WITHDRAWN

University of Memphis Libraries

American Men & Women of Science

1998-99 • 20th Edition

The 20th edition of *AMERICAN MEN & WOMEN OF SCIENCE* was
prepared by the R.R. Bowker Database Publishing Group in
collaboration with the Publication Systems Department.

Senior Staff of the Database Publishing Group includes:

Senior Vice President & Chief Operating Officer, R.R. Bowker
Neal Goff

Publisher
Nan Hudes

Vice President, Database Publishing
Leigh Yuster-Freeman

Editorial:
Director: *Owen O'Donnell*
Managing Editor: *Karen Hallard*
Senior Editor: *Alison J. Butkiewicz*
Associate Editors: *Angela Krakow*
Elizabeth McCarthy

Research:
Director: *Judy Redel*
Senior Managing Editor: *Tanya Hurst*
Senior Editor: *Beverly Heath*

Tampa Division:
Director: *Valerie Harris*
Production Manager: *Debra Wilson*
Associate Coordinator: *Jennifer Rodgers*

American Men & Women of Science

1998-99 • 20th Edition

A Biographical Directory of Today's Leaders in Physical, Biological and Related Sciences.

Volume 6 • Q-S

R.R. BOWKER
A Unit of Reed Elsevier Business Information
New Providence, New Jersey

Published by R.R. Bowker, A Unit of Reed Elsevier Business Information

Copyright© 1998 by Reed Elsevier Inc. All rights reserved. Except as permitted under the Copyright Act of 1976, no part of *American Men and Women of Science* may be reproduced or transmitted in any form or by any means stored in any information storage and retrieval system, without prior written permission of R.R. Bowker, 121 Chanlon Road, New Providence, New Jersey, 07974.

International Standard Book Number
        Set: 0-8352-3748-6
   Volume 1:   0-8352-3749-4
   Volume 2:   0-8352-3775-3
   Volume 3:   0-8352-3776-1
   Volume 4:   0-8352-3778-8
   Volume 5:   0-8352-3779-6
   Volume 6:   0-8352-3781-8
   Volume 7:   0-8352-3782-6
   Volume 8:   0-8352-3783-4

International Standard Serial Number: 0192-8570
Library of Congress Catalog Card Number: 6-7326
Printed and bound in the United States of America.

R.R. Bowker has used its best efforts in collecting and preparing material for inclusion in this publication but does not warrant that the information herein is complete or accurate, and does not assume, and hereby disclaims, any liability to any person for any loss or damage caused by errors or omissions in *American Men and Women of Science*, whether such errors or omissions result from negligence, accident or any other cause.

8 Volume Set

ISBN 0-8352-3748-6

Contents

Advisory Committee vi

Preface vii

Major Honors & Awards ix

Statistics xi

Sample Entry xvii

Abbreviations xviii

Biographies 1

Advisory Committee

Dr. Charles Henderson Dickens
Former Executive Secretary, Federal Coordinating Council for Science, Engineering & Technology
Office of Science & Technology Policy

Dr. Oscar Nicolas Garcia
NCR Distinguished Professor & Chair, Department of Computer Science & Engineering
Wright State University

Dr. Michael J. Jackson
Executive Director
Federation of American Societies for Experimental Biology

Dr. Shirley Mahaley Malcom
Head, Directorate for Education and Human Resources Programs
American Association for the Advancement of Science

Ms. Beverly Fearn Porter
Assistant to the Executive Director for Society Relations
American Institute of Physics

Dr. William Eldon Splinter
Former Vice Chancellor for Research
University of Nebraska-Lincoln

Dr. Dael Lee Wolfle
Professor Emeritus, Graduate School of Public Affairs
University of Washington

Dr. Ahmed H. Zewail
Linus Pauling Professor of Chemistry & Physics
California Institute of Technology

Preface

American Men and Women of Science remains without peer as a chronicle of North American and Canadian scientific endeavor and achievement. The present work is the twentieth edition since it was first compiled as *American Men of Science* by J. McKeen Cattell in 1906. In its ninety-two year history, *American Men and Women of Science* has profiled the careers of over 300,000 scientists and engineers. Since the first edition, the number of American scientists and the fields they pursue has grown immensely. This edition alone lists full biographies for 119,618 engineers and scientists, 4184 of which are listed for the first time. Although the book has grown, our stated purpose is the same as when Dr. Cattell first undertook the task of producing a biographical directory of active American scientists. It was his intention to record educational, personal and career data which would make "a contribution to the organization of science in America" and "make men [and women] of science acquainted with one another and with one another's work." It is our hope that this edition will fulfill these goals.

The biographies of engineers and scientists constitute seven of the eight volumes and provide birthdate, birthplace, field of specialty, education, honorary degrees, current position, professional and concurrent experience, awards, memberships, research information and addresses for each entrant when applicable. The eighth volume, the discipline index, organizes biographees by field of activity. This index, adapted from the National Science Foundation's Taxonomy of Degree and Employment Specialties, classifies entrants by 192 subject specialties listed in the table of contents of Volume 8. The index lists scientists and engineers by state within each subject specialty, allowing the user to easily locate a scientist in a given area. Also included are statistical information and charts showing the distribution of *AMWS* listees by age and discipline and and annotated listing of the recipients of the Nobel Prizes, the Craaford Prize, the Charles Stark Draper Prize, the National Medals of Science and Technology, the Fields Medal and the Alan T. Waterman Award since the last edition.

While the scientific fields covered by *American Men and Women of Science* are comprehensive, no attempt has been made to include all American scientists. Entrants are meant to be limited to those who have made significant contributions in their field. The names of new entrants were submitted for consideration at the editors' request by current entrants and by leaders of academic, government and private research programs and associations. Those included met the following criteria:

1. Distinguished achievement, by reason of experience, training or accomplishment, including contributions to literature, coupled with continuing activity in scientific work;

or

2. Research activity of high quality in science as evidenced by publication in reputable scientific journals; or, for those whose work cannot be published due to governmental or industrial security, research activity of high quality in science as evidenced by the judgement of the individual's peers;

or

3. Attainment of a position of substantial responsibility requiring scientific training and experience.

This edition profiles living scientists in the physical and biological fields, as well as public health scientists, engineers, mathematicians, statisticians, and computer scientists. The information is collected by means of direct communication whenever possible. All entrants receive forms for corroboration and updating. New entrants receive questionnaires and verification proofs before publication. The information submitted by entrants is included as completely as possible within the boundaries of editorial and space restrictions. If an entrant does not return the form and his or her current location can be verified in secondary sources, the full entry is repeated. References to the previous edition are given for those who do not return forms and cannot be located, but who are presumed to be still active in science or engineering. Entrants known to be deceased are noted as such and a reference to the previous edition is given. Scientists and engineers who are not citizens of the United States or Canada are included if a significant portion of their work was performed in North America.

The information in *American Men & Women of Science* is available on magnetic tape. For information, contact Bowker Electronic Publishing (888-BOWKER-2). *American Men and Women of Science* is also available for online searching through Lexis®-Nexis® (800-227-4908) and through DIALOG, a service of Knight-Ridder Information, Inc. (800-334-2564). The online products allow fielded as well as key word searches of all elements of a record, including field of interest, experience, and location. An ERL-compliant CD-ROM is available through SilverPlatter Information (800-343-0064). Mailing lists are available through Reed Elsevier Business Information Lists (John Panza, Account Manager, Bowker Files, 245 W 17th St, New York, NY, 10011; 212-337-7164).

A project as large as publishing *American Men and Women of Science* involves the efforts of a great many people. The editors take this opportunity to thank the twentieth edition advisory committee for their guidance, encouragement and support. Appreciation is also expressed to the many scientific societies who provided their membership lists for the purpose of locating former entrants whose addresses had changed, and to the tens of thousands of scientists across the country who took time to provide us with biographical information. We also wish to thank Donna Brinkmann and Carol Carr of Reed Technology & Information Services, Inc. for their assistance in the successful production of this directory.

Comments, suggestions and nominations for the twenty-first edition are encouraged and should be directed to The Editors, *American Men and Women of Science*, R.R. Bowker, 121 Chanlon Road, New Providence, New Jersey, 07974.

Karen Hallard
Managing Editor

Major Honors & Awards

Nobel Prizes
Nobel Foundation, Royal Swedish Academy of Sciences & Nobel Assembly of the Karolinska

The Nobel Prizes were established in 1900 (and first awarded in 1901) to recognize those people who "have conferred the greatest benefit on mankind."

1995 Recipients

Chemistry:
Paul Josef Crutzen, Mario Jose Molina & Frank Sherwood Rowland
Awarded "for their work in atmospheric chemistry, particularly concerning the formation and decomposition of ozone."

Physics:
Martin Lewis Perl
Frederick Reines
Awarded to Perl "for the discovery of the tau lepton" and to Reines "for the detection of the nutrino."

Physiology or Medicine:
Edward B. Lewis, Christiane Nusslein-Volhard & Eric F. Wieschaus
Awarded "for their discoveries concerning the genetic control of early embryonic development."

1996 Recipients

Chemistry:
Robert Floyd Curl, Harold Walter Kroto & Richard Errett Smalley
Awarded "for their discovery of fullerenes, carbon atoms bound in the form of a ball."

Physics:
David Morris Lee, Douglas Dean Osheroff & Robert Coleman Richardson
Awarded "for their discovery of superfluidity in helium-3."

Physiology or Medicine:
Peter Charles Doherty & Rolf Martin Zinkernagel
Awarded "for their discoveries of how the immune system recognizes virus-infected cells."

1997 Recipients

Chemistry:
Paul Delos Boyer, Jens Christian Skou & John Ernest Walker
Awarded to Boyer & Walker "for their elucidation of the enzymatic mechanism underlying the synthesis of adenosine triphosphate (ATP)" and to Skou "for the first discovery of an ion-transporting enzyme, NA$^+$, K$^+$-ATPase."

Physics:
Claude Nessin Cohen-Tannoudji, Steven Chu & William Daniel Phillips
Awarded "for their development of methods to cool and trap atoms with laser light."

Physiology or Medicine:
Stanley Ben Prusiner
Awarded to Prusiner for his discovery of prions, a new genre of infectious agents.

Craoord Prize
Royal Swedish Academy of Sciences

The Crafoord Prize was introduced in 1982 to award scientists in disciplines not covered by the Nobel Prize, namely mathematics, astronomy, geosciences and biosciences.

1995 Recipients

Willi Dansgaard & Nicholas John Shackleton
Awarded "for their fundamental work on developing and applying isotope geological analysis methods for the study of climatic variations during the Quaternary period."

1996 Recipient

Robert McRedie May
Awarded to May "for his pioneering ecological research concerning theoretical analysis of the dynamics of populations, communities and ecosystems."

1997 Recipients

Fred Hoyle & Edwin Ernest Salpeter
Awarded "for their pioneering contributions involving the study of nuclear reactions in stars and stars' development."

Charles Stark Draper Prize
National Academy of Engineering

The Draper Prize, awarded biennially, was introduced in 1989 to recognize engineering achievement.

1995 Recipients

John Robinson Pierce & Harold A. Rosen
Awarded for developing communications satellite technology.

1997 Recipients
Vladimir Haensel
Awarded to Haensel for inventing "Platforming" — platinum reforming to convert petroleum into high-performance fuels.

National Medal of Science
National Science Foundation

The National Medals of Science were established by the United States Congress in 1959 and have been awarded by the President of the United States since 1962. The National Science Foundation's selection criteria are based on the "total impact of an individual's work on the present state of physical, biological, mathematical, engineering, behavioral, or social sciences."

1995 Recipients

Thomas Robert Cech
Hans Georg Dehmelt
Peter Goldreich
Hermann A(nton) Haus
Isabella Lugoski Karle
Louis Nirenberg
Alexander Rich
Roger N. Shepard

1996 Recipients

Wallace Broecker
Norman Ralph Davidson
James L(oton) Flanagan
Richard M. Karp
Chandra Kumar Naranbhai Patel
Ruth Patrick
Paul Anthony Samuelson
Stephen Smale

1997 Recipients

William K. Estes
Darleane Christian Hoffman
Harold Sledge Johnston
Marshall N. Rosenbluth
Martin Schwarzschild (deceased)
James Dewey Watson
Robert A. Weinberg
George West Wetherill
Shing-Tung Yau

Fields Medal
International Mathematical Union

The Fields Medals were established in 1936 by Canadian mathematician John Fields to acknowledge outstanding research by young mathematicians. The medals are awarded every four years at the International Congress of Mathematicians.

1994 Recipients

Jean Bourgain
Pierre Louis Lions
Jean-Christophe Yoccoz
Efim Isaakovich Zelmanof

Awarded to Bourgain for his insights into the geometry of infinite dimensional spaces. Awarded to Lions for advances in non-linear partial differential equations. Awarded to Yoccoz for analyzing the end results of complicated sequences of circle maps. Awarded to Zelmanov for solving the unrestricted Burnside problem.

National Medal of Technology
U.S. Department of Commerce

The National Medals of Technology were created as part of the 1980 Stevenson-Wydler Technology Innovation Act and were first awarded in 1985. They are bestowed by the President of the United States to recognize individuals and companies for their development or commercialization of technology or for their contributions to the establishment of a technologically-trained workforce.

1995 Recipients

Praveen Chaudhari
Jerome John Cuomo
Richard Joseph Gambino
Edward R. McCracken
Sam B. Williams
Alejandro Zaffaroni
Procter & Gamble Company
3M

1996 Recipients

Charles Huron Kaman
Stephanie Louise Kwolek
James C. Morgan
Peter Henry Rose
Johnson & Johnson

1997 Recipients

Norman R. Augustine
Vinton Gray Cerf
Ray Milton Dolby
Robert Elliot Kahn
Robert Steven Ledley

Alan T. Waterman Award
National Science Foundation & National Science Board

Established by the United States Congress in 1975, the Waterman Award is given annually to an outstanding researcher, aged 35 or younger, in any field of science or engineering supported by the National Science Foundation.

1995 Recipient

Matthew P.A. Fisher
Awarded to Fisher "for his pioneering contributions to the theory of disordered superconductors."

1996 Recipient

Robert Mebane Waymouth
Awarded to Waymouth for discovering new ways to make polymers.

1997 Recipient

Eric Allin Cornell
Awarded to Cornell for creation of Bose-Einstein condensate (BEC).

Statistics

Statistical distribution of entrants in *American Men & Women of Science* with U.S. mailing addresses is illustrated on the following five pages. The regional scheme for geographical analysis is diagrammed in the map below. A table enumerating the geographic distribution can be found on page xvi, following the charts. The statistics are compiled by tallying all occurrences of a major index subject. Each scientist may choose to be indexed under as many as four categories; thus, the total number of subject references is greater than the number of entrants in *AMWS*.

All Disciplines

	Number	Percent
Northeast	56,006	34%
Southeast	41,313	25%
North Central	19,699	12%
South Central	12,169	7%
Mountain	11,675	7%
Pacific	25,703	15%
TOTAL	**166,565**	**100%**

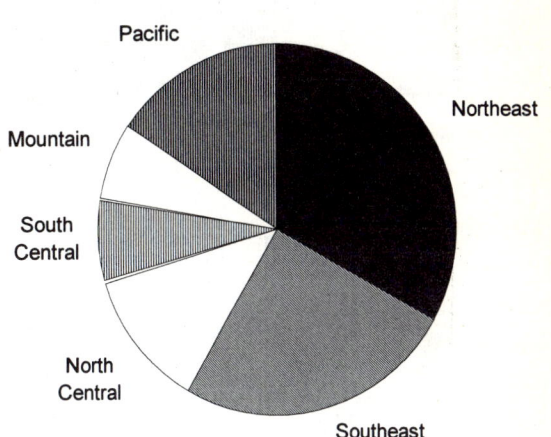

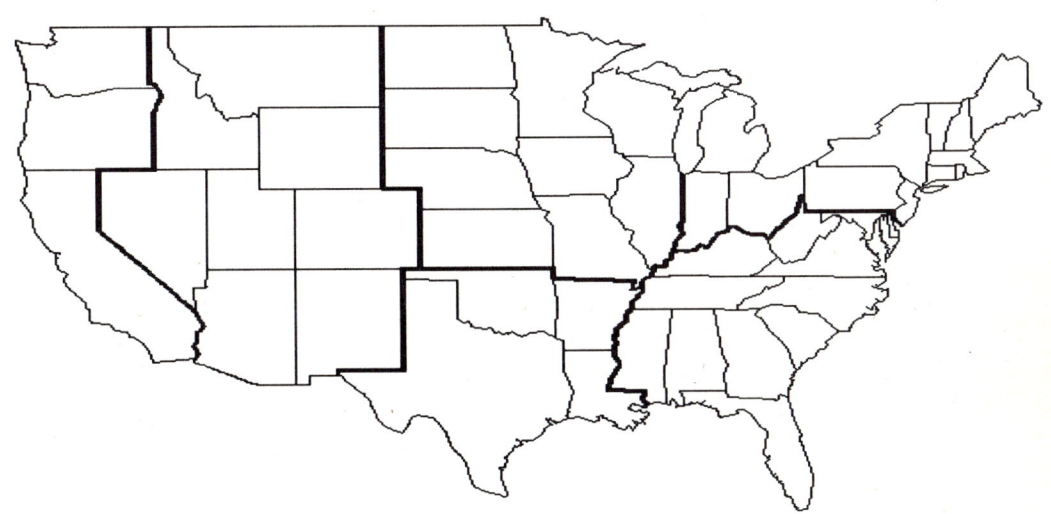

Age Distribution of American Men & Women of Science

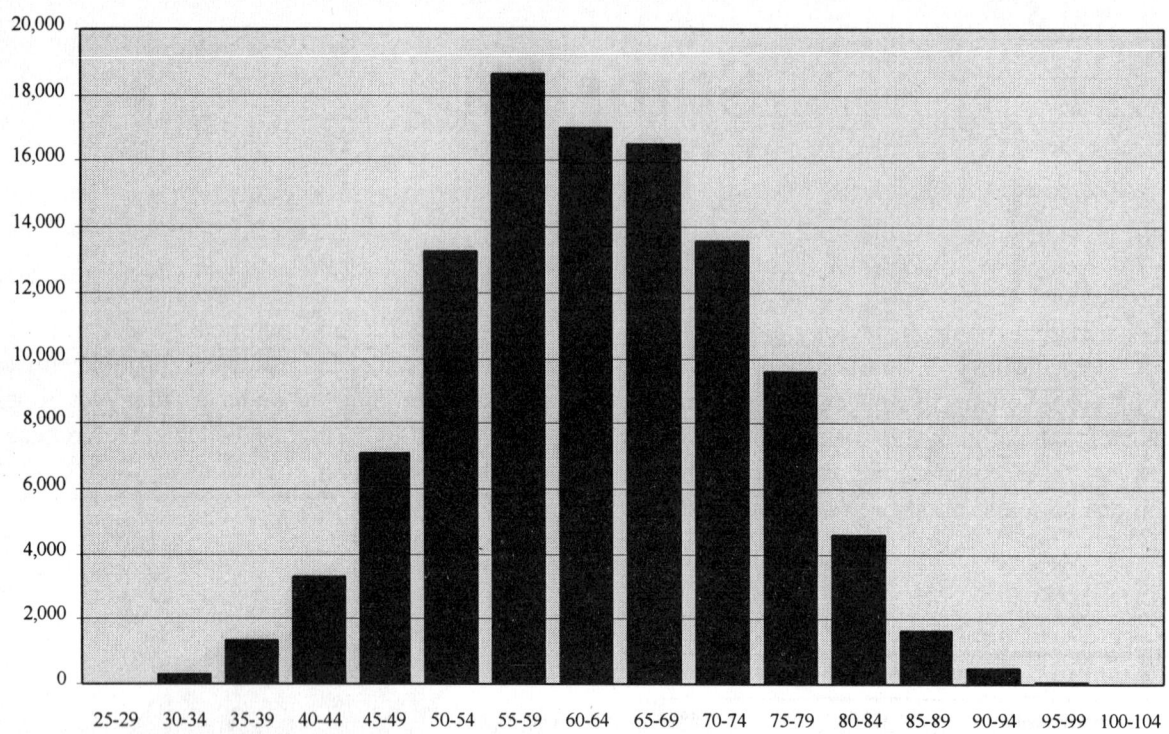

Number of Scientists in Each Discipline of Study

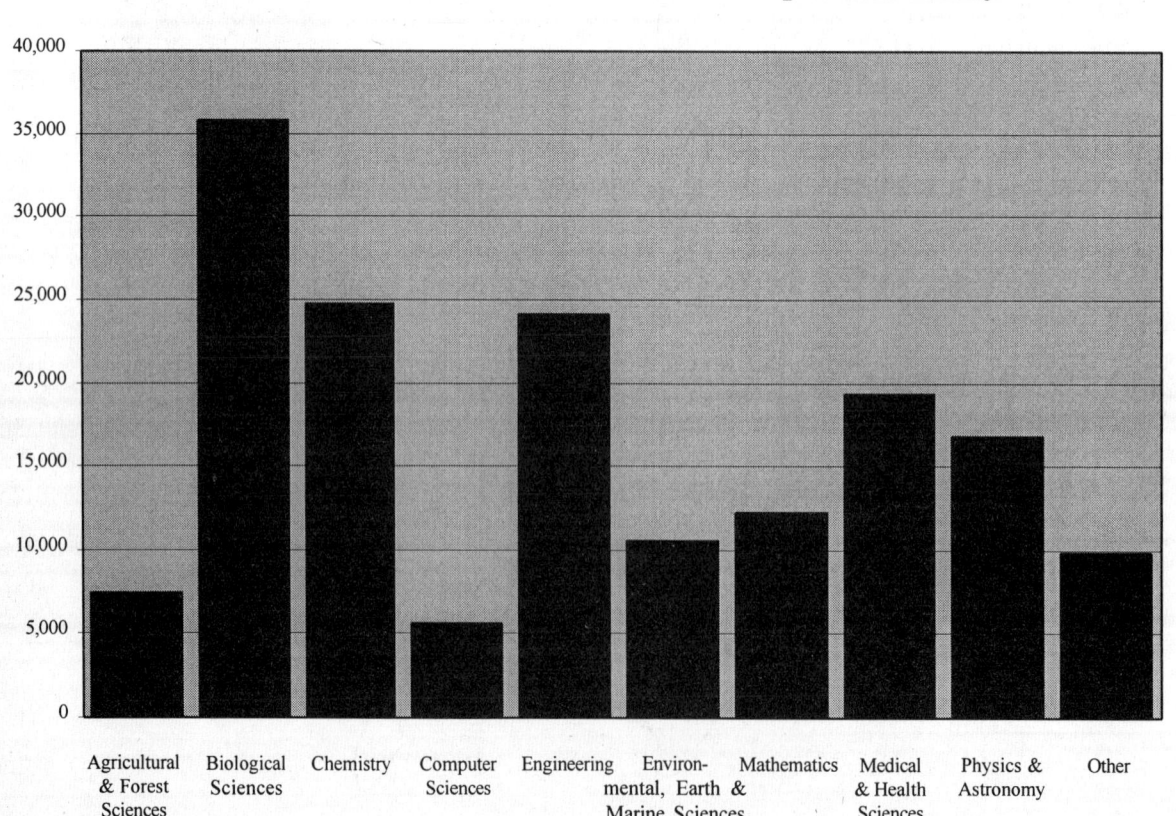

Agricultural & Forest Sciences

	Number	Percent
Northeast	1,585	21%
Southeast	2,053	27%
North Central	1,171	16%
South Central	635	8%
Mountain	739	10%
Pacific	1,305	17%
TOTAL	**7,488**	**100%**

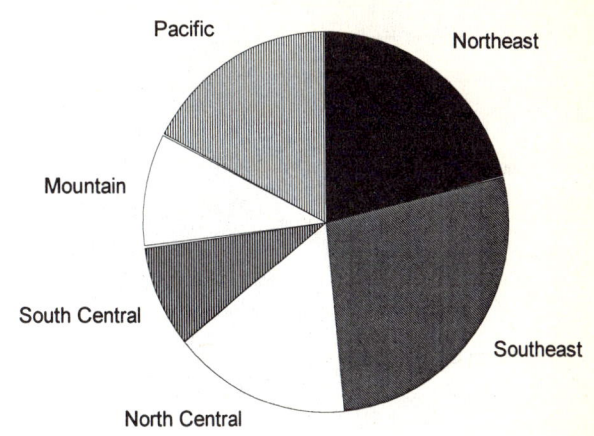

Biological Sciences

	Number	Percent
Northeast	11,671	33%
Southeast	9,045	25%
North Central	4,918	14%
South Central	2,741	8%
Mountain	2,125	6%
Pacific	5,277	15%
TOTAL	**35,777**	**100%**

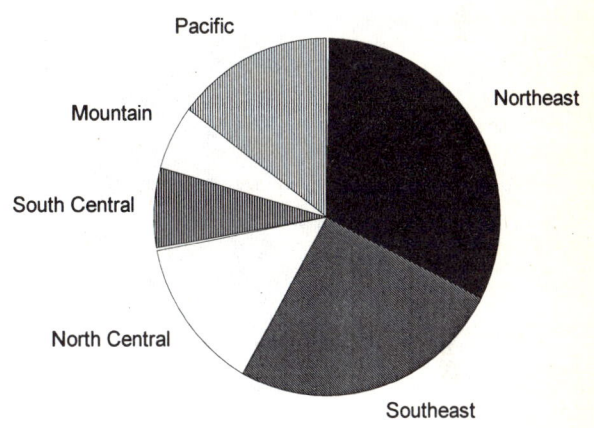

Chemistry

	Number	Percent
Northeast	9,296	38%
Southeast	6,196	25%
North Central	2,964	12%
South Central	1,724	7%
Mountain	1,381	6%
Pacific	3,139	13%
TOTAL	**24,700**	**100%**

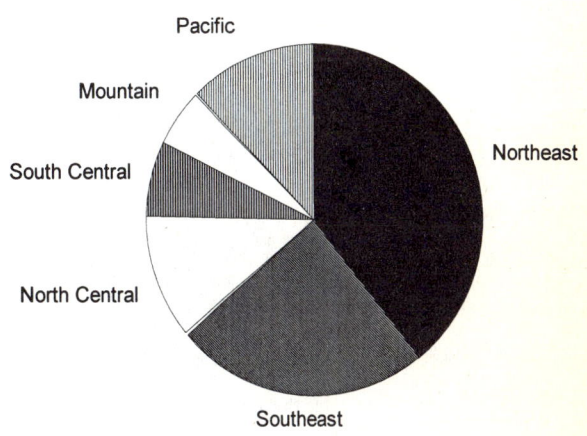

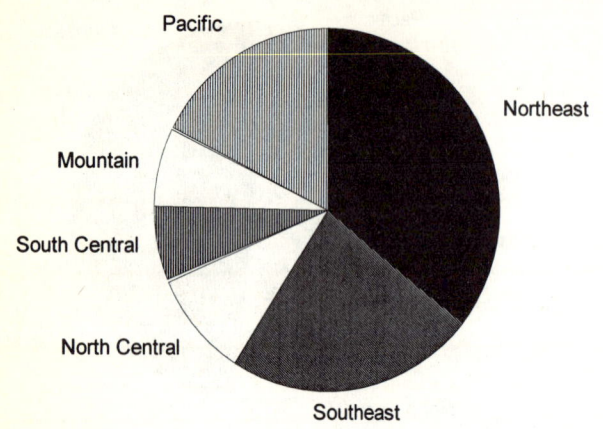

Computer Sciences

	Number	Percent
Northeast	1,983	35%
Southeast	1,278	23%
North Central	556	10%
South Central	378	7%
Mountain	423	7%
Pacific	1,034	18%
TOTAL	**5,652**	**100%**

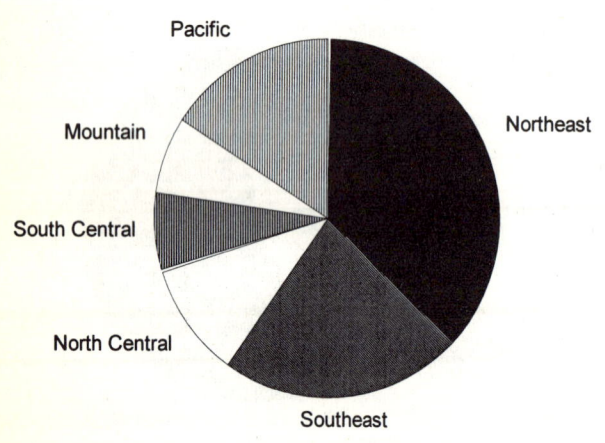

Engineering

	Number	Percent
Northeast	8,780	36%
Southeast	5,487	23%
North Central	2,501	10%
South Central	1,742	7%
Mountain	1,760	7%
Pacific	3,883	16%
TOTAL	**24,153**	**100%**

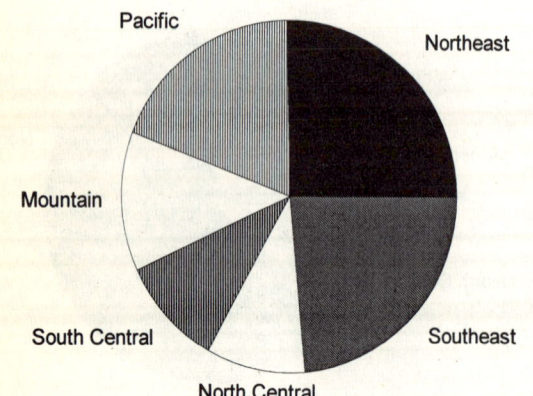

Environmental, Earth & Marine Sciences

	Number	Percent
Northeast	2,654	25%
Southeast	2,507	24%
North Central	984	9%
South Central	1,008	10%
Mountain	1,365	13%
Pacific	2,008	19%
TOTAL	**10,526**	**100%**

Mathematics

	Number	Percent
Northeast	4,292	35%
Southeast	2,865	23%
North Central	1,552	13%
South Central	933	8%
Mountain	760	6%
Pacific	1,901	15%
TOTAL	**12,303**	**100%**

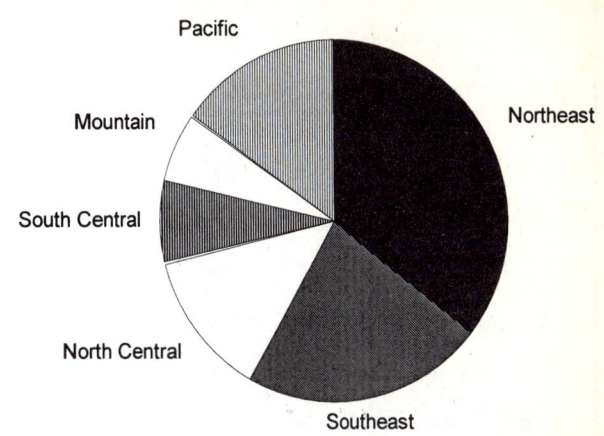

Medical & Health Sciences

	Number	Percent
Northeast	6,883	36%
Southeast	5,139	27%
North Central	2,471	13%
South Central	1,494	8%
Mountain	804	4%
Pacific	2,501	13%
TOTAL	**19,292**	**100%**

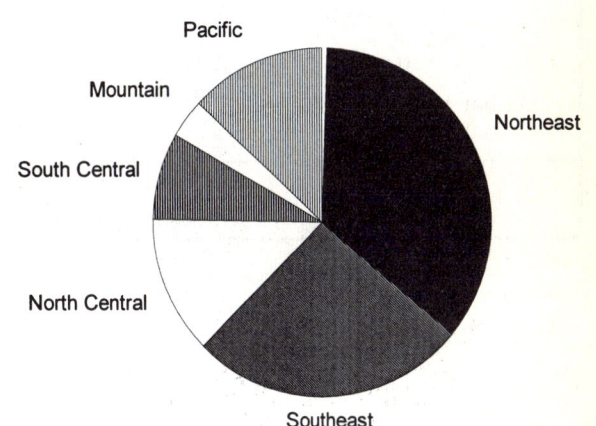

Physics & Astronomy

	Number	Percent
Northeast	5,603	33%
Southeast	3,776	22%
North Central	1,545	9%
South Central	904	5%
Mountain	1,674	10%
Pacific	3,307	20%
TOTAL	**16,809**	**100%**

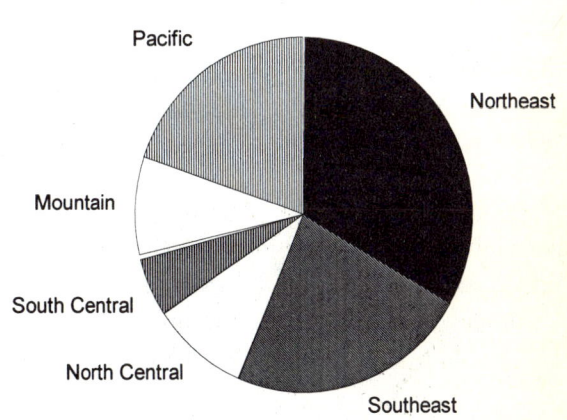

Geographic Distribution of Scientists by Discipline

	Northeast	Southeast	North Central	South Central	Mountain	Pacific	TOTAL
Agricultural & Forest Sciences	1,585	2,053	1,171	635	739	1,305	**7,488**
Biological Sciences	11,671	9,045	4,918	2,741	2,125	5,277	**35,777**
Chemistry	9,296	6,196	2,964	1,724	1,381	3,139	**24,700**
Computer Sciences	1,983	1,278	556	378	423	1,034	**5,652**
Engineering	8,780	5,487	2,501	1,742	1,760	3,883	**24,153**
Environmental, Earth & Marine Sciences	2,654	2,507	984	1,008	1,365	2,008	**10,526**
Mathematics	4,292	2,865	1,552	933	760	1,901	**12,303**
Medical & Health Sciences	6,883	5,139	2,471	1,494	804	2,501	**19,292**
Physics & Astronomy	5,603	3,776	1,545	904	1,674	3,307	**16,809**
Other Professional Fields	3,259	2,967	1,037	610	644	1,348	**9,865**
TOTAL	**56,006**	**41,313**	**19,699**	**12,169**	**11,675**	**25,703**	**166,565**

Geographic Definitions

Northeast
Connecticut
Indiana
Maine
Massachusetts
Michigan
New Hampshire
New Jersey
New York
Ohio
Pennsylvania
Rhode Island
Vermont

Southeast
Alabama
Delaware
District of Columbia
Florida
Georgia
Kentucky
Maryland
Mississippi
North Carolina
South Carolina
Tennessee
Virginia
West Virginia

North Central
Illinois
Iowa
Kansas
Minnesota
Missouri
Nebraska
North Dakota
South Dakota
Wisconsin

South Central
Arkansas
Louisiana
Texas
Oklahoma

Mountain
Arizona
Colorado
Idaho
Montana
Nevada
New Mexico
Utah
Wyoming

Pacific
Alaska
California
Hawaii
Oregon
Washington

Sample Entry

American Men & Women of Science (AMWS) is an extremely useful reference tool. The book is most often used in two ways: to find more information about a particular scientist and to locate a scientist in a specific field.

To locate information about an individual, the biographical section is most helpful. It encompasses the first seven volumes and lists scientists and engineers alphabetically by last name. The fictitious biographical listing shown below illustrates every type of information an entry may include.

The Discipline Index, volume 8, can be used to easily find a scientist in a specific subject specialty. This index is first classified by area of study; within each specialty entrants are divided further by state of residence.

Name	
Birthdate	
Children's Name(s)	
Honors & Awards	
Concurrent Experience	
Memberships	
E-Mail Address	

REED, SAMANTHA J(EAN), OCEANOGRAPHY, MARINE BIOLOGY. *Current Pos:* SR ASSOC OCEANOGRAPHER, DEPT NAVY, 86- *Personal Data:* b Brooklyn, NY, Nov 9, 42; m 67, James A. Mayer; c Steven C & Lillian M. *Educ:* Univ Notre Dame, BS, 63, MS, 65, Fla State Univ, PhD(oceanog), 70. *Hon Degrees:* DSc, Univ Calif, Davis, 79. *Honors & Awards:* Henry Bryant Bigelow Medal, Oceanog, 92; *Prof Exp:* Asst prof oceanog, 71-73, assoc prof oceanog & biol, Harvard Univ, 73-75. *Concurrent Pos:* Consult, New England Aquarium, 74-78; vis lect, Wash Univ, 77. *Mem:* AAAS, Am Soc Naval Engrs, Sigma Xi, Oceanog Soc (vpres 82-83). *Res:* Ocean pollution prevention, water treatment and analysis, ecology of marine plankton and sponges, author of 13 publications. *Mailing Address:* 121 102 Smithfield Way, Boca Raton, FL 33431. *Fax:* 407-555-5939; *E-Mail:* sreed@usnavy.mil.fla

Labels on right: Field of Specialty, Current Position, Marriage/Spouse data, Education, Honorary Degrees, Professional Experience, Research and Publications, Mailing Address, Fax Number

Abbreviations

AAAS—American Association for the Advancement of Science
abnorm—abnormal
abstr—abstract
acad—academic, academy
acct—account, accountant, accounting
acoust—acoustic(s), acoustical
ACTH—adrenocorticotrophic hormone
actg—acting
activ—activities, activity
addn—addition(s), additional
Add—Address
adj—adjunct, adjutant
adjust—adjustment
Adm—Admiral
admin—administration, administrative
adminr—administrator(s)
admis—admission(s)
adv—adviser(s), advisory
advan—advance(d), advancement
advert—advertisement, advertising
AEC—Atomic Energy Commission
aerodyn—aerodynamic
aeronaut—aeronautic(s), aeronautical
aerophys—aerophysical, aerophysics
aesthet—aesthetic
AFB—Air Force Base
affil—affiliate(s), affiliation
agr—agricultural, agriculture
agron—agronomic, agronomical, agronomy
agrost—agrostologic, agrostological, agrostology
agt—agent
AID—Agency for International Development
Ala—Alabama
allergol—allergological, allergology
alt—alternate
Alta—Alberta
Am—America, American
AMA—American Medical Association
anal—analysis, analytic, analytical
analog—analogue
anat—anatomic, anatomical, anatomy
anesthesiol—anesthesiology
angiol—angiology
Ann—Annal(s)
ann—annual
anthrop—anthropological, anthropology
anthropom—anthropometric, anthropometrical, anthropometry

antiq—antiquary, antiquities, antiquity
antiqn—antiquarian
apicult—apicultural, apiculture
APO—Army Post Office
app—appoint, appointed
appl—applied
appln—application
approx—approximate(ly)
Apr—April
apt—apartment(s)
aquacult—aquaculture
arbit—arbitration
arch—archives
archaeol—archaeological, archaeology
archit—architectural, architecture
Arg—Argentina, Argentine
Ariz—Arizona
Ark—Arkansas
artil—artillery
asn—association
assoc(s)—associate(s), associated
asst(s)—assistant(s), assistantship(s)
assyriol—Assyriology
astrodyn—astrodynamics
astron—astronomical, astronomy
astronaut—astronautical, astronautics
astronr—astronomer
astrophys—astrophysical, astrophysics
attend—attendant, attending
atty—attorney
audiol—audiology
Aug—August
auth—author
AV—audiovisual
Ave—Avenue
avicult—avicultural, aviculture

b—born
bact—bacterial, bacteriologic, bacteriological, bacteriology
BC—British Colombia
bd—board
behav—behavior(al)
Belg—Belgian, Belgium
Bibl—Biblical
bibliog—bibliographic, bibliographical, bibliography
bibliogr—bibliographer
biochem—biochemical, biochemistry
biog—biographical, biography
biol—biological, biology
biomed—biomedical, biomedicine

biomet—biometric(s), biometrical, biometry
biophys—biophysical, biophysics
bk(s)—book(s)
bldg—building
Blvd—Boulevard
Bor—Borough
bot—botanical, botany
br—branch(es)
Brig—Brigadier
Brit—Britain, British
Bro(s)—Brother(s)
byrol—byrology
bull—Bulletin
bur—bureau
bus—business
BWI—British West Indies

c—children
Calif—California
Can—Canada, Canadian
cand—candidate
Capt—Captain
cardiol—cardiology
cardiovasc—cardiovascular
cartog—cartographic, cartographical, cartography
cartogr—cartographer
Cath—Catholic
CEngr—Corp of Engineers
cent—central
Cent Am—Central American
cert—certificate(s), certification, certified
chap—chapter
chem—chemical(s), chemistry
chemother—chemotherapy
chg—change
chmn—chairman
citricult—citriculture
class—classical
climat—climatological, climatology
clin(s)—clinic(s), clinical
cmndg—commanding
Co—County
Co—Companies, Company
co-auth—co-author
co-dir—co-director
co-ed—co-editor
co-educ—co-education, co-educational
col(s)—college(s), collegiate, colonel
collab—collaboration, collaborative
collabr—collaborator

xviii

ABBREVIATIONS

Colo—Colorado
com—commerce, commercial
Comdr—Commander
commun—communicable, communication(s)
comn(s)—commission(s), commissioned
comndg—commanding
comnr—commissioner
comp—comparitive
compos—composition
comput—computation, computer(s), computing
comt(s)—committee(s)
conchol—conchology
conf—conference
cong—congress, congressional
Conn—Connecticut
conserv—conservation, conservatory
consol—consolidated, consolidation
const—constitution, constitutional
construct—construction, constructive
consult(s)—consult, consultant(s), consultantship(s), consultation, consulting
contemp—contemporary
contrib—contribute, contributing, contribution(s)
contribr—contributor
conv—convention
coop—cooperating, cooperation, cooperative
coord—coordinate(d), coordinating, coordination
coordr—coordinator
corp—corporate, corporation(s)
corresp—correspondence, correspondent, corresponding
coun—council, counsel, counseling
counr—councilor, counselor
criminol—criminological, criminology
cryog—cryogenic(s)
crystallog—crystallographic, crystallographical, crystallography
crystallogr—crystallographer
Ct—Court
Ctr—Center
cult—cultural, culture
cur—curator
curric—curriculum
cybernet—cybernetic(s)
cytol—cytological, cytology
Czech—Czechoslovakia, Czech Republic

DC—District of Columbia
Dec—December
Del—Delaware
deleg—delegate, delegation
delinq—delinquency, delinquent
dem—democrat(s), democratic
demog—demographic, demography
demogr—demographer
demonstr—demontrator
dendrol—dendrologic, dendrological, dendrology
dent—dental, dentistry
dep—deputy
dept—department
dermat—dermatologic, dermatological, dermatology

develop—developed, developing, development, developmental
diag—diagnosis, diagnostic
dialectol—dialectological, dialectology
dict—dictionaries, dictionary
Dig—Digest
dipl—diploma, diplomate
dir(s)—director(s), directories, directory
dis—disease(s), disorders
Diss Abst—Dissertation Abstracts
dist—district
distrib—distributed, distribution, distributive
distribr—distributor(s)
div—division, divisional, divorced
DNA—deoxyribonucleic acid
doc—document(s), documentary, documentation
Dom—Dominion
Dr—Drive

E—East
ecol—ecological, ecology
econ(s)—economic(s), economical, economy
economet—econometric(s)
ECT—electroconvulsive or electroshock therapy
ed—edition(s), editor(s), editorial
ed bd—editorial board
educ—education, educational
educr—educator(s)
EEG—electroencephalogram, electroencephalographic, electroencephalography
Egyptol—Egyptology
EKG—electrocardiogram
elec—electric, electrical, electricity
electrochem—electrochemical, electrochemistry
electroph—electrophysical, electrophysics
elem—elementary
embryol—embryologic, embryological, embryology
emer—emeriti, emeritus
employ—employment
encour—encouragement
encycl—encyclopedia
endocrinol—endocrinologic, endocrinology
eng—engineering
Eng—England, English
engr(s)—engineer(s)
enol—enology
Ens—Ensign
entom—entomological, entomology
environ—environment(s), environmental
enzym—enzymology
epidemiol—epidemiologic, epidemiological, epidemiology
equip—equipment
ERDA—Energy Research & Development Administration
ESEA—Elementary & Secondary Education Act
espec—especially
estab—established, establishment(s)
ethnog—ethnographic, ethnographical, ethnography
ethnogr—ethnographer

ethnol—ethnologic, ethnological, ethnology
Europ—European
eval—evaluation
Evangel—Evangelical
eve—evening
exam—examination(s), examining
examr—examiner
except—exceptional
exec(s)—executive(s)
exeg—exegeses, exegesis, exegetic, exegetical
exhib(s)—exhibition(s), exhibit(s)
exp—experiment, experimental
exped(s)—expedition(s)
explor—exploration(s), exploratory
expos—exposition
exten—extension

fac—faculty
facil—facilities, facility
Feb—February
fed—federal
fedn—federation
fel(s)—fellow(s), fellowship(s)
fermentol—fermentology
fertil—fertility, fertilization
Fla—Florida
floricult—floricultural, floriculture
found—foundation
FPO—Fleet Post Office
Fr—French
Ft—Fort

Ga—Georgia
gastroenterol—gastroenterological, gastroenterology
gen—general
geneal—genealogical, genealogy
geod—geodesy, geodetic
geog—geographic, geographical, geography
geogr—geographer
geol—geologic, geological, geology
geom—geometric, geometrical, geometry
geomorphol—geomorphologic, geomorphology
geophys—geophysical, geophysics
Ger—German, Germanic, Germany
geriat—geriatric
geront—gerontological, gerontology
Ges—Gesellschaft
glaciol—glaciology
gov—governing, governor(s)
govt—government, governmental
grad—graduate(d)
Gt Brit—Great Britain
guid—guidance
gym—gymnasium
gynec—gynecologic, gynecological, gynecology

handbk(s)—handbook(s)
helminth—helminthology
hemat—hematologic, hematological, hematology
herpet—herpetologic, herpetological, herpetology
HEW—Department of Health, Education & Welfare

ABBREVIATIONS

Hisp—Hispanic, Hispania
hist—historic, historical, history
histol—histological, histology
HM—Her Majesty
hochsch—hochschule
homeop—homeopathic, homeopathy
hon(s)—honor(s), honorable, honorary
hort—horticultural, horticulture
hosp(s)—hospital(s), hospitalization
hq—headquarters
HumRRO—Human Resources Research Office
husb—husbandry
Hwy—Highway
hydraul—hydraulic(s)
hydrodyn—hydrodynamic(s)
hydrol—hydrologic, hydrological, hydrologics
hyg—hygiene, hygienic(s)
hypn—hypnosis

ichthyol—ichthyological, ichthyology
Ill—Illinois
illum—illuminating, illumination
illus—illustrate, illustrated, illustration
illusr—illustrator
immunol—immunologic, immunological, immunology
Imp—Imperial
improv—improvement
Inc—Incorporated
in-chg—in charge
incl—include(s), including
Ind—Indiana
indust(s)—industrial, industries, industry
Inf—Infantry
info—information
inorg—inorganic
ins—insurance
inst(s)—institute(s), institution(s)
instnl—institutional(ized)
instr(s)—instruct, instruction, instructor(s)
instrnl—instructional
int—international
intel—intellligence
introd—introduction
invert—invertebrate
invest(s)—investigation(s)
investr—investigator
irrig—irrigation
Ital—Italian

J—Journal
Jan—January
Jct—Junction
jour—journal, journalism
jr—junior
jurisp—jurisprudence
juv—juvenile

Kans—Kansas
Ky—Kentucky

La—Louisiana
lab(s)—laboratories, laboratory
lang—language(s)
laryngol—larygological, laryngology
lect—lecture(s)

lectr—lecturer(s)
legis—legislation, legislative, legislature
lett—letter(s)
lib—liberal
libr—libraries, library
librn—librarian
lic—license(d)
limnol—limnological, limnology
ling—linguistic(s), linguistical
lit—literary, literature
lithol—lithologic, lithological, lithology
Lt—Lieutenant
Ltd—Limited
m—married
mach—machine(s), machinery
mag—magazine(s)
maj—major
malacol—malacology
mammal—mammalogy
Man—Manitoba
Mar—March
Mariol—Mariology
Mass—Massechusetts
mat—material(s)
mat med—materia medica
math—mathematic(s), mathematical
Md—Maryland
mech—mechanic(s), mechanical
med—medical, medicinal, medicine
Mediter—Mediterranean
Mem—Memorial
mem—member(s), membership(s)
ment—mental(ly)
metab—metabolic, metabolism
metall—metallurgic, metallurgical, metallurgy
metallog—metallographic, metallography
metallogr—metallographer
metaphys—metaphysical, metaphysics
meteorol—meteorological, meteorology
metrol—metrological, metrology
metrop—metropolitan
Mex—Mexican, Mexico
mfg—manufacturing
mfr—manufacturer
mgr—manager
mgt—management
Mich—Michigan
microbiol—microbiological, microbiology
micros—microscopic, microscopical, microscopy
mid—middle
mil—military
mineral—mineralogical, mineralogy
Minn—Minnesota
Miss—Mississippi
mkt—market, marketing
Mo—Missouri
mod—modern
monogr—monograph
Mont—Montana
morphol—morphological, morphology
Mt—Mount
mult—multiple
munic—municipal, municipalities
mus—museum(s)
musicol—musicological, musicology
mycol—mycologic, mycology

N—North
NASA—National Aeronautics & Space Administration
nat—national, naturalized
NATO—North Atlantic Treaty Organization
navig—navigation(al)
NB—New Brunswick
NC—North Carolina
NDak—North Dakota
NDEA—National Defense Education Act
Nebr—Nebraska
nematol—nematological, nematology
nerv—nervous
Neth—Netherlands
neurol—neurological, neurology
neuropath—neuropathological, neuropathology
neuropsychiat—neuropsychiatric, neuropsychiatry
neurosurg—neurosurgical, neurosurgery
Nev—Nevada
New Eng—New England
New York—New York City
Nfld—Newfoundland
NH—New Hampshire
NIH—National Institute of Health
NIMH—National Institute of Mental Health
NJ—New Jersey
NMex—New Mexico
No—Number
nonres—nonresident
norm—normal
Norweg—Norwegian
Nov—November
NS—Nova Scotia
NSF—National Science Foundation
NSW—New South Wales
numis—numismatic(s)
nutrit—nutrition, nutritional
NY—New York State
NZ—New Zealand

observ—observatories, observatory
obstet—obstetric(s), obstetrical
occas—occasional(ly)
occup—occupation, occupational
oceanog—oceanographic, oceanographical, oceanography
oceanogr—oceanographer
Oct—October
odontol—odontology
OEEC—Organization for European Economic Cooperation
off—office, official
Okla—Oklahoma
olericult—olericulture
oncol—oncologic, oncology
Ont—Ontario
oper(s)—operation(s), operational, operative
ophthal—ophthalmologic, ophthalmological, ophthalmology
optom—optometric, optometrical, optometry
ord—ordnance
Ore—Oregon
org—organic

ABBREVIATIONS

orgn—organization(s), organizational
orient—oriental
ornith—ornithological, ornithology
orthod—orthodontia, orthodontic(s)
orthop—orthopedic(s)
osteop—osteopathic, osteopathy
otol—otological, otology
otolaryngol—otolaryngological, otolaryngology
otorhinol—otorhinologic, otorhinology

Pa—Pennsylvania
Pac—Pacific
paleobot—paleobotanical, paleobotany
paleont—paleontology
Pan-Am—Pan-American
parasitol—parasitology
partic—participant, participating
path—pathologic, pathological, pathology
pedag—pedagogic(s), pedagogical, pedagogy
pediat—pediatric(s)
PEI—Prince Edward Islands
penol—penological, penology
periodont—periodontal, periodontic(s)
petrog—petrographic, petrographical, petrography
petrogr—petrographer
petrol—petroleum, petrologic, petrological, petrology
pharm—pharmacy
pharmaceut—pharmaceutic(s), pharmaceutical(s)
pharmacog—pharmacognosy
pharamacol—pharmacologic, pharmacological, pharmacology
phenomenol—phenomenologic(al), phenomenology
philol—philological, philology
philos—philosophic, philosophical, philosophy
photog—photographic, photography
photogeog—photogeographic, photogeography
photogr—photographer(s)
photogram—photogrammetric, photogrammetry
photom—photometric, photometrical, photometry
phycol—phycology
phys—physical
physiog—physiographic, physiographical, physiography
physiol—physiological, phsysiology
Pkwy—Parkway
Pl—Place
polit—political, politics
polytech—polytechnic(s)
pomol—pomological, pomology
pontif—pontifical
pop—population
Port—Portugal, Portuguese
Pos—Position
postgrad—postgraduate
PQ—Province of Quebec
PR—Puerto Rico
pract—practice
practr—practitioner
prehist—prehistoric, prehistory

prep—preparation, preparative, preparatory
pres—president
Presby—Presbyterian
preserv—preservation
prev—prevention, preventive
prin—principal
prob(s)—problem(s)
proc—proceedings
proctol—proctologic, proctological, proctology
prod—product(s), production, productive
prof—professional, professor, professorial
Prof Exp—Professional Experience
prog(s)—program(s), programmed, programming
proj—project(s), projection(al), projective
prom—promotion
protozool—protozoology
Prov—Province, Provincial
psychiat—psychiatric, psychiatry
psychoanal—psychoanalysis, psychoanalytic, psychoanalytical
psychol—psychological, psychology
psychomet—psychometric(s)
psychopath—psychopathologic, psychopathology
psychophys—psychophysical, psychophysics
psychophysiol—psychophysiological, psychophysiology
psychosom—psychosomatic(s)
psychother—psychoterapeutic(s), psychotherapy
Pt—Point
pub—public
publ—publication(s), publish(ed), publisher, publishing
pvt—private

Qm—Quartermaster
Qm Gen—Quartermaster General
qual—qualitative, quality
quant—quantitative
quart—quarterly
Que—Quebec

radiol—radiological, radiology
RAF—Royal Air Force
RAFVR—Royal Air Force Volunteer Reserve
RAMC—Royal Army Medical Corps
RAMCR—Royal Army Medical Corps Reserve
RAOC—Royal Army Ordnance Corps
RASC—Royal Army Service Corps
RASCR—Royal Army Service Corps Reserve
RCAF—Royal Canadian Air Force
RCAFR—Royal Canadian Air Force Reserve
RCAFVR—Royal Canadian Air Force Volunteer Reserve
RCAMC—Royal Canadian Army Medical Corps
RCAMCR—Royal Canadian Army Medical Corps Reserve
RCASC—Royal Canadian Army Service Corps

RCASCR—Royal Canadian Army Service Corps Reserve
RCEME—Royal Canadian Electrical & Mechanical Engineers
RCN—Royal Canadian Navy
RCNR—Royal Canadian Naval Reserve
RCNVR—Royal Canadian Naval Volunteer Reserve
Rd—Road
RD—Rural Delivery
rec—record(s), recording
redevelop—redevelopment
ref—reference(s)
refrig—refrigeration
regist—register(ed), registration
registr—registrar
regt—regiment(al)
rehab—rehabilitation
rel(s)—relation(s), relative
relig—religion, religious
REME—Royal Electrical & Mechanical Engineers
rep—represent, representative
Repub—Republic
req—requirements
res—research, reserve
rev—review, revised, revision
RFD—Rural Free Delivery
rhet—rhetoric, rhetorical
RI—Rhode Island
Rm—Room
RM—Royal Marines
RN—Royal Navy
RNA—ribonucleic acid
RNR—Royal Naval Reserve
RNVR—Royal Naval Volunteer Reserve
roentgenol—roentgenologic, roentgenological, roentgenology
RR—Railroad, Rural Route
Rte—Route
Russ—Russian
rwy—railway

S—South
SAfrica—South Africa
SAm—South America, South American
sanit—sanitary, sanitation
Sask—Saskatchewan
SC—South Carolina
Scand—Scandinavia(n)
sch(s)—school(s)
scholar—scholarship
sci—science(s), scientific
SDak—South Dakota
SEATO—Southeast Asia Treaty Organization
sec—secondary
sect—section
secy—secretary
seismog—seismograph, seismographic, seismography
seismogr—seismographer
seismol—seismological, seismology
sem—seminar, seminary
Sen—Senator, Senatorial
Sept—September
ser—serial, series
serol—serologic, serological, serology
serv—service(s), serving

xxi

ABBREVIATIONS

silvicult—silvicultural, silviculture
soc(s)—societies, society
soc sci—social science
sociol—sociologic, sociological, sociology
Span—Spanish
spec—special
specif—specification(s)
spectrog—spectrograph, spectrographic, spectrography
spectrogr—spectrographer
spectrophotom—spectrophotometer, spectrophotometric, spectrophotometry
spectros—spectroscopic, spectroscopy
speleol—speleological, speleology
Sq—Square
sr—senior
St—Saint, Street(s)
sta(s)—station(s)
stand—standard(s), standardization
statist—statistical, statistics
Ste—Sainte
steril—sterility
stomatol—stomatology
stratig—stratigraphic, stratigraphy
stratigr—stratigrapher
struct—structural, structure(s)
stud—student(ship)
subcomt—subcommittee
subj—subject
subsid—subsidiary
substa—substation
super—superior
suppl—supplement(s), supplemental, supplementary
supt—superintendent
supv—supervising, supervision
supvr—supervisor
supvry—supervisory
surg—surgery, surgical
surv—survey, surveying
survr—surveyor
Swed—Swedish
Switz—Switzerland
symp—symposia, symposium(s)
syphil—syphilology
syst(s)—system(s), systematic(s), systematical

taxon—taxonomic, taxonomy
tech—technical, technique(s)
technol—technologic(al), technology
tel—telegraph(y), telephone

temp—temporary
Tenn—Tennessee
Terr—Terrace
Tex—Texas
textbk(s)—textbook(s)
text ed—text edition
theol—theological, theology
theoret—theoretic(al)
ther—therapy
therapeut—therapeutic(s)
thermodyn—thermodynamic(s)
topog—topographic, topographical, topography
topogr—topographer
toxicol—toxicologic, toxicological, toxicology
trans—transaction(s)
transl—translated, translation(s)
translr—translator(s)
transp—transport, transportation
treas—treasurer, treasury
treat—treatment
trop—tropical
tuberc—tuberculosis
TV—television
Twp—Township

UAR—United Arab Republic
UK—United Kingdom
UN—United Nations
undergrad—undergraduate
unemploy—unemployment
UNESCO—United Nations Educational Scientific & Cultural Organization
UNICEF—United Nations International Childrens Fund
univ(s)—universities, university
UNRRA—United Nations Relief & Rehabilitation Administration
UNRWA—United Nations Relief & Works Agency
urol—urologic, urological, urology
US—United States
USAAF—US Army Air Force
USAAFR—US Army Air Force Reserve
USAF—US Air Force
USAFR—US Air Force Reserve
USAID—US Agency for International Development
USAR—US Army Reserve
USCG—US Coast Guard
USCGR—US Coast Guard Reserve

USDA—US Department of Agriculture
USMC—US Marine Corps
USMCR—US Marine Corps Reserve
USN—US Navy
USNAF—US Naval Air Force
USNAFR—US Naval Air Force Reserve
USNR—US Naval Reserve
USPHS—US Public Health Service
USPHSR—US Public Health Service Reserve
USSR—Union of Soviet Socialist Republics

Va—Virginia
var—various
veg—vegetable(s), vegetation
vent—ventilating, ventilation
vert—vertebrate
Vet—Veteran(s)
vet—veterinarian, veterinary
VI—Virgin Islands
vinicult—viniculture
virol—virological, virology
vis—visiting
voc—vocational
vocab—vocabulary
vol(s)—voluntary, volunteer(s), volume(s)
vpres—vice president
vs—versus
Vt—Vermont

W—West
Wash—Washington
WHO—World Health Organization
WI—West Indies
wid—widow, widowed, widower
Wis—Wisconsin
WVa—West Virginia
Wyo—Wyoming

Yearbk(s)—Yearbook(s)
YMCA—Young Men's Christian Association
YMHA—Young Men's Hebrew Association
Yr(s)—Year(s)
YT—Yukon Territory
YWCA—Young Women's Christian Association
YWHA—Young Women's Hebrew Association

zool—zoological, zoology

AMERICAN MEN & WOMEN OF SCIENCE

Q

QADRI, SYED M HUSSAIN, medical microbiology, for more information see previous edition

QASBA, PRADMANN K, BIOCHEMISTRY. *Current Pos:* cancer expert, Lab Pathophysiol, Div Cancer Biol & Diag, Nat Cancer Inst, NIH, 79-82, sr res chemist, 82-84 & Lab Tumor Immunol & Biol, 85-86, SR RES CHEMIST, LAB MATH BIOL, DIV CANCER BIOL & DIAG, NAT CANCER INST, NIH, 86- *Personal Data:* b India, Feb 19, 38; US citizen; m; c 2. *Educ:* Birla Col Pilani, India, BPharm, 58; Munich Univ, WGer, PhD, 65. *Prof Exp:* Max-Planck fel, Max-Planck Inst Biochem, Munich, WGer, 65-68; asst prof, Dept Cell Biol & Pharmacol, Sch Med, Md Univ, Baltimore, 70-72. *Concurrent Pos:* Vis assoc, Lab Biol & Viruses, Nat Inst Allergy & Infectious Dis, NIH, 68-70; vis scientist, Lab Biochem, Div Cancer Biol & Diag, Nat Cancer Inst, NIH, 72-74 & Lab Pathophysiol, 74-79; dir, Inst Biotechnol, New Delhi, India, 85; consult recombinant DNA technol, Nat Chem Lab, Poona, India, 86 & 87. *Mem:* Am Cancer Soc; Am Soc Biol Chemists; AAAS. *Res:* Cancer biology and diagnosis. *Mailing Add:* 9300 Cedarcrest Dr Bethesda MD 20814-2810

QASIM, MOHAMMAD A, PROTEIN PROTEINASE INHIBITORS, PROTEIN STRUCTURE & FUNCTION. *Current Pos:* postdoctoral fel, 87-90, RES ASSOC, PURDUE UNIV, 94- *Personal Data:* b Aligarh, India, Feb 26, 51; m 83, Sabiha; c Maliha & Sadia. *Educ:* Am Univ, India, BSc, 71, MSc, 73, MPhil, 75, PhD(biochem), 78. *Prof Exp:* Danida fel, Danish Inst Protein Chem, 79-80; lectr biochem, Am Univ, 81-87, reader, 90-94. *Concurrent Pos:* Daad fel, Westfalische Wilhems Univ, 92-93. *Mem:* Protein Soc; Am Soc Biochem & Molecular Biol; Sigma Xi. *Res:* Dissect the inhibitor-protease interaction in terms of the individual contact residues of the inhibitor. *Mailing Add:* Dept Chem Purdue Univ West Lafayette IN 47907. *Fax:* 765-494-0239; *E-Mail:* gasim@ommi.ec.purdue.edu

QASIM, SYED REAZUL, SANITARY & ENVIRONMENTAL ENGINEERING. *Current Pos:* assoc prof, 73-78, PROF CIVIL ENG, UNIV TEX, ARLINGTON, 78- *Personal Data:* b Allahabad, India, Dec 1, 38; m 67, Yasmin Rizvi; c 2. *Educ:* Aligarh Muslim Univ, India, BScEng, 57; WVa Univ, MSCE, 62; US citizen; m 68, Mamoona Shafiq; c Zubaida M, Sulaiman M, Amin M, Ibrahim M, Hajira M & Haleema M. *Educ:* Panjab Univ, Lahore, BS, 58, MS, 60; Imp Col, Eng, MS, 60; London Univ, PhD(chem eng), 66. *Prof Exp:* Lectr chem eng, Panjab Univ, 60-61, Univ Baghdad, Iraq, 68- 70; sr res officer, W R Lab, Lahore, 66-68; instr chem, City Col, Chicago, 70-71; chemist, Chicago Etching Corp, 71-72; process engr, A D Singh Co, 72-73, Austin Co, 73-74; sr process engr, Procon Int, 78-83; asst prof appl chem eng, Univ PM Dhahran, Saudi Arabia, 74- 78; sr consult,

Chem & Indust Consult, 83-88; prin engr, Ambitech Eng Corp, 88-93. *Concurrent Pos:* GMD Found fel, 62; PCSIR grant, 63; part time lectr plant design, Panjab Univ, 66-68; adj fac chem, Triton Col, 83-84. *Mem:* Inst Chem Engrs; Am Inst Chem Engrs; Am Chem Soc; AAAS; Soc Chem Indust; Hazardous Mat Control Res Inst. *Res:* Segregation of particles in granular masses, power technology; plasma arc techology; nitrem process evaluation; pink water treatment technology research. *Mailing Add:* 2807 Bedord St PO Box 5192 Johnstown PA 15904. *Fax:* 814-269-2798, 266-9371; *E-Mail:* qazi@.ctc.com

QAZI, QUTUBUDDIN H, PEDIATRICS, GENETICS. *Current Pos:* asst prof, 69-73, assoc prof, 73-84, PROF PEDIAT, STATE UNIV NY, DOWNSTATE MED CTR, 84- *Personal Data:* b Pavas, India, June 15, 31; m 62; c 3. *Educ:* Grant Med Col, Bombay, MB, BS, 56; Univ Toronto, MA, 65, PhD(genetics), 70. *Prof Exp:* House physician med & psychiat, J J Group Hosps, Bombay, 57-58; intern, Coney Island Hosp, Brooklyn, 59-60; from jr resident to chief resident pediat, King's Co Hosp, Brooklyn, 60-63; fel genetics, Res Inst, Hosp Sick Children, Toronto, 63-68. *Concurrent Pos:* Attend pediat, King's Co Hosp, Brooklyn, 69- & State Univ Hosp, 69-; consult pediat, Methodist Hosp, Brooklyn, 74- *Mem:* Soc Pediat Res; fel Am Acad Pediat; Am Soc Human Genetics; Sigma Xi; Am Pediat Soc; Am Col Med Genetics. *Res:* Microcephaly and mental retardation; congenital adrenal hyperplasia; lead poisoning; dermatoglyphics; cytogenetic disorders; congenital malformations. *Mailing Add:* Dept Pediat Downstate Med Ctr State Univ NY 450 Clarkson Ave Brooklyn NY 11203. *Fax:* 718-270-1985

QI, QUAN, VIBRATIONS & DYNAMICS, NONLINEAR ACOUSTICS. *Current Pos:* DEVELOP ENGR, HEWLETT PACKARD CO, 96- *Personal Data:* b Xian, China; US citizen; m, Sharon L Horstman; c Madeline N. *Educ:* Xian Jiaotong Univ, BS, 82; Univ Ill, MS, 90, PhD(theoret & appl mech), 92. *Prof Exp:* Hunt fel, Univ Ill, Urbana, 92-94; res assoc, Univ Colo, Boulder, 94-96. *Concurrent Pos:* Consult, Arjo Inc, Ill, 92-94. *Mem:* Acoust Soc Am; Am Soc Mech Engrs. *Res:* Modeling and testing of advanced electronics packages. *Mailing Add:* Develop Engr 3404 E Harmony Rd Ft Collins CO 80525-9544

QIN, JIANGUANG, FISH-PLANKTON INTERACTION, PLANKTON COMMUNITY STRUCTURE & TROPHIC DYNAMICS. *Current Pos:* POSTDOCTORAL FEL, 94- *Personal Data:* b Hebei, China, Nov 21, 60; m 86, Ranming Liu; c Stephanie Y & Sarah W. *Educ:* Dalian Fisheries Col, China, BS, 81; Okla Univ, MS, 88; Ohio State Univ, PhD, 94. *Prof Exp:* Res asst, Okla Univ, 86-88. *Mem:* Am Soc Limnol & Oceanog; Am Fisheries Soc. *Res:* Plankton community ecology; growth and survival of larval fish; fertilization and water quality management, fish genetics, aquaculture. *Mailing Add:* PO Box 1346 Kaneohe HI 96744. *Fax:* 808-236-7443; *E-Mail:* qin@hawaii.edu

QIN, SHU, SEMICONDUCTOR DEVICE & FABRICATION, PLASMA THEORY & PROCESSING. *Current Pos:* RES SCIENTIST ELEC ENG, NORTHEASTERN UNIV, 92-; CONSULT, EATON CORP, 93- *Personal Data:* b Beijing, China, May 21, 50; US citizen; m 78, Fuping Zhai; c Zhen. *Educ:* Beijing Polytech Univ, BSEE, 76; Tsinghua Univ, MSEE, 82; Northeastern Univ, PhD(elec eng), 92. *Prof Exp:* Asst prof, Tsinghua Univ, 76-82; sr lectr, Beijing Inst Post & Telecommun, 82-86; res scientist, Lehigh Univ, 86-87. *Mem:* AAAS; Inst Elec & Electronics Engrs Electron Device Soc; Mat Res Soc; sr mem Inst Elec & Electronics Engrs. *Res:* Research and teaching on microelectronics, semiconductor processing plasma theory and processing; author of over 80 publications and granted 2 US patents. *Mailing Add:* 47 Francis St No 2 Malden MA 02148. *Fax:* 781-397-2482; *E-Mail:* shuqin@neu.edu

QIU, CHANG H, SEMICONDUCTOR MATERIALS & DEVICES, OPTOELECTRONICS. *Current Pos:* PRIN INVESTR, ASTRALUX, INC, 94- *Personal Data:* b Hubei, China, Dec 26, 63. *Educ:* Wuhan Univ, BS, 83; Colo Sch Mines, PhD(appl physics), 92. *Prof Exp:* Staff scientist, Inst Physics,

1

Chinese Acad Sci, 83-88; res assoc, Dept Elec Eng, Univ Colo, Boulder, 92-94. *Mem:* Am Phys Soc; Mat Res Soc. *Res:* Photoconductive properties of III-V nitride semiconductors; performed original work on erbium-doped gallium nitrid for light source. *Mailing Add:* 362 Riverside Dr No 6B7 New York NY 10025. *E-Mail:* qiu@colorado.edu, chq1@columbia.edu

QIU, XIAOPING, OIL FIELD CHEMICAL PRODUCTS & PROCESSES, OIL AGGLOMORATION PROCESS. *Current Pos:* SR DEVELOP ENGR, SCHLUMBERGER DOWELL, 97- *Personal Data:* b Sichuan, China, May 19, 63. *Educ:* Chengdu Univ Sci & Technol, BS, 82, MS, 87; Iowa State Univ, PhD(chem eng), 92. *Prof Exp:* Chengdu, Sichuan Inst Indust Antibiotics, 82-84; design engr, Chengdu Chem Eng Corp, 87-88. *Mem:* Am Inst Chem Engrs. *Res:* Develop chemical products used in oilfield to stimulate well production, such as polymer fluids and fluid loss control additives; develop new process of making fluids; optimize manufacturing process; develop waste minimization processes. *Mailing Add:* 110 Schlumberger Dr Sugar Land TX 77477. *Fax:* 918-250-4707; *E-Mail:* xpqiu@slb.com

QUACKENBUSH, FORREST WARD, BIOCHEMISTRY. *Current Pos:* prof, 43-74, head dept, 43-65, EMER PROF BIOCHEM, PURDUE UNIV, WEST LAFAYETTE, 74- *Personal Data:* b Melrose, Wis, Aug 18, 07; m 37; c 2. *Educ:* Univ Wis, BS, 32, PhD(biochem), 37. *Prof Exp:* Asst biochem, Univ Wis, 34 & 36-37; Rockefeller Found fel, Kaiser-Wilhelm Inst & Univ Heidelberg, 38 & Rijk's Univ, Utrecht, 39; res fel, Univ Wis, 39-42. *Mem:* Am Chem Soc; Am Oil Chemist's Soc; Am Soc Biochem & Molecular Biol; Asn Off Anal Chem. *Res:* Biochemistry and nutrition of lipids; chemistry of carotenoids; biosynthesis of lipids. *Mailing Add:* Dept Biochem Purdue Univ 2911 Browning St West Lafayette IN 47906-1307

QUACKENBUSH, ROBERT LEE, microbial genetics, extrachromosomal elements, for more information see previous edition

QUADE, CHARLES RICHARD, MOLECULAR PHYSICS. *Current Pos:* from asst prof to assoc prof, 65-70, PROF PHYSICS, TEX TECH UNIV, 70- *Personal Data:* b Glasgow, Mont, June 18, 36; m 58; c 5. *Educ:* Univ Okla, BS, 58, MS, 60, PhD(physics), 62. *Prof Exp:* Asst prof physics, Univ Del, 62-65. *Concurrent Pos:* Res grants, NSF, Res Corp & Univ Del Res Found, 63-65, Welch Found, Advan Res Proj Agency. *Mem:* Fel Am Phys Soc; Sigma Xi. *Res:* Vibration rotation interactions; microwave spectroscopy; magnetic susceptibilities; crystal field theory. *Mailing Add:* Dept Physics Tex Tech Univ Lubbock TX 79409

QUADE, DANA EDWARD ANTHONY, NONPARAMETRIC, STATISTICS. *Current Pos:* from asst prof to assoc prof, 62-70, PROF BIOSTATIST, UNIV NC, CHAPEL HILL, 70- *Personal Data:* b Cardston, Alta, Jan 11, 35; US citizen; m 62, Erna Goetz; c Jonathan, Christopher & Ingrid (Rojas). *Educ:* Univ Calif, Los Angeles, BA, 55; Univ NC, PhD, 60. *Prof Exp:* Statistician, Communicable Dis Ctr, USPHS, Ga, 60-61 & Nat Inst Neurol Dis & Blindness, 61-62. *Mem:* Fel Am Statist Asn; Inst Math Statist; Biomet Soc; Inter Statist Inst. *Res:* Statistical theory, especially nonparametric. *Mailing Add:* UNC-SPH-Biostat CB No 7400 McGavran-Greenberg Hall Chapel Hill NC 27599-7400. *Fax:* 919-966-3804; *E-Mail:* dana_quade@unc.edu

QUADER, ATHER ABDUL, MECHANICAL ENGINEERING. *Current Pos:* from assoc res engr to staff res engr, 68-83, sr staff res engr, 83-93, PRIN RES ENGR, FUELS & LUBRICANTS DEPT, GEN MOTORS RES LABS, 93- *Personal Data:* b Hyderabad, India, Oct 10, 41; m 68; c Samsena, Salmaan, Saheche. *Educ:* Osmania Univ, India, BE, 62; Univ Wis, PhD(mech eng), 69. *Honors & Awards:* Horning Mem Award, Soc Automotive Engrs, 74, Arch T Colwell Award, 77, 83 & 93, Oral Presentation Award, 76, 78, & 89 & Teetor Ind Lectr, 85. *Prof Exp:* Res asst mech eng, Univ Wis, 63-68. *Mem:* Fel Soc Automotive Engrs; Combustion Inst; Sigma Xi. *Res:* Combustion; internal combustion engines; spectroscopic studies of engine combustion and pollutant formation; lean misfire limit in engines; stratified charge engines; cold start; alternate fuels; reformulated gasoline. *Mailing Add:* Fuels & Lubricants Dept MC-480-106-160 Gen Motors Res Labs Tech Ctr Warren MI 48090-9055

QUADIR, TARIQ, TOUGHENED ZIRCONIA MATERIAL, SILICON NITRIDE MATERIAL. *Current Pos:* VPRES, ENG FUSITE, DIV EMERSON ELECT, 97- *Personal Data:* b Karachi, Pakistan, Aug 26, 53; US citizen; m, Laurie Sharaba; c Dean P, Amber S & Jarrad A. *Educ:* NED Univ Eng & Technol, BE, 78; Ohio State Univ, MS, PhD(ceramic eng), 84. *Prof Exp:* Sr ceramic engr, AC Spark Plug, Gen Motors, 84-87; staff engr, W R Grace, Columbia, MD, 87-93; eng mgr, Alsimag Tech Ceramics, 93-96. *Mem:* Sigma Xi; Am Ceramic Soc; Am Soc Metals; Metall Soc. *Res:* Structural ceramics; developing toughened zirconia, zirconia toughened alumina composites, and silicon nitride for wear and high temperature applications; processing, forming techniques sintering, hiping of the above materials; novel brimdey systems for dry pressing; injection molding. *Mailing Add:* 6000 Fernview Ave Cincinnati OH 45212

QUADRI, SYED KALEEM, NEUROENDOCRINOLOGY. *Current Pos:* ASSOC PROF PHYSIOL, KANS STATE UNIV, 77- *Personal Data:* b Bidar, India. *Educ:* Osmania Univ, India, DVM, 60; Kans State Univ, MS, 66; Mich State Univ, MS, 70, PhD(neuroendocrinol), 73. *Prof Exp:* Vet asst surgeon, State Govt India, 60-64; res Ore Regional Primate Res Ctr, assoc, asst scientist neuroendocrinol, 76-77; asst prof physiol, Univ Ore Health Sci Ctr, 75-77. *Mem:* Sigma Xi; Soc Study Reproduction. *Res:* Primate and rodent neuroendocrinology, with special emphasis on prolactin, aging and breast cancer. *Mailing Add:* Dept Anat & Physiol VMS 228 Kans State Univ Manhattan KS 66506

QUADT, R(AYMOND) A(DOLPH), PHYSICAL METALLURGY. *Current Pos:* RETIRED. *Personal Data:* b Perth Amboy, NJ, Apr 16, 16; m 40; c Brian. *Educ:* Rutgers Univ, BS, 39; Stevens Inst Technol, MS, 47. *Honors & Awards:* Meritorious Pub Serv Citation, USN, 55. *Prof Exp:* Teacher high sch, NJ, 39-42; res metallurgist, Am Smelting & Refining Co, 42-48, mgr aluminum div, 48-50; dir res, Hunter Douglas Aluminum Co, 50-54, vpres res & develop, 54- 57, vpres res & develop, Bridgeport Brass Co, 57-60; pres, Reactive Metals, Inc, 60-65; vpres, Pascoe Steel Corp, 65-73; pres, Phoenix Cement Co, 73-80, consult, 80-84. *Concurrent Pos:* Vchmn, Sunstate Bansshares Inc, Casa Grande, Ariz. *Mem:* Am Soc Metals. *Res:* Physical and process metallurgy of aluminum, titanium, zirconium, columbium and tantalum. *Mailing Add:* 6454 S Willow Dr Tempe AZ 85283

QUAGLIANO, JAMES VINCENT, INORGANIC CHEMISTRY. *Current Pos:* HUDSON PROF CHEM, AUBURN UNIV, 75- *Personal Data:* b New York, NY, Nov 9, 15; m 61; c 2. *Educ:* Polytech Inst Brooklyn, BS, 38, MS, 40; Univ Ill, PhD(inorg chem), 46. *Prof Exp:* Instr chem, Villanova Col, 40-43 & Univ Ill, 44-45; asst prof, Univ Md, 46-48; from asst prof to assoc prof, Univ Notre Dame, 48-58; from assoc prof to prof chem, Fla State Univ, 58-75. *Mem:* AAAS; Am Chem Soc; Am Inst Chemists; fel Royal Soc Chem; NY Acad Sci. *Res:* Inorganic complex compounds; reduction potentials of some inorganic coordination compounds; infrared absorption of inorganic coordination complexes. *Mailing Add:* 1009 West Ave Richmond VA 23220

QUAID, KIMBERLY ANDREA, PSYCHOSOCIAL ASSESSMENT OF NEW MEDICAL TECHNOLOGIES, PREDICTIVE GENETIC TESTING FOR LATE-ONSET DISORDERS. *Current Pos:* clin asst prof, 90-95, CLIN ASSOC PROF MED & MOLECULAR GENETICS & PSYCHIAT, IND UNIV, 95- *Personal Data:* b Elizabeth, NJ, Oct 25, 55. *Educ:* Brown Univ, BA, 77; Johns Hopkins Univ, MA, 82, PhD(psychol), 86. *Prof Exp:* Res assoc, Johns Hopkins Univ Sch Med, 86-89, instr, 89-90. *Concurrent Pos:* Mem, Bd Trustees, Huntington's Dis Soc Am, 91-93; mem, Predictive Testing Comt, World Fedn Neurol; sr adv, Proj Genetic Privacy, Dept Energy, 93-95. *Mem:* Am Soc Human Genetics; Asn Practical & Prof Ethics. *Res:* Psychological and social consequences of predictive genetic testing for late onset disorders; establishing testing protocols and methods of handling the complicated ethical issues that arise from this testing. *Mailing Add:* Dept Med Genetics Ind Univ Med Ctr 975 W Walnut St Indianapolis IN 46202. *E-Mail:* iroe@indyvax.iupui.edu

QUAIFE, MARY LOUISE, BIOCHEMISTRY. *Current Pos:* RETIRED. *Personal Data:* b Madison, Wis; m 69, William H Tuttle. *Educ:* Univ Mich, AB, 38, MS, 39; Univ Ill, PhD(anal chem), 42; Am Bd Clin Chem, dipl, 52. *Prof Exp:* Clin chemist, Univ Hosp, Vanderbilt, 39-40; asst chem, Univ Ill, 41-42, asst physiol, 42-43; sr res chemist, Distillation Prod Industs Div, Eastman Kodak Co, 43-54; res assoc nutrit, Sch Pub Health, Harvard Univ, 56-57, assoc, 57-59; res asst environ health, Sch Pub Health, Univ Mich, 60-61, res assoc obstet & gynec, Med Sch, 61-62; biochemist, Div Toxicol Eval, US Food & Drug Admin, 62-70; biochemist, Toxicol Br, Hazard Eval Div, US Environ Protection Agency, 70-82. *Concurrent Pos:* Consult chem & toxicol, 82- *Mem:* Am Chem Soc; Am Soc Biol Chemists; Am Inst Nutrit; fel Am Inst Chemists; Soc Toxicol. *Res:* Toxicological evaluation of pesticides and food additives; analysis and biochemistry of vitamin E; modern analytical techniques. *Mailing Add:* 1506 33rd St NW Washington DC 20007

QUAIL, JOHN WILSON, CRYSTALLOGRAPHY. *Current Pos:* from asst prof to assoc prof, 64-83, PROF CHEM, UNIV SASK, 83- *Personal Data:* b Brooklyn, NY, Mar 19, 36; Can citizen; m 59, Florence A Nowik; c 4. *Educ:* Univ BC, BSc, 59, MSc, 61; McMaster Univ, PhD(inorg chem), 63. *Prof Exp:* Fel inorg chem, McMaster Univ, 63-64. *Concurrent Pos:* Sabbatical leave, Univ Chem Lab, Cambridge Univ, 72-73, Dept Chem, Univ Alta, Edmonton, 81-82, Dept Crystallog, Birkbeck Col, Univ London, 88-89, Dept Chem & Biochem, Massey Univ, NZ, 93 & Dept Biochem, 96- *Mem:* Chem Inst Can; Am Crystallog Asn. *Res:* Protein crystallography; crystallography of drug molecules. *Mailing Add:* Dept Chem Univ Sask 110 Science Pl Saskatoon SK S7N 5C9 Can. *Fax:* 306-966-4730; *E-Mail:* quail@sask.usask.ca

QUAIL, PETER HUGH, PLANT MOLECULAR BIOLOGY, MOLECULAR PHOTOBIOLOGY. *Current Pos:* RES DIR, PLANT GENE EXPRESSION CTR, ALBANY, CA, 87- *Personal Data:* b Cooma, New SWales, Australia, Feb 4, 44; c 1. *Educ:* Univ Sydney, BSc, 64, PhD(plant physiol), 68. *Prof Exp:* Res assoc, plant res lab, Mich State Univ, 68-71, Biol Inst, Univ Freiburg, 71-73; res fel, Res Sch Biol Sci, Australian Nat Univ, 73-77; sr fel, dept biol, Carnegie Inst Stanford, 77-79; assoc prof bot, Univ Wis-Madison, 79-84, prof bot & genetics, 84-87; prod molecular plant biol, Univ Calif Berkeley, 87- *Mem:* Int Soc Plant Molecular Biol; Am Soc Plant Physiologists; Am Soc Photobiologists. *Res:* Molecular mechanism by which the plant regulatory photoreceptor, phytochrome, controls gene expression in response to light; structural studies on the phytochrome molecule and characterization of regulatory sequences in phytochrome-controlled genes. *Mailing Add:* 416 Vista Heights Rd Richmond CA 94805

QUAILE, JAMES PATRICK, MECHANICAL ENGINEERING, ENERGY SCIENCES. *Current Pos:* Pro engr transp, Transp Tech Ctr, 72-73, syst engr energy, 74-76, mgr, 76-77, liaison scientist consumer prod, 77-82, SYSTS ENGR INFO SYSTS LAB, CORP RES & DEVELOP, GEN ELEC CO, 82- *Personal Data:* b Philadelphia, Pa, Jan 16, 43; m 68; c 2. *Educ:* NJ Inst Technol, BS, 68; Lehigh Univ, MS, 69, PhD (mech eng) 72; State Univ NY, MBA, 85. *Honors & Awards:* Fel, NSF. *Concurrent Pos:* Adj prof, Union Col State Univ of NY. *Mem:* Am Soc Mech Engrs; fel NSF. *Res:* Energy; thermodynamics; heat transfer; fluid dynamics; interdisciplinary systems approach to the conception and development of novel computer systems for decision support and productivity improvement in engineering, manufacturing, marketing and financial areas; use of leading edge technologies such as artificial intelligence/expert systems combined with relational database concepts to implement these systems. *Mailing Add:* 87 St Stephens Lane W Scotia NY 12302

QUALLS, CLIFFORD RAY, MATHEMATICAL STATISTICS. *Current Pos:* asst prof, 67-74, assoc prof, 74-80, PROF MATH, UNIV NMEX, 80- *Personal Data:* b Duncan, Okla, Oct 31, 36; m 59; c 2. *Educ:* Calif State Col Long Beach, BA, 61; Univ Calif, Riverside, MA, 64, PhD(math), 67. *Prof Exp:* Mathematician, US Naval Ord Lab, Calif, 56-61; reliability engr, Autonetics Div, NAm Aviation, Inc, 61-64; instr math, Calif State Col Fullerton, 64-67. *Mem:* Math Asn Am; Inst Math Statist; Inst Elec & Electronics Engrs. *Res:* Crossing problems for stationary stochastic processes; life testing; prediction theory for stochastic processes. *Mailing Add:* 416 Solano SE Albuquerque NM 87108

QUALLS, ROBERT GERALD, BIOGEOCHEMISTRY, SOIL ORGANIC CHEMISTRY. *Current Pos:* ASST PROF, UNIV NEV, 97- *Personal Data:* b May 20, 52. *Educ:* Univ NC, BS & MS; Univ Ga, PhD(ecol), 89. *Honors & Awards:* Founders Award, Int Assoc Water Pollution, 86; Eugene & William Odum Found Res Award, Inst Ecol, 92. *Concurrent Pos:* Res assoc, Duke Univ, 89-92, res prof ecol, 92-96; Consult, J M Montgomery Consult Engrs, 92. *Mem:* Int Humic Substances Soc; AAAS; Ecol Soc Am; Soil Sci Soc Am. *Res:* Reasons why some ecosystems are efficient in recycling and storing nutrients while others are leaky and susceptible to loss of fertility. *Mailing Add:* 5020 Ambrose Dr Reno NY 89509. *E-Mail:* qualls@earth.ers.unr.edu

QUALSET, CALVIN ODELL, AGRONOMY, CONSERVATION BIOLOGY. *Current Pos:* from asst prof to assoc prof, Univ Calif, Davis, 67-74, chmn, Dept Agron & Range Sci, 75-81, assoc dean, Col Agr & Environ Sci, 81-86, chmn, Dept Agron & Range Sci, 91-94, PROF AGRON, UNIV CALIF, DAVIS, 74-; DIR, CALIF GENETIC RESOURCES CONSERV PROG, 85- *Personal Data:* b Newman Grove, Nebr, Apr 24, 37; m 57; c 3. *Educ:* Univ Nebr, BS, 58; Univ Calif, Davis, MS, 60, PhD(genetics), 64. *Prof Exp:* Lab technician agron, Univ Calif, Davis, 60-64; asst prof, Univ Tenn, Knoxville, 64-67. *Concurrent Pos:* Fulbright sr scholar, Australia, 76 & Yugoslavia, 84; ed-in-chief, Crop Sci Soc Am, 80-83; mem, Nat Plant Genetic Resources Bd, 82-87, Res Adv Comt, US AID, 89-92, Nat Res Coun Comt Alternative Farming Pract, 86-88, Nat Res Coun Comt Global Mgt Genetics Resources Workshop, chair, Rev Nat Plant Germplasm Syst, 87-89, Nat Res Coun Comt Sci Eval Introd Genetically Modified Microrganisms & Plants Into Environment; consult, ed bd Plant Breeding, Ger, 85-; chair, Agr Sect AAAS, 92. *Mem:* Fel AAAS; Am Genetics Asn; Genetics Soc Am; Genetics Soc Can; fel Am Soc Agron; fel Crop Sci Soc Am (pres, 89, 94). *Res:* Analysis of quantitative genetic variation in plants; breeding for improvement in agronomic and quality characteristics in barley, wheat, oats, triticale and rye; genetic resources conservation in plants. *Mailing Add:* 478 Floral Way Rohnert Park CA 94928

QUAM, DAVID LAWRENCE, AERODYNAMICS, CONTROL SYSTEMS. *Current Pos:* AEROSPACE ENG CONSULT & PRES, QUAMAERO RES INC, 83- *Personal Data:* b Minneapolis, Minn, June 5, 42. *Educ:* Univ Minn, BAE, 65; Univ Wash, MSAA, 70, PhD(aeronaut & astronaut), 75. *Prof Exp:* Assoc engr, Lockheed-Calif Co, 65; teaching assoc, Univ Wash, 68-75; assoc prof aerospace eng, Univ Dayton, 75-82. *Concurrent Pos:* Sr aerodynamicist, Boeing Commercial Airplane Co, 68-69; control systs analyst, Marine Systs Div, Honeywell, 72-75; fac researcher, Fac Res Prog, USAF-Am Soc Eng Educ, 77; chmn, Flight Simulation Course, Univ Dayton, 79-80; math modeling consult, Technol, Inc, 79-85; vis prof, Frank J Seiler Res Lab, USAF Acad, 80-81. *Mem:* Am Inst Aeronaut & Astronaut; Am Helicopter Soc; Am Soc Eng Educ. *Res:* Perception studies and myoelectric feedback for flight simulation; missile aerodynamics and control; digital control of spacecraft; experimental and theoretical work in unsteady aerodynamics; aircraft and ship simulator design. *Mailing Add:* 37 Seminary Ave Dayton OH 45403

QUAMME, GARY ARTHUR, MEDICINE. *Current Pos:* from asst prof to assoc prof, 76-86, PROF, DEPT MED, UNIV BC, 86- *Personal Data:* b Moose Jaw, Sask, Oct 26, 44; c 3. *Educ:* Univ Sask, BSc, 65, DVM, 69; Univ Ottawa, MSc, 70; McGill Univ, PhD(physiol), 74. *Prof Exp:* Res investr, Toxicol Res Div, Health Protection Br, Health & Welfare Can, 69-70; instr, Dept Physiol, Western Col Vet Med, Sask, 70-71; Med Res Coun fel, Centre d'Etudes Nucleaires de Saclay, Gif-sur-Yvette, France, 74-75; asst prof, Dept Physiol, McGill Univ, Montreal, 75-76. *Concurrent Pos:* Med Res Coun scholar, Dept Physiol, McGill Univ, 75-76 & Dept Med, Univ BC, 76-80; mem, Prog Comt, Am Soc Nephrology, 82 & 89, Grants Comt, Med Res Coun Can, 83 & Sci Coun, Kidney Found Can, 87-90; chmn, Symp Magnesium, Am Col Nutrit, 85 & Scanning Electron Micros Conf, Ont, 87; assoc ed, Can J Physiol & Pharmacol, 85-90; Med Res Coun vis scientist & prof, Inst Physiol, Univ Zurich, 87-88; Schering travel award, Can Soc Clin Invest, 87; vis scientist, Roche Res Found, 87-88; Izaak Walton Killam fac res fel, 88; ed, Magnesium Res, 88-; clin investr, Can Asn Gastroenterol, 89-; distinguished lectr, Fac Med, Univ BC, 89. *Mem:* Can Soc Nephrology; Can Physiol Soc; Am Fedn Clin Res; Am Soc Nephrology; Fedn Am Socs Exp Biol; Am Soc Clin Invest; Can Soc Clin Invest; Int Soc Nephrology; Am Physiol Soc; Int Union Physiol Sci. *Mailing Add:* Dept Med Vancouver Hosp & Health Sci Ctr Univ BC Koerner Pavilion 2211 Westbrook Mall Rm S-154 Vancouver BC V6T 1W5 Can

QUAMME, HARVEY ALLEN, HORTICULTURE. *Current Pos:* From res officer fruit res to res scientist, Can Dept Agr, 63-74, res scientist I, 74-77, res scientist II, 78-82, res scientist III, 88-91, MEM STAFF, RES STA, CAN DEPT AGR, 74-, RES SCIENTIST IV, 91- *Personal Data:* b Browniee, Sask, Apr 23, 40; m 63, Sonya L MacKenzie; c Darcie L & Heather A. *Educ:* Univ Sask, BSA, 62, MSc, 64; Univ Minn, PhD(hort), 71. *Honors & Awards:* Gourley Award Res Pomol, Am Soc Hort Sci, 73 & 83; Carroll R Miller Award, Nat Peach Coun, 79; Westdale Award, Can Soc Hort Sci, 87, Hoechst Award, 89, C J Bishop Award, 91. *Mem:* Am Soc Hort Sci; Can Soc Hort Sci; Int Soc Hort Sci; Agr Inst Can. *Res:* Evaluation and development of new rootstock varieties of tree fruits with emphasis on dwarfing precocity, cold hardiness and disease resistance; investigation of mechanisms of winter survival in fruit crops which involve deep supercooling; breeding new apple varieties. *Mailing Add:* Pac Agr Food Res Sta Agr Summerland BC V0H 1Z0 Can. *Fax:* 250-494-0755; *E-Mail:* quammh@cm.agr.ca

QUAN, STUART F, CRITICAL CARE MEDICINE, SLEEP DISORDERS. *Current Pos:* fel pulmonary, Univ Ariz, 79-80, instr med, 80-81, asst prof, 81-86, assoc prof med, 86-92, assoc prof anesthesiol, 87-92, PROF MED & ANESTHESIOL, UNIV ARIZ, TUCSON, 92- *Personal Data:* b San Francisco, Calif, May 16, 49; m 71; c 2. *Educ:* Univ Calif, Berkeley, AB, 70, San Francisco, MD, 74. *Prof Exp:* Med intern internal med, Univ Wis-Madison, 74-75, med resident, 75-77; fel critical care, Univ Calif, San Francisco, 77-78, fel emergency med, 78-79. *Concurrent Pos:* Mem, Anesthesiol & Respiratory Therapy Devices Panel, US Food & Drug Admin, 86-89, chmn, 88-89, consult, 89-93; mem, Am Bd Sleep Med, 90- *Mem:* Am Thoracic Soc; Soc Critical Care Med; Am Col Chest Physicians; Clin Sleep Soc; Am Fedn Clin Res; Nat Asn Med Dirs Respiratory Care. *Res:* Mechanisms responsible for bronchial hyperreactivity after viral infections; epidemiology of sleep disorders; mechanical ventilation in acute respiratory failure. *Mailing Add:* Univ Ariz Col Med AHSC 1501 N Campbell Ave PO Box 245030 Tucson AZ 85724-0001

QUAN, WEILUN, COMPUTATIONAL ELECTROPHYSIOLOGY, CELLULAR ELECTROPHYSIOLOGY. *Current Pos:* CHIEF BIOMED ENGR, WINTHROP UNIV HOSP, STATE UNIV NY, STONEY BROOK, 96-; ADJ ASSOC PROF, HOFSTRA UNIV, 96- *Personal Data:* b Shanghai, China, Aug 10, 47; m 87, Suhua Jin; c Cindy. *Educ:* Qinghua Univ, BS, 70; SChina Inst Technol, MS, 81; Case Western Res Univ, PhD(biomed eng), 88. *Prof Exp:* Sr res assoc, Case Western Res Univ, 90-92; electrophysiol engr & instr bioeng, N Shore Univ Hosp, Cornell Univ Med Col, 92-94; sr scientist, Long Island Jewish Hosp, Einstein Med Col, 94-96. *Concurrent Pos:* Fel, Am Heart Asn, 87-89; prin investr, Whitaker Found, 90-, Cornell Supercomputer Ctr, NSF, 93-; co-prin investr, NIH, 93- *Mem:* Am Heart Asn; NAm Soc Pacing & Electrophysiol; Inst Elec & Electronics Engrs. *Res:* Cardiac electrophysiology and computer application in cardiology; methodology used includes theoretical computer modeling and signal processing. *Mailing Add:* 22 Surrey Lane Plainview NY 11803. *Fax:* 516-663-8546; *E-Mail:* eggwza@vaxd.hofstra.edu

QUAN, WILLIAM, ENVIRONMENTAL SCIENCE. *Current Pos:* proj mgr, Solid Waste Mgt Prog, 88-92, PROG MGR, HAZARDOUS WASTE MGT PROG, 92- *Personal Data:* b Aug 1, 48. *Educ:* Univ Calif, Berkeley, BS, 70; Ohio State Univ, MS, 72; Golden Gate Univ, MPA, 92. *Prof Exp:* Chief formulating chemist, Lee Pharmaceut, S El Monte, Calif, 73-75; mem tech staff, Rocketdyne Div, Rockwell Int, Canoga Park, Calif, 75-77; pub health chemist, Air & Indust Hyg Lab, 77-80, coordr, State's Indust Waste Recycling Prog, 80-83, chief, Environ Assessment Unit, Toxic Substances Control Div, Calif Dept Health Serv, 83-88. *Res:* Pollution prevention and environmental chemistry; polymer and analytical chemistry; environmental fate of contaminants; plastic mineral composite technology. *Mailing Add:* 640 Brooklyn Ave Oakland CA 94606. *Fax:* 510-554-3434

QUAN, XINA SHU-WEN, POLYMER ENGINEERING. *Current Pos:* from assoc mem to mem, AT&T Bell Labs, 80-91, distinguished mem tech staff, 91-94, tech mgr, 94, DEPT HEAD, AT&T BELL LABS, 94- *Personal Data:* b Gloucester, NJ, Dec 23, 57; m 80; c 1. *Educ:* Mass Inst Technol, SBChE, 80, SMChE, 80; Princeton Univ, PhD(chem eng), 86. *Mem:* Am Phys Soc; Am Chem Soc. *Res:* Multiphase polymer characterization; block copolymers; polymer blends; mechanical properties; small-angle scattering; plastic liquid crystal displays; polymers for passive optical components. *Mailing Add:* AT&T Bell Labs Rm 7F 212 PO Box 636 Murray Hill NJ 07974

QUANDT, EARL RAYMOND, JR, CHEMICAL ENGINEERING. *Current Pos:* res coordr appl mech, USN Marine Eng Lab, 63-67, HEAD POWER SYSTS DIV, USN SHIP RES & DEVELOP CTR, 67- *Personal Data:* b Washington, DC, Feb 5, 34; m 56; c 4. *Educ:* Univ Cincinnati, ChE, 56; Univ Pittsburgh, PhD(chem eng), 61. *Prof Exp:* Sr engr, Bettis Atomic Power Lab, Westinghouse Elec Corp, 56-63. *Mem:* Am Inst Chem Engrs; Sigma Xi. *Res:* Two phase flow; heat transfer; systems dynamics; reliability; marine propulsion. *Mailing Add:* 1605 Riverside Dr Annapolis MD 21401-5803

QUANSTROM, WALTER ROY, ANIMAL BEHAVIOR. *Current Pos:* staff ecologist, Stand Oil Co, Ind, 74-77, dir ecol, 77-79, dir environ & energy conserva, 79-81, MGR INDUST HYGIENE, TOXICOL & SAFETY, STANDARD OIL CO, IND, 81-; VPRES, ENVIRON AFFAIRS & SAFETY, AMOCO CORP, GEN MGR, 84- *Personal Data:* b Gary, Ind, Nov 20, 42; m 63, Harriet F Sheldon; c 2. *Educ:* Bethany Nazarene Col, BS, 64; Univ Okla, PhD(zool), 68. *Prof Exp:* NASA trainee, Univ Okla, 65-67; asst prof biol, Olivet Nazarene Col, 68-70; assoc prof & chmn dept, Northwest Nazarene Col, 70-74, chmn div natural sci & math, 72-74. *Concurrent Pos:* Mem, Exec Develop Prog, Northwestern Univ, 80; adj prof, Kellogg Grad

Sch Bus, Northwestern Univ; vchmn, Keystone Ctr, Keystone Sci Sch. *Mem:* Am Soc Mammalogists. *Res:* Ethoecology of Richardson's ground squirrel, Spermophilus richardsonii. *Mailing Add:* 923 Maryknoll Circle Glen Ellyn IL 60137

QUARLES, CARROLL ADAIR, JR, ATOMIC PHYSICS, GEOPHYSICS. *Current Pos:* from asst prof to assoc prof, Tex Christian Univ, 67-74, assoc dean, 74-78, chmn dept, 78-84, PROF PHYSICS, TEX CHRISTIAN UNIV, 74-, HOLDER W A MONCRIEF CHAIR PHYSICS, 87-, CHAIR, PHYSICS DEPT, 96- *Personal Data:* b Abilene, Tex, Nov 24, 38; m 71, Sonja Bandy; c Jennifer & John. *Educ:* Tex Christian Univ, BA, 60; Princeton Univ, MA, 62, PhD(physics), 64. *Prof Exp:* Res fel physics, Brookhaven Nat Lab, 64-65, asst physicist, 65-67. *Mem:* AAAS; Am Phys Soc; Am Asn Physics Teachers. *Res:* Electron and atomic collisions; bremsstrahlung; inner shell ionization; coincidence experiments in electron collisions, positron annihilation studies of rocks and porous materials, chemical effects in x-ray production. *Mailing Add:* Dept Physics Tex Christian Univ Ft Worth TX 76129. *Fax:* 817-921-7110; *E-Mail:* c.quarles@tcu.edu

QUARLES, GILFORD GODFREY, PHYSICS. *Current Pos:* RETIRED. *Personal Data:* b Charlottesville, Va, Dec 24, 09; m 34; c 3. *Educ:* Univ Va, BS, 30, MS, 33, PhD(physics), 34. *Prof Exp:* Instr physics, Univ Va, 31-33; actg prof, Mercer Univ, 34-35 & Univ Ala, 35-41; assoc prof, Furman Univ, 41-43; res assoc, Harvard Univ, 44-45; from assoc prof to prof eng res, Pa State Univ, 45-56; tech & sci consult to commanding gen, Ballistic Missile Agency, US Dept Army, 56-58, chief scientist, Ord Missile Command, Redstone Arsenal, Ala, 58-59, chief sci adv, CEngrs, 59-60; dir long-range mil planning, Bendix Corp, 60-61; chief sci adv, Off Chief Engrs, US Army CEngrs, 61-75. *Concurrent Pos:* Asst dir, Ord Res Lab, Pa State Univ, 47-52, dir, 52-56. *Mem:* AAAS. *Res:* Photographic latent image; electrooptical Kerr effect; underwater ordnance; sonic and ultrasonic vibrations; ballistic missiles. *Mailing Add:* 1244 Westerly Pkwy State College PA 16801

QUARLES, JOHN MONROE, MEDICAL MICROBIOLOGY, VIROLOGY. *Current Pos:* dir grad studies, 89-92, PROF MICROBIOL, COL MED, TEX A&M UNIV, 91-, DIR, CTR FLOW CYTOMETRY & IMAGE ANALYSIS, HEALTH SCI CTR, 94- *Personal Data:* b Chattanooga, Tenn, May 24, 42; c Bryan Stephen. *Educ:* Fla State Univ, BS, 63, MS, 65; Mich State Univ, PhD(microbiol), 73; Am Bd Microbiol, cert pub health & med lab microbiol, 75. *Prof Exp:* Res microbiologist, Ctr Dis Control, USPHS, 65-66; head, Serol-Virol Lab, Naval Med Sch, Nat Naval Med Ctr, USN, 66-69; fel, Univ Tenn & Oak Ridge Nat Lab, 73-74 & Nat Cancer Inst & Oak Ridge Nat Lab, 74-76. *Mem:* Am Soc Microbiol; Am Soc Virol. *Res:* Transformation of mammalian cells by chemical carcinogens; rapid techniques for diagnosis of microorganisms; flow cytometry; dialysis culture of microorganisms and mammalian cells; animal virology; antiviral agents and vaccines; influenza; distance learning. *Mailing Add:* Dept Med Microbiol Col Med Tex A&M Univ College Station TX 77843-1114. *Fax:* 409-845-3479; *E-Mail:* jmquarles@tamu.edu

QUARLES, RICHARD HUDSON, BIOCHEMISTRY, NEUROCHEMISTRY. *Current Pos:* From staff fel to sr staff fel biochem, 68-73, res chemist, 73-77, HEAD, SECT MYELIN & BRAIN DEVELOP, NAT INST NEUROL & COMMUNICATIVE DIS & STROKE, 77- *Personal Data:* b Baltimore, Md, Sept 23, 39; m 64; c 3. *Educ:* Swarthmore Col, AB, 61; Harvard Univ, PhD(biochem), 66. *Concurrent Pos:* NSF fel, Inst Animal Physiol, Cambridge, Eng, 66-67, Nat Inst Neurol Dis & Stroke fel, 67-68. *Mem:* AAAS; Am Chem Soc; Am Soc Neurochem; Int Soc Neurochem. *Res:* Metabolism of phospholipids, glycolipids, and glycoproteins; roles of lipids and proteins in membrane structure and function; developing brain; myelination. *Mailing Add:* NINDS NIH Bldg 49 Rm 2A28 Bethesda MD 20892-0001

QUARLES, RICHARD WINGFIELD, polymer chemistry; deceased, see previous edition for last biography

QUARONI, ANDREA, DEVELOPMENTAL BIOLOGY. *Current Pos:* DEPT PHYSIOL, CORNELL UNIV, 81- *Personal Data:* b Milano, Italy, Aug 9, 46; m 75; c 1. *Educ:* Univ Pavia, Italy, PhD(biochem), 70. *Prof Exp:* Asst volontario biochem, Univ Pavia, Italy, 70-71; asst I biochem, Swiss Fed Inst Technol, Zurich, 72-75; res fel biochem, Harvard Med Sch & Mass Gen Hosp, 75-78; instr biochem, Harvard Med Sch, 78-80, asst prof, 80-81. *Concurrent Pos:* Asst biochem, Mass Gen Hosp, 78-80. *Mem:* Soc Complex Carbohydrates; Swiss Biochem Soc; Swiss Biochem Soc; Tissue Culture Asn. *Res:* Structure and function of the intestinal epithelium; identification, purification and biosynthesis of surface membrane proteins and glycoproteins and cultured intestinal epithelial cells; structure and composition of the intestinal basement membrane. *Mailing Add:* Dept Physiol Cornell Univ T8 024A Vet Res Tower Ithaca NY 14853-0001

QUARRY, MARY ANN, ANALYTICAL CHEMISTRY. *Current Pos:* RES MGR, DUPONT MERCK PHARMACEUT, 91- *Personal Data:* b Philadelphia, Pa; m 89, John W Dolan. *Educ:* Villanova Univ, BS, 75, PhD(anal chem), 84. *Prof Exp:* Anal chemist, Arco Chem, 79-80; applications specialist, DuPont Instrument Systs, 81-84; res chemist, E I Du Pont de Nemours & Co, Inc, 84-89, group leader, 89-91. *Mem:* Sigma Xi; Am Chem Soc. *Res:* Pharmaceutical analysis; separation optimization by gradient elution HPLC; expert systems. *Mailing Add:* DuPont Merck Pharmaceut PO Box 80353 Wilmington DE 19880-0353

QUARTARARO, IGNATIUS NICHOLAS, DENTISTRY. *Current Pos:* RETIRED. *Personal Data:* b Brooklyn, NY, July 26, 26; m 52; c 4. *Educ:* NY Univ, DDS, 52; Am Bd Endodont, dipl, 59. *Prof Exp:* Asst endodontia, NY Univ, 52-54, from instr to assoc prof, 54-73. *Concurrent Pos:* Consult, Dept Surg, New York Infirmary Hosp, 61-66; dir endodont, Cath Med Ctr, Brooklyn & Queens, 72-85; pres, DSSNY, 89. *Mem:* Fel Am Asn Endodont; fel Am Col Dent; Am Acad Oral Med; Sigma Xi; fel Int Col Dentists. *Res:* Temporo-mandibular joint; fluoroscopy of sealing properties of endodontic cements; pathology of the periapical lesion. *Mailing Add:* 246 Westminster Rd West Hempstead NY 11552

QUARTERMAN, ELSIE, BOTANY, ECOLOGY. *Current Pos:* from instr to assoc prof biol, Vanderbilt Univ, 43-66, chmn div bact, bot & zool, 60-61, prof biol, 66-76, PROF EMER, VANDERBILT UNIV, 76- *Personal Data:* b Valdosta, Ga, Nov 28, 10. *Educ:* Ga State Col, AB, 32; Duke Univ, MA, 41, PhD(bot), 49. *Honors & Awards:* Oakleaf Award, Nature Conservancy, 81; Sol Feinstone Environ Award, 82. *Prof Exp:* Pub sch teacher, Ga, 32-43. *Concurrent Pos:* Mem bd dirs, Tenn Bot Gardens, 71-72; US Fish & Wildlife Serv Tenn Coneflower Recovery Team, 80-83; mem bd, Tenn Nature Conservancy, 93-95; Tenn State Comt Natural Areas; Tenn Protection Planning Comt. *Mem:* Asn Southeastern Biologists; Sigma Xi. *Res:* Distribution of the Compositae in South Georgia; composition and structure of limestone cedar glade plant communities in middle Tennessee; ecology of bryophytes; climax forests of the coastal plain of southeastern United States; autecology of middle Tennessee endemics; conservation of ecosystems. *Mailing Add:* 1313 Belmont Park Ct Nashville TN 37215

QUASS, LA VERNE CARL, INORGANIC CHEMISTRY. *Current Pos:* assoc prof, 76-80, PROF CHEM, GRAND VIEW COL, 80-, CHMN, DIV NATURAL SCI, 86- *Personal Data:* b Beloit, Wis, Jan 17, 37; m 59; c 3. *Educ:* Luther Col, BA, 59; Univ Wis-Madison, MS, 64, PhD(chem), 69. *Prof Exp:* Instr chem, Univ Wis-Fox Valley Ctr, 63-66; asst prof chem, Univ Wis, Parkside, 69-76. *Mem:* AAAS; Am Chem Soc; Chem Soc. *Res:* Organometallic and organosilicon chemistry. *Mailing Add:* 901 26th St West Des Moines IA 50265-3263

QUAST, JAY CHARLES, ICHTHYOLOGY. *Current Pos:* RETIRED. *Personal Data:* b San Francisco, Calif, Sept 17, 23; m 49. *Educ:* Univ Calif, BA, 48, MA, 50 & 51, PhD(ichthyol), 60. *Prof Exp:* High sch teacher, Calif, 51-53; asst, Univ Calif, Los Angeles, 53-57; res biologist, Scripps Inst, Univ Calif, 58-61; supvry fishery biologist, Nat Marine Fisheries Serv, Nat Oceanic & Atmospheric Admin, 61-74, proj scientist, Environ Res Labs, 74-76, nat sci ed, 77-80, res biologist, 81-83. *Mem:* Am Fisheries Soc; Am Soc Ichthol & Herpet. *Res:* Fish ecology, taxonomy, variation, osteology and population dynamics; research management. *Mailing Add:* 1565 Jamestown St SE Salem OR 97302

QUASTEL, D M J, PHYSIOLOGY. *Current Pos:* assoc prof, 69-77, PROF PHARMACOL, UNIV BC, 77- *Personal Data:* b Cardiff, UK, June 7, 36; Can citizen; m 59; c 2. *Educ:* McGill Univ, BS, 55, MD, CM, 59, PhD(physiol), 63. *Prof Exp:* Med Res Coun Can fel, 61-63; Muscular Dystrophy Asn Can fel, 63-65; asst prof physiol, Dalhousie Univ, 65-69. *Mem:* Can Physiol Soc; Soc Neurosci. *Res:* Mechanisms of synaptic transmission. *Mailing Add:* Dept Pharmacol Univ BC 2176 Health Sci Mall Vancouver BC V6T 1Z3 Can

QUATE, CALVIN F(ORREST), APPLIED PHYSICS, ELECTRICAL ENGINEERING. *Current Pos:* prof appl physics & elec eng, 61-95, LELAND T EDWARDS PROF ELEC ENG, STANFORD UNIV, 86- *Personal Data:* b Baker, Nev, Dec 7, 23; m 46; c 4. *Educ:* Univ Utah, BS, 44; Stanford Univ, PhD(elec eng), 50. *Honors & Awards:* Morris N Liebmann Award, Inst Elec & Electronics Engrs, 81, Rank Prize for Opto-Electronics, 82, Achievement Award, 86 & Medal of Hon, 88; Nat Medal Sci, 92. *Prof Exp:* Tech staff mem, Bell Tel Labs, NJ, 49-58; dir & vpres res, Sandia Corp, NMex, 59-61. *Concurrent Pos:* Guggenheim fel & Fulbright scholar, Fac Sci, Montpellier, France, 68-69; chmn, Dept Appl Physics, Stanford Univ, 69-72 & 78-81, assoc dean, Sch Humanities & Sci, 72-74 & 82-83; sr res fel, Xerox Palo Alto Res Ctr, 84- *Mem:* Nat Acad Sci; Nat Acad Eng; Am Phys Soc; fel Inst Elec & Electronics Engrs; fel Acoust Soc Am; fel AAAS; fel Am Acad Arts & Sci; hon fel Royal Micros Soc. *Res:* Microwave electronics and solid state devices; physical acoustics; imaging microscopy and the storage of digital information; holder or co-holder of 42 patents; author or co-author of over 160 publications. *Mailing Add:* Dept Appl Physics MS 4090 Stanford Univ Stanford CA 94305

QUATRANO, RALPH STEPHEN, CELL BIOLOGY, DEVELOPMENTAL BIOLOGY. *Current Pos:* chmn, Dept Biol, 92-97, JOHN N COUCH PROF BIOL, UNIV NC, CHAPEL HILL, 89- *Personal Data:* b Elmira, NY, Aug 3, 41; m, Barbara Bishico; c Stephen, Elisabeth & Carolyn. *Educ:* Colgate Univ, AB, 62; Ohio Univ, MS, 64; Yale Univ, PhD(biol), 68. *Prof Exp:* From asst prof to prof bot, Ore State Univ, 68-86, dir, Ctr Gene Res & Biotechnol, 84-86; mgr molecular biol, Cent Res, Dupont, 86-92. *Concurrent Pos:* Vis prof, Marine Biol Lab, Woods Hole, Stanford Univ & Friday Harbor Lab, Univ Wash. *Mem:* Soc Develop Biol; Am Soc Plant Physiologists; Int Plant Molecular Biol Soc; Am Soc Cell Biol. *Res:* Studies in physiology, cell and molecular biology of plant cell differentiation and embryogenesis in algae and angiosperms. *Mailing Add:* Dept Biol Univ NC Chapel Hill NC 27599-3280. *E-Mail:* rsq@unc.edu

QUATTROCHI, DALE ANTHONY, REMOTE SENSING & LANDSCAPE ECOLOGY. *Current Pos:* geographer, Sci & Technol Lab, John C Stennis Space Ctr, 80-92, GEOGRAPHER GLOBAL HYDROL, MARSHALL SPACE FLIGHT CTR, NASA, 92- *Personal Data:* b Cleveland, Ohio, Dec 3, 50; m 77. *Educ:* Ohio Univ, BS, 73; Univ Tenn, MS, 78; Univ Utah, PhD, 90. *Prof Exp:* Res assoc, Miss Remote Sensing Ctr, Miss State Univ, 77-80. *Concurrent Pos:* Adj asst prof, Dept Geog, Univ New Orleans, 88-, Univ Southern Miss, 90- *Mem:* Asn Am Geographers; Am Soc Photogram & Remote Sensing; Sigma Xi; Int Asn Landscape Ecol. *Res:* Analysis of landscape environmental interrelationships; remote sensing data analysis and modeling of urban biophysical interrelationships; author of numerous articles and papers. *Mailing Add:* NASA/Global Hydrol & Climate Ctr George C Marshall Space Flight Ctr MS-ES42 Huntsville AL 35812

QUAY, PAUL DOUGLAS, GEOCHEMISTRY, LIMNOLOGY. *Current Pos:* Res assoc geol, Quaternary Res Ctr, 77-80, ASST PROF, DEPT GEOL SCI & OCEANOG, UNIV WASH, 80- *Personal Data:* b New York, NY, Oct 10, 49. *Educ:* City Univ New York, BA, 71; Columbia Univ, PhD(geol), 77. *Res:* Determining ocean mixing rates by using radiocarbon distribution; modeling global carbon dioxide and radiocarbon distributions in nature; studying the geochemistry of lakes, rivers and marine systems using naturally occurring radioisotopes; chemical oceanography. *Mailing Add:* 304 N 41st St Seattle WA 98103

QUAY, PAUL MICHAEL, causation, isomorphisms in physics; deceased, see previous edition for last biography

QUAY, THOMAS LAVELLE, ANIMAL ECOLOGY. *Current Pos:* ENVIRON CONSULT, 80- *Personal Data:* b Mt Holly, NJ, Aug 23, 14; m 39; c 1. *Educ:* Univ Ark, BS, 38; NC State Col, MS, 40, PhD(zool), 48. *Prof Exp:* Asst, Univ Ark, 35-38; instr zool & entom, 46-48, from asst prof to assoc prof zool, 48-57, prof zool, NC State Univ, 57-80. *Mem:* AAAS; Ecol Soc Am; Am Inst Biol Sci; Am Ornithologists Union; Wildlife Soc. *Res:* Ecological succession of birds; habitat associations and niche relationships of animals; animal behavior. *Mailing Add:* 2720 Vanderbuilt Ave Raleigh NC 27607

QUAY, WILBUR BROOKS, NEUROENDOCRINOLOGY, HISTOPHYSIOLOGY. *Current Pos:* INDEPENDENT RES WRITING & CONSULT, 90- *Personal Data:* b Cleveland, Ohio, Mar 7, 27; m 53, 76; c 1. *Educ:* Harvard Univ, AB, 50; Univ Mich, Ann Arbor, MS & PhD(zool), 52. *Honors & Awards:* Bissendorf Lectr, 87. *Prof Exp:* Instr anat, Med Sch, Univ Mich, 52-56; from asst prof to prof zool, Univ Calif, Berkeley, 56-73, Miller prof, 64-65 & 71-72; prof, Waisman Ctr Ment Retardation & Human Develop, Dept Zool & Endocrinol Reprod Physiol Prog. Univ Wis-Madison, 73-77; prof anat, Dept Anat & grad div biochem, Dept Human Biol Chem & Genetics, Univ Tex Med Br, 77-83; Sr scientist, Advan Develop Div, Healthdyne, Inc, 83-84; vis scholar & res assoc, Dept Physiol & Anat, Univ Calif, Berkeley, 83-90. *Concurrent Pos:* Fel, Neth Orgn Advan Pure Res, Cent Inst Brain Res, Amsterdam, 66; res grants, NSF, NIH, Univ Wisc Sea Grant Prog & Fisheries Res Bd Can; mem ment retardation res & training comt, Nat Inst Child Health & Human Develop, 70-73; co-founder & assoc ed, J Pineal Res, 83-; independant researcher, writer & consult, Bio-Res Lab, Napa, Calif, 83-90. *Mem:* Endocrine Soc; Am Physiol Soc; Am Chem Soc; Am Asn Anat; Int Brain Res Orgn; Soc Neurosci. *Res:* Neuroendocrinology; chronobiology; regulatory, rhythmic and adaptive mechanisms in nervous, glandular, and reproductive systems; vertebrate pineal complex; biogenic amines; interrelations of pineal, retina and central nervous system; analytical methods and evaluations of avian male reproduction. *Mailing Add:* 1627 State Rd Y New Bloomfield MO 65063-9719

QUAZI, AZIZUL H(AQUE), ELECTRICAL ENGINEERING. *Current Pos:* res electronic engr, Info Processing Div, US Navy Underwater Sound Lab, Conn, New London Lab, 65-69, team leader, 69-85, br head, 85-88, SR RES ENGR & CONSULT, INFO PROCESSING BR, NAVAL UNDERSEA WARFARE CTR, NEWPORT, RI. *Personal Data:* b Rahimpur, Bangladesh, Jan 1, 35; m 67; Suraiya S Chowdhury; c Abu S & Shakil A. *Educ:* Univ Dacca, BSEE, 56; Munich Tech Univ, DrEng, 63. *Prof Exp:* Asst engr, Govt Bangladesh & Utah Int Inc, USA, Chittagong H T, Bangladesh, 56-58; res assoc eng, Munich Tech Univ, 64-65. *Concurrent Pos:* Lectr, Dept Elec Eng, Univ RI, 66-68, Univ Conn, Hartford Grad Ctr, Univ New Haven; Ger Acad exchange scholar, 58-63. *Mem:* Sr mem AAAS; Inst Elec & Electronics Engrs; fel Acoust Soc Am. *Res:* Research and development in the field of statistical theory of communication, especially in detection, localization and classification of underwater targets; semiconductor devices; high frequency; underwater acoustics; advanced systems technology, digital signal processing, underwater communications, sonar systems developments, and advanced concept developments. *Mailing Add:* Naval Undersea Warfare Ctr Code 3124 Bldg 1320 Newport RI 02841. *Fax:* 860-440-6228; *E-Mail:* quazi@a1.vsdec.nl.nuwc.navy.mil

QUE, LAWRENCE, JR, BIOINORGANIC CHEMISTRY, METALLOBIOCHEMISTRY. *Current Pos:* assoc prof, 83-87, PROF CHEM, UNIV MINN, 87- *Personal Data:* b Manila, Philippines; US citizen. *Educ:* Ateneo Manila Univ, BSCH, 69. *Prof Exp:* Asst prof chem, Cornell Univ, 77-83. *Res:* Bioinorganic chemistry; metallobiochemistry; oxygen activation; nonheme iron enzymes; biomimetic chemistry. *Mailing Add:* Chem Dept Univ Minn 207 Pleasant St SE Minneapolis MN 55455-0431

QUEBBEMANN, ALOYSIUS JOHN, TOXICOLOGY. *Current Pos:* asst prof, 69-75, ASSOC PROF PHARMACOL, SCH MED, UNIV MINN, MINNEAPOLIS, 75- *Personal Data:* b Chicago, Ill, Jan 19, 33; m 67; c 5. *Educ:* Univ Alaska, BS, 60; NMex Highlands Univ, MS, 64; State Univ NY, Buffalo, PhD(pharmacol), 68. *Prof Exp:* USPHS res fel pharmacol, Sch Med, State Univ NY, Buffalo, 68-69; Merck Found fac develop award, 69. *Mem:* Am Soc Nephrol. *Res:* Pharmacology of renal transport mechanisms. *Mailing Add:* 1564 Fulham St St Paul MN 55108

QUEDNAU, FRANZ WOLFGANG, ENTOMOLOGY, TAXONOMIC ENTOMOLOGY. *Current Pos:* RES SCIENTIST II ENTOM, CAN FORESTRY SERV, DEPT AGR, 64- *Personal Data:* b Dresden, Ger, Apr 27, 30; m 69; c 2. *Educ:* Free Univ, Berlin, BSc, 51, PhD(zool), 53. *Prof Exp:* Res asst entom, Biologische Bundesanstalt, Berlin, 53-60; prof officer, Plant Protection Res Inst, Pretoria, SAfrica, 60-63. *Concurrent Pos:* Fulbright fel travel grant & Ger Res Coun fel, Dept Biol Control, Univ Calif, Riverside, 58-59. *Mem:* Entom Soc Can. *Res:* Biological control of insect pests; ecology of hymenopterous parasites; toxonomy of trichogramma; taxonomy of aphids. *Mailing Add:* Laurentian Forest Res Ctr PO Box 3800 1055 Du PEPS Ste Foy PQ G1V 4C7 Can

QUEEN, DANIEL, ELECTRONICS ENGINEERING, ACOUSTICS. *Current Pos:* PRES, DANIEL QUEEN ASSOCS, 70- *Personal Data:* b Boston, Mass, Feb 15, 34; m 57; c 1. *Prof Exp:* Engr, Magnecord Inc, Ill, 55-57; proj engr, 3M-Revere-Wollensak, 57-62; dir eng, Perma-Power Div, Chamberlain Mfg Co, 63-70. *Concurrent Pos:* Rep, Am Nat Standards Comt, 73-; standards mgr, Audio Eng Soc, 81-, chmn tech coun, 86-96. *Mem:* Acoust Soc Am; Inst Elec & Electronics Engrs; fel Audio Engr Soc; AAAS; Soc Motion Picture & TV Engr. *Res:* Development of sound reinforcement technology for small meeting and teaching rooms; human factors research involving acoustical conditions and noise. *Mailing Add:* Daniel Queen Associates 239 W 23rd St New York NY 10011. *Fax:* 212-645-5436; *E-Mail:* master@dqueen.com

QUEENAN, JOHN T, OBSTETRICS & GYNECOLOGY. *Current Pos:* PROF OBSTET & GYNEC & CHMN DEPT, SCH MED, GEORGETOWN UNIV, 80- *Personal Data:* b Aurora, Ill, May 5, 31; m 57; c 2. *Educ:* Univ Notre Dame, BS, 54; Cornell Univ, MD, 58; Am Bd Obstet & Gynec, dipl, 66. *Prof Exp:* From clin instr to clin assoc prof obstet & gynec, Med Col, Cornell Univ, 62-72; prof obstet & gynec & chmn dept, Univ Louisville, 72-80. *Concurrent Pos:* Dir Rh-clin & Lab, New York Hosp, 62-72; from asst attend to sr attend, Greenwich Hosp, Conn, 63-71; chief obstet & gynec, Norton-Childrens Hosp, Louisville, 73-80; obstet & gynec-in-chief, Georgetown Univ Hosp, 80-; ed, Contemp Obstet-Gynec. *Mem:* Fel Am Col Obstetricians & Gynecologists; fel Am Col Surgeons; affil Royal Soc Med; fel Am Fertil Soc; NY Acad Sci. *Res:* Treatment of erythroblastosis fetalis by aminicentesis and in intrauterine transfusions; care of the immunized obstetrical patient and treatment to prevent future immunization; perinatal medicine; management of the high risk pregnancy; perinatal ultrasound; study of intrauterine growth retardation. *Mailing Add:* Dept Obstet & Gynec Georgetown Univ Sch Med 3800 Reservoir Rd NW Washington DC 20007-2196

QUEENER, SHERRY FREAM, BIOCHEMISTRY, PHARMACOLOGY. *Current Pos:* From instr to assoc prof, 71-84, PROF PHARMACOL, SCH MED, IND UNIV, INDIANAPOLIS, 84- *Personal Data:* b Muskogee, Okla, July 8, 43; m 67, Stephen W Queener; c 2. *Educ:* Okla Baptist Univ, BS, 65; Univ Ill, Urbana, MS, 68, PhD(biochem), 70. *Concurrent Pos:* Woodrow Wilson scholar, 65. *Mem:* AAAS; Am Chem Soc; Am Soc Clin Res; NY Acad Sci; Am Soc Biol Chemists. *Res:* Regulation of metabolic pathways; enzyme regulation at the genetic level and as mediated by effector molecules; antibiotic therapy of Pneumocystis carinii. *Mailing Add:* Dept Pharmacol Ind Univ Sch Med, 635 Barnhill Dr Indianapolis IN 46202-5120. *Fax:* 317-274-1560

QUEENER, STEPHEN WYATT, MICROBIOLOGY. *Current Pos:* Sr scientist, 70-74, res scientist, 74-80, group leader cell res & develop, 89-94, SR RES SCIENTIST, ASSAY TECHNOL DEVELOP, ELI LILLY & CO, 81- *Personal Data:* b Indianapolis, Ind, Jan 31, 43; m 67; c 2. *Educ:* Wabash Col, BA, 65; Univ Ill, MS, 68, PhD(biochem), 70. *Honors & Awards:* Serv Award Int Br, Am Soc Microbiol. *Concurrent Pos:* Guest lectr, Czechoslovak Acad Sci & Europ Fedn Microbiol Sci, 81; mem, Int Sci Coun, World Congress Microbiol, 94. *Mem:* Am Soc Microbiol; Am Chem Soc; Soc Indust Microbiol (secy, 89-); Sigma Xi; Mycol Soc. *Res:* Development and application of techniques for efficient mutation and selection, strain breeding, and recombinant DNA manipulations. *Mailing Add:* Eli Lilly & Co MC 625 Bldg 88 Indianapolis IN 46285

QUE HEE, SHANE STEPHEN, ANALYTICAL & ENVIRONMENTAL CHEMISTRY, ENVIRONMENTAL SCIENCES. *Current Pos:* assoc prof, 89-94, PROF ENVIRON HEALTH SCI, UNIV CALIF, LOS ANGELES, 94- *Personal Data:* b Sydney, Australia, Oct 11, 46. *Educ:* Univ Queensland, BSc, 68, MSc, 71; Univ Sask, PhD(org chem), 76. *Honors & Awards:* Cert Outstanding Achievement, US Environ Protection Agency, 81. *Prof Exp:* Res & teaching fel, McMaster Univ, 76-78; from asst prof to assoc prof environ health, Univ Cincinnati, 78-89. *Concurrent Pos:* Mem TOXNET, Nat Library Med, 85-89. *Mem:* Fel Am Inst Chemists; AAAS; Am Chem Soc; Am Indust Hyg Asn; Am Col Toxicol; Air Pollution Control Asn; NY Acad Sci; Am Conf Govt Indust Hyg; Am Publ Health Asn. *Res:* Microanalytical techniques; chemiluminescence; bioluminescence; industrial hygiene; pesticide chemistry; lipid chemistry; photochemistry; analytical chemistry; ecology; biological monitoring; clinical chemistry; ecotoxicology, environmental health, hazard waste chemistry. *Mailing Add:* Univ Calif Dept Environ Health Sci Sch Publ Health 10833 Le Conte Ave Los Angeles CA 90095-1772. *Fax:* 310-794-2106; *E-Mail:* squehee@uda.edu

QUEK, FRANCIS K H, COMPUTER SCIENCE, ELECTRICAL ENGINEERING. *Current Pos:* ASST PROF ELEC ENG & COMPUT SCI & CO-DIR, VISION INTERFACES & SYSTS LAB, UNIV ILL, CHICAGO. *Mem:* Inst Elec & Electronics Engrs; Asn Comput Mach. *Res:* Computer vision, dynamic vision, object recognition, human computer interaction; video analysis for multi-media database access and robot navigation. *Mailing Add:* Dept Elec Eng & Comput Sci Univ Ill 851 S Morgan Chicago IL 60607

QUELLER, DAVID CHARLES, EVOLUTION OF SOCIAL BEHAVIOR. *Current Pos:* Huxley res instr, Rice Univ, 84-87, res assoc, 87-89, asst prof, 89-94, ASSOC PROF, DEPT ECOL & EVOLUTIONARY BIOL, RICE UNIV, 94- *Personal Data:* b Madison, Wis, May 20, 54; m 88, Joan E Strassmann; c Anna, Daniel & Philip. *Educ:* Univ Ill, BA, 76; Univ Mich, MS, 76, PhD(biol scis), 83. *Honors & Awards:* Young Investr Award, Am Soc Naturalists, 85. *Prof Exp:* NATO fel, Univ Sussex, 83-84. *Concurrent Pos:* J S Guggenheim Mem Found fel, Rice Univ, 88-89. *Mem:* Soc Study Evolution; Am Soc Naturalists; Int Union Study Social Insects; Behav Ecol Soc; Soc Syst Biol; Animal Behav Soc. *Res:* Evolution of social interactions; theoretical studies of kin selection; lab and field studies of the evolution of altruistic behavior in eusocial wasps. *Mailing Add:* Dept Ecol & Evolutionary Biol Rice Univ 6100 Main St Houston TX 77005-1827. *Fax:* 713-285-5232; *E-Mail:* queller@pop.rice.edu

QUENEAU, PAUL E(TIENNE), EXTRACTIVE METALLURGY, MINERAL ENGINEERING. *Current Pos:* prof eng, 71-87, EMER PROF ENG & RES, THAYER SCH ENG, DARTMOUTH COL, 87- *Personal Data:* b Philadelphia, Pa, Mar 20, 11; m 39; c 2. *Educ:* Columbia Univ, BA, 31, BSc, 32, EM, 33; Delft Univ Technol, DSc, 71. *Honors & Awards:* Egleston Medal, Columbia, 65; Douglas Gold Medal, Am Inst Mech Engrs, 68; Extractive Metall Lect Award, Am Inst Mining, Metall & Petrol Engrs, 77; Gold Medal, Brit Inst Mining & Metall, 80; Henry Krumb lectr, Am Inst Mining & Eng, 84. *Prof Exp:* Metall engr, Int Nickel Co, WVa, 34-37, res engr, Ont, 38-40, dir res, 41 & 46-48, metall engr, Exec Dept, NY, 49-57, vpres, 58-69, tech asst to pres, 60-66, asst to chmn & consult engr, 67-69; vis scientist, Delft Univ Technol, 70-71. *Concurrent Pos:* Geogr, Perry River Arctic Exped, 49; chmn, Adv Comt Arctic Res, US Navy, 57; chmn, Int Symp Extractive Metall Copper, Nickel & Cobalt, Am Inst Mining, Metall & Petrol Engrs, 60, dir, 67-70; mem, Columbia Eng Coun, 65-70; mem, Vis Comt, Mass Inst Technol, 67-70, dir, Eng Found, 66-76, chmn, 73-75; consult engr, 72-; vis prof, Inst Technol, Univ Minn, 74-75 & Univ Utah, 87-91. *Mem:* Nat Acad Eng; fel Metall Soc (pres, 69); Nat Soc Prof Engrs; Can Inst Mining & Metall; Am Inst Mining, Metall & Petrol Engrs (vpres, 67-70); Australasian Inst Mining & Metall; Brit Inst Mining & Metall. *Res:* Utilization of mineral resources; patentee processes and apparatus employed in the pyrometallurgy, hydrometallurgy and vapometallurgy of nickel, copper, cobalt, lead and iron; extractive metallurgy oxygen technology; INCO oxygen flash smelting; oxygen top-blow rotary converter; lateritic ore matte smelting; nickel high pressure carbonyl and iron ore recovery processes; Lurgi QSL lead-making and Dravo oxygen sprinkle smelting copper processes. *Mailing Add:* Thayer Sch Eng Dartmouth Col Hanover NH 03755

QUENON, ROBERT HAGERTY, MINING ENGINEERING. *Current Pos:* RETIRED. *Personal Data:* b Clarksburg, WVa, Aug 2, 28; m 53, Jean Bowling; c Evan, Ann & Richard. *Educ:* WVa Univ, BS, 51; George Washington Univ, LLB, 64. *Hon Degrees:* PhD, Univ Mo, 79, Blackburn Col, 83 & WVa Univ, 88. *Honors & Awards:* Eavenson Award, Soc Mining Metall & Explor, 94. *Prof Exp:* Mine supt, Consol Coal Co, WVa, 56-61; mgr deep mines, Pittston Co, Va, 64-66; gen mgr, Riverton Coal Co, WVa, 66-67; mgr opers, Coal & Shale Oil Dept, Exxon Co, Houston, 67-69; pres, Monterey Coal Co, Houston, 69-76; sr vpres, Carter Oil Co, Houston, 76-77; exec vpres, Peabody Coal Co, 77-78, pres & chief exec officer, 78-83; pres & chief exec officer, Peabody Holding Co Inc, St Louis, 83-90, chmn, 90-91. *Concurrent Pos:* Bd dirs, Newmont Gold Co & St Louis, Laclede Steel Co; trustee, Blackburn Col, Ill, 75-83 & St Louis Univ, 81-91; chmn bd, Nat Coal Asn, 78-80; chmn, Bituminous Coal Operator's Asn, 80-83 & 89-91; vchmn, Am Mining Cong, 80-91. *Mem:* Am Mining Cong; Nat Coal Asn. *Mailing Add:* 6 Upper Ladue Rd St Louis MO 63124-1675

QUENTIN, GEORGE HEINZ, CHEMICAL ENGINEERING. *Current Pos:* PROJ MGR, GENERATION & STORAGE DIV, ELEC POWER RES INST, 77- *Personal Data:* b Rome, NY, Jan 25, 34; m 60; c 5. *Educ:* Rensselaer Polytech Univ, BChE, 55; Iowa State Univ, MS, 62, PhD(chem eng), 65. *Prof Exp:* Chem engr, Ind Ord Works, E I du Pont de Nemours & Co, Inc, 55-57, process engr, 57-58; technologist, US Indust Chem Div, Nat Distillers & Chem Corp, Ill, 58-60; sr engr cent eng dept, Monsanto Co, Mo, 65-66, eng specialist, 66-69; asst prof chem eng, Univ NMex, 69-73; assoc prof control eng, Univ Tex, 73-77. *Concurrent Pos:* Consult process control, 70-77. *Mem:* Am Inst Chem Engrs; Am Chem Soc; Instrument Soc Am; Soc Comput Simulation. *Res:* Coal gasification research and development for electric power generation; experimental pilot plant studies of process dynamics; control analysis of advanced power plant technology by computer simulation; gas turbine advanced diagnostic instrumentation development and testing; expert systems for gas turbine operation and maintenance; knowledge-based interactive video training systems. *Mailing Add:* Elec Power Res Inst 3412 Hillview Ave Palo Alto CA 94303-0813

QUERFELD, CHARLES WILLIAM, ATMOSPHERIC OPTICS. *Current Pos:* SCIENTIST, BALL AEROSPACE SYSTS, 82-88 & 90- *Personal Data:* b Bloomington, Ill, Mar 29, 33; m 95, Judith A Hall; c Edward C. *Educ:* Harvard Univ, BA, 55; Clarkson Col Technol, MS, 69, PhD(physics), 70. *Honors & Awards:* Victor K LaMer Award, Am Chem Soc, 70. *Prof Exp:* Field engr, Darin & Armstrong, 55-56; physicist, US Army Atmospheric Sci Lab, 56-66; res asst physics, Clarkson Col Technol, 66-69; scientist solar physics, High Altitude Observ, Nat Ctr Atmospheric Res, 70-81; scientist, E-Systs, 88-90. *Concurrent Pos:* Consult, Atmospheric Sci Lab, White Sands, NMex, 72-73. *Mem:* AAAS; Am Phys Soc; Sigma Xi. *Res:* Atmospheric optics. *Mailing Add:* 7183 Dry Creek Ct Longmont CO 80503-8581

QUERINJEAN, PIERRE JOSEPH, BIOTECHNOLOGY, MULTIMEDIA REMOTE TEACHING. *Current Pos:* GEN MGR BIOTECHNOL INFO, NPMA BIOCLUB, 89- *Personal Data:* b Spa, Belg, Jan 13, 42; m 65, Antoine N; c Genevieve & Didier. *Educ:* Univ Louvain, PhD(biochem), 66; Inst Pasteur, Paris, cert immunol, 69. *Prof Exp:* IRSIA fel biochem, Univ Louvain, 63-66, FNRS res fel immunol, 67-75, res fel cancerology, 75-89. *Concurrent Pos:* Europ Molecular Biol Orgn fel immunol, Med Res Coun Lab, Cambridge Univ, 71-72; Int Union Against Cancer Fel immunol, Mt Sinai Sch Med, NY & Southern Med Sch, Dallas, 73-74; conceptor, Remote Teaching in Biol, 91- *Mem:* Belg Soc Biochem; Belg Soc Immunol; Am Asn Immunol; Brit Biochem Soc. *Res:* Systemic approach of biological problems with the help of computer science tools; cancer's reversibility including diagnostic and therapeutic approaches-biomatics, health systemic approach. *Mailing Add:* NMPA Bioclub Ave Des Fauvettes 15 Ottignies B-1341 Belgium

QUERRY, MARVIN RICHARD, OPTICAL PHYSICS. *Current Pos:* from asst prof to prof, 68-87, prof physics, 75-87, CURATOR'S PROF PHYSICS, 87-, CHMN DEPT PHYSICS, UNIV MO, KANSAS CITY, 87- *Personal Data:* b Butler, Mo, Nov 7, 35; m 57; c 3. *Educ:* Univ Kansas City, BS(math) & BS(physics), 61; Kans State Univ, MS, 64, PhD(physics), 68. *Prof Exp:* Asst prof physics, Kans State Univ, 66-67, res assoc, 67-68. *Concurrent Pos:* Res grants & contracts, Univ Mo, US Dept Interior, USAF, US Army, Dept Com & NASA, 69-; pres, Sci Metrics Inc, 75-; Univ Mo, Kansas City Trustees Fac Fel, 85-86. *Mem:* AAAS; fel Optical Soc Am; Am Phys Soc; Am Asn Physics Teachers. *Res:* Measurement of the optical properties and optical constants of liquids, solids and biological materials. *Mailing Add:* Chancellor Academics Univ Mo 5115 Oak Ave Kansas City MO 64110-2446

QUERTERMUS, CARL JOHN, JR, ANIMAL BEHAVIOR, AQUATIC ECOLOGY. *Current Pos:* from asst prof to assoc prof, 72-82, PROF BIOL, WGA COL, 83- *Personal Data:* b Chicago, Ill, June 28, 43; m 84, Polly Holmes; c Kristin, Sonny, Lisa & Christy. *Educ:* Ill State Univ, BS, 65, MS, 67; Mich State Univ, PhD(zool), 72. *Prof Exp:* Instr biol, Ill High Sch, 67-69. *Concurrent Pos:* Consult lakes & wetlands; mem bd dirs, Ga Wildlife Fedn, 91- *Mem:* Am Fisheries Soc; NAm Lake Mgt Soc. *Res:* Habitat selection and movement patterns of largemouth bass in reservoirs; assessment of black bass fisheries and fishing quality in Georgia reservoirs. *Mailing Add:* Dept Biol WGa Col Carrollton GA 30118

QUESADA, ANTONIO F, APPLIED MATHEMATICS. *Current Pos:* MATHEMATICIAN, AIR FORCE GEOPHYS LAB, 70- *Personal Data:* b San Jose, Costa Rica, Feb 25, 25; nat US; m 54. *Educ:* Mass Inst Technol, SB, 47; Harvard Univ, MS, 58, PhD, 64. *Prof Exp:* Instr physics, Univ Costa Rica, 42-44; sr res mathematician, Baird Atomic, Inc, 49-68 & Dynarand, Inc, 68-69. *Concurrent Pos:* Consult, Govt Costa Rica, 54-55. *Mem:* Am Math Soc; Soc Indust & Appl Math; Math Asn Am. *Res:* Differential equations; noise theory; magnetodydrodynamics. *Mailing Add:* PO Box 111 Cambridge MA 02138

QUESENBERRY, CHARLES P, STATISTICS, QUALITY CONTROL. *Current Pos:* assoc prof, 66-69, PROF STATIST, NC STATE UNIV, 69- *Personal Data:* b Dugspur, Va, Apr 13, 31; m 53; c 4. *Educ:* Va Polytech Inst, 57, MS, 58, PhD(statist), 60. *Honors & Awards:* Brumbaugh Award, Am Soc Qual Control, 88. *Prof Exp:* From asst prof to assoc prof math, Mont State Univ, 60-66. *Concurrent Pos:* NASA grant, 64-66; NSF grant, 77-79; indust consult, Gen Motors, Union Carbide & Interalia. *Mem:* Fel Am Statist Asn; Int Statist Inst; Am Soc Qual Control. *Res:* Statistical inference; nonparametric discrimination, goodness-of-fit, model discrimination and validity; quality control, particularly statistical process control. *Mailing Add:* 224 Northbrook Dr Raleigh NC 27609

QUESENBERRY, KENNETH HAYS, PLANT BREEDING & GERMPLASM, CYTOGENETICS. *Current Pos:* from asst prof to assoc prof agron, 75-86, PROF AGRON, UNIV FLA, 86- *Personal Data:* b Springfield, Tenn, Feb 28, 47; m 69, Joyce; c James K & Kendra J. *Educ:* Western Ky Univ, BS, 69; Univ Ky, PhD(crop sci), 75. *Prof Exp:* D F Jones fel cytogenetics, Univ Ky, 72-75. *Concurrent Pos:* Vis prof agron dept, Univ Wis-Madison, 86; vis prof, Crop Sci Dept, Ore State Univ, 94. *Mem:* Fel Am Soc Agron; fel Crop Sci Soc Am; Am Forage & Grassland Coun. *Res:* Breeding and cytogenetics of temperate and tropical forage legumes; selection of varieties producing greater yield, digestibility and animal performance; germplasm evaluation for response to root-knot nematodes, soil flooding tolerance, disease resistance, seed production potential and drought stress tolerance; development of protocols for tissue culture and genetic transformation of forage legumes. *Mailing Add:* Dept Agron 304 Newell Hall Univ Fla Gainesville FL 32611-0500. *Fax:* 352-392-1840; *E-Mail:* clover@gnv.ifas.ufl.edu

QUESNEL, DAVID JOHN, MATERIALS SCIENCE, MECHANICAL METALLURGY. *Current Pos:* From asst prof to assoc prof, 77-89, PROF MECH ENG & MAT SCI, RIVER CAMPUS, UNIV ROCHESTER, 89- *Personal Data:* b Plattsburg, NY, Apr 5, 50; m 73, Alicia M; c 1. *Educ:* State Univ NY, Stony Brook, BE, 72; Northwestern Univ, MS, 74, PhD(mat sci), 77. *Honors & Awards:* Ralph Teetor Educ Award, Soc Advan Educ, 89. *Concurrent Pos:* NSF res initiation grant, 78-; Alexander Von Humboldt fel,

85-86. *Mem:* Sigma Xi; Metall Soc; Am Soc Mech Engrs; Am Soc Metals; Mat Res Soc. *Res:* Mechanical metallurgy with emphasis on fracture and fatigue of metals; cyclic response of metals to repetitive strain; author of technical papers in general area of mechanical behavior of materials. *Mailing Add:* Dept Mech Eng Univ Rochester Rochester NY 14627-0001

QUEST, KEVIN B, NUMERAL METHODS, ASTROPHYSICS. *Current Pos:* PROF, ELECTRO & COMPUT ENG DEPT, UNIV CALIF, SAN DIEGO, 88- *Personal Data:* b Scott AFB, Ill, Sept 18, 52. *Educ:* Drexel Univ, BS, 75; Univ Calif, Los Angeles, PhD(space plasma physics), 82. *Honors & Awards:* Macelware Medal, Am Geophys Union, 88. *Prof Exp:* Staff mem, Los Alamos Nat Lab, 82-88. *Mem:* Fel Am Geophys Union. *Mailing Add:* Univ Calif San Diego 9500 Gilman Dr La Jolla CA 92093. *Fax:* 619-534-2487; *E-Mail:* kquest@ucsd.edu

QUESTAD, DAVID LEE, POLYMER SCIENCE. *Current Pos:* ASST PROF ENG SCI & MECH, PA STATE UNIV, 81- *Personal Data:* b Muskegon, Mich, Aug 22, 52. *Educ:* Pa State Univ, BS, 74; Rutgers Univ, MS, 78, PhD(mech & mat sci), 81. *Prof Exp:* Anal eng, Pratt & Whitney Aircraft, 74-75; asst, Rutgers Univ, 76-78, teaching asst statics & dynamics, 78-79. *Mem:* Am Phys Soc; Soc Plastics Engrs; Sigma Xi; NY Acad Sci. *Res:* Effects of hydrostatic pressure on physical and mechanical properties of polymers, specifically pressure, volume, temperature and dielectric measurements; large scale deformation and thermal aging of polymers. *Mailing Add:* 1317 Hillside Dr Vestal NY 13850

QUEVEDO, WALTER COLE, JR, ANIMAL GENETICS. *Current Pos:* from asst prof to assoc prof, 61-70, PROF BIOL, BROWN UNIV, 70- *Personal Data:* b Brooklyn, NY, Jan 7, 30; m 55, Mercedes H. *Educ:* St Francis Col, BS, 51; Marquette Univ, MS, 53; Brown Univ, PhD(biol), 56. *Prof Exp:* Asst, Marquette Univ, 51-53; teaching assoc, Brown Univ, 53-55; resident res assoc, Argonne Nat Lab, 56-58; sr cancer res scientist, Roswell Park Mem Inst, 58-61. *Mem:* AAAS; Am Soc Photobiol; Soc Develop Biol; Genetics Soc Am; Soc Exp Biol & Med; Soc Investigative Dermat. *Res:* Mammalian genetics; radiation biology; physiological genetics of coat and skin coloration in mice; regulation of melanin formation in normal and neoplastic pigmented tissues. *Mailing Add:* Div Biol & Med Brown Univ Providence RI 02912

QUIBELL, CHARLES FOX, PLANT ANATOMY, PLANT SYSTEMATICS. *Current Pos:* Asst prof, 70-73, assoc prof, 73-81, PROF BIOL, SONOMA STATE UNIV, 81- *Personal Data:* b Fresno, Calif, Jan 29, 36; m 70; c 2. *Educ:* Pomona Col, BA, 58; Univ Calif, Berkeley, PhD(bot), 72. *Mem:* AAAS; Bot Soc Am; Am Soc Plant Taxonomists; Am Inst Biol Sci; Soc Econ Bot; Sigma Xi. *Res:* Systematic anatomy of woody saxifrages; comparative wood anatomy of dicotyledonous plants. *Mailing Add:* 4682 Hidden Oaks Rd Santa Rosa CA 95404-9541

QUICK, GRAEME R, AGRICULTURAL ENGINEERING. *Current Pos:* CONSULT ENGR. *Personal Data:* b Mar 10, 36; m, Marlene Robertson; c Peter, Tim & Steve. *Educ:* Iowa State Univ, MS, 70, PhD, 72. *Honors & Awards:* Urrbrae Medal, 83. *Concurrent Pos:* Exprt, UN/Food & Agr Orgn & UN Int Develop Orgn; head, Agr Eng Div, Int Rice Res Inst; res engr, White Farm Equip; dir eng, Dept Agr, Univ NSW; ed, J Soc Eng Agr, Australia. *Mem:* Fel Am Soc Agr Engrs; fel Inst Engrs Australia; Soc Eng Agr Australia. *Res:* Grain harvesting equipment design and evaluation; farm equipment development. *Mailing Add:* 292 David Lowe Way Peregian Beach Qld 4573 Australia. *Fax:* 61-754-48-2174

QUICK, JAMES S, PLANT BREEDING, GENETICS. *Current Pos:* PROF WHEAT BREEDING, COLO STATE UNIV, 81- *Personal Data:* b Devils Lake, NDak, Oct 20, 40; m 68; c 3. *Educ:* NDak State Univ, BA, 62; Purdue Univ, MS, 65, PhD(plant breeding, genetics), 66. *Prof Exp:* Asst geneticist, Rockefeller Found, prof, 66-69; assoc prof durum wheat breeding, NDak State Univ, 69-76, prof, 76-81. *Mem:* Fel Crop Sci Soc Am; Coun Agr Sci & Technol. *Res:* Development of new varieties of wheat, improved breeding methods and genetic, pathological, physiological, entomological and agronomic research. *Mailing Add:* 2545 Orchard Pl Ft Collins CO 80521. *Fax:* 970-491-0564

QUICK, NATHANIEL RICHARD, LASER SYNTHESIS OF MATERIALS, ACCELERATED LIFE OF TESTING MATERIALS. *Current Pos:* VPRES RES & DEVELOP, MEMTEC AM CORP, 96-; PRES & CHIEF SCIENTIST, APPLICOTE ASSOC, 89-;. *Personal Data:* b Brooklyn, NY, Apr 20, 49; m, Lauralee Wickens; c Andrea, Jelani, Anthony & Erica. *Educ:* Cornell Univ, BS, 71, MS, 74, PhD(mat sci & eng), 76. *Prof Exp:* Mat scientist, Eastman Kodak, 75-77; vpres lab opers, Washburn Wire Prod, 77-80; supvr technol appln, AT&T Technol/Bell Labs, 80-85; technol mgr, EG&G/ Kaiser-Hill, LLC, 90-96. *Concurrent Pos:* NSF fel, 73; guest researcher, Nat Inst Stand & Technol, 91-; prin investr, US Dept Energy, 93- *Mem:* Am Soc Metals Int; Laser Inst Am; Inst Elec & Electronics Engrs; Am Soc Testing & Mat; NY Acad Sci. *Res:* Laser synthesis of ceramic electro-conductors and semi-conductors as a second phase in dielectric ceramics; laser etching and laser reflowing of dielectric ceramics for fabrication of high power integrating substrates; in-situ materials characterization during accelerated life testing using optical spectroscopy techniques; 23 domestic and foreign patents. *Mailing Add:* 894 Silverado Ct Lake Mary FL 32746. *Fax:* 303-966-7383; *E-Mail:* 104630.100@compuserve.com

QUICK, WILLIAM ANDREW, BOTANY. *Current Pos:* assoc prof, 67-82, PROF BIOL, UNIV REGINA, 82 - *Personal Data:* b Senlac, Sask, July 18, 25; m 53; c 3. *Educ:* Univ Sask, BA, 46, BEd, 51, MA, 60, PhD(plant physiol), 63. *Prof Exp:* Asst prof plant physiol, Univ Guelph, 63-67. *Mem:* AAAS; Am Soc Plant Physiologists; Can Soc Plant Physiologists; Weed Sci Soc Am. *Res:* Dormancy mechanisms in seeds; wild oat (Avena fatua L) seed dormancy and environmental constraints; physiology of herbicides. *Mailing Add:* Dept Biol Univ Regina Regina SK S4S 0A2 Can

QUIE, PAUL GERHARDT, PEDIATRICS. *Current Pos:* resident, Dept Pediat, Univ Minn, Minneapolis, 54-57, res fel, Univ Hosp, 57-58, from instr to assoc prof pediat, 58-68, consult physician, Inst Child Develop Nursery Sch, 60-90, prof microbiol & Am Legion Mem Heart res prof, 74-91, PROF PEDIAT & LAB MED, UNIV MINN, MINNEAPOLIS, 68-, PROF MICROBIOL, 74-, REGENTS PROF PEDIAT, 90- *Personal Data:* b Dennison, Minn, Feb 3, 25; m 51, Elizabeth Holmes; c Katherine A, William L, Paul J & David A. *Educ:* St Olaf Col, BA, 50; Yale Univ, MD, 53; Am Bd Pediat, dipl. *Hon Degrees:* MD, Univ Lund, Swed, 93. *Honors & Awards:* Mead Johnson Award, Am Acad Pediat, 71; James W McLaughlin Lectr, Univ Tex, 73; Alexis F Hartman Sr Lectr, Wash Univ, 78; Lori Haker Mem Lectr, Milwaukee Children's Hosp, 79; Bristol Lectr, Univ Calif, Los Angeles-Harbor Hosp, 80; Davidson Lectr, Univ Aberdeen, Scotland, 80; Sir Almroth Wright Mem Lectr, St Mary's Med Sch, 82; Maxwell Finland Lectr, Infectious Dis Soc Am, 83; Bristol Award, 94; Alton Goldbloom Mem Lectr, McGill Univ & Montreal Children's Hosp Res Inst, 83; Stephen I Morse Mem Lectr, State Univ NY, 84; Joseph F Mulach Lect, St Clair Hosp, Pittsburgh, 85; Herbert C Miller Lectr, Univ Kans, 85; Lewis W Wannamaker Mem Lectr, Univ Minn, 90; Henry J Kaiser Lect, Univ Hawaii, 94; Amberg-Helmholz Lect, Mayo Clin, 96. *Prof Exp:* Intern, Minneapolis Gen Hosp, 53-54. *Concurrent Pos:* Attend physician, Minneapolis Gen Hosp, 59-; USPHS res fel, 60-61 & career develop award, 62-; John & Mary R Markle scholar med sci, 61-66; guest investr, Rockefeller Inst, 62-64, Radcliffe Infirmary, Oxford, Eng, 71-72, Univ Cologne, Ger, 86 & 88 & Univ Bergen, Norway, 91; assoc mem, Comn Streptococcal & Staphylococcal Dis, Armed Forces Epidemiol Bd, 65-; mem, Comt Control Infectious Dis, 70-76, Adv Comt, Inst Allergy & Infectious Dis, 72-74, Adv Coun, 75-79 & Bd Sci Counrs, 82-86; John Simon Guggenheim fel, 71; Alexander von Humboldt US sr scientist award, 85. *Mem:* Inst Med-Nat Acad Sci; Am Fedn Clin Res; Am Soc Microbiol; NY Acad Sci; Infectious Dis Soc Am (pres, 85); Am Pediat Soc (pres, 88); AAAS; Asn Am Physicians. *Res:* Infectious diseases; author of numerous scientific publications. *Mailing Add:* Univ Minn Hosp Dept Pediat 420 Delaware St SE Mayo Mem Bldg Box 296 Minneapolis MN 55455

QUIGG, CHRIS, HIGH ENERGY PHYSICS, THEORETICAL PHYSICS. *Current Pos:* head, Theoret Physics Dept, 77-87, dep dir SSC Cent Design Group, 87-89, PHYSICIST, FERMI NAT ACCELERATOR LAB, 74- *Personal Data:* b Bainbridge, Md, Dec 15, 44; m 67, Elizabeth Kelley; c David M & Katherine K. *Educ:* Yale Univ, BS, 66; Univ Calif, Berkeley, PhD(physics), 70. *Prof Exp:* Res assoc physics, State Univ NY, Stony Brook, 70-71, from asst prof to assoc prof, 71-74. *Concurrent Pos:* Sloan Found fel, 74-78; vis scholar, Enrico Fermi Inst, Univ Chicago, 74-78; mem prog adv comt, Stanford Linear Accelerator Ctr, 75-77; mem high energy adv comt, Brookhaven Nat Lab, 78-80 & Lawrence Berkley Lab, 78-81; prof lectr, Univ Chicago, 78-82, prof, 82-94; div assoc ed, Particles & Fields, Phys Review Lett, 81-83, assoc ed, Reviews Mod Physics, 81-93; vis prof, Ecole Normale Superieure, Paris, 81-82; mem, Bd Overseers Superconducting Super Collider, 85-87; vis scientist, Lawrence Berkeley Lab, 89-90; scholar-in-residence, Bellagio Ctr, 90; vis prof, Cornell Univ, 95, Princeton Univ, 97. *Mem:* Fel Am Phys Soc; fel AAAS. *Res:* Phenomenology of elementary particles; supercollider physics. *Mailing Add:* Theoret Physics MS106 Fermilab PO Box 500 Batavia IL 60510-0500. *E-Mail:* quigg@fnal.gov

QUIGG, RICHARD J, PHYSICAL METALLURGY. *Current Pos:* vpres mkt, 80-90, vpres, 90-96, CONSULT, RES INT CANNON-MUSKEGON CORP, 96- *Personal Data:* b Bethlehem, Pa, Nov 12, 30; div, Linda J Hoffman; c Richard J, Daniel H & Laura J. *Educ:* Va Polytech Inst, BS, 52; Lehigh Univ, MS, 54; Case Inst Technol, PhD(phys metall), 59; Cleveland State Univ, JD, 66. *Prof Exp:* Metallurgist, E I du Pont de Nemours & Co, Inc, 52-53; res asst, Lehigh Univ, 53-54; res metallurgist, Rem-Cru Titanium, Inc, 54-56; res asst, Case Inst Technol, 56-59; res metallurgist, TRW Inc, 59-63, res supvr, 63-64, wrought metall mgr, Metals Div, 64-65, res sect mgr, 65-67, mgr mat & processes, 67-68, mgr res & develop, Metals Div, 68-70; exec vpres, Jetshapes, Inc, 70-73, pres, 73-78; sr staff engr, Pratt & Whitney Aircraft, 78-80. *Mem:* Am Inst Mining, Metall & Petrol Engrs; fel Am Soc Metals; Am Soc Testing & Mat; fel Am Soc Metals Int. *Res:* Titanium alloy development; hydrogen embrittlement; superalloy development; phase changes in nickel-base superalloys; law; casting and solidification. *Mailing Add:* Cannon-Muskegon Corp PO Box 506 Muskegon MI 49443. *Fax:* 616-453-1178; *E-Mail:* grigg@alliance.net

QUIGLEY, FRANK DOUGLAS, mathematics; deceased, see previous edition for last biography

QUIGLEY, GARY JOSEPH, MOLECULAR BIOPHYSICS. *Current Pos:* PROF CHEM, HUNTER COL, CUNY, 88- *Personal Data:* b Syracuse, NY, Aug 1, 42; div. *Educ:* State Univ NY Col Environ Sci & Forestry, 64, PhD(chem), 69. *Prof Exp:* Fel & res assoc molecular biophys, 69-78, prin res scientist, Mass Inst Technol, 78-88. *Mem:* Am Crystallog Asn; Am Inst Physics; Am Chem Soc. *Res:* Determination of crystal structures of nucleic acids including transfer-RNA, Z-DNA and drug DNA complexes; ion, water and drug interactions with nucleic acids; molecular mechanics to understand nucleic acid structure and structure-function relationships; development of

X-ray area detector for X-ray crystallographic data collection for macromolecules; DNA sequence analysis; RNA secondary structure. *Mailing Add:* Dept Chem Hunter Col CUNY 695 Park Ave New York NY 10021-0367

QUIGLEY, GERARD PAUL, LASER CHEMISTRY, LASER PHYSICS. *Current Pos:* asst group leader laser photochem, 75-86, PROJ LEADER LASER PROPOGATION, LOS ALAMOS SCI LAB, 86- *Personal Data:* b Boston, Mass, Jan 3, 42; m 66; c 2. *Educ:* Northeastern Univ, BSEE, 64, MS, 66; Polytech Inst Brooklyn, MS, 70; Cornell Univ, PhD(appl physics), 74. *Concurrent Pos:* US Steel fel, Cornell Univ, 74. *Mem:* Am Phys Soc; AAAS; Am Chem Soc. *Res:* Laser photochemistry and isotope separation; physics and kinetics of laser systems; optoacoustic spectroscopy of laser excited systems. *Mailing Add:* 620 Navajo St Los Alamos NM 87544

QUIGLEY, HERBERT JOSEPH, JR, PATHOLOGY, CHEMISTRY. *Current Pos:* from asst prof to assoc prof, 68-72, PROF PATH, CREIGHTON UNIV, 72-; STAFF PATHOLOGIST, VET ADMIN HOSP, 88- *Personal Data:* b Philadelphia, Pa, Mar 6, 37; m 64; c Amelia. *Educ:* Franklin & Marshall Col, BS, 58; Univ Pa, MD, 62; Am Bd Path, dipl, 68. *Honors & Awards:* Borden Prize for Med Res, Borden Corp, 62. *Prof Exp:* Resident path, Presby Hosp, New York, 62-66; chief path serv, Vet Admin Med Ctr, Omaha, Nebr, 68-88. *Concurrent Pos:* NIH acad path career develop trainee, Col Physicians & Surgeons, Columbia Univ, 62-66; chief path serv, Monroe Co Gen Hosp & US Naval Hosp, Key West, 66-68; porpoise pathologist & res consult, Off Naval Res Cetacean Lab, Key West, 66-68. *Mem:* Fel Col Am Path; fel Am Inst Chem; Am Chem Soc; fel Am Soc Clin Path. *Res:* Blood coagulation; disseminated intravascular coagulation; fibrinolysis; instrumental analytical chemistry. *Mailing Add:* Path Serv Vet Admin Hosp 4101 Woolworth Ave Omaha NE 68105-1873

QUIGLEY, JAMES P, TUMOR CELL BIOLOGY, ENZYMOLOGY. *Current Pos:* asst prof, 74-77, ASSOC PROF MICROBIOL & IMMUNOL, DOWNSTATE MED CTR, STATE UNIV NY, 78- *Personal Data:* b New York, NY, Mar 18, 42; m 67; c 2. *Educ:* Manhattan Col, BS, 65; Johns Hopkins Univ, PhD(physiol chem), 69. *Prof Exp:* Fel chem biol, Rockefeller Univ, 70-73, asst prof, 73-74. *Concurrent Pos:* Fel, Leukemia Soc Am, 70-72; scholar, Sinsheimer Found Scholar, 77; vis prof, Sch Path, Oxford Univ, 80-81. *Mem:* Am Asn Cancer Res; Am Soc Cell Biol; Harvey Soc; NY Acad Sci. *Res:* Biochemical examination of normal and malignant cells; role of tumor viruses in malignant transformation; mechanism of tumor cell invasion and metastasis. *Mailing Add:* Path Dept State Univ NY BHS Tower 9 Rm 168 Stonybrook NY 11794-8691

QUIGLEY, NEIL BENTON, PHYTOBACTERIOLOGY OF PLANT-PATHOGENIC BACTERIA, BACTERIAL MOLECULAR GENETICS. *Current Pos:* Adj asst prof, 93, RES ASST PROF, DEPT MICROBIOL, UNIV TENN, 93- *Personal Data:* b Vancouver, BC, May 23, 56; Can & NZ citizen; m 88, Bonnie H Ownely; c Benjamin R. *Educ:* Univ Auckland, NZ, BSc, 78, MSc, 80, PhD(cell biol), 84. *Prof Exp:* Res assoc, Univ Sydney, Australia, 84-87, Wash State Univ, 87-92. *Mem:* Am Phytopath Soc; Am Soc Microbiol; Int Soc Plant Microbe Interactions. *Res:* Virulence determinants in plant pathogenic bacteria; mechanism of secretion of a phytotoxin by strains of pseudomonas syringae pathover syringae. *Mailing Add:* Univ Tenn Dept Microbiol M409 Walters Life Sci Knoxville TN 37996-0001

QUIGLEY, ROBERT JAMES, VARIABLE STARS. *Current Pos:* from asst prof to assoc prof, 70-83, PROF PHYSICS & ASTRON, WESTERN WASH UNIV, 83- *Personal Data:* b Cord, Ark, Feb 18, 40; div. *Educ:* Calif Inst Technol, BS, 61, MS, 62; Univ Calif, Riverside, MA, 64, PhD(physics), 68. *Prof Exp:* Res asst solid state physics, Univ Calif, Riverside, 65-68; asst prof, Ill Inst Technol, 68-70. *Concurrent Pos:* Vis lectr, Inst Physics, Univ Frankfurt, 69-70; vis scholar astron, Univ Tex & McDonald Observ, 76-77; vis scientist, Sacramento Peak Observ, 80-81 & Steward Observ, Univ Ariz, 84-85. *Mem:* Am Astron Soc; Astron Soc Pac. *Res:* Photoelectric photometry of cataclysmic variable stars. *Mailing Add:* Dept Physics & Astron Western Wash Univ M/S 9064 Bellingham WA 98225-9064

QUIGLEY, ROBERT MURVIN, soil mechanics, engineering geology; deceased, see previous edition for last biography

QUILLEN, DANIEL G, MATHEMATICS. *Current Pos:* PROF MATH, MATH INST, OXFORD UNIV, 88- *Personal Data:* b June 27, 40. *Educ:* Harvard Univ, PhD(math), 69. *Prof Exp:* Norbert Wiener prof math, Mass Inst Technol, 73-88. *Mem:* Nat Acad Sci; Am Math Soc. *Mailing Add:* Math Inst Oxford Univ 24 St Giles Oxford England

QUILLEN, EDMOND W, JR, NEUROHUMORAL REGULATIONS, REFLEX CONTROL. *Current Pos:* ASSOC PROF, UNIV ILL, CHICAGO, 94- *Personal Data:* b Feb 9, 53; m; c 3. *Educ:* Univ Miss, PhD(physiol), 81. *Prof Exp:* From asst prof to assoc prof obstet & gynec, McGill Univ, 86-94. *Mem:* Am Physiol Soc. *Res:* Arterial pressure regulation; fluid and electrolyte balance; pregnancy; sheep; surgical techniques; computer science. *Mailing Add:* Univ Ill M/C808 820 S Wood St Chicago IL 60612

QUILLIGAN, JAMES JOSEPH, JR, VIROLOGY. *Current Pos:* assoc prof, 54-59, RES PROF PEDIAT, SCH MED, LOMA LINDA UNIV, 59-, DIR VIRUS LAB, 54- *Personal Data:* b Philadelphia, Pa, Oct 18, 12; m 41; c 4. *Educ:* Ohio State Univ, BA, 36; Univ Cincinnati, MD, 40. *Prof Exp:* Instr pediat & res assoc epidemiol, Sch Pub Health, Univ Mich, 46-49, asst prof pediat, Univ & asst prof epidemiol, Sch Pub Health, 50; assoc prof pediat, Univ Tex Southwestern Med Sch Dallas, 51-54. *Concurrent Pos:* Dir Labs, Children's Med Ctr, Dallas, 51-54; res career investr, Nat Inst Allergy & Infectious Dis, 63- *Mem:* Am Acad Microbiol; Soc Pediat Res; Am Acad Pediat; Am Asn Immunol; Infectious Dis Soc Am. *Res:* Influenza; herpes; hepatitis viruses; tumor viruses. *Mailing Add:* 11234 Anderson St PO Box 2000 Loma Linda CA 92354-0200

QUILLIN, CHARLES ROBERT, CYTOLOGY, EVOLUTIONARY BIOLOGY. *Current Pos:* from asst prof to assoc prof, 75-88, DEAN STUDENT DEVELOP, POINT PARK COL, 75-, EXEC OFF, 86-, PROF, 88- *Personal Data:* b Crawfordsville, Ind, Jan 14, 38. *Educ:* Wabash Col, AB, 60; Brown Univ, ScM, 63, PhD(bot), 66. *Prof Exp:* Sr asst, Wabash Col, 60; asst bot, Brown Univ, 60-62, asst biol, 62-65; from instr to asst prof, Colby Col, 65-70, assoc dean students, 67-70; fel, Off Inst Res, Mich State Univ, 70-71; dean students, Marshall Univ, 72-73, asst to vpres student affairs, 73-75. *Concurrent Pos:* NSF vis scientist's prog lectr, 66- *Mem:* Sigma Xi. *Res:* Study of histone as related to deoxyribose nucleic acid, acid cycle in a cell. *Mailing Add:* Off Dean Student Develop Point Park Col Pittsburgh PA 15222. *Fax:* 412-261-5303

QUIMBY, FRED WILLIAM, LYMPHOCYTE DIFFERENTIATION ANTIGENS, IMMUNE MEDIATED DISEASES IN DOGS. *Current Pos:* assoc prof, 79-93, PROF PATH, CORNELL UNIV, 93- *Personal Data:* b Providence, RI, Sept 19, 45; m 65, Cynthia Connelly; c Cynthia J & Kelly A. *Educ:* Univ Pa, VMD, 70, PhD(path), 74. *Honors & Awards:* Trum Award, New Eng Br, Am Asn Lab Animal Sci, 79; Silver Jubilee Speaker, Lab Animals Ltd, 94; Charles River Prize, Am Vet Med Asn, 95. *Prof Exp:* Fel hemat, New Eng Med Ctr, 74-75; from instr to asst prof path, Tufts Med Sch, 75-79. *Concurrent Pos:* Vet, Springfield Animal Hosp, 70-74; consult, St Elizabeth Hosp, 74-79, Concord Field Sta, Harvard, 75-79 & Sidney Farber Cancer Ctr, Harvard, 78-79; dir, Lab Animal Med, Tufts New Eng Med Ctr, 75-79, Ctr Res Animal Resources, Cornell Univ, 79-; mem, Nat Acad Sci Comt on the Guide, 84-85, & Comt on Immunodeficient Rodents, 85-88, comt Animal Welfare, World Vet Asn; ed, Lab Animal Sci, 91-92 & consult ed, 92-; focused giving award, Johnson & Johnson, 86-90; chmn cmt stand dogs, Nat Acad Sci. *Mem:* NY Acad Sci; Soc Vet Immunol; Am Vet Med Asn; Am Asn Lab Animal Sci (pres NE Br, 78-79); World Vet Asn (treas, 90-92, secy, 92). *Res:* Differentiation antigens on canine lymphocytes and immmunological abnormalities in autoimmune disease; the etipathogenesis of bacterial toxic shock syndromes. *Mailing Add:* 115 Terraceview Dr Ithaca NY 14850. *Fax:* 607-253-3527; *E-Mail:* ma36@cornell.edu

QUIMPO, RAFAEL GONZALES, CIVIL ENGINEERING, HYDROLOGY. *Current Pos:* from asst prof to assoc prof, 66-75, PROF CIVIL ENG, UNIV PITTSBURGH, 75- *Personal Data:* b Aklan, Philippines, Mar 23, 39; m 63, Vanida; c Rafael Jr, Veronica, Carlos & Vanessa. *Educ:* Feati Univ, Philippines, BS, 59; Seato Grad Sch Eng, Bangkok, ME, 62; Colo State Univ, PhD(civil eng), 66. *Prof Exp:* Civil engr, Am-Asia Eng Assocs, 62-63; res asst, Colo State Univ, 63-66. *Concurrent Pos:* Res grants, Off Water Resources, US Dept Interior, Univ Pittsburgh, 67-70 & NSF, 70-72, 73-76, 79-80 & 84-86; consult, Mobay Chem Co, 72; vis prof, Fed Univ Rio de Janiero, Brazil, 72-73; vis scientist, Philippine Nat Sci Develop Bd, 75-76; NSF int travel grant, 76, 78, 80, 83 & 85; consult, US Army CEngrs, 79-80, J T Boyd Co, 85-86, USX Corp, 86-; NSF res grant, 86-88 & 90-91. *Mem:* AAAS; Am Geophys Union; Am Soc Civil Engrs; Am Soc Eng Educ; Int Asn Hydraul Res; Am Water Works Asn. *Res:* Water resources development; applied statistics; stochastic processes; stochastic hydrology; non-conventional energy sources; reliability of water distribution systems; remote sensing of the environment. *Mailing Add:* 5010 Impala Dr Pittsburgh PA 15239. *Fax:* 412-624-0135; *E-Mail:* rgq1@vms.cis.pitt.edu

QUIN, LOUIS DUBOSE, ORGANIC CHEMISTRY, ORGANOPHOSPHORUS CHEMISTRY. *Current Pos:* ADJ PROF & DISTINGUISHED VIS PROF, UNIV NC WILMINGTON, 96- *Personal Data:* b Charleston, SC, Mar 5, 28; c Gordon, Howard & Carol. *Educ:* The Citadel, BS, 47; Univ NC, MA, 49, PhD(org chem), 52. *Prof Exp:* Res chemist, Am Cyanamid Co, 49-50; res proj leader, Westvaco Chem Div, Food Mach & Chem Corp, 52-54 & 56; from res assoc to prof chem, Duke Univ, 56-81, chmn dept, 70-76, James B Duke prof, Duke Univ, 81-86; prof chem & head dept, Univ Mass, 86-96. *Concurrent Pos:* Ford Found fel, Woods Hole Oceanog Inst, 63-64; prof, distinguished vis prof, Univ NC, Wilimington, 96- *Mem:* Fel AAAS; Am Chem Soc. *Res:* Organophosphorus and heterocyclic compounds; synthesis, stereochemistry, and spectral properties of cyclic phosphorus compounds; spectra-structure correlations of organophosphorus compounds; carbon-phosphorus compounds in nature. *Mailing Add:* 124 White Oak Bluffs Stella NC 28582

QUINAN, JAMES ROGER, INDUSTRIAL CHEMISTRY. *Current Pos:* RETIRED. *Personal Data:* b Watervliet, NY, June 27, 21; m 50, Shirley M O'Brien; c Jay R. *Educ:* State Univ NY Albany, AB, 42, AM, 48; Rensselaer Polytech Inst, PhD(infrared & Raman spectroscopy), 54. *Prof Exp:* Chemist & foreman, Adirondack Foundries & Steel, 42-45; res assoc biochem, Sterling-Winthrop Res Inst, 48-52; sr chemist, Behr-Manning Div, Norton Co, 54-57, group leader abrasive grain & electrostatics, 57-70, sr res prof, Coated Abrasive Div, 70-75; tech dir, mach div, Albany Int Corp, 77-79, proj engr, eng systs div, 79-83. *Concurrent Pos:* Consult, 75-77 & 83- *Mem:* Am Chem Soc; NY Acad Sci. *Res:* Chemical and physical properties of abrasives as related to coated abrasive products; electrostatics as applied to coated abrasives; metallurgical and high temperature materials research. *Mailing Add:* 57 Upper Loudon Rd Loudonville NY 12211

QUINE, WILLARD V, LOGIC, PHILOSOPHY OF SCIENCE. *Current Pos:* EMER PROF, HARVARD UNIV, 78- *Personal Data:* b Akron, Ohio, June 25, 08; m 30, 48; c Elizabeth (Roberts), Norma, Douglas & Margaret (McGovern). *Educ:* Oberlin Col, AB, 30; Harvard Univ, AM, 31, PhD(philos), 32. *Hon Degrees:* Numerous from US & foreign univs, 55-89. *Honors & Awards:* N M Butler Gold Medal, Columbia Univ, 70; Bronze Medal, Col France, 69; F Polacky Medal, Prague, 71, Charles Univ Silver Medal, 93; R Schock Prize, Royal Swed Acad, 93; Kyoto Prize, 96. *Concurrent Pos:* Vis prof, Oxford, Paris, Tokyo, Sao Paulo, Uppsala, Gerona. *Mem:* Nat Acad Sci; Am Philos Soc; Am Acad Arts & Sci; Brit Acad; Norweg Acad; Institut de France. *Mailing Add:* Emerson Hall Harvard Univ Cambridge MA 02138

QUINLAN, DANIEL A, NOISE CONTROL, PERCEPTION OF NOISE. *Current Pos:* MEM TECH STAFF, AT&T BELL LABS, 86- *Personal Data:* b Glen Ridge, NJ, Oct 8, 58; m 84, Patricia F; c Noah & Anna. *Educ:* Univ NH, BS, 80; Pa State Univ, MS, 85. *Prof Exp:* Acoust engr, Genesis Physics Corp, 81-83; acoust consult, Bolt, Beranek & Newman Inc, 85-86. *Concurrent Pos:* Bd dirs, Inst Noise Control Eng. *Mem:* Inst Noise Control Engrs; Acoust Soc Am; Am Inst Aeronaut & Astronaut. *Res:* Physics of air-moving devices; measurement of acoustic and structural intensity; perception of noise and active control of sound. *Mailing Add:* Lucent Technol Inc Bell Labs Rm 2D-340 600 Mountain Ave PO Box 636 Murray Hill NJ 07974-0636. *Fax:* 908-582-7308; *E-Mail:* dbq@bell_labs.com

QUINLAN, DENNIS CHARLES, CELL BIOLOGY, BIOCHEMISTRY. *Current Pos:* asst prof, 76-80, ASSOC PROF BIOL, WVA UNIV, 80- *Personal Data:* b Detroit, Mich, Jan 29, 43; m 69; c 1. *Educ:* Wayne State Univ, BS, 65, MS, 66; Univ Rochester, PhD(microbiol), 73. *Prof Exp:* Sr res assoc cell biol, Worcester Found Exp Biol, 73-76. *Concurrent Pos:* Prin investr, Am Cancer Soc grant, 77-79 & NIH grant, WVa Univ, 78-81. *Mem:* Am Soc Biol Chemists; Am Soc Zoologists; Develop Biol Soc; Int Soc Differentiation; AAAS; Sigma Xi. *Res:* Cell cycle regulation in cultured, mammalian cells; membrane dynamics of normal and tumor cells. *Mailing Add:* Dept Biol WVa Univ Brooks Hall PO Box 6057 Morgantown WV 26506-6057

QUINLAN, JOHN EDWARD, PHYSICAL CHEMISTRY. *Current Pos:* From instr to assoc prof, 58-69, dean admis & financial aid, 69-81, ASSOC PROF CHEM, & DIR ADMIN COMPUT POMONA COL, 69- *Personal Data:* b Milwaukee, Wis, Aug 6, 30; m 57; c 3. *Educ:* Marquette Univ, BS, 52; Univ Ark, MS, 55; Univ Wis, PhD(chem), 59. *Concurrent Pos:* NSF fac fel, 64-65. *Mem:* AAAS. *Res:* Chemical kinetics and mechanisms of gas phase reactions. *Mailing Add:* Dir Admin Comput Pomona Col 333 N College Way Claremont CA 91711-6301

QUINLAN, KENNETH PAUL, INORGANIC CHEMISTRY. *Current Pos:* PHYS CHEMIST, AIR FORCE CAMBRIDGE RES LABS, 60- *Personal Data:* b Somerville, Mass, Jan 13, 28; m 64, Margo Welch; c Ellen, Marueen, Kenneth & Joseph. *Educ:* Boston Univ, BA, 51; Tufts Univ, MS, 52; Univ Notre Dame, PhD(inorg chem), 55; Northeastern Univ, MS, 81. *Prof Exp:* Res chemist, US Army CEngrs, 52-53, Am Cyanamid Co, 53-54 & Nat Lead Co, Inc, 54-56. *Mem:* AAAS; Am Chem Soc; Electrochem Soc. *Res:* Photosynthesis; solar energy; solid state chemistry. *Mailing Add:* 70 Grasmere Newton MA 02158

QUINLIVAN, WILLIAM LESLIE G, OBSTETRICS & GYNECOLOGY. *Current Pos:* RETIRED. *Personal Data:* b Waunfawr, Wales, Dec 20, 21; US citizen; m 50; c 3. *Educ:* Univ London, MB, BS, 46, MD, 65; FRCS, 65; FRCOG, 66. *Prof Exp:* Asst prof obstet & gynec, Univ Pittsburgh, 62-65; from assoc prof to prof obstet & gynec, Univ Calif, Irvine, 65-91. *Concurrent Pos:* NIH res fel obstet & gynec, Cancer Res Inst, Univ Calif, San Francisco, 60-62; Health, Res & Serv Found grants, 62-65; NIH res grants, 63-72. *Mem:* Am Physiol Soc; fel Am Col Obstet & Gynec; Am Fertil Soc. *Res:* Methods for the pre-selection of sex in humans; immunological cause of infertility in the human female. *Mailing Add:* 660 W Via De Suenos Green Valley AZ 85614-1726

QUINN, BARRY GEORGE, AQUATIC BIOLOGY. *Current Pos:* From asst prof to assoc prof, 62-72, PROF BIOL, WESTMINSTER COL, UTAH, 72-, HEAD DEPT, 63- *Personal Data:* b Rochelle Park, NJ, Dec 2, 34; div; c 2. *Educ:* Univ Utah, BS, 57, MA, 58; Univ Colo, PhD(biol), 62. *Concurrent Pos:* Scripps Inst Oceanography, 58-59; NIH fel, Marine Lab, Univ Miami, 63-66; chmn, Div Natural Sci & Math, Westminster Col, 66-71 & 74-77; mem, Eval Panel, NSF Undergrad Instr Sci Equip Prog, 65 & Steering Comt, Utah Conf Higher Educ, 72-74; partic, NSF Summer Inst Comp Anat, Univ Wash, 68. *Mem:* AAAS; Ecol Soc Am; Am Soc Limnol & Oceanog; Sigma Xi. *Res:* Comparative limnology of mountain lakes and streams; limnology of Great Salt Lake; ecology of coral reefs; behavior of marine invertebrates. *Mailing Add:* 1605 E Lakewood Dr Salt Lake City UT 84117-7517

QUINN, C JACK, ENERGY CONSERVATION & ALTERNATE ENERGY SOURCES, RECOVERY OF WASTE ENERGY. *Current Pos:* from assoc prof to prof mech eng technol, 69-84, PROF & CHMN MFG TECHNOL, PURDUE UNIV FT WAYNE, 84- *Personal Data:* b Westbaden, Ind, June 4, 29; m 53; c 4. *Educ:* Ind Inst Technol, BSME, 56; Ball State Univ, MS, 61. *Prof Exp:* From instr to assoc prof mech eng, Ind Inst Technol, 56-69. *Concurrent Pos:* Sr engr, Int Harvester, 63-66; consult, Franklin Elec Co, 68-70, Defense Civil Preparedness Agency, 71-81, Phelps Dodge, Inc, 82 & Kemtune, Inc, 83-; nat deleg, Am Soc Mech Engrs, 74 & 75; team chmn accreditation, Am Soc Heating, Refrigeration & Air-Conditioning Engrs, 82-89; prog evaluator for accreditation, Soc Mfg Engrs. *Mem:* Am Soc Mech Engrs; Am Soc Eng Educ; Am Soc Heating, Refrigeration & Air-Conditioning Engrs; Nat Soc Prof Engrs; Soc Mfg Engrs. *Res:* Energy conservation; waste heat recovery and utilization of alternate energy resources; environmental pollution. *Mailing Add:* 4726 N Webster Rd New Haven IN 46774-9558

QUINN, DAVID LEE, NEUROENDOCRINOLOGY, REPRODUCTIVE PHYSIOLOGY. *Current Pos:* assoc prof, 66-77, PROF BIOL, MUSKINGUM COL, 77- *Personal Data:* b Steubenville, Ohio, Nov 28, 38; m 59; c 3. *Educ:* Washington & Jefferson Col, BA, 60; Purdue Univ, MS, 62, PhD(brain & ovulation), 64. *Prof Exp:* NIH fel neuroendocrinol, Sch Med, Duke Univ, 64-66. *Mem:* AAAS; Sigma Xi; Endocrine Soc. *Res:* Comparative analysis of brain mechanisms controlling ovulation and prolactin secretion. *Mailing Add:* 180 Foxcreek Rd New Concord OH 43762-9601

QUINN, DENNIS WAYNE, APPLIED MATHEMATICS. *Current Pos:* appl mathematician res, Flight Dynamics Lab, 75-80, from asst prof to assoc prof, 80-86, PROF MATH & STATIST, AIR FORCE INST TECHNOL, WRIGHT-PATTERSON AFB, 87- *Personal Data:* b West Grove, Pa, Apr 20, 47; c Meghen & Adam. *Educ:* Univ Del, BA, 69, MS, 71, PhD(math), 73. *Prof Exp:* Mathematician/programmer, E I du Pont de Nemours, 69-70; from res assoc to appl mathematician, Aerospace Res Lab, 74-75. *Concurrent Pos:* Nat Res Coun resident res assoc, Nat Acad Sci, 73-74. *Mem:* Soc Indust Appl Math. *Res:* Analysis of the behavior of solutions of singular, elliptic, partial differential equations; numerical solution of partial differential equations, particularly those arising in pharmacokinetics and air pollution; parameter identification of physiological parameters in pharmacokinetics. *Mailing Add:* Dept Math Air Force Inst Technol Wright-Patterson AFB OH 45433

QUINN, EDWIN JOHN, ORGANIC CHEMISTRY, POLYMER CHEMISTRY. *Current Pos:* res chemist, 64-81, SR RES SCIENTIST, ARMSTRONG WORLD INDUSTS, 81- *Personal Data:* b Geneva, Ill, July 20, 27; m 64; c 3. *Educ:* St Procopius Col, BSc, 51; Univ Ill, Urbana, MSc, 55; State Univ NY Col Forestry, Syracuse, PhD(org polymer chem), 62. *Prof Exp:* Res asst, US Govt Synthetic Rubber Prog, Univ Ill, Urbana, 53-55; res chemist, Blockson Chem Co div, Olin Mathieson Chem Corp, 55-57 & Naugatuck Chem Div, US Rubber Co, 60-64. *Mem:* Am Chem Soc. *Res:* Synthetic polymer chemistry; surfactants; carbohydrates and synthetic polyols; photochemistry; inorganic polymers and polyphosphazenes; polymer flammability and smoke evolution; polyvinyl chloride. *Mailing Add:* 1730 Santa Barbara Dr Lancaster PA 17601-4122

QUINN, FRANK HUGH, HYDROLOGY OF LARGE LAKES & RIVER BASINS. *Current Pos:* head, Lake Hydrol Group, 74-88, HEAD, PHYS SCI DIV, GREAT LAKES ENVIRON RES LAB, NAT OCEANIC & ATMOSPHERIC ADMIN, 89- *Personal Data:* b Detroit, Mich, Nov 22, 37; m 60; c 3. *Educ:* Wayne State Univ, BS, 60, MS, 66; Univ Mich, PhD(civil eng), 71. *Honors & Awards:* Silver Medal, US Dept Com, 87. *Prof Exp:* Civil engr, Los Angeles Dist, US Army CEngrs, 60-62; hydraul engr, Lake Surv Dist, 62-65, chief, Spec Studies Sect, 66-70. *Concurrent Pos:* Consult, World Meteorol Orgn, 75-; mem, Int Great Lakes Levels & Flows Adv Bd, 80-, Int Great Lake Info Network Bd, 80- *Mem:* Am Soc Civil Engrs; Int Asn Great Lakes Res (pres, 85); Am Geophys Union; Am Meteorol Soc; AAAS; Am Water Resources Asn. *Res:* Hydrologic water balance and water resource studies for large lakes and river basins; primary emphasis on the North American Great Lakes. *Mailing Add:* 2205 Commonwealth Blvd Great Lakes Environ Res Lab Ann Arbor MI 48105-1593. *Fax:* 313-741-2055; *E-Mail:* quinn@glerl.noaa.gov

QUINN, FRANK S, TOPOLOGY OF MANIFOLDS. *Current Pos:* prof, 77-85, DISTINGUISHED PROF MATH, VA POLYTECH INST, 85- *Personal Data:* b Havana, Cuba, June 3, 46; c 2. *Educ:* Princeton Univ, PhD(math), 70. *Prof Exp:* Prof math, Princeton Univ, 71-73; Yale Univ, 73-76 & Rutgers Univ, 76-77. *Concurrent Pos:* Ed, Bull Am Math Soc. *Mem:* Am Math Soc. *Res:* Topology of manifolds. *Mailing Add:* Va Polytech Inst Va Polytech Inst & State Univ Blacksburg VA 24061-0123

QUINN, GALEN WARREN, ORTHODONTICS. *Current Pos:* RETIRED. *Personal Data:* b Tama, SDak, Jan 28, 22; wid; c 8. *Educ:* Creighton Univ, DDS, 52; Univ Tenn, MS, 55; Am Bd Orthod, dipl, 69. *Honors & Awards:* Pierre Fauchard Award. *Prof Exp:* Elem sch teacher, 40-41; dep supply officer, Vet Admin, 45-47; pvt pract, 52-54; asst prof pedodontics, head dept & dir, postgrad & grad prog, Univ Tenn, 55-58, from assoc prof to prof orthod, 58-92, div chief, 64-84. *Concurrent Pos:* Dean, Sch Dent, Creighton Univ, 61-62; ed, Cleft Palate Bull, 59-62; NC Dent J, 78-80; consult, Vet Admin Hosp, Durham, NC, State Bd Health, Voc Rehab, Site visits, Nat Inst Dent Res & US Army, Ft Benning, Ga & Ft Bragg, NC; mem, Craniofacial Biol Group, Int Asn Dent Res, 74. *Mem:* Am Soc Dent Children; Am Dent Asn; assoc mem Am Asn Orthod; Am Cleft Palate Asn; fel AAAS; Int Asn Dent Res; Col Am Bd Orthod; fel Am Col Dentists; fel Int Col Dentists; Am Bd Orthod. *Res:* Etiology and treatment of congenital and acquired craniofacialorodental anomolies, i.e. cleft lip/palate, burns, tumors, trauma, arthritis, scoliosis, polio, caries, eruption, TMJ problems, etc; effects of soft tissue on growth, shape, position and posture of bone-especially face, jaws and causes of malocclusion; etiology and results of upper airway obstruction to cause mouth breathing treatment of upper airway; effect of mouthbreathing on muscle balance as a cause of orodentofacial deformities; non-surgical and surgical treatments of effects of mouthing; mandible and maxillahypo and hyperplasia-sinus blockage from nasal obstruction; a dental articulator and a rotational cineradiographic unit; author of numerous publications. *Mailing Add:* Duke Univ Med Ctr Baker House PO Box 3945 Durham NC 27710

QUINN, GEORGE DAVID, FAILURE ANALYSIS, HEAT TRANSFER. *Current Pos:* CERAMICS ENGR, NIST, DEPT COM, 91- *Personal Data:* b Boston, Mass, Nov 28, 50; m 73; c 2. *Educ:* Northeastern Univ, BS, 73. *Prof Exp:* Ceramic engr, US Army Mat & Mech Res Ctr, 73-85; ceramic engr, US Army Mat Technol Lab, 85-87; Ger Aerospace Lab DFVLR, 87-88. *Concurrent Pos:* Consult, Mat Res Coun, Army Res Proj Agency, 72-73 & Tech Coop Prog, 84-85. *Mem:* Am Ceramic Soc; US Naval Inst; Am Soc Testing & Mat. *Res:* Mechanical testing of ceramic materials; failure analysis of ceramic materials. *Mailing Add:* 12721 War Admiral Way Potomac MD 20878-3729

QUINN, GERTRUDE PATRICIA, biochemical pharmacology; deceased, see previous edition for last biography

QUINN, HELEN RHODA ARNOLD, ELEMENTARY PARTICLE PHYSICS. *Current Pos:* STAFF MEM, STANFORD LINEAR ACCELERATOR CTR, 79-, ASST TO DIR FOR EDUC & PUB OUTREACH, 93- *Personal Data:* b Melbourne, Australia, May 19, 43; US citizen; m 66, Daniel J; c Elizabeth H & James A. *Educ:* Stanford Univ, BS, 63, MS, 64, PhD(physics), 67. *Prof Exp:* Res assoc physics, Stanford Linear Accelerator Ctr, 67-68; guest scientist, Ger Electron Synchrotron, Hamburg, Ger, 68-70; res fel, Harvard Univ, 71-72, from asst prof to assoc prof, 72-77; vis scientist, Stanford Linear Accelerator Ctr, 77-78, res assoc, 78-79. *Concurrent Pos:* Alfred P Sloan fel, 74-77; vis assoc prof physics, Stanford Univ, 76-78. *Mem:* Fel Am Phys Soc. *Res:* Particle and theoretical physics; gauge field theories and their applications. *Mailing Add:* Stanford Linear Accelerator Ctr-Bin 81 PO Box 4349 Stanford CA 94305. *E-Mail:* quinn@slac.stanford.edu

QUINN, JAMES AMOS, PLANT ECOLOGY, POPULATION BIOLOGY. *Current Pos:* From asst prof to assoc prof, Rutgers Univ, 66-77, assoc chair personnel, dept biol sci, 81-82, dir grad prog bot & mem exec coun, Grad Sch, 83-86, PROF BOT, RUTGERS UNIV, 77- *Personal Data:* b Chickasha, Okla, Aug 12, 39. *Educ:* Panhandle State Univ, BS, 61; Colo State Univ, MS, 63, PhD(bot sci), 66. *Concurrent Pos:* Travel grants, Rockefeller Found, Int Grassland Cong, 70, Bot Soc Am, Int Bot Cong, 75 & 87, Am Forage & Grassland Coun, Int Grassland Cong, 85 & 89; Rutgers Univ Res Coun fac fel, Australia, 72-73; vchmn, ecol sect, Bot Soc Am, 77, chmn, 78; vis scientist, Div Land Resources Mgt, CSIRO, Australia & Univ New Eng, Australia, 80-81; consult, Ont Coun Grad Studies, 82; assoc ed, Bull Torrey Bot Club, 83-85; sr ecologist, Bd Prof Cert, Ecol Soc Am, 90; external reviewer, City Univ, NY, Queens Col, Dept Biol Sci, 93 & Ohio Univ, Dept Environ & Plant Biol, 95. *Mem:* Torrey Bot Club (pres, 82-83); Ecol Soc Am; Bot Soc Am; Am Inst Biol Sci; Soc Range Mgt; Am Forage & Grassland Coun. *Res:* Grassland ecology; population ecology; genetic differentiation within plant species; species interactions; evolutionary biology; reproductive biology of amphicarpic species; life histories and sex ratios in populations of dioecious species; phenotypic plasticity. *Mailing Add:* Dept Biol Sci Rutgers Univ Piscataway NJ 08855-1059. *Fax:* 732-445-5870; *E-Mail:* quinn@biology.rutgers.edu

QUINN, JAMES GERARD, MARINE ORGANIC CHEMISTRY. *Current Pos:* from asst prof to assoc prof, 68-78, PROF CHEM OCEANOG, UNIV RI, 78- *Personal Data:* b Providence, RI, Oct 28, 38; m 65; c 3. *Educ:* Providence Col, BS, 60; Univ RI, MS, 64; Univ Conn, PhD(biochem), 67. *Prof Exp:* USPHS training prog fel steroid biochem, Worcester Found Exp Biol, 67-68. *Mem:* AAAS; Am Chem Soc; Am Soc Limnol & Oceanog; Int Asn Geochem & Cosmochem; Geochem Soc; Sigma Xi. *Res:* Marine organic chemistry; organic geochemistry of seawater and sediments; metal-organic and mineral-organic interactions; the biogeochemistry of organic pollutants in the marine environment. *Mailing Add:* Grad Sch Oceanog Univ RI 15 S Ferry Rd Narragansett RI 02882-1197

QUINN, JARUS WILLIAM, OPTICS. *Current Pos:* RETIRED. *Personal Data:* b West Grove, Pa, Aug 25, 30; m 53; c 5. *Educ:* St Joseph's Col, Pa, BS, 52; Cath Univ Am, PhD(physics), 64. *Prof Exp:* Res assoc physics, Johns Hopkins Univ, 54-55; staff scientist, Res Inst Advan Study, Inc, 56-57; res assoc physics, Cath Univ Am, 58-60, from instr to asst prof, 61-69; exec dir, Optical Soc Am, 69-93. *Concurrent Pos:* Mem, Gov Bd, Am Inst Physics, 73- *Mem:* Am Phys Soc; fel Optical Soc Am; Coun Eng & Sci Soc Executives. *Res:* Science administration; optics. *Mailing Add:* 357 Fearrington Post Pittsboro NC 27312

QUINN, JOHN A(LBERT), CHEMICAL ENGINEERING. *Current Pos:* dept chmn, 80-85, PROF CHEM ENG, UNIV PA, 71-, ROBERT D BENT PROF, 78- *Personal Data:* b Springfield, Ill, Sept 3, 32; m 57; c 3. *Educ:* Univ Ill, Urbana, BS, 54; Princeton Univ, PhD(chem eng), 59. *Honors & Awards:* Colburn Award, Am Inst Chem Engrs, 66; Mason Lectr, Stanford Univ, 81; D L Katz Lectr, Univ Mich, 85; Reilly Lectr, Univ Notre Dame, 87. *Prof Exp:* Mem fac, Univ Ill, Urbana, 58-70, prof chem eng, 66-70. *Concurrent Pos:* NSF sr fel, 65; vis prof, Imp Col, Univ London, 65-66 & 86, Univ Rome, 92; mem, Eng Res Bd, Comn Eng & Tech Systs & Comt Surv Chem Eng, Comn Phys Sci, Math & Resources, Nat Res Coun, 84-; Sherman Fairchild distinguished scholar, Calif Inst Technol, 85; bd chem sci & technol, Nat Res Coun, 86-; sci adv comt, Whitaker Found, 87- *Mem:* Nat Acad Eng; fel AAAS; Am Inst Chem Engrs; Am Chem Soc; Am Acad Arts & Scis. *Res:* Interfacial phenomena; biotechnology; transport in biological systems; membrane structure and function. *Mailing Add:* Dept Chem Eng 311A Towne Bldg Univ Pa Philadelphia PA 19104-6393

QUINN, JOHN JOSEPH, THEORETICAL PHYSICS, CONDENSED MATTER PHYSICS. *Current Pos:* prof physics & eng & chancellor, 89-92, LINCOLN CHAIR EXCELLENCE, UNIV TENN, 92- *Personal Data:* b New York, NY, Sept 25, 33; m 58, Betsy Vincent; c Daniel, Elizabeth, Heather & Jennifer. *Educ:* St John's Univ, NY, BS, 54; Univ Md, PhD(physics), 58. *Hon Degrees:* ScD, Purdue Univ, 92. *Honors & Awards:* Res Achievement Award, NRL, 72 & 84. *Prof Exp:* Res assoc, Univ Md, 58-59; mem tech staff, RCA Labs, 59-64; vis prof, Purdue Univ, 64-65; prof physics, Brown Univ, 65-91, Ford Found prof, 85-91, dean fac, 86-89. *Concurrent Pos:* Vis lectr, Univ Pa, 61-62; vis prof, State Univ NY, Stony Brook, 68-69, Univ Rome, 71, Univ Calif, Irvine, 77-78 & Univ Md, 88; vis scientist, Max Planck Inst, Stuttgart, 72. *Mem:* Am Phys Soc; Inst Elec & Electronics Engrs. *Res:* Solid state theory; electronic properties of solids; many body effects; semiconductor physics. *Mailing Add:* 210 S College Univ Tenn Knoxville TN 37996. *E-Mail:* jjquinn@utkux.utk.edu

QUINN, LEBRIS SMITH, CELL DIFFERENTIATION, MUSCLE GROWTH & DEVELOPMENT. *Current Pos:* Grad res myogenesis, Med Sch, Univ Wash, 78-82, postdoctoral res myogenesis, 82-83, cellular aging, 84-85, res assoc biochem, 85-86, RES ASST PROF MYOGENESIS & ANAT, MED SCH, UNIV WASH, 86- *Personal Data:* b Norwalk, Conn, Apr 13, 54; m 85, Travis C Gamble. *Educ:* Swarthmore Col, BA, 76; Univ Wash, PhD(cell biol & anat), 82. *Concurrent Pos:* Prin investr grants, indust & USDA, 86- *Mem:* Am Soc Cell Biol; AAAS; Am Soc Animal Sci. *Res:* Factors whih control proliferation of vertebrate skeletal muscle precursor cells; cell lineage of myoblasts in development. *Mailing Add:* VA Med Ctr GRECC American Lake Tacoma WA 98493. *Fax:* 253-543-1524

QUINN, LOUISE ANNE, CLASTIC SEDIMENTOLOGY, PROVENANCE STUDIES. *Current Pos:* lectr, 89-93, asst prof, 93-95, ASSOC PROF & CHAIR GEOL, BRANDON UNIV, 95- *Personal Data:* b Glasgow, Scotland, July 19, 59; Brit citizen. *Educ:* Cambridge Univ, BA, 80; Mem Univ, MSc, 85, PhD(geol), 93. *Prof Exp:* Lectr geol, Univ Sask, 88-89. *Concurrent Pos:* Adj prof geol, Univ Sask, 96- *Mem:* Can Soc Petrol Geologists; Can Sedimentol Res Group; Geol Asn Can; Soc Sedimentary Geol. *Res:* Provenance studies of clastic units in Western Newfoundland, ranging in age from Ordovician to Devonian; clastic sedimentology of the Triassic Montney formation, Western Canada sedimentary basin. *Mailing Add:* Dept Geol Brandon Univ Box 270 Brandon MB R7A 6A9 Can. *Fax:* 204-728-7346; *E-Mail:* quinn@brandonu.ca

QUINN, LOYD YOST, BACTERIOLOGY. *Current Pos:* RETIRED. *Personal Data:* b Cutler, Ind, June 16, 17; m 45; c 4. *Educ:* Purdue Univ, BS, 41, MS, 47, PhD(bact), 49. *Prof Exp:* From asst prof to prof bact, Iowa State Univ, 49-86, actg head dept, 57-59. *Mem:* Tissue Cult Asn; Am Soc Microbiol. *Res:* Antibody production by tissue cells grown in continuous culture; computerized feedback control of tissue cell culture conditions; aging in tissue cell cultures; effects of heavy metals on in vivo and tissue cell culture modes of immune response; genetic control of immune responses; computer graphics of protein structures. *Mailing Add:* 3423 Clinton St Ames IA 50010-4371

QUINN, MARY ELLEN, SCIENCE EDUCATION, PUBLICATION CONSULTING. *Current Pos:* RETIRED. *Personal Data:* b Chicago, Ill, Sept 24, 23. *Educ:* St Mary-of-the-Woods Col, BS, 56; Depaul Univ, MS, 64; Univ Tex, San Antonio, MA, 80; Univ Pa, EdD,71. *Prof Exp:* Teacher physics, math & sci, Schs Archdioceses Chicago & Indianapolis, 44-68; lectr & doctoral fel, Univ Pa, 68-70; asst prof physics, St Mary-of-the-Woods Col, 71-72; dir curric & inservice, Archdiocese San Francisco, 72-73; assoc prof chem & math, Immaculata Col Wash, 73-75; dir curric, Edgewood Sch Dist, 75-80-; teacher physics & english as second language, Alamo Heights Sch Dist, 80-88; vis prof math, Our Lady of the Lake Univ, 88-95. *Concurrent Pos:* Res partic, Oak Ridge Inst Nuclear Studies, 65, Lawrence Radiation Labs, Berkeley, 68; lectr, Trinity Univ, San Antonio, 75-78, Providence Col, Taiwan, 83; consult & lectr, Univ Tex, San Antonio, 75-97 & St Mary's Univ, San Antonio, 76-80; consult, NY City Bd Educ, 85 & 88, Ctr Appl Linguistics, Washington, DC, 86-90. *Mem:* AAAS; Am Asn Physics Teachers; Nat Asn Res Sci Teaching; Nat Sci Teachers Asn; Nat Coun Teachers Math. *Res:* Why and how teaching science and mathematics to second language learners accelerates learning that language; research, consult and publish materials for inclusion of science and math in textbooks for teachers and students. *Mailing Add:* 3123 Clearfield Dr San Antonio TX 78230-3413. *Fax:* 210-690-4414; *E-Mail:* mquinn@lonestar.utsa.edu

QUINN, MICHAEL H, POLYMER SYNTHESIS, COATING. *Current Pos:* GROUP MGR, WESLEY-JESSEN SCHERING PLOUGH, 86- *Personal Data:* b S Fork, Pa, Feb 28, 43. *Educ:* Duquesne Univ, BS, 65; WVa Univ, MS, 67; Akron Univ, PhD(polymer sci), 73. *Prof Exp:* Sr chemist, Monsanto, 73-77; tech mgr, St Regis Paper Co, 77-80; tech dir, Frye Copysysts, Allied Signal, 80-84 & Coated Film Co, 84-86. *Mem:* Am Chem Soc. *Res:* Contact lenses; synthesis of new polymers and modification of existing polymers. *Mailing Add:* 4302 Walden Lane Valparaiso IN 46383

QUINN, PATICIA K, ATMOSPHERIC CHEMISTRY. *Current Pos:* RES CHEMIST, NAT OCEANIC & ATMOSPHERIC ADMIN, 93- *Personal Data:* b Los Alamos, NMex, Nov 13, 60. *Educ:* Reed Col, BS, 82; Univ Wash, PhD(chem), 88. *Honors & Awards:* Excellence Citation, J Geophys Res, 93. *Prof Exp:* Oceangr, Univ Wash, 89-93. *Mem:* Am Geophys Union; Am Aerosol Res; Asn Women Sci. *Mailing Add:* Nat Oceanic & Atmospheric Admin PMEL 7600 Sand Point Way NE Seattle WA 98115. *Fax:* 206-526-6744; *E-Mail:* quinn@pmel.noaa.gov

QUINN, RICHARD PAUL, IMMUNOCHEMISTRY. *Current Pos:* PRES, Q CONSULT INC, 95- *Personal Data:* b Modesto, Calif, Oct 22, 42; m 64, Joan A Marzell; c Timothy J, Susan A & Kate E. *Educ:* Univ San Francisco, BS, 64; Ore State Univ, PhD(biochem), 68. *Prof Exp:* USPHS fel, Biol Div, Oak Ridge Nat Lab, 68-70; res biochemist, Wellcome Res Labs, Burroughs Wellcome Co, 70-75, sr res biochemist, 75-95. *Mem:* Am Asn Immunologists; Am Chem Soc; Sigma Xi. *Res:* Immunosuppressive and immunomodulating agents; immunochemical approaches to drug action; immunoassay development; metabolism of serum proteins; use of monoclonal antibodies for drug development. *Mailing Add:* Q Consult Inc 809 Ellynn Dr Cary NC 27511. *Fax:* 919-315-8597; *E-Mail:* usbwcprc@ibmmail.com

QUINN, ROBERT GEORGE, PLASMA PHYSICS, SPACE SCIENCES. *Current Pos:* assoc prof, Ionosphere Res Lab, 66-71, dean acad instr commonwealth campuses, 71-74, PROF ENG, PA STATE UNIV, 72- *Personal Data:* b Beaver Falls, Pa, June 14, 36; m 61; c 5. *Educ:* Drexel Inst, BSEE, 59; Cath Univ, MS, 60, PhD(physics), 62. *Prof Exp:* Res assoc, Princeton Univ, 62-63; from asst prof to assoc prof, Dept Space Sci & Appl Physics, Cath Univ, 63-66. *Concurrent Pos:* Res assoc, Goddard Space Flight Ctr, NASA, 65-66. *Mem:* Am Geophys Union; Am Phys Soc; Am Soc Testing & Mat; Int Elec & Electronics Engrs; Am Soc Eng Educ. *Res:* Ionospheric physics; dielectrics. *Mailing Add:* Dept Elec & Comp Engr Drexel Univ 32nd & Chestnut Sts Philadelphia PA 19104

QUINN, ROBERT M(ICHAEL), ELECTRICAL ENGINEERING, ELECTROPHYSICS. *Current Pos:* sr scientist/engr, 95-96, SR MFG ENG MGR, IRVINE SENSOR CORP, 96- *Personal Data:* b Bedford, Ind, July 7, 41; m 61, Judith DeForge; c Bruce, Brian, Kerry, Amy & Ethan. *Educ:* Rensselaer Polytech Inst, BEE, 63, MEE, 65, PhD(elec eng), 68. *Prof Exp:* Staff engr, IBM Corp, 68-76, adv engr, 76-82, sr eng, 82-87, sr engr process mgr, 87-89, engr device design mgr, 89-91, consult, 91-95. *Res:* Instabilities in magnetoplasmas; integrated circuit device design and process technology; semiconductor manufacturing engineering. *Mailing Add:* 3 Deborah Dr South Burlington VT 05403

QUINN, THOMAS PATRICK, IONOSPHERIC PHYSICS. *Current Pos:* DEP ASST SECY, DEPT DEFENSE, 79- *Personal Data:* b Freeland, Pa, Mar 20, 30; m 62; c 2. *Educ:* Pa State Univ, BS, 57, MS, 58, PhD(physics of ionosphere), 64. *Honors & Awards:* Arthur S Flemming Award, Wash Jr Chamber Com, 67; Presidential Distinguished Exec Award, 84; Presidential Meritorious Exec Award, 89. *Prof Exp:* Instr elec eng, Ionosphere Res Lab, Pa State Univ, 58-64; consult commun, Off Naval Res, 64-77, spec asst systs, Off Asst Secy Navy, 77-79. *Concurrent Pos:* Asst prof, Pa State Univ, 64-66; mem, Int Sci Radio Union, 64-; US mem, NATO Air Defense Electronics Environ Comt, 80-81, Commun & Info Systs Comt, 80-81, 84-, Sci Comt Nat Reps, 80-81, NATO Sr Nat Reps, 83-; chmn, NATO Panel Air Space Mgt & Control, 83-88, Sci Comt of Nat Rep; bd, Supreme Hq, Allied Powers Europe Tech Ctr, 81-86. *Mem:* Sigma Xi; Am Geophys Union; sr mem Inst Elec & Electronics Engrs; Armed Forces Commun & Electronics Asn. *Res:* Electromagnetic wave propagation; communications theory; radar systems; modulation and detection techniques. *Mailing Add:* 5399 Temple Hill Rd Temple Hills MD 20748-3525

QUINN, TIMOTHY SEAN, SOLID, FLUID & FRACTURE MECHANICS, DATABASE DESIGN & DEVELOPMENT. *Current Pos:* PROJ ENGR, BIRD MACHINE CO, 97- *Personal Data:* b Cincinnati, Ohio, June 20, 68. *Educ:* Univ Dayton, BS, 90; Mass Inst Technol, MS, 92, PhD(mech eng), 94. *Prof Exp:* Proj mgr, Resources Eng Systs, 94-97. *Mem:* Nat Soc Prof Engrs; Am Soc Mech Engrs; Soc Petrol Engrs. *Res:* Analytical and experimental analysis of solid and fluid interactions in permeable materials. *Mailing Add:* 395 Broadway Cambridge MA 02139. *E-Mail:* tspquinn@aol.com

QUINN, WARREN EUGENE, ATOMIC & NUCLEAR PHYSICS. *Current Pos:* Staff mem, Los Alamos Nat Lab, 57-65, from assoc group leader to group leader, 65-77, from assoc div leader to dep div leader, 77-91, LAB ASSOC, LOS ALAMOS NAT LAB, 91- *Personal Data:* b Chehalis, Wash, July 17, 26. *Educ:* Wash State Univ, BS, 51, MS, 52; Harvard Univ, PhD(atomic & nuclear physics), 57. *Mem:* Fel Am Phys Soc; AAAS; Sigma Xi. *Res:* Magnetic fusion energy research and program development; participant in theta-pinch fusion device which produced the first laboratory thermonuclear plasma; magnetic fusion confinement experiments. *Mailing Add:* 98 Navajo Los Alamos NM 87544

QUINNAN, GERALD VINCENT, JR, BIOLOGY. *Current Pos:* PROF PREV MED & BIOMETRICS, UNIFORMED SERVS, UNIV HEALTH SCIS, BETHESDA, MD, 93- *Personal Data:* b Boston, Mass, Sept 7, 47; m 90, Leigh A Sawyer; c Kevin, Kylie, Kathleen & John. *Educ:* Col Holy Cross, Worcester, AB, 69; St Louis Univ Med Sch, MD, 73; Am Bd Internal Med, dipl. *Prof Exp:* Resident & fel, Boston Univ Med Ctr, 73-77; med officer, Bur Biologics, Food & Drug Admin, 77-80, dir, Herpes Virus Br, 80-81, dir, Div Virol, 81-88, dep dir, Ctr Biologics Eval & Res, 88-90, actg dir, 90-92, dep dir, 92-93. *Mem:* Fel Infectious Dis Soc Am; Am Soc Clin Invest; Am Fedn Clin Res; Am Soc Microbiol; AAAS; Int AIDS Soc. *Res:* Immunology and pathogenesis of viral diseases with emphasis on cell mediated immunity; herpes viruses; retroviruses; vaccine safety. *Mailing Add:* 14508 Manor Park Dr Rockville MD 20853-1954

QUINNEY, PAUL REED, ANALYTICAL CHEMISTRY. *Current Pos:* RETIRED. *Personal Data:* b Haverhill, Mass, May 11, 24; m 47; c 4. *Educ:* Univ NH, BS & MS, 49; Iowa State Col, PhD(chem), 54. *Prof Exp:* Fel chem, Mellon Inst, 54; sr chemist, Brown Co, 54-56 & Koppers Co, 56-58; from asst prof to prof, Butler Univ, 58-74, John Hume Reade prof chem, 74-88, head dept, 72-88. *Mem:* AAAS; Am Chem Soc; Am Inst Chemists. *Res:* Instrumental analysis. *Mailing Add:* Dept Chem 5350 N Illinois St Indianapolis IN 46208

QUINONES, FERDINAND ANTONIO, plant breeding, for more information see previous edition

QUINONES, MARK A, PREVENTIVE MEDICINE, PUBLIC HEALTH. *Current Pos:* coordr, Develop Dept, 69, adminr, Div Drug Abuse, 69-71, asst prof, 71-75, dir, Div Drug Abuse, 74-80, assoc prof, 76-80, PROF PREV MED & DIR, DIV GERIAT & SOCIAL MED, COL MED & DENT NJ, 80- *Personal Data:* b New York, NY, Jan 13, 31; m 52; c 2. *Educ:* Southeastern La Univ, BA, 53; La State Univ, MA, 55, PhD(med sociol), 71; Wayne State Univ, MHA, 56; Columbia Univ, MPH, 73. *Prof Exp:* Health educr, Tuberculosis League of Pittsburgh, 56-57; consult, NJ Tuberculosis & Health Asn, 57-62; exec dir, Passaic County Heart Asn, NJ, 62-66; managing dir, Northwest Area Tuberculosis & Respirator Dis Asn, NJ, 66-69. *Concurrent Pos:* Vis prof, Sch Educ, Fairleigh Dickinson Univ, 71-74; health consult, PR Cong of NJ, 72- *Mem:* Am Pub Health Asn; Asn Teachers Prev Med; Soc Pub Health Educrs; Am Sociol Asn. *Res:* Areas concerned with the social aspects of health and medicine, particularly migrant health, criminal offenders, tuberculosis, asthma and allied health. *Mailing Add:* Dept Psychol/ Prev Med/Community Health Univ Med & Dent NJ 185 S Orange Ave Newark NJ 07103-2714

QUINSEY, VERNON LEWIS, BEHAVIOR MODIFICATION, FORENSIC PSYCHOLOGY. *Current Pos:* PROF PSYCHOL, QUEENS UNIV, KINGSTON, ONT, 88-, PROF PSYCHIAT, 92- *Personal Data:* b Flin Flon, Man, Oct 10, 44; Can Citizen; m 92, Jill Atkinson; c Heidi, Ira, Al & Aaron. *Educ:* Univ NDak, BSc, 66; Univ Mass, Amherst, MSc, 69, PhD (psychol), 70. *Prof Exp:* Fel, Dalhousie Univ, Halifax, NS, 70-71; psychologist, Mental Health Ctr, Penetanguishene, Ont, 71-75, dir res, 76-84 & 86-88. *Concurrent Pos:* Vis scientist, Philippe Pinel Inst, Montreal, 84-86; adj assoc prof psychol dept, Concordia Univ, Montreal, 84-86; assoc prof psychiat dept, Univ Toronto, 86-88; chair, Nat Inst Mental Health Criminal & Violent Behav Res Comt, 86-88; chair, Ont Mental Health Found Res Comt, 80-82, Ont Mental Health Found Community & Social Serv Res Rev Comt, 87-; consult, Am Psychiat Asn Comt, 85-87. *Mem:* Fel Can Psychol Asn; Am Psychol Asn; Asn Treatment of Sexual Abusers; Int Acad Sex Res; Int Acad Law & Mental Health. *Res:* Antisocial behavior, applied decision making modification and program evaluation; psychophysiological assessment; sex offenders; forensic psychology. *Mailing Add:* Psychol Dept Queens Univ Kingston ON K7L 3N6 Can. *E-Mail:* quinsey@parlor.psyc.queensu.ca

QUINTANA, RONALD PRESTON, MEDICINAL CHEMISTRY. *Current Pos:* prin scientist, 83-84, ASST DIR, CONTACT LENS CARE RES, ALCON LABS INC, 85- *Personal Data:* b New Orleans, La, Feb 23, 36; m 57; c 2. *Educ:* Loyola Univ, New Orleans, BS, 56; Univ Wis, MS, 58, PhD(pharmaceut chem), 61. *Prof Exp:* From instr to prof med chem, Col Pharm, Ctr Health Sci, Univ Tenn, 60-71, vchmn dept, 65-83, distinguished serv prof med chem, 71-83, prof periodont, Col Dent, 72-74. *Mem:* Acad Pharm Sci; Am Chem Soc; Am Pharmaceut Asn; The Chem Soc. *Res:* Synthesis of, and surface-chemical studies on, compounds with biological significance. *Mailing Add:* Alcon Labs Inc 6201 S Freeway M/S Q-137 Ft Worth TX 76134-2099

QUINTANILHA, ALEXANDRE TIEDTKE, OXYGEN TOXICITY, AGING. *Current Pos:* PROF BIOPHYSICS & DEAN, BIOMEDICAL SCH, DIR, INST BIOL MOLECULAR CELL, UNIV PORTO, 91- *Personal Data:* b Maputo, Mozambique, Aug 9, 45. *Educ:* Witwatersrand Univ, BSc Hons, 68, PhD(solid state physics), 72; Univ Porto, Agregacao, 81. *Prof Exp:* Lectr physics, Witwatersrand Univ, 72-73; assoc prof physiol, Lawrence Berkeley Nat Lab, Univ Calif, Berkeley, 73-90, dir, Ctr Environ Studies, 84-90. *Concurrent Pos:* Gulbenkian Found fel, 71; Nat Acad Sci-Nat Res Coun fel, 78; ed, John Wiley & Sons, 83-, CRC Press, 85- & Plenum Press, 86. *Mem:* Am Soc Biochem & Molecular Biol; Biophys Soc; AAAS; Am Soc Photobiol; Int Soc Magnetic Resonance; NY Acad Sci; Int Cell Res Orgn; Nat Delegate Biotechnol; fel World Acad Srts & Sci; Acad Europ. *Res:* Oxidative and free radical mechanism of damage to biological systems. *Mailing Add:* Inst Biol Molec & Cell Univ Porto R Campo Alegre 823 Porto Portugal 4150. *Fax:* 351-2-6099157

QUINTIERE, JAMES G, FIRE CONTROL. *Current Pos:* PROF, FPE, UNIV MD, 90- *Personal Data:* b Passaic, NJ, May 5, 40; c 2. *Educ:* Newark Col Eng, BS, 62; NY Univ, MS, 66, PhD(mech eng), 70. *Honors & Awards:* Bronze Medal, Nat Bur Standards, 76; Silver Medal, US Dept Com, 82; Emmans lectr in Fire, 86. *Prof Exp:* Mech engr, nuclear rocket res, NASA Lewis Lab, 62-63; instr mech eng, NY Univ, 67-69; res scientist heat transfer, Am Standard Res & Develop Lab, 69-71; mech engr, Nat Inst Standards & Technol, 71-80, prog analyst, 85-86, group head, fire res, 80-85, chief, Fire Sci & Eng Div, 86-90. *Mem:* Combustion Inst; Am Soc Mech Engrs. *Res:* Uncontrollable fire; enclosure fires, ignition and flame spread of materials and flammability test methods; natural convection heat transfer. *Mailing Add:* Dept FPE Eng Bldg 0147A Univ Md College Park MD 20742-0001

QUINTING, GREGORY, NUCLEAR MAGNETIC RESONANCE, COATINGS SCIENCE. *Current Pos:* RES CHEMIST, SHERWIN WILLIAMS AUTOMOTIVE, 88- *Personal Data:* b Mich, Dec 22, 56. *Educ:* Univ Mich, BS, 79; Univ Wis, PhD(anal chem), 85. *Prof Exp:* Postdoctoral res fel, Colo State Univ, 85-88. *Mem:* Am Chem Soc. *Res:* Spectroscopic characterization of polymers and coatings; product development. *Mailing Add:* Sherwin-Williams Automotive 10909 S Cottage Grove Ave Chicago IL 60628-3812

QUINTO, ERIC TODD, RADON TRANSFORMS, COMPUTED TOMOGRAPHY. *Current Pos:* Lectr, 77-78, asst prof, 78-84, ASSOC PROF MATH, TUFTS UNIV, 84- *Personal Data:* b Indianapolis, Ind, May 10, 51. *Educ:* Ind Univ, AB, 73; Mass Inst Technol, PhD(math), 78. *Concurrent Pos:* Vis scholar, Dept Math, Mass Inst Technol, 78-79; res grants, NSF, NIH; Humboldt res fel, 85, vis assoc prof, Univ Munster, Ber Ilan Univ. *Mem:* Am Math Soc; Math Asn Am; Asn Women Math. *Res:* Generalized radon transforms, a field of mathematics applicable to partial differential equations and computed tomography; when and how organs (functions) can be recovered from given tomographic data (integrals over surfaces). *Mailing Add:* Dept Math Tufts Univ Medford MA 02155-7049

QUINTON, ARTHUR ROBERT, EXPERIMENTAL NUCLEAR PHYSICS. *Current Pos:* PROF PHYSICS, UNIV MASS, AMHERST, 66- *Personal Data:* b Lowestoft, Eng, July 1, 24; m 46, Rose Trebilcock; c Hebe (Avery), Keith & Tracy (Farnham). *Educ:* Univ London, BSc, 44; Univ Western Ont, MSc, 51; Yale Univ, PhD, 54. *Prof Exp:* Res physicist, Mullard Radio Valve Co, 46-48; from instr to asst prof physics, Yale Univ, 54-63; assoc prof, Univ Fla, 63-66. *Concurrent Pos:* Vis fel, Australian Nat Univ, 61-62 & vis prof, 72-73; mem Publ Comt, Am Asn Physics Teachers, 71-74. *Mem:* Am Phys Soc; Am Asn Physics Teachers. *Res:* Nuclear structure; low energy nuclear physics; fission; heavy ions; x-ray excitation by ion bombardment. *Mailing Add:* 75 Red Gate Lane Amherst MA 01002. *E-Mail:* quinton@phast.umass.edu

QUINTON, DEE ARLINGTON, RANGE NUTRITION, SECONDARY PRODUCTIVITY. *Current Pos:* RES SCIENTIST RANGE ECOL, AGR CAN, 76- *Personal Data:* b Cardston, Alta, May 17, 39; m 66, Doreen Hirschi; c Arlin, Deanne, Doren, Dorianne, Dalen & Devon. *Educ:* Weber State Col, BS, 69; Colo State Univ, PhD(range sci), 72. *Prof Exp:* Res assoc range sci, Colo State Univ, 72-73; asst prof wildlife mgt, Tex Tech Univ, 73-75. *Mem:* Soc Range Mgt. *Res:* Secondary productivity of range lands; range improvements; range trend studies; beef production. *Mailing Add:* Res Sta Agr Can 3015 Ord Rd Kamloops BC V2B 8A9 Can

QUIOCHO, FLORANTE A, BIOCHEMISTRY. *Current Pos:* from asst prof to assoc prof, 72-81, PROF BIOCHEM, RICE UNIV, 81- *Personal Data:* b Philippines, Oct 26, 37; m 59; c 3. *Educ:* Cent Philippines Univ, BS, 59; Howard Univ, MS, 61; Yale Univ, PhD(biochem), 66. *Honors & Awards:* Asian Chemist Award, Am Chem Soc, 61. *Prof Exp:* Mem res staff molecular biophys, Yale Univ, 64-66; res fel chem, Harvard Univ, 66-72. *Concurrent Pos:* Mem, Cellular & Mollecular Basis Dis Rev Comt, Nat Inst Gen MedSci, NIH, 78-82; USPHS training fel biochem, Yale Univ, 62-64, res fel, European Molecular Biol Orgn, 80, fel, John Simon Guggenheim Mem Found, 80-81; vis scientist, Lab Molecular Biophysics, Oxford Univ, 80. *Mem:* Am Soc Biol Chemists; Sigma Xi. *Res:* Physical chemistry of biological macromolecules, especially proteins; x-ray crystallographic studies of proteins; mechanisms of enzyme action; chemical behavior of enzymes in the solid state. *Mailing Add:* Howard Hughes Med Inst Baylor Col Med 1 Baylor Plaza Rm T517 Houston TX 77030

QUIRK, JOHN THOMAS, TREE PHYSIOLOGY, FOREST PRODUCTS. *Current Pos:* RES TECHNOLOGIST, FOREST PROD LAB, USDA, 60- *Personal Data:* b Dubuque, Iowa, Jan 21, 33; m 58; c 4. *Educ:* Iowa State Univ, BS, 56; Syracuse Univ, MS, 60; Univ Wis, PhD(forestry & forest prod), 67. *Prof Exp:* Res forester, Cent State Forest Exp Sta, USDA, 56-58. *Mem:* AAAS; Soc Wood Sci & Technol; Soc Am Foresters; Electron Micros Soc Am; Am Inst Biol Sci. *Res:* Anatomy and morphology; structure-function; physiology-structure; structure-strength. *Mailing Add:* 117 N Franklin Ave Madison WI 53705

QUIRK, RODERIC P, ORGANIC CHEMISTRY, SYNTHETIC INORGANIC & ORGANOMETALLIC CHEMISTRY. *Current Pos:* PROF POLYMER SCI, INST POLYMER SCI, UNIV AKRON, 83-, DISTINGUISHED PROF, 96-, KUMHO PROF POLYMER SCI, 96. *Personal Data:* b Detroit, Mich, Mar 26, 41; m 62, Donna Duncan; c Scott, Brian & Marion. *Educ:* Rensselaer Polytech Inst, BS, 63; Univ Ill, MS, 65, PhD(chem), 67. *Prof Exp:* Anal chemist, Ethyl Corp, 63; res chemist, Minn Mining & Mfg Co, 64; res assoc, Univ Pittsburgh, 67-69; from asst prof to assoc prof chem, Univ Ark, 69-78; sr res scientist, Mich Molecular Inst, 79-83. *Concurrent Pos:* Res chemist, Phillips Petrol Co, 74; vis prof, Inst Polymer Sci, Univ Akron, 76-77, Tokyo Inst Technol, 90 & Inst Charles Sadron, Nat Ctr Sci Res, Strasbourg, France, 91; adj assoc prof polymer chem, Case Western Reserve Univ, 79-83 & Cent Mich Univ, 80-83; NAm ed, Polymer Int; fel, Japan Soc Promotion Sci, 90. *Mem:* Am Chem Soc; Sigma Xi. *Res:* synthesis of functionalized polymers; solvation of alkyllithium compounds; synthesis of block copolymers; anionic polymerization; synthesis of star polymers; group transfer polymerization. *Mailing Add:* Dept Polymer Sci Univ Akron Akron OH 44325-3909. *Fax:* 330-972-5290; *E-Mail:* quirk@polymer.uakron.edu

QUIRKE, TERENCE THOMAS, JR, EXPLORATION GEOLOGY, COMPUTER APPLICATIONS IN EXPLORATION. *Current Pos:* RETIRED. *Personal Data:* b Minneapolis, Minn, Aug 18, 29; m 58, Ruth Mary Carter; c Grace Anne. *Educ:* Univ Ill, BS, 51; Univ Minn, MS, 53, PhD, 58. *Prof Exp:* Asst geol, Univ Minn, 52-53, asst & instr, 55-58; asst prof geol, Univ NDak, 58-60; geologist, Int Nickel Co Can, Ltd, 60-65, res geologist, 65-69, asst mgr, Western Region, Field Explor Dept, 69-71, regional mgr, 71-73, regional geologist, 73-75; dist geologist, Eastern US Region, Am Copper & Nickel Co, Inc, 75-79, supvr sr staff geologist, 79-90. *Concurrent Pos:* Proprietor, Quirke, Quirke & Assoc, Res Consults. *Mem:* Soc Econ Geologists; Geol Soc Am; Geol Asn Can; Irish Geneal Res Soc; Soc Genealogists; Ont Geneal Soc; Sigma Xi. *Res:* Iron, copper and nickel in Canada; uranium, base and precious metal exploration; computer applications in exploration; genealogy: Canada, Ireland, United Kingdom. *Mailing Add:* 2310 Juniper Ct Golden CO 80401-8087

QUIROS, CARLOS F, PLANT GENETICS, PLANT BREEDING. *Current Pos:* assoc prof genetics & breeding, 83-90, PROF, GENETICS BREEDING, DEPT VEG CROPS, UNIV CALIF, DAVIS, 90- *Personal Data:* b Lima, Peru, Mar 17, 46; m 70; c 2. *Educ:* Agrarian Univ, Peru, BSc, 68; Univ NH, MS, 72; Univ Calif, Davis, PhD(genetics), 75. *Prof Exp:* Fel tomato genetics, Univ Calif, Davis, 75-76; res assoc breeding & genetics, Nat Inst Agr Res, Mex, 76-77; fel genetics, Univ Sherbrooke, 77-78; res assoc genetics & breeding, Univ Alta, 78-81; res scientist genetics & breeding, Int Plant Res Inst, 81-83. *Mem:* Sigma Xi; Am Soc Hort Sci; Econ Bot. *Res:* Evolution, genetics and breeding of crop plants, specifically solanaceas and cool season vegetables; germplasm collection and preservation. *Mailing Add:* 946 K St Davis CA 95616

QUIROZ, RODERICK S, METEOROLOGY. *Current Pos:* CONSULT, 85- *Personal Data:* b Ajo, Ariz, Nov 6, 23. *Educ:* Univ Calif, Los Angeles, BA, 50; Univ Md, College Park, MS, 70; Georgetown Univ, MS, 91. *Prof Exp:* Res meteorologist, US Air Weather Serv, 59-66 & Nat Meteorol Ctr, Nat Weather Serv, Nat Oceanic & Atmospheric Admin, 66-85; res meteorologist, Nat Meteorol Ctr, Nat Weather Serv, Nat Oceanic & Atmospheric Admin, 66-85. *Concurrent Pos:* Mem, US Comt Exten to Standard Atmosphere, 62-85; comt chmn, Atmospheric Problems Aerospace Vehicles, 68-72; lectr, Von Karman Inst Fluid Dynamics, Brussels, 70; chmn, Am Meteorol Soc Comt Upper Atmosphere, 73-78. *Mem:* Fel Am Meteorol Soc; Am Geophys Union. *Res:* Structure and circulation of upper atmosphere, emphasizing interaction with the troposphere on long-wave and climatic time-scales; analysis of atmospheric measurements with rockets and satellites. *Mailing Add:* 4520 Yuma St NW Washington DC 20016

QUISENBERRY, DAN RAY, HEALTH PHYSICS. *Current Pos:* asst prof, 68-80, chmn dept, 81-89, ASSOC PROF PHYSICS, MERCER UNIV, 80- *Personal Data:* b Lake Co, Ind, Jan 3, 38; m 58; c 1. *Educ:* Univ Ky, AB, 61; Col William & Mary, MS, 66; World Open Univ, PhD(physics), 79. *Prof Exp:* Teacher sci & math, Ft Knox Dependent Schs, 61-66; asst prof sci, Brevard Jr Col, 66-67. *Mem:* Am Asn Physics Teachers; Am Phys Soc; Nat Geog Soc; Planetary Soc. *Res:* Environmental pollution, chiefly environmental effects of tritium; environmental monitoring of nuclear energy facilities; radon levels in buildings. *Mailing Add:* Dept Physics Mercer Univ Main Campus 1400 Coleman Ave Macon GA 31201

QUISENBERRY, KARL SPANGLER, JR, PHYSICS. *Current Pos:* RETIRED. *Personal Data:* b Washington, DC, Apr 4, 26; m 49; c 3. *Educ:* Univ Nebr, BS, 49; Univ Minn, MA, 52, PhD(physics), 55. *Prof Exp:* Asst physics, Univ Minn, 49-55, res assoc, 55-57; from asst prof to assoc prof, Univ Pittsburgh, 57=62; physicist, Knolls Atomic Power Lab, Gen Elec Co, 61-65, mgr advan exp physics, 65-74, spec critical facilities opers & safety, 71-74, mgr exp physics, 74-76, mgr advan develop activity, 76-77; dir nuclear, Schlumberger-Doll Res Ctr, 77-81, dir Houston Eng, Schlumberger Well Serv, 81-85; wireline coordr, EMR Photoelect, 85-86; consult, Sci Consult, 86-89. *Mem:* Am Phys Soc. *Res:* Nuclear physics and spectroscopy; neutron and nuclear reactor physics; oil well logging; nuclear fuel. *Mailing Add:* 43 Shady Ridge Lane Asheville NC 28805

QUISENBERRY, RICHARD KEITH, SYNTHETIC POLYMERS, FINISHES. *Current Pos:* EXEC DIR, AMTEX PARTNERSHIP, DEL, 93- *Personal Data:* b Springfield, Ill, July 27, 34; m 57; c 4. *Educ:* Millikin Univ, BA, 56; Univ Utah, PhD(chem), 61. *Prof Exp:* Res chemist, Dacron Res Lab, E I DuPont de Nemours & Co, Inc, Del, 60-62, sr res chemist, 62-63, supvr tech plant, 63-64, supvr res, 64-66, sr supvr, Nylon Technol Sect, Del, 66-68, res mgr, Benger Lab, 68-72, tech supt, Va, 72-74, prod supt, 74-75, prin consult, Corp Plans Dept, 75-77, mgr bus planning, Spunbonded Prod, 77-78, prod mgr indust fibers, 78-79, dir, Feedstock Res Div, 79-80, dir pioneering res-fibers, 80-81, dir res & develop, Fabrics & Finishes Dept, 81-84, vpres res, Cent Res Dept, 84-93. *Mem:* Am Chem Soc; Sigma Xi; Indust Res Inst. *Res:* Synthesis and evaluation of polymeric materials for fibers, plastics, packaging, electronics and finishes; advanced materials; biotechnology. *Mailing Add:* PO Box 3635 Greenville DE 19807

QUISENBERRY, VIRGIL L, SOIL PHYSICS. *Current Pos:* From asst prof to assoc prof, 74-83, PROF SOIL PHYSICS, CLEMSON UNIV, 83- *Personal Data:* b Patesville, Ky, Sept 25, 46; m 67; c 1. *Educ:* Univ Ky, BSA, 69, MS, 71, PhD(soil sci), 74. *Mem:* Am Soc Agron; Soil Sci Soc Am. *Res:* Flow of water and solutes in field soils with particular emphasis on macropore flow. *Mailing Add:* Dept Agron Clemson Univ Clemson SC 29632-0001

QUISENBERRY, WALTER BROWN, PREVENTIVE MEDICINE, CANCER. *Current Pos:* RETIRED. *Personal Data:* b Purman, Mo, June 24, 12; m 40; c 3. *Educ:* Loma Linda Univ, MD, 41; Westmont Col, BA, 42; Johns Hopkins Univ, MPH, 45; Am Bd Prev Med, dipl, 50. *Prof Exp:* Prof chem & sch health physician, Westmont Col, 41-42; venereal dis control officer, Southside Health Dist, Va, 42-44; asst med, Johns Hopkins Hosp, 44-45; dir div venereal dis, Nebr State Dept Health, 45-46; asst prof prev med & pub health, Sch Med, Loma Linda Univ, 46-54, actg head dept, 46-47; chief venereal dis & cancer control, Territorial Dept Health, Hawaii, 47-51, dir div prev med, 51-54; exec dir, Hawaii Cancer Soc, 54-58; dir div prev med, Hawaii State Dept Health, Straub Clin & Hosp, Honolulu, 58-63, dep dir health, 63-66, dir health, 66-74, assoc physician, 75-82, physician, 75-83; res physician, Cancer Pac Health Res Inst, 83-84. *Concurrent Pos:* Rockefeller Found fel, Johns Hopkins Univ, 44-45; pvt pract, Long Beach, Calif, 41-42; staff physician, Coleman Med Group, Alhambra, Calif, 46-47; jr attend physician, Los Angeles County Hosp, 46-48; mem teaching staff pub health, Univ Hawaii, 47-75; attend staff, Queens, Kuakini, Kapiolani & Kauikeolani Children's Hosp, Honolulu, 49-; deleg, Nat Cancer Conf, Mich, 56, Int Cancer Cong, Eng, 58, Int Conf Cancer Probs, Japan, 60; assoc clin prof, Sch Med, Loma Linda Univ, 60-75; lectr, Int Cancer Cong, Moscow, USSR, 62; lectr oncol, Univ Sydney, Sydney, Adelaide, Melbourne & Brisbane, Australia & Auckland, NZ, 63; US rep int conf nasopharyngeal cancer, Int Union Against Cancer, Singapore, 64; chmn, Chronic Illness & Aging Comt, 82-92. *Mem:* Fel Am Pub Health Asn; AMA; fel Am Col Prev Med; fel Am Col Physicians; Royal Soc Health; Am Geriat Soc. *Res:* Cytologic diagnosis of cancer by the smear technique; ethnic differences in the incidence of cancer; methadone treatment of heroin addiction; epidemiology of cancer of the stomach, breast, liver and lung; epidemiology of venereal diseases; treatment of venereal diseases with antibiotics; twinning; sociocultural factors in cancer. *Mailing Add:* 2128 Kamehameha Ave Honolulu HI 96822-2103

QUISMORIO, FRANCISCO P, JR, RHEUMATOLOGY, CLINICAL IMMUNOLOGY. *Current Pos:* fel clin immunol, 68-70, from asst prof to assoc prof, 72-83, PROF, MED, UNIV SOUTHERN CALIF, 83-, PROF, PATH, 86- *Personal Data:* b Philippines, Jan 21, 41; m, Violeta Consolacion; c James & Anne. *Educ:* Univ Philippines, BS, 60, MD, 64; Am Bd Internal Med, cert internal med, 75, diagnostic lab immunol, 87. *Prof Exp:* Fel rheumatology, Univ Pa Hosp, 66-68. *Concurrent Pos:* Mem, med & sci comt, Arthritis Found, 79-86; assoc ed, Lupus Erythematosus; dir clin Rheumatology Lab, Univ Southern Calif Med Ctr, 80-; comn, Med Bd Calif, 81- *Mem:* Am Asn Immunologists; fel Am Col Physicians; Clin Immunol Soc; NY Acad Med; Am Col Rheumatol. *Res:* Immunopathology of systemic connective tissue diseases; significance of circulating auto antibodies; clin features and treatment of systemic lupus erythematosus and other rheumatic diseases. *Mailing Add:* Univ Southern Calif Sch Med HMR-715 2025 Zonal Ave Los Angeles CA 90033. *Fax:* 213-342-2874

QUISSELL, DAVID OLIN, REGULATORY BIOLOGY, METABOLIC REGULATION. *Current Pos:* asst prof pharmacol, 77-80, ASST PROF BIOCHEM, SCH MED, UNIV COLO, 80- *Personal Data:* b Pipestone, Minn, Oct 25, 44; m 72; c 1. *Educ:* Augustana Col, BA, 66; Univ Wis-Madison, PhD(biochem), 72. *Prof Exp:* Fel oncol & path, Univ Wis-Madison, 71-73; asst prof biochem, Univ Mo, Columbia, 73-77. *Concurrent Pos:* Res scholar award, Nat Cystic Fibrosis Found, 79. *Mem:* Am Chem Soc; Am Soc Cell Biol; Soc Complex Carbohydrates; Int Asn Dent Res; Sigma Xi. *Res:* Stimulus-secretion coupling mechanism in exocrine tissue; role of cyclic adenosine monophosphate, cyclic guanosine monophosphate, and calcium in the regulation of secretion; pathogenesis of cystic fibrosis. *Mailing Add:* Dept Basic Sci Univ Colo Health Sci Ctr 4200 E Ninth Ave Box C286 Denver CO 80262-0001

QUIST, ARVIN SIGVARD, PHYSICAL CHEMISTRY. *Current Pos:* CLASSIFICATION OFFICER, LOCKHEED MARTIN ENERGY SYST, INC, 85- *Personal Data:* b Blair, Nebr, Nov 15, 33; m 57, 92, Joan C Edie; c Erik, Brian & Mark. *Educ:* Dana Col, Nebr, BS, 54; Univ Nebr, MS, 57, PhD(chem), 59, Univ Tenn, JD, 75. *Prof Exp:* Asst, Univ Nebr, 54-56; res assoc & instr, Univ Pittsburgh, 59-60; instr chem, Univ Nebr, 60-61; mem res staff, Oak Ridge Nat Lab, 61-76; staff mem, Off Waste Isolation, Union Carbide Corp, 76-78; staff mem, Gas Centrifuge Proj, Nuclear Div, 78-85. *Mem:* Nat Classification Mgt Soc. *Res:* Physical chemistry of aqueous electrolyte solutions and molten salts; electrical conductances and Raman spectroscopy of aqueous solutions and molten salts at high temperatures and pressures; environmental and safety impacts of nuclear facilities. *Mailing Add:* 104 Neville Lane Oak Ridge TN 37830

QUIST, OREN PAUL, DEFECT PROPERTIES. *Current Pos:* PROF PHYSICS, SDAK STATE UNIV, 86- *Personal Data:* b St Peter, Minn, Aug 26, 43; m 65, Karen L Gunderson; c Peter, Scot & Eric. *Educ:* Gustavus Adolphus Col, BA, 65; Univ Denver, MS, 67, PhD(physics),73. *Prof Exp:* Res assoc, Minn Mining & Mfg, 65; instr physics, Bemidji State Univ, 67-71; prof physics & math, Bethany Lutheran Col, 73-86. *Mem:* Am Asn Physics Teachers; Am Soc Engrs Educ. *Res:* Determining the role played by defects in determining physical properties of materials. *Mailing Add:* 120 Pine Ridge Rd Brookings SD 57006. *Fax:* 605-688-5878; *E-Mail:* quisto@mg.sdstate.edu

QUIST, RAYMOND WILLARD, SPEECH PATHOLOGY. *Current Pos:* assoc prof, 74-77, PROF SPEECH PATH, IND STATE UNIV, TERRE HAUTE, 77- *Personal Data:* b Minneapolis, Minn, Nov 26, 34; m 57; c 2. *Educ:* Hamline Univ, BA, 52; Univ Minn, Minneapolis, MA, 66, PhD(speech path), 71. *Prof Exp:* Assoc prof speech path, Calif State Col (Pa), 68-71; assoc prof speech path, Madison Col, 71-74. *Mem:* Am Speech & Hearing Asn; Coun Except Children; Am Asn Univ Professors. *Res:* Behavior modification; stuttering; voice. *Mailing Add:* Spec Educ Ind State Univ 217 N Sixth St Terre Haute IN 47809-0001

QUIST, WILLIAM EDWARD, ALUMINUM ALLOY FATIGUE & FRACTURE. *Current Pos:* PRIN ENGR, BOEING COM AIRPLANE CO, 59- *Personal Data:* b Seattle, Wash, May 13, 35; m 66; c 2. *Educ:* Univ Wash, BS, 57, MS, 63, PhD(metall eng), 74. *Prof Exp:* Engr corrosion, Farwest Corrosion Control, 57; metallurgist, Pacific Car & Foundry Co, 58-59. *Concurrent Pos:* NSF res assoc grant, 67-68; lectr, Univ Wash, 72-73; co-chmn, Pac Northwest Metals & Minerals Conf, Am Soc Metals & Am Inst Mech Engrs, 77; co-prin investr, Study Develop Low Density Alloys, USAF & Boeing, 81-; gen chmn, Pac Northwest Mat Conf, Am Soc Metals, Am Welding Soc, Soc Advan Mat & Process Eng & Soc Nondestructive Testing, 83; chmn, Develop Al-Li Alloys, West IC-85, Am Soc Metals & Am Soc Mech Engrs, 85. *Mem:* Fel Am Soc Metals. *Res:* Phase transformation, fracture, fatigue, and corrosion studies in aluminum, titanium, and nickel base systems; aluminum alloy development, strengthening mechanisms and engineering property microstructural relationships. *Mailing Add:* 18215 NE 27th St Redmond WA 98052

QUISTAD, GARY BENNET, AGRICULTURAL BIOCHEMISTRY, ORGANIC CHEMISTRY. *Current Pos:* PRIN SCIENTIST, SANDOZ CROP PROTECTION CORP, 88- *Personal Data:* b Riverside, Calif, Jan 17, 47; m 82; c 3. *Educ:* Univ Calif, Riverside, BS, 69; Univ Calif, Los Angeles, PhD(chem), 72. *Prof Exp:* Sr chemist, Zoecon Corp, 73-80, group leader metab, 80-81, sect head, 82-85, sr sect head, 85-87. *Mem:* Am Chem Soc; Sigma Xi; AAAS. *Res:* Pesticide metabolism and environment degradation photochemistry; spider venoms, arthropod toxins; terpenoid biosynthesis. *Mailing Add:* 2645 La Salle Dr Mountain View CA 94040

QUITEVIS, EDWARD LEON, ULTRAFAST LASER SPECTROSCOPY, PHOTOPHYSICS & LIQUID STATE DYNAMICS. *Current Pos:* asst prof chem, 84-90, JOINT PROF PHYSICS, TEX TECH UNIV, 89-, ASSOC PROF CHEM & BIOCHEM, 90- *Personal Data:* b San Francisco, Calif, Apr 2, 52; m 86, Jackie A Wright. *Educ:* Univ Calif, Berkeley, BS, 74; Harvard Univ, AM, 76, PhD(chem physics), 81. *Prof Exp:* Fel, Univ Toronto, 81-82, res assoc, 82-84, vis asst prof chem, 84. *Concurrent Pos:* Chem tutor, Univ Toronto, 82-83; prin investr, Petrol Res Fund, 84-87, Robert A Welch Found, 85-, Res Corp, 85-88, NIH, 89-92, Tex Tech Univ, 92-, Tex Advan Res Prog, 94- *Mem:* Am Chem Soc; Am Phys Soc; Sigma Xi. *Res:* Ultrafast laser spectroscopy; photophysics in model biomembranes, polymeric media and colloidal dispersions; solute solvent interactions in the photophysical properties of molecules; linear and nonlinear optical dynamics of molecular aggregates; artificial photosynthesis. *Mailing Add:* Dept Chem Tex Tech Univ Lubbock TX 79409. *Fax:* 806-742-1289

QUITTNER, HOWARD, PATHOLOGY. *Current Pos:* RETIRED. *Personal Data:* b Brooklyn, NY, Feb 1, 22; m 66, Carolyn Ward; c 5. *Educ:* Tulane Univ La, BS, 42, MD, 44; Am Bd Path, dipl, 51. *Prof Exp:* Adj pathologist, Beth Israel Hosp, 51-52; dir labs, Washington Hosp, Pa, 52-64; prof clin path, Sch Med & dir clin labs, Univ Ark, Little Rock, 64-76; prof path, Sch Med, Tulane Univ, 76-78, dir clin labs, Med Ctr, 76-78; prof path, Sch Med, Marshall Univ, 78-94. *Concurrent Pos:* Levy Found res fel, Beth Israel Hosp, NY, 49-52; adj prof biochem, Tulane Univ, 76-78; dir lab serv, Vet Admin Med Ctr, Huntington, 80-94. *Mem:* Can Asn Pathologists; Asn Clin Sci (pres, 67). *Res:* Clinical pathology diagnostic techniques. *Mailing Add:* 51A Neron Pl New Orleans LA 70118-4267

QUOCK, RAYMOND MARK, NEUROPHARMACOLOGY. *Current Pos:* assoc prof, 89-93, PROF PHARMACOL, COL MED, UNIV ILL, ROCKFORD, 93- *Personal Data:* b San Francisco, Calif, June 9, 48; m 75, Lina Chiu; c Lauren R, Daniel G & Lindsay P. *Educ:* Univ San Francisco, BS, 70; Univ Wash, PhD(pharmacol), 74. *Honors & Awards:* Dr Elwood Molseed Award, 70; Dr Leo Pinsky Award, 83, 86; Raymond B Allen Award, 90, 91, 92, 93 & 96. *Prof Exp:* Lab asst pharmacol, Sch Med, Univ Calif, San Francisco, 63-70; instr, Sch Med, Univ Wash, 74-75; asst prof physiol & pharmacol, Sch Pharm, Univ Pac, 75-79; from asst prof to prof pharmacol, Sch Dent, Marquette Univ, 79-89. *Concurrent Pos:* Exam consult, Calif State Bd Pharm, 76-79; adj asst prof pharmacol & toxicol, Med Col Wis, 80-89; res assoc toxicol, C J Zablocki Vet Admin Med Ctr, 81-89, consult dent, 82-89; consult, Systems Res Labs, Inc, 96- *Mem:* Soc Neurosci; Western Pharmacol Soc; Am Soc Pharmacol & Exp Therapeut; Int Brain Res Orgn; Bioelectromagnetic Soc; Int Behav Neurosci Soc. *Res:* Mechanisms of pain and anxiety control; nitrous oxide; bioeffects of microwaves. *Mailing Add:* Dept Biomed Sci Col Med Univ Ill 1601 Parkview Ave Rockford IL 61107-1897. *Fax:* 815-395-5666; *E-Mail:* raymondq@uic.edu

QUON, CHECK YUEN, DRUG METABOLISM & PHARMACOKINETICS, BIOANALYTICAL CHEMISTRY. *Current Pos:* res mgr, Du Pont Pharmaceut, 88-90, DIR, DRUG METAB & PHARMAKINETICS, DU PONT MERCK PHARMACEUT CO, 91- *Personal Data:* b Canton, China, Nov 15, 49; US citizen; m 74, Wailan Louie; c Nicole, Daniel & Justin. *Educ:* Univ Calif, Los Angeles, BS, 72, PhD(pharmacol), 77. *Prof Exp:* Res assoc, McArdle Lab Cancer Res, 77-79; res investr, Arnar-Stone, 79-81; sr res investr, Am Crit Care, 81-83, group leader, 83-85, sect head, 85-88. *Mem:* Am Soc Pharmacol & Exp Therapeut; Int Soc Study Xenobiotics; Am Asn Pharmaceut Scientists; Pharmaceut Mfrs Asn. *Res:* Clinical and preclinical drug metabolism and pharmacokinetics; clinical pharmacology; bioanalytical chemistry; n-oxidation. *Mailing Add:* Du Pont Merck Pharmaceut Co Elkton Rd Newark DE 19713

QUON, DAVID SHI HAUNG, MINERALOGY. *Current Pos:* RETIRED. *Personal Data:* b Canton, China, Dec 26, 31; Can citizen; m 60; c 2. *Educ:* Sun Yat Sen Univ, BSc, 49; Ohio State Univ, MSc, 59; Univ Mich, PhD(mineral), 65. *Prof Exp:* Geologist, Geotech Develop Co, 54-58; res asst mineral, Univ Mich, 60-64; mem sci staff, Res & Develop Labs, Northern Elec Co, 64-67 & 68-75; asst prof, Lakehead Univ, 67-68; mem sci staff, Bell Northern Res, 68-75; sr res scientist, Canmet Energy, Mines & Resources, Can, 75-96. *Concurrent Pos:* Nat Res Coun Can res grant, 68-69. *Mem:* Mineral Soc Am; Soc Econ Geologists; Am Ceramic Soc; Mineral Soc Can. *Res:* Mineralogy and geochemistry of carbonatites; crystallochemistry; mineralog synthetic ceramic materials; growing single crystals; mineral processing, extraction of alumina from non-bauxitic minerals and building materials research; solid electrolyte for energy storage; advanced ceramic materials. *Mailing Add:* 10 Sherk Cresent Kanata Ottawa ON K2K 2L4 Can

QURAISHI, MOHAMMED SAYEED, AIDS & INFECTIOUS DISEASES, PESTICIDE TOXICOLOGY. *Current Pos:* entomologist-toxicologist chief, Pest Control & Consult Sect, NIH, 76-84, health scientist adminr, exec secy, MIDRC, 84-88, sci rev admin, spec rev, Nat Inst Allergy & Infectious Dis, 88-96, SCI REV ADMIN, AIDS CLIN & EPIDEMIOL RES REV BR, NIH. *Personal Data:* b Jodhpur, Rajasthan, India, June 23, 24; m 53, Akhtar Imtiaz; c Rana, Naveed & Sabah. *Educ:* St John's Col, Agra Univ, BSc, 42; Aligarh Muslim Univ, MSc, 44; Univ Mass, PhD(entom), 48. *Prof Exp:* Sr mem, UN WHO Team, Pakistan, 49-51; entomologist, Malaria Inst Pakistan, 51-55; sr res officer, Pakistan Coun Sci & Indust Res, 55-60; sr sci officer, Pakistan Atomic Energy Comm, 60-64; assoc prof entom, Univ Man, 64-66; assoc prof entom, NDak State Univ, 66-70, prof, 70-74; chief sci biol, NY State Sci Serv, 74-75; vis scientist, Harvard Sch Pub Health, 95. *Concurrent Pos:* Assoc secy, Sci Comn Pakistan, 59-60; sr scientist, Cent Treaty Orgn, Inst Nuclear Sci, Tehran, Iran, 60-64; prog mgr, Interdept Contract, Proj Themis, Dept of Defense, 68-74; mem, Publ Comt, Soc Environ Toxicol & Chem, 80-83. *Mem:* Entom Soc Am; Am Chem Soc; Soc Environ Toxicol & Chem; Sigma Xi. *Res:* Chemicals showing transient interference with vital phases of insect development; infectious diseases. *Mailing Add:* NIH Solar Bldg Rm 4C22 Bethesda MD 20892. *Fax:* 301-402-2638; *E-Mail:* mq2b@nih.gov

QURESHI, A H, ELECTRICAL ENGINEERING. *Current Pos:* PROF, CLEVELAND STATE UNIV. *Personal Data:* b Dagi, Pakistan, Oct 28, 32; m 61; c 3. *Educ:* Univ Peshawar, BEng, 55; Aachen Tech Univ, PhD(elec eng), 61. *Prof Exp:* Guest res collabr, Nuclear Res-Centre, Juelich, Ger, 58-61; asst prof elec eng, Univ Waterloo, 61-64; head dept, Col Eng, Riyadh, Saudi Arabia, 64-65; sessional lectr, Univ Calgary, 65-66; from asst prof to assoc prof, Univ Windsor, 66-70, prof elec eng & head dept, 70- *Res:* Magnetic and solid state materials; high voltage technology. *Mailing Add:* Dept Elec Eng Cleveland State Univ Euclid Ave & E 24th Cleveland OH 44115-1123

QURESHI, IQBAL HUSSAIN, NUCLEAR CHEMISTRY. *Current Pos:* officer spec training, Pakistan Atomic Energy Comn, Karachi, 60-63, sr sci officer, Lahore, 63-68, prin sci officer, 69-76, chief sci officer, Islamabad, 76-88, CHIEF SCIENTIST, PAKISTAN ATOMIC ENERGY COMN, ISLAMABAD, 88- *Personal Data:* b Ajmer, India, Sept 27, 36; m 65, 87, Khurshid; c Adnan I & Imran I. *Educ:* Govt Col, Hyderabad, Pakistan, BS, 56; Univ Sind, Pakistan, MS, 58; Univ Mich, MS, 62; Tokyo Univ, PhD, 63. *Honors & Awards:* Gold Medal for Phys Sci, Pakistan Acad Sci, 88; Star of Distinction Sci Award, Gov Pakistan, 92. *Prof Exp:* Lectr, Govt Col, 56-60; res chemist, US Nat Bur Stand, 67-68. *Concurrent Pos:* Vis scientist, AEC, Denmark, 70-72; dir, Pakistan Inst Nuclear Sci & Technol, Islamabad, 84-91; tech mem, Pakistan AEC, 91. *Mem:* Int Union Elementologists. *Res:* Nuclear science and technology. *Mailing Add:* House 211 St No 18 F-10/2 PO Box 1114 Islamabad Pakistan

QURESHI, NILOFER, LIPOPOLYSACCHARIDES, MYCOBACTERIAL LIPIDS. *Current Pos:* RES BIOCHEMIST, VET ADMIN HOSP, MADISON, 81- *Personal Data:* b Karachi, Pakistan, July 31, 47; US citizen; m 70, Asaf A; c Arif. *Educ:* St Joseph's Col, BS, 67; Karachi Univ Pakistan, MS, 69; Univ Wis-Madison, PhD(physiol chem), 75. *Prof Exp:* Res assoc biochem, Univ Wis-Madison & Vet Admin Hosp, 76-77, proj assoc, 77-81. *Concurrent Pos:* Adj assoc prof, Dept Bact, Univ Wis-Madison. *Mem:* Am Soc Biol Chemists; Am Soc Microbiol; Am Chem Soc; Int Edotoxin Soc. *Res:* Purification and structure of lipopolysaccharides and lipid A from Salmonella and E coli; lipid A, structure and function; structure and biosynthesis of mycolic acids in Mycobacteria; long-chain fatty acids in Mycobacteria structure and biosynthesis; purification and mechanism of action of B-hydroxy B-methylglutaryl-coenzyme A reductase (yeast); mechanisms involved in the septic shock syndrome. *Mailing Add:* Vet Admin Hosp D-2215 2500 Overlook Terr Madison WI 53705. *Fax:* 608-262-7685

QUTUB, MUSA Y, WATER RESOURCES, GEOLOGY. *Current Pos:* asst prof, 69-72, assoc prof earth sci, 72-80, PROF HYDROGEOL, NORTHEASTERN ILL UNIV, 80- *Personal Data:* b Jerusalem, Palestine, June 2, 40; US citizen; m 70; c 4. *Educ:* Simpson Col, BA, 64; Colo State Univ, MS, 66; Iowa State Univ, PhD(geol & higher educ), 69. *Prof Exp:* Instr earth sci, Iowa State Univ, 66-69. *Concurrent Pos:* NSF & NDEA fels, Northeastern Ill Univ, 69-72; NSF grants, 70-; consult, NSF, 72-, mem aerospace educ comt, 72; Off Environ Educ grant, 73-74; chmn, Six Nat Symposia Environ & Water Resources; Ministry Planning, Saudi Arabia, 77-78; leader, USA Environ Sci Deleg, People's Repub China, 84. *Mem:* AAAS; Int Asn Advan Earth & Environ Sci (pres); Nat Asn Geol Teachers (pres); Nat Sci Teacher Asn. *Res:* Geological education; science learning; ground water and application to city planning in northern Illinois. *Mailing Add:* Dept Geog & Environ Studies Northeastern Ill Univ Chicago IL 60625

QUYNN, RICHARD GRAYSON, POLYMER PHYSICS. *Current Pos:* RETIRED. *Personal Data:* b Newport News, Va, Jan 23, 28; m 53, Louise; c Jennifer & Katelyn. *Educ:* Col William & Mary, BS, 47; Inst Textile Technol, MS, 49; Princeton Univ, AM, 52, PhD(physics, phys chem), 57. *Prof Exp:* Res physicist, Summit Res Labs, Celanese Corp Am, 53-54, sr res physicist, 57-63, res assoc physics, 63-65, sect head mat sci, Celanese Res Co, Celanese Corp, 65-70; mgr mat sci, Res Ctr, Burlington Industs, 70-72; asst dir mat sci, FRL Div, Albany Int Corp, 72-79; mem tech staff, Jet Propulsion Lab, Calif Inst Technol, 79; sr ed, High Technol Mag, 81; sr specialist engr, Boeing Mil Airplane Co, 82-85; res physicist, Res Develop Eng Ctr, US Army, Natick, 86-96. *Mem:* Am Phys Soc; Fiber Soc. *Res:* Physical structure of fibers and films; high polymer physics; spectroscopy; electro-optics. *Mailing Add:* 424 Lincoln St Duxbury MA 02332

R

RAAB, FREDERICK HERBERT, RADIO FREQUENCY POWER AMPLIFIERS, COMMUNICATIONS. *Current Pos:* PRES-OWNER, GREEN MOUNTAIN RADIO RES, 80- *Personal Data:* b Ft Crook, Nebr, Feb 4, 46; m 70, Rebecca Staude; c Hans F. *Educ:* Iowa State Univ, Ames, BS, 68, MS, 70, PhD(elec eng), 72. *Prof Exp:* Engr, Collins Radio Co, Rockwell, 66-69; technologist, NASA Marshall Space Flight Ctr, 70; mem tech staff, Cincinnati Electronics Corp, 72-75; sr systs engr, Polhemus Navig Sci, Inc, 75-80. *Concurrent Pos:* Prog chmn, Radio Frequency Expo E Conf, Radio Frequency Design Mag, 90. *Mem:* Sigma Xi; sr mem Inst Elec & Electronics Engrs; Asn Old Crows; Inst Navig. *Res:* Radio frequency power amplifiers, especially high-efficiency; transmitters; communications, especially through-the-earth; signal processing; author and co-author of over 70 technical publications; reducing new theory to working prototype. *Mailing Add:* 240 Stanford Rd Burlington VT 05401

RAAB, HARRY FREDERICK, JR, REACTOR DESIGN, EXPERIMENTAL REACTOR PHYSICS. *Current Pos:* RETIRED. *Personal Data:* b Johnstown, Pa, May 9, 26; m 51, Phebe Duerr; c Harry F III, Constance D & Cynthia (Morgenthaler). *Educ:* Mass Inst Technol, SB & SM, 51; Oak Ridge Sch Reactor Technol, Dr(pile eng), 55. *Prof Exp:* Control systs engr, Bettis Atomic Power Lab, Westinghouse Elec Corp, 51-55, mgr surface ship physics, 55-62, mgr light water breeder physics, 62-72; chief physicist, Navy Nuclear Propulsion Directorate, US Dept Energy, 72-95. *Concurrent Pos:* Pediat chaplain, Fairfax Hosp, Va, 95- *Mem:* Fel Am Nuclear Soc; AAAS; Sigma Xi. *Res:* Developed light water breeder reactor; direct reactor physics development for the Navy; granted five patents involving breeder reactors. *Mailing Add:* 8202 Ector Ct Annandale VA 22003

RAAB, JACOB LEE, PHYSIOLOGY. *Current Pos:* RES SYST ANALYST, CIBA-GIEGY, 82- *Personal Data:* b Elkhart, Ind, Nov 29, 38; m 65; c 3. *Educ:* Univ Chicago, BS, 60, MS, 65; Duke Univ, PhD(zool), 71. *Prof Exp:* Instr biol, Franklin & Marshall Col, 66-69; asst prof physiol, Rutgers Univ, Newark, 71-; sci dir, West Mountain Sch, Inc. *Mem:* Am Physiol Soc; AAAS. *Res:* Relationship of the energetics of exercise to variables of temperature, humidity, terrain and the time of day. *Mailing Add:* 19 Laurel Ave Summit NJ 07901

RAAB, JOSEPH A, MATHEMATICS. *Current Pos:* chmn dept math, 72-75, asst vpres acad affairs, 78-79, PROF MATH, METROP STATE COL, 69- *Personal Data:* b Oshkosh, Wis, Dec 20, 34; m 55; c 6. *Educ:* Wis State Univ, Oshkosh, BS, 57; Univ Ill, MS, 60; Univ Wis, PhD(math), 67. *Prof Exp:* Teacher pub schs, Wis, 57-59; assoc prof math, Wis State Univ, Oshkosh, 60-69. *Concurrent Pos:* Teacher, Univ N Colo, 68; rep, Colo State Col & Univ Consortium, 75-77; coordr acad progs, Consortium State Cols in Colo, 77-78. *Mem:* Math Asn Am. *Res:* Fibonacci sequences; Pascal's triangle higher order continued fractions and associated algorithms; number theory; abstract algebra; analysis. *Mailing Add:* PO Box 323 Pine CO 80470

RAABE, HERBERT P(AUL), ELECTRICAL ENGINEERING. *Current Pos:* CONSULT, 74- *Personal Data:* b Halle, Ger, Aug 15, 09; nat US; m 56, Hildegard Zumbusch; c Angelika, Eleonore, Bertram & Hans. *Educ:* Berlin Tech Univ, dipl, 36, Dr Ing, 39. *Prof Exp:* From instr to asst prof elec commun technol, Berlin Tech Univ, 36-45; mgr & tech consult, Asn Microfilm, Ger, 45-47; tech consult, Wright Air Develop Ctr, Ohio, 47-56; sr tech specialist, Litton Industs, Inc, 56-66 & Int Bus Mach Corp, NY, 66-68; sr engr, Fed Systs Div, IBM Corp, Gaithersburg, 68-74. *Concurrent Pos:* Res engr, Heinrich Hertz Inst, 37-45; sci consult, Bur Commun Tech, 46-47. *Mem:* Sr mem Inst Elec & Electronics Engrs; sr mem Am Inst Aeronaut & Astronaut; hon mem Ger Soc Rocket Technol & Travel; Inst Navigation. *Res:* Electrical communication technique and radar; information theory; microwave theory and technique; antennas; propagation; electrical countermeasures; infrared technique; military reconnaissance; systems analysis. *Mailing Add:* 10121 Lloyd Rd Potomac MD 20854-1946

RAABE, ROBERT DONALD, plant pathology, for more information see previous edition

RAAEN, VERNON F, ORGANIC CHEMISTRY. *Current Pos:* RETIRED. *Personal Data:* b Plentywood, Mont, Nov 8, 18; m 49; c 1. *Educ:* Concordia Col, BA, 41; Univ Minn, MS, 50, PhD(chem) 58. *Prof Exp:* Chemist & opers supt, Columbia Powder Co, Olin Mathieson Chem Corp, 42-44; chemist,

Union Carbide Nuclear Co Div, Oak Ridge Nat Lab, 50-79. *Mem:* AAAS; Am Chem Soc; Sigma Xi. *Res:* Organic reactions studies with the help of radiocarbon and tritium as tracers. *Mailing Add:* 111 Scenic Dr Oak Ridge TN 37830

RAAM, SHANTHI, ONCOLOGY, BREAST CANCER. *Current Pos:* RES ASSOC, CANCER RES CTR, TUFTS UNIV, 73-, ASSOC PROF RES, SCH MED. *Personal Data:* b Madras, India, Nov 26, 41; US citizen. *Educ:* Univ Madras, India, BS, 60, MS, 62; Univ Ga, PhD(immunol & microbiol), 73. *Honors & Awards:* Kenneth Dodgson Mem Lectr, Univ Ga, Athens, 91. *Prof Exp:* Dir, Oncol Lab, Lemuel Shattuck Hosp, 77-93. *Concurrent Pos:* Consult radioimmunoassay, Leary Labs, Boston, Mass, 73-74; consult steroid receptors, New Eng Nuclear, Boston, Mass; researcher estrogen receptor breast cancer, Tufts Med Cancer Unit, Lemuel Shattuck Hosp, Jamaica Plain, Mass, 75-; prin investr, Am Cancer Soc NY res grants, 79-80 & 80-81; invited speaker consensus comt for steroid receptors in breast cancer, Nat Cancer Inst, 79; prin investr, Nat Cancer Inst, 83-, chmn ad hoc rev comt, 89, 90; mem, Peer Rev Comt, 91- *Mem:* Am Asn Cancer Res; AAAS; Am Asn Clin Oncologists; Am Asn Immunologists; Endocrine Soc. *Res:* Significance of steroid hormone receptors in cancer; search for tumor markers which may prove to be of prognostic and/or diagnostic value in cancer; study of functionally defective hormone receptors in hormone-therapy resistant breast cancers; immunoendocrinology; breast cancer research. *Mailing Add:* 827 Oak Hill Ave Attleboro MA 02703. *Fax:* 617-524-9599

RAAMOT, TONIS, CIVIL ENGINEERING. *Current Pos:* PARTNER, RAAMOT ASSOCS, CONSULT ENGRS, 69- *Personal Data:* b Tartu, Estonia, Jan 6, 32; US citizen; m 58; c 1. *Educ:* Columbia Univ, BA, 53, BS, 54, MS, 56; Univ Ill, PhD(civil eng), 62. *Honors & Awards:* Arthur Wellington Award, Am Soc Civil Engrs, 65. *Prof Exp:* From asst prof to prof civil eng & asst chmn dept, Newark Col Eng, 62-67; chief civil eng, RCP Div, Raymond Int Inc, NY, 67-69; prof civil eng, NJ Inst Technol, 70- *Concurrent Pos:* Soils consult, Raymond Int Inc, 64; NSF res initiation grant, 64-66. *Mem:* Am Soc Civil Engrs; Nat Soc Prof Engrs; Am Soc Eng Educ; Am Concrete Inst; Am Soc Testing & Mat. *Res:* Soil mechanics; foundation engineering; behavior of deep foundations; pile driving analysis. *Mailing Add:* 9995 Shore Rd Brooklyn NY 11209

RAAPHORST, G PETER, MEDICAL PHYSICS, RADIATION & HYPERTHERMIA BIOLOGY. *Current Pos:* res officer radiation biol, 77-85, HEAD RADIATION BIOL, WHITESHELL DIV, ATOMIC ENERGY CAN, 85-; CHIEF, MED PHYSICS, OTTAWA REGIONAL CANCER CTR, 85- *Personal Data:* b Holland; Can citizen; m 74; c 2. *Educ:* Univ Waterloo, BSc, 72, MSc, 74, PhD(physics), 76. *Prof Exp:* Med Res Coun Can res fel, Colo State Univ, 76-78. *Concurrent Pos:* Prof, Dept Radiol, Univ Ottawa, 85-, Dept Biol, 88- & Dept Physiol, 95-; adj prof physics, Carleton Univ, Ottawa, 86-; mem, Allied Sci Staff, Dept Radiol, Civic Hosp, Ottawa, 86- *Mem:* Radiation Res Soc; Can Fedn Biol Sci; NAm Soc Hyperthermia; Can Asn Radiation Oncol; Am Asn Physicists Med; Can Orgn Med Physics. *Res:* The effects of radiation chemotherapeutic agents and hyperthemia on cellular systems in vitro; flow cytometry; electron microscopy; high-performance liquid chromatography of normal and malignant cells given radiation drug hyperthemia or combined treatments; optimizing cancer treatment and determining mechanisms of cellular injury; molecular biology of repair of radiation damage. *Mailing Add:* 1054 Deauvill Crescent Orleans ON K1C 5M1 Can. *E-Mail:* graaphorst@octrf.on.ca

RAASCH, GILBERT O, geology, paleontology, for more information see previous edition

RAASCH, LOU REINHART, ANALYTICAL CHEMISTRY. *Current Pos:* ENVIRON SERV MGR, NAM RAYON CORP, 83- *Personal Data:* b Republican City, Nebr, Apr 27, 44; m 68; c 2. *Educ:* Univ Nebr, Lincoln, BS, 65, PhD(chem), 71. *Prof Exp:* Asst prof chem, MacMurray Col, 69-75; asst prof chem, ETenn State Univ, 75-83. *Mem:* Am Chem Soc. *Res:* Electrochemistry of coordination compounds; voltammetry involving charge transfers followed by chemical reactions; non-aqueous solvents for electrochemical investigations. *Mailing Add:* 505 Sunnyvale Dr Johnson City TN 37601

RAASCH, MAYNARD STANLEY, ORGANIC CHEMISTRY. *Current Pos:* RETIRED. *Personal Data:* b Castlewood, SDak, Feb 27, 15. *Educ:* SDak Sch Mines, BS, 37; Ohio State Univ, MS, 38, PhD(org chem), 41. *Prof Exp:* Lab instr chem, SDak Sch Mines, 35-37; asst gen & org chem, Ohio State Univ, 37-39; res chemist, Exp Sta, E I Du Pont de Nemours Co, Inc, 41-80. *Concurrent Pos:* Res assoc, Stetson Univ, 84; consult, 85-86; res scientist, Univ Ala, 87. *Mem:* Am Chem Soc. *Res:* Organic fluorine compounds; organic sulfur compounds; synthetic biologically active chemicals. *Mailing Add:* 2300 Inglewood Dr Wilmington DE 19803

RAB, PAUL ALEXIS, ZOOLOGY. *Current Pos:* instr, 72-80, PROF BIOL, SINCLAIR COMMUNITY COL, 80- & DEPT CHMN LIFE SCI, 80- *Personal Data:* b Dayton, Ohio, Mar 2, 44; m 67; c 1. *Educ:* Ohio State Univ, BSc, 66, MSc, 70, PhD(zool), 72. *Res:* Social behavior; genetics of behavior. *Mailing Add:* Dept Biol Sinclair Community Col 444 W Third St Dayton OH 45402-1421

RABA, CARL FRANZ, JR, GEOTECHNICAL ENGINEERING, CONSTRUCTION MATERIALS SCIENCE. *Current Pos:* pres, 79-80, CHMN, RABA-KISTNER CONSULT, INC, 80- *Personal Data:* b San Antonio, Tex, Dec 24, 37; c 5. *Educ:* Tex A&M Univ, BS, 61, ME, 62, PhD(civil eng), 68. *Prof Exp:* Res asst geotech, Tex Transp Inst Tex A&M Univ, 61-62; pres, Raba & Assoc Consult Engrs, Inc, 67-78. *Concurrent Pos:* Mem comt, Am Soc Test & Mat, 72-; pres, Tex Coun Eng Labs, 74-75; chmn, Nat Comt Geotech Eng, Exam, Inst Cert Eng Technicians, 75-78. *Mem:* Sigma Xi; Am Soc Civil Engrs; Am Geophys Union; Am Soc Lubrication Engrs. *Res:* Geotechnical considerations of drilled pier and pile foundation systems, and stabilization aspects of fly ash in pavements and embankments. *Mailing Add:* 12821 W Golden Lane San Antonio TX 78249

RABALAIS, FRANCIS CLEO, PARASITOLOGY. *Current Pos:* assoc prof, 68-93, EMER PROF BIOL, BOWLING GREEN STATE UNIV, 93- *Personal Data:* b Bunkie, La, Aug 16, 37; m 59; c 2. *Educ:* Univ Southwestern La, BS, 61; La State Univ, MS, 63, PhD(zool), 67. *Prof Exp:* Instr zool, La State Univ, 66-67 & parasitol, Sch Med, Tulane Univ, 67-68. *Concurrent Pos:* Adj assoc prof microbiol, Med Col Ohio; fel, Sch Trop Med, Tulane Univ, 67; assoc prof, Health & Community Serv, 73-94. *Mem:* Am Soc Trop Med & Hyg; Am Soc Parasitol. *Res:* Biology of trematodes of lower vertebrates; biology of filarial nematodes; host-parasite relationships of filarial nematodes. *Mailing Add:* 192 Shortt Rd Rogersville TN 37857

RABALAIS, JOHN WAYNE, PHYSICAL CHEMISTRY. *Current Pos:* ASSOC PROF PHYS CHEM, UNIV HOUSTON, 75- *Personal Data:* b Bunkie, La, Sept 7, 44; m 66. *Educ:* Univ Southwestern La, BS, 66; La State Univ, PhD(phys chem), 70. *Prof Exp:* NATO fel electron spectros, Univ Uppsala, 70-71; asst prof phys chem, Univ Pittsburgh, 71-75. *Mem:* Am Chem Soc; AAAS. *Res:* Ultraviolet and x-ray photoelectron spectroscopy and its applications to surfaces, catalysis, chemisorption, and adsorption; visible and ultraviolet absorption and emission spectroscopy; secondary ion mass spectrometry; applied quantum chemistry. *Mailing Add:* Dept Chem Univ Houston Houston TX 77204-5641

RABAN, MORTON, ORGANIC CHEMISTRY, NUCLEAR MAGNETIC RESONANCE. *Current Pos:* from asst prof to assoc prof, 67-74, fac res fel, 68, PROF CHEM WAYNE STATE UNIV, 74- *Personal Data:* b St Louis, Mo, Oct 18, 40; m 64. *Educ:* Harvard Univ, AB, 62; Princeton Univ, MS, 66, PhD(org chem), 67. *Prof Exp:* Chemist, Res Inst Med & Chem, 62-63; instr chem, Princeton Univ, 66-67. *Concurrent Pos:* Petrol Res Fund grant, 67-69 & 72-74; Res Corp grant-in-aid, 68-70; NIH res grant, 69-72; NSF res grant, 70-74; Sloan fel, 72-76. *Mem:* AAAS; Am Chem Soc; The Chem Soc. *Res:* Stereochemistry, including optical rotary dispersion-circular dispersion spectroscopy; asymmetric synthesis and determination of absolute configuration; organic chemistry and stereochemistry of sulfur and nitrogen compounds; dynamic nuclear magnetic resonance spectroscopy. *Mailing Add:* 6888 W Dartmoor Rd West Bloomfield MI 48322

RABB, GEORGE BERNARD, CONSERVATION BIOLOGY. *Current Pos:* cur & coordr res, Chicago Zool Park, 56-64, assoc dir res & educ, 64-69, dept dir, 69-75, DIR, CHICAGO ZOOL PARK, 76- *Personal Data:* b Charleston, SC, Jan 2, 30; m 53, Mary Sughrue. *Educ:* Col Charleston, BS, 51; Univ Mich, MA, 52, PhD(zool), 57. *Hon Degrees:* Col Charleston, DHL, 95. *Honors & Awards:* Heine Hediger Award, World Zoo Orgn, 96; Peter Scott Award, Species Survival Comn, 96. *Prof Exp:* Ed asst, Charleston Mus, 49. *Concurrent Pos:* Herpet ed, Copeia, Am Soc Ichthyol & Herpet, 64-68; res assoc, Univ Chicago, 60-67; mem, Comt Evolutionary Biol, 69-; chmn, Int Union Conserv Nature's Species Survival Comn, 89-96, vice-chair, 97-; bd mem, Ill State Mus, 95- *Mem:* Fel AAAS; Am Soc Ichthyol & Herpet (pres, 78); Animal Behav Soc; Am Soc Mammal; Soc Conserv Biol; Sigma Xi. *Res:* Vertebrate behavior; systematics of reptiles; species extinction; amphibians. *Mailing Add:* Chicago Zool Park Brookfield IL 60513

RABB, ROBERT LAMAR, ENTOMOLOGY, POPULATION BIOLOGY. *Current Pos:* RETIRED. *Personal Data:* b Lenoir, NC, Aug 6, 19; m 46; c 2. *Educ:* NC State Univ, BS, 47, MS, 50, PhD(entom), 53. *Honors & Awards:* Ciba-Geigy Recognition Award, Entom Soc Am, 73, Founders Mem Award, 77, W N Reynolds Dist Prof, 81. *Prof Exp:* Asst entom, NC State Univ, 47-50, asst to exten entomologist, 51-52, from asst prof to assoc prof, 53-63, prof entom, 63-83. *Mem:* Entom Soc Am; Ecol Soc Am; AAAS; Am Inst Biol Sci; Int Orgn Biol Control; Sigma Xi. *Res:* Insect ecology and management of agricultural insect pests. *Mailing Add:* 203 Carolina Meadows Villa Chapel Hill NC 27514

RABBANY, SINA Y, BIOSENSORS-KINETICS OF ANTIBODY ANTIGEN INTERACTIONS & CARDIAC MECHANICS, CELL BIOMECHANICS & INTRAMYOCARDIAL DYNAMICS. *Current Pos:* asst prof bioeng, 90-93, ASSOC PROF ENG & DIR BIOENG, HOFSTRA UNIV, 93- *Personal Data:* b Tehran, Aug 8, 63; US citizen. *Educ:* Univ Pa, BS, 85, MS, 86, PhD(bioeng), 91. *Honors & Awards:* Sagawa Young Investr Award, Cardiovasc Syst Dynamic Soc, 92. *Prof Exp:* Res assoc, Cardiovasc Studies Unit, Univ Pa, 84-90, teaching asst biomed instrumentation, Bioeng Dept, 86-89. *Concurrent Pos:* Res intern, Likoff Cardiovasc Inst, Hahnemann Univ, 87-90; fel, Georgetown Univ/Naval Res Lab, 90; Navy fac res fel, Ctr Bio Molecular Sci & Eng, 91-93; res fel, Am Soc Eng Educ, 91-93; presidential res award, Hofstra Univ, 92-96; prin investr, Off Naval Res, 93. *Mem:* Biomed Eng Soc; Inst Elec & Electronics Engrs; Cardiovasc Syst Dynamic Soc. *Res:* Biosensors nonequilibrium kinetics of antibody-antigen interactions at solid-liquid interfaces; role of immobilization on antibody function; cardiovascular mechanics; genesis of intramyocardial pressure; intracellular pressure, force and length relations in isolated muscle cells; mathematical modelling of the heart. *Mailing Add:* 2 Beverly Rd Great Neck NY 11021. *Fax:* 516-565-0183; *E-Mail:* eggsyr@hofstra.edu

RABE, ALLEN E, CHEMICAL ENGINEERING. *Current Pos:* SR RES ENGR, E I DU PONT DE NEMOURS & CO, INC, 62 - *Personal Data:* b New Holstein, Wis, Nov 12, 31; m 56; c 5. *Educ:* Univ Wis, BS, 54, MS, 55, PhD(chem eng), 58. *Prof Exp:* Develop engr, Linde Co, Union Carbide Corp, 58-60; chem engr, Elec Boat Div, Gen Dynamics Corp, 60-62. *Mem:* Am Chem Soc; Am Inst Chem Engrs; Sigma Xi. *Res:* Development of research apparatus for reaction rate constants; measurement of reaction rate constants; analysis and interpretation of kinetic data. *Mailing Add:* Old Carrcroft 104 Glennside Ave Wilmington DE 19803-4221

RABE, AUSMA, PSYCHOBIOLOGY. *Current Pos:* vis scientist, 73-76, RES SCIENTIST VII, NY STATE INST BASIC RES DEVELOP DISABILITIES, 77-, CHMN DEPT PSYCHOBIOL, 85- *Personal Data:* b Daugavpils, Latvia, Jan 26, 26; Can citizen. *Educ:* Queen's Univ (Ont), BA, 53, MA, 54; Univ Mich, PhD(physiol psychol), 60. *Prof Exp:* Res scientist, Bur Res Neurol & Psychiat, NJ Neuropsychiat Inst, 60-72. *Concurrent Pos:* Vis prof, Grad Fac, New Sch Social Res, 63-81. *Mem:* AAAS; Am Psychol Asn; Can Psychol Asn; Soc Neurosci; Int Soc Develop Psychobiol; Teratology Soc. *Res:* Neural mechanisms of behavior; neuroteratology; behavioral teratology. *Mailing Add:* NY State Inst Basic Res Ment Retardation 1050 Forest Hill Rd Staten Island NY 10314

RABE, EDWARD FREDERICK, PEDIATRIC NEUROLOGY. *Current Pos:* RETIRED. *Personal Data:* b Watsontown, Pa, Nov 7, 18; m 43; c 4. *Educ:* Bucknell Univ, BS, 39; Yale Univ, MD, 43. *Prof Exp:* Instr pediat, Sch Med, Yale Univ, 47-49; instr, Sch Med, Univ Kans, 49-50, asst prof, 50-51; chief dept, Geisinger Mem Hosp, Danville, Pa, 51-58; from asst prof to prof pediat, Sch Med, Tufts Univ, 61-86; consult & head sect pediat neurol, King Faisal Specialist Hosp & Res Ctr, Riyadh, Saudi Arabia, 86-89. *Concurrent Pos:* Fel neurol, Mass Gen Hosp, 58-61; dir seizure clin, Pa State Dept Health, 57-58; head sect pediat neurol, New Eng Med Ctr Hosps; pediat neurologist, Boston Floating Hosp; asst pediatrician, Mass Gen Hosp; consult, Paul A Dever State Sch, Mass & New Eng Rehab Inst, Woburn; mem, Task Force II-Minimal Brain Dysfunction, Nat Progs Learning Disabilities in Children, Comt Med & Health Related Servs, 66-69; mem neurol sci res training comt A, Nat Inst Neurol Dis & Stroke, 69-73; mem bd trustees, Easter Seal Res Found, 72-78, chmn, 74-78. *Mem:* Am Acad Pediat; Soc Pediat Res; Am Pediat Soc; Am Acad Neurol. *Res:* Cerebrospinal fluid dynamics; neurological aspects of minimal brain dysfunction; subdural fluid dynamics and treatment of cerebral dysrhythmia; pharmacokinetics of anticonvulsant drugs. *Mailing Add:* PO Box 36 North Whitefield ME 04353-0036

RABEL, FREDRIC M, ANALYTICAL CHEMISTRY. *Current Pos:* PROD MGR, E M SEPARATIONS TECHNOL, 90- *Personal Data:* b Mansfield, Ohio, May 29, 38. *Educ:* Ohio Univ, BS, 60; Univ Wis-Madison, MS, 62; Univ Pa, PhD(chem), 67. *Prof Exp:* Sr chemist, J T Baker Chem Co, 67-71; sr scientist, H Reeve Angel & Co, Inc, 71-74, tech serv mgr, Whatman, Inc, 74-87; pres, ChromHELP, Inc, 87-90. *Concurrent Pos:* Lectr, Sadtler Res Labs, 70-75, Ctr Prof Advan, 78- & Am Chem Soc, 81-84. *Mem:* AAAS; Am Chem Soc; Am Soc Testing & Mat. *Res:* Thin layer, column and high performance liquid chromatography, especially applications and materials development; extraction techniques; organometallic syntheses and bonding; development of analytical systems. *Mailing Add:* 480 S Democrat Rd Gibbstown NJ 08027

RABEN, IRWIN A(BRAM), CHEMICAL ENGINEERING. *Current Pos:* CONSULT, 86- *Personal Data:* b New Orleans, La, Oct 26, 22; m 45; c 4. *Educ:* Tulane Univ, BE, 42; La State Univ, MS, 47. *Prof Exp:* Chem engr, New Orleans Water Purification Plant, La, 42; sr process engr, Cities Serv Refining Corp, 47-55; sr process engr & supvr, Wyatt C Hedrick Corp, 55-58; mgr process develop & design, Southwest Res Inst, 58-60, mgr chem eng res, 60-64; supvr process eng, Bechtel Corp, 64-69, mgr air pollution control eng, 69-73; vpres, Western Opers, Combustion Equip Assocs, Inc, 73-79; pres, Iar Technol, Inc, 79-85. *Mem:* Am Inst Chem Engrs; Air Pollution Control Asn; Am Chem Soc; Sigma Xi. *Res:* Development and design of chemical processes and equipment; heat transfer; economics; development and design of commercial size flue-gas desulphurization systems for utility boilers; process design of air quality control systems. *Mailing Add:* 130 Sandringham S Moraga CA 94556-1931

RABENSTEIN, ALBERT LOUIS, GENERAL COMPUTER SCIENCES. *Current Pos:* assoc prof, 72-75, prof, 75-90, EMER PROF MATH, WASHINGTON & JEFFERSON COL, 90- *Personal Data:* b East Liverpool, Ohio, May, 20, 31. *Educ:* Washington & Jefferson Col, AB, 52; Univ WVa, MS, 53; Mass Inst Technol, PhD(math), 58. *Prof Exp:* Asst prof math, Allegheny Col, 59-61 & Pa State Univ, 61-64; asst prof, Macalester Col, 64-68, assoc prof, 68-72. *Concurrent Pos:* consult, 90- *Mem:* Math Asn Am. *Res:* Ordinary differential equations. *Mailing Add:* 632 E Beau St Washington PA 15301

RABENSTEIN, DALLAS LEROY, BIOANALYTICAL CHEMISTRY. *Current Pos:* chmn dept chem, 89-92, PROF CHEM, UNIV CALIF, RIVERSIDE, 85-, DEAN, COL NATURAL & AGRI SCI, 93- *Personal Data:* b Portland, Ore, June 13, 42; m 64, Gloria Duncan; c Mark & Lisa. *Educ:* Univ Wash, BS, 64; Univ Wis, PhD(anal chem), 68. *Honors & Awards:* Fisher Sci Award, Can, 84. *Prof Exp:* Res asst nuclear magnetic resonance, Univ Wis, 65-66, lectr, 67-68; res chemist, Chevron Res Co, 68-69; from asst prof to prof chem, Univ Alta, 69-85. *Concurrent Pos:* Res grants, NIH, NSF. *Mem:* Fel AAAS; Am Chem Soc; fel Chem Inst Can. *Res:* Nuclear magnetic resonance spectroscopy; solution chemistry of metal-complexes; application of nuclear magnetic resonance to biochemistry; analytical biochemistry; nuclear magnetic resonance studies of peptides, proteins and red blood cells. *Mailing Add:* Dept Chem Univ Calif Riverside CA 92521. *Fax:* 909-787-4713; *E-Mail:* dlrab@mail.ucr.edu

RABER, DOUGLAS JOHN, CHEMISTRY. *Current Pos:* DIR, BD CHEM SCIS & TECHNOL, NAT RES COUN, 90- *Personal Data:* b New York, NY, Nov 13, 42; m 94, Linda Ross; c Wendy & Jessica. *Educ:* Dartmouth Col, AB, 64; Univ Mich, PhD(org chem), 68. *Prof Exp:* NIH fel, Princeton Univ, 68-70; from asst prof to prof chem, Univ SFla, 70-90. *Mem:* AAAS; Am Chem Soc. *Res:* Physical organic chemistry; computational chemistry. *Mailing Add:* Nat Res Coun 2101 Constitution Ave Washington DC 20418. *E-Mail:* draber@nas.edu

RABER, MARTIN NEWMAN, MEDICINE. *Current Pos:* PROF MED & CHMN, DEPT CLIN INVEST, M D ANDERSON HOSP & TUMOR INST, HOUSTON, 85- *Personal Data:* b New York, NY, Mar 29, 47; m 78; c 3. *Educ:* Washington Univ, St Louis, AB, 68; Cath Univ Louvain, MD, 75; FRCPC, 79. *Prof Exp:* Intern resident internal med, Sch Med, Dalhousie Univ, 75-78; fel med oncol, M D Anderson Hosp, 78-80; from asst prof to assoc prof med, Sch Med, Univ Tex, Houston, 80-85. *Mem:* Fel Am Col Physicians; Am Soc Clin Oncol; NY Acad Sci; Soc Anal Cytol. *Res:* Clinical evaluation of new drugs and other therapeutic modalities in patients with cancer; evaluation and management of patients with unknown primary cancers. *Mailing Add:* Univ Tex M D Anderson Cancer Ctr PO Box 318 Houston TX 77030-4095

RABIDEAU, PETER W, ORGANIC CHEMISTRY. *Current Pos:* PROF CHEM, LA STATE UNIV, BATON ROUGE, 89-, DEAN, COL BASIC SCI, 89- *Personal Data:* b Johnstown, Pa, Mar 4, 40; m 62, 86, Jennifer Mooney; c Steven, Michael, Christine, Susan, Mark & Leah. *Educ:* Loyola Univ, BS, 64; Case Inst Technol, MS, 67; Case Western Res Univ, PhD(org chem), 68. *Prof Exp:* Res assoc org chem, Ben May Lab Cancer Res, Univ Chicago, 68-69, instr, 69-70; from asst prof to prof chem, Ind Univ-Purdue Univ, Indianapolis, 70-89, chmn dept, 85-89. *Mem:* Am Chem Soc; AAAS. *Res:* Stereochemistry of cyclic hydrocarbons by nuclear magnetic resonance; metal ammonia reduction of aromatic compounds; synthesis of polynuclear aromatics with curved surfaces. *Mailing Add:* Off Dean Col Basic Sci La State Univ Baton Rouge LA 70803-1802. *Fax:* 504-388-8826; *E-Mail:* cxrab@lsuvm.sncc.lsu.edu

RABIDEAU, SHERMAN WEBBER, PHYSICAL CHEMISTRY. *Current Pos:* CONSULT, 82- *Personal Data:* b Cloquet, Minn, May 9, 20; m 43; c 3. *Educ:* Univ Minn, BChem, 41; Univ Iowa, MS, 47, PhD(phys chem), 49. *Honors & Awards:* Clark Medal, Am Chem Soc. *Prof Exp:* Chemist, Firestone Tire & Rubber Co, 41-42; res chemist electrochem, US Naval Res Lab, 42-46; instr chem, Univ Iowa, 47-49; mem staff chem res, Los Alamos Nat Lab, Univ Calif, 49-82. *Mem:* Fel AAAS; fel Am Inst Chemists; Am Chem Soc; Sigma Xi. *Res:* Laser induced chemistry; gas phase reaction kinetics; isotope separations. *Mailing Add:* 5913 Cubero Dr NE Albuquerque NM 87107

RABIGER, DOROTHY JUNE, ORGANIC CHEMISTRY. *Current Pos:* INDEP RES CHEM 1ST, 74- *Personal Data:* b Philadelphia, Pa, May 30, 35. *Educ:* Ursinus Col, BS, 57; Univ Pa, MS, 60, PhD(org chem), 62. *Prof Exp:* Res chemist, Nat Renderers Asn-USDA, 57-58 & Rohm & Haas Co, 62-64; fel org chem & cancer chemother, Ravdin Inst, Hosp Univ Pa, 64-67, res assoc, 67-69; res chemist, Borden Chem Co, 69; instr pharmaceut chem, Sch Pharm, Temple Univ, 69-70, asst prof, 70-74. *Concurrent Pos:* Res grant-in-aid, Temple Univ, 70-71. *Mem:* AAAS; Am Chem Soc; Sigma Xi. *Res:* Cancer chemotherapy; effects of substituents and structural modifications on the properties of organic molecules; synthesis of novel organic compounds for biological applications; chemical topology. *Mailing Add:* 517 Boyer Rd Cheltenham PA 19012

RABII, JAMSHID, ENDOCRINOLOGY, NEUROENDOCRINOLOGY. *Current Pos:* asst prof physiol, 77-83, ASSOC PROF BIOL SCI, RUTGERS UNIV, 83- *Personal Data:* b Tehran, Iran, July 12, 46; m 68; c 3. *Educ:* Univ Calif, Berkeley, BA, 70; Univ Calif, San Francisco, PhD(endocrinol), 75. *Prof Exp:* Res anatomist, Dept Anat & Brain Res, Univ Calif, Los Angeles, 75-76, fel, Mental Health Training Prog, 76-77. *Concurrent Pos:* Prin investr grants, NIH, 78-83 & Rutgers Univ, 80- *Mem:* Endocrine Soc; Soc Neurosci; Int Soc Neuroendocrinol; Soc Study Reproduction. *Res:* Neuroendocrinology: longterm influences of opiates on various neuroendocrine phenomena; hypothalamic control of anterior pituitary hormone secretion; involvement of biogenic amines in the regulation of anterior pituitary hormone secretion in mammalian and avian species. *Mailing Add:* Dept Biol Sci Rutgers State Univ New Brunswick NJ 08903

RABII, SOHRAB, THEORETICAL SOLID STATE PHYSICS. *Current Pos:* from asst prof to assoc prof, 69-78, chmn dept, 77-82, PROF ELEC ENG, MOORE SCH ELEC ENG, UNIV PA, 78--, CHMN DEPT, 94- *Personal Data:* b Ahwaz, Iran, Dec 30, 37; div, Susan Hunt; c Susan & Elizabeth. *Educ:* Univ Southern Calif, BS, 61; Mass Inst Technol, MS, 62, PhD(solid state physics), 66. *Hon Degrees:* MA, Univ Pa, 75. *Prof Exp:* Res fel solid state physics, Mass Inst Technol, 66-67; sr res physicist, Monsanto Co, Mo, 67-69. *Concurrent Pos:* Fel, Max Planck Soc Advan Sci, Repub Ger, 75. *Mem:* Inst Elec & Electronics Engrs; Am Phys Soc; Col Art Asn Am; Am Soc Anesthetists. *Res:* Theoretical calculation of energy band structure and electronic properties of crystalline solids and disordered alloys; electronic structure of molecules and localized state in solids; relativistic effects in atoms molecules and solids; electronic structure of low dimensional solids, solid-solid interface. *Mailing Add:* Dept Elec Eng Univ Pa Philadelphia PA 19104. *Fax:* 215-573-2045; *E-Mail:* rabii@ee.upenn.edu

RABIN, BRUCE S, IMMUNOLOGY, PATHOLOGY. *Current Pos:* PROF PATH, UNIV PITTSBURGH PRESBY HOSP, 72- *Educ:* State Univ NY, MD & PhD, 69. *Mailing Add:* Dept Clin Immunopath CLSI Univ Pittsburgh Med Ctr 200 Lothrop St Pittsburgh PA 15213-2582

RABIN, ELIJAH ZEPHANIA, INTERNAL MEDICINE, BIOCHEMISTRY. *Current Pos:* ASSOC PROF MED, UNIV OTTAWA, 74- *Personal Data:* b Ottawa, Ont, Jan 30, 37; m 65; c 2. *Educ:* Queen's Univ, Ont, MD, 61; McGill Univ, PhD(biochem), 71. *Prof Exp:* Assoc med officer, Prudential Assurance Eng, 68-74; asst prof med, Montreal Gen Hosp, McGill Univ, 70-74. *Concurrent Pos:* Med Res Coun Can scholar, 70-74; chief med dir, Montreal Life Ins Co, 73-74. *Mem:* Can Soc Clin Invest; Am Soc Nephrology; Int Soc Nephrology. *Res:* Ribonuclease activity in renal failure; role of ribonuclease in uremic toxicology; biochemical structure of human urinary ribonuclease. *Mailing Add:* 1919 Riverside Dr Suite 204 Ottawa ON K1H 1A2 Can

RABIN, ERWIN R, PATHOLOGY, VIROLOGY. *Current Pos:* DIR PATH, HURON RD HOSP, OHIO, 76- *Personal Data:* b St Louis, Mo, Oct 22, 30; m 54; c 3. *Educ:* Wash Univ, AB, 52, MD, 56. *Prof Exp:* Intern path, Sch Med, Yale Univ, 56-57, resident, 57-59; asst pathologist, Sinai Hosp Baltimore, Inc, 61-62; asst prof path, Baylor Col Med, 62-66, assoc prof, 66-68; assoc prof path, Sch Med, Wash Univ, 68-74; mem staff, Lattimore-Fink Labs, Inc, 74-76. *Concurrent Pos:* Life Ins Med Res Fund fel, 57-58 & USPHS trainee, 58-59; from asst to assoc pathologist, Jewish Hosp St Louis, 68-70, actg dir, 71-74. *Mem:* Col Am Pathologists; Am Asn Pathologists; Int Acad Path; Sigma Xi. *Res:* Ultrastructural changes in in-vivo viral infections as related to viral-host interaction and pathogenesis of the disease. *Mailing Add:* Dept Path Meridia Huron Hosp 13951 Terrace Rd Cleveland OH 44112-4399

RABIN, HARVEY, EXPERIMENTAL BIOLOGY. *Current Pos:* SR VPRES, PRO-NEURON, ROCKVILLE, MD, 92- *Educ:* Temple Univ, PhD, 58. *Prof Exp:* assoc dir viral dis res, E I Du Pont De Nemours & Co, Inc, 89-92. *Mailing Add:* Pro-Neuron 1530 E Jefferson St Rockville MD 20852

RABIN, HERBERT, QUANTUM OPTICS, SOLID STATE PHYSICS. *Current Pos:* DIR, ENG RES CTR, PROF ELEC ENG & ASSOC DEAN, COL ENG, UNIV MD, COLLEGE PARK, MD, 83- *Personal Data:* b Milwaukee, Wis, Nov 14, 28; m 62; c 2. *Educ:* Univ Wis, BS, 50; Univ Ill, MS, 51; Univ Md, PhD(physics), 59. *Honors & Awards:* E O Hulburt Award, 70; NASA Cert Commendation; Centennial Medal, Univ Md Col Eng. *Prof Exp:* Physicist, Elec Div, Naval Res Lab, 52-54, Solid State Physics Div, 54-62, head, Radiation Effects Sect, Dielec Br, 62-65, mat sci staff, 65-66, head, Radiation Physics Sect, Optical Mat Br, Optical Physics Div, 66-67, actg head, Appl Optics Br, 67-68, head, Quantum Optics Br, 68-70, assoc dir space & commun sci & technol, Naval Res Lab, 70-79; dep asst secy navy, res, appl & space technol, Dept Navy, Washington, DC, 79-83. *Concurrent Pos:* Vis scientist, Univ Stuttgart, 60-61; consult, Dept Physics, Univ Sao Paulo, 64 & 70; prof lectr, Dept Physics, George Washington Univ, 55-73; adv panel, NASA, 72-75; mem, Space Panel, Naval Studies Bd, Nat Acad Sci, 78-, Naval Studies Bd, 93-; trustee, Nat Technol Univ, 84-; bd dir, Gen Res Corp Int, 88-, Yurie Systs Inc, 95- *Mem:* Corresp mem Brazilian Acad Sci; fel Am Inst Aeronaut & Astronaut; sr mem Inst Elec & Electronics Engrs; fel Am Phys Soc; fel Optical Soc Am; fel AAAS. *Res:* Characterization of defect structure in insulating crystals; elucidation of nonlinear optical phenomena; space research and system developments. *Mailing Add:* 7109 Radnor Rd Bethesda MD 20817. *Fax:* 301-403-4105; *E-Mail:* hr1@umail.umd.edu

RABIN, JEFFREY MARK, STRING THEORY, GEOMETRY OF SUPERMANIFOLDS. *Current Pos:* asst prof, 87-91, ASSOC PROF, DEPT MATH, UNIV CALIF, SAN DIEGO, 91- *Personal Data:* b Los Angeles, Calif, Aug 29, 55. *Educ:* Univ Calif, Los Angeles, BS, 76; Stanford Univ, MS, 78, PhD(physics), 81. *Prof Exp:* Res staff physicist & lectr physics, Yale Univ, 81-83; Enrico Fermi fel, Enrico Fermi Inst, Univ Chicago, 83-87. *Mem:* Am Math Soc. *Res:* Topology, geometry and integration theory on supermanifolds; string theory; integrable systems. *Mailing Add:* Dept Math Univ Calif-San Diego La Jolla CA 92093-0112

RABIN, MICHAEL O, THEORY OF ALGORITHMS. *Current Pos:* THOMAS J WATSON SR PROF COMPUT SCI, HARVARD UNIV, 83- *Personal Data:* b Breslau, Ger, Sept 1, 31. *Educ:* Hebrew Univ, Israel, MSc, 53; Princeton Univ, PhD(math), 56. *Honors & Awards:* C Weizmann Prize Exact Sci, 60; Rothschild Prize Math, 74; Turing Award Comput Sci, Asn Comput Mach, 76; Harvey Prize Sci & Technol, 80. *Prof Exp:* H B Fine instr, Princeton Univ, 56-58, mem, Inst Advan Study, 58; assoc prof, Hebrew Univ, Jerusalem, 58-65, prof, 65-, Albert Einstein chair, 80- *Concurrent Pos:* Consult, IBM, 57- & Bell Tel Labs, 60; vis assoc prof math, Univ Calif, Berkeley, 61-62, Mass Inst Technol, 62-63; chmn, Inst Math, Hebrew Univ, 64-66 & Comput Sci Dept, 70-71; lectr comput sci, Paris Univ, 65; vis prof math, Yale Univ, 67, math & comput sci, NY Univ, 70-71, appl math, Mass Inst Technol, 72-78, comput sci, Wash State Univ, 79 & Harvard Univ, 80-81; Gordon McKay prof comput sci, Harvard Univ, 81-83; Fairchild scholar, Calif Inst Technol, 87. *Mem:* Foreign assoc Nat Acad Sci; foreign hon mem Am Acad Arts & Sci; Israel Acad Sci & Humanities; foreign mem Am Philos Soc. *Res:* Theory of algorithms; randomized algorithms; complexity of computations; computer security. *Mailing Add:* Div Eng & Appl Sci Harvard Univ 33 Oxford St Cambridge MA 02138. *E-Mail:* rabin@deas.harvard.edu

RABIN, MONROE STEPHEN ZANE, ELEMENTARY PARTICLE PHYSICS, MEDICAL PHYSICS. *Current Pos:* assoc prof, 72-81, PROF PHYSICS, UNIV MASS, 81- *Personal Data:* b Brooklyn, NY, Dec 19, 39; m 65, Joan Greenblatt; c Carolyn & Elaine. *Educ:* Columbia Col, AB, 61; Rutgers Univ, MS, 64, PhD(physics), 67. *Prof Exp:* Physicist, Univ Calif, Lawrence Berkeley Lab, 67-72. *Concurrent Pos:* Vis physicist, Stanford Linear Accelerator Ctr, 79-80; vis scholar physics, Harvard Univ, 86-87; first Soriano res scholar radiol physics, Dept Radiation Med, Mass Gen Hosp, 86-87. *Mem:* Am Phys Soc; Fedn Am Scientists; Sigma Xi. *Res:* Elementary particle physics: search for strange quark matter, lifetimes of charmed particles, electromagnetic interactions; hadronic production of heavy flavors; use of protons and other ionizing particles in cancer therapy. *Mailing Add:* Dept Physics & Astron Univ Mass Amherst MA 01003-4525. *Fax:* 413-545-0648; *E-Mail:* rabin@phast.umass.edu

RABINER, LAWRENCE RICHARD, ELECTRICAL ENGINEERING, COMMUNICATIONS. *Current Pos:* Mem tech staff, Bell Tel Labs, 67-72, supvr, 72-85, dept head, 85-90, dir, 90-95, VPRES, BELL LABS, 95-; VPRES, AT&T LABS, 96- *Personal Data:* b Brooklyn, NY, Sept 28, 43; m 68, Suzanne Login; c Sheri, Wendi & Joni. *Educ:* Mass Inst Technol, BS & MS, 64, PhD(elec eng), 67. *Honors & Awards:* Biennial Award, Acoust Soc Am, 74; Piori Award & Soc Award, Inst Elec & Electronics Engrs, 80, Centennial Award, 84. *Concurrent Pos:* Fel, Bell Labs, 90, AT&T, 96. *Mem:* Nat Acad Sci; Nat Acad Eng; fel Inst Elec & Electronics Engrs; fel Acoust Soc Am. *Res:* Speech communications including recognition, synthesis, perception and analysis; digital filtering and computer applications. *Mailing Add:* Rm 2C-562 AT&T Labs Murray Hill NJ 07974. *Fax:* 908-582-6758; *E-Mail:* research.att.com!lrr

RABINO, ISAAC, BIOLOGICAL & HEALTH SCIENCES, SCIENCE EDUCATION. *Current Pos:* ASSOC PROF BIOL & HEALTH SCI, EMPIRE STATE COL, STATE UNIV NY, 85- *Personal Data:* b Haifa, Israel, Dec 2, 38; m 70, Linda L Urie; c Tahli. *Educ:* Hebrew Univ, Jerusalem, Israel, BSc, 62; Col Agr & Life Sci, Cornell Univ, Ithaca, NY, MS, 65; State Univ NY, Stony Brook, DPhil(biol sci), 76. *Prof Exp:* Asst prof biol, physiol, microbiol & environ sci, St Peter's Col, Jersey City, NJ, 77-81; asst prof embryol & develop biol, State Univ NY, Stony Brook, 81-82; sci assoc environ affairs, Scientists & Engrs for Secure Energy, New York, 82-83; asst prof biol, Dept Natural Sci, Baruch Col, City Univ New York, 83-85. *Concurrent Pos:* NSF Summer Res Grant, Columbia Univ, New York, 78-81; res grant, Richard Lounsbery Found, 87-90 & 87-, surv perceptions US scientists in genetic-eng/biotech res, 94. *Mem:* NY Acad Sci; AAAS; Am Inst Biol Sci; Asn Politics & Life Sci; Soc Social Studies of Sci. *Res:* Impact of political advocacy on biotechnology research in the United States; AIDS and society; author of numerous scientific journal articles and publications; drugs and society; perceptions of European genetic-engineering researchers; follow up study of 15,000 scientists in the United States; perceptions and concerns on policy, ethical, regulatory issues vis-a-vis genetic engineering research and development, United States Competitiveness. *Mailing Add:* Sci Dept State Univ NY Metropolitan Ctr 225 Varick St New York NY 11014-4303

RABINOVICH, DANIEL, SYNTHETIC INORGANIC & ORGANOMETALLIC CHEMISTRY, INORGANIC CHEMISTRY. *Current Pos:* ASST PROF CHEM, UNIV NC, CHARLOTTE, 96- *Personal Data:* b Lima, Peru, Dec 19, 65; m 92, Miryam M Melo; c Deborah N. *Educ:* Cath Univ, Lima, Peru, BSc, 90; Columbia Univ, MA, 90, PhD(inorg chem), 94. *Prof Exp:* Postdoctoral res assoc, Los Alamos Nat Lab, 94-96. *Mem:* Am Chem Soc. *Res:* Synthetic, mechanistic and structural inorganic and organometallic chemistry. *Mailing Add:* Dept Chem Univ NC Charlotte NC 28223. *Fax:* 704-547-3151; *E-Mail:* drabinov@email.uncc.edu

RABINOVICH, ELIEZER M, GLASS CERAMICS SCIENCE. *Current Pos:* MEM TECH STAFF & PRIN INVESTR, GLASS & CERAMIC SCI, BELL LABS, MURRAY HILL, NJ, 81-; ADV, LUCENT TECHNOL. *Personal Data:* b Moscow, Russia, Apr 4, 37, US citizen; m 65, 67, Jesya Asinovsky; c Irina & Asya. *Educ:* Moscow Mendeleev Inst Chem Technol, MSc, 59, PhD(ceramic sci), 64. *Prof Exp:* Res engr glass for electronics, Res Inst Vacuum Electronics, Moscow, USSR, 59-64, sr res fel, 64-68, group supvr, 68-73; sr & prin investr, glass & ceramic sci, Israel Ceramic & Silicate Inst, Technion City, Haifa, Israel, 74-80. *Concurrent Pos:* Adj prof glass & ceramics, Technion-Israel Inst Technol, Haifa, Israel, 76-80; mem, Ed Adv Comt, Am Ceramic Soc, 89-94. *Mem:* Fel Am Ceramic Soc. *Res:* Broad experience in research and development of a variety of glass and ceramic materials, study of their properties, designing new materials and technological processes; extensive research in sol-gel preparation of materials, in glass ceramics, glasses for electronics; author of 90 papers and recipient of 9 patents; strengthening of glass. *Mailing Add:* Bell Lab Rm 1D-441 600-700 Mountain Ave PO Box 636 Murray Hill NJ 07974-0636

RABINOVICH, SERGIO ROSPIGLIOSI, INTERNAL MEDICINE, INFECTIOUS DISEASES. *Current Pos:* chmn dept, 74-88, PROF MED & CHMN DIV INFECTIOUS DIS, SCH MED, SOUTHERN ILL UNIV, 73- *Personal Data:* b Lima, Peru, Apr 4, 28; m 53, Nelly Vasques-Solis; c Regina, Sergio Jr, Egla & Norka. *Educ:* Univ Lima, BM & MD, 54. *Prof Exp:* Intern, Grasslands Hosp, Valhalla, NY, 54, asst med resident, 55- 56, chief med resident, 56-57; resident gastroenterol, Henry Ford Hosp, Detroit, 57-58; pvt pract, Peru, 58-59; prof med & head dept, Univ San Agustin, Peru, 60-61; physician-in-chg, Hosp Arzobispo Loayza, Lima, Peru, 63; assoc, Col Med, Univ Iowa, 63, from asst prof to assoc prof med, 65-73. *Concurrent Pos:* Consult, Arequipa Gen Hosp, Peru, 60-61; res fel med, Col Med, Univ Iowa, 63-65, fel infectious dis, 65; res fel, Sch Med, Univ Kans, 64-65. *Mem:* Am Soc Microbiol; AMA; Sigma Xi; fel Am Col Physicians; fel Infectious Dis Soc Am; Am Thoracic Soc. *Res:* Infectious disease, mycology, virology and antibiotics. *Mailing Add:* Sch Med Southern Ill Univ PO Box 3926 Springfield IL 62708. *Fax:* 217-788-5880

RABINOVITCH, B(ENTON) S(EYMOUR), PHYSICAL CHEMISTRY. *Current Pos:* from asst prof to prof, 48-85, EMER PROF CHEM, UNIV WASH, 85- *Personal Data:* b Montreal, Que, Feb 19, 19. *Educ:* McGill Univ, BSc, 39, PhD(phys chem), 42. *Hon Degrees:* DSc Israel Inst Technol, Haifa, 91. *Honors & Awards:* Du Pont lect, Univ Rochester, 64; Reilly lectr, Univ

Notre Dame, 68; Debye lectr, Cornell Univ, 78; King lectr, Kans State Univ, 80; Res Prize, Sigma Xi, 81; Debye Award, Am Chem Soc, 84; Polanyi Medal, Royal Soc Chem London, 84. *Prof Exp:* Res chemist, Chem Warfare Labs, 42; Royal Soc Can fel, Harvard Univ, 46-47, Milton fel, 47-48. *Concurrent Pos:* Chmn, Puget Sound Sect, Am Chem Soc, 58 & Phys Chem Div, 67; Guggenheim fel, 61; vis scientist, Nat Res Coun Can, 62; mem, var comts, Nat Acad Sci-Nat Res Coun, 65-; vis Sloan prof, Harvard Univ, 66; distinguished vis prof, Univ Ariz, 68 & Israel Inst Technol-Technion, 78; vis fel, Trinity Col, Oxford Univ, 71; ed, Ann Rev Phys Chem, 75-85; Frontiers Chem lectr, Wayne State Univ, 81, Frontiers Phys Chem lectr, Cambridge Univ, 83; hon res fel, Univ Col, London, 85-90. *Mem:* Fel Am Phys Soc; Am Chem Soc; Royal Soc Chem; fel Am Acad Arts & Sci; fel Royal Soc London. *Res:* Chemical kinetics; unimolecular reactions; chemical activation; non-equilibrium systems; energy transfer and relaxation; silver surfaces. *Mailing Add:* Dept Chem Univ Wash Box 351700 Seattle WA 98195. *Fax:* 206-685-8665

RABINOVITCH, MARLENE, PEDIATRICS, PATHOLOGY. *Current Pos:* asst prof pediat & path, 82-88, GRAD FAC DEPT PATH, UNIV TORONTO, 82-, PROF PEDIAT & PATH, 88- *Personal Data:* b Montreal, Can, July 14, 46. *Educ:* McGill Univ, BS, 67, MD, 71. *Honors & Awards:* Cushing Award, McGill Univ Sch Med. *Prof Exp:* Instr pediat, Children's Hosp Med Ctr, Harvard Med Sch, Boston, 77-78, asst prof, 79-82. *Concurrent Pos:* Asst, Dept Cardiol, Children's Hosp Med Ctr, Boston, 77-78, assoc, 78-82, sr assoc pediat & path, Hosp Sick Children, Toronto, 82-, actg dir cardiovasc res, Res Inst, 86-88, dir, 88-; reviewer, numerous journals; mem, Study Sect Young Investr, NIH, 81-, Pathobiochem, 90-93, Parent Comt Appln 90-91. *Mem:* Am Col Cardiol; Soc Pediat Res; Am Asn Path; Am Thoracic Soc; Am Soc Clin Invest. *Res:* Pulmonary circulation in congenital heart disease; pulmonary hypertension; vascular cellular and molecular biology; numerous publications. *Mailing Add:* Dept Pediat & Path Cardiovasc Res Univ Toronto Hosp Sick Children 555 University Ave Toronto ON M5G 1X8 Can

RABINOVITCH, MICHEL PINKUS, CELL BIOLOGY, EXPERIMENTAL MEDICINE. *Current Pos:* Res assoc cellular immunol, 64-65, from asst prof to assoc prof, 65-73, PROF CELL BIOL, SCH MED, NY UNIV, 73-; PROF CELL PHYSIOL & IMMUNOL, ROCKEFELLER UNIV, 90- *Personal Data:* b Sao Paulo, Brazil, Mar 22, 26; m 67; c 2. *Educ:* Univ Sao Paulo, MD, 49, Livre Docente, 53. *Concurrent Pos:* Rockefeller Found fel, Univ Chicago, Marine Biol Lab & Univ Calif, Berkeley, 53-54. *Mem:* Am Asn Immunol; Am Soc Cell Biol; Harvey Soc. *Res:* Nucleic acids content of tissues; RNA synthesis in amoeba; control of serum ribonuclease by the kidneys; phagocytic recognition by macrophages, tissue culture cells, insect hemocytes, Acanthamoeba; cell adhesion and spreading. *Mailing Add:* Steinman Lab Rockefeller Univ 1230 York Ave New York NY 10021 France

RABINOVITCH, PETER S, MITOTIC CELL CYCLE, CELL ACTIVATION. *Current Pos:* ASST PROF PATH, UNIV WASH, 80- *Educ:* Univ Wash, MD, 79, PhD (genetics), 80. *Mailing Add:* Dept Path Univ Wash Sch Med 3900 Seventh Ave NE Seattle WA 98195

RABINOVITZ, MARCO, PHARMACEUTICAL CHEMISTRY, BIOCHEMISTRY. *Current Pos:* RETIRED. *Personal Data:* b Braila, Rumania, Dec 12, 23; US citizen; m 57, Edith Kisch; c Alice & Michael. *Educ:* Univ Pa, BS, 44; Univ Minn, PhD(biochem), 50. *Prof Exp:* Am Cancer Soc fel, Comt on Growth, Nat Res Coun, Univ Calif, 50-52, res biochemist, Dept Physiol Chem, 52-58; res biochemist, Nat Cancer Inst, 58-95. *Mem:* AAAS; Am Chem Soc; Am Soc Biol Chem; Soc Exp Biol & Med; Am Asn Cancer Res; Am Soc Cell Biol. *Res:* Protein biosynthesis; antimetabolites; biosynthetic control mechanisms; biochemical basis for experimental cancer chemotherapy; cell biology. *Mailing Add:* 4504 Traymore St Bethesda MD 20814-3965

RABINOW, JACOB, ENGINEERING. *Current Pos:* chief res engr, Nat Eng Lab, Nat Bur Stand, 72-75, CONSULT, NAT INST STAND & TECHNOL, 75- *Personal Data:* b Karkov, Russia, Jan 8, 10; nat US; m 43, Gladys Lieder; c Clare & Jean. *Educ:* City Col New York, BS, 33, EE, 34. *Hon Degrees:* LHD, Towson State Univ, 83. *Honors & Awards:* Pres Cert Merit, 48; Edward Longstreth Medal, Franklin Inst, 69; Harry Diamond Award, Inst Elec & Electronics Engrs, 77. *Prof Exp:* Radio technician, Sheffield Radio Co, NY, 34; radio engr, Sterling Radio Co, 34-35 & Halson Radio Mfg Co, 35-37; jr elec engr, Fed Power Comn, 37; eng draftsman, Gibbs & Hill Eng Co, 37-38; mech engr, Nat Bur Stand, 38-53; consult, Diamond Ord Fuze Labs, 53-54; pres, Rabinow Electronics Inc, Control Data Corp, 54-68, vpres, 68-72. *Mem:* Nat Acad Eng; Sigma Xi; fel Inst Elec & Electronics Engrs; fel AAAS. *Res:* Design of electronic equipment; design and development of ordnance devices such as guided missiles and fuses; patents on special cameras, watch regulators, headlight dimmers; inventor of magnetic fluid clutch; optical character recognition machines; post office machinery. *Mailing Add:* Nat Inst Stand & Technol Bldg 820 Rm 264 Gaithersburg MD 20878

RABINOWICZ, ERNEST, MECHANICAL ENGINEERING. *Current Pos:* Mem staff, Div Indust Coop, 50-54, from asst prof to assoc prof, 54-67, PROF MECH ENG, MASS INST TECHNOL, 67- *Personal Data:* b Berlin, Ger, Apr 22, 26; US citizen; m 53; c 3. *Educ:* Cambridge Univ, BA, 47, PhD(phys chem), 50. *Honors & Awards:* Hodson Award, Am Soc Lubrication Engrs, 57; Ragnar Holm Award, Inst Elec & Electronics Engrs-Holm Conference on Elect Contacts, 83; Mayo D Hersey Award, Am Soc Mech Engr, 85; Nat Award, Soc Tribologists & Lubrication Engrs, 88. *Concurrent Pos:* Consult, IBM Corp, 61-75 & Asn Am Railroads, 75-83; vis prof, Israel Inst Technol, 69. *Mem:* Am Phys Soc; fel Soc Tribologists & Lubrication Engrs; fel Am Soc Mech Engrs. *Res:* Tribology; surface properties of solids; experimentation and measurement techniques; accelerated testing. *Mailing Add:* Rm 35-010 Mass Inst Technol Cambridge MA 02139

RABINOWITCH, VICTOR, SCIENCE ADMINISTRATION. *Current Pos:* vpres prog, 91-92, SR VPRES, JOHN D & CATHERINE T MACARTHUR FOUND, 93- *Personal Data:* b London, Eng, 1934; US citizen; m 58, 92, Mary M Bennett; c Nikolai, Peter & Alexander. *Educ:* Univ Ill, BS, 65: Univ Wis, MS, 61, PhD(zool & int rels), 65. *Prof Exp:* Staff dir, Org Develop Bd, Nat Acad Sci, 65-68, Bd Sci & Technol Int Develop, Nat Res Coun, 70-82; dir, Ctr Study Sci & Soc, assoc prof sci & pub admin, State Univ, NY 69-70; exec dir, Off Int Affairs, Nat Res Coun, 81- *Concurrent Pos:* Ed, sci & technol, World Develop, 72-; dir, Comt Int Security & Arms Control, Nat Acad Sci, 85-91. *Mem:* Fel AAAS; Asn Advan Agr Sci Africa; Fedn Am Scientists; Int Ctr Insect Physiol & Ecol; Sigma Xi. *Res:* Numerous publications. *Mailing Add:* 1212 N Lake Shore Dr No 10 A S Chicago IL 60610-2371. *Fax:* 312-920-6258

RABINOWITZ, ISRAEL NATHAN, AGRICULTURAL & FOOD CHEMISTRY, CHEMICAL & BIOLOGICAL ENGINEERING. *Current Pos:* PRES, CERECHEM CORP, 91- *Personal Data:* b New York, NY, Jan 24, 35; m 59, Lynn Schneiderman; c Mirle D & Joshua P. *Educ:* City Col New York, BS, 56; Univ Wash, MS, 62; Rutgers Univ, PhD(biochem), 65. *Prof Exp:* Damon Runyon fel, King's Col, London, 65-66; USPHS fel, Sch Med, Stanford Univ, 67-69, res assoc biophys, 69-70, physiol, 71-72, res assoc physiol, 72-74; consult, Vet Admin Hosp, Palo Alto, 74-76; pres, ITD Corp, 87-91. *Concurrent Pos:* Lectr, Col Notre Dame, Calif, 70-; vpres res & develop, M & T Labs, 80; lectur, biochem eng, Univ Calif, Santa Barbara, 81; consult, ISTI, 93- *Mem:* AAAS; Am Crystallog Asn; Sigma Xi; Am Chem Soc; Inst Food Technol; Am Soc Biochem & Molecular Biol. *Res:* Biological structure and function; metal complexes; membrane biophysics; agricultural biotechnology. *Mailing Add:* 2534 Foothill Rd Santa Barbara CA 93105

RABINOWITZ, JACK GRANT, RADIOLOGY. *Current Pos:* chmn dept, 78-95, PROF RADIOL, MT SINAI SCH MED, 78- *Personal Data:* b New York, NY, July 9, 27; m 51, 72, Rica Guedalia; c Antoine, Anne, Pierre, Yaron & Tal. *Educ:* Univ Calif, BA, 49; Univ Berne, MD, 55. *Prof Exp:* Instr radiol, Downstate Med Ctr, State Univ NY, 60-61, prof, 70-74; asst radiologist, Mt Sinai Hosp, 62-65; assoc prof radiol, Mt Sinai Sch Med, 65-67; radiologist-in-chief, Brooklyn-Cumberland Med Ctr, 67-70; prof radiol, Downstate Med Ctr, State Univ NY, 70-74; prof diag radiol & chmn dept, Univ Tenn, Memphis, 74-78. *Concurrent Pos:* Dir, Dept Radiol, Kings County Hosp Ctr, 70-74; consult, US Vet Admin, Bronx. *Mem:* Fel Am Col Radiol; Radiol Soc NAm; Asn Univ Radiol. *Mailing Add:* Dept Radiol Mt Sinai Sch Med New York NY 10029

RABINOWITZ, JAMES ROBERT, MOLECULAR MODELING OF ENVIRONMENTAL CHEMICALS IN BIOLOGICAL SYSTEMS. *Current Pos:* RES PHYSICIST, HEALTH EFFECTS RES LAB, US ENVIRON PROTECTION AGENCY, 80- *Personal Data:* b New York, NY, Apr 7, 42. *Educ:* Alfred Univ, BA, 62; State Univ NY, Buffalo, PhD(physics), 72. *Prof Exp:* Res assoc, Ctr Theoret Biol, State Univ NY, Buffalo, 70-72, fel, 72-73; assoc res scientist, Inst Environ Med, New York Univ Med Ctr, 73-77; res scientist, NY Inst Technol, 77-80. *Concurrent Pos:* NATO fel, Uppsala Univ, 69; guest scientist, Northeast Radiol Health Lab, Bur Pub Health, Food & Drug Admin, Dept Health, Educ & Welfare, 73. *Mem:* AAAS; Radiation Res Soc; Bioelectromagnetics Soc; Sigma Xi; Int Soc Quantum Biol. *Res:* The use of molecular modeling methods to predict chemical toxicity; structure activity in environmental health. *Mailing Add:* Genetic Toxicol Div MD-68 Health Effects Res Lab US Environ Protection Agency Triangle Park NC 27711-0001

RABINOWITZ, JESSE CHARLES, BIOCHEMISTRY, ONE-CARBON METABOLISM. *Current Pos:* from assoc prof to prof, 57-91, chmn dept, 78-83, EMER PROF BIOCHEM, UNIV CALIF, BERKELEY, 91- *Personal Data:* b New York, NY, Apr 28, 25. *Educ:* Polytech Inst Brooklyn, BS, 45; Univ Wis, MS, 47, PhD(biochem), 49. *Prof Exp:* Nat Heart Inst trainee, Univ Wis, 50-51; USPHS fel, Univ Calif, Berkeley, 51-53; chemist, Nat Inst Arthritis & Metab Dis, Md, 53-57. *Mem:* Nat Acad Sci; Am Soc Biol Chemists; Am Soc Microbiol. *Res:* Enzymology; purine fermentation; folic acid coenzymes; iron-sulfur proteins; protein biosynthesis. *Mailing Add:* Barker Hall Univ Calif Berkeley CA 94720. *E-Mail:* panisse@mendel.berkley.edu

RABINOWITZ, JOSEPH LOSHAK, BIOCHEMISTRY, LIPIDS. *Current Pos:* From res assoc to assoc prof, 53-70, PROF BIOCHEM, SCH DENT MED, UNIV PA, 70-; CHIEF RADIOISOTOPE RES, VET ADMIN HOSP, PHILADELPHIA, 58- *Personal Data:* b Odessa, Ukraine, Nov 4, 23; US citizen; m 46, Josephine Fledmark; c Malva, Lois & Martin. *Educ:* Philadelphia Col Pharm, BS, 44; Univ Pa, MSc, 48, PhD(org chem), 50. *Hon Degrees:* DSc, Univ Bordeaux, France, 79. *Concurrent Pos:* Fulbright fel, Carlsberg Lab, Copenhagen, Denmark, 58; fel, Eng, 68; prin scientist, Radioisotope Serv, Vet Admin Hosp, Philadelphia, 53-58; ed, Topics Med Chem; prof biochem, UNAM, Mexico, 89. *Mem:* Am Chem Soc; Am Soc Biol Chem; Soc Nuclear Med; Soc Exp Biol & Med; Am Nuclear Soc. *Res:* Biochemistry of lipids, thyroid function, obesity and alcoholism; isotope methodology; transdermal delivery of medicinals; development and testing of hypocholesterolemic compounds; hypocholesterolemic agents; isotope effects; auhor of 305 publications and 5 books. *Mailing Add:* 127 Juniper Rd Havertown PA 19083-5409. *Fax:* 215-823-5171

RABINOWITZ, LAWRENCE, PHYSIOLOGY. *Current Pos:* from asst prof to assoc prof, 68-76, PROF HUMAN PHYSIOL, SCH MED, UNIV CALIF, DAVIS, 76- *Personal Data:* b San Francisco, Calif, Apr 9, 33; m 59; c 3. *Educ:* Univ Calif, Berkeley, AB, 56; Univ Calif, San Francisco, PhD(renal physiol), 61. *Prof Exp:* NIH res fel, 61-63; asst prof physiol, Univ NC, Chapel Hill,

63-68. *Mem:* AAAS; Am Physiol Soc; Am Soc Nephrology. *Res:* Renal physiology, particularly the excretion of urea and related organic nonelectrolytes. *Mailing Add:* Dept Human Physiol Univ Calif Sch Med Davis CA 95616

RABINOWITZ, MARIO, LOW TEMPERATURE PHYSICS, ELECTRICAL ENGINEERING. *Current Pos:* CHIEF EXEC OFFICER, ARMOR ASSOCS, 96- *Personal Data:* b Mexico City, Mex, Oct 24, 36; US citizen; c Benjamin M, Lisa B & Daniel L. *Educ:* Univ Wash, BS, 59, MS, 60; Wash State Univ, PhD(physics), 64. *Prof Exp:* Electronics engr, Collins Radio Co, 57; res engr, Nuclear Physics Dept, Boeing Co, 58-61; res asst physics, Wash State Univ, 61-63; sr physicist, Plasma Prog, Westinghouse Res Labs, 63-66; mgr gas discharges & vacuum pump physics, Varian Assocs, 66-67; res physicist, Stanford Linear Accelerator Ctr, 67-74; mgr superconductivity & cryogenics, Elec Power Res Inst, 74-80, sr scientist, 80-95. *Concurrent Pos:* George F Baker scholar, 56-57; assoc prof, San Jose State Univ, 73-76; adj prof, Boston Univ & Case Western Reserve Univ, 75-77, Ga Inst Technol, 88-, Univ Houston, 90- & Va Commonwealth Univ, 90- *Mem:* Am Phys Soc; Am Vacuum Soc; NY Acad Sci; Am Asn Physics Teachers; Inst Elec & Electronics Engrs; Sigma Xi. *Res:* High temperature superconductivity; electron and photodesorption of gases; electron emission; gas and metal-vapor arcs and plasmas; electrical discharges in vacuum; electrical explosion of metals; ultrahigh vacuum; superconducting generation, transmission; electric power; cryoresistive transmission; superconducting trapped magnetic fields; nuclear electromagnetic pulse; amorphous metals; superfluidity; physical electronics; classical tunneling. *Mailing Add:* 715 Lakemead Way Redwood City CA 94062

RABINOWITZ, PAUL H, NON-LINEAR FUNCTIONAL ANALYSIS. *Current Pos:* PROF MATH, UNIV WIS, 71- *Personal Data:* b Newark, NJ, Nov 15, 39. *Educ:* NY Univ, BA, 61, PhD(math), 66. *Concurrent Pos:* Guggenheim fel, 78-79. *Mem:* Am Math Soc; Soc Indust & Appl Math. *Res:* Non-linear ordinary and partial differential equations; non-linear functional analysis. *Mailing Add:* Univ Wis 480 Lincoln Dr Madison WI 53706-1313

RABINOWITZ, PHILIP, NUMERICAL INTEGRATION, APPROXIMATION THEORY. *Current Pos:* from assoc prof to prof, 67-91, EMER PROF APPL MATH, WEIZMANN INST SCI, 91- *Personal Data:* b Philadelphia, Pa, Aug 14, 26; m 51, Esther Sichel; c Yehoshua, Yaffa, Yehuda, Yona & Yoel. *Educ:* Univ Pa, AB, 46, AM, 48, PhD(math), 51. *Honors & Awards:* Info Processing Asn Israel Prize, 68. *Prof Exp:* Mathematician, Nat Bur Stand, 51-55 & 59-60; sr scientist, Weizmann Inst, 55-59, 60-64 & 65-67; vis assoc prof appl math, Brown Univ, 64-65. *Concurrent Pos:* Vis prof, Hebrew Univ, Jerusalem, 67-68, Latrobe Univ, Australia, 77, Univ Witwatersrand, SAfrica, 78, 90 & Univ NSW, Australia, 80, 86, 89; prof, Bar-Illan Univ, Israel, 70-72. *Mem:* Fel Japanese Soc Prom Sci. *Res:* Numerical integration, theory and practice; approximation by splines and Hermite-Fejer interpolation. *Mailing Add:* Dept Appl Math Weizmann Inst Sci Rehovot 76100 Israel. *Fax:* 972-8-9344122; *E-Mail:* maweintr@weizmann.weizmann.ac.il

RABINOWITZ, RONALD, PEDIATRIC SURGERY, UROLOGY. *Current Pos:* from asst prof to assoc prof, 76-87, PROF UROL SURG & PEDIAT, SCH MED, UNIV ROCHESTER, 87-; CHIEF UROL, ROCHESTER GEN HOSP, 76- *Personal Data:* b Pittsburgh, Pa, Feb 24, 43; m 67, Sally Miller; c Marui L, Tara A & Aaron D. *Educ:* Univ Pittsburgh, BS, 64, MD, 68. *Honors & Awards:* Prize for Clin Res, Am Urol Asn, 77 & 90, Walter S Kerr Prize, 91; Prize for Res, Northeastern Sect Am Urol Asn, 89. *Prof Exp:* Intern surg, Hosps Univ Health Ctr, Pittsburgh, 68-69, resident, 69-70, resident urol surg, 72-75; resident & clin fel pediat urol surg, Hosp Sick Children, Toronto, 75-76. *Concurrent Pos:* Attend pediat urologist, Rochester Gen Hosp, 76-; attend pediat urologist, Birth Defects Ctr, Univ Rochester & Strong Mem Hosps, 76- *Mem:* Am Urol Asn; Am Acad Pediat; Am Col Surgeons; Soc Pediat Urol; Soc Univ Urologists; Can Urol Asn; Am Soc Laser Surg & Med. *Res:* Laser welding in urinary tract reconstruction; experimental testis torsion. *Mailing Add:* 144 S Portland Ave Suite 309 Rochester NY 14641-3008. *Fax:* 716-338-1227

RABINS, MICHAEL J, MECHANICAL ENGINEERING, CONTROL SYSTEMS. *Current Pos:* head mech eng dept, Tex A&M Univ, 87-89, Halliburton prof, 87-88, Tex eng exp sta res prof, 89-91, COORDR ENG ETHICS PROG, TEX A&M UNIV, 91- *Personal Data:* b New York, NY, Feb 24, 32; m 56; c Andrew W, Evan S & Alexandra L. *Educ:* Mass Inst Technol, BS, 53; Carnegie Inst Technol, MS, 54; Univ Wis, PhD(mech eng), 59. *Honors & Awards:* Silver Serv Award, US Dept Transportation, 77; Leadership Award, Am Soc Mech Engrs, 96. *Prof Exp:* Design engr, M W Kellogg Co, 53-54; hydraul engr, Repub Aviation Corp, 55; design engr, Atlantic Design Co, 55-56; asst prof mech eng, Univ Wis, 59-60; from asst prof to assoc prof, NY Univ, 60-70; prof syst eng & prog dir, Polytech Inst Brooklyn, 70-75; vis prof, Polytech Inst Grenoble, France, 75; dir, Off Univ Res, Off Secy Transp, Washington, DC, 75-77; chmn, Dept Mech Eng, Wayne State Univ, 77-85, assoc dean eng res & grad progs, 85-87. *Concurrent Pos:* NSF sci fac fel, Univ Calif, Berkeley, 67-68. *Mem:* Fel Am Soc Mech Engrs; sr mem Inst Elec & Electronics Engrs. *Res:* Nonlinear automatic controls; system engineering and design; engineering ethics; engineering ethics and professionalism. *Mailing Add:* Mech Eng Dept Tex A&M Univ College Station TX 77843-3123. *Fax:* 409-862-2418; *E-Mail:* mlr6609@acs.tamu.edu

RABITZ, HERSCHEL ALBERT, PHYSICAL CHEMISTRY. *Current Pos:* from asst to assoc prof, 71-79, PROF CHEM, PRINCETON UNIV, 80- *Personal Data:* b Los Angeles, Calif, Apr 10, 44; m 70. *Educ:* Univ Calif, Berkeley, BS, 66; Harvard Univ, PhD(chem physics), 70. *Concurrent Pos:* Dreyfus Found teacher/scholar, 74; Sloan Found fel, 75. *Mem:* AAAS; Sigma Xi. *Res:* Theoretical chemistry; molecular collisions; time-dependent processes; chemical kinetics. *Mailing Add:* Dept Chem Princeton Univ Princeton NJ 08540

RABJOHN, NORMAN, ORGANIC CHEMISTRY. *Current Pos:* from assoc prof to prof, 48-83, chmn dept chem, 58-61 & 66-69, EMER PROF CHEM, UNIV MO, COLUMBIA, 83- *Personal Data:* b Rochester, NY, May 1, 15; m 43, Dora Taylor; c James Norman. *Educ:* Univ Rochester, BS, 37; Univ Ill, MS, 39, PhD(org chem), 42. *Prof Exp:* Chemist, Eastman Kodak Co, NY, 37-38; instr org chem, Univ Ill, 42-44; chemist, Goodyear Tire & Rubber Co, 44-48. *Mem:* Fel AAAS; Am Chem Soc; Sigma Xi. *Res:* Synthesis; pharmaceuticals; hydrocarbons. *Mailing Add:* Dept Chem Univ Mo 53 Chemistry Columbia MO 65211

RABKIN, MITCHELL T, MEDICINE. *Current Pos:* pres, 66-96, PHYSICIAN, BETH ISRAEL HOSP, 66-; PROF MED, HARVARD MED SCH, 83-; CHIEF EXEC OFFICER, CAREGROUP, 96- *Personal Data:* b Boston, Mass, Nov 27, 30; m 56; c 2. *Educ:* Harvard Col, AB, 51; Harvard Med Sch, MD, 55; Am Bd Internal Med, cert, 63. *Hon Degrees:* DSc, Brandeis Univ & Mass Col Pharm & Allied Health Sci, 83, Curry Col, 89, Northeastern Univ, 94; DHH, Salem State Col, 95. *Prof Exp:* From intern to chief resident internal med, Mass Gen Hosp, 55-62; from instr to assoc prof, Harvard Med Sch, 62-82. *Concurrent Pos:* Clin assoc, Nat Inst Arthritis & Metab Dis, NIH, 57-59; clin fel med, Endocrine Unit, Mass Gen Hosp, 60-62, asst med, 63-71, actg chief, Endocrine Clin, 64-66; dir, Mass Hosp Asn, 70-73, Med Found, 70-76 & Blue Cross Mass, Inc, 70-80; mem, Conf Boston Teaching Hosp, 74-, chmn, 75-76 & 80-81; vis lectr health serv, Sch Pub Health, Harvard Univ, 76-; mem, Study Group Grad Med Educ Joshiah Macy, Jr Found, 77-80; secy, Coun Teaching Hosp, Asn Am Med Col, 79-80, chmn, 82; vpres, Commonwealth Health Care Corp, Inc, 81-82 & pres, 82-83; mem, Med Adv Bd, Hadassah Med Orgn, 81-; med div chmn, United Way Mass Bay, 82; mem, Adv Comt, Clin Nurse Scholars Prog & Prog Prepaid Managed Health, Robert Wood Johnson Found, 82- & Off Technol Assessment, US Cong, 79-83; mem, Task Force Organ Transplantation, Commonwealth Mass, 83-84; bd dirs, Dead River Group, Portland, 84-86 & 88- & UST Corp, Boston, 88-; co rep, Harvard Med Ctr, Asn Acad Health Ctr, 85-; bd dirs, Partnership Inc, co-chmn, 85-88; affil, Bd Health Sci Policy, Inst Med, 86-; mem, Coun Res & Develop, Am Hosp Asn, 86-; mem, Health Adv Comt, US Gen Acct Off, 87-; mem, Vis Comt Sch Mgt, Suffolk Univ, Boston, 87- *Mem:* Inst Med-Nat Acad Sci; fel AAAS; fel Am Col Physician Execs; Soc Med Adminr; fel Royal Soc Med; Am Fedn Clin Res; AMA; Boylston Med Soc. *Res:* Author of over 25 publications in medicine. *Mailing Add:* Chief Exec Officer Care Group 375 Longwood Ave Boston MA 02215. *Fax:* 617-667-2356

RABL, ARI, ENERGY CONVERSION, ENVIRONMENTAL IMPACTS. *Current Pos:* RESPONSABLE SCIENTIFIQUE, ECOLE DES MINES DE PARIS, 88- *Personal Data:* b Ger, Feb 21, 42. *Educ:* Beloit Col, BSc, 63; Univ Calif, Berkeley, MA, 66, PhD(physics), 69. *Prof Exp:* Res assoc physics, Int Ctr Theoret Physics, Trieste, Italy, 69; res assoc, Weizmann Inst, Israel, 70-71; res assoc, Ohio State Univ, 72-73; asst physicist, Argonne Nat Lab, 74-77, engr, 77-78; prin scientist, Solar Energy Res Inst, Golden, Colo, 78-80; lectr & res scientist, Princeton Univ, 82-88. *Concurrent Pos:* Sr res assoc, Univ Chicago, 76-81; adj prof civil eng, Univ Colo, 92-97, res prof, 97- *Mem:* Am Phys Soc; Solar Energy Soc; Am Soc Heating, Refrig & Air-Conditioning Engrs. *Res:* Solar energy conversion; environmental problems; nonimaging optics. *Mailing Add:* Centre d' Energetique Ecole des Mines 60 Bd St Michel Paris 75272 Cedex 06 France

RABL, VERONIKA ARIANA, ELECTRIC UTILITIES, ENERGY UTILIZATION. *Current Pos:* subprog mgr, Elec Power Res Inst, 81-88, prog mgr demand-side planning, 89-90, sr prog mgr demand-slide mgt, 91, DIR CUSTOMER SYSTS, ELEC POWER RES INST, 91- *Personal Data:* b Michalovce, Czech, Dec 16, 45. *Educ:* Weizmann Inst Sci, Israel, MSc, 71; Ohio State Univ, PhD(physics), 74. *Prof Exp:* Jr scientist physics, Weizmann Inst Sci, Israel, 71; res assoc, Syracuse Univ, 74-75; res assoc, Argonne Nat Lab, 75-77, asst scientist energy res, 77-81. *Mem:* Am Soc Heating, Refrig & Air Conditioning Engrs; Inst Elec & Electronics Engrs. *Res:* Energy/environment; demand-side management; utility planning; energy markets; demand forecasting and analysis; energy storage systems; load management. *Mailing Add:* Elec Power Res Inst 3412 Hillview Ave Palo Alto CA 94304

RABO, JULE ANTHONY, CHEMICAL ENGINEERING. *Current Pos:* Res assoc, Union Carbide Corp, 57-60, res mgr, 60-72, corp fel, 69-82, SR CORP RES FEL, UNION CARBIDE CORP, 82-, UNIV PAC, 88- *Personal Data:* b Budapest, Hunagary; m, Sheelagh Ennis; c Benedict & Sebastian. *Educ:* Polytech Univ, BS, 46, DSc, 49. *Hon Degrees:* Dr, Polytech Univ, 86. *Honors & Awards:* Kossuth Award, Govt Hungary, 53; E V Murphree Award, Am Chem Soc, 88; Eugene J Houdry Award, Am Catalysis Soc, 89; Humboldt Award, Fed Repub Ger, 90; Varga Medal, Hungarian Acad Sci, 91; Chem Pioneer Award, Am Inst Chemists, 93. *Concurrent Pos:* Consult, Chem & Catalysis, Armonk, NY. *Mem:* Am Chem Soc; Am Catalysis Soc; Am Inst Chemists; Hungarian Acad Sci. *Res:* Patentee in field. *Mailing Add:* 19 Windmill Rd Armonk NY 10504-2612

RABOLD, GARY PAUL, INDUSTRIAL CHEMISTRY. *Current Pos:* INDUST CHEMIST PROD DEVELOP, DOW CHEM CO, 67- *Personal Data:* b Providence, RI, July 10, 39; m 66; c 3. *Educ:* Harvard Univ, AB, 60; Northeastern Univ, PhD(org chem), 65. *Prof Exp:* Fel biophys, Univ Hawaii, 65-67. *Mem:* Am Chem Soc. *Res:* New product development for organic chemicals; solvents and hydraulic fluids. *Mailing Add:* Dow Chem Co 1801 Bldg Midland MI 48674

RABOLT, JOHN FRANCIS, POLYMER PHYSICS, CHEMICAL PHYSICS. *Current Pos:* RES STAFF MEM POLYMERS, IBM RES LAB, 78- *Personal Data:* b New York, NY, May 14, 49; m 90; c 1. *Educ:* State Univ NY Col, Oneonta, BS, 70; Southern Ill Univ, Carbondale, PhD(physics), 74. *Honors & Awards:* Coblentz Award, 85; Williams-Wright Award, 90. *Prof Exp:* Postdoctoral fel physics, Univ Mich, 74-75; Nat Res Coun/Nat Acad Sci res assoc, Nat Bur Stand, 76-77. *Mem:* Fel Am Phys Soc; Soc Appl Spectros; Am Chem Soc. *Res:* Use of Fourier transform (FT) infrared and FT and Conventional Raman spectroscopy to investigate crystal and molecular structure of long chain molecules and polymers; integrated optical techniques in conjunction with Raman Spectroscopy to investigate submicron polymer films and polymer surfaces; FTIR studies of self assembled and Langmoir-Blodgett films on metals & dielectrics; FT-Raman spectroscopy co-developer. *Mailing Add:* 1519 Barley Mill Rd Greenville DE 19807

RABOVSKY, JEAN, ENVIRONMENTAL & OCCUPATIONAL HEALTH. *Current Pos:* TOXICOLOGIST, OFF ENVIRON HEALTH HAZARD ASSESSMENT, SACRAMENTO, CALIF, 89- *Personal Data:* b Baltimore, Md. *Educ:* Univ Md, BS, 59; Brandeis Univ, PhD(biochem), 64. *Prof Exp:* Res biologist, Univ Calif, Irvine, 72-76; assoc, Univ Fla, Gainesville, 76-78; chemist, Nat Inst Occup Safety & Health, Morgantown, WVa, 78-89. *Mem:* Am Chem Soc; AAAS; NY Acad Sci; Sigma Xi; Soc Toxicol. *Res:* Detoxication/bioactivation mechanisms; pulmonary cytochrome P450; environmental/occupational health issues related to chemical exposure. *Mailing Add:* Off Environ Health Hazard Assessment 2151 Berkeley Way Annex 11 Berkeley CA 94704-1011. *Fax:* 510-540-2923; *E-Mail:* berkeley.jrabovsk@hw1.cahwnet.gov

RABOY, SOL, NUCLEAR PHYSICS, CONDENSED MATTER PHYSICS. *Current Pos:* chmn dept, 66-77, PROF PHYSICS, STATE UNIV NY, BINGHAMTON, 65- *Personal Data:* b Ambridge, Pa, Feb 11, 20; m 48, Marguerite Marvin; c Naomi Elka, Nathan Harman, Sara Rose, David Geoffrey, Ashen Samuel, Adley Chaim & Dara Ruth. *Educ:* Brooklyn Col, BA, 41; Carnegie Inst Technol, DSc(physics), 50. *Prof Exp:* Instr physics, Carnegie Inst Technol, 49-50, res assoc, 50-51; assoc physicist, Argonne Nat Lab, 51-65. *Mem:* Fel Am Phys Soc. *Res:* Mobility of electrons in insulators; angular distributions of nuclear radiation; spectroscopy of gamma rays; variation of electron mass with velocity; measurements of magnetic moments of excited states of nuclei; measurement of quadrupole moments of nuclei; nuclear structure; muonic x-rays; optics, quantum electronics and photonics. *Mailing Add:* 605 Valleyview Dr Endwell NY 13760

RABSON, ALAN S, PATHOLOGY. *Current Pos:* PATHOLOGIST, NAT CANCER INST, 55- *Personal Data:* b New York, NY, July 1, 26; m 50; c 1. *Educ:* Univ Rochester, AB, 47; Long Island Col Med, MD, 50. *Res:* Oncogenic viruses and viral tumors. *Mailing Add:* Nat Cancer Inst 9000 Rockville Pike Bethesda MD 20892. *Fax:* 301-402-0338; *E-Mail:* rabsona@ud.nci.nih.gov

RABSON, GUSTAVE, MATHEMATICS. *Current Pos:* RETIRED. *Personal Data:* b New York, NY, Sept 28, 20; m 58; c 3. *Educ:* Cornell Univ, AB, 41; Univ Mich, MA, 48, PhD(math), 52. *Prof Exp:* Engr, Tank-Automotive Ctr, Univ Mich, 42-44, mathematician, Ballistics Res Lab, 44-45; instr math, Purdue Univ, 49-53; from asst prof to assoc prof, Antioch Col, 53-57; sr mathematician, Am Optical Co, 57-59; res mathematician, Inst Sci & Technol, Univ Mich, 59-66; prof math, Tech Inst Aeronaut, Brazil, 66-67; emer prof, Clarkson Univ, 67-85. *Concurrent Pos:* NSF grant, 56; vis scientist, Mass Inst Technol, 78. *Mem:* Am Math Soc; Math Asn Am. *Res:* Topological groups; mathematical statistics; applied mathematics. *Mailing Add:* 67 King St Oberlin OH 44074-1321. *E-Mail:* prabson@alpha.oberlin.edu

RABSON, ROBERT, PLANT PHYSIOLOGY. *Current Pos:* RETIRED. *Personal Data:* b Brooklyn, NY, Mar 4, 26; m 50; c 3. *Educ:* Cornell Univ, BS, 51, PhD(plant physiol), 56. *Honors & Awards:* Adoph Gude Award, Am Soc Plant Physiol, 86. *Prof Exp:* Biologist, Oak Ridge Nat Lab, 56-58; from asst prof to assoc prof biol, Univ Houston, 58-64; biochemist, Div Biol & Med, US AEC, 63-67, asst chief, Biol Br, 67-73, first officer, Food & Agr Orgn-Int Atomic Energy Agency Joint Div, Plant Breeding & Genetics Sect, Int Atomic Energy Agency, Vienna, Austria, 73-76; mem staff, Div Biomed & Environ Res, Energy Res & Develop Admin, US Dept Energy, 76-78, dir, Div Energy Biosci, Off Basic Energy Sci, 78-95. *Mem:* Am Soc Plant Physiol; Crop Sci Soc; fel AAAS; Am Soc Photobiol; Am Soc Microbiol. *Res:* Genetics and biochemistry of protein synthesis in developing seeds. *Mailing Add:* 2269 Glenmore Terr Rockville MD 20850

RABSON, THOMAS A(VELYN), FERROELECTRIC THIN FILMS, SEMICONDUCTOR NONVOLATILE MEMORIES. *Current Pos:* From asst prof to assoc prof, 59-70, chmn dept, 79-84, PROF ELEC ENG, RICE UNIV, 70- *Personal Data:* b Houston, Tex, July 31, 32; m 57, Sylvia; c Tamara, William & Robert. *Educ:* Rice Univ, BA, 54, BS, 55, MA, 57, PhD(nuclear physics), 59. *Concurrent Pos:* NSF sci fac fel, 65-66; vis prof elec eng, Univ Colo, Colo Springs, 92-93. *Mem:* Am Phys Soc; Inst Elec & Electronics Engrs; Optical Soc Am; Soc Photo-Optical Instrumentation Engrs. *Res:* Semiconductor physics; lasers; nonvolatile memory arrays; ferroelectric thin film applications. *Mailing Add:* Dept Elec & Comput Eng Rice Univ 6100 S Main St Houston TX 77005

RABUCK, DAVID GLENN, HISTOLOGY-HISTOCHEMISTRY, BIOLOGY OF REPRODUCTION. *Current Pos:* ADJ FAC ANAT, PHYSIOL & BIOL, OAKTON COMMUNITY COL, 87-; ADJ FAC ANAT & PHYSIOL, TRITON COL, 93- *Personal Data:* b Geneva, Ill; m 64; c 1. *Educ:* NCent Col, BA, 63; Loyola Univ, MS, 66, PhD(anat), 76. *Prof Exp:* Instr anat, Pritzker Sch Med, Univ Chicago, 76; asst prof anat, Col Dent, Marquette Univ, 77-78 & Chicago Col Osteop Med, 78-82; vis asst prof embryol & histol, Univ Calif, Riverside, 82-83; sci tutor, 85-87 & 92-93. *Concurrent Pos:* Teaching assoc anat, Med Sch, Rush Univ, 76; assoc anat, Med Col, Univ Ill, Chicago, 77, instr oral anat, Dent Sch, 90-91; anat & physiol tutor, Oakton Community Col, 89; instr physiol, Nat Col Educ, 89; fac anat & physiol, Northeastern Ill Univ, 91, Rosary Col, 91 & 93 & Morton Col, 92-93; fac, Du Page Univ, Glen Ellyn, Ill & Naprapathy Univ, Chicago, 96- *Mem:* AAAS; Am Soc Zoologists; assoc mem Soc Study Reproduction; Nat Educ Asn; Nat Space Soc. *Res:* Origin, morphogenesis, structure and endocrine mechanisms of gonadal tissues, especially the changes in the right gonad of overiectomized birds. *Mailing Add:* 3352 Crain St Skokie IL 60076-2408

RABUNG, JOHN RUSSELL, NUMBER THEORY. *Current Pos:* PROF COMPUT SCI, RANDOLPH MACON COL, ASHLAND, VA, 84- *Personal Data:* b Elyria, Ohio, July 22, 43; m 67; c 3. *Educ:* Univ Akron, BA, 65; Wash State Univ, MA, 67, PhD(number theory), 69. *Prof Exp:* Res mathematician number theory, Math Res Ctr, US Naval Res Lab, 69-70; instr & opers res analyst statist & oper res, US Army Logistics Mgt Ctr, 70-72; asst prof math, Randolph-Macon Col, 72-74; from asst prof to assoc prof math sci, Va Commonwealth Univ, 74-84. *Mem:* Am Math Soc; Math Asn Am. *Res:* Combinatorial problems in number theory, specifically, some aspects of Van der Waerden's theorem on arithmetic progressions. *Mailing Add:* Dept Computer Sci Randolph Macon Col Ashland VA 23005

RABUSSAY, DIETMAR PAUL, GENE REGULATION. *Current Pos:* sect head, 81-82, res dir, 82-83, VPRES, BETHESDA RES LABS, LIFE TECHNOLOGIES INC, 83- *Personal Data:* b Wolfsberg, Austria, Aug 9, 41; m 66; c 2. *Educ:* Tech Univ Graz, Austria, MSc, 67; Univ Munich, PhD(biochem), 71. *Prof Exp:* Wissensch asst molecular biol, Max Planck Inst Biochem, 71-72; fel, Univ Calif, San Diego, 72-75, asst res biologist, 75-79; vis scientist, Max Planck Inst Biochem, 78-79; asst prof microbiol, Fla State Univ, 79-81. *Concurrent Pos:* Adj prof, Univ Md, 81-86. *Mem:* AAAS; Am Soc Microbiol; Europ Molecular Biol Orgn; Am Soc Biol Chemists. *Res:* In vitro protein synthesis; mechanism and regulation of transcription; development of bacterial viruses; DNA enzymology; genetic engineering. *Mailing Add:* 518 N Rios Ave Solano Beach CA 92075

RABY, BRUCE ALAN, TECHNICAL MANAGEMENT. *Current Pos:* CONSULT CHEM & TECHNOL, 80-83 & 88- *Personal Data:* b Seattle, Wash, Aug 22, 30; m 54; c 4. *Educ:* Univ Wash, BS, 52; Univ Calif, Berkeley, MS, 54; Iowa State Univ, PhD(anal chem), 63. *Prof Exp:* Proj engr, Wright Air Develop Ctr, Wright-Patterson AFB, Ohio, 53-56; res asst anal chem, Inst Atomic Res, Ames Nat Lab, Iowa State Univ, 56-63; scientist, Rocketdyne Div, NAm Aviation, Inc, Calif, 63-64; chemist, Lawrence Radiation Lab, Univ Calif, Berkeley, 64-70; mem staff, Uthe Technol Int, 70-75, admin mgr res & applications, 75-80; supvr, Anal & Vacuum, Conductimer Corp, 83-85; group leader, Lockheed, 86-87; sr engr, Perkin-Elmer, 87-88. *Mem:* Soc Appl Spectros; Am Chem Soc; Am Soc Mass Spectros; Sigma Xi; Am Vacuum Soc; Electrochem Soc. *Res:* Fluorescence; halogen fluorides as reagents; rocket fuels; magnesium alloys; nuclear reactors; production and separation of trans-lead isotopes; mass spectrometry; analytical chemistry; chemical vapor deposition; instrument design and fabrication; analytical software. *Mailing Add:* 1547 Arata Ct San Jose CA 95125-1802

RABY, STUART, SUPERSYMMETRY, PHYSICS BEYOND THE STANDARD MODEL. *Current Pos:* PROF PHYSICS, OHIO STATE UNIV, 89- *Personal Data:* b Bronx, NY, May 18, 47; m 73, Elaine M Neal; c Eric Y & Liat. *Educ:* Univ Rochester, BS, 69; Tel Aviv Univ, MS, 73, PhD(physics), 76. *Prof Exp:* Res assoc, Cornell Univ, 76-78; actg asst prof physics, Stanford Univ, 78-80, res assoc, Stanford Linear Accelerator Ctr, 80-81; staff mem, Los Alamos Nat Lab, 81-85, group leader, 85-89. *Concurrent Pos:* Vis scientist, Univ Mich, 82-83. *Mem:* Fel Am Phys Soc. *Res:* High energy physics and particle; astrophysics; construct particle physics models to explain experimental data. *Mailing Add:* Dept Physics 4024 Smith Lab Ohio State Univ 174 W 18th Ave Columbus OH 43210. *Fax:* 614-292-7557; *E-Mail:* raby@mps.ohio-state.edu

RACANIELLO, VINCENT RAIMONDI, MICROBIOLOGY VIROLOGY. *Current Pos:* asst prof, 82-88, assoc prof & dir grad prog, Dept Microbiol, 88-90, PROF, DEPT MICROBIOL, COL PHYSICIANS & SURGEONS, COLUMBIA UNIV, 90-, HIGGINS PROF, 94- *Personal Data:* b Paterson, NJ, Jan 2, 53; m 82, Doris F Cully; c Aidan. *Educ:* Cornell Univ, BA, 74; Mt Sinai Sch Med, PhD, 79. *Honors & Awards:* Career Scientist Award, I T Hirschl Trust, 83; Eli Lilly & Co Res Award Microbiol & Immunol, Am Soc Microbiol, 92; Harvey Soc lectr, 91. *Prof Exp:* Fel, Mass Inst Technol, 79-82. *Concurrent Pos:* NIH fel, 80; Searle scholar, 84; consult, Lederle Labs, 88-; mem, Virol Study Sect, NIH, 89-; lectr, Harvey Soc, 91; ed, J Virol, 92-; chair, Virol Study Sect, NIH, 95-97. *Mem:* Am Soc Microbiol; AAAS; Am Soc Virol. *Res:* Microbiology; molecular descriptio of the replication and pathogenesis of poliovirus. *Mailing Add:* Columbia Univ 701 W 168th St New York NY 10032-2704. *Fax:* 212-305-5106; *E-Mail:* vrr1@columbia.edu

RACCAH, PAUL M(ORDECAI), material science, quantum electronics; deceased, see previous edition for last biography

RACE, GEORGE JUSTICE, PATHOLOGY, IMMUNOLOGY. *Current Pos:* PROF PATH & ASSOC DEAN CONTINUING EDUC, UNIV TEX SOUTHWESTERN MED SCH, 73- *Personal Data:* b Everman, Tex, Mar 2, 26; m 46, Anne Rinker; c G William, J Clark, Mark C & Elizabeth M. *Educ:* Univ Tex Southwestern, MD, 47; Univ NC, MSPH, 53; Baylor Univ, PhD(anat-microbiol), 69. *Honors & Awards:* Caldwell Hon Award, Tex Soc Path, 73. *Prof Exp:* Instr & path, Duke Univ, 51-53 & instr, Harvard Med Sch, 53-54; from asst prof to prof, Cancer Ctr, 55-73, dir, 73-76; pathologist-in-chief & dir labs, Baylor Univ Med Ctr, 59-86, prof path & microbiol, Grad & Dent Sch, 62-68, prof & chmn dept path, 69-73; prop anat, Baylot Univ Grad Sch, 71-, adj prof biol, 81-; dean continuing educ health sci, Baylor Univ Med Ctr, 73- *Concurrent Pos:* Asst path, Peter Bent Brigham Hosp, Boston, 53-54; pathologist, St Anthony's Hosp, Fla, 54-55; consult path, Vet Admin Hosp, Dallas, 55-75; from asst to assoc pathologist, Children's Med Ctr, Dallas, Terrell's labs, & Parkland Mem Hosp, 55-59; lectr law, 71-75, Southern Methodist Univ, adj prof anthro & biol, 74-; vis pathologist, Guy's Hosp Med & Dent Sch, London, 72; chmn, bd dir, Baylor Res Found, 86-89. *Mem:* Soc Med Educ Dirs Continuing Med Educ (secy-treas, 80-81, pres, 82-83); Sigma Xi; fel Col Am Pathologists; fel Am Soc Clin Pathologists; fel AAAS; fel Acad Clin Lab Physicians & Scientists. *Res:* Adrenal cortex functional zonation and hypertension; immunopathology of Trichinella spiralis and other parasites; anthropology. *Mailing Add:* 3429 Beverly Dr Dallas TX 75205-2928. *Fax:* 214-526-8607

RACE, STUART RICE, ENTOMOLOGY. *Current Pos:* RETIRED. *Personal Data:* b Glen Ridge, NJ, Sept 20, 26; m 57; c 4. *Educ:* Gettysburg Col, AB, 51; Rutgers Univ, MS, 55, PhD(entom), 57. *Prof Exp:* Asst prof, NMex State Univ, 57-65; assoc prof, Rutgers Univ, New Brunswick, 65-70, exten specialist entom, 70-93. *Mem:* Entom Soc Am. *Res:* Fruits, forage and field crops; livestock, poultry, and stored grain. *Mailing Add:* 576 Country Club Rd Bridgewater NJ 08807

RACETTE, GEORGE WILLIAM, AEROSPACE MATERIALS, SPACE CRAFT CONTAMINATION. *Current Pos:* physicist semiconductor detectors, Photovoltaics & Aerospace Mat, Valley Forge Space Ctr, 74-92, CONTAMINATION CONTROL ENG, MARTIN MARIETTA ASTRO SPACE, 92- *Personal Data:* b Schenectady, NY, June 2, 29; m 56; c 4. *Educ:* Siena Col, NY, BS, 51; Univ Rochester, MS, 54. *Prof Exp:* From jr to sr engr semiconductor devices, Philco Corp Res Div, 53-57, proj scientist infrared & photodevices, 57-64; proj scientist lasers, Philco-Ford Res Div, Ford Sci Lab, 64-66, eng specialist automotive electronics, Philco-Ford Res Div, 66-70; mgr, Whitemarsh Township, 70-74. *Mem:* Am Phys Soc; Am Inst Aeronaut & Astronaut. *Res:* Semiconductor materials; infrared; photo detectors; lasers; high intensity light effects; vidicons; solar cells; vacuum deposition; aerospace materials; space environment; spacecraft contamination. *Mailing Add:* 2292 Mulberry Lane Lafayette Hill PA 19444

RACEY, THOMAS JAMES, QUASI-ELASTIC LIGHT SCATTERING, SURVEILLANCE OF SPACE. *Current Pos:* from asst prof to assoc prof, 83-92, head dept, 96-97, PROF PHYSICS, ROYAL MIL COL CAN, 92- *Personal Data:* b Woodstock, Ont, Apr 27, 52. *Educ:* Univ Waterloo, BSc, 75; Univ Guelph, MSc, 76, PhD(biophys), 82; Queen's Univ, BEd, 77. *Prof Exp:* Teacher physics & math, Frontenac County Bd Ed, 77-79; software specialist, Andyne Computing Ltd, 82-83. *Mem:* Can Asn Physicists. *Res:* Optical signal processing; particle sizing from scattering information; analysis of Fourier transform information and time correlation techniques; satellite tracking. *Mailing Add:* Royal Mil Col Can Kingston ON K7L 2W3 Can. *Fax:* 643-541-6040

RACHFORD, HENRY HERBERT, JR, MATHEMATICS, ENGINEERING. *Current Pos:* PROF MATH & COMPUT SCI, RICE UNIV, 64- *Personal Data:* b El Dorado, Ark, June 14, 25; m 57; c 2. *Educ:* Rice Inst, BS, 45, AM, 47; Mass Inst Technol, ScD, 50. *Prof Exp:* Res engr, Humble Oil & Ref Co, 49-56, asst div petrol engr, 56-57, res supvr, 57-64. *Mem:* Am Math Soc; Soc Petrol Eng; Am Inst Mining, Metall & Petrol Eng; Am Inst Chem Eng. *Res:* Numerical techniques, especially for partial differential equations; use of digital computers; solution of engineering problems with mathematical methods. *Mailing Add:* 6150 Chevy Chase Houston TX 77057-3514

RACHFORD, THOMAS MILTON, CIVIL ENGINEERING. *Current Pos:* PRIN ENGR, GANNETT FLEMING, CORDDRY & CARPENTER, 74- *Personal Data:* b Bellevue, Ky, Mar 14, 42; m 64; c 2. *Educ:* Univ Ky, BS, 64, MS, 66; Stanford Univ, PhD(civil eng), 72. *Prof Exp:* Asst prof civil eng, Pa State Univ, 69-73. *Mem:* Water Pollution Control Fedn. *Res:* Civil engineering; hydrology and water resources; sanitary and environmental engineering. *Mailing Add:* 466 Woodcrest Dr Mechanicsburg PA 17055

RACHINSKY, MICHAEL RICHARD, science education, biochemistry; deceased, see previous edition for last biography

RACHLIN, JOSEPH WOLFE, AQUATIC BIOLOGY, GISHERY SCIENCE & ICHTHYOLOGY. *Current Pos:* from instr to assoc prof, 67-77, PROF BIOL, LEHMAN COL, CITY UNIV NY, 77-, ACTG DEAN, DIV NATURAL & SOC SCI; RES ASSOC, DEPT ICHTHYOL, AM MUS NATURAL HIST, NY, 80- *Personal Data:* b New York, NY, Jan 23, 36; m 60, Jetti Bruk; c David & Adam. *Educ:* City Col New York, BS, 57; NY Univ, MS, 62, PhD(aquatic biol), 67. *Prof Exp:* Lab technician chemother, Sloan-Kettering Inst Cancer Res, 57-58; biol sci asst instr med, US Army Med Res Lab, Ky, 58-60; biol sci trainee endocrinol, Sch Med, NY Univ, 60-64, fel radiol health, 64-65, trainee environ health, 65-66. *Mem:* Am Soc Ichthyol & Herpet; Am Fisheries Soc; Sigma Xi; Am Inst Fishery Res Biologists; Willi Hennig Soc; Soc Systemic Zoologists. *Res:* Fish cytogenetics; fish ecology-population dynamics and niche overlap. *Mailing Add:* Dept Biol Sci Lehman Col Bedford Park Blvd W Bronx NY 10468. *Fax:* 718-960-8929; *E-Mail:* jwrlc@cunyvm.cuny.edu

RACHMELER, MARTIN, MICROBIOLOGY, GENETICS. *Current Pos:* DIR TECHNOL TRANS, UNIV CALIF, SAN DIEGO, 89- *Personal Data:* b Brooklyn, NY, Nov 21, 28; m 56, Betty Karkalis; c Susan, Ann & Helen. *Educ:* Ind Univ, AB, 50; Western Reserve Univ, PhD(microbiol), 60. *Prof Exp:* Asst geneticist, Univ Calif, Berkeley, 61-62; from asst prof to assoc prof microbiol, Med Sch, Northwestern Univ, Chicago, 62-89, dir, Res Serv Admin, Evanston, 77-89. *Concurrent Pos:* USPHS fel, Univ Calif, Berkeley, 59-61; vis fac, Baylor Col Med, 71-72. *Mem:* AAAS; Am Soc Microbiol; Sigma Xi. *Res:* Biochemistry of human genetic diseases; role of tumor viruses in cell transformation; regulation of cell growth. *Mailing Add:* 10695 Loire Ave San Diego CA 92131-1532. *Fax:* 619-534-7245; *E-Mail:* mrochmeler@ucd.edu

RACHUBINSKI, RICHARD ANTHONY, ORGANELLE BIOGENESIS, GENE REGULATION. *Current Pos:* PROF & CHAIR CELL BIOL & ANAT, UNIV ALTA, 93- *Personal Data:* b Montreal, PQ, Mar 7, 54; m 85, Franquoise Fernandez; c Dorian A & Ariane I. *Educ:* McGill Univ, BSc, 76, MSc, 78, PhD(cell biol), 80. *Prof Exp:* Fel, Med Res Coun, McGill Univ, 80-82 & Rockefeller Univ, 82-84; from asst prof to prof, McMaster Univ, 84-93. *Concurrent Pos:* Scientist, Med Res Cooun, 92; panel mem, path & morphol, Med Res Coun Can, 94-97, sr scientist, 97. *Mem:* Am Soc Cell Biol; Am Soc Microbiol; AAAS; Can Soc Biochem & Cell Biol. *Res:* Molecular cascade leading to assembly of peroxisome, an organelle involved in lipid metabolism; mechanism of action of the peroxisome proliferator-activated receptor, a member of the steroid receptor superfamily. *Mailing Add:* Cell Biol & Anat Med Sci Bldg 5-14 Univ Alta Edmonton AB T6G 2H7 Can. *Fax:* 403-492-9278; *E-Mail:* rrachubi@anat.med.ualberta.ca

RACINE, MICHEL LOUIS, ALGEBRA. *Current Pos:* from asst prof to assoc prof, 74-86, PROF MATH, UNIV OTTAWA, 86- *Personal Data:* b Casselman, Ont, Jan 19, 45; c 1. *Educ:* Univ Ottawa, BSc, 60; Yale Univ, MPhil, 69, PhD(math), 71. *Prof Exp:* Res assoc math, Carleton Univ, 71-72; Nat Res Coun fel, Univ Wis-Madison, 72-73, MacDuffee fel, 73-74. *Concurrent Pos:* Alexander von Humboldt fel, Univ Munster, 80-81, SSHN fel, Univ Paris, 87-88. *Mem:* Am Math Soc; Math Asn Am; Can Math Soc. *Res:* Structure of Jordan algebras and related questions. *Mailing Add:* Univ Ottawa PO Box 450 Ottawa ON K1N 6N5 Can

RACINE, RENE, ASTRONOMY. *Current Pos:* PROF, UNIV MONTREAL, 76- *Personal Data:* b Quebec City, Que, Oct 16, 39; m 63; c 2. *Educ:* Laval Univ, BA, 58, BSc, 63; Univ Toronto, MA, 65, PhD(astron), 67. *Prof Exp:* Carnegie fel, Hale Observs, Calif, 67-69; from asst prof to assoc prof astron, Univ Toronto, 69-76. *Concurrent Pos:* Dir, Can-Fran-Haw Tel Corp, 80-84 & Observ Astron, Mont Megantic, 76-80 & 84-90. *Mem:* AAAS; Am Astron Soc; Can Astron Soc (pres, 74-76); Royal Astron Soc Can. *Res:* Galactic structure; galaxies; open and globular clusters; optical instrumentation/telescopes. *Mailing Add:* Dept Physics Univ Montreal CP 6128 Succ A Montreal PQ H3C 3J7 Can. *Fax:* 514-343-2071

RACISZEWSKI, ZBIGNIEW, POLYMER CHEMISTRY. *Current Pos:* RETIRED. *Personal Data:* b Uchanie, Poland, Jan 20, 22. *Educ:* Univ Sask, MSc, 52; Univ Notre Dame, PhD(chem), 56. *Prof Exp:* Instr food technol, Agr Col Warsaw, Poland, 47-49; sr res chemist, Explor Org Chem Group, Pittsburgh Plate Glass Co, 55-60; res chemist, Consumer Prod Div, Union Carbide Corp, 60-63, Chem Div, WVa, 63-69; assoc ed, 69-74, sr assoc ed, 74-80, sr ed, Macromolecular Sect, Chem Abstr Serv, 80-85. *Res:* Mechanism of organic reactions; polymer chemistry. *Mailing Add:* 6619 Brock St Dublin OH 43017

RACK, EDWARD PAUL, chemistry, radiochemistry; deceased, see previous edition for last biography

RACK, HENRY JOHANN, MATERIAL SCIENCE, METALLURGY. *Current Pos:* PROF MECH ENG & METALL, CLEMSON UNIV, 85- *Personal Data:* b New York, NY, Nov 1, 42; c 2. *Educ:* Mass Inst Technol, SB, 64, SM, 65, ScD(metall), 68. *Prof Exp:* Scientist, Lockheed Ga Co, 68-72; mem tech staff, Sandia Labs, 72-81; prof, NMex Inst Mining & Technol, 75-81; mgr, metall dept mat div, Exxon Enterprises, 81-82; mgr, metall silage opers, Arco Metals, 82-85, mgr, advan mat compos, 85. *Mem:* Am Soc Metals; Am Inst Mining, Metall & Petrol Engrs; Am Soc Testing & Mat. *Res:* Metal matrix composites; structural materials; fracture; structural reliability; nuclear waste management and transportation; solar materials and applications. *Mailing Add:* 322 Sleepy Hollow Pendleton SC 29670

RACKE, KENNETH DAVID, ENVIRONMENTAL CHEMISTRY. *Current Pos:* sr res chemist, 89-91, tech leader, 91-93, SR SCIENTIST, DOW CHEM CO, 93- *Personal Data:* b Evergreen Park, Ill, July 6, 59; m 81; c 2. *Educ:* Trinity Christian Col, BA, 81; Univ Wis, MS, 84; Iowa State Univ, PhD(entom), 87. *Honors & Awards:* Am Chem Soc Award, 87. *Prof Exp:* Res assoc, Iowa State Univ, 85-87; asst soil scientist, Conn Agr Exp Sta, 87-88. *Concurrent Pos:* Chmn, Comn Agrochem, 95-97. *Mem:* Am Chem Soc; Am Sci Affil; Soil Sci Soc Am; Soc Environ Toxicol & Chem. *Res:* Fate and degradation of pesticides and other organic chemicals in soil, water, and waste materials; interaction between microorganisms and environmental pollutants. *Mailing Add:* Environ Chem Lab Dow Elanco Indianapolis IN 46268-1053. *Fax:* 317-337-4649; *E-Mail:* kracke@dowelanco.com

RACKIS, JOSEPH JOHN, BIOCHEMISTRY, FOOD SCIENCE. *Current Pos:* RETIRED. *Personal Data:* b Somersville, Conn, July 29, 22; m 54; c 2. *Educ:* Univ Conn, BS, 50; Univ Iowa, PhD(biochem), 55. *Honors & Awards:* Bond Award, Am Oil Chemists Soc, 65. *Prof Exp:* Chemist, Northern Regional Res Ctr, Agr Res Serv, USDA, 55-60, prin chemist, 61-84; consult, 84-90. *Mem:* Am Chem Soc; Am Soc Biol Chemists; Inst Food Technol; Am Asn Cereal Chem; Am Soybean Asn. *Res:* Plant biochemistry; physical organic chemistry of soybean proteins; chromatography; amino acids; plant analysis; lipids; nutritional, toxicological and physiological evaluation; food and feed uses of soybean products. *Mailing Add:* 3411 N Elmcroft Terr Peoria IL 61604

RACKOFF, JEROME S, VERTEBRATE PALEONTOLOGY. *Current Pos:* asst prof biol, 75-78, found & govt rels officer, 78-82, assoc dir develop, 82-88, ASSOC VPRES, UNIV RELATIONS ADMIN, BUCKNELL UNIV, 88- *Personal Data:* b Brooklyn, NY, Nov 14, 46; m 71; c 3. *Educ:* Brooklyn Col, BS, 68; Yale Univ, MPhil, 73, PhD(geobiol), 76. *Prof Exp:* Teacher earth sci, Brooklyn Friends Sch, NY, 69-70; teacher biol, Friends Sem, NY, 70-72. *Mem:* Sigma Xi. *Res:* Functional morphology and evolution of Paleozoic fishes, particularly Crossopterygii and lower tetrapods; the origin of tetrapod limbs and terrestrial locomotion. *Mailing Add:* Univ Relations Admin Bucknell Univ Cooley Hall Lewisburg PA 17837

RACKOW, ERIC C, MEDICINE, CRITICAL CARE MEDICINE. *Current Pos:* CHMN, DEPT MED, ST VINCENT'S HOSP & MED CTR, NY, 89- *Educ:* Franklin & Marshall Col, BA, 67; State Univ NY, MD, 71; Am Bd Internal Med, dipl, 75, dipl cardiovasc, 77, dipl critical care, 87. *Prof Exp:* Resident internal med, State Univ NY, Downstate Med Ctr & Kings County Hosp Ctr, 71-72, chief resident, 72-73, fel cardiol, 73-75. *Concurrent Pos:* Exec vpres, Inst Critical Care Med, Rancho Mirage, Calif, 90-; prof med & vchmn, Dept Med, NY Med Col, 89- *Mem:* Fel Am Col Physicians; fel Am Col Cardiol; fel Am Col Chest Physicians; fel Am Col Critical Care Med. *Res:* Critical care medicine; circulatory shock; sepsis and septic shock; fluid resuscitation; pulmonary edema; cardiopulmonary resuscitation; author of 300 technical publications. *Mailing Add:* Dept Med St Vincent's Hosp & Med Ctr 153 W 11th St New York NY 10011-8397

RACKOW, HERBERT, ANESTHESIOLOGY. *Current Pos:* RETIRED. *Personal Data:* b New York, NY, June 17, 17; m 42. *Educ:* Pa State Univ, BS, 39; Howard Univ, MD, 46. *Prof Exp:* Fel biochem, NY Univ, 48-50; from instr to assoc prof, Columbia Univ, 52-70, prof anesthesiol, Col Physicians & Surgeons, 70-77. *Res:* Respiratory physiology. *Mailing Add:* 147-01 Third Ave Whitestone NY 11357

RACLE, FRED ARNOLD, NATURAL SCIENCE. *Current Pos:* RETIRED. *Personal Data:* b Columbus, Ohio, Dec 16, 32; m 62. *Educ:* Ohio State Univ, BSc, 60, MSc, 62, PhD(bot), 65. *Prof Exp:* From assoc prof to prof natural sci, Mich State Univ, 65-90. *Mem:* Sigma Xi. *Res:* Curriculum devlopment in general education, science. *Mailing Add:* 9928 Alliston Dr NW Pickerington OH 43147

RACOTTA, RADU GHEORGHE, CONTROL OF FOOD INTAKE, METABOLIC REGULATION. *Current Pos:* TEACHING & RES PHYSIOL, NAT SCH BIOL SCI, IPN, MEXICO CITY, 70- *Personal Data:* b Bucarest, Romania, Jan 5, 30; Mex citizen. *Educ:* Univ Bucarest, BSc, 63; Inst Politech Nacional, Mex, DSc, 75. *Prof Exp:* Res agron, Inst Cult Corn, Romania, 59-62; res & diag phtisiol, Inst Phtisiol, Bucarest, Romania, 62-66; res physiol, Inst Biol, Bucarest, Romania, 66-69. *Mem:* Am Physiol Soc; Soc Study Ingestive Behav; NY Acad Sci; Mex Soc Physiol Sci. *Res:* Food and water intake physiological control, specifically through hepatic receptors; catecholamines and energy metabolism; nervous control of the testes. *Mailing Add:* Dept Physiol ENCB Carpio Y Plan de Ayala Mexico City 11340 Mexico. *Fax:* 52-5-396-35-03

RACUNAS, BERNARD J, CHEMICAL ENGINEERING. *Current Pos:* Engr, 66-74, sr engr, 74-76, staff engr, 76-78, SECT HEAD, ALCOA LABS, 78- *Personal Data:* b June 12, 43; US citizen. *Educ:* Univ Pittsburgh, BS, 65, MS, 67. *Mem:* Am Inst Chem Engrs; Am Inst Metall Engrs; Sigma Xi. *Res:* Aluminum smelting; carbon technology; molten salt technology. *Mailing Add:* 1075 Woodberry Rd New Kensington PA 15068

RACUSEN, DAVID, plant biochemistry, for more information see previous edition

RACUSEN, RICHARD HARRY, PLANT PHYSIOLOGY. *Current Pos:* ASST PROF BOT, UNIV MD, 78- *Personal Data:* b Geneva, NY, July 26, 48; m 70. *Educ:* Univ Vt, BS, 70, MS, 72, PhD(cell biol), 75. *Prof Exp:* Res fel cell biol, Unit Vt, 70-75; res fel plant physiol, Yale Univ, 75-78. *Mem:* AAAS; Sigma Xi; Am Soc Plant Physiol. *Res:* Ion transport, morphogenesis and plant bioelectric phenomena. *Mailing Add:* Dept Bot Univ Md College Park MD 20742-0001

RAD, FRANZ N, STRUCTURAL ENGINEERING. *Current Pos:* From asst prof, to assoc prof, 71-79, PROF CIVIL ENG & DEPT HEAD, PORTLAND STATE UNIV, 79- *Personal Data:* b Zabol, Iran, Sept 25, 43; m 64; c 3. *Educ:* Univ Tex, Austin, BS, 68, MS, 69, PhD(civil eng), 73. *Concurrent Pos:* Consult, industrialization, 72-; Western Elec Fund Award, Am Soc Eng Educ, 79; pres, Struct Eng Asn, Ore, 85-86. *Mem:* Fel Am Soc Civil Engrs; fel Am Concrete Inst; Am Soc Eng Educ; Nat Soc Prof Engrs; Post Tension Inst. *Res:* Limit states behavior of reinforced concrete members and structures. *Mailing Add:* Dept Civil Eng Portland State Univ Portland OR 97207-0751

RADABAUGH, DENNIS CHARLES, BEHAVIOR OF PREDATORS & PREY, PHYSIOLOGICAL ECOLOGY. *Current Pos:* Vis asst prof, 70-72, from asst prof to assoc prof, 70-81, PROF ZOOL, OHIO WESLEYAN UNIV, 82- *Personal Data:* b Detroit, Mich, Sept 27, 42; m 67, Joan Maxwell; c John & Carrie. *Educ:* Albion Col, BA, 64; Ohio State Univ, MSc, 67, PhD(animal behav), 70. *Mem:* AAAS; Animal Behav Soc; Sigma Xi; Am Soc Arachnologists. *Res:* Predator-prey behavioral interactions; effects of parasites on intermediate host behavior; behavior of fish; behavior and physiology of spiders. *Mailing Add:* Dept Zool Ohio Wesleyan Univ Delaware OH 43015. *E-Mail:* dcradaba@cc.owu.edu

RADANOVICS, CHARLES, FOOD SCIENCE, NUTRITION. *Current Pos:* DIR RES & DEVELOP, RYKOFF-SEXTON, INC, 74- *Personal Data:* b Budapest, Hungary, Aug 9, 32; US citizen; m 60, Margaret McCormeck; c Mari (Bynne), Kathrina (Reed) & Anthony. *Educ:* Univ Budapest, BS, 56; Univ Calif, Davis, MS, 63; Mich State Univ, PhD(food sci), 69. *Prof Exp:* Mgr qual control, Model Dairy, Melbourne, Australia, 57-60; sr chemist, Tarax Ale Co, Melbourne, 60-62; proj leader food res, Carnation Co, Calif, 63-65; sect mgr food res, Quaker Oats Co, 69-74. *Concurrent Pos:* Adv panel, Univ Minn Food Sci Dept. *Mem:* Fel Inst Food Technol; Am Chem Soc; Res & Develop Assoc (pres, 79); Sigma Xi; Nat Food Processors Asn. *Res:* Food service; new product development; regulatory activities; formulation of fabricated foods; process innovation; nutrition of foods; teaching food science. *Mailing Add:* 4976 Tudor Pl Carmel IN 46033

RADBILL, JOHN R(USSELL), NUMERICAL ANALYSIS, FLUID MECHANICS. *Current Pos:* MEM TECH STAFF APPL MATH, JET PROPULSION LAB, CALIF INST TECHNOL, 70- *Personal Data:* b Upland, Pa, Apr 22, 32. *Educ:* Mass Inst Technol, BS & MS, 55, MechE, 56, ScD(mech eng), 58. *Prof Exp:* Asst mech eng, Mass Inst Technol, 54-58; develop engr ionic propulsion, Aerojet-Gen Corp, Gen Tire & Rubber Co, 58-61; tech specialist, Space & Info Systs Div, N Am Aviation, Inc, 61-66, sr tech specialist, Ocean Systs Opers, 66, mem tech staff, Autonetics Div, N Am Rockwell Corp, 66-70. *Concurrent Pos:* Instr, Citrus Jr Col, 59-60; consult, Technol Assocs of Southern Calif, Inc, 72- *Mem:* Assoc Am Soc Mech Engrs; Am Inst Aeronaut & Astronaut; Asn Comput Mach; Sigma Xi. *Res:* Fluid mechanics; numerical analysis; numerical solution of nonlinear partial differential equations; tornado lifted missiles; blood flow in diseased arteries. *Mailing Add:* 10413 Haines Canyon Ave Tujunga CA 91042-2031

RADCLIFFE, ALEC, PHYSICS, SYSTEMS ANALYSIS. *Current Pos:* RETIRED. *Personal Data:* b Cleethorpes, Eng, Aug 28, 17; nat US; m 46. *Educ:* Univ London, BSc, 39. *Prof Exp:* Temp exp asst & exp officer, Mine Design Dept, Brit Navy, 40-46; from sci officer to prin sci officer, Nat Gas Turbine Estab, 46-54; physicist & asst dept supvr, Appl Physics Lab, Johns Hopkins Univ, 55-87. *Mem:* Fel Brit Inst Physics. *Res:* Magnetism; acoustics; combustion; propulsion; fuel injection; unsteady gas dynamics; operations research. *Mailing Add:* 1710 Highland Dr Silver Spring MD 20910-2219

RADCLIFFE, EDWARD B, ENTOMOLOGY. *Current Pos:* Res fel, 63-64, res assoc, 64-65, from asst prof to assoc prof, 65-76, PROF ENTOM, UNIV MINN, ST PAUL, 76- *Personal Data:* b Rapid City, Man, Oct 25, 36; US citizen; m 64; c 2. *Educ:* Univ Man, BSA, 59; Univ Wis, MS, 61, PhD(entom), 63. *Concurrent Pos:* Vis prof, Beijing Agr Univ & Jilin Agr Univ, 82, Univ PR, Mayaguez, 84-85; adj prof, IAV-Hassan II, Rabat, 87- *Mem:* AAAS; Entom Soc Am; Entom Soc Can; Potato Asn Am. *Res:* Resistance of plants to insect attack; integrated pest management. *Mailing Add:* Dept Entom 219 Hodson Hall Univ Minn 1980 Folwell Ave St Paul MN 55108-1037

RADD, F(REDERICK) J(OHN), ABSTRACT MEDICAL ETIOLOGY, ENVIRONMENTAL CHEMISTRY & GEOLOGY. *Current Pos:* RETIRED. *Personal Data:* b Greenfield, Mass, July 28, 21; m, Barbara Elizabeth; c David, Margaret & Victoria. *Educ:* Univ Mo, BS, 43; Mass Inst Technol, ScD(metall), 49. *Prof Exp:* Asst metall, Res Lab, Gen Elec Co, 43; staff mem, Div Indust Coop, Mass Inst Technol, 43-45; res metallurgist, AEC, 49-51; supvr, Boeing Airplane Co, 51-52; staff scientist, Continental Oil Co, 52-77, sr res assoc, 78-85. *Mem:* Am Soc Metals; Nat Asn Corrosion Engrs; Am Chem Soc; Am Inst Mining, Metall & Petrol Engrs; AAAS. *Res:* Primary causes of certain unsolved illnesses; petroleum reservoir characteristics; hydrogen-magnetics in ferromagnetic metals. *Mailing Add:* PO Box 2428 Ponca City OK 74602-2428

RADDING, CHARLES MEYER, BIOCHEMISTRY, GENETICS. *Current Pos:* assoc prof med, molecular biophys & biochem, 67-72, prof, 72-79, PROF GENETICS, YALE UNIV, 79- *Personal Data:* b Springfield, Mass, June 18, 30; m 54; c 3. *Educ:* Harvard Univ, AB, 52, MD, 56. *Prof Exp:* Intern, Harvard Med Serv, Boston City Hosp, Mass, 56-57; res assoc metab, Nat Heart Inst, 57-59; Am Heart Asn advan res fel biochem, Sch Med, Stanford Univ, 59-62; asst prof human genetics, Univ Mich, 62-65, assoc prof, 65-67. *Concurrent Pos:* Miller vis prof, Univ Calif, Berkeley, 77. *Mem:* Nat Acad Sci; Am Soc Biol Chemists. *Res:* Genetic recombination; molecular virology. *Mailing Add:* Dept Genetics Sch Med Yale Univ 333 Cedar St PO Box 3333 New Haven CT 06510. *Fax:* 203-785-7023; *E-Mail:* charles-raddii8@quickmail.yale.edu

RADEBAUGH, RAY, CRYOGENICS, REFRIGERATION. *Current Pos:* assoc, 66-68, PHYSICIST CRYOG, NAT BUR STANDARDS, 68- *Personal Data:* b South Bend, Ind, Nov 4, 39; div; c Michael, Keith, Carol & James C. *Educ:* Univ Mich, BSE, 62; Purdue Univ, MS, 65, PhD(physics), 66. *Honors & Awards:* Nat Bur Stand Superior Performance Award, 68, 84-87; R & D 100 Award, 90. *Prof Exp:* Res asst physics, Purdue Univ, 62-66. *Concurrent*

Pos: Vis prof, Univ Tokyo, 72-73. *Mem:* Am Phys Soc; Sigma Xi. *Res:* Heat transfer, refrigeration, and thermometry at cryogenic temperatures. *Mailing Add:* MS 838 09 Nat Inst Stand & Technol 325 Broadway Boulder CO 80303. *Fax:* 303-497-5044

RADEKA, VELJKO, INSTRUMENTATION SCIENCE. *Current Pos:* res assoc, 62-64, assoc scientist, 66-69, scientist, 69-73, SR SCIENTIST INSTRUMENTATION, BROOKHAVEN NAT LAB, 73-, DIV HEAD, 72- *Personal Data:* b Zagreb, Yugoslavia, Nov 21, 30; m 58, Jelena Horvat; c Dejan & Dina. *Educ:* Univ Zagreb, Dipl Ing, 55, Dr Eng Sci(electronics), 61. *Honors & Awards:* Merit Award, Inst Elec & Electronics Engrs, 83, Centennial Medal, 89. *Prof Exp:* Scientist instrumentation, Ruder Boskovic Inst, Zagreb, 55-66. *Mem:* Fel Inst Elec & Electronics Engrs; Am Phys Soc. *Res:* Scientific instrumentation; nuclear detector signal processing. *Mailing Add:* Instrumentation Div Brookhaven Nat Lab Upton NY 11973. *Fax:* 516-282-7586; *E-Mail:* radeka@bnl.gov

RADEL, STANLEY ROBERT, SCIENCE EDUCATION. *Current Pos:* from instr to assoc prof, 64-91, PROF CHEM, CITY COL NY, 91- *Personal Data:* b New York, NY, July 6, 32; m 54; c 2. *Educ:* NY Univ, AB, 53, MS, 56, PhD(phys chem), 63. *Hon Degrees:* FGS. *Prof Exp:* Tutor chem, Queens Col, NY, 57-59, lectr, 59-64. *Mem:* Am Chem Soc; Am Phys Soc; AAAS. *Res:* Intramolecular forces; molecular dynamics; quantum mechanics and spectroscopy. *Mailing Add:* 66 Hillcrest Ave Yonkers NY 10705-1508

RADER, CHARLES ALLEN, SURFACE CHEMISTRY. *Current Pos:* group leader, 67-72, mgr biochem sci dept, 72-76, mgr, Phys Sci Dept, 77-80, DIR, GILLETTE RES INST, 80- *Personal Data:* b Washington, DC, Sept 30, 32; m 56, Carole Herbert; c William, Steven & Susan. *Educ:* Univ Md, BS, 55. *Prof Exp:* Chemist, Nat Bur Stand, 55-58; from chemist to sr chemist, Harris Res Labs, Inc, 58-64, res supvr, 64-67. *Mem:* Am Chem Soc; Am Asn Textile Chemists & Colorists; Am Inst Chemists; Fiber Soc; Soc Cosmetic Chemists. *Res:* Surface chemistry; detergents and surfactants; actinic degradation of polymers; cosmetic and personal products; aerosols; chemical and physical properties of skin and hair; textiles; chemical warfare. *Mailing Add:* Gillette Res Inst 401 Professional Dr Gaithersburg MD 20879-3400. *Fax:* 301-590-1656

RADER, CHARLES GEORGE, CHEMISTRY. *Current Pos:* Sr res engr, Occidental Chem Corp, Grand Island, NY, 74-77, group leader, 77-78, tech mgr, Niagara Falls, 78-81, tech dir, Grand Island, 81-84, DIR TECHNOL, OCCIDENTAL CHEM CORP, GRAND ISLAND, NY, 84- *Personal Data:* b Niagara Falls, NY, Apr 9, 46; m 71, Sheila A Dunlop; c Carla B & Kevin A. *Educ:* Rensselaer Polytech Inst, BSChemE, 68; Univ Rochester, MS, 70; State Univ NY, PhD, 74. *Concurrent Pos:* Vpres, DS Ventures, Dallas, 87-; mem, Indust Adv Bd, State Univ NY, Buffalo. *Mem:* Am Inst Chem Engrs; Am Chem Soc; Electrochem Soc; Sigma Xi. *Res:* Chemical engineering. *Mailing Add:* 180 Spicer Creek Run Grand Island NY 14072-1244

RADER, CHARLES PHILLIP, THERMOPLASTIC ELASTOMERS, RUBBER CHEMISTRY. *Current Pos:* MKT TECH SERV PRIN, ADVAN ELASTOMER SYSTS, LP, 91- *Personal Data:* b Greeneville, Tenn, Apr 9, 35; m 58, Clarita A Morgan; c Charles M & Charles A. *Educ:* Univ Tenn, BS, 57, MS, 60, PhD(chem), 61. *Honors & Awards:* Chmn, Rubber Div, Am Chem Soc, 86. *Prof Exp:* Instr chem, Univ Tenn, 59; sr res chemist, Monsanto Co, 61; org chemist, US Army Chem Ctr, 61-63; sr res chemist, Monsanto Co, 63-69, com develop proj mgr, 69-70, res group leader, 70-82, sr tech serv rep, 83-87, mkt tech serv prin, 88-90. *Concurrent Pos:* Asst prof, Univ Md, 62-63; counr, Am Chem Soc, 76- *Mem:* Am Chem Soc; NY Acad Sci; Soc Plastic Engrs; Soc Automotive Engrs; Am Soc Testing & Mats; Int Stand Orgn. *Res:* Applications of physical methods to organic chemistry; structure elucidation; conformational analysis; natural products; catalytic hydrogenation; rubber technology and tire technology; polymer chemistry; thermoplastic rubbers. *Mailing Add:* Advan Elastomer Systs LP 388 S Main St Akron OH 44311

RADER, LOUIS T(ELEMACUS), ELECTRICAL ENGINEERING. *Current Pos:* prof elec eng & bus admin, 69-82, EMER PROF BUS ADMIN, UNIV VA, 82-; SR FEL, OLSSON CTR APPL ETHICS. *Personal Data:* b Frank, Alta, Aug 24, 11; nat US; m 38; c 2. *Educ:* Univ BC, BSc, 33; Calif Inst Technol, MS, 35, PhD(elec eng), 38. *Prof Exp:* Test engr, Gen Elec Co, NY, 37-38, adv, Eng Prog, Gen Eng Dept, 38-39, sect head, Control Eng Dept, 43-45, div engr, Control Lab Div, 47-49, asst to mgr, 49-50, asst to mgr, Eng Div, 50-51, mgr eng, Control Div, 51-53, gen mgr, Specialty Control Dept, 53-59; dir, Elec Eng Dept & consult, Armour Res Found, Ill Inst Technol, 45-47; vpres, US Commercial Group & mem bd dirs, Int Tel & Tel Corp, 59-62; pres, Univac Div, Sperry Rand Corp, 62-64; vpres & gen mgr, Info Systs Div, Gen Elec Co, Charlottesville, 64-68; gen mgr, Indust Process Control Div, 68-69. *Concurrent Pos:* Bd visitors & gov, St Johns Col, Md, 61-70; trustee, Robert A Taft Inst Govt, NY, 63-80. *Mem:* Nat Acad Eng; Am Soc Eng Educ; fel Inst Elec & Electronic Engrs; Sigma Xi. *Res:* Principles of magnetic design; arc interruption. *Mailing Add:* PO Box 1721 Waynesboro VA 22980

RADER, RONALD ALAN, ANTIVIRAL DRUG & VACCINE DEVELOPMENT, BIOMEDICAL INFORMATION RESOURCES DEVELOPMENT. *Current Pos:* PRES, BIOTECHNOL INFO INST, 90- *Personal Data:* b Newark, NJ, May 28, 51; m 83, Sally A Young. *Educ:* Univ Md, BS, 73, MLS, 79. *Honors & Awards:* Rittenhouse Award, Med Libr Asn, 78. *Prof Exp:* User support coordr, Comput Sci Corp, 83-84; info scientist, Biospherics, Inc, 84; proj mgr, Expand Assoc, 84-85; ed & proj leader, Omec Int Inc, 85-90. *Concurrent Pos:* Mgr info serv, Porton Int Inc, 85-90; chem ed, Tech Resources Inc, 85; ed, Antiviral Agents Bull, 88- *Mem:* Am Chem Soc; Int Soc Antiviral Res; Drug Info Asn; Soc Indust Microbiol; Am Soc Microbiol; Am Soc Info Sci. *Res:* Biotechnology and pharmaceutical information resources design and development; acquired immunodeficiency syndrome and antiviral drug and vaccine development information resources; market and technology assessments. *Mailing Add:* Biotechnol Info Inst 1700 Rockville Pike Suite 400 Rockville MD 20852. *Fax:* 301-424-0257

RADER, WILLIAM AUSTIN, VETERINARY TOXICOLOGY. *Current Pos:* RETIRED. *Personal Data:* b Detroit, Mich, Aug 27, 16; m 42; c 4. *Educ:* Mich State Univ, DVM, 41. *Prof Exp:* Pvt practr vet med, 42-46 & 52-64; pub health off, Mich Dept Health, 46-47; dir res & develop, Vita-Vet Labs, Ind, 64-65; vet toxicologist, Petitions Rev Br, Bur Sci, Food & Drug Admin, US Dept Health, Educ & Welfare, 65-67; vet med off, Div Vet Med Rev, Bur Vet Med, 67-68, chief investr, New Animal Drug Br, New Animal Drugs Div, 68-73; chief toxicologist, Residue Planning & Eval Staff, Animal & Plant Health Inspection Serv, USDA, 73-75. *Concurrent Pos:* Pvt consult animal & plant health, 75-88. *Mem:* Am Vet Med Asn; Am Pub Health Asn; fel Am Col Vet Toxicologists; Am Soc Vet Physiologists & Pharmacologists; Soc Toxicologists. *Res:* Toxicological significance of pesticides, herbicides, fungicides, industrial environmental contaminants and chemicals and of oral and injectible drugs under conditions of use. *Mailing Add:* 4638 Bay Shore Rd Sarasota FL 34234

RADER, WILLIAM ERNEST, PLANT PATHOLOGY, MICROBIOLOGY. *Current Pos:* RETIRED. *Personal Data:* b Ellensburg, Wash, Aug 21, 16; m 38, Bernice Rubin; c William E Jr & Evelyn (Bentley). *Educ:* State Col Wash, BS, 39; Utah State Col, MS, 42; Cornell Univ, PhD(plant path), 46. *Prof Exp:* Asst, Utah State Col, 39-42 & Cornell Univ, 44-46; microbiologist, Biol Sci Res Ctr, Agr Lab, Shell Develop Co, 46-81. *Mem:* Am Phytopath Soc; Soc Nematol. *Res:* Pesticides and agricultural chemicals; biochemistry of fungicidal action; physiology and biochemistry of plant disease; chemical control of nematodes; biotreatment of industrial wastes. *Mailing Add:* 3325 Printemps Dr Modesto CA 95356-9311. *Fax:* 209-543-8589

RADERMACHER, REINHARD, REFRIGERATION, HEAT TRANSFER. *Current Pos:* vis prof, 83-84, from asst prof to assoc prof, 84-95, PROF MECH ENG, UNIV MD, 95- *Personal Data:* b Heidelberg, Ger, Dec 21, 52. *Educ:* Tech Univ Munich, Ger, MS, 77, PhD(physics), 81. *Prof Exp:* NATO scholar res, Nat Inst Standards & Technol, 81-83. *Concurrent Pos:* Prin investr, Nat Inst Stands & Technol, 83-, Sundstrand Corp, 84-87, Dept Energy, 86-89, NSF, 86-, GRI, 87 & 88 Environ Protection Agency, 89-93 & Elec Power Res Inst, 92-, Whirlpool Corp, 89-93 & Trane Co, 92-93, Samsung 96- *Mem:* Am Soc Heating Refrig & Air Conditioning Eng; Int Inst Refrig; Am Soc Eng Educ; Int Inst Refrig; Am Soc Med Engr; Soc Automobile Engr. *Res:* Energy conversion cycles, working fluid mixtures, environmentally safe fluids, household refrigerators; thermodynamics, heat transfer; residential air-conditioners/heat pumps; natural refrigerants. *Mailing Add:* Dept Mech Eng Univ Md College Park MD 20742-3035

RADFORD, ALBERT ERNEST, BOTANY. *Current Pos:* From instr to prof, 47-87, EMER PROF BOT, UNIV NC, CHAPEL HILL, 87- *Personal Data:* b Augusta, Ga, Jan 25, 18; m 41; c 3. *Educ:* Furman Univ, BS, 39; Univ NC, PhD(bot), 48. *Res:* Taxonomy of vascular plants; vascular flora of southeastern North America. *Mailing Add:* V-201 Carolina Meadows Chapel Hill NC 27514

RADFORD, DAVID CLARKE, HIGH-SPIN STATES, GAMMA-RAY SPECTROSCOPY. *Current Pos:* RETIRED. *Personal Data:* b Wellington, NZ, Mar 14, 54; c 2. *Educ:* Univ Auckland, BSc, 75, PhD(physics), 79. *Prof Exp:* Res staff physicist, Wright Nuclear Structure Lab, Yale Univ, 78-81; vis res scientist, Nuclear Res Ctr, Strasbourg, France, 81-83; res assoc, Argonne Nat Lab, 83-84; asst res officer, Chalk River Nuclear Lab, Atomic Energy Can Ltd, 85, assoc res officer, 86-97. *Res:* Nuclear structure reseach; high-spin states of nuclei using the techniques of Gamma-Ray spectroscopy. *Mailing Add:* Chalk River Labs AECL Res Chalk River ON K0J 1J0 Can. *E-Mail:* radfordd@crl.aecl.ca

RADFORD, DAVID EUGENE, MATHEMATICS. *Current Pos:* assoc prof, 76-82, PROF MATH, UNIV ILL, CHICAGO CIRCLE, 82- *Personal Data:* b Plattsburg, NY, June 4, 43; m 66; c 3. *Educ:* Univ NC, Chapel Hill, BS, 65, MA, 68, PhD(math), 70. *Prof Exp:* Asst prof math, Lawrence Univ, 70-76. *Concurrent Pos:* Vis lectr, Rutgers Univ, 75-76, vis assoc prof, 79-80. *Mem:* Am Math Soc. *Res:* Algebra; Hopf algebras, algebraic groups and co-algebras; quantum groups. *Mailing Add:* Dept Math Statist & Comput Sci M/C 249 Univ Ill Chicago IL 60680. *E-Mail:* radford@math.uic.edu

RADFORD, DIANE MARY, BREAST SURGERY, SURGICAL ONCOLOGY. *Current Pos:* PARK CREST SURG. *Personal Data:* b Irvine, Ayrshire, Scotland, Nov 14, 57. *Educ:* Glasgow Univ, Scotland, BSc Hons, 78, MB chB, 81, MD, 91. *Prof Exp:* Jr house officer med, Gartnavel Gen Hosp, Glasgow, 81-82; jr house officer surg, Monklands Dist Gen Hosp, Airdrie, 82; sr house officer surg specialties, Western Infirmary, Glasgow, 82-83; sr house officer surg, Royal Infirmary, Edinburgh, 83-84; registrar, Crosshouse Hosp, Kilmarnock, 84-85; surg oncol fel, Roswell Park Cancer Inst, 85-87; resident surg, St Louis Univ, 87-88, chief resident, 88-91; instr, Wash Univ, 91-92, asst prof surg, 91- *Mem:* Am Asn Cancer Res; Soc Surg Oncol; Europ Soc Surg Oncol; Am Med Asn; Asn Acad Surg; AAAS. *Res:* Molecular events in the oncogenesis of breast cancer. *Mailing Add:* Park Crest Surg 675 Old Ballas Rd Suite 200 St Louis MO 63141. *Fax:* 314-361-4197

RADFORD, HERSCHEL DONALD, ORGANIC CHEMISTRY. *Current Pos:* CONSULT, 76- *Personal Data:* b Butler, Mo, June 21, 11; m 39; c 2. *Educ:* Park Col, AB, 33; Univ Mo, AM, 44, PhD(chem), 49. *Prof Exp:* Chemist, Res & Develop Dept, Pan-Am Refining Corp, Stand Oil Co, Ind; 41-44, group leader, Chem Res Sect, 44-51, head, Process Develop Sect, 51-57, dir, Process Div, Am Oil Co, 57-60, tech dir, Process Develop Labs, 60-62, asst dir res & develop dept, 62-73, dir process & eng develop, Amoco Oil Co, Stand Oil Co, Ind, 73-76. *Mem:* Am Chem Soc; Am Inst Chem Engrs. *Res:* Alkylation of aromatic and aliphatic hydrocarbons; dealkylation of aromatic hydrocarbons, catalytic hydrogenation of substituted carbonyl and carbinol compounds; organic reactions catalyzed by anhydrous hydrofluoric acid; catalytic reforming; hydrocracking; desulfurization; isomerization; coking; catalytic cracking; synthetic fuels. *Mailing Add:* 1375 Dartmouth Rd PO Box 208 Flossmoor IL 60422-1904

RADFORD, KENNETH CHARLES, METALLURGY. *Current Pos:* sr scientist, 68-78, fel engr, 78-84, adv eng mgr ceramics, 84-, ENGR, WESTINGHOUSE ELEC CORP. *Personal Data:* b Manchester, Eng, July 1, 41; m 65, Janice Salesky; c Amanda, Joanna & Celia. *Educ:* Univ London, BSc, 63; Imp Col, dipl & ARSM, 63, PhD(metall), 67. *Prof Exp:* Staff, Imp Col, London, 67-68. *Mem:* Inst Metall; Am Ceramic Soc. *Res:* Dielectric properties; ceramics; nuclear fuel; electrical properties of ceramics; physical properties of ceramic powders; ceramic fabrication; optical ceramics diamond; ceramic matrix composites. *Mailing Add:* Sci & Technol Ctr Northrop Grumman 1350 Beulah Rd Pittsburgh PA 15235-5080. *Fax:* 412-256-1267

RADFORD, TERENCE, ORGANIC CHEMISTRY. *Current Pos:* res scientist, 68-80, SR RES SCIENTIST MASS SPECTROS, COCA-COLA CO, 80- *Personal Data:* b Sheffield, Eng, Apr 1, 39; m 72. *Educ:* Liverpool Col Technol, ARIC, 62; Sheffield Univ, PhD(org chem), 65. *Prof Exp:* Asst lectr org chem, Sheffield Col Technol, 65-66; res fel, Ohio State Univ, 66-67 & Wayne State Univ, 67-68. *Mem:* Royal Soc Chem; Am Chem Soc. *Res:* The application of instrumental techniques, especially combined gas chromatography/mass spectrometry to the identification of natural products. *Mailing Add:* 423 Tara Trail NW Atlanta GA 30327-4925

RADFORTH, NORMAN WILLIAM, PALEOBOTANY. *Current Pos:* CONSULT, RADFORTH & ASSOCS, 77- *Personal Data:* b Lancashire, Eng, Sept 22, 12; nat Can; m 39; c 2. *Educ:* Univ Toronto, BA, 36, MA, 37; Univ Glasgow, Scotland, PhD(paleobot), 39. *Honors & Awards:* Silver Medal, Royal Soc Arts, 58. *Prof Exp:* Lectr bot, Univ Toronto, 42-46; prof, McMaster Univ, 46-68, head dept, 46-53, chmn dept biol, 60-66, chmn org & assoc terrain res unit, 61-68, coordr acad develop, 65-66; prof biol & Muskeg Studies, Univ NB, 68-77, head dept biol, 68-70, dir, Muskeg Res Inst, 68-73. *Concurrent Pos:* Dir, Royal Bot Gardens, Can, 46-53; mem, Assoc Comt Geotech Res, Nat Res Coun Can, 48-; prog chmn & secy, Int Cong Bot, 59; vpres, Int Orgn Paleont, 59. *Mem:* Royal Soc Can; fel Royal Soc Arts. *Res:* Experimental morphology and embryology of higher plants applying in vitro methods; micropaleobotany and northern peatland interpretation. *Mailing Add:* Radforth & Assocs Muskeg Lab Limbert Rd RR 3 Parry Sound ON P2A 2W9 Can. *Fax:* 705-746-5190

RADHAKRISHNAMURTHY, BHANDARU, BIOCHEMISTRY. *Current Pos:* PROF APPL HEALTH SCI, TULANE SCH PUB HEALTH & TROP MED, 92- *Personal Data:* b Andhra Pradesh, India, July 1, 28; m 53, 83, Sulochana Y Pragada; c Rajeswararao, Umakalagnanam, Hema & Srinivas. *Educ:* Osmania Univ, India, BS, 51, MS, 53, PhD(chem), 58. *Prof Exp:* Res chemist, Sirsilk, Ltd, India, 53-54; lectr chem, Osmania Univ, 55-61; from res assoc to prof med & biochem, La State Univ Med Ctr, New Orleans, 61-92. *Concurrent Pos:* Fulbright fel med & biochem, Sch Med, La State Univ, New Orleans, 61-62; mem, Coun Atherosclerosis, Am Heart Asn, 71- *Mem:* NY Acad Sci; Am Chem Soc; Soc Exp Biol & Med; Am Soc Biol Chem; AAAS. *Res:* Biochemistry of connective tissue; proteoglycans and glycoproteins. *Mailing Add:* Dept Appl Health Sci Tulane Sch Pub Health & Trop Med 1430 Tulane Ave SL29 New Orleans LA 70112

RADHAKRISHNAN, CHITTUR VENKITASUBHAN, VETERINARY MICROBIOLOGY. *Current Pos:* VET MED OFFICER, BUR CONTAGIOUS & INFECTIOUS DIS, FLA DEPT AGR, 72- *Personal Data:* b Mannuthy, India, June 6, 37; m 65, Jaya Lakshmy; c Raja, Nila & Siva. *Educ:* Univ Kerala, India, BVSc, 59; Univ Fla, PhD(vet parasitol), 71. *Prof Exp:* Lectr vet med, Col Vet Med, Univ Kerala, 59-64; sci officer parasitol, Hindustan Antibiotics Res Ctr, 64-68; res asst, Dept Vet Sci, Univ Fla, 68-71, teaching asst parasitol, 71-72. *Concurrent Pos:* Assoc prof pathobiol, Col Vet Med, Pahlavi Univ, Shiraz, Iran, 73-75. *Mem:* Am Oil Chemists' Soc; Am Asn Avian Pathologists; Am Asn Vet Lab Diagnosticians; Am Soc Parasitologists. *Res:* Symbiotic and competitive nature of microorganisms; pathobiology of sporozoa infection; avian respiratory viruses; brucellosis; tuberculosis. *Mailing Add:* 12151 Jeffrey Lane Dade City FL 33525-5923

RADHAKRISHNAN, VENKATARAMAN, ASTRONOMY. *Current Pos:* dir, 72-94, EMER DIR, RAMAN RES INST, BANGALORE, 94- *Personal Data:* b Madras, India, May 18, 29. *Educ:* Mysore Univ, BSc, 50. *Prof Exp:* Res scholar, Indian Inst Sci, Bangalore, 50-51; res assoc, Chalmers Inst Technol, Sweden, 55-58; sr res fel, Calif Inst Technol, 59-64; prin res scientist, Commonwealth Sci & Indust Res Orgn, Australia, 65-71. *Mem:* Foreign assoc Nat Acad Sci; fel Indian Acad Sci; Royal Astron Soc. *Mailing Add:* Raman Res Inst CV Roman Ave Sadashivanager Bangalore 560 080 India

RADICE, GARY PAUL, MUSCLE DEVELOPMENT, MORPHOGENESIS. *Current Pos:* RES ASSOC, UNIV RICHMOND, 90- *Personal Data:* b Bay Village, OH, April 9, 52. *Educ:* Yale Univ, PhD(biol), 79. *Prof Exp:* Res assoc, Ind Univ, 81-90. *Mailing Add:* Dept Biol Univ Richmond Richmond VA 23173

RADIMER, KENNETH JOHN, INORGANIC CHEMISTRY. *Current Pos:* RETIRED. *Personal Data:* b Clifton, NJ, Mar 31, 20. *Educ:* Mass Inst Technol, SB, 42, PhD(inorg & anal chem), 47. *Prof Exp:* Res chemist, Nat Res Corp, Mass, 42; asst physics & chem, Mass Inst Technol, 43-44; res chemist chg anal lab, Kellex Corp, NJ, 44-45; res asst, SAM Labs, Carbide & Carbon Chem Corp, 45-46; instr anal chem, Lehigh Univ, 47-48; asst prof inorg & anal chem, Ind Univ, 48-50; res chemist, Gen Chem Div, Allied Chem & Dye Corp, 50-51; sect leader, Vitro Corp Am, 51-54; res chemist, M W Kellog Co Div, Pullman, Inc, 54-57 & 59-62 & Minn Mining & Mfg Co, 57-58; chief chemist, CBS Labs, 58-59; mgr metals applns, FMC Corp, Princeton, 62-69, res assoc, Indust Chem Div, 69-82. *Mem:* Electrochem Soc. *Res:* Microrefractometry; fluorine; fluorocarbon analysis; freon synthesis; molten salt electrolysis; reactions of metals with chemicals; chemistry of hydrogen peroxide; electrolytic persulfate processes; production of soda ash, phosphorus and phosphates; corrosion. *Mailing Add:* 12 Martin Pl Little Falls NJ 07424

RADIN, CHARLES LEWIS, MATHEMATICAL PHYSICS. *Current Pos:* from asst prof to assoc prof, 76-90, PROF MATH, UNIV TEX, AUSTIN, 90- *Personal Data:* b New York, NY, Jan 15, 45; m 69; c 1. *Educ:* City Col New York, BS, 65; Univ Rochester, PhD(physics), 70. *Prof Exp:* Fel math physics, Univ Nijmegen, 70-71; res assoc, Princeton Univ, 71-73 & Rockefeller Univ, 73-74; instr math, Univ Pa, 74-76. *Mem:* Am Math Soc; Am Phys Soc; Int Asn Math Physics. *Res:* Qualitative dynamics of quantum systems, especially many-body systems; automorphisms of operator algebras; classical ground states; neural networks. *Mailing Add:* Dept Math Univ of Tex Austin TX 78712. *E-Mail:* radin@math.utexas.edu

RADIN, ERIC LEON, ORTHOPEDICS, BIOMEDICAL ENGINEERING. *Current Pos:* CLIN PROF ORTHOP SURG, UNIV MICH, 89- *Personal Data:* b New York, NY, Sept 14, 34; c 3. *Educ:* Amherst Col, BA, 56; Harvard Univ, MD, 60. *Prof Exp:* Teaching fel orthop surg, Med Sch, Harvard Univ, 65-66, instr, 68-70, from asst prof to assoc prof, 70-79; prof & chmn, dept orthop surg, Med Sch, WVa Univ, 79-89; DIR BONE & JOINT CTR, HENRY FORD HOSP, DETROIT, 89- *Concurrent Pos:* Co-chief, arthritis clins, US Air Force Hosp, Andrews AFB, 66-68; instr orthop surg, Med Sch, George Washington Univ, 67-68; consult, Liberty Mutual Rehab Ctr, 69-79 & Ctr Law & Health Sci, Boston Univ, 71-79; lectr mech eng, Mass Inst Technol, 69-79; assoc, active staff, orthop surg, Beth Israel Hosp, 70-74 & Children's Hosp Med Ctr, 70-79; mem, active orthop staff, Mt Auburn Hosp, 74-79 & dir, orthop res, 78-79; assoc, Mus Comp Zool, Harvard Univ, 75-79; mem, Surg & Rehab Devices Panel, US Food & Drug Admin, 83-87, chmn, 85-87; mem, Orthop Study Sect, NIH, 87-90, bd trustees, Clin Orthop on Related Res, 87-90; mem, orthop residency rev comt, 89- *Mem:* Orthop Res Soc; Am Soc Mat & Testing; Sigma Xi; Int Soc Surg, Orthop & Trauma; Soc Biomat; Biomed Eng Soc; Am Bd Orthop Surg; Am Acad Orthop Surg; Am Orthop Asn; Asn Bone Joint Surg. *Res:* Joint degeneration; joint lubrication; biomechanics of the degenerative process. *Mailing Add:* Bone & Joint Ctr Henry Ford Hosp 2799 W Grand Blvd Detroit MI 48202-2608

RADIN, JOHN WILLIAM, PLANT PHYSIOLOGY. *Current Pos:* plant physiologist, Western Cotton Res Lab, 71-93, NAT PROG LEADER PLANT PHYSIOL & COTTON PROD, AGR RES SERV, USDA, 93- *Personal Data:* b New York, NY, Jan 8, 44; m 65; c 2. *Educ:* Univ Calif, Davis, BS, 65, PhD(plant physiol), 70. *Prof Exp:* Assoc agron, Univ Calif, Davis, 70-71. *Mem:* Am Soc Plant Physiologists; Crop Sci Soc Am. *Res:* General plant physiology; root physiology; nitrogen metabolism, especially nitrate reduction; hormonal control of growth and development in plants. *Mailing Add:* USDA Agr Res Serv NPS PNRS, Plant Physiol Bldg 005 Rm 336 BARC/W 10300 Baltimore Ave Beltsville MD 20705

RADIN, NATHAN, CLINICAL CHEMISTRY. *Current Pos:* CLIN CHEM CONSULT, 86- *Personal Data:* b Brooklyn, NY, Jan 22, 19; m 46, Galla H Solomon; c Jared P & Rachel A. *Educ:* Univ Calif, BA, 41; Columbia Univ, MA, 47; Purdue Univ, PhD(anal chem), 51. *Prof Exp:* Proj engr, Eng Res & Develop Labs, US Army, 51-52; chemist, Lederle Labs, Am Cyanamid Co, 53-54; biochemist, Mt Sinai Hosp, New York, 55-56; instr chem, Rochester Inst Technol, 56-59; chief biochemist, Rochester Gen Hosp, 58-66; clin chemist, Harrisburg Hosp Inst Path & Res, Penn, 66-67; res chemist, Ctr Dis Control, 67-86. *Concurrent Pos:* Ed, Newsletter Am Asn Clin Chem. *Mem:* Am Chem Soc; Am Asn Clin Chem; Sigma Xi. *Res:* Quality control, standards; reference materials; training. *Mailing Add:* 28215 Plantation Dr NE Atlanta GA 30324-2941. *E-Mail:* natradin@mindspring.com

RADIN, NORMAN SAMUEL, BIOCHEMISTRY. *Current Pos:* RETIRED. *Personal Data:* b New York, NY, July 20, 20; m 47; c 2. *Educ:* Columbia Univ, BA, 41, PhD(biochem), 49. *Prof Exp:* Asst res chemist, Off Sci Res & Develop, Pa, 42-45; fel, Univ Calif, 49-50; res scientist, Biochem Inst, Univ Tex, 50-52; res assoc, Med Sch, Northwestern Univ, 52-55, from asst prof to assoc prof, 55-60; prof biol chem in psychiat, Univ Mich, Ann Arbor, 73-84, prof neurochem in psyciat 84-94, res biochem, ment health res inst, 60-94. *Concurrent Pos:* Prin scientist, Radioisotope Unit, Vet Admin Hosp, Hines, Ill, 52-54 & Res Hosp, Chicago, 54-57; ed, Analytical Biochem; Sen Jacob Javits Res Investr, 84. *Mem:* Am Soc Biol Chemists; Am Soc Neurochem; Int Soc Neurochem. *Res:* Brain lipids; lipid methodology; glycolipid metabolism; sphingolipid enzyme inhibitors; Gaucher's disease. *Mailing Add:* 350 Sharon Park Dr Apt C3 Menlo Park CA 94025-6810

RADIN, SHELDEN HENRY, PLASMA PHYSICS. *Current Pos:* From asst prof to assoc prof, 63-74, assoc chair, 84-86, PROF PHYSICS, LEHIGH UNIV, 74-,. *Personal Data:* b Hartford, Conn, Dec 24, 36; m 60, Ruth Yaffe; c Naomi, Sari & Samuel. *Educ:* Worcester Polytech Inst, BS, 58; Yale Univ, MS, 59, PhD(physics), 63. *Concurrent Pos:* Mem, Exam Comt, Physics Achievement Test, Col Entrance Exam Bd, 70-78, chmn, 72-78; vis prof, Univ Rochester, 86-87; reviewer, ACT, 82-, GRE, 84, MCAT, 89-; vis comt, NJ Inst Technol, 83, Univ Cincinnati, 90-91. *Mem:* Am Phys Soc; Am Asn Univ Profs; Am Asn Physics Teachers. *Res:* Statistical mechanics of plasmas; kinetic theory of nonequilibrium situations; numerical simulations of plasmas. *Mailing Add:* Dept Physics Lehigh Univ 16 Mem Dr E Bethlehem PA 18015. *Fax:* 610-758-5730; *E-Mail:* shr0@lehigh.edu

RADKE, LAWRENCE FREDERICK, ATMOSPHERIC SCIENCE, CLOUD PHYSICS. *Current Pos:* MGR, NCAR, 91- *Personal Data:* b Seattle, Wash, Mar 19, 42. *Educ:* Univ Wash, BSc, 64, MSc, 66, PhD(atmospheric sci), 68. *Prof Exp:* Res assoc, Univ Wash, 68-70, res asst prof, 70-72, res assoc prof, 72-80, res prof atmospheric sci, 80-91. *Mem:* Am Meteorol Soc; AAAS; Sigma Xi. *Res:* Aircraft measurments and instrumental development; meteorology; cloud physics; atmospheric chemistry; air pollution. *Mailing Add:* 2503 Norwood Ave Boulder CO 80304-1364

RADKE, RODNEY OWEN, WEED SCIENCE. *Current Pos:* OWNER & PRIN CONSULT, AGR TECHNOL SYSTS, 93- *Personal Data:* b Ripon, Wis, Feb 5, 42; m 63, Jean M Rutsch; c Cheryl L, Lisa D & Daniel E. *Educ:* Univ Wis, Madison, BS, 63, MS, 65, PhD(soil biochem), 67. *Prof Exp:* Plant physiologist, US Army Biol Res Labs, 67-69; sr res biologist, Agr Div, Monsanto Co, 69-74, res specialist, Monsanto Agr Prods Co, 74-75, sr res group leader, 75-78, mgr, 78-81, mgr res, 81-92. *Mem:* N Cent Weed Sci Soc; Weed Sci Soc Am; Environ Assessment Asn. *Res:* Discovery and development of crop protection chemicals for control of weeds and plant diseases; evaluation of bioengineered crops; operation of research farms. *Mailing Add:* 1119 Grand Prix Dr St Charles MO 63303

RADKE, WILLIAM JOHN, COMPARATIVE & HUMAN ANATOMY. *Current Pos:* PROF BIOL, UNIV CENT OKLA, 75- *Personal Data:* b Mankato, Minn, June 8, 47; m 84, Christine Albasi; c Sarah & Julia. *Educ:* Mankato State Univ, BS, 70, MA, 72; Univ Ariz, PhD(zool), 75. *Concurrent Pos:* Post doctorate, Wolfson Inst, Univ Hull, 82-83, Univ Ariz, 90-91. *Mem:* Sigma Xi. *Res:* Hypothalamic-hypophyseal-thyroid axis of the bird; avian integument, avian adrenal regulation. *Mailing Add:* Dept Biol Univ Cent Okla Edmond OK 73034-0177. *E-Mail:* wradke@aix1.ucok.edu

RADKOWSKY, ALVIN, REACTOR PHYSICS. *Current Pos:* PROF NUCLEAR ENG, TEL AVIV UNIV & BEN GURION UNIV, 72- *Personal Data:* b Elizabeth, NJ, June 30, 15; m 50; c 1. *Educ:* City Col New York, BSE, 35; George Washington Univ, AM, 42; Cath Univ Am, PhD(physics), 47. *Honors & Awards:* Abromowitz-Zeitlin Award, 86. *Prof Exp:* Chief scientist, US Naval Reactor Hq, Washington, DC, 50-72. *Mem:* Nat Acad Eng; fel Am Phys Soc; fel Am Nuclear Soc; Sigma Xi. *Res:* Reactor physics; nuclear reactor design and concepts. *Mailing Add:* Dept Interdisciplinary Studies Sch Eng Tel-Aviv Univ Ramat Aviv Tel-Aviv 69978 Israel

RADLOFF, HAROLD DAVID, DAIRY SCIENCE, BIOCHEMISTRY. *Current Pos:* MGR MKT, CONTINENTAL GRAIN, 88- *Personal Data:* b Mellen, Wis, Aug 25, 37; m 60; c 2. *Educ:* Univ Wis, BS, 59, MS, 61, PhD(dairy sci, biochem), 64. *Prof Exp:* Res fel dairy sci, Univ Wis, 64-66; asst prof dairy husb, Univ Wyo, 66-70, assoc prof, 70-77, prof, 77-81, prof animal sci, 81-88, exten animal scientist, 81-88. *Mem:* Am Dairy Sci Asn; Am Soc Animal Sci. *Res:* Lipid metabolism in ruminants; milk fat synthesis; general dairy cow nutrition. *Mailing Add:* 309 Melbourne Modesto CA 95357

RADLOFF, ROGER JAMES, VIROLOGY. *Current Pos:* asst prof, 72-81, ASSOC PROF, MICROBIOL, SCH MED, UNIV NMEX, 82- *Personal Data:* b Mason City, Iowa, Oct 16, 40; m 68; c 2. *Educ:* Iowa State Univ, BS, 62; Calif Inst Technol, PhD(biophys & chem), 68. *Prof Exp:* Fel, Biophys Lab, Univ Wis, 68-72. *Concurrent Pos:* NIH fel, 68-70; NSF & NIH res grant, 74-83. *Mem:* Am Soc Microbiol; Am Soc Virol. *Res:* Structure and synthesis of encephalomyocarditis virus and DNA repair in neurospora; medical virology diagnostics. *Mailing Add:* Dept Microbiol Univ NMex Med Sch One University Campus Albuquerque NM 87131-0001. *Fax:* 505-277-6029; *E-Mail:* rradloff@medusa.unm.edu

RADLOW, JAMES, DIFFRACTION THEORY, SINGULAR INTEGRAL EQUATIONS. *Current Pos:* prof appl math, 65-89, RES PROF, UNIV NH, 89- *Personal Data:* b New York, NY. *Educ:* NY Univ, PhD(math), 57. *Prof Exp:* Assoc prof math, Adelphi Univ, 59-62 & Purdue Univ, 62-65. *Res:* Diffraction by a quarter-plane multi-dimensional singular integral equation toeplitz operators fitering at high noise levels; singular integral equations; Hilbert space; partial differential equations; magnetohydrodynamics. *Mailing Add:* 47 Maple St Somersworth NH 03878. *E-Mail:* jgradlow@concentric.net

RADNER, ROY, MATHEMATICAL ECONOMICS. *Current Pos:* prof econ & info syst, 95-96, PROF BUS, STERN SCH, NY UNIV, 96- *Personal Data:* b Chicago, Ill, June 29, 27; m, Charlotte V Kuh; c 4. *Educ:* Univ Chicago, PhB, 45, BS, 50, MS, 51, PhD(math statist), 56. *Prof Exp:* Res asst, Cowles Comn Res Econ, Univ Chicago, 51, res assoc, 51-54, asst prof, 54-55; asst prof, Dept Econ, Yale Univ, 55-57; from assoc prof to prof econ & statist, Univ Calif, Berkeley, 57-79, chmn, Dept Econ, 66-69; mem tech staff, AT&T Bell Labs, 79-85, distinguished mem tech staff, 79-85, 85-95. *Concurrent Pos:* Fel, Ctr Advan Study Behav Sci, 55-56; consult, Boeing Airplane Co, 56-57, Kaiser Found Psychol Res, 57-58, Rand Corp, 59-70, Soc Econ & Appl Math, 61-62, Syst Develop Corp, 62-65 & Mathematica, 56-66; consult, Maritime Cargo Transp Conf, Nat Acad Sci, 58-60, Comt Utilization of Sci & Eng Manpower, 62-63; assoc ed, Mgt Sci, 59-70, Econometrica, 61-68, J Econ Theory, 68- & Am Econ Rev, 79-82; Guggenheim Found fel, 61-62 & 65-66; mem, Econ Adv Panel, NSF, 63-65; mem, Tech Adv Comt, Carnegie Comn Future Higher Educ, 67-73, consult, 67-73; mem, Comt Status Teaching Asst, Am Asn Univ Profs, 68-70; overseas fel, Churchill Col, Cambridge, 69-70 & 90; mem math sci bd, Social Sci Res Coun, 70-74; mem, Nat Bur Econ Res Comt Econometrics & Math Econ, 71-; mem, Adv Comt Econ Educ, Nat Acad Educ, 72-73; mem, Adv Bd Off Math Sci, Nat Res Coun-Nat Acad Sci, 72-76, Comn Human Resources, 76-79, Comt Fundamental Res Relevant to Educ, 76-77, Assembly Behav & Social Sci, Nat Res Coun, 79-82, Comt Risk & Decision Making, 80-81, Comt Basic Res in Behav & Social Sci, Working Group Markets & Orgns, 85, Comt Contrib of Behav & Social Sci to Prev Nuclear War, 85-90; Taussig prof econ, Harvard Univ, 77-78; vis prof, Kennedy Sch Govt, Harvard Univ, 78-79, res prof econ, NY Univ, 83-95. *Mem:* Nat Acad Sci; fel Am Acad Arts & Sci; fel AAAS; distinguished fel Am Econ Asn; fel Econometric Soc (vpres, 71-72, pres, 72-73); Inst Math Statist. *Res:* Decentralization, incentives, transfer pricing and budgeting; sequential games with uncertainty; economics of information. *Mailing Add:* Stern Sch MEC 9-68 NY Univ 44 W 4th St New York NY 10012. *Fax:* 212-995-4228; *E-Mail:* rradner@stern.nyu.edu

RADNITZ, ALAN, MATHEMATICS. *Current Pos:* Asst prof, 70-75, assoc prof, 75-82, PROF MATH, CALIF STATE POLYTECH UNIV, POMONA, 82- *Personal Data:* b Miami Beach, Fla, Dec 16, 44; m 68, Rena Savetz; c Todd & Scott. *Educ:* Univ Calif, Los Angeles, AB, 66, PhD(math), 70. *Mem:* Am Math Soc; Math Asn Am. *Res:* Differential equations in banach spaces; partial differential equations; functional analysis. *Mailing Add:* Dept Math Calif State Polytech Univ 3801 W Temple Ave Pomona CA 91768. *Fax:* 909-869-4369; *E-Mail:* aradnitz@csupomona.edu

RADO, GEORGE TIBOR, SOLID STATE PHYSICS. *Current Pos:* RES PROF, JOHNS HOPKINS UNIV, 83- *Personal Data:* b Budapest, Hungary, July 22, 17; nat US; wid; c Lisa & Anita. *Educ:* Mass Inst Technol, SB, 39, SM, 41, PhD(physics), 43. *Honors & Awards:* Pure Sci Award, Naval Res Lab-Sci Res Soc Am, 57; E O Hulburt Sci Award, 65; Distinguished Achievement Sci Award, USN, 71. *Prof Exp:* Res assoc, Div Indust Coop, Mass Inst Technol, 42-43 & Radiation Lab, 44-45; physicist, Naval Res Lab, 45-55, head, Magnetism Br, 55-82, chief scientist magnetism, 82-83. *Concurrent Pos:* Adj prof Univ Md, 62-83; mem comn magnetism, Int Union Pure & Appl Physics, 66-75, secy, 69-72, chmn, 72-75. *Mem:* Fel Am Phys Soc; Sigma Xi. *Res:* Light scattering; microwave propagation; saturation magnetization; magnetic spectra; domain theory; ferrites; Faraday effect; ferromagnetic resonance; magnetocrystalline anisotropy; magnetoelectric effects; ultra-thin magnetic films; magnetic surface anisotropy. *Mailing Add:* 818 Carrie Ct McLean VA 22101

RADOMSKI, JACK LONDON, CHEMICAL CARCINOGENESIS. *Current Pos:* CONSULT, 87- *Personal Data:* b Milwaukee, Wis, Dec 10, 20; m 47, 70, Teresa Pascual; c Mark S, Linda, Eric P, Janet (Balinger) & Mayte (Matranca). *Educ:* Univ Wis, BS, 42; George Washington Univ, PhD, 50. *Honors & Awards:* Acad Toxicol, Award 82. *Prof Exp:* Chemist, Gen Aniline & Film Corp, 42-44; pharmacologist, Food & Drug Admin, Fed Security Agency, 44-53; from asst prof to assoc prof pharmacol, Sch Med, Univ Miami, 53-59, prof, 59-82; pres, Covington Chemtox, 82-87. *Concurrent Pos:* Consult toxicol, WHO, 78-82. *Mem:* Am Soc Pharmacol & Exp Therapeut; Soc Toxicol; Am Asn Cancer Res; NY Acad Sci; Acad Toxicol Sci. *Res:* Toxicology and metabolism of drugs, chemicals and insecticides; environmental and occupational toxicology and carcinogenesis. *Mailing Add:* 6432 Driftwood Dr Hudson FL 34667

RADONOVICH, LEWIS JOSEPH, STRUCTURAL CHEMISTRY. *Current Pos:* from asst prof to assoc prof, 73-84, PROF CHEM, UNIV NDAK, 84- *Personal Data:* b Curtisville, Pa, July 2, 44; m 66; c 2. *Educ:* Thiel Col, BA, 66; Wayne State Univ, PhD(phys chem), 70. *Prof Exp:* Res assoc inorg chem, Cornell Univ, 70-73. *Concurrent Pos:* Res supvr inorg anal, Univ NDak Energy Res Ctr, 84-86; chmn, Dept Chem, 88- *Mem:* Am Chem Soc; Am Crystallog Asn. *Res:* Organometallic chemistry, x-ray crystallography and the structural chemistry of compounds of biological interest. *Mailing Add:* Univ N Fla Arts & Sci 4567 St Johns Bluff Rd S Jacksonville FL 32224-2646

RADOSEVICH, JAMES A, TUMOR IMMUNOLOGY, TUMOR CELL BIOLOGY. *Current Pos:* Asst prof, 85-90, ASSOC PROF & STAFF RES SCIENTIST, NORTHWESTERN UNIV, 90- *Personal Data:* b Peoria, Ill, June 18, 56; m 80, Cynthia A Swearingen; c Catherine & Teresa. *Educ:* Bradley Univ, BS, 78; Univ Ill, PhD(exp path), 83. *Concurrent Pos:* Staff res scientist, Dept Vet Affairs, 85- *Mem:* AAAS; NY Acad Sci; Am Fedn Clin Res; Am Soc Microbiol; Int Union Against Cancer. *Res:* Vaccines against cancer; cloned an adenocarcinoma related antigen. *Mailing Add:* 7135 Sentinel Rd Rockford IL 61107-2706. *Fax:* 312-503-4943

RADOSEVICH, LEE GEORGE, ENERGY CONVERSION, SOLID STATE PHYSICS. *Current Pos:* MEM STAFF PHYSICS, SANDIA LABS, 69- *Personal Data:* b Milwaukee, Wis, Nov 5, 38. *Educ:* Marquette Univ, BS, 60, MS, 62; Northwestern Univ, Ill, PhD(physics), 68. *Prof Exp:* Physicist, Allis-Chalmers Mfg Co, 62; res assoc physics, Univ Ill, Urbana, 67-69. *Mem:* Am Phys Soc. *Res:* Solar thermal power conversion. *Mailing Add:* 1614 Vancouver Way Livermore CA 94550

RADOSKI, HENRY ROBERT, SPACE PHYSICS, PLASMA PHYSICS. *Current Pos:* res physicist, Space Physics Lab, Geophys Lab, 68-76, PROG MGR, OFF SCI RES, USAF, 76- *Personal Data:* b Jersey City, NJ, Aug 18, 36; m 59, Elizabeth A Patton; c Raymond R, Henry Z & Derek P. *Educ:* Col Holy Cross, BS, 58; Mass Inst Technol, PhD(physics), 63. *Prof Exp:* Res asst plasma physics, Res Lab Electronics, Mass Inst Technol, 59-63; res assoc prof geophys, Weston Observ, Boston Col, 63-68. *Mem:* Am Geophys Union. *Res:* Magnetospheric physics; solar physics; astrophysics; solar-terrestrial physics. *Mailing Add:* 2603 Turbridge Lane Alexandria VA 22308

RADOVSKY, FRANK JAY, ACAROLOGY, MEDICAL ENTOMOLOGY. *Current Pos:* COURTESY PROF ENTOM, ORE STATE UNIV, 94- *Personal Data:* b Fall River, Mass, Jan 5, 29; div; c Susan & Judith. *Educ:* Univ Colo, AB, 51; Univ Calif, Berkeley, MS, 59, PhD(parasitol), 64. *Prof Exp:* Actg asst prof entom, Univ Calif, Berkeley, 62-63; asst res parasitologist, Hooper Found, Med Ctr, Univ Calif, San Francisco, 63-69, lectr parasitol, Dept Int Health, 69; acarologist, Bishop Mus, 70-85, chmn, Dept Entom, 72-85, asst to dir res, 73-76, actg dir, 76-77, asst dir, 77-85, L A Bishop distinguished chair zool, 84-86; vis prof entom, Ore State Univ, Corvallis, 87; dir res & collections, NC State Mus Natural Sci, 87-92; field agt, NC Food & Drug Protection, 92-94. *Concurrent Pos:* Ed, J Med Entom, 70-85 & 87-88; secy, Int Cong Acarology, 71-78; mem bd mgt, Wau Ecol Inst, Papua, New Guinea, 72-85; mem, Hawaii Animal Species Adv Comn, 72-80, Sci Comt Entom, Pac Sci Asn, 82-87 & Hawaiian Natural Area Res Syst Comn, 85; managing ed, Pac Insects, 78-85; assoc ed/ed, Ann Rev Entom, 78-97. *Mem:* AAAS; Entom Soc Am; Acarology Soc Am; Sigma Xi; Am Soc Trop Med & Hyg; Soc Vector Ecologists. *Res:* Biology and systematics of acarine parasites; adaptation and evolution of relationships between arthropod parasites and their hosts; arthropod vectors of disease agents. *Mailing Add:* Dept Entom Ore State Univ Cordley Hall 2046 Corvallis OR 97331-2907. *Fax:* 541-737-3643; *E-Mail:* adovskf@bcc.orst.edu

RADSPINNER, JOHN ASA, PHYSICAL CHEMISTRY. *Current Pos:* assoc prof, 57-62, actg dean, 69-70, chmn dept, 70-72, PROF CHEM, LYCOMING COL, 62- *Personal Data:* b Vincennes, Ind, May 14, 17; m 42; c 2. *Educ:* Univ Richmond, BS, 37; Va Polytech Inst, MS, 38; Carnegie Inst Technol, DSc(phys chem), 42. *Prof Exp:* Res chemist, Pan-Am Refining Corp, Div Stand Oil Co Ind, 42-44; supvr operating dept, 44-54, asst dir indust rels, Am Oil Co Div, 54-56, personnel dir, Yorktown Refinery, 56-57. *Mem:* Am Chem Soc; AAAS. *Mailing Add:* 432 Oakland Ave Williamsport PA 17701-2132

RADTKE, DOUGLAS DEAN, PHYSICAL INORGANIC CHEMISTRY. *Current Pos:* Asst prof, 66-69, assoc prof, 69-77, PROF CHEM, UNIV WIS, STEVENS POINT, 77- *Personal Data:* b New London, Wis, Nov 6, 38; m 62; c 2. *Educ:* Wis State Univ, Stevens Point, BS, 61; Univ Wis, PhD(phys chem), 66. *Mem:* Am Chem Soc. *Res:* Molecular orbital calculations for transition metal complexes; preparation and structure of simple divalent rare earth compounds. *Mailing Add:* Dept Chem Univ Wis Stevens Pt Stevens Point WI 54481

RADTKE, RICHARD LYNN, HANDICAPPED & COMPUTER ACCESS, SCANNING ELECTRON MICROSCOPE & MICROPROBE TECHNIQUES. *Current Pos:* instr, Col Continuing Ed, 81, RES PROF OCEANIC BIOL, HAWAII INST GEOPHYS, UNIV HAWAII, MANOA, 83- *Personal Data:* b North Judson, Ind, July 9, 52; m 92, Judith Echavez; c David & Ocean. *Educ:* Wabash Col, BA, 74; Univ SC, PhD (marine sci), 78. *Prof Exp:* Staff mem, Jean-Michel Cousteau Inst, 78; Can vis fel, St John's, Nfld, 78-80; res scientist, Pac Gamefish Found, 81-82. *Concurrent Pos:* Bd dirs, Multiple Sclerosis Soc, ALOHA Spec Technol Access Ctr Inc, Hawaii, Ctrs Independent Living & AAAS Diplomacy. *Mem:* Am Soc Ichthyologists & Herpetologists; Sigma Xi; Am Soc Zoologists. *Res:* Use of otolith structures in fish to determine demographic data, life history information and migrational insights; designed unique methodologies to examine history of species temperative, tropic and arctic climates in many migratory species. *Mailing Add:* Univ Hawaii-Hawaii Inst Geophys 1000 Pope Rd MSB 632 Honolulu HI 96822. *Fax:* 808-956-9516; *E-Mail:* radtke@hawaii.edu

RADWAN, MOHAMED AHMED, PLANT PHYSIOLOGY. *Current Pos:* plant physiologist, 60-68, PRIN PLANT PHYSIOLOGIST, US FOREST SERV, 68- *Personal Data:* b Dakahlia, Egypt, Apr 16, 26; nat US; m 57. *Educ:* Cairo Univ, Egypt, BSc, 46, MS, 50; Univ Calif, PhD(plant physiol), 56. *Prof Exp:* Asst lectr chem, Cairo Univ, 47-52; lectr plant physiol, 56-57; sr lab technician, Univ Calif, 57-58; instr chem, Sacramento City Col, 58-60. *Mem:* Am Chem Soc; Am Soc Plant Physiol; Bot Soc Am; Am Soc Agron; Soc Am Foresters. *Res:* Nutrition; fertilization; forest tree physiology. *Mailing Add:* 9130 Blomberg SW Olympia WA 98512

RADWAN, NABIL, INTEGRATED PEST MANAGEMENT FOR PACKAGING, PAPERMAKING. *Current Pos:* sr staff engr, 89-90, prin eng, 90-93, DIR TECHNOL, TENNECO INC, 93- *Educ:* Univ Alexandria, BSc, 67; Univ Cairo, MSc, 72; Univ Ottawa, PhD(chem eng), 88. *Prof Exp:* Lectr, Nat Res Coun, Egypt, 72-73; proj scientist, Domtar Inc, 80-88; mgr, Profit Increase Serv, Valmet-Dominion Inc, 88-89. *Mem:* Can Pulp & Paper Asn; Tech Asn Pulp & Paper Indust; Int Asn Sci Papermakers. *Res:* Development and application of integrated pest management and functional barriers to fats and moisture vapor for wood fibre based packagings. *Mailing Add:* Tenneco Packaging 100 Industrial Ave Rittman OH 44270-1573

RADWANSKA, EWA, OBSTETRICS & GYNECOLOGY, ENDOCRINOLOGY. *Current Pos:* MEM STAFF, DEPT OBSTET & GYNEC, RUSH MED COL, CHICAGO, 81- *Personal Data:* b Wilno, Poland, Oct 24, 38; c 1. *Educ:* Med Acad, Warsaw, MD, 62, Dr Med Sci, 69; Univ London, MPhil, 75. *Prof Exp:* Resident & instr obstet, gynec & endocrinol, Med Acad, Warsaw, 64-70; fel endocrinol, Univ Col Hosp, London, 70-75; registr, Hillingdon Hosp, London, 75-76; asst prof obstet, gynec & endocrinol, Univ NC, Chapel Hill, 77-79; mem staff, Univ Ark, Little Rock, 79-81. *Concurrent Pos:* Med officer, City Clin, Warsaw, 64-70, Family Planning Asn, London, 70-76 & Marie Stopes Mem Birth Control Ctr, London, 70-76. *Mem:* Polish Endocrine Soc; Am Med Soc; Royal Col Obstetricians & Gynecologists; Am Fertil Soc; Soc Study Reprod. *Res:* Reproductive endocrinology, particularly induction of ovulation, ovarian failure, luteal deficiency, spontaneous abortions, infertility, progesterone assay, tubal sterilization. *Mailing Add:* Obstet & Gynec Rush Univ Med Col 600 S Paulina St Chicago IL 60612-3832

RADWIN, HOWARD MARTIN, UROLOGY. *Current Pos:* PROF UROL & CHMN DEPT, UNIV TEX, HEALTH SCI CTR, SAN ANTONIO, 68- *Personal Data:* b New York, NY, Mar 13, 31; m 58; c 3. *Educ:* Princeton Univ, AB, 52; Columbia Univ, MD, 56. *Prof Exp:* Asst prof urol, Tulane Univ, 64-68. *Concurrent Pos:* Nat Cancer Inst fel, Tulane Univ, 61-62; consult, Brooke Army Hosp & Air Force Wilford Hall Hosp, 69- *Mem:* Fel Am Col Surg; Am Urol Asn; Soc Univ Urologists. *Res:* Prostate physiology; pyelonephritis; urologic cancer; application of renal physiology to urologic disease. *Mailing Add:* Urol Cons 8042 Wurzbach Suite 430 San Antonio TX 78229-3807

RADZIALOWSKI, FREDERICK M, PHARMACOLOGY, BIOCHEMISTRY. *Current Pos:* SR RES INVESTR METAB, G D SEARLE & CO, 68- *Personal Data:* b Detroit, Mich, Mar 25, 39; m 60; c 2. *Educ:* Wayne State Univ, BS, 60, MS, 64; Purdue Univ, PhD(pharmacol), 68. *Mem:* AAAS; Am Pharmaceut Asn. *Res:* Drug and lipid metabolism; obesity; circadian rhythms. *Mailing Add:* FMR Res Assocs Inc 3700 Winnetka Stello Glenview IL 60025-1354

RADZIEMSKI, LEON JOSEPH, ATOMIC SPECTROSCOPY. *Current Pos:* DEAN, COL SCI, WASH STATE UNIV, 90- *Personal Data:* b Worcester, Mass, June 18, 37; m 83, Barbara Woodruff; c Michael & Timothy. *Educ:* Col Holy Cross, BS, 58; Purdue Univ, MS, 61, PhD(physics), 64. *Prof Exp:* Lectr physics, Inst Technol, USAF, 65-67; staff mem, Los Alamos Nat Lab, Univ Calif, 67-83; head, Physics Dept, NMex State Univ, 83-88, assoc dean, Col Arts & Sci & dir, Arts & Sci Res Ctr, 88-90. *Concurrent Pos:* Lectr, Wright State Univ, 66-67; vis scientist, Lab Aime Cotton, France, 74-75; mem, Comt Line Spectra Elements, Nat Res Coun, 75-81; vis mem fac, Univ Fla, 78-79; vis scientist, Sandia Nat Lab, Livermore, 84-88. *Mem:* Fel Optical Soc Am; Am Phys Soc; Soc Appl Spectros; fel Laser Inst Am (pres, 91); fel AAAS; Coun Col Arts & Sci Deans. *Res:* Atomic spectroscopy; spectrochemical applications of lasers; remote, point, and in situ detection of toxic substances; laser-induced breakdown spectroscopy; laser guiding of electron beams; optical spectroscopy (conventional & laser); editor of 2 books, holds 2 patents and 70 publications. *Mailing Add:* Col Sci 208 Morrill Hall Wash State Univ Pullman WA 99164-3520. *Fax:* 509-335-3295; *E-Mail:* lradziemski@wsu.edu

RADZIKOWSKI, M ST ANTHONY, INORGANIC CHEMISTRY. *Current Pos:* dean women, 55-58, chmn chem dept, 61-86, ASSOC PROF CHEM, MARYWOOD COL, 61- *Personal Data:* b Jermyn, Pa, Mar 10, 19. *Educ:* Marywood Col, AB, 39; Univ Notre Dame, MS, 57, PhD(chem), 61. *Prof Exp:* Teacher parochial sch, Pa, 45-55. *Mem:* Am Chem Soc; Coblentz Soc. *Res:* Complexes of methyl esters of proline and sarcosine; infrared spectra of coordination compounds of amines with metal halides; spectroscopic studies of reactions with organic donor compounds. *Mailing Add:* Marywood Col Scranton PA 18509-1598

RAE, PETER MURDOCH MACPHAIL, CELL BIOLOGY. *Current Pos:* sr res scientist, Miles Inc, 83-85, prin staff scientist, Molecular Diagnostics Inc, 85-90, prin staff scientist, 90-93, DIR, INST RES TECHNOL, BAYER CORP, 94- *Personal Data:* b Alexandria, Scotland, Jan 7, 44; US citizen; m 71, Margaret Engel; c Andrew. *Educ:* Univ Calif, Davis, AB, 65, MA, 66; Univ Chicago, PhD(biol), 70. *Prof Exp:* Lectr biol, Harvard Univ, 70; Max-Planck Inst Biol, Tubingen, WGer, 71-72, vis scientist, 73; from asst prof to assoc prof biol, Yale Univ, 73-83. *Res:* Molecular biology of metabolic, central nervous systems and autoimmune diseases. *Mailing Add:* Bayer Res Ctr 400 Morgan Lane West Haven CT 06516

RAE, STEPHEN, ENVIRONMENTAL PHYSICS. *Current Pos:* ASST PROF PHYSICS, WELLS COL, 76- *Personal Data:* b New York, NY, May, 44; m 65. *Educ:* Stevens Inst Technol, BS, 65; Univ Vt, MS, 69, PhD(physics), 73. *Prof Exp:* Eng physicist noise abatement, US Naval Marine Eng Lab, 65-66; anal physicist nuclear reactors, Knolls Atomic Power Lab, 66-67; teaching asst, 69-73, lectr physics, Univ Vt, 75-76. *Concurrent Pos:* Pres sci & tech consult serv, N&R Assoc Inc, 75- *Mem:* Am Asn Physics Teachers; Fedn Am Scientists. *Res:* Application and teaching of physics related to environmental problems, currently in the area of energy; theoretical description of atomic collision processes. *Mailing Add:* Dept Math Sci 1 Wells Col Aurora NY 13026-1100

RAE, WILLIAM J, AERONAUTICAL ENGINEERING, HEAT TRANSFER. *Current Pos:* vis prof, 83-84, res prof, 84-85, PROF, DEPT MECH & AEROSPACE ENG, STATE UNIV NY, BUFFALO, 85- *Personal Data:* b Buffalo, NY, Sept 3, 29; m 57; c 4. *Educ:* Canisius Col, BA, 50; Cornell Univ, PhD(aeronaut eng), 60. *Prof Exp:* Computer, Cornell Aeronaut Lab, Inc, 50-53, jr mathematician, 53-54, jr aerodynamicist, 54-55, res asst, Cornell Univ, 55-59, res aerodynamicist, Cornell Aeronaut Lab, Inc, 59-63, prin aerodynamicist, 63-64; prin res engr, Advan Technol Ctr, Calspan Corp, 64-83. *Concurrent Pos:* Lectr, Medaille Col, 61-67, trustee, 69-76. *Mem:* Am Inst Aeronaut & Astronaut; Sigma Xi; Am Soc Mech Engrs; Nat Soc Prof Engrs. *Res:* Wing-body interference; viscous acoustics; boundary-layer flow; impact-generated shock-wave propagation in solids; low-density flow, environmental fluid mechanics; turbomachinery; computational fluid dynamics. *Mailing Add:* Buffalo Dept Mech Eng State Univ NY Buffalo NY 14260-0001

RAE-GRANT, QUENTIN A, PSYCHIATRY. *Current Pos:* prof & dept chmn, 87-94, EMER PROF PSYCHIAT, UNIV WESTERN ONT, 94- *Personal Data:* b Aberdeen, Scotland, Apr 5, 29; Can citizen; m 55, Naomi Penfold; c Alexander & John. *Educ:* Aberdeen Univ, MB, ChB, 51; Univ London, dipl psychiat med, 58; FRCPsych(C), 71; FRCP(C), 73. *Prof Exp:* Intern med & surg, Aberdeen Univ, 52-53, resident psychiat, 53-54; resident, Maudsley Hosp, London, Eng, 55-58; dir child psychiat, Jewish Hosp, St Louis, Mo, 58-60; instr pediat & psychiat, Univ & psychiatrist, Univ Hosp, Johns Hopkins Univ, 60-61; dir, Ment Health Div, St Louis Co Health Dept, 62-64; chief, Social Psychiat Sect, Community Res & Serv Br, NIMH, 65-66, dir & chief, Ment Health Study Ctr, Md, 66-68; psychiatrist-in-chief, Hosp Sick Children, Toronto, 68-87, hon consult. *Concurrent Pos:* Consult, Sinai Hosp, Baltimore & Rosewood State Hosp, Md, 60-61 & St Louis State Hosp, 62-64; asst prof, Wash Univ, 62-64; lectr, Sch Nursing, St Louis Univ, 62-64; asst prof, Johns Hopkins Univ, 65-68; consult, Clarke Inst Psychiat, 68-, St Michael's Hosp, Toronto, 68-87, assoc prof pediat, 73-81, prof, 81-87; prof & head, Div Child Psychiat, Univ Toronto, 68-87, vchmn, Dept Psychiat, 71-82, prof & chmn, Dept Behav Sci, 84-87; chief examr, Royal Col Physicians & Surgeons, Can, 81-86; chmn, Nucleus Comt Psychiat, Royal Col Physicians & Surgeons Can, 86-92; consult psychiat, Univ Hosp, St Josephs Health Centre, Victoria Hosp, London Psychiat Hosp; Can rep, World Psychiat Asn, 89- *Mem:* Am Psychiat Asn; Am Orthopsychiat Asn; Can Psychiat Asn (pres elect, 81-82, pres, 82-83); Royal Col Psychiat; Can Acad Child Psychiat (pres, 84-86); Can Med Asn; World Psychiat Asn. *Res:* Child and adolescent psychiatry; consultation service; new patterns of psychiatric service; evaluation of health care delivery system effectiveness; prevention of sexual abuse. *Mailing Add:* Dept Psychiat Univ Western Ont London ON N6A 5A5 Can

RAEL, EPPIE DAVID, IMMUNOLOGY, MICROBIOLOGY. *Current Pos:* from asst prof to assoc prof, 75-90, PROF IMMUNOL, UNIV TEX, EL PASO, 90- *Personal Data:* b Cochiti, NMex, Jan 17, 43; m 71; c 2. *Educ:* Univ Albuquerque, BS, 65; NMex Highlands Univ, MS, 70; Univ Ariz, PhD(microbiol), 75. *Prof Exp:* Res asst clin immunol, Med Sch, Univ NMex, 69-71; asst microbiol, Univ Ariz, 71-75. *Concurrent Pos:* Prin investr, Minority Biomed Support, Nat Cancer Inst, 75-77 & Minority Biomed Support, HEW, 77-; prog dir, Minority Biomed Support, 84-90; counr, Coun Undergrad Res. *Mem:* Am Soc Microbiol; AAAS; Sigma Xi; Int Asn Toxinologists; Am Asn Immunologists. *Res:* Monoclonal antibodies; complement; rattlesnake venom. *Mailing Add:* Dept Biol Sci Univ Tex El Paso 500 W University Ave El Paso TX 79968-0519

RAEMER, HAROLD R, PHYSICS, ELECTRICAL ENGINEERING. *Current Pos:* from assoc prof to prof elec eng, 63-93, chmn dept, 67-77, EMER PROF & ADJ PROF, CTR ELECTROMAGNETICS RES, NORTHEASTERN UNIV, 94- *Personal Data:* b Chicago, Ill, Apr 26, 24; m 47, Paulgne Barkin; c Daniel, Liane (Brodsky) & Diane (MacConnell). *Educ:* Northwestern Univ, BS, 48, MS, 49, PhD(physics), 59. *Prof Exp:* Asst math, Ind Univ, 49-50; asst physics, Northwestern Univ, 50-52; physicist, Res Labs, Bendix Aviation Co, Mich, 52-54, sr physicist, 54-55; sr engr, Cook Res Labs, Ill, 55-57, staff engr, 57-60; asst prof elec eng, Ill Inst Technol, 60; sr eng specialist, Appl Res Labs, Sylvania Electronic Systs, Gen Tel & Electronics Corp, 60-63. *Concurrent Pos:* Vis lectr, Harvard Univ, 62, hon res assoc, 72-73; consult, Sylvania Appl Res Labs, 63-71 & US Naval Res Lab, 69-; vis scientist, Mass Inst Technol, 84-85. *Mem:* AAAS; Am Phys Soc; sr mem Inst Elec & Electronics Engrs. *Res:* Electromagnetic radio wave propagation theory; statistical communication theory; plasma physics, particularly wave propagation in plasma; physical mathematics; radar systems theory. *Mailing Add:* Dept Elec & Comput Eng Northeastern Univ 360 Huntington Ave Boston MA 02115. *Fax:* 617-373-8627

RAESE, JOHN THOMAS, AGRONOMY, PLANT PHYSIOLOGY. *Current Pos:* res plant physiologist, Field Lab Tung Invests, La, 63-68, Tung Trees Lab, Fla, 68-71 & Pome Fruit Lab, Wash, 71-73, plant physiologist, 71-89, COOLABR, AGR RES SERV, USDA, WASH, 90- *Personal Data:* b West Chester, Pa, Apr 3, 30; m 53, Joan M Keeney; c John C, David S, Carolyn K & Mary A. *Educ:* WVa Univ, BS, 52, MS, 59; Univ Md, PhD(agron), 63. *Prof Exp:* Instr agron, WVa Univ, 58-59; teacher high sch, Md, 62-63. *Concurrent Pos:* Adj prof, Wenatchee Valley Col, 97. *Mem:* Soc Cryobiol; Am Soc Hort Sci; Sigma Xi. *Res:* Chemical analyses of soils and plant tissues; pasture and forage management; physiological and nutritional studies of the tung tree; plant nutrition, growth regulators, and cold hardiness of pome trees. *Mailing Add:* 1104 N Western Wenatchee WA 98801

RAESIDE, JAMES INGLIS, PHYSIOLOGY. *Current Pos:* prof, 58-91, EMER PROF PHYSIOL, ONT VET COL, UNIV GUELPH, 92- *Personal Data:* b Saskatoon, Sask, May 21, 26; m 54, Margaret McLaren; c David, Janet, William & Marion. *Educ:* Glasgow Univ, BSc, 47; Univ Mo, MS, 50, PhD, 54. *Prof Exp:* Sr lectr animal physiol, NZ, 54-57; res fel, McGill Univ, 57-58. *Concurrent Pos:* Vis scientist, Karolinska Inst, Sweden, 64-65, Weizmann Inst, Israel, 82, INSERM U307, Lyon, France, 87. *Mem:* Can Biochem Soc; Brit Soc Study Fertil; Soc Study Reprod; AAAS. *Res:* Comparative physiology of reproduction; endocrinology; steroid metabolism; hormone assay; animal production and behavior. *Mailing Add:* Dept Biomed Sci Ont Vet Col Univ Guelph Guelph ON N1G 2W1 Can. *Fax:* 519-767-1450; *E-Mail:* jraeside@ovenet.uoguelph.ca

RAETHER, MANFRED, PLASMA PHYSICS. *Current Pos:* res asst prof, Coord Sci Lab, Univ Ill, Urbana, 59-61, assoc prof, Dept Physics & Coord Sci Lab, 61-67, prof, 67-92, assoc head dept, 80-92, EMER PROF PHYSICS, UNIV ILL, URBANA, 92- *Personal Data:* b Stettin, Ger, Jan 22, 27; m 56; c 2. *Educ:* Univ Bonn, Dr rer nat(physics), 58. *Prof Exp:* Asst physics, Univ Bonn, 57-58; res engr, US Army Ballistic Missile Agency, Ala, 58-59. *Mem:* Fel Am Phys Soc. *Res:* Plasma instabilities; plasma turbulence. *Mailing Add:* Dept Physics 215 Loomis Lab Univ Ill 1110 W Green St Urbana IL 61801

RAETZ, CHRISTIAN RUDOLF HUBERT, BIOCHEMISTRY, MEDICINE. *Current Pos:* EXEC DIR, BIOCHEM, MERCK SHARP & DOHME RES LABS, 87- *Personal Data:* b Berlin, Ger, Nov 17, 46; US citizen; m 71; c 2. *Educ:* Yale Univ, BS, 67; Harvard Univ, PhD(biochem) & MD, 73. *Honors & Awards:* Harry & Evelyn Steenbock Award, Univ Wis, 76. *Prof Exp:* House officer, Peter Bent Brigham Hosp, Boston, Mass, 73-74; res assoc, NIH, 74-76; from asst prof to assoc prof, 76-82, prof biochem & dir, ctr membrane biosynthesis res, Univ Wis-Madison, 82-87. *Concurrent Pos:* Life Ins Found med scientist fel, 69-72; sr comn officer student training & extern prog fel, NIH, 72-73; res career develop award, 78-83, mem, physiol chem study sect, 78-81 & biochem study sect, 85; chmn, Membrane Lipid Metab, Gordon Conf, 83; H I Romnes fac fel, Univ Wis, 84. *Mem:* Fel Japanese Soc Prom Sci; Am Soc Biol Chemists. *Res:* Synthesis and function of biological membranes; metabolism of phospholipids; genetics of bacteria and animal cells grown in tissue culture. *Mailing Add:* Dept Biochem Duke Univ Med Ctr Box 3711 Durham NC 27710

RAE-VENTER, BARBARA, BIOCHEMISTRY, MOLECULAR BIOLOGY. *Current Pos:* PARTNER, FISH & RICHARDSON, 93- *Personal Data:* b Auckland, NZ, July 17, 48; US citizen; m 68, 81, 90; c 1. *Educ:* Univ Calif, San Diego, BA, 72, PhD(biol), 76; Univ Tex, Austin, JD, 85. *Prof Exp:* Fel, Roswell Park Mem Inst, 76-77, cancer res scientist II, 77-79; asst prof, Univ Tex Med Br, Galveston, 79-83; law clerk, Davis & Davis, Austin, Tex, 84-85; assoc patent atty, Richard, Harris, Medlock & Andrews, Dallas, 85-86; assoc patent atty, Leydig, Voit & Mayer, Palo Alto, Calif, 86-89; spec coun, Cooley Godward Castro Huddleson & Tatum, Calif, 90-93. *Concurrent Pos:* Vis asst prof, Stanford Univ, 88-90. *Mem:* Endocrine Soc; Am Bar Asn. *Res:* The role of steroid and peptide hormones in tumorigenesis; control of peptide hormone receptor synthesis; elucidation of the subcellular events consequent to peptide hormone receptor binding. *Mailing Add:* PO Box 61016 Palo Alto CA 94306

RAFAJKO, ROBERT RICHARD, VIROLOGY. *Current Pos:* PRES, BIOFLUIDS INC, 75- *Personal Data:* b Chicago, Ill, Sept 3, 31; div; c 6. *Educ:* Coe Col, BA, 53; Univ Iowa, MS, 58, PhD(bact), 60. *Prof Exp:* Res assoc biol, Merck Sharp & Dohme, Inc, Pa, 60-61; virologist, Microbiol Assocs, Inc, Md, 61-66; vpres & gen mgr biol res, Med Res Consults Div, NAm Mogul Prod, Inc, 66-69, dir res & develop, Diag Div, 69-71; dir & vpres res & develop, NAm Biologicals, Inc, 71-74. *Concurrent Pos:* Pres, Tysan Serum, Inc, 74- *Mem:* AAAS; NY Acad Sci; Tissue Cult Asn; Am Soc Microbiol. *Res:* Interferon induction and assay systems; development of killed equine virus vaccine; adenovirus strain differences and relatedness to oncogenicity; adeno-associated viruses; adenovirus induced transformation of mammalian cells; cell growth factors. *Mailing Add:* Biofluids Inc 1146 Taft St Rockville MD 20850

RAFANELLI, KENNETH R, THEORETICAL PHYSICS. *Current Pos:* From asst prof to assoc prof, 64-73, PROF PHYSICS, QUEENS COL, NY, 73- *Personal Data:* b New York, NY, Nov 11, 37; m 61; c 1. *Educ:* Stevens Inst Technol, ME, 58, MS, 60, PhD(physics), 64. *Concurrent Pos:* Consult, TRW Systs, Calif, 65-68. *Mem:* Sigma Xi. *Res:* Theoretical research on the elementary particles. *Mailing Add:* Dept Physics Queens Col City Univ NY Flushing NY 11367. *Fax:* 718-997-3349

RAFELSKI, JOHANN, NUCLEAR & VACUUM STRUCTURE, HEAVY IRON COLLISIONS. *Current Pos:* PROF PHYSICS, UNIV ARIZ, 87- *Personal Data:* b Krakow, Poland, May 19, 50; Ger citizen; m 73, Helga; c Susanne & Marc. *Educ:* Univ Frankfurt, DPhilNat, 73. *Prof Exp:* Sci assoc, Univ Frankfurt, 71-73, assoc prof theoret physics, 79-83; sci assoc, Univ Pa, 73-74; staff, Argonne Nat Lab, 74-78; fel, Cern-Geneva, 77-79; chair theoret physics, Univ Cape Town, 83-87. *Concurrent Pos:* Vis prof, Univ Paris, 93-94. *Mem:* Am Phys Soc; Europ Phys Soc. *Res:* Subnuclear theoretical physics; vacuum structure; nuclear collisions; neural nets. *Mailing Add:* Dept Physics Univ Ariz Tucson AZ 85721

RAFELSON, MAX EMANUEL, JR, BIOCHEMISTRY, MOLECULAR BIOLOGY. *Current Pos:* chmn dept, 61-70, prof biochem, 70-88, EMER PROF & CHMN BIOCHEM, RUSH MED COL, 88-; PROF BIOL CHEM, UNIV ILL COL MED, 60- *Personal Data:* b Detroit, Mich, June 17, 21; m 47, 73, Trudy Hellem; c Mark T & Anne E. *Educ:* Univ Mich, BS, 43; Univ

Southern Calif, PhD(biochem), 51. *Honors & Awards:* Res Award, Sigma Xi, 70; Jane Nugent Cochems Award, 71. *Prof Exp:* From asst prof to assoc prof, 53-60; chmn, Dept Biochem, Presby-St Luke's Hosp, 61-70. *Concurrent Pos:* USPHS res fel, Wenner Grens Inst, Stockholm, Sweden, 51-53; vis prof, Univ Paris, 61, 77-78 & Univ Ulm, 86; assoc dean biol & behav sci & serv, Rush Med Col, 70-72, vpres, mgt info sci, 72-78; vpres, Rush-Presby-St Luke's Med Ctr, 72-78. *Mem:* AAAS; Am Chem Soc; Am Soc Biol Chem; Brit Biochem Soc; Nat Acad Clin Biochem; Soc Chem Biol France. *Res:* Protein chemistry; enzymology; blood; platelets; endothelial cells; prostaglandins; virus structure. *Mailing Add:* Dept Biochem Rush-Presbyterian-St Lukes Med Ctr 2246 N Seminary Chicago IL 60614-3507

RAFF, HERSHEL, NEUROENDOCRINOLOGY, SYSTEMS PHYSIOLOGY. *Current Pos:* DIR ENDOCRINE RES, ST LUKE'S HOSP, MILWAUKEE, 83- *Personal Data:* b Paterson, NJ, May 23, 53; m 76; c 1. *Educ:* Union Col, BA, 75; Johns Hopkins Univ, PhD(physiol), 81. *Prof Exp:* Teaching fel endocrinol, Univ Calif, San Francisco, 80-83. *Concurrent Pos:* Asst prof med & physiol, Med Col Wis, 83- *Mem:* Am Physiol Soc; Endocrine Soc; Sigma Xi. *Res:* Neuroendocrine control; neuroendocrine responses to cardiopulmonary stimuli; control of vasopressin, ACTH and adrenal cortex. *Mailing Add:* Dept Med & Physiol Med Col Wisc 2901 W Kinnickinnic River Pkwy Suite 503 Milwaukee WI 53215-3660

RAFF, HOWARD V, INFECTIOUS DISEASE THERAPY, BIOPROCESS DEVELOPMENT. *Current Pos:* asst prof, 80-90, ASSOC PROF, DEPT MICROBIOL & IMMUNOL, UNIV WASH, SEATTLE, 91-; PROJ MGR, CHIRON CORP, EMERYVILLE, CALIF, 94- *Personal Data:* b Chicago, Ill, Aug 8, 50; c 1. *Educ:* Univ Ill, Urbana, BS, 72; Wash State Univ, MS, 73, PhD, 77. *Prof Exp:* Postdoctoral fel clin immunol, Univ Calif, San Francisco, 77-78, res assoc, Howard Hughes Med Inst, 78-80; assoc dir biol res, Bristol-Myers Squibb, Pharmaceut Res Inst, 91-94. *Concurrent Pos:* Pres bd, Food-Wise Nutrit Serv, Inc, 82-; Am Asn Immunologists travel award, 3rd Int Cong Immunol, Kyoto, Japan, 83; sr res investr, Bristol-Myers Squibb, Pharmaceut Res Inst, 84-90. *Mem:* Am Soc Microbiol; Am Asn Immunologists; Am Asn Lab Animal Sci; AAAS; Am Chem Soc. *Res:* Author of 38 technical publications. *Mailing Add:* Dept Proj Mat Chiron Corp 4560 Horton St Emeryville CA 94608. *Fax:* 206-727-3605

RAFF, LIONEL M, CHEMICAL PHYSICS, PHYSICAL CHEMISTRY. *Current Pos:* from asst prof to prof phys chem, 64-78, REGENTS PROF CHEM, OKLA STATE UNIV, 78- *Personal Data:* b Mich, Nov 4, 34; m 55, Murna J Christofferson; c Aaron M & Debra A (Katcher). *Educ:* Univ Okla, BS, 56, MS, 57; Univ Ill, PhD(phys chem), 62. *Prof Exp:* Chemist, Dow Chem Co, 57; NSF fel, Columbia Univ, 63-64. *Concurrent Pos:* Assoc ed, J Chem Physics, 80-83; Phys Chem Exam Comt, Am Chem Soc, 86-88. *Mem:* Am Chem Soc; Am Phys Soc. *Res:* Classical, quasiclassical, and quantum mechanical scattering calculations of inelastic and reactive gas-phase processes; classical and statistical mechanical studies of gas-surface interactions and of chemical processes under matrix-isolated conditions. *Mailing Add:* Chem Okla State Univ Stillwater OK 74078-0001. *Fax:* 405-744-6007

RAFF, MARTIN JAY, INFECTIOUS DISEASES. *Current Pos:* From asst prof to prof med, 71-80, asst prof microbiol & immunol, 77-86, chief, Div Infectious Dis, 71-92, ASSOC PROF MICROBIOL & IMMUNOL & PROF MED, SCH MED, UNIV LOUISVILLE, 86- *Personal Data:* b Brooklyn, NY, Mar 20, 37; m; c Eric, Lori, Stacy, Jason, Evan & Joshua. *Educ:* Brandeis Univ, BA, 58; Univ Vt, MS, 60; Univ Tex Med Br Galveston, MD, 65; Univ Louisville, JD, 88. *Concurrent Pos:* NIH fel infectious dis, Col Med, Cornell Univ & New York Hosp, 66-67; consult, Vet Admin, Norton Childrens, Audubon, Methodist, Suburban, Baptist East, Sts Mary & Elizabeth, Floyd County & Clark County Hosps, Southwest Hosp, Louisville, KY, 71- & Ireland Army Hosp, Ft Knox, KY, 71-; staff physician, Jewish Hosp, Louisville, Ky & Univ Louisville Hosp, 71-; chief, clin internal med, Univ Louisville, 87-, chmn infection control. *Mem:* Fel Am Col Physicians; fel Infectious Dis Soc Am; Am Soc Microbiol; AAAS; fel Am Col Chest Physicians; fel Am Col Legal Medicine. *Res:* Effects of steroids on the products of bacterial metabolism and on infection in animals; metabolic factors altering humoral and cellular host resistance mechanisms; antibiotic pharmacokinetics and therapeutic efficiency; infections of bones and joints; leukocyte function. *Mailing Add:* Sect Infectious Dis Sch Med Univ Louisville Louisville KY 40292

RAFF, MORTON SPENCER, STATISTICS. *Current Pos:* RETIRED. *Personal Data:* b Chicago, Ill, Jan 12, 23; m 47, Miriam Gore; c Daniel & Michael. *Educ:* Swarthmore Col, BA, 43; Yale Univ, cert, 48; Am Univ, MA, 55. *Prof Exp:* Physicist, US Naval Res Lab, 43-44; physicist & mathematician, US Naval Ord Lab, 44-47; res asst hwy traffic, Yale Univ, 48-49; traffic res engr, Eno Found Hwy Traffic Control, 49-50; mathematician, US Bur Pub Roads, 50-55; math statistician, US Bur Lab Statist, 55-67 & 72-78 & Nat Heart & Lung Inst, 67-72. *Concurrent Pos:* Lectr, Johns Hopkins Univ, 56-59, USDA Grad Sch, 61-70 & Georgetown Univ, 67. *Res:* Medical and labor statistics; seasonal adjustment; probability theory applied to traffic behavior; approximations to the binomial distribution. *Mailing Add:* 3803 Montrose Driveway Chevy Chase MD 20815-4701

RAFF, RUDOLF ALBERT, DEVELOPMENTAL BIOLOGY, EVOLUTION. *Current Pos:* assoc prof biol, 71-80, PROF, DEPT BIOL, IND UNIV, 80-, DIR, IND MOLECULAR BIOL INST, 83- *Personal Data:* b Shawinigan, Que, Nov 10, 41; US citizen; m 65, Elizabeth Craft; c Amanda C & Aaron R. *Educ:* Pa State Univ, BS, 63; Duke Univ, PhD(biochem), 67. *Prof Exp:* Officer, Armed Forces Radiobiol Res Inst, USN, 67-69; fel develop biol, Mass Inst Technol, 69-71. *Concurrent Pos:* Instr-in-chief embryol, Marine Biol Lab, Woods Hole, Mass, 80-82. *Mem:* Soc Develop Biol; Soc Study Evolution. *Res:* Molecular biology of early development; molecular systematics; role of developmental processes in evolution. *Mailing Add:* Dept Biol Ind Univ Jordan Hall Rm 142 Bloomington IN 47405. *Fax:* 812-855-6082; *E-Mail:* rraff@bio.indiana.edu

RAFF, SAMUEL J, OCEAN ACOUSTICS, NAVAL WARFARE. *Current Pos:* CONSULT, JOHNS HOPKINS APPL PHYSICS LAB, 85- *Personal Data:* b New York, NY, Nov 4, 20; m 85, Barbara McKenzie; c Melvin, Brian, Nina, Terri, Sara & Franklin. *Educ:* City Univ NY, BME, 43; Univ Md, MS, 50, PhD(physics), 57. *Prof Exp:* Head staff, USN Undersea Warfare Res & Develop Coun, 62-64; pres, Raff Assocs, 64-74; prog mgr, US NSF, 74-78; pres, Bethesda Corp, 78-86; prof elec eng & computer sci, George Washington Univ, 86-90; ed-in-chief, Int J Computers & Opers Res, 73- *Concurrent Pos:* Ed-in-chief, Int J Computers & Opers Res, 73- *Mem:* Opers Res Soc Am; sr mem Inst Elec & Electronics Engrs; Soc Automotive Engrs. *Res:* Signal processing underwater acoustics and sonar. *Mailing Add:* 8312 Snug Hill Lane Potomac MD 20854. *Fax:* 301-299-3163; *E-Mail:* sraffcor@aol.com

RAFFA, ROBERT B, ANALGESIA, BIOLOGY. *Current Pos:* sr scientist, 90-91, PRIN SCIENTIST, R W JOHNSON PHARMACEUT RES INST, 91- *Personal Data:* b July 24, 48; m 78, Linda Miller; c Jonathan & Kimberlee. *Educ:* Univ Del, BA & BChE, 71; Drexel Univ, MS, 79; Temple Univ, PhD(pharmacol), 82; Thomas Jefferson Univ, MS, 86. *Honors & Awards:* J&J Philip B Hofmann Award Outstanding Sci Achievement. *Prof Exp:* Res asst prof, Jefferson Med Col, 85-86; res scientist, McNeil Pharmaceut, 86-87; res scientist, Janssen Res Found, 87-88, sr scientist, 88-90. *Concurrent Pos:* Adj assoc prof, Dept Pharmacol, Med Sch, Temple Univ; adj asst prof, Dept Pharmacol, Jefferson Med Col; co-ed, Pharmacol Lett; Nat Res Serv awards, 83 & 84. *Mem:* Soc Neurosci; Am Soc Pharmacol & Exp Therapeut. *Res:* Author of more than 80 technical publications. *Mailing Add:* R W Johnson Pharmaceut Res Inst Welsh & McKean Rds Spring House PA 19477-0776. *Fax:* 215-628-2452

RAFFAUF, ROBERT FRANCIS, ORGANIC CHEMISTRY. *Current Pos:* prof, 69-84, EMER PROF PHARMACOG, COL PHARM, NORTHEASTERN UNIV, 84- *Personal Data:* b Buffalo, NY, Jan 8, 16; m 50, Heidi Jenni; c Martin & Mark. *Educ:* City Col New York, BS, 36; Columbia Univ, MA, 37; Univ Minn, PhD(org chem), 44. *Prof Exp:* Anal chemist, Tex Co, NY, 38-40; asst org chem, Univ Minn, 42-44; sr res chemist, Eaton Labs, Inc, NY, 44-47; asst, Univ Zurich, 47; res asst, Univ Basel, 47-48, fel, 49; res chemist, Nat Drug Co, 50-51; res assoc, Smith Kline & French Labs, 51-53; sr chemist, 53, lit scientist, 54-69. *Concurrent Pos:* Prof, Harvard Univ Exten, 77-85; res assoc, Bot Mus, Harvard Univ, 80-; vis prof, Univ PR, 81-82, Nat Polytech Inst, Mex; consult, Shaman Pharmaceut, Inc, South San Francisco, Calif. *Mem:* Fel AAAS; Am Chem Soc; Swiss Chem Soc. *Res:* Natural products. *Mailing Add:* Col Pharm Northeastern Univ Boston MA 02115

RAFFEL, JACK I, INTEGRATED CIRCUITS. *Current Pos:* Res asst digital comput lab, 52-54, staff mem, Lincoln Lab, 54-62, GROUP LEADER, LINCOLN LAB, MASS INST TECHNOL, 62- *Personal Data:* b New York, NY, Apr 1, 30; m 59; c 2. *Educ:* Columbia Univ, AB, 51, BS, 52; Mass Inst Technol, MS, 54. *Mem:* Inst Elec & Electronics Engrs. *Res:* Digital computer research and development; design and fabrication of very large-scale integrated circuits. *Mailing Add:* 23 Eliot Rd Lexington MA 02173

RAFFEL, SIDNEY, MEDICAL BACTERIOLOGY, IMMUNOLOGY. *Current Pos:* RETIRED. *Personal Data:* b Baltimore, Md, Aug 24, 11; m 38; c 5. *Educ:* Johns Hopkins Univ, AB, 30, ScD(immunol), 33; Stanford Univ, MD, 43. *Prof Exp:* Asst immunol, Sch Hyg & Pub Health, Johns Hopkins Univ, 33-35; from asst to assoc prof, Sch Med, Stanford Univ, 35-48, consult physician, Student Health Serv, 42-44, prof bact & exp path, Sch Med, 48-76, chmn dept med microbiol, 53-76, actg dean, 64-65, emer chmn dept med microbiol, 76-80, emer prof dermat, 77-80. *Concurrent Pos:* Guggenheim fel, 49-50; lab dir, Palo Alto Hosp, 45-47; consult, Vet Admin, 47-71; chmn study sect allergy & immunol, NIH, 56-59, mem training grant comt, 60-84. *Mem:* Am Soc Microbiol; Am Soc Exp Path; Am Thoracic Soc; Am Asn Immunol; Sigma Xi. *Res:* Immunology of tuberculosis; hypersensitivity; cellular immunity. *Mailing Add:* 770 Santa Ynez St Stanford CA 94305-8441

RAFFELSON, HAROLD, PHARMACEUTICAL CHEMISTRY, ORGANIC CHEMISTRY. *Current Pos:* RETIRED. *Personal Data:* b Sheboygan, Wis, Oct 29, 20; m 48; c 1. *Educ:* Univ Wis, BS, 47; Univ Mich, PhD(pharmaceut chem), 51. *Prof Exp:* Org res chemist, Frederick Stearns & Co, 47; res chemist, Monsanto Co, 51-59, group leader, 59-61, res specialist, 61-73, sr res specialist, 73-85. *Concurrent Pos:* Consult, 85- *Mem:* Am Chem Soc. *Res:* Synthetic antispasmodics; steroid synthesis; organo-phosphorus compounds; process development; catalysis. *Mailing Add:* Seven Planters Dr Olivette MO 63132-3441

RAFFENETTI, RICHARD CHARLES, SOFTWARE SYSTEMS, ORACLE DATABASE ADMINISTRATION. *Current Pos:* asst chemist quantum chem, Chem Div, 76-79, COMPUT SCIENTIST, ELECTRONICS COMPUT TECHNOL DIV, ARGONNE NAT LAB, 79- *Personal Data:* b Springfield, Mass, Oct 15, 42; m 78, Mimi A Coconato; c 2. *Educ:* Tufts Univ, BS, 64; Iowa State Univ, PhD(phys chem), 71. *Honors & Awards:* Pacesetter Award. *Prof Exp:* Res assoc quantum chem, Battelle Mem Inst, 71-73 & Johns Hopkins Univ, 73-74; vis scientist quantum chem, Inst Comput Applns Sci & Eng, NASA Langley Res Ctr, 74-76. *Concurrent Pos:* Consult, VMS

Comput Syst. *Mem:* Sigma Xi. *Res:* Virtual Address Extension and Virtual Memory Operating Systems computing service project management and systems management and Virtual Address Extension cluster management; design and maintenance of networking applications software; system configuration and analysis; VAX/VMS system management. *Mailing Add:* 817 Columbia Lane Darien IL 60561. *E-Mail:* rraffenetti@anl.gov

RAFFENSPERGER, EDGAR M, ENTOMOLOGY. *Current Pos:* assoc prof, 61-77, PROF ENTOM, CORNELL UNIV, 77- *Personal Data:* b Gettysburg, Pa, June 13, 26; m 53; c 3. *Educ:* Pa State Univ, BS, 51, MS, 52; Univ Wis, PhD(entom), 55. *Prof Exp:* From asst prof to assoc prof entom, Va Polytech Inst, 55-61. *Concurrent Pos:* Vis scientist, Norweg Agr Res Coun, Vollebekk, Norway, 68-69; lectr, Univ Oslo, 69; consult, stored prod insect control & arthropod pests in indust sites; instr trop insects, Insect Pop Mgt Res Unit, USDA, Kenya, Latin Am. *Mem:* AAAS; Entom Soc Am. *Res:* Taxonomy of Diptera and Mallophaga; insect transmission of fowl diseases; pesticides in agriculture; teaching in general entomology and cultural entomology; insect morphology and control; control of stored products insects; insect integrated pest management; management of the clusterfly (pollenia rudis). *Mailing Add:* 139 Pine Tree Rd Ithaca NY 14850

RAFFENSPERGER, EDWARD COWELL, GASTROENTEROLOGY. *Current Pos:* Instr gastroenterol, Grad Sch Med, 48-58, assoc, Sch Med, 53-62, from asst prof to assoc prof, 62-71, PROF MED, SCH MED, UNIV PA, 71- *Personal Data:* b Dickinson, Pa, July 9, 14; m 49. *Educ:* Dickinson Col, BS, 36; Univ Pa, MD, 40. *Concurrent Pos:* Res fel gastroenterol, Grad Hosp, Univ Pa, 46-48; consult, Vet Admin Hosp, Philadelphia & Polyclin Hosp, Harrisburg, 62-, Children's Hosp, Philadelphia, 64- & Lankenau Hosp, 69- *Mem:* Am Gastroenterol Asn; Am Fedn Clin Res. *Res:* Amino acids in nutrition; inflammatory bowel diseases. *Mailing Add:* 290 St James Pl Philadelphia PA 19106

RAFFERTY, KEEN ALEXANDER, JR, EMBRYOLOGY, CELL CULTURE. *Current Pos:* head dept, 70-77, prof, dept anat, 70-88, EMER PROF ANAT & CELL BIOL, UNIV ILL MED CTR, 88- *Personal Data:* b Robinson, Ill, Mar 6, 26; m 53, Nancy Schwarz; c Burns A & Katherine L. *Educ:* Univ NMex, BS, 50; Univ Ill, MS, 51, PhD(zool), 55. *Prof Exp:* Asst zool, Univ Ill, 50-54; instr microbiol, Yale Univ, 57-58; from asst prof to assoc prof anat, Sch Med, Johns Hopkins Univ, 58-70. *Concurrent Pos:* NIH fel microbiol, Yale Univ, 55-57; Fogarty sr fel, 77-78; libr reader, Marine Biol Lab, Woods Hole, Mass, 95- *Res:* Cellular differentiation and aging of cultured cells. *Mailing Add:* 59 Harbor Hill Rd Woods Hole MA 02543-1219

RAFFERTY, NANCY S, CELL BIOLOGY, ANATOMY. *Current Pos:* RETIRED. *Personal Data:* b New York, NY, June 11, 30; m 53, Keen A; c Burns Arthur & Katherine Louisa. *Educ:* Queens Col, NY, BS, 52; Univ Ill, MS, 53, PhD(zool), 58. *Prof Exp:* From instr to asst prof anat, Johns Hopkins Univ, 63-70; from asst prof to assoc prof, Northwestern Univ, 72-76, prof anat, Med & Dent Sch, 76-94, scientist, Marine Biol Lab, 91-94. *Concurrent Pos:* NIH res fel, Johns Hopkins Univ, 58-60, fel anat, Sch Med, 60-63; NIH res grants, Johns Hopkins Univ, 65-71 & Northwestern Univ, 70-; mem, VISA study sect, 78-82; vis prof, Guy's Hosp, London, UK, 77-78 & 88-89. *Mem:* AAAS; Asn Res Vision & Ophthal; Am Asn Anat; Fedn Am Socs Exp Biol; Int Soc Eye Res; Sigma Xi. *Res:* Experimental cataract; wound healing; cell population kinetics; electron microscopy of lens; cellular dynamics of the proliferative response in injured frog, mouse and squirrel lens epithelium; etiology of senile cataract; lens aging; mechanism of lens accommodation; cytoskeleton of lens cells. *Mailing Add:* Marine Biol Lab 59 Harbor Hill Rd Woods Hole MA 02543-1219. *E-Mail:* kraff.rol.com

RAFFERTY, TERENCE DAMIEN, CARDIAC ANESTHESIA, TRANSESOPHAGEAL ECHOCARDIOGRAPHY. *Current Pos:* from asst prof to assoc prof, 77-93, PROF ANESTHESIOL, YALE UNIV, SCH MED, 93- *Personal Data:* b Dublin, Ireland, Nov 9, 47; US citizen; m 72, Jacinta Power; c Deirdre, Colm & Sinead. *Educ:* Nat Univ Ireland, MB BCh BAO, 72, MD, 83. *Hon Degrees:* MA, Yale Univ, 94. *Honors & Awards:* Bird Respiratory Care Award, Am Asn Respiratory Ther, 80. *Prof Exp:* Instr anesthesiol, Harvard Med Sch, 76-77. *Concurrent Pos:* Jr assoc anesthesia, Peter Bent Brigham Hosp, 76-77; assoc, Yale-New Haven Hosp, 77-79, attending, 79- *Mem:* Am Soc Anesthesiologists; Int Anesthesia Res Soc; fel Am Col Angiol; fel Int Col Angiol; hon mem Int Soc Study Hypertension Pregnancy; Soc Cardiovasc Aneshtesiologists. *Res:* Transesophageal two-dimensional echocardiographic and saline-contrast evaluation of cardiac function; color flow doppler evaluation of valvular dysfunction; estimation of thermodilution right ventricular ejection fraction; definition of transcutaneous-arterial oxygen and carbon dioxide tension relationships. *Mailing Add:* 17 E Wharf Rd Madison CT 06443-3117

RAFLA, SAMEER, RADIATION MEDICINE, ONCOLOGY. *Current Pos:* DIR RADIATION THER, METHODIST HOSP, 69-; DIR RADIOTHER, LUTHERAN MED CTR, 77-; DIR RADIOTHER, MAIMONIDES MED CTR, 79-; MED DIR CANCER, NY INST BROOKLYN, 90-; CHMN RADIATION ONCOL, 96- *Personal Data:* b Cairo, Egypt, Sept 3, 30; m 65; c 5. *Educ:* Univ Cairo, BS, 47, MB & BCh, 53; London Univ, PhD(radiation med), 70. *Concurrent Pos:* Radiotherapist, Manitoba Cancer Found, 67-69; prin investr, Cancer & Leukemia Group B, State Univ, NY, Downstate, Oncol Prog, Brooklyn Community Hosp, Nat Cancer Inst, Continuing Ed Radiotherapists, Am Cancer Soc Grant; clin prof radiation oncol, Downstate Med Ctr, State Univ NY, 81-; dir radiother, Wyckhoff Heights, 93-96. *Mem:* Am Radium Soc; Royal Col Radiol; Am Soc Therapeut Radiologists; Soc Surg Oncol; Radiol Soc NAm. *Res:* The effect of radiation on the malignant and normal cell as well as its possible effect on the immune response; the treatment of certain cancers especially head and neck, kidney and lymphoma. *Mailing Add:* NY Methodist Hosp 506 Sixth St Brooklyn NY 11215

RAFOLS, JOSE ANTONIO, ANATOMY. *Current Pos:* From instr to asst prof, 70-73, ASSOC PROF ANAT, SCH MED, WAYNE STATE UNIV, 73- *Personal Data:* b Guantanamo, Cuba, July 7, 43; US citizen. *Educ:* St Procopius Col, BS, 65; Univ Kans, PhD(anat), 69. *Concurrent Pos:* NIH trainee, Cajal Inst, Madrid, Spain, 71. *Mem:* AAAS; Pan-Am Asn Anat. *Res:* Golgi and electron microscopic analysis of the mammalian visual system and basal ganglia. *Mailing Add:* Dept Anat & Cell Biol Sch Med Wayne State Univ 540 E Canfield Ave Detroit MI 48201

RAFTER, GALE WILLIAM, BIOCHEMISTRY. *Current Pos:* assoc prof, 65-71, PROF BIOCHEM, SCH MED, WVA UNIV, 71- *Personal Data:* b Seattle, Wash, Nov 3, 25; m 57; c 3. *Educ:* Univ Wash, BS, 48, PhD(biochem), 53. *Prof Exp:* Asst prof biochem, Sch Hyg & Pub Health, Johns Hopkins Univ, 55-59, asst prof microbiol, Sch Med, 59-65. *Concurrent Pos:* Fel, McCollum-Pratt Inst, Johns Hopkins Univ, 53-55. *Mem:* Am Soc Biol Chem; Hist Sci Soc. *Res:* Mode of action of antirheumatic drugs; role of protein sulfhydryl groups in action of enzymes. *Mailing Add:* Dept Biochem WVa Univ Sch Med Morgantown WV 26506-9142

RAFTOPOULOS, DEMETRIOS D, ENGINEERING MECHANICS, BIOENGINEERING & BIOMEDICAL ENGINEERING. *Current Pos:* from assoc prof to prof mech eng, 73-93, SUPER ANNUATE EMER PROF BIOENG, UNIV TOLEDO, 93- *Personal Data:* b Argostolion, Greece, May 30, 26; US citizen; m 59, Eugenia Mallas; c Michael J. *Educ:* Widener Univ, BSCE, 59; Univ Del, MCE, 63; Pa State Univ, PhD(eng mech), 66. *Honors & Awards:* Outstanding Sigma Xi Serv Award, 81, Sigma Xi Outstanding Res Award, 83; Plato Award, Am Hellinic Educ Progressive Asn, 84. *Prof Exp:* Sr engr, Del State Hwy Dept, 59-61; instr eng, PMC Cols, 61-64; res asst eng mech, Pa State Univ, 64-67. *Concurrent Pos:* Jr investr, Ballistic Res Lab, Aberdeen Proving Ground, Md, 64-67, proj dir, 67-68; prin investr, Naval Res Labs, Washington, DC, 67-69 & AEC, Md, 68-71; reviewer, Appl Mech Res, 69-; vis prof mech, Nat Tech Univ Athens, 73-74 & Univ Mich, Ann Arbor, 86-87; Fulbright Award, 95. *Mem:* Am Soc Eng Educ; Am Soc Civil Engrs; fel Am Soc Mech Engrs; Am Acad Mech; Sigma Xi; Orthop Res Soc. *Res:* Elasto-plastic stress waves; analysis of foundation interaction with nuclear power plants during earthquake loading; structure interaction with underwater shock waves; fracture mechanics; bio-mechanics. *Mailing Add:* 2801 W Bancroft St Univ Toledo Toledo OH 43606. *Fax:* 419-530-8076

RAFUSE, ROBERT P(ENDLETON), ELECTRICAL ENGINEERING. *Current Pos:* mem staff, 75-78, MEM SR STAFF, LINCOLN LAB, MASS INST TECHNOL, 78- *Personal Data:* b Newton, Mass, Dec 7, 32; div; c 2. *Educ:* Tufts Col, BSEE, 54; Mass Inst Technol, SM, 57, ScD(elec eng), 60. *Prof Exp:* Teaching asst elec eng, Mass Inst Technol, 54-57, instr, Res Lab Electronics, 57-60, from asst prof to assoc prof, 60-70; pres, Rafuse Assocs, 70-75. *Concurrent Pos:* Adv, NASA, NIH & Dept Defense, 54-66; Consult to many govt & indust orgns; mem, Nat Defense Exec Reserve, 69-, vchmn gov's comn emergency commun, Commonwealth Mass, 70-, mem gov's energy emergency comn, 71; chmn, Nat Acad Sci-Nat Res Coun eval panel for Nat Bur Standards-EMD, 72-78. *Mem:* AAAS; Soc Am Mil Engrs; Inst Elec & Electronics Engrs; Am Defense Preparedness Asn. *Res:* Sensor systems; microwave solid state circuits; space communications; management of energy resources. *Mailing Add:* 167 Willow Rd Nahant MA 01908

RAGAINI, RICHARD CHARLES, ENVIRONMENTAL PROTECTION. *Current Pos:* chemist, Lawrence Livermore Nat Lab, 71-75, sect leader, Radiochem Div, 75-77, dept div leader, 77-81, actg div leader, Environ Sci Div, 81-82, assoc div leader, Mech Eng Dept, 82-86, dept head, Environ Protection Dept, 86-90, assoc dept head environ protection res & develop, 90-94, SR SCIENTIST, LAWRENCE LIVERMORE NAT LAB, 95- *Personal Data:* b Danbury, Conn, Feb 7, 42; div; c Karen Ann & Christine Lynn. *Educ:* Clark Univ, BA, 63; Mass Inst Technol, PhD(nuclear chem), 67. *Prof Exp:* Fel radiochem, Los Alamos Sci Lab, 67-69; res assoc chem, Brookhaven Nat Lab, 69-70; asst prof chem, Wash State Univ, 70-71. *Concurrent Pos:* Course dir, Innovative Cleanup Contaminated Soils & Groundwater, Ettore Majorana Ctr Sci Cult, Erice, Sicily, 90, 92 & 95. *Mem:* Am Physics Soc; Am Chem Soc; Sigma Xi; fel Am Nuclear Soc. *Res:* Effects of trace elements and organics in the environment; methods for trace element and organic analysis; trace elements and organics from energy production; developing innovative technologies for characterization and cleaning up contaminated soil and groundwater. *Mailing Add:* L-626 Lawrence Livermore Lab Livermore CA 94550. *Fax:* 510-423-9987; *E-Mail:* rragaini@llnl.gov

RAGAN, CHARLES ELLIS, III, NUCLEAR PHYSICS. *Current Pos:* STAFF MEM NUCLEAR PHYSICS, LOS ALAMOS NAT LAB, 72- *Personal Data:* b Charleston, SC, Oct 19, 44; div; c 2. *Educ:* The Citadel, BS, 66; Duke Univ, PhD(nuclear physics), 71. *Prof Exp:* Res assoc nuclear physics, NC State Univ, 70; physicist, USAF Weapons Lab, 70-72. *Mem:* Am Phys Soc; Sigma Xi. *Res:* Precise equation-of-state measurements at pressures of 10-100 mega-bar using shock waves produced by underground nuclear explosions; nuclear physics experiments using neutrons produced by reactors, Van de Graaff linear accelerators, computer graphics and animation of 3-D data; nuclear explosions. *Mailing Add:* MS B226 Group XTM Los Alamos Sci Lab PO Box 1663 Los Alamos NM 87545

RAGAN, DONAL MACKENZIE, STRUCTURAL GEOLOGY, ENGINEERING GEOLOGY. *Current Pos:* assoc prof, 67-70, PROF GEOL, ARIZ STATE UNIV, 70- *Personal Data:* b Los Angeles, Calif, Oct 4, 29; m 52; c 2. *Educ:* Occidental Col, BA, 51; Univ Southern Calif, MS, 54; Univ Wash, PhD(geol), 61; Univ London, DIC, 69. *Prof Exp:* From instr to assoc prof geol, Univ Alaska, 60-67. *Concurrent Pos:* NSF res grants, 64-66;

fac fel, Imp Col, London, 66-67. *Mem:* AAAS; Int Soc Rock Mech; Am Geophys Union; fel Geol Soc Am; fel Geol Soc London; Sigma Xi. *Res:* Structural geology; engineering geology. *Mailing Add:* Dept Geol Ariz State Univ Tempe AZ 85287-1404

RAGAN, HARVEY ALBERT, TOXICOLOGY & HEMATOLOGY, RADIOBIOLOGY. *Current Pos:* sr res scientist hemat, Battelle Mem Inst, 69-72, staff scientist hemat, 72-77, mgr, Exp Path Sect, Pac Northwest Labs, 77-91, MGR, TOXICOL DEPT, BATTELLE MEM INST, 91- *Personal Data:* b Boise, Idaho, July 11, 29; m 51, Carma Bigler; c Daryl S, Jennie L & Kari A. *Educ:* Wash State Univ, BS, 56, DVM, 59; Am Bd Toxicol, dipl. *Prof Exp:* Pvt pract, 59-62; scientist radiobiol, Hanford Labs, Gen Elec Co, 62-65; res scientist radiobiol, Pac Northwest Labs, Battelle Mem Inst, 65-66, sr res scientist radiotoxicol, 66-67; NIH spec fel exp hemat, Col Med, Univ Utah, 67-69. *Concurrent Pos:* Mem, Nat Coun Radiation Protection, 78-; adj prof, Joint Ctr Grad Studies, 81- *Mem:* Am Soc Vet Clin Path (pres 81-82); Int Soc Animal Biochem; Am Soc Hemat. *Res:* Effects of chemical and physical insults on the hematopoietic system; carcinogenesis; blood cell kinetics; immunology; iron metabolism; clinical pathology; inhalation toxicology. *Mailing Add:* 1616 Butternut Ave Richland WA 99352. *Fax:* 509-325-3701

RAGAN, MARK ADAIR, PROTISTOLOGY, MARINE BIOLOGY. *Current Pos:* res assoc, Inst Marine Biosci, Nat Res Coun Can, NS, 78-80, asst res officer, 80-83, assoc res officer, 83-88, SR RES OFFICER, INST MARINE BIOSCI, NAT RES COUN CAN, 88- *Personal Data:* b Kokomo, Ind, July 1, 50; m 87, Chikako Oki; c Alicia M & Wesley M. *Educ:* Univ Chicago, BA, 72; Dalhousie Univ, PhD(biol), 76. *Prof Exp:* NATO fel, Inst Marine Biochem, Trondheim, Norway, 76-78. *Concurrent Pos:* Vis lectr, Acad Sinica, China, 83 & USSR Acad Sci, 90; guest prof, Inst Pharmaceut Biol, Univ Bonn, Ger, 84; co-ed, Appl Phycol Forum, 88-92; hon res assoc, Dept Biol, Dalhousie Univ, 89-93, hon adj prof, 93- *Mem:* Int Seaweed Asn (pres, 92-95); Int Soc Evolutionary Prostistology (pres, 94-96); fel Can Inst Advan Res; fel Linnean Soc London. *Res:* Gene structure and evolution of marine algae and other protists; theoretical phylogenetics; sequencing the genome of the thermophilic archaebacterium Sulfolobus solfataricus. *Mailing Add:* Nat Res Coun Inst Marine Biosci 1411 Oxford St Halifax NS B3H 3Z1 Can. *Fax:* 902-426-9413; *E-Mail:* mark.ragan@nrc.ca

RAGAN, ROBERT MALCOLM, HYDROLOGY. *Current Pos:* assoc prof, 67-68, head dept, 69-76, PROF CIVIL ENG, UNIV MD, COL PARK, 69- *Personal Data:* b San Antonio, Tex, Dec 19, 32; m 55; c 3. *Educ:* Va Mil Inst, BS, 55; Mass Inst Technol, MS, 59; Cornell Univ, PhD(civil eng), 65. *Prof Exp:* Designer, Whitman Requardt & Assocs, Md, 56-57; res asst sanit eng, Mass Inst Technol, 57-59; from asst prof to assoc prof, Univ Vermont, 59-67. *Mem:* Am Soc Civil Engrs; Am Geophys Union. *Res:* Watershed hydrology. *Mailing Add:* Dept Civil Eng Univ Md College Park MD 20742-0001

RAGENT, BORIS, PHYSICS. *Current Pos:* SR RES ASSOC, SAN JOSE STATE UNIV FOUND, 87- *Personal Data:* b Cleveland, Ohio, Mar 2, 24; m 49; c 3. *Educ:* Marquette Univ, BEE, 44; Univ Calif, Berkeley, PhD(physics), 54. *Prof Exp:* Engr electronics, Victoreen Instrument Co, Cleveland, 46-48; engr & res scientist electronics & physics, Radiation Lab, Univ Calif, Berkeley, 48-53, res scientist physics, Livermore, 53-56; res scientist, Broadview Res Corp, Burlingame, 56-59; staff scientist, Vidya Div, Itek Corp, Palo Alto, 59-66; chief electronic instrument develop br, 66-80, sr staff scientist, Space Sci Div, Ames Res Ctr, NASA, 80-87. *Concurrent Pos:* Lectr, Stanford Univ, 62 & 79. *Mem:* Am Phys Soc; AAAS. *Res:* Nuclear physics; instrumentation; plasma physics; planetary atmospherics. *Mailing Add:* NASA Ames Res Ctr Moffett Field CA 94035

RAGEP, F JAMIL, ISLAMIC SCIENCE, HISTORY OF ASTRONOMY. *Current Pos:* asst prof, 90-93, ASSOC PROF HIST SCI, UNIV OKLA, 93- *Personal Data:* b WVa, June 19, 50; m 73, Sally Palchik; c Anwar & Lina. *Educ:* Univ Mich, BA, 72, MA, 73; Harvard Univ, PhD(hist sci), 82. *Prof Exp:* Instr math, Long Island Univ, 82; instr hist sci, Stonehill Col, 89; asst prof hist sci, Brown Univ, 89-90. *Concurrent Pos:* Lectr hist sci, Harvard Univ, 83-84 & 87-88. *Mem:* Hist Sci Soc. *Res:* History of ancient, medieval and early modern science, particularly in the way ancient astronomy was transformed in Islam and the repercussions of this for subsequent astronomy. *Mailing Add:* Dept Hist Sci Rm 622 Univ Okla 601 Elm Norman OK 73019-0315. *Fax:* 405-325-2213; *E-Mail:* jragep@uoknor.edu

RAGHAVA, RAM S, INTERFACES IN TWO PHASE MATERIALS. *Current Pos:* POLYMER SCIENTIST, AUTOMOTIVE COMPONENTS DIV, FORD MOTOR CO, 90- *Personal Data:* m 76, Kasuma Rani Singh; c Swasti & Smit. *Educ:* Univ Mich, PhD(mech eng), 72. *Prof Exp:* Lectr & postdoctoral fel, Univ Mich, 72-73; mat engr, Am Cyanamid Co, 73-78, Kelsey Hayes Res & Develop, 78-81; sr scientist, Westinghouse Res & Develop Ctr, 81-86; sr res & develop assoc, BF Goodrich Res & Develop Ctr, 86-89. *Mem:* Soc Plastics Engrs; Soc Automotive Engrs. *Res:* Polymer composites and polymer blends, with emphasis on interphase tailoring; polymer deformation and fracture; patentee in field. *Mailing Add:* 3118 Fawnmeadow Ct Ann Arbor MI 48105

RAGHAVACHARI, KRISHNAN, ELECTRONIC STRUCTURE OF MATERIALS, SEMICONDUCTOR CLUSTERS. *Current Pos:* DISTINGUISHED MEM TECH STAFF, MAT SCI, BELL LABS, MURRAY HILL, NJ, 81- *Personal Data:* b Madras, India, Apr 3, 53; m 78, Akola Krishnan; c Ranjani & Meera. *Educ:* Madras Univ, India, BSc, 73; Indian Inst Technol, MSc, 75; Carnegie-Mellon Univ, PhD(chem), 80. *Mem:* Am Chem Soc; Am Physics Soc. *Res:* Development and application of new molecular orbital methods in quantum chemistry; theoretical study of atomic and molecular clusters; electronic structure of materials. *Mailing Add:* Bell Labs 1A 362 700 Mountain Ave Murray Hill NJ 07974-2008. *Fax:* 908-582-3958; *E-Mail:* krish@allwise.att.com

RAGHAVAN, PRAMILA, SOLAR NEUTRINOS, NUCLEAR PROPERTIES & HYPERFINE INTERACTIONS. *Current Pos:* RESIDENT VISITOR, BELL LABS, 72- *Personal Data:* b Bangalore, India; US citizen; m 67. *Educ:* Univ Mysore, India, BSc, 54, MSc, 56; Saha Inst, Univ Calcutta, India, assoc dipl, 58; Mass Inst Technol, PhD(physics), 67. *Prof Exp:* Lectr, Univ Mysore, India, 54-55 & 56-57; res assoc, Tata Inst Fundamental Res, India, 58-61; commonwealth scholar, Nuclear Physics Lab, Oxford Univ, 61-62; res asst, Mass Inst Technol, 62-67; guest prof, Univ Munchen, WGer, 67-69; asst, Technol Univ Munich, WGer, 70-72; fel, Rutgers Univ, 72-80, res assoc physics, 80-85, res prof, 85-87. *Mem:* Am Phys Soc. *Res:* Nuclear structure; nuclear moments using radioactivity and nuclear reactions; interaction of nuclei with its environment; hyperfine interactions; applications to solid state physics, atomic physics and material science; solar neutrino detection. *Mailing Add:* 54 Rutherford Rd Berkeley Heights NJ 07922. *E-Mail:* pram@physics.alt.com

RAGHAVAN, RAJAGOPAL, PETROLEUM ENGINEERING. *Current Pos:* SR STAFF ASSOC RESERVOIR ENG, PHILLIPS PETROL CO, 90- *Personal Data:* b Tiruchirappalli, India, July 26, 43. *Educ:* Birla Inst Technol, Mesra, India, BSc, 66; Univ Birmingham, dipl, 67; Stanford Univ, PhD(petrol & mech eng), 70. *Honors & Awards:* Distinguished Fac Award, Soc Petrol Engrs, 81, Reservoir Eng Award, 88. *Prof Exp:* Res assoc petrol eng, Stanford Univ, 70-71, asst prof, 71-72; sr res engr, Amoco Prod Co, 72-75; from assoc prof to prof, Univ Tulsa, 75-80, prof, 80-82, Mcman prof, 82-89; Adams prof, Tex A&M, 89-90. *Concurrent Pos:* Tech ed, Soc Petrol Engrs, 78-79 & 80-82, distinguished lectr, 90. *Mem:* Soc Petrol Engrs; assoc fel Brit Inst Petrol; NY Acad Sci; Sigma Xi; Am Geophys Union. *Res:* Unsteady state fluid flow and heat transfer in porous media, including well test analysis, stability of liquid interfaces, compaction and subsidence, geothermal energy and application of computers. *Mailing Add:* Phillips Petrol Co 232 GB Bartlesville OK 74004. *Fax:* 918-662-5304; *E-Mail:* rara@ppco.com

RAGHAVAN, RAMASWAMY SRINIVASA, NEUTRINO ASTROPHYSICS, NUCLEAR PHYSICS. *Current Pos:* mem staff, 72-89, DISTINGUISHED MEM STAFF PHYSICS, AT&T BELL LABS, 89- *Personal Data:* b Tanjore, India, Mar 31, 37; m 67, Pramila. *Educ:* Univ Madras, India, MA, 57, MSc, 58; Purdue Univ, PhD(physics), 65. *Prof Exp:* Res asst, Tata Inst Fundamental Res, 59-62 & Purdue Univ, 62-65; fel, Bartol Res Found, 65-66; vis prof, Univ Bonn, Ger, 66-67; res assoc, Tech Univ, Munich, 67-72. *Concurrent Pos:* Assoc grad fac, Rutgers Univ, 74- *Mem:* Fel Am Phys Soc. *Res:* Neutrino physics; detection of solar neutrinos; nuclear electronics and detector hardware; nuclear structure; nuclear interactions with matter; solid state physics; application of nuclear techniques to microelectronics device technology. *Mailing Add:* AT&T Bell Labs 600 Mountain Ave 1E 432 Murray Hill NJ 07974. *Fax:* 908-582-4228; *E-Mail:* raju@physics.att.com

RAGHAVAN, SRINIVASA, BIOCHEMISTRY. *Current Pos:* RES ASST PROF, DEPT NEUROL, NY UNIV, MED CTR, 91- *Personal Data:* b Madras, India, July 1, 40; nat US; m 77, Vijaya; c 2. *Educ:* Univ Madras, India, BSc, 60, MSc, 63; Indian Inst Sci, PhD(biochem), 70. *Prof Exp:* Res fel, Mass Gen Hosp, Boston, 70-73; res assoc, E K Shriver Ctr, Mass, 73-74, sr res fel, 74-77, sr res assoc, 77-78, asst biochemist, 78-82, assoc biochemist, 82-91. *Concurrent Pos:* Asst biochemist, neurol res, Mass Gen Hosp, 79-87, assoc biochemist, 88- *Mem:* Am Soc Neurochem. *Res:* Inherited neurological diseases of glycorphingolipid metabolism resulting from genetic deficiency of specific lysosomal hydrolases; animal models to understand the function of glycolipids in cell development differentiation myclination and demyelination in the nervous system. *Mailing Add:* 92 Princess Dr New Brunswick NJ 08902. *Fax:* 212-263-7721

RAGHAVAN, THIRUKKANNAMANGAI E S, MATHEMATICS, GAME THEORY. *Current Pos:* from asst prof to assoc prof, 69-79, PROF MATH, UNIV ILL, CHICAGO CIRCLE, 79- *Personal Data:* b Madras, India, Aug 5, 40; m 67, Usha; c Deepa, Tara & Ramanujan. *Educ:* Loyola Col, Madras, India, BSc, 60; Presidency Col, Madras, India, MSc, 62; Indian Statist Inst, Calcutta, PhD(statist, math), 66. *Prof Exp:* Lectr math, Univ Essex, 66-69. *Res:* Stochastic games, algorithms and existence theorems; optimization methods in matrices; shapley value and nucleolus in cooperative games; applied statistics; complementarity in programming. *Mailing Add:* Dept Math Statist & Comput Sci Univ Ill 851 S Morgan Chicago IL 60607-7045. *E-Mail:* u20833@uicvm.bitnet

RAGHAVAN, VALAYAMGHAT, PLANT MORPHOGENESIS. *Current Pos:* from asst prof to assoc prof, 70-77, PROF BOT, OHIO STATE UNIV, 77- *Personal Data:* b Edavanakad, Cochin, India, Mar 19, 31; m 62, Lakshmi; c Anita. *Educ:* Univ Madras, BS, 50; Benares Hindu Univ, MS, 52; Princeton Univ, PhD(biol), 61. *Prof Exp:* Res assoc biol, Harvard Univ, 61-63; reader bot, Univ Malaya, 63-70; guest investr biol, Rockefeller Univ, 66-67; vis prof, Dartmouth Col, 69-70. *Concurrent Pos:* Vis prof, Nat Univ Singapore, 93. *Mem:* Bot Soc Am; Am Soc Plant Physiologists. *Res:* Developmental physiology of lower plants; photomorphogenesis and biochemical cytology of spore germination; experimental plant embryogenesis. *Mailing Add:* 3020 N Star Rd Columbus OH 43221. *Fax:* 614-292-6345; *E-Mail:* raghavan.1@osu.edu

RAGHEB, HUSSEIN S, MICROBIOLOGY, BIOCHEMISTRY. *Current Pos:* ASSOC PROF BIOCHEM, PURDUE UNIV, LAFAYETTE, 61- *Personal Data:* b Cairo, Egypt, Jan 30, 24; m 56; c 1. *Educ:* Cairo Univ, BS, 44, MS, 50; Mich State Univ, PhD(fermentation), 56. *Prof Exp:* Res asst microbiol, Mich State Univ, 53-56, res assoc, 57; fel food tech, Iowa State Univ, 56; asst prof biochem & microbiol, Ferris State Col, 57-61. *Mem:* Am Soc Microbiol; Asn Official Anal Chemists. *Res:* Microbial chemistry; mode of action, methods of assay and characterization of antibiotics. *Mailing Add:* 509 N 30th St Lafayette IN 47904

RAGHOW, RAJENDRA, GENE REGULATION, EXTRACELLULAR MATRIX. *Current Pos:* from asst prof to assoc prof, 82-89, PROF PHARMACOL, UNIV TENN, MEMPHIS, 90- *Personal Data:* b Haryana, India, Apr 1, 47; US citizen; m 76, Gursharan Dhaliwal; c Sandeep & Rajeev. *Educ:* Panjab Univ, BS, 68, MS, 69; Australian Nat Univ, PhD(biochem), 74. *Prof Exp:* Leon Journey fel, St Jude Hosp, 75-77, asst mem, 77-82. *Concurrent Pos:* Assoc career scientist, Vet Admin Med Ctr, 88-94, res career scientist, 94-; ed, Molecular & Cellular Biochem, 89-; Am Cancer Soc vis prof, Univ Calif, San Diego, 93-94; mem, Pathobiochem Study Sect, NIH, 94-98. *Mem:* Am Soc Microbiol; Am Soc Pharmacol & Exp Therapeut; AAAS. *Res:* Mechanisms by which extracellular matrix, growth factors and homeobox genes regulate wound healing and early embryogenesis. *Mailing Add:* Dept Pharmacol Univ Tenn 1030 Jefferson Ave Memphis TN 38104. *Fax:* 901-577-7273; *E-Mail:* rraghow@utmem1.utmem.edu

RAGHUNATHAN, SRIKANTH, NANOCRYSTALLINE & REFRACTORY MATERIALS. *Current Pos:* SR TECH STAFF, CONCURRENT TECHNOLOGIES CORP, 96- *Personal Data:* b Karaikudi, India, Dec 23, 63; m 94, Padmashri Sampathkumar. *Educ:* Anna Univ, India, BS, 85; Univ Tex, Austin, MS, 88, PhD(mat sci & eng), 91. *Prof Exp:* Mfg engr, Sundaram Clayton, India, 85-86; postdoctoral fel, Inst Advan Technol, 91-93; sr scientist, Mat Modification Inc, 94-95; res & develop mgr, Valenite Inc, 95-96. *Mem:* Am Soc Metals; Am Ceramic Soc; Metal Powder Indust Fedn; Mat Res Soc; Minerals, Metals & Mat Soc; Am Powder Metall Inst. *Res:* Synthesis, consolidation and evaluation of nanocrystalline refractory and high-temperature structural and non-structural materials; processing and evaluation of particulate materials for cutting tools, mining, die/wear parts and armor/anti-armor (ballistic) materials. *Mailing Add:* Concurrent Technologies Corp 1450 Scalp Ave Johnstown PA 15904-3374. *Fax:* 814-269-2799, 445-8152; *E-Mail:* raghunas@ctc.com, nanomaterials@juno.com

RAGHUVEER, MYSORE R, SIGNAL & IMAGE PROCESSING, COMMUNICATIONS. *Current Pos:* ASSOC PROF SIGNAL & IMAGE PROCESSING, ROCHESTER INST TECHNOL, 87- *Personal Data:* b Bangalore, India, June 17, 57; m 87; c 1. *Educ:* Mysore Univ, India, BE, 79; Indian Inst Sci, ME, 81; Univ Conn, PhD(elec eng), 84. *Prof Exp:* Mem tech staff, Advanced Micro Devices Inc, 85-87. *Concurrent Pos:* Prin investr, NSF grant, 89-91; assoc ed, Inst Elec & Electronics Engrs Trans on Signal Processing, 91-93; consult, RIT Res Corp & Orincon Corp & Analog Simulator Res & Develop Ctr; mem, Tech Comt Statist Signal & Array Processing, Inst Elec & Electronics Engrs Signal Processing Soc. *Mem:* Inst Elec & Electronics Engrs; Inst Elec & Electronics Engrs Signal Processing Soc. *Res:* Digital image coding; digital image restoration and reconstruction; spectral analysis, especially with higher-order statistics; biomedical applications of signal processing; wavelet analysis. *Mailing Add:* Dept Elec Eng Rochester Inst Technol One Lomb Memorial Dr Rochester NY 14623

RAGHUVIR, NUGGEHALLI NARAYANA, ENTOMOLOGY. *Current Pos:* from instr to assoc prof biol, 63-91, ASSOC PROF, COL CHIROPRACT UNIV, BRIDGEPORT, 91- *Personal Data:* b Bangalore, India, July 12, 30; m 57, Swarna Raghavachari; c Nina & Veena. *Educ:* Univ Poona, India, BSc, 50; Karnatak Univ, MSc, 55; Utah State Univ, PhD(entom), 62. *Prof Exp:* Malaria supvr, Pub Health Dept, Poona, 50-51; res asst entom, Cent Food Tech Res Inst, Mysore, 56-58; instr zool, Duke Univ, 62-63. *Concurrent Pos:* Acad Year Exten res award, 64-65; consult entom, 78-91. *Mem:* Entom Soc Am; Sigma Xi. *Res:* Basic and applied aspects of insect physiology; general entomology, agricultural entomology and animal physiology. *Mailing Add:* Col Chiropract No 220 Univ Bridgeport Bridgeport CT 06101

RAGINS, HERZL, SURGERY. *Current Pos:* instr, 60-62, from asst prof to assoc prof, 62-75, clin prof surg, 75-, PROF SURG, ALBERT EINSTEIN COL MED. *Personal Data:* b Tel Aviv, Israel, July 27, 29; US citizen; m 59; c 3. *Educ:* Univ Ill, BS, 47, MS & MD, 51; Univ Chicago, PhD(surg, gastric physiol), 56. *Prof Exp:* Instr surg, Univ Chicago, 59-60; attend surg, Bronx Munic Hosp Ctr, 68- *Concurrent Pos:* Am Cancer Soc fel, 57-58. *Mem:* Am Col Surg; Am Physiol Soc; Soc Surg Alimentary Tract; Am Gastroenterol Asn; Sigma Xi. *Res:* Gastric physiology; histochemistry of gastric mucosa; histamine metabolism; mast cells and parietal cell turn over in gastric mucosa; radiation effects on gastric mucosa; effect of intrajejunal amino acids on pancreatic secretion. *Mailing Add:* 55 Hamptom Oval New Rochelle NY 10805-2901

RAGINS, NAOMI, ADULT & CHILD PSYCHIATRY, PSYCHOANALYSIS. *Current Pos:* Asst prof psychiat, 57-63, clin asst prof, 63-71, CLIN ASSOC PROF CHILD PSYCHIAT, SCH MED, UNIV PITTSBURGH, 71- *Personal Data:* b Chicago, Ill; m 55, Mark Goldsmith. *Educ:* Univ Chicago, PhB, 46, BS, 47, MD, 51; Am Bd Psychiat & Neurol, dipl, 59, cert child psychiat, 61; Am Psychoanal Assoc, cert adult & child psychoanal, 71. *Concurrent Pos:* Fac psychoanal, Pittsburgh Psychoanal Inst, 67-, supv child analyst, 71-, training & supv analyst, 77-; teaching consult, Children's Hosp, Pittsburgh, 72-; consult, Child Develop Prog, Head Start, Pittsburgh Child Guid Ctr, 73-76. *Mem:* Am Psychoanal Asn; Am Psychiat Asn; Am Acad Child Psychiat; Asn Child Psychoanal; Am Orthopsychiat Asn. *Res:* Ego development in infancy and childhood. *Mailing Add:* 6627 Forest Glen Rd Pittsburgh PA 15217

RAGLAND, JOHN LEONARD, SOIL CHEMISTRY, PLANT NUTRITION. *Current Pos:* RETIRED. *Personal Data:* b Beaver Dam, Ky, Oct 30, 31; m 56; c 3. *Educ:* Univ Ky, BS, 55, MS, 56; NC State Univ, PhD(soil sci), 59. *Honors & Awards:* Thomas Poe Cooper Award Distinguished Agr Res, Univ Ky, 67. *Prof Exp:* Asst prof soil technol, Pa State Univ, 59-61; from asst prof to prof agron, Univ Ky, 61-95, chmn, Dept Agron, 66-69, assoc dean exten & assoc dir coop exten serv, 69-86. *Concurrent Pos:* Chmn, State Comt Rural Community Develop, USDA, 70- *Mem:* Soil Sci Soc Am; Am Soc Agron; Int Soc Soil Sci. *Res:* Interaction of plant nutrient availability with the microclimatic; cation exchange equilibria in soils. *Mailing Add:* Dept Agr-Agron Univ Ky Agr Sci Ctr N Bldg Off N122 Lexington KY 40546-0091

RAGLAND, PAUL C, GEOCHEMISTRY, PETROLOGY. *Current Pos:* chmn natural sci area, 80-82, PROF GEOL & CHMN DEPT, FLA STATE UNIV, 78- *Personal Data:* b Lubbock, Tex, June 28, 36; m 58; c 2. *Educ:* Tex Tech Col, BS, 58; Rice Univ, MA, 61, PhD(geol), 62. *Prof Exp:* From asst prof to prof geol, Univ NC, Chapel Hill, 62-78. *Concurrent Pos:* Consult, Sinclair Res, 65, US Naval Ord Labs, 68-69, Va Div Mineral Resources, 70-71, Dames & Moore, 73-77, E I du Pont de Nemours, 75-77, Ebasco, Inc, 75- & NUS Corp, 78; Adv Res Projs Agency Mat Res Ctr grant, 66-74; vis prof, Duke Univ, 68 & 75, Mineral Mus, Oslo, Norway, 69-70 & Univ Ky, 75; assoc dean res admin, Univ NC, 71, assoc chmn dept geol, 75; Dept Energy grant, 76-78 & NSF grant, 79-81. *Mem:* Fel Geol Soc Am; Geochem Soc. *Res:* Application of analytical chemical data to petrogenesis of igneous and metamorphic rocks; geochemical prospecting; trace elements in chemical weathering and diagenesis. *Mailing Add:* Dept Geol Fla State Univ 600 W College Ave Tallahassee FL 32306-1096

RAGLAND, WILLIAM LAUMAN, III, IMMUNOPHARMACOLOGY. *Current Pos:* assoc prof, 70-76, PROF, DEPTS AVIAN MED, PATH & MED MICROBIOL, COL VET MED, UNIV GA, 76- *Personal Data:* b Richmond, Va, Aug 24, 34; div; c Karen R, Alexander S, & Amy E. *Educ:* Col William & Mary, BS, 56; Univ Ga, DVM, 60; Wash State Univ, PhD(vet path & biochem), 66. *Prof Exp:* Res asst path, Tulane Univ, 60-61, instr, 61-62; Nat Cancer Inst spec res fel, 66-68, asst prof path & vet sci, McArdle Lab, Univ Wis, 68-70. *Concurrent Pos:* Pres, Ragland Res Inc, Athens, Ga, 80-86; adj prof, Dept Path & Lab Med, Emory Univ, 84-; vis prof, Vet Fac, Univ Zagreb, Yugoslavia, 89, Croatia, 91 & adj prof, 91- *Mem:* AAAS; Int Acad Path; Am Asn Pathologists; Am Asn Immunologists; Am Asn Avian Pathologists. *Res:* Avian thymic hormones; immunoregulation and immunomodulation of chickens. *Mailing Add:* Poultry Dis Res Ctr 953 College Station Rd Athens GA 30602-4875. *Fax:* 706-542-5630; *E-Mail:* wragland@uga.cc.uga.edu

RAGLE, JOHN LINN, PHYSICAL CHEMISTRY. *Current Pos:* assoc prof, 64-69, PROF CHEM, UNIV MASS, AMHERST, 70- *Personal Data:* b Colorado Springs, Colo, Feb 4, 33; m 69. *Educ:* Univ Calif, BS, 54; Wash State Univ, PhD(chem), 57. *Prof Exp:* Asst prof chem, Univ Mass, 57-60; fel, Cornell Univ, 60-62; mem res staff, Northrop Space Labs, 62-64. *Concurrent Pos:* Vis assoc prof chem, Univ BC, Vancouver, 69-70; preistrager, Alexander von Humboldt stiftung award, 75. *Mem:* Am Phys Soc. *Res:* Chemistry and physics of molecular structure. *Mailing Add:* Dept Chem Lgrt 102 Univ Mass Amherst MA 01003

RAGLE, RICHARD HARRISON, GEOLOGY. *Current Pos:* CONSULT, 79- *Personal Data:* b Boston, Mass, June 11, 23; m 74, Harriet Paine; c 3. *Educ:* Middlebury Col, BA, 52; Dartmouth Col, MA, 58. *Prof Exp:* Geologist, Cold Regions Res & Eng Lab, US Army Corps Engrs, Greenland & Antarctic, 54-60; res scientist, Arctic Inst NAm, 60-64, staff scientist, 64-74; sr geologist, Dames & Moore, 74-77; mem staff, Naval Arctic Res Lab, 77-79; sr hydrogeologist, Northern Tech Serv, 80-81. *Concurrent Pos:* Field sci leader, Icefield Ranges Res Proj, St Elias Mt, Yukon Terr, Can, 63-70, dir, 70-74. *Mem:* Fel Arctic Inst NAm; sr fel Geol Soc Am; Glaciol Soc; Am Inst Prof Geologists (pres-elect, 91-92, pres, 92-93). *Res:* Glaciology, glacio-meteorology and climatology; ice and snow stratigraphy and metamorphism; sea ice mechanics and engineering. *Mailing Add:* 2419 Telequana Dr Anchorage AK 99517-1026

RAGONE, DAVID VINCENT, TEACHING, CONSULTING. *Current Pos:* SR LECTR, DEPT MAT SCI & ENG, MASS INST TECHNOL, CAMBRIDGE, 87-; PARTNER, AMPERSAND VENTURES, 92- *Personal Data:* b New York NY, May 16, 30; m 54, Katherine H Spaulding; c Christine M & Peter V. *Educ:* Mass Inst Technol, SB, 51, SM, 52, ScD, 53. *Prof Exp:* From asst prof to prof, Dept Chem & Metall Eng, Univ Mich, Ann Arbor, 53-61; chmn, Metall Dept, John J Hopkins Lab Pure & Appl Sci Gen Atomic Div, Gen Dynamics, La Jolla, Calif, 62-67, asst dir, 65; Alcoa prof metall, Carnegie Mellon Univ, Pittsburgh, Pa, 67-69, assoc dean & prof eng, Sch Urban & Pub Affairs, 69-70; dean, Thayer Sch Eng, Dartmouth Col, 70-72; dean eng, Univ Mich, Ann Arbor, 72-80; pres, Case Western Res Univ & prof metall & mat sci, Cleveland, Ohio, 80-87. *Concurrent Pos:* Mem bd dirs, var corp, 68-; mem bd trustees, Mitre Corp, 70-, Henry Luce Found, 84-; mem, adv comt Advan Automotive Power Systs, Coun Environ Qual, 70-76, chmn, 71-76, ad hoc panel Unconventional Engines, 69-70, US Dept Com Tech Adv Bd, 67-75, Panel on Automotive Air Pollution, 67-68, panel housing technol, chmn, 68-69, panel automotive fuels, chmn, 70-71; mem, Nat Sci Bd, 78-84;

mem, White House Sci Coun Study Health of Univ, Exec Off President, 84-86; gen partner, Ampersand Ventures, Wellesley, 88-92; bd dirs, Sifco Inc, Cabot Corp. *Mem:* Fel Am Soc Metals; Am Inst Mining & Metall Eng; Am Chem Soc; AAAS; Nat Soc Prof Engrs. *Res:* Metallurgical and chemical engineering. *Mailing Add:* Dept Mat Sci & Eng Mass Inst Technol Rm 8-405 Cambridge MA 02139

RAGOTZKIE, ROBERT AUSTIN, METEOROLOGY, OCEANOGRAPHY. *Current Pos:* RETIRED. *Personal Data:* b Albany, NY, Sept 13, 24; m 49; c 3. *Educ:* Rutgers Univ, BS, 48, MS, 50; Univ Wis-Madison, PhD(zool & meteorol), 53. *Honors & Awards:* Nat Sea Grant Award, 93. *Prof Exp:* Proj assoc meteorol, Univ Wis-Madison, 53; coord marine biol lab & asst prof biol, Univ Ga, 54-57, dir marine inst & assoc prof biol, 57-59; from asst prof to assoc prof, Univ Wis-Madison, 59-65, chmn dept meteorol, 64-67, prof meteorol, 65-89, dir, Marine Studies Ctr, 67-69, dir sea grant prog, 68-8,, prof environ sci, 71-89, dir, Sea Grant Inst, 80-90. *Mem:* Fel AAAS; Am Meteorol Soc; Am Geophys Union; Int Asn Gt Lakes Res. *Res:* Physical limnology of Great Lakes, thermal structure and currents; Great Lakes as systems. *Mailing Add:* Dept Atmospheric & Oceanic Sci Univ Wis-Madison 1225 W Dayton St Madison WI 53706

RAGOZIN, DAVID LAWRENCE, NUMERICAL ANALYSIS, APPROXIMATIONS. *Current Pos:* from asst prof to assoc prof, 69-85, PROF MATH, UNIV WASH, 85- *Personal Data:* b Brooklyn, NY, Apr 20, 41; m 70, Arlene Schwazreich; c Michael & Dylan. *Educ:* Reed Col, BA, 62; Harvard Univ, AM, 63, PhD(math), 67. *Prof Exp:* Instr math, Mass Inst Technol, 67-69. *Concurrent Pos:* NSF grant, Mass Inst Technol, 68-69, res assoc & NSF grant, 70-71; NSF grant, Univ Wash, 71-77 & 83-87; consult statist sci, 87- *Mem:* Am Math Soc; Math Asn Am. *Res:* Harmonic analysis on Lie groups and homogeneous spaces; applications of differential geometry; numerical analysis; wavelets as tools for efficient computational approximations, computation of smoothness from approximate data. *Mailing Add:* Dept Math Univ Wash Box 354350 Seattle WA 98195. *Fax:* 206-543-0397; *E-Mail:* rag@math.washington.edu

RAGSDALE, DAVID WILLARD, INTEGRATED PEST MANAGEMENT. *Current Pos:* ASST PROF ENTOM, UNIV MINN, 81- *Personal Data:* b Boise, Idaho, Nov 8, 52; m 73; c 1. *Educ:* Pt Loma Col, BA, 74; La State Univ, MS, 77, PhD(entom), 80. *Prof Exp:* Res assoc, La State Univ, 79-81. *Mem:* Entom Soc Am; Sigma Xi. *Res:* Insects as vectors of plant disease agents; integrated pest management of field crops; use of serology in determining predator-prey relationships; production of monoclonal antibodies. *Mailing Add:* Dept Entom 219 Hodson Hall Univ Minn 1980 Folwell Ave St Paul MN 55108-1037

RAGSDALE, HARVEY LARIMORE, ECOLOGY, BOTANY. *Current Pos:* Asst prof, 68-72, ASSOC PROF BIOL, EMORY UNIV, 72- *Personal Data:* b Atlanta, Ga, Mar 6, 40. *Educ:* Emory Univ, AB, 62; Univ Tenn, MS, 64, PhD(bot), 68. *Concurrent Pos:* Consult, Allied Gen Nuclear Serv, 70-78 & Environ Div, Tex Instruments, Inc, 78; co-prin investr grants, US Energy Res & Develop Admin, 70-76 & NSF, 76-78; prin investr grants, US Dept Energy, 76-79. *Mem:* Am Inst Biol Sci; AAAS; Ecol Soc Am; Sigma Xi. *Res:* Ecological chemical element cycling; ecosystem modeling and simulation; radiation effects and cycling; deciduous forest community studies; solar energy from woody biomass fuel species. *Mailing Add:* 48 Kansasgowa Dr Brevard NC 28712

RAGSDALE, NANCY NEALY, PESTICIDE CHEMISTRY, CELL PHYSIOLOGY. *Current Pos:* pesticide assessment specialist, Sci & Educ Admin-Chem Res, 78-80, pesticide coordr, Coop State Res Serv, 80-89, DIR, NAT AGR PESTICIDE IMPACT ASSESSMENT PROG, USDA, 91- *Personal Data:* b Griffin, Ga, Feb 5, 38; m 59, William C; c Nancy V & Elizabeth R (Howard). *Educ:* Cent Conn State Col, BS, 62; Univ Md, MS, 66, PhD(bot), 74. *Prof Exp:* Res assoc fungal physiol, Dept Bot, Univ Md, 74-78, environ coordr, 89-91. *Mem:* AAAS; Soc Toxicol; Am Chem Soc; Sigma Xi. *Res:* Mode of action of pesticides and environmental toxicology. *Mailing Add:* 13903 Overton Lane Silver Spring MD 20904. *Fax:* 202-720-1767; *E-Mail:* nragsdale@ars.usda.gov

RAGSDALE, RONALD O, INORGANIC CHEMISTRY. *Current Pos:* from asst prof to assoc prof, 63-72, PROF CHEM, UNIV UTAH, 72- *Personal Data:* b Boise, Idaho, Dec 10, 32; m 56; c 3. *Educ:* Brigham Young Univ, BS, 57; Univ Ill, MS, 59, PhD(chem), 60. *Prof Exp:* Res chemist, Gen Chem Div, Allied Chem Corp, 60-63. *Mem:* Am Chem Soc; Royal Soc Chem. *Res:* Metal ion complexes; Lewis acid-base interactions; nuclear magnetic resonance. *Mailing Add:* Chem Dept Univ Utah Salt Lake City UT 84112-1102

RAGSDELL, KENNETH MARTIN, MECHANICAL ENGINEERING & QUALITY ENGINEERING. *Current Pos:* assoc vchancellor & prof eng mgt, 92, PROF, DESIGN ENG CTR, UNIV MO-ROLLA, 92- *Personal Data:* b Jacksonville, Ill, Sept 3, 42; m 62; c 3. *Educ:* Univ Mo, Rolla, BS, 66, MS, 67; Univ Tex, Austin, PhD(mech eng), 72. *Prof Exp:* Instr eng, Okla State Univ, 67-68; mech engr, IBM Corp, 68-70; instr eng, Univ Tex, Austin, 70-72; asst prof mech eng, Purdue Univ, West Lafayette, 72-76, assoc prof, 76-, grad chmn, 76; prof mech & aerospace eng, Univ Ariz, Tucson, 82-84; dir, Design Optimization Lab, 84-89; chmn mech & aerospace eng, Columbia, Mo, 89-92. *Concurrent Pos:* Consult; pres, CAD Serv, Inc. *Res:* Computational aspects of design; optimization theory dynamics; computer aided design; engineering computation; optimization theory; design of dynamic mechanical systems. *Mailing Add:* 1807 Belmont Ct Rolla MO 65401

RAHA, CHITTA RANJAN, organic chemistry, biochemistry, for more information see previous edition

RAHAL, LEO JAMES, NUCLEAR ENGINEERING, PLASMA PHYSICS. *Current Pos:* SR PHYSICIST, GEO-CENTER INC, 93- *Personal Data:* b Detroit, Mich, July 22, 39; m 71; c 2. *Educ:* Univ Detroit, BS, 62, MS, 64; Univ NMex, PhD(physics), 78. *Prof Exp:* Physicist, LTV Aerospace, 68-73, Kirtland Weapons Lab, 73-76, Los Alamos Nat Lab, 76-77, Los Alamos tech assoc, 77-81; physicist, Los Alamos Nat Lab, 76-77, tech assoc, 77-81; physicist, Dikewood Corp, 81-93. *Res:* Plasma physics microinstability analysis: in the area of high density plasmas; nuclear waste management including waste disposal and air dispersion; nuclear reactor safety-hydrogen buildup in reactors and consequences. *Mailing Add:* 8720 Madre Ave NE Albuquerque NM 87111-6610

RAHE, JAMES EDWARD, PLANT PATHOLOGY. *Current Pos:* Asst prof, 69-77, assoc prof, 77-85, PROF BIOL SCI, SIMON FRASER UNIV, 85- *Personal Data:* b Muncie, Ind, Mar 12, 39; m 66; c Jason, Susan, Matthew & Jonathan. *Educ:* Purdue Univ, BS, 61, PhD(biochem), 69. *Mem:* Am Phytopath Soc; Can Phytopath Soc; Sigma Xi; NY Acad Sci. *Res:* Biochemistry and physiology of host-parasite interaction; biological and integrated control of plant disease. *Mailing Add:* Dept Biol Sci Simon Fraser Univ 8888 University Dr Burnaby BC V5A 1S6 Can. *Fax:* 604-291-3496

RAHE, MAURICE HAMPTON, MATHEMATICS. *Current Pos:* asst prof, 78-85, ASSOC PROF MATH, TEX A&M UNIV, 85- *Personal Data:* b Tucumcari, NMex, Jan 17, 44; m 73; c 2. *Educ:* Pomona Col, BA, 65; Stanford Univ, MS, 70, PhD(math), 76. *Prof Exp:* Lectr & fel, Univ Toronto, 76-78. *Concurrent Pos:* Vis asst prof, Rice Univ, 81. *Mem:* Am Math Soc; Inst Elec & Electronics Engrs. *Res:* Ergodic theory; information theory; probability. *Mailing Add:* 3807 Westerman St Houston TX 77005-1137

RAHE, RICHARD HENRY, PSYCHIATRY. *Current Pos:* PROF PSYCHIAT & DIR NEV STRESS CTR, UNIV NEV, SCH MED, 86- *Personal Data:* b Seattle, Wash, May 28, 36; m 60, Laurie Ann Davies; c Richard Bradley & Annika Lee. *Educ:* Univ Wash, MD, 61. *Honors & Awards:* McDonnell Prize, Univ Wash, 61; Hans Selye MD Award, Am Inst Stress, 97. *Prof Exp:* Intern med, Bellevue Hosp, New York, 61-62; from resident to chief resident psychiat, Univ Wash, 62-65; res psychiatrist, US Navy Neuropsychiat Res Univ, 65-68; head stress med div, US Naval Health Res Ctr, 70-76, comndg officer, 76-80; comndg officer, US Naval Hosp, Guam, 81-84; prof, US Univ Health Sci, Bethesda, 84-86. *Concurrent Pos:* NIH spec fel, Karolinska Inst, Sweden, 68-69; adj prof psychiat, Neuropsychiat Inst; adj prof psychiat, Univ Calif, Los Angeles, 75-; adj assoc prof psychiat, Univ Calif, San Diego & Univ Calif, Los Angeles, 70-74. *Mem:* Fel Am Psychiat Asn; Am Psychosom Soc; Pavlovian Soc; Acad Behav Med; Res Am Inst Stress. *Res:* Life changes and illness onset; psychosocial aspects of physical illnesses; computer applications of stress and coping measures; expert on post-traumatic stress disorders. *Mailing Add:* 638 St Lawrence Reno NV 89509-1440

RAHEEL, MASTURA, TEXTILE SCIENCE, POLYMER CHEMISTRY. *Current Pos:* asst prof, 78-84, assoc prof & div chmn, 84-90, PROF TEXTILE SCI, UNIV ILL, URBANA, 91- *Personal Data:* b Lahore, Pakistan, Mar 1, 38; m 59; c 2. *Educ:* Punjab Univ, Pakistan, BSc, 57, MSc, 59; Okla State Univ, MS, 62; Univ Minn, St Paul, PhD(textile sci), 71. *Honors & Awards:* Res Excellence Award, Am Textile Mfrs Asn, 89. *Prof Exp:* Asst prof & head textiles & clothing, Col Home Econ, Lahore, 60-77; lectr, Univ Minn, St Paul, 77-78. *Mem:* Am Asn Textile Chemists & Colorists; Int Textile & Apparel Asn; Sigma Xi; Am Chem Soc. *Res:* Textile physics; textile chemistry; barrier properties of textiles toward toxic chemicals; author of six books & more than 50 technical research articles. *Mailing Add:* Dept Natural Resources & Environ Sci Univ Ill 239 Bevier Hall Urbana IL 61801

RAHIMTOOLA, SHAHBUDIN HOOSEINALLY, CARDIOLOGY, INTERNAL MEDICINE. *Current Pos:* PROF MED & CHIEF SECT CARDIOL, UNIV SOUTHERN CALIF, 80-, GEORGE C GRIFFITH PROF CARDIOL, 84- *Personal Data:* b Bombay, India, Oct 17, 31; US citizen; m 67; c 3. *Educ:* Univ Karachi, MB & BS, 56; MRCPE, 63; FRCP, 72. *Prof Exp:* Sr house officer, Barrowmore Chest Hosp, Chester, Eng, 56-57 & Whittington Hosp, London, 58-59; house physician, Cardiac Unit, London Chest Hosp, 59-60; Locum med registr, Whittington Hosp, London, 60; registr, Cardiac Unit, Wessex Reg Hosp, Southampton Eng, 60-63; co-dir, Cardiac Lab, Mayo Clin, Rochester, Minn, 65-66; sr registr cardiopulmonary dis, Dept Med, Queen Elizabeth Hosp, Birmingham, Eng, 66-67; res asst & hon sr registr, Dept Med, Royal Postgrad Med Sch & Hammersmith Hosp, London, 67-68; assoc prof med, Abraham Lincoln Sch Med, Col Med, Univ Ill, 69-72; prof med, Health Sci Ctr, Univ Ore, 72-80, dir res, 73-78. *Concurrent Pos:* Co-dir, Dept Adult Cardiol, Cook Co Hosp, Chicago, 69-70, dir, 70-72; consult cardiol, Madigan Gen Army Hosp, Ft Lewis, Wash, 72-; NIH grant, 72-77, 78-; Ore Heart Asn & Med Res Found Ore grants, 73-77; rep for Ore, Coun Clin Cardiol, Am Heart Asn, 75-77, mem exec comt, 77-, mem long range planning comt & mem nominating comt, 78-; consult, Nat Coop Study Valvular Heart Dis, 76-77; mem planning comt, Vet Admin, Washington, DC, 76-77, mem exec comt, 77-; mem circulatory systs devices panel, Food & Drug Admin, HEW, 76-80, chmn dept, 77-80; vis scientist, Cardiovasc Res Inst & vis prof med, Sch Med, Univ Calif, San Francisco, 78-79; grants, Coun Clin Cardiol, Am Heart Asn & Coun Circulation; mem adv panel cardiovascular drugs, US Pharmacopia, Nat Forumlary, 81-; ed, Newsletter, Coun Clin Cardiol, Am Heart Asn, 79-, Clin Cardiol, Am Med Asn, 80-83, Mod Concepts Cardiovasc Dis, Am Heart Asn, 85-88. *Mem:* Fel Am Col Cardiol; fel Am Col Chest Physicians; fel Am Col Physicians; Asn Univ Cardiologists. *Res:* Left ventricular performance in various disease states; coronary artery disease; valvular heart disease; cardiac electrophysiology. *Mailing Add:* Dept Med Cardiol Univ SCalif Sch Med 1200 North State St Los Angeles CA 90033-4525

RAHLMANN, DONALD FREDERICK, GRAVITATIONAL PHYSIOLOGY. *Current Pos:* RETIRED. *Personal Data:* b San Francisco, Calif, July 21, 23; m 49; c 3. *Educ:* Univ Calif, Davis, BS, 55, MS, 56, PhD(animal physiol), 62. *Honors & Awards:* Cosmos Achievement Award, NASA, 81. *Prof Exp:* Jr specialist, Dept Animal Husbandry, Univ Calif, Davis, 49-50, asst specialist reproductive physiology, 50-62; jr res physiologist, dept physiol & anat, Univ Calif, Berkeley, 62-63, asst res physiologist space physiol, 63-81, assoc res physiologist, Environ Physiol Lab, 81-85. *Concurrent Pos:* Consult, Lawrence Hall Sci, Univ Calif, Berkeley, 66-67; Int Govt Personnel Act, Ames Res Ctr, NASA, Moffett Field, Calif, 75-76; participant, Joint US-USSR Cosmos 1129 Flight Exp, 78-79. *Mem:* Am Physiol Soc; Sigma Xi; AAAS; Am Asn Lab Animal Sci; Int Primatological Soc. *Res:* Animal experimentation in metabolism related to environmental changes; physiology of non-human primates; development of equipment and instrumentation for measurement of physiological response. *Mailing Add:* 1144 Nogales St Lafayette CA 94549-3252

RAHM, DAVID CHARLES, PHYSICS. *Current Pos:* From asst physicist to assoc physicist, 55-62, physicist, 62-82, SR PHYSICIST, BROOKHAVEN NAT LAB, 82- *Personal Data:* b Ironwood, Mich, Dec 1, 27; m 51; c 2. *Educ:* Univ Chicago, SB, 49; Univ Mich, MS, 51, PhD(physics), 56. *Concurrent Pos:* Physicist, Nuclear Res Ctr, Saclay, France, 60-61; vis scientist, Europ Orgn Nuclear Res, Geneva, 68-69, 75-80 & 85-88. *Mem:* Fel Am Phys Soc. *Res:* Particle physics; particle detectors; particle beams; superconducting magnets; accelerators. *Mailing Add:* Physics Dept Bldg 510 Brookhaven Nat Lab Upton NY 11973. *Fax:* 516-344-5568; *E-Mail:* rahm@bnl.gov

RAHMAN, MD AZIZUR, PERMANENT MAGNET MACHINES, DIGITAL PROTECTION. *Current Pos:* assoc prof, 76-80, PROF ELEC ENG, MEM UNIV NFLD, 80-, UNIV RES PROF, 93- *Personal Data:* b Santahar, Bangladesh, Jan 9, 41; Can citizen; m 63, Alta; c Diana, Proton & Adam. *Educ:* Bangladesh Univ Eng, BSc, 62; Univ Toronto, MASc, 65; Carleton Univ, PhD(elec eng), 68. *Honors & Awards:* G E Centennial Award; Outstanding Achievement Award, Inst Elec & Electronics Engrs Indust Applns Soc; Outstanding Eng Educator Medal, Inst Elec & Electronics Engrs Can; Merit Award, Asn Prof Engrs & Geoscientist Nfld. *Prof Exp:* Res scientist, Can Gen Elec Co, 68-69; from asst prof to assoc prof elec eng, Bangladesh Univ Eng, 69-74; Nuffield acad visitor, Imp Col Sci & Technol, London, 74-75; sr engr & consult, Man Hydro, 75-76. *Concurrent Pos:* Lectr elec eng, Bangladesh Univ Eng, 62-64; mem, Tech Educ Comn, E Pakistan, 69-70; res fel, Tech Univ, Eindhoven, Neth, 73-74; lectr, Univ Man, 75-76; consult, Nfld & Labrador Hydro, 77-78, 80-81 & 88-, Gen Elec Co, Schnectady, NY, 78-79; res prof, Univ Toronto, 84-85; vis prof, Nayang Technol Univ, 91-92; centennial vis prof, Tokyo Inst Technol, 92. *Mem:* Fel Inst Engrs Bangladesh; Can Elec Asn; fel Inst Elec & Electronics Engrs; fel Inst Elec Engrs; Inst Elec Engrs Japan. *Res:* Design analysis of hysteresis, permanent magnet and bearing less motors; applications of supermagnets and superconductors in power apparatus and devices; delta pulse width modulated inverters and converters; digital protection of power transformers, generators, lines and reactors; published 282 papers. *Mailing Add:* Fac Eng & Appl Sci Mem Univ Nfld St John's NF A1B 3X5 Can. *Fax:* 709-737-4042; *E-Mail:* rahman@engr.mun.ca

RAHMAN, MIZANUR, BASIC HYPERGEOMETRIC SERIES, ORTHOGONAL POLYNOMIALS. *Current Pos:* from asst prof to assoc prof, 65-78, PROF MATH, CARLETON UNIV, OTTAWA, 78- *Personal Data:* b Dhaka, Bangladesh, Sept 16, 32; Can citizen; m 61, Shamsun Nahar; c Babu & Raja. *Educ:* Dhaka Univ, BSc, 53, MSc, 54; Cambridge Univ, BA, 58; Univ NB, PhD(math), 65. *Prof Exp:* Lectr math, Dhaka Univ, Bangladesh, 58-62; lectr, Univ NB, 62-65. *Mem:* Am Math Soc; Am Phys Soc; Can Math Soc; Can Appl Math Soc; Soc Inst Advan Mat. *Res:* Basic hypergeometric series; statistical mechanics and stochastic processes; author of approximately 75 publications in refereed journals in North America and United Kingdom; co-author of the book "Basic Hypergeometric Series", Cambridge University Press, 1990. *Mailing Add:* Dept Math & Statist Carleton Univ 1125 Colonel By Dr Ottawa ON K1S 5B6 Can. *Fax:* 613-788-3536; *E-Mail:* mizan.rahman@carleton.ca

RAHMAN, TALAT SHAHNAZ, SOLID STATE PHYSICS. *Current Pos:* AT DEPT PHYSICS, KANS STATE UNIV, 83- *Personal Data:* b Calcutta, India, Feb 5, 48; Pakistan citizen; c 1. *Educ:* Univ Karachi, BSc, 68, MSc, 69; Univ Rochester, PhD(physics), 77. *Prof Exp:* Res asst physics, Univ Rochester, 71-76, teaching asst, 73 & 76-77; res physicist, Univ Calif, Irvine, 77-82. *Concurrent Pos:* Alexander von Humboldt Fel, 87-88. *Mem:* Am Phys Soc; Asn Women Sci. *Res:* Surface physics and optical properties of solids. *Mailing Add:* Dept Physics Kans State Univ Cardwell Hall Manhattan KS 66506

RAHMAN, YUEH ERH, MEDICINE, HEALTH SCIENCES. *Current Pos:* dir grad studies, 88-92, head, Dept Pharmaceut, 91-96, PROF, COL PHARM, DEPT PHARMACEUT, UNIV MINN, MINNEAPOLIS, 85- *Personal Data:* b Canton, China, June 10, 30; m 56, Aneesur; c Aneesa. *Educ:* Univ Louvain, MD, 56. *Honors & Awards:* Indust Res 100 Award, 76. *Prof Exp:* Med officer, Belg Leprosy Ctr, India, 57-58; asst res officer, Indian Cancer Res Ctr, 58-59; res assoc biochem cytol, Univ Louvain, 59-60; res assoc, Biol Div, Argonne Nat Lab, 60-63, asst biologist, 63-72, biologist, 72-81, sr biologist, 81-85. *Concurrent Pos:* Vis scientist, Dept Biochem, Univ Utrecht, 68-69; adj assoc prof, Dept Biol Sci, Northern Ill Univ, 71-; mem rev group, Exp Therapeut Study Sect, NIH, 79-83; pres, Chicago Chap, Asn Women Sci, 79-80. *Mem:* Am Soc Cell Biol; Radiation Res Soc; NY Acad Sci; AAAS; Asn Women Sci; Am Asn Pharmaceut Scientists. *Res:* Cellular biochemistry; cell membranes; radiation and lysosomes; chemotherapy by use of liposome encapsulation of drugs, such as chelating agents, anti-tumor drugs and immunosuppressants. *Mailing Add:* Col Pharm Health Sci Unit F Univ Minn 308 Harvard St SE Minneapolis MN 55455. *Fax:* 612-626-2125; *E-Mail:* rahma001@maroon.tc.umn.edu

RAHMAT-SAMII, YAHYA, SATELLITE COMMUNICATION ANTENNAS, ELECTROMAGNETIC SCATTERING. *Current Pos:* PROF ELEC ENG, UNIV CALIF, LOS ANGELES, 88- *Personal Data:* b Tehran, Iran, Aug 20, 48; US citizen. *Educ:* Tehran Univ, BS, 70; Univ Ill, Urbana-Champaign, MS, 72, PhD(elec eng), 75. *Prof Exp:* Vis asst prof elec eng, Univ Ill, Urbana-Champaign, 75-78; sr res scientist, Jet Propulsion Lab, 78-88. *Concurrent Pos:* Dir, Electromagnetic Soc, 84- & Antennas Measurement Tech Asn, 90-; vis prof elec eng, Tech Univ Denmark, 86. *Mem:* Fel Inst Elec & Electronics Engrs; fel Int Union Radio Sci; fel Inst Advan Eng; Inst Elec & Electronics Engrs Antennas & Propagation Soc; Inst Elec & Electronics Engrs Microwave Theory & Tech Soc; Electromagnetics Soc; Antennas Measurement Tech Asn. *Res:* Novel space and ground antenna concepts; satellite communications; advanced antenna measurement and diagnostic techniques; radar cross section; asymptotic and high frequency diffraction methods; numerical modeling in electromagnetic scattering; author of over 180 technical publications. *Mailing Add:* Eng IV Bldg Univ Calif Los Angeles CA 90024

RAHN, JOAN ELMA, PLANT MORPHOLOGY. *Current Pos:* SCI WRITING, 67- *Personal Data:* b Cleveland, Ohio, Feb 5, 29. *Educ:* Western Res Univ, BS, 50; Columbia Univ, AM, 52, PhD, 56. *Prof Exp:* From asst prof to assoc prof biol, Thiel Col, 56-59; instr bot, Ohio State Univ, 59-60; instr biol, Int Sch Am, 60-61; asst prof, Lake Forest Col, 61-67. *Mem:* AAAS; Bot Soc Am; Am Inst Biol Sci; Sigma Xi. *Mailing Add:* 5475 Market Rd Bellingham WA 98226

RAHN, KENNETH A, ATMOSPHERIC CHEMISTRY. *Current Pos:* PROF CTR ATMOSPHERIC CHEM STUDIES, UNIV RI, 80- *Personal Data:* b Hackensack, NJ, Aug 10, 40; wid; c 2. *Educ:* Mass Inst Technol, BS, 62; Univ Mich, PhD(meteorol), 71. *Prof Exp:* Sci/math teacher, Classical High Sch, Barrington College, 63-68; res assoc atmospheric chem, Inst Nuclear Sci, Univ Ghent, 71-73; res assoc, Grad Sch Oceanog, Univ RI, 73-75; vis scientist, Max Planck Inst Chem, 75-76; res assoc atmospheric chem, grad sch oceanog, Univ RI, 76- *Mem:* Am Chem Soc; AAAS; Am Meteorol Soc; Gesellschaft Fur Aerosolforschung. *Res:* Aerosols; arctic air chemistry; long-range transport. *Mailing Add:* Sch Oceanog Univ RI Narragansett RI 02882-1197

RAHN, PERRY H, HYDROLOGY, GEOMORPHOLOGY. *Current Pos:* from asst prof to assoc prof, 68-78, PROF GEOL, SDAK SCH MINES & TECHNOL, 78- *Personal Data:* b Allentown, Pa, Oct 27, 36; m 62; c 4. *Educ:* Lafayette Col, BS & BA, 59; Pa State Univ, PhD(geol), 65. *Honors & Awards:* Claire P Holdredge Award, Asn Eng Geol, 87; E B Burwell Award, Geol Soc Am, 90. *Prof Exp:* Civil engr, Calif Dept Water Resources, 59-61; asst prof geol, Univ Conn, 65-68. *Concurrent Pos:* Hydrogeologist, Argonne Nat Lab, 77 & Bucknell Univ, 88. *Mem:* Fel Geol Soc Am; Int Asn Hydrogeol; Nat Water Well Asn; Am Quaternary Asn; Sigma Xi; Nat Soc Prof Engr. *Res:* Engineering geology; hydrology of glacial and limestone terranes; uranium tailing pond contamination; engineering geology. *Mailing Add:* SDak Sch Mines & Technol Rapid City SD 57701

RAHN, RONALD OTTO, PHOTOCHEMISTRY OF DNA, IODINE CHEMISTRY. *Current Pos:* PROF ENVIRON HEALTH, UNIV ALA, BIRMINGHAM, 85- *Personal Data:* b Bridgeport, Conn, Feb 7, 35; m 63; c 2. *Educ:* Univ Conn, BA, 57; Brandeis Univ, PhD(chem), 63. *Prof Exp:* Res staff biophys, Bell Tel Labs, 63-65; res scientist biol div, Oak Ridge Nat Lab, 65-85. *Concurrent Pos:* Prof, Biomed Sch, Univ Tenn. *Res:* Quantitative analysis of the damage caused to DNA by exposure to a variety of environmental agents including ultra violet, ionizing radiation, carcinogens and anti tumor agents; use of halogenated pyrimidines as radiation sensitizers; binding of small molecules to DNA. *Mailing Add:* Univ Ala TH314 1717 7th Ave Birmingham AL 35294-0001

RAHWAN, RALF GEORGE, TOXICOLOGY. *Current Pos:* from asst prof to assoc prof, 72-80, PROF PHARMACOL, COL PHARM, OHIO STATE UNIV, 80- *Personal Data:* b Egypt; Feb 28, 41; US citizen; c 1. *Educ:* Cairo Univ, BS, 61; Butler Univ, MS, 70; Purdue Univ, PhD(pharmacol), 72. *Prof Exp:* Retail pharmacist, 61-64; head, Sci Doc & Training Dept, Hoechst Orient Pharmaceut Co, 64-67; assoc pharmacologist, Human Health Res & Develop Labs, Dow Chem Co, 67-70. *Mem:* Am Soc Pharmacol & Exp Therapeut; Soc Toxicol; Sigma Xi; Am Soc Clin Pharmacol Therapeut. *Res:* Endocrine pharmacology, toxicology, calcium antagonists. *Mailing Add:* Div Pharmacol & Toxicol Ohio State Univ Col Pharm 500 W 12th Ave Columbus OH 43210-1214

RAI, AMARENDRA KUMAR, ION BEAM PROCESSING OF MATERIALS, SCANNING TRANSMISSION ELECTRON MICROSCOPY. *Current Pos:* scientist, 81-83, SR SCIENTIST, MATS RES DIV, UNIVERSAL ENERGY SYSTS, 83- *Personal Data:* b Varanasi, UP, India, Oct 20, 52; m 71, Singh. *Educ:* Gorakhpur Univ, BSc, 70; Banaras Hindu Univ, MSc, 72, PhD(physics), 77. *Prof Exp:* Jr res fel physics, Coun Sci & Indust Res, India, 72-75, sr res fel, 76-77, fel, 78-79; fel mats eng, NC State Univ, Raleigh, 79-81. *Concurrent Pos:* Vis scientist, Solid State Div, Oak Ridge Nat Lab, 81; prin investr, Dept Defense, 85-86 & 86-87. *Mem:* Am Phys Soc; Am Ceramic Soc; Mats Res Soc. *Res:* Surface modification of various materials employing ion beam processing; microstructural characterization of materials using scanning transmission electron microscopy; author of over 90 research papers in various scientific journals. *Mailing Add:* UES Inc 4401 Dayton Xenia Rd Dayton OH 45432

RAI, CHARANJIT, CHEMICAL ENGINEERING, CHEMISTRY. *Current Pos:* MEM FAC, DEPT CHEM & NATURAL GAS ENG, TEX A&I UNIV, 80- *Personal Data:* b Barabanki, India, July 19, 29. *Educ:* Univ Agra, BSc, 48; Lucknow Univ, MSc, 50; Indian Inst Sci, Bangalore, dipl, 52, PhD(chem), 59; Univ Ill, MS, 56; Ill Inst Technol, PhD(chem eng), 60. *Prof Exp:* Res asst chem eng, Univ Ill, 54-56; instr, Ill Inst Technol, 56-58; sr res scientist, Pure Oil Co, 59-65; sr res suprv, Richardson Co, Ill, 65-66; dept head prod & process res, Cities Serv Oil Co, 66-76; prof, US Energy Res & Develop Agency, Morgantown Energy Res, 77-80. *Concurrent Pos:* Prof chem eng & chmn dept, Indian Inst Technol, Kanpur, 63-64. *Mem:* AAAS; Am Inst Chem Engrs; Am Chem Soc; Indian Inst Chem Engrs. *Res:* Mass transfer; thermodynamics; oxidation of hydrocarbons; petrochemicals; fuels and lubricants. *Mailing Add:* Dept Chem & Natural Gas Eng Tex A&M Univ Kingsville TX 78363-8203

RAI, DHANPAT, SOIL CHEMISTRY, SOIL MINERALOGY. *Current Pos:* sr res scientist, 75-81, staff scientist, 81-90, SR STAFF SCIENTIST, BATTELLE, PAC NORTHWEST LABS, 90- *Personal Data:* b June 12, 43; US citizen; m 72; c 2. *Educ:* Panjab Agr Univ, BSc, 63; MSc, 65; Ore State Univ, PhD(soil sci), 70. *Prof Exp:* Res assoc soil sci, Ore State Univ, 70-71; fel, Colo State Univ, 72-73; res assoc & asst prof, NMex State Univ, 74-75. *Mem:* Am Soc Agron; Soil Sci Soc Am; Int Soc Soil Sci; Res Soc NAm; Am Chem Soc. *Res:* Soil chemistry; environmental chemistry of actinides; geochemistry. *Mailing Add:* Pac Northwest Lab PO Box 999 Richland WA 99352-0999

RAI, KANTI R, HEMATOLOGY, ONCOLOGY. *Current Pos:* assoc prof med, 72-80, PROF MED, SCH MED, STATE UNIV NY, STONY BROOK, 80-90; CHIEF, DIV HEMAT-ONCOL, LONG ISLAND JEWISH-HILLSIDE MED CTR, 81-; PROF MED, ALBERT EINSTEIN COL MED, 91- *Personal Data:* b Jodhpur, India, May 10, 32; m 68, Susan Segal; c Samantha & Joshua. *Educ:* Med Col, Univ Rajasthan, MB & BS, 55; Am Bd Pediat, dipl, 61. *Prof Exp:* Head exp med, Inst Nuclear Med, Delhi, India, 62-66; assoc scientist, Brookhaven Nat Lab, 66-70. *Concurrent Pos:* Leukemia res scholar, Nat Leukemia Asn, 66-67 & 75-77; attending physician hemat-oncol, Long Island Jewish-Hillside Med Ctr, 70-80. *Mem:* Am Soc Hemat; Am Soc Clin Oncol. *Res:* Natural history and biology of leukemias; cell kinetics in leukemias; new therapeutic approaches in the malignancies of blood. *Mailing Add:* Long Island Jewish Hillside Med Ctr 270-05 76th Ave New Hyde Park NY 11040. *E-Mail:* rai@aecom.yu.edu

RAI, KARAMJIT SINGH, VECTOR GENETICS, GENOME EVOLUTION. *Current Pos:* res assoc, Radiation Lab & Dept Biol, Univ Notre Dame, 60-62, sr staff mem radiation lab, 62-77, from asst prof to assoc prof, 62-66, dir Mosquito Biol Training Prog, 69-75, PROF BIOL, UNIV NOTRE DAME, 70-, DIR, PARASITOL, VECTOR BIOL TRAINING PROG, 94- *Personal Data:* b Moranwali, Punjab, India, Mar 24, 31; m 56; c 5. *Educ:* Panjab Univ, India, BSc, 53, MSc, 55; Univ Chicago, PhD(bot), 59. *Prof Exp:* Lectr bot, Khalsa Col, Amritsar, 55-56; head dept bot, Deshbandhu Col, Delhi, 56-58; Charles Hutchinson fel & Coulter res fel, Univ Chicago, 58-60; assoc, Chicago Natural Hist Mus, Ill, 60. *Concurrent Pos:* Consult, Ill Inst Technol, 64-68, Int Atomic Energy Agency, Vienna, 66 & 69 & WHO, Geneva, 66-75; adv, Govt Ceylon, 66 & Govt Brazil, 69; mem Int Atomic Energy Agency panels, 68 & 70; mem US-Japan panels on parasitic dis, 70,72,73; mem, planning & rev group, World Health Orgn, Res Unit Genetic Control Mosquitoes, New Delhi, 71-75; vis prof, Univ Pernambuco, Brazil, 69 & Guru Nanak Dev Univ, India, 73-74; co-prin investr, Mosquito Biol Unit, Mombasa, Nairobi, Kenya, 71-76; mem, Rockfeller Found, Conf Genetics Dis Vectors, Bellagio, Italy, 81; chmn, Conf Genetics & Molec Biol, Entomal Soc Am, 84; Ernest Oppenheimer Mem Trust W D Wilson fel, SAfrica, 90. *Mem:* AAAS; Genetics Soc Am; Entom Soc Am; Am Mosquito Control Asn; Am Inst Biol Sci; fel Nat Acad Sci India. *Res:* Cytogenetics and molecular genetics of Aedes mosquitoes, molecular organization and evolution of mosquito genomes; chromosomal rearrangements and insect population control; genetics of speciation in Aedes; mutagenesis; vector competence; genetic control of cell division; genetic control of vectors. *Mailing Add:* Dept Biol Sci Univ Notre Dame Notre Dame IN 46556-0369

RAIBLE, ROBERT H(ENRY), ELECTRICAL ENGINEERING. *Current Pos:* PROF ELEC ENG, UNIV CINCINNATI, 77- *Personal Data:* b Cincinnati, Ohio, Aug 27, 35; m 58; c 1. *Educ:* Univ Cincinnati, EE, 58; Purdue Univ, PhD(elec eng), 64. *Prof Exp:* Proj engr, Cincinnati Milling Mach, 57-58; instr, Purdue Univ, 59-64; from asst prof to assoc prof, 64-76. *Concurrent Pos:* Consult, Spot Industs; Metcut Assoc. *Mem:* Inst Elec & Electronics Engrs. *Res:* Analysis and design of automatic control systems; theory and application of adaptive and learning systems. *Mailing Add:* Elec & Comput Eng Dept Rhodes Hall Mail Lac Univ Cincinnati Cincinnati OH 45221

RAICH, HENRY, PHYSICAL CHEMISTRY. *Current Pos:* RETIRED. *Personal Data:* b Philadelphia, Pa, June 11, 19; m 43; c 2. *Educ:* Rensselaer Polytech Inst, BS, 40 & 44, PhD, 49. *Prof Exp:* Chemist, Am Smelting & Refining Co, 40-43 & Los Alamos Sci Lab, 44-46; fel, Mellon Inst, 49-52; chemist, Nuodex Prod Co, Inc, 52-54; res assoc lubricants, Mobil Oil Corp, 54-83. *Concurrent Pos:* Consult, 83- *Mem:* Am Chem Soc; Am Soc Lubrication Engrs; Am Soc Testing & Mat; Nat Lubricating Grease Inst. *Res:* Lubricants; colloids; rheology; metal soaps. *Mailing Add:* 1620 Aster Dr Cherry Hill NJ 08003-2598

RAICH, JAMES W, TERRESTRIAL PLANT ECOLOGY, TROPICAL FOREST ECOSYSTEMS. *Current Pos:* ASST PROF, DEPT BOT, IOWA STATE UNIV, 92- *Personal Data:* b Nebr, Dec 21, 53. *Educ:* Mich State Univ, BS, 77; Univ Fla, MS, 80, Duke Univ, PhD(forestry), 87. *Prof Exp:* Postdoctoral res assoc, Ecosysts Ctr, Marine Biol Lab, Woods Hole, Mass, 87-89, res assoc, 89-90; postdoctoral fel, Dept Biol Sci, Stanford Univ, 90-92. *Concurrent Pos:* Res grantee, Nat Geog Soc, 86, Iowa State Univ, 93-95, Iowa Sci Found, 94-95, Iowa Dept Natural Resources, 94-97, Iowa Ctr Global & Regional Environ Res, 95-97 & USDA, 95-; Fulbright grantee, Jawaharlal Univ, New Delhi, India, 96-97. *Mem:* AAAS; Am Inst Biol Sci; Ecol Soc Am; Int Soc Trop Foresters; Soil Sci Soc Am; Asn Trop Biol. *Res:* Terrestrial plant ecology; environmental controls over carbon cycling, plant productivity, diversity, and nutrient cycling in plant communities; global carbon cycle modeling. *Mailing Add:* Dept Bot 353 Bessey Hall Iowa State Univ Sci & Technol Ames IA 50011-1020

RAICH, JOHN CARL, SOLID STATE PHYSICS, CHEMICAL PHYSICS. *Current Pos:* from asst prof to prof physics, 61-78, chmn dept, 72-78, assoc dean, 78-85, DEAN, COL NAT SCI, COLO STATE UNIV, 85- *Personal Data:* b Badgastein, Austria, May 9, 37; US citizen; m 63, Mary Deagle; c Paul & Brenda. *Educ:* Iowa State Univ, BS, 59, PhD(physics), 63. *Prof Exp:* Res assoc physics, Iowa State Univ, 64 & Purdue Univ, 64-66. *Concurrent Pos:* Consult, Los Alamos Sci Lab, 71-; NATO sr fel sci, NSF, 75, Humboldt fel, 77. *Mem:* Am Phys Soc. *Res:* Statistical mechanics of molecular crystals. *Mailing Add:* 1413 Osprey Ct Ft Collins CO 80525

RAICHEL, DANIEL R(ICHTER), THEORETICAL PHYSICS & ACOUSTICS, THERMAL & FLUID SCIENCES. *Current Pos:* PRIN, RAICHEL TECHNOL GROUP, 79-; PROF MECH ENG, COOPER UNION, 90- *Personal Data:* b Paterson, NJ, Aug 22, 35; m 67, Geri Wahrman; c Adam M & Dina K. *Educ:* Rensselaer Polytech Inst, BME, 57; Mass Inst Technol, SM, 58; Columbia Univ, MechEngr, 62; NY Univ, EngScD, 70. *Prof Exp:* Asst proj engr, Curtiss-Wright Corp, 61-62; instr, Wind Tunnel Lab, Case Inst Technol, 62-63; eng consult, Polytech Design Corp, 63-64; asst res scientist aeronaut & astronaut, NY Univ, 64-65; instr mech eng, Newark Col Eng, 65-67; independent consult, 67-68; consult advan develop eng, Electro-Nucleonics, Inc, 69-71; pres & chief scientist med & lab instrumentation, Dathar Corp, 71-75; prin, Ingenieurs Int, 75-79; prof mech eng, Pratt Inst, 83-91. *Concurrent Pos:* Adj prof mech eng, NJ Inst Technol, 78-82; vis prof, Grad Ctr, City Univ NY, 95- *Mem:* Fel Am Soc Mech Engrs; Am Phys Soc; Acoust Soc Am; Audio Eng Soc; Sigma Xi; Am Soc Eng Educr. *Res:* Acoustics; fluid mechanics; materials science; molecular physics. *Mailing Add:* 532 Spencer Dr Wyckoff NJ 07481. *E-Mail:* raichel@juno.com

RAICHLE, MARCUS EDWARD, NEUROLOGY. *Current Pos:* res instr neurol, Sch Med, Washington Univ, 71-72, asst prof neurol & radiol, 72-75, asst prof biomed eng, 74-75, assoc prof neurol, 75-78, assoc prof radiol & biomed eng, 75-79, PROF NEUROL & RADIATION SCI, SCH MED, WASHINGTON UNIV, 78-, PROF BIOMED ENG, 79-, SR MCDONNELL FEL, 82-, PROF NEUROBIOL, 93- *Personal Data:* b Hoquiam, Wash, Mar 15, 37; m 64, Mary E Rupert; c Marcus E, Timothy S, Sarah E & Katherine A. *Educ:* Univ Wash, BS, 60, MD, 64. *Honors & Awards:* E O Jones Scholar Prize, Univ Wash Sch Med, 64; Numerous lectureships, 78-94; Sarah L Poiley Mem Award, NY Acad Sci, 84. *Prof Exp:* Intern, Baltimore City Hosp, 64-65; resident med, 65-66; from asst neurologist to neurologist, NY Hosp, Cornell Med Ctr, 66-69, instr neurol, 68-69; consult, Sch Aerospace Med, USAF, 69-71. *Concurrent Pos:* NIH teacher-investr award, Nat Inst Neurol & Commun Dis & Stroke, 71-; from asst neurologist to neurologist, Barnes Hosp, 71-78, neurologist, 78-; mem, Neurol A Study Sect, NIH, 75 & Cardiovasc D Res Study Comt, Am Heart Asn, 75-; consult neurologist, St Louis Children's Hosp, 75-; neurologist, Jewish Hosp, 84-, St Louis Regional Hosp, 85- *Mem:* Nat Acad Sci; Inst Med-Nat Acad Sci; Am Physiol Soc; Soc Neuroscience; Am Neurol Asn; AAAS; Am Heart Asn; hon foreign mem Asn Brit Neurologists; Int Soc Cerebral Blood Flow & Metab (secy, 85-89, pres-elect, 89-91, pres, 91-93); Soc Nuclear Med; Am Acad Neurol. *Res:* In vivo measurement of brain hemodynamics, metabolism and exchange processes using trace kinetic techniques and positron-emitting, cyclotron-produced radioisotopes. *Mailing Add:* 4525 Scott Ave 2nd Floor Rm 2116 E Bldg Washington Univ Med Sch 510 S Kingshighway St Louis MO 63110. *Fax:* 314-362-6110; *E-Mail:* marc@npg.wustl.edu

RAICHLEN, FREDRIC, HYDRAULICS. *Current Pos:* from asst prof to assoc prof, 62-72, PROF CIVIL ENG, CALIF INST TECHNOL, 72- *Personal Data:* b Baltimore, Md, Oct 12, 32. *Educ:* Johns Hopkins Univ, BE, 53; Mass Inst Technol, SM, 55, SCD, 62. *Prof Exp:* Fel & asst prof civil eng, Mass Inst Technol, 62. *Mem:* Nat Acad Eng; Int Asn Hydraulic Res; Sigma Xi; fel Am Soc Civil Engrs. *Mailing Add:* Calif Inst Technol MC 138-78 1200 E California Ave Pasadena CA 91125

RAIDER, STANLEY IRWIN, MATERIALS SCIENCE, SURFACE & INTERFACE CHEMISTRY. *Current Pos:* chemist, East Fishkill Facil, IBM Components Div, Hopewell Junction, NY, 67-75, CHEMIST, T J WATSON RES CTR, IBM CORP, 75- *Personal Data:* b New York, NY, July 21, 34; m 60; c 2. *Educ:* Brooklyn Polytech Inst, BChE, 57; State Univ NY, Syracuse, MS, 62; State Univ NY Stony Brook, PhD(chem), 67. *Honors & Awards:* T D Callinan Award, Electrochem Soc, 93. *Prof Exp:* Chem engr, US Naval Powder Plant, 56 & Hooker Chem Co, 58-59. *Concurrent Pos:* Assoc ed, J Electrochem Soc. *Mem:* Electrochem Soc; Mat Res Soc. *Res:* Surface and interface chemistry; failure mechanisms in thin dielectric films; spectroscopy; superconducting materials; superconducting devices; technical editing. *Mailing Add:* IBM T J Watson Res Ctr PO Box 218 Yorktown Heights NY 10598. *Fax:* 914-945-2018; *E-Mail:* raider@watson.ibm.com

RAIFORD, MORGAN B, ophthalmology; deceased, see previous edition for last biography

RAIJMAN, LUISA J, MITOCHONDRIAL METABOLISM, BIOGENESIS. *Current Pos:* ASSOC PROF PATH & ANAT, THOMAS JEFFERSON UNIV, 90- *Personal Data:* b Cordoba, Argentina, Nov 2, 34; div. *Educ:* Nat Univ Cordoba, MD, 57. *Prof Exp:* Assoc prof, Dept Biochem, Sch Med, Univ Southern Calif, 81-90. *Concurrent Pos:* Prin investr, 75, vis assoc prof, Univ NC, Chapel Hill, 85-; comt mem, NSF, 80-85. *Mem:* Am Soc Biol Chemists; AAAS; Am Asn Univ Profs; Sigma Xi; Biochem Soc UK. *Res:* Structural and functional organization of enzymes in kinetic properties of enzymes in situ studies in fermeahilized cells and intochondria mammalian mitochondrial biogenesis. *Mailing Add:* 4036 MacNiff Dr Lafayette Hill PA 19444

RAIKHEL, NATASHA V, PLANT CELL & MOLECULAR BIOLOGY. *Current Pos:* ASST RES SCIENTIST, UNIV GA, 68- *Educ:* Inst Cytol, Russia, PhD(biol), 75. *Res:* Tissue specificity of gene expression. *Mailing Add:* Dept Energy Plant Res Lab Mich State Univ Wilson Blvd Rm 122C East Lansing MI 48824-0001

RAIKOW, RADMILA BORUVKA, AUTOIMMUNITY, CANCER BIOLOGY. *Current Pos:* fel cancer biol, 75-78, RES SCIENTIST, CANCER RES, ALLEGHENY-SINGER RES INST, PITTSBURGH, 78- *Personal Data:* b Prague, Czech, Mar 20, 39; US citizen; m 66; c 2. *Educ:* NY Univ, BA, 60; Brooklyn Col, MA, 65; Univ Calif, Berkeley, PhD(genetics), 70. *Prof Exp:* Res assoc genetics, Univ Hawaii, 70-71; fel biochem, Univ Pittsburgh, 71-72. *Concurrent Pos:* Instr biol, Univ Pittsburgh, 83- *Mem:* AAAS; Sigma Xi; Am Asn Cancer Res; Clin Immunol Soc; Soc Exp Biol & Med; NY Acad Sci. *Res:* Autoimmunity in ophthalmopathy and immune functions in cancer etiology. *Mailing Add:* 1229 Winterton St Pittsburgh PA 15206-1733

RAIKOW, ROBERT JAY, ANATOMY, ORNITHOLOGY. *Current Pos:* from asst prof to assoc prof, 71-86, PROF BIOL SCI, UNIV PITTSBURGH, 86- *Personal Data:* b Detroit, Mich, May 28, 39; m 66; c 2. *Educ:* Wayne State Univ, BS, 61, MS, 64; Univ Calif, Berkeley, PhD(zool), 69. *Prof Exp:* Actg asst prof zool, Univ Calif, Berkeley, 69-70; NIH fel, Univ Hawaii, 70-71. *Concurrent Pos:* Rev ed, Wilson Bulletin, 74-84; prin investr NSF res grants, 74 -; res assoc, Carnegie Mus Natural Hist, 75 - *Mem:* Fel AAAS; Soc Syst Zool; Am Soc Zool; fel Am Ornith Union; Cooper Orinth Soc; Wilson Orinth Soc. *Res:* Avian anatomy and systematics; vertebrate functional anatomy; phylogenetic studies of birds based on cladistic analysis of morphology, primarily appendicular myology; systematic methodology. *Mailing Add:* Dept Biol Sci Univ Pittsburgh Pittsburgh PA 15260

RAILSBACK, LOREN BRUCE, SEDIMENTARY PETROLOGY & GEOCHEMISTRY. *Current Pos:* asst prof, 89-94, ASSOC PROF GEOL, UNIV GA, 94- *Personal Data:* b Richmond, Ind, Nov 22, 57; m 78, Celeste M Condit. *Educ:* Univ Iowa, BA, 80, BS, 81, MS, 83; Univ Ill, PhD(geol), 89. *Prof Exp:* Explor geologist, Shell Oil Co, 83-85. *Concurrent Pos:* Vis assoc prof, Univ New Orleans, 97. *Mem:* Am Asn Petrol Geologists; Int Asn Sedimentologists; fel Geol Soc Am; Geochem Soc; Sigma Xi; Soc Sedimentary Geol. *Res:* Carbonate petrology, sedimentary geochemistry and pre-Cretaceous paleoceanography; stylolites and pressure dissolution; speleothems and climate records. *Mailing Add:* Dept Geol Univ Ga Athens GA 30602-2501. *Fax:* 706-542-2425

RAIMI, RALPH ALEXIS, MATHEMATICAL ANALYSIS. *Current Pos:* from asst prof to prof, Univ Rochester, 56-94, prof math, 66-94, assoc dean grad studies, Col Arts & Sci, 67-75, chmn dept sociol, 83-86, EMER PROF MATH, UNIV ROCHESTER, 94- *Personal Data:* b Detroit, Mich, July 25, 24; m 47, Sonya Drews; c Jessica & Diana. *Educ:* Univ Mich, BS, 47, MS, 48, PhD(math), 54. *Prof Exp:* Instr math, Univ Rochester, 52-55; Lloyd fel, Univ Mich, 55-56. *Concurrent Pos:* Fac ed, Coun Lib Learning, Asn Am Col, 85-86. *Mem:* Math Asn Am. *Res:* Functional analysis; topological linear spaces; invariant measures and means; mathematics education. *Mailing Add:* Dept Math Univ Rochester Rochester NY 14627. *Fax:* 716-244-6631; *E-Mail:* rarm@db2.cc.rochester.edu

RAIMONDI, ALBERT ANTHONY, TRIBOLOGY. *Current Pos:* RETIRED. *Personal Data:* b Plymouth, Mass, Mar 29, 25; m 89, Doris A Polliti. *Educ:* Tufts Col, BS, 45; Univ Pittsburgh, MS, 63, PhD(mech eng), 68. *Honors & Awards:* Hunt Mem Award, Soc Lubrication Engrs, 59, Nat Award, 68. *Prof Exp:* Fel res engr, Mech Dept, Res Labs, Westinghouse Elec Corp, 46-68, mgr lubrication mech, 68-78, mgr tribol & exp struct mech, Westinghouse Res & Develop Ctr, 78-90, consult engr, Westinghouse Sci & Technol Ctr, 90-94. *Concurrent Pos:* Ed, Soc Lubrication Engrs, 71. *Mem:* Am Soc Mech Engrs; fel Soc Lubrication Engrs. *Res:* Tribology; experimental mechanics; bearing and seal design and application; mechanical design. *Mailing Add:* 125 Eighth St Turtle Creek PA 15145-1805

RAIMONDI, ANTHONY JOHN, NEUROSURGERY, NEUROANATOMY. *Current Pos:* PROF NEUROSURG & CHMN DIV, SCH MED, NORTHWESTERN UNIV, CHICAGO, 69-, PROF ANAT, 74- *Personal Data:* b Chicago, Ill, July 16, 28; m 54; c 3. *Educ:* Univ Ill, BA & BS, 50; Univ Rome, MD, 54. *Prof Exp:* Instr neurosurg, Univ Chicago, 61-62; instr, Northwestern Univ, 62-64; clin asst prof, Univ Chicago, 64-66, clin assoc prof, 66-67; assoc prof neurosurg , Univ Ill Col Med, 67-69. *Concurrent Pos:* Attend neurosurg, Children's Mem Hosp, 62-63; chmn div neurosurg, 69-; prof, Cook County Grad Sch Med, 63-70, chmn dept, Cook County Hosp, 63-70; mem fac adv bd, Chicago Med Sch Quart, 64-66; chmn neurosurg, Vet Res Hosp, Chicago, 72-; attend neurosurgeon, Passavant Mem Hosp, 69- & Northwestern Mem Hosp, 74-; attend physician neurosurg, Surg Serv, Vet Admin Hosp; consult-lectr, Great Lakes Naval Hosp; chmn med adv comt, Am Spina Bifida Asn, Epilepsy Fund Am & Asn Brain Tumor Res. *Mem:* Am Col Surg; Am Asn Neurosurg; Am Asn Neuropath; Int Soc Pediat Neurosurg (secy); Am Asn Surg of Trauma. *Res:* Ultrastructural characteristics of normal edematous, neoplastic and toxic glia; cerebral angiography in the newborn and infant; pediatric neurosurgery; pediatric neuroradiology. *Mailing Add:* 1820 S Clarence Berwyn IL 60402-1915

RAIMONDI, PIETRO, CHEMICAL ENGINEERING. *Current Pos:* From proj chem engr to sr res engr, 57-70, SECT SUPVR, GULF RES & DEVELOP CO, 70- *Personal Data:* b Acqui, Italy, Feb 18, 29; m 56; c 6. *Educ:* Univ Notre Dame, BS, 52, MS, 53; Carnegie Inst Technol, PhD(chem eng), 57. *Mem:* Am Inst Chem Engrs; Am Inst Mining, Metall & Petrol Engrs. *Res:* Single and multiphase flow and diffusion and mixing of fluids in porous media; oil reservoir mechanics; synthetic fuel by in-situ method. *Mailing Add:* 6721 Quincy Dr Verona PA 15147

RAINA, ASHOK K, BEHAVIORAL PHYSIOLOGY, INSECT-PLANT INTERACTIONS & BIORATIONAL CONTROL. *Current Pos:* RES ENTOMOLOGIST, INSECT BIOCONTROL LAB, RES SERV, USDA, BELTSVILLE, MD, 86- *Personal Data:* b Srinagar, Kashmir, India, Feb 28, 42; US citizen; m 60; c Rakesh & Seema. *Educ:* Jammu & Kashmir Univ, India, BSc, 61; Aligarh Muslim Univ, India, MSc, 67; NDak State Univ, PhD(entom), 74. *Honors & Awards:* L O Howard Distinguished Achievement Award Entom, 91; Biol & Commun Award, Jean Marie Delwart Found & Royal Belg Sci Acad, 96. *Prof Exp:* Res asst, Commonwealth Inst Biol Control, Bangalore, India, 62-65; sr res asst, Regional Pulse Improv Proj, USAID, New Delhi, India, 67-70; res asst, NDak State Univ, 70-74; asst prof biol & elec micros, Minot State Col, Minot, NDak, 74-75; assoc entom, Va State Univ, 76-77; res scientist, Int Ctr Insect Physiol & Ecol, 78-79, prog coordr, 80-81; sr res assoc, Dept Entom, Univ Md, 81-85. *Concurrent Pos:* Adj prof, Dept Entomol, Univ Md, 87- *Mem:* Entom Soc Am; fel Entom Soc India; Int Soc Chem Ecol. *Res:* Behavioral physiology, hormones and pheromones of insects; insect-plant interactions; endocrinology; electron microscopy; discovery of new insect hormones; insect viruses; biorational pest control. *Mailing Add:* Insect Biocontrol Lab Bldg 306 USDA-Agr Res Serv Beltsville Agr Res Ctr-E Beltsville MD 20705. *E-Mail:* araina@asrg.arsusda.gov

RAINAL, ATTILIO JOSEPH, NOISE THEORY & RANDOM PROCESSES, ELECTRICAL INTERCONNECTIONS & THEIR PERFORMANCE LIMITS. *Current Pos:* mem tech staff, 64-83, DISTINGUISHED MEM TECH STAFF, AT&T BELL LABS, 83- *Personal Data:* b Marion Heights, Pa, Feb 14, 30; m 57, Violet D Robel; c Valery & Eric. *Educ:* Pa State Univ, BS, 56; Drexel Univ, MS, 59; Johns Hopkins Univ, PhD(elec eng), 63. *Prof Exp:* Engr, Martin Co, Baltimore, 56-59; staff mem res, Carlyle Barton Lab, Johns Hopkins Univ, 59-64. *Mem:* Sr mem Inst Elec & Electronics Engrs; Inst Elec & Electronics Engrs Info Theory Soc; Inst Elec & Electronics Engrs Components Hybrids & Mfg Technol Soc; Sigma Xi. *Res:* Noise theory; signal detection and estimation; radiometry; radar; FM; first passage times of random processes; crosstalk; voltage breakdown; current carrying capacity of printed conductors; performance limits of electrical interconnections; balanced interconnections and laser intensity modulation. *Mailing Add:* 28 Woodruff Rd Morristown NJ 07960

RAINBOLT, MARY LOUISE, BIOLOGY. *Current Pos:* RETIRED. *Personal Data:* b Cleveland, Okla, June 21, 25. *Educ:* Okla Baptist Univ, BS, 46; Okla State Univ, MS, 48; Univ Okla, PhD, 63. *Prof Exp:* Prof biol, Southwestern State Col, Okla, 48-65; prof, Ill Col, 64-81, head dept, 64-85, Hitchcock prof, 81-85. *Mem:* Am Soc Zool. *Res:* Physiology; endocrinology. *Mailing Add:* 710 Stolfa St SE Ardmore OK 73401-6065

RAINBOW, ANDREW JAMES, DNA REPAIR, RADIOBIOLOGY. *Current Pos:* from asst prof to assoc prof radiol, McMaster Univ, 72-84, assoc mem, Dept Biol, 73-85, prof radiol & dir Regional Radiol Sci Prog, 84-93, ASSOC MEM PHYSICS, MCMASTER UNIV, 83-, PROF BIOL, 85-, CHAIR, DEPT BIOL, 96- *Personal Data:* b Essex, Eng, Dec 18, 43; Can citizen; m 72, Anna Omeluck; c Joanna & Michael. *Educ:* Univ Manchester, BSc, 65; Univ London, MSc, 67; McMaster Univ, PhD(biol), 70. *Prof Exp:* Fel biol, McMaster Univ, 70-71; radiol hosp physicist & assoc scientist, Royal Victoria Hosp, Montreal, 71-72. *Concurrent Pos:* Lectr radiol, McGill Univ, 71-72; lectr radiography, Dawson Col, 71-72; radiol physicist, Hamilton & Dist Hosps, 72-80; teaching master radiation physics, radiobiol & protection, Mohawk Col, Ont, 72-87; dir, Regional Radiol Sci Prog, Chedoke-McMaster Hosps, 80-84; vis scholar, Dept Zool, Univ Cambridge, UK, 83; chmn, Div Med & Biol Physics, Can Asn Physicists, 85-86; vis prof, Flinders Univ SAustralia, 88-89; vis scientist, QIMR, Brisbane, Queensland Australia, 94; actg dir, Inst Molecular Biol & Biotechnol, 94-95. *Mem:* Fel Can Col Physicists Med; Radiation Res Soc; Am Soc Photobiol; Genetics Soc Can. *Res:* Role of DNA damage and DNA repair in human cancer; radiobiology of viruses; patient exposure and quality assurance measurements in diagnostic radiology; medical physics. *Mailing Add:* Dept Biol McMaster Univ/Life Sci Bldg Rm 218A Hamilton ON L8S 4K1 Can. *Fax:* 905-522-6066; *E-Mail:* rainbow@mcmail.cis.mcmaster.ca

RAINE, CEDRIC STUART, NEUROPATHOLOGY. *Current Pos:* from asst prof to assoc prof path, 69-78, PROF PATH, ALBERT EINSTEIN COL MED, 78-, PROF NEUROSCI, 79- *Personal Data:* b Eastbourne, Eng, May 11, 40; m 63; c 1. *Educ:* Univ Durham, BSc, 62; Univ Newcastle, PhD(med), 67, DSc(med), 75; FRCPath, 88. *Honors & Awards:* Weil Award, Am Asn Neuropath, 69 & 75, Moore Award, 76. *Prof Exp:* Sci officer neuropath, Demyelinating Dis Unit, Med Res Coun, Eng, 64-68. *Concurrent Pos:* NIH interdisciplinary fel, Albert Einstein Col Med, 68-69; NIH career develop award, 72-77; Javits Award 85-92; mem Neuro C Study Sect NIH, Nat MS Soc study sect, 87-92. *Mem:* AAAS; Assoc Am Asn Neuropath; Soc Neurosci; NY Acad Sci; Brit Soc Neuropath; Am Soc Neurochem ARNMD; Soc Neuroimmunol. *Res:* Demyelinating conditions; nervous system development; ultrastructure; viral infections of nervous tissue; multiple sclerosis; in vitro studies of organized nervous tissue; myelin pathology; neuroimmunology. *Mailing Add:* Dept Path Albert Einstein Col Med 1300 Morris Park Ave Bronx NY 10461-1924

RAINER, JOHN DAVID, PSYCHIATRY, MEDICAL GENETICS. *Current Pos:* CO-CHMN, INST REV BD. *Personal Data:* b Brooklyn, NY, July 13, 21; m 44, Barbara Antin; c Jeffrey & Peter. *Educ:* Columbia Univ, AB, 41, MA, 44, MD, 51. *Hon Degrees:* LittD, Gallaudet Col, 68. *Prof Exp:* Assoc res scientist, NY State Psychiat Inst, 56-65, actg chief psychiat res, 65-68, chief, 68-91. *Concurrent Pos:* From asst to assoc prof, Columbia Univ, 59-72, prof clin psychiat, 72- *Mem:* Asn Res Nerv Ment Dis; Am Soc Human Genetics; fel Am Psychiat Asn; fel Am Psychoanal Asn; Am Psychopath Asn. *Res:* Application of human genetics to psychiatry on molecular, cellular, chemical, psychological and social levels; psychiatric treatment of the deaf. *Mailing Add:* NY State Psychiat Inst 722 W 168th St New York NY 10032. *E-Mail:* jdr1@columbia.edu

RAINER, NORMAN BARRY, APPLIED CHEMISTRY. *Current Pos:* SR SCIENTIST CATALYSIS & NATURAL PRODS, RES & DEVELOP, PHILIP MORRIS CORP, 68- *Personal Data:* b New York, NY, May 14, 29. *Educ:* Univ Chicago, MS, 50; Univ Del, PhD(phys org chem), 56. *Prof Exp:* Res chemist polymers, Textile Fibers Div, E I du Pont de Nemours & Co, Inc, 56-61; res mgr polymers, Fibers Div, Allied Chem Corp, 61-68. *Mem:* Am Chem Soc. *Res:* Catalysis; fast organic reactions; inorganic chemistry; pyrolysis of cellulose. *Mailing Add:* 2008 Fon-Du-Lac Rd Richmond VA 23229

RAINES, ARTHUR, NEUROPHARMACOLOGY, CARDIOVASCULAR PHARMACOLOGY. *Current Pos:* PROF PHARMACOL & ACTG DEPT CHMN, SCH MED & DENT, GEORGETOWN UNIV, 69- *Educ:* Cornell Univ, PhD(pharmacol), 65. *Mailing Add:* Pharmacol Dept Georgetown Univ Sch Med 3900 Reservoir Rd Washington DC 20007-2195

RAINES, GARY L, ECONOMIC GEOLOGY. *Current Pos:* DEPUTY CHIEF, MINERAL RESOURCES, US GEOL SURV, 83-, GEOLOGIST, 88- *Personal Data:* b Pocatello, Idaho, Jan 21, 46. *Educ:* Univ Calif, Los Angeles, BA, 69; Colo Sch Mines, MA & PhD(geol), 71. *Mem:* Geol Soc Am. *Mailing Add:* US Geol Surv Reno Field Off Mackay Sch Mines Univ Nevada Reno NV 89557

RAINES, JEREMY KEITH, ELECTROMAGNETIC ENGINEERING. *Current Pos:* CONSULT ANTENNAS, 73- *Personal Data:* b Washington, DC, Nov 25, 47. *Educ:* Mass Inst Technol, BS, 69, PhD(electromagnetics), 74; Harvard Univ, MS, 70. *Prof Exp:* Instr elec eng, Mass Inst Technol, 69-73. *Concurrent Pos:* Elec engr commun, Naval Electronics Systs Command, 70; elec engr opers res, Naval Ship Res & Develop Ctr, Carderock, 71; elec engr electronics, Naval Electronics Lab Ctr, San Diego, 72; lectr antennas, George Washington Univ, 75- *Mem:* Asn Fed Commun Consult Engrs; Am Phys Soc; Fedn Am Scientists; Inst Elec & Electronics Engrs; Soc Am Mil Engrs. *Res:* Mathematical modeling of antennas and antenna arrays; analysis and design of communication and data transmission networks; radio wave propagation; electromagnetic theory; biological hazards of electromagnetic fields. *Mailing Add:* 13420 Cleveland Dr Rockville MD 20850-3603

RAINES, RONALD T, PROTEIN DESIGN & ENGINEERING. *Current Pos:* ASST PROF, DEPT BIOCHEM, UNIV WIS-MADISON, 89- *Personal Data:* b Montclair, NJ, Aug 13, 58. *Educ:* Mass Inst Technol, BS(chem) & BS(biol), 80; Harvard Univ, MA, 82, PhD(chem), 86. *Prof Exp:* Postdoctoral fel, Univ Calif, San Francisco, 86-89. *Concurrent Pos:* Searle scholar, Chicago Community Trust, 90; NSF presidential young investr, 90. *Mem:* Sigma Xi; Am Soc Biochem & Molecular Biol; AAAS; Am Chem Soc. *Res:* Protein design and engineering; protein folding; molecular recognition; heterologous gene expression. *Mailing Add:* Dept Biochem Univ Wis-Madison 420 Henry Mall Madison WI 53706-1569

RAINES, THADDEUS JOSEPH, polymer chemistry, for more information see previous edition

RAINEY, DONALD PAUL, AGRICULTURE. *Current Pos:* RES ASSOC, ELI LILLY & CO, 67- *Personal Data:* b Indianapolis, Ind, June 29, 40; m 79; c 3. *Educ:* Butler Univ, BS, 62; Univ Wis-Madison, MS, 65, PhD(biochem), 67. *Mem:* Am Chem Soc; Sigma Xi. *Res:* Environmental fate of agricultural chemicals in soil, water, plants and animals; pathways by which agricultural chemicals are degraded in the environment. *Mailing Add:* 7361 W 100 N Greenfield IN 46140-9666

RAINEY, JOHN MARION, JR, ANXIETY DISORDERS, FORENSIC PSYCHIATRY. *Current Pos:* asst prof psychiat, & dir res, Lafayette Clin, 74-87, DIR MED CONTINUING EDUC, DEPT BEHAV & NEUROSCI, DETROIT MED CTR, WAYNE STATE UNIV, 74-, ASSOC PROF PSYCHIAT, 87- *Personal Data:* b Atlanta, Ga, June 20, 42; m 69; c 2. *Educ:* Vanderbilt Univ, BA, 63, MD, 69, PhD(biochem), 72. *Honors & Awards:* William C Menninger Award, Cent Neuropsychiat Asn, 74. *Prof Exp:* Intern path, Vanderbilt Univ Hosp, 70-71, from resident to chief resident psychiat, 71-74. *Concurrent Pos:* Consult, Vet Admin, Sci Adv Comn, 80-, Allen Park Vet Admin Hosp, 84-, NIMH, 84- & Mich Bd Pharm, 85- *Mem:* Soc Biol Psychiat; Sigma Xi; Am Psychiat Asn; AMA. *Res:* Biological psychiatry and biochemistry; neurophysiology and psychobiology of sudden death in psychiatric disorders; cardiovascular effects of psychotropic drugs; physiology and biochemistry of anxiety disorders. *Mailing Add:* 766 Balfour St Grosse Pointe Park MI 48230

RAINEY, MARY LOUISE, ANALYTICAL CHEMISTRY. *Current Pos:* res spec, Analysis Labs, Dow Chem, 74-79, group leader, designed latexes & resins res, 79-84, mgr Fed Drug Admin Compliance, 84- 89, MGR HEALTH, ENVIRON & REGULATORY AFFAIRS, DOW CHEM, 89- *Personal Data:* b Flagler, Colo, Jan 20, 43; m 67; c 2. *Educ:* Knox Col, BA, 64; Univ Md, PhD(analytical chem), 74. *Prof Exp:* Teacher math, Cardozo High Sch, Washington, DC, 67-69; master teacher, Urban Teacher Corps, Washington, DC, 68-69; teacher math, Walt Whitman High Sch, Bethesda, Md, 69-71. *Mem:* Sigma Xi; Asn Women Sci; Am Chem Soc. *Res:* High performance liquid chromatography, gas chromatography. *Mailing Add:* 1320 Waldo Ave Dow Chem Midland MI 48642

RAINEY, ROBERT HAMRIC, RADIOCHEMISTRY. *Current Pos:* RETIRED. *Personal Data:* b Charleston, Miss, Mar 23, 18; m 47, Margaret W; c 3. *Educ:* Memphis State Univ, BS, 42. *Prof Exp:* Chemist, Oak Ridge Gaseous Diffusion Plant, 45-51; group leader process develop, Oak Ridge Nat Lab, 51-78, consult, 85-86; Oak Ridge Assoc Univs, 78-84. *Concurrent Pos:* Consult, through pvt co & Ger res lab. *Mem:* Am Nuclear Soc; Sigma Xi. *Res:* Nuclear reactor fuel recovery process development, separation and isolation of thorium, uranium, plutonium, protactinium, and americium by solvent extraction and ion exchange; environmental impact studies of nuclear reactors and nuclear fuel reprocessing facilities; fuel cycle economics. *Mailing Add:* 3635 Taliluna Ave Knoxville TN 37919

RAINIS, ALBERT EDWARD, RADIATION PHYSICS. *Current Pos:* PHYSICIST, OFFICE SECY DEFENSE, 86- *Personal Data:* b Chicago, Ill, May 15, 41; m 63; c 2. *Educ:* DePaul Univ, BS, 63, MS, 65; Univ Notre Dame, PhD(nuclear physics), 71, Cent Mich Univ, MBA, 81. *Prof Exp:* Asst prof physics, Tri-State Col, 70-72 & WVa Univ, 72-75; physicist, Ballistics Res Lab, 75-86. *Concurrent Pos:* Geothermal consult, WVa Univ, 75-79. *Mem:* Am Phys Soc; Sigma Xi. *Res:* Nuclear radiation transport; geothermal phenomena; shielding calculations. *Mailing Add:* 522 Colecroft Ct Alexandria VA 22314

RAINIS, ANDREW, SURFACE CHEMISTRY, COAL PREPARATION. *Current Pos:* SR RES CHEMIST, CHEVRON RES CO, 80- *Personal Data:* b Riga, Latvia, June 6, 40; Australian citizen; m 68; c 2. *Educ:* Univ New South Wales, Australia, BSc, 65, PhD(phys chem), 69. *Prof Exp:* Res assoc phys chem, Columbia Univ, 69-70 & Col Environ Sci & Forestry, State Univ NY, Syracuse, 70-75; proj mgr, Otisca Indust Ltd, 75-80. *Mem:* Am Chem Soc; AAAS. *Res:* Mineral beneficiation; fossil fuel recovery and upgrading. *Mailing Add:* Chevron Res Co PO Box 1627 Richmond CA 94802-1792

RAINS, DONALD W, PLANT NUTRITION, SOIL SCIENCE. *Current Pos:* asst soil scientist, 66-70, assoc prof agron & range sci, 74-77, AGRONOMIST, UNIV CALIF, DAVIS, 70-, PROF AGRON, 77- *Personal Data:* b Fairfield, Iowa, Dec 16, 37; m 59; c 3. *Educ:* Univ Calif, Davis, BS, 61, MS, 63, PhD(soil sci), 66. *Prof Exp:* NSF fel, 65-66. *Concurrent Pos:* Consult, 65; lectr soil sci, 68-74; dir, Plant Growth Lab, 79-81; Chmn, Agron & Range Sci, 81-87. *Mem:* AAAS; Am Soc Plant Physiol; Am Soc Agron; Crop Sci Soc Am. *Res:* Ion transport and translocation in plants; plant nutrition and salinity; mineral cycling; heavy metal nutrition in soil-plant ecosystems; plant cell culture. *Mailing Add:* Dept Agron & Range Sci Univ Calif Davis CA 95616-8515

RAINS, ROGER KERANEN, CHEMICAL PROCESS RESEARCH, RESEARCH MANAGEMENT. *Current Pos:* Sr res engr, Technol Dept, Monsanto Indust Chem Co, 68-72, res group leader, 72-78, sr res group leader, 78-82, res sec mgr, 83-85, RES MGR, MONSANTO CHEM CO, 86- *Personal Data:* b Ann Arbor, Mich, May 11, 40; m 67; c 2. *Educ:* Univ Mich, BSE, 63, MSE, 64, MS, 65, PhD(chem eng), 68. *Mem:* Am Chem Soc; Am Inst Chem Engrs. *Res:* Process research and development, primarily separation processes and chemical reaction engineering; process research and development; rubber chemicals. *Mailing Add:* 3453 Timberwood Trail Richfield OH 44286-9755

RAINS, THEODORE CONRAD, ANALYTICAL CHEMISTRY. *Current Pos:* PRES, HIGH PURITY STAND, 90- *Personal Data:* b Pleasureville, Ky, Jan 10, 25; m 47; c 3. *Educ:* Eastern Ky Univ, BS, 50. *Honors & Awards:* Cert Recognition, E2 & E3, Am Soc Testing & Mat, 68. *Prof Exp:* Teacher pub sch, Ky, 50-51; chemist, Ky Synthetic Rubber Co, 51-52 & Union Carbide Nuclear Co, 52-65; res chemist, Nat Bur Stand, 65-90. *Concurrent Pos:* Vis prof, Univ Md, College Park, 75; column ed, J Appl Spectros, 75- *Mem:* Am Chem Soc; Soc Appl Spectros (pres, 82). *Res:* Solvent extraction with applications for analytical chemistry; atomic absorption; emission and fluorescence spectrometry. *Mailing Add:* High Purity Stand PO Box 86609 Charleston SC 29416-0609

RAINVILLE, DAVID PAUL, ORGANOTELLURIUM CHEMISTRY. *Current Pos:* asst prof, 82-86, ASSOC PROF, INORG CHEM, UNIV WIS, RIVER FALLS, 86- *Personal Data:* b Dover, NH, June, 21, 52. *Educ:* Univ NH, BA, 74; Tex A&M Univ, PhD(chem), 79. *Prof Exp:* Res assoc, Tex A&M

Univ, 79 & Univ NH, 80; asst prof chem, Austin Col, 81-82. *Mem:* Am Chem Soc. *Res:* Synthesis of selenium and tellurium containing heterocycles for use in charge-transfer systems; electrolysis plating of metals via organometallics. *Mailing Add:* Chem Univ Wis River Falls WI 54022-5099

RAINWATER, DAVID LUTHER, LIPOPROTEINS. *Current Pos:* postdoctoral scientist, SW Found Biomed Res, 84-87, asst scientist, 87-91, assoc scientist, 91-94, HEAD, LIPOPROTEIN GENETICS LAB, SOUTHWEST FOUND BIOMED RES, 89-, SCIENTIST, 94- *Personal Data:* b Phoenix, Ariz, Feb 13, 47; m 70, Catherine Bomberger; c Elizabeth & Emily. *Educ:* Chapman Col, Orange, Calif, BA, 69; Univ Southern Calif, Los Angeles, PhD(cellular & molecular biol), 79. *Prof Exp:* Postdoctoral res assoc, Inst Biol Chem, Wash State Univ, 79-84. *Mem:* Fel Am Heart Asn; Am Soc Biochem & Molecular Biol; AAAS; Am Asn Clin Chem. *Res:* Genetic and dietary effects on primate lipoprotein phenotypes; lipoprotein chemistry and metabolism; animal models of atherosclerosis. *Mailing Add:* Dept Genetics SW Found Biomed Res PO Box 760549 San Antonio TX 78245-0549. *Fax:* 210-670-3317; *E-Mail:* david@darwin.sfbr.org

RAINWATER, JAMES CARLTON, STATISTICAL MECHANICS, KINETIC THEORY. *Current Pos:* res fel, 76-78, PHYSICIST, NAT INST STANDARDS & TECHNOL, BOULDER, COLO, 78- *Personal Data:* b New York, NY, Jan 9, 46; m *Educ:* Univ Colo, BA, 67, PhD(physics), 74. *Prof Exp:* Lectr physics, Univ Colo, Denver, 74; res fel chem, Univ BC, 75-76. *Concurrent Pos:* Vis physicist, Nat Bur Standards, Washington, DC, 79; assoc adj prof physics, Univ Colo, 85-94, lectr, 94- *Mem:* Am Phys Physics Teachers. *Res:* Classical and quantum statistical mechanics; kinetic theory; phase transitions and critical phenomena in mixtures; non-Newtonian liquids. *Mailing Add:* Nat Inst Standards & Technol Boulder CO 80303-3328

RAIRDEN, JOHN RUEL, III, METALLURGICAL ENGINEERING. *Current Pos:* RETIRED. *Personal Data:* b Denver, Colo, Apr 9, 30; m 50; c 2. *Educ:* Colo Sch Mines, MetE, 51; Rensselaer Polytech Inst, MMetE, 58. *Prof Exp:* Trainee engr, Gen Elec Co, 51-53, specialist, Res Lab, 53-57, metall engr, Res & Develop Ctr, 57-90. *Res:* Anodizing and surface treatment of metals; vacuum deposition and sputtering of thin films; oxidation and corrosion resistant coatings for high temperature alloys and plasma spray processing. *Mailing Add:* 2675 County Rd 1 Montrose CO 81401

RAISBECK, BARBARA, DEVELOPMENTAL BIOLOGY, INSECT PHYSIOLOGY. *Current Pos:* SCIENCE WRITER, 79- *Personal Data:* b Arlington, Mass, Feb 7, 28; m 48, Gordon Raisbeck; c Michael N, Lucy M (Trombley), Alison J (Lanman), Timothy G & James G. *Educ:* Boston Univ, BS, 51; Brandeis Univ, PhD(biol), 69. *Prof Exp:* Res assoc biol, Tufts Univ, 69-71; Nat Res Coun vis scientist, Pioneering Res Labs, US Army Natick Labs, 71-73; instr, 70-71, asst prof, 73-74, res assoc biol, Northeastern Univ, 75-76; mem fac, Middlesex Community Col, 78-79. *Concurrent Pos:* Consult, Arthur D Little, 74-76. *Res:* Insect development; tissue culture; insect behavior; human anatomy and physiology. *Mailing Add:* 40 Deering St Portland ME 04104-2212. *E-Mail:* 71742.1031@compuserve.com

RAISBECK, GORDON, MANAGEMENT OF TECHNOLOGICAL INNOVATION. *Current Pos:* RETIRED. *Personal Data:* b New York, NY, May 4, 25; m 48, Barbara Wiener; c Michael N, Lucy M (Trombley), Alison J (Lanman), Timothy G & James G. *Educ:* Stanford Univ, BA, 44; Mass Inst Technol, PhD(math), 49. *Honors & Awards:* Distinguished Serv Award, Oceanic Eng Soc, Inst Elec & Electronics Engrs, 92. *Prof Exp:* Asst, Stanford Univ, 43-44; instr math, Mass Inst Technol, 46-47 & 48-49; mem tech staff, Bell Tel Labs, Inc, 49-54, dir transmission line res, 54-61; sr staff mem systs eng, Arthur D Little, Inc, 61-64, dir systs eng, 65-72, dir phys sensor systs res, 72-75, vpres, 73-86. *Concurrent Pos:* Mem, Inst Defense Anal, 59-60. *Mem:* Fel Inst Elec & Electronics Engrs; Math Asn Am; fel Acoust Soc Am; Oceanic Eng Soc (secy, 87-91); Eng Mgt Soc. *Res:* Information theory; communication technology and system analysis; transmission lines; underwater acoustics; research and development planning; management of technological innovation. *Mailing Add:* 40 Deering St Portland ME 04101-2212. *E-Mail:* 71742.1031@compuserve.com

RAISEN, ELLIOTT, INORGANIC CHEMISTRY, PHYSICAL CHEMISTRY. *Current Pos:* PRES, CARDIO-RESPIRATORY HOME CARE INC, 79- *Personal Data:* b New York, NY, Apr 24, 28; m 50; c 3. *Educ:* City Col New York, BS, 50; Univ Cincinnati, MS, 52, PhD(inorg chem), 60. *Prof Exp:* Asst, Univ Cincinnati, 50-52; res chemist, Bell Aircraft Corp, NY, 54-56; res chemist, Ill Inst Technol Res Inst, 56-62, sr scientist, 62-72, mgr phys chem sect, 72-76; dir chem res div, Toth Aluminum Corp, New Orleans, 76-77; pres, E&S Enterprises, Inc, 77- *Mem:* Am Chem Soc; Am Inst Aeronaut & Astronaut; Am Ordnance Asn; Sigma Xi; NY Acad Sci. *Res:* Inorganic complexes; phosphate and high temperature chemistry; high temperature reactions; visible and infrared radiation from chemical reactions; water treatment; oxygen production. *Mailing Add:* 4721 Taft Park Metairie LA 70002-1438

RAISZ, LAWRENCE GIDEON, INTERNAL MEDICINE, ENDOCRINOLOGY. *Current Pos:* PROF MED & HEAD DIV ENDOCRINOL & METAB, SCH MED, UNIV CONN HEALTH CTR, FARMINGTON, 74- *Personal Data:* b New York, NY, Nov 13, 25; m 48, Helen Martin; c Stephen, Matthew, Jonathan, Katherine & Nicholas. *Educ:* Harvard Med Sch, MD, 47. *Hon Degrees:* Dr, Univ Umea, Sweden, 90. *Honors & Awards:* E B Astwood Lectr Award; Andre Lichtwitz Prize, 80; William F Neuman Award, 86. *Prof Exp:* Instr physiol, Col Med, NY Univ-Bellevue Med Ctr, 48-50; resident med, Vet Admin Hosp, Boston, 52-54; instr, Sch Med, Boston Univ, 54-56; asst prof, Col Med, State Univ NY Upstate Med Ctr, 56-61; assoc prof pharmacol & med, Sch Med & Dent, Univ Rochester, 61-66, assoc prof med, 66-68, prof pharmacol & toxicol, 66-74. *Concurrent Pos:* USPHS spec fel, Strangeways Res Lab, Cambridge, Eng, 60-61, Nat Inst Dent Res, NIH, 71-72; asst chief radioisotopes, Vet Admin Hosp, Syracuse Univ, 56-57, clin investr, 57-61; physician, Strong Mem Hosp, 68-74. *Mem:* AMA; Am Fedn Clin Res; Am Soc Pharmacol & Exp Therapeut; Am Soc Clin Invest; Asn Am Physicians; Am Soc Bone & Mineral Res. *Res:* Parathyroid and calcium metabolism; clinical pharmacology; endocrinology and metabolism; laboratory studies on the hormonal and local regulation of bone formation and resorption and clinical studies on the pathogenesis; prevention and treatment of osteoporosis. *Mailing Add:* Div Endocrinol & Metab Sch Med Univ Conn Health Ctr Farmington CT 06032-9984. *Fax:* 860-679-1258; *E-Mail:* raisz@nso.uchc.edu

RAITT, RALPH JAMES, JR, VERTEBRATE ZOOLOGY. *Current Pos:* RETIRED. *Personal Data:* b Santa Ana, Calif, Feb 9, 29; m 53; c 2. *Educ:* Stanford Univ, AB, 50; Univ Calif, Berkeley, PhD(zool), 59. *Prof Exp:* Technician, Mus Vert Zool, Univ Calif, Berkeley, 53-55, teaching asst zool, 56-58; from instr to prof biol, NMex State Univ, 58- *Concurrent Pos:* Guggenheim Mem fel, 67; ed, The Condor, 69-71. *Mem:* Soc Study Evolution; Soc Syst Zool; Animal Behav Soc; Cooper Ornith Soc; Am Ornith Union. *Res:* Ecology, behavior, evolution and systematics of birds, especially those of southwestern United States and Latin America. *Mailing Add:* 3257 Fairway Dr Las Cruces NM 88011

RAITZER, CYNTHIA CARILLI, PROTEIN CHEMISTRY. *Current Pos:* VPRES SCI AFFAIRS, SCICLONE PHARMACEUT INC, 91- *Personal Data:* b San Jose, Calif, Jan 22, 58. *Educ:* Harvard Univ, BS, 79; Univ Calif, Berkeley, PhD(biochem), 84. *Prof Exp:* Sr scientist, Seicas, Nova, 84-90; mgr prod develop, Beckton-Dickerson, 90-91. *Mem:* AAAS; Am Soc Biochem & Molecular Biol. *Res:* Protein chemistry. *Mailing Add:* SciClone Pharmaceut Inc 901 Mariners Island Blvd Suite 315 San Mateo CA 94404

RAIZADA, MOHAN K, CELLULAR ENDOCRINOLOGY, CELLULAR BIOLOGY. *Current Pos:* res assoc, 76-78, from asst prof to assoc prof physiol & biochem, 79-86, PROF PHYSIOL, UNIV FLA, 86- *Personal Data:* b Fatehpur, India, Oct 21, 48; m 79, Laura; c Kristen & Keely. *Educ:* Univ Lucknow, India, BS, 64, MSc, 66; Univ Kanpur, PhD(biol sci), 72. *Honors & Awards:* Young Scientist Medal, Institut Nat de Systematique Appliquee Can, 74; Outstanding Scientist Award, Sigma Xi, 88. *Prof Exp:* Fel biochem, Med Col Wis, 73-74; assoc cell biol, Lady Davis Inst, Montreal, 74-76. *Mem:* Endocrine Soc; Am Soc Cell Biol; Am Physiol Soc; AAAS. *Res:* Regulation of insulin receptors in cells cultured from nondiabetic and diabetic animals and humans; role of the central nervous system angiotensin-effector system in the development and maintenance of hypertension; molecular physiology and endocrinology of CNS mediated hypertension. *Mailing Add:* Dept Physiol Box 100274 Col Med Univ Fla Gainsville FL 32610-0001

RAIZEN, MARK GEORGE, ATOM OPTICS, QUANTUM CHAOS. *Current Pos:* asst prof, 91-96, ASSOC PROF, DEPT PHYSICS, UNIV TEX, AUSTIN, 96- *Personal Data:* b New York, NY, June 13, 55. *Educ:* Tel-Aviv Univ, BSc, 80; Univ Tex, Austin, PhD(physics), 89. *Prof Exp:* Fel, Nat Inst Sci & Technol, Boulder, Colo, 89-91. *Mem:* Am Phys Soc; Optical Soc Am. *Res:* Experimental study of quantum chaos with ultra-cold atoms; quantum transport of atoms in optical lattices. *Mailing Add:* Dept Physics Univ Tex Austin TX 78712. *Fax:* 512-471-9637; *E-Mail:* raizen@physics.utexas.edu

RAIZEN, SENTA AMON, PHYSICAL CHEMISTRY. *Current Pos:* DIR, NAT CTR IMPROVING SCI EDUC, 88- *Personal Data:* b Vienna, Austria, Oct 28, 24; US citizen; m 48; c 3. *Educ:* Guilford Col, BS, 44; Bryn Mawr Col, MA, 45. *Prof Exp:* Res chemist, Sun Oil Co, Pa, 45-48; staff asst chem, Nat Acad Sci-Nat Res Coun, 60-62; prof asst sci educ & admin, NSF, 62-65, asst prog dir, 65-68, assoc prog dir, 68-69, spec tech asst, 69-71; sr prog planner, Nat Inst Educ, 71-72; sr researcher, Domestic Prog Ctr, Rand Corp, 72-74; assoc dir, Nat Inst Educ, 74-78; independent consult, 78-80; study dir, Nat Acad Sci, 80-88. *Concurrent Pos:* Abstractor, Chem Abstr, 46-60; consult, US Off Educ, NSF, pvt res firms. *Mem:* Fel AAAS; Am Chem Soc; Am Educ Res Asn. *Res:* Critical data compilations; strategies for educational and other domestic sector research, dissemination and utilization of research and development; federal education policy and support of research; evaluation of research and development programs; mathematics and science education; educational assessment and testing. *Mailing Add:* Nat Ctr Improving Sci Ed 2000 L St NW Suite 603 Washington DC 20036. *Fax:* 202-467-0659; *E-Mail:* seutar@gwuvm.gwu.edu

RAIZMAN, PAULA, organic chemistry; deceased, see previous edition for last biography

RAJ, BALDEV, BOTANY. *Current Pos:* from asst prof to assoc prof, 69-76, PROF BIOL, JACKSON STATE UNIV, 76- *Personal Data:* b DI Kahn, Pakistan, Jan 8, 35; m 62; c 3. *Educ:* Panjab Univ, BSc, 57, MSc, 59; Univ Delhi, PhD(bot), 65. *Prof Exp:* Asst prof bot, Univ Delhi, 64-68; fel biol, Univ SC, 68-69. *Res:* Embryology of vascular plants; isolation of plant protoplasts. *Mailing Add:* Dept Biol Jackson State Univ 1400 Jr Lynch St Jackson MS 39217-0001

RAJ, HARKISAN D, microbial physiology & systematics; deceased, see previous edition for last biography

RAJ, PRADEEP, COMPUTATIONAL AERODYNAMICS. *Current Pos:* res & develop engr, Burbank, 79-91, TECH FEL, LOCKHEED AERONAUT SYSTS CO, BURBANK, MARIETTA, 92- *Personal Data:* b Meerut, India, Dec 15, 49; m 80, Mary J Phillips; c 2. *Educ:* Indian Inst Sci, BE, 71, ME, 73; Ga Inst Technol, PhD(aerospace eng), 76. *Prof Exp:* Asst prof, Iowa State Univ, 76-78; asst prof mech & aerospace eng, Univ Mo-Rolla, 78-79. *Mem:* Am Inst Aeronaut & Astronaut; Am Helicopter Soc. *Res:* Applied computational aerodynamics; simulation of inviscid and viscous flow problems. *Mailing Add:* Dept 73-07 Zone 0685 Lockheed Martin Aeronaut Systs Marietta GA 30063-0685. *E-Mail:* raj@mar.lmco.com

RAJ, RISHI S, WAKES, TURBULENCE MODELING. *Current Pos:* dean admin, Sch Eng, 87-88, PROF MECH ENG & DIR, TURBO LAB, CITY UNIV NEW YORK, 75- *Personal Data:* b Moga, Punjab, India; US citizen; m 70, Swadesh; c Rashmi S & Vishwa S. *Educ:* Punjab Univ, BS Hons, 64; People's Friendship Univ, MS Hons, 69; Pa State Univ, PhD(aerospace), 74. *Concurrent Pos:* Consult, Curtis-Wright Corp, 76-84; distinguished fel, Exxon, 81, Gen Elec, Teledyne & US Army, 83, US Navy, 91-93; fel, Langley Res Ctr, NASA, 89-90; UN consult. *Mem:* Am Soc Mech Engrs; Am Inst Aeronaut & Astronaut. *Res:* All aspects of steam and gas turbines; power plants; thermodynamics; deposition; erosion; applied turbulence; weapon launching; electrostatic charge; transients; liquid propellant gun. *Mailing Add:* Dept Mech Eng City Univ NY City Col 138th St & Convent Ave New York NY 10031-9198

RAJA, RAJENDRAN, HIGH ENERGY PHYSICS. *Current Pos:* Res assoc, Fermi Lab, 74-78, staff physicist, 78-83, scientist I, 83-88, SCIENTIST II, FERMI LAB, 88- *Personal Data:* b Guruvayur, India, July 14, 48; m 76, Selitha; c Anjali. *Educ:* Univ Cambridge, Eng, MA, 70, PhD, 75. *Concurrent Pos:* Fel Trinity Col, Cambridge, 73-79. *Mem:* Am Phys Soc; AAAS; Int Platform Asn. *Res:* Co-discoverer of the top quark; author of over 130 publications; editor of conference proceedings; D0 experiment at the tevation. *Mailing Add:* Dept Physics Fermi Lab PO Box 500 Batavia IL 60510. *Fax:* 630-840-8481; *E-Mail:* raja@fnal.gov

RAJAGOPAL, ATTIPAT KRISHNASWAMY, THEORETICAL PHYSICS. *Current Pos:* RES PHYSICIST, NAVAL RES LAB, 85- *Personal Data:* b Mysore City, India, June 3, 37; m 64, Jayashree; c Ashoka & Sumana. *Educ:* Lingaraj Col, India, BSc, 57; Indian Inst Sci, Bangalore, MSc, 60; Harvard Univ, PhD(appl physics), 65. *Honors & Awards:* Distinguished Res Master Award, La State Univ Coun Res, 84. *Prof Exp:* Res fel, Harvard Univ, 64-65; asst prof physics, Univ Calif, Riverside, 65-68; fel & reader theoret physics, Tata Inst Fundamental Res, India, 68-70; assoc prof, 70-72, prof physics, La State Univ, Baton Rouge, 72-84. *Concurrent Pos:* Prof, Ctr Theoret Studies, Indian Inst Sci, Bangalore, India, 74-75; consult, Naval Res Lab, Washington, DC, 80-81 & Oak Ridge Nat Lab, 81-85. *Mem:* Fel Am Phys Soc. *Res:* Quantum mechanics of two, three and many particle systems; solid state physics; mathematical physics; nonequilibrium quantum statistical mechanics. *Mailing Add:* Code 6860-1 Naval Res Lab Washington DC 20375

RAJAGOPAL, K R, MECHANICAL ENGINEERING. *Current Pos:* PROF MECH ENG, TEX A&M UNIV, 96- *Personal Data:* b New Delhi, India, Nov 24, 50; m 75, Chandrika Iyengar; c Keshava & Sudarshan. *Educ:* Indian Inst Technol, Madras, BTech, 73; Ill Inst Technol, MS, 74; Univ Minn, PhD(mech), 78. *Prof Exp:* Fel lectr mech, Univ Mich, Ann Arbor, 78-80; asst prof mech eng, Cath Univ Am, 80-82; from asst prof to prof mech eng, Univ Pittsburgh, 82-96; math prof & statist, 86-96. *Concurrent Pos:* Vis prof, Indian Inst Technol, Madras, 84; mem, Constitutive Equations Comt, Appl Math Div, Am Soc Mech Engrs, 85 & Fluid Mechs Comt, 85; dir, Inst Appl & Comput Mech, Univ Pittsburgh, 85. *Mem:* Fel Am Soc Mech Engr; Soc Natural Philos; Soc Rheology; Am Acad Mech; Soc Indust Appl Math. *Res:* Non-linear mechanics and applied non-linear analysis. *Mailing Add:* Dept Mech Eng Tex A&M Univ College Station TX 77843. *Fax:* 409-862-3989; *E-Mail:* krajagopal@mengr.tamu.edu

RAJAGOPAL, P K, FISH BIOLOGY. *Current Pos:* BIOLOGIST, STATE FISHERY EXP STA, 75- *Personal Data:* b India, June 18, 36; m 65, Remani; c Rajiv. *Educ:* Annamalai Univ, Madras, BS, 57, MS, 58; Utah State Univ, PhD(fish biol), 75. *Prof Exp:* Sr res scholar, Zool Res Lab, Univ Madras, 58-62; res fel zool, Univ Col Rhodesia & Nyasaland, 62-65; sr res officer, Ghana Acad Sci, 66-71, instr gen biol for lab technicians, Inst Aquatic Biol, 66-70; res technologist, US-IBP Desert Biomed Prog, Utah Coop Fishery Unit, Utah State Univ, 71-72, res asst, 72-75, instr fish biol, 74-75. *Concurrent Pos:* Res assoc, Biol Dept, Univ Nev, Las Vegas, 69. *Mem:* Am Fisheries Soc; Am Inst Fishery Res Biologists; Am Inst Biol Sci; Freshwater Biol Asn UK. *Res:* General and aquatic biology; ecology and ecological physiology; fishery science; effects of pollution on aquatic animals; respiratory metabolism. *Mailing Add:* 1540 N 1600 E Logan UT 84341

RAJAGOPALAN, K V, BIOCHEMISTRY. *Current Pos:* fel biochem, Med Sch, 59-66, from asst prof to assoc prof, 67-77, PROF BIOCHEM, MED SCH, DUKE UNIV, 77- *Personal Data:* b Mysore, India, Apr 11, 30; m 58; c 3. *Educ:* Presidency Col, Madras, BSc, 51; Univ Madras, MSc, 54, PhD(biochem), 57. *Prof Exp:* Asst res officer, Indian Coun Med Res, Madras, 58-59. *Res:* Enzymology; metalloenzymes. *Mailing Add:* Dept Biochem Duke Univ 234 MSIA Bldg Durham NC 27710-0001

RAJAGOPALAN, PARTHASARATHI, ORGANIC CHEMISTRY, MEDICINAL CHEMISTRY. *Current Pos:* MEM STAFF, EXP STA, E I DU PONT DE NEMOURS & CO, INC, 80- *Personal Data:* b Mannargudi, India, Mar 13, 30; m 51; c 2. *Educ:* Univ Madras, BS, 49; Univ Delhi, MS, 51; NY Univ, PhD(org chem), 60. *Prof Exp:* USPHS fel, Sch Med, NY Univ, 59-60; inst fel, Rockefeller Inst, 60-61; sr res scientist med chem, Ciba Res Ctr, Ciba India Ltd, Bombay, 62-67; sr res scientist, Endo Labs Inc, 67-73, res assoc, 73-80. *Concurrent Pos:* Adj assoc prof, Queens Col, City Univ New York, 72- *Mem:* Am Chem Soc. *Res:* Heterocyclic chemistry; new, 1,3-dipolar cycloaddition reactions. *Mailing Add:* 4655 Norwood Dr Wilmington DE 19803-4811

RAJAGOPALAN, RAJ, TRANSPORT PHENOMENA, STATISTICAL PHYSICS. *Current Pos:* PROF CHEM ENG, UNIV HOUSTON, TEX, 86-, PROF PHYSICS, 93- *Educ:* Indian Inst Technol, Madras, BS, 69; Syracuse Univ, MS, 71, PhD(chem eng), 75. *Prof Exp:* Asst prof chem eng, Syracuse Univ, NY, 75-76; from asst prof to prof, Rensselaer Polytech Inst, Troy, NY, 76-86. *Concurrent Pos:* Prin investr, numerous res progs, 76-; consult, Gen Elec, Conn, 80, NSF, 83-85 & 87, T S Assocs, Md, 85-; adv, Comt Frontiers Chem Eng, Nat Res Coun, 85-86; prog dir, NSF, Washington, DC, 86- *Mem:* Am Chem Soc; Am Inst Chem Engrs; Sigma Xi; Am Phys Soc; Soc Indust & Appl Math; NY Acad Sci. *Res:* Statistical physics of supramolecular fluids; transport phenomena; condensed matter physics of colloids; separation and membrane phenomena; complex fluids. *Mailing Add:* Dept Chem Eng & Physics Univ Houston Houston TX 77204-4792

RAJAN, PERIASAMY KARIVARATHA, DIGITAL SIGNAL PROCESSING, CIRCUITS & SYSTEMS. *Current Pos:* assoc prof elec eng, 83-85, PROF ELEC ENG, TENN TECHNOL UNIV, COOKEVILLE, 85-, GRAD PROG DIR, DEPT ELEC ENG, 87-, CHAIR ELEC ENG, 91- *Personal Data:* b Tamil Nadu, India, Sept 20, 42; nat US; m 71, Visalakshi Gounder; c Rajkumar. *Educ:* Univ Madras, India, BS, 66; Indian Inst Technol, Madras, India, MTech, 69, PhD(elec eng), 75. *Prof Exp:* Lectr elec eng, Regional Eng Col, Trichy, India, 69-70; assoc lectr elec eng, Indian Inst Technol, Madras, India, 70-75, fel elec eng, 77-78; asst prof elec eng, State Univ NY Col, Buffalo, 78-80; assoc prof elec eng, NDak State Univ, Fargo, 80-83. *Concurrent Pos:* Part time fac, Concordia Univ Montreal, 77-78, vis res asst prof, 79. *Mem:* Int Elec & Electronic Engrs; Am Soc Eng Educ; Sigma Xi; Int Soc Optical Eng. *Res:* Applications of symmetry for the design and application of two and three dimensional digital filters; spectral analysis and multidimensional fast fourier transform algorithm development; general digital signal processing algorithms and applications; design of pattern recognition filters; optical pattern recognition. *Mailing Add:* Dept Elec Eng Tenn Technol Univ Cookeville TN 38505. *Fax:* 615-372-6172; *E-Mail:* pkr1259@tntech.edu

RAJAN, THIRUCHANDURAI VISWANATHAN, SOMATIC CELL GENETICS, IMMUNOGENETICS. *Current Pos:* PROF PATH & INTERIM CHAIR, UNIV CONN HEALTH CTR, 88- *Personal Data:* b Tanjore, India, Oct 1, 45; US citizen; m 77, Sandra Winkler; c Meena H, Chandrika M & Tara M. *Educ:* All India Inst Med Sci, MB & BS, 68; Albert Einstein Col Med, PhD(cell biol), 74. *Prof Exp:* From asst prof to prof path, Albert Einstein Col Med, 80-88. *Concurrent Pos:* Attending pathologist, Bronx Municipal Hosp Ctr, 75- *Mem:* Am Soc Trop Med & Hyg; Am Asn Immunol. *Res:* Host-parasite interactions in human lymphatic filariasis. *Mailing Add:* Dept Path Univ Conn 263 Farmington Ave Farmington CT 06030-3105. *Fax:* 860-679-2936; *E-Mail:* rajan@cortex.uchc.edu

RAJANNA, BETTAIYA, TOXICOLOGY, ENVIRONMENT POLLUTION. *Current Pos:* assoc prof biol, 75-77, prof & chmn, Div Natural & Appl Sci, 77-87, ACAD DEAN & PROF, SELMA UNIV, 87- *Personal Data:* b Bangalore, India; m 67; c 2. *Educ:* Mysore Univ, India, BS, 59 & 63; Miss State Univ, MS, 70, PhD(physiol), 72. *Hon Degrees:* DLett, Selma Univ, 89. *Honors & Awards:* White House Award Excellence in Sci & Technol. *Prof Exp:* Res asst hort, Hort Dept, Mysore State, India, 63-64, asst dir, 64-67; res asst plant sci, Agron Dept, Miss State Univ, 67-72, fel ecol, Dept Zool, 73-75. *Concurrent Pos:* Panelist, Sci Educ, NSF, 77-81 & NIH, 86-90; prin investr, MBS, Res Prog, NIH, 79-, consult, 80; consult, NIH, 80- *Mem:* Am Soc Agron; Am Soc Crop Sci; Am Soc Plant Physiologists; Indian Soc Seed Technologists; Sigma Xi. *Res:* Interaction of heavy metals, cadmium, lead and mercury, with catecholamines uptake by rat brain and heart; biochemical changes due to aging in plant seeds; pollution ecology: effects of air pollutants on plants; seed physiology; 46 published papers and 81 presentations. *Mailing Add:* Acad Dean Selma Univ 1501 Lapsley St Selma AL 36701-5232

RAJARAM, SANJAYA, wheat breeding, genetics of host-parasite interaction, for more information see previous edition

RAJARAMAN, SRINIVASAN, IMMUNOPATHOLOGY, NEPHROPATHOLOGY. *Current Pos:* from asst prof to assoc prof, 80-93, PROF PATH, UNIV TEX MED BR, GALVESTON, 94- *Personal Data:* b India, July 10, 43; US citizen; m 72, Chitra Venkateswaran; c Anupama & Shiva. *Educ:* Univ Madras, India, MB & BS, 65. *Prof Exp:* Med officer, captain, Indian Armed Forces, 65-69; res fel gen surg, Stanley Med Col, Madras, India, 69-71, asst surgeon, Govt Stanley Hosp, 71-74; resident gen surg, NJ Sch Med, Newark, 74-75 & resident path, Sch Med, WVa Univ, Morgantown, 75-79; spec fel immunopath, Cleveland Clin, Ohio, 79-80. *Mem:* Am Asn Pathologists; Int Acad Path; Am Soc Clin Pathologists; Am Soc Nephrology; AAAS; NY Acad Sci; Int Soc Nephrology; Am Asn Cancer Res. *Res:* Molecular pathobiology of cell injury and regeneration; tumor biology; immunopathophysiology of progressive renal injury; glut and renal endocrinology. *Mailing Add:* Renal Immunopath Univ Tex Med Br Galveston TX 77555-0848. *Fax:* 409-772-9377; *E-Mail:* srajaram@.med.utmb.edu

RAJARATNAM, N(ALLAMUTHU), HYDRAULIC ENGINEERING, FLUID MECHANICS. *Current Pos:* Nat Res Coun Can fel, 63-65, session lectr, 65-66, from asst prof to assoc prof, 66-71, PROF HYDRAUL, UNIV ALTA, 71- *Personal Data:* b Mukuperi, India, Dec 18, 34; m 61; c 2. *Educ:* Univ Madras, BE, 57, MSc, 58; Indian Inst Sci, Bangalore, PhD(hydraul), 61. *Prof Exp:* Jr res engr, Irrig Res Sta, Madras, India, 58-59; sr sci officer hydraul, Indian Inst Sci, 60-63. *Concurrent Pos:* Nat Res Coun Can res grants, 65- *Mem:* Am Soc Civil Engrs; Eng Inst Can; Int Asn Hydraul Res. *Res:* Open channel flow; hydraulics of energy dissipations; turbulent boundary layers, jets and wakes; non-Newtonian flow; rivers; thermal and oil pollution problems; fishways. *Mailing Add:* Dept Civil Eng Univ Alta Edmonton AB T6G 2G7 Can

RAJENDRAN, VAZHAIKKURICHI M, HORMONE REGULATION OF ION TRANSPORT, MOLECULAR IDENTIFICATION OF TRANSPORTER. *Current Pos:* assoc res scientist, 85-90, RES SCIENTIST, YALE UNIV SCH MED, 90- *Personal Data:* b Vazhaikkurichi, India, Dec 2, 52; m 84; c 2. *Educ:* Univ Madras, BS, 74, MS, 77, MPhil, 88, PhD(biochem), 81. *Prof Exp:* Postdoctoral fel, Med Col Wis, 83-85. *Mem:* Am Physiol Soc. *Res:* Novel transport system localized in baselateral membranes; transport physiology; enzyme kinetics. *Mailing Add:* Dept Internal Med 92 LMP Yale Univ Sch Med 333 Cedar St New Haven CT 06510-3219

RAJESHWAR, KRISHNAN, ELECTROCHEMISTRY. *Current Pos:* from asst prof to assoc prof, 83-89, PROF CHEM, TEX, ARLINGTON, 89- *Personal Data:* b Trivandrum, India, Apr 15, 49; m 77, Rohini Chidambaram; c Reena & Rebecca. *Educ:* Univ Col, India, BSc, 69; Indian Inst Technol, Sc, 71; Indian Inst Sci, PhD(chem), 74. *Honors & Awards:* Doherty Award, Am Chem Soc. *Prof Exp:* Res chemist, Prods Formulation Group Foseco Int, India, 74-75; res fel chem, St Francis, Xavier Univ, Can, 75-76; res fel, Colo State Univ, 76-78, vis respt prof, 78-79 sr res assoc, 79-83. *Concurrent Pos:* Consult, Univ Wyo Res Corp & Forensic Labs, Tex, Edwards Aerospace Inc, Sid Richardson Carbon Co, Ft Worth. *Mem:* Am Chem Soc; Electrochem Soc. *Res:* Charge storage and transport mechanisms in a variety of materials; semiconductors and polymers; environmental electrochemistry and photoelectrochemistry. *Mailing Add:* Dept Chem & Biochem Univ Tex Arlington TX 76019-0065. *Fax:* 817-273-3808; *E-Mail:* rajeshwar@uta.edu

RAJHATHY, TIBOR, plant genetics & cytology; deceased, see previous edition for last biography

RAJLICH, VACLAV THOMAS, SOFTWARE SYSTEMS MAINTENANCE, COMPREHENSION OF LEGACY SOFTWARE. *Current Pos:* chair, 85-90, PROF COMPUT SCI, WAYNE STATE UNIV, 85- *Personal Data:* b Praha, Czech, May 3, 39; m 68, Ivana; c Vasik, Paul, John & Luke. *Educ:* Czech Tech Univ, MS, 62; Case Western Res Univ, PhD(math), 71. *Prof Exp:* Grad fel, Res Inst Math Mach, Prague, 66-68, res scientist software eng, 71-74, mgr, Dept Algorithms, 74-79; teaching asst math, Case Western Res Univ, 69-71; vis assoc prof comput sci, Calif State Univ, Fullerton, 80-81; assoc prof comput sci & eng, Univ Mich, 82-85. *Concurrent Pos:* Mem fac, Dept Cybernet, Charles Univ, Prague, 74-79; prin investr grant, Int Bus Mach, 83-85, Chrysler Challenge Fund, 86-90; consult, Software Eng Develop Corp, 84 & Epcom, 93; grantee, Inst Mfg Res, Wayne State Univ, 85-90; vis scientist, Carnegie-Mellon Univ, 87, Harvard Univ, 88 & NASA Goddard Space Flight Ctr, 92; prog comt chair, Inst Elec & Electronics Engrs Conf on Software Maintenance, 91, gen chair, 92. *Mem:* Inst Elec & Electronics Engrs Comput Soc; Asn Comput Mach. *Res:* Tools for maintenance and comprehension of legacy software systems; parallel and graph grammars. *Mailing Add:* Dept Comput Sci Wayne State Univ Detroit MI 48202. *Fax:* 313-577-6868; *E-Mail:* rajlich@cs.wayne.edu

RAJNAK, KATHERYN EDMONDS, ATOMIC PHYSICS. *Current Pos:* RETIRED. *Personal Data:* b Kalamazoo, Mich, Apr 30, 37; m 61, Stanley. *Educ:* Kalamazoo Col, BA, 59; Univ Calif, Berkeley, PhD(chem), 63. *Prof Exp:* Fel chem, Lawrence Radiation Lab, 62-65; asst prof physics, Kalamazoo Col, 67-70; physicist, Lawrence Livermore Lab, 74-75, consult, 75-89; adj assoc prof, Kalamazoo Col, 85-96. *Concurrent Pos:* Consult, Argonne Nat Lab, 66-89; adj lectr physics, Kalamazoo Col; vis prof, Univ Paris, IV, 79 & 80 & Univ Paris, Orsay, 79 & 81. *Mem:* Am Phys Soc. *Res:* Theory and analysis of lanthanide and actinide spectra. *Mailing Add:* 1841 South Fourth St Kalamazoo MI 49009. *E-Mail:* krajnak@hobbes.kzoo.edu

RAJNAK, STANLEY L, MATHEMATICS. *Current Pos:* From asst prof to assoc prof, 65-77, PROF MATH, KALAMAZOO COL, 77- *Personal Data:* b Richmond, Calif, Apr 23, 36; m 61. *Educ:* Univ Calif, Berkeley, AB, 60, PhD(math), 66. *Mem:* Am Math Soc; Math Asn Am. *Res:* Analysis; linear topological spaces; distribution theory. *Mailing Add:* Kalamazoo Col Kalamazoo MI 49006-3295

RAJOTTE, RAY V, BIOMEDICAL ENGINEERING. *Current Pos:* fel, Dept Med, Univ Alta, Edmonton, 75-76, res assoc, 77-79, asst prof, 79-82, asst prof, Dept Med & Surg, 83-84, assoc prof, 84-88, DIR, ISLET CELL LAB, UNIV ALTA, EDMONTON, 82-, PROF, DEPT MED & SURG, 88-, DIR, DIV EXP SURG, 88- *Personal Data:* b Wainwright, Alta, Dec 5, 42; m 66, Gloria A Yackimetz; c Brian, Michael & Monique. *Educ:* Univ Alta, BSc, 71, MSc, 73, PhD(biomed eng), 75. *Prof Exp:* Fel, Oak Ridge Nat Lab, 76-77, Washington Univ, St Louis, 77, Univ Calif, Los Angeles, 77. *Concurrent Pos:* Assoc dir, Surg-Med Res Inst, Univ Alta, 84-87, dir, 87-, co-dir, Juvenile Diabetes Fund Diabetes Interdisciplinary Res Prog, 92- *Mem:* Cell Transplantation Soc; Int Pancreas & Islet Transplant Asn; Can Transplantation Soc; Europ Asn Study Diabetes; Soc Cryobiol; Am Diabetes Asn; Can Soc Clin Invest; NY Acad Sci; Transplantation Soc; Can Diabetes Asn; Acad Surg Res; Int Diabetes Fedn. *Res:* Granted one patent for glucose sensor. *Mailing Add:* Surg-Med Res Inst Rm 1074 Dent Pharm Ctr Univ Alta Edmonton AB T6G 2N8 Can

RAJSUMAN, ROCHIT, COMPUTER ENGINEERING. *Current Pos:* ASST PROF COMPUTER ENG & SCI, CASE WESTERN RES UNIV, 88-, ASST PROF ELEC ENG, 91- *Personal Data:* b Meerut City, India, Mar 13, 64. *Educ:* KN Inst Technol, India, BTech, 84; Univ Okla, MS, 85; Colo State Univ, PhD(elec eng), 88. *Prof Exp:* Grad teaching asst elec eng, Colo State Univ, 86-88. *Concurrent Pos:* Gen chair, Int Workshop Memory Testing, Inst Elec & Electronics Engrs, 93 & 94. *Mem:* Inst Elec & Electronics Engrs Computer Soc Circuits & Syst Soc; Asn Computer Mach. *Res:* Digital hardware testing; design for testability; vlsi design; design automation; fault tolerant design; fault modeling; computer architecture; computer networks; published 2 books and more than 50 technical articles. *Mailing Add:* 1362 Lakeshore Circle San Jose CA 95131. *E-Mail:* rajsuman@alpha.ces.cwru.edu

RAJU, GOVINDA, HIGH VOLTAGE ENGINEERING, DIELECTRIC MATERIALS & APPLICATIONS. *Current Pos:* PROF ELEC ENG, UNIV WINDSOR, 81-, HEAD DEPT, 89- *Personal Data:* m 67, Padmini; c Anand. *Educ:* Univ Mysore, BE, 57; Univ Liverpool, UK, PhD(elec eng), 63. *Prof Exp:* Res engr, Assoc Elec Industs, UK, 63-65; asst prof high voltage eng, Indian Inst Sci, 65-73, prof, 73-81, head, Dept High Voltage Eng, 75-80. *Concurrent Pos:* Commonwealth fel, Brit Coun, 72; vis lectr, Univ Sheffield, UK, 74. *Mem:* Sr mem Inst Elec & Electronics Engrs; Inst Elec Engrs UK; fel Inst Engrs. *Res:* Gas discharges, discharges in electric and magnetic fields, high voltage engineering, vacuum breakdown, high temperature polymer insulating materials. *Mailing Add:* 2435 Delmar St Windsor ON N9H 1L4 Can. *Fax:* 519-973-7062; *E-Mail:* raju@uwindsor.ca

RAJU, IVATURY SANYASI, ENGINEERING, AERONAUTICS. *Current Pos:* SR SCIENTIST & VPRES, ANALYTICAL SERVS & MATS, INC, 84- *Personal Data:* b Kakinada,India, Aug 9, 44; m 71; c 1. *Educ:* Andhra Univ, India, BE, 65; Indian Inst Sci, ME, 67, PhD(aeronaut eng), 73; MEA, George Wash Univ, 82. *Prof Exp:* Sr eng, Vikram Sarabhai Space Ctr, Trivandrum, 71-75; res assoc, Nat Res Coun, 75-77, res assoc, 77-79, asst res prof, 79-82, assoc res prof, Joint Inst Flight Sciences, George Wash Univ, Langley Res Ctr, NASA, 82-83; sr scientist, Vigyan Res Assoc, Inc, 83-84. *Concurrent Pos:* Leverhulme overseas fel, Univ Liverpool, Eng, 73-74. *Mem:* Am Inst Aeronaut & Astronaut; Am Soc Testing & Mat. *Res:* Static; dynamic and stability analysis of aerospace structures; fracture mechanics; finite element methods; laminated composite structures; boundary element methods. *Mailing Add:* 10 Oxford Mew SW Poquoson VA 23662

RAJU, MUDUNDI RAMAKRISHNA, RADIATION BIOPHYSICS, RADIOTHERAPY. *Current Pos:* staff mem biophys, 71-79, FEL, LOS ALAMOS NAT LAB, 80- *Personal Data:* b Bhimavaram, India, July 15, 31. *Educ:* Univ Madras, BSc, 52, MA, 54; Andhra Univ, India, MSc, 55,. *Hon Degrees:* DSC, Andhra Univ, 60. *Prof Exp:* Lectr nuclear instruments, Andhra Univ, India, 57-61; fel biophys, Mass Gen Hosp, Mass Inst Technol & Harvard Univ, 61-63; Donner fel, Donner Lab, Univ Calif, Berkeley, 63-64, biophysicist, 64-65; from asst prof to assoc prof biophys, Univ Tex, Dallas, 65-71. *Concurrent Pos:* Vis scientist, Hammersmith Hosp, London, 67-68; guest scientist, Lawrence Radiation Lab, Univ Calif, 65- *Mem:* Radiation Res Soc. *Res:* Physics and radiobiology of new radiations, pi mesons, heavy charged particles and neutrons, and their potential applications in radiation therapy. *Mailing Add:* 1479 Big Rock Loop Los Alamos NM 87544

RAJU, NAMBOORI BHASKARA, FUNGAL GENETICS, FUNGAL CYTOLOGY. *Current Pos:* res assoc, 74-83, SR RES SCIENTIST, CYTOGENETICS, STANFORD UNIV, 84- *Personal Data:* b Pothumarru, India, Jan 1, 43; m 64, Swarajya Rudraraju; c Geeta, Suja & Meena. *Educ:* Banaras Hindu Univ, BSc, 65, MSc, 67; Univ Guelph, PhD(genetics), 72. *Prof Exp:* Scientist, Coun Sci & Indust Res, India, 73-74. *Res:* Cytology of fungi, especially Neurospora: meiotic and mitotic processes, including ascus development, behavior of chromosomes, nucleolus and spindle pole bodies; cytogenetic behavior of Neurospora mutants that affect ascus and ascospore differentiation, chromosome rearrangements that involve the nucleolus organizer region, and spore killers. *Mailing Add:* Dept Biol Sci Stanford Univ Stanford CA 94305-5020. *Fax:* 650-723-6132

RAJU, PALANICHAMY PILLAI, ENGINEERING MECHANICS, STRUCTURAL ENGINEERING. *Current Pos:* SR RELIABILITY ENG MGR, DIGITAL EQUIP CORP, 87- *Personal Data:* b Theni, India, June 15, 37; US citizen; m 62, Dhanam; c Prabhakar, Manohar & Rita. *Educ:* Madras Univ, BE, 60, MSc, 61; Univ Del, PhD(eng mech), 68. *Honors & Awards:* Cert Appreciation, Am Soc Mech Engrs Bd Gov. *Prof Exp:* Design engr, Larson & Toubro, 61-64; res fel aerospace, Univ Del, 64-68; lead engr, Westinghouse Nuclear Energy Systs, 68-76; consult engr, Teledyne Eng Serv, Teledyne Inc, 76-84; sr consult, Cygna Energy Servs, 84-87. *Concurrent Pos:* Mem pressure vessel res comts & nuclear code comts, Am Soc Mech Engrs. *Mem:* Fel Am Soc Mech Engrs; Am Soc Civil Engrs; Sigma Xi; Inst Elec & Electronics Engrs; Am Soc Qual Control. *Res:* Shell theory of composite materials known for their anisotropic properties, both mechanical and thermal; safety and reliability of nuclear power plant components and piping systems; new analysis techniques; vibration and 3D analysis; fracture mechanics evaluation; reliability of computer hardware; life extension studies; reliability engineering; concurrent engineering; total quality management. *Mailing Add:* 26 Harvard Dr Sudbury MA 01776

NARAYANA G V, ENGINEERING, ELECTRICAL ENG. *Current Pos:* PROF & DIR, DIV ENG, UNIV TEX, SAN ANTONIO, 91- *Personal Data:* b Undi, India, Jan 8, 34; m 55, Nagamani; c Jaya. *Educ:* Andhra Univ, BS, 55; Banaras Univ, MS, 57; Indian Inst Technol, MTech, 59; Polytech Inst Brooklyn, PhD(elec eng), 65. *Honors & Awards:* Outstanding Res Contribs & Exemplary Leadership Award, Inst Elec & Electronics Engrs Systs Mgt & Cybernet Soc. *Prof Exp:* Res asst electronics, Phys Res Labs, Polytech Inst Brooklyn, 59-61, fel, 61-65; asst prof elec eng, Clarkson Col Technol, 65-67; from asst prof to prof, Ohio Univ, 67-90, chmn dept, 73-84. *Mem:* Fel Inst Elec & Electronics Engrs; Sigma Xi; Am Soc Elec Engrs. *Res:* Control systems; design of control systems; adaptive control; system identification; pattern recognition; stability theory; robotics; fuzzy logic control. *Mailing Add:* Div Eng Univ Tex San Antonio TX 78249-0665. *Fax:* 210-691-5589

RAKA, EUGENE CD, physics, for more information see previous edition

RAKE, ADRIAN VAUGHAN, GENETICS, MOLECULAR BIOLOGY. *Current Pos:* from prof, 76-94, EMER PROF BIOL, WRIGHT STATE UNIV, 94- *Personal Data:* b New York, NY, Mar 27, 34; m 61; c 3. *Educ:* Swarthmore Col, BA, 56; Univ Pa, PhD(microbiol), 64; Pa State Univ, BS, 75. *Prof Exp:* NIH res fel biochem, Univ BC, 64-66; fel, Carnegie Inst, 66-68; asst prof biophys, Pa State Univ, 68-75. *Concurrent Pos:* Red Cross health vol, nat & int disaster. *Mem:* AAAS; NY Acad Sci; Genetics Soc Am; Sigma Xi; Biophys Soc. *Res:* Genome size in trisomy; altered nuclear organization. *Mailing Add:* 3824 Fowler Rd Springfield OH 45502

RAKES, ALLEN HUFF, DAIRY NUTRITION. *Current Pos:* from asst prof to assoc prof, 63-73, PROF ANIMAL SCI, NC STATE UNIV, 73- *Personal Data:* b Floyd, Va, Aug 19, 33; m 58; c 2. *Educ:* Va Polytech Inst, BS, 56, MS, 57; Cornell Univ, PhD(animal nutrit), 60. *Honors & Awards:* Honors Award, Am Dairy Sci Asn. *Prof Exp:* Asst prof dairy sci, WVa Univ, 60-63. *Mem:* Am Dairy Sci Asn; Am Soc Animal Sci. *Res:* Energy utilization of ruminants; voluntary feed intake control mechanisms. *Mailing Add:* Animal Sci NC State Univ PO Box 7621 Raleigh NC 27695-0001

RAKES, JERRY MAX, ANIMAL SCIENCE. *Current Pos:* RETIRED. *Personal Data:* b Bentonville, Ark, Dec 7, 32; m 49; c 3. *Educ:* Univ Ark, BS, 54, MS, 55; Iowa State Univ, PhD(physiol), 58. *Prof Exp:* Asst prof dairy physiol, Iowa State Univ, 56-58; assoc prof, Univ Ark, Fayetteville, 58-63, prof dairy genetics, 63- *Mem:* Am Soc Animal Sci; Am Dairy Sci Asn. *Res:* Dairy physiology and biochemistry; dairy cattle genetics. *Mailing Add:* 3019 S Johnson Visalia CA 93277

RAKESTRAW, JAMES WILLIAM, electronic systems, for more information see previous edition

RAKESTRAW, ROY MARTIN, MATHEMATICS, COMPUTER SCIENCES. *Current Pos:* AT DEPT MATH, PHILLIPS UNIV. *Personal Data:* b Redding, Calif, Jan 31, 42; m 62; c 2. *Educ:* Okla State Univ, BS, 65, MS, 66, PhD(math), 69. *Prof Exp:* asst prof math, Univ Mo-Rolla, 69-76; assoc prof math, Wheaton Col, 76- *Mem:* Math Asn Am; Am Math Soc; Am Sci Affil. *Res:* Convex sets; functional analysis. *Mailing Add:* 2704 S Lions Ave Broken Arrow OK 74012

RAKHIT, GOPA, BIOCHEMISTRY, PHARMACOLOGY. *Current Pos:* HEALTH SCIENTIST ADMINR, NIH, 84- *Personal Data:* b India; US citizen; m 77. *Educ:* Univ Calcutta, BSc, 65, MSc, 67; Univ Utah, PhD(chem physics), 76. *Prof Exp:* Vis fel, Nat Heart, Lung & Blood Inst, 76-78; sr staff fel, Off Drugs, Food & Drug Admin, 78-84. *Mem:* Biophys Soc; Am Chem Soc; AAAS. *Res:* Spectroscopic studies of enzyme-substrate, protein-ligand, and drug-biomolecular interaction; structure-function relation in proteins, nucleic acids and membranes; effects of radiation and the role of free radicals in drug-toxicty. *Mailing Add:* NIH Rm 4154 6701 Rockledge Dr Bethesda MD 20892-7806

RAKHIT, SUMANAS, ORGANIC CHEMISTRY. *Current Pos:* DIR CHEM, BIOMEGA, INC, 84- *Personal Data:* b Banaras, India, Oct 17, 30; m 59; c 1. *Educ:* Banaras Hindu Univ, MPharm, 53, PhD(pharmaceut), 57. *Prof Exp:* Coun Sci & Indust Res India sr res fel org chem, Cent Drug Res Inst, Univ Lucknow, 57-59; res assoc, Laval Univ, 59-60, Nat Res Coun Can fel, 60-62; staff scientist, Worcester Found Exp Biol, 62-65; sr res chemist, Ayerst Res Labs, 65-83; assoc prof, Univ Louis Pasteur, Strasbourg, France, 83-84. *Concurrent Pos:* Mem grants selection comt chem sect, Nat Sci & Eng Res Coun, Can, 81- *Mem:* Am Chem Soc; Chem Inst Can. *Res:* Structural determination; synthesis of steroids and other natural products; phospholipids; biosynthesis of steroids; synthesis of pharmacologically active compounds; antibiotics; peptide chemistry. *Mailing Add:* Allelix Biopharmaceut 6850 Goreway Dr Mississauga ON L4V 1P1 Can

RAKIC, PASKO, NEUROSCIENCES, DEVELOPMENTAL BIOLOGY. *Current Pos:* chmn, Sect Neuroanat, 77-90, PROF NEUROSCI, SCH MED, YALE UNIV, 77-, DORYS MCCONNELL DUBERG CHAIR, 78-, CHMN, SECT NEUROBIOL, 90- *Personal Data:* b Ruma, Yugoslavia, May 15, 33; m 69. *Educ:* Univ Belgrade, MD, 59, ScD(neuroembryol), 69. *Hon Degrees:* MS, Yale Univ, 78. *Honors & Awards:* Grass Found Award & Lectr, 85; Karl Spencer Lashley Award, Am Philos Soc, 86; Pattison Award in Neurosci, 86. *Prof Exp:* Intern, Univ Hosp, Belgrade Univ Med Sch, 59-60, resident neurosurg, 61-62, asst prof path physiol, Belgrade Univ, 60-61; res fel neurosurg, Harvard Med Sch, 62-66, from asst prof to assoc prof neuropath, 69-77; asst prof, Inst Biol Res, Belgrade, 67-69. *Concurrent Pos:* Prin investr grants, Nat Inst Neurol & Commun Dis & Stroke, NIH, 70-, Nat Eye Inst, 77-; mem study sects, NIH, 72-; consult, NSF, Atomic Energy Control Bd, Can, Med Res Coun, Can, March of Dimes, J S Guggenheim Mem Found, Huntington Chorea Found; assoc, Neurosci Res Prog, 80-89; Jacob K Javits Neurosci Investr Award, 84; dir, Sen Jacob Javits Ctr Excellence Neurosci, Yale Univ, 85-90; numerous invited lectrs. *Mem:* Nat Acad Sci; AAAS; Am Asn Anatomists; Am Asn Neuropathologists; Int Brain Res Orgn; Int Soc Develop Neurosci; NY Acad Sci; Sigma Xi; Soc Neurosci. *Res:* Developmental neurobiology; cellular and molecular mechanisms of neuronal migration, axonal navigation and synaptogenesis; genetic and epigenetic regulation of neuronal interactions during development. *Mailing Add:* Dept Neurobiol Sch Med Yale Univ PO Box 3333 New Haven CT 06510-8001. *Fax:* 203-785-5263

RAKITA, LOUIS, CARDIOVASCULAR DISEASES, INTERNAL MEDICINE. *Current Pos:* from instr to prof, 54-93, EMER PROF MED, CASE WESTERN RES UNIV, 93- *Personal Data:* b Montreal, Que, US citizen; m 45, Blance Michlin; c Robert M. *Educ:* Sir George Williams Univ, BA, 42; McGill Univ, MD, CM, 49; Am Bd Internal Med, dipl, 56; Royal Col Physicians & Surgeons, Can, cert, 56; FRCPC, 72. *Honors & Awards:* Gold Heart Award, Am Heart Asn, Cert of Merit. *Prof Exp:* Intern, Montreal Gen Hosp, 49-50; resident med, Jewish Gen Hosp, Montreal, 50-51; fel, Alton Ochsner Med Found, 51-52; chief resident, Cleveland City Hosp, 52-53; dir cardiol, Cleveland Metrop Gen Hosp, 66-87. *Concurrent Pos:* Am Heart Asn fel, Inst Med Res, Cedars Lebanon Hosp, Los Angeles, 53-54; Am Heart Asn Fel, Cleveland City Hosp, 54-55, advan fel, 59-61; USPHS sr res fel, Cleveland City Hosp, 61-62; USPHS res career develop award, Cleveland Metrop Gen Hosp, 62-69; asst vis physician, Cleveland City Hosp, 54-57, vis physician, 57-; vis cardiologist, Sunny Acres Hosp, 73- *Mem:* AAAS; Am Fedn Clin Res; Am Heart Asn; fel Am Col Physicians; fel Am Col Cardiol. *Res:* Electrophysiology and biochemistry of cardiac hypertrophy. *Mailing Add:* Cardiol Metrohealth Med Ctr 2500 Metrohealth Dr Cleveland OH 44109-1998. *Fax:* 216-459-3927

RAKITA, PHILIP ERWIN, ORGANOMETALLIC CHEMISTRY & CHEMICAL TECHNOLOGY, MANAGEMENT & DEVELOPMENT. *Current Pos:* BUS MGR, ELF ATOCHEM NA, 96- *Personal Data:* b Cleveland, Ohio, Sept 4, 44; m; c 2. *Educ:* Case Inst, BSc, 66; Mass Inst Technol, PhD(chem), 70. *Prof Exp:* Asst prof inorg chem, Univ NC, Chapel Hill, 70-75; grants officer, Indust Environ Res Lab, US Environ Protection Agency, 75-76; sr Fulbright prof, Moscow State Univ, USSR, 76; prof inorg chem, Univ Minn, 76-77; sr res chemist, Ferro Corp, 77-78, int prod mgr, 79-80; tech mgr, 81-83, mkt mgr, M&T Chem Inc, 84-89; dept head, Atochem, Paris, 89-92; dir technol, Elf Atochem, Japan, Tokyo, 93-95. *Concurrent Pos:* Sr Fulbright, NSF & NIH fels; dir, Americuros, 95- & Armour Assocs, 95- *Mem:* Am Chem Soc; Soc Plastics Engrs. *Res:* Organometallic chemistry; polymer additives; technology transfer; grignard chemistry. *Mailing Add:* 222 Delancey St Philadelphia PA 19107. *E-Mail:* armour_associates@msn.com

RAKOFF, HENRY, ORGANIC CHEMISTRY. *Current Pos:* RETIRED. *Personal Data:* b Brooklyn, NY, Nov 13, 24; m 50, 83, Nancy H Safford; c Alan C, Steven B & Tracy A. *Educ:* City Col New York, BS, 44; Purdue Univ, MS, 48, PhD(chem), 50; Bradley Univ, MLS, 93. *Prof Exp:* Asst chem, Purdue Univ, 46-48; petrol chemist, Natural Resources Res Inst, Univ Wyo, 50-52; sr res chemist, Velsicol Corp, Ill, 52-53; from asst prof to assoc prof chem, Tex A&M Univ, 53-66; prof, Parsons Col, 66-73, chmn dept, 67-73; res assoc, Univ Mo, Columbia, 73-74; res chemist, Nat Ctr Agr Utilization Res, Agr Res Serv, USDA, 74-92. *Mem:* Fel AAAS; Am Chem Soc. *Res:* Synthesis of pharmacologically active compounds; chemistry of fatty acids and glycerides. *Mailing Add:* 302 E Glen Ave Peoria IL 61614-5106. *E-Mail:* hrakoff@bradley.bradley.edu

RAKOFF, VIVIAN MORRIS, PSYCHIATRY. *Current Pos:* from assoc prof to prof psychiat, 68-74, dir postgrad educ, 68-71, PROF PSYCHIAT EDUC, UNIV TORONTO, 74- *Personal Data:* b Capetown, SAfrica, Apr 28, 28; Can citizen; m 59; c 3. *Educ:* Univ Capetown, BA, 47, MA, 49; Univ London, MB, BS, 57; McGill Univ, DPsych, 63; FRCP(C), 64. *Honors & Awards:* Schonfeld Award, Am Soc Adolescent Psychiat, 88. *Prof Exp:* Psychologist, Tavistock Clin, 50-51; house officer surg, St Charles Hosp, 57; house officer med, Victoria Hosp, 58; registr, Groote Schuur Hosp, 58-61; resident psychiat, McGill Univ, 61-63; assoc dir res, Jewish Gen Hosp, 63-67, asst prof & dir res, 67-68. *Concurrent Pos:* Prof & chmn dept psychiat, Univ Toronto, 80; dir & psychiatrist in chief, Clarke Inst Psychiat. *Mem:* Am Psychiat Asn; Can Psychiat Asn; Am Col Psychiatrists. *Res:* Patterns of mutual perception within the family; neurophysiological substrates of addictive behavior; adolescence and the family. *Mailing Add:* Univ Toronto Fac Med 1 Kings Col Circle Toronto ON M5S 1R8 Can

RAKOSKY, JOSEPH, JR, FOOD SCIENCE, SANITATION. *Current Pos:* FOOD INDUST CONSULT, J RAKOSKY SERV INC, 78- *Personal Data:* b Harrisburg, Pa, Apr 17, 21; m 44; c 4. *Educ:* Univ Md, BS, 49, MS, 50; Pa State Univ, PhD(bact), 53. *Prof Exp:* Dairy technician, Univ Md, 49-50; asst bact, Pa State Univ, 50-51; sr microbiologist & group leader, Baxter Labs, Inc, 53-55; res microbiologist & group leader, Glidden Co, 55-58; res microbiologist, Cent Soya Co Inc, Chicago, leader, 58-64, asst div prod mgr, 64-65, tech serv mgr, 65-70, dir tech mkt, 70-76; sr consult, Bernard Wolnak & Assoc, 76-77. *Mem:* AAAS; Am Chem Soc; Am Soc Microbiol; Inst Food Technol; Am Pub Health Asn. *Res:* Soy products, manufacture and use; regulatory matters, government liaison, technical literature and manuals, technical sales training; nutrition; marketing feasibility studies and surveys; plant sanitation. *Mailing Add:* 5836 Crain St Morton Grove IL 60053

RAKOW, ALLEN LESLIE, BIORHEOLOGY, BIOSEPARATION. *Current Pos:* ASSOC PROF CHEM ENG, COLO STATE UNIV, 90- *Personal Data:* m 71, Anne M Schroeder; c Elen K, Neal A & Alexi Schroeder. *Educ:* Rensselaer Polytech Inst, BChE, 64; Stevens Inst Technol, MEng, 66; Wash Univ, ScD, 74. *Prof Exp:* Res engr, Esso Res & Eng, 66-68; peace corps vol, Peace Corps, 68-70; develop engr, Dyno Industs, 71-72; assoc prof, Cooper Union, 75-81, NMex State Univ, 81-90. *Concurrent Pos:* Res consult, Columbia Univ, Col Physicians & Surgeons, 75-78; NASA/Am Soc Eng Educ fac fel, 78, 79, 82, 83, 94 & 95; prin investr, NSF, 79-81, 87-88, 89-92 & 94-97, Dept Energy, 79-80, Nat Livestock & Meat Bd, 89, IAMS Co, 96-97; consult, Phillips 66, 89, Meadowlark Optics, 95, Novacor, 95; vpres, Eng Sect, NY Acad Sci, 89. *Mem:* Am Inst Chem Engrs; Am Chem Soc; Am Soc Eng Educ; NY Acad Sci. *Res:* Fundamental rheological phenomena in the lateral migration of bioparticles in laminar flow including recovery of cells from fermentable broths; viscoelastic properties of erythrocytes and marine polysaccharides; nori product and process development; microalgal processes and products food extrusion. *Mailing Add:* 2224 Wakefield Dr Ft Collins CO 80526. *E-Mail:* allen@longs.engr.colostate.edu

RAKOWSKI, KRZYSZTOF J, plant morphogenesis, environmental biology, for more information see previous edition

RAKOWSKI, ROBERT F, MEMBRANE BIOPHYSICS, IONIC CHANNELS & PUMPS. *Current Pos:* assoc prof, 84-89, PROF PHYSIOL, UNIV HEALTH SCI, CHICAGO MED SCH, 89-, CHMN, DEPT PHYSIOL & BIOPHYS. *Personal Data:* b Rahway, NJ, Oct 8, 41; m 64, Linda Eakin; c 3. *Educ:* Cornell Univ, BChE, 64, MEng, 66; Univ Rochester, PhD(physiol), 72. *Prof Exp:* Asst prof physiol, Wash Univ, 75-84. *Concurrent Pos:* Vis scientist, Max-Planck Inst Biophys, Frankfurt, Ger; bd of trustees res award, Univ Health Sci, Chicago Med Sch. *Mem:* Am Soc Zoologists; Biophys Soc; Soc Gen Physiologists; AAAS; NY Acad Sci. *Res:* Mechanism of voltage-dependent ion conductance changes in excitable cells; voltage-clamp studies of sodium pump activity in cells. *Mailing Add:* Univ Health Sci Chicago Med Sch 3333 Greenbay Rd North Chicago IL 60064-3095. *Fax:* 847-578-3265

RAKOWSKY, FREDERICK WILLIAM, PHYSICAL CHEMISTRY. *Current Pos:* RETIRED. *Personal Data:* b Cleveland, Ohio, Aug 24, 28; m 53; c 2. *Educ:* Baldwin-Wallace Col, BS, 50; Ohio State Univ, MS, 51, PhD(chem), 54. *Prof Exp:* Asst, Ohio State Univ, 50-54; res assoc, Amoco Oil Co, 54-88. *Mem:* Am Chem Soc; Am Soc Testing & Mat. *Res:* Corrosion in hydrocarbon and water systems; hydrocarbon oxidation; air pollution. *Mailing Add:* 1008 Trout Lilly Lane Darien IL 60561

RAKSIS, JOSEPH W, DESIGN & SYNTHESIS OF POLYMERIC MATERIALS. *Current Pos:* dir, 77-82, VPRES, RES DIV, W R GRACE & CO, 82- *Personal Data:* b Wilkes-Barre, Pa, March 9, 42; m 82; c 3. *Educ:* Wilkes Col, BS, 63; Univ Calif, Irvine, PhD(chem), 67. *Prof Exp:* Res chemist, Dow Chem Co, USA, 67-71, res mgr, 72-77. *Mem:* Am Chem Soc; Indust Res Inst. *Res:* Design and synthesis of polymeric materials having specific functional properties. *Mailing Add:* 5216 Woodam Ct Columbia MD 21044-3310

RAKUSAN, KAREL JOSEF, PHYSIOLOGY. *Current Pos:* assoc prof, 69-74, PROF PHYSIOL, UNIV OTTAWA, 74- *Personal Data:* b Slany, Czech, Jan 28, 35; Can citizen; m 61, Jaromira; c 2. *Educ:* Charles Univ, Prague, MD, 60; Czech Acad Sci, PhD(physiol), 64. *Honors & Awards:* Czech Acad Sci Award, 66. *Prof Exp:* Asst prof pathophysiol, Charles Univ, Prague, 60-64, assoc prof, 67-68. *Concurrent Pos:* Mem, Int Study Group Res Cardiac Metab; NIH fel cardiol, Wayne State Univ, 65-66; Med Res Coun grantee, Univ Ottawa, 69-; vis scientist, Univ Ottawa, 68-69. *Mem:* Am Physiol Soc; Can Physiol Soc; Int Soc Heart Res; Int Soc Oxygen Transport Tissue (pres). *Res:* Microcirculatory aspects of the oxygen supply; experimental cardiomegaly; oxygen in the heart muscle; developmental physiology and angiogenesis. *Mailing Add:* Dept Physiol Univ Ottawa Ottawa ON K1H 8M5 Can. *Fax:* 613-562-5434; *E-Mail:* krakusau@labsunl.med.uottawa.ca

RALAPATI, SURESH, BIOCHEMISTRY, ORGANIC CHEMISTRY. *Current Pos:* SCIENTIST, US DEPT TREAS, NAT LAB CTR, 91-; ADJ PROF, BOWMAN-GRAY SCH MED, WAKE FOREST UNIV. *Personal Data:* b Secunderabad, India, 1949. *Educ:* AP Agr Univ, Hyderabad, India, BS, 71; Univ Mo, MS, 74, PhD(biochem), 78. *Prof Exp:* Scientist, J R Nabisco Inc. *Mem:* AAAS; Am Chem Soc. *Mailing Add:* US Dept Treas Nat Lab Ctr 1401 Research Blvd Rockville MD 20850-3188

RALEIGH, CECIL BARING, GEOPHYSICS. *Current Pos:* DEAN, SCH OCEAN & EARTH SCI & TECH, UNIV HAWAII, 89- *Personal Data:* b Little Rock, Ark, Aug 11, 34; m 76, 81; c 4. *Educ:* Pomona Col, BA, 56, MA, 59; Univ Calif, Los Angeles, PhD(geol), 63. *Honors & Awards:* Interdisciplinary Award, Intersoc Coun Rock Mech, 69 & 74; Meritorious Serv Award, Dept Interior, 79. *Prof Exp:* Res fel geophys, Inst Advan Studies, Australian Nat Univ, 63-65, fel, 65-66; res geophysicist, Nat Ctr Earthquake Res, US Geol Surv, 66-73, br chief earthquake tectonics; dir, Lamont-Doherty Geol Observ & prof, Dept Geol Sci, Columbia Univ, 81-89. *Mem:* Fel Geol Soc Am; fel Am Geophys Union. *Res:* Experimental deformation of rocks at high pressure and temperature; studies of earthquakes triggered by fluid injection; plastic deformation of rock forming minerals; rock mechanics. *Mailing Add:* Sch Ocean & Earth Sci & Technol Univ Hawaii 1680 East West Rd Honolulu HI 96822

RALEIGH, DOUGLAS OVERHOLT, ELECTROCHEMISTRY. *Current Pos:* RETIRED. *Personal Data:* b New York, NY, Aug 19, 29; m 60, 76; c 1. *Educ:* Rensselaer Polytech Inst, BS, 51; Columbia Univ, MA, 55, PhD(chem), 60. *Prof Exp:* Res chemist, Sylvania Elec Prod Corp, NY, 51-52; sr chemist, Atomics Int Div, Rockwell Int, 58-62, mem tech staff, 62-84, independent res & develop mgr, Sci Ctr, 84-93. *Concurrent Pos:* Invited lectr, Gordon Conf Electrochem, 68, Solid State, 73, Electrochem, 74 & high temperature chem, 78; vis assoc prof, Univ Utah, 69; invited tutorial lectr, NATO Advan Study Insts, Belgirate, Italy, 72 & Ajaccio, Corsica, 75, mem sci comt, 75; mem steering & prog comts, NBS Workshop on Electrocatalysis, 75; US-Japan Joint Sem, Defects & Diffusion in Solids, Tokyo, 76. *Res:* Electrochemical processes in molten salts and solid ionic conductors. *Mailing Add:* 22460 Venido Rd Woodland Hills CA 91364

RALEIGH, JAMES ARTHUR, ORGANIC CHEMISTRY, RADIATION BIOCHEMISTRY. *Current Pos:* assoc prof, 88-92, PROF RADIATION ONOCOL, UNIV NC, CHAPEL HILL, 92- *Personal Data:* b Vancouver, BC, Feb 21, 38; m 62, Donna Mary Macleod; c 4. *Educ:* Univ BC, BSc, 60, MSc, 62; Mass Inst Technol, PhD(org chem), 67. *Prof Exp:* Fel, Univ Sussex, 66-68; res off med biophys, Whiteshell Nuclear Res Estab, Atomic Energy Can Ltd, 68-78; sr scientist, Cross Cancer Inst, 78-88. *Concurrent Pos:* Assoc ed, radiation res, 83-86; mem, NIH radiation study sect, 83-86; mem, chem coun, Radiation Res Soc, 86-89; adj prof, NCar State Univ, 96-; consult, Natural Pharmaceut Int, Inc, Research Triangle Park, NC. *Mem:* Am Chem Soc; Radiation Res Soc; Chem Inst Can; Royal Soc Chem; Soc Free Radical Res. *Res:* Radiation chemistry of biologically important compounds; biochemistry of nitroaromatic compounds; tumor physiology; tumor hypoxia. *Mailing Add:* Dept Radiation Oncol CB No 7512 Univ NC Sch Med Chapel Hill NC 27599-7512. *Fax:* 919-966-7681; *E-Mail:* raleigh@radonc.unc.edu

RALEY, CHARLES FRANCIS, JR, ORGANIC CHEMISTRY. *Current Pos:* RETIRED. *Personal Data:* b Baltimore, Md, May 8, 23; m 47, Jane A Davis; c Charles C, Lelia E & Amy J. *Educ:* Univ Notre Dame, BS, 43, MS, 47; Univ Del, PhD(org chem), 50. *Prof Exp:* Org chemist, Southwest Res San Antonio, Tex, 50-56; org chemist, Dow Chem USA, 57-64, sr res chemist, 63-73, sr res specialist, Dow Chem Co, 73-75, assoc scientist, 75-82. *Concurrent Pos:* Adj instr chem, Saginaw Valley State Col, 84-87. *Mem:* Am Chem Soc; Sigma Xi. *Res:* Ignition-resistant plastics; thermal halogenations; high temperature reactions; free radical chemistry; halomethylation; Friedel-Crafts bromination. *Mailing Add:* 830 N Saginaw Rd Midland MI 48640

RALEY, JOHN HOWARD, PHYSICAL ORGANIC CHEMISTRY. *Current Pos:* RETIRED. *Personal Data:* b Salt Lake City, Utah, Sept 28, 16; m 41, Patricia Patterson; c John P & Richard. *Educ:* Univ Utah, AB, 37, AM, 39; Univ Rochester, PhD(chem), 42. *Prof Exp:* Chemist, Shell Develop Co, Calif, 42-51, refinery technologist, Shell Oil Co, Tex, 51-52, res supvr, Shell Develop Co, Calif, 52-68, dir phys sci, 68-69, res supvr, 69-72; chemist, Lawrence Livermore Nat Lab, Univ Calif, 75-81. *Concurrent Pos:* Chmn, Gordon Res Conf Hydrocarbon Chem, 63; consult, 81-90. *Mem:* Am Chem Soc. *Res:* Exploratory research petroleum and petrochemical processes products; hydrocarbon chemistry; oxidation; chemistry of reactive intermediates; metal complexes; homogeneous, heterogeneous catalysis; oil shale; shale oil. *Mailing Add:* 1040 Homestead Ave Walnut Creek CA 94598-4744

RALL, DAVID PLATT, ENVIRONMENTAL HEALTH. *Current Pos:* RETIRED. *Personal Data:* b Aurora, Ill, Aug 3, 26; m 89, Mary Monteiro; c 2. *Educ:* NCent Col (Ill), BA, 46; Northwestern Univ, MD & PhD(pharmacol), 51. *Hon Degrees:* MD, Med Col Ohio, 91. *Honors & Awards:* Arnold J Lehman Award, Soc Toxicol, 83; Ramazzini Award, 88. *Prof Exp:* Res assoc pharmacol, Northwestern Univ, 51-52; intern, 2nd Med Div, Bellevue Hosp, Cornell Univ, 52-53; pharmacologist, Lab Chem Pharmacol, Nat Cancer Inst, 53-55, clin pharmacol & exp ther serv, 55-58, head, 58-63, chief, Lab Chem Pharmacol, 63-71, assoc sci dir exp therapeut, 65-71, dir, Nat Inst Environ Health Sci, 71-90, dir, Nat Toxicol Prog, 78-90. *Concurrent Pos:* Asst surgeon gen, USPHS, 90- *Mem:* Soc Toxicol; Am Soc Pharmacol & Exp Therapeut; Inst Med-Nat Acad Sci; Am Asn Cancer Res; Soc Occup & Environ Health. *Res:* Bacterial pyrogens; toxicology; drug distribution; cancer chemotherapy; environmental health. *Mailing Add:* 5302 Reno Rd NW Washington DC 20015

RALL, JACK ALAN, MEDICAL PHYSIOLOGY, MUSCLE CONTRACTION. *Current Pos:* from asst prof to assoc prof, 74-85, PROF PHYSIOL, OHIO STATE UNIV, 85- *Personal Data:* b Detroit, Mich, Apr 12, 44; m 67, Bonnie Gee; c Caroline & Jennifer. *Educ:* Olivet Col, Mich, BA, 66; Univ Iowa, PhD(physiol), 72. *Prof Exp:* Fel, Univ Calif, Los Angeles, 72-74. *Concurrent Pos:* Fel, Muscular Dystrophy Asns Am, 72; hon res fel, dept Physiol, Univ Col, London. *Mem:* Am Physiol Soc; Biophys Soc; Soc Gen Physiol. *Res:* Elucidation of the mechanism of muscle contraction with emphasis on the energetics of the contractile process. *Mailing Add:* Dept Physiol 1645 Neil Ave Ohio State Univ Columbus OH 43210

RALL, JONATHAN ANDREW REILEY, ATMOSPHERIC REMOTE SENSING OF TRACE SPECIES, ELECTRO-OPTICAL INSTRUMENTS BASED ON ALUMINUM GALLIUM ARSENIDE DIODES. *Current Pos:* Student coop, Mat Br, 84-85, electronics engr, Instrument Electro-Optics Br, 85-90, SR ELECTRONICS ENGR, EXP INSTRUMENTS BR, NASA GODDARD SPACE FLIGHT CTR, 90- *Personal Data:* b Washington, DC, Apr 9, 63; m 91, Allison F Young. *Educ:* Am Univ, BS, 85, MS, 89, PhD(phys), 94; Wash Univ, BS, 86. *Res:* Developing remote sensing instruments based on aluminum gallium arsenide laser diodes and silicon avalanche photo diodes; making measurements of atmospheric constituents with these compact instruments. *Mailing Add:* 9334 Copernicus Dr Lanham MD 20706. *E-Mail:* jarrall@elb.1.gsfc.nasa.gov

RALL, JOSEPH EDWARD, ENDOCRINOLOGY, THYROIDOLOGY. *Current Pos:* chief, Clin Endocrinol Br, NIH, 55-62, dir intramural res, Nat Inst Arthritis, Diabetes, Digestive & Kidney Dis, 62-83, actg dep dir sci, 81-82, dep dir intramural res, 83-91, EMER SCIENTIST, NAT INST ARTHRITIS, DIABETES, DIGESTIVE & KIDNEY DIS, NIH, 91- *Personal Data:* b Naperville, Ill, Feb 3, 20; m 44, 78, Caroline Domm; c Priscilla & Edward. *Educ:* NCent Col, BA, 40; Northwestern Univ, MS, 44, MD, 45; Univ Minn, PhD(med), 52. *Hon Degrees:* DSc, NCent Col, 66; Dr, Free Univ Brussels, 75; MD, Univ Naples, 85. *Honors & Awards:* Van Meter Prize, Am Thyroid Asn, 50, Distinguished Service Award, 67; Fleming Award, 59; Robert H Williams Distinguished Leadership Award, 83; Super Serv Award, Dept Health, Educ & Welfare, 65, Distinguished Serv Award, 86. *Prof Exp:* Asst pharmacol, Northwestern Univ, 41-44; asst prof med, Med Col, Cornell Univ, 50-55. *Concurrent Pos:* Asst mem, Sloan-Kettering Inst, 50-51, assoc mem, 51-55; from asst attend physician to assoc attend physician, Med Serv, Mem Hosp, New York, 50-55; consult, Brookhaven Nat Lab, 50-; mem, Nat Res Coun, 60-; chmn, Coun Scientists, Human Frontier Sci Prog, 89. *Mem:* Nat Acad Sci; Endocrine Soc; Asn Am Physicians; Fr Soc Biol; Am Thyroid Asn; Am Acad Arts & Sci; Sigma Xi; Am Soc Clin Invest; AAAS; Am Physiol Soc; Radiation Effects Res Found. *Res:* Endocrinology; molecular biology. *Mailing Add:* NIH Bldg 10 Rm 8N307 Bethesda MD 20892. *Fax:* 301-402-0387

RALL, LLOYD L(OUIS), ENGINEERING. *Current Pos:* RETIRED. *Personal Data:* b Galesville, Wis, Dec 7, 16; m 52, Mary M Moller; c Lauris, David, Christopher & Jonathan. *Educ:* Univ Wis, BSCE, 40. *Prof Exp:* Dept Engr forward area, US Army Strategic Air Force, Corps Engrs, US Army, 44-45, chief construct div, Far East Air Forces, Tokyo, 45-47, engr mem, Mil Surv Mission to Turkey, 47, Off Joint Chief Staff, Pentagon, 47-49, exec officer, Res & Develop Off, Chief Engrs, 49-51, asst dist engr, Seattle Dist, Wash, 52-54, dep engr, Commun Zone, France, 54-56, commanding officer, 540th combat engr group, 56-57, prof mil sci & tactics, Mo Sch Mines & Metall, 57-60, dep dir topog, Off Chief Engrs, 60-64, dir, Geod Intel & Mapping Res & Develop Agency, Ft Belvoir, Va, 64-66, dep asst dir, Defense Intel Agency Mapping, Charting & Geod, 66-69, asst dir, Defense Intel Agency Mapping & Charting, 69-72; dir, Wash Off, Optical Systs Div, ITEK Corp, 77-92. *Concurrent Pos:* Mem, Nat Tech Adv Comt, Antarctica Mapping, 60-64. *Mem:* Am Soc Photogram; Am Cong Surv & Mapping; Am Inst Aerospace & Astronaut; Nat Space Club. *Res:* Mapping, charting and geodesy; geographic intelligence data. *Mailing Add:* 301 Cloverway Dr Alexandria VA 22314. *Fax:* 703-751-4021

RALL, LOUIS BAKER, NUMERICAL ANALYSIS. *Current Pos:* from asst dir to assoc dir, 65-73, res mem, Math Res Ctr, 62-86, PROF MATH, UNIV WIS-MADISON, CTR MATH SCI, 86- *Personal Data:* b Kansas City, Mo, Aug 1, 30; m 52; c 2. *Educ:* Col Puget Sound, BS, 49; Ore State Col, MS, 54, PhD(math), 56. *Prof Exp:* Asst, Ore State Col, 53-56; mathematician, Shell Develop Co, 56-57; assoc prof math, Lamar State Col Technol, 57-60; from assoc prof to prof, Va Polytech Inst & State Univ, 60-62. *Concurrent Pos:* Vis prof, Innsbruck Univ, 70, Oxford Univ, 72-73, Univ Copenhagen & Tech Univ Denmark, 80 & Univ Karlsruhe, 85. *Mem:* Soc Indust & Appl Math; Am Math Soc; Math Asn Am; Inst Math & Its Appln; Int Asn Math & Comput in Simulation. *Res:* Functional and numerical analysis; integral equations; machine computing; interval analysis; theory of interval analysis and its applications to efficient, self-validating numerical solution of scientific and technological problems. *Mailing Add:* 5101 Odana Rd Madison WI 53711-1013

RALL, RAYMOND WALLACE, EXPLORATION GEOLOGY. *Current Pos:* INDEPENDENT GEOLOGIST, 86- *Personal Data:* b Hanover, Ill, Mar 23, 26; m 49; c 4. *Educ:* Univ Ill, BS, 50, MS, 51. *Prof Exp:* Res asst, Ill State Geol Surv, 50-51; geologist & stratigrapher, Pure Oil Co, 51-59; sr geologist, Tenneco Oil Co, 59-67, sr geologist, Tenneco Oil & Minerals Ltd, 67-74, geol specialist, Tenneco Oil Co, 74-78, sr geol specialist, 78-86. *Mem:* Soc Econ Paleont & Mineral; Am Asn Petrol Geologists; Can Soc Petrol Geologists. *Res:* Paleozoic stratigraphy of Texas, upper midwest United States, Williston Basin, northern Canada, east coast United States and Canada, Great Basin, Alaska and western interior basins of the United States. *Mailing Add:* 450 Shadycroft Dr Littleton CO 80120

RALL, STANLEY CARLTON, JR, PROTEIN CHEMISTRY. *Current Pos:* CONSULT, 93- *Personal Data:* b Seattle, Wash, May 18, 43; m 69. *Educ:* Whitman Col, AB, 65; Univ Calif, Berkeley, PhD(biochem), 70. *Prof Exp:* Res asst biochem, Univ Calif, Berkeley, 65-70, fel, 71-74; fel biochem, Los Alamos Nat Lab, 75-78; sr scientist, Gladstone Found Labs, Univ Calif, San Francisco, 79-93. *Concurrent Pos:* Fel, Am Cancer Soc, 71-73; Dernham Jr fel, 73. *Mem:* Fel Am Heart Asn; fel Am Soc Biochem & Molecular Biol; Protein Soc. *Res:* Structure and function of apolipoproteins. *Mailing Add:* Gladstone Found Labs for Cardiovasc Dis Univ Calif PO Box 419100 San Francisco CA 94141-9100

RALL, THEODORE WILLIAM, PHARMACOLOGY. *Current Pos:* PROF PHARMACOL, SCH MED, UNIV VA, 75- *Personal Data:* b Chicago, Ill, Apr 7, 28; m 49. *Educ:* Univ Chicago, SB, 48, PhD(biochem), 52. *Prof Exp:* From res assoc to prof, Case Western Res Univ, 54-73, dir dept pharmacol, Sch Med, 73-75. *Mem:* Am Soc Pharmacol & Exp Therapeut; Am Soc Biol Chemists; Soc Neurosci. *Res:* Hormonal regulatory mechanisms; neuropharmacology. *Mailing Add:* Dept Pharmacol Box 395 Univ Va Sch Med Med Ctr 0 Hospital Dr Charlottesville VA 22908-0001

RALL, WALDO, PHYSICS, RESEARCH ADMINISTRATION. *Current Pos:* RETIRED. *Personal Data:* b Los Angeles, Calif, Mar 20, 24; m 85, Andree Fortier; c Richard A & Victoria (John). *Educ:* Wash Univ, BA, 44; Ind Univ, MS, 48, PhD, 50. *Prof Exp:* Asst cyclotron lab, Wash Univ, 43-44; asst metall lab, Univ Chicago, 44; jr scientist, Clinton Lab, Tenn, 44-45; jr scientist, Los Alamos, NMex, 45-46; nuclear studies, 46-47; asst physics. Ind Univ, 47-49; from instr to asst prof, Yale Univ, 49-56; from asst div chief to div chief, Res Lab, US Steel Corp, 56-75, mgr anal & planning, 75-80, dir contract res, 80-85. *Concurrent Pos:* Consult, 85- *Mem:* AAAS; fel Am Phys Soc; Am Soc Metals; Sigma Xi. *Res:* Nuclear, instrumental, vacuum and metal physics; research planning and budgeting; marketing of research; research administration. *Mailing Add:* 100 Oxford Dr A-702 Monroeville PA 15146

RALL, WILFRID, BIOPHYSICS, NEUROPHYSIOLOGY. *Current Pos:* res biophysicist, 57-67, sr res physicist, 67-94, EMER SCIENTIST, MATH RES BR, NAT INST DIABETES, DIGESTIVE & KIDNEY DIS, NIH, 94- *Personal Data:* b Los Angeles, Calif, Aug 29, 22; m 46, 83, Mary E Condon; c Sara E & Madelyn R (Badger). *Educ:* Yale Univ, BS (Hons), 43; Univ Chicago, MS, 48; Univ NZ, PhD(physiol), 53. *Honors & Awards:* Sr Scientist Performance Award, NIH, 83. *Prof Exp:* Jr physicist, Manhattan Proj, Chicago, 43-46; lectr biophys, Med Sch, Otago, NZ, 49-51, sr lectr physiol, 51-56; head biophys div, Naval Med Res Inst, Nat Naval Med Ctr, 56-57. *Concurrent Pos:* Rockefeller Found fel, Univ Col London, 54, Rockefeller Inst, 54-55; mem neurocommun & biophys panel, Int Brain Res Orgn, 60-, rep, Cent Coun, 68-73; mem nat comt, Nat Res Coun, 72-76; comt brain sci, Nat Res Coun, 68-73. *Mem:* Emer mem Soc Neurosci; Biophys Soc; Physiol Soc UK; Am Physiol Soc; fel AAAS. *Res:* Theoretical and experimental neurophysiology; dendritic branching; synaptic structure, function and integration; intracellular and extracellular potentials; computation with mathematical models; neurosciences. *Mailing Add:* Math Res Br NIH NIDDK 9190 Rockville Pike Suite 350 Bethesda MD 20814. *Fax:* 301-402-0535; *E-Mail:* wilrall@helix.nih.gov

RALL, WILLIAM FREDERICK, CRYOBIOLOGY, EMBRYOLOGY. *Current Pos:* Nat res coun fel, Vet Resources Prog, Nat Ctr Res Resources, 92-96, CRYOBIOLOGIST, PHYSIOLOGIST, VET RESOURCES PROG, NAT CTR RES RESOURCES, NIH, 97- *Personal Data:* b Bayshore, NY, May 31, 51; m 74; c 2. *Educ:* State Univ NY, BA, 73; Univ Tenn, Oak Ridge Grad Sch Biomed Sci, PhD(biomed sci), 79. *Prof Exp:* Vis scientist, Div Cell Path, Clin Res Ctr, Med Res Coun, UK, 79-80; sr sci off, Animal Res Sta, Inst Animal Physiol, Agr Res Coun, UK, 80-83; sr res fel, Cryobiol Lab, Am Red Cross Blood Res Lab, 83-84; sr scientist, Res & Develop Div, Rio Vista Int Inc, 84-88; assoc scientist, Am Type Cult Collection, Rockville, Md, 88-96. *Concurrent Pos:* Vis scientist, Health & Technol Div, Mass Inst Technol, 78-79; mem, Darwin Col, Cambridge, UK, 80-83; guest researcher, Embryo Cryopreserv Prog, Vet Resources Br, NIH, 84-86; adj assoc scientist, Southwest Found Biomed Res, San Antonio, Tex, 86-90; cryobiologist, Nat Zool Park, Smithsonian Inst, 88-96. *Mem:* AAAS; Soc Cryobiol; Soc Low Temp Biol; Int Embryo Transfer Soc; Soc Study Fertil. *Res:* Cryobiology of mammalian embryos, spermatozoa and cell lines; low-temperature light microscopy; development and physiology of preimplantation mammalian embryos; germ plasm banking. *Mailing Add:* Vet Resources Prog Bldg 14F Rm 101 NIH Bethesda MD 20892

RALLEY, THOMAS G, MATHEMATICS. *Current Pos:* Asst prof, 67-73, ASSOC PROF MATH, OHIO STATE UNIV, 73- *Personal Data:* b Chicago, Ill, July 10, 39; m 61; c 2. *Educ:* Ill Inst Technol, BS, 61; Univ Ill, MS, 63, PhD(math), 66. *Mem:* Am Math Soc. *Res:* Representations of finite groups and associative algebras. *Mailing Add:* Portland State Univ PO Box 751 Portland OR 97207

RALLS, JACK WARNER, CHEMISTRY. *Current Pos:* RETIRED. *Personal Data:* b Los Angeles, Calif, Feb 1, 20; m 46, Nancy J Lindberg; c David, Karen, Janet L & Martin W. *Educ:* Univ Calif, Los Angeles, BA, 43, MA, 44; Northwestern Univ, PhD(chem), 49. *Prof Exp:* Proj assoc, Univ Wis, 49-51; res chemist, G D Searle & Co, Ill, 51-55; res chemist, Calif Res Corp, 55-58; res chemist, Nat Canners Assn, 58-67; collabr, 58-64, res coordr, 64-67, res mgr, Western Utilization Res & Develop Div, USDA, 67-73; sr res scientist, Eng Exp Sta, Ga Inst Technol, 77-78; gen mgr, Temp Tech Assocs, Kensington, 78-80; dir, Org Labs, Univ SC, 80-81. *Concurrent Pos:* Lectr exten div, Univ Calif, Berkeley, 58-71. *Mem:* Am Chem Soc; Inst Food Technol. *Res:* Food processing; organic chemistry of thermally processed foods; flavor chemistry of fruits and vegetables; canned food technology; environmental chemistry. *Mailing Add:* Six Highgate Rd Kensington CA 94707-1141

RALLS, KATHERINE SMITH, MAMMALOGY, CONSERVATION BIOLOGY. *Current Pos:* fel, 73-75, RES ZOOLOGIST, SMITHSONIAN INST, 76-; ADJ PROF ENVIRON STUDIES, UNIV CALIF, SANTA CRUZ, 91- *Personal Data:* b Oakland, Calif, Mar 21, 39; div; c Robin, Tamsen & Kristin. *Educ:* Stanford Univ, AB, 60; Radcliffe Col, MA, 62; Harvard Univ, PhD(biol), 65. *Honors & Awards:* C Hart Merriam Award, Am Soc Mammalogists, 96; Edward T LaRoe Award, Soc Conserv Biol, 96. *Prof Exp:* Fel animal behav, Univ Calif, Berkeley, 65-67; guest investr, Rockefeller Univ, 68-70; asst prof, Sarah Lawrence Col, 70-73; fel, Radcliffe Inst, 73-74. *Concurrent Pos:* Adj asst prof animal behav, Rockefeller Univ, 70-76; Am Asn Univ Women, 75-76; mem psychobiol adv comt, NSF, 81-83; sci adv comt, Marine Mammal Comn, 79-82; consult, Int Union Conserv Nature, Natural Res, Survival Serv Comn, Captive Breeding Specialist Group, 79-, Otter specialist group, 89-, reintroduction specialist group, 92-; Species Survival Plan Subcomt, Am Asn Zool Parks & Aquaria, 81-88; bd dir, Am Soc Mammalogists, 83-93, second vpres, 90-93; mem gov bd, Soc Conserv Biol, 85-90; mem, Sea Otter Recovery Team, US Fish & Wildlife Serv, 89-, Condor

Recovery Team, 90-, comt on sci issues in endangered species Act, Nat Res Coun, 93; mem, Hawaiian monk seal recovery team, Nat Marine Fisheries Serv, 97- *Mem:* Am Soc Mammal; fel Animal Behav Soc; Asn Women Sci; Soc Marine Mammal; Soc Conserv Biol; fel AAAS; Wildlife Soc. *Res:* Mammalian social behavior; genetics of small populations; marine mammals; scientific approaches to solving conservation problems. *Mailing Add:* DZR Nat Zoo Smithsonian Inst Washington DC 20008. *Fax:* 202-673-4686; *E-Mail:* nzpzro12@sium.si.edu

RALLS, KENNETH M(ICHAEL), MATERIALS SCIENCE, PHYSICAL METALLURGY. *Current Pos:* from asst prof to assoc prof, 67-76, PROF MECH ENG, UNIV TEX, AUSTIN, 76- *Personal Data:* b Salt Lake City, Utah, Feb 14, 38; m 78; c 4. *Educ:* Stanford Univ, BS, 60; Mass Inst Technol, SM, 62, ScD(phys metall), 64. *Prof Exp:* Res assoc metall, Mass Inst Technol, 64-65; fel, Inorg Mat Res Div, Lawrence Radiation Lab, Calif, 65-67. *Mem:* Am Inst Mining, Metall & Petrol Engrs (Metall Soc); Am Soc Metals; Am Phys Soc; fel Am Inst Chemists; Metal Soc Gr Brit; Sigma Xi. *Res:* Physical metallurgy of high magnetic field superconductive materials; fabrication and preparation of multifilamentary superconducting composites. *Mailing Add:* Dept Mech Eng ETC 5-160 Univ Tex Austin TX 78712

RALPH, C(LEMENT) JOHN, AVIAN ECOLOGY. *Current Pos:* RES ECOLOGIST, US FOREST SERV, 76- *Personal Data:* b Oakland, Calif, Sept, 3, 40; m 73; c 2. *Educ:* Univ Calif, Berkeley, AB, 63; Calif State Univ, San Jose, MS, 69; Johns Hopkins Univ, ScD(pathobiol), 74. *Honors & Awards:* Tucker Award, Cooper Ornith Soc, 67; Wilson Award, Wilson Ornith Soc, 73; Roberts Award, Am Ornith Soc. *Prof Exp:* Dir, Point Reyes Bird Observ, 66-69; asst prof ecol/behav, Dickinson Col, 73-76. *Concurrent Pos:* Comnr, Animal Species Adv Comn, Hawaii, 80-82; ed, Elepaio. *Mem:* Am Ornithologists Union; Ecol Soc Am; Animal Behav Soc; Wilson Ornith Soc; Sigma Xi; Cooper Ornith Soc (pres, 85-87). *Res:* Life history and ecological relationships of Hawaiian and Pacific Northwest forest birds, especially rare and endangered species. *Mailing Add:* Redwood Scis Lab-US Forest Serv 1700 Bayview Dr Arcata CA 95521

RALPH, CHARLES LELAND, PHYSIOLOGY. *Current Pos:* PROF ZOOL & ENTOM & CHMN DEPT, COLO STATE UNIV, 74- *Personal Data:* b Flint, Mich, Aug 16, 29; m 80; c 2. *Educ:* Southeast Mo State Col, BS, 52; Northwestern Univ, MS, 53, PhD(biol), 55. *Prof Exp:* Spec prof personnel corps, US Army Chem Ctr, Md, 55-57; physiologist, USDA, 57-59; from asst prof to prof biol, Univ Pittsburgh, 59-74, chmn dept, 72-74. *Mem:* Fel AAAS; Am Soc Zool; Am Physiol Soc; Am Asn Anat; Am Inst Biol Sci. *Res:* Comparative physiology; neuroendocrinology; physiology of the pineal body; vertebrate color change. *Mailing Add:* 1249 Oak Island Ct Ft Collins CO 80525

RALPH, PETER, HEMATOLOGY, CANCER. *Current Pos:* DIR IMMUNOL, GENENTECH INC, S SAN FRANCISCO, 92- *Personal Data:* b Brandon, Vt, Oct 7, 36. *Educ:* Yale Univ, BA, 58; Univ Cal, Berkeley, MA, 60; Mass Inst Technol, PhD(biol), 68. *Prof Exp:* Asst res prof, Salk Inst, 68-75; dir cell biol, Cetus Corp, 84-91. *Concurrent Pos:* Assoc mem, Sloan Kettering Inst Cancer Res, NY, 75-84. *Mem:* AAAS; Am Asn Immunologists; Soc Leuk Biol. *Res:* Cellular immunology; phagocytes; hematology. *Mailing Add:* Genentech Inc 460 Point San Bruno Blvd MS38 South San Francisco CA 94080-4980

RALPHS, MICHAEL H, POISONOUS PLANTS, LIVESTOCK GRAZING BEHAVIOR. *Current Pos:* RANGE SCIENTIST, POISONOUS PLANT RES LAB, AGR RES SERV, USDA, 83- *Personal Data:* b Price, Utah, July 25, 50; m 77, Diana Alldredge; c Marian, Jesse, Kimberly, Jeanette & Matthew. *Educ:* Utah State Univ, BS, 74, MS, 77; Tex A&M Univ, PhD(range sci), 83. *Honors & Awards:* Cert of Merit, Agr Res Serv, USDA, 86, 92. *Prof Exp:* Exten specialist, Utah Coop Exten Serv, 74-77; ranch mgr, Saval Ranching Co, 78-79; res asst, Tex A&M Univ, 80-83. *Concurrent Pos:* Pres, Utah Sect, Soc Range Mgt, 98. *Mem:* Am Soc Animal Sci; Weed Sci Soc Am; Western Soc Weed Sci. *Res:* Determine toxin levels in plants; determine the conditions under which livestock graze these plants; develop management recommendations to reduce livestock loss and deaths. *Mailing Add:* 1150 E 1400 N Logan UT 84341

RALSTON, ANTHONY, MATHEMATICS EDUCATION. *Current Pos:* prof math, 65-95, prof comput sci, 67-95, EMER PROF COMPUT SCI, STATE UNIV NY, BUFFALO, 95- *Personal Data:* b New York, NY, Dec 24, 30; m 58; c 4. *Educ:* Mass Inst Technol, SB, 52, PhD(math), 56. *Honors & Awards:* Distinguished Service Award, Asn Comput Mach, 82. *Prof Exp:* Mem tech staff, Bell Tel Labs, Inc, 56-59; lectr math, Univ Leeds, 59-60; mgr tech comput, Am Cyanamid Co, 60-61; from assoc prof to prof math, Stevens Inst Technol, 60-65, dir, Comput Ctr, 60-65, dir comput serv, 65-70, chmn, Comput Sci Dept, 67-80. *Concurrent Pos:* Vis prof, Univ London, 71-72, 78-79, 85-86 & 92-93; ed, Abacus, 83-88; mem, Bd Govs, Math Asn Am, 84-87 & Bd Math Sci Educ, Nat Res Coun, 85-89; acad vis, Imp Col, London, 95- *Mem:* Fel Asn Comput Mach (vpres, 70-72, pres, 72-74); Soc Indust & Appl Math; Am Fedn Info Processing Socs (pres, 75-76); Math Asn Am; fel AAAS. *Res:* Discrete mathematics; education in computer science and mathematics. *Mailing Add:* Flat 4 58 Prince Consort Rd London SW7 2BA England. *Fax:* 44-171-581-8024; *E-Mail:* ar9@doc.ic.al.uk

RALSTON, DOUGLAS EDMUND, BIOCHEMISTRY. *Current Pos:* ASSOC PROF BIOCHEM, MANKATO STATE UNIV, 62- *Personal Data:* b Cherokee, Iowa, July 9, 32; m 53; c 2. *Educ:* Wayne State Col. BS, 55, MS, 57; SDak State Univ, MA, 59; Univ Minn, Minneapolis, PhD(biochem), 69. *Prof Exp:* Asst prof chem, Wayne State Col, 59-60. *Concurrent Pos:* Chmn, Nat Educ Asn Higher Educ Coun, 78-80. *Mem:* Am Chem Soc. *Res:* Membrane transport. *Mailing Add:* Dept Chem & Geol Mankato State Univ 515 Main St Mankato MN 56001-6001

RALSTON, ELIZABETH WALL, COMPUTER ALGEBRA. *Current Pos:* SR CONSULT, INFERENCE CORP, 84- *Personal Data:* b Urbana, Ill, June 26, 45; m 69. *Educ:* Stanford Univ, BS, 66; Yale Univ, PhD(math), 70. *Prof Exp:* Instr math, Fordham Univ, 70-71; asst prof, Calif State Col, Dominguez Hills, 71-73; adj asst prof, Univ Calif, Los Angeles, 73-75; asst prof math, Fordham Univ, 75-77; mem technol staff, Aerospace Corp, 77-83; comput scientist, Transaction Technol, Inc, 83-84. *Mem:* Am Math Soc. *Res:* Computer algebra. *Mailing Add:* 2044 Kerwood Ave Los Angeles CA 90025

RALSTON, HENRY JAMES, III, NEUROANATOMY, ELECTRON MICROSCOPY. *Current Pos:* PROF ANAT & CHMN DEPT, UNIV CALIF, SAN FRANCISCO, 73- *Personal Data:* b Berkeley, Calif, Mar 12, 35; m 60, Diane Daly; c Rachel A & Amy S. *Educ:* Univ Calif, Berkeley, AB, 56; Univ Calif, San Francisco, MD, 59. *Honors & Awards:* Borden Award, 59. *Prof Exp:* Intern med, Mt Sinai Hosp, New York, 59-60; resident, Univ Calif, San Francisco, 60-61; asst prof anat, Sch Med, Stanford Univ, 65-69; assoc prof anat, Univ Wis-Madison, 69-73. *Concurrent Pos:* Nat Inst Neurol Dis & Blindness spec fel neuroanat, Univ Col, Univ London, 63-65; prin investr, Nat Inst Neurol & Communicative Dis & Stroke res grants, 65-; mem neurol A study sect, NIH, 77-81; mem, Nat Bd Med Examrs, 82-96, chmn, Anat Test Comt, 85-88; chmn, Acad Senate, Univ Calif, San Francisco, 86-88; Jacob Javits investr award, 88-95; chmn, Step I Comt, US Med Licensing Exam, 93-96. *Mem:* AAAS; Anat Soc Gt Brit & Ireland; Am Asn Anat (pres, 87-88); Soc Neurosci; Int Asn Study Pain. *Res:* Fine structural organization of mammalian nervous system; mechanisms of somatic sensation; neural circuitry serving pain mechanisms in the primate. *Mailing Add:* Dept Anat Univ Calif 513 Parnassus Ave San Francisco CA 94143-0452. *Fax:* 415-476-4845; *E-Mail:* hjr@phy.ucsf.edu

RALSTON, JAMES VICKROY, JR, MATHEMATICS. *Current Pos:* from asst prof to assoc prof, 71-77, PROF MATH, UNIV CALIF, LOS ANGELES, 77- *Personal Data:* b Elyria, Ohio, June 26, 43; m 69. *Educ:* Harvard Univ, BA, 64; Stanford Univ, PhD(math), 69. *Prof Exp:* Vis mem, Courant Inst Math Sci, 68-70; asst prof math, NY Univ, 70-71. *Concurrent Pos:* Fel, Alfred Sloan Found, 74-76. *Mem:* Am Math Soc. *Res:* Hyperbolic partial differential equations; scattering theory. *Mailing Add:* Univ Calif Los Angeles CA 90095-1555

RALSTON, JOHN PETER, HIGH ENERGY THEORY. *Current Pos:* from asst prof to assoc prof, 84-93, PROF HIGH ENERGY THEORY, PHYSICS DEPT, UNIV KANS, 93- *Personal Data:* b Reno, Nev, Aug 8, 51. *Educ:* Univ Nev, Reno, BS, 73; Univ Ore, PhD(physics), 80. *Prof Exp:* Engr instrument design, Hamilton Co, Reno, 74; res assoc high energy theory, McGill Univ, 80-82; fac lectr, 82; res assoc high energy theory, Argonne Nat Lab, 82-84; sci assoc, GLAC, CERN, Fermilab, Los Alamos & Argonne Nat Labs, 84-90. *Mem:* Sigma Xi. *Res:* Theoretical high energy physics; applications of quantum field theory to particle structure and interactions; particle astrophysics; interface of particle and nuclear physics. *Mailing Add:* 940 Rhode Island St Lawrence KS 66044. *Fax:* 785-864-5262; *E-Mail:* ralston@kuphsx.phsx.ukans.edu

RALSTON, MARGARETE A, ELECTROMAGNETIC FIELD THEORY, TELECOMMUNICATIONS. *Current Pos:* ASSOC PROF ELEC ENG, METROP STATE COL, DENVER, 87- *Personal Data:* b Denver, Colo, July 15, 54. *Educ:* Univ Denver, BA, 74; Univ Colo, MS, 77. *Prof Exp:* Proj engr, Vir James PC, 74-77; occup engr, Western Elec, 77-78; antenna design engr, Jampro Antennas, 78-79; engr, Broadcast Prod Div, Harris Corp, 79-80; sr engr, RCA Corp, 80-81 & Sci Atlanta, 82-84; staff engr, Martin Marietta Corp, 85-87. *Concurrent Pos:* Rep, 2 degree spacing comt, space sta working group, Fed Commun Comn, 86; adj fac, Univ Denver, 89-; fac assoc, Inst Telecommun Sci, Nat Telecommun & Info Admin, 88-89. *Mem:* Sr mem Inst Elec & Electronic Engrs; Nat Soc Prof Engrs; Am Soc Eng Educ. *Res:* Communications, both analog and digital; satellites, antenna design and telecommunications; data communication networks; awarded one United States patent. *Mailing Add:* US W Advan Technol 4001 Discovery Dr Suite 390 Boulder CO 80303

RAM, BUDH, PHYSICS. *Current Pos:* from asst prof to assoc prof, 66-77, PROF PHYSICS, NMEX STATE UNIV, 77- *Personal Data:* b Delhi, India, Jan 12, 35; m 64; c 2. *Educ:* Univ Delhi, BS, 55, MS, 57; Univ Colo, PhD(physics), 63. *Prof Exp:* Lectr physics, Univ Delhi, 57-58, lectr, Panjab Univ, India, 58-59; teaching asst, Univ Colo, 59-62; res fel, Battersea Col Technol, Univ London, 63-64; res assoc, Univ NC, 64-66. *Mem:* Am Phys Soc. *Res:* Elementary particles; theoretical physics. *Mailing Add:* 3333 Majestic Ridge Las Cruces NM 88011

RAM, C VENKATA S, HYPERTENSION, CARDIOVASCULAR DISEASE. *Current Pos:* fac assoc, 77-78, asst prof, 78-83, ASSOC PROF INTERNAL MED, UNIV TEX HEALTH SCI CTR, SOUTHWESTERN MED SCH, DALLAS, 84- *Personal Data:* b Machilipatnam, India, Oct 24, 48; US citizen; m 79; c 2. *Educ:* Govt Med Col-Marathwada Univ, BS, 66; Osmania Med Col, MD, 71; Am Bd Internal Med, cert. *Prof Exp:* Intern, Mercer Hosp, Trenton, NJ, 73; med intern, Brown Univ & RI Hosp, 74, resident internal med & teaching fel, Div Biol Sci, 75-76. *Concurrent Pos:* Instr, Univ Pa Sch Med, 76-77; attend physician, Parkland Mem Hosp, Dallas, Tex, 78-, dir, Hypertension Clin, 80-; attend physician, St Paul's Hosp,

Dalllas, Tex, 79-, dir, Hypertension Clin, 79- *Mem:* Am Heart Asn; Am Col Chest Physicians; Am Col Physicians; Am Col Cardiol; Am Col Clin Pharmacol; AMA; Am Fedn Clin Res; Int Soc Hypertension; Am Soc Hypertension. *Res:* Clinical research mechanism and management of hypertension; development and application of new cardiovascular drugs. *Mailing Add:* Univ Tex Health Sci Ctr 5939 Harry Hines Blvd No 600 Dallas TX 75235-6243

RAM, J SRI, BIOCHEMISTRY, IMMUNOLOGY. *Current Pos:* actg chief, 76-78, Nat Heart, Lung & Blood Inst, NIH, chief, Airways Dis Br, 78-89, spec asst to dir, Div Lung Dis, 89-94, HEALTH SCIENTIST ADMINR, NAT HEART, LUNG & BLOOD INST, NIH, 94- *Personal Data:* b India, Apr 5, 28; m 50, Devasena Chavali; c Prasad & Kalpana. *Educ:* Andhra Univ, India, BSc, 48; Univ Bombay, PhD(biochem), 52. *Prof Exp:* Res assoc, Columbia Univ, 54-55; res assoc immunochem, Univ Pittsburgh, 55-59, asst prof biochem, 59-61; asst prof biol chem, Univ Mich, 61-65; res biochemist, Nat Inst Arthritis, Metab & Digestive Dis, 65-74; exec secy, Pathobiol Chem Study Sect, Div Res Grants, Grants, NIH, 74-76. *Concurrent Pos:* Lady Tata scholar biochem, Indian Inst Sci, Bangalore, 52-53 & Fordham Univ, 53-54; Fulbright-Hays vis prof, India, 71; consult, UN Develop Prog, Patel Chest Inst, India, 90-91; Woodrow Wilson Found vis fel, 93-94. *Mem:* Am Asn Path; Am Soc Biochem & Molecular Biol; Am Asn Immunol; AAAS; Soc Exp Biol & Med. *Res:* Immunochemistry; mechanism of enzyme action; antigen-antibody interactions; protein modification; antigenicity of hormones and drugs; immunology and biochemistry of disease; aging; science policy; pulmonary disease research administration. *Mailing Add:* 6701 Rockledge Dr Two Rockledge Ctr Ste 10018 Bethesda MD 20892. *Fax:* 301-480-3559; *E-Mail:* rams@nih.gov

RAM, JEFFREY L, INVERTEBRATE NEUROPHYSIOLOGY, ENDOCRINOLOGY. *Current Pos:* from asst prof to assoc prof, 77-93, PROF NEUROPHYSIOL, WAYNE STATE UNIV, 93- *Personal Data:* b Newark, NJ, Sept 25, 45; m 77; c 3. *Educ:* Univ Pa, BA, 67; Calif Inst Technol, PhD(biochem), 74. *Prof Exp:* Fel neurosci, Univ Calif, Santa Cruz, 73-77. *Concurrent Pos:* Stipendiary fel, Marine Biol Lab, Woods Hole, Mass, 75; vis prof, Technion, Haifa, Israel, 84-85; Picchione vis scholar, Dalhousie Univ, Halifax, NS, Can, 96-97. *Mem:* AAAS; Am Physiol Soc; Soc Int Comp Biol; Soc Develop Biol; Int Soc Invert Reproduction; Int Asn Great Lakes Res. *Res:* Comparative aspects of gastropod egg hormones; modulatory effects of serotonin; activation of neurons by peptides; biophysics membranes; vascular smooth muscle physiology; zebra mussel reproduction. *Mailing Add:* Dept Physiol Sch Med Wayne State Univ Detroit MI 48201

RAM, MICHAEL, ATMOSPHERIC PHYSICS, THEORETICAL PHYSICS. *Current Pos:* from asst prof assoc prof, 67-93, PROF PHYSICS, STATE UNIV NY BUFFALO, 93- *Personal Data:* b Alexandria, Egypt, Dec 18, 36; m 59, Edna; c Alan, Dorrit & Shelley. *Educ:* Israel Inst Technol, BSc, 60, MSc, 62; Columbia Univ, PhD(physics), 65. *Prof Exp:* Res assoc physics, Johns Hopkins Univ, 65-67. *Concurrent Pos:* Chmn physics dept, State Univ NY, 74-77. *Mem:* Am Geophys Union. *Res:* Theoretical physics; atmospheric physics. *Mailing Add:* 111 Dan Troy Dr Buffalo NY 14221. *Fax:* 716-645-2507; *E-Mail:* phymram@ice.physics.buffalo.edu

RAM, MICHAEL JAY, MEDICAL DEVICES, PATENT LAW. *Current Pos:* GEN COUN, PHARMACIA OPHTHALMICS INC, 85- *Personal Data:* b Newark, NJ, Dec 18, 40; m 64; c 3. *Educ:* Lafayette Col, BS, 62; Newark Col Eng, MS, 63, DSc(chem eng), 66; Seton Hall Univ, JD, 72. *Prof Exp:* Sr res engr, Celanese Res Co, Summit, 67-73; patent atty, Brooks, Haidt, Haffner, 73-74; dir tech liason, C R Bard Inc, 73-84. *Mem:* Am Chem Soc; Am Inst Chem Engrs; Am Bar Asn. *Res:* Synthetic fibers; plastics; medical products; patent law; medical devices and the patent protection of products. *Mailing Add:* 650 E Huntington Dr PO Box 5036 Monrovia CA 91017-7136

RAM, NEIL MARSHALL, HAZARDOUS WASTE ASSESSMENT, CHEMICAL FATE & TRANSPORT. *Current Pos:* VPRES & DIST MGR, FLUOR DANIEL GTI, 91- *Personal Data:* b New York, NY, Feb 6, 52; m 74, Jan S Pevar; c Jesse & Jonah. *Educ:* Rutgers Univ, BS, 73, MS, 75; Harvard Univ, MS, 77 & PhD(environ eng), 79. *Prof Exp:* Fel environ eng, Technion Inst Sci, 79-80; asst prof environ eng, Univ Mass, 80-84; lab mgr, Alliance Technol Corp, 84-87; sr prod mgr, Stone & Webster Eng Corp, 87-89 & ICF Kaiser Engrs, 89-91. *Concurrent Pos:* Co-ed, Assoc Environ Eng Profs, 82-84, Stand Methods Comt, Stand Methods for Water & Wastewater, 84-83, proj adv comt, Am Water Works Asn Res Found, 87-88; mgr, Envirologic Data Inc, 91-93. *Mem:* Hazardous Mat & Control Res Inst; Am Chem Soc; Licensed Site Prof Asn. *Res:* Assessment, management and remediation of toxic or hazardous substances; occurence, treatment and significance of organic compounds in drinking water; determination of fate and transport for hazardous substances in environmental matrices; waste treatment technology development. *Mailing Add:* Fluor Daniel GTI 100 River Ridge Rd Norwood MA 02062. *Fax:* 781-769-7785; *E-Mail:* nram@gtionline.com

RAMACHANDRAN, BANUMATHI, GENE REGULATION & EXPRESSION. *Current Pos:* RES ASSOC, CHILDREN'S HOSP PHILADELPHIA, 88- *Personal Data:* b Vellore, Tamilnadu, India, July 25, 56; m 85, Ram; c Jyotsna. *Educ:* Madras Univ, BS, 77, MS, 79; Indian Inst Sci, PhD(microbiol & cell biol), 85. *Prof Exp:* Fel Univ Med & Dent NJ, Robert Wood Johnson Med Sch, 87-88. *Mem:* Am Soc Biochem & Molecular Biol. *Res:* Locate cis and trans-acting elements required for the regulation of the platelet specific gene platelet factor 4; understanding the nuclear and cytoplasmic factors involved in differential expression of specific genes during megakaryocytic differentiation. *Mailing Add:* 20 Aberdeen Circle Flemington NJ 08822. *Fax:* 215-590-3893

RAMACHANDRAN, CHITTOOR KRISHNA, LIPID BIOCHEMISTRY. *Current Pos:* RES BIOCHEM CELL BIOL, VET ADMIN MED CTR, KANSAS CITY, MD, 79- *Personal Data:* b Edavanakkad, Kerala, India, Nov 12, 45; US citizen; m 79; c 2. *Educ:* Univ Kerala, India, BSc, 66; Univ Baroda, India, MSc, 70; V P Chest Inst, Univ Delhi, India, PhD(biochem), 74. *Prof Exp:* Jr lectr chem, St Alberts Col, Ernakulam, 66-68; teaching fel neurochem, Brain Behav Res Ctr, Sonoma, Univ Calif, San Francisco, 74-76; res assoc cell biol, Univ Kans Med Ctr, 76-79. *Concurrent Pos:* Adj asst prof microbiol, Univ Kans Med Ctr, Kansas City, Kans, 80- *Mem:* Am Soc Biol Chem; Tissue Cult Asn; Soc Exp Biol & Med. *Res:* Mode of action of glucocorhioids on plasma membrane components; lipid metabolism enzymes in cultured cells; cholesterol synthesis and dolichol-mediated glycosylation of proteins. *Mailing Add:* 1394 Embassy Way Salt Lake City UT 84108

RAMACHANDRAN, JANAKIRAMAN, ENDOCRINOLOGY, BIOCHEMISTRY. *Current Pos:* VPRES RES, NEUREX CORP, 88- *Personal Data:* b Bombay, India, June 12, 35; m 67; c 1. *Educ:* Univ Madras, MA, 56; DePaul Univ, MS, 59; Univ Calif, Berkeley, PhD(biochem), 62. *Prof Exp:* Jr res biochemist, Hormone Res Lab, Univ Calif, Berkeley, 62-63, asst res biochemist, 63-68; lectr, Sch Med, Univ Calif, San Francisco, 64-68, from asst prof to prof biochem, Med Ctr, 68-83; sr scientist, Genentech, 83-88. *Concurrent Pos:* Weizmann Mem fel biophys, Weizmann Inst, 65-66; adj prof biochem, Univ Calif, San Francisco, 83-88, adj prof physiol, 88-; dir, Astra Res Ctr India, Bangalore, 86- *Mem:* AAAS; NY Acad Sci; Endocrine Soc; Tissue Cult Asn; Am Soc Biol Chemists. *Res:* Study of the mode of action of polypeptide hormones. *Mailing Add:* 3279 Emerson St Palo Alto CA 94306

RAMACHANDRAN, MUTHUKRISHNAN, SICKLE CELL DISEASE, RED CELL METABOLISM. *Current Pos:* DIR NEWBORN SCREENING PROG, DIV PUB HEALTH, STATE GA, ATLANTA, 94- *Personal Data:* b Sivaganga, India, Feb 12, 43; m 74; c 2. *Educ:* Univ Madras, India, BS, 63, MS, 69; Univ Kerala, India, PhD(red cell metab), 81. *Prof Exp:* Demonstr & lectr biochem, Med Col, Kotcayam-8, Kerala, India, 70-74; lectr & biochemist, Jawaharlal PG Med Inst, Pondicherry-6, India, 74-80; sr lectr biochem, Col Med Sci, Univ Calabar, Nigeria, 80-85; sr res fel, Med Col Ga, Augusta, 85-89, tech supvr & asst res scientist, Dept Cell & Molecular Biol, 89-92; res assoc, Bowman Gray Sch Med, Winston-Salem, NC, 92-94. *Concurrent Pos:* Co-investr red cell membrane res, NIH, 85- *Mem:* Am Asn Clin Chemists; Am Soc Biochem & Molecular Biol; NY Acad Sci. *Res:* Abnormal hemoglobins; red cell membrane proteinkinase-c and its role in the pathogenesis of sickle cell disease; red cell metabolism; medical biochemistry; protein chemistry; DNA-protein interactions; post translational modifications. *Mailing Add:* Clin Prog 47 Trinity Ave Atlanta GA 30334

RAMACHANDRAN, NARAYANAN, MICROGRAVITY FLUID MECHANICS MODELING, EXPERIMENTAL FLUID MECHANICS. *Current Pos:* res assoc, 87-88, ASSOC SCIENTIST, UNIVS SPACE RES ASN, 88- *Personal Data:* b Bombay, India, Jan 6, 58; m, Geetha Chandra; c Nina. *Educ:* Univ Madras, India, BEHons, 80; Univ Mo, Rolla, MS, 83, PhD (mech eng), 87. *Prof Exp:* Teaching asst thermodyn, Univ Mo, Rolla, 80-83, res asst, 84-87. *Concurrent Pos:* Prin investr, NASA Advan Tech Develop Proj, 87-91; coinvestr, US Microgravity Lab-I Space Shuttle Mission, 92. *Mem:* Sigma Xi; Am Inst Aeronaut & Astronaut; Am Soc Mech Engrs. *Res:* Computation fluid dynamics associated with microgravity materials experiments, effects of g-jitter on fluids; experimental fluids mechanics associated with space shuttle main engine and related components; hot wire and laser doppler measurements in air and water flows. *Mailing Add:* ES75 State Sci Lab NASA Marshall Space Flight Ctr Huntsville AL 35812. *E-Mail:* ramachandran@ssl.msfc.nasa.gov

RAMACHANDRAN, PALLASSANA N, PHYSICAL CHEMISTRY, SURFACE CHEMISTRY. *Current Pos:* sr res chemist, Colgate-Palmolive Res Ctr, 67-80, res assoc, 80-85, sr res assoc, 85-88, assoc res fel, 88-94, sr assoc dir, 94-96, DIR TECHNOL, COLGATE PALMOLIVE RES CTR, 96- *Personal Data:* b Palghat, India; US citizen; m 66, Sundya; c Sondya. *Educ:* Univ Bombay, BSc, 56; Temple Univ, MA, 62, PhD(phys chem), 65. *Prof Exp:* Fel chem, Textile Res Inst, Princeton, NJ, 65-67. *Mem:* Am Chem Soc; Am Oil Chemists Soc; Fiber Soc. *Res:* Development and processing of household products; clinical evaluations of skin and hair care products. *Mailing Add:* Colgate-Palmolive Res Ctr 909 River Rd Piscataway NJ 08855-1343. *Fax:* 732-878-6031

RAMACHANDRAN, SUBRAMANIA, ORGANIC CHEMISTRY, BIOCHEMISTRY. *Current Pos:* from asst mgr to mgr, Biochem Dept, 69-72, vpres res & develop, 72-74, MGR RES & DEVELOP, APPL SCI LABS, INC, 74- *Personal Data:* b Madras, India, Jan 8, 38; m 68; c 1. *Educ:* Annamalai Univ, Madras, 57, Hons, 59, MSc, 60; Ohio State Univ, MS, 64, PhD(biochem), 68. *Prof Exp:* Asst chem, Ohio State Univ, 61-68, fel physiol chem, 68-69. *Mem:* Am Oil Chem Soc. *Res:* Synthesis of lipids, including steroids; metabolism of lipids; chromatographic separation of organic compounds; analytical methods in clinical chemistry and pharmacology. *Mailing Add:* 26 Crickelwood Circle State College PA 16803

RAMACHANDRAN, VANGIPURAM S, CONCRETE TECHNOLOGY, CLAY MINERALOGY. *Current Pos:* res fel bldg sci, Nat Res Coun Can, 62-65, res officer bldg sci, 68-79, head, Bldg Mat Sect, 79-89, DISTINGUISHED RESEARCHER, NAT RES COUN CAN, 89- *Personal Data:* b Bangalore, India, Dec 30, 29; m 57; c 2. *Educ:* Mysore Univ, India, BSc, 49, DSc(cement chem), 81; Banaras Hindu Univ, MSc, 51; Calcutta Univ, PhD(catalysis), 56. *Hon Degrees:* DSc, Internation Univ Found, US, 87. *Honors & Awards:* Pres Award, Nat Res Coun, 89. *Prof Exp:* Sr res officer clay mineral, Cent Bldg Res Inst, Roorkee, India, 56-62, 65-68. *Concurrent*

Pos: Mem bd, Ceramic Soc Abstracts, 63-; contrib ed, Cements Res Progress, Am Ceramic Soc, 74-83; chmn, Cements Div, Am Ceramic Soc, 81 & mem, Int Union Testing & Res Labs for Mat & Struct, France, 83-85; ed, J Mat & Struct, France, 81-; consult ser ed, Noyes Publ, NJ, 85-; res adv, Am Biog Inst, 86-; chief ed, J Mat Civil Eng, USA, 89- *Mem:* Fel Am Ceramic Soc; fel Royal Soc Chem, UK; fel Inst Ceramics UK; Int Union Testing & Res Labs for Mat Struct France; Can Stand Asn; Am Soc Testing & Mat. *Res:* Clay mineralogy; gypsum and cement chemistry; author of seven books and 20 chapters in books. *Mailing Add:* 1079 Elmlea Dr Ottawa ON K1J 6W3 Can

RAMACHANDRAN, VENKATANARAYANA D, ELECTRICAL ENGINEERING. *Current Pos:* assoc prof, 69-71, PROF ELEC ENG, CONCORDIA UNIV, 71- *Personal Data:* b Mysore City, India, May 3, 34; m 60, Kamala; c Ravi Prakash. *Educ:* Cent Col, Bangalore, BSc, 53; Indian Inst Sci, Bangalore, BE, 56, ME, 58, PhD(elec eng), 65. *Honors & Awards:* Western Elec Fund Award, Am Soc Eng Educ, 83. *Prof Exp:* Sr res asst elec eng, Indian Inst Sci, Bangalore, 58-59, lectr, 59-65; asst prof, NS Tech Col, 66-69. *Concurrent Pos:* Assoc ed, Can Elec Eng J, 81-83, ed, 83-85. *Mem:* Fel Inst Elec & Electronics Engrs; fel Inst Elec Engrs UK; fel Inst Elec & Telecommun Engrs India; fel Inst Eng India; fel Eng Inst Can. *Res:* Circuit theory; active, lumped and multivariable networks. *Mailing Add:* Dept Elec Eng Concordia Univ Montreal PQ H3G 1M8 Can. *E-Mail:* kamala@ece.concordia.ca

RAMACHANDRAN, VENKATARAMAN, FAILURE ANALYSIS & ACCIDENT INVESTIGATION, MECHANICAL BEHAVIOR OF MATERIALS. *Current Pos:* EMER SCIENTIST, NAT AEROSPACE LABS, 92- *Personal Data:* b Tamil, Nadu, India, Feb 15, 32; m 60, Lakshmi; c R Guruprasad & R Krishnaprasad. *Educ:* Univ Madras, BSc, 51; India, Inst Sci, BE, 55; Mich State Univ, MS, 62; Univ Fla, PhD(metall & mat eng), 70. *Honors & Awards:* Biren Roy Trust Award, Aeronaut Soc India, 84; IT Mirchandani Mem Award, India, Inst Welding, 88. *Prof Exp:* Res asst metall, Indian Inst Sci, 56-59, lectr, 59-64, asst prof, 64-66; Nat Res Coun res assoc, US Army Mat & Mech Res Ctr, 70-72; asst dir I, Nat Aeronaut Lab, 72-79, asst dir II, 79-83, dep dir I, 83-90, dep dir II, 90-92. *Concurrent Pos:* Vis scientist, Univ Md, 89-91, Elec Power Res Inst, Palo Alto, Calif, 96 & Failure Anal Assocs, Menlo Park, Calif, 96. *Mem:* Fel Am Soc Metals Int; fel Inst Engrs India; fel Aeronaut Soc India; Mat Res Soc India; fel Indian Inst Metals; fel Indian Nat Acad Eng. *Res:* Mechanical behavior of metals over a wide range of temperature and strain rate; dynamic plasticity of metals; failure analysis; investigation of aircraft and industrial accidents. *Mailing Add:* Mat Sci Div Nat Aerospace Labs Bangalore 560017 India. *Fax:* 91-80-5260862; *E-Mail:* viman@cmmacs.ernet.in

RAMACHANDRAN, VILAYANUR SUBRAMANIAN, VISUAL PERCEPTION, NEUROPSYCHOLOGY. *Current Pos:* PROF PSYCHOL, UNIV CALIF, SAN DIEGO, 83- *Personal Data:* b Madras, India, Aug 10, 51; m 87. *Educ:* Stanley Med Col, MD, 74; Trinity Col, Eng, PhD(neurosci), 78. *Prof Exp:* Sr Rouse-Ball, Trinity Col, Cambridge Univ, Eng, 77-78; res fel, Calif Inst Technol, Pasadena, 79-81. *Concurrent Pos:* Vis assoc biol, Calif Inst Technol, 83- *Mem:* Asn Res Vision & Opthalmol. *Res:* Neuropsychology; visual perception; author of over 50 research papers. *Mailing Add:* Psychol Dept 0109 Univ Calif-San Diego 9500 Gilman Dr La Jolla CA 92093-0109

RAMADHYANI, SATISH, MECHANICAL ENGINEERING, HEAT TRANSFER. *Current Pos:* from asst prof to assoc prof, 83-91, PROF MECH ENG, PURDUE UNIV, WEST LAFAYETTE, 91-, DIR, GRAD STUDIES MECH ENG, 96- *Personal Data:* b Bangalore, India, Aug 1, 49; m 79. *Educ:* Indian Inst Tech, Madras, BTech, 71; Univ Minn, MS, 77, PhD(mech eng), 79. *Honors & Awards:* President's Gold Medal, Indian Inst Technol, 71. *Prof Exp:* Engr, Motor Industs Co, India, subsid Robert Bosch, 71-75; asst prof mech eng, Tufts Univ, Medford, Mass, 79-83. *Concurrent Pos:* Lectr, Mass Inst Technol, 82; prin investr, United Eng Found, 82-83, IBM, 84-92, Whirlpool Corp, 85-87, NSF, 87-92, Gas Res Inst, 86-95. *Mem:* Am Soc Mech Engrs; Am Inst Aeronaut & Astronaut; Am Soc Eng Educ; AAAS; NY Acad Sci. *Res:* Development of novel numerical techniques for prediction of heat transfer; experimental and numerical studies of solid-liquid phase change, compact heat exchangers and heat transfer augmentation in electronic packages; mathematical modeling of human thermal comfort. *Mailing Add:* Sch Mech Eng Purdue Univ West Lafayette IN 47907

RAMAGE, COLIN STOKES, METEOROLOGY. *Current Pos:* RETIRED. *Personal Data:* b Napier, NZ, Mar 3, 21; nat US; c 2. *Educ:* Victoria Univ, NZ, BSc, 40, DSc, 61. *Prof Exp:* Meteorologist, Meteorol Serv. NZ, 41, sci officer, 46-53; dep dir, Royal Observ, Hong Kong, 54, actg dir, 55-56, assoc meteorologist, 56; assoc prof, Univ Hawaii, 57, prof meteorol, 58-88, chmn dept, 71-87. *Concurrent Pos:* Meteorol & oceanog, 60-62, geosci, 64-69, assoc dir, Hawaii Inst Geophys, 64-71; Commonwealth Fund fel, 53-54; consult, USAF, 56-61, US Navy, 69-71; sci dir, Indian Ocean Exped, 62-73; consult. *Mem:* Fel Am Meteorol Soc; Am Geophys Union. *Res:* Meteorology of the tropics, south and southeast Asia; monsoons. *Mailing Add:* 1420 Acadia St Durham NC 27701-1302

RAMAGE, MICHAEL P, CHEMICAL ENGINEERING. *Current Pos:* EXEC VPRES & CHIEF TECHNOL OFFICER, MOBIL OIL CORP; PRES, MOBIL TECHNOL CO, 95- *Personal Data:* m, Ann; c 3. *Educ:* Purdue Univ, BS, 66, MS, 69, PhD(chem eng), 71. *Hon Degrees:* DEng, Purdue Univ, 96. *Prof Exp:* Staff mem, Paulsboro Res Lab, Mobil Res & Develop Corp, 71-80, mgr, 82-87, vpres planning, 87-89; mgr process develop, Mobil Chem Co, 80, mgr planning coord, 81-82; mgr, Mobil Dallas Res Lab, 89-92; gen mgr, Mobil Explor & Producing Tech Ctr, 92-94, vpres eng, 94-95. *Mem:* Nat Acad Eng; Am Inst Chem Engrs; Soc Petrol Engrs; Am Asn Petrol Geologists; Indust Res Inst Inc. *Mailing Add:* Mobil Technol Co 3225 Gallows Rd Fairfax VA 22037

RAMAGOPAL, SUBBANAIDU, PLANT MOLECULAR BIOLOGY, CELL BIOLOGY. *Current Pos:* PLANT PHYSIOLOGIST & LEAD SCIENTIST, PLANT MOLECULAR & CELL BIOL, AGR RES SERV, USDA, 83- *Personal Data:* b Madras, India, July 5, 41; US citizen; div; c 2. *Educ:* Univ Madras, India, BS, 64; Utah State Univ, MS, 68; Univ Calif, Davis, PhD(plant biochem & physiol), 72. *Honors & Awards:* Gold Medal, Food & Agr Orgn, 63. *Prof Exp:* Res fel molecular biol, Harvard Univ, 72-74; res assoc molecular biol & cell biol, Inst Cancer Res, Philadelphia, 74-77; sr res fel molecular biol, Roche Inst Molecular Biol, Nutley, NJ, 77-79; res scientist molecular biol & immunol, Sch Med, NY Univ & NJ Med Sch, 79-81; sr scientist molecular biol, cell biol & genetic eng, Armos Corp & Univ Calif, Berkeley, 81-83. *Concurrent Pos:* Adj grad prof, Univ Hawaii, 86-89, Univ Idaho, 90- *Mem:* AAAS; Int Soc Plant Molecular Biol. *Res:* Plant molecular and cellular biology; plant genetic engineering and crop improvement; molecular bases of growth and development; cell differentiation; gene expression in response to abiotic stresses. *Mailing Add:* 4409 Samar St Beltsville MD 20705. *Fax:* 301-504-5320

RAMAKER, DAVID ELLIS, AUGER SPECTROSCOPY, STIMULATED DESORPTION. *Current Pos:* from asst prof to assoc prof, 75-83, PROF PHYS CHEM, GEORGE WASHINGTON UNIV, 83-, CHAIR, DEPT CHEM, 88- *Personal Data:* b Sheboygan, Wis, Aug 11, 43; m 66, Beverly A Back; c Julie, Jacqueline, Jan & Jason. *Educ:* Univ Wis-Milwaukee, BS, 65; Univ Iowa, MS, 68, PhD(phys chem), 71. *Honors & Awards:* Hildebrand Award, Am Chem Soc, 89. *Prof Exp:* Res physics, Sandia Labs, 70-72; res assoc & assoc instr, Univ Utah, 72-74; vis asst prof, Calvin Col, 74-75. *Concurrent Pos:* Consult res chem, Naval Res Lab, 76-; consult, Nat Bur Stand, 82-90. *Mem:* Am Chem Soc; Am Vacuum Soc; Combustion Inst. *Res:* Theoretical studies of surfaces and chemisorption; auger spectroscopy; electron and photon stimulated desorption. *Mailing Add:* Dept Chem George Washington Univ Washington DC 20052-0001. *Fax:* 202-994-5873; *E-Mail:* ramaker@gwuvm.gwu.edu

RAMAKRISHAN, S, IMMUNOTOXINS, CANCER THERAPY. *Current Pos:* ASSOC PROF PHARMACOL, UNIV MINN. *Personal Data:* b Apr 11, 49. *Educ:* All India Inst Med Sci, New Delhi, PhD(biochem), 80. *Prof Exp:* Res assoc biochem, Univ Kans, 81-84; scientist, Protein Chem Dept, Cetus Corp, Emeryville, Calif, 85-86; asst med res prof, Med Ctr, Duke Univ, Durham, NC, 87- *Mem:* Am Soc Biochem & Molecular Biol; Am Asn Immunologists; NY Acad Sci. *Mailing Add:* Dept Pharmacol 3-249 Milard Hall 435 Delaware St SE Minneapolis MN 55455

RAMAKRISHNA, KILAPARTI, BRIDGING THE GAP BETWEEN SCIENCE & PUBLIC AFFAIRS. *Current Pos:* SR ASSOC, INT ENVIRON LAW, WOODS HOLE RES CTR, 87-, DIR, PROF SCI PUB AFFAIRS, 91-; ADJ PROF INT LAW, FLETCHER SCH LAW & DIPLOMACY, TUFTS UNIV, MEDFORD, MA. *Personal Data:* b Rajahmundry, Andhra Pradesh, Oct 13, 55; m 83, Anjali Malwade. *Educ:* Andra Univ, SIndia, BSc, 73, BL, 76; Jawaharlal Nehru Univ, New Delhi, India, MPhil, 78, PhD(int environ law), 85. *Prof Exp:* Assoc ed, Indian J Int Law, 80-86; asst prof int law, Indian Soc Int Law, New Delhi, India, 80-85; vis scholar, Harvard Law Sch, 85-87; marine policy fel, Woods Hole Oceanog Inst, 86-89. *Concurrent Pos:* Vis prof int law, Boston Univ, Mass, 87-88 & 91; mem, Comn Environ Law, Int Union Conserv Nature & Natural Resources. *Mem:* Sigma Xi; Am Soc Int Law. *Mailing Add:* Woods Hole Res Ctr PO Box 296 Woods Hole MA 02543. *Fax:* 508-540-9700; *E-Mail:* kramakrishna@whrc.org

RAMAKRISHNAN, DINAKAR, MATHEMATICS. *Current Pos:* PROF MATH, CALIF INST TECHNOL, 88- *Personal Data:* b Madras, India. *Educ:* Univ Madras, BE, 70; Brooklyn Polytech, MS, 73; Columbia Univ, MA, 77, PhD(math), 80. *Prof Exp:* L E Dickson instr math, Univ Chicago, 80-82; mem, Sch Math, Inst Advan Study, Princeton, NJ, 82-83; asst prof math, Johns Hopkins Univ, 83-85; from asst prof to assoc prof, Cornell Univ, 85-88. *Concurrent Pos:* Alfred P Sloan fel, 86-90; vis prof, Univ Crete, Greece, 92, Hebrew Univ, Jerusalem, 92, Tata Inst Fundamental Res, Bombay, 93; vis mem, Issac Newton Inst Math Sci, Cambridge, 93. *Mailing Add:* Calif Inst Technol 253-37 Pasadena CA 91125-0001

RAMAKRISHNAN, RAGHU, DATABASE SYSTEMS & THEORY, LOGIC PROGRAMMING & RULE-BASED SYSTEMS. *Current Pos:* ASST PROF COMPUTER SCI, UNIV WIS-MADISON, 87- *Personal Data:* b Pudukkottai, India, Dec 2, 61; m 90; c 1. *Educ:* Indian Inst Technol, Madras, BTech, 83; Univ Tex, Austin, PhD(computer sci), 87. *Concurrent Pos:* Vis fac mem, Int Bus Mach Almaden Res Ctr & T J Watson Res Ctr, 88; prin investr, NSF & Int Bus Mach, 88-90; fac fel sci & technol, David & Lucille Packard Found, 89; NSF presidential young investr, 90. *Mem:* Asn Comput Mach; Inst Elec & Electronic Engrs; Asn Logic Prog. *Res:* Theory and implementation techniques to efficiently support declarative languages; extended query languages for relational databases and logic programming languages. *Mailing Add:* Computer Sci Dept Univ Wis 1210 W Dayton St Madison WI 53706

RAMAKRISHNAN, TERIZHANDUR S, FLUID DYNAMICS, TRANSPORT PHENOMENA. *Current Pos:* Res scientist, 85-95, PROG LEADER, SCHLUMBERGER-DOLL RES, 94-, SR RES SCIENTIST, 96- *Personal Data:* b Madras, India. *Educ:* Indian Inst Technol, New Delhi, BTech, 80; Ill Inst Technol, Chicago, PhD(chem eng), 85. *Honors & Awards:* Silver Medal, Indian Inst Technol, 80; P C Ray Award, Indian Inst Chem Engrs, 80; Henri Doll Award, 95. *Mem:* Am Inst Chem Engrs; Soc Petrol Engrs; Sigma Xi. *Res:* Creeping flow in porous media; chemically enhanced oil recovery; immiscible displacement in porous media; petrophysical properties of rocks; pressure transient analysis of petroleum formations; carbonate reservoirs. *Mailing Add:* Schlumberger-Doll Res Old Quarry Rd Ridgefield CT 06877. *Fax:* 203-438-3819

RAMAKRISHNAN, VENKATASWAMY, STRUCTURAL ENGINEERING. *Current Pos:* prof civil eng, 70-87, dir res, 87, DISTINGUISHED PROF, SDAK SCH MINES & TECHNOL, 96- *Personal Data:* b Coimbatore, India, Feb 27, 29; m 62; c 2. *Educ:* Govt Col Technol, Coimbatore, India, BE, 52; PSG Col Technol, Coimbatore, dipl soc sci, 53; Univ London, PhD(civil eng), 60, Imp Col, dipl hydraul power, 56 & concrete technol, 57. *Honors & Awards:* Cert Appreciation in Recognition of Serv & Advan of Fiber Reinforced Concrete Indust, Can Ctr Mineral & Energy Technol, 91; Nat Achievement Award, Am Concrete Inst, 94. *Prof Exp:* Jr engr, Madras Pub Works Dept, India, 52; asst lectr civil eng, PSG Col Technol, Coimbatore, 52-53, lectr, 53-60, asst prof, 60-61, prof & head dept, 61-69. *Concurrent Pos:* Partic, Sem Recent Trends Struct Design, 61, Ind Cong Appl of Math in Eng, Weimar, Ger, 67 & Int Conf Struct, Solid Mech & Eng Design Civil Eng Mar, Southampton, Eng, 69; visitor, Bldg Res Inst, Prague Tech Univ, 67, Asian Inst Technol, Bangkok, SDak Sch Mines & Technol, Univ Colo, Ill, Chicago Circle & Mo, Columbia, 69, Norwegian Inst Tech, Swed Cement & Concrete Res Inst, Univ WI & Inst Technol, Stockholm; coordr, Advan Summer Schs Struct Eng for Eng Col Teachers, India, 68 & 69; organizing secy & ed proc, Int Conf Shear, Torsion & Bond Reinforced & Prestressed Concrete, 69; chmn, Comt Mech Properties Concrete, Transp Res Bd, Nat Acad Sci-Nat Res Coun, Comt Admixtures & Cementitious Mat for Concrete; archit & struct eng consult; founding dir & guide prof, World Open Univ, 74-, vpres, 79- *Mem:* fel Am Concrete Inst; Am Soc Civil Engrs; Nat Soc Prof Engrs; Am Soc Eng Educ; Sigma Xi. *Res:* Concrete technology, particularly ultimate behavior and strength of reinforced concrete; materials technology; structural engineering and mechanics. *Mailing Add:* 1809 Sheridan Lake Rd Rapid City SD 57702

RAMAKUMAR, RAMACHANDRA GUPTA, POWER ENGINEERING, ENERGY. *Current Pos:* vis assoc prof, 67-70, from assoc prof to prof, 70-91, DIR, ENG ENERGY LAB, OKLA STATE UNIV, 87-, PSO/ALBRECHT NAETER PROF ELEC ENG, 91- *Personal Data:* b Coimbatore, India, Oct 17, 36; m 63, Tallam Gokula; c Sanjay & Malini. *Educ:* Univ Madras, India, BE, 56; Indian Inst Technol, Kharagpur, India, MTech, 57; Cornell Univ, PhD(elec eng), 62. *Prof Exp:* From asst lectr to lectr elec eng, Coimbatore Inst Technol, India, 57-62, asst prof, 62-67. *Concurrent Pos:* Consult, Jet Propulsion Lab, Calif, 78-79, Nat Sci Found, Washington, DC, 80, Fla Solar Energy Ctr, 81, Kuwait Univ, 82, Mariah Inc, 84 & Dowell Schlumberger, 87-88; mem, Expert Group Energy Storage Develop Countries, UN Environ Prog, 83. *Mem:* Fel Inst Elec & Electronics Engrs; Int Solar Energy Soc; Am Soc Eng Educr; Sigma Xi; Global Energy Soc. *Res:* Alternate energy sources development and application in developing countries for rural development; energy storage; energy conversion and power engineering; solar and wind energy systems. *Mailing Add:* 216 Eng S Okla State Univ Stillwater OK 74078-5034. *Fax:* 405-744-9198; *E-Mail:* ramakum@master.ceat.okstate.edu

RAMALEY, JAMES FRANCIS, MATHEMATICS. *Current Pos:* mgr info systs, 74-76, budget dir circulation, 76-82, VPRES, CIRCULATION SERV, ZIFF-DAVIS PUBL CO, 82- *Personal Data:* b Columbus, Ohio, Oct 10, 41; m 67; c 2. *Educ:* Ohio State Univ, BSc, 62; Univ Calif, Berkeley, MA, 64; Univ NMex, PhD(math), 67. *Prof Exp:* Reader math, Univ Calif, 63-64; res asst, Univ NMex, 64-65; lectr, Carnegie Inst Technol, 65-66; asst prof math, Bowling Green State Univ, 66-70; asst prof, Univ Pittsburgh, 70-73; systs analyst, On-Line Systs, Inc, 73-74. *Concurrent Pos:* Vis mem, Math Res Inst, Swiss Fed Inst Technol, 69; adj prof math, Univ Pittsburgh, 73-76. *Mem:* Am Math Soc; Math Asn Am; Opers Res Soc Am; Asn Comput Mach. *Res:* Category theory; logic; systems software; applications software. *Mailing Add:* Ziff-Davis Publ Co 1 Park Ave New York NY 10016-5801. *E-Mail:* jramaley@zd.com

RAMALEY, JUDITH AITKEN, ENDOCRINOLOGY, REPRODUCTIVE BIOLOGY. *Current Pos:* PRES, PORTLAND STATE UNIV, ORE, 90- *Personal Data:* b Vincennes, Ind, Jan 11, 41; m 66; c 2. *Educ:* Swarthmore Col, BA, 63; Univ Calif, Los Angeles, PhD(anat), 66. *Prof Exp:* Asst prof anat & physiol, Ind Univ, Bloomington, 69-72; from asst prof to prof physiol & biophys, Univ Nebr Med Ctr, Omaha, 72-82, asst vpres acad affairs, 81-82; vpres acad affairs, 82-87, State Univ NY, Albany, 82-87, actg pres, 84-85, exec vpres academic affairs, 85-87; exec vchancellor, Univ Kans Lawrence, 87-90. *Concurrent Pos:* NIH fel, Ctr Neurol Sci, Ind Univ, Bloomington, 67-68, NIH fel chem, 68; mem, NSF, Regulatory Biol Panel, 78-81; mem, Biochem Endocrinol Study Sect, NIH, 81-84; chair, Acad Affairs Coun, Nat Asn State Univ & Land Grant Col, & Comm Women Higher Educ, Am Coun Educ, 87-88. *Mem:* Am Physiol Soc; Am Asn Anat; Soc Neurosci; Endocrine Soc; Soc Study Reproduction. *Res:* Physiology of puberty; control of male and female fertility. *Mailing Add:* 11650 SW Military Rd Portland OR 97219-8378

RAMALEY, LOUIS, MASS SPECTROMETRY, INSTRUMENTATION. *Current Pos:* assoc prof, 70-92, PROF CHEM, DALHOUSIE UNIV, 92- *Personal Data:* b El Paso, Tex, Oct 7, 37; m 64, Linda G Pullen; c Caroline E & Janelle S. *Educ:* Univ Colo, BA, 59; Princeton Univ, MA. 61, PhD(electrochem), 64. *Prof Exp:* Assoc, Univ Ill, 63-64; asst prof chem, Univ Ariz, 64-70. *Mem:* Sigma Xi; Am Chem Soc; Am Soc Mass Spectrometry; fel Chem Inst Can. *Res:* Chemical instrumentation; mass spectrometry; environmental chemical analysis. *Mailing Add:* Dept Chem Dalhousie Univ Halifax NS B3H 4J3 Can. *Fax:* 902-494-1310; *E-Mail:* lramaley@is.dal.ca

RAMALEY, ROBERT FOLK, BIOCHEMISTRY, MICROBIOLOGY. *Current Pos:* assoc prof, 72-78, PROF BIOCHEM, UNIV NEBR MED CTR, OMAHA, 78-, PROF PATH & MICROBIOL, 83- *Personal Data:* b Colorado Springs, Colo, Dec 15, 35; m 66, 95; c Andrew & Alan. *Educ:* Ohio State Univ, BS, 59, MS, 62; Univ Minn, PhD, 64. *Prof Exp:* Asst prof microbiol, Ind Univ, Bloomington, 66-72. *Concurrent Pos:* USPHS fel, 64-66; lectr, Am Soc Microbiol Found; res grants, NIH & NSF; vis scientist, NIH & DuPont. *Mem:* Am Soc Microbiol; Am Soc Biol Chem. *Res:* Physiology of sporulation; control of intermediate metabolism and enzyme intermediates; thermophilic microorganism and medical microbiology. *Mailing Add:* Dept Biochem & Molecular Biol Univ Nebr Med Ctr Omaha NE 68198-4525. *Fax:* 402-559-6650; *E-Mail:* rramaley@unmcvm.unmc.edu

RAMALINGAM, MYSORE LOGANATHAN, ENERGY CONVERSION SCIENCES, HEAT TRANSFER & MATERIAL CHARACTERISTICS. *Current Pos:* res scientist, 86-89, sr scientist, 89-92, PRIN RES SCIENTIST, UNIVERSAL ENERGY SYSTS, INC, 92- *Personal Data:* b Mysore, Karnataka, India, Dec 12, 54; m 81, Samyuktha; c Suraj & Shyma. *Educ:* Bangalore Univ, India, BE, 75; Indian Inst Sci, India, ME, 77; Ariz State Univ, PhD(mech eng), 86. *Prof Exp:* Asst engr, Jyoti Pumps, Inc, India, 77; engr SC/SD, Indian Space Res Orgn, India, 77-82; grad asst thermodyn, Ariz State Univ, 82-83, res asst, 83-86. *Concurrent Pos:* Heat pipe expert, Gujarat Rotating Mach Corp, India, 77, Gas Turbine Res Est, India, 81-82; thermal consult, Vikran Sarabhai Space Ctr, India, 79-80, K-tron Int, Inc, Phoenix, 83-84; res assoc, Ariz State Univ, 85-86; thermionics expert, Wright Patterson AFB, 87-; mem, ASME/AESD thermionics, Thermoelectrics Comt, 90- *Mem:* Assoc mem Inst Engrs India; assoc fel Am Inst Aeronaut & Astronaut; Am Soc Metals; Am Soc Mech Engrs. *Res:* Thermionic, thermophysical and material properties at high temperature of refractory metals and alloys slated for applications in thermionic fuel elements; performance characteristics of low and high temperature heat pipes with emphasis on boiling heat transfer at the evaporator. *Mailing Add:* Universal Energy Systs 4401 Dayton-Xenia Rd Dayton OH 45432-1894

RAMALINGAM, SUBBIAH, MECHANICAL ENGINEERING, MATERIALS ENGINEERING. *Current Pos:* PROF MECH ENG, UNIV MINN, 81- *Personal Data:* b Udumalpet, India, June 15, 35; m 67. *Educ:* Indian Inst Technol, Khapagpur, India, BTech Hons, 56; Univ Ill, Urbana, MS, 61, PhD(mech eng), 67. *Prof Exp:* Instr, Univ Ill, Urbana, 61-67, asst prof, 67-68; from asst prof to prof mech eng, State Univ NY, Buffalo, 68-77; prof mech eng, Ga Inst Technol, 77-81. *Concurrent Pos:* Vis prof, Monash Univ, Australia, 75-76. *Mem:* Am Inst Mining, Metall & Petrol Engrs; Am Soc Metals; Soc Mfg Engrs; Japan Soc Precision Engrs; Am Soc Mech Engrs. *Res:* Machining theory; theory of tool wear; tribology; deformation processing; alloy design for processing; thin film science and technology; materials conservation through thin film technology; electron microscopy of metals; magnetron melting and plasma processing. *Mailing Add:* 1715 Eldridge Ave St Paul MN 55113

RAMAMOORTHY, CHITTOOR V, COMPUTER SCIENCES, ELECTRICAL ENGINEERING. *Current Pos:* PROF ELEC ENG & COMPUT SCI, UNIV CALIF, BERKELEY, 72- *Personal Data:* b Henzada, Burma, May 5, 26; US citizen; m 57; c 3. *Educ:* Univ Madras, India, BS, 49; Univ Calif, Berkeley, MS, 51, MechEng, 53; Harvard Univ, AM & PhD(appl math & comput theory), 64. *Prof Exp:* Res engr, Honeywell Inc, 56-57, sr engr, Electronic Data Processing Div, 58-60, staff engr, 61-65, sr staff scientist, 65-67; prof elec eng, Univ Tex, Austin, 67-72, prof comput sci, 68-72. *Concurrent Pos:* Res fel appl math, Harvard Univ, 66-67. *Mem:* Asn Comput Mach; fel Inst Elec & Electronics Engrs. *Res:* Computer theory, design, use and applications information sciences. *Mailing Add:* Comput Sci Div Univ Calif Berkeley CA 94720

RAMAMOORTHY, PANAPAKKAM A, DIGITAL SIGNAL PROCESSING, NEURAL NETWORKS. *Current Pos:* from asst prof to assoc prof, 82-91, dir grad studies, 91-93, PROF, UNIV CINCINNATI, 91- *Personal Data:* b India, Dec 20, 49; m 72; c 2. *Educ:* Univ Madras, India, BS, 71; Indian Inst Technol, MS, 74; Univ Calgary, PhD(elec eng), 77. *Honors & Awards:* Elec & Comput Eng Res Award, Dept Elec & Comput Eng, Univ Cincinnati, 88. *Prof Exp:* Fel, Elec Eng Dept, Univ Calgary, 77-79; asst prof elec & comput eng, New Eng Col, Mass, 79-81; asst prof, Elec & Comput Eng Dept, Wayne State Univ, 81-82. *Concurrent Pos:* Consult, M B Electronics, 79-82; fac fel, NASA Lewis Res Ctr, Cleveland, 84-85, Rome Air Develop Ctr, Rome, NY, 87, Wright Patterson Svionics Lab, Dayton, Ohio, 88; prog dir, Circuits & Signal Processing, NSF, 89-90. *Mem:* Inst Elec & Electronics Engrs; Soc Photo-Instrumentation Engrs. *Res:* Digital signal and image processing algorithms, architectures and applications; optical signal processing and computing; neural networks; research administration; technical management; science policy. *Mailing Add:* Dept Elec & Comput Eng Univ Cincinnati Cincinnati OH 45221

RAMAMRITHAM, KRITHI, COMPUTER SCIENCE. *Current Pos:* PROF, DEPT COMPUT SCI, UNIV MASS, 81-; CO-DIR, REAL TIME SYSTS LAB. *Educ:* Indian Inst Technol, BTech, 76, MTech, 78; Univ Utah, PhD(comput Sci), 81. *Concurrent Pos:* Consult, Lucent Bell Labs; ed, Int J Real-Time Systs, Distrib Systs Eng J & Int J Appl Software Technol; vchair, Int Conf Data Eng, 95. *Mem:* Sr mem Inst Elec & Electronics Engrs. *Res:* Computer aided design/computer aided manufacturing design and workflow systems; development of scheduling algorithms, specification and programming languages, operating system support, architectural support, and design strategies for distributed real-time applications; transaction processing support for real-time applications that utilize databases. *Mailing Add:* Dept Comput Sci Univ Mass Amherst MA 01003. *Fax:* 413-545-1249; *E-Mail:* krithi@cs.umass.edu

RAMAMURTHY, AMURTHUR C, electrochemistry & electrodeposition, impedance spectroscopy, for more information see previous edition

RAMAMURTI, KRISHNAMURTI, cement chemistry, asphalt deterioration, for more information see previous edition

RAMAN, ARAVAMUDHAN, CORROSION, PHYSICAL METALLURGY. *Current Pos:* PROF MAT SCI, LA STATE UNIV, BATON ROUGE, 66- *Personal Data:* b Madras, India, Oct 13, 37; m 65, Edelgard; c Vasu, Padhma & Kala. *Educ:* St Joseph's Col, India, MA, 58; Indian Inst Sci, Bangalore, BEng, 60; Tech Univ Stuttgart, Dr rer Nat(phys metall), 64. *Prof Exp:* Assoc lectr metall, Indian Inst Technol, Bombay, 61; res assoc phys metall, Univ Ill, Urbana, 64-65; fel mat sci, Univ Tex, Austin, 65-66. *Concurrent Pos:* NASA res grant, 66-68; Sea res grant, 78-81; transportation res grant, 83-86; vis scientist, Univ Calif Los Angeles, 69, Russ Acad Sci, 91, IIT, Bombay, 94. *Mem:* Nat Asn Corrosion Engrs. *Res:* X-ray metallography; crystal and alloy chemistry of metallic phases; physical properties of alloys; corrosion science and engineering; metallic coatings; high temperature composites; solar energy devices and appliances. *Mailing Add:* 6919 N Rothmer Dr La State Univ Baton Rouge LA 70808. *Fax:* 504-388-5924; *E-Mail:* meraman@me.lsu.edu

RAMAN, JAY ANANTH, INFORMATION SCIENCE & SYSTEMS, PHARMACOLOGY. *Current Pos:* SR PRIN SCIENTIST, SCHERING PLOUGH RES INST, 81- *Personal Data:* m 74, Kamakshi Krishnamurthy; c Laxmi & Priya. *Educ:* Madras Univ, India, BS; Univ NH, MS, 68; Cornell Univ, PhD(biochem), 73. *Honors & Awards:* Pres Spec Award, Schering-Plough, 88. *Prof Exp:* Sr sci asst, Cent Food Technol Res Inst, Mysore, India, 60-66; res asst, Univ NH, 66-68 & Cornell Univ, 68-73; mgr, Specialty Foods Inc, 72-74; dir, Loblaws, Inc, 74-77; asst dir, Pennwalt Corp, 77-81. *Mem:* AAAS; Am Chem Soc; NY Acad Sci; Sigma Xi. *Res:* Isolation, purification and characterization recombinant proteins. *Mailing Add:* 25 Highmont Dr West Windsor NJ 08691-9562. *Fax:* 908-820-6995

RAMAN, SUBRAMANIAN, NUCLEAR PHYSICS. *Current Pos:* Res staff mem, 66-80, SR RES STAFF MEM, OAK RIDGE NAT LAB, 80- *Personal Data:* b North Parur, India, Apr 2, 38; US citizen; m 67, Judith S Slutsky; c Anand, Manya & Jay. *Educ:* Univ Madras, BE, 59; Rensselaer Polytech Inst, MEE, 61; Pa State Univ, University Park, PhD(physics), 66. *Mem:* fel Am Phys Soc. *Res:* Nuclear spectroscopy and reactions; data compilations; nuclear science applications. *Mailing Add:* Physics Div Bldg 6010 MS 6354 Oak Ridge Nat Lab PO Box 2008 Oak Ridge TN 37831-6354. *Fax:* 423-576-8746; *E-Mail:* ram@ornl.gov

RAMAN, VARADARAJA VENKATA, THEORETICAL PHYSICS, HISTORY OF SCIENCE. *Current Pos:* assoc prof, 66-77, PROF PHYSICS, ROCHESTER INST TECHNOL, 77- *Personal Data:* b Calcutta, India; m 62; c 2. *Educ:* St Xavier's Col, India, BS, 52; Univ Calcutta, MS, 54; Univ Paris, PhD(theoret physics), 58. *Prof Exp:* Res assoc physics, Saha Inst Nuclear Physics, India, 59-60; assoc prof, Univ PR, Mayaguez, 60-63; chmn dept, Inst Telecommun, Columbia, 63-64; UNESCO expert appl math, Nat Polytech Sch, Univ Algiers, 64-66. *Mem:* Am Asn Physics Teachers; Hist Sci Soc. *Res:* Historical aspects of physics. *Mailing Add:* 20 Sutton Pl Pittsford NY 14534

RAMANAN, V R V, FERROMAGNETISM, AMORPHOUS MATERIALS. *Current Pos:* RES ASSOC, METALS & CERAMICS LAB, ALLIED-SIGNAL INC, 79- *Personal Data:* b Madras, India, July 5, 52; m 83; c 1. *Educ:* Univ Delhi, BSc, 71, MSc, 73, Carnegie-Mellon Univ, MS, 75, PhD(physics), 79. *Mem:* Inst Elec & Electronics Engrs; Am Phys Soc; Mat Res Soc; Am Soc Metals; Metall Soc; Am Inst Mining, Metall & Petrol Engrs. *Res:* Ferromagnetic behavior, thermal and magnetic stabilities; structure-property relationships in metallic glasses; design and optimization of new magnetic materials for specific applications; stability of intermetallic phases in Al-based alloys. *Mailing Add:* 1021 Main Campus Dr Raleigh NC 27606

RAMANARAYANAN, MADHAVA, CLINICAL BIOCHEMISTRY, IMMUNOLOGY. *Current Pos:* PRES & CONSULT CLIN DIAG, WINDSOR PARK LAB INC, 89- *Personal Data:* b Varapuzaha, India, Feb 5, 45. *Educ:* Am Col, Maduri, India, BS, 64, MS, 66; Indian Inst Sci, Bangalora, PhD(biochem), 68. *Prof Exp:* Vpres res & develop, Visual Diag Inc, 85-89. *Mem:* NY Acad Sci; fel Am Inst Chemists; fel Nat Acad Clin Biochem; Am Chem Soc. *Mailing Add:* Windsor Park Lab Inc 190 W Englewood Ave Teaneck NJ 07666-3512

RAMANATHAN, GANAPATHIAGRAHARAM V, APPLIED MATHEMATICS, STATISTICAL MECHANICS. *Current Pos:* assoc prof, 70-83, PROF MATH, UNIV ILL, CHICAGO, 83- *Personal Data:* b Madras, India; m 74; c 1. *Educ:* Madras Univ, BE, 57; Princeton Univ, PhD(aerospace), 66. *Prof Exp:* Asst lectr mech eng, Govt Col Technol, Coimbatore, 57-58; sci officer nuclear eng, Atomic Energy Estab, Bombay, 59-60; assoc res scientist math, Courant Inst Math Sci, NY Univ, 65-66; Nat Acad Sci res assoc plasma physics, Goddard Space Flight Ctr, 66-68; assoc res scientist math, Courant Inst Math Sci, NY Univ, 68-69, asst prof, 69-70. *Res:* Singular and secular perturbation theories. *Mailing Add:* 1513 W Adams St Chicago IL 60607

RAMANATHAN, VEERABHADRAN, ATMOSPHERIC SCIENCE. *Current Pos:* DIR, CTR CLOUDS, CHEM & CLIMATE, SCRIPPS INST OCEANOG, UNIV CALIF, SAN DIEGO, 90-, ALDERSON PROF OCEAN SCI, 90-, DIR, CTR ATMOSPHERIC SCI, 96-; CHIEF SCIENTIST, CENT EQUATORIAL PAC EXPER, 92- *Personal Data:* b Madras, India, Nov 24, 44; m 73; c 3. *Educ:* Annamalai Univ, India, BE, Hons, 65; Indian Inst Sci, Bangalore, India, MSc, 70; State Univ NY, Stony Brook, PhD(atmospheric sci), 74. *Honors & Awards:* Medal Exceptional Sci Achievement, NASA, 89; Buys Ballot Medal, Royal. *Prof Exp:* Nat Acad Sci-Nat Res Coun fel atmospheric sci, NASA Langley Res Ctr, 74-75, vis scientist, 75-76; sr scientist & leader, Cloud-Climate Interactions Group, Nat Ctr Atmospheric Res, Boulder, Colo, 82-86; prof, Dept Geophys Sci, Univ Chicago, 86-90. *Concurrent Pos:* Mem panel, Comt Impacts Stratospheric Change, AMPS, Nat Acad Sci, 78- & Comt Solar-Terrestrial Res, Geophys Res Bd, 78-; assoc ed, J Atmospheric Sci, 79-82; mem sci team, Earth Radiation Budget Satellite Exp, NASA, 79-84; mem, Comt Earth Sci, Nat Res Coun, 81-84; mem, Climate Res Comt, Nat Acad Sci, 83-, Panel Int Satellite Cloud Climate Proj, 84-; fac affil, Colo State Univ, Ft Collins, 85-; prof, Univ Chicago, 86; vis prof, Cath Univ Louvain, Belg, 88; co-chief scientist, Indoex, 96- *Mem:* Fel Am Meteorol Soc; fel AAAS; fel Am Geophys Union; fel Am Acad Arts & Sci; foreign mem Acad Europaea. *Res:* Climate dynamics; radiative transfer; greenhouse effect; clouds; aerosols; satellite radiation measurements; global climate models. *Mailing Add:* Scripps Inst Oceanog Calif Space Inst Univ Calif San Diego Nierenberg Hall Rm 325 8605 La Jolla Shores Dr La Jolla CA 92093

RAMANI, KARTHIK, MANUFACTURING & MATERIAL PROCESSING, COMPOSITE & POLYMER PROCESSING. *Current Pos:* Asst prof mech eng, 91-97, ASSOC PROF MECH ENG, PURDUE UNIV, 97- *Personal Data:* Madras, India, Feb 2, 64; m 90; c 1. *Educ:* Indian Inst Technol, BTech, 85; Ohio State Univ, MS, 86; Stanford Univ, PhD(mech eng), 91. *Honors & Awards:* Ralph R Teetor Award, Soc Automotive Engrs, 96; Career Award, NSF, 96, Res Initiation Award, 96. *Mem:* Assoc Am Soc Mech Engrs; assoc Soc Plastics Engrs; Adhesion Soc. *Res:* Composites and polymer processing; process design and development of associated process equipment; processes and machines for polymer bonded systems; interphases and durability of interphases, adhesive joining for structural applications. *Mailing Add:* Sch Mech Eng Purdue Univ West Lafayette IN 47907-1288. *E-Mail:* ramani@ecn.purdue.edu

RAMANI, RAJA VENKAT, MINING, ENVIRONMENTAL. *Current Pos:* from asst prof to assoc prof, 70-78, CHMN, MINERAL ENG MGT, PA STATE UNIV, UNIVERSITY PARK, 74-, PROF MINING ENG, 78-, HEAD DEPT, 87- *Personal Data:* b Madras, India, Aug 4, 38; US citizen; m 72, Geetha V Chalam; c Deepak & Gautam. *Educ:* Ranchi Univ, India, BS, 62; Indian Sch Mines, Dhanbad, AISM, 62; Pa State Univ, University Park, MS, 68, PhD(mining), 70. *Honors & Awards:* Distinguished Mem Award, Soc Mining Engrs, USA, 89; APCOM Distinguished Achievement Award, Int Coun Appln of Computers to Mineral Indust, 89; Fulbright Lectr Award Soviet Union, Ctr Int Exchange Scholars, 89-90; Environ Conserve Award, Am Inst Mining, Metall & Petrol Engrs, 90, Percy W Nichols Award, 92; Howard N Eavenson Award, Soc Mining, Metall & Explor, Inc, 91; Henry Krumb Lectr, 94. *Prof Exp:* Safety officer, vent officer & prod mgr, Bengal Coal Co, Andrew Yule, India, 62-66; license, first class mine mgr, India, 65. *Concurrent Pos:* Proj dir develop mine vent similator, US Bur Mines, 73-77, proj dir appln total syts simulator to surface coal mining, 75-78; proj dir, Premining Planning Manual Eastern Surface Coal Mining, Environ Protection Agency, 75-78; chmn, Comt Underground Mine Disaster Survival & Rescue, Nat Acad Sci, 79-81; proj dir, Integration Surface Mining & Lane Use Planning, US Off Surface Mining, 79-82; vis prof, Mo Sch Mines, Rolla, 80, Tech Univ Berlin, 88, Univ Rome, 88, Univ Queensland, 88; dir, Ctr Excellence Longwall Mining, SOHIO, 83-89, Generic Technol Ctr Respirable Dust, 83-; consult, UN, 84-; co-dir, Nat Mined Land Res Ctr, 89-; mem expert panel, US Dept Labor, 92 & 96, US Dept Health & Human Serv, 92-, US Dept Interior, 95-96 & Nat Acad Sci, 95. *Mem:* Am Inst Mining, Metall & Petrol Engrs; Inst Mgt Sci; Sigma Xi; Mine Ventilation Soc SAfrica; Soc Mining, Metall & Explor Inc (pres, 95); Am Soc Surface Mining & Reclamation. *Res:* Surface mining and underground mining methods; ventilation; health and safety; computer-oriented planning and control; management; resource management; technical management; cost analysis and control, human resource training; environmental planning. *Mailing Add:* 285 Oakley Dr State College PA 16803. *Fax:* 814-865-3248

RAMANUJAM, V M SADAGOPA, ORGANIC CHEMISTRY, ENVIRONMENTAL CHEMISTRY. *Current Pos:* Robert A Welch Found fel, 74-78, asst prof, 79-84, ASSOC PROF, DEPT PREV MED & COMMUNITY HEALTH, ENVIRON HEALTH LAB, UNIV TEX MED BR, GALVESTON, 84- *Personal Data:* b July 2, 46; m 74; c 2. *Educ:* Univ Madras, India, BSc, 66, MSc, 68, PhD(org chem), 73. *Honors & Awards:* Merit Award, Govt India, 66-68. *Prof Exp:* Instr chem, Vivekananda Col, Madras, India, 68-72; develop chemist, Res Div, Greaves Foseco, Ltd, Calcutta, India, 73. *Concurrent Pos:* Consult, Nat Acad Sci, 79-; sci adv, US Environ Protection Agency, 80-81. *Mem:* Sigma Xi; Am Chem Soc. *Res:* Physico-chemical characterization of toxins from Gymnodinium breve Davis; structure-activity relationship studies on drugs; carcinogens and mutagens; development of analytical methods for drugs, toxins and environmental pollutants; mutagenicity studies on atomatic hydrocarbons and amines; oxidation reaction mechanisms and syntheses. *Mailing Add:* PO Box 20856 Beaumont TX 77720-0856

RAMANUJAN, MELAPALAYAM SRINIVASAN, MATHEMATICS. *Current Pos:* from instr to assoc prof, 59-72, PROF MATH, UNIV MICH, ANN ARBOR, 72- *Personal Data:* b Coimbatore, India, July 16, 31; m 65. *Educ:* Annamalai Univ, Madras, BS, 51, MA, 52, MSc, 53, DSc(math), 58. *Honors & Awards:* Narasinga Rao Gold Medal, Indian Math Soc, 53. *Prof Exp:* Res assoc math, Ramanujan Inst Math, 57-58; lectr, Aligarh Muslim Univ, India, 58-59. *Concurrent Pos:* Reader, Ramanujan Inst Math, 61-63; Humboldt fel, Univ Frankfurt, 69-70, 83 & 87. *Mem:* Am Math Soc; Math Asn Am; Indian Math Soc (secy, 62-63). *Res:* Summability; moment problems; topological vector spaces; duality theory; abstract sequence spaces. *Mailing Add:* 2435 Prairie St Ann Arbor MI 48105

RAMAPRASAD, K R (RAM), SPECTROSCOPY, POLYMERS. *Current Pos:* SR SCIENTIST, CHRONAR CORP, PRINCETON, NJ, 79-; SR SCIENTIST, TRI/PRINCETON, 93- *Personal Data:* b Bangalore, India, Dec 8, 38; m 68, Rukmani Raghavachari; c Saroja & Venkat. *Educ:* Univ Mysore, Bangalore, India, BSc(hons), 58; NY Univ, MS, 71, PhD(phys chem), 72. *Prof Exp:* Teaching asst, Univ Geneva, 72-73; chemist, Fed Sch Polytech, Lausanne, 74; res assoc, Dept Chem, Princeton Univ, 74-77, mem res staff, Dept Chem Eng, 77-79; sr scientist, Electron Transfer Tech, 90-93. *Concurrent Pos:* Adj instr chem, Bucks Co Community Col, 91- *Mem:* Am Chem Soc; Sigma Xi. *Res:* Photochemistry; spectroscopy; polymers; surface studies; spectroscopy; photochemistry; textile fibers; hair; thin films. *Mailing Add:* 4 Cresthill Rd Lawrenceville NJ 08648-3204. *Fax:* 609-683-7836; *E-Mail:* ramaprasadk@bucks.edu

RAMASASTRY, SAI SUDARSHAN, microsurgery, hand surgery, for more information see previous edition

RAMASWAMI, DEVABHAKTUNI, CHEMICAL ENGINEERING. *Current Pos:* RETIRED. *Personal Data:* b Pedapudi, India, Apr 4, 33; m, Vijayalakshmi; c Srikrishna. *Educ:* Andhra, India, BSc, 53, MSc, 54, DSc, 58; Univ Wis, PhD(chem eng), 61. *Honors & Awards:* Am Chem Soc Award, 60. *Prof Exp:* Res scholar chem eng, Andhra, India, 54-56; Indian Inst Technol, Kharagpur, 56-57; asst prof, Banaras Hindu Univ, 57-58; res asst, Univ Wis, 58-61; res engr, Int Bus Mach Corp, 61-62; res assoc, Argonne Nat Lab, 62, chem engr, 62-85. *Mem:* Fel Am Inst Chem Engrs. *Res:* Nuclear reactor core; development; engineering; author or coauthor of over 93 publications; industrial chemical reactions and petroleum refining. *Mailing Add:* 50 Craigie St Apt 15 Somerville MA 02143-2446

RAMASWAMI, VAIDYANATHAN, OPERATIONS RESEARCH, STATISTICS. *Current Pos:* ASST PROF MATH, DREXEL UNIV, 78- *Personal Data:* b Kerala, India, Feb 24, 50; m 77; c 2. *Educ:* Univ Madras, BSc, 69, MSc, 71; Purdue Univ, MS, 76, PhD(opers res), 78. *Prof Exp:* Lectr statist, Loyola Col, Madras, India, 71-74. *Concurrent Pos:* Statist consult, Madras, Ctr Soc Med & Community Health, Jawaharlal Nehru Univ, New Delhi, India, 72-74. *Mem:* Opers Res Soc Am. *Res:* Stochastic processes; computational probability; queueing theory; mathematical programming; discrete optimization. *Mailing Add:* Bellcore NVC 2X-151 331 Newman Springs Rd Red Bank NJ 07701

RAMASWAMY, C, CHEMISTRY, PHYSICAL CHEMISTRY. *Current Pos:* DIR, PROPELLANT DIV, BREED TECHNOL INC, 88- *Personal Data:* b Bangalore, India, 1924. *Educ:* Univ Mysore, BS, 43; Univ Poona, MS, 53, PhD(chem), 60. *Prof Exp:* Chemist, IDL Chem Co, India, 67-80; chief chemist, Action Group Indust, 80-87. *Mem:* Fel Am Inst Chemists; fel Royal Soc Chemists. *Mailing Add:* PO Box 95023 Lakeland FL 33804-5023

RAMASWAMY, H N, INORGANIC CHEMISTRY, ANALYTICAL CHEMISTRY. *Current Pos:* CONSULT CHEM, 96- *Personal Data:* b Honnavally, India, Oct 30, 37; m 66; c 2. *Educ:* Univ Mysore, BSc, 58; Karnatak Univ, India, MSc, 61; Tulane Univ, PhD(inorg chem), 67. *Prof Exp:* Teacher, Govt High Sch, India, 58-59; lectr chem, APS Col, Bangalore, 61-63; lectr, Tulane Univ, 63-67; res assoc, Southern Regional Res Lab, USDA, La, 67-69; sr chemist, Thiokol Chem Corp, Ga, 69-70; head anal labs, AZS Chem Corp, 70-79, supt process eng & process develop, 79-86; develop assoc, Nat Starch & Chem Co, 86-94. *Concurrent Pos:* NSF fel, 67-69. *Mem:* Am Chem Soc; Sigma Xi. *Res:* Spectroscopy; infrared chemical analysis; pyrolysis and gas-liquid chromatography; textile chemicals and polymers; liquid chromatography, amines, alkyd resins, hydrogenation, distillation product and process development, thermal analysis, glycidyl ethers; process improvement and development; scale-up. *Mailing Add:* 5030 Green Forest Pkwy Smyrna GA 30082

RAMASWAMY, KIZHANATHAM V, industrial engineering, for more information see previous edition

RAMASWAMY, KRISHNAMURTHY, GASTROENTEROLOGY, MEMBRANE PHYSIOLOGY. *Current Pos:* PROF PHYSIOL MED, UNIV ILL, CHICAGO, 91- *Personal Data:* m 69, Jaya Natarajan; c Akila. *Educ:* Univ Madras, India, PhD(biochem), 68. *Prof Exp:* Asst prof med, Univ Tex Med Sch, 76-80, Univ SC Sch Med, 80-83; assoc prof med & biochem, Med Col Wis, 83-90, prof, 90-91. *Mem:* Am Physiol Soc; Am Gastroenterol Asn. *Res:* Mechanisms of intestinal absorption of nutrients and electrolytes in man; studies using human intestinal membrane vesicles, biochemical and molecular biology techniques to determine the specific membrane transport pathways for protein digestion products. *Mailing Add:* Univ Ill 840 S Wood St MC 787 Chicago IL 60612. *E-Mail:* kramaswa@uic.edu

RAMASWAMY, SONNY B, INSECT PHEROMONES, INSECT-PLANT INTERACTIONS. *Current Pos:* PROF ENTOM, MISS STATE UNIV, 92- *Personal Data:* b Hyderabad, India, June 1, 52; US citizen; m 79, Gita Narasimhan; c Megha. *Educ:* Univ Agr Sci, India, BSc, 73, MSc, 76; Rutgers Univ, PhD(entom), 80. *Prof Exp:* Res asst, Univ Agr Scis, India, 73-76 & Rutgers Univ, 76-80; res assoc, Mich State Univ, 80-82; from asst prof to assoc prof, Miss State Univ, 82-92; assoc prof, Cornell Univ, 92. *Concurrent Pos:* Prin investr, USDA-Competitive Res Grants Off, 85-88; co-prin investr, NSF, 89; vis assoc prof, Cornell Univ, 92; prin investr, USAID, 92- *Mem:* Entom Soc Am; Int Soc Chem Ecol; Am Asn Univ Profs. *Res:* Sex pheromones of insects to understand the chemistry of pheromones and insect behavior. *Mailing Add:* Dept Entom Miss State Univ Mississippi State MS 39762-9999

RAMASWAMY, VENKATACHALAM, ATMOSPHERIC RADIATION, CLIMATE PROCESSES. *Current Pos:* res staff mem, 85-89, RES SCIENTIST, GEOPHYS FLUID DYNAMICS LAB, PRINCETON UNIV, 89- *Personal Data:* b Madras, India, Apr 28, 55; m 86, M Khantha. *Educ:* Univ Delhi, India, BSc, 75, MSc, 77; State Univ Ny, Albany, PhD(atmospheric sci), 82. *Honors & Awards:* Henry A Houghton Award, Am Meteorol Soc, 94. *Prof Exp:* Res assoc, State Univ NY, 83, fel, Advan Study Prog, Nat Ctr Atmospheric Res, 83-85. *Concurrent Pos:* Mem, World Meteorol Orgn Proj Intercomparison Radiation Codes Climate Models, 83-, Ozone Assessment, World Meteorol Soc, 88, 92 & 94, Earth Observ Systs Mission, 88-; assoc ed, J Geophys Res, 92-; mem, Comt Middle Atmosphere, Am Meteorol Soc, 92-94; chair, Stratospheric Temperature Trends Assessment, 93-; panel mem, Aerosols & Climate, Nat Acad Sci, 94; lead author, Intergovt Panel on Climate Change, UN, 92, 94 & 95. *Mem:* Am Geophys Union; Am Meteorol Soc. *Res:* Transfer of radiation in scattering-absorbing atmospheres; radiative and climatic effects of aerosols, clouds and gases; interaction of radiation with microphysical, chemical and dynamical processes; cloud-climate interactions; general circulation modeling of the earth's atmosphere and atmospheric transport of species; investigation of past, present and future natural and anthropogenic climate perturbations. *Mailing Add:* Nat Oceanic Atmospheric Admin/Geophys Fluid Dynamics Lab Princeton Univ PO Box 308 Princeton NJ 08542. *Fax:* 609-987-5063; *E-Mail:* vr@gfdl.gov

RAMATY, REUVEN, ASTROPHYSICS. *Current Pos:* Nat Res Coun resident res assoc astrophys, Goddard Space Flight Ctr, NASA, 67-69, astrophysicist, 69-80, head, Theory Off, 80-93, SR SCIENTIST, LAB HIGH ENERGY ASTROPHYS, GODDARD SPACE FLIGHT CTR, NASA, 93- *Personal Data:* b Timisoara, Rumania, Feb 25, 37; m 61, Vera Klein; c Daphne & Deborah. *Educ:* Tel-Aviv Univ, BSc, 61; Univ Calif, Los Angeles, PhD(space sci), 66. *Honors & Awards:* Lindsay Award, Goddard Space Flight Ctr, NASA, 80, Exceptional Sci Achievement Medal, 81; Sr US Scientist Award, Alexander von Humboldt Found, Fed Repub Ger, 75. *Prof Exp:* Asst res geophysicist, Inst Geophys & Planetary Physics, Univ Calif, Los Angeles, 66-67. *Concurrent Pos:* Vis scientist, Stanford Univ, 72; vis prof physics, Wash Univ, 78; Fairchild scientist, Calif Inst Technol, 79; vis prof, Nagoya Univ, Japan, 93. *Mem:* Am Astron Soc; Int Astron Union; fel Am Phys Soc. *Res:* High energy astrophysics; solar physics; gamma-ray astronomy; nuclear astrophysics. *Mailing Add:* Goddard Space Flight Ctr NASA Code 665 Greenbelt MD 20771. *Fax:* 301-286-1682; *E-Mail:* ramaty@lheavx.gsfc.nasa.gov

RAMAYYA, AKUNURI V, EXPERIMENTAL NUCLEAR PHYSICS. *Current Pos:* res assoc, Vanderbilt Univ, 64-70, asst prof, 70-75, assoc prof, 75-80, PROF NUCLEAR PHYSICS, VANDERBILT UNIV, 80- *Personal Data:* b Bezwada, India, Aug 15, 38; m 65, Krishna Palacodeti; c Radhika A & Sarat A. *Educ:* Andhra Univ, India, BSc, 57, MSc, 58; Ind Univ, PhD(physics), 64. *Prof Exp:* Asst physics, Ind Univ, Bloomington, 60-64. *Concurrent Pos:* Alexander von Humboldt fel, 81-82. *Mem:* Sigma Xi; fel Am Phys Soc. *Res:* Experimental heavy ion nuclear physics; spectroscopy of neutron deficient and neutron vicer nuclei; nuclear structure; cold fission; tornary fission processes; cluster radioactivity. *Mailing Add:* Box 1807 Stat B Vanderbilt Univ Nashville TN 37235

RAMAZZOTTO, LOUIS JOHN, PHYSIOLOGY. *Current Pos:* DIR, RES SERV, LONG ISLAND JEWISH MED CTR, 88- *Personal Data:* b New York, NY, Dec 18, 40; m 66, Virginia Dama; c Robert H & John D. *Educ:* Fairleigh Dickinson Univ, BS, 62; Fordham Univ, MS, 64, PhD(physiol), 66. *Honors & Awards:* Cert of Achievement, Am Asn Lab Animal Sci. *Prof Exp:* Lab instr biol, Fairleigh Dickinson Univ, 62-63; lectr, St Peters Col, NJ, 63-64; lectr physiol, Hunter Col, 64-66; asst prof, Marymount Col, NY, 66-67; from asst prof to prof physiol, Sch Dent & Grad Sch, Fairleigh Dickinson Univ, 74-88, chmn dept, 67-88. *Concurrent Pos:* Coun Accrediation, Am Asn Accrediation Lab Animal Care. *Mem:* AAAS; NY Acad Sci; Am Phys Soc; Fed Am Soc Exp Biol; Int Asn Dent Res; Am Asn Lab Animal Sci. *Res:* Effects of nitrous oxide and other inhalation anesthetics on blood and reproductive system. *Mailing Add:* Long Island Jewish Med Ctr Res Serv Rm 133 New Hyde Park NY 11042. *Fax:* 516-354-8931

RAMBERG, CHARLES F, JR, BIOMEDICAL ENGINEERING. *Current Pos:* PROF NUTRIT, DEPT CLIN STUDIES, SCH VET MED, UNIV PA, 82- *Educ:* Rutgers Univ, BS; Univ Pa, VMD. *Concurrent Pos:* Chief Sect Nutrit, Sch Vet Med, Univ Pa, dir, Ctr Animal Health & Productivity, lectr, course organizer; chair, Computerization Task Force, New Bolton Ctr. *Res:* Mathematical modeling; kinetic analysis; computer applications in veterinary medicine, agriculture and biology; mineral and trace element nutrition; disorders of metabolism and homeostasis; numerous publications. *Mailing Add:* 378 W Street Rd Kennett Square PA 19348

RAMBERG, EDWARD G, physics; deceased, see previous edition for last biography

RAMBERG, STEVEN ERIC, MECHANICAL ENGINEERING, FLUID MECHANICS. *Current Pos:* RES MGR OCEAN ENG, OFF NAVAL RES, 88- *Personal Data:* b Boston, Mass, Jan 4, 48; m 67; c 2. *Educ:* Univ Lowell, BS, 70, MS, 72; Cath Univ Am, PhD(mech eng), 78. *Honors & Awards:* Moisseif Award, Am Soc Civil Engrs, 79. *Prof Exp:* Res engr fluid mech, Naval Res Lab, 72-88. *Mem:* Am Soc Mech Engrs; Sigma Xi. *Res:* Flow-induced vibrations; bluff body wakes; ocean wave forces; cable dynamics; wind-wave growth; stratified flows. *Mailing Add:* 7611 Range Rd Alexandria VA 22306-2425

RAMBOW, FREDERICK H K, ROCK PHYSICS & PETROGRAPHIC IMAGE ANALYSIS, BOREHOLE ACOUSTICS & BOREHOLE IMAGING. *Current Pos:* res physicist, 78-80, sr res physicist, 80-85, STAFF RES PHYSICIST, SHELL DEVELOP CO, 86- *Personal Data:* b Kansas City, Mo, Dec 16, 48. *Educ:* Univ Mo Rolla, PhD(physics), 76. *Prof Exp:* Exchange scientist, Royal Dutch Shell res, Neth, 85-86. *Concurrent Pos:* Distinguished lectr, Soc Prof Well Log Analysis, 87. *Mem:* Soc Prof Well Log Analysts; Am Inst Physics; AAAS. *Res:* Petrographic image analysis and the fractal behavior of rocks; devising better ways to measure petrophysical properties, including acousto-mechanical properties of oil-bearing formations from microscopic samples; subsidiary activities continue to include research into applications of acoustic borehole imaging and cement evaluation for zonal fluid isolation. *Mailing Add:* 5526 Darnell Houston TX 77096

RAMDAS, ANANT KRISHNA, SOLID STATE PHYSICS, OPTICS. *Current Pos:* Res assoc physics, 56-60, from asst prof to assoc prof, 60-67, PROF PHYSICS, PURDUE UNIV, LAFAYETTE, 67- *Personal Data:* b Poona, India, May 19, 30; m 56. *Educ:* Univ Poona, BSc, 50, MSc, 53, PhD(physics), 56. *Concurrent Pos:* Alexander von Humboldt US sr scientist, 77-78. *Mem:* Fel Am Phys Soc; fel Indian Acad Sci. *Res:* Spectroscopy; application of spectroscopic techniques to solid state physics; electronic and vibrational spectra of solids studied by absorption and emission spectra in the visible and the infrared and by laser Raman spectroscopy. *Mailing Add:* Dept Physics Purdue Univ West Lafayette IN 47907

RAMER, LUTHER GRIMM, ACOUSTICS. *Current Pos:* RETIRED. *Personal Data:* b Pawpaw, Ill, May 24, 08; m 35; c 1. *Educ:* Univ Ill, BS, 30, MS, 34. *Prof Exp:* Engr, Bell Tel Labs, 30-32; res engr, Univ Ill, 34-36; res physicist, Riverbank Acoust Labs, Armour Res Found, 36-47, lab supvr acoust, 47-54; res engr, Mech Div, Gen Mills, Inc, 54-60; mgr acoust lab, Wood Conversion Co, 60-62; sr res engr, Trane Co, 62-74; acoustical consult, 74-93. *Mem:* Acoust Soc Am; Sigma Xi. *Res:* Developmental research in architectural acoustics and acoustical materials; acoustics related to sounds of air conditioning equipment. *Mailing Add:* 373 Lunar Dr Ft Myers FL 33908

RAMESH, NAGARAJAH, PATTERN RECOGNITION, OBJECT & DEFECT RECOGNITION. *Current Pos:* SR RES SCIENTIST, TENCOR INSTRUMENTS, 95- *Personal Data:* m, Lakshmi Swaminathan. *Educ:* Regional Eng Col, BE, 86; Wayne State Univ, MS, 89, PhD(comput sci), 95. *Prof Exp:* Res engr, Ctr Develop Telematics, 86-87, IBM-Thomas J Watson Res Ctr, 91-92. *Mem:* Asn Comput Mach; Inst Elec & Electronics Engrs; Int Soc Optical Eng. *Res:* Object recognition, automatic defect classification, pattern recognition; clustering, develop, prototype and implement software and hardware systems to solve specific application problems for the industrial section. *Mailing Add:* 1074 Valencia Ave No 5 Sunnyvale CA 94086. *E-Mail:* rajramesh@tencor.com

RAMESH, SUNDARAM K, OPTOELECTRONICS, ELECTRONICS ENGINEERING. *Current Pos:* from asst prof to assoc prof, 87-92, PROF ELEC ENG, CALIF STATE UNIV, SACRAMENTO, 92-, CHMN DEPT, 94- *Personal Data:* b Madras, India, July 20, 60; US citizen; m 87, Utpala Kamath; c Arvind S. *Educ:* Univ Madras, India, BE, 81; Southern Ill Univ, Carbondale, MS, 83, PhD(optical commun), 86. *Prof Exp:* Vis instr, Southern Ill Univ, Carbondale, 83-86, vis asst prof, 86-87. *Concurrent Pos:* Prin investr, NSF, 90-92, tech reviewer, 91; grad coordr, Calif State Univ, Sacramento, 91-94. *Mem:* Sr mem Inst Elec & Electronics Engrs; Sigma Xi. *Res:* Coherent optical communication systems; modeling and simulation of optical communication systems; optical fiber communications for terahertz applications. *Mailing Add:* Elec Eng Dept Calif State Univ Sacramento CA 95819-6019. *E-Mail:* s.ramesh@ieee.org

RAMETTE, RICHARD WALES, COULOMETRY, SOLUBILITY. *Current Pos:* From asst prof to prof chem, Carleton Col, 54-90, chmn dept, 60-72, dir, Off Sci Activ, 69-72, EMER PROF CHEM, CARLETON COL, 65- *Personal Data:* b Stafford Springs, Conn, Oct 9, 27; m 49; c 5. *Educ:* Wesleyan Univ, BA, 50; Univ Minn. PhD(chem), 54. *Honors & Awards:* Col Chem Teachers Award, Mfr Chemists Asn, 66. *Concurrent Pos:* Vis scholar, St Olaf Col, 62-63; resident res assoc, Argonne Nat Lab, 66-67; sci adv, US Food & Drug Admin, 69-80 & Oak Ridge Nat Lab, 83-84; vis prof, Univ Fla, 75-76; chmn, Am Chem Soc, Div Chem Educ, 77. *Mem:* Am Chem Soc. *Res:* Aqueous equilibria; solution thermodynamics. *Mailing Add:* 805 Highland Ave Northfield MN 55057

RAMEY, CHESTER EUGENE, ORGANIC CHEMISTRY. *Current Pos:* TECH MGR, NEW VENTURES GROUP, LUBRIZOL CORP, 88- *Personal Data:* b Santa Maria, Calif, Jan 15, 43; m 64; c 3. *Educ:* Univ Calif, Berkeley, BS, 64; Univ Ore, PhD(org chem), 68. *Prof Exp:* Sr res chemist, Plastics & Additives Div, Ciba-Geigy Corp, 68-76; group leader synthesis, Ferro Corp, 76-82, res mgr, Bedford Chem Div, 82-84, tech dir, Bedford Chem Div, 84-88. *Mem:* Am Chem Soc; Soc Plastics Engrs. *Res:* Polymer additives; antioxidants; ultraviolet stabilizers; heat stabilizers; stabilization and degradation of polymers. *Mailing Add:* 8222 Bainbridge Rd Chagrin Falls OH 44023-4720

RAMEY, CRAIG T, CHILD DEVELOPMENT, PSYCHOLOGY. *Current Pos:* DIR, CIVILAN INT RES CTR, UNIV ALA, BIRMINGHAM, 90-, DIR, SPARKS CTR DEVELOP & LEARNING DIS, 90-, PROF, DEPTS PSYCHOL, PEDIAT & PUB HEALTH, 90- *Personal Data:* b Aug 16, 43; m, Sharon Landesman; c Lee, Ann, Jane & Samuel. *Educ:* WVa Univ, BA, 65, MA, 67, PhD(develop psychol), 69. *Honors & Awards:* Head Start Res Award, Am Psychol Asn. *Prof Exp:* Fel develop psychol, Univ Calif, Berkeley, 69; asst prof, Wayne State Univ, 69-71; assoc prof, Univ NC, Chapel Hill, 71-78, sr investr & dir infant res, Frank Porter Graham Child Develop Ctr, 71-74, dir res, 75-89, assoc dir, 78-89, prof psychol, 79-90, prof pediat, 84-90. *Mem:* Am Psychol Asn; Soc Res Child Develop; Am Pub Health Asn; Am Asn Ment Retardation. *Res:* Prevention and treatment of disabilities in childhood. *Mailing Add:* Univ Ala Civitan 1719 Sixth Ave Birmingham AL 35294-0021. *Fax:* 205-975-6330; *E-Mail:* cramey.civitan@civmail.circ.uab.edu

RAMEY, ESTELLE R, PHYSIOLOGY, ENDOCRINOLOGY. *Current Pos:* from asst prof to assoc prof, 56-66, prof biophys, 80-87, PROF PHYSIOL, SCH MED, GEORGETOWN UNIV, 66-, EMER PROF BIOPHYS, 87- *Personal Data:* b Detroit, Mich, Aug 23, 17; m 41; c 2. *Educ:* Columbia Univ, MA, 40; Univ Chicago, PhD(physiol), 50. *Hon Degrees:* Numerous from US univs. *Prof Exp:* Tutor chem, Queens Col, NY, 38-41; lectr, Univ Tenn, 42-47; instr physiol, Univ Chicago, 51-54, asst prof, 54-58. *Concurrent Pos:* USPHS fel, Univ Chicago, 50-51; Mem adv bd, Planned Parenthood, Dir of NIH & Health & Human Serv; mem bd dirs, Asn Women Sci & Admiral H G Rickover Found; pres, Asn Women Sci, 72-74; founder & pres, Asn Women Sci Educ Found; mem, Comt for Women Vet, US Vet Admin, President's Adv Comt Women, Exec Adv Panel to the Chief of Naval Opers & Gen Med Study Sect, NIH; vis prof & lectr at several universities. *Mem:* Am Physiol Soc; Am Chem Soc; Endocrine Soc; Am Diabetes Asn; Am Acad Neurol. *Res:* Endocrinology metabolism chiefly in the field of adrenal function; sex hormones and longevity. *Mailing Add:* 6817 Hillmead Rd Bethesda MD 20817

RAMEY, HARMON HOBSON, JR, FIBER SCIENCE. *Current Pos:* AGR MKT SPECIALIST, AGR MKT SERV, USDA, 84- *Personal Data:* b Russell, Ark, Dec 4, 30; m 54, Jenell Bostater; c Joseph W & Deborah A. *Educ:* Univ Ark, BSA, 51, MS, 52; NC State Col, PhD(plant breeding, genetics), 59. *Prof Exp:* Asst, Univ Ark, 51-52; asst cotton geneticist, Delta Br Exp Sta, Miss State Univ, 55-57 & 59-61; asst, NC State Col, 57-59; geneticist & fiber scientist, Nat Cotton Coun Am, Tenn, 61-70; res geneticist, Agr Res Serv, USDA, 70-84. *Concurrent Pos:* Adj prof, Univ Tenn, Knoxville, 71-80. *Mem:* Am Soc Qual Control; Fiber Soc; Sigma Xi. *Res:* fiber & textiles technology; relationship of fiber properties to processing performance and product quality; fiber property measurement. *Mailing Add:* 2756 Stage Park Dr Memphis TN 38134. *Fax:* 901-766-2915

RAMEY, MELVIN RICHARD, CIVIL ENGINEERING, BIOMECHANICS. *Current Pos:* from asst prof to assoc prof, 67-73, dept chair, 91-96, PROF CIVIL ENG, UNIV CALIF, DAVIS, 73- *Personal Data:* b Pittsburgh, Pa, Sept 13, 38; m 64; c 2. *Educ:* Pa State Univ, BS, 60; Carnegie-Mellon Univ, MS, 65, PhD(civil eng), 67. *Prof Exp:* Bridge design engr, Pa State Dept Hwys, 60-63; res asst, Carnegie-Mellon Univ, 63-67. *Concurrent Pos:* Consult, Calif State Div Hwys, 68-69, Murray & McCormick Consult Engrs, 69, Fireman's Fund Am Ins Co, 70 & var archit design firms, 71-; consult, various architectural design firms, 70- *Mem:* Am Soc Civil Engrs; Am Concrete Inst; Int Soc Biomech in Sports; Am Soc Eng Educ; Am Asn Higher Educ. *Res:* Structural design and analysis; materials behavior and testing; biomechanics with applications to human movement and sports; computer aided structural design; fiber reinforced concrete. *Mailing Add:* Dept Civil Eng Univ Calif Davis CA 95616-5224

RAMEY, ROBERT LEE, ENGINEERING PHYSICS. *Current Pos:* assoc prof elec eng, 56-62, PROF ELEC ENG, UNIV VA, 62- *Personal Data:* b Middletown, Ohio, June 26, 22; m 46; c 2. *Educ:* Duke Univ, BSEE, 45; Univ Cincinnati, MS, 47; NC State Col, PhD(elec eng, physics), 54. *Prof Exp:* Asst elec eng, Univ Cincinnati, 46-48; instr, NC State Col, 49-54; res lab dir, Wright Mach Div, Sperry-Rand Corp, 54-56. *Concurrent Pos:* Ed, Encycl Sci & Technol, 59; NASA res grant, 62-70. *Mem:* Am Phys Soc; Inst Elec & Electronics Engrs. *Res:* Physical electronics, including vacuum, gaseous and solid state. *Mailing Add:* 1709 Essex Rd Charlottesville VA 22901

RAMEZAN, MASSOOD, THERMAL FLUID SCIENCE, ADVANCED POWER SYSTEM. *Current Pos:* PRIN ENGR, BURNS & ROE SERV CORP, 88- *Personal Data:* b Iran, 56; US citizen; m 87, Sara Hejazs; c Sherwin & Armin. *Educ:* WVa Univ, BS, 77, MS, 79, PhD(mech eng), 84. *Prof Exp:* Res fel engr, WVa Univ, 77-79 & 81-84, asst prof, 84-86; consult engr, Hosp Utility Inc, 79-81; res engr, ORAU/METC, 86-88. *Mem:* Fel Am Soc Mech Engrs; Soc Automotive Engrs. *Res:* Conducted research in areas of fluid, heat transfer, combustion and its engineering applications; numerical modeling and computer simulation. *Mailing Add:* 116 Copperwood Dr Bethel Park PA 15102. *E-Mail:* ramezan@petc.doe.gov

RAMHARACK, ROOPRAM, ADHESIVES, RHEOLOGY. *Current Pos:* RES ASSOC, NAT STARCH & CHEM CO, 89- *Personal Data:* b Berbice, Guyana, Aug 26, 52; US citizen. *Educ:* Univ Guyana, BS, 76; Polytech Univ, PhD(polymer chem), 83. *Honors & Awards:* Carl Dahlquist Award, Pressure Sensitive Tape Coun, 93. *Prof Exp:* Res aide, Cornell Med Ctr, 79-82; sr chemist, 3M, 84-87; scientist, Polaroid, 87-89. *Concurrent Pos:* Team leader drug delivery, Nat Starch, 92-93, team leader radiation processing. *Mem:* Am Chem Soc; NY Acad Sci; Pressure Sensitive Tape Coun. *Res:* Several areas of polymers including elastomers for pressure sensitive adhesives and polymers for transdermal drug delivery; radiation processing of polymers by ebeam and ultra violet. *Mailing Add:* 5901 Carnegie Blvd Charlotte NC 28209. *Fax:* 908-685-7785

RAMIG, ROBERT E, SOIL CONSERVATION, SOIL FERTILITY. *Current Pos:* RETIRED. *Personal Data:* b McGrew, Nebr, June 22, 22; m 43, Lois F Franklin; c Robert F, Mary K & John C. *Educ:* Univ Nebr, BSc, 43, PhD(soils), 60; Wash State Univ, MSc, 48. *Prof Exp:* Asst agronomist, Exp Sta, Univ Nebr, 48-51; coop agent, Exp Sta, Univ Nebr & USDA, 51-57; soil scientist, Agr Res Serv, USDA, 57-71, dir, Columbia Plateau Conserv Res Ctr, 71-81, res soil scientist, 81-91; emer assoc prof soils, Ore State Univ. *Mem:* Am Soc Agron; Soil Sci Soc Am; Soil Conserv Soc Am; AAAS. *Res:* Soil and water conservation using balanced fertility to give maximum production per unit of water. *Mailing Add:* 1208 NW Johns Ave Pendleton OR 97801-1261

RAMIREZ, ARTHUR P, SOLID STATE PHYSICS. *Current Pos:* Postdoctoral mem tech staff, 84-86, MEM TECH STAFF, AT&T BELL LABS, MURRAY HILL, NJ, 86- *Personal Data:* b Amityville, NY, Aug 4, 56; m 86; c 1. *Educ:* Yale Univ, BS, 78, PhD(physics), 84. *Mem:* Am Phys Soc. *Res:* Condensed matter experimental physics, especially in the field of magnetism and superconductivity in novel materials; heavy fermion systems; low-dimensional magnetism; spin glass; high-Tc superconductivity. *Mailing Add:* Lucent Technol Rm 1B-120 600 Mountain Ave Murray Hill NJ 07974-2070

RAMIREZ, DONALD EDWARD, ABSTRACT HARMONIC ANALYSIS, COMPUTATIONAL STATISTICS. *Current Pos:* asst prof, 67-71, ASSOC PROF MATH, UNIV VA, 71- *Personal Data:* b New Orleans, La, May 21, 43; div; c 3. *Educ:* Tulane Univ, BS, 63, PhD(math), 66. *Prof Exp:* Off Naval Res fel & res assoc, Univ Wash, 66-67. *Mem:* Am Status Asn. *Res:* Measure algebras factor analysis. *Mailing Add:* 1284 Maple View Dr Charlottesville VA 22902

RAMIREZ, FRANCESCO, HUMAN MOLECULAR GENETICS, GENE EVOLUTION. *Current Pos:* PROF MOLECULAR BIOL, MT SINAI HOSP. *Educ:* Univ Sci, Palarmo, Italy, PhD(genetics), 69. *Prof Exp:* Assoc prof molecular genetics, Rutgers Univ, 79-86; prof human genetics, State Univ NY Health Sci Ctr, 86- *Res:* Connective tissue disorders. *Mailing Add:* Brookdale Ctr Molecular Biol Mount Sinai Sch Med Box 1126 Gustave Levy Pl New York NY 10029-6504

RAMIREZ, GUILLERMO, ONCOLOGY. *Current Pos:* ASSOC PROF HUMAN ONCOL, SCH MED, UNIV WIS-MADISON, 71- *Personal Data:* b Bogota, Colombia, Sept 19, 34; US citizen; m 57; c 2. *Educ:* Nat Col St Bartholomew, BS, 51; Nat Univ Colombia, MD, 58. *Concurrent Pos:* Consult, Vet Admin Hosps, 68-; prin investr, Cent Oncol Group, 72- *Mem:* Am Asn Cancer Res; Am Soc Clin Oncol; Int Asn Study Lung Cancer; NY Acad Sci; Am Asn Study Neoplastic Dis. *Res:* Clinical-pharmacological studies; phase I, II and III drug studies. *Mailing Add:* Calle 103 23 A-57 Apt 401 Santa Fe De Bogota Colombia

RAMIREZ, J ROBERTO, BIO-ORGANIC CHEMISTRY. *Current Pos:* CHMN & ASSOC PROF CHEM, UNIV PR, RIO PIEDRAS CAMPUS, 75-; PRES HIGH TECHOL, 97- *Personal Data:* b Ponce, PR, Feb 17, 41; US citizen; m 72; c 1. *Educ:* Univ Notre Dame, BSc, 63; Univ PR, MSc, 66; Univ Karlsruhe, Ger, Dr rer nat, 70. *Prof Exp:* Fel, Swiss Fed Inst Technol, 71-72. *Mem:* Soc Chemists PR (secy, 73-74, pres-elect, 74-75, pres, 75-); Am Chem Soc. *Res:* Biosynthesis of acyclic carotenes; synthesis of carotenoids and model compounds. *Mailing Add:* PO Box 366950 San Juan PR 00936-6950

RAMIREZ, W FRED, CHEMICAL ENGINEERING. *Current Pos:* From asst prof to assoc prof, 65-75, chmn dept, 71-79, Croft res prof, 80, PROF CHEM ENG, UNIV COLO, BOULDER, 75- *Personal Data:* b New Orleans, La, Feb 19, 41; m 63, Marion Kneipp; c 3. *Educ:* Tulane Univ, BS, 62, MS, 64, PhD(chem eng), 65. *Honors & Awards:* Dow Award, Am Soc Eng Educ, 74; Levey Award, Tulane Univ, 74; Western Elec Award, Am Soc Eng Educ, 80; Col Eng Fac Res Award, Univ Colo, 86. *Concurrent Pos:* Fulbright res fel, France, 76; fac fel, Univ Colo, 85-86 & 92-93; vis scientist, Mass Inst Technol, 85-; fel, Acad Sci Exchange, to Soviet Union, 87; vis prof, Cambridge Univ, 92-93. *Mem:* Fel Am Inst Chem Engrs; Am Soc Eng Educ. *Res:* Optimal control of chemical, biochemical energy and environmental processes. *Mailing Add:* Dept Chem Eng Univ Colo Boulder CO 80309-0424. *Fax:* 303-492-4341; *E-Mail:* ramirez@cubldr.colorado.edu

RAMIREZ-RONDA, CARLOS HECTOR, INFECTIOUS DISEASES. *Current Pos:* Assoc chief staff res & develop, 75-90, CHIEF, INFECTIOUS DIS RES LAB, VET ADMIN MED CTR, 76-, CHIEF DEPT MED, 90-; DIR INFECTIOUS DIS, SCH MED, UNIV PR, 78-, PROF MED, 84- *Personal Data:* b Mayaquez, PR, Jan 24, 43; US citizen; m 63, Crimilda; c Carlos R & Ivana. *Educ:* Northwestern Univ, Chicago, BSM, 64, MD, 67. *Prof Exp:* Res fel infectious dis, Southwestern Med Sch, Univ Tex, 73-75. *Concurrent Pos:* ASST PROF MED, sCH mED, uNIV pr, 75-78; consult infectious dis, San Juan City Hosp, 76-; investr, Am Heart Asn & PR Heart Asn, 77-; assoc ed, PR Med Asn J, 78-; prog dir infectious dis, Univ Hosp, San Juan, 78-; assoc prof med, Sch Med, Vet Admin Hosp, 78-84, dir infectious dis, 78-; vis prof, Autonomous Univ, Mex, 78, 79 & 80; mem, Bact & Mycol Study Sect, NIH, 81-85; vis prof, Univ Cent Columbia, Bogotta, 88; mem, Adv Comt Immunization Pract, 90-94. *Mem:* Infectious Dis Soc; Am Fedn Clin Res; Am Soc Microbiol; Am Col Physicians; Int Soc Infectious Dis; Asn Panam Infectol; Am Med Asn; NY Acad Sci; AAAS; Am Pub Health Asn. *Res:* Pathogenesis of bacterial diseases especially adherence and bacterial endocarditis; clinical microbiology; microbial susceptibility and resistance; antibiotic pharmacology; seroepidemiology; clinical studies on new antimicrobials; clinical studies with HIV-AIDS, epidemiology of AIDS, antiretroviral therapy. *Mailing Add:* 81 Mirador St, Paseo Alto Rio Piedras PR 00926

RAMKE, THOMAS FRANKLIN, SR, FORESTRY. *Current Pos:* RETIRED. *Personal Data:* b Bancker, La, Jan 1, 17; m 41, Thelma Moist; c Geraldine, Rachael, Roslyn & Thomas F Jr. *Educ:* La State Univ, BS, 40. *Prof Exp:* Forester, La Dept Conserv, 40-41, asst dist forester, 41-42; forester, Tenn Valley Auth, 42-61, asst dist forester, 48-49, chief, Forestry Field Br, 61-66, Forest Mgt Br, Norris, 66-67, tributary area rep, 67-74, dist mgr, Off Tributary Area Develop, 74-79. *Mem:* Soc Am Foresters. *Res:* Factors related to the application of forest and watershed management and skillful use of forest reserves; elements related to improving community structure for effective citizen participation; community planning, evaluation and development. *Mailing Add:* 4107 Fulton Dr Knoxville TN 37918-4314

RAMLER, EDWARD OTTO, ORGANIC CHEMISTRY. *Current Pos:* RETIRED. *Personal Data:* b Washington, DC, Sept 25, 16; m 42; c 3. *Educ:* Cath Univ Am, BS, 38; Pa State Col, MS, 40, PhD(org chem), 42. *Prof Exp:* Asst chem, Pa State Col, 39-41, instr, 41-42; res chemist, Plastics Dept, E I du Pont de Nemours & Co, Inc, 42-46, tech investr, Textile Fibers Dept, 46-53, supvr, Patent Div, 53-60, patent adminr, Int Dept, 60-70, mgr, Patents Trademarks & Contracts Sect, 70-80. *Mem:* Am Chem Soc. *Res:* Organic chemistry of fluorine; synthesis of vinyl type monomers and polymers; plastics technology; reactions catalyzed by hydrogen fluoride. *Mailing Add:* Stonegates 65 4031 Kennett Pike Greenville DE 19807

RAMLER, W(ARREN) J(OSEPH), INDUSTRIAL RADIATION SYSTEMS. *Current Pos:* PRES, WJR CONSULT, 86- *Personal Data:* b Joliet, Ill, Jan 1, 21; m 43, Ruth Wilder; c John W, Barbara A & Richard W. *Educ:* Ill Inst Technol, BS, 43, MS, 51. *Honors & Awards:* Radtech Int Award. *Prof Exp:* Student engr, Westinghouse Elec Corp, 43; instr elec eng, Carnegie Inst Technol, 43-44 & 46; asst, Tenn Eastman Corp, 44-46; assoc, Argonne Nat Lab, 46-49, asst group leader, Cyclotron Proj, 49-56, group leader, 56-59, sr scientist, 59, group leader low energy accelerators, 59-73; gen mgr, PPG Industs, 73-81; sr vpres, RPC Industs, Inc, 81-86; PRES, WJR CONSULTS, 86- *Concurrent Pos:* Consult, Argonne Nat Lab, 73-; pres, Aetek Int Inc, 88-93. *Mem:* Inst Elec & Electronics Engrs; Am Phys Soc; NY Acad Sci; Am Mgt Asn. *Res:* Development and systems design and construction of radiation generating equipment for industrial use and laboratory research; Dc and cyclic accelerators, linacs and ultraviolet processors. *Mailing Add:* 70 Moons View Rd Sedona AZ 86351

RAMM, ALEXANDER G, GEOPHYSICS, ELECTROMAGNETICS. *Current Pos:* PROF MATH, KANS STATE UNIV, 81- *Personal Data:* b Leningrad, USSR, Jan 13, 40; US citizen; m, Lubov L; c Olga & Yuliya. *Educ:* Univ Leningrad, BS, 59, MS, 61; Univ Moscow, PhD(math physics), 64; Inst Math Acad Sci, Minsk, DrSci, 72. *Prof Exp:* Prof math, Univ Mich, 79-81. *Concurrent Pos:* Vis scientist, Schlumberger Doll Res, 83; vis prof math, Univ Goteborg, 82, Univ Manchester, 84, Univ London, 85, Acad Sinica, Taipei, 86, Univ Bonn, Ger, 84, Univ Stuttgart, Ger, 83, Univ Heidelberg, Ger, 87, Indian Inst Sci, Bangalore, 87, Univ Uppsala, Royal Inst Technol, 87, Concordia Univ, 90, Complutense Univ, Madrid, 95, Milan Polytech, 95 & Univ J Fourier, Grenoble, 95 & 97; consult, Dikewood Corp, 84; Stand Oil Prod Co, 85 & Los Alamos Nat Lab, 94; elected mem, Electromagnetic Acad, Mass Inst Technol, 90; sr Fulbright res prof, 91-92, Technion, Israel; assoc ed, J Math Anal Appl, J Inverse & Ill Posed Prob, Appl Anal. *Mem:* Am Math Soc; NY Acad Sci. *Res:* Spectral and scattering theory in classical physics and quantum mechanics; inverse problems, theoretical numerical analysis and ill posed problems; random fields estimation and signal processing; wave propagation and nonlinear passive networks; tomography and integral geometry, image processing; awarded 2 patents. *Mailing Add:* Dept Math Kans State Univ Manhattan KS 66506. *Fax:* 785-532-7004; *E-Mail:* ramm@math.ksu.edu

RAMM, DIETOLF, COMPUTER SCIENCE. *Current Pos:* Assoc community health sci, Duke Med Ctr, Duke Univ, 69-70, asst prof community health sci, univ, 70-71, asst prof info sci in psychiat, 70-76 & comput sci, 71-76, ASSOC MED RES PROF PSYCHIAT, MED CTR, DUKE UNIV, 76-, DIR GERIAT COMPUT CTR, CTR STUDY AGING & HUMAN DEVELOP, 69- *Personal Data:* b Berlin, Ger, June 17, 42; US citizen; m 66. *Educ:* Cornell Univ, BA, 64; Duke Univ, PhD(physics), 69. *Concurrent Pos:* Lectr comput sci, Duke Univ, 76- *Mem:* AAAS; Asn Comput Mach; Geront Soc; Am Phys Soc. *Res:* Medical applications for computing; micro-computers in the laboratory; human-machine interface problems; interactive computing; computers in psychiatry and the study of aging. *Mailing Add:* 234 Crawford Rd Hillsborough NC 27278-9493

RAMMER, IRWYN ALDEN, PESTICIDE DEVELOPMENT. *Current Pos:* AGR CONSULT, 86- *Personal Data:* b Stockton, Calif, Aug 15, 28; m 56, Ann Palazzolo; c Peter, Ronald & Lori. *Educ:* Univ Calif, BS, 51, MS, 52, PhD(entom), 60. *Prof Exp:* Res asst entom, Univ Calif, 56-59; res assoc, Agr Chem Group, FMC CORP, 59-86. *Mem:* Entom Soc Am. *Res:* Pesticides for control of agricultural pests. *Mailing Add:* 2682 Moraga Dr Pinole CA 94564

RAMMING, DAVID WILBUR, PLANT BREEDING. *Current Pos:* res leader fruit breeding, Western Region, Sci & Educ Admin, 75-86, RES HORTICULTURIST, AGR RES, USDA, 86- *Personal Data:* b Oklahoma City, Okla, Oct 31, 46; m 75; c 3. *Educ:* Okla State Univ, BA, 68, MA, 72; Rutgers Univ, PhD(hort), 76. *Prof Exp:* Teaching asst crop sci, Okla State Univ, 68-69, asst hort, 71-72; asst fruit breeding, Rutgers Univ, 72-75. *Mem:* Am Soc Hort Sci; Am Pomol Soc. *Res:* Fruit breeding, development of improved stone fruit and grape varieties; embryo culture of early-ripening prunes and seedless vitis; transformation of grape plants. *Mailing Add:* 207 N Locan Ave Fresno CA 93727. *Fax:* 209-453-3088

RAM-MOHAN, L RAMDAS, SOLID STATE PHYSICS. *Current Pos:* from asst prof to assoc prof, 78-85, PROF, WORCESTER POLYTECH INST, 85- *Personal Data:* b Poona, India, July 21, 44; US citizen. *Educ:* Univ Delhi, BSc, 64; Purdue Univ, MS, 67, PhD(physics), 71. *Prof Exp:* Instr physics, Purdue Univ, 75-78. *Concurrent Pos:* Consult, Mass Inst Technol, Purdue Univ, Univ Notre Dame, Univ Mo & NEC Res Inst; pres, Quantum Semiconductor Algorithms Inc. *Mem:* Am Phys Soc; Inst Elec & Electronics Engrs. *Res:* Theory of electromagnetic properties of metals; optical properties of semiconductors; many-body theory; quantum field theory; quantum semiconductor heterostructures. *Mailing Add:* Dept Physics Worcester Polytech Inst Worcester MA 01609. *E-Mail:* lrram@wpi.wpi.edu

RAMO, SIMON, ELECTRICAL ENGINEERING, PHYSICS. *Current Pos:* RETIRED. *Personal Data:* b Salt Lake City, Utah, May 7, 13; m 37; c 2. *Educ:* Univ Utah, BS, 33; Calif Inst Technol, PhD(elec eng, physics), 36. *Hon Degrees:* DEng, Case Western Reserve Univ, 60, Univ Mich, 66 & Polytech Inst New York, 71; DSc, Univ Utah, 61, Union Col, 63, Worcester Polytech Inst, 68, Univ Akron, 69 & Cleveland State Univ, 76; LLD, Carnegie-Mellon Univ, 70 & Univ Southern Calif, 72, Gonzaga Univ, 83, Occidental Col, 84, Claremont Univ, 85. *Honors & Awards:* Kayan Medal, Columbia Univ, 72; Delmar S Fahrney Award, Franklin Inst, 78; Nat Medal of Sci; Founders Medal, Inst Elec & Electronics Engrs, 80, Centennial Medal, 84; Arthur M Bueche Medal, Nat Acad Eng, 83; Durand Lectr, Am Inst Aeronaut & Astronaut, 84; John Fritz Medal, 86; Nat Eng Award, Am Asn Eng Socs, 88; Howard Hughes Mem Award, 89. *Prof Exp:* Res engr, Gen Elec Co, NY, 36-46; vpres & dir develop, Hughes Aircraft Co, 46-53; co-founder, vpres, Ramo-Wooldridge Corp, 53-58, sci dir, US Intercontinental Ballistic Missile Prog, 54-58; exec vpres, TRW Inc, 58-61, vchmn bd, 61-78, chmn exec comt, 69-78, dir, 54-85, chmn bd, TRW-Fujitsu Co, 80-83. *Concurrent Pos:* Pres & dir, Bunker Ramo Corp, 64-66; dir, Union Bank, Times Mirror, Atlantic Richfield; mem, White House Energy Res & Develop Coun, 73-75 & bd dirs, Los Angeles World Affairs Coun, 73-85; trustee, Calif Inst Technol; chmn, President's Comt Sci & Technol, 76-77, co-chmn, Transition Task Force Sci & Technol, 80-81; mem, Secy's Adv Coun, Dept Com, 76-77, consult to adminr, ERDA, 76-77; vis prof mgt sci, Calif Inst Technol, 78-; fac fel, John F Kennedy Sch Govt, Harvard Univ, 80-84; Regent's lectr, Univ Calif, Los Angeles, 81-82; mem bd adv sci & technol, Repub China, 81-84. *Mem:* Nat Acad Sci; Nat Acad Eng; fel Am Inst Aeronaut & Astronaut; fel Am Phys Soc; fel Inst Elec & Electronics Engrs; Am Philos Soc; Am Acad Arts & Sci; Int Acad Astronaut; fel AAAS; fel Inst Advan Eng. *Res:* Electronics; microwaves. *Mailing Add:* 9200 Sunset Blvd Suite 801 Los Angeles CA 90069

RAMOHALLI, KUMAR NANJUNDA RAO, COMBUSTION, ACOUSTICS. *Current Pos:* PROF, DEPT AEROSPACE & MECH ENG, UNIV ARIZ, 82-; PRIN INVESTR, SPACE ENG RES CTR, NASA, 88- *Personal Data:* b Karnataka, India, Nov 12, 45; m 77. *Educ:* Univ Col Eng, BE, 67; Indian Inst Sci, ME, 68; Mass Inst Technol, PhD(propulsion), 71. *Honors & Awards:* Exceptional Serv Medal, NASA, 84. *Prof Exp:* Res fel propulsion, Guggenheim Jet Propulsion Ctr, Calif Inst Technol, 71-74, sr res fel, 74-75, sr sect mem tech staff advan technol, 75-79, group leader & group supvr thermal & chem, Jet Propulsion Lab, 79-, res engr, 81- *Concurrent Pos:* Vis scientist, Indian Inst Sci, Indian Space Res Orgn, 78; mgr, Sunfuels, Jet Propulsion Lab, Calif Inst Technol, 80-81; vis scientist, Beijing Inst Technol, 87; vis scientist, Northwestern Polytech Univ, Xiam, China, 87; adj prof, Penn State Univ, 89; vis assoc, Harvard Univ, 89-90. *Mem:* Assoc fel Am Inst Aeronaut & Astronaut; Combustion Inst; Sigma Xi. *Res:* Combustion involving solids and gases; theory of hybrid combustion; composite solid propellant combustion including nitramines; novel perforated porous plate analogue for heterogeneous combustion; acoustic diagnostics of burners; graphite composts and their hazards alleviation through gasification; space junk cleanup; light weight, deployable solar collectors; nine certificates of recognition from NASA; production of propellants & other useful materials extraterrestrially for cost effectiveness of future space missions. *Mailing Add:* NASA Ctr Utilization Aerospace Mech Eng Univ Ariz 301 AME Tucson AZ 85721-0001

RAMON, SERAFIN, CYTOGENETICS. *Current Pos:* assoc prof biol, Panhandle State Univ, 67-71, head dept, 69-85, head dept sci, 73-75, PROF BIOL, PANHANDLE STATE UNIV, 71-, HEAD DEPT, 77- *Personal Data:* b Feb 3, 34; US citizen; m 58; c 3. *Educ:* Panhandle Agr & Mech Col, BS, 57; Univ N Mex MS, 62; Univ Kans, PhD(bot), 67. *Prof Exp:* From instr to asst prof biol, Panhandle Agr & Mech Col, 59-65. *Concurrent Pos:* NSF sci fel, 66-67. *Mem:* AAAS; Genetics Soc Am; Bot Soc Am; Am Genetical Asn. *Res:* Plant morphology and root anatomy; cytogenetic and biosystematics of selected Compositae. *Mailing Add:* Dept Math Sci Panhandle State Univ PO Box 430 Goodwell OK 73939-0430

RAMOND, PIERRE MICHEL, ELEMENTARY PARTICLE PHYSICS. *Current Pos:* PROF PHYSICS, UNIV FLA, 80- *Personal Data:* b Neuilly-Seine, France, Jan 31, 43; US citizen; m 67, Lillian; c Tanya, Lisa & Jennifer. *Educ:* Newark Col Eng, BSEE, 65; Syracuse Univ, PhD(physics), 69. *Honors & Awards:* B Pregel Prize, NY Acad Sci, 92. *Prof Exp:* Res assoc physics, Fermi Lab, 69-71; instr, Yale Univ, 71-73, asst prof, 73-76; Millikan fel, Calif Inst Technol, 75-80. *Concurrent Pos:* Trustee, Aspen Ctr Physics, Univ Fla, 80-; div assoc ed, Phys Rev Letts, 84-87; Guggenheim fel, 85; dir, Inst Fundamental Theory, 88-; pres, Aspen Ctr Physics, 96- *Mem:* Fel Am Phys Soc. *Res:* Grand unified theories; unification of gravity with elementary particles; superstrings. *Mailing Add:* Dept Physics Univ Fla Gainesville FL 32611. *E-Mail:* ramond@phys.ufl.edu

RAMON-MOLINER, ENRIQUE, NEUROANATOMY. *Current Pos:* RETIRED. *Personal Data:* b Murcia, Spain, July 11, 27; Can citizen; m 57; c 4. *Educ:* Inst Cajal, Madrid, MD, 56; McGill Univ, PhD, 59. *Prof Exp:* Asst res prof anat, Univ Md, 59-63; from asst prof to assoc prof physiol, Laval Univ, 63-68; from assoc prof to prof anat, Sch Med, Univ Sherbrooke, 74. *Concurrent Pos:* Assoc, Med Res Coun Can, 63-81. *Mem:* Am Asn Anat; Can Asn Anat; Can Physiol Soc; Int Brain Res Orgn; Soc Neurosci. *Res:* Histology and cytology of the central nervous system; structure of the cerebral cortex; morphological varieties and classification of nerve cells; correlation between dendritic morphology and function of nerve cells; ultrastructure of the central nervous system; neurohistochemistry; corticothalamic connections. *Mailing Add:* PO Box 422 North Hatley PQ G0B 2C0 Can

RAMOS, HAROLD SMITH, MEDICINE. *Current Pos:* PROF MED, SCH MED, EMORY UNIV, 75-, ASST DEAN SCH MED, 72- *Personal Data:* b Atlanta, Ga, July 20, 28; m 54, Barbara T Lavender; c Mary C, Ralph & Steven. *Educ:* Johns Hopkins Univ, AB, 48; Med Col Ga, MD, 54. *Prof Exp:* From asst prof to assoc prof med, Sch Med, Emory Univ, 63-75; chief med & dir med educ, 63-85, med dir , Crawford W Long Mem Hosp, 85- *Concurrent Pos:* Fel hemat & renal dis, Walter Reed Army Inst Res, Washington, DC, 58-59. *Mem:* AMA; Am Col Physicians; NY Acad Sci. *Res:* Medical education; cardiology. *Mailing Add:* 550 Peachtree St Atlanta GA 30365. *Fax:* 404-686-4951

RAMOS, JUAN, SOCIAL WELFARE. *Current Pos:* spec asst to dir, Off Prog Coord, NIMH, 68-72, chief, Interagency Liaison Br, 72-74, dep dir, 74-75, dir, Div Prev & Spec Ment Health Prog, 75-85, dep dir, 85-92, ASSOC DIR PREV, NIMH, 92-; ADJ PROF, SCH SOCIAL WORK, UNIV MD & VA COMMONWEALTH UNIV, 90- *Educ:* Sul Ross State Col, BS, 56; Univ Southern Colif, Los Angeles, MSW, 60; Brandeis Univ, PhD(social welfare), 68. *Honors & Awards:* Knee-Whitman Ment Health Award, 93. *Prof Exp:* Child welfare worker, Santa Clara Co Welfare Dept, 60-62, supvr, 62-65. *Concurrent Pos:* Soc worker, Bur Pub Assistance, Los Angeles Co, 56-58 & 59; regents lectr, Sch Social Welfare, Univ Calif, Los Angeles, 87. *Mem:* Nat Asn Social Workers. *Mailing Add:* Off Dir NIMH Parklawn Bldg Rm 9-C25 5600 Fishers Lane Rockville MD 20857

RAMOS, JUAN IGNACIO, MECHANICAL ENGINEERING, APPLIED MATHEMATICS. *Current Pos:* from instr to assoc prof, 80-89, PROF MECH ENG, CARNEGIE MELLON UNIV, 89- *Personal Data:* b Bernardos, Spain, Jan 28, 53; m 89, Mercedes Naveiro; c Juan & Fernando. *Educ:* Madrid Polytech Univ, BAEng, 75; Princeton Univ, MA, 79, PhD(mech eng), 80, Madrid Polytech Univ, PhD(eng), 83. *Honors & Awards:* Ralph R Teetor Award, Soc Automotive Engrs, 81; Aeronaut Eng Medal, 77. *Prof Exp:* Res engr, Aeronaut Constructs Ltd, Spain, 76-77. *Concurrent Pos:* Consult, PPG Industs, 82-84; prin investr, NASA Lewis Res Ctr, 80-, NSF, 81-84, AFOSR 84-86; Guggenheim fel, 77-78; Van Ness Lothrop fel, 79-80; NASA fac fel, 82, 88; consult, Software Eng Inst, 86; vis prof, Univ Rome, 88; vis prof, Univ Malaga, Spain, 90-91, prof, 92. *Mem:* Soc Indust & Appl Math. *Res:* Numerical modeling of internal combustion engines and gas turbines (combustion and fluid mechanics); numerical analysis finite elements; heat transfer and ignition, thermal sciences; applied mathematics, wave propagation; liquid curtains; chemical reactors. *Mailing Add:* Dept Mech Eng Carnegie-Mellon Univ Pittsburgh PA 15213-3890

RAMOS, LILLIAN, CHEMISTRY, SCIENCE EDUCATION. *Current Pos:* Prof chem, biol, phys sci & math, 55-70, prof educ, 70-78, dir grad studies educ, 71-77, PROF SCH ADMIN, CATH UNIV PR, 90- *Personal Data:* b Ponce, PR; US citizen. *Educ:* Cath Univ PR, BS, 54; Fordham Univ, MSEd, 60, PhD, 71. *Mem:* Am Chem Soc; Col Chem PR. *Res:* School administration. *Mailing Add:* Pontifical Cath Univ PR 2250 Las America Ave Ponce PR 00731-6389

RAMP, FLOYD LESTER, ORGANIC CHEMISTRY. *Current Pos:* RETIRED. *Personal Data:* b Newman, Ill, Mar 6, 23; m 48; c 4. *Educ:* Univ Ill, BS, 44; Univ Minn, PhD, 50. *Prof Exp:* Du Pont fel, Mass Inst Technol, 51; res chemist, B F Goodrich Co, Brecksville, 51-62, sr res assoc, 62-69, res fel chem, Res Ctr, 69-84. *Mem:* Am Chem Soc. *Res:* Chemical reactions of high polymers; electrochemistry. *Mailing Add:* 225 Hollywood St Oberlin OH 44074-1011

RAMP, WARREN KIBBY, BONE METABOLISM, ORAL BIOLOGY. *Current Pos:* SR SCIENTIST, ORTHOPEDIC SURG, CAROLINA MED CTR, 91- *Personal Data:* b New York, NY, Aug 19, 39; m 63, Anita Decker; c Nancy & Marjorie. *Educ:* State Univ NY, Oneonta, BS, 63; Colo State Univ, MS, 64; Univ Ky, PhD(physiol, biochem), 67. *Prof Exp:* From asst prof to assoc prof oral biol & pharmacol, Univ NC, Chapel Hill, 70-79; assoc prof, Univ Louisville, 79-82, chmn oral biol, 83-86, prof oral biol, Pharmacol & Toxicol, 82-91. *Concurrent Pos:* Nat Inst Dent Res fel, Univ Rochester, 67-70; adj scientist, Emory Univ, 87-88; vis scientist, Univ NC, Wilmington, 89-92; adj prof biol, Univ NC, Charlotte, 92-; adj asst prof bioeng, Clemson Univ, 97- *Mem:* Am Physiol Soc; Soc Exp Biol & Med; Am Soc Bone & Mineral Res; AAAS; Int Asn Dent Res; Sigma Xi. *Res:* Calcium metabolism; bone metabolism; effects of humoral, nutritional and physical factors on calcium homeostasis and connective tissue cells. *Mailing Add:* Orthopedic Surg Carolina's Med Ctr PO Box 32861 Charlotte NC 28232-2861. *Fax:* 704-355-2845; *E-Mail:* wkramp@juno.com

RAMPACEK, CARL, METALLURGY, MINERAL RESOURCES. *Current Pos:* dir, Mineral Resources Inst, Univ Ala, 76-83, assoc dir, 83-89, EMER DIR, MINERAL RESOURCES INST, UNIV ALA. *Personal Data:* b Omaha, Nebr, Aug 7, 13; m 39; c 2. *Educ:* Creighton Univ, BS, 35, MS, 37. *Honors & Awards:* Henry Krumb Lectr Metall, Am Inst Mining & Metall Engrs, 77; Robert Earll McConnell Award, Am Inst Mining, Metall & Petrol Engrs, 78. *Prof Exp:* Chemist, Phillips Petrol Co, Okla, 39-41; mineral technologist, US Bur Mines, Ala, 41-43, phys chemist, 43-45, metallurgist, Ariz, 45-51, chief, Process Develop & Res Br, Metall Div, 51-54, supvry metallurgist, Southwest Exp Sta, 54-60, res dir, Tuscaloosa Metall Res Ctr, 60-63, asst dir admin, 63-67, res dir, Col Park Metall Res Ctr, 67-69, asst dir metall, US Bur Mines, 69-75. *Mem:* Am Chem Soc; Am Inst Mining, Metall & Petrol Engrs; AAAS; Fedn Mat Soc (vpres-pres elect, 78). *Res:* Metallurgical research. *Mailing Add:* 5005 Old Montgomery Hwy No 14 Tuscaloosa AL 35405-6417

RAMPHELE, MAMPHEIA ALEETA, SOCIAL ANTHROPOLOGY. *Current Pos:* Sr researcher, Dept Social Anthrop, 86-91, dep vchancellor, 91-96, VCHANCELLOR, UNIV CAPE TOWN, SAFRICA, 96- *Personal Data:* b Pietersburg, SAfrica, Dec 28, 47. *Educ:* Univ Cape Town, PhD(social anthrop), 91. *Hon Degrees:* DSc, Tufts Univ, 91. *Mem:* Inst Med-Nat Acad Sci. *Res:* Western Cape hostel dwellers; social anthropology; adolescent research in Western Cape African townships. *Mailing Add:* Univ Cape Town Private Bag Cape Town 7701 South Africa

RAMPINO, MICHAEL ROBERT, CLIMATE CHANGE, GEOPHYSICS. *Current Pos:* asst prof, 85-90, ASSOC PROF, EARTH SYSTS GROUP, DEPT APPL SCI, NY UNIV, 91-; RES CONSULT, GODDARD INST SPACE STUDIES, NASA, 85- *Personal Data:* b Brooklyn, NY, Feb 8, 48. *Educ:* Hunter Col, BA, 68; Columbia Univ, PhD(geol), 78. *Prof Exp:* Instr geol, Hunter Col, 72-74 & Rutgers Univ, 76-78; Nat Acad Sci res assoc, NASA, 78-80, res assoc climatol, 80-85. *Concurrent Pos:* Adj instr geol, Lehman Col, NY, 74-77; instr, Earth Sci Dept, Fairleigh-Dickinson Univ, 78-79; vis asst prof, Dartmouth Col, 80, 82; lectr geol, Columbia Univ, 79-83; adj instr, Sch Visual Arts, 80-86; adj asst prof, Barnard Col, 82-83; ed, Climate History, Periodicity & Predictability, 87; adj asst prof, Sch Continuing Educ, NY Univ, 83-; res consult, Ctr Study Global Habitability, Columbia Univ, 85-; chair, Geol Sci Sect, NY Acad Sci, 89-90; rep, Int Climate Comn, Int Geosphere-Biosphere Proj, 87; mem, Nat Oceanic & Atmospheric Admin Joint US-USSR Working Group VIII on Climate Change, 89- *Mem:* AAAS; Am Geophys Union; Geol Soc Am; Soc Sedimentary Geol; NY Acad Sci; Int Soc Study Origin Life; Sigma Xi. *Res:* Climatic change especially the effects of volcanic eruptions and extraterrestrial impactors on climate and the environment; causes of mass extinctions, comet showers, and episodic volcanism; periodicity in the geologic record. *Mailing Add:* Earth & Environ Sci Prog/Dept Biol New York Univ New York NY 10003. *Fax:* 212-995-3820; *E-Mail:* rampin@is3.nyu.edu

RAMPONE, ALFRED JOSEPH, PHYSIOLOGY. *Current Pos:* from instr to prof, 55-71, actg chmn, Dept Physiol, 79-81, PROF PHYSIOL, MED SCH, UNIV ORE, 71- *Personal Data:* b Kelowna, BC, May 21, 25; nat US; m 57; c 4. *Educ:* Univ BC, BA, 47, MA, 50; Northwestern Univ, PhD, 54. *Prof Exp:* Res assoc physiol, Sch Med, Northwestern Univ, 54-55; instr, St Louis Univ, 55. *Mem:* Am Physiol Soc; Soc Exp Biol & Med. *Res:* Intestinal transport of lipids; energy metabolism. *Mailing Add:* Dept Physiol Sch Med Ore Health Sci Univ 3181 SW Sam Jackson Park Rd Portland OR 97201

RAMPP, DONALD L, SPEECH PATHOLOGY. *Current Pos:* PROF & HEAD, DEPT AUDIOL & SPEECH PATH, LA STATE UNIV MED CTR, NEW ORLEANS, 74- & PROF, DEPT OTOLARYNGOL & BIOCOMMUN & DEPT COMMUN DISORDERS, SCH MED, 74- *Personal Data:* b Meramac, Okla, Feb 10, 35; c 2. *Educ:* Northeastern State Col, BAEd, 57; Ohio State Univ, MA, 58; Univ Okla, PhD(speech path), 67. *Prof Exp:* Speech pathologist, Pub Sch, Okla, 57-58; asst prof speech path, Northeastern State Col, 58-62; chief speech path & audiol, Child Develop Ctr, Med Units, Univ Tenn, 66-69; assoc prof speech path & coordr med serv, Memphis State Univ, 69-74. *Concurrent Pos:* Speech pathologist, Med Ctr, Univ Okla, 66-68; supvr speech, lang & hearing, Collaborative Perinatal Res Proj, Med Units, Univ Tenn, Memphis, 69-, prof, 71-; consult, Vet Admin Hosp, Memphis, Tenn, 70- *Mem:* Am Cleft Palate Asn; Am Speech & Hearing Asn. *Res:* Auditory processing of verbal stimuli and its relationship to learning disabilities in children; voice quality characteristics of cleft palate persons. *Mailing Add:* 1116 Phosphor Ave Metairie LA 70005

RAMRAS, MARK BERNARD, MATHEMATICS. *Current Pos:* ASSOC PROF MATH, NORTHEASTERN UNIV, 75- *Personal Data:* b Brooklyn, NY, May 18, 41. *Educ:* Cornell Univ, BA, 62; Brandeis Univ, MA, 64, PhD(math), 67. *Prof Exp:* Asst prof math, Harvard Univ, 67-70 & Boston Col, 70-74; assoc prof math, Univ Mass, Boston, 74-75. *Mem:* Am Math Soc; Math Asn Am. *Res:* Ring theory; homological algebra. *Mailing Add:* Dept Math Northeastern Univ 02115-5096 MA 02115

RAMSAY, ARLAN (BRUCE), GROUPOIDS, REPRESENTATION THEORY. *Current Pos:* assoc prof, 68-72, PROF MATH, UNIV COLO, BOULDER, 72- *Personal Data:* b Dodge City, Kans, July 1, 37; m 58; c 2. *Educ:* Univ Kans, BA, 58; Harvard Univ, AM, 59, PhD(math), 62. *Prof Exp:* Instr math, Mass Inst Technol, 62-64; vis asst prof, Brandeis Univ, 64-65; asst prof, Univ Rochester, 65-68. *Mem:* Am Math Soc. *Res:* Locally compact groups; representation theory; groupoids in analysis; orthmodular lattices. *Mailing Add:* Campus Box 395 Univ Colo Boulder CO 80309-0395

RAMSAY, DAVID JOHN, medical physiology, for more information see previous edition

RAMSAY, DONALD ALLAN, MOLECULAR SPECTROSCOPY. *Current Pos:* RETIRED. *Personal Data:* b London, Eng, July 11, 22; Can citizen; m 46, Nancy Brayshaw; c Shirley M, Wendy K & Catharine J. *Educ:* Cambridge Univ, BA, 43, MA & PhD, 47, ScD, 76. *Hon Degrees:* Dr, Univ Reims, 69; Fil Hed Dr, Univ Stockholm, 82. *Honors & Awards:* Queen Elizabeth II Silver Jubilee Medal, 77; Centenary Medal, Royal Soc Can, 82; Chem Inst Can Medal, 92; Commemorative Medal, 125th Anniversary Confedn Can, 92. *Prof Exp:* Jr res officer, Nat Res Coun Can, 47-49, asst res officer, 50-54, assoc res officer, 55-60, sr res officer, 61-67, prin res officer, 68-87. *Concurrent Pos:* Guest lectr, Univ Ottawa, 55-67; vis prof, Univ Minn, 64, Univ Orsay, 66 & 75, Univ Stockholm, 67, 71 & 74, Univ Sao Paulo, 72 & 78, Univ Bologna, 73, Univ Western Australia & Australian Nat Univ, 76, Univ Wuppental, 88, Univ Christchurch, NZ, 91 & Univ Ulm, 92; regents lectr, Univ Calif, Irvine, 70; adv prof, EChina Normal Univ, Shanghai, 87. *Mem:* Fel Am Phys Soc; fel Chem Inst Can; Royal Soc Can (vpres acad sci, 75-76, hon treas, 76-79 & 88-91); fel Royal Soc; Can Asn Physicists. *Res:* Molecular spectroscopy, especially the spectra of free radicals. *Mailing Add:* 1578 Drake Ave Ottawa ON K1G 0L8 Can

RAMSAY, JOHN BARADA, DETONATION PHYSICS, PHYSICAL CHEMISTRY. *Current Pos:* RETIRED. *Personal Data:* b Phoenix, Ariz, Dec 28, 29; m 53, Barbara Hisenhoff; c Bryan, Kathleen, Carol & David. *Educ:* Univ Tex, El Paso, BS, 50; Univ Wis, PhD(anal chem), 55. *Prof Exp:* Staff mem anal chem, Los Alamos Sci Lab, 54-57, staff mem detonation physics, 57-70; assoc prof anal chem, Univ Petrol & Minerals, Saudi Arabia, 70-73; mem staff detonation physics, Los Alamos Nat Lab, 73-93. *Concurrent Pos:* Lectr, Univ NMex, Los Alamos Campus, 80-85. *Mem:* AAAS; Sigma Xi; Archaeol Inst Am. *Res:* Explosive initiation and related phenomena; saline deposits of arid areas. *Mailing Add:* Six Erie Lane Los Alamos NM 87544

RAMSAY, JOHN MARTIN, ANIMAL BREEDING. *Current Pos:* RETIRED. *Personal Data:* b Bethlehem, Pa, Apr 9, 30; m 94, Bernice Hollaway Meier; c Martin, Loren & Paige. *Educ:* Berea Col, BS, 52; Iowa State Univ, MS, 64, PhD(animal breeding), 66. *Prof Exp:* Instr agr, Warren Wilson Jr Col, 52-55; assoc dir rural life, John C Campbell Folk Sch, 66-67, dir, 67-73; asst prof recreation exten, Berea Col, 74-76, dir recreation & asst prof animal sci, Dept Animal Sci, 76-95. *Res:* Use of identical twins in dairy breeding research; genetic interpretation of heterogeneous variance of milk production; economic feasibility of crossing and upgrading a Jersey herd to Holsteins. *Mailing Add:* 520 Mapleview Dr University City MO 63130. *E-Mail:* johnberni@aol.com

RAMSAY, MAYNARD JACK, ENTOMOLOGY. *Current Pos:* plant quarantine inspector, Plant Quarantine Div, Agr Res Serv, USDA, 43-50, port entomologist, Plant Importations Br, 50-56, training off, 56-66, head post-entry quarantine sect, 66-67, AGRICULTURIST, ANIMAL & PLANT HEALTH INSPECTION SERV, PLANT PROTECTION & QUARANTINE PROGS, PLANT QUARANTINE DIV, AGR RES SERV, USDA, 67-; STAFF OFFICER NAT PROG PLANNING STAFF, 75- *Personal Data:* b Buffalo, NY, Nov 22, 14; m 41, Alberta J Wentworth; c Paul, Carolyn, Craig, Leigh & Bruce. *Educ:* Univ Buffalo, AB, 36, AM, 38; Cornell Univ, PhD, 42. *Honors & Awards:* Superior Serv Award, USDA, 56. *Prof Exp:* Asst zool, Univ Buffalo, 36-38; asst insect morphol & insect physiol, Cornell Univ, 39-40, biol, 40-42; hort inspector, Bur Plant Indust, State Dept Agr & Mkts, NY, 42-43. *Concurrent Pos:* Head publ coop econ insect rep weekly, Nat Econ Insect Surv, 73- *Mem:* Entom Soc Am. *Res:* Coleoptera of Allegany State Park, NY; Mexican bean beetle control; Dutch elm disease control; international plant quarantine; survey methods for economic insects; losses due to pests. *Mailing Add:* 3806 Viser Ct Bowie MD 20715

RAMSAY, OGDEN BERTRAND, ORGANIC CHEMISTRY, HISTORY OF CHEMISTRY. *Current Pos:* RETIRED. *Personal Data:* b Baltimore, Md, Sept 24, 32; m 62, Patricia Leyden; c Sean. *Educ:* Washington & Lee Univ, BS, 55; Univ Pa, PhD(org chem), 60. *Prof Exp:* Fel org chem, Ga Inst Technol, 59-61; asst prof chem, Univ Pac, 61-63; res fel org chem, Northwestern Univ, 63-64, inst chem, 64-65; from asst prof to prof chem, Eastern Mich Univ, 65-95, actg head dept, 80-82, head dept, 82-86. *Concurrent Pos:* NSF sci fac fel, Dept Chem, Univ Wis-Madison, 68-69. *Mem:* Am Chem Soc. *Res:* History of chemistry; chemical information retrieval; chemical education. *Mailing Add:* 1203 Sherman Ypsilanti MI 48197. *E-Mail:* c3@bizserve.com

RAMSAY, WILLIAM CHARLES, RESOURCE MANAGEMENT. *Current Pos:* CONSULT & WRITER, 86- *Personal Data:* b Jamaica, NY, Nov 6, 30; m 51, 66, 88; c 4. *Educ:* Univ Colo, BA, 52; Univ Calif, Los Angeles, MA, 57, PhD(physics), 62. *Prof Exp:* NSF fel, Univ Calif, San Diego, 62-63, res assoc physics, 63-64; asst prof, Univ Calif, Santa Barbara, 64-67; sr staff scientist, Systs Assocs, Inc, 67-72; sr environ economist, Atomic Energy Comn, 72-75; tech adv, Nuclear Regulatory Comn, 75-76; sr fel, Resources for the Future, 76-83; sr fel, Ctr for Stategic & Int Studies, Georgetown Univ, 83-85; sr staff officer, Nat Acad Sci, 85-86. *Mem:* Am Phys Soc; Am Astron Soc; Int Asn Energy Economists. *Res:* Energy strategies; environmental management. *Mailing Add:* 2930 Foxhall Rd NW Washington DC 20016

RAMSDALE, DAN JERRY, UNDERWATER ACOUSTICS, SIGNAL PROCESSING. *Current Pos:* res physicist, Acoust Div, Naval Res Lab, Washington, DC, 74-77, sr prin investr, Array Effects Br, Naval Ocean Res & Develop Activ, Stennis Space Ctr, Miss, 77-85, head, Arctic Acoust Br & tech prog mgr, Arctic Environ Acoust Prog, 85-88, asst dir ocean acoust & technol directorate, Naval Oceanog & Atmospheric Res Lab, 88-91, HEAD, OCEAN ACOUST BR, NAVAL RES LAB, STENNIS SPACE CTR DETACHMENT, MISS, 91- *Personal Data:* b El Paso, Tex, Dec 12, 42; m

69, Portia Rissler; c Jerry & Stuart. *Educ:* Univ Tex, El Paso, BS, 64; Kans State Univ, PhD(physics), 69. *Prof Exp:* Res dir, Gus Mfg, Inc, Globe Universal Sci, Inc, 69-74. *Concurrent Pos:* Adj prof, El Paso Community Col, 71-74; adj prof physics, Univ New Orleans, 81-; past chmn, Tech Comt Underwater Acoust, Oceanic Eng Soc, Inst Elec & Electronics Engrs. *Mem:* Acoust Soc Am; Sigma Xi; Am Geophys Union; Inst Elec & Electronics Engrs; Am Inst Physics. *Res:* Atmospheric acoustics, infrasonics, acoustic echo-sounding and the acoustic grenade sounding technique; electroacoustics and electrostatic transducer design; theoretical atomic physics, Auger and x-ray transition rates; seismic waves; underwater acoustics, especially low frequency propagation studies and fluctuations; the use of acoustic arrays as measurement tools; propagation and scattering of underwater acoustic energy in the Arctic Ocean; high frequency acoustics in shallow waters. *Mailing Add:* Naval Res Lab Ocean Acoust Br Stennis Space Center MS 39529

RAMSDELL, ROBERT COLE, GEOLOGY. *Current Pos:* RETIRED. *Personal Data:* b Trenton, NJ, July 8, 20; m 46; c 1. *Educ:* Lehigh Univ, BA, 43; Rutgers Univ, MS, 48; Princeton Univ, MA, 50. *Prof Exp:* With State Bur Mineral Res, NJ, 48-50; from instr to asst prof geol, Williams Col, 50-61; asst prof, Rutgers Univ, 61-66; assoc prof, Geosci Div, Montclair State Col, 66-*Mem:* AAAS; Geol Soc Am; Paleont Soc; Soc Econ Paleont & Mineral; Nat Asn Geol Teachers. *Res:* Paleontology and stratigraphy of Atlantic coastal plain; Silurian and Devonian Appalachian paleontology and stratigraphy. *Mailing Add:* 226 Winding Way Morrisville PA 19067-4825

RAMSDEN, HUGH EDWIN, ORGANIC CHEMISTRY. *Current Pos:* RETIRED. *Personal Data:* b Amesbury, Mass, May 30, 21; m 46; c 3. *Educ:* Mass Inst Technol, SB, 43, PhD(org chem), 46. *Prof Exp:* Res chemist, E I du Pont de Nemours & Co, NJ, 46-48; res chemist, Metal & Thermit Corp, 49-52, res suprv & head, Dept Org Chem, 52-59; res chemist, Esso Res & Eng Co, 59-61, res assoc, 61-70, Esso Agr Prod Lab Div, 66-70; res assoc, R T Vanderbilt Co, 70-71; mem staff, Rhodia Inc, 71-79; scientist, J T Baker Chem Co, 79-85, prin scientist, 85-87. *Mem:* Am Chem Soc; AAAS; NY Acad Sci. *Res:* Sugars; organoalkali reagents; fluorine chemistry; condensation polymers; plasticizers; coordination compounds; rubber; reaction of rubbers with organometallic compounds; organic synthesis; vinyl grignards; gasoline additives; pesticides synthesis; terpenes, perfume and flavor, fine chemicals; solid phases for L C of bioengineered products, proteins, RNA, DNA, and monoclonals. *Mailing Add:* 1556 Scholar Pl Toms River NJ 08755

RAMSEUR, GEORGE SHUFORD, BOTANY. *Current Pos:* RETIRED. *Personal Data:* b Burke Co, NC, July 19, 26; m 53; c 3. *Educ:* Elon Col, AB, 48; Univ NC, MEd, 53, PhD(bot), 59. *Prof Exp:* Teacher high sch, NC, 49-54; from instr to prof bot, Univ of the South, 58-93. *Mem:* AAAS; Bot Soc Am; Am Soc Plant Taxon. *Res:* Taxonomy of vascular plants; southern Appalachian flora. *Mailing Add:* Univ of the South Univ Ave Box 1218 Sewanee TN 37383

RAMSEY, ALAN T, PLASMA SPECTROSCOPY. *Current Pos:* RES SCIENTIST, PRINCETON PLASMA PHYSICS LAB, 79- *Personal Data:* b Madison, Wis, May 23, 38; m 60; c 2. *Educ:* Princeton Univ, AB, 60; Univ Wis, MS, 62, PhD(physics), 64. *Prof Exp:* Physicist, Lawrence Radiation Lab, Univ Calif, 64-67; asst prof physics, Brandeis Univ, 67-73; proj scientist, Am Sci & Eng, 74-76; res scientist, Mass Inst Technol, 76-78. *Res:* Optical pumping and atomic beam research on atomic and nuclear structure; x-ray astronomy; plasma diagnostics; spectroscopic instrumentation; medical instrumentation and research. *Mailing Add:* Princeton Plasma Physics Lab PO Box 451 Princeton NJ 08543. *Fax:* 609-243-2418; *E-Mail:* aramsey@pppl.gov

RAMSEY, ARTHUR ALBERT, PESTICIDE CHEMISTRY. *Current Pos:* Sr res chemist, Agr Chem Div, 68-77, mgr, compound acquisition, 77-88, SR METAB CHEMIST, AGR CHEM GROUP, FMC CORP, 88- *Personal Data:* b Schenectady, NY, Apr 11, 40; m 62; c 3. *Educ:* Albany Col Pharm, BS, 62; Univ Kans, PhD(med chem), 68. *Mem:* Am Chem Soc. *Res:* Metabolism and environmental fate studies of agricultural chemicals; physiological chemistry of plants, fungi and insects. *Mailing Add:* Agr Chem Group FMC Corp Box 8 Princeton NJ 08540. *Fax:* 602-951-3670; *E-Mail:* arthur_ramsey@fmc.com

RAMSEY, BRIAN GAINES, PHYSICAL ORGANIC CHEMISTRY, MOLECULAR SPECTROSCOPY. *Current Pos:* PROF CHEM, ROLLINS COL, 80- *Personal Data:* b Union, SC, Mar 17, 37; m 76; c 3. *Educ:* Univ SC, BSc, 56; Univ Wis, MSc, 58; Fla State Univ, PhD(chem), 62. *Prof Exp:* Fel, Pa State Univ, 62-64; asst prof, Univ Akron, 64-69; from assoc prof to prof chem, San Francisco State Univ, 69-80. *Concurrent Pos:* Sr Fulbright res fel, Ger, 72-73; Alexander von Humboldt Award, Germany, 72 & 73. *Mem:* Am Chem Soc. *Res:* Spectroscopic investigations of reactive intermediates in organic chemistry; electronic transitions in organometallics; chemistry of organoboranes. *Mailing Add:* Chem Rollins Col 1000 Holt Ave PO Box 2743 Winter Park FL 32789-4499

RAMSEY, CLOVIS BOYD, ANIMAL SCIENCE. *Current Pos:* PROF MEAT SCI, TEX TECH UNIV, 68- *Personal Data:* b Sneedville, Tenn, Aug 1, 34; m 58; c 2. *Educ:* Univ Tenn, BS, 56; Univ Ky, MS, 57, PhD(meats), 60. *Prof Exp:* Asst prof meat sci, Univ Tenn, 60-68. *Mem:* Am Meat Sci Asn; Am Soc Animal Sci; Inst Food Technol; Sigma Xi. *Res:* Physical, chemical and organoleptic properties of beef, lamb and pork; live-animal carcass evaluation; meat processing methods; factors affecting meat quality and quantity. *Mailing Add:* Animal Sci Tex Tech Univ Lubbock TX 79409-0001

RAMSEY, DERO SAUNDERS, DAIRY SCIENCE. *Current Pos:* From asst prof to prof, 56-90, EMER PROF DAIRY SCI, MISS STATE UNIV, 91- *Personal Data:* b Starkville, Miss, June 17, 28; m 50, Adelaide; c Lawrence A & Dero S Jr. *Educ:* Miss State Univ, BS, 50, MS, 53; Univ Wis, PhD(dairy husb), 57. *Mem:* AAAS; Am Dairy Sci Asn; Am Soc Animal Sci. *Res:* Physiology and nutrition of dairy cattle; animal waste management. *Mailing Add:* 1103 S Montgomery St Starkville MS 39759

RAMSEY, FRED LAWRENCE, MATHEMATICAL STATISTICS. *Current Pos:* asst prof, 66-72, assoc prof, 72-, PROF STATIST, ORE STATE UNIV. *Personal Data:* b Ames, Iowa, Mar 3, 39; m 66. *Educ:* Univ Ore, BA, 61; Iowa State Univ, MS, 63, PhD(statist), 64. *Prof Exp:* Asst prof statist, Iowa State Univ, 64; NIH fel, Johns Hopkins Univ, 65-66. *Mem:* Inst Math Statist. *Res:* Time series analysis; non-parametric statistics. *Mailing Add:* Dept Statist Ore State Univ Corvallis OR 97331-1801

RAMSEY, GORDON PAUL, HIGH ENERGY SPIN PHYSICS. *Current Pos:* PROF PHYSICS, LOYOLA UNIV, CHICAGO, 82- *Personal Data:* b Gary, Ind, Oct 7, 48; m 68, Dale Mooth; c Gordon Jr. *Educ:* Southern Ill Univ, BA, 70; Ill Inst Technol, MS, 72, PhD(physics), 82. *Prof Exp:* Lectr math, Europ Div, Univ Md, 74-77. *Concurrent Pos:* Vis assoc scientist, Argonne Nat Lab, 87; chair, Comt Int Educ, Am Asn Physics Teachers, 95-97. *Mem:* Am Asn Physics Teachers; Am Phys Soc; Sigma Xi. *Res:* Spin structure of elementary particles; provide theoretical background for interpreting high energy polarization experiments; planning and predicting outcomes of future related experiments. *Mailing Add:* Loyola Physics 6525 N Sheridan Chicago IL 60626. *Fax:* 773-508-3534; *E-Mail:* gpr@hep.anl.gov

RAMSEY, GWYNN W, PLANT SYSTEMATICS. *Current Pos:* chmn dept, 68-71 & 83-85, PROF BIOL, LYNCHBURG COL, 65-, CUR HERBARIUM, 66- *Personal Data:* b Drexel, NC, Nov 13, 31; m 52; c 3. *Educ:* Appalachian State Teachers Col, BS, 55, MA, 58; Univ Tenn, PhD(bot), 65. *Prof Exp:* Teacher high sch, NC, 55-58; instr biol & bot, Lees-McRae Col, 58-61. *Mem:* Bot Soc Am; Am Soc Plant Taxon. *Res:* Biosystematics of the genus Cimicifuga; Virginia flora. *Mailing Add:* Dept Biol Lynchburg Col 1501 Lakeside Dr Lynchburg VA 24501

RAMSEY, HAROLD ARCH, ANIMAL NUTRITION. *Current Pos:* assoc & prof animal sci, 63-65, prof animal sci & head dairy husb sect, 65-70, PROF ANIMAL SCI, NC STATE UNIV, 70- *Personal Data:* b Ft Scott, Kans, Sept 16, 27; m 51; c 3. *Educ:* Kans State Univ, BS, 50; NC State Univ, MS, 53, PhD(animal nutrit), 55. *Prof Exp:* From asst prof to assoc prof animal sci, NC State Univ, 55-62; vis assoc prof dairy sci, Univ Ill, 62-63. *Mem:* Am Dairy Sci Asn; Am Inst Nutrit. *Res:* Nutritional requirements of ruminants; nutritional value of soy protein for newborn calves. *Mailing Add:* 610 Ralph Dr Cary NC 27511

RAMSEY, JAMES MARVIN, ENERGY METABOLISM. *Current Pos:* PRE-MED ADV, 92- *Personal Data:* b Wilmington, Ohio, May 21, 24; m 92, Mildred Gorsuch; c 3. *Educ:* Wilmington Col, BS, 48; Miami Univ, MS, 51. *Prof Exp:* Instr biol sci, Cedarville Col, 48-52; res assoc skin allergy & toxicol, Col Med, Univ Cincinnati, 52-53; instr physiol, Miami Univ, 55-60; assoc prof biol sci, Univ Dayton, 64-80, prof, 80-88, emer prof, 92. *Concurrent Pos:* NSF instnl res grants, 66-68 & 71-; NIH res grant, 68-71. *Mem:* AAAS; Sigma Xi; Physiol Soc. *Res:* Carbon monoxide toxicology; red blood cell metabolism; the response of erythrocyte 2, 3-diphosphoglycerate to hypoxic stress; the relation of non-specific stress to asthmatic bronchoconstriction; regulation of plasma glucose and lipoproteins; author of textbook on pathophysiology. *Mailing Add:* 11138 W Cove Harbor Dr Crystal River FL 34428

RAMSEY, JED JUNIOR, ZOOLOGY. *Current Pos:* assoc prof, 65-72, PROF BIOL, LAMAR UNIV, 72- *Personal Data:* b Dighton, Kans, Oct 17, 25; m 48; c 4. *Educ:* Kans State Univ, BS, 49; Kans State Teachers Col, MS, 62; Okla State Univ, PhD(zool), 66. *Prof Exp:* Teacher high schs, Kans, 50-63. *Mem:* Sigma Xi; Am Ornith Union; Wilson Ornith Soc; Cooper Ornith Soc. *Res:* Metabolic changes in Chimney Swifts at lowered environmental temperatures; ecology and behavior of ciconiiform birds; avifauna of the Beaumont unit of the Big Thicket. *Mailing Add:* 875 Belvedere Beaumont TX 77706-4301

RAMSEY, JERRY DWAIN, ERGONOMICS, HUMAN FACTORS & SAFETY ENGINEERING. *Current Pos:* from asst prof to assoc prof, 67-75, assoc vpres acad affairs, 77-89, PROF INDUST ENG, TEX TECH UNIV, 75-, ASSOC VPRES OPER, 89- *Personal Data:* b Tulia, Tex, Nov 6, 33; wid; c Randall, Randa, Rachel & Richard. *Educ:* Tex A&M Univ, BS, 55, MS, 60; Tex Tech Univ, PhD(indust eng), 67. *Honors & Awards:* Citation, Outstanding Contrib Ergonomics, Inst Indust Eng, 85. *Prof Exp:* Indust eng trainee, Square D Co, Wis, 53, Mich, 54; engr, Great Western Drilling Co, Tex, 55; indust engr, Collins Radio Co, Tex, 57-58; instr indust eng, Tex A&M Univ, 58-60, asst prof, 60-61; tech staff mem, Sandia Corp, NMex, 61-65. *Concurrent Pos:* Mem, President's Comt Employment of Handicapped; consult, Occup Health & Safety Admin, 72-, Nat Inst Occup Health & Safety, 73-, Us Bureau Int Labor Affairs, 74-, US Consumer Prod Safety Comn, 76-; chmn, Nat Stand Adv Comt Heat Stress, 73-74; exec comt, Nat Safety Coun Pub Employees, 74-90; bd dirs, Tex Safety Asn, 76- & Southwest Lighthouse for the Blind, 82-91; ed, Int J Indust Ergonomics, 85- *Mem:* Nat Soc Prof Engrs; Inst Indust Engrs; Human Factors Soc; Am Indust Hyg Asn; Am Soc Safety Engrs; Syst Safety Soc. *Res:* Ergonomics; human factors engineering; product safety; occupational safety and health; management systems and optimization techniques; effects of environmental stressors on human performance; safety behavior and psychology, ergonomics applications for the disabled. *Mailing Add:* Dept Indust Eng Tex Tech Univ Lubbock TX 79409-3061

RAMSEY, JOHN CHARLES, TOXICOLOGY. *Current Pos:* RETIRED. *Personal Data:* b Yakima, Wash, June 19, 33. *Educ:* Univ Puget Sound, BS, 55; Ore State Univ, PhD(plant biochem), 64; Am Bd Toxicol, dipl. *Prof Exp:* Res chemist pesticide residues, Dept Agr-Chemicals, Dow Chem Co, 64-71, res toxicologist indust & agr chem, 71-83, toxicologist, anal & environ chem, dept Toxicol, 83-88. *Mem:* Soc Toxicol. *Res:* Pharmacokinetics and toxicology of agricultural and industrial chemicals; mathematical modeling of chemicals in biological systems. *Mailing Add:* 2261 S Diamond Barr Lane Tucson AZ 85713

RAMSEY, JOHN SCOTT, fish biology, for more information see previous edition

RAMSEY, KATHLEEN SOMMER, toxicology, for more information see previous edition

RAMSEY, LAWRENCE WILLIAM, ASTRONOMICAL SPECTROSCOPY, ASTRONOMICAL INSTRUMENTATION. *Current Pos:* from asst prof to assoc prof astron, 76-88, PROF ASTRON & ASTROPHYS, PA STATE UNIV, 88- *Personal Data:* b Louisville, Ky, Mar 14, 45; m 70, Mary E Gessling. *Educ:* Univ Mo, St Louis, BA, 68; Kans State Univ, MS, 72; Ind Univ, PhD(astron), 76. *Prof Exp:* Simulation systs design engr, Kitt Peak Nat Observ, 66-70, res asst solar physics, 72-73. *Concurrent Pos:* Proj scientist, Spectros Surv Telescope, joint proj between Univ Tex, Pa State, Stanford and others, 90- *Mem:* Am Astron Soc; Int Astron Union; Astron Soc Pac. *Res:* Solar-like phenomenon on other stars; stellar spectroscopy precision radial velocities and astronomical instrumentation. *Mailing Add:* Pa State Univ 525 Davey Lab University Park PA 16802. *Fax:* 814-865-3399; *E-Mail:* lwr@astro.psu.edu

RAMSEY, LLOYD HAMILTON, MEDICAL ADMINISTRATION, INTERNAL MEDICINE. *Current Pos:* instr, 54-55, asst prof, 55-63, investr, Howard Hughes Med Inst, 55-65, assoc prof, 63-78, PROF MED, SCH MED, VANDERBILT UNIV, 78-, ASSOC DEAN, 75- *Personal Data:* b Lexington, Ky, June 10, 21; wid; c 4. *Educ:* Univ Ky, BS, 42; Wash Univ, MD, 50; Am Bd Internal Med, dipl, 59. *Prof Exp:* Intern med, Duke Univ, 50-51; asst resident, Peter Bent Brigham Hosp, Boston, 51-52, asst, 52-53. *Concurrent Pos:* Fel, Harvard Med Sch, 52-53; res fel, Sch Med, Vanderbilt Univ, 53-54; chief resident physician, Univ Hosp, Vanderbilt Univ, 54-55; consult, Mid Tenn State Tuberc Hosp, Nashville, 55-65. *Mem:* AAAS; fel Am Col Physicians; Am Clin & Climat Asn; Sigma Xi. *Res:* Pulmonary physiology, especially gas diffusion and relationships of external respiration to blood flow. *Mailing Add:* Vanderbilt Univ Sch Med Nashville TN 37232

RAMSEY, MAYNARD, III, BIOMEDICAL ENGINEERING. *Current Pos:* vpres res & develop, 79-82, VPRES SCI & TECHNOL, CRITIKON, 82- *Personal Data:* b Birmingham, Ala, Aug 28, 43; m 69; c 2. *Educ:* Emory Univ, BA, 65; Duke Univ, MD, 69, PhD(biomed eng), 75. *Prof Exp:* Dir res, Appl Med Res Corp, 75-79. *Mem:* Inst Elec & Electronics Engrs; Asn Advan Med Instrumentation. *Res:* Principles and mechanism of indirect and direct measurement of blood pressure; body surface electrocardiography and its implementation for clinical use. *Mailing Add:* 2423 Sunset Dr Tampa FL 33629

RAMSEY, NORMAN FOSTER, JR, PHYSICS, MOLECULAR BEAMS. *Current Pos:* from assoc prof to prof, Harvard Univ, 47-66, dir nuclear lab, 48-50 & 52, Higgins prof, 66-87, EMER HIGGINS PROF PHYSICS, HARVARD UNIV, 87- *Personal Data:* b Washington, DC, Aug 27, 15; m 40, 85, Elinor Jameson & Ellie Welch; c Margaret (Kasschau), Patty (Ramsey), Winifred (Swarr) & Janet (Farrell). *Educ:* Columbia Univ, AB, 35, PhD(physics), 40; Cambridge Univ, AB, 37, MA, 41, DSc, 54. *Hon Degrees:* MA, Harvard Univ, 47; DSc, Case Western Reserve Univ, 68, Middlebury Col, 69, Oxford Univ, 73, Rockefeller Univ, 86, Univ Chicago, 89, DCL Oxford Univ, 89, Univ Houston, 91, Carleton Coll, 92 & Univ Mich, 93. *Honors & Awards:* Nobel Prize, 89; Lawrence Award & Medal, 60; Davisson-Germer Prize, Am Phys Soc, 74; Medal Hon, Inst Elec & Electronics Engrs, 84; Rabi Prize, 85; Monie Ferst Prize, Sigma Xi, 85; Karl Compton Prize, Am Inst Physics, 85; Rumford Prize, 88; Nat Medal Sci, 89; Oersted medal, Am Asn Physics Teachers, 88; Pupin Medal, 92; Einstein Medal, 93; Erice Science Peace Prize, 92; Vannevar Bush Award, Nat Sci Bd, 95; Alexander Hamilton Award, 95. *Prof Exp:* Assoc physics, Univ Ill, 40-42; assoc prof, Columbia Univ, 42-47. *Concurrent Pos:* Consult, Off Sci Res & Develop & Nat Defense Res Comt, 40-45; consult, US Secy War, 42-45; res assoc, Radiation Lab, Mass Inst Technol, 40-42; group leader & assoc div head, Atomic Energy Proj Lab, Los Alamos Sci Lab, Univ Calif, 43-45; head, Physics Dept, Brookhaven Nat Lab, 46-47; mem sci adv bd, US Dept Air Force, 49-56 & US Dept Defense, 54-58; trustee, Brookhaven Nat Lab, 52-56, Carnegie Endowment Int Peace, 63- & Rockefeller Univ, 76-; Guggenheim fel, 54-55; sci adv, NATO, 58-59; mem gen adv comt, AEC, 60-72; chmn high energy physics panel, Sci Adv Bd, Off President, 63; dir, Varian Assocs, 63-66, sr fel, Harvard Soc Fels, 69-81; pres, Univs Res Asn, 66-81 & chmn physics sect, AAAS, 77-78; Eastman prof, Oxford Univ, 73-74; chmn bd govrs, Am Inst Physics, 80-86; vis prof, Colo, 86-87, Chicago, 88, Mich, 89-92. *Mem:* Nat Acad Sci; AAAS; fel Am Phys Soc (pres, 78-79); Am Philos Soc; Fr Acad Sci. *Res:* Nuclear moments; molecular beams; high energy particles; nuclear interactions in molecules; deuteron quadrupole moment; molecular structure atomic clocks; diamagnetism; thermodynamics; proton-proton scattering; high energy accelerators; atomic masers; electron scattering; neutrons. *Mailing Add:* Lyman Physics Lab Harvard Univ Cambridge MA 02138. *Fax:* 617-496-5144; *E-Mail:* ramsey@physics.harvard.edu

RAMSEY, PAUL ROGER, POPULATION BIOLOGY, GENETICS. *Current Pos:* assoc prof, 75-78, PROF ZOOL, LA TECH UNIV, 78- *Personal Data:* b Lake Charles, La, July 27, 45; m 67, 93, Dagmara Sreckovic; c 2. *Educ:* Tex Tech Univ, BS, 67, MS, 69; Univ Ga, PhD(zool & ecol), 74; La Tech Univ, BA, 89. *Prof Exp:* Asst prof biol, Presby Col, 73-75. *Concurrent Pos:* Adj asst prof biol, Fla Inst Technol, 78-; vis prof, Livestock Res Inst, Univ Novi Sad, Yugoslavia, 89-90; Fulbright fel, Yugoslavia. *Mem:* Am Soc Mammalogists; Soc Study Evolution. *Res:* Ecological genetics and protein variation of marine fish and small mammals. *Mailing Add:* Dept Biol Sci La Tech Univ 305 Wisteria St Ruston LA 71272-0001. *E-Mail:* pramsey@vm.cc.latech.edu

RAMSEY, PAUL W, METALLURGY. *Current Pos:* RETIRED. *Personal Data:* b Wilkinsburg, Pa, Feb 17, 19; m 42; c 3. *Educ:* Carnegie Inst Technol, BS, 40; Univ Wis, MS, 56. *Honors & Awards:* Nat Award, Am Welding Soc, 71; S W Miller Mem Award, Am Welding Soc, 80. *Prof Exp:* Sr investr, NJ Zinc Co, Pa, 40-51; proj engr, A O Smith Corp, 51-56, supvr, 56-65, mgr weiding, 65-81, mgr welding & metall res & develop, 81- *Mem:* Am Welding Soc (vpres, 72-75, pres, 75-76); Am Inst Mining, Metall & Petrol Eng; fel Am Soc Metals; Soc Automotive Engrs; Soc Metall Engrs. *Res:* Welding metallurgy, mechanical testing; welding controls; power sources; physical metallurgy. *Mailing Add:* 3016 E Newport Ct Milwaukee WI 53211

RAMSEY, RICHARD HAROLD, PHYTOPATHOLOGY, MYCOLOGY. *Personal Data:* b San Francisco, Calif, Nov 21, 36; m 60; c 2. *Educ:* Univ Calif, Davis, 58, PhD(phytopath), 66. *Prof Exp:* From asst prof to prof biol, Rocky Mountain Col, 75-85; vpres & dean, Northland Col, 85-90. *Res:* Genetics of Pleospora herbarum. *Mailing Add:* 86 E 15th St Arcata CA 95521

RAMSEY, ROBERT BRUCE, COMPUTATIONAL CHEMISTRY, NEUROCHEMISTRY. *Current Pos:* ASSOC CLIN PROF, ST LOUIS UNIV, 79-, SR CONSULT, MATTSON JACK GROUP, 93- *Personal Data:* b Moline, Ill, Jan 4, 44; m 67, Penny T Germain; c Anne & Sarah. *Educ:* Augustana Col, BA, 66; St Louis Univ, PhD(biochem), 71, MBA, 84. *Prof Exp:* From asst prof to assoc prof neurol, Sch Med, St Louis, 72-79; prod mgr, Sherwood Med, 79-85; mgr planning & develop, McDonnell Douglas Health Systs, Co, 85-87, mgr, mergers & acquisitions, Info Syst Group, 87-88, mgr planning & mkt res, 88-90; mgr mkt planning, Asian Sales & Mkt, Tripos Assoc, 90-93. *Concurrent Pos:* NIH fel, Inst Neurol, Univ London, 71-73. *Mem:* AAAS; Am Chem Soc; Brit Biochem Soc; Am Soc Biol Chemists. *Res:* Pharmaceutical market modeling. *Mailing Add:* 1133 Ridgelynn Dr St Louis MO 63124-1219. *Fax:* 314-469-6794

RAMSHAW, JOHN DAVID, STATISTICAL MECHANICS, FLUID DYNAMICS. *Current Pos:* PHYSICIST, LAWRENCE LIVERMORE NAT LAB, 96- *Personal Data:* b Salt Lake City, Utah, Mar 20, 44; div; c 2. *Educ:* Col Idaho, BS, 65; Mass Inst Technol, PhD(chem physics), 70. *Prof Exp:* Res assoc & assoc instr, Univ Utah, 71-72; staff scientist physics & eng, Appl Theory Inc, 72-73; assoc scientist, Aerojet Nuclear Co, 73-75; staff mem theoret div, Los Alamos Nat Lab, 75-86; sci & eng fel, Idaho Nat Eng Lab, 86-96. *Concurrent Pos:* Air Force Off Sci Res-Nat Res Coun res award chem physics, Univ Md, 70-71. *Mem:* Am Phys Soc. *Res:* Equilibrium and nonequilibrium statistical mechanics; dielectrics; liquids; nonlinear stochastic processes; transport far from equilibrium; analytical and numerical fluid dynamics; turbulence; multicomponent flow; chemically reactive flow; two-phase flow; thermal plasmas. *Mailing Add:* 5236 Felicia Ave Livermore CA 94550-2305. *E-Mail:* ramshaw@llnl.gov

RAMSLEY, ALVIN OLSEN, PHYSICAL CHEMISTRY. *Current Pos:* RETIRED. *Personal Data:* b North Bergen, NJ, Feb 6, 20; m 49, Florence Jensen; c Walter C & Kenneth R. *Educ:* Houghton Col, BS, 43; Columbia Univ, MA, 48. *Prof Exp:* Chemist, Gen Elec Co, 48-50; chemist, Gen Test Labs, 50-53, res chemist, Natick Labs, US Army QM, 53-84, chief Countersurveillance Sect, Natick Res & Develop Command, 74-84. *Mem:* Am Chem Soc; Inter-Soc Color Coun; Sigma Xi. *Res:* Physical chemistry of excited states as related to chemical structure, absorption spectra, and luminescence; photodegradation of dyes; materials research for visual and non-visual counter-surveillance measures; vision, color measurement and colorant formulation. *Mailing Add:* PO Box 358 Sherborn MA 01770

RAMSPOTT, LAWRENCE DEWEY, STRATEGIC PLANNING. *Current Pos:* SR STAFF, TRW ENVIRON SAFETY SYSTS, INC, 93- *Personal Data:* b Jacksonville, Fla, Dec 9, 34. *Educ:* Principia Col, BS, 56; Pa State Univ, PhD(geol), 62. *Prof Exp:* Asst prof geol, Univ Ga, 62-67; sr geologist, Lawrence Livermore Nat Lab, 67-70, group leader geol & geophys, 70-74, sect leader geol, 74-75, sr scientist, 75-76, proj leader nuclear waste mgt, 76-88, assoc prog leader, Energy Prog, 88-93. *Concurrent Pos:* NSF grant, 63-66. *Mem:* AAAS; Geol Soc Am; Am Nuclear Soc. *Res:* Petrology, mineralogy and structural geology; applied geology and geophysics; relation between site geology and containment of radioactivity and seismic coupling from an underground nuclear explosion; underground radionuclide migration; high-level nuclear waste disposal. *Mailing Add:* 1243 Sail Ct Byron CA 94514

RAMSTAD, PAUL ELLERTSON, FOOD SCIENCE. *Current Pos:* CONSULT, 78- *Personal Data:* b Minneapolis, Minn, Jan 30, 18; m 41, 88; c 4. *Educ:* Univ Minn, BS, 39, PhD(agr biochem), 42. *Prof Exp:* Soybean agent, USDA, 39-42; res chemist, Gen Mills, Inc, Minn, 42-46, head cereal res sect, 47-48; assoc prof biochem, Sch Nutrit, Cornell Univ, 48-53; asst dir res, Oscar Mayer & Co, Wis, 53-55; tech dir dept qual control, Gen Mills, Inc, 55-65; vpres res & develop, Am Maize-Prod Co, 65-68, pres, Corn Processing Processing Div, 69-75, pres, Co, 76-78. *Concurrent Pos:* Ed, Cereal Sci

Today, 57-62; sci ed, Cereal Chem, 78-84. *Mem:* AAAS; Am Chem Soc; Am Asn Cereal Chemists (pres, 64-65); Inst Food Technol. *Res:* Research administration; cereal chemistry and technology; grain storage; starches; syrups; vegetable gums; packaged foods; nutrition. *Mailing Add:* PO Box 841 Ithaca NY 14851-0841

RAMULU, MAMIDALA, MECHANICS OF COMPOSITE MACHINING, MECHANICS OF ABRASIVE WATERJET. *Current Pos:* Postdoctoral fel mech eng, Univ Wash, 82, res asst prof, 82-85, asst prof, 85-90, ASSOC PROF MECH ENG, UNIV WASH, 90- *Personal Data:* b Andhra Pradesh, India, Sept 19, 49; m 85; c 2. *Educ:* Osmania Univ, India, BE, 74; Indian Inst Technol, New Delhi, MTech, 77; Univ Wash, PhD(mech eng), 82. *Honors & Awards:* Ralph R Teetor Award, Soc Automotive Engrs, 87. *Concurrent Pos:* Mem, Fracture Tech Activ Comt & Res Papers Rev Comt, Soc Exp Mech, 86-; lectr, Indian Inst Metals, Am Soc Metals, 86; chmn, Fatigue Tech Comt, Soc Exp Mech, 88-, Mat Processing Comt, Am Soc Mech Engrs, 89-; NSF Presidential Young Investr Award, 89; AT&T Found award, Am Soc Eng Educ, 89. *Mem:* Am Soc Eng Educ; Am Soc Mech Engrs; Soc Exp Mech; Soc Mfg Engrs; Soc Automotive Engrs; Am Soc Metals. *Res:* Development of production methods, modeling, and optimization of production processes; traditional and nontraditional machining methods to process engineered materials; EDM and ultrasonic machining process; fracture mechanics; author of numerous technical publications. *Mailing Add:* Dept Mech Eng Box 352600 Univ Wash Seattle WA 98195-0001

RAMUS, JOSEPH S, ALGAE, PHYSIOLOGY. *Current Pos:* assoc prof, 78-85, asst dir, 81-89 actg dir, 89-90, PROF BOT, DUKE UNIV, 85-, DIR MARINE LAB, 90- *Personal Data:* b Detroit, Mich, May 7, 40; m 81; c 3. *Educ:* Univ Calif, Berkeley, AB, 63, PhD(bot), 68. *Prof Exp:* From asst prof to assoc prof biol, Yale Univ, 68-78. *Mem:* Am Soc Limnol & Oceanog; Phycol Soc Am; Am Soc Univ Prof; Am Geophys Union. *Res:* Algal ecological physiology; estuarine dynamics; carbon partitioning. *Mailing Add:* Dept Bot Duke Univ Durham NC 27706-8001

RAMWELL, PETER WILLIAM, PHARMACOLOGY, PHYSIOLOGY. *Current Pos:* PROF PHYSIOL & BIOPHYS, SCH MED, GEORGETOWN UNIV, 74- *Personal Data:* b US citizen. *Educ:* Univ Sheffield, BS, 51; Univ Leeds, PhD(physiol), 58. *Prof Exp:* Mem sci staff, Med Res Coun, Univ Leeds, 55-58; sr lectr pharmacol, Univ Bradford, 58-60; mem sci staff, Med Res Coun, Univ Birmingham & Oxford Univ, 60-64; sr scientist, Worcester Found Exp Biol, Mass, 64-69; assoc prof physiol, Stanford Univ, 69-74. *Concurrent Pos:* Indust consult, UK & US; dir, NIMH Postdoctoral Training Prog, 67-69; ed, Prostaglandins J, 74- *Mem:* Am Physiol Soc; Physiol Soc; Am Pharmacol Soc; Brit Pharmacol Soc. *Res:* Sex steroids and cardiovascular disease; eicosanoids. *Mailing Add:* Dept Physiol Georgetown Univ Med Ctr 3900 Reservoir Rd NW Washington DC 20007-2187

RANA, MOHAMMAD A, PLANT CYTO-HISTOCHEMISTRY, BOTANY-ECOLOGY. *Current Pos:* ASST PROF ECOL, ST JOSEPH'S COL, 90- *Personal Data:* b Lahore, Pakistan, May 1, 49; US citizen; m 89; c 2. *Educ:* Punjab Univ, Pakistan, BSc, 69, MSc, 71; Univ London, Eng, PhD(cell biol), 82. *Hon Degrees:* MIB, Inst Biol London, 81. *Prof Exp:* Lectr biol, Shiraz Univ, Sharaz, Iran, 73-79; demonstr biol, Univ London, Eng, 79-81; sr lectr bot, Univ Port Harcourt, Nigeria, 82-86; chairperson, Sci Dept, Mother Cabrini Inst, 86-90. *Concurrent Pos:* Environ consult, Univ Port Harcourt, Nigeria, 83-86. *Res:* Identification of plant secondary products and their interaction with plant and animal life; searching resistant varieties of halophytes, a possible solution for oil spill problem. *Mailing Add:* Dept Biol St Josephs Col 2V5 Clinton Ave Brooklyn NY 11205-3602

RANA, MOHAMMED WAHEEDUZ-ZAMAN, HUMAN ANATOMY. *Current Pos:* From instr to asst prof, 68-78, ASSOC PROF ANAT, SCH MED, ST LOUIS UNIV, 78- *Personal Data:* b Lahore, Pakistan, May 28, 34; US citizen; m 65; c 4. *Educ:* Olivet Col, BA, 64; Wayne State Univ MS, 66, PhD(anat), 68. *Mem:* Am Asn Anat; Soc Exp Biol & Med. *Res:* Study of RPE-retinal complex. *Mailing Add:* Dept Anat & Neurobiol St Louis Sch Med 1402 S Grand Blvd St Louis MO 63104

RANA, RAM S, solid state physics, spectroscopy, for more information see previous edition

RANADE, MADHAV (ARUN) BHASKAR, CHEMICAL ENGINEERING, PARTICLE TECHNOLOGY. *Current Pos:* PRES & OWNER, PARTICLE TECH INC, 87- *Personal Data:* b Indore City, India, Sept 27, 42; m 68; c 1. *Educ:* Nagpur Univ, BTech, 6; Ill Inst Technol, MS, 68, PhD(chem eng), 74. *Prof Exp:* Res engr chem eng, Chicago Bridge & Iron Co, 68-70; res engr particle technol, IIT Res Inst, 72-77; sr engr, Res Triangle Inst, 77-78, sect head particle technol, 78-87, mgr, Environ Technol Dept, 80, dir, Ctr Separation Processes, 84-87. *Concurrent Pos:* Adj assoc prof, dept environ eng, Univ NC, 80- *Mem:* Fine Particle Soc; Am Inst Chem Engrs; Am Chem Soc; Sigma Xi; Air Pollution Control Asn; AAAS; Int Asn Colloid & Interface Scientists. *Res:* Fine particles technology; aerosol science; air pollution measurement and control; particle size measurement; powder technology; colloid and surface science. *Mailing Add:* 9705 Cedar Lane Bethesda MD 20814

RANADE, MADHUKAR G, PROCESS METALLURGY, TECHNOLOGY DEVELOPMENT & OPERATIONS TECHNOLOGY. *Current Pos:* engr, Inland Steel Co, 77-79, res engr, 79-82, sr res engr, 82-85, sect mgr, 85-89, MGR, INLAND STEEL CO, 89- *Personal Data:* b Bombay, India, Sept 8, 53; m 79, Karen; c Brian & Erica. *Educ:* Indian Inst Technol, Bombay, BTech, 75; Univ Calif, Berkeley, MS, 77. *Honors & Awards:* Silver Medal, Indian Inst Technol, Bombay, India, 75; J E Johnson Award, Iron & Steel Soc, 89. *Prof Exp:* Res asst, Univ Calif, 75-77. *Concurrent Pos:* Reviewer, Ironmaking & Steelmaking J, 80-82; leader US deleg, ISO Meeting, Ottawa, Can, 82; key reader, Transactions of Iron & Steel Soc, 83-85; prog comt, Iron & Steel Soc, Am Inst Mining, Metall & Petrol Engrs, 83-; invited lectr, Univ Minn, Duluth, 87; direct steelmaking prog adv, Am Iron & Steel Inst, 89- *Mem:* Am Soc Testing & Mat; Iron & Steel Inst Japan; Iron & Steel Soc. *Res:* Development of new processes and improvement of existing processes for production of raw materials, iron and steel; responsible for leading and managing process research and development, and technology transfer and implementation for a major steel manufacturer; operations technology iron and steelmaking. *Mailing Add:* Inland Steel 2-975 East Chicago IN 46312. *Fax:* 219-399-4835

RANADE, VINAYAK VASUDEO, MEDICINAL CHEMISTRY. *Current Pos:* SR PHARMACOLOGIST, ABBOTT LABS, 75- *Personal Data:* b Wani, India, Feb 5, 38; m 64, Meghana; c Tanuja. *Educ:* Univ Bombay, BSc, 58, MSc, 61, PhD(org chem), 65. *Honors & Awards:* GC Prize for Nuclear Med & Radio Pharmacol, Tel-Aviv Univ, Israel, 74. *Prof Exp:* Res assoc med chem, Col Pharm, Univ Mich, Ann Arbor, 65-75, univ fel, 65-68. *Mem:* Am Chem Soc; Am Pharmaceut Asn; Acad Pharmaceut Sci; fel Am Inst Chemists; Sigma Xi. *Res:* Synthetic medicinal chemistry and synthesis of radio pharmaceuticals; drug metabolism, biotransformation. *Mailing Add:* 1219 Deer Trail Libertyville IL 60048-1394

RANADIVE, NARENDRANATH SANTURAM, IMMUNOLOGY, EXPERIMENTAL PATHOLOGY. *Current Pos:* RETIRED. *Personal Data:* b Bombay, India, Sept 9, 30; m 60, Kishori; c Salil & Madhuvanti. *Educ:* Univ Bombay, BSc, 52, MSc, 57; McGill Univ, PhD(biochem), 65. *Prof Exp:* Res asst biophys, Indian Cancer Res Ctr, Bombay, India, 58-59; analyst, Glaxo Labs, Bombay, 59-60; from asst prof to assoc prof, Univ Toronto, 69-78, tenured prof path, Dept Path, 78-96. *Concurrent Pos:* Fel, Scripps Clin & Res Found, Calif, 66-69; Med Res Coun Can scholar, 69-72. *Mem:* Am Asn Pathologists; Am Asn Immunol; Am Soc Photobiol; Int Pigment Cell Soc; NY Acad Sci. *Res:* Cellular mechanism in anaphylaxis; immunologic tissue injury; chemical mediators in neutrophil lysosomes; mechanism of the release of lysosomal constituents; free radicals in phototoxic reactions; phototoxic cutaneous reactions. *Mailing Add:* Dept Path Med Sci Bldg Univ Toronto Toronto ON M5S 1A8 Can. *Fax:* 416-978-5959

RANALLI, ANTHONY WILLIAM, FOOD TECHNOLOGY. *Current Pos:* VPRES QUAL ASSURANCE, PEPPERIDGE FARMS INC, 79- *Personal Data:* b Portchester, NY, Jan 13, 30; m 64; c 3. *Educ:* Syracuse Univ, BS, 52, MS, 53, PhD(microbiol), 59. *Prof Exp:* Res supvr, Continental Baking Co, 59-63; tech dir refined syrups & sugars div, CPC Int, Inc, 63-70; asst to pres, Pepperidge Farm, Inc, 70-73, dir qual control, 70-77; dir qual assurance, Quaker Oats Co, Chicago, 77-79. *Mem:* Am Chem Soc; Inst Food Technol; fel Am Inst Chem. *Res:* Chemistry; product development; quality control. *Mailing Add:* 46 Undercliff Rd Pepperidge Farms Inc Trumbull CT 06611-2547

RANCK, JAMES BYRNE, JR, NEUROSCIENCE, SPATIAL BEHAVIOR. *Current Pos:* PROF NEUROSCI, STATE UNIV NY, DOWNSTATE MED CTR, 75- *Educ:* Columbia Univ, MD, 55. *Res:* Hippocampus. *Mailing Add:* Dept Physiol State Univ NY Health Sci Ctr 450 Clarkson Ave Brooklyn NY 11203-2012

RANCK, JOHN PHILIP, MOLECULAR STRUCTURE. *Current Pos:* from asst prof to assoc prof, 63-69, PROF CHEM, ELIZABETHTOWN COL, 69- *Personal Data:* b Needmore, Pa, Aug 20, 36; m 61, Henrietta Kohr; c Laura (White) & Sara A. *Educ:* Elizabethtown Col, BS, 58; Princeton Univ, MA, 60, PhD(chem), 62. *Prof Exp:* Instr chem, Upsala Col, 62-63. *Concurrent Pos:* NSF partic, Univ Calif, Berkeley, 64; res guest, H C Orsted Inst, Copenhagen Univ, 70-71 & 94. *Mem:* AAAS; Am Chem Soc; Am Asn Physics Teachers; fel Sigma Xi. *Res:* Molecular orbital theory; molecular spectroscopy; equilibria of transition metal ions with asymmetric ligands; computers in chemistry; molecular visualization and chemical education. *Mailing Add:* Dept Chem Elizabethtown Col One Alpha Way Elizabethtown PA 17022-2298. *E-Mail:* ranck@acad.etown.edu

RANCOURT, JAMES DANIEL, OPTICAL ENGINEERING. *Current Pos:* ENGR, OPTICAL COATING LAB INC, 74- *Educ:* Bowdoin Col, BA, 63; Carnegie Inst Technol, MS, 65; Univ Ariz, PhD(optical sci), 74. *Prof Exp:* Engr, Itek Corp, 65-69; res assoc, Optical Sci Ctr, Univ Ariz, 69-74. *Mem:* Int Soc Optical Eng; Optical Soc Am. *Res:* Optical thin films; granted 12 patents. *Mailing Add:* 129 Sherwood Dr Santa Rosa CA 95405

RAND, A STANLEY, evolutionary biology, for more information see previous edition

RAND, ARTHUR GORHAM, JR, FOOD SCIENCE. *Current Pos:* instr animal & dairy sci, Univ RI, 63-65, from asst prof to assoc prof animal sci & food & resource chem, 65-75, chmn dept, 81-90, PROF FOOD SCI & NUTRIT, UNIV RI, 75- *Personal Data:* b Boston, Mass, Sept 29, 35; m 60, Cynthia Pollard; c Wesley, Douglas & Karen. *Educ:* Univ NH, BS, 58; Univ Wis, MS, 61, PhD(dairy & food indust, biochem), 64. *Prof Exp:* Res asst dairy & food indust, Univ Wis, 58-63. *Concurrent Pos:* Vis prof, Univ NSW, 71 & Rutgers Univ, 90. *Mem:* Int Asn Milk, Food & Enviorn Sanitarians; Inst Food

Technologists; NY Acad Sci. *Res:* Food enzyme technology; seafood quality; food biosensors. *Mailing Add:* Food Sci & Nutrit Res Ctr Univ RI 530 Liberty Lane West Kingston RI 02892. *Fax:* 401-874-2994; *E-Mail:* enzyme@uriacc.uri.edu

RAND, CYNTHIA LUCILLE, PHARMACEUTICALS PROCESS RESEARCH, SCALEUP OF ORGANOMETALLIC CHEMISTRY. *Current Pos:* sr res chemist/proj leader, 82-89, RES LEADER PHARMACEUT PROCESS RES, DOW CHEM CO, 91- *Personal Data:* m, William J Kruper Jr; c William R Kruper. *Educ:* State Univ NY, Binghamton, BS, 76; Purdue Univ, PhD(org chem), 82. *Mem:* Am Chem Soc. *Res:* Development of chemical technology that is efficient, scalable, economical and environmentally feasible. *Mailing Add:* 230 Barden Rd Sanford MI 48657-9534

RAND, DAVID MCNEAR, MOLECULAR EVOLUTION, POPULATION GENETICS. *Current Pos:* ASST PROF, BROWN UNIV, 91- *Personal Data:* m 86, Kristi Wharton; c Katie & Laura. *Educ:* Harvard Col, BA, 80; Yale Univ, PhD(biol), 87. *Honors & Awards:* Nat Res Serv Award, NIH, 88-91. *Prof Exp:* Teaching fel biol, Phillips Andover Acad, 80-81; teacher, St Albans Sch, 81-83; fel, Inst Marine Biol, Crete, Greece, 87, pop genetics, Harvard Univ, 88-91. *Concurrent Pos:* Prin investr pop biol, NSF, 92-; expert witness DNA forensic, Brown Univ, 93. *Mem:* Soc Study Evolution; Soc Molecular Biol & Evolution; Genetics Soc Am; AAAS; Soc Syst Biol. *Res:* Molecular approaches to evolution, ecology and population biology; co-evolution of nuclear and mitochondrial genomes; genetics of species boundaries; molecular population genetics of drosophila; molecular ecological genetics of barnacles. *Mailing Add:* Dept Ecol & Evolutionary Biol Brown Univ Providence RI 02912. *Fax:* 401-863-2166; *E-Mail:* david_rand@brown.edu

RAND, JAMES LELAND, AEROSPACE ENGINEERING, MECHANICAL ENGINEERING. *Current Pos:* PRES, WINZEN ENG INC, 94- *Personal Data:* b Ft Worth, Tex, Dec 23, 35; m 74; c 6. *Educ:* Univ Md, College Park, BS, 61, MS, 63, PhD(mech eng), 67. *Prof Exp:* Instr eng, Univ Md, College Park, 61-62; res engr, Naval Ord Lab, 62-68; from asst prof to prof struct mech, Tex A&M Univ, 68-78; mgr, Dynamic Anal Southwest Res Inst, 78-83; pres, Winzen Int Inc, 83-94. *Concurrent Pos:* Dir, Balloon Eng Lab, 77-78; vis mem, Grad Fac, Tex A&M Univ, 78- *Mem:* Am Inst Aeronaut & Astronaut; Am Soc Mech Engrs; Am Acad Mech; Am Soc Eng Educ; Soc Plastics Eng. *Res:* Design and analysis of thin polymeric film stratospheric balloons; nonlinear viscoelasticity; biaxial stress analysis; long term prediction of polyethylene sheets and films. *Mailing Add:* Winzen Eng Inc 12001 Network Blvd Suite 200 San Antonio TX 78249

RAND, LEON, ORGANIC CHEMISTRY. *Current Pos:* CHANCELLOR, IND UNIV SOUTHEAST, 85- *Personal Data:* b Boston, Mass, Oct 8, 30; m 59; c 3. *Educ:* Northeastern Univ, BS, 53; Univ Tex, MA, 56, PhD(chem), 58. *Prof Exp:* Fel, Purdue Univ, 58-59; from asst prof to assoc prof chem, Univ Detroit, 59-68; prof chem, Youngstown State Univ, 68-81, dean grad studies & res, 73-81; prof chem & vchancellor acad affairs, Pembroke State Univ, 81-85. *Mem:* Am Chem Soc; Am Inst Chemists. *Res:* Steric effects and use of potassium fluoride in organic chemistry; anodic oxidation reactions; urethane chemistry; carbonium ion processes; halide catalysis. *Mailing Add:* Ind Univ SE 4201 Grant Line Rd New Albany IN 47150

RAND, PATRICIA JUNE, PLANT ECOLOGY. *Current Pos:* GEN PARTNER & PRES, SARA ASSOCS, PASADENA, CALIF, 85- *Personal Data:* b St Paul, Minn, June 6, 26. *Educ:* Univ Minn, Minneapolis, BS, 47, MS, 53; Duke Univ, PhD(bot), 65. *Prof Exp:* Teaching asst, res asst & instr bot, Univ Minn, Minneapolis, 47-53; instr biol, Hamline Univ, 53-58; teaching asst bot, Duke Univ, 58-60; from instr to asst prof, Univ Ark, Fayetteville, 62-66; asst prof, Univ Nebr, Lincoln, 66-73; sr sci adv ecol, Atlantic Richfield Co, 73-88. *Concurrent Pos:* Seed technologist, Northrup, King & Co, 51-52; collabr, US Nat Park Serv, 59-70; adj prof, Univ Nebr, Lincoln, 73-76. *Mem:* Fel AAAS; Ecol Soc Am; Bot Soc Am; Am Inst Biol Sci; Soc Ecol Restoration. *Res:* Reclamation of disturbed areas; land use management; physiological ecology of woody plants. *Mailing Add:* 1710 S 58th St Lincoln NE 68506

RAND, PETER W, ENVIRONMENTAL HEALTH. *Current Pos:* intern, Maine Med Ctr, 55-56, resident internal med, 56-57 & 59-60, dir, Res Dept, 65-89, assoc vpres res, 89-95, RES ASSOC, MAINE MED CTR RES INST 95-; ASST PROF MED, COL MED, UNIV VT, 81- *Personal Data:* b Boston, Mass, Oct 26, 29; m 53, Alice Hildreth; c Elizabeth R (Algeo) & Peter W, Jr. *Educ:* Harvard Univ, AB, 51, MD, 55. *Concurrent Pos:* Fel cardiol, Maine Med Ctr, 60-61, USPHS fel, 61-63, NIH grant, 63; asst clin prof med, Col Med, Univ Vt, 72-80; adj prof, appl immunol, Univ SMaine, 88- *Mem:* Entom Soc Am; Am Physiol Soc; Health Physics Soc. *Res:* Environmental health; lyme disease research; vector borne diseases ecology/epidemiology. *Mailing Add:* Maine Med Ctr Res Inst 125 John Roberts Rd Unit 5 South Portland ME 04106

RAND, PHILLIP GORDON, BIOCHEMISTRY. *Current Pos:* SR DEVELOP SCIENTIST, ENVIRON TEST SYSTS, INC, 94- *Personal Data:* b Meredith, NH, Nov 5, 34; m 55, Joyce Magouirk; c Bruce, Brenda & Steven. *Educ:* John Brown Univ, BA, 56; Univ Wyo, MS, 58; Purdue Univ, PhD(biochem), 63. *Prof Exp:* Res biochemist, Miles Inc, 63-71, sr res biochemist & sect head, 71-73, prod develop mgr, 73-77, prin res scientist, 77-83, sr develop scientist, 83-89. *Mem:* Am Chem Soc. *Res:* Nutritional effects of fats; cholesterol metabolism; clinical diagnosis of disease. *Mailing Add:* 1320 W Lexington Ave Elkhart IN 46514-2048

RAND, RICHARD PETER, MEMBRANE BIOLOGY, PHYSICAL BIOCHEMISTRY. *Current Pos:* from asst prof to assoc prof, 66-73, PROF BIOL SIC, BROCK UNIV, 73- *Personal Data:* b Can, Jan 31, 37; m 62, Cynthia Knight; c Marc L, Thomas P & Gordon N. *Educ:* Carleton Univ, BSc, 59; Univ Western Ont, MSc, 61, PhD(biophys), 65. *Prof Exp:* Fel, Med Res Coun Can, Nat Ctr Sci Res, Paris, 64-66. *Concurrent Pos:* Chmn, Brock Univ, 73-; assoc mem, Dept Biol, McMaster Univ & Dept Physics, Guelph Univ, 76-; mem, Grant Selection Comt, Natural Sci & Eng Res Coun Can, 78-80, grants & scholar comt, Nat Sci & Eng Res Coun Can, 86-89; Killam res fel, 93- *Mem:* Biophys Soc; AAAS; fel Royal Soc Can. *Res:* Measurements of the forces of interaction between model and biological cell membranes and mechanisms of membrane fusion; role of water in molecular assembly and macromolecular conformation; enzyme activity. *Mailing Add:* Dept Biol Sci Brock Univ St Catharines ON L2S 3A1 Can

RAND, ROBERT COLLOM, MATHEMATICS. *Current Pos:* RETIRED. *Personal Data:* b Pittsburgh, Pa, Aug 24, 17; m 42; c 3. *Educ:* Duke Univ, AB, 39, AM, 40; Univ Md, PhD(math), 43. *Prof Exp:* Asst, Univ Md, 40-43; stress analyst, Eng & Res Corp, 42-44; instr math, US Naval Acad, 46-48; sr mathematician, Appl Physics Lab, Johns Hopkins Univ, 48-82. *Mem:* Math Asn Am. *Res:* Shock waves in non-steady flow; supersonic aerodynamics and shock waves; rectilinear motion of a gas subsequent to an internal explosion; dynamics of guided missiles; radar countermeasures; reliability; transportation systems. *Mailing Add:* 7018 Pindell School Rd Fulton MD 20759

RAND, SALVATORE JOHN, ANALYTICAL CHEMISTRY, PHYSICAL CHEMISTRY. *Current Pos:* CONSULT LIQUID FUELS, 94- *Personal Data:* b Brooklyn, NY, Dec 1, 33; m 56; c 5. *Educ:* Fordham Univ, BS, 56; Rensselaer Polytech Inst, PhD(phys chem), 60. *Prof Exp:* Sr res chemist, Colgate-Palmolive Co, 60-62; res scientist, Res Labs, United Technols, 62-67; res chemist, Texaco Inc, 67-70, consult, fuels res, Res & Develop Dept. *Concurrent Pos:* Mem adj fac, Grad Sch Chem, St Joseph Col, Conn, 64-67. *Mem:* AAAS; Am Chem Soc; Am Phys Soc; Am Soc Testing & Mat. *Res:* Specifications and testing for motor gasoline; aviation gasoline; diesel fuel and jet fuel; laboratory certification; hydrocarbon analysis; gas and liquid chromatography; fuels analysis and distribution. *Mailing Add:* 7 Americana Blvd Hopewell Junction NY 12533. *Fax:* 914-221-2130

RAND, STEPHEN COLBY, QUANTUM ELECTRONICS, LASER SPECTROSCOPY. *Current Pos:* assoc prof, 87-96, PROF, UNIV MICH, 96- *Personal Data:* b Seattle, Wash, Nov 20, 49; m 75, Paula D Fraser; c Spencer & Kevin. *Educ:* McMaster Univ, BSc, 72; Univ Toronto, MSc, 74, PhD(physics), 78. *Prof Exp:* Res assoc, Varian Labs, Stanford Univ, 80-82; mem tech staff, Hughes Res Lab, 82-87. *Concurrent Pos:* Topical ed, J Optical Soc; Fulbright sr scholar, Paris. *Mem:* Am Phys Soc; Optical Soc Am. *Res:* Upconversion and color center lasers; cooperative nonlinear dynamics in rare earth materials; four-wave mixing spectroscopy; growth and characterization of diamond-like materials; numerous patents for optical fiber and solid state laser devices, including invention of the diamond laser and a mode-locked, visible upconversion laser. *Mailing Add:* 3725 Dines Ct Ann Arbor MI 48105

RAND, WILLIAM MEDDEN, BIOSTATISTICS. *Current Pos:* PROF BIOSTATIST, TUFTS UNIV SCH MED, 88-, PROF COMP MED, TUFTS UNIV SCH VET MED, 95- *Personal Data:* b Seneca Falls, NY, June 26, 38; m 67, Patricia Gooding; c Toby Stewart. *Educ:* Ind Univ, BA, 59; Brandeis Univ, MA, 61; Univ Calif, Los Angeles, PhD(biostatist), 69. *Prof Exp:* Engr, Jet Propulsion Labs, 62-64; res assoc med, Univ Southern Calif, 65-68; from asst prof to assoc prof biostatist, Mass Inst Technol, 69-77, lectr, 77-88, dir, Infoods, 83-88. *Mem:* Biomet Soc; Am Statist Asn; Am Inst Nutrit. *Res:* Mathematical and statistical biomedicine. *Mailing Add:* Tufts Univ Sch Med 136 Harrison Ave Boston MA 02111

RANDA, JAMES P, THEORETICAL PHYSICS. *Current Pos:* PHYSICIST, ELECTROMAGNETIC FIELDS DIV, NAT INST STANDS & TECHNOL, BOULDER, 83- *Personal Data:* b Chicago, Ill, Jan 26, 47; m 70, Susan Bulmann; c David. *Educ:* Ill Benedictine Col, BSc, 69; Univ Ill, Urbana, MSc, 70, PhD(physics), 74. *Honors & Awards:* Bronze Medal, Us Dept Com, 92. *Prof Exp:* Vis asst prof, Dept Physics, Tex A&M Univ, 74-75; res fel, Dept Theoret Physics, Univ Manchester, 75-78; vis asst prof, Dept Physics, Univ Colo, Boulder, 78-80, asst prof, 80-83. *Concurrent Pos:* Lectr, Dept Physics, Univ Colo, Boulder, 85-89. *Mem:* Am Phys Soc; Inst Elec & Electronics Engrs; Int Union Radio Sci. *Res:* Metrology of electromagnetic noise. *Mailing Add:* Nat Inst Standards & Technol 813 06 325 Broadway Boulder CO 80303-3328. *Fax:* 303-497-3970; *E-Mail:* randa@boulder.nist.gov

RANDALL, BARBARA FEUCHT, PHYSIOLOGY. *Current Pos:* asst prof, 69-88, EMER PROF PHYSIOL, IND UNIV, BLOOMINGTON, 88- *Personal Data:* b Buffalo, NY, Jan 7, 25; m 49; c 4. *Educ:* State Univ NY, BS, 45; Univ Iowa, MS, 48, PhD, 51. *Prof Exp:* Asst physiol, Univ Iowa, 47-52; res assoc phys med, Ohio State Univ, 53-55; instr med, Med Ctr, Univ Mo, 55-62; lectr phys med, Med Sch, Northwestern Univ, 64-69. *Mem:* Am Phys Ther Asn. *Mailing Add:* 609 S Jordan Ave Bloomington IN 47401-5121

RANDALL, CHARLES ADDISON, JR, COSMIC RAY PHYSICS, ASTROPHYSICS. *Current Pos:* from asst prof to assoc prof, 50-60, PROF PHYSICS, OHIO UNIV, 60- *Personal Data:* b Daytona Beach, Fla, Sept 12, 15; m 41; c 2. *Educ:* Kalamazoo Col, AB, 36; Cornell Univ, MA, 39; Univ Mich, PhD(physics), 51. *Prof Exp:* Instr physics, Allen Acad, Tex, 39-40; instr, Wayland Jr Col & Acad, 40-42; res physicist, Fairbanks Morse & Co, 42-45; asst, Univ Mich, 46-50. *Concurrent Pos:* Off Europ Econ Coop sr sci fel, NSF Europ Orgn Nuclear Res Lab, 60-61; res partic, Oak Ridge Nat Lab, 52; instr, Goodyear Atomic Corp, 54; consult, Los Alamos Sci Lab, 56-; consult nuclear emulsion inst, Univ Chicago, 56; US rep, Int Conf Nuclear Educ, Buenos Aires, Arg, 64; on sabbatical leave, Sandia Corp, NMex & Atomic Energy Res Estab, Eng, 68-69; mem int comt of the forum on physics & soc, Am Phys Soc, 75-; consult, Skylab, NASA Ames Lab, Mountainview, Calif. *Mem:* AAAS; Am Geophys Union; fel Am Phys Soc; Am Asn Physics Teachers; Sigma Xi. *Res:* Cosmic rays; fundamental particles; cosmology. *Mailing Add:* 14 Palmer Lane Palm Coast FL 32164

RANDALL, CHARLES CHANDLER, MICROBIOLOGY. *Current Pos:* prof & chmn dept, 57-78, EMER PROF MICROBIOL, SCH MED, UNIV MISS, 78- *Personal Data:* b Cedar Rapids, Iowa, Mar 27, 13; m 41, Virginia G Smith; c Gillette & Stephen. *Educ:* Univ Ky, BS, 36; Vanderbilt Univ, MD, 40; Am Bd Path, dipl. *Prof Exp:* NIH fel, Vanderbilt Univ, 48-49, instr path, Sch Med, 49-51, asst prof path & bact, 51-52, assoc prof bact, 52-55, prof microbiol & actg head dept, 55-57. *Concurrent Pos:* Chmn, Assoc Med Sch Microbiol. *Mem:* Am Asn Immunologists; hon mem Am Soc Microbiol; Am Asn Pathol; Am Soc Cell Biol; fel Am Acad Microbiol. *Res:* Virology. *Mailing Add:* Dept Microbiol Univ Miss Med Ctr 2500 N State St Jackson MS 39216-4505

RANDALL, CHARLES MCWILLIAMS, atmospheric physics; deceased, see previous edition for last biography

RANDALL, CLIFFORD W(ENDELL), POLLUTION CONTROL. *Current Pos:* from asst prof to prof sanit eng, 68-81, CHMN, OCCOQUAN WATERSHED MONITORING PROG, VA POLYTECH INST & STATE UNIV, 72-, CHARLES LUNSFORD PROF CIVIL ENG & CHMN, ENVIRON ENG & SCI PROGS, 81- *Personal Data:* b Somerset, Ky, May 1, 36; m 59, Phyllis Amis; c Andrew A & William O. *Educ:* Univ Ky, BSCE, 59, MSCE, 63; Univ Tex, Austin, PhD(environ health eng), 66. *Honors & Awards:* Bedell Award, Water Pollution Control Fedn, 83, Phillip F Morgan Cert, 81; Acad Achievement Award, Am Waterworks Asn, 80 & 89, Mathias Medal, Chesapeake Res Consortiom, 96. *Prof Exp:* Asst prof civil eng, Univ Tex, Arlington, 65-68. *Concurrent Pos:* Res specialist, Aerobiol Lab, Southwest Med Sch, Univ Tex, 66-68; res dir, San Antonio River Auth, 67; consult pollution control, United Piece Dye Works, Inc, 69-, Blue Ridge Winkler, 76-89, Hester Industs, 78-82, Holly Farms Inc, 79-82 & Celanese Inc, 81-; consult waste treatment & munitions, Hercules, Inc, & Radford Army Ammunitions Plant, Va, 70-74; consult munic, Wiley & Wilson, Inc, Lynchburg, 70-71 & Harwood Beebe, Inc, Spartanburg, SC; consult indust, E I du Pont de Nemours & Co, Inc, Martinsville, 70, 72 & 78, Waynesboro, Va, 77-; consult, Mead Corp, Lynchburg, 70-71, & Belding Corticelli Fiber Glass Fabrics Co, Bedford, Va, 71-73; res & training grant consult, Environ Protection Agency, 70-71; chmn watershed monitoring subcomt & dir, Occoquan Watershed Water Qual Monitoring Prog, State Water Control Bd Va, 71-; affiliated consult, George A Jeffreys & Co, Inc, Salem, Va, 72-78, Black & Veatch Inc, 86-, & Innovatech, Inc, 84-; consult indust waste treat, Am Cyanamid, 72-78, Va Bd Cert Water & Wastewater Works Operators, 78-86, Va-NC Chowan River Basin Tech Panel; proj anal water supply, Southern Baptist Foreign Mission Bd, Kenya, 83; lectr, Nat Environ Eng Res Inst, Nagpur, India, 83; vis prof, Univ Cape Town, SAfrica, 83; consult, WHO, New Delhi, India, 83-84, Wastewater Res Inst Can, 92-, NY City Pub Works, 91-, Daewoo Construct Res Inst, Seoul, Korea, 96- & Harza Int, Seoul, Korea, 96-; mem, Sci & Tech Adv Comt, Chesapeake Bay Prog, 85-, chmn, 93-; chmn, US Nat Comt Int Asn Water Pollution Res & Control, 86-88, mem, gov. *Mem:* Water Pollution Control Fedn; Am Soc Civil Engrs; Am Water Works Asn; Int Asn Water QualCRes; Asn Environ Eng Prof (secy-treas, 79-80, vpres, 94-95, pres, 95-96). *Res:* Reservoir eutrophication; sanitary microbiology, stormwater runoff pollution control, industrial waste treatment; biological nutrient removal wastewater treatment. *Mailing Add:* Dept Civil Eng Va Polytech Inst & State Univ Blacksburg VA 24061

RANDALL, DAVID CLARK, AUTONOMIC NERVOUS SYSTEMS, BEHAVIORAL MEDICINE. *Current Pos:* from asst prof to assoc prof, 75-85, PROF PHYSIOL, SCH MED, UNIV KY, 85- *Personal Data:* b St Louis, Mo, Apr 23, 45; m 85; c Christopher C, Matthew F & Benjamin W. *Educ:* Taylor Univ, AB, 67; Univ Wash, PhD(physiol & biophys), 71. *Prof Exp:* Asst prof behav biol, Sch Med, Johns Hopkins Univ, 72-75. *Mem:* Am Physiol Soc; Fedn Am Soc Exp Biol; Am Sci Affil; Soc Exp Biol & Med; Pavlovian Soc NAm; Soc Neurosci. *Res:* Nervous control of the heart and coronary circulation during periods of behavioral and environmental stress in unanesthetized non-human primates and dogs; gravitational effects on circulation; behavioral medicine. *Mailing Add:* Dept Physiol Univ Ky Sch Med Lexington KY 40536-0084

RANDALL, DAVID JOHN, ZOOLOGY, PHYSIOLOGY. *Current Pos:* From asst prof to associate prof, 63-73, PROF ZOOL, UNIV BC, 73-, ASSOC DEAN GRAD STUDIES, 90- *Personal Data:* b London, Eng, Sept 15, 38; Can citizen; div; c 5. *Educ:* Univ Southampton, BSc, 60, PhD(physiol), 63; FRSC, 81. *Honors & Awards:* Fry Medal, 93. *Concurrent Pos:* Vis lectr, Bristol Univ, 68-69; Guggenheim Found fel, 68-69; vis scientist, Marine Labs, Univ Tex, 70 & Zool Sta, Naples, 73; chmn animal biol comt, Nat Res Coun, Can, 74; NATO vis scientist, Acadia Univ, 75 & Marine Lab, Univ Tex, 77; chief scientist, Alpha Helix Amazon Exped, 76; mem adv bd, J Comp Physiol, 77- & J Exp Biol, 81-84; assoc ed, Marine Behavior Physiol. *Mem:* Can Soc Zoologists; Soc Exp Biologists; fel Royal Soc Can, 81. *Res:* Respiration and circulation in fish and amphibia with an emphasis on oxygen and carbon dioxide transfer and hydrogen ion regulation across the gills of fish. *Mailing Add:* Univ BC Dept Zool 6270 University Blvd Vancouver BC V6T 1Z4 Can. *Fax:* 604-822-2416; *E-Mail:* davidrandall@mtsg.ubc.ca

RANDALL, ERIC A, BRYOLOGY, AGROFORESTRY. *Current Pos:* from asst prof to assoc prof biol, 73-85, chmn, Dept Biol, 91-93, PROF BIOL, STATE UNIV NY BUFFALO, 85-, ASSOC DEAN, FAC NAT & SOC SCI, 93- *Personal Data:* b Silver Springs, NY, June 12, 46; m 71; c 2. *Educ:* State Univ NY Oswego, BS, 68; Pa State Univ, PhD(bot), 73. *Mem:* Am Bryol & Lichenological Soc; Am Soc Plant Taxon; Int Asn Plant Taxon; Sigma Xi. *Res:* Bryological and phytogeographic studies of Atlantic northern United States and Canada; microfiltration of maple (Acer saccharum) sap. *Mailing Add:* State Univ NY Col 1300 Elmwood Ave HA113 Buffalo NY 14222. *Fax:* 716-878-4009; *E-Mail:* randalea@snygufua

RANDALL, FRANCIS JAMES, POLYMER CHEMISTRY. *Current Pos:* CHEMIST PROD DEVELOP, S C JOHNSON & SON, INC, 69-, SR RES ASSOC, S C JOHNSON WAX. *Personal Data:* b Williston, NDak, Feb 17, 42. *Educ:* Dickinson State Col, NDak, BA, 63; Univ Sask, MS, 68; Univ NDak, PhD(chem), 70. *Mem:* Am Chem Soc; AAAS; Sigma Xi. *Res:* Polymer coatings. *Mailing Add:* 724 Hilaeah Dr Racine WI 53403-2158

RANDALL, GYLES WADE, SOIL SCIENCE. *Current Pos:* from asst prof to assoc prof, 72-80, PROF SOILS, FAC SOIL SCI, SOUTHERN EXP STA, UNIV MINN, 80- *Personal Data:* b Rochester, Minn, Jan 3, 42; m 66; c 2. *Educ:* Univ Minn, St Paul, BS, 63, MS, 68; Univ Wis-Madison, PhD(soils), 72. *Prof Exp:* Res asst soils, Univ Minn, 64-65, res fel, 65-69; res asst, Univ Wis, 69-72. *Mem:* Am Soc Agron; Soil Sci Soc Am; Soil Conserv Soc Am; Sigma Xi; Coun Agr Sci & Technol. *Res:* Tillage, soil fertility and plant nutrition with emphasis on nutrient accumulation and movement. *Mailing Add:* 123 Eighth St SE Waseca MN 56093-3849

RANDALL, HENRY THOMAS, nutrition; deceased, see previous edition for last biography

RANDALL, HOWARD M, PHYSIOLOGY. *Current Pos:* Instr, 65-68, from asst prof to assoc prof, 68-83, PROF PHYSIOL, SCH MED, LA STATE UNIV MED CTR, NEW ORLEANS, 83- *Personal Data:* b Rockville Ctr, NY, May 5, 36; m 62, 78; c 2. *Educ:* Univ RI, BS, 58; Univ Rochester, PhD(physiol), 65. *Concurrent Pos:* La Heart Asn grant, 66-67; NIH grant, 68-; assoc dean student affairs & records, Sch Med, La State Univ. *Mem:* AAAS; Am Physiol Soc; Biophys Soc; Am Asn Med Cols; Sigma Xi. *Res:* Relationships between physiological functions and metabolism in the kidney. *Mailing Add:* Dept Physiol La State Univ Med Sch 1542 Tulane Ave New Orleans LA 70112-2865

RANDALL, J MALCOM, HEALTH CARE ADMINISTRATION. *Current Pos:* assoc prof, 66-74, PROF HEALTH & HOSP ADMIN, COL HEALTH RELATED PROFESSIONS, UNIV FLA, 75-; DIR, VET ADMIN MED CTR, GAINESVILLE, 66-; CHMN, FLA NETWORK, VET ADMIN HOSPS & OUTPATIENT CLINS, 90- *Personal Data:* b East St Louis, Ill, Aug 9, 16; m 72. *Educ:* McKendree Col, Lebanon, Ill, AB, 39; St Louis Univ, MHA, 56. *Honors & Awards:* Presidential Rank Award, 83. *Prof Exp:* Chief spec serv, Vet Admin Hosp, St Louis, 53-56; asst dir, Vet Admin Hosp, Spokane, 56-57, Vet Admin Res Hosp, Chicago, 57-58, Vet Admin Hosp, Indianapolis, 58-60 & Vet Admin Ctr, Milwaukee, 60-64; dir, Vet Admin Hosp, Miles City Mont, 64-66. *Concurrent Pos:* Mem, Bd Dirs, Am Health Planning Asn, Coun Teaching Hosps, Asn Am Med Cols, Coun Regents, Am Col Hosp Adminr & Nat Adv Comts, Vet Admin; med dist dir, Vet Admin Med Ctrs & Outpatient Clins Fla, 73-90; partic, US-Yugoslavia Health Scientist Exchange Prog, Univ Clin Ctr, Ljubljana, Yugoslavia, 83, 84, 85, 86, 87, 88 & 89, US-Hungary Health Scientist Exchange Prog, 89 & 90. *Mem:* Inst Med-Nat Acad Sci; fel Am Col Hosp Adminr; Am Hosp Asn; Am Soc Pub Admin. *Res:* Numerous published articles in med journals. *Mailing Add:* Vet Affairs Med Ctr 1601 SW Archer Rd Gainesville FL 32608-1197

RANDALL, JAMES CARLTON, JR, physical chemistry, for more information see previous edition

RANDALL, JAMES EDWIN, BIOPHYSICS, PHYSIOLOGY. *Current Pos:* prof physiol, 68-89, EMER PROF, IND UNIV, BLOOMINGTON, 89- *Personal Data:* b Bloomington, Ind, July 23, 24; m 49; c 4. *Educ:* Purdue Univ, BSEE, 47; State Univ Iowa, 52; Ohio State Univ, PhD(biophys), 55. *Prof Exp:* Electronics eng, Collins Radio Co, Cedar Rapids, 47-49; from asst prof to assoc prof physiol, Univ Mo, 55-63; prof, Northwestern Univ, 63-68. *Concurrent Pos:* Consult, Nat Health & Lung Prog Proj Comt, 70-74. *Mem:* Am Physiol Soc. *Res:* Physiological variables as statistical signals; physiological simulations with microcomputers; physiological time series; laboratory digital computation. *Mailing Add:* 609 S Jordan Ave Bloomington IN 47401

RANDALL, JANET ANN, COMMUNICATION, SOCIAL ORGANIZATION. *Current Pos:* ASSOC PROF BIOL, SAN FRANCISCO STATE UNIV, 87- *Personal Data:* b Twin Falls, Idaho, July 3, 43; m 85. *Educ:* Univ Idaho, BS, 65; Univ Wash, MEd, 69; Wash State Univ, PhD(zool), 77. *Prof Exp:* Postdoctoral fel biopsychol, Univ Tex, Austin, 77-79; from asst prof to asoc prof biol, Cent Mo State Univ, 79-87. *Concurrent Pos:* Vis assoc prof psychol, Cornell Univ, 84-85; prin investr grants, NSF, 86- *Mem:* Animal Behav Soc; Am Soc Zoologists; Am Soc Mammalogists; Int Soc Behav Ecol. *Res:* Comparison of communications and social organization of desert rodents-kangaroo rats. *Mailing Add:* Dept Biol San Francisco State Univ 1600 Holloway Ave San Francisco CA 94132

RANDALL, JOHN DOUGLAS, APPLIED MATHEMATICS, SOFTWARE SYSTEMS. *Current Pos:* SR PROG MGR, US NUCLEAR REGULATORY COMN, 80- *Personal Data:* b Corning, NY, July 23, 42; m 69, Catherine Frisch; c Ian, Trevor & Elise. *Educ:* Cornell Univ, BMchE, 65, PhD(fluid dynamics), 72; Clarkson Col, MSME, 67. *Prof Exp:* Instr thermodyn, Clarkson Col, 66-67; sr engr, Appl Physics Lab, Johns Hopkins Univ, 73-80. *Mem:* AAAS; Am Soc Mech Engrs; Am Geophys Union; Sigma Xi. *Res:* Management of development and coordination of research projects to provide information for regulation of radioactive waste disposal. *Mailing Add:* 6318 Dry Stone Gate Columbia MD 21045-2888. *E-Mail:* vdr@cu.nih.gov

RANDALL, JOHN ERNEST, MARINE BIOLOGY, ICHTHYOLOGY. *Current Pos:* marine zoologist & sr ichthyologist, 65-96, SR ICHTHYOLOGIST EMER, BERNICE P BISHOP MUS, 97- *Personal Data:* b Los Angeles, Calif, May 22, 24; m 51, Helen Au; c Loreen R (O'Hara) & Rodney D. *Educ:* Univ Calif, Los Angeles, BA, 50; Univ Hawaii, PhD(marine zool), 55. *Honors & Awards:* Stoye Award Ichthyol, Am Soc Ichthyol & Herpet; Gibbs Award, Syst Ichthyol, 90. *Prof Exp:* Asst zool, Univ Calif, Los Angeles, 50; Bishop Mus fel, Yale Univ, 55-56; res asst prof ichthyol, Marine Lab, Univ Miami, 57-61; prof biol & dir inst marine biol, Univ PR, 61-65. *Concurrent Pos:* Dir, Oceanic Inst, Waimanalo, 65-66; marine biologist, Inst Marine Biol, Univ Hawaii, 67-69; mem, Subcomt Conserv Ecosyts, Int Biol Prog; mem, Great Barrier Reef Comt; Distinguished fel, Am Sco Ichthyol & Herpet. *Mem:* Am Soc Ichthyol & Herpet; Ichthyol Soc Japan; Australian Coral Reef Soc; Europ Ichthyol Union; Int Soc Reef Studies; Explorers Club. *Res:* Tropical marine ichthyology and biology. *Mailing Add:* Natural Sci/Ichthyology 1525 Bernice St Bernice P Bishop Mus Honolulu HI 96817-0916. *Fax:* 808-841-8968; *E-Mail:* johne@bishop.bishop.hawaii.org

RANDALL, JOHN FRANK, BIOLOGY. *Current Pos:* RETIRED. *Personal Data:* b Walnut, NC, Aug 2, 18; m 50; c 1. *Educ:* Univ NC, AB, 41; Univ Mich, MS, 50; Univ SC, PhD(biol), 57. *Prof Exp:* Instr biol, Alpena Community Col, 52-55; from assoc prof to prof zool, Appalachian State Univ, 57-77, prof biol, 77-90. *Mem:* AAAS; Ecol Soc Am; Sigma Xi. *Res:* Vertebrate ecology; ornithology; ichthyology. *Mailing Add:* 142 Blanwood Dr Boone NC 28607

RANDALL, JOSEPH LINDSAY, LASERS, COMMUNICATIONS. *Current Pos:* res physicist, 62-67, BR CHIEF, TECHNOL DIV, ASTRIONICS LAB, MARSHALL SPACE FLIGHT CTR, NASA, 67-, DIR, INFO & ELECTRONICS SYST LAB. *Personal Data:* b Clanton, Ala, Dec 7, 32; m 54; c 4. *Educ:* Univ Ala, BS, 54, MS, 56, PhD(physics), 60. *Honors & Awards:* NASA Exceptional Sci Achievement Medal. *Prof Exp:* Res physicist, Lockheed Aircraft, 60-61 & Redstone Arsenal, 61-62. *Mem:* Am Phys Soc; Optical Soc Am. *Res:* Laser communication systems for space application; atmospheric effects on optical communication. *Mailing Add:* 2212 Shadecrest Rd SE Huntsville AL 35801

RANDALL, KAREN T, COMPUTER & COMMUNICATIONS SECURITY. *Current Pos:* MEM TECH STAFF, AT&T BELL LABS, 88- *Personal Data:* b Bidiford, Maine. *Educ:* Case Western Res Univ, BS, 84; Univ NC, Chapel Hill, MS, 86, PhD(biomed eng), 87. *Mem:* Inst Elec & Electronics Engrs; Biomed Eng Soc. *Mailing Add:* AT&T Universal Card Serv IM-313 101 Crawfords Corner Rd Holmdel NJ 07733

RANDALL, LINDA LEA, PROTEIN EXPORT, CHAPERONES. *Current Pos:* assoc prof, 81-83, PROF BIOCHEM, WASH STATE UNIV, 83- *Personal Data:* b Montclair, NJ, Aug 7, 46; m 70, Gerald L Hazelbauer. *Educ:* Colo State Univ, BS, 68; Univ Wis-Madison, PhD(molecular biol), 71. *Honors & Awards:* Eli Lilly Award, 84; Parke-Davis Award, 95. *Prof Exp:* Fel, Inst Pasteur, France, 71-73; res assoc molecular biol, Univ Uppsala, 73-75, asst prof, 75-81. *Mem:* Nat Acad Sci; AAAS; Am Soc Biol Chemists; Protein Soc; Am Soc Microbiol. *Res:* Molecular mechanism of export of protein through biological membranes; recognition of nonnative protein by chaperones. *Mailing Add:* Dept Biochem & Biophys Wash State Univ Pullman WA 99164-4660. *Fax:* 509-335-9688

RANDALL, MICHAEL STEVEN, ELECTROACTIVE DEVICES, ACTUATORS. *Current Pos:* PRIN ENGR, AVX CORP, 92- *Personal Data:* b Hornell, NY, June 25, 63; m 90, Sara Pittman Elder. *Educ:* Alfred Univ, BS, 85; Univ Fla, MS, 87, PhD(mat sci & eng), 93. *Prof Exp:* Res engr, Univ Fla, 85, grad res asst, 85-91; eng consult, Gould Lewis & Proctor, 91-92. *Mem:* Am Ceramic Soc; Mat Res Soc; Int Soc Hybrid Microelectronics. *Res:* Corporate research and product development on electro-active devices; stack actuators, chip actuators and pad actuators; thecnolysis and green processing. *Mailing Add:* AVX Corp PO 867 Myrtle Beach SC 29578. *Fax:* 803-347-0873

RANDALL, PETER, PLASTIC SURGERY. *Current Pos:* instr, Sch Med, Univ Pa, 53-56, assoc, Hosp, 53-59, assoc, Sch Med, 56-59, from asst prof to assoc prof, 59-70, chief div, 80-89, PROF PLASTIC SURG, SCH MED & HOSP, UNIV PA, 70- *Personal Data:* b Philadelphia, Pa, Mar 29, 23; m 48; c 4. *Educ:* Princeton Univ, AB, 44; Johns Hopkins Univ, MD, 46; Am Bd Plastic Surg, dipl, 55. *Prof Exp:* Intern, Union Mem Hosp, Baltimore, Md, 46-47; resident, US Naval Hosp, Philadelphia, 47-48; asst instr surg, Sch Med & resident, Hosp, Univ Pa, 49-50; asst instr surg, Sch Med, Wash Univ, 50-53. *Concurrent Pos:* Resident, Barnes & St Louis Children's Hosp, 52-53; from asst surgeon to sr surgeon, Children's Hosp, Philadelphia, 53-; chief Div Plastic Surg, 62-81; attend plastic surgeon, Vet Admin Hosp, 54-; chief dept plastic surg, Lankenau Hosp, 71; bd mem, Am Bd Plastic Surg, 71. *Mem:* Am Soc Plastic & Reconstruct Surg (secy, 66-69, vpres, 75-76, pres, 77-78); Am Asn Plastic Surg; Am Col Surg; Am Cleft Palate Asn (pres, 66-67); Plastic Surg Res Coun (pres, 64-65). *Res:* Cleft lip and palate. *Mailing Add:* Plastic Surg G12 Univ Pa 10 Penn Tower 3400 Spruce St Philadelphia PA 19104-4219

RANDALL, RAYMOND VICTOR, MEDICINE, ENDOCRINOLOGY & METABOLISM. *Current Pos:* instr, Univ Minn, 54-59, from asst prof to assoc prof, 59-70, head sect internal med & endocrinol, 63-74, prof, 70-97, EMER PROF MED, MAYO GRAD SCH MED, UNIV MINN, 97- *Personal Data:* b Washington, DC, Aug 1, 20; m 46, Priscilla Richmond; c Raymond R, Priscilla (Middleton) & Susan (Geery). *Educ:* Harvard Univ, AB, 42, MD, 45; Univ Minn, MS, 51. *Prof Exp:* House officer med, Mass Gen Hosp, 45-46. *Concurrent Pos:* Clin & res fel, Mass Gen Hosp, 51-52; teaching fel pediat, Harvard Med Sch, 51, teaching fel med, 52; resident physician, House of the Good Samaritan, Boston, 51; asst to staff, Mayo Clin, 52; consult, St Mary's Hosp & Rochester Methodist Hosp, 53-; consult, Mayo Clin, 53-74, sr consult 74- *Mem:* Endocrine Soc; Am Fedn Clin Res; Int Endocrine Soc; Int Soc Neuroendocrinol; Int Soc Psychoneuroendocrinol. *Res:* Endocrine and metabolic diseases. *Mailing Add:* Mayo Clin Rochester MN 55905

RANDALL, WALTER CLARK, physiology; deceased, see previous edition for last biography

RANDALL, WILLIAM CARL, PHYSICAL CHEMISTRY. *Current Pos:* Res fel, 67-80, SR RES FEL, MERCK SHARP & DOHME RES LABS, WEST POINT, 80- *Personal Data:* b Hampton, Iowa, Jan 27, 41. *Educ:* Iowa State Univ, BS, 63; Univ Wis, PhD(phys chem), 67. *Mem:* AAAS; Am Chem Soc. *Res:* Kinetics of reactions in solution and the application of physical chemistry to medicinal chemistry. *Mailing Add:* 1735 Supplee Rd Lansdale PA 19446-5457

RANDAZZO, ANTHONY FRANK, GEOLOGY, HYDROGEOLOGY. *Current Pos:* From asst prof to assoc prof, Univ Fla, 67-77, asst dir, 77-80, assoc dean sponsored res, 80-82, dir res admin, 82-88, chmn, Dept Geol, 88-95, PROF GEOL, UNIV FLA, 77- *Personal Data:* b Staten Island, NY, Sept 20, 41; m 65, Lynne Schmeiser; c Kirk & Jeff. *Educ:* City Col New York, BS, 63; Univ NC, Chapel Hill, MS, 65, PhD(geol), 68. *Concurrent Pos:* Vis prof, Brigham Young Univ, 72; bd mem prof geol Bd, State Fla, 87-; bd dirs, Oak Ridge Assoc Univ, 88-95; J William Fulbright sr res fel, 95-96. *Mem:* Fel Geol Soc Am; Soc Econ Paleont & Mineral; Sigma Xi; Am Asn Petrol Geologists; Am Geophys Union. *Res:* Petrography and geohydrology of limestones of Florida and the Caribbean; carbonate sedimentology. *Mailing Add:* Dept Geol Univ Fla Gainesville FL 32611

RANDEL, WILLIAM JOHN, STRATOSPHERIC DYNAMICS, TRANSPORT & CHEMISTRY. *Current Pos:* Postdoctoral fel, 85-87, from scientist I to scientist II, 87-94, SCIENTIST III, NAT CTR ATMOSPHERIC RES, 94- *Personal Data:* m 83, Sharon L Gutche; c Matthew, Katherine & Gregory. *Educ:* Univ Cincinnati, BS, 78; Iowa State Univ, PhD(physics), 84. *Concurrent Pos:* Prin investr, NASA, 90-97, Nat Oceanic & Atmospheric Admin, 93-95; ozone trends panels, World Meteorol Orgn, 93-97, temperature trends panel, 95-97; vis res fel, Monash Univ, Melbourne, 95-96. *Mem:* Am Meteorol Soc; Am Geophys Union. *Res:* Analysis of satellite and ground-based data to study dynamic variability and long-term trends in stratospheric meteorological and constituent data. *Mailing Add:* Nat Ctr Atmospheric Res PO Box 3000 Boulder CO 80307-3000. *Fax:* 303-497-1492; *E-Mail:* randel@ucar.edu

RANDELL, RICHARD, MANIFOLD THEORY, SINGULARITY THEORY. *Current Pos:* From asst prof to assoc prof, 81-87, dept chmn, 91-94, PROF MATH, UNIV IOWA, 87- *Personal Data:* b Fairfield, Iowa, Aug 23, 46. *Educ:* Univ Wis, PhD(math), 73. *Mem:* Am Math Soc. *Res:* Topology of varieties, singularities and manifolds; topology of arrangements. *Mailing Add:* Dept Math Univ Iowa Iowa City IA 52242

RANDELS, JAMES BENNETT, COMPUTER SCIENCE. *Current Pos:* RETIRED. *Personal Data:* b Detroit, Mich, June 13, 31; m 56; c 2. *Educ:* Univ Calif, Los Angeles, BA, 53; Ohio State Univ, MA, 58, PhD(math), 65. *Prof Exp:* Res engr, Univ Calif, Los Angeles, 54; instr math, Univ Dayton, 56-57; res asst, Ohio State Univ, 57-58, res assoc, 61-63, chief systs programmer, 63-65, asst prof math, 65-66, asst prof comput sci, 66-70, chmn, Comput Coord Comt, 70-73, asst dir, Learning Resources Comput Ctr, 70-72, asst dir univ systs, 72-75, assoc prof comput & info sci, 70-80, assoc dir comput systs programming, 75-80, sr programmer analyst, Comput Ctr & sr comput specialist univ systs, 82-89. *Concurrent Pos:* Mem tech staff comput & data reduction, Space Tech Labs, Inc, 58-60, head spec proj group, 60-61; assoc prof, Denison Univ, 80-81. *Mem:* Asn Comput Mach; Math Asn Am; Sigma Xi. *Res:* Digital computer programming; computer operating systems; simulation of systems. *Mailing Add:* 999 Greenridge Rd Columbus OH 43235-3417

RANDERATH, KURT, BIOCHEMISTRY. *Current Pos:* from assoc prof to prof pharmacol, 71-89, PROF & HEAD, DIV TOXICOL, BAYLOR COL MED, 89- *Personal Data:* b Dusseldorf, Ger, Aug 2, 29; m 62. *Educ:* Univ Heidelberg, DrMed, 55, dipl, 58. *Prof Exp:* Asst org chem, Darmstadt Tech, 59-62; from res assoc to asst prof, Harvard Med Sch, 64-71. *Concurrent Pos:* Res fel biol chem, Harvard Med Sch, 63-64; Nat Cancer Inst res career develop award, 69; Am Cancer Soc fac res award, 72. *Mem:* AAAS; Am Soc Biol Chem; Am Asn Cancer Res; Am Chem Soc. *Res:* Analysis of nucleic acids and derivatives; drug effects on nucleic acids; separation methods, particularly thin-layer chromatography; chemical carcinogenesis; DNA damage and repair. *Mailing Add:* Div Toxicol Dept Pharmacol Baylor Col Med 1 Baylor Plaza Houston TX 77030-3498. *Fax:* 713-798-3145

RANDERSON, DARRYL, METEOROLOGY, EMERGENCY RESPONSE CAPABILITY. *Current Pos:* res meteorologist, Nat Weather Serv Nuclear Support Off, 69-81, supvr meteorologist, 81-84, dep meteorologist-in-charge, 85-93, DIR ARL/SORD, NAT WEATHER SERV NUCLEAR SUPPORT OFF, 94- *Personal Data:* b Houston, Tex, July 8, 37; m 61; c 2. *Educ:* Tex A&M Univ, BS, 60, MS, 62, PhD(meteorol), 68. *Honors & Awards:* NASA Group Achievement Award, Johnson Space Ctr, Houston, Tex, 74; Nat Oceanic & Atmospheric Admin Spec Achievement Award, Nat Weather Serv, Las Vegas, Nev, 75. *Prof Exp:* Instr meteorol, Tex A&M Univ, 62-65; res scientist air pollution, Tex A&M Res Found, 67-68, res assoc, 68-69. *Concurrent Pos:* Res asst, Tex A&M Univ, 61-65; traineeship, NIH, 65-67; vis prof meteorol, Univ Nev, Las Vegas, 70- *Mem:* Fel Am Meteorol Soc. *Res:* Numerical modeling; thunderstorms; weather forecasting; satellite meteorology; air pollution meteorology; radar meteorology. *Mailing Add:* Air Resources Lab Spec Opers & Res Div PO Box 94227 Las Vegas NV 89193-4227

RANDHAWA, JAGIR SINGH, PHYSICS. *Current Pos:* RETIRED. *Personal Data:* b Vahila, India, Nov 1, 22; US citizen; m 54; c 2. *Educ:* Univ Punjab, WPakistan, BS, 45, MS, 46; Univ Colo, Boulder, MS, 59; NMex State Univ, PhD(physics), 64. *Prof Exp:* Lectr physics, Educ Dept, Univ Punjab, India, 50-57; teaching asst, Univ Colo, Boulder, 57-59; res assoc, NMex State Univ, 59-64; res physicist, Atmospheric Sci Lab, White Sands Missile Range, 64-91. *Concurrent Pos:* Spec Act Award, US Army, 67-72. *Mem:* Am Phys Soc; Am Geophys Union; Am Meteorol Soc; Am Inst Aeronaut & Astronaut; Sigma Xi. *Res:* Physics of upper atmosphere; aeronomy; meteorology; photochemistry of ozone. *Mailing Add:* 5830 S Bethel Ave Del Rey CA 93616

RANDIC, MILAN, CHEMICAL GRAPH THEORY, CHEMICAL STRUCTURE DOCUMENTATION. *Current Pos:* from assoc prof to prof, 80-87, DISTINGUISHED PROF MATH, DRAKE UNIV, 88- *Personal Data:* b Belgrade, Yugoslavia, Oct 1, 30; US citizen; m 60; c 2. *Educ:* Univ Zagreb, Yugoslavia, BA, 54; Univ Cambridge, Eng, PhD(spectros), 58. *Honors & Awards:* Boris Kidric Found Award, Slovene Nat Assembly, 87. *Prof Exp:* Assoc theoret chem, Inst Rugjer Boskovic, 60-65; from assoc prof to prof chem, Univ Zagreb, 65-70; vis prof physics, Univ Utah, 71-72; fac guest, dept chem, Harvard Univ, 72-73; vis prof chem, Tufts Univ, 73-74. *Concurrent Pos:* Mem adv bd, Croatica Chem Act & J Math Chem. *Mem:* Int Soc Math Chem (pres); Math Asn Am; Am Chem Soc; Croatian Chem Soc. *Res:* Mathematical modeling of chemical structure with an emphasis on combinatorial and topological aspects of a structure; structure-property and structure-activity studies; drug design. *Mailing Add:* Dept Math & Comp Sci Dept Drake Univ Des Moines IA 50311

RANDIC, MIRJANA, NEUROPHYSIOLOGY. *Current Pos:* assoc prof, 75-77, PROF PHARMACOL, DEPT VET ANAT PHARMACOL & PHYSIOL, IOWA STATE UNIV, 77- *Personal Data:* b Ogulin, Yugoslavia, Oct 12, 34; m 60; c 1. *Educ:* Univ Zagreb, MD, 59, PhD(pathophysiol), 62. *Prof Exp:* From asst to assoc prof neurophysiol, Rudjer Boskovic Inst, Yugoslavia, 59-70; asst prof, McGill Univ, 64-65; assoc prof neuropharmacol, Dept Biochem & Pharmacol, Sch Med, Tufts Univ, 72-75. *Mem:* Int Asn Study Pain; Brit Physiol Soc; Brit Pharmacol Soc; Int Brain Res Orgn; Soc Neurosci. *Res:* Chemical synaptic transmission; the physiological role of peptides, especially substance P, endorphins and somatostatin in nociceptive pathways. *Mailing Add:* 3225 Kingman Rd Ames IA 50014

RANDINITIS, EDWARD J, BIOPHARMACEUTICS. *Current Pos:* res pharmacist, 69-72, res scientist, 72-76, RES ASSOC PHARM, PARKE-DAVIS & CO, WARNER-LAMBERT, 76- *Personal Data:* b Scranton, Pa, Apr 7, 40; m 72; c 2. *Educ:* Wayne State Univ, Detroit, BS, 62, MS, 64, PhD(pharm), 69. *Prof Exp:* Asst pharm, Wayne State Univ, 62-69. *Mem:* Am Pharmaceut Asn; Acad Pharmaceut Sci; Sigma Xi; Am Asn Pharmaceut Scientists. *Res:* Assessment of pharmaceutical formulations regarding bioavailability; assay of biological fluids for drugs and metabolites; development of assay for such. *Mailing Add:* 11943 Beacon Hill Plymouth MI 48170

RANDLE, ROBERT JAMES, physiological optics, statistical procedures; deceased, see previous edition for last biography

RANDLES, RONALD HERMAN, STATISTICS. *Current Pos:* PROF STATIST, UNIV FLA, 81-, DEPT CHAIR, 89- *Personal Data:* b Canton, Ohio, Sept 4, 42; m 68; c 2. *Educ:* Col Wooster, BA, 64; Fla State Univ, MS, 66, PhD(statist), 69. *Prof Exp:* From asst prof to assoc prof, Univ Iowa, 69-78, prof statist, 78-81. *Concurrent Pos:* Assoc ed, Am Statistician, 74-76, J Am Statist Asn, 79-85, Comn Statist, 86- & J Nonpar Statist, 90- *Mem:* Fel Am Statist Asn; Inst Math Statist. *Res:* Nonparametrics and large sample distribution theory. *Mailing Add:* 4430 NW 20th Pl Gainesville FL 32605

RANDLETT, HERBERT ELDRIDGE, JR, COMPUTER SYSTEMS, CHEMICAL ENGINEERING. *Current Pos:* RETIRED. *Personal Data:* b Centralia, Wash, July 17, 17; m 46; c 2. *Educ:* Univ Calif, BS, 39. *Prof Exp:* Mgr exp lab, Shell Oil Co, 54-64, systs mgr mfg, 64-74, staff systs rep, Rep Opers, 47-79. *Res:* Computer systems applications. *Mailing Add:* 1324 Chardonnay Dr Houston TX 77077

RANDOL, BURTON, MATHEMATICS. *Current Pos:* assoc prof, 69-74, PROF MATH, GRAD CTR, CITY UNIV NY, 75- *Personal Data:* b New York, NY, Sept 16, 37; m 64. *Educ:* Rice Univ, BA, 59; Princeton Univ, PhD(math), 62. *Prof Exp:* Instr math, Princeton Univ, 62-63; lectr, Yale Univ, 63-64, asst prof, 64-69. *Mem:* Am Math Soc; Soc Math France. *Res:* Analysis. *Mailing Add:* Dept Math City Univ NY Grad Ctr New York NY 10036

RANDOLPH, ALAN DEAN, CHEMICAL ENGINEERING. *Current Pos:* assoc prof, 68-70, PROF CHEM ENG, UNIV ARIZ, 70- *Personal Data:* b Muskogee, Okla, Mar 25, 34; m 57; c 3. *Educ:* Univ Colo, BSChE, 56; Iowa State Univ, MSChE, 59, PhD(crystallization), 62. *Prof Exp:* Asst technologist, Shell Chem Corp, 56-58; res proj engr, Am Potash & Chem Corp, Calif, 62-65, head crystallization sect, Res Dept, 65; assoc prof chem eng, Univ Fla, 65-68. *Concurrent Pos:* NSF res grant crystallization, 66-; consult, Dow Chem Co, 68-70 & Kerr-McGee Corp, 69-; mem, Consult Comt Nuclear Waste Immobilization, Atlantic Richfield Hanford Co, 71-79; consult, Los Alamos Sci Lab, 78-81, US Borax, 78-82 & E I DuPont de Nemours & Co Inc, 78-83; vis prof, Univ Col, London, 81. *Mem:* Am Inst Chem Engrs; Am Chem Soc. *Res:* Mathematical simulation, description and control of particulate systems, especially crystallization processes, theoretical and experimental study of nucleation-growth rate kinetics and residence-time distributions of particulate systems. *Mailing Add:* 2131 Rainbow Vista Dr Tucson AZ 85712-2910

RANDOLPH, CARL LOWELL, CHEMISTRY. *Current Pos:* TRUSTEE, CHMN BD & EMER PROF, WHITTIER COL, 69-; BD DIRS & CHMN, IND COL, SOUTHERN CALIF, 82- *Personal Data:* b Pasadena, Calif, May 30, 22; m 43, Jane Taber; c Margaret & Stephen. *Educ:* Whittier Col, BA, 43; Univ Southern Calif, MS, 47, PhD, 49. *Hon Degrees:* LLD, Whittier Col, 82; DPS, Univ Alaska, 83. *Prof Exp:* Prin chemist, Aerojet-Gen Corp, 49-57; vpres, US Borax Res Corp, Calif, 57-63, asst to pres, Los Angeles, 63-66, vpres, 66-68, exec vpres, 68-69, pres, 69-86, vchmn, 83-87. *Mem:* Sigma Xi. *Mailing Add:* 1407 Seaview Way Anacortes WA 98221-9794

RANDOLPH, JAMES COLLIER, ECOLOGY. *Current Pos:* from asst prof to assoc prof, 74-82, assoc dean, 86-90, PROF BIOL, SCH PUB & ENVIRON AFFAIRS, IND UNIV, BLOOMINGTON, 82-; DIR, MIDWESTERN CTR GLOBAL ENVIRON CHANGE, 90- *Personal Data:* b Knox City, Tex, Mar 26, 44; m 68, 85, Mary Broihier. *Educ:* Univ Tex, Austin, BA, 66, MA, 68; Carleton Univ, PhD(biol), 71. *Prof Exp:* Res scientist, Ecol Sci Div, Oak Ridge Nat Lab, 72-74. *Mem:* AAAS; Am Inst Biol Sci; Ecol Soc Am; Am Soc Mammal; Soc Am Foresters; Am Soc Photo Rem Sensing. *Res:* Physiological ecology and forest ecology. *Mailing Add:* Sch Pub & Environ Affairs Ind Univ Bloomington IN 47405. *Fax:* 812-855-7547; *E-Mail:* randolph@indiana.edu

RANDOLPH, JAMES EUGENE, AEROSPACE MISSION & SYSTEM DESIGN, AEROSPACE MISSION MANAGEMENT. *Current Pos:* mem tech staff, 64-77, SOLAR PROBE STUDY MGR, JET PROPULSION LAB, CALIF INST TECHNOL, 77- *Personal Data:* b Los Angeles, Calif, Jan 19, 40; m 86, Gail Farrar; c John, Julie & Jane. *Educ:* Calif State Univ, Los Angeles, BS, 64; Univ Southern Calif, MS, 67. *Prof Exp:* Systs engr, Viking Mars Studies, 70-72, leader, Mission Planning Team, 72-75, mission engr & sci integration team mgr, Voyager, 75-77, mgr, Starprobe Mission Study, 76-91. *Concurrent Pos:* Systs engr, Viking Mars Studies, 70-72, leader, Mission Planning Team, 72-75, mission engr & sci integration team mgr, Voyager, 75-77, mgr, Starprobe Mission Study, 76-91; mgr, Solar Probe Pre-Proj Develop, NSAS Hq, 89-91, Adv Progs Chief, Space Physics Div, 91. *Mem:* Assoc fel Am Inst Aeronaut & Astronaut; Am Geophys Union. *Res:* Application of advanced science, mission and systems engineering techniques to the design, implementation, and management of interplanetary missions to optimize the return of scientific data. *Mailing Add:* Jet Propulsion Lab Calif Inst Technol 4800 Oak Grove Dr MS301-170U Pasadena CA 91109

RANDOLPH, JUDSON GRAVES, SURGERY. *Current Pos:* SURGEON-IN-CHIEF, CHILDREN'S HOSP, WASHINGTON, DC, 64-; assoc prof, 64-68, PROF SURG, SCH MED, GEORGE WASHINGTON UNIV, 68-, PROF CHILD HEALTH & DEVELOP, 71- *Personal Data:* b Macon, Ga, July 19, 27; m 52; c 5. *Educ:* Vanderbilt Univ, BA, 50, MD, 53. *Prof Exp:* Teaching fel, Harvard Med Sch, 60-61; asst surgeon, Children's Hosp Med Ctr, Boston, 61-63. *Concurrent Pos:* Instr, Harvard Med Sch, 62-63; consult, Nat Naval Med Ctr, Bethesda, 64- & Walter Reed Army Med Ctr, DC, 65-; mem staff, NIH, 65- *Mem:* Am Col Surg; Am Acad Pediat; Am Asn Thoracic Surg; Am Pediat Surg Asn; Soc Univ Surg. *Res:* Burns in children; surgical metabolism in infants; jejunoileal bypass in adolescents; esophageal surgery in infants and children. *Mailing Add:* 3800 Whitland Ave Nashville TN 37205-2432

RANDOLPH, LYNWOOD PARKER, HIGHER EDUCATION ADMINISTRATION. *Current Pos:* CONSULT, 97- *Personal Data:* b Richmond, Va, May 21, 38; m 60, Judith Howard; c Leslie P, Lynwood P II, Leonard P & Lemuel P. *Educ:* Va State Univ, BS, 59; Howard Univ, MS, 64, PhD(physics), 72. *Prof Exp:* Physicist, Harry Diamond Labs, 64-68, res physicist, 68-75; prog mgr, NASA, 75-80, mgr, 80-82, dep dir productivity, 82-85, chief mgt progs, 85-90, dir, Info Technol Stand, 90-95; dir, Qual Inst, Clark Atlanta Univ, 95-96. *Concurrent Pos:* Lectr, Univ DC, 72-80; adj prof, Univ DC & Howard Univ, 80-82; colloquium speaker, Am Phys Soc, 90-97. *Mem:* Assoc fel Am Inst Aeronaut & Astronaut; Am Phys Soc; AAAS; sr mem Inst Elec & Electronics Engrs; Am Soc Qual Control; Nat Soc Black Physicists. *Res:* Solar cells and other devices which convert sunlight into electrical energy; lasers to be used in the future to transmit power or propel spacecraft into space; radiation-induced effects in optoelectronic materials. *Mailing Add:* 3000 Fairhill Ct Suitland MD 20746. *Fax:* 202-358-3745; *E-Mail:* lrandolp@hq.nasa.gov

RANDOLPH, MALCOLM LOGAN, biophysics, radiobiology; deceased, see previous edition for last biography

RANDOLPH, PAUL HERBERT, OPERATIONS RESEARCH. *Current Pos:* PROF, INFO SYSTS & QUANT SCI, COL BUS ADMIN, TEX TECH UNIV, 81- *Personal Data:* b Jamestown, NY, Jan 14, 25; m 48, Dorothy Overn; c Karl, Elizabeth, Nancy, David, Erica & Jon. *Educ:* Univ Minn, BA, 48, MA, 49, PhD(statist), 55. *Prof Exp:* Instr math, Bethany Lutheran Col, 49-50; instr bus admin, Univ Minn, 50-53; asst prof indust eng, Ill Inst Technol, 54-57; assoc prof math & statist, Purdue Univ, 57-66; from assoc prof to prof math, NMex State Univ, 66-74; prof eng, Iowa State Univ, 74-76; opers res anal, Dept Energy, 76-77; vpres energy econ, Chase Manhattan Bank, 77-79; sr assoc engr, Mobil Res & Develop Corp, 79-81. *Concurrent Pos:* Guest prof, Univ Heidelberg, 64-65; sci adv, Norsk Regnesentral, 65-66; consult, Braddock, Dunn & McDonald, 66-69, White Sands Missile Range, 69-73; vis prof, Mid East Tech Univ, Turkey, 70-71; vis prof, Inst Math, Univ Oslo, 73-74; sr Fulbright prof, Mid East Tech Univ, Ankara, Turkey, 90-91 & 95-96; vis distinguished prof, Opers Res, US Army Logistics Mgt Col, Ft Lee, VA, 86-87. *Mem:* Opers Res Soc Am; Inst Mgt Sci; Am Inst Indust Engrs; Asn Comput Mach; Sigma Xi; Am Prod Inventor Control Soc. *Res:* Optimization techniques; expert systems; decision support systems; distance education; optimal stopping rules. *Mailing Add:* Info Systs & Quant Sci Tex Tech Univ Lubbock TX 79409-2101. *Fax:* 806-742-2099; *E-Mail:* odphr@coba.ttu.edu

RANDOLPH, PHILIP L, PHYSICS, RESEARCH ADMINISTRATION. *Current Pos:* assoc dir, 77-79, DIR UNCONVENTIONAL SUPPLY RES, INST GAS TECHNOL, 79- *Personal Data:* b Casper, Wyo, Feb 25, 31; m 52; c 2. *Educ:* Univ Wash, BS, 52, PhD(physics), 58. *Prof Exp:* Physicist, Lawrence Radiation Lab, Univ Calif, Livermore, 58-61, dep tech dir, Proj Gnome, 61-62, tech dir salmon event, Proj Dribble, 62-63 & 64-66, assoc div leader, 66-68; mgr nuclear group, El Paso Natural Gas Co, 68-74, dir res, 74-77. *Mem:* Am Phys Soc; Am Nuclear Soc; Soc Petrol Engr. *Res:* Nuclear explosive test execution; use of nuclear explosives to stimulate natural gas production and produce underground storage for natural gas; massive hydraulic fracturing of tight natural gas reservoirs; improving quantitative understanding of natural gas well completions and reservoir rock properties; producing natural gas from aquifers and coal seams; underground gas storage. *Mailing Add:* 1713 Crestwood Dr Texas City TX 77591

RANDRUP, JORGEN, HEAVY-ION REACTIONS, NUCLEAR DYNAMICS. *Current Pos:* div fel, 78-81, SR PHYSICIST, NUCLEAR SCI DIV, LAWRENCE BERKELEY LAB, UNIV CALIF, BERKELEY, 81-, HEAD, NUCLEAR THEORY PROG, 93- *Personal Data:* b Aarhus, Denmark, Sept 23, 46. *Educ:* Univ Aarhus, Cand Scient, 70, Lic Scient, 72. *Honors & Awards:* Sr Scientist Award, Alexander von Humboldt Found, 89. *Prof Exp:* Res fel, Physics Dept, Univ Aarhus, Denmark, 72-75; res fel, Niels Bohr Inst, Copenhagen, 75-76, Nordita, 76-79. *Concurrent Pos:* Vis researcher, Nuclear Sci Div, Lawrence Berkeley Lab, Univ Calif, Berkeley, 72-73; fel, Nuclear Sci Div, Lawrence Berkeley Lab, 73-75; vis prof, GSI, Darmstadt, Ger, 74-75 & Nordita, Copehagen, 84-85; res assoc, Caltech, Pasadena, Calif, 77-78; sci dir, Nuclear Theory & Data Eval, Nuclear Sci Div, Lawrence Berkeley Lab, 87-91; lectr, Physics Dept, Univ Calif Berkeley, 88; assoc div ed, Physics Rev Lett, 89-91; vis scientist, GSI, Darmstadt, Ger, 91-92. *Mem:* Am Phys Soc. *Res:* Theoretical nuclear physics especially heavy ion reactions; nuclear physics. *Mailing Add:* Nuclear Sci Div 70A-3307 Lawrence Berkeley Lab One Cyclotron Rd Berkeley CA 94720

RANDT, CLARK THORP, neurology; deceased, see previous edition for last biography

RANDTKE, STEPHEN JAMES, DRINKING WATER QUALITY & TREATMENT, PHYSICAL & CHEMICAL PROCESSES FOR WATER & WASTEWATER TREATMENT. *Current Pos:* assoc prof, 83-89, res engr, Air/Ecosyst Interactions Res Lab 86-92, PROF, CIVIL & ENVIRON ENG, UNIV KANS, 89-, CO-DIR, ENVIRON ENG & SCI RES LAB & CO-DIR, ENVIRON ENG & SCI GRAD PROG, 92- *Personal Data:* b Rochester, NY, Oct 3, 50; m 76, Jessie L Luke; c Stacy, S Joseph, John & Mark. *Educ:* Loyola Univ, BS, 72, Stanford Univ, MS, 73; PhD(civil/environ eng), 77. *Prof Exp:* Student engr, Los Angeles Dept Water & Power, 73, asst engr, 74; asst prof, Univ Ill, 77-83. *Concurrent Pos:* Consult, Black & Veatch, 88-, Jordan, Jones & Goulding, 89-91 & 94-, Johnson Co Water Dist No 1, 92 & 95, E Bay Munic Utility Dis, Oakland, Calif, 95- & CH2M-Hill, 96-; bd trustee, Res Div, Am Water Works Asn, 91-, vchair, 94-95, chair, 95-; bd dirs, Asn Environ Eng Profs, 92-96. *Mem:* Am Acad Environ Engrs; AAAS; Am Water Works Asn; Asn Environ Eng Profs (vpres, 93-94, pres, 94-95); Water Environ Fedn; Int Asn Water Qual. *Res:* Control of naturally occuring and synthetic chemical contaminants in public water supplies through source control, conventional treatment and advanced treatment technology; sources and transformations of chemical contaminants in water supplies; formation of trihalomethanes and other halogenated byproducts during chlorination of drinking water;; natural and airborne sources of water contaminants; lime softening of water supplies, particularly in regard to removal of trace contaminants; authored over 90 technical publications. *Mailing Add:* Dept Civil & Environ Eng Univ Kans Lawrence KS 66045

RANEY, GEORGE NEAL, MATHEMATICS. *Current Pos:* assoc prof, 63-66, prof, 66-85, EMER PROF MATH, UNIV CONN, 85- *Personal Data:* b Portland, Ore, Oct 14, 22; m 52, Barbara Robinson; c Rebecca & Patricia. *Educ:* Queens Col, NY, BS, 43; Columbia Univ, PhD(math), 53. *Prof Exp:* Instr math, Mass Inst Technol, 43-44; lectr, Columbia Univ, 46-50, instr, 50-53; instr, Brooklyn Col, 53-55; from asst prof to assoc prof, Pa State Univ, 55-61; vis assoc prof, Wesleyan Univ, 61-63. *Mem:* Am Math Soc. *Res:* Lattice theory; combinatorial analysis; automata theory; continued fractions. *Mailing Add:* Dept Math Univ Conn Storrs CT 06268

RANEY, RUSSELL KEITH, REMOTE SENSING. *Current Pos:* chief radar scientist, Radarsat, 84-89, RES SCIENTIST, DEPT ENERGY, MINES & RESOURCES, FED GOVT CAN, 76-, CHIEF RADAR SCIENTIST, CAN CENTRE FOR REMOTE SENSING. *Personal Data:* b Auburn, NY, Dec 26, 37; Can citizen. *Educ:* Harvard Univ, BS, 60; Purdue Univ, MS, 62; Univ Mich, Ann Arbor, PhD(comput, info & control eng), 68. *Honors & Awards:* Distinguished Achievement & Outstanding Serv Award, Geosci & RSM Sensing Soc, Inst Elec & Electronic Engrs. *Prof Exp:* Asst engr, Zenith Radio Corp, Ill, 60; engr, Systs Div, Bendix Corp, Mich, 62-63; res engr, Willow Run Labs, Univ Mich, Ann Arbor, 62-74, res engr, Environ Res Inst Mich, 74-76. *Concurrent Pos:* Consult, NASA, 74- & Europ Space Agency, 77. *Mem:* Can Remote Sensing Soc; fel Inst Elec & Electronic Engrs; Int Remote Sensing Soc. *Res:* Application of radar remote sensing systems to environmental surveillance, synthetic aperture radar research; dissemination and utilization of scientific knowledge; oceanic reflectivity; systems development; planetary radar. *Mailing Add:* Johns Hopkins Univ Appl Physics Lab Johns Hopkins Rd Laurel MD 20723

RANEY, WILLIAM PERIN, PHYSICS, ACOUSTICS. *Current Pos:* RETIRED. *Personal Data:* b Neenah, Wis, June 27, 27; m 53, Carol Burnell; c Jennifer, Christopher, Anneke & Gillian. *Educ:* Harvard Univ, AB, 50; Brown Univ, ScM, 53, PhD(physics), 55. *Hon Degrees:* DSc, Lawrence Univ, 77. *Prof Exp:* Res assoc physics, Brown Univ, 54-55; res fel acoustics, Harvard Univ, 55-56, asst prof appl physics, 56-60; assoc prof elec eng, Univ Minn, 60-62; exec secy, Comt Undersea Warfare, Nat Acad Sci-Nat Res Coun, 62-64; spec asst to asst secy navy for res & develop, 64-72; dep & chief scientist, Off Naval Res, 72-76; sr policy analyst, Off Sci & Tech Policy, NASA, 77-78, asst assoc admin space sci & appln, 78-84, dir utilization & req, 84-87, spec asst dir, Space Sta, 87-94. *Concurrent Pos:* Mem tech staff, Bell Tel Labs, 59-60. *Mem:* AAAS; Acoust Soc Am; Am Phys Soc; Sigma Xi. *Res:* Physical acoustics; sound propagation in inhomogeneous media; finite amplitude effects; propagation at hypersonic frequencies; linear systems analysis. *Mailing Add:* 5946 Wilton Rd Alexandria VA 22310-2150. *E-Mail:* wraney@compuserve.com

RANFTL, ROBERT M(ATTHEW), TECHNOLOGICAL PRODUCTIVITY & CREATIVITY. *Current Pos:* PRES, RANFTL ENTERPRISES INC, 81- *Personal Data:* b Milwaukee, Wis, May 31, 25; m 46. *Educ:* Univ Mich, BSEE, 46. *Prof Exp:* Prod engr, Russell Elec Co, 46-47; head, Eng Dept, Radio Inst Chicago, 47-50; sr proj engr, Webster Chicago Corp, 50-51; prod design engr, 51-53, head equip design group, 53-54, head electronic equip sect, 54-55, mgr, Prod Eng Dept, 55-58, mgr reliability & qual control, 58-59, mgr admin, 59-61, mgr, Prod Effectiveness Lab, 61-77; corp dir configuration mgt, data mgt & design rev, Hughes Aircraft Co, 64-74, corp dir eng & design mgt, 74-84, asst dir prod integrity, 77-84, corp dir managerial prod, 84-86. *Concurrent Pos:* Teacher res & develop mgt & prod, Hughes Aircraft Co, 75-86; consult, res & develop mgt, creativity & prod, 78-; instr eng & mgt prog, Univ Calif, Los Angeles, 87- *Mem:* AAAS; Am Inst Aeronaut & Astronaut; sr mem Inst Elec & Electronics Eng; NY Acad Sci. *Res:* Means of improving creativity and productivity in technology-based organizations. *Mailing Add:* Ranftl Enterprises Inc PO Box 49892 Los Angeles CA 90049

RANG, EDWARD ROY, APPLIED MATHEMATICS, GENERAL COMPUTER SCIENCES. *Current Pos:* PROF MATH & COMPUT, UNIV WIS-RIVER FALLS, 86- *Personal Data:* b Milwaukee, Wis, Dec 23, 27; m 87; c 2. *Educ:* Univ Wis-Madison, BS, 49, MS, 50; Univ Minn, Minneapolis, PhD(math), 57. *Prof Exp:* Asst prof mech, Univ Minn, 57-60; res eng, Honeywell, 60-86. *Concurrent Pos:* Prof, US Naval Postgrad Sch, 68-69. *Mem:* Soc Indust & Appl Math; Inst Elec & Electronics Engrs; Math Asn Am; Sigma Xi; Asn Comput Mach. *Res:* Automatic control theory; applied mathematics. *Mailing Add:* 505 Tower Rd Hudson WI 54016-8120

RANGACHARI, PATANGI SRINIVASA KUMAR, EPITHELIAL PHYSIOLOGY, GASTRO-INTESTINAL PHARMACOLOGY. *Current Pos:* Can Heart Found fel, 81-83, PROF, DEPT MED, MCMASTER UNIV, 83- *Personal Data:* b Tiruchirapalli, India, Jan 15, 43; Can citizen; m 77, Usha Ranganathan; c Manu. *Educ:* All-India Inst Med Sci, MBBS, 66; Univ Alta, Edmonton, PhD(pharmacol), 72. *Honors & Awards:* Annual Award, Pharamacol Soc Can, 86. *Prof Exp:* Fel, Cardiovasc Res Inst, Univ Calif, San Francisco, 72-76; res asst, Hosp Necker, Paris, France, 74-76; reader pharmacol, Delhi Univ, India, 76-80; res worker, Hosp Bichat, Paris, 80-81; res assoc, Harvard Dept Anat, Beth Israel Hosp, 83. *Mem:* Sigma Xi; Am Physiol Soc; Am Soc Pharmacol & Exp Therapeut; Biophys Soc; Can Asn Gastroenterol; Can Soc Clin Pharmacol. *Res:* Study the effects of inflammatory mediators and neurotransmitters on epithelial ion transport (principally the stomach, colon). *Mailing Add:* Dept Med McMaster Univ Hamilton ON L8N 3Z5 Can. *Fax:* 905-522-3454; *E-Mail:* chair@fls.memastu.ca

RANGACHARYULU, CHILAKAMARRI, DISCRETE SYMMETRIES, NUCLEAR STRUCTURE. *Current Pos:* res assoc, 79-83, from asst prof to assoc prof, 83-88, PROF PHYSICS, UNIV SASK, 94- *Personal Data:* b Rajahmundry, India, Aug 15, 47; Can citizen. *Educ:* Andhra Univ, BS, 66, MS, 68; Indian Inst Kanpur, PhD(nuclear physics), 72. *Prof Exp:* Mombusho foreign res fel, Osaka Univ, Japan, 72-75; fel, Univ Laval, Que, 75-79. *Mem:* Am Phys Soc; Can Asn Physicists. *Res:* Subatomic physics with experiments on discrete symmetries and nuclear structure by decay and reaction studies; investigation of signatures of chaos in microwave cavities and other physical systems; nuclear reactions; instrumentation for particle detection; quantum chaos; physics education. *Mailing Add:* Dept Physics & Eng Physics Univ Sask 116 Sci Pl Saskatoon SK S7N 0W0 Can. *Fax:* 306-966-6400; *E-Mail:* chary@sask.usask.ca

RANGANATHAN, BRAHMANPALLI NARASIMHAMURTHY, METALLURGICAL ENGINEERING. *Current Pos:* mgr, 92-93, PROG MGR, A O SMITH CORP TECH CTR, 94- *Personal Data:* b Madras, India, Feb 14, 45; US citizen; m 72, Aruna; c Vishnu. *Educ:* Indian Inst Sci, BE, 68; Ga Tech, PhD(metall), 72. *Prof Exp:* Group engr, Martin Marietta Michoud Aerospace, 81-84, chief res progs, Advan Qual Technol, 84-90, sr scientist, Martin Marietta Corp Labs, 90-92. *Mem:* Am Soc Metals; Am Soc Nondestructive Testing. *Res:* Physical metallurgy; characterization of materials; composites. *Mailing Add:* A O Smith Corp Tech Ctr PO Box 23990 Milwaukee WI 53223

RANGANATHAN, SUBRAMANIAN, NON-EQUILIBRIUM & EQUILIBRIUM STATISTICAL MECHANICS, MOLECULAR DYNAMICS SIMULATION & KINETIC THEORY OF FLUIDS. *Current Pos:* res assoc, Royal Mil Col, 68-69, from asst prof to assoc prof, 69-83. head, Dept Math & Comput Sci, 85-94, dir res admin, 94-95, PROF, ROYAL MIL COL, 83-, DIR, CTR SPACE RES, 95- *Personal Data:* b Madras, India, Apr 12, 41; Can citizen; m 70, Muthulakshmi Kalyanakrishnan; c Shoba. *Educ:* Delhi Univ, BSc, 60, MSc, 62, Indian Inst Technol, MTech, 63; Cornell Univ, PhD(appl physics), 67. *Prof Exp:* Res assoc, Cornell Univ, 67-68. *Concurrent Pos:* Res grants, Acad Res Prog Nat Defense, 75-; vis assoc, Calif Inst Technol, 79; vis scientist, Mass Inst Technol, 78, Atomic Energy Res Estab, 81-82; exchange prof, Royal Mil Col Sci, 81-82, distinguished prof, 94; vis prof, Univ BC, 86; vis fel, Australian Nat Univ, 92. *Mem:* Am Phys Soc; Can Asn Physicists; Can Inst Neutron Scattering. *Res:* Investigation of static, dynamic and transport properties of two and three-dimensional classical systems-fluids, electron gas, yukawa, liquid metals-by molecular dynamics and theoretical methods. *Mailing Add:* Dept Physics Royal Mil Col PO Box 17000 Stn Forces Kingston ON K7K 7B4 Can. *Fax:* 613-541-6040; *E-Mail:* ranganathan-s@rmc.ca

RANGANAYAKI, RAMBABU POTHIREDDY, GEOPHYSICS. *Current Pos:* sr staff geophysicist, Mobil Res & Develop Corp, 80-84, res geophysicist, 84-85, sr res geophysicist, 85-89, ASSOC, MOBIL RES & DEVELOP CORP, 89- *Personal Data:* b Secunderabad, India, Jan 15, 42; m 68; c Anita & Anuja. *Educ:* Osmania Univ, India, MSc, 64; Univ Hawaii, Honolulu, MS, 72; Mass Inst Technol, PhD(geophys), 78. *Prof Exp:* Sr sci asst geomagnetism, Nat Geophys Res Inst, India, 64-69, scientist, 69-70; res asst geophys, Mass Inst Technol, 72-78; res assoc geophys, Carnegie Inst Washington, 78-80. *Mem:* Am Geophys Union; Soc Explor Geophysicists; Sigma Xi. *Res:* Magnetotelluric depth sounding; geomagnetic depth sounding; data analysis and interpretation; model development; paleomagnetism; induced polarization; vertical seismic profiling; enhanced oil recovery monitoring; prestack migration. *Mailing Add:* 3212 Executive Circle Farmers Branch TX 75234. *E-Mail:* rprangan@dal.mobil.com

RANGE, R MICHAEL, CAUCHY-RIEMANN EQUATIONS, INTEGRAL REPRESENTATIONS. *Current Pos:* from asst prof to assoc prof, 73-83, chmn, Dept Math, 92-94, PROF MATH, STATE UNIV NY, ALBANY, 83- *Personal Data:* b WGer, Aug 7, 44; m 69, Alexandria Villegas; c Ofelia, Marisa & Roberto. *Educ:* Univ Gottingen, dipl, 68; Univ Calif, Los Angeles, PhD(math), 71. *Prof Exp:* J W Gibbs instr math, Yale Univ, 71-73. *Concurrent Pos:* Vis asst prof, Univ Wash, Seattle, 75-76; res prof, Univ Bonn, WGer, 80, Max Planck Inst Math, 84 & 86, Ctr de Recerca Maths, Univ Autonoma Barcelona, 89. *Mem:* Am Math Soc; Ger Math Soc; Math Asn Am. *Res:* Multidimensional complex analysis; analytic methods and problems involving integral representations. *Mailing Add:* Dept Math State Univ NY Albany NY 12222. *Fax:* 518-442-4731; *E-Mail:* range@math.albany.edu

RANGEL ALDAO, RAFAEL, MOLECULAR BIOLOGY, DEVELOPMENT OF DIAGNOSTIC METHODS FOR MICROBES THAT CONTAMINATE FOODS. *Current Pos:* PROF CELLULAR BIOL, SIMON BOLIVAR UNIV, 87-; NAT MGR BIOTECHNOL, CERVECERIA POLAR CA, 87- *Personal Data:* b Caracas, Venezuela, May 5, 46; m 70, Doris Serrano de Rangel; c Dorella R & Rafael E. *Educ:* Cent Univ Venezuela, MD, 69; Yeshiva Univ, MS, 75, PhD, 77. *Honors & Awards:* Interam Prize of Sci & Technol, Orgn Am States, 85. *Prof Exp:* Instr biochem, Cent Univ Venezuela, 69-72; res assoc, Albert Einstein Col Med, 77-78; from asst prof to prof biochem, Carabobo Univ, 78-87. *Concurrent Pos:* chmn, Iberoam Biotechnol, 87; consult, WHO, Geneva, 87; sr adv, Inst Advan Studies, 92. *Mem:* NY Acad Sci; Am Soc Biochem & Molecular Biol; Am Soc Microbiol; Am Soc Parasitologists; Soc Protozoologists; Am Soc Trop Med & Hyg. *Mailing Add:* Buzoom A-CCS A-0074 PO Box 028537 Miami FL 33102. *Fax:* 305-202-3065

RANGER, KEITH BRIAN, APPLIED MATHEMATICS. *Current Pos:* lectr, 61-63, from asst prof to assoc prof, 63-70, PROF MATH, UNIV TORONTO, 70- *Personal Data:* b Salisbury, Eng, Aug 11, 35; m 59; c 2. *Educ:* Univ London, BSc, 56, PhD, 59. *Prof Exp:* Asst lectr math, Bedford Col, London, 58-61. *Mem:* Am Math Soc; Soc Indust & Appl Math; Can Math Cong. *Res:* Axially symmetric potentials; slow motion of a viscous fluid; magnetohydrodynamics. *Mailing Add:* Dept Math Univ Toronto 100 St George St Toronto ON M5S 3G3 Can

RANGO, ALBERT, WATERSHED MANAGEMENT, REMOTE SENSING. *Current Pos:* sr hydrologist, 72-80, head, Hydrological Sci Br, 80-83, CHIEF, HYDROL LAB, AGR RES SERV, NASA, 83- *Personal Data:* b Cleveland, Ohio, Nov 7, 42; m 66; c 1. *Educ:* Pa State Univ, BS, 65, MS, 66; Colo State Univ, PhD(watershed mgt), 69. *Prof Exp:* Asst prof meteorol, Pa State Univ, University Park, 69-72; *Concurrent Pos:* Consult, Environ Serv Oper, E G & G, 68-69; vis instr, State Univ NY Col Buffalo, 70. *Mem:* Am Meteorol Soc; Am Geophys Union; Am Water Resources Asn. *Res:* Weather modification effects; fluvial geomorphology; snow hydrology; bioclimatology; watershed modelling; watershed physiography; floodplain mapping; soil moisture; meteorology; snowmelt-runoff modeling. *Mailing Add:* 127 Southwood Ave Silver Spring MD 20901

RANHAND, JON M, HEALTH SCIENCE ADMINISTRATION. *Current Pos:* SR SCIENTIST, USPHS, 73- *Personal Data:* b New York, NY, Feb 11, 39; m 63, Barbara Oidick; c Sharon & Carla. *Educ:* City Col New York, BS, 61; Johns Hopkins Univ, MS, 64; Univ Cincinnati, PhD(microbiol), 68. *Prof Exp:* Fel, Lab Microbiol, NIH, 68-69, staff fel, 69-73. *Mailing Add:* 17 Barrington Fare Rockville MD 20850. *Fax:* 301-480-3541; *E-Mail:* jr57x@nih.gov

RANHOTRA, GURBACHAN SINGH, NUTRITIONAL BIOCHEMISTRY. *Current Pos:* group leader, 69-80, DIR NUTRIT RES, AM INST BAKING, 81- *Personal Data:* b Abbotabad, India, Aug 8, 35; m 60; c 2. *Educ:* Agra Univ, BS, 58, MS, 60; Univ Minn, PhD(nutrit), 64. *Prof Exp:* Fel nutrit biochem, Univ Ill, Urbana, 64-65; assoc prof nutrit, Punjab Agr Univ, 65-68; assoc mem biochem, Univ Okla, 68-69. *Concurrent Pos:* Adj prof foods & nutrit, Kans State Univ; assoc ed, Cereal Chem, 79-83, J Food Science, 84-87, ed tech bulletins, Am Inst Baking, 88- *Mem:* Am Inst Nutrit; Am Asn Cereal Chem; Inst Food Technologists. *Res:* Fiber lipids; minerals; cereal-based foods. *Mailing Add:* Nutrit Res Am Inst Baking 1213 Bakers Way Manhattan KS 66502. *Fax:* 785-537-1493

RANIERI, RICHARD LEO, ORGANIC CHEMISTRY. *Current Pos:* AT SANDOZ CHEM CORP. *Personal Data:* b Chicago Heights, Ill, Oct 30, 43; m 71. *Educ:* Univ Ill, BS, 65; Univ Toledo, PhD(chem), 73. *Prof Exp:* Fel, Dept Med Chem & Pharmacog, Purdue Univ, 73-76; res chem, Wash Res Ctr, W R Grace & Co, 76-80; mem staff, Sodyeco Div, Martin Marietta Co, 80- *Mem:* Am Soc Pharmacog; Am Chem Soc. *Res:* Structure elucidation by spectroscopy; tetrahydrolsoquinoline synthesis; chromatography; organophosphorus chemistry; natural products chemistry. *Mailing Add:* 3238 Sunnybrook Dr Charlotte NC 28210-3229

RANK, GERALD HENRY, GENETICS MOLECULAR BIOLOGY, FOOD SCIENCE & TECHNOLOGY. *Current Pos:* PROF BIOL, UNIV SASK, 75- *Personal Data:* b Man, Sept 30, 40; m 68; c 2. *Educ:* Univ Man, BScAg, 63, MSc, 64; Univ BC, PhD(genetics), 70. *Mem:* Can Soc Genetics. *Res:* Molecular evolution; breeding of the alfalfa leafcutter bee; gene transfer in industrial Saccaromyces yeasts; expression of antisense RNA; genome sequencing. *Mailing Add:* Dept Biol Univ Sask 112 Science Pl Saskatoon SK S7N 5E2 Can

RANK, ROGER GERALD, IMMUNOLOGY OF CHLAMYDIA INFECTIONS. *Current Pos:* From asst prof to assoc prof, 76-89, PROF, UNIV ARK MED SCI, 89-, CHMN, 92- *Personal Data:* b W Reading, Pa, Mar 24, 49; m 86, Sigrun Simons; c Timothy M & Christopher J. *Educ:* Albright Col, BS, 71; Hahnemann Med Col, MS, 73, PhD(microbiol & immunol), 75. *Mem:* Am Soc Microbiol. *Res:* Immunology and pathogenesis of genital and ocular infections caused by Chlamydia. *Mailing Add:* Dept Microbiol & Immunol Univ Ark Med Sci 4301 W Markham St Little Rock AR 72205-7101. *Fax:* 501-686-5359; *E-Mail:* rgrank@biom.ed.uams.edu

RANKEL, LILLIAN ANN, INORGANIC CHEMISTRY. *Current Pos:* ASSOC CHEM CATALYSIS, MOBIL RES & DEVELOP CORP, 77- *Personal Data:* b New York, NY; m 81, Andrew Jackson; c 3. *Educ:* Molloy Col, BS, 66; Fordham Univ, MS, 68; Princeton Univ, PhD(inorg chem), 77. *Prof Exp:* Assoc mem technol staff chem, Bell Labs, Murray Hill, NJ, 68-73; res asst, Princeton Univ, 73-77. *Mem:* Am Chem Soc. *Res:* Catalyst characterization of zeolites and other materials for ability to crack, hydrogenate, isomerize, aromatize, etc., model compounds and/or refinery feed streams to yield more valuable products; automated testing equipment is designed, built, and used for these catalyst characterization methods. *Mailing Add:* 4 Walking Purchase Dr Pennington NJ 08534

RANKEN, WILLIAM ALLISON, ENERGY CONVERSION. *Current Pos:* RETIRED. *Personal Data:* b Amityville, NY, Jan 18, 28; m 51; c 3. *Educ:* Yale Univ, BS, 49; Rice Univ, MS, 56, PhD(physics), 58. *Prof Exp:* Res asst weapons develop, Los Alamos Sci Lab, 50-52, staff mem, 52-54; res physicist, Union Carbide Nuclear Co, NY, 57-58; staff mem, Advan Propulsion Group, Los Alamos Sci Lab, 58-62, from asst group leader to group leader, 62-73, group leader, Advan Heat Transfer Group, 73-77, alt group leader, Reactor & Advan Heat Transfer Technol Group, 77-91. *Mem:* AAAS; Am Phys Soc; Sigma Xi. *Res:* Heat pipe technology; thermionic conversion; radiation damage; low energy nuclear physics; nuclear reactor development. *Mailing Add:* 1031 Colusa Ave Berkeley CA 94707-2515

RANKER, TOM A, BOTANY. *Current Pos:* PROF, DEPT BOT, UNIV COLO. *Honors & Awards:* Edgar T Wherry Award, Bot Soc Am, 92. *Res:* Botany. *Mailing Add:* Dept Bot Univ Colo Box 334 Boulder CO 80309-0334

RANKIN, DOUGLAS WHITING, TECTONICS, VOLCANOLOGY. *Current Pos:* CONSULT, 83- *Personal Data:* b Wilmington, Del, Sept 9, 31; m 56, Mary L Backus; c Katharine N & Andrea L. *Educ:* Colgate Univ, BA, 53; Harvard Univ, MA, 55, PhD, 61. *Prof Exp:* Field asst, US Geol Surv, Colo, 54; asst prof geol, Vanderbilt Univ, 58-61; geologist & teacher, AID, Washington, DC, 61-62; geologist, US Geol Surv, 62-78, supvry geologist, 78-83. *Concurrent Pos:* Staff scientist, Lunar Sample Off, NASA, 72; coordr,

Charleston Invests, SC, 76-78; chief, Br Eastern Regional Geol, 78-83. *Mem:* AAAS; fel Geol Soc Am; fel Mineral Soc Am; Am Geophys Union. *Res:* Paleovolcanology and tectonics of the Appalachian orogenic belt; geology of the Absaroka volcanic field in Wyoming; intraplate earthquakes; geology of the US Virgin Islands. *Mailing Add:* US Geol Surv Stop 926 Nat Ctr Reston VA 20192

RANKIN, GARY O'NEAL, CHEMICAL-INDUCED TOXICITY, NEPHROTOXICITY. *Current Pos:* from asst prof to assoc prof, 78-86, assoc dean biomed grad educ & res develop, 89-92, PROF & CHMN DEPT PHARMACOL, MARSHALL UNIV SCH MED, 86- *Personal Data:* b Little Rock, Ark, Oct 6, 49; m 92, Monica Valentovic. *Educ:* Univ Ark, Little Rock, BS, 72; Univ Miss, PhD(med chem), 76. *Honors & Awards:* Res Award, Am Heart Asn, WVa affil. *Prof Exp:* Teaching assoc, pharmacol, Med Col Ohio, 76-78. *Concurrent Pos:* Mem subcomt, Prof Utilization & Training, Am Soc Pharmacol & Exp Therapeut, 86-, chair, 89, prof Affairs Comt, 93-; ad hoc rev, Toxicol Study Sect, NIH, 87 & 93, mem, 94-; mem, group educ affairs, Asn Am Med Cols, 90-92; toxicol 90's educ issues task force, Soc Toxicol, 91-94, chair, 92-94; assoc ed, Toxicol Appl Pharmacol, 95-; jour reviewer. *Mem:* Am Soc Pharmacol & Exp Therapeut; Soc Toxicol; NY Acad Sci; Soc Exp Biol & Med; Int Soc Study Xenobiotics; Genetic Toxicol Asn; Sigma Xi; Am Chem Soc; AAAS; Asn Med Sch Pharmacol. *Res:* Increasing understanding of why chemicals are toxic, examining chemical structure and its relationship to toxicity with select kidney toxins. *Mailing Add:* Dept Pharmacol Marshall Univ Sch Med Huntington WV 25755-9310. *E-Mail:* rankin@marshall.edu

RANKIN, JOANNA MARIE, RADIO ASTRONOMY. *Current Pos:* assoc prof, 80-88, PROF PHYSICS & ASTRON, UNIV VT, 88- *Personal Data:* b Denver, Colo. *Educ:* Southern Methodist Univ, BS, 65; Tulane Univ, MS, 66; Univ Iowa, PhD(astrophys), 70. *Prof Exp:* Res assoc radio astron, Univ Iowa, 70-74; asst prof astron, Cornell Univ, 74-78, sr res assoc hist, 78-80. *Concurrent Pos:* Vis scientist, Arecibo Observ, PR, 69-78; Am Philos Soc res grant, Radiophys Div, Commonwealth Sci Indust Res Orgn, Sydney, Australia, 72; grants, NSF & Res Corp, 73-; actg head, Arecibo Observ Comput Dept, 75; Indo-Am fel, Raman Res Inst, Bangalore, India, 90-91; Fulbright fel, 93-94. *Mem:* Int Union Radio Sci; Int Astron Union; Am Astron Soc. *Res:* Observational properties of pulsars and the interstellar medium; history and philosophy of contemporary physical science; feminist perspectives on contemporary science. *Mailing Add:* Dept Physics Cook Bldg A405 Univ Vt Burlington VT 05401

RANKIN, JOEL SENDER, OBSTETRICS & GYNECOLOGY, ENDOCRINOLOGY. *Current Pos:* ASSOC PROF OBSTET & GYNEC, SCH MED, BOSTON UNIV, 69-, UNIV MASS, 80- *Personal Data:* b Brockton, Mass, Sept 13, 31; wid; c Danielle & Jonathan. *Educ:* Yale Univ, BA, 53; Boston Univ, MD, 57; Am Bd Obstet & Gynec, dipl, 65. *Prof Exp:* Intern med, Beth Israel Hosp, Boston, 57-58; resident surg, Mass Mem Hosp, 58-59; resident obstet & gynec, Boston City Hosp, 59-62; officer in chg, Castle AFB Hosp, Calif, 62-64; asst clin prof obstet & gynec, Western Res Univ, 66-69; dir obstet & gynec, Framingham Union Hosp, 75-96; chmn, Dept Obstet & Gynec, Metrowest Med Ctr, 92-96. *Concurrent Pos:* USPHS fel endocrinol, Jefferson Med Col, 64-66; asst dir obstet & gynec, Mt Sinai Hosp Cleveland, Ohio; asst obstetrician & gynecologist, Cleveland Metrop Gen Hosp, dir endocrine-steril clin, 66-69, asst vis obstetrician & gynecologist, 67-69; dir gynec-infertility clin, Boston City Hosp, Mass, 69-75, assoc vis surg, 69-90; assoc vis gynecologist, Univ Hosp, Boston, 69-90; lectr, Harvard Med Sch, 95- *Mem:* Am Col Obstet & Gynec; Am Soc Reprod Med. *Mailing Add:* 115 Lincoln St Framingham MA 01701

RANKIN, JOHN CARTER, CEREAL CHEMISTRY. *Current Pos:* Chemist carbohydrate & starch chem, USDA, 46-58, res chemist, 58-67, prof leader cereal chem, Northern Regional Res Lab, Agr Res Serv, 67-79, CONSULT STARCH CHEM, USDA, 80- *Personal Data:* b Knoxville, Tenn, Dec 21, 19; m 43, Ruth E Kirk; c Christine K (Yutrzenka), Mark K & Ellen E (Mallory). *Educ:* Bradley Univ, BS, 42, MS, 55. *Honors & Awards:* Fed Inventors Award, US Dept Com, 80. *Mem:* Am Chem Soc; Sigma Xi; Tech Asn Pulp & Paper Indust; NY Acad Sci. *Res:* Reactions of carbohydrates; structure of starch and dextrans; starch and flour derivatives; utilization of cereal grains and fractions therefrom in films, paper, and textiles. *Mailing Add:* 1734 E Maple Ridge Dr Peoria IL 61614

RANKIN, JOSEPH EUGENE, PSYCHIATRY. *Current Pos:* PROF PSYCHIAT, SCH MED, GEORGE WASHINGTON UNIV, 56- *Personal Data:* b Washington, DC, Jan 13, 20; m 43; c 3. *Educ:* Cath Univ Am, BS, 42; George Washington Univ, MD, 46; Wash Psychoanal Inst, grad, 66. *Prof Exp:* Intern, US Naval Hosp, Oakland, Calif, 47; intern, US Naval Hosp, Bethesda, Md, 47, resident neurol, 48; resident psychiat, St Elizabeth's Hosp, Washington, DC, 50-52; mem staff, Child Guid Clin, Cath Univ Am, 52-56. *Concurrent Pos:* Mem psychother dept, St Elizabeth's Hosp, Washington, DC, 52-56, consult, 57-62; consult, DC Gen Hosp, 57-61 & Crownsville State Hosp, Md, 62-81; pvt pract psychiat & psychoanal, 72-; mem bd dirs, Psychiat Inst Found, Washington, DC. *Mem:* Fel Am Psychiat Asn; Am Psychoanal Asn. *Res:* Psychoanalysis; adolescence. *Mailing Add:* Beacon HL Annapolis MD 21401

RANKIN, SIDNEY, CHEMICAL ENGINEERING. *Current Pos:* CONSULT, 84- *Personal Data:* b Baltimore, Md, Dec 18, 31; m 60; c 1. *Educ:* Johns Hopkins Univ, BE, 53; Univ Del, MChE, 55, PhD(chem eng), 61. *Prof Exp:* Sr process engr, Kordite Co, NY, 57-60; chem engr, Monsanto Chem Co, Mass, 60-62; process develop & design engr, Silicone Prod Dept, Gen Elec Co, NY, 62-70; process supt, Borden Chem Co, Mass, 71-74; dir res & eng, Dacor Inc, 74-75; sr staff engr, GAF Corp, 75-77; sr res engr, Celanese Res Co, Summit, NJ, 77-84; asst res prof, Rutgers Univ, 84-92. *Mem:* Am Inst Chem Engrs; Soc Plastic Engrs. *Res:* Product and process development, especially aspects of commercial development and process design for chemicals, polymers, specialties and agricultural products; solid waste management and recycling technology. *Mailing Add:* 3006 Fallstaff Manor Ct Baltimore MD 21209

RANNELS, DONALD EUGENE, JR, PHYSIOLOGY. *Current Pos:* Res assoc, 71-73, from instr to assoc prof, 73-83, SR RES ASSOC ANESTHESIA, HERSHEY MED CTR, PA STATE UNIV, 78-, PROF CELLULAR & MOLECULAR PHYSIOL, 83- *Personal Data:* b Lancaster, Pa, Apr 5, 46; m 67; c 1. *Educ:* Pa State Univ, BS, 68, PhD(physiol), 72. *Concurrent Pos:* Vis prof, Duke Univ Col Med, 85-86; pres, assembly cell biol, Am Lung Asn, 88-89; ed bd, Biochem J, 85- & numerous physiol journals; assoc ed, Am J Physiol, Endocrinol & Metab, 88-; mem res training rev comt, Nat Heart Liver Blood Inst, 90- *Mem:* Am Soc Biol Chem; Am Thoracic Soc; Am Physiol Soc; Am Heart Asn; Am Lung Asn; Biochem Soc; Am Soc Cell Biol. *Res:* Regulation of lung growth and development role of type II pulmonary epithelial cells in these processes and in the response of the lung injury, role of extracellular matrix in cellular differentiation, metabolic consequences of membrane defarmation or stretch regulation of protein turnover; effects of oxygen deprivation on myocardial metabolism; control of protein metabolism in pulmonary aviolar macrophages; compartmentation of intracellular amino acids; lung growth and metabolism. *Mailing Add:* Dept Cell & Molecular Physiol Pa State Univ 500 University Dr C4723 Hershey PA 17033-0850

RANNEY, BROOKS, OBSTETRICS & GYNECOLOGY. *Current Pos:* chmn, Dept Obstet & Gynec, Univ SDak, Yankton Clinic, 48-83, clin asst prof, 48-51, clin prof, 51-76, chmn dept, Sch Med, 51-76, PROF OBSTET & GYNEC, UNIV SDAK, YANKTON CLIN, 76- *Personal Data:* b Daytona Beach, Fla, Jan 31, 15; m 81, Viona Thum Voy; c Robert L, David F & Carol E. *Educ:* Oberlin Col, AB, 36; Northwestern Univ, BM, 40, MD, 41, MS, 48. *Prof Exp:* Lab instr physiol, Med Sch, Northwestern Univ, 47-48; gynec consult, SDak Human Serv Ctr, 48-75. *Mem:* Am Col Obstet & Gynec (pres, 81-82); Am Col Surg; Cent Asn Obstet & Gynec (pres, 74-75); Sigma Xi. *Res:* Obstetric analgesia and anesthesia; congenital incompetence of the cervix; paracervical block analgesia for primigravidas; diagnosis and treatment of enterocele; family planning and sex education; external cephalic version; prenatal care studies; clinical studies of endometriosis; advantages of local anesthesia for cesarean section; ovarian function after hysterectomy; volume reduction of uterus during hysterectomy; decreasing numbers of patients for vaginal hysterectomy; sequeae of incomplete gynecological operations. *Mailing Add:* Yankton Med Clin-AC PO Box 590 Yankton SD 57078

RANNEY, CARLETON DAVID, PLANT PATHOLOGY, AGRONOMY. *Current Pos:* ASST DIR & HEAD DELTA RES & EXTEN CTR, MISS AGR & FORESTRY EXP STA, 87- *Personal Data:* b Jackson, Minn, Jan 23, 28; m 49, Mary K Ransleben; c David C & Mary E. *Educ:* Agr & Mech Col, Tex, BS, 54, MS, 55, PhD(plant path), 59. *Prof Exp:* Asst plant path, Agr & Mech Col, Tex, 54-55; agent, Field Crops Res Br, 55-57, plant pathologist, Crops Res Div, Cotton & Cordage Fibers Res Br, Tex, 57-58, plant pathologist, Delta Exp Sta, Miss, 58-70, leader cotton path invest, Plant Indust Sta, Md, 70-72, asst area dir, Agr Res Serv, Ala-N Miss Area, 72-74, area dir, Delta States Area, 74-82, area dir, Mid South Area, Agr Res Serv, USDA, 82-87. *Concurrent Pos:* Adj prof, Dept Agron, Miss State Univ, 74-; chmn, Cotton Dis Coun, 61-62. *Mem:* Cotton Dis Coun; Am Soc Agron; Crop Sci Soc Am; Sigma Xi; Coun Agr Sci & Technol. *Res:* Chemical control of plant diseases; physiology of disease resistance; nature of host parasite relationships. *Mailing Add:* Delta Res/Exten Ctr Miss State Univ PO Box 197 Stoneville MS 38776. *Fax:* 601-686-7336

RANNEY, DAVID FRANCIS, IMMUNOBIOLOGY, ONCOLOGY. *Current Pos:* ASST PROF PATH, MED SCH, UNIV TEX HEALTH SCI CTR, DALLAS, 78- *Personal Data:* b Chicago, Ill, Feb 14, 43. *Educ:* Oberlin Col, BA, 65; Case Western Reserve Univ, MD, 69. *Prof Exp:* From intern to resident surg, Stanford Univ Hosp, 69-71; res assoc immunol, Nat Inst Dent Res, 71-73; res assoc immunol, Dent Surg, 73-75, asst prof microbiol-immunol & surg, Med Sch, Northwestern Univ, 75-78. *Concurrent Pos:* Consult, Natural Prod Sect, Drug Res & Develop Br, NIH, 75- *Res:* Regulation of the immune response by natural products from normal and malignant tissues and by synthetic drugs; regulation of lymphoid neoplasias and autoimmunity by natural products; surgery. *Mailing Add:* Access Pharmaceut Inc 2600 N Stemmmons Suite 210 Dallas TX 75207-2107

RANNEY, HELEN M, INTERNAL MEDICINE, HEMATOLOGY. *Current Pos:* RETIRED. *Personal Data:* b Summer Hill, NY, Apr 12, 20. *Educ:* Barnard Col, AB, 41; Columbia Univ, MD, 47. *Hon Degrees:* DSc, Univ Southern Calif, 79, State Univ NY, Buffalo, 96. *Honors & Awards:* Joseph Mather Smith Prize, Columbia Univ, 55; Gold Medal, Col Physicians & Surgeons Alumni Asn, Columbia Univ, 78; May H Soley Res Award, Western Soc Clin Invest, 87. *Prof Exp:* Asst prof clin med, Columbia Univ, 58-60; from assoc prof to prof med, Albert Einstein Col Med, Yeshiva Univ, 60-70; prof, State Univ NY Buffalo, 70-73; chmn dept med, Univ Calif, San Diego, 73-86, prof med, 73-90; distinguished physician, Vet Admin Med Ctr, San Diego, 86-91. *Concurrent Pos:* Mem bd dirs, Squibb Corp, 75-89; consult, Alliance Pharmaceut Corp, 91- *Mem:* Nat Acad Sci; Asn Am Physicians; Am Acad Arts & Sci; master Am Col Physicians; Am Soc Clin Invest; Am Soc Hemat. *Res:* Relationship of hemoglobin and red cell membranes in sickle cell disease and red cell survival. *Mailing Add:* 6229 La Jolla Mesa Dr San Diego CA 92037. *Fax:* 619-558-4333

RANNEY, J BUCKMINSTER, COMMUNICATIONS SCIENCE, AUDIOLOGY. *Current Pos:* RETIRED. *Personal Data:* b Brattleboro, Vt, Dec 26, 19; m 80. *Educ:* NY Univ, BA, 46, MA, 47; Ohio State Univ, PhD(speech), 57. *Prof Exp:* From asst prof to assoc prof speech, Ohio Northern Univ, 48-57; clin dir commun sci, Auburn Univ, 57-69; exec secy, Critical Design Rev Com, NIH, 69-75, chief, Sci Eval Br, 75-78, dep dir commun dis prog, Nat Inst Neurol & Commun Dis & Stroke Admin, 78- *Concurrent Pos:* Nat Inst Neurol & Commun Disorders & Stroke Spec fel, Johns Hopkins Univ Hosp, 62-63; audiol consult, State Ala Maternal & Child Health, 64-69; chief audio & speech path, Vet Admin Hosp, San Juan, PR, 66-67; assoc ed, Deafness, Speech, Hearing Abstr, 68-82; actg dir, HEW/NIH/Nat Inst Neurol & Commun Disorders & Stroke/Extramural Activ Prog, 78. *Mem:* Fel Am Speech & Hearing Asn; AAAS; Alexander Graham Bell Asn. *Res:* Deafness; language pathology and speech pathology. *Mailing Add:* 6646 Hillandale Ave Chevy Chase MD 20815

RANNEY, RICHARD RAYMOND, PERIODONTOLOGY, DENTAL EDUCATION. *Current Pos:* PROF & DEAN, DENT SCH, UNIV MD, BALTIMORE, 91- *Personal Data:* b Atlanta, Ga, July 11, 39; m 69, Patricia Denoto; c Christine (Vlahcevic), Kathleen Anne, Maureen Frances & Russell Christopher. *Educ:* Univ Iowa, DDS, 63; Univ Rochester, MS, 69; Eastman Dent Ctr, cert, 69. *Hon Degrees:* Dr, Univ Buenos Aires, 95. *Honors & Awards:* Balint Orban Prize, Am Acad Periodontol; Basic Res Award, Periodontol Int Asn Dent Res. *Prof Exp:* Asst prof periodont, Univ Ore Dent Sch, 69-72, assoc prof, Va Commonwealth Univ, 72-78, dir grad periodont, 72-76, chmn periodont, 74-77, asst dean res, Sch Dent, 77-86, prof periodont, Va Commonwealth Univ, 78-86, prof & dean, 86-89; prof periodont, Univ Ala, Birmingham Sch Dent, 86-91. *Concurrent Pos:* Intern, USPHS Hosp, San Francisco, 63-64, chief officer, USPHS Outpatient Clin, 64-66, prin investr, NIH grants res, 70-86, dir, Clin Res Ctr, Va Commonwealth Univ, 78-86, bd sci counselors, Nat Inst Dent Res, 81-85, consult, Coun Dent Therapeut, Am Dent Asn, 84-, grants & allocations comn, Am Fund Dent Health, 86-90, Nat Affairs Comn, bd dir, Am Asn Dent Res, 87-91, bd dir Int Asn Dent Res, 93-97. *Mem:* Am Acad Periodontol; Int Asn Dent Res; Am Asn Dent Res (pres, 90-91); Am Asn Dent Sch; Am Dent Asn; Am Soc Microbiol; Int Col Dentists; Am Col Dentists; fel AAAS. *Res:* Etiology and pathogenesis of periodontal diseases particularly in relating microbiology, immunology and other host defense mechanisms, and human genetics to clinical disease. *Mailing Add:* Univ Md Baltimore Dent Sch 666 W Baltimore St Baltimore MD 21201-1586. *E-Mail:* rrr001@dental3.ab.umd.edu

RANSFORD, GEORGE HENRY, BROMINE CHEMISTRY. *Current Pos:* SR PT SPECIALIST, ALBEMARLE CORP, 95- *Personal Data:* b Detroit, Mich, Oct 26, 41; m 66, Barbara Pearson; c Carolyn & G Andrew. *Educ:* Albion Col, BA, 63; Wayne State Univ, PhD(org chem), 70. *Prof Exp:* Res chemist, Ash Stevens, Inc, 64-65, sr res chemist, 70-76; res chemist, Ethyl Corp, 76-83, sr res chemist, 83-88, res & develop specialist, 88-89, sr res & develop specialist, 89-95. *Concurrent Pos:* Secy & treas, Ouachita Valley Sect, Am Chem Soc, 91-92, chmn elect, 92-93, chmn, 93-94. *Mem:* Am Chem Soc; Sigma Xi. *Res:* Organic synthesis; nucleoside, nucleotide, cardiac glycoside synthesis; halogen chemicals; process research; carbohydrate chemistry; phase transfer catalysis; heterocycles; condensed aromatics; technical service to manufacturing. *Mailing Add:* Albemarle Corp PO Box 729 Magnolia AR 71753-0729

RANSIL, BERNARD J(EROME), RESEARCH METHODOLOGY. *Current Pos:* dir, Core Lab Clin Res Ctr, Beth Israel Hosp, 74-96, ASST PHYSICIAN TO SR PHYSICIAN, BETH ISRAEL DEACONESS MED CTR, 74- *Personal Data:* b Pittsburgh, Pa, Nov 15, 29. *Educ:* Duquesne Univ, BS, 51; Cath Univ Am, PhD(phys chem), 55; Univ Chicago, MD, 64. *Prof Exp:* Res assoc, Lab Molecular Struct & Spectra, Univ Chicago, 56-62; intern, Harbor Gen Hosp, Univ Calif, Los Angeles, 64-65; staff, Boston City Hosp, 66-74; from assoc med to assoc prof med, Harvard Med Sch, 66-96. *Concurrent Pos:* Nat Res Coun-Nat Acad Sci fel, Nat Bur Stand, 55-56; Guggenheim fel, 65-66; consult, exobiol proj, NASA & Nat Bur Standards, 56-62; consult, prophet proj, NIH, 71-88; consult, Howard Hughes Med Inst, 79-80; consult, Cooperative Cataract Res Group, 81-83; vis scientist, Rockefeller Univ, 85, Scripps Found, 86, Calif State Univ, 86, Univ Pittsburgh Med Sch, 87 & Dept Neurol, Beth Israel Deaconess Med Ctr, 96- *Mem:* Am Chem Soc; AMA; Sigma Xi; NY Acad Sci; AAAS. *Res:* Computation of the structure and properties of diatomic molecules (computational chemistry); development of biostatistical software (computational statistics); biomedical data analysis and inference in many medical fields; research methodology; medical ethics. *Mailing Add:* 226 Calumet St Boston MA 02120

RANSLEBEN, GUIDO E(RNST), JR, AERONAUTICAL ENGINEERING. *Current Pos:* RETIRED. *Personal Data:* b Comfort, Tex, Oct 19, 25; m 51; c 4. *Educ:* Tex A&M Col, BS, 50. *Prof Exp:* Traffic analyst, US AF Security Serv, 50-51; draftsman, Douglas Aircraft Corp, 51; engr, Reynolds Andricks Consult Eng, 51-52; res engr, Southwest Res Inst, 52-56; aircraft eng supvr, Mfg Div, Howard Aero, Inc, 56-58; sr res engr, SW Res Inst, 58-85, staff engr, 85-95. *Mem:* Am Inst Aeronaut & Astronaut. *Res:* Vibrations; dynamics; aeroelasticity; hydro-elasticity; wind tunnel and towing tank testing; instrumentation; flow component testing. *Mailing Add:* 119 Lafayette Ave San Antonio TX 78229

RANSOHOFF, JOSEPH, NEUROSURGERY. *Current Pos:* RETIRED. *Personal Data:* b Cincinnati, Ohio, July 1, 15; m 37; c 2. *Educ:* Harvard Univ, BS, 38; Univ Chicago, MD, 41; Am Bd Neurol Surg, dipl, 51. *Prof Exp:* Instr surg, Med Sch, Univ Cincinnati, 43-44; asst neurol surg, Col Physicians & Surgeons, Columbia Univ, 49-50, instr neurol surg & assoc neurol surgeon, 50-52, asst prof clin neurol surg, 54-58, assoc prof, 59-61; prof neurosurg & chmn dept, Med Ctr, NY UNIV, 61-90; dir neurosurg, Bellevue Hosp Ctr, 61-90. *Concurrent Pos:* From asst attend neurol surgeon to attend neurol surgeon, Neurol Inst, Presby Hosp, New York, 49-61, chief clin neurosurg, Vanderbilt Clin, 53-55; consult, St John's Riverside & Yonkers Gen Hosps, 61-; consult, St Francis Hosp, Port Jervis; chief consult, Manhattan Vet Admin Hosp. *Mem:* Am Acad Neurol; Cong Rehab Med; AMA; Am Acad Neurol Surg; Soc Neurol Surg (pres). *Res:* Surgery of intracranial tumors, vascular malformations and aneurysms; epilepsy and hydrocephalus. *Mailing Add:* James A Haley Vet Admin Hosp 13000 Bruce B Downs Blvd Tampa FL 33612-4745

RANSOM, BRUCE DAVIS, PHYSICAL CHEMISTRY. *Current Pos:* VPRES, SKAARLAND HOMES, 80- *Personal Data:* b Binghamton, NY, Apr 15, 51; m 78. *Educ:* State Univ NY, Binghamton, BA, 73, PhD(chem), 78. *Prof Exp:* Assoc chem, Rensselaer Polytech Inst, 78-80. *Mem:* Am Chem Soc; Sigma Xi. *Res:* Excited electronic states of large polyatomic molecules; excited states of butadiene and pyridazine; naphthalene type heterocyles. *Mailing Add:* 466 W Lykers Rd Canajoharie NY 13317-9346

RANSOM, BRUCE R, NEUROLOGY, NEUROSCIENCE. *Current Pos:* WARREN & JERMAINE MAGNUSON PROF & CHAIR, DEPT NEUROL, UNIV WASH, 95- *Personal Data:* b Santa Fe, NMex, Aug 5, 45; m, Joanne Elmore; c 2. *Educ:* Univ Minn, BA, 67; Washington Univ, St Louis, MD, 72, PhD(neurophysiol), 72. *Honors & Awards:* Hans Berger Award, Am Electroencephalographic Soc, 73. *Prof Exp:* Straight med internship, Dept Med, Washington Univ, Jewish Hosp St Louis, 72-73; res assoc, Behav Biol Br, Nat Inst Child Health & Human Develop, NIH, 73-76; neurol residency, Med Ctr, Stanford Univ, Calif, 76-79, asst prof neurol, Sch Med, 79-87, Hume fac scholar, 79-84; assoc prof, Sch Med, Yale Univ, 87-94. *Concurrent Pos:* Javits neurosci investr award, 91-98; prof cellular & molecular physiol, Sch Med, Yale Univ, Conn, 94-, prof neurol, 94- *Mem:* Am Acad Neurol; Soc Neurosci; AAAS; Soc Cerebral Blood Flow & Metab. *Res:* Physiology, anatomy and function of mammalian glial cells; ionic and volume homeostasis in brain extracellular space, especially the role of glial cells; intracellular ion homeostasis in glial and neurons; pathophysiology of anoxic/ischemic injury in the adult and developing CNS; the mechanisms of action of antiepileptic drugs; the role of pH in controlling neural excitability and epiletic discharge. *Mailing Add:* Dept Neurol Box 356465 Univ Wash Seattle WA 98195

RANSOM, C J, COMPUTER INTEGRATED MANUFACTURING, COMPUTER AIDED ENGINEERING. *Current Pos:* MGR, CAD/CAM ANAL, BELL HELICOPTER TEXTRON, 85- *Personal Data:* b Denison, Tex, June 26, 40. *Educ:* Univ Tex Austin, BSc, 62, MS, 65, PhD(plasma physics), 68. *Prof Exp:* Asst prof physics, Univ Tex, 67-68; chief, Comput Mfg, Gen Dynamics, 68-85. *Concurrent Pos:* Lectr, Nat Mgt Asn, 72-85. *Mem:* Am Phys Soc; Am Helicopter Soc. *Res:* Computer integrated manufacturing and mathematical analysis for aerospace. *Mailing Add:* Bell Helicopter Textron 0126 A87 PO Box 482 Ft Worth TX 76101

RANSOM, J(OHN) T(HOMPSON), PHYSICAL METALLURGY. *Current Pos:* RETIRED. *Personal Data:* b Philadelphia, Pa, Aug 4, 20; m 45, Audrey Lawrence; c Shirley, Doris & John III. *Educ:* Lehigh Univ, BS, 42; Carnegie Inst Technol, DSc(metall), 50. *Prof Exp:* Instr metall, Carnegie Inst Technol, 46-48; res engr, 48-55, res supvr, 55-62, res mgr, 62-63, res sect mgr, 63-66, sr eng assoc, 66-81, Du Pont res fel, E I du Pont de Nemours & Co, Inc, 81; consult, 81-82. *Mem:* Am Soc Metals. *Res:* Materials engineering and fabrication. *Mailing Add:* PO Box 5 Yorklyn DE 19736

RANSOM, PRESTON LEE, ELECTRICAL ENGINEERING. *Current Pos:* res asst, Antenna Lab, 63-67, instr, 67-69, res assoc, 69-70, from asst prof to assoc prof, 70-87, PROF ELEC ENG, UNIV ILL, 87- *Personal Data:* b Peoria, Ill, Jan 2, 36; m 62; c 2. *Educ:* Univ Ill, Urbana, BS, 62, MS, 65, PhD(elec eng), 69. *Prof Exp:* Technician electronics, Res Div, Caterpillar Tractor Co, Peoria, 59-60; student technician, Antenna Lab, Univ Ill, 60-62; elec engr microwave antennas, Raytheon Co, Bedford, 62-63. *Concurrent Pos:* Paul V Galvin teaching fel, Univ Ill, 67-68; prin investr, NSF Grant, 71-72 & 73-74; hon res fel, Univ Col London, 76; mem adv comt, USSR & Eastern Europe, Nat Acad Sci, 76- *Mem:* Inst Elec & Electronics Engrs; Optical Soc Am; Am Soc Eng Educ; Sigma Xi. *Res:* Coherent optical processing; holography; diffraction theory; frequency independent antennas. *Mailing Add:* 2609 Lakeview Champaign IL 61821

RANSOME, RONALD DEAN, INTERMEDIATE ENERGY NUCLEAR PHYSICS. *Current Pos:* asst prof, 85-91, ASSOC PROF PHYSICS, RUTGERS UNIV, 91- *Personal Data:* b Pueblo, Colo, June 9, 54; m 86; c 1. *Educ:* Colo Sch Mines, BS, 76; Univ Tex, Austin, PhD(physics), 81. *Prof Exp:* Res assoc, Max-Planck Inst Physics, 81-85. *Mem:* Am Phys Soc. *Res:* Nucleon-nucleon and antinucleon-nucleon interaction; pion absorption; delta resonance in nuclei. *Mailing Add:* Physics Dept Rutgers Univ New Brunswick NJ 08903

RANT, WILLIAM HOWARD, MATHEMATICS. *Current Pos:* ASST PROF MATH, LINCOLN UNIV, MO, 74- *Personal Data:* b Dothan, Ala, May 24, 45. *Educ:* Univ Ala, BS, 66, MA, 68, PhD(math), 70. *Prof Exp:* Asst prof, Jacksonville State Univ, 70-74. *Mem:* Math Asn Am. *Res:* Ring theory with emphasis on perfect rings and theory of modules. *Mailing Add:* 201 City View Dr Jefferson City MO 65101

RANU, HARCHARAN SINGH, ORTHOPEDIC & SPINE BIOMECHANICS, BIOTRIBOLOGY & BIOMATERIALS. *Current Pos:* ADJ PROF BIOMED, COL PHYSICIANS & SURGEONS, COLUMBIA UNIV, 88-; PROF & EXEC ASST TO PRES & DIR DOCTORAL PROG, LIFE COL, MARIETTA, GA, 93- *Personal Data:* b India. *Educ:* Leicester Polytech, Eng, BSc, 63; Univ Surrey, Eng, MSc, 68; Middlesex Hosp Med Sch & Polytech Cent London, PhD(biomed eng), 76. *Honors & Awards:* Clayton Award, Inst Mech Eng, London; President's Award, Biol Eng Soc, London; IOC Third World Cong Sports Sci Award, Atlanta, 95. *Prof Exp:* Demonstr mech eng, Leicester Polytech, Eng, 63-64; asst to chief engr, Fabricom, Belg, 65-66; biomed res scientist, Med Res Coun, London, 67-70 & Plastics Res Asn Gt Brit, 77; asst prof bioeng & mech eng, Wayne State Univ, 77-81; prof biomed eng, La Tech Univ, 82-85; dir, Rehab Res & Develop Ctr, 83-85; chmn & prof orthop biomech, NY Col Osteop Med, 89-93. *Concurrent Pos:* Biomed scientist, NATO, 82-; consult, Lincoln Gen Hosp, 82-85, La State Univ Med Ctr, 82-, St Luke's & Roosevelt Hosp Ctr, 88- & NY Scientists' Inst Pub Info, 89-; mem, grad fac, La Tech Univ, 82-85 & NY Inst Technol, 89-; vis biomed scientist, Dryburn Hosp, Eng, 86-87; vis prof, Indian Inst Technol, New Delhi, Postgrad Inst Med Educ, Chandigarh, India & King's Col Hosp Med Sch, Univ London, 89-, USSR Acad Sci, Moscow, 90 & Polytech Cent, London, 91-; guest ed, Inst Elec & Electronics Engrs Eng Med & Biol, 90-92; mem staff, Nassau County Med Ctr, 89-; vis prof, Univ Westiminster, London, 95-, All India Inst Med Sci, New Delhi, 94, Banaras Hindu Univ, Aranas, 94-, Nat Inst Sports, Patiala, 94- & Univ Istanbul, 82- *Mem:* Fel Am Soc Mech Engrs; Am Soc Biomech; Orthop Res Soc; fel Inst Mech Eng London; fel Biol Eng Soc London; Biomed Eng Soc; fel Ints Physics & Eng Med; Int Soc Biomechanics. *Res:* Orthopedic and spine biomechanics; biomaterials; biotribology; human gait analysis; laser applications; modeling in biomechanics; blood flow mechanics; skin biomechanics; rehabilitation biomedical sciences; author of over 160 publications; research administration; sports biomechanics; coined the term "Laserectomy". *Mailing Add:* PO Box 724441 Atlanta GA 31139-1441

RANU, RAJINDER S, MICROBIOLOGY. *Current Pos:* assoc prof microbiol, 79-88, ASSOC PROF PLANT PATH, COLO STATE UNIV, 88- *Personal Data:* b Jallan, India, July 26, 40; US citizen; m 70; c 2. *Educ:* Punjab Univ, DVM, 61; Univ Pa, MS, 66, PhD(microbiol), 71. *Prof Exp:* Spec Fel Biochem, Univ Chicago, 71-73; res assoc biol, Mass Inst Technol, 74-78. *Concurrent Pos:* Veterinarian; Am Career Soc young & talented investr award, Univ Chicago, 73. *Mem:* Am Soc Microbiol; Am Soc Genetics; NY Acad Sci; Am Soc Biochem & Molecular Biol. *Res:* Translational regulation of gene expression using rabbit reticulocyte lysates and caulimovirusu as model systems. *Mailing Add:* Plant Path Dept Colo State Univ Ft Collins CO 80523-0001

RANZ, WILLIAM E(DWIN), CHEMICAL ENGINEERING. *Current Pos:* PROF CHEM ENG, UNIV MINN, MINNEAPOLIS, 58- *Personal Data:* b Blue Ash, Ohio, June 3, 22; m 52, Virginia L Horricks; c Beth, Christina, Roger & Jennifer. *Educ:* Univ Cincinnati, ChE, 47; Univ Wis, PhD(chem eng), 50. *Prof Exp:* Res assoc, Univ Ill, 50-51, asst prof chem eng, 51-53; from assoc prof to prof eng res, Pa State Univ, 53-58. *Concurrent Pos:* NSF fel, Cambridge Univ, 52-53. *Mem:* Am Chem Soc; Am Inst Chem Engrs; fel AAAS. *Res:* Aerosols; sprays; heat and mass transfer; fluid mechanics. *Mailing Add:* Dept Chem Eng & Mat Sci Univ Minn Minneapolis MN 55455-0132

RANZONI, FRANCIS VERNE, MYCOLOGY. *Current Pos:* RETIRED. *Personal Data:* b Los Angeles, Calif, Nov 29, 16; c 2. *Educ:* Univ Calif, PhD(mycol), 50. *Prof Exp:* Asst prof biol, Eastern Wash Col, 50-53; asst res botanist, Univ Calif, 53-55; from asst prof bot to assoc prof plant sci, Vassar Col, 55-62, chmn, Dept Plant Sci, 60-63, chmn, Dept Biol, 65-68, prof, 62-82, emer prof biol, 82- *Concurrent Pos:* NSF sci fac fel, 64-65. *Mem:* Bot Soc Am; Mycol Soc Am; Ecol Soc Am; NY Acad Sci; Sigma Xi. *Res:* Fungi imperfecti; ascomycetes; plant physiology. *Mailing Add:* 6176 Henderson Rd Sanibel FL 33957

RAO, ANANDA G, BIOCHEMISTRY, NUTRITION. *Current Pos:* RES BIOCHEMIST, VET ADMIN MED CTR, MARTINEZ, 71- *Personal Data:* b Quilon, India, Dec 27, 30; US citizen; m 62, Syamala; c Gita, Veena & Vivek. *Educ:* Univ Kerala, BSc, 52, MSc, 54; Univ Tex Southwestern Med Sch Dallas, 62-66, PhD(biochem), 66. *Prof Exp:* Lectr chem, Sree Sankara Col, Kalady, India, 54-55; res scholar, Univ Kerala, 55-58; asst res off biochem, Indian Coun Med Res, 58-59; res asst, Wellcome Res Lab, Vellore, 59-62; Welch Found fel, Univ Tex Southwestern Med Sch, Dallas, 62-67; res assoc, Tex A&M Univ, 67-69, res scientist, 69-71. *Concurrent Pos:* NIH res grant, 70-73; Vet Admin res grant, 71-; assoc ed, Biochem Archives, 86-88, ed, 89-; mem ed bd, J Optimal Nutrit. *Mem:* Am Inst Nutrit; Int Soc Biomed Res Alcoholism. *Res:* Lipid metabolism; hematology, erythropoiesis; role of drugs and diet fat on tissue lipid composition; iron deficiency; alcoholic fatty liver damage; dietary control of alcoholic liver damage; role of inadequate nutrition on effects attributed to chronic alcoholism. *Mailing Add:* 10 Hargate Court Pleasant Hill CA 94523. *Fax:* 510-228-5738

RAO, ATAMBIR, NUCLEAR ENGINEERING. *Current Pos:* Prin engr, BWR Prog, PROD MGR, ESBWR, GEN ELEC ENERGY, SAN JOSE. *Honors & Awards:* George Westinghouse Silver Medal, Am Soc Mech Engrs, 90. *Res:* Nuclear engineering. *Mailing Add:* GE Nuclear Energy 175 Curtner Ave MC 365 San Jose CA 95125

RAO, B SESHAGIRI, SPECTROSCOPY, OPTICS. *Current Pos:* from asst prof to assoc prof, 66-78, PROF PHYSICS, UNIV NDAK, 78-, CHMN DEPT, 87- *Personal Data:* b Masulipatam, India, Apr 18, 36; US citizen; m 63; c 3. *Educ:* Andhra Univ, BSc, 53; Banaras Hindu Univ, MSc, 56; Pa State Univ, PhD(physics), 63. *Prof Exp:* Instr physics, Pa State Univ, 64; sr scientist, Warner & Swasey Co, 64-65; asst prof, Duquesne Univ, 65-66. *Mem:* Am Phys Soc; Optical Soc Am. *Res:* Dipole moment functions of simple molecules; optical properties of matter. *Mailing Add:* Physics Dept PO Box 7129 Univ NDak Grand Forks ND 58202. *E-Mail:* serao@vm1.nodak.edu

RAO, BALAKRISHNA RAGHAVENDRA, INSECT PHYSIOLOGY. *Current Pos:* from assoc prof entom to prof entom, 67-80, PROF BIOL, EAST STROUDSBURG UNIV, 80- *Personal Data:* b Udupi, India, Sept 15, 36; m 65; c 3. *Educ:* Banaras Hindu Univ, BScAg, 57; Karnatak Univ, India, MScAgr, 59; Ohio State Univ, PhD(entom), 64. *Prof Exp:* Lectr agr entom, Col Agr, Dharwar, India, 59-60; res assoc, Johns Hopkins Univ, 64-65 & Univ Conn, 65-67. *Concurrent Pos:* Res fel, Marine Biol Lab, Woods Hole, Mass, 64-67. *Mem:* Entom Soc Am. *Res:* Reproductive physiology of cockroaches. *Mailing Add:* Dept Biol Sci East Stroudsburg Univ East Stroudsburg PA 18301

RAO, CALYAMPUDI R, STATISTICS. *Current Pos:* EBERLY PROF STATIST & DIR, CTR MULTIVARIATE ANALYSIS, PA STATE UNIV, 88- *Personal Data:* b Hadagali, India, Sept 10, 20; m 48, Bhargavi. *Educ:* India, MA, 41, MA, 43; Cambridge Univ, PhD(statist), 48; Cambridge Univ, ScD, 65. *Hon Degrees:* Numerous honorary degrees from US, Can & foreign univs, 67-97. *Honors & Awards:* Guy Medal Silver, Royal Statist Soc UK, 65; Maghnad Saha Medal, Indian Nat Sci Acad, 69; J C Bose Gold Medal, Inst Sci India, 79; Wilks Medal, Am Statist Asn, 89, Distinguished Achievement Medal, Statist Environment Sect, 97; Mahalanosbis Barth Centenary Gold Medal, Indian Sci Cong Asn, 96. *Prof Exp:* Dir, Indian Statist Inst, Calcutta, 45-80; prof, Univ Pittsburgh, 80-88. *Concurrent Pos:* Pres, Int Biomet Soc, 73-75, Inst Math Statist, US & Int Statist Inst, 77-79; nat prof, India, 87-92; adj prof, Univ Pittsburgh, 88- *Mem:* Nat Acad Sci; Indian Nat Sci Acad; fel Royal Soc UK; fel Third World Acad Sci 0. *Res:* Estimation; multivariate analysis; design of experiments; matrix algebra and its applications; differential geometric methods in inference. *Mailing Add:* Statist Dept Pa State Univ 326 Thomas Bldg University Park PA 16802. *Fax:* 814-863-7114

RAO, CHALAMALASETTY VENKATESWARA, MOLECULAR REPRODUCTIVE BIOLOGY. *Current Pos:* from asst prof to assoc prof, 72-79, PROF OBSTET & GYNECOL, SCH MED, UNIV LOUISVILLE, 79-, DIR ENDOCRINE LAB & RES, 72-, PROF BIOCHEM, 91- *Personal Data:* b Bantumelli, India, Dec 26, 41; m 71, Vijayalakshmi; c Naveen & Satish. *Educ:* Sri Venkateswara Univ, BVSc, 64; Wash State Univ, MS, 66, PhD(animal sci), 69. *Prof Exp:* Res asst animal sci, Wash State Univ, 66-69; res fel biochem & assoc urol, Albert Einstein Col Med, 69-70; res fel reproductive endocrinol, Med Col, Cornell Univ, 70-72. *Mem:* Am Soc Biol Chemists & Molecular Biol; Endocrine Soc; Soc Study Reproduction; Am Fertil Soc; Am Physiol Soc; Soc Gynec Invest; Am Soc Cell Biol. *Res:* Molecular Mechanisms of action of prostaglandins, gonadotropins, and growth factors in reproductive tissues; identification and characterization of receptors; nuclear protein hormone receptors, eicosanoid biosynthetic enzymes and eicosanoid receptors; nongonadal expression of luteinizing hormone/human chorionic gonadotropin receptor gene. *Mailing Add:* Dept Obstet & Gynec Univ Louisville Sch Med Louisville KY 40292. *Fax:* 502-852-0881; *E-Mail:* curaoo01@ulkyumlouisville.edu

RAO, DESIRAJU BHAVANARAYANA, ATMOSPHERIC DYNAMICS, OCEANOGRAPHY. *Current Pos:* chief, marine prediction br, Nat Meteorol Ctr, 84-96, CHIEF, OCEAN MODELING BR, ENVIRON MODELING CTR, NAT CTR ENVIRON PREDICTION, NAT OCEANICS & ATMOSPHERIC ADMIN, 96- *Personal Data:* b Visakhapatnam, India, Dec 8, 36; US citizen; m 89, Padmavati Kavuru; c Pramila & Kavitha. *Educ:* Andhra Univ, India, BSc, 56, MSc, 59; Univ Chicago, MS, 62, PhD(geophys), 65. *Prof Exp:* Fel, Nat Ctr Atmospheric Res, Boulder, 65-67; res scientist oceanog, Marine Sci Br, Dept Energy, Mines & Resources, Ottawa, 67-68; asst prof meteorol, Dept Atmospheric Sci, Colo State Univ, 68-71; vis assoc prof oceanog, Dept Physics, Univ Wis-Milwaukee, 71-72, assoc prof, Dept Energetics, 72-74, prof, 74-75; head phys limnol & meteorol, Great Lakes Environ Res Lab, Nat Oceanic & Atmospheric Admin, Ann Arbor, 75-80; head oceans & ice br, Goddard Space Flight Ctr, Md, 80-84. *Concurrent Pos:* Consult, Can Ctr Inland Waters, Burlington, Ont, 71 & Marine Environ Data Serv, Dept Environ, Ottawa, 74; adj prof limnol & meteorol, Univ Mich, 77-80; adj prof meteorol, Univ Md, Col Park, 81- *Mem:* Sigma Xi; fel Am Meteorol Soc; Am Soc Limnol & Oceanog; Oceanog Soc; Am Geophys Union. *Res:* Oscillations and circulations in lakes; numerical modeling of lake and atmospheric phenomena; waves on continental shelves. *Mailing Add:* Nat Meteorol Ctr Rm 206 Washington DC 20233. *Fax:* 301-763-8545; *E-Mail:* wd21dr@sunl.wwb.noaa.gov

RAO, DEVULAPALLI V G L N, SOLID STATE PHYSICS, LASERS. *Current Pos:* assoc prof, 68-75, chmn dept, 78-81, PROF PHYSICS, UNIV MASS, BOSTON, 75- *Personal Data:* b Pithapuram, India, July 6, 33; m 62, Voruganti; c Radhika, Sandhya & Sudhamsu. *Educ:* Andhra Univ, India, BSc(Hons), 53, MSc, 54, DSc, 58. *Prof Exp:* Lectr physics, Andhra Univ, India, 57-59 & 61-63; res assoc, Duke Univ, 59-61; sr scientist, Solid State Physics Lab, Govt India, Delhi, 63-66; res physicist, Maser Optics Inc, 66-68; mgr, Spacerays Inc, 68. *Concurrent Pos:* Res fel eng & appl physics, Harvard Univ, 67-69; dir, Laser Nucleonics Inc, 68-75; NSF res grant, Univ Mass, Boston, 70-74, grad prog dir, 86-88 & 92-95, adj prof, Amherst, 94-; Battelle res contract, 90, 91, 92 & 95-96; mem, US Army Natick Res, Develop & Eng

Centre Res Contract Third Order Nonlinear Optical Interactions, 92- *Mem:* Am Phys Soc; Optical Soc Am; Mat Res Soc. *Res:* Nonlinear optics; liquid crystals; polymers; optical computers; information processing. *Mailing Add:* Dept Physics Univ Mass Boston MA 02125

RAO, GANDIKOTA V, METEOROLOGY. *Current Pos:* NSF fel & asst prof, 71-74, assoc prof, 74-79, PROF METEOROL, ST LOUIS UNIV, 79-, DIR METEOROL & ASSOC CHMN, 80- *Personal Data:* b Vizianagram, India, July 15, 34; m 65; Vidya Gollapudi; c Madhu & Anita. *Educ:* Andhra Univ, BS, 54, MSc, 55; Indian Inst Technol, Kharagpur, MTech, 58; Univ Chicago, MS, 61, PhD(meteorol), 65. *Prof Exp:* Res assoc meteorol, Univ Chicago, 65; Environ Sci Serv Admin fel & asst prof, Nat Hurricane Res Labs, Univ Miami, 65-68; Nat Res Coun Can fel, Can Meteorol Serv, 68-70 & Univ Waterloo, 70-71. *Mem:* Fel Am Meteorol Soc; Sigma Xi; Am Geophys Union; Royal Meteorol Soc. *Res:* Mesometeorology, tropical meteorology land processes; attacking meteorological problems with sound dynamical and numerical techniques; analyzing structure of convection over the Indian Ocean during a southwest monsoon season. *Mailing Add:* 3507 Laclede Ave St Louis MO 63103. *Fax:* 314-977-3117; *E-Mail:* rao@eas.slu.edu

RAO, GIRIMAJI J SATHYANARAYANA, ENZYMOLOGY, GENETICS. *Current Pos:* RES ASSOC BIOCHEM GENETICS, CHILDREN'S MEM HOSP, 69-; asst prof pediat, 71-76, ASSOC PROF PEDIAT, MED SCH, NORTHWESTERN UNIV, CHICAGO, 76-; ASST PROF PATH, BROWN UNIV, 80- *Personal Data:* b Bethamangala, India, Feb 13, 34; m 64; c 2. *Educ:* Univ Mysore, BSc, 53; Indian Inst Sci, MSc, 59, PhD(biochem), 64. *Prof Exp:* Lectr chem, Univ Mysore, 53-55. *Concurrent Pos:* W B Lawson fel, NY State Dept Health, Albany, 64-67; S M & O M Rosen fel, Albert Einstein Col Med, 67-69; Robert & Mary Wood innovative res fel in cystic fibrosis, 72; trainer in biochem, Prog in Human Biochem Genetics, Children's Mem Hosp, 70-; asst dir clin chem, RI Hosp, 80- *Mem:* AAAS; Soc Pediat Res; Am Chem Soc; Am Soc Human Genetics. *Res:* Enzymology of cystic fibrosis; control mechanisms in cultured cells; chemical modification of enzymes and proteins. *Mailing Add:* 40 Dartmouth Dr Cranston RI 02920

RAO, GOPAL SUBBA, PERIODONTAL DISEASES, ORAL BIOLOGY. *Current Pos:* PRES & CHIEF EXEC OFFICER, MULTITEK, MELROSE PARK, ILL. *Personal Data:* b India, Aug 12, 38; US citizen; m 72, Harsha Udeshi; c Raveen. *Educ:* Madras Univ, India, BSc, 58; Howard Univ, MS, 65; Univ Mich, Ann Arbor, PhD(pharmaceut chem), 69. *Prof Exp:* Chemist forensic chem, Lab Chem & examiner to the Govt Mysore, Pub Health Inst, Bangalore, 58-61; instr biomed chem, Col Pharm, Howard Univ, 62-65; res asst, Dept Pharmaceut, Col Pharm, Univ Mich, Ann Arbor, 65-69; NIH fel, Lab Chem, Nat Heart, Lung & Blood Inst, NIH, 69-72, NIH fel, Lab Chem Pharmacol, 72-74; dir & chief res scientist, Div Biochem, Am Dent Asn Health Found, Chicago, 78-85, chief, Lab Pharmacol, Res Inst, 74-85; clin prof, Dept Biochem, Dent Sch, Loyola Univ, Maywood, Ill, 85-93. *Concurrent Pos:* Prin investr grants & contracts, NIH & Am Fund Dent Health, 74-; Sigma Xi lectr, Med Ctr, Univ Miss, 82. *Mem:* Am Soc Pharmacol & Exp Therapeut; Soc Toxicol; Am Chem Soc; Am Pharmaceut Asn; Am & Int Asn Dent Res; Am Col Toxicol; AAAS; Am Soc Pharmacog; Sigma Xi; Int Soc Study Xenobiotics. *Res:* Biochemical etiology of periodontal and oral diseases; development of new diagnostic methods and novel drugs and procedures useful in the treatment of oral diseases; salivary nitrite and carcinogenic nitrosamine formation; occupational hazards in dental practice; oral health effects of smokeless tobacco usage. *Mailing Add:* 1221 Hialeah Lane Hanover Park IL 60103. *Fax:* 708-343-3858; *E-Mail:* rao@super-highway.net

RAO, GOPALAKRISHNA M, ELECTROCHEMISTRY, TECHNICAL MANAGEMENT. *Current Pos:* HEAD, ENERGY STORAGE SECT, NASA/GODDARD SPACE FLIGHT CTR, GREENBELT, MD, 89- *Personal Data:* b Udupi, India, Mar 17, 44; US citizen; m 75, Kavitha G; c India G. *Educ:* Mysore Univ, India, BSc, 64, MSc, 66; Mem Univ Nfld, St John's, PhD(phys chem & electrochem), 73. *Prof Exp:* Fel metall eng, Queen's Univ, Kingston, Ont, 77-78; res assoc, Ctr Mat Res, Stanford Univ, 78-81; res specialist inorg & metals res, Dow Chem Co, Freeport, Tex, 81-86, res specialist inorg chem, 85-86; Welch vis scholar, Rice Univ, Dept Chem, Houston, Tex, 86-87; consult, Advan Clin Prod, Inc, League City, Tex, 87-88; guest scientist, Nat Res Coun, USAF Acad, Colorado Springs, Colo, 88-89. *Concurrent Pos:* Welch vis fel, 86-87; fel, Coun Sci Indust Res, India, 87; sr res assoc, Nat Res Coun, 88-89. *Mem:* Electrochem Soc; Interagency Advan Power Group; Am Chem Soc. *Res:* Electrochemistry of fused salts; electrosyntheses of metals and semi-conductors; electro deposition and dissolution of metals, semi-conductors and minerals; chlor-alkali technology; bioelectrochemistry and energies of electron transfer processes in living systems; charge transfer at metal-solution interface; diffusion and permeation of hydrogen isotopes through metals; aqueous and non-aqueous batteries; fuel cell; clinical chemistry; aerospace battery; aeronautical and astronautical engineering; author of numerous technical publications; granted 2 patents. *Mailing Add:* 11812 Backus Dr Bowie MD 20720. *Fax:* 301-286-1751; *E-Mail:* gopalakrishn.m.rao.1@gsfc.nasa.gov

RAO, GUNDU HIRISAVE RAMA, BIOCHEMICAL PHARMACOLOGY. *Current Pos:* res fel, Univ Minn, St Paul, 70-71, NIH fel, Minneapolis, 71-72, asst scientist, 72-73, scientist, 73-75, from asst prof to assoc prof, 75-88, PROF, DEPT LAB MED & PATH, UNIV MINN, MINNEAPOLIS, 88- *Personal Data:* b Tumkur, India, Apr 17, 38; US citizen; m 65; c 2. *Educ:* Univ Mysore, India, BS, 57; Univ Poona, India, BS Hons, 58, MS, 59; Kans State Univ, PhD(entom), 68. *Prof Exp:* Res fel, Commonwealth Inst Biol Control, 59-61 & Cent Food Technol Res Inst, 61-65; res asst, Kans State Univ, 65-68; res fel, Tex A&M Univ, 68-70. *Concurrent Pos:* Coun Sci Ind Res fel, India, 60, sr fel, 62; mem Nat Thrombosis Coun, Am Heart Asn. *Mem:* Am Asn Pathologists; Int Soc Thrombosis & Haemostasis; Am Heart Asn; Am Soc Hemat; NY Acad Sci; Am Assoc Biol Chem & Molecular Biol; Biochem Soc London. *Res:* Elucidation of mechanisms involved in cell signalling pathways; experimental pathology. *Mailing Add:* Dept Lab Med & Path Box 198 Univ Minn Hosp & Clins Univ Minn Med Sch Minneapolis MN 55455

RAO, JAGANMOHAN BOPPANA LAKSHMI, ANTENNAS, RADAR SYSTEMS. *Current Pos:* ELECTRONICS ENGR RADAR, NAVAL RES LAB, 74- *Personal Data:* b Raghavapuram, India, Aug 6, 36; US citizen; m 60; c Ravi, Madhu & Sushma. *Educ:* Andhra Univ, India, BSc, 56; Madras Inst Technol, DMIT, 59; Univ Wash, MS, 63, PhD(elec eng), 66. *Prof Exp:* Asst res engr antennas, Univ Mich, 66-68; staff engr microwave antennas, Northrop Corp, 68-70; asst prof elec eng, Savannah State Col, 70-71; res assoc, NASA, 71-73. *Concurrent Pos:* Asst prof elec eng, Howard Univ, 73. *Mem:* Sr mem Inst Elec & Electronics Engrs. *Res:* Antennas; electromagnetic theory; radar systems and radar signal processing. *Mailing Add:* Radar Div Code 5317 Naval Res Lab Washington DC 20375-5000

RAO, JONNAGADDA NALINI KANTH, SURVEY SAMPLING, LINEAR MODELS. *Current Pos:* PROF STATIST, CARLETON UNIV, 73- *Personal Data:* b Eluru, India, May 16, 37; m 65; c 2. *Educ:* Andhra Univ, India, BA, 54; Univ Bombay, MA, 58; Iowa State Univ, PhD(statist), 61. *Honors & Awards:* Gold Medal, Statist Soc Can, 93. *Prof Exp:* Asst prof statist, Iowa State Univ, 61-63; assoc prof, Grad Res Ctr Southwest, 64-65; from assoc prof to prof, Tex A&M Univ, 65-69; prof, Univ Man, 69-73. *Concurrent Pos:* Consult, Statist Can, 74-; mem, Comt Poverty Stats Small Areas, Nat Acad Sci. *Mem:* Fel Inst Math Statist; elected mem Int Statist Inst; Can Statist Asn; Biomet Soc; fel Am Statist Asn; fel Royal Soc Can. *Res:* Sample survey theory and practice; linear models and variance components; time series. *Mailing Add:* Dept Math & Statist Carleton Univ Ottawa ON K1S 5B6 Can

RAO, K V N, PHYSICS, ELECTRICAL ENGINEERING. *Personal Data:* b Visakhapatnam, India, June 27, 33; US citizen; m 67, Laksmi Prabhavati; c Aparna & Chetan. *Educ:* Andhra Univ, India, BSc, 52; Indian Inst Sci, dipl, 55; Univ Ill, Urbana, PhD(elec eng), 62. *Prof Exp:* From res asst to res assoc elec eng, Univ Ill, Urbana, 55-63; res physicist, Air Force Cambridge Res Labs, 63-76; res physicist, Rome Air Develop Ctr-Electromagnetic Sci Div, Hanscom AFB, 76-93. *Concurrent Pos:* Adj prof, Northeastern Univ, 65-69; adv, Rensselaer Polytech Inst, 70- *Mem:* Inst Elec & Electronics Engrs; Am Inst Physics. *Res:* Reentry plasma physics; gaseous electronics; microwave interaction with gyrotropic media; propagation in ionosphere; basic atomic and molecular physics; laser interaction with solid dielectrics radar systems, EM transmission; radar systems; environmental effects; EM scattering; land, sea terrain features. *Mailing Add:* One Old Bellerica Rd Bedford MA 01730

RAO, KALIPATNAPU NARASIMHA, EXPERIMENTAL NUTRITION. *Current Pos:* instr, 71-76, ASST PROF PATH, UNIV PITTSBURGH, 76-; ASSOC MEM CANCER RES, PITTSBURGH CANCER INST, 86- *Personal Data:* b Naraspur, India, Mar 7, 37; US citizen; m 65; c 3. *Educ:* Bombay Univ, BS, 58; Nagpur Univ, MS, 60; Indian Agr Res Inst, PhD(biochem), 65. *Prof Exp:* Res officer biochem, Nat Inst Commun Dis, India, 64-71. *Concurrent Pos:* NIH res grant, 80; vis prof, Univ Cagliari, Sardinia, Italy, 83; Nat Dairy Coun res grant, 85. *Mem:* Am Pancreatic Asn; Am Inst Nutrit; Am Asn Pathologists; Soc Toxicol Pathologists. *Res:* Biochemical pathology of gastrointestinal tract; chemical carcinogenesis; experimental nutrition; regulation of cholesterol metabolism. *Mailing Add:* Toxicol Lab Clin Chem Lab CLSI Univ Pittsburgh Med 200 Lothrop St Rm 5835 MT Pittsburgh PA 15213-2582

RAO, KAMESWARA KOLLA, DESIGN OF MOS INTEGRATED CIRCUITS, DESIGN OF PROGRAMMABLE LOGIC CIRCUITS. *Current Pos:* proj engr signetics, 81-93, mgr intel, mgr & dir catalyst semi-conductors, 86-94, DIR & SR STAFF ENGR, XILINX, 94- *Personal Data:* b Kasimkota, India, July 28, 44; m 72, Namburi Vasavi; c Swathi, Sandhya, Preethi & Srinivas. *Educ:* Andhra Univ, BSc, 63, MSc, 64, PhD(physics), 68; Univ Wis-Madison, MS, 73, PhD(physics), 75. *Prof Exp:* Asst prof physics, Western Mich Univ, 75-79; staff engr, Nat Semiconductor, 79-81. *Concurrent Pos:* Asst prof, San Jose State Univ, 80-81. *Mem:* Inst Elec & Electronics Engrs. *Res:* Identify and evaluate new ideas, architectures and technology for field programmable gate arrays; complimentary metal-oxide semiconductor transistor scaling, technology, circuit design applied to programmable logic devices, in particular field programmable gate array - field programmable logic arrays. *Mailing Add:* 1172 Arlington Lane San Jose CA 95129-3740. *Fax:* 408-559-7114; *E-Mail:* kamesh.rao@xilinx.com

RAO, KANDARPA NARAHARI, PHYSICS, ASTROPHYSICS. *Current Pos:* res assoc, Ohio State Univ, 54-60, lectr, 59-60, from assoc prof to prof, 60-92, EMER PROF, OHIO STATE UNIV, 93- *Personal Data:* b Kovvur, India, Sept 5, 21; m 52; c 1. *Educ:* Andhra Univ, India, BSc, 41, MSc, 42; Univ Chicago, PhD, 49. *Prof Exp:* With Govt Meteorol Serv, India, 42-46; with sci off, Nat Phys Lab, 50-52; res assoc physics, Duke Univ, 52-53; res assoc & asst prof, Univ Tenn, 53-54. *Concurrent Pos:* Consult, Nat Oceanic & Atmospheric Admin, 73-; ed J Molecular Spectros. *Mem:* Am Astron Soc; fel Optical Soc Am; fel Am Phys Soc; Int Astron Union; Coblentz Soc. *Res:* Structures of molecules, especially their electronic spectra in the ultraviolet and high resolution absorption and emission spectra in the infrared. *Mailing Add:* 1000 Urlin Ave Apt 1614 Columbus OH 43212

RAO, KROTHAPALLI RANGA, CRUSTACEAN PHYSIOLOGY, INVERTEBRATE ENDOCRINOLOGY. *Current Pos:* from asst prof to assoc prof, 72-78, PROF BIOL, UNIV W FLA, 78-, DISTINGUISHED UNIV RES PROF, 86- *Personal Data:* b Amartaluru, India, Sept 24, 41; m 65; c 2. *Educ:* Andhra Univ, India, BS, 58, MS, 61, PhD(zool), 67. *Prof Exp:* Demonstr biol, Andhra Christian Col, India, 58-59,demonstr zool, Andhra Univ, 61-62, res fel, 62-65; res assoc biol, Tulane Univ, 66-72. *Concurrent Pos:* Assoc ed, J exper zool, 86-88; mem NSF rev panel for Presidential Young Invest Award prog cellular biol; mem EPA Environ Biol rev panel, 88. *Mem:* Am Soc Zool; fel AAAS; Crustacean Soc; Int Pigment Cell Soc; Sigma Xi. *Res:* Biochemistry and functions of invertebrate neuropeptides; control of color changes and molting in crustaceans; pollution physiology of marine animals; isolation and characterization of the crustacean neurohormones; comparative endocrinology. *Mailing Add:* 9709 Stillbrook Rd Pensacola FL 32514-5751

RAO, M S(AMBASIVA), SURGICAL PATHOLOGY. *Current Pos:* From asst prof to assoc prof, 77-87, PROF PATH, NORTHWESTERN UNIV MED SCH, 87- *Personal Data:* b Chiluvur, India, Oct 19, 42; m 68; c 2. *Educ:* Osmania Univ, MB & BS, 65; Andhra Univ, MD, 72. *Concurrent Pos:* Prin investr, NIH, 83-90. *Mem:* Am Asn Cancer Res; Int Acad Path; Am Asn Path. *Res:* Peroxisome proliferators-induced hepatocarcinogenesis and transdifferentiation of pancreatic cells into hepatocytes. *Mailing Add:* Dept Path Northwestern Univ Med Sch Chicago IL 60611. *Fax:* 312-503-8247

RAO, MALEMPATI MADHUSUDANA, MATHEMATICAL ANALYSIS. *Current Pos:* PROF MATH, UNIV CALIF, RIVERSIDE, 72- *Personal Data:* b June 6, 29; Indian citizen; m, Durgamba Kolluru; c Leela & Uma. *Educ:* Andhra Univ, India, BA, 49; Univ Madras, MA, 52, MSc, 55; Univ Minn, PhD, 59. *Prof Exp:* Lectr math, Univ Col Andhra Univ, India, 52-53; res mathematician, Carnegie-Mellon Univ, 59-60, from asst prof to prof, 60-72. *Concurrent Pos:* NSF grants, 60-62, 63-65 & 66-79; Air Force grant award, 68-69; vis mem, Inst Advan Study, 70-72, 84-85 & 91-92; res awards, Off Naval Res, 80-93; mem, Math Sci Res Inst, 92. *Mem:* Am Math Soc; fel Inst Math Statist; fel AAAS; Int Statist Inst. *Res:* Probability; function spaces; related areas in analysis; stochastic integration; harmonic analysis; harmonizable processes and random fields. *Mailing Add:* Dept Math Univ Calif Riverside CA 92521

RAO, MAMIDANNA S, BIOSTATISTICS. *Current Pos:* assoc prof, 76-88, PROF BIOSTATIST, COL MED, HOWARD UNIV, 88- *Personal Data:* b Kaikalur, India, June 21, 31; US citizen; m 76, Jayasheela; c Suryasatyasree & Gayatriveena. *Educ:* Univ Madras, BSc, 51; Univ Punjab, MA, 60; Univ Pittsburgh Sch Pub Health, MSHyg, 68, ScD(biostatist), 70. *Prof Exp:* Statistician biostatist, Venereal Dis Training Ctr, 55-64 & Indian Coun Med Res, 64-67; biostatistician, St Francis Gen Hosp, Community Ment Health Ctr, 69-70; asst prof biostatist, Univ Tex Med Br, 70-71; asst dir biostatist, Montefiore Hosp & Med Ctr, 71-72; statistician biostatist, Pan Am Health Orgn, WHO, 72-76. *Concurrent Pos:* Biostatistician & liaison officer, USAID & Govt Sudan proj schistosomiasis control Sudan, Africa, 82-84. *Mem:* Sigma Xi; Am Pub Health Asn; fel Royal Soc Trop Med & Hyg; Am Statist Asn; Biomet Soc. *Res:* Teaching of biostatistics; consultation and research; design of experiments; sample surveys; computer applications. *Mailing Add:* Howard Univ Col Med 520 W St NW Rm 2400 Washington DC 20059-2337. *Fax:* 202-806-4898; *E-Mail:* mrao@fac.howard.edu or msgirirao@aol.com

RAO, MENTREDDI ANANDHA, FOOD ENGINEERING. *Current Pos:* from asst prof to assoc prof, 73-86, PROF FOOD SCI, CORNELL UNIV, 86- *Personal Data:* b Dornakal, India, July 4, 37; US citizen; m 70, Jan; c 1. *Educ:* Osmania Univ, India, BChE, 58; Univ Cincinnati, MS, 63; Ohio State Univ, PhD(chem eng), 69. *Prof Exp:* Res assoc chem eng, USAF, Dayton, Ohio, 63-65; proj engr, Am Standards, Inc, 69-71; prof & head food eng, Univ Campinas, Brazil, 71-73. *Concurrent Pos:* Fulbright res scholar, Brazil, 80-81, Portugal, 88-89. *Mem:* Inst Food Technologists; Am Soc Agr Engrs; Am Inst Chem Engrs; Soc Rheology; AAAS. *Res:* Energy use and conservation for foods; rheology of fluid foods; heat transfer in food processing; recovery and concentration of juice aromas. *Mailing Add:* Dept Food Sci Cornell Univ Geneva NY 14456. *Fax:* 315-787-2397; *E-Mail:* mar2@cornell.edu

RAO, MRINALINI CHATTA, MEMBRANE TRANSPORT, HORMONE ACTION. *Current Pos:* asst prof, 84-89, ASSOC PROF, UNIV ILL, CHICAGO, 89- *Personal Data:* b Bangalore, India; m; c 2. *Educ:* Univ Delhi, BSC, 69, MSC, 71; Univ Mich, MS, 74, PhD(cell & molecular biol), 77. *Prof Exp:* Fel, Univ Chicago, 77-80, asst prof & res assoc, 80-83. *Concurrent Pos:* Teaching asst fel, Univ Mich, 74. *Mem:* Am Soc Cell Biologists; Am Physiol Soc; Am Gastroenterol Asn. *Res:* Molecular mechanisms involved in agonist (hormone) and mediator dependent regulation of cell function; regulation of ion transport in epithelial cells; role of protein phosphorylation; signal transduction. *Mailing Add:* Dept Physiol & Biophys Univ Ill Chicago Rm 270 835 S Mollcott Chicago IL 60612-7342

RAO, MUKUND CHANNAGIRI, TRIBOLOGY, MATERIALS CHARACTERIZATION & FAILURE ANALYSIS. *Current Pos:* SR STAFF DEVELOP ENGR, SEAGATE TECHNOL, 95- *Personal Data:* b Madras, India, Aug 1, 57; US citizen; m, Usha Vasudevan. *Educ:* Indian Inst Technol, Madras, India, BTech, 79; Univ Notre Dame, MS, 87, PhD(metall eng & mat sci), 85. *Prof Exp:* Sr scientist, Control Data Corp, 85-88; postdoctoral res assoc, Oakridge Nat Lab, 88-89; consult, Martin Marietta Energy Systs, 89-95. *Concurrent Pos:* Vis asst prof, Univ Notre Dame, 89-90. *Mem:* Soc Tribologists & Lubrication Engrs. *Res:* Understand effects of micro-contamination, surface physical and chemical phenomena on nano-tribological phenomena in hard disc drives. *Mailing Add:* Seagate Technol 10323 W Reno Ave M-SOKM259 Oklahoma City OK 73127. *Fax:* 405-324-4222; *E-Mail:* mukund__rao@notes.seagate.com

RAO, NUTAKKI GOURI SANKARA, TOXICOLOGY. *Current Pos:* CHIEF, TOXICOL BUR, DEPT HEALTH, NMEX, 93- *Personal Data:* b Tenali, India, Dec 2, 33; m 60; c Srinivas, Swati & Ranga. *Educ:* Univ Saugar, BSc, 55, MSc, 57, BPharm, 58; St Louis Col Pharm, MS, 62; NDak State Univ, PhD(pharmaceut chem), 66; dipl, Am Bd Forensic Toxicol. *Prof Exp:* Chemist, Ciba Pharmaceut Ltd, 58-59; from assoc prof to prof toxicol, NDak State Univ, 70-93, chmn, Dept Toxicol, 73-93. *Concurrent Pos:* State toxicologist, NDak, 73-93. *Mem:* Am Acad Clin Toxicologists; Am Acad Forensic Sci; Int Asn Forensic Toxicologists; Sigma Xi; Soc Forensic Toxicologists; Am Soc Crime Lab Dirs. *Res:* Detection and quantitation of drugs and metabolites from biological tissues; analytical and clinical toxicology. *Mailing Add:* 6149 Via Corta Del Sur NW Albuquerque NM 87120. *Fax:* 505-841-2543

RAO, P KRISHNA, METEOROLOGY, OCEANOGRAPHY. *Current Pos:* DIR, OFF RES & APPL NAT ENVIRON SATELLITE SERV, NAT OCEANIC & ATMOSPHERIC ADMIN, 61- *Personal Data:* b Kapileswarapuram, India, Mar 26, 30; m 54; c 2. *Educ:* Andhra Univ, India, BS, 50, MS, 52; Fla State Univ, MS, 57; NY Univ, PhD(meteorol, oceanog), 68. *Prof Exp:* Asst res scientist, NY Univ, 56-60; meteorologist, Can Meteorol Serv, 60-61. *Concurrent Pos:* Dept Com sci & technol fel & mem, Rann Prog, NSF, 71-72; expert meteorol satellites, World Meteorol Orgn, Geneva, 74-76; Fullbright fel, 85-86. *Mem:* Fel Am Meteorol Soc; fel Royal Meteorol Soc; fel NY Acad Sci. *Res:* Satellite meteorology and oceanography. *Mailing Add:* 15824 Buena Vista Dr Rockville MD 20855

RAO, PALAKURTHI SURESH CHANDRA, ENVIRONMENTAL CHEMISTRY, CONTAMINANT HYDROLOGY. *Current Pos:* Asst res scientist, Univ Fla, 77-79, from asst prof to prof, 79-93, GRAD RES PROF SOIL SCI, UNIV FLA, 93- *Personal Data:* b Warangal, India, Feb 15, 47; m; c 1. *Educ:* Andhra Pradesh Agr Univ, Hyderabad, India, BSc, 67; Colo State Univ, MS, 69; Univ Hawaii, PhD(soil sci), 74. *Honors & Awards:* Sci & Technol Achievement Award, US Environ Protection Agency, 90; Environ Qual Res Award, Am Soc Agron, 91. *Concurrent Pos:* Assoc ed, J Environ Qual, 80-83, Water Resources Res, 90-93; ed, J Contaminant Hydrol, 85-93; mem, Water Sci & Technol Bd, Nat Acad Sci, 88-91; chmn, Environ Qual Div, Am Soc Agron, 93. *Mem:* Fel Soil Sci Soc Am; fel Am Soc Agron; Int Soil Sci Soc; Am Geophys Union; Am Chem Soc; Soc Environ Toxicol Chem; Sigma Xi. *Res:* Environmental quality; environmental remediation technologies; groundwater contamination. *Mailing Add:* Soil & Water Sci Dept Univ Fla 2169 McCarty Hall Gainesville FL 32611-0290. *Fax:* 904-392-3902; *E-Mail:* pscr@gnv.ifas.ufl.edu

RAO, PAPINENI SEETHAPATHI, REPRODUCTIVE PHYSIOLOGY. *Current Pos:* assoc prof, 79-85, PROF GYNEC, OBSTET & PHYSIOL, UNIV S FLA, 85- *Personal Data:* b Vetapalam, India, Apr 19, 37; m 67, Nayani; c Karuna, Rajani & Sobha. *Educ:* Andhra Vet Col, India, BVSc, 59; Univ Mo, Columbia, MS, 61, PhD(reproductive physiol), 65. *Honors & Awards:* Kiepe Scholar, Univ MO, 61-62. *Prof Exp:* Vet asst surgeon, Dept Vet Med, Andhra, India, 59-60; res asst, Univ Mo, Columbia, 62-65, res assoc, 65-66; from instr to assoc prof gynec, obstet & physiol, Sch Med, St Louis Univ, 66-79. *Mem:* AAAS; Soc Study Reproduction; Am Physiol Soc; Shock Soc; Am Asn Univ Prof; Int Endotoxin Soc. *Res:* Clinical veterinary medicine; conception and contraception; endotoxic shock; toxemia of pregnancy; cardiovascular physiology. *Mailing Add:* Dept Obstet/Gynec Box 18 Univ SFla Col Med Tampa FL 33612. *Fax:* 813-254-0940

RAO, PEJAVER VISHWAMBER, NONPARAMETRICS, BIOSTATISTICS. *Current Pos:* from asst prof to assoc prof, 64-72, PROF STATIST, UNIV FLA, 72- *Personal Data:* b Udipi, India, June 11, 35; m 62; c 2. *Educ:* Univ Madras, BA, 54; Univ Bombay, MA, 56; Univ Ga, PhD(statist), 63. *Prof Exp:* Lectr statist, Col Sci, Univ Nagpur, 56-60; asst statistician, Univ Ga, 62-64, asst prof math, 63-64. *Concurrent Pos:* Vis fel, Australian Nat Univ, 85. *Mem:* Inst Math Statist; Biomet Soc; Am Statist Asn; Int Statist Inst. *Res:* Nonparametric estimation; censored data analysis. *Mailing Add:* Dept Statist Univ Fla 103 Griffin-Floyd Hall Box 118545 Gainesville FL 32611-2002

RAO, PEMMARAJU NARASIMHA, STEROID SYNTHESIS & IMMUNOASSAY DEVELOPMENT. *Current Pos:* res assoc steroid chem, Southwest Found Biomed Res, 58-62, asn found scientist org chem, 62-67, found scientist, 67-77, CHMN, DEPT ORG CHEM, SOUTHWEST FOUND BIOMED RES, 77- *Personal Data:* b Rajahmundry, India, Dec 20, 28; m 53, Suvarna Rani; c Uma D, Ramakrishna & Sankar. *Educ:* Andhra Univ, India, BSc, 48, MSc, 50; Univ Calcutta, PhD(chem), 54. *Prof Exp:* Fulbright travel grant & fel steroid chem, Sch Med, Univ Rochester, 54-55; res assoc org chem, Indian Inst Sci, Bangalore, 55-56; jr sci officer, Nat Chem Lab, Poona, India, 55-58. *Concurrent Pos:* Res prof, St Mary's Univ, Tex, 60- *Mem:* Am Chem Soc; Royal Soc Chem; Endocrine Soc; Am Inst Chemists; Am Asn Clin Chem; NY Acad Scis; AAAS; Int Isotope Soc; Clin Ligand Assay Soc. *Res:* Organic synthesis; natural products chemistry, particularly steroids and diterpenes; synthesis of polycyclic hydrocarbons; steroid radioimmunoassays; synthesis of unnatural aminoacids; steroid metabolism. *Mailing Add:* Southwest Found Biomed Res Dept Org Chem PO Box 760549 San Antonio TX 78245-0549. *Fax:* 210-670-3321

RAO, PEMMARAJU VENUGOPALA, NUCLEAR PHYSICS, ATOMIC PHYSICS. *Current Pos:* asst prof, 67-71, ASSOC PROF PHYSICS, EMORY UNIV, 71- *Personal Data:* b Tirupatipuram, India, Sept 1, 32; m 58, Lakshmi; c Nalini & Saleena. *Educ:* Andhra Univ, India, BSc, 53, MSc, 54; Univ Ore, PhD(physics), 64. *Prof Exp:* Demonstr physics, Andhra Univ, India, 55-57, lectr, 58-59; res assoc, Univ Ore, 64-66; res assoc, Ga Inst Technol, 66-67.

Concurrent Pos: Ed, Vijnana Patrika, 70-76. *Mem:* AAAS; Sigma Xi; Am Phys Soc; Am Asn Physics Teachers. *Res:* Nuclear spectroscopy; fast neutron reactions, atomic fluorescence yields and inner shell ionization. *Mailing Add:* Dept Physics Emory Univ Atlanta GA 30322-2430. *Fax:* 404-727-0873; *E-Mail:* phspvr@physics.emory.edu

RAO, PEMMASANI DHARMA, MINERAL ENGINEERING. *Current Pos:* from asst prof to prof, 66-90, assoc dir, Mineral Indust Res Lab, 85-90, EMER PROF COAL TECHNOL, UNIV ALASKA, FAIRBANKS, 90- *Personal Data:* b Burripalem, Andhra Pradesh, Apr 15, 33; m, Vijayalakshmi Sakhamuri; c Ravishankar, Sreenivas & Umabala. *Educ:* Andhra Univ, India, BSc, 52, MSc, 54; Pa State Univ, MS, 59, PhD(mineral prep), 61. *Prof Exp:* Jr sci asst petrol, Ore Dressing Div, Nat Metall Lab, Jamshedpur, India, 55-57; asst mineral prep, Pa State Univ, 58-61; tech adv coal & mineral processing, McNally-Bird Eng Co Ltd, India, 62-66. *Mem:* Am Inst Mining, Metall & Petrol Engrs; Soc Mech Engrs; Minerals Metals & Mat Soc. *Res:* Coal petrology; coal characterization and utilization; ore microscopy; mineral processing. *Mailing Add:* Mineral Indust Res Lab Univ Alaska 212 E O'Neill Resources Bldg Fairbanks AK 99775-1180

RAO, PODURI S R S, STATISTICS & BIOSTATISTICS, APPLIED STATISTICS. *Current Pos:* assoc prof statist, 67-73, PROF STATIST, UNIV ROCHESTER, 74- *Personal Data:* b Kakinada, India, Dec 13, 34; m 70, Kanakadurga Ayyagari; c Anna (Purna) & Gopals. *Educ:* Andhra Univ, India, BA, 55; Karnatak Univ, India, MA, 57; Harvard Univ, PhD(statist), 65. *Prof Exp:* Demonstr & lectr statist, Univ Bombay, 57-60; asst prof, Univ Rochester, 64-66; sr math statistician, Info Res Assocs Inc, 66-67. *Concurrent Pos:* Fulbright travel grant, 60; J N Tata endowment; elect mem, Int Statist Inst. *Mem:* Fel Am Statist Asn; Int Statist Asn. *Res:* Sampling; linear models; mullivariate analysis; variance components. *Mailing Add:* Dept Statist Univ Rochester Rochester NY 14627-0136

RAO, POTU NARASIMHA, CELL BIOLOGY, CYTOGENETICS. *Current Pos:* assoc prof cell biol, 71-77, CHIEF SECT CELLULAR PHARMACOL, UNIV TEX M D ANDERSON CANCER CTR, 76-, PROF CELL BIOL, 77- *Personal Data:* b Muppalla, India, July 1, 30; m 57; c 3. *Educ:* Andhra Univ, India, BSc, 52; Univ Ky, PhD(cytogenetics), 63. *Prof Exp:* Instr cellular physiol, Univ Ky, 64-66, asst prof, 66-68; asst prof cell biol, Sch Med, Univ Colo, 68-71. *Mem:* AAAS; Am Asn Cancer Res; Am Soc Cell Biol. *Res:* Biochemical processes related to the regulation of DNA synthesis and mitosis in mammalian cells in culture; monoclonal antibodies specific to Mitotic cells. *Mailing Add:* 4114 Durness Way Houston TX 77025

RAO, PRASAD YARLAGADDA, NUCLEIC ACIDS, ENZYMOLOGY. *Current Pos:* SCIENTIST, FOOD & DRUG ADMIN, 90- *Personal Data:* b Pamarru, India, June 5, 45; US citizen; m 76, Kimeera Uppaluri; c Jasmine & Neil. *Educ:* Andhra Univ, BS, 66; Banaras Hindu Univ, MS, 68; Indian Inst Sci, dipl, 70, PhD(biochem), 74. *Honors & Awards:* David Coffin Award, Dexter Corp, 87. *Prof Exp:* Fel, Columbia Univ, 74-78; dir res & develop, ENZO-Biochem Inc, 78-79; staff scientist, Bethesda Res Labs, 79-87; vis prof, Georgetown Univ, 87-88; scientist, NIH, 88-90. *Mem:* Fel Am Inst Chemists; AAAS; Regulatory Affairs Prof Soc; Soc Toxicol. *Res:* Safety evaluation of biomaterials implanted in humans as medical devices; toxicology of silicone products; use of biotechnology derived products in molecular diagnostics for detection of cancer and genetic disorders. *Mailing Add:* Food & Drug Admin 15681 Radwick Lane Silver Spring MD 20906-1033

RAO, PURUSHOTHAMA, ELECTROCHEMICAL ENGINEERING, LEAD METALLURGY. *Current Pos:* Res metallurgist, Gould Nat Batteries, 66-75, mgr advan eng, 75-82, dir, Res & Develop, 82-85, VPRES RES & DEVELOP, GOULD NAT BATTERIES TECHNOL, 85- *Personal Data:* b India, Oct 3, 40; nat US; m 64, Rama P; c Veena & Sridhar. *Educ:* Indian Inst Sci, BE, 62, Univ Minn, MS, 66; Mankato State Univ, MBA, 84. *Honors & Awards:* IR 100 Award, 83. *Mem:* Electrochem Soc. *Res:* Development of corrosion resistant lead alloys for various electrolyte MF-lead acid batteries and sealed lead acid batteries; holds 13 US patents in field; developed major processes for the manufacturing of Pb-Acid batteries. *Mailing Add:* 2630 Hariston Dr Aurora IL 60504-9028. *Fax:* 630-691-7876

RAO, R(AMACHANDRA) A, HYDROLOGY, WATER RESOURCES. *Current Pos:* from asst prof to assoc prof, 68-79, PROF CIVIL ENG, PURDUE UNIV, WEST LAFAYETTE, 79- *Personal Data:* b Kanakapura, India; m 71, Mamatha Shama; c Malini, Karthik & Siddhartha. *Educ:* Univ Mysore, BE, 60; Univ Minn, MSCE, 64; Univ Ill, PhD(civil eng), 68. *Prof Exp:* Lectr civil eng, Univ Mysore, 60-62; instr lang, Univ Minn, 62-63, res asst hydraul, 63-64; res asst hydrol, Univ Ill, 64-68. *Concurrent Pos:* Consult to several orgns. *Mem:* AAAS; Am Geophys Union; Am Soc Civil Engrs; Int Asn Hydraul Res; Int Asn Sci Hydrol. *Res:* Urban and stochastic hydrology. *Mailing Add:* Sch Civil Eng Purdue Univ West Lafayette IN 47907. *Fax:* 765-494-0395

RAO, R(ANGAIYA) A(SWATHANARAYANA), ELECTRONICS & MICROWAVES, SOLID STATE PHYSICS. *Current Pos:* asst prof solid state electronics, 68-74, assoc prof elec eng, 74-80, PROF ELEC ENG, CALIF STATE UNIV, SAN JOSE, 80- *Personal Data:* b Bangalore, India, Feb 27, 34; m 67. *Educ:* Univ Mysore, BSc, 53; Indian Inst Sci, Bangalore, dipl elec commun eng, 57; Univ Calif, Berkeley, MS, 61, PhD(elec eng), 66. *Prof Exp:* Sir Dorabji Tata scholar, Indian Inst Sci, Bangalore, 56-57; jr sci officer microwave tubes. Cent Electronic Eng Res Inst, Pilani, India, 57-59; grad res engr, Electronics Res Lab, Univ Calif, Berkeley, 59-66; mem tech staff, Fairchild Semiconductor Res & Develop Lab, Calif, 66-68. *Concurrent Pos:* Vis scholar, Stanford Univ, 77-78; consult, SKE Power Interface Devices, 79, Avantek Inc, Santa Clara, 84; USAF fel & res grant, Wright Patterson AFB, 79-80; fel, Lawrence Livermore Nat Labs, AWU-Dept Energy, 82, Japan Soc Prom Sci, Kyoto Univ, 88-89, fac res fel, Naval Ocean Systs Ctr, San Diego, 89, 90. *Mem:* Inst Elec & Electronics Engrs; Am Soc Eng Educ. *Res:* Electron beams and guns; microwave tubes; solid state devices; microwave semiconductor devices; device and circuit modeling and simulation; monolithic microwave integrated circuits. *Mailing Add:* Dept Elec Calif State Univ San Jose CA 95192

RAO, RAMACHANDRA M R, FOOD SCIENCE & TECHNOLOGY. *Current Pos:* asst prof food sci, 67-70, assoc prof, Food Preservation, 70-80, PROF FOOD SCI, LA STATE UNIV, BATON ROUGE, 80- *Personal Data:* b Bangalore City, India, Oct 30, 31. *Educ:* Univ Mysore, BSc, 59; Univ Houston, BS, 62; La State Univ, Baton Rouge, MS, 63, PhD(food sci), 66. *Honors & Awards:* US AEC Award, 66. *Prof Exp:* Chemist, Savage Labs, Houston, 60-62; dir res, AME Enterprises, NJ, 66-67. *Concurrent Pos:* Allen Prod grant, La State Univ, Baton Rouge, 67-68; fel, Int Atomic Energy Agency, SVietnam & adv, Vienna, Austria, 70. *Mem:* Assoc Am Inst Chem Eng; Inst Food Technol; Can Inst Food Sci & Technol. *Res:* Food processing and preservation; water and air pollution; waste utilization and disposal; fermentation technology. *Mailing Add:* 921 Woodstone Dr Baton Rouge LA 70808

RAO, RAMGOPAL P, OPHTHALMIC INSTRUMENTATION, SCIENTIFIC INSTRUMENTATION. *Current Pos:* CHIEF EXEC OFFICER, TOMEY SCI INC, 91- *Personal Data:* b India, Aug 15, 42; US citizen; m 69, Sandhya Kulkarni; c Sameer, Sushant & Neeraj. *Educ:* Regional Eng Col, India, BSEE, 65; Okla State Univ, Stillwater, MSEE, 66; Northeastern Univ, MBA, 72. *Prof Exp:* Sr syst engr, Honeywell Inc, 66-70; proj engr, Digilab Inc, 70-72, dir res & develop, 72-75, dir customer serv, 75-77, vpres mfg, 77-79; div mgr, Ophthalmic Div, Biorad Labs Inc, 81-90. *Concurrent Pos:* Pres, Techland Corp. *Mem:* Inst Elec & Electronics Engrs. *Mailing Add:* 31 Stewart Rd Needham MA 02192

RAO, SALEM S, MICROBIOLOGY, BACTERIOLOGY. *Current Pos:* RES SCIENTIST, NAT WATER RES INST, CAN, 73- *Personal Data:* b Bangalore, India, Apr 12, 34; Can citizen; m 64, Uma; c Anita & Shaila. *Educ:* Univ Mysore, PhD(zool), 64; Royal Soc London, FRSH, 65. *Prof Exp:* Res microbiologist, Rensselaer Polytech Inst, 61-64; res scientist, Ont Res Found, 64-65; scientist bacteriol, Ont Dept Health, 65-73. *Concurrent Pos:* Teacher environ microbiol/ecol; hon res assoc & adj prof, Brock Univ & Univ Toronto. *Mem:* Royal Soc Health London; Sigma Xi; Am Soc Testing & Mat; Royal Soc Can. *Res:* Limnology of aquatic ecosystems; cold water bacteriology; assimilation under low temperatures; bacterial nutrient relationships under different temperatures; acid rain-stress bacteriology (biodegradation and bioassimilation); acid lake recovery study; contaminat-biotic interactions and transport in flurial systems; ecotoxicology; microbiology toxicity; genotoxicity. *Mailing Add:* Aquatic Ecosystem Conserv Br Ecosystem Health Assessment Nat Water Res Inst Burlington ON L7R 4A6 Can. *Fax:* 905-336-4989

RAO, SAMOHINEEVEESU TRIVIKRAMA, AIR POLLUTION METEOROLOGY, ATMOSPHERIC MODELING. *Current Pos:* res fel, State Univ NY, Albany, 69-72, res assoc atmospheric sci, 73-74, res scientist air pollution & meteorol & chief atmospheric modeling sect & math modeling sect, 74-84, dir res, 84-96, ASST COMNR, OFF SCI & TECHNOL, DEPT ENVIRON CONSERV, 96- *Personal Data:* b India, July 2, 44; US citizen; m 74, Marcia L Neiss; c Manjula & Leela. *Educ:* Andhra Univ, India, BSc, 62, MSc, 65; State Univ NY, Albany, PhD(atmospheric sci), 73. *Prof Exp:* Lectr physics, Govt Arts Col, Nizamabad, India, 65-66; sr sci asst meteorol, Inst Trop Meteorol, Govt India, 66-69. *Concurrent Pos:* Prin investr, Funded Res Proj, US Environ Protection Agency & other fed & state agencies, 75-; consult, State Univ NY, Albany, 75-76, M B Assoc, San Francisco, 77-78, Indian Inst Technol, New Delhi & Bombay, India; res prof atmospheric sci, State Univ NY, Albany, 76-; panel mem, Nat Coop Hwy Res Prog, Nat Acad Sci, 78-82; mem, Tech Coun Meteorol, Atmospheric Chem & Deposition & Educ, Air & Waste Mgt Asn, 79-, Comt Meteorol Aspects Air Pollutions, Am Meteorol Soc, 93-; cert consult meteorologist, Am Meteorol Soc, 80-; consult, Indian Inst Technol, New Delhi, India. *Mem:* Am Meteorol Soc; Air & Waste Mgt Asn. *Res:* Mathematical modeling of transport and diffusion of pollutants in the atmosphere; develop and validate air pollution dispersion models; statistical analysis of air pollution and meteorological data. *Mailing Add:* 49 Timberwick Dr Clifton Park NY 12065-6206

RAO, SHANKARANARAYANA RAMOHALLINANJUNDA, CIVIL ENGINEERING, SOIL MECHANICS. *Current Pos:* RETIRED. *Personal Data:* b Hiriyur, India, July 11, 23; m 58. *Educ:* Univ Mysore, BE, 46; Univ Roorkee, ME, 58; Univ Conn, MS, 61; Rutgers Univ, PhD(soil mech), 64. *Prof Exp:* Supvr irrig-works, Mysore Pub Works Dept, 46-50; tech asst, River Valley Projs, 50-57; asst engr, Mysore Eng Res Sta, 58-59; from assoc prof to prof civil eng, Prairie View A&M Univ, 64-92, chmn dept, 64-84, assoc dean eng, 85-92. *Mem:* Am Soc Civil Engrs; Am Soc Eng Educ; Am Soc Testing & Mat; Concrete Inst; Sigma Xi; Int Soc Soil Mech & Found Eng; Nat Soc Prof Engrs. *Res:* Field study of restriction of evaporation from open water surfaces; problem of canal lining; phenomena of frost action in highways; permeability of soils; structural strength of brick masonry prisms; correlation of data from field for remote sensing of wheat canopy; nature of fracture failure in composite materials. *Mailing Add:* PO Box 936 Prairie View TX 77446

RAO, SREEDHAR P, PEDIATRICS, HEMATOLOGY-ONCOLOGY. *Current Pos:* resident pediat, State Univ NY Downstate Med Ctr, 68-71, fel pediat-hemat-oncol, 71-73, fel pediat-oncol, 73-74, instr pediat, 74-75, asst prof pediat, 75-81, assoc prof, 81-93, PROF CLIN PEDIAT, STATE UNIV NY DOWNSTATE MED CTR, 93- *Personal Data:* b Jan 2, 43; US citizen; m, Sarojini Ambatpalli; c Sanjay & Sheilaja. *Educ:* Kakatiya Med Col, Warangal, India, MBBS, 66; Am Bd Pediat, 72; cert pediat hemat-oncol, 76. *Prof Exp:* Internship med-surg, Bergen Pines Co Hosp, Paramus, NJ, 67-68. *Concurrent Pos:* Attend physician pediat, Kings Co Hosp, 73-; consult pediat-hemat-oncol, Staten Island Hosp, NY, 83; dir hematol/oncol, State Univ NY-Health Sci Ctr, Brooklyn, 92- *Mem:* Assoc fel Am Acad Pediat; Am Soc Hemat; Am Soc Pediat Hemat-Oncol; Am Soc Clin Oncol. *Res:* Sickle cell disease in children; infections; osteomyelitis versus bone infarction in sickle cell disease; leukemia in children; neutropenia in children; parvovirus B19 infection in children with sickle cell disease, leukemia, solid tumor or with AIDS; platelet function in children with Aids; role of erythropoietin in term infants with anemia in the newborn period. *Mailing Add:* Dept Pediat Box 49 450 Clarkson Ave Brooklyn NY 11203. *Fax:* 718-270-1985; *E-Mail:* spulluru@pol.net

RAO, SURYANARAYANA K, TOXICOLOGY. *Current Pos:* GLOBAL PROD REGIST MGR, DOWELANCO, 92- *Personal Data:* b Hyderabad, India, Feb 20, 39; c 2. *Educ:* Osmania Univ, India, DVM, 61; Magadh Univ, India, MS, 63, PhD(toxicol), 68. *Prof Exp:* Res fel toxicol, Magadh Univ, India, 64-67; asst res officer, Nutrit Res Labs, Hyderabad, 67-68; fel physiol, Case Western Res Univ, 68-69; res assoc pharmacol, Mich State Univ, 69-71; res investr, Dept Path-Toxicol, Searle Labs, 71-72, sr res investr toxicol, 72-77; res specialist, Dow Chem Co, 77-80, res leader teratology & reproduction, Dept Toxicol, 80-89, mgr regulatory affairs, 89-92. *Mem:* Soc Toxicol; Teratology Soc. *Res:* Carbon tetrachloride hepatotoxicity in the rat; aflatoxin induced hepatotoxicity in the Rhesus monkey; physical examination procedures, teratology, reproduction and mutagenicity testing, monitoring cardiovascular parameters and data recording methodology employed in safety studies. *Mailing Add:* 9330 Zionsville Rd Indianapolis IN 46268-1054

RAO, TADIMETI SEETAPATI, NEUROPHARMACOLOGY, INFLAMATION RESEARCH. *Current Pos:* sr res scientist, 93-95, SR RES FEL, SALK INST BIOTECHNOL INDUST ASSOCS, 95- *Personal Data:* b Munjuluru, India, Apr 15, 59; m 93, Krishna K Meduri. *Educ:* Andhra Univ, India, BPharm, 80, MPharm, 82; Univ Alta, Can PhD(pharmaceut sci/ neurochem), 87. *Honors & Awards:* Gold Medal, Indian Pharmaceut Asn, 80. *Prof Exp:* Prod develop scientist, Sarabhai Res Ctr, India, 83; vis scientist, Ciba-Geigy Corp, 87-88; res investr, G D Searle & Co, 88-90, sr res investr, 91-92, res scientist, 92-93. *Concurrent Pos:* Travel award, Alta Heritage Found, 84-86, Western Pharmacol Soc, 86, Can Bur Int Educ, Univ Alta. *Mem:* Soc Neurosci; Can Col Neuropsychol & Pharmacol; Int Brain Res Org; Inflammation Res Asn; Int Soc Neurochem; Am Soc Mass Spectrometry. *Res:* Dynamics of transmitter function; excitatory amino acids; neurodegeneration. *Mailing Add:* Salk Inst Biotechnol/Indust Assocs Inc 505 Coast Blvd S La Jolla CA 92037-4641. *Fax:* 619-452-9279; *E-Mail:* tsrao@salk_sc2.sdsc.edu

RAO, UDIPI RAMACHANDRA, SPACE TECHNOLOGY, SPACE APPLICATION. *Current Pos:* chmn, Space Comn & secy, Dept Space, 84-94, MEM SPACE COMN & DR VIKRAM SARABHAI DISTINGUISHED PROF, DEPT SPACE, GOVT INDIA, 94- *Personal Data:* b Admar, India, Mar 10, 32; m 56, Yashoda; c Madan & Mala. *Educ:* Madras Univ, India, BSc, 51; Banars Hindu Univ, MSc, 53; Gujarat Univ, PhD, 60. *Hon Degrees:* Numerous from various univs. *Honors & Awards:* Karnataka Rajyotsava Award, 75 & 83; Hari Om Vikram Sarabhai Award, 75; Shanti Swarup Bhatnagar Award, 75; Medal Hon, USSR Acad Sci, 75; Padma Bhushan Award, 76; Nat Design Award, 80; P C Mahalnobis Medal, 87; Yuri Gagarin Medal, Govt USSR, 91; Aryabhata Award, 93 & 95; Meghnad Saha Medal, 93; PC Chandra Puraskar Award, 94; Frank J Maline Award, Int Astronaut Fedn, 94; Jawaharlal Nehru Award, 95. *Prof Exp:* Postdoctoral fel, Mass Inst Technol, 61-63; asst prof, SW Ctr Advan Res, 63-66; from assoc prof to prof, Phys Res Lab, India, 66-72; proj dir, Indian Sci Satellite Proj, 72-75; dir, Indian Space Res Orgn Satellite Ctr, 75-84. *Concurrent Pos:* Pres, Comt Liaison Int Orgns & Developing Nations, 88-; chmn, UN-Comt Peaceful Uses Outer Space, 97- *Mem:* Fel Indian Acad Sci; fel Inst Electronics & Telecom Engrs; fel Nat Sci Acad; fel Indian Nat Sci Acad; fel Indian Nat Acad Eng; fel Astronaut Soc India (pres, 84-); fel Third World Acad Sci; Int Astronaut Fedn (vpres, 86-94). *Res:* Father of Indian satellite program; applications in meteorology, communications, television broadcast, education and management of natural resources; operational rockets for launching remote sensing satellites; contributed over 250 articles to science journals. *Mailing Add:* Indian Space Res Orgn ISRO Hq Antariksh Bhavan New BEL Rd Bangalore 560 094 Karnataka India. *Fax:* 3410705; *E-Mail:* urrao@isro.ernet.in

RAO, V UDAYA S, CATALYSIS, COAL LIQUEFACTION. *Current Pos:* res chemist, 78-85, br chief, 85-88, PROJ MGR, US DEPT ENERGY, 89- *Personal Data:* b Visakhapatnam, India, Aug 4, 38; m 66, Cecilia Sequeita; c Vivek. *Educ:* Andhra Univ, BS, 58; Tata Inst Fundamental Res, PhD(physics), 67. *Prof Exp:* Res fel, Tata Inst Fundamental Res, India, 59-68; res assoc, 69-71, asst prof superconductivity intermetallics, Univ Pittsburgh, 71-78. *Mem:* Am Chem Soc; Catalysis Soc. *Res:* Liquefaction of coal; conversion of syngas to liquid fuels. *Mailing Add:* Advan Crosscutting Technol Div Fed Energy Technol Ctr DOE PO Box 10940 Pittsburgh PA 15236

RAO, VALLURU BHAVANARAYANA, ALGORITHMS, QUEUEING THEORY. *Current Pos:* from asst prof to assoc prof math, 67-83, chmn dept math & co-chmn dept comput sci, 77-79, assoc prof comput sci, 84-89, PROF COMPUT SCI, UNIV BRIDGEPORT, 84- *Personal Data:* b Tenali, India, June 27, 34; m 56; c 1. *Educ:* Andhra, India, BSc, 54, MSc, 56; Univ Ill, Urbana, MS, 65; Wash Univ, DSc(appl math & comput sci), 67. *Prof Exp:* Sr res investr, directorate econ & statist, Ministry Food & Agr, India, 57-62. *Concurrent Pos:* Res grant, Univ Bridgeport, 68-70; consult, Glendinning Co, 67-69, Marena Systs, 79, Honeywell Info Systs, 81 & Philips Med Systs, 84; Monsanto fel, Wash Univ, 65-67. *Mem:* Math Asn Am; Inst Opers Res Mgt Sci; fel AAAS; Asn Comput Mach. *Res:* Algorithms, computation; integer, dynamic and stochastic programming; turbo C plus plus; neural networks and fuzzy logic. *Mailing Add:* Univ Bridgeport Bridgeport CT 06601. *E-Mail:* rao@cse.bridgeport.edu

RAO, VASANTH N, ELECTRON OPTICS, THIN FILMS. *Current Pos:* CONSULT, IMAGING & DISPLAY SYSTS, 91- *Personal Data:* b India, Mar 19, 29; m 65; c 2. *Educ:* Univ Madras, India, BSc, 49; Univ Bombay, MSc, 52; Univ Tubingen, WGer, DSc, 64. *Prof Exp:* Tech supvr, Elec & Mech Engrs Corp, 53-58; asst prof eng, Pa State Univ, 66-67; mgr develop eng, NAm Philips, 67-83, tech mgr, 83-91. *Mem:* Inst Elec & Electronics Engrs; Electron Microscope Soc WGer. *Res:* Imaging using electron and ion beams used in microlithography; thermal imaging; invention of the diode gun used in tv camera tubes. *Mailing Add:* 123 Central Pike Foster RI 02825

RAO, VIJAY MADAN, DIAGNOSTIC RADIOLOGY. *Current Pos:* resident diagnostic radiol, 75-78, from instr to assoc prof, 78-87, PROF RADIOL, MED COL, THOMAS JEFFERSON UNIV HOSP, 87- *Personal Data:* b Delhi, India, Sept 15, 50; m 74; c 2. *Educ:* Hindu Col, Univ Delhi, BA, 68; All India Inst Med Sci, MD, 73. *Prof Exp:* Intern surg med, Albert Einstein Med Ctr, 73-75. *Mem:* Radiol Soc NAm; Am Roentgen Ray Soc; Am Asn Univ Radiologists; Sigma Xi; AMA; Am Soc Head & Neck Radiologists; fel Am Col Radiol. *Res:* Radiographic manifestations of sickle cell disease; diagnostic imaging of head and neck diseases. *Mailing Add:* Dept Radiol 1092 Main Bldg Thomas Jefferson Univ Hosp Philadelphia PA 19107. *Fax:* 215-955-5329; *E-Mail:* raol@jefflin.tju.edu

RAO, VITTAL SRIRANGAM, ELECTRICAL ENGINEERING. *Current Pos:* assoc prof, 81-88, PROF, UNIV MO, ROLLA, 88-; DIR, INTEL SYSTS CTR, 91- *Personal Data:* b Inampamula, India, June 8, 44; m 65, Vijaya Morishetti; c Asha & Ajay. *Educ:* Indian Inst Technol, MTech, 72, PhD, 75. *Honors & Awards:* Centennial Medal, Inst Elec & Electronics Engrs. *Prof Exp:* Asst prof, Indian Inst Technol, New Delhi, 75-79; vis prof, Tech Univ, Halifax, 80-81. *Concurrent Pos:* Consult, Delco Remy, 85-87, Allison Gas Turbines, 86-87 & US Army Picatinny Arsenal, 88-91. *Mem:* Fel Am Inst Aeronaut & Astronaut; sr mem Inst Elec & Electronics Engrs. *Res:* Development of reduced order modeling techniques for large space structures; interdisciplinary approach for control of smart structures. *Mailing Add:* Dept Elec Eng Univ Mo Rolla MO 65401

RAO, YALAMANCHILI A K, ALLERGY, IMMUNOLOGY. *Current Pos:* Resident pediat, Long Island, Col Hosp, 71-73, fel allergy & immunol, 73-75, resident internal med, 75-77, ASST DIR ALLERGY & IMMUNOL, LONG ISLAND COL HOSP, 77- *Personal Data:* b Godavarru, India, Sept 15, 43; m 70; c 2. *Educ:* Guntur Med Col, India, MD, 69; Columbia Univ, MS, 71. *Concurrent Pos:* Asst clin prof, Downstate Med Ctr, Brooklyn. *Mem:* Fel Am Acad Allergy & Immunol; fel Am Col Allergists; assoc Am Col Physicians; fel Am Acad Pediat. *Res:* Pharmacology of theophylline; AIDS research; chronic asthma; environmental health. *Mailing Add:* 565 Bay Ridge Pkwy Brooklyn NY 11209-3309

RAO, YALAMANCHILI KRISHNA, METALLURGICAL ENGINEERING, PHYSICAL CHEMISTRY. *Current Pos:* assoc prof, 76-80, PROF, UNIV WASH, 80- *Personal Data:* b India, May 9, 41; US citizen; m 69, Padmavathi Tathineni; c Ram, Vijay & Rupa. *Educ:* Banaras Hindu Univ, BS, 62; Univ Pa, PhD(metall), 65. *Honors & Awards:* Fel Inst of Mining & Metall, 84. *Prof Exp:* Res engr, Inland Steel Co, 65-67; res metallurgist, Corning Glass Works, 67-68; from asst prof to assoc prof extractive metall, Columbia Univ, 68-76. *Mem:* Am Inst Mining, Metall & Petrol Engrs; Am Chem Soc; Inst Min Metall; Indian Inst Metals; fel SAfrican Inst Mining & Metall. *Res:* Physical chemistry of metal extraction; reaction kinetics and mass transfer; thermodynamics of metallurgical systems; research publications in the fields of catalysis, carbon gasification, intrinsic rates and effectiveness factors, thermodynamics of complex systems, Gibbs Phase rule, diffusion and equilibria. *Mailing Add:* Dept Mat Sci & Eng Univ Wash Roberts Hall 352120 Seattle WA 98195. *Fax:* 206-543-3100

RAO, YEDAVALLI SHYAMSUNDER, ORGANIC CHEMISTRY. *Current Pos:* assoc prof chem, 70-77, PROF CHEM, KENNEDY-KING COL, 77- *Personal Data:* b Rajahmundry, India, Nov 15, 30; m 52; c 4. *Educ:* Andhra Univ, India, BSc, 50; Osmania Univ, India, MSc, 54; Ill Inst Technol, PhD(org chem), 63. *Prof Exp:* USPHS fel, Ill Inst Technol, 62-63; res chemist, Richardson Co, Melrose Park, 63-65 & CPC Int Co, Argo, 68-70. *Concurrent Pos:* USPHS fel, Ill Inst Technol, 67-68, asst prof, Eve Div, 67- *Mem:* Am Chem Soc; Royal Soc Chem. *Res:* Heterocycles; fluorine chemistry; amino acids. *Mailing Add:* 6800 S Wentworth Ave Chicago IL 60621

RAOUF, ABDUL, industrial engineering, for more information see previous edition

RAPACZ, JAN, IMMUNOGENETICS. *Current Pos:* vis prof, 70-71, assoc prof, 72-78, PROF IMMUNOGENETICS, UNIV WIS-MADISON, 78- *Personal Data:* b Lubien, Poland, Jan 21, 28; US citizen; m 69, Judith Hasler; c Jan & Wanda. *Educ:* Jagiellonian Univ, BS, 53, MS, 55, PhD(immunogenetics), 59. *Hon Degrees:* Dr, Agr Univ, Krakow, Poland, 91. *Prof Exp:* Res assoc, Jagiellonian Univ, 58-61; fel, Univ Wis-Madison, 61-63; head, Polish Zootech Inst, Krakow, 63-65; vis prof immunogenetics, Univ Wis-Madison, 65-68; dir, Polish Zootech Inst, 68-70. *Mem:* Am Genetic Asn; Am Heart Asn; Am Soc Biochem & Molecular Biol. *Res:* Serum protein polymorphisms; immunogenetics of immunoglobulins; active and passive immunity; lipoprotein immunogenetics and atherogenesis; genetic susceptibility to pathogens and cell receptors; genetics of dislipidemios and atherosclerosis. *Mailing Add:* Dept Genetics & Meat & Animal Sci Univ Wis 1675 Observatory Dr Madison WI 53706-1205. *Fax:* 608-262-5157

RAPAKA, RAO SAMBASIVA, PHARMACEUTICAL CHEMISTRY. *Current Pos:* PROG ADMIN, NAT INST DRUG ABUSE, ROCKVILLE, MD, 84- *Personal Data:* b Rapaka, India, June 16, 43; US citizen; m 71; c 3. *Educ:* Andhra Univ, India, BS, 63, MS, 64; Univ Calif, San Francisco, MS, 68, PhD(pharmaceut chem), 70. *Prof Exp:* Res chemist, Univ Calif, San Francisco, 70, asst res biochemist, 71-75; res assoc radiation biol, Albert Einstein Med Ctr, Philadelphia, 75-76; res assoc, Lab Molecular Biophys, Med Ctr, Univ Ala, Birmingham, 76-78; mem staff, Biopharmaceut Lab, Food & Drug Admin, 78-84. *Mem:* Am Chem Soc; Am Asn Pharmaceut Scientists. *Res:* Synthesis of polymeric peptides as models for enzymes, and as models for collagen; studies on collagen chemistry, biochemistry and radiobiology; synthesis of peptides as models for elastin and mechanisms of arterial wall calcification; gas chromatographic, high-performance liquid chromatography, studies on thyroidal amino acids; studies on bioequivalency of drugs; drug analysis; opioid peptides; edit books; organize conferences; medical chemistry of drugs and abuse. *Mailing Add:* 15109 Gravenstein Way Gaithersburg MD 20878

RAPAPORT, ELLIOT, CARDIOLOGY. *Current Pos:* PROF MED & ASSOC DEAN CARDIOL, UNIV CALIF, SAN FRANCISCO, 60- *Personal Data:* b Los Angeles, Calif, Nov 22, 24; m 43; c 3. *Educ:* Univ Calif, Berkeley, AB, 44; Univ Calif, San Francisco, MD, 46. *Prof Exp:* Intern, San Francisco Gen Hosp, 46-47; asst resident med, Univ Hosp, Univ Calif, 47-50; instr, Albany Med Col, 55-56, asst prof, 56-57; dir cardiopulmonary lab, Mt Zion Hosp, San Francisco, Calif, 57-60. *Concurrent Pos:* Res fel, Med Sch, Univ Calif, 50-51 & Harvard Med Sch, 53-55; dir res, Vet Admin Hosp, Albany, NY, 55-57; consult, USPHS Hosp, San Francisco, 58- & Letterman Army Hosp, 59-; chief cardiol, San Francisco Gen Hosp, 60-91; coordr regional med progs, Area I, Calif, 67-73. *Mem:* Am Heart Asn (pres, 74-75); Am Fedn Clin Res; Am Soc Clin Invest; Am Physiol Soc; Asn Am Physicians; fel Am Col Cardiol. *Res:* Cardiovascular physiology, particularly blood flows and regional volumes; coronary artery disease; creatine kinase. *Mailing Add:* San Francisco Gen Hosp Dept Med Cardiol Div 1001 Potrero Ave Rm 5G1 San Francisco CA 94110

RAPAPORT, FELIX THEODOSIUS, SURGERY, TRANSPLANTATION IMMUNOLOGY. *Current Pos:* PROF SURG, DIR TRANSPLANTATION DIV & ATTEND SURGEON SURG SERV, STATE UNIV NY, STONY BROOK, 77- *Personal Data:* b Munich, Ger, Sept 27, 29; m 69, Margaret Bresner; c Max, Benjamin, Simon, Michael & Adelaide. *Educ:* NY Univ, AB, 51, MD, 54. *Honors & Awards:* Comdr, Order of Sci Merit of France, 68; Chevalier, Nat Order of Merit of France, 70; Gold Medal, City Paris, 79; Grand Croix, Palmes Acad France, 81; Honig Award, Nat Kidney Found, 90. *Prof Exp:* Asst med, Med Ctr, NY Univ, 58-60, from instr to prof surg, 60-77, dir, Transplantation & Immunol Div, 65-77. *Concurrent Pos:* Res fel med & surg, Sch Med, NY Univ, 54-55, res fel path, 56; intern, Mt Sinai Hosp, New York, 55-56; asst resident & chief resident, Med Ctr, NY Univ, 58-62; USPHS res career develop award, 61-62; City of New York Health Res Coun career scientist award, 63-72; mem, adv comt collab res in transplantation & immunol, Nat Inst Allergy & Infectious Dis, 64-68, chmn, arthritis & metab dis prog proj adv comt, Div Res Grants, NIH, Md, 68-72; consult, Vet Admin Hosp, Manhattan, 64-77; assoc attend surg, NY Univ Hosp, 69-77; vis surgeon, NY Univ Surg Div, Bellevue Hosp, NY, 70-77; mem, sci adv bd, Nat Kidney Found, 72-; mem, Am Inst Biol Sci Adv Bd to Off Naval Res, 74-76; mem, merit rev bd immunol, Vet Admin, 74-78; mem, sci adv bd, Am Cancer Soc, 75-77; mem, Surg Study Sect B, Div of Res Grants, NIH, Md, 75-76 & Surg Study Sect A, 76-79; ed-in-chief, Transplantation Proc, 76-79; consult surgeon, Vet Admin Hosp, Northport, NY, 77-; attend surg & dir, Transplantation Serv, Univ Hosp, State Univ NY, Stony Brook, 77- *Mem:* AAAS; Transplantation Soc (secy, 66-74, vpres, 74-76, pres elect, 76-78, pres, 78-); Am Burn Asn; Am Asn Immunol; Soc Univ Surg; Am Surg Asn; Am Asn Transplant Surg; Am Asn Transplant Physicians; Soc for Exp Biol & Med; Sigma Xi; Soc Organ Sharing. *Res:* Transplantation biology and medicine; trauma; burns. *Mailing Add:* Health Sci Ctr Stony Brook NY 11790-2354

RAPAPORT, IRVING, MINING GEOLOGY. *Current Pos:* OWNER, FOUR CORNERS EXPLOR CO, 53- *Personal Data:* b New York, NY, May 21, 25; m 52; c 4. *Educ:* Univ Minn, BS, 49; Grad Studies, Columbia Univ, 55-56. *Honors & Awards:* Small Mining Co Award, Mining World, 59. *Prof Exp:* Explor geologist, AEC, Colo, 49-50, proj chief explor, Utah & NMex, 50-52; mgr, Hanosh Mines Corp, 52. *Concurrent Pos:* Consult, Chilean Nitrate Corp, 52-53, J H Whitney & Co, Kerr McGee Corp, Santa Fe Railway Corp, Spencer Chem Corp & others, 53- *Mem:* Am Inst Mining, Metall & Petrol Engrs; fel Geol Soc Am. *Res:* Exploration and development of uranium ore bodies. *Mailing Add:* 4301 Chinlee Ave NE Albuquerque NM 87110

RAPAPORT, JACOBO, EXPERIMENTAL NUCLEAR PHYSICS. *Current Pos:* assoc prof, 69-73, prof, 73-81, DISTINGUISHED PROF PHYSICS, OHIO UNIV, 81- *Personal Data:* b Santiago, Chile, Nov 30, 30; m 58; c 2. *Educ:* Univ Chile, Engr, 56; Univ Fla, MSc, 57; Mass Inst Technol, PhD(physics), 63. *Prof Exp:* Instr physics, Univ Chile, 57-60, prof, 63-65, dir inst physics, 64; asst prof, Mass Inst Technol, 65-69. *Mem:* Fel Am Phys Soc. *Res:* Experimental information on nuclear spectroscopy obtained by means of low energy nuclear reactions; nuclear reaction studies induced with high energy neutrons; charge exchange (pion, muon); reactions at intermediate energies. *Mailing Add:* Dept Physics Ohio Univ Athens OH 45701-2979. *Fax:* 740-593-1436

RAPAPORT, WILLIAM JOSEPH, COGNITIVE SCIENCE, ARTIFICIAL INTELLIGENCE. *Current Pos:* asst prof, 84-88, ASSOC PROF COMPUT SCI, STATE UNIV NY, BUFFALO, 88- *Personal Data:* b Brooklyn, NY, Sept 30, 46; m 93, Mary E DiPirro; c Sheryl, Laura, Robert & Michael. *Educ:* Univ Rochester, BA, 68; Ind Univ, AM, 74, PhD(philos), 76; State Univ NY, Buffalo, MS, 84. *Prof Exp:* Teacher math, Inwood Jr High Sch, 68-69 & Walden Sch, 69-71; assoc instr philos, Ind Univ, 71-72 & 75, asst ed, 72-75; from asst prof to assoc prof philos, State Univ NY, Fredonia, 76-84. *Concurrent Pos:* Prin investr, NSF, NEH & State Univ NY Res Found, 86-89; Master's scholar award, Northeastern Asn Grad Schs, 87; Steelman vis scientist, Lenoir-Rhyne Col, 88. *Mem:* Am Asn Artificial Intel; Am Philos Asn; Asn Comput Ling; Asn Comput Mach; Cognitive Sci Soc; Soc Mach & Mentality (pres, 93-95). *Res:* Knowledge representation; natural-language understanding; philosophical foundations of cognitive science. *Mailing Add:* Dept Comput Sci State Univ NY Buffalo NY 14260. *Fax:* 716-645-3464; *E-Mail:* rapaport@cs.buffalo.edu

RAPER, CARLENE ALLEN, MYCOLOGY, DEVELOPMENTAL GENETICS. *Current Pos:* res asst prof, Dept Microbiol, 83-87, RES ASSOC PROF, DEPT MICROBIOL & MOLECULAR GENETICS, UNIV VT, 87- *Personal Data:* b Plattsburgh, NY, Jan 9, 25; m 49, John R; c Linda Carlene & Jonathan Arthur. *Educ:* Univ Chicago, BS, 46, MS, 48; Harvard Univ, PhD(biol), 77. *Prof Exp:* Res scientist radiation biol, Argonne Nat Labs, Chicago, 47-53; res scientist fungal genetics develop, Dept Biol, Harvard Univ, 61-74, lectr & res assoc, 74-78; lectr microbiol, Bridgewater State Col, Mass, 78; asst prof biol & genetics develop biol, Dept Biol Sci, Wellesley Col, Mass, 78-83. *Concurrent Pos:* Coop investr, US-Israel Binat Sci Orgn, 74-77; res grants, Campbell Inst Agr Res, 74-78, Maria Moores Cabot Fount, Harvard Univ, 75-77, Neth Orgn Advan Pure Res, 77 & Res Corp, 77-81; res fel, Univ Groningen, Neth, 77, NSF, 83-87, 92-, NIH, 87-90, USDA, 91-92 & NSF Study Panel, 93-96; assoc ed, Exp Mycol, 79-96 & Mycologia, 87-92; co-vice-chmn, Gordon Conf Fungal Metab, 82, co-chmn, 84; chair, Policy Comt Fungal Genetics, 93. *Mem:* Genetics Soc Am; Mycol Soc Am. *Res:* Genetic regulation of morphogenesis in the sexual cycle of higher fungi; comparative biology, sexuality and breeding of edible fungi, especially Agaricus species; molecular genetics of mating in schizophyllum commune. *Mailing Add:* Dept Microbiol & Molecular Genetics Stafford Hall Univ Vt Burlington VT 05405. *Fax:* 802-656-8749; *E-Mail:* craper@zoo.uvm.edu

RAPHAEL, LOUISE ARAKELIAN, MATHEMATICAL ANALYSIS, APPLIED MATHEMATICS. *Current Pos:* assoc prof, 82-86, PROF MATH, HOWARD UNIV, 86- *Personal Data:* b New York, NY, Oct 24, 37; div; c Therese & Marc. *Educ:* St Johns Univ, BS, 59; Cath Univ Am, MA, 62, PhD(math), 67. *Prof Exp:* Asst prof math, Howard Univ, 66-70; assoc prof math, Clark Col, 71-82. *Concurrent Pos:* NSF res grant, 75-76 & 89-91, Army Res Off Grants, 81-88; vis assoc prof math, Mass Inst Technol, 77-78 & prof, 89-90; actg admin officer, Conf Bd Math Sci, 85-86; NSF fel, 63, 64, NASA fel, 65-66; assoc prog dir, Sci & Math Directorate, NSF, 86-87, prog dir, Div Math Sci, 87-88; Courant Inst Math Sci, NY Univ, 96-97. *Mem:* Am Math Soc; Math Asn Am; AAAS; Sigma Xi; Nat Coun Teachers Math; Soc Indust Appl Math. *Res:* Wavelets, signal processing and multi-variate box splines from theoretical and applied views. *Mailing Add:* Seven Thompson St Annapolis MD 21401. *Fax:* 202-806-6831; *E-Mail:* lar@scs.howard.edu

RAPHAEL, THOMAS, APPLIED CHEMISTRY, PHOTOGRAPHIC CHEMISTRY. *Current Pos:* CONSULT. *Personal Data:* b Somerville, Mass, June 9, 22; m 48, Elva W Holmes; c 4. *Educ:* Harvard Univ, AB, 44; Univ Chicago, PhSc, 45. *Prof Exp:* Div res mgr, Dewey & Almy Chem Co, W R Grace & Co, 46-56; group leader, Arthur D Little, Inc, 56-66; asst mgr, Tech Control Ctr, Polaroid Corp, 66-69, mgr spec projs, 69-74, sr tech mgr, Appl Technol Div, 74-81, sr mgr mat develop, Tech Photo Div, 81-85. *Concurrent Pos:* Regist prof eng, Mass. *Mem:* Electrochem Soc; Am Chem Soc; Soc Plastics Indust; Soc Plastics Eng; Tech Asn Pulp & Paper Indust; Am Nat Stand Inst; Int Stand Orgn. *Res:* Process and product development in photographic products, plastics, rubber, paper and textiles; chemical engineering research administration. *Mailing Add:* 90 Grove St Winchester MA 01890-3845

RAPIN, ISABELLE (MRS HAROLD OAKLANDER), NEUROLOGY, PEDIATRIC NEUROLOGY. *Current Pos:* instr neurol, 58-61, from asst to assoc prof neurol & pediat, 61-72, dir pediat neurol training prog, 60-68, 70-74, PROF NEUROL & PEDIAT, ALBERT EINSTEIN COL MED, 72- *Personal Data:* b Lausanne, Switz, Dec 4, 27; US citizen; m 59; c 4. *Educ:* Univ Lausanne, Swiss Fed physician dipl, 52, Dr(med), 55. *Honors & Awards:* Hower Award, Child Neurol Soc, 87; Frank R Ford Mem lectr, Int Child Neurol Asn, 89. *Prof Exp:* Intern pediat, NY Univ, Bellevue Med Ctr, 53-54; asst resident neurol, Columbia-Presby Med Ctr, 54-57. *Concurrent Pos:* Fel pediat neurol & asst neurologist, Columbia-Presby Med Ctr, 57-58; asst vis physician, Bronx Munic Hosp Ctr, 58-63, assoc vis physician, 63-69, vis neurologist, 69-; prin investr, Nat Inst Neurol Dis & Blindness res grant, 59-74 & 85-; prin investr, Children's Bur, USPHS grant, 68-74; adj vis physician, Montefiore Hosp, 64-; assoc vis pediatrician, Lincoln Hosp, 64-74; vis physician, Hosp, Albert Einstein Col Med, 66-, vis neurologist, 69-; mem nat adv coun, Nat Inst, Neurol Commun Disorders & Stroke, 84-88; prin investr, Nat Inst, Commun Disorders & Stroke, 85- *Mem:* AAAS; Int Neuropsychol Soc; Am Neurol Asn (vpres, 81-82); Child Neurol Soc; Int Child Neurol Asn (secy gen, 79-82, vpres, 82-86); fel Am Acad Neurol. *Res:* Deaf and nonverbal children; brain damage in children; degenerative diseases of the nervous system in children. *Mailing Add:* Albert Einstein Col Med Bronx NY 10461-2896

RAPISARDI, SALVATORE C, NEUROSCIENCE, ANATOMY. *Current Pos:* ASST PROF ANAT, COL MED, HOWARD UNIV, 77- *Personal Data:* b New York, NY, July 8, 41; m 79. *Educ:* Duke Univ, BA, 63; Temple Univ, MA, 66; Univ Calif, Riverside, PhD(physiol psychol), 71. *Prof Exp:* Fel anat, Dept Neurol & Anat, Stanford Univ, Sch Med, 72-74; instr, Univ Calif, Berkeley, 77; fel, Med Sch, Univ Calif, San Francisco, 74-77. *Concurrent Pos:* Prin investr, Nat Eye Inst, 79-82 & Biomed Interdisplinary Proj, NIH, 79- *Mem:* Am Soc Neurosci; AAAS; Am Asn Anatomists; Europ Soc Neurosci. *Res:* Synaptology of the dorsal lateral geniculate in cat and monkey by analysis of series of consecutive thin sections; reconstruction of neural processes from consecutive thin sections. *Mailing Add:* Dept Anat Col Med Howard Univ 520 W St NW Washington DC 20059

RAPKIN, MYRON COLMAN, CLINICAL CHEMISTRY, REAGENT STRIPS. *Current Pos:* DIR RES & DEVELOP, ALPHATEST, INC, 94- *Personal Data:* b Rochester, NY, Nov 24, 38; m 66, Joan; c Liorah & Ariana. *Educ:* Rochester Inst Technol, BS, 63. *Prof Exp:* Clin chemist, Genesee Hosp, 65-66; med lab technologist, Wilson Mem Hosp, 66-68; develop chemist emulsions & color photog, Gen Aniline & Film, 68-70; sr assoc res scientist, Prod Res & Develop, Ames Co Div, Miles Lab, 70-82; mgr res & develop, Smithkline Beckman, 82-87; res investr, Boehringer-Mannheim, 87-94. *Concurrent Pos:* chmn, Indianapolis sect, CDIC. *Mem:* Fedn Socs Coatings Technol; Tech Asn Pulp & Paper Indust; Technol Transfer Soc. *Res:* Diagnostic systems; confirmatory tests; clinical and urinalysis control systems; performance and proficiency testing; solid phase or dry chemistry systems; patents; technology transfer. *Mailing Add:* 6231 Oakland Ave N Indianapolis IN 46220. *Fax:* 603-532-6644

RAPOPORT, ABRAHAM, medicine, for more information see previous edition

RAPOPORT, ANATOL, EXPERIMENTAL SOCIAL PSYCHOLOGY, THEORY OF GAMES. *Current Pos:* PROF PSYCHOL, UNIV TORONTO, 96- *Personal Data:* b Lozovaya, Russia, May 22, 11; US citizen; m 49; c Anya, Alexander & Anthony. *Educ:* Univ Chicago, SB, 38, SM, 40 & PhD(math), 41. *Hon Degrees:* LHD, Univ Western Mich, 86; LLD, Univ Toronto, 86; DSc, Royal Mil Col, 95, Ehrendaktor Univ Bern, 96. *Honors & Awards:* Lenz Int Peace Res Award, 75; Harold Lasswell Award, 86. *Prof Exp:* Instr math, Ill Inst Technol, 46-47; res assoc math biol, Univ Chicago, 47-48, asst prof, 48-54; from assoc prof to prof, math biol, Univ Mich, 55-70; prof psychol & math, Univ Toronto, 70-80; dir, Inst Adv Studies, Vienna, 80-84; prof peace studies, Univ Toronto, 84-96. *Mem:* Am Math Soc; Soc Math Biol; Int Soc Gen Semantics (pres, 53-55); Soc Gen Systs Res (pres, 65-66); Can Peace Res & Educ Asn (pres, 72-75); Sci Peace (pres, 84-86). *Res:* Strategic aspects of conflict and cooperation using experimental games in studying behavior in situations including choice between individually rational and collectively rational strategies. *Mailing Add:* 38 Wychwood Park Toronto ON M6G 2V5 Can

RAPOPORT, HENRY, ORGANIC CHEMISTRY. *Current Pos:* from instr to assoc prof, 46-57, PROF CHEM, UNIV CALIF, BERKELEY, 57- *Personal Data:* b Brooklyn, NY, Nov 16, 18; m 44; c 3. *Educ:* Mass Inst Technol, SB, 40, PhD(org chem), 43. *Honors & Awards:* Res Achievement Award, Acad Pharmaceut Sci, 72. *Prof Exp:* Chemist, Heyden Chem Corp, NJ, 43-45; Nat Res Coun fel, NIH, 46. *Mem:* Am Chem Soc. *Res:* Alkaloids; heterocyclic compounds; natural products; pigments; biosynthesis. *Mailing Add:* Dept Chem Univ Calif Berkeley CA 94720

RAPOPORT, JUDITH LIVANT, CHILD PSYCHIATRY, PSYCHIATRY. *Current Pos:* MEM STAFF, NIMH, 77- *Personal Data:* b New York, NY, July 12, 33; m 61, Stanley I; c Erik & Stuart. *Educ:* Swarthmore Col, BA, 55; Harvard Univ, MD, 59; Am Bd Psychiat & Neurol, dipl & cert child psychiat, 69. *Honors & Awards:* Res Prize, Am Psychiat Asn, 92. *Prof Exp:* Intern, Mt Sinai Hosp, 59-60; resident psychiat, Mass Ment Health Ctr, Boston, 60-61 & St Elizabeth's Hosp, Washington, DC, 61-62; NIMH health fel, Psychol Inst, Uppsala & Karolinska Hosp, Stockholm, Sweden, 62-64; NIMH fel child psychiat, Children's Hosp, Washington, DC, 64-66; spec fel, Lab Psychol, NIMH, 66-67; clin assoc prof pediat & psychiat, Med Sch, Georgetown Univ, 67-77. *Concurrent Pos:* Prin investr, USPHS grant biol factors in hyperactivity, 72-76; chief, Child Psychiat BR, NIMH. *Mem:* Inst Med-Nat Acad Sci; Am Col Neuropsychopharmacol; Psychiat Res Soc; fel Am Acad Child Psychiat; fel Am Psychiat Asn; Soc Neurosci. *Res:* Biological child psychiatry; pediatric psychopharmacology; obsessive compulsive disorder. *Mailing Add:* NIMH Bldg 10 Rm 6N240 Bethesda MD 20892

RAPOPORT, LORENCE, ORGANIC POLYMER CHEMISTRY. *Current Pos:* dir, Res Sect, 64-67, dir, Res & Develop Sect, 67-70, dir new prod res & develop, 70-75, MGR PROD & PROCESS DEVELOP, OLIN CORP, 75- *Personal Data:* b Springfield, Mass, Oct 8, 19; m 46; c 3. *Educ:* Harvard Univ, AB, 41; Duke Univ, PhD(org chem), 44. *Prof Exp:* Asst, Boston Woven Hose & Rubber Co, 41; lab instr, Duke Univ, 41-44; B F Goodrich fel, Ohio State Univ, 44-45, Upjohn fel, 45-46; res chemist, Am Cyanamid Co, 46-54, group leader, 54-63. *Concurrent Pos:* Res assoc, Off Sci Res & Develop, Ohio State Univ, 45; vis scientist, Cath Univ Louvain, 60-61. *Mem:* Am Chem Soc. *Res:* Synthesis of detergents; carcinogenic hydrocarbons; acrylonitrile and derivatives; nitrogen compounds; s-triazines; cellophane; cellulose derivatives; polymers; coatings; plastic films. *Mailing Add:* 175 Windsor Rd Asheville NC 28804-1610

RAPOPORT, STANLEY I, MEDICINE, PHYSIOLOGY. *Current Pos:* CHIEF LAB NEUROSCI, GERONT RES CTR, NAT INST AGING, BALTIMORE, MD, 78- *Personal Data:* b New York, NY, Nov 24, 32; m 61; c 2. *Educ:* Princeton Univ, AB, 54; Harvard Med Sch, MD, 59. *Prof Exp:* Intern med, Bellevue Hosp, New York, 59-60; res scientist neurophysiol, NIMH, 60-62, res scientist physiol, 64-78. *Concurrent Pos:* NSF fel biophys, Physiol Inst, Uppsala, Sweden, 62-64; prof lectr, Georgetown Univ Sch Med, 71- *Mem:* AAAS; Biophys Soc; Soc Neurosci; Soc Gen Physiol; Am Physiol Soc. *Res:* Physiology of blood brain barrier; aging of nervous system membrane phenomena; excitation-contraction coupling in muscle. *Mailing Add:* Nat Inst Aging NIH 10 Center Dr MSC 1582 Bethesda MD 20892-1582

RAPP, DONALD, SPACECRAFT TECHNOLOGY, ASTROPHYSICS. *Current Pos:* SR RES SCIENTIST & DIV TECHNOLOGIST, JET PROPULSION LAB, CALIF INST TECHNOL, 79- *Personal Data:* b Brooklyn, NY, Sept 27, 34; m 56, Zolita Sverdlove; c Erica & Melissa. *Educ:* Cooper Union, BS, 55; Princeton Univ, MS, 56; Univ Calif, Berkeley, PhD(phys chem), 60. *Prof Exp:* Staff scientist, Lockheed Palo Alto Res Labs, 59-65; assoc prof chem, Polytech Inst Brooklyn, 65-69; assoc prof chem, Univ Tex, Dallas, 69-73, prof physics, 73-79. *Concurrent Pos:* Consult, Grumman Aircraft Corp, 65-69, Solar Energy Proj, Am Technol Univ, 74-79. *Mem:* Fel Am Phys Soc. *Res:* Technology for advanced telescopes in space; IR astronomy; inflatable optics; Mars environment; conversion of planetary materials to useful products. *Mailing Add:* 1445 Indiana Ave South Pasadena CA 91030. *Fax:* 818-393-4868; *E-Mail:* donald_rapp@ccmail.jpl.nasa.gov

RAPP, DOROTHY GLAVES, EXPERIMENTAL CANCER METASTASIS. *Current Pos:* CANCER RES SCIENTIST, NY STATE DEPT HEALTH, ROSWELL PARK CANCER INST, 72- *Personal Data:* b Sheffield, Eng, Aug 14, 43; m 78. *Educ:* Univ London, BSc, 65; Univ Nottingham, PhD(tumor immunol), 69. *Prof Exp:* Res officer, Cancer Res Campaign, Univ Nottingham, 69-72. *Concurrent Pos:* Asst prof fac microbiol & Immunol, & Fac Exp Path State Univ NY, Buffalo. *Mem:* AAAS; NY Acad Sci; Sigma Xi; Am Asn Cancer Res. *Res:* Characterization of host and tumor related factors which determine the fate of cancer cells during the post-intravasation phases of metastasis; Pre-clinical development of anti-cancer therapies. *Mailing Add:* Dept Med Roswell Park Cancer Inst Elm & Carlton Sts Buffalo NY 14263

RAPP, FRED, VIROLOGY. *Current Pos:* assoc provost, dean Health Affairs & dir, Specialized Cancer Res Ctr, Pa State Univ, 73-84, prof, 69-78, Evan Pugh prof microbiol, Col Med, 78-91, assoc dean acad affairs, Res & Grad Studies, 87-91, EMER PROF MICROBIOL, PA STATE UNIV, 91- *Personal Data:* b Fulda, Ger, Mar 13, 29; nat US; c 3. *Educ:* Brooklyn Col, BS, 51; Union Univ, NY, MS, 56; Univ Southern Calif, PhD(med microbiol), 58; Am Bd Med Microbiol, dipl. *Prof Exp:* Jr bacteriologist, Div Labs & Res, NY State Dept Health, 52-53, bacteriologist, 53-55; instr med microbiol, Sch Med, Univ Southern Calif, 56-59; virologist, Philip D Wilson Res Found, 59-61; asst prof microbiol & immunol, Med Col, Cornell Univ, 61-62; from assoc prof to prof virol & epidemiol, Baylor Col Med, 62-69. *Concurrent Pos:* Consult supvry microbiologist, Hosp Spec Surg, NY, 59-62; res career prof virol, Am Cancer Soc, 66-69, prof, 77-; sr mem grad sch & mem res ref reagents comt, Nat Inst Allergy & Infectious Dis, NIH, 67-71, chmn, Atlantic Coast Tumor Virol Group, 71, mem, Virol Study Sect, 72-76 & Virol Task Force, 76-; consult, Virus Cancer Prog, Nat Cancer Inst, NIH, 71-75; mem, Nat Bladder Cancer Proj, 73-76; chmn, Gordon Res Conf Cancer, 75, Herpes Simplex Virus Vaccine, Nat Inst Allergy & Infections Dis, 81; mem, deleg viral oncol, US-USSR Joint Comt Health Coop & US-France & adv bd, Cancer Info Dissemination & Anal Ctr, 76-; mem viral oncol, US-USSR Joint Comt Health Coop; chmn, DNA Viruses Div, Am Soc Microbiol, 81-82, mem Med Microbiol & Immunol Comt Pub & Sci Affairs Bd, 86-88; mem, Herpesviruses Study Group, NIH, 81-84, Herpes Resource Ctr, Am Soc Health Asn, 83-, coun, Soc Exp Biol & Med, 83-, Coun Res & Clin Invest, Am Soc Virol, 84-; Am Soc Microbiol rep, US Nat Comt, Int Union Microbiol Soc, 86-90. *Mem:* AAAS; Am Soc Microbiol; Am Asn Immunol; Am Asn Cancer Res; Soc Exp Biol; Soc Gen Microbiol; Am Asn Univ Prof; Sigma Xi. *Res:* Replication of viruses; transformation of mammalian cells by viruses; viral genetics and immunology; tumor viruses; herpes viruses; measles virus. *Mailing Add:* c/o Lissa Olbeter 68 Azalea Dr Hershey PA 17033

RAPP, GEORGE ROBERT, JR, GEOARCHAEOLOGY. *Current Pos:* dean, Col Lett & Sci, Univ Minn, 75-84, prof geol & archaeol, 75-95, dean, Col Sci & Eng, 84-89, REGENTS' PROF GEOARCHAEOL, UNIV MINN, DULUTH, 95- *Personal Data:* b Toledo, Ohio, Sept 19, 30; wid; c Kathryn & Karen. *Educ:* Univ Minn, BA, 52; Pa State Univ, PhD(geochem), 60. *Honors & Awards:* Archaeol Geol Award, Geol Soc Am; Nat Award, Am Fedn Mineral Soc; Pomerance Medal, Archaeol Inst Am. *Prof Exp:* Asst prof mineral, SDak Sch Mines & Technol, 57-60, assoc prof & cur mineral, 61-65; assoc prof mineral, Univ Minn, Minneapolis, 65-75, assoc chmn dept, 69-72; Fulbright sr scholar, Fulbright-Hays Prog, 72-73. *Concurrent Pos:* NSF fel, 63-64; assoc dir, Minn Messenia Exped, 69-78; chmn, Coun Educ Geol Sci, 69-73; archaeometry dir, Tel Michal Excavation, 77-80; nat lectr, Sigma Xi, 79-81; res prof archaeol, Boston Univ, 89-; Bd Dirs Sigma Xi, 91-; mem, Nat Coun, AAAS, 92-94. *Mem:* Fel Geol Soc Am; fel Mineral Soc Am; Nat Asn

Geol Teachers (pres, 69-70); Archaeol Inst Am; Asn Field Archaeol (pres, 79-81); Soc Prof Archaeologists; fel AAAS; Soc Archaeol Sci (pres, 83-84); Sigma Xi; Soc Am Archaeol. *Res:* Archaeological geoarchaeology; archaeological geology; environmental geology and geochemistry. *Mailing Add:* Archaeometry Lab Univ Minn Duluth MN 55812-2496. *Fax:* 218-726-6979; *E-Mail:* qrapp@d.umn.edu

RAPP, JOHN P, PATHOLOGY, GENETICS. *Current Pos:* assoc prof, 76-80, prof, Dept Med, 80-, PROF & CHMN, DEPT PHYSIOL & MOLEC MED, MED COL OHIO. *Personal Data:* b New York, NY, Dec 22, 34; m 65. *Educ:* Cornell Univ, DVM & MS, 59; Univ Pa, PhD(path), 64. *Prof Exp:* Res assoc physiol, Penrose Res Lab, Zool Soc Philadelphia, 62-76. *Concurrent Pos:* NIH fels, Univ Pa, 62-63 & Univ Utah, 64-65; mem, Coun High Blood Pressure Res, Am Heart Asn. *Mem:* Am Physiol Soc; Am Heart Asn; Endorine Soc; AAAS; Am Soc Hypertension. *Res:* Biomedical research in experimental hypertension; biochemical genetics of blood pressure regulation. *Mailing Add:* Dept Physiol & Molecular Med Med Col Ohio PO Box 10008 Toledo OH 43699-0008. *E-Mail:* rapp%milo@cutter.mco.edu

RAPP, PAUL ERNEST, THEORETICAL NEUROPHYSIOLOGY. *Current Pos:* from asst prof to assoc prof, 79-91, PROF PHYSIOL, ALLEGHENY UNIV, PA, 91- *Personal Data:* b Chicago, Ill, Sept 2, 49; m 91, Tanya Schmah. *Educ:* Univ Ill, Urbana-Champaign, BS(physiol) & BS(physics), 72; Cambridge Univ, Eng, PhD(math), 75. *Prof Exp:* Fel math, Caius Col, Cambridge Univ, 75-79. *Concurrent Pos:* Vis fac, Dept Math, Rutgers Univ, 78, Dept Math, Univ Western Australia, 85, 86, 88, 93; Winston Churchill scholar, Cambridge Univ; mem bd dirs, Soc Math Biol, 84-87; ed, Physica D. *Mem:* Am Math Soc; Soc Math Biol; Soc Psychoanal Psychother. *Res:* Mathematical investigations of biochemical and biophysical control systems; large dimension nonlinear differential equations; theoretical neurobiology; analysis EEGs and event related potentials. *Mailing Add:* Dept Physiol Allegheny Univ Health Sci 2900 Queen Lane Philadelphia PA 19129. *Fax:* 215-843-0155; *E-Mail:* prapp@cc.brynmawr.edu

RAPP, RICHARD HENRY, GEODESY. *Current Pos:* Res assoc, Ohio State Univ, 61-65, asst supvr, 65-66, from instr to prof geod sci, 63-92, RES SUPVR, RES CTR, OHIO STATE UNIV, 66-, EMER PROF GEOD SCI, 92- *Personal Data:* b Danbury, Conn, Aug 26, 37; m 65, Patricia Hallabrin; c Richard H Jr & Christopher M. *Educ:* Rensselaer Polytech Inst, BS, 59; Ohio State Univ, MSc, 61, PhD(geod sci), 64. *Honors & Awards:* W H Heiskanen Award, 65. *Concurrent Pos:* Assoc ed, J Geophys Res, 77-79; pres, Sect 5, Int Asn Geod, 79-83; chmn, Comt Geod, Nat Acad Sci, 84-87. *Mem:* Fel Am Geophys Union (pres, geod sect, 82-84). *Res:* Improving knowledge of the gravity field of the Earth for geodetic, geophysical and oceangraphic applications. *Mailing Add:* Dept Civil Ohio State Univ 470 Hitchcock Columbus OH 43210-1275. *Fax:* 614-292-2957; *E-Mail:* rapp.1@osu.edu

RAPP, ROBERT, pediatric dentistry, histology, for more information see previous edition

RAPP, ROBERT, RADIOLOGY. *Current Pos:* From instr to assoc prof, 53-80, EMER ASSOC PROF RADIOL, UNIV MICH, ANN ARBOR, 80- *Personal Data:* b Reading, Pa, Apr 22, 21; m 45, Anne Baird. *Educ:* Ursinus Col, BS, 42; Temple Univ, MD, 46; Am Bd Radiol, dipl. *Mem:* Am Col Radiol; Radiol Soc NAm. *Res:* Clinical radiology; teaching. *Mailing Add:* 1460 Cedar Bend Dr Ann Arbor MI 48105

RAPP, ROBERT ANTHONY, METALLURGY. *Current Pos:* from asst prof to prof, 63-95, EMER PROF METALL ENG, OHIO STATE UNIV, 95- *Personal Data:* b Lafayette, Ind, Feb 21, 34; m 60, Heidi B Sartorius; c Kathleen (Raymand), Thomas, Stephen & Stephanie (Surface). *Educ:* Purdue Univ, BS, 56; Carnegie Inst Technol, MS, 59, PhD(metall eng), 60. *Hon Degrees:* Dr Inst Polytech Tonlouse, 95. *Honors & Awards:* Stoughton Young Teacher Award, Am Soc Metals, 67, Howe Gold Medal, 73; Campbell Lectr, Am Soc Metals, 83, Nat Acad Eng, 88; Willis R Whitney Award, Nat Asn Corrosion Engr, 86; Acta/Scripta Met Lectr, 91-93; UR Evans Award, Brit Corrosion Soc, 92. *Prof Exp:* Fulbright fel, Max Planck Inst Phys Chem, 59-60; Res Metall 1st Lt, USAF, WPAFB, 60-63. *Concurrent Pos:* Guggenheim fel, Univ Grenoble, 72-73; Fulbright fel, ENS Chimie, Toulouse, 85-86. *Mem:* Fel Am Inst Mining, Metall & Petrol Engrs; fel Am Soc Metals; fel Electrochem Soc; fel Nat Asn Corrosion Engrs; hon mem, French Soc Metals & Mat; hon fel, British Inst Corrosion. *Res:* Oxidation of metals and alloys; thermodynamics; electrochemistry, point defects in compounds, hot corrosion of materials, kinetics; fused salts; protective coatings; aluminum metallurgy. *Mailing Add:* 1379 Southport Dr Columbus OH 43235. *Fax:* 614-292-1537

RAPP, ROBERT DIETRICH, ORGANIC CHEMISTRY. *Current Pos:* from asst prof to prof, 67-93, EMER PROF CHEM, ALBRIGHT COL, 93- *Personal Data:* b Reading, Pa, Dec 21, 30; m 53, Grace M Miller; c Johanna & Ilsa. *Educ:* Tufts Univ, BS, 55; Lehigh Univ, PhD(org chem), 67. *Prof Exp:* Chemist, Glidden Co, 55-57 & Polymer Corp, 57; biochemist, Reading Hosp, 57-64; asst chem, Lehigh Univ, 64-65, res asst, 65-66; instr, Lafayette Col, 66-67. *Concurrent Pos:* Sigma Xi res grant, 67; vis scientist, Lehigh Univ, 93- *Mem:* AAAS; Am Chem Soc; Am Soc Pharmacog; NY Acad Sci. *Res:* Synthesis of psoralens and coumarins; preparation of drug delivery systems. *Mailing Add:* Dept Chem Albright Col Reading PA 19612-5234

RAPP, WALDEAN G, BIOCHEMISTRY, FOOD SCI & TECHNOLOGY. *Current Pos:* tech dir, Cargill, Inc, Corn Starch & Syrup, 70-82, MGR, BIOTECHNOL RES & ANALYTIC SERV, CARGILL, INC, 82- *Personal Data:* b Oakley, Kans, Mar 30, 36; m 57; c 3. *Educ:* Univ Ottawa, BS, 59; Univ Ark, MS, 61, PhD(chem), 63. *Prof Exp:* Res chemist, Chem Res Dept, Food Div, Anderson, Clayton & Co, 63-67; chief chemist, Hubinger Co, Iowa, 67-70. *Mem:* Am Chem Soc; Am Asn Cereal Chem; Am Soc Brewing Chemists; Am Oil Chem Soc; Inst Food Technol; Soc Soft Drink Technologists. *Res:* Hormonal effects on the acid soluble nucleotides of liver; flavor studies of various food and food products, including sensory evaluation of foods; basic food science; corn wet-milling; biotechnology and fermentation research. *Mailing Add:* Cargill Anal Serv 2301 Crosby Rd Wayzata MN 55391-2397

RAPP, WILLIAM RODGER, PATHOLOGY. *Current Pos:* DIAG PATHOLOGIST, 87- *Personal Data:* b Dover, NJ, May 18, 36; m 66; c 2. *Educ:* Kans State Univ, BS, 64, DVM, 66, MS, 70. *Prof Exp:* Res assoc neuropath, Kans State Univ, 66-67; instr path, 67-72; dir path, Bio Dynamics Inc, East Millstone, NJ, 72-76; consult pathologist, 76-87. *Mem:* Am Vet Med Asn; Am Asn Vet Lab Diagnosticians. *Res:* Comparative pathology; veterinary pathology; experimental toxicology and neoplasia epidemiology. *Mailing Add:* PO Box 279 Arden NC 28704

RAPPAPORT, CAREY M, MATHEMATICS. *Current Pos:* asst prof, 87-93, ASSOC PROF ELEC & COMPUT ENG NORTHEASTERN UNIV, 93- *Personal Data:* b Tokyo, Japan, Jan 9, 59; m 89, Ann W Morgenthaler; c Sarah & Brian. *Educ:* Mass Inst Technol, SB(elec eng) & SB(math), 82, MS, 82, PhD(elec eng & comput sci), 87. *Honors & Awards:* H A Wheeler Award, Inst Elec & Electronics Engrs Antenna & Propagation Soc, 95. *Prof Exp:* Mem tech staff, Commun Satellite Corp, 78-83 & Aerospace Corp, 84. *Concurrent Pos:* Consult microwave antenna design & modeling. *Mem:* Sr mem Inst Elec & Electronics Engrs; Sigma Xi. *Res:* Novel antenna designs for wide field of view communications; biomedical heating applications; ground penetrating radar; computational electromagnetics; developing new absorbing bounday conditions. *Mailing Add:* Dept Elec & Comput Eng Northeastern Univ 235 Forsyth Bldg Boston MA 02115. *Fax:* 617-373-8627; *E-Mail:* rappaport@neu.edu

RAPPAPORT, DAVID, MATHEMATICS EDUCATION. *Current Pos:* PROF MATH EDUC, NORTHEASTERN ILL UNIV, 57- *Personal Data:* b Kiev, Russia, June 13, 07; m 33; c 2. *Educ:* Univ Chicago, BS, 28; Northwestern Univ, MA, 54, EdD(educ), 57. *Prof Exp:* Teacher, Pub Schs, Ill, 37-40; teacher high school, 40-56. *Concurrent Pos:* Math consult, Am Educ Publs, 71-72. *Res:* Problems of teaching elementary school mathematics. *Mailing Add:* 2747 W Coyle Ave Chicago IL 60645

RAPPAPORT, HARRY P, BIOLOGY. *Current Pos:* assoc prof biol, 65-71, PROF BIOL, TEMPLE UNIV, 71- *Personal Data:* b Los Angeles, Calif, Oct 9, 27. *Educ:* Mass Inst Technol, BS, 51; Yale Univ, PhD(physics), 56. *Prof Exp:* USPHS fel, Yale Univ, 56-58, asst prof biophys, 59-65. *Mem:* Am Chem Soc; Am Soc Biol Chem. *Res:* Ligand-protein interactions; bacterial secretion of proteins. *Mailing Add:* Dept Biol Temple Univ Philadelphia PA 19122

RAPPAPORT, IRVING, IMMUNOLOGY. *Current Pos:* PROF IMMUNOL, BENNINGTON COL, 92- *Personal Data:* b New York, NY, Sept 4, 23; m 48, Helen Magid; c Glenn, Jeffrey & Paul. *Educ:* Cornell Univ, AB, 48; Calif Inst Technol, PhD(immunol, biochem), 53. *Prof Exp:* Res botanist, Univ Calif, Los Angeles, 53-61; asst prof microbiol, Univ Chicago, 61-64; actg chmn dept, New York Med Col, 66-67, prof, 64-91, emer prof, 91-92. *Mem:* Fel AAAS; Am Asn Immunol; Reticuloendothelial Soc; Genetics Soc Am; Am Soc Microbiol; Sigma Xi. *Res:* Antigenic structure of viruses; antibody synthesis in vitro. *Mailing Add:* PO Box 721 North Bennington VT 05257

RAPPAPORT, LAWRENCE, PLANT PHYSIOLOGY, HORTICULTURE. *Current Pos:* From appointment at jr olericulturist to assoc olericulturist, Univ Calif, Davis, 56-68, actg dir, Plant Growth Lab, 74-76, dir, 78-79, chmn, Dept Veg Crops, 78-84, prof, 68-91, EMER PROF & OLERICULTURIST VEG CROPS, UNIV CALIF, DAVIS, 91- *Personal Data:* b New York, NY, May 28, 28; m 53, Norma Horowitz; c Meryl, Debra & Craig. *Educ:* Univ Idaho, BS, 50; Mich State Univ, MS, 51, PhD(hort), 56. *Concurrent Pos:* Res fel, Calif Inst Technol, 58; Fulbright & Guggenheim fels, Hebrew Univ & Univ Tokyo, 63-64; NIH spec vis prof & fel org chem, Univ Bristol, 70-71; vis prof, Dept Biol, Univ Calif, San Diego, 78, Div Hort, Commonwealth Sci Indust Res Orgn, Adelaide, S Australia, 84 & Dept Chem, City Univ London, 85; vis scientist, Friedrich-Miescher Inst, Basel, 85; chmn bot group, Univ Calif, Davis, 86-90; McMaster fel, Australia, 91. *Mem:* Fel Am Soc Hort Sci; Am Soc Plant Physiol. *Res:* Growth and development; plant growth regulators; gibberellins; plant cell culture; somatic cell biology; cell and plant selection for disease resistance; hormonal regulation; mode of action of plant hormones. *Mailing Add:* Dept Veg Crops Univ Calif Plant Growth Lab Davis CA 95616. *E-Mail:* rappaport@vegmail.ucdavis.edu

RAPPAPORT, MAURICE, PSYCHIATRY, NEUROPSYCHOLOGY. *Current Pos:* RESEARCHER PSYCHIAT, UNIV CALIF, 72- *Personal Data:* b New York, NY, Feb 9, 26; c 6. *Educ:* Stanford Univ, MD, 62; Ohio State Univ, PhD(psychol), 54. *Prof Exp:* Chief res, Agnews State Hosp, 62-72. *Mem:* AAAS; Am Med Asn; Human Factors Soc; Am Psychiat Asn. *Res:* Neuropsychiatry; psychopharmacology. *Mailing Add:* 1120 McKendrie St San Jose CA 95126-1406

RAPPAPORT, RAYMOND, EMBRYOLOGY, CELL BIOLOGY. *Current Pos:* from asst prof to assoc prof biol, 52-89, EMER PROF, UNION COL, NY, 89-; SR RES SCIENTIST, MT DESERT ISLAND BIOL LAB, 89- *Personal Data:* b North Bergen, NJ, May 21, 22; m 48, Barbara Nolan; c Ann, Peter & Jean. *Educ:* Bethany Col, WVa, BS, 48; Univ Mich, MS, 48; Yale Univ, PhD, 52. *Prof Exp:* Lab instr gen biol, Yale Univ, 51-52. *Concurrent Pos:* Trustee, Mt Desert Island Biol Lab, 54-70, dir 56-59, pres, 79-81. *Mem:* Fel AAAS; Am Soc Zool; Am Micros Soc; Am Soc Cell Biol; Soc Develop Biol; Sigma Xi. *Res:* Animal cell division; role of water in growth and differentiation; mechanics of animal cell division, emphasis on experiments with living invertebrate eggs, including geometrical rearrangement of asters, mitotic apparatuses, and shape changes of the cells. *Mailing Add:* Mt Desert Island Biol Lab Salisbury Cove ME 04672-0035. *Fax:* 207-288-2130

RAPPAPORT, SAUL A, ASTROPHYSICS. *Current Pos:* PROF PHYSICS, MASS INST TECHNOL, 70- *Personal Data:* b Philadelphia, Pa, 42. *Educ:* Mass Inst Technol, PhD(physics), 68. *Honors & Awards:* Res fel Alfred P Sloan, 74-78. *Mem:* Am Astrol Soc; Am Physical Soc. *Mailing Add:* 62 Chandler Rd Burlington MA 01803

RAPPAPORT, STEPHEN MORRIS, INDUSTRIAL HYGIENE. *Current Pos:* from asst prof to assoc prof indust hyg, 76-90, PROF OCCUP HEALTH, SCH PUB HEALTH, UNIV CALIF, BERKELEY, 90- *Personal Data:* b San Antonio, Tex, Jan 6, 48; m 70. *Educ:* Univ Ill, BS, 69; Univ NC, Chapel Hill, MSPH, 73, PhD(indust hyg), 74; Am Bd Indust Hyg, cert, 75. *Prof Exp:* Anal chemist, Hazleton Labs, Inc, 69-71; staff mem indust hyg, Los Alamos Sci Lab, Univ Calif, 74-76. *Mem:* Am Indust Hyg Asn; Am Acad Indust Hyg; Am Conf Gov Indust Hygienists; Am Chem Soc. *Mailing Add:* Dept Environ Sci & Eng Sch Pub Health Univ NC Chapel Hill NC 27599-8140

RAPPAPORT, STEPHEN S, COMMUNICATIONS AND SYSTEMS ENGINEERING. *Current Pos:* from asst prof to prof eng, 68-91, dir grad prog, 72-73, 78-79 & 84-85, LEADING PROF, STATE UNIV NY, STONY BROOK, 91- *Personal Data:* b New York, NY, Sept 26, 38; m 66; c 2. *Educ:* Cooper Union, BEE, 60; Univ Southern Calif, MSEE, 62; NY Univ, PhD(elec eng), 65. *Prof Exp:* Mem tech staff, Hughes Aircraft Co, 60-62; instr elec eng, NY Univ, 64-65; mem tech staff, Bell Tel Labs, 65-68. *Concurrent Pos:* Indust consult, 69-; NSF grant commun tech, 76-85; chmn, Undergrad Prog Comt, Col Eng, State Univ NY, Stony Brook, 77-78, Data Commun Syst Comt, Inst Elec & Electronics Engrs, 84-86; assoc ed, Inst Elec & Electronics Engrs Trans Commun, 82-85; prin investr, Off Nav Res, 85-; mem bd gov, Inst Elec & Electronics Engrs Commun Soc, 87-90; chmn, Awards Comt, Long Island Sect Inst Elec & Electronics Engrs, 88-91; Mountbotten premium, Inst Elec Engrs, UK, 95. *Mem:* Fel Inst Elec & Electronics Engrs. *Res:* Communications systems and theory; analytical modelling and simulation; network architecture, multiple access techniques, and communications traffic; mobile communication systems; data, voice, and computer communications; personal communication networks; spread spectrum techniques; 8c code division multi-access; mobile wireless communications. *Mailing Add:* Dept Elec Eng State Univ NY Stony Brook NY 11794-2350

RAPPERPORT, EUGENE J, METALLURGY, MECHANICAL ENGINEERING. *Current Pos:* CONSULT, E RAPPERPORT & ASSOCS, 74- *Personal Data:* b St Louis, Mo, Mar 13, 30; m 50; c 3. *Educ:* Mass Inst Technol, BS, 52, ScD(metall), 55. *Prof Exp:* Group leader metall, Nuclear Metals, Inc, 51-6; sr scientist, Ledgemont Labs, Kennecott Copper Corp, 63-73; prof, New Col, 73-74. *Mem:* Am Inst Mining, Metall & Petrol Engrs; Am Welding Soc; Am Soc Metals; Am Soc Testing & Mat; AAAS. *Res:* Diffusion; x-ray physics; refractory metal technology; phase equilibrium and electron microprobe studies; deformation of metals; chemical thermodynamics and kinetics; computer applications; mass spectrometry; nuclear fusion engineering; magnetohydrodynamics engineering; magnet design and construction. *Mailing Add:* Old County Rd Lincoln MA 01773

RAPPORT, DAVID JOSEPH, ECOLOGY, THEORETICAL BIOLOGY. *Current Pos:* PROF, UNIV GUELPH, ONT, 94- *Personal Data:* b Omaha, Nebr, Feb 16, 39; m 65, 86; c 3. *Educ:* Univ Mich, BBA, 60, MA, 66, PhD(econ), 67. *Prof Exp:* Res assoc econ, Univ Mich, 67-68; fisheries res bd fel, Univ Toronto, 68-69, fel ecol, 69-70; vis asst prof & Can Coun Killam sr res fel, Simon Fraser Univ, 70-74; environmentalist, Statist Can, 74-81; Titular prof zool, Univ Toronto, 77-81; sci adv, Statist Can, 82-89; res coordr, Inst Res Environ & Ecol, Univ Ottawa, 89-94. *Concurrent Pos:* Vis scientist, Statistics Sweden, Stockholm; tri-coun eco-res chair, Eco Syst Health, 94-; pres, Int Soc Econ Syst Health & Med, 94-; ed & chief, J Eco-Syst Health & Med, Blackwell Sci, 94- *Mem:* Inst Ecol; Soc Am Naturalists; fel Linwean Soc (London). *Res:* Data for development; common foundations for economics and society; behavior of ecosystems under stress; framework for environmental statistics; state of environment reporting; economic environment linkages. *Mailing Add:* Fac Environ Sci Univ Guelph Ottawa ON N1G 2W1 Can

RAPPORT, MAURICE M, BIOCHEMISTRY. *Current Pos:* prof biochem, 58-67, AM CANCER SOC PROF, ALBERT EINSTEIN COL MED, 62-67, 76-, VIS PROF NEUROL, 86-; EMER PROF BIOCHEM, COL PHYSICIANS & SURGEONS, COLUMBIA UNIV, 86- *Personal Data:* b New York, NY, Sept 23, 19; m 42, 94, Nancy B Reich; c Erica (Gringle) & Ezra. *Educ:* City Col New York, BS, 40; Calif Inst Technol, PhD(org chem), 46. *Prof Exp:* Technician, Rockefeller Inst, 40-41; asst, Off Sci Res & Develop, Calif Inst Technol, 42-45; mem res staff, Cleveland Clin Found, 46-48; res assoc, Col Physicians & Surgeons, Columbia Univ, 48-51; assoc res scientist immunol, Div Labs & Res, State Dept Health, NY, 51-58; prof biochem, Col Physicians & Surgeons, Columbia Univ, 67-86; chief, Div Neurosci, NY State Psychiat Inst, 68-86. *Concurrent Pos:* Fulbright scholar, Inst Superiore Sanita, Italy, 52; head, Immunol Sect, Sloan-Kettering Inst, 54-58. *Mem:* Am Chem Soc; Am Soc Neurochem; fel AAAS; fel NY Acad Sci; Biochem Soc; Int Soc Neurochem; Am Soc Biochem & Molecular Biol. *Res:* Serotonin; lipid haptens; brain proteins; plasmalogens; lipid-protein interactions; gangliosides; antibodies as interventive agents in studies of central nervous system function; regulated secretion. *Mailing Add:* Dept Neurol F314 Albert Einstein Col Med 1300 Morris Park Ave Bronx NY 10461-1975

RAPUNDALO, STEPHEN T, CARDIOVASCULAR. *Current Pos:* scientist, 87-90, SR SCIENTIST PHARMACOL, PARKE-DAVIS PHARMACEUT RES, 90- *Personal Data:* b Sudbury, Ont, Aug 22, 58; m 82; c 2. *Educ:* Laurentian Univ, Sudbury, BSc Hons, 79; Med Col Va, PhD(physiol), 83. *Prof Exp:* Postdoctoral fel pharmacol, Col Med, Univ Cincinnati, 83-85, res assoc, 85-87. *Mem:* Am Physiol Soc; Biophys Soc; Am Soc Pharmacol & Exp Therapeut; Cardiac Muscle Soc; AAAS. *Res:* Cellular mechanisms related to cardiac pathophysiology; characterization of membrane receptor structure and function, signal transduction, cellular and molecular actions, and processing enzymes of vasoactive peptides; development and evaluation of discovery strategies for cardiovascular therapies. *Mailing Add:* Dept Biochem Parke-Davis Pharmaceut Res 2800 Plymouth Rd Ann Arbor MI 48105-2430

RARD, JOSEPH ANTOINE, PHYSICAL CHEMISTRY, CHEMICAL THERMODYNAMICS. *Current Pos:* CHEMIST THERMODYN & TRANSP PROPERTIES, LAWRENCE LIVERMORE NAT LAB, UNIV CALIF, 79- *Personal Data:* b St Louis, Mo, Sept 29, 45; m 71, Deborah Allen; c Elizabeth M & Joseph D. *Educ:* Southern Ill Univ, Edwardsville, BA, 67; Iowa State Univ, PhD(phys chem), 73. *Prof Exp:* Fel, Ames Lab, Dept Energy, 73-76; vis res asst prof geol, Univ Ill, Urbana-Champaign, 77-78. *Concurrent Pos:* Chmn, Nuclear Engergy Agency Specialist Team, Technetium Thermochem Data Base, 88- *Mem:* Am Chem Soc. *Res:* Experimental determination of thermodynamic and transport properties of aqueous solutions, especially brine salts, sulfuric acid, rare earth electrolytes and transition metal electrolytes; critical reviews of chemical thermodynamics for rare earths and second transition series (fission products) elements. *Mailing Add:* Lawrence Livermore Nat Lab PO Box 808 Livermore CA 94550. *Fax:* 510-422-0208; *E-Mail:* rard1@llnl.gov

RARIDEN, ROBERT LEE, INFORMATION SYSTEM MODELING & ANALYSIS, BUSINESS PROCESS IMPROVEMENT. *Current Pos:* ASSOC PROF, INFO SYST, ILL STATE UNIV, 88-; RES PROJ COORDR, ARMY CENGRS, 92- *Personal Data:* b Flint, Mich, Mar 7, 49. *Educ:* Cent Mich Univ, BA, 71; Univ Miami, MA, 78, PhD(philos), 83. *Prof Exp:* Asst prof info syst, Grambling State Univ, 87-88. *Mem:* Inst Elec & Electronics Engrs; Am Chem Soc; Data Processing Mgt & Asn. *Res:* Identifying useful and accurate methods of requirements analysis; this involves the development and application of computer assisted tools for model development, management and analysis. *Mailing Add:* 1602 Baumgart Normal IL 61761. *Fax:* 309-438-5113; *E-Mail:* rariden@ilstu.edu

RARIDON, RICHARD JAY, PHYSICAL CHEMISTRY. *Current Pos:* CONSULT, 92- *Personal Data:* b Newton, Iowa, Oct 25, 31; m 56, Mona Herndon; c Susan G & Ann C. *Educ:* Grinnell Col, BA, 53; Vanderbilt Univ, MA, 55, PhD(chem), 59. *Prof Exp:* Assoc prof physics, Memphis State Univ, 58-62; res chemist, Oak Ridge Nat Lab, 62-71, comput specialist, 72-92. *Concurrent Pos:* Res specialist, Coop Sci Educ Ctr, 71-72. *Mem:* Fel AAAS; Sigma Xi; Asn Acad Sci (secy-treas, 71-75, pres, 77). *Res:* Temperature dependence of chemical equilibria; physical properties of solutions; water desalination; plasma physics; environmental modeling. *Mailing Add:* 111 Columbia Dr Oak Ridge TN 37830-7721. *E-Mail:* rjr@fed.ornl.gov

RARITA, WILLIAM ROLAND, ELEMENTARY PARTICLE PHYSICS. *Current Pos:* res physicist, Space Sci Lab, 62-63, VIS SCIENTIST, LAWRENCE BERKELEY LAB, UNIV CALIF, 63- *Personal Data:* b Bordeaux, France, Mar 21, 07; nat US; m 49; c 1. *Educ:* City Col New York, BS, 27, EE, 29; Columbia Univ, MA, 30, PhD(physics), 37. *Prof Exp:* From instr to prof physics, Brooklyn Col, 30-62. *Concurrent Pos:* Sr scientist, Manhattan Proj, 44-46; consult, Res Inst Advan Study, 56-62. *Mem:* Fel Am Phys Soc. *Res:* Photoelectric effect; beta activity; deuteron and triton; high energy nucleon-nucleon interaction; Regge poles. *Mailing Add:* 752 Grizzly Peak Blvd Berkeley CA 94708

RAS, ZBIGNIEW WIESLAW, KNOWLEDGE REPRESENTATION, INTELLIGENT INFORMATION SYSTEMS. *Current Pos:* PROF COMPUT SCI, UNIV NC, CHARLOTTE, 81- *Personal Data:* b Warsaw, Poland, June 17, 47; m 87, Joanna Wapinska; c Anna. *Educ:* Univ Warsaw, MS, 70, PhD(computer sci), 73. *Prof Exp:* Programmer, Polish Acad Sci, 73-74; asst prof math & computer sci, Univ Warsaw, 73-83 & Jagiellonian Univ, Poland, 76-78; res assoc, Columbia Univ, 75-76; assoc prof, Univ Tenn, Knoxville, 85-86. *Concurrent Pos:* Vis asst prof math, Univ Fla, Gainesville, 78-79; vis prof, Univ Bonn, Ger, 87 & Linkoping Univ, Sweden, 80; ed-in-chief, J Intel Info Systs, Kluwest, 92 & assoc ed, Fundamenta Informaticae J, 92- *Mem:* Asn Comput Mach; Am Asn Artificial Intel; Sigma Xi; Inst Elec & Electronics Engrs Computer Soc. *Res:* Knowledge representation; distributed information systems; logic for artificial intelligence; machine learning. *Mailing Add:* 6628 Morrowick Circle Charlotte NC 28226. *Fax:* 704-547-3516

RASAIAH, JAYENDRAN C, PHYSICAL CHEMISTRY, THEORETICAL CHEMISTRY. *Current Pos:* from asst prof to assoc prof, 69-78, PROF CHEM, UNIV MAINE, ORONO, 78- *Personal Data:* b Colombo, Ceylon, Apr 1, 34. *Educ:* Univ Ceylon, BSc, 57; Univ Pittsburgh, PhD(chem), 65. *Prof Exp:* Off Saline Water fel, State Univ NY, Stony Brook, 65-68, instr chem, 68-69. *Concurrent Pos:* Sr vis fel, Sci Res Coun, Oxford Univ & London Univ, 75-76; vis fel, Dept Appl Math, Australian Nat Univ, Canberra; vis prof, Dept Chem, Univ NSW, Australia, 80. *Mem:* Am Chem Soc; Am Phys Soc. *Res:* Statistical mechanics of electrolyte solutions; perturbation theories of polar and non-polar fluids; computer simulation studies of fluids and solutions; non linear effects in polar fluids; solvent dynamical effects on electron transfer and ion mobilities; structure of DNA triplet repeats. *Mailing Add:* Dept Chem Univ Maine Orono ME 04469-0105. *Fax:* 207-581-1191; *E-Mail:* rasaiah@maine.edu

RASBAND, S NEIL, PHYSICS. *Current Pos:* from asst prof to assoc prof, 72-88, PROF PHYSICS, BRIGHAM YOUNG UNIV, 88- *Personal Data:* b Ogden, Utah, June 21, 39; m 63; c 3. *Educ:* Univ Utah, BA, 64, PhD(physics), 69. *Prof Exp:* AEC fel, Princeton Univ, 69-70; res assoc physics, La State Univ, Baton Rouge, 70-71, vis asst prof, 71-72. *Mem:* Am Phys Soc; Am Astron Soc. *Res:* Plasma physics; magnetic confinement fusion. *Mailing Add:* Dept Physics Brigham Young Univ Provo UT 84602

RASBERRY, STANLEY DEXTER, METROLOGY. *Current Pos:* Physicist, 63-75, exec asst, 75-79, dept chief, 79-83, CHIEF, NAT BUR STAND, 83- *Personal Data:* b Lubbock, Tex, July 23, 41; m 61; c 2. *Educ:* Johns Hopkins Univ, BA, 63. *Concurrent Pos:* Ed, Ref Mat Column, Am Lab, 80-; deleg, US Pharmacopoeial Conv, 80-; lectr, Montgomery Col, 82-85. *Mem:* Am Phys Soc; Am Chem Soc; Soc Appl Spectros; Am Soc Testing & Mat; Int Stand Orgn. *Res:* Development of spectrometric methods for materials analysis including co-development of Rasberry-Heinrich correction for interelement effects in x-ray fluorescence analysis; development of standard reference materials as calibrants for chemical analysis or for physical measurement. *Mailing Add:* 818 Crystal Ct Gaithersburg MD 20878

RASCH, ELLEN M, CYTOCHEMISTRY, CYTOPHOTOMETRY. *Current Pos:* chmn, 86-94, PROF BIOPHYS, JAMES H QUILLEN COL MED, ETENN STATE UNIV, 78-, PROF ANAT, 94- *Personal Data:* b Chicago Heights, Ill, Jan 31, 27; m 50, Robert W; c Martin. *Educ:* Univ Chicago, PhB, 45, BS, 47, MS, 48, PhD(bot), 50. *Prof Exp:* Asst histologist, Am Meat Inst Found, Chicago, Ill, 50-51; USPHS fel zool, Univ Chicago, 51-53, from res asst to res assoc, 53-59; instr civil defense, Milwaukee Civil Defense Dept, 60-62; res assoc prof biol, Marquette Univ, 62-78, Todd C Wehr distinguished prof biophys, 75-78. *Concurrent Pos:* Nat Inst Gen Med Sci Res Career Develop Award, 67-72. *Mem:* Fel AAAS; Am Soc Zool; Royal Micros Soc; Am Soc Cell Biol; Histochem Soc (secy, 75-79, treas, 84-86); Sigma Xi; Am Soc Ichthyologists & Herpetologists. *Res:* Quantitative cytophotometry; nucleoprotein synthesis in dipteran polytene chromosomes; evolutionary biology of unisexual fish; chromatin diminution in copepods. *Mailing Add:* Dept Anat & Cell Biol Quillen Col Med ETenn State Univ Johnson City TN 37614-0421. *Fax:* 423-439-6249

RASCH, ROBERT, PHYSIOLOGY. *Current Pos:* prof & chmn, 77-87, EMER PROF PHYSIOL, QUILLEN-DISHNER COL MED, 87- *Personal Data:* b Chicago, Ill, Nov 19, 26; m 50, Ellen M Myrberg; c Martin K. *Educ:* Univ Chicago, PhB, 46, PhD(physiol), 59; Northwestern Univ, MD, 51. *Prof Exp:* Instr, Med Col Wis, 59-61, from asst prof to assoc prof physiol, 61-77. *Mem:* AAAS; Am Soc Cell Biol; NY Acad Sci. *Res:* Chromosome structure and nucleocytoplasmic interaction; compensatory physiological mechanisms, chromosome structure and nucleocytoplasmic interaction; physiological simulations on microprocessors. *Mailing Add:* Dept Physiol Quillen-Dishner Med Col Box 19780A Johnson City TN 39614. *E-Mail:* 74634.2745@compuserve.com

RASCHE, JOHN FREDERICK, STATISTICAL PROCESS CONTROL. *Current Pos:* Assoc develop chem engr, 58-61, develop engr, 61-65, sr develop engr, 65-75, group leader process res & develop, 75-79, process engr mgr, 79-87, ENG FEL, A E STALEY MFG CO, 87-, MGR, STATIST PROCESS ANALYSIS, 88- *Personal Data:* b Bonne Terre, Mo, Apr 14, 36; m 58, Judith Rodgers; c Jeffrey, Kay & David. *Educ:* Univ Mo, Rolla, BS, 58. *Mem:* Am Inst Chem Engrs. *Res:* Catalysis of carbohydrates using soluble and immobilized enzymes; purification and separation processes applied to corn and soybean processing. *Mailing Add:* 1821 Burning Tree Dr Decatur IL 62521. *Fax:* 217-421-2901; *E-Mail:* therasches@juno.com

RASCO, BARBARA A, FOOD REGULATIONS, FISHERIES TECHNOLOGY. *Current Pos:* asst prof, 84-89, ASSOC PROF FOOD SCI, INST FOOD SCI & TECHNOL, SCH FISHERIES, UNIV WASH, 89- *Personal Data:* b Pittsburgh, Pa, Apr 3, 57; m 84. *Educ:* Univ Pa, BSE, 79; Univ Mass, PhD(food sci & nutrit), 83; Seattle Univ, JD, 95. *Prof Exp:* Biochem engr, Cargill Inc, 82-83, res chemist, 83-84. *Mem:* Inst Food Technologists; Am Chem Soc; Pac Fisheries Technologists; Am Bar Asn. *Res:* Development of rapid analytical methods for fisheries technology and aquaculture; applied enzymology; food product/process development, food adulteration; food laws and regulations. *Mailing Add:* 12043 Sixth Ave NW Seattle WA 98177

RASE, HOWARD F, CHEMICAL ENGINEERING, CATALYSIS. *Current Pos:* from asst prof to prof, 52-74, chmn dept, 63-68, W A CUNNINGHAM PROF CHEM ENG, UNIV TEX, AUSTIN, 74- *Personal Data:* b Buffalo, NY, Oct 18, 21; m 54, Beverly Bonelli; c Carolyn V & Howard F Jr. *Educ:* Univ Tex, BS, 42; Univ Wis, MS, 50, PhD(chem eng), 52. *Honors & Awards:* Fulbright lectr, Tech Univ Denmark, 57. *Prof Exp:* Chem engr res & develop, Dow Chem Co, 42-44; process engr, Eastern State Petrol Co, 44; process engr & proj engr, Foster Wheeler Corp, 44-49. *Concurrent Pos:* Consult, catalysis & reactor design. *Mem:* Am Inst Chem Engrs. *Res:* Applied kinetics and reactor design; homogeneous and heterogeneous catalysis; catalyst development; process design techniques; enzyme catalysis. *Mailing Add:* Dept Chem Eng Univ Tex Austin TX 78712. *Fax:* 572-471-7060

RASEMAN, CHAD J(OSEPH), CHEMICAL & NUCLEAR ENGINEERING. *Current Pos:* vpres, 67-88, PRES, SOLAR SUNSTILL, INC, 88- *Personal Data:* b Detroit, Mich, Aug 29, 18; m 45; c 5. *Educ:* Wayne State Univ, BS, 41; Univ Mich, MS, 44; Cornell Univ, PhD(chem eng), 51. *Hon Degrees:* EngD, Wayne State Univ, 58. *Prof Exp:* Chief chem engr, R P Scherer Corp, 41-44 & Boyle-Midway, Inc, 46-47; head, Oak Ridge Chem Eng Div, Kellex Corp, 47-48; fel, Brookhaven Nat Lab, 48-51, group leader, Nuclear Eng Dept, 51-58, asst div head, 58-65, tech asst to dept chmn, Dept Appl Sci, 65-70, group leader rotating fluidized bed reactor, Space Nuclear Propulsion Proj, 70-73. *Concurrent Pos:* Asst, Cornell Univ, 48-49; chief eval sect, Div Reactor Develop, US AEC, 60-62; dir, Nat Agr Plastics Asn, 72-76. *Mem:* AAAS; Am Chem Soc; fel Am Inst Chem; Am Nuclear Soc; Int Solar Energy Soc. *Res:* Design, evaluation and testing of the fluidized bed concept for space nuclear propulsion and unique chemical reactions; co-inventor of solar distillation units and special coatings that control condensation and light transmission. *Mailing Add:* 644 W San Francisco Santa Fe NM 87501-1490

RASENICK, MARK M, NEUROBIOLOGY, NEUROTRANSMITTER RESPONSE. *Current Pos:* from asst prof to assoc prof, 83-92, PROF PHYSIOL & BIOPHYS, COL MED, UNIV ILL, 93- *Personal Data:* b Chicago, Ill, Sept 5, 49; m 74, Helene J Shambelar; c Elliot S, Matthew M & Emily A. *Educ:* Case Western Res Univ, BA; Wesleyan Univ, PhD(develop biol), 77. *Honors & Awards:* Res Scientist Develop Award, NIMH. *Prof Exp:* Assoc res scientist, Dept Neurol, Sch Med, Yale Univ, 81-83. *Concurrent Pos:* Mem staff, Ill State Psychiatric Inst, 83-86; fel, Yale Univ, 81; mem, Cellular Neurosci Panel, NSF. *Mem:* NY Acad Sci; Soc Neurosci; AAAS; Am Soc Biol Chemists; Union Concerned Scientists; Sigma Xi. *Res:* Neurotransmitter receptors, cyclic nucleotides and G proteins in synaptic function; influence of the cytoskeleton on neurotransmitter responsiveness in synaptic membranes and cultured neural cells; cellular and molecular basis of mental and neurological dysfunction; molecular basis of antidepressant and other neuroleptic drug action. *Mailing Add:* Dept Physiol & Biophys Col Med Univ Ill 901 Wolcott M/C 901 Chicago IL 60612-7342. *Fax:* 312-996-1414; *E-Mail:* v20133@uicvm

RASERA, ROBERT LOUIS, SOLID STATE PHYSICS, NUCLEAR PHYSICS. *Current Pos:* assoc prof, 71-81, PROF PHYSICS, UNIV MD, BALTIMORE CO, 81-, ASSOC CHAIR, 96- *Personal Data:* b New York, NY, July 25, 39; m 61, Paula Schlundt; c 2. *Educ:* Wheaton Col, BS, 60; Purdue Univ, PhD(physics), 65. *Prof Exp:* Res assoc, Purdue Univ, 65; guest prof, Inst Radiation & Nuclear Physics, Univ Bonn, 65-66; asst prof, Univ Pa, 66-71. *Mem:* Am Phys Soc; Am Asn Physics Teachers; Sigma Xi. *Res:* Perturbed angular correlations of nuclear radiations; hyperfine fields in solids. *Mailing Add:* Dept Physics Univ Md Baltimore Co Baltimore MD 21250. *E-Mail:* rasera@umbc.edu

RASEY, JANET SUE, CANCER & CANCER IMAGING, RADIOBIOLOGY. *Current Pos:* assoc prof, 72-83, PROF TUMOR RADIATION & CELL BIOL, DEPT RADIATION ONCOL, MED SCH, UNIV WASH, 83-, DIR, RES FUNDING SERV, 89- *Personal Data:* b Fremont, Mich, June 13, 42; m 91, Frank C Jackson. *Educ:* Univ Mich, BS, 64; Ore State Univ, MS, 65; Univ Ore, PhD(biol), 70. *Prof Exp:* NIH fel, Cell & Radiation Biol Lab, Allegheny Gen Hosp, Pittsburgh, 70-72. *Mem:* Nat Coun Univ Res Adminr; Radiation Res Soc (secy-treas); Am Soc Therapeut Radiol & Oncol. *Res:* Tumor radiation response; nuclear imaging of tumors; effects of tumor micro environment on gene expression; hypoxia and gene expression. *Mailing Add:* Dept Radiation Oncol Univ Wash Med Sch 1959 NE Pacific St Seattle WA 98195

RASGADO-FLORES, HECTOR, CELL VOLUME REGULATION. *Current Pos:* asst prof, 89-93, ASSOC PROF PHYSIOL, CHICAGO MED SCH, FINCH UNIV HEALTH SCI, 94- *Personal Data:* b Mexico City, Mex, Nov 2, 54; m 91, Cecilia Pena; c Hector & Cecilia. *Educ:* Cinvestav-IPN, Max, MSc, 79; Univ Md, PhD(neurosci), 84. *Prof Exp:* Postdoctoral fel, Md Am Heart Asn, 84-86; res asst prof, Chicago Med Sch, 87-88, Med Sch, Univ Md, 88-89. *Concurrent Pos:* Prin investr, Bressler Res Found, 87-88, NIH, 88-97 & Chicago Am Heart Asn, 90-; ed, Soc Latin Am Biophysicists, 90-; estab investr, Am Heart Asn, 91-96; mem, Int Comt, Am Physiol Soc, 96-, Minority Affairs Comt, Biophys Soc, 97- *Mem:* Soc Latin Am Biophysicists (secy, 85-86); Am Physiol Soc; Biophys Soc. *Res:* Study mechanisms of regulation of volume in muscle cells; study transport of calcium, magnesium chloride and amino acids in excitable cells. *Mailing Add:* Dept Physiol Chicago Med Sch 3333 Green Bay Rd North Chicago IL 60064. *Fax:* 847-578-3265; *E-Mail:* floresh@mis.finchcms.edu

RASH, FRED HOWARD, INDUSTRIAL CHEMICALS RESEARCH DEVELOPMENT & MANUFACTURING. *Current Pos:* Chemist, Tenn Eastman Co, 66-72, sr chemist, 73-77, group leader, 77-89, RES ASSOC, EASTMAN CHEM CO, 81- *Personal Data:* b Elkin, NC, Jan 21, 41; m 67, Judith Adcock; c 2. *Educ:* Wake Forest Univ, BS, 62; Duke Univ, PhD(chem), 67. *Mem:* Am Chem Soc; AAAS. *Res:* Product and process research and development in industrial chemicals; external technology sourcing. *Mailing Add:* Eastman Chem Co PO Box 1972 Bldg 150B Kingsport TN 37662-5150. *Fax:* 423-229-3665; *E-Mail:* frash@eastman.com

RASH, JAY JUSTEN, METABOLISM. *Current Pos:* Res scientist metab, Cent Res Labs, 72-81, DIR REGULATORY AFFAIRS, PFIZER, INC, 81- *Personal Data:* b Iowa Falls, Iowa, Dec 26, 41; m 61; c 3. *Educ:* Northwest Mo State Univ, BS, 66; Univ Mo-Columbia, MS, 67, PhD(anal biochem), 71. *Mem:* Am Chem Soc; Sigma Xi. *Res:* Development of analytical methods in tissues and biological fluids for drugs, metabolites and important biological compounds; the determination of the metabolic pathways of xenobiotics in biological systems. *Mailing Add:* 340 Stoney Hill Rd Quarryville PA 17566

RASH, JOHN EDWARD, NEUROBIOLOGY. *Current Pos:* assoc prof anat, 79-86, PROF ANAT & NEUROBIOL, COLO STATE UNIV, 86- *Personal Data:* b Dallas, Tex, Feb 16, 43; m 65. *Educ:* Univ Tex, BA, 65, MA, 67, PhD(zool), 69. *Prof Exp:* Teaching asst biol, Univ Tex, 66-67; fel surg & cancer res, Sch Med, Johns Hopkins Univ, 69-70; asst investr, Dept Embryol, Carnegie Inst Wash, 70-72; res assoc, Univ Colo, 72-74; asst prof, 74-77, assoc prof pharmacol & exp therapeut, Sch Med, Univ Md, 77-79. *Concurrent Pos:* Muscular Dystrophy Asn grant-in-aid, 75; prin investr, NIH grants; instr, Marine Biol Lab, Woods Hole, Mass. *Mem:* AAAS; Am Soc Cell Biol; Soc Neurosci. *Res:* Myogenesis; membrane differentiation; electron microscopy; freeze-fracture of mammalian neuromuscular junctions and spinal cord neurons. *Mailing Add:* Dept Anat & Neurobiol Colo State Univ Ft Collins CO 80523-0001

RASHBA, EMMANUEL IOSIF, SYMMETRY OF SOLIDS & ELECTRONIC PROPERTIES, SPECTROSCOPY OF EXCITONS IN CRYSTALS. *Current Pos:* RES PROF PHYSICS, UNIV UTAH, 92- *Personal Data:* b Kiev, Ukraine, Oct 30, 27; m 57, Erna Kelman; c Julia. *Educ:* Kiev Univ, Ukraine, dipl, 49; Ukraine Acad Sci, PhD(physics), 56. *Hon Degrees:* Dr(sci), Ioffe Inst Physics & Technol, Leningrad, 63. *Honors & Awards:* Lenin Prize for Sci, Govt USSR, 66; A F Ioffe Prize, USSR, Acad Sci, 87. *Prof Exp:* From jr & sr scientist to head, Theoret Dept, Ukrainian Acad Sci, 54-66; head, Dept Theory Semiconductors, Landau Inst Theoret Physics, Moscow, 66-91. *Concurrent Pos:* mem, Sci Coun, USSR, Acad Sci, 60-80; prof, Moscow Inst Physics & Technol, 67-82; vis scholar, Nat Ctr Sci Res, France, 87, Univ Stuttgart, Ger, 88, Inst Sci Interchange & Int Ctr Theoret Physics, Italy, 90 & Res Inst Physics, Hebrew Univ, Israel, 91. *Mem:* Fel Am Phys Soc. *Res:* Electron theory of solids, especially prediction of the electric-dipole spin resonance, giant oscillator strengths and coexistence of free and self-trapped states; initiating mechanics of growing elastic bodies in civil engineering. *Mailing Add:* Phys Dept Univ Utah 201 James Fletcher Bldg Salt Lake City UT 84112. *E-Mail:* rashba@physics.utah.edu

RASHEED, SURAIYA, GENETICS & MOLECULAR BIOLOGY, VIROLOGY & AIDS. *Current Pos:* instr path, 70-72, from asst prof to assoc prof 72-82, PROF PATH, UNIV SOUTHERN CALIF, SCH MED, 82-, DIR, VIRAL ONCOL & AIDS RES. *Personal Data:* b Hyderabad, India; US citizen; m, Nasir; c 2. *Educ:* Osmania Univ, India, BSc, 53, MSc, 55, PhD, 58; London Univ, PhD, 64; FRCPath, 93. *Prof Exp:* Res assoc, Dept Cancer Res, Mt Vernon Hosp, Eng, 64-70. *Concurrent Pos:* Consult, Int Ctr Med Res & Training, 85-, Abbott Lab, Diag Div, Ill, Prince Agha Khan Univ, 86-, Alpha Therapeut, Los Angeles, 86-; mem, Comt Rev Res Grants & Res Career Grant Appl, Nat Cancer Inst, NIH, 80-, spec reviewer, Nat Large Bowel Projs, 81, Cancer Biol-Immunol Contract Rev Comt, 86-90, spec tech sci rev group, Small Bus Innovation Res Prog, 86-90; mem, Int Adv Bd, Future Trends Chemother, Italy, 87-, Spec Adv Comt, NCI-NIH AIDS-Antiviral Drug Screening Prog, 86-90, Virol Core Comt, AIDS Clin Trials Group, Nat Inst Allergy & Infectious Dis, NIH, 86-91; hon professorships, People's Repub China, 88-92. *Mem:* Int Asn Comp Res Leukemia & Related Dis; Am Soc Microbiol; Am Soc Virologists; AAAS; Am Asn Univ Professors; Int AIDS Soc. *Res:* Molecular interactions of viruses with host cellular genomes; pathogenisis of HIV disease; mechanisms of oncogene transduction by retroviruses; molecular characterization of HIV genotypes; evaluation of vaccines and antiviral drug effects in AIDS clinical trials and identification of HTLV-I and HTLV-II-related viruses associated with leukemia and other diseases. *Mailing Add:* Lab Viral Oncol & Aids Res Sch Med Univ Southern Calif 1840 N Soto St Los Angeles CA 90032-3626

RASHID, KAMAL A, BIOTECHNOLOGY. *Current Pos:* SR RES ASSOC BIOTECHNOL & VIS PROF, PA STATE UNIV, 83-, DIR BIOTECH TRAINING PROG, 89-, RES ASSOC PROF BIOCHEM & MOLECULAR BIOL, 92- *Personal Data:* b Sulaimania, Iraq, Sept 11, 44; m 70, Afifa B Sabir; c Niaz K, Neian K & Suzanne K. *Educ:* Univ Baghdad, BS, 65, Pa State Univ, MS, 74, PhD, 78. *Honors & Awards:* Fac Serv Award, Nat Continuing Educ Asn, 97. *Prof Exp:* Lab instr, Univ Baghdad, 66-72; mem fac, Univ Basrah, 78-80, Univ Sulaimania, 80-83. *Concurrent Pos:* Vpres, Cogenic Inc, Pa State Col, 89-90; consult & speaker, Biotech Training Prog, Pa State Univ; exec dir, Int Biotechnol Assocs, 96- *Mem:* Am Chem Soc; Environ Mutagen Soc; Am Soc Cell Biol. *Res:* Investigated the impact of environmental pollutants on human health and the mechanisms involved in DNA damage due to these pollutants; contributed articles to professional journals. *Mailing Add:* Pa State Univ 203 S Frear University Park PA 16802. *Fax:* 814-863-7024; *E-Mail:* kxr9@psu.edu

RASHID, MUHAMMAD HARUNUR, POWER ELECTRONICS & MOTOR DRIVES, INDUSTRIAL CONTROL. *Current Pos:* PROF ELEC ENG & DIR, UNIV FLA, 97- *Personal Data:* b Comilla, Bangladesh, Feb 15, 45; US citizen; m 70, Fatema; c Faeza, Farzana & Hasan. *Educ:* Bangladesh Univ Eng & Technol, BSc, 67; Univ Birmingham, Eng, MSc, 71; PhD(electronic & elec eng), 75. *Honors & Awards:* Outstanding Engr Award, Inst Elec & Electronics Engrs, 91. *Prof Exp:* Sr develop engr, Brush Elec Mach Ltd, Eng, 74-76; res officer, Lucas Group Res Ctr, Eng, 76-77; lectr & head control eng, Higher Inst Electronics, Malta, 77-80; vis asst prof, Univ Conn, 80-81; assoc prof, Concordia Univ, Montreal, 81-85; prof elec eng, Purdue Univ, Calumet, 85-89, prof & chair, Ft Wayne, 89-97. *Concurrent Pos:* External Examr, Ngee Ann Polytech, Singapore, 87-97; curric consult polytech develop, Malaysia, 95; vis prof elec eng, Univ Petrol & Minerals, 95-96. *Mem:* Sr mem Inst Elec & Electronics Engrs; fel Inst Elec Engrs. *Res:* Power electronics; published more than 100 technical papers. *Mailing Add:* 11000 University Parkway Pensacola FL 32514-5754. *Fax:* 850-474-3412; *E-Mail:* mrashid@uwf-uf.ee.uwf.edu

RASHIDBAIGI, ABBAS, IMMUNOLOGY, PROTEIN CHEMISTRY. *Current Pos:* DIR CELL BIOL, INTERFERON SCI INC, 90- *Personal Data:* b Tehran, Iran, Nov 30, 48; US citizen; m 75, Zahra Azizi; c Ali, Rouzbeh & Omid. *Educ:* Tehran Univ, PharmD, 75; Univ Wis-Madison, MS, 78, PhD(pharmacol), 82. *Prof Exp:* Proj assoc, Univ Wis, 82-83; fel, Roche Inst Molecular Biol, 83-86; asst prof, Univ Med & Dent NJ, 86-90. *Concurrent Pos:* Adj asst prof, Univ Med & Dent NJ, 92- *Mem:* Sigma Xi; Am Soc Biochem & Molecular Biol; Int Soc Interferon Res; AAAS; Am Soc Biochem & Molecular Biol. *Res:* Synthesis of photoaffinity ligand for characterization of beta-adrenergic receptors and sodium, potassium ATPase; molecular structure of interferon gamma receptor and its mode of signal transduction. *Mailing Add:* Interferon Sci Inc 783 Jersey Ave New Brunswick NJ 08901-3605. *Fax:* 732-249-6895

RASHKIN, JAY ARTHUR, PHYSICAL CHEMISTRY. *Current Pos:* ASSOC PROF CHEM, SULLIVAN COUNTY COMMUNITY COL, 86- *Personal Data:* b New York, NY, Sept 21, 33; div; c 2. *Educ:* NY Univ, BA, 55; Princeton Univ, MA, 57, PhD(phys chem), 61. *Prof Exp:* Res chemist, E I du Pont de Nemours & Co, 59-62; mem tech staff, Space Tech Labs, 62-64; res specialist, Monsanto Co, 64-66; sr res chemist, Cities Serv Oil Co, 66-76; res assoc, Halcon Catalyst Indust, 77-82 & Halcon Res, 82-86. *Mem:* Am Chem Soc; Am Phys Soc; AAAS. *Res:* Heterogeneous catalysis; differential thermal analysis and x-ray structure studies of catalysts; catalytic oxidation of hydrocarbons; catalytic processes in petroleum refining and petrochemicals; surface chemistry; electron spectroscopy for chemical analysis; surface analysis; chemisorption; temperature programmed desorption. *Mailing Add:* Sullivan County Comm Col Loch Sheldrake NY 12759

RASK, NORMAN, AGRICULTURAL ECONOMICS. *Current Pos:* from asst prof to prof, 65-95, EMER PROF AGR ECON, OHIO STATE UNIV, 95- *Personal Data:* b Duanesburg, NY, June 26, 33; m 55; c 4. *Educ:* Cornell Univ, BS, 55, MS, 60; Univ Wis, PhD(agr econ), 64. *Prof Exp:* Exten assoc agr econ, Cornell Univ, 59-60; asst prof, Univ Wis, 64-65. *Concurrent Pos:* Consult, World Bank, Food & Agr Orgn & US Agency Int Develop. *Res:* Energy policy; energy from biomass; economics of farm size, and world food population problems. *Mailing Add:* 1250 Carron Dr Columbus OH 43220

RASKA, KAREL FRANTISEK, JR, PATHOLOGY, MICROBIOLOGY. *Current Pos:* CHMN, DEPT LAB MED & PATH, UNIV MED & DENT NJ, NJ MED SCH, NEWARK, 89- *Personal Data:* b Prague, Czech, May 26, 39; US citizen; m 60; c 2. *Educ:* Charles Univ, MD, 62; Czech Acad Sci, PhD(biochem), 65. *Honors & Awards:* Prize, Czech Acad Sci, 65. *Prof Exp:* Commonwealth Fund res fel pharmacol, Sch Med, Yale Univ, 65-66; res assoc, Inst Microbiol, Rutgers Univ, New Brunswick, 66-67; scientist, Inst Org Chem & Biochem, Czech Acad Sci, 67-68; from asst prof to assoc prof microbiol, Univ Med & Dent NJ, Robt Wood Johnson, 71-78, from assoc prof to prof path, 73-89, prof microbiol, 78-89. *Concurrent Pos:* Pathologist, Robt Wood Johnson Univ Hosp 77-; dir, Univ Diag Lab, 82-; chief serv, Univ Hosp, Newark, 89- *Mem:* Am Soc Virology; Am Soc Microbiol; Am Asn Pathologists; Am Asn Immunologists; Am Asn Cancer Res; Soc Clin Immunol; Col Am Path; Soc Exp Biol Med; Sigma Xi. *Res:* Molecular biology of animal viruses; cell transformation by oncogenic viruses; cancer chemotherapy; immunopathology. *Mailing Add:* Dept Path St Peter's Med Ctr 254 Easton Ave New Brunswick NJ 08903-0591

RASKAS, HESCHEL JOSHUA, BIOCHEMISTRY. *Current Pos:* PRES, RASKAS FOODS, INC, 82- *Personal Data:* b St Louis, Mo, June 11, 41; m 62, Adinah Waltuch; c Jonathan, Daniel, Aviva, Ruth & Mordechai. *Educ:* Mass Inst Technol, BS, 62; Harvard Univ, PhD(biochem, molecular biol), 67. *Prof Exp:* Res fel, Inst Molecular Virol, St Louis Univ, 67-69, asst prof molecular virol & path, Sch Med, Inst Molecular Virol & Dept Path, 69-73; assoc prof, Sch Med, Wash Univ, 73-77, dir, Ctr Basic Cancer Res, 77-80, prof path & microbiol, 77-85, vis prof path, 85-86. *Mem:* AAAS; Am Soc Microbiol. *Res:* Regulation of oncogenic viral gene expression in eukaryotic cells. *Mailing Add:* 722 Brittany Lane St Louis MO 63130

RASKI, DEWEY JOHN, NEMATOLOGY. *Current Pos:* Instr & jr nematologist, 48-50, from lectr & asst nematologist to lectr & assoc nematologist, 50-60, PROF NEMATOL & NEMATOLOGIST, UNIV CALIF, DAVIS, 60- *Personal Data:* b Kenilworth, Utah, Dec 12, 17; m 43; c 3. *Educ:* Univ Calif, BS, 41, PhD(nematol), 48. *Mem:* Am Phytopath Soc; Am Soc Nematol; Soc Europ Nematol. *Res:* Plant parasitic nematodes; virus-nematode vector relationships; biology, control and systematics. *Mailing Add:* 1912 Alpine Pl Davis CA 95616

RASKIN, BETTY LOU, plastics engineering, consumer behavior, for more information see previous edition

RASKIN, DONALD, PHYSICS. *Current Pos:* PRIN ENGR, NEXT LEVEL SYSTS, 94- *Educ:* Univ Chicago, BS, 61; Columbia Univ, MA, 63, PhD(physics), 68. *Prof Exp:* Asst dir transp res, Metrop Transp Authority, New York, 71-78; mgr prod appln, New Ventures Group, Allied-Signal Corp, 79-86; marketing-prog mgr non-linear optics, Adv Technol Group, Hoechst Celanese Cor, 86-90; vpres eng, Commun Prod Div, Texscan Corp, 90-94. *Mem:* Am Phys Soc; Inst Elec & Electronics Engrs; Sigma Xi. *Res:* Fiberoptics-based products; granted 5 US patents. *Mailing Add:* Next Level Systs 2200 Byberry Rd Hatboro PA 19040

RASKIN, JOAN, MEDICINE, DERMATOLOGY. *Current Pos:* assoc med, Sch Med, 60-63, lectr, Sch Phys Ther, 61-66, asst prof, Sch Med, 63-66, ASSOC PROF MED, DIV DERMAT, SCH MED, UNIV MD, BALTIMORE CITY, 66- *Personal Data:* b Baltimore, Md, Aug 11, 30. *Educ:* Goucher Col, BA, 51; Univ Md, MD, 55; Am Bd Dermat, dipl, 61. *Prof Exp:* Intern, Hosp, Univ Md, 55-56, asst resident med, 56-57, resident dermat, 57-58. *Concurrent Pos:* Fel, Hosp, Univ Md, 58-59; fel, Hosps, Univ Minn, 59-60; NIH grants, 61-65; Bressler Fund grant, 62-66; mem courtesy staff, South Baltimore Gen Hosp, 61-71, sr staff, 72-, head, Div Dermat, 80-; mem courtesy staff, Sinai Hosp, 61-64, active staff, 64-86; mem staff, Mercy Hosp, 74-; dermatologist, Md Sch for Blind, 74-; active staff, Union Mem Hosp, 75-; consult, 86- *Mem:* Am Acad Dermat; Am Med Asn; Am Med Women's Asn. *Res:* Dermatologic areas of autoimmune diseases and virology. *Mailing Add:* 3506 Calvert St N Baltimore MD 21218-2800

RASKIN, NEIL HUGH, NEUROLOGY, NEUROCHEMISTRY. *Current Pos:* from asst prof to assoc prof, 68-79, PROF NEUROL & VCHMN DEPT, UNIV CALIF, SAN FRANCISCO, 79- *Personal Data:* b New York, NY, Jan 16, 35. *Educ:* Dartmouth Col, AB, 56; Harvard Med Sch, MD, 59. *Prof Exp:* Resident neurol, Columbia Univ Col Physicians & Surgeons, 61-64, res fel cerebral metab, 64-65; chief of serv neurol, US Naval Hosp, Philadelphia, 65-66; res assoc cerebral metab, NIH, 66-68. *Concurrent Pos:* Res career develop award, NIH, 68-73; res grant, Nat Inst for Alcohol Abuse & Alcoholism, 68-73; mem, Res Group Migraine & Headache, World Fedn Neurol, 76-; dir neurol outpatient & consult serv, Sch Med, Univ Calif, San Francisco, 77- *Mem:* Am Neurol Asn; Am Soc Neurochem; Asn Res Nerv & Ment Dis; Int Asn Study Pain; Am Acad Neurol. *Res:* Biochemical effects of alcohol upon the nervous system; mechanisms of migraine; metabolic neurologic disorders. *Mailing Add:* Dept Neurol Univ Calif San Francisco CA 94143

RASKIND, WENDY H, MEDICINE, GENETICS. *Current Pos:* ASSOC PROF, UNIV WASH, 91- *Personal Data:* b New York, NY, Dec 13, 42; m, Murray; c 3. *Educ:* Brown Univ, BA, 64; Univ Wash, PhD(genetics), 77, MD, 78. *Mem:* Am Soc Human Genetics; Am Col Physicians. *Res:* Medical genetics; cancer genetics; pathogenesis of cancer. *Mailing Add:* Dept Med RG-25 Univ Wash Seattle WA 98195. *Fax:* 206-543-3050; *E-Mail:* wendyrun@u.washington.edu

RASKOVA, JANA D, PATHOLOGY, MEDICINE. *Current Pos:* res assoc immunol, Inst Microbiol, Rutgers Univ, 69-70, asst prof path, 70-78, assoc prof path, 78-87, PROF PATH, UNIV MED & DENT NJ, ROBERT WOOD JOHNSON MED SCH, 87- *Personal Data:* b Prague, Czech, Oct 18, 40; US citizen; m 60; c 2. *Educ:* Charles Univ, Prague, MD, 63. *Prof Exp:* Res fel pharmacol, Sch Med, Yale Univ, 65-66; vis investr immunol, Inst Microbiol, Rutgers Univ, 66-67; fel genetics, Inst Exp Biol & Genetics, Czech Acad Sci, Prague, 67-68. *Mem:* AAAS; Am Asn Pathologists; Am Soc Cell Biol; Int Acad Path. *Res:* Immunopathology and pathology of chronic renal failure. *Mailing Add:* Dept Path Univ Med & Dent NJ Robert Wood Johnson Med Sch 675 Hoes Lane Piscataway NJ 08845-5635

RASLEAR, THOMAS G, PSYCHOPHYSICS, HUMAN FACTORS. *Current Pos:* ENG PSYCHOLOGIST, FED RAILROAD ADMIN, 93- *Personal Data:* b New York, NY, Nov 25, 47; m 71, Lois T Keck. *Educ:* City Col NY, BS, 69; Brown Univ, ScM, 72, PhD(psychol), 74. *Prof Exp:* Asst prof psychol, Boston Univ, 74-75 & Wilkes Col, Wilkes-Barre, 75-79; res psychologist, Dept Microwave Res, Walter Reed Army Inst Res, 79-89, sr psychologist, 89-93. *Concurrent Pos:* Dep chief, Physiol & Behav Br, Dept Med Neurosci, Walter Reed Inst Res, 85-89. *Mem:* Am Psychol Soc; Am Psychol Asn; Acoust Soc Am; AAAS; Inst Elec & Electronics Engrs. *Res:* Manage research projects on human factors caused accidents and safety in the railroad industry; fatigue, workload, stress, fitness-for-duty; information processing aspects of railroad jobs are addressed. *Mailing Add:* Off Res & Develop RDV-32 Fed Railroad Admin 400 Seventh St SW Washington DC 20590. *Fax:* 202-632-3854; *E-Mail:* thomas.raslear@fra.dot.gov

RASMUSSEN, ARLETTE IRENE, NUTRITION. *Current Pos:* asst prof, 61-65, ASSOC PROF NUTRIT, UNIV DEL, 65- *Personal Data:* b Thief River Falls, Minn. *Educ:* Northwestern Univ, Ba, 56; Univ Wis, MS, 58, PhD(human nutrit & biochem), 61. *Prof Exp:* Res asst, Univ Wis, 56-61. *Concurrent Pos:* Sr fel, Dept Med, Hematol Div, Sch Med, Univ Wash, 70-71; co-chair, Northeast Res Prog, Steering Comt Nutrit & Food Safety, US Dept Agr & State Agr Exp Sta, 77-82; exec bd mem, Nat Nutrit Consortium 77-80; actg chair, Dept Food Sci & Human Nutrit, Univ Del, 78-79; nutritionist, Coop State Res Serv, US Dept Agr, 79-80. *Mem:* Am Inst Nutrit; Am Dietetic Asn; Soc Nutrit Educ; Sigma Xi; AAAS. *Res:* Protein evaluation; amino acid utilization; vitamin B-6; mineral nutrition; human nutrition and metabolism; nutrient interactions. *Mailing Add:* Dept Nutrit & Dietetics Univ Del Alison Hall Newark DE 19716-0001

RASMUSSEN, CHRIS ROYCE, MEDICINAL CHEMISTRY. *Current Pos:* R W JOHNSON PHARM, 94- *Personal Data:* b Trenton, Nebr, Feb 19, 31; m 52; c 4. *Educ:* Ft Hays Kans State Col, AB, 54; Univ Kans, PhD(org & pharmaceut chem), 62. *Prof Exp:* Res assoc, Ind Univ, 62-63; res scientist, McNeil Labs, Inc, 64-70, group leader, 70-76, res fel, 76-94. *Mem:* Am Chem Soc. *Res:* Hypoglycemic agents; central nervous system drugs, specifically muscle relaxants, anticonvulsants, anti-anxiety agents, cardiovascular-anti-anginal, antihypertensive and antiarrhythmic drugs; gastro-intestinal-antisecretory agents; anti-irritable bowel. *Mailing Add:* 124 Pine Crest Lane Lansdale PA 19446

RASMUSSEN, DAVID IRVIN, genetics, for more information see previous edition

RASMUSSEN, DAVID TAB, PRIMATOLOGY, VERTEBRATE PALEONTOLOGY. *Current Pos:* ASSOC PROF ANTHROP, WASH UNIV, ST LOUIS, 91-, GRAD COORDR, 93- *Personal Data:* b Salt Lake City, Utah, June 17, 58; m 87, Asenath Bernhardt. *Educ:* Colo Col, BA, 80; Duke Univ, PhD(anthrop), 86. *Prof Exp:* Res assoc paleont, Primate Ctr, Duke Univ, 86-87; vis asst prof anthrop, Rice Univ, 87-88; asst prof anthrop, Univ Calif, Los Angeles, 88-91. *Concurrent Pos:* Res assoc, Natural Hist Mus Los Angeles Co, 88-, Carnegie Mus Natural Hist, Pittsburgh, 93- *Mem:* Am Asn Phys Anthropologists; Am Soc Naturalists; Soc Avian Paleont & Evolution; Soc Vertebrate Paleont. *Res:* Primate evolution and paleontology; prosimian adaptations and life history studies; anthropoid origins; field paleontology in Africa and North America; comparative anatomy and biology of primates; mammalian and avian paleontology; hyracoid evolution. *Mailing Add:* Dept Anthrop Washington Univ Campus Box 1114 1 Brookings Dr St Louis MO 63130-4862

RASMUSSEN, DON HENRY, CHEMICAL METALLURGY, MATERIALS SCIENCE. *Current Pos:* asst prof, 78-80, PROF CHEM ENG, CLARKSON UNIV, 80- *Personal Data:* b Wild Rose, Wis, Sept 20, 44; m 66; c 3. *Educ:* Univ Wis-Madison, BA, 67, MS, 71, PhD(mat sci), 74. *Prof Exp:* Res assoc, Cryobiol Res Inst of Am Found, Madison, 67-75; res assoc metall, Dept Metals & Minerals Eng, Univ Wis-Madison, 75-78. *Mem:* Am Chem Soc; Am Inst Mining, Metall & Petrol Engrs; Am Inst Chem Engrs. *Res:* Surface properties of metals; phase transformations; nucleation phenomena; chemical vapor deposition of metals. *Mailing Add:* 4 Earmer Canton NY 13617

RASMUSSEN, HARRY PAUL, PLANT PHYSIOLOGY, PLANT NUTRITION. *Current Pos:* DIR, UTAH AGR EXP STA, UTAH STATE UNIV, 89-, ASSOC VPRES RES, 92- *Personal Data:* b Tremonton, Utah, July 18, 39; m 58, Mary J Dalley; c Randy, Lorianne, Trent & Rachelle. *Educ:* Utah State Univ, BS, 61; Mich State Univ, MS, 62, PhD(hort), 65. *Honors & Awards:* Alex Laurie Award, 75. *Prof Exp:* Asst prof plant physiol, Conn Agr Exp Sta, 65-66; from asst prof to prof hort, Mich State Univ, 66-80; chmn, Dept Hort & Landscape Archit, Wash State Univ, 80-89. *Mem:* Fel Am Soc Hort Sci; Coun Agr Sci & Technol. *Res:* Leaf and fruit abscission; botanical histochemistry; electron microprobe x-ray analysis and scanning electron microscopy of plant tissues and cells. *Mailing Add:* Plant & Earth Sci Utah State Univ Logan UT 84322-0001. *Fax:* 435-750-3321

RASMUSSEN, HOWARD, MEDICINE, CELL BIOLOGY. *Current Pos:* PROF MED & CELL BIOL, SCH MED, YALE UNIV, 77- *Personal Data:* b Harrisburg, Pa, Mar 1, 25; m 50; c 4. *Educ:* Gettysburg Col, AB, 48; Rockefeller Inst, PhD, 59; Gettysburg Col, DSc, 66. *Hon Degrees:* MA, Univ Pa, 71. *Honors & Awards:* Andre Lichwitz Prize, France, 71. *Prof Exp:* Asst prof physiol, Rockefeller Inst & assoc physician, Hosp, 59-61; assoc prof biochem, Univ Wis, 61-64, prof, 64-65; chmn dept biochem, Med Sch, Univ Pa, 65-71, prof pediat, biochem & biophys, 65-77. *Concurrent Pos:* NSF sr fel, Cambridge Univ, 71-72; mem endocrine study sect, NIH, 63-65, mem cardiovasc study sect, 73-74; mem fel panel, NSF, 69; sr physician, Children's Hosp Philadelphia, 70-77; trustee, Gettysburg Col, 71-77; mem, Gen Med B Study Sect, 74-77; assoc endocrinologist, Children's Hosp, 75-; consult metab bone dis, Hosp Lariboisiere, Paris. *Mem:* AAAS; Endocrine Soc; Soc Gen Physiol; Am Soc Cell Biol; Am Soc Biol Chem. *Res:* Biochemistry and physiology of ion transport and of peptide and steroid hormone action; cellular basis of oxygen-2 toxicity. *Mailing Add:* Inst Molecular Med & Genet Med Col Ga 1120 15th St CB2803 Augusta GA 30912-3175

RASMUSSEN, JEWELL J, ceramics; deceased, see previous edition for last biography

RASMUSSEN, JOHN OSCAR, JR, NUCLEAR CHEMISTRY. *Current Pos:* from instr to prof, 52-69, prof, 73-91, EMER PROF CHEM, UNIV CALIF, BERKELEY, 91- *Personal Data:* b St Petersburg, Fla, Aug 8, 26; m 50, Louise Brooks; c Nancy, Jane, David & Stephen. *Educ:* Calif Inst Technol, BS, 48; Univ Calif, Berkeley, PhD(chem), 52. *Hon Degrees:* AM, Yale Univ, 69. *Honors & Awards:* E O Lawrence Award, 67; Am Chem Soc Award for Nuclear Applns in Chem, 76. *Prof Exp:* Prof chem, Yale Univ, 69-73. *Concurrent Pos:* Vis prof, Nobel Inst Physics, Stockholm, Sweden, 53; NSF sr fel, Niels Bohr Inst, Copenhagen, Denmark, 61-62; vis prof, Fudan Univ, Shanghai, 79, 84, hon prof, 84; sr sci, Von Humboldt, Munich, 91. *Mem:* Am Chem Soc; fel Am Phys Soc; fel AAAS; Fedn Am Scientists. *Res:* Nuclear structure theory and experiment; heavy ion nuclear reactions. *Mailing Add:* MS 70A-3307 Lawrence Berkeley Lab Berkeley CA 94720. *Fax:* 510-486-6707; *E-Mail:* jorasmussen@lbl.gov

RASMUSSEN, KATHLEEN GOERTZ, endocrinology-immune system interactions, virus-induced neurological damage, for more information see previous edition

RASMUSSEN, KATHLEEN MAHER, REPRODUCTIVE PHYSIOLOGY. *Current Pos:* res fel, Cornell Univ, 78-80, res assoc, 81, instr, 81-83, asst prof, 83-88, assoc prof nutrit, 88-96, PROF NUTRIT, CORNELL UNIV, 96- *Personal Data:* b Dayton, Ohio, Mar 1, 48; div; c 1. *Educ:* Brown Univ, AB, 70; Harvard Univ, ScM, 75, ScD(nutrit), 78. *Prof Exp:* Teacher sci, Cape Hatteras Sch, 71-72; anal chemist, Berkley Mach Works & Foundry Co, Inc, 72-73; res fel, Harvard Univ, 78. *Concurrent Pos:* Assoc dir grad affairs, Div Nutrit Sci, Cornell Univ, 92-95. *Mem:* Am Inst Nutrit; Am Soc Clin Nutrit; Int Soc Res Human & Milk & Lactation; Brit Nutrit Soc. *Res:* Nutrition and reproduction; maternal and child nutrition; pregnancy; lactation. *Mailing Add:* Div Nutrit Sci 111 Savage Hall Cornell Univ Ithaca NY 14853-6301. *Fax:* 607-255-2290; *E-Mail:* kmr5@cornell.edu

RASMUSSEN, LOIS E LITTLE, ANIMAL PHEROMONE, NEUROCHEMISTRY. *Current Pos:* assoc prof, 90-94, SR SCIENTIST, ORE GRAD CTR, 77-, MEM FAC, 85- *Personal Data:* b Summit, NJ, Nov 11, 38; m 61; c 2. *Educ:* Stanford Univ, BA, 60; Washington Univ, PhD(neurochem), 64. *Prof Exp:* NIH fel, Dept Psychiatry, Med Sch, Washington Univ, 61-64; NIH staff fel, Sect Chem Neuropath, Nat Inst Neurol Dis & Blindness, NIH, 64-66; proj biochemist, Dow Corning Corp, 66-68; adj scientist, Dept Zool, Wash State Univ, 70-77. *Concurrent Pos:* Instr, invertebrate & vertebrate embryol & fresh water ecol, Saginaw Valley Col, 68-69; res assoc & consult, Dept Zool, Wash State Univ, 75-77; mem, Asian elephant spec group, Species Survival Comn, Int Union Conserv Nature & Natural Resources; res scientist, Sea World, Orlando & Washington Park Zoo; Guggenheim fel, 93. *Mem:* Am Fisheries Soc; Am Soc Mammologists; AAAS; Am Soc Neurochem; Soc Protection Old Fishes; Asn Chemoreception Sci. *Res:* Elephant pheromone study; comparative study of temporal gland secretions in Asian and African elephants; chemical characterization of the sex pheromones in Asian elephants. *Mailing Add:* Ore Grad Inst PO Box 91000 Portland OR 97291

RASMUSSEN, LOWELL W, AGRONOMY. *Current Pos:* from asst prof & asst agronomist to prof & agronomist, 47-56, from asst dir res to assoc dir res, 56-75, EMER ASSOC DIR RES, COL AGR, WASH STATE UNIV, 75- *Personal Data:* b Redmond, Utah, Mar 21, 10; m 38; c 2. *Educ:* Utah State Univ, BS, 40, MS, 41; Iowa State Univ, PhD(plant physiol), 47. *Prof Exp:* Field supvr, Exp Sta, Utah State Col, 37-41; asst county supvr, Farm Security Admin, 41; jr agronomist, Soil Conserv Serv, USDA, 41-42; county agr agent, Exten Serv, Univ Utah, 42-45. *Concurrent Pos:* Ford Found adv, Ministry Agr, Saudi Arabia, 65-67. *Mem:* AAAS; Weed Sci Soc Am; Am Soc Plant Physiol. *Res:* Weed control; action of growth regulator herbicides; techniques in weed research; research administration. *Mailing Add:* SE 910 Glen Echo Rd Pullman WA 99163

RASMUSSEN, MAURICE L, AERONAUTICS, ASTRONAUTICS. *Current Pos:* assoc prof, 67-70, PROF GAS DYNAMICS, UNIV OKLA, 70-, LA COMP CHAIR, 94- *Personal Data:* b Coon Rapids, Iowa, June 2, 35; m 61, Barbara; c Eric & Mathew. *Educ:* Ore State Univ, BS, 57, MS, 59; Stanford Univ, PhD(aeronaut, astronaut), 64. *Honors & Awards:* Halliburton Distinguished Lectr Award. *Prof Exp:* Res engr, Ames Res Ctr, NASA, 58-59; res asst aeronaut & astronaut, Stanford Univ, 59-64; lectr & res assoc gas dynamics, 64-65, actg asst prof, 64-67. *Concurrent Pos:* Vis res scientist, Air Force Armaments Lab, 80-81; distinguished vis prof, Air Force Inst Technol, 84-85; assoc ed, Am Inst Aeronaut & Astronaut J, 87-90; David Ross Boyd prof, 88- *Mem:* Am Inst Aeronaut & Astronaut; Am Soc Mech Engr. *Res:* Gas dynamics; nonlinear oscillations; hypersonic aerodynamics. *Mailing Add:* Dept Mech Eng Main Campus Univ Okla 865 Asp Ave Norman OK 73019-0601

RASMUSSEN, NORMAN CARL, RISK ANALYSIS. *Current Pos:* From instr to nuclear eng, Mass Inst Technol, 56-94, dept head, 75-81, McAfee prof eng, 83-94, EMER PROF, MASS INST TECHNOL, 94- *Personal Data:* b Harrisburg, Pa, Nov 12, 27; m 54, Thalia Tichenor; c Neil & Arlene (Soule). *Educ:* Gettysburg Col, BA, 50; Mass Inst Technol, PhD(physics), 56. *Hon Degrees:* Dr, Gettysburg Col, 79; Cath Univ, Leuven, Belg, 80. *Honors & Awards:* Theos Thompson Award, Am Nuclear Soc, 81-; Enrico Fermi Award, US Dept Energy, 85; Ahlstrom Prize, 92. *Concurrent Pos:* Consult, Nuclear Regulatory Comn, 72-82, Cabot Corp, 73-93, EG&G Idaho, Inc, 76-84 & Nuclear Utility Serv Corp, 77-84; mem, Defense Sci Bd, 74-77, Presidential Adv Group on Contrib Technol Econ Strength, 75 & bd trustees, NE Utilities, 77-; mem, Nat Sci Bd, 82-88. *Mem:* Nat Acad Sci; Nat Acad Eng; AAAS; fel Am Nuclear Soc; Health Physics Soc; fel Am Acad Arts & Sci; Soc Risk Anal. *Res:* Early research in activation analysis; low-level counting techniques and gamma-ray spectroscopy; nuclear safety and environmental impact of nuclear power; reliability analysis and risk assessment. *Mailing Add:* 80 Winsor Rd Sudbury MA 01776

RASMUSSEN, PAUL G, INORGANIC POLYMER CHEMISTRY. *Personal Data:* b Chicago, Ill, Jan 27, 39; m 60; c 3. *Educ:* St Olaf Col, BA, 60; Mich State Univ, PhD, 64. *Prof Exp:* From asst prof to assoc prof chem, Univ Mich, Ann Arbor, 64-75, assoc dean res & facil, prof, 75-82. *Mem:* Am Chem Soc. *Res:* Electron delocalization in transition metal complexes; polymers based on cyanoimidazoles. *Mailing Add:* Dept Chem 3100 Chem Bldg Univ Mich 930 N University Ave Ann Arbor MI 48109-1001

RASMUSSEN, REINHOLD ALBERT, PLANT PHYSIOLOGY, CHEMICAL ENGINEERING. *Current Pos:* PROF ENVIRON TECHNOL, ORE GRAD CTR, 77- *Personal Data:* b Brockton, Mass, Nov 4, 36; m 61. *Educ:* Univ Mass, BS, 58, MEd, 60; Wash Univ, PhD(bot), 64. *Prof Exp:* Plant biochemist, Agr Div, Monsanto Co, 62-63; clin biochemist, Walter Reed Army Med Ctr, 64-67; res proj chemist & head plant sci sect, Biomed Res Lab, Dow-Corning Corp, 67-69; assoc plant physiologist, Air Pollution Res Sect, Col Eng, 69-74, prof, 74-75, sect head, Ar Resources Sect, Chem Eng Br, Wash State Univ, 75-77. *Concurrent Pos:* Consult, US Army Tropic Test Ctr, 64-67 & Nat Ctr Atmospheric Res, 67-; lectr, Saginaw Valley Col, 67-; consult, Vapor Phase Org Air Pollutants from Hydrocarbons, Nat Acad Sci-Nat Res Coun, 72, consult, Panel Ammonia; consult, Air Pollution Physics & Chem Adv Comt, Environ Protection Agency, 72-75; mem, Intersoc Comt D-5 Hydrocarbon Anal; affil prof, Inst Environ Studies, Univ Wash, 75- *Mem:* Am Chem Soc; Am Meteorol Soc. *Res:* Role of naturally occurring organic volatiles in the atmosphere, especially their chemical identification, photochemistry and biological interactions with the environment and man. *Mailing Add:* 17010 NW Skyline Portland OR 97231

RASMUSSEN, ROBERT A, PHYCOLOGY. *Current Pos:* from asst prof to assoc prof, 66-77, PROF BOT, HUMBOLDT STATE UNIV, 77- *Personal Data:* b St Peter, Minn, Aug 31, 33; m 61, Frances Stewart; c 4. *Educ:* Col St Thomas, BS, 56; Univ Minn, Minneapolis, MS, 62; Univ Canterbury, PhD(zool), 65; Humboldt State Univ, MATW, 85. *Prof Exp:* Res assoc, Friday Harbor Marine Labs, Univ Wash, 65-66. *Concurrent Pos:* Mem Environ Consults, Pac Marine Eng, Inc, 72-74; vpres, Environ Res Consults, 73-78. *Mem:* Int Phycol Soc; Phycol Soc Am; Brit Phycol Soc. *Res:* Seaweed autoecology. *Mailing Add:* Dept Biol Humboldt State Univ 1 Harps St Arcata CA 95521-8299. *Fax:* 707-826-3201; *E-Mail:* rasmussenr@humboldt.axe.edu

RASMUSSEN, RUSSELL LEE, ORGANIC CHEMISTRY, BIO-ORGANIC CHEMISTRY. *Current Pos:* from asst prof to assoc prof, 69-74, head, Dept Phys Sci, 72-74, PROF CHEM, WAYNE STATE COL, 74- *Personal Data:* b Allen, Nebr; m 65, Charlene K Shuey; c Eric & Claire. *Educ:* Univ Nebr, BS, 60, PhD(inorg biochem), 70. *Prof Exp:* Asst prof chem, Stout State Univ, 66-67. *Concurrent Pos:* Vis prof, Univ Nebr, Lincoln, 81 & 92, Utah State Univ, 85-86 & 88-90. *Mem:* Chem Heritage Found; Am Chem Soc. *Res:* Model enzyme systems; coordination compounds; thiol esters of amino acids; pyridoxal containing enzymes; relationship of verbal ability and scientific achievement; the two cultures. *Mailing Add:* Div Math Sci Wayne State Col Wayne NE 68787-1486. *Fax:* 402-375-7204; *E-Mail:* rrasmus@wscgate.wsc.edu

RASMUSSEN, THEODORE BROWN, NEUROLOGY, NEUROSURGERY. *Current Pos:* prof, 54-80, EMER PROF NEUROL & NEUROSURG, MCGILL UNIV, 80- *Personal Data:* b Provo, Utah, Apr 28, 10; m 47; c 4. *Educ:* Univ Minn, BS & MB, 34, MD, 35, MS, 39; FRCS(C). *Hon Degrees:* DrMed, Edinburgh Univ, 80, Umea Univ, Sweden, 88. *Honors & Awards:* Ambassador Award, Epilepsy Int, 79; Penfield Award, Can League Against Epilepsy, 82; Lennox Award, Am Epilepsy Soc, 86; Distinguished Serv Award, Soc Neurol Surg, 89. *Prof Exp:* Lectr neurol & neurosurg, McGill Univ, 46-47; prof neurol surg, Univ Chicago, 47-54; neurosurgeon, Montreal Neurol Inst, 54-80. *Concurrent Pos:* Assoc neurosurgeon, Montreal Neurol Inst, 46-47, dir, 60-72, sr neurosurg consult, 72-; mem, Int Brain Res Orgn. *Mem:* AAAS; Neurosurg Soc Am; Am Asn Neurol Surg; Soc Neurol Surg; AMA; Am Neurol Asn. *Res:* Cerebral circulation; localization of cortical function; effects of radiation on cerebral tissue; focal epilepsy; surgical treatment of epilepsy. *Mailing Add:* 29 Surrey Dr Montreal PQ H3P 1B2 Can

RASMUSSEN, V PHILIP, JR, SOILS & SOIL SCIENCE. *Current Pos:* assoc prof soil physics, Utah State Univ, 81-89, prof & asst dept head, 90-92, prof & head, 92-96, PROF & ASST DIR, UTAH STATE UNIV, 96- *Personal Data:* b Logan, Utah, Apr 3, 50; m 74, Linda; c Angela, Bryan, Jennifer, Neal & Katie. *Educ:* Utah State Univ, BS, 74, MS, 76; Kans State Univ, PhD(agron), 79. *Prof Exp:* Res assoc soil physics, Utah State Univ, 74-76, crop modeling, Kans State Univ, 76-78; asst prof, Ricks Col, 78-81. *Concurrent Pos:* Consult, Campbell Sci, Inc, 76-81, Omnidata Int, 80-; lectr, Prof Farmers Inst, Data Processing Mgt Asn & Farmers Home Admin, USDA. *Mem:* Sigma Xi; Am Soc Agron; Soil Sci Soc Am; Int Soc Soil Sci. *Res:* On farm microcomputers; plant growth modelling. *Mailing Add:* Dept Plant Soil & Biomet Utah State Univ Logan UT 84322-4820

RASMUSSEN, WILLIAM OTTO, MODELING, COMPUTER SIMULATION. *Current Pos:* asst res prof comput mapping & remote sensing, 73-82, dir Western Computor Consortium, 82-87, ASSOC PROF BIOSYSTS ENG, UNIV ARIZ, 87- *Personal Data:* b Burley, Idaho, Jan 29, 42; m 64; c 2. *Educ:* Univ Idaho, BS, 64, MS, 66; Univ Ariz, PhD(watershed mgt), 73. *Prof Exp:* Explor geophysicist, Heinrichs Geoexplor Co, 68-70; dir Lab Remote Sensing & Comput Mapping, Univ Ariz, 73-82; sr scientist, Bell Tech Oper, Tucson, 81-87. *Concurrent Pos:* Dir remote sensing & comput mapping, Univ Ariz, 73-, remote sensing exten specialist, 75- *Mem:* Am Water Resources Asn; AAAS; Sigma Xi; Am Asn Univ Prof. *Res:* Simulation of electromagnetic radiation-environment interaction; scene synthesis; simulation of natural resource systems; water resources quality and quantity; atmospheric optics; ecosystem modeling; simulation and prediction of strip mine resources, mass balance, and reclamation; development of geographic data analysis and display systems; visibility analysis in vegetated scenes; computer software design and development; electronic warfare simulation. *Mailing Add:* Dept Agr & Bio Systs Eng State Bldg Rm 507 Univ Ariz 1200 E South Campus Dr Tucson AZ 85721

RASMUSSON, DONALD C, PLANT GENETICS, PLANT BREEDING. *Current Pos:* Res assoc, 58-72, PROF PLANT GENETICS, UNIV MINN, ST PAUL, 72- *Personal Data:* b Ephraim, Utah, May 28, 31; m 50; c 5. *Educ:* Utah State Univ, BS, 53, MS, 56; Univ Calif, PhD(genetics), 58. *Honors & Awards:* Agron Achievement Award, Am Soc Agron, 90. *Mem:* Fel Am Soc Agron; Crop Sci Soc Am. *Res:* Plant breeding and genetics. *Mailing Add:* Agron Plant Gen 411 Borlaug Hall Univ Minn 1991 Upper Buford Cr St Paul MN 55108-6024

RASMUSSON, DOUGLAS DEAN, NEUROPHYSIOLOGY, SOMATOSENSORY SYSTEM. *Current Pos:* from asst prof to assoc prof, 77-91, PROF PHYSIOL & BIOPHYS, DAHOUSIE UNIV, 91- *Personal Data:* b Denver, Colo, Aug 4, 46; Can citizen; m 96, Susan; c Timothy. *Educ:* Colo Col, BA, 68; Dalhousie Univ, MA, 70, PhD(physiol), 75. *Prof Exp:* Fel neurophysiol, Univ Toronto, 75-77. *Mem:* Can Physiol Soc; Soc Neurosci; Can Asn Neuroscientists; Int Res Orgn. *Res:* Organization and function of somatosensory cortex; plasticity due to changes in peripheral nervous system; control of cortical acetylocholine. *Mailing Add:* Dept Physiol & Biophysics Dalhousie Univ Halifax NS B3H 4H6 Can. *Fax:* 902-494-1685; *E-Mail:* rasmus@is.dal.ca

RASMUSSON, EUGENE MARTIN, METEOROLOGY. *Current Pos:* SR RES SCIENTIST, UNIV MD, 86- *Personal Data:* b Lindsborg, Kans, Feb 27, 29; m 60, Georgene R Sachfleben; c Hary J, Ruth A, Elizabeth A & Kristin M. *Educ:* Kans State Univ, BS, 50; St Louis Univ, MS, 63; Mass Inst Technol, PhD(meteorol), 66. *Honors & Awards:* Silver Medal, Dept Com; Jule Charney Award, Am Meteorol Soc, Robert H Horton, lectr, Am Meteor Soc; Victor Starr Mem Lectr, Mass Inst Tech. *Prof Exp:* Design engr, Kans State Hwy Comn, 50-51; meteorologist, USAF, 51-55; engr, Pac Tel Co, 55-56; meteorologist & hydrologist, US Weather Bur, 56-60, meteorologist forecaster, 60-63; res meteorologist, Nat Oceanic & Atmospheric Admin, Rockville, Md, 63-86. *Concurrent Pos:* Mem steering comt, Int Field Year for Great Lakes, 67-71, US co-chmn lake meteorol panel, 69-79; mem, Trop Ocean & Global Atmosphere panel, Nat Acad Sci, 83-85, Sci Steering Group, World Climate Res Prog, 85-88, Nat Res Coun Comt on US Geol Surv Water Res, 88-93, Nat Res Coun Expert Task Group, Strategic Hwy Res Prog, 90-93, GEWEX continental Scale Sci Panel, 91-, Steering Group, Atlantic Climate Chg Prog, 91-93; counr, Am Meteorol Soc, 93-96, NAS Bd Atmosphere Sci & Climate, 92-97. *Mem:* AAAS; Am Geophys Union; fel Am Meteorol Soc (pres elect, 97, pres, 98). *Res:* Atmospheric general circulation; large scale water balance; air-sea interactions; tropical meteorology; climate variability. *Mailing Add:* Dept Meteorol Univ Md College Park MD 20742. *Fax:* 301-314-9482

RASMUSSON, GARY HENRY, MEDICINAL CHEMISTRY. *Current Pos:* CONSULT, 96- *Personal Data:* b Clark, SDak, Aug 2, 36; m 58, Nancy Torkelson; c Randall, Korise, Tamara (Olson) & Todd. *Educ:* St Olaf Col, BA, 58; Mass Inst Technol, PhD(org chem), 62. *Prof Exp:* NSF res fel, Stanford Univ, 62-63; NIH res fel, 63-64; sr chemist, Merck Sharp & Dohme Res Labs, 64-72, res fel, 72-77, sr res fel, 77-85, sr investr, 85-94. *Concurrent Pos:* Vpres chem, Biofor, Inc, 96. *Mem:* Am Chem Soc; AAAS. *Res:* Synthetic organic and medicinal chemistry in the areas of heterocycles, steroids and pharmaceutically active compounds; mechanism of intracellular hormone action and development of agents to combat deleterious effects of steroid hormones. *Mailing Add:* 155 Park Pl Watchung NJ 07060-5936. *Fax:* 732-594-4773

RASNAKE, MONROE, SOIL FERTILITY, ANIMAL WASTE MANAGEMENT. *Current Pos:* EXTEN AGRON SPECIALIST, UNIV KY, 78- *Personal Data:* b Buchanan County, Va, Feb 8, 42; m 65, Florence Long; c Sara, Matthew & Javan. *Educ:* Berea Col, BS, 65; Va Polytech Inst, MS, 67; Univ Ky, PhD(soil chem), 73. *Honors & Awards:* Merit Cert Award, Am Forage & Grasslands Coun, 88. *Prof Exp:* High sch teacher math sci & biol, Grundy, Va, 67-70; grad asst res lab instr, Univ Ky, 70-73; asst prof, Va Polytech Inst & State Univ, 73-77; supvry mgt agronomist, Dept Army, Blackstone, Va, 77-78. *Mem:* Coun Agr Sci & Technol; Am Soc Agron; Sigma Xi; Am Forage & Grasslands Coun. *Res:* Fire-cured tobacco information; effect of soil fertility level on ozone injury of tobacco; effect of agricultural drainage on water quality; effect of tobacco nutrition on occurrence of insect pests; soil erosion as related to soybean production practices; no-till corn fertilization; effect of soil pH and lime on crop rotations. *Mailing Add:* 106 W Hillcrest Dr Princeton KY 42445. *E-Mail:* mrasnake@ca.uky.edu

RASOR, NED S(HAURER), energy conversion, cardiovascular devices, for more information see previous edition

RASPINI, ANDREA, MASSLESS DIRAC PARTICLES, RELATIVISTIC ZEEMAN EFFECT. *Current Pos:* asst prof, 85-91, ASSOC PROF PHYSICS, STATE UNIV NY, FREDONIA, 92- *Personal Data:* b Florence, Italy, Oct 5, 53. *Educ:* Univ Florence, Italy, Laurea physics, 78; Univ Mass, PhD(physics), 84. *Prof Exp:* Researcher, Fermilab, Ill, 80-81; asst prof physics, Ball State Univ, Ind, 84-85. *Concurrent Pos:* Vis prof physics, Univ Salamanca, Spain, 91-92. *Res:* Relativistic corrections to magnetic interactions in atoms and nuclei (first researcher to apply relativistic center of mass variables to this study); modifications to the Dirac equation for massless particles. *Mailing Add:* Dept Physics State Univ NY Fredonia NY 14063. *Fax:* 716-673-3347; *E-Mail:* raspini@fredonia.edu

RASSIN, DAVID KEITH, NEUROCHEMISTRY, NUTRITION. *Current Pos:* assoc prof, 80-85, PROF, UNIV TEX MED BR, GALVESTON, 85- *Personal Data:* b Liverpool, Eng, Dec 1, 42; m 65, Glennda McConnell; c Meya G, Keith D & Heather K. *Educ:* Columbia Univ, AB, 65; City Univ New York, PhD(pharmacol), 74. *Prof Exp:* Asst res scientist, NY State Inst Basic Res Ment Retardation, 67-70, res scientist, 70-74, sr res scientist human develop & nutrit, 74-77, res scientist IV, 77-79, res scientist V, 79-80. *Concurrent Pos:* Adj asst prof Mt Sinai Sch Med, 76-80 & adj assoc prof, Col Staten Island, City Univ New York, 79-80. *Mem:* Int Soc Neurochem; Am Soc Neurochem; Am Soc Clin Nutrit; Soc Pediat Res; Am Soc Exp Pharmacol & Therapeut; Soc Neurosci. *Res:* Neurochemistry of amino acids, especially sulfur containing amino acids, as they relate to inborn errors of metabolism and nutrition in children. *Mailing Add:* Dept Pediat Univ Tex Med Br Galveston TX 77555-0344. *Fax:* 409-772-4599; *E-Mail:* drassin@pedi.utmb.edu

RAST, HOWARD EUGENE, JR, SOLID STATE SCIENCE, FIBER OPTICS. *Current Pos:* res physicist, 70-80, supvry scientist, 80-86, MGR, SOLID STATE ELECTRONICS DIV, NAVAL COMMAND, CONTROL & OCEAN SURVEILLANCE CTR, RDT & E DIV, 86- *Personal Data:* b Mexia, Tex, June 8, 34; m 58, Yoko Watanabe; c David E & Dieter E. *Educ:* Univ Tex, BA, 56; Univ Ore, PhD(phys chem), 64, Univ Southern Calif, MS, 77. *Prof Exp:* Res chemist, Calif Ink Co, Div Tenneco Inc, 58-60; res asst chem, Univ Ore, 60-64; phys chemist, US Naval Weapons Ctr, 64-70. *Mem:* Am Phys Soc; Optical Soc Am; AF Commun & Electronics Asn. *Res:* Spectra and optical properties of materials; lattice dynamics; military optical counter-measures; electro-optics and optical technology; fiber optics; semiconductors; optical electronics. *Mailing Add:* Code D89 53560 Hull St San Diego CA 92152-5001. *E-Mail:* rast@nosc.mil

RAST, NICHOLAS, STRUCTURAL GEOLOGY. *Current Pos:* chmn dept, 81-89, HUDNALL PROF GEOL, UNIV KY, LEXINGTON, 79- *Personal Data:* b Teheran, Iran, June 20, 27; c 5. *Educ:* Univ Col, London, BSc, 52; Univ Glasgow, PhD(geol), 56. *Prof Exp:* Lectr geol, Univ Wales, 55-59; lectr, 59-61, sr lectr, 61-65, reader, Univ Liverpool, 65-71; chmn dept, Univ NB, Can, 71-79. *Concurrent Pos:* Prof geol, Univ Mex, 70; asst lectr, Univ Wales, 54-55, Univ Glasgow, 52-54. *Mem:* AAAS; Geol Soc Am; Geol Asn Can; Hist Earth Sci Soc; Nat Asn Geol Teachers; Sigma Xi; Am Geophys Union. *Res:* Structural and tectonic geology of the Scottish Highlands, England and Wales and the Appalachian Chain of North America - both Canada and the USA; volcanic rocks of Wales; seismites in the Appalachians. *Mailing Add:* Dept Geol Sci Univ Ky Slone Bldg Lexington KY 40506

RASTALL, PETER, THEORETICAL PHYSICS. *Current Pos:* lectr physics, 57-58, from instr to assoc prof, 58-71, PROF PHYSICS, UNIV BC, 71- *Personal Data:* b Washingborough, Eng, Nov 18, 31. *Educ:* Univ Manchester, BSc, 52, PhD(theoret physics), 55. *Prof Exp:* staff mem, Aerodyn Dept, Rolls Royce, Ltd, 55-57. *Res:* Field theory; quantum mechanics; gravitation. *Mailing Add:* Dept Physics Univ BC Vancouver BC V6T 1Z1 Can

RASTOGI, PRABHAT KUMAR, material science, metallurgy, for more information see previous edition

RASTOGI, SURESH CHANDRA, MATHEMATICAL STATISTICS, BIOSTATISTICS. *Current Pos:* supvry math statistician, Ctr Biologics, 73-90, DEP DIR, DIV BIOSTATIST & EPIDERMIOLOGY CTR BIOLOGICS, FOOD & DRUG ADMIN, 90- *Personal Data:* b Sambhal, India, July 7, 37; US citizen; m 66, Geeta Kshatriya; c Vineeta, Tanuja, Anuja & Mohit. *Educ:* Univ Lucknow, BSc, 57, MSc, 60; Univ Iowa, PhD(statist), 65. *Prof Exp:* Lectr statist, Univ Lucknow, 60-62; statistician, Univ Md, Baltimore City, 66-67; asst prof statist, Univ Md, College Park, 67-72; mgr statist, Hq, US Postal Serv, 72-73. *Concurrent Pos:* Consult, Div Biologics Stand, NIH, 67-70. *Mem:* Am Statist Asn; Biomet Soc; Int Statist Inst; Soc CLin Trials. *Res:* Multivariate statistical methods; regression and analysis of variance used in applied fields; bioassay; clinical trial design and evaluation. *Mailing Add:* Div 6 Native Dancer Ct 1401 N Potomac Rockville MD 20878-3709. *Fax:* 301-594-1972

RASWEILER, JOHN JACOB, IV, REPRODUCTIVE PHYSIOLOGY, PLACENTATION. *Current Pos:* asst prof anat, Cornell Univ, 78-84, asst prof, 84-86, dir, Invitro Fertil Labs, 87-88, ASSOC PROF REPRODUCTIVE BIOL, MED COL, CORNELL UNIV, 86- *Personal Data:* b Newport, RI, June 4, 43; m 64, Margaret Rex; c John. *Educ:* Colgate Univ, BA, 65; Cornell Univ, PhD(physiol), 70. *Prof Exp:* Vis asst prof morphol, Div Health, Univ Valle, Colombia, 70-72; asst prof anat, Col Physicians & Surgeons, Columbia Univ, 72-78. *Concurrent Pos:* Pop Coun fel, Univ Valle, Colombia, 70-72; NIH grant, Int Ctr Med Res & Training, Tulane Univ, 71-72, vis scientist, 72-74. *Mem:* Soc Study Reproduction; Am Asn Anatomists; Am Soc Mammal; Soc Study Mammalian Evolution. *Res:* Reproductive physiology; development of bats as laboratory models; studies of implantation, placentation and trophoblast-uterine interactions. *Mailing Add:* Dept Obstet & Gynec Med Col Cornell Univ New York NY 10021. *Fax:* 212-746-8799

RATAJCZAK, HELEN VOSSKUHLER, CELL MEDIATED IMMUNITY, IMMUNOTOXICOLOGY. *Current Pos:* res immunologist, 83-86, staff mem immunol, 86-88, SR IMMUNOLOGIST, IIT RES INST, 88-, GROUP LEADER IMMUNOL, 90- *Personal Data:* b Tucson, Ariz, Apr 9, 38; div; c Lorraine, Eric, Peter & Eileen. *Educ:* Univ Ariz, BS, 59, MS, 70, PhD(molecular biol), 76. *Prof Exp:* Asst res, SW Clin & Res Inst, Univ Ariz, 67-72, NIH trainee, Health Sci Ctr, 73-74, Am Thoracic Soc fel, 74-76; asst res scientist, Col Med, Univ Iowa, 76-78; instr, Eye & Ear Hosp, Univ Pittsburg, 78-80, res assoc, Med Sch, 80-81; asst prof, Med Sch, Loyola Univ, 81-83. *Concurrent Pos:* Lectr, Occup Safety & Health Admin, 84-; instr, Ill Inst Technol, 88- *Mem:* Sigma Xi; Am Thoracic Soc; Am Asn Immunologists; NY Acad Sci; AAAS; Soc Toxicol. *Res:* Definition of alteration of immune competence by the interactions of foreign substances with the host or a modification of self. *Mailing Add:* IIT Res Inst 10 W 35th St Chicago IL 60616-3799. *Fax:* 312-567-4466

RATCHES, JAMES ARTHUR, ELECTRO-OPTICS, SYSTEMS ANALYSIS. *Current Pos:* Res physicist, Ctr for Night Vision & Electro-Optics, 69-81, dir, Visionics Div, 81-87, dir, Spec Proj Off, 87-88, assoc dir sci & technol, 88-92, CHIEF SCIENTIST, CTR FOR NIGHT VISION & ELECTRO-OPTICS, 92- *Personal Data:* b Hartford, Conn, May 12, 42; m 73, Kristina Edberg; c Zoe, Nathaniel & Eve. *Educ:* Trinity Col, Conn, BS, 64; Worcester Polytech Inst, MS, 66, PhD(physics), 69. *Res:* Development of target acquisition models for thermal imaging devices; analysis and design evaluation of electro-optical sensors; atmospheric propagation effects on electro-optical devices. *Mailing Add:* CECOM RDEC Night Vision Electronic Sensors Directorate Ft Belvoir VA 22060-5677

RATCHFORD, JOSEPH THOMAS, TRADE & TECHNOLOGY POLICY, INTERNATIONAL SCIENCE & TECHNOLOGY POLICY. *Current Pos:* PROF INT SCI & TECHNOL POLICY, GEORGE MASON UNIV, 93-, DIR, CTR SCI, TRADE & TECHNOL POLICY, 94- *Personal Data:* b Kingstree, SC, Sept 30, 35; m 60, Joanne W Causey; c Joseph T Jr, Laura L, James R & David A. *Educ:* Davidson Col, BS, 57; Univ Va, MA, 59, PhD(physics), 61. *Prof Exp:* Staff mem, Sandia Corp, 59; asst prof physics, Washington & Lee Univ, 61-64; proj scientist, Solid State Sci Div, Air Force Off Sci Res, Arlington, 64-70; sci consult, Comt Sci & Technol, US House Rep, 70-77; assoc exec officer, AAAS, Washington, DC, 77-89; assoc dir policy & int affairs, White House Off Sci & Technol Policy, Washington DC, 89-93. *Concurrent Pos:* Res physicist, US Naval Ord Lab, 63-64; Am Polit Sci Asn cong fel, 68-69; res scholar, Int Inst Appl Systs Anal, Laxenburg, Austria, 76; chmn, Res Coord Panel, Gas Res Inst, Chicago, Ill, 76-79, mem, 76-; bd mem, Int Develop Conf, 77-89, Korea-US Sci Coop Ctr, 96-; chmn, Adv Panels to US Congressional Off Technol Assessment, Solar Energy, Energy Conserv & Energy Biol Processes, 78-80; chmn, Adv Comt Int Progs, NSF, 84-87; consult int trade & technol, 93-; mem, Int Affairs Comn, Am Asn Eng Soc, 93-; Chair, Forum Int Physics, Am Phys Soc, 95-96. *Mem:* Fel AAAS; Am Phys Soc; Sigma Xi; Coun Foreign Rels; NY Acad Sci. *Res:* Science and government; materials sciences; energy technology and policy; international science cooperation and policy; international trade and technology policy; education and training. *Mailing Add:* 8804 Fircrest Pl Alexandria VA 22301. *Fax:* 703-993-8211

RATCHFORD, ROBERT JAMES, PHYSICAL CHEMISTRY. *Current Pos:* RETIRED. *Personal Data:* b Firesteel, SDak, Nov 16, 24. *Educ:* Spring Hill Col, BS, 53; Cath Univ, PhD(chem), 58. *Prof Exp:* Res asst, Max Planck Inst Phys Chem & Karlsruhe Tech Univ, 62-63; asst prof chem, Loyola Univ, La, 64-80, dean arts & sci, 75-79. *Mem:* Am Chem Soc; Electrochem Soc. *Res:* Solution electrochemistry; electrochemistry of solid state electrolytes. *Mailing Add:* 6363 St Charles Ave New Orleans LA 70118-6195

RATCLIFF, BLAIR NORMAN, ELEMENTARY PARTICLE PHYSICS. *Current Pos:* res assoc, 75-79, STAFF PHYSICIST, STANFORD LINEAR ACCELERATOR CTR, 74- *Personal Data:* b Grinnell, Iowa, Sept 26, 44; m 76, Ruth Cronkite; c Bryce & Collin. *Educ:* Grinnell Col, BA, 66; Stanford Univ, MS, 68, PhD(physics), 71. *Prof Exp:* Res assoc, Rutherford High Energy Lab, 71-74. *Concurrent Pos:* Vis scientist, Europ Orgn Nuclear Res, 71-74. *Mem:* Am Phys Soc; AAAS. *Res:* Experimental high energy physics; meson and strange baryon spectroscopy; strange baryon spectroscopy; electroweak physics at the Z-CP violation in B-mesons; lepton pair production. *Mailing Add:* 475 Glenwood Ave Redwood City CA 94062. *Fax:* 650-926-3587; *E-Mail:* blair@slac.stanford.edu

RATCLIFF, KEITH FREDERICK, ASTROPHYSICS, THEORETICAL PHYSICS. *Current Pos:* from asst prof to assoc prof, 69-90, PROF PHYSICS, STATE UNIV NY, ALBANY, 90- *Personal Data:* b Drexel Hill, Pa, Nov 15, 38; m, Glenis R deMeza; c Jennifer, Hillary & Karin. *Educ:* Northwestern Univ, Evanston, BA, 60; Univ Pittsburgh, PhD(physics), 65. *Prof Exp:* Res assoc physics, Univ Rochester, 65-67; res assoc, Mass Inst Technol, 67-68, instr, 68-69. *Concurrent Pos:* Vis assoc prof, State Univ NY, Stony Brook, 72-73; scientist, Space Astron Lab, 75-89. *Mem:* AAAS; Am Phys Soc; Am Asn Physics Teachers. *Res:* Neutron star evolution; cosmic dust problems; many-body theory; astronautics and space science; creation of general science curriculum on space exploration. *Mailing Add:* Univ Albany Physics 312 1400 Washington Ave Albany NY 12222

RATCLIFF, MILTON, JR, ANALYTICAL CHEMISTRY, ORGANIC CHEMISTRY. *Current Pos:* PROJ LEADER COMPUT SCI, NELSON ANAL INC, 80- *Personal Data:* b Memphis, Tenn, Apr 19, 44; m 73. *Educ:* Southwestern at Memphis, BS, 66; Case Western Reserve Univ, PhD(org chem), 70. *Prof Exp:* Fel geochem, Indiana Univ, 70-72; proj leader chem, Jet Propulsion Lab, Calif Inst Technol, 72-74; sr chemist geochem, US Geol Surv, 74-76; mgr anal res & residue methods anal chem, Zoecon Corp-Subsid Hooker Chem Co, 76-80. *Mem:* Am Chem Soc; Asn Comput Mach. *Res:* Gas chromatography; mass spectrometry; trace analysis; chemical applications of data processing; instrument interfacing; capillary column development. *Mailing Add:* PE Nelson Systems 3833 N First St San Jose CA 95134-1701

RATCLIFFE, BRETT CHARLES, SYSTEMATICS, COLEOPTERA-SCARABAEIDAE. *Current Pos:* cur insects, 68-76 & 78-92, PROF, UNIV NEBR STATE MUS, 68-, CURATOR INSECTS & ASST DIR RES, 92- *Personal Data:* b Bedford, Eng, Mar 18, 46; US citizen. *Educ:* Univ Nebr, BS, 68, MS, 70, PhD(entom), 75. *Prof Exp:* Chief, Div Entom, Nat Inst Amazon Res, 76-78. *Concurrent Pos:* Vis researcher, Nat Acad Sci & Mus Nature, Ger, 80 & Inst Ecol, Mex, 87; counr, Coleopterists Soc, 89-90. *Mem:* Entom Soc Am; Sigma Xi; Coleopterists Soc (pres, 83-84); Soc Syst Biol; Asn Trop Biol. *Res:* Systematics, phylogeny and biogeography of Scarabaeidae, especially those of neotropics. *Mailing Add:* Univ Nebr W436 Nebr Hall Lincoln NE 68588-0514. *Fax:* 402-472-8949

RATCLIFFE, CHARLES THOMAS, INORGANIC CHEMISTRY. *Current Pos:* SUPVR, PROC RES, UNION OIL OF CALIF. *Personal Data:* b Malad, Idaho, Nov 18, 38; m 64; c 2. *Educ:* Univ Idaho, BS, 61, MS, 63, PhD(inorg chem), 67. *Prof Exp:* Sci Res Coun fel chem, Glasgow Univ, 67-68; res chemist, Corp Res Ctr, Allied Chem Corp, 68-72; sr res chemist, 72-76, res group leader, 76-80, with Exxon Res Eng Co, 80- *Concurrent Pos:* Sci Res Coun fel, Great Britain, 67-68. *Mem:* Sigma Xi; Am Chem Soc; fel NY Acad Sci. *Res:* Catalysis reactions with coal, sulfur; coal chemistry; heterogeneous sulfur containing catalysts; reduction reactions. *Mailing Add:* 14141 Southwest Freeway Sugar Land TX 77478

RATEAVER, BARGYLA, CONSERVATION, SOIL FERTILITY. *Current Pos:* CONSULT, 80- *Personal Data:* b Ft Dauphin, Madagascar, Aug 3, 16; US citizen; c Gylver. *Educ:* Univ Calif, Berkeley, AB, 43, MSLS, 59; Univ Mich, Ann Arbor, MS, 50, PhD(bot), 51, Eminence Credential, Einstein Clause, Calif educ code, 69. *Honors & Awards:* Am Acad Arts & Sci Award, 55. *Prof Exp:* Specialist lima bean maturity stand, Univ Calif, Davis, 51-52, technician photo period determinations floral crops, Hort Dept, Los Angeles, 53-54; pvt plant propagator, 55-56; organizer, Biol Libr, Kaiser Labs, Univ Calif, Berkeley, 58-59; tech abstractor, G C Rocket Co, 59-60; organizer & dir, Histol Lab, Univ Alta, 59-64; librn, D Victor Co, 61 & Marin County Sch Syst, Calif, 67-68; regional rep sci & technol books, J S Stacey, 63; automation analyst, Space & Info Systs, NAm Aviation, 64; Instr, Manpower Develop Training Prog, 65-67; instr org gardening & farming, Jr Cols, Univ Calif & Calif State Univs, 70-78; ed & publ, Conserv Gardening & Farming Series, The Rateavers, 73-94. *Concurrent Pos:* Longwood Gardens grant, 55; lit res, Libr Sch, Univ Calif, Berkeley, 58-59; lectr org gardening, 65-; assoc prof, Calif State Univ, Sacramento, 72-73, instr, Long Beach, 75; organizer, First Int Conf Org Method Farm & Garden, San Francisco, 73; mem, Coord Comt, Int Fedn Org Agr Movements & Working Groups Info Educ, 78-82. *Mem:* Int Fedn Org Agr Movements. *Res:* Development and introduction of first US course in organic gardening and farming; madagascar plants; tropical agriculture; world literature on tropical plants; biological agriculture and horticulture; science education in conservation; soil fertility of field crops, tree and vegetable crops; utilization of weeds; fertilizer comparisons; author of publications and books on organic method of gardening and farming. *Mailing Add:* Int Consult 9049 Covina St San Diego CA 92126. *E-Mail:* brateaver@aol.com

RATH, BHAKTA BHUSAN, METALLURGY. *Current Pos:* supt, Mat Sci Div, 77-82, HEAD, MAT SCI & COMP TECH DIRECTORATE & ASSOC DIR RES, US NAVAL RES LAB, 82- *Personal Data:* b Banki, India, Oct 28, 34; m 63, Sushama; c Minati, Manesh & Manik. *Educ:* Utkal, India, BSc, 55; Mich Technol Univ, MS, 58; Ill Inst Technol, PhD(metall), 62. *Honors & Awards:* Alan Berman Award; Charles S Barrett Award; George Kimball Burgess Award; Leadership Award, Minerals, Metals & Mat Soc. *Prof Exp:* Res assoc metall, Ill Inst Technol, 60-61; asst prof & res metallurgist, Wash State Univ, 61-65; res scientist, E C Bain Lab Fundamental Res, US Steel Corp, 65-71; mem res staff, McDonnell Douglas Res Labs, St Louis, 72-76. *Concurrent Pos:* Adj fac mem, Carnegie-Mellon Univ, Colo Sch Mines. *Mem:* AAAS; fel Am Soc Metals; fel Am Inst Mining, Metall & Petrol Engrs; Brit Inst Metals; Phys Soc Japan; Mat Res Soc India; Sigma Xi; fel Indian Nat Acad Eng. *Res:* Recovery, recrystallization and grain growth in metals; teaching physics of metals; x-ray diffraction; theory of solids; crystallography; deformation and recrystallization textures; micro-calorimetry; solid state physics; defects in solids; phase transformations. *Mailing Add:* Mat Sci & Comp Tech Directorate US Naval Res Lab Code 6000 Washington DC 20375-5000

RATH, CHARLES E, HEMATOLOGY. *Current Pos:* RETIRED. *Personal Data:* b Philippines, Aug 14, 19; m 41, Betty Kate; c Charles III, Elizabeth K, Frederick D & Robert K. *Educ:* Col Wooster, AB, 40; Western Res Univ, MD, 43; Am Bd Internal Med, dipl, 51. *Hon Degrees:* DSc, Georgetown Univ, 83. *Prof Exp:* From instr to prof med, Univ Hosp, Georgetown Univ, 49-84, dir hemat & blood bank, 49-61, univ & dir labs, 61-84. *Concurrent Pos:* Consult, NIH Clin Ctr, 53- & Bethesda Naval Hosp, 54- *Mem:* Am Soc Hemat; AMA; Am Fedn Clin Res; fel Am Col Physicians; Int Soc Hemat. *Res:* Iron metabolism. *Mailing Add:* Rte 2 Box 515 Harpers Ferry WV 25425

RATH, NIGAM PRASAD, SINGLE CRYSTAL X-RAY CRYSTALLOGRAPHY, SYNTHETIC ORGANOMETALLIC CHEMISTRY. *Current Pos:* RES ASST PROF CHEM, UNIV MO, ST LOUIS, 89- *Personal Data:* b Berhampur, India, Mar 24, 58; m 85; c 1. *Educ:* Berhampur Univ, India, BSc Hons, 77, MSc, 79; Okla State Univ, Stillwater, PhD(chem), 85. *Prof Exp:* Postdoctoral res assoc chem, Univ Notre Dame, 86-87, asst fac fel, 87-89. *Mem:* Am Crystallog Asn; Am Phys Soc. *Res:* Single crystal x-ray diffraction studies; synthesis and characterization of organometallic compounds; use of crystallographic data bases and molecular modelling studies; structure-activity relationships. *Mailing Add:* Chem Dept Univ Mo 8001 Natural Bridge Rd St Louis MO 63121-4401

RATHBUN, TED ALLAN, PHYSICAL & FORENSIC ANTHROPOLOGY, PATHOLOGY. *Current Pos:* from instr to assoc prof, 70-84, chmn, 87-89, PROF ANTHROP, UNIV SC, 84- *Personal Data:* b Ellsworth, Kans, Apr 11, 42; m 64, Babette Cowley; c Joel. *Educ:* Univ Kans, BA, 64, MA, 66, PhD(anthrop), 71. *Prof Exp:* Instr eng, Ahwaz Agr Col, Peace Corps, 66-68. *Concurrent Pos:* Res assoc, Inst Archaeol, Univ SC, 71-; comt res & prod scholar grant, 71 & 78; consult phys anthropologist, Off State Med Examr, Med Univ SC, 72-; Field Res Projs grant, Field Mus Natural Hist & Univ SC, 72-73; dipl, Am Bd Forensic Anthrop, 82- & mem bd Am Bd Anthrop; biomed grant, Afroamerican biohistory, Univ SC, 85; Dep State Archaeologist Forensics, NSF Grant, 87, Venture Fund, 90. *Mem:* Am Anthrop Asn; Am Asn Phys Anthrop; dipl Am Bd Forensic Anthropol; Am Acad Forensic Sci; Paleopath Asn; Int Asn Identification. *Res:* Osteology; Bronze and Iron Ages in Southwest Asia; social structure and fertility; physical anthropology of groups in Southwest Asia; forensic anthropology; paleopathology; non-metric variation; colonial and 19th century South Carolina; Egypt-early dynastic; forensic video superimposition; bone chemistry; pathology; forensic skeletal identification. *Mailing Add:* Dept Anthrop Univ SC Columbia SC 29208-0001. *Fax:* 803-772-0259

RATHBUN, WILLIAM B, LENS BIOCHEMISTRY. *Current Pos:* Res assoc, 64-67, asst prof, 67-73, ASSOC PROF OPHTHAL BIOCHEM, UNIV MINN, MINNEAPOLIS, 73-, DEPT SMALL ANIMAL CLIN SCI, 84- *Personal Data:* b Wisconsin Dells, Wis, June 20, 32; m 86, Joan Luschei; c 2. *Educ:* Univ Wis, BS, 54, MS, 55; Univ Minn, Minneapolis, PhD(biochem), 63. *Honors & Awards:* Sr Investr Award, Res Prevent Blindness, 93. *Concurrent Pos:* NIH fel ophthal biochem, Univ Minn, Minneapolis, 63-64, grants, 69-71, 72-86, 87-92 & 92-96. *Mem:* Asn Res Vision & Ophthal; Sigma Xi; Int Soc Eye Res; Asn Eye Res; Int Soc Ocular Toxicol. *Res:* Lens enzymes; biochemistry of cataracts; biosynthesis and metabolism of glutathione; biochemistry of cornea; gilutathione prodrugs; anti-cataract drugs. *Mailing Add:* Dept Ophthal Univ Minn 2001 Sixth St SE Minneapolis MN 55455. *Fax:* 612-626-0781; *E-Mail:* rath001@maroon.tc.umn.edu

RATHBURN, CARLISLE BAXTER, JR, PUBLIC HEALTH ENTOMOLOGY. *Current Pos:* RETIRED. *Personal Data:* b Fulton, NY, Apr 23, 24; wid; c Margaret L & Carlisle B III. *Educ:* Syracuse Univ, AB, 46; Univ Fla, BSA, 50, MAg, 51; Cornell Univ, PhD(entom), 64. *Honors & Awards:* Maurice W Provost Mem Award, 90. *Prof Exp:* Res asst entom, Cornell Univ, 53-57; entomologist, Entom Res Ctr, Fla State Dept Health & Rehab Serv, 57-64, entomologist, W Fla Arthropod Res Lab, 64-86; biol adminr, John A Mulrennan Sr Res Lab, 86-90. *Concurrent Pos:* Prin investr, USPHS res grant, 60-66; ed, J Florida Mosquito Control Asn, 79-94. *Mem:* Sigma Xi; Entom Soc Am; Am Mosquito Control Asn. *Res:* Biology and control of mosquitoes and other insects of medical importance; author of more than 100 scientific papers. *Mailing Add:* 3340 Robinson Bayou Circle Panama City FL 32405

RATHCKE, BEVERLY JEAN, ECOLOGY. *Current Pos:* asst prof, 78-85, ASSOC PROF BIOL, UNIV MICH, 85- *Personal Data:* b Wadena, Minn, July 12, 45. *Educ:* Gustavus Adolphus Col, BA, 67; Imp Col, Univ London, MSc, 68; Univ Ill, Urbana-Champaign, PhD(ecol), 73. *Prof Exp:* Student ecol, Cornell Univ, 73-75; res assoc ecol, Brown Univ, 75-78. *Concurrent Pos:* Ed, J Ecol Soc Am, 75-82; NATO fel, Univ Col NWales, 79. *Mem:* Ecol Soc Am; Brit Ecol Soc; Soc Study Evolution; Soc Am Naturalists. *Res:* Animal-plant interactions and community ecology. *Mailing Add:* 810 Fifth St Ann Arbor MI 48103

RATHER, JAMES B, JR, CHEMICAL ENGINEERING. *Current Pos:* PRES, SCH HOUSE ENTERPRISES LTD, 72- *Personal Data:* b Bryan, Tex, Feb 2, 11; m 35; c 3. *Educ:* Lehigh Univ, ChE, 32. *Prof Exp:* Asst chief chemist, Magnolia Petrol Co, 35-37, supvr eng, Tech Serv Div, Socony Mobil Oil Co, 38-41, asst mgr div, 43-56, admin dir, 56-60, mgr toxicol & pollution, Res Dept, Mobil Oil Corp, 60-67, corp asst air & water conserv coord, 67-72. *Concurrent Pos:* Mem, Ny State Action for Clean Air Comt. *Mem:* Air Pollution Control Asn; Am Nat Stand Insts; Am Soc Testing & Mat (vpres, 64, pres, 66); Am Chem Soc. *Res:* Petroleum technology; air and water pollution control; standardization; toxicology. *Mailing Add:* Grindstone Ave Winter Harbor ME 04693-2232

RATHKE, JEROME WILLIAM, CATALYSIS. *Current Pos:* chemist, 75-95, SR CHEMIST, ARGONNE NAT LAB, 95- *Personal Data:* b Humboldt, Iowa, July 10, 47; m 68; c 2. *Educ:* Iowa State Univ, BS, 69; Ind Univ, PhD(inorg chem), 73. *Honors & Awards:* R&D 100 Award, 94. *Prof Exp:* Fel chem, Cornell Univ, 73-75. *Concurrent Pos:* Group leader, Argonne Nat Lab, 81- *Mem:* Am Chem Soc; NY Acad Sci; AAAS; Sigma Xi; Am Inst Chemists. *Res:* Catalysis; organometallic chemistry; coal conversion chemistry. *Mailing Add:* Chem Eng Div Argonne Nat Lab Argonne IL 60439. *Fax:* 630-252-9373; *E-Mail:* rathke@cmt.anl.gov

RATHKE, MICHAEL WILLIAM, ORGANIC CHEMISTRY. *Current Pos:* from asst prof to assoc prof, 68-78, PROF CHEM, MICH STATE UNIV, 78- *Personal Data:* b Humboldt, Iowa, Aug 13, 41; m 65; c 1. *Educ:* Iowa State Univ, BS, 63; Purdue Univ, PhD(chem), 67. *Prof Exp:* NSF fel, Purdue Univ, 67-68. *Mem:* Am Chem Soc. *Res:* Synthetic organic chemistry; organometallic chemistry, particularly boron organic chemistry. *Mailing Add:* 6125 Horizon Dr East Lansing MI 48823-2238

RATHMANN, CARL ERICH, THERMODYNAMICS, CHAOTIC DYNAMICS. *Current Pos:* PROF MECH ENG, DIR & ASSOC DEAN, ENG GRAD STUDIES, COL ENG, CALIF STATE POLYTECH UNIV, 79- *Personal Data:* b Chicago, Ill, June 27, 45; m 68; c 3. *Educ:* Northwestern Univ, BS, 68, MS, 70, PhD(mech eng), 75. *Prof Exp:* Engr, Res Div, Gen Am Transp Corp, 65-75; vis asst prof mech eng, Northwestern Univ, 76-77; staff mem, Mission Res Corp, 77-78; asst prof physics, Westmont Col, 79. *Concurrent Pos:* Instr mech eng, Univ Calif, Santa Barbara, 79; consult, Gen Dynamics Corp, 80-84; adj assoc prof, Harvey Mudd Col, 81-86. *Mem:* Sigma Xi; Am Soc Mech Engrs; Am Phys Soc; Am Soc Eng Educ. *Res:* Numerical simulation of plasma phenomena including development of methods for simulation long-time-scale wave-particle (resonance) interactions; investigation of spectral decomposition techniques appropriate to plasma parameters; investigation of chaotic transition to turbulence. *Mailing Add:* 1272 Celia Ct Upland CA 91784-1748

RATHMANN, GEORGE B, PHYSICAL CHEMISTRY. *Current Pos:* CHMN, PRES & CHIEF EXEC OFFICER, ICOS CORP, 90- *Personal Data:* b Milwaukee, Wis, Dec 25, 27. *Educ:* Northwestern Univ, BS, 48; Princeton Univ, MS, 50, PhD(phys chem), 52. *Mem:* Nat Acad Eng. *Mailing Add:* 22021 20th Ave SE Bothell WA 98021. *Fax:* 425-485-1911

RATHNAM, PREMILA, BIOCHEMISTRY, ENDOCRINOLOGY. *Current Pos:* fel endocrinol in med, Cornell Univ, 66-69, instr biochem in med, 69-71, asst prof, 71-78, ASSOC PROF BIOCHEM IN MED & ENDOCRINOL IN OBSTET & GYNEC, MED COL, CORNELL UNIV, 78- *Personal Data:* b India, Jan 7, 36; m. *Educ:* Univ Madras, BSc, 55; Univ Wis, MS, 62; Seton Hall Univ, PhD(biochem), 66. *Prof Exp:* Res asst biochem & home econ, Univ Wis, 61-62; res asst chem, Seton Hall Univ, 62-66. *Concurrent Pos:* Lalor Found fel, Med Col, Cornell Univ, 66-68, USPHS trainee, 66-69; Int Cong Biochem travel awards, 70, 73 & 88, Endocrine Soc travel award, 76, 80 & 88. *Mem:* NY Acad Sci; Am Chem Soc; Endocrine Soc; Am Soc Biol Chemists. *Res:* Isolation, characterization and structure function relationships of human anterior pituitary hormones and its receptors; one patent. *Mailing Add:* Dept Biochem & Endocrinol Cornell Univ Med Col 1300 York Ave New York NY 10021-4896

RATHOD, MULCHAND S, HEAT TRANSFER, MECHANICAL ENGINEERING. *Current Pos:* DIR & PROF, DIV ENG TECHNOL, WAYNE STATE UNIV, 87- *Personal Data:* b Pathri, India, Mar 3, 45; US citizen; m 71, Damayanti D Thankor; c Prerana, Falgun & Sejal. *Educ:* Sardar Patel Univ, BE, 70; Miss State Univ, MS, 72, PhD(mech eng), 75. *Prof Exp:* Consult engr, B&B Consult Engrs, 75-76; asst prof, Tuskegee Univ, 76-78; assoc prof & coordr, State Univ NY, 79-87. *Concurrent Pos:* Staff insulation optimization studies, Bowron & Butler Consult Engrs, 76-80; redesign wood-gas generator, Interpine, 77-79; staff geometric tolerancing & dimensioning, Savin, 80-81; tech staff, Jet Propulsion Lab, 80-81; consult, IBM, 82-86. *Mem:* Am Soc Mech Engrs; Am Soc Eng Educ; Am Soc Heating, Refrig & Air Conditioning Engrs; Soc Mfg Engrs; Prof Order Eng Technol. *Res:* Artificial heart; centrifugal pump; energy conversion and conservation; engineering technology education; electronic cooling and packaging; cardiac pump. *Mailing Add:* Dept Eng Technol Wayne State Univ 4855 Fourth Detroit MI 48202-3919. *E-Mail:* rathod@etl.eng.wayne.edu

RATIU, TUDOR S, MATHEMATICS, GEOMETRIC MECHANICS. *Current Pos:* PROF MATH, DEPT MATH, UNIV CALIF, SANTA CRUZ, 87- *Personal Data:* b Timisoara, Romania, Mar 18, 50; m 78, Lillian Massoud; c Victor I, Marius M & Julia L. *Educ:* Univ Timisoara, BA, 73, MA, 74; Univ Calif, Berkeley, PhD(math), 80. *Honors & Awards:* Alexander von Humboldt Found Prize, 97. *Prof Exp:* T H Hildebrandt res asst prof math, Univ Mich, Ann Arbor, 80-83; assoc prof, Univ Ariz, Tucson, 83-87. *Concurrent Pos:* NSF fel, 83-86; fel, A P Sloan Found, 84-87; Miller res prof, Univ Calif, Berkeley, 94; Fulbright scholar, Inst Advan Study Sci, Bures Sur Yvette, France, 94-95. *Mem:* Am Math Soc; Am-Romanian Acad Arts & Sci. *Res:* Geometric methods in the study of the dynamics of classical mechanical systems, continuum mechanics, integrable systems, stability and bifurcations. *Mailing Add:* Dept Math Univ Calif Santa Cruz CA 95064. *Fax:* 408-459-3260; *E-Mail:* ratiu@math.ucsc.edu

RATKOWSKI, DONALD J, FDA REGULATORY AFFAIRS. *Current Pos:* PRES, DJR RESOURCES INC, 90- *Personal Data:* b Cleveland, Ohio, July 29, 38; m 62, Joyce Kotlarczyk; c Rhonda, Tamyra, Cheryl & Randall. *Hon Degrees:* DSc, Alliance Col, 86. *Honors & Awards:* Trailblazer Award, Contact Lens Mfrs Asn, 87; Leonardo DaVinci Award, Contact Lens Mfrs Asn, 90. *Prof Exp:* Sr engr, Motorola Semiconduct Prod Div, 60-70, 75-76; vpres, Danker & Wohlk, 70-75; pres, Paragon Optical, 76-90. *Concurrent Pos:* Lectr, Contact Lens Mfrs Asn, 78-90; adv & assoc mem, Opticians Asn Am, 87-88; steering comt, Optometry Col, Poland, 89-91; prog chmn & chmn educ fund, Contact Lens Soc Am, 89-91. *Mem:* Contact Lens Soc Am; Contact Lens Mfrs Asn. *Res:* Invented and patented formulas and process for rigid gas permeable contact lens materials; designed compression, injection and cast molding as well as manufacturing equipment for the contact lens industry. *Mailing Add:* 31 Oakwood Hills Dr Chandler AZ 85248

RATLIFF, FLOYD, NEUROPHYSIOLOGY, VISION. *Current Pos:* RETIRED. *Personal Data:* b La Junta, Colo, May 1, 19; m 42, Orma V Priddy; c Merry. *Educ:* Colo Col, AB, 47; Brown Univ, MSc, 49, PhD(psychol), 50. *Hon Degrees:* DSc, Colo Col, 75. *Honors & Awards:* Warren Medal, Soc Exp Psychol, 66; Tillyer Award, Optical Soc Am, 76; Pisart Vision Award, NY Asn Blind, 83; Distinguished Sci Contrib Award, Am Psychol Asn, 84; William James fel, Am Psychol Asn, 89. *Prof Exp:* Nat Res Coun fel, Johns Hopkins Univ, 50-51; instr psychol, Harvard Univ, 51-52, asst prof, 52-54; from asst to assoc prof biophys, Rockefeller Univ, 54-66, prof, 66-89, pres, Harry Frank Guggenheim Found, 83-89. *Mem:* Nat Acad Sci; fel Am Acad Arts & Sci; Am Psychol Soc; Am Philos Soc. *Res:* Neurophysiology of vision. *Mailing Add:* 2215 Calle Cacique Santa Fe NM 87505-4944. *E-Mail:* redcliff@aol.com

RATLIFF, FRANCIS TENNEY, PAPER TECHNOLOGY. *Current Pos:* RETIRED. *Personal Data:* b Bogalusa, La, Oct 6, 19; m 44; c 1. *Educ:* La State Univ, BS, 40; Lawrence Col, MS, 42, PhD(paper chem), 48. *Prof Exp:* Res chemist, Standard Oil Develop Co, La, 42-45 & Johns-Manville Co, 48-51; paper technologist, Personal Prod Co, 51-54, tech dir, Paper Div, 54-57; asst res dir, Rhinelander Paper Co, 57-60, res dir, Rhinelander Div, St Regis Paper Co, 60-71, prod develop mgr, 71-73, asst tech dir, 73-74, res dir, 74-83, asst tech dir, 77-83. *Mem:* Tech Asn Pulp & Paper Indust; Am Soc Qual Control; Can Pulp & Paper Asn; Brit Paper & Bd Makers' Asn. *Res:* Physical properties of wood pulps; roofing papers; creped tissues; glassine, greaseproof, reprographic and packaging papers. *Mailing Add:* 534 S Eastern Ave Rhinelander WI 54501

RATLIFF, HUGH DONALD, INDUSTRIAL ENGINEERING. *Current Pos:* PROF ENG, GA INST TECHNOL. *Honors & Awards:* Baker Distinguished Res Award, Am Inst Indust Engrs, 91. *Mem:* Nat Acad Eng. *Mailing Add:* Dept Indust Eng Ga Inst Technol Atlanta GA 30332. *Fax:* 404-894-2301; *E-Mail:* don.ratliff@ifye.gatech.edu

RATLIFF, LOUIS JACKSON, JR, MATHEMATICS. *Current Pos:* lectr, 63-64, from asst prof to assoc prof, 64-69, PROF MATH, UNIV CALIF, RIVERSIDE, 69- *Personal Data:* b Cedar Rapids, Iowa, Sept 1, 31; m 96, Georgia Hawkes. *Educ:* Univ Iowa, BA, 53, MA, 58, PhD(math), 61. *Prof Exp:* Lectr math, Ind Univ, 61-63. *Concurrent Pos:* NSF grants, 64-68, 70-72 & res grant, 72-86. *Mem:* Am Math Soc. *Res:* Commutative algebra; local ring theory. *Mailing Add:* Dept Math Univ Calif Riverside CA 92521. *E-Mail:* ratliff@urcmath.ucr.edu

RATLIFF, NORMAN B, JR, PATHOLOGY. *Current Pos:* PATHOLOGIST & HEAD, AUTOPSY SERV, CLEVELAND CLIN, 79- *Personal Data:* b Winchester, Ky, Aug 28, 38. *Educ:* Duke Univ, MD, 62. *Mem:* Am Asn Pathol. *Mailing Add:* Dept Path Cleveland Clin Found 9500 Euclid Ave Cleveland OH 44195-0001

RATLIFF, PRISCILLA N, CHEMICAL INFORMATION SCIENCE, BUSINESS INTELLIGENCE. *Current Pos:* res chemist, 76-78, SUPVR LIBR & INFO SERV, ASHLAND CHEM CO, 78- *Personal Data:* b Uniontown, Pa, Dec 26, 40; m 69, Wendell L; c Jason K. *Educ:* Maryville Col, BS, 62; Vanderbilt Univ, MS, 64. *Prof Exp:* Asst ed, Chem Abstr Serv, 64-67; info scientist, Battelle Columbus Labs, 67-73; tech writer, Warren-Teed Pharmaceut, Inc, 73-76. *Mem:* Am Chem Soc; Soc Competitive Intel Profs; Spec Libr Asn. *Res:* Computerized and manual information retrieval systems; patent searching; competitive intelligence using online systems and the internet. *Mailing Add:* Ashland Chem Co PO Box 2219 Columbus OH 43216. *Fax:* 614-793-6223

RATLIFF, RAYMOND DEWEY, RANGE CONDITION & TREND ANALYSIS, MOUNTAIN MEADOW ECOLOGY & MANAGEMENT. *Current Pos:* Range conservationist res, 61-65, RANGE SCIENTIST, USDA FOREST SERV, PAC SW RES STA, 65- *Personal Data:* b Salt Fork, Okla, Aug 7, 31; m 54, 70, Donna M Kinzel; c Trixine A (Peart), Andrew J, Cosette E (Cantrell) & Kristen L. *Educ:* Univ Calif, BS, 59, MS, 61; NMex State Univ, PhD(range mgt), 79. *Mem:* Soc Range Mgt. *Res:* Evaluation of rest-rotation grazing; ecology and management of meadows; defoliation effects on California poppy; management of annual grass rangeland; range condition and trend evaluation methods; sensitive plants; conifer plantation grazing. *Mailing Add:* 4703 E San Gabriel Ave Fresno CA 93726

RATLIFF, ROBERT L, BIOCHEMISTRY. *Current Pos:* STAFF MEM BIOMED RES GROUP ENZYM, LOS ALAMOS NAT LAB, 63- *Personal Data:* b Shawnee, Okla, Dec 1, 31; m 59; c 2. *Educ:* Univ Santa Clara, BS, 56; St Louis Univ, PhD(biochem), 60. *Prof Exp:* Am Cancer Soc fel enzymol, Univ Wis, 60-63. *Mem:* Fedn Am Soc Exp Biol; AAAS; Am Soc Biol Chem; Sigma Xi. *Res:* Steroid--metabolism of bile acids; enzymes--purification of enzymes nucleoside diphosphokinases; nucleic acids; enzymatic synthesis of DNA and RNA. *Mailing Add:* 252 LaCueva Los Alamos NM 87544-2522

RATNASWAMY, MARY JOSANNE, WILDLIFE CONSERVATION, MAMMOLOGY. *Current Pos:* ASST PROF, UNIV MO, 95- *Personal Data:* b St Paul, Minn, Aug 28, 54; m 88, Vincent Burke; c Selena R. *Educ:* Carleton Col, BS, 76; Univ RI, MS, 82; Univ Ga, PhD(wildlife ecol), 95. *Mem:* Am Soc Mammologists; Soc Conserv Biol; Wildlife Soc; Soc Marine Mammal. *Res:* Conservation biology of mammals; conservation of fin whales; reintroduction of otters, small mammal ecology in agriculturally impacted flood plains; ecology of nest predators; community. *Mailing Add:* Sch Natural Resources Univ Mo 112 Stephens Hall Columbia MO 65211. *Fax:* 573-884-5070; *E-Mail:* mary_ratnaswamy@muccmail.missouri.edu

RATNAYAKE, WALISUNDERA MUDIYANSELAGE NIMAL, FATS & OILS CHEMISTRY, LIPID CHEMISTRY. *Current Pos:* RES SCIENTIST, FOOD DIRECTORATE HEALTH & WELFARE CAN, OTTAWA, 89- *Personal Data:* b Kandy, Sri Lanka, Feb 22, 49; Can citizen; m 76, Udula Herath; c Lakmal N & Ayesha D. *Educ:* Univ Sri Lanka, BSc, 72; Dalhousie Univ, MSc, 78, PhD(org chem), 80. *Prof Exp:* Asst lectr phys chem, Univ Sri Lanka, 72-73; res officer lipid chem, Ceylon Inst Sci & Indust Res, Sri Lanka, 73-82; res assoc Lipid Chem, Can Inst Fisheries Technol, Tech Univ NS, Halifax, 82-88. *Concurrent Pos:* Vis lectr, lab technician course, Chem Inst Sri Lanka, 74-76; Can Commonwealth scholar, 76-80. *Mem:* Can Inst Chem; Chem Inst Sri Lanka; Chemists Soc. *Res:* Vegetable and marine oils chemistry; partial hydrogenation of fats and oils; heated and oxidized oils; directed interesterification of marine oils; large scale isolation of n3-polyunsaturated fatty acids in fish oils; analytical techniques in lipid chemistry; lipid nutrition. *Mailing Add:* Bur Nutrit Sci Food Directorate Health Protection Br Tunney's Pasture Ottawa ON K1A 0L2 Can. *Fax:* 613-941-6182

RATNER, ALBERT, ENDOCRINOLOGY, PHYSIOLOGY. *Current Pos:* PROF PHYSIOL, SCH MED, UNIV NMEX, 67- *Personal Data:* b Brooklyn, NY, Sept 10, 37; m 67; c 2. *Educ:* Brooklyn Col, BS, 59; Mich State Univ, 62, PhD(physiol), 65. *Concurrent Pos:* NIH fel physiol, Univ Tex Southwestern Med Sch Dallas, 65-67; NSF grant, 68-75. *Mem:* Psychoneuroendocrine Soc; Am Physiol Soc; Biol Reprod Soc; Am Neurosci Soc; Endocrine Soc; Am Fertil Soc. *Res:* Neuroendocrine control of anterior pituitary and gonadal function. *Mailing Add:* 1408 Bluebell Pl NE Albuquerque NM 87122

RATNER, BUDDY DENNIS, BIOMATERIALS SCIENCE ENGINEERING, SURFACE SCIENCE. *Current Pos:* From res assoc to res asst prof, 72-84, assoc prof, 84-86, PROF BIOENG & CHEM ENG, UNIV WASH, 86- *Personal Data:* b Brooklyn, NY, Jan 19, 47; m 68, Teri Stoller; c Daniel. *Educ:* Brooklyn Col, BS, 67; Polytech Inst Brooklyn, PhD(polymer chem), 72. *Honors & Awards:* Perkin Elmer Phys Electronics Award for Excellence in Surface Sci. *Concurrent Pos:* Asst ed, J Biomed Mat Res; consult; ed, Plasmas & Polymers; dir, Univ Wash Engineered Biomat Eng Res Ctr. *Mem:* Am Chem Soc; AAAS; Soc Biomat; Adhesion Soc; Am Inst Med & Biol Eng; Am Inst Chem Eng. *Res:* Interaction of biological systems with biologically recognized surfaces; materials for blood-contact and ophthalmologic applications; surface analysis of materials; plasma deposition. *Mailing Add:* Dept Bioeng Box 351750 Univ Wash Seattle WA 98195. *E-Mail:* ratner@cheme.washington.edu

RATNER, LAWRENCE THEODORE, MATHEMATICS. *Current Pos:* from asst prof to assoc prof, 49-87, EMER PROF MATH, VANDERBILT UNIV, 87- *Personal Data:* b Philadelphia, Pa, Feb 16, 23; m 47. *Educ:* Univ Calif, Los Angeles, AB, 44, MA, 45, PhD(math), 49. *Prof Exp:* Asst math, Univ Calif, Los Angeles, 44-45 & 47-49. *Mem:* Am Math Soc; Math Asn Am; Sigma Xi. *Res:* Analysis in abstract spaces; topology; probability. *Mailing Add:* 102 Emma Neuhoff Ct Nashville TN 37205

RATNER, LAZARUS GERSHON, HIGH ENERGY PHYSICS, ACCELERATOR PHYSICS. *Current Pos:* RES SCIENTIST, UNIV MICH 93- *Personal Data:* b Chicago, Ill, Sept 14, 23; m 53, Joyce Rosenberg; c Toni, Daniel & Joseph. *Educ:* Univ Calif, Berkeley, AB, 48, MA, 50. *Prof Exp:* Asst physicist accelerator physics, Lawrence Berkeley Lab, Univ Calif, 50-60; physicist accelerator & high energy physics, Argonne Nat Lab, 60-81; physicist accelerator, Brookhaven Nat Lab, 81-93. *Concurrent Pos:* Vis scientist, Ctr Europ Nuclear Res, Geneva, Switz, 71-72. *Mem:* AAAS; Sigma Xi. *Res:* Strong interaction physics; polarization phenomena in high energy scattering acceleration of polarized beams; design of high energy accelerators. *Mailing Add:* Brookhaven Nat Lab 911-B Upton NY 11973

RATNER, MARINA, PURE & APPLIED MATH. *Current Pos:* from actg asst prof to assoc prof, 75-82, PROF PURE & APPL MATH, UNIV CALIF, 82- *Personal Data:* b Moscow, Russ. *Educ:* Moscow State Univ, MA, PhD. *Prof Exp:* Asst, High Tech Eng Sch, Moscow, 69-71; lectr, Hebrew Univ, Jerusalem, 71-74; sr teacher pre acad sch, 74-75. *Concurrent Pos:* Alfred P Sloan res fel, 77-79; Miller res prof, 85-86; John Simon Guggenheim fel, 87-88. *Mem:* Nat Acad Sci; AAAS. *Mailing Add:* Ctr Pure & Appl Math Univ Calif Berkeley CA 94720. *Fax:* 510-642-8204; *E-Mail:* ratner@math.berkeley.edu

RATNER, MARK A, PHYSICAL CHEMISTRY. *Current Pos:* assoc prof, 75-80, PROF CHEM, NORTHWESTERN UNIV, 80- *Personal Data:* b Cleveland, Ohio, Dec 8, 42; m 69, Nancy. *Educ:* Harvard Univ, AB, 64; Northwestern Univ, Evanston, PhD(chem), 69. *Prof Exp:* Amanuensis chem, Aarhus Univ, Denmark, 69-70; asst, Munich Tech Univ, 70; from asst prof to assoc prof, NY Univ, 70-75. *Concurrent Pos:* A P Sloan fel; fel, Jerusalem Advan Study Inst. *Mem:* AAAS; fel Am Phys Soc; NY Acad Sci; Chem Soc; Am Chem Soc. *Res:* Theoretical chemistry; nonadiabatic problems; hydrogen bonding; kinetics; spectra; green functions; electron transfer; reaction dynamics, non-linear optics. *Mailing Add:* Dept Chem Northwestern Univ Evanston IL 60208. *Fax:* 847-491-7713; *E-Mail:* ratner@mercury.chem.nwu.edu

RATNER, MICHAEL IRA, RADIO ASTRONOMY. *Current Pos:* RES ASSOC, RADIO & GEOASTRON DIV, HARVARD-SMITHSONIAN CTR ASTROPHYS, 83- *Personal Data:* b New York, NY, June 30, 49; m 75; c 2. *Educ:* Yale Col, BS, 71; Univ Colo, PhD(astro-geophysics), 76. *Prof Exp:* Res assoc radio astron, Dept Earth & Planetary Sci, Mass Inst Technol, 76-82. *Mem:* Am Astron Soc. *Res:* Computerized analyses of interferometric observations of radio signals from spacecraft and natural radio sources; observational tests of gravitation theory; motions and natures of radio sources. *Mailing Add:* Ctr Astrophys Harvard Univ Cambridge MA 02138

RATNER, ROBERT (STEPHEN), TRANSPORTATION, SYSTEMS ENGINEERING. *Current Pos:* PRES, RATNER ASSOC, INC. *Personal Data:* b Newark, NJ, Apr 13, 41; m 64; c 1. *Educ:* Mass Inst Technol, BS; Stanford Univ, MS, 65, PhD(elec eng), 68. *Prof Exp:* Res engr & sr res engr, Stanford Res Inst, SRI Int, 68-71; group mgr, Transp Eng & Control, 71-76, dir, Transp & Indust Systs Ctr, 76-81, vpres, Systs Consult Div, 82-86. *Mem:* Opers Res Soc Am. *Res:* Air transportation and railroad operations and management consulting; air traffic control; transportation systems. *Mailing Add:* Ratner Assocs Inc 1 First St Suite 14 PO Box AJ Los Altos CA 94022

RATNER, SARAH, BIOCHEMISTRY. *Current Pos:* RETIRED. *Personal Data:* b New York, NY, June 9, 03. *Educ:* Cornell Univ, BA, Columbia Univ, MA, 27, PhD(biochem), 37. *Hon Degrees:* DSc, Univ NC, 81, Northwestern Univ, Evanston, Ill, 82 & State Univ NY, Stony Brook, 84. *Honors & Awards:* Schoenheimer Lectr, 56; Neuberg Medal, 59; Garvan Medal, Am Chem Soc, 61; L & B Freedman Found Award, NY Acad Sci, 75. *Prof Exp:* Asst biochem, Col Physicians & Surgeons, Columbia Univ, 30-31, 32-34, Macy res fel, 37-39, from instr to asst prof, 39-46; asst prof pharmacol, Col Med, NY Univ, 46-53, assoc prof, 53-54; assoc mem, Div Nutrit & Physiol, Pub Health Res Inst City New York Inc, 54-57, mem, Dept Biochem, 57-90,. *Concurrent Pos:* Ed, J Biol Chem, 59- & Anal Biochem, 74-; res prof, Col Med, NY Univ; Fogarty scholar-in-residence, NIH, 78-79. *Mem:* Nat Acad Sci; Am Acad Arts & Sci; Am Soc Biol Chem; fel Harvey Soc; fel NY Acad Sci; Am Chem

Soc; Sigma Xi; fel AAAS. *Res:* Metabolism and chemistry of amino acids; application of isotopes to intermediary metabolism; enzymatic mechanisms of arginine biosynthesis and urea formation and other nitrogen transferring reactions; regulation and structure function relationships in enzymes of arginine biosynthesis from citrulline. *Mailing Add:* 70 E Tenth St New York NY 10003

RATNEY, RONALD STEVEN, INDUSTRIAL HYGIENE. *Current Pos:* TECH DIR, ENVIRON HEALTH SERV, MABBETT & ASSOCS, 95- *Personal Data:* b Brooklyn, NY, June 1, 32; m 57, Tanya Kanter; c Eugene, Catherine & Michael. *Educ:* Calif Inst Technol, BS, 54; Yale Univ, PhD(chem), 59; Harvard Sch Pub Health, MS, 72. *Prof Exp:* Chemist, Trubek Labs, 58-60; from asst prof to assoc prof chem, Hood Col, 60-67; assoc prof, Bentley Col, 67-71; chemist, Mass Div Occup Hyg, 72-75; indust hygienist, Occup Safety & Health Admin, 75-84, asst regional admin, 84-95. *Concurrent Pos:* Mem, Am Conf Govt Indust Hygienists Threshold Limit Value Comt. *Mem:* Am Acad Indust Hyg; Sigma Xi; Am Indust Hyg Soc; Am Conf Govt Indust Hygienists; NY Acad Sci. *Res:* Toxicology; industrial hygiene. *Mailing Add:* 167 Old Billerica Rd Bedford MA 01730. *E-Mail:* rratney@tiac.net

RATNOFF, OSCAR DAVIS, INTERNAL MEDICINE. *Current Pos:* from asst prof to assoc prof, 50-61, asst vis physician 52-57, assoc vis physician, 57-67, PROF MED, SCH MED, CASE WESTERN RESERVE UNIV, 61-, VIS PHYSICIAN, UNIV HOSPS, 67- *Personal Data:* b New York, NY, Aug 23, 16; m 45, Marian Foreman; c William & Martha. *Educ:* Columbia Univ, AB, 36, MD, 39. *Hon Degrees:* LLD, Univ Aberdeen, Scotland, 80; SciD, Case Western Reserve Univ, 96. *Honors & Awards:* Thelin Award, Nat Hemophilia Found, 71; Dameshek Award, Am Soc Hemat, 72; John Phillips Award, Am Col Physicians, 74; John Smith Prize, Columbia Univ, 76; Grant Award, Int Soc Thrombosis, 81; Kovalenko Award, Nat Acad Sci, 85; Kober Medal, Asn Am Physicians, 88. *Prof Exp:* Intern, Med Serv, Johns Hopkins Hosp, 39-40; asst resident med, Montefiore Hosp, New York, 42; asst med, Col Physicians & Surgeons, Columbia Univ, 42-46; instr, Johns Hopkins Univ, 48-50. *Concurrent Pos:* Austin teaching fel physiol, Harvard Med Sch, 40-41; resident, Res Serv Chronic Dis, Goldwater Mem Hosp, 42-43; fel, Sch Med, Johns Hopkins Univ, 46-48; assoc, Mt Sinai Hosp, Cleveland, Ohio, 50-52; career investr, Am Heart Asn, 60-86. *Mem:* Nat Acad Sci; Am Soc Hemat (pres, 75); master, Am Col Physicians; Cent Soc Clin Res (pres, 70-71); Asn Am Physicians; fel AAAS. *Res:* Hemostatic mechanisms. *Mailing Add:* 2916 Sedgewick Rd Shaker Heights OH 44120. *Fax:* 216-844-3000

RATTAN, KULDIP SINGH, ELECTRICAL ENGINEERING COMPUTER ENGINEERING. *Current Pos:* from asst prof to assoc prof, 79-89, PROF ELEC ENG, WRIGHT STATE UNIV, 89- *Personal Data:* b India, Apr 25, 48; m 76; c 2. *Educ:* Punjab Eng Col, India, BSc, 69; Univ Ky, MS, 72, PhD(elec eng), 75. *Prof Exp:* Fel bioeng, Univ Ky, 76, res assoc, 77-78. *Concurrent Pos:* Res assoc & SCEE fel, SCEEE Res Prog, USAF, 80-84; prin investr, USAF Off Sci Res, 81-; vis prof, Carnegie-Mellon Univ, 87-88. *Mem:* Inst Elec & Electronics Engrs. *Res:* Design and analysis of digital control systems; robotics and computer control; computer aided design; fuzzy control, neural networks. *Mailing Add:* Dept Elec Systs Eng Wright State Univ Dayton OH 45435. *Fax:* 937-775-5009; *E-Mail:* krattan@cs.wright.edu

RATTAN, SATISH, PATHOPHYSIOLOGY OF GASTROINTESTINAL MOTILITY DISORDERS, NEUROHUMORAL CONTROL OF RECTOANAL SPHINCTERS. *Current Pos:* PROF MED & PHYSIOL & DIR, GASTGOENTEROL RES, THOMAS JEFFERSON UNIV, 89- *Personal Data:* b Hoshiarpur, India, Oct 2, 46; US Citizen; m 74, Shashi Bala; c Neeru & Neha. *Educ:* Punjab Agr Univ, India, BVSc & AH, 68; Univ Houston, MS, 70. *Prof Exp:* Instr pharmacol, Univ Houston, 70-71; res scientist med, Baylor Col Med, Houston, 71-73; instr med, Univ Tex SW Med Sch, Dallas, 73-78; asst prof, Univ Tex, 78-81; from asst prof to assoc prof med, Harvard Univ, 81-89. *Concurrent Pos:* Prin investr, NIH, 85-; vis prof, numerous univs US & overseas, 85-; assoc ed, Gastroenterol, 86-89; ed bd, J Pharmacol & Exp Therapeuts & Am J Physiol 94- *Mem:* Am Gastroenterol Asn; Am Fedn Clin Res; Am Motility Soc; Fedn Socs Exp Biol & Med; Am Soc Pharmacol & Exp Therapeut. *Res:* Investigate the basic mechanisms responsible for the maintenance of basal tone in the internal anal sphincter and its relaxation; application of physiology, pharmacology, biochemistry and molecular biology to identify the regulatory mechanisms of gastrointestinal sphincteric function and dysfunction. *Mailing Add:* 43 Lakeside Ct Devon PA 19333

RATTAZZI, MARIO CRISTIANO, HUMAN GENETICS, BIOCHEMICAL GENETICS. *Current Pos:* PROF PEDIAT, NORTH SHORE UNIV HOSP, CORNELL UNIV, MED COL, 84- *Personal Data:* b Naples, Italy, Oct 1, 35; m 62; c 1. *Educ:* Univ Naples, MD, 61. *Prof Exp:* Res asst prof human genetics, Univ Leiden, Neth, 62-69; from res asst prof to prof pediat, State Univ NY, Buffalo, 69-84. *Concurrent Pos:* Adv, WHO, 63; res career develop award, Nat Inst Gen Med Sci, 73; co-ed, Isozymes: Current Trends Biol & Med Res, 76-88; mem, exec comt, NY State Genetic Dis Prog, 82-87; mem, Ment Retardation Res Comt, Nat Inst Child Health & Human Develop, NIH, 84-88, chmn, 87-88; prog dir & prin investr, biomed res support grant, NIH, North Shore Univ Hosp, 85- *Mem:* Am Soc Human Genetics; AAAS; NY Acad Sci; Soc Pediat Res; Soc Inherited Metab Dis. *Res:* Human lysosomal storage diseases; biochemical genetic diagnostic and therapeutic aspects; animal models of human diseases. *Mailing Add:* Mt Sinai Sch Med Fifth Ave & 99th St Box 120 New York NY 10029

RATTE, JAMES C, VOLCANIC GEOLOGY, ASSOCIATED MINERAL DEPOSITS. *Current Pos:* geologist, 52-59, chief var projs, 59-93, EMER GEOLOGIST, US GEOL SURV, 93- *Personal Data:* b Hartford, Conn, Nov 21, 25; m 49, Frances Burt; c Kathryn, Judith, Margaret, Mary & Jennifer. *Educ:* Mich State Univ, BS, 50; Darthmouth Col, MA, 52. *Prof Exp:* Explor geologist, Noranda Mines Ltd, Lebrador Trough, New Que, 51. *Mem:* Fel Geol Soc Am; Soc Econ Geol; Colo Sci Soc; Am Geophys Union. *Res:* Mid-tertiary volcanic rocks, caldera complexes and associated ore deposits. *Mailing Add:* US Geol Surv Fed Ctr Mail Stop 905 Box 25046 Denver CO 80225. *Fax:* 303-236-3200; *E-Mail:* jrattle@usgs.gov

RATTI, JOGINDAR SINGH, ANALYTICAL MATHEMATICS. *Current Pos:* assoc prof, 67-69, chmn dept, 69-77, PROF MATH, UNIV S FLA, 69- *Personal Data:* b Rajoya, India, Jan 1, 35; m 62; c 2. *Educ:* Univ Bombay, BSc, 55, MSc, 58; Wayne State Univ, PhD(math), 66. *Prof Exp:* Lectr math, Khalsa Col, India, 58-60 & Nat Col, Bombay, India, 60-61; instr, Nev Southern Univ, 63-65 & Wayne State Univ, 65-66; asst prof, Oakland Univ, 66-67. *Mem:* Am Math Soc; Math Asn Am. *Res:* Graph theory; summability; univalent functions; polynomials; graphs of semigroups and semirings. *Mailing Add:* Dept Math Phy 114 Univ SFla 4202 E Fowler Ave Tampa FL 33620-9951

RATTIEN, STEPHEN, NATIONAL RESEARCH POLICY, ENERGY TECHNOLOGIES & POLICY. *Current Pos:* dep exec dir, Comn Eng & Tech Systs, 87-89, EXEC DIR COMN GEOSCI, ENVIRON & RESOURCES, NAT RES COUN, 89- *Personal Data:* b Dec 12, 42; m 69, Josephine A Sturniolo; c Lisa & Daniel. *Educ:* Cooper Union, BEE, 63; Univ Rochester, MSEE, 65; Cornell Univ, PhD(regional environ planning), 70. *Prof Exp:* Asst res prof, Grad Sch Pub Health, Univ Pittsburgh, 67-71; staff mem, Pres Coun Environ Qual, 71-73; dep dir, Off Energy Res & Develop Policy, NSF, 73-74, exec officer planning, 74-75; pres, DHR Inc, 76-85; vpres technol develop & transfer, Ctr Innovative Technol, 86-87. *Mem:* Inst Elec & Electronics Engrs; AAAS. *Res:* National disaster mitigation and research policy; environmental management; energy/environment analysis. *Mailing Add:* Nat Res Coun Washington DC 20418. *Fax:* 202-334-3362; *E-Mail:* srattien@nas.edu

RATTNER, BARNETT ALVIN, BIOMARKERS OF TOXICANT EXPOSURE & EFFECT. *Current Pos:* res physiologist, Physiol Sect, Patuxent Wildlife Res Ctr, 78-85, leader, Wildlife Toxicol Sect, 85-88, dep chief, Environ Contaminants Res Br, 88-96, GROUP LEADER, PATUXENT WILDLIFE RES CTR, 96- *Personal Data:* b Washington, DC, Oct 4, 50; m 78, Francine Koplin; c Alexander S. *Educ:* Univ Md, BS, 72, MS, 74, PhD(environ & reprod physiol), 77. *Prof Exp:* Teaching asst zool, Univ Md, 72-76, instr, 76-77; Nat Res Coun res assoc, Naval Med Res Inst, Nat Naval Med Ctr, Bethesda, Md, 77-78. *Concurrent Pos:* Adj assoc prof, Dept Poultry Sci, Univ Md. *Mem:* Am Physiol Soc; Am Soc Zoologists; Soc Study Reprod; Soc Exp Biol & Med; Soc Environ Toxicol & Chem; Soc Toxicol. *Res:* Biochemical indicators of pollutant exposure in wildlife; toxicology; environmental and nutritional effects on endocrine and reproductive function; biomonitoring pollution in estuaries. *Mailing Add:* Patuxent Wildlife Res Ctr US Dept Interior Laurel MD 20708-4041. *Fax:* 301-497-5675; *E-Mail:* barnett_rattner@nbs.gov

RATTNER, JEROME BERNARD, ANATOMY, MOLECULAR BIOLOGY. *Current Pos:* asst prof, 81-85, ASSOC PROF ANAT, DEPT MED BIOCHEM, UNIV CALGARY, 85- *Personal Data:* b Cincinnati, Ohio, Aug 12, 45; m 73, Eileen; c John P & Nathalie. *Educ:* Miami Univ, BS, 67; Univ Tex, MS, 69; Washington Univ, PhD(biol), 73. *Prof Exp:* Fel cell biol, Univ Calif, Irvine, 73-75, res asst, 76-81; NATO fel biol, Nat Ctr Sci Res, France, 75-76. *Concurrent Pos:* Ed, Chromosoma. *Mem:* Am Soc Cell Biol; Genetics Soc Can. *Res:* Organization of chromatin and chromosomes in eukaryotic cells with special reference to the kinetochore. *Mailing Add:* Dept Med Biochem & AnaT Univ Calgary 3330 Hosp Dr NW Calgary AB T2N 4N1 Can. *Fax:* 403-270-0737; *E-Mail:* rattner@acs.ucalgary.ca

RATTO, PETER ANGELO, PHARMACEUTICAL CHEMISTRY. *Current Pos:* MEM FAC SCH PHARM, SOUTHWESTERN OKLA STATE UNIV, 80- *Personal Data:* b San Francisco, Calif, Jan 31, 30; m 66; c 1. *Educ:* Univ Calif, BS, 51, MS, 56, PhD(pharmaceut chem), 58. *Prof Exp:* Asst prof pharm & pharmaceut chem, Loyola Univ, 58-63; sr res scientist, Bristol Labs, 63-71; res pharmacist, Norwich-Eaton Pharmaceut Co, 71-80. *Mem:* Am Pharmaceut Asn; Am Soc Hosp Pharmacist; Sigma Xi; Am Asn Col Pharmacist. *Res:* Synthesis of organic medicinal agents; physical chemical evaluation and preparation of pharmaceutical dosage formulations. *Mailing Add:* Pharm Southwestern Okla State Univ 100 Campus Dr Weatherford OK 73096-3001

RATTRAY, BASIL ANDREW, MATHEMATICS. *Current Pos:* RETIRED. *Personal Data:* b Iron Hill, Que, Nov 16, 27; m 55. *Educ:* McGill Univ, BSc, 48, MSc, 49; Princeton Univ, PhD(math), 54. *Prof Exp:* Lectr math, Univ NB, 52-54; from asst prof to prof math, McGill Univ, 54-92. *Mem:* Am Math Soc; Can Math Cong. *Res:* Topology. *Mailing Add:* Dept Math McGill Univ 805 Sherbrooke St W Montreal PQ H3A 2K6 Can

RATTRAY, MAURICE, JR, HYDRODYNAMICS, PHYSICAL OCEANOGRAPHY. *Current Pos:* From asst prof to prof, 50-85, chmn dept, 68-78, EMER PROF OCEANOG, UNIV WASH, 85- *Personal Data:* b Seattle, Wash, Sept 16, 22; m 51, Mary L Walsey; c Julie (Westwood), Maurice III, Gordon W. *Educ:* Calif Inst Technol, BS, 44, MS, 47, PhD(physics), 51. *Concurrent Pos:* Rossby fel, Woods Hole Oceanog Inst, 66-67; mem, Adv Panel Earth Sci, NSF, 66-68; consult, US Naval Oceanog

Off, 68-74; consult sci adv comt, US Coast Guard, 69-72; mem ocean sci comt, Nat Acad Sci, 71-74; mem environ pollutant movement & transformation adv comt, Environ Protection Agency, 76-78; mem, comt rev outer continental shelf, Environ Studies Prog, Nat Acad Sci-Nat Res Coun, 87-91, chmn phys oceanog panel. *Mem:* Am Soc Limnol & Oceanog (vpres, 63-64, pres-elect, 64-65, pres, 65-66); Am Geophys Union. *Res:* Dynamics of estuarine and oceanic current systems. *Mailing Add:* Dept Oceanog Univ Wash Box 357940 Seattle WA 98195-7940. *E-Mail:* rattray@ocean.washington.edu

RATTS, KENNETH WAYNE, ORGANIC CHEMISTRY. *Current Pos:* RETIRED. *Personal Data:* b Martinsville, Ill, July 7, 32; m 59, Rosemary Circle; c Valerie S, Andrew W & Eric B. *Educ:* Univ Eastern Ill, BS, 54; Ohio State Univ, PhD, 59. *Prof Exp:* Asst chem, Ohio State Univ, 54-55, asst org chem, 55-57, asst instr, 57-59; res chemist, Monsanto Co, 59-62, sr res specialist, 63-65, sr group leader, 66, sci fel, 66-75, mgr res, 75-78, res dir process technol, 78-80, dir chem res, 80-83, dir prod res, 83-87, dir environ sci & support technol, 87-90. *Mem:* NY Acad Sci; Sigma Xi; Am Chem Soc. *Res:* 5-halobenzo (a) biphenylenes and transformations; agricultural chemicals; ylid and phosphorus chemistry; sulfur chemistry. *Mailing Add:* 15194 Strollways Dr Chesterfield MO 63017-7754

RATTY, FRANK JOHN, JR, GENETICS. *Current Pos:* from instr to assoc prof zool, 55-62, prof biol, 62-89, EMER PROF BIOL, SAN DIEGO STATE UNIV, 89- *Personal Data:* b San Diego, Calif, June 26, 23; wid; c 1. *Educ:* San Diego State Col, BA, 48; Univ Utah, MS, 49, PhD(genetics), 52. *Prof Exp:* Instr biol, Univ Utah, 52-53; res geneticist poultry husb, Univ Calif, 53-54. *Mem:* AAAS; Genetics Soc Am. *Res:* Mutation; cytogenetics. *Mailing Add:* 899 Van Horn Rd El Cajon CA 92019

RATZ, H(ERBERT) C(HARLES), ELECTRICAL ENGINEERING. *Current Pos:* from assoc prof to prof, Univ Waterloo, 63-86, assoc dean, 68-71 & 87-89, prof elec eng & dir exchange progs, 89-92, EMER PROF & DIR EXCHANGE PROGS, UNIV WATERLOO, 93- *Personal Data:* b Hamilton, Ont, July 23, 27; m 55, Jean Fairles; c 3. *Educ:* Univ Toronto, BASc, 50; Mass Inst Technol, SM, 52; Univ Sask, PhD(elec eng), 63. *Prof Exp:* Res engr, Ferranti-Electronics, Ltd, Ont, 52-55, proj engr, 56-57; design engr, Fischer & Porter (Can) Ltd, 57-59; asst prof elec eng, Univ Sask, 60-63. *Concurrent Pos:* Nat Res Coun Can res grants, 62-72; consult, Ferranti-Electronics, Ltd, 64-66, Can Westinghouse Co, 65 & Naval Res Estab, 67-71; vis prof, NS Tech Col, 71; sr indust fel, Nat Sci Eng Res Coun Can, Bell Northern Res, Can, 84-85. *Mem:* Sr Mem Inst Elec & Electronics Engrs. *Res:* Signal analysis and communications; computer communications networks; safety of computer control. *Mailing Add:* Univ Waterloo Waterloo ON N2L 3G1 Can. *Fax:* 519-725-9970; *E-Mail:* hratz@uwaterloo.ca

RATZ, JOHN LOUIS, DERMATOLOGY. *Current Pos:* DIR, DERMAT SURG, OCHSNER CLIN, 92- *Personal Data:* b Aurora, Ill, May 18, 47; m 69; c 3. *Educ:* Aurora Col, BS, 70; Case Western Reserve, MD, 75. *Prof Exp:* Intern, Cleveland Clin Found, 75-76, resident dermat, 76-79, fel dermat surg & oncol & supvr, Psoriasis Ctr, 79-80; from asst prof to assoc prof dermat, Univ Cincinnati Med Ctr, 80-83; staff dermatologist, Dept Dermat, Cleveland Clin Found, 84-92. *Concurrent Pos:* Chief dermat sect, Vet Admin Med Ctr, 80-82; med staff, dept dermat, Jewish Hosp, 81-83; mem, Comt Mohs Surg Facil, Am Col Chemosurg, 86-88, Sci Prog Comt, 86-88, & comt Public Info, Am Soc Dermat Surg, 86-87; vis prof, Billings Clinic, 87, Northwestern Univ Med Sch, 87, Mayo Clinic, 87, & Ohio State Univ, 88. *Res:* Clinical evaluation of dermatologic conditions; dermatologic surgery; laser surgery. *Mailing Add:* Ochsner Clinic 1514 Jefferson Hwy New Orleans LA 70121

RATZLAFF, KERMIT O, PHYSIOLOGY, ZOOLOGY. *Current Pos:* asst prof physiol & zool, 62-74, ASSOC PROF BIOL SCI, SOUTHERN ILL UNIV, EDWARDSVILLE, 74- *Personal Data:* b Hillsboro, Kans, Dec 26, 21; m 44; c 5. *Educ:* Univ Calif, Los Angeles, AB, 49, MA, 51, PhD(zool), 62. *Prof Exp:* Res technician, White Mem Hosp, Los Angeles, Calif, 52-56; teaching asst zool, Univ Calif, Los Angeles, 56-58; res physiologist, Sch Med, Univ Calif, 59-62. *Concurrent Pos:* Instr, Biola Col, 50-54; consult, Vet Admin Ctr, Los Angeles, 60-62 & Vet Admin Hosp, Long Beach, 62. *Mem:* AAAS; Am Sci Affil; Sigma Xi. *Res:* Mechanisms of functioning of sense organs, particularly regeneration of visual pigments; problems related to ocular metabolism. *Mailing Add:* 17 Shell Lane Edwardsville IL 62025

RATZLAFF, MARC HENRY, ANATOMY, VETERINARY MEDICINE. *Current Pos:* assoc prof anat, 76-92, PROF ANAT, WASH STATE UNIV, 92- *Personal Data:* b Bakersfield, Calif, Feb 21, 42; m 63; c 2. *Educ:* Univ Calif, Davis, AB, 64, MA, 66, PhD(anat), 69; Mich State Univ, DVM, 74. *Prof Exp:* Asst prof anat, Mich State Univ, 69-74; pvt vet pract, Eagle, Idaho, 74-75. *Mem:* Am Asn Vet Anatomists; Am Vet Med Asn. *Res:* Equine locomotion; biomechanics; international veterinary medical education directed towards the Soviet block countries. *Mailing Add:* Dept Vet Comp Anat Pharm & Physiol Wash State Univ Pullman WA 99164

RATZLAFF, WILLIS, limnology, for more information see previous edition

RAU, A RAVI PRAKASH, ATOMIC PHYSICS. *Current Pos:* from asst prof to assoc prof, 74-81, PROF PHYSICS, LA STATE UNIV, BATON ROUGE, 81- *Personal Data:* b Calcutta, India, Aug 9, 45; m 69, 85; c 2. *Educ:* Univ Delhi, BSc, 64, MSc, 66; Univ Chicago, PhD(atomic physics), 70. *Honors & Awards:* Hannan Rosenthal Mem lectr, Yale & Columbia Univs, 85; distinguished res master, La State Univ, 88. *Prof Exp:* Res assoc physics, Univ Chicago, 70; assoc res scientist physics, NY Univ, 70-72; vis fel theoret physics, Tata Inst Fundamental Res, Bombay, India, 72-73. *Concurrent Pos:* Conf fel, III Int Conf Atomic Physics, Boulder, Colo, 72; vis assoc prof, Yale Univ, 78-79; Alfred P Sloan Found fel; vis fel, Joint Inst Lab Astrophys, Univ Colo, 84 & Australian Nat Univ, 87-88. *Mem:* Sigma Xi; fel Am Phys Soc. *Res:* Two-electron phenomena, structure and properties of atoms in intense magnetic fields, such as those on pulsars; development and application of general variational principles in atomic physics and in other areas of physics. *Mailing Add:* Dept Physics La State Univ Baton Rouge LA 70803-4001. *Fax:* 504-388-5855; *E-Mail:* phravi@lsuvm.sncc.lsu.edu

RAU, ALLEN H, SURFACTANT CHEMISTRY, TABLET PROCESSING. *Current Pos:* sr proj mgr, Andrew Jergens Co, 85-87, dir prod develop, 87-90, sr res scientist, 90-94, DIR RES & DEVELOP, ANDREW JERGENS CO, 94- *Personal Data:* b Pittsburgh, Pa, Apr 6, 58; m 89, Edyce D Solomon; c Seth B & Justin A. *Educ:* Rutgers Univ, BS, 79; Univ Cincinnati, MBA, 83. *Prof Exp:* Staff engr, Procter & Gamble, 79-81, group leader, 81-85. *Mem:* Soc Cosmetic Chemists; Am Inst Chem Engrs; Am Chem Soc. *Res:* Development of new and improved consumer products; surfactant-based and emulsion products; tablet products; specializing in effervescent tablets. *Mailing Add:* 8681 Twilight Tear Lane Cincinnati OH 45249. *E-Mail:* ahrau@ix.netcom.com

RAU, BANTWAL RAMAKRISHNA, COMPUTER SCIENCE, COMPUTER ENGINEERING. *Current Pos:* SR RES SCIENTIST, HEWLETT PACKARD LABS. *Personal Data:* b Lucknow, India, Feb 13, 51; m 75; c 1. *Educ:* Indian Inst Technol, Madras, BTech, 72; Stanford Univ, MS, 73, PhD(elec eng), 77. *Prof Exp:* Mem tech staff comput design, Palyn Assocs, Inc, 73-74; res asst elec eng, Stanford Univ, 75-77; asst prof elec eng, Univ Ill, Urbana-Champaign, 77; mgr performance accelerators, Elxsi, Santa Clara, Calif. *Concurrent Pos:* Assoc consult, Palyn Assocs, Inc, 78. *Mem:* Inst Elec & Electronics Engrs; Asn Comput Mach. *Res:* Computer architecture; computer performance evaluation; applied queueing theory. *Mailing Add:* Hewlett Packard Labs 1501 Page Mill Rd Bldg 3L Palo Alto CA 94304

RAU, CARL, CONDENSED MATTER PHYSICS. *Current Pos:* assoc prof, 83-84, PROF PHYSICS, RICE UNIV, 84- *Educ:* Tech Univ Munich, Ger, BS, 63, dipl physics, 67, PhD(physics), 70. *Prof Exp:* Asst & res scientist, Ludwigs-Maximilians Univ, 71-76, head, Res Group Solid State Physics, 71, fac bd mem natural sci, 72, sr res scientist, & directive head, Res Group Surface Physics, 76-79; res scientist ion scattering neutralization & optical spectroscopy, Bell Labs, 79-80. *Concurrent Pos:* Mem res coun, Rice Univ, 84, Rice Quantum Inst, 85; organizer ion & atom-surface interactions in metals, Am Phys Soc, 92, magnetic interfaces, Mat Res Soc, 93. *Mem:* Ger Phys Soc; Am Phys Soc; Am Vacuum Soc; Mat Res Soc. *Res:* Physics; author of over 100 publications. *Mailing Add:* Rice Univ Dept Physics Weiss Sch Natural Sci PO Box 1892 Houston TX 77251

RAU, ERIC, INDUSTRIAL CHEMISTRY, QUALITY ASSURANCE. *Current Pos:* PRES, ERA CONSULT, 96- *Personal Data:* b Weissenfels, Ger, Sept 25, 28; US citizen; m 55, Anita D Goldrich; c Allen H & Gerald S. *Educ:* NY Univ, BA, 51, PhD(phys chem), 55. *Prof Exp:* Chemist, US Naval Air Rocket Test Sta, 50-52; from engr to sr engr, Bettis Atomic Power Lab, Westinghouse Elec Corp, 55-60; res chemist, Cent Res FMC Corp, Princeton, NJ, 60-63, supvr, Inorg Chem Div, 63-65, mgr, Phys Chem Sect, Inorg Res & Develop Dept, 65-74, asst dir process develop, Indust Chem Div, Res & Develop Dept, 74-78; dir res & develop, Technol, Conversion Systs Inc, 78-81, vpres, 81-84, dir technol, 81; dir, Chem Div, Spex Indust, 85; asst vpres, EA Labs, 86; asst dir, lab & qual assurance, NJ Dept Environ Protection, 87-96. *Concurrent Pos:* Mem, Fed Adv Comt, Nat Accreditation Environ Labs, 92-93, State Focus Group Environ Lab Accreditation, 93-95, dir, 95- *Mem:* Am Chem Soc; Asn Res Dirs; fel Am Inst Chemists. *Res:* Phosphorus; alkali salts; corrosion; high temperature reactions; coal; electrochemistry; waste management and ultimate disposal; pozzalanic reactions; alkaline earth salts; quality assurance; environmental analysis laboratory certification. *Mailing Add:* 17 Pine Knoll Lawrenceville NJ 08648. *Fax:* 609-882-6072; *E-Mail:* yippee2345@aol.com

RAU, GREGORY HUDSON, BIOGEOCHEMISTRY, ISOTOPES. *Current Pos:* RES ASSOC, AMES RES CTR, NASA, 81-; RES SCIENTIST, UNIV CALIF, SANTA CRUZ, 85-; PARTICIPATING GUEST, LAWRENCE LIVERMORE NAT LAB, LIVERMORE, 91- *Personal Data:* b Tacoma, Wash, Dec 14, 48; m 91, Verena Carol. *Educ:* Western Wash Univ, BA, 71; Univ Wash, MS, 74, PhD(ecol), 79. *Honors & Awards:* Antarctic Serv Medal, NSF, 86. *Prof Exp:* Res asst, Western Wash Univ, 71 & Univ Wash, 73-78; res assoc, Ore State Univ, 79; postdoctoral scholar, Univ Calif, Los Angeles, 79-81. *Concurrent Pos:* Consult, Coop Fisheries Unit, Univ Wash, 72, Global Geochem Corp, 80-81, Southern Calif Coastal Water Res Proj, 81, Aqua Resources Inc, 84, Us Geol Surv, 85, Westec Serv Inc, 85 & Intl Atomic Energy Agency, 86-88; assoc res scientist, Tiburon Ctr Environ Studies, 83-85. *Mem:* Am Soc Limnol & Oceanog; Am Geophys Union; AAAS; Oceanog Soc; Sigma Xi. *Res:* Carbon and nitrogen flow and cycling in past and present environments; microbial, plant, animal and human biology, ecology, and nutrition; interpretation of preceding based on stable isotope natural abundances. *Mailing Add:* L-256 LLNL 7000 East Ave Livermore CA 94550-9900. *Fax:* 510-422-6339; *E-Mail:* rau4@llnl.gov

RAU, LISA FAY, natural language processing, information retrieval, for more information see previous edition

RAU, MANFRED ERNST, PARASITOLOGY, BEHAVIORAL ECOLOGY. *Current Pos:* Fel, 69-70, res assoc, 70-75, asst prof, 75-79, ASSOC PROF, INST PARASITOL, MCGILL UNIV, 79- *Personal Data:* b May 30, 42; m 69; c 1. *Educ:* Univ Western Ont, BSc, 65, PhD(parasitol), 70. *Mem:* Can Soc Zool; Am Soc Parasitologists; Am Mosquito Control Asn. *Res:* Behavioral ecology of parasite transmission; biological control of mosquitoes. *Mailing Add:* Dept Natural Res Sci MacDonald Campus McGill Univ 21111 Ste Anne de Bellevue PQ H9X 3V9 Can

RAU, R RONALD, PHYSICS, ACCELERATORS. *Current Pos:* RETIRED. *Personal Data:* b Tacoma, Wash, Sept 1, 20; m 44, Maryjane Uhrlaub; c Whitney & Liltie. *Educ:* Col Puget Sound, BS, 41; Calif Inst Technol, MS, 43, PhD(physics), 48. *Honors & Awards:* Alexander von Humboldt Sr US Scientist Award, Hambur, Ger, 88. *Prof Exp:* Physicist, Calif Inst Technol, 43-45; from instr to asst prof physics, Princeton Univ, 47-56; from assoc physicist to sr physicist, Brookhaven Nat Lab, 56-70, sr physicist, 62-90, chmn dept physics, 66-70, assoc dir high energy physics, 70-81. *Concurrent Pos:* Fulbright res prof, Ecole Polytech, France, 54-55; mem policy comt, Stanford Linear Accelerator Ctr, 67-73; mem prog comt, Los Alamos Meson Physics Fac, 70-74; chmn high energy adv comt, Brookhaven Nat Lab, 70-81; mem high energy physics adv panel, AEC, 70-74; adj prof, Univ Wyo, 70-84; mem bd trustees, Univ Puget Sound, 78-84; vis prof, Desy Lab, Hamburg, Ger, 84-85 & Mass Inst Technol, 84-85. *Mem:* Am Phys Soc; NY Acad Sci. *Res:* Cloud chamber studies of cosmic rays at high altitudes and of heavy mesons; experimental high energy particle physics; bubble chambers; strong interactions; resonance production; particle accelerators; superconducting magnets. *Mailing Add:* Brookhaven Nat Lab Upton NY 11973. *E-Mail:* rau@bnldag.ags.bnl.gov

RAU, RICHARD RAYMOND, PHYSICS, COMPONENT ENGINEERING. *Current Pos:* SR STAFF ENGR COMPONENTS & CIRCUITS, PERKIN-ELMER CO, DANBURY, 78- *Personal Data:* b Philadelphia, Pa, Apr 17, 28; m 54; c 4. *Educ:* Muhlenberg Col, BS, 49; Yale Univ, MS, 50; Univ Pa, PhD(solid state physics), 55. *Prof Exp:* Sr engr semiconductor develop, Sperry Rand Corp, 56-59; dir eng, Nat Semiconductor Corp, 59-67; mgr, Eng Digital Integrated Circuit, Transitron Electronic Corp, 67-70; mgr prod procurement electronic components, Raytheon Co, 71-72; mgr, Eng Hybrid Circuits, Control Prod Div, Bell & Howell Co, 72-78. *Concurrent Pos:* Asst instr, Univ Bridgeport, 59; lectr, Univ Conn, 65-67. *Mem:* Am Phys Soc; Inst Elec & Electronics Engrs; Res Soc Am; Int Soc Hybrid Mfrs. *Res:* Silicon devices. *Mailing Add:* Optical Systs Hughes Danbury 100 Wooster Heights Rd Danbury CT 06810

RAU, WELDON WILLIS, MICROPALEONTOLOGY, BIOSTRATIGRAPHY. *Current Pos:* CONSULT, PAC, NORTHWEST & ALASKA BIOSTRATIG, 82- *Personal Data:* b Tacoma, Wash, Jan 20, 21; m 44, Jane F Hudson; c Gregory H. *Educ:* Col Puget Sound, BS, 43; Univ Iowa, MS, 46, PhD(paleont), 50. *Prof Exp:* Asst geol, Univ Iowa, 43-47; from instr to asst prof, Col Puget Sound, 47-50; geologist stratig micropaleont, Geol Div, US Geol Surv, 50-60, consult geol, 60-82; geologist, Div Geol & Earth Resources, Wash State Dept Natural Resources, 60-92. *Concurrent Pos:* Consult, Wash State Dept Natural Resources, 92- *Mem:* Paleont Soc; Geol Soc Am; Soc Econ Paleont & Mineral; Am Asn Petrol Geol. *Res:* Tertiary Foraminifera of the Pacific Northwest and Southeast Alaska; stratigraphic micropaleontology of West Coast Tertiary rocks. *Mailing Add:* 3035 Edgewood Dr Olympia WA 98501

RAUB, HARRY LYMAN, III, PHYSICS. *Current Pos:* from asst prof to prof, 47-84, EMER PROF PHYSICS, MUHLENBERG COL, 84. *Personal Data:* b Lancaster, Pa, Oct 22, 19; m 47, Sedora E Locke; c Thomas G & David A. *Educ:* Franklin & Marshall Col, 41; Cornell Univ, PhD(exp physics), 47. *Prof Exp:* Asst, Cornell Univ, 41-47, res assoc, 47. *Concurrent Pos:* Vis prof, Wesleyan Univ, 65-70, Ariz State Univ, 71. *Mem:* Am Phys Soc; Am Asn Physics Teachers; Sigma Xi. *Res:* Elastic losses in high polymers; study of sound velocities with acoustic interferometer; x-ray diffraction. *Mailing Add:* 2872 Reading Rd Allentown PA 18103

RAUB, THOMAS JEFFREY, MEMBRANE PROTEIN, ENDOCYTOSIS. *Current Pos:* RES SCIENTIST, DRUG DELIVERY SYSTS RES, UPJOHN CO, 85- *Educ:* Univ Fla, PhD(cell biol), 82. *Res:* Protein sorting. *Mailing Add:* Upjohn Co 301 Henrietta St Kalamazoo MI 49007-4940

RAUB, WILLIAM F, PHYSIOLOGY, COMPUTER SCIENCE. *Current Pos:* SCI ADV TO ADMINR, US ENVIRON PROTECT AGENCY, 92- *Personal Data:* b Alden Station, Pa, Nov 25, 39; m 64; c 3. *Educ:* Wilkes Col, AB, 61; Univ Pa, PhD(physiol), 65. *Prof Exp:* NSF predoctoral fel, Univ Pa, 61-64, Pa Plan fel, 64-66; health sci adminr, Div Res Facil & Resources, NIH, Bethesda, Md, 66-69, chief, Biotechnol Resources Br, Div Res Resources, 69-75, assoc dir extramural & collab progs, Nat Eye Inst, 75-78, assoc dir extramural res, 78-83, dep dir extramural res, 83-86, dep dir, 86-92. *Res:* Automated information-handling in biology and medicine and respiratory physiology. *Mailing Add:* Dept Health & Human Servs 200 Independence Ave SW Washington DC 20201

RAUBER, LAUREN A, THEORETICAL PHYSICS, SOLID STATE PHYSICS. *Current Pos:* COMPUT PHYSICIST, APPL THEORET PHYSICS, LOS ALAMOS NAT LAB, 85- *Personal Data:* b St Louis, Mo, May 18, 46. *Educ:* Emory Univ, BS, 68; Univ Md, MS, 72, PhD(solid state physics), 76. *Prof Exp:* Staff scientist, G&G Corp, 77-85. *Mem:* Am Phys Soc; Am Asn Physics Teachers. *Mailing Add:* Los Alamos Nat Lab Div F669 PO Box 1663 Los Alamos NM 87545

RAUCH, ALBERT LEE, RECEPTOR & ENZYME REGULATION, CARDIOVASCULAR DISEASES. *Current Pos:* VPRES RES DEPT, EVEREN SECURITES. *Personal Data:* b Chicago, Ill, Oct 14, 53; m 75, Colleen E Lennon; c Sarah E, David A & Rebecca A. *Educ:* Univ SDak, BS, 76, MA, 78; Emory Univ, PhD(exp pathol), 83; Rensselaer Polytech Inst, MBA, 93. *Prof Exp:* Res assoc, Dept Med, Sect Nephrol, Bowman Gray Sch Med, Wake Forest Univ, 85-86, res instr, 86-87, res asst prof, 87-89; sr res scientist, Dept Metab Dis, Pfizer Cent Res, 91-, group leader, 92- *Concurrent Pos:* Lee Talley fel, Emory Univ, 82-83; NIH fel, Bowman Gray Sch Med, Wake Forest Univ, 83-85. *Mem:* Am Heart Asn; Am Chem Soc; Am Soc Physiol. *Res:* Identify new therapeutic targets, non-peptide ligands of inhibitors of these targets and develop these agents into treatments for the treatment of cardiovascular disease; author of over 23 publications; granted 2 patents. *Mailing Add:* 715 Meadows Rd Geneva IL 60134

RAUCH, DONALD J(OHN), ELECTRICAL ENGINEERING. *Current Pos:* PRES, EVOLVING TECHNOL CO, 79- *Personal Data:* b St Peters, Mo, Oct 20, 35; m 58; c 2. *Educ:* Washington Univ, St Louis, BS, 57; Mich State Univ, MS, 60, PhD(elec eng), 63. *Prof Exp:* Radar engr, Emerson Elec Mfg Co, 57-58; sr lectr elec eng, SDak State Col, 58-59; systs res assoc, Planning Res Corp, 63-67; sr engr guid & control systs, Litton Industs, 67-71; vpres & dir, Sysdyne, Inc, 71-76, pres, 76-78. *Concurrent Pos:* Sr lectr, Univ Southern Calif, 65-; chmn session on state space synthesis, Asilomar Conf Circuits & Systs, 70; mem tech prog comt, Joint Nat Conf Major Systs, 71; chmn, Los Angeles Prof Group Circuit Theory. *Mem:* Sr mem Inst Elec & Electronics Engrs. *Res:* Radar cross sections, extended diffraction scattering model for electromagnetic waves to include plasma or multilayered media; adaptive control processes; development of techniques for synthesizing physical systems from a time domain model. *Mailing Add:* Evolving Tech Co PO Box 60010 San Diego CA 92166

RAUCH, EMIL B(RUNO), ORGANIC CHEMISTRY. *Current Pos:* RETIRED. *Personal Data:* b Friedland, Czech, mar 19, 19; nat US; m 47, Erika H Hoffmann; c Michele & Annette. *Educ:* Univ Heidelberg, PhD, 53. *Prof Exp:* Res assoc org chem, Wash Univ, 53-55; res chemist, Indust Photo Div, GAF Corp, 55-64, res assoc, 64-67, mgr color res & develop, 67-74, dir res & develop, 74-77, sr scientist, 77-80; sr scientist, Anitec Image Corp, 80-88. *Mem:* Am Chem Soc; Soc Ger Chem; Soc Photog Sci & Engr. *Mailing Add:* 5 Perkins Ave Binghamton NY 13901-1822

RAUCH, FRED D, HORTICULTURE, PLANT PHYSIOLOGY. *Current Pos:* RETIRED. *Personal Data:* b Rainier, Ore, Jan 17, 31; m 58; c 2. *Educ:* Ore State Univ, BS, 56, MS, 63; Iowa State Univ, PhD(hort, plant physiol), 67. *Prof Exp:* Exp farm technician, Ore State Univ, 58-60, asst hort, Mid-Columbia Exp Sta, Hood River, 60-63; instr, Iowa State Univ, 63-67; asst prof, Miss State Univ, 67-70; from asst specialist to specialist, Dept Hort, Univ Hawaii, 70-96. *Mem:* Int Plant Propagators Soc; Am Soc Hort Sci; Int Palm Soc. *Res:* Stock-scion relationships; plant nutrition; growth regulators; herbicides. *Mailing Add:* 20301 NE 10094th Ave Battleground WA 98604

RAUCH, HAROLD, ZOOLOGY. *Current Pos:* From instr to assoc prof, 50-60, chmn dept, 71-74, PROF ZOOL, UNIV MASS, AMHERST, 60- *Personal Data:* b New York, NY, Oct 13, 25; m 52; c 3. *Educ:* Queens Col, NY, BS, 44; Univ Ill, MS, 47; Brown Univ, PhD(biol), 50. *Mem:* Genetics Soc Am; Am Soc Zool. *Res:* Mammalian physiological genetics; nervous system, pigmentation and copper metabolism in the mouse. *Mailing Add:* 101 Red Gate Lane Amherst MA 01002

RAUCH, HELENE COBEN, IMMUNOLOGY, NEUROIMMUNOLOGY. *Current Pos:* ASSOC PROF IMMUNOL, WAYNE STATE UNIV, 75- *Personal Data:* b Los Angeles, Calif; c 4. *Educ:* Univ Calif, Los Angeles, BA, 51, PhD(microbiol), 58. *Prof Exp:* Bacteriologist, Los Angeles Co Dept Pub Health, 51-52; part-time asst, Univ Calif, Los Angeles, 53-57; res assoc, Dept Allergy & Immunol, Palo Alto Med Res Found, 57-60; res assoc, Div Infectious Dis, Sch Med, Stanford Univ, 60-61, prin investr, Nat Inst Neurol Dis & Stroke Grant & res assoc, Dept Med Microbiol, 64-75. *Concurrent Pos:* Nat Multiple Sclerosis Soc fel, Sch Med, Stanford Univ, 61-64. *Mem:* AAAS; Am Soc Microbiol; Sigma Xi; Am Asn Immunologists; Tissue Cult Asn. *Res:* Auto-allergic diseases, especially experimental allergic encephalomyelitis; immunopathology; cellular hypersensitivity; multiple sclerosis. *Mailing Add:* Dept Immunol & Microbiol Wayne State Univ 540 E Camfield Detroit MI 48201-1928

RAUCH, HENRY WILLIAM, HYDROGEOLOGY, GEOCHEMISTRY. *Current Pos:* PROF GEOL, WVA UNIV, 70- *Personal Data:* b Amsterdam, NY, Oct 23, 42; m 71; c 1. *Educ:* Alfred Univ, BA, 65; Pa State Univ, PhD(geochem), 72. *Concurrent Pos:* Hydrogeol consult; mem, WVa Reclamation Bd Rev, 78-84 & 90- *Mem:* Geol Soc Am; Int Asn Hydrogeol; Nat Groundwater Asn; fel Nat Speleol Soc. *Res:* Ground water hydrology and aqueous geochemistry; karst hydrogeology; ground water pollution; ground water exploration; effects of coal mining on ground water; hydrogeologic methods for natural gas exploration; lineaments. *Mailing Add:* Geog & Geol White Hall Morgantown WV 26506-0001

RAUCH, HERBERT EMIL, SIGNAL PROCESSING, OPTIMAL CONTROL. *Current Pos:* CONSULT SCIENTIST & SR MEM RES LAB, LOCKHEED PALO ALTO RES LAB, 62- *Personal Data:* b St Louis, Mo, Oct 6, 35; m 61; c 4. *Educ:* Calif Inst Technol, BS, 57; Stanford Univ, MS, 58, PhD(elec eng), 62. *Honors & Awards:* Centennial Medal, Inst Elec & Electronics Engrs, 84; Space Shuttle Award, Am Inst Aeronaut & Astronaut, 84. *Prof Exp:* Mem tech staff, Hughes Aircraft Co, 58-62. *Concurrent Pos:*

Assoc prof, San Jose State Univ, 68-70; ed, J Astronaut Sci, 80-86 & Inst Elec & Electronics Engrs Control Systs Magazine, 85-93; chmn, Math Control Comt, Int Fedn Automatic Control, 84-87; mem publ comt, Am Inst Aeronaut & Astronaut, 80-91; founding ed, Inst Elec & Electronics Engrs Transactions on Neural Networks, 89-91. *Mem:* Fel Inst Elec & Electronics Engrs; fel Am Inst Aeronaut & Astronaut; fel Am Astronaut Soc (vpres, 80-84); fel AAAS; Inst Elec & Electronics Engrs Control Systs Soc (pres, 95). *Res:* Optimal estimation and control; signal processing; astrodynamics; guidance; expert systems; neural networks. *Mailing Add:* 401 Dracena Lane Los Altos CA 94022

RAUCH, JEFFREY BARON, MATHEMATICAL PHYSICS. *Current Pos:* from asst prof to assoc prof, 71-81, chmn, Dept Math, 90-91, PROF MATH, UNIV MICH, ANN ARBOR, 81- *Personal Data:* b New York, NY, Nov 29, 45; c 1. *Educ:* Harvard Univ, AB, 67; NY Univ, PhD(math), 71. *Prof Exp:* Instr math, NY Univ, 68-71. *Concurrent Pos:* Vis mem, Inst Advan Study, 75-76, Inst Advan Sci Studies, France, 78-79 & Ecole Polytech, Paris, 92-93; assoc prof, Higher Normal Sch, France, 85-86. *Mem:* Am Math Soc. *Res:* Hyperbolic partial differential equations. *Mailing Add:* Dept Math Angell Hall Univ Mich Ann Arbor MI 48104

RAUCH, LAWRENCE L(EE), APPLIED MATHEMATICS. *Current Pos:* from asst prof to prof aeronaut eng, Univ Mich, 49-79, chmn nuclear eng prog, 51-52, instrumentation prog, 52-63 & mgt sci prog, 58-59, chmn comput, info & control eng, 71-76, assoc chmn, dept Elec & Comput Eng, 72-76, EMER PROF ENG, UNIV MICH, ANN ARBOR, 79- *Personal Data:* b Los Angeles, Calif, May 1, 19; m 61, Norma Cable; c Lauren & Maury. *Educ:* Univ Southern Calif, AB, 41; Princeton Univ, MA, 48, PhD(math), 49. *Honors & Awards:* Spec Award, Inst Elec & Electronics Engrs, 57; Annual Award, Nat Telemetering Conf, 60; Eckman Award, Instrument Soc Am, 66; Pioneer Award, Int Telemetering Conf, 85. *Prof Exp:* Asst, Uranium Separation Proj, Princeton Univ, 42, & anti-aircraft fire control, 42-43; instr math, 42-49, instr pre-radar sch, 43-44, res supvr radio telemetering systs for aircraft, 44-46, supvr air blast telemetering, Oper Crossroads, Bikini, 46, nonlinear differential equations proj, US Off Naval Res, 47-49. *Concurrent Pos:* Consult, 45-; mem res adv comt commun, instrumentation & data processing, NASA, 63-70; vis prof, Ecole Nationale Superieure de l'Aeronautique et de l'Espace, Toulouse, France, 70, Univ Tokyo, 78 & Calif Inst Technol, 77-85. *Mem:* Fel AAAS; Am Math Soc; fel Inst Elec & Electronics Engrs; Am Inst Aeronaut & Astronaut. *Res:* Radio telemetry and communication theory; mathematical models and physical realizations of communication operations; communications engineering; deep space communications. *Mailing Add:* 759 N Citrus Ave Los Angeles CA 90038-3401. *Fax:* 213-934-7504; *E-Mail:* lawrence.l.rauch@jpl.nasa.gov

RAUCH, RICHARD TRAVIS, GRAVITATION THEORY & COSMOLOGY, SYSTEMS ENGINEERING-ANALYSIS & ADVANCED CONCEPT DEVELOPMENT. *Current Pos:* SR SCIENTIST, DEFENSE GROUP INC, 88- *Personal Data:* b New Orleans, La, Nov 18, 55. *Educ:* La State Univ, Baton Rouge, BS, 77; State Univ NY, Stony Brook, MA, 79, PhD(theoret physics), 82. *Honors & Awards:* Sustained Serv Award, Am Inst Aeronaut & Astronaut, 86. *Prof Exp:* Exp res asst, Dept Physics & Astron, La State Univ, 74-77; teaching asst, Dept Physics, State Univ NY, Stony Brook, 77-78, res asst physics, Inst Theoret Physics, 78-82; physicist, R&D Assocs, 83-88. *Concurrent Pos:* Consult to R&D Assocs, Space Shuttle Prog, Rockwell Int, 87-88, independent consult, 88. *Mem:* Am Phys Soc; Am Inst Aeronaut & Astronaut; Space Studies Inst. *Res:* Systems engineering-analysis and advanced concept development for a variety of space, strategic and tactical systems; development of extended theories of gravitation and an assessment of their astrophysical and cosmological consequences and their general experimental viability. *Mailing Add:* 429 Santa Monica Blvd Suite 420 Santa Monica CA 90401

RAUCH, SOL, APPLY TECHNOLOGY TO DEFINE PRODUCT DEVELOPMENT OPPORTUNITIES, SIGNAL PROCESSING IN RADIO NAVIGATION SYSTEMS. *Current Pos:* Design engr, Avionics Div, Can Marconi Co, 62-65, proj engr, 66-71, prod mgr, 71-78, group mgr, 78-90, gen mgr, 90-93, VPRES AEROSPACE, CAN MARCONI CO, 93- *Personal Data:* b Horodenko, Poland, Apr 22, 40; Can citizen; m 71, Helen Bergman; c Karen. *Educ:* McGill Univ, BS, 62, MS, 66. *Concurrent Pos:* Lectr, Loyola Col, Montreal, 73-78; auxilary prof, McGill Univ, 75-78. *Mem:* Inst Elec & Electronics Engrs; Soc Info Displays; Asn Prof Engrs Ont. *Res:* Display systems for high ambient illumination environments; ruggedness, small size, intelligence and high brightness and contrast ratio. *Mailing Add:* 16 Parkmount Crescent Nepean ON K2H 5T4 Can. *Fax:* 613-592-7467; *E-Mail:* sravch@kan.marconi.ca

RAUCH, STEWART EMMART, JR, ORGANIC CHEMISTRY. *Current Pos:* RETIRED. *Personal Data:* b Bethlehem, Pa, Aug 29, 21; m 47; c 4. *Educ:* Moravian Col, BSc, 42; Lehigh Univ, MS, 47. *Prof Exp:* Instr meteorol, Univ Va, 42-43; from asst prof to assoc prof chem, Moravian Col, 47-62; res engr, Bethlehem Steel Corp, 62-77. *Concurrent Pos:* Consult, 77-88. *Mem:* AAAS. *Res:* Antimalarials; developments commercially marketed; photoelectric colorimeter; portable potentiometer; portable wheatstone bridge; self-contained portable gas chromatograph; electronic clinical thermometer; chemical instrumentation; internal ballistics. *Mailing Add:* 5521 Old Bethlehem Pike Bethlehem PA 18015

RAUCHER, STANLEY, SYNTHETIC ORGANIC CHEMISTRY. *Current Pos:* Asst prof, 75-81, ASSOC PROF CHEM, UNIV WASH, 81- *Personal Data:* b St Paul, Minn, Nov 4, 48. *Educ:* Univ Minn, BA, 70, PhD(chem), 73. *Mem:* Am Chem Soc. *Res:* Synthesis of natural products. *Mailing Add:* Dept Chem BG10 Univ Wash Seattle WA 98195

RAUCHFUSS, THOMAS BIGLEY, INORGANIC CHEMISTRY, CATALYSIS. *Current Pos:* PROF CHEM, UNIV ILL, 78- *Personal Data:* b Baltimore, Md, Sept 11, 49; m 77; c 2. *Educ:* Univ Puget Sound, BS, 71; Wash State Univ, PhD(inorg chem), 75. *Prof Exp:* Res fel chem, Australian Nat Univ, 75-77. *Concurrent Pos:* Fel, A P Sloan Found, 83; vis prof, Univ Auckland, 85, Univ Louis Pasteur-Strasbourg, 92, Univ Karlsruhe, 93; J S Guggenheim fel, 92. *Mem:* Am Chem Soc; Royal Soc Chem; Mat Res Soc. *Res:* Preparative inorganic; homogeneous catalysis; organometallic; ligand design and synthesis; organic synthesis with metal ions; phosphorus and sulfur chemistry; desulfurization chemistry; metal clusters. *Mailing Add:* Univ Ill Box 21-1 Noyes Lab 600 S Matthews Urbana IL 61801-3617

RAUCKHORST, WILLIAM H, LOW TEMPERATURE PHYSICS. *Current Pos:* ASSOC PROVOST & PROF PHYSICS, MIAMI UNIV, 85- *Personal Data:* b Covington, Ky, Sept 9, 40; m 64, Elaine Krager; c Cynthia, Jane & Julie. *Educ:* Thomas More Col, BA, 62; Univ Cincinnati, PhD(physics), 67. *Prof Exp:* Asst prof physics & chmn dept, Bellarmine Col, Ky, 67-71, assoc prof physics & chmn div natural sci, 71-72; planner phys sci prog, Sangamon State Univ, 72-73, coordr, 73-75, assoc prof phys sci, 72-76; prog mgr, Fac Develop Prog, US Dept Energy, Washington, DC, 76-78; head, Col/Univ Progs Sect, Argonne Nat Lab, 78-85; prog dir, Undergrad Sci, Eng & Math Educ, NSF, 90-92. *Mem:* Am Asn Physics Teachers; Sigma Xi. *Res:* Specific heat studies; superconductivity; energy education. *Mailing Add:* Miami Univ Oxford OH 45056

RAUDORF, THOMAS WALTER, PHYSICS, NUCLEAR INSTRUMENTATION. *Current Pos:* staff physicist, 75-85, MGR, DETECTOR RES & DEVELOP, EG&G ORTEC INC, 85- *Personal Data:* b Berlin, Ger, May 6, 43; m 75, Claudia Ditchburn; c Thomas J. *Educ:* Concordia Univ, BSc, 64; McGill Univ, MSc, 67, PhD(physics), 71. *Prof Exp:* Staff physicist, Simtec Industs Ltd, 71-73 & Electronic Assocs Can Ltd, 73-75. *Mem:* Can Asn Physicists; Am Phys Soc; sr mem Inst Elec & Electronics Engrs. *Res:* Rectifying and ohmic contacts on semiconductors; charge carrier transport in semiconductors; semiconductor surface physics; deep levels in semiconductors; semiconductor crystal growth. *Mailing Add:* 110 E Morningside Dr Oak Ridge TN 37830

RAUFF, JAMES VERNON, FORMAL LANGUAGE THEORY. *Current Pos:* dir, Writing Across the Disciplines, 92-94, PROF MATH, MILLIKIN UNIV, 88- *Personal Data:* b Detroit, Mich, Dec 21, 46; m 85; c 1. *Educ:* Albion Col, BA, 69; Univ Wyo, MA, 71; Loyola Univ, Chicago, MA, 81; Northwestern Univ, PhD(ling), 88. *Prof Exp:* Prof math, Col Lake Co, 73-88. *Mem:* Europ Asn Theoret Comput Sci; Am Math Soc; Nat Coun Teachers Math; Asn Comput Mach; Asn Comput Ling. *Res:* Regulated rewriting in formal languages; epistemic logic and constructivist learning; machine translation; DNA computing. *Mailing Add:* 111 S Westdale Decatur IL 62522. *E-Mail:* rauff@millikin.edu

RAUH, ROBERT DAVID, JR, ELECTROCHEMISTRY, PHOTOCHEMISTRY. *Current Pos:* sr scientist, 74-76, prin scientist chem, 76-79, DIR RES, EIC LAB, INC, 79- *Personal Data:* b Medford, Mass, Nov 15, 43; m 69; c 1. *Educ:* Bowdoin Col, AB, 65; Wesleyan Univ, MA, 68; Princeton Univ, PhD(chem), 72. *Prof Exp:* Fel chem, Brandeis Univ, 72-74. *Mem:* Am Chem Soc; Electrochem Soc; Sigma Xi. *Res:* Chemical aspects of energy conversion; high energy density batteries; photochemical storage of solar energy; photovoltaic devices; chemical sensors. *Mailing Add:* 17 Converse Ave Newton MA 02158-2503

RAUHUT, MICHAEL MCKAY, ORGANIC CHEMISTRY, PHOSPHORUS & PHOTO CHEMISTRY. *Current Pos:* Chemist, Cent Res Div, Am Cyanamid Co, Conn, 55-62, sr res chemist, 62, group leader, 63-70, res mgr, Chem Res Div, 70-81, mgr venture technol, Bound Brook, 81-82, mgr, plastics additives & resins res, Stamford Labs, 83-84, mgr regulatory affairs, 85-89, MGR NEW TECHNOL APPRAISAL, AM CYANAMID CO, 90- *Personal Data:* b New York, NY, Dec 4, 30; m 57; c 3. *Educ:* Univ Nev, BS, 52; Univ NC, PhD(chem), 55. *Honors & Awards:* IR-100 Award, Indust Res, Inc, 70. *Mem:* Am Chem Soc. *Res:* Physical organic chemistry; mechanisms of aromatic nucleophilic substitution and organophosphorus reactions; mechanisms of chemiluminescent reactions. *Mailing Add:* 201 Range Rd Wilton CT 06897-3923

RAUK, ARVI, CHEMISTRY. *Current Pos:* asst prof chem, 70-77, assoc prof, 77-80, PROF CHEM, UNIV CALGARY, 80- *Personal Data:* b Estonia, Sept 30, 42; Can citizen; m 68; c 2. *Educ:* Queen's Univ, Ont, BSc, 65, PhD(chem), 68. *Prof Exp:* Nat Res Coun Can fel, Princeton Univ, 68-70. *Mem:* Am Chem Soc; Am Phys Soc; Chem Inst Can. *Res:* Theoretical and experimental studies of optical activity of organic and organometallic systems. *Mailing Add:* Dept Chem Univ Calgary Calgary AB T2N 1N4 Can

RAULET, DAVID HENRI, T-CELL ACTIVATION & DEVELOPMENT. *Current Pos:* ASSOC PROF BIOL, MASS INST TECHNOL, 83- *Personal Data:* b June 3, 54. *Educ:* Mass Inst Technol, PhD(biol), 81. *Concurrent Pos:* Cancer Res Inst investr award. *Mem:* Am Asn Immunologists. *Mailing Add:* Dept Immunol 489LSA Univ Calif Berkeley CA 94720-3200

RAULINS, NANCY REBECCA, ORGANIC CHEMISTRY. *Current Pos:* from instr to prof, 48-79, EMER PROF CHEM, UNIV WYO, 80- *Personal Data:* b Dickson, Tenn, Oct 17, 16. *Educ:* Tulane Univ, BA, 36, MS, 38; Univ Wyo, PhD(chem), 53. *Prof Exp:* Teacher high sch, La, 38-39, sci & math, All Saints Col, 39-41; teacher physics & chem, Spartanburg Jr Col, 41-42;

chemist, Chickasaw Ord Works, 42-43; head dept chem, Lambuth Col, 43-46. *Mem:* Am Chem Soc. *Res:* Physical and chemical analytical methods in organic research; mechanism of reactions; hydrogen bonding in heterocyclic systems. *Mailing Add:* 466 N Ninth St Laramie WY 82070

RAULSTON, JAMES CHESTER, HORTICULTURE. *Current Pos:* PROF ORNAMENTAL HORT, NC STATE UNIV, 76- *Personal Data:* b Enid, Okla, Nov 24, 40. *Educ:* Okla State Univ, BS, 62; Univ MD, MS, 66, PhD(hort), 69. *Prof Exp:* Instr plant sci, Inst Appl Agr, Univ Md, 65-66; asst prof ornamental hort, Agr Res & Educ Ctr, Univ Fla, 69-72; assoc prof ornamental hort, Tex A&M Univ, 72-75. *Mem:* Am Soc Hort Sci; Int Soc Hort Sci. *Res:* Research in production and utilization of perennial landscape plants, including production, marketing and establishment of woody plants; production and use of native plants; physiology of landscape plants. *Mailing Add:* Dept Hort NC State Univ Box 7609 Raleigh NC 27695-0001

RAUN, ARTHUR PHILLIP, ANIMAL NUTRITION. *Current Pos:* RETIRED. *Personal Data:* b Upland, Nebr, Apr, 28, 34; m 58; c 2. *Educ:* Univ Nebr, BS, 55; Iowa State Univ, MS, 56, PhD(animal nutrit), 58. *Prof Exp:* Asst prof chem & physiol, USAF Acad, 59-62; sr scientist, Eli Lilly & Co, 62-68, res scientist, 69-70, head animal sci field res, 71-72, head animal nutrit res, Lilly Res Labs, 72-92. *Mem:* Am Soc Animal Sci. *Res:* Ruminant nutrition, specifically action of anabolic compounds in ruminants; ruminant bloat and rumen microbial metabolism. *Mailing Add:* 26255 County Rd 25/ 41 Elbert CO 80106-9751

RAUN, EARLE SPANGLER, ENVIRONMENTAL SCIENCE GENERAL, AGRICULTURE GENERAL. *Current Pos:* OWNER & PRES, PEST MGT CO, 83- *Personal Data:* b Sioux City, Iowa, Aug 28, 24; m 46, Georgia A Hart; c Michele A, Nancy L & Patricia A. *Educ:* Iowa State Col, BS, 46, MS, 50, PhD, 54. *Honors & Awards:* Distinguished Entomologist, Am Registry Prof Entomologists, 86. *Prof Exp:* Entomologist, Bur Entom & Plant Quarantine, USDA, Fla, 46-48; exten entomologist, Iowa State Univ, 48-60; res entomologist corn borer invests, Entom Res Div, Agr Res Serv, USDA, 61-66; prof entom, Univ Nebr, Lincoln, 66-74, assoc dir, Nebr Coop Exten Serv, 70-74, chmn dept entom, 66-70; entomologist, Pest Mgt Consults, Inc, 74-83, pres, 80-83. *Concurrent Pos:* Consult, Off Technol Assessment, US Cong, 78-80; Pesticide Users Adv Comt, Environ Protection Agency, 81-; pres, Registry Prof Entom, 81; pres, Entom Soc Am, 83-84. *Mem:* Entom Soc Am; Nat Alliance Independent Crop Consults (pres, 78-80); Am Registry Prof Entomologists (pres, 80). *Res:* Integration of insect population management techniques for grower use in corn, alfalfa, soybeans, and grain sorghum. *Mailing Add:* 3036 Prairie Rd Lincoln NE 68506. *E-Mail:* pm31648@narix.net

RAUN, NED S, ANIMAL NUTRITION, AGRICULTURE. *Current Pos:* vpres progs, Winrock Inst, 78-84, actg pres, 84-85, regional rep Wash, 85-92, SR ASSOC, WINROCK INST, 93- *Personal Data:* b Upland, Nebr, Feb 10, 25; m 46, Esther Zangger; c 6. *Educ:* Univ Nebr, BS, 48; Iowa State Univ, PhD(nutrit), 61. *Hon Degrees:* DSc, Univ Nebr, 84. *Honors & Awards:* Int Animal Agr Award, Am Soc Animal Sci, 84. *Prof Exp:* Animal scientist, Rockefeller Found, 61-64; assoc prof animal nutrit, Okla State Univ, 64-65; animal scientist, Rockefeller Found, 65-76, dir animal sci, Int Ctr Trop Agr, Cali, Colombia, 69-76; chief livestock div, AID, Dept State, 76-78. *Mem:* Fel Am Soc Animal Sci; Latin Am Asn Animal Prod; fel AAAS. *Res:* Ruminant nutrition; pasture and forage utilization. *Mailing Add:* 919 S Woodcrest Stillwater OK 74074-1464. *Fax:* 405-372-1267

RAUP, DAVID MALCOLM, INVERTEBRATE PALEONTOLOGY. *Current Pos:* RETIRED. *Personal Data:* b Boston, Mass, Apr 24, 33; m 56, 87; c 1. *Educ:* Univ Chicago, SB, 53; Harvard Univ, AM, 55, PhD(geol), 57. *Honors & Awards:* Schuchert Award, Paleont Soc, 73. *Prof Exp:* Instr invert paleont, Calif Inst Technol, 56-57; from asst prof to assoc prof geol, Johns Hopkins Univ, 57-65; from assoc prof to prof, Univ Rochester, 66-78, chmn dept, 69-71; res assoc, Univ Chicago, 78-80, prof geophys sci, 80-94, prof conceptual found sci, 81-94, chmn dept, 82-85, prof evolutionary biol, 82-94. *Concurrent Pos:* Grants, Am Asn Petrol Geol, 57, Am Philos Soc, 59, NSF, 61-64, 66-67, 75-81 & Am Chem Soc, 65-71, NASA, 83-; resident mem staff, Morgan State Col, 58; vis prof, Univ Tubingen, 65 & 72 & Univ Chicago, 77 & 78; mem adv panel earth sci, NSF, 70-73 & adv bd syst biol, 82-83; mem vis comt geol sci, Harvard Univ, 77-81 & Univ Colo, 83 & vis comt organismic & evolutionary biol, Harvard Univ, 81-82; cur & chmn, dept geol, Field Mus Hatural Hist, 78-80, dean sci, 80-82; mem, Geol Sci Bd, Nat Acad Sci-Nat Res Coun, 80-82, Space Sci Bd, 86-89, Comt Biodiversity, 87-90, Comn Phys Sci, Math & Resources, 87-90; Swell L Avery distinguished serv prof, Univ Chicago, 84- *Mem:* Nat Acad Sci; Soc Study Evolution; Paleont Soc (pres, 76-77); fel AAAS; Am Soc Naturalists (vpres, 83); Paleont Asn; Sigma Xi; Soc Syst Zool. *Res:* Skeletal mineralogy and crystallography; theoretical morphology; paleoecology; computer applications; evolution; extinction. *Mailing Add:* RR 1 Box 1684 Washington Island WI 54246

RAUP, HUGH MILLER, botany; deceased, see previous edition for last biography

RAUP, OMER BEAVER, GEOLOGY, GEOCHEMISTRY. *Current Pos:* Geologist, 53-72, chief, Chem Resources Br, 72-76, RES GEOLOGIST, US GEOL SURVEY, 76- *Personal Data:* b Washington, DC, July 14, 30; m 60; c 2. *Educ:* Am Univ, BS, 52; Univ Colo, PhD(geol), 62. *Mem:* Am Asn Petrol Geologists; Geol Soc Am; Soc Econ Paleont & Mineral. *Res:* Geology of plateau uranium deposits; quadrangle and reconnaissance mapping of Washington and Oregon; clay mineralogy of redbeds; geology and mineralogy of marine evaporites. *Mailing Add:* 12295 W Applewood Knolls Dr Lakewood CO 80215

RAUP, ROBERT BRUCE, JR, GEOLOGY. *Current Pos:* Geologist, Geol Div, 52-70, asst chief geologist environ geol, 70-74, GEOLOGIST, GEOL DIV, US GEOL SURV, 74- *Personal Data:* b New York, NY, Nov 4, 29; m 55; c 3. *Educ:* Columbia Univ, BA, 51; Univ Mich, MA, 52. *Mem:* Geol Soc Am. *Res:* Geology of uranium in Precambrian rocks of central Arizona; geology and mineral deposits of southern Arizona; environmental geologic aspects of coal and oil shale, northwestern Colorado. *Mailing Add:* 6570 Crestbrook Dr Morrison CO 80465

RAUSCH, DAVID JOHN, ORGANIC CHEMISTRY, BIOCHEMISTRY. *Current Pos:* from asst prof to assoc prof, 66-71, chmn dept, 77-82, PROF CHEM, ILL BENEDICTINE COL, 71- *Personal Data:* b Aurora, Ill, Oct 24, 40; m 62; c 6. *Educ:* St Procopius Col, BS, 62; Iowa State Univ, PhD(org chem), 66. *Prof Exp:* Res assoc chem, Univ Wis, 65-66. *Concurrent Pos:* Consult, Continental Can Co, 66-67, Argonne Nat Lab, 67-78, Res Corp, 70-72, Amoco Chem Co, 87-, McIntyre Chem, 89- *Mem:* AAAS; Am Chem Soc; Royal Soc Chem. *Res:* Organic reaction mechanisms, including beta-elimination reactions, free radical substitution reactions and pyrolysis reactions; photochemistry of aromatic compounds; nuclear magnetic resonance and spectral interpretation; stereochemistry and conformational analysis. *Mailing Add:* Benedictine Univ Chem Dept Lisle IL 60532-0900

RAUSCH, DOUGLAS ALFRED, ORGANIC CHEMISTRY. *Current Pos:* res mgr, 56-79, DIR PROD STEWARDSHIP, DOW CHEM CO, 79- *Personal Data:* b Ft Wayne, Ind, July 26, 28; m 53; c 3. *Educ:* Univ Ind, BS, 50; Univ Colo, PhD(chem), 54. *Prof Exp:* Asst, Univ Colo, 50-53; res chemist, E I du Pont de Nemours & Co, 53-54. *Mem:* AAAS; Am Chem Soc; Sigma Xi. *Res:* Fluorine and inorganic chemistry. *Mailing Add:* 4518 James Dr Midland MI 48642-3782

RAUSCH, DOYLE W, METAL FIBERS, WIRE REINFORCEMENT. *Current Pos:* asst dir res, 73-76, DIR RES, NAT-STAND CO, 76- *Personal Data:* b Dover, Ohio, May 3, 31; m 64; c 2. *Educ:* Ohio State Univ, BMetE, 61, PhD(metall eng), 65. *Prof Exp:* Asst to plant mgr, US Ceramic Tile Co, 51-56, res asst, 58; tech asst process metall, Battelle Mem Inst, 59-60; res fel metall eng, Ohio State Univ Res Found, 60-64; asst prof, Ill Inst Technol, 65-68; assoc div chief, Mat Processing Div, Battelle Mem Inst, 68-73. *Mem:* Am Soc Metals; Am Inst Mining, Metall & Petrol Engrs; Am Soc Testing & Mat; Nat Asn Corrosion Engrs; Electrochem Soc. *Res:* Teflon processing; thermochemical and metallurgical process development; wire technology, metal fibers, wire reinforcement of polymeric materials; inorganic coating technology. *Mailing Add:* Nat-Stand Co 1618 Terminal Rd Niles MI 49120-1243

RAUSCH, GERALD, ORGANIC CHEMISTRY. *Current Pos:* from asst prof to assoc prof, 65-69, PROF ORG & ANALYTICAL CHEM, UNIV WIS-LA CROSSE, 69- *Personal Data:* b New Hampton, Iowa, Mar 18, 38; m 60; c 1. *Educ:* Univ Iowa, MS, 62, PhD(org chem), 63. *Prof Exp:* Res chemist, Chem Div, Union Carbide Corp, 63-65. *Mem:* Am Chem Soc. *Res:* Organic synthesis; N-acyl lactam chemistry; amines and amine derivatives; analytic separations, alcohols. *Mailing Add:* W 5722 Sherwood Dr La Crosse WI 54601-8442

RAUSCH, JAMES PETER, PHYSIOLOGY, BIOMATERIALS RESEARCH. *Current Pos:* from asst prof to assoc prof, 69-82, PROF BIOL, ALFRED UNIV, 82-, CHMN, BIOL DIV, 81- *Personal Data:* b Ravenna, Ohio, Aug 17, 38; m 65; c 3. *Educ:* Kent State Univ, BA, 64, MA, 66, PhD(physiol), 71. *Prof Exp:* Instr physiol, Kent State Univ, 68-69. *Mem:* Soc Biomat. *Res:* Ceramic-tissue interface response; physiology of marine and freshwater invertebrates; respiratory physiology. *Mailing Add:* Dept Biol Alfred Univ 26 N Main St Alfred NY 14802-1232

RAUSCH, MARVIN D, ORGANOMETALLIC CHEMISTRY, ORGANIC CHEMISTRY. *Current Pos:* assoc prof, 63-68, PROF CHEM, UNIV MASS, AMHERST, 68- *Personal Data:* b Topeka, Kans, June 27, 30; m 83; c 1. *Educ:* Univ Kans, BS, 52, PhD, 55. *Prof Exp:* NSF fel, Univ Munich, 57-59; sr res chemist, Monsanto Co, 59-63. *Concurrent Pos:* Alexander von Humboldt fel & vis prof, Univ Munich, 69-70 & 77, US Sr Scientist Award, Univ Bayreuth, 84-85, 90. *Mem:* Royal Soc Chem; Am Chem Soc. *Res:* Organic derivatives of transition metals; metallocene chemistry; organometallic catalysis; organometallic polymers; functionally substituted cyclopentadienyl-metal compounds. *Mailing Add:* Dept Chem Univ Mass Amherst MA 01003-0001

RAUSCH, ROBERT LLOYD, VETERINARY PARASITOLOGY. *Current Pos:* assoc dir, Div Animal Med, 86-89, prof, 78-92, EMER PROF PATHOBIOL & COMP MED, UNIV WASH, 92- *Personal Data:* b Marion, Ohio, July 20, 21; m 53, Virginia R Sacressen; c 1. *Educ:* Ohio State Univ, BA, 42, DVM, 45; Mich State Col, MS, 46; Univ Wis, PhD(parasitol), 49. *Hon Degrees:* LLD, Univ Alaska, 85; DSc, Univ Alaska, Fairbanks, 87; DVM, Univ Zurich, 92. *Honors & Awards:* Henry Baldwin Ward Medal, Am Soc Parasitol, 61; K F Meyer Award, Am Vet Epidemiol Asn, 79; Distinguished Serv Award, Wildlife Dis Asn, 83; Arctic Sci Prize, 84. *Prof Exp:* Asst, Ohio State Univ, 43-45 & Mich State Col, 45-46; from asst to instr, Univ Wis, 46-49; parasitologist, Arctic Health Res Ctr, USPHS, Alaska, 49-51, chief, Infectious Dis Sect, 51-74; prof parasitol, Western Col Vet Med, Univ Sask, 75-78. *Concurrent Pos:* Field work, Arctic & Subarctic, 49-, Siberia, 75-77 & 79, China, 85 & 89. *Mem:* AAAS; Am Soc Parasitol; Am Micros Soc; Am Soc Mammal; Am Soc Trop Med Hyg; Am Vet Med Asn. *Res:* Host-parasite ecology and epizootiology of helminths and diseases in wildlife; diseases of wildlife in relation to public health; hydatid disease. *Mailing Add:* 737 Ferncliff Ave NE Bainbridge Island WA 98110. *Fax:* 206-685-3006

RAUSCH, STEVEN K, BIOPROCESSING RESEARCH. *Current Pos:* SR RES SCIENTIST, BIOPROCESSING RES DEPT, PITMAN-MOORE INC, 82- *Personal Data:* b Aurora, Ill, Nov 17, 55. *Educ:* Purdue Univ, BA, 77; Univ Ill, PhD(biochem), 82. *Mem:* Am Chem Soc; AAAS; Am Soc Biochem & Molecular Biol; Protein Soc; Sigma Xi. *Mailing Add:* Somatogen Inc 2545 Central Ave Boulder CO 80301

RAUSCHER, TOMLINSON GENE, SOFTWARE ENGINEERING MANAGEMENT. *Current Pos:* MGR, SOFTWARE, XEROX CORP, 78- *Personal Data:* b Oneida, NY, May 27, 46; c 4. *Educ:* Yale Univ, BS, 68; Univ NC, MS, 71; Univ MD, PhD(comput sci), 75; Univ Rochester, MBA, 84. *Prof Exp:* Software engr, Naval Res Lab, 72-75; mgr, software, Nat Cash Regist Corp, 75-76; sr comput archit, Amdahl Corp, 76-77; mgr, software, Gen Tel Elec, 77-78. *Mem:* Inst Elec & Electronics Engrs; Asn Comput Mach. *Res:* Software engineering management; author of two books based on microcomputing. *Mailing Add:* Xerox Corp Cross Keys Park Bldg 815 Pittsford Palmyra Rd Fairport NY 14540

RAUSCHKOLB, ROY SIMPSON, SOIL FERTILITY. *Current Pos:* at Dept Soils, Water & Eng, at MARICOPA AGR CTR, UNIV ARIZ. *Personal Data:* b St Louis, Mo, Apr 18, 33; m 53; c 3. *Educ:* Ariz State Univ, BA, 61; Univ Ariz, MS, 63, PhD(agr chem, soils), 68. *Prof Exp:* Cotton specialist, Agr Exten, Univ Ariz, 65-66, supt exp sta & adminr exp farms opers, Col Agr, 66-67, soil specialist, Agr Exten 67-69; soil specialist, Agr Exten & res assoc, Exp Sta, Univ Calif, Davis, 69-77, asst dir, 77-81, assoc dean, Col Agr & dir, coop exten resource sci & eng, 81- *Concurrent Pos:* Consult, UN Food & Agr Orgn, 71, 74; mem intergovt personnel act assignment staff, US Environ Protection Agency, R S Kerr Lab, 76-77. *Mem:* Fel Soil Sci Soc Am; Am Soc Agron. *Res:* Soil-plant relationships; plant nutrition; soil and plant tissue testing; soil pollution; soil incorporation and recycling of plant residues and animal wastes; reactions and movement of plant nutrients in soils. *Mailing Add:* 37697 W Smith Enke Rd Maricopa AZ 85239

RAUSEN, AARON REUBEN, PEDIATRICS, HEMATOLOGY & ONCOLOGY. *Current Pos:* PROF PEDIAT & DIR PEDIAT ONCOL, NY UNIV MED CTR, 81-; DIR, STEPHEN D HASSENFELD CHILDREN'S CTR CANCER & BLOOD DIS, 90- *Personal Data:* b Jersey City, NJ, June 30, 30; m 68, Emalou Watkins; c David, Susan & Elisabeth. *Educ:* Dartmouth Col, 47-50; State Univ NY Downstate Med Ctr, MD, 54. *Prof Exp:* USPHS fel pediat hemat, Children's Hosp, Boston & Harvard Med Sch, 59-61; from assoc prof to prof pediat, Mt Sinai Sch Med, 66-81; dir pediat, Beth Israel Med Ctr, 73-81. *Concurrent Pos:* Chief pediat, Greenpoint Hosp, 62-64 & City Hosp Ctr, Elmhurst, 64-73; from asst attend pediatrician to attend pediatrician, Mt Sinai Hosp, 63-81; mem acute leukemia study group B, NIH, 64-81; consult, USPHS Hosp, 71-81, Beekman-Downtown Hosp, 78- & Hackensack Hosp, 78-; vis physician, Rockefeller Univ Hosp, 78-; consult pediat hemat, Lenox Hill Hosp, 81-; prin investr, Children Cancer Group, 92- *Mem:* Am Asn Cancer Res; Am Soc Hemat; Am Acad Pediat; Am Soc Clin Oncol; Am Soc Pediat Hemat Oncol. *Res:* Disorders of blood in children and cancer in childhood; oncology. *Mailing Add:* NY Univ Med Ctr 550 First Ave New York NY 10016. *Fax:* 212-263-8410

RAUSER, WILFRIED ERNST, PLANT PHYSIOLOGY, PLANT BIOCHEMISTRY. *Current Pos:* asst prof plant physiol, 67-72, assoc prof, 72-82, PROF BOT, UNIV GUELPH, 82- *Personal Data:* b Arlesheim, Switz, Oct 11, 36; Can citizen; m 61, J Stephanie Fry; c Erick & Ivan. *Educ:* Univ Toronto, BSA, 59, MSA, 61; Univ Ill, Urbana, PhD(agron), 65. *Prof Exp:* Res officer agron, Exp Farm, Can Dept Agr, Sask, 61-62, res scientist plant physiol, Res Sta, Man, 65-66. *Concurrent Pos:* Fel, Div Biosci, Nat Res Coun Can, 66-67. *Mem:* Am Soc Plant Physiol; Can Soc Plant Physiol. *Res:* Physiological effects of excess metal ions on plants; mechanisms of metal ion toxicity and tolerance; plant metal binding proteins. *Mailing Add:* Dept Bot Univ Guelph Guelph ON N1G 2W1 Can. *Fax:* 519-767-1991

RAUSHEL, FRANK MICHAEL, ENZYMOLOGY, REACTION MECHANISMS. *Current Pos:* Assoc prof, 86-89, PROF ORG CHEM, TEX A&M UNIV, 89- *Personal Data:* b Hibbing, Minn, Dec 12, 49; m 75; c 3. *Educ:* Univ Wis-Madison, PhD(biochem), 76. *Mem:* Sigma Xi; Am Chem Soc. *Res:* Analysis of enzyme reaction mechanisms by kinetic, magnetic resonance and genetic techniques. *Mailing Add:* Dept Chem Tex A&M Univ College Station TX 77843-3255

RAUT, KAMALAKAR BALKRISHNA, ORGANIC CHEMISTRY. *Current Pos:* PROF CHEM, SAVANNAH STATE COL, 64- *Personal Data:* b Bombay, India, Aug 10, 20; m 45; c 5. *Educ:* Univ Bombay, BSc, 41, BA, 42, MSc, 46; Univ Okla, PhD(chem, pharmaceut chem), 59; Univ Ga, certs, 65, 66 & 67. *Honors & Awards:* Outstanding Chem award, Am Chem Soc, 87. *Prof Exp:* Res chemist, India Pharmaceut Labs, 46-55; asst, Univ Okla, 55-59; vis instr org chem, ETex State Univ, 59-60; sci officer, Cent Drug Res Inst, Govt India, Lucknow, 60-61; asst prof, Indian Inst Technol, Kanpur, 62-64. *Concurrent Pos:* Abstractor, Chem Abstr Serv, 59-; counr, Am Chem Soc, 71-73 & cong sci counr, 73-75, 80-88. *Mem:* Am Chem Soc; Indian Sci Cong Asn; Int Union Pure & Appl Chem. *Res:* Synthetic dyes; natural products; flavons; chalcones; chromones; synthetic medicinal products; reaction mechanisms; computer programming; chemical education; use of computers in chemical education; air pollution; water pollution. *Mailing Add:* 708 Pennwaller Rd Savannah GA 31410-3104

RAUTENBERG, THEODORE HERMAN, PHYSICS. *Current Pos:* RETIRED. *Personal Data:* b Cleveland, Ohio, May 14, 30; m 54, Joann Johnston. *Educ:* Amherst Col, BA, 52. *Prof Exp:* Physicist, Light Prod Physics Br, Res & Develop Ctr, Gen Elec Co, 53-72, physicist, Plasma Physics Br, 72-74, physicist, Electronic Power Systs Br, 74-81, physicist, Lighting Systs Prog, 81-90; consult, 90-92. *Mem:* Am Phys Soc; Optical Soc Am; Inst Elec & Electronics Engrs; Audio Eng Soc. *Res:* Fundamental studies of chemical and gas discharge light sources; experimental optical spectroscopy and photometry; electrooptical devices, application to light control systems; electroacoustics, design of sound reinforcement systems. *Mailing Add:* 8 Hill St PO Box 125 Alplaus NY 12008

RAUTENSTRAUCH, CARL PETER, APPLIED MATHEMATICS. *Current Pos:* asst prof, 68-72, ASSOC PROF & ASST CHMN MATH, UNIV CENT FLA, 72- *Personal Data:* b New York, NY, Sept 19, 36; m 59; c 2. *Educ:* Univ Fla, BS, 58; Univ Ala, MA, 60; Auburn Univ, PhD(math), 67. *Prof Exp:* Instr math, Auburn Univ, 63-66; asst prof, Univ Tex, Arlington, 67-68. *Mem:* Am Math Soc; Soc Indust & Appl Math. *Res:* Special functions; complex analysis; differential equations. *Mailing Add:* Dept Math Univ Cent Fla PO Box 25000 Orlando FL 32816-0001

RAUTENSTRAUS, R(OLAND) C(URT), CIVIL ENGINEERING. *Current Pos:* Instr civil eng, 47-50, from asst prof to assoc prof, 50-57, head, Dept Civil Eng, 59-64, assoc dean fac, 64-68, vpres educ & student rels, 68-70, vpres univ rels, 70-73, exec vpres, 73-74, PROF CIVIL & ENVIRON ENG, UNIV COLO, BOULDER, 57-, PRES, 74- *Personal Data:* b Gothenburg, Nebr, Feb 27, 24; m 46; c 1. *Educ:* Univ Colo, BS, 46, MS, 49. *Hon Degrees:* DL, Univ NMex, 76. *Honors & Awards:* Lincoln Gold Medal, Am Welding Soc; Robert L Stearns Award; Norlen Medal. *Concurrent Pos:* Consult, Travelers Ins Co, 58-59; mem educ panel, Esso Refining Humble Oil Co, 60; mem bd dirs, Northwest Eng Co, 69-; mem, Gov's Energy Task Force, 73-74; mem, Regional Adv Bd, Inst Int Educ, 75- *Mem:* Am Soc Photogram; Am Soc Eng Educ; Am Soc Civil Engrs. *Res:* Altimetry; photogrammetry; highway engineering. *Mailing Add:* Dept Civil & Environ Eng Univ Colo Campus Box 428 Boulder CO 80309-0428

RAUTH, ANDREW MICHAEL, BIOPHYSICS. *Current Pos:* asst prof biophys, 65-74, assoc prof, 74-79, PROF BIOPHYS, UNIV TORONTO, 79-; PHYSICIST, ONT CANCER INST, TORONTO, 65- *Personal Data:* b Rochester, NY, Oct 8, 35; m 68; c 2. *Educ:* Brown Univ, BSc, 58; Yale Univ, PhD(biophys), 62. *Prof Exp:* Nat Cancer Inst grant, Ont Cancer Inst, Toronto, 62-65. *Mem:* Radiation Res Soc; Can Soc Cell Biol; Sigma Xi. *Res:* Radiation biology; mechanisms of drug action; somatic cell genetics; mutational processes in mammalian cells in vitro; radiobiology of solid tumors. *Mailing Add:* Exp Therapeut Ont Cancer Inst 610 University Ave Toronto ON M5G 2M9 Can. *Fax:* 416-926-6529

RAVAL, DILIP N, PHYSICAL BIOCHEMISTRY. *Current Pos:* RETIRED. *Personal Data:* b Bombay, India, June 3, 33; US citizen; m 61. *Educ:* Univ Bombay, BS, 53, MS, 55; Univ Ore, PhD(chem), 62. *Prof Exp:* NIH fel, Univ Ore, 61-62; fel virus res, Univ Calif, Berkeley, 62-64; res scientist, Palo Alto Med Res Inst, 64-66; mgr res, Varian Assocs, 66-68; dir clin labs, Med Ctr, Univ Calif, San Francisco, 68-70; dir res, Alcon Labs, 70-72, gen mgr, Sci & Technol Div, 72-73, vpres, 73-91, exec vpres, Res & Develop Div, 91-96. *Mem:* Acad Clin Lab Physicians & Sci. *Res:* Enzyme kinetics protein structure; medical instrument development; pharmaceutical drug development. *Mailing Add:* 4405 Overton Terr Ft Worth TX 76109

RAVE, TERENCE WILLIAM, SYNTHETIC POLYOLEFIN PULPS, PAPER CHEMISTRY. *Current Pos:* VPRES TECHNOL, AET PACKAGING FILMS, 94- *Personal Data:* b Mendota, Ill, Aug 23, 38; m 65, Ann Bowers; c 3. *Educ:* Bradley Univ, BS, 60; Univ Wis, PhD(org chem), 65. *Prof Exp:* Res chemist, Procter & Gamble Co, 65-67; from res chemist to sr res chemist, Hercules Inc, 67-76, res scientist, 76-80, res assoc, 80-84, mkt dir, 84-87, dir res, 88-89, vpres technol, 89-94. *Mem:* Am Chem Soc; Tech Asn Pulp & Paper Indust. *Res:* Organic nitrogen and phosphorous chemistry; paper chemistry; polymer synthesis and modification, synthetic polyolefin pulps; preparation, modification and applications of synthetic polyolefin pulps; paper wet and dry strength resins; polyolefin films; polyolefin fibers; polyproylene films. *Mailing Add:* 2523 Blackwood Rd Wilmington DE 19810

RAVECHE, ELIZABETH MARIE, AUTOIMMUNITY, CELL CYCLE KINETICS. *Current Pos:* PROF, DEPT PATH, MED SCH, UNIV MED & DENT NJ, 89- *Personal Data:* b Stuttgart, Ger, Nov 21, 50; US citizen; m 74; c 4. *Educ:* Seton Hill Col, BS, 72; George Washington Univ, PhD(genetics), 77. *Prof Exp:* Res scientist immunol, NIH, 77-85; assoc prof, Albany Med Col, 85-89. *Mem:* Am Asn Immunologists; Am Rheumatism Asn; Am Asn Pathologists; Tissue Cult Asn. *Res:* Murine models of autoimmunity; modes of inheritance of immunologic abnormalities and modulation by sex hormones; the study of mechanisms of B cell activation using flow cytometric techniques; abnormal lymphocyte differentiation and the development of aneuploidy in autoimmunity. *Mailing Add:* Dept Path UMDNJ Med Sch 185 S Orange Ave Newark NJ 07103-2714

RAVECHE, HAROLD JOSEPH, CHEMICAL PHYSICS. *Current Pos:* PRES, STEVENS INST TECHNOL, 88- *Personal Data:* b New York, NY, Mar 18, 43; m 74; c 4. *Educ:* Hofstra Univ, BA, 63; Univ Calif, San Diego, PhD(chem physics), 68. *Honors & Awards:* Electroendosmosis Award, Nat Bur Standards. *Prof Exp:* Nat Res Coun-Nat Acad Sci assoc statist physics, Nat Bur Standards, 68-70, res chemist, 70-78, chief, thermophysics div, 78-85; dean sci, Rensselaer Polytech Inst, 85-88. *Mem:* Soc Indust & Appl Math; Am Phys Soc; AAAS. *Res:* Statistical mechanics of equilibrium and non-equilibrium phenomena; computer simulation. *Mailing Add:* Stevens Inst Technol Castle Point on the Hudson Hoboken NJ 07030

RAVEED, DAN, PLANT PHYSIOLOGY, BIOCHEMISTRY. *Current Pos:* TECH DIR LAB PACK, HERITAGE ENVIRON SERV, 89- *Personal Data:* b Baltimore, Md, Aug 12, 21; m 46; c 2. *Educ:* Univ Calif, Berkeley, BS, 56; Univ Calif, Davis, PhD(plant physiol), 65. *Prof Exp:* Lab head soil & water relations, Water Authority, Israel, 54-55; lab technician, Univ Calif, Davis, 56-59, res chemist, 59-61, teaching asst plant physiol, 61-64, fel ion uptake, 67-68; assoc biochemist, Negative Inst, Beer Sheva, Israel, 64-67; staff scientist, Photobiol Br, C F Kettering Res Lab, 68-72, head, Electron Micros Lab, 72-77; asst prof path, Dept Electron Microscope Lab, Ind Sch Med, 77-80; pesticide chem, Ind State Bd Health, 80-86; qual assurance officer, Off Ind Dept Environ Mgt, 86-89. *Mem:* AAAS; Am Soc Cell Biologists; Japanese Soc Plant Physiol; Scand Soc Plant Physiol; Electron Micros Soc Am. *Res:* Biochemical ultrastructure of functional enzyme complexes from membranes of chloroplasts, bacterial chromatophores, retinas; immuno-electron microscopy; membrane response to stress, pollutants and inhibitors; physiology of photosynthesis; ion uptake by plants. *Mailing Add:* 4536 Dickson Rd Indianapolis IN 46226

RAVEL, JOANNE MACOW, BIOCHEMISTRY, MOLECULAR BIOLOGY. *Current Pos:* Res scientist, Clayton Found Biochem Inst, 44-53, Hite fel, 54-56, res scientist, 56-70, asst dir, 70-85, from assoc prof to prof chem, Univ Tex, Austin, 72-85, RES SCIENTIST, CLAYTON FOUND BIOCHEM INST, UNIV TEX, AUSTIN, 85- *Personal Data:* b Austin, Tex, July 28, 24; m 46; c 2. *Educ:* Univ Tex, BS, 44, MA, 46, PhD(chem), 54. *Mem:* Am Soc Biochem & Molecular Biol; Am Chem Soc; Am Soc Plant Physiologists; Am Soc Microbiol. *Res:* Eukaryotic protein synthesis and its regulation; biological control mechanisms. *Mailing Add:* Dept Chem & Biochem Univ Tex Austin 7115 Las Ventanas Austin TX 78731

RAVEN, BERTRAM H(ERBERT), PSYCHOLOGY, SOCIAL PSYCHOLOGY. *Current Pos:* PROF & CHMN, DEPT PSYCHOL, UNIV CALIF, LOS ANGELES, 56- *Personal Data:* b Youngstown, Ohio, Sept 26, 26; m 61, Celia Cutler; c Michelle G & Jonathan H. *Educ:* Ohio State Univ, BA, 48, MA, 49; Univ Mich, PhD, 53. *Prof Exp:* Res assoc, Res Ctr Group Dynamics, 52-54; lectr psychol, Univ Mich, Ann Arbor, 53-54; vis prof, Univ Nijmegen & Univ Utrecht, Neth, 54-55; psychologist, Rand Corp, 55-56. *Concurrent Pos:* Fulbright scholar, Neth, 54-55, Israel, 62-63 & Britain, 69-70; Guggenheim fel, Israel, 62-63; vis prof, Hebrew Univ, Jerusalem, 62-63, Univ Wash, Seattle & Polit Sci, 69-70, London Sch Econ, 69-70; ed, J Social Issues, 69-74; Consult & expert witness on eyewitness testimony, 73-; chair, Bd Social & Ethical Responsibility, Am Psychol Asn, 78-82; consult psychologist, 79-; co-dir, Training Prog Health Psychol, Univ Calif, Los Angeles, 79-88; consult, WHO, Manila, 85-86; NATO sr fel, Italy, 89. *Mem:* Fel Am Psychol Asn; fel Am Psychol Soc; fel Soc Psychol Study Social Issues (pres, 73-74); AAAS; Am Sociol Asn; Int Asn Appl Psychol; Soc Exp Social Psychol; Asn Advan Psychol; Int Soc Polit Psychol; Inter-Am Psychol Soc; Am Psychol-Law Soc; Int Soc Polit Psychol. *Res:* Social psychology theory and research on interpersonal influence and social power relationships. *Mailing Add:* Dept Psychol UCLA Los Angeles CA 90095-1563. *Fax:* 310-206-5895; *E-Mail:* raven@ucla.edu

RAVEN, CLARA, forensic pathology, bacteriology, for more information see previous edition

RAVEN, FRANCIS HARVEY, MECHANICAL ENGINEERING. *Current Pos:* from asst prof to assoc prof, 58-66, PROF MECH ENG, UNIV NOTRE DAME, 66- *Personal Data:* b Erie, Pa, July 29, 28; m 52, Therese Strobel; c Betty, Ann, Paul, John, Mary, Cathy & Linda. *Educ:* Gannon Col, BS, 48; Pa State Univ, BS, 50, MS, 51; Cornell Univ, PhD(mech eng), 58. *Prof Exp:* Anal design engr, Hamilton Standard Div, United Technologies, 50-54; instr mech eng, Cornell Univ, 54-58. *Concurrent Pos:* Consult, McCauley Accessory Div, Cessna Aircraft Co, S Bend Lathe. *Mem:* Assoc Am Soc Mech Engrs; Am Soc Eng Educ; Sigma Xi. *Res:* Kinematics, robotics and automatic control systems. *Mailing Add:* Dept Aerospace & Mech Eng Univ Notre Dame Notre Dame IN 46556

RAVEN, PETER BERNARD, CARDIOVASCULAR RESPONSES. *Current Pos:* Assoc prof, 77-86, PROF PHYSIOL, TEX COL OSTEOP MED, 86- *Educ:* Univ Ore, Eugene, PhD(phys educ), 69. *Res:* Exercise physiology; work physiology; cardiovascular responses to exercise. *Mailing Add:* Dept Integrative Physiol Univ NTex Health Sci Ctr 3500 Camp Bowie Blvd Ft Worth TX 76106-2699

RAVEN, PETER HAMILTON, BOTANY, POPULATION BIOLOGY. *Current Pos:* DIR, MO BOT GARDEN, 71-; ENGELMANN PROF BOT, WASHINGTON UNIV. *Personal Data:* b Shanghai, China, June 13, 36; US citizen; m 58, 68, Tamra Engelhorn; c 4. *Educ:* Univ Calif, Berkeley, AB, 57; Univ Calif, Los Angeles, PhD(bot), 60. *Hon Degrees:* DSc, St Louis Univ, 82, Knox Col, 83, Southern Ill Univ, Edwardsville, 83, Miami Univ, 86, Univ Gutenberg, 87, Rutgers Univ, 88, Univ Mass, 88, Leiden Univ, Neth, 90, Nat Univ La Plata, Arg, 91, Westminster Col, 92, Univ Mo, 92, Wash Univ, 93, Univ Conn, 93 & Univ Cordoba, Arg, 93; LHD, Webster Univ, 84. *Honors & Awards:* Merit Award, Bot Soc Am, 77; Distinguished Serv Award, Am Inst Biol Sci, 81; Int Environ Leadership Medal, UN Environ Prog, 82; John D & Catherine T MacArthur Found Fel, 85-90; Intern Prize Biol, Govt Japan, 86; Tyler Prize Environ Achievement, 95; Sasakawa Environ Prize, 95; Liberty Hyde Bailey Medal, Am Hort Soc, 96; Merit Award, Am Asn Bot Gardens & Arboreta, 96; Asa Gray Award, Am Soc Plant Taxonomists, 96. *Prof Exp:* NSF fel, Brit Mus Natural Hist, 60-61; taxonomist & cur, Rancho Santa Ana Bot Garden, 61-62; from asst prof to assoc prof biol sci, Stanford Univ, 62-71. *Concurrent Pos:* NSF grants, 61-; Guggenheim fel & sr res fel, Dept Sci, Indust Res, NZ, 69-70; res assoc, Calif Acad Sci, 70-; hon cur phanerogans, Nat Mus Costa Rica, 80-; mem, Comt Res & Explor, Nat Geog Soc, 82-; mem bd dirs, World Wildlife Fund-US, 83-; res assoc bot, Bernice P Bishop Mus, 85-; hon dir, Inst Bot Acad Sinica, Beijing, 88- *Mem:* Nat Acad Sci; Am Acad Arts & Sci; Soc Study Evolution (vpres, 68, 72, pres, 78); Am Soc Naturalists (pres, 83); Am Soc Plant Taxon (pres, 72); fel AAAS; Am Inst Biol Sci (pres, 83-84); foreign mem Royal Danish Acad Sci & Lett; Orgn Trop Studies (treas, 81-84, vpres, 84-85, pres, 85-86); foreign mem Royal Swed Acad Sci; Am Philos Soc. *Res:* Taxonomy, especially Onagraceae; general botany; biogeography; taxonomic theory; biosystematics; cytogenetics; geography; ethnobotany; conservation biology; cytogenetics; pollination systems; flora of North America; flora of China; tropical botany; author of over 450 scientific papers. *Mailing Add:* Mo Bot Garden PO Box 299 St Louis MO 63166

RAVENEL, DOUGLAS CONNER, MATHEMATICS. *Current Pos:* PROF MATH, UNIV ROCHESTER, 88- *Personal Data:* b Alexandria, Va, Feb 17, 47; m 83; c 4. *Educ:* Oberlin Col, BA, 69; Brandeis Univ, MA, 69, PhD(math), 72. *Prof Exp:* Instr math, Mass Inst Technol, 71-73; asst prof, Columbia Univ, 73-76; mem staff, Inst Advan Study, 74-75; from asst prof to prof math, Univ Wash, 76-88. *Concurrent Pos:* Alfred P Sloan Found res fel, 77-79. *Mem:* Am Math Soc. *Res:* Algebraic topology; complex cobordism theory; homotopy theory. *Mailing Add:* Dept Math Univ Rochester Rochester NY 14627-0001

RAVENHALL, DAVID GEOFFREY, THEORETICAL PHYSICS. *Current Pos:* from asst prof to assoc prof, 57-63, PROF THEORET PHYSICS, UNIV ILL, URBANA, 63- *Personal Data:* b Birmingham, Eng, Mar 4, 27; US citizen; m 52; c Katherine. *Educ:* Univ Birmingham, BSc, 47, PhD(electrodynamics), 50. *Prof Exp:* Dept Sci & Indust Res sr fel theoret physics, Univ Birmingham, 50-51; res physicist, Carnegie Inst Technol, 51-52; mem, Inst Advan Study, 52-53; res assoc theoret physics, Stanford Univ, 53-57. *Concurrent Pos:* NSF sr fel, 63-64. *Mem:* Am Phys Soc. *Res:* Theoretical nuclear physics at intermediate energies; particle physics, mesoscopic physics, dense matter. *Mailing Add:* Dept Physics Loomis Lab Univ Ill 1110 W Green St Urbana IL 61801. *E-Mail:* ravenhal@uiuc.edu

RAVENHOLT, REIMERT THOROLF, EPIDEMIOLOGY, PUBLIC HEALTH. *Current Pos:* RETIRED. *Personal Data:* b Milltown, Wis, Mar 9, 25; m 48, 81; c 4. *Educ:* Univ Minn, BS, 48, MB, 51, MD, 52; Univ Calif, Berkeley, MPH, 56; Am Bd Prev Med, dipl & cert pub health, 60. *Honors & Awards:* John J Sippy Mem Award, Am Pub Health Asn, 61, Carl Schultz Award, 79; Distinguished Honor Award, AID, 72; Hugh Moore Mem Award, 74. *Prof Exp:* Intern, USPHS Hosp, San Francisco, 51-52; mem staff, Epidemic Intel Serv, Nat Commun Dis Ctr, USPHS, Ga, 52-54; dir, Epidemiol & Commun Dis Div, Seattle-King Co Dept Pub Health, 54-61; epidemiol consult, Europ Area, USPHS, Am Embassy, Paris, France, 61-63; assoc prof prev med, Sch Med, Univ Wash, 63-66; chief, Pop Br, Health Serv, Off Tech Coop & Res, Develop Support Bur, 66-67, dir pop serv, Off War Hunger, 67-69, dir, Off Pop, Tech Assistance Bur, 69-72, dir, Off Pop, Pop & Humanitarian Assistance, 72-77, dir, Off Pop, 77-79; dir, World Health Surv, Ctrs Dis Control, Rockville, Md, 80-82; asst dir res, Nat Inst Drug Abuse, Rockville, Md, 82-84; chief, Epidemiol Br, Off Epidemiol & Biostatist, Food & Drug Admin, Rockville, Md, 84-87. *Concurrent Pos:* Originator & mem prog steering comn, World Fertil Surv, 71- *Mem:* AAAS; fel Am Pub Health Asn; fel Am Col Epidemiol. *Res:* Population; preventive medicine; infectious diseases; immunization; diseases of smoking and ionizing radiation; malignant cellular evolution; mortality and fertility patterns; contraceptive development; population dynamics. *Mailing Add:* 3156 E Laurelhurst NE Seattle WA 98105

RAVENTOS, ANTOLIN, IV, RADIATION ONCOLOGY. *Current Pos:* chmn dept, 70-80, prof, 70-91, EMER PROF RADIOL, SCH MED, UNIV CALIF, DAVIS, 91- *Personal Data:* b Wilmette, Ill, June 3, 25; m 76, Anne Gray. *Educ:* Univ Chicago, SB, 45, MD, 47; Univ Pa, MSc, 55. *Prof Exp:* From asst instr to prof radiol, Sch Med, Univ Pa, 51-70. *Concurrent Pos:* Spec consult, Nat Cancer Inst, Surgeon Gen Army, 61-62 & Armed Forces Radiobiol Res Inst, 64-67; consociate mem, Nat Coun Radiation Protection & Measurements; pres, Am Registry Radiol Technol, 66. *Mem:* Am Med Writers Asn; Am Radium Soc (pres, 72); Radiol Soc NAm; Radiation Res Soc; Am Soc Cancer Educ. *Res:* Radiation therapy; radioactive isotopes in medicine; radiobiology. *Mailing Add:* 44434 Country Club Dr El Macero CA 95618

RAVENTOS-SUARAZ, CARMEN ELVIRA, ANALYTICAL CYTOLOGY, CELL CYCLE ANALYSIS. *Current Pos:* RES SCIENTIST ONCOL & IMMUNOL, MED RES DIV, AM CYANAMID CO, 85- *Personal Data:* b Lima, Peru, May 27, 47; m 81; c 1. *Educ:* San Marcos Univ, Lima, Peru, BASc, 70, biologist, 73, PhD(biol), 85; Univ Chile, Santiago, lic in sci, 76. *Prof Exp:* Tech assoc, Bact Inst Chile, 70-71; vol virol, Virol Unit, Sch Med, Univ Chile, 72-73; instr, 74-77; researcher exp hemat, Albert Einstein Col Med, NY, 78-79, assoc, 79-85. *Concurrent Pos:* Vol neoplastic dis, Atran Labs, Mt Sinai, NY, 78; researcher, NY Blood Ctr, 78. *Mem:* Int Soc Anal Cytol; Am Asn Immunologists. *Res:* Characterization of early progenitor cells from the mouse bone marrow and their interaction with cytokines by fluorescence activated cell sorter methodology, response and activation by cytotoxic and immunomodulator drugs. *Mailing Add:* Bristol Meyers Squibb Box 4000 K2201 Princeton NJ 08543

RAVI, NATARAJAN, BIO-INORGANIC CHEMISTRY, METALLOPROTEINS. *Current Pos:* PROF CHEM, SPELMAN COL, 95- *Personal Data:* b Mayuram, India, June 18, 54; m, Kokila; c Aparna & Anusha. *Educ:* Univ Hyderabad India, PhD(chem), 82. *Prof Exp:* Vis fel, Univ Groningen, Neth, 83-84; sci officer, Indira Gandhi Ctr Atomic Res,

Kalpakkam India, 85-87; res assoc, Emory Univ, 87-93; res assoc, Carnegie Mellon Univ, 93-95. *Mem:* Am Chem Soc; Am Phys Soc. *Res:* Investigations of a variety of metal containing proteins and enzymes by spectroscopy; understanding structure-function relationship of the biological systems by quantum mechanical treatment. *Mailing Add:* Dept Chem Spelman Col 350 Spelman Lane Box 1134 Atlanta GA 30314-4399. *Fax:* 412-268-1061; *E-Mail:* nr27@andrew.cmu.edu

RAVICZ, ARTHUR EUGENE, CHEMICAL ENGINEERING, DISTILLATION. *Current Pos:* Res engr, Calif Res Corp, 52 & 58-63, sr res engr, 63-67, sr eng assoc, 67-81, supv process engr, 81-88, SR STAFF PROCESS ENGR, CHEVRON CORP, 88- *Personal Data:* b New Rochelle, NY, Oct 28, 30; m 57, Patricia Wagonjack; c Michael, Anne & Catherine. *Educ:* Univ Colo, BS, 52; Univ Tex, MS, 55; Univ Mich, PhD(chem eng), 59. *Concurrent Pos:* Instr, Exten Div, Univ Calif, 63-64, lectr, 70; chmn, tech comts, Fractionation Res, Inc, 91- *Mem:* Am Inst Chem Engrs. *Res:* Distillation; applications of automatic computers in chemical engineering; petroleum and petrochemical process design. *Mailing Add:* 45 Mendocino Lane Novato CA 94947

RAVILISETTY, RAO PADMANABHA, PHOSPHORS FOR DISPLAY DEVICES, DISPLAY MATERIALS. *Current Pos:* SR SCIENTIST, PLASMACO, INC, 96- *Personal Data:* b Chirala, India, July 10, 51; m 80, Rama Devi Pasupuleti; c Pavan Kumar & Sai Krishna. *Educ:* Andhra Univ, BS, 72, MSc, 75; Indian Inst Technol, PhD(mat sci), 81. *Prof Exp:* Sr res asst, Indian Inst, Technol, 81-82; res scientist, Cent Electrochem Res Inst, 85-90; vis scientist, Univ Waterloo, 90-92; mat scientist, Thomas Electronics, Inc, 92-94; sr scientist, Coloray Display Corp, 94-96. *Concurrent Pos:* Vis fel, Univ Montpellier, 82-84; consult, Anapurna Agroprod, 84-86; joint ed, Bull Electrochem, 85-90; mem, Dept Electronics, Govt India, 87-90, prin investr, Dept Sci & Technol Proj, 87-91, Dept Electronics Proj, 87-92, investr, Dept Sci & Technol Proj, 89-94. *Mem:* Inst Elec & Electronics Engrs; Am Chem Soc; Electrochem Soc; Soc Info Display; Soc Radiation Physists. *Res:* Development of phosphor materials for various applications such as plasma displays, field emission display devices, cathode ray tubes, lamps and radiology; authored 68 papers published in various international scientific journals; phosphors for ac plasma display devices; granted 5 patents on phosphor materials. *Mailing Add:* Plasamaco Inc 180 South St Highland NY 12528. *Fax:* 914-883-5179; *E-Mail:* raor@plasmaco.com

RAVILLE, MILTON E(DWARD), ENGINEERING. *Current Pos:* PROF & DIR SCH ENG SCI & MECH, GA INST TECHNOL, 62- *Personal Data:* b Malone, NY, July 12, 21; m 43; c 6. *Educ:* Norwich Univ, BS, 43; Kans State Univ, MS, 47; Univ Wis, PhD(mech), 55. *Prof Exp:* Instr appl mech, Kans State Univ, 47-50, from asst prof to assoc prof, 50-56, prof & head dept, 56-62. *Concurrent Pos:* Res engr, Forest Prod Lab, Wis, 54-55 & Gen Dynamics, 63. *Mem:* Am Soc Eng Educ; Nat Soc Prof Engrs; Soc Eng Sci; Am Acad Mech. *Res:* Stress analysis and vibrations of solid bodies; analysis of sandwich structures. *Mailing Add:* 6009 Dee Ct Stone Mountain GA 30087

RAVINDRA, NUGGEHALLI MUTHANNA, MICROELECTRONICS & OPTOELECTRONICS. *Current Pos:* ASSOC PROF PHYSICS, NJ INST TECHNOL, 87- *Personal Data:* b Hyderabad, India, Oct 1, 55; m 84, Pushpa Seetharam; c Krishna, Pradeep & Jayant. *Educ:* Bangalore Univ, BS Hons, 74, MS, 76; Roorkee Univ, PhD(physics), 82. *Prof Exp:* Res scientist, Ctr Nat Res Sci, 82-85 & Int Ctr Theoret Physics, 83-85; vis scientist, Microelectronics Ctr NC & NC State Univ, 85-86; res assoc prof mat sci, Vanderbilt Univ, 86-87. *Concurrent Pos:* Prin investr, Bell Commun Res, 88-, Sematech Ctr Excellence, 88-90 & NJ Comn Sci & Technol, 90-92; co-prin investr, Advan Res Proj Agency, 92- *Mem:* Inst Elec & Electronics Engrs; Soc Photo-Optical Instrumentation Engrs; Mat Res Soc; Sigma Xi; Electrochem Soc. *Res:* Material science and technology; applications in infra-red detectors, solar cells, mos devices and cmos device technology; silicon processing and technology; temperature and infra-red sensors; superconduction. *Mailing Add:* Dept Physics NJ Inst Technol Microelectronics Newark NJ 07102. *Fax:* 973-596-5794; *E-Mail:* ravindra@hertz.njit.edu

RAVINDRA, RAVI, GEOPHYSICS, COSMOLOGY. *Current Pos:* assoc prof, 75-79, PROF PHYSICS & RELIG DALHOUSIE UNIV, 79- *Personal Data:* b Patiala, India, Jan 14, 39; m 65, Sally Bambridge; c Munju M & Kabir P. *Educ:* Indian Inst Technol, Kharagpur, BSc, 59, MTech, 61; Univ Toronto, MSc, 62, PhD(physics), 65; Dalhousie Univ, MA, 68. *Prof Exp:* From asst prof to assoc prof physics & philos, Dalhousie Univ, 66-73; vis fel, Hist & Philosophy of Sci, Princeton Univ, 68-69; vis scholar, Dept Relig, Columbia Univ, 73-74. *Concurrent Pos:* Res grants, Nat Res Coun Can, 66-72, Geol Surv Can, 66- & Dom Observ Can, 66-; Can Coun fel philos & Killam res fel, 68-69; vis fel philos sci, Princeton Univ, 68-69; Can Coun res grant, 72-77; cross-disciplinary fel, Soc Relig Higher Educ, Columbia Univ, 73-74; Can Coun fel, 73-74; Can Coun Leave fel, 77-78; Shastri Indo-Can Inst sr fel, 77-78; Soc Sci & Humanities Res Coun Can res grant, 77-82; dir, Threshhold Award, 78-80; vis mem Inst Advan Study, Princeton Univ, 77. *Mem:* Am Asn Physics Teachers; Am Soc Study Relig; Can Soc Study Relig. *Res:* Relativistic cosmology; yoga and consciousness; philosophy of religion, particularly spiritual traditions; philosophy and history of science; comparative study of cultures, science and spirituality. *Mailing Add:* Depts Physics & Relig Dalhousie Univ Halifax NS B3H 3J5 Can. *Fax:* 902-479-1070; *E-Mail:* ravi.ravindra@dal.ca

RAVINDRAN, COMONDORE, METALLURGY & PHYSICAL METALLURGY ENGINEERING. *Current Pos:* PROF ADVAN MAT & MFG PROCESSES, RYERSON POLYTECH UNIV, 89- *Personal Data:* b Madras, India, Nov 4, 45; Can citizen; m 75, Shanti Parthasarathi; c Nikila, Vikram & Shobita. *Educ:* Univ Madras, BSc, 64; Indian Inst Sci, BEng, 67; Univ Man, PhD(mat sci & eng), 82. *Honors & Awards:* G MacDonald Young Award, Am Soc Mat Can Coun, 95. *Prof Exp:* Process & prod develop engr, Man Steel Rolling Mills Inc, 73-76, chief indust engr, 76-80, chief metallurgist, 80-85; vpres, Galtaco Castings Inc, 85-88. *Concurrent Pos:* Adj prof, Univ Western Ont, 92-, Univ Toronto, 93- *Mem:* Fel Am Soc Mat Int; Am Foundrymen's Soc. *Res:* Casting of ferrous and non-ferrous materials mainly for automotive and aerospace industries. *Mailing Add:* Dept Mech Eng Ryerson Polytech Univ 350 Victoria St Toronto ON M5B 2K3 Can. *Fax:* 416-979-5265; *E-Mail:* rrarindr@acs.ryerson.ca

RAVINDRAN, NAIR NARAYANAN, ORGANIC CHEMISTRY. *Current Pos:* RETIRED. *Personal Data:* b Vechoor, India, Nov 25, 34; m 66; c 1. *Educ:* Univ Kerala, India, BS, 58, MS, 60; Purdue Univ, PhD(chem), 72. *Prof Exp:* Sci officer radiochem, Bhabha Atomic Res Ctr, Bombay, 58-67; res assoc org chem, Purdue Univ, 72-74; res chemist, Eastman Kodak Co, 74-80, sr res chemist, 80-91. *Mem:* Am Chem Soc. *Res:* Design and synthesis of photographically useful organic compounds to meet the needs of future photographic products of the company; design and building of color photographic film products. *Mailing Add:* 401 Pennels Dr Rochester NY 14626-4914

RAVIOLA, ELIO, ANATOMY, NEUROBIOLOGY. *Current Pos:* from assoc prof to prof anat, 70-89, BULLARD PROF NEUROBIOL, HARVARD UNIV MED SCH, 89-, PROF OPHTHAL, 89- *Personal Data:* b Asti, Italy, June 15, 32; m 90, Trude Kleinschmidt; c Giuseppe. *Educ:* Univ Pavia, Italy, MD, 57, PhD(anat), 63. *Prof Exp:* Resident neurol & psychiat, Univ Pavia, asst prof, 58-70. *Concurrent Pos:* Assoc ed, Anat Record, 72- *Mem:* Am Soc Cell Biol; Am Asn Anatomists; Soc Neurosci; Am Acad Arts & Sci. *Res:* Mechanism of vision. *Mailing Add:* Dept Neurobiol Harvard Univ Med Sch 220 Longwood Ave Boston MA 02115-6092

RAVIS, WILLIAM ROBERT, BIOPHARMACEUTICS, PHARMACOKINETICS. *Current Pos:* From asst prof to assoc prof 77-87, PROF PHARMACOKINETICS, SCH PHARM, AUBURN UNIV, 87-, HEAD PHARMACOL SCI, 90- *Personal Data:* b Phoenixville, Pa, July 1, 49; m 70, Vicki A Glisson; c Nicole E & Julie A. *Educ:* Temple Univ, BS, 72; Univ Houston, PhD(pharmaceut), 77. *Concurrent Pos:* adj prof, Col Vet Med, 87-; consult, FDA Ctr Vet Med, 93- *Mem:* Fel Am Col Clin Pharmacol; Am Asn Pharmaceut Scientist; Acad Pharmaceut Sci; Sigma Xi; Am Asn Col Pharm. *Res:* Preclinical and clinical studies of the biopharmaceutics and pharmacokinetics of drugs and on their dosage forms; author of 85 research publications and 5 book chapters. *Mailing Add:* Sch Pharm Auburn Univ Auburn AL 36849-3501

RAVISHANKAR, SATHANJHERI A, COMPOSITE PIGMENT TECHNOLOGY, KAOLIN RESEARCH. *Current Pos:* SCIENTIST, DRY BRANCH KAOLIN CO, 97- *Educ:* Roorkee Univ, India, MS, 83; Indian Inst Technol, India, MTech, 85; Va Inst Technol, PhD(mat sci), 95. *Prof Exp:* Res engr, Tata Res & Develop Ctr, 86-90; scientist, Nort Kaolin Co, 95-97. *Mem:* Soc Mining Engrs; Am Chem Soc; AAAS; Tech Asn Pulp & Paper Indust. *Res:* Stability of colloid system by classical and non-classical surface forces; Kaolin based composite pigments for coating industry. *Mailing Add:* 3896 Riverside Dr No 3812 Macon GA 31210. *Fax:* 912-945-3155; *E-Mail:* saravish@aol.com

RAVITSKY, CHARLES, APPLIED PHYSICS, OPTICS & OPTOELECTRONICS. *Current Pos:* PRIN ENGR, GRC INT, INC, 95- *Personal Data:* b New York, NY, May 25, 17; m 40, Charlotte Epstein; c Carol J (Spar) & Cynthia L. *Educ:* City Col NY, BS, 38, MS, 39. *Honors & Awards:* US Naval Ord Develop Award, 45; Outstanding Performance, Defense Advan Res Proj Agency, 75. *Prof Exp:* Teacher high sch, NY, 38; from jr physicist to prin physicist, Nat Bur Stand, 41-53; prin physicist, Diamond Ord Fuze Labs, 53-54, chief, Systs Res Sect, 54-58, res supvr, 58-62; chief scientist & chief, Physics Br, US Army Res & Develop Group, Europe, 62-67; sr prog mgr, Off Secy Defense, 67-72, asst to dir tactical technol, Defense Advan Res Projs Agency, 72-75; physicist, Cerberonics, Inc, 77-78; staff scientist, SWL Inc, 78-95. *Concurrent Pos:* Assoc physics, George Washington Univ, 43-50, lectr, 50-54; asst chmn electronic scientist panel, Bd Civil Serv Exam, Nat Bur Stand, 50-55, chmn, 55-59, mem bd, 55-61; mem, US Deleg, NATO Panel IV Optics & Infrared, 71-75; consult, Battelle Columbus Labs, 75-88. *Mem:* Am Phys Soc; Optical Soc Am. *Res:* Administration of research and development programs; communications research and development; surveillance; military systems utilizing infrared or visible radiation; development of submersible vehicles; remote sensors; anti-submarine warfare; intrusion detection sensors; airborne reconnaissance systems. *Mailing Add:* 1505 Drexel St Takoma Park MD 20912-7032. *Fax:* 703-416-0034

RAVITZ, LEONARD J, JR, ELECTROMAGNETIC FIELD MEASUREMENTS, HYPNOSIS. *Current Pos:* CLIN ASST PROF PSYCHIAT, STATE UNIV, NY HEALTH SCI CTR & DOWNSTATE MENT HYG ASN, 83- *Personal Data:* b Cuyahoga Co, Ohio, Apr 17, 25. *Educ:* Case Western Res Univ, BS, 44; Wayne State Univ, MD, 46; Yale Univ, MS, 50. *Prof Exp:* Am Bd Psychiat & Neurol, cert, 52. *Prof Exp:* Intern, St Elizabeths Hosp, Washington, DC, 46-47; asst resident psychiat, Yale-New Haven Hosp, 47-49; res fel Neuro-Anat Sect, Yale Med Sch, 49-50; sr resident neuropsychiat, Duke Univ Hosp, Durham, NC, 50-51, assoc, Pvt Diag Clin, 51-53; asst dir, prof educ, Dorrey Vet Admin Hosp, North Chicago, Ill, 53-54; assoc, Dept Psychiat, Sch Med & Hosp, Univ Pa, 55-58; dir training & res, Eastern State Hosp, Williamsburg, Va, 58-60; psychiatrist & consult, Div Alcohol Studies & Rehab, Va Dept Mental Health & Ment Retardation,

Norfolk Alcohol Serv, 61-81; consult, Nat Inst Rehab Therapy, Butler, NJ, 82-83. *Concurrent Pos:* Pvt consult, Cleveland, Ohio, 60-69; mem staff Med Ctr Hosp, Norfolk Gen Div, Va, 61-; lectr, Int Conf Rhythmic Functions in the Living Systs, NY Acad Sci, 61; lectr sociol, Old Dominion Univ, Norfolk, Va, 61-62, consult Nutrit Res Proj & res prof psychol, 78-90; consult, Tidewater Epilepsy Found, Chesapeake, 62-68, spec med consult, Frederick Mil Acad, Portsmouth, 63-71, US Pub Health Hosp Alcohol Unit, Norfolk, VA, 80-81; guest lectr, Fourth Int Conf Hypn & Paychosom Med, Guttenburg Univ, Mainz, WGer, 70; featured lectr, Significance Field Measurements in Hypn, Health & Dis, 14th Ann Meeting, Am Soc Clin Hypn, Chicago, 71; asst ed, J Am Soc Psychosom, Dent & Med, Brooklyn, 80-83; psychiatrist, Greenpoint Multiserv Ctr, Brooklyn, 83-87, 17th St Clin, Manhattan, 87-91; teacher, Nursing Sch Affil, Univ Wyo. *Mem:* Fel NY Acad Sci; fel AAAS; fel Am Psychiat Asn; Sigma Xi; fel Am Soc Clin Hypn; fel Royal Soc Health. *Res:* Discovery of electromagnetic field correlates of hypnosis, emotions, psychiatric/medical disorders, aging and electric phenomena in humans which parallel those of other life forms. *Mailing Add:* Dept Psychiat Med Sch State Univ NY Health Sci Ctr 450 Clarkson Ave PO Bos 1203 Brooklyn NY 11203. *Fax:* 718-287-0337

RAVIV, JOSEF, APPLIED MATHEMATICS, COMPUTER SCIENCE. *Current Pos:* Res staff mem, T J Watson Res Ctr, 64-72, mgr, IBM Israel Sci Ctr, 72-85, MGR, IBM ISRAEL SCI & TECHNOL, HAIFA, 85- *Personal Data:* b Slonim, Poland, Mar 11, 34; US citizen; m 56; c 3. *Educ:* Stanford Univ, BS, 55, MS, 60; Univ Calif, Berkeley, MA, 63, PhD(elec eng), 64. *Concurrent Pos:* Lectr, Univ Conn, 65-; assoc prof, Technion, Israel, 71-86; pres, Info Processing Asn Israel. *Mem:* Fel Inst Elec & Electronics Engrs; Asn Comput Mach. *Res:* Decision making; pattern recognition; data compaction; recognition of continuous speech. *Mailing Add:* IBM Israel & Haifa Res Lab Matam Advan Technol Ctr Haifa 31905 Israel

RAW, CECIL JOHN GOUGH, PHYSICAL CHEMISTRY. *Current Pos:* from asst prof to prof, 60-95, chmn dept, 83-88, EMER PROF CHEM, ST LOUIS UNIV, 95- *Personal Data:* b Ixopo, SAfrica, Oct 20, 29; US citizen; m 56, Gillian Galt; c Jeremy, Timothy, Matthew & Rebecca. *Educ:* Univ Natal, BSc, 51, MSc, 52, PhD(phys chem), 56. *Prof Exp:* Lectr chem, Univ Natal, 54-57, sr lectr, 58-59; res assoc, Univ Minn, 59-60. *Concurrent Pos:* African Explosives & Chem Industs res fel, 57-59; summer vis asst prof, Univ Minn, 60 & Univ Md, 62. *Mem:* Am Chem Soc; Am Asn Univ Professors; Sigma Xi. *Res:* Microcomputers in chemistry; chaotic and oscillating chemical systems. *Mailing Add:* Dept Chem St Louis Univ St Louis MO 63103

RAWAL, KANTI M, CROP IMPROVEMENT, SCIENTIFIC INFORMATION SYSTEMS. *Current Pos:* PLANT BREEDER, DEL MONTE CORP, R J REYNOLDS INDUST, 80- *Personal Data:* b Karachi, Pakistan, Sept 25, 40; m 72; c 2. *Educ:* Gujarat Univ, India, BSc, 61, MSc, 64; Univ Ill, PhD(genetics), 69. *Prof Exp:* Fel biochem & genetics, Univ Ill, 69-70; asst prof genetics, Univ Ibadan, Nigeria, 70-72; geneticist plant genetics, Int Inst Trop Agr, Nigeria, 72-75; chief scientist theory orgn, Lab Info Sci & Genetic Resources, Univ Colo, Boulder, 75-78, plant breeding, 78-80. *Concurrent Pos:* Mem, Int Wheat Descriptor Comt, Food & Agr Orgn, Rome, 75-80, Int Sorghum Germplasm Comt, 76-80 & Tech Adv Comt Wheat, Sorghum, Peas, Beans & Tomatoes, Sea Sci & Educ Admin, Agr Res, USDA, 78-80. *Mem:* Fel Linnaean Soc; Am Genetic Asn; Am Soc Agron; Crop Sci Soc Am; Soc Econ Bot. *Res:* Plant breeding of tomatoes, dry legumes, cucumbers; germplasm resources exploration, utilization and management; population biology of native plants; computerized information management for agriculture; statistics; biosystematics; crop evolution and tropical agricultural ecosystems. *Mailing Add:* 571 Mitchell Ave San Leandro CA 94577

RAWAT, ARUN KUMAR, BIOCHEMISTRY. *Current Pos:* PROF PHARMACOL, UNIV TOLEDO, 78- *Personal Data:* b Uttar Pradesh, India, Sept 19, 45; m 74. *Educ:* Univ Lucknow, BSc, 62, MSc, 64; Univ Copenhagen, DSc(biochem), 69. *Prof Exp:* NIH fel, 69-70; instr med, City Univ New York, 70; asst prof psychiat, State Univ NY Downstate Med Ctr, 70-72; assoc prof psychiat & biochem, Med Col Ohio, 73-78. *Concurrent Pos:* Dir div neurochem, Dept Psychiat, State Univ NY Downstate Med Ctr, 70-72; dir, Alcohol Res Ctr, 73- *Mem:* Am Soc Biol Chemists; Am Soc Neurochem; Am Soc Clin Res. *Res:* Neurochemistry of alcoholism; effects of alcohol on fetus; mechanisms of addiction; effect of alcohol on protein synthesis in brain. *Mailing Add:* Midwest Inst Treat & Study Alcoholism Univ Toledo PO Box 5888 Toledo OH 43613-0888

RAWAT, BANMALI SINGH, MICROWAVES, OPTICAL FIBER COMMUNICATIONS. *Current Pos:* prof & head elec eng, 88-91, PROF, ELEC ENG DEPT, UNIV NEV, RENO, 88- *Personal Data:* b Garhwal, UP, India, July 2, 47; US citizen; m 77, Shanti Parmar; c Manita & Sahit. *Educ:* Banaras Hindu Univ, India, BS, 68, MS, 70; Sri Venkasteswara Univ, India, PhD(elec eng), 76. *Prof Exp:* Instr engr, W Coast Paper Mills, India, 71-72; sr res fel, BITS-Pilani, SV Univ Tirupati, 72-75; sr scientist res, Defense Res & Develop, Govt India, 75-78; assoc prof elec eng, Univ Gorakhpur, India, 78-80, prof & head, 80-81; assoc prof elec eng, Univ NDak, 81-86, prof, 86-88. *Concurrent Pos:* Prin investr, IBM, E F Johnson Co, II Morrow Projs, 82-90; consult, E F Johnson Co, Waseca, Minn, 82-88, UPS/II Morrow Inc, Salem, Ore, 89-90; chmn adv comt, ISRAMT, 89-92, 92-; chmn Northern Nev Sect, Inst Elect & Electronics Engrs, 90-91, 93-94 & 94-95. *Mem:* Sr mem Inst Elec & Electronics Engrs; Int Soc Optical Engrs; Electromagnetics Acad; Soc Photo-optical Instrumentation Engrs; Sigma Xi. *Res:* Microwave integrated circuits; mm-waves; dielectric waveguides; microstrip antennas; mobile communication filters; dielectric resonators; EM numerical techniques; optical fibers; optical fiber sensors. *Mailing Add:* Elec Eng Dept Univ Nev Reno NV 89557

RAWITCH, ALLEN BARRY, BIOCHEMISTRY, FORENSIC CHEMISTRY. *Current Pos:* assoc prof, 75-82, PROF BIOCHEM, MED SCH, UNIV KANS, 82- *Personal Data:* b Chicago, Ill, Dec 29, 40; m 62, Patricia N Karlan; c Bruce & David. *Educ:* Univ Calif, Los Angeles, BS, 63, PhD(biochem), 67. *Honors & Awards:* Res Career Develop Award, NIH, 72. *Prof Exp:* Res chemist, Wadsworth Vet Admin Hosp, Los Angeles, 62-63; res assoc biochem, Univ Ill, Urbana, 67-69; from asst prof to assoc prof chem, Kent State Univ, 69-75. *Concurrent Pos:* Fel, Univ Ill, Urbana, 67-69; scientist, Mid Am Cancer Ctr Prog; dir Med Biochem, Univ Kans Med Ctr, 76-87, vchmn, 81-; dir, Biotech Support Facil, 88-91 & Med Biochem, 93- *Mem:* Endocrine Soc; Am Soc Biol Chemists; Sigma Xi; Am Thyroid Asn. *Res:* Physical and chemical properties of proteins; application of fluorescence spectroscopy to study macromolecules; structure of thyroid proteins; thyroid hormone biosynthesis; structure of pancreatic hormones; comparative endocrinology; drug analyses techniques; gas-phase micro sequencing of peptide and proteins; solid-phase peptide synthesis. *Mailing Add:* Dept Biochem & Molecular Biol Univ Kans Med Ctr 3901 Rainbow Blvd Kansas City KS 66160-7421. *Fax:* 913-588-7440

RAWITSCHER, GEORGE HEINRICH, THEORETICAL NUCLEAR PHYSICS. *Current Pos:* assoc prof, 66-72, PROF PHYSICS, UNIV CONN, 72- *Personal Data:* b Freiburg, Ger, Feb 27, 28; US citizen; m 57, 82; c 2. *Educ:* Univ Sao Paulo, Brazil, AB, 49; Stanford Univ, PhD(physics), 56. *Prof Exp:* Instr physics, Brazil Ctr Invest Physics, 50-52; asst, Stanford Univ, 53-56; instr, Univ Rochester, 56-58; instr, Yale Univ, 58-61, asst prof, 61-64. *Concurrent Pos:* Alexander V Humboldt Found fel, Max Planck Inst Nuclear Physics, 64-66; Brazilian Army Res, 50-71. *Mem:* Am Phys Soc. *Res:* Elementary particle and nuclear physics; mu mesons; scattering and reaction theory in nuclear physics. *Mailing Add:* Dept Physics U46 Univ Conn 2152 Hillside Rd Storrs CT 06269

RAWLING, FRANK L(ESLIE), JR, CHEMICAL ENGINEERING. *Current Pos:* res engr, E I Du Pont de Nemours & Co, Inc, 64-68, sr res engr, Textile Fibers Dept, 68-80, proj engr, 81-83, consult, 83-91, SR CONSULT, ENG DEPT, E I DU PONT DE NEMOURS & CO, INC, 91- *Personal Data:* b Lowell, Mass, Dec 2, 35; m 66; c 2. *Educ:* Lowell Tech Inst, BS, 59; Univ Maine, MS, 61; Iowa State Univ, PhD(chem eng), 64. *Prof Exp:* Res asst chem eng, Iowa State Univ, 61-64. *Mem:* Am Inst Chem Engrs. *Res:* Polymer processing, especially with regard to man-made fibers; mass transfer; mixing technology, process design. *Mailing Add:* 32 Carriage Lane Newark DE 19711

RAWLINGS, CHARLES ADRIAN, INSTRUMENTATION. *Current Pos:* from lectr to assoc prof, 64-92, PROF, DEPT ELEC ENG, SOUTHERN ILL UNIV, CARBONDALE, 77-, DIR, BIOMED ENG, 81- *Personal Data:* b Paducah, Ky, Nov 11, 36. *Educ:* Univ Ill, BS, 59; Southern Ill Univ, MS, 65, PhD(eng & physiol), 74. *Prof Exp:* Engr, Sperry Utah Eng Labs, div Sperry Rand Corp, 59-61; field eng training rep, Autonetics Div, NAm Aviation, 61-65, mem tech staff, clin eng, 66-69, sr logistics field engr, Space & Info Syst, 65. *Concurrent Pos:* Mem, Bd Examrs Cert Biomed Equip Technicians, 73-75, chmn, 75-79, chmn Cert Comn, 79-81; qualified instr, Defense Civil Preparedness Agency, 70-; mem bd dir, Asn Advan Med Instrumentation Foundations, 79-81, pres, Asn Advan Med Instrumentation, 81-83, chmn bd dir, 83-84, ed, Med Instrumentation, 87-89; dir Sem Biomed Instrumentation, 72-; asst chmn, Dept Elec Eng, Southern Ill Univ, Carbondale, 87-; mem, bd trustees, Mensa Educ & Res Found, 96- *Mem:* Sr mem Instrument Soc Am; Inst Elec & Electronics Engrs; Asn Advan Med Instrumentation (pres, 81-83); Am Soc Hosp Eng. *Res:* Medical instrumentation, especially that related to cardiovascular system; rehabilitation engineering; sensory physiology; electro cardiography on humans; electric safety. *Mailing Add:* Elect Eng Southern Ill Univ Carbondale IL 62901

RAWLINGS, CLARENCE ALVIN, VETERINARY SURGERY. *Current Pos:* ASSOC PROF SURG, UNIV GA, 72- *Personal Data:* b Olney, Ill, Apr 18, 43; m 67; c 2. *Educ:* Univ Ill, BS, 65, DVM, 67; Colo State Univ, MS, 69; Univ Wis, PhD(vet med), 74; Am Col Vet Surgeons, dipl. *Prof Exp:* Staff vet, Humane Soc Mo, St Louis, 67-68; Nat Defense Educ Act fel surg, Col Vet Med, Colo State Univ, 68-69; chief & asst chief exp surg, USAF Sch Aerospace Med, Brooks AFB, Tex, 69-72; fel phsyiol, Univ Wis, 72-74. *Mem:* Am Vet Med Asn; Acad Vet Cardiol; Am Soc Vet Anesthesiol; Am Soc Vet Physiologists & Pharmacologists; Am Heart Asn. *Res:* Understanding cardiopulmonary function in clinical conditions; heartworm disease, anesthesia, shock, cardiac tamponade, and congenital heart disease; prospective clinical studies involve soft tissue surgery. *Mailing Add:* Dept Small Animal Med Col Vet Med Univ Ga Athens GA 30602

RAWLINGS, GARY DON, ENVIRONMENTAL SCIENCE, PHYSICS. *Current Pos:* contract mgr & eng specialist environ res & develop, Dayton Lab, Monsanto Corp, 74-83, int mkt mgr, nuclear sources, 83-84, bus develop mgr, phosphate fiber, 84-87, mkt develop mgr specialty chem, Monsanto Corp, 87-92, DIR COM DEVELOP, MONSANTO GROWTH ENTERPRISE, 92- *Personal Data:* b Houston, Tex, Feb 6, 48; m 69, 82, Marilyn S Mooney; c Lisa K, M Brent & C Jason. *Educ:* Southwest Tex State Univ, BS, 70, MS, 71; Tex A&M Univ, PhD(environ sci, eng), 74. *Prof Exp:* Res asst & grant, Tex Exp Sta, Tex A&M Univ, 73-74. *Mem:* Air Pollution Control Asn; Am Inst Chem Engrs; Sigma Xi; Soc Advan Mat & Process Eng; Soc Plastic Indust. *Res:* Solution to environmentally related problems; detection systems; analytical techniques; control technology alternatives; new business development for high performance specialty chemicals and materials; establish new high tech businesses for corporation. *Mailing Add:* Monsanto 800 N Lindbergh Blvd St Louis MO 63167

RAWLINGS, JOHN OREN, BIOMETRICS. *Current Pos:* RETIRED. *Personal Data:* b Archer, Nebr, July 26, 32; m 52, Mary R Reichardt; c 3. *Educ:* Univ Nebr, BS, 53, MS, 57; NC State Col, PhD, 60. *Prof Exp:* Geneticist, Agr Res Serv, USDA, 59-60; asst statist, NC State Univ, 60-61, from asst prof to prof statist, Dept Statist, 68-94. *Concurrent Pos:* Assoc ed, Biometrics, Biomet Soc, 75; statist consult, Nat Crop Loss Assessment Network, 81-89; chmn, Environ Protection Agency Acid Precipation Rev, Am Statist Asn, 83-84. *Mem:* Fel Am Soc Agron; Crop Sci Soc Am; Biomet Soc; fel Am Statist Asn. *Res:* Design and analysis of experiments. *Mailing Add:* 6216 Splitrock Trail Apex NC 27502

RAWLINGS, SAMUEL CRAIG, BEHAVIORAL SCIENCES, VISION RESEARCH. *Current Pos:* Glaucoma & training, Nat Eye Inst, NIH, 75-77, exec secy, humaN develop & aging study, Sect Div Grants, NIH, 80-86, CHIEF, BEHAV & NEUROL SCI REV SECT, DIV RES GRANTS, NIH, 86- *Personal Data:* b Wichita, Kans, Sept 7, 38; m, Kathy Bowers; c Megan, Chainy & Ryan. *Educ:* Calif State Univ, Fullerton, BS, 64; Univ Miami, MS, 68 & PhD(psychol), 70. *Prof Exp:* Asst prof, Univ Houston, 71-74; asst prof & dir res, ophthal, Univ Tex Health Sci Ctr, 77-80. *Concurrent Pos:* Ed bd, Peer Rev Notes, Nat Inst Health, 86- *Mem:* Am Psychol Asn. *Res:* Supervise behavioral and neurosciences review section which is composed of 18 Nat Inst Health study sections. *Mailing Add:* 6535 Farmingdale Ct Rockville MD 20855

RAWLINS, NOLAN OMRI, AGRICULTURAL ECONOMICS. *Current Pos:* from asst prof to assoc prof, 68-81, PROF AGR, MID TENN STATE UNIV, 81- *Personal Data:* b McRae, Ga, Nov 30, 38; m 64; c 4. *Educ:* Univ Ga, BSA, 61, MS, 63; Tex A&M Univ, PhD(agr econ), 68. *Prof Exp:* Asst prof econ & sociol, Middle Ga Col, 67-68. *Mem:* Nat Asn Col & Teachers Agr. *Mailing Add:* Dept Agr Mid Tenn State Univ Box 5 Murfreesboro TN 37132

RAWLINS, WILSON TERRY, PHYSICAL CHEMISTRY, CHEMICAL KINETICS. *Current Pos:* head aeronomy & surface sci group, Aerospace Sci Area, 86-87, PRIN SCIENTIST, PHYS SCI INC, 77-, MGR CHEM SCI, 87- *Personal Data:* b Edinburg, Tex, Nov 8, 49; m 75, Elizabeth Brown; c Kyle G & Adriana F. *Educ:* Univ Tex, Austin, BS & BA, 72; Univ Pittsburgh, PhD(chem), 77. *Mem:* Am Geophys Union; Combustion Inst; Soc Photo-Optical Instrumentation Engrs. *Res:* Gas phase kinetics, photochemistry and spectroscopy; chemistry of planetary atmospheres; combustion chemistry; gas-surface interactions. *Mailing Add:* Phys Sci Inc 20 New Eng Bus Ctr Andover MA 01810. *Fax:* 978-689-3232; *E-Mail:* rawlins@psicorp.com

RAWLINSON, DAVID JOHN, ORGANIC CHEMISTRY. *Current Pos:* from asst prof to assoc prof, 68-77, PROF CHEM, WESTERN ILL UNIV, 77- *Personal Data:* b Manchester, Eng, May 14, 35. *Educ:* Oxford Univ, BA, 57, PhD(chem), 63. *Prof Exp:* Res assoc, Univ Ore, 59-61; tech officer, Plant Protection Ltd, Eng, 61-63; chemist, Agr Chem Div, Shell Develop Co, US, 63-65; fel, Ill Inst Technol, 65-66; fel & lectr, Univ Wis-Milwaukee, 66-68. *Res:* Free radical chemistry; chemistry of peroxides. *Mailing Add:* Chem Western Ill Univ 900 W Adams St Macomb IL 61455-1396

RAWLINSON, JOHN ALAN, MEDICAL PHYSICS. *Current Pos:* clin physicist, 65-68, sr clin physicist, 70-77, PHYSICIST-IN-CHG HIGH ENERGY SECT & HEAD CLIN PHYSICIST, ONT CANCER INST, 78- *Personal Data:* b Liverpool, Eng, Nov 30, 40; Can citizen; m 67; c 3. *Educ:* Univ London, BSc Hons, 63; Univ Toronto, MSc, 70. *Prof Exp:* Head physicist, Inst Radiother, Brazil, 77-78. *Concurrent Pos:* Mem tech comt, 62, Can Nat Comt, Int Electrotech Comn, 76- *Mem:* Can Asn Physicists; Am Asn Physicists Med; Brazilian Asn Med Physics. *Res:* Improvement in the radiation characteristics of equipment used in radiation therapy; improvements in treatment techniques in radiation therapy. *Mailing Add:* 32 St Cuthberts Rd Toronto ON M4G 1V1 Can

RAWLS, HENRY RALPH, BIOMEDICAL MATERIALS, CONTROLLED RELEASE. *Current Pos:* PROF, UNIV TEX HEALTH SCI CTR, SAN ANTONIO, 87- *Personal Data:* b Chattahoochee, Fla, Nov 19, 35; m 78, Andrea Geoffray; c Randall G. *Educ:* La State Univ, BS, 57; Fla State Univ, PhD(phys chem), 64. *Prof Exp:* Res chemist, Unilever Res Lab, Unilever NV, Holland, 64-67; res chemist, Gulf S Res Inst, 68-73, sr res chemist & mgr, Physics Dept, 73-76; from asst prof to assoc prof biomat, Sch Dent, La State Univ, 77-85; staff res & develop scientist, Gillette Co, Boston, 85-87. *Concurrent Pos:* Vis scientist, Forsyth Dent Ctr, Boston, 78 & staff assoc, 85-87; Fogarty sr fel, Mat Tech Lab, Univ Groningen, Holland, 80; consult, Johnson & Johnson, 72-79, Gulf Res Inst, 76-85, Univ Mich Dent Sch, 79-84, Bausch & Lomb Co, 89-90 & Oral-B Labs, 90-95; prin investr res grants, NIH, 74-, res career awardee, 77-79; adj prof biomed eng, Tulane Univ, 80-84; res assoc, Polymer Res Inst, State Univ NY, Syracuse, 82-; consult, Biomed Develop Corp, San Antonio, Tex, 88. *Mem:* Adhesion Soc; Am Chem Soc; Int Asn Dent Res; fel Acad Dent Mat; Europ Orgn Caries Res; Controlled Release Soc. *Res:* Applications of physical, surface and polymer chemistry to biomedical problems; oral diseases; development of restorative polymer resin materials and oral-care products for dentistry. *Mailing Add:* Div Biomat Univ Tex Health Sci Ctr 7703 Floyd Curl Dr San Antonio TX 78284-7890. *Fax:* 210-567-6354; *E-Mail:* rawls@uthscsa.edu

RAWLS, JOHN MARSHALL, ACCELERATORS. *Current Pos:* DIR, ELECTROMAGNETIC SYST DIV, GEN ATOMICS, 74- *Personal Data:* b Washington, DC, June 29, 44; m 66, Dawn; c Diana & Alicia. *Educ:* Mich State Univ, BS, 65; Brandeis Univ, PhD(particle physics), 70. *Mem:* Am Phys Soc. *Res:* High average power accelerator technology. *Mailing Add:* PO Box 85608 San Diego CA 92186-9784. *Fax:* 619-455-3334; *E-Mail:* john.rawls@gat.com

RAWLS, JOHN MARVIN, JR, GENE STRUCTURE & EXPRESSION. *Current Pos:* from asst prof to assoc prof, 75-90, PROF BIOL SCI, T H MORGAN SCH BIOL SCI, UNIV KY, 90- *Personal Data:* b Madison, Tenn, May 12, 46; m 69, Carol Shumock; c John & Anna. *Educ:* Univ S Ala, BS, 69; Univ NC, Chapel Hill, PhD(zool), 73. *Prof Exp:* Postdoctoral fel genetics, Univ Calif, Berkeley, 73-75. *Concurrent Pos:* Vis scientist, Eucaryotes Molecular Genetics Lab, Strasbourg, France, 81-82; Sch Biol Sci, Univ Sussex, UK, 88; dir, Sch Bio! Sci, Univ Ky, 88- *Mem:* Genetics Soc Am. *Res:* Molecular genetics of coordinate gene expression in animal cells, using the pyrimidine biosynthesis genes in Drosophila melanogaster as a model experiment station. *Mailing Add:* 101 Morgan Bldg Univ Ky Lexington KY 40506. *Fax:* 606-257-1717; *E-Mail:* bio145@ukcc.uky.edu

RAWLS, WALTER CECIL, JR, GENERAL ENVIRONMENTAL SCIENCES, MEDICAL PHYSICS. *Current Pos:* Assoc res dir, 72-84, RES DIR, DAVIS RES LABS, 84-; PRES, BIOMAGNETICS INT INC, 72-; VPRES, BIOMAGNETICS SYSTS, INC, 84- *Personal Data:* b Richmond, Va, Sept 13, 28; m, Sheila Kitsch; c Richard W & James D. *Educ:* Washington Univ, JD, 58; Davis Col, DSc, 73. *Hon Degrees:* PhD, McGill Univ, 78. *Mem:* AAAS; NY Acad Sci; Fedn Am Scientists. *Res:* Biomagnetics; development of medical, agricultural, environmental and industrial products. *Mailing Add:* Biomagnetics Int Inc 2301 Park Ave Orange Park FL 32073

RAWNSLEY, HOWARD MELODY, PATHOLOGY. *Current Pos:* RETIRED. *Personal Data:* b Long Branch, NJ, Nov 20, 25; m 67; c 2. *Educ:* Haverford Col, AB, 49; Univ Pa, MD, 52; Am Bd Path, cert anat path, 57, clin path, 58. *Prof Exp:* From assoc to assoc prof clin path, Sch Med, Univ Pa, 57-69, prof path, 69-75, from asst dir to dir, William Pepper Lab, 60-75, assoc dir, Clin Res Ctr, Univ Hosp, 62-70; vchmn dept, Dartmouth Med Sch, 75-79, prof path, 75-94, chmn dept, 79-94. *Concurrent Pos:* Trustee, Am Bd Path. *Mem:* AAAS; AMA; Am Asn Clin Chem; Col Am Path; Am Soc Clin Path; Am Bd Path. *Res:* Clinical chemistry; liver disease; serum proteins; interpretation of laboratory information. *Mailing Add:* 7 Haskins Rd Hanover NH 03755

RAWSON, ERIC GORDON, OPTICS. *Current Pos:* PRES, RAWSON OPTICS, 95- *Personal Data:* b Saskatoon, Sask, Mar 4, 37; m 66; c 3. *Educ:* Univ Sask, BA, 59, MA, 60; Univ Toronto, PhD(physics), 66. *Prof Exp:* Mem tech staff optics, Bell Tel Labs, 66-73; mem res staff optics, Xerox Palo Alto Res Ctr, 73-80, mgr, I&TT Area Optics, 80-95. *Mem:* Fel Optical Soc Am; Inst Elec & Electronics Engrs; Soc Photo Instrumentation Engrs. *Res:* Fiber-optical waveguides and systems; optics of display systems; light scattering; 3-dimensional displays. *Mailing Add:* 20887 Maureen Way Saratoga CA 95070

RAWSON, JAMES RULON YOUNG, PLANT MOLECULAR BIOLOGY. *Current Pos:* res assoc, 84-89, SR RES ASSOC, BP AM, 89- *Personal Data:* b Boston, Mass, July 28, 43; m 70; c 2. *Educ:* Cornell Univ, BS, 65; Northwestern Univ, PhD(biol), 69. *Prof Exp:* NIH fel, Univ Chicago, 69-71, trainee biophys, 71-72; from asst prof to assoc prof bot & biochem, Univ Ga, 72-83, prof bot & genetics, 83-84. *Concurrent Pos:* NSF res grants, 73-75, 75-77, 77-79, 79-81, 80-82 & 82-85; Res Corp grant, 75-76; USDA grant, 80-82. *Mem:* Am Soc Biochem & Molecular Biol; Am Chem Soc. *Res:* Microbial genetics; biochemistry. *Mailing Add:* 60 Timberwick Dr Clifton Park NY 12065

RAWSON, RICHARD RAY, GEOLOGY. *Current Pos:* RETIRED. *Personal Data:* b Loma Linda, Calif, Dec 31, 28; m 52, Helen J Ashman; c Dawn, Ron, Mary, Brian, Carol & David. *Educ:* Brigham Young Univ, BS, 56, MS, 57; Univ Wis, PhD(geol), 66. *Prof Exp:* Res geologist, Continental Oil Co, 57-63; asst prof geol, Emory Univ, 66-67; from asst prof to assoc prof geol, Northern Ariz Univ, 67-80; sr geologist, Marathon Oil Co, 80-82, dist geologist, 82-84, div staff geologist, 84-88, regional staff geologist, 88-92. *Mem:* Am Asn Petrol Geol. *Res:* Depositional environments carbonate sediments; stratigraphy; sedimentation; basin analysis; petroleum exploration. *Mailing Add:* 2156 Mesa Hills Dr Cedar City UT 84720

RAWSON, ROBERT ORRIN, PHYSIOLOGY. *Current Pos:* RETIRED. *Personal Data:* b East St Louis, Ill, Apr 25, 17; m 87, Carolyn Kneen; c 3. *Educ:* Univ Ill, Urbana, BS, 40; Loyola Univ, Ill, PhD(physiol), 60. *Prof Exp:* Res metallurgist, Am Zinc Co, Ill, 40-44; radio & TV broadcasting, St Louis & Chicago, 44-56; instr biol, Univ Ill, Chicago Circle, 56-58; instr physiol, Sch Med, Yale Univ, 61-68, asst prof epidemiol, 68-75, sr res assoc & lectr, 75-82. *Concurrent Pos:* Fel physiol, Loyola Univ, Ill, 60-61; from asst fel physiol to fel, John B Pierce Found, Conn, 61-82, fel emer, 82. *Mem:* Am Physiol Soc. *Res:* Physiology of temperature regulation; nervous control of circulation; physiology and pharmacology of the autonomic nervous system. *Mailing Add:* 273 Legend Hill Madison CT 06443

RAY, AJIT KUMAR, applied mathematics, fluid dynamics, for more information see previous edition

RAY, ALDEN E(ARL), PHYSICAL METALLURGY. *Current Pos:* RETIRED. *Personal Data:* b Centralia, Ill, Feb 14, 31; m 52; c 4. *Educ:* Southern Ill Univ, BA, 53; Iowa State Univ, PhD(metall), 59. *Prof Exp:* Jr chemist, Ames Lab, Iowa State Univ, 53-56, res asst, 56-59; res metallurgist, Res & Eng Div, Monsanto Chem Co, 59-61; assoc prof, Univ Dayton, 61-71, sr metallurgist, Res Inst, 61-91, dir grad prog mat sci, 71-76, prof, Sch Eng, 71-91, supvr, Metals & Ceramics Div, 74-87, dir, Magnetics Lab, 89-91. *Mem:* Fel Am Soc Metals; Sigma Xi; Am Soc Testing & Mat; sr mem Inst Elec

& Electronics Engrs; Magnetics Soc. *Res:* Structure-property relationships of intermetallic phases, especially of rare earth transition metal alloys; magnetic properties; phase stability; phase diagrams. *Mailing Add:* 950 S Garcia St No 220 Port Isabel TX 78578

RAY, ALLEN COBBLE, VETERINARY TOXICOLOGY, ANALYTICAL TOXICOLOGY. *Current Pos:* vet toxicologist, 73-87, HEAD DRUG TESTING LAB, TEX VET MED DIAG LAB, TEX A&M UNIV, 87- *Personal Data:* b Jacksonville, Tex, Nov 17, 41; m 73, Betty Pharr. *Educ:* Univ Tex, Austin, BS, 64, PhD(chem), 71. *Prof Exp:* Teaching asst chem, Univ Tex, Austin, 64-67; res scientist, Clayton Found, Biochem Inst, Univ Tex, 67-71, res assoc, 72-73. *Concurrent Pos:* Vis mem, Dept Vet Physiol & Pharmacol, Tex A&M Univ, 78-; mem safety, Am Asn Vet Diag Comm, 87-89, anal toxicol, 88-90; assoc ref, Asn Off Anal Chem, 87-89; chair, SW Asn Toxicol, 87-90, pres, 93-94. *Mem:* Am Chem Soc; Am Asn Vet Lab Diag; Soc Toxicol; Am Inst Chem; Asn Off Anal Chem; Asn Off Racing Chem. *Res:* Development of analytical and diagnostic methods in veterinary and human toxicology; chemistry modes of action and metabolism of naturally occurring and environmental toxins; analytical methods for drugs of abuse in racing animals. *Mailing Add:* TV MDL PO Drawer 3040 College Station TX 77841. *Fax:* 409-845-1794

RAY, ALOKE K, COST REDUCTION TECHNIQUES FOR PROTOTYPE DEVELOPMENT, ADVANCED LASER MANUFACTURING PROCESS. *Current Pos:* SR PROJ ENGR, DELCO ELECTRONICS, 95- *Educ:* Gauhati Univ, BSME, 77; Calcutta Univ, MSME, 80; Marquette Univ, MSME, 86; Iowa State Univ, PhD(advan mfg), 95. *Prof Exp:* Engr exec design, Tata Eng Co, 80-83; proj engr, Artos Eng, 85-88, Systems Inc, 88-90; sr develop engr, Buehler Prods Inc, 95. *Concurrent Pos:* Vpres mkt & sales, Develop Consults, Inc, 90- *Mem:* Am Soc Mech Engrs. *Res:* Applied reverse engineering techniques; cost effective prototype product design; fatigue life predictions. *Mailing Add:* 4715 Wexmore Dr Kokomo IN 46902

RAY, APURBA KANTI, HIGH INTENSITY SWEETENERS. *Current Pos:* res scientist gum & emulsions, 79-82, SR SCIENTIST, GUMS, EMULSIONS & SWEETENERS, COCA-COLA CO, ATLANTA, 82- *Personal Data:* b Calcutta, India, Sept 9, 43; US citizen; m 81; c 1. *Educ:* Jadavpur Univ, Calcutta, BSc, 61, MSc, 63, PhD(kinetics & solution chem), 69. *Prof Exp:* Instr chem, Pratt Inst, 69-70 & Brooklyn Col, City Univ NY 70-71-; interdisciplinary res fel neurol, Albert Einstein Col Med, Bronx, NY, 71-73, res assoc lung surfactant physico-chem, 73-79. *Mem:* Am Chem Soc; fel Am Inst Chemists; Inst Food Technologists; Int Asn Colloid & Interface Scientists. *Res:* Emulsion science and technology; sensory analyses of high intensity sweeteners relevant to beverage systems. *Mailing Add:* Corp Res & Develop Coca-Cola Co PO Drawer 1734 Atlanta GA 30301

RAY, ASIT KUMAR, MATHEMATICAL MODELING, HEAT & MASS TRANSFER. *Current Pos:* from asst prof to assoc prof, 80-88, PROF CHEM ENG, UNIV KY, 88- *Personal Data:* b Calcutta, India, Jan 23, 54; m 85. *Educ:* Indian Inst Technol, BTech, 75; Clarkson Col Technol, MS, 77, PhD(chem eng), 80. *Honors & Awards:* Kenneth T Whitby Award, Am Asn Aerosol Res, 84; Presidential Young Investr Award, NSF, 84. *Prof Exp:* Fel, Univ NMex, 80. *Mem:* Sigma Xi; Am Inst Chem Engrs; NY Acad Sci; Am Asn Aerosol Res; Fine Particle Soc; Sigma Xi. *Res:* Formation and growth of aerosol particles; experimental and theoretical studies on single particle systems to understand mass transfer phenomena in continuum and non-continuum regimes. *Mailing Add:* 2044 Vonlist Way Lexington KY 40502

RAY, CHARLES, JR, GENETICS. *Current Pos:* RETIRED. *Personal Data:* b Baltimore, Md, Dec 6, 11; m 37; c 1. *Educ:* Lafayette Col, AB, 37; Univ Va, PhD(genetics), 41. *Prof Exp:* Geneticist, Plant Res Dept, Cent Fibre Corp, 41-52; from asst prof to prof, biol, Emory Univ, 52-80, emer prof, 80,. *Concurrent Pos:* Mem, Marine Biol Lab, Woods Hole Oceanog Inst. *Mem:* Genetics Soc Am. *Res:* Population genetics; computer simulation. *Mailing Add:* 1993-L N Williamsburg Dr Decatur GA 30033-3510

RAY, CHARLES DEAN, NEUROSURGERY, SURGERY OF THE SPINE. *Current Pos:* ASSOC DIR SPINE SURG, INST LOW BACK CARE, 80-; PRES & CHMN BD RES & DEVELOP, SPINE, CEDAR SURG, INC, 86- *Personal Data:* b Americus, Ga, Aug 1, 27; m 92, Nancy Newhard; c 4. *Educ:* Emory Univ, AB, 50; Univ Miami, MS, 52; Med Col Ga, MD, 56; Am Col Surgeons, FACS, 69. *Hon Degrees:* FRSH, Royal Soc Health, London, 70. *Honors & Awards:* Sci Award, Bausch & Lomb, Inc, 47; Golden Spine Award, Challenge of the Lumbar Spine Soc, 87. *Prof Exp:* Res fel bioeng, Mayo Found Clin, 62-64; asst prof, neurosurg & lectr bioeng, Johns Hopkins Hosp & Univ, 64-68; vdir, med eng, Roche, Inc, Basel, Switz, 68-73; vpres, neurol devices, Medtronic, Inc, 73-80; assoc prof neurosurg, Univ Minn, 73-83. *Concurrent Pos:* Ed, Med Eng, 68-74, Med Progress Through Technol, 69-74; lectr, Univ Basel, Switz, 68-72; consult, WGer Armed Forces Med Soc, 69-71; Europ Reg dir, Inst Elec & Electronics Engrs, 69-72; indust rep, Food & Drug Admin Panel on Neurol Devices, 76-79; chief deleg, ISO Comt on Neurol Devices, 76-80; comt chair, World Fedn Neurosurg Socs, 80-91. *Mem:* AMA; fel Am Col Surgeons; fel Royal Soc Health Eng; sr mem Inst Elec & Electronics Engrs; Sigma Xi; fel NAm Spine Soc (pres, 91-92). *Res:* Author of 265 publications; granted 32 patents; spinal surgical devices and methods; artificial human disc. *Mailing Add:* 880 Kempsvielle Rd Norfolk VA 23502

RAY, CLARENCE THORPE, INTERNAL MEDICINE. *Current Pos:* chmn dept, 75-82, PROF MED, SCH MED, TULANE UNIV, 75- *Personal Data:* b Hutto, Tex, July 17, 16; m 42; c 1. *Educ:* Univ Tex, BA, 37, MD, 41; Am Bd Internal Med & Am Bd Cardiovasc Dis, dipl. *Prof Exp:* Intern, Scott & White Hosp, Temple, Tex, 41-42; resident, Parkland Hosp, Dallas, 42-44, dir outpatient dispensary, 43-44; from instr to assoc prof med, Sch Med, Tulane Univ, 45-58, dir heart sta, 47-58; prof med & chmn dept, Sch Med & physician & chief med serv, Hosp, Univ Mo-Columbia, 58-67; dir educ & res, Alton Ochsner Med Found, 67-75. *Concurrent Pos:* Instr, Southwestern Med Found, Inc, 43-44; from asst vis physician to sr vis physician, Charity Hosp, 45-58; consult, Vet Admin, 53-58, USPHS, 55-58 & Vet Admin Hosps, New Orleans & Alexandria, La, 57-58; head sect cardiol, Dept Med, Ochsner Clin, New Orleans, La, 68-75, trustee & vpres, Alton Ochsner Med Found, 70-75. *Mem:* Am Soc Clin Invest; AMA; fel Am Col Physicians. *Res:* Cardiovascular disease. *Mailing Add:* 473 Woodvine Ave Metairie LA 70005-4459

RAY, CLAYTON EDWARD, VERTEBRATE PALEONTOLOGY. *Current Pos:* assoc cur later cenozoic mammals, 64-68, CUR QUATERNARY & MARINE MAMMALS, NAT MUS NATURAL HIST, SMITHSONIAN INST, 69- *Personal Data:* b New Castle, Ind, Feb 6, 33; m 53; c 4. *Educ:* Harvard Univ, BA, 55, MA, 58, PhD(geol), 62. *Prof Exp:* Asst cur vert paleont, State Mus & asst prof biol, Univ Fla, 59-63. *Mem:* Am Soc Mammal; Soc Vert Paleont. *Res:* Systematics, morphology, distribution and evolution of Cenozoic mammals including living ones; emphasis on pinnipeds. *Mailing Add:* Nat Mus Nat Hist MRC 121 Smithsonian Inst 10th & Constitution Ave NW Washington DC 20560

RAY, DALE C(ARNEY), ELECTRICAL ENGINEERING, SOLID STATE PHYSICS. *Current Pos:* assoc prof, 66-77, assoc dean, Div Grad Studies & Res, 69-77, PROF ELEC ENG, GA INST TECHNOL, 77- *Personal Data:* b Highland Park, Mich, Aug 31, 33; m 53; c 4. *Educ:* Univ Mich, BSE, 56, MSE, 57, PhD(cryomagnetics), 62. *Prof Exp:* Res asst comput design & technol, Eng Res Inst, Univ Mich, 56-57, instr elec eng, Univ, 57-62, admin dir solid state devices lab, 60-61, asst prof elec eng, Univ, 62-66. *Concurrent Pos:* Consult, Off Res Admin, Univ Mich, 57-, Power Equip Div, Lear Siegler, Inc, 62-63, Sensor Dynamics, Inc, 63-64 & Lockheed-Ga Co, 67-; Ford Found fel, 62-63; prin engr, Raytheon Corp, 63-64. *Mem:* AAAS; Am Phys Soc; Inst Elec & Electronics Engrs; Am Asn Physics Teachers; Am Soc Eng Educ. *Res:* Cryomagnetics; magnetic measurements and application; heat transfer; non-electromechanical energy conversion; microwave integrated circuit technology and studies in sociotechnology. *Mailing Add:* Sch Elec & Comput Eng 777 Atlantic Dr Ga Inst Technol Atlanta GA 30332-0250

RAY, DAN S, MOLECULAR BIOLOGY, BIOPHYSICS. *Current Pos:* from asst prof to assoc prof, 66-73, PROF MOLECULAR BIOL, UNIV CALIF, LOS ANGELES, 73- *Personal Data:* b Memphis, Tenn, Dec 27, 37; c 2. *Educ:* Memphis State Univ, BS, 59; Western Reserve Univ, MS, 61; Stanford Univ, PhD(biophysics), 65. *Prof Exp:* USPHS fel, biochem virol, Max Planck Inst Biochem, 65-66. *Concurrent Pos:* USPHS res grants, 67-70 & 72-89, Am Cancer Soc grant, 78-80, WHO grant, 80-82; found scientist, Int Genetic Eng, Inc, 81; USPHS res grants, 82-97; NSF grant, 94-97. *Mem:* AAAS; Biophys Soc; Am Soc Microbiol; Am Soc Biochem & Molecular Biol. *Res:* Structure and replication of DNA; genetic control of DNA replication; molecular cloning of DNA; molecular parasitology; DNA sequence analysis; replication mechanisms of small viruses; genetic and biochemical analysis of trypanosomes; structure and replication of kinetoplast DNA. *Mailing Add:* Dept Molecular Cell & Develop Biol Univ Calif 405 Hilgard Ave Los Angeles CA 90095-1570

RAY, DAVID SCOTT, MATHEMATICS. *Current Pos:* assoc prof, 64-70, PROF MATH & CHMN DEPT, BUCKNELL UNIV, 70- *Personal Data:* b New Haven, Conn, Oct 5, 30; m 56; c 4. *Educ:* Washington & Jefferson Col, AB, 52; Univ Mich, MA, 56; Univ Tenn, PhD(math), 64. *Prof Exp:* Teaching fel math, Univ Mich, 56-58; instr, Univ Tenn, 58-64. *Mem:* Am Math Soc; Math Asn Am. *Res:* Topology, especially problems associated with the imbedding of Peano continua in Euclidean spaces. *Mailing Add:* Dept Math Bucknell Univ Lewisburg PA 17837

RAY, EARL ELMER, MEAT SCIENCE. *Current Pos:* asst prof, 61-72, assoc prof, 72-74, PROF ANIMAL SCI, NMEX STATE UNIV, 74- *Personal Data:* b Burnsville, NC, Aug 5, 29; m 55; c 1. *Educ:* NC State Col, BS, 52, MS, 54; Ore State Col, PhD(genetics), 58. *Prof Exp:* Asst, NC State Col, 52-54; animal husbandman sheep breeding, Agr Res Serv, USDA, NMex, 59-61. *Res:* Improvement of beef tenderness by postmortem treatments; palatability characteristics of hot-boned, prerigor meat. *Mailing Add:* 1805 Halfmoon Dr Las Cruces NM 88005

RAY, EVA K, BIOTECHNOLOGY, DEFENSE RELATED BIOLOGICAL CHEMICAL TECHNOLOGIES. *Current Pos:* TECHNOL CONSULT, STEG, RAY & ASSOCS, 85- *Personal Data:* b Zagreb, Croatia; US citizen; c Jude, Diane, David & Jean. *Educ:* Cornell Univ, BA, 55; Bryn Mawr Col, MA, 65, PhD(biochem), 73. *Prof Exp:* Instr, Med Sch, Univ Pa, 73-76; asst prof bio chem, Med Col Pa, 76-82, dir, off prog women, 80-83; vpres opers, Organica, Inc, 94. *Concurrent Pos:* Vchmn, gravitational effects living systs, Gordon Res Conf, 88, chmn, 90; consult, Aging & Spaces Res Prog, Lew Evans Found, 90, NASA, 90-91; consult, Defense Dept, Dual-use Technol Prog. *Mem:* Am Soc Microbiol; Sigma Xi; AAAS; Asn Women Sci; Geront Soc Am; Am Asn Gravitational Biol. *Res:* Lipid biochemistry - effects of lipoproteins on cholesterol metabolism; chemotherapy of herpes virus; biogenesis of herpes simplex virus envelope (glycosylation); basic and applied research in space related living systems; cell biology. *Mailing Add:* 1222 Prospect Hill Rd Villanova PA 19085. *Fax:* 215-520-0810

RAY, FREDERICK KALB, FOOD SCIENCE & TECHNOLOGY. *Current Pos:* EXTEN ANIMAL FOODS SPECIALIST MEAT & DAIRY PROD, DEPT ANIMAL SCI, OKLA STATE UNIV, 78- *Personal Data:* b Zanesville, Ohio, Mar 23, 44; m 71; c 3. *Educ:* Ohio State Univ, BScAg, 67, MS, 74; Purdue Univ, PhD(animal sci), 78. *Prof Exp:* Prod supvr meat packing, Dinner Bell Foods, Defiance, Ohio, 70-72. *Mem:* Am Soc Animal Sci; Inst Food Technologists; Am Meat Sci Asn. *Res:* Emulsion technology; factors effecting emulsion stability; evaluation of meat emulsions using scanning electron microscopy to observe the structure of fat and protein. *Mailing Add:* Dept Animal Sci Okla State Univ Stillwater OK 74078-0001

RAY, G CARLETON, ZOOLOGY, ECOLOGY. *Current Pos:* RES PROF, UNIV VA, 79- *Personal Data:* b New York, NY, Aug 15, 28; m 59; c Gwen Karen & Carleton Trimble. *Educ:* Yale Univ, BS, 50; Univ Calif, MA, 53; Columbia Univ, PhD(zool), 60. *Prof Exp:* Asst to dir, NY Aquarium, 57-59, cur, 60-66; from asst prof to assoc prof pathobiol, Sch Hyg & Pub Health, Johns Hopkins Univ, 67-79. *Concurrent Pos:* adj fac, Col William & Mary. *Mem:* Soc Marine Mammal; Am Soc Limnol & Oceanog; Am Soc Naturalists; Ecol Soc Am; Soc Conserv Biol; fel AAAS. *Res:* Role of large organisms, especially marine mammals and fish in marine ecosystems; marine ecology, especially related to marine conservation; biodiversity of coasts and oceans; land-seascape ecology. *Mailing Add:* Dept Environ Sci Clark Hall Univ Va Charlottesville VA 22903. *Fax:* 804-982-2137; *E-Mail:* cr@virginia.edu

RAY, JAMES ALTON, veterinary pathology, veterinary microbiology, for more information see previous edition

RAY, JAMES P, CORAL REEF ECOLOGY, CRUSTACEAN SYSTEMATICS. *Current Pos:* Environ adv marine biol, 74-94, MGR ENVIRON SCI, HS&E, SHELL OIL CO, 82- *Personal Data:* b New York, NY, Jan 16, 44; m 66. *Educ:* Univ Miami, BS, 66; Tex A&M Univ, MS, 70, PhD(biol oceanog), 74. *Concurrent Pos:* Contrib author, Petrol in the Marine Environ, Nat Acad Sci, 81; panel mem, Fate & Effects of Drilling Muds in the Marine Environ, Nat Acad Sci, 81-83; mem, Arctic Marine Sci Comt, Polar Res Bd, Nat Acad Sci, 84-85; Task Force on Particulate Dispersion in Oceans, 86-87; mem, Sci Adv Comt, Mineral Mgt Serv, 87-93; mem, Ocean Studies Bd, Nat Res Coun, 95- *Mem:* Int Soc Petrol Indust Biologists (pres, 81-82); Soc Environ Toxicol & Chem. *Res:* Petroleum industry research on fate and effects of drilling fluids and petroleum hydrocarbons in marine environment; fate and effects of produced water. *Mailing Add:* HS&E Shell Oil Co PO Box 4320 Houston TX 77210

RAY, JESSE PAUL, EDUCATIONAL ADMINISTRATION, ANALYTICAL CHEMISTRY. *Current Pos:* RETIRED. *Personal Data:* b Central Lake, Mich, Nov 8, 16; m 39, 82, Elsaleen Blakeley; c 1. *Educ:* Asbury Col, AB, 39; Univ Syracuse, PhD(anal chem), 47. *Prof Exp:* Teacher high sch, Ill, 39-42; chief chemist, Chem & Metall Lab, Remington Arms Co, Inc, 42-44; asst chem, Univ Syracuse, 44-45; res engr, Battelle Mem Inst, 46-47; from assoc prof to prof, Asbury Col, 47-82. *Concurrent Pos:* Consult chemist, 47-80; educ adminr, 82-92. *Mem:* Fel Am Chem Soc. *Res:* Physical chemistry of metals; determination of metal phase diagrams; development of analytical methods of steel analysis; instrumentation. *Mailing Add:* Shell Point Village 308 Nautilus Ct Ft Myers FL 33908-1610. *Fax:* 941-454-1929; *E-Mail:* jpray@prodigy.com

RAY, JOHN DELBERT, MECHANICAL ENGINEERING. *Current Pos:* DEAN, HEFF COL, 89- *Personal Data:* b Murphysboro, Ill, Aug 21, 30; m 56; c 3. *Educ:* Univ Ill, BS, 56, MS, 57; Univ Okla, PhD(mech eng), 68. *Prof Exp:* Engr, McDonnell Aircraft Corp, 57-62; res dir, Res Inst, Univ Okla, 62-68; from asst prof to prof mech eng, Col Eng, Memphis State Univ, 68-89, chmn dept & dir grad studies & res, 77-89. *Mem:* Am Soc Mech Engrs. *Res:* Vibrations; structural dynamics; design; high temperature metal erosion and fatigue; composite material. *Mailing Add:* Herff Col Eng Univ Memphis Memphis TN 38152

RAY, JOHN ROBERT, PHYSICS. *Current Pos:* from asst prof to assoc prof, 66-77, PROF PHYSICS, CLEMSON UNIV, 77- *Personal Data:* b Beckley, WVa, Jan 27, 39; m 65; c 2. *Educ:* Rose-Hulman Inst Technol, BS, 61; Univ Ohio, PhD(physics), 64. *Prof Exp:* Asst prof physics, Auburn Univ, 64-65; res assoc, Coord Sci Lab, Univ Ill, 65-66. *Concurrent Pos:* Res fel, Marshall Space Flight Ctr, Huntsville, Ala, 81-82; res partic, Argonne Nat Lab, Ill, 83-85. *Mem:* Am Phys Soc. *Res:* Relativity; field theory; theoretical physics; molecular dynamic computer simulation of solids. *Mailing Add:* Dept Physics & Astron Clemson Univ 303 Kinard Lab Clemson SC 29634-1911

RAY, JOHN ROBERT, GEOGRAPHIC INFORMATION SYSTEMS. *Current Pos:* from instr to prof, 64-84, chmn dept, 74-84, EMER PROF GEOG, WRIGHT STATE UNIV, 84- *Personal Data:* b Alderson, WVa, Aug 27, 21; m 48. *Educ:* Ind Univ, AB, 54, MA, 55; Ohio State Univ, PhD(geog), 72. *Prof Exp:* From instr to asst prof geog, Univ Miami, 55-64. *Concurrent Pos:* Wright State Univ Res Coun grant, 74-75; vis prof civil eng, Ohio State Univ, 80-81; mem bd dirs, Am Soc Photogram & Remote Sensing, 81-84; mem bd trustees, Soc Photog Scientists & Engrs, 85-86 & Int Geog Info Found. *Mem:* Am Soc Photogram & Remote Sensing; Asn Am Geogrs; Int Geog Info Found (pres, 87-91, vpres 92-). *Res:* Analysis of environmental problems with remote sensing techniques; terrain analysis, using aerial photo interpretation; measuring human attitudes toward environmental insults; conservation of resources, geographic information systems applications; remote sensing of Earth Resources. *Mailing Add:* 710 Leisure Lane Waverly OH 45690

RAY, OAKLEY S, PSYCHOPHARMACOLOGY. *Current Pos:* PROF PSYCHOL, VANDERBILT UNIV, 70-, ASSOC PROF PHARMACOL, MED CTR, 70-, PROF PSYCHIAT, 82- *Personal Data:* b Altoona, Pa, Feb 6, 31; m 53; c 4. *Educ:* Cornell Univ, BA, 52; Univ Pittsburgh, MEd, 54, PhD(psychol), 58. *Prof Exp:* Assoc prof psychol pharmacol, Univ Pittsburgh, 60-70; chief ment health unit patient care, Vet Admin Ctr, Nashville, 73-87. *Concurrent Pos:* Fel, Neuropharmacol Res Labs, NIMH, Pittsburgh, 58-60; chief psychol serv, Vet Admin Med Ctr, Nashville, 70-; chief, Psychol Res Lab, Vet Admin Med Ctr, Nashville, 70-; mem, Grad Neurobiol Res Training Progs, NIMH, 74-78. *Mem:* Fel Am Col Neuropsychopharmacol; fel Am Psychol Asn; Am Soc Pharmacol & Exp Therapeut. *Res:* Research centers around the genetic and developmental determinants of brain function in animals, and on the effects of CNS drugs on behavior during development and at maturity. *Mailing Add:* 2100 Hampton Ave Nashville TN 37215-1402

RAY, PAUL DEAN, BIOCHEMISTRY. *Current Pos:* from asst prof to assoc prof, 67-73, PROF BIOCHEM, SCH MED, UNIV NDAK, 73-, CHESTER FRITZ DISTINGUISHED PROF, 92- *Personal Data:* b Monmouth, Ill, Dec 7, 34; m 57, Annette M Thrift; c Debra A, Kenneth A, Michael E & Linda M. *Educ:* Monmouth Col, Ill, AB, 56; St Louis Univ, PhD(biochem), 62. *Prof Exp:* Am Cancer Soc fel, Enzyme Inst, Univ Wis-Madison, 62-65, univ fel, 65-67. *Concurrent Pos:* Estab investr, Am Heart Asn, 67-72, mem Great Plains regional res rev & adv comn, 74-78; mem study sect arthritis metab & digestive dis, NIH, 69-73. *Mem:* Sigma Xi; Am Chem Soc; Am Soc Biol Chem. *Res:* Carbohydrate metabolism, gluconeogenesis, and metabolic regulation; endocrinology. *Mailing Add:* Dept Biochem Univ NDak Sch Med Grand Forks ND 58202. *Fax:* 701-777-3894; *E-Mail:* paulray@mail.med.und.nodak.edu

RAY, PETER MARTIN, PLANT PHYSIOLOGY. *Current Pos:* PROF BIOL SCI, STANFORD UNIV, 68- *Personal Data:* b San Jose, Calif, Dec 17, 31; m 54; c 2. *Educ:* Univ Calif, AB, 51; Harvard Univ, PhD(biol), 55. *Honors & Awards:* Charles Albert Schull Award, Am Soc Plant Physiol, 71. *Prof Exp:* Jr fel, Soc Fels, Harvard Univ, 55-58; from asst prof to prof bot, Univ Mich, Ann Arbor, 58-65; prof biol, Univ Calif, Santa Cruz, 66-68. *Mem:* Am Soc Plant Physiol. *Res:* Physiology and biochemistry of plant growth and development; plant hormones. *Mailing Add:* Dept Biol Sci Stanford Univ Gilbert Hall Stanford CA 94305-9991

RAY, PETER SAWIN, METEOROLOGY. *Current Pos:* CHMN, METEOROL DEPT, FLA STATE UNIV, 94- *Personal Data:* b Iowa City, Iowa, July 26, 44; m 70; c 1. *Educ:* Iowa State Univ, BS, 66; Fla State Univ, MS, 70, PhD(meteorol), 73. *Prof Exp:* Res meteorologist, Nat Oceanic & Atmospherics Admin, 73-80, chief meteorol res group, Nat Severe Storms Lab, 80-85. *Concurrent Pos:* Nat Res Coun fel, Nat Severe Storms Lab, 73-74; adj asst prof, Depts Meteorol & Elec Eng, Univ Okla, 74-85. *Mem:* Am Meteorol Soc; Am Geophys Union; Am Inst Physics. *Res:* Scattering physics of radiation and hydrometeors; using models and observations, the study of the morphology and dynamics of severe storms. *Mailing Add:* Dept Meteorol Fla State Univ Tallahassee FL 32306-1096

RAY, RICHARD SCHELL, VETERINARY PHARMACOLOGY. *Current Pos:* From instr to assoc prof, 55-73, prof vet clin sci & dir, pre & post race testing labs, 73-84, EMER PROF, OHIO STATE UNIV, 84- *Personal Data:* b Antwerp, Ohio, May 21, 28; m 54; c 3. *Educ:* Ohio State Univ, BA, 50, DVM, 55, MSc, 58, PhD(physiol, pharmacol), 63. *Concurrent Pos:* Grants, NY Racing Asn & Jockey Club, 65-66, Harness Racing Inst, 66-67 & Thoroughbred Racing Fund, 68- *Mem:* Am Asn Equine Practitioners; Am Soc Vet Physiol & Pharmacol; World Asn Physiologists, Pharmacologists, Biochemists; Asn Drug Detection Labs; fel Am Col Vet Pharmacol & Therapeut. *Res:* Intermediate metabolism and diseases related to metabolism; detection of illegally used drugs; serum transaminase changes related to disease; research and development of drug detection methods in biological fluids; general physiology. *Mailing Add:* 2752 Folkstone Rd Columbus OH 43220

RAY, ROBERT ALLEN, CLINICAL CHEMISTRY. *Current Pos:* RES CHEMIST, HDI, 91-; EXEC VPRES, FLEXSITE INC, 97- *Personal Data:* b Scottsbluff, Nebr, Dec 19, 39; m 60; c 4. *Educ:* Univ Nebr, BS, 61, MS, 63, PhD(biochem), 66. *Prof Exp:* Res chemist, Beckman Instruments, 66-74, eng mgr, 74-78, prog mgr, 81-91. *Mem:* AAAS; Am Chem Soc; Am Asn Clin Chemists. *Res:* Chemical and biomedical instrumentation for the assay of enzymes or their substrates. *Mailing Add:* 3307 SW Villa Pl Palm City FL 34990-8117

RAY, ROBERT DURANT, ORTHOPEDIC SURGERY. *Current Pos:* RETIRED. *Personal Data:* b Cleveland, Ohio, Sept 21, 14; m 53; c 5. *Educ:* Univ Calif, BA, 36, MA, 38, PhD(anat), 48; Harvard Univ, MD, 43. *Hon Degrees:* MedDrSci, Royal Univ Umea, 72. *Prof Exp:* Asst anat, Med Sch, Univ Calif, 37-38; intern surg, Peter Bent Brigham Hosp, Boston, 43; asst orthop surg, Harvard Med Sch, 44-45; instr anat, Med Sch, Univ Calif, 47-48; asst prof orthop surg, Sch Med, Wash Univ, 48-51, assoc prof & head dept, 54-56; prof orthop surg & head dept, Col Med, Univ Ill, Chicago, 56-81. *Concurrent Pos:* Mem staff, Ravens Wood Hosp, 71- *Mem:* Am Orthop Res Soc (pres, 59); Am Asn Anat; Am Orthop Asn; Am Col Surg; Am Acad Orthop Surg. *Res:* Bone growth, maturation and metabolism; influence of intrinsic and extrinsic factors on these processes including endocrines and radiation; kinetics of bone-seeking radioactive isotopes. *Mailing Add:* Dept Orthop Univ Ill 2200 Laguna Vista Dr Rm 209 Box 6998 Chicago IL 60680

RAY, ROBERT LANDON, MEDIUM ENERGY PHYSICS. *Current Pos:* RES SCIENTIST, DEPT PHYSICS, UNIV TEX, 79- *Mem:* Fel Am Phys Soc. *Res:* Medium energy physics. *Mailing Add:* Dept Physics RLM Bldg Rm 5 Univ Tex Austin TX 78712

RAY, ROSE MARIE, MATHEMATICAL STATISTICS. *Current Pos:* managing scientist, 88-93, SR MANAGING SCIENTIST, FAILURE ANALYSIS ASSOC, MENLO PARK, 93- *Personal Data:* b Hayward, Calif, Mar 30, 43; m 73, Robert E Kroll; c C Stephen, Bodhi D & Allegheny M. *Educ:* Univ Calif, Berkeley, BA, 65, PhD(statist), 72. *Honors & Awards:* Evelyn Fix Biostatist Award, 70. *Prof Exp:* From actg instr to actg asst prof statist, Univ Calif, Berkeley, 71-72; asst prof math, Northwestern Univ, 72-74; asst prof statist, Univ Fla, 74-76; statist consult, 76; personnel res statistician, Pac Gas & Elec Co, San Francisco, 78-88. *Concurrent Pos:* Consult mkt res, Montgomery Ward Co, Chicago, 74; consult, Biostatist Unit, J Hillis Miller Health Ctr, Univ Fla, 74-76; sr statistician, Sci Comput Serv, Univ Calif, San Francisco, 76-78; sr biostatistician, Contraceptive Drug Study, Kaiser Found Hosp, Walnut Creek, Calif, 76-78; lectr, Dept Statist, Univ Calif, Berkeley, 77- *Mem:* Inst Math Statist; Am Statist Asn; AAAS; Sigma Xi; Biomet Soc; Soc Automotive Engrs. *Res:* Traffic safety research; fire safety research; risk analysis development and application of special stochastic models for research in medicine, biology, marketing, manpower planning and cost analysis; research in the theory of C-alpha tests. *Mailing Add:* Failure Analysis Assoc 149 Commonwealth Dr PO Box 3015 Menlo Park CA 94025. *Fax:* 650-688-7269

RAY, SAMMY MEHEDY, MARINE BIOLOGY. *Current Pos:* asst prof oceanog & meterol, Tex A&M Univ, 59-63, assoc prof oceanog, dir, Marine Lab, 63-90, prof biol, Oceanog, Marine Sci & Wildlife Fisheries Sci, 69-90, head, Dept Marine Sci, 74-90, dir, Sch Marine Technol, 77-90, EMER PROF, TEX A&M UNIV, 90-, DIR COMMUNITY & YOUTH EDUC, 92- *Personal Data:* b Mulberry, Kans, Feb 25, 19; m 43; c 4. *Educ:* La State Univ, BS, 42; Rice Inst, MA, 52, PhD(biol), 54. *Prof Exp:* Fishery res biologist, US Fish & Wildlife Serv, 54-59. *Mem:* AAAS; Nat Shellfisheries Asn; Am Soc Limnol & Oceanog; Phycol Soc Am; Am Inst Fishery Res Biol. *Res:* Oyster biology; marine microbiology, phytoplankton and pollution. *Mailing Add:* 18 Legas Dr Galveston TX 77551-1568

RAY, SIBA PRASAD, MATERIALS SCIENCE, METALLURGY. *Current Pos:* scientist, Alcoa Labs, 77-78, sr scientist mat sci, 78-82, sci assoc, 82-90, SR SCI ASSOC, ALCOA LABS, 91- *Personal Data:* b Dinhata, India, Jan 4, 44; m 77, Lipika; c Souran & Leena. *Educ:* Univ Calcutta, BE, 64; Columbia Univ, MS, 70, DEngSc, 74. *Prof Exp:* Sci officer, Bhabha Atomic Res Ctr, India, 65-69; res assoc, Pa State Univ, 74-77. *Concurrent Pos:* Krumb fel, Columbia Univ, 69- *Mem:* Am Ceramic Soc; Sigma Xi; Am Inst Mining, Metall & Petrol Engrs. *Res:* High temperature materials; conducting ceramics; aluminum smelting process development; refractory electrodes; oxygen sensors; ceramic engineering; solid state chemistry; ceramic composites, squeeze casting; ceramic matrix composites. *Mailing Add:* Alcoa Tech Ctr 100 Technical Dr Alcoa Center PA 15069

RAY, STEVE, INDUSTRIAL & MANUFACTURING ENGINEERING. *Current Pos:* GROUP LEADER, NAT INST STAND & TECHNOL, 94- *Personal Data:* b Mar 15, 56. *Educ:* Princeton Univ, PhD(mech & aerospace eng), 81. *Concurrent Pos:* Postdoctoral fel, Nat Res Coun, 81. *Mailing Add:* Nat Inst Stand & Technol Mfg Systs Integration Div Rte 270 Bldg 220 Gaithersburg MD 20899. *E-Mail:* ray@mst.gov

RAY, SYLVIAN RICHARD, NEURAL NETWORKS, BIOMEDICAL SYSTEMS. *Current Pos:* res assoc elec eng, 60-61, from asst prof to assoc prof, 61-72, PROF ELEC ENG, UNIV ILL, URBANA, 72- *Personal Data:* b Pineville, La, Aug 26, 31; m 59, Emily L Belleff; c Tane S & Leland E. *Educ:* Southwestern La Inst, BS, 51; Univ Ill, MS, 57, PhD(elec eng), 60. *Prof Exp:* Elec scientist, Naval Res Lab, 51-54. *Mem:* Sigma Xi; Asn Comput Mach; Int Neural Network Soc. *Res:* Artificial intelligence; biomedical applications of computers; intelligent signal interpretation. *Mailing Add:* Dept Comput Sci 2323 DCL Univ Ill Urbana IL 61801. *Fax:* 217-333-3501; *E-Mail:* ray@cs.uiuc.edu

RAY, THOMAS SHELBY, EVOLUTION, TROPICAL BIOLOGY. *Current Pos:* asst prof, 81-90, ASSOC PROF BIOL, UNIV DEL, 90-, ASSOC PROF COMPUT SCI, 93- *Personal Data:* b Norman, Okla, Sept 21, 54; m 82, Isabel Arias; c Ariel I. *Educ:* Fla State Univ, BS(biol) & BS(chem), 76; Harvard Univ, AM, 80, PhD(plant ecol), 81. *Prof Exp:* Sta mgr, Finca LaSelva, Orgn Trop Studies, 78-79. *Concurrent Pos:* Environ consult, Fla State Univ, 72-73; owner & operator, Finca El Bejuco Biol Sta, Costa Rica, 82; vis prof, Santa Fe Inst, 91-92; consult, Inter-Am Develop Bank, 93-94; invited researcher, Advan Telecommun Res Inst, Japan, 93-; external fac, Sante Fe Inst, 93- *Res:* Study of evolution through the synthesis of naturally evolving artificial systems; evolution in the broadest context, including outside of the medium of carbon chemistry, particularly in the digital medium. *Mailing Add:* Univ Del Biol Dept Newark DE 19717-0001. *Fax:* 302-831-2281; *E-Mail:* ray@udel.edu

RAY, VERNE A, MICROBIOLOGY, BIOCHEMISTRY. *Current Pos:* Sr res scientist, Chas Pfizer & Co, 59-67, proj leader, 67-72, mgr, 72-75, asst dir, Dept Drug Safety Eval, 75-90, SR TECH ADV, CENT RES, PFIZER INC, 90- *Personal Data:* b Portsmouth, NH, July 28, 29; m 52; c 2. *Educ:* Univ NH, BS, 51, MS, 55; Univ Tex, PhD(bact), 59. *Honors & Awards:* Alexander Hollander Award, Environ Mutagen Soc, 79. *Concurrent Pos:* Chmn, Drinking Water Comt, US Environ Protection Agency. *Mem:* Am Soc Microbiol; Soc Toxicol; Environ Mutagen Soc. *Res:* Molecular biology of virus infectious process; factors controlling induced mutation frequency in microorganisms; elaboration products of microorganisms and methods of increasing yield; genetic toxicology, in vitro toxicology; alternative toxicological methods to animal testing. *Mailing Add:* Med Res Lab Pfizer Inc Eastern Point Rd Groton CT 06340

RAY, W(ILLIS) HARMON, CHEMICAL ENGINEERING. *Current Pos:* chmn dept, 81-83, Steenbock chair eng, 86, PROF CHEM ENG, UNIV WIS-MADISON, 76-, STEENBOCK PROF ENG, 86- *Personal Data:* b Washington, DC, Apr 4, 40; m 62; c 3. *Educ:* Rice Univ, BA, 62, BSChE, 63; Univ Minn, PhD(chem eng), 66. *Honors & Awards:* Eckman Award, Am Automatic Control Coun, 69; A K Doolittle Award, Am Chem Soc, 81; Prof Prog Award, Am Inst Chem Eng, 82; Distinguished Reilly Lect Award, Univ Notre Dame, Ind, 84; W N Lacey Lectr, Calif Inst Technol, Pasadena, 88; Educ Award, Am Automatic Control Coun, 89. *Prof Exp:* Asst prof chem eng, Univ Waterloo, 66-69, assoc prof, 69-70; from assoc prof to prof, State Univ NY Buffalo, 70-76. *Concurrent Pos:* Indust consult, 67-; vis prof, Rijksuniversiteit Gent & Univ Leuven, 73-74, Tech Univ Stuttgart, WGer, 74, Dept Chem Eng, Univ Minn, 86 & Cornell Univ, 91; Guggenheim mem fel, Europe, 73-74; C-I-L distinguished vis lectr, Univ Alta, Can, 82 & McMaster Univ, Ont, 85. *Mem:* Nat Acad Eng; Am Chem Soc; Am Soc Eng Educ; Soc Indust & Appl Math; Chem Inst Can; fel Am Inst Chem Engrs; Am Asn Artificial Intel; Inst Elec & Electronics Engrs; Sigma Xi. *Res:* Chemical reactor engineering including polymerization processes; process modeling, optimization, dynamics and control. *Mailing Add:* Dept Chem Eng Univ Wis Madison WI 53706

RAY, WILLIAM J, CLINICAL PSYCHOLOGY, PSYCHOPHYSIOLOGY. *Current Pos:* PROF PSYCHOL, PA STATE UNIV, 72- *Personal Data:* b Birmingham, Ala, Sept 3, 45; m, Judith Mebanc; c Jen, David, Adam, Lauren & Katy. *Educ:* Eckerd Col, St Petersburg, Fla, BA, 67; Vanderbilt Univ, MA, 69, PhD(clin psychol), 71. *Honors & Awards:* Nat Media Award, Am Psychol Found, 76 & 78. *Prof Exp:* Fel med psychol, Langley Porter Neuropsychiat Inst, 71-72. *Concurrent Pos:* Vis prof, Univ Hawaii, 87, Univ Tubingen, WGer, 89; dir, Health Psychol Prog, 85-, Clin Training Prog. *Mem:* AAAS; Am Psychosomatic Soc; Am Psychol Asn; Soc Res Psychopath. *Res:* Psychophysiological assessment-brain/behavior relationships; chaos and EEG; behavioral medicine; interdependence of mental, emotional and physiological/motor activities. *Mailing Add:* Pa State Univ 416 Psychol Bldg University Park PA 16802. *Fax:* 814-863-7002; *E-Mail:* wjr@psuvm.psu.edu

RAY, WILLIAM JACKSON, JR, ORGANIC CHEMISTRY. *Current Pos:* from asst prof to assoc prof, 61-70, PROF BIOCHEM, PURDUE UNIV, LAFAYETTE, 70- *Personal Data:* b Bradenton, Fla, Mar 19, 32; m 54; c 2. *Educ:* Bethany-Nazarene Col, BS, 49; Purdue Univ, PhD(org chem), 57. *Prof Exp:* Res assoc biochem, Brookhaven Nat Lab, 57-59; asst prof, Rockefeller Inst, 59-61. *Mem:* Am Chem Soc; Am Soc Biol Chem. *Res:* Mechanism of enzyme action. *Mailing Add:* Purdue Univ Lily Hall Life Sci West Lafayette IN 47907-1392

RAYBON, GREGORY, ELECTRICAL ENGINEERING, OPTICS. *Current Pos:* MEM TECH STAFF, AT&T BELL LABS, 85- *Personal Data:* b Port Arthur, Tex, Dec 29, 61; m 87; c 1. *Educ:* Pa State Univ, BS, 84; Stevens Inst Technol, MS, 90. *Prof Exp:* Prod engr, Nat Semiconductor, 84-85. *Mem:* Optical Soc Am. *Res:* Short optical pulse generation from semiconductor photonic devices, such as lasers, novel modulation schemes and optical thin films, which are directly applicable to future optical communication systems for long haul and local loop exchange. *Mailing Add:* Lucent Technols Rm M229 E 1791 Holmdel-Keyport Rd Holmdel NJ 07733

RAYBORN, GRAYSON HANKS, ATOMIC PHYSICS. *Current Pos:* from asst prof to assoc prof, 70-79, PROF PHYSICS, UNIV SOUTHERN MISS, 79-, DIR SCH MATH SCI, 91- *Personal Data:* b Columbia, Miss, May 26, 39; m 65. *Educ:* Rensselaer Polytech Inst, BS, 61; Univ Fla, PhD(physics), 69. *Prof Exp:* Asst engr, Sperry Rand Corp, 61-62; res asst physics, Univ Fla, 68-69; asst prof physics, Old Dominion Univ, 69-70. *Concurrent Pos:* Consult, Langley Res Ctr, NASA, 71. *Mem:* Am Asn Physics Teachers; Am Phys Soc; Fedn Am Scientists; Am Chem Soc. *Res:* Photoionization and dissociative photoionization; deconvolution and inverse digital filtering; free electron magnetometer; development of novel apparatus for use by undergraduate physics majors. *Mailing Add:* 231 Balboa Dr Hattiesburg MS 39402-9591

RAYBURN, MARLON CECIL, JR, TOPOLOGY. *Current Pos:* from asst prof to assoc prof, 69-82, PROF MATH, UNIV MAN, 83- *Personal Data:* b Clay, Ky, Sept 29, 31; m 62; c 3. *Educ:* Evansville Col, BA, 52; Auburn Univ, MS, 56; Univ Ky, PhD(math), 69. *Prof Exp:* Instr math & physics, Earlham Col, 59-62; asst prof math, State Univ NY Col Geneseo, 65-68. *Mem:* Can Math Cong; Am Math Soc; Math Asn Am. *Res:* General topology; compactifications and realcompactifications; uniformities; proximities; applications to analysis; sigma algebras. *Mailing Add:* Univ Manitoba Rm 319 Machray Hall Winnipeg MB R3T 2N2 Can

RAYBURN, WILLIAM REED, BOTANY & MICROBIOLOGY. *Current Pos:* Instr, Wash State Univ, 67-69, asst prof bot & gen biol, 69-78, assoc prof bact, pub health & bot, 78-85, chair gen biol, 82-87, assoc dean, Grad Sch, 87-89, PROF MICROBIOL, BOT & GEN BIOL, WASH STATE UNIV, 85-, ASSOC VPROVOST RES, 89-; ASSOC DIR, WASH TECHNOL CTR, 89- *Personal Data:* b St Louis, Mo, Apr 7, 40; m 67, Barbara J Lindbloni; c Jennifer A & Christine E. *Educ:* Washington Univ, BA, 63; Ind Univ, Bloomington, MA, 67, PhD(bot, microbiol), 71. *Concurrent Pos:* Interim dir, Nuclear Radiation Ctr, Wash State Univ, 89-90; interim dir, Plant Biotechnol Ctr, Wash Technol Ctr, 90-93, dir, Biotechnol Group, 93; exec dir, Intellectual Property Admin, 96-; pres, Wash State Univ Res Found, 96- *Mem:* Bot Soc Am; Phycol Soc Am; Soc Res Admin; Int Phycol Soc; Am Inst Biol Sci. *Res:* Sexuality of algae; ecology of soil algae; microbial extra-cellular polysaccharides. *Mailing Add:* Grad Sch Wash State Univ Pullman WA 99164-1030. *Fax:* 509-335-1949; *E-Mail:* rayburnw@wsuvm1.csc.wsu.edu

RAYCHAUDHURI, ANILBARAN, IMMUNOLOGY, INFLAMMATION. *Current Pos:* STAFF SCIENTIST IMMUNOL & INFLAMMATION, CIBA-GEIGY CORP, SUMMIT, NJ, 78- *Personal Data:* b Tipperah, India; m 64, Purnima Bardhan; c Raka, Renee & Neil. *Educ:* Univ Calcutta, BSc, 51; Univ Rangoon, MS, 58; Univ Cincinnati, PhD(biol sci), 63. *Prof Exp:* Res chemist geront, Vet Admin Hosp, Baltimore, Md, 65-67; res assoc, Georgetown Univ, 67-70; sr scientist, Merrell-Nat Lab, Cincinnati, 70-78. *Concurrent Pos:* Vis fel, NIH, Bethesda, Md, 63-65; consult, Vet Admin Hosp, Baltimore, 64-65. *Mem:* NY Acad Sci; AAAS; Sigma Xi. *Res:* Immunology in general and cell-mediated immunity in particular; application of chemotherapy to rheumatoid arthritis involving a unique type of compound designated as disease modifying anti-rheumatic drugs; more emphasis on in vivo & ex vivo animal models for various human inflammatory diseases including arthritis. *Mailing Add:* Arthritis Biol Res Novartis Pharmaceut Corp 556 Morris Ave LSB 2329 Summit NJ 07901. *Fax:* 908-277-2577

RAY-CHAUDHURI, DILIP K, POLYMER CHEMISTRY, ORGANIC CHEMISTRY. *Current Pos:* proj supvr org chem res, Nat Starch & Chem Co, 64-67; sect leader, 67-72, mgr cent res, 72-77, dir corp res, 77-81, div vpres & dir corp res, 81-93, DIV VPRES TECHNOL DEVELOP, NAT STARCH & CHEM CO, 93- *Personal Data:* b Dacca, E Pakistan, Sept 4, 29; m 61; c Trishna & Avijit. *Educ:* Univ Dacca, BSc, 48, MSc, 49; Univ Calcutta, PhD(chem), 56. *Prof Exp:* Jr res asst chem jute cellulose, Tech Res Lab, India, 56-58; fel, Cellulose Res Inst, State Univ NY Col Forestry, Syracuse, 58-61; res assoc, Ont Res Found Can, 61-64. *Mem:* Am Chem Soc; NY Acad Sci; Sigma Xi; fel Inst Chemists. *Res:* Polyelectrolytes; adhesives; wet strength additives; polyurethanes and polyesters. *Mailing Add:* Nat Starch & Chem Co 10 Finderne Ave Bridgewater NJ 08807. *Fax:* 908-707-3722

RAY-CHAUDHURI, DWIJENDRA KUMAR, DISCRETE MATHEMATICS, COMBINATORICS. *Current Pos:* chmn dept, 80-83, PROF MATH, OHIO STATE UNIV, 66- *Personal Data:* b Narayangang, Bangladesh, Nov 1, 33; m 62; c 3. *Educ:* Presidency Col, Calcutta, BSc, 53; Calcutta Univ, MSc, 55; Univ NC, Chapel Hill, PhD(math statist), 59. *Honors & Awards:* Alexander von Humboldt Award, WGer, 84. *Prof Exp:* Res assoc, Case Inst Technol, 59-60; asst prof math statist, Univ NC, Chapel Hill, 60-61; reader, Indian Statist Inst, 61-62; mem res staff math, T J Watson Res Ctr, IBM Corp, NY, 62-64; consult statist & math, Cornell Med Ctr & Sloan-Kettering Inst, 64-65; vis assoc prof math, Math Res Ctr, Univ Wis-Madison, 65-66. *Concurrent Pos:* Invited speaker, Int Math Cong, 70; vis prof, Gottingen Univ, WGer, 72 & Erlangen Univ, 76; sr Sci Res Coun fel, Univ London, 84; assoc ed, J Comb Theory B, Combinatorica & J Statist Inference & Planning. *Mem:* Am Math Soc; Math Asn Am. *Res:* Combinatorial mathematics; finite geometry; graph and information theory; error-correcting codes; statistical design experiments. *Mailing Add:* 231 W 18th Ave Ohio State Univ Columbus OH 43210

RAYCHAUDHURI, KAMAL KUMAR, TELECOMMUNICATIONS. *Current Pos:* DISTINGUISHED MEM TECH STAFF, AT&T BELL LABS, 83- *Personal Data:* b Dinapore, India, Nov 11, 47; m 74, Shampa Sen; c Koeli & Samudra. *Educ:* Univ Calcutta, India, BSc, 67, MSc, 69; Univ Pa, PhD(physics), 77, MSE, 78. *Prof Exp:* Assoc, Saha Inst Nuclear Physics, Calcutta, India, 71; res fel physics, Univ Pa, 77-78; res assoc, Univ Mass, Amherst, 78-79, asst prof physics, 80-83. *Mem:* Sr mem Inst Elec & Electronics Engrs. *Res:* Experimental high energy physics: hyperon studies and studies of new particles using high speed electronic detectors. *Mailing Add:* AT&T Bell Labs 101 Crawfords Corner Rd Holmdel NJ 07733

RAYCHOWDHURY, PRATIP NATH, applied mathematics, mathematical physics, for more information see previous edition

RAYFIELD, GEORGE W, PHYSICS. *Current Pos:* ASSOC PROF PHYSICS, UNIV ORE, 68- *Personal Data:* b San Francisco, Calif, Feb 17, 36; m 59; c 1. *Educ:* Stanford Univ, BS, 58; Univ Calif, Berkeley, MA & PhD(physics), 64. *Prof Exp:* Res asst eng sci, Univ Calif, Berkeley, 60-61; physics, 61-64; asst prof, Univ Pa, 64-68. *Mem:* Am Phys Soc. *Res:* Solid state physics; liquid helium; ionic probes in liquid helium; microwave tubes; electron beams. *Mailing Add:* 4024 Alder St Eugene OR 97405

RAYFORD, PHILLIP LEON, PHYSIOLOGY, ENDOCRINOLOGY. *Current Pos:* PROF & CHMN DEPT PHYSIOL, UNIV ARK SCH MED, LITTLE ROCK, 80- *Personal Data:* b Roanoke, Va, July 25, 27; m 52. *Educ:* NC A&T State Univ, BS, 49; Univ Md, College Park, MS, 69, PhD(reproductive endocrinol), 73. *Hon Degrees:* LHD, NC A&T State Univ, 85. *Prof Exp:* Supvry biologist endocrinol, Nat Cancer Inst, 55-62, supvry biologist, NIHMR, 62-64, supvry biologist radioimmunoassay, Nat Cancer Inst, 64-70, supvry biology, NICHO, 70-73; from asst prof to assoc prof biochem, Div Human Cell Biol & Genetics, Univ Tex Med Br Galveston, 73-77, prof & dir, Biochem Lab, Dept Surg, 77-80. *Mem:* Endocrinol Soc; Am Physiol Soc; Am Gastroenterol Asn; Soc Exp Biol & Med; NY Acad Sci. *Res:* Metabolism and catabolism of gastrointestinal and pancreatic hormones in man and dogs; research and development of radioimmunoassay systems for measuring hormones of gastrointestinal, pancreatic and pituitary origin. *Mailing Add:* Dept Physiol & Biophys Univ Ark Med Sch 4301 W Markham Slot 505 Little Rock AR 72205-7101

RAYKHMAN, ALEKSANDR, FORECASTING OF NON-STATIONARY DYNAMIC OBJECTS BEHAVIOR, SYNTHESIS OF ACOUSTIC & ELECTRO-DYNAMIC MEASURING SYSTEMS. *Current Pos:* CHIEF SCIENTIST, CONTROL SYSTS ENG, 92- *Personal Data:* b Feb 11, 51; m 85, Inesa Vinarskaya; c Victoria, Rodion & David. *Educ:* Donetsk Polytech Inst, USSR, BS, 70, MS, 73; Moskow Mining Inst, PhD(automatic control theory), 88. *Prof Exp:* Staff researcher, Inst Physics in Siberian Div Russian Acad Sci, USSR, 73-75; sr scientist, Donetsk Mining Mach Automation Inst, USSR, 76-90; res & develop dept head, Am-Soviet JV, Amsovindustries, USSR, 90-91. *Concurrent Pos:* Consult, ACSSYN Ltd, Israel, 92- *Res:* Nonlinear dynamic objects mathematical analysis, both analytical and numerical; cause-effect models building for complex nonlinear with nonstationary parameters systems; developing of technical diagnostics methods for industrial objects and theory of predictions for economical applications. *Mailing Add:* 45 Sussex St Providence RI 02908. *Fax:* 401-727-2542

RAYLE, DAVID LEE, PLANT PHYSIOLOGY. *Current Pos:* from asst prof to assoc prof, 70-75, chmn dept, 74-80, PROF BOT, SAN DIEGO STATE UNIV, 80- *Personal Data:* b Pasadena, Calif, Oct 22, 42; m 67; c 2. *Educ:* Univ Calif, Santa Barbara, BA, 64, PhD(biol), 67. *Prof Exp:* NSF fel & res assoc bot, Mich State Univ-Atomic Energy Comn Plant Res Lab, Mich State Univ, 67-68; res assoc, Univ Wash, 68-70. *Mem:* Am Soc Plant Physiol. *Res:* Mechanism of action of plant growth hormones; physical properties of plant cell walls; plant growth and development. *Mailing Add:* Dept Bot San Diego State Univ San Diego CA 92182-0001

RAYLE, RICHARD EUGENE, GENETICS. *Current Pos:* ASST PROF ZOOL, MIAMI UNIV, 70- *Personal Data:* b Freesoil, Mich, Apr 5, 39; m 63; c 1. *Educ:* Mich State Univ, BS, 62; Univ Ill, Urbana, PhD(genetics), 67. *Prof Exp:* NIH trainee, Univ Calif, Davis, 67-69; res assoc zool, Univ NC, Chapel Hill, 69-70, vis asst prof, 70. *Mem:* AAAS; Genetics Soc Am. *Res:* Structural and functional organization of eukaryotic genetic systems. *Mailing Add:* 405 W Chestnut St Oxford OH 45056

RAYMAN, MOHAMAD KHALIL, FOOD MICROBIOLOGY. *Current Pos:* RES SCIENTIST HEALTH & WELFARE & CHIEF RES BLDG, CAN, 73- *Personal Data:* b Guyana, SAm, Feb 23, 38; Can citizen; m 59; c 2. *Educ:* McGill Univ, BSc, 66, PhD(microbiol), 70. *Prof Exp:* Med Res Coun Can fel, Univ Toronto, 70-73. *Mem:* Can Soc Microbiol; Asn Off Anal Chem. *Res:* Methodology related to isolation and identification of food poisoning organisms; mechanism of succinate transport into membrane vesicles of Escherichia coli; mechanism of thermal injury in Salmonella; testing replacement for nitrite in food preservation, development of genetic probes for identification of food-borne microorganisms. *Mailing Add:* Health Protection Br-Microbiol Res Div PL 2204A2 Tunney's Pasture Sir FG Banting Bldg Ottawa ON K1A 0L2 Can

RAYMON, LOUIS, MATHEMATICS. *Current Pos:* From asst prof to assoc prof, 66-77, PROF MATH, TEMPLE UNIV, 77- *Personal Data:* b New Brunswick, NJ, Oct 17, 39; m 62; c 4. *Educ:* Yeshiva Col, BA, 60; Yeshiva Univ, MA, 61, PhD(math), 66. *Mem:* Am Math Soc. *Res:* Classical problems in real and complex analysis, especially approximation theory. *Mailing Add:* 1405 Westwood Lane Wynnewood PA 19096

RAYMOND, ARTHUR E(MMONS), AEROSPACE ENGINEERING. *Current Pos:* RETIRED. *Personal Data:* b Boston, Mass, Mar 24, 99; m 21; c 1. *Educ:* Harvard Univ, BS, 20; Mass Inst Technol, MS, 21. *Hon Degrees:* DSc, Polytech Inst Brooklyn, 47. *Prof Exp:* Engr, Douglas Aircraft Co, 25-34, vpres eng, 34-60; consult, Rand Corp, 60-85. *Concurrent Pos:* Mem, Nat Adv Comt Aeronaut, NASA, 46-56, consult, 62-68; trustee, Aerospace Corp, 60-71 & Res Anal Corp, 65-71. *Mem:* Nat Acad Sci; Nat Acad Eng; hon fel Am Inst Aeronaut & Astronaut. *Res:* Aeronautics; astronautics. *Mailing Add:* 65 Oakmont Dr Los Angeles CA 90049

RAYMOND, CHARLES FOREST, GEOPHYSICS. *Current Pos:* From asst prof to assoc prof, 69-79, PROF GEOPHYS, UNIV WASH, 79- *Personal Data:* b St Louis, Mo, Oct 31, 39; m 65. *Educ:* Univ Calif, Berkeley, BA, 61; Calif Inst Technol, PhD(geophys), 69. *Mem:* Am Geophys Union; Int Glaciol Soc. *Res:* Rheology of earth materials; flow and structure of glaciers. *Mailing Add:* Geol Sci A J-20 Univ Wash 3900 Seventh Ave NE Seattle WA 98195-0001

RAYMOND, DALE RODNEY, CHEMICAL ENGINEERING, TECHNICAL MANAGEMENT. *Current Pos:* Res scientist, Papermaking Prog, 73-79, group leader papermaking, 79-83, sect head eng areas, 83-85, TECH DIR PROCESS, ENVIRON & TECH SERV, RES & DEVELOP, UNION CAMP, 85- *Personal Data:* b Farmington, Maine, Mar 8, 49; m 74; c 3. *Educ:* Univ Maine, BS, 71, MS, 73, PhD(chem eng), 75. *Prof Exp:* Instr chem eng, Univ Maine, Orono, 73-75. *Mem:* Sigma Xi; Tech Asn Pulp & Paper Indust; Am Inst Chem Engrs. *Res:* Forming, pressing and drying on the paper machine and in the chemical recovery area to develop high solids firing; process engineering and environmental engineering. *Mailing Add:* 148 Crescent Dr Franklin VA 23851-1228

RAYMOND, DAVID JAMES, PHYSICS, METEOROLOGY. *Current Pos:* res assoc, 73-75, asst prof, 75-79, ASSOC PROF PHYSICS, NMEX INST MINING & TECHNOL, 79- *Personal Data:* b Hammond, Ind, Oct 24, 43. *Educ:* Rensselaer Polytech Inst, BS, 65; Stanford Univ, PhD(physics), 70. *Prof Exp:* Asst prof meteorol, Univ Hawaii, 70-73. *Mem:* Am Phys Soc; Am Meteorol Soc. *Res:* Mesoscale meteorology; turbulence in geophysical flows. *Mailing Add:* Dept Physics NMex Inst Mining & Technol Socorro NM 87801

RAYMOND, GERALD PATRICK, CIVIL ENGINEERING. *Current Pos:* from asst prof to assoc prof, 61-72, prof, 72-, chmn grad studies, 75-77, EMER PROF CIVIL ENG, QUEEN'S UNIV, ONT. *Personal Data:* b Bagdad, Iraq, June 25, 33; Can citizen; m 59; c 2. *Educ:* Univ London, BSc, 56, PhD(soil mech), 65, DSc(eng), 73; Princeton Univ, MSE, 57. *Honors & Awards:* Walmsley Mem Prize, 56. *Prof Exp:* Eng asst, Howard Humphries & Sons, 51-54 & Kennedy & Donkin, 54-56; engr, Procter & Redfern, 57-58; dep city engr, North Bay, Ont, 58-59; lectr civil eng, Univ Sydney, 59-61. *Concurrent Pos:* Mem, Comts Soil & Roc Properties, Mech of Earth Masses & Layered Systs & Track Struct Syst Design, Transp Res Bd, Nat Res Coun; chmn, Comt Geotextiles, Can Geotech Soc; mem, Comt Track Maintenance, Asn Am Railways. *Mem:* Am Soc Civil Engrs; Am Rwy Eng Asn; Can Geotech Soc. *Res:* Consolidation of clays and settlement of foundations on clays; bearing capacity of peat; stresses and deformations under dynamic and static load systems in railroad track structure and support. *Mailing Add:* Dept Civil Eng Queen's Univ Kingston ON K7L 3N6 Can

RAYMOND, HOWARD LAWRENCE, FISHERIES. *Current Pos:* RETIRED. *Personal Data:* b Seattle, Wash, Aug 2, 29; m 70; c 2. *Educ:* Univ Wash, BS, 53. *Prof Exp:* Fishery biologist res, Bur Com Fisheries, 54-57; design engr statist, Boeing Co, 57-60; supvry fishery biologist res, Nat Marine Fisheries Serv, 60-61. *Concurrent Pos:* Consult, Tech Adv Comt, Columbia Basin Fisheries, 75- *Mem:* Am Fisheries Soc; Am Inst Fisheries Res Biologists. *Res:* Development of methodology for protecting migrating anadromous fish in dammed and impounded rivers. *Mailing Add:* 1813 Ginamarie Lane Burlington WA 98233-5202

RAYMOND, JOHN CHARLES, ASTROPHYSICS. *Current Pos:* RES FEL ASTROPHYS, HARVARD COL OBSERV, 76- *Personal Data:* b Edgerton, Wis, Nov 28, 48; m 75; c 1. *Educ:* Univ Wis, Madison, BA, 70, PhD(physics), 76. *Mem:* Am Astron Soc. *Res:* Ultraviolet astronomy; solar physics; interstellar medium. *Mailing Add:* 15 Harvard Smithsonian CFA 60 Garden St Harvard Univ Observ Cambridge MA 02138

RAYMOND, KENNETH NORMAN, INORGANIC CHEMISTRY, CRYSTALLOGRAPHY. *Current Pos:* From asst prof to assoc prof, 68-78, chmn, Dept Chem, 93-96, PROF INORG CHEM, UNIV CALIF, BERKELEY, 78- *Personal Data:* b Astoria, Ore, Jan 7, 42; m 65, 75, 77, Barbara G Sternitzke; c Mary K, Alan, Gabriella & Christopher. *Educ:* Reed Col, BA, 64; Northwestern Univ, Evanston, PhD(chem), 68. *Honors & Awards:* E O Lawrence Award, 84; Humboldt Res Award, Sr US Scientists, 92; Alfred Bader Award, Bioinorganic of Bioorganic Chem, 93. *Concurrent Pos:* Vis prof, Stanford Univ, Australian Nat Univ, Univ Sydney, Univ Strasbourg, Univ Rennes, Queensland Univ; Miller prof, Univ Calif, 77-78; Guggenheim fel, 80-81. *Mem:* Nat Acad Sci; Am Chem Soc; Am Crystallog Asn; Sigma Xi; AAAS. *Res:* Chemistry of transition metal coordination compounds. *Mailing Add:* Dept Chem Univ Calif Berkeley CA 94720. *E-Mail:* raymond@garnet.berkeley.edu

RAYMOND, LAWRENCE W, MEDICINE. *Current Pos:* asst med dir, 79-84, med dir res & eng, 84-90, ASSOC MED DIR, EXXON CO USA, 90- *Personal Data:* b Buffalo, NY, Feb 14, 35. *Educ:* Manhattan Col, BCE, 56; Harvard Univ, SM, 57; Cornell Univ, MD, 64. *Prof Exp:* Res & engr, Exxon, 51-60; intern, Georgetown Med Ctr, 64-65; res physician, Naval Med Res Inst, 65-67 & 72-74; resident med, Bethesda Naval Hosp, 67-70, chief pulmonary med, 74-77; pulmonary fel, Univ Calif, San Francisco, 70-72; assoc prof med, Yale Univ, 77-79. *Mem:* AMA; Am Thoracic Soc; fel Am Col Physicians; fel Am Col Occup Med; Am Physiol Soc; Am Asn Accredited Scientists; Sigma Xi. *Mailing Add:* 2539 Summerlake Rd Charlotte NC 28226-5623

RAYMOND, LOREN ARTHUR, STRUCTURAL GEOLOGY, PETROLOGY. *Current Pos:* instr, Appalachian State Univ, 72-73, asst prof, 73-76 & 77-78, assoc prof, 78-82, PROF GEOL, APPALACHIAN STATE UNIV, 82-, CHAIRPERSON, 95- *Personal Data:* b Sebastopol, Calif, Nov 23, 43; m 65, Margaret Pyne; c Matthew. *Educ:* San Jose State Col, BS, 67, MS, 69; Univ Calif, Davis, PhD(geol), 73. *Prof Exp:* Asst prof geol, SOre State Col, 76-77. *Concurrent Pos:* Pres, Geol Servs Int, 76- *Mem:* Geol Soc Am; Am Geophys Union; Mineral Soc Am; Asn Geoscientists Int Develop; Soc Sedimentary Geologists. *Res:* Understanding the deformational and metamorphic processes in subduction and convergent zones as revealed by the Franciscan Complex of California and Ashe Metamorphic Suite of North Carolina. *Mailing Add:* Dept Geol Appalachian State Univ Boone NC 28608-0001. *Fax:* 704-262-6503; *E-Mail:* raymondla@appstate.edu

RAYMOND, LOUIS, METALLURGY. *Current Pos:* prof, Calif State Univ, Long Beach, 79- *Personal Data:* b Natrona, Pa, Nov 18, 34; m 57; c 4. *Educ:* Carnegie Inst Technol, BS, 56, MS, 58; Univ Calif, Berkeley, PhD(metall), 63. *Honors & Awards:* Am Soc Testing & Mat Award, 63-64; Space Processing Invention Award, NASA, 78. *Prof Exp:* Methods engr mat process, Pittsburgh Plate Glass Co, 55; res engr stainless steel, Allegheny Ludlum Steel Co, 56-58; mech metall, Inst Eng Res, Univ Calif, Berkeley, 58-63; sr res engr strength mech, Aeronutronic Div, Ford Motor Co, 63-65; MEM TECH STAFF, AEROSPACE CORP, 65-, HEAD METALL RES, 67-, STAFF SCIENTIST, 77- *Concurrent Pos:* Mem fac, Calif State Univ, Long Beach, 63-; spec consult, UNESCO-UN Develop Prog Proj, Higher Mining Eng Sch, Oviedo, Spain; lectr exten course, Univ Calif, Los Angeles; consult failure anal, Dept Transp, USCG, 75-77; consult struct integrity offshore platforms, US Geol Surv, Dept Interior, 76; consult life prediction anal, Dept Transp, Fed Railroad Admin, 77-; mem fracture toughness testing comt, Nat Mat Adv Bd-Nat Acad Sci, 75-76, mem fracture toughness requirements in design comt, 77- *Mem:* Am Inst Mining, Metall & Petrol Engrs; fel Inst Advan Eng; Sigma Xi; Am Soc Testing & Mat; AAAS. *Res:* Mechanical metallurgy; thermal mechanical processing; strengthening mechanisms; fracture toughness; hydrogen embrittlement; corrosion-fatigue; space processing; failure analysis. *Mailing Add:* 915 Celtis Pl Eastbluff Newport Beach CA 92660

RAYMOND, MATTHEW JOSEPH, drug metabolism & pharmacokinetic analysis, pharmaceutical stabilization formulation & delivery, for more information see previous edition

RAYMOND, MAURICE A, ORGANIC CHEMISTRY, POLYMER CHEMISTRY. *Current Pos:* DIR RES, RHONE-POULENC, INC, 90- *Personal Data:* b New Bedford, Mass, Jan 8, 38; m 63, E Beatty; c Catherine & Elizabeth. *Educ:* Providence Col, BS, 58; Univ Fla, PhD(org chem), 62. *Prof Exp:* Sr res chemist, Olin Corp, New Haven, 62-64, group supvr, 64-67, sect mgr, 67-70, tech mgr, 70-77, mkt mgr rigid urethanes, 77-78, bus mgr chem specialties, 78-85; corp dir res & develop, TREMCO, Inc, 85-90. *Mem:* Am Chem Soc; Sigma Xi; Soc Cosmetics Chemists; Soc Plastics Eng. *Res:* Cyclopolymerization; fluoroaromatics; nitrenes and carbenes; plasticizers; functional fluids; thermally stable elastomers; homogeneous catalysis; urethane foam machinery and chemical systems. *Mailing Add:* 107 Sayre Dr Princeton NJ 08540. *Fax:* 609-860-0165

RAYMOND, SAMUEL, MEDICINE, COMPUTERS. *Current Pos:* RETIRED. *Personal Data:* b Chester, Pa, Feb 7, 20; m 51; c 2. *Educ:* Swarthmore Col, BA, 41; Univ Pa, MA & PhD(chem), 45; Columbia Univ, MD, 57. *Prof Exp:* Asst instr, Univ Pa, 41-45; asst, Col Physicians & Surgeons, Columbia Univ, 47-48, instr, 49-52; from asst prof to assoc prof clin path, Univ Pa, 58-90. *Concurrent Pos:* Dir, Am Bd Clin Chem, 71-76; mem lab adv bd, Pa State Dept Health. *Mem:* AAAS; Am Chem Soc; Am Asn Clin Chem. *Res:* Electrophoresis; medical applications of computers. *Mailing Add:* 31 Bar Neck Rd Woods Hole MA 02543

RAYMONDA, JOHN WARREN, PHYSICAL CHEMISTRY. *Current Pos:* RES CHEMIST, HIGH ENERGY LASER TECHNOL DEPT, BELL AEROSPACE TEXTRON, 76- *Personal Data:* b Wickenburg, Ariz, May 2, 39; m 63; c 2. *Educ:* Cornell Univ, BA, 61; Univ Wash, Seattle, PhD(chem), 66. *Prof Exp:* Res assoc molecular beam spectros, Harvard Univ, 66-68; asst prof phys chem, Univ Ariz, 68-72; prin chemist, Aerodyn Res Dept, Calspan Corp, 72-76. *Mem:* Sigma Xi. *Res:* Electronic spectroscopy of sigma bonded systems; molecular beam spectroscopy of high temperature species; primary events in photochemical processes; chemical lasers, laser induced chemical reactions, high temperature thermodynamics, laser radar; chemical laser modeling and development, laser diagnostics using nonlinear optics. *Mailing Add:* 901 Lantana Ave Las Cruces NM 88005

RAYMOND-SAVAGE, ANNE, MARINE BIOLOGY. *Current Pos:* ASSOC PROF SCI EDUC & MARINE BIOL, OLD DOMINION UNIV, NORFOLK, VA, 71-, ASSOC VPRES ACAD AFFAIRS, 85; ASSOC VPRES, LIFELONG LEARNING & ACAD TV SERV, 91- *Personal Data:* b Scituate, RI, Apr 10, 39; div; c 4. *Educ:* Univ RI, BS, 59, MA, 69; Ore State Univ, PhD(sci educ), 71. *Prof Exp:* Teacher sci, Coventry Schs, RI, 59-61 & West Warwick Schs, 64-66; instr sci educ, Univ RI, 67-69; A. *Concurrent Pos:* Consult, WHRO-TV, Norfolk, Va, 73- & Corp Pub Broadcasting, Dept Defense. *Mem:* Nat Univ Teleconference Network; Nat Sci Teachers Asn; Asn Educ Commun Technol. *Res:* Marine biology education models; coral reef ecology. *Mailing Add:* New Admin Bldg Rm 217 Old Dominion Univ Norfolk VA 23529

RAYMUND, MAHLON, FRACTURE, FINITE ELEMENTS. *Current Pos:* SR LECTR MATH & STATIST DEPT, UNIV PITTSBURGH, 86- *Personal Data:* b Columbus, Ohio, June 10, 32; m 56; c 3. *Educ:* Univ Chicago, AB, 51, SB, 54, SM, 60, PhD(physics), 63. *Prof Exp:* Res assoc hyperfragments, Enrico Fermi Inst, Univ Chicago, 63-64, Kaonproton scattering, 65-68; sr scientist, Nutron Cross Sect Data & Reactor Comput, Nuclear Energy Systs, Westinghouse Elec Corp, 68-81, fel scientist methods, supercomput, 81-86. *Concurrent Pos:* Dept Sci & Indust Res sr vis fel, Univ Col, Univ London, 64-65; res collabr, Nat Neutron Cross Sect Ctr, Brookhaven Nat Lab, 70-71. *Mem:* Am Phys Soc; Soc Indust & Appl Math. *Res:* Finite element methods for fracture and seismic analysis; computer applications; computational fluid dynamics. *Mailing Add:* 5526 Raleigh St Pittsburgh PA 15217

RAYNAL, DUDLEY JONES, PLANT ECOLOGY. *Current Pos:* from asst prof to prof, 74-92, DISTINGUISHED TEACHING PROF BOT, COL ENVIRON SCI & FORESTRY, STATE UNIV NY, SYRACUSE, 92- *Personal Data:* b Greenville, SC, Jan 1, 47; m 71, Georgia Pender; c Ann E & George D. *Educ:* Clemson Univ, SC, BS, 69; Univ Ill, Urbana, PhD(bot), 74. *Honors & Awards:* Outstanding Res Award, Sigma Xi. *Prof Exp:* Vis lectr bot, Univ Ill, Urbana, 74. *Concurrent Pos:* Chmn tech comt, Nat Atmospheric Deposition Prog, NADP, 85-86; exec chair fac, State Univ NY-Environ Sci & Forestry, Syracuse, 90-92. *Mem:* Ecol Soc Am; Bot Soc Am; Brit Ecol Soc; fel AAAS; Sigma Xi; Am Inst Biol Sci. *Res:* Plant population and community ecology; plant succession plant life history studies; role of man-induced disturbance on terrestrial ecosystems; atmospheric deposition effects on forests. *Mailing Add:* Environ/Forest Biol Dept State Univ NY Syracuse NY 13210. *Fax:* 315-470-6934; *E-Mail:* djr@suvm.acs.syr.edu

RAYNAUD, MICHEL, MATHEMATICS. *Current Pos:* PROF, DEPT MATH, UNIV PARIS XI-SUD. *Honors & Awards:* Frank Nelson Cole Algebra Prize, Am Inst Prof Geologists, 96. *Mailing Add:* Univ Paris XI SUD 15 rue G Clemenceau Orsay 91405 Cedex France

RAYNE, JOHN A, PHYSICS. *Current Pos:* from assoc prof to prof physics, 64-90, CONSULT, CARNEGIE-MELLON UNIV, 90- *Personal Data:* b Sydney, Australia, Mar 22, 27; m 54; c 3. *Educ:* Univ Sydney, BSc, 48, BE, 50; Univ Chicago, MS, 51, PhD, 54. *Prof Exp:* Sci officer, Commonwealth Sci & Indust Res Orgn, Australia, 54-56; res engr, Westinghouse Elec Co, Pa, 56-61, adv engr, 61-64. *Mem:* Am Phys Soc. *Res:* Cryogenics; physics of metals; alloy theory. *Mailing Add:* Dept Physics Carnegie-Mellon Univ 5000 Forbes Ave Pittsburgh PA 15213-3816

RAYNER, JOHN NORMAN, DYNAMIC CLIMATOLOGY, EXPLANATION OF CLIMATE THROUGH COMPUTER MODELING. *Current Pos:* res assoc, Inst Polar Studies, Ohio State Univ, 66, from asst prof to assoc prof geog, 66-71, assoc prof physics, 68, chair, dept geog, 75-95, dir atmospheric sci, 85-95, PROF GEOG & ATMOSPHERIC SCI, OHIO STATE UNIV, 68- *Personal Data:* b Worstead, Eng, Mar 12, 36; m 57; c 3. *Educ:* Univ Birmingham, Eng, BA, 58; McGill Univ, MS, 61; Univ Canterbury, NZ, PhD(geog), 65. *Honors & Awards:* Honors Award, Asn Am Geographers, 90. *Prof Exp:* Lectr geog, Univ Canterbury, NZ, 61-65. *Concurrent Pos:* State Climatologist, Ohio, 77-86. *Mem:* Am Meteorol Soc; Royal Meteorol Soc; Asn Am Geographers; Nat Weather Asn. *Res:* Computer modelling of atmospheric systems; quantitative analysis of form-shape and of N-dimensional patterns; use of linux operating system. *Mailing Add:* Dept Geog Ohio State Univ 154 N Oval Mall Columbus OH 43210-1321. *Fax:* 614-292-6213; *E-Mail:* jnr@osu.edu

RAYNER-CANHAM, GEOFFREY WILLIAM, CHEMICAL EDUCATION, HISTORY OF CHEMISTRY & ENVIRONMENTAL CHEMISTRY. *Current Pos:* asst prof, 75-80, assoc prof, 80-88, PROF INORG CHEM, MEM UNIV, NFLD, 88- *Personal Data:* b London, Eng, 1944; Can citizen. *Educ:* Univ London, BSc, 66, DIC, 69, PhD(inorg chem), 69. *Honors & Awards:* Polysar Award, Chem Inst Can, 80; Catalyst Award, 85. *Prof Exp:* Fel, Simon Fraser Univ, 69-71 & 72-73 & York Univ, 71-72; vis asst prof inorg chem, Univ Victoria, 73-74; vis asst prof, Bishop's Univ, 74-75. *Concurrent Pos:* Vis assoc prof, Colo Sch Mines, 81-82; res assoc, Univ Calif, Santa Cruz, 81; vis scholar, New Col, Univ SFla, 90 & Univ York, Eng, 95. *Mem:* Fel Chem Inst Can; Royal Soc Chem. *Res:* Program development for college chemistry students; development of chemistry in late 18th and early 19th century; women in the history of science. *Mailing Add:* Dept Chem Sir Wilfred Grenfell Col Corner Brook NF A2H 6P9 Can. *E-Mail:* grcanham@beothuk.swgc.mun.ca

RAYNES, BERTRAM C(HESTER), CHEMICAL ENGINEERING. *Current Pos:* CONSULT CHEM ENG, 72- *Personal Data:* b Jersey City, NJ, Mar 12, 24; m 44, Margaret Schaeffer. *Educ:* Pa State Univ, BS, 44; Union Univ, NY, MS, 49. *Prof Exp:* Asst res lab, Gen Elec Co, 44-50; develop engr, Brush Beryllium Co, 50-51; head process eng, Horizons, Inc, 51-62; vpres appl res, Rand Develop Corp, 62-70; head environ eng, Trygve Hoff & Assocs Consult Engrs, 70-72. *Concurrent Pos:* Natural sci columnist, Jadison Hale News. *Mem:* Am Chem Soc; Am Inst Chem Engrs; Water Pollution Control Fedn. *Res:* Process research and development; fused salt electrolysis of refractory metals; high temperature ceramics; water pollution control; nonbiologic waste water treatment; land use management; environmental controls. *Mailing Add:* PO Box LL Jackson WY 83001

RAYNIE, DOUGLAS EDWARD, CHROMATOGRAPHIC SEPARATIONS & THEORY, SUPERCRITICAL FLUID TECHNOLOGY. *Current Pos:* STAFF RES CHEMIST, PROCTER & GAMBLE CO, 90- *Personal Data:* b Hawarden, Iowa, Jan 4, 59. *Educ:* Augustana Col, BA, 81; SDak State Univ, MS, 83; Brigham Young Univ, PhD(anal chem), 90. *Prof Exp:* Res assoc, Univ NDak Energy Res Ctr, 84-86. *Concurrent Pos:* Asst to ed, J Microcolumn Separations, 90-91. *Mem:* Am Chem Soc; AAAS; Sigma Xi. *Res:* Development of analytical uses of supercritical fluids; development of high resolution chromatographic techniques and application to the separation of complex organic mixtures; chromatographic and separations theory. *Mailing Add:* Procter & Gamble Miami Valley Labs PO Box 538707 Cincinnati OH 45253-8707. *E-Mail:* raynie.de@pg.com

RAYNOLDS, PETER WEBB, COLLOID CHEMISTRY. *Current Pos:* res chemist, 79-82, sr res chemist, 82-90, ASSOC RES CHEMIST, TENN EASTMAN CO, 90- *Personal Data:* b East Orange, NJ, Feb 3, 51; m 81; c 2. *Educ:* Hope Col, Holland, Mich, BS, 72; Ohio State Univ, PhD(org chem), 77. *Prof Exp:* Res asst, Univ Groningen, Neth, 73 & Univ Zurich, Switz, 73-74; res fel, Univ Minn, 77-79. *Mem:* Am Chem Soc. *Res:* Emulsion polymerization chemistry; colloid chemistry. *Mailing Add:* 878 Canton Rd Kingsport TN 37663

RAYNOLDS, STUART, ORGANIC CHEMISTRY, POLYMER CHEMISTRY. *Current Pos:* RETIRED. *Personal Data:* b Chicago, Ill, Oct 29, 27; m 85, Joanne May Wilber; c 3. *Educ:* Cornell Univ, AB, 50; Univ Pittsburgh, MS, 55, PhD(org chem), 59. *Prof Exp:* Asst assayer, US Bur Mint, DC, 50-51; jr fel, Mellon Inst, 51-55; chemist, Jackson Labs, E I DuPont de Nemours & Co, Inc, 59-65, res supvr, 65-69, res assoc, 69-72, res fel, 72-84, sr res fel, 84-89, consult, DuPont & Ducon, 89-93. *Mem:* AAAS; Am Chem Soc. *Res:* Tar base and textile chemistry; polymers; colloid chemistry. *Mailing Add:* 2415 Ramblewood Dr Wilmington DE 19810-1245

RAYNOR, SUSANNE, CHEMICAL DYNAMICS. *Current Pos:* res asst prof, 82-88, ASSOC PROF CHEM, RUTGERS UNIV, NEWARK, 88- *Personal Data:* b Philadelphia, Pa, May 18, 48; m 72, Louis H Kipnis. *Educ:* Duke Univ, BS, 70; Georgetown Univ, PhD(chem), 76. *Prof Exp:* Res assoc chem, Univ Toronto, 76-78; res assoc, Harvard Univ, 78-82. *Concurrent Pos:* Lectr, Univ Toronto, New Col, 78; collabr, Los Alamos Nat Lab, 86-91. *Mem:* Am Phys Soc; Am Chem Soc. *Res:* Ab initio quantum mechanics of molecules and solids; theoretical study of the dynamics and kinetics of molecular energy transfer and reaction. *Mailing Add:* Dept Chem Olsen Hall Rutgers Univ 73 Warren St Newark NJ 07102. *Fax:* 973-648-1264; *E-Mail:* raynor@draco.rutgers.edu

RAYPORT, MARK, NEUROSURGERY, EPILEPSY & STEREOTAXIC NEUROSURGERY. *Current Pos:* co-chmn neurosci, Med Col Ohio, 69-85, prof, 69-93, chmn, 85-89, EMER PROF NEUROL SURG, MED COL OHIO, 93- *Personal Data:* b Kharkov, Ukraine, Sept 6, 22; US citizen; m 51, Shirley M Ferguson; c Stephen G, Jeffrey F & Jennifer S. *Educ:* Earlham Col, BA, 43; McGill Univ, MD, CM, 48, PhD(neurophysiol), 58. *Prof Exp:* Neurosurg resident, Montreal Neurol Inst, 54-57; asst prof neurosurg, Albert Einstein Col Med, 58-61, assoc prof, 61-68, asst prof physiol, 58-68; asst chief surg, Neurol Inst, Mt Zion Hosp & Med Ctr, San Francisco, 68-69. *Concurrent Pos:* Duggan fel neuropath, Montreal Neurol Inst, 53, res fel, 55-56 & 58; res fel, USPHS, 55-56 & 58; spec sr fel, Interdisciplinary Prog, NIMH, 58-61; career scientist award, Health Res Coun NY, 62-68; vis prof, Univ Paris, 67-68 & 86. *Mem:* Am Asn Neurol Surgeons; Am Epilepsy Soc; Am Col Surgeons; Am Electroencephalog Soc; Soc Neurosci. *Res:* Basic approaches to clinical problems; neurosurgical treatment of epilepsy and pain; neurophysiology of mammalian and human cortex; interdisciplinary studies of brain and behavior. *Mailing Add:* Dept Neurosurg CS 10008 Med Col Ohio Toledo OH 43699

RAYSON, BARBARA M, kidneys, ion transport, for more information see previous edition

RAYSON, GARY D, GRAPHITE FURNACE ATOMIC ABSORPTION SPECTROMETRY, SOLID STATE LUMINESCENCE. *Current Pos:* ASSOC PROF ANALYTICAL CHEM, NMEX STATE UNIV, 86- *Personal Data:* b Oklahoma City, Okla, Apr 27, 57; m 88, Jenny Moorer. *Educ:* Baker Univ, BS, 79; Univ Tex, Austin, PhD(chem), 83. *Prof Exp:* Res assoc, Ind Univ, Bloomington, 83-86. *Mem:* Am Chem Soc; Soc Appl Spectros; Optical Soc Am. *Res:* Chemical processes occurring in high temperature sources used in atomic spectroscopy; metal ion bindings to biogenic materials. *Mailing Add:* 19 Bishop's Cap Rd Mesquite NM 88048. *E-Mail:* grayson@nmsu.edu

RAYUDU, GARIMELLA V S, NUCLEAR CHEMISTRY, NUCLEAR MEDICINE. *Current Pos:* from asst prof to assoc prof, 68-88, PROF NUCLEAR MED, MED SCH, RUSH UNIV, 88- *Personal Data:* b Andhra Pradesh, India, Oct 1, 36; m 65; c 4. *Educ:* Andhra Univ, India, BSc, 56, MSc, 57; McGill Univ, PhD(nuclear chem), 61; Am Bd Radiol, cert, 77; Am Bd Nuclear Med, cert, 79. *Prof Exp:* Res asst health physics, Atomic Energy Estab, Bombay, India, 57-58; res assoc, Carnegie Inst Technol, 61-65; sr res assoc nuclear activation anal, Univ Toronto, 65-67; asst prof radiochem & nuclear chem, Loyola Univ, La, 67-68. *Concurrent Pos:* US AEC grant nuclear & cosmochem, Carnegie Inst Technol, 61-65; Food & Drug Directorate Can pub health grant, Univ Toronto, 65-67; sr scientist, Rush-Presby St Luke's Med Ctr, 68- *Mem:* AAAS; Am Chem Soc; Royal Soc Chem; Am Asn Physicists Med; Soc Nuclear Med. *Res:* Organ imaging radiopharmaceuticals; trace elements in liver, lung, pancreas, muscle and kidney; radiochemistry; cosmochemistry; instrumental analytical chemistry. *Mailing Add:* 1008 Clinton Ave Oak Park IL 60304

RAZ, AVRAHAM, HUMAN METASTASIS. *Current Pos:* MEM & DIR CANCER METASTASIS, MICH CANCER FOUND, DETROIT, MICH, 87-; PROF RADIATION ONCOL & PATH, WAYNE STATE UNIV SCH MED, DETROIT, MICH, 92- *Personal Data:* b Bucharest, Romania, Mar 3, 45; m, Tirza; c Yuval, Yosef & Yaron. *Educ:* Ben-Gurion Univ, BSc, 70, MSc, 72; Weismann Inst Sci, Rehovot, Israel, PhD, 78. *Honors & Awards:* Bondi Mem Award, Weismann Inst, 76, H Dudley Wright Res Award, 85. *Prof Exp:* Vis scientist, Frederick Cancer Res, Nat Cancer Inst, 78-80; res fel, Dept Cell Biol, Weismann Inst, 80-81; sr scientist, 81-86, assoc prof, 86-88. *Concurrent Pos:* Adj prof, Dept Radiol Oncol, Wayne State Univ, 88; ad hoc mem, Path H Study Sect, NIH, Bethesda, Md, 88, consult, 89; dir, Tumor Biol Prog, M L Prentis Comprehensive Cancer Ctr, 92. *Mem:* Am Asn Cancer Res; Am Asn Cell Biol; AAAS; Europ Asn Cancer Res; Int Metastasis Soc; Israel Biochem Soc. *Res:* Role of tumor ecell antigens and genes in the spread of cancer in the body. *Mailing Add:* Michigan Cancer Found 110 E Warren Ave Detroit MI 48201-1379. *Fax:* 313-831-7518

RAZAK, CHARLES KENNETH, FORENSIC ENGINEERING, ENGINEERING & MANAGEMENT CONSULTING. *Current Pos:* ENG & MGT CONSULT, 70- *Personal Data:* b Collyer, Kans, Sept 15, 18; m 40, Lilian B McCall; c Nancy L & Jeanne M. *Educ:* Univ Kans, BS, 39, MS, 42. *Prof Exp:* From instr to asst prof aeronaut eng, Univ Kans, 39-43; 39-43; assoc prof & head dept, Wichita Univ, 43-48, prof, 48-64, dir dept eng, 48-51, actg dean col bus admin, 51-53, dean sch eng & dir eng res, 53-64; prof eng & dir indust exten serv, Kans State Univ, 66-70, adj prof eng, 70-71. *Concurrent Pos:* Pres, Razak Eng, Inc, Educ Rec Serv, Inc & Educ Data, Inc. *Mem:* Soc Automotive Engrs; Am Asn Automotive Med; Int Asn Automotive Med; Rotary Int. *Res:* Expert testimony; lowspeed aerodynamics; aircraft design; transportation safety; educational consulting. *Mailing Add:* 7717 Killarney Ct Wichita KS 67206. *Fax:* 316-265-8005

RAZDAN, MOHAN KISHEN, COMBUSTION, FLUID MECHANICS. *Current Pos:* STAFF ENGR, EXXON RES & ENG CO, 80- *Personal Data:* b Srinagar, India. *Educ:* Regional Eng Col, India, BE, 71; Indian Inst Technol, Kanpur, MTech, 74; Pa State Univ, MS, 76, PhD(mech eng), 79. *Prof Exp:* Res asst, Pa State Univ, 77-79, asst prof mech eng, 79-80. *Mem:* Combustion Inst; assoc mem Am Soc Mech Engrs; Am Inst Aeronaut & Astronaut; Sigma Xi. *Res:* Effects of fluid mechanics on combustion processes and heat transfer in turbulent reacting flows with an emphasis on reduction of pollutants; fluidized bed reactor modeling; design of solid-fluid systems. *Mailing Add:* 7005 Andre Dr Indianapolis IN 46278-1533

RAZDAN, RAJ KUMAR, ORGANIC CHEMISTRY, MEDICINAL CHEMISTRY. *Current Pos:* AFFIL PROF, DEPT PHARMACOL & TOXICOL, MED COL VA, RICHMOND, 86-; CHIEF EXEC OFFICER, ORGANIX INC, 86- *Personal Data:* b Simla, India, Dec 19, 29; m 56, Janet Ritchie; c Rikki & Roma. *Educ:* Univ Delhi, BSc, 48; Indian Inst Sci, Bangalore, dipl, 51; Univ Glasgow, PhD(chem), 54. *Prof Exp:* Jr sci officer, Nat Chem Lab, India, 54-56; sci officer, Glaxo Labs, Ltd, Eng, 56-58, joint works mgr fine chem prod, India, 58-63; res assoc org chem, Univ Mich, 63-64; sr staff scientist, Arthur D Little, Inc, Mass, 64-70; vpres res, 70-80, pres, SISA Inst Res & SISA Inc, 81-83, dir toxicol, SISA Inc, 81-83, prin scientist, SISA Pharmaceut Labs Inc, 84-86. *Concurrent Pos:* Consult, Nat Inst Drug Abuse. *Mem:* Am Chem Soc; Royal Soc Chem; AAAS. *Res:* Cannabinoids; terpenes; steroids; central nervous system active drugs; molecular rearrangements; morphine chemistry; narcotic antagonists; lysergic acid chemistry. *Mailing Add:* 34 Salt Island Rd Gloucester MA 01930. *Fax:* 781-933-6695

RAZGAITIS, RICHARD A, MECHANICAL ENGINEERING. *Current Pos:* VPRES TECHNOL COMMERCIALIZATION, BELLCORE, 95- *Personal Data:* b Chicago, Ill, Jan 13, 44; m 67; c 5. *Educ:* Univ Ill, BS, 65; Univ Fla, MS, 69; Southern Methodist Univ, PhD(mech eng), 74; Ohio State Univ, MBA, 90. *Prof Exp:* Mem, Apollo Launch Team, Cape Kennedy Space Ctr, McDonnell-Douglas Corp, 65-69; asst prof, Univ Portland, 69-72; asst prof eng, Ohio State Univ, 74-81; mgr vpres com develop, Battelle, 81-95. *Concurrent Pos:* Dresser fel, Southern Methodist Univ, 72-74; Dupont asst prof, Ohio State Univ, 75-76. *Mem:* Am Soc Mech Engrs; Am Soc Eng Educ; Licensing Exec Soc. *Res:* Swirl flow heat transfer; aerosol mechanics; cyclonic separation techniques of particulates and steam; thermal and fluid sciences. *Mailing Add:* 589 Sweet Hollow Rd Bloomsbury NJ 08804

RAZNIAK, STEPHEN L, ORGANIC CHEMISTRY. *Current Pos:* from asst prof to assoc prof, 61-64, head dept, 74-79, PROF ORG CHEM, ETEX STATE UNIV, 64- *Personal Data:* b Detroit, Mich, May 23, 34; m 65; c 3. *Educ:* Wayne State Univ, BS, 55; Wash State Univ, PhD(chem), 59. *Prof Exp:* NSF fel org chem, Brown Univ, 59-60, instr, 60-61. *Mem:* Am Chem Soc; Sigma Xi. *Res:* Organic sulfur chemistry; environmental chemistry. *Mailing Add:* Dept Chem ETex State Univ Commerce TX 75429-3011

RAZOUK, RASHAD ELIAS, CHEMISTRY. *Current Pos:* prof, 68-78, EMER PROF CHEM, CALIF STATE UNIV, LOS ANGELES, 79- *Personal Data:* b Dumiat, Egypt, Aug 22, 11; US citizen; m 46, 90, Henrietta Doche; c Reda & Rami. *Educ:* Cairo Univ, BSc, 33, MSc, 36, PhD(chem), 39. *Prof Exp:* Asst prof chem, Cairo Univ, 39-47, assoc prof, 47-50; prof & chmn dept, Ain Shams Univ, Cairo, 50-66, vdean, 54-60; prof, Am Univ Cairo, 66-68. *Concurrent Pos:* Actg dir, Div Colloid & Surface Chem, Nat Res Ctr, Cairo, 50-68. *Mem:* Am Inst Chem; Am Chem Soc; Royal Soc Chem. *Res:* Surface chemistry; adsorption on carbons and active solids; solid reactions; surface tension and contact angles; wetting and wettability. *Mailing Add:* 1140 Keats St Manhattan Beach CA 90266-6810

RE, RICHARD N, CELL BIOLOGY. *Current Pos:* chmn clin invests comt, Alton Ochsner Med Found, 80-86, HEAD SECT HYPERTENSIVE DIS, OCHSNER CLIN, 81-, VPRES & DIR RES, ALTON OCHSNER MED FOUND, 85-, STAFF MEM, 79- *Personal Data:* b Palisade, NJ, Sept 4, 44; m 79, Martha MacDonald; c Richard M, Christopher M & Gregory N. *Educ:* Harvard Col, AB, 65; Harvard Med Sch, MD, 69; cert, Am Bd Internal Med, Am Bd Endocrinol & Metab. *Prof Exp:* Med intern & resident, Mass Gen Hosp, 69-71; clin & res fel endocrinol, 71-74; clin asst med, 74-76; asst prof med, Harvard Med Sch, 77-79. *Concurrent Pos:* Res fel, Harvard Med Sch, 71-74; instr med, 75-76; chief, Hypertension Clinic, Mass Gen Hosp, 75-79, & asst in med, 76-79; assoc clin prof med, Tulane Univ Sch Med, & assoc prof med, La State Univ Sch Med, 80-; fel Coun High Blood Pressure, Am Heart Asn; assoc ed, Hypertension, J Am Heart Asn, 94-99. *Mem:* Fel, Am Col Physicians; Am Heart Asn; Int Soc Hypertension; Am Fed Clin Res; AAAS; NY Acad Sci; Soc Exp Biol & Med. *Res:* Cellular biology of the Renin-angiotensin systems and the sequeiae of hypertension. *Mailing Add:* Alton Ochsner Med Found 1514 Jefferson Hwy New Orleans LA 70121-2483

REA, DAVID KENERSON, GEOLOGICAL OCEANOGRAPHY. *Current Pos:* from asst prof to prof, Dept Atmospheric & Oceanic Sci, 75-87, PROF, DEPT GEOL SCI, UNIV MICH, 87-, CHAIR, 95- *Personal Data:* b Pittsburgh, Pa, June 2, 42; m 67, Donna Harshbarger; c Gregory K & Margaret M. *Educ:* Princeton Univ, AB, 64; Univ Ariz, MS, 67; Ore State Univ, PhD(oceanog), 74. *Prof Exp:* Asst prof oceanog, Sch Oceanog, Ore State Univ, 74-75. *Concurrent Pos:* Assoc dir, Climate Dynamics Prog, NSF, Wash, DC, 86-87; interim dir, Ctr Great Lakes & Aquatic Sci, Univ Mich, 88-89. *Mem:* Geol Soc Am; Am Geophys Union; AAAS; Sigma Xi; Oceanog Soc. *Res:* Paleoclimatology and paleoceanography; marine and lacustrine sediments and sedimentation; history of oceans and ocean basins. *Mailing Add:* Dept Geol Sci Univ Mich Ann Arbor MI 48109-1063. *Fax:* 313-763-4690

REA, DAVID RICHARD, CHEMICAL ENGINEERING. *Current Pos:* TECH SUPT, PLASTIC PRODS & RESINS DEPT, E I DU PONT DE NEMOURS & CO, INC, 66- *Personal Data:* b Indianapolis, Ind, May 4, 40; m 64; c 4. *Educ:* Purdue Univ, BS, 62; Princeton Univ, MA, 64, PhD(chem eng), 67. *Mem:* Am Inst Chem Engrs; Am Chem Soc. *Res:* Rheology as applied to plastics; process development of fluorocarbon chemistry products; low-density polyethylene; nylon intermediates work; engineering thermoplastics. *Mailing Add:* 119 Rockland Circle Wilmington DE 19803

REA, DONALD GEORGE, PLANETARY SCIENCES. *Current Pos:* CONSULT SCIENTIST, MITRE CORP, VA, 91- *Personal Data:* b Portage La Prairie, Man, Sept 21, 29; nat US. *Educ:* Univ Man, BSc, 50, MSc, 51; Mass Inst Technol, PhD(chem), 54. *Hon Degrees:* DSc, Univ Man, 80. *Honors & Awards:* Exceptional Sci Achievement Award, NASA, 69 & Outstanding Leadership Medal, 85. *Prof Exp:* Nat Res Coun Can fel, Oxford Univ, 54-55; res chemist, Calif Res Corp, 55-61; assoc res chemist, Space Sci Lab, Univ Calif, Berkeley, 61-68; dep dir, Planetary Progs, Off Space Sci & Appln, NASA Hq, 68-70; asst lab dir sci, Jet Propulsion Lab, Calif Inst Technol, 70-76, dept asst lab dir, 76-80, asst lab dir, Technol & Space Prog Develop, 80-91. *Concurrent Pos:* Res fel, John F Kennedy Sch Govt, Harvard Univ, 79-80. *Mem:* Am Chem Soc; Am Phys Soc; Optical Soc Am; Am Astron Soc; Am Geophys Union; AAAS. *Res:* Molecular spectroscopy of planetary atmospheres; remote sensing of planetary surfaces; space exploration advancement. *Mailing Add:* 118 Gresham Pl Falls Church VA 22046

REA, KENNETH HAROLD, PLANT SYNECOLOGY, COMPUTER SCIENCE. *Current Pos:* MEM STAFF ECOL, LOS ALAMOS NAT LAB, 76- *Personal Data:* b Red Oak, Iowa, Aug 20, 46; m 67; c 4. *Educ:* NMex State Univ, BS, 69, MS, 72; Utah State Univ, PhD(ecol), 76. *Mem:* AAAS; Soc Range Mgt. *Res:* Plant demography; impacts of geothermal energy development; hazardous waste management. *Mailing Add:* Los Alamos Nat Lab PO Box 1663 Mail Stop J495 Los Alamos NM 87545

READ, ALBERT JAMES, PHYSICS, SCIENCE EDUCATION. *Current Pos:* from assoc prof to prof physics, 57-85, DIR SCI DISCOVERY CTR, STATE UNIV NY COL ONEONTA, 85- *Personal Data:* b Albany, NY, June 8, 20; m 53; c 1. *Educ:* State Univ NY Col Educ, Albany, BA, 47, MA, 54. *Prof Exp:* Instr physics, Rensselaer Polytech Inst, 47-50; asst prof, Morrisville Agr & Tech Inst, 52-57. *Mem:* Int Solar Energy Soc; Am Asn Physics Teachers; Nat Sci Teachers Asn; Hist Sci Soc; Soc Hist Technol. *Mailing Add:* 45 Woodside Ave Oneonta NY 13820

READ, CHARLES H, PEDIATRICS, ENDOCRINOLOGY. *Current Pos:* from asst prof to assoc prof, 54-59, prof, 59-87, EMER PROF PEDIAT, COL MED, UNIV IOWA, 87- *Personal Data:* b Amherst, NS, July 22, 18; m 42; c Charles, Patricia, Judith, Susan & Connie. *Educ:* Acadia Univ, BSc, 39; McGill Univ, MD & CM, 43. *Prof Exp:* Rutherford Caverhill fel, Fac Med, McGill Univ, 47-49; Commonwealth Fund fel, Harvard Med Sch & Mass Gen Hosp, Boston, 49-51; asst prof pediat, Fac Med, Univ Man, 51-52, assoc prof, 52-54. *Mem:* Soc Pediat Res; Endocrine Soc; Am Diabetes Asn; Am Acad Pediat. *Res:* Adrenal cortical activity of newborns; endocrinological studies of infants of diabetic mothers; immunological assay of human pituitary growth hormone; thirty year follow-up of children and adolescents with hyperthyroidism treated with radio-active iodine 131. *Mailing Add:* 3 Glenview Knoll NE Iowa City IA 52240

READ, DAVID HADLEY, PHYSICAL ORGANIC CHEMISTRY. *Current Pos:* assoc prof, 54-65, PROF CHEM, SEATTLE UNIV, 65- *Personal Data:* b Seattle, Wash, May 20, 21; m 51, 63; c 5. *Educ:* Seattle Univ, BS, 42; Univ Ill, MS, 44; Univ Notre Dame, PhD(org chem), 49. *Prof Exp:* Asst prof chem, Univ Seattle, 48-51; res chemist, Am-Marietta Co, 51-54. *Mem:* AAAS; Am Chem Soc; The Chem Soc. *Res:* Vinyl polymerization; electronic effects in rigid systems; clinical separations by high-performance liquid chromatography. *Mailing Add:* 911 11th E Seattle WA 98102-4513

READ, DAVID THOMAS, FRACTURE MECHANICS, PHYSICAL METALLURGY. *Current Pos:* PHYSICIST MECH PROPERTIES, US NAT BUR STANDARDS, 75- *Personal Data:* b Seattle, Wash, Sept 17, 47; m 72; c 4. *Educ:* Univ Santa Clara, BS, 69; Univ Ill, MS, 71, PhD(physics), 75. *Concurrent Pos:* Nat Res Coun fel, Nat Bur Standards, 75-76. *Mem:* Am Phys Soc; Am Soc Testing & Mat. *Res:* Low-temperature mechanical properties of metals; fracture mechanics; measurements of the J contour integral; mechanical properties of thin films. *Mailing Add:* Mat Reliability Div 853 Nat Inst Standards & Technol 325 Broadway Boulder CO 80303-3328

READ, DOROTHY LOUISE, PROMOTER STRUCTURE & ACTIVATION OF TRANSCRIPTION IN PROKARYOTES. *Current Pos:* assoc prof, 88-94, PROF BIOL, UNIV MASS, DARTMOUTH, 94- *Personal Data:* b Racine, Wis, July 18, 38; div; c Rachel & Joshua. *Educ:* Antioch Col, BS, 61; Univ Calif, Berkeley, PhD(biophys), 66. *Prof Exp:* Fel biochem, Brandeis Univ, 66-67, res assoc, 68-69 & 74-78; lectr biol, Northeastern Univ, 78; vis lectr biol, Southeastern Mass Univ, 78-79, asst prof biol, 79-82 & 85-88, vis asst prof med microbiol, Stanford Univ, 82-83 & 85; res assoc microbiol, Univ Southern Calif Sch Med, 83-84. *Concurrent Pos:* Consult, Stanford Res Inst, 85; prin investr, NIH, 88-91; vis prof microbiol & immunol, Stanford Univ, 90-91. *Mem:* Am Soc Microbiol; Am Soc Molecular Marine Biol & Biotechnol; Soc Indust Microbiol; AAAS; Asn Women Sci. *Res:* Genetic control of carbon starvation gene in Escherichia coli, primarily with regard to promoter activation; physical nature of plasmids; recombination in lambda bacteriophage; conjugation in thiobacilli. *Mailing Add:* Biol Dept Univ Mass Dartmouth 285 Old Westport Rd Dartmouth MA 02747

READ, FLOYD M, PHYSICS. *Current Pos:* Asst prof phys sci, 57-60, from asst prof to assoc prof physics, 60-75, PROF PHYSICS, E CAROLINA UNIV, 75-, AT DEPT SCI EDUC. *Personal Data:* b Ray City, Ga, Oct 4, 24; m 43; c 1. *Educ:* Univ Fla, BSEd, 52, MEd, 56; NY Univ, PhD, 69. *Mem:* Nat Sci Teachers Asn; Am Asn Physics Teachers; Nat Asn Res Sci Teaching; Sigma Xi. *Res:* Solar radiometry; teaching of physics. *Mailing Add:* 1804 Fairview Way Greenville NC 27858-4627

READ, GEORGE WESLEY, DRUG ABUSE. *Current Pos:* res asst, 64-68, from asst prof to assoc prof, 68-86, PROF PHARMACOL, UNIV HAWAII, MANOA, 86- *Personal Data:* b Los Angeles, Calif, June 24, 34; div; c Gregory C & Bonnie A. *Educ:* Stanford Univ, BA, 59, MS, 62; Univ Hawaii, PhD, 69. *Prof Exp:* Instr gen sci, Univ Hawaii, Hilo, 63-64. *Concurrent Pos:* Vis scientist, Univ Tex, Dallas, 75 & 84, Univ Washington, 76, NIH, 78, St Louis Univ, 83 & Ctr Nat Res, Rome, Italy, 91. *Mem:* Am Soc Pharmacol & Exp Therapeut. *Res:* Pharmacology of histamine release,; drug abuse, especially policy review. *Mailing Add:* Dept Pharmacol Univ Hawaii Sch Med Honolulu HI 96822-2319. *Fax:* 808-956-3165; *E-Mail:* read@uhccmvs. its.hawaii.edu

READ, JOHN FREDERICK, KINETICS. *Personal Data:* b Reading, Eng, Apr 11, 40; m 63; c 3. *Educ:* Univ Nottingham, BSc, 61, PhD(phys chem), 64. *Prof Exp:* Fel chem, Northwestern Univ, 64-65; teaching fel, Hope Col, 65-66; from asst prof to prof, Mt Allison Univ, 66-74, from asst dean to assoc dean, 70-78, dean, Col Arts & Sci, 78-90. *Mem:* fel Chem Inst Can. *Res:* Oxidation of sulfur compounds by potassium ferrale. *Mailing Add:* Dept Chem Mt Allison Univ Sackville NB E0A 3C0 Can. *E-Mail:* jread@mta

READ, JOHN HAMILTON, PEDIATRICS, PREVENTIVE MEDICINE. *Current Pos:* prof & head, Div Community Health Sci & prof pediat, Fac Med, 68-89, EMER PROF PEDIAT, FAC MED, UNIV CALGARY, 89- *Personal Data:* b Joliette, Que, Feb 20, 24; m 48; c 3. *Educ:* McGill Univ, BSc, 48, MD, CM, 50; Univ Toronto, DPH, 52. *Prof Exp:* Med officer, Simcoe Co, Ont, 52-54; resident pediat, Univ Mich, 54-56, instr, 56-58; asst prof pediat & prev med, Univ BC, 58-62; prof prev med & head dept & asst prof pediat, Queen's Univ, Ont, 62-68. *Mem:* Am Pub Health Asn. *Res:* Preventive pediatrics. *Mailing Add:* 3712 Underhill Dr NW Calgary AB T2N 4G1 Can

READ, KENNETH FRANCIS, JR, RELATIVISTIC HEAVY ION PHYSICS, SPIN STRUCTURE PHYSICS. *Current Pos:* STAFF MEM & COLLABORATING SCIENTIST, OAK RIDGE NAT LAB, 91- *Personal Data:* b Annapolis, Md, Apr 24, 59. *Educ:* Stanford Univ, BS, 81; Cornell Univ, MS, 84, PhD(physics), 87. *Prof Exp:* Postdoctoral res assoc, Princeton Univ, 87-90, res staff mem, 90. *Concurrent Pos:* Asst prof, Univ Tenn, 91- *Mem:* Sigma Xi; Am Phys Soc. *Res:* Experimental nuclear physics; measuring and understanding the properties of hot, dense nuclear matter and the spin structure of the nucleon; numerous measurements in experimental high energy physics. *Mailing Add:* Bldg 6003 MS 6372 Oak Ridge Nat Lab PO Box 2008 Oak Ridge TN 37831

READ, MARSHA H, NUTRITION. *Current Pos:* From instr to assoc prof, 69-84, PROF NUTRIT, UNIV NEV, RENO, 84- *Personal Data:* b Salt Lake City, Utah. *Educ:* Univ Nev, BS, 68, MS, 69; Utah State Univ, PhD(nutrit), 77. *Mem:* Am Diet Asn; Am Inst Nutrit. *Res:* Micronutrient supplementation patterns and effects; nutrition and physical performance; dietary compliance. *Mailing Add:* Dept Nutrit 142 Univ Nev Reno NV 89557-0001

READ, MERRILL STAFFORD, BIOCHEMISTRY, NUTRITION. *Current Pos:* PROF & CHMN, DEPT HUMAN NUTRIT & FOOD SYSTS, COL HUMAN ECOL, UNIV MD, 85- *Personal Data:* b Baltimore, Md, June 3, 28; div; c 2. *Educ:* Northwestern Univ, BS, 49; Ohio State Univ, MS, 51, PhD(biochem), 56. *Honors & Awards:* Dir Award Nutrit, NIH, 76. *Prof Exp:* Asst biochem, Ohio State Univ, 49-52; chief, Irradiated Food Br, Med Res & Nutrit Lab, Fitzsimons Army Hosp, Denver, 54-59; tech coordr, Radiation Preservation of Food Prog, Off Surgeon Gen, US Army, 59; vis prof biochem & nutrit, Va Polytech Inst & State Univ, 59-60; dir nutrit res, Nat Dairy Coun, 60-65, exec asst to pres, 64-66; nutrit prog admnr, Nat Inst Child Health & Human Develop, 66, dir, Growth & Develop Br, 66-76, actg dep dir, Ctr Res Mothers & Children, 74-76; adv nutrit res, Div Family Health, Nutrit Unit, Pan Am Health Orgn, 76-79; chief, Clin Nutrit & Early Develop Br, Nat Inst Child Health & Human Develop, 80-85. *Concurrent Pos:* Mem adv comt food irradiation, Am Inst Biol Sci-AEC, 60-62; mem comn Ill, Int Union Nutrit Sci, 67-76; vis scientist, Mass Inst Technol, 70; mem & chmn, Nat Adv Coun, NY State Col Human Ecol, Cornell Univ, 71-76; mem subcomt malnutrit, brain develop & behav, Nat Acad Sci-Nat Res Coun, 75-81; mem, Gov Coun, Am Pub Health Asn, 81-83; chmn, Comt Nutrit Educ & Training, Am Soc Clin Nutrit, 80-84, mem, 85-87. *Mem:* AAAS; Am Inst Nutrit; Am Soc Clin Nutrit; Am Pub Health Asn; Soc Nutrit Educ; Latin Am Soc Nutrit. *Res:* Child growth and development; mental development; maternal health; nutritional surveillance; nutrition education. *Mailing Add:* 1701 Hobart St NW Washington DC 20009-2907

READ, NICHOLAS, CONDENSED MATTER PHYSICS, QUANTUM HALL EFFECT. *Current Pos:* from asst to ASSOC PROF PHYSICS, YALE UNIV, 88- *Personal Data:* b London, UK, Nov 22, 58. *Educ:* Cambridge Univ, BA, 80, cert advan study, 81; Imp Col, DIC & PhD(theoret physics), 86. *Honors & Awards:* Presidential Young Investr Award, 91. *Prof Exp:* Res fel, Brown Univ, 85-86, Mass Inst Technol, 86-87. *Concurrent Pos:* Res fel, A P Sloan Found, 89-93. *Mem:* Fel Am Phys Soc. *Res:* Condensed matter theory; quantum hall effect; quantum magnetism; disordered systems. *Mailing Add:* Appl Physics Yale Univ PO Box 208284 New Haven CT 06520

READ, PAUL EUGENE, HORTICULTURE, PLANT TISSUE CULTURE. *Current Pos:* PROF & HEAD DEPT HORT, UNIV NEBR, LINCOLN, 87- *Personal Data:* b Canandaigua, NY, July 13, 37; m 89; c Sharon A, Nancy B, Norman A, Emma J & Peter A. *Educ:* Cornell Univ, BS, 59, MS, 64; Univ Del, PhD(Biol sci), 67. *Prof Exp:* Co 4-H Club agent, Fulton Co Exten Serv Asn, NY, 59-62; teaching asst hort, Cornell Univ, 62-64; res assoc, Univ Del, 64-67; from asst prof to assoc prof, 67-78, prof hort, Univ Minn, St Paul, 78-87. *Concurrent Pos:* Consult, Teaching & Res, People's Repub China, Zambia, Morocco, Australia, Eastern Europe. *Mem:* Fel Am Soc Hort Sci (vpres, 86-87); Int Asn Plant Tissue Cult; Am Hort Soc; Bot Soc Am; Soc Invitro Biol; Plant Growth Regulator Soc Am. *Res:* Plant tissue culture; plant propagation; chemical plant growth regulation; nutrition of horticultural plants; administration; biotechnology. *Mailing Add:* Dept Hort Univ Nebr 377 Plant Sci Bldg Lincoln NE 68583-0724

READ, PHILIP LLOYD, PHYSICS, INSTRUMENTATION. *Current Pos:* CONSULT, 88- *Personal Data:* b Flint, Mich, Jan 9, 32; m 56, Ann Goodall; c Thomas E, Elizabeth A & Jane C. *Educ:* Oberlin Col, AB, 53; Univ Mich, MS, 54, PhD(physics), 61. *Prof Exp:* Physicist, Res Lab, Gen Elec Co, NY, 60-67, mgr x-ray components eng, X-Ray Dept, Wis, 67-70, mgr cardio-surg systs sect, Med Systs Div, 70-75; vpres & gen mgr, Prod Systs Div, 75-81, chief oper officer, 81-83, sr vpres, Computervision Corp, Bedford, 81-88. *Mem:* Am Phys Soc. *Res:* Ionic conduction in solids; circuit theory; thermionic emission; ultrahigh vacuum; electrical transport properties of insulator surfaces; biophysics; computer graphics; Computer-Aided Design/ Computer-Aided Manufacturing. *Mailing Add:* 80 Witherell Dr Sudbury MA 01776

READ, RAYMOND CHARLES, SURGERY. *Current Pos:* CHIEF SURG SERV & STAFF SURGEON, VET ADMIN HOSP, 66-; PROF SURG, UNIV ARK, LITTLE ROCK, 66- *Personal Data:* b London, Eng, Jan 26, 24; nat US; m 46; c 3. *Educ:* Cambridge Univ, MA, 44, MB, BCh, 47; Univ Minn, MB, 46, MD, 51, MS, 57, PhD, 58. *Prof Exp:* Intern & resident surg, Kings Col, Univ London, Harvard Univ & Univ Hosps, Univ Minn, 46-51; Harvey Cushing res fel, Harvard Med Sch, 51-53; Life Ins Med res fel, Med Sch, Univ Minn, Minneapolis, 56-58, asst prof surg, 58-61; assoc prof, Wayne State Univ, 61-66. *Concurrent Pos:* Staff surgeon, Vet Admin Hosp, Minneapolis, 58-61; mem sr staff, Detroit Gen Hosp, 61-66. *Mem:* AAAS; Soc Exp Biol & Med; AMA; Sigma Xi. *Res:* Fundamental and surgical cardiovascular physiology. *Mailing Add:* JLM Vet Hosp 112 LR 4300 W Seventh St Little Rock AR 72205-5411

READ, ROBERT E, ORGANIC CHEMISTRY. *Current Pos:* CONSULT, 94- *Personal Data:* b Stoke on Trent, Eng, Jan 30, 33; US citizen; m 55, Majory Fair; c 2. *Educ:* Haverford Col, BS, 55; Univ Del, MS, 57, PhD(org chem), 60. *Prof Exp:* Chemist, Chem Dyes & Pigments Dept, E I DuPont de Nemours & Co, Inc, 60-80, tech prog mgr, Cent Res & Develop Dept, 81-85, tech prog mgr, Biomed Prod Dept, 85-90, mgr support & develop, Med Prod Dept, 90-91; at Terumo Med Corp, 91-94. *Mem:* Am Chem Soc; Am Asn Textile Chemists & Colorists; Sigma Xi; Asn Advan Brit Biotechnol. *Res:* Urethanes, organic carbodiimides and isocyanate related chemistry; polymer chemistry; development of chemical finishing agents for textiles; development of medical instrumentation. *Mailing Add:* 1537 Old Coach Rd Newark DE 19711. *Fax:* 302-737-4194; *E-Mail:* robobr@aol.com

READ, ROBERT G, METEOROLOGY, OCEANOGRAPHY. *Current Pos:* from asst prof to prof, 61-88, EMER PROF METEOROL, SAN JOSE STATE UNIV, 88- *Personal Data:* b Kingston, NY, Apr 2, 18; m 47; c 6. *Educ:* US Naval Postgrad Sch, BS, 53, MS, 61. *Prof Exp:* Instr meteorol & oceanog, US Naval Postgrad Sch, 59-61. *Concurrent Pos:* Assoc dir, NSF Summer Inst Earth Sci, 64 & Partic in-serv inst oceanog, Moss Landing Marine Labs & instnl grant marine influences on potential evaporation in coastal Calif, 68-69; investr, Sea Trout Prog, Moss Landing Marine Labs, Calif, 70-71; estab environ measurement network on Barro Colorado Island, CZ, Smithsonian Inst Trop Res, 71; joint researcher with Mid Am Res Unit, NIH, 73-79; meteorol consult, Fed Univ Rio de Janeiro & Fed Univ Rio Grande do Sol, 82; vis scholar, Smithsonian Trop Res Inst, Panama, 84; Fulbright scholar, Univ Panama, 85. *Mem:* AAAS; Am Meteorol Soc; Am Geophys Union. *Res:* Problems in evaporation in the tropics and in the marine coastal atmosphere; marine meteorology and the energy transport across the air-ocean interface; general synoptic meteorology; author numerous publications. *Mailing Add:* 156 Robles Del Rio Carmel Valley CA 93924

READ, ROBERT H, METALLURGY, PHYSICS. *Current Pos:* PRES, SECOND OPINION INC, 95- *Personal Data:* b Jacksonville, Ill, Feb 15, 28; m 50; c 3. *Educ:* Ill Col, AB, 52; Pa State Univ, MS, 53, PhD(metall), 55. *Prof Exp:* Res metallurgist, Armour Res Found, Ill Inst Technol, 56-57, supvr powder metals res, 57-58, supvr phys metall, 59-62; dir res, Atlas Steels Co, Rio Algom Mines Ltd, Ont, 62-64, mgr technol, 64-69, vpres res & metall, 69-72, mgr corp planning, 72-73; sr vpres technol & sales, Teledyne Vasco, 73-76, exec vpres, 76-80, pres, Teledyne Portland Forge, 80-90, group exec. *Mem:* Am Iron & Steel Inst; Am Soc Metals; Am Inst Mining, Metall & Petrol Engrs; Can Inst Mining & Metall. *Mailing Add:* 2060 S New Mt Pleasant Rd Portland IN 47371

READ, ROBERT RICHARD, MATHEMATICAL STATISTICS. *Current Pos:* assoc prof, 61-71, PROF PROBABILITY & STATIST, NAVAL POSTGRAD SCH, 71- *Personal Data:* b Columbus, Ohio, Oct 5, 29; m 63; c Christopher, Steven & Darren. *Educ:* Ohio State Univ, BS, 51; Univ Calif, PhD(math statist), 57. *Prof Exp:* Asst res statistician, Univ Calif, 57-60; vis asst prof statist, Univ Chicago, 60-61. *Concurrent Pos:* Lectr, Univ Calif,

58-59; consult, Maritime Cargo Transportation Conf, Nat Acad Sci-Nat Res Coun, Lockheed Calif Co & ARRO Res Corp. *Mem:* Inst Math Statist; Am Statist Asn; Sigma Xi. *Res:* Probability; statistics; operations research. *Mailing Add:* Naval Post Grad Sch Oper Analysis Code 55Re Monterey CA 93943. *Fax:* 408-656-2595

READ, RONALD CEDRIC, MATHEMATICS, COMPUTER SCIENCE. *Current Pos:* prof, 70-90, ADJ PROF MATH, UNIV WATERLOO, 90- *Personal Data:* b London, Eng, Dec 19, 24; m 49, 87, Marie Barson; c Helen & Colin. *Educ:* Cambridge Univ, BA, 48, MA, 53; Univ London, PhD(math), 58. *Prof Exp:* Lectr math, Univ WI, 50-60, sr lectr, 60-66, reader, 66-67, prof, 67-70. *Concurrent Pos:* USAF Off Sci Res grant, Univ WI, 65-68; Nat Res Coun Can grant, Univ Waterloo, 71-95; ed, J Asn Comput Mach, 71-75. *Mem:* Fel Inst Combinatorics & Its Appln. *Res:* Enumerative graph theory; applications of computers to graph theoretical and combinatorial problems. *Mailing Add:* Dept Combinatorics & Optimization Univ Waterloo Waterloo ON N2L 3G1 Can. *E-Mail:* rcread@math.uwaterloo.ca

READ, THOMAS THORNTON, DIFFERENTIAL EQUATIONS. *Current Pos:* From asst prof to assoc prof, 67-76, PROF MATH, WESTERN WASH UNIV, 76- *Personal Data:* b Philadelphia, Pa, Jan 24, 43; m 67; c 1. *Educ:* Oberlin Col, BA, 63; Yale Univ, MA, 65, PhD(math), 69. *Concurrent Pos:* Vis lectr, Chalmers Univ Technol, Gothenburg, Sweden, 73-74; vis prof, Univ Groningen, Neth, 78-80. *Mem:* Am Math Soc; London Math Soc. *Res:* Linear differential equations, especially spectral theory. *Mailing Add:* Dept Math Western Wash Univ Bellingham WA 98225-9063

READ, VIRGINIA HALL, BIOCHEMISTRY, ENDOCRINOLOGY. *Current Pos:* Instr biochem, Sch Med, Univ Miss, 65-66, asst prof, 66-68, asst prof biochem, 70-74, assoc prof clin lab sci, 79-88, ASSOC PROF BIOCHEM, SCH MED, UNIV MISS, 74-, ASSOC PROF PATH, 88- *Personal Data:* b Louisville, Miss, Oct 15, 37; m 60, Dale G; c Laura (Sprabery), Dale G Jr & Eva (Warden). *Educ:* Univ Miss, BS, 59, PhD(biochem), 64. *Concurrent Pos:* NIH spec fel endocrinol, Sch Med, Univ Ala, Birmingham, 68-70; Miss Heart Asn fel, 65-67. *Mem:* Sigma Xi; Am Chem Soc; Endocrine Soc; Am Asn Clin Chem. *Res:* Control of aldosterone secretion; mechanism of aldosterone action and its relationship to diseases; relationship of adrenal steroids and thyroid hormones to electrolyte and water metabolism; radioimmunoassay of hormones. *Mailing Add:* Dept Path Div Lab Med Univ Miss Med Sch Jackson MS 39216-4505. *Fax:* 601-984-5008

READ, WILLIAM GEORGE, NUCLEAR PHYSICS. *Current Pos:* from asst prof to prof, 49-59, head dept, 59-70, vpres acad affairs & dean of fac, 70-78, PROF, MURRAY STATE UNIV, 78- *Personal Data:* b Stratton, Colo, Apr 13, 21; m 48. *Educ:* Kans State Teachers Col, Ft Hays, BS, 43, MS, 48; Univ Kans, PhD(physics), 56. *Prof Exp:* Instr physics, Kans State Teachers Col, Ft Hays, 47-48. *Mem:* AAAS; Am Phys Soc; Nat Asn Physics Teachers; Sigma Xi. *Res:* Experimental nuclear physics and physical properties of soils; electronics. *Mailing Add:* 4644 Rockland Pl La Canada CA 91011

READDY, ARTHUR F, JR, PHYSICAL CHEMISTRY, MATERIALS SCIENCE ENGINEERING. *Current Pos:* CONSULT, MAT UTILIZATION DEGRADATION, 88- *Personal Data:* b Jersey City, NJ, Mar 4, 28; m 60, Mary Szabo; c Margaret, Andrew & Christine. *Educ:* St Peters Col, BS, 49; Stevens Inst Technol, MS, 57. *Prof Exp:* Res chemist, Onyx Oil & Chem Co, 49-51; Theobald Industs, 51-53 & Colgate-Palmolive Co, 53-56; head chem sect, Appl Sci Br, Naval Supply Res & Develop Facility, 56-66; scientist, Plastics Tech Eval Ctr, Armament Res & Develop Command, US Dept Defense, Dover, 66-88. *Concurrent Pos:* Vis prof, Jersey City State Col, 59-61. *Res:* Surface chemistry and physics; radiations effects and applications; composite materials; protection-decontamination of equipment; electrical, electronic and other properties of materials; nuclear, chemical, biological agents decontamination. *Mailing Add:* 9 Lenox Ave Cranford NJ 07016

READDY, MARGARET ANNE, ALGEBRAIC COMBINATORICS, CONVEX POLYTOPES. *Current Pos:* ASST PROF MATH, CORNELL UNIV, 95- *Personal Data:* b Elizabeth, NJ, Aug 10, 64; m 96, Richard Ehrenborg. *Educ:* Rutgers Univ, BA, 86; Univ Mich, MS, 89; Mich State Univ, PhD(math), 93. *Prof Exp:* Res analyst, Blue Cross & Blue Shield NJ, Inc, 86-87; postdoctoral fel, Univ Que, Montreal, 93-95. *Mem:* Am Math Soc; Asn Women Math; Math Asn Am; Swedish Math Soc. *Res:* Algebraic techniques to polytope theory; properties and combinatorial aspects of convex polytopes. *Mailing Add:* 701 N Aurora St Ithaca NY 14853-7901. *Fax:* 607-255-7149; *E-Mail:* readdy@math.cornell.edu

READE, MAXWELL OSSIAN, MATHEMATICS. *Current Pos:* from asst prof to prof, 46-86, EMER PROF MATH, UNIV MICH, ANN ARBOR, 86- *Personal Data:* b Philadelphia, Pa, Apr 11, 16; m 66; c 3. *Educ:* Brooklyn Col, BS, 36; Harvard Univ, MA, 37; Rice Inst, PhD(math), 40. *Prof Exp:* Instr math, Ohio State Univ, 40-42 & Purdue Univ, 42-44 & 46. *Mem:* AAAS; assoc Am Math Soc; assoc Math Asn Am. *Res:* Theory of functions of one complex variable. *Mailing Add:* 3220 Angell Hall Univ Mich Ann Arbor MI 48109-1109

READER, GEORGE GORDON, MEDICINE & PUBLIC HEALTH, DELIVERY OF HEALTH SERVICES. *Current Pos:* from instr to prof med, 49-72, Livingston Farrand Prof Pub Health & Chmn Dept, 72-92, EMER LIVINGSTON FARRAND PROF PUB HEALTH & EMER PROF MED, MED COL, CORNELL UNIV, 92- *Personal Data:* b Brooklyn, NY, Feb 8, 19; m 42, Helen C Brown; c Jonathan, David, Mark & Peter. *Educ:* Cornell Univ, BA, 40, MD, 43. *Hon Degrees:* DSc, Drew Univ, 88. *Prof Exp:* Intern med, NY Hosp, 44, res fel, 46-47, asst res physician, 47-49. *Concurrent Pos:* Chmn human ecol study sect, NIH, 61-65; ed, Milbank Mem Fund Quart, Health & Soc, 71-88. *Mem:* Sr mem Inst Med-Nat Acad Sci; fel Am Pub Health Asn; fel Am Col Physicians; fel Am Col Prev Med; Am Sociol Asn. *Res:* Medical education and medical care; medical sociology. *Mailing Add:* NY Hosp Cornell Med Ctr 1300 York Ave PO Box 73 New York NY 10021

READER, JOSEPH, PHYSICS. *Current Pos:* STAFF PHYSICIST, NAT INST STANDARDS & TECHNOL, 63- *Personal Data:* b Chicago, Ill, Dec 1, 34; m 56, Evelyn Rosendorff; c Jack, Michael & Cheryl (Snechter). *Educ:* Purdue Univ, BS, 56, MS, 57; Univ Calif, Berkeley, PhD(physics), 62. *Honors & Awards:* Gold Medal, Dept Com; W F Meggers Award, Optical Soc Am. *Prof Exp:* Res assoc physics, Argonne Nat Lab, 62-63. *Mem:* Fel Am Phys Soc; fel Optical Soc Am. *Res:* Experimental atomic physics; optical spectroscopy; hyperfine structure; electronic structure of highly ionized atoms; wave length standards; ionization energies of atoms and ions. *Mailing Add:* Phys A163 Nat Inst Standards & Technol Gaithersburg MD 20899. *Fax:* 301-975-3038; *E-Mail:* jreader@nist.gov

READER, WAYNE TRUMAN, acoustical materials; deceased, see previous edition for last biography

READHEAD, ANTHONY C S, ASTRONOMY, ASTROPHYSICS. *Current Pos:* sr res fel, Calif Inst Technol, 77-79, res assoc, 79-81, prof radio astron, 81-90, exec officer, Dept Astron, 90-92, PROF ASTRON, CALIF INST TECHNOL, 90- *Educ:* Univ Witwatersrand, Johannesburg, BSc(math & physics) & BSc(theoret physics), 68; Univ Cambridge, PhD, 72. *Prof Exp:* Royal Soc Weir res fel, Cavendish Lab, Cambridge Univ, 72-77; dir, Owens Valley Radio Observ, 81-86. *Concurrent Pos:* Weir res fel, Royal Soc London, 73-77; mem, Comt Spaces Astron & Astrophysics, Nat Acad Sci, 82-95. *Mem:* Nat Acad Sci; Am Acad Arts & Sci; Am Astron Soc; Royal Astron Soc; Int Union Radio Sci. *Mailing Add:* Dept Radio Astron Calif Inst Technol Pasadena CA 91109

READHEAD, CAROL WINIFRED, BIOLOGY. *Current Pos:* fel biol, 77-79, sr res fel, 80-83, STAFF SCIENTIST, CALIF INST TECHNOL, 83- *Personal Data:* b Johannesburg, SAfrica, Sept 9, 47; m 69; c 2. *Educ:* Univ Witwatersrand, BSc hons, 70; Cambridge Univ, PhD(biol), 77. *Prof Exp:* Res asst biochem, Cambridge Univ, 70-72. *Concurrent Pos:* Asst prof, Univ Southern Calif, 79-80. *Mem:* Sigma Xi. *Res:* Recombinant DNA research on immunoglobulin genes; molecular biology of neurological mouse mutants, genetic engineering. *Mailing Add:* 2185 San Pasqual St Pasadena CA 91107

READING, ANTHONY JOHN, PSYCHOSOMATIC MEDICINE. *Current Pos:* PROF & CHAIRPERSON PSYCHIAT, UNIV SFLA, TAMPA, 75-, ASSOC DEAN, 93- *Personal Data:* b Sydney, Australia, Sept 10, 33; m 75, Elisabeth Hoffman; c Wendy (England) & Sarah. *Educ:* Univ Sydney, MB & BS, 57; Johns Hopkins Univ, MPH, 61, ScD, 64; Am Bd Psychiat & Neurol, cert, 71. *Prof Exp:* Jr resident med officer, Sydney Hosp, Australia, 57-58, sr resident med officer, 58-59; pvt pract, 59-60; instr pathobiol & ment hyg, Johns Hopkins Univ, Sch Med, 62-65, asst prof pathobiol, 64-65, asst resident psychiat, 65-68, instr med, 68-69, from asst prof to assoc prof psychiat, 68-75, asst prof med, 69-75, dir, Psychiat Liaison Serv, Johns Hopkins Hosp, 74-75 & Comprehensive Alcoholism Prog, 72-75. *Concurrent Pos:* Physician-in-charge, Alcoholism Clin, Johns Hopkins Hosp, 69-75 & Psychosomatic Clin, 74-75. *Mem:* AAAS; Am Psychosomatic Soc; AMA; Am Psychiat Asn. *Res:* Psychosocial aspects of illness; psychobiology. *Mailing Add:* Univ SFla TGH Univ Psychiat Ctr 3515 E Fletcher Ave Tampa FL 33613-4706. *Fax:* 813-972-7055

READING, JAMES CARDON, BIOSTATISTICS, MATHEMATICAL STATISTICS. *Current Pos:* instr, 70-72, asst prof biostatist & adj asst prof math, 72-76, ASSOC PROF BIOSTATIST & ADJ ASSOC PROF MATH, 76-, CHMN DIV BIOSTATIST, 77- *Personal Data:* b Ogden, Utah, Dec 7, 37; m 64; c 4. *Educ:* Stanford Univ, BS, 60, MS, 66, PhD(statist), 70. *Prof Exp:* Comput programmer & math analyst, Lockheed Missiles & Space Co, 62-67. *Mem:* Inst Math Statist; Am Statist Asn; Biomet Soc; Soc Clin Trials. *Res:* Methodological aspects of the analysis of clinical trials including design, conduct and statistical methods; classification problems. *Mailing Add:* PO Box 925 Centerville UT 84014

READING, JOHN FRANK, THEORETICAL PHYSICS. *Current Pos:* assoc prof, 71-81, PROF THEORET PHYSICS, TEX A&M UNIV, 81- *Personal Data:* b West Bromwich, Eng, Oct 19, 39; m 63; c 4. *Educ:* Christ Church, Oxford Univ, BA, 60, MA, 63; Univ Birmingham, dipl math physics, 61, PhD(physics), 64. *Prof Exp:* Instr theoret physics, Mass Inst Technol, 64-66; sr res assoc, Univ Wash, 66-68; Harwell fel, Atomic Energy Res Estab, Harwell, Eng, 68-69; assoc prof, Northeastern Univ, 69-71. *Concurrent Pos:* Consult, Oak Ridge Nat Lab; ed, Bienneal Conf, cross sect fusion & other applns. *Mem:* Fel Am Phys Soc. *Res:* Scattering theory in atomic, nuclear and solid state physics; numerical calculations of ion-atom collisions producing excitation, charge transfer and ionization. *Mailing Add:* Dept Physics Tex A&M Univ College Station TX 77843. *Fax:* 409-845-2590; *E-Mail:* reading@ tamphys.bitnet

READING, ROGERS W, physiological optics, optometry; deceased, see previous edition for last biography

READNOUR, JERRY MICHAEL, PHYSICAL INORGANIC CHEMISTRY, CHEMICAL EDUCATION. *Current Pos:* From asst prof to assoc prof, 68-79, PROF CHEM, SOUTHEAST MO STATE UNIV, 79- *Personal Data:* b Muncie, Ind, Oct 19, 40; m 62; c 2. *Educ:* Ball State Teachers Col, BS, 62; Purdue Univ, PhD(chem), 69. *Concurrent Pos:* Mem, Gen Chem Test Comt, Am Chem Soc, 79-89. *Mem:* Am Chem Soc. *Res:* Thermodynamic properties of aqueous solutions; stability constants; learning theory. *Mailing Add:* 427 N Sunset Cape Girardeau MO 63701-5219

READY, JOHN FETSCH, LASERS & ELECTRO-OPTICS. *Current Pos:* From res scientist to sr res scientist, Honeywell Corp Res Ctr & Mat Sci Ctr, 58-66, sr prin res scientist, 66-78, staff scientist, 78-79, group leader, Honeywell Corp Technol Ctr, 79-82, sect chief, 82-86, SR RES FEL, HONEYWELL SYSTS & RES CTR, 86- *Personal Data:* b St Paul, Minn, July 13, 32; m 53; c 6. *Educ:* Col St Thomas, BS, 54; Univ Minn, MS, 56. *Mem:* Am Phys Soc; Laser Inst Am. *Res:* Nuclear radiation damage; infrared materials and components; lasers, particularly effects of laser radiation and laser applications; laser based material processing and sensors. *Mailing Add:* 4401 Gilford Dr Edina MN 55435

REAGAN, DARYL DAVID, PHYSICS. *Current Pos:* RETIRED. *Personal Data:* b Longview, Wash, Apr 29, 25; m 59, Gertrude Burke King; c Jeffrey Philip & Russell Lawrence. *Educ:* Stanford Univ, MS, 49, PhD(physics), 55. *Prof Exp:* Sr physicist plasma physics, Lawrence Livermore Lab, 55-63; res assoc, Oxford Univ, 58-59; physicist accelerator physics, Stanford Univ, 63-93. *Mem:* Am Phys Soc. *Res:* Photonuclear physics; shock hydrodynamics; plasma physics; accelerator physics; magnetic measurements; synchrotron radiation. *Mailing Add:* 967 Moreno Ave Palo Alto CA 94303

REAGAN, JAMES OLIVER, MEAT SCIENCES. *Current Pos:* EXEC DIR SCI & TECHNOL, NAT CATTLEMEN BEEF ASN, 96- *Personal Data:* b Lampasas, Tex, Nov 13, 45; m 82; c 2. *Educ:* Tex A&M Univ, BS, 68, MS, 70, PhD(animal sci), 74. *Honors & Awards:* Creative Res Award, Outstanding Young Scientist, AGHON. *Prof Exp:* Instr animal sci, Tex A&M Univ, 72-73; asst prof, Ore State Univ, 73-74; from asst prof to prof animal & dairy sci, Univ Ga, 74-91; res prof, Nat Livestock & Meat Bd, 91-96. *Concurrent Pos:* Mem, Coun Agr Sci & Technol. *Mem:* Am Meat Sci Asn; Am Soc Animal Sci; Inst Food Technologists; Sigma Xi; Coun Agr Sci & Technol. *Res:* Quantitative and qualitative evaluation of meat animals, methods of extending the caselife of fresh meats; biochemical and physical attributes of pre- and post-rigor meat. *Mailing Add:* Nat Cattlemen Beef Asn PO Box 3469 Englewood CO 80155

REAGAN, JAMES W, pathology; deceased, see previous edition for last biography

REAGAN, JOHN ALBERT, ATMOSPHERIC RADIOMETRY. *Current Pos:* CONSULT, 76- *Personal Data:* b Grandview, Mo, May 2, 41; m 66; c 2. *Educ:* Univ Mo, Rolla, BS, 63, MS, 64; Univ Wis, PhD(elec eng), 67. *Honors & Awards:* Outstanding Serv Award, Geosci & Remote Sensing Soc, Inst Elec & Electronics Engrs, 88. *Prof Exp:* Elec engr, IBM Systs Develop Div, 64; from asst prof to assoc prof elec eng, Univ Ariz, 67-70, prof, 76. *Concurrent Pos:* Vis scientist, NASA Langley Res Ctr, aerosol measurement res branch, 78-79; mem, NASA LITE P, 85-89, Nat Oceanic & Atmospheric Admin Profiler Adv Comt, 87-88; vis prof, dept meteorol, Pa State Univ, 88-89; NASA Lite Sci Steering Group, 89-91; guest ed, Opt Engr Lidar Special Issue, 91; mem adv comt, Geosci & Remote Sensing Soc, Inst Elec & Electronics Engrs, 80-93, secy-treas, 84-87, vpres, 88-89, pres, 90-91. *Mem:* Fel Inst Elec & Electronics Engrs; Am Meteorol Soc; Int Soc Optical Eng. *Res:* Atmospheric remote sensing of aerosols and trace gases by laser radar; solar radiometry and microwave radiometry including both experimental implentation and signal processing. *Mailing Add:* Dept Elec & Comput Eng ECE Bldg 104 Univ Ariz Tucson AZ 85721

REAGAN, THOMAS EUGENE, INTEGRATED PEST MANAGEMENT. *Current Pos:* from asst prof to assoc prof, 77-85, PROF ENTOM, LA STATE UNIV, 85- *Personal Data:* b Tylertown, Miss, Jan 12, 47; m 68, Sheila B; c William, Joy & Jill. *Educ:* La State Univ, Baton Rouge, BS, 70, MS, 72; NC State Univ, PhD(entom, ecol, statist), 75. *Prof Exp:* Asst prof & exten specialist entom, NC State Univ, 75-77. *Concurrent Pos:* Expert witness, US & foreign consult. *Mem:* Sigma Xi; Entom Soc Am; Nat Asn Cols & Teachers Agr. *Res:* Applied and basic research on ecology and pest management of sugar cane insects; interdisciplinary aspects of pest management; pest/beneficial arthropod interactions with cultural practices; management of plant virus disease transmission by insect vectors; pesticide impact assesment, insecticide resistance; predictive mathematical modeling; imported fire ant ecology; sugarcane. *Mailing Add:* 402 Life Sci Bldg Entom Dept La State Univ Baton Rouge LA 70803. *Fax:* 504-388-1643; *E-Mail:* treagan@unix1.sncc.lsu.edu

REAGAN, WILLIAM JOSEPH, INORGANIC CHEMISTRY. *Current Pos:* RES CHEMIST, AMOCO OIL RES & DEVELOP, 88- *Personal Data:* b Salem, Mass, Nov 16, 43; m 65; c 3. *Educ:* Boston Col, BS, 65; Mich State Univ, PhD(inorg chem), 70. *Prof Exp:* Res asst, Mich State Univ, 66-69; res assoc, Univ Southern Calif, 70; sr res chemist, Mobil Res & Develop Corp, 70-78; group leader catalyst res, Englehard Minerals & Chem Corp, 78-88, res assoc, Englehard Corp, 81-88. *Mem:* Am Chem Soc. *Res:* Synthesis and characterization of molybdenum and tungsten compounds and fluorocarbon phosphine transition element compounds; transition metals in catalysis; solid state chemistry of heterogeneous catalysts; zeolite synthesis and catalysis. *Mailing Add:* Amoco Oil Co PO Box 3011 Naperville IL 60566-7011

REAGOR, JOHN CHARLES, TOXICOLOGY, BIOCHEMISTRY. *Current Pos:* Asst prof biochem, 65-71, VIS MEM, DEPT VET PHYSIOL & PHARMACOL, UNIV & HEAD DEPT TOXICOL, TEX VET MED DIAG LAB, TEX A&M UNIV, 69- *Personal Data:* b Llano, Tex, Mar 25, 38; m 61; c 2. *Educ:* Tex A&M Univ, BS, 60, MS, 63, PhD(biochem, nutrit), 66. *Mem:* Asn Off Anal Chemists; Am Asn Vet Lab Diagnosticians. *Res:* Development of analytical methods and techniques for forensic analyses of biological materials; study of poisonous plants including diagnostic methods. *Mailing Add:* 1400 Village Dr College Station TX 77840

REAL, LESLIE ALLAN, ECOLOGY, POPULATION BIOLOGY. *Current Pos:* ASST PROF ZOOL & BIOMATH, NC STATE UNIV, 78-; PROF BIOL, UNIV NC, CHAPEL HILL. *Personal Data:* b Philadelphia, Pa, June 22, 50. *Educ:* Ind Univ, BA, 72; Univ Mich, MS, 75, PhD(zool), 77. *Honors & Awards:* Prof Develop Award, NC State Univ, 78. *Prof Exp:* Fel biol, Univ Miami, 77-78. *Concurrent Pos:* Rosenstiel fel, Univ Miami, 77. *Mem:* Soc Study Evolution; Ecol Soc Am; AAAS. *Res:* Theoretical population biology; pollination ecology; animal behavior; ecological genetics. *Mailing Add:* Jordan Hall Bloomington IN 47405

REALS, WILLIAM JOSEPH, PATHOLOGY. *Current Pos:* PATHOLOGIST & DIR LABS, ST JOSEPH'S HOSP & PROF PATH & DEAN, SCH MED, UNIV KANS, 50- *Personal Data:* b Hot Springs, SDak, June 22, 20; m 44; c 5. *Educ:* Creighton Univ, BS, 44, MD, 45, MS, 49. *Prof Exp:* Instr path, Sch Med, Creighton Univ, 49-50. *Concurrent Pos:* Asst pathologist, Creighton Mem-St Joseph's Hosp, Omaha, Nebr, 49-50; consult, Wichita Vet Admin Hosp, 50-; lectr, Med Ctr, Univ Kans, 55-72; consult, Surgeon Gen, USAF, DC, 59-77 & Civil Air Surgeon, Fed Aviation Agency, 60-75. *Mem:* Am Soc Clin Path; Asn Mil Surg US; Aerospace Med Asn; Col Am Path (pres, 71-73). *Res:* Oncology; hormone chemistry, especially thyroid diseases; forensic pathology related to aircraft accidents. *Mailing Add:* Pathol Univ Kans Med Ctr Sch Med 3901 Rainbow Blvd Kansas City KS 66160-0001

REAM, BERNARD CLAUDE, ORGANIC CHEMISTRY, CATALYSIS. *Current Pos:* Res chemist, 66-76, proj scientist, 76-80, res scientist, 80-87, SR RES SCIENTIST, UNION CARBIDE CORP, 87- *Personal Data:* b Johnstown, Pa, Jan 30, 39; m 67; c 2. *Educ:* Seton Hall Univ, BS, 61; Ohio State Univ, MS, 63, PhD(org chem), 65. *Mem:* Am Chem Soc. *Res:* Metal-catalyzed synthesis of organic compounds; ethylene oxide/ethylene glycol process chemistry; syn-gas chemistry, catalysis; ethyleneamines and ethanolamines process chemistry. *Mailing Add:* 1807 Rolling Hills Rd Charleston WV 25314-2272

REAM, LLOYD WALTER, JR, MICROBIAL GENETICS, PLANT MOLECULAR BIOLOGY. *Current Pos:* ASSOC PROF, ORE STATE UNIV, 88-, ASSOC DIR, GENETICS PROG, 93- *Personal Data:* b Chester, Pa, Mar 20, 53; m 75, Nancy J Smith. *Educ:* Vanderbilt Univ, BA, 75; Univ Calif, Berkeley, PhD(molecular biol), 81. *Prof Exp:* Sr res fel microbiol, Dept Microbiol, Univ Wash, 80-83; asst prof molecular biol, Dept Biol, Ind Univ, 83-88. *Concurrent Pos:* Res asst molecular genetics, Inst Genetics, Univ Koln, Ger, 75; grad student molecular biol, Univ Calif, Berkeley, 75-80; consult ed, Plant Molecular Biol, 84-; inst fel, Inst Molecular & Cellular Biol, Ind Univ, 84-87. *Mem:* Genetics Soc Am; Am Soc Microbiol; AAAS; Int Soc Plant Molecular Biol; Am Cancer Soc. *Res:* The mechanism of T-DNA transmission during crown gall tumorigenesis; inducible virus resistance in plants; bateria-plant interactions; responses of plants to stress; genetic recombination. *Mailing Add:* 6005 NW Vineyard Dr Corvallis OR 97330. *Fax:* 541-737-0497; *E-Mail:* reamw@bcc.orgt.edu

REAME, NANCY E K, INFERTILITY RESEARCH, MATERNITY NURSING. *Current Pos:* assoc prof, 80-89, PROF NURSING, SCH NURSING, UNIV MICH, 90-, DIR, NAT CTR INFERTILITY RES, 91- *Educ:* Mich State Univ, BSN, 69; Wayne State Univ, MSN, 74, PhD(nursing), 77. *Prof Exp:* Asst prof, Col Nursing & assoc fac, Dept Physiol, Wayne State Univ, Mich, 77-80. *Concurrent Pos:* Postdoctoral fel, Univ Mich, 83; Comt Tech Bulletins, Am Col Obstetricians & Gynecologists, 84-87; prin investr, NIH, 86-90, 90-95, 91-92, 91-96 & 92-93; elected mem, Reprod Sci Prog, Univ Mich, 87-, res scientist, 91-; vis scholar, Stanford Univ, 89; pres, Univ Mich Res Club, 94-95; Am Acad Nursing sr nurse scholar, Inst Med, 96-97. *Mem:* Inst Med-Nat Acad Sci; Soc Menstrual Cycle Res (pres, 87-89); Fel Am Acad Nursing. *Res:* Reproductive physiology; gender and health; physiology of pain; psychobiology of stress; infertility; women's health. *Mailing Add:* Sch Nursing Rm 2238 Univ Mich 400 N Ingalls Bldg Ann Arbor MI 48109-0482

REAMES, DONALD VERNON, ASTROPHYSICS, PHYSICS. *Current Pos:* ASTROPHYSICIST COSMIC RAYS, NASA, GODDARD SPACE FLIGHT CTR, 64- *Personal Data:* b West Palm Beach, Fla, Dec 30, 36; wid; c Deborah. *Educ:* Univ Calif, Berkeley, AB, 58, PhD(physics), 64. *Mem:* Am Phys Soc; Inst Elec & Electronics Engrs Comput Soc; Am Geophys Union. *Res:* Cosmic rays, solar physics; interplanetary particles and fields; particle detectors; nuclear physics; microprocessor controlled experiments. *Mailing Add:* 11306 Sherrington Ct Upper Marlboro MD 20772-2317. *Fax:* 301-286-1682; *E-Mail:* reqmes@lheavx.gsfc.nasa.gov

REAMS, MAX WARREN, GEOMORPHOLOGY, SEDIMENTARY PETROLOGY. *Current Pos:* From asst prof to assoc prof, 67-77, CHMN DEPT GEOL SCI, OLIVET NAZARENE UNIV, 69-, PROF GEOL, 77-, CHMN DIV NATURAL SCI, 75- *Personal Data:* b Virgil, Kans, Mar 10, 38; m 61, Carol Cushard; c Brian, Anne & Kayla. *Educ:* Univ Kans, BA & BS,

61, MS, 63; Wash Univ, PhD(geol), 68. *Mem:* Geol Soc Am; Am Quaternary Asn; Clay Minerals Soc; Sigma Xi. *Res:* Geology and geochemistry of caves and cave sediments; weathering zone precipitates; mineralogy and petrology of speleothems; fractals in Karst; global ionospheric studies applications. *Mailing Add:* Dept Geol Sci Olivet Nazarene Univ Kankakee IL 60901. *Fax:* 815-939-5071; *E-Mail:* mreams@olivet.edu

REAP, JAMES JOHN, ORGANIC CHEMISTRY. *Current Pos:* RES CHEMIST BIOCHEM DEPT, E I DU PONT DE NEMOURS & CO, INC, 75- *Personal Data:* b Hazelton, Pa, Jan 22, 48; m 70; c 2. *Educ:* Villanova Univ, BS, 69; Univ Pittsburgh, PhD(org chem), 75. *Prof Exp:* Teacher physics & chem, Gloucester Cath Sr High Sch, 69-70. *Mem:* Am Chem Soc. *Res:* Synthesis of novel biologically active organic chemicals. *Mailing Add:* 2505 Bona Rd Wilmington DE 19810-2219

REARDEN, CAROLE ANN, IMMUNOHEMATOLOGY, TRANSPLANTATION. *Current Pos:* res pediat, 74, res clin path, 75-76, fel immunohemat, 76-79, asst prof path, 79-86, ASSOC PROF PATH, UNIV CALIF, SAN DIEGO, 86-, DIR, HISTOCOMPATIBILITY & IMMUNOGENETICS LAB, 79-, HEAD, DIV LAB MED, 89- *Personal Data:* b Belleville, Ont, June 11, 46; US citizen. *Educ:* McGill Univ, BSc, 69, MSc, 71, MDCM, 71. *Prof Exp:* Intern pediat, Children's Mem Hosp, Chicago, 71-72; fel biochem genetics, 72-73. *Concurrent Pos:* Prin investr, NIH grant, 83-86; mem, comt transplantation, Am Asn Blood Banks, 82-86. *Mem:* Am Asn Path; Am Fedn Clin Res; Am Soc Hemat; Am Asn Blood Banks; Am Asn Histocompatability & Immunogenetics; Int Soc Blood Transfusion. *Res:* Immunogenetics of major red cell membrane proteins (glycophorins). *Mailing Add:* Dept Path 0612 Univ Calif San Diego 9500 Gilman Dr La Jolla CA 92093-0612

REARDON, ANNA JOYCE, PHYSICS. *Current Pos:* from instr to prof & head dept, 41-75, EMER PROF PHYSICS, UNIV NC, GREENSBORO, 75- *Personal Data:* b East St Louis, Ill, Jan 22, 10. *Educ:* Col St Teresa, BA, 30; St Louis Univ, MS, 33, PhD(physics), 37. *Prof Exp:* High sch instr, Minn, 30-31 & Mo, 32-35; instr physics & Math, Ursuline Col, La, 36-37, Mt St Scholastica Col, 37-39, Col St Teresa 39-40 & Loretto Heights Col, 40-41. *Concurrent Pos:* Chmn, NC Comt High Sch Physics, 67-76, instr spec course in physics for x-ray technician students, Moses Cone Hosp. *Mem:* Am Phys Soc; Am Asn Physics Teachers; Sigma Xi; Asn Women Sci. *Res:* Theoretical photography. *Mailing Add:* 1105 Dover Rd Greensboro NC 27408-7313

REARDON, EDWARD JOSEPH, JR, RADIATION CURED COATINGS, PHOTORESISTS. *Current Pos:* sr chemist, 76-77, group leader, 78-79, res mgr, 79-84, tech dir, 84-86, VPRES TECH OPERS, DYNACHEM ELECTRONIC MAT GROUP, MORTON INT INC, 86- *Personal Data:* b Southbridge, Mass, Apr 24, 43; m 78, Dianne Fabian. *Educ:* Brown Univ, ScB, 65; Seton Hall Univ, MS, 67, PhD(org chem), 69. *Prof Exp:* NIH fel, Ind Univ, Bloomington, 69-70; assoc, Univ NC, Chapel Hill, 70-72; vis asst prof org chem, Bucknell Univ, 72-73; sr res assoc, Photohorizons Div, Horizons Res, 74-75. *Mem:* Am Chem Soc; Soc Photographic Scientists & Engrs. *Res:* Applied research and development of radiation sensitive coatings, primarily resists for fabrication of electronic circuits; synthesis of polymers and sensitizers; formulation, applications, manufacturing, and quality control methodologies. *Mailing Add:* Morton Electronic Mat 2631 Michelle Dr Tustin CA 92680-7018

REARDON, FREDERICK H(ENRY), COMBUSTION & PROPULSION, ENGINEERING EDUCATION. *Current Pos:* asst prof mech eng, Calif State Univ, 66-68, assoc prof eng, 68-73, chmn dept, 76-81, assoc dean, 81-86, PROF ENG, CALIF STATE UNIV, SACRAMENTO, 73- *Personal Data:* b Philadelphia, Pa, Oct 22, 32; m 56, Dorothy Hoeppner; c Kenneth F, Joy R (Moreton) & Steven E. *Educ:* Univ Pa, BS, 54, MS, 56; Princeton Univ, PhD(aeronaut eng), 61. *Prof Exp:* Instr mech eng, Univ Pa, 54-56; res engr, Princeton Univ, 56-61; supvr, Liquid Rocket Opers, Aerojet-Gen Corp, Sacramento, 61-64; tech specialist, 64-65; sr res engr, 65-66. *Concurrent Pos:* Mem working group combustion, Joint Army-Navy-NASA-Air Force, 64-; consult, Liquid Rocket Oper, Aerojet-Gen Corp, 66-; USAF, 76-86 & Chem Systs Div, United Technol Corp, 80-85. *Mem:* Sigma Xi; fel Am Soc Mech Engrs; assoc fel Am Inst Aeronaut & Astronaut; Combustion Inst; Am Soc Eng Educ. *Res:* Combustion and flow processes in engines, furnaces and waste recovery systems; automobile economy and emissions control; impact of scientific technology on society; development of educational simulations and games. *Mailing Add:* 5619 Haskell Ave Carmichael CA 95608-1203. *Fax:* 916-278-5949; *E-Mail:* freardon@csus.edu

REARDON, JOHN JOSEPH, ecology. biology, for more information see previous edition

REARDON, JOSEPH DANIEL, PHYSICAL CHEMISTRY. *Current Pos:* SUPVR MAT ENG, METCO INC, 77- *Personal Data:* b Buffalo, NY, Aug 24, 44; m 68. *Educ:* Univ Rochester, BS, 66; Univ Conn, PhD(phys chem), 70. *Prof Exp:* Res & develop engr, GTE Sylvania Inc, 70-73; assoc dir res, Quantum, Inc, 73-77. *Mem:* Am Soc Metals; Am Chem Soc. *Res:* Development of composite powders for plasma and vacuum plasma flame spray applications especially for sprayed abradable coatings; mass spectrometry and high vacuum technology; processing parameters for high performance plastics; development of synthetic membranes. *Mailing Add:* Sulzer Metco 1101 Prospect Ave Westbury NY 11590-2724

REARDON, JOSEPH EDWARD, ORGANIC CHEMISTRY, POLYMER CHEMISTRY. *Current Pos:* res chemist, Plastics Dept, 66-67, res chemist, Electrochem Dept, 67-72, res chemist, Plastics Dept, 72-80, RES ASSOC, F & FP DEPT, E I DU PONT DE NEMOURS & CO, INC, 85- *Personal Data:* b Albany, NY, Jan 25, 38; m 60; c 4. *Educ:* Canisius Col, BS, 61; Univ Notre Dame, PhD(org chem), 67. *Prof Exp:* Chemist, Carborundum Co, 61-63. *Mem:* Am Chem Soc. *Res:* Dispersion chemistry and polymer synthesis, primarily methacrylates. *Mailing Add:* Nine Lyells Ct Wilmington DE 19808

REARDON, JOSEPH PATRICK, PHYSICAL CHEMISTRY, MATERIALS SCIENCE. *Current Pos:* MGR MAT PROCESS & DEVELOP, DEXTER COMPOSITES, 86- *Personal Data:* b Pittston, Pa, Sept 26, 40; m 69; c 2. *Educ:* Spring Hill Col, BS, 65; Am Univ, MS, 69, PhD(chem), 75. *Prof Exp:* Instr chem, Georgetown Prep Sch, 65-67; res chemist, Naval Res Lab, 71-79; mgr mat develop, Pure Carbon Co, 79-80; mgr mat process & develop, Tribon Bearing Co, 80-86. *Concurrent Pos:* Chmn, N Ohio chap, Soc Aerospace Mat & Process Engrs, 89-90. *Mem:* Soc Aerospace Mat & Process Engrs. *Res:* Low surface energy polymers; adhesives; carbon fibers and graphite intercalation chemistry; electrets and piezoelectric polymers; electrically conductive organic polymers; high temperature composites; solid self-lubricating bearing materials; novel chemical modifications and processing techniques for polyimide resins, molding compounds and molded components, in order to reduce the cost of advanced composites to feasible industrial levels. *Mailing Add:* 21125 S Park Dr Cleveland OH 44126

REARICK, DAVID F, MATHEMATICS. *Current Pos:* asst prof, 61-66, ASSOC PROF MATH, UNIV COLO, BOULDER, 66- *Personal Data:* b Danville, Ill, Aug 5, 32; div. *Educ:* Univ Fla, BS, 54; Adelphi Univ, MS, 56; Calif Inst Technol, PhD(math), 60. *Prof Exp:* Instr math, Univ BC, 60-61. *Mem:* Am Math Soc; Math Asn Am. *Res:* Analytic number theory; arithmetic functions. *Mailing Add:* Dept Math Univ Colo PO Box 395 Boulder CO 80309

REASENBERG, ROBERT DAVID, ASTRONOMICAL OPTICAL INTERFEROMETRY, ASTROMETRY. *Current Pos:* PHYSICIST, SMITHSONIAN ASTROPHYS OBSERV, 83- *Personal Data:* b New York, NY, Apr 27, 42; m 65, Wendy Schoenbach; c Suzanne. *Educ:* Polytech Inst Brooklyn, BS, 63; Brown Univ, PhD(physics), 70. *Honors & Awards:* Newcomb Cleveland Award, AAAS, 77. *Prof Exp:* Res assoc, Mass Inst Technol, 69-71, res staff mem, 71-79, prin res scientist, 81-82. *Concurrent Pos:* Consult, Lincoln Lab, Mass Inst Technol, 70-76, C S Draper Lab, Inc, 78-80 & Ames Res Ctr, NASA Space, 81-83; assoc mem, Viking Radio Sci Team, Mariner-Venus-Mercury Radio Sci Team, Mariner-9 Celestial Mech Team & Pioneer Venus Science Steering Group; lectr, Int Sch Cosmology & Gravitation, 77, 79, 82 & 85; consult, NASA Ames Res Ctr, 81-83; chmn, Comt Gravitation & Relativity, Starprobe Mission, 80-81; mem, Planetary Systs Sci Working Group, 88-92, Ad Hoc Comt Gravitation Physics & Astron, 89-91 & Interferometry Panel, Astron & Astrophys Surv, 89-90. *Mem:* Am Phys Soc; AAAS; Am Astron Soc; Sigma Xi; Int Astron Union; Int Soc Gen Relativity & Gravitation. *Res:* Optical interferometry and space astrometry; author of over 100 publications; gravity research, especially tests of theories of gravitation, determination of solar-system constants and planetary ephermerides, and determination of the structure, gravitational potential and rotational motion of planets. *Mailing Add:* 16 Garfield St Lexington MA 02173. *Fax:* 617-495-7109; *E-Mail:* reasenberg@cfa.harvard.edu

REASER, DONALD FREDERICK, STRUCTURAL GEOLOGY, PHYSICAL STRATIGRAPHY. *Current Pos:* ASSOC PROF STRUCT GEOL & TECTONICS, UNIV TEX, ARLINGTON, 68- *Personal Data:* b Wichita Falls, Tex, Sept 30, 31; m 75, Bette J Forrest; c David. *Educ:* Southern Methodist Univ, BS, 53, MS, 58; Univ Tex, Austin, PhD(geol), 74. *Prof Exp:* Geol asst, De Golyer & MacNaughton, Dallas, 56-57; instr introductory & struct geol, Arlington State Col, 61-64; petrol geologist, Humble Oil & Refining Co, 65-66; asst prof, WTex State Univ, 67-68. *Concurrent Pos:* Grant-in-aid res, Sigma Xi, 60; field trip consult, Shell Develop Co, 64-; res asst, Bur Economic Geol, Austin, 67-68; consult geologist, Cor Labs, Dallas, 74-79, Gearhart Indust, Ft Worth, 82-84; instr, Inst Energy Develop, Ft Worth, 78-79; at Tex Elec Serv Co, 81-85, Ebasco Serv, Austin, 87, Southwest Labs, Dallas, 87, Earth Technol Corp, Long Beach, Calif, 89-90, Chem Lime Co, Ft Worth, 92. *Mem:* Am Asn Petrol Geologists; Geol Soc Am; Soc Econ Paleontologists & Mineralogists; Sigma Xi. *Res:* Structure and regional tectonics of West Texas and Northern Mexico; stratigraphy and structure of Upper Cretaceous rocks in North-central Texas; petroleum possibilities of subsurface Mesozoic rocks in Northeast Texas; landslide potential of Cretaceous rocks in northeast Texas. *Mailing Add:* PO Box 19049 Arlington TX 76019-0001. *Fax:* 817-794-5653

REASONER, JOHN W, PHOTOCHEMISTRY, FUEL SCIENCE. *Current Pos:* PROF CHEM, WESTERN KY UNIV, 65- *Personal Data:* b Winona, Mo, Feb 28, 40; m 61, Sandra M Schott; c David, Kenneth & Martha. *Educ:* Southeast Mo State Col, BS, 61; Iowa State Univ, PhD(org chem), 65. *Mem:* Am Chem Soc; Royal Soc Chem; Sigma Xi; InterAm Photochem Soc. *Res:* Organic structure of coal and coal plasticity; technique of analytical pyrolysis as a tool for the study of plastic coals. *Mailing Add:* Dept Chem Western Ky Univ Bowling Green KY 42101. *E-Mail:* john.reasoner@wku.edu

REASONS, KENT M, PLANT PHYSIOLOGY. *Current Pos:* RES & FIELD DEVELOP, MKT & BUS MGT, DOMESTIC & OVERSEAS, AGR PROD DEPT, E I DU PONT DE NEMOURS & CO, INC, 64- *Personal Data:* b Dyersburg, Tenn, June 24, 40. *Educ:* Univ Tenn, MS, 64. *Mem:* Wheat Sci Soc Am; Agron Soc; Nat Agr Chem Asn; Entom Soc Am; Coun Agr Sci & Technol. *Mailing Add:* Agr Prod Dept E I du Pont de Nemours & Co Inc Stein Haskey Bldg 1090 Elkton Rd Newark DE 19714

REASOR, MARK JAE, PULMONARY TOXICOLOGY, IMMUNOTOXICOLOGY. *Current Pos:* from asst prof to assoc prof, 76-84, PROF PHARMACOL & TOXICOL, MED CTR, WVA UNIV, 84- *Personal Data:* b Evansville, Ind, Nov 3, 45; m 67, Mary Comer; c Michael & Meredith. *Educ:* Purdue Univ, BS, 67; Duke Univ, MA, 69; Johns Hopkins Univ, PhD(toxicol), 75; Am Bd Toxicol, dipl, 81. *Prof Exp:* Res fel pharmacol, Nat Inst Environ Health Sci, NIH, 75-76. *Concurrent Pos:* Prin investr, NIH res grant, 79-83; vis scholar, Univ Calif, San Diego, 83; assoc ed, Toxicol Environ Health. *Mem:* Soc Toxicol; Am Soc Pharmacol & Exp Therapeut; Int Soc Built Environ. *Res:* Toxicity of cationic amphiphilic drugs in humans and animals with an emphasis on impairment in pulmonary and immune functions. *Mailing Add:* Dept Pharmacol & Toxicol Health Sci Ctr WVa Univ Morgantown WV 26506. *Fax:* 304-293-6854; *E-Mail:* mreasor2@wvu.edu

REAVEN, EVE P, CELL SECRETION, ELECTRON MICROSCOPY. *Current Pos:* AT VET ADMIN HOSP, PALO ALTO, 70- *Personal Data:* b Kosice, Czech, Jan 18, 28. *Educ:* Univ Chicago, PhD(anat), 52. *Mem:* Am Soc Cell Biol; Am Soc Endocrinol; Europ Asn Study Diabetes. *Mailing Add:* Dept Med Endocrinol Gerent & Metab Va Palo Alto Health Care Syst 3801 Miranda Ave 182-B Palo Alto CA 94304-1207

REAVES, GIBSON, ASTRONOMY. *Current Pos:* RETIRED. *Personal Data:* b Chicago, Ill, Dec 26, 23; m 55, Mary Kerr; c Benjamin K. *Educ:* Univ Calif, Los Angeles, BA, 47; Univ Calif, Berkeley, PhD(astron), 52. *Prof Exp:* From instr to assoc prof, Univ Southern Calif, 52-65, chmn dept, 69-74, prof astron, 65-94. *Concurrent Pos:* Assoc meritus, Lowell Observ, 85- *Mem:* Am Astron Soc; fel Royal Astron Soc; Int Astron Union; fel AAAS; Hist Sci Soc. *Res:* Extragalactic problems; history of astronomy, especially discovery of Pluto and Leonardo da Vincis astronomy; orbits of asteroids. *Mailing Add:* Dept Physics & Astron Univ Southern Calif Los Angeles CA 90089-1342

REAVES, HARRY LEE, physics, mathematics; deceased, see previous edition for last biography

REAVEY-CANTWELL, NELSON HENRY, MEDICINE. *Current Pos:* asst prof, 68-71, ASSOC PROF CLIN MED, THOMAS JEFFERSON UNIV, 71- *Personal Data:* b Buffalo, NY, May 8, 26; m; c 3. *Educ:* Canisius Col, BS, 44; Fordham Univ, MSc, 48, PhD(phys org chem), 52; Columbia Univ, MD, 59; Henry George Sch, dipl, 58. *Hon Degrees:* HCD, Univ Tokyo, 81; ScD, Univ Philippines, 81. *Honors & Awards:* Merck Award, 66. *Prof Exp:* From asst to instr chem, Fordham Univ, 47-52; from instr to asst prof, Yale Univ, 52-55; intern, Bellevue Hosp & Mem Ctr Cancer & Allied Dis, 59-60; resident internal med, Vet Admin Hosp, Manhattan, NY, 60-61; asst dir med res, Merck Inst, 61-68. *Concurrent Pos:* Fel, Harvard Univ, 49; attend physician, Curtis Clin, Thomas Jefferson Univ Hosp, 68-; dir div res, William H Rorer, Inc, 68-69, vpres res, 69-78, vpres med & sci affairs, Rorer Int, 78- *Mem:* Am Soc Clin Pharmacol & Therapeut; Am Soc Internal Med; fel Am Col Clin Pharmacol; Am Fedn Clin Res; fel Royal Soc Med. *Res:* Internal medicine; endocrinology and immunology; kinetics and mechanisms of metabolic reactions; steroid and electrolyte metabolism. *Mailing Add:* Spring Valley Rd Box 258 Furlong PA 18925-0258

REAY, JOHN R, MATHEMATICS. *Current Pos:* Assoc prof, 63-68, PROF MATH, WESTERN WASH UNIV, 68- *Personal Data:* b Pocatello, Idaho, Oct 27, 34; m 58; c 3. *Educ:* Pac Lutheran Univ, BA, 56; Univ Idaho, MS, 58; Univ Wash, PhD(math), 63. *Mem:* Am Math Soc; Math Asn Am. *Res:* Convexity and geometry. *Mailing Add:* Dept Math Western Wash Univ Bellingham WA 98225-5996

REAZIN, GEORGE HARVEY, JR, PLANT PHYSIOLOGY, BIOCHEMISTRY. *Current Pos:* RETIRED. *Personal Data:* b Chicago, Ill, Feb 3, 28; m 50; c 3. *Educ:* Northwestern Univ, BS, 49; Univ Mich, MS, 51, PhD(plant physiol), 55. *Honors & Awards:* Guymon Mem Lectr, Am Soc Enologists, 81. *Prof Exp:* Res assoc, Brookhaven Nat Lab, 54-56; res scientist, Joseph E Seagram & Sons, Inc, White Plains, NY, 56-62, head biochem sect, 62-71, head chem sect, 71-82, mgr chem res & serv, 82-92. *Mem:* Bot Soc Am; Am Chem Soc; Am Soc Plant Physiologists. *Res:* Chemistry of flavors and biochemistry of their formation; chemistry laboratory management using computer laboratory information management systems (LIMS). *Mailing Add:* 1604 Reidinger Ridge New Albany IN 47150-9656

REBA, RICHARD CHARNEY, MEDICINE, NUCLEAR MEDICINE. *Current Pos:* PROF RADIOL, UNIV CHICAGO, 91, CHIEF, NUCLEAR MED SECT, 91-, CHIEF, BIOL SCI DIV, 91- *Personal Data:* b Milwaukee, Wis, July 1, 32; m 54, 83, Diane E Cameron; c Lori T & Lee B. *Educ:* Univ Md, MD, 57; Am Bd Internal Med, dipl, 64; Am Bd Nuclear Med, dipl, 72. *Prof Exp:* Asst resident med, Univ Hosp, Baltimore, Md, 59-61; fel nuclear med, Johns Hopkins Univ, 61-62; sr investr, Walter Reed Army Inst Res, 62-65, actg chief dept isotope metab, 64, chief, 64-65, chief med serv, 85th Evacuation Hosp, Vietnam, 65-66; from asst prof to assoc prof radiol & radiol sci, Sch Hyg & Pub Health, Johns Hopkins Univ, 66-70, asst prof internal med, 67-70, assoc radiol sci, 70-78; chmn dept nuclear med, Wash Hosp Ctr, 70-76; prof radiol, Sch Med, George Washington Univ, 71-91, prof med, Sch Med, 76-91, dir, Div Nuclear Med, Med Ctr, 76-91. *Concurrent Pos:* Asst chief gen med, Sect Four, Walter Reed Army Gen Hosp, 64-65; chief clin nuclear med sect, Johns Hopkins Med Insts, 68-70; clin prof med, Sch Med, Georgetown Univ, 71-79. *Mem:* AAAS; Soc Nuclear Med (pres); fel Am Col Nuclear Physicians (pres, 77-); fel Am Col Physicians; Am Fedn Clin Res. *Res:* Diagnostic and research applications of radioisotopes in medicine. *Mailing Add:* Dept Radio/MC 2026 Univ Chicago 5841 S Maryland Ave Chicago IL 60637-1463. *Fax:* 773-702-1161; *E-Mail:* r__reba@uchicago.edu

REBACH, STEVE, OPTIMAL FORAGING, BIOLOGICAL RHYTHMS. *Current Pos:* from asst prof to assoc prof, 72-85, PROF BIOL, UNIV MD, EASTERN SHORE, 85- *Personal Data:* b New York, NY, Nov 15, 42; s; c Benjamin & Ari. *Educ:* City Col New York, BS, 63; Univ RI, PhD(oceanog), 70. *Prof Exp:* Instr oceanog, Grad Sch Oceanog, Univ RI, 69-70; asst prof, St Mary's Col Md, 70-72. *Concurrent Pos:* Chmn, Grad Prog Marine, Estuarine & Environ Sci, Univ Md, 81-; prin investr, Crustacean Ecol & Mariculture Inst; US Forest Serv res grants, dimilin sensitivity. *Mem:* AAAS; Animal Behav Soc; Atlantic Estuarine Res Soc; Sigma Xi. *Res:* Foraging behavior, sensory perception, molting in Crustacea; effects of diflubenzuron (dimilin) on molt; orientation and migration of marine organisms; biological rhythms. *Mailing Add:* Dept Biol Univ Md Eastern Shore Princess Anne MD 21853. *Fax:* 410-651-7739; *E-Mail:* srebach@umes.umd.edu

REBBI, CLAUDIO, PARTICLE THEORY, QUANTUM FIELD THEORY. *Current Pos:* PROF, BOSTON UNIV, 86- *Personal Data:* b Trieste, Italy, Mar 1, 43; m 67; c 2. *Educ:* Univ Torino, Italy, Laurea, 65, PhD(nuclear physics), 67. *Prof Exp:* Prof, Univ Trieste, 70-72; res assoc, Europ Orgn Nuclear Res, 72-74; vis assoc prof, Mass Inst Technol, 74-77; scientist, Brookhaven Nat Lab, 77-87. *Concurrent Pos:* Fel, Calif Inst Technol, 68-69; vis, Europ Orgn Nuclear Res, 80-81 & 84-85. *Mem:* Fel Am Phys Soc. *Res:* Elementary particle theory; quantum field theory; computational physics. *Mailing Add:* Physics Dept Boston Univ 590 Commonwealth Ave Boston MA 02215

REBEC, GEORGE VINCENT, NEUROPHARMACOLOGY, NEUROBIOLOGY. *Current Pos:* from asst prof to assoc prof, 77-85, PROF & DIR PROG NEURAL SCI, IND UNIV, BLOOMINGTON, 85- *Personal Data:* b Harrisburg, Pa, Apr 6, 49. *Educ:* Villanova Univ, AB, 71; Univ Colo, Boulder, MA, 74, PhD(biopsych), 75. *Honors & Awards:* Lilly Award, Lilly Endowment, 79. *Prof Exp:* NIMH res fel, Univ Calif, San Diego, 75-77. *Concurrent Pos:* Prin investr, Nat Inst Drug Abuse grant, 79-, NSF grant, 85- *Mem:* Soc Neurosci; Int Brain Res Orgn; AAAS; Am Psychol Soc; Int Basal Ganglia Soc. *Res:* Neurochemical and neurophysiological systems underlying the behavioral response to certain drugs of abuse and to the antipsychotic drugs; electrochemical and electrophysiological recordings obtained from specific regions of the central nervous system. *Mailing Add:* Dept Psychol Prog Neural Sci Ind Univ Bloomington IN 47405. *Fax:* 812-855-4520; *E-Mail:* Rebec@Indiana.edu

REBEIZ, CONSTANTIN ANIS, BIOLOGICAL SCIENCE, PLANT PHYSIOLOGY. *Current Pos:* assoc prof, 72-76, PROF PLANT PHYSIOL, UNIV ILL, URBANA- CHAMPAIGN, 76- *Personal Data:* b Beirut, Lebanon, July 11, 36; nat US; m 62, Carole L Conness; c Paul A, Natalie & Mark J. *Educ:* Am Univ, Beirut, BS, 59; Univ Calif, Davis, MS, 60, PhD, 65. *Honors & Awards:* Beckman Res Award, 82 & 85; Funk Award, 85; John P Trebellas Res Endowment, 86. *Prof Exp:* Dir, Dept Biol Sci, Agr Res Inst, Beirut, 65-69; res assoc biol, Univ Calif, Davis, 69-71. *Mem:* Am Soc Plant Physiologists; Int Comt Photobiol; Am Soc Photobiol; AAAS; Lebanese Asn Advan Sci; Sigma Xi. *Res:* Pathway of chlorophyll biosynthesis; chloroplast development; bioengineering of photosynthetic reactors; biosynthesis of chlorophyll in vitro; duplication of greening process of plants in test tube; operation of multibranched chlorophyll biosynthetic pathway in nature; formulation and design of laser herbicides, insecticides and cancer chemotherapeutic agents. *Mailing Add:* Hort Univ Ill Urbana 1301 W Gregory Dr Urbana IL 61801-3608

REBEK, JULIUS, JR, ORGANIC CHEMISTRY. *Current Pos:* PROF CHEM, SCRIPPS RES INST, 96- *Personal Data:* b Beregszasz, Hungary, Apr 11, 44; US citizen; c 2. *Educ:* Univ Kans, BA, 66; Mass Inst Technol, PhD(chem), 70. *Prof Exp:* Am Chem Soc-Petrol Res Fund fel, 70-73; Eli Lilly res fel, 72-74, asst prof chem, Univ Calif, Los Angeles, 70-76; assoc prof, Univ Pittsburgh, 76-80, prof, 80-89; prof, Mass Inst Technol, 89-96. *Concurrent Pos:* A P Sloan fel, 76-78, Alexander von Humboldt fel, 81; Guggenheim fel, 86. *Mem:* Nat Acad Sci; AAAS; Am Chem Soc. *Res:* Enzyme models; organic reaction mechanisms; molecular recognition; self-replicating systems. *Mailing Add:* Scripps Res Inst 10550 N Torrey Pines La Jolla CA 92037

REBEL, WILLIAM J, POLYMER CHEMISTRY. *Current Pos:* RETIRED. *Personal Data:* b Troy, NY, Mar 15, 34. *Educ:* State Univ NY Albany, BS, 57, MS, 59; Univ Alta, PhD(org chem), 63. *Prof Exp:* Fel org chem, Univ Rochester, 63-64; chemist, Chem Div, Union Carbide Corp, 64-66; chemist, Polymer Technol Div, Eastman Kodak Co, 66-74, tech assoc, Mfg Technol Div, 74-91. *Mem:* Am Chem Soc; NY Acad Sci. *Res:* Decomposition of iodonium salts; characterization and synthesis of cellulose esters; synthesis of addition polymers; preparation of new polymers; dispersion of pigments and radiation curing of monomer/polymer systems. *Mailing Add:* 770 Vanvoorhis Ave Rochester NY 14617-2170

REBENFELD, LUDWIG, STRUCTURE AND PROPERTIES OF POLYMERIC FIBERS. *Current Pos:* sr chemist, Textile Res Inst, 54-55, group leader, 55-60, assoc res dir, 60-65, vpres educ & res, 66-70, pres & dir, 71-93, EMER PRES & RES ASSOC, TEXTILE RES INST, 93- *Personal Data:* b Czech, July 10, 28; nat US; m 56, Ellen Vogel. *Educ:* Lowell Tech Inst, BS, 51; Princeton Univ, MA, 53, PhD(org chem), 55. *Hon Degrees:* DSc, Philadelphia Col, 79; PhD, Tech Univ Liberec, Czech Repub, 93. *Honors & Awards:* Distinguished Achievement Award, Fiber Soc, 68; Smith Medal, Am Soc Testing & Mat, 74; Inst Medal, Textile Inst Eng, 76; Olney Medal, Am Asn Textile Chemists & Colorists, 87. *Prof Exp:* Asst instr chem, Lowell Tech Inst, 49-51. *Concurrent Pos:* Vis prof, Princeton Univ, 65-; chmn bd & life trustee, Philadelphia Col Textiles & Sci; ed, Textile Res J, 92- *Mem:* Fiber Soc (secy-treas); Am Chem Soc; Am Asn Textile Chemists & Colorists; fel Brit

Textile Inst; Am Inst Chem Engrs. *Res:* Chemistry of cellulose and cellulose derivatives; chemical and physical properties of textile fibers; cotton fiber technology; keratin fiber deformation processes; structure and properties of synthetic polymers; crystallization phenomena in thermoplastic composites. *Mailing Add:* 49 Pardoe Rd Princeton NJ 08540

REBER, ELWOOD FRANK, NUTRITION, BIOCHEMISTRY. *Current Pos:* prof nutrit & dean col nutrit, textiles & human develop, 74-78, prof nutrition & food sci, 78-86, EMER PROF NUTRIT & FOOD SCI, TEX WOMAN'S UNIV, 86- *Personal Data:* b Reading, Pa, June 24, 19; m 42; c 3. *Educ:* Berea Col, AB, 44; Cornell Univ, MNS, 48; Okla State Univ, MS, 50, PhD(chem), 51. *Prof Exp:* Food inspector, Kroger Grocery & Baking Co, 44-45; lab asst biochem, Okla State Univ, 48-49, asst microbiol assays, 49-51; res chemist, Swift & Co, 51-52; from asst prof to prof vet physiol & pharmacol, Univ Ill, 52-64; prof foods & nutrit & head dept, Univ Mass, Amherst, 64-68 & Purdue Univ, Lafayette, 68-74. *Concurrent Pos:* Fulbright res fel, Col Agr & Vet Med, Copenhagen, Denmark, 61-62. *Mem:* Am Chem Soc; Inst Food Technologists; Am Inst Nutrit. *Res:* Human nutrition and foods; food science; wholesomeness of irradiated foods; nutrition and disease; metabolic disorders; use of cottonseed in foods for humans. *Mailing Add:* 1824 Concord Lane Denton TX 76205-5452

REBER, JERRY D, NUCLEAR PHYSICS. *Current Pos:* assoc prof, State Univ NY Col Geneseo, 69-79, chmn dept, 69-96, prof, 80-96, DISTINGUISHED PROF TEACHING, STATE UNIV NY COL GENESEO, 96- *Personal Data:* b Lebanon, Pa, May 25, 39; m 63, Dixie Hill; c Ellen M & Matthew H. *Educ:* Franklin & Marshall Col, AB, 61; Univ Ky, MS, 64, PhD(nuclear physics), 67. *Prof Exp:* NSF fel, Univ Ky, 65; res assoc & asst prof physics, Univ Va, 68-69. *Mem:* Am Phys Soc; Am Asn Physics Teachers. *Res:* Neutron scattering studies of calcium, potassium, lanthanum and holmium; isobaric spin impurities of fluorine; ion induced x-ray fluorescence; neutron-proton scattering; ion beam lithography. *Mailing Add:* Dept Physics & Astron State Univ NY Col 1 College Circle Geneseo NY 14454. Fax: 716-245-5288

REBER, RAYMOND ANDREW, ADSORPTION SEPARATION SYSTEMS DEVELOPMENT, TECHNOLOGY LICENSING. *Current Pos:* EXEC VPRES & CHIEF OPERATING OFFICER, BOLCHEM CORP, 94- *Personal Data:* b Apr 16, 42; m 63, Anita Roe; c Laura, Paul & Jill. *Educ:* NY Univ, BS, 63, MS, 66. *Prof Exp:* Process develop engr, M W Kellogg, 66-70; supvr process develop, Union Carbide, 70-75, mgr, licensing petrol refinery technol, 75-77, molecular sieve process, 77-82, molecular sieve catalysis, 82-85 & molecular sieve adsorption technol, 85-89; dir, new ventures develop, Univ Pac, 89-93. *Concurrent Pos:* Comnr, Montrose Improvement Dist. *Mem:* Am Inst Chem Engrs; Nat Soc Prof Engrs; Com Develop Asn. *Res:* New applications for molecular sieves including processes and products involving heterogeneous catalysis, molecular separations; currently overseeing company involved in food additive encapsulates. *Mailing Add:* 10 Bonnie Hollow Lane Montrose NY 10548

REBERS, PAUL ARMAND, IMMUNOCHEMISTRY, ENVIRONMENTAL CHEMISTRY. *Current Pos:* RETIRED. *Personal Data:* b Minneapolis, Minn, Jan 24, 23; m 52, Louise Burrell; c Michael, John & Joseph. *Educ:* Univ Minn, Minneapolis, BS, 43, MS, 46; Univ Minn, St Paul, PhD(agr biochem), 53. *Prof Exp:* Process engr, Rohm & Haas, 46-49; res chemist, Nat Animal Disease Lab, 61-88; mem grad fac, Iowa State Univ, 66-88, assoc prof biochem, 70-88. *Mem:* AAAS; Am Chem Soc; Am Soc Microbiol; Am Asn Immunol; Soc Exp Biol & Med; Sigma Xi. *Res:* Purification, isolation and structure of carbohydrate antigens; colorimetric analysis of sugars; immunology of fowl cholera. *Mailing Add:* 627 14th Street Pl Nevada IA 50201

REBHUHN, DEBORAH, APPLIED MATHEMATICS. *Current Pos:* mem tech staff, Bell Labs, 80-83, DIST MGR, BELL COMMUN RES, 84- *Personal Data:* b Heidenheim, Ger, Oct 23, 46; US citizen; m 80; c 1. *Educ:* Cornell Univ, AB, 68; Univ Ill, MS, 70, PhD(math), 74. *Prof Exp:* Teaching asst math, Univ Ill, 68-73; asst prof math, Vassar Col, NY, 73-79. *Mem:* Asn Women Math. *Res:* Qualitative properties of control systems, particularly the study of properties of control systems that are stable under sufficiently small perturbations; systems engineering and systems analysis to support development of large software systems. *Mailing Add:* 10 Landing Lane New Brunswick NJ 08901

REBHUN, LIONEL ISRAEL, ZOOLOGY, CELL BIOLOGY. *Current Pos:* prof, 69-77, COMMONWEALTH PROF BIOL, UNIV VA, 77- *Personal Data:* b Bronx, NY, Apr 19, 26; m 49; c 2. *Educ:* City Col New York, BS, 49; Univ Chicago, MS, 51, PhD(zool), 55. *Prof Exp:* From instr to asst prof anat, Col Med, Univ Ill, 55-58; from asst prof to assoc prof biol, Princeton Univ, 58-69. *Concurrent Pos:* Lalor fel, 56; Guggenheim fel, 62. *Mem:* Am Soc Cell Biologists; Biophys Soc; Electron Micros Soc Am; Soc Develop Biol; Soc Gen Physiologists. *Res:* Control of cell division; cellular motility; cell ultrastructure; cryobiology. *Mailing Add:* Dept Biol Gilmer Hall Rm 43 Univ Va Charlottesville VA 22903-2453

REBICK, CHARLES, PHYSICAL CHEMISTRY. *Current Pos:* res chemist, Exxon Res Eng Co, 73-82, proj leader, Exxon Res & Develop Labs, Baton Rouge, La, 80-82, lab dir, Catalysis Sci Lab, 84-86, sr staff assoc planning, 86-88, sr res assoc sensors & analyzers, 88-93, SECT HEAD HEAVY HYDROCARBON SCI, CORP RES, EXXON RES ENG CO, 93- *Personal Data:* b Halifax, NS, Oct 21, 44; m 71, Suzanne Waters; c Sarah & Joshua. *Educ:* Univ Toronto, BSc, 67; Mass Inst Technol, PhD(phys chem), 71. *Honors & Awards:* Sigma Xi Award, 71. *Prof Exp:* Fel phys chem, Hebrew Univ, Jerusalem, 72 & Theoret Chem Inst, Univ Wis-Madison, 73. *Mem:* Am Chem Soc. *Res:* Kinetics and mechanisms of free radical reactions, especially thermal reactions of hydrocarbons; heterogeneous catalysis; sensors and analyzers; heavy hydrocarbon conversion and characterization. *Mailing Add:* 5 Whispering Hills Dr Annandale NJ 08801. *E-Mail:* crebick@erenj.com

REBMAN, KENNETH RALPH, EDUCATIONAL ADMINISTRATION. *Current Pos:* From asst prof to assoc prof, 69-77, dept chmn, 80-85, PROF MATH & COMPUT SCI, CALIF STATE UNIV, HAYWARD, 77-, DEAN, SCH SCI, 87- *Personal Data:* b Mishawaka, Ind, Oct 4, 40; m 64. *Educ:* Oberlin Col, AB, 62; Univ Mich, Ann Arbor, MA, 64, PhD(math), 69. *Concurrent Pos:* Bd gov, Math Asn Am, 78-81. *Mem:* Math Asn Am; Sigma Xi. *Res:* Mathematical optimization; combinatorics. *Mailing Add:* VCAA-CU PO Box 7150 Colorado Springs CO 80933-7150

REBOUCHE, CHARLES JOSEPH, METABOLISM. *Current Pos:* asst prof, 84-88, ASSOC PROF PEDIAT, UNIV IOWA, 88- *Personal Data:* b New Orleans, La, Dec 27, 48. *Educ:* Tulane Univ, BS, 70; Vanderbilt Univ, PhD(biochem), 74. *Prof Exp:* Post-doctoral res assoc biochem, Univ Tex, 74-75; res fel, Mayo Found, 75-80, assoc consult neurol, 80-84. *Concurrent Pos:* Pfizer travelling fel, Clin Res Inst, Montreal, 83. *Mem:* Am Chem Soc; Am Inst Nutrit; Am Soc Biochem & Molecular Biol. *Res:* Carnitine biosynthesis, metabolism and function; amino acid metabolism; human nutrition. *Mailing Add:* Dept Pediat Univ Hosp Univ Iowa 100 Oakdale Res Park Rm A138 Iowa City IA 52242-5000

REBOUL, THEO TODD, III, SOLID STATE PHYSICS. *Current Pos:* RETIRED. *Personal Data:* b New Orleans, La, Oct 3, 22; m 52; c 2. *Educ:* Tulane Univ, BS, 44, MS, 48; Univ Pa, PhD(physics), 53. *Prof Exp:* Instr, Gen & Intermediate Physics Labs, Tulane Univ, 46-48; instr gen physics, Univ Pa, 48-50 & Drexel Inst, 51-53; physicist, Photo Prod Dept, E I du Pont de Nemours & Co, 53-59; sr engr, Radio Corp Am, 59-63, staff engr, 63-69; staff tech adv, RCA Corp, 69-74, chmn, Educ Aid Comt, 74-87, dir, Corp Contrib Progs, 80-87. *Concurrent Pos:* Mem, Overseas Schs Adv Coun, US State Dept, 74-86. *Mem:* Am Phys Soc; Sigma Xi. *Res:* Photographic properties; plasma physics; electro-optics; imaging sensors; administration. *Mailing Add:* 655 Willow Valley Sq L-308 Lancaster PA 17602-4873

REBSTOCK, THEODORE LYNN, PLANT BIOCHEMISTRY. *Current Pos:* RETIRED. *Personal Data:* b Elkhart, Ind, June 24, 25; m 57; c 2. *Educ:* NCent Col, BA, 49; Mich State Univ, MS, 51, PhD(chem), 56. *Prof Exp:* From asst to asst prof agr chem, Mich State Univ, 49-59; from assoc prof to prof chem, Westmar Col, 59-84, chmn dept, 63-84, dir nat sci div, 80-83; lab mgr, Harkers Inc, 85-90. *Mem:* AAAS; Am Chem Soc; Sigma Xi. *Res:* Mechanism of action and synthesis and isolation of plant growth regulators. *Mailing Add:* 1026 Sixth Ave SE LeMars IA 51031-2673

REBUCK, JOHN WALTER, HEMATOLOGY. *Current Pos:* RETIRED. *Personal Data:* b Minneapolis, Minn, Nov 24, 14; m 43. *Educ:* Creighton Univ, AB, 35; Univ Minn, MA, 40, MB, MD, 43, PhD(hemat), 47. *Honors & Awards:* H P Smith Award, Am Soc Clin Path, 82. *Prof Exp:* Asst hemat, Univ Minn, 38-42; intern, Henry Ford Hosp, 43; hematopathologist, Army Inst Path, 46; pathologist & chief Div Lab Hemat, Henry Ford Hosp, 47-76, sr hematopathologist, Labs, 76-84. *Concurrent Pos:* Ed, R E S, 65-74; prof, Wayne State Univ, 70-81, emer prof, 81-; prof, Univ Mich, 71-81. *Mem:* Fel Am Soc Hemat (secy, 58-61); Am Soc Clin Path; Reticuloendothelial Soc (pres, 58-60); Am Asn Pathologists & Bacteriologists; fel Int Soc Hemat. *Res:* Electron microscopy of blood cells; functions of leukocytes; cytology of inflammatory exudate; ultrastructure of sickle cells; hematopathology. *Mailing Add:* 22447 N Nottingham Dr Birmingham MI 48025

REBUFFE-SCRIVE, MARIELLE FRANCOISE, STEROID HORMONES, ADIPOSE TISSUE METABOLISM. *Current Pos:* RES SCIENTIST, DEPT PSYCHOL, YALE UNIV, NEW HAVEN, 91- *Personal Data:* b Paris, France. *Educ:* Univ Paris VI, France, MSc, 69, PhD(biochem), 77; Univ Goteborg, Sweden, PhD(med sci), 86. *Prof Exp:* Asst biol, Hotel-Dieu Med Clin, Paris, 71-82; res fel, Dept Med, Salgren's Hosp, Goteborg, Sweden, 82-88. *Concurrent Pos:* Vis res scientist, Dept Psychol, Yale Univ, New Haven, 88-91. *Mem:* Am Inst Nutrit; Europ Soc Clin Invest. *Res:* Hormonal and behavioral determinants of regional fat distribution and metabolism and its associated diseases. *Mailing Add:* Servier Amerique 22 Rue Garnier Neuilly-sur-Seine 92200 06520 France

RECANT, LILLIAN, MEDICINE. *Current Pos:* PROF MED, SCH MED, GEORGETOWN UNIV, 66-; CHIEF DIABETES RES LAB, VET ADMIN HOSP, 66- *Personal Data:* b New York, NY, Mar 7, 22; m 55. *Educ:* Hunter Col, BA, 41; Columbia Univ, MD, 46. *Prof Exp:* Intern med, Col Physicians & Surgeons, Columbia Univ & Presby Hosp, 46-48; asst med & endocrinol, Peter Bent Brigham Hosp, 48-49; asst resident, Col Physicians & Surgeons, Columbia Univ & Presby Hosp, 49-50, Commonwealth fel biochem, 50-51; Commonwealth fel biochem, Sch Med, Washington Univ, 51-53, from asst prof to assoc prof med & prev med, 53-66. *Mem:* Am Soc Clin Invest; Endocrine Soc; Asn Am Physicians; Asn Teachers Prev Med; Soc Exp Biol & Med; Am Diabetes Asn. *Res:* Diabetes, metabolism and endocrinology; nephrosis; liver diseases. *Mailing Add:* 3802 Alton Pl NW Washington DC 20016

RECH, RICHARD HOWARD, NEUROPHARMACOLOGY, PSYCHOPHARMACOLOGY. *Current Pos:* PROF PHARMACOL, MICH STATE UNIV, 71-, PROF TOXICOL, 77- *Personal Data:* b Irvington, NJ, Mar 20, 28; m 52, Barbara; c Sharon, Michelle & Charles. *Educ:* Rutgers Univ, BSc, 52; Univ Mich, MSc, 55, PhD(pharmacol), 60. *Prof Exp:* Pharmacist, Univ Hosp, Univ Mich, 55-56, asst pharmacol, Univ, 57-58; from instr to assoc prof, Dartmouth Med Sch, 61-71. *Concurrent Pos:* USPHS fel, Univ Utah, 59-61; NIH Fogarty fel (sr res fel), Mario Negri, Milan, Italy, 78-79. *Mem:* AAAS; Am Soc Pharmacol & Exp Therapeut; fel Am Col Neuropsychopharmacol; Soc Neurosci. *Res:* Pharmacology. *Mailing Add:* Dept Pharmacol Mich State Univ Life Sci 1 East Lansing MI 48824-0001. *Fax:* 517-353-8915

RECHARD, OTTIS WILLIAM, COMPUTER SCIENCE, MATHEMATICS. *Current Pos:* dir comput serv, 76-79, PROF MATH & COMPUT SCI, UNIV DENVER, 76- *Personal Data:* b Laramie, Wyo, Nov 13, 24; m 43, Dorothy Duble; c 4. *Educ:* Univ Wyo, BA, 43; Univ Wis, MA, 46, PhD(math), 48. *Prof Exp:* Asst, Alumni Res Found, Univ Wis, 45-48, instr math, 48; from instr to asst prof, Ohio State Univ, 48-51; staff mem, Los Alamos Sci Lab, Univ Calif, 51-56; assoc prof math, Wash State Univ, 56-61, dir comput ctr, 56-68, prof comput sci & math, 61-76, chmn dept comput sci, 63-76, dir systs & comput, 68-70. *Concurrent Pos:* Consult, Los Alamos Sci Lab, Univ Calif, 56-59, 75-79, vis staff mem, 74-75; consult, Atomic Energy Div, Phillips Petrol Co, 59-70; consult, NSF, 63-64 & 65-, dir comput sci prog, 64-65. *Mem:* Fel AAAS; Am Math Soc; Soc Indust & Appl Math; Math Asn Am; Asn Comput Mach; Inst Elec & Electronics Engrs Comput Soc. *Res:* Electronic computers; computer architecture and operating systems; design and analysis of algorithms. *Mailing Add:* Dept Math & Comput Sci Univ Denver Denver CO 80208-0001. *E-Mail:* ovechard@cs.du.edu

RECHARD, PAUL A(LBERT), HYDROLOGIC ENGINEERING, CIVIL ENGINEERING. *Current Pos:* PRES, WESTERN WATER CONSULTS, INC, 80- *Personal Data:* b Laramie, Wyo, June 4, 27; m 49, Mary L Roper; c Robert P & Karen A (Davis). *Educ:* Univ Wyo, BS, 48, MS, 49, CE, 55. *Prof Exp:* Civil engr, US Bur Reclamation, 48-49, hydraul engr, 49-54, asst proj hydrologist, 53-54; dir water resources & interstate streams comnr, Wyo Natural Resource Bd, 54-58; prin hydraul engr, Upper Colo River Comn, 58-64; water resources res engr, Univ Wyo, 64-66, asst dir, Natural Resources Res Inst, 66-71, dir, Water Resources Res Inst, 66-81, prof civil eng, 64-82. *Concurrent Pos:* Off Water Resources Res grants, 66-81; grants, Environ Protection Agency, 73-81. *Mem:* Int Comn Irrig & Drainage; Am Water Works Asn; Am Geophys Union; fel Am Soc Civil Engrs; Am Water Resources Asn; Nat Soc Prof Engrs; Nat Water Well Asn; Sigma Xi. *Res:* Hydrologic research dealing with precipitation-runoff relationships; consumptive use by agricultural and municipal and users; water planning criteria; hydrologic aspects of surface mining; snow hydrology; precipitation measurement. *Mailing Add:* Western Water Consults Inc 611 Skyline Rd Laramie WY 82070. *Fax:* 307-721-2913; *E-Mail:* wwclar@wyoming.com

RECHCIGL, JOHN E, SOIL FERTILITY, ENVIRONMENTAL QUALITY. *Current Pos:* asst prof, 86-91, assoc prof, 91-96, PROF DEPT SOIL & WATER SCI, UNIV FLA, 96- *Personal Data:* b Washington, DC, Feb 27, 60; m 83, Nancy A Palko; c Gregory J, Kevin T & Lindsey N. *Educ:* Univ Del, BS, 82; Va Polytech Inst & State Univ, MS, 83, PhD(soil crop & environ sci), 86. *Prof Exp:* Res assoc, Va Polytech Inst & State Univ, 83-86. *Concurrent Pos:* Prin investr, Fla Inst Phosphate Res, USDA, SFla Water Mgt Dist, Allied Chem & Tenn Valley Authority, 86-; assoc ed, J Environ Qual, 93-97. *Mem:* Soil Sci Soc Am; Am Soc Agron; Sigma Xi; Am Chem Soc. *Res:* Related to the impact of soil amendments on water and air quality; efforts have concentrated on ways to alleviate detrimental effects of over fertilization on the environment; have published articles, chapters, authored and edited 4 books dealing with fertilizers and environmental quality. *Mailing Add:* 13511 Fourth Plaza E Bradenton FL 34202. *Fax:* 941-735-1930; *E-Mail:* rechcigl@gnv.ifas.ufl.edu

RECHCIGL, MILOSLAV, JR, NUTRITIONAL BIOCHEMISTRY, RESEARCH MANAGEMENT. *Current Pos:* RETIRED. *Personal Data:* b Mlada Boleslav, Czech, July 30, 30; nat US; m 53, Eva Edwards; c Jack E & Karen M. *Educ:* Cornell Univ, BS, 54, MNS, 55, PhD, 58. *Honors & Awards:* Josef Hlavka Commenorative Medal, Czechoslovak Acad Scis, Prague, 91. *Prof Exp:* USPHS fel, Lab Biochem, Nat Cancer Inst, 58-60, chemist, Enzyme & Metab Sect, 60-61, res biochemist, Tumor-Host Rels Sect, 62-64, sr investr, 64-68, sr investr, Biosynthesis Sect, 68, USPHS grants assoc, 68-69; spec asst nutrit & health, Off Dir, Regional Med Progs Serv, Health Serv & Ment Health Admin, 69-70; nutrit adv, USAID, US Dept State, Washington, DC 70, chief, Res & Inst Grants Div, 70-73, asst dir, Off Res & Inst Grants, 73-74, actg dir, 74-75, dir interrgional res staff, 75-78, chief, Res & Methodology Div, 79-83, res dir, Off Sci Adv, AID, 83-91, Off Res, 92-96. *Concurrent Pos:* Nat Acad Sci travel grant, 62; mem, Educ Comn, Nat Cancer Inst Assembly Scientists, 62-63, chmn commun, mem comn & mem coun, 63-65; deleg, White House Conf Food, Nutrit & Health, 69; consult, Off Secy, USDA, 69-70, US Dept Treas, 73-74, Off Technol Assessment, 77-79, Food & Drug Admin, 79-81 & Nat Acad Sci & Nat Res Coun, 85-; exec secy, Nutrit Prog Adv Comt, Health Serv & Ment Health Admin, 69-70; exec secy, Res & Inst Grants Coun, Res Adv Comn, 71-83 & Rep, Consult Group Gen Res, US Dept State, 71-78; AID rep to USC/FAR Comt, 72-78; ed-in-chief, Series in Nutrit & Food, 77- *Mem:* Am Chem Soc; Am Soc Biol Chem; Am Inst Nutrit; Soc Int Develop; hon mem Czech Soc Arts & Sci (pres, 74-78, 94-96, 96-); Am Inst Biol Sci. *Res:* Amino acid nutrition; vitamin A and protein metabolism; tumor-host relationship; regulatory mechanisms of enzyme activity; enzyme degradation and turnover; catalase; biblography, history and historiography of science; research management; science administration; international development; biotechnology. *Mailing Add:* 1703 Mark Lane Rockville MD 20852

RECHNITZ, GARRY ARTHUR, ANALYTICAL BIOCHEMISTRY. *Current Pos:* PROF CHEM, UNIV HAWAII, 89- *Personal Data:* b Berlin, Ger, Jan 1, 36; US citizen; m 58, Harriet L Jones. *Educ:* Univ Mich, BS, 58; Univ Ill, MS, 59, PhD(chem), 61. *Honors & Awards:* Van Slyke Award, 78; Am Chem Soc Award, 83, Electrochem Award, 92; Iddles Lectr, 88; Gardinier Lectr Award, 89. *Prof Exp:* Asst prof chem, Univ Pa, 61-66; from assoc prof to prof, State Univ NY, Buffalo, 66-77, assoc provost natural sci & math, 67-69; prof chem & biotechnol, Univ Del, 78-89. *Concurrent Pos:* Sloan Found res fel, 66-68; vis prof path, Scripps Clin & Res Found, La Jolla, Calif, 87-88. *Mem:* AAAS; Am Chem Soc. *Res:* Biosensors membrane electrodes; ion selectivity in liquid and crystal membranes; clinical instrumentation. *Mailing Add:* Dept Chem Univ Hawaii Honolulu HI 96822

RECHNITZER, ANDREAS BUCHWALD, BUSINESS MANAGEMENT, ADVANCED TECHNOLOGIES CONSULTING. *Current Pos:* ADJ PROF OCEANOG, SAN DIEGO STATE UNIV, 86-; RES ASSOC, CALIF ACAD SCI, 90- *Personal Data:* b Escondido, Calif, Nov 30, 24; m 46; c 3. *Educ:* Mich State Univ, BS, 47; Univ Calif, Los Angeles, MA, 51, PhD(oceanog), 56. *Honors & Awards:* Nogi Award for Sci; Lockheed Award for Sci & Eng. *Prof Exp:* Adj prof oceanog, USN Post Grad Sch, 87-88. *Concurrent Pos:* Sci & technol adv, Oceanogr Navy Off, Wash, DC, 73-85; sr scientist, Sci Applications Int Corp, 85-; pres, Viking Oceanog, 85-; consult, Unique Mobility, Inc, Marine Develop Assocs & Int Maritime, Inc, 85- *Mem:* Marine Technol Soc; Am Geophys Union; Cedam Int (pres, 67-76). *Res:* Scientist-in-charge of the world's record descent by man to 35,800 feet into the Marianas Trench, January 23, 1960; specialist on the effects of explosions and hyperbaric pressure on marine life; marine ecology; animal behavior; consulting in the field of ocean engineering, including materials, power sources, navigation and controls, field operations and advanced systems. *Mailing Add:* 1345 Lomita Rd El Cajon CA 92020

RECHT, HOWARD LEONARD, WATER CHEMISTRY, ELECTROCHEMISTRY. *Current Pos:* supvr electrochem, 62-70, proj engr water technol, Atomics Int Div, NAm Rockwell Corp, 70-77, MEM TECH STAFF, ENERGY SYSTS GROUP, ROCKWELL INT CORP, 77- *Personal Data:* b Pittsburgh, Pa, July 16, 27; m 52; c 4. *Educ:* Carnegie Inst Technol, BS, 48; Cornell Univ, PhD(phys chem), 54. *Prof Exp:* Res chemist, Res & Develop Div, Consol Coal Co, Pa, 54-59; sr chemist, Atomics Int Div, NAm Aviation, Inc, Calif, 59-60, res specialist, 60-61; head electrochem, Astropower, Inc, Douglas Aircraft Corp, 61-62. *Mem:* AAAS; Am Chem Soc; Am Phys Soc; Electrochem Soc; Sigma Xi. *Res:* Electrochemical energy conversion, including high temperature fuel cells, radiation effects on batteries; sodium vapor-graphite interaction; corrosion, water and wastewater treatment; phosphate removal; nuclear waste disposal. *Mailing Add:* 11002 Garden Grove Ave Northridge CA 91326-2838

RECHTIEN, RICHARD DOUGLAS, GEOPHYSICS. *Current Pos:* asst prof, 66-70, ASSOC PROF GEOPHYS, UNIV MO, ROLLA, 70- *Personal Data:* b St Louis, Mo, Sept 10, 33; m 53; c 2. *Educ:* Wash Univ, BS, 58, MA, 59, PhD(geophys), 64. *Prof Exp:* Engr, McDonnell Aircraft Corp, Mo, 59-62; fluid dynamicist, Marshall Space Flight Ctr, NASA, 62-66. *Mem:* Soc Explor Geophys; Acoust Soc Am. *Res:* Noise generation in turbulent flow; rocket acoustics; random noise theory; nonlineal wave propagation; geomagnetism; magnetohydrodynamics of the earth's core; interplanetary magnetic fields. *Mailing Add:* 1100 Lynwood Dr Rolla MO 65401

RECHTIN, EBERHARDT, SYSTEMS ARCHITECTING. *Current Pos:* RETIRED. *Personal Data:* b Orange, NJ, Jan 16, 26; m 51, Dorothy D; c Andrea, Nina, Julie, Erica & Mark. *Educ:* Calif Inst Technol, BS, 46, PhD, 50. *Honors & Awards:* NASA Medal Sci, 65; Aerospace Commun Award, Am Inst Aeronaut & Astronaut, 69, von Karman Lectureship in Astronaut, 85; Alexander Bell Award, Inst Elec & Electronics Engrs, 77; Gold Medal Eng, Armed Forces Commun & Electronics Asn; C & C Prize, Japan, 92; Robert H Goddard Astronaut Award, 91. *Prof Exp:* Res engr, Jet Propulsion Lab, Calif Inst Technol, 49-52, group supvr secure commun, 52-54, sect chief commun res, 54-57, dir chief guid res, 57-59, dir chief telecommun, 59-60, dir, NASA Deep Space Instrumentation Prog, 60-63, asst dir tracking & data acquisition, 63-67; dir, Advan Res Projs Agency, US Dept Defense, 67-70, prin dep dir defense res & eng, 70-72, asst secy defense telecommun, 72-73; chief engr, Hewlett-Packard, 73-77; pres, Aerospace Corp, 77-87; emer prof elec eng, Univ Southern Calif, 88-94. *Concurrent Pos:* Var govt & Nat Res Coun comts, 56-88. *Mem:* Nat Acad Eng; fel Am Inst Aeronaut & Astronaut; fel Inst Elec & Electronics Engrs; Int Acad Astronaut; hon fel Inst Environ Sci; fel AAAS. *Res:* Information and communication theory; space and secure communication; international cooperative space research; systems architecture; electronics engineering; systems architecting. *Mailing Add:* 1665 Cataluna Pl Palos Verdes Estates CA 90274

RECHTSCHAFFEN, ALLAN, SLEEP, DREAMS. *Current Pos:* instr, 57-58, from asst prof to assoc prof, 58-68, PROF PSYCHOL, UNIV CHICAGO, 68- *Personal Data:* b New York, NY, Dec 8, 27; m 80; c 3. *Educ:* City Col New York, BSS, 49, MA, 51; Northwestern Univ, PhD(psychol), 56. *Honors & Awards:* Kleitman Award, Asn Sleep Dis Clins, 85; Distinguished Scientist Award, Sleep Res Soc, 89. *Prof Exp:* Psychologist, Fergus Falls State Hosp, 51-53; lectr psychol, Northwestern Univ, 56-57; researcher, Vet Admin, 56-57. *Mem:* Sleep Res Soc (pres, 79-82). *Res:* Function and physiology of sleep; psychophysiology of dreaming. *Mailing Add:* 5800 S Harper Ave Chicago IL 60637

RECK, GENE PAUL, PHYSICAL CHEMISTRY. *Current Pos:* from asst prof to assoc prof, 65-75, PROF PHYS CHEM, WAYNE STATE UNIV, 75- *Personal Data:* b Chicago, Ill, Sept 12, 37; c Ronald & Cathrine. *Educ:* Univ Ill, Urbana, BS, 59; Univ Minn, PhD(phys chem), 63. *Prof Exp:* Instr phys chem, Univ Minn, 63-64; res assoc, Brown Univ, 64-65. *Mem:* Am Phys Soc; Am Chem Soc; Sigma Xi. *Res:* Atomic and molecular scattering; laser driven chemistry; laser spectroscopy in combustion, ablation and atmospheric pressure chemical vapor deposition. *Mailing Add:* Dept Chem Wayne State Univ Detroit MI 48202-3489

RECK, RUTH ANNETTE, ATMOSPHERIC PHYSICS, ATMOSPHERIC CHEMISTRY. *Current Pos:* DIR GLOBAL CLIMATE CHANGE PROGS, ARGONNE NAT LABS, 92- *Personal Data:* b Rolla, Mo; div; c 2. *Educ:* Mankato State Univ, BA, 54; Univ Minn, PhD(phys chem), 64. *Honors & Awards:* Gold Award Eng. *Prof Exp:* Instr physics & chem, Wis State Univ, River Falls, 59-61; res assoc chem, Brown Univ, 64-65; assoc sr res physicist, Gen Motors Res Labs, 65-70, assoc sr res chemist, 71-74, sr res chemist, 74-76, sr scientist, 76-79, staff res scientist, 79-92. *Concurrent Pos:* Consult, Environ Movement & Transformation Adv Comt, Environ Protection Agency, 75-76, mem comt, 76-81, mem adv bd, 77-; mem, Climate Modeling Group VIII Exchange with USSR, 76; US rep CO2 Workshop, Int Inst Appl Systs Anal, Austria, 78, Workshop Extended Clouds, World Meterol Orgn, Oxford Univ, 78, Int Asn Meterol & Atmospheric Physics, 81 & ad hoc working group aerosols, Lille, France, 82; mem, comt chem & biol sensors, Nat Res Coun, 83 & sci adv bd, Int Joint Comn, 85-86, chmn, air pollution indicators task force, 83-84; mem, Radiol & Environ Rev Bd, Argonne Nat Lab, 83-86; mem, panels climatic effects trace gases & surface radiation budget climate appln, NASA, 85. *Mem:* AAAS; Am Chem Soc; Am Phys Soc; Sigma Xi; Am Geophys Union. *Res:* Statistics of climate change, atmospheric radiative transfer and related thermal effects from trace gases and particles; statistical properties of polymeric and magnetic materials; transport-limited rate processes in random systems. *Mailing Add:* 1257 Hobson Oaks Dr Naperville IL 60540-8135

RECKASE, MARK DANIEL, ITEM RESPONSE THEORY, PSYCHOMETRICS. *Current Pos:* dir resident prog, 81-84, asst vpres, Assessment Prog, 84-91, ASST VPRES ASSESSMENT INNOVATIONS, ACT, 91- *Personal Data:* b Chicago, Ill, Aug 31, 44; m 68, Charlene Repetny; c Erik & Debra. *Educ:* Univ Ill, Urbana, BA, 66; Syracuse Univ, MS, 71 & PhD(psychol), 72. *Prof Exp:* Res assoc statist, Adult Develop Study, Syracuse Univ, 70-71; 1st lieutenant, US Army, 71-72; from asst prof to assoc prof educ psychol, Univ Mo, Columbia, 72-81. *Concurrent Pos:* Consult, Multipurpose Arthritis Ctr, Univ Mo Sch Med, 80-81; mem, CAT & DAC adv comt, Dept Defense, 81-84 & 89-, tech adv comt, Calif Assessment Prog, 84, Nat Coun Measurement Educ & Mgt Comt, J Educ Statist, 91-; ed, J Educ Measurement, 93- *Mem:* Fel Am Psychol Soc; Am Educ Res Asn; Psychometric Soc (secy, 86-91); Brit Psychol Soc; Soc Multivariate Exp Psychol. *Res:* Modeling of the interaction of persons and test items; multidimensional models of the persons item interaction; computer applications to measurement of cognitive skills. *Mailing Add:* 51 Earling Dr Iowa City IA 52246

RECKEL, RUDOLPH P, immunology, biochemistry; deceased, see previous edition for last biography

RECKHOW, DAVID ALAN, PHYSICAL & CHEMICAL TREATMENT PROCESSES FOR DRINKING WATER, OXIDATIVE PROCESSES IN NATURAL & ENGINEERED SYSTEMS. *Current Pos:* ASSOC PROF CIVIL & ENVIRON ENG, UNIV MASS, AMHERST, 85- *Personal Data:* b Buffalo, NY, June 20, 55; m 86, Catherine Wanat; c 2. *Educ:* Tufts Univ, BS, 77; Stamford Univ, MS, 78; Univ NC, Chapel Hill, PhD(environ eng), 84. *Honors & Awards:* Presidential Young Investr, NSF, 88. *Prof Exp:* Res assoc, Compagnie Generale des Eaux, 84-85. *Concurrent Pos:* Asst ed, Environ Sci & Eng, 93- *Mem:* Am Water Works Asn; Am Chem Soc; Am Soc Civil Engrs; Int Ozone Asn; Water Environ Fedn; Int Asn Water Pollution Control. *Res:* Oxidation process and oxidation by-products in water and wastewater; coagulation processes and removal of natural organic matter; nature of organics in water and fate of organics. *Mailing Add:* Dept Civil & Environ Eng Univ Mass Marston Hall Rm 18 Amherst MA 01003. *Fax:* 413-545-2202; *E-Mail:* reckhow@ecs.umass.edu

RECKHOW, KENNETH HOWLAND, WATER QUALITY MODELING, APPLIED STATISTICS. *Current Pos:* PROF, SCH ENVIRON, DEPT CIVIL ENG, INST STATIST & DECISION SCI, DUKE UNIV, 80-; DIR, WATER RESOURCES RES INST, UNIV NC, 96- *Personal Data:* b San Francisco, Calif, Feb 7, 48; m 75, Ellen Waldman; c Sarah & Michael. *Educ:* Cornell Univ, SB, 71; Harvard Univ, SM, 72, PhD(environ systs), 77. *Prof Exp:* Asst prof water resources, Dept Resource Develop, Mich State Univ, 77-80. *Concurrent Pos:* Assoc ed, J Water Resources Res, 80-85, Water Resources Bull, 84-89; consult, US Army CEngr, US Environ Protection Agency, 79- & US Soil Conserv Serv; prin investr, Nat Oceanic & Atmospheric Admin, 79-83, US Environ Protection Agency, 85-88 & NSF, 90-92. *Mem:* Am Geophys Union; Am Water Resources Asn; Am Statist Asn; Soc Risk Anal; NAm Lake Mgt Soc (secy, 85, pres, 95). *Res:* Mathematical and statistical methods employed in water quality management, including techniques for mathematical model confirmation, risk analysis, uncertainty analysis and statistical descriptions of space-time variability. *Mailing Add:* Sch Environ Duke Univ Durham NC 27708-0328. *Fax:* 919-684-8741; *E-Mail:* reckhow@duke.edu

RECKHOW, WARREN ADDISON, ORGANIC CHEMISTRY, INFORMATION SCIENCE. *Current Pos:* Chemist, 46-47, res chemist, 50-55, RES ASSOC, RES LAB, EASTMAN KODAK CO, 55- *Personal Data:* b Brooklyn, NY, Mar 29, 21; m 45; c 4. *Educ:* Drew Univ, BA, 43; Univ Rochester, PhD(chem), 50. *Concurrent Pos:* Lectr, Univ Rochester, 51-52. *Mem:* Am Chem Soc. *Res:* Fries rearrangement reactions; synthetic curariform compounds; color photographic chemistry; the use of microform in scientific information. *Mailing Add:* 54 Coronado Dr Rochester NY 14617-4406

RECKLEY, JOHN S(TEVEN), PHYSICAL CHEMISTRY, CHEMICAL KINETICS. *Current Pos:* LAB TECHNICIAN CHEM, WASTEWATER TREATMENT PLANT, MD, 94- *Personal Data:* b Sept 28, 55. *Educ:* Frostburg Univ, BA, 77; WVa Univ, PhD(chem), 88. *Prof Exp:* Researcher, Morgantown Energy Technol Ctr, US Dept Energy, 90-92. *Mem:* Am Chem Soc; Am Inst Chemists. *Mailing Add:* 14111 Smouses Mill Rd NE Cumberland MD 21502. *E-Mail:* jsreckley@bix.com

RECKTENWALD, GERALD WILLIAM, PHYSICAL CHEMISTRY, RESEARCH ADMINISTRATION. *Current Pos:* RETIRED. *Personal Data:* b Lexington, Ky, June 28, 29; m 55; c 2. *Educ:* Univ Ky, BS, 49, MS, 50; Ind Univ, PhD(phys chem), 55. *Prof Exp:* Asst chem, Ind Univ, 52-54; radio chemist, Dow Chem Co, Mich, 54-55; chemist, Major Appliance Lab, Gen Elec Co, 55-65; mgr res & develop rigid foams, Olin Mathieson Chem Corp, 65-69, plant mgr plastics div, Cellular Prod Dept, Olin Corp, 69-72; proj mgr, Air Prod & Chem, 72-74, mgr new ventures, 74-78, dir com develop, 78-81, mgr r&d facil, 81-87. *Concurrent Pos:* Lectr, Ind Univ, 57-58, Univ Louisville, 58 & Nazareth Col, Ky, 59-60. *Mem:* Am Chem Soc; Soc Plastics Indust; Soc Plastic Engrs. *Res:* Polyurethane foams and hermetic systems; surface active agents; wire enamels; radiochemistry; chemical instrumentation; barrier properties of plastics; medical instrumentation. *Mailing Add:* 314 N 28th St Allentown PA 18104-4837

RECORD, M THOMAS, JR, BIOPHYSICAL CHEMISTRY. *Current Pos:* from asst prof to prof chem, 70-82, PROF CHEM & BIOCHEM, UNIV WIS-MADISON, 82- *Personal Data:* b Exeter, NH, Dec 18, 42; c 2. *Educ:* Yale Univ, BA, 64; Univ Calif, San Diego, PhD(chem), 67. *Prof Exp:* NSF fel biochem, Stanford Univ, 68-70. *Concurrent Pos:* NSF & NIH grants. *Mem:* AAAS; Am Chem Soc; Biophys Soc; Am Soc Biol Chemists. *Res:* Physical chemistry of nucleic acids and proteins; protein-nucleic acid interactions, physical chemical basis of control of gene expression. *Mailing Add:* Dept Biochem Univ Wis-Madison 420 Henry Mall Madison WI 53706-1569

RECORDS, RAYMOND EDWIN, HUMAN EYE. *Current Pos:* PROF OPHTHAL & CHMN DEPT, COL MED, UNIV NEBR, 70- *Personal Data:* b Ft Morgan, Colo, May 30, 30; div; c 1. *Educ:* Univ Denver, BS, 56; St Louis Univ, MD, 61. *Prof Exp:* Instr ophthal surg, Sch Med, Univ Colo, 65-67, asst prof, 67-70. *Concurrent Pos:* Consult & sect chief, Vet Admin Ctr, 70-; consult, Bishop Clarkson Mem Hosp, 73- *Mem:* Am Acad Ophthal; Asn Res Vision & Ophthal; Asn Univ Prof Ophthal. *Res:* Physiology of the human eye and visual system. *Mailing Add:* 21919 Riverside Ctr Elkhorn NE 68022-1708

RECSEI, ANDREW A, ORGANIC CHEMISTRY. *Current Pos:* PRES, RECSEI LABS, 46- *Personal Data:* b Kula, Yugoslavia, July 22, 02; nat US; m 42; c 3. *Educ:* Univ Vienna, Austria, BA, 22; Univ Brno, Czech, MA, 24, PhD, 26. *Prof Exp:* Res chemist, Dr Honsig Chem Lab, 26-30; plant mgr, Pharmador Pty Ltd, SAfrica, 31-39; pres, Recsei Labs, Calif, 40-42; res assoc, Univ Calif, Los Angeles, 42-43; res chemist, Calif Inst Technol, 43-44 & Printing Arts Res Lab, 44-46. *Concurrent Pos:* Instr, Univ Calif, Santa Barbara, 54-56, assoc, 56-65. *Mem:* Am Chem Soc. *Res:* Antihistamines; allergy; nutrition; antimitotic compounds and anti-tumor agents. *Mailing Add:* 633 Tabor Lane Santa Barbara CA 93108-1536

RECSEI, PAUL ANDOR, BIOCHEMISTRY. *Current Pos:* OWNER, RECSCI LABS, 75- *Personal Data:* b Santa Barbara, Calif, Feb 24, 45. *Educ:* Harvard Univ, BS, 67; Univ Calif, PhD(biochem), 72. *Prof Exp:* Fel biochem, Univ Calif, 73-75; vpres pharmaceut, Recsei Labs, 75-; res scientist, Dept Plasmid Biol, Pub Health Res Inst. *Res:* Development and design of pharmaceuticals. *Mailing Add:* 330 S Kellogg Ave Goleta CA 93117

RECTOR, CHARLES WILLSON, SOLID STATE PHYSICS. *Current Pos:* assoc prof, 66-75, PROF PHYSICS, US NAVAL ACAD, 75- *Personal Data:* b Sioux City, Iowa, Apr 29, 26; m 54, Gwendolyn Griffith; c Frederick & Alicia. *Educ:* Univ Chicago, PhB, 46, SB, 49; Franklin & Marshall Col, MS, 59; Johns Hopkins Univ, PhD(physics), 66. *Prof Exp:* Design engr, Tube Div, Radio Corp Am, 54-59, mem tech staff, RCA Labs, 60-62. *Concurrent Pos:* Instr, Elizabethtown Col, 57-59; res assoc physics, Johns Hopkins Univ, 66. *Mem:* Am Asn Physics Teachers; Am Phys Soc. *Res:* Photoconductivity; semiconductor smokes; rare earth ions in crystals; electron paramagnetic resonance; optical spectroscopy; laser damage effects. *Mailing Add:* Dept Physics US Naval Acad Annapolis MD 21402

RECTOR, FLOYD CLINTON, JR, NEPHROLOGY. *Current Pos:* sr scientist, Cardiovasc Res Inst, & prof, 77-95, EMER PROF MED & PHYSIOL & DIR, DIV NEPHROLOGY, UNIV CALIF, SAN FRANCISCO, 95- *Personal Data:* b Slaton, Tex, Jan 28, 29; m 50; c 3. *Educ:* Tex Tech Univ, BS, 50; Univ Tex, MD, 54. *Prof Exp:* Intern, Parkland Mem Hosp, Dallas, 55, resident, 56; instr internal med, SWestern Med Sch, Univ

Tex, 58-59, asst prof, 59-63, assoc prof nephrol, 63-66, prof & dir div, 66-73. Concurrent Pos: Mem & chmn, Cardiovasc Study Sect, NIH, 65-69, mem, Nephrol & Urol Fel & Training Grants Comt, 71-76, chmn, 72-73; chmn, Fel & Res Grants Comt, Nat Kidney Found, 68-71, chmn, Sci Adv Bd, 71-73. Mem: Am Soc Clin Invest; Am Asn Physicians; Am Physiol Soc; Am Soc Nephrol (secy-treas, 73-76, pres, 76-77); Biophys Soc. Res: Mechanisms of ion and water transport by renal tubules. Mailing Add: Dept Med & Philos Univ Calif San Francisco CA 94143-0532

REDALIEU, ELLIOT, DRUG METABOLISM, MEDICINAL CHEMISTRY. Current Pos: sr scientist, Ciba-Geigy Corp, 71-80, sr scientist II, 75-80, mgr, bioavailability & pharmacokinetics, 80-86, ASST DIR BIOANALYTICS & PHARMACOKINETICS, PHARMACEUT DIV, CIBA-GEIGY CORP, 87- Personal Data: b Bronx, NY, Dec 12, 39; m 62; c 3. Educ: Fordham Univ, BS, 61; Univ Mich, MS, 63, PhD(pharmaceut chem), 66. Prof Exp: Teaching asst pharmaceut anal, Univ Mich, 61-62; fel, Stanford Res Inst, 66-68; res biochemist, Pharmaceut Div, Geigy Chem Corp, 68-71. Mem: AAAS; Am Chem Soc; NY Acad Sci; Am Asn Pharmaceut Scientists; Int Soc Study Xenobiotics. Res: Metabolism of drugs; organic synthesis; analgesics; cardiovascular compounds; radiotracer techniques; gas chromatography; liquid chromatography; bioavailability; pharmacokinetics. Mailing Add: 32 Hickory Lane Garnerville NY 10923

REDDAN, JOHN R, CELL PHYSIOLOGY. Current Pos: NIH fel cell biol, 65-67, from asst prof to assoc prof, 67-78, PROF BIOL, OAKLAND UNIV, 78- Personal Data: b Trenton, NJ, Apr 18, 39; m 62; c 4. Educ: St Michaels Col, BA, 61; Univ Vt, PhD(zool), 66. Mem: AAAS; Am Soc Cell Biol; Asn Res Vision & Ophthal; Am Soc Zool. Res: Metabolic and cytological, light and electron microscopic changes which precede and accompany the initiation of cell division in normal, injured and cultured mammalian lenses epithelial cells. Mailing Add: Dept Biol Oakland Univ Rochester MI 48309-4401

REDDAN, WILLIAM GERALD, PHYSIOLOGY. Current Pos: res asst physiol, 60-62, proj assoc pulmonary physiol, 62-64, instr, 64-65, asst prof environ physiol, 65-72, ASSOC PROF PREV MED, MED SCH, UNIV WIS-MADISON, 72-, ASSOC PROF ANAT, 77- Personal Data: b St Louis, Mo, Aug 29, 27; m 52; c 3. Educ: Univ Mo-Columbia, BS, 51; Univ Wis-Madison, MS, 55, PhD(biodynamics), 65. Prof Exp: Teacher, Spring Green Pub Schs, 55-60. Mem: Am Physiol Soc. Res: Gas exchange in the lung; pulmonary physiology applied to occupational and environmental lung disease; physical education. Mailing Add: 5526 Country Rd M Oregon WI 53575

REDDELL, DONALD LEE, GROUND WATER HYDROLOGY & QUALITY. Current Pos: from asst prof to assoc prof, Tex A&M Univ, 69-77, prof, 77-89, head 89-93, PROF, TEX A&M UNIV, 93- Personal Data: b Tulia, Tex, Sept 28, 37; m 57, Minnie E Cox; c Revis, Cheryl & Stephen. Educ: Tex Technol Col, BS, 60; Colo State Univ, MS, 61, PhD(agr eng), 69. Prof Exp: Jr engr, High Plains Underground Water Conserv Dist, Lubbock, Tex, 60-62, agr engr, 62-64, engr, 64-65. Mem: Am Soc Agr Engrs; Am Geophys Union; Soil & Water Conserv Soc. Res: Groundwater hydrology, hydraulics and quality; heat transfer in groundwater aquifers; mathematical modeling of hydrological systems; irrigation and drainage; pollution problems in agriculture; contaminant transport in ground water; operation of farm irrigation systems. Mailing Add: 3808 Courtney Circle Bryan TX 77802. Fax: 409-845-3932

REDDEN, JACK A, GEOLOGY. Current Pos: dir eng & mining exp sta, 69-83, PROF GEOL, SDAK SCH MINES & TECHNOL, 69- Personal Data: b Rossville, Ill, Sept 24, 26; m 51; c 2. Educ: Dartmouth Col, AB, 48; Harvard Univ, MA, 50, PhD, 55. Prof Exp: Assoc prof geol, Va Polytech Inst & State Univ, 58-64; assoc prof geol & dir, Wright State Univ, 64-68, assoc dean sci & eng, 68-69. Concurrent Pos: Geologist, US Geol Surv, 48- Mem: Geol Soc Am; Mineral Soc Am. Res: Petrology; structure and ore deposits; specialist on stratigraphy, structure and ore deposits of Precambrian rocks of the Black Hills including uraniferous conglomerates. Mailing Add: 1214 West Blvd Rapid City SD 57701

REDDEN, PATRICIA ANN, PHYSICAL CHEMISTRY, EDUCATION. Current Pos: Asst prof anal chem, 68-74, assoc prof chem, 74-80, PROF CHEM, ST PETER'S COL, NJ, 80-, CHMN DEPT, 77- Personal Data: b New York, NY, Sept 10, 41. Educ: Cabrini Col, BS, 62; Fordham Univ, PhD(phys chem), 68. Mem: Am Chem Soc; Am Asn Univ Professors; Sigma Xi; NY Acad Sci. Res: Food analysis; lab safety. Mailing Add: Chem Dept St Peter's Col 2641 Kennedy Blvd Jersey City NJ 07306-4694

REDDI, A HARI, ORTHOPEDICS, BIOLOGICAL CHEMISTRY. Current Pos: PROF, DEPT ORTHOP & BIOL CHEM, JOHNS HOPKINS MED SCH, 91-, DIR, LAB MUSCULOSKELETAL CELL BIOL, 91- Personal Data: b Madras, India, Oct 20, 42; m 72, Anu H Reddy; c Ajoy, Amit & Anand. Educ: Annamalai Univ, India, MSc, 62; Univ Delhi, India, PhD, 66. Honors & Awards: Kappa Delta Award, Am Acad Orthop Surgeons, 91. Prof Exp: Fel, Johns Hopkins Med Sch, 68-69; res assoc, Univ Chicago, 69-72, asst prof, 72-76; res biologist, NIH, 76-78, chief, Bone Cell Biol Sect, 78-91. Res: Bone cell biology. Mailing Add: Johns Hopkins Univ Sch Med Ross Res Bldg Rm 225 720 Rutland Ave Baltimore MD 21205-2196

REDDICK, BRADFORD BEVERLY, PLANT VIROLOGY. Current Pos: ASST PROF PLANT VIROL, DEPT ENTOM & PLANT PHYSIOL, UNIV TENN, KNOXVILLE, 83- Personal Data: b Portsmouth, Va, May 28, 54; m 76. Educ: Randolph Macon Col, BS, 76; Clemson Univ, MS, 78, PhD(plant path), 81. Prof Exp: Res assoc, dept plant path, Univ Wis-Madison, 81-83. Mem: Am Phytopath Soc; AAAS. Res: Plant virus problems on basic and applied levels. Mailing Add: Dept Entom Univ Tenn 1345 Circle Pk Knoxville TN 37996-0001

REDDICK-MITCHUM, RHODA ANNE, MEDICAL MICROBIOLOGY. Current Pos: dir, Div Diag Microbiol, Bur Labs, 70-75, DIR, DIV LAB IMPROV, SC DEPT HEALTH & ENVIRON CONTROL, 75- Personal Data: b Waynesboro, Ga, Nov 2, 37; m 70. Educ: Ga Col, AB, 58; Emory Univ, cert med technol, 59; Med Col Ga, MS, 65, PhD(med microbiol), 68; Am Bd Med Microbiol, dipl, 73. Prof Exp: Med technologist, Emory Univ Hosp, 59-61 & Eugene Talmadge Hosp, Med Col Ga, 62-64; fel med microbiol, Ctr Dis Control, USPHS, Atlanta, Ga, 68-70. Mem: Am Soc Microbiol; Am Pub Health Asn; fel Am Acad Microbiol; Am Veneral Dis Asn; NY Acad Sci. Res: Development of new diagnostic procedures in medical microbiology and evaluation of products available to diagnostic microbiology laboratories. Mailing Add: 2605 Pine Lake Dr W Cola West Columbia SC 29169

REDDING, FOSTER KINYON, NEUROLOGY, NEUROPHYSIOLOGY. Current Pos: prof neurol, Sch Med, Wayne State Univ, 73-82. Personal Data: b Owatonna, Minn, July 22, 29; m 60; c 4. Educ: Univ Pa, MD, 54; McGill Univ, PhD(neurophysiol), 64. Prof Exp: Physician & surgeon, Palen Clin, Minneapolis, 55-56; asst prof neurol, Sch Med, Univ Ill, 64-67; neurologist & neurophysiologist, Henry Ford Hosp, Detroit, 67-73, chief neurol, 72-73. Concurrent Pos: USPHS res grant, Sch Med, Univ Ill, 66-69. Mem: Am Acad Neurol; Am EEG Soc; Am Epilepsy Soc. Res: Relationship of rhinencephalon with brain stem reticular formation. Mailing Add: 18424 Mack Ave Grosse Pointe MI 48236-3221

REDDING, JOSEPH STAFFORD, ANESTHESIOLOGY. Current Pos: PROF ANESTHESIOL & HEAD, DIV RESPIRATORY/CRIT CARE, MED UNIV SC, 74- Personal Data: b Macon, Ga, May 29, 21; m 49; c 5. Educ: Univ NC, Chapel Hill, BA, 43; Univ Md, Baltimore City, MD, 48. Prof Exp: Resident anesthesiol, Univ NC, 56-58; from instr to assoc prof anesthesiol, Johns Hopkins Univ, 58-70; prof anesthesiol, Univ Nebr Med Ctr, Omaha, 70-74. Concurrent Pos: Nat Heart Inst res grant, Baltimore City Hosps, 60-69, from asst chief to chief anesthesiol, Baltimore City Hosps, 58-70; assoc prof, Univ Md, 63-67, prof, 67-70. Mem: Am Soc Anesthesiol; Int Anesthesia Res Soc; Soc Crit Care Med; fel Am Col Physicians; Royal Soc Med. Res: Cardiopulmonary resuscitation; physiology of sudden death; life support measures; critical care medicine. Mailing Add: 236 Hobcaw Mt Pleasant SC 29464

REDDING, RICHARD WILLIAM, VETERINARY PHYSIOLOGY, PHARMACOLOGY. Current Pos: RETIRED. Personal Data: b Toledo, Ohio, Mar 18, 23; m 46; c 3. Educ: Ohio State Univ, DVM, 46, MSc, 50, PhD(vet physiol & pharmacol), 57. Prof Exp: Instr vet surg, Ohio State Univ, 48-50; asst prof, Univ Calif, 50-51 & Univ Ga, 51-53; from instr to assoc prof vet physiol & pharmacol, Ohio State Univ, 53-63, prof, Col Vet Med & Grad Sch, 63-68; prof small animal surg & med & physiol & pharmacol, Auburn Univ, 68-85. Concurrent Pos: Consult, Martin Co, 63 & USN Radiol Defense Labs, 66- Mem: AAAS; Am Vet Med Asn; Am Soc Vet Physiol & Pharmacol; Am Asn Vet Neurol (secy-treas, 72-). Res: Techniques, application and use of electroencephalograph in canine diagnosis; surgical control of behavior in the canine species. Mailing Add: 449 Camellia Dr Auburn AL 36830

REDDING, ROGERS WALKER, PHYSICAL CHEMISTRY, PHYSICS. Current Pos: DEAN, COL ART & SCI, NORTHERN KY UNIV, 95- Personal Data: b Louisville, Ky, July 15, 42; m 66, Shirley Berry; c Jeff, Jon, Chris & MacKenzie. Educ: Ga Inst Technol, BS, 65; Vanderbilt Univ, PhD(chem), 69. Prof Exp: Nat Acad Sci fel, Nat Bur Stand, Washington, DC, 69-70; from asst prof to prof physics, Tex Acad Math & Sci, Univ NTex, 70-95, chmn dept, 80-87, dir, 87-89, assoc dean sci, Col Arts & Sci, 90-95. Concurrent Pos: Distinguished vis prof physics, USAF Acad, 89-90. Mem: AAAS; Am Phys Soc; Am Asn Physics Teachers. Res: Theoretical molecular physics; molecular spectroscopy. Mailing Add: Col Arts & Sci Northern Ky Univ BEP 222 Highland Heights KY 41099. Fax: 817-565-4517; E-Mail: redding@cas.unt.edu

REDDINGTON, JOHN, AGRICULTURE ECONOMICS. Current Pos: DIR, DAIRY LIVESTOCK & POULTRY DIV, FOREIGN AGR SERV, 95- Personal Data: b Woburn, Mass, Nov 13, 47. Educ: Univ Mass, BS, 75; Purdue Univ, MS, 77. Mailing Add: Foreign Agr Serv 14th & Independence Ave SW Rm 5935 Washington DC 20250

REDDOCH, ALLAN HARVEY, CHEMICAL PHYSICS, SEMICONDUCTOR MATERIALS. Current Pos: CONSULT, 91- Personal Data: b Montreal, Que, Jan 19, 31; m 70, Joyce M Dunston. Educ: Queen's Univ, Ont, BSc, 53, MSc, 55; Univ Calif, Berkeley, PhD(phys chem), 60. Prof Exp: Fel chem, Nat Res Coun Can, 59-61, from asst res officer to assoc res officer, Div Chem, 61-74, sr res officer, 74-86, sr res officer, Inst Microstruct Sci, 86-91. Concurrent Pos: Lectr, Univ Ottawa, 61-65; adj prof, Univ Waterloo, 86-90. Mem: Sigma Xi; Am Phys Soc; Chem Inst Can. Res: Electron spin resonance of organic radicals in solution; organic charge-transfer crystals; hydrogen-bonded ferroelectrics; semimagnetic semiconductors; spin dynamics phase transitions; floristics and taxonomy of North American orchids. Mailing Add: 548 Rivershore Crescent Gloucester ON K1J 7Y7 Can

REDDY, BANDARU SIVARAMA, BIOCHEMISTRY, CANCER PREVENTION. *Current Pos:* chief nutrit, 71-83, assoc chief, Div Nutrit Endocrinol, 83-88, CHIEF NUTRIT CARCINOGENESIS, AM HEALTH FOUND, 89-, ASSOC DIR RES, 94-; RES PROF MICROBIOL, NY MED COL, 76- *Personal Data:* b Nellore, India, Dec 30, 32; m 62; c 3. *Educ:* Madras Univ, BVSc, 55; Univ NH, MS, 60; Mich State Univ, PhD(biochem), 63. *Honors & Awards:* Tana Award, 85; Tokten Prog, United Nations, 87. *Prof Exp:* Vet surg & med, Andhra Pradesh Govt, India, 55-58; res assoc biochem, Lobund Lab, Univ Notre Dame, 63-65, res scientist, 65-68, assoc res prof, 68-72. *Concurrent Pos:* NIH res grants, 65; Burrows-Welcome vis prof, 94. *Mem:* Am Inst Nutrit; Am Asn Pathologists; Asn Gnotobiotics; Am Asn Cancer Res; Soc Toxicol; Am Soc Prev Oncol. *Res:* Effect of intestinal microflora on the nutritional biochemistry of host; role of bile acids and microflora on the etiology of colon cancer; chemical carcinogenesis; nutrition and cancer; nutritional toxicology; mechanism of carcinogenesis; primary and secondary prevention of colon cancer; chemoprevention of cancer. *Mailing Add:* Am Health Found Mo One Dana Rd Valhalla NY 10595

REDDY, CHILEKAMPALLI ADINARAYANA, MICROBIAL ECOLOGY, MICROBIAL PHYSIOLOGY. *Current Pos:* from asst prof to assoc prof, 72-85, dir grad studies, Dept Microbiol, 80-84, PROF MICROBIOL, MICH STATE UNIV, EAST LANSING, 85- *Personal Data:* b Nandimandalan, Andhra Pradesh, India, July 1, 41; US citizen; m 72, Sasikala C; c Sumabala C. *Educ:* Sri Venkateswara Univ, Tirupati, India, BVSc, 62; Univ Ill, Urbana, MS, 67, PhD(microbiol), 70. *Honors & Awards:* Res Excellence Award, Smith Kline-Beecham. *Prof Exp:* Vet asst surgeon, Animal Husbandry Dept, Andhra Pradesh, India, 62-65; res asst, Univ Ill, Urbana, 65-70; res assoc, Univ Ga, Athens, 70-72. *Concurrent Pos:* Prin investr res grants, USDA, NSF, NIH, Dept Energy, Dept Environ Qual, State Mich & Mich State Univ, 72-; consult, Dow Chem Co, Midland, Mich, 73-80 & Food & Agr Orgn, UN, 83 & 89; vis scientist, Nat Animal Dis Ctr, Ames, Iowa, 79 & Tamil Nadu Agr Univ, India. *Mem:* Fel Am Acad Microbiol; Am Col Vet Microbiol; Am Vet Med Asn; AAAS; Am Soc Microbiol; Sigma Xi. *Res:* Physiology and molecular biology of lignin degradation by wood-degrading basidiomycetous fungi; biodegradation of chlorocromatic compounds and other toxic environmental pollutants; pathogenic corynebacteria-actinomyces; gastrointestinal anaerobes. *Mailing Add:* Dept Microbiol Mich State Univ East Lansing MI 48824-1101. *E-Mail:* reddy@pilot.msu.edu

REDDY, CHURKU MOHAN, PEDIATRIC ENDOCRINOLOGY. *Current Pos:* from asst prof to assoc prof, 75-82, PROF PEDIAT, MEHARRY MED COL, 82-, DIR DIV ENDOCRINOL & METAB, 75- *Personal Data:* b Kothapalli, India, Aug 3, 42; c Latha & Raju. *Educ:* Osmania Univ, India, MB, BS, 66; Am Bd Pediat, dipl, 75, cert endocrinol, 83. *Prof Exp:* Med officer, Primary Health Ctr, India, 68-70; asst instr pediat, State Univ NY, Downstate Med Ctr, 71-75. *Concurrent Pos:* Fel pediat endocrinol & metab, State Univ NY, Downstate Med Ctr, Kings County Hosp Ctr, 73-75. *Mem:* Fel Am Acad Pediat; AMA. *Res:* Clinical research. *Mailing Add:* Dept Pediat Meharry Med Col Nashville TN 37208

REDDY, ERAGAM PREMKUMAR, MOLECULAR BIOLOGY. *Current Pos:* DIR, FELS INST CANCER RES & MOLECULAR BIOL, PA, 92-; LAURA H CARNELL PROF MED, TEMPLE UNIV, 93- *Personal Data:* b Madanapalli, India, Jan 2, 44; c 2. *Educ:* Osmania Univ, BS, 62, MS, 65, PhD(molecular biol), 71. *Honors & Awards:* Sci Achievement Award, Am Cancer Soc, 93. *Prof Exp:* Res scholar, Indian Coun Sci & Indust Res, Hyderabad, 65-72; NIH fel, Univ Calif, Los Angeles, 72-73; Fogarty Int fel, Nat Cancer Inst, 74-75, vis scientist, Lab Cellular & Molecular Biol, 78-82, chief, Molecular Genetics Sect, 82-84; head, Viral Immunol Prog, Microbiol Assocs, Md, 75-78; res leader, Dept Molecular Oncol, Hoffman-LaRoche Inc, NJ, 84-85; mem, Roche Inst Molecular Biol, NJ, 85-86; prof, Wistar Inst, 86-91, dep dir, 91-92. *Concurrent Pos:* Mem, Cell Biol & Physiol Study Sect-2, 84-89; Wistar prof path, Univ Pa, 87-91; bd dirs, Nat Inst Environ Health Sci, NIH, 90-95; assoc ed, J Cellular Biochem, 94. *Mem:* AAAS; Int Asn Comp Res Leukemia & Related Dis. *Mailing Add:* Fels Inst Cancer Res 3420 N Broad St Philadelphia PA 19140

REDDY, GADE SUBBARAMI, PHYSICAL CHEMISTRY. *Current Pos:* res chemist, Eastern Lab, 62-66, RES CHEMIST, CENT RES DEPT, EXP STA, E I DU PONT DE NEMOURS & CO, INC, 66- *Personal Data:* b Aluru, India, May 20, 35; m 56; c 4. *Educ:* Andhra Univ, India, BSc, 54; Benares Hindu Univ, MSc, 56; Emory Univ, PhD(phys chem), 60. *Prof Exp:* Govt India sr res scholar phys chem, Benares Hindu Univ, 56-57; res assoc spectros, Emory Univ, 60-62. *Mem:* Am Chem Soc. *Res:* Nuclear magnetic resonance spectroscopy; nuclear magnetic resonance in liquid crystals; kinetics and reaction mechanisms by nuclear magnetic resonance; nuclear magnetic resonance in biological systems. *Mailing Add:* 714 Morris Rd Hockessin DE 19707

REDDY, GUNDA, ENTOMOLOGY, PHARMACOLOGY. *Current Pos:* RES TOXICOLOGIST, METAB MUNITION COMPOUNDS, HEALTH & ENVIRON EFFECTS, US ARMY, FT DETRICK, MD, 83- *Personal Data:* b Cheekodu, India; US citizen; m 76, Vijaya; c Samatha. *Educ:* Osmania Univ, India, BSc, 60, MSc, 62, PhD(zool, entom), 68; Am Bd Toxicol, dipl, 84. *Prof Exp:* Fel pesticide & residues, dept entom, Univ Ky, 69-70; res assoc metab ammonia & calcium, dept biol, Rice Univ, 70-71; vis scholar insect hormones, dept biol, Marquette Univ, 71-73; res pesticide metab, dept biol, Univ Ill, 73-76; res assoc insect hormones, Marquette Univ, 76-78; res assoc PCB metab & path, dept path, Univ Wis-Madison, 78-83. *Mem:* Am Soc Pharmacol & Exp Therapeut; Soc Toxicol; Asn Govt Toxicologists; Indian Sci Cong; Am Col Toxicol; Soc Environ Toxicol & Chem. *Res:* Action and metabolism of pesticides; insect endocrine interactions; environmental and health effect of pollutants and munition chemicals; biochemical toxicology. *Mailing Add:* US Army Ctr Health Prom & Prev Med Ft Detrick Bldg 568 Frederick MD 21702-5010. *Fax:* 301-619-2569

REDDY, JANARDAN K, PATHOLOGY. *Current Pos:* PROF PATH, NORTHWESTERN UNIV MED SCH, CHICAGO, 76- *Personal Data:* b India, Oct 7, 38; m 62; c 2. *Educ:* Osmania Univ, India, MB, BS, 61; All India Inst Med Sci, MD, 65. *Honors & Awards:* Fel Yamagina-Yoshida Cancer; NIH Merit Award. *Prof Exp:* From asst prof to assoc prof path & oncol, Univ Kans Med Ctr, Kansas City, 70-76. *Concurrent Pos:* United Nations Tokten Scholar to India; Assoc Ed, Cancer Res, J Toxicol, Env Health. *Mem:* AAAS; Am Asn Pathologists; Soc Exp Biol & Med; Histochem Soc; Am Soc Cell Biol; Biochemical Soc, UK. *Res:* Experimental chemcial carcinogenesis; effect of drugs and carcinogens on the structure and function of liver and pancreas; role of hypolipidemic drugs on the induction of peroxisome proliferation in liver cells. *Mailing Add:* Dept Path Ward Mem Bldg Sch Med Northwestern Univ 303 E Chicago Ave Chicago IL 60611-3072

REDDY, JUNUTHULA N, MECHANICAL ENGINEERING, APPLIED MECHANICS. *Current Pos:* OSCAR S WYATT ENDOWED PROF, TEX A&M UNIV, 92- *Personal Data:* b Warangal, India, Aug 12, 45; m 68, Aruna; c Anita & Anil. *Educ:* Osmania Univ, India, BE, 68; Okla State Univ, MS, 70; Univ Ala, Huntsville, PhD(appl mech), 73. *Honors & Awards:* Teetor Award Res & Teaching, Soc Automotive Engrs, 76; Univ Okla Res Award, 79; Huber Prize, Am Soc Civil Engrs, 84; Worcester Reed Warner Medal, Am Soc Mech Engrs, 92. *Prof Exp:* Res assoc mech, Univ Ala, 70-73; fel, Univ Tex, Austin, 73-74; res assoc aeromech, Lockheed Missiles & Space Co, 74-75; from asst prof to assoc prof mech eng, Univ Okla, 75-80; prof, Va Polytech Inst, 80-85, Clifton C Garvin prof, 85-92. *Concurrent Pos:* Consult, Battelle Columbus Labs, Ohio, Alcoa Tech Labs & Gen Dynamics; res grants, NSF, Off Naval Res, NASA, Army Res Off & Air Force Off Sci Res. *Mem:* Am Acad Mech; fel Am Soc Mech Engrs; Soc Eng Sci; Am Soc Civil Engrs. *Res:* Analysis of composite structural components; computational fluid mechanics; theory and application of the finite element method in solid and fluid mechanics; variational methods and composite materials. *Mailing Add:* Texas A&M Univ MS 3123 College Station TX 77843. *Fax:* 409-845-3081; *E-Mail:* jneddy@tamvm1.tamu.edu

REDDY, KALLURU JAYARAMI, GENE EXPRESSION, BIOLOGICAL NITROGEN FIXATION. *Current Pos:* ASST PROF MICROBIOL, STATE UNIV NY, BINGHAMTON, 90- *Personal Data:* b Pidugupalli, Andhra Pradesh, Apr 15, 53; m 84; c 1. *Educ:* Sri Venkateswara Univ, BSc, 72, MSc, 74; Univ Miami, PhD(marine biol), 84. *Prof Exp:* Jr res fel, Indian Inst Technol, 74-76; jr plant physiologist, Indian Agr Res Inst, New Delhi, 76-80; res asst, Univ Miami, 80-84; fel molecular biol, Univ Mo, Columbia, 85-89; res scientist, Purdue Univ, West Lafayette, 89-90. *Mem:* Am Soc Microbiol; Am Soc Plant Physiol. *Res:* Molecular genetics of nitrogen fixation in unicellular cyanobacteria. *Mailing Add:* Dept Biol Sci State Univ NY PO Box 6000 Binghamton NY 13902-6000

REDDY, KAPULURU CHANDRASEKHARA, APPLIED MATHEMATICS, FLUID MECHANICS. *Current Pos:* from asst prof to assoc prof, 66-75, PROF MATH, SPACE INST, UNIV TENN, TULLAHOMA, 75-, DEAN, ACAD AFFAIRS, 90- *Personal Data:* b Nellore, India, Aug 20, 42; m 67, Leena; c Sunil & Gautham. *Educ:* V R Col, India, BA, 59; Sri Venkateswara Univ, india, MSc, 61; Indian Inst Technol, Kharagpur, MTech, 62, PhD(appl math), 65. *Prof Exp:* Assoc lectr math, Indian Inst Technol, Kharagpur, 64-65; instr aerospace eng, Univ Md, College Park, 65-66. *Concurrent Pos:* Staff engr, Lockheed Electronics Co, Houston, 69 & 70; consult, US Army Res Off, Durham, 73 & Lockheed Ga Co, Marietta, Ga, 76; res engr, ARO, Inc & Calspan, Arnold Eng Develop Ctr, 77-90. *Mem:* Am Inst Aeronaut & Astronaut; Sigma Xi; Soc Indust & Appl Math. *Res:* Computational fluid mechanics; transonic flow problems; numerical analysis; boundary layers. *Mailing Add:* Dean's Off Space Inst Univ Tenn Tullahoma TN 37388. *Fax:* 615-393-7346; *E-Mail:* kreddy@utsi.edu

REDDY, MOHAN MUTHIREVAL, IMMUNOLOGY, AIDS. *Current Pos:* DIR, ALLERGY & CLIN IMMUNOL, ST LUKES ROOSEVELT HOSP CTR, 79- *Personal Data:* b Chittor, India, Apr 25, 42; US citizen; m 72; c 2. *Educ:* Univ Chicago, PhD(biol), 69. *Mem:* Am Asn Immunologist; Am Asn Clin Pathologists; Am Acad Allergy. *Res:* Role of immunology in diseases. *Mailing Add:* Dept Allergy & Immunol St Lukes Roosevelt Hosp Ctr 1000 Tenth Ave New York NY 10019

REDDY, NARENDER PABBATHI, BIOMEDICAL ENGINEERING, MECHANICAL ENGINEERING. *Current Pos:* assoc prof, 81-89, PROF, DEPT BIOMED ENG, UNIV AKRON, 89- *Personal Data:* b Karimnagar, India, May 5, 47; m 76, Swarna Latha; c Haricharan & Vishnukrupa. *Educ:* Osmania Univ, India, BE, 69; Univ Miss, MS, 71; Tex A&M Univ, PhD(bioeng), 74. *Prof Exp:* Res asst, Tex A&M Univ, 71-74, res assoc bioeng, 74-75; res assoc rehab eng, Baylor Col Med, 75-76; res physiologist, Univ Calif, San Francisco, 77-78; sr res scientist, Biomech Res Unit, Helen Hays Hosp, NY, 78-81. *Concurrent Pos:* Res fel, Cardiovasc Res Inst, Univ Calif, San Francisco, 77-78; adj assoc prof, Rensselaer Polytech Inst, 79-81; adj staff, Edwin Shaw Hosp, Akron, Ohio, 84-; chmn, tech sessions, numerous nat & int sci meetings & confs; chmn, Biomed Eng Div Prog, Am Soc Eng Educ, 94. *Mem:* Biomed Eng Soc; Am Soc Mech Engrs; Am Soc Eng Educ; Rehab Eng Soc NAm; Am Soc Eng Educ. *Res:* Biomechanical engineering; medical devices; rehabilitation engineering; virtual reality; noninvasive diagnosis, telepresence. *Mailing Add:* Biomed Eng Dept Col Eng Univ Akron 302 Buchtel Mall Akron OH 44325-0001. *Fax:* 330-374-8834

REDDY, PARVATHAREDDY BALARAMI, CONTROL SYSTEMS, ELECTRICAL ENGINEERING. *Current Pos:* PRES, APEX TECHNOL INC, 85- *Personal Data:* b Nellore, India, Dec 1, 42; US citizen; m 67, Devasena; c 2. *Educ:* Sri Venkateswara Univ, BE hons, 65; Indian Inst Technol, MTech, 67; Rutgers Univ, PhD(elec eng controls), 73. *Honors & Awards:* Siromani Award, Outstanding Engr, Am Telugu Asn. *Prof Exp:* Res & teaching asst elec eng, Rutgers Univ, 69-73; sr systs analyst control & navig, Dynamics Res Corp, 73-78; mem tech staff navig & guid, Litton Guid & Control Systs, 78-80; res scientist, Teledyne Systs Co, 80-85. *Concurrent Pos:* Convener, Indo-Am Trade Fair, 94. *Mem:* Inst Elec & Electronics Engrs. *Res:* Guidance, navigation, statistical modeling; modeling and simulation with general modeling interest; strapdown systems using ring laser gyros. *Mailing Add:* Apex Tech Inc 1735 Jefferson Davis Hwy Stuite 907 Arlington VA 22202. *Fax:* 818-591-7970

REDDY, RAJ, COMPUTER SCIENCE. *Current Pos:* From assoc prof to prof, Carnegie-Mellon Univ, 69-84, Univ prof, 84-86, dir, Robotics Inst, 80-86, DEAN COMPUT SCI, CARNEGIE-MELLON UNIV, 86- *Personal Data:* b Katoor, India, June 13, 37; US citizen; m 66; c 2. *Educ:* Univ Madras, BE, 58; Univ NSW, MTech, 61; Stanford Univ, PhD(conput sci), 66. *Concurrent Pos:* Consult, Litton Indust, 68-69, Stanford Res Inst, 70-71, Palo Alto Res Ctr, Xerox Corp, 70-78, NSF, 72-76, ITT, 78-79, Jet Propulsion Labs, 78-79, Gen Motors, 78-80, Rand Corp, 78-80 & var other co, 78-; John Guggenheim fel, 75-76; chmn, bd trustees, Int Joint Coun Artificial Intel, 77-79; mem, gov bd, Cognitive Sci Soc, 79-84, adv bd, Trans Pattern Anal & Mach Intel, Inst Elec & Electronics Engrs, 79-80, bd dirs, Robot Inst Am, 82 & mfg studies bd, Nat Res Coun, 83-86; vchmn, Study Group Mach Intel & Robotics, NASA, 79-80; vpres & chief scientist, World Ctr Comput Sci & Human Resources, 82-; pres, Am Asn Artificial Intel, 87-89. *Mem:* Nat Acad Eng; fel Acoust Soc Am; fel Inst Elec & Electronics Engrs; Asn Comput Mach; Asn Comput Ling. *Res:* Speech and visual input to computers; graphics; man-machine communication; artificial intelligence; robotics; computer science. *Mailing Add:* Sch Comput Sci Carnegie-Mellon Univ Pittsburgh PA 15213

REDDY, RAMAKRISHNA PASHUVULA, animal health, immunology; deceased, see previous edition for last biography

REDDY, RAMANA G, MATERIALS PROCESSING, WASTE TREATMENT & ENVIRONMENTAL ENGINEERING. *Current Pos:* ACIPCO PROF & ADJ PROF CHEM, MAT & MECH ENG, UNIV ALA, 96- *Personal Data:* b Warangal, India, Feb 4, 51; m 83, Rama; c Bharat. *Educ:* Osmania Univ, BE, 73; Indian Inst Technol, Bombay, MTech, 75; Univ Utah, PhD(metall eng), 80. *Honors & Awards:* Serv Award Light Metals, Metall Soc, 97. *Prof Exp:* from asst prof to assoc prof, Univ Nev, Reno, 81-91, chmn & prof, 93, prof, 91-95. *Concurrent Pos:* Vis assoc prof, Indian Inst Technol, 89; vis res scientist, Lawrence Berkeley Lab, Univ Calif, 89-94; secy, Process Fundamentals Comn, Minerals, Metals & Mat Soc, 95- *Mem:* Soc Mining & Metall Eng; Am Foundryment Soc; fel Am Soc Metals Int. *Res:* Thermodynamics and kinetics of reactions; phase stability; fused salt electrolysis; synthesis and processing of advanced materials molten metal processing; industrial waste treatment and processing. *Mailing Add:* Dept Metall & Mat Eng Univ Ala PO Box 870202 Rm A129 Bevill Bldg Tuscaloosa AL 35487-0202. *Fax:* 205-348-2164; *E-Mail:* rreddy@coe.eng.ua.edu

REDDY, REGINALD JAMES, MOLECULAR SPECTROSCOPY. *Current Pos:* asst prof, 73-89, ASSOC PROF PHYSICS, SIENA COL, NY, 89- *Personal Data:* b Staten Island, NY, July 16, 34. *Educ:* St Bonaventure Univ, BA, 57; Holy Name Col, STM, 61; Univ SC, PhD(physics), 77. *Prof Exp:* Instr physics & math, Archbishop Walsh High Sch, 61-65; teaching asst, Univ SC, 68-73. *Mem:* Am Asn Physics Teachers; Nat Sci Teachers Asn; Sigma Xi. *Res:* Flash photolysis studies of various polycyclic hydrocarbons including triplet-triplet transitions, quenching of the triplet states by various impurities, energy transfer between triplets. *Mailing Add:* Dept Physics Siena Col 515 Louden Rd Loudonville NY 12211-1462

REDDY, SATTI PADDI, PHYSICS, MOLECULAR SPECTROSCOPY. *Current Pos:* res fel, 63-64, from asst prof to assoc prof, 64-72, PROF PHYSICS, MEM UNIV NFLD, 72-, HEAD, DEPT PHYSICS & OCEANOG, 95- *Personal Data:* b Sept 1, 32; Can citizen; m 55, Parvati Mallidi; c Sethu-Kumar, Bharati & Suresh. *Educ:* Andhra Univ, India, BSc, 54, MSc, 55, DSc(physics), 59. *Prof Exp:* Lectr physics, Andhra Univ, India, 59-61; res assoc, Univ Toronto, 61-63. *Concurrent Pos:* Sr res fel, Andhra Univ, India, 60-61; vis prof physics, Ohio State Univ, 77-78; chmn, Div Atomic & Molecular Physics, Can Asn Physicists, 92-93. *Mem:* Fel Brit Inst Physics; Can Asn Physicists; fel Am Phys Soc. *Res:* Molecular physics; infrared, laser and optical spectroscopy. *Mailing Add:* Dept Physics Mem Univ Nfld St John's NF A1B 3X7 Can. *Fax:* 709-737-8739; *E-Mail:* spreddy@kehoin.physics.mun.ca

REDDY, SUDHAKAR M, ELECTRICAL ENGINEERING. *Current Pos:* Asst prof elec eng, 68-77, PROF ELEC & COMPUT ENG, UNIV IOWA, 77-, FOUND DISTINGUISHED PROF, 90- *Personal Data:* b Gadwal, India, Jan 5, 38; m 63, Bharathi; c Kartik & Svath. *Educ:* Osmania Univ, India, BS, 58 & 62; Indian Inst Sci, MS, 63; Univ Iowa, PhD(elec eng), 68. *Concurrent Pos:* Chmn, Dept Elec & Comput Eng, Univ Iowa. *Mem:* Fel Inst Elec & Electronics Engrs; Sigma Xi. *Res:* Coding theory; digital systems. *Mailing Add:* Dept Elec Eng Univ Iowa Iowa City IA 52242. *E-Mail:* reddy@eng.uiowa.edu

REDDY, THOMAS BRADLEY, BATTERY TECHNOLOGY, ELECTROCHROMIC DISPLAYS. *Current Pos:* VPRES ENG, YARDNEY TECH PRODUCTS, PAWCATUCK, CT, 94- *Personal Data:* b Amesbury, Mass, Sept 11, 33; m 88, Mary E Scarborough; c David P, Peter J & Josina C. *Educ:* Yale Univ, BS, 55; Univ Minn, PhD(phys chem), 60. *Prof Exp:* Res assoc chem, Univ Ill, 59-61; mem tech staff electrochem, Bell Tel Labs, 61-65; proj leader, Am Cyanamid Co, 65-74, prin res chemist, Stamford Res Labs, 74-79; dir-battery-technol, Stonehart Assocs, Inc, Madison, Conn, 79-80; dir technol Power Conversion ,Inc, Elmwood Park, NJ, 80-88, dir mil mkt, 88-89, vpres 89-94. *Concurrent Pos:* Rice fel, G E Educ & Charilabe Found, 58-59. *Mem:* Am Chem Soc; Electrochem Soc; Sigma Xi. *Res:* Lithium battery technology; lithioum ion battery technol; electrochromic display devices; alkaline battery technology. *Mailing Add:* 30 Elm Rock Rd Bronxville NY 10708. *Fax:* 860-599-5903; *E-Mail:* treddy@yardney.com

REDDY, VENKAT N, BIOCHEMISTRY. *Current Pos:* asst prof ophthalmic biochem, Kresge Eye Inst, 57-61, assoc ophthal, 61-77, PROF BIOMED SCI & DIR EYE RES INST, OAKLAND UNIV, 75- *Personal Data:* b Hyderabad, India, Nov 4, 22; nat US; m 55; c 2. *Educ:* Madras Univ, BSc, 45; Fordham Univ, MS, 49, PhD(biochem), 52. *Honors & Awards:* Fight for Sight Citation, Nat Coun Combat Blindness, 68; Friedenwald Award, Asn Res Vision & Ophthal, 79. *Prof Exp:* Asst chem, Fordham Univ, 48-50, sr asst biochem, 50-52; res asst obstet & gynec, Columbia Univ, 52-54, res assoc, 54-56, res fel, Banting & Best Inst, Can, 56. *Concurrent Pos:* Mem visual sci study sect, NIH, 66-70, consult, Cataract Workshop, 73; asst dir inst biol sci, Oakland Univ, 68-75; Nat Acad Sci-Nat Res Coun Comt Vision, 71-; consult, Nat Adv Eye Coun Vision Res Prog Planning Comt, 74; bd sci counr, Nat Eye Inst, 78-82. *Mem:* AAAS; Am Soc Biol Chemists; NY Acad Sci; Asn Res Vision & Ophthal; Brit Biochem Soc; Sigma Xi. *Res:* Transport mechanisms; aqueous humor dynamics; metabolism of ocular tissues; cataract; biochemistry of the lens; monoclonal antibodies. *Mailing Add:* Oakland U, Eye Rsch Inst Rochester MI 48309-4401

REDDY, VILAMBI N R K, NEW PRODUCT DEVELOPMENT IN DRUG DELIVERY, ELETROCHEMICAL ENGINEERING. *Current Pos:* mgr electrode technol, 93-96, ASSOC DIR RES & DEVELOP, BECTON DICKINSOL, 96- *Personal Data:* m 81, Indra; c Yogesh V & Yuvaram V. *Educ:* Madras Univ, India, BS, 81; Clarkson Univ, MS, 82, PhD(chem eng), 87. *Prof Exp:* Prin scientist, Phys Sci Inc, 87-90; sr staff engr, Hughes Aircraft Co, 90-93. *Concurrent Pos:* Consult, Univ Ariz, 92, Phys Sci Inc, 93, Technic Inc, 94-96. *Mem:* Am Chem Soc; Am Electroplate & Surface Finisher Soc; Electrochem Soc. *Res:* Research and engineering development of novel transdermal controlled programmable drug delivery systems. *Mailing Add:* 70 Hillside Dr Bloomingdale NJ 07403. *Fax:* 201-703-2295

REDDY, WILLIAM L, TOPOLOGY. *Current Pos:* from asst prof to assoc prof, Wesleyan Univ, 68-75, chmn dept, 74 & 77-80, assoc dir, Grad Summer Sch, 76-79, PROF MATH, WESLEYAN UNIV, 75-, ACTG CHMN, COMPUT CTR, 80- *Personal Data:* b Albany, NY, Dec 15, 38; div; c 1. *Educ:* Siena Col, BS, 60; Syracuse Univ, MA, 62, PhD(math), 64. *Prof Exp:* Asst prof math, Webster Col, 64-65 & State Univ NY Albany, 67-68. *Concurrent Pos:* Mem, Inst Advan Study, 69. *Mem:* AAAS; Math Asn Am; Am Math Soc. *Res:* Branched coverings; topological dynamics. *Mailing Add:* 37 Straits Rd Chester CT 06412

REDEI, GYORGY PAL, GENETICS, GENETIC ENGINEERING. *Current Pos:* from asst prof to prof, 57-91, chmn, Genetics Prog, 90-91, EMER PROF GENETICS, UNIV MO, COLUMBIA, 91- *Personal Data:* b Vienna, Austria, June 14, 21; m 53, Magdolna M Nagy; c Mari. *Educ:* Magyarovar Acad Agr, Hungary, dipl, 48; Univ Agr Sci, Hungary, dipl, 49; Hungarian Acad Sci, CSc, 55. *Honors & Awards:* Sr Res Award, Sigma Xi, 89. *Prof Exp:* Res asst, Nat Inst Plant Breeding, Magyarovar, Hungary, 48, Inst Genetics, Hungarian Acad Sci, 49 & Agr Exp Sta, Kisvarda, 50; res adminr, Ministry Agr, Budapest, 51; res assoc, Inst Genetics, Hungarian Acad Sci, 52-56. *Concurrent Pos:* Grants, NSF, 59, 61, 63, 65, 69 & 89, NIH, 63 & 64, AEC, 66, 67 & 68, NATO, 75 & 79 & Environ Protection Agency, 79, 80, 83, 85, USDA, 86; vis prof, Max-Planck Inst, Cologne, Ger, 86, 92 & 93. *Mem:* Genetics Soc Am; foreign mem Hungarian Nat Acad Sci; AAAS. *Res:* Genetics of Arabidopsis; thiamine auxotrophy; regulation of gene activity by metabolites and antimetabolites; genetics of organelles; mutation; detection of carcinogens and mutagens; transformation; author of one textbook; developmental genetics. *Mailing Add:* 3005 Woodbine Ct Columbia MO 65203-0906

REDEKER, ALLAN GRANT, MEDICINE. *Current Pos:* From instr to assoc prof, 58-69, PROF MED, UNIV SOUTHERN CALIF, 69- *Personal Data:* b Lincoln, Nebr, Sept 10, 24; m 50, 79; c 3. *Educ:* Northwestern Univ, BS, 49, MD, 52. *Concurrent Pos:* Schweppe Found res fel, Sch Med, Univ Southern Calif, 54-56; Bank of Am-Giannini Found res fel, 56-57; Bank of Am-Giannini Found traveling res fel, Minn, London & Malmo Clins, Sweden, 57; Lederle med fac award, 59-62; USPHS career develop award, 62-69; mem attend staff, Los Angeles County Hosp, 55- & Rancho Los Amigos Hosp. *Mem:* Am Fedn Clin Res; Am Soc Clin Invest; Am Asn Study Liver Dis (pres, 71); Int Soc Study Liver; Asn Am Physicians; Am Gastroenterol Asn. *Res:* Hepatic physiology and diseases of the liver; bilirubin and pyrrole pigment metabolism. *Mailing Add:* 9323 Samoline Ave Downey CA 90240-2716

REDEKOPP, LARRY G, AERODYNAMICS & FLUID DYNAMICS. *Current Pos:* PROF AERO ENG, UNIV SOUTHERN CALIF, 71- *Personal Data:* b Wolf Point, Mont, Apr 10, 41. *Educ:* Mont State Univ, BS, 62; Univ Calif, Los Angeles, MS, 66, PhD(eng), 69. *Mem:* Am Phys Soc; Am Inst Aeronaut & Astrophys. *Res:* Aerodynamics and fluid dynamics. *Mailing Add:* Dept Aero Eng Univ Southern Calif Los Angeles CA 90089

REDENTE, EDWARD FRANCIS, LAND RESTORATION, PLANT ECOLOGY. *Current Pos:* res assoc, 76-79, instr, 79-80, asst prof mined land reclamation, 80-87, PROF RANGE SCI, RANGE SCI DEPT, COLO STATE UNIV, 88- *Personal Data:* b Derby, Conn, Feb 18, 51; m 73; c 3. *Educ:* Western Mich Univ, BA, 72; Colo State Univ, MS, 74, PhD(range ecol), 80. *Prof Exp:* Environ engr, Utah Int Inc, 74-76. *Concurrent Pos:* Consult, Thorne Ecol Inst, 76-77, Colo State Dept Natural Resources, 80-81; prin investr, Oil Shale Reclamation Proj, 80-84, mechanisms of secondary succession, US Dept Energy, 84- *Mem:* Soc Range Mgt; Ecol Soc Am; Sigma Xi; Am Soc Surface Mining & Reclamation. *Res:* Primary and secondary successional processes that occur on arid and semiarid land disturbed by energy development; determine effects of revegetation practices on rate and direction of plant succession and interaction between succession and soil microbial processes. *Mailing Add:* Dept Range Sci Colo State Univ Ft Collins CO 80523-0001

REDER, FRIEDRICH H, PHYSICS. *Current Pos:* CONSULT, OMEGA RADIO NAVIG, 80- *Personal Data:* b Garsten, Austria, Dec 9, 19; US citizen; m 52; c 1. *Educ:* Graz Univ, MS, 47, PhD(physics), 49. *Honors & Awards:* Res & Develop Ann Achievement Award, Army Materiel Command, 70. *Prof Exp:* Asst physics, Graz Univ, 48-52; physicist, Frequency Control Div, US Army Electronics Labs, 53-62, sr scientist, Inst Explor Res, 62-71, chief antennas & geophys res area, Electronics Technol & Devices Lab, 71-73, chief commun res technol area, Commun/ADP Lab, 73-78; res physicist, Ctr Commun Systs, Commun Res & Develop Command, 78-80. *Concurrent Pos:* UNESCO fel plasma physics, Radiation Lab Electronics, Mass Inst Technol, 50-51, US Indust fel, 51; mem laser comt, US Dept Defense, 61-62. *Res:* Atomic frequency, time control and propagation of very low frequency electromagnetic waves. *Mailing Add:* 480 Marvin Dr Long Branch NJ 07740

REDETZKI, HELMUT M, PHARMACOLOGY. *Current Pos:* prof pharmacol & head dept, 68-86, EMER PROF PHARMACOL, SCH MED, LA STATE UNIV, SHREVEPORT, 86- *Personal Data:* b Memel, Lithuania, Sept 23, 21; nat US; m 57. *Educ:* Univ Hamburg, MD, 48; Am Bd Med Toxicol, dipl, 75. *Honors & Awards:* Dehnecke Medal & Award, Univ Hamburg, 55; H M Hub Cotton Faculty Excellence Award, 75. *Prof Exp:* Intern, Med Sch, Univ Hamburg, 47-48, res assoc biochem, 48-51, res assoc virol, Poliomyelitis Res Inst, 51-52; resident internal med, St George Hosp, Hamburg, Ger, 52-56; instr pharmacol, Univ Tex Med Br Galveston, 59-60, asst prof, 60-61; assoc prof, Sch Med, La State Univ, New Orleans, 61-66, prof 66-68. *Concurrent Pos:* McLaughlin Found fel, Tissue Metab Res Lab, Univ Tex Med Br Galveston, 56-59; proj & med dir, La Regional Poison Control Ctr, 77- *Mem:* Fel Am Acad Clin Toxicol; Soc Exp Biol & Med; Am Heart Asn; fel Am Col Physicians; Am Soc Clin Pharmacol & Therapeut; Am Acad Clin Toxicol (pres, 84-86). *Res:* Alcohol metabolism; cancer chemotherapy; drug-enzyme interactions; clinical toxicology. *Mailing Add:* Dept Pharmacol & Therapeut Sch Med La State Univ PO Box 33932 Shreveport LA 71130

REDFEARN, PAUL LESLIE, JR, BRYOLOGY. *Current Pos:* PROF LIFE SCI, SOUTHWEST MO STATE UNIV, 57- *Personal Data:* b Sanford, Fla, Oct 5, 26; m 49; c 2. *Educ:* Fla Southern Col, BS, 48; Univ Tenn, MS, 49; Fla State Univ, PhD, 57. *Honors & Awards:* Burlington Res Award, Southwest Mo State Univ, 87. *Prof Exp:* Instr bot, Univ Fla, 50-51. *Concurrent Pos:* Res assoc, Mo Bot Garden, 74. *Mem:* Fel AAAS; Am Bryol & Lichenological Soc (pres, 71-73); Ecol Soc Am; Am Soc Plant Taxonomists. *Res:* Taxonomy and ecology of bryophytes; interior highlands of NA, China. *Mailing Add:* Dept Life Sci Southwest Mo State Univ Springfield MO 65802

REDFEARN, RICHARD DANIEL, POLYMER MICROSTRUCTURAL ANALYSIS, NEW POLYMER FORMULATIONS. *Current Pos:* SR CHEMIST, ICI ACRYLICS INC, 93- *Personal Data:* b El Paso, Tex, Oct 26, 52; m 91, Violet Trosper; c Gillian & Joshua. *Educ:* Lander Univ, BS, 77; Duke Univ, PhD(org chem), 83. *Prof Exp:* Res chemist, E I du Pont de Nemours & Co, 82-86, sr res chemist, 86-89, sr chemist, 89-93. *Concurrent Pos:* Instr org chem, Memphis State Univ, 90-93, gen chem, State Tech Inst Memphis, 94- *Mem:* Am Chem Soc. *Res:* Obtaining basic information about structure-property relationships in polymers, primarily acrylic polymers; characterize target polymers at the microstructural level. *Mailing Add:* ICI Acrylics 7275 Goodlett Farms Pkwy Cordova TN 38018-4909

REDFERN, ROBERT EARL, ENTOMOLOGY. *Current Pos:* RETIRED. *Personal Data:* b Blackburn, Ark, July 29, 29; m 55; c 4. *Educ:* Univ Ark, BS, 59, MS, 61. *Prof Exp:* Entomologist, Fruit & Veg Res Br, Ind, USDA, 60-62, entomologist-in-charge, Pesticide Chem Res Br, Tex, 63-68, Md, 68-72, chief biol eval chem lab, 72-74, res entomologist, biol eval chem lab, Agr Environ Qual Inst, 74-89. *Mem:* Entom Soc Am. *Res:* Insects affecting deciduous fruits; primary screening of juvenile and molting hormones. *Mailing Add:* 5508 Taylor Rd Riverdale MD 20737

REDFIELD, ALFRED GUILLOU, PHYSICAL BIOCHEMISTRY. *Current Pos:* PROF PHYSICS & BIOCHEM, BRANDEIS UNIV, 72-, PROF, ROSENSTIEL BASIC MED SCI RES CTR, 77- *Personal Data:* b Boston, Mass, Mar 11, 29; m 60, Sarah Cossum; c 3. *Educ:* Harvard Univ, BA, 50; Univ Ill, MA, 52, PhD(physics), 53. *Honors & Awards:* Patterson lectr, Inst Cancer Res, 81; Ismar Prize, Int Soc Magnetic Resonance, 96. *Prof Exp:* Univ fel appl sci, 54-55; physicist, Watson Lab, IBM Corp, 55-71. *Concurrent Pos:* Assoc, Columbia Univ, 55-61, adj asst prof, 61-63, adj prof, 63-71; vis physicist, AEC, Saclay, France, 60-61; Miller vis prof, Univ Ill, Urbana, 61; mem corp, Woods Hole Oceanog Inst, 64-74; vis physicist, Univ Calif, Berkeley, 70-71, NSF sr fel, 71-72; Little vis prof, Mass Inst Technol, 72. *Mem:* Nat Acad Sci; fel Am Phys Soc; Am Soc Biol Chemists; Am Chem Soc; Am Acad Sci. *Res:* Nuclear magnetic resonance and relaxation; protein catalysis and electronic structure; superconductivity. *Mailing Add:* MS 09 Brandeis Univ 415 South St Waltham MA 02154

REDFIELD, CAROL ANN LUCKHARDT, INTELLIGENT TUTORING SYSTEMS, GAME PLAYING & THEORY. *Current Pos:* SR SCIENTIST, MEI TECHNOL CORP, 95- *Personal Data:* b Greencastle, Ind, July 19, 58; m 90, Joe B; c Neil M. *Educ:* Univ Mich, BS, 80, MS(math) & MS(comput), 82, PhD, 89. *Prof Exp:* Sr res engr, SW Res Inst, 87-94. *Concurrent Pos:* Adj prof math & comput sci, Univ Tex, San Antonio, 89 & 94-; chair, Space Educ Comt, Nat Space Soc, 97- *Mem:* Am Asn Artificial Intel; Nat Space Soc; Space Studies Inst; Nat Coun Teachers Math; Artificial Intel Educ. *Res:* Intelligent tutoring systems; computer-based training and educational games; expert systems, knowledge engineering, search and game playing/theory, software engineering, space colonization and applications of artificial intelligence. *Mailing Add:* 609 Ridge View Dr San Antonio TX 78253. *E-Mail:* carol@meitx.com

REDFIELD, DAVID, OPTOELECTRONIC MATERIALS, SOLAR ENERGY. *Current Pos:* CONSULT PROF, STANFORD UNIV, 85- *Personal Data:* b New York, NY, Sept 20, 25; m 50; c 2. *Educ:* Univ Calif, Los Angeles, AB, 48; Univ Md, MS, 53; Univ Pa, PhD(physics), 56. *Prof Exp:* Electronic scientist, Nat Bur Stand, 49-52; sr res physicist, Union Carbide Corp, 55-64; assoc prof elec eng, Columbia Univ, 64-67; res physicist, RCA Corp, 67-85. *Concurrent Pos:* Mem, Solar Photovoltaics Energy adv comt, US Dept Energy, 80-81; vchmn, Am Nat Stand Photovoltaics Subcomt, 80-81. *Mem:* AAAS; fel Am Phys Soc; sr mem Inst Elec & Electronics Engrs; Fedn Am Scientists. *Res:* Optical and electronic properties of solids; effects of surfaces, defects; optical and transport properties of disordered semiconductors; solar energy. *Mailing Add:* Dept Mat Sci & Eng Stanford Univ Stanford CA 94305-2205

REDFIELD, JOHN A(LDEN), NUCLEAR ENGINEERING. *Current Pos:* Assoc engr, 57-59, from engr to sr engr, 59-66, fel engr, 66-69, adv engr, 69-71, mgr thermal-hydraulic develop, 71-73, mgr A4W reactor eng, 73-75, mgr LWBR technol, 75-77, mgr reactor technol, 77-78, mgr advan water breeder, 78, MGR LIGHT WATER BREEDER REACTOR, BETTIS ATOMIC POWER LAB, WESTINGHOUSE ELEC CORP, 78- *Personal Data:* b Orange, NJ, Mar 18, 33; m 54; c 3. *Educ:* Univ Cincinnati, BS, 55; Univ Pittsburgh, MS, 60, PhD(chem eng), 63. *Mem:* Am Inst Chem Engrs; Am Nuclear Soc; Inst Elec & Electronics Engrs; Sigma Xi. *Res:* Heat transfer; fluid flow; systems analysis; reactor plant kinetics; dynamics of physical systems. *Mailing Add:* 2620 Quail Hill Dr Pittsburgh PA 15241-2931

REDFIELD, ROSEMARY JEANNE, EVOLUTION OF SEX, MOLECULAR EVOLUTION. *Current Pos:* ASST PROF ZOOL, UNIV BC, CAN, 90- *Personal Data:* b Vancouver, BC, Aug 26, 48. *Educ:* Monash Univ, Australia, BSc, 77; McMaster Univ, Can, 80; Stanford Univ, PhD(biol sci), 86. *Prof Exp:* Postdoctoral evol, Harvard Univ, 87; postdoctoral molecular biol, Sch Med, Johns Hopkins Univ, 88-90. *Concurrent Pos:* Scholar, Can Inst Advan Res, 90- *Mem:* Genetics Soc Am; Am Soc Microbiol. *Res:* Regulation of competence in naturally transformable bacteria; mechanisms of genetic exchange and recombination in bacteria; chromosome structure and organization; evolution of sex; deep phylogeny. *Mailing Add:* Dept Zool Univ BC Vancouver BC V6T 1Z4 Can. *Fax:* 604-822-2416; *E-Mail:* redfield@unixg.ubc.ca

REDFORD, JOHN W B, REHABILITATION MEDICINE. *Current Pos:* CONSULT, 88- *Personal Data:* b Victoria, BC, Aug 7, 28; m 54; c 6. *Educ:* Univ BC, BA, 49; Univ Toronto, MD, 53; Mayo Clin & Mayo Found, MS, 58; Am Bd Phys Med & Rehab, dipl, 62. *Prof Exp:* From instr to asst prof phys med & rehab, Sch Med, Univ Wash, 58-63; prof & chmn dept, Med Col Va, 63-67; prof rehab med & dir sch, Univ Alta, 67-72, chmn dept phys med & rehab, Univ Hosp, 67-74; prof rehab med & chmn dept, Univ Kans Med Ctr, Kansas City, 74-88. *Mem:* Am Geriat Soc; AMA; Am Acad Phys Med & Rehab; Am Cong Rehab Med; Am Asn Electrodiag. *Mailing Add:* 2231 W 63rd St Shawnee Mission KS 66208

REDGATE, EDWARD STEWART, NEUROPHYSIOLOGY, NEUROENDOCRINOLOGY. *Current Pos:* ASSOC PROF PHYSIOL, SCH MED, UNIV PITTSBURGH, 62- *Personal Data:* b Yonkers, NY, Mar 13, 25; div; c 3. *Educ:* Bethany Col, BS, 49; Univ Minn, MS, 52, PhD(physiol), 54. *Prof Exp:* Asst, Univ Minn, 49-54; instr, Western Res Univ, 57-59, asst prof physiol, 59-62. *Concurrent Pos:* Fel neurophysiol, Univ Minn, 55-56; USPHS fel, Western Res Univ, 56-57. *Mem:* Am Physiol Soc; Endocrine Soc. *Res:* Brain stem regulations; cardiovascular, respiratory and autonomic nervous systems; viscera; norepinephrine; physiology of the hypothalamus; neural control of adrenocorticotropic hormone release; interaction of hypothalamic neuropeptides; neurochemistry; polyamines and brain tumor growth. *Mailing Add:* Dept Cell Biol & Physiol Univ Pittsburgh Sch Med Pittsburgh PA 15261. *Fax:* 412-648-8330

REDHEAD, PAUL AVELING, SURFACE PHYSICS, VACUUM PHYSICS. *Current Pos:* from res officer to prin res officer, Nat Res Coun Can, 47-71, dir prog planning & anal, 70-72, dir gen planning, 72-73, dir, Div Physics, 73-86, group dir, Phys & Chem Sci Lab, 74-83, chmn, Comt Dirs, 81-86, secy, Sci & Technol Policy Comt, 86-89, EMER RESEARCHER, NAT RES COUN CAN, 89- *Personal Data:* b Brighton, Eng, May 25, 24; m 48, Doris Pickman; c Janet R (Randall) & Patricia J. *Educ:* Cambridge Univ, BA, 44, MA, 48, PhD, 69. *Honors & Awards:* Welch Award, Am Vacuum Soc, 75; Jubilee Medal, 77; Achievement in Physics Medal, Can Asn Physicists, 89. *Prof Exp:* Sci officer, Serv Electronics Res Lab, Brit Admiralty, 44-47. *Concurrent Pos:* Ed, J Vacuum Sci & Technol, 69-74; asst ed-in-chief, Can J Res, 74-87; dir, Ont Ctr Mat Res, 89-91. *Mem:* Fel Am Phys Soc; Can Asn Physicists; fel Inst Elec & Electronics Engrs; hon mem Am Vacuum Soc (pres, 68); fel Royal Soc Can. *Res:* Electron physics; chemical adsorption and interaction of electrons with adsorbed layers; vacuum physics; ion trapping; electron-plasmas. *Mailing Add:* Inst Microstruct Sci Nat Res Coun Ottawa ON K1A 0R6 Can. *Fax:* 613-990-0202

REDHEAD, SCOTT ALAN, TAXONOMY, ECOLOGY. *Current Pos:* Biologist, 77-79, res scientist, Ctr Land & Biol Resources Res, 79-85, RES SCIENTIST, EASTERN CEREAL & OIL FEED RES CTR, AGR CAN, 85- *Personal Data:* b Regina, Sask, Can, Dec 26, 50; c 4. *Educ:* Univ BC, BSc, 72, MSc, 74; Univ Toronto, PhD(mycol), 79. *Honors & Awards:* Alexopoulos Prize, Mycol Soc Am, 89. *Mem:* Mycol Soc Am; Mycol Soc Japan; Int Asn Plant Taxon; NAm Mycol Asn. *Res:* The biogeography, taxonomy, nomenclature, ecology (pathogenicity, mycorrhizal associations, symbioses and wood decay types) and the influences on human affairs (legality, toxicity, edibility, drug production) of the mushroom flora of Canada. *Mailing Add:* Eastern Cereal & Oil Feed Res Ctr Agr Can Ottawa ON K1A 0C6 Can

REDHEFFER, RAYMOND MOOS, MATHEMATICS. *Current Pos:* from instr to assoc prof, 50-60, PROF MATH, UNIV CALIF, LOS ANGELES, 60- *Personal Data:* b Chicago, Ill, Apr 17, 21; m 51; c 1. *Educ:* Mass Inst Technol, SB, 43, SM, 46, PhD(math), 48. *Hon Degrees:* DSc, Univ Karlsruhe, 91. *Honors & Awards:* Humboldt Found Sr US Scientist Award, 76 & 85. *Prof Exp:* Mem staff, Radiation Lab, Mass Inst Technol, 42-46, res assoc, Lab Electronics, 46-48; instr math, Harvard Univ, 48-50. *Concurrent Pos:* Peince fel, Harvard Univ, 48-50; NSF sr fel, Univ Gottingen, 56; Fulbright fel, Univ Vienna, 57; Fulbright res fel, Univ Hamburg, 61-62, guest prof, 66; guest lectr, Tech Univ Berlin, 62; guest prof, Univ Karlsruhe, 71-72, 81, 85 & 88. *Mem:* Math Asn Am; Am Math Soc. *Res:* Differential and integral inequalities. *Mailing Add:* Univ Calif Los Angeles CA 90095-1555

REDI, MARTHA HARPER, PLASMA PHYSICS. *Current Pos:* fel quantum chem, Princeton Univ, 76-77, vis res fel physics, 77-80, res staff mem, Dept Physics, 80, Geophys Fluid Dynamics Lab, 80-82, prof sci & eng staff mem, Plasma Physics Lab, 82-90, staff res physicist, 90-93, RES PHYSICIST, PLASMA PHYSICS LAB, PRINCETON UNIV, 93- *Personal Data:* b Bryn Mawr, Pa; m 63; c 1. *Educ:* Mass Inst Technol, BS, 64; Rutgers Univ, MS, 66, PhD(physics), 69. *Prof Exp:* Fel physics, Rutgers Univ, 69-70. *Concurrent Pos:* NIH vis res fel, 77-80. *Mem:* Am Phys Soc; AAAS; Am Geophys Union. *Res:* Transport modeling in plasma physics; oceanographic modeling; superconductivity; magnetic interactions; biophysics of electron transfer; hemaglobin action; oceanography. *Mailing Add:* Plasma Physics Lab Forrestal Campus Princeton Univ Box 451 Princeton NJ 08544

REDI, OLAV, EXPERIMENTAL ATOMIC PHYSICS. *Current Pos:* MEM FAC PHYSICS, NY UNIV, 71- *Personal Data:* b Tallinn, Estonia, May 29, 38; US citizen; m 63; c 1. *Educ:* Rensselaer Polytech Inst, BS, 60; Mass Inst Technol, PhD(physics), 65. *Prof Exp:* Res assoc physics, Princeton Univ, 64-66, from instr to asst prof, 66-71. *Mem:* Am Phys Soc. *Res:* Nuclear moments and isotope shifts; atomic level-crossing spectroscopy; optical and atomic beam hyperfine structure studies. *Mailing Add:* 124 Fisher Pl Princeton NJ 08540-6432

REDICK, MARK LANKFORD, ENDOCRINOLOGY, ELECTRON MICROSCOPY. *Current Pos:* RES ASSOC, VET ADMIN MED CTR, 86- *Personal Data:* b Seattle, Wash, Nov 30, 54. *Educ:* Southwest Mo Univ, BA; Univ Kans, PhD(anat), 85. *Mailing Add:* 448 Aberdeen Shawnee Mission KS 66205

REDICK, THOMAS FERGUSON, PHYSIOLOGY. *Current Pos:* PROF PHYSIOL & BIOL, FROSTBURG STATE COL, 66- *Personal Data:* b Youngstown, Ohio, Oct 20, 21; m 52. *Educ:* Miami Univ, BA, 48; Univ Pittsburgh, MS, 52, PhD, 55. *Prof Exp:* Asst zool, Univ Pittsburgh, 50-52; jr fel, Mellon Inst, 52-54; from instr to asst prof physiol, Sch Med, Univ Pittsburgh, assoc prof, State Univ NY, 63-66. *Concurrent Pos:* Dept HEW fel neuropharmacol, Leech Farm Vet Hosp, Pittsburgh, Pa, 62-63; vis investr, Radiobiol Lab, US Bur Fisheries, NC, 70-72; mem staff marine sci, Univ La Laguna, Spain, 71-72, res prof, 72- res fel, NASA Langley Field, 77; unicate res, La Laguna Tenerife, 84. *Mem:* Soc Syst Zool. *Res:* Mollusks; cardiovascular research; neuropharmacology in tunicates. *Mailing Add:* 54 Bealls Ln Frostburg MD 21532

REDIKER, ROBERT HARMON, ELECTRO-OPTIC DEVICES, SEMICONDUCTOR LASERS. *Current Pos:* Asst physics, Mass Inst Technol, 48-50, res assoc, 50-51, mem staff, Lincoln Lab, 51-57, asst group leader, 57-59, group leader appl physics, 59-66, prof, Dept Elec Eng, 66-76, assoc head, Optics Div, 70-72, head, Dept Elec Eng, 76-82, adj prof, Dept Elec Eng, 76-82, sr staff, Lincoln Lab, 80-91, sr res scientist, Dept Elec Eng, 82-96, RES SCIENTIST, MASS INST TECHNOL, 96-; CONSULT, 96- *Personal Data:* b Brooklyn, NY, June 7, 24; m 80, Barbara Zenn; c Richard J & Donald E. *Educ:* Mass Inst Technol, BS, 47, PhD(physics), 50. *Honors & Awards:* David Sarnoff Award, Inst Elec & Electronics Engrs, 69. *Concurrent Pos:* Res assoc, Ind Univ, 52-53; mem, Nat Acad Sci eval panel for Nat Bur Stand; sr vpres advan res & develop, Cynosure Inc, Bedford Mass, 91-96. *Mem:* Nat Acad Eng; fel Optical Soc Am; fel Inst Elec & Electronics Engrs; fel Am Phys Soc. *Res:* Solid state devices; optics; guided-wave optics; semiconductor lasers and light emitters; semiconductor devices; medical applications of semiconductor. *Mailing Add:* 151 Coolidge Ave Apt 305 Watertown MA 02172-2865. *E-Mail:* redikerbob@msn.com

REDIN, ROBERT DANIEL, THERMAL & ELECTRICAL CONDUCTIVITY. *Current Pos:* PROF PHYSICS, SDAK SCH MINES & TECHNOL, 62- *Personal Data:* b Rockford, Ill, Jan 18, 28. *Educ:* Iowa State Univ, BS, 52, MS, 55, PhD(physics), 57. *Prof Exp:* Asst physics, Iowa State Univ, 54-57; physicist, Electronics Lab, US Dept Navy, 57-62. *Mem:* Am Asn Physics Teachers; Am Phys Soc; Sigma Xi; Mat Res Soc. *Res:* Thermal conductivity in solids; semiconductors; alloys; transport properties of solids. *Mailing Add:* 1414 Clark St Rapid City SD 57701-4430

REDINBO, G ROBERT, ELECTRICAL ENGINEERING. *Current Pos:* PROF, DEPT ELEC ENG & COMPUTER SCI, UNIV CALIF, DAVIS, 84- *Personal Data:* b Lafayette, Ind, July 11, 39; m 61; c 3. *Educ:* Purdue Univ, BS, 62, MS, 66, PhD(elec eng), 70. *Prof Exp:* Instr elec eng, Purdue Univ, 65-70; asst prof, Univ Wis-Madison, 70-76; assoc prof elec & systs eng, Rensselaer Polytechnic Inst, 76- *Concurrent Pos:* Trustee, Nat Electronics, Inc, 72-; NASA-Am Soc Eng Educ fel, Goddard Space Flight Ctr, 72; NSF fel, Univ Wis, 72-73; adv comt, Inst Elec & Electronics Engrs Signal Processing Soc, 76-80. *Mem:* Inst Elec & Electronics Engrs; Asn Comput Mach; Sigma Xi. *Res:* Algebraic coding theory; communication theory; generalized transforms; digital filtering in communications systems. *Mailing Add:* Dept Elec & Comput Eng Univ Calif Davis CA 95616

REDINGER, RICHARD NORMAN, GASTROENTEROLOGY. *Current Pos:* PROF MED, DEPT MED, UNIV LOUISVILLE, 81-, ASSOC PROF DEPT BIOCHEM, 81-, VCHMN DEPT MED, 84- *Personal Data:* b E Windsor, Sandwich, Ont, Feb, 18, 38; m 65; c 4. *Educ:* Univ Western Ont, BA, 60, MD, 62; FRCP(C), 68 & 75. *Prof Exp:* Res assoc med, Sch Med, Boston Univ, 68-71; mem med staff, Univ Hosp, 72-78, dir gastrointestinal lab, 73-78; chief gastrointestinal res, Univ Hosp, 78-81, assoc prof, Dept Med, Boston Univ Med Ctr, 78-81, assoc vis physician & assoc mem, Evans Mem, 78-81. *Concurrent Pos:* Consult gastrointestinal dis, Westminster Hosp, 71-; asst prof med, Univ Western Ont, 71, assoc prof, 75-78; NIH res grant, 78-81 & 84-; chief digestive dis & nutrit, Univ Louisville, 81- *Mem:* Can Med Asn; Can Soc Clin Invest; Am Fedn Clin Res; Am Gastroenterol Asn; Am Asn Study Liver Dis; Am Soc Gastrointestinal Endoscopy; AMA. *Res:* Effects of phenobarbital and cholesterol lowering agents on biliary lipid composition and gallstone formation and/or dissolution; hepatobiliary disposal of cholesterol in baboons. *Mailing Add:* Dept Med ACB-3rd Floor Univ Louisville Sch Med 2301 S Third St Louisville KY 40292-0001

REDINGTON, CHARLES BAHR, PLANT PHYSIOLOGY, APPLIED ENVIRONMENTAL ASSESSMENTS. *Current Pos:* from asst prof to assoc prof, 69-83, PROF BIOL, SPRINGFIELD COL, 83-, DIR, ENVIRON HEALTH TECH PROG, 85- *Personal Data:* b Elyria, Ohio, Mar 20, 42; m 64; c 2. *Educ:* Baldwin-Wallace Col, BS, 64; Rutgers Univ, MS, 66, PhD(plant physiol, path), 69. *Prof Exp:* Teaching & res fel biol, Rutgers Univ, 64-66, res fel plant path, physiol, 66-69. *Concurrent Pos:* Vis prof, Western New Eng Col, 84-; consult environ biol, Baystate Environ Consults, 85-; exped leader, Springfield Col & EAfrican Safaris, Ltd, 85- *Mem:* Sigma Xi. *Res:* Use of atomic absorption spectrophotometry in assessing nutrient deficiency in bud blasting; plant communication; bomb calorimetric evaluation of factors increasing crop yield. *Mailing Add:* Bemis Hall Off 107 Springfiled Col Springfield MA 01109

REDINGTON, RICHARD LEE, PHYSICAL CHEMISTRY. *Current Pos:* from asst prof to assoc prof, 67-73, PROF CHEM, TEX TECH UNIV, 73- *Personal Data:* b Minneapolis, Minn, May 16, 33; m 57, Theresa Weinzettel; c Norman H. *Educ:* Univ Minn, BA, 55; Univ Wash, PhD(phys chem), 61. *Prof Exp:* Res fel, Mellon Inst, 61-64; asst prof chem, Utah State Univ, 64-67. *Concurrent Pos:* Vis scientist, Mass Inst Technol, 83-93. *Mem:* Am Chem Soc; Optical Soc Am; Am Phys Soc. *Res:* Molecular spectroscopy; molecular structure. *Mailing Add:* Dept Chem Tex Tech Univ Lubbock TX 79412. *Fax:* 806-742-1289; *E-Mail:* redingtn@proton.chem.ttu.edu

REDINGTON, ROWLAND WELLS, medical diagnostic imaging; deceased, see previous edition for last biography

REDISH, EDWARD FREDERICK, PHYSICS EDUCATION RESEARCH, USE OF COMPUTERS IN PHYSICS EDUCATION. *Current Pos:* Fel, Ctr Theoret Physics, Univ Md, 68-70, from asst prof to assoc prof, 70-79, chmn, Dept Physics & Astron, 82-85, PROF PHYSICS, UNIV MD, COLLEGE PARK, 79- *Personal Data:* b New York, NY, Apr 1, 42; m 67, Janice Copen; c A David & Deborah M. *Educ:* Princeton Univ, AB, 63; Mass Inst Technol, PhD(physics), 68. *Honors & Awards:* Inst Medal, Cent Res Inst Physics, Budapest, Hungary, 79; Leo Schubert Award, Wash Acad Sci, 88. *Concurrent Pos:* Vis scientist, Saclay Nuclear Res Ctr, France, 73-74; Nat Acad Sci-Nat Res Coun sr resident res assoc, Goddard Space Flight Ctr, NASA, 77-78; vis prof, Ind Univ & Cyclotron Facil, 85-86; prin investr, Md Univ, Proj Physics & Educ Technol, 85-; mem, Cyclotron Facil Prog Adv Comt, Ind Univ, 85, chmn, 86, Nuclear Sci Adv Comt, 87-89, Steering Comt, Am Phys Soc Trop Group on Few Body Syst & Multiparticle Dynamics, 87-89, chmn, 89-90; mem, Bonner Prize Comt, Div Nuclear Physics, Am Phys Soc, 88-90, chmn, 89-90; co-chair, Conf Comput Physics Instr, Raleigh, NC, 88; vis prof, Univ Wash, 92-93 & Univ Sydney, Australia, 93; mem, Int Comn Physics Educ, 93; exec comt, form educ, Am Phys Soc, 93-96; co-chair, Int Conf Undergrad Physics Educ, Col Park, Md, 96. *Mem:* Fel AAAS; Sigma Xi; fel Am Phys Soc; Am Asn Physics Teachers. *Res:* Physics education; development and testing of software for physics education; many-body quantum scattering-theory and few body problems. *Mailing Add:* Dept Physics Univ Md College Park MD 20742-4111. *Fax:* 301-314-9525; *E-Mail:* redish@quark.umd.edu

REDISH, JANICE COPEN, LINGUISTICS & PLAIN ENGLISH, USABILITY OF SOFTWARE INTERFACES. *Current Pos:* PRES, REDISH & ASSOCS, INC, 94- *Personal Data:* b Newark, NJ, Aug 12, 41; m 67, Edward F; c A David & Deborah. *Educ:* Bryn Mawr Col, AB, 63; Harvard Univ, PhD(ling), 69. *Honors & Awards:* Rigo Award, Spec Interest Group Doc, Asn Comput Mach, 96- *Prof Exp:* Res assoc, Ctr Appl Ling, 71-72, Educ Study Ctr, 72-73, Asn Renewal Educ, 75-77; res scientist, Am Inst Res, 77-79, dir, Doc Design Ctr, 79-90, vpres, 84-92. *Concurrent Pos:* Fulbright Hayes scholar Slavic ling, Univ Amsterdam, 63-64; vis lectr, George

Washington Univ, 74; vis scholar, Univ Wash, Seattle, 92-93. *Mem:* Ling Soc Am; assoc fel Soc Tech Commun; Asn Comput Mach; Asn Teachers Tech Writing; Usability Prof Asn. *Res:* Writing in the workplace; readability and usability of technical documents; development of usable software interfaces and online documentation; testing products and manuals for usability. *Mailing Add:* Redish & Assocs Inc 6820 Winterberry Lane Bethesda MD 20817. *Fax:* 301-229-2971; *E-Mail:* redish@ari.net

REDISH, KENNETH ADAIR, COMPUTER SCIENCE. *Current Pos:* ASSOC PROF COMPUT SCI & SYST, MCMASTER UNIV, 67- *Personal Data:* b London, Eng, May 6, 26; m 50; c 7. *Educ:* Univ London, BSc, 53. *Prof Exp:* Asst lectr math, Woolwich Polytech Inst Eng, 53-55; lectr, Battersea Col Adv Technol, 55-59; lectr comput, Univ Birmingham, 60-62, sr lectr, 62-67, dir comput serv, 64-67. *Mem:* Asn Comput Mach; fel Brit Comput Soc. *Res:* Numerical analysis. *Mailing Add:* Dept Comput Sci & Systs GS Rm 415A McMaster Univ 1280 Main St W Hamilton ON L8S 4L8 Can

REDLICH, FREDRICK CARL, PSYCHIATRY. *Current Pos:* EMER PROF PSYCHIAT & NEUROPSYCHIAT, YALE UNIV, 77-; MEM STAFF, NEUROPSYCHIAT INST, UNIV CALIF, LOS ANGELES, 82- *Personal Data:* b Vienna, Austria, June 2, 10; nat US; m 37, 55; c 2. *Educ:* Univ Vienna, MD, 35. *Prof Exp:* Intern, Allgem Krankenhaus, Vienna, 35-36; resident, Univ Psychiat Clin, Univ Vienna, 36-38; asst physician, State Hosp, Iowa, 38-40; resident, Neurol Unit, Boston City Hosp, 40-42; from instr to assoc prof psychiat, Sch Med, Yale Univ, 42-50, exec officer, 47-50, prof psychiat & chmn dept, 50-67, assoc provost med affairs & dean, 67-72, prof psychiat, Sch Med, 72-77, dir, Behav Sci Study Ctr, 73-77; assoc chief of staff educ, Vet Admin Med Ctr, Brentwood, 77-82. *Concurrent Pos:* Teaching fel, Harvard Med Sch, 41-42; dir, Conn Ment Health Ctr, 64-67; consult, NIMH & Off Surgeon Gen, US Army. *Mem:* Inst Med-Nat Acad Sci; Am Psychosom Soc; fel Am Psychiat Asn; Am Orthopsychiat Asn; AAAS. *Res:* Personality theory; social structure and mental disorder; scientific methodology in psychiatry. *Mailing Add:* 1529 Belair Rd Los Angeles CA 90077

REDLICH, MARTIN GEORGE, PHYSICS. *Current Pos:* res, 61-62, MEM NUCLEAR THEORY GROUP, LAWRENCE BERKELEY LAB, UNIV CALIF, 62- *Personal Data:* b Vienna, Austria, Dec 1, 28; US citizen. *Educ:* Univ Calif, Berkeley, AB, 48; Princeton Univ, PhD(physics), 54. *Prof Exp:* Res asst physics, Princeton Univ, 54; proj assoc, Univ Wis-Madison, 54-56; res assoc, Wash Univ, 56-57; res, Mass Inst Technol, 57-59. *Concurrent Pos:* NSF fel, 57-58. *Mem:* Am Phys Soc. *Res:* Theory of the structure of the nucleus. *Mailing Add:* Bldg 70A Nuclear Sci Div Univ Calif Berkeley CA 94720. *Fax:* 510-486-4794

REDLICH, ROBERT WALTER, ELECTRONICS ENGINEERING, ELECTROMAGNETISM. *Current Pos:* CONSULT, 79- *Personal Data:* b Lima, Peru, Sept 20, 28; US citizen; m 60; c 2. *Educ:* Rensselaer Polytech Inst, BS, 50, PhD(physics), 60; Mass Inst Technol, MS, 51. *Prof Exp:* Develop engr gyroscopes, Gen Elec Co, 51-52; res & develop engr inertial navig, US Army Ballistic Missiles Agency, 54-56; from asst prof to assoc prof elec eng, Clarkson Tech Univ, 60-65; sr res fel, Univ Sydney, 65-68; from assoc prof to prof, Ohio Univ, 68-75; chief engr, Gorman-Redlich Mfg Co, 74-87. *Concurrent Pos:* Adj prof, Ohio Univ, 81-85. *Mem:* Inst Elec & Electronics Engrs; NY Acad Sci; Sigma Xi. *Res:* Electromagnetic theory, especially radiation from aerials and moving charges; electronics; linear electric motors and generators; linear motion transducers; control systems. *Mailing Add:* Nine Grand Park Blvd Athens OH 45701

REDLINGER, LEONARD MAURICE, COMMODITY CHEMICAL PROTECTANTS, FUMIGATION & STORED PRODUCTS INSECTS. *Current Pos:* RETIRED. *Personal Data:* b Keota, Iowa, Dec 4, 22; m 49; c 6. *Educ:* Iowa Wesleyan Col, BS, 46; Kans State Col, MS, 47. *Honors & Awards:* Golden Peanut Res & Educ Award, USDA, 87. *Prof Exp:* Lab instr zool & cur insect collection, Iowa Wesleyan Col, 43-46; entomologist, Mosquito Control Proj, Bur Entom & Plant Quarantine, USDA, Alaska, 47, Stored-Prod Insects Sect, 48-54 & Mkt Res Div, Agr Mkt Serv, 54-56; entomologist, Pfeffer & Son Warehouse Co, Tex, 56-60; sta leader, Stored-Prod Insects Br, Mkt Qual Res Div, USDA, 60-65; leader, Peanut & Southern Corn Insects Invests, 65-73, res entomologist, Stored-Prod Insects Res & Develop Lab, Chem Control Res Unit, 73-86. *Concurrent Pos:* Secy-treas, Ga Entom Soc, 64-70, pres, 71-72, mem, bd dirs, 72-73. *Mem:* Entom Soc Am; Am Peanut Res & Educ Soc; Sigma Xi. *Res:* Applied and developmental research to improve existing and to devise new chemical methods of controlling or preventing insect infestations of post harvest agricultural commodities in the marketing channels. *Mailing Add:* 3910 Doster Rd Monroe NC 28112-9684

REDMAN, CHARLES EDWIN, BIOLOGY, STATISTICS. *Current Pos:* PRES, HCA MED RES CO, 84- *Personal Data:* b Pawtucket, RI, Aug 1, 31; m 53; c 4. *Educ:* Univ Mass, BS, 54, MS, 56; Univ Minn, PhD(statist), 60. *Prof Exp:* Sr biometrician, Eli Lilly & Co, 60-62; dept head statist, 62-64, asst head, 64-65, head statist & rec, 65-69, asst dir sci serv, 69-72, dir sci info, 72-80, dir med info systs, 80-83. *Mem:* Am Statist Asn; Biomet Soc; Drug Info Asn; Pharmaceut Mfrs Asn; Sigma Xi. *Res:* Population genetics and associated statistical design problems; design, analysis and interpretation of screening and physiology studies; clinical research management, phases I, II, III, and IV. *Mailing Add:* 4403 Charleston Pl Circle Nashville TN 37215

REDMAN, COLVIN MANUEL, BIOCHEMISTRY, MOLECULAR BIOLOGY. *Current Pos:* assoc investr, 67-70, investr, 70-76, SR INVESTR & MEM, NY BLOOD CTR, 76- *Personal Data:* b Dominican Repub, Jan 26, 35; US citizen; m 65; c 3. *Educ:* McGill Univ, BS, 57; Univ Wis-Madison, PhD(physiol chem), 62. *Prof Exp:* Fel biochem, Univ Wis-Madison, 62-63 & Rockefeller Univ, 63-65; staff fel, Addiction Res Ctr, NIMH, Ky, 65-66, res biochemist, 67. *Mem:* Am Soc Biol Chem; Am Soc Cell Biol; Harvey Soc; Am Chem Soc; Int Soc Thrombosis Halvostosis. *Res:* Membrane structure and function; kell blood group system; fibrinogen; expression and assembly. *Mailing Add:* NY Blood Ctr 310 E 67th St New York NY 10021-6295

REDMAN, DONALD ROGER, VETERINARY MEDICINE, VETERINARY SURGERY. *Current Pos:* Clin instr 62-73, from asst prof to assoc prof, 72-82, PROF PREV MED, OHIO AGR RES & DEVELOP CTR, OHIO STATE UNIV, 82- *Personal Data:* b Eaton, Ohio, Jan 21, 36; m 61; c 3. *Educ:* Ohio State Univ, BS, 58, DVM, 62, MS, 66, PhD(prev med), 73. *Mem:* Am Vet Med Asn; Int Embryo Transfer Soc; Am Asn Swine Practitioners. *Res:* Developmental and immune response of porcine fetus exposed to viral agents; reproductive efficiency of domestic animals; embryo transfer techniques; enteric diseases of neonatal calves and cryptosporidiosis in animals. *Mailing Add:* 1733 E Messner Rd Wooster OH 44691

REDMAN, ROBERT SHELTON, EMBRYOLOGY. *Current Pos:* STAFF ORAL PATHOLOGIST & CHIEF, ORAL PATH RES LAB, DEPT VET AFFAIRS MED CTR, WASHINGTON, DC, 78-; CLIN ASSOC PROF PATH, BALTIMORE COL DENT SURG, UNIV MD, BALTIMORE, 89- *Personal Data:* b Fargo, NDak, Aug 1, 35; m 58, Barbara Klug; c Melissa. *Educ:* Univ Minn, Minneapolis, BS & DDS, 59, MSD, 63; Univ Wash, PhD (exp path), 69; Am Bd Oral Maxillotarial Path, cert, 73. *Prof Exp:* First Lt-Capt, US Army Dent Corps, Ft Lewis, Wash, 59-61; clin asst prof oral diag, Sch Dent, Univ Minn, Minneapolis, 63-64; instr oral biol, Sch Dent, Univ Wash, 68-69; assoc prof oral biol, Sch Dent, Univ Minn, Minneapolis, 69-75; res oral pathologist, Vet Admin Med Ctr, Denver, Colo, 75-78. *Concurrent Pos:* Am Cancer Soc Clin fels, 62-64; Nat Inst Dent Res trainee path, Univ Wash, 64-68, Nat Inst Dent Res career develop award oral biol, 68-69; consult, Children's Orthop Hosp, Seattle, Wash, 66-69; Nat Inst Dent Res career develop award, Sch Dent, Univ Minn, Minneapolis, 71-75; assoc prof oral biol, Sch Dent, Univ Colo Med Ctr, Denver, 75-78; Vet Admin Res Career Prog Clin Investr, Vet Admin Med Ctr, Denver Colo, 76-78; prog chmn, Salivary Res Group, Int Asn Dent Res, 82-86; prog spec oral biol, Vet Admin Dept Med Surg, 83-87; prof lectr oral path, Georgetown Univ, Sch Dent, Washington, DC, 86-88; secy-treas, Salivary Res Group, Int, Asn Dent Res, 95-; adj sci, Nat Inst Dent Res, NIH, Bethesda, Mdd, 97- *Mem:* Am Dent Asn; fel Am Acad Oral Path; Int Asn Dent Res; Am Inst Nutrit; Soc Invitro Biol. *Res:* Salivary gland growth and development; morphogenesis of salivary gland neoplasms; etiology of tongue diseases; etiology of dental caries; experimental carcinogenesis; gene transfer; cell culture. *Mailing Add:* 12425 Bobbink Ct Potomac MD 20854-3005. *Fax:* 202-462-2006

REDMAN, WILLIAM CHARLES, REACTOR PHYSICS, MAGNETOHYDRODYNAMICS. *Current Pos:* RETIRED. *Personal Data:* b Washington, DC, June 19, 23; m 48, Eileen Keenan; c Timothy, Brian & Marilyn. *Educ:* Georgetown Univ, BS, 43; Yale Univ, MS, 47, PhD(physics), 49. *Prof Exp:* Jr physicist, Dept Terrestrial Magnetism, Carnegie Inst & Nat Bur Standards, 43; asst instr physics, Yale Univ, 43-44; jr physicist, Manhattan Dist, Argonne Nat Lab, Univ Chicago, 44-46; asst instr physics, Yale Univ, 47-48; assoc physicist, Argonne Nat Lab, 49-54; pres, Fournier Inst Technol, 54-55; assoc physicist, Argonne Nat Lab, 55-59, sr physicist, 59-63, assoc dir, Appl Physics Div, 63-72, sr physicist, 72-74, dep dir Energy Conversion Progs, 74-85, consult, Energy Systs, 85-87. *Concurrent Pos:* Lectr, Fournier Inst Technol, 52-54. *Mem:* Fel Am Phys Soc; fel Am Nuclear Soc. *Res:* Physics of neutrons and nuclear reactors; instrumentation; environmental planning and impact, and energy conversion systems; atomic and molecular physics. *Mailing Add:* 608-S Monroe St Hinsdale IL 60521

REDMANN, ROBERT EMANUEL, PLANT ECOLOGY, PHYSIOLOGICAL PLANT ECOLOGY. *Current Pos:* From asst prof to assoc prof, 68-78, PROF PLANT ECOL, UNIV SASK, 78- *Personal Data:* b Jamestown, NDak, Nov 24, 41; m 63, Elaine Mayer; c John, Jennifer, Susan & Paul. *Educ:* Univ NDak, BA, 64; Univ Ill, Urbana, MS & PhD(bot), 68. *Concurrent Pos:* Vis assoc prof, Utah State Univ, 77-78; exchange scientist, Czech Acad Sci, 78; adj prof, Mont State Univ, 84; vis prof, NE Norm Univ, Changchun, People's Repub China, 85. *Mem:* Sigma Xi; Ecol Soc Am; Soc Range Mgt. *Res:* Grassland ecology; plant carbon dioxide exchange; plant water relations; salt tolerance in plants; pollution ecology. *Mailing Add:* Dept Crop Sci & Plant Ecol Univ Sask 51 Campus Dr Saskatoon SK S7N 5A8 Can

REDMON, JOHN KING, ELECTRICAL ENGINEERING, POWER. *Current Pos:* CONSULT EDUC, REDMON ASSOCS, 81- *Personal Data:* b Lexington, Ky, Nov 4, 20; m 67, Emilie E Monroe; c John R, Alan L, Martha L (Cureton) (deceased), Carol A (Northup) & Carl K Monroe. *Educ:* Newark Col Eng, BS, 42; Stevens Inst Technol, MS, 49; Worcester Polytech Inst, MS, 70. *Prof Exp:* Sales engr, Westinghouse Elec Corp, 45-51, consult & appln engr, 53-60; from asst prof to assoc prof elec eng, Newark Col Eng, 60-70; assoc adminr, Pa Power & Light Co, 70-81; prof, Grad Sch, Lehigh Univ, 70-82. *Concurrent Pos:* Consult, Pub Serv Elec & Gas Co, 61-66; adj prof, Northampton Co Area Community Col, 75-85. *Mem:* Inst Elec & Electronics Engrs; Am Soc Eng Educ. *Res:* Application of power equipment to industrial use; electrical distribution and lightning protection; power systems and circuit analysis. *Mailing Add:* 325 N Cool Spring St Fayetteville NC 28301-5160

REDMON, MICHAEL JAMES, PHYSICAL CHEMISTRY, ATOMIC PHYSICS. *Current Pos:* PRES, CALVERT INST, 90- *Personal Data:* b Long Beach, Calif, Oct 3, 41; m 75. *Educ:* Fla State Univ, BS, 63; Rollins Col, MS, 68; Univ Fla, PhD(chem), 73. *Prof Exp:* Res engr physics, Orlando Div, Martin Co, 63-67; asst prof, Valdosta State Col, 67-73; res assoc chem, Univ Tex, Austin, 74-77; res scientist chem physics, Columbus Labs, Battelle Mem Inst, 77-80; at Chem Dynamics Corp, 80-90. *Concurrent Pos:* Res asst, Univ Fla, 68-74; Robert Welch Found fel, 75. *Mem:* Am Phys Soc; Am Chem Soc. *Res:* Atomic and molecular collisions; quantum chemistry; chemical physics. *Mailing Add:* 732 Lazy River Red Lusby MD 20657

REDMOND, BILLY LEE, ENTOMOLOGY, ELECTRON MICROSCOPY. *Current Pos:* from asst prof to assoc prof, 73-87, PROF BIOL, STATE UNIV NY NEW PALTZ, 87-, DIR, ELECTRON MICROS LAB, 77- *Personal Data:* b Franklin, Tenn, May 25, 42. *Educ:* Univ Tenn, Martin, BS, 64; Univ Ill, Urbana, MS, 67; Cornell Univ, PhD(zool), 71. *Prof Exp:* Lab instr zool, Univ Tenn, Martin, 64-65; NIH fel entom & zool, Ohio State Univ, 71-72; asst prof gen biol & anat, Otterbein Col, 72-73. *Concurrent Pos:* Ed, NAm Registry Electron Micros Courses, 80- *Mem:* Electron Micros Soc Am; Entom Soc Am; Acarological Soc Am; Sigma Xi; Nat Sci Teachers Asn. *Res:* Developmental morphology and fine structure of tissues, especially those of the arthropods; electron microscopy. *Mailing Add:* Dept Biol State Univ NY 75 S Manheim Blvd New Paltz NY 12561-2400

REDMOND, DONALD EUGENE, JR, BIOLOGICAL PSYCHIATRY, NEUROPHARMACOLOGY. *Current Pos:* from asst prof to assoc prof, 74-87, PROF, MED SCH, YALE UNIV, 87-, HEAD, NEUROBEHAV LAB, 85- *Personal Data:* b San Antonio, Tex, June 17, 39. *Educ:* Southern Methodist Univ, BA, 61; Baylor Col Med, MD, 68; Am Bd Psychiat & Neurol, cert, 77. *Hon Degrees:* MA, Yale Univ, 87. *Honors & Awards:* Res Found Kent Prize, Am Psychiat Asn, 81. *Prof Exp:* Intern, Ben Taub Hosp, 68-69; resident res, Ill State Psychiat Inst, 69-72; clin assoc, NIMH, 72-74. *Concurrent Pos:* Falk fel, Am Psychiat Asn, 70-71; mem fac biol sci training grant, NIH, 74-; Guggenheim Found grant, 77-85; NIMH grant, 78- & Nat Inst Drug Abuse grant, 79-86; career develop award, Nat Inst Drug Abuse, 80-85; career res scientist, NIMH, 86-, prog dir, neural grafts prog proj, 86-89. *Mem:* Am Psychiat Asn; Am Psychosomatic Med Soc; Soc Neurosci; Am Soc Primatologists; Am Col Neuropsychopharmacol. *Res:* Biology of depression, anxiety, opioid drugs; two neurochemically defined brain systems, norepinephrine and dopamine; role of central norepinephrine in anxiety and drug-withdrawal syndromes; the dopamine system work aims to determine the causes of Parkinson's disease and possible treatment using transplanted brain dopamine cells; growth factors; gene therapy; transplantation and regeneration. *Mailing Add:* PO Box 208068 New Haven CT 06520-8068

REDMOND, DONALD MICHAEL, MATHEMATICS, NUMBER THEORY. *Current Pos:* Asst prof, 77-83, ASSOC PROF MATH, SOUTHERN ILL UNIV, 83- *Personal Data:* b San Francisco, Calif, Feb 5, 48; m 77, Charlotte Keller. *Educ:* Univ Santa Clara, BS, 70; Univ Ill, MS, 73, PhD(math), 76. *Mem:* Am Math Soc; Math Asn Am; Sigma Xi; Nat Coun Teachers Math. *Res:* Analytic number theory, particularly the properties of Dirichlet series satisfy functional equation involving gamma factors. *Mailing Add:* Dept Math Neckers A 0259 Southern Ill Univ Carbondale IL 62901-4408

REDMOND, DOUGLAS ROLLEN, FORESTRY. *Current Pos:* RETIRED. *Personal Data:* b Upper Musquodoboit, NS, Aug 30, 18; m 43; c 4. *Educ:* Univ NB, BScF, 49; Yale Univ, MF, 50, PhD(forest path), 54. *Honors & Awards:* Fernow Award, Am Forestry Asn, 75. *Prof Exp:* Prov forest pathologist, NS, 50-51; officer chg forest path invests, Sci Serv, Can Dept Agr, 51-57; chief forest res div, Forestry Br, Dept Northern Affairs & Nat Resources, 57-60; dir forest res br, Dept Forestry, 60-65, sci adv, 65-69, dir forestry rels, Dept Fisheries & Forestry, 69-71; dir forestry rels, Dept Environ, 71-75, dir, Nat Forestry Insts, 75-79; consult forestry, 79-90. *Concurrent Pos:* Hon lectr, Univ NB, 51-57; mem permanent comt, Int Union Forest Res Orgn, 61-71, vpres, 72-76. *Mem:* Can Inst Forestry (pres, 78-79); hon mem Int Union Forest Res Orgn; Can Forestry Asn (pres, 80-82). *Res:* Forest ecology. *Mailing Add:* 643 Tillbury Ave Ottawa ON K2A 0Z9 Can

REDMOND, JAMES RONALD, COMPARATIVE PHYSIOLOGY. *Current Pos:* RETIRED. *Personal Data:* b Ohio, July 14, 28; m 49; c Cleve & Jill. *Educ:* Univ Cincinnati, BS, 49; Univ Calif, Los Angeles, PhD(zool), 54. *Prof Exp:* Asst prof biol, Univ Fla, 56-62; assoc prof, Iowa State Univ, 62-67, actg chmn, 83-84, prof zool, 67-93. *Concurrent Pos:* Chief scientist, Alpha Helix Nautilus Expedition, 74. *Mem:* Fel AAAS; Am Soc Zoologists; Sigma Xi. *Res:* Blood pigments; circulatory and respiratory physiology of invertebrates. *Mailing Add:* 4907 Utah Dr Ames IA 50014

REDMOND, JOHN PETER, PLASTICS CHEMISTRY. *Current Pos:* res assoc, Res Div, Amp, Inc, 69-73, mgr, Plastics Lab, 79, Anal Lab, 83, SR RES ASSOC, AMP, INC, 76-, MGR SPEC PRODS. *Personal Data:* b Camden, NJ, Aug 1, 25; m 50; c 6. *Educ:* Cath Univ Am, BS, 50, MS, 55; Pa State Univ, PhD(fuel tech), 59. *Prof Exp:* Phys chemist, Chem Div, US Naval Res Lab, 51-55; asst, Pa State Univ, 55-59; sr chemist, Appl Physics Lab, Johns Hopkins Univ, 59-65; sr scientist, Gen Tech Corp, 65-66; res dir & vpres, Commonwealth Sci Corp, 66-69. *Mem:* Am Chem Soc; Soc Plastics Engrs. *Res:* Chemical kinetics; vapor deposition; plastics, injection and transfer molding; rheology studies; resin selection and compounding for electronic industry; electrical connector development; 15 patents. *Mailing Add:* 750 Boros Rd Southport NC 28461-9770

REDMOND, ROBERT F(RANCIS), NUCLEAR ENGINEERING, ENERGY CONVERSION. *Current Pos:* prof nuclear eng & chmn dept,70-77, ASSOC DEAN, COL ENG, OHIO STATE UNIV, 77-, DIR ENG EXP STA, 77-, ACTG DEAN, 90- *Personal Data:* b Indianapolis, Ind, July 15, 27; m 52; c 5. *Educ:* Purdue Univ, BS, 50; Univ Tenn, MS, 55; Ohio State Univ, PhD(physics), 61. *Prof Exp:* Engr, Oak Ridge Nat Lab, 50-53; fel, Anal Physics Div, Battelle Mem Inst, 53-70. *Concurrent Pos:* Mem bd trustees, Argonne Univs Asn, 72-80; mem, Ohio Power Siting Comn, 78-82; mem bd dir, Nat Regulatory Res Inst, 87-, Edison Welding Inst, 87-; pres & mem bd dirs, TRC, Inc, 90- *Mem:* Am Nuclear Soc; Am Soc Eng Educ; AAAS. *Res:* Nuclear and reactor physics and engineering; research engineering. *Mailing Add:* 4621 Nugent Dr Columbus OH 43220

REDMORE, DEREK, ORGANIC CHEMISTRY. *Current Pos:* res chemist, Petrolite Corp, 65-67, sect leader, 67-76, sect mgr org chem, Tretolite Div, 76-90, dir technol support, 90-93, VPRES TECHNOL, PETROLITE CORP, 93- *Personal Data:* b Horncastle, Eng, Aug 8, 38; m 65; c 2. *Educ:* Univ Nottingham, BSc, 59, PhD(org chem), 62. *Honors & Awards:* St Louis Award, Am Chem Soc, 82. *Prof Exp:* Res assoc chem, Wash Univ, 62-65. *Mem:* Am Chem Soc; Royal Soc Chem; AAAS. *Res:* Organic, organophosphorus, alicyclic and heterocyclic chemistry. *Mailing Add:* 300 Park Rd St Louis MO 63119-2533

REDMOUNT, IAN H, GRAVITATION THEORY, COSMOLOGY. *Current Pos:* ASST PROF SCI & MATH, PARKS COL, ST LOUIS UNIV, 93- *Personal Data:* b New York, NY, Sept 25, 56; m 96, Hisako Matsuo. *Educ:* Mich State Univ, BS, 78; Calif Inst Technol, MS, 81, PhD(physics), 84. *Prof Exp:* Fel, Harvard Col Observ, Harvard Univ, 83-86; res assoc, Inst Astron, Univ Cambridge, 86-89, McDonnell Ctr Space Sci & Dept Physics, Washington Univ, St Louis, 89-91, Dept Physics, Univ Wis-Milwaukee, 91-93. *Concurrent Pos:* Assoc, Dept Physics, Harvard Univ, 83-86; vis res fel, Res Inst Fundamental Physics, Kyoto Univ, Japan, 84-85; assoc lectr physics, Univ Wis-Milwaukee, 93; adj asst prof, Dept Physics, Washington Univ, St Louis, 94- *Mem:* Am Phys Soc; Am Astron Soc; Sigma Xi; NY Acad Sci; Math Asn Am. *Res:* Classical and quantum gravitation theory; black-hole physics, cosmological structure, particle physics in curved spacetime and the quantum dynamics of spacetime geometry. *Mailing Add:* Dept Sci & Math Parks Col St Louis Univ PO Box 56907 St Louis MO 63156-0907. *Fax:* 314-977-8390; *E-Mail:* redmount@hypatia.slu.edu

REDMOUNT, MELVIN B(ERNARD), CHEMICAL ENGINEERING, ECONOMICS. *Current Pos:* PRES, MBR ASSOCS, 88- *Personal Data:* b Lakewood, Pa, Oct 11, 26; m 52, Florence Schweitzer; c Esther, Ian & Joel J. *Educ:* Pa State Univ, BChE, 48; Polytech Inst Brooklyn, MChE, 52. *Prof Exp:* Chem engr, Develop Dept, Tidewater Oil Co, 51-53; group leader & res chem engr, Columbia Univ, 53-57; resident supvr develop, Speer Carbon Co, 57-64, resident mgr develop, 64-66, mgr new prod com develop, 66-70, mgr planning, Airco Speer Carbon-Graphite Div, Boc Group, Inc, 70-74, dir planning, 74-88. *Mem:* Am Chem Soc; Am Inst Mining, Metall & Petrol Engrs. *Res:* Carbon; graphite; high temperature materials; continuous fermentation; minerals processing; economics analyses. *Mailing Add:* 310 Jackson Ave Ridgway PA 15853-1916

REDNER, SIDNEY, PHYSICS, THEORETICAL PHYSICS. *Current Pos:* Vis asst prof, Boston Univ, 78-79, from asst prof to assoc prof, 79-89, assoc chmn 92-94, PROF PHYSICS, BOSTON UNIV, 89-, ASSOC CHMN, 92-94 & 96- *Personal Data:* b Hamilton, Can, Nov 10, 51; m 77, Anita Zetlan; c Gabriel & Rebecca. *Educ:* Univ Calif, Berkeley, AB, 72; Mass Inst Technol, PhD(physics), 77. *Concurrent Pos:* Fel, Univ Toronto, 77-78; vis scientist, Schlumberger-Doll Res, 84-85. *Mem:* Am Phys Soc. *Res:* Chemical kinetics, phase transitions and critical phenomena; percolation theory; polymers; computer simulations. *Mailing Add:* Dept Physics Boston Univ Boston MA 02215. *Fax:* 617-353-9393; *E-Mail:* redner@buphyk.bu.edu

REDO, SAVERIO FRANK, SURGERY, PEDIATRIC SURGERY. *Current Pos:* From intern to resident surg, 50-57, asst attend surgeon, 59-60, ASSOC ATTEND SURGEON & DIR DEPT PEDIAT SURG, NY HOSP, 60-; PROF SURG, MED COL, CORNELL UNIV, 73- *Personal Data:* b Brooklyn, NY, Dec 28, 20; m 48, Maria Lappano; c Philip & Martha. *Educ:* Queens Col, NY, BS, 42; Cornell Univ, MD, 50; Am Bd Surg & Am Bd Thoracic Surg, dipl. *Concurrent Pos:* Ledyard fel, NY Hosp, 57-59; asst prof surg, Med Col, Cornell Univ, 59-61, clin assoc prof, 61- *Mem:* Soc Univ Surg; fel Am Col Surg; Am Acad Pediat; Am Fedn Clin Res; Am Surg Asn; Sigma Xi. *Res:* Etiology and methods of surgical management of peptic esophagitis and esophageal pathology; cardiovascular research, including development of an artificial heart and procedures for myocardial revascularization. *Mailing Add:* Dept Surg 525 E 68th St New York NY 10021

REDONDO, ANTONIO, SURFACE SCIENCE. *Current Pos:* STAFF MEM, LOS ALAMOS NAT LAB, 83- *Personal Data:* b Guatemala City, Guatemala, Dec 10, 48; US & Span citizen; m 71, Shelby Dinteman; c Tomas, Michael & Rebecca. *Educ:* Utah State Univ, BSc, 71; Calif Inst Technol, MSc, 72, PhD(appl physics), 77. *Prof Exp:* Asst prof physics & surface sci, Univ Los Andes, Merida, Venezuela, 77-80; vis assoc, 80-81, res assoc chem, Calif Inst Technol, 81-83. *Mem:* Am Phys Soc; Am Chem Soc. *Res:* Applications of quantum mechanics to the study of surfaces, interfaces and solids. *Mailing Add:* Los Alamos Nat Lab Mail Stop B268 Los Alamos NM 87545. *E-Mail:* redondo@lanl.gov

REDSHAW, PEGGY ANN, MICROBIAL GENETICS. *Current Pos:* PROF BIOL, AUSTIN COL, 79- *Personal Data:* b Beardstown, Ill, Sept 4, 48; m 85, Jerry B Lincecum. *Educ:* Quincy Col, BS, 70; Ill State Univ, PhD(biol sci), 74. *Prof Exp:* Fel microbiol, Sch Med, St Louis Univ, 74-77; asst prof biol, Wilson Col, 77-79. *Concurrent Pos:* Primary researcher, Cottrell Col Sci grant, Res Corp, 78-83; mem, Action/Adv Comt, Proj Kaleidoscope, 91- Undergrad Educ Task Area, Bd Educ & Training, Am Soc Microbiol, 92-95. *Mem:* Am Soc Microbiol; AAAS; Coun Undergrad Res; Asn Biol Lab Educ. *Res:* Genetics of streptomyces; isozyme analysis of ferns. *Mailing Add:* Dept Biol Austin Col 900 N Grand Sherman TX 75090-4440. *E-Mail:* predshaw@austinc.edu

REDWINE, ROBERT PAGE, NUCLEAR PHYSICS, PARTICLE PHYSICS. *Current Pos:* from asst prof to assoc prof, 79-90, PROF PHYSICS, MASS INST TECHNOL, 90-, DIR, LAB NUCLEAR SCI, 92- *Personal Data:* b Raleigh, NC, Dec 3, 47; m 86; c 2. *Educ:* Cornell Univ, BA, 69; Northwestern Univ, PhD(physics), 73. *Prof Exp:* Res assoc physics, Los Alamos Sci Lab, 73-74 & Univ Bern, 74-75; res assoc, Los Alamos Sci Lab, 75-77; staff scientist, 77-79. *Mem:* Am Phys Soc; AAAS. *Res:* Intermediate energy nuclear and particle physics. *Mailing Add:* Dept Physics Mass Inst Technol Cambridge MA 02139. *Fax:* 617-253-0111; *E-Mail:* redwine@mitlns.mit.edu

REDWOOD, R(ICHARD) G(EORGE), CIVIL ENGINEERING, STRUCTURAL ENGINEERING. *Current Pos:* from asst prof to assoc prof, 65-70, chmn, 84-89, PROF CIVIL ENG, MCGILL UNIV, 74- *Personal Data:* b Dorset, Eng, May 1, 36; Can citizen; m 68; c 2. *Educ:* Bristol Univ, BSc, 57, PhD(civil eng), 64; Univ Toronto, MASc, 60. *Prof Exp:* Asst engr, Shawinigan Eng Co, 57-58 & W S Atkins & Assoc, 58-59; lectr civil eng, Bristol Univ, 64-65. *Mem:* Fel Can Soc Civil Eng; fel Brit Inst Struct Eng; Brit Inst Civil Eng. *Res:* Structural engineering; behaviour and design of metal structures; seismic response. *Mailing Add:* Dept Civil Eng McGill Univ 817 Sherbrooke St W Montreal PQ H3A 2K6 Can

REE, BUREN RUSSEL, ORGANIC CHEMISTRY. *Current Pos:* Sr res chemist, 69-73, RES SPECIALIST, 3M CO, 73- *Personal Data:* b Bentley, Alta, Feb 15, 43; m 66; c 1. *Educ:* Univ Alta, BSc, 64; Univ Ill, MS, 66, PhD(chem), 69. *Mem:* Am Chem Soc. *Res:* Molecular weight modification in vinyl polymers. *Mailing Add:* 1790 Neal Ave N Stillwater MN 55082-1704

REE, FRANCIS H, CHEMICAL PHYSICS. *Current Pos:* RES PHYSICIST, LAWRENCE LIVERMORE LAB, UNIV CALIF, 60- *Personal Data:* b Kyoto, Japan, Sept 6, 36; US citizen; m 68, Clara U; c Christina Y & Peter Y. *Educ:* Univ Utah, BA, 57, PhD(physics), 60. *Mem:* Am Phys Soc; Biophys Soc. *Res:* Classical statistical mechanics, thermodynamics; theoretical studies on thermodynamic and statistical mechanical properties of gases, liquids and solids; high pressure physics; quantum chemistry. *Mailing Add:* Lawrence Livermore Lab Univ Calif L-299 PO Box 808 Livermore CA 94550

REE, WILLIAM O(SCAR), CIVIL ENGINEERING. *Current Pos:* RETIRED. *Personal Data:* b South Milwaukee, Wis, Mar 13, 13; m 48, Mary E James; c William O Jr. *Educ:* Univ Wis, BS, 35. *Honors & Awards:* Hancor Award, Am Soc Agr Engrs, 92. *Prof Exp:* Draftsman, Bucyrus Erie Co, Wis, 29-31; draftsman, Soil Conserv Serv, USDA, 35-37, jr engr, SC, 37-38, proj supvr, 38-41, proj supvr, Okla, 41-54, proj supvr, Agr Res Serv, 54-64, res invest leader, 64-75; hydraul eng consult, 75-78. *Mem:* Am Soc Agr Engrs; Am Soc Civil Engrs. *Res:* Hydraulics; hydraulics of conservation structures, hydrology and sedimentology. *Mailing Add:* 2015 W Tenth Stillwater OK 74074

REEBER, ROBERT RICHARD, MATERIALS ENGINEERING, MINERAL PHYSICS. *Current Pos:* MAT ENGR, ARMY RES OFF, 81- *Personal Data:* b Flushing, NY, Jan 22, 37; m 72, Waltraud Brendt; c Ursula F, Andrew B, Meri K & Joy E. *Educ:* NY Univ, BE, 58, MS, 60; Ohio State Univ, PhD(indust mineral), 68. *Prof Exp:* Mat engr transistors, Radio Corp Am, Somerville, Mass, 59-60; mat engr ceramics, Aerospace Res Labs, 60-63, vis res assoc phase transformations, 63-69; asst prof mat sci, Mich State Univ, 69-70; asst prof metall eng, Arya-Mehr Indust Univ, 70-71; res assoc crystallog, T H Aachen, 72-73; sr res asst mineral, Cambridge Univ, 73-74; prog mgr geochem eng, Dept Energy, 76-81. *Concurrent Pos:* Adj asst prof, Mich State Univ, 71-73; sr res Fulbright, Inst Crystallog, T H Aachen, Ger, 72; vis sr researcher, Electron Micros Inst, Fritz Haber Inst Max Planck Soc, Berlin, 75, 86; vis researcher, Inorg Mat Div, Nat Bur Stand, 78-80; joint adj assoc prof geol & physics, Univ NC-Chapel Hill, 83-89, adj prof geol, 90-97; adj prof mat sci, NC State Univ, 96- *Mem:* Fel AAAS; Mat Res Soc; Mineral Soc Am; Am Ceramic Soc; Am Crystallog Asn; Am Geophys Union. *Res:* Crystal chemistry; thermal expansion; phase transformations in solids; materials engineering; research management; thermophysical properties of materials at high temperatures/pressures; theory of materials. *Mailing Add:* Army Res Off PO Box 12211 Research Triangle Park NC 27709-2211. *Fax:* 919-549-4399; *E-Mail:* reeber@aro.ncren.net

REEBURGH, WILLIAM SCOTT, CHEMICAL OCEANOGRAPHY, BIOGEOCHEMISTRY & METHANE GEOCHEMISTRY. *Current Pos:* PROF EARTH SYST SCI, UNIV CALIF, IRVINE, 93- *Personal Data:* b Port Arthur, Tex, Feb 25, 40; m 63, Carelyn Yerkes; c Scott L, Nancy E & Peter W. *Educ:* Univ Okla, BS, 61; Johns Hopkins Univ, MA, 64, PhD(oceanog), 67. *Prof Exp:* Res asst, Chesapeake Bay Inst, Johns Hopkins Univ, 61-67, res staff asst, 67-68; from asst prof to prof marine sci, Univ Alaska, 68-93. *Mem:* Am Chem Soc; Geochem Soc; Am Soc Limnol & Oceanog; Am Soc Microbiol; Am Geophys Union; Sigma Xi. *Res:* Physical and chemical properties of sea water; gases in natural waters; composition of interstitial waters, microbial ecology, marine and terrestrial methane biogeochemistry. *Mailing Add:* Dept Earth Syst Sci Univ Calif Irvine CA 92697-3100. *Fax:* 714-824-3256; *E-Mail:* reeburgh@uci.edu

REECE, JOE WILSON, MECHANICAL ENGINEERING, APPLIED MATHEMATICS. *Current Pos:* PRES, REECE ENG ASSOC, 70- *Personal Data:* b Elkin, NC, Mar 1, 35; m 55, 92, Ellen Miller; c James T, Joel W & Joe W Jr. *Educ:* NC State Univ, BSNE, 57, MS, 61; Univ Fla, PhD(eng mech), 63. *Prof Exp:* Instr eng mech, NC State Univ, 58-61; from asst prof to prof mech eng, Auburn Univ, 64-83. *Concurrent Pos:* Prof eng, Surry Comm Col, 73-97; Dep dir, Div Oper Reactors, US Nuclear Regulatory Comn, 76-78; consult combustion eng, US Army, E I du Pont de Nemours & Co, US Nuclear Regulatory Comn & Westinghouse. *Mem:* Soc Eng Educ; Am Soc Mech Engrs. *Res:* Inviscid unsteady flow; steam generator mechanics; reactor hydraulics. *Mailing Add:* 402 North Carolina Ave Boonville NC 27011

REECE, ROBERT WILLIAM, ZOOLOGY. *Current Pos:* DIR ZOOL, WILD ANIMAL HABITAT, 77; EXEC DIR, WILD INT CTR PRESERV WILD ANIMALS, 92- *Personal Data:* b Saginaw, Mich, Jan 21, 42; m 65, Jill Whetstone; c William C, Gregory S & Mark A. *Educ:* Mich State Univ, BS, 64. *Prof Exp:* Fel, Univ Western Fla, 69-71, Univ SFla, 71-74; dir, NW Fla Zool Gardens, Pensacola, 70-72; zool dir, Lion Co Ga, 72-73; asst dir, Salisbury Zoo, 76-77. *Concurrent Pos:* Assoc ed, Sci J Zool Biol, 82-; prof fel, Am Asn Zool Parks & Aquariums. *Mem:* Am Soc Mammalogists; Am Behav Soc; Int Union Conserv Nature & Natural Resources. *Res:* Zoological administration. *Mailing Add:* The Wilds Inc 14000 Int Rd Cumberland OH 43732-9500

REECK, GERALD RUSSELL, BIOCHEMISTRY. *Current Pos:* asst prof, 74-78, assoc prof biochem, 78-, PROF BIOCHEM, KANS STATE UNIV, MANHATTAN, KANS. *Personal Data:* b Tacoma, Wash, Dec 28, 45; m 67; c 2. *Educ:* Seattle Pac Col, Wash, BA, 67; Univ Wash, PhD(biochem), 71. *Prof Exp:* Res assoc develop biochem, Lab Nutrit & Endocrinol, Nat Inst Arthritis, Metab & Digestive Dis, NIH, Bethesda, Md, 71-74. *Mem:* Am Chem Soc. *Res:* Structure and function of chromatin proteins, especially the nonhistone chromatin proteins; trypsin inhibitors. *Mailing Add:* Dept Biochem 104 Willard Hall Kans State Univ Manhattan KS 66506-3702

REED, A THOMAS, INORGANIC CHEMISTRY. *Current Pos:* MEM STAFF, DEPT CHEM, MIAMI UNIV, OXFORD, 76- *Personal Data:* b Anderson, Ind, Apr 10, 46. *Educ:* Ball State Univ, Ind, BS, 69. *Prof Exp:* Asst city chemist, Anderson Munic Water Works, Anderson, Ind, 65-69; NSF grant chem, Univ Nebr, Lincoln, 75-76. *Mem:* Am Chem Soc; Am Crystallog Asn; Sigma Xi. *Res:* Crystal and molecular structure of metal-dicarboxylate including the synthesis of compounds, growth of single crystals and x-ray determination. *Mailing Add:* 2633 McLain Ct Grove City OH 43123-2699

REED, ALLAN HUBERT, ELECTROCHEMISTRY, ELECTRODEPOSITION. *Current Pos:* SR RES ELECTROCHEMIST, TECHNIC INC, 90- *Personal Data:* b Youngstown, Ohio, Jan 4, 41; m 66, Rose Ogden; c David M & Michael S. *Educ:* Thiel Col, AB, 63; Case Western Reserve Univ, MS, 64, PhD(phys chem), 68. *Prof Exp:* Res asst phys chem, Case Western Reserve Univ, 66-68; res chemist, Columbus Labs, Battelle Mem Inst, 68-73; eng scientist res div, AMP, Inc, 73-81; res mgr, Electrochem Inc, 81-90. *Mem:* Electrochem Soc; Am Chem Soc; Am Electroplaters Soc; Sigma Xi. *Res:* Electrode processes; electrodeposition of precious metals; electroless plating; high-rate electrochemical processes; electroforming; batteries; electrochemical synthesis. *Mailing Add:* 27 Lillian Ct Warwick RI 02886

REED, BRENT C, INSULIN RECEPTOR METABOLISM, PROTEIN TRAFFICKING. *Current Pos:* ASSOC PROF BIOCHEM, DEPT BIOCHEM & MOLECULAR BIOL, MED CTR, LA STATE UNIV, 88- *Educ:* Univ Utah, PhD(biochem), 76. *Prof Exp:* Asst prof biochem, Health Sci Ctr, Univ Tex, 80-88. *Mailing Add:* Dept Biochem & Molecular Biol La State Univ 1501 Kings Hwy Shreveport LA 71130-3922

REED, CHARLES ALLEN, AGRICULTURAL ORIGINS. *Current Pos:* actg head dept, 67-70, prof, 67-80, EMER PROF ANTHROP, UNIV ILL, CHICAGO, 80- *Personal Data:* b Portland, Ore, June 6, 12; m 51; c 3. *Educ:* Univ Ore, BS, 37; Univ Calif, PhD(zool), 43. *Honors & Awards:* Archaeol Inst Am Sci Contrib Archaeol, 85. *Prof Exp:* Instr zool, Univ Ore, 36-37; asst, Univ Calif, 37-42, asst anat, Med Sch, 43; instr biol, Reed Col, 43-46; from instr to asst prof zool, Univ Ariz, 46-49; from asst prof to assoc prof, Col Pharm, Univ Ill, 49-61; assoc prof biol, Yale Univ & cur mammal & herpet, Peabody Mus, 61-66; prof anthrop & biol sci, Univ Ill, Chicago, 66-67. *Concurrent Pos:* Mem, Univ Ore Archaeol Exped, Catlow Caves, 37, John Day Archaeol Exped, 46 & Univ Chicago Oriental Inst Prehist Proj, Iraq, 54-55, Iran, 60 & Turkey, 70; dir, Yale Prehist Exped, Nubia, 62-65; res assoc vert anat, Field Mus, 66- *Mem:* AAAS; Am Asn Phys Anthropologists; Am Anthrop Asn; Am Soc Zoologists; Soc Vert Paleont; Sigma Xi. *Res:* Origins of agriculture, human evolution; evolutionary anatomy; prehistory of Near East. *Mailing Add:* Dept Anthrop Univ Ill 1007 W Harrison M/C 027 Chicago IL 60607

REED, CHARLES E(LI), chemistry, chemical engineering; deceased, see previous edition for last biography

REED, CHARLES E, INTERNAL MEDICINE, ALLERGY. *Current Pos:* PROF MED MAYO GRAD SCH MED, UNIV MINN, ROCHESTER, 78- *Personal Data:* b Boulder, Colo, Mar 13, 22. *Educ:* Columbia Univ, MD, 45. *Prof Exp:* Intern, Sch Med, Univ Colo, 45-46; resident med, Roosevelt Hosp, 48-51; clin instr med, Med Sch, Univ Ore, 51-58, clin asst prof, 58-61; from asst prof to prof med, Univ Wis-Madison, 61-78. *Concurrent Pos:* Pvt pract, Ore, 51-61. *Mem:* Am Acad Allergy (pres, 76); Am Col Physicians; Am Asn Immunol; Am Fedn Clin Res; Cent Soc Clin Res. *Res:* Bronchial asthma; nonasthmatic allergic diseases of the lung. *Mailing Add:* Mayo Clinic 200 First St SW Rochester MN 55905

REED, CHRISTOPHER ALAN, BIOINORGANIC, COORDINATION & ORGANOMETALLIC CHEMISTRY. *Current Pos:* from asst prof to assoc prof, 73-81, PROF CHEM, UNIV SOUTHERN CALIF, LOS ANGELES, 81- *Personal Data:* b Auckland, NZ, Feb 25, 47; m, Barbara K Burgess; c 3. *Educ:* Auckland Univ, NZ, BSc, 68, MSc hon, 69, PhD(chem), 71. *Prof Exp:* Res assoc chem, Stanford Univ, 71-73. *Concurrent Pos:* A P Sloan fel, 76. *Mem:* Am Chem Soc; NZ Inst Chem. *Res:* Bioinorganic chemistry of the transition metals particularly the structure and the reactivity of hemes, oxygen carriers and cytochromes; organo-transition metal chemistry and coordination chemistry; magnetic interactions; fullerene chemistry; carborane chemistry. *Mailing Add:* Dept Chem Univ Southern Calif Los Angeles CA 90089-0744. *Fax:* 213-740-0930; *E-Mail:* careed@usc.edu

REED, COKE S, MATHEMATICS. *Current Pos:* asst prof, 67-75, assoc prof, 75-81, PROF MATH, AUBURN UNIV, 81- *Personal Data:* b Austin, Tex, Mar 8, 40; m 61; c 1. *Educ:* Univ Tex, BS, 62, MA, 65, PhD(math), 66. *Prof Exp:* Asst prof math, Ga Inst Tech, 66-67. *Mem:* Am Math Soc. *Res:* Real variables; topological dynamics. *Mailing Add:* Ctr Comput Sci 17100 Science Dr Bowie MD 20715-4374

REED, DALE HARDY, EXPLORATION GEOPHYSICS, ELECTRICAL ENGINEERING. *Current Pos:* RETIRED. *Personal Data:* b Houston, Tex, Aug 5, 30; m 54, Marva A Cunningham; c 4. *Educ:* Rice Univ, BA, 52, BSEE, 53. *Prof Exp:* Res engr, Atlantic Richfield Co, 53-72, res dir, 64-72, res assoc, 72-82, mgr explor spec projs, 82-85. *Concurrent Pos:* Consult geophys & expert witness, UN; consult, Independent Oil & Gas Prod. *Mem:* Soc Explor Geophysicists; Europ Asn Explor Geophysicists. *Res:* Borehole logging; reflection seismic; magnetics; geochemistry; planning and evaluation; marine seismic systems; exploration on basalt covered terrain; shear wave seismology. *Mailing Add:* 10415 Coleridge Dallas TX 75218

REED, DANIEL A, PARALLEL PROCESSING, PERFORMANCE ANALYSIS. *Current Pos:* from asst prof to assoc prof, 84-91, sr software engr, Ctr Supercomput Res & Develop, 86-93, PROF COMPUT SCI, UNIV ILL, URBANA-CHAMPAIGN, 91- *Personal Data:* b Wichita, Kans, June 12, 57; m 87, Andrea Krupa. *Educ:* Univ Mo, Rolla, BS, 78; Purdue Univ, MS, 80, PhD(comput sci), 83. *Prof Exp:* Asst prof comput sci, Univ NC, Chapel Hill, 83-84. *Concurrent Pos:* Prin investr, NSF, 84-92; consult, ICASE, NASA Langley Res Ctr, 84-; IBM fac develop award, 84-85; NSF presidential young investr award, 87-92; mem, Sigmetrics Bd Dirs, Asn Comput Mach, 91-93; vis scientist, IBM Res, 91. *Mem:* Asn Comput Mach (secy & treas, 93-); Inst Elec & Electronics Engrs Comput Soc; AAAS. *Res:* Interaction of architecture, software, and application algorithms across a range of high performance computing systems and performance analysis techniques of these systems; parallel computer design. *Mailing Add:* Dept Comput Sci Univ Ill 1304 W Springfield Ave Urbana IL 61801. *E-Mail:* reedr@cs.uiuc.edu

REED, DAVID DOSS, ECOLOGICAL MODELLING, STATISTICAL DESIGN OF ECOLOGICAL STUDIES. *Current Pos:* asst prof, 82-86, assoc prof, 86-90, PROF FOREST BIOMET, MICH TECHNOL UNIV, 90- *Personal Data:* b Jonesboro, Ark, Sept 14, 56; m 82, Elizabeth A Jones; c 3. *Educ:* Univ Ark, Monticello, BS, 77; Va Polytech Inst & State Univ, MS, 79, MS & PhD(forest biomet), 82. *Prof Exp:* Forest biometrician, Weyerhaeuser Co, 80-81. *Concurrent Pos:* Assoc ed, Forest Sci, 93-95; Forest Ecol Mgmt, 96-; Fulbright fel dept Engenharia Florestal, Tech Univ, Lisbon, Portugal, 96. *Mem:* AAAS; Soc Am Foresters; Am Forestry Asn; Am Statist Asn; Sigma Xi. *Res:* Effects of stress factors on the health and productivity of forest ecosystems, design and analysis of ecological monitoring studies, modeling of forest production. *Mailing Add:* Mich Technol Univ Sch Forestry & Wood Prods 1400 Townsend Dr Houghton MI 49931

REED, DAVID WILLIAM, HORTICULTURE, FLORICULTURE. *Current Pos:* ASST PROF HORT, TEX A&M UNIV, 78- *Personal Data:* b Opelousas, La, Dec 7, 52; m 74; c 1. *Educ:* Univ Southwestern La, BS, 74; Cornell Univ, MS, 77, PhD(hort), 79. *Mem:* Am Soc Hort Sci. *Res:* Penetration of foliar-applied compounds into the leafs of plants; structure, development and function of the plant cuticle of leaves; mineral nutrition of plants. *Mailing Add:* Dept Hort Sci Tex A&M Univ College Station TX 77843-0100

REED, DONAL J, PHARMACOLOGY. *Current Pos:* from instr to prof pharmacol, 62-88, actg chmn dept, 80-88, EMER PROF, COL MED, UNIV UTAH, 88- *Personal Data:* b Riverdale, Calif, Apr 24, 24; m 45; c 5. *Educ:* Col Idaho, BA, 48; Univ Calif, PhD(physiol), 59. *Prof Exp:* Asst physiol, Univ Calif, 56-57 & 58-59. *Concurrent Pos:* NIH res fel pharmacol, Col Med, Univ Utah, 59-62. *Mem:* AAAS; Am Soc Pharmacol & Exp Therapeut; Am Physiol Soc. *Res:* Mechanism and kinetics of distribution of electrolytes and other substances among the blood, cerebrospinal fluid and the brain; neuropharmacology; pharmaco-kinetics; adrenal steroids. *Mailing Add:* 50 E 1800 S Bountiful UT 84010-5239

REED, DONALD JAMES, BIOCHEMISTRY, ENVIRONMENTAL HEALTH. *Current Pos:* from asst prof to assoc prof, 62-72, PROF BIOCHEM, ORE STATE UNIV, 72-, DIR ENVIRON HEALTH SCI CTR, 81- *Personal Data:* b Montrose, Kans, Sept 26, 30; m 49; c 6. *Educ:* Col Idaho, BS, 53; Ore State Univ, MS, 55, PhD(chem), 57. *Prof Exp:* Asst, Ore State Univ, 53-55; assoc biochemist cereal invests, Western Regional Res Lab, Agr Res Serv, USDA, Calif, 57-58; asst prof chem, Mont State Univ, 58-62. *Concurrent Pos:* USPHS spec res fel, NIH, 69-70, mem toxicol study sect, 71-75, mem, Ad Hoc Rev Comt, Nat Cancer Inst, 75-87; Eleanor Roosevelt Am Cancer Soc Int Cancer fel, Karolinska Inst, Stockholm, 76-77; environ sci review panel health res, Environ Protection Agency, 81; environ health sci review comt, Nat Inst Environ Health Sci, 82-85; assoc ed, J Toxicol & Environ Health, 80-84, Toxicol & Appl Pharmacol, 81-84, Cancer Res, 87- & ed, Cell Biol & Toxicol; Burroughs Wellcome Toxicol Scholar Award Selection Comt, 84-87; vis prof, Burroughs Wellcome Travel Grant, MRC Toxicol Unit, Carshalton, Eng, 84; sabbatical scientist, Nat Cancer Inst, NIH, Bethesda, Md, 84-85; mem, Task Group Health Criteria, Int Prog Chem Safety, WHO, 86 & Biochem & Carcinogenesis Rev Comt, Am Cancer Soc, 84-; consult, Univ Calif, San Francisco, 85- *Mem:* Am Soc Biol Chem; Am Soc Pharmacol & Exp Therapeut; Soc Toxicol; Am Asn Cancer Res; Sigma Xi. *Res:* Biological oxidations; environmental toxicology; biochemical anticancer drugs; protective mechanisms of glutathione functions; vitamin E status. *Mailing Add:* Dept Biochem & Biophys Ore State Univ Agr & Life Sci 2011 Corvallis OR 97331-7305

REED, DWAYNE MILTON, GERONTOLOGY. *Current Pos:* SR EPIDEMIOLOGIST, BUCK CTR RES AGING, 93- *Personal Data:* b Kinsley, Kans, Dec 10, 33; c Colin & Heather. *Educ:* Univ Calif, Berkeley, BA, 55, MPH, 62, PhD(epidemiol), 69; Univ Calif, San Francisco, MD, 60. *Honors & Awards:* Commendation Medal, USPHS, 87 & 92. *Prof Exp:* Asst chief, epidemiol br, Nat Inst Neurol Dis & Blindness, NIH, Guam, 62-64; chief, field unit, Arctic Health Res Ctr, Anchorage, 64-66; assoc res epidemiol, Sch Pub Health, Univ Calif, 66-69; assoc prof, Sch Pub Health, Univ Tex, 69-71; Dep chief, Nat Inst Neurol Dis & Stroke, NIH, 71-74; epidemiologist, SPac Comm, 74-75; chief, epidemiol br, Nat Inst Child Health & Human develop, NIH, 75-78; med epidemiologist, Calif State Dept Health, 78-79; dir, Honolulu Heart Prog, Nat Heart, Blood, Lung Inst, NIH, 80-92. *Concurrent Pos:* Consult, Hawaii Heart Asn, 83-, Japan Heart Found, 84, Int Soc Hypertension, 84, WHO, Philippines, 86, Brunei, 87; liaison officer, US Japan Agreement Cardiovasc Dis, 82-92. *Mem:* Am Pub Health; Soc Epidemiol Res; Am Epidemiol Soc; fel Am Heart Asn. *Res:* Public health and research in epidemiology. *Mailing Add:* Buck Ctr Res Aging 505-A San Marin Dr Novato CA 94945. *Fax:* 415-899-1810

REED, EDWARD BRANDT, LIMNOLOGY, ECOLOGY. *Current Pos:* RETIRED. *Personal Data:* b Longmont, Colo, Jan 11, 20; m 46; c 2. *Educ:* Colo State Univ, BS, 53, MS, 55; Univ Sask, PhD(biol), 59. *Prof Exp:* Fisheries biologist, Sask Dept Natural Resources, 56-59; from asst prof to prof zool, 59-74, mem affil fac zool, Colo State Univ, Pres Ecol Consults, Inc, 74-81. *Concurrent Pos:* Dir, NSF Summer Inst, 60-64; environ consult, Nat Park Serv, 67 & Western Solo Resource Study, 70-71; Environ Protection Agency res grant, 70-71. *Mem:* Fel AAAS; Int Asn Theoret & Appl Limnol; Am Soc Limnol & Oceanog. *Res:* Application of limnological principles to problems associated with water resource use; abatement of ecological problems associated with disturbed lands and resource development; systematics of freshwater cyclopoid copepeds. *Mailing Add:* 1901 Stover St Ft Collins CO 80525

REED, ELIZABETH WAGNER, human genetics; deceased, see previous edition for last biography

REED, ELLEN ELIZABETH, MATHEMATICS. *Current Pos:* CONSULT, 80- *Personal Data:* b Covina, Calif, Sept 16, 40. *Educ:* Gonzaga Univ, BA, 62; Univ Colo, Boulder, MA, 64, PhD(math), 66. *Prof Exp:* From asst prof to assoc prof math, Univ Mass, Amherst, 66-77; mem staff, Dept Math, St Mary's Col, 77-80. *Concurrent Pos:* Lectr, Smith Col, 72; mem staff, Dept Math, Notre Dame, 77 & Col Eng, 79-81. *Mem:* Am Math Soc. *Res:* Uniform spaces and generalizations; extensions and compactifications of topological spaces and convergence spaces. *Mailing Add:* Trinity Sch 107 S Greenlawn South Bend IN 46617

REED, EUGENE D, ELECTRICAL ENGINEERING. *Current Pos:* RETIRED. *Personal Data:* b Vienna, Austria, Oct 12, 19; nat US. *Educ:* Univ London, BSEE, 42; Columbia Univ, PhD(elec eng), 53. *Prof Exp:* Exec, Bell Labs, 47-75. *Mem:* Nat Acad Eng; Inst Elec & Electronics Engrs. *Mailing Add:* 3125 Middle Ranch Rd Pebble Beach CA 93953

REED, F(LOOD) EVERETT, MECHANICAL & MARINE ENGINEERING. *Current Pos:* PRES & TREAS, LITTLETON RES & ENG CORP, 62- *Personal Data:* b North Stonington, Conn, Aug 23, 14; m 39, Anna E Shiphard; c Theordore L, David E, Eleanor J & Esther E. *Educ:* Webb Inst Naval Archit, BS, 36; Mass Inst Technol, MS, 51. *Prof Exp:* From asst marine engr to sr marine engr, US Maritime Comn, 39-46; asst prof mech eng, Mass Inst Technol, 46-49; mech engr, Arthur D Little, Inc, 49-51, leader, Appl Mech Group, 51-55, sr mech engr & head appl mech, Tech Opers, Inc, 55-59; partner, Conesco Consults, 59-61, tech vpres, Conesco, Inc & Flow Corp, 62. *Concurrent Pos:* Chmn, SNAME M20 Mach Vibr Panel. *Mem:* Am Soc Lubrication Engrs; Am Soc Mech Engrs; Soc Exp Mech; Soc Naval Archit & Marine Engrs; Soc Eng Educ; fel AAAS. *Res:* Vibration; stress analysis; applied mechanics; hydrodynamics; ship structure vibration; mechanical vibration; applied mechanics. *Mailing Add:* 95 Russell St PO Box 128 Littleton MA 01460

REED, FRED DEWITT, JR, medicinal chemistry, for more information see previous edition

REED, GEORGE FARRELL, otolaryngology, medical education; deceased, see previous edition for last biography

REED, GEORGE HENRY, BIOPHYSICS, BIOCHEMISTRY. *Current Pos:* PROF, INST FOR ENZYME RES, UNIV WIS. *Personal Data:* b Muncie, Ind, Aug 29, 42. *Educ:* Purdue Univ, BS, 64; Univ Wis, PhD(chem), 68. *Prof Exp:* Lectr chem, Univ Wis, 67-68; asst prof biophys, Univ Pa, 71-76, assoc prof biochem & biophys, 76-- *Concurrent Pos:* NIH fel, Univ Pa, 69-71 & USPHS career develop award, 72-77. *Mem:* Am Chem Soc; Am Soc Biol Chemists; Sigma Xi. *Res:* Spectroscopic investigation of enzyme-substrate complexes; applications of electron paramagnetic resonance and nuclear magnetic resonance spectroscopy in biological chemistry; interactions of inorganic cations in biological processes. *Mailing Add:* Inst Enzyme Res Univ Wisc 1710 University Ave Madison WI 53705-4087

REED, GEORGE W, JR, RADIO CHEMISTRY, METEORITICS. *Current Pos:* assoc chemist, 52-68, SR SCIENTIST, ARGONNE NAT LAB, 68- *Personal Data:* b Washington, DC, Sept 25, 20; m 45; c 4. *Educ:* Howard Univ, BS, 42, MS, 44; Univ Chicago, PhD(chem), 52. *Prof Exp:* Asst chemist, SAM Labs, Columbia Univ & Metall Labs, Univ Chicago, 44-47. *Concurrent Pos:* Sr res assoc, Univ Chicago, 74. *Mem:* Am Chem Soc; Am Geophys Union; Sigma Xi; Meteoritical Soc; Geochem Soc. *Res:* Lunar and meteoritic science; radiochemistry; geocosmochemistry. *Mailing Add:* 5227 University Ave Chicago IL 60615-4405

REED, HAZELL, HORTICULTURE. *Current Pos:* instr hort, Univ Ark, Pine Bluff, 73-76, exten horticulturist specialist, Coop Exten, 76-79 & 83-85, instr horticulture, 79-83, exten horticulturist, Coop Exten Serv, 85, dean agr & home econ, 85-89, VCHANCELLOR, UNIV ARK, PINE BLUFF, 89- *Personal Data:* b Heth, Ark. *Educ:* AM&N Col, BS, 68; Pa State Univ, MS, 73; Univ Ark, PhD(plant sci), 83. *Prof Exp:* Instr ornamental hort, Ark AM&N Col, 68-71. *Concurrent Pos:* Mem, exec comt, SE Consortium Int Develop, 87-, chmn bd, 89-90; comt mem, Int Comt Orgn & Policy, 87- & State Found & Agr Coun, 88- *Mem:* Sigma Xi; Am Soc Hort Sci; Southern Region Am Soc Hort Sci; Southern Asn Agr Scientists. *Mailing Add:* 48 Lexington Dr Pine Bluff AR 71602

REED, HORACE BEECHER, MEDICAL ENTOMOLOGY, INSECT ECOLOGY. *Current Pos:* RETIRED. *Personal Data:* b Etowah, Tenn, July 8, 23; m 64, Helen V Weaks. *Educ:* Univ Tenn, AB, 46, MS, 48, PhD(entom), 53; Univ Mich, MA, 52. *Prof Exp:* Instr zool, Univ Maine, 48-49; asst, Univ Tenn, 52-53, asst entom, 54, asst, bact, 57; head sci dept high sch, Ga, 59; prof biol & head dept, Shorter Col, Ga, 59-63; from asst prof to assoc prof biol, Mid Tenn State Univ, 64-84. *Res:* Ecology of medically important arthropods. *Mailing Add:* 215 City View Dr Murfreesboro TN 37130

REED, IRVING STOY, ELECTRICAL ENGINEERING, COMPUTER SCIENCE. *Current Pos:* prof, 63-94, EMER PROF ELEC ENG & COMPUT SCI, UNIV SOUTHERN CALIF, 94- *Personal Data:* b Seattle, Wash, Nov 12, 23. *Educ:* Calif Inst Technol, BS, 44, PhD(math), 49. *Honors & Awards:* Hamming Arold Medal, Inst Elec & Electronics Engrs, 79. *Prof Exp:* Staff mem, Lincoln Lab, Mass Inst Technol, 51-60; sr staff mem, RAND Corp, 60-63. *Concurrent Pos:* Consult, RAND, MITRE Corp; dir, Adaptive Sensors Inc. *Mem:* Nat Acad Eng; fel Inst Elec & Electronics Engrs; Soc Indust & Appl Math; Am Math Soc. *Res:* Mathematics; computer design; coding theory; stochastic processes; information theory; developer of the Reed-Soloman error-correcting code used in compact disc technology. *Mailing Add:* Dept Elec Eng Univ Southern Calif Los Angeles CA 90089-0272

REED, JACK WILSON, METEOROLOGY. *Current Pos:* CONSULT METEOROLOGIST, JWR, INC, 89- *Personal Data:* b Corning, Iowa, Sept 24, 23; m 44; c 1. *Educ:* Univ NMex, MBS, 48. *Prof Exp:* Meteorologist, Sandia Nat Labs, 48-51; USAF Air Weather Serv, 51-53; meteorologist, Sandia Nat Labs, 53-89. *Concurrent Pos:* Chmn working group, Atmospheric Blast Effects, Am Nat Stand Inst, 52; chmn working group (WG-22), Int Stand Orgn; mem tech comt shock & vibration (TC-108), Atmospheric Blast Effects, 93- *Mem:* AAAS; Am Meteorol Soc; Am Geophys Union; Am Nuclear Soc; Acoust Soc Am; Air & Waste Mgt Asn. *Res:* Atmospheric propagation of explosion effluents; wind power climatology; meteorological statistics. *Mailing Add:* 1128 Monroe SE Albuquerque NM 87108

REED, JAMES ROBERT, JR, FISH BIOLOGY, AQUATIC ECOLOGY. *Current Pos:* PRES, JAMES R REED & ASSOCS, INC, 77- *Personal Data:* b Wayland, NY, Apr 29, 40; m 65; c 2. *Educ:* Harvard Univ, AB, 62; Cornell Univ, MS, 64; Tulane Univ, PhD(biol), 66. *Prof Exp:* Fel environ sci, Oak Ridge Nat Lab, 66-68; asst prof, Va Commonwealth Univ, 68-73, assoc prof biol, 73-77. *Mem:* Am Soc Ichthyologists & Herpetologists; Am Fisheries Soc; Ecol Soc Am; Am Coun Independent Labs; Am Soc Testing & Mat. *Res:* Ecology of fishes with respect to effects of pollution; aquaculture; fish behavior; environmental monitoring. *Mailing Add:* 40 Finns Point Lane Hampton VA 23669

REED, JAMES STALFORD, CERAMICS. *Current Pos:* from asst prof to assoc prof, 66-78, chairperson div, 87-90, PROF CERAMIC ENG, NY STATE COL CERAMICS, ALFRED UNIV, 78-, DEAN CERAMIC ENG. *Personal Data:* b Jamestown, NY, June 7, 38; m 61; c 1. *Educ:* Pa State Univ, BS, 60; Alfred Univ, PhD(ceramic sci), 65. *Prof Exp:* Res engr, Harbison-Walker Refractories Co, 60-62. *Mem:* Am Ceramic Soc; Nat Inst Ceramic Engrs; Soc Coating Technol. *Res:* Mechanics of fabrication processes; mechanical properties of ceramics; firing whiteware ceramics. *Mailing Add:* NY State Col Ceramics Alfred Univ Pine St Alfred NY 14802-1296

REED, JOEL, ADVANCED EDUCATION. *Current Pos:* Dir univ commun educ prog, Col Art & Sci, 75-86, DIR ORIENTATION & RECRUTMENT & INSTR MATH, COL GEN STUDIES, UNIV PITTSBURGH, 86- *Personal Data:* b Pittsburgh, Pa, Nov 6, 42. *Educ:* Pa State Univ, BA, 65, Univ Pittsburgh, MED, 70, PhD, 72. *Mem:* Am Educ Res Asn; Nat Coun Educ Opportunity Prog. *Res:* Familiarized minority children with the educational project. *Mailing Add:* 8935 Eastwood Rd Pittsburgh PA 15235

REED, JOHN CALVIN, JR, STRUCTURAL GEOLOGY, REGIONAL GEOLOGY. *Current Pos:* Geologist, US Geol Surv, 54-55 & 57-74, chief, Eastern States Br, 65-69, chief, Off Environ Geol, 74-79, geologist, 79-94, chief, Br Cent Regional Geol, 94-95, GEOLOGIST, CENT REGION GEOL MAPPING TEAM, US GEOL SURV, 95- *Personal Data:* b Erie, Pa, July 24, 30; m 60, Linda Hassel; c Rebecca & Robert. *Educ:* Johns Hopkins Univ, PhD, 54. *Concurrent Pos:* Mem, Adv Comn Basic Res, Nat Res Coun-US Army, 73-; mem, Comt Stratigraphic Names, US Geol Surv, 74-86; ed, Map & Chart Series, Geol Soc Am; vpres 28th Int Geol Cong; G K Gilbert Fel, US Geol Surv, 84-86; mem, Sci Adv Comt, Geol Div, US Geol Surv, 91-93, mem, Strategic Planning Team, 93-95. *Mem:* Fel Geol Soc Am; Am Geophys Union; Colo Sci Soc (pres, 94). *Res:* Geology of crystalline rocks of central and southern Appalachians; geology of central Alaska Range; Appalachian structure and tectonics; geochronology; Precambrian crystalline rocks of Wyoming, Colorado and New Mexico; Precambrian rocks of US; geologic map of North America. *Mailing Add:* US Geol Surv Fed Ctr MS 913 Box 25046 Denver CO 80225

REED, JOHN FREDERICK, BOTANY. *Current Pos:* RETIRED. *Personal Data:* b Rockport, Maine, Nov 18, 11; m 34, 79, Beatrice C; c 3. *Educ:* Dartmouth Col, AB, 33; Duke Univ, MA, 35, PhD(bot), 36. *Prof Exp:* Asst bot, Duke Univ, 33-34; instr natural sci, Amarillo Col, 36-38; from instr to assoc prof biol, Baldwin-Wallace Col, 38-46, dean men, 42-46; from asst prof to prof bot, Univ Wyo, 46-56; prof, Univ NH, 56-62, dean grad sch, 56-60 & col lib arts, 58-60, vpres, 61, actg pres, 61-62; prof bot & pres, Ft Lewis Col, 62-69; sect head ecol & syst biol, Div Biol & Med Sci, NSF, 69-70; prof ecosyst anal & chmn dept, Univ Wis-Green Bay, 70-75, dean acad affairs, 75-77, prof 75-82, emer prof environ sci, 82-83. *Concurrent Pos:* Technician Pedo Bot Mission to Ruanda-Urundi, Africa, Econ Coop Admin, 51-52; mem environ biol panel, NSF, 56-59; mem coun, Nat Inst Dent Res, 59-63; comn plans & objectives higher educ, Am Coun Educ, 63-66; comt radioactive waste mgt, Nat Res Coun, 70-74; chmn, US Nat Comt Int Biol Prog, 72-74; mem, US Nat Comt Man & the Biosphere, 73-75; mem, US Nat Comn, UNESCO, 73-78. *Mem:* Fel AAAS; Brit Ecol Soc; Am Soc Range Mgt; Ecol Soc Am (secy, 53-57, pres, 63); fel Explorers Club. *Res:* Plant ecology; forest ecology of the Rocky Mountains. *Mailing Add:* 201 W Park Ave Durango CO 81301

REED, JOHN J R, analytical chemistry; deceased, see previous edition for last biography

REED, JOSEPH, ORGANOMETALLIC CHEMISTRY. *Current Pos:* PROG DIR, CHEM RES INSTRUMENTATION PROG CHEM DIV, NSF, 86- *Personal Data:* b Bradenton, Fla, Jan 18, 44; m 66, Beverly Surcy; c Joseph S. *Educ:* Lincoln Univ, AB, 66; Temple Univ, MA, 71; Brown Univ, PhD(chem), 74. *Prof Exp:* Chemist, E I du Pont de Nemours & Co, Inc, 66-70, Rohm & Haas, 70, Bell Labs, 74-77, Exxon Res & Eng Co, 77-86. *Concurrent Pos:* Adj prof chem, Lincoln Univ, 79-86; Comsci fel, 92-93; Legis Fel, 96. *Mem:* Am Chem Soc; Nat Orgn Prof Advan Black Chemist & Chem Engrs; Orgn Black Scientists. *Res:* Chemistry and homogeneous catalytic approach to hydrodesulfurization with organometallic complexes. *Mailing Add:* NSF 4201 Wilson Blvd Rm 1055 Arlington VA 22230. *Fax:* 800-338-3128; *E-Mail:* jreed@nsf

REED, JOSEPH, CIRCUIT DESIGN, SERVO-MECHANISM. *Current Pos:* TECH DIR, ITT DEFENSE INC, 86- *Personal Data:* b New York, NY, Dec 11, 20; m 51; c 4. *Educ:* Cooper Union, BEE, 44; Polytech Inst Brooklyn, MEE, 51; Polytech Inst NY, DEE (control physics & math), 75. *Prof Exp:* Asst plant supt, RCA Commun Inc, 47-53; servo-lab head, AM Mach & Foundry Lab, 53-54; head, Radar Dept, Gen Precision Labs, 54-62; vpres res & dir eng, Litcom Div, Litton Syst Inc, 62-72; tech dir, ITT Corp, 72-86. *Concurrent Pos:* Lectr, Col City New York, 63-68. *Mem:* Fel Inst Elec & Electronics Engrs; fel AAAS. *Mailing Add:* 668 Westover Rd Stamford CT 06902-1321

REED, JOSEPH RAYMOND, HYDRAULIC ENGINEERING. *Current Pos:* instr fluids & surv, Dept Civil Eng, Pa State Univ, 53-55 & 59-60, asst prof, 60-64 & 67-72, assoc prof, 72-87, prof, 87-95, acad officer, 89-95, EMER PROF CIVIL ENG, PA STATE UNIV, 96. *Personal Data:* b Pittsburgh, Pa, Aug 15, 30; wid; c Michelle, Stephanie & David. *Educ:* Pa State Col, BS, 52; Pa State Univ, MS, 55; Cornell Univ, PhD(civil eng), 71. *Prof Exp:* Asst fluid mech, dept civil eng, Pa State Col, 52-53; capt & liaison engr, US Army CEngr, Southwestern Div, Dallas, Tex, USAF, 56-59; res asst civil eng, Cornell Univ, 64-66. *Concurrent Pos:* Asst engr, George H McGinness Assocs, 52-55; consult, Ketron Inc, Westvaco, McGraw-Hill Bk Co & others, 63-; publ referee, Hydraul Div, Am Soc Civil Engrs, 69-95; prin investr projs, Fed Hwy Admin, Fed Aviation Admin, Pa Coal Res Bd & others, 71-; chmn, Storm Water Authority, State Col Borough, Pa, 74-78; proposal reviewer, NSF, 80-81. *Mem:* Am Soc Civil Engrs; Am Soc Eng Educ; Int Asn Hydraul Res; Sigma Xi. *Res:* Rainfall runoff from highways and runways as it affects the hydroplaning potential of the pavements; dredging mechanics of large river dredges, friction slope modeling in steady nonuniform channel flow. *Mailing Add:* 1394 Penfield Rd State College PA 16801

REED, JUTA KUTTIS, BIOCHEMISTRY. *Current Pos:* asst prof, 75-81, ASSOC PROF CHEM, ERINDALE COL, UNIV TORONTO, 81- *Personal Data:* Can citizen. *Educ:* Queen's Univ, BA, 66; Univ Western Ont, MSc, 67; Univ Wis, PhD(biochem), 72. *Prof Exp:* Res fel, Calif Inst Technol, 73-75. *Mem:* Am Chem Soc; Can Biochem Soc. *Res:* Pharmacology of purines in the cns and pns; membrane proteins and developmental control mechanisms in neurogenesis; fluorescence spectroscopy of biopolymers and molecular assemblies. *Mailing Add:* Dept Chem Univ Toronto Mississauga Erinlake Campus 3359 Mississauga Rd N Mississauga ON L5L 1C6 Can

REED, KENNARD, ORDINARY DIFFERENTIAL EQUATIONS, PARTIAL DIFFERENTIAL EQUATIONS. *Current Pos:* INSTR MATH, HOUSTON COMMUNITY COL SYST, 79- *Personal Data:* b Houston, Tex, Jan 20, 39; m 74, Marjorie A Radoff; c Naomi B & Rebecca J. *Educ:* Fisk Univ, BA, 58; NY Univ, MS, 60, PhD(math), 63. *Prof Exp:* J W Young res instr math, Dartmouth Col, 63-64; assoc prof, Tex Southern Univ, 64-65; vis asst prof, Rice Univ, 65-66; asst prof, Georgetown Univ, 66-68, Polytech Inst Brooklyn, 69-70; postulant holy orders, Philadelphia Divinity Sch, 71-72; teacher, Houston Independent Sch Dist, 73-79. *Mem:* Math Asn Am. *Res:* Finding solutions to complex mathematical problems; math education. *Mailing Add:* 16030 Logan Rock Rd Missouri City TX 77489

REED, KENNETH PAUL, ANALYTICAL CHEMISTRY, INDUSTRIAL HYGIENE. *Current Pos:* PRES, KENNETH P REED & ASSOCS, 80- *Personal Data:* b Covington, Ky, Aug 30, 37; m 66; c 3. *Educ:* Thomas More Col, AB, 57; Xavier Univ, MS, 59; La State Univ, PhD(chem), 68; Am Bd Indust Hyg, dipl, 91. *Prof Exp:* From instr to prof chem, Thomas More Col, 59-78, chmn dept, 68-72; dir freshman studies prog, 72-75, dir develop, 75-78; staff consult, Actus Environ Serv, Florence, 78-80, gen mgr, 80. *Concurrent Pos:* NSF Sci Fac Fel, 66-67. *Mem:* Am Chem Soc; Am Indust Hyg Asn; Am Conf Govt Indust Hygienists; Sigma Xi; Am Acad Indust Hygienists; Asn Off Anal Chemists. *Res:* Analytical separations; fractional entrainment sublimation; metal chelates; organic synthesis of chelating agents; sampling methods for industrial toxicology; environmental chemistry; environmental health; emmissions of carpets and building materials; indoor air quality; pollution reduction for adhesive using industries. *Mailing Add:* 3027 Dixie Hwy Suite 317 Edgewood KY 41017

REED, L WHETTEN, AGRICULTURAL ECONOMICS. *Current Pos:* DIR, RES & SCI EXCHANGES DIV, USDA, 95. *Personal Data:* b Snowflake, Ariz, Feb 27, 43. *Educ:* Ariz State Univ, BA, 63, MS, 65. *Mailing Add:* Res & Sci Exchanges Div USDA 14th & Independence Ave SW Washington DC 20250

REED, LESTER JAMES, ENZYMOLOGY. *Current Pos:* assoc dir, 62-63, dir, 63-96, RES SCIENTIST, CLAYTON FOUND BIOCHEM INST, 49-; PROF CHEM, UNIV TEX, AUSTIN, 58-, ASHBEL SMITH PROF, 84- *Personal Data:* b New Orleans, La, Jan 3, 25; m 48, Janet L Gruschow; c Pamela, Sharon, Richard & Robert. *Educ:* Tulane Univ, BS, 43; Univ Ill, PhD(chem), 46. *Hon Degrees:* DSc, Tulane Univ, 77. *Honors & Awards:* Lilly Award, Am Chem Soc, 58; Merck Award, Am Soc Biochem & Molecular Biol, 94. *Prof Exp:* Asst, Nat Defense Res Comt, Univ Ill, 44-46; res assoc biochem, Med Col, Cornell Univ, 46-48; from asst prof to prof, Univ Tex, Austin, 48-58. *Mem:* Nat Acad Sci; AAAS; Am Chem Soc; Am Soc Biochem & Molecular Biol; Am Acad Arts & Sci. *Res:* Chemistry and function of lipoic acid; enzyme chemistry; structure, function and regulation of multienzyme complexes. *Mailing Add:* 3502 Balcones Dr Austin TX 78731-5802

REED, LESTER W, soil chemistry, mineralogy, for more information see previous edition

REED, MARION GUY, SOIL CHEMISTRY. *Current Pos:* res chemist, Chevron Res Co, Calif, 62-69, sr res chemist, 69-73, sr res assoc, Chevron Oil Field Res Co, 73-92, CONSULT, CHEVRON PETROL TECHNOL CO, 92- *Personal Data:* b Osceola, Iowa, June 26, 31; m 51; c 2. *Educ:* Iowa State Univ, BS, 57, PhD(soil chem), 63. *Prof Exp:* Res assoc soils, Iowa State Univ, 57-62. *Mem:* Am Soc Agron; Soil Sci Soc Am; Clay Minerals Soc (vpres, 85, pres, 86); Soc Petrol Eng; Am Chem Soc; Soc Core Analysts. *Res:* Physical chemistry of clays and clay-fluid interactions as related to petroleum, uranium and geothermal energy production; kinetics and mechanism of potassium release from micaceous minerals. *Mailing Add:* Chevron Petrol Technol Co PO Box 446 La Habra CA 90633-0446

REED, MARK ARTHUR, NANOELECTRONICS, ARTIFICIALLY STRUCTURED MATERIALS. *Current Pos:* PROF ELEC ENG & APPL PHYSICS, YALE UNIV, 90-, CHMN ELEC ENG, 95- *Personal Data:* b Suffern, NY, Jan 4, 55; m, Elizabeth J Schaffer; c Victor. *Educ:* Syracuse Univ, BS, 77, MS, 79, PhD(physics), 83. *Honors & Awards:* Kilby Young Innovator's Award, 94. *Prof Exp:* Univ fel, Physics Dept, Syracuse Univ, 81-83; sr mem tech staff, Cent Res Lab, Tex Instruments, 83-90. *Concurrent Pos:* Jour referee, Appl Physics Lett, J Appl Physics, 85-, Electron Device Lett, NSF, 85-; adj prof physics, Tex A&M Univ, 86-90; co-chair, Int Conf Nanostructure Physics & Fabrication, 89 & 91. *Mem:* Sr mem Inst Elec & Electronics Engrs; Am Phys Soc; Optical Soc Am; Sigma Xi. *Res:* Investigating ultra-submicron quantum size effect devices; physics of mesoscopic systems, tunneling, heterostructures, quantum wells and superlattices; novel quantum confined semiconductor structures; author of articles to professional publication; granted 8 US and foreign patents. *Mailing Add:* Dept Elec Eng Yale Univ PO Box 208284 New Haven CT 06520-8284. *Fax:* 203-432-6420

REED, MELVIN LEROY, INTERNAL MEDICINE, ONCOLOGY. *Current Pos:* ASSOC PROF ONCOL, SCH MED, WAYNE STATE UNIV, 63- *Personal Data:* b Kalamazoo, Mich, Oct 28, 29; m; c 2. *Educ:* Kalamazoo Col, AB, 51; Univ Mich, MD, 55. *Prof Exp:* Intern med, City Mem Hosp, Winston-Salem, NC, 55-56; resident, Henry Ford Hosp, Detroit, 58-60, assoc physician med oncol, 62-63. *Concurrent Pos:* Nat Cancer Inst fel clin cancer res, Henry Ford Hosp, Detroit, 60-62; assoc dir, Darling Mem Ctr, Mich Cancer Found, 63-75; dir, Southeastern Mich Regional Cancer Prog, 71-76. *Mem:* Am Fedn Clin Res; Am Soc Clin Oncol; fel Am Col Physicians; Am Asn Cancer Res. *Res:* Experimental drugs and methods in therapy of human malignant diseases. *Mailing Add:* 785 N Lapeer Rd Lake Orion MI 48361

REED, MICHAEL CHARLES, MATHEMATICAL PHYSICS. *Current Pos:* chmn dept, 82-89, PROF MATH, DUKE UNIV, 74- *Personal Data:* b Kalamazoo, Mich, May 7, 42; m 92, Rhonda Jo Weisberg; c David, Isaac, Jacob & Hannah. *Educ:* Yale Univ, BS, 63; Stanford Univ, MS, 66, PhD(math), 69. *Prof Exp:* From instr to asst prof math, Princeton Univ, 68-74. *Concurrent Pos:* Ed, Duke J Math, 74-80; Dir, Ctr Math & Comput in Life Sci & Med, 86- *Mem:* Am Math Soc; Soc Indust & Appl Math; Asn Women Math. *Res:* Problems in nonlinear harmonic analysis and partial differential equations, especially scattering theory and propagation of singularities; applications of mathematics to physiology and medicine. *Mailing Add:* Dept Math Duke Univ Durham NC 27708

REED, MICHAEL ROBERT, INTERNATIONAL TRADE, MARKETING & AGRIBUSINESS. *Current Pos:* From asst prof to assoc prof, 78-89, exec dir, Ctr Export Develop, 88-95, PROF, UNIV KY, LEXINGTON, 89- *Personal Data:* b Lawrence, Kans, July 11, 53; m 73, Patricia G Gurtler; c Laura G & Brian M. *Educ:* Kans State Univ, BS, 74; Iowa State Univ, MS, 76, PhD, 79. *Concurrent Pos:* Grantee, Farm Coop Servs, 82-84 & 87-88, Tenn Valley Authority, 82-85, Fed Crop Ins Co, 85-87, USDA, 86-95, US Dept Educ, 93-96; consult, USAID, 83-86. *Mem:* Am Agr Econs Asn; Southern Agr Econs Asn. *Res:* International trade in agricultural and food products; foreign investment activities of US food firms. *Mailing Add:* Dept Agr Econ Univ Ky 308 Agr Eng Lexington KY 40546-0215. *Fax:* 606-323-1913; *E-Mail:* aec003@ukcc.uky.edu

REED, NORMAN D, IMMUNOLOGY. *Current Pos:* from asst prof to assoc prof, 70-76, head dept, 77-91, PROF MICROBIOL, MONT STATE UNIV, 76- *Personal Data:* b Lyons, Kans, July 6, 35; m 62; c 4. *Educ:* Kans State Univ, BS, 59, MS, 62; Mont State Univ, PhD(microbiol), 66. *Honors & Awards:* Sigma Xi res award, Kans State Univ, 62. *Prof Exp:* Bacteriologist, Kans State Bd Health, 61-62; res virologist, Mont Vet Res Lab, 62-63; asst prof microbiol, Univ Nebr, Lincoln, 66-70. *Concurrent Pos:* Consult, Dorsey Labs, Nebr, 66-68; career develop award, USPHS, Nat Inst Allergy & Infectious Dis, Dept HEW, 72-77. *Mem:* Fel AAAS; Am Soc Microbiol; fel Am Acad Microbiol; Am Asn Pathologists; Am Asn Immunol. *Res:* Immunological tolerance; functions of thymus gland; generation and regulation of immune responses; immunoparasitology. *Mailing Add:* Dept Microbiol Mont State Univ Bozeman MT 59717

REED, PETER WILLIAM, PHARMACOLOGY, GRADUATE STUDIES. *Current Pos:* ASSOC PROF PHARMACOL, MED SCH, 75-, ASSOC DEAN GRAD STUDIES & RES, VANDERBILT UNIV, 84- *Personal Data:* b White Plains, NY, July 1, 39. *Educ:* Syracuse Univ, BA, 61; State Univ NY Upstate Med Ctr, PhD(pharmacol), 68. *Prof Exp:* Asst res prof, Inst Enzyme Res, Univ Wis-Madison, 70-73; from asst prof to assoc prof physiol, Med Ctr, Univ Mass, 73-75. *Concurrent Pos:* NIH fel, Inst Enzyme Res, Univ Wis-Madison, 68-70; estab investr, Am Heart Asn, 72-77. *Mem:* Am Soc Biol Chemists; Am Soc Pharmacol & Exp Therapeut. *Res:* Leukocyte metabolism; mitochondria and antibiotics; calcium and magnesium in metabolism; toxic antibiotic effects on cells. *Mailing Add:* 411 Kirkland Hall Vanderbilt Univ Nashville TN 37240

REED, RANDALL R, animal physiology, for more information see previous edition

REED, RAYMOND EDGAR, ANIMAL PATHOLOGY. *Current Pos:* From asst prof to assoc prof, 52-59, actg head dept, 64-65, head dept, 65-77, PROF VET SCI, UNIV ARIZ, 59- *Personal Data:* b Kankakee, Ill, May 11, 22; m 46; c 2. *Educ:* Wash State Univ, BS, 50, DVM, 51; Am Col Vet Path, dipl. *Mem:* Am Vet Med Asn; Am Col Vet Path; Sigma Xi. *Res:* Pathology of animal diseases. *Mailing Add:* 3441 N Olsen Ave Tucson AZ 85719-2350

REED, RICHARD JAY, MEDICINE, PATHOLOGY. *Current Pos:* STAFF MEM, REED LAB SKIN PATH, 90- *Personal Data:* b Gilmer, Tex, July 23, 28; m 53, Peggy J Bivins; c Lauralee & Robert. *Educ:* Tulane Univ, MD, 52; Am Bd Path, dipl, 61. *Prof Exp:* Gen pract, Tex, 53-55; from instr to prof, Tulane Univ, Sch Med, 57-75, clin prof, 75-85, prof path, 85-90. *Concurrent Pos:* Fel, Tulane Univ, 57-60; fel surg path, Barnes Hosp, St Louis, Mo, 60-61; consult, USPHS Hosp, New Orleans, 62-; consult, Ochsner Found Hosp, 65-; fel, Warren Found Path Lab, Tulsa, Okla, 70-71; physician, Charity Hosp, New Orleans, 71-90; surg path, Touro Infirmary & partner, Dermatopath Lab, New Orleans, 75-85. *Mem:* Fel Col Am Path; AMA; Int Acad Path; Am Soc Clin Pathologists; Am Soc Dermatopath. *Res:* Dermatopathology; orthopedic and surgical pathology. *Mailing Add:* Reed Lab Skin Path 1401 Foucher St New Orleans LA 70115. *Fax:* 504-897-8275

REED, RICHARD JOHN, METEOROLOGY. *Current Pos:* from asst prof to prof, 54-91, EMER PROF METEOROL, UNIV WASH, 91- *Personal Data:* b Braintree, Mass, June 18, 22; m 50, Joan Murray; c Ralph Murray, Richard Cobden & Elizabeth Ann. *Educ:* Calif Inst Technol, BS, 45; Mass Inst Technol, ScD(meteorol), 49. *Honors & Awards:* Meisinger Award, Am Meteorol Soc, 64, 2nd Half Century Award, 72; Charles Franklin Brooks Award, Am Meteorol Soc, 84, Carl Gustaf Rossby Res Medal, 89. *Prof Exp:* Mem staff, Mass Inst Technol, 49-54. *Concurrent Pos:* Consult, US Weather Bur, 61-62, Europ Ctr Medium Range Weather Forecasts, 85-86; ed, J Appl Meteorol, 66-68; exec scientist, US Global Atmospheric Prog, Nat Acad Sci/ Nat Res Coun, 68-69. *Mem:* Nat Acad Sci; Am Meteorol Soc (pres, 72); Am Geophys Union. *Res:* Weather analysis and forecasting; stratospheric and tropical meteorology. *Mailing Add:* Dept Atmospheric Sci Box 351640 Univ Wash Seattle WA 98195-1640. *Fax:* 206-543-0308; *E-Mail:* reed@atmos.washington.edu

REED, RICHARD P, PHYSICAL METALLURGY. *Current Pos:* CONSULT, 90- *Personal Data:* b Hammond, Ind, May 17, 34; m 80; c 3. *Educ:* Purdue Univ, BS, 56; Univ Colo, MS, 58; Colo Sch Mines, MS, 62; Univ Denver, PhD(metall), 66. *Honors & Awards:* Silver Medal & Gold Medal, Nat Bur Standards. *Prof Exp:* Supvry metallurgist, Nat Bureau Standards, 57-79, chief, Fracture & Deformation Div, 79-90. *Concurrent Pos:* Ed, Advances Cryog Eng Mat & Cryogenic Mat Series. *Mem:* Am Phys Soc; Am Inst Mining, Metall & Petrol Engrs; Am Soc Testing & Mat; Am Welding Soc. *Res:* Deformation, fracture, phase transformations, materials at low temperatures. *Mailing Add:* 2625 Iliff St Boulder CO 80303

REED, ROBERT MARSHALL, PLANT ECOLOGY. *Current Pos:* res assoc, 77-80, staff res mem, 80-83, GROUP LEADER, OAK RIDGE NAT LAB, 83- *Personal Data:* b Berea, Ohio, June 29, 41; m 66. *Educ:* Duke Univ, BA, 63; Wash State Univ, PhD(plant ecol), 69. *Prof Exp:* Asst prof biol, Univ Ottawa, 69-77. *Mem:* Ecol Soc Am; Am Inst Biol Scientists; Soil Conserv Soc Am; AAAS. *Res:* Synecology, with emphasis on forest communities and relationship of vegetation to soil; environmental assessment of energy and defense-related projects; environmental regulatory analysis. *Mailing Add:* 104 E Morningside Dr Oak Ridge TN 37830-8312

REED, ROBERT WILLARD, nondestructive evaluation, low temperature physics, for more information see previous edition

REED, ROBERTA GABLE, BIOCHEMISTRY. *Current Pos:* RES BIOCHEMIST, MARY IMOGENE BASSETT HOSP, COOPERSTOWN, NY, 73- *Personal Data:* b Baltimore, Md, Sept 18, 45. *Educ:* Lebanon Valley Col, Pa, BS, 67; Wesleyan Univ, MA, 69, PhD(org chem), 71. *Prof Exp:* Res asst chem, Res Triangle Inst, NC, 71-72; instr chem, State Univ NY Col Oneonta, 72-73. *Concurrent Pos:* Vis biologist, Ind Univ, Bloomington, 79-80; vis scientist, John Hopkins Univ Sch Med, Baltimore, 87; res scientist, Dept Med, Columbia Univ. *Mem:* Am Soc Biol & Molecular Biology; Am Chem Soc; Am Asn Clin Chem; Protein Soc. *Res:* Dynamic and structural relationships in binding of ions and small organic molecules to serum transport proteins; fatty acid transport and turnover. *Mailing Add:* Mary Imogene Bassett Hosp Cooperstown NY 13326-1394

REED, RONALD KEITH, OCEANOGRAPHY. *Current Pos:* Oceanogr, Coast & Geodetic Surv, 58-65, OCEANOGR, US DEPT COM, NAT OCEANIC & ATMOSPHERIC ADMIN, 65- *Personal Data:* b Mountain Top, Ark, May 6, 32; c Chris & Mark. *Educ:* Ark Polytech Col, BS, 58; Ore State Univ, MS, 73. *Mem:* Am Geophys Union; Am Meteorol Soc. *Res:* Circulation of offshore and inshore currents in the subarctic Pacific and Gulf of Alaska; relation of flow to important ecosystems. *Mailing Add:* Pac Marine Environ Lab 7600 Sand Point Way NE Seattle WA 98115. *Fax:* 206-526-6485

REED, RUSSELL, JR, PROPELLANT CHEMISTRY, ORGANIC CHEMISTRY. *Current Pos:* head appl res & processing div, 72-76, SR RES SCIENTIST, US NAVAL WEAPONS CTR, NWC, 76- *Personal Data:* b Glendale, Calif, Dec 25, 22; m 56, Leslie Parry; c 3. *Educ:* Univ Calif, Los Angeles, BS, 44, PhD(org chem), 50. *Honors & Awards:* William B McLean Award. *Prof Exp:* Res chemist, US Naval Ord, China Lake Test Sta, 51-58; head org & polymer res sect, Hughes Tool Co, Culver City, Calif, 58-59; head, Dept Chem, Rocket Power Inc, Mesa, Ariz, 59-64; head propellant res sect, Thiokol Corp, Brigham City, Utah, 64-72. *Mem:* Am Chem Soc; Am Inst Aeronaut & Astronaut; sr fel Naval Weapons Ctr. *Res:* Propellant chemistry combustion; pyrotechnic and explosive chemistry; processing of energetic materials; polymer chemistry; extinguishable propellants; fire suppressing and air bag gas generators. *Mailing Add:* 2026 S Mono Ridgecrest CA 93555-4977

REED, RUTH ELIZABETH, CHEMISTRY EDUCATION. *Current Pos:* from asst prof to assoc prof, 76-88, PROF CHEM, JUNIATA COL, 88- *Personal Data:* b Ames, Iowa, Dec 14, 46; m 72, Tom Lyons Fisher. *Educ:* Winthrop Col, BA, 68; Va Polytech Inst & State Univ, PhD(biochem), 74. *Prof Exp:* Fel biochem, Dept Physiol Chem, Sch Med, Johns Hopkins Univ, 74-76. *Concurrent Pos:* Nat Heart, Lung & Blood Inst res fel, Johns Hopkins Univ, 75-76; Fulbright award, Univ Gottingen, 68-69; Fulbright inter-univ exchange, Polytech de Lille, France, 81; vis assoc prof chem, Univ NC, Chapel Hill, 85, 86. *Mem:* Am Chem Soc. *Res:* Regulation of carbon and nitrogen metabolism in photosynthetic tissue of higher plants. *Mailing Add:* Dept Chem Juniata Col 1700 Moore St Huntingdon PA 16652. *E-Mail:* reed@juniata.edu

REED, SHERMAN KENNEDY, AGRICULTURAL CHEMISTRY, CHEMICAL ENGINEERING. *Current Pos:* CONSULT, 84- *Personal Data:* b Chicago, Ill, Apr 11, 19; m 43, Octavia Bailey; c Martin Bailey, Holly Anne & Jule Marie. *Educ:* Univ Ill, BS, 40, Cornell Univ, PhD(chem), 49. *Prof Exp:* Asst chem, Cornell Univ, 40-43, Nat Defense Res Comt, 43; res scientist, SAM Labs, Columbia Univ, 43-46; from instr to asst prof chem, Bucknell Univ, 46-50; group leader, Res & Develop Dept, Westvaco Chem Div, FMC Corp, 50-53, asst dir res, Niagara Chem Div, 53-57, dir res & develop, Chem & Plastics Div, 57-60, dir cent res dept, 60-72, vpres technol, Chem Group, 72-74, vpres, 74-84. *Concurrent Pos:* Consult, Smith Kline Corp, 47-50; dir, Franklin Inst, Birkett Mills, Avicon, Inc & Indust Res Inst; chmn, Franklin Res Ctr. *Mem:* Am Chem Soc. *Res:* Fluorine phosphorus and agricultural chemistry; plastics; computer applications to chemistry; toxicology. *Mailing Add:* 14 Sailfish Rd Vero Beach FL 32960-5279

REED, STUART ARTHUR, ZOOLOGY, PHYSIOLOGY. *Current Pos:* RETIRED. *Personal Data:* b Erie, Pa, Jan 29, 30; m 53; c 4. *Educ:* Kent State Univ, BS, 51, MS, 53; Mich State Univ, PhD(zool), 62. *Prof Exp:* Instr physiol, Mich State Univ, 57-58, zool, 59-60, biol, 61-63, asst prof, 63-69; assoc prof zool, Univ Hawaii, 69-73, prof, 73- *Concurrent Pos:* NSF sci fac fel, 66-67. *Mem:* AAAS; Nat Asn Biol Teachers; Am Soc Zoologists; Sigma Xi; Am Inst Biol Sci. *Res:* Invertebrate zoology; curriculum developmental in marine biology. *Mailing Add:* Dept Zool Univ Hawaii Edmondson Hall Honolulu HI 96822

REED, TERRY EUGENE, MEDICAL GENETICS, EPIDEMIOLOGY. *Current Pos:* Fel, 71-72, from instr to assoc prof, 72-91, PROF MED GENETICS, SCH MED, IND UNIV, 91- *Personal Data:* b Mechanicsburg, Pa, Oct 7, 45; m 73, Dianne Bartram; c Matthew, Samantha & Alycia. *Educ:* Juniata Col, BS, 67; Ind Univ, PhD(med genetics), 71; Univ Pittsburgh. MPh, 82; Am Bd Med Genetics, dipl, 82. *Concurrent Pos:* Dir, Genetic Serv, Indianapolis Comprehensive Sickle Cell Ctr, 73-77; bd dir, Am Dermatoglyphics Asn, 76-79; consult, Genetic Dis Sect, Maternal & Child Health Div, Ind State Bd Health, 85-87, birth defects surveillance comt, Great Lakes Regional Serv Network, 86-; data base mgr, Vet Twin Study Coord Ctr, Nat Heart, Lung & Blood Inst, 85-91. *Mem:* Am Soc Human Genetics; Am Dermatoglyphics Asn; Sigma Xi. *Res:* Longitudinal epidemiologic studies of twin cohorts; role of environmental factors and genetic predisposition to inherited disease; dermatoglyphics as a developmental marker in twins and individuals with congenital abnormalities. *Mailing Add:* Dept Med & Molecular Genetics Sch Med Ind Univ Indianapolis IN 46202-5251. *Fax:* 317-274-2387; *E-Mail:* treed@medgen.iupui.edu

REED, THEODORE H(AROLD), VETERINARY MEDICINE. *Current Pos:* RETIRED. *Personal Data:* b Washington, DC, July 25, 22; m 80; c 2. *Educ:* Kans State Col, DVM, 45. *Honors & Awards:* Arthur S Flemming Award, 62. *Prof Exp:* Instr vet path, Kans State Col, 45-46; asst state vet, Ore, 46-48; vet, Portland Zoo, 49-55; vet, Nat Zool Park, 55-56, actg dir, 56-58, dir, 58-87. *Concurrent Pos:* Pvt pract, Idaho & Ore, 49-55; mem, Mayor's Zoo Comn, Portland Zoo, 51-55. *Mem:* Fel Am Asn Zool Parks & Aquariums (pres, 63-64). *Res:* Zoo administration and zoo veterinary medicine. *Mailing Add:* 104 Cherry St Milford DE 19963

REED, THOMAS BINNINGTON, SYNTHETIC FUEL TECHNOLOGY. *Current Pos:* sr staff, Biochem Conversion Br, 77-80, PRIN SCIENTIST, THERMOCHEM & ELECTROCHEM RES BR, NAT SOLAR ENERGY RES INST, 80-; RES PROF, DEPT CHEM ENG, COLO SCH MINES, 86- *Personal Data:* b Chicago, Ill, Jan 2, 26; m 47; c 4. *Educ:* Northwestern Univ, BS, 47; Univ Minn, PhD(phys chem), 52. *Honors & Awards:* R&D 100 Award, 82 & 93. *Prof Exp:* Chemist, Oil Explor & Develop Lab, Shell Oil Co, 47-48; res chemist, Linde Air Prod Co, Union Carbide & Carbon Corp, 52-59; mem staff, Solid State Div, Lincoln Lab, Mass Inst Technol, 59-77. *Concurrent Pos:* Sci Res Coun sr fel inorg chem, Oxford Univ, 65-66; mem high temperature chem comt, NSF; grant, Methanol as a Synthetic Fuel, J B Hawley Found, 74-; mem renewable resources comt, NSF, 75-; pres, Biomass Energy Found. *Mem:* Am Chem Soc. *Res:* X-ray crystallography; thermal plasmas; solid state chemistry; high temperature processes; heat mirrors for solar insulation; synthetic fuel manufacture and use, biomass conversion processes; oil spill control. *Mailing Add:* 1810 Smith Rd Golden CO 80401. *Fax:* 303-273-3730; *E-Mail:* 73002.1213@compuserve.com

REED, THOMAS EDWARD, HUMAN GENETICS, BEHAVIORAL GENETICS. *Current Pos:* RETIRED. *Personal Data:* b Gadsen, Ala, Nov 12, 23; m 49, Maria Zenzes; c Christopher & Thomas. *Educ:* Univ Calif, AB, 48; Univ London, PhD(zool), 52. *Prof Exp:* Jr geneticist, Univ Mich, 52-56, asst prof, 56-57, res assoc, 57-60; assoc prof zool & pediat, Univ Toronto, 60-69, prof zool & anthrop, 69-89. *Concurrent Pos:* Vis assoc prof, Sch Pub Health, Univ Calif, Berkeley, 65-66; sabbatical, Inst Behav Genetics, Univ Colo, Boulder, Inst Behav Genetics, Univ Heidelberg & Dept Educ Psychol, Univ Calif, Berkeley. *Mem:* AAAS; Am Soc Human Genetics; Behav Genetics Asn. *Res:* Human genetics; genetics of responses to alcohol. *Mailing Add:* Dept Zool Univ Toronto Toronto ON M5S 1A1 Can

REED, THOMAS FREEMAN, polymer chemistry, rubber chemistry, for more information see previous edition

REED, WILLIAM, CELL BIOLOGY, CYTOSKELETON. *Current Pos:* FEL BIOPHYSICS, UNIV NC, 86- *Educ:* Univ Calif, San Francisco, PhD(biophysics), 84. *Prof Exp:* Fel, Ctr Neural Biol & Behav Col Physicians & Surgeons, Columbia Univ, NY, 84-86. *Res:* Cell surface receptors. *Mailing Add:* CEMLB Univ NC CB 7310 104 Mason Farm Rd Chapel Hill NC 27599

REED, WILLIAM ALFRED, OPTICAL FIBER DESIGN & CHARACTERIZATION. *Current Pos:* DISTINGUISHED MEM TECH STAFF, OPTICAL FIBER RES DEPT, AT&T BELL LABS, 86- *Personal Data:* b Rochester, NY, Jan 5, 36; m 58, Patricia Hawley; c Catherine & Susan. *Educ:* Oberlin Col, BA, 57; Northwestern Univ, PhD(physics), 62. *Prof Exp:* Mem tech staff, Metal Physics Dept, Bell Labs, 61-71, mem staff, Condensed State Res Dept, 71-79, Glass Res Dept, 79-85. *Mem:* Am Phys Soc; Am Optical Soc. *Res:* Galvanomagnetic effects; Fermi surface studies; resistive behavior of superconductors; Compton scattering of x-rays; optical fiber design and characterization. *Mailing Add:* Bell Tel Labs Rm 6D 209 600 Mountain Ave Murray Hill NJ 07974

REED, WILLIAM DOYLE, entomology; deceased, see previous edition for last biography

REED, WILLIAM EDWARD, SOIL CHEMISTRY. *Current Pos:* RETIRED. *Personal Data:* b Columbia, La, July 15, 14; m 42; c 3. *Educ:* Southern Univ, BS, 37; Iowa State Univ, MS, 41; Cornell Univ, PhD(soil sci), 46. *Prof Exp:* Asst agr engr, Soil Conserv Serv, USDA, 36-37; county agent, La State Univ, 37-40; instr soil sci & chem, Southern Univ, 42-47; agr res specialist, US Dept State, Liberia, 47-49; dean, Sch Agr, Agr & Tech Col NC, 48-57; chief field staff, Int Coop Admin contract, Int Develop Serv, Inc, Ghana, 57-59, Int Coop Admin rep, Lome, 61, opers officer, Ibadan, 61, asst dir, Lagos, 61-68, dep dir mission to Ethiopia, 68-72, officer-in-residence, USAID, 72-74, spec asst to chancellor int progs, 74-76, assoc dean res & spec projs, 78, dir, int progs & spec projs, NC A&T State Univ, 78-84. *Concurrent Pos:* Mem US deleg, Soviet Union, 55; mem US deleg, UN Conf Sci & Technol, 63. *Mem:* AAAS; Am Chem Soc; Am Soc Agron; Am Foreign Serv Asn; Soil Sci Soc Am. *Res:* Soil genesis, fertility and morphology; agronomy. *Mailing Add:* 2711 McConnell Rd Greensboro NC 27401-4534

REED, WILLIAM J, STOCHASTIC MODELLING, OPTIMIZATION. *Current Pos:* PROF STATIST, UNIV VICTORIA, 79- *Personal Data:* b Hastings, UK, Jan 19, 46; Can citizen; m 74; c 2. *Educ:* Imp Col, Univ London, BSc, 68; McGill Univ, MSc, 70; Univ BC, PhD(appl math), 75. *Prof Exp:* Res assoc ecol, Univ BC, 77-79. *Concurrent Pos:* Lectr statist, Portmouth Polytech, 70-71. *Mem:* Resource Modeling Asn; Soc Indust & Appl Math; Biomet Soc; Inst Math Statist; Statist Soc Can. *Res:* Resource management modelling; management modeling and statistics in forestry and fisheries; resource economics. *Mailing Add:* Dept Statist Univ Victoria PO Box 1700 Victoria BC V8W 3P4 Can. *Fax:* 250-721-8962; *E-Mail:* reed @uvvm.uvic.ca

REEDER, CHARLES EDGAR, PHYSICAL CHEMISTRY, ORGANIC CHEMISTRY. *Current Pos:* RETIRED. *Personal Data:* b Fairfield, Iowa, July 20, 27; m 56; c 3. *Educ:* Wheaton Col, BS, 51; Iowa State Col, PhD(chem), 55. *Honors & Awards:* Am Inst Chemists Award. *Prof Exp:* Draftsman, Louden Mach Co, 45-47; asst, Parsons Col, 48, Wheaton Col, 49-50 & Iowa State Col, 51-55; instr chem, Bates Col, 55-57; from asst prof to assoc prof chem, Baylor Univ, 57-92. *Mem:* Am Chem Soc; Sigma Xi. *Res:* Reaction mechanisms; catalysis; molecular structure; coordination compounds; chemistry teaching methods and effectiveness. *Mailing Add:* 717 Falcon Dr Waco TX 76712

REEDER, CLYDE, CHEMICAL ENGINEERING. *Current Pos:* RETIRED. *Personal Data:* b Huntingdon, Pa, Mar 2, 24; m 46; c 3. *Educ:* Juniata Col, BS, 48; Ohio State Univ, PhD(chem eng), 51. *Prof Exp:* Res engr, Org Chem Dept, Jackson Lab, E I du Pont de Nemours & Co, 51-60, sr res engr, Elastomer Chem Dept, Exp Sta, 60-63; mgr process develop, Agr Chem, Atlanta Res Ctr, Armour Agr Chem Co, 63-68, lab mgr, USS Agrichem, Inc, 68-69; technologist, Mobay Chem Co, 69-87; consult, 87-89. *Mem:* Am Chem Soc; Am Inst Chem Engrs. *Res:* Fluorinated elastomers; process development; kinetics; economic analyses of chemical processes; elastomer chemical and engineering technology; urethanes; agricultural chemicals. *Mailing Add:* Four Hartle Lane Pittsburgh PA 15228

REEDER, DON DAVID, HIGH ENERGY PHYSICS. *Current Pos:* from asst prof to assoc prof, 66-72, PROF PHYSICS, UNIV WIS-MADISON, 72- *Personal Data:* b Dubuque, Iowa, Aug 18, 35; m 58, Carol Bender; c Julia A & Linda S. *Educ:* Univ Ill, BS, 58; Univ Wis, MS, 62, PhD(physics), 66. *Prof Exp:* Ltjg, USN. *Concurrent Pos:* Fel, NATO, 74. *Mem:* Fel Am Phys Soc; AAAS; Inst Elec & Electronics Engrs. *Res:* Experimental elementary particle physics. *Mailing Add:* Dept Physics Sterling Hall Univ Wis Madison WI 53706. *Fax:* 608-263-0800

REEDER, JOHN HAMILTON, MATHEMATICS. *Current Pos:* ASST PROF MATH, UNIV MO, COLUMBIA, 73- *Personal Data:* b Baltimore, Md, Jan 25, 44; m 74. *Educ:* Stevens Inst Technol, BS, 66; Northwestern Univ, MS, 67, PhD(math), 72. *Prof Exp:* Vis asst prof math, Ore State Univ, 71-72; vis scholar, Univ Victoria, 72-73. *Mem:* Am Math Soc. *Res:* Water waves; kinetic theory of fluids; Wiener-Hopf operators. *Mailing Add:* Dept Math Univ Mo 205 Math Sci Bldg Columbia MO 65211-0002

REEDER, JOHN RAYMOND, BOTANY. *Current Pos:* SCHOLAR, UNIV ARIZ, 76- *Personal Data:* b Grand Ledge, Mich, July 29, 14; m 41, Charlotte Goodding. *Educ:* Mich State Col, BS, 39; Northwestern Univ, MS, 40; Harvard Univ, MA, 46, PhD(syst bot), 47. *Prof Exp:* From instr to assoc prof, Cur Herbarium, Yale Univ, 47-68; prof & cur, Rocky Mountain Herbarium, Univ Wyo, 68-76. *Concurrent Pos:* Vis prof, Univ Venezuela, 64, hon prof, 66-; ed, Brittonia, 67-71. *Mem:* Am Soc Naturalists; Int Asn Plant Taxon; Torrey Bot Club; Sigma Xi; fel Linnean Soc London; Am Soc Plant Taxon; Botanical Soc Am. *Res:* Taxonomy of vascular plants; taxonomy and phylogeny of Gramineae. *Mailing Add:* Herbarium Rm 113 Shantz Bldg Univ Ariz Tucson AZ 85721

REEDER, PAUL LORENZ, NUCLEAR CHEMISTRY, FISSION PRODUCTS. *Current Pos:* STAFF SCIENTIST NUCLEAR CHEM, PAC NORTHWEST LABS, BATTELLE MEM INST, RICHLAND, WASH, 70- *Personal Data:* b Dayton, Ohio, Sept 28, 36; m 84, Rachel Miller; c David, Eric, Douglas & Katherine. *Educ:* Col Wooster, Ohio, AB, 58; Univ Calif, Berkeley, PhD(nuclear chem), 63. *Prof Exp:* Fel nuclear chem, Brookhaven Nat Lab, Upton, NY, 63-65; asst prof chem, Washington Univ, St Louis, 65-70. *Concurrent Pos:* NATO fel, Orsay, France, 68; sabbatical, Lawrence Berkeley Lab, 90. *Mem:* Am Phys Soc; Am Chem Soc; AAAS. *Res:* Instruments for radiation detection; nuclear decay properties of short-lived isotopes; on-line mass spectrometry. *Mailing Add:* MS P8-08 Pac Northwest Labs Battelle Mem Inst PO Box 999 Richland WA 99352

REEDER, RAY R, PHYSICAL CHEMISTRY, INORGANIC CHEMISTRY. *Current Pos:* From instr to assoc prof chem, 69-76, interim dean fac, 76-77, dir, Ctr Community Educ, 76-78, dept chmn, 81-89, ASSOC PROF CHEM, ELIZABETHTOWN COL, 78- *Personal Data:* b Cleveland, Ohio, July 18, 43; m 65; c 1. *Educ:* Case Inst Technol, BS, 65; Brown Univ, PhD(chem), 70. *Mem:* Am Chem Soc. *Res:* Inorganic systems through use of physical techniques; computer applications in undergraduate chemical education; computer simulation and graphics. *Mailing Add:* Dept Chem Elizabethtown Col One Alpha Dr Elizabethtown PA 17022-2298

REEDER, RONALD HOWARD, MOLECULAR BIOLOGY. *Current Pos:* MEM & SECT CHIEF, HUTCHINSON CANCER RES CTR, 78- *Personal Data:* b Denver, Colo, Sept 7, 39; m 54. *Educ:* Columbia Union Col, Md, BS, 61; Mass Inst Technol, PhD(biol), 65. *Prof Exp:* Staff mem, dept embryol, Carnegie Inst Washington, 69-78. *Concurrent Pos:* Mem, NIH Cell Biol Study Sect, 75-77; ed, J Cell Biol, 77- & J Biol Chem, 79- *Mem:* Am Soc Cell Biol; Am Soc Biol Chemists. *Res:* Study of the primary structure of the ribosomal genes and the proteins which bind to them. *Mailing Add:* Fred Hutchinson Cancer Res Ctr 1100 Fairview Ave N Seattle WA 98109

REEDER, WILLIAM GLASE, ANIMAL ECOLOGY, VERTEBRATE PALEONTOLOGY. *Current Pos:* DIR, TEX MEM MUS, 78-; PROF ZOOL, UNIV TEX, AUSTIN, 78- *Personal Data:* b Los Angeles, Calif, Feb 4, 29; m 51; c 4. *Educ:* Univ Calif, Los Angeles, BA, 50; Univ Mich, MS, 53, PhD(zool), 57. *Prof Exp:* Instr zool, Univ Calif, Los Angeles, 55-56; from instr to prof zool, Univ Wis-Madison, 56-78. *Mem:* AAAS; Am Soc Mammal; Am Soc Archnology. *Res:* Vertebrate ecology, especially of North American deserts, the Arctic and tropics, especially Galapagos Islands; problems of thermoregulation; paleoecology, especially of rodents; human ecology; biogeography and ecology of arachnids. *Mailing Add:* 7014 Greenshores Dr Austin TX 78730

REED-HILL, ROBERT E(LLIS), METALLURGY. *Current Pos:* RETIRED. *Personal Data:* b Detroit, Mich, Nov 19, 13; m 38; c 2. *Educ:* Univ Mich, BS, 36, MS, 38; Yale Univ, DEng, 56. *Prof Exp:* From instr to assoc prof eng, USCG Acad, 39-60; from assoc prof to prof metall, Dept Mat Sci & Eng, Univ Fla, 60-84. *Mem:* Am Inst Mining Metall & Petrol Engrs; fel Am Soc Metall; Brit Inst Metals; Am Soc Testing & Mat; Sigma Xi. *Res:* Mechanical metallurgy; deformation twinning; dynamic strain aging; slow strain-rate embrittlement. *Mailing Add:* 11100 NW 11th Ave Gainesville FL 32606-5496

REEDS, LLOYD GEORGE, AGRICULTURAL GEOGRAPHY. *Current Pos:* prof, 48-85, EMER PROF GEOG, MCMASTER UNIV, 85- *Personal Data:* b Lindsay, Ont, July 11, 17; m 49, Marguerite Fallis; c Gregory, Barbara & Judy. *Educ:* Univ Toronto, BA, 40, MA, 42, PhD(geog), 56. *Honors & Awards:* Senvile Award, Can Asn Geog, 80. *Prof Exp:* Soil survr, Ont Agr Col, 42-43; lectr geog, Univ Toronto, 45-48. *Mem:* Asn Am Geog; Can Asn Geog (pres, 61-62); fel Royal Can Geog Soc. *Res:* Agricultural land-use problems in Southern Ontario. *Mailing Add:* Dept Geog McMaster Univ 1280 Main St W Hamilton ON L8S 4K1 Can

REEDY, JOHN JOSEPH, BIOLOGY. *Current Pos:* PROF ZOOL, NIAGARA UNIV, 60- *Personal Data:* b Buffalo, NY, May 14, 27; m 52, Joann Walsh; c Kerry, Susan, Mary & Tim. *Educ:* Niagara Univ, BSNS, 48; Notre Dame Univ, MS, 50, PhD(zool), 52; Bridgewater State Col, MEd, 60. *Prof Exp:* Instr, Univ Detroit, 52-53; from asst prof to prof zool, Stonehill Col, 53-60. *Mem:* AAAS; Soc Syst Zool; Am Genetics Soc; Soc Study Evolution; Sigma Xi. *Res:* Human genetics; radiobiology; Drosophila genetics dealing with Epistasis. *Mailing Add:* Dept Biol Niagara Univ Box 121 Niagara Falls NY 14109

REEDY, MICHAEL K, CELL BIOLOGY. *Current Pos:* assoc prof, 69-86, prof anat, 86-88, PROF CELL BIOL, SCH MED, DUKE UNIV, 88- *Personal Data:* b Seattle, Wash, June 19, 34; m 74; c 3. *Educ:* Univ Wash, BA, 58, MD, 62. *Honors & Awards:* Newcomb S Cleveland Prize, AAAS, 67. *Prof Exp:* Intern path, Univ Hosp, Seattle, Wash, 62-63; NIH res fel, 63-66; asst prof physiol, Med Ctr, Univ Calif, Los Angeles, 66-68, assoc prof, 68-69. *Concurrent Pos:* NIH res career develop award, 67-69 & 72-75; Alexander von Humboldt US Sr Scientist Award & Guggenheim fel, 78. *Mem:* AAAS; Am Soc Cell Biol; Biophys Soc. *Res:* Ultrastructure of myofibrils; mechanisms of contractility; preparative methods for biological electron microscopy; mass measurements by microscopy. *Mailing Add:* Dept Cell Biol Duke Univ Med Ctr Box 3011 Sands Bldg Rm 458 Durham NC 27710-0001

REEDY, ROBERT CHALLENGER, NUCLEAR CHEMISTRY & COSMOCHEMISTRY, SPACE PHYSICS. *Current Pos:* STAFF MEM, LOS ALAMOS NAT LAB, 72- *Personal Data:* b Summit, NJ, Mar 5, 42; m 69, Maria Homs; c Anne & John. *Educ:* Colgate Univ, BA, 64; Columbia Univ, PhD(chem physics), 69. *Prof Exp:* Res assoc nuclear chem, Columbia Univ, 64-69; res chemist, Univ Calif, San Diego, 69-72. *Concurrent Pos:* Consult, NASA, 74-76; guest scientist, Max-Planck Inst, Mainz, WGer, 82-83. *Mem:* Fel Meteoritical Soc; Am Geophys Union. *Res:* Nuclear interactions and nuclear reactions in the moon and other extraterrestrial matter; chemistry of planets from orbit by gamma-ray spectroscopy; energetic particles in space. *Mailing Add:* Group NIS-2 Mail Stop D 436 Los Alamos Nat Lab Los Alamos NM 87545. *E-Mail:* rreedy@lanl.gov

REEKE, GEORGE NORMAN, JR, CRYSTALLOGRAPHY, NEUROBIOLOGY. *Current Pos:* asst prof biochem, 70-76, ASSOC PROF BIOL MODELLING, ROCKEFELLER UNIV, 76- *Personal Data:* b Green Bay, Wis, Oct 16, 43; m 69. *Educ:* Calif Inst Technol, BS, 64; Harvard Univ, MA, 66, PhD(chem), 69. *Prof Exp:* Res asst chem, Harvard Univ, 69-70. *Concurrent Pos:* Res fel, Alfred P Sloan Found, 75-77. *Mem:* AAAS; Am Soc Biol Chemists; Am Crystallog Asn; Soc Neurosci. *Res:* Synthetic neural modelling protein crystallography. *Mailing Add:* Rockefeller Univ Box 253 New York NY 10021. *E-Mail:* reeke@lobimo.rockefeller.edu

REEKER, LARRY HENRY, COMPUTER SCIENCE & COMPUTATIONAL LINGUISTICS, KNOWLEDGE & DATA MANAGEMENT, LEARNING. *Current Pos:* RES STAFF, INST DEFENSE ANALYSIS, 89-; PROG DIR, KNOWLEDGE MODELS & COGNITIVE SYSTS, NSF, 94- *Personal Data:* b Spokane, Wash, Feb 2, 43; m 64, 89, Gail Bleach; c Philip, David, Christina, Greg & Seth. *Educ:* Yale Univ, BA, 64; Carnegie-Mellon Univ, PhD(comput sci), 74. *Prof Exp:* Asst prof comput & info sci & ling, Ohio State Univ, 68-73; asst prof comput sci, Univ Ore, 73-75; assoc prof, Univ Ariz, 75-78; reader & head comput sci, Univ Queensland, 78-82; prof & head comput sci, Tulane Univ, 82-85; vpres & sr prin scientist, BDM Corp, 85-89. *Concurrent Pos:* Consult, Tech/Ops Corp, 67-68; vis lectr comput sci, Univ Pittsburgh, 68; asst dir, Ling Inst, Ling Soc Am, 70; ed consult, Barnes & Noble Inc, 70-71; ed, SIGACT News, Asn Comput Mach, 70-78; vis res scientist, Chemical Abstracts Serv, 82; vis scientist, Naval Res Lab, 84-85; coun rep, Capital Region, Asn Comput Mach, 86-89. *Mem:* Asn Comput Mach; Asn Comput Ling; Am Asn Artificial Intel; Inst Elec & Electronics Engrs Computer Soc. *Res:* Computer modeling of language acquisition; formal language theory and related theory of computing; programming languages and environments; automatic information extraction from texts; knowledge acquisition and representation. *Mailing Add:* 11001 Lockwood Dr Silver Spring MD 20901. *Fax:* 703-306-0599; *E-Mail:* reeker@ida.org, lreeker@nsf.gov

REEL, JERRY ROYCE, ENDOCRINOLOGY & TOXICOLOGY. *Current Pos:* VPRES SCI, BIOQUAL, INC, ROCKVILLE, MD, 91- *Personal Data:* b Washington, Ind, May 4, 38; m 65, Joan Wedberg; c Justine J. *Educ:* Ind State Univ, BA, 60; Univ Ill, MS, 63, PhD(physiol), 66. *Prof Exp:* USPHS fel, Oak Ridge Nat Lab, 66, Am Cancer Soc fel, 66-68; res scientist, 68, endocrinologist biochemist, 68-70, sect dir endocrinol, 70-75, sr res scientist, Parke Davis & Co, 75-78; sect mgr endocrinol, 78-80, dir life sci & toxicol, div, Res Triangle Inst, 80-85; dir, Endocrinol Dept, Sterling-Winthrop Res Inst, 85-87, dir endocrine pharmacol, 87-89, asst dir, Dept Pharmacol, 87-89; vpres, res & admin, Integrated Lab Systs, Inc, 89-90; sr toxicologist, Exp Path Labs, 91. *Concurrent Pos:* Adj assoc prof, Wayne State Univ Sch Med, 74-78; diplomate, Am Bd Toxicol, 80- *Mem:* Am Chem Soc; Soc Biol Reproduction; Endocrine Soc; Am Physiol Soc; Tissue Cult Asn; Soc Toxicol. *Res:* Reproduction; cell culture; hormone and drug action; hypothalamic releasing factors and their antagonists; reproductive toxicology; contraceptive research and development. *Mailing Add:* Diagnon Corp 9600 Med Ctr Dr Rockville MD 20850-3300

REEMTSMA, KEITH, SURGERY. *Current Pos:* DIR SURG SERV, PRESBY HOSP, 71- *Personal Data:* b Madera, Calif, Dec 5, 25; m; c 2. *Educ:* Idaho State Univ, BS, 48; Univ Pa, MD, 49; Am Bd Surg, dipl, 58; Am Bd Thoracic Surg, dipl, 60. *Hon Degrees:* DSc, Columbia Univ, 58. *Prof Exp:* From intern to resident, Presby Hosp, New York, 50-57; asst, Col Physicians & Surgeons, Columbia Univ, 57; asst prof, Sch Med, Tulane Univ, 57-62, assoc prof surg, 62-66; prof & head dept, Sch Med, Univ Utah, 66-71; PROF SURG & CHMN DEPT, COL PHYSICIANS & SURGEONS, COLUMBIA UNIV, 71- *Concurrent Pos:* Mem study sect A, Surg, NIH, 65- *Mem:* Soc Clin Surg; Am Surg Asn; Soc Univ Surgeons; Am Col Surgeons; Am Fedn Clin Res. *Res:* Transplantation; cardiovascular surgery. *Mailing Add:* 622 W 168th St New York NY 10032-3702

REENSTRA, ARTHUR LEONARD, ELECTRICAL ENGINEERING, SOLID STATE ELECTRONICS. *Current Pos:* DIR ENG, PACKAGING & WEIGHT DIV, FRANKLIN ELEC CO, 80- *Personal Data:* b Clifton, NJ, Mar 5, 36; m 59; c 3. *Educ:* Bucknell Univ, BS, 59; Carnegie Inst Technol, MS, 60; Purdue Univ, PhD(elec eng), 67. *Prof Exp:* Res engr, Res Labs, US Rubber Co, 60-62; instr elec eng, Purdue Univ, 62-64; mem tech staff, Res & Develop Dept, Mat & Electronic Controls Group, Tex Instruments, Inc, 67-76; dir prod develop, Beede Elec Instrument Co, 76-77, dir eng, 77-78, vpres, 79-80. *Mem:* Soc Automotive Engrs; Inst Elec & Electronics Engrs. *Res:* Positive temperature coefficient thermistor; thermistoic networks; control sensors and actuators. *Mailing Add:* 5078 Bunch Rd Summerfield NC 27358

REENTS, WILLIAM DAVID, JR, MASS SPECTROMETRY, GAS PHASE CLUSTER CHEMISTRY. *Current Pos:* Mem tech staff, 80-87, DISTINGUISHED MEM TECH STAFF, AT&T BELL LABS, 87- *Personal Data:* b Portsmouth, Va, Jan 18, 54; m 77; c 2. *Educ:* Monmouth Col, BS, 76; Purdue Univ, PhD(chem), 80. *Mem:* Am Soc Mass Spectrometry; Am Chem Soc. *Res:* Ion-molecule reactions of gas phase clusters using Fourier transform mass spectrometry; purity of hazardous reagents for semiconductor device manufacture; detection and characterization of sub-micron particles. *Mailing Add:* 18 Glen Gary Rd Middlesex NJ 08846-1262

REES, ALLAN W, PHYSICAL BIOCHEMISTRY. *Current Pos:* asst prof biochem, Univ Tex Health Sci Ctr, 69-77, ASST PROF, UNIV TEX DIV EARTH SCI, SAN ANTONIO, 77- *Personal Data:* b Piqua, Ohio, Dec 23, 33; m 59; c 2. *Educ:* Univ Cincinnati, ChE, 56, MS, 63, PhD(biochem), 67. *Prof Exp:* Res chemist, Cincinnati Milling Mach Co, 56-62. *Concurrent Pos:* Nat Cancer Inst res fel, 67-68. *Mem:* AAAS; Fedn Am Soc Exp Biol; Am Chem Soc; Biophys Soc. *Res:* Structure and conformation of DNA and nucleoproteins; centrifugal and hydrodynamic techniques. *Mailing Add:* 14319 123rd Ave NE No D Kirkland WA 98034-1440

REES, ALUN HYWEL, ORGANIC CHEMISTRY, PHARMACEUTICAL CHEMISTRY. *Current Pos:* assoc prof, 66-74, prof, 74-92, chmn, Dept Chem, 89-91, EMER PROF, TRENT UNIV, 92- *Personal Data:* b Pontypridd, Wales, Aug 30, 28; m 51; c 2. *Educ:* Cambridge Univ, BA, 49, MA, 53, PhD(chem), 68; Univ London, PhD(org chem), 58; Oxford Univ, MA, 65. *Prof Exp:* Res chemist, Roche Prod Ltd, Eng, 49-53; lectr chem, Univ Ibadan, 53-62, sr lectr, 62-64; res fel, Oxford Univ, 64-66. *Concurrent Pos:* Fulbright scholar & res fel, Harvard Univ, 59 & 63; vis prof pharmaceut chem, Univ Ife, Nigeria, 74-75; vis prof org & appl chem, Univ Port, Harcourt, Nigeria, 81; vis res fel, Yale Univ, 85, Univ Wales, Cardiff, 74 & 89. *Mem:* Chem Inst Can; Am Chem Soc; Royal Soc Chem. *Res:* Heterocyclic, medicinal and natural product chemistry; azepines. *Mailing Add:* Dept Chem Trent Univ Peterborough ON K9J 7B8 Can

REES, CHARLES SPARKS, MATHEMATICS. *Current Pos:* from asst prof to assoc prof math, 70-77, PROF MATH, UNIV NEW ORLEANS, 77- *Personal Data:* b Dallas, Tex, Nov 21, 40; m 62; c 2. *Educ:* La State Univ, BS, 62; Univ Kans, MA, 63, PhD(math), 67. *Prof Exp:* Asst prof math, Univ Tenn, Knoxville, 67-70. *Mem:* Am Math Soc; Math Asn Am. *Res:* Integration and summability of Fourier series. *Mailing Add:* Dept Math Univ New Orleans New Orleans LA 70148-0001

REES, EBERHARD F M, AEROSPACE TECHNOLOGY. *Current Pos:* RETIRED. *Personal Data:* b Trossingen, Ger, Apr 28, 08; US citizen; m 47. *Educ:* Stuttgart Techn Univ, BS; Dresden Inst Technol, MS, 34. *Hon Degrees:* DSc, Rollins Col, 59, Univ Ala, Huntsville, 72. *Honors & Awards:* Medal Outstanding Leadership, NASA, 66. *Prof Exp:* Tech asst, Meier & Weichelt Foundry & Steel Mill, Leipzig, 34-40; plant mgr, Guided Missile Ctr, Peenemuende, Ger, 40-45; aerodyn develop engr, Ord Res & Develop, Ft Bliss, 45-50; dep chief, Guided Missile Develop Div, NASA, Huntsville, Ala, 50-56, dep dir, Army Ballistic Missile Agency, 56-60, dep dir, G C Marshall Space Flight Ctr, 60-70, dir, 70-73. *Mem:* Nat Acad Eng; fel Am Astronaut Soc; hon mem Hermann Oberth Soc; fel Am Inst Aeronaut & Astronaut. *Res:* Rocketry; space flight technology. *Mailing Add:* 400 E Howry Ave Deland FL 32724

REES, HORACE BENNER, JR, VIROLOGY. *Current Pos:* RETIRED. *Personal Data:* b Big Lake, Tex, July 25, 26; m 54, Helen H Scott; c 1. *Educ:* Univ Tex, BA, 49, MA, 50; George Washington Univ, PhD, 66. *Prof Exp:* Asst immunologist, Tex State Dept Health, 50-52; asst dir, Regional Lab, San Antonio City Health Dept, 52; dir, Abilene-Taylor County Health Unit Lab, 53; asst dir, Wene's Poultry Labs, Pleasantville, NJ, 54; microbiologist, Viral & Rickettsial Div, US Army Biol Ctr, Ft Detrick, Md, 54-66; chief, Ecol & Technol Br, Life Sci Lab Div, US Army Biol Labs, 66-83. *Concurrent Pos:* Author & consult, 83- *Mem:* Am Soc Microbiol; Tissue Cult Asn; NY Acad Sci; Sigma Xi. *Res:* Rickettsiae; medical bacteriology. *Mailing Add:* 3584 Millstream Lane Salt Lake City UT 84109-3254

REES, JOHN, ECONOMIC DEVELOPMENT-SCIENCE BASED. *Current Pos:* PROF GEOG & HEAD DEPT, UNIV NC, GREENSBORO, 87- *Personal Data:* b Bangor, Wales, Mar 25, 48; m 71, Janet Siegrist; c David, Mark & Catherine. *Educ:* Univ Wales, BA Hons, 69; Univ Cincinnati, MA, 71; London Sch Econ, PhD(geog), 77. *Prof Exp:* From asst prof to assoc prof polit econ, Univ Tex, Dallas, 75-83; assoc prof geog, Syracuse Univ, 83-87. *Concurrent Pos:* Prin investr, NSF, 76-90; consult, Joint Econ Comt, US Cong, 78-84, President Carter's Comn, Nat Agenda US, 79-80 & Off Technol Assessment, US Cong, 83-85; Nat Res Coun fel, 82-83; vis scientist, Int Inst Appl Systs Anal, Austria, 82; mem, Tissot Econ Found, Switz, 87- & Gov Hunt Task Force Indust Incentives, NC, 93-; sr fel, Kenan Inst, Univ NC, Chapel Hill, 89-; adv, Urban Policy, Carter & Bush Admin. *Mem:* Asn Am Geographers; Regional Sci Asn; Sigma Xi. *Res:* Impact of industry and government policy on regional development; science and technology policy in US, Europe and Asia. *Mailing Add:* Dept Geog Univ NC Greensboro NC 27412. *Fax:* 910-334-5864

REES, JOHN DAVID, BIOGEOGRAPHY, CULTURAL GEOGRAPHY. *Current Pos:* Asst prof, 65-66 & 68-77, ASSOC PROF GEOG, CALIF STATE UNIV, LOS ANGELES, 77- *Personal Data:* b Los Angeles, Calif, Mar 16, 32. *Educ:* Univ Calif, Los Angeles, BA, 55, MA, 61, PhD(geog), 71. *Mem:* AAAS; Asn Am Geographers; Soc Econ Botanists. *Res:* Peasant utilization of biotic resources in middle America; rural economy; neotropical biogeography and conservation; regional geography of middle America. *Mailing Add:* 424 S Holt Ave Los Angeles CA 90048-4004

REES, JOHN ROBERT, PARTICLE ACCELERATORS. *Current Pos:* staff mem, Stanford Linear Accelerator Ctr, 65-67, adj prof physics, 69-94, assoc dir, 76-91, Superconducting Super Collider, 91-94, EMER PROF, STANFORD LINEAR ACCELERATOR CTR, 94- *Personal Data:* b Peru, Ind, Feb 17, 30; m 56, Marion Janet Heimert; c Carol Ellen & John Alton. *Educ:* Ind Univ, AB, 51, MS, 54, PhD(physics), 57. *Prof Exp:* Res fel physics, Harvard Univ, 56-65; chief, Advan Accelerators Br, High Energy Physics Prog Div Res, US AEC, DC, 67-69. *Concurrent Pos:* Instr, Northeastern Univ, 59-60; Chmn, Div Physics Beams, Am Phys Soc, 94-95. *Mem:* Fel Am Phys Soc. *Res:* Design and construction of high energy particle accelerators including technical management and project management. *Mailing Add:* 1340 Sunrise Ct Los Altos CA 94024. *E-Mail:* jrr@slac.stanford.edu

REES, MANFRED HUGH, AERONOMY. *Current Pos:* prof, 75-92, EMER PROF GEOPHYS, UNIV ALASKA, 92- *Personal Data:* b Ger, June 29, 26; nat US; m 49; c 2. *Educ:* WVa Univ, BSEE, 48, Univ Colo, MS, 56, PhD(physics), 58. *Prof Exp:* Engr, Nat Adv Comt Aeronaut, 48-49; proj engr, Sperry Gyroscope Co, 51-53; instr physics, Univ Colo, 53-58; asst prof geophys, Geophys Inst, Univ Alaska, 58-60; sr res fel appl math, Queen's Univ, Belfast, 60-61; res physicist, Univ Colo, 61-65; assoc prof physics & head dept, Univ Alaska, 65-66; mem staff, Lab Atmospheric & Space Physics, Univ Colo, Boulder, 66-75, lectr astro-geophys, 70-75. *Concurrent Pos:* Physicist, Nat Bur Stand, 56-58; vis prof, Univ Southhampton. *Mem:* Am Geophys Union. *Res:* Upper atmosphere physics; aurora and airglow; zodiacal light; spectroscopy; atomic and molecular collision processes; solar-terrestrial relations. *Mailing Add:* Dept Physics Univ Southampton Southampton S0171BJ England. *Fax:* 44-170-359-3910; *E-Mail:* mhr@phys.zotom.ac.uk

REES, MARTIN J, ASTROPHYSICS. *Current Pos:* prof astron & exp philos, 73-92, dir, Inst Astron, 77-92, ROYAL SOC RES PROF, CAMBRIDGE UNIV, 92-, ASTRONOMER, ROYAL, 95. *Personal Data:* b York, Eng, June 23, 42. *Educ:* Cambridge Univ, BA, 63, MA & PhD(astrophys), 67. *Hon Degrees:* DSc, Sussex, 90, Leicester, 93, Keele New Castle, Uppsalm, 95, Copenhagen 96, Toronto, 97. *Honors & Awards:* Heinemann Prize, Am Inst Physics, 84; Gold Medal, Royal Astron Soc, 87; Balzan Prize, 89; Robinson Prize, 90; Bruce Medal, Astron Soc Pac. *Prof Exp:* Prof astron, Sussex Univ, 72-73. *Concurrent Pos:* Vis assoc, Calif Tech Inst, 70; vis prof, Harvard Univ, 72, 86-88 & Inst Astrophys, Princeton Univ, 82; Regents fel, Smithsonian Inst, 84-88; prim Brit Asn Adv Sci 95-96. *Mem:* Foreign mem Nat Acad Sci; foreign hon mem Am Acad Arts & Sci; Royal Astron Soc (pres, 92-94); fel Royal Soc; hon mem Royal Swed Acad Sci; hon mem Am Philos Soc; hon mem Indian Acad Sci; Pontifical Acad Sci; foreign mem Acad Lincei Rome. *Res:* Astrophysics; cosmology; space research. *Mailing Add:* Inst Astron Madingley Rd Cambridge CB3 OHA England

REES, MINA S, MATHEMATICS. *Current Pos:* dean grad studies, 61-68, provost, Grad Div, 68-69, pres grad sch, 69-72, EMER PROF MATH, CITY UNIV NEW YORK, 72-, EMER PRES GRAD SCH, 72- *Personal Data:* b Cleveland, Ohio, Aug 2, 02; m 55. *Educ:* Hunter Col, AB, 23; Columbia Univ, AM, 25; Univ Chicago, PhD(math), 31. *Hon Degrees:* Eighteen from US cols & univs. *Honors & Awards:* Pub Welfare Medal, Nat Acad Sci, 83. *Prof Exp:* From instr to prof math, Hunter Col, 26-61, dean fac, 53-61. *Concurrent Pos:* Tech aide & exec asst to chief appl math panel, Nat Defense Res Comt, Off Sci Res & Develop, 43-46; head math br, Off Naval Res, 46-49, dir math sci div, 49-52, dep sci dir, 52-53; mem math div, Nat Res Coun, 53-56, mem exec comt, 54-56, comt surv math in US, 54-57; chmn adv comt math, Nat Bur Standards, 54-57, mem, 54-58; adv panel math, NSF, 55-58; Nat Sci Bd, 64-70; subcomt, Sci & Tech Manpower, Nat Manpower Adv Comt; mem, NY State Adv Coun Grad Educ, 62-72; chmn, Coun Grad Sch United States, 70; bd dir, NY Assoc Hosp Serv, 62-74, Health Serv Improvement Fund, 74-83; dir, Inst Math & Soc, 73- *Mem:* Fel AAAS; Am Math Soc; Math Asn Am (second vpres, 63-65); Soc Indust & Appl Math; fel NY Acad Sci; Sigma Xi. *Res:* Linear algebras; numerical analysis; history of computers. *Mailing Add:* 301 E 66th St New York NY 10021-6205

REES, PAUL KLEIN, MATHEMATICS. *Current Pos:* from assoc prof to prof, 46-67, actg head dept, 47-48, EMER PROF MATH, LA STATE UNIV, BATON ROUGE, 67- *Personal Data:* b Center Point, Tex, June 10, 02; m 35, Mary Boone; c Tom B & Charles S. *Educ:* Southwestern Univ, Tex, AB, 23; Univ Tex, MA, 25; Rice Inst, PhD(math), 33. *Prof Exp:* Teacher high sch, Tex, 23-26; instr math, Tex Tech Col, 26-28; asst prof, Univ Miss, 28-30; instr math, Tex Tech Col, 34-35; asst prof, NMex Col, 35-39; from asst prof to assoc prof, Southern Methodist Univ, 39-43; prof, Southwestern La Inst, 43-46. *Mem:* Am Math Soc; Math Asn Am. *Res:* Fuchsian groups; automorphic functions; algebra; trigonometry; analytic geometry; mathematics of finance; calculus. *Mailing Add:* 345 Centenary Dr Baton Rouge LA 70808-4702

REES, REES BYNON, PHARMACOLOGY, THERAPEUTICS. *Current Pos:* From instr to prof dermat, 43-86, chmn, Dept Dermat, 54-66, EMER CLIN PROF DERMAT & RADIOL, UNIV CALIF, SAN FRANCISCO, 86- *Personal Data:* b Bakersville, Calif, Feb 2, 15; m 57, Natalia E Kuznetsova; c Daniel L & David W. *Educ:* Univ Calif, Berkeley, AB, 36; Univ Calif, San Francisco, MD, 40. *Honors & Awards:* Finnerud Award, Dermat Found, 74; Taub Int Mem Award Res Psoriasis; Gold Medal, Am Acad Dermat, 87. *Concurrent Pos:* Consult, St Luke's Hosp, 46-, Shriners Hosp, 47-80, Mt Zion Hosp, 54-80, Am Bd Dermat, 64-74, US Army, 66-80 & Santa Rosa Mem Hosp, 83-; vis prof, Tulane Univ & La State Univ, 63-83, Henry Ford Hosp & Wayne State Univ, 67-82 & Emory Univ & Miami Univ, 78-82; hon staff mem, St Luke's Hosp, 80- *Mem:* Hon mem Am Dermat Asn (pres, 75); hon mem Am Acad Dermat (pres, 78); AMA; hon mem Danish Dermat Soc; hon mem Bulgarian Dermat Soc; hon mem Polish Dermat Soc. *Res:* Antifolics for psoriasis; antimalarials in dermatology; biology and treatment of warts. *Mailing Add:* 214 Oak Shadow Dr Santa Rosa CA 95409-6225

REES, ROBERTS M, MEDICINE. *Current Pos:* VPRES, MED & REGULATORY AFFAIRS, CLIN RES INT, 89- *Personal Data:* b Akron, Ohio, Mar 15, 20; m 45; c 2. *Educ:* Temple Univ, MD, 45. *Prof Exp:* Pvt pract, Akron, Ohio & Beverly Hills, Calif, 52-58; med dir, Pfizer Labs, 60-64, dir clin res, Chas Pfizer & Co Inc, 61-64; dir clin res, Winthrop Prod Inc, 64-66; dir clin res, Winthrop Labs, Sterling Drug Inc, 66-68, vpres, 67-73, dir med res div, Sterling-Winthrop Res Inst, 68-73, corp med officer, Sterling Drug Inc, 70-73; pres, Clin Resources, 78-84; vpres, Med Affairs, Zenith Lab, 84-88. *Concurrent Pos:* Spec consult to Exec Off of President, Spec Action Off Drug Abuse Prev, 71-72. *Mem:* AMA; Am Soc Clin Pharmacol & Therapeut; Drug Info Asn; AMA. *Mailing Add:* 557 Weathersfield Pittsboro NC 27312

REES, ROLF STEPHEN, COMBINATORICS & FINITE MATHEMATICS. *Current Pos:* ASSOC PROF MATH, DEPT MATH & STATIST, MEM UNIV NFLD, 90- *Personal Data:* b St Johns, Nfld, Jan 30, 60. *Educ:* Mem Univ Nfld, 80, B Med Sc, 82; Queens Univ, PhD(math), 86. *Prof Exp:* Fel dept combinatorics & optimization, Univ Waterloo, 86-87; asst prof math, Dept Math & Comput Sci, Mt Allison Univ, 87-90. *Mem:* Can Math Soc. *Res:* Construction and uses of pairwise balanced designs. *Mailing Add:* Dept Math & Statist Mem Univ Nfld Elizabeth Ave St John's NF A1C 5S7 Can

REES, THOMAS CHARLES, ORGANIC CHEMISTRY. *Current Pos:* MGR POLYMER CHEM, PMC SPECIALTIES GROUP, CHICAGO, 85-, BUS DEVELOP MGR, POLYMER ADDITIVES, 95- *Personal Data:* b Pottsville, Pa, June 6, 39; m 65, Patricia O'Neal; c Michael, Brian & Erin. *Educ:* Mt St Mary's Col, Md, BS, 61; Pa State Univ, PhD(org chem), 66. *Prof Exp:* Fel, Radiation Chem Div, Max Planck Inst Coal Res, 65-66; sr chemist, Sherwin-Williams Co, Chicago, 67-72, group leader pigment dispersions, 72-76, group leader plastics additives, 76-81, mgr, Polymer Additives Lab, 81-85. *Mem:* Soc Plastics Engrs; Am Chem Soc. *Res:* Ultraviolet and heat stabilization of polymers; organometallic chemistry, including Grignard and lithium reagents and transition metal organometallics; photochemistry and color properties of pigments; flame retardants. *Mailing Add:* 3641 W Stuenkel Rd Crete IL 60417-9711

REES, WILLIAM JAMES, MEDICINE, DERMATOLOGY. *Current Pos:* PRES & MANAGING DIR, RHYS INT ASSOCS, 88- *Personal Data:* b Kansas City, Mo, July 13, 22; m 50, Marybeth Smith; c Virginia, Diane, Carolyn, Karen & Mary N. *Educ:* Rockhurst Col, AB, 42; St Louis Univ, MD, 46; Univ Minn, MPH, 50. *Prof Exp:* Pvt pract, Mo, 50-52; scientist admin med, Sci Liaison & Adv Group, DC, 52-57; Europ rep, Upjohn Co, 57-58; scientist admin med, Sci Liaison & Adv Group, Ger, 58-61; clin investr, Abbott Labs, Ill, 61-63; resident dermat, Med Ctr, Univ Calif, San Francisco, 63-65; assoc exec dir life sci res & chmn biomed res, Stanford Res Inst, 65-69, dir life sci activ, Europ Off, Switz, 69-71, asst dir, DC Off, 71-72; dir clin res, Int Med Affairs, G D Searle & Co, 72-83; dir clin res, Chemex Pharmaceuts, Denver, 83-86. *Concurrent Pos:* Consult, Div Occup Health, Calif Dept Pub Health, 63-68; clin instr dermat, Med Ctr, Univ Calif, San Francisco, 65-69, asst clin prof, 69-71; colonel, Med Corps, USAR, 42-87; mem, Am Med Soc Vienna. *Mem:* Am Acad Clin Toxicol; Am Acad Dermat; Am Pub Health Asn; Asn Mil Surgeons US; Am Soc Trop Med & Hyg. *Res:* Dermatology, especially occupational and tropical aspects. *Mailing Add:* 550 Seamont Lane Edmonds WA 98020

REES, WILLIAM SMITH, JR, SYNTHETIC MECHANISTIC & STRUCTURAL MAIN GROUP CHEMISTRY, ELECTRONIC MATERIALS BY CHEMICAL VAPOR DEPOSITION. *Current Pos:* assoc prof 94-95, FULL PROF MAT SCI & ENG & DIR, MOLECULAR DESIGN INST, GA INST TECHNOL, 95- *Personal Data:* b Quanah, Tex, Nov 2, 59; m 86, Phyllis A Waite; c Bryce A & Aerryn E. *Educ:* Tex Tech Univ, BS, 80; Univ Calif, Los Angeles, PhD(inorg chem), 86. *Prof Exp:* From teaching asst to res asst chem, Tex Tech Univ, 78-81; res chemist, Cosden Oil & Chem Co, 81; teaching consult chem, Off Instrnl Develop, Univ Calif, Los Angeles, 82-83, instr chem, Exten, 82-83, teaching assoc chem, 82-83, vis instr chem, 83 & res assoc chem, 83-86; postdoctoral fel chem, Mass Inst Technol, 86-89; from asst prof to assoc prof, Fla State Univ, 89-93. *Concurrent Pos:* John von Neumann fel, NSF, 76; univ scholar, Tex Tech Univ, 77; mem, Fla High Technol & Indust Coun, Microelectronics & Mat Subcomt, 90-94; co-organizer, Advan Mat Chem Conf, 91- *Mem:* Am Chem Soc; Mat Res Soc; Am Ceramic Soc; Int Union Pure & Appl Chem; AAAS; Sigma Xi. *Res:* Synthetic, mechanistic and structural study of main group inorganic and organometallic compounds useful for the chemical vapor deposition of thin films of electronic materials-superconductors, conductors, semiconductors and insulators. *Mailing Add:* Molecular Design Inst Dept Chem & Biochem & Dept Mat Sci & Eng Ga Inst Technol Atlanta GA 30332-0400. *Fax:* 404-894-1144; *E-Mail:* will.rees@chemistry.gatech.edu

REES, WILLIAM WENDELL, ORGANIC CHEMISTRY. *Current Pos:* res chemist, 58-60, photog scientist, 60-65, admin asst, Gen Mgt Staff, 65-67, lab head, Res Labs, 67-69, sr lab head, 69-72, asst div dir, 72-77, DIV DIR, RES LABS, EASTMAN KODAK CO, 77- *Personal Data:* b Albany, NY, Dec 21, 33; m 80; c 3. *Educ:* Amherst Col, BA, 55; Mass Inst Technol, PhD(chem), 58. *Prof Exp:* Asst, Amherst Col, 53-55 & Mass Inst Technol, 55-57. *Mem:* Soc Photog Sci & Eng; Am Chem Soc; Sigma Xi. *Res:* Physical organic chemistry; kinetics and mechanisms of organic reactions; photographic process; research administration. *Mailing Add:* 35 N Country Club Dr Rochester NY 14618-3723

REESE, ANDY CLARE, IMMUNOLOGY, COMPUTER ASSISTED INSTRUCTION. *Current Pos:* asst prof, 75-81, dir, MD-PhD Prog, 91-95, ASSOC PROF IMMUNOL, MED COL GA, 81- *Personal Data:* b Wann, Okla, June 22, 42; m 65, Alice L Burt. *Educ:* Univ Okla, BS, 64; Univ Mo, PhD(biochem), 71; Augusta Col, MBA, 90. *Prof Exp:* Assoc chemist, Skelly Oil Co, 64-66; res assoc med, Sch Med, Case Western Res Univ, 66-72, fel microbiol, 72-74; asst res prof path, Mt Sinai Sch Med, 74-75. *Concurrent Pos:* Pres, Multimedia Learning Resources, Inc. *Mem:* Am Asn Immunologists; Soc Leukocyte Biol; Soc Exp Biol & Med; Sigma Xi; AAAS. *Res:* Development of computer based instructional modules in immunology and biomedical ethics; corporation of technology in curriculum design, learning theory. *Mailing Add:* Dept Cell Biol & Anat Med Col Ga Augusta GA 30912. *Fax:* 706-721-9197; *E-Mail:* areese@mail.mcg.edu

REESE, BRUCE ALAN, AEROSPACE ENGINEERING, PROPULSION. *Current Pos:* dep comdr eng, 83-86, CONSULT AEROSPACE ENG, US ARMY STRATEGIC DEFENSE COMMAND, 86- *Personal Data:* b Provo, Utah, Aug 3, 23; m 45, Barbara Taylor; c Bruce Taylor, Michael D & Pamela K. *Educ:* Univ NMex, BS, 44; Purdue Univ, MS, 48, PhD(mech eng), 53. *Prof Exp:* From asst prof to prof mech eng, Purdue Univ, 53-73, dir, Jet Propulsion Ctr, 65-73, head, Sch Aeronaut & Astronaut, 73-79; chief scientist, USAF Arnold Eng Develop Ctr, Tullahoma, Tenn, 79-83. *Concurrent Pos:* Consult, Aerospace Govt Agencys & Indust, 53-; dep dir, Nike Zeus Res & Develop, US Army, 61-62 & tech dir, Nike X Proj Off, US Army, 62-63; consult, Sci Adv Panel, US Army, 67-79; mem, Sci Adv Bd, US Air Force, 69-76, Adv Group Foreign Tech Div, 70-74 & Div Adv Group Aeronaut Systs Div, 73-76; chmn, Tank & Automotive Command Sci Adv Grp, 70-74; mem, Missile Command Adv Cmt, 72-79 & Navel Res Adv Cmt, 78-79; adv, Assembly Engrs, Nat Res Coun, 77. *Mem:* Fel Am Inst Aeronaut & Astronaut; Sigma Xi. *Res:* Heat transfer; gas dynamics; hybrid fueled rockets; laser diffusers; slurry fuel combustion. *Mailing Add:* 5804 Macon Dr SE Huntsville AL 35802-1934

REESE, CECIL EVERETT, POLYMER CHEMISTRY. *Current Pos:* RETIRED. *Personal Data:* b Benson, Utah, July 3, 21; m 46, Ethel M Fox; c Cecile (Peterson), Dennis E, Pamela (Mortensen), Bruce L & Andrea (Brady). *Educ:* Univ Utah, BS, 45, MS, 47, PhD(chem), 49. *Prof Exp:* Asst prof chem, Kans State Col, 49-50; res chemist, E I DuPont de Nemours & co, Inc, 50-59, res assoc, 59-67, res fel, 67-91. *Mem:* Am Chem Soc. *Res:* Specific heats of organic liquids; diffusion and membrane permeability; visco-elastic properties of hair and other fibers; mechanical behavior of polyacrylonitrile fibers in the presence of an external plasticizer. *Mailing Add:* 1211 Stockton Rd Kinston NC 28504

REESE, ELWYN THOMAS, MYCOLOGY. *Current Pos:* mycologist lab, Qm Res & Develop Ctr, Mass, 48-72, MYCOLOGIST SATD LAB, US ARMY NATICK LABS, 72- *Personal Data:* b Scranton, Pa, Jan 16, 12; m 40; c 2. *Educ:* Pa State Col, BS, 33, MS, 38, PhD(mycol), 46. *Prof Exp:* Teacher high sch, Pa, 34-39; mycologist, Knaust Bros Mushroom Co, NY, 42-43; bacteriologist, Phila Qm Corps Depot, 44-45; mycologist, J T Baker Chem Co, 46-48. *Concurrent Pos:* Secy Army fel, 64-65. *Mem:* Mycol Soc Am; Am Chem Soc. *Res:* Decomposition of cellulose by microorganisms; physiology of fungi; polysaccharases. *Mailing Add:* Seven Charles St Wayland MA 01778-4711

REESE, ERNST S, ANIMAL BEHAVIOR, ECOLOGY. *Current Pos:* Assoc prof, 60-71, PROF ZOOL, UNIV HAWAII, 71-, NSF RES GRANT, 63- *Personal Data:* b Madison, Wis, Jan 26, 31; m 61. *Educ:* Princeton Univ, AB, 53; Univ Calif, Los Angeles, PhD(zool), 60. *Concurrent Pos:* NSF fel, Univ Groningen, 61-62; mem adv sci comt, Charles Darwin Found for Galapagos Isles, 66- *Mem:* AAAS; Ecol Soc Am; Animal Behav Soc (pres-elect). *Res:* Ecology and behavior of marine animals, especially crustacea and fish; emphasis on comparative developmental aspects and ecological significance behavior. *Mailing Add:* Edmondson Hall 2538 The Mall Honolulu HI 96822

REESE, FLOYD ERNEST, BIOCHEMISTRY, ORGANIC CHEMISTRY. *Current Pos:* RETIRED. *Personal Data:* b Ransomville, NY, Nov 8, 17; m 43; c 3. *Educ:* Greenville Col, BS, 41; Purdue Univ, MA, 44, PhD(biochem), 47. *Prof Exp:* Res chemist biochem, Upjohn Co, Mich, 47-48; from assoc prof to prof chem, Houghton Col, 48-56; from asst prof to assoc prof, Calif State Univ, Chico, 56-65, head dept, 63-67, prof chem, 65-81. *Mem:* Am Chem Soc. *Res:* Metabolism of amino acids and guanidino acids; gamma irradiation of proteins. *Mailing Add:* 5081 Wilderness Way Paradise CA 95969-6649

REESE, LYMON C(LIFTON), CIVIL ENGINEERING. *Current Pos:* from asst prof to assoc prof, Univ Tex, Austin, 55-64, prof civil eng, 64-87, chmn dept, 65-72, T U Taylor prof & assoc dean res, 72-79, Rashid chair, 81-84, EMER NASSER I AL-RASHID CHAIR, UNIV TEX, AUSTIN, 87-; OWNER, LCRNA, INC & ENSOFT, INC, 87- *Personal Data:* b Murfreesboro, Ark, Apr 27, 17; m 48; c 3. *Educ:* Univ Tex, BS, 49, MS, 50; Univ Calif, PhD, 55. *Honors & Awards:* Middlebrooks Award, Am Soc Civil Engrs, 58; Karl Terzaghi Lectr, 76. *Prof Exp:* Res scientist, Univ Tex, 48-50; asst prof civil eng, Miss State Col, 50-51, 53-55. *Concurrent Pos:* Consult var co & govt agencies, 55- *Mem:* Nat Acad Eng; Am Soc Eng Educ; fel Am Soc Civil Engrs; Sigma Xi. *Res:* Soil mechanics; interaction between soils and structures; analysis and design of foundations for offshore structures; behavior of laterally loaded piles. *Mailing Add:* LCRNA Inc PO Box 180348 Austin TX 78718

REESE, MILLARD GRIFFIN, JR, ORGANIC CHEMISTRY. *Current Pos:* RETIRED. *Personal Data:* b Dinwiddie, Va, Aug 14, 31; m 58, Margaret A Terrell; c Millard G III. *Educ:* Randolph-Macon Col, BS, 52; Univ Va, MS, 55, PhD(org chem), 57. *Prof Exp:* Sr res chemist, Dacron Res Lab, E I du Pont de Nemours & Co, Inc, 57-85. *Mem:* Sigma Xi; Am Chem Soc. *Res:* Unsaturated diketones, reactions; reaction mechanisms and derivatives; condensation polymerization; properties of high polymers; textile fibers. *Mailing Add:* 2705 Carey Rd Kinston NC 28501-1431

REESE, ROBERT TRAFTON, immunology, biochemistry &biophysics, for more information see previous edition

REESE, RONALD MALCOLM, SHIP PROTECTION, SHIP DESIGN. *Current Pos:* HEAD SYSTS ANALYSIS BR, NKF ENG, INC, 80-, HEAD, SYSTS ENG DIV, 80- *Personal Data:* b Oakland, Calif, Oct 2, 38; m 60; c 2. *Educ:* US Naval Acad, BS, 60; Mass Inst Technol, MS, 70, PhD(ocean eng), 72. *Prof Exp:* Chief engr, US Naval Destroyer, 62-64, mat officer, USN Destroyer Squadron, 65-67; ship design mgr patrol hydrofoil, Naval Ship Eng Ctr, Hyattsville, Md, 72-73, ship design mgr aircraft carriers, Newport News, Va, 75, supvr shipbuilding, conversion & repair, 75-79; force maintenance officer, Naval Surface Force, Atlantic Fleet, Norfolk, Va, 79-80. *Mem:* Sigma Xi; Soc Naval Architects & Marine Engrs; Am Soc Naval Engrs. *Res:* Design of propulsion plants for deep submersibles; engineering design of complex warships and application of new technology to ship design. *Mailing Add:* 11424 Vale Rd Oakton VA 22124

REESE, THOMAS SARGENT, CELL BIOLOGY, NEUROSCIENCE. *Current Pos:* res assoc, 63-65, res med officer, 66-70, CHIEF, LAB NEUROBIOL, NAT INST NEUROL DIS & STROKE, NIH, 83- *Personal Data:* b Cleveland, Ohio, May 20, 35; m 75; c 2. *Educ:* Harvard Univ, BS, 57; Columbia Univ, MD, 62. *Honors & Awards:* C Judson Herrick Award; Mathilde Solowey Award. *Prof Exp:* Res asst, Psycho-Acoust Lab, Harvard Univ, 57-58; intern, Boston City Hosp, 62-63; res fel anat, Sch Med, Harvard Univ, 65-66. *Concurrent Pos:* Instr neurobiol, Marine Biol Labs, Woods Hole, Mass, 75-; co-instr-in-chief neurobiol, Marine Biol Lab, 80-84; assoc, Neurosci Res Prog, Rockefeller Univ, 86- *Mem:* Nat Acad Sci; Am Soc Cell Biol; Soc Neurosci; Biophys Soc. *Res:* Membrane structure and function in neural cells, axonal transport synapses; cellular neurobiology. *Mailing Add:* 10605 Belfast Pl Potomac MD 20854. *Fax:* 301-480-1485; *E-Mail:* tsr@codon.nih.80v

REESE, WELDON HAROLD, POLLUTION BIOLOGY, PHYCOLOGY. *Current Pos:* assoc prof, 66-77, PROF BIOL, WAYLAND COL, 77-, HEAD DEPT BIOL & CHMN DIV SCI, 66- *Personal Data:* b Stonewall Co, Tex, May 5, 27; m 48; c 2. *Educ:* Tex Tech Col, BS, 52, MS, 61; Ore State Univ, PhD(pollution biol, phycol), 66. *Prof Exp:* Teacher sec schs, 52-61; NSF fel pollution res, 61-62; res assoc, Ore State Univ, 62-63, fel pollution res & res asst, 63-64. *Concurrent Pos:* Lectr, Jamaica, 67-68; Terra-Rite Corp res grant, 67-; res grant, Tex Agr Exp Sta, 68-; mem int comn inter-col educ, Southern Asn Baptist Col & Schs, 68- *Mem:* AAAS; Am Soc Limnol & Oceanog; Phycol Soc Am. *Res:* Effects of community imbalance in lentic and lotic environments caused by organic enrichment and other pollutants; periphyton community. *Mailing Add:* 1000 E US 380 Bus Decatur TX 76234

REESE, WILLIAM, THERMAL PHYSICS. *Current Pos:* RETIRED. *Personal Data:* b Kansas City, Mo, Feb 24, 37; m 58; c 1. *Educ:* Reed Col, BA, 58; Univ Ill, MS, 60, PhD(physics), 62. *Prof Exp:* Res assoc physics, Univ Ill, 62-63; from asst prof to assoc prof, US Naval Postgrad Sch, 63-73, prof physics, 73-82, tech dir, Naval Intel, 91-93. *Mem:* Am Phys Soc; Sigma Xi. *Res:* Low temperature physics; thermal properties of polymers; second order phase transitions; military systems analysis. *Mailing Add:* 325 Melrose St Pacific Grove CA 93950-3824

REESE, WILLIAM DEAN, BIOLOGY. *Current Pos:* from asst prof to assoc prof, 57-66, chmn dept, 74-77, PROF BIOL, UNIV SOUTHWESTERN LA, 66-, HEAD DEPT, 81- *Personal Data:* b Baltimore, Md, Sept 10, 28; m 50; c 4. *Educ:* Univ Md, BS, 53; Fla State Univ, MS, 55, PhD(bot), 57. *Prof Exp:* Asst bot, Fla State Univ, 53-55. *Concurrent Pos:* Ed, The Bryologist, 70-74. *Mem:* AAAS; Soc Bot Mex; Am Bryol & Lichenological Soc (vpres, 77-79, pres, 79-81); Int Asn Plant Taxon; Brit Bryol Soc. *Res:* Taxonomy, distribution and ecology of Musci. *Mailing Add:* Dept Biol Univ Southwestern La PO Box 42451 Lafayette LA 70504

REESE, WILLIAM GEORGE, PSYCHIATRY. *Current Pos:* prof, 51-85, EMER PROF PSYCHIAT & CHMN DEPT, COL MED, UNIV ARK MED SCH, LITTLE ROCK, 87- *Personal Data:* b Lewiston, Utah, Apr 2, 17; m 42; c 3. *Educ:* Univ Idaho, BS & MS, 38; Wash Univ, MD, 42. *Hon Degrees:* DSc, Univ Ariz. *Prof Exp:* Intern internal med, Barnes Hosp, St Louis, 42-43; resident psychiat, Johns Hopkins Hosp, 46-48, instr psychiatrist, 48-51. *Concurrent Pos:* Commonwealth fel, Johns Hopkins Univ, 46-48; dir prof educ, Vet Admin Hosp, Perry Point, Md, 48-51, consult, North Little Rock. *Mem:* AMA; fel Am Psychiat Asn; Pavlovian Soc; fel Am Col Psychiat; Sigma Xi. *Res:* Basic psychophysiology. *Mailing Add:* 14300 Chenal Pkwy 7437 Little Rock AR 72211

REESMAN, ARTHUR LEE, GEOLOGY. *Current Pos:* asst prof, 68-70, chmn, 76-79, ASSOC PROF GEOL, VANDERBILT UNIV, 70- *Personal Data:* b Eldorado, Ill, Feb 20, 33; m 63; c 3. *Educ:* Eureka Col, BS, 55; Univ Mo-Columbia, AM, 61, PhD(geol), 66. *Prof Exp:* Asst geol, Univ Mo-Columbia, 59-62; asst prof, Univ NDak, 62-63 & Western Mich Univ,

66-67. *Mem:* Clay Minerals Soc; Geochem Soc. *Res:* Chemical weathering of rocks and minerals; genesis of clay minerals; evolution of landscapes through weathering. *Mailing Add:* Dept Geol Vanderbilt Univ 2201 W End Ave Nashville TN 37240-0001

REESOR, JOHN ELGIN, GEOLOGY. *Current Pos:* RETIRED. *Personal Data:* b Saskatoon, Sask, June 2, 20; m 54; c 3. *Educ:* Univ BC, BASc, 49; Princeton Univ, PhD(geol), 52. *Prof Exp:* Geologist, Can Geol Surv, 52-85. *Mem:* Fel Geol Soc Am. *Mailing Add:* 1166 Bonnie Crescent Ottawa ON K2C 1Z5 Can

REETHOF, GERHARD, MECHANICAL ENGINEERING, ACOUSTICS. *Current Pos:* RETIRED. *Personal Data:* b Teplice, Czech, July 1, 22; US citizen; m 56; c 3. *Educ:* Mass Inst Technol, SB, 47, SM, 49, ScD(mech eng), 54. *Prof Exp:* Proj engr, Sperry Gyroscope Co, NY, 49-50; asst prof fluid power & mech eng, Dynamic Anal & Controls Lab, Mass Inst Technol, 50-55; chief res, Vickers Inc, Mich, 55-58; mgr acoust eng, Flight Propulsion Div, Gen Elec Co, Ohio, 58-67; Alcoa prof mech eng, Pa State Univ, 67-76, prof mech eng & dor, Noise Control Lab, 76-88; res prof, Drexel Univ, 88-94. *Concurrent Pos:* Fulbright prof, Finland Inst Technol, Helsinki, 53-54; consult, Electronics Div, Gen Dynamics Corp, 67-70, US Nuclear Regulatory Comn, 68-80 & Army Mat Command, 71-82; expert witness, du Pont Atomic Energy Div, 75-85. *Mem:* Fel Am Soc Mech Engrs; Acoust Soc Am; Inst Noise Control; Am Soc Eng Educ; Am Inst Aeronaut & Astronaut. *Res:* Acoustics and noise control; jet noise; fan noise; propagation and attenuation of complex acoustic waves in ducts; valve noise; high intensity acoustics; acoustic agglom of submicro wave particles; transportation noise; probabilistic methods in design and reliability. *Mailing Add:* 4503 Northhampton Dr New Port Richey FL 34653

REETZ, HAROLD FRANK, JR, CROP PRODUCTION, COMPUTER SIMULATION. *Current Pos:* REGIONAL DIR, POTASH & PHOSPHATE INST, 82-; VPRES, FOUND AGRON RES, 96- *Personal Data:* b Watseka, Ill, Mar 10, 48; m 73, Christine Kaiser; c Carrie, Wesley & Anthony. *Educ:* Univ Ill, BS, 70; Purdue Univ, MS, 72, PhD(agron, crop physiol), 76. *Prof Exp:* Exten res agronomist grain crop prod, Dept Agron, Purdue Univ, 74-82. *Concurrent Pos:* Consult, Monsanto, Control Data Corp & Int Harvester, 78-82. *Mem:* Fel Am Soc Agron; fel Crop Sci Soc Am; Coun Agr Scientists & Technologists; Soil Sci Soc Am. *Res:* Computer simulation of crop production; physiological reactions and production impact of environmental stresses; cultural practices in grain crop production; computer applications in agribusiness and in farming; intensive, site-specific crop and soil management. *Mailing Add:* Potash & Phosphate Inst 1497 N 1050 East Rd Monticello IL 61856. *E-Mail:* hreetz@ppi-far.com

REEVE, AUBREY C, ENVIRONMENTAL CONTROL, CHEMICAL ENGINEERING. *Current Pos:* RETIRED. *Personal Data:* b Staines, Eng, June 23, 37; m 59; c 3. *Educ:* Univ Birmingham, BSc, 58, PhD(gasification of hydrocarbons), 61. *Prof Exp:* Res fel movement of particles, McGill Univ & Pulp & Paper Res Inst Can, 61-63; sr chem engr, Res Div, Carrier Corp, 63-73, mgr systs develop, 73-74, proj control coordr, 74-75; res engr, Amoco Chem Corp, 75-78, sr res engr, 78-94. *Mem:* Assoc mem Am Inst Chem Engrs. *Res:* By-product aromatics during gasification of hydrocarbons; motion of particles through force fields; removal of odors; air pollution control; gas absorption in packed columns; process development. *Mailing Add:* 899 Baver Rd Hiawassee GA 30546

REEVE, ERNEST BASIL, PHYSIOLOGY. *Current Pos:* from assoc prof to prof, 53-83, EMER PROF MED, SCH MED, UNIV COLO, DENVER, 83- *Personal Data:* b Liverpool, Eng, May 5, 12; m 84; c 2. *Educ:* Oxford Univ, BA, 35, BM, BCh, 38. *Prof Exp:* Clin asst & mem staff, Clin Res Unit, Guys Hosp, London, 40-52; mem permanent staff, Med Res Coun, London, 46-52; vis prof of physiol, Columbia Univ, 53. *Mem:* Am Physiol Soc; Brit Physiol Soc. *Res:* Metabolism of plasma proteins, especially clotting proteins; regulation of body water, sodium, calcium and phosphate; systems analysis of physiological functions. *Mailing Add:* 182 Race Denver CO 80206

REEVE, JOHN, ELECTRICAL ENGINEERING. *Current Pos:* from assoc prof to prof, 67-96, ADJ PROF ELEC ENG, UNIV WATERLOO, CAN, 96- *Personal Data:* b Nelson, Eng, Oct 11, 36; Can citizen; c 2. *Educ:* Univ Manchester, BSc, 58, MSc, 59, PhD(elec eng), 66, DSc, 74. *Honors & Awards:* Uno Lamm High Voltage Direct Current Award & Medal, Inst Elec & Electronics Engrs, 66. *Prof Exp:* Develop engr, Eng Elec Protection Co, Stafford, Eng, 58-61; lectr elec eng, Univ Manchester Inst Sci Technol, 61-67. *Concurrent Pos:* Pres, John Reeve Consult Ltd, 71-; vis prof, Monash Univ, Australia, 74-75 & Univ Canterbury, NZ, 75; proj mgr elec syst, Elec Power Res Inst, 80-81; mem, Hydro-Que Inst Res, 89-90. *Mem:* Fel Inst Elec & Electronics Engrs. *Res:* Transmission power by direct current, control, protection, system analysis and simulation; high power electronics. *Mailing Add:* Elec & Comput Eng Dept Univ Waterloo Waterloo ON N2L 3G1 Can

REEVE, MARIAN ENZLER, PLANT ANATOMY. *Current Pos:* RETIRED. *Personal Data:* b Placerville, Calif, Aug 28, 20; m 41, Roger; c Paul, James, Andrew & Terell. *Educ:* Univ Calif, Berkeley, AB, 40, PhD(bot), 49. *Prof Exp:* Prof biol, Merritt Col, 55-81. *Mem:* Bot Soc Am; Sigma Xi. *Mailing Add:* 4325 Mountain View Ave Oakland CA 94605

REEVE, RONALD C(ROPPER), AGRICULTURAL ENGINEERING. *Current Pos:* RETIRED. *Personal Data:* b Hinckley, Utah, Mar 27, 20; m 40; c 3. *Educ:* Utah State Univ, BS, 43; Iowa State Univ, MS, 49. *Prof Exp:* Engr, Boeing Aircraft Co, Wash, 43-45; irrig & drainage engr, Salinity Lab, USDA, 46-55, tech staff specialist, Salinity Lab & Western Soil & Water Mgt Br, Soil & Water Conserv Res Div, Agr Res Serv, 55-57, agr engr, Salinity Lab, 57-64, res invests leader, 64-74, staff scientist water mgt, Nat Prog Staff, Soil, Water & Air Sci, 73-77; Tech dir, Advan Drainage Systs, Inc, 77-82. *Concurrent Pos:* Consult, Abaca invests, div cotton & other fiber crops & dis, Bur Plant Indust, Soils & Agr Eng, Costa Rica, 51; drainage res proj consult, PR Agr Exp Sta & Univ PR, 55 & 56; consult, Col Agr Eng, Punjab Agr Univ, 66, Int Eng Co, Inc, Ankara, Turkey, 66 & Food & Agr Orgn, UN, Mexico City, 68; adj prof agr eng, Ohio State Univ, 70-74. *Mem:* Fel Am Soc Agr Engrs; Am Soc Civil Engrs; Int Comn Irrig & Drainage. *Res:* Water management, especially irrigation, drainage and salinity control. *Mailing Add:* 1222 Southport Dr Columbus OH 43235

REEVER, RICHARD EUGENE, COSMETIC & TOILETRIES, DRUGS. *Current Pos:* VPRES RES & DEVELOP, MINNETONKA INC, 77- *Educ:* Millersville State Univ, BS, 70. *Prof Exp:* Assoc dir res & develop, Alberto Culver Co, 73-77. *Mem:* Am Chem Soc; Soc Cosmetic Chemists. *Res:* Drugs: research and development; quality assurance. *Mailing Add:* 5935 Howards Pt Rd Excelsior MN 55331-7402

REEVES, ANDREW LOUIS, TOXICOLOGY OF ASBESTOS, BARIUM & BERYLLIUM. *Current Pos:* Res assoc indust med & hyg, 55-63, from asst prof to prof, 63-92, EMER PROF OCCUP & ENVIRON HEALTH, WAYNE STATE UNIV, 92- *Personal Data:* b Budapest, Hungary, Oct 13, 24; nat US; m 51, Shirley M Roe; c 3. *Educ:* Univ Munich, dipl, 51-53; Wayne State Univ, PhD(physiol chem), 59. *Concurrent Pos:* Sr sci fel, Univ Milan, 73; mem permanent comn, Int Asn Occup Health; vis prof, Univ Wurzburg, 80-81. *Mem:* AAAS; Am Chem Soc; Am Indust Hyg Asn; NY Acad Sci; Soc Toxicol; Int Comn Occup Health. *Res:* Biochemical aspects of industrial toxicology; mechanism of action of air pollutants; etiology of pulmonary carcinogenesis; toxicology of arsenic, asbestos, barium, beryllium. *Mailing Add:* 573 Pemberton Grosse Pointe MI 48230-1711. *Fax:* 313-822-4651

REEVES, BARRY L(UCAS), REENTRY PHYSICS, HYPERSONIC GAS DYNAMICS. *Current Pos:* PRIN SCIENTIST, TEXTRON DEFENSE SYSTS, 85- *Personal Data:* b St Louis, Mo, Jan 11, 35; m 54, Marilyn Riester; c Katherine, Michael & Janet. *Educ:* Washington Univ, St Louis, BS, 56, MS, 58, DSc(eng, physics), 60. *Prof Exp:* Res assoc, McDonnell Aircraft Corp, Mo, 59-60; Air Force Off Sci Res fel, Aeronaut Dept, Calif Inst Technol, 60-64; sr research scientist, Avco Systs Div, Avco Corp, 64-72, sr consult scientist, 72-78, prin scientist, 78-85. *Concurrent Pos:* Fel, Convair, 58, NSF, 59-60, Air Force Off Sci Res, 60-62; consult, Space Gen Corp, 62-63 & Nat Eng & Sci Co, 63-64; consult, High Q Co, 91-92. *Mem:* Sigma Xi; Am Phys Soc. *Res:* Hypersonic wakes and boundary layers; laminar and turbulent separated flows; massive turbulent ablation; shock wave-boundary layer interactions; reentry physics and reentry vehicle plasma environments; gas-dynamic lasers; boundary layer transition; aero-optics; reentry vehicle ablation and aerodynamic performance. *Mailing Add:* 10 Hillcrest Pkwy Winchester MA 01890

REEVES, C C, JR, GEOLOGY. *Current Pos:* FROM INSTR TO PROF GEOL, TEX TECH UNIV, 72- *Personal Data:* b Cincinnati, Ohio, May 19, 30; div; c 6. *Educ:* Univ Okla, BS, 55, MS, 57; Tex Tech Univ, PhD(geol), 70. *Prof Exp:* Geologist, Texaco, Inc, 56-57. *Mem:* Am Inst Prof Geol; Geol Soc Am. *Res:* Hydrogeology of Ogallala of WTex; tertiary-quaternary of Tex-NMex; qualified expert witness; experienced well driller. *Mailing Add:* PO Box 4516 Lubbock TX 79409

REEVES, DALE LESLIE, PLANT BREEDING, AGRONOMY. *Current Pos:* asst prof, 70-74, assoc prof, 74-80, PROF PLANT BREEDING, SDAK STATE UNIV, 80- *Personal Data:* b Norton, Kans, Mar 24, 36; m 57, JoAnne Foley; c Theresa, Bruce & Richard. *Educ:* Kans State Univ, BS, 58, MS, 63; Colo State Univ, PhD(plant genetics), 69. *Prof Exp:* Asst county agent, Kans State Univ, 62-63. *Concurrent Pos:* Mem, USAID Proj, Botswana, Africa. *Mem:* Am Soc Agron; Crop Sci Soc Am. *Res:* Oat improvement; improving yield, straw strength and rust resistance in oats; increasing protein levels by breeding; rye variety development; semi dwarf rye. *Mailing Add:* Dept Plant Sci SDak State Univ Brookings SD 57007. *Fax:* 605-688-4452

REEVES, EDMOND MORDEN, SPACEFLIGHT INSTRUMENTATION, SOLAR PHYSICS. *Current Pos:* chief, Astrophys Br, Spacelab Flight Div, 82-88, dep dir, Flight Systs Div, Off Space Sci & Applns, 88-93, DIR, FLIGHT SYSTS DIV, OFF LIFE & MICROGRAVITY SCIS & APPLNS, NASA, 93- *Personal Data:* b London, Ont, Jan 14, 34; m 56, Vivian Irvine; c 2. *Educ:* Western Ont Univ, BSc, 56, MSc, 57, PhD(physics), 59. *Honors & Awards:* Except Sci Achievement Medal, NASA, 74. *Prof Exp:* Nat Res Coun Can overseas fel, Imp Col, Univ London, 59-61; res physicist & lectr astron, Harvard Univ, 61-78, sr res assoc, Harvard Col Observ, 68-78, assoc, 78-80, sect head, Nat Ctr Atmospheric Res, High Altitude Observ, 78-82. *Concurrent Pos:* Mem, Solar Physics Panel, Astron Missions Bd, NASA, 68-71, consult, 68-77 & 79-81, mem, Space Shuttle Opers Mgt Working Group, 72-76; physicist, Smithsonian Astrophys Observ, 73-78. *Mem:* Int Astron Union; Am Astron Soc; Int Acad Astronautics. *Res:* Vacuum ultraviolet spectroscopy of the sun from rockets and satellites; related problems in laboratory astrophysics using laboratory plasmas from the far ultraviolet to the visible. *Mailing Add:* NASA Hq Code US Washington DC 20546. *E-Mail:* ereeves@hq.nasa.gov

REEVES, FONTAINE BRENT, JR, MYCOLOGY. *Current Pos:* From asst prof to assoc prof bot, 66-79, PROF PLANT PATH, COLO STATE UNIV, 79- *Personal Data:* b Eufaula, Ala, May 16, 39; m 64; c 2. *Educ:* Tulane Univ, BS, 61, MS, 63; Univ Ill, PhD(bot), 66. *Mem:* AAAS; Mycol Soc Am; Bot Soc Am; Sigma Xi. *Res:* Cytology and evolution of fungi; ultrastructure of fungi; mycorrhizae. *Mailing Add:* Dept Bot & Plant Path Colo State Univ Ft Collins CO 80523-0001

REEVES, GEOFFREY D, SPACE PLASMA PHYSICS, MAGNETOSPHERIC PHYSICS. *Current Pos:* STAFF SCIENTIST, LOS ALAMOS NAT LAB, 89- *Personal Data:* b Boston, Mass, Dec 23, 61; m 91. *Educ:* Univ Colo, BA, 83; Stanford Univ, PhD(appl physics), 88. *Honors & Awards:* Group Achievement Award, NASA, 83. *Concurrent Pos:* Assoc, Comt Space Res, Int Coun Sci Unions. *Mem:* Am Geophys Union; Am Inst Physics. *Res:* Space plasma physics, shuttle-based electron beam-plasma-wave interactions in the ionosphere; energetic particle data in the investigation of magnetospheric substorms. *Mailing Add:* Mail Stop D-436 Los Alamos Nat Lab Los Alamos NM 87545. Fax: 505-665-4414; E-Mail: reeves@lanl.gov

REEVES, HENRY COURTLAND, BIOCHEMISTRY, BACTERIAL PHYSIOLOGY. *Current Pos:* chmn dept bot & microbiol, 72-77, vpres res, 85-91, PROF MICROBIOL, ARIZ STATE UNIV, 69- *Personal Data:* b Camden, NJ, Nov 25, 33; m 52, Florence Rockwell; c 2. *Educ:* Franklin & Marshall Col, BS, 55; Vanderbilt Univ, MA, 56, PhD(biochem), 59. *Prof Exp:* USPHS fels bact physiol, Walter Reed Army Inst Res, Washington, DC, 60-61 & biochem, Albert Einstein Med Ctr, 61-63, USPHS res career develop awardee, 62-69; vis investr, Max Planck Inst Cell Chem, 65-66; mem fac biochem, Albert Einstein Med Ctr, 66-69. *Concurrent Pos:* Vis investr, Biochem Inst, Freiburg, Ger, 75-76; dir, Div Physiol, Cell & Molecular Biol, NSF, 77-79. *Mem:* Sigma Xi; AAAS; Am Soc Biol Chem; Am Chem Soc; Am Soc Microbiol; Am Soc Cell Biol. *Res:* Enzymology; intermediary metabolism; bacterial genetics. *Mailing Add:* Dept Microbiol Ariz State Univ 3108 S Golf Dr Tempe AZ 85282-4033. Fax: 602-820-5744; E-Mail: iadhcr@asuacad.inre.edu

REEVES, HOMER EUGENE, AGRONOMY. *Current Pos:* RETIRED. *Personal Data:* b Atoka, Okla, Dec 4, 28; m 60, Loretta Ann; c Renett G (Bullard), Cynthia A (Maloy) & Henry D. *Educ:* Okla State Univ, BS, 55, MS, 57; Kans State Univ, PhD, 71. *Prof Exp:* Asst, Okla State Univ, 55-57; from asst prof to prof agron, Panhandle State Univ, 57-91, prof biol sci, 73-91, chmn agribus, 83-91, chmn agron, 85-91, prof agron, 85- *Concurrent Pos:* Asst, Kans State Univ, 65-67, vis asst prof, 70-72; mem, Coun Agr Sci & Technol. *Mem:* Am Soc Agron. *Res:* Crop ecology; crop and soil management; water management. *Mailing Add:* 2201 N James St Guymon OK 73942

REEVES, JAMES BLANCHETTE, medical microbiology; deceased, see previous edition for last biography

REEVES, JERRY JOHN, ENDOCRINOLOGY, REPRODUCTIVE PHYSIOLOGY. *Current Pos:* from asst prof to assoc prof, 70-80, PROF ANIMAL SCI, WASH STATE UNIV, 80- *Personal Data:* b Watsonville, Calif, Oct 5, 43; m 66; c 2. *Educ:* Ore State Univ, BS, 65, MS, 67; Univ Nebr, Lincoln, PhD(reprod physiol & animal sci), 69. *Honors & Awards:* Young Sci Award, Am Soc Animal Sci, 77. *Prof Exp:* Res asst animal sci, Univ Nebr, Lincoln, 67-69; instr med & NIH fel, Med Sch, Tulane Univ, La & endocrine & polypeptide lab, Vet Admin Hosp, New Orleans, La, 69-70. *Concurrent Pos:* Consult, Int Atomic Energy Agency, 84, W R Grace & Co, 85-, Monoclonal Anti-bodies Inc, 84- & Norden Labs, 85-; feature teacher agr, Wash State Univ, 76. *Mem:* Am Soc Animal Sci; Soc Study Reproduction; Endocrine Soc; Soc Exp Biol & Med; Domestic Animal Endocrinol. *Res:* Neuroendocrinology concerning hypothalamic control of reproduction, growth and lactation; immunization of animals against their own hormones to control reproduction. *Mailing Add:* Dept Animal Sci Wash State Univ 1 SE Stadium Way Pullman WA 99164-0001

REEVES, JOHN PAUL, BIOCHEMISTRY, PHYSIOLOGY. *Current Pos:* ASSOC RESEARCHER, ROCHE INST MOLECULAR BIOL, NJ, 81- *Personal Data:* b Bryn Mawr, Pa, June 16, 42; m 67; c 3. *Educ:* Juniata Col, BS, 64; Mass Inst Technol, PhD(biol), 69. *Prof Exp:* Asst prof biol, Allen Univ, 69-70; NIH fel, Rutgers Univ, 70-72; guest worker biochem, Roche Inst Molecular Biol, 72-73; from asst prof to assoc prof physiol, Univ Tex Health Sci Ctr, Dallas, 73-81. *Concurrent Pos:* NIH grantee, 74-81 & NSF, 78-80. *Mem:* AAAS; Biophys Soc; Am Physiol Soc; Soc Gen Physiol; Physiol Soc Eng. *Res:* Permeability properties and transport activities of biological membranes; Na-Ca exchange in heart cell membranes. *Mailing Add:* Dept Physiol UMDNJ New Jersey 185 S Orange Ave Newark NJ 07103-2714

REEVES, JOHN T, CARDIOLOGY. *Current Pos:* PROF MED, UNIV COLO MED CTR, DENVER, 72- *Personal Data:* b Hazard, Ky, Nov 17, 28; c 2. *Educ:* Mass Inst Technol, BS, 50; Univ Pa, MD, 54. *Prof Exp:* USPHS res fel cardiol, Univ Colo, 57-58, Colo Heart Asn res fel, 58-59, Am Heart Asn advan res fel, 59-61; from asst prof to prof med, Univ Ky, 61-72. *Mem:* Am Physiol Soc; Soc Exp Biol Med; Am Col Chest Physicians; Am Thoracic Soc. *Mailing Add:* Dept Med & Pediat Univ Colo Health Sci Ctr Develop Lung Biol Lab B-131 Denver CO 80262

REEVES, LEONARD WALLACE, PHYSICAL CHEMISTRY. *Current Pos:* chmn dept, 69-71, PROF CHEM, UNIV WATERLOO, 69- *Personal Data:* b Bristol, Eng, Feb 8, 30; m 54. *Educ:* Bristol Univ, BSc, 51, PhD(phys chem), 54. *Hon Degrees:* DSc, Bristol Univ, 65. *Prof Exp:* Res asst, Univ Calif, 54-56; fel, Nat Res Coun Can, 56-57; fel, Mellon Inst, 57-58; from asst prof to prof chem, Univ BC, 58-69. *Concurrent Pos:* Vis prof, Univ Sao Paulo, 67-; Noranda lectr, 69. *Mem:* AAAS; Am Chem Soc; fel Chem Inst Can; Am Phys Soc; Int Soc Magnetic Resonance; fel Royal Soc Can; corresp mem Nat Acad Sci Brasil. *Res:* Metal ions in aqueous and ordered environments; lyotropic liquid crystals and membranes; chemical exchange and reaction mechanisms; pulsed and continuous wave nuclear magnetic resonance; molecular structure and intermolecular forces. *Mailing Add:* 15111 Russell Ave Apt 709 White Rock BC V4B 2P4 Can

REEVES, PERRY CLAYTON, CHEMISTRY. *Current Pos:* dean, Col Natural & Appl Sci, 81-87, PROF CHEM, ABILENE CHRISTIAN UNIV, 80-, CHAIR, 91- *Personal Data:* b Brady, Tex, Nov 9, 42; m 64, Judy Allen; c Amy & Mark. *Educ:* Abilene Christian Col, BS, 65; Univ Tex, Austin, PhD(chem), 69. *Prof Exp:* From asst prof to prof chem, Southern Methodist Univ, 69-80. *Mem:* Am Chem Soc; Sigma Xi. *Res:* Organic synthesis via organometallic compounds; photocatalytic destruction of hazardous organic compounds. *Mailing Add:* 810 Green Valley Abilene TX 79601-4519

REEVES, R C, cardiovascular medicine, for more information see previous edition

REEVES, RAYMOND, NUCLEIC ACID BIOCHEMISTRY. *Current Pos:* PROF BIOCHEM, BIOPHYS, MOLECULAR GENETICS & CELL BIOL, WASH STATE UNIV, 79- *Personal Data:* b St Louis, Mo, June 29, 43; div; c 2. *Educ:* Univ Calif, Berkeley, BA, 66, PhD, 71. *Prof Exp:* Fel, Oxford Univ, Eng, 71-72; fel, Med Res Coun Lab Molecular Biol, Cambridge, 72-73; asst prof, Univ BC, 73-78. *Mem:* Am Soc Biol Chemists; Soc Develop Biol; Am Soc Cell Biol; Int Soc Develop Biol. *Res:* Biochemistry of eukaryotic gene regulation; lymphokine regulation of lymphocyte growth and response of lymphokine genes to viral infections; chromatin structure and function. *Mailing Add:* Dept Biochem & Biophysics Genetics & Cell Biol Wash State Univ Fulmer Synth Bldg Rm 664 Pullman WA 99164-4660

REEVES, RICHARD ALLEN, AEROSPACE. *Current Pos:* Atty, Marshall Space Flight Ctr, NASA, 74-77, NASA Hq, 77-80, dep chief counsel, Goddard Space Flight Ctr, 80-82, dep dir mgt, 82-85, assoc dir, Ames Res Ctr, 85-88, dir planning, NASA Hq, 88-90, asst dir, NASA Hq Space Explor, 90-91, DIR INSTS, NASA HQ, 91- *Personal Data:* b Chicago, Ill, July 10, 44; m 67, 80, Elizabeth M Litkowski; c Garth K, Blakely C & Janice E. *Educ:* Ga State Univ, BBA, 70; Univ Tenn, JD, 73. *Mem:* Am Inst Aeronaut & Astronaut. *Res:* Aerospace management. *Mailing Add:* 7811 Custer Rd Bethesda MD 20814

REEVES, RICHARD EDWIN, organic chemistry, for more information see previous edition

REEVES, ROBERT BLAKE, PHYSIOLOGY. *Current Pos:* res assoc biophysics, 60-61, assoc prof, 66-76, PROF PHYSIOL, STATE UNIV NY, BUFFALO, 76- *Personal Data:* b Philadelphia, Pa, July 26, 30; m 67; c 2. *Educ:* Swarthmore Col, AB, 52; Harvard Univ, PhD(physiol), 59. *Prof Exp:* Res assoc physiol, Univ Pa, 59-60; asst prof physiol, Cornell Univ, 61-66. *Concurrent Pos:* Jr fel, Soc Fels, Harvard Univ, 57-60. *Mem:* Am Physiol Soc. *Res:* Acid-base balance; oxygen transport; red cell gas kinetics. *Mailing Add:* Dept Physiol State Univ NY Sch Med Buffalo NY 14214

REEVES, ROBERT DONALD, NUTRITION, BIOCHEMISTRY. *Current Pos:* assoc prof, 77-86, PROF NUTRIT, DEPT FOODS & NUTRIT, KANS STATE UNIV, 86- *Personal Data:* b Lubbock, Tex, Jan 14, 42; m 67, Sue Sloan; c Alan & Sherman. *Educ:* Tex Tech Univ, BA, 64, MS, 65; Iowa State Univ, PhD(nutrit), 71. *Prof Exp:* Res assoc nutrit, Agr Exp Sta, Iowa State Univ, 65-71; res & teaching nephrology med, Vet Admin Hosp, Little Rock, Ark, 71-77; from instr to asst prof med & biochem, Med Sci, Univ Ark, Little Rock, 74-77. *Concurrent Pos:* Scientist nutrit, Agr Exp Sta, Kans State Univ, 77- *Mem:* Am Inst Nutrit; Am Fedn Clin Res; Am Dietetic Asn; Sigma Xi; fel Am Col Nutrit; Am Soc Clin Nutrit. *Res:* Clinical nutrition and nutritional aspects of metabolic disease; nutritional factors influencing somatomedin activity; dietary fiber and lipid metabolism. *Mailing Add:* Dept Foods & Nutrit Kans State Univ Manhattan KS 66506. Fax: 785-532-3132; E-Mail: rdreeves@ksuvm.ksu.edu

REEVES, ROBERT GRIER (LEFEVRE), economic geology, geophysics; deceased, see previous edition for last biography

REEVES, ROBERT R, physical chemistry, chemical engineering, for more information see previous edition

REEVES, ROBERT WILLIAM, TROPICAL METEOROLOGY. *Current Pos:* METEOROLOGIST, CTR ENVIRON ASSESSMENT SERV, 69- *Personal Data:* b Morristown, NJ, Aug 12, 39; m 64; c 2. *Educ:* NY Univ, BS, 61, MS, 65; Univ Wash, PhD(meterol), 80. *Prof Exp:* Res meteorologist, Nat Hurricane Res Lab, 65-69. *Concurrent Pos:* Coordr aircraft opers, Barbados Oceanog & Meteorol Exp, 69; Rawinsonda data qual expert, Workshop Global Atmospheric Res Prog, Atlantic Trop Exp, 77. *Mem:* Am Meteorol

Soc. *Res:* Investigation of the dynamics of the disturbed and undisturbed tradewind atmosphere; implementation of existing coastal ocean circulation modeling to aid in marine environmental assessment. *Mailing Add:* 5400 Waneta Rd Bethesda MD 20816

REEVES, ROGER MARCEL, entomology, acarology; deceased, see previous edition for last biography

REEVES, ROY FRANKLIN, MATHEMATICS. *Current Pos:* PROF MATH SCI, OTTERBEIN COL, 81- *Personal Data:* b Warrensburg, Mo, July 8, 22; m 51; c 5. *Educ:* Univ Colo, BS, 47; Iowa State Col, PhD(math), 51. *Prof Exp:* Instr math, Univ Colo, 47-48; instr elec eng, Iowa State Col, 48-50, instr math, 50-51; prof math, Ohio State Univ, 51-81, dir, Computer Ctr, 55-81. *Mem:* Am Mgt Asn; NY Acad Sci; AAAS; Am Math Soc; Math Asn Am. *Res:* Numerical analysis and computing; computer science. *Mailing Add:* 16321 Lewis Rd Sunbury OH 43074

REEVES, STUART GRAHAM, immunoassay of contaminants, international agriculture, for more information see previous edition

REEVES, T JOSEPH, CARDIOVASCULAR PHYSIOLOGY, MEDICINE. *Current Pos:* PVT PRACT, SE CARDIOL, BEAUMONT, TEX, 86- *Personal Data:* b Waco, Tex, Apr 22, 23;; c 3. *Educ:* Baylor Univ, BS, 43, MD, 46. *Prof Exp:* Intern med, Parkland Hosp, Dallas, Tex, 46-47, resident, 49-51; pvt pract, Beaumont, Tex, 52-54; from asst prof to prof med, Sch Med, Univ Ala, Birmingham, 54-73, dir cardiovasc div, 58-66, assoc prof physiol & biophys, 58-73, dir cardiovasc res & training prog, 66-73, chmn dept med, 70-73; dir cardiovasc lab, St Elizabeth Hosp, 73-81; clin prof med, Univ Tex, Houston, 81-86. *Concurrent Pos:* Fel heart dis, Univ Ala, 51-52; Nat Heart Inst spec fel, Queen Elizabeth Hosp, Birmingham, Eng, 57-58; chief med serv, Vet Admin Hosp, Birmingham, Ala, 54-55, consult, 56-73; mem exec comt, Coun Circulation, Am Heart Asn, 63-66; mem nat adv comt, Heart Dis Control Prog & chmn prog proj comt, Nat Heart Inst, 65-67; chmn adv comt cardiol, Nat Heart & Lung Inst, 74-77. *Mem:* Am Soc Clin Invest; Am Physiol Soc; Am Fedn Clin Res; Sigma Xi. *Res:* Myocardial contraction; physiology of muscular exercise; cardiac diagnosis. *Mailing Add:* Dept Med Univ Tex Med Br 2955 Harrison Suite 207 Beaumont TX 77702

REEVES, W PRESTON, ORGANIC CHEMISTRY. *Current Pos:* from asst prof to assoc prof, 65-77, PROF CHEM, TEX LUTHERAN COL, 77- *Personal Data:* b Handley, Tex, Sept 22, 35; m 60, Lynda R Arthur; c Wylie E. *Educ:* Tex Christian Univ, BS, 57, MA, 59; Univ Tex, Austin, PhD(chem), 66. *Prof Exp:* Instr chem, Arlington State Col, 61-62. *Mem:* Am Chem Soc. *Res:* Thermal reactions of strained rings; allene chemistry; phase transfer catalysis; ultrasound. *Mailing Add:* Dept Chem Tex Lutheran Univ Seguin TX 78155. *Fax:* 830-372-8096; *E-Mail:* reeves_p@txlutheran.edu

REEVES, WILLIAM CARLISLE, EPIDEMIOLOGY. *Current Pos:* Lab asst, Entom Div, Univ Calif, 38-42, entomologist, Hooper Found, 41-42, asst epidemiol, Entom Div, 42-46, asst, Med Sch, 45-48, res asst, 46-49, lectr, Sch Pub Health, 47-54, assoc prof pub health, 49-54, from actg dean to dean, Sch Pub Health, 67-71, prof, 54-87, EMER PROF EPIDEMIOL, SCH PUB HEALTH, UNIV CALIF, BERKELEY, 87- *Personal Data:* b Riverside, Calif, Dec 2, 16; m 40, Mary J Maulton; c William C II, Robert R & Terrence M. *Educ:* Univ Calif, BS, 38, PhD(entom), 43, MPH, 48. *Honors & Awards:* Walter Reed Medal, Am Soc Trop Med Hyg, Harry Haogstraal Medal; John Snow Award, Am Pub Health Soc. *Mem:* Am Soc Trop Med & Hyg; Entom Soc Am; Am Mosquito Control Asn. *Res:* Epidemiology of the arthropod-borne virus encephalitides; mosquito biology and systematics. *Mailing Add:* Sch Pub Health Univ Calif Berkeley CA 94720

REEVES, WILSON ALVIN, TEXTILE CHEMISTRY. *Current Pos:* RETIRED. *Personal Data:* b Mittie, La, July 14, 19; m 42; c 4. *Educ:* Southwestern La Inst, BS, 41; Tulane Univ, La, MS, 50;. *Hon Degrees:* DSc, Clemson Univ, 69. *Honors & Awards:* John Scott Award, 65; Olney Medal, 66; Honor Award, Am Inst Chem, 70, 76, 78. *Prof Exp:* Chemist, Southern Regional Res Lab, Agr Res Serv, USDA, 42-75; prof, La State Univ, 76-85. *Concurrent Pos:* Consult, 75-76. *Mem:* Am Chem Soc; Sigma Xi; Am Asn Textile Chem & Colorists; Fiber Soc. *Res:* Organic, polymer and cellulose chemistry; fire retardant textiles. *Mailing Add:* 145 Devon St Mandeville LA 70448-3405

REFFES, HOWARD ALLEN, ANALYTICAL CHEMISTRY. *Current Pos:* DIR, TECH SERV, NESTLE ENTERPRISES LTD, 84- *Personal Data:* b New York, NY, Sept 18, 28. *Educ:* Queens Col, NY, BS, 50; Stevens Inst Technol, MS, 56. *Prof Exp:* Res analytical chemis, Colgate-Palmolive Co, 52-57; sr chemist & head analytical develop, Wallace & Tiernan, Inc, 57-61; mgr qual control, Flavor Div, Int Flavors & Fragrances, Inc, NJ, 61-68, plant mgr, 68-73; indust mgr, North Am Dairy Industs, 73-81; vpres & gen mgr, Food Div, Goodhost Foods, Ltd, 81-84. *Concurrent Pos:* Instr, NY Community Col, 56-68. *Mem:* AAAS; Am Chem Soc; Inst Food Technol; Am Soc Qual Control; fel Am Inst Chem. *Res:* Methods development for food additives and residues, pharmaceuticals, plasticizers and fatty acids; analytical research in condensed phosphates; polymeric anhydrides; analytical instrumentation; quality control of flavors; flavor manufacturing. *Mailing Add:* 330 Spadina Rd Suite 1901 Toronto ON M5R 2V9 Can

REFFNER, JOHN A, CHEMICAL MICROSCOPY, INFRARED SPECTROSCOPY. *Current Pos:* CORP FEL, SPECTRA-TECH INC, 86- *Personal Data:* b Akron, Ohio, Jan 5, 35; m 57, Sally E Messner; c John R & Elaine M (Teeters). *Educ:* Univ Akron, BS, 56; Ill Inst Technol, MS, 60; Univ Conn, PhD(polymer sci), 75. *Prof Exp:* Mat engr, B F Goodrich Co, 55-57; dir res, W C McCrone Assoc, 58-66; asst dir, Inst Mat Sci, Univ Conn, 66-77; prin res scientist, Am Cyanamid Res Labs, 77-86. *Concurrent Pos:* Sci consult, Conn State Police, 74-; adj fac, John Jay Col, 85- *Mem:* Am Chem Soc; Electron Micros Soc Am; Northeastern Asn Forensic Sci; Am Soc Testing & Mat; Microbeam Soc Am; Am Acad Forensic Sci. *Res:* Chemical microscopy; infrared spectroscopy; ultramicro analysis; polymer science; forensic science; failure analysis. *Mailing Add:* 97 Ocean Dr Expressway Stamford CT 06906. *Fax:* 203-357-1713

REFOJO, MIGUEL FERNANDEZ, BIOMATERIALS, OPHTHALMOLOGY. *Current Pos:* SR SCI, SCHEPEMS EYE RES INST, 71-; ASSOC PROF OPHTHAL, HARVARD MED SCH, 82- *Personal Data:* b Santiago, Spain, July 6, 28; US citizen; m 59, 81, 86, Svetlana Bernaldo; c Carla & Michael. *Educ:* Univ Santiago, Spain, Lic Sc, 53, DSc(org chem), 56. *Hon Degrees:* Dr hon causa (med), Univ Santiago, Spain, 88. *Honors & Awards:* Hon Mem, Academia Medico-Quirurgica, Santiago, Spain, 88; Emilio Diaz Caneja Award Res Ophthal, Univ Valladolid, Spain, 96. *Prof Exp:* Fel, Yale Univ, 56-59; res chemist, Tech Dept, DuPont Can, Ont, 59-63; res assoc, Mass Eye & Ear Infirmary, Boston, 63-64; res assoc, Eye Res Inst Retina Found, 64-70, assoc, 70-71, head polymer chem unit, 71-93. *Concurrent Pos:* Dir, Corneal Sci, Inc, Boston, 72-79; prin assoc ophthal & biochem, Harvard Med Sch, 75-82; vis prof, Col Optom, Univ Houston, 84; adj assoc prof, Sch Optom, Univ Mo, St Louis, 90-91; vis prof, Univ Jaime I, Castellon, Spain, consult FDA, 70-92; study sect, NIH, 73, 76, 82, 83 & 84; mem study sect NRC, NAS, 86-87 & 88-90; acad corresp, Royal Acad Pharm, Madrid, 96. *Mem:* AAAS; Am Chem Soc; Asn Res Vision & Ophthal; Sigma Xi; Soc Biomat; Int Soc Contact Lens Res (pres, 84-86). *Res:* Ophthalmology; synthetic polymers in medicine and surgery; hydrogels, silicones; contact lenses; drug delivery. *Mailing Add:* The Schepens Eye Res Inst 20 Staniford St Boston MA 02114

REFT, CHESTER STANLEY, MEDICAL PHYSICS, RADIATION DOSIMETRY. *Current Pos:* res assoc, 80-88, ASST PROF PHYSICS, UNIV CHICAGO, 88- *Personal Data:* b Pittsburgh, Pa, Sept 29, 44; m 68; c 3. *Educ:* Carnegie-Melon Univ, BS, 66; Univ Pittsburgh, PhD(physics), 73. *Prof Exp:* Res physicist, US Army-Harry Diamond Lab, 72-75; res assoc, Old Dominion Univ, 75-77, asst prof physics, 77-78, res assoc, 78-79, asst prof, 79-80. *Mem:* Am Phys Soc; Am Asn Physicists Med. *Res:* Improving the dosimetry of electron, photon and neutron teletheupy units for radyation therapy. *Mailing Add:* 246 Indiana St Park Forest IL 60466

REGAL, JEAN FRANCES, ALLERGY, LUNG PATHOLOGY. *Current Pos:* ASSOC PROF PHARMACOL, UNIV MINN, 85- *Educ:* Univ Minn, PhD(pharmacol), 77. *Res:* Immediate hypersensitivity. *Mailing Add:* Dept Pharmacol Univ Minn Duluth MN 55812-2487

REGAL, PHILIP JOE, BEHAVIORAL BIOLOGY, EVOLUTION. *Current Pos:* assoc prof ecol & behav biol & cur herpet, Mus Natural Hist, Univ Minn, Minneapolis, 70-, PROF ECOL, EVOLUTION & BEHAV, UNIV MINN, ST PAUL. *Personal Data:* b Los Angeles, Calif, Dec 2, 39. *Educ:* San Diego State Col, BA, 62; Univ Calif, Los Angeles, MA, 66, PhD(zool), 68. *Prof Exp:* Trainee, NIMH Brain Res Inst-Univ Calif, Los Angeles-Univ Calif, San Diego-Scripps Inst Oceanog, 68-70. *Concurrent Pos:* Mem US directorate UNESCO Man in Biosphere Prog. *Mem:* AAAS; Animal Behav Soc; Am Soc Ichthyologists & Herpetologists; Soc Study Amphibians & Reptiles; Ecol Soc Am. *Res:* Behavioral and physiological adaptations; behavioral temperature regulation; evolutionary processes; evolutionary trends in vertebrates, particularly amphibians and reptiles, evolutionary ecology of plants. *Mailing Add:* Dept Ecol Evolution Behav 1987 Upper Buford Circle 100 Ecology Bldg St Paul MN 55108

REGAN, DAVID M, VISION & HEARING RESEARCH, RECORDING ELECTRIC & MAGNETIC FIELDS OF THE HUMAN BRAIN. *Current Pos:* PROF OPHTHAL, UNIV TORONTO, 87-; PROF PSYCHOL, YORK UNIV, 87-, PROF BIOL & NSERC/CAE INDUST RES PROF AVIATION, 93- *Personal Data:* b Scarborough, Yorkshire, Eng, May 5, 35; Can & Brit citizen; m 59; c 2. *Educ:* London Univ, BSc, ARCS, 57, MSc, DIC, 58, PhD(physics), 64, DSc, 74. *Honors & Awards:* Prentice Medal, Am Acad Optom, 90. *Prof Exp:* Lectr physics, London Univ, 60-65; reader neurosci, Keele Univ, 65-75; prof med, Dalhousie Univ, 78-87, dir, Ctr Res Vision & Hearing, 78-87, prof physiol, 80-84, prof otolaryngol, 80-84, prof ophthal, 81-87. *Concurrent Pos:* Hon appt, Birmingham Hosp Bd, UK, 68-75; consult med physics, Camp Hill Hosp, Halifax; mem sensory dis panel, Nat Eye Inst, NIH, 81; vis prof, Univ Amsterdam, 85; co-dir, Human Performance in Space Lab, Inst Space Terrestrial Sci, 87-; I W Killam fel, 91-93. *Mem:* Fel Royal Soc Can; fel Optical Soc Am; fel Am Acad Optom. *Res:* Visual psychophysics; auditory psychophysics; visual factors in aviation, driving and sport; visual disorders (multiple sclerosis, amblyopia, cataract); recording electric and magnetic fields of the human brain. *Mailing Add:* York Univ Rm 375 BSB 4700 Keele St North York ON M3J 1P3 Can. *Fax:* 416-736-5814; *E-Mail:* regan@vm1.yorku.ca

REGAN, FRANCIS, mathematics; deceased, see previous edition for last biography

REGAN, GERALD THOMAS, ECOLOGY. *Current Pos:* from asst prof to assoc prof, 72-82, PROF BIOL, SPRING HILL COL, 82- *Personal Data:* b Omaha, Nebr, Apr 19, 31. *Educ:* St Louis Univ, AB, 55, PhL, 57, MS, 62; Univ Kans, PhD(zool), 72. *Prof Exp:* Instr biol, Creighton Univ, 68-71. *Concurrent Pos:* Chmn, sci div, 82-85, prog comt Marine Environ Sci Consortium, 85-86; Coord, Ala Marine Mammal Stranding Network, 90- *Mem:* Soc Marine Mammal; Am Cetacean Soc. *Res:* Evolution; ecological biogeography. *Mailing Add:* Dept Biol Spring Hill Col Mobile AL 36608-1791

REGAN, RAYMOND WESLEY, BIOLOGICAL WASTE TREATMENT SYSTEMS, INDUSTRIAL WASTE ABATEMENT & BENEFICIAL USE. *Current Pos:* asst prof, 72-78, assoc prof civil eng, 78-96, PROF ENVIRON ENG, 96-, DIR, OFF HAZARDOUS & TOXIC WASTE MGT, INST RES LAND & WATER RESOURCES, PA STATE UNIV, 81- *Personal Data:* b New York, NY, Aug 30, 43; m 68; c 8. *Educ:* Manhattan Col, BEChE, 65, ME, 66; Kans Univ, Lawrence, PhD(environ health eng), 72. *Honors & Awards:* Gabriel Narutowicz Medal, Inst Meteorol & Water Mgt, Warsaw, 91. *Prof Exp:* Proj engr, Environ Eng Grad Prog, Manhattan Col, 66-70. *Concurrent Pos:* Assoc, Environ Sci Div, Oak Ridge Nat Lab, Tenn, 82, Toxic & Hazardous Mat Agency, US Army, Aberdeen, Md, 85 & Appl Res Lab, 93. *Mem:* Am Soc Civil Engrs; Water Environ Fedn; Am Foundrymen's Soc. *Res:* Advancing technologies for improved hazardous and residual solid waste management for industries, including electroplaters-metal finishers, plastics and synthetics, paint and allied products; foundries; tanneries; pulp and paper. *Mailing Add:* Pa State Univ 134 Land & Water Bldg University Park PA 16802. *Fax:* 814-865-3378; *E-Mail:* rwri@psuvm.psu.edu

REGAN, THOMAS M(ICHAEL), CHEMICAL ENGINEERING, BIOENGINEERING. *Current Pos:* From asst prof to assoc prof, 66-76, PROF CHEM ENG, UNIV MD, COLLEGE PARK, 76- *Personal Data:* b New Orleans, La, Nov 28, 41; m 64; c 2. *Educ:* Tulane Univ, BS, 63, PhD, 67. *Mem:* Am Inst Chem Engrs; Am Chem Soc. *Res:* Optimization of artificial kidney systems; membrane test cell design; testing of blood-gas exchangers; ionic and membrane diffusion. *Mailing Add:* Dept Chem Eng Univ Md Rm 2105 JM Patterson Bldg College Park MD 20742-0001

REGAN, TIMOTHY JOSEPH, INTERNAL MEDICINE, CARDIOLOGY. *Current Pos:* from asst prof to assoc prof, 60-66, DIR, DIV CARDIOVASC DIS, UNIV MED & DENT NJ, 65-, PROF MED, 66- *Personal Data:* b Boston, Mass, July 24, 24; c 4. *Educ:* Boston Col, AB, 48; Boston Univ, MD, 52; Am Bd Internal Med, dipl, 60. *Prof Exp:* Rotating intern, City Detroit Receiving Hosp, 56-57; instr med, Sch Med, Wayne State Univ, 57-59, asst prof, 59-60. *Concurrent Pos:* Jr assoc med, City Detroit Receiving Hosp, 57-60; assoc in med, Children's Hosp, Detroit, 59-60; assoc dir, T J White Cardiopulmonary Inst, B S Pollak Hosp, Jersey City, 60-65, dir, 65-71, attend physician, Hosp, 60-71; estab investr, Am Heart Asn, 61-66; attend physician, Vet Admin Hosp, East Orange, NJ & Univ Med & Dent NJ-Univ Hosp, Newark, 65-; chmn subcomt diag procedures in heart dis, NJ Regional Med Prog, 69-; mem cardiovasc study sect, Nat Adv Coun & Comts, NIH, 69-73. *Mem:* Am Fedn Clin Res; Am Physiol Soc; Am Heart Asn; Am Soc Clin Invest; Am Diabetes Asn; Asn Am Physicians. *Res:* Myocardial metabolism in disease. *Mailing Add:* Dept Med/Div Cardiovasc Dis Univ Med & Dent NJ Med Sch 185 S Orange Ave Newark NJ 07103-2714

REGE, AJAY ANAND, ANTISENSE OLIGONUCLEOTIDES IN THERAPY, CARDIOVASCULAR BIOLOGY. *Current Pos:* SR SCIENTIST, TEX BIOTECHNOL CORP, 91- *Personal Data:* b Karwar, India, May 27, 58; c 2. *Educ:* Poona Univ, India, BSc, 77; Tex A&M Univ, PhD(microbiol), 84. *Prof Exp:* Res assoc, Baylor Col Med, 84-87, res instr, 87-89, instr, 89-91. *Mem:* Am Soc Biochem & Molecular Biol; Am Soc Microbiol; AAAS; Sigma Xi. *Res:* Structure-function analysis of enzymes from tropical parasites; use of antisense oligonucleotides as therapeutic agents for vascular disease. *Mailing Add:* Tex Biotechnol Corp 7000 Fannin St Suite 1920 Houston TX 77030. *Fax:* 713-796-8232

REGELSON, WILLIAM, MEDICINE. *Current Pos:* chief, Div Med Oncol, Va Commonwealth Univ, 67-76, PROF MED, MED COL VA, VA COMMONWEALTH UNIV, 67-, ADJ PROF MICROBIOL, 80-, ADJ PROF BIOMED ENG, 91- *Personal Data:* b New York, NY, July 12, 25; m 48, Sylvia Phillips; c 6. *Educ:* Univ NC, AB, 48; State Univ NY, MD, 52. *Prof Exp:* Intern med, Maimonides Hosp, Brooklyn, NY, 52-53; from asst resident to sr resident, Mem Ctr Cancer & Appl Dis, New York, 53-55; spec fel cancer res, Roswell Park Mem Inst, 55-56, sr cancer res internist, 56-57, assoc cancer res internist, 57-59, assoc chief med, 59-67; asst res prof med, State Univ NY, Buffalo, 65-67. *Concurrent Pos:* Consult, Monsanto Chem Co, 59, A H Robins Co, Inc, 69-71, Hercules, Inc, 71-74 & Merrell-Nat Labs, 71-76, Pitarmacia, 79-86, Phoenix Adv Tech, 88-91, Cobra, 91- & Neurocrine, 93-; sci dir, Fund Int Biomed Res, 80-85. *Mem:* Fel NY Acad Sci; Am Asn Cancer Res; Am Soc Clin Oncol. *Res:* Effect of polyelectrolytes on cell growth and differentiation and on enzyme and virul function; effects of various chemotherapeutic and immunotherapeutic agents on cancer in man and animal; production and prevention of tumor growth; aging; pineal, melatonin and hormonal effects on aging and immune response; ultrasonic hearing; low frequency vibratory effects. *Mailing Add:* Med Col Va PO Box 273 Richmond VA 23202-0273

REGEN, DAVID MARVIN, PHYSIOLOGY, BIOCHEMISTRY. *Current Pos:* from asst prof to assoc prof, 64-76, PROF PHYSIOL, VANDERBILT UNIV, 76- *Personal Data:* b Nashville, Tenn, Mar 18, 34; m 58; c 3. *Educ:* Davidson Col, BS, 56; Vanderbilt Univ, PhD(physiol), 62. *Prof Exp:* Instr physiol, Vanderbilt Univ, 62-63; guest investr, Max Planck Inst Cell Chem, 63-64. *Concurrent Pos:* Howard Hughes Med Inst fel, 63-64, investr, 64-71; NIH res grant, 65- *Mem:* Am Physiol Soc. *Res:* Mechanism and kinetics of glucose transport; regulatory effects of insulin, diabetes, anoxia and work on glucose utilization in muscle; control of hepatic cholesterol synthesis; monocarboxylate transport; regulation of glucose transport in lymphocytes; brain glucose metabolism; brain ketone-body metabolism; cardiac dynamics. *Mailing Add:* Dept Molecular Physiol & Biophys Vanderbilt Univ Sch Med Nashville TN 37232-0615

REGENBRECHT, D(OUGLAS) E(DWARD), SPACE THERMAL SYSTEMS, OPTICAL THERMAL STABILITY. *Current Pos:* CONSULT, 89. *Personal Data:* b Bryan, Tex, June 8, 24; m 58; c 3. *Educ:* Tex A&M Univ, BSME, 48; Purdue Univ, MSME, 51, PhD(mech eng), 62. *Prof Exp:* Instr mech eng, Purdue Univ, 50-57; asst prof, Univ Tulsa, 57-63, assoc prof & head dept, 63-67; sr mem tech staff, Ball Bros Res Corp, 67-77, staff scientist, 77-80; prin thermal engr, Ball Aerospace Systs Group, 80-89. *Concurrent Pos:* Consult, Space & Info Systs Div, NAm Aviation, Inc, Tulsa, 62-66. *Mem:* Am Soc Mech Engrs; Am Soc Eng Educ; Am Inst Aeronaut & Astronaut; Soc Packaging & Handling Engrs; Sigma Xi. *Res:* Fluid mechanics; convective and radiative heat transfer; thermal energy conversion systems; mathematical modeling. *Mailing Add:* 870 Gilpin Dr Boulder CO 80303-2523

REGENER, VICTOR H, PHYSICS. *Current Pos:* OWNER, VHR SYSTS, 79- *Personal Data:* b Berlin, Ger, Aug 25, 13; nat US; m 41, Birgit Hamilton; c Eric & Vivian (Rose). *Educ:* Stuttgart Inst Technol, Dr-Ing, 38. *Prof Exp:* Res fel, Padova Univ, 38-40; res fel, Univ Chicago, 40-42, instr physics, 42-46; from assoc prof to prof physics, Univ NMex, 46-57, chmn dept, 46-57 & 62-79, res prof, 57-76. *Concurrent Pos:* Assoc cur, Mus Sci & Indust, Univ Chicago, 45-46; hon prof, Univ Mayor de San Andres, La Paz, Bolivia. *Mem:* Fel Am Phys Soc; Am Astron Soc; fel NY Acad Sci; Int Soc Optical Eng. *Res:* Atmospheric ozone; cosmic radiation; zodiacal light; balloon and satellite experiments; optical studies of pulsars; electronics; optics. *Mailing Add:* 532 Solano NE Albuquerque NM 87108

REGENSTEIN, JOE MAC, FOOD SCIENCE, RELIGIOUS FOODS. *Current Pos:* asst prof poultry sci, Cornell Univ, 74-80, from asst prof to assoc prof food sci, 75-87, prof poultry sci & food sci, 87- 91, DIR, CORNELL KOSHER FOOD INITIATIVE, CORNELL UNIV, 91-, PROF FOOD SCI, 91- *Personal Data:* b Brooklyn, NY, Sept 22, 43; m 66, Carrie Forsheit; c Elliot & Scott. *Educ:* Cornell Univ, BA, 65, MS, 66; Brandeis Univ, PhD(biophys), 72. *Honors & Awards:* Earl P McFee Award, Atlantic Fisheries Technol Soc. *Prof Exp:* Fel muscle, Children's Cancer Res Ctr, Boston, 73 & Brandeis Univ, 73-74. *Concurrent Pos:* Sabbatical leave, Torry Res Sta, Aberdeen, Scotland, 80-81; guest fel, New Zealand Inst Food Sci & Technol; counr, Inst Food Technologists; nat lectr, Inst Food Technologies. *Mem:* Am Chem Soc; Poultry Sci Asn; Inst Food Technologists; AAAS; Am Meat Sci Asn; Nat Kosher Food Trade Asn. *Res:* Functional properties of muscle proteins, especially water retention properties and emulsification; frozen storage changes in gadoid fish; shelf-life extension of fresh poultry and fish; new product development from minced fish and poultry; kosher foods; waste management in fisheries. *Mailing Add:* Food Sci Dept Stocking Hall Cornell Univ Ithaca NY 14853-7201. *Fax:* 607-257-2871; *E-Mail:* jmr9@cornell.edu

REGER, BONNIE JANE, plant physiology, for more information see previous edition

REGER, DANIEL LEWIS, COORDINATION CHEMISTRY. *Current Pos:* From asst prof to assoc prof, 72-84, PROF CHEM, UNIV SC, 84- *Personal Data:* b Mineral Wells, Tex, Sept 16, 45; m 68, Cheryl S; c Jill E & Lance B. *Educ:* Dickinson Col, BS, 67; Mass Inst Technol, PhD(chem), 72. *Mem:* Am Chem Soc; Sigma Xi. *Res:* Transition metal organometallic synthesis; coordination chemistry of main group elements. *Mailing Add:* Dept Chem Univ SC Columbia SC 29208-0001

REGER, JAMES FREDERICK, CYTOLOGY. *Current Pos:* RETIRED. *Personal Data:* b Norway, Iowa, Oct 27, 24; m 46; c 3. *Educ:* Univ Iowa, PhD(zool), 54. *Prof Exp:* Asst, Univ Iowa, 50-54; asst prof zool, Ariz State Univ, 54-55; from res assoc to asst prof anat, Sch Med, Univ Colo, 55-65; from assoc prof to prof, Med Units, Univ Tenn, Memphis, 65-95. *Concurrent Pos:* USPHS career develop award, 59-65. *Mem:* AAAS; Am Soc Zoologists; Soc Protozool; Am Asn Anatomists; Am Soc Cell Biol. *Res:* Cytology of spinal ganglion cells; electron microscopy of euglena, myoneural junction, the synapse, kidney, muscle, oocytes; spermatozoa. *Mailing Add:* 830 Poplar Acres Rd Collierville TN 38017

REGER, RICHARD DAVID, GLACIAL GEOLOGY, QUATERNARY GEOLOGY. *Current Pos:* GEOLOGIST III, ALASKA DIV GEOL & GEOPHYS SURV, 75- *Personal Data:* b Chico, Calif, May 10, 39; m 68; c 2. *Educ:* Univ Alaska, Fairbanks, BS, 63, MS, 64; Ariz State Univ, PhD(geol), 75. *Prof Exp:* Instr geol, Ariz State Univ, 72-73; sr geologist, R&M Consult, Inc, 73-75. *Res:* Mapping surficial deposits, especially glacial deposits, throughout Alaska for a comprehensive environmental evaluation. *Mailing Add:* Box 638 La Grande OR 97850

REGEZI, JOSEPH ALBERTS, ORAL PATHOLOGY. *Current Pos:* PROF ORAL PATH/PATH, UNIV CALIF, SAN FRANCISCO, 90- *Personal Data:* b Grand Rapids, Mich, May 14, 43; m 64; c 2. *Educ:* Univ Mich, DDS, 68, MS, 71. *Prof Exp:* Chmn dept path, David Grant Med Ctr, USAF, 71-73; asst prof oral path, Univ Mich, Ann Arbor, 73-77, asst prof dent, Dept Hosp

Dent, Univ Mich Hosp, 73-90, assoc prof oral path, Sch Dent, 77-90, asst prof path, Med Sch, 76-90. *Mem:* Fel Am Acad Oral Path; Int Asn Dent Res. *Res:* Light and electron microscopic studies of head and neck neoplasms, especially salivary gland and odontogenic tumors, in regard to their classification, diagnosis, and histogenesis. *Mailing Add:* Univ Calif 513 Parnassus Suite 512 San Francisco CA 94143

REGIER, HENRY ABRAHAM, ECOLOGY, FISHERIES. *Current Pos:* from asst prof to assoc prof, 66-73, PROF ZOOL, UNIV TORONTO, 73- *Personal Data:* b Brainerd, Alta, Mar 5, 30; m 56; c 3. *Educ:* Queen's Univ, BA, 54; Cornell Univ, MS, 59, PhD(fishery biol), 62. *Honors & Awards:* Centenary Medal, Royal Soc Can, 86. *Prof Exp:* Teacher sci, Stamford Collegiate Inst, Ont, 55-57; res scientist, Ont Dept Lands & Forests, 61-63; res assoc biomet, Cornell Univ, 63-64, asst prof conserv & asst leader, NY Coop Fish Unit, 64-66. *Concurrent Pos:* Chief resource eval br fisheries, Food & Agr Orgn, UN, Rome, 70-71; trustee, Inst Ecol, 73-75; res plan consult, Fisheries Res Bd Can, 73-76; comnr, Great Lakes Fishery Comn, 80- *Mem:* Int Union Theoret & Appl Limnol; Int Asn Gt Lakes Res; Am Fisheries Soc (pres, 78-79); Int Asn Ecol. *Res:* Ecology of aquatic ecosystems, particularly large-scale responses of fish communities to major cultural stresses; screening and assessing ecological models and methods for interdisciplinary application; sustainable redevelopment of the Great Lakes Basin. *Mailing Add:* Dept Zool Univ Toronto 25 Harbard St Toronto ON M5S 1A1 Can

REGISTER, RICHARD ALAN, MULTIPHASE POLYMERS, POLYMER MORPHOLOGY. *Current Pos:* Asst prof, 90-96, ASSOC PROF CHEM ENG, PRINCETON UNIV, 96- *Personal Data:* b Cheverly, Md, Sept 6, 63; m 89, Jean Tom. *Educ:* Mass Inst Technol, BS, 83, BS, 84, MS, 85; Univ Wis-Madison, PhD(chem eng), 89. *Honors & Awards:* Unilever Award, Am Chem Soc, 92. *Concurrent Pos:* Fac mem, Princeton Mat Inst, 90-; res assoc, TRI/Princeton, 94-; fac mem, ATC/POEM, 95- *Mem:* Am Chem Soc; Am Phys Soc; Am Inst Chem Engrs; Mat Res Soc; Soc Plastics Engrs. *Res:* Morphology, properties, and dynamics of multiphase polymeric materials, particularly block copolymers, polymer blends, semicrystalline polymers and ionomers; electroluminescent polymers; applications of small-angle scattering. *Mailing Add:* Dept Chem Eng Princeton Univ Princeton NJ 08544. *Fax:* 609-258-0211; *E-Mail:* register@pucc.princeton.edu

REGISTER, ULMA DOYLE, BIOCHEMISTRY, NUTRITION. *Current Pos:* from instr to assoc prof biochem, Loma Linda Univ, 51-67, chmn grad prog nutrit, 69, chmn dept nutrit, dietetics, 72-82, prof nutrit & chmn dept, 67-84, PROF NUTRIT, LOMA LINDA UNIV, 84- *Personal Data:* b West Monroe, La, Feb 4, 20; m 42, Helen Hite; c Rebecca A, Dorothy L & Deborah J. *Educ:* Madison Col, BS, 42; Vanderbilt Univ, MS, 44; Univ Wis, PhD(biochem), 50. *Prof Exp:* Fel, Sch Med, Tulane Univ, 50-51. *Concurrent Pos:* Commonwealth Fund fel, Karolinska Inst, Sweden, 63-64. *Mem:* Am Inst Nutrit; Am Dietetic Asn; Am Soc Clin Nutrit. *Res:* Assessment of vitamin B12 status in total vegetarians. *Mailing Add:* Dept Nutrit Loma Linda Univ Sch Pub Health Loma Linda CA 92350-0001

REGNA, PETER P, ORGANIC BIOCHEMISTRY, ANTIBIOTIC RESEARCH. *Current Pos:* sr partner, 70-72, MANAGING PARTNER, HARRINGTON RES CO, 72- *Personal Data:* b Hoboken, NJ, May 26, 09; m, Barbara E Kellner; c Peter J & Robert E. *Educ:* Polytech Inst NY, BS, 32, MS, 37, PhD(phys org chem), 42. *Honors & Awards:* Perkin Medalist, Am Sect, Soc Chem Indust, 86; Kohnstamm Award, Columbia Univ, 88; Hon Scroll Award, Am Inst Chemist, 72, 86. *Prof Exp:* Res group leader, Pfizer, Inc, 45-50, tech asst to dir res, 50-54, coordr cancer prog, 54-57, spec projs officer, 57-61; dir res planning, Squibb Inst Med Res, NJ, 61-70. *Concurrent Pos:* Consult; pres, Indust Chem Soc. *Mem:* AAAS; Am Chem Soc; fel Am Inst Chemists; fel NY Acad Sci; fel Am Col Clin Pharmacol. *Res:* Kinetic reactions; carbohydrate chemistry; synthetic vitamins; structure antibiotics; chemotherapeutic agents; development of pharmaceuticals; antineoplastic substances; physical chemistry; physical organic; author of 40 scientific papers and holder of 35 US and foreign patents. *Mailing Add:* PO Box 932 Harrington Res Co Englewood Cliffs NJ 07632-0932

REGNAULT, WILLIAM F, MATERIAL ENGINEERING. *Current Pos:* mat scientist, Ctr Devices & Radiol Health, 86-91, GROUP LEADER DEPT MAT ENG, FOOD & DRUG ADMIN, 91- *Personal Data:* b New Brunswick, NJ, Aug 17, 46. *Educ:* Drew Univ, BA, 68; Pa State Univ, 77. *Prof Exp:* Solar mat scientist, Solarex, 79-86. *Mailing Add:* Dept Mat Eng Food & Drug Admin 12200 Wilkins Ave Rockville MD 20852. *Fax:* 301-443-5259

REGNER, JOHN LAVERNE, NUCLEAR PHYSICS, SYSTEMS ANALYSIS. *Current Pos:* MISSION/SYST ANALYST, TELEDYNE BROWN ENG, 83- *Personal Data:* b Columbus, Ohio, Oct 24, 46; m 68; c 2. *Educ:* Ohio State Univ, BS, 69, MS, 69, PhD(physics), 76. *Prof Exp:* Systs analyst missile systs, NAm Rockwell, 69-73; res assoc nuclear physics, Ohio State Univ, 73-76, assoc, Van de Graaff Lab, 76-77; systs analyst defense systs, Inst Defense Anal, 77-83. *Concurrent Pos:* Adj asst prof physics, Univ Ala-Huntsville, 84- *Mem:* Am Phys Soc. *Res:* Nuclear physics utilizing polarized particles; nuclear spectroscopy; communication systems for command and control; strategic force exchange analysis; ballistic missile defense analysis. *Mailing Add:* 132 Thomas Rd Madison AL 35758

REGNERY, DAVID COOK, BIOLOGY. *Current Pos:* From instr to assoc prof, 47-53, PROF BIOL, STANFORD UNIV, 53- *Personal Data:* b La Grange, Ill, June 26, 18; m 45; c 3. *Educ:* Stanford Univ, AB, 41; Calif Inst Technol, PhD(genetics), 47. *Res:* Wildlife diseases, pox viruses, myxomatosis. *Mailing Add:* 488 Westridge Dr Menlo Park CA 94028

REGNIER, FREDERICK EUGENE, BIOCHEMISTRY. *Current Pos:* from asst prof to assoc prof, 68-76, PROF BIOCHEM, PURDUE UNIV, LAFAYETTE, 76- *Personal Data:* b Fairbury, Nebr, July 7, 38; m 60; c 1. *Educ:* Nebr State Teachers Col, Peru, BS, 60; Okla State Univ, PhD(chem), 65. *Prof Exp:* Fel, Okla State Univ, 65-66 & Univ Chicago, 66-68. *Mem:* Am Chem Soc; Am Soc Biol Chemists; Sigma Xi. *Res:* Pheromones; hormones; instrumental analysis. *Mailing Add:* Dept Biochem Purdue Univ Lafayette IN 47907

REGO, VERNON J, PERFORMANCE, SIMULATION. *Current Pos:* Asst prof, 85-91, ASSOC PROF COMPUTER SCI, DEPT COMPUTER SCI, PURDUE UNIV, 91- *Educ:* Mich State Univ, MS, 83, PhD(computer sci), 85. *Concurrent Pos:* Res visitor computer sci, Univ Stuttgart, Ger, 88; fac visitor computer sci, Oak Ridge Nat Lab, Tenn, 90 & 91. *Mem:* Inst Elec & Electronics Engrs. *Res:* Performance evaluation; stochastic modelling; simulation; parallel simulation; computer networks; distributed systems; software engineering and reliabilty. *Mailing Add:* Dept Comput Sci Purdue Univ West Lafayette IN 47907

REGOLI, DOMENICO, PEPTIDES. *Current Pos:* PROF & CHMN PHARMACOL, UNIV SHERBROOKE, 68-, CAREER INVESTR, MED RES COUN CAN, 73- *Personal Data:* b Lucca, Italy, May 16, 33; Can citizen; m 68; c 4. *Educ:* Liceo Classico Carducci Grosseto-Baccal, 53; Univ Siena, Italy, MD, 59; Univ Lausanne, Switz, Priv Docent(pharmacol), 67. *Honors & Awards:* M Sarrazin Prize, Med Res, 87; UpJohn Prize, Can Pharmacol Soc, 92. *Prof Exp:* Asst prof med, Univ Siena, 59-60; fel pharmacol, Ciba Biol Labor, 60-63; fel, Royal Col Surgeons, 63-64; from asst prof to assoc prof, Univ Lausanne, 65-68. *Concurrent Pos:* Pharmaceut co consult; prof pharmacol, Univ Ferrara, Italy. *Mem:* Am Soc Pharmacol & Therapeut; Brit Pharmacol Soc; Pharmacol Soc Can; Int Soc Hypertension; NY Acad Sci. *Res:* Pharmacology of peptide hormones and antagonists; isolation and identification of naturally occurring peptides; chemical synthesis and purification of peptide analogues; development of anti-hypertensive, anti-inflammatory and analgesic drugs. *Mailing Add:* Dept Pharmacol Univ Sherbrooke Sch Med Sherbrooke PQ J1H 5N4 Can

REGULSKI, THOMAS WALTER, POLYMER CHEMISTRY. *Current Pos:* SR RES CHEMIST, DOW CHEM CO, 73- *Personal Data:* b Detroit, Mich, Dec 13, 43; m 63; c 3. *Educ:* Wayne State Univ, BS, 67; Univ Nebr, PhD(org chem), 71. *Prof Exp:* Assoc, Univ Toronto, 71-73. *Mem:* Am Chem Soc. *Res:* Area of polymer synthesis for industrial and biomedical applications. *Mailing Add:* 4844 Valley Way Antioch CA 94509

REGUNATHAN, PERIALWAR, WATER PURIFICATION, WATER FILTRATION. *Current Pos:* supvr res, Everpure Inc, Beatrice Co, Westmont, Ill, 68-70, mgr res, 70-78, res & develop, 78-80, VPRES RES & DEVELOP, EVERPURE, INC, BEATRICE, CO, WESTMONT, ILL, 80- *Personal Data:* b Samugarengapuram, Tamil Nadu, India, Feb 23, 40; m 63; c 3. *Educ:* Univ Madras, India, BE, 61, MSc, 63; Iowa State Univ, MS, 65, PhD(sanit eng), 67. *Honors & Awards:* Spes Hominum Award, Nat Sanit Found, 85. *Prof Exp:* Asst lectr civil eng, Col Eng, Univ Madras, India, 62-63; instr sanit eng, Iowa State Univ, 67; engr-scientist, Eng-Sci, Inc, Oakland, 67-68. *Concurrent Pos:* Mem, Sci Adv Comn, Water Qual Asn, 80-, chmn, Drinking Water Comt, 85-; indust rep, Environ Protection Agency, 77-80 & 84-86. *Mem:* Am Water Works Asn; Filtration Soc; Am Soc Testing & Mat; Water Qual Asn. *Res:* Development of processes and products employing advanced ideas in filtration adsorption, disinfection and destabilization areas of water treatment for use by final user in home or other establishments such as restaurants. *Mailing Add:* 1490 Jasper Dr Wheaton IL 60187

REH, JOHN W, AGRICULTURAL ENGINEERING. *Current Pos:* PRES, REH & ASSOCS, 92- *Personal Data:* b Saline Co, Kans, July 2, 35; m 57, Judith A Kirkland; c Elaine M (Edwards), Jeffrey K & Kirk W. *Educ:* Kans State Univ, BS, 58. *Prof Exp:* Hydraul engr, Soil Conserv Serv, USDA, Salina, Kans, 58-61 & 63-70, construct engr, Cheney, Kans, 61-63, leader water resources planning staff, Salina, Kans, 70-84, asst state conservationist, 84-91. *Concurrent Pos:* Conserv & watershed adv, Kans Water Plan, Kans Water Authority, 80-91. *Mem:* Nat Soc Prof Engrs; Soil & Water Conserv Soc. *Res:* Development of hydrologic procedures. *Mailing Add:* 2267 Leland Way Salina KS 67401

REH, THOMAS ANDREW, DEVELOPMENTAL NEUROBIOLOGY. *Current Pos:* ASSOC PROF BIOL STRUCT, UNIV WASH, SEATTLE, 88- *Personal Data:* b Chicago, Ill, Feb 17, 55; m 81. *Educ:* Univ Ill, Champaign, BS(biochem) & BS(physiol), 77; Univ Wis-Madison, PhD(neurosci), 81. *Honors & Awards:* Jerzy Rose Award, Univ Wis-Madison, 82; Recipient AHFMR Scholar; Recipient Alfred East Sloan Scholar, 87-88. *Prof Exp:* vis fel, Neurosci, Princeton Univ, 81-84; prof med physiol, Univ Calgary, 88. *Concurrent Pos:* Reviewer ad hoc grant, NSF, 82- *Mem:* Am Soc Cell Biol. *Res:* Development of the retina. *Mailing Add:* Dept Biol Struct SM-20 Univ Wash Sch Med 3900 7th Ave NE Seattle WA 98195-0001

REHAK, MATTHEW JOSEPH, CLINICAL CHEMISTRY, TOXICOLOGY. *Current Pos:* RETIRED. *Personal Data:* b Baltimore, Md, Apr 24, 29; m 53; c 5. *Educ:* Loyola Col, AB, 50; Univ Md, MS, 55, PhD(biochem, pharmacol), 58. *Prof Exp:* Chemist, Off Chief Med Exam, Md, 50-51, asst, 53-54; asst pharmacol, Med Sch, Univ Md, 54-57; state toxicologist, Conn State Health Dept, 57-60; clin chemist, St Agnes Hosp, 60-94. *Concurrent Pos:* Consult clin chem, Dept of State, Washington, DC, 68-73. *Mem:* Nat Acad Clin Biochem; Clin Radioassay Soc; Am Chem Soc; Am Asn Clin Chem. *Res:* New analytical methods for drugs and metabolites; detection and determination of drug effects on enzyme systems. *Mailing Add:* 1029 Hart Rd Baltimore MD 21286

REHAK, PAVEL, HIGH ENERGY PHYSICS, ELECTRODYNAMICS. *Current Pos:* RES PHYSICIST PARTICLE PHYSICS, BROOKHAVEN NAT LAB, 76- *Personal Data:* b Prague, Czech, Dec 5, 45; m 77. *Educ:* Charles Univ, Prague, RNDr(nuclear physics), 69; State Univ Col Pisa, PhD(elem particle physics), 72. *Prof Exp:* Res physicist particle physics, Kernforschungscentrum, Karlsruhe, WGer, 72-73; res assoc, Yale Univ, 73-76. *Res:* Experiments in elementary particle physics; detector and particle detection system development; electrodynamics in strong magnetic field. *Mailing Add:* 436 Bay Ave Patchogue NY 11772

REHA-KRANTZ, LINDA J, DNA POLYMERASE STRUCTURE-FUNCTION STUDIES, DNA REPLICATION. *Current Pos:* from asst prof to assoc prof genetics, 81-94, PROF BIOL SCI, UNIV ALTA, 94- *Personal Data:* b Tacoma, Wash, Feb 11, 49; c Matthew J Krantz. *Educ:* Univ Wash, BSc(chem) & BSc(molecular biol), 71; Johns Hopkins Univ, PhD(biol & biochem), 75. *Prof Exp:* Postdoctoral fel, Albert Einstein Col Med, NIH, 75-77 Nat Cancer Inst Can, 77-79. *Concurrent Pos:* Vis assoc prof molecular biophys & biochem, Yale Univ, 90-91; scientist, Alta Heritage Found Med Res, 81-; professorship for women, NSF, 90-91. *Mem:* Protein Soc; Genetics Soc Am; Am Soc Biochem & Molecular Biol; Can Soc Biochem, Molecular & Cellular Biol. *Res:* Genetic, biochemical and biophysical techniques used to probe structure-function relationships of the bateriophage T4 DNA polymerase; DNA sequence methods and techniques. *Mailing Add:* Dept Biol Sci Univ Alta Edmonton AB T6G 2E9 Can. *Fax:* 403-492-9234; *E-Mail:* ireha@gpu.srv.ualberta.ca

REHBERG, CHESSIE ELMER, organic chemistry; deceased, see previous edition for last biography

REHDER, HARALD ALFRED, INVERTEBRATE ZOOLOGY. *Current Pos:* Sr sci aide, 32-34, from asst cur to assoc cur, 34-46, actg cur, 46, cur, 46-65, sr zoologist, Div Mollusks, 65-76, EMER ZOOLOGIST, DEPT INVERT ZOOL, NAT MUS NATURAL HIST, SMITHSONIAN INST, 76- *Personal Data:* b Boston, Mass, June 5, 07; m 38; c 2. *Educ:* Bowdoin Col, AB, 29; Harvard Univ, AM, 33; George Washington Univ, PhD(zool), 34. *Concurrent Pos:* Co-ed, Indo-Pac Mollusca; mem field expeds to French Polynesia, Yucatan & Marshall Islands; adj prof biol sci, George Washington Univ, 70- *Mem:* AAAS; Paleont Soc; Soc Syst Zool; fel Am Malacol Union (pres, 40); Unitas Malacologica; Int Soc Reef Studies. *Res:* Systematic malacology; geographical distribution of mollusks; marine mollusks of Indo-Pacific, especially Polynesia. *Mailing Add:* 3900 Watson Pl No G Washington DC 20016

REHDER, KAI, ANESTHESIOLOGY, PHYSIOLOGY. *Current Pos:* asst prof anesthesiol, Mayo Grad Sch Med, Univ Minn & consult, Mayo Clin & Mayo Found, 66-77, PROF PHYSIOL & ANESTHESIOL, MAYO CLIN, 77-, PROF MAYO GRAD SCH, 76- *Personal Data:* b Hohenwestedt, WGer, Dec 17, 28; m 58; c 4. *Educ:* Univ Freiburg, MD, 53. *Prof Exp:* Intern pediat, Univ Hosp, Freiburg, 53-54, resident pharmacol, 56-57; resident oncol, Jeanes Hosp, Philadelphia, Pa, 54-55; resident internal med, Mayo Grad Sch Med, Univ Minn & Mayo Clin, 57-58, resident anesthesiol, 58-60, res asst physiol, 60-61, docent anesthesiol, Univ Wurzburg, 62, head dept, Univ Hosp, 62-65. *Mem:* Am Soc Anesthesiologists; Am Physiol Soc. *Res:* Pulmonary physiology. *Mailing Add:* Anesthesiol Res Mayo Clin & Found 200 First St SW Rochester MN 55905-0002

REHFIELD, DAVID MICHAEL, BETA-RAY SPECTROSCOPY, HIGHER EDUCATION. *Current Pos:* ASST PROF PHYSICS, LAFAYETTE COL, 82- *Personal Data:* b Mason City, Iowa, Aug 19, 42. *Educ:* Seattle Univ, BSc, 64; Univ Ariz, MSc, 67; McGill Univ, PhD(physics), 77. *Prof Exp:* Fel, II Physikalisches Inst Justus Liebig Univ, Ger, 77-79; res assoc, Foster Radiation Lab, McGill Univ, 79-81; instr, Vanier Col, Montreal, 81-82; asst prof, Swarthmore Col, 81-82. *Concurrent Pos:* Vis scientist, Brookhaven Nat Lab, 80-; res collabr, Nat Res Coun Can, 81-83. *Mem:* Sigma Xi; Am Asn Physics Teachers; Am Phys Soc; Am Nuclear Soc. *Res:* Nuclear physics, with emphasis on beta-ray spectroscopy, involving solid-state detectors and the development of superconducting-solenoid beta-ray spectrometers, and data-analysis programs; study of short-lived fission products. *Mailing Add:* Highline Col PO Box 98000 MS 15-1 Des Moines WA 98198

REHFIELD, LAWRENCE WILMER, AEROSPACE ENGINEERING. *Current Pos:* PROF AEROSPACE ENG, UNIV CALIF, DAVIS, 89- *Personal Data:* b Miami, Fla, Feb 1, 38. *Educ:* Ga Inst Technol, BAeroE, 61; Mass Inst Technol, MS, 62; Stanford Univ, PhD(aeronaut, astronaut), 65. *Prof Exp:* Res asst aeronaut & astronaut, Stanford Univ, 63-65; asst prof aeronaut & astronaut & fel eng, Mass Inst Technol, 65-67; from asst prof to prof aerospace eng, Ga Inst Technol, 67-89. *Mem:* Am Inst Aeronaut & Astronaut; Soc Exp Stress Analysis; Am Inst Ultrasonics Med. *Res:* Structural mechanics as applied to vehicle technology; stability of shell structures. *Mailing Add:* Dept Mech Eng Univ Calif Davis CA 95616

REHFUSS, MARY, ORGANIC CHEMISTRY. *Current Pos:* Instr, 49-50, 53-54, from asst prof to assoc prof, 58-65, PROF CHEM, COL ST ROSE, 65- *Personal Data:* b Albany, NY, Sept 16, 27. *Educ:* Col St Rose, BS, 49; St Louis Univ, PhD(org chem), 58. *Mem:* Sigma Xi; Am Chem Soc. *Res:* Kinetics of molecular rearrangements; applications of chemistry to conservation of art objects. *Mailing Add:* 93 Park Ave Albany NY 12202

REHKUGLER, GERALD E(DWIN), AGRICULTURAL & BIOLOGICAL ENGINEERING. *Current Pos:* RETIRED. *Personal Data:* b Lyons, NY, Apr 11, 35. *Educ:* Cornell Univ, BS, 57, MS, 58; Iowa State Univ, PhD, 66. *Honors & Awards:* Paper Awards, Am Soc Agr Engrs, 65, 75, 77, 79 & 87. *Prof Exp:* from asst prof to assoc prof, Cornell Univ, 58-77, prof agr & biol eng, 77-, chmn dept, 84-90, assoc dean, Col Eng, 90- *Concurrent Pos:* NSF sci fac fel, 64; vis prof, Mich State Univ, 74. *Mem:* Fel Am Soc Agr Engrs; Am Soc Eng Educ; fel Am Inst Med & Biol Eng. *Res:* Design and development of machinery for handling, harvesting and processing of food and agricultural products; dynamics of agricultural vehicles; computer control and simulation in agricultural and food processing machinery. *Mailing Add:* Col Eng Cornell Univ 221 Carpenter Hall Ithaca NY 14853-2201. *Fax:* 607-255-9606

REHM, ALLAN STANLEY, POLITICO-MILITARY GAMING & SIMULATIONS, MODELING COMBAT. *Current Pos:* LEAD SCIENTIST, MITRE CORP, 90- *Personal Data:* b Chicago, Ill, May 2, 36; m 59; c 2. *Educ:* Univ Ill, BS, 58, MS, 59, PhD(math), 64. *Prof Exp:* Grad asst math, Univ Ill, 58-63; sr res engr, NAm Aviation, 63-85; asst prof math, Clarkson Col Technol, 65-67; tech staff, Ketron, Inc, 73-75; br chief, US Cent Intel Agency, 75-83; div mgr, SAIC, 83-85; tech staff, Ctr Naval Anal, 67-73 & 85-90. *Concurrent Pos:* Instr, Dept Admin & Bus, Col Continuing Educ, Johns Hopkins Univ, 80-94; consult, Independent Consult, 83-90; distinguished vis analyst, US Army Concepts Anal Agency, 88-89. *Mem:* Am Math Soc; Math Asn Am; Soc Indust & Appl Math; Inst Mgt Sci; Opers Res Soc Am. *Res:* Political-military gaming and simulations; Soviet military applications of operations research; graphical techniques of information display; quantitative data from historical combat, battles, campaigns; engineering economics and costs. *Mailing Add:* 13320 Tuckaway Dr Fairfax VA 22033-1104. *E-Mail:* arehm@mitre.org

REHM, GEORGE W, SOIL FERTILITY, AGRONOMY. *Current Pos:* EXTEN SCIENTIST SOIL FERTIL, UNIV MINN, 83- *Personal Data:* b St Clairsville, Ohio, Oct 1, 41; m 64; c 3. *Educ:* Ohio State Univ, BS, 63; Univ Minn, MS, 65, PhD(soil sci), 69. *Prof Exp:* Teaching asst soil sci, Univ Minn, 63-69; dist exten agronomist, Univ Nebr, 69-80, exten soils specialist, 80-83. *Mem:* Am Soc Agron; Soil Sci Soc Am. *Res:* Soil fertility, particularly nitrogen-sulfur interactions; plant nutrition; soil-plant relationships; plant nutrition research with corn and forage crops. *Mailing Add:* Dept Soil Sci Univ Minn St Paul MN 55108

REHM, LYNN P, CLINICAL PSYCHOLOGY, COGNITIVE-BEHAVIOR THERAPY. *Current Pos:* PROF PSYCHOL, UNIV HOUSTON, 79- *Personal Data:* b Chicago, Ill, May 20, 41; m 64, Susan Higginbotham; c Elizabeth S & Sarah A (Roberts). *Educ:* Univ Southern Calif, BA, 63; Univ Wis-Madison, MA, 66, PhD(clin psychol), 70. *Hon Degrees:* Dipl, Nat Autonomous Univ, Mex. *Prof Exp:* From asst prof to assoc prof psychol, Univ Pittsburgh, 70-79, assoc prof psychiat, 77-79. *Concurrent Pos:* Intern, Wood Vet Admin, Milwaukee, Wis, 67-68; actg instr psychol, Dept Psychiat, Univ Calif, Los Angeles, 68-69, asst prof, 69-70; ed, The Tex Psychologist, 85-88; consult, Tex Dept Corrections, 86-93; chmn bd, Coun Univ Dirs Clin Psychol, 86-88; coun rep, Am Psychol Asn, 91-93, bd educ affairs, 93- *Mem:* Fel Am Psychol Asn; Asn Advan Behav Ther; Soc Psychother Res; Soc Res Psychopath; Behav Ther & Res Soc. *Res:* Psychotherapy and psychopathology theory and research; treatment of depression. *Mailing Add:* Dept Psychol Univ Houston Houston TX 77204-5341. *E-Mail:* lprehm@uhupumi.uh.edu

REHM, RONALD GEORGE, APPLIED MATHEMATICS, FLUID DYNAMICS. *Current Pos:* mathematician appl math & fluid dynamics, Nat Bur Stand, 75-87, FEL, NAT INST STAND & TECHNOL, 87- *Personal Data:* b Chicago, Ill, Nov 6, 38; m 59, Marcia Moucka; c Jeffrey R, Scott R, Jennifer (Daniels), Stephanie (Gelin) & Julie (Sullivan). *Educ:* Purdue Univ, BS, 60; Mass Inst Technol, PhD(appl math), 65. *Honors & Awards:* Gold Medal, US Dept Com, 85. *Prof Exp:* Prin engr appl math & fluid dynamics, Cornell Aeronaut Lab, Buffalo, NY, 65-75. *Mem:* Am Phys Soc; Soc Indust Appl Math; AAAS; Combustion Inst; Sigma Xi. *Res:* Waves in stratified fluids; buoyancy-induced fluid flows; fire research, combustion; fire-induced fluid flows. *Mailing Add:* Nat Inst Stand & Technol Bldg 820 RM 667 Gaithersburg MD 20899. *Fax:* 301-216-2075; *E-Mail:* rehmro@cam.nist.gov

REHM, THOMAS R(OGER), CHEMICAL ENGINEERING. *Current Pos:* from asst prof to assoc prof, 66-76, PROF CHEM ENG, UNIV ARIZ, 76- *Personal Data:* b Los Angeles, Calif, Nov 11, 29; m 57; c 1. *Educ:* Univ Wash, BSChE, 52, PhD(chem eng), 60. *Prof Exp:* From asst prof to assoc prof chem eng, Univ Denver, 60-66. *Concurrent Pos:* Res engr, Denver Res Inst, 60-66; consult, Walvoord, Inc, Colo, 61; Thermo-Tech, Inc, 62-65; Monsanto Co, 73 & Criterion Anal, 77-78; dir property develop, Rehm & Condon, Inc, 65-; abstr nuclear sci, Chem Abstr, 65-76. *Mem:* Am Inst Chem Engrs. *Res:* Boiling heat transfer; suspended solid-liquid mass transfer; turbulent fluid dynamics. *Mailing Add:* Dept Chem Eng Univ Ariz Harshbarger Bldg Rm 108C 1235 E North Campus Dr Tucson AZ 85721-0001

REHN, LYNN EDUARD, PHYSICS, MATERIALS SCIENCE. *Current Pos:* asst physicist, 76-80, physicist mat sci, 80-82, GROUP LEADER, IRRADIATION & KINETIC EFFECTS, ARGONNE NAT LAB, 82-, ASSOC DIR MAT SCI DIV, 92- *Personal Data:* b Detroit, Mich, Sept 12, 45; m 75; c 4. *Educ:* Albion Col, BA, 67; Univ Ill, Urbana, MS, 69, PhD(physics), 73. *Honors & Awards:* Sustained Outstanding Res, US Dept Energy, 84. *Prof Exp:* Scientist solid state, Kernforschungsanlage, Julich, WGer, 73-76. *Mem:* Fel Am Phys Soc; Sigma Xi; Mat Res Soc; Am Soc Metals. *Res:* Defects in metals; ultrasonics; Auger electron spectroscopy; internal friction; radiation damage; ion implantation. *Mailing Add:* Mat Sci Div Argonne Nat Lab 9700 S Cass Ave Argonne IL 60439

REHR, JOHN JACOB, SOLID STATE THEORY. *Current Pos:* from asst prof to assoc prof, 75-85, PROF PHYSICS, UNIV WASH, 85- *Educ:* Univ Mich, BSE, 67; Cornell Univ, PhD(theoret physics), 72. *Prof Exp:* NATO fel, King's Col, London, Eng, 72-73; scholar physics, Univ Calif, San Diego, 73-75. *Concurrent Pos:* NATO fel, King's Col, London, Eng, 72-73; Humboldt fel, Max Planck Inst Solid State, Stuttgart, WGer, 78; vis scientist, Cornell Univ, Ithaca, NY, 87-88 & Freie Univ, Berlin, 93; consult prof, Standord Synchrotron Radiation Lab, 93-; affil staff scientist, Pac NW Nat Lab, 95- *Mem:* Am Phys Soc. *Res:* Condensed matter theory; x-ray spectroscopy theory. *Mailing Add:* Dept Physics Univ Wash Box 351560 Seattle WA 98195-1560. *Fax:* 206-685-0635; *E-Mail:* jjr@phys.washington.edu

REHWALDT, CHARLES A, GENETICS, PLANT PHYSIOLOGY. *Current Pos:* head dept, 68-78, prof, 65-86, EMER PROF BIOL, ST CLOUD STATE UNIV, 86- *Personal Data:* b Kewanee, Ill, Sept 7, 25; m 52; c 2. *Educ:* Mankato State Univ, BA, 51; Univ Minn, MS, 53; State Univ NY Col Forestry, Syracuse Univ, PhD(genetics), 65. *Prof Exp:* Teacher high sch, Minn, 55-57; instr biol, Austin Community Col, 57-62. *Concurrent Pos:* Lectr, NSF Summer Insts, 67, 68. *Mem:* Genetics Soc Am; Am Soc Human Genetics; Sigma Xi. *Res:* Genetics and physiology of seed dormancy. *Mailing Add:* 1759 14th St St Cloud MN 56301

REIBEL, KURT, PHYSICS. *Current Pos:* from asst prof to prof, 61-92, EMER PROF PHYSICS, OHIO STATE UNIV, 92- *Personal Data:* b Vienna, Austria, May 23, 26; nat US; m 54, Eleanor Mannino; c Linda, Michael & David. *Educ:* Temple Univ, BA, 54; Univ Pa, MS, 56, PhD(physics), 59. *Prof Exp:* Jr res assoc physics, Brookhaven Nat Lab, 57-59; res assoc, Univ Pa, 59-61. *Mem:* AAAS; Am Phys Soc; Fedn Am Sci. *Res:* High energy physics; particle detectors; instrumentation; polarized targets. *Mailing Add:* Dept Physics Ohio State Univ Columbus OH 43210-1106. *Fax:* 614-292-8261; *E-Mail:* reibel@mps.ohio_state.edu

REIBEL-SHINFELD, DIANE KAREN, CARDIAC HYPOTROPHY, MYOCARDIAL ISCHEMIA. *Current Pos:* ASST PROF CARDIOVASC PHYSIOL, THOMAS JEFFERSON UNIV, 81- *Educ:* Thomas Jefferson Univ, PhD(physiol), 78. *Mailing Add:* Jefferson Med Col 111 S 11th St Philadelphia PA 19107-5083

REIBLE, DANNY DAVID, EXPOSURE ASSESSMENT, BEHAVIOR OF CONTAMINANTS. *Current Pos:* PROF CHEM ENG, LA STATE UNIV, 81-, DIR, HAZARDOUS SUBSTANCE RES CTR, 95- *Personal Data:* b Rantoul, Ill, Dec 21, 54; m 79, Susanne C Schulte; c Kristin & Monica. *Educ:* Lamar Univ, BS, 77; Calif Inst Tech, MS, 79, PhD(chem eng), 82. *Concurrent Pos:* AAAS fel, US Environ Protection Agency, 87; sr vis, Cambridge Univ, 91; Shell prof environ engr, Univ Sydney, 93-95. *Mem:* Am Inst Chem Eng; Am Chem Soc; Sigma Xi; Am Soc Eng Educ; Am Geophys Union. *Res:* Exposure assessment-fate and transport of organic chemicals as a result of physical, chemical and biological processes in sediments and adjacent media. *Mailing Add:* Dept Chem Eng La State Univ Baton Rouge LA 70803. *Fax:* 504-388-5043; *E-Mail:* reible@che.lsu.edu

REICE, SETH ROBERT, STREAM ECOLOGY, DECOMPOSITION. *Current Pos:* Asst prof, 73-79, ASSOC PROF BIOL, UNIV NC, CHAPEL HILL, 79- *Personal Data:* b Brooklyn, NY, June 30, 47; m 71; c 1. *Educ:* Univ Rochester, BA, 69; Mich State Univ, PhD(zool), 73. *Honors & Awards:* Hamilton Award & Charles Award, 69. *Concurrent Pos:* Vis prof zool, Hebrew Univ, Jerusalem, 81. *Mem:* Ecol Soc Am; Am Inst Biol Sci; Sigma Xi; Int Limnol Asn. *Res:* Regulation of benthic community structure and litter decomposition in woodland streams; roles of substrate type, disturbance and predation. *Mailing Add:* Coker Hall CB-3280 Univ NC Chapel Hill NC 27599-3280

REICH, BRIAN M, CIVIL ENGINEERING, HYDROLOGY. *Current Pos:* MEM STAFF DEPT HYDROL & WATER RES, UNIV ARIZ. *Personal Data:* b Pretoria, SAfrica, May 16, 27; m 52; c 3. *Educ:* Univ Witwatersrand, BSc, 51; Iowa State Univ, MS, 59; Colo State Univ, PhD(civil eng), 62. *Prof Exp:* Conserv officer, Dept Conserv, SRhodesia, 51-53; engr, Dept Agr Tech Serv, SAfrica, 53-62; invests leader hydrol res, Natal Region, SAfrica, 62-64; asst prof civil eng, Colo State Univ, 64-66; from assoc prof to prof, Pa State Univ, 66-74; flood plain engr, City Tucson, 75-77; flood plain mgr, Pima Co, 78-80; flood plain engr, City Tucson, 80-84. *Concurrent Pos:* Mem, US working group floods & their comput, Int Hydrol Decade; consult engr & hydrologist, 84-; mem, US deleg on estimation of extreme floods, People's Repub China. *Mem:* Fel Am Soc Civil Engrs; Am Soc Agr Engrs; Am Geophys Union; Am Water Resources Asn. *Res:* Rainstorms; floods from rural area; urban hydrology; planning of open space in suburban watersheds; personal programmable calculators. *Mailing Add:* 2635 E Cerrada Adelita Tucson AZ 85718

REICH, CHARLES, RESEARCH ADMINISTRATION. *Current Pos:* res specialist, Org Chem Res Lab, 3M Co, 68-74, tech mgr, 74-78, tech dir, Bldg Servs & Cleaning Prods Div, 78-82, managing dir, 3M Switz, 82-87, exec dir res & develop, 87-89, VPRES DENT PROD DIV, 3M CO, 89- *Personal Data:* b Minneapolis, Minn, Aug 2, 42; m 63; c 3. *Educ:* Univ Minn, Minneapolis, BS, 64; Univ Wis-Madison, PhD(org chem), 68. *Prof Exp:* NIH fel, Mass Inst Technol, 68. *Mem:* Am Chem Soc. *Res:* Organometallic synthesis; polymer chemistry; catalyst synthesis. *Mailing Add:* 1292 Sylvandale Rd Mendota Heights MN 55118-1720

REICH, CHARLES WILLIAM, NUCLEAR PHYSICS. *Current Pos:* sect chief, Nuclear Struct Sect, EG&G Idaho, Inc, 76-83, prin scientist, 81-82, sci & eng fel, 82-92, EMER, EG&G IDAHO, INC, 92- *Personal Data:* b Oklahoma City, Okla, Sept 12, 30; m 52, Juana S Woods; c Paul W, Jane K & Donna K. *Educ:* Univ Okla, BS, 52; Rice Univ, MA, 54, PhD(physics), 56. *Prof Exp:* Group leader, Radioactivity & Decay Schemes Group, Atomic Energy Div, Phillips Petrol Co, 59-66; group leader, Idaho Nuclear Corp, 66-71; group leader, Radioactivity & Decay Schemes Group, Aerojet Nuclear Co, 71-74, sect chief, 74-76. *Concurrent Pos:* Prin investr, Dept Energy Res Progs, 60-92, mem, Transplutonium Prog Comt, 78-86; guest scientist, Niels Bohr Inst, Copenhagen, Denmark, 64-65; chmn, Decay-Data Subcomt, Cross Sect Eval Working Group, 73-92; US coordr & rep, Int Atomic Energy Agency Coord Res Prog, Measurement Actinide Decay Data, 77-86; mem, Transplutonium Prog Comt, US Dept Energy, 78-84, Task Force on Decay Heat Predictions, Nuclear Energy Agency, Nuclear Data Comt, 88-90; adj prof, Utah State Univ, 68-82; physics curric coordr, Idaho Nat Eng Lab Educ Prog, Univ Idaho, 79-92; mem grad fac, Univ Idaho, 86- *Mem:* fel Am Phys Soc; Sigma Xi; NY Acad Sci. *Res:* Experimental investigation and analysis of nuclear level energy structure; compilation and evaluation of nuclear data. *Mailing Add:* 2837 Snowflake Dr Boise ID 83706. *Fax:* 208-334-9575

REICH, CLAUDE VIRGIL, MEDICAL MICROBIOLOGY, LEPROLOGY. *Current Pos:* RES PROF, DEPT MICROBIOL, GEORGE WASHINGTON UNIV, 81- *Personal Data:* b Reading, Pa, May 18, 21; m 48, Vallie Moyer; c Kimber L. *Educ:* Pa State Univ, BS, 53, PhD(bact), 58; Univ Wis, MS, 54. *Prof Exp:* Instr vet sci, Pa State Univ, 54-58; instr bact, Col Med, Univ Ill, 58-59; assoc bacteriologist, Johns Hopkins Univ, 59-62, lab dir & microbiologist, Leonard Wood Mem Lab, Cebu, Philippines, 62-83, chief lab br, Philippines Div, 63-83, asst prof pathobiol, Sch Hyg, 59-72, chief opers, 73-83. *Concurrent Pos:* Mem leprosy expert panel, WHO, 68- *Mem:* Am Soc Microbiol; Conf Res Workers Animal Dis; Int Leprosy Asn. *Res:* Immunologic and nutritional aspects of bacteria related to infectious infertility; factors associated with non-cultivable states of mycobacteria; clinical chemistry and bacteriology of leprosy; animal transmission of mycobacterial diseases; leprosy immunology. *Mailing Add:* 1516 N 14th St Reading PA 19604

REICH, DANIEL, MATHEMATICS. *Current Pos:* ASST PROF MATH, TEMPLE UNIV, 70- *Personal Data:* b New York, NY, June 25, 41; m 65; c 1. *Educ:* Cornell Univ, AB, 62; Princeton Univ, MA, 64, PhD, 66. *Prof Exp:* Instr math, Johns Hopkins Univ, 66-68, asst prof, 68-70. *Mem:* Am Math Soc. *Res:* Number theory; algebraic geometry. *Mailing Add:* Dept Math Temple Univ Philadelphia PA 19122-2585

REICH, DANIEL H, PHYSICS. *Current Pos:* ASST PROF, DEPT PHYSICS, JOHNS HOPKINS UNIV. *Honors & Awards:* Packard fel, David & Lucile Packard Found, 93. *Mailing Add:* Dept Physics Johns Hopkins Univ 3400 N Charles St Baltimore MD 21218-2608

REICH, DONALD ARTHUR, ORGANIC CHEMISTRY. *Current Pos:* Supvr org chem, Chem Div, Pittsburgh Plate Glass Co, Ohio, 56-81, SR SUPVR ORG RES, PPG INDUSTS, INC, 67- *Personal Data:* b Quincy, Ill, Dec 14, 29; m 51; c Susan. *Educ:* Millikin Univ, BA, 52; Univ Mo, PhD(chem), 56. *Mem:* Am Chem Soc; Am Soc Testing Mats. *Res:* Application research; process and product development; use and stabilization of chlorinated hydrocarbons. *Mailing Add:* PPG Indust Chem Div 3501 Kingston Lake Charles LA 70605. *Fax:* 318-491-4248

REICH, EDGAR, MATHEMATICS. *Current Pos:* from asst prof to assoc prof, 56-61, PROF MATH, UNIV MINN, MINNEAPOLIS, 61- *Personal Data:* b Vienna, Austria, June 7, 27; nat US; m 49; c 2. *Educ:* Polytech Inst Brooklyn, BEE, 47; Mass Inst Technol, MS, 49; Univ Calif, Los Angeles, PhD(math), 54. *Prof Exp:* Asst servomech lab, Mass Inst Technol, 47-49; mathematician, Rand Corp, 49-56. *Concurrent Pos:* NSF fel, 54-55; mem, Inst Advan Study, 54-55, Math Res Inst, Zurich, Switz, 71-72 & 78-79; consult, Rand Corp, 56-66; Guggenheim fel & Fulbright res grant, Math Inst, Aarhus Univ, 60-61; vis prof, Israel Inst Technol, 65-66, Swiss Fed Inst Technol, Zurich, 82-83. *Mem:* Am Math Soc; foreign mem Finnish Acad Sci & Letters. *Res:* Complex analysis. *Mailing Add:* Sch Math Inst Technol Univ Minn Minneapolis MN 55455. *E-Mail:* reich@math.umn.edu

REICH, GEORGE ARTHUR, MEDICINE, EPIDEMIOLOGY. *Current Pos:* RETIRED. *Personal Data:* b Los Angeles, Calif, Jan 18, 33; m 57; c 7. *Educ:* Univ Fla, BS, 56; Univ Iowa, MD, 62; Univ NC, MPH, 69. *Prof Exp:* Intern, Hosp, USPHS, Norfolk, Va, 62-63, staff physician, Outpatient Clin, Miami, Fla, 63-64, chief med serv, 64-65, field epidemiologist, Commun Study on Pesticides, Bur State Serv, 65-66, asst chief commun studies, Pesticides Prog, Nat Commun Dis Ctr, 66-69; chief epidemiologist, Div Commun Studies, Food & Drug Admin, 69-70; dir health maintenance orgn serv, Polk Co, Fla, 71-73, dir, PSRO Prog, 73-74, dir div qual & stand, 74, regional health adminr, region IV, 74-85, health officer, 85-88; med dir, Polk Co Dept Human Serv, Bartow, Fla, 88-93; dir, Office Substance Abuse, Bartow, 89-90. *Mem:* AMA. *Res:* Delivery of health care. *Mailing Add:* 1040 W Lake Hamilton Dr Winter Haven FL 33881-9222

REICH, HANS JURGEN, ORGANIC CHEMISTRY, MAIN GROUP ORGANOMETALLIC CHEMISTRY. *Current Pos:* from asst prof to assoc prof, 70-79, PROF CHEM, UNIV WIS-MADISON, 79- *Personal Data:* b Danzig, Ger, May 6, 43; Can citizen; m 69, Ieva Lazdins. *Educ:* Univ Alta, BSc, 64; Univ Calif, Los Angeles, PhD(org chem), 68. *Prof Exp:* Nat Res Coun Can fel, Calif Inst Technol, 68-69 & Harvard Univ, 69-70. *Concurrent*

Pos: Res grants, Petrol Res Found, 70, 73, 76, 81, 85 & 90, Res Corp, 72, NSF, 74, 77, 81, 85, 88 & 94 & NIH, 78 & 81; Alfred P Sloan Found fel, 75; vis prof, Phillips-Univ, Marburg, WGer, 79, Univ Louis Pasteur, Strasbourg, France, 87; Woodrow Wilson fel. *Mem:* Am Chem Soc; Royal Soc Chem; Sigma Xi. *Res:* Organic and organometalloid chemistry; synthetic applications, stereochemistry and mechanism in organosulfur-selenium-iodine and silicon chemistry; synthesis of theoretically interesting molecules; nuclear magnetic resonance spectroscopy; organolithium chemistry. *Mailing Add:* Dept Chem Univ Wis 1101 University Ave Madison WI 53706

REICH, HERBERT JOSEPH, ELECTRONICS, ELECTRICAL ENGINEERING. *Current Pos:* prof elec eng, 46-64, prof eng & appl sci, 64-69, EMER PROF ENG & APPL SCI, YALE UNIV, 69- *Personal Data:* b Staten Island, NY, Oct 25, 00; wid; c Robert J & Donald E. *Educ:* Cornell Univ, BE, 24, PhD(physics), 28. *Prof Exp:* Instr mach design, Cornell Univ, 24-25, instr physics, 25-29; from asst prof to prof elec eng, Univ Ill, 29-46. *Concurrent Pos:* Spec res assoc, Radio Res Lab, Harvard Univ, 44-46; mem adv group electron tubes, Off Asst Secy Defense, Res & Develop, 51-59; US deleg tech comt electron tubes, Int Electrotech Comn, 60-71, chmn subcomt microwave tubes, 65-72; prof physics & math, Deep Springs Col, Calif, 76-79. *Mem:* Fel Am Phys Soc; fel Inst Elec & Electronics Engrs. *Res:* Electron devices and electron-device circuits; microwave devices and microwave-device circuits electronics; stabilized cathode ray oscilloscope, coinventor; author of three college textbooks and co-author and editor of four textbooks. *Mailing Add:* 8 Park St Groveland MA 01834

REICH, IEVA LAZDINS, ORGANIC CHEMISTRY. *Current Pos:* res assoc org chem, 70-80, lectr gen chem, 81-82, ASSOC SCIENTIST, UNIV WIS-MADISON, 82-, LECTR ORG CHEM, 85- *Personal Data:* b Riga, Latvia, June 30, 42; US citizen; m 69, Hans J. *Educ:* Univ Wash, BS, 64; Univ Calif, Los Angeles, PhD(org chem), 69. *Prof Exp:* NIH fel, Harvard Univ, 69-70. *Concurrent Pos:* Consult, Miles Labs, Madison, 74-79. *Mem:* Am Chem Soc. *Res:* Synthesis of polychlorinated biphenyl arene oxides; synthetic methods involving organo-selenium, organo-sulfur and organo-tin compounds; mechanism of lithium-organometalloid exchange; functional group manipulation involving steroids. *Mailing Add:* Dept Chem Univ Wis Madison WI 53706. *Fax:* 608-265-4534; *E-Mail:* ilreich@facstaff.wisc.edu

REICH, ISMAR M(EYER), CHEMICAL ENGINEERING, FOOD TECHNOLOGY. *Current Pos:* RETIRED. *Personal Data:* b New York, NY, Aug 13, 24; m 56, Diane Wechsler; c Haley M, Arnold S & Andrew W. *Educ:* City Col New York, BChE, 45; Polytech Inst Brooklyn, MChE, 55. *Prof Exp:* Chem engr, Fleischmann Labs, Standard Brands, Inc, 45-48, head pilot plant dept, 48-53, head process develop div, 53-60, dir res, Coffee Instants, Inc, 60-65, dir mfg & res, 65-66, vpres mfg, 66-69; vpres, Chock Full O'Nuts Corp, New York, 69-80, gen mgr, Sol Cafe Div, 76-80, tech dir, 80-82, vpres, res & develop, 82-93. *Mem:* AAAS; Am Chem Soc; Am Inst Chem Engrs; NY Acad Sci; fel Am Inst Chem. *Res:* Food technology; extraction; dehydration; instrumentation; agglomeration. *Mailing Add:* 2136 Holland Way Merrick NY 11566

REICH, JAMES HARRY, personality disorder validation, anxiety disorder research, for more information see previous edition

REICH, LEO, POLYMER CHEMISTRY. *Current Pos:* adj prof, 72-93, RES PROF, STEVENS INST TECHNOL, 93- *Personal Data:* b Brooklyn, NY, June 23, 24; m 54, Doris; c Margery. *Educ:* Polytech Inst Brooklyn, MS, 49; Stevens Inst Technol, PhD(chem), 59. *Prof Exp:* Sr develop chemist, Nepera Chem Co, Inc, 49-57; instr chem eng, Stevens Inst Technol, 57-59; sr res chemist, Air Reduction Co, Inc, 59-61; polymer res chemist, Picatinny Arsenal, Dover, 61-74. *Mem:* Am Chem Soc; Sigma Xi; Amer Inst Chemists. *Res:* Reaction kinetics; electric discharge phenomena; photochemistry; thermal and thermooxidative degradation of polymers. *Mailing Add:* Three Wessman Dr West Orange NJ 07052

REICH, MARVIN FRED, MEDICINAL CHEMISTRY. *Current Pos:* res chemist, Bound Brook Res Labs, 79-80, SR RES CHEMIST, LEDERLE LAB DIV, AM CYANAMID CO, 80- *Personal Data:* b Brooklyn, NY, Dec 30, 47. *Educ:* Polytech Inst, Brooklyn, BS, 68; NY Univ, MS, 72; Univ Ill, PhD(org chem), 78. *Prof Exp:* Chemist, Lederle Labs Div, Am Cyanamid Co, 69-73; teaching asst org chem, Univ Ill, 73-75, res asst, 75-78; staff fel, NIH, 78-79. *Mem:* Am Chem Soc. *Res:* Medicinal and organic chemistry; design, synthesis and characterization of new pharmaceutical agents; anti-inflammatory, anti-allergy and anti-fungal agents; cardiovascular drugs. *Mailing Add:* 3 Somerset Dr Apt 10M Suffern NY 10901-6937

REICH, MELVIN, MICROBIOLOGY, BIOCHEMISTRY. *Current Pos:* asst res prof pharmacol, 60-64, asst prof microbiol, 64-68, assoc prof, 68-79, PROF MICROBIOL, SCH MED, GEORGE WASHINGTON UNIV, 79- *Personal Data:* b New York, NY, July 17, 32; m 63; c 2. *Educ:* City Col New York, BS, 53; Rutgers Univ, PhD(biochem, physiol), 60. *Prof Exp:* Asst biochem, Rutgers Univ, 55-60. *Mem:* AAAS; Am Soc Microbiol; Sigma Xi; Am Asn Univ Professors. *Res:* Bacterial physiology; mycobacteria; antimicrobials. *Mailing Add:* Dept Microbiol Sch Med George Washington Univ 2300 I St NW Washington DC 20037-2337

REICH, MURRAY H, POLYMER CHEMISTRY. *Current Pos:* res chemist, Princeton Chem Res, Inc, 62-64, lab mgr, Res & Develop Lab, 64-70 & 74-76, tech dir, 76-77, consult, 77-81 & 85-89, DEVELOP CHEMIST, PRINCETON CHEM RES, INC, 70-; ACTG PRES, TYNDALE PLAINS HUNTER, 93- *Personal Data:* b Brooklyn, NY, May 29, 22; m 49, Naomi A Pollack; c Michael, Leslie & Pamela. *Educ:* City Col New York, BS, 43; Univ Akron, MS, 54; Trenton State Col, MED, 74; Columbia Univ, DEd, 82. *Prof Exp:* Process engr elastomers, US Govt Labs, 47-52, group leader, 52-55, chief engr, 55-56; res chemist, FMC Corp, 56-62; vpres, Biolan Corp, 89-93. *Concurrent Pos:* Preretirement counr, gerontologist & dir, Premac Assocs; adj prof, gerontology; consult, Div Aging, Off Ombudsmen. *Mem:* Am Chem Soc; Soc Plastics Eng. *Res:* Emulsion and solution polymerization of dienes; rubber and epoxy development; polyacetal and polyolefin research and degradable plastics; role of mentors in the careers of executives, both men and women; commercialization of degradable plastics, work has resulted in a commercial degradable agriculture mulch film, called Biolan film; hydrophilic polymers. *Mailing Add:* 184 Loomis Ct Princeton NJ 08540-3439

REICH, NATHANIEL EDWIN, MEDICINE. *Current Pos:* RETIRED. *Personal Data:* b New York, NY, May 19, 07; m 43; c 2. *Educ:* NY Univ, BS, 27; Univ Chicago, MD, 32; Am Bd Internal Med, dipl, 42. *Honors & Awards:* Am Col Angiol Res Awards, 57 & 58. *Prof Exp:* Instr phys diag, Col Med, State Univ NY Downstate Med Ctr, 38-42, assoc prof clin med, 52-74, prof, 74-77, emer prof, 77-94. *Concurrent Pos:* Asst attend physician, NY Postgrad Med Sch, Columbia Univ, 38-40; attend physician, Kings County Hosp, 47- & State Univ NY Downstate Med Ctr; impartial specialist, NY State Dept Labor, 52-58; consult, Long Beach Mem Hosps, 54-; vis prof, Fac Med, San Marcos Univ, Peru, 68, Medico, Afghanistan, 70 & Indonesia, 72; consult, US Dept Health & Health Serv, US RR Retirement Bd, & NY State Disability Determ. *Mem:* Fel Royal Soc Med; fel Am Col Physicians; fel Am Col Chest Physicians; fel Am Col Cardiol. *Res:* Cardiology. *Mailing Add:* 1620 Ave I Brooklyn NY 11230

REICH, SIMEON, NONLINEAR FUNCTIONAL ANALYSIS, NONLINEAR EVOLUTION EQUATIONS. *Current Pos:* assoc prof, 84-85, PROF MATH, TECHNION-ISRAEL INST TECHNOL, 85- *Personal Data:* b Cracow, Poland, Aug 12, 48; US & Israeli citizen; m 74, Hayuta Cohen; c Uri, Daphna & Shelley. *Educ:* Israel Inst Technol, BSc, 70, DSc, 73. *Prof Exp:* Lectr math, Tel Aviv Univ, 73-75; Dickson instr, Univ Chicago, 75-77; from asst prof to prof math, Univ Southern Calif, 77-95. *Concurrent Pos:* Vis scientist, Argonne Nat Lab, 78; consult, Math Res Ctr, Madison, Wis, 78 & 80; vis assoc prof, Univ Calif, Berkeley, 81; actg chmn, Math Dept, Univ Southern Calif, 83-84; grantee, NSF, 76-84 & 93-96. *Mem:* Am Math Soc; Math Asn Am; Soc Indust & Appl Math; Israel Math Union. *Res:* Nonlinear analysis: fixed point theory, asymptotic behavior of nonlinear semigroups, constructive solvability of nonlinear equations, properties of accretive and monotone operators in Banach spaces, integral equations, nonlinear identification problems; infinite-dimensional holomorphy. *Mailing Add:* Dept Math Technion-Israel Inst Technol Haifa 32000 Israel. *Fax:* 972-4-8324654; *E-Mail:* sreich@tx.technion.ac.il

REICH, THEOBALD, VASCULAR SURGERY. *Current Pos:* fel surg, 59-61, PROF EXP SURG, NY UNIV, 80-; DEP CHIEF SURGEON, NY POLICE DEPT, 82- *Personal Data:* b Czech, Jan 1, 27. *Educ:* NY Univ, BA, 47; St Louis Univ, MD, 51. *Prof Exp:* Med officer infectious dis, US Army, 53-55; asst prof vascular surg, Mt Sinai Hosp, 65-67; co-dir, Biomed Rehab Res Eng, 81-87. *Mem:* NY Acad Sci; Am Physiol Soc; Am Heart Asn; Biomed Eng Soc. *Mailing Add:* Dept Surg & Rehab NY Univ Med Ctr 400 E 34th St New York NY 10016

REICH, VERNON HENRY, AGRONOMY, STATISTICS. *Current Pos:* asst prof agron, 68-76, ASSOC PROF PLANT & SOIL SCI, UNIV TENN KNOXVILLE, 76- *Personal Data:* b Rushville, Ill Apr 30, 39; m 66, Martha Jones. *Educ:* Univ Ill, BS, 61, MS, 65; Iowa State Univ, PhD(agron, plant breeding), 68. *Prof Exp:* Res assoc agron, Iowa State Univ, 65-68. *Mem:* Am Soc Agron; Crop Sci Soc Am; Genetics Soc Am; Am Genetic Asn. *Res:* Plant breeding and genetics. *Mailing Add:* Plant & Soil Sci Univ Tenn 1345 Circle Park Knoxville TN 37996-0001. *Fax:* 423-974-7997

REICHARD, GRANT WESLEY, ELECTROMECHANICAL DESIGN, INSTRUMENTATION. *Current Pos:* QUAL ASSURANCE MGR, HUMBOLDT MFG CO, 94- *Personal Data:* b Chicago, Ill, Apr 9, 38; m 61, Mariett McCall; c Judy & Nancy. *Educ:* Univ Ill, Urbana, BS, 61, MS, 64; Univ Chicago, MBA, 69; Univ Ill, Chicago, MSEE, 93. *Prof Exp:* Eng trainee, Borg-Warner Corp, 63-66; proj engr, Bastian-Blessing Corp, 66-72; sr prof engr, Stewart-Warner Corp, 72-74; chief engr, Dickson Co, 74-91; consult, Reichard & Assoc, 91-94. *Mem:* Am Soc Mech Engrs; Instrument Soc Am. *Res:* Emissive properties of materials; infrared thermal applications; quality assurance. *Mailing Add:* 1708 S Clifton Ave Park Ridge IL 60068

REICHARD, H(AROLD) F(ORREST), CHEMICAL ENGINEERING. *Current Pos:* RETIRED. *Personal Data:* b Easton, Pa, Apr 15, 20; m 44, Miriam C; c Thomas, Mark & Janet K. *Educ:* Lafayette Col, BS, 41. *Prof Exp:* Develop chem engr, E I du Pont de Nemours & Co, 41-44 & 46-48; supvr chem eng res, prod contracts, US AEC, 48-51; proj & group leader & supvr lab & pilot res, Vitro Corp, 51-56; asst dir res & develop, Mining & Mat Dept, Mining & Metals Div, Union Carbide Corp, 56-68, prod mgr spec alloys, 68-71, gen mgr alloys prod, 71-81; mgr prod spec metals, Elkem Metals Co, 81-83. *Concurrent Pos:* Ord officer, US Navy, World War II. *Mem:* Fel Am Inst Chemists; Am Inst Mining, Metall & Petrol Engrs; Am Inst Chem Engrs. *Res:* Unit operations of distilling, drying, grinding, crystallizing and extracting; process development in dyestuffs, vitamins, fine chemicals, resin polymerization, organic chlorination, uranium chemistry and physical metallurgy; hydrometallurgy, ion exchange, adsorption, industrial minerals processing and applications; electrolytic process metallurgy. *Mailing Add:* 4 Gen Howard Rd South Yarmouth MA 02664

REICHARD, RONNAL PAUL, SMALL CRAFT DESIGN, COMPOSITE MATERIALS & STRUCTURES. *Current Pos:* Chmn & chief exec officer, STRUCT COMPOSITES INC, 87-; CHIEF EXEC OFFICER, COMPSYS INC, 93- *Personal Data:* b Troy, NY, Nov 25, 50; c 1. *Educ:* Univ NH, BS, 73, MS, 76, PhD(eng mech), 80. *Prof Exp:* From asst prof to assoc prof ocean eng, Fla Inst Technol, 81-92, dir Struct Composites Lab, 85-92, chmn ocean eng, 86-88; res fel, Univ Wash, 79-81. *Concurrent Pos:* Tech dir, USN Marine Composites Technol Ctr, 94- *Mem:* Soc Naval Architects & Marine Engrs; Am Soc Naval Engrs; Am Soc Mat. *Res:* Composite materials; measurement, analysis, and design of composite material structures. *Mailing Add:* 788 Acacia Ave Melbourne FL 32904

REICHARD, SHERWOOD MARSHALL, RADIOBIOLOGY, PHYSIOLOGY. *Current Pos:* assoc prof, 64-69, dir, Div Radiobiol, 69-76, PROF RADIOL & PHYSIOL, MED COL GA, 69-, REGENTS PROF, 79- *Personal Data:* b Easton, Pa, June 24, 28; m 54; c 3. *Educ:* Lafayette Col, BA, 48; NY Univ, MS, 50, PhD(endocrine physiol), 55. *Honors & Awards:* Founders Day Award, NY Univ, 56; Zool Medal, Int Cong Zool, 63; Fred Conrad Koch Travel Award, Endocrine Soc, 65. *Prof Exp:* Res collabr, Dept Biol, Brookhaven Nat Lab, 53-55, res assoc, 55; Muscular Dystrophy Asn Am Lilienthal Mem fel, McCollum-Pratt Inst, Johns Hopkins Univ, 57-58, advan res fel, Am Heart Asn, 58-60; asst prof physiol, Fla State Univ, 60-64. *Concurrent Pos:* Vis investr, Dept Radiobiol, Armed Forces Inst Path, 58-60; consult, Off Tech Utilization, NASA. *Mem:* Fel AAAS; Am Physiol Soc; Am Soc Zoologists; Radiation Res Soc; Endocrine Soc; Sigma Xi. *Res:* Physiology of reticuloendothelial system; endocrine inter-relations; protection against traumatic shock and x-irradiation; radiation effects; vitamin E and electron transport; hormones and enzymes and terminal respiration. *Mailing Add:* 1021 15th St Suite 9 Augusta GA 30901

REICHARDT, JOHN WILLIAM, PHYSICS, DEVICE ENGINEERING. *Current Pos:* staff scientist, 73-75, prod mgr neutron gererators, 75-84, DIR ENG, KAMAN INSTRUMENTATION CORP, 84-, VPRES, ENG & QUAL ASSURANCE, 87- *Personal Data:* b Imperial, Nebr, Nov 18, 40. *Educ:* Univ Denver, BS, 62; Univ Wichita, MS, 64; Univ Va, PhD(physics), 67. *Prof Exp:* Staff scientist res & develop, Sandia Labs, 67-73. *Res:* Neutron production and instrumentation for borehole geophysics; neutron activation analysis; small accelerator design; vacuum tube design; vacuum technology; materials and process technology; physics and chemistry of solid surface. *Mailing Add:* MF Physics 5074 List Colorado Springs CO 80919

REICHART, CHARLES VALERIAN, entomology; deceased, see previous edition for last biography

REICHBERG, SAMUEL BRINGEISSEN, CLINICAL LABORATORY MEDICINE, CELL BIOLOGY. *Current Pos:* ASST PROF PATH, NY MED COL, 78- *Personal Data:* b Santiago, Chile, Aug 30, 46; m 72; c 2. *Educ:* Univ Chile, LicMed, 70, MD, 71; Yale Univ, MPhil, 73, PhD(biochem), 75. *Prof Exp:* Fel human genetics, Med Sch, Yale Univ, 72-74, med, 74-76, residency lab med, 76-78. *Concurrent Pos:* Dir, Clin Lab Dept, Brookdale Hosp, 83-; fac, Med Sch, NY Univ, Downstate, 82- *Mem:* AAAS; NY Acad Sci. *Res:* Regulation of cell plasma membrane transport activity; correlation between transport effects and chemical changes in membrane composition produced by the hormones insulin and glucocorticoids and by growth regulatory compounds. *Mailing Add:* 22 Lakeview Ave North Tarrytown NY 10591-1113

REICHE, LUDWIG P(ERCY), SATELLITE TELECOMMUNICATIONS, ELECTRONICS INSTRUMENTATION. *Current Pos:* mem staff, Huges Aircraft Co, 64-72, sr proj engr, 72-80, proj mgr, 80-94, scientist, 94-96, CONSULT, HUGHES AIRCRAFT CO. *Personal Data:* b Germany, Dec 26, 19; m 51; c 3. *Educ:* NY Univ, BEE, 48. *Prof Exp:* Proj engr, Victor Div, Radio Corp Am, Calif, 50-52; staff engr, Int Telemeter Corp, 52-53; sr proj engr, Hoffman Labs, 53-54; sr res engr, Radio Systs Lab, Stanford Res Inst, 54-60; mgr microwave commun, Melabs, 60-64. *Concurrent Pos:* Coordr, Indonesian Pub Tel Enterprise, 75-77. *Mem:* Inst Elec & Electronics Engrs. *Mailing Add:* 843 Via Campobello Santa Barbara CA 93111

REICHEL, WILLIAM LOUIS, ENVIRONMENTAL CHEMISTRY. *Current Pos:* RETIRED. *Personal Data:* b Philadelphia, Pa, July 10, 27; m 53; c 2. *Educ:* Philadelphia Col Pharm, BSc, 52. *Prof Exp:* Org chemist, Philadelphia Naval Shipyard, 52-59; res chemist, Bur Sport Fisheries & Wildlife, US Fish & Wildlife Serv, 59-66, chief chemist, 66-83. *Mem:* Am Chem Soc. *Res:* Development of procedures for isolation, identification and quantitative measurement of pesticide residues in animal tissues and their environment. *Mailing Add:* 9145 Winding Way Ellicott City MD 21043

REICHELDERFER, THOMAS ELMER, PEDIATRICS, PUBLIC HEALTH. *Current Pos:* assoc prof, 73-85, EMER ASSOC PROF PEDIAT, JOHNS HOPKINS UNIV, 85- *Personal Data:* b Newark, NJ, Aug 31, 16; m 43; c 3. *Educ:* Rutgers Univ, BS, 39; Johns Hopkins Univ, MD, 50, MPH, 56. *Prof Exp:* From asst to instr pediat, Johns Hopkins Univ, 51-54, instr pediat & pub health admin, 54-56; asst prof pediat, Univ Minn, 56-57; chief gen study unit, Lab Infectious Dis, Nat Inst Allergy & Infectious Dis, 57-58; chief med officer, DC Gen Hosp, 58-72. *Concurrent Pos:* Asst resident, Johns Hopkins Hosp, Baltimore, Md, 51-52, resident pediatrician, 52-54; consult, Nat Naval Med Ctr, 53-54; pediatrician, Johns Hopkins Hosp, Baltimore, Md, 54-56 & 73-; clin prof pediat, Howard Univ, 58-72; assoc prof pediat, George Washington & Georgetown Univs, 58-72. *Mem:* AMA; fel Am Acad Pediat. *Res:* Infectious diseases; newborn infants. *Mailing Add:* 2029 Chesapeake Rd Annapolis MD 21401

REICHENBACH, GEORGE SHERIDAN, MECHANICAL ENGINEERING. *Current Pos:* vpres, 86-88, sr vpres, 88-96, MANAGING DIR, ADVENT INT, 96- *Personal Data:* b Waterbury, Conn, May 25, 29; m 56, Mary L Littlefield; c Heidi, John & Frederick. *Educ:* Yale Univ, BME, 51; Mass Inst Technol, MS, 52, ScD, 56. *Honors & Awards:* Alfred Noble Prize, Joint Eng Socs, 60; Yale Eng Award, 61. *Prof Exp:* From asst prof to assoc prof mech eng, Mass Inst Technol, 56-66; asst dir res, Norton Co, 66-69, dir res & develop, 69-74, vpres & gen mgr org prod, Grinding Wheel Div, 74-79, vpres & gen mgr, Mat Div, 79-81, vpres bonded abrasives, 81-86. *Concurrent Pos:* Mem vis comt, Dept Mech Eng, Mass Inst Technol. *Mem:* Am Soc Mech Engrs; Am Ceramic Soc; Nat Venture Capital Asn; Am Soc Metals. *Res:* Materials, lubrication and metal processing; venture investing in high technology forms. *Mailing Add:* 123 West St Carlisle MA 01741. *Fax:* 617-951-0566

REICHENBACHER, PAUL H, REINFORCED PLASTICS, ORGANIC CHEMISTRY. *Current Pos:* Res chemist, Corp Res Ctr, Allied Signal Inc, 67-72, group leader, 72-77, dir technol, 77-91, MGR TECH STRATEGY, ALLIED SIGNAL INC, 91- *Personal Data:* b Aurora, Ill, Feb 4, 40; m 63, Patricia A McGrath; c Bill, Mark, Tom & Dave. *Educ:* St Mary's Col, BA, 62; Pa State Univ, PhD(chem), 67. *Concurrent Pos:* Adj prof, Ill Benedictine Col, 69-70 & Concordia Teachers Col, 70-71; dir, Alumni Bd, St Mary's Col, 78-84, pres, 80-82. *Mem:* Am Chem Soc; Inst Interconnecting & Packaging Electronic Circuits; Sigma Xi; Int Electronic Packaging Soc. *Res:* Reinforced thermoset laminates; electronic interconnects; composite materials; electrical properties of materials; polymerization reactions; specialty organic chemicals; physical organic chemistry; printed circuits. *Mailing Add:* Allied Signal Inc 230 N Front St PO Box 1448 La Crosse WI 54602-1448. *Fax:* 608-791-2484

REICHENBECHER, VERNON EDGAR, JR, MONOCLONAL ANTIBODY PRODUCTION. *Current Pos:* asst prof, 81-86, ASSOC PROF BIOCHEM, SCH MED, MARSHALL UNIV, 86- *Personal Data:* b Meyersdale, Pa, Mar 29, 48; m 76, Linda Jernigan; c Jennifer L & Rebecca A. *Educ:* WVa Univ, BS, 70; Duke Univ, PhD(biochem), 76. *Prof Exp:* Fel med genetics, Baylor Col Med, 76-79, res assoc, 80-81. *Concurrent Pos:* Mem grad fac, WVa Univ, 82- *Mem:* Am Soc Cell Biol; Genetics Soc Am; Sigma Xi; AAAS. *Res:* Production of monoclonal antibodies; structure and function of mammalian ribosomes; toxic plant lectins; hypertension; somatic cell genetics. *Mailing Add:* Dept Biochem & Molecular Biol Marshall Univ Sch Med 1542 Spring Valley Dr Huntington WV 25704-9588

REICHERT, JOHN DOUGLAS, THEORETICAL PHYSICS, OPTICAL PHYSICS. *Current Pos:* STAFF MEM, UNIV NMEX-NMERI, 85- *Personal Data:* b Cameron, Tex, Nov 29, 38; m 61, Linda Bartlett; c Lance W, Jay G & Cynthia A. *Educ:* Univ Tex, Austin, BS & BA, 61; Calif Inst Technol, PhD(theoret physics), 65. *Prof Exp:* Fel theoret physics, Relativity Ctr, Univ Tex, Austin, 65-66; res assoc, Univ Southern Calif, 66-67, asst prof physics, 67-71; assoc prof elec eng, Tex Tech Univ, 71-79, prof, 80-85. *Concurrent Pos:* Adj prof, Optical Sci Ctr, Univ Ariz, 71-; pres, Radtech, Inc, 83-84; mgr, ABQ Off SRS Tech, Inc, 84-86. *Mem:* Optical Soc Am; Am Phys Soc; Sigma Xi. *Res:* Laser beam propagation; optical resonators; diffraction and scattering theory; nonlinear interactions of light with matter; Fourier optics; quantum theory. *Mailing Add:* 1003 Warm Sands Trail SE Albuquerque NM 87123. *E-Mail:* reichert@flash.net

REICHERT, JONATHAN F, SOLID STATE PHYSICS, MAGNETIC RESONANCE. *Current Pos:* assoc prof, 70-90, PROF PHYSICS, STATE UNIV NY BUFFALO, 91. *Personal Data:* b Cincinnati, Ohio, Aug 29, 31; m 53; c 3. *Educ:* Case Western Reserve Univ, BS, 53; Wash Univ, PhD(physics), 62. *Prof Exp:* Fel physics, Harvard Univ, 63-65; asst prof, Case Western Reserve Univ, 65-70. *Concurrent Pos:* Air Force res grant, 66-69; NY State Res Found grant, 72; NSF grant ions in liquid helium, 74-76 & 76-78; NY Res Found grant, 75-76; chmn fac senate, State Univ NY Buffalo, 76-78; vis assoc prof, Princeton Univ, 78-79; dir, Nuclear War Prev Studies, 87-91. *Mem:* Am Phys Soc; Am Asn Physics Teachers; Union Concerned Scientists. *Res:* Mossbauer spectroscopy and liquid helium; nuclear and electronic magnetic resonance and solid state physics of defects; science education. *Mailing Add:* Physics Rm 128 Fronczak Hall State Univ NY North Campus Amherst NY 14260

REICHERT, LEO E, JR, BIOCHEMISTRY, ENDOCRINOLOGY. *Current Pos:* chmn, 79-89, PROF, ALBANY MED COL, 79- *Personal Data:* b New York, NY, Jan 9, 32; m 57, Gerda Sihler; c Christine, Leo, Linda & Andrew. *Educ:* Manhattan Col, BS, 55; Loyola Univ Chicago, MS, 57, PhD(biochem), 60. *Honors & Awards:* Ayerst Award, Endocrine Soc, 71. *Prof Exp:* From instr to prof biochem, Emory Univ, 60-79. *Concurrent Pos:* Secy gonadotropin subcomt, Nat Pituitary Agency, 68-74, mem med adv bd, Agency, 71-74; mem reproductive biol study sect, NIH, 71-75; mem Adv Panel Cellular Physiol, NSF, 83-86; mem Expert Adv Panel Biol Standardization, WHO, 84- *Mem:* AAAS; Am Soc Biol Chemists; Endocrine Soc; Soc Study Reproduction. *Res:* Biochemistry and physiology of gonadotropin hormones and their receptors; relationship of structure to function; authored 300 original articles, chapters, abstracts; granted various US patents. *Mailing Add:* 10 Laurel Dr Albany NY 12211-1618

REICHES, NANCY A, EPIDEMIOLOGY, BIOSTATISTICS. *Current Pos:* PVT CONSULT, 90- *Personal Data:* b Cleveland, Ohio, Jan 26, 49. *Educ:* Univ Colo, Boulder, BA, 71, MA, 72; Ohio State Univ, PhD(prev med), 77. *Prof Exp:* Lectr commun theory, Univ Nev, Las Vegas, 72-73; res asst biostatist, Biomet, Ohio State Univ, 73-76, res assoc epidemiol, Comprehensive Cancer Ctr, 76-77, res asst epidemiol & biostatist, 77-84; dir res, Riverside Methodist Hosp, 84-90. *Concurrent Pos:* Consult, Battelle Mem Inst, Columbus, Ohio, 77- *Mem:* Am Pub Health Asn; Soc Epidemiol Res; Am Soc Prev Oncol. *Res:* Cancer epidemiology; environmental epidemiology; biostatistical methods; biomedical computing. *Mailing Add:* 91 S Roosevelt Columbus OH 43209

REICHGOTT, MICHAEL JOEL, MEDICINE, CLINICAL PHARMACOLOGY. *Current Pos:* asst dean, 84-89, ASSOC DEAN, STUDENTS & CLIN EDUC, ALBERT EINSTEIN COL MED, 89- *Personal Data:* b Newark, NJ, July 26, 40; m 62; c 3. *Educ:* Gettysburg Col, AB, 61; Albert Einstein Col Med, MD, 65; Univ Calif, San Francisco, PhD(pharmacol), 73. *Prof Exp:* Trainee clin pharmacol, Med Ctr, Univ Calif, San Francisco, 69-72; assoc med, 72-73, asst prof med, 73-81, dir, Outpatient Clins, 75-78, dir, Dept Pract, 78-80, assoc chief staff ambulatory care, Med Ctr, 80-81, assoc prof med, Hosp, Univ Pa, 73-, chief, Sect Gen Med, Med Ctr, 81-84; med die, Bronx Municipal Hosp Ctr, 84-89. *Mem:* Fel Am Col Physicians; AAAS; Am Soc Pharmacol & Exp Therapeut; Am Fedn Clin Res; Soc Gen Internal Med. *Res:* Compliance, health services delivery; ambulatory care; medical education. *Mailing Add:* Off Educ Albert Einstein Col Med 1300 Morris Park Ave Blefer Bldg Rm 210 Bronx NY 10461

REICHLE, ALFRED DOUGLAS, PETROLEUM REFINING, CATALYSIS. *Current Pos:* engr, EXXON RES & DEVELOP CO, 59-60, sr res engr, 60-62, eng assoc, 62-63, sect head, 63-67, sr eng assoc, 67-71, ENG ADV PETROL REFINING, EXXON RES & DEVELOP CO, 71- *Personal Data:* b Port Arthur, Tex, Dec 19, 20; m 43; c 2. *Educ:* Rice Univ, BS, 42, MS, 43; Univ Wis, PhD(chem eng), 48. *Prof Exp:* Chemist petrol refining, Shell Develop Co, 43-57; staff asst process develop, Phillips Petrol Co, 57-59. *Mem:* Am Inst Chem Engrs. *Res:* Petroleum process development; catalytic refining processes; catalyst development. *Mailing Add:* 1025 Broadmoor Circle Baton Rouge LA 70815

REICHLE, DAVID EDWARD, ENVIRONMENTAL SCIENCES. *Current Pos:* US AEC fel, Oak Ridge Nat Lab, 64-66, ecologist, 66-72, assoc div dir, 72-86, dir, 86-90, ASSOC DIR LIFE SCI & ENVIRON TECHNOL, OAK RIDGE NAT LAB, 90- *Personal Data:* b Cincinnati, Ohio, Oct 19, 38; m 61, Donna R Haubrick; c John, Deborah & Jennifer. *Educ:* Muskingum Col, BS, 60; Northwestern Univ, MS, 61, PhD(biol sci), 64. *Honors & Awards:* Sci Achievement Award, Int Union Forest Res Orgn, 76. *Concurrent Pos:* Prof grad prog ecol, Univ Tenn; Danforth fel, 61-; vchmn, Tenn Chap, Nature Conservancy; bd dirs, Int Asn Radioecol & Oak Ridge Boys Club; bd vis, Sch Pub & Environ Affairs, Ind Univ; chmn bd, Joint Inst Energy & Environ, Oak Ridge Nat Lab, Tenn Valley Authority, Univ Tenn; chap pres, Sigma Xi, 84-85. *Mem:* AAAS; Ecol Soc Am; Am Inst Biol Sci; Nature Conservancy; Int Asn Radio Ecol; Asn Women in Sci; Sigma Xi. *Res:* Environmental geochemistry and health; terrestrial invertebrate ecology, bioenergetics, structure and function of arthropod communities; radioecology, movement of radioisotopes through food chains, effects of ionizing radiation upon natural arthropod communities; mineral cycling; ecosystem analysis. *Mailing Add:* Life Sci & Environ Technol Directorate Oak Ridge Nat Lab PO Box 2008 Oak Ridge TN 37831-6253. *Fax:* 423-574-9869; *E-Mail:* der@ornl.gov

REICHLE, FREDERICK ADOLPH, GENERAL & VASCULAR SURGERY. *Current Pos:* resident, 62-66, from instr to assoc prof, 66-76, PROF SURG, HEALTH SCI CTR, TEMPLE UNIV, 76-, CHIEF, SECT PERIPHERAL VASC SURG, 74-; CHMN & PROF SURG, PRESBY-UNIV PA MED CTR, 80-; CHIEF SURG, JOHN F KENNEDY HOSP, 90- *Personal Data:* b Neshaminy, Pa, Apr 20, 35. *Educ:* Temple Univ, BA, 57, MS, 61 & 66, MD, 61. *Prof Exp:* Intern med, Abington Mem Hosp, 61-62. *Concurrent Pos:* Fel vascular surg, Health Sci Ctr, Temple Univ, 66-67; asst attend surgeon, Episcopal & St Christopher's Hosps, 66-; mem coun thrombosis, Am Heart Asn, 71-; mem, Nat Kidney Found, 72; consult, Vet Admin Hosp, Wilkes-Barre. *Mem:* Fel Am Col Surgeons; Am Surg Asn; Soc Surg Alimentary Tract; AAAS; Int Soc Thrombosis & Haemostasis; Soc Univ Surgeons. *Res:* Vascular surgery; liver metabolism; amino acid metabolism; cancer; thrombosis. *Mailing Add:* PO Box 42891 Philadelphia PA 19101-2891

REICHLE, WALTER THOMAS, CHEMISTRY, CATALYSIS. *Current Pos:* Res chemist, Res Labs, Plastics Div, 58-68, sr res scientist chem & plastics, Res & Develop Lab, 69-84, CORP FEL, UNION CARBIDE CORP, 84- *Personal Data:* b Cleveland, Ohio, Aug 2, 28; m 53, Janice Gardner; c Thomas, Anne & Jean. *Educ:* NJ Inst Technol, BS, 53; Ohio State Univ, PhD(chem), 58. *Honors & Awards:* Co-recipient Thomas Alva Edison Patent Award, 92. *Concurrent Pos:* Vis fel, Princeton Univ, 73-74. *Mem:* Am Chem Soc; Sci Res Soc Am; Catalysis Soc. *Res:* Organo-metallic and inorganic chemistry; catalytic agents; homogeneous and heterogeneous catalysis. *Mailing Add:* Tech Ctr Union Carbide Corp PO Box 670 Bound Brook NJ 08805-0670. *Fax:* 732-563-5123

REICHLER, ROBERT JAY, CHILD PSYCHIATRY, OBSESSIVE & COMPULSIVE DISORDERS. *Current Pos:* BD, CRISIS CLIN, 90- *Personal Data:* b Bronx, NY, Nov 22, 37; c 2. *Educ:* Univ Chicago, BA & BS, 57; Albert Einstein Col Med, MD, 61; Am Bd Psychiat & Neurol, dipl, 71. *Honors & Awards:* Gold Achievement Award, Am Psychiat Asn, 72. *Prof Exp:* Instr psychiat, Strong Mem Hosp, Univ Rochester, 64-65; clin asst prof, Med Col Charleston, 68-69; asst prof, Univ NC, Sch Med, Chapel Hill, 69-72, assoc prof child psychiat & co-dir, Div Teach, 72-76; prof psychiat & head, Div Child Psychol, Univ Wash, Sch Med, 76-79; prof psychiat, Harborview Med Ctr, 76-93, dir res, 86-90. *Concurrent Pos:* NIMH fel psychiat, Strong Mem Hosp, Univ Rochester, 62-65; NIMH fel child psychiat, NC Mem Hosp, Univ NC, 65-67; from asst surgeon to sr surgeon, USPHS, 67-69; mem, Child & Family Develop Res Rev Comt, Off Child Develop, Dept HEW, 72-74; mem prof adv bd, Nat Soc Autistic Children, 72-, chmn, 77-; mem intervention comt, NC Coun Develop Disabilities, 72-75; consult, Div Neuropharm, Food & Drug Admin, 76-, Off Sci Eval, Bur Drugs, Food & Drug Admin & Div Neuropharmacol, & NIMH, 76-79; dir, Dept Behav Sci, Children's Orthop Hosp & Med Ctr, 76-79; adj prof pediat, Sch Med, Univ Wash, 77-93; actg head inpatient psychiat treat div, Children's Orthop Hosp & Med Ctr, 78; dir, Child at Risk Proj, 84-89; mem, Fac Senate Exec Comt, 87-89; co-dir, Ctr Anxiety & Depression, 87-90; pres, Wash State Coun Child Psychiat, 88-89. *Mem:* Autistc Soc Am; Am Psychopathol Asn; Am Psychiat Asn; Am Acad Child Psychiat. *Res:* Psychotic and communication disordered children; parent and professional estimates of current and future abilities; psychophysiological parameters in childhood psychosis; nosology for child psychopathology; developmental psychopharmacology; anxiety and depression disorders; high risk children. *Mailing Add:* 2150 N 107th St Suite 200 Seattle WA 98133-9009

REICHLIN, MORRIS, MEDICINE, CLINICAL IMMUNOLOGY. *Current Pos:* MEM & HEAD, ARTHRITIS & IMMUNOL LAB, OKLA MED RES FOUND, PROF & CHIEF, IMMUNOL SECT, COL MED, OKLA HEALTH SCI CTR, 81- *Personal Data:* b Toledo, Ohio, Feb 2, 34; m 58, Marianne Wolfson; c Michele E & Hershel P. *Educ:* Washington Univ, AB, 55, MD, 59. *Prof Exp:* Fel biochem, Brandeis Univ, 61-63 & Univ Rome, 63-64; instr med, Col Med, Univ Vt, 64-65; from asst prof to assoc prof med & biochem, State Univ NY Buffalo, 65-71, prof, 71-81. *Mem:* Am Soc Biol Chemists; Am Asn Immunologists. *Res:* Autoimmunity and chemistry of autoantigens; rheumatology. *Mailing Add:* Okla Med Res Found 825 NE 13th St Oklahoma City OK 73104-5097. *Fax:* 405-271-4110

REICHLIN, SEYMOUR, INTERNAL MEDICINE, PHYSIOLOGY. *Current Pos:* PROF MED, SCH MED, TUFTS UNIV, 72- *Personal Data:* b New York, NY, May 31, 24; m 51; c 3. *Educ:* Antioch Col, AB, 45; Washington Univ, MD, 48; Univ London, PhD, 54. *Honors & Awards:* Eli Lilly Award, Endocrine Soc, 72; Berthold Award, Ger Endocrine Soc, 83. *Prof Exp:* Commonwealth Fund fel, 52-54; instr med & psychiat, Sch Med, Washington Univ, 54-56, asst prof, 56-61; assoc prof med, Sch Med & Dent, Univ Rochester, 62-66, prof, 66-69; prof med & chmn, Dept Med & Pediat Specialties, Sch Med, Univ Conn, 69-71, prof physiol & head dept, 71-72. *Concurrent Pos:* Palmer Fund fel, 54-56; mem endocrinol study sect, USPHS, 66-70. *Mem:* Endocrine Soc (pres, 75-76); Am Physiol Soc; Am Psychosom Soc; Asn Res Nerv & Ment Dis (pres, 77); Asn Am Physicians. *Res:* Endocrinology; neuroendocrinology; thyroid and pituitary physiology. *Mailing Add:* Univ Ala health Sci Ctr 750 Washington St Tucson AZ 85721

REICHMAN, OMER JAMES, ECOLOGY, BEHAVIOR. *Current Pos:* from asst prof to assoc prof, 81-86, assoc vprovost res & dir, Off Res & Sponsored Progs, 91-93, PROF, KANS STATE UNIV, 90- *Personal Data:* b Tampa, Fla, Jan 4, 47; m 82, Jessica Hagemann. *Educ:* Tex Tech Univ, BA, 68, MS, 70; Northern Ariz Univ, PhD(biol), 74. *Prof Exp:* Instr biol, Northern Ariz Univ, 72-74; res asst prof biol, Univ Utah, 74-75; res ecologist, Mus Northern Ariz, 75-81. *Concurrent Pos:* Fel, Univ Utah, 74-75; bd dirs, Am Soc Mammalogists, 88-; ecol prog dir, NSF, 90-91; bd trustees, Biosis Corp, 92-; coun, Ecol Soc Am, 93- *Mem:* Ecol Soc Am; Am Soc Mammal; Am Soc Nat; Sigma Xi; AAAS; Animal Behav Soc. *Res:* Plant and animal interactions; resource distribution particularly seeds; pocket gopher ecology; resource utilization by rodents; food catching behavior. *Mailing Add:* Dept Ecol Evolution & Marine Biol Univ Calif Santa Barbara CA 93106. *Fax:* 785-532-6653; *E-Mail:* jreichma@ksuvm.ksu.edu

REICHMAN, SANDOR, PHYSICAL CHEMISTRY. *Current Pos:* asst prof, 68-72, assoc prof, 72-76, PROF PHYS CHEM, CALIF STATE UNIV, NORTHRIDGE, 76- *Personal Data:* b Nov 24, 41; US citizen; m 66; c 3. *Educ:* City Col NY, BS, 63; NY Univ, PhD(phys chem), 67. *Prof Exp:* Fel infrared spectros, Univ Minn, 66-68. *Concurrent Pos:* Vis prof, Hebrew Univ, Jerusalem, 80. *Mem:* Am Phys Soc. *Res:* Infrared spectroscopy; molecular dynamics; high resolution infrared spectroscopy; anharmonicity calculations. *Mailing Add:* Dept Chem Calif State Univ 1811 Nordhoff St Northridge CA 91330

REICHMANIS, ELSA, LITHOGRAPHIC MATERIALS. *Current Pos:* mem tech staff org chem, AT&T Bell Labs, 78-84, supvr, radiation sensitive mat & appln group, 84-94, HEAD POLYMER AND ORG MAT RES DEPT, AT&T BELL LABS, LUCENT TECH, 94- *Personal Data:* b Melbourne, Australia, Dec 9, 53; US citizen; m 79, Francis J Purcell; c Patrick W, Elizabeth A, Edward A, Thomas A. *Educ:* Syracuse Univ, BS, 72, PhD(org chem), 75. *Honors & Awards:* R&D 100 Award, Res & Develop Mag, 92; Achievement Award, Soc Women Engrs, 93; Eng Mat Award, Am Soc Metals, 96. *Prof Exp:* Intern org chem, Syracuse Univ, 75-76, Chaim Weizmann fel sci res, 76-78. *Concurrent Pos:* Mem, Comt Surv Mat Res Opportunities & Needs for Electronics Indust, Nat Res Coun, 87; secy, Div Am Chem Soc, 91-92, vchair, 93 & chair-elect, 94; chair, 95; fel, Bell Labs, 94; assoc ed, Chem of Mat, 96-; mem, US Nat Comt Int Union Pure & Appl Chem, 96- *Mem:* Nat Acad Eng; AAAS; Soc Photo-Optical Instrumentation Engrs; fel Soc Women Engrs; Am Chem Soc. *Res:* Chemistry; properties and application of radiation sensitive materials; electronic materials; microlithography; photochemistry; synthesis; polymers for electronic applications. *Mailing Add:* 550 St Marks Ave Westfield NJ 07090

REICHMANN, MANFRED ELIEZER, VIROLOGY. *Current Pos:* prof bot, 64-71, PROF MICROBIOL, UNIV ILL, URBANA, 71- *Personal Data:* b Trencin, Czech, Apr 16, 25; m 57; c 3. *Educ:* Hebrew Univ, Israel, MSc, 49, PhD(biochem), 51. *Prof Exp:* USPHS fel, Harvard Univ, 51-53; Nat Res Coun Can fel, 53-55; res officer, Plant Virus Inst, Res Br, Can Dept Agr, 55-64. *Concurrent Pos:* Prof biochem, Univ BC, 62-64; assoc mem, Ctr Adv Studies, Univ Ill, 77-78; scholar, Am Cancer Soc, 77-78. *Mem:* Am Soc Biol Chemists; Am Soc Microbiol; AAAS. *Res:* Physiochemical studies of viruses; chemical composition of viral proteins and nucleic acids; defective interfering particles; mechanism of autointerference; Vesicular Stomatitis virus, Papilloma viruses; molecular biology; biochemistry. *Mailing Add:* Dept Microbiol Univ Ill 506 S Mathews Ave Urbana IL 61801-3618

REICHSMAN, FRANZ KARL, PSYCHOSOMATIC MEDICINE. *Current Pos:* RETIRED. *Personal Data:* b Vienna, Austria, Sept 26, 13; nat US; m 45; c 5. *Educ:* Univ Vienna, MD, 38; Am Bd Internal Med, dipl. *Prof Exp:* Res asst, Johns Hopkins Hosp, 39-40; intern med, Sinai Hosp, Baltimore, 40-41, asst path, 41-42, asst resident med, 42-43; asst prof, Univ Tex, Southwestern Med Sch, Dallas, 46-49, clin asst prof, 49-52; from instr to assoc prof med & psychiat, Sch Med, Univ Rochester, 52-64; prof med & psychiat, State Univ NY, Downstate Med Ctr, 64- *Concurrent Pos:* Dazian Found fel, Bowman Gray Sch Med, 43-44 & Univ Tex, Southwestern Med Sch, Dallas, 44-45; Commonwealth Fund fel, Sch Med, Univ Rochester, 52-54; chief chest serv, Vet Admin Hosp, McKinney, Tex, 47-50, asst chief med serv, 50-52; Commonwealth Fund fel, Sch Med, Univ Rochester; career investr, USPHS, 56-61; vis physician, Kings Co Hosp, 64-; vis prof, Oxford Univ, 71-72; assoc physician & assoc psychiatrist, Strong Mem Hosp. *Mem:* Royal Soc Med; Am Psychiat Asn; Group Advan Psychiat; Am Psychosom Soc (pres elect, 80-81). *Res:* Dynamics of congestive heart failure; arterial hypertension; adaptation to hemodialysis; emotions and gastric function. *Mailing Add:* PO Box 380 Cowpath 40 Marlboro VT 05344-0380

REICHSTEIN, TADEUS, botany; deceased, see previous edition for last biography

REID, ALLEN FRANCIS, BIOPHYSICS. *Current Pos:* RETIRED. *Personal Data:* b Deer River, Minn, July 31, 17; m 43, Dorothy Cullen; c Sally & David. *Educ:* Univ Minn, BCh, 40; Columbia Univ, AM, 42, PhD(chem), 43; Southwest Sch Med, Univ Tex, MD, 59. *Prof Exp:* Asst chem, Columbia Univ, 40-42, res scientist in chg radioactivity labs, 42-46; indust consult, Sun Oil Co, Pa, 46-47; from assoc prof to prof biophys, Southwest Med Sch, Univ Tex, 47-60; chmn dept, 47-60; prof biol & chmn dept, Univ Dallas, 60-68; dir, Clin Biochem, Brooklyn-Cumberland Med Ctr, 68-74; prof biol & chmn dept, State Univ NY, Geneseo, 74-82. *Concurrent Pos:* Prof & chmn dept biophys & phys chem, Grad Res Inst, Baylor Univ, 47-50, biophysicist, Univ Hosp, 47-50; consult, Oak Ridge Inst Nuclear Studies, 50-52; biophysicist, Parkland Mem Hosp, Dallas, 50-58; consult, US Vet Admin, 50-67; clin prof path, State Univ NY Downstate Med Ctr, 68-74; dir path, Brooklyn-Cumberland Med Ctr, 70-74. *Mem:* Am Asn Cancer Res; Am Chem Soc; Am Phys Soc; Am Physiol Soc; AMA. *Res:* Energy recovery; tracer work in chemical and biological systems; radioactivity; methods of fractionation; reaction and biologic mechanisms; desalination. *Mailing Add:* 4736 Reservoir Rd Geneseo NY 14454

REID, ARCHIBALD, IV, PLANT ECOLOGY. *Current Pos:* from assoc prof to prof, 68-91, EMER PROF BIOL, STATE UNIV NY COL, GENESEO, 91- *Personal Data:* b Janesville, Wis, Nov 23, 30; m 57, Jane Kiudschi; c Scott & Jill. *Educ:* Univ Wis-Platteville, BS, 57; Univ Wis-Madison, MS, 59, PhD(bot), 62. *Prof Exp:* Asst prof bot, Univ Wyo, 61-66; assoc prof landscape archit & regional planning, Univ Pa, 66-68. *Concurrent Pos:* Mem, Rochester Acad Sci. *Mem:* Am Mus Natural Hist; Ecol Soc Am; Wilderness Soc; Nature Conservancy. *Res:* Growth inhibitors produced by vascular plants; ecology as the base for landscape architecture and regional planning; structure of plant communities; environmental measurements; ecology of old fields. *Mailing Add:* Six Haley Ave Geneseo NY 14454. *Fax:* 716-245-5007

REID, AUSTIN HENRY, JR, PHOTOCHEMISTRY OF METAL OXIDES, SURFACE CHEMISTRY OF METAL OXIDES. *Current Pos:* res & develop chemist, DuPont, 85-88, develop supvr, 89-90, res supvr, 90-93, SR RES SUPVR, DUPONT, 94- *Personal Data:* b Birmingham, Ala, Mar 18, 57. *Educ:* Univ Montevallo, BS, 78; Auburn Univ, PhD(chem), 82. *Prof Exp:* Postdoctoral fel, Tex A&M Univ, 82-85. *Mem:* Am Chem Soc; Am Crystallog Asn; Soc Plastics Engrs. *Res:* Process and product development for the manufacture and commercial application of pigmentary metal oxides; surface and colloid chemistry as applied to the paint, paper and polymer industries. *Mailing Add:* 952 Dogwood Dr New Johnsonville TN 37134

REID, BOBBY LEROY, biochemistry, nutrition; deceased, see previous edition for last biography

REID, BRIAN ROBERT, BIOCHEMISTRY, STRUCTURAL CHEMISTRY. *Current Pos:* PROF CHEM, DEPT CHEM & BIOCHEM, UNIV WASH, 80- *Personal Data:* b Gillingham, Eng, Nov 14, 38; m 61; c 2. *Educ:* Cambridge Univ, BA, 60; Univ Calif, Berkeley, PhD(biochem), 65. *Prof Exp:* Jane Coffin Childs Mem fel biochem, Dartmouth Med Sch, 64-66; from asst prof to assoc prof, 66-75, prof biochem, Univ Calif, Riverside, 75-80. *Concurrent Pos:* Guggenheim Found fel, Med Res Coun Lab Molecular Biol, Cambridge Univ, 72-73; Fogarty sr int fel, Univ Oxford, 79-80. *Mem:* Am Soc Biol Chemists; Am Chem Soc. *Res:* Protein biosynthesis; nucleic acids; structure and function of transfer RNA and DNA. *Mailing Add:* Dept Chem & Biochem Box 351700 Univ Wash Seattle WA 98195-1700

REID, C GLENN, PHYSICAL ORGANIC CHEMISTRY, RESIN MANUFACTURING. *Current Pos:* DEVELOP SCIENTIST, UNION CARBIDE CORP, 84- *Personal Data:* b Louisville, KY, Apr 24, 43; m 83, Wanda; c Jenny, Cindy & Will. *Educ:* Bellarmine Col, BA, 65; Case Western Res Univ, PhD(phys org chem), 69. *Prof Exp:* Chemist II, Celanese Corp, 69-78, group leader, 78-81, sr chemist, 81-83. *Mem:* Am Chem Soc; Soc Plastics Industs. *Res:* Low profile additives for composites application in automotive, sanitary ware, and general industrial end uses. *Mailing Add:* 1214 Dudley Rd Charleston WV 25314-1416

REID, CHARLES PHILLIP PATRICK, FOREST ECOLOGY, ECOLOGICAL PHYSIOLOGY. *Current Pos:* PROF & DIR, SCH RENEWABLE NATURAL RESOURCES, UNIV ARIZ, 92- *Personal Data:* b Columbia, Mo, Jan 8, 40; m 61, Miriam Davis; c Clayton P & Miriam. *Educ:* Univ Mo, BSF, 61; Duke Univ, MF, 66, PhD(forest ecol), 68. *Prof Exp:* Nat Acad Sci-Nat Res Coun assoc herbicide res, Plant Sci Lab, Ft Detrick, Dept Army, 67-69; from asst prof to prof, Colo State Univ, 69-85; prof & chmn, Dept Forestry, Univ Fla, 86-92. *Concurrent Pos:* Mem, US-Australia Coop Sci Prog, S Australia, 76-77; Fulbright lectr, Univ Innsbruck, Austria, 85-86; sr Fulbright scholar, 85. *Mem:* AAAS; Soc Am Foresters; Ecol Soc Am. *Res:* Mycorrhizae of forest trees; plant-microbiol interactions; ecosystem nutrient cycling; plant-water relations; iron nutrition of plants. *Mailing Add:* Sch Renewable Natural Resources Univ Ariz 325 Biosci E Tucson AZ 85721

REID, CLARICE D, SICKLE CELL DISEASE RESEARCH. *Current Pos:* actg dir, Div Blood Dis & Resources, 88-89, NAT COORDR, SICKLE CELL DIS PROG & CHIEF SICKLE CELL DIS BR, NAT HEART LUNG & BLOOD INST, NIH, 76- *Personal Data:* b Birmingham, Ala; m; c 4. *Educ:* Talledega Col, BS, 52; Univ Cincinnati, MD, 59; Am Bd Pediat, dipl, 64. *Prof Exp:* Pvt pract pediat, 62-68; dir pediat educ, Jewish Hosp, 68-69, chmn, Dept Pediat, 69-70; med consult, Pub Health Serv, Nat Ctr Family Planning, Health Serv & Ment Health Admin, 72-73; dep dir, Sickle Cell Dis Prog, Bur Commun Health Serv, Health Serv Admin, 73-76. *Concurrent Pos:* Assoc attend pediat, Jewish Hosp, Cincinnati, 62-68, Childrens Hosp Med Ctr, 62-70, Catherine Booth Hosp, 62-68; attend pediat, Bethesda Hosp, 63-70; pediatrician, Maternal & Child Health-Babies Milk Fund, Cincinnati, 63-70, Hamilton County Welfare Dept, 64-69; clin instr pediat, Univ Cincinnati, Col Med, 64-68; pediat consult, Ohio Dept Health, 66-70; asst prof pediat & asst chief, Family Care Prog, Univ Cincinnati, Sch Med, 68-70; clin asst prof pediat, Howard Univ Col Med, 79- *Mem:* Fel Am Soc Pediat; Am Acad Pediat; Nat Med Asn; AAAS; Am Soc Hemat; NY Acad Sci. *Res:* Sickle cell disease; pediatrics. *Mailing Add:* 9715 Fernwood Rd Bethesda MD 20817

REID, DAVID MAYNE, PLANT PHYSIOLOGY. *Current Pos:* from asst prof to assoc prof, 68-76, PROF BOT, UNIV CALGARY, 76- *Personal Data:* b Belfast, Northern Ireland, Dec 7, 40; m 67. *Educ:* Queen's Univ, Belfast, BSc, 64, PhD(plant physiol), 67. *Prof Exp:* Asst lectr bot, Queen's Univ, Belfast, 67-68. *Mem:* Brit Photobiol Soc; Can Soc Plant Physiol; Am Soc Plant Physiol; Sigma Xi; Soc Exp Biol. *Res:* Sites of synthesis of hormones in plants; interactions of hormones and phytochrome; root-shoot relations. *Mailing Add:* Biol Dept Univ Calgary Calgary AB T2N 1N4 Can

REID, DONALD HOUSE, AVIATION & SPACE PHYSIOLOGY, ENVIRONMENTAL ENGINEERING & ADMINISTRATION. *Current Pos:* RETIRED. *Personal Data:* b Phillipsburg, Pa, May 31, 35; m 64, Mary A Rush; c Douglas C & Joan E. *Educ:* Cornell Univ, BS, 58; SDak State Univ, MS, 60; Univ Southern Calif, PhD(physiol), 68. *Honors & Awards:* Fred A Hitchcock Award Excellence Aerospace Physiol, 73. *Prof Exp:* Res asst nutrit, SDak State Univ, 58-60; Aerospace physiologist, USN, 60-80; mgr sci mgt, Gen Elec Co, 80-84; sr life scientist, Boeing Corp, 84-93, environ eng & admin, 93-95. *Mem:* Fel Aerospace Med Asn; Soc Fed Med Agencies; Am Physiol Soc. *Res:* Stress physiology of humans particularly related to space flight and to the physiology of flying high performance aircraft, physiology of parachuting, and the development of aeromedically more acceptable aircrew life support equipment; physiology of parachuting; development of aeromedically more acceptable aircrew life support equipment for military and civilian aircraft. *Mailing Add:* 9293 N Montierra Pl Tucson AZ 85742-8774. *Fax:* 253-657-9459

REID, DONALD J, AGRONOMY, FIELD CROPS. *Current Pos:* ASSOC PROF AGRON, ETEX STATE UNIV, 81- *Personal Data:* b Whitney, Tex, Jan 29, 38; m 61; c 2. *Educ:* Calif State Polytech Inst, BS, 59; Cornell Univ, MS, 61, PhD(agron), 64. *Prof Exp:* Tech rep, Agr Chem Div, Shell Chem Co, 64-66; asst prof crop & soil sci, Mich State Univ, 66-75; assoc prof & exten agronomist-crops, SDak State Univ, 75-80, prof, 80-81. *Mem:* Am Soc Agron; Crop Sci Soc Am. *Res:* Information dissemination on small grains and row crops in the eastern half of South Dakota. *Mailing Add:* Agr ETex State Univ ETex Sta Commerce TX 75428

REID, EVANS BURTON, ORGANIC CHEMISTRY. *Current Pos:* actg dean fac, Colby Col, 67-68, dir, NSF Summer Inst Sci, 58-60, 61-67 & 68-73, Merrill prof & chmn, Dept Chem, 54-78, EMER PROF, COLBY COL, 78- *Personal Data:* b Brock Twp, Ont, Mar 29, 13; nat US; m 42, 63, Dorothy; c 1. *Educ:* McGill Univ, BSc, 37, PhD(org chem), 40. *Prof Exp:* Grad asst chem eng, McGill Univ, 37-38, demonstr org chem, 38-40; res chemist, Dominion Tar & Chem Co, Montreal, 40-41; instr chem, Middlebury Col, 41-43, asst prof, 43-46; asst prof chem, Johns Hopkins Univ, 46-54. *Concurrent Pos:* Consult, Tainton Prod, Baltimore, 51-54; chmn, Maine Sect, Am Chem Soc, 56, 62, 71; Smith-Mundt vis prof, Univ Baghdad, 60-61; consult, Comt Educ & Personnel, NSF, 63-65; corporator, Maine Med Care Develop, Inc, 68-76. *Res:* Chemistry of tetronic acids; Michael condensation; cyclobutane acids; plant growth hormones; chemistry of neurospora; dimeric ketenes and cyclobutanediones; sesquiterpenes; organic alicyclics; natural products. *Mailing Add:* 11 Highland Ave Waterville ME 04901

REID, F JOSEPH, SOLID STATE PHYSICS. *Current Pos:* RETIRED. *Personal Data:* b Lancaster, Ohio, Mar 19, 30; m 54; c 6. *Educ:* Ohio State Univ, BS, 52, MS, 57. *Prof Exp:* Prin physicist, Phys Chem Div, Battelle Mem Inst, Ohio, 56-59, proj leader, 59-62, assoc chief, 62-67; group mgr, GTE Corp, 67-69, dept mgr, 69-72, res mgr, 72-78, dir GTE Labs, Inc, 78-88. *Mem:* Electrochem Soc; Am Phys Soc; Am Ceramic Soc. *Res:* Materials science. *Mailing Add:* 619 Kings Trail Sunset Beach NC 28468

REID, GEORGE C, ATMOSPHERIC PHYSICS, METEOROLOGY. *Current Pos:* SR SCIENTIST, AERONOMY LAB, NAT OCEANIC & ATMOSPHERIC ADMIN. *Personal Data:* b Edinburgh, Scotland, Sept 13, 29. *Educ:* Edinburgh Univ, BSc, 50, PhD(physics), 54. *Mem:* Fel Am Geophys Union; Am Meteorol Soc. *Mailing Add:* Aeronomy Lab Nat Oceanic & Atmospheric Admin 325 Broadway Boulder CO 80303. *Fax:* 303-497-5373; *E-Mail:* reid@al.noaa.gov

REID, GEORGE KELL, AQUATIC ECOLOGY. *Current Pos:* prof biol, 60-83, EMER PROF BIOL, ECKERD COL, 83- *Personal Data:* b Fitzgerald, Ga, Mar 23, 18; m 49; c 2. *Educ:* Presby Col, BS, 40; Univ Fla, MS, 49, PhD(zool), 52. *Prof Exp:* Instr biol sci, Univ Fla, 49-52; asst prof biol, Col William & Mary, 52-53; asst prof wildlife mgt, Tex A&M Univ, 53-56; asst prof zool, Rutgers Univ, 56-60. *Concurrent Pos:* Prin investr, Va Inst Marine Sci, 53 & Marine Lab, Tex Game & Fish Comn, 54-56; consult, Fla Dept Conserv, Marine Lab, 60-63, Nat Marine Mammal Comn, 93 & wetlands & aquatic ecol, pvt pract, 89-; writer, Reinhold Publ, 61, Van Nostrard Reinhold Publ, 66 & 74, Western Publ, 66 & Rand McNally Publ, 67; chmn, Aquatic Ecol Sect, Ecol Soc Am, 64-66. *Mem:* Ecol Soc Am; Am Soc Limnol & Oceanog; fel AAAS; Sigma Xi; Nat Audubon Soc. *Res:* Ichthyology; limnology; ecology of mangrove communities; intertidal zones, lakes and streams. *Mailing Add:* 6079 Town Colony Dr No 1022 Boca Raton FL 33433

REID, H(ARRY) F(RANCIS), JR, METALLURGY. *Current Pos:* RETIRED. *Personal Data:* b Coshocton, Ohio, Sept 15, 17; m 60; c 2. *Educ:* Geneva Col, BS, 39; Ohio State Univ, MS, 48. *Prof Exp:* Chemist, Ceramic Color & Chem Mfg Co, Pa, 39-42; res engr, Battelle Mem Inst, 42-51; mgr tech serv dir, McKay Co, 51-68, asst to vpres mkt, 68-73, asst vpres tech serv, 73-81, sr staff engr, Am Welding Soc, 81-94. *Mem:* Am Welding Soc; Am Soc Metals. *Res:* Development of coating for ferrous and nonferrous arc welding electrodes. *Mailing Add:* 2107 Hershey Ct York PA 17404

REID, HAY BRUCE, JR, PLANT PHYSIOLOGY, BOTANY. *Current Pos:* ASSOC PROF BIOL, KEAN COL, NJ, 73- *Personal Data:* b Hyannis, Mass, Sept 15, 39; m 74; c 2. *Educ:* Drew Univ, AB, 61; Univ Mass, Amherst, MA, 63; Univ Calif, Los Angeles, PhD(bot), 66. *Prof Exp:* Scholar, Univ Calif, Los Angeles, 66-67; asst prof bot, Rutgers Univ, New Brunswick, 67-73. *Mem:* Am Asn Plant Physiologists. *Res:* Photoperiodism; physiology of flowering. *Mailing Add:* Dept Biol Kean Col 1000 Morris Ave Union NJ 07083-7133

REID, IAN ANDREW, PHYSIOLOGY. *Current Pos:* fel physiol, Univ Calif, San Francisco, 70-72, lectr & asst res physiologist, 72-73, adj asst prof, 73-77, ASSOC PROF PHYSIOL, UNIV CALIF, SAN FRANCISCO, 77- *Personal Data:* b Hobart, Australia, Aug 31, 43; m 71; c 2. *Educ:* Univ Melbourne, BAgSc, 65; Monash Univ, PhD(renal physiol), 69. *Prof Exp:* Sr teaching fel physiol, Monash Univ, 69-70. *Concurrent Pos:* NIH res career develop award, 75; consult, Hypertension Task Force, Nat Heart & Lung Inst, 76-77. *Mem:* Am Physiol Soc; Endocrine Soc; AAAS; Am Fedn Clin Res; Soc Exp Biol Med. *Res:* Regulation of fluid and electrolyte balance and blood pressure with emphasis on the role of the renin-angiotensin system. *Mailing Add:* Dept Physiol Univ Calif San Francisco Box 0444 San Francisco CA 94143-0444

REID, JACK RICHARD, ORGANIC CHEMISTRY, MEDICINAL CHEMISTRY. *Current Pos:* sr res chemist org chem, Lorillard Div, Loews Theatre, Inc, 75-87, mgr org chem, 87-92, DIR RES, LORILLARD TOBACCO CO, 93- *Personal Data:* b Youngstown, Ohio, Oct 31, 47; m 69, Linda Newton; c Lara & Jonathan. *Educ:* Lebanon Valley Col, Pa, BS, 69; Lehigh Univ, MS, 72, PhD(chem), 73. *Prof Exp:* Air pollution chemist analytical chem, US Army Environ Hyg Agency, 70-72. *Concurrent Pos:* Res assoc med chem, Univ Kans, 73-75. *Mem:* Am Chem Soc; Sigma Xi. *Res:* Natural products, terpenes, alkaloids; heterocyclic chemistry; phosphorous chemistry; flavor chemistry. *Mailing Add:* 6052 Ingold Rd Whitsett NC 27377-9731. *Fax:* 910-373-6640

REID, JAMES CUTLER, ORGANIC CHEMISTRY. *Current Pos:* SR CHEMIST, PHYSIOL LAB, NAT CANCER INST, 49- *Personal Data:* b Akron, Ohio, Apr 17, 18. *Educ:* Univ Pa, BS, 39; Pa State Col, MS, 40; Univ Calif, PhD(org chem), 44. *Prof Exp:* Instr chem, Bowling Green State Univ, 40-42; asst, Univ Calif, 42-44, res assoc, 44-45, mem sci staff, Radiation Lab, 45-49. *Mem:* AAAS; Am Chem Soc; Am Soc Biol Chem. *Res:* Metabolism of compounds labeled with carbon 14 with special reference to cancer; tracer and other metabolic studies with special reference to tumor-host relationships. *Mailing Add:* 6330 Annapolis Lane Dallas TX 75214-2105

REID, JAMES DOLAN, MATHEMATICS. *Current Pos:* assoc prof, 69-71, PROF MATH, WESLEYAN UNIV, 71- *Personal Data:* b Augusta, Ga, June 24, 30; m 59; c 3. *Educ:* Fordham Univ, BS, 52, MA, 53; Univ Wash, PhD(math), 60. *Hon Degrees:* MA, Wesleyan Univ, 72. *Prof Exp:* Instr math, Univ Wash, 59-60; asst prof, Syracuse Univ, 60-61 & Amherst Col, 62-63; from asst prof to assoc prof, Syracuse Univ, 63-69. *Concurrent Pos:* Off Naval Res res fel, Yale Univ, 61-62. *Mem:* Soc Indust & Appl Math; Am Math Soc; Math Asn Am. *Res:* Algebra. *Mailing Add:* Dept Math Wesleyan Univ Middletown CT 06459-0128

REID, JOHN DAVID, TEXTILE CHEMISTRY. *Current Pos:* CONSULT TEXTILE CHEM, 75- *Personal Data:* b Portland, Ore, Feb 19, 09; m 31; c 2. *Educ:* State Col Wash, BS, 30; George Washington Univ, MA, 32; American Univ, PhD(chem), 37. *Prof Exp:* Jr chemist, Color & Farm Waste Div, Bur Chem & Soils, USDA, 30-37, asst chemist, Agr By-prods Lab, Iowa State Col, 37-40, assoc chemist, Southern Regional Res Lab, Bur Agr & Indust Chem, 40-42, chemist, 42-44, sr chemist, 44-45, in charge, Finishing Unit, Cotton Chem Processing Sect, Southern Utilization Res Br, 54-58, head chem finishing invests, Cotton Chem Lab, Southern Utilization Res & Develop Div, 58-75. *Mem:* Am Chem Soc; Am Inst Chem. *Res:* Chemical modification of cotton fibers; creative problem solving; creative thinking and efficiency in research. *Mailing Add:* 4519 Banks St New Orleans LA 70119

REID, JOHN MITCHELL, MEDICAL IMAGING, ELECTRICAL ENGINEERING. *Current Pos:* Calhoun prof, 82-94, CALHOUN EMER PROF ELEC & BIOMED ENG & RES PROF, DREXEL UNIV, 94-; PROF RADIOL, THOMAS JEFFERSON UNIV, 83- *Personal Data:* b Minneapolis, Minn, June 8, 26; m 83, Shadi Wang; c Helen Hu. *Educ:* Univ Minn, BS, 50, MS, 57; Univ Penn, PhD(elec eng), 65. *Honors & Awards:* Pioneer Award, Am Inst Ultrasound Med; Lifetime Achievement Award, Inst Elec & Electronics Engrs; Pioneer Award, Soc Vascular Technologists. *Prof Exp:* Res fel surg, Univ Minn, 50-51, res fel elec eng, 51-53; chief res engr, St Barnabas Hosp, 54-57; res assoc biomed, Univ Penn, 57-65; res assoc prof physiol & biomed engr, Univ Wash, 66-71; asst dir physiol res, Inst Appl Physiol Med, 71-81, Providence Hosp, Seattle, 73-79. *Concurrent Pos:* Reviewer, NIH, 64-; affil assoc prof elec eng, Univ Wash, 73-79; mem, Int Electrotech Comn, 79-, subcomt ultrasonics. *Mem:* Fel Acoust Soc Am; fel Am Inst Ultrasound Med; fel Inst Elec & Electronics Engrs; fel Am Inst Med & Biol Engrs. *Res:* Wave energy for imaging and diagnosis, particularly ultrasonic energy; development of transducers & circuits; extraction of parameters that characterize the medium being imaged. *Mailing Add:* Sch Biomed Eng & Sci & Health Syst Drexel Univ Philadelphia PA 19104. *E-Mail:* reid@coe.drexel.edu

REID, JOHN REYNOLDS, JR, GEOMORPHOLOGY, GLACIOLOGY. *Current Pos:* from asst prof to assoc prof, 61-71, assoc dean, Col Arts & Sci, 67-78, PROF GEOL, UNIV NDAK, 71- *Personal Data:* b Melrose, Mass, Jan 4, 33; m 56; c Valerie, William, Karen & Linda. *Educ:* Tufts Univ, BS, 55; Univ Mich, MS, 57, PhD(geol), 61. *Prof Exp:* Asst prof geol, Mt Union Col, 59-60; lectr, Univ Mich, 60-61. *Concurrent Pos:* Res geologist, Great Lakes Res Div, Inst Sci Technol, 60-61; fel, Quaternary Res Ctr, Univ Wash, 69-70; assoc dir, NDak Regional Environ Assessment Prog, 75-77, Interim Dir, 77-78; consult, US Army Corp Eng, 80-; vis prof, Univ Bergen, Norway, 86 & Edinburg Univ, Scotland, 87. *Mem:* Fel Geol Soc Am; Nat Asn Geol Teachers; Am Quaternary Asn; Sigma Xi. *Res:* Glacial geology; geomorphology of North Dakota and Alaska; glacial deposits; regimen of Alaska glaciers; structural glaciology of Antarctic firn folds; environmental geology of potential impact areas; shoreline erosion processes of Lakes Sakakawea and Oahe. *Mailing Add:* PO Box 8358 Univ Sta Grand Forks ND 58202-8358. *Fax:* 701-777-4449; *E-Mail:* joreid@badlands.nodak.edu

REID, JOSEPH LEE, OCEANOGRAPHY. *Current Pos:* Res oceanographer & lectr, Scripps Inst Oceanog, Univ Calif, San Diego, 50-74, DIR MARINE LIFE RES GROUP, 74-87, prof oceanog, 74-92, EMER PROF OCEANOG, SCRIPPS INST OCEANOG, UNIV CALIF, SAN DIEGO, 92- *Personal Data:* b Franklin, Tex, Feb 7, 23; m 53; c 2. *Educ:* Univ Tex, BA, 42; Univ Calif, MS, 50. *Honors & Awards:* Nat Oceanog Data Ctr Award, Washinton, DC, 84; Spec Creativity Award, NSF, 88-90; Alexander Agassiz Medal, Nat Acad Sci, 93; Henry Stommel Res Award, Am Meteorol Soc, 96. *Mem:* Fel Am Geophys Union; Am Soc Limnol & Oceanog; fel AAAS. *Res:* Ocean circulation; distribution of temperature, salinity, oxygen, phosphate and marine life; wind-driven and thermohaline circulation; exchange between oceans; Antarctic Ocean circulation; California current; descriptive physical oceanography; world ocean. *Mailing Add:* Scripps Inst Oceanog Univ Calif 9500 Gilman Dr La Jolla CA 92093-0230

REID, KARL NEVELLE, JR, MECHANICAL ENGINEERING. *Current Pos:* from asst prof to assoc prof, 64-70, dir, Ctr Systs Sci, 68-72, PROF MECH & AERO-ENG, OKLA STATE UNIV, 70-, HEAD SCH, 72- *Personal Data:* b Fayetteville, Ark, Oct 10, 34; m 56; c 2. *Educ:* Okla State Univ, BS, 56, MS, 58;. *Hon Degrees:* DSc, Mass Inst Technol, 64. *Prof Exp:* Asst mech eng, Mass Inst Technol, 58-60, instr, 60-64, lab coordr, 61-62. *Concurrent Pos:* Tech consult, Scovill Mfg, Westinghouse Elec Co; educ consult to NSF & USAID; assoc ed, Trans/J Dynamic Systs, Measurements & Control, 71-73, ed, 74-76, sr tech ed, 76-; US mem, Tech Comt Components, Int Fedn Automatic Control; chmn, Components Comt, Am Automatic Control Coun, 72- *Mem:* Am Soc Mech Engrs; Am Soc Eng Educ; Fluid Power Soc; Nat Soc Prof Engrs. *Res:* Systems dynamics; analysis and design of fluid control systems; automatic control systems; fluidics; biomedical engineering. *Mailing Add:* Dept Eng 111 Engineering Okla State Univ Stillwater OK 74078-2095

REID, KENNETH BROOKS, MATHEMATICS. *Current Pos:* From asst prof to assoc prof math, LA State Univ, Baton Rouge, 68-89, chmn, 87-89, dir, honors prog, 92-95, EMER CHAIR MATH, LA STATE UNIV, BATON ROUGE, 89-, EMER PROF, 89- *Personal Data:* b Jacksonville, Fla, Mar 2, 43; m 66; Marion Taylor; c Kathryn Margaret & Kristina Brooks. *Educ:* Univ Calif, Berkeley, BA, 64; Univ Ill, Urbana, MA, 66, PhD(math), 68. *Concurrent Pos:* Vis assoc prof, Univ Waterloo, Can, 74; vis fel, Inst Advan Studies, Australian Nat Univ, 75; vis prof, Johns Hopkins Univ & Ga Inst Technol, 82; W K Kellogg Nat fel, 81-84; vis lectr, Math Asn Am, 75- *Mem:* Am Math Soc; Math Asn Am; Soc Indust & Appl Math; Combinatorial Soc Australia; Soc Social Choice & Welfare; fel Inst Combinatorics & Appln. *Res:*

Combinatorial theory, particularly graph theory; enumeration of various discrete structures; existence problems concerning structure in graphs and directed graphs, particularly tournaments; extremal problems in graphs and directed graphs; combinatorics of permutation groups; special voting problems. *Mailing Add:* Founding Fac Calif State Univ San Marcos San Marcos CA 92096-0001. *E-Mail:* kb_reid@mailhost1.csusm.edu

REID, LLOYD DUFF, FLIGHT SIMULATION, FLIGHT MECHANICS. *Current Pos:* From asst prof to assoc prof, 69-82, PROF & ASSOC DIR, INST AEROSPACE STUDIES, UNIV TORONTO, 82- *Personal Data:* b North Bay, Ont, Jan 6, 42; m 64, Lynda; c 3. *Educ:* Univ Toronto, BASc, 64, MASc, 65, PhD(aerospace), 69. *Honors & Awards:* De Florez Award Flight Simulation, Am Inst Aeronaut & Astronaut, 92. *Concurrent Pos:* Engr oper res, deHavilland Aircraft Can, 69; consult, var co, 69-; first vpres, Aerospace Eng & Res Consults Ltd, 73-75, pres, 75-82; vis prof, Delft Univ Technol, 78-79. *Mem:* Assoc fel Am Inst Aeronaut & Astronaut; fel Can Aeronaut & Space Inst. *Res:* Flight simulator motion and visual systems; human pilot performance; aircraft flight through wind shear and turbulence; car driver-vehicle interaction; mathematical models of human operators. *Mailing Add:* Inst Aerospace Studies Univ Toronto 4925 Dufferin St Downsview ON M3H 5T6 Can. *Fax:* 416-667-7799

REID, LOIS JEAN, MATHEMATICS. *Current Pos:* MATHEMATICIAN, NAVAL SURFACE WEAPONS CTR, DAHLGREN LAB, 74- *Personal Data:* b Portsmouth, Va, Sept 23, 37. *Educ:* Col William & Mary, BS, 59; Duke Univ, MA, 61, PhD(math), 67. *Prof Exp:* Instr math, Duke Univ, 60-61; from instr to asst prof, Mary Wash Col, Univ Va, 63-66; asst prof, Univ NC, Greensboro, 67-70; assoc prof, Longwood Col, 70-74. *Mem:* Math Asn Am. *Res:* Algebra and number theory, particularly symmetric q-polynomials, their generalizations and applications. *Mailing Add:* Box 628 Dahlgren VA 22448

REID, LOLA CYNTHIA MCADAMS, BIOCHEMISTRY. *Current Pos:* PROF, DEPT PHYSIOL & MED, UNIV NC, 94- *Personal Data:* b Charlotte, NC, May 25, 45; m 82. *Educ:* Univ NC, BA, 68, PhD(neuroendocriol), 74. *Honors & Awards:* Sinsheimer Career Develop Award, 77. *Prof Exp:* Technician physiol ecol, Univ NC, Chapel Hill, 68, teaching asst, 73; fel cancer biol, Univ Calif, San Diego, 74-77; asst prof differentiation, Albert Einstein Col, 77-, assoc prof, Dept Molecular Pharmacol, Microbiol & Immunol, 94. *Concurrent Pos:* Res fel, Bar Harbor, Maine, 75, Pasteur Inst, 76; prin investr, var res proj, 77-; consult, var co, 76- *Mem:* Am Asn Cancer Res; AAAS; Am Soc Zoologists. *Res:* Regulation of differentiation in normal and neoplastic cells especially by the synergistic interactions of hormones and exgracellular matrix. *Mailing Add:* Univ NC Rm 34 Glaxo Bldg CB 7038 Mason Farm Rd Chapel Hill NC 27599. *Fax:* 919-419-0048

REID, MACGREGOR STEWART, SPACE SYSTEMS & OPERATIONS, SPACE COMMUNICATIONS. *Current Pos:* res engr, 69-82, mgr prog planning, 82-87, TECH EXEC ASST TO DIR, JET PROPULSION LAB, 87- *Personal Data:* b Johannesburg, SAfrica, June 11, 32; US citizen; m 62, Anita C Menke; c Stewart, Warwick & Matthew. *Educ:* Univ Witwatersrand, SAfrica, BSc, 53, BSc, 56, MSc, 62, PhD(radio physics), 69. *Prof Exp:* Sr res engr, Nat Inst Telecommun Res, SAfrica, 60-69. *Concurrent Pos:* Invited vis res eng, Jet Propulsion Lab, 65-66; dep vpres, Int Astronaut Fedn, 92-; mem, US Deleg, Com Aircraft & Space Vehicles, Int Orgn Stand, 93-, chmn subcomt Space Systs & Opers, 93-; chmn, Comt Qual, Int Acad Astronaut, 95- *Mem:* Fel Royal Aeronaut Soc; Int Acad Astronaut; fel Am Inst Aeronaut & Astronaut (vpres, 91-94). *Res:* Microwave antennas including standards and high precision calibrations, space communications including low-noise receivers; international cooperation in standards for space operations and space systems; granted one patent. *Mailing Add:* Jet Propulsion Lab 4800 Oak Grove Dr Pasadena CA 91109. *Fax:* 818-393-4218; *E-Mail:* macgregor.s.reid@jpl.nasa.gov

REID, MICHAEL BARON, RESPIRATORY MUSCLES, CHEST WALL MECHANICS. *Current Pos:* asst prof, 89-93, ASSOC PROF MED, BAYLOR COL MED, 93- *Personal Data:* b Ft Worth, Tex, Aug 28, 52; m 84; c 2. *Educ:* Univ Tex, Arlington, BS, 74, Dallas, PhD(physiol), 80. *Prof Exp:* Res fel, Health Sci Ctr, Univ Tex, Dallas, 80-81; res fel, Sch Pub Health, Harvard Univ, 81-83, res assoc, 83-87, asst prof pysiol, 87-89. *Concurrent Pos:* Respiratory therapist, Harris Hosp, Ft Worth, 70-75, St Paul's Hosp, Dallas, 75-76, Presby Hosp, Dallas, 77-81 & Beth Israel Hosp, Boston, 81-83; adj fac, Simmons Col, Boston, 81-83; res physiologist, Vet Admin, 84-89; vis prof, Cath Univ Leuven, Belg; mem, Cardiopulmonary Coun, Am Heart Asn. *Mem:* Am Physiol Soc; Am Thoracic Soc; Am Heart Asn; Oxygen Soc; AAAS. *Res:* Physiology and pathophysilogy of nitric oxide and reactive oxygen species in skeletal muscle. *Mailing Add:* Pulmonary Med Rm 520B Baylor Col Med One Baylor Plaza Houston TX 77030. *Fax:* 713-798-3619; *E-Mail:* reid@bcm.tmc.edu

REID, PARLANE JOHN, BIOCHEMISTRY, MICROBIAL GENETICS. *Current Pos:* ASST PROF BIOCHEM, SCH MED, UNIV CONN, 68- *Personal Data:* b Long Beach, Calif, Apr 14, 37; m 59; c 2. *Educ:* Univ Calif, Santa Barbara, BA, 60, MA, 61, PhD(biol), 66. *Prof Exp:* Res assoc genetics, Univ Calif, Santa Barbara, 60-61; instr biol, Calif State Polytech Col, 61-62; fel biochem, Sch Med, Stanford Univ, 66-68. *Res:* Mechanisms of RNA and protein synthesis in microbes and bacteriophage. *Mailing Add:* 1524 Danforth Lane Osprey FL 34229

REID, PHILIP DEAN, PLANT PHYSIOLOGY, AGRICULTURE & PLANT BIOCHEMISTRY. *Current Pos:* from asst prof to prof biol sci, Smith Col, 71-91. asst to pres campus planning, 79-88, chmn, Dept Biol Sci, 86-89, LOUISE C HARRINGTON PROF BOT SMITH COL, 92- *Personal Data:* b Ypsilanti, Mich, Mar 6, 37; m 84, Cathy Hofer; c Taylor C & Aloma B. *Educ:* Eastern Mich Univ, BA, 62; Univ Mo, MS, 64; Univ Mass, PhD(bot), 70. *Prof Exp:* Res biol, Uniroyal Corp, 64-66; res fel, Univ Calif, Riverside, 70-71. *Mem:* Fel AAAS; Sigma Xi; Am Soc Plant Physiologists; Bot Soc Am; Am Inst Biol Sci. *Res:* Hormonal control of plant metabolism and development; special emphasis on abscission and cellulase as well as programmed cell death. *Mailing Add:* Dept Biol Sci Smith Col Northampton MA 01063. *Fax:* 413-5585-3786; *E-Mail:* preid@science.smith.edu

REID, PRESTON HARDING, SOIL CHEMISTRY, SOIL FERTILITY. *Current Pos:* RETIRED. *Personal Data:* b Akron, Colo, Nov 15, 23; m 48; c 1. *Educ:* Colo State Univ, BS, 49; NC State Univ, MS, 51, PhD(soils), 56. *Prof Exp:* Res asst prof soils, NC State Univ, 56-60, assoc prof, 60-66, prof soil sci, 66-69, dir soil test div, NC Dept Agr, 65-69; dir, Tidewater Res & Continuing Educ Ctr, Va Polytech Inst & State Univ, 69-86. *Concurrent Pos:* Soils adv to Peru, 61-63; ed, Peanut Science, J Am Peanut Res & Educ Asn, 74-75; exten specialist, soybeans, Va Polytech Inst & State Univ, 75- *Mem:* Am Soc Agron; Soil Sci Soc Am; Am Soybean Asn; Sigma Xi. *Res:* Soil Testing. *Mailing Add:* 3104 SE Balboa Dr Vancouver WA 98683

REID, RALPH R, RADAR SYSTEMS, MICROWAVE RECEIVING. *Current Pos:* sr vpres eng, Loral Defense Systs, 87-96, TECH CONSULT, LOCKHEED MARTIN, 96- *Personal Data:* b Topeka, Kans, Nov 19, 34; m 57, Gloria A Cook; c Terri & Jeffrey. *Educ:* Washburn Univ, BS, 56. *Prof Exp:* Vpres eng, Goodyear Aerospace Corp, 63-87. *Res:* Radar systems. *Mailing Add:* Lockheed Martin PO Box 85 Litchfield Park AZ 85340

REID, RICHARD J(AMES), ELECTRICAL ENGINEERING. *Current Pos:* from instr to assoc prof, 56-70, PROF COMPUTER SCI, MICH STATE UNIV, 70- *Personal Data:* b Burlington, Iowa, Oct 29, 32; m 52; c 5. *Educ:* Iowa State Univ, BS, 55, MS, 56; Mich State Univ, PhD, 59. *Prof Exp:* Instr elec eng, Iowa State Univ, 55-56. *Mem:* Inst Elec & Electronics Engrs; Asn Comput Mach. *Res:* Artificial intelligence. *Mailing Add:* Dept Computer Sci Mich State Univ East Lansing MI 48824

REID, ROBERT C(LARK), CHEMICAL ENGINEERING. *Current Pos:* From asst prof to assoc prof, Mass Inst Technol, 54-64, prof chem eng, 64-81, Chevron prof, 81-87, EMER PROF, MASS INST TECHNOL, 87- *Personal Data:* b Denver, Colo, June 11, 24; m 50; c 2. *Educ:* Purdue Univ, BS, 50, MS, 51; Mass Inst Technol, ScD(chem eng), 54. *Honors & Awards:* Warren K Lewis Award, Am Inst Chem Engrs, 76, Founders Award, 86. *Concurrent Pos:* Am Soc Eng Educ lectr chem eng, 77; Olaf A Hougen prof, Univ Wis-Madison, 80-81. *Mem:* Nat Acad Eng; Am Inst Chem Engrs. *Res:* Thermodynamics; cryogenics; liquefied natural gas and petroleum gas; safety; critical point extraction; migration of chemicals from polymer food wraps to food; superheated liquid explosions; botanical engineering. *Mailing Add:* Dept Chem Eng 66-544 Mass Inst Technol Cambridge MA 02139

REID, ROBERT LELON, SOLAR ENERGY, HEAT TRANSFER. *Current Pos:* DEAN, COL ENG, MARQUETTE UNIV, 87- *Personal Data:* b Detroit, Mich, May 20, 42; m 62, Judy Nestell; c Robert, Bonnie & Matthew. *Educ:* Univ Mich, BSE, 63; Southern Methodist Univ, MSE, 66, PhD(mech eng), 69. *Honors & Awards:* Centennial Medallion, Am Soc Mech Engrs. *Prof Exp:* Res engr, Atlantic Richfield Corp, 64-65; staff engr, Linde Div, Union Carbide Corp, 66-68; assoc prof mech eng, Univ Tenn, Knoxville, 69-75, Cleveland State Univ, 75-77; prof mech eng & asst dir, Energy, Environ & Resources Ctr, Univ Tenn, Knoxville, 77-82; chmn, Mech & Indust Eng Dept, Univ Tex, El Paso, 82-87. *Concurrent Pos:* Prof, NASA, 70 & 76, prin investr, 77-78; prof, Exxon Corp, 72 & 73, prin investr, 72-73; prin investr contracts, Union Carbide, 74-82, NSF, 77-79, Tenn Valley Authority, 79-82, US Bur Reclamation, 87-, consult, Oak Ridge Nat Lab, 80-81, Modine Mfg Co, 91- & State Wis, 93-; assoc ed, J Solar Energy Eng, Am Soc Mech Engrs, 81-90, tech ed, 90- *Mem:* Fel Am Soc Mech Engrs; Am Soc Heating, Refrig & Air Conditioning Engrs; Int Solar Energy Soc; Am Soc Engr Educ. *Res:* Solar energy; energy conservation; heat transfer; author or coauthor of over 100 publications. *Mailing Add:* Marquette Univ Dean Eng Col 201 Olin Eng PO Box 1881 Milwaukee WI 53201-1881. *Fax:* 414-288-7082; *E-Mail:* reidr@vms.csd.mu.edu

REID, ROBERT LESLIE, RUMINANT NUTRITION, FORAGE UTILIZATION. *Current Pos:* RETIRED. *Educ:* Aberdeen Univ, Scotland, PhD(agr biochem), 57. *Prof Exp:* Prof animal sci, Div Animal & Vet Sci, WVa Univ, 69-93. *Res:* Mineral metabolism. *Mailing Add:* Rte 10, Box 9 Morgantown WV 26505

REID, ROBERT LESLIE, REPRODUCTIVE ENDOCRINOLOGY & INFERTILITY. *Current Pos:* from asst prof to assoc prof, 81-90, PROF, DEPT OBSTET & GYNEC, QUEEN'S UNIV, KINGSTON, 90- *Personal Data:* b Belleville, Ont, Jan 26, 51; m 76; c 3. *Educ:* Queen's Univ, MD, 74. *Prof Exp:* Fel reproductive endocrinol, Dept Obstet & Gynec, Univ Calif, San Diego, 79-81. *Concurrent Pos:* Chmn, Joint Can Fertil & Andrology Soc & Soc Obstetricians & Gynecologists, Can Ethics Comt New Reproductive Technologies, 87-91; pres, Can Fertil & Andrology Soc, 88-89; FIGO 1944 Organizing Comt mem, Fedn Int Gynecologie Obstetrie, 88-94. *Mem:* Soc Gynec Invest; Soc Obstetricians & Gynecologists Can; Can Fertil & Andrology Soc; Am Fertil Soc. *Res:* Menstrual cycle related mood and physical disorders; hormonal effects on mood in menopausal hormone replacement therapy; photodynamic ablation of endometrim/endometriosis. *Mailing Add:* Kingston en Hosp Obstet & Gynec Victory 4 Kingston ON K7L 2V7 Can

REID, ROBERT OSBORNE, OCEANOGRAPHY. *Current Pos:* from asst prof to assoc prof oceanog & meteorol, Tex A&M Univ, 51-59, prof oceanog & civil eng, 59-78, distinguished prof oceanog, 78-87, EMER DISTINGUISHED PROF OCEANOG, TEX A&M UNIV, 87- *Personal Data:* b Milford, Conn, Aug 24, 21; m 47; c 6. *Educ:* Univ Southern Calif, BE, 46; Univ Calif, MS, 48. *Hon Degrees:* DSc, Old Dominion Univ, 88. *Honors & Awards:* Spec Award, Am Meteorol Soc, 75. *Prof Exp:* Asst, Scripps Inst, Univ Calif, 46-47, oceanogr, 48-51; meteorologist, US Naval Electronics Lab, Calif, 47-48. *Concurrent Pos:* Assoc ed, J Geophys Res, 61-73 & J Marine Res, 61-73 & 83-85; consult, US Army CEngrs, 65-78 & Hydraul Div, Waterways Exp Sta, Vicksburg, 75-; ed-in-chief, J Phys Oceanog, Am Meteorol Soc, 70-80; mem, Ad Hoc Panel Comput Resources & Facil Ocean Circulation Modeling, Nat Acad Sci, 79-80, Comt Coastal Flooding, 80-84, US Nat Comt Int Union Geod & Geophys, 80-84, Storm Surge Prog Rev Bd, Nat Oceanic & Atmospheric Admin, 81-83, subcomt, Nat Marine Bd, Nat Acad Sci, 86-88 & Coastal Eng Res Bd, US Army CEngr, 88- *Mem:* Nat Acad Eng; fel Am Meteorol Soc; fel Am Geophys Union; Int Asn Hydraul Res; Sigma Xi. *Res:* Physical oceanography, especially problems in ocean waves; storm tides and circulation; author of numerous technical publications. *Mailing Add:* Dept Oceanog Tex A&M Univ College Station TX 77843

REID, RODERICK VINCENT, JR, THEORETICAL PHYSICS. *Current Pos:* asst prof, 69-74, ASSOC PROF PHYSICS, UNIV CALIF, DAVIS, 74- *Personal Data:* b Charlotte, NC, Oct 17, 32; m 59, Virginia Haffner; c Katherine, Valerie & Roderick. *Educ:* Univ Denver, AB, 58, MS, 59; Cornell Univ, PhD(physics), 68. *Prof Exp:* Physicist, Mass Inst Technol, 67-69. *Mem:* Am Inst Physics; NY Acad Sci. *Res:* Nuclear theory. *Mailing Add:* Dept Physics Univ Calif Davis CA 95616. *E-Mail:* rvreid@ucdphy.ucdavis.edu

REID, ROLLAND RAMSAY, GEOLOGY. *Current Pos:* asst prof, Univ Idaho, 55-60, assoc prof geol & head, Dept Geol & Geog, 60-65, actg dean, 63-65, actg head, Dept Geol & Geog, 59-60, dean, Col Mines, 65-74, prof, 65-94, EMER PROF GEOL, UNIV IDAHO, 94- *Personal Data:* b Wilbur, Wash, Nov 12, 26; m 47, 75; c 3. *Educ:* Univ Wash, PhD(geol), 59. *Prof Exp:* Instr geol, Mont Sch Mines, 53-55. *Concurrent Pos:* NSF fac fel, 58-59; dep asst secy, Energy & Minerals, US Dept Interior, 75-76. *Mem:* Geol Soc Am; Soc Econ Geologists. *Res:* Metamorphic and structural petrology; structural geology. *Mailing Add:* 621 East Moscow ID 83843

REID, RUSSELL MARTIN, PHYSICAL ANTHROPOLOGY, BIOLOGICAL ANTHROPOLOGY. *Current Pos:* chair, 83-92, PROF DEPT ANTHROP, UNIV LOUISVILLE, 83- *Personal Data:* b St Louis, Mo, July 30, 41; m 64, Mary T Parmalee; c Julie A & Theodore R. *Educ:* Univ Ill, BS, 63, PhD(anthrop), 71. *Prof Exp:* Asst prof anthrop, Univ Tex, Austin, 69-76; asst prof, Univ Houston, 76-78, assoc prof anthrop & chmn, Dept Anthrop, 78-83. *Concurrent Pos:* NSF-Univ Sci Develop Prog grant, Univ Tex, Austin Field Res, Ceylon, 69-73, Haiti, 78. *Mem:* Am Anthrop Asn; Am Asn Phys Anthrop; Brit Soc Study Human Biol; Soc Study Social Biol. *Res:* Human population genetics, especially the role of social organization on genetic structure of populations, particularly consanguinity and inbreeding in human populations; dietary behavior and nutrition. *Mailing Add:* Dept Anthrop New Acad Bldg Univ Louisville Box 35260 Louisville KY 40292. *Fax:* 502-852-4560; *E-Mail:* rmreid@ulkyvm

REID, SIDNEY GEORGE, ORGANIC CHEMISTRY. *Current Pos:* RETIRED. *Personal Data:* b Glamis, Scotland, Sept 21, 23; Can citizen; m 51; c 2. *Educ:* Univ St Andrews, BSc, 44, PhD(chem), 49. *Prof Exp:* Fel, Univ Edinburgh, 48-51; res fel lignin chem, Ont Res Found, 51, asst dept dir, 57-63, dir dept appl chem, 63-85. *Mem:* Fel Chem Inst Can; Can Pulp & Paper Asn; Tech Asn Pulp & Paper Inst. *Res:* Wood, cellulose and lignin chemistry; paper additives; utilization of pulp and paper wastes and industrial wastes. *Mailing Add:* 291 Balsam Dr Oakville ON L6J 3X7 Can

REID, STANLEY LYLE, ORGANIC CHEMISTRY. *Current Pos:* DIR SCI LABS, HILLSDALE COL, HILLSDALE, MICH, 87- *Personal Data:* b Royal Oak, Mich, June 8, 30; m 54, Norma Pifer; c David & Janet. *Educ:* Univ Mich, PhD(chem), 57. *Prof Exp:* From chemist to sr res specialist, Monsanto Co, 57-85. *Mem:* Am Chem Soc. *Res:* Natural products; organic synthesis; oxidation. *Mailing Add:* 333 Grant St Jonesville MI 49250-1017

REID, TED WARREN, BIOCHEMISTRY. *Current Pos:* VCHMN, DEPT OPHTHAL & VISUAL SCI, TEX TECH UNIV HEALTH SCI CTR, 90- *Personal Data:* b Cayuga, Ind, Sept 26, 39; m 61, Nancy C Greve; c Wayne & Wendy. *Educ:* Occidental Col, BS, 61; Univ Ariz, MS, 63; Univ Calif, Los Angeles, PhD(chem), 67. *Prof Exp:* Asst prof molecular biophys & biochem, Med Sch, Yale Univ, 70-75, assoc prof molecular biophys & biochem, ophthal & visual sci, 75-84; dir res, Dept Opthal, Sch Med, Univ Calif, 84-90. *Concurrent Pos:* res prof, Prevent Blindness, 74; vis fel, Imp Cancer Res Found, London, 80. *Mem:* Am Chem Soc; Asn Res Vision & Ophthal; Am Soc Cell Biol. *Res:* Biochemistry of the retina, cornea and cell growth factors; wound healing in the eye. *Mailing Add:* Ophthal Dept Tex Tech Univ Health Sci Ctr Thompson Hall Lubbock TX 79430. *Fax:* 806-743-1782; *E-Mail:* hwtwr@ttacs.ttu.edu

REID, THOMAS S, ORGANIC CHEMISTRY. *Current Pos:* res chemist, Minn Mining & Mfg Co, 44-51, sect leader, Org Sect, 51-55, assoc dir, Cent Res Dept, 55-60, coordr, Div Res, 60-62, mgr biochem res, 62-64, dir biochem res, 64-71, dir biosci res lab, 71-77, CONSULT, MINN MINING & MFG CO, 77- *Personal Data:* b Trenton, NJ, Dec 20, 11; m 42; c 2. *Educ:* Rutgers Univ, BS, 36, MS, 38; Univ Minn, PhD(biochem), 42. *Prof Exp:* Res chemist, Eastern Regional Res Lab, USDA, Pa, 42-44. *Mem:* AAAS; Am Chem Soc; Am Ceramic Soc. *Res:* Biochemistry, polymer and fluorine chemistry; medicinal and health sciences. *Mailing Add:* 735 County Rd B2E St Paul MN 55117-1800

REID, WILLIAM BRADLEY, PHARMACEUTICALS. *Current Pos:* RETIRED. *Personal Data:* b Indianapolis, Ind, Aug 2, 20; m 45; c 2. *Educ:* Butler Univ, BS, 42; Ind Univ, MA, 44, PhD(org chem), 46. *Prof Exp:* res chemist, Upjohn Co, 46-51, sect head, 52-83. *Concurrent Pos:* Mgr, Facilities Planning & Environ Regulatory Afffairs, 74- *Mem:* Am Chem Soc; Am Soc Testing & Mat. *Res:* Synthetic organic chemistry; bacteriology; administration. *Mailing Add:* 1821 Nichols Rd Kalamazoo MI 49006

REID, WILLIAM HILL, APPLIED MATHEMATICS. *Current Pos:* from assoc prof to prof, 63-89, EMER PROF APPL MATH, UNIV CHICAGO, 89-; PROF MATH SCI, IND UNIV-PURDUE UNIV, INDIANAPOLIS, 89- *Personal Data:* b Oakland, Calif, Sept 10, 26; m 62; c 1. *Educ:* Cambridge Univ, PhD(math), 55; Brown Univ, AM ad eundem, 61. *Hon Degrees:* ScD, Cambridge Univ, 67. *Prof Exp:* NSF fel math, Yerkes Observ, Univ Chicago, 57, res assoc astron, 58; from asst prof to assoc prof appl math, Brown Univ, 58-63. *Concurrent Pos:* Lectr, Johns Hopkins Univ, 55-56; consult, Gen Motors Corp, 60-73; Fulbright res grant math, Australian Nat Univ, 64-65. *Mem:* Fel Am Phys Soc; Am Meteorol Soc; Am Math Soc; Soc Indust & Appl Math. *Res:* Fluid mechanics; hydrodynamic stability; asymptotic analysis. *Mailing Add:* 7554 Ballinshire N Dr Indianapolis IN 46254-9772

REID, WILLIAM JAMES, SCIENCE EDUCATION. *Current Pos:* pres, Fac Senate, 71-72, 76-77 & 88-89, prof physics & head dept, 68-91, HEAD DEPT PHYS SCI & ENG, JACKSONVILLE STATE UNIV, 91- *Personal Data:* b Abbeville, SC, Nov 2, 27; m 64, Nancy L Edwards; c Laura L, William J III & Sandra S. *Educ:* Erskine Col, AB, 49; Duke Univ, MA, 58; Clemson Univ, PhD(physics), 67. *Prof Exp:* Instr chem, Erskine Col, 49-51, field rep, 51-52, asst prof physics & math, 56-62, assoc prof physics, 66-68. *Concurrent Pos:* NSF Coop Grad fel, 63-66; adj, Presby Col, 67-68. *Mem:* Am Phys Soc; Sigma Xi; Am Asn Physics Teachers. *Res:* Superconductivity in thin films; pedagogy of physics; physics lecture demonstrations; anthropology, Route of Hernando de Soto. *Mailing Add:* Dept Phys Scis & Eng Jacksonville State Univ Jacksonville AL 36265. *Fax:* 205-782-5228; *E-Mail:* Bitnet: wjr@jsumus

REID, WILLIAM JOHN, POLYMER CHEMISTRY, PHYSICAL CHEMISTRY. *Current Pos:* MEM STAFF CONLIAM RESOURCES PTY LTD, AUSTRALIA. *Personal Data:* b Dublin, Ireland, Jan 29, 45; Can citizen; m 69; c 2. *Educ:* Univ Dublin, BS, 67; Univ BC, MS, 70, PhD(chem), 72. *Prof Exp:* Res assoc polymer chem, Ecoplastics, Univ Toronto, 72-73; res chemist, Res Lab, Uniroyal Ltd, 73-76, res chemist, Uniroyal Inc, 76-78; technol mgr, Plastics & Additives Div, Ciba-Geigy Corp, 78- *Mem:* Am Chem Soc. *Res:* Stabilization and degradation mechanisms in polymers; relationship of properties of polymers to molecular structure and morphology. *Mailing Add:* Plastic Ser PTD Ltd 13 Salisbury St Cottesloe WA 6011 Australia

REID, WILLIAM SHAW, SOIL FERTILITY. *Current Pos:* from asst prof to assoc prof, 66-79, dept agron ext leader, 75-87, PROF SOIL SCI, CORNELL UNIV, 79- *Personal Data:* b Slate Springs, Miss, Feb 24, 38; m 60, Charlotte Miller; c William Shaw Jr, Rhonda Sue & Julie Lynne. *Educ:* Miss State Univ, BS, 59, MS, 61, PhD(agron, soils), 65. *Prof Exp:* Proj officer radiation biol, Air Force Weapons Lab, Kirtland AFB, NMex, 63-66. *Mem:* Am Soc Agron; Soil Sci Soc Am. *Res:* Interactions of fertilizers and climate on the uptake of plant nutrients and plant growth with respect to efficient agricultural production. *Mailing Add:* 333 Snyder Hill Rd Ithaca NY 14850

REID, WILLIAM T(HOMAS), energy conversion; deceased, see previous edition for last biography

REIDENBERG, MARCUS MILTON, PHARMACOLOGY, MEDICINE. *Current Pos:* assoc prof med, 76-80, PROF PHARMACOL & HEAD DIV, MED COL, CORNELL UNIV, 76-, PROF MED, 80-, ASST DEAN, 80- *Personal Data:* b Philadelphia, Pa, Jan 3, 34; m 57; c 3. *Educ:* Temple Univ, MD, 58. *Honors & Awards:* Rawls Palmer Award, Am Soc Clin Pharmacol & Therapeut, 81; Exp Therapeut Award, Am Soc Pharmacol, 83. *Prof Exp:* From instr to asst prof pharmacol, Temple Univ, 62-72, assoc prof pharmacol & med, 72-75, chief sect clin pharmacol, 72-75. *Concurrent Pos:* NIH fel, Temple Univ, 59-60, NIH res career develop award, 71-74. *Mem:* Am Soc Pharmacol & Exp Therapeut; Am Col Physicians; Am Soc Clin Invest; Am Soc Clin Pharmacol & Therapeut; Am Fedn Clin Res; Asn Am Physicians. *Res:* Clinical pharmacology; drug metabolism; adverse drug reactions; clinical pharmacology of contraception. *Mailing Add:* Cornell Univ Med Col 1300 York Ave New York NY 10021. *E-Mail:* mmreid@cumc.cornell.edu

REIDER, PAUL JOSEPH, SYNTHETIC ORGANIC CHEMISTRY. *Current Pos:* SR RES CHEMIST, MERCK, SHARP & DOHME RES LABS, 80- *Personal Data:* b New York, NY, June 7, 51; m 74. *Educ:* Washington Square Col, AB, 72; Univ Vt, PhD(org chem), 78. *Prof Exp:* NIH fel, Colo State Univ, 78-80. *Mem:* Am Chem Soc. *Res:* Synthesis of complex organic molecules of pharmacological interest; development of viable processes for such synthesis. *Mailing Add:* 621 Kimball Ave Westfield NJ 07090-2446

REIDER, RICHARD GARY, PHYSICAL GEOGRAPHY. *Current Pos:* from asst prof to assoc prof, 69-83, PROF GEOG, UNIV WYO, 83- *Personal Data:* b Denver, Colo, Feb 7, 41. *Educ:* Univ Northern Colo, BA, 63, MA, 65; Univ Nebr, PhD(geog), 71. *Prof Exp:* Instr geog, Ind Univ, Pa, 65-66; instr, Univ Nebr, Lincoln, 66-69. *Concurrent Pos:* NSF grant & Sigma Xi grant, 74-83; soils consult, Dept Anthrop, Univ Wyo & Smithsonian Inst, 75-85; ed, Great Plains-Rocky Mountain Geog J, 76-80. *Mem:* Am Quaternary Asn; Sigma Xi; Geol Soc Am. *Res:* Geomorphology and soils geography; geoarchaeology. *Mailing Add:* Dept Geog Univ Wyo Laramie WY 82071-3371. *Fax:* 307-766-2697

REIDIES, ARNO H, INDUSTRIAL ELECTROCHEMISTRY. *Current Pos:* Res chemist, 54-58, chief res chemist, 58-64, res mgr, 64-68, dir res, 68-83, div technologist & consult, 83-90, PRIN SCIENTIST, CARUS CHEM CO, 90- *Personal Data:* b Tilsit, Ger, July 31, 25; US citizen; m 53; c 3. *Educ:* Univ Freiburg, Dipl, 54. *Mem:* Am Chem Soc; Electrochem Soc; Ger Chem Soc; Am Asn Textile Chemists & Colorists. *Res:* Chemistry of manganese, specifically manganese oxides, manganates and permanganates, quinones and hydroquinones; environmental chemistry of manganese and other transition metals. *Mailing Add:* 1137 Fourth St LaSalle IL 61301-2215

REIDINGER, RUSSELL FREDERICK, JR, FISH & WILDLIFE SCIENCES. *Current Pos:* DIR, CTR EXCELLENCE NATURAL RESOURCES MGT, LINCOLN UNIV, 93- *Personal Data:* b Reading, Pa, June 19, 45; m 73, Carol Jean Wieman; c Alysia, Michael, Stephanie & Benjamin. *Educ:* Albright Col, BS, 67; Univ Ariz, PhD(zool), 72. *Prof Exp:* Asst prof biol, Augustana Col, 71-74; res physiologist, US Fish & Wildlife Serv, Philippines, 74-78; asst mem, Monell Chem Senses Ctr & wildlife biologist, 78-86, dir, Denver Wildlife Res Ctr, Philadelphia, 87-93. *Concurrent Pos:* Vis prof, Dept Zool, Univ Philippines, 75-78; consult, Bangladesh Agr Res Coun, USAID, 77, Ministry Agr Develop & Agrarian Reform, Nicaragua, 81 & Makerere Univ, Biol Field Sta, Uganda, 95. *Mem:* Am Soc Mammalogists; Wildlife Soc; Nat Animal Damage Control Asn. *Res:* Chemical senses in relation to wildlife damage management. *Mailing Add:* Dept Agr Natural Resources & Home Econ Lincoln Univ Jefferson City MO 65102-0029. *Fax:* 573-681-5548; *E-Mail:* reidingr@lincolnu.edu

REIDLINGER, ANTHONY A, GENERAL CHEMISTRY. *Current Pos:* from assoc prof to prof, 60-89, chmn dept chem, 66-80, EMER PROF ORG CHEM, LONG ISLAND UNIV, 89- *Personal Data:* b Islip, NY, Nov 30, 26; m 59. *Educ:* Hofstra Univ, BA, 49; NY Univ, MS, 51, PhD(org chem), 55. *Prof Exp:* Assoc eng scientist, Res Div, Col Eng, NY Univ, 55-57; assoc prof org chem, Grad Sch St John's Univ, NY, 56-60. *Concurrent Pos:* Consult, Evans Chemetics, 59-60. *Mem:* Am Chem Soc; Electrochem Soc; Sigma Xi. *Res:* Polarography of organic compounds; nitro derivatives of naphthalene. *Mailing Add:* Dept Chem 24-71 Bellmore Ave Bellmore NY 11710-4301

REIDY, JAMES JOSEPH, ANTIPROTON INTERACTIONS. *Current Pos:* assoc prof, 72-82, PROF PHYSICS, UNIV MISS, 82-, ACTG CHMN, 87- *Personal Data:* b Tulsa, Okla, June 12, 36; m 62; c 3. *Educ:* Univ Notre Dame, BS, 58, PhD(nuclear physics), 63. *Prof Exp:* Instr physics, Univ Notre Dame, 62-63; res assoc, Univ Mich, 63-65, asst prof, 65-71; vis prof, Franklin & Marshall Col, 71-72. *Concurrent Pos:* Vis prof, Tech Univ, Munich, Ger, 76-77; vis staff mem, Los Alamos Nat Lab, 72-; res assoc, Cern, Geneva, Switz, 85; mem, Working Group on State Initiatives in Appl Res, Nat Gov Assoc, 88- *Mem:* Am Asn Physicists Med; Am Phys Soc; Am Asn Physics Teachers; Sigma Xi. *Res:* Physics of negative muon and pion capture by atoms; interaction of negative pions and antiprotons at near rest with nuclei; chemical effects in negative pion and muon atomic capture; determination of nuclear decay schemes. *Mailing Add:* Dept Physics & Astron Univ Miss University MS 38677

REIERSON, JAMES (DUTTON), NUCLEAR PHYSICS, OPERATIONS RESEARCH. *Current Pos:* LEAD ENGR, MITRE CORP, 78- *Personal Data:* b Seward, Nebr, Oct 14, 41; m 75. *Educ:* Univ Nebr, Lincoln, BS, 63; Iowa State Univ, PhD(physics), 69; Marymont Univ, Va, MBA, 84. *Prof Exp:* Systs analyst, Analytical Serv, Inc, 69-73; lectr physics, Univ South Pac, 73-75; comput scientist, Comput Sci Corp, 76-78. *Concurrent Pos:* Mem, Inst Phys, George Mason Univ, 79. *Mem:* Am Phys Soc. *Res:* Systems engineering; analysis and application of artificial intelligence for air traffic control, energy and military problems. *Mailing Add:* 3311 N George Mason Dr Arlington VA 22207

REIF, ARNOLD E, IMMUNOLOGY. *Current Pos:* res prof, 75-89, EMER PROF PATH, SCH MED, BOSTON UNIV, 89- *Personal Data:* b Vienna, Austria, July 15, 24; US citizen; m 50, 79, Katherine E Hume; c 3. *Educ:* Cambridge Univ, BA, 45, MA, 49; Univ London, BSc, 46; Carnegie-Mellon Univ, MS, 49, DSc, 50; Harvard Univ, MTS, 93. *Prof Exp:* From jr sci officer to sci officer, Dept Sci & Indust Res, Gt Brit, 44-47; res fel, Carnegie-Mellon Univ, 47-50; McArdle Mem Lab Cancer Res fel oncol, Sch Med, Univ Wis, 50-53; res assoc, Lovelace Found, NMex, 53-57; asst prof surg & biochem, 57-69, assoc prof surg, Sch Med, Tufts Univ, 69-75. *Concurrent Pos:* Res pathologist, Mallory Inst Path, Boston City Hosp, 73-89; pres, Boston Cancer Res Asn, 96-97. *Mem:* Am Asn Immunol; Am Asn Cancer Res; NY Acad Sci. *Res:* Cancer research; immunology; health education; life-time research work in cancer immunology, immunotherapy, protective vaccines & causation of cancer. *Mailing Add:* 39 College Rd Wellesley MA 02181-5703

REIF, CHARLES BRADDOCK, ZOOLOGY. *Current Pos:* from asst prof to prof, 42-85, EMER PROF ZOOL, WILKES COL, 85- *Personal Data:* b Washington, DC, July 31, 12; wid. *Educ:* Univ Minn, BA, 35, MA, 38, PhD(zool), 41. *Prof Exp:* Asst zool, Univ Minn, 35-41; cur educ, Mus Natural Hist, Minn, 41-42. *Concurrent Pos:* At US Forest Serv, 36 & 38. *Mem:* Am Soc Limnol & Oceanog; Phycol Soc Am; Micros Soc Am; Sigma Xi. *Res:* Limnology; biology; plankton of many lakes in northeastern Pennsylvania. *Mailing Add:* 112 N Franklin St Wilkes-Barre PA 18701

REIF, DONALD JOHN, NUCLEAR CHEMISTRY. *Current Pos:* RETIRED. *Personal Data:* b Oshkosh, Wis, Feb 6, 31; m 52, Marilyn Tuttle; c Susan G & Thomas. *Educ:* Univ Wis, BS, 53; Mass Inst Technol, PhD(org chem), 57. *Prof Exp:* res chemist, E I Du Pont de Nemours & Co, Inc, 57-65, sr res chemist, Old Hickory, Tenn, 65-77, staff chemist, Res & Develop Labs, 77-83, res staff chemist, Savannah River Lab, Aiken, SC, 83-89; sr scientist, Westinghouse Savannah River, 89-91. *Res:* Spent nuclear fuel reprocessing. *Mailing Add:* 722 Ravenel Rd Augusta GA 30909

REIF, FREDERICK, PHYSICS, SCIENCE EDUCATION. *Current Pos:* PROF PHYSICS & PSYCHOL, CARNEGIE-MELLON UNIV, 89- *Personal Data:* b Vienna, Austria, Apr 24, 27; nat US; m 69. *Educ:* Columbia Univ, AB, 48; Harvard Univ, AM, 49, PhD(physics), 53. *Prof Exp:* From instr to asst prof physics, Univ Chicago, 53-60; assoc prof, Univ Calif, Berkeley, 60-64, Miller prof, 64-65, prof, 64-89, prof educ, 83-89. *Concurrent Pos:* Alfred P Sloan fel, Univ Chicago, 55-59. *Mem:* AAAS; Am Phys Soc; Am Educ Res Asn; Cognitive Sci Soc. *Res:* Nuclear magnetic resonance; solid state and low temperature physics; superconductivity; superfluidity of liquid helium; educational research and development; cognitive science. *Mailing Add:* CDEC Carnegie-Mellon Univ Pittsburgh PA 15213

REIF, JOHN H, COMBINATORIAL ALGORITHMS, PARALLEL ALGORITHMS. *Current Pos:* PROF COMPUT SCI, DUKE UNIV, 86- *Personal Data:* b Madison, Wis, Aug 4, 51; m. *Educ:* Harvard Univ, PhD(comput sci), 77. *Prof Exp:* Assoc prof comput sci, Harvard Univ, 79-86. *Mem:* Am Math Soc; fel Asn Comput Mach; Soc Indust & Appl Math; fel Inst Elec & Electronics Engrs. *Res:* Games, robotics, combinatorics, graphs and program optimization; algorithms for real time synchronization of parallel distributed computer systems, using probabilistic methods; parallel algorithms for sorting, searching and solution of linear systems; optical computing; robotic movement planning; data compression. *Mailing Add:* Comput Sci Dept Duke Univ PO Box 90129 Durham NC 27708-0129

REIF, L RAFAEL, SEMICONDUCTORS, INTEGRATED CIRCUITS. *Current Pos:* from asst prof to assoc prof, 80-88, PROF ELEC ENG, MASS INST TECHNOL, 88-, DIR, MICROSYSTS TECHNOL LABS, 90- *Personal Data:* b Maracaibo, Venezuela, Aug 21, 50; div; c Jessica H. *Educ:* Univ Carabobo, Venezuela, Ingeniero Electrico, 73; Stanford Univ, MS, 75, PhD(elec eng), 79. *Prof Exp:* Asst prof elec eng, Univ Simon Bolivar, Venezuela, 73-74; vis asst prof, Stanford Univ, 78-79. *Concurrent Pos:* Consult, Mass Inst Technol, Lincoln Lab, SPIRE Corp, Digital Infrared Industs, Aerodyne Res, Gen Motors Res Labs, M/A Com & Advantage Corp; Presidential Young Investr Award, NSF, 84-89. *Mem:* Electrochem Soc; fel Inst Elec & Electronics Engrs; Metall Soc-Am Inst Mining, Metall & Petrol Engrs; Mat Res Soc. *Res:* Fabrication technology of advanced integrated circuits, e g low temperature thin film epitaxial technology for Si, Si-Ge, GaAs, GaP, IC manufacturing equipment; polysilicon thin film transistor technology. *Mailing Add:* Mass Inst Technol Rm 39-321 60 Vassar St Cambridge MA 02139. *Fax:* 617-253-9622; *E-Mail:* reif@mtl.mit.edu

REIF, VAN DALE, PHARMACEUTICAL CHEMISTRY. *Current Pos:* sect leader, 90-92, ASSOC DIR, ANALYTICAL RES & DEVELOP, SCHERING-PLOUGH RES INST, 92- *Personal Data:* b Burlington, Iowa, Feb 18, 47; m 81, Merry C L Lee; c Bryan & Jillian. *Educ:* Univ Iowa, BS, 70; Univ Mich, MS, 71, PhD(pharmaceut chem), 75. *Prof Exp:* Sr sci assoc pharmaceut anal, Drug Res & Testing Lab, US Pharmacopeia, 75-78; unit suprv, Anal Res & Develop, Wyeth Labs, 78-85, mgr, 85-88; dir, Anal Res & Develop, Controlled Therapeutics, 88-90. *Mem:* Am Chem Soc; Am Asn Pharmaceut Scientists. *Res:* Pharmaceutical analysis, analytical chemistry, chromatography; drug characterization. *Mailing Add:* K 11 3 Schering Plough 2000 Galloping Hill Rd Kenilworth NJ 07033-1310

REIFENBERG, GERALD H, ORGANOMETALLIC CHEMISTRY. *Current Pos:* res chemist, Pennwalt Corp, 73-78, tech mgr plastic additives, 79-91, staff chemist, Org Res & Develop, 91-93, RES SCIENTIST, ORG RES & DEVELOP, ELF ATOCHEM N AM, 93- *Personal Data:* b Brooklyn, NY, Jan 18, 31; m 60; c 2. *Educ:* City Col New York, BS, 55; NY Univ, PhD(chem), 62. *Prof Exp:* Anal chemist, Refining Unincorp, 55-57; chemist, NY Naval Shipyard, 57-58; teaching fel org chem, NY Univ, 58-59; chemist, Gen Chem Div, Allied Chem Corp, 61-62; res chemist, M&T Chem, Inc, NJ, 63-68, supvr specialty chem, 68-69; scientist, Am Cyanamid Co, 69-71; dir res, Magic Marker Corp, 71-73. *Concurrent Pos:* Instr, Rutgers Univ, 64-65 & Newark Col Eng, 65-67. *Mem:* Am Chem Soc; Sigma Xi. *Res:* Organometallic chemistry, especially organotins; radioisotopes in tracer work; organofluorine, organophosphorus and flame retardant chemistry; organic synthesis (amises, thio compounds). *Mailing Add:* 393 Dutch Neck Rd Hightstown NJ 08520

REIFENRATH, WILLIAM GERALD, DERMATOLOGY. *Current Pos:* RES CHEMIST, DIV CUTANEOUS HAZARDS, LETTERMAN ARMY INST RES, 76- *Personal Data:* b Crofton, Nebr, Mar 2, 47; m 79. *Educ:* Univ Nebr-Lincoln, BS, 69, MS, 72, PhD(med chem), 75. *Mem:* Am Chem Soc. *Res:* Interaction of chemicals with skin; animal and in vitro models and analytical procedures for studying mechanisms of percutaneous penetration. *Mailing Add:* Six Christopher Ct Novato CA 94947-2831

REIFF, GLENN AUSTIN, ELECTRONICS ENGINEERING. *Current Pos:* PROF IN RESIDENCE ENG TECH, UNIV SOUTHERN COLO, 78- *Personal Data:* b Newton, Kans, Nov 18, 23; m 47; c 2. *Educ:* US Naval Acad, BS, 45; US Naval Postgrad Sch, BS, 52, MS, 53. *Honors & Awards:* Except Serv Award, NASA, 71. *Prof Exp:* Officer, USN, 42-61; prog mgr & engr, NASA, 62-70; engr, US Dept Transp, 71-78. *Mem:* Sr mem Inst Elec & Electronics Engrs. *Mailing Add:* Garmark Serv 59 Villa Dr Pueblo CO 81001

REIFF, HARRY ELMER, ORGANIC CHEMISTRY. *Current Pos:* RETIRED. *Personal Data:* b Allentown, Pa, Apr 19, 24; m 47, Helen White; c Harry, David & Thomas. *Educ:* Lehigh Univ, BSChE, 49, MS, 50; Univ Minn, PhD(org chem), 55. *Prof Exp:* Asst, Lehigh Univ, 49-50; jr chemist, Merck & Co, Inc, 50-52,; asst, Univ Minn, 52-54; sr chemist, Smith Kline & French Labs, 55-58, group leader, 58-60, asst sect head, 60-62, head org chem sect, 62-67, dir chem support & lab animal sci, Res & Develop Div, 67-72, dir phys sci mfg & planning, 72-78, dir tech planning, 78-81, dir tech assurance, 81-84; consult, 84-86. *Mem:* Fel AAAS; Am Chem Soc; fel Am Inst Chem; Sigma Xi. *Res:* Physical sciences research and development involving pharmaceuticals and drugs, particularly synthetic organic chemistry. *Mailing Add:* 1601 Clair Martin Pl Ambler PA 19002

REIFF, PATRICIA HOFER, MAGNETOSPHERIC PHYSICS. *Current Pos:* asst prof magnetospheric physics, 76-81, ASSOC RES SCIENTIST, CTR SPACE PHYSICS, RICE UNIV, 81-, ASST CHMN, DEPT SPACE PHYSICS & ASTRON, 79- *Personal Data:* b Oklahoma City, Okla, Mar 14, 50; m 76. *Educ:* Okla State Univ, BS, 71; Rice Univ, MS, 74, PhD(space physics, astron), 75. *Prof Exp:* Res assoc magnetospheric physics, Rice Univ, 75; Nat Acad Sci-Nat Res Coun resident res assoc magnetospheric physics, Marshall Space Flight Ctr, NASA, 75-76. *Concurrent Pos:* US deleg, Int Union Geod & Geophys, 75 & 81; fac assoc, Nat Res Coun-Nat Acad Sci, 79, mem comt solar-terrestrial res, 79- *Mem:* Am Geophys Union; AAAS; Sigma Xi; Audubon Soc. *Res:* Study of solar wind, magnetosphere and ionosphere interactions, theoretically and using on atmosphere explorer satellites -C and -D; low-energy electron experiment data and Apollo 14 charged particle data; co-investigator on high altitude plasma instrument on dynamic explorer spacecraft; computer simulation of magnetospheric convertion. *Mailing Add:* 4214 Southwestern St Houston TX 77005

REIFF, WILLIAM MICHAEL, INORGANIC CHEMISTRY. *Current Pos:* asst prof, 70-77, PROF CHEM, NORTHEASTERN UNIV, 78- *Personal Data:* b Binghamton, NY, Mar 9, 42; m 67; c 2. *Educ:* State Univ NY Binghamton, AB, 64; Syracuse Univ, PhD(chem), 68. *Prof Exp:* NSF fel & fac assoc chem & physics, Univ Tex, Austin, 68-70. *Concurrent Pos:* Vis scientist, Francis Bitter Nat Magnetic Lab. *Mem:* Am Chem Soc. *Res:* Physical inorganic chemistry; magnetically perturbed Mossbauer spectroscopy; magnetochemistry; electronic structure of coordination compounds and solid state materials. *Mailing Add:* Dept Chem Northeastern Univ Boston MA 02115-5096

REIFFEL, LEONARD, PHYSICS. *Current Pos:* CHIEF EXEC OFFICER, EXELAR CORP, 92- *Personal Data:* b Chicago, Ill, Sept 30, 27; m 71; c 2. *Educ:* Ill Inst Technol, BSc, 47, MSc, 48, PhD, 53. *Honors & Awards:* IR-100 Award, 70, 72, 73, 85. *Prof Exp:* Physicist, Perkin-Elmer Corp, 48; eng physicist, Univ Chicago, Inst Nuclear Studies, 48-49; dir, Physics Res, Ill Inst Technol Res Inst, 49-63, vpres, Physics Div, 63-65; chmn bd, Instruct Dynamics Inc, 65-81; chmn bd, Interand Corp, 69-91. *Concurrent Pos:* Consult & dep dir Apollo Pro, NASA Headquarters, 65-70, tech dir, Manned Space Flight Exper Bd, 66-70; sci ed, WBBM-CBS Radio Chicago, 71-72; host Backyard Safari, WBBM-TV, 71-73; sci ed & feature broadcaster, WEEI-CBS Radio, Boston, 65-75; syndicated news columnist, Universal Sci News, 66-72, Los Angeles Times Syndicate, 72-78; sci consult, CBS Network, 67-71; consult, Korean Govt Estab Atomic Energy Res Prog, 58-60, US Army, 79. *Mem:* Fel Am Phys Soc; AAAS; Sigma Xi. *Res:* Research and development of science. *Mailing Add:* 602 Deming Pl Chicago IL 60614. *Fax:* 773-871-0171

REIFFEN, BARNEY, ELECTRICAL ENGINEERING. *Current Pos:* staff mem, 55-61, group leader, 61-73, DIV HEAD, LINCOLN LAB, MASS INST TECHNOL, 73- *Personal Data:* b Brooklyn, NY, Oct 5, 27; m 50; c 2. *Educ:* Cooper Union, BS, 49; Polytech Inst Brooklyn, MS, 53; Mass Inst Technol, PhD(elec eng), 60. *Prof Exp:* Engr, Harvey-Wells Electronics, Inc, 51-53 & Balco Res Labs, 53-55. *Concurrent Pos:* Prin assoc med, Beth Israel Hosp, Harvard Med Sch, 69-73. *Mem:* Sr mem Inst Elec & Electronics Engrs. *Res:* Satellite communications systems; information systems. *Mailing Add:* 26 Peacock Farm Rd Lexington MA 02173

REIFFENSTEIN, RHODERIC JOHN, pharmacology; deceased, see previous edition for last biography

REIF-LEHRER, LIANE, BIOCHEMISTRY. *Current Pos:* PRES, ERIMON ASSOCS, 85- *Personal Data:* b Vienna, Austria, Nov 14, 34; US citizen; m 60, Sherwin; c Damon & Erica. *Educ:* Barnard Col, Columbia Univ, BA, 56; Univ Calif, Berkeley, PhD(phys org chem), 60. *Prof Exp:* Staff scientist, Res & Adv Develop Div, Avco Corp, Mass, 60-62; res fel, Harvard Med Sch, 63-66, instr ophthal res, 66-71, from asst to assoc prof biochem ophthal, 71-85, dir, Off Acad Careers, 81-82. *Concurrent Pos:* NIH fel, 64-66, res grant, 68-85; staff scientist, Boston Biomed Res Inst, Harvard Univ, 72-75; sr scientist, Eye Res Inst, 75-85; mem grant rev bd, NIH, 76-78; consult; vis scientist, Inst Ophthal, London, 78-79. *Res:* Effects of excitotoxic amino acids on neural retina; control mechanisms in animal cells; biochemical controls in the normal and diseased retina; effects of ingestion of excess monosodium glutamate on humans; grant application writing, expository writing, time management, and author of over 50 publications. *Mailing Add:* Erimon Assocs PO Box 645 Belmont MA 02178

REIFLER, CLIFFORD BRUCE, PSYCHIATRY, MEDICAL ADMINISTRATION. *Current Pos:* prof health serv, psychiat, prev med & community health & dir, 70-94, EMER PROF PSYCHIAT & HEALTH SERV & EMER DIR UNIV HEALTH SERV, UNIV ROCHESTER, 94- *Personal Data:* b Chicago, Ill, Dec 28, 31; m 54, Barbara Karmuth; c Margery (Kimbrough), Cindy & Angela (Jones). *Educ:* Univ Chicago, AB, 51; Northwestern Univ, Evanston, BS, 53; Yale Univ, MD, 57; Univ NC, Chapel Hill, MPH, 67. *Honors & Awards:* Edward Hitchcock Award, Am Col Health Asn, 81, Ruth Boynton Award, 88. *Prof Exp:* USPHS fel & resident psychiat, Strong Mem Hosp, Rochester, NY, 58-61; from instr to assoc prof, Sch Med, Univ NC, Chapel Hill, 63-70, from asst prof to assoc prof ment health, Sch Pub Health, 68-70. *Concurrent Pos:* Assoc physician-in-chg psychiat, Student Health Serv, Univ NC, Chapel Hill, 63-67, sr psychiatrist, 67-70; consult psychiat, Rochester Inst Technol, 76-83; interim vpres student affairs, Univ Rochester, 80-81; mem, Vis Comt, Harvard Univ Health Serv, 78-84; med dir, Strong Mem Hosp, 83-85; assoc dean clin affairs, Sch Med & Dent, Univ Rochester, 83-85, actg chmn, Dept Health Serv, 83-85. *Mem:* Fel Am Col Physician Execs; fel Am Pub Health Asn; fel Am Psychiat Asn; fel Am Col Health Asn (pres, 76-77); Am Acad Med Dirs; Int Union Sch & Univ Health & Med (vpres, 85-88). *Res:* Psychiatric epidemiology; health care delivery systems. *Mailing Add:* Univ Rochester Rochester NY 14642. *Fax:* 716-275-5353; *E-Mail:* reifler@medinfo.rochester.edu

REIFSCHNEIDER, WALTER, ORGANIC CHEMISTRY. *Current Pos:* CONSULT, 93- *Personal Data:* b Vienna, Austria, July 29, 26; nat US; m 59, Hertha Eder; c Martin. *Educ:* Univ Vienna, PhD(chem), 53. *Prof Exp:* Res assoc, Univ Ill, 53-57; res chemist, Dow Chem Co, 57-61, group leader, 61-70, assoc scientist, 70-81, res scientist, 81-90; fel, Dowelanco, 91-93. *Mem:* AAAS; Am Chem Soc; fel Sci Res Soc Am. *Res:* General organic synthesis; heterocycles; sulfur compounds; pesticide chemistry; natural products. *Mailing Add:* 3538 Bayberry Dr Walnut Creek CA 94598

REIFSNIDER, KENNETH LEONARD, MATERIAL SCIENCE, MECHANICS. *Current Pos:* From asst prof to assoc prof eng mech, 68-75, PROF ENG MECH, VA POLYTECH INST & STATE UNIV, 75-, CHMN MAT ENG SCI PROG, 71- *Personal Data:* b Baltimore, Md, Feb 19, 40; m 63; c 2. *Educ:* Western Md Col, BA, 63; Johns Hopkins Univ, BES, 64, MSE, 65, PhD(metall), 68. *Concurrent Pos:* NATO mat sci consult, 69 & 78; sabbatical leave, Univ Calif, Livermore, 81. *Mem:* Am Inst Mining, Metall & Petrol Engrs; Am Soc Metals; Am Soc Testing & Mat. *Res:* Composite materials; nondestructive testing and evaluation; mechanics of inhomogeneous deformation including fatigue and fracture; continuum theories of material defects. *Mailing Add:* 2127 Woodland Hills Dr Blacksburg VA 24060

REIFSNYDER, WILLIAM EDWARD, FOREST METEOROLOGY. *Current Pos:* from asst prof to assoc prof, Yale Univ, 55-65, prof forest meteorol, 65-90, pub health, 67-90, EMER PROF FOREST METEOROL, YALE UNIV, 90- *Personal Data:* b Ridgway, Pa, Mar 29, 24; wid; c Rita, Cheryl & Gawain. *Educ:* NY Univ, BS, 44; Univ Calif, MF, 49; Yale Univ, PhD(forest meteorol), 54. *Honors & Awards:* Achievement Award, Am Meteorol Soc. *Prof Exp:* Meteorologist, Calif Forest & Range Exp Sta, 51-54. *Concurrent Pos:* Mem & chmn, Adv Comt Climate, US Weather Bur, Nat Acad Sci-Nat Res Coun, 57-63, mem sci task force atmospheric sci, 61, panel educ, Comt Atmospheric Sci, 62-64, chmn, Adv Comt Biometeorol; vis scientist, Soc Am Foresters-NSF, 61-65 & 70, assoc ed, Can J Forest Res, 71-; vis prof, Univ Munich, 68; consult forest meteorol, World Meteorol Orgn, 73, chmn working group on the appln of meteorol to forestry, 75-80; ed-in-chief, Agr & Forest Metrol Int J, 80-94; vis scientist, Swed Univ Agr Sci, 81; sr res sci, Nat Oceanic & Atmospheric Admin, 84-85, vpres, Int Soc Biometrol, 84-88. *Mem:* Fel AAAS; Soc Am Foresters; Am Meteorol Soc; Int Soc Biometeorol; Sigma Xi. *Res:* Energy budgets; air pollution meteorology; climate variability and change. *Mailing Add:* HC 81 Questa NM 87556. *Fax:* 505-586-1151; *E-Mail:* william.reifsnyder@yale.edu

REIGEL, EARL WILLIAM, COMPUTER ARCHITECTURE, SYSTEM INTEGRATION. *Current Pos:* PVT CONSULT, 92- *Personal Data:* b Summit Hill, Pa, Aug 18, 35; m 55, Joan C Fair; c Daryl, Craig, Doug, Kevin, Sean & Melissa. *Educ:* Pa State Univ, BS, 59, MS, 61; Univ Pa, PhD, 69. *Prof Exp:* Res asst comput software & hardware, Pa State Univ, 59-61; sr engr, Burroughs Corp, 61-64; sr programmer comput software, Gen Elec, 64-67; mgr comput archit, Adv Develop, Burroughs Unisys Syst Eng, 67-80, dir comput res, Paoli Res Ctr, 80-86, dir comput eng, 86-88, dir advan technol, 88-92. *Concurrent Pos:* Adj prof, Univ Pa, 72-82 & Villanova Univ, 78-82; bd adv, Widener Univ, 81-87; eval bd, Adv Tech Ctr Southeast Pa, 85-88; nat lectr, Asn Comput Mach, 72; distinguished visitor, Inst Elec & Electronics Engrs, 72. *Mem:* Asn Comput Mach; fel Inst Elec & Electronics Engrs. *Res:* Computer architecture: parallelism-algorithms and software to identify parallelism and hardware to exploit it; microprogramming-hardware architectures and their use: emulation and application adaptation; artificial intelligence and application specific languages. *Mailing Add:* RR 1 Downingtown PA 19335

REIHER, HAROLD FREDERICK, ACOUSTICS. *Current Pos:* res engr, 57-64, vpres, 64-89, PRES, GEIGER & HAMME, INC, 89- *Personal Data:* b Detroit, Mich, July 8, 27; m 53, Marvel Sackett; c Linda G, Laura M & Lisa M. *Educ:* Univ Mich, BS, 50. *Prof Exp:* Lab asst, Eng Res Inst, Univ Mich, 49-51, res assoc, 51-56, assoc res engr, 56-57. *Mem:* Inst Elec & Electronics Engrs; Am Soc Test & Mat. *Res:* Architectural acoustics; measurement and control of sound and vibration; evaluation of acoustical properties and performance of materials, structures and equipment; electronic instrumentation. *Mailing Add:* 1835 Knight Rd Ann Arbor MI 48103-9303

REILING, GILBERT HENRY, ENGINEERING PHYSICS. *Current Pos:* RETIRED. *Personal Data:* b St Paul, Minn, Sept 19, 28; m 51; c 8. *Educ:* Col St Thomas, BS, 51; Univ NDak, MS, 52; Univ Mo, PhD(physics), 57. *Prof Exp:* Instr physics, Univ Mo, 53; physicist, Gen Elec Co, 57-61, mgr eng, Lighting Res & Tech Serv, 61-90. *Concurrent Pos:* Lectr, Siena Col, 58- *Mem:* Am Phys Soc; Inst Elec & Electronics Engrs; fel Illum Eng Soc. *Res:* Optical properties of solid state materials; fundamental processes in low pressure arcs. *Mailing Add:* 12370 Raymond Dr Chardon OH 44024

REILLY, BERNARD EDWARD, PLASMID BIOLOGY, VIROLOGY. *Current Pos:* vis prof genetics, 69-71, asst prof, 72-75, ASSOC PROF MICROBIOL, UNIV MINN, SCH DENT, MINNEAPOLIS, 75- *Personal Data:* b Meadville, Pa, June 9, 35; m 70. *Educ:* Westminster Col, BS, 58; Case Western Reserv Univ, PhD(microbiol), 65. *Prof Exp:* Res fel microbiol, Univ Minn, Minneapolis, 62-65; res assoc microbiol, Scripps Clin & Res Found, 65-68; asst prof biol, NMex State Univ, 68-69. *Res:* Bacteriophage and microbial genetics, viral and post transcriptional function modification of proteins; viral assemlidy; viral assemlidy. *Mailing Add:* 632 SE Third Ave Minneapolis MN 55414

REILLY, CHARLES AUSTIN, CHEMICAL PHYSICS. *Current Pos:* RETIRED. *Personal Data:* b Summerside, PEI, May 18, 16; nat US; m 42, Helen Warner. *Educ:* Dalhousie Univ, BSc, 39, MSc, 40; Harvard Univ, AM, 46, PhD(chem physics), 50. *Prof Exp:* Asst res physicist, Nat Res Coun Can, 40-43; asst prof chem, Dalhousie Univ, 48-51; physicist, Belleaire, Shell Develop Co, 51-80, sr staff res physicist, 80-85. *Mem:* Fel Am Phys Soc; Am Chem Soc; fel Am Inst Chemists. *Res:* Molecular beams; nuclear magnetic resonance; field emission spectroscopy. *Mailing Add:* 1754 S Pebble Beach Blvd Sun City Center FL 33573-5751

REILLY, CHARLES BERNARD, ORGANIC CHEMISTRY, POLYMER CHEMISTRY. *Current Pos:* RETIRED. *Personal Data:* b New York, NY, Dec 7, 29; m 55; c 6. *Educ:* Queen's Col, NY, BS, 53; Univ Cincinnati, MS, 55, PhD(chem), 57. *Prof Exp:* Res & develop chemist, Gen Elec Co, 57-65, sr chemist, 65-66, mgr process develop, 66-69; group leader, Goodyear Tire & Rubber Co, 69-80, sr chemist rubber compoundings, urethane applns, 80-91. *Mem:* Am Chem Soc; AAAS. *Res:* Polymer chemistry specializing in thermoset resins as epoxies and urethanes; organic synthesis of polymer intermediates; physical properties of polymers. *Mailing Add:* 3256 Linden St Uniontown OH 44685-9353

REILLY, CHARLES CONRAD, HOST-PARASITE INTERACTIONS. *Current Pos:* RES PLANT PATHOL, USDA, SOUTHEASTERN FRUIT & TREE NUT RES LAB, BYRON, GA, 80- *Personal Data:* b Cornwall, NY, Dec 3, 40; m 61; c 5. *Educ:* Auston Peay State Univ, BS, 71; Univ Ill, MS, 74, PhD(plant path), 77. *Prof Exp:* Grad Res Asst plant path, dept plant path, Univ Ill, 71-77, res assoc, dept hort, 77-78; res assoc, USDA, Am Res Serv, Metab & Radiation Res Lab, 78-80. *Concurrent Pos:* Adj fac, Fort Valley State Col, Ga, 80-; Adj prof, dept plant path, Univ Ga, Athens, 83- *Mem:* Sigma Xi; Am Phytopath Soc. *Res:* Production limiting problems of pecan trees; chemical or biological control of diseases and insects; physiological interactions of the host and parasites; diseases of pecan. *Mailing Add:* USDA-ARS Southeastern Fruit & Tree Nut Res Lab 111 Dunbar Rd Byron GA 31008

REILLY, CHRISTOPHER ALOYSIUS, JR, VIROLOGY. *Current Pos:* Fel virol, Argonne Nat Lab, 68-69, asst microbiologist, 69-73, dep prog mgr, Synfuels Environ Res Prog, 80-85, assoc div dir & dir, Ctr Environ Res, 87-89, MICROBIOLOGIST, ARGONNE NAT LAB, 73- & DIV DIR, ENVIRON RES DIV, 89- *Personal Data:* b Tucson, Ariz, Aug 8, 42; m 68, Georgia K Cole; c Colleen, Megan & Erin. *Educ:* Loyola Univ, Los Angeles, BS, 64; Univ Ariz, MS, 66, PhD(microbiol), 68. *Concurrent Pos:* Adj assoc prof biol sci, Northern Ill Univ, 75- *Mem:* Am Soc Microbiol; Soc Toxicol; Sci Exp Biol & Med; AAAS; Sigma Xi. *Res:* Characterization of the environmental effects of chemical pollutants, with particular emphasis on carcinogenesis and chemical toxicology. *Mailing Add:* Environ Res Div Bldg 203 Argonne Nat Lab 9700 S Cass Ave Argonne IL 60439

REILLY, CHRISTOPHER F, pharmacology, for more information see previous edition

REILLY, DOROTHEA ELEANOR, FERMENTATION PROCESS DEVELOPMENT FOR THE PRODUCTION OF HETEROLOGOUS PROTEINS, IDENTIFYING AND CHARACTERIZING ECHERICHIA COLI PROTEASES. *Current Pos:* sr res assoc, 83-91, SCIENTIST, GENENTECH, INC, 91- *Personal Data:* b Hackensack, NJ, May 26, 16. *Educ:* Univ Va, BA, 78, MS, 80. *Prof Exp:* Scientist, Genex Corp, 80-83. *Mem:* Am Chem Soc; Am Soc Microbiol. *Res:* Fermentation processes for the production of heterologous proteins in Echerichia coli; identifying and characterizing proteases from Echerichia coli. *Mailing Add:* 334 Mt Vernon Ave San Francisco CA 94112-3634

REILLY, EDWIN DAVID, JR, COMPUTER SCIENCE, PHYSICS. *Current Pos:* dir, Comput Ctr, State Univ NY, 65-70, chmn dept, 67-73, assoc prof, 67-91, EMER ASSOC PROF COMPUT SCI, STATE UNIV NY, ALBANY, 91- *Personal Data:* b Troy, NY, Apr 27, 32; m 54, Jean M Sayers; c David, Michael, Ellen, Daniel, Peter & Diane. *Educ:* Rensselaer Polytech Inst, BS, 54, MS, 58, PhD(physics), 69. *Prof Exp:* Mathematician, Knolls Atomic Power Lab, Gen Elec Co, 56-61, mgr digital anal & comp, 61-65. *Concurrent Pos:* Supvr, Town of Niskayuna, NY, 70-79, 89-; pres, Cybernetic Info Systs, 80- *Mem:* AAAS; Am Phys Soc; Sigma Xi. *Res:* Application of computers to the humanities; computer language; cryptography; scattering of electromagnetic waves from nonspherical targets. *Mailing Add:* 870 Cunningham Ct Niskayuna NY 12309-6302

REILLY, EMMETT B, PATHOLOGY, HEMATOLOGY. *Current Pos:* CLIN PROF, UNIV SOUTHERN CALIF, 65- *Personal Data:* b Los Angeles, Calif, Aug 19, 20; m 55, Betty Wicks; c David, Margaret, Eliz, John & Kathleen. *Educ:* Loyola Univ, Calif, BS, 42; Univ Southern Calif, MD, 46; Am Bd Path, dipl, 52, cert clin path, 56, cert hemat, 63, cert radioisotopic path, 74. *Prof Exp:* Chief clin path, Vet Admin Hosp, Long Beach, 50-57; chief pathologist, Orange County Hosp, 57-65, Daniel Freeman Hosp, 65-90; pathologist, Harbor Univ Calif, Los Angeles, Med Ctr, 91- *Concurrent Pos:* Consult, Vet Admin Hosp, Long Beach, Calif, 57- *Mem:* Fel Am Soc Clin Pathologists; NY Acad Sci; fel Col Am Pathologists. *Res:* Coagulation of blood; neoplasia. *Mailing Add:* Dept Path Harbor UCLA Med Ctr Torrance CA 90501

REILLY, EUGENE PATRICK, ORGANIC CHEMISTRY. *Current Pos:* SR RES SCIENTIST RESOURCE RECOVERY, AM CAN CO, 76- *Personal Data:* b New York, NY, Mar 12, 39; m 69; c 2. *Educ:* St Peter's Col, NJ, BS, 63; Fordham Univ, PhD(org chem), 68. *Prof Exp:* Res chemist plastics, acrylics & acetals, E I du Pont de Nemours Co, Inc, Wilmington, 67-71; develop chemist polyesters, Plastics Dept, Gen Elec Co, Pittsfield, Mass, 71-73; res scientist terpen chem, Union Camp Corp, Princeton, 73-76. *Mem:* Am Inst Chem Engrs; Tech Asn Pulp & Paper Indust. *Res:* Plastics especially acrylics, acetals, polyesters, thermosets; laboratory to plant scale; upgrading of natural products especially terpenes and talloils to useful products; resource recovery, utilization of natural organic waste materials from paper making processes. *Mailing Add:* 243 Glenn Ave Trenton NJ 08648

REILLY, FRANK DANIEL, HUMAN ANATOMY, MEDICAL PHYSIOLOGY. *Current Pos:* assoc prof, 78-85, PROF ANAT, SCH MED, WVA UNIV, 85- *Personal Data:* b Fairborn, Ohio, Aug 20, 49; m 69; c 1. *Educ:* Ohio State Univ, BS, 71; Univ Cincinnati, PhD(anat), 75. *Prof Exp:* Asst prof anat, Col Med, Univ Cincinnati, 75-78. *Mem:* Am Asn Anatomists; Microvascular Soc; Sigma Xi; AAAS. *Res:* Hematology and microvascular physiology; morphology and pharmacology. *Mailing Add:* Dept Anat WVa Univ Sch Med Byrd Health Sci Ctr PO Box 9128 Morgantown WV 26505-9128

REILLY, HUGH THOMAS, PHYSICAL CHEMISTRY, CHEMICAL ENGINEERING. *Current Pos:* PRIN INVESTR, RES ENG CORP, 87- *Personal Data:* b New York, NY, Apr 19, 25. *Educ:* St Peter's Col, NJ, BS, 50; Polytech Inst NY, MS, 53. *Prof Exp:* Res & teaching fel, Polytech Inst Brooklyn, 50-51; proj engr, Thiokol Chem Corp, Elkton, Md, 57-59, mgr Space Propulsion Systs, 59-60, mgr New Prod Develop, 60-63; tech adv & proj engr, Land Warfare Lab, US Army Chem & Armaments Mat Command, 63-74, chief lethal group, Edgewood Arsenal, 74-76, team leader pipeline gas prog, 76-78, chief, Dept Energy Support Off & Supvry Chem Engr, 78-81, dir, Environ Technol Chem Res & Develop Ctr, 81-87. *Mem:* Fel Am Inst Aeronaut & Astronaut; Am Chem Soc; fel Am Inst Chemists. *Res:* Atmospheric sensing; chemical process; chemical detection; pollution; cloud physics, coal process. *Mailing Add:* 115 Eleanor St Elkton MD 21921-6150

REILLY, JAMES PATRICK, PHYSICAL CHEMISTRY, ANALYTICAL CHEMISTRY. *Current Pos:* from asst prof to assoc prof, 79-86, PROF CHEM, IND UNIV, 87- *Personal Data:* b Mt Vernon, NY, Aug 29, 50. *Educ:* Princeton Univ, AB, 72; Cambridge Univ, CPGS, 73; Univ Calif, Berkeley, PhD(chem), 77. *Prof Exp:* Guest researcher, Max Planck Inst, Garching, 77-79. *Concurrent Pos:* Alfred P Sloan fel, Alfred P Sloan Found, 82. *Mem:* Sigma Xi; Am Chem Soc; Am Phys Soc; Am Soc Mat Sci. *Res:* Probing optical transitions in transient species and excited molecular states; investigation of the chemistry of excited molecules; ultrasensitive methods of laser spectroscopy. *Mailing Add:* Dept Chem Ind Univ Bloomington IN 47405. *Fax:* 812-855-8300; *E-Mail:* reilly@indiana.edu

REILLY, JAMES PATRICK, AERONAUTICAL & ASTRONNAUTICAL ENGINEERING. *Current Pos:* VPRES SCI & ENG, W J SCHAFER ASSOC INC, 78- *Personal Data:* b Jersey City, NJ, Nov 17, 37; m 62; c 4. *Educ:* Univ Detroit, BAE, 61; Mass Inst Technol, MS(aeronaut & astronaut) & MS(mech eng), 63, ScD, 67. *Honors & Awards:* Consejo Superior Investigaciones Cientificas, Spain, 90. *Prof Exp:* Res staff mem, Div Sponsored Res, Mass Inst Technol, 67-68; vpres appl technol, Avco Everett Res Lab, 68-78. *Concurrent Pos:* Lectr, Mass Inst Technol, 72- *Mem:* Assoc fel Am Inst Aeronaut & Astronaut; Sigma Xi; Soc Photo Optical Instrumentation Engrs. *Res:* Experimental & theoretical aspects of high power repetitively; pulsed electrically excited gas lasers; charged particle accelerator technology; free electron lasers; particle beam technology; high power microwave emitters; radiometric sensors; laser radars; gas discharges. *Mailing Add:* Appl Phys Lab Johns Hopkins Univ John Hopkins Rd Laurel MD 20723

REILLY, JAMES PATRICK, GEODESY, SURVEYING. *Current Pos:* PROF & DEPT HEAD SURV, NMEX STATE UNIV, 90- *Personal Data:* b Barnesboro, Pa, Nov 30, 33; m 56, Faith; c James, Michael, Jeffrey & Sean. *Educ:* Pa State Univ, BS, 56; Ohio State Univ, MS, 69, PhD(geodetic sci), 74. *Prof Exp:* Assoc prof civil eng, Iowa State Univ, 74-77; nat prod mgr, Wild Heerbrugg Inst, Inc, 77-83; pres, Dudley-Reilly Assocs, 83-86 & Geodetic Enterprises, Inc, 86-90. *Mem:* Am Cong Surv & Mapping; Am Soc Photogram & Remote Sensing; Inst Navig. *Res:* Surveying; author of various publications. *Mailing Add:* 960 Maple St Las Cruces NM 88001. *Fax:* 505-646-3549

REILLY, JAMES WILLIAM, CHEMICAL ENGINEERING, PHYSICAL CHEMISTRY. *Current Pos:* MGR RES & DEVELOP, ABB LUMMUS CREST INC, 87- *Personal Data:* b Jersey City, NJ, Oct 18, 35; m 56; c 4. *Educ:* Seton Hall Col, BS, 56; Stevens Inst Technol, MS, 59, ScD(chem eng), 65. *Prof Exp:* Develop engr, Turbomotor Div, Curtiss-Wright Corp, 56-57; sr res engr, Tex-US Chem Co, 57-60; proj engr, Plastics Div, Koppers Co, 60;

teaching asst, Mass Inst Technol, 60-61; asst prof chem & chem eng, Newark Col Eng, 61-65; sr develop engr, Bloomfield Div, Eng Develop Ctr, Lummus Co, Combustion Eng, Inc, 65-74, prin engr, 74-81, mgr proj eng, 81-86. *Mem:* Am Inst Chem Engrs; Sigma Xi. *Res:* Engineering process research and development for proprietary processes in catalyst, hydrogenation and process design/scale up. *Mailing Add:* 69 Woodland Dr Roselle NJ 07203-2466

REILLY, JOSEPH F, PHARMACOLOGY, TOXICOLOGY. *Current Pos:* RETIRED. *Personal Data:* b Waucoma, Iowa, May 14, 15; m 48, Joan M Cowie; c Joseph, Joan, John, Elizabeth & Andrew. *Educ:* Univ Ill, BA, 37; Harvard Univ, MA, 39; Univ Chicago, PhD(pharmacol), 47. *Prof Exp:* Chemist, Chem Res Dept, Armour Labs, Ill, 39-43; res assoc, Anti-Malarial Prog & asst pharmacol, Univ Chicago, 43-47; pharmacologist, US Army Chem Ctr, Md, 47-48; res fel, Med Sch, Cornell Univ, 48-49, from instr to asst prof pharmacol, 49-54, asst prof pharmacol & psychiat, 54-62; chief, Pharmacodyn Sect, Div Pharmacol, Bur Sci, US Food & Drug Admin, DC, 63-70, chief, Drug Bioanalysis Br, Div Res & Testing, Ctr Drug Eval & Res, 70-92. *Concurrent Pos:* Chief pharmacologist, Payne Whitney Clin, NY Hosp-Cornell Med Ctr, 54-62; consult, Coun Drugs, AMA, 58 & 65; collabr, US Pharmacopoeia Stand, 70; actg dep dir, Div Drug Biol, Bur Drugs, US Food & Drug Admin, Washington, DC, 78-79. *Mem:* Am Soc Pharmacol & Exp Therapeut; Soc Toxicol; Soc Exp Biol & Med; Harvey Soc; Sigma Xi. *Res:* Anti-malarials; plasma enzymes; diethylstilbestrol-enzymes; acetylstrophanthidin-fluoroacetate-heart; experimental arrythmias; catecholamines-psychiatric patients; reserpine; glutathione reductase-carbon tetrachloride; shellfish toxin; desmethylimipramine toxicity; age, sex, ulcers; age-catecholamines; organochlorine and monosodium glutamate effects. *Mailing Add:* 9623 Alta Vista Terr Bethesda MD 20814

REILLY, KEVIN DENIS, SOFTWARE SYSTEMS & ARTIFICIAL INTELLIGENCE, BIOMATHEMATICS. *Current Pos:* PROF COMPUT & INFO SCI, UNIV ALA, BIRMINGHAM, 70- *Personal Data:* b Omaha, Nebr, Sept 12, 37; m 61; c 3. *Educ:* Creighton Univ, BS, 59; Univ Nebr, Lincoln, MS, 62; Univ Chicago, PhD(math biol), 66. *Prof Exp:* Res scientist, Univ Calif, Los Angeles, 66-70, lectr comp sci, 69-70. *Concurrent Pos:* Sr lectr, Sch Bus, Univ Southern Calif, 69-70; adj prof, Develop Psychol; mem, Ling Prog. *Mem:* Inst Elec & Electronics Engrs; Asn Comput Mach; Soc Comput Simulation Int. *Res:* Digital modeling and simulation, discrete-event programming systems; artificial intelligence systems, natural intelligence; software systems; programming systems; mathematical biology; biophysics. *Mailing Add:* Dept Comput & Info Sci Univ Ala UAB Sta Birmingham AL 35294

REILLY, MARGARET ANNE, NEUROPHARMACOLOGY, PSYCHOPHARMACOLOGY. *Current Pos:* RES SCIENTIST, NATHAN KLINE INST PSYCHIAT RES, 66- *Personal Data:* b Port Chester, NY, 1937. *Educ:* Col New Rochelle, BA, 59; NY Med Col, MS, 78, PhD(pharmacol), 81. *Prof Exp:* Sr lab technician, Sloan-Kettering Inst, 59-64; lab & teaching biol asst, Hunter Col, City Univ NY, 65. *Concurrent Pos:* Adj assoc prof pharmacol, Sch Nursing, Col New Rochelle, 78-92; adj asst prof pharmacol, Concordia Col, Bronxville, 88-; mem, Coun Res Scientists, NY State Off Ment Health; instr pharmacol, Phillips Beth Israel Sch Nursing, New York, 92- *Mem:* Histamine Res Soc NAm (secy-treas, 80-); Asn Women Sci; Am Soc Pharmacol & Exp Therapeut; NY Acad Sci; Women Neurosci. *Res:* Investigations of the interactions of various substances such as aspartame and acetyl-L-carnitine with binding characteristics at central nervous system neurotransmitter receptor systems. *Mailing Add:* Nathans Kline Psychiat Res Inst Orangeburg NY 10962. *Fax:* 914-365-6107; *E-Mail:* reilly@nki

REILLY, MARGUERITE, protozoology, microbiology, for more information see previous edition

REILLY, MICHAEL HUNT, IONOSPHERIC RADIO PROPAGATION, DATA ANALYSIS. *Current Pos:* RES PHYSICIST MATH PHYSICS, NAVAL RES LAB, 66- *Personal Data:* b Rochester, NY, Dec 23, 39; m 65; c Daniel & Karen. *Educ:* Univ Rochester, BS, 61, PhD(solid state physics), 67. *Concurrent Pos:* Nat Acad Sci-Nat Res Coun fel, Naval Res Lab, 66-68. *Mem:* Inst Elect & Electronic Engrs; Am Geophys Union. *Res:* Software development of ionospheric propagation models and discrete inverse theory analysis of radio system data. *Mailing Add:* Code 8111 Naval Res Lab Washington DC 20375. *Fax:* 202-404-7234

REILLY, NORMAN RAYMUND, SEMIGROUPS, ORDERED ALGEBRAIC SYSTEMS. *Current Pos:* asst prof, 66-69, assoc prof, 69-74, chmn, 76-78, actg assoc vpres, 78-79, PROF MATH, SIMON FRASER UNIV, 74- *Personal Data:* b Glasgow, Scotland, Jan 30, 40; m 66; c 3. *Educ:* Univ Glasgow, BSc Hons, 61, PhD(math), 65. *Prof Exp:* Asst lectr math, Univ Glasgow, 64-65; vis asst prof math, Newcomb Col, Tulane Univ, New Orleans, 65-66. *Concurrent Pos:* Vis prof math, Monash Univ, Melbourne, Australia, 71. *Mem:* Can Math Soc; Am Math Soc; Soc Actuaries. *Res:* Algebra especially in the structure, representations and varieties of algebras. *Mailing Add:* Dept Math Simon Fraser Univ Burnaby BC V5A 1S6 Can

REILLY, PARK MCKNIGHT, STATISTICS, CHEMICAL ENGINEERING. *Current Pos:* prof 67-, DISTINGUISHED EMER PROF CHEM ENG, UNIV WATERLOO, 94- *Personal Data:* b Welland, Ont, May 14, 20; m 45; c 4. *Educ:* Univ Toronto, BASc, 43; Univ London, PhD(statist) & dipl, Imp Col, 62. *Prof Exp:* Jr chem engr, Welland Chem Works, 41-45; lectr chem eng, Ajax Div, Univ Toronto, 45-47; prin chem engr, Polysar Ltd, 47-67. *Concurrent Pos:* Adj prof, Univ Waterloo, 64-67; consult several chem industs, 67- *Mem:* Fel Can Soc Chem Eng; fel Royal Statist Soc. *Res:* Application of statistical methods to chemical engineering research and plant operation; design of experiments; model discrimination. *Mailing Add:* 48 Culpepper Dr Waterloo ON N2L 5L1 Can

REILLY, PATRICK J, RADIATION POLYMERIZATION, RADIATION GRAFTING. *Current Pos:* RES SCIENTIST, GOODYEAR TIRE & RUBBER CO, 63- *Personal Data:* b New York, NY, May 1, 36; m, Katherine; c Siobham, Nicholas & Ian. *Educ:* Mass Inst Technol, BS, 58; Trinity Col, Dublin, PhD(phys chem), 63; Akron Univ, MBA, 72. *Res:* Kinetics of polymerization, radiation induced polymerization, cationic polymerization and radiation curing of rubber; urethane chemistry, ultrasonic curing and rubber extrusion; polymer composites. *Mailing Add:* 275 Afton Ave Akron OH 44313

REILLY, PETER JOHN, CHEMICAL ENGINEERING. *Current Pos:* from assoc prof to prof, 74-92, DISTINGUISHED PROF CHEM ENG, IOWA STATE UNIV, 92- *Personal Data:* b Newark, NJ, Dec 26, 38; m 65, 76, Rae Messer; c Diane & Karen. *Educ:* Princeton Univ, AB, 60; Univ Pa, PhD(chem eng), 64. *Prof Exp:* Res engr, Org Chem Dept, Jackson Lab, E I du Pont de Nemours & Co, Inc, 64-68; asst prof chem eng, Univ Nebr, Lincoln, 68-74. *Concurrent Pos:* Invited prof, Swiss Fed Inst Tech, Lausanne, Switz, 83-84 & 92-93. *Mem:* fel Am Inst Chem Engrs. *Res:* Biochemical engineering; enzyme kinetics; agricultural residue utilization; carbohydrate chromatography. *Mailing Add:* Dept Chem Eng Iowa State Univ Ames IA 50011. *Fax:* 515-294-2689; *E-Mail:* reilly@iastate.edu

REILLY, RICHARD J, HEAT TRANSFER. *Current Pos:* VPRES BUS DEVELOP, KAVOURAS INC, 88- *Personal Data:* b La Crosse, Wis, Jan 15, 30; m 54, Betty A Neas; c Timothy. *Educ:* Univ Minn, BS, 51. *Honors & Awards:* USAF Systs Command Award, 63. *Prof Exp:* Jr res engr, Rosemount Res Facility, Univ Minn, 51; res engr, Aeronaut Res Div, Gen Mills, Inc, 51-54, Northrop Aircraft Inc, 54-57; sr develop engr, Aeronaut Div, Honeywell Inc, Minn, 57-60, sr res scientist fluid mech, Mil Prod Res, 60-63, prin res scientist, 63-64, supvr res, 64-65, res sect head, Systs & Res Ctr, 65-67, fluid sci res mgr, 67-69; exec vpres, Cytec Corp, 69-74; pres, Galileo Co, 74-88, Cuyuna Corp, 78- *Concurrent Pos:* Pvt consult, 59-64; consult lectr, Adv Group Aerospace Res & Develop, NATO, 66-70; dir, BMT, Inc, 76-79; adj instr, St Thomas Univ Bus Sch, 88-89. *Mem:* Assoc fel Am Inst Aeronaut & Astronaut. *Res:* Aerodynamics; compressible flow; boundary layer flows; supersonic inlets; fluidics; alternate energy sources; aircraft propulsion; flight testing techniques. *Mailing Add:* 1759 Venus Ave St Paul MN 55112. *Fax:* 612-882-4500; *E-Mail:* rjreilly@delphi.com

REILLY, THOMAS E, GROUND-WATER HYDROLOGY. *Current Pos:* HYDROLOGIST, US GEOL SURV, 75- *Personal Data:* b New York, NY. *Educ:* Villanova Univ, BCE, 74; Princeton Univ, MSE, 75; Polytech Univ, PhD(civil eng), 86. *Mem:* Am Geophys Union; Asn Ground Water Scientists & Engrs; Geol Soc Am. *Res:* Three-dimensional simulation; aquifer test analysis; solute transport; salt water - fresh water interaction in ground-water systems. *Mailing Add:* US Geol Surv 411 Nat Ctr Reston VA 20192

REILY, WILLIAM SINGER, ORGANIC CHEMISTRY, POLYMER CHEMISTRY. *Current Pos:* RETIRED. *Personal Data:* b Chicago, Ill, June 13, 24; m 51, Barbara; c David, Donald, Daniel, Diane, Dean & Dennis. *Educ:* Roosevelt Univ, BS, 48; De Paul Univ, MS, 50. *Prof Exp:* Develop chemist, Bauer & Black Lab, Kendall Co, 52-53; res chemist, Baxter Labs, Inc, 53-54; develop chemist, G D Searle Co, 54-57; proj engr, Amphenol Electronics Co, 57-58; develop chemist, Du Kane Corp, 58-67; proj leader, US Gypsum, 67-87. *Mem:* Am Chem Soc. *Res:* Applied and industrial chemistry; process and product development; trouble shooting and environmental testing. *Mailing Add:* 884 Horne Terr Des Plaines IL 60016-5971

REIM, ROBERT E, ELECTROCHEMISTRY. *Current Pos:* SR RES CHEMIST, DOW CHEM CO, 74- *Personal Data:* b Abrams, Wis. *Educ:* Univ Wis, OshKosh, BS, 71, Milwaukee, MS, 74. *Mem:* Am Chem Soc; Soc Appl Spectros; Sigma Xi. *Res:* Development and application of analytical techniques including electroanalytical chemistry, spectroscopy and chromatography. *Mailing Add:* 1307 Whitehall St Midland MI 48642

REIMAN, ALLAN H, THREE-DIMENSIONAL MAGNETOHYDRODYNAMICS, NUMERICAL ALGORITHM DEVELOPMENT. *Current Pos:* staff physicist II, 82-84, res physicist, 84-91, PRIN RES PHYSICIST, PLASMA PHYSICS LAB, PRINCETON UNIV, 91- *Personal Data:* b New York, NY, June 6, 49; c Jonathan. *Educ:* Harvard Univ, BA, 71; Princeton Univ, PhD(physics), 77. *Prof Exp:* Res assoc, Cornell Univ, 78-80, Univ Md, 80-81. *Concurrent Pos:* Consult, Sci Applns Inc, McLean, Va, 80-82; lectr prof, Dept Astrophys Sci, Princeton Univ, 94- *Mem:* Fel Am Phys Soc. *Res:* Theoretical and computational investigations of nonlinear three-dimensional magnetohydrodynamics. *Mailing Add:* 64 Cambridge Way Princeton Junction NJ 08550. *E-Mail:* reiman@pppl.gov

REIMANN, BERNHARD ERWIN FERDINAND, GENERAL BIOLOGY, GENERAL GEOLOGY. *Current Pos:* ENVIRON ADV, VILLAGE CAPITAN, LINCOLN CO, NMEX, 88- *Personal Data:* b Berlin, Ger, May 30, 22; m 49, Beate E Hedwig; c Joachim O. *Educ:* Free Univ Berlin, Dr rer nat, 59. *Prof Exp:* Scientist asst, Bot Inst, Marburg, 58-60; asst res biologist, Scripps Inst, Univ Calif, San Diego, 61-67, supvr electron microscope facil, 64-67; chief electron micros, William Beaumont Army Med Ctr, US Army, 67-87. *Concurrent Pos:* NSF grant, 65-67 & 68-69; assoc prof, NMex State Univ, 67-; assoc, Grad Fac, Univ Tex, El Paso, 68-71; assoc clin prof path, Tex Tech Med Sch. *Mem:* Emer fel AAAS; emer mem Electron Micros Soc Am. *Res:* Cytology and ultrastructure of mineral deposition in biological systems; histopathology diagnostic at ultrastructure level. *Mailing Add:* PO Box 44 Capitan NM 88316

REIMANN, ERWIN M, BIOCHEMISTRY. *Current Pos:* from asst prof to assoc prof, 70-82, PROF BIOCHEM, MED COL OHIO, TOLEDO, 82- *Personal Data:* b Parkston, SD, July 26, 42; m 61; c 2. *Educ:* Augustana Col, SDak, BA, 64; Univ Wis-Madison, PhD(biochem), 68. *Prof Exp:* Fel biochem, Univ Calif, Davis, 68-70. *Concurrent Pos:* Vis asst prof physiol, Vanderbilt Univ, Nashville, 74; vis scientist, Univ Wash, Seattle, 82-83 & 87. *Mem:* Sigma Xi; Am Chem Soc; AAAS; Am Soc Biol Chem; Protein Soc. *Res:* The role of protein kinases and phosphatases in cellular function, especially their roles in glycogen metabolism. *Mailing Add:* Dept Biochem & Molecular Biol Med Col Ohio Toledo OH 43699-0008. *Fax:* 419-382-7395; *E-Mail:* ereimann@opus.1arc.mco.edu

REIMANN, HANS, ORGANIC CHEMISTRY, REGULATORY AFFAIRS. *Current Pos:* RETIRED. *Personal Data:* b Vienna, Austria, Dec 4; nat US; m 57, Arline Robbins; c Robert M. *Educ:* Univ Calif, Los Angeles, BS, 51, PhD(chem), 57. *Prof Exp:* from chemist to sr chemist, Schering Corp, 57-68, unit head, 68-71, asst to dir, Chem & Microbiol Develop, 71-73, coordr, Corp Prod Develop, 73-74, mgr prod planning & control, 74-77, assoc dir, Tech Regulatory Doc & Actives Control, 78-80, dir, Regulatory Affairs-Tech, 80-87, assoc dir, Regulatory Affairs, 87-94. *Mem:* Am Chem Soc; Am Soc Microbiol; Regulatory Affairs Prof Soc. *Res:* Natural products; steroids; antibiotics. *Mailing Add:* 8 Rande Dr Wayne NJ 07470-5931

REIMCHEN, THOMAS EDWARD, FUNCTIONAL MORPHOLOGY. *Current Pos:* ADJ PROF, DEPT BIOL, UNIV VICTORIA, 85- *Personal Data:* b Wetaskiwin, Alta, July 25, 46; m, Sheila Douglas. *Educ:* Univ Alta, BSc, 70; Univ Liverpool, UK, PhD(marine ecol), 74. *Concurrent Pos:* Sessional lectr evolution & ichthyol, Univ Alta, 85-89, adj prof, 85-89. *Mem:* Soc Study Evolution. *Res:* Ecological and evolutionary causes for intrapopulation variability in morphological traits; evolution of Queen Charlotte Island biota. *Mailing Add:* 131 Thomas Rd Salt Spring Island BC V8K 1R2 Can. *Fax:* 250-559-8648; *E-Mail:* reim@uvvm.uvic.ca

REIMER, DAVID, MATHEMATICS. *Current Pos:* RESEARCHER MATH, RUTGERS UNIV. *Honors & Awards:* George Polya Prize, Soc Indust & Appl Math, 96. *Mailing Add:* Dept Math Middlesex County Col 155 Mill Rd Edison NJ 08837-3675

REIMER, DENNIS D, MATHEMATICS, COMPUTER SCIENCE. *Current Pos:* SR SYSTS ANALYST, 3-M CO, 83- *Personal Data:* b Corn, Okla, May 20, 40; m 61; c 2. *Educ:* Southwestern Okla State Univ, BSEd, 62; Okla State Univ, MS, 64; NTex State Univ, EdD(math), 69. *Prof Exp:* Instr, Southwestern Okla State Univ, 63-65, prof math, 67-83. *Mem:* Nat Coun Teachers Math; Math Asn Am. *Mailing Add:* 1526 Mockingbird Lane Weatherford OK 73096-2738

REIMER, DIEDRICH, GENETICS, ANIMAL SCIENCE. *Current Pos:* RETIRED. *Personal Data:* b Altona, Man, May 6, 25; US citizen; m 51; c 3. *Educ:* Univ Man, BScA, 50; Univ Minn, MS, 55, PhD(genetics, animal sci), 59. *Prof Exp:* Vet agr instr, US Dept Vet Affairs, 50-53; from instr to assoc prof, Univ Minn, 55-64; assoc prof animal sci, Univ Hawaii, 64-72, prof, 72-, animal scientist, Hawaii Inst Trop Agr & Human Resources, 74- *Concurrent Pos:* Supt, Hawaii Agr Exp Sta, Hawaii Br, 78-80. *Mem:* AAAS; Am Genetic Asn; Am Soc Animal Sci. *Res:* Improvement of beef cattle, swine and sheep through breeding methods; swine nutrition and livestock management; improvement of beef cattle production under tropical range conditions through the application of breeding methods; development of a synthetic line of beef cattle selected for improved reproduction, growth rate, carcass quality and adaptability to tropical environments. *Mailing Add:* PO Box 366 Kurtistown HI 96760

REIMER, KEITH A, CARDIAC PATHOLOGY, MYOCARDIAL ISCHEMIA & REPERFUSION. *Current Pos:* from asst prof to assoc prof, 75-88, head, cardiovasc path, 89-94, PROF PATH, DUKE UNIV MED CTR, 88- *Personal Data:* b Beatrice, Nebr, Apr 10, 45; m 66, Susan K Stucky. *Educ:* Northwestern Univ, PhD(exp path), 71, MD, 72. *Prof Exp:* Instr path, Northwestern Univ Med Sch, 72-75. *Concurrent Pos:* Coun mem, Int Soc Heart Res, 89-, secy, Am Sect, 85-94. *Mem:* Int Soc Heart Res; Soc Cardiovasc Path; Am Heart Asn; US & Can Asn Path. *Res:* Mechanism(s) of myocardial responses to lethal or sublethal cell injury caused by ischemia and/or reperfusion. *Mailing Add:* Dept Path Box 3712 Duke Univ Med Ctr Durham NC 27710. *Fax:* 919-684-3324; *E-Mail:* reime002@mc.duke.edu

REIMERS, ROBERT T, ENVIRONMENTAL ENGINEERING & SCIENCE. *Current Pos:* PROF, DEPT ENVIRON HEALTH & SCI, SCH PUB HEALTH & TROP MED, 75- *Personal Data:* b Burlington, Iowa, June 9, 43. *Educ:* Cornell Col, BA, 66; Univ Tex, Austin, MS, 68; Vanderbilt Univ, PhD(environ eng), 73. *Prof Exp:* Res scientist & process technician, Battelle Lab, 73-75. *Mem:* Fel Am Inst Chemists; Sigma Xi. *Mailing Add:* 4705 Clearview Pkwy Metairie LA 70006-2311

REIMERS, THOMAS JOHN, ENDOCRINOLOGY, REPRODUCTIVE PHYSIOLOGY. *Current Pos:* ASST PROF ENDOCRINOL, COL VET MED, CORNELL UNIV, 78- *Personal Data:* b West Point, Nebr. *Educ:* Univ Nebr, BS, 67; Univ Ill, MS, 69, PhD(animal sci), 74. *Prof Exp:* Res asst animal sci, Univ Ill, 67-69 & 71-74; fel physiol, Colo State Univ, 74-75, res assoc, 75-78. *Mem:* Soc Study Reproduction; Am Soc Animal Sci; AAAS; Sigma Xi. *Res:* Reproduction physiology in domestic animals; clinical endocrinology in large and small domestic animals. *Mailing Add:* 3 Wildflower Dr Ithaca NY 14850

REIMOLD, ROBERT J, ENVIRONMENTAL SCIENCE. *Current Pos:* VPRES & NAT DIR ENVIRON QUAL, METCALF & EDDY, INC, 82- *Personal Data:* b Greenville, Pa, Nov 15, 41; m 63, Mardith Osborne; c Elizabeth, Katherine & Ray. *Educ:* Thiel Col, BA, 63; Univ Del, MA, 65, PhD(biol sci), 68. *Prof Exp:* Teaching asst biol, Thiel Col, 62-63; res asst salt marsh ecol, Marine Labs, Univ Del, 63-68; res assoc, Marine Inst, Univ Ga, 68-69, asst prof zool & marine inst, 69-74, ecologist, Marine Resources Ext Ctr, 75-77; dir, Coastal Resources Div, Ga Dept Natural Resources, 77-81. *Concurrent Pos:* Univ Ga Marine Inst res fel, 68-69; vis prof, W I Lab, Fairleigh Dickinson Univ; sci consult, Encycl Britannica Corp, 74-; ecol comt, Water Environ Fedn, marine water qual comt. *Mem:* AAAS; Am Fisheries Soc; Ecol Soc Am; Brit Ecol Soc; Estuarine Res Fedn (past pres); Water Pollution Control Fedn; Sigma Xi. *Res:* Applied environmental engineering specializing in coastal, aquatic and wetland sciences supporting major infrastructure engineering projects. *Mailing Add:* 175 Cushing St Hingham MA 02043-4841. *Fax:* 781-245-6293

REIMSCHUSSEL, ERNEST F, HORTICULTURE. *Current Pos:* RETIRED. *Personal Data:* b Poischwitz, Germany, July 21, 17; US citizen; m 40; c 5. *Educ:* Brigham Young Univ, BA, 40, MS, 51. *Prof Exp:* Gardner, Brigham Young Univ, 41-42, asst land archit, 42-47, instr, 47-54, asst hort, 47-54, from instr to assoc prof 54-72, chmn dept, 58-66, assoc prof agron & hort, 72-82. *Mem:* Sigma Xi. *Res:* Ornamental woody plants; landscape architecture; trees. *Mailing Add:* 835 No 300 W Provo UT 84604

REIN, ALAN JAMES, PHYSICAL CHEMISTRY, SPECTROSCOPY. *Current Pos:* VPRES TECH OPER, APPLIED SYSTEMS, INC, 87- *Personal Data:* b New York, NY, Nov 1, 48; m 80, Ronnie Draisin; c Jessica. *Educ:* Rutgers Univ, BA, 70, MS, 73, PhD(phys chem), 74. *Prof Exp:* Sr res chemist phys & anal chem, Merck Sharp & Dohme Res Labs, 73-77, res fel phys chem, 77-79; adv scientist, IBM Instruments, 79-80, sr scientist & prod mgr, 80-87. *Mem:* AAAS; Soc Appl Spectros; Am Chem Soc. *Res:* Vibrational spectroscopy of inorganic, organometallic and biochemical species; laser raman spectroscopy; Fourier transform infrared spectroscopy; reaction analysis and monitoring of chemical processes by FTIR spectroscopy. *Mailing Add:* 25 Laurie Dr Englewood Cliffs NJ 07632-1862

REIN, DIANE CARLA, ENZYMOLOGY, BIOCHEMISTRY. *Current Pos:* SR RES ASSOC, UNIV CINCINNATI, 79- *Educ:* Univ Cincinnati, PhD(develop biol), 77. *Res:* Molecular genetics. *Mailing Add:* Dept Biol Sci Univ Cincinnati Cincinnati OH 45221-0006

REIN, ROBERT, QUANTUM CHEMISTRY, BIOPHYSICS. *Current Pos:* asst prof theoret biol, 65-66, assoc res prof theoret biol & biophys, 66-68, RES PROF BIOPHYS SCI, SCH PHARM, STATE UNIV NY BUFFALO, 68-, PRIN CANCER RES SCIENTIST, ROSWELL PARK MEM INST, 67-, REF PROF & CHMN, BIOMET DEPT, 80- *Personal Data:* b Ada, Yugoslavia, June 1, 28; m 70. *Educ:* Hebrew Univ, Israel, MSc, 55, PhD(phys chem), 60. *Prof Exp:* Res asst, Weizmann Inst, 56-60; sr res scientist, Quantum Chem Group, Univ Uppsala, 63-65. *Mem:* AAAS; Am Chem Soc; Biophys Soc; Int Soc Quantum Biol. *Res:* Molecular orbital theory of organic and biomolecules; quantum theory of intermolecular interactions and their application to molecular recognition in biology; electronic and physicochemical aspects of biopolymers. *Mailing Add:* Roswell Park Cancer Inst Elm & Carlton St Buffalo NY 14263-0002

REIN, ROBERT G, JR, chemical engineering, rheology, for more information see previous edition

REINBERG, ALAN R, SEMICONDUCTOR PROCESSING, THIN FILMS. *Current Pos:* INDEPENDENT CONSULT, 91- *Personal Data:* b New York, NY, Oct 19, 31; m 54, Linda Blumenthal; c Debra, Susan, Julie (Porter) & Melissa. *Educ:* Univ Chicago, BA, 52; Ill Inst Technol, BS, 57, MS, 59, PhD(physics), 61; Univ Conn, MBA, 93. *Honors & Awards:* Tegal Thinker Award. *Prof Exp:* Res physicist, Res Inst, Ill Inst Technol, 60-63; sr physicist, Lear Siegler Inc, 63-64; mem tech staff physics, Tex Instruments Inc, 64-80; Perkin Elmer Corp, 80-90. *Mem:* Inst Elec & Electronics Engrs. *Res:* Properties of point defects by magnetic resonance; optical properties; plasma chemistry; x-ray lithography. *Mailing Add:* 1910 Lake Heron Rd Boise ID 83706

REINBERGS, ERNESTS, PLANT BREEDING. *Current Pos:* Lectr field husb, 54-57, from asst prof to prof, 57-85, EMER PROF CROP SCI, ONT AGR COL, UNIV GUELPH, 86- *Personal Data:* b Latvia, Mar 1, 20; nat Can; m 44, Daina Sulcs; c Marts & Anne. *Educ:* Univ Toronto, MSA, 54; Univ Man, PhD(cytogenetics, plant breeding), 57. *Hon Degrees:* Dr, Agr Univ Latria, 96. *Honors & Awards:* Grindley Medal, Agr Inst Can, 77; Outstanding Res Award, Can Soc Agron, 87. *Mem:* Can Soc Agron; Genetics Soc Can; Agr Inst Can; Sigma Xi. *Res:* Barley, oat and triticale breeding; double haploids and breeding methods in barley; cytogenetics; disease resistance. *Mailing Add:* Dept Crop Sci Ont Agr Col Univ Guelph Guelph ON N1G 2W1 Can

REINBOLD, GEORGE W, BACTERIOLOGY, DAIRY INDUSTRY. *Current Pos:* VPRES RES & DEVELOP, LEPRINO FOODS, 74- *Personal Data:* b Williamsport, Pa, Apr 10, 19; m 42; c 3. *Educ:* Pa State Univ, BS, 42; Univ Ill, MS, 47, PhD(dairy mfg), 49. *Honors & Awards:* Pfizer Cheese Res Award, 70; Dairy Res Inc Award, 77. *Prof Exp:* Proj dir bact, Kraft Foods Co, Nat Dairy Prod Corp, 49-53, prod technician dairy indust, 53-58; prod mgr, Tolibia Cheese Mfg Corp, 58-59; exten specialist, Iowa State Univ, 59-60, from assoc prof to prof dairy bact, 60-74. *Mem:* Am Dairy Sci Asn;

Am Soc Microbiol; Int Asn Milk, Food & Environ Sanitarians. *Res:* Dairy microbiology, especially indicator organisms, sanitation and cheese microbiology and manufacture. *Mailing Add:* 4180 Dudley St Wheat Ridge CO 80033

REINBOLD, PAUL EARL, ANALYTICAL CHEMISTRY, INORGANIC CHEMISTRY. *Current Pos:* from asst prof to assoc prof, Bethany Nazarene Col, 70-76, PROF CHEM & HEAD DEPT, SOUTHERN NAZARENE UNIV, 76- *Personal Data:* b Vincennes, Ind, Oct 21, 43; m 65, Janice Kay Folsom; c Sheila Kay (deceased). *Educ:* Olivet Nazarene Col, AB, 65; Purdue Univ, West Lafayette, Ind, 68; Tex A&M Univ, PhD (analytical chem), 70. *Prof Exp:* Analytical chemist, Armour Pharmaceut Co, Ill, 64-65; Robert A Welch-Tex A&M Res Coun fel, Tex A&M Univ, 69-70. *Mem:* Am Chem Soc. *Res:* Optically active inorganic coordination complexes; kinetics and mechanisms of inorganic exchange reactions; kinetics of electrode deposition processes from metal ion complexes; microcomputers in chemical education. *Mailing Add:* Dept Chem Southern Nazarene Univ 6729 NW 39th Expressway Bethany OK 73008-2694. *E-Mail:* paulrein@snu.edu

REINDERS, VICTOR A, chemistry, for more information see previous edition

REINECCIUS, GARY (AUBREY), FOOD SCIENCE. *Current Pos:* Assoc prof, 70-80, PROF FOOD SCI, UNIV MINN, ST PAUL, 80- *Personal Data:* b Webster, Wis, Jan 12, 44; m 64; c 2. *Educ:* Univ Minn, BS, 64, MS, 67; Pa State Univ, PhD(food sci), 70. *Mem:* Am Chem Soc; Inst Food Technol; hon mem Soc Flavor Chemists. *Res:* Chemistry of food flavor, including biogenesis and chemical composition of flavor. *Mailing Add:* Minn Univ Food Sci Dept 1334 Eckles Ave St Paul MN 55108-1040

REINECKE, KENNETH J, ECOLOGY & MANAGEMENT OF WATER FOWL, STATUS OF WETLANDS. *Current Pos:* Wildlife res biologist, 80-93, STAFF MEM, PATUXENT WILDLIFE RES CTR, 97- *Personal Data:* b May 14, 48. *Educ:* Ripon Col, AB, 70; Univ Maine, PhD(wildlife ecol), 78. *Honors & Awards:* Ducks Unlimited Wetland Conserv Achievement Award, 93. *Prof Exp:* Wildlife res biologist, Nat Wetlands Res Ctr, 93-97. *Concurrent Pos:* Adj prof, Miss State Univ, 88- *Mem:* Am Ornithologists Union; Wildlife Soc; Wilson Ornith Soc; Cooper Ornith Soc. *Res:* Ecology and management of North American waterfowl and their habitats. *Mailing Add:* Commodore Apts Vicksburg MS 39180. *Fax:* 601-634-7296

REINECKE, MANFRED GORDON, ORGANIC CHEMISTRY, MEDICINAL PLANTS. *Current Pos:* from asst prof to assoc prof, 64-74, PROF ORG CHEM, TEX CHRISTIAN UNIV, 74- *Personal Data:* b Milwaukee, Wis, May 19, 35; m 57, Marlene Zwisler; c Kurt, Kryn & Claire. *Educ:* Univ Wis, BS, 56; Univ Calif, Berkeley, PhD(org chem), 60. *Honors & Awards:* W T Doherty Award, Am Chem Soc. *Prof Exp:* Asst org chem, Univ Calif, Berkeley, 56-57, instr, 59-60; asst prof, Univ Calif, Riverside, 60-64. *Concurrent Pos:* NSF fac fel, Univ Tubingen, 71-72; Nat Acad Sci exchange scientist, Acad Wissenschaften, Ger Dem Repub, 79 & 90; vis prof, Univ BC, Vancouver Can, 87. *Mem:* Am Soc Pharmacognosy; Am Chem Soc; Royal Soc Chem; Phytochem Soc NAm. *Res:* Organic synthesis, mechanisms, reactive intermediates; natural products; medicinal herbs; heterocyclic compounds. *Mailing Add:* Dept Chem Tex Christian Univ Ft Worth TX 76129. *Fax:* 817-921-7110; *E-Mail:* m.reinecke@gamma.is.tcu.edu

REINECKE, ROBERT DALE, OPHTHALMOLOGY, SURGERY. *Current Pos:* ophthal-in-chief, Wills Eye Hosp, 81-85, chmn ophthal, Thomas Jefferson Med Col, 81-85, PROF OPHTHAL, THOMAS JEFFERSON MED COL, 81-, DIR, FOERDERER EYE MOVEMENT CTR, WILLS EYE HOSP, 85- *Personal Data:* b Ft Scott, Kans, Mar 26, 29; m 52, Mary; c Karen. *Educ:* Ill Col Optom, OD, 51; Univ Kans, AB, 55, MD, 59; Am Bd Ophthal, cert, 65. *Honors & Awards:* Howe Award, 81; Sr Honor Award, Am Acad Ophthal, 86. *Prof Exp:* From asst instr to asst prof, Harvard Univ, 64-69, sci dir, Vision Info Ctr, 67-70; prof ophthal & chmn dept, Albany Med Col, 70-81. *Concurrent Pos:* Instr eye anat, Simmons Col, 62-68; resident ophthal, Mass Eye & Ear Infirmary, 63; teaching fel ophthal, Harvard Med Sch, 63-64; chief instr Infirmary, 63-67, dir ocular motility clin, 67-69, asst instr, Infirmary, 63-69; asst instr, Mass Gen Hosp, 63-69; asst instr, Mass Gen Hosp, 63-69; mem bd dirs, Cononad Berens Int Eye Film Libr, 70-; mem visual sci study sect, NIH, 71-75; chmn med adv comt, Comn Blind & Visually Handicapped, 71-76; grant, Albany Med Col, 72-; chmn panel ophthal devices, Food & Drug Admin, 74-78; mem comt vision, Nat Acad Sci-Nat Res Coun, 77-80; trustee, Asn Res Vision & Ophthal, 86-91. *Mem:* AAAS; AMA; Asn Res Vision & Ophthal; Am Acad Ophthal (pres, 89); Am Asn Pediat Ophthal & Strobisms. *Res:* Eye movement; visual acuity; stereopsis; nystagmus; amblyopia. *Mailing Add:* Wills Eye Hosp Ninth & Walnut St Philadelphia PA 19107. *Fax:* 215-928-3474; *E-Mail:* reineck1@jeflin.tju.edu

REINECKE, THOMAS LEONARD, ELECTRONIC & OPTICAL PROPERTIES OF SOLIDS, LOW DIMENSIONAL SYSTEMS, SURFACES & INTERFACES. *Current Pos:* res assoc, 74-76, res physicist, 76-80, head, Theory Sect Semiconductors Br, 80-90, HEAD, ELEC & OPTICAL PROPERTIES SECT, NAVAL RES LAB, 90- *Personal Data:* b Park Falls, Wis, Sept 14, 45. *Educ:* Ripon Col, Wis, BA, 68; Oxford Univ, PhD(physics), 72. *Honors & Awards:* Prize in Pure Sci, Sigma Xi, 82. *Prof Exp:* Res assoc & lectr, Dept Physics, Brown Univ, Providence, RI, 72-74. *Concurrent Pos:* Panel mem, NSF Res Initiation & Support Prog, 76-77; mem steering comt, Greater Wash Solid State Physics Colloquia, 78-, secy, 83-85; guest scientist, Max Planck Inst Solid State Res, Stuttgart, W Ger, 79; panel on artificially structured mat, Nat Acad Sci, 84-85; selection comt for Rhodes Scholars, Va, 84-, Fla, 94; mem, Solid State Sci Comt, Forum Nat Res Coun Nat Acad Sci, 84-; mem, NSF Eval Comt, Ctr Sci & Technol, 88-89; guest scientist, Tech Physics Inst, Univ Wuerzburg, Ger, 93; mem, organizing comt, workshop on Surface Dynamics, Tenn, 93, workshop on Mesoscopic Systs, Moscow, 94. *Mem:* Fel Am Phys Soc; Sigma Xi. *Res:* Solid state theory including interacting electronic systems, phase transitions, surfaces interfaces and low dimensional systems; various systems including semiconductors, and magnetic and ferroelectric materials. *Mailing Add:* Code 6877 Naval Res Lab Washington DC 20375-5347. *Fax:* 202-767-1165; *E-Mail:* reinecke@estd.nrl.navy.mie

REINECKE, WILLIAM GERALD, AERODYNAMICS. *Current Pos:* PRIN RES SCIENTIST, PHYS SCI INC, 90-; DIR, INST ADVAN TECHNOL, 93- *Personal Data:* b Indianapolis, Ind, July 21, 35; m 59, Sandra Wright; c Kathryn & Sheryl. *Educ:* Purdue Univ, BS, 57; Princeton Univ, MA & PhD(aeronaut eng), 61. *Prof Exp:* Sr staff scientist, Res & Develop Div, Avco Corp, 64-65; group leader exp aerodyne Ballistic Range Group, Res & Technol Labs, 65-66, sect chief, Exp Fluid Physics Sect, 66-71, sr consult, Technol Directorate, 71-77, mgr ballistics lab, Avco Systs Div, 77-78, dir Ballistics & Ordnance Technol, 78-82; dir eng, Textron Defense Systs, 83-89; area mgr, Phys Sci Inc, 90-92. *Concurrent Pos:* Mem, Aeroballistic Range Asn. *Mem:* Assoc fel Am Inst Aeronaut & Astronaut; Am Defense Preparedness Asn. *Res:* Aerodynamics, especially high speed flows, high speed erosion and internal and terminal ballistics. *Mailing Add:* 4030-2 W Braker Lane Austin TX 78759

REINEMUND, JOHN ADAM, GEOLOGY. *Current Pos:* Geologist, Strategic Mineral Invests, US Geol Serv, 42-44, Oceanog Res, Off Sci Res & Develop, 44-45, Mineral Fuel Invests, 46-49, Coal Surv, Econ Coop Admin, Korea, 49-50, asst chief, Eastern Invest Sect, Fuels Br, 51-53, regional supvr, Midcontinent Region, 53-56, geol adv, AID, Geol Surv, Pakistan, 56-64, chief, Br Foreign Geol, DC, 64-69, chief, Off Int Geol, 69-84, EXEC DIR, CIRCUM-PACIFIC COUN ENERGY & MINERAL RESOURCES, US GEOL SURV, 84- *Personal Data:* b Muscatine, Iowa, Jan 14, 19; m 43. *Educ:* Augustana Col, BA, Augustana Col, BA, 42, 51. *Hon Degrees:* DHumL, Augustana Col, 67. *Honors & Awards:* Distinguished Serv Award, US Dept of Interior, 88. *Concurrent Pos:* Bd mem, Int Geol Corr Prog, 73-79; treas, Int Union Geol Sci, 79-89. *Mem:* Geol Soc Am; Am Asn Petrol Geol; Am Geophys Union. *Res:* Structural geology; sedimentary petrology; geology of fuels; origin of mineral and fuel resources in relation to sedimentary and tectonic processes; principal research has dealt with structural and sedimentational controls for the origin and distribution of fossil fuels in tectonic basins and continental margin belts; recent activity has been mainly concerned with organizing programs for the Pacific and Atlantic Basins. *Mailing Add:* PO Box 890 Leesburg VA 22075

REINER, ALBEY M, MICROBIOLOGY, GENETICS. *Current Pos:* asst prof, 71-77, ASSOC PROF MICROBIOL, UNIV MASS, AMHERST, 77- *Personal Data:* b Brooklyn, NY, Aug 11, 41; m 65; c 2. *Educ:* Princeton Univ, BS, 62; Oxford Univ, cert math statist, 63; Univ Wis-Madison, MS, 64; Harvard Univ, PhD(molecular biol), 69. *Prof Exp:* Rothschild Found fel, Hebrew Univ, Israel, 68-69; NIH fel, Univ Calif, Berkeley, 69-70. *Res:* Microbial genetics. *Mailing Add:* Dept Microbiol Univ Mass Amherst MA 01003-0002

REINER, CHARLES BRAILOVE, PATHOLOGY, PEDIATRICS. *Current Pos:* RETIRED. *Personal Data:* b Ellenville, NY, Dec 3, 20; m 51, Elaine V Mayson; c Alan L, Janet L & Barbara L (Graymountain). *Educ:* Temple Univ, AB, 42, MD, 45, MSc, 53; Am Bd Path, dipl, 54; Am Bd Path, dipl, 66. *Prof Exp:* Fel histochem, Univ Chicago, 52; physician-in-chg, Pediat Outpatient Clin, Univ Hosp, Temple Univ, 52-55; asst prof path, Col Med, State Univ NY Downstate Med Ctr, 56-59; from asst prof to assoc prof path & pediat, Col Med, Ohio State Univ, 59-86; chief, Div Anod Path, Dept Lab Med, Children's Hosp, Columbus, 72-85, pathologist, 85-88. *Concurrent Pos:* Assoc pathologist, Children's Hosp, Columbus, 59-72; pathologist, Inst Perinatal Studies, 60-64; consult, pediat path, 88- *Mem:* Soc Pediat Path; Int Acad Path. *Res:* Pediatric pathology; perinatal problems, especially hyaline membrane syndrome; heparin in human tissues; laboratory aspects of blood coagulation; sudden infant death syndrome. *Mailing Add:* 3555 Piatt Rd Delaware OH 43015-9622

REINER, IRMA MOSES, MATHEMATICS, EDUCATION. *Current Pos:* RETIRED. *Personal Data:* b Newburgh, NY, Mar 3, 22; wid; c David & Peter. *Educ:* Cornell Univ, AB, 42, AM, 44, PhD(algebra, geom, physics), 46. *Prof Exp:* Instr math, Temple Univ, 46-48 & Danville Community Col, Ill, 49-50; instr math, Univ Ill, Urbana, 48-49 & 56-57, asst prof, 57-92. *Concurrent Pos:* Erastus Brooks fel, Cornell Univ, 42. *Mem:* Am Math Soc; Math Asn Am; Asn Women Math; Sigma Xi. *Res:* Theory of numbers and matrix theory. *Mailing Add:* Dept Math Univ Ill 1409 W Green St Urbana IL 61801-2917

REINER, LEOPOLD, MEDICINE. *Current Pos:* vis assoc prof, 56-72, prof, 72-79 EMER PROF PATH, ALBERT EINSTEIN COL MED, 79- *Personal Data:* b Leipzig, Ger, Jan 22, 11; nat US; m 46, Lillian Myers. *Educ:* Univ Vienna, MD, 36; Am Bd Path, dipl, 52. *Prof Exp:* Intern, Rothschild Hosp, Vienna, Austria, 36-38; from resident path to asst pathologist, W Jersey Hosp, Camden, NJ, 41-46; instr path, Harvard Med Sch, 50-53, clin assoc, 53-56. *Concurrent Pos:* From resident path to actg pathologist, Beth Israel Hosp, Boston, 46-56; pathologist & dir labs, Bronx Lebanon Hosp Ctr, 56-82. *Mem:* Histochem Soc; Am Asn Path; NY Acad Med; Int Acad Path; Am Soc Clin Path. *Res:* Pathology, especially cardiovascular pathology; coronary arterial and mesenteric arterial circulation; cardiac hypertrophy. *Mailing Add:* 277 Old Colony Rd Hartsdale NY 10530-3620

REINERS, JOHN JOSEPH, JR, MECHANISMS OF CHEMICAL CARCINOGENS, IMMUNOMODULATION BY CHEMICALS. *Current Pos:* assoc prof, 92-96, PROF TOXICOL, INST CHEM TOXICOL & PROF PHARMACOL, SCH MED, WAYNE STATE UNIV, 96- *Personal Data:* b St Paul, Minn, Dec 3, 49. *Educ:* Univ Minn, BS, 71; Purdue Univ, PhD(biochem), 77. *Prof Exp:* Fel, Dept Pharmacol, Baylor Col Med, 77-80; res asst prof, Oak Ridge Grad Sch Biomed Sci, Univ Tenn, 80-83; from asst prof to assoc prof carcinogenesis, Sci Park-Res Div, M D Anderson Cancer Ctr, Univ Tex, 83-92. *Concurrent Pos:* Mem chem path study sect, NIH, 91-95; assoc prof pharmacol, Wayne State Med Sch, 92-96. *Mem:* Am Asn Cancer Res; Soc Invest Dermat; Soc Toxicol. *Res:* Characterization of proteins involved in xenobiotic metabolism and the signal transduction pathways that regulate their expression as a function of tissue differentiation and chemical exposure. *Mailing Add:* Inst Chem Toxicol Rm 4000 Wayne State Univ 2727 Second Ave Detroit MI 48201. *Fax:* 313-577-0082

REINERS, WILLIAM A, ECOLOGY, REMOTE SENSING. *Current Pos:* PROF BOT, UNIV WYO, 83-, J E WARREN PROF ENERGY & ENVIRON, 96- *Personal Data:* b Chicago, Ill, June 10, 37; m 62, Norma M Miller; c Peter William & Derek Seth. *Educ:* Knox Col, BA, 59; Rutgers Univ, MS, 62, PhD(bot), 64. *Honors & Awards:* Henry J Oosting lectr, Duke Univ, 81. *Prof Exp:* From instr to asst prof bot, Univ Minn, 64-67; from asst prof to prof biol, Dartmouth Col, 76-83. *Concurrent Pos:* Fel, Wissenschaftskolleg zu Berlin, 89-90. *Mem:* AAAS; Ecol Soc Am (treas, 81-). *Res:* Biogeochemistry of terrestrial ecosystems with special emphasis on succession and landscape relations; global ecology; landscape ecology. *Mailing Add:* Dept Bot Univ Wyo Laramie WY 82071-3165. *Fax:* 307-766-2851; *E-Mail:* reiners@uwyo.edu

REINERT, JAMES A, TURFGRASS ENTOMOLOGY & ORNAMENTAL PLANT ENTOMOLOGY, HOST-PLANT RESISTANCE. *Current Pos:* prof entom & resident dir res, 89-94, PROF ENTOM, TEX A&M UNIV RES & EXTEN CTR, TEX AGR EXP STA, 94- *Personal Data:* b Enid, Okla, Jan 26, 44; m 63; c 6. *Educ:* Okla State Univ, BS, 66; Clemson Univ, MS, 68, PhD(entom), 70. *Honors & Awards:* Porter Henninger Mem Hort Award, Southern Nurseryman Asn. *Prof Exp:* Res asst entom, Clemson Univ, 66-70; entomologist, State Bd Agr, Univ Md, College Park, 70; from asst prof to prof entom, Ft Lauderdale Res & Educ Ctr, Univ Fla, 70-84. *Concurrent Pos:* UNIX Comput Sch. *Mem:* Entom Soc Am; Int Turfgrass Soc. *Res:* Urban agriculture with specialty in insects and mites in turfgrass and ornamental plants; host plant resistance and pest management of turfgrass insects and mites; biology, behavior and control by chemical or biological agents of insect and mite pests; research administration. *Mailing Add:* 3805 Covinton Ln Plano TX 75023-7731. *Fax:* 972-783-1723; *E-Mail:* jreinert@dallas-ctr.tamu.edu

REINERT, RICHARD ALLYN, PLANT PATHOLOGY, HORTICULTURE. *Current Pos:* adj assoc prof, Univ NC, 69-73, assoc prof, Sci & Admin Agr Res, 73-77, PROF PLANT PATH, SOUTHERN REGION, AGR RES SERV, USDA & NC STATE UNIV, 77-, PROF, USDA, AIR QUAL EFFECTS. *Personal Data:* b Elkhorn, Wis, June 3, 35; m 59; c 3. *Educ:* Univ Wis, BS, 58, PhD(plant path, hort), 62. *Prof Exp:* Asst prof plant path, Univ Ky, 62-67; res plant pathologist, R A Taft Sanit Eng Ctr, USDA-USPHS, Ohio, 67-69, Nat Environ Res Ctr, Plant Sci Res Div, USDA-Environ Protection Agency, 69-73. *Mem:* AAAS; Am Phytopath Soc; Am Soc Hort Sci. *Res:* Plant virology and tissue culture; physiology of growth and development; effects of air pollutants on cultivated plants and diseases of horticulture and ornamental crops. *Mailing Add:* Dept Plant Path Gardner Hall NC State Univ Box 7616 Raleigh NC 27695-7616

REINES, DANIEL, GENETICS, ENZYMOLOGY. *Current Pos:* Fel biochem, Univ Calif, Berkeley, 85-90. *Educ:* Albert Einstein Col Med, PhD(molecular biol), 85. *Mailing Add:* Dept Biochem Sch Med Emory Univ 1510 Clifton Rd NE Atlanta GA 30322

REINES, FREDERICK, ELEMENTARY PARTICLE PHYSICS, COSMIC RAY PHYSICS. *Current Pos:* dean phys sci, 66-74, prof physics, 66-88, PROF, RADIOL SCI, MED SCH, UNIV CALIF, IRVINE, 70-, DISTINGUISHED EMER PROF PHYSICS, 88- *Personal Data:* b Paterson, NJ, Mar 16, 18; m 40; c 2. *Educ:* Stevens Inst Technol, ME, 39, MS, 41; NY Univ, PhD(theoret physics), 44. *Hon Degrees:* DSc, Univ Witwatersrand, 66; Dr, Stevens Inst Technol, 84. *Honors & Awards:* Nobel Prize Physics, 95; Steven Honor Award, 71; J Robert Oppenheimer Mem Prize, 81; Nat Medal of Sci, 86; L L Schiff Mem Lectr, Stanford Univ, 88; Albert Einstein Mem Lectr, Israel Acad Sci & Humanities, 88; Rossi Prize, 89; Michelson-Morley Award, 90; Goud Schmidt Mem Lectr, 90; W K H Panofsky Prize, 92; Franklin Medal, 92. *Prof Exp:* Mem staff & group leader, Theoret Div, Los Alamos Sci Lab, 44-59, dir exp, Operation Greenhouse Eniwetok, 51; prof physics & head dept, Case Western Inst Technol & chmn, Joint Case, Western Res High Energy Physics Prog, 59-66. *Concurrent Pos:* Lectr, Exten Div, Univ Calif, 49; consult, Armed Forces spec weapons proj, 49-53 & Rand Corp, 50; centennial lectr, Univ Md, 56; fels, Guggenheim Found, 58-59 & Sloan Found, 59-63; trustee, Argonne Univ Assocs, 61-64; mem, NASA Electrophys Adv Comt, 63-64, Fulbright Physics Screening Comt, 64-66, consult, Inst Defense Anal, 65-69 & Los Alamos Sci Lab. *Mem:* Nat Acad Sci; fel Am Phys Soc; fel Am Acad Arts & Sci; Am Soc Physics Teachers; fel AAAS; Nat Medal Sci; Sigma Xi. *Res:* Nuclear fission; physics of nuclear weapons and effects; scintillation detectors; free neutrino; cosmic rays; baryon conservation test; charge conservation; atmospheric neutrinos; low level counting. *Mailing Add:* 18 Perkins Ct Irvine CA 92612

REINESS, GARY, NEURAL DEVELOPMENT & PLASTICITY. *Current Pos:* PROF & CHAIR BIOL, LEWIS & CLARK COL, 94- *Personal Data:* b Pittsburgh, Pa, Aug 20, 45; div; c 1. *Educ:* Johns Hopkins Univ, BA, 67; Columbia Univ, MPhil, 74, PhD(biol), 75. *Prof Exp:* Fel, Dept Neurobiol, Harvard Med Sch, 75-76; scholar, Dept Physiol, Univ Calif, San Francisco, 76-81; from asst prof to prof biol, Pomona Col, 81-93, chair, 88-90, assoc dean, 90-93. *Concurrent Pos:* Vis assoc prof, Dept Anat & Neurobiol, Wash Univ Med Sch, 87-88; biol counr, Coun Undergrad Res, 89-94; mem, Neurosci grad Prog, Ore Health Sci Univ, 96- *Mem:* Soc Neurosci; AAAS; Am Soc Cell Biol; Coun Undergrad Res. *Res:* Regulation of acetylcholine receptor and acetylcholinesterase during development of the neuromuscular junction; plasticity of adult neuromuscular junction induced by injury or toxins; synthesis and secretionof neuronal growth factors. *Mailing Add:* Dept Biol Lewis & Clark Col Portland CA 97219. *E-Mail:* reiness@lclark.edu

REINFELDS, JURIS, PROGRAMMING METHODOLOGY, PROGRAMMING LANGUAGE. *Current Pos:* PROF COMPUT SCI, NMEX STATE UNIV, 89- *Personal Data:* b Riga, Latvia, Apr 1, 36; Australian citizen; m 62, Lauma Petersons; c Peteris M, Ivars V & Martins N. *Educ:* Univ Adelaide, Australia, BSc, 59, PhD(math physics), 63. *Prof Exp:* ICI postdoctoral fel, Univ Edinburgh, Scotland, 61-64; NSF res assoc, Marshall Space Flight Ctr, 65-66; asst prof comput sci, Univ Ga, 66-74; vis scientist, Europ Orgn Nuclear Res, Switz, 72-75; found prof comput sci, Univ Wollongong, Australia, 75-91. *Concurrent Pos:* Consult, Australian Int Develop Prog, Phillippines, 83-90, Thailand, 83-91. *Mem:* Asn Comput Mach; Inst Elec & Electronics Engrs; Australian Comput Soc. *Res:* Author of over 20 scientific publications and over 50 technical reports; author of interactive programming languages AMTRAN and SIGMA. *Mailing Add:* Klipsel Sch Elec Eng & Comput Eng PO Box 30001 Dept 3-0 Las Cruces NM 88003. *Fax:* 505-646-1435; *E-Mail:* juris@nmsu.edu

REINFURT, DONALD WILLIAM, APPLIED STATISTICS. *Current Pos:* Staff assoc, 68-80, assoc dir, anal studies, 81-93, DEP DIR, HWY SAFETY RES CTR, UNIV NC, 80-, ADJ ASSOC PROF, DEPT BIOSTATIST, 78- *Personal Data:* b Wilkes-Barre, Pa, Aug 30, 38; m 65, Karen Hillix; c Kristin E & David W. *Educ:* State Univ NY Albany, BS, 60; State Univ NY Buffalo, MA, 63; NC State Univ, PhD(statist), 70. *Mem:* Asn Advan Automotive Med; Am Statist Asn; Am Pub Health Asn. *Res:* Application of statistical methods, particularly categorical data analysis, to traffic safety problems. *Mailing Add:* 403 Highview Dr Chapel Hill NC 27514

REINGOLD, EDWARD MARTIN, ANALYSIS ALGORITHMS, DATA STRUCTURES. *Current Pos:* From asst prof to assoc prof, 70-82, PROF COMPUT SCI, UNIV ILL, URBANA-CHAMPAIGN, 82- *Personal Data:* b Chicago, Ill, Nov 12, 45; m 68, Ruth E Nothmann; c Leah S, Deborah H, Rachel N & Eve M. *Educ:* Ill Inst Technol, BS, 67; Cornell Univ, MS, 69, PhD(comput sci), 71. *Mem:* Asn Comput Mach; Soc Indust & Appl Math; Am Math Soc; Math Asn Am. *Res:* Design and analysis of algorithms and data structures for non-numerical problems such as sorting, searching, graph and tree manipulation and exhaustive search. *Mailing Add:* Dept Comput Sci Univ Ill 1304 W Springfield Ave Urbana IL 61801-2910. *Fax:* 217-333-3501; *E-Mail:* reingold@cs.uiuc.edu

REINGOLD, HAIM, MATHEMATICS. *Current Pos:* supvr instr, Signal Corps Training Schs, 42-43, from asst prof to assoc prof, 43-56, PROF MATH, ILL INST TECHNOL, 56-, DIR EVE DIV, 46-, CHMN DEPT MATH, 54-; PROF MATH, MUNDELEIN COL, 84- *Personal Data:* b Lodz, Poland, Mar 16, 10; nat US; m 66; c 3. *Educ:* Univ Cincinnati, AB, 33, AM, 34, PhD(math), 38. *Prof Exp:* Instr math, Univ Cincinnati, 35-36; prof & head dept, Our Lady Cincinnati Col, 38-42. *Concurrent Pos:* Actg chmn dept math, Ill Inst Technol, 51-54; prof math, Ind Univ Northwest & 75-82, Purdue Univ Calumet, 82-84. *Mem:* AAAS; Am Math Soc; Am Soc Eng Educ; Math Asn Am. *Res:* Invariants of a system of linear homogeneous differential equations of the second order; generalized determinants of Vandermonde; basic mathematics for engineers and scientists. *Mailing Add:* 1329 E 55th St Chicago IL 60615-5301

REINGOLD, I(VER) DAVID, ORGANIC CHEMISTRY. *Current Pos:* assoc prof, 88-92, PROF CHEM, 92- *Personal Data:* b Concord, NH, Aug 29, 49; m 74, Kay Balmer; c Colin & Alison. *Educ:* Dartmouth Col, AB, 71; Univ Ore, PhD(chem), 76. *Prof Exp:* Res assoc chem, Univ Alta, 77-78; asst prof, Haverford Col, 78-79 & Middlebury Col, 79-86; vis assoc prof chem, Lewis & Clark Col, 86-88. *Concurrent Pos:* Vis asst prof, Univ Chicago, 83-84; vis scholar, Dartmouth Col, 93-94. *Mem:* Am Chem Soc. *Res:* Synthetic organic chemistry; theoretically interesting molecules; strained molecules. *Mailing Add:* Dept Chem Juniata Col Huntingdon PA 16652. *Fax:* 814-641-3685; *E-Mail:* reingold@juniata.edu

REINGOLD, IRVING, ELECTRONICS ENGINEERING. *Current Pos:* VIS RES PROF, MONMOUTH UNIV, 94- *Personal Data:* b Newark, NJ, Nov 13, 21; m 48, Marilyn Cooper; c Lynne (Hoo) & Robin (Menell). *Educ:* Newark Col Eng, BS, 42, BS (eng), 48. *Honors & Awards:* Tech Leadership Award, US Army Electronic Res & Develop Lab, 62; Soc Info Francis Rice Darne Mem Award, 78; Commander's Award, Dept Army, 85, Medal Meritorious Civilian Serv; Region One Award, Elec Eng Mgt, Inst Elec & Electronics Engrs, 85, Prof Achievement Award, 90, Microwave Theory & Techniques Soc Applns Award, 93; Beatrice Winner Mem Award, Soc Info Display, 88. *Prof Exp:* Elec mfg engr, Westinghouse Elec Co, NJ, 43-45; proj engr, Air Force Watson Labs, NJ, 45-51; proj engr, Chief Switching Devices Sect, Microwave Tubes Br, Electronics Technol & Devices Lab, NJ, 51-60, dep br chief, 60-66, br chief, Pickup, Display & Storage Devices Br, 66-75, dir, Beam Plasma & Display Div, 75-81, dep dir, elec technol & devices lab,

US Army elec res & develop command, 81-85; adj prof & consult, SE Ctr Elec Eng Educ, 85-89, Geo-Ctrs Inc, 89-92; consult, Questechnic, 93-94. *Concurrent Pos:* Mem adv group on electron devices, US Dept Defense, 81-85; chmn, NJ Coast Sect, Hons & Awards Comt, Inst Elec & Electronics Engrs, 85-90; mem, MIT Electromagnetics Acad, 90-, NJ Inst Technol Workforce 2000 Action Coun, 90- *Mem:* Fel Inst Elec & Electronics Engrs; fel Soc Info Display; Sigma Xi. *Res:* Research and development in the fields of microwave tubes and devices, pulsers and display devices; microelectronics; integrated circuits; solid state microwave devices; engineering, program and project management. *Mailing Add:* 409 Runyon Ave Deal Park Deal NJ 07723. *E-Mail:* menell@aol.com

REINHARD, EDWARD HUMPHREY, HEMATOLOGY. *Current Pos:* from instr to prof, 43-80, EMER PROF MED, SCH MED, WASHINGTON UNIV, 81- *Personal Data:* b St Louis, Mo, Dec 9, 13; m 40, 76, Barbara Miller; c Julia Barbley (Hofmann), Thomas Edward, John D'Arey & Mary J (Schawacker). *Educ:* Washington Univ, AB, 35, MD, 39. *Concurrent Pos:* Dir pvt med serv, Barner Hosp, St Louis, 48-79. *Mem:* Am Soc Hemat; fel Am Col Physicians; Asn Am Physicians; Int Soc Hemat. *Res:* Hematology; therapy of malignant diseases; treatment of leukemia; anemia associated with malignant diseases. *Mailing Add:* 42 Frederick Lane St Louis MO 63122

REINHARD, JOHN FREDERICK, JR, NEUROCHEMISTRY, BIOCHEMISTRY. *Current Pos:* SR BIOCHEMIST, WELLCOME RES LABS, 82- *Personal Data:* b Bronxville, NY, Sept 2, 51; m 76; c 2. *Educ:* Mass Inst Technol, MS, 77, PhD(neural & endocrine regulation), 80. *Prof Exp:* Res fel pharmacol, Sch Med, Yale Univ, 80-82. *Concurrent Pos:* Vis scientist, Wellcome Res Labs, Kent, UK, 91-92; adj assoc prof, Sch Pharm, Univ NC, Chapel Hill. *Mem:* Int Soc Neurochem; Soc Neurosci; Am Soc Pharmacol & Exp Therapeut. *Res:* Compensatory neuronal mechanisms which occur in response to damage within the central nervous system; disorders of amino acid metabolism. *Mailing Add:* Dept Pharmacol Wellcome Res Labs 3030 Cornwallis Rd Research Triangle Park NC 27705-5206. *Fax:* 919-315-8890

REINHARD, KARL RAYMOND, VETERINARY MEDICINE. *Current Pos:* LECTR, DEPT FAMILY & COMMUNITY MED, UNIV ARIZ, 70- *Personal Data:* b Coplay, Pa, Jan 13, 16; m 45, Janet E Correll; c Eric J, Karen J & Karl J. *Educ:* Muhlenberg Col, BS, 36; Pa State Univ, MA, 40; Cornell Univ, DVM, 49, PhD(microbiol), 50. *Honors & Awards:* Borden Award, 49. *Prof Exp:* Asst animal path res, Pa State Univ, 39-41; bacteriologist, Med Dept, US Army, 41-45; prof bact, Univ Ky, 50-51; chief leptospirosis res, Rocky Mountain Lab, USPHS, 51-54, chief infectious dis prog, Arctic Health Res Ctr, Alaska, 54-60, exec secy, Gen Med Study Sect, Div Res Grants, NIH, 60-63, asst to chief, 63-66, chief eval staff, Bur Dis Prev & Environ Control, 66-67, chief prog eval, Div Indian Health, 67-68; prof microbiol & dean col vet med, Okla State Univ, 68-69; chief health status surveillance, Health Prog Systs Ctr, Indian Health Serv, USPHS, 69-79. *Concurrent Pos:* Consult, WHO, 73, 75, 76, 77, 80 & 81; res fel, NIH; mem task force, Revising Statement On Smoking & Health, USPHS, Develop Policy Ethics Human Subj Res. *Mem:* Arctic Inst NAm. *Res:* Zoonotic disease leptospirosis; epidemiology of disease in Artic populations; epidemiological surveillance by lay reporting; epidemiological surveillance using computerized health records; semantics of lay reporting of disease. *Mailing Add:* 4911 Hidden Valley Rd Tucson AZ 85750

REINHARDT, CHARLES FRANCIS, OCCUPATIONAL MEDICINE, TOXICOLOGY. *Personal Data:* b Spring Grove, Ind, Nov 25, 33; m 56; c 4. *Educ:* Wabash Col, BA, 55; Ind Univ, MD, 59; Ohio State Univ, MSc, 64; Am Bd Prev Med, dipl & cert occup med, 67; Am Bd Toxicol, dipl & cert gen toxicol, 80. *Prof Exp:* Plant physician, Chambers Works, E I Du Pont de Nemours & Co Inc, 64-66, physiologist, 66-69, chief, Physiol Sect, 69-70, res mgr environ sci, 70-71, asst dir, 71-74, assoc dir, 74-76, dir, Haskell Lab Toxicol & Indust Med, 76-96. *Mem:* AMA; Am Indust Hyg Asn; Am Occup Med Asn; Am Acad Occup Med; Soc Toxicol. *Mailing Add:* Haskell Lab E I du Pont de Nemours & Co Inc PO Box 50 Elkton Rd Newark DE 19714-0050

REINHARDT, DONALD JOSEPH, MICROBIOLOGY, MYCOLOGY. *Current Pos:* asst prof, 66-69, ASSOC PROF MICROBIOL, GA STATE UNIV, 69- *Personal Data:* b New York, NY, Dec 6, 38; m 68, Betty Carter; c 3. *Educ:* Manhattan Col, BS, 60; Columbia Univ, MA, 62, PhD(microbiol), 66; Am Bd Microbiol, dipl. *Prof Exp:* Teaching asst mycol, Columbia Univ, 61-66. *Concurrent Pos:* Res fel med microbiol, Ctr Dis Control, USPHS, Ga, 66-69; expert witness, indust consult, trouble shooting infection control indust settings. *Mem:* Am Soc Microbiol; fel Am Soc Microbiol; fel Am Acad Microbiol. *Res:* Medical devices and disinfectants, sterilants, quality control; clinical medical microbiology; chemical and medical microbiology; epidemiology and infection control in hospitals; forty publications, two books, excellence in speaking/teaching. *Mailing Add:* Dept Biol Ga State Univ PO Box 4010 Atlanta GA 30302-4010. *Fax:* 404-651-2509

REINHARDT, HOWARD EARL, MATHEMATICAL STATISTICS. *Current Pos:* from asst prof to prof math, Univ Mont, 57-82, chmn dept, 66-73, dean arts & sci, 82-85, CONSULT, UNIV MONT, 85- *Personal Data:* b Nezperce, Idaho, Mar 16, 27; m 56; c 3. *Educ:* Univ Idaho, BS, 49; State Col Wash, MA, 51; Univ Mich, PhD(math), 59. *Prof Exp:* Instr math, State Col Wash, 52-53. *Mem:* Math Asn Am. *Res:* Statistical inference, particularly parametric and non-parametric hypothesis testing techniques. *Mailing Add:* Dept Math Univ Mont Missoula MT 59812-0001

REINHARDT, RICHARD ALAN, INORGANIC CHEMISTRY. *Current Pos:* from asst prof to prof, 54-86, EMER PROF CHEM, NAVAL POSTGRAD SCH, 86- *Personal Data:* b Berkeley, Calif, Oct 18, 22. *Educ:* Univ Calif, BS, 43, PhD(chem), 47. *Prof Exp:* Asst chem, Univ Calif, 43-44; jr scientist, Univ Chicago, 44-45; jr scientist, Los Alamos Sci Lab, 45-46; asst chem, Univ Calif, 46; instr chem, Cornell Univ, 47-51; res chemist, Wright Air Develop Ctr, Wright-Patterson AFB, 51-53. *Mem:* Am Chem Soc; Sigma Xi. *Res:* Kinetics of inorganic redox reactions; transition-metal complexes; thermodynamics of internal explosions. *Mailing Add:* 25045 Valley Pl Carmel CA 93923-8304

REINHARDT, ROBERT MILTON, ORGANIC CHEMISTRY. *Current Pos:* Chemist, Chem Properties Sect, Cotton Fiber Div, Southern Regional Res Ctr, USDA, 47-54, chemist, Chem Finishing Invests, Cotton Chem Lab, 54-61, Wash-Wear Invests, Cotton Finishes Lab, 61-76, sr res chemist, Cotton Textile Chem Lab, 76-85, LEAD SCIENTIST, DYEING & FINISHING, TEXTILE FINISHING CHEM RES, SOUTHERN REGIONAL RES CTR, USDA, 85- *Personal Data:* b New Orleans, La, 1927; m 51; c 2. *Educ:* Tulane Univ, BS, 47. *Mem:* Am Chem Soc; Sigma Xi; Am Asn Textile Chemists & Colorists. *Res:* Chemical modification and finishing of cotton and cellulose derivatives; chemistry of crosslinking agents for cellulose; properties of chemically modified cottons; free radical modification of cellulose; dyeing crosslinked cotton. *Mailing Add:* S Reg Res Ctr PO Box 19687 New Orleans LA 70179-0687

REINHARDT, WILLIAM NELSON, MATHEMATICS. *Current Pos:* Asst prof, 67-73, ASSOC PROF MATH, UNIV COLO, BOULDER, 73- *Personal Data:* b Bartlesville, Okla, May 12, 39; div; c 2. *Educ:* Col Wooster, BA, 61; Univ Calif, Berkeley, PhD(math), 67. *Concurrent Pos:* NSF grants, 67-73; vis prof, Univ Amsterdam, 72-73; mem, Inst Advan Study, 73-74. *Mem:* Am Math Soc; Math Asn Am. *Res:* Set theory and foundations of mathematics; logic; model theory; philosophical logic. *Mailing Add:* 740 17th St Boulder CO 80302-7602

REINHARDT, WILLIAM PARKER, CHEMICAL PHYSICS. *Current Pos:* PROF CHEM, UNIV WASH, 91-, ASSOC CHAIR, 93- *Personal Data:* b San Francisco, Calif, May 22, 42; m 79, Katrina Currens; c James W & Alexander H. *Educ:* Univ Calif, Berkeley, BS, 64; Harvard Univ, AM, 66, PhD(chem physics), 68. *Hon Degrees:* MA, Univ Pa, 85. *Prof Exp:* From instr to assoc prof chem, Harvard Univ, 67-74; prof chem, Univ Colo, Boulder, 74-84, chmn dept, 77-80; prof, Dept Chem, Univ Pa, 84-91, chmn dept, 85-88, D M Crow prof, 86-91. *Concurrent Pos:* Vis fel, Joint Inst Lab Astrophys, 72, fel, 74-; Sloan Found fel, 72, Dreyfus Found teacher scholar, 72-77; Guggenheim Mem fel, 78; fac fel, Coun Res & Creative Work, Univ Colo, 78; nat lectr, Sigma Xi, 80-82. *Mem:* Am Chem Soc; fel AAAS; fel Am Phys Soc; Sigma Xi. *Res:* Atomic and molecular structure; scattering processes; many-body theory as applied to chemical problems; classical and semiclassical theories of highly excited electronic and vibrational states; atoms in intense fields; classical and quantum chaos; simulation of molecular fluids and surfaces. *Mailing Add:* Dept Chem BF-10 Univ Wash Seattle WA 98195-0001. *Fax:* 206-685-8665; *E-Mail:* rein@chem.washington.edu

REINHART, GREGORY DUNCAN, BIOCHEMISTRY. *Current Pos:* ASST PROF, DEPT CHEM, UNIV OKLA, 83- *Personal Data:* b Chicago, Ill, Nov 1, 51; m 76; c 1. *Educ:* Univ Ill, BS, 73; Univ Wis, Madison, PhD(biochem), 79. *Prof Exp:* Res fel, Mayo Clin Found, 79-80, res assoc, 80-81, assoc consult biochem, 81-83; instr biochem, Mayo Med Sch, 81-83. *Mem:* Biophys Soc; NY Acad Sci; Sigma Xi; Am Soc Biol Chemists; Am Chem Soc. *Res:* Regulation of enzyme activity; biophysical properties of enzymes; regulation of carbohydrate metabolism. *Mailing Add:* TX A&M Univ Dept Biochem & Biophys College Station TX 77843

REINHART, JOHN BELVIN, PSYCHIATRY, PEDIATRICS. *Current Pos:* CONSULT CHILD PSYCHIAT, TREND MENT HEALTH SERV, 83- *Personal Data:* b Merrill, Wis, Dec 22, 17; m 49, Helen E; c 6. *Educ:* Duke Univ, AB, 39; Wake Forest Col, MD, 43. *Honors & Awards:* Simon Wile Award, Am Acad Child Adolescent Psychiat, 90. *Prof Exp:* Instr pediat, Bowman Gray Sch Med, Wake Forest Col, 50-52; dir pediat psychiat, Children's Hosp, 56-74; dir div behav sci, Children's Hosp, Pittsburgh, 74-83; from asst prof to prof, 56-83, emer prof pediat & child psychiat, Sch Med, Univ Pittsburgh, 83- *Mem:* Am Psychiat Asn; Am Acad Pediat; Am Acad Child Psychiat. *Res:* Child abuse and neglect; consultation-liaison to psychiatry; failure to thrive; psychosomatic disease in children; brief pediatric-child psychiatry liaison. *Mailing Add:* 34 Hunters Lane Hendersonville NC 28791

REINHART, MICHAEL P, biochemistry, for more information see previous edition

REINHART, ROY HERBERT, GEOLOGY, VERTEBRATE PALEONTOLOGY. *Current Pos:* from asst prof to assoc prof, 51-62, actg chmn dept, 64-65, PROF GEOL, MIAMI UNIV, 62- *Personal Data:* b Cincinnati, Ohio, Sept 11, 19; m 41; c 3. *Educ:* Miami Univ, AB, 41; Univ Chicago, MS, 49; Univ Calif, Berkeley, PhD(paleont), 52. *Prof Exp:* Asst geol, WTex State Univ, 50-51. *Concurrent Pos:* Fel, Miami Univ, 59; res assoc, Univ Fla, 61-66. *Mem:* Soc Vert Paleont. *Res:* Fossil marine mammals, especially orders Sirenia and Desmostylia of world; correlation of Cenozoic stratigraphy of world. *Mailing Add:* 841 S Maple Ave Oxford OH 45056

REINHART, STANLEY E, JR, ELECTRICAL ENGINEERING. *Current Pos:* RETIRED. *Personal Data:* b Cincinnati, Ohio, Apr 25, 28; m 52; c 5. *Educ:* US Mil Acad, BS, 50; Ga Inst Technol, MS, 64, PhD(electromagnetic theory), 66. *Prof Exp:* US Army, 46-90; from instr to assoc prof elec eng, US Mil Acad, 53-77, prof & actg head dept, 77-90. *Mem:* Inst Elec & Electronics Engrs; Am Soc Eng Educ. *Res:* Electromagnetic theory; near fields of antennas; numerical calculation of fields; undergraduate electrical engineering curricula. *Mailing Add:* 134 Forest View Dr Flat Rock NC 28731

REINHEIMER, JOHN DAVID, ORGANIC CHEMISTRY. *Current Pos:* RETIRED. *Personal Data:* b Springfield, Ohio, Dec 23, 20; m 44; c 5. *Educ:* Kenyon Col, AB, 42; Johns Hopkins Univ, AM, 44, PhD(chem), 48. *Prof Exp:* From instr to prof chem, Col Wooster, 48-85. *Concurrent Pos:* Vis prof, Univ NC, 58-59, Univ Munich, 62-63; Von Humboldt fel, 63; vis scientist, UCSB, 68-69, 73-74, 79-80 & 85. *Mem:* Am Chem Soc; Sigma Xi. *Res:* Qualitative and physical organic chemistry; kinetics of organic reactions; kinetics of the aromatic nucleophilic substitution reaction; nuclear magnetic resonance studies on simple molecules and biochemical systems; ring opening reactions. *Mailing Add:* 5750 Vial Real No 303 Carpinteria CA 93013-2612

REINHEIMER, JULIAN, PHYSICS. *Current Pos:* sect mgr, Aerospace Corp, 64-68, assoc dept head, 68-72, assoc prog dir, 72-76, syst dir, 76-86, sr proj engr, 86-91, CONSULT, AEROSPACE CORP, EL SEGUNDO, 91- *Personal Data:* b Philadelphia, Pa, Oct 19, 25; m 56, Olga Deutsch; c 1. *Educ:* Pa State Col, BS, 49; Univ Minn, MS, 50; NY Univ, PhD(physics), 68. *Prof Exp:* Physicist, 3M Co, 50-52; proj engr, Fisher Sci Co, 52-53; res physicist, Inst Coop Res, Univ Pa, 53-58; from staff scientist to sect head, Repub Aviation Corp, 58-64. *Concurrent Pos:* Ed staff, Siam J, 54-56; lectr, Univ Calif, Riverside, Exten, 67. *Mem:* Am Phys Soc; Optical Soc Am; Am Asn Physics Teachers. *Res:* Optics; mathematical physics; solid state physics, radiation effects; technology development. *Mailing Add:* 4112 Quinlin Dr Palos Verdes Peninsula CA 90274

REINHOLD, VERNON NYE, ANALYTICAL BIOCHEMISTRY. *Current Pos:* LECTR DEPT BIOL CHEM, HARVARD MED SCH, 76- *Personal Data:* b Beverly, Mass, May 13, 31; m 53; c 5. *Educ:* Univ NH, BS, 59, MS, 61; Univ Vt, PhD(biochem), 65. *Prof Exp:* AEC fel protein chem, Brookhaven Nat Lab, NY, 65-67; Helen Hay Whitney fel, Mass Inst Technol & Harvard Med Sch, 67-71, jr res assoc chem, Mass Inst Technol, 71-76. *Mem:* AAAS; Soc Complex Carbohydrates; Am Chem Soc. *Res:* Gas chromatography-mass spectrometry; computer assisted analysis of biochemical components; glycoprotein structure and carbohydrate sequence analysis via gas liquid chromatography-mass spectrometry; protein and organic chemistry. *Mailing Add:* Dept Microbiol & Immunol Boston Univ Sch Med 80 E Concord St Boston MA 02118-2394

REINIG, JAMES WILLIAM, MAGNETIC RESONANCE IMAGING, DIAGNOSTIC RADIOLOGY. *Current Pos:* CLIN DIR, MAGENTIC RESONANCE IMAGING, 86-, CHIEF, DEPT RADIOL, ANNE ARUNDEL MED CTR, 93- *Personal Data:* b Augusta, Ga, May 20, 54; m 80, Ellen M Tinkler; c Margaret & Ann. *Educ:* Harvard Col, AB, 76; Med Univ SC, MD, 80; Am Bd Radiol, cert radiol, 84; Am Bd Nuclear Med, cert nuclear med, 84. *Prof Exp:* Fac diag radiol, NIH, 84-86. *Concurrent Pos:* Vis fac, Dept Diag Radiol, NIH, 86- *Mem:* Soc Magnetic Resonance Med; Radiol Soc of NAm; Am Col Radiol; Am Roentgen Ray Soc; AMA. *Res:* Application of clinical magnetic resonance imaging of the body. *Mailing Add:* Anne Arundel MRI 235 Jennifer Rd Annapolis MD 21401

REINIG, WILLIAM CHARLES, HEALTH PHYSICS. *Current Pos:* RETIRED. *Personal Data:* b New York, NY, June 5, 24; m 49, Marion Borgstrom; c James W & Christine (Flournoy). *Educ:* Polytech Inst Brooklyn, BME, 45; Am Bd Health Physics, dipl. *Prof Exp:* Med engr, Hanford Works, Gen Elec Co, 46-48; assoc health physicist, Brookhaven Nat Lab, 48-51; area supvr health physics, Savannah River Plant, E I du Pont de Nemours & Co, Inc, 51-61, chief tech supvr, 61-65, sr res supvr environ effects, 65-76, res mgr environ anal & planning, 76-78, supt health protection dept, 78-88, gen supt tech dept, 88-89, dep gen mgr, Savannah River Site, Westinghouse Savannah River Co, 89-94. *Concurrent Pos:* Chmn, Am Bd Health Physics, 74-76; chmn comt tritium measurement & comt nuclear decommissioning, Nat Coun Radiation Protection & Measurements. *Mem:* Health Physics Soc (secy, 64-66, pres, 80-81); Am Acad Health Physics (dir, 85-87). *Res:* Environmental radiation and radioactivity; radiological health. *Mailing Add:* 1014 Stanton Dr North Augusta SC 29841

REINING, PRISCILLA COPELAND, ANTHROPOLOGY, AGRARIAN SYSTEMS. *Current Pos:* ADJ PROF, UNIV FLA, 90- *Personal Data:* b Chicago, Ill, Mar 11, 23; m 44, 84; c Robert, Anne & Conrad. *Educ:* Univ Chicago, AB, 45, AM, 49, PhD(anthrop), 67. *Honors & Awards:* Distinguished Serv Award, Am Anthrop Asn, 90; Res Explor Award, Nat Geog Soc, 93. *Prof Exp:* Sr res fel, EAfrican Inst Social Res, 51-55; lectr, Univ Minn, 56-59 & Howard Univ, 60-65; res assoc, Cath Univ, 66-68, Smithsonian Inst, 66 & 68-70; consult, proj res, Int Bank Reconstuct & Develop, 72 & AID, 73; res assoc, AAAS, 74, prog dir, admin, 75-90. *Concurrent Pos:* Lectr, Comt Space Res, Brazil, 74; mem, US deleg UN Conf Desertification, Nairobi, Kenya, 77; mem, Bd Sci & Technol Int Develop, Nat Acad Sci, 78-80 & adv comt Sahel, 79-81; mem, experts group desertification, UN Environ Prog, 79 & 81, IV Int Conf AIDS, Stockholm, 88; bd dirs, Renewable Natural Resources Found, 91- *Mem:* Fel AAAS; fel African Studies Asn; fel Am Anthrop Asn; Am Pub Health Asn. *Res:* Africa land tenure and land use, population and kinship; desertification processes in Africa and other Third World countries; decentralized energy systems in villages; use of remote sensing methodology in the social sciences; transmission, care, consequences of human immunodeficiency virus/acquired immune deficiency syndrome in sub-Saharan Africa. *Mailing Add:* 3601 Rittenhouse St NW Washington DC 20015. *Fax:* 202-966-5492; *E-Mail:* pacr3601@gwuvm

REININGER, EDWARD JOSEPH, PHYSIOLOGY, CARDIOVASCULAR RESPIRATORY PHYSIOLOGIST. *Current Pos:* RETIRED. *Personal Data:* b Chicago, Ill, Dec 30, 29; c David J & Jonathan T. *Educ:* Univ Ill, BS, 50, MS, 52; Ohio State Univ, PhD(physiol), 57. *Prof Exp:* From asst to instr physiol, Ohio State Univ, 52-58; lectr, McGill Univ, 58-60, asst prof, 60-71; assoc prof, Sch Med, Ind Univ, Terre Haute, 71-74; prof physiol, Sch Med, Southern Ill Univ, Springfield, 74-76; prof & chmn dept physiol & pharm, Sch Med, Univ Cent Caribe, 77-78, prof physiol, 78-86. *Concurrent Pos:* Grants, Que Heart Found, 59-65 & Med Res Coun Can, 66-70; res prog, Minority Hypertension, Univ Fla, 81-83. *Mem:* Am Physiol Soc; Natural Hist Soc PR (treas, 84-85 & vpres, 86). *Res:* Cardiovascular effects of cardiac pacing and feeding; sighing in man and spontaneous gasps and post-gasp apnea in dogs; mechanism that prevents atelectasis; measurement of cardiac output; minicomputer programming for teaching and research. *Mailing Add:* 330 SE Second St No 403G Hallandale FL 33009-5608

REINISCH, BODO WALTER, ELECTRICAL ENGINEERING. *Current Pos:* assoc prof elec eng, 80-83, DIR, CTR ATMOSPHERIC RES, UNIV MASS, LOWELL, 75-, PROF ELEC ENG, 83-, DEPT HEAD, 88- *Personal Data:* b Beuthen, Ger, Nov 26, 36; m 63, Gerda Seidenschwand; c Karin & Ulrike. *Educ:* Univ Freiburg, Ger, MS, 63; Lowell Tech Inst, PhD, 70. *Prof Exp:* Res asst, Ionospharen Inst, Ger, 61-63, physicist, 63-65; physicist, Lowell Tech Inst, 65-75. *Concurrent Pos:* Consult, Royal Meteorol Inst, Brussels, 70-71; guest prof physics, Univ Linz, Austria, 78-79; grantee, USAF, NASA & NSF. *Mem:* Sr mem Inst Elec & Electronics Engrs; Am Geophys Union; Int Union Radio Sci. *Res:* Development of global network of digisonde sounders; established high frequency Doppler observations for ionospheric drift studies; granted two patents. *Mailing Add:* 14 Overlook Dr Bedford MA 01730-1331

REINKE, DAVID ALBERT, PHARMACOLOGY, PHYSIOLOGY. *Current Pos:* ASSOC PROF PHARMACOL & TOXICOL, MICH STATE UNIV 64-, VICE CHAIRPERSON, DEPT PHARMACOL & TOXICOL, 87- *Personal Data:* b Manitowoc, Wis, May 15, 33; m 56; c 2. *Educ:* Univ Wis, BS, 55; Univ Mich, MA, 60, PhD(pharmacol), 64. *Prof Exp:* Res chemist, Dow Corning Corp, 55-58. *Concurrent Pos:* Mem, Medicinal Chem Div, Am Chem Soc. *Mem:* Am Soc Pharmacol & Exp Therapeut. *Mailing Add:* 1916 N Harrison Rd East Lansing MI 48823-1304

REINKE, LESTER ALLEN, ALCOHOL, FREE RADICALS. *Current Pos:* prof pharmacol, Col Med, 80-94, PROF PHARMACOL & TOXICOL, COL PHARM, UNIV OKLA HEALTH SCI CTR, 94- *Personal Data:* b Davenport, Nebr, Sept 29, 46; m 68, Carol Sue Paulsen; c Jonathan Paul & Lisa Sue. *Educ:* Univ Nebr-Lincoln, BS, 69, MS, 75; Univ Nebr Med Ctr-Omaha, PhD(biomed chem), 77. *Prof Exp:* Fel pharmacol, Univ NC, 77-80, res asst prof, 80. *Concurrent Pos:* Provost res award, Univ Okla Health Sci Ctr, 84; hon lectr, Mid-Am State Univ Asn, 86-87. *Mem:* Am Soc Pharmacol & Exp Therapeut; Int Soc Biomed Res Alcoholism; Int EPR Soc; Oxygen Soc; Res Soc Alcoholism. *Res:* Detection of free radical intermediates in biological samples, their biological effects; mechanisms of cellular protection against radicals; alcohol and free radicals. *Mailing Add:* Dept Pharmacol & Toxicol Univ Okla Health Sci Ctr Oklahoma City OK 73190

REINKE, WILLIAM ANDREW, BIOSTATISTICS. *Current Pos:* asst dean, 74-76, assoc dean, 76-77, PROF INT HEALTH, SCH HYG, JOHNS HOPKINS UNIV, 70- *Personal Data:* b Cleveland, Ohio, Aug 10, 28; div; c 4. *Educ:* Kenyon Col, BA, 49; Univ Pa, MBA, 50; Case Western Reserve Univ, PhD(statist), 61. *Prof Exp:* Staff asst to controller, Warner & Swasey Co, 50-55; syst analyst, US Steel Corp, 55-56; statistician, Union Carbide Corp, 56-59; instr statist, Case Western Reserve Univ, 59-61; sr res mathematician, Corning Glass Works, 61-63; asst prof biostatist, Univ Md, 63-64. *Concurrent Pos:* Assoc ed, Opers Res, 71-74; treas, Univ Assoc for Int Health Inc, 73-; mem comt tech consult, Nat Ctr Health Statist, 73; mem, Nursing Res & Educ Adv Comt, 74-78. *Mem:* Inst Mgt Sci; fel Am Pub Health Asn; Am Statist Asn. *Res:* Health planning methodology; health practice research in relation to health services delivery. *Mailing Add:* 9 Airway Circle No 4B Baltimore MD 21286

REINKING, LARRY NORMAN, STOMACH-RENAL INTERACTION. *Current Pos:* ASSOC PROF BIOL, MILLERSVILLE UNIV, 81- *Educ:* Univ Mont, PhD(zool), 78. *Res:* Upper urinary tract. *Mailing Add:* Dept Biol Millersville Univ PO Box 1002 Millersville PA 17551-0302

REINMUTH, OSCAR MCNAUGHTON, NEUROLOGY, INTERNAL MEDICINE. *Current Pos:* PROF & CHMN DEPT NEUROL, SCH MED, UNIV PITTSBURGH, 77- *Personal Data:* b Lincoln, Nebr, Oct 23, 27; m 51, 80; c 3. *Educ:* Univ Tex, AB, 48; Duke Univ, MD, 52. *Prof Exp:* Intern, Duke Hosp, 52-53; asst resident, New Haven Med Ctr, 53-55; asst resident to chief resident, Boston City Hosp, 55-57; from assoc prof to prof neurol, Sch Med, Univ Miami, 58-77. *Concurrent Pos:* NIH trainee, Med Sch, Yale Univ, 54-55; lectr neurol, Sargent Col, Boston Univ, 55-56; teaching fel, Harvard Med Sch, 56-57; NIH spec trainee, Nat Hosp, Queen's Square, London, 57-58; consult, Nat Inst Neurol Dis & Stroke, 68-; consult adv comt, Sect Head Injury & Stroke, NIH, 73-; mem coun stroke, Am Heart Asn, ed, Stroke, 87- *Mem:* Am Acad Neurol (vpres, 71-75); Am Neurol Asn (vpres, 78-79); fel Am Col Physicians; fel Am Heart Asn; Soc Neurosci; Sigma Xi. *Res:* Cerebral circulation and metabolism in humans and experimental animals; cerebral vascular disease; movement disorders. *Mailing Add:* Dept Neur Univ Ariz Health Sci Ctr 1501 N Campbell Ave Tucson AZ 85724-5023

REINSBOROUGH, VINCENT CONRAD, PHYSICAL CHEMISTRY. *Current Pos:* from asst prof to assoc prof, 70-83, PROF CHEM, MT ALLISON UNIV, 83-, DEPT HEAD, 87- *Personal Data:* b Buctouche, NB, May 14, 35; m 77, Anne Kiefl; c Michelle, Marie & Laura. *Educ:* Univ Toronto, BA, 58, MA, 59, STB, 64; Univ Tasmania, PhD(chem), 69. *Prof Exp:* Teacher high sch, Ont, 59-61; lectr chem, Univ St Michael's Col, 61-65; Nat Res Coun Can fel, Univ Toronto, 69-70. *Concurrent Pos:* Vis prof Fritz-Haber Inst, Berlin, 84-85, NMex State Univ, 91-92. *Mem:* Chem Inst Can; Royal Soc Chem; Am Chem Soc; fel Can Soc Chem. *Res:* Solubilization, kinetics and catalysis in micellar solutions; dynamics in solution of cyclodextrin inclusions. *Mailing Add:* Dept Chem Mt Allison Univ Sackville NB E0A 3C0 Can. *Fax:* 506-364-2313; *E-Mail:* vcreinsb@mta.ca

REINSCHMIDT, KENNETH F(RANK), CIVIL ENGINEERING, COMPUTER-AIDED ENGINEERING & DESIGN. *Current Pos:* INDEPENDENT CONSULT, 96- *Personal Data:* b Cincinnati, Ohio, Mar 26, 38; m 67. *Educ:* Mass Inst Technol, SB, 60, SM, 62, PhD(civil eng), 65. *Honors & Awards:* Thomas Fitch Rowland Prize, Am Soc Civil Engrs, 91. *Prof Exp:* From asst prof to assoc prof civil eng, Mass Inst Technol, 65-73, sr res assoc, 73-75; consult engr, Stone & Webster Eng Corp, 75-80, vpres & sr consult engr, 80-88, sr vpres, 88-92, pres, Stone & Webster Advan Systs Develop Serv, Inc, 88-96, sr vpres, 92-96. *Mem:* Nat Acad Eng; Am Soc Civil Engrs; Opers Res Soc Am; Inst Mgt Sci; Sigma Xi; fel AAAS. *Res:* Historical development of building science; expert systems and artificial intelligence; computer modeling and operations research; mathematical programming and optimization; computer-aided design; neural networks; three-dimensional computer graphics; engineering, manufacturing, construction, production planning, scheduling, plant operations and control. *Mailing Add:* 20 Tahattawan Rd Littleton MA 01460-1605

REINSEL, GREGORY CHARLES, STATISTICAL TIME SERIES ANALYSIS, MULTIVARIATE STATISTICAL METHODS. *Current Pos:* From asst prof to assoc prof, 76-87, PROF STATIST, UNIV WIS-MADISON, 87- *Personal Data:* b Wilkinsburg, Pa, Mar 10, 48; m 76; c 2. *Educ:* Univ Pittsburgh, BS, 70, MA, 72, PhD(math & statist), 76. *Concurrent Pos:* Prin investr, NASA, Nat Oceanic & Atmospheric Admin & Chem Mfrs Asn, 81-; res assoc, Grad Sch Bus, Univ Chicago, 84. *Mem:* Am Statist Asn; Inst Math Statist; Royal Statist Soc; Am Geophys Union. *Res:* Development of useful statistical methods and related theory for the analysis of time series data, especially multivariate time series; trend analysis of atmospheric ozone and temperature time series data for global changes. *Mailing Add:* 6326 Shoreham Dr Madison WI 53711

REINSTEIN, LAWRENCE ELLIOT, MEDICAL PHYSICS. *Current Pos:* MEM STAFF DEPT RADIATION MED, BROWN UNIV. *Personal Data:* b New York, NY, Apr 18, 45; m 68; c 3. *Educ:* Brooklyn Col, BS, 66; Yale Univ, MS, 68; Boston Univ, PhD(physics), 75. *Prof Exp:* Fel med physics, Mem Sloan-Kettering Cancer Inst, 75-76; physicist radiation oncol, RI Hosp, Providence, 76- *Concurrent Pos:* Asst prof bio-med, Brown Univ, 76- *Mem:* Am Phys Soc; Am Asn Physicists Med. *Res:* Electron beam radiation as used in treatment of cancer; 3-dimensional treatment planning. *Mailing Add:* Dept Radiation Med SUNY Health Sci Ctr 100 Nicolls Rd Stony Brook NY 11794-0001

REINTJES, J FRANCIS, ELECTRICAL ENGINEERING. *Current Pos:* prof, 47-77, EMER PROF & SR LECTR ELEC ENG, MASS INST TECHNOL, 77- *Personal Data:* b Troy, NY, Feb 19, 12; m 42, Elizabeth A Walsh; c William F, John F & Ellen E. *Educ:* Rensselaer Polytech Inst, BS, 33, ME, 34. *Prof Exp:* Elec engr, Gen Motors Corp, 36-37; asst prof elec eng, Manhattan Col, 37-43; vis asst prof elec eng, Mass Inst Technol, 43-45; elec engr, Gen Elec Co, 46-47. *Concurrent Pos:* Dir, Electronic Systs Lab, Mass Inst Technol, 53-73 & Co-Op Prog Elec Eng, 60-69. *Mem:* Fel Inst Elec & Electronics Engrs; Am Soc Eng Educ. *Res:* Pulse doppler radar; information storage and retrieval; digital encoding of images. *Mailing Add:* Mass Inst Technol Rm 35-418 77 Massachusetts Ave Cambridge MA 02139

REINTJES, JOHN FRANCIS, JR, LASERS, QUANTUM OPTICS. *Current Pos:* res physicist, 73-81, head, Nonlinear Optics Sect, Laser Physics Br, 82-95, SR SCIENTIST QUANTUM ELECTRONICS, NAVAL RES LAB, 95- *Personal Data:* b Boston, Mass, Dec 7, 45; m 71, Maura Carol Burns; c Christopher J. *Educ:* Mass Inst Technol, BS, 66; Harvard Univ, PhD(appl physics), 72. *Prof Exp:* Postdoctoral fel nonlinear optics res, Int Bus Mach Corp Watson Res Ctr, 71-73. *Concurrent Pos:* Consult, Lawrence Livermore Lab, 71; lectr, Catholic Univ, 84- *Mem:* Am Phys Soc; fel Optical Soc Am; Sigma Xi; Inst Elec & Electronics Engrs. *Res:* Nonlinear optics for extreme ultraviolet generation, higher order harmonic generation, Raman beam cleanup and optical phase conjugation; low light level image amplification; sensors for mechanical diagnostics. *Mailing Add:* Naval Res Lab Code 5600-2 Washington DC 20375. *Fax:* 202-404-7530; *E-Mail:* reintjes@ccf.nrl.navy.mil

REINTJES, MARTEN, ORGANIC CHEMISTRY. *Current Pos:* from res chemist to res group leader, ITT Rayonier Inc, 68-73, sect leader, 73-77, sect supvr, Olympic Res Div, 78-82, res assoc, 83, mgr tech admin, res ctr, 84-88 & PROD SAFETY ADMINR, ITT RAYONIER INC, 89- *Personal Data:* b Meeden, Netherlands, Mar 13, 32; US citizen; m 57, Elsie Siegert; c Maurice & Eric. *Educ:* Univ Calif, Riverside, BA, 59, PhD(chem), 66. *Prof Exp:* Analyst, Chemische Fabriek Flebo, Netherlands, 49-52; asst chemist, Orange Co Sanit Dist, Calif, 55-57; res chemist, Sunkist Growers, Inc, 59-62 & Arapahoe Chem Div, Syntex Corp, Colo, 65-68. *Mem:* Can Pulp & Paper Asn; Am Chem Soc. *Res:* Organic synthesis and natural products; process development; organo-boron, boron-hydride and carborane chemistry; silvichemicals. *Mailing Add:* PO Box 417 Shelton WA 98584. *Fax:* 206-426-7537

REIS, ARTHUR HENRY, JR, INORGANIC CHEMISTRY. *Current Pos:* adminr chem dept, Brandeis Univ, 79-82, assoc prof chem, 80-83, dir, 82-86, assoc dean, sci resources & planning, 86-89, assoc provost, 90-91, proj dir, Nat Ctr Complex Systs, 87-95, acting proviost & dean fac, 91-92, ASSOC PROVOST, BRANDEIS UNIV, 92-, ASSOC VPRES DEVELOP, 94- *Personal Data:* b Chicago, Ill, Nov 6, 46; m 70, 92, Debra-Ann Sowul; c Sally (Wessell) & Rodger H. *Educ:* Cornell Col, Iowa, BA, 68; Harvard Univ, MA, 69, PhD(chem), 72. *Prof Exp:* Teaching fel org chem, Harvard Univ, 72; space systs analyst satellite tracking, US Air Force, Ent AFB, Colo, 72-73; space oper officer satellite tracking, USAF, Thule AFB, Greenland, 73-74; appointee, Argonne Nat Lab, Argonne, Ill, 74-75, res assoc inorg chem, 75-76, asst chemist, 76-79. *Concurrent Pos:* Consult, Picker X-Ray Corp, 71-72; assoc proj dir, Undergrad Res Particip Proj, NSF-GTE Corp, 81; Nat Coun Univ Res Adminr, 81; dir forefront topics in sci proj, Brandeis Univ, 83-; New Eng Coun, 84. *Mem:* Am Chem Soc; Am Crystallog Asn; Coun Chem Res. *Res:* Synthesis and structural characterization by x-ray and neutron diffraction of one-dimensional transition metal conductors, pulsed neutron diffraction and exafs studies of metal complexes in zeolites. *Mailing Add:* Off Provost Brandeis Univ MS-134 Waltham MA 02254-9110. *Fax:* 781-736-3457; *E-Mail:* reis@brandeis.edu

REIS, DONALD J, NEUROLOGY, NEUROBIOLOGY. *Current Pos:* from asst prof to prof neurol, 63-81, GEORGE C COTIAS DISTINGUISHED PROF NEUROL, CORNELL UNIV, 81- *Personal Data:* b New York, NY, Sept 9, 31. *Educ:* Cornell Univ, AB, 53, MD, 56. *Honors & Awards:* CIBA Medal, Am Heart Asn, 87. *Prof Exp:* Res anatomist, Univ Calif, Los Angeles, 54-55; intern med, New York Hosp, 56-57; resident neurol, Boston City Hosp, 57-59; res assoc neurophysiol, NIMH, 60-62. *Concurrent Pos:* Teaching fel, Harvard Med Sch, 57-59; United Cerebral Palsy Found fel brain res, Nat Hosp, London, Eng, 59-60; mem, Karolinska Inst, Sweden, 59-60; Nat Inst Neurol Dis & Blindness spec fel, Nobel Neurophysiol Inst, Karolinska Inst, Sweden, 62-63; vis scientist, Chiba Univ Med Sch, Japan, 63; Nat Inst Neurol Dis & Blindness career develop res award, 66-; USPHS career develop award; vis scientist, Lab Clin Sci, NIMH, 70. *Mem:* Am Acad Neurol; Am Physiol Soc; Am Soc Pharmacol & Exp Therapeut; Am Soc Clin Invest; Am Soc Neurochem; Sigma Xi; Am Asn Physicians. *Res:* Central neural autonomic regulation; molecular mechanisms in central nervous regulation of cardiovascular function; neural mechanisms of emotive behavior; central neurotransmitters; brain monoamines and behavior. *Mailing Add:* Dept Neurol & Neurosci Cornell Univ Med Col 411 E 69th St Rm KB410 New York NY 10021-5603

REIS, IRVIN L, MECHANICAL & INDUSTRIAL ENGINEERING. *Current Pos:* RETIRED. *Personal Data:* b Lincoln, Nebr, Oct 5, 26; m 51; c 2. *Educ:* Univ Nebr, BSME, 49, MSME, 50; Univ Ill, PhD(indust eng), 57. *Prof Exp:* Job analyst, Univ Nebr, 49, supvr insts, 50-53, assoc prof mech eng, 57-59; lectr indust eng, Univ Ill, 53-57; res engr, Lincoln Steel Corp, 57; prof indust eng & head dept, Kans State Univ, 59-62; prof, Univ Ark, 62-64; vis prof mech eng, Univ Tex, 64-66; prof mech eng & head dept, Mont State Univ, 66-70, mem fac, Indust Eng Dept, 80-84; prof mech eng, Lamar Univ, 70-80, dept head, 77-80. *Concurrent Pos:* Indust training consult, 50-62; consult, City of Lincoln, Nebr, 58-59 & Bayer & McElrath, Mich, 64-; prof indust eng & head dept, Mont State Univ, 66-67; partner, Mgt Insts Unlimited, 75- *Mem:* Am Soc Eng Educ; Am Inst Indust Engrs; Am Soc Mech Engrs. *Res:* Probabilistic models; conveyer theory; economics. *Mailing Add:* 15881 Sunrise Rd Gravette AR 72736

REIS, PAUL G(EORGE), CHEMICAL ENGINEERING. *Current Pos:* CHEM ENGR PROCESS DEVELOP, PIGMENTS DEPT, E I DUPONT DE NEMOURS & CO, INC, 54- *Personal Data:* b St Cloud, Minn, May 3, 25; m 53; c 6. *Educ:* Northwestern Univ, BS, 45, MS, 49; Univ Wis, PhD(chem eng), 54. *Prof Exp:* Chem engr, process develop, E I du Pont de Nemours & Co, 45 & 47-48; asst, Univ Wis, 49-52. *Mem:* Am Inst Chem Engrs; Am Chem Soc. *Res:* Chemical equilibrium and kinetics. *Mailing Add:* Four Toby Ct Sherwood Park II Wilmington DE 19808-3019

REIS, VICTOR H, MEHCANICAL ENGINEERING. *Current Pos:* ASST SECY, DEPT ENERGY DEFENSE PROGS, 93- *Educ:* Princeton Univ, PhD(mech eng). *Prof Exp:* Sr vpres stategic planning, Sci Applns Int Corp; security adv, Off Sci & Technol Policy; spec asst to dir, Lincoln Labs, Mass Inst Technol; dep dir, Defense Advan Res Projs Agency, 89-90, dir, 90-93. *Res:* Energy defense. *Mailing Add:* Asst Secty US Dept Energy, Dept Energy Def Progs 1000 Independence Ave SW Washington DC 20585

REIS, WALTER JOSEPH, PSYCHIATRY, CLINICAL PSYCHOLOGY. *Current Pos:* clin instr psychiat, 59-63, clin asst prof, 63-69, CLIN PROF PSYCHIAT, SCH MED, UNIV PITTSBURGH, 90-; PSYCHIATRIST & PSYCHOANALYST, PSYCHIAT ASSOCS, 69- *Personal Data:* b Worzburg, Ger, Aug 5, 18; nat US; m 43; c Alan, Judy & Claude. *Educ:* Univ Gonzaga, BPh, 47; City Col New York, BS, 47; Western Res Univ, PhD(psychol), 51; Emory Univ, MD, 55; Am Bd Psychiat & Neurol, dipl, 62. *Prof Exp:* Intern, USPHS Hosp, Norfolk, Va, 55-56; fel, Western Psychiat Inst, Pa, 56-59. *Concurrent Pos:* Mem fac, Pittsburgh Psychoanal Inst, 67-, pvt practr psychiat, 59-; consult, Dixmont State Hosp, Sewickley, Pa, 68-73; training analyst, Pittsburgh Psychoanal Inst, Pa, 72-; clin assoc prof, Sch Med, Univ Pittsburgh, 74-90. *Mem:* Fel Am Psychiat Asn; Am Psychol Asn; Soc Personality Assessment. *Res:* Psychotherapy; psychoanalysis; psychopharmacology. *Mailing Add:* 226 S Maple Ave Greensburg PA 15601-3234. *Fax:* 412-687-1880

REISA, JAMES JOSEPH, JR, ENVIRONMENTAL BIOLOGY, TOXICOLOGY. *Current Pos:* assoc dir, 86-88, DIR, BD ENVIRON STUDIES & TOXICOL, NAT RES COUN, NAT ACAD SCI, 88- *Personal Data:* b Oak Park, Ill, Dec 13, 41; div. *Educ:* Loyola Univ, Chicago, BS, 66; Northwestern Univ, Evanston, Ill, MS, 68, PhD(biol sci), 71. *Honors & Awards:* Bronze Medal, US Environ Protection Agency, 80. *Prof Exp:* US Environ Protection Agency res fel, Dept Biol Sci, Northwestern Univ, 71-72; staff biologist, Argonne Nat Lab, Argonne, Ill, 72-74; staff mem, Coun Environ Qual, Exec Off President, Washington, DC, 74-75, coordr, Environ Monitoring Prog, 75-77, sr staff mem, 77-78; dir environ rev div, Off Toxic Substances, US Environ Protection Agency, 78-79, assoc dep asst adminr for toxic substances, 79-81, dir, Off Explor Res, 81-82; vpres, IDEA Tech Assoc, Alexandria, Va, 82-86. *Concurrent Pos:* Vis lectr biol, Mundelein Col, Chicago, 70-71, vis asst prof, 71-72; chmn, Fed Interagency Task Force Air Qual Indicators, 75-77, President's Task Force Environ Data Monitoring, 77-78, Toxics Res Comt, US Environ Protection Agency, 79-81 & Appl Ecol Sect, Ecol Soc Am, 80-82; mem, Bd Dir, Soc Environ Toxicol & Chem, 81-82. *Mem:* Ecol Soc Am; AAAS; Am Inst Biol Sci; Sigma Xi; Soc Environ Toxicol & Chem. *Res:* Assessment of environmental fate and effects of toxic chemicals; science policy and regulatory decision making; environmental data systems. *Mailing Add:* Bd Environ Studies & Toxicol MH354 Nat Acad Sci 2101 Constitution Ave NW Washington DC 20418. *Fax:* 202-334-2752; *E-Mail:* jreisa@nas.edu

REISBERG, BORIS ELLIOTT, MEDICINE, INFECTIOUS DISEASES. *Current Pos:* assoc, 68-69, ASST PROF INTERNAL MED, NORTHWESTERN UNIV, CHICAGO, 69- *Personal Data:* b New York, NY, Dec 12, 35. *Educ:* Brown Univ, AB, 57; State Univ NY, MD, 61; Am Bd Internal Med, dipl, 68, cert infectious dis, 74. *Prof Exp:* Instr internal med, New Eng Ctr Hosp, Tufts Univ, 64-66; NIH fel, 66-67. *Mailing Add:* 251 E Superior St Chicago IL 60611-2913

REISBERG, JOSEPH, CHEMISTRY. *Current Pos:* RETIRED. *Personal Data:* b New York, NY, May 10, 21; m 53. *Educ:* City Col New York, BS, 43. *Prof Exp:* Res chemist, SAM Lab, Columbia Univ, 43-44; Los Alamos Sci Lab, Univ Calif, 44-47 & Colgate-Palmolive-Peet Corp, NJ, 47-48; res chemist, explor & prod res lab, 49-66, res assoc, 66-70, Shell Lab, Rijswijk, Holland, 70-71, sr res assoc, 71-74, res assoc, Shell Develop Co, Tex, 74- *Mem:* AAAS; Am Chem Soc; Am Inst Mining, Metall & Petrol Engrs; NY Acad Sci. *Res:* Surface and colloid chemistry; unconventional methods for petroleum recovery. *Mailing Add:* 5508 Shadowcrest Houston TX 77096

REISBIG, RONALD LUTHER, MECHANICAL ENGINEERING, THERMODYNAMICS. *Current Pos:* dean, 84-85, vchancellor acad affairs, 85-89, PROF AEROSPACE ENG, COL ENG & AVIATION, EMBRY-RIDDLE UNIV, 89- *Personal Data:* b Kalamazoo, Mich, Jan 31, 38; m 58; c 4. *Educ:* Mich State Univ, BSME, 60, PhD(mech eng), 66; Univ Wash, MSME, 63. *Prof Exp:* Res engr, Boeing Co, 60-63; asst teaching, Mich State Univ, 63-64; asst prof eng, Western Mich Univ, 65-66; asst prof mech eng, Wayne State Univ, 66-69; assoc prof, Univ Mo, Rolla, 69-75; prof & dean, Victoria Campus, Univ Houston, 75-77; dean eng, Western New Eng Col, 77-84. *Concurrent Pos:* Westinghouse scholar, Mich State Univ, 59-60; Consult, Nat Waterlift Co, Mich, 65-66. *Mem:* Am Soc Mech Engrs; Am Soc Eng Educ; Instrument Soc Am; Sigma Xi; Soc Automotive Engrs. *Res:* Thermal science; interferometric holography; solar energy; thermography. *Mailing Add:* Col Eng-Aviation Embry-Riddle Aeronaut Univ Daytona Beach FL 32114

REISCH, BRUCE IRVING, PLANT BREEDING, GENETICS & TISSUE CULTURE. *Current Pos:* From asst prof to assoc prof, 80-94, PROF, NY STATE AGR EXP STA, CORNELL UNIV, 95- *Personal Data:* b New York, NY, July 23, 55; m 84, Kim Stone; c Maren, Jacob & Lucas. *Educ:* Cornell Univ, BS, 76; Univ Wis, Madison, MS, 78, PhD(plant breeding), 80. *Concurrent Pos:* Chmn, Grape Crop Germplasm Comt, Nat Plant Germplasm Syst; invited lectr, NATO Advan Study Inst Plant Biotechnol, 87; vis prof, Univ Calif, Riverside, 90. *Mem:* Int Asn Plant Tissue Cult; Am Soc Enol; Crop Sci Soc Am; Am Soc Hort Sci; Sigma Xi. *Res:* Application of new technology to plant breeding, including gene transformation, tissue culture, genome mapping, grape genetics and grape breeding. *Mailing Add:* 57 High St Geneva NY 14456

REISCH, KENNETH WILLIAM, HORTICULTURE. *Current Pos:* From instr to assoc prof, 53-66, PROF HORT, OHIO STATE UNIV, 66-, ASSOC DEAN COL AGR & HOME ECON, 72- *Personal Data:* b Southington, Conn, Oct 7, 29; m 52; c 4. *Educ:* Univ Conn, BSc, 52; Ohio State Univ, MSc, 53, PhD(hort), 56. *Concurrent Pos:* Chmn, Res Instr, Comt Org & Policy, Nat Asn State Univ, & Land Grant Col, 86. *Mem:* Am Soc Hort Sci; Sigma Xi. *Res:* Physiological and taxonomical studies with woody ornamental plants, especially growth, reproduction and nutrition. *Mailing Add:* 6528 Masefield St Columbus OH 43085

REISCHMAN, MICHAEL MACK, RESEARCH ADMINISTRATION. *Current Pos:* ASSOC DEAN, RES & GRAD STUDIES, PA STATE UNIV, 90- *Personal Data:* b Barnesville, Ohio, Sept 26, 42; m 84, Debbrah Freimiller; c Stacy, Todd & Kristi. *Educ:* NMex State Univ, BS, 67, MS, 69; Okla State Univ, PhD(mech engr), 73. *Prof Exp:* Res assoc, Nat Res Coun, Nat Acad Sci, 73-74; res engr, Naval Ocean Systs Ctr, 74-78, br head, 78-83; prog mgr, Off Naval Res, 83-88, div dir, 89-90. *Concurrent Pos:* Coun Educ, Am Soc Mech Engrs; Eng Res Coun, Am Soc Eng Educ. *Mem:* Am Soc Mech Engrs; Am Phys Soc; Am Soc Eng Educ; AAAS. *Res:* Experimental fluid dynamics; laser anemometry; turbulence; drag reduction; hydroacoustics; flow visualization; image processing. *Mailing Add:* Pa State Univ Col Eng 101 Hammond Bldg University Park PA 16802. *Fax:* 814-863-0497; *E-Mail:* mmrdo@engr.psu.edu

REISCHMAN, PLACIDUS GEORGE, ZOOLOGY. *Current Pos:* RETIRED. *Personal Data:* b South Bend, Wash, Sept 15, 26. *Educ:* St Martin's Col, BA, 50; Cath Univ Am, MSc, 57, PhD, 60. *Prof Exp:* Instr, St Martin's Col, 55-56, prof biol, 59- *Mem:* AAAS. *Res:* Marine invertebrate zoology; parasitic Crustacea; Rhizocephala. *Mailing Add:* Dept Math & Sci St Martins Col 5300 Pacific Ave SE Lacey WA 98503

REISEL, ROBERT BENEDICT, MATHEMATICS. *Current Pos:* From instr to asst prof, 54-63, ASSOC PROF MATH, LOYOLA UNIV CHICAGO, 63- *Personal Data:* b Chicago, Ill, Apr 27, 25; m 61; c 3. *Educ:* DePaul Univ, BS, 49; Univ Chicago, MS, 51; Northwestern Univ, PhD(math), 54. *Mem:* Am Math Soc; Math Asn Am. *Res:* Associative algebras. *Mailing Add:* 5052 N Nordica Ave Chicago IL 60656-3604

REISEN, WILLIAM KENNETH, MEDICAL ENTOMOLOGY, VECTOR ECOLOGY. *Current Pos:* RES ENTOMOLOGIST & DIR, ARBOVIRUS FIELD ST, SCH PUB HEALTH, UNIV CALIF, BERKELEY, 80- *Personal Data:* b Jersey City, NJ, Feb 11, 46; m 71; c 2. *Educ:* Univ Del, BS, 67; Clemson Univ, MS, 68; Univ Okla, PhD(zool), 74. *Prof Exp:* Teaching asst zool, Dept Entomol & Zool, Clemson Univ, 67-68; Capt US Armed Forces & med entomologist, 1st Med Serv Wing, Clark Air Base, Philippines, 69-71; teaching asst, Dept Zool, Univ Okla, 71-74; asst prof int med, Int Health Prog, Sch Med, Univ Md, 74-80. *Concurrent Pos:* Investr ecol & control arboviruses, NAIAD, NIH, 84-; consult mosquito vector field studies, Bd Sci & Technol Int Develop & US Agency Int Develop, 83-, Nepal Malaria Eradication Orgn, Vector Biol & Control Proj, USAID, 86-, SCalif Mosquito Control Orgn, 87-; co-ed, J Med Entomol, 88-; co-investr epidemiol & control arboviruses, Univ Calif Mosquito Res Funds. *Mem:* Royal Soc Trop Med Hyg; Am Soc Trop Med & Hyg; Entomol Soc Am; Soc Vector Ecologists; Am Mosquito Control Asn. *Res:* Ecological relationships among environmental factors, mosquito bionomics and the prevalence of mosquito-borne disease (malaria and encephalitis); range of specific topics, from mosquito demography to disease surveillance and control. *Mailing Add:* Arbovirus Field Sta 4705 Allen Rd Bakersfield CA 93312

REISENAUER, HUBERT MICHAEL, SOIL SCIENCE. *Current Pos:* PROF SOIL SCIENCE & SOIL SCIENTIST, UNIV CALIF, DAVIS, 62- *Personal Data:* b Portland, Ore, Mar 11, 20; m 45; c 2. *Educ:* Univ Idaho, BS, 41; NC State Univ, PhD(agr), 49. *Prof Exp:* Prof soils, Wash State Univ, 49-62. *Mem:* AAAS; Am Soc Agron; Soil Sci Soc Am; Int Soil Sci Soc; Sigma Xi. *Res:* Plant nutrition; micronutrients; soil fertility and soil-plant interrelationships. *Mailing Add:* Land Air & Water Res Univ Calif Davis CA 95616

REISER, CASTLE O, CHEMICAL & NUCLEAR ENGINEERING. *Current Pos:* prof eng & chmn dept, 58-78, EMER PROF, DEPT CHEM ENG, ARIZ STATE UNIV, 80- *Personal Data:* b Berthoud, Colo, Dec 21, 12; m 35; c 2. *Educ:* Colo Agr & Mech Col, BS, 34; Colo Sch Mines, PE, 38; Univ Wis, PhD(chem eng), 45. *Prof Exp:* Res engr, Pilot Plant, Stand Oil Develop Co, 38-41; instr & res assoc chem eng, Univ Wis, 41-45; asst prof, Univ Colo, 45-46; assoc prof, Okla Agr & Mech Col, 46-47; prof & head dept, Univ Idaho, 47-53; pilot plant suprv, Chem Res Ctr, Food Mach & Chem Corp, 53-55; sr res engr, Atomics Int Div, NAm Aviation, Inc, 55-56; prof chem eng & chmn dept, Univ Seattle, 56-58. *Concurrent Pos:* Consult, Water Planning for Israel, 67-68. *Mem:* Am Chem Soc; fel Am Inst Chem Engrs; Am Soc Eng Educ; Am Nuclear Soc. *Res:* Industrial wastes; nitrogen fixation; process design; evaporation control; pollution abatement; environmental control; nuclear fuel cycle. *Mailing Add:* 4224 E Mitchell Dr Phoenix AZ 85018

REISER, H JOSEPH, RESEARCH ADMINISTRATION, MEDICAL SCIENCES. *Current Pos:* EXEC DIR RES & DEVELOP, BERLEX LABS, INC, 85- *Personal Data:* b Bad Kissingen, WGer, July 1, 46; m 70; c 2. *Educ:* Ind Univ, MS, 74, PhD(physiol), 76. *Concurrent Pos:* Adj assoc prof med & physiol, Likoff CV Inst, Hahnemann Univ, 82-; mem circulation coun, Am Heart Asn. *Mem:* Am Col Cardiol; Am Heart Asn; Int Soc Heart Res; Am Physiol Soc; Am Heart Asn. *Mailing Add:* Schering-Berlin 300 Fairfield Rd Wayne NJ 07470

REISER, MORTON FRANCIS, PSYCHIATRY, PSYCHOANALYSIS. *Current Pos:* dir res psychiat, Albert Einstein Col Med, Yale Univ & from assoc prof to prof, 55-69, prof psychiat & Chem Dept, 69-86, Albert E Kent prof, 86-90, EMER ALBERT E KENT PROF PSYCHIAT, SCH MED, YALE UNIV, 90- *Personal Data:* b Cincinnati, Ohio, Aug 22, 19; m 76, Lynn Whisnant; c David, Barbara & Linda. *Educ:* Univ Cincinnati, BS, 40, MD, 43. *Hon Degrees:* MA, Yale Univ, 69. *Honors & Awards:* Seymour Vestermark Award, Am Psychiat Asn, 86; William Meninger Award, Am Col Physicians, 88. *Prof Exp:* Instr psychiat & internal med, Med Sch, Cincinnati Gen Hosp, 49-50, asst prof, 50-52; res psychiatrist, Neuropsychiat Div, Walter Reed Army Inst Res, 54-55. *Concurrent Pos:* Fel psychiat, Cincinnati Gen Hosp, 47-50; vis psychiatrist, Bronx Munic Hosp, 54-69; mem small grants comt, NIMH, 56-58, mem career investr comt, 59-63; consult, Walter Reed Army Inst Res, Washington, DC, 57-58; prof lectr, State Univ NY Downstate Med Ctr, 59-65; chief, Div Psychiat, Montefiore Hosp & Med Ctr, 65-69; mem fac, Western New Eng Inst Psychoanal, 69- *Mem:* Am Psychosom Soc (secy-treas, 56-59, pres, 60); Am Soc Clin Invest; fel Am Psychiat Asn; fel Am Col Psychiatrists; Int Col Psychosom Med (pres, 75-77); Am Psychoanal Asn (pres, 82-84); Benjamin Rush Soc. *Res:* Psychoanalysis and psychophysiology; psychosomatic medicine. *Mailing Add:* Dept Psychiat Yale Univ Sch Med 25 Park St New Haven CT 06519. *Fax:* 203-562-2103

REISER, PETER JACOB, CARDIAC MUSCLE & DEVELOPING SKELETAL MUSCLE PHYSIOLOGY. *Current Pos:* ASST PROF PHYSIOL, UNIV ILL, 88- *Personal Data:* b Feb 6, 53. *Educ:* Ohio State Univ, PhD(physiol), 81. *Prof Exp:* NIH fel Physiol, Univ Wis-Madison, 84-86, assoc researcher, 86-88. *Concurrent Pos:* Am Heart Asn Postdoctoral Fel, Case Western Reserve Univ, 81-83. *Mem:* Am Physiol Soc; Biophys Soc. *Mailing Add:* 2216 Aspenwood Lane Columbus OH 43235

REISER, RAYMOND, BIOCHEMISTRY. *Current Pos:* from asst chemist to assoc chemist, Div Chem Exp Sta, Tex A&M Univ, 40-48, from assoc prof to prof, 48-65, distinguished prof, 65-76, DISTINGUISHED EMER PROF BIOCHEM & BIOPHYS, TEX A&M UNIV, 76- *Personal Data:* b Philadelphia, Pa, July 28, 06; m 39; c 2. *Educ:* Western Reserve Univ, BA, 29; Ohio State Univ, PhD(agr chem), 36. *Honors & Awards:* Glycerine Producer's Asn Award, 52; Southwest Regional Award, Am Chem Soc, 64; Can Award, Am Oil Chem S No, 63; Dr Norman E Borlaug Award, 73; Alton Bailey Medal, Am Oil Chemists' Soc, 76. *Prof Exp:* Hanes fel med, Duke Univ, 36-40. *Concurrent Pos:* NIH res career award, 62, mem, Nutrit Study Sect, 63-67. *Mem:* AAAS; Am Chem Soc; Am Oil Chem Soc (vpres, 66, pres, 67); Am Soc Biol Chemists; fel Am Inst Nutrit. *Res:* Fat absorption; glyceride and essential fatty acid metabolism; lipid analysis; fats in nutrition. *Mailing Add:* Dept Biochem & Biophys Tex A&M Univ College Station TX 77843-2128

REISER, SHELDON, BIOCHEMISTRY, ANIMAL NUTRITION. *Current Pos:* LAB CHIEF, NUTRIT INST, USDA, 73-, RES BIOCHEMIST, 77- *Personal Data:* b New York, NY, Oct 13, 30; m 55; c 2. *Educ:* City Col New York, BS, 53; Univ Wis, MS, 57, PhD(biochem), 60. *Prof Exp:* Assoc prof biochem & med, Med Ctr, Ind Univ, Indianapolis, 60-73. *Concurrent Pos:* Mem staff, Vet Admin Hosp, Indianapolis, 60-73. *Mem:* Am Inst Nutrit; Am Chem Soc; Biophys Soc; Am Soc Biol Chem. *Res:* The effects of the type and amount of dietary carbohydrate consumed by animals and humans on carbohydrate and lipid metabolism, intestinal absorption and digestion, and hormone responses. *Mailing Add:* 11308 Cedar Lane Beltsville MD 20705

REISERT, PATRICIA, MICROBIOLOGY, BOTANY & IMMUNOLOGY. *Current Pos:* from asst prof to assoc prof natural sci, 75-86, chair div, 88-91, PROF BIOL, ASSUMPTION COL, 86- *Personal Data:* b New York, NY, July 2, 37; m 62; c 2. *Educ:* Manhattanville Col, BA, 59; Brown Univ, MA, 61, PhD(bot), 65. *Prof Exp:* Instr biol, St Joseph's Col, Pa, 65-66, asst prof, 66-68; asst prof, Villanova Univ, 69-71 & Worcester Polytech Inst, 74-75. *Concurrent Pos:* Fac res fel, St Joseph's Col, Pa, 67; affil asst prof life sci, Worcester Polytech Inst, 75-80; sabbatical leave, Med Sch Pharmacol, Univ Mass, 81-82, 88-89, affil prof pharmacol, 84-; NSF fac develop fel, 81-82; NSF planning grant, 89-90 & NSF ILI grants, 89 & 91. *Mem:* AAAS; Tissue Cult Asn; Am Inst Biol Sci. *Res:* Cell surface phenomena in plants; untigen processing and presentation. *Mailing Add:* Assumption Col 500 Salisbury St Worcester MA 01609-1294

REISFELD, RALPH ALFRED, IMMUNOCHEMISTRY, BIOCHEMISTRY. *Current Pos:* mem dept exp path, 70-74, MEM DEPT MOLECULAR IMMUNOL, SCRIPPS CLIN & RES FOUND, 74- *Personal Data:* b Suttgart, Ger, Apr 23, 26; US citizen; m 56; c 2. *Educ:* Rutgers Univ, BS, 52; Ohio State Univ, PhD, 57. *Prof Exp:* Biochemist, Endocrinol Br, Nat Cancer Inst, 57-59; sr chemist, Merck & Co, 59-63; biochemist, Immunol Lab, Nat Inst Allergy & Infectious Dis, Md, 63-70. *Concurrent Pos:* Adj prof, Univ Calif, San Diego, 72. *Mem:* AAAS; Am Chem Soc; Soc Exp Biol & Med; Am Asn Immunol. *Res:* Isolation and biological characterization of transplantation antigens from inbred guinea pigs; isolation and biochemical characterization of human lencocyte-a, b, c and human leucocyte-DR antigens; expression and biosynthesis of cell surface antigens on human and murine lymphoid cells; biosynthesis and structure of human melanoma associated antigens. *Mailing Add:* Dept Immunol IMM13-R218 Scripps Res Inst 10666 N Torrey Pines Rd La Jolla CA 92037-1092

REISH, DONALD JAMES, MARINE ZOOLOGY. *Current Pos:* from asst prof to prof, 58-66, EMER PROF BIOL, CALIF STATE UNIV, LONG BEACH, 66- *Personal Data:* b Corvallis, Ore, June 15, 24; m 52; c 3. *Educ:* Univ Ore, BS, 46; Ore State Col, MA, 49; Univ Southern Calif, PhD(zool), 52. *Prof Exp:* Res asst, Hancock Found, Univ Southern Calif, 53, res assoc, 53-58. *Concurrent Pos:* Mem staff, Arctic Res Lab, 53 & Eniwetok Marine Biol Lab, 57-58; mem Pac expeds, Hancock Found, Univ Southern Calif, 49 & 53, res assoc, Univ, 73-88. *Mem:* AAAS; Soc Toxicol Chem; Water Pollution Control Fedn; Marine Biol Asn UK. *Res:* Systematics and biology of polychaetous annelids; marine ecology and pollution. *Mailing Add:* 3092 Blume Dr Los Alamitos CA 90720

REISING, RICHARD F, RADIOISOTOPIC METHODS. *Current Pos:* RETIRED. *Personal Data:* b St Louis, Mo, Nov 18, 34; m 59; c 4. *Educ:* Princeton Univ, BA, 56; Wash Univ, PhD(chem), 63. *Prof Exp:* Mem staff, Argonne Nat Lab, 63-65; res scientist, McDonnell Aircraft Corp, Mo, 65-67; assoc sr res chemist, Gen Motors Res Labs, 67-76, sr staff res scientist, 76- *Res:* Radioisotope applications: use of radioisotopes in solving unique scientific and engineering problems. *Mailing Add:* 2308 Atlas Dr Troy MI 48083

REISKIN, ALLAN B, RADIOLOGICAL SCIENCES, ONCOLOGY. *Current Pos:* CONSULT, 90- *Personal Data:* b New York, NY, Apr 24, 36; m 62; c 2. *Educ:* City Col New York, BA, 63; Univ Pa, DDS, 63; Oxford Univ, DPhil, 66. *Prof Exp:* Am Cancer Soc Brit-Am fel 63-66; from asst biologist to assoc biologist, Argonne Nat Lab, 68-70; prof oral radiol, Univ Conn, 70-90. *Concurrent Pos:* Res assoc, Zoller Dent Clin & asst prof path, Univ Chicago, 68-70; consult clin assoc prof, Loyola Univ Chicago, 70; consult, Am Dent Asn. *Mem:* Am Asn Cancer Res; Radiol Soc NAm; Am Acad Dent Radiol; Radiation Res Soc; Brit Inst Radiol. *Res:* Diagnostic imaging; carcinogenesis; radiation safety. *Mailing Add:* 25 Highwood Dr Avon CT 06001

REISKIND, JONATHAN, ARACHNOLOGY. *Current Pos:* Asst prof, 67-72, ASSOC PROF ZOOL, UNIV FLA, 72-, ASSOC DIR, UNIV HONORS PROG, 88- *Personal Data:* b Staten Island, NY, May 27, 40; m 66, Julia Barth; c Julia A & Michael H. *Educ:* Amherst Col, AB, 62; Harvard Univ, MA, 65, PhD(biol), 68. *Concurrent Pos:* Res assoc, Fla State Collection Arthropods, 68- *Mem:* AAAS; Soc Study Evolution; Am Arachnol Soc (pres, 81-83); Asn Trop Biol; Soc Syst Zool. *Res:* Systematics and biology of spiders; mimicry in spiders; spider-plant associations; ethology of arachnids; tropical biology; ecology; biogeography; amber (fossils). *Mailing Add:* Dept Zool Univ Fla Gainesville FL 32611. *Fax:* 352-392-3704; *E-Mail:* jon@zoo.ufl.edu

REISLER, DONALD LAURENCE, INFORMATION SCIENCE, PHYSICS. *Current Pos:* PRES & CHMN BD, DBS CORP, 73- *Personal Data:* b Brooklyn, NY, May 28, 41; m 64; c 1. *Educ:* Rutgers Univ, AB, 63; Yale Univ, MS, 65, PhD(physics), 67. *Prof Exp:* Staff analyst, Res Analysis Corp, 67-70 & Lambda Corp, Va, 70-73. *Mem:* Inst Elec & Electronics Engrs; NY Acad Sci. *Res:* Design and installation of information systems; mathematical formulation and solution of organizational problems and decisions. *Mailing Add:* 360 Glyndon St NE Vienna VA 22180. *Fax:* 703-938-9057

REISLER, HANNA, CHEMICAL KINETICS, PHOTOCHEMISTRY. *Current Pos:* res scientist elec eng, 77-79, res asst prof elec eng & chem, 79-83, res assoc prof chem, 78-87, ASSOC PROF CHEM, UNIV SOUTHERN CALIF, 87- *Personal Data:* b Tel-Aviv, Israel, July 12, 43; m 66; c 1. *Educ:* Hebrew Univ, BSc, 64, MSc, 66; Weizmann Inst Sci, PhD(phys chem), 72. *Prof Exp:* Fel chem, Johns Hopkins Univ, 72-74; sr scientist, Soreg Nuclear Res Ctr, 74-77. *Mem:* Am Phys Soc; Am Chem Soc. *Res:* Kinetics and dynamics of elementary processes in the gas phase; laser kinetic spectroscopy of free radicals; multi photon ionization and dissociation; unimolecular reactions of molecules and ions. *Mailing Add:* SSC 619 University Park 0482 Univ Southern Calif Los Angeles CA 90089-0482

REISMAN, ABRAHAM JOSEPH, POLYMER CHEMISTRY. *Current Pos:* SR RES CHEMIST, MONSANTO CO, INDIAN ORCHARD, 59- *Personal Data:* b Springfield, Mass, Dec 28, 25; m 49; c 2. *Educ:* Univ Mass, BS, 59, MS, 73. *Mem:* Am Chem Soc. *Res:* Color technology. *Mailing Add:* 51 Emerson St Springfield MA 01118-1732

REISMAN, ARNOLD, CHEMICAL VAPOR DEPOSITION, INSULATOR DEFECTS. *Current Pos:* PROF, ELECTROCHEM ENGR, NC STATE UNIV, 82- *Personal Data:* b New York, NY, June 12, 27; m 48, Hilda Rabinowitz; c Richard, Robert, David & Daniel. *Educ:* City Col NY, BS, 49; Brooklyn Col, MA, 53; Polytech Inst Brooklyn, PhD(chem), 58. *Honors & Awards:* Electronics Div Award, Electrochem Soc; Donald Fink Award, Inst Elec & Electronics Engrs. *Prof Exp:* Control chemist, City New York, 49-51; res staff mem, US Govt, 51-53; mem res staff, T J Watson Res Ctr, Int Bus Mach Corp, 53-82; vpres, Semiconductor Res & Technol, Microelectronics Ctr NC, 82-90. *Concurrent Pos:* Assoc ed, J Electronics Mat, J Electrochem Soc, J Vacuum Sci & J Supercomput; Solid State Sci Panel, Nat Res Coun; consult, Indust Develop Authority. *Mem:* Fel Electrochem Soc; fel Inst Elec & Electronics Engrs. *Res:* Materials science of semiconductors and solid-gas reaction phenomena; epitaxial growth via chemical transport reactions; high pressure reactions; plasma enhanced reactions; radiation induced insulator defects; semiconductor processing. *Mailing Add:* 816 Thatcher Way Raleigh NC 27615. *Fax:* 919-515-3027; *E-Mail:* reisman@eos.ncsu.edu

REISMAN, ARNOLD, OPERATIONS RESEARCH, INDUSTRIAL ENGINEERING. *Current Pos:* PROF OPERS RES, CASE WESTERN RES UNIV, 68- *Personal Data:* b Lodz, Poland, Aug 2, 34; nat US; m 54, 81; c 4. *Educ:* Univ Calif, Los Angeles, BS, 55, MS, 57, PhD(eng), 63. *Honors & Awards:* Engr of Year Award, var eng socs, 73. *Prof Exp:* Asst mech engr, Los Angeles Dept Water & Power, 55-57; from asst prof to assoc prof eng, Calif State Col Los Angeles, 57-66; vis prof eng & bus admin, Univ Wis-Milwaukee, 66-68. *Concurrent Pos:* Consult, 57-; NSF fac fel, 62-63; assoc res engr, Western Mgt Sci Inst, Univ Calif, Los Angeles, 64-65; vpres, Univ Assocs, Inc, 69-74; mem, Coun AAAS & prog coordr, AAAS-Inst Mgt Sci, 73-75; vis prof, Hebrew Univ of Jerusalem, 74-75; mem, Japan-Am Inst Mgt Sci, Honolulu & mem, Inst Planning Comt & Bd Trustees, 75-; mem, Rev Bd, Lake Erie Regional Transp Authority, 75-76. *Mem:* Opers Res Soc Am; Inst Mgt Sci; fel AAAS; sr mem Am Inst Indust Engrs; NY Acad Sci. *Res:* Engineering economy; systems analysis applications to operations management problems in health care delivery, industry and educational institutions; basic research in manpower planning, decision analysis and countertrade analysis; authored 13 books in engineering economy, systems analysis, materials management, health care planning, history and epistemology of management science and one nonfiction-Wellcome Tomorrow. *Mailing Add:* Reisman & Assoc 18428 Parkland Dr Shaker Heights OH 44122. *Fax:* 216-561-2842

REISMAN, ELIAS, EXPERIMENTAL PHYSICS. *Current Pos:* RETIRED. *Personal Data:* b New York, NY, Mar 12, 26; m 48; c 3. *Educ:* Cornell Univ, AB, 50, PhD(exp physics), 57. *Prof Exp:* Asst mass spectros, Cornell Univ, 50-55; sr physicist, Radiation Lab, Univ Calif, 57-60; sr scientist,

Aeronutronic Div, Philco-Ford Corp, 60- *Mem:* Am Phys Soc; Sigma Xi; Optical Soc Am. *Res:* Atmospherics; propagation and scattering; quantum electronics and laser applications. *Mailing Add:* 839 E Palmdale Ave Orange CA 92865

REISMAN, HAROLD BERNARD, BIOCHEMICAL ENGINEERING, BIOLOGICAL ENGINEERING. *Current Pos:* PRIN, BIOTECHNOLOGY RESULTS, 95- *Personal Data:* b Brooklyn, NY, Oct 29, 35; m 60, Miriam Fish; c Jocelyn & Joseph. *Educ:* Columbia Univ, BS, 56, PhD(chem eng), 65; Cornell Univ, MS, 59. *Prof Exp:* Chem engr, Merck & Co, 61-64, sr chem eng, Merck Sharp & Dohme Res Labs, Rahway, 64-67, sect mgr biochem eng, 67-73; dir, Bioeng Lab, Stauffer Chem Co, 73-75, plant mgr, 75-76, dir mfg, Food Ingredients Div, 76-89; vpres opers, Organogenesis Inc, 89-95. *Concurrent Pos:* Auth, Economic Anal Fermentation Processes, 88. *Mem:* Am Inst Chem Engrs; Am Chem Soc; fel Am Inst Med & Biol Eng; Inst Food Technologists. *Res:* Biochemical engineering, especially fermentation, tissue engineering; natural product isolation and purification; design of fermentors and auxiliaries; pilot plant operations; process development; operations management; plant design; aseptic processing; GMP. *Mailing Add:* 15 October Dr Weston CT 06883. *Fax:* 203-226-1445; *E-Mail:* hbreisman@aol.com

REISMAN, HOWARD MAURICE, ICHTHYOLOGY. *Current Pos:* asst prof biol, 69-73, assoc prof, 75-80, PROF BIOL & MARINE SCI, SOUTHAMPTON COL, LONG ISLAND UNIV, 80- *Personal Data:* b Syracuse, NY, May 23, 37; m 64; c 3. *Educ:* Syracuse Univ, BA, 59, MA, 61; Univ Calif, Santa Barbara, PhD(biol), 67. *Prof Exp:* NIH fel, Cornell Univ, 67-69. *Concurrent Pos:* Vis res prof, Tiergarten Schonbrunn, Vienna, Austria, 87-89. *Mem:* AAAS; Am Soc Ichthyol & Herpet; Animal Behav Soc; Am Inst Biol Sci. *Res:* Ichthyology; general marine biology. *Mailing Add:* Div Natural Sci Southampton Col Southampton NY 11968-4198

REISMAN, OTTO, NUCLEAR ENGINEERING, PHYSICS. *Current Pos:* ASST PROF PHYSICS, NJ INST TECHNOL, 62- *Personal Data:* b Vienna, Austria, July 29, 28; US citizen; m 58; c 2. *Educ:* City Col New York, BS, 58; NY Univ, MS, 60, PhD(nuclear eng), 73. *Prof Exp:* Jr engr physics, Weston Elec Instruments, 57-58; proj engr elec eng, Bendix Aviation, 58-61; instr physics, St Peter's Col, 61-62. *Mem:* Sigma Xi; Am Nuclear Soc. *Res:* Nuclear reactor heat transfer. *Mailing Add:* Dept Physics NJ Inst Technol 323 Martin Luther King Jr Newark NJ 07102-1824

REISMAN, STANLEY S, ELECTRICAL ENGINEERING, BIOENGINEERING. *Current Pos:* from instr to assoc prof, 68-85, PROF ELEC ENG, NJ INST TECHNOL, 85- *Personal Data:* b New York, NY, June 11, 41; m 64, Loretta; c Karen & David. *Educ:* Polytech Inst NY, BS, 62, PhD(bioeng), 74; Mass Inst Technol, MS, 63. *Prof Exp:* Mem tech staff, Bell Tel Labs Inc, 63-68. *Concurrent Pos:* Lectr elec eng, City Col New York, 68. *Mem:* Inst Elec & Electronics Engrs. *Res:* Mathematical and computer simulation of physiologic systems; biomedical instrumentation; biomedical signal processing. *Mailing Add:* 59 Eastbrook Terr Livingston NJ 07039. *Fax:* 973-596-5680; *E-Mail:* reisman@admin1.njit.edu

REISMANN, HERBERT, SOLID MECHANICS, AERONAUTICAL ENGINEERING. *Current Pos:* PROF ENG, STATE UNIV NY, BUFFALO, 64-, DIR AEROSPACE PROG, 80- *Personal Data:* b Vienna, Austria, Jan 26, 26; US citizen; m 53, Edith Falber; c 2. *Educ:* Ill Inst Technol, BS, 47, MS, 49; Univ Colo, PhD(eng mech), 62. *Honors & Awards:* Outstanding Aerospace Achievement Award, Am Inst Aeronaut & Astronaut, 88. *Prof Exp:* Instr mech, Ill Inst Technol, 47-50; proj struct engr, Gen Dynamics Corp, 51-53; prin systs engr, Repub Aviation Corp, 54-56; sect chief solid mech, Martin-Marietta Corp, 57-64. *Concurrent Pos:* Grants shell dynamics, USAF Off Sci Res & Army Res Off, 65-, Praxair, 96-; consult, Bell Aerosysts Co, 65- *Mem:* AAAS; assoc fel Am Inst Aeronaut & Astronaut; Am Soc Mech Engrs; Int Asn Bridge & Struct Engrs; Sigma Xi. *Res:* Elasticity theory, particularly the dynamics of plates and shells; aeroelasticity; elastokinetics; dynamics of elastic bodies; geophysics. *Mailing Add:* 71 Chaumont Dr Williamsville NY 14221

REISNER, GERALD SEYMOUR, MICROBIOLOGY. *Current Pos:* asst prof, 58-65, assoc prof microbiol, 63-70, PROF BIOL, ALLEGHENY COL, 70- *Personal Data:* b Brooklyn, NY, Apr 10, 26; m 49; c 4. *Educ:* State Univ NY Col Educ Albany, AB, 49, MA, 51; Cornell Univ, MS, 55, PhD(plant physiol), 56. *Prof Exp:* Teacher high sch, NY, 49-52; plant physiologist, Plant, Soil & Nutrit Lab, Soil & Water Conserv Res Div, Agr Res Serv, USDA, 52-56; mem fac biol, Goddard Col, 56-58. *Concurrent Pos:* Nat Acad Sci res assoc, USDA, 64-65; NIH fel, Ctr Biol Natural Systs, Wash Univ, 71-72; bacteriologist, Bd Health, City Meadville, Pa, 58-75; chmn, microbiol dept, Allegheny Col, 81-86. *Mem:* Sigma Xi; Am Soc Microbiol; NY Acad Sci; Am Asn Univ Professors. *Res:* The application of asymbiotic nitrogen fixing bacteria to the growth of crop plants; effects of cations on bacterial enzymes. *Mailing Add:* Dept Biol Allegheny Col Meadville PA 16335

REISNER, JOHN H, PHYSICS. *Current Pos:* RETIRED. *Educ:* Davidson Col, BS, 39; Univ Va, MS, 41, PhD(physics), 43. *Prof Exp:* Sr scientist, RCA Lab, Princeton, 42-83. *Mem:* Fel Am Phys Soc. *Mailing Add:* 671 Euclid Ave Haddonfield NJ 08033

REISNER, RONALD M, DERMATOLOGY. *Current Pos:* from asst prof to assoc prof dermat, 62-73, coordr dermat, Complex Affil Insts, 73-77, PROF & CHIEF DIV, SCH MED, UNIV CALIF, LOS ANGELES, 73-; DIR, COMBINED UNIV CALIF-VET ADMIN WADSWORTH MED CTR DERMAT PROG, 77- *Personal Data:* b Buffalo, NY, May 2, 29; m 72, Ellen S; c David Alan & Andrew Evan. *Educ:* Univ Calif, Los Angeles, BA, 52, MD, 56; Am Bd Dermat, dipl, 61. *Prof Exp:* From asst resident to resident dermat, UCLA, 57-59, res trainee, 60, chief div dermat, Harbor San Pedro, 62-73. *Concurrent Pos:* Consult, USAF Ballistics Missile Div Med Facil, 62-72, US Naval Regional Hosp, San Diego, Calif, 76-80; chief dermat serv, Vet Admin Wadsworth Med Ctr, Los Angeles, 77-; pres, Pac Dermat Asn, 85-86; mem bd dirs, Soc Invest Dermat, 74-79. *Mem:* Fel Am Acad Dermat; Soc Invest Dermat; Am Dermat Asn; Am Asn Prof Dermat (secy-treas, 74-76); Int Soc Trop Dermat; fel Pan-Am Med Asn; Am Dermat Asn. *Res:* Pathogenesis of acne. *Mailing Add:* Div Dermat Sch Med Univ Calif Los Angeles CA 90024. *E-Mail:* rreisner@ucla.edu

REISS, CAROL S, VIRAL IMMUNITY, PATHOGENESIS. *Current Pos:* PROF, NY UNIV, 91- *Personal Data:* b Boston, Mass, Mar 14, 50; c Joshua & Steven. *Educ:* City Univ New York, PhD(biomed sci), 78. *Prof Exp:* Fel, Harvard Med Sch, 78-81, from instr to assoc prof, 81-91. *Concurrent Pos:* Dir, Animal Facil, Dana-Farber Cancer Inst, 81-89. *Mem:* Am Soc Virol; Am Soc Cell Biol; Asn Women Sci; Am Soc Microbiologists; Am Asn Immunologists; Soc Neurosci. *Res:* Study of antigen processing and presentation, pathogenesis of a neutotropic viral infection, cytokines and vaccine development. *Mailing Add:* Biol Dept NY Univ 100 Washington Sq E New York NY 10003-6688. *Fax:* 212-995-4015; *E-Mail:* carol.reiss@nyu.edu

REISS, DIANA, BIOACOUSTICS, ANIMAL COGNITION. *Current Pos:* PRIN INVESTR & PROJ DIR, DOLPHIN COMT RES, MARINE WORLD FOUND, 81- *Personal Data:* b Philadelphia, Pa, Nov 1, 48. *Educ:* Temple Univ, BS, 72, PhD(commun & speech), 81. *Prof Exp:* Admin asst, Animal Sonar Systs Symp, NATO, 78-79; lectr speech & commun, Temple Univ, 79-80; researcher biomed res, Stanford Res Inst Int, 81-82; fac mem animal commun, human commun & speech, San Francisco State Univ, 83-88. *Concurrent Pos:* Dir & bd mem, Marine World Found, 85-88; consult, Time-Life Books-Bioastron Series, 88- *Mem:* AAAS; Soc Marine Mammal; Am Asn Zool Parks & Aquariums. *Res:* Dolphin communication and cognition; ontogeny of dolphin behavior and communication in a captive environment. *Mailing Add:* Marine World Marine World Pkwy Vallejo CA 94589

REISS, ERROL, MICROBIAL IMMUNOCHEMISTRY. *Current Pos:* res microbiologist, 74-80, HEAD IMMUNOCHEM LABS, DIV MYCOTIC DIS, CTR DIS CONTROL, ATLANTA, 80- *Personal Data:* b New York, NY, Jan 16, 42; m 68; c 2. *Educ:* City Col New York, BSc, 63; Rutgers Univ, PhD(microbiol), 72. *Prof Exp:* Bacteriologist, Vet Admin Hosp, Washington, DC, 66-67; NIH fel, 68 & 72-74. *Concurrent Pos:* Instr, grad prog, NIH, 72-74, & dept biol, Atlanta Univ, 80-82; adj prof, dept lab pract, Sch Pub Health, Univ NC, Chapel Hill, 78-, dept biol, Ga State Univ, Atlanta, 83- & Med Sch, Emory Univ, 87-; guest lectr, Morehouse Med Sch, Atlanta, 81-83. *Mem:* Am Asn Immunol; Am Chem Soc; Am Acad Microbiol; Am Soc Microbiol; Int Soc Human Animal Mycol; Med Mycol Soc Am. *Res:* Molecular immunology and molecular biology of microbial infections; mycotic infections; microbial immunochemistry; monoclonal antibodies; genetic probes; enzyme immunoassays; animal models of infection and immunity cellular immunology; cell wall chemistry; immunity to respiratory infections. *Mailing Add:* 3642 Castaway Ct Chamblee GA 30341-4602

REISS, HOWARD, PHYSICAL CHEMISTRY. *Current Pos:* PROF CHEM, UNIV CALIF, LOS ANGELES, 68- *Personal Data:* b New York, NY, Apr 5, 22; m 45, Phyllis Kohn; c Gloria R & Steven C. *Educ:* NY Univ, AB, 43; Columbia Univ, PhD(phys chem), 49. *Honors & Awards:* Tolman Medal, Am Chem Soc, 73; Herbert Newby McCoy Award, 74; Colloid & Surface Chem Prize, Am Chem Soc, 80, J H Hildebrand Award, 91. *Prof Exp:* Chemist, Tenn Eastman Corp, Tenn, 44-45; instr chem, Boston Univ, 49-51; chemist, Celanese Corp Am, 51-52 & Bell Tel Labs, Inc, 52-60; from assoc dir to dir res dept, Atomics Int Div, NAm Aviation, Inc, 60-62, pres & dir sci ctr & vpres NAm Aviation, Thousand Oaks, 62-68. *Concurrent Pos:* Corp rep, Am Inst Physics, 63-66; mem, Physics Res Eval Group, Air Force Off Sci Res, 66-, Reactor Chem Eval Comt, Oak Ridge Nat Lab, 66-68, Mat Res Coun, Advan Res Proj Agency, 68- & Adv Comt Math & Phys Sci, NSF, 70-74; Guggenheim fel, 78-79; mem comn socio-tech systs, Nat Res Coun; ed, J Statist Physics, 68-78. *Mem:* Nat Acad Sci; fel Am Phys Soc; Sigma Xi; fel AAAS; Am Chem Soc. *Res:* Semiconductors; statistical mechanics; solid state chemistry; thermodynamics; nucleation theory; information theory; electrochemistry; polymers science. *Mailing Add:* 16656 Oldham St Encino CA 91436-3706

REISS, HOWARD R, INTENSE-FIELD PHENOMENA. *Current Pos:* PROF PHYSICS, AM UNIV, 69- *Personal Data:* b Brooklyn, NY, July 29, 29; m 83, Janet Bideaux; c Stephanie (Drake) & John. *Educ:* Polytech Inst Brooklyn, BAE, 50, MAE, 51; Univ Md, PhD(physics), 58. *Prof Exp:* Asst, Polytech Inst Brooklyn, 51; physicist, David W Taylor Model Basin, Bur Ships, US Dept Navy, 51-55, Naval Ord Lab, 55-58, chief nuclear physics div, 58-69; mem fac, Dept Physics, 78-81, res prof, Ariz Res Lab, Univ Ariz, 81-86. *Concurrent Pos:* Lectr, Univ Md, 59-63; vis scientist, Univ Torino, Italy, 63-64; adj prof physics, Am Univ, 67-69; vis prof, Univ Ariz, 75-81; consult, Naval Res Lab, Washington DC, 74-75, Stand Oil Co, Ind, 80-82, Los Alamos Nat Lab, 85-87, Naval Surface Weapons Ctr, White Oak, Md, 86-90; long-term visitor, Harvard-Smithsonian Ctr Astrophys, 93-94. *Mem:* Fel Am Phys Soc; Optical Soc Am. *Res:* Development of theoretical methods for very intense electromagnetic fields, and applications to interaction of intense fields with atoms, nuclei and solids. *Mailing Add:* Dept Physics Am Univ Washington DC 20016-8058. *E-Mail:* reiss@american.edu

REISS, KEITH WESTCOTT, MICROWAVE PHYSICS, ENGINEERING PHYSICS. *Current Pos:* PHYSICIST USN SUPPORT, VITRO LABS DIV, AUTOMATION INDUST, 73- *Personal Data:* b Washington, DC, July 22, 45; m 66; c 1. *Educ:* Univ Va, BS, 66; Wake Forest Univ, MA, 68; Duke Univ, PhD(physics), 71. *Prof Exp:* Chmn natural sci & math div & dept head phys sci, Truett-McConnell Col, 71-73. *Mem:* Am Phys Soc; Sigma Xi. *Res:* Development and analysis of US Navy surface-to-surface missile systems. *Mailing Add:* 3522 Laurel Leaf Lane Fairfax VA 22031-3213

REISS, OSCAR KULLY, BIOCHEMISTRY. *Current Pos:* asst prof, 59-67, ASSOC PROF BIOCHEM, SCH MED, UNIV COLO, DENVER, 67- *Personal Data:* b Bad-Duerkheim, Ger, May 6, 21; nat US; m 44; c 3. *Educ:* Univ Chicago, BS, 50, PhD(biochem), 54. *Prof Exp:* Instr physiol chem, Sch Med, Johns Hopkins Univ, 57-58, asst prof, 58-59. *Mem:* Am Soc Biol Chemists; Am Chem Soc; Brit Biochem Soc. *Res:* Intermediary and lipid metabolism of lung and other tissues; structure and function of membranes; effects of organothiophosphates on pulmonary enzyme systems. *Mailing Add:* 775 Carr St Lakewood CO 80215

REISS, WILLIAM DEAN, AGRONOMY. *Current Pos:* TECH SERV CONSULT, ASGRON SEED CO, 79- *Personal Data:* b Breese, Ill, July 24, 37; m 61, Dixie E Mauck; c Roger D, David W & John A. *Educ:* Southern Ill Univ, BS, 60, MS, 61; Univ Ill, PhD(crop prod), 67. *Prof Exp:* Res asst crop prod, Southern Ill Univ, 60-61; teaching asst, Univ Ill, 61-62, res asst, 62-65, Lafayette, 65-74, 78, res agronomist, 74-77; exten agronomist, Purdue Univ, West. *Concurrent Pos:* Mem, Bd Dirs, Asn Off Seed Certifying Agencies, 67-73; mem soybean prog comt, Am Seed Trade Asn. *Mem:* Am Soc Agron. *Res:* Influence of density of stand, row width, planting date and plant nutrients on behavior of corn, sorghum and soybeans; factors affecting seed quality of soybeans and corn; seed certification; liaison between research and sales; assembles and disseminates product information for grower meetings, field days and training sessions. *Mailing Add:* 30 Oriole Ct Lafayette IN 47905

REISSE, ROBERT ALAN, PHYSICS. *Current Pos:* PRIN SCIENTIST, SCI INQUIRIES, INC, 91- *Personal Data:* b Philadelphia, Pa, Apr 9, 46; m 73, Dana Meiggs; c Andrew & Benjamin. *Educ:* Wesleyan Univ, BA, 67; Univ Md, MS, 70, PhD(physics), 76. *Honors & Awards:* NASA Medal Except Sci Achievement, 94. *Prof Exp:* Res assoc, Physics Dept, Univ Md, 76-77; mem tech staff physics, Sperry Res Ctr, Sperry Rand Corp, 77-81; res asst prof & mem staff, Ariz Res Labs & Santa Catalina Lab Exp Relativity By Astrometry, Univ Ariz, 81-82; at CGR Med Corp, Baltimore, Md, 82-85; mem staff, ITE Inc, Beltsville, Md, 85-88; mentor, Technologies Inc, Rockville, Md, 88-91. *Mem:* Am Phys Soc; Optical Soc Am. *Res:* Optical information processing; quantum electronics; experimental general relativity; solar astrophysics; space optical instruments. *Mailing Add:* 312 Patleigh Rd Catonsville MD 21228-5630. *Fax:* 410-788-0472; *E-Mail:* rareisse@postoffice.worldnetintt.net

REISSIG, MAGDALENA, ELECTRON MICROSCOPY, VIROLOGY. *Current Pos:* from asst prof to assoc prof pathobiol, 61-82, assoc prof, 83-88, EMER PROF IMMUNOL & INFECTIOUS DIS, JOHNS HOPKINS UNIV, 88- *Personal Data:* b Buenos Aires, Arg, Sept 1, 23. *Educ:* Univ Buenos Aires, Arg, MD, 50. *Prof Exp:* Res asst cell ultrastruct, Inst Biol Sci, Uruguay, 50-53; res asst prev med, Sch Med, Yale Univ, 53-56, res assoc, 56-58; res assoc microbiol, Albert Einstein Med Ctr, 58-61. *Mem:* Electron Micros Soc Am; Am Asn Immunologists; Am Soc Cell Biol. *Res:* Cytology; cytopathology and pathogenesis of virus infections; ultrastructure of parasitic helminths. *Mailing Add:* Dept Molecular Immunol & Microbiol Johns Hopkins Univ 615 N Wolfe St Baltimore MD 21205-2103

REISSMANN, THOMAS LINCOLN, ANALYTICAL CHEMISTRY. *Current Pos:* RETIRED. *Personal Data:* b Wilmington, Del, Feb 12, 20; m 51, Maria A Robinson; c Alan & Elizabeth (Eagan). *Educ:* Pa State Univ, BS, 42, MS, 47, PhD(chem), 49. *Prof Exp:* Chemist, Atlas Powder Co, 42 & 45-46; asst chief chemist, Ky Ord Works, 42-45; asst chem, Pa State Col, 46-49; res chemist, Ethicon Inc, 49-58, dept mgr collagen res, 58-69, absorbable suture res & develop, 70-72, dept mgr chem, 73-80, asst to corp dir, Qual Assurance, 80-82. *Concurrent Pos:* Consult, 82- *Mem:* AAAS; Am Chem Soc; Am Soc Qual Control; NY Acad Sci. *Res:* Collagen chemistry; fibers and films; medical products; chemical quality of drugs; application of computerized systems to the quality assurance function. *Mailing Add:* 24 Hillcrest Rd Martinsville NJ 08836

REISSNER, ERIC, APPLIED MECHANICS, APPLIED MATHEMATICS. *Current Pos:* prof, 70-78, EMER PROF APPL MECH, UNIV CALIF, SAN DIEGO, 78- *Personal Data:* b Aachen, Ger, Jan 5, 13; nat US; m 38; c John & Eva M. *Educ:* Tech Univ, Berlin, Dipl Ing, 35, Dr Ing(civil eng), 36; Mass Inst Technol, PhD(math), 38. *Hon Degrees:* Dr Ing(mech eng), Hannover Univ, 64. *Honors & Awards:* Theodore von Karman Medal, Am Soc Civil Eng, 64; Timoshenko Medal, Am Soc Mech Eng, 73, Medal, 88; Struct & Mat Award, Am Inst Aeronaut & Astronaut, 84. *Prof Exp:* From instr to prof appl math, Mass Inst Technol, 39-69. *Concurrent Pos:* Managing ed, J Math & Physics, 45-67; assoc ed, Quar Appl Math, 46-95, Studies Appl Math, 70-, Int J Solids & Structures, 83-95; Aeronaut res scientist, NASA, Langley Field, 48 & 51, Ramo, Woolridge, 54 & 55, Lockheed, Palo Alto, 56 & 57; vis prof, Univ Mich, Ann Arbor, 49 & Univ Calif, San Diego, 67; Guggenheim fel, 62; NSF sr fel, 67. *Mem:* Nat Acad Eng; fel Am Acad Arts & Sci; hon mem & fel Am Soc Mech Eng; fel Am Inst Aeronaut & Astronaut; Am Math Soc; fel Am Acad Mech; Int Acad Astronaut; hon mem Soc Appl Math & Mech Ger. *Res:* Theory of elasticity, especially development of variational methods, and behavior of beams, plates and shells. *Mailing Add:* Dept Appl Mech Eng Univ Calif San Diego South La Jolla CA 92039-0411

REIST, ELMER JOSEPH, ORGANIC CHEMISTRY. *Current Pos:* asst dir, 56-80, ASSOC DIR BIOORG CHEM, STANFORD RES INST INT, 80- *Personal Data:* b Can, Aug 29, 30; nat US; m 54; c 2. *Educ:* Univ Alta, BSc, 52; Univ Calif, PhD(org chem), 55. *Prof Exp:* Fel, Nat Res Coun Can, 55-56. *Mem:* Am Chem Soc; AAAS; Am Soc Microbiol. *Res:* Carbohydrates; synthesis; nitrogen mustards; neuraminic acid; enzyme chemistry; nitrosamines; chemical carcinogenesis; nucleic acids; antiviral agents. *Mailing Add:* 581 Berkeley Ave Menlo Park CA 94025-3446

REIST, PARKER CRAMER, AEROSOL SCIENCE. *Current Pos:* PROF AIR & INDUST HYG, SCH PUB HEALTH, UNIV NC, CHAPEL HILL, 72- *Personal Data:* b Williamsport, Pa, Mar 3, 33; m 55, Janet Stanislawsky Aston; c Adam & Sophia. *Educ:* Pa State Univ, BS, 55; Mass Inst Technol, SM, 57; Harvard Univ, SMHyg, 63, ScD(radiol health), 66. *Prof Exp:* Lectr indust hyg, Harvard Univ, 65-66, from asst prof to assoc prof, 66-72. *Concurrent Pos:* Mem, NC State Bd Refrig Examrs, 75-96; Fulbright res scholarship, 84; vis prof, Univ Col, Galway, Ireland, 84-85. *Mem:* Am Asn Aerosol Res; Am Indust Hyg Asn; hon mem Irish Occup Physcians Soc. *Res:* Industrial hygiene; air pollution control; aerosol technology and particle behavior; radiation protection; disposal of hazardous particulate wastes. *Mailing Add:* Sch Pub Hyg Univ NC Chapel Hill NC 27599. *Fax:* 919-966-4711; *E-Mail:* reist@sphvax.sph.unc.edu

REISTAD, GORDON MACKENZE, THERMODYNAMICS, ENERGY HEATING & AIR CONDITIONING. *Current Pos:* from asst prof to assoc prof, 70-81, PROF MECH ENG, ORE STATE UNIV, 81-, HEAD DEPT, 86- *Personal Data:* b Philipsburg, Mont, Oct 21, 44; m 65, Kathleen; c Brian & Brett. *Educ:* Mont State Univ, BS, 66; Univ Wis-Madison, MS, 67, PhD(mech eng), 70. *Honors & Awards:* EK Campbell Merit Award, Am Soc Heating, Refrig & Air Conditioning Engrs. *Prof Exp:* Instr mech eng, Univ Wis-Madison, 69-70. *Concurrent Pos:* Consult, Battelle Northwest, Lawrence Livermore Labs, Elec Power Res Inst, Nat Bur Stand, Int Dist Heating Asn & others; chmn, Nat Prog Comt, Am Soc Heating & Air-Conditioning Engrs. *Mem:* Fel Am Soc Mech Engrs; fel Am Soc Heating, & Air-Conditioning Engrs; Am Soc Eng Educ. *Res:* Energy systems evaluation and design; second law of thermodynamics; geothermal energy systems analysis and design. *Mailing Add:* 4370 NW Queens Ave Corvallis OR 97330. *Fax:* 541-737-2600; *E-Mail:* reistadg@ccmail.orst.edu

REISTER, DAVID B(RYAN), ROBOTICS, GLOBAL OPTIMIZATION. *Current Pos:* SCIENTIST, OAK RIDGE NAT LAB, 85- *Personal Data:* b Los Angeles, Calif, Feb 22, 42; m 63, Willa Fletcher; c Austen & Fletcher. *Educ:* Univ Calif, Berkeley, BS, 64, MS, 66, PhD(eng sci), 69. *Prof Exp:* Lectr eng sci, State Univ NY Buffalo, 68-69, asst prof, 69-74; scientist, Inst Energy Anal, 74-85. *Mem:* Inst Elec & Electronics Engrs; Sigma Xi. *Res:* Planning and control of robotic systems; global optimization of large non linear systems. *Mailing Add:* PO Box 2008 Oak Ridge TN 37831. *Fax:* 423-574-7860; *E-Mail:* dbr@ornl.gov

REISWIG, HENRY MICHAEL, INVERTEBRATE ZOOLOGY, BIOLOGY OF SPONGES. *Current Pos:* asst prof, Dept Biol, 72-77, ASSOC PROF BIOL, REDPATH MUS, MCGILL UNIV, 77- *Personal Data:* b St Paul, Minn, July 8, 36; m 63, Ann Latusek; c Jennifer, Eric & May. *Educ:* Univ Calif, Berkeley, BA, 58, MA, 66; Yale Univ, MSc, 68, PhD(biol), 71. *Prof Exp:* Staff res, Dept Biol, Yale Univ, 71, asst res, Peabody Mus, 71-72. *Mem:* Am Soc Zoologists; Can Soc Zool; Am Soc Limnol & Oceanog; Asn Marine Labs Caribbean; Sigma Xi. *Res:* Anatomy and taxonomy of hexactinellida and spongillidae (porifera). *Mailing Add:* Redpath Mus McGill Univ 859 Sherbrooke St W Montreal PQ H3A 2K6 Can. *Fax:* 514-398-3185; *E-Mail:* inhr@musicb.mcgill.ca

REISWIG, ROBERT D(AVID), METALLURGY. *Current Pos:* STAFF MEM, LOS ALAMOS SCI LAB, 55- *Personal Data:* b Wichita, Kans, July 14, 29; m 51; c 2. *Educ:* Univ Kans, BS, 51; Univ Wis, MS, 53, PhD, 56. *Prof Exp:* Res engr, Battelle Mem Inst, 51-52. *Mem:* Am Inst Mining, Metall & Petrol Engrs; Am Soc Metals. *Res:* Titanium casting; pyrophoric alloys; transformations; phase equilibria; thermal conductivity; temperature measurement; microstructures; carbons and graphites; carbide-carbon composites; corrosion; shaped charge liners. *Mailing Add:* 90 Tecolote Los Alamos NM 87544

REIT, ERNEST MARVIN I, PHARMACOLOGY. *Current Pos:* Asst prof, 66-69, ASSOC PROF PHARMACOL, COL MED, UNIV VT, 69- *Personal Data:* b New York, NY, July 3, 32; m 56; c 4. *Educ:* Cornell Univ, BS, 53, DVM, 57; Yale Univ, PhD(pharmacol), 64. *Concurrent Pos:* Spec fel, Nat Inst Med Res, Mill Hill, Eng, 64-65; USPHS career develop award, 67-72. *Mem:* AAAS; Am Soc Pharmacol & Exp Therapeut; Brit Pharmacol Soc. *Res:* Neuropharmacology, especially chemical mediation and modulation of the transmission of nerve impulses. *Mailing Add:* Dept Pharmacol Univ Vt Col Med Given Med Bldg Burlington VT 05405-0068

REITAN, DANIEL KINSETH, COMPUTER APPLICATIONS. *Current Pos:* PVT CONSULT, 83- *Personal Data:* b Duluth, Minn, Aug 13, 21; m 46; c 2. *Educ:* NDak State Univ, BSEE, 46, Univ Wis, MSEE, 49, PhD(elec & comput engr), 52. *Honors & Awards:* Centennial Medal & Cert, Inst Elec & Electronics Engrs. *Prof Exp:* Res engr, Gen Eng & Res Lab, Gen Elec Co, Schenectady, 46-48; toll line engr, Gen Telephone Co, Madison, Wis, 49-50; prof, elec & comput eng, Univ Wis-Madison, 52-83. *Concurrent Pos:* Chmn, Basic Sci Comt, Inst Elec & Electronics Engrs, 55; dir, Wis Utilities AC Network Calculator Lab, 58-68, Univ Wis Power Syst Simulation Lab, 68-83, wind energy res, Univ Wis Energy Ctr, 72-83; consult, Nat Inst Stand & Technol, 79-83. *Mem:* Sigma Xi; fel Inst Elec & Electronics Engrs; Am Soc Eng Educ. *Res:* Published fifty articles in various journals. *Mailing Add:* PO Box 213 Pelican Rapids MI 56572

REITAN, PAUL HARTMAN, GEOCHEMISTRY, PETROLOGY. *Current Pos:* assoc prof, State Univ NY, Buffalo, 66-69, assoc provost, Fac Natural Sci & Math, 70-75, dir, Natural Sci & Math Res Inst, 70-80, actg provost, 75-76, provost, Fac Natural Sci & Math, 76-78, dean, Fac Natural Sci & Math, 78-80, PROF GEOL, STATE UNIV NY, BUFFALO, 69- *Personal Data:* b Kanawha, Iowa, Aug 18, 28; m 62, Reidun Engebretsen; c Kirsten & Eric. *Educ:* Univ Chicago, AB, 53; Univ Oslo, PhD(geol), 59. *Prof Exp:* Geologist, US Geol Surv, 53-56; state geologist, Geol Surv Norway, 56-60; asst prof mineral, Stanford Univ, 60-66. *Concurrent Pos:* Fulbright sr lectr, Indian Sch Mines, Dhanbad, India, 86; Consult, Geol Survey Norway, 86-90, 92-93. *Mem:* AAAS; fel Geol Soc Am; fel Mineral Soc Am; Int Asn Geochem & Cosmochem; fel Geol Soc India; Norwegian Geol Soc; foreign mem Royal Norwegian Soc Scis & Letters. *Res:* Metamorphic petrology and recrystallization; fractionation of elements between coexisting minerals; temperatures of metamorphism; cycling of elements in earth's crust; sustainability of human society. *Mailing Add:* Dept Geol State Univ NY Buffalo NY 14260-3050. *Fax:* 716-645-3999; *E-Mail:* preitan@acsu.buffalo.edu

REITAN, PHILLIP JENNINGS, ZOOLOGY. *Current Pos:* assoc prof, 62-67, chmn dept, 62-72, PROF BIOL, LUTHER COL, IOWA, 67- *Personal Data:* b Grove City, Minn, July 14, 29; m 53; c 5. *Educ:* Concordia Col, Moorhead, Minn, BA, 52; Univ Wis, MS, 54, PhD(zool), 58. *Prof Exp:* Teacher pub sch, NDak, 49-50; from instr to assoc prof biol, Wagner Col, 57-62. *Concurrent Pos:* Co-prin investr, NIH res grant, 58-63; NSF sci fac fel, Harvard Univ, 65-66; vis scholar, Hopkins Marine Sta, 73; Pac Lutheran Univ, 80; hon fel zool, Univ Wis, 81; volunteer, Page Mus, Los Angeles, 88. *Mem:* AAAS; Am Soc Zoologists; Am Asn Univ Profs; Sigma Xi. *Res:* Drosophila development, especially the relationship between inherited abnormalities and normal embryology; relationship between dehydration and radiation effects in Drosophila embryology; function of avian amnion in development; impact of Darwinism. *Mailing Add:* 606 Center St Decorah IA 52101

REITAN, RALPH MELDAHL, NEUROPSYCHOLOGY. *Current Pos:* PRES, REITAN NEUROPSYCHOL LABS INC. *Personal Data:* b Beresford, SDak, Aug 29, 22; div; c Ellen, Jon, Ann, Richard & Erik. *Educ:* Univ Chicago, PhD(psychol), 50. *Honors & Awards:* Gordon Barrows Mem Award, 65; 1st Distinguished Clin Neuropsychologist Award, Nat Acad Neuropsychol, 88; Margaret Bancroft Award, 92; Inaugural Distinguished Contrib Award, Nat Acad Neuropsychol, 94. *Prof Exp:* Lectr psychol, South Bend Exten Ctr, Ind Univ, Indianapolis, 48-51; from asst prof to assoc prof surg, Sch Med, 51-60, prof psychol & dir sect neuropsychol, 60-70; prof psychol & neurol surg, Univ Wash, 70-77; prof psychol, Univ Ariz, 77-86. *Concurrent Pos:* Instr, Univ Chicago, 49-51; consult, Space Med Adv Group, NASA, 64-65, Off Assoc Dir, Nat Inst Neurol Dis & Blindness, 61-76 & Vet Admin Hosp, Tucson, 77-85. *Mem:* Nat Acad Neuropsychol; Am Psychol Asn; Am Neurol Asn; Am Acad Neurol. *Res:* Brain localization of abilities, neuropsychology; brain-behavior relationships. *Mailing Add:* Neuropsychol Lab 2920 S Fourth Ave South Tucson AZ 85713

REITEMEIER, RICHARD JOSEPH, GASTROENTEROLOGY, ONCOLOGY. *Current Pos:* RETIRED. *Personal Data:* b Pueblo, Colo, Jan 2, 23; m 51; c 7. *Educ:* Univ Denver, AB, 43; Univ Colo, MD, 46; Univ Minn, MS, 54; cert, Am Bd Intern Med, 54. *Honors & Awards:* Irving S Cutter Gold Medal, 86; Alfred Stengel Award, Am Col Physicians, 90. *Prof Exp:* From instr to assoc prof med, Mayo Med Sch, 57-67, chmn, Dept Internal Med, Mayo Clin, 67-74, emer prof med, 71-87, consult, Mayo Med Sch & Found, 54-87; med dir, Phoenix Alliance, Inc, St Paul, Minn, 91-93. *Concurrent Pos:* Vis prof, Univ Iowa, 71, Scott White Clin, Temple Tex, 76; mem, Bd Develop, Mayo Found, 86; exec & sci dir, Ludwig Inst Cancer Res, 88- *Mem:* Inst Med-Nat Acad Sci; Am Col Physicians (pres, 83-84); Am Gastroenterol Asn; AMA; Am Clin & Climotol Asn; Am Fedn Clin Res; Am Soc Clin Oncol. *Mailing Add:* 707 12th Ave SW Rochester MN 55902

REITER, ELMAR RUDOLF, CLIMATOLOGY. *Current Pos:* RETIRED. *Personal Data:* b Wels, Austria, Feb 22, 28; m 54; c 3. *Educ:* Univ Innsbruck, PhD(meteorol, geophys), 53. *Honors & Awards:* Advan Sci Award, Govt Upper Austria, 62; Robert M Losey Award, Am Inst Aeronaut & Astronaut, 67; Silver Anniversary Medal Distinguished Serv, Univ Innsbruck, 70. *Prof Exp:* Res asst meteorol, Univ Chicago, 52-53, res assoc & instr, 54-56; instr, NATO Officer's Sch, Ger, 53-54; res assoc meteorol & geophys, Univ Innsbruck, 56-59, asst prof, 59-61; assoc prof, Colo State Univ, 61-65, head dept, 68-74, prof atmospheric sci, 65-88, prof civil eng, Colo State Univ, 85-88; pres, Wels Res Corp, 88- *Concurrent Pos:* Res fel, Deutscher Wetterdienst, Repub Ger, 59; lectr, SEATO Grad Sch, Bangkok, 63; consult, Ger Lufthansa Airlines, 59-61, Meteorol Res Inc, Calif, 63-65, Univ Melbourne, 63, Litton Industs, Minn, 64, Boeing Aircraft Co, Seattle, 65, NASA-Marshall Space Flight Ctr, Huntsville & US Army Missile Commmand, 65-, Nat Comt Clear Turbulence, 66, Inst Defense Analysis, 73-75 & Nat Acad Sci, 73-75; pres, Meteorol Sect, Am Geophys Union, 80-82; mem adv bd, Geophys Inst, Univ Alaska. *Mem:* Fel Am Meteorol Soc; fel Am Geophys Union; Am Inst Aeronaut & Astronaut; Royal Meteorol Soc; Meteorol Soc Japan; Math Soc Austria; Austrian Acad Sci. *Res:* Numerical and heuristic computer modeling; aviation meteorology, especially clear-air turbulence; computerized decision support systems. *Mailing Add:* 7223 Four Rivers Rd Boulder CO 80301

REITER, HAROLD BRAUN, MATHEMATICS. *Current Pos:* ASSOC PROF MATH, UNIV NC, CHARLOTTE, 72- *Personal Data:* b Jackson, Tenn, Oct 14, 42; m 66, Betty Baker; c Ashley. *Educ:* La State Univ, Baton Rouge, BS, 64; Clemson Univ, MS, 65, PhD(math), 69. *Prof Exp:* Asst prof math, Univ Hawaii, 69-72. *Concurrent Pos:* Assoc chmn, dept comput sci, Univ Md, College Park; chmn, Am High Sch Math Exam, 94- *Mem:* Am Math Soc; Math Asn Am. *Res:* Comparison of topologies; function algebras; convexity; game theory; recreational mathematics, including magic geograms, knight interchange problems and teacher education. *Mailing Add:* Dept Math Univ NC Charlotte NC 28223. *E-Mail:* hbreiter@email.uncc.edu

REITER, MARSHALL ALLAN, GEOPHYSICS. *Current Pos:* geophysicist, 75-79, SR GEOPHYSICIST, NMEX BUR MINES & MINERAL RESOURCES, 79- *Personal Data:* b Pittsburgh, Pa, Sept 11, 42; m 64; c 3. *Educ:* Univ Pittsburgh, BS, 65; Va Polytech Inst, PhD(geophys), 70. *Prof Exp:* From asst prof to assoc prof geophys, NMex Inst Mining & Technol, 70-75. *Concurrent Pos:* Adj assoc prof geophys, NMex Inst Mining & Technol, 75-80, adj prof, 80- *Mem:* Am Geophys Union; fel Geol Soc Am; Soc Explor Geophysicists; Sigma Xi. *Res:* Geothermal studies; define the geographic variation of terrestrial heat flux in the Southwestern United States with borehole temperature measurements, locate geothermal areas, thermal conditions in the crust and upper mantle. *Mailing Add:* 1307 North Dr Socorro NM 87801

REITER, RAYMOND, computer science, for more information see previous edition

REITER, RUSSEL JOSEPH, NEUROENDOCRINOLOGY, CELL & MOLECULAR BIOLOGY. *Current Pos:* assoc prof, 71-73, PROF NEUROENDOCRINOL, UNIV TEX HEALTH SCI CTR, SAN ANTONIO, 73- *Personal Data:* b St Cloud, Minn, Sept 22, 36; m 62, 90; c 2. *Educ:* St John's Univ, Minn, BA, 59; Bowman Gray Sch Med, MS, 61, PhD(anat), 64. *Prof Exp:* Exp endocrinologist, Edgewood Arsenal, Md, 66; asst prof anat, Med Ctr, Univ Rochester, 66-69, assoc prof, 69-71. *Concurrent Pos:* NIH career develop award, 69-74; ed, J Pineal Res, Neurosci Lett & Pineal Res Rev. *Mem:* Endocrine Soc; Am Physiol Soc; NY Acad Sci; Soc Neurosci; Int Soc Chronobiol; Sigma Xi. *Res:* Neuroendocrinology, especially the pineal gland, cell biology and reproductive physiology; brain chemistry and behavior; author of six books. *Mailing Add:* Dept Cellular & Struct Biol Univ Tex Health Sci Ctr 7703 Floyd Curl Dr San Antonio TX 78284-7762

REITER, STANLEY, MATHEMATICS, ECONOMICS. *Current Pos:* MORRISON PROF ECON & MATH, NORTHWESTERN UNIV, 67- *Personal Data:* b Apr 26, 25; m 44, Nina Breger; c Carla Frances & Frank Joseph. *Educ:* Queens Col, AB, 47; Univ Chicago, MA, 50, PhD(econ), 55. *Prof Exp:* Instr econ, Stanford Univ, 50-53; from asst prof to prof econ & math, Purdue Univ, 54-67. *Concurrent Pos:* From res asst to res assoc, Cowles Comt, Res in Econ, Univ Chicago, 48-50; res assoc, Appl Math & Statist Lab, Stanford Univ, 53-54; prin investr, Off Naval Res Contract Math Econ, Purdue Univ, 58-67; vis fel, Churchill Col, Cambridge Univ, 61-62; chmn, Managerial Econ & Decision Sci, Northwestern Univ, 73-74, dir, Ctr Math Studies Econ & Mgt Sci, 74-; sr mem, Inst Math & Applications, Univ Minn, 83-84; Morrison prof econ & math, Col Arts & Sci, Dept Managerial Econ & Decision Sci, Grad Sch Mgt, Northwestern Univ, 78-; vis fac assoc, Calif Inst Technol. *Mem:* AAAS; fel Econometric Soc; Am Acad Arts & Sci; Am Math Soc; Math Asn Am. *Mailing Add:* 2138 Orrington Ave Evanston IL 60201-2914. *Fax:* 847-491-2530; *E-Mail:* s-reiter@nwu.edu

REITER, WILLIAM FREDERICK, JR, MECHANICAL ENGINEERING. *Current Pos:* PROF MECH ENG, ORE STATE UNIV, 93- *Personal Data:* b Egg Harbor City, NJ, July 20, 38; m 72; c 2. *Educ:* Rutgers Univ, BS, 61; Auburn Univ, MS, 66; NC State Univ, PhD(mech eng), 73. *Prof Exp:* Instr mech eng, Auburn Univ, 66-69; from asst prof to assoc prof, NC State Univ, 78-82; staff mem, IBM, 83-92; staff mem, Boeing, 93. *Mem:* Am Soc Mech Engrs; Soc Automotive Engrs. *Res:* Dynamics of rotating machinery; vibration and sound radiation from structures; sound and vibration signal processing. *Mailing Add:* Dept Mech Eng 204 Rogers Hall Col Eng Ore State Univ Corvallis OR 97331

REITH, MAARTEN E A, NEUROCHEMISTRY, NEUROPHARMACOLOGY. *Current Pos:* assoc prof, 91-95, PROF, UNIV ILL COL MED, PEORIA, 95- *Personal Data:* b Utrecht, Neth, Dec 29, 46; m 80, Irma Vara; c Catherina. *Educ:* State Univ Utrecht, Neth, BS, 68, MS, 71, PhD(neurochem-pharmacol), 75. *Prof Exp:* Res fel neurochem, Ctr Neurochem, Fac Med, Strasbourg, France, 71; res scientist biochem, Rudolf Magnus Inst Pharmacol, State Univ Utrecht, Neth, 71-74; sr res scientist biochem, Int Molecular Biol, 74-78; sr res scientist, Ctr Neurochem, N S Kline Inst, New York, 78-91. *Concurrent Pos:* Prin investr, NY State Health Res Coun, 81-82 & Nat Inst Drug Abuse, 83-; adj prof, Ill State Univ, Normal, 96- *Mem:* Am Soc Biol Chemists; Am Soc Neurochem; Int Soc Neurochem; Soc Neurosci; NY Acad Sci. *Res:* Receptors for neurotransmitters and psychoactive drugs; monoamine uptake, release and storage; action of drugs of abuse. *Mailing Add:* Dept Biomed & Therapeut Sci Univ 211 Col Med PO Box 1649 Wards Island Peoria IL 61656. *Fax:* 309-671-8403; *E-Mail:* maartenr@uic.edu

REITMAN, MARC LIONEL, MOLECULAR BIOLOGY OF OBESITY & METABOLIC REGULATION. *Current Pos:* Med staff fel, 86-89, SR STAFF FEL, DIABETES BR, NAT INST DIABETES & DIGESTIVE & KIDNEY DIS, NIH, 89-, INVESTR, 97- *Personal Data:* b New Rochelle, NY, Oct 3, 55; m 80, Ann M Ginsberg; c Nadine & Jason. *Educ:* Mass Inst Technol, BS(chem) & BS(biol), 77; Washington Univ, St Louis, MD & PhD(molecular biol), 83. *Concurrent Pos:* Resident internal med, Presby Hosp, NY, 83-96; Lucille P Markey scholar biomed sci, Markey Charitable Trust, 89-97. *Mem:* Am Diabetes Asn; Endocrine Soc; Am Soc Biochem & Molecular Biol; NAm Soc Biochem & Molecular Biol. *Res:* Genetics of diabetes and obesity. *Mailing Add:* 10 Center Dr Bldg 10 Rm 8N-250 Bethesda MD 20892-1770. *E-Mail:* mlr@helix.nih.gov

REITNOUR, CLARENCE MELVIN, ANIMAL NUTRITION. *Current Pos:* assoc prof, 68-80, PROF, UNIV DEL, 81-, EQUINE SPECIALIST, 68- *Personal Data:* b Spring City, Pa, Oct 17, 33; m 69. *Educ:* Pa State Univ, BS, 59; Univ Ky, MS, 62, PhD, 68. *Prof Exp:* Res asst, Univ Ky, 60-62 & Univ Md, 62-64; exten specialist, Univ Ky, 64-66, res asst, 66-68. *Mem:* Am Soc Animal Sci. *Res:* Equine nitrogen metabolism. *Mailing Add:* Dept Animal & Food Scis Univ Del Newark DE 19711

REITSEMA, HAROLD JAMES, SOLAR SYSTEM STUDIES, SPACE INSTRUMENTATION. *Current Pos:* sr engr, Systs Div, Ball Aerospace, 82-86, prin engr, 86-89, staff consult, 89-96, DIR ADVAN PROGS, SYSTS DIV, BALL AEROSPACE, 96- *Personal Data:* b Kalamazoo, Mich, Jan 19, 48; m 70, Mary Jo Gunnink; c Ellen C & Laurie J. *Educ:* Calvin Col, AB, 72; NMex State Univ, PhD(astron), 77. *Honors & Awards:* Engr of Yr, Am Inst Aeronaut & Astronaut, 89. *Prof Exp:* Sr res assoc, Univ Ariz, 77-81. *Concurrent Pos:* Vis scientist, Univ Ariz, 82-96; chmn, Space Sci & Astron Tech Comt, Inst Aeronaut & Astronaut, 90-91. *Mem:* Am Astron Soc; Am Inst Aeronaut & Astronaut; Am Astronaut Soc; Int Astron Union. *Res:* Occultation observations of solar system bodies; studies of Comet 5; searching for other planetary systems. *Mailing Add:* Ball Aerospace PO Box 1062 Boulder CO 80303. *E-Mail:* hreitsem@ball.com

REITSEMA, ROBERT HAROLD, geochemistry; deceased, see previous edition for last biography

REITZ, ALLEN BERNARD, STEREOSELECTIVE SYNTHESIS METHODOLOGY, CENTRAL NERVOUS SYSTEM RESEARCH. *Current Pos:* Fel, McNeil Pharmaceut, Johnson & Johnson, 82-83, res scientist, 83-84, sr scientist, 84-87, prin scientist, Janssen Res Found, 87-89, prin scientist, 90-92, RES FEL, R W JOHNSON PHARMACEUT RES INST, 92- *Personal Data:* b Alameda, Calif, Apr 7, 56; m 78, Evelyn McCullough; c Darryl & Meredith. *Educ:* Univ Calif, Santa Barbara, BA, 77; Univ Calif, San Diego, MS, 79, PhD(chem), 82. *Concurrent Pos:* Lectr, numerous univs & res conferences; reviewer, J Org Chem, Carbohydrate Res, Heteroatom Chem, Tetrahedron Lett & J Med Chem. *Mem:* Am Chem Soc; Sigma Xi; AAAS. *Res:* Systematic development of structure-activity relationships, attempting to maximize a desired biological profile; discovery of new and useful stereoselective synthetic methodology in organic chemistry, including cycloadditions and novel methods for aminosugar synthesis; author of numerous publications; ten US patents. *Mailing Add:* 109 Greenbriar Rd Lansdale PA 19446-1519. *Fax:* 215-628-4985

REITZ, HERMAN J, HORTICULTURE. *Current Pos:* RETIRED. *Personal Data:* b Belle Plaine, Kans, July 5, 16; m 45; c 2. *Educ:* Kans State Col, BS, 39; Ohio State Univ, MS, 40, PhD(hort), 49. *Prof Exp:* From assoc horticulturist to horticulturist, Fla Agr Res & Educ Ctr, 46-56, horticulturist chg, 57-65, dir, 65-82. *Mem:* Fel AAAS; Int Soc Citricult (pres, 73-77); Int Soc Hort Sci; fel Am Soc Hort Sci. *Res:* Mineral nutrition of citrus; citrus growing, harvesting and processing. *Mailing Add:* 290 Park Lane W Lake Alfred FL 33850

REITZ, JOHN RICHARD, THEORETICAL PHYSICS. *Current Pos:* RETIRED. *Personal Data:* b Lakewood, Ohio, Feb 7, 23; m 47; c 4. *Educ:* Case Inst Technol, BS, 43; Univ Chicago, MS, 47, PhD(physics), 49. *Prof Exp:* Res assoc acoust, Underwater Sound Lab, Harvard Univ, 43-45; mem staff theoret physics, Los Alamos Sci Lab, Univ Calif, 49-52; sci liaison officer physics, Off Naval Res, London, 52-54; from asst prof to prof, Case Inst Technol, 54-65; mgr physics dept, Sci Lab, Ford Motor Co, 65-87. *Mem:* Fel Am Phys Soc. *Res:* Cohesion of solids; imperfection in alkalihalide crystals; electronic structure and transport properties of solids; plasma physics; high speed ground transportation; electricity and magnetism. *Mailing Add:* 2260 Chaucer Ct Ann Arbor MI 48103

REITZ, MARVIN SAVIDGE, JR, MOLECULAR VIROLOGY. *Current Pos:* ASSOC DIR, BASIC SCI DIV, INST HUMAN VIROL, UNIV MD, BALTIMORE, 96- *Personal Data:* m 80, Kathleen Whalen; c Petra, Theresa & Andrew. *Educ:* Western Md Col, BA, 65; Purdue Univ, PhD(biochem). *Prof Exp:* Res asst, Purdue Univ, 65-69; fel, Retina Found, 69-71; staff scientist, Lifton Bionetics, 71-74, chief sect molecular virol, 74-78; chief, Sect Molecular Hemat Cells, Lab Tumor Cell Biol, Nat Cancer Inst, NIH;, 89-96. *Concurrent Pos:* Sr investr, Lab Tumor Cell Biol, Nat Cancer Inst, NIH, 78-, acting deputy chief, 90-; instr, Tech Site Directed Mutagenesis, Ctr Advan Training Cellular & Molecular Biol, 89-; consult, Inst Biotech & Molecular Med, 93- *Mem:* Am Soc Microbiol. *Res:* Molecular biology of human retroviruses (human immunovirus I, human t-cell lymphotropic virus I; co-discoverer of human t-cell lymphotropic virus I. *Mailing Add:* 17833 Bowie Mill Rd Derwood MD 20855

REITZ, RICHARD ELMER, ENDOCRINOLOGY, CALCIUM METABOLISM. *Current Pos:* MED DIR, NICHOLS INST, 91- *Personal Data:* b Buffalo, NY, Sept 18, 38; m 60; c 2. *Educ:* Heidelberg Col, Tiffin, Ohio, BS, 60; State Univ NY, Buffalo, MD, 64. *Prof Exp:* Intern med, Hartford Hosp, Conn, 64-65; resident, Yale Univ Hosp, 65-66 & Hartford Hosp, 66-67; res assoc endocrinol, Nat Heart Inst, NIH, Bethesda, Md, 67-68; res fel endocrinol, Harvard Med Sch, 67-69 & Mass Gen Hosp, 68-69; asst dir, Clin Invest Ctr, Naval Regional Med Ctr, Oakland, Calif, 69-71; asst prof, Univ Calif-San Francisco, 71-76, assoc clin prof, 76-86, clin prof med, Univ Calif, Davis, 86-; dir, Endocrine Metab Ctr, Oakland, Calif, 73-91. *Concurrent Pos:* Chief endocrinol, Providence Hosp, Oakland, 73- *Mem:* Endocrine Soc; Am Soc Bone & Mineral Res; Am Fedn Clin Res; Am Fertil Soc; AAAS; Am Soc Int Med. *Res:* Cytoreceptor assay for 1,25 dihydroxy vitamin D; metabolic bone disease of renal failure. *Mailing Add:* Quest-Nichols Inst 33608 Ortega Hwy San Juan Capistrano CA 92690

REITZ, RICHARD HENRY, BIOCHEMISTRY, TOXICOLOGY. *Current Pos:* Res biochemist drug develop, Human Health Res & Develop, 66-74, sr res biochemist fermentation, Cent Res Lab, 74-78, RES SPECIALIST, TOXICOL RES LAB, DOW CHEM CO, 78- *Personal Data:* b Minneapolis, Minn, Sept 1, 40; m 63; c 1. *Educ:* DePauw Univ, BS, 62; Northwestern Univ, Evanston, PhD(biochem), 66, Am Bd Toxicol, dipl. *Mem:* Am Chem Soc; Am Soc Microbiol; AAAS. *Res:* Chemical carcinogenesis and mutagenesis; microbiological production of chemicals; asthma and hypersensitivity; psychopharmacology. *Mailing Add:* 4105 Chelsea Midland MI 48640

REITZ, ROBERT ALAN, PHYSICS. *Current Pos:* from asst prof to assoc prof, 54-65, chmn dept, 57-71, PROF PHYSICS, CARLETON COL, 65- *Personal Data:* b Lakewood, Ohio, Sept 8, 26; m 48; c 4. *Educ:* Case Inst Technol, BS, 49; Univ Ill, MS, 51, PhD(physics), 55. *Prof Exp:* Asst physics, Univ Ill, 49-51 & 52-54. *Concurrent Pos:* NSF fac fel, Ger, 63-64; vis scholar, Stanford Univ, 71-72 & Univ Calif, San Diego, 79-80. *Mem:* Am Phys Soc; Am Asn Physics Teachers; Sigma Xi. *Res:* Solid state physics. *Mailing Add:* 11 Bundy Ct Northfield MN 55057-2607

REITZ, ROBERT REX, ORGANIC CHEMISTRY. *Current Pos:* RES CHEMIST, ELASTOMER CHEM DEPT, E I DU PONT DE NEMOURS & CO, INC, 73- *Personal Data:* b Oklahoma City, Okla, Dec 18, 43; m 67; c 2. *Educ:* Austin Col, BA, 66; Kans State Univ, PhD(chem), 71. *Prof Exp:* Assoc org chem, Ohio State Univ, 72-73. *Mem:* Am Chem Soc. *Res:* Research and development of new synthetic rubber and rubber chemicals. *Mailing Add:* 727 Folly Hill Rd West Chester PA 19382-6909

REITZ, RONALD CHARLES, BIOCHEMISTRY. *Current Pos:* assoc prof, 75-80, PROF BIOCHEM, UNIV NEV, RENO, 80- *Personal Data:* b Dallas, Tex, Feb 27, 39; m 65, Jeanne M Geiger; c Erica A & P Brett. *Educ:* Tex A&M Univ, BS, 61; Tulane Univ, PhD(biochem), 66. *Prof Exp:* USPHS fel, Univ Mich, Ann Arbor, 66-69; asst prof biochem, Univ NC, Chapel Hill, 69-75. *Concurrent Pos:* Vis scientist, Unilever Res Lab, Frythe, Welwyn, Eng, 68, Du Pont de Nemours & Co, Del, 84; sci consult, NC Ctr Alcohol Studies, 74-76; vis prof, Nagoya City Univ, Japan, 90, Max Planck Inst Biophys Chem, Gottingen, Ger, 90-91. *Mem:* Am Soc Biol Chemists; Am Soc Pharmacol & Exp Ther; AAAS; Am Oil Chemists Soc; Res Soc Alcoholism. *Res:* Lipid metabolism; effects of chronic alcoholism on membrane lipids and on membrane function; membrane lipids of tumor tissue; relationships between sphingo lipids turnover and apoptosis; affects of W3 fatty acids on turn or growth. *Mailing Add:* Dept Biochem Univ Nev 153 Howard Med Sci Bldg Reno NV 89577. *Fax:* 702-784-1419; *E-Mail:* reitz@unssurv.scs.unr.edu

REITZE, DAVID H, PHYSICS. *Current Pos:* ASST PROF PHYSICS, UNIV FLA, 93- *Personal Data:* b Jan 6, 61. *Educ:* North Western, Univ, BS, 83; Univ Tex, PhD(physics), 90. *Honors & Awards:* Res Initiation Award, NSF, 94. *Mailing Add:* Dept Physics/Univ Fla PO Box 118440 Gainesville FL 32611. *Fax:* 352-392-3591; *E-Mail:* reitze@phys.ufl.edu

REIVICH, MARTIN, NEUROLOGY. *Current Pos:* instr, Univ Pa, 62-65, instr pharmacol, 63-64, asst prof neurol, 66-68, assoc prof, 68-72, dir, Cerebrovascular Res Lab, 66-73, PROF NEUROL, SCH MED, UNIV PA, 72-, DIR, CEREBROVASCULAR RES CTR, 73- *Personal Data:* b Philadelphia, Pa, Mar 2, 33; m 60; c 2. *Educ:* Univ Pa, BS, 54, MD, 58. *Hon Degrees:* Dr, Semmelweis Med Univ, 90. *Honors & Awards:* Semmelweis Award, 77. *Prof Exp:* Intern med, King County Hosp, Seattle, Wash, 58-59; resident neurol, Hosp Univ Pa, 59-61; clin clerk, Nat Hosp, London, Eng, 61-62. *Concurrent Pos:* NIH res fel, 60-61, training grant, 63; Fulbright fel, 61-62; USPHS career res develop award, 66-75; vis assoc physiol, NIMH, 64-65; mem coun cerebrovascular dis, Am Heart Asn, 67-; mem, Int Study Group Cerebral Circulation, 68-; mem neurol A study sect, NIH, 71-75; consult, Vet Admin Hosp, Philadelphia, 68- & US Naval Air Develop Ctr, 70-72; co-dir stroke ctr, Philadelphia Gen Hosp, 71-72; mem task force stroke, Nat Heart, Blood Vessel, Lung & Blood Prog; mem, NSP-A study sect, NIH, 86-90. *Mem:* Am Neurol Asn; Am Physiol Soc; Soc Neurosci; Am Acad Neurol; Asn Res Nerv & Ment Dis; Soc Nuclear Med; Fedn Neurol. *Res:* Cerebral circulation and metabolism; cerebrovascular disease. *Mailing Add:* Dept Neurol Univ Pa Sch Med 429 Johnson Pavilion 36th & Hamilton Walk Philadelphia PA 19104-6063

REIZER, JONATHAN, REGULATION OF SUGAR TRANSPORT, METABOLIC PATHWAYS OF SUGAR METABOLISM. *Current Pos:* RES BIOLOGIST, UNIV CALIF, SAN DIEGO, 88- *Personal Data:* b Haifa, Israel, Feb 16, 40; US citizen; m 68; c 2. *Educ:* Hebrew Univ, Jerusalem, BSc, 64, MSc, 67, PhD(microbiol), 78. *Prof Exp:* Res assoc, Thomas Jefferson Univ, 79-80, Brown Univ, 80-81 & Univ Calif, San Diego, 82-85; sr staff fel, NIH, 85-88. *Mem:* Am Soc Microbiol; Am Soc Biochem & Molecular Biol. *Res:* Biochemistry and physiology of transmembrane sugar transport in bacteria; contributed articles to scientific journals. *Mailing Add:* 13613 Boquita Dr Del Mar CA 92014-3407

REJ, ROBERT, BIOCHEMISTRY. *Prof Exp:* Int fel, Am Asn Clin Chem, 95. *Mailing Add:* NY State Dept Health Wadsworth Ctr Labs & Res Empire State Plaza PO Box 509 Albany NY 12201

REJALI, ABBAS MOSTAFAVI, RADIOLOGY, NUCLEAR MEDICINE. *Current Pos:* assoc prof radiol & nuclear med, 63-68, asst prof radiol, 68-76, ASSOC PROF RADIOL, CASE WESTERN RESERVE UNIV, 76-, DIR DEPT NUCLEAR MED, 74- *Personal Data:* b Aug 19, 21; US citizen; m 54; c 1. *Educ:* State Univ NY Downstate Med Ctr, MD, 51; Am Bd Radiol, dipl,

55. *Prof Exp:* Intern med, Grasslands Hosp, Valhalla, NY, 51-52; resident radiol, Univ Hosps, Cleveland, 52-55; teaching fel radiation ther & actg dir radiation ther, 56-57; assoc chief radiol, Roswell Park Mem Inst, 59-61. *Concurrent Pos:* Atomic Energy Proj fel, Case Western Reserve Univ, 55-57, sect assoc radiation biol, 56-57; US rep, Int Atomic Energy Agency, 68 & 70; consult radiologist, Highland View Hosp, Metrop Gen Hosp & Huron Rd Hosp. *Mem:* Radiol Soc NAm; fel Am Col Nuclear Med; Soc Nuclear Med; fel Am Col Radiol. *Res:* Diagnostic use of radioisotope tracer; development of radioisotopic instrumentation. *Mailing Add:* 2853 Montgomery Rd Cleveland OH 44122

REJTO, PETER A, MATHEMATICS. *Current Pos:* asst prof, 65-77, PROF MATH, SCH MATH, UNIV MINN, MINNEAPOLIS, 77- *Personal Data:* b Budapest, Hungary, Apr 28, 34; US citizen; m 60; c 1. *Educ:* NY Univ, PhD(math), 59. *Prof Exp:* Asst prof, NY Univ, 60-64 & Math Res Ctr, Univ Wis, 64-65. *Mem:* Am Math Asn; Am Math Soc; Soc Indust & Appl Math. *Res:* Spectral theory of operators in Hilbert space. *Mailing Add:* 1539 E River Terr Minneapolis MN 55414

REKASIUS, ZENONAS V, ELECTRICAL ENGINEERING. *Current Pos:* assoc prof, 64-68, PROF ELEC ENG, TECHNOL INST, NORTHWESTERN UNIV, 68- *Personal Data:* b Lithuania, Jan 1, 28; m 60; c 3. *Educ:* Wayne State Univ, BS, 54, MS, 56; Purdue Univ, PhD(elec eng), 60. *Prof Exp:* From asst prof to assoc prof elec eng, Purdue Univ, 60-64. *Mem:* Inst Elec & Electronics Engrs. *Res:* Control systems; stability; optimization. *Mailing Add:* Northwestern Univ Evanston IL 60201

REKERS, ROBERT GEORGE, ANALYTICAL CHEMISTRY. *Current Pos:* RETIRED. *Personal Data:* b Rochester, NY, Feb 1, 20; m 51; c William E, Martha N & Sandra K. *Educ:* Univ Rochester, BSc, 42; Univ Colo, PhD(chem), 51. *Prof Exp:* Asst foundry chemist, Gen Rwy Signal Co, 41; anal chemist & group leader, Eastman Kodak Co, 42-47; asst phys chem, Univ Colo, 47-51; spectroscopist, US Naval Ord Test Sta, Calif, 51-55; from asst prof to assoc prof chem, Text Tech Univ, 55-86 asst chmn dept, 69-75. *Mem:* AAAS; Am Chem Soc; Colbentz Soc; Sigma Xi. *Res:* Spectroscopy of flames; instrumental methods of analysis. *Mailing Add:* 1717 Norfolk Ave No 2479 Lubbock TX 79416

REKLAITIS, GINTARAS VICTOR, COMPUTER AIDED DESIGN, PROCESS OPERATIONS. *Current Pos:* from asst prof to assoc prof, 70-80, PROF CHEM ENG, PURDUE UNIV, WEST LAFAYETTE, 80-, ASST DEAN ENG, 85-, HEAD CHEM ENG, 87- *Personal Data:* b Posen, Poland, Oct 20, 42; US citizen; m 66; c 2. *Educ:* Ill Inst Technol, BS, 65; Stanford Univ, MS, 69, PhD(chem eng), 69. *Honors & Awards:* Comput Chem Eng Award, Am Inst Chem Engrs, 84. *Prof Exp:* NSF fel, Inst Opers Res, Zurich, Switz, 69-70. *Concurrent Pos:* Fulbright sr lectr, Lithuania, 80; dir, Comput & Systs Technol Div, Am Inst Chem Engrs, 80-83, chmn, Prog Bd, 86-89, div 2nd vchmn, 89, 1st vchmn, 90, chmn, 91; secy, Comput Aids Chem Eng Educ Corp, 82-84, vpres, 84-86, pres, 86-88. *Mem:* Am Chem Soc; Math Prog Soc; Opers Res Soc Am; Am Inst Chem Engrs; AAAS. *Res:* Optimization theory; process simulation; computer aided design; scheduling and design of batch processes; computer aided process operations. *Mailing Add:* Sch Chem Eng Purdue Univ West Lafayette IN 47906

REKOFF, M(ICHAEL) G(EORGE), JR, ELECTRICAL ENGINEERING, PROCESS CONTROL. *Current Pos:* RETIRED. *Personal Data:* b Galveston, Tex, July 27, 29; m 51, Virginia Larsen; c Caroline, Michael & Paul. *Educ:* Agr & Mech Col, Tex, BSEE, 51, MSEE, 55; Univ Wis, PhD(elec eng), 61. *Prof Exp:* Instr elec eng, Agr & Mech Col, Tex, 54-56 & Univ Wis, 56-59; from asst prof to prof, Tex A&M Univ, 59-69; mem tech staff, TRW Systs Group, 69-70, staff engr, Telelyn Brown Eng, 70-76; dir elec res & develop, Onan Corp, 76-79; prof, Univ Tenn, Chattanooga, 79-82; prof, Univ Ala, Birmingham, 83. *Mem:* Fel Instrument Soc Am. *Res:* Servo-mechanisms; computing; machines; systems engineering. *Mailing Add:* Dept Elec Eng Univ Ala Birmingham AL 35294

RELLER, L BARTH, MICROBIOLOGY. *Current Pos:* PROF, MED CTR, DUKE UNIV. *Honors & Awards:* Becton Dickinson & Co Award in Clin Microbiol, Am Soc Microbiol, 91. *Res:* Microbiology. *Mailing Add:* 2616 McDowell Rd Durham NC 27705

RELLES, HOWARD, POLYMERS & PLASTICS. *Current Pos:* PRES, RELLES ASSOC, 92- *Personal Data:* b Newark, NJ, Feb 21, 39. *Res:* Polymers and plastics. *Mailing Add:* 15 Carolyn Terr Schenectady NY 12309-2531

RELMAN, ARNOLD SEYMOUR, MEDICINE. *Current Pos:* prof med, 77-91, prof med & social med, 91-93, SR PHYSICIAN, BRIGHAM & WOMEN'S HOSP, BOSTON, 77-; EMER PROF MED & SOCIAL MED, HARVARD MED SCH, 93- *Personal Data:* b New York, NY, June 17, 23; m 53; c 3. *Educ:* Cornell Univ, AB, 43; Columbia Univ, MD, 46; Am Bd Internal Med, dipl, 52, 74. *Hon Degrees:* MA, Univ Pa, 75; ScD, Med Col Wis, 80, Albany Med Col, 83, Med Col Ohio, 90, Mt Sinai Sch Med, 91; DMSc, Brown Univ, 81; LHD, State Univ NY, 83, Temple Univ, 86. *Honors & Awards:* John Phillips Medal, Am Col Physicians, 85; William C Menninger Lectr, Am Psychiat Asn, 85; McGovern Award Lectr, Med Library Asn, 85; Charles V Chapin Orator, RI Med Soc, 85; Distinguished Serv Award, Am Col Cardiol, 87; John Peters Award, Am Soc Nephrol, 92; Kober Medal, Am Asn Physicians, 93. *Prof Exp:* From intern to assoc resident med, New Haven Hosp, 46-49; asst med, Boston Univ, 49-50, from asst prof to prof med, Sch Med, 51-67, Conrad Wesselhoeft prof med, 67-68; Frank Wister Thomas prof med & chmn dept, Sch Med, Univ Pa, 68-77. *Concurrent Pos:* Asst med, Sch Med, Yale Univ, 47-49; Nat Res Coun fel med sci, Evans Mem Dept Clin Res, Mass Mem Hosps, 49-50, head, Renal & Electrolyte Sect, 50-67; res career award, NIH, 61-67; ed, J Clin Invest, Am Soc Clin Invest, 62-67, New Eng J Med, 77-88, ed-in-chief, 88-91, emer ed-in-chief, 94-; res assoc biol chem, Harvard Med Sch, 65-66; dir, V & VI Med Serv, Boston City Hosp, 67-68; dir med serv, Hosp Univ Pa, 68-77; vis prof numerous Am & foreign univs, 70-85; mem, Adv Panel, Study Cost Educ Health Prof, Nat Acad Sci, 72-73, mem comt, Biomed Res Vet Admin, 74-75, chmn, Comt Study Health-Related Effects Cannabis & Derivatives, 80-82; consult, Coun Int Exchange Sch, Nat Acad Sci, 73-75, Food & Drug Admin Adv Rev Panel Over-the-Counter-Antacid Drugs, HEW, Pub Health Serv, 72-73, dir med, Bur Health Manpower, 76-77; vis mem, Merton Col, Univ Oxford, 75-76; attend physician, Brigham & Women's Hosp, Boston. *Mem:* Inst Med-Nat Acad Sci; fel Am Acad Arts & Sci; master Am Col Physicians; Am Fedn Clin Res (vpres, 59-60, pres, 60-61); Am Soc Clin Invest (pres, 68-69); fel AAAS; fel Royal Col Physicians; Am Soc Nephrol; Asn Am Physicians. *Res:* Kidney physiology and disease; acid-base and electrolyte physiology; internal medicine and medical education; author of numerous publications. *Mailing Add:* 181 Longwood Ave Boston MA 02115-5804. *Fax:* 617-525-2186

RELYEA, DOUGLAS IRVING, ORGANIC CHEMISTRY. *Current Pos:* res assoc corp res & develop, Oxford Mgt & Res Ctr, 72-80, RES ASSOC CORP PROTECTION CHEM RES, UNIROYAL CHEM, 80- *Personal Data:* b Rochester, NY, Sept 20, 30; m 57; c 4. *Educ:* Clarkson Tech, BS, 51; Cornell Univ, MS, 53; Univ SC, PhD(chem), 54. *Prof Exp:* Proj assoc org chem, Univ Wis, 54-56; res scientist, Gen Labs, US Rubber Co, 56-57 & Res Ctr, 57-64, sr res scientist, 64-70. *Mem:* Am Chem Soc; Royal Soc Chem. *Res:* Chemistry of sulfur compounds; chemistry of nitrogen compounds; biological activity of organic compounds; chemical structure retrieval; molecular geometry and computer graphics. *Mailing Add:* 25 Brookwood Rd Bethany CT 06524-3148

RELYEA, JOHN FRANKLIN, SOIL SCIENCE. *Current Pos:* RES SCIENTIST ENVIRON CHEM, WESTINGHOUSE, 83- *Personal Data:* b Stuttgart, Ark, Oct 25, 47; m 74; c 1. *Educ:* Univ Ark, BS, 69, MS, 72, PhD(agron), 78. *Prof Exp:* Res scientist environ chem, Battelle Pac Northwest Labs, 77-83. *Mem:* AAAS; Am Soc Agron. *Res:* Soil chemistry and soil physics; environmental chemistry; radionuclide chemistry in geologic media. *Mailing Add:* 7702 W 13th Ave Kennewick WA 99337

RELYEA, KENNETH GEORGE, ICHTHYOLOGY, ECOLOGY. *Current Pos:* MEM STAFF, DEPT BIOL, OHIO DOMINICAN COL. *Personal Data:* b New York, NY, Oct 24, 41; m 62; c 1. *Educ:* Fla State Univ, BA, 62, MS, 65; Tulane Univ, PhD(ichthyol), 67. *Prof Exp:* Asst prof biol, Jacksonville Univ, 67-72, assoc prof, 72- *Mem:* AAAS; Am Soc Ichthyol & Herpet; Ecol Soc Am. *Res:* Systematics, ecology and behavior of Ictalurid catfishes and killifishes. *Mailing Add:* Biol Dept Armstrong State Col Savannah GA 31419

REMAR, JOSEPH FRANCIS, ORGANIC CHEMISTRY. *Current Pos:* Sr res chemist, 66-90, PRIN SCIENTIST, ARMSTRONG CORK CO, 90- *Personal Data:* b Bridgeport, Pa, Oct 2, 38; m 67, Marcella Wernick; c Glenn & Craig. *Educ:* Villanova Univ, BS, 60; Pa State Univ, PhD(chem), 66. *Mem:* Am Chem Soc. *Res:* Urethane foams and coatings; ultraviolet curable systems; polymer synthesis; organic synthesis. *Mailing Add:* 801 Stonebridge Dr Lancaster PA 17601

REMBERT, DAVID HOPKINS, JR, PLANT PHYLOGENY. *Current Pos:* from asst prof to assoc prof, Univ SC, 67-81, asst dean, 72-76, actg dean, 75, assoc chmn biol, 87-93, PROF BIOL, UNIV SC, 81-, ASSOC DEAN, COL SCI & MATH, 93- *Personal Data:* b Columbia, SC, Jan 14, 37; m 60, Margaret Rainey; c Rainey, Augusta, Llewellyn & David III. *Educ:* Univ SC, BS, 59, MS, 64; Univ Ky, PhD(biol), 67. *Prof Exp:* Instr biol, Converse Col, 64-65; instr bot, Univ Ky, 67. *Mem:* Bot Soc Am; fel Linnean Soc London. *Res:* Embryology and phylogeny in legumes; floristics in the southeastern United States; botanical history and garden history; eighteenth century botanical history. *Mailing Add:* Dept Biol Univ SC Columbia SC 29208. *Fax:* 803-777-2451; *E-Mail:* rembert@cosm.psc.sc.edu

REMEDIOS, E(DWARD) C(HARLES), CHEMICAL ENGINEERING. *Current Pos:* PRIN, BLANCHET, HARAAL, REMEDIOS & ASSOC, 93- *Personal Data:* b Vengurla, India, Nov 17, 41; c 1. *Educ:* Univ Edinburgh, BSc, 65, PhD(chem eng), 69; Univ Calif, Berkeley, MBA, 79. *Prof Exp:* Res engr, Chevron Res Co, 69-73; sr resource engr, Pac Gas & Elec, 73-78, supv resource engr, 78-80, coordr, 80-86, mgr econ & forecasting, 87-93. *Mem:* Pac Coast Gas Asn; Pac Coast Elec Asn. *Res:* Technical and economic evaluations for the utility industries. *Mailing Add:* 33 Toledo Way San Francisco CA 94123. *Fax:* 920-474-7253

REMENYIK, CARL JOHN, FLUID MECHANICS. *Current Pos:* asst prof fluid mech, 64-66, assoc prof fluid mech, 66-80, PROF DEPT ENG SCI & MECH, UNIV TENN, KNOXVILLE, 80- *Personal Data:* b Budapest, Hungary, May 5, 27; US citizen; m 68; c 1. *Educ:* Swiss Fed Inst Technol, Dipl, 51; Johns Hopkins Univ, PhD(aeronaut), 62. *Prof Exp:* Asst fluid dynamics, Swiss Fed Inst Technol, 51-52, asst mach tools, 52-53; sr aeronaut engr, Convair Div, Gen Dynamics, Tex, 57; eng specialist, Martin-Marietta, Md, 61-64. *Concurrent Pos:* Consult, Reactor Div, Oak Ridge Nat Labs, 64- & molecular anat prog, 72- *Mem:* Am Phys Soc; Sigma Xi. *Res:* Aerodynamically generated sound in boundary layers; heat transfer in hypersonic boundary layers; mechanics of biological fluids; centrifugation; dynamics of oscillating liquids and bubbles; magnetohydrodynamic vortex flow. *Mailing Add:* 8240 Corteland Dr Knoxville TN 37909-2115

REMER, DONALD SHERWOOD, ENGINEERING ECONOMICS & MANAGEMENT, CHEMICAL & BIOCHEMICAL ENGINEERING. *Current Pos:* assoc prof, 75-80, dir energy inst, 81-83, PROF ENG, HARVEY MUDD COL ENG & SCI, CLAREMONT, 80-; COFOUNDER & PARTNER, CLAREMONT CONSULT GROUP, 79- *Personal Data:* b Detroit, Mich, Feb 16, 43; m 69, Louise; c Tanya, Candace & Miles. *Educ:* Univ Mich, Ann Arbor, BS, 65; Calif Inst Technol, MS, 66, PhD(chem eng, bus econ), 70. *Honors & Awards:* First Pl Nat Pub Rels Award, Am Inst Chem Engrs, 76; Outstanding Res Award, NASA, 83; Centennial Award, Am Soc Eng Educ, 93. *Prof Exp:* Tech contact engr, Exxon Chem Co, USA, 70-71, chem raw mat div coordr, 72, startup engr new ethylene unit, 72-73, sr proj engr, 72-73, econ & forecast coordr, 73-75, task force mgr, 74-75. *Concurrent Pos:* Sr eng consult, Caltech's Jet Propulsion Lab, 75-80, mem tech staff, 80-92 & 97-, mgr planning analysis, 92-98; Westinghouse Found grant eng econ & Shelby Cullum Found grant eng mgt, Harvey Mudd Col, 78-; case study ed, The Eng Economist 78-89; mem adv coun, Nat Energy Found, 81-86; dir, Eng Econ Div, Am Soc Eng Educ, 80-83, Am Soc Eng Mgt, 81-83; econ chairperson, Nat Tech Prog Comt, Fuels & Petrochemicals Div, Am Inst Chem Engrs. *Mem:* Am Inst Chem Engrs; Am Soc Eng Mgt; Am Soc Eng Educ; Am Asn Cost Engrs. *Res:* Industrial process and project cost estimation, venture, and risk analysis; engineering management and engineering economic analysis and optimization of capital projects, biotechnology, biochemical process economics; energy management and planning; air and water pollution abatement; solar energy and cogeneration; life cycle cost economic analysis. *Mailing Add:* Dept Eng Harvey Mudd Col Eng & Sci 301 E 12th St Claremont CA 91711-2834

REMERS, WILLIAM ALAN, ORGANIC CHEMISTRY, MEDICINAL CHEMISTRY. *Current Pos:* head dept, 80-85, PROF MED CHEM, COL PHARM, UNIV ARIZ, 76- *Personal Data:* b Cincinnati, Ohio, Oct 14, 32; m 61; c 2. *Educ:* Mass Inst Technol, BS, 54; Univ Ill, PhD, 58. *Prof Exp:* USPHS res fel org chem, Oxford Univ, 58-59; org chemist, Lederle Labs, Am Cyanamid Co, NY, 59-70; assoc prof, Sch Pharm & Pharmaceut Sci, Purdue Univ, 70-76, assoc head dept, 74-76. *Concurrent Pos:* Res grants, Nat Cancer Inst, 71-, Bristol Labs, 75-83 & AmpliMed Corp, 90- *Mem:* Acad Pharmaceut Sci; Am Chem Soc; Am Pharmaceut Asn; Am Asn Cancer Res. *Res:* Antibiotics; heterocycles; synthetic methods; cancer chemotherapeutic agents; molecular mechanics. *Mailing Add:* Col Pharm Univ Ariz Tucson AZ 85721-0001. *Fax:* 520-626-4063

REMICK, FORREST J(EROME), NUCLEAR ENGINEERING, MECHANICAL ENGINEERING. *Current Pos:* dir, Off Policy Eval, US Nuclear Regulatory Comn, 81-82, prof nuclear engr & assoc vpres res, 82-89, COMNR, US NUCLEAR REGULATORY COMN, 89- *Personal Data:* b Lock Haven, Pa, Mar 16, 31; m 53, Grace L Grove; c Beth A (Gillio) & Eric F. *Educ:* Pa State Univ, BS, 55, MS, 58, PhD, 63. *Prof Exp:* Design engr, Bell Tel Labs, Inc, 55; nuclear engr, Nuclear Reactor Facil, Pa State Univ, 56-59, dir, 59-65, assoc prof, 63-67, actg dir, Ctr Air Environ Studies, 76-78, dir, Inst Sci & Eng & asst to vpres res & grad studies, 67-79, prof nuclear eng, 67-81, asst vpres res & grad studies & dir inter-col res progs, 79-81. *Concurrent Pos:* Dir, Curtiss-Wright Nuclear Res Lab, 60-65; mem res reactor subcomt, Nat Acad Sci-Nat Res Coun, 63-65; mem, Atomic Safety & Licensing Bd Panel, 72-82; consult, US Nuclear Regulatory Comn, USAF, Dept Energy, Inst Nuclear Power Opers, Nat Nuclear Accrediting Bd, 82-88, Sci Adv Comt, Idaho Nat Eng Lab, 84-89 & Adv Comt Reator Safeguards, 82-89; chmn, Adv Comt Reactor Safeguards, 89 & Reactor Safety Adv Comt, Savannah River Site, 86-89. *Mem:* Fel Am Nuclear Soc; Am Soc Mech Engrs; Am Soc Eng Educ; Sigma Xi. *Res:* Reactor design and operation; heat transfer and fluid flow in reactor systems. *Mailing Add:* 305 E Hamiliton Ave State College PA 16801

REMILLARD, MARGUERITE MADDEN, REMOTE SENSING, GEOGRAPHIC INFORMATION SYSTEMS. *Current Pos:* res asst, Ctr Remote Sensing & Mapping Sci, Dept Geog, Univ Ga, 85-90, res assoc, 90-91, asst res scientist, 91-93, ASSOC RES SCIENTIST, CTR REMOTE SENSING & MAPPING SCI, DEPT GEOG, UNIV GA, 93- *Personal Data:* b Burlington, Vt, Apr 4, 56; m 80; c 2. *Educ:* State Univ NY, Plattsburg, BA, 79, MA, 84; Univ Ga, PhD(ecol), 90. *Prof Exp:* Nat Wetlands inventory analyst, Lab Remote Sensing, State Univ NY, 82, teaching asst, Dept Biol, 82-84, wetlands res analyst, 84-85. *Concurrent Pos:* Geog info systs specialist, R-Wel, Inc, 88-; co-prin investr, Nat Oceanic & Atmospheric Admin, 89-90, 90-91, & 93-94, NSF, 92-94, Nat Park Serv, 93- *Mem:* Am Soc Photogram & Remote Sensing; Int Asn Landscape Ecol; Sigma Xi; NAm Lake Mgt Soc. *Res:* Use of geographic information systems and remote sensing technologies for natural resource mapping and landscape ecology applications; aquatic vegetation mapping from aerial photographs and satellite image data; database development; spatial analysis with a geographic information system. *Mailing Add:* 1091 Skipstone Ct Watkinsville GA 30677

REMILLARD, STEPHEN PHILIP, CELL & MOLECULAR BIOLOGY. *Current Pos:* RES ASSOC, BRANDEIS UNIV, 81- *Educ:* Princeton Univ, PhD(biol), 81. *Mem:* Am Soc Cell Biol. *Mailing Add:* Dept Biol MS 008 Brandeis Univ 313 Kossow Waltham MA 02254

REMINE, WILLIAM HERVEY, SURGERY. *Current Pos:* RETIRED. *Personal Data:* b Richmond, Va, Oct 11, 18; m 43; c William H, Stephen G, Gary C & Walter J. *Educ:* Univ Richmond, BS, 40; Med Col Va, MD, 43; Univ Minn, MS, 52; Am Bd Surg, dipl. *Hon Degrees:* DSc, Univ Richmond, 65. *Prof Exp:* Surgeon, Mayo Found, 52-83, from asst prof to prof surg, Univ Minn, Mayo Grad Sch Med, 59-83. *Concurrent Pos:* Consult, Surgeon Gen, 53-83. *Mem:* Fel Am Col Surgeons; Am Pancreatic Asn; Soc Surg Alimentary Tract; hon fel Venezuelan Soc Surg; hon fel Colombian Soc Surg; Sigma Xi; Am Surg Asn. *Res:* Surgery of the gastrointestinal tract; head and neck surgery; endocrine surgery. *Mailing Add:* 8212 Seven Mile Dr Ponte Vedra Beach FL 32082

REMINGTON, BRUCE A, PLASMA PHYSICS, HYDRODYNAMICS. *Current Pos:* RES SCIENTIST & HYDRODYN GROUP LEADER, LAWRENCE LIVERMORE NAT LAB, 95- *Educ:* Mich State Univ, PhD(nuclear physics), 86. *Honors & Awards:* Excellence in Plasma Physics Award, Am Phys Soc, 95. *Mem:* fel Am Phys Soc. *Res:* Hydrodynamic instabilities and shock physics relevant to plasma physics, inertial confinement fusion, high energy-density physics, astrophysics and solid-state physics. *Mailing Add:* Lawrence Livermore Nat Lab MS L473 PO Box 808 Livermore CA 94550

REMINGTON, C(HARLES) R(OY), JR, MECHANICAL ENGINEERING. *Current Pos:* RETIRED. *Personal Data:* b Webster Groves, Mo, July 15, 24; m 46; c 2. *Educ:* Mo Sch Mines, BSME, 49, MSME, 50. *Prof Exp:* From instr to prof mech eng, Univ Mo, Rolla, 50-89. *Concurrent Pos:* Asst dir indust res ctr, Univ Mo, 65-66. *Mem:* Am Soc Eng Educ; Soc Automotive Engrs; Am Soc Mech Engrs; Nat Soc Prof Engrs; Sigma Xi. *Res:* Heat transfer by conduction in solids, liquids and gases; thermal contact resistance; automotive emission studies and control. *Mailing Add:* 649 Salem Ave Rolla MO 65401-3451

REMINGTON, CHARLES LEE, EVOLUTIONARY GENETICS, PALEOENTOMOLOGY. *Current Pos:* From instr to assoc prof zool, Yale Univ, 48-56, fel Pierson Col, 50-92, res assoc, Peabody Mus, 53-56, assoc cur entom, 56-74, assoc prof biol, 56-83, prof forest entom, 79-83, cur entom, Peabody Mus, 74-92, prof biol, entom environ studies & museology, 83-92, EMER PROF, YALE UNIV, 92-, EMER CUR, PEABODY MUS, 92- *Personal Data:* b Reedville, Va, Jan 19, 22; m 46, 88, Ellen Meneilly; c Eric, Janna & Sheldon T C. *Educ:* Principia Col, BS, 43; Harvard Univ, AM, 47, PhD(biol), 48. *Concurrent Pos:* Ed, J Lepidopterists Soc, 47-64; entom ed, Conn Geol & Natural Hist Surv, 51-76; secy, Rocky Mountain Biol Lab, 55-59, trustee, 62-63, Guggenheim fel, 58-59; dir, Zero Pop Growth, 68-71, vpres, 69-71; dir, Coun Pop & Environ, 69-76, prog chmn, First Nat Cong; dir, Equil Fund, 70-76, pres, 73-75; mem study panel, Food Producing Ecosyst Changed Climates, 75-76; res fel entom, CSIRO, Australia, 76; res fel zool, Campinas Univ, Brazil, 81; mem, Survival Serv Comn, Int Union Conserv Nature & Natural Resources, 79-; res assoc entom, Univ Calif, Berkeley, 81; dir, New Haven Ecol Proj, 94-, Philacicada Soc, 96- *Mem:* Soc Study Evolution; Am Soc Naturalists; Ecol Soc Am; Soc Syst Biol; Lepidopterists Soc (pres, 71); Entom Soc Am. *Res:* Animal interspecific hybridization; island biology; genetics and biology of mimicry; systematics and caryology of Lepidoptera, Thysanura and Entotrophi; museology; world population and environment; ecology periodical cicadas; cola-vision in butterflies. *Mailing Add:* 165 Prospect St 455 OML New Haven CT 06520-8104. *Fax:* 203-432-3854

REMINGTON, JACK SAMUEL, INTERNAL MEDICINE. *Current Pos:* from instr to assoc prof, 62-74, PROF MED, DIV INFECTIOUS DIS & GEOG MED, STANFORD UNIV, 74-; CHMN, DEPT IMMUNOL & INFECTIOUS DIS, RES INST & CHIEF CONSULT INFECTIOUS DIS, MED CLIN, PALO ALTO MED FOUND, 62- *Personal Data:* b Chicago, Ill, Jan 19, 31; div; c Lynne & David. *Educ:* Univ Ill, BS, 54, MD, 56; Am Bd Internal Med, dipl, 65. *Hon Degrees:* Dr, Univ Paul Sabatier, Toulouse, France, 92. *Honors & Awards:* Maxwell Finland Award, Infectious Dis Soc Am, 82; Marcus A Krupp Res Chair, Palo Alto Med Found, 86; Alexander Von Humboldt Sci Award, 88. *Prof Exp:* Intern, Univ Calif Serv, San Francisco County Hosp, 56; res assoc, Nat Inst Allergy & Infectious Dis, 57-59; asst resident med, Med Ctr, Univ Calif, San Francisco, 59-60; sr res fel, Nat Inst Allergy & Infectious Dis, Harvard Med Sch & Thorndike Mem Lav, 60-62. *Concurrent Pos:* Scientist under US-Soviet Health Exchange, 66, 69; consult, Vet Admin Hosp, Palo Alto, 62-; spec consult, Proctor Found, Med Ctr, Univ Calif, San Francisco, 66-; infectious dis consult, WHO, 67-, Pan-Am Health Orgn, 67- & Dept Army, Ft Ord, Calif, 71-; mem bd, Gorgas Mem Inst, 72-78. *Mem:* Am Asn Immunol; Am Soc Microbiol; Infectious Dis Soc Am (pres, 87-88); Immunocompromised Host Soc (pres, 88-89). *Res:* Congenital infection; acquired toxoplasmosis; compromised host and infection; immunoglobulins in body secretions; defense mechanisms of the host; role of cellular immunity in resistance to infections with intracellular organisms; tumor immunology. *Mailing Add:* Res Inst Palo Alto Med Found 860 Bryant St Palo Alto CA 94301-2799

REMINGTON, LLOYD DEAN, ANALYTICAL CHEMISTRY. *Current Pos:* from asst prof to prof, 65-86, EMER PROF CHEM, UNIV NC, ASHEVILLE, 86- *Personal Data:* b Jackson, Mich, Dec 29, 19; m 44, Violet Givoux; c Connie (Hamilton), Ronda (Camfield), Linda (Herrmann) & Kay (Brown). *Educ:* Univ Mich, BS, 42; Univ Fla, MEd, 54, PhD(anal chem), 66; Cornell Univ, MST, 62. *Honors & Awards:* Am Chem Soc Award, 61. *Prof Exp:* Chemist, Buick Motors Div, Gen Motors Corp, 42-45; teacher jr high schs & jr cols, Pinellas County, Fla, 46-66. *Concurrent Pos:* Sci adv, Ford Found Univ Chicago Proj, EPakistan Exten Ctr, 69-71. *Mem:* fel Am Inst Chemists. *Res:* Chemistry; comparison of British and North American practices in teaching science. *Mailing Add:* 46 Dortch Ave Asheville NC 28801

REMINGTON, PAUL JAMES, STRUCTURAL ACOUSTICS & VIBRATION, ACTIVE NOISE & VIBRATION CONTROL. *Current Pos:* Sr engr, Bolt Beranek & Newman Inc, 70-82, PRIN ENGR, BBN TECHNOLOGIES, 82- *Personal Data:* b Plainfield, NJ, Mar 19, 43; m 65, Lynne Harris; c Christopher & Alexander. *Educ:* Mass Inst Technol, BS, 66, MS, 66, PhD(mech eng), 70. *Honors & Awards:* Excellence in Presentation Award, Soc Automotive Engrs, 84. *Concurrent Pos:* Vis lectr, Tufts Univ, 79; assoc ed, J Acoust Soc Am, 82-; vis scientist, Tech Univ Berlin, 90; adj prof mech eng, Boston Univ, 95. *Mem:* Fel Acoust Soc Am; Am Soc Mech Engrs. *Res:* Transportation noise especially from rail vehicles; control of rolling noise, propulsion system noise, noise inside transit cars and noise from elevated structures; structural acoustics and vibration including both active and passive noise and vibration control. *Mailing Add:* BBN Technol 10 Moulton St Cambridge MA 02138. *Fax:* 617-873-2918; *E-Mail:* premington@bbn.com

REMINGTON, WILLIAM ROSCOE, organic chemistry; deceased, see previous edition for last biography

REMLER, EDWARD A, PHYSICS. *Current Pos:* from asst prof to assoc prof, 67-77, PROF PHYSICS, COL WILLIAM & MARY, 77- *Personal Data:* b Vienna, Austria, Dec 26, 34; US citizen; m 61; c 2. *Educ:* Mass Inst Technol, BS, 55; Columbia Univ, MS, 60; Univ NC, PhD(physics), 63. *Prof Exp:* Res assoc physics, Univ NC, 63-64; instr, Princeton Univ, 64-66; fel, Lawrence Livermore Lab, Univ Calif, 66-67. *Mem:* Am Phys Soc. *Res:* Quantum mechanics; particle physics. *Mailing Add:* Dept Physics Small Hall Rm 177 Col William & Mary Williamsburg VA 23187-8795

REMLEY, MARLIN EUGENE, PHYSICS. *Current Pos:* RETIRED. *Personal Data:* b Walcott, Ark, Apr 25, 21; m 43, Ruth Evens; c Carol (Bothwell), Nancy & Barbara (Taylor). *Educ:* Southeast Mo State Col, AB, 41; Univ Ill, MS, 48, PhD(physics), 52. *Prof Exp:* Instr physics & math, Southeast Mo State Col, 46-47; asst physics, Univ Ill, 47-52; res engr exp physics, NAm Aviation, Inc, 52-55, supvr exp physics, Atomics Int Div, 55-56, group leader reactor kinetics, 56-58, actg chief reactor develop, 58, dir spec projs, 59-60, reactor physics & instrumentation, 60-61, dir health safety & radiation serv, Energy Systs Group, 67-84, dir, Nuclear Safety & Licensing, 84-89, consult nuclear eng & safety, 89-92. *Mem:* Am Phys Soc; fel Am Nuclear Soc; Atomic Indust Forum; Sigma Xi. *Res:* Nuclear and reactor physics; nuclear scattering; scintillation counters; reactor design and development; reactor dynamics and safety; radiological safety; nuclear materials management and safeguards; author or coauthor of over 50 publications. *Mailing Add:* 19112 Halsted St Northridge CA 91324

REMMEL, RANDALL JAMES, MATERNAL & CHILD EPIDEMIOLOGY, INFORMATION SYSTEMS. *Current Pos:* lectr, 87-93, PROG DIR, UNIV SFLA, 93- *Personal Data:* b Peoria, Ill, Aug 23, 49; m 81, Toni A Mitchell; c Staci R. *Educ:* Ill State Univ, BS, 71; Ohio State Univ, PhD(inorg chem), 75; Univ SFla, MBA, 86. *Prof Exp:* Res assoc, Mat Lab, Polymer Br, USAF, 75-76; asst prof chem, Univ Ala, Birmingham, 76-82; dir, Gulf Stream Res Corp, 82-87. *Mem:* Am Chem Soc; Am Pub Health Asn; Decision Sci Inst. *Res:* Development of data systems for material and child health studies. *Mailing Add:* 818 Chipaway Dr Apollo Beach FL 33572. *E-Mail:* rremmel@frodo.coph.usf.edu

REMMEL, RONALD SYLVESTER, NEUROPHYSIOLOGY, NEUROANATOMY. *Current Pos:* OWNER, REMMEL LABS. *Personal Data:* b West Bend, Wis, July 18, 43; m 72; Effie L Lan; c Charlotte, Joseph & Ryan. *Educ:* Calif Inst Technol, BS, 65; Princeton Univ, PhD(physics), 71. *Prof Exp:* Res assoc physics, Princeton Univ, 71-72; fel physiol, Univ Calif, Berkeley, 72-74; fel ophthal, Med Sch, Johns Hopkins Univ, 74-75; from asst prof to assoc prof physiol, Univ Ark Med Sci, 75-83; assoc prof, Dept Biomed Eng, Boston Univ, 84-91. *Concurrent Pos:* NIH fel, 72-75; fel, Fight for Sight Inc, NY, 75; NIH gen res grant, Univ Ark Med Sci, 75-76; prin investr, Nat Eye Inst res grant, 76-79 & 85-89; grants, NIMH, 79-81 & NSF, 80- *Mem:* Asn Res Vision & Ophthal. *Res:* Eye movement monitors which measure where people or animals are looking to an accuracy of about 1 arc second movements. *Mailing Add:* Remmel Labs 26 Bay Colony Dr Ashland MA 01721-1840

REMMELE, RICHARD L, DIRECT DELIVERY & FORMULATION SPECTROSCOPY. *Current Pos:* STAFF SCIENTIST, IMMUNEX CORP, 93- *Personal Data:* b Pomona, Calif, Feb 26, 56. *Educ:* Oral Roberts Univ, BS, 78; Calif Polytech State Univ, MS, 83; Ariz State Univ, PhD(biophys chem), 88. *Prof Exp:* Fel, Biochem & Hort Dept, Colo State Univ, 88-93. *Mem:* Am Chem Soc; Am Inst Chemists. *Mailing Add:* 3120 153rd Pl SW Lynwood WA 98037-2428

REMMENGA, ELMER EDWIN, STATISTICS. *Current Pos:* from asst prof to assoc prof math, Colo State Univ, 55-62, sta statistician, 55-64, chief comput ctr, 57-62, PROF APPL STATIST, COLO STATE UNIV, 62- *Personal Data:* b Douglas, Nebr, Jan 9, 27; m 53; c 5. *Educ:* Univ Nebr, BS, 50; Purdue Univ, MS, 53, PhD, 55. *Prof Exp:* Asst statistician, Exp Sta, Purdue Univ, 50-55. *Concurrent Pos:* Math consult, Bur Mines Res Ctr, Colo, 58-; vis biometrician, Waite Agr Res Inst, Univ Adelaide, 61-62; vis prof, Univ Colo, 62-65; statist consult, Nat Water Qual Lab, Environ Protection Agency, Minn, 70-; vis prof, Swiss Fed Forestry Res Inst. *Mem:* Biomet Soc; Am Statist Asn; Inst Math Statist. *Res:* Application of statistical methods to biological sciences; design sampling; computing. *Mailing Add:* 42515 Weld Co Rd 15 Ft Collins CO 80524

REMO, JOHN LUCIEN, LASER RESONATOR OPTICS, ENERGY EXPERT SYSTEMS. *Current Pos:* CHIEF SCIENTIST QUANTAMETICS INC, OPTIC SYSTS, INC, 87- *Personal Data:* b Brooklyn, NY, Dec 13, 41; m 77, Claudia J Kyser; c John & Allison. *Educ:* Manhattan Col, BS, 63; State Univ NY, Stony Brook, MS, 71; Polytech Inst NY, MS, 73, PhD(physics), 79. *Honors & Awards:* Nininger Meteorite Award, 72-73; Cert Recognition, NASA, 96. *Prof Exp:* Res scientist astrophysics, Copenhagen Univ Observ, 69-70 & Bartol Res Found Franklin Inst, 70-71; prof energy, Ctr Energy Policy & Res, NY Inst Technol, 84-87, prof mech eng, Dept Eng, 85-87, prof physics, 86-88. *Concurrent Pos:* Pres & sr scientist, Quantametrics Inc. *Mem:* Am Phys Soc; Optical Soc Am; Meteoritical Soc; Am Geophys Union; Sigma Xi; Intrp Soc Optical Eng. *Res:* Development of integral operator methods to describe active laser resonator dynamics; utilization of solar energy for electricity generation and interior daylighting; development of expert system software for micro computers; near earth objects analysis of imaging characteristics for extreme ultraviolet laser systems; optical computing systems designs; developed energy conservation and alternate energy software; developed laser resonator design optics; developed sub aperture interferometry; numerous publications in optics, astrophysics, geophysics and energy systems & numerous patents in interferometry, quantum optics instrumentation, high powered laser design and materials synthesis. *Mailing Add:* Brackenwood Path Head of the Harbor St James NY 11780. *Fax:* 516-584-4213; *E-Mail:* jremo@aol.com

REMOLD, HEINZ G, IMMUNOLOGY. *Current Pos:* Assoc prof, 75-83, PROF MED, SCH MED, HARVARD UNIV, 83- *Personal Data:* b Bad Reichenhall, Germany, May 27, 37. *Educ:* Univ Munich, PhD(zool), 64. *Mem:* Am Asn Immunol; Am Fedn Clin Res; Am Asn Biol Chemists; Am Soc Pathologists. *Mailing Add:* Dept Rheumatologl/Immunol Harvard Med Sch LMRC Brigham & Women's Hosp 221 Longwood Ave Rm 513 Boston MA 02115-5817

REMOLE, ARNULF, PHYSIOLOGICAL OPTICS, OPTOMETRY. *Current Pos:* from asst prof to prof, 69-93, EMER PROF OPTOM, UNIV WATERLOO, 93- *Personal Data:* b Melhus, Norway, July 1, 28; Can citizen; m 65; c 1. *Educ:* Univ Man, BFA, 58; Ont Col Optom, OD, 62; Ind Univ, Bloomington, MS, 67, PhD(physiol optics), 69. *Prof Exp:* Instr optom, Sch Optom, Ont Col Optom, 62-66; teaching assoc physiol optics, Ind Univ, Bloomington, 68-69. *Mem:* Fel Am Acad Optom; Can Asn Optom; Optical Soc Am. *Res:* Psychophysics of vision; border effects; visual pattern responses arising from temporal modulations of the stimulus; binocular vision; visual performance evaluation; optics of the eye; optometrical instrumentation; aniseikonia. *Mailing Add:* Sch Optom Univ Waterloo Waterloo ON N2L 3G1 Can. *Fax:* 519-725-0784; *E-Mail:* aremole@sciborg

REMONDINI, DAVID JOSEPH, GENETICS, EVOLUTION. *Current Pos:* EXEC SECY GENETICS STUDY SECT, DIV RES GRANTS, NIH, DHHS, 77- *Personal Data:* b Deming, NMex, Dec 27, 31; m 52, Earnestine M Williamson; c Thomas D, Denise M (Gerhauser), Stephen J, Theresa A (Wickman), Suzanne E (Sasdelli) & John E. *Educ:* Univ Calif, Santa Barbara, BA, 55; Univ Utah, MS, 64; Utah State Univ, PhD(zool-genetics), 68. *Prof Exp:* Asst prof biol, Gonzaga Univ, 67-74; assoc prof biol sci, Mich Technol Univ, 74-77. *Concurrent Pos:* Jesuit Res Coun res grant, Gonzaga Univ, 67-71, dir summer sessions & spec progs, 71-73; consult genetics, Sacred Heart Med Ctr, Spokane, 73-74. *Mem:* AAAS; Genetics Soc Am; Am Soc Human Genetics; Genetics Soc Can. *Res:* Human cytogenetics; Drosophila genetics; temperature sensitivity; maternal effects. *Mailing Add:* 2101 Campfire Ct NIH Silver Spring MD 20906. *Fax:* 301-594-7059; *E-Mail:* drb@cu.nih.gov

REMPEL, ARTHUR GUSTAV, ZOOLOGY. *Current Pos:* from instr to prof, 38-75, cur, Mus Natural Hist, 38-46 & 53-71, EMER PROF BIOL, WHITMAN COL, 75- *Personal Data:* b Russia, Jan 5, 10; nat US; m 34, Lucile E Sommerfield; c Herbert F, Margaret L (Cook), Roland R, Robert A (deceased) & Paul L (deceased). *Educ:* Oberlin Col, AB, 34; Univ Calif, PhD(zool), 38. *Hon Degrees:* DSc, Whitman Col, 87. *Prof Exp:* Actg cur, Mus Zool & Anthrop, Oberlin Col, 31-34; custodian, Dept Zool, Univ Calif, 34-35, asst, 35-38. *Mem:* Fel AAAS; Sigma Xi. *Res:* Embryology. *Mailing Add:* 635 University St Walla Walla WA 99362

REMPEL, GARRY LLEWELLYN, CATALYSIS, POLYMER MODIFICATION & PROCESSING. *Current Pos:* asst prof, Univ Waterloo, 69-73, assoc prof, 73-80, chmn dept, 88-96, PROF CHEM ENG, UNIV WATERLOO, 80- *Personal Data:* b Regina, Sask, Aug 20, 44; m 75, Flora T Ng. *Educ:* Univ BC, BSc, 65, PhD(phys inorg chem), 68. *Honors & Awards:* Thomas W Eadie Medal, Royal Soc Can, 93; Indust Pract Award, Can Soc Chem Eng, 94. *Prof Exp:* Nat Res Coun Can fel, Imp Col, Univ London, 68-69. *Concurrent Pos:* Consult, Polysar Ltd, 81-95, Inst Polymer Res, Univ Waterloo, 84-, Ortho McNeil Inc, 92- & Bayer Inc, 95- *Mem:* Fel Royal Soc Can; fel Chem Inst Can; Am Chem Soc; Can Soc Chem Eng; Am Inst Chem Engrs; Soc Chem Indust. *Res:* Coordination chemistry and homogeneous catalysis; organometallic chemistry; physical chemistry of hydrometallurgical processes; polymer supported and entrapped metal catalysts; catalysts for waste water treatment; chemical modification of polymers; polymer processing; metallocene catalysts; catalytic distillation. *Mailing Add:* 532 Sandbrooke Ct Waterloo ON N2T 2H4 Can. *Fax:* 519-746-4979; *E-Mail:* grempel@cape.uwaterloo.ca

REMPEL, HERMAN G, chemistry; deceased, see previous edition for last biography

REMPEL, WILLIAM EWERT, ANIMAL BREEDING. *Current Pos:* asst, 48-49, from instr to assoc prof, 50-64, PROF ANIMAL HUSB, UNIV MINN, ST PAUL, 64- *Personal Data:* b Man, Can, July 6, 21; nat US; m 48; c 2. *Educ:* Univ Man, BSA, 44, MSc, 46; Univ Minn, PhD(animal breeding), 52. *Prof Exp:* Instr animal husb, Univ Man, 46-47; agr rep, Man Dept Agr, 47-48. *Concurrent Pos:* Dir genetics ctr, Univ Minn, 65-67. *Mem:* Fel AAAS; Am Soc Animal Sci; Genetics Soc Am; NY Acad Sci; Am Genetic Asn; Can Soc Animal Sci. *Res:* Genetics. *Mailing Add:* 1424 Belmont Lane W St Paul MN 55113

REMPFER, GERTRUDE FLEMING, PHYSICS. *Current Pos:* assoc prof, 59-68, prof, 68-77, EMER PROF PHYSICS, PORTLAND STATE UNIV, 77- *Personal Data:* b Seattle, Wash, Jan 30, 12; m 42; c 4. *Educ:* Univ Wash, BS, 34, PhD(physics), 39. *Prof Exp:* Instr physics, Mt Holyoke Col, 39-40 & Russell Sage Col, 40-42; physicist, Naval Res Lab, 42-43 & SAM Lab, Columbia Univ, 44; proj engr, Farrand Optical Co, 45-51; assoc prof eng, Antioch Col, 51-52; assoc prof physics, Fisk Univ, 53-57; assoc prof, Pac Univ, 57-59. *Concurrent Pos:* Consult, AMP, Inc, 51-57, Tektronix, 60-70 & Elektros, 70-75; NSF grant, 79-82; pres, E-scope, 75-. *Mem:* Am Phys Soc; Am Asn Physics Teachers; Electron Micros Soc Am; Sigma Xi. *Res:* Electron physics; electron and ion optics; electron microscopy. *Mailing Add:* Dept Physics Portland State Univ PO Box 751 Portland OR 97207

REMPFER, ROBERT WEIR, MATHEMATICS. *Current Pos:* assoc prof, 57-58, PROF MATH, 58-, EMER PROF MATH SCI, PORTLAND STATE UNIV. *Personal Data:* b Parkston, SDak, Apr 14, 14; m 42; c 4. *Educ:* Univ SDak, BA, 33; Northwestern Univ, MA, 34, PhD(math), 37. *Prof Exp:* Instr math, Rensselaer Polytech Inst, 37-44; physicist, SAM Labs, Columbia Univ, 44-45 & Farrand Optical Co, 45-50; prof math, Antioch Col, 50-53; assoc prof, Fisk Univ, 53-57. *Concurrent Pos:* Chmn dept math, Portland State Univ, 58-67. *Mem:* Am Math Soc; Sigma Xi. *Res:* Gaseous diffusion; electron optical design; interference optics; probability; information theory; geometry. *Mailing Add:* 45230 NW David Hill Rd Forest Grove OR 97116

REMPT, RAYMOND DOAK, FIBEROPTIC SENSORS, LOW RESISTANCE MEASUREMENTS. *Current Pos:* PRIN ENGR, BOEING DEFENSE & SPACE GROUP, 84- *Personal Data:* b Los Angeles, Calif, Mar 20, 43. *Educ:* Univ Calif, Los Angeles, BS, 64, MS, 66, PhD(physics), 69. *Prof Exp:* Chief scientist, Space Environ Test Labs, Martin Marietta, 80-84. *Mailing Add:* 16325 NE 203rd Pl Woodinville WA 98072. *Fax:* 253-773-3698; *E-Mail:* raymond.d.rempt@boeing.com

REMSBERG, ELLIS EDWARD, ATMOSPHERIC PHYSICS. *Current Pos:* aerospace technologist, 73-80, SR RES SCIENTIST, LANGLEY RES CTR, NASA, 80-; PROJ SCI, UARS HALOE EXP, 96- *Personal Data:* b Buckeystown, Md, Oct 24, 43; m 67, Judy Perdue; c Mark & Karen. *Educ:* Va Polytech Inst, BS, 66; Univ Wis-Madison, MS, 68, PhD(meteorol), 71. *Honors & Awards:* Floyd Thompson fel, NASA, 83-84. *Prof Exp:* Jr res asst, Nat Radio Astron Observ, 62-65; geophysicist, US Coast & Geod Surv, 66; res asst chem, Univ Minn, 69-70; lectr meteorol, Univ Wis-Madison, 71; res asst prof chem, Col William & Mary, 71-72; res asst prof & NASA res grant geophys, Old Dom Univ, 72-73. *Concurrent Pos:* Fel, Univ Wash, Seattle, 83-84; prin investr, NASA, 85- *Mem:* Am Geophys Union; Am Meteorol Soc. *Res:* Air chemistry; remote sensing; satellite meteorology; processes in the stratosphere. *Mailing Add:* Langley Res Ctr NASA M/S 401B Hampton VA 23681-0001

REMSBERG, LOUIS PHILIP, JR, NUCLEAR CHEMISTRY. *Current Pos:* CHEMIST, BROOKHAVEN NAT LAB, 61- *Personal Data:* b Rupert, Idaho, Sept 14, 33; m 57; c 3. *Educ:* Univ Idaho, BS, 55, MS, 56; Columbia Univ, PhD(phys chem), 61. *Prof Exp:* Actg instr chem, Univ Idaho, 55-56. *Mem:* Am Chem Soc. *Res:* Nuclear reactions and properties. *Mailing Add:* Brookhaven Nat Lab Upton NY 11973

REMSEN, CHARLES C, III, MICROBIOLOGY, LIMNOLOGY. *Current Pos:* assoc prof zool & assoc scientist, Ctr Great Lake Studies, Univ Wis, Milwaukee, 75-83, coordr zool & microbiol, 76-84, actg dir, 87-89, PROF & SR SCIENTIST, UNIV WIS-MILWAUKEE, 83-, DIR, CTR GREAT LAKE STUDIES, 89-, DIR, GREAT LAKES RES FACIL, UNIV WIS SYST, 89- *Personal Data:* b Newark, NJ, May 16, 37; m 60, 76, Margaret Fairchild; c David P, Linda R (Brandenberg), Stephen D, Andrew W, Elizabeth H (Herzog) & Jennifer H (Jonas). *Educ:* Nat Agr Col, BS, 60; Syracuse Univ, MS, 63, PhD(microbiol), 65. *Prof Exp:* NIH fel, 65-67; asst scientist biol, Woods Hole Oceanog Inst, 67-71, assoc scientist, 71-75. *Concurrent Pos:* Spec serv appointment, Grad Sch, Boston Univ; NSF rep, 2nd US-Japan Conf Microbiol; chmn, joint comt biol oceanog, Mass Inst Technol, WHOI PhD Prog, 71-74; deleg, Coun Ocean Affairs, 90-; bd trustees, Wis Chap, Nature Conserv. *Mem:* Int Asn Great Lakes Res; Am Soc Limnol Oceanog; Electron Micros Soc Am; Am Geophys Union; Am Soc Microbiol. *Res:* Aquatic microbiology, microbial ecology, ultrastructure of autotrophic procaryotes, methane oxidations, biogeochemistry, freshwater hydrothermal vent communities. *Mailing Add:* Biol Sci Univ Wis Milwaukee WI 53201. *Fax:* 414-382-1705; *E-Mail:* ccremsen@csd4.csd.uwm.edu

REMSEN, JAMES VANDERBEEK, JR, NEOTROPICAL BIRD BIOLOGY. *Current Pos:* Asst prof, 78-83, assoc prof, 83-89, PROF DEPT ZOOL & PHYSIOL, LA STATE UNIV, 89-, CUR BIRDS, MUS ZOOL, 78- *Personal Data:* b Newark, NJ, Sept 21, 49; m 88, Catherine Cummins; c Kenneth William. *Educ:* Stanford Univ, BA & MA, 71; Univ Calif, Berkeley, PhD(zool), 78. *Mem:* AAAS; Am Ornithologists Union; Ecol Soc Am; Am Soc Naturalists; Cooper Ornith Soc; Wilson Ornith Soc; Asn Field Ornithologists. *Res:* Ecology and evolution of neotropical birds; aspects in which they differ from birds of the temperate zone; birds of the Andes and western Amazonia. *Mailing Add:* Mus Nat Sci La State Univ Baton Rouge LA 70803. *Fax:* 504-388-3075; *E-Mail:* najames@lsuvm.sncc.lsu.edu

REMSON, IRWIN, HYDROLOGY, ENVIRONMENTAL GEOLOGY. *Current Pos:* chmn dept appl earth sci, 75-82, Barney & Estell Morris prof earth sci, 81, PROF GEOL, STANFORD UNIV, 68- *Personal Data:* b New York, NY, Jan 23, 23; m 48; c 2. *Educ:* Columbia Univ, AB, 46, AM, 49, PhD, 54. *Honors & Awards:* Birdsall lectr geol, Geol Soc Am. *Prof Exp:* Asst geol, Columbia Univ, 47-49; geologist, US Geol Surv, 49-60; assoc prof civil eng, Drexel Inst, 60-65, prof & chief marshal fac, 65-68. *Concurrent Pos:* Lectr, Drexel Inst, 54-60; Lindback Found Award, 66. *Mem:* Geol Soc Am; Am Geophys Union; Soil Sci Soc Am; Sigma Xi. *Res:* Ground water geology; soil moisture movement; ground water recharge. *Mailing Add:* 1016 Cathcart Way Palo Alto CA 94305-2210

REMY, CHARLES NICHOLAS, BIOCHEMISTRY. *Current Pos:* assoc prof, 62-68, PROF BIOCHEM, BOWMAN GRAY SCH MED, 68- *Personal Data:* b Hudson, NY, May 31, 24; m 52; c 4. *Educ:* Syracuse Univ, PhD(biochem), 52. *Prof Exp:* Am Cancer Soc fel, Sch Med, Univ Pa, 52-53 & Div Biochem, Mass Inst Technol, 53-54; instr biochem, State Univ NY Upstate Med Ctr, 54-60, asst prof biochem, 60-62. *Concurrent Pos:* Biochemist, Res Div, Vet Admin Hosp, Syracuse, NY, 54-56; prin scientist, 56-62. *Mem:* AAAS; Am Soc Biol Chemists; Am Chem Soc; Soc Exp Biol & Med; Am Soc Microbiol; Sigma Xi. *Res:* Biomethylation of nucleic acids; biosynthesis of ribosomes; biological regulation of nucleic acids and protein synthesis; taurine biosynthesis and transport. *Mailing Add:* Dept Biochem Bowman Gray Sch Med Ctr Med Ctr Blvd Winston-Salem NC 27157-1016

REMY, DAVID CARROLL, MEDICINAL CHEMISTRY. *Current Pos:* RETIRED. *Personal Data:* b Waco, Tex, July 17, 29; m 63, Nancy Wagner; c Eric & Cynthia. *Educ:* Univ Calif, Los Angeles, BS, 51, MS, 52; Univ Wis, PhD, 58. *Prof Exp:* Res chemist, Elastomer Chem Dept, E I du Pont de Nemours & Co, 58-60; fel oncol, McArdle Mem Lab, Med Sch, Univ Wis, 60-62; sr res fel, Merck, Sharp & Dohme Res Labs, 62-80, sr invest, 80-93. *Mem:* Am Chem Soc; AAAS. *Res:* Medicinal chemistry; CNS drugs; blood coagulation. *Mailing Add:* 607 Jenkins Lane MR 1 North Wales PA 19454

REN, PETER, TECHNICAL MANAGEMENT. *Current Pos:* SECT HEAD, COLGATE PALMOLIVE, 89- *Personal Data:* b Macau, Mar 12, 48; US citizen; m 78; c 2. *Educ:* Adelphia Univ, BA, 71; Univ RI, PhD(biochem), 76, Rutgers Univ, MBA, 85. *Prof Exp:* Res asst, Univ RI, 71-76; res assoc biochem, Sch Med, Univ Md, 76-78; res biochem, Beecham Prod, 78-82, group leader, 82-85; mgr, Oral B Labs, 85-87, dir mfg, 87-89. *Concurrent Pos:* Assoc, over the counter prod develop, Food & Drug Admin, Prod Scheduling, Clin Testing. *Mem:* AAAS; Am Asn Dental Res. *Res:* Mechanism of action of vitamin K; anticoagulant drugs; clotting proteins synthesis; basement membrane metabolism; collagen metabolism; oral hygiene; bacterial adhesion; caries formation; inflammations; chemotaxis. *Mailing Add:* 19 Davis Ct Martinsville NJ 08836

REN, SHANG YUAN, SEMICONDUCTOR PHYSICS, SEMICONDUCTOR DEVICE PHYSICS. *Current Pos:* PROF PHYSICS, UNIV SCI & TECH, CHINA, 85-; RES PROF, ARIZ STATE UNIV, 91-; PROF PHYSICS, PEKING UNIV, 94- *Personal Data:* b Chongqin, Sichuan, China, Jan 10, 40; m 68, Weimin Hu; c Yujian & Yuhui. *Educ:* Peking Univ, BS, 63, PhD(physics), 66. *Prof Exp:* Engr, Beijing Second Semiconductor Factory, 68-73; teacher, Univ Sci & Tech, China, 73-78; vis scholar appl physics, Stanford Univ, 78-80; res assoc solid state physics, Univ Ill, 80-81; lectr physics, Univ Sci & Tech, China, 78-83, assoc prof, 83-85. *Concurrent Pos:* Mem, All China Acad Comt, Condensed Matter Theory & Statist Physics, 82-86; prin investr, Chinese Acad Sci, 83-85, Chinese Nat Educ Comt, 86-88, Chinese NSF, 86-88; vis prof, Univ Notre Dame, 86-90; res prof, Ariz State Univ, 91-94. *Mem:* Chinese Phys Soc; Am Phys Soc. *Res:* Theory condensed matter; electronic structure, optical, transport, vibrational and mechanical properties of semiconductors, semiconductor superlattices, semiconductor quantum dots and possible device applications. *Mailing Add:* Dept Physics Peking Univ Beijing 100871 China. *Fax:* 86-10-6275-1615; *E-Mail:* syren@bimp.pku.edu.cn

REN, SHANG-FEN, SEMICONDUCTORS, ELECTRONIC STATES. *Current Pos:* ASST PROF PHYSICS, ILL STATE UNIV, 94- *Personal Data:* b Hunan, China. *Educ:* Beijing Univ, China, BS, 70; Tex A&M Univ, PhD(physics), 86. *Prof Exp:* Ed, Inst Sci & Technol Changsha, Hunan, China, 72-77; teaching & res asst physics, Univ Sci & Technol China, 77-81 & Tex A&M Univ, 83-86; res assoc, 81-83, res physicist, 86-94. *Concurrent Pos:* Vpres, Women Acad Prof Group, Univ Ill, Urbana-Champaign, 88-90; founder & co-pres Asn Women Sci, Heart Ill Chapt 94-97, mem Int Relations Comt. *Mem:* Am Phys Soc; Am Asn Women Sci. *Res:* Theoretical studies on electrons and phonons in semiconductors and their alloys, at semiconductor surfaces, in superlattices and other heterostructures; vibrational properties. *Mailing Add:* Ill State Univ Campus Box 4560 Normal IL 61790-4560. *Fax:* 309-438-5413; *E-Mail:* ren@phyilstu.edu

RENARD, JEAN JOSEPH, management of research & development projects in wood chemistry & pulping & bleaching technology, management of research & development projects in environmental sciences & technology, for more information see previous edition

RENARD, KENNETH G, CIVIL ENGINEERING, HYDROLOGY & WATER RESOURCES. *Current Pos:* Hydraul engr, Agr Res Serv, USDA, Wis, 57-59, res hydraul engr, Ariz, 59-64, res hydraul engr, Southwest Watershed Res Ctr, 64-68, dir, 68-88, DIR, ARIDLAND WATERSHED MGT RES CTR, AGR RES SERV, USDA, 88-, HYDRAUL ENGR, 88- *Personal Data:* b Sturgeon Bay, Wis, May 5, 34; m 56; c 3. *Educ:* Univ Wis, BS, 57, MS, 59; Univ Ariz, PhD(civil eng), 72. *Honors & Awards:* Arid Lands Hydraulic Eng Award, Am Soc Civil Engrs, 92. *Concurrent Pos:* Adj prof, Univ Ariz; ed, J Irrig & Drainage Eng, 83-85; mem exec comt, Irrig & Drainage Div, Am Soc Civil Engrs. *Mem:* Soil Conserv Soc Am (pres, 79); fel Am Soc Civil Engrs; AAAS; Am Soc Agr Engrs; Am Geophys Union; fel

Soil & Water Conserv Soc. *Res:* Watershed hydrology relating land practices to water yields and peak rates of discharge; sediment transport phenomenon in ephemeral stream beds; erosion prediction from varying land use. *Mailing Add:* Arid Land Watershed Mgt Res Unit 2000 E Allen Rd Tucson AZ 85719. *Fax:* 520-670-5550; *E-Mail:* renard@tucson.ars.ag.gov

RENARD, ROBERT JOSEPH, METEOROLOGY. *Current Pos:* from asst prof to prof meteorol, 52-90, chmn dept, 80-90, EMER PROF, US NAVAL POSTGRAD SCH, 90- *Personal Data:* b Green Bay, Wis, Dec 22, 23; m 47, Dorothy; c 4. *Educ:* Univ Chicago, MS, 52; Fla State Univ, PhD(meteorol), 70. *Honors & Awards:* John Campanills Holm Award, Dept Com, Nat Oceanic & Atmospheric Admin, Thomas Jefferson Award. *Prof Exp:* Asst meteorol, Univ Chicago, 51-52. *Mem:* Fel Am Meteorol Soc; Int Weather Watchers. *Res:* Synoptic, polar and satellite meteorology; emphasis on observations, marine fog, visibility, Antarctic and model output statistics. *Mailing Add:* Dept Meteorol Naval Postgrad Sch 589 Dyer Rd Monterey CA 93943-5114. *Fax:* 408-656-3061; *E-Mail:* jonespa@met.nps.navy.mil

RENARDY, MICHAEL, VISCOELASTIC FLUIDS. *Current Pos:* assoc prof, 86-89, PROF MATH, VA POLYTECH INST & STATE UNIV, 89- *Personal Data:* b Stuttgart, Ger, Apr 9, 55; m 81, Yuriko Yamamuro; c Sylvia, David & Marissa. *Educ:* Univ Stuttgart, dipl, 77 & 78 & PhD(math), 80. *Honors & Awards:* Fed Victor, Fed Competition, Found Ger Sci, 73. *Prof Exp:* Res assoc, Univ Stuttgart, 78-80; post doc fel, Univ Wis, 80-81 & Univ Minn, 81-82; from asst prof to assoc prof math, Univ Wis, 82-86. *Concurrent Pos:* Pres Young Investr Award, 85. *Mem:* Am Math Soc; Soc Indust & Appl Math; Int Soc Interaction Mech & Math; Soc Natural Philos; Soc Rheology. *Res:* Problems in nonlinear partial different equations, in particular, equations modelling viscoelastic fluids. *Mailing Add:* Dept Math Va Polytech Inst & State Univ Blacksburg VA 24061-0123. *Fax:* 540-231-5960; *E-Mail:* renardym@math.vt.edu

RENARDY, YURIKO, FLUID DYNAMICS, COMPUTATIONAL FLUID DYNAMICS. *Current Pos:* from asst prof to assoc prof, 86-92, PROF MATH, VA POLYTECH INST & STATE UNIV, 93- *Personal Data:* b Sapporo, Japan, Jan 15, 55; m 81; c 3. *Educ:* Australian Nat Univ, BSc, 77; Univ Western Australia, PhD(math), 81. *Honors & Awards:* Career Advan Award, NSF, 88. *Prof Exp:* Res assoc, Math Res Ctr, Univ Wis-Madison, 80-83, lectr, 82-83, prog coordr, 83-86. *Concurrent Pos:* Lectr math, Univ Minn, 81-82; vis fel, Australian Nat Univ, 84, 88. *Mem:* Soc Indust & Appl Math; Am Phys Soc. *Res:* Fluid dynamics, with emphasis on stability and numerical methods. *Mailing Add:* Dept Math Va Polytech Inst & State Univ 460 McBride Hall Blacksburg VA 24061-0123

RENAUD, LEO P, NEUROSCIENCE, NEUROENDOCRINOLOGY. *Current Pos:* PROF MED, UNIV OTTAWA, 90-; CHIEF, DIV NEUROL, OTTAWA CIVIC HOSP, 90-; ASSOC DIR, LOEB RES INST, 90- *Personal Data:* Can citizen. *Educ:* Univ Ottawa, BA, 61, MD, 65; McGill Univ, PhD(physiol), 72. *Honors & Awards:* Gold Medal, Royal Col Physicians & Surgeons, Can, 85. *Prof Exp:* From asst prof to assoc prof neurol, McGill Univ, 73-81; asst physician, Montreal Univ Hosp, 73-78, assoc physician med, 78-90; prof neurol, McGill Univ, 81-90. *Concurrent Pos:* Scholar, Med Res Coun, Can, 73-78 & Found Health Res Que, 78-85. *Mem:* Am Physiol Soc; Can Physiol Soc; Endocrine Soc; Soc Neurosci. *Res:* Electrophysiology of mammalian neurosecretory neurons; neurotransmitter regulation of their excitability and hormone (vasopressin and oxytocin) release using in-vivo and in-vitro approaches; central neural processing of cardiovascular inputs to the brain. *Mailing Add:* Div Neurol Ottawa Civic Hosp 1053 Carling Ave D712 Ottawa ON K1Y 4E9 Can

RENAUD, SERGE, EXPERIMENTAL PATHOLOGY. *Current Pos:* RES DIR, UNIV 330, NIH, BORDEAUX. *Personal Data:* b Cartelegue, France, Nov 21, 27; Can citizen; m 84, Helen Kogut; c Louise. *Educ:* Univ Bordeaux, BA, 47; Univ Montreal, VMD, 57, PhD(exp med), 60, PhD(hematol) 78. *Honors & Awards:* Borden Award for Nutrit, 67; Award of the Found Francaise de Nutrit, 83; Nestle Award Nutrit, 97. *Prof Exp:* Res assoc, Montreal Heart Inst, 60-63, chief lab exp path, 63-73; dir, Unit 63, NIH & Med Res, France, 73-94; prof nutrit, Univ Montreal, 75-81. *Concurrent Pos:* Med Res Coun Can & Que Heart Found grants, 61-; vis prof, Boston Univ, 71-72; prof path, Univ Montreal, 72-73, dir, Dept Nutrit, 75-80. *Mem:* Soc Exp Biol & Med; Am Heart Asn; Nutrit Soc Can; Am Soc Exp Path; Int Acad Path; Europ Soc Cardiol. *Res:* Influence of nutrition, stress, hormones on the pathogenesis of thrombosis, atherosclerosis and coronary heart disease. *Mailing Add:* Res Unit 330 NIH & Med Res Bordeax II University 146-Rve Leo-Saignat 33076 Bordeaux Cedex France. *Fax:* 33-05-56-99-13-60

RENAULT, JACQUES ROLAND, GEOCHEMISTRY, PETROLOGY. *Current Pos:* geologist, 64-80, sr geologist, 80-95, EMER SR GEOLOGIST, STATE BUR MINES & MINERAL RESOURCES, NMEX INST MINING & TECHNOL, 95- *Personal Data:* b Alameda, Calif, July 26, 33; m 56, Magali Larose; c 2. *Educ:* Stanford Univ, BS, 57; NMex Inst Mining & Technol, MS, 59; Univ Toronto, PhD(geol), 64. *Prof Exp:* Explor geologist, Bear Creek Mining Co, 59-60, Southwest Potash Corp, 61, F R Joubin & Assoc, 62-63. *Concurrent Pos:* Grant, Geol Surv Can, 62-63, NMex Energy Inst, 76, 78; exec bd, NMex Energy Inst, NMex State Univ, 78-80; adj prof, geosci dept, NMex Tech. *Mem:* AAAS; fel Geol Soc Am; fel Mineral Soc Am; Am Geophys Union; Sigma Xi. *Res:* Statigraphic geochemistry; mineral physics, especially x-ray diffraction and thermoluminescence; ingeous petrology; x-ray flourescence spectroscopy. *Mailing Add:* 1210 South Dr Socorro NM 87801. *E-Mail:* jacquesr@nmt.edu

RENCHER, ALVIN C, LINEAR MODELS, MULTIVARIATE ANALYSIS. *Current Pos:* chmn dept, 80-85, assoc dean, 85-92, PROF STATIST, BRIGHAM YOUNG UNIV, 63- *Personal Data:* b St Johns, Ariz, Dec 21, 34; m 62, LaRue Drechsel; c David A, Michael A & Ashley A. *Educ:* Brigham Young Univ, BS, 59, MA, 62; Va Polytech Inst, PhD(statist), 68. *Prof Exp:* Statistician, Hercules Inc, 62-63. *Concurrent Pos:* NSF fac fel, 67-68; epidemiol consult, Kennecott Copper Corp, 70-71. *Mem:* Am Statist Asn. *Res:* Best subset regression; discriminant analysis; effect of individual variables in multivariate analysis. *Mailing Add:* 206 TMCB Brigham Young Univ Provo UT 84602

RENCRICCA, NICHOLAS JOHN, HEMATOLOGY, MALARIOLOGY & INTERNAL MEDICINE. *Current Pos:* from assoc prof to prof biol sci, Univ Lowell, 70-84, actg dean, Col Pure & Appl Sci, 84-86, EMER PROF, UNIV MASS-LOWELL, 94-; MED DIR, PALM BEACH CO DETENTION CTR, 96- *Personal Data:* b New York, NY, Mar 22, 41; m; c Daniel, Nicholas, Karen, Matthew, Nicole & Gina. *Educ:* St Francis Col, NY, BS, 62; St John's Univ, NY, MS, 64; Boston Col, PhD(physiol), 67; Univ Mass Med Sch, MD, 91. *Prof Exp:* Teaching asst physiol, anat & zool, St John's Univ, NY, 62-64; NIH-Nat Heart Inst res fel hematol, Sch Med, Tufts Univ, 67-70. *Concurrent Pos:* Res assoc, Dept Army & Univ Lowell, 73-75; ref ed, J Hematol, 75; NSF fel, Boston Univ, 78-80. *Mem:* AMA. *Res:* Control of hematopoiesis; stem cell proliferation and differentiation; erythropoiesis in rodent malaria; hyperbaric oxygen-induced toxicity; effects on stress of erythropoiesis. *Mailing Add:* 720 Sanctuary Cove Dr North Palm Beach FL 33410. *Fax:* 561-688-4671

RENDA, FRANCIS JOSEPH, SOLID STATE PHYSICS. *Current Pos:* RETIRED. *Personal Data:* b Brooklyn, NY, June 16, 39; m 63; c 2. *Educ:* Brooklyn Col, BS, 62; Syracuse Univ, MS, 65, PhD(physics), 69. *Prof Exp:* Mem tech staff physics, Santa Barbara Res Ctr, Hughes Aircraft Co, 69-96. *Mem:* Am Inst Physics. *Res:* Photoconductivity. *Mailing Add:* 270 Savona Ave Goleta CA 93117

RENDELL, DAVID H, THEORETICAL PHYSICS. *Current Pos:* RETIRED. *Personal Data:* b St John's, Nfld, July 28, 35; m 61; c 3. *Educ:* Dalhousie Univ, BSc, 56, MSc, 57; Univ BC, PhD(physics), 62. *Prof Exp:* From asst prof to prof physics, Mem Univ Nfld, 59-95, asst dean sci, 71-74, assoc dean sci, 74-83, head dept, 82-90. *Mem:* Am Asn Physics Teachers; Can Asn Physicists; Sigma Xi. *Res:* Atomic and molecular physics; quantum mechanics. *Mailing Add:* Dept Physics Mem Univ Nfld St John's NF A1B 3X7 Can. *E-Mail:* drendell@morgan.ucs.mun.ca

RENDIG, VICTOR VERNON, SOIL FERTILITY, CROP QUALITY. *Current Pos:* From jr soil chemist to assoc prof, 49-63, prof, 63-88, PROF EMER SOILS & PLANT NUTRIT, UNIV CALIF, DAVIS, 88- *Personal Data:* b Wis, July 4, 19; m 44; c 2. *Educ:* Univ Wis, BS, 42, PhD(soil sci, biochem), 49. *Mem:* Soil Sci Soc Am; Am Soc Agron; Am Soc Plant Physiologists; Am Chem Soc. *Res:* Effects of soil fertility and plant nutrition on plant composition and metabolism: nitrogen in cereal grain crops; sulfur(s) and S/Seienium in forages. *Mailing Add:* 601 Oeste Dr Davis CA 95616

RENDINA, GEORGE, BIOCHEMISTRY. *Current Pos:* from assoc prof to prof, 67-84, EMER PROF CHEM, BOWLING GREEN STATE UNIV, 84- *Personal Data:* b New York, NY, July 1, 23; m 48, Irma C Esner; c Alan Ralph, Steven Jeremy, David Nathan & Frederic Thomas. *Educ:* NY Univ, AB, 49; Univ Kans, MA, 53, PhD, 55. *Prof Exp:* Instr biochem, Univ Kans, 54-55; Nat Found Infantile Paralysis fel, Univ Mich, 55-56, sr biochemist, 57; sr fel, E B Ford Inst Med Res, 57-58; instr physiol chem, Sch Med, Johns Hopkins Univ, 58-61; res biochemist, Training Sch, 62-63, chief biochemist, 64-66, dir, Isotope Lab, Cent Wis Colony, 66-67. *Concurrent Pos:* Adj assoc prof, Med Col Ohio, 70-77; grants, NSF & NIH. *Mem:* AAAS; Am Chem Soc; Sigma Xi. *Res:* Neurochemistry; protein synthesis; kinetics; enzymology. *Mailing Add:* 30 Brier Lane Brewster MA 02631

RENDINA, RODNEY A, SOLID STATE PHYSICS. *Current Pos:* RES SCIENTIST, PHILIPS LAB, 94- *Personal Data:* b Union Town, Pa, Sept 6, 47. *Educ:* WVa Univ, BS, 70, MS, 72. *Prof Exp:* USAF, 72-93. *Mem:* Am Phys Soc. *Mailing Add:* 15 Barisano Way Nashua NH 03063

RENDTORFF, ROBERT CARLISLE, TROPICAL MEDICINE. *Current Pos:* from asst prof to assoc prof, Col Med, 55-66, prof community med, 66-79, EMER PROF, UNIV TENN, MEMPHIS, 79- *Personal Data:* b Carlisle, Pa, Mar 22, 15; m 37; c 1. *Educ:* Univ Ill, AB, 37, MS, 39; Johns Hopkins Univ, ScD(protozool), 44, MD, 49. *Prof Exp:* Instr epidemiol, Virol Lab, Mich, 42-44; med entomologist, Ministry Sanit & Social Assistance, Venezuela, 46; sr asst scientist, USPHS, 48, from asst surgeon to surgeon, 49-55. *Concurrent Pos:* Ed, Tenn Med Alumnus; consult epidemiologist infection control, 79-88. *Res:* Medical parasitology; epidemiology of human protozoan diseases, venereal diseases and respiratory viruses. *Mailing Add:* Four N Ashlawn Memphis TN 38112-4308

RENDU, JEAN-MICHEL MARIE, ORE RESERVES, GEOSTATISTICS. *Current Pos:* VPRES, NEWMONT GOLD CO, COLO, 88- *Personal Data:* b Tunis, Tunisia, Feb 25, 44; m 73, Karla M Meyer; c Yannick P & Mikael P. *Educ:* Sch Mines St Etienne, Ingenieur des Mines, 66; Columbia Univ, MS, 68, D(eng sci), 71. *Honors & Awards:* Henry Krumb Lectr, Soc Mining Metall & Explor, 92, Jackling Award Medal, 94. *Prof Exp:* Mgr opers res, Anglovaal, Johannesburg, 72-76; assoc prof, Univ Wis-Madison, 76-79; assoc, Golder Assocs, Denver, 79-84; dir technol & sci systs, Newmont Mining Corp, Conn, 84-88. *Mem:* Nat Acad Eng; NY Acad Sci; Int Asn Math Geol; Soc Mining

Engrs; Sigma Xi; fel SAfrican Inst Mining & Metall. *Res:* Geostatistical methods of mineral evaluation; contributed technical papers to professional journals. *Mailing Add:* Newmont Gold Co 1700 Lincoln St Denver CO 80203-4501. *Fax:* 303-837-5922

RENEAU, DANIEL DUGAN, JR, CHEMICAL ENGINEERING. *Current Pos:* from asst prof to assoc prof chem eng, La Tech Univ, 67-77, prof biomed eng & head dept, 77-80, vpres acad affairs, 80-87, PRES, LA TECH UNIV, 87- *Personal Data:* b Woodville, Miss, June 11, 40; m 61; c 2. *Educ:* La Polytech Inst, BS, 63, MS, 64; Clemson Univ, PhD(chem eng), 66. *Prof Exp:* Res engr, Com Solvents Corp, 62-63; actg instr chem eng, La Polytech Inst, 63-64; res engr, Esso Res & Eng Co, 66-67. *Concurrent Pos:* Res engr, Humble Oil & Refining Co, 64; NIH fel, 66. *Mem:* Am Chem Soc; Am Inst Chem Engrs. *Res:* Chemical and biomedical engineering, especially mathematical modeling, dynamic system behavior, transport phenomena, mass transport and oxygen diffusion in brain; iron metabolism; oxygen transport in placenta. *Mailing Add:* Pres Off La Tech Univ PO Box 3168 Ruston LA 71272

RENEAU, JOHN, AUDIOLOGY, SPEECH PATHOLOGY. *Current Pos:* RETIRED. *Personal Data:* b Beloit, Wis, May 1, 27; m 55; c 3. *Educ:* Univ Wis, BS, 51; Univ Denver, MS, 58, PhD(audiol, speech path), 60. *Honors & Awards:* Rosemary Dybwad Int Award, 67. *Prof Exp:* Dir speech & hearing, State Home & Training Sch, Denver, Colo, 56-60; dir speech & hearing, Cent Wis Colony, 64-92. *Concurrent Pos:* Fel med audiol, Med Sch, Univ Iowa, 60-63; NIH spec fel neurophysiol, Inst Med Physics, Utrecht, Neth, 63-64; lectr, Univ Wis-Madison, 71-; mem comt hearing, bioacoust & biomech, Nat Acad Sci, 71; mem sensory study sect, Social & Rehab Serv, Dept HEW, 71- *Mem:* Fel Am Speech & Hearing Asn. *Res:* Study of sensory electroneurophysiology using averaged evoked responses; research audiology. *Mailing Add:* 5410 Russett Rd Madison WI 53711

RENEAU, RAYMOND B, JR, SOIL CHEMISTRY. *Current Pos:* from asst prof to assoc prof soil pollution, 71-86, PROF SOIL ENVIRON QUAL, VA POLYTECH INST & STATE UNIV, 86- *Personal Data:* b Burkesville, Ky, Sept 11, 41. *Educ:* Berea Col, BS, 64; Univ Ky, MS, 66; Univ Fla, PhD(soil chem), 69. *Prof Exp:* Asst prof agron, Tex Tech Univ, 70-71. *Concurrent Pos:* Consult, Jamaica Sch Agr, 70- *Mem:* AAAS; Am Soc Agron. *Res:* Movement of septic pollutants through natural soil systems and the potential contamination of ground and surface waters. *Mailing Add:* Crop & Soil Sci Va Polytech Inst & State Univ PO Box 0404 Blacksburg VA 24063-0001

RENEKE, JAMES ALLEN, MATHEMATICAL ANALYSIS. *Current Pos:* asst prof, 66-71, ASSOC PROF MATH, CLEMSON UNIV, 71- *Personal Data:* b Jacksonville, Fla, Sept 21, 37; m 61; c 4. *Educ:* Univ Fla, BA, 58, MA, 60; Univ NC, Chapel Hill, PhD(math), 64. *Prof Exp:* Assoc prof math, Newberry Col, 64-66. *Concurrent Pos:* Vis assoc prof, Univ Houston, 72-73. *Mem:* Am Math Soc. *Res:* Mathematical system theory, in particular, system problems of realization, identification and control. *Mailing Add:* Dept Math Sci Clemson Univ Clemson SC 29634-1907

RENEKER, DARRELL HYSON, PHYSICS, SOLID STATE PHYSICS. *Current Pos:* DIR, INST POLYMER SCI, 89-94; PROF POLYMER SCI, UNIV AKRON, 89- *Personal Data:* b Birmingham, Iowa, Dec 5, 29; m 53; c 2. *Educ:* Iowa State Univ, BS, 51; Univ Chicago, MS, 55, PhD, 59. *Prof Exp:* Mem tech staff, Bell Tel Labs, Inc, 51-53; physicist, Polychems Dept, Exp Sta, E I du Pont de Nemours & Co, 59-63, eng mat lab, 63-64, cent res dept, 64-69; chief polymer crystal physics sect, Polymers Div, Nat Bur Stand, 75, dep chief polymer sci & standards div, 75-80, dep dir, Ctr Mat Sci, 80-85. *Concurrent Pos:* Exec secy, Comt Mat, Off Sci & Technol Policy, Off Pres, Wash, 85-89. *Mem:* Am Phys Soc; Soc Plastics Engrs; Micros Soc Am; Mat Res Soc; Am Chem Soc. *Res:* Ultra-sonic waves in metals; electronic properties of metals; physical properties of polymers and molecular solids; scanning probe microscopy; electrical properties of polymers. *Mailing Add:* Univ Akron Akron OH 44325

RENFREW, ANDREW COLIN, ARCHAEOLOGY. *Current Pos:* DISNEY PROF ARCHAEOL, CAMBRIDGE UNIV, 81- *Personal Data:* b Stockton-on-Tees, Eng, July 25, 37; m 65; Jane Margaret Ewbank; c Helen, Alan & Magnus. *Educ:* Cambridge Univ, BA, 62, MA, 64, PhD, 65, ScD, 76. *Honors & Awards:* George Grant McCurdy Lectr, Harvard Univ, 77; Rivers Mem Medal, Royal Anthrop Inst, 79, Huxley Mem Medal, 91; Patten Lectr, Ind Univ, 82. *Prof Exp:* Lectr archaeol, Univ Sheffield, 65-72; prof, Univ Southampton, 72-81. *Concurrent Pos:* Field excavations, Saliagos, 64-65, Sitagroi, 68-70, Quanterness, Orkney, 72-74, Phylakopi, Melos, 74-76; vis lectr, Univ Calif, Los Angeles, 67; fel, St Johns Col, 81-86; master, Jesus Col, Cambridge, 86-97. *Mem:* Foreign assoc Nat Acad Sci; Fel Brit Acad. *Res:* Excavations, archaeology; problem in European prehistory. *Mailing Add:* Dept Archaeol Cambridge Univ Downing St Cambridge CB2 3DZ England

RENFREW, EDGAR EARL, INDUSTRIAL ORGANIC CHEMISTRY. *Current Pos:* RETIRED. *Personal Data:* b Colfax, Wash, Apr 8, 15; m 43; c 2. *Educ:* Univ Idaho, BS, 36; Univ Minn, PhD(org chem), 44. *Prof Exp:* Chemist, Bunker Hill & Sullivan Mining Co, Idaho, 36-38; asst, Univ Minn, 39-43; res chemist, Gen Aniline & Film Corp, Pa, 44-58; mgr dyestuffs res, Koppers Co, Inc, 58-62; res chemist, 3M Co, 62-66; dir res & develop, Am Aniline Prod, Inc, 66-72; vpres res & develop, Am Color & Chem Co, 72-80. *Concurrent Pos:* Consult, 80-83. *Mem:* Am Chem Soc; Am Asn Textile Chemists & Colorists. *Res:* Dyestuffs and intermediates; aromatic intermediates. *Mailing Add:* 1189 S Hillview St Lock Haven PA 17745-2390

RENFREW, MALCOLM MACKENZIE, SCIENCE EDITOR. *Current Pos:* head, Phys Sci Div, Univ Idaho, 59-68, head dept, 68-73, prof chem, 68-76, EMER PROF, UNIV IDAHO, 76- *Personal Data:* b Spokane, Wash, Oct 12, 10; m 38. *Educ:* Univ Idaho, BS, 32, MS, 34; Univ Minn, PhD(phys chem), 38. *Hon Degrees:* DSc, Univ of Idaho, 76. *Honors & Awards:* Harry & Carol Mosher Award, 86 & CHAS Award, Am Chem Soc, 85. *Prof Exp:* Asst physics, Univ Idaho, 32-33, chem, 33-35; asst chem, Univ Minn, 35-37; res chemist, E I du Pont de Nemours & Co, 38-44, res supvr, 44-49; dir chem res, Gen Mills Inc, 49-54; dir res & develop, Spencer Kellog & Sons, Inc, 54-58; prof chem & head div phys sci, Univ Idaho, 59-67; staff assoc, Adv Coun Col Chem, Stanford Univ, 67-68. *Concurrent Pos:* Consult, Mat Adv Bd, Nat Acad Sci-Nat Res Coun, 62-67; dir, Col Chem Consult Serv; exec vpres, Idaho Res Found, 77-78, patent mgr, 78-88, safety ed, J Chem Educ, 77-90. *Mem:* Am Chem Soc; Am Inst Chemists; Am Inst Chem Engrs; Soc Chem Indust. *Res:* Polymer chemistry; organic coatings and plastics. *Mailing Add:* Dept Chem Univ Idaho Moscow ID 83843. *E-Mail:* renfrew@uidaho.edu

RENFREW, ROBERT MORRISON, TRANSPORTATION SYSTEM DESIGN. *Current Pos:* AT ACER, UK, 92- *Personal Data:* b Glasgow, Scotland, Mar 11, 38; Can citizen; m 60; c 4. *Educ:* Univ Toronto, Can, BASc, 60. *Prof Exp:* Chief engr, Husky Mfg & Tool Works, 69-73; sr prog engr, Govt Toronto, 73-75; prog dir, Urban Transp Develop Corp, 75-78, vpres eng, 78-80, sr vpres, 80-82, exec vpres, Res & Develop Ltd, 82-83; exec dir, Can Inst Guided Ground Transp, 83-86; sr vpres eng & technol, UTDC Inc, 86-92. *Res:* Transportation systems and related technologies; control systems; propulsion technology; urban transit market research; materials technology; civil infrastructure related to transportation. *Mailing Add:* Hyder Consult Ltd 2 Cornwall Terr London Nw1 4QP England

RENFRO, J LARRY, RENAL PHYSIOLOGY, COMPARATIVE OSMO REGULATION. *Current Pos:* PROF PHYSIOL, UNIV CONN, 74- *Educ:* Univ Okla, PhD(zool), 70. *Mailing Add:* Dept Physiol & Neurobiol Univ Conn 65 N Eagleville Rd Rm CSA 712 Storrs CT 06269-3042

RENFRO, WILLIAM CHARLES, BIOLOGICAL OCEANOGRAPHY, MARINE RADIOECOLOGY. *Current Pos:* RETIRED. *Personal Data:* b Hillsboro, Tex, Jan 16, 30; m 55, Patricia Wagner; c 4. *Educ:* Univ Tex, BA, 51, MA, 58; Ore State Univ, PhD(oceanog), 67. *Prof Exp:* Marine biologist, Tex Game & Fish Comn, 58-59; fishery res biologist, US Bur Com Fisheries, 59-64; asst prof oceanog, Ore State Univ, 67-71; chief radiobiol group, Int Atomic Energy Agency, Lab Marine Radioactivity, Monaco, 71-73; chief environ progs, NE Utilities Co, 73-80, dir environ progs, 80-92. *Concurrent Pos:* Dir, Conn Acad Sci & Eng. *Mem:* AAAS; Am Nuclear Soc; Am Soc Limnol & Oceanog. *Res:* Marine and aquatic radioecology; estuarine ecology; marine pollution; radiochemistry; shrimp life history and ecology; fish physiology. *Mailing Add:* 270 Highcrest Rd Wethersfield CT 06109

RENFROE, HARRIS BURT, ORGANIC & PHARMACEUTICAL CHEMISTRY. *Current Pos:* dir new drug coord, 89-91, exec dir res support, 91-93, VPRES, PLANNING & PROD DEVELOP DIV, NITRO MED, INC, 93- *Personal Data:* b Meridian, Miss, Nov 22, 36; m 64; c 2. *Educ:* Miss State Univ, BS, 58; Univ Ill, PhD(org chem), 61. *Prof Exp:* NIH fel org chem, Zurich, 61-62; chemist, Lederle Labs, Am Cyanamid Co, 63-65; res chemist, Geigy Res Labs, Ciba-Geigy Corp, 65-69, proj leader, 69-71, group leader, Dept Org Chem, 72-81, dir chem res, 81-86, assoc dir drug dis coord, 86-89. *Mem:* Am Chem Soc; Sigma Xi. *Res:* Synthesis of pharmacologically active compounds; exploratory organic synthesis; preclinical and non-clinical development of drug candidates; IND and NDA stages. *Mailing Add:* 90 Bristol Rd Wellesley MA 02181

RENGAN, KRISHNASWAMY, NUCLEAR CHEMISTRY, ANALYTICAL CHEMISTRY. *Current Pos:* assoc prof, 70-79, PROF CHEM, EASTERN MICH UNIV, 79- *Personal Data:* b Varalotti, India, Aug 9, 37; m 69; c 2. *Educ:* Univ Kerala, BSc, 57, MSc, 58; Univ Mich, PhD (chem), 66. *Honors & Awards:* Res Award, Sigma Xi. *Prof Exp:* Sci off radiochem div, Bhabha Atomic Res Ctr, Bombay, 58-70. *Mem:* Am Phys Soc; Am Chem Soc; fel AAAS; Health Phys Soc; Sigma Xi. *Res:* Decay scheme studies; radiochemical separations; application of activation analysis to environmental problems. *Mailing Add:* Dept Chem Eastern Mich Univ Ypsilanti MI 48197

RENICH, PAUL WILLIAM, CHEMISTRY. *Current Pos:* ADJ PROF, BETHEL COL, 84- *Personal Data:* b La Junta, Colo, May 5, 19; m 43, Roberta Enns; c Rebekah, Stephen & Thomas. *Educ:* Bethel Col Kans, AB, 42; Univ Kans, MA, 44, PhD(phys chem), 49. *Prof Exp:* Prof chem, Kans Wesleyan Univ, 48-74, dean, 51-69, pres, 69-73; instr, Haskell Indian Jr Col, 74-84. *Concurrent Pos:* Ford Found fel, Mass Inst Technol, 54-55; assoc, NCent Asn Cols, 59-60, consult-examr, 60-74. *Mem:* Am Chem Soc; AAAS. *Res:* Physical chemistry, including electrodeposition and physiochemical properties. *Mailing Add:* 720 W 17th St CT Newton KS 67114-1465

RENIS, HAROLD E, VIROLOGY, BIOCHEMISTRY. *Current Pos:* RES ASSOC VIROL, SR SCIENTIST, UPJOHN CO, 84- *Personal Data:* b Highland Park, Ill, Jan 1, 30; m 51; c 3. *Educ:* Elmhurst Col, BS, 51; Bradley Univ, MS, 54; Purdue Univ, PhD(biochem), 56. *Prof Exp:* Instr chem, Bradley Univ; res asst biochem, Purdue Univ, Nat Heart Inst fel microbiol. *Mem:* AAAS; Am Chem Soc; Am Microbiol Soc; Tissue Cult Asn; Soc Exp Biol Med; Sigma Xi; Int Soc Antiviral Res. *Res:* Tissue culture; nucleic acid antagonists; virus chemotherapy; animal virology; immunomodulators. *Mailing Add:* 6631 Trotwood St Kalamazoo MI 49002-3256

RENKA, ROBERT JOSEPH, NUMERICAL ANALYSIS, MATHEMATICAL SOFTWARE. *Current Pos:* asst prof, 84-89, ASSOC PROF COMPUTER SCI, UNIV NTEX, 89- *Personal Data:* b Summit, NJ, Dec 28, 47. *Educ:* Univ Tex, Austin, BA & BS, 76, MA, 79, PhD(comput sci) 81. *Prof Exp:* Numerical analyst, Oak Ridge Nat Lab, 81-84. *Concurrent Pos:* Ed-in-chief, Collected Algorithms Asn Comput Mach, CALGO, 89-93; prin investr, NSF grant, 90-91, 91-93. *Mem:* Asn Comput Mach; Soc Indust & Appl Math. *Res:* Numerical analysis; mathematical software; curve and surface fitting; computational geometry; scattered data interpolation and smoothing. *Mailing Add:* 1700 Kendolph Dr Denton TX 76205-6940. *E-Mail:* renka@ponder.csci.unt.edu

RENKEN, JAMES HOWARD, COMPUTATIONAL PHYSICS. *Current Pos:* RETIRED. *Personal Data:* b El Paso, Tex, July 1, 35; m 78, Patricia Cazier; c Catherine, Stephanie & John. *Educ:* Ohio State Univ, BSc & MSc, 58; Calif Inst Technol, PhD(physics), 63. *Prof Exp:* Staff mem, Theory & Anal Div, Sandia Nat Labs, 64-67, supvr, Theoret Div, 67-80, supvr, Hostile Environ Div, 80-83, mgr, Radiation Effects Dept, 83-92, mgr, Radiation & Electromagnetic Dept, 92-94, dep dir, Ctr Appl Physics, 94-96. *Concurrent Pos:* Secy, Radiation & Shielding Div, Am Nuclear Soc, 92-94. *Mem:* Am Phys Soc; Am Nuclear Soc. *Res:* Transport theory; interaction of radiation with matter; mathematical physics. *Mailing Add:* MS 1166 Sandia Nat Labs PO Box 5800 Albuquerque NM 87185-1166. *Fax:* 505-845-3471; *E-Mail:* jhrenke@sandia.gov

RENKEY, EDMUND JOSEPH, JR, MECHANICAL ENGINEERING. *Current Pos:* Procurement specialist, Westinghouse Elec Co, 72-74, sect mgr, 74-78, sr engr, 78-81, PRIN ENGR, WESTINGHOUSE HANFORD CO, WESTINGHOUSE ELEC CO, 81- *Personal Data:* b Pittsburgh, Pa, May 19, 40. *Educ:* Pa State Univ, BS, 63, MBA, 66. *Prof Exp:* Assoc engr, Wright Aero Div, Curtiss-Wright Corp, 63-65; sr contract adminr, Marvel-Schebler Div, Borg Warner Corp, 67-71; proposal adminr power generation, Babcock & Wilcox Co, 71-72. *Concurrent Pos:* Adj prof, Cent Wash Univ, 76 & 78. *Mem:* Am Soc Mech Engrs. *Res:* Diaphragm compressor development; auxiliary equipment/systems for testing space-based nuclear reactors. *Mailing Add:* 1963 Marshall Ave Richland WA 99352

RENKIN, EUGENE MARSHALL, PHYSIOLOGY, ANIMAL PHYSIOLOGY. *Current Pos:* chmn dept, 74-91, prof, 74-94, EMER PROF HUMAN PHYSIOL, SCH MED, UNIV CALIF, DAVIS, 94- *Personal Data:* b Boston, Mass, Oct 21, 26; m 55, 67, Elizabeth Russell; c Miriam, Hadley, Joshua & Daniel. *Educ:* Tufts Col, BS, 48; Harvard Univ, PhD(med sci), 51. *Honors & Awards:* Bowditch lectr, Am Physiol Soc, 63; E M Landis Award, 77; B W Zweifach Award, 84; C J Wiggers Award, 85. *Prof Exp:* Assoc biologist, Brookhaven Nat Lab, 51-55; sr asst scientist, Nat Heart Inst, 55-57; from asst prof to prof physiol & chmn dept, Sch Med, George Washington Univ, 57-63; prof pharmacol & head div, Sch Med, Duke Univ, 63-69, prof physiol, 69-74. *Concurrent Pos:* NSF sr fel, 60-61; Wellcome vis prof physiol, 78. *Mem:* Am Physiol Soc; Am Heart Asn; Microcirculatory Soc (pres, 75); Sigma Xi. *Res:* Peripheral circulation; capillary and membrane permeability; lymph circulation. *Mailing Add:* Dept Human Physiol Univ Calif Sch Med Davis CA 95616

RENN, DONALD WALTER, BIOTECHNOLOGY, NATURAL PRODUCT ISOLATION & CHARACTERIZATION. *Current Pos:* OWNER/CONSULT, CREATIVE SOLUTIONS, 95- *Personal Data:* b East Rutherford, NJ, Mar 23, 32; m 55, Patricia Eaby; c Lori, Lisa & Carrie. *Educ:* Franklin & Marshall Col, BS, 53; Mich State Univ, PhD(org chem), 57. *Prof Exp:* Res chemist, John L Smith Mem Cancer Res, Pfizer, Inc, 57-65, asst dept head chem, 61-65, group leader immunochem cancer & viral chem, 62-65; sr chemist, Marine Colloids, Inc, 65-68, res scientist, 68-69, sr scientist, 69-79, dir spec proj res group, 70-72, dir res, MCI Biomed, 72-75; mgr, Biotechnol Venture, Marine Colloids Div, FMC Corp, 77-79, dir biomed res, 79-80, corp res fel, 79-81, sr res fel, 81-95, dir, Corp Explor Lab, 83-85, dir explor technol group, 87-95. *Mem:* Am Chem Soc; Sigma Xi; AAAS; fel Am Inst Chemists; Am Asn Clin Chem; Int Plant Molecular Biol Asn. *Res:* Natural product chemistry and biochemistry particularly polysaccharides and their life science applications; immunochemical and electrophoretic (including DNA) methods for disease detection; biotechnology tools and techniques. *Mailing Add:* 4 Brewster Pt Glen Cove ME 04846-0088

RENNAT, HARRY O(LAF), MECHANICAL ENGINEERING. *Current Pos:* ASSOC PROF MECH ENG, COLO STATE UNIV, 56- *Personal Data:* b Estonia, Aug 6, 22; nat US; m 51; c 3. *Educ:* Univ Wis, BS, 53, MS, 54, PhD(mech eng), 56. *Prof Exp:* Res asst, Bjorksten Res Labs, Inc, Wis, 51-56. *Mem:* Am Soc Mech Engrs. *Res:* Heat transfer; materials science. *Mailing Add:* 6015 S County Rd 11 Ft Collins CO 80525

RENNE, DAVID SMITH, METEOROLOGY. *Current Pos:* TECHNOL MGR, NAT RENEWABLE ENERGY LAB, 92- *Personal Data:* b Harvey, Ill, Nov 27, 43; m 66; c 2. *Educ:* Kalamazoo Col, BA, 66; Colo State Univ, MS, 69, PhD(earth resources), 75. *Prof Exp:* Meteorologist, US Weather Bur, Lansing, 66; res asst atmospheric sci, Colo State Univ, 66-71; meteorologist air pollution, Environ Qual Bd, San Juan, PR, 71-72; res asst earth resources, Colo State Univ, 72-74; res scientist meteorol, Pac Northwest Labs, Battelle Mem Inst, 75-92. *Concurrent Pos:* Consult air pollution, Marlatt & Assoc, Ft Collins, Colo, 72-75 & Inst Ecol-Urban Secondary Impacts Workshop, 74; consult hydrol, City of Ft Collins Planning Dept, 73-74. *Mem:* Am Meteorol Soc; Sigma Xi; Air Pollution Control Asn. *Res:* Research and project management in wind characteristics for wind energy utilization; long range transport and wet and dry deposition of pollutants. *Mailing Add:* 1617 Cole Blvd Golden CO 80401. *Fax:* 303-275-4675

RENNEKE, DAVID RICHARD, PHYSICS, COMPUTER SCIENCE. *Current Pos:* Asst prof, 68-77, assoc prof, 77-86, PROF PHYSICS, AUGUATANA COL, ILL, 86- *Personal Data:* b Gaylord, Minn, June 29, 40; m 63, Donna Mueller; c Linda, Sharon & John. *Educ:* Gustavus Adolphus Col, BS, 62; Iowa State Univ, MS, 64; Univ Kans, PhD(physics), 70. *Concurrent Pos:* Consult comput graphics, John Deere Tech Ctr, Moline, 77-86. *Mem:* Am Asn Phys Teachers; Sigma Xi. *Res:* Computer applications in education; mathematical modeling of physical systems; holography; optical reflection from solids; photoconductivity in ionic crystals; atomic imperfections in solids; cryogenic gas storage systems; computer graphics; x-ray diffraction of titanium nitrate. *Mailing Add:* Dept Phys Augustana Col Rock Island IL 61201. *E-Mail:* phrenneke@augustana.edu

RENNELS, MARGARET BAKER, PEDIATRIC INFECTIOUS DISEASES, VACCINE DEVELOPMENT. *Current Pos:* Resident pediat, Sch Med, Univ Md, 73-76, chief resident, 76-77, fel infectious dis, 77-79, from asst prof to assoc prof, 79-96, PROF PEDIAT, SCH MED, UNIV MD, 96- *Personal Data:* b Easton, Md, Oct 30, 45; m 71, Marshall L. *Educ:* Skidmore Col, BA, 67; Univ Md, MD, 73. *Concurrent Pos:* Clin head, Div Pediat Infectious Dis, Sch Med, Univ Md, 81-, dir fel training prog, 96-; prin investr, 84-; chief, Pediat Clin Studies Sect, Ctr Vaccine Develop, 85- *Mem:* Fel Am Acad Pediat; Am Soc Microbiol; fel Pediat Infectious Dis Soc; fel Infectious Dis Soc Am; Am Pediat Soc. *Res:* Design, conduct, analyze and publish clinical evaluation of new and improved vaccines for children. *Mailing Add:* 5434 Landing Rd Elkridge MD 21227

RENNELS, MARSHALL L, NEUROANATOMY. *Current Pos:* Asst prof anat, Univ Md, Baltimore, 66-71, asst prof neurol, 69-71, assoc prof anat, 71-79, dir MD/PhD prog, Sch Med & Grad Sch, 89-96, PROF ANAT & ASSOC PROF NEUROL, SCH MED, UNIV MD, BALTIMORE, 79- *Personal Data:* b Marshall, Mo, Sept 2, 39; m 71. *Educ:* Eastern Ill Univ, BS, 61; Univ Tex Med Br Galveston, MA, 64, PhD(neuroendocrinol, neurocytol), 66. *Mem:* AAAS; Electron Micros Soc Am; Am Asn Anatomists; Soc Neurosci; Int Soc Cerebral Blood Flow & Metab; Sigma Xi. *Res:* Ultrastructural and histochemical investigations of the cerebrovascular system and its innervation by autonomic and central neurons; related studies examine the characteristics of the cerebral microcirculatory system and its relationships to the cerebral parenchyma. *Mailing Add:* Sch Med Univ Md 655 W Baltimore St Baltimore MD 21201. *Fax:* 410-706-2512

RENNER, DARWIN S(PRATHARD), ELECTRICAL ENGINEERING. *Current Pos:* vpres, 47-50, PRES, GEOTRONIC LABS, INC, 50- *Personal Data:* b Powell, Ohio, Oct 15, 10; m 44; c 3. *Educ:* Ohio State Univ, BEE, 32, MSc, 33. *Prof Exp:* Comput, Geophys Serv, Tex, 35-37, res engr, 37-42, supt electronics div, 42-45, sr engr, 45-47. *Mem:* Am Phys Soc; Soc Explor Geophys; Inst Elec & Electronics Engrs; Am Geophys Union; Sigma Xi. *Res:* Automatic amplifiers; servomechanisms; filter systems; magnetic detectors; test sets-fault locators; mixing systems; noise meters; interference eliminators; cameras; recording oscillographs; inductive and capacitive components; computers. *Mailing Add:* 1314 Cedar Hill Ave Dallas TX 75208-2403

RENNER, GERARD W, physics, acoustics & underwater sound; deceased, see previous edition for last biography

RENNER, RUTH, NUTRITION. *Current Pos:* RETIRED. *Personal Data:* b Lewistown, Mont, Nov 17, 25. *Educ:* Univ Alta, BSc, 48, MSc, 50; Cornell Univ, PhD(animal nutrit), 60. *Honors & Awards:* Borden Award, Nutrit Soc Can, 70. *Prof Exp:* Res asst soils, Univ Alta, 50-52, res asst poultry, 52-55; res assoc nutrit & poultry, Cornell Univ, 55-58, asst, 58-60; from asst prof to prof nutrit, Sch Household Econ, Univ Alta, 60-81. *Mem:* Am Inst Nutrit; Poultry Sci Asn; Nutrit Soc Can. *Res:* Nutritive value of proteins; energy and fat metabolism. *Mailing Add:* RR 1 Priddis AB T0L 1W0 Can

RENNER, TERRENCE ALAN, PHYSICAL CHEMISTRY. *Current Pos:* RES SCI, AMOCO OIL CO, 82- *Personal Data:* b Evergreen Park, Ill, Dec 1, 47. *Educ:* DePaul Univ, Chicago, BS, 69; Yale Univ, PhD(phys chem), 72. *Prof Exp:* Asst chemist phys chem, Chem Eng Div, Argonne Nat Lab, Argonne, Ill, 73-82. *Concurrent Pos:* Fel, Argonne Nat Lab, Argonne, Ill, 72-73. *Mem:* Sigma Xi. *Res:* Transport properties of reacting gas mixtures; thermal conductivity; nucleation of superheated liquids; tritium and hydrogen transport in sodium-cooled fast breeder reactors; tritium permeation through reactor construction materials; sodium cold trap optimization. *Mailing Add:* 22706 Fossil Creek Circle Katy TX 77450-8679

RENNERT, JOSEPH, PHOTOCHEMISTRY. *Current Pos:* from asst prof to prof, 62-86, EMER PROF CHEM, CITY COL NEW YORK, 86- *Personal Data:* b Mannheim, Ger, July 26, 19; nat US; m 47; c 2. *Educ:* City Col New York, BS, 48; Syracuse Univ, MS, 52, PhD(chem), 53. *Prof Exp:* Asst anal chem, Syracuse Univ, 48-50 & phys chem, 50-52; res chemist, Ozalid div, Gen Aniline & Film Corp, 52-54 & Chas Bruning Co, 54-55; proj engr, Balco Res Labs, 55-56; from res scientist to sr res scientist, Inst Math Scis, NY Univ, 56-62. *Concurrent Pos:* Lectr, City Col New York, 56-; consult, Itek Corp, 60-62. *Mem:* AAAS; Am Chem Soc; fel Am Inst Chemists; NY Acad Sci; Am Soc Photobiol. *Res:* Photochemistry; mechanisms of photo-cyclo-addition, photo- scission, photo-redox and photosensitized reactions; photochemical and photophysical imaging and information storage systems; solid state photochemistry; photobiology. *Mailing Add:* 525 Fordham Pl Paramus NJ 07652-5637

RENNERT, OWEN M, PEDIATRICS, BIOCHEMISTRY. *Current Pos:* PROF & CHMN, DEPT PEDIAT, SCH MED, GEORGETOWN UNIV, 88- *Personal Data:* b New York, NY, Aug 8, 38; m 63, Sandra Strota; c Laura J, Rachel L & Ian P. *Educ:* Univ Chicago, BS & BA, 57, MD, 61, MS, 63; Am Bd Pediat, dipl, 67. *Honors & Awards:* Gitlitz lectr, Am Asn Clin Sci, 80; Gerber lectr, Am Col Nutrit, 82. *Prof Exp:* Res & clin assoc neurol, Nat Inst Neurol Dis & Blindness, Md, 64-66; instr pediat & chief resident, Univ Chicago, 66-67, asst prof pediat, 67-68; from assoc prof to prof pediat & biochem, Col Med, Univ Fla, 68-78, head, Inst Div Genetics, Endocrinol & Metab, 70-77; prof pediat & biochem, Col Med, Univ Okla, 77-88, head, Dept Pediat, 77-88. *Concurrent Pos:* Mem bd med examr, Ill, 61, Fla, 70 & Nat Bd Med Examr, 62; mem adv comt inborn errors of metab, Bd Health, Fla; NIH & Nat Cystic Fibrosis Fedn fels, 71-76; Fla Heart Asn fel, 72-73; James C Overall vis prof, Vanderbilt Univ, 84. *Mem:* AAAS; fel Am Acad Pediat; Soc Pediat Res; Am Pediat Soc; Am Soc Biochem & Molecular Biol; Am Soc Human Genetics; Asn Clin Scientists; Am Fedn Clin Res; Am Chem Soc; NY Acad Sci; Sigma Xi; AMA; Am Inst Nutrit; Biochem Soc; Endocrine Soc; Am Pub Health Asn; Am Soc Microbiol; Am Col Nutrit; Asn Med Sch Pediat Dept Chmn; fel Am Col Med Genetics. *Res:* Inborn errors of metabolism; human genetics. *Mailing Add:* Dept Pediat Georgetown Univ Hosp 3800 Reservoir Rd NW Washington DC 20007. *Fax:* 202-687-7161

RENNHARD, HANS HEINRICH, ORGANIC CHEMISTRY, METABOLISM OF FOOD ADDITIVES. *Current Pos:* RETIRED. *Personal Data:* b Aarau, Switz, Sept 26, 28; nat US; m 55; c 2. *Educ:* Swiss Fed Inst Technol, dipl, 52, DSc, 55. *Prof Exp:* Fel, Mass Inst Technol, 55-57; from res chemist to sr res chemist, Pfizer Inc, 57-73, sr res investr, 74-79, prin res investr, 80-92. *Mem:* Swiss Chem Soc; Am Chem Soc. *Res:* Antibiotics; tetracyclines; flavor enhancers; pharmacology of food additives; carbohydrate chemistry and metabolism; radiobiology; analytical methods development. *Mailing Add:* 205 Blood St Old Lyme CT 06371-3511

RENNICK, BARBARA RUTH, PHYSIOLOGY. *Current Pos:* RETIRED. *Personal Data:* b Ashtabula, Ohio, Oct 23, 19. *Educ:* Wayne State Univ, BSc, 42, MSc, 44; Univ Mich, MD, 50. *Prof Exp:* Pharmacologist, Ciba Pharmaceut Prod, 44-46; instr physiol, State Univ NY Upstate Med Ctr, 50-54, asst prof, 54-61; assoc prof, Mt Holyoke Col, 61-64; prof pharmacol, Med Sch, State Univ NY Buffalo, 65-82. *Concurrent Pos:* USPHS spec fel, Oxford Univ, 54-55; Wellcome Found traveling fel, 58. *Mem:* AAAS; Am Physiol Soc; Am Soc Pharmacol & Exp Therapeut; Am Soc Nephrology. *Res:* Renal tubular function; membrane transport; autonomic pharmacology; newborn physiology; general physiology. *Mailing Add:* 3304 Dominica Ct Punta Gorda FL 33950. *E-Mail:* rennickb@suno.com

RENNIE, DONALD ANDREWS, SOIL CHEMISTRY. *Current Pos:* RETIRED. *Personal Data:* b Medicine Hat, Alta, Apr 21, 22; m 48; c 3. *Educ:* Univ Sask, BSA, 49; Univ Wis, PhD(soils), 52. *Honors & Awards:* Award, Am Chem Soc, 67; Centennial Medal, Can, 67; Agr Hall Fame, 82. *Prof Exp:* From asst prof to prof, 52-64, head dept, 64-81, dean col agr, Univ Sask, 84-89. *Concurrent Pos:* Dir, Sask Inst Pedology, 65-81; head soils irrig & crop prod sect, Int Atomic Energy Agency, Vienna, Austria, 68-70. *Mem:* Fel Can Soc Soil Sci (secy-treas, 56-58, pres, 76-77); fel Agr Inst Can (vpres, 59-60); fel Soil Sci Soc Am; fel Am Soc Agron; fel Can Soc Soil Sci. *Res:* Soil chemistry and fertility. *Mailing Add:* 134 Highbury Pl Saskatoon SK S7H 4X7 Can

RENNIE, JAMES CLARENCE, ANIMAL BREEDING. *Current Pos:* RETIRED. *Personal Data:* b Ont, Sept 14, 26; m 50; c 2. *Educ:* Univ Toronto, BS, 47; Iowa State Col, MS, 50, PhD, 52. *Honors & Awards:* Award of Merit, Can Soc Animal Sci. *Prof Exp:* Asst agr rep, Dept Agr, Ont, 47-49; tech off, Cent Exp Farm, Ottawa, 49; assoc prof animal husb, Ont Agr Col, Univ Guelph, 52-56, chmn dept, 65-71, prof, 56-74; exec dir educ & res, 74-78, asst dep minister technol & field serv, 85-90, asst dep minister educ, res & spec serv, Ont Ministry Agr & Food, 78-91, dir, Agr Res Inst Ont, 90-91. *Concurrent Pos:* Coordr exten, dept animal & poultry sci, Ont Agr Col, Univ Guelph, 71-73, actg dean res, 73-74. *Mem:* Fel Agr Inst Can; Ont Inst Agrologists. *Mailing Add:* 18 Forest Hill Dr Guelph ON M1G 2E3 Can

RENNIE, PAUL STEVEN, PROSTATE CANCER, ANDROGEN ACTION. *Current Pos:* dir res, 92-97, RES SCIENTIST, BC CANCER AGENCY, 79-; PROF SURG, UNIV BC, 86- *Personal Data:* b Toronto, Ont, Feb 9, 46; m 68, Carol Andrews; c Jan. *Educ:* Univ Western Ont, BSc, 69; Univ Alta, PhD(biochem), 73. *Prof Exp:* Res assoc, Univ Alta, 75-76, asst prof med, 76-79, assoc prof, 79. *Concurrent Pos:* Med Res Coun res fel, Imp Cancer Res Fund, 73-75; res scholar, Nat Cancer Inst Can, 76-79. *Mem:* Endocrine Soc; Can Soc Clin Invest; Biochem Soc. *Res:* Biochemical control of growth in androgen responsive organs and neoplasms; genetic markers in prostate cancer. *Mailing Add:* BC Cancer Agency 600 W Tenth Ave Vancouver BC V5Z 4E6 Can. *Fax:* 604-877-6011; *E-Mail:* prennie@bccancer.bc.ca

RENNIE, ROBERT JOHN, SOIL MICROBIOLOGY. *Current Pos:* VPRES NEW PROD RES & DEVELOP, AGRIUM INC, 94- *Personal Data:* b Prince Albert, Sask, Sept 12, 49; m 70; c 2. *Educ:* Univ Sask, BSA Hons, 71; Laval Univ MSc, 72; Univ Minn, PhD(soil microbiol), 75. *Prof Exp:* Res scientist dinitrogen fixation, Agr Res Coun, nit Nitrogen Fixation, UK, 75-76; assoc officer, Food & Agr Orgn, Int Atomic Energy Agency, Div Atomic Energy Food & Agr, UN, 76-78; res scientist dinitrogen fixation, Agr Can, 78-85; mgr, Agr Sci Progs, Exxon Chem, 85-90, AGR BIOL, 90-94. *Concurrent Pos:* Nat Res Coun Can fel, Agr Res Coun Unit Nitrogen Fixation, UK, 75-76; mem, Can Comt Nitrogen Fixation, Agr Can, 78-85; bd mem, Alta Sci Res Authority, 96- *Mem:* Am Soc Microbiol; Am Soc Agron; Agr Inst Can; Can Soc Microbiologists. *Res:* Dinitrogen fixing bacteria associated with legumes and non-legumes such as spring wheat and temperate prairie grasses; isotope techniques and immunofluorescent procedures are applied throughout. *Mailing Add:* 1926 14th St SW Lethbridge AB T1K 1V1 Can

RENNIE, THOMAS HOWARD, HAZARDOUS WASTES, POLLUTION PREVENTION. *Current Pos:* REGIONAL ENVIRON MGR HAZARDOUS WASTES, CTR ENVIRON EXCELLENCE, CENT ENVIRON REGION OFF, USAF, DALLAS, TEX, 93- *Personal Data:* b Coral Gables, Fla, Nov 26, 43; m 68, Sandra Rummel; c Marcail, Elsa, Tristan & Allison. *Educ:* Univ Miami, BS, 65; Tex A&M Univ, MS, 67, PhD(biol), 75. *Prof Exp:* Instr zool, Ohio State Univ, 72-73; asst prof biol, Augustana Col, Rock Island, Ill, 74-79; sr biologist, Wapora, 79-80; environ specialist, Savannah, Ga, US Army CEngrs, 80-82, New Orleans, La, 82-83, Galveston, Tex, 83-88, chief, Environ & Anal Br, Chicago, Ill, 88-89, staff mgr, Coastal Planning Br, Galveston, Tex, 89-93. *Res:* Freshwater and marine invertebrate ecology, mainly of zooplankton and benthos; copepod taxonomy and physiology. *Mailing Add:* 2304 Brown Deer Trail Plano TX 75023-1468. *Fax:* 214-767-4661; *E-Mail:* trennie@afceeb1.brooks.af.mil

RENNILSON, JUSTIN J, PHOTOMETRY, SPECTRORADIOMETRY. *Current Pos:* VPRES RES & ENG, GAMMA SCI, INC, 74- *Personal Data:* b Berkeley, Calif, Dec 10, 26; m 54; c 3. *Educ:* Univ Calif, AB, 50; Tech Univ, Berlin, 55. *Prof Exp:* Assoc engr, Visibility Lab, Univ Calif, San Diego, 55-61; sr scientist, Jet Propulsion Lab, Calif Inst Technol, 61-69, sr res fel, 69-74. *Concurrent Pos:* Instr, San Diego State Col, 56-58; co-investr, NASA Surveyor TV Exp, 63-68; consult, Cohu Electronics Co, 68-74 & Photo Res Co, 71-74; co-investr, NASA Apollo Geol Exp 11-17. *Mem:* Optical Soc Am; Sigma Xi; Am Soc Testing & Mat. *Res:* Photometry, colorimetry; optical instrument design; spectroradiometric standards; specroradiometry; retroreflection. *Mailing Add:* 4141 S Tropico Dr La Mesa CA 91941

RENO, FREDERICK EDMUND, PRODUCT SAFETY. *Current Pos:* CONSULT, 88- *Personal Data:* b Reno, Nev, July 20, 39; m 64; c 2. *Educ:* Univ San Francisco, BS, 61; Univ Nev, Reno, MS, 63; Utah State Univ, PhD(toxicol), 67. *Prof Exp:* Lab instr human anat & physiol, Univ Nev, 63-64; res assoc emergency med servs, State of Nev, 64; assoc res coordr toxicol, Hazleton Labs, 67-68, proj mgr toxicol, 68-72, dir toxicol dept, 72-80, dir sci develop, 80-81, vpres, Hazleton Labs Am, Inc, 82-87. *Mem:* AAAS; Soc Toxicol; Am Col Vet Toxicol; Europ Soc Toxicol; Am Col Toxicol. *Res:* Toxicological and teratological evaluation of new drugs, agricultural chemicals, food additives, cosmetics and industrial chemicals; reproductive physiology; consultant to industry on product safety issues, toxicology, and toxic tort cases. *Mailing Add:* 3725 Ridgelea Dr Fairfax VA 22031

RENO, HARLEY W, HAZARDOUS WASTES MANAGEMENT, ENVIRONMENTAL MANAGEMENT. *Current Pos:* mgr environ monitoring, 78-80, prof eng sci, 80-96, PROF ENG & ENVIRON SCI, IDAHO NAT ENG LAB, UNIV IDAHO, 80-, PRIN ENG SPECIALIST, 80-, QUAL ENGR RES & DEVELOP, 92-; PRIN PROG PROJ ENGR & CONSULT, EG+G IDAHO, INC, 78- *Personal Data:* b Oakland, Calif, Feb 13, 39; m; c Robin V & Katy C. *Educ:* Okla State Univ, BS, 61, MS, 63, PhD, 67. *Honors & Awards:* Stoye Award, Am Soc Ichthyol & Herpet, 64. *Prof Exp:* Asst biol fishes, Okla State Univ, 62-67; from asst prof to assoc prof biol, Baylor Univ, 67-74; vis prof, Pan Am Univ, 74-75; tech coordr & supvr ecol sci, Williams Bros Environ Serv, Williams Bros Eng Co, Resource Sci Corp, 75-78; environ mgr, Nuclear Waste Prog, EG+G Idaho, 78-81. *Concurrent Pos:* Resident surg path, Scott & White Mem Hosp, Temple, Tex, 68-83; postdoctoral fel, Univ Okla, 74; adj prof environ sci, Univ Tulsa, 76-78. *Mem:* AAAS; Am Soc Zoologists; Am Soc Study Evolution; Sigma Xi; Ecol Soc Am; Am Nuclear Soc; Am Numismatic Asn; Am Soc Ichthyologists & Herpetologist. *Res:* Environmental transport of radioactive isotopes; hydrocarbon transport systems; surface coal mining; biological morphomechanics and systems evolution; environmental planning; risk and mechanics of communication. *Mailing Add:* Syst Eng Dept Box 1625 Lockheed Martin Idaho Technol Co Idaho Falls ID 83415. *Fax:* 208-526-9822; *E-Mail:* hwr@ingl.gov

RENO, MARTIN A, CHEMICAL PHYSICS. *Current Pos:* asst dean natural & soc sci, 70-72, PROF PHYSICS, HEIDELBERG COL, 66-, DIR, COMPUT CTR, 75- *Personal Data:* b Erie Co, Pa, July 14, 36; m 55; c 3. *Educ:* Edinboro State Col, BS, 55; Harvard Univ, EdM, 58; Rensselaer Polytech Inst, MS, 60; Western Res Univ, PhD(chem), 66. *Prof Exp:* Teacher high sch, Ohio, 58-66. *Concurrent Pos:* Dir, Col Sci Improv Prog, Heidelberg Col, 69-73. *Mem:* Am Chem Soc; Am Asn Physics Teachers; Nat Sci Teachers Asn. *Res:* Low temperature calorimetry; thermodynamic properties of fluorine containing gases; x-ray structure determination of biologically important molecules. *Mailing Add:* 80 Gross St Tiffin OH 44883-2468

RENO, ROBERT CHARLES, SOLID STATE PHYSICS, NUCLEAR SPECTROSCOPY. *Current Pos:* asst prof, 73-78, ASSOC PROF PHYSICS, UNIV MD, BALTIMORE COUNTY, 78- *Personal Data:* b New York, NY, Feb 26, 43; m 65; c 2. *Educ:* Manhattan Col, BS, 65; Brandeis Univ, MA, 67, PhD(physics), 71. *Prof Exp:* Nat Res Coun res assoc physics, Nat Bur Standards, 71-73. *Concurrent Pos:* Consult, Nat Bur Standards, 74-; prin investr, Petrol Res Fund grant, 77- *Mem:* Am Phys Soc. *Res:* Hyperfine interactions in solids; perturbed angular correlations; Mossbauer spectroscopy; physics of metals and alloys; positron annihilation; electron microscopy. *Mailing Add:* 5413 Killingworth Way Columbia MD 21044

RENOLL, ELMO SMITH, AGRICULTURAL ENGINEERING. *Current Pos:* RETIRED. *Personal Data:* b Glen Rock, Pa, Jan 25, 22; m 45, Margaret Waid; c Lynn & Jean. *Educ:* Auburn Univ, BS, 47; Iowa State Univ, MS, 49. *Honors & Awards:* Outstanding Serv Cert, Am Soc Agr Engrs, 64. *Prof Exp:* Engr agr eng, USDA, 45-49; from asst prof to assoc prof, 49-72, prof agr eng, Auburn Univ, 72-81. *Mem:* Sr mem Am Soc Agr Engrs; Am Soc Eng Educ; AAAS. *Res:* Agricultural power and machinery; machinery use and selection; programming, modeling and simulation; hay and forage machinery utilization; alcohol and other alternative fuel utilization. *Mailing Add:* 939 S Gay St Auburn AL 36830

RENOLL, MARY WILHELMINE, CHEMISTRY. *Current Pos:* RETIRED. *Personal Data:* b St Petersburg, Pa, June 26, 06. *Educ:* Grove City Col, AB, 27; Ohio State Univ, MS, 30. *Prof Exp:* Chemist, Midgley Found, Ohio State Univ, 30-38; res chemist, Monsanto Chem Co, Ohio, 39-44; res assoc chem, Res Found, Ohio State Univ, 45-57, from asst supvr to assoc supvr, 58-67, res assoc, 68, independent researcher chem, food sci & nutrit, 69-73, res assoc, Res Found, 73-76. *Concurrent Pos:* Vol, Dept Food Sci Technol, Ohio State Univ, 76- *Mem:* AAAS; Am Chem Soc; fel Am Inst Chemists; NY Acad Sci; Sigma Xi. *Res:* Organic fluorine compounds; nucleoproteins; organic and rubber chemistry; nucleic acids. *Mailing Add:* 886 W Tenth Ave Columbus OH 43212

RENSCHLER, CLIFFORD LYLE, OPTICAL SPECTROSCOPY. *Current Pos:* Mem tech staff, 81-89, MGR, SANDIA NAT LABS, 89- *Personal Data:* b Evansville, Ind, Sept 20, 55; m 78, Karen Brown; c 2. *Educ:* Univ Evansville, BS, 77; Univ Ill, PhD(chem), 81. *Mem:* Am Chem Soc; Mat Res Soc. *Res:* Radio luminescent light and scintillator development; photo degradation kinetics; photoresists and other materials for microlithography; carbon formation by organic pyrolysis. *Mailing Add:* Sandia Natl Lab Org 1812 Albuquerque NM 87185-0367. *Fax:* 505-844-9624; *E-Mail:* clrensc@sandia.gov

RENSE, WILLIAM A, SPACE PHYSICS. *Current Pos:* from assoc prof to prof physics, 49-80, co-dir lab atmospheric & space physics, 56-78, EMER PROF, UNIV COLO, BOULDER, 80- *Personal Data:* b Massillon, Ohio, Mar 11, 14; m 42, Wanda E Childs; c William Childs, John Alexander Luther & Charles Edward Easton. *Educ:* Case Western Reserve Univ, BS, 36; Ohio State Univ, MS, 37, PhD(physics), 39. *Prof Exp:* Instr physics, La State Univ, 39-40; asst prof, Univ Miami, 40; vis asst prof, Rutgers Univ, 41-42; from asst prof to assoc prof, La State Univ, 43-49. *Mem:* Am Geophys Union; Am Phys Soc; Sigma Xi; Am Astron Soc. *Res:* Vacuum spectroscopy; solar ultraviolet and stellar spectroscopy; upper air physics; space science, rocket and satellite experiments. *Mailing Add:* 204 Birch Dr Lafayette LA 70506

RENSINK, MARVIN EDWARD, MAGNETIC FUSION ENERGY. *Current Pos:* PHYSICIST, LAWRENCE LIVERMORE NAT LAB, 67- *Personal Data:* b Mason City, Iowa, Jan 29, 39; m 61, Nancy Williams; c 3. *Educ:* St Johns Univ, BS, 60; Univ Calif, Los Angeles, MS, 62, PhD(physics), 67. *Prof Exp:* Physicist, Hughes Aircraft Co, 60-63; res asst, Univ Calif, Los Angeles, 65-67. *Mem:* Am Phys Soc. *Res:* Computational modeling of plasma confinement in magnetic fusion devices. *Mailing Add:* Lawrence Livermore Nat Lab PO Box 808 L-637 Livermore CA 94550. *E-Mail:* rensink@velo.llnl.gov

RENTHAL, ROBERT DAVID, PROTEIN CHEMISTRY. *Current Pos:* asst prof, 75-80, assoc prof, 80-87, PROF BIOCHEM, UNIV TEX, SAN ANTONIO, 87- *Personal Data:* b Chicago, Ill, Oct 29, 45; m 77, Ann R Lomax; c William & Katherine. *Educ:* Princeton Univ, BA, 67; Columbia Univ, PhD(biochem), 72. *Prof Exp:* NIH fel molecular biophys, Yale Univ, 72-74; Nat Res Coun assoc life sci, Ames Res Ctr, NASA, 74-75. *Concurrent Pos:* Vis scientist, Cardiovasc Res Inst, Univ Calif, San Francisco, 79-80; NIH sr fel, Biochem Dept, Univ Tex Health Sci Ctr, San Antonio, 91-92. *Mem:* AAAS; Am Chem Soc; Biophys Soc; Am Soc Biochem & Molecular Biol; NY Acad Sci. *Res:* Structure and function of membrane proteins; mechanisms of energy transduction by photoreceptor membranes; rhodopsin and bacteriorhodopsin; structure and function of retinal rod cell connecting cilium. *Mailing Add:* Div Earth & Phys Sci Univ Tex San Antonio TX 78249. *Fax:* 210-458-4469; *E-Mail:* rrenthal@lonestar.utsa.edu

RENTMEESTER, KENNETH R, ORGANIC CHEMISTRY. *Current Pos:* CONSULT, INT EXEC SERV CORP, 82- *Personal Data:* b Green Bay, Wis, Apr 26, 31; m 67; c 1. *Educ:* St Norbert Col, BS, 52; Northwestern Univ, MS, 61. *Prof Exp:* Res assoc, Res Ctr, Am Can Co, 50-80, sr res assoc, 50-82, chemist, 52-82. *Mem:* AAAS; Am Chem Soc. *Res:* Protective organic coatings for glass, metal and plastic packages; high strength adhesive bonding systems; coil and sheet applied precoatings for deep prawn food containers with formulation and application. *Mailing Add:* 736 Highland Ave Barrington IL 60010-4521

RENTON, JOHN JOHNSTON, GEOCHEMISTRY. *Current Pos:* from asst to assoc prof, 65-75, PROF GEOL GEOCHEM, WVA UNIV, 75-, COOP GEOCHEMIST, WVA GEOL & ECON SURV, 65- *Personal Data:* b Pittsburgh, Pa, Nov 25, 34; m 61; c 2. *Educ:* Waynesburg Col, BS, 56; WVa Univ, MS, 59, PhD(geol), 65. *Prof Exp:* Mem staff solid state physics, Res & Develop Off, USAF, 60-63. *Concurrent Pos:* NSF grant exp diagenesis, WVa Univ, 65-67. *Mem:* AAAS; Geol Soc Am; Am Asn Petrol Geol. *Res:* Geochemistry of coal; acid mine drainage. *Mailing Add:* WVa Geol Survey White Hall Morgantown WV 26506-0001

RENTON, KENNETH WILLIAM, PHARMACOLOGY. *Current Pos:* from asst prof to assoc prof, 77-81, PROF PHARMACOL, 81- , HEAD DEPT, DALHOUSIE UNIV, 88- *Personal Data:* b Galashiels, Scotland, Apr 6, 44; Can citizen; m 66; c 2. *Educ:* Sir George Williams Univ, BSc, 72; McGill Univ, PhD(pharmacol), 75. *Honors & Awards:* Merck Award Pharmacol, 87. *Prof Exp:* Fel pharmacol, Univ Minn, 75-77. *Concurrent Pos:* Can Med Res Coun fel, 75-77, scholar, 77-82. *Mem:* Can Fedn Biol Sci; Am Soc Pharmacol & Exp Therapeut; Can Soc Clin Pharamcol. *Res:* Drug biotransformation by cytochrome P-450; drug metabolism during infectious disease; drug interaction; drug toxicity; marine environ toxicol. *Mailing Add:* Dept Pharmacol Dalhousie Univ Sir Charles Tupper Med Bldg Halifax NS B3H 4H7 Can

RENTZ, DAVID CHARLES, systematic entomology, for more information see previous edition

RENTZEPIS, PETER M, CHEMICAL PHYSICS. *Current Pos:* PROF CHEM, PRESIDENTIAL CHAIR, UNIV CALIF, IRVINE, 86- *Personal Data:* b Kalamata, Greece, Dec 11, 34; US citizen; m 60; c 2. *Educ:* Denison Univ, BS, 58; Syracuse Univ, MS, 60; Cambridge Univ, PhD(phys chem), 63. *Hon Degrees:* PhD, Syracuse Univ, 80; DSc, Carnegie-Mellon Univ, 83, Tech Univ, Greece, 95. *Honors & Awards:* Langmuir Prize in Chem Physics, Am Phys Soc, 73; Peter Debye Award, Am Chem Soc, 79,; A Cressy Morrison Award, NY Acad Sci, 78. *Prof Exp:* Mem tech staff phys chem, Gen Elec Res Labs, 60-61; mem tech staff, Bell Labs, 63-73, head, Phys Chem Dept, 73-86. *Concurrent Pos:* Adj prof, Univ Pa, 69-; exec mem, Comt Phys Chem Div, Am Chem Soc; prof, Yale Univ, 81. *Mem:* Nat Acad Sci; fel Am Phys Soc; fel NY Acad Sci; Royal Soc Chem. *Res:* Lasers; photochemistry; kinetics; picosecond spectroscopy. *Mailing Add:* Dept Chem Univ Calif Irvine CA 92717

RENUART, ADHEMAR WILLIAM, PEDIATRIC NEUROLOGY, NEUROCHEMISTRY. *Current Pos:* ASSOC CLIN PROF NEUROL, UNIV NC, MED CTR, CHAPEL HILL, 76- *Personal Data:* b Miami, Fla, Aug 10, 31; m 52; c 9. *Educ:* Duke Univ, BS, 52, MD, 56. *Prof Exp:* Assoc, Duke Univ, 61-71; from asst prof to assoc prof pediat, Med Ctr, 72-76, assoc clin prof pediat, 72-76. *Concurrent Pos:* Dir res, Murdoch Ctr, 61-76. *Mailing Add:* Rte 1 Box 184A Franklinton NC 27525

RENWICK, J ALAN A, INSECT BEHAVIOR, PHYTOCHEMISTRY. *Current Pos:* res asst, 60-66, from asst chemist to assoc chemist, 66-83, CHEMIST, BOYCE THOMPSON INST, CORNELL UNIV, 83- *Personal Data:* b Dundee, Scotland, May 7, 36; m 83; c 2. *Educ:* Dundee Tech Col, HNC, 60; City Col New York, MA, 64; Univ Gottingen, DF, 70. *Prof Exp:* Lab asst, Scottish Hort Res Inst, 58-60. *Concurrent Pos:* Adj prof entom, Cornell Univ, 87- *Mem:* Am Chem Soc; Entom Soc Am; Int Soc Chem Ecol; Phytochem Soc NAm. *Res:* Chemical factors affecting oviposition and feeding behavior of phytophagous insects; positive stimuli (recognition of suitable host plants) and negative stimuli involved in host selection; plant-insect interactions. *Mailing Add:* Boyce Thompson Inst Cornell Univ Ithaca NY 14853. *Fax:* 607-254-1242; *E-Mail:* jar14@cornell.edu

RENZEMA, THEODORE SAMUEL, experimental solid state physics; deceased, see previous edition for last biography

RENZETTI, ATTILIO D, JR, PULMONARY DISEASES, PHYSIOLOGY. *Current Pos:* chmn Pulmonary Dis Div, 61-87, from assoc prof to prof, 61-90, EMER PROF MED, UNIV UTAH, 90- *Personal Data:* b New York, NY, Nov 11, 20; m 47, Mabel; c Patricia, Laurence, Pamela & David. *Educ:* Columbia Univ, AB, 41, MD, 44. *Prof Exp:* Asst prof indust med, Postgrad Med Sch, NY Univ, 49-51; asst prof med, Sch Med, Univ Utah, 52-53; asst prof, Col Med, State Univ NY Upstate Med Ctr, Syracuse Univ, 53-59, assoc prof, 59-60; assoc prof, Johns Hopkins Univ & Univ Md, 60-61. *Concurrent Pos:* Fel cardio-pulmonary physiol, Bellevue Hosp Chest Serv, 49-51; Nat Heart & Lung Inst grantee, Univ Utah, 61-; mem, Subspecialty Bd Pulmonary Dis, Am Bd Internal Med, 65-72, chmn, 70-72; mem, Epidemiol & Biomet Adv Comt, Nat Heart & Lung Inst, 70-73, mem, Comt Spec Ctr Res, 71; consult, Vet Admin Hosp, Salt Lake City, Utah, 70-85. *Mem:* Am Lung Asn; Am Fedn Clin Res; Am Thoracic Soc (pres-elect, 74-75, pres, 75-76); fel Am Col Physicians; NY Acad Sci; Sigma Xi. *Res:* Pulmonary function in disease; applied respiratory physiology. *Mailing Add:* 1801 London Plane Rd Salt Lake City UT 84124-3531

RENZETTI, NICHOLAS A, PHYSICS. *Current Pos:* sect chief telecommun, 59-63, mgr, Tracking & Data Systs for Planetary Projs, 64, tech mgr, eng, 64-80, PROG MGR, JET PROPULSION LAB, CALIF INST TECHNOL, 80- *Personal Data:* b New York, NY, Sept 30, 14; m 45; c 4. *Educ:* Columbia Univ, AB, 35, AM, 36, PhD(physics), 40. *Honors & Awards:* NASA Outstanding Leadership Medal. *Prof Exp:* Asst physics, Columbia Univ, 37-40, res assoc, 40; physicist, Bur Ord, US Navy, 40-44; sci res administr, Naval Ord Test Sta, Calif, 44-54; sr physicist, Air Pollution Found, Calif, 54-59. *Concurrent Pos:* Consult, US Naval Ord Test Sta, Pasadena, Calif, 54-62, Gen Motors Corp, Mich, 56-59 & Air Pollution Found, 59-61. *Mem:* Sigma Xi. *Res:* Telecommunications science and engineering with space vehicles; air pollution; underwater technology. *Mailing Add:* 1321 Virginia Rd San Marino CA 91108

RENZI, ALFRED ARTHUR, PHYSIOLOGY, ENDOCRINOLOGY. *Current Pos:* RETIRED. *Personal Data:* b Rochester, NY, July 20, 25; m 54; c 5. *Educ:* Fordham Univ, BS, 47; Syracuse Univ, MS, 49, PhD(zool), 52. *Prof Exp:* Asst endocrinol, Syracuse Univ, 47-51; from assoc endocrinologist to sr endocrinologist, Ciba Pharmaceut Co, NJ, 52-60, assoc dir physiol, 60-62, head endocrine-pharmacol sect, 62-67; head, Pharmacol Dept, Dow Human Health Res & Develop Labs, Ind, 67-71, assoc scientist, Dow Chem Co, 71-80, assoc scientist, Med Dept, 80-88, assoc scientist, Toxicol Dept, Merrell Dow Res Inst, 88-90. *Mem:* Am Physiol Soc; Am Soc Pharmacol & Exp Therapeut; Endocrine Soc. *Res:* Steroid hypertension; water metabolism; kidney function; adrenal cortex; inflammation; reproduction; atherosclerosis; lipid metabolism. *Mailing Add:* 40 Staten Pl Zionsville IN 46077-1140

REPA, BRIAN STEPHEN, BIOENGINEERING. *Current Pos:* sr prof engr impaired driver countermeasures, 72-73, proj mgr driver physiol, 73-74, staff res engr driver-vehicle performance, 74-82, prog mgr, safety res, 82-84, ACTIV HEAD, HUMAN FACTORS, PROJ TRILBY, GEN MOTORS RES LABS, 84- *Personal Data:* b Detroit, Mich, Apr 5, 42; m 70; c 3. *Educ:* Univ Mich, Dearborn Campus, BS, 65, Ann Arbor, MS, 66, PhD(bioeng), 72. *Prof Exp:* Co-op & res engr elec eng, Eng & Res Ctr, Ford Motor Co, 62-65; res asst manual-mach syts, Univ Mich, 68-70, lab instr analog comput, 70-71. *Concurrent Pos:* Mem road user characteristics comt, Transp Res Bd, 74-, mem simulation & measurement of driving comt, 75-; mem passenger car safety comt, Soc Automotive Engrs, 75-, mem vehicle dynamics comt, 78- *Mem:* Soc Automotive Engrs. *Res:* Mathematical modeling of the driver-vehicle system; effects of vehicle characteristics on driver-vehicle performance; perceptual cues used by drivers in controlling their vehicles; driving simulators; driver impairment detection. *Mailing Add:* 22868 ShagBark Rd Beverly Hills MI 48025-4770

REPAK, ARTHUR JACK, PROTOZOOLOGY. *Current Pos:* from asst prof to assoc prof, 70-79, PROF BIOL, QUINNIPIAC COL, 79- *Personal Data:* b New York, NY, Mar 19, 40; m 66, Diane Mendelson; c Bonnie & Stefanie. *Educ:* Univ Mich, Ann Arbor, BS, 61; LI Univ, MS, 64; NY Univ, PhD(biol), 67. *Prof Exp:* Dir clin lab, 801st Med Group, Griffiss AFB, Rome, NY, 68-70. *Concurrent Pos:* Consult, Ecol Consults, 70-, Examr fac, Charter Oak Col, 90-93 & Int Bus Mach Corp; Yale-Lilly fel, 77-78; vis fac fel, Yale Univ, 78-82, res assoc, 71-82; mem Comn Water Pollution Control Authority, Cheshire, Conn, 84-; dir, Conn Jr Acad Sci & Eng, 84-; mem bd dirs, Conn Sci Fair Asn, 86-92; northeast regional dir, Sigma Xi, 90-96. *Mem:* Am Micros Soc; Sigma Xi; Soc Protozoologists. *Res:* Taxonomy and morphology of heterotrichous ciliates; encystment and excystment of protozoa; nutritional and physiological studies of marine and freshwater heterotrichous ciliates; studies of the physiology of slugs. *Mailing Add:* Dept Biol Sci Quinnipiac Col Box 185 Hamden CT 06518-0569. *Fax:* 203-281-8706; *E-Mail:* repak@quinnipiac.edu

REPASKE, ROY, MOLECULAR BIOLOGY, MICROBIAL BIOCHEMISTRY. *Current Pos:* chemist, Lab Microbiol, 59-74 & Off Sci Dir, 74-80, CHEMIST, LAB MOLECULAR MICROBIOL, INST ALLERGY & INFECTIOUS DIS, NIH, 80-, ASST LAB CHIEF, 91- *Personal Data:* b Cleveland, Ohio, Mar 17, 25; m 50; c 3. *Educ:* Western Reserve Univ, BS, 48; Univ Mich, MS, 50; Univ Wis, PhD(bact, biochem), 54. *Prof Exp:* Res assoc bact metab, Univ Wis, 53; from instr to assoc prof bact, Ind Univ, 54-59. *Concurrent Pos:* Consult, NASA, 62-65 & Naval Med Res Inst, 90-; chmn gen div, Am Soc Microbiol, 63-64; instr, Found Advan Studies Sci, 66-73; prog dir biochem, NSF, 73-74. *Mem:* Fel AAAS; Am Soc Microbiol; Am Soc Biol Chem; Sigma Xi; Am Soc Virol. *Res:* Molecular biology of retroviruses, recombinant DNA. *Mailing Add:* Nat Inst Allergy & Infectious Dis Bldg 4 Rm 303 NIH Bethesda MD 20892-0001

REPASKY, ELIZABETH ANN, CYTOSKELETAL SYSTEMS, T & B CELLS. *Current Pos:* cancer res scientist II, 83-89, cancer res scientist III, 89-92, CANCER RES SCIENTIST IV, DEPT MOLECULAR IMMUNOL, ROSWELL PARK CANCER INST, 92-; ASSOC PROF, ROSWELL PARK DIV, STATE UNIV NY, BUFFALO, 89-, DIR GRAD STUDIES, 91- *Personal Data:* b Greensburg, Pa, Mar 29, 54; m, John Subjeck; c Joey & Elizabeth. *Educ:* Seton Hill Col, BA, 76; State Univ NY, Buffalo, MS, 77, PhD(anat & cell biol), 81. *Prof Exp:* NIH fel, Calif Inst Technol, 80-82; asst prof, Dept Microbiol & Immunol, State Univ NY, Buffalo, 85-88. *Concurrent Pos:* Prin investr, Muscular Dystrophy Asn, 83-85, NIH, 84-85, 88-93 & Am Cancer Soc, 86-91; adj asst prof, Dept Anat Sci, State Univ NY, Buffalo, 83-; supvr, Electron Micros Facil, Cancer Cell Ctr, Roswell Park Cancer Inst, 86-90. *Mem:* Am Asn Cell Biol; Am Asn Anatomists. *Res:* Plasma membrane structure; membrane/cytoskeletal interactions; differentiation and maturation-related changes associated with the lymphocyte plasma membrane as related to the immune response and the cytoskeleton; membrane lipid organization and the immune response; tumor cell markers and role of integrin receptors in tumor metastasis. *Mailing Add:* Dept Molecular Immunol Roswell Park Cancer Inst Elm & Carlton Sts Buffalo NY 14263-0001. *Fax:* 716-845-8906

REPINE, JOHN E, LUNG, PHAGOCYTE & OXYGEN RADICAL RESEARCH. *Current Pos:* assoc prof med, Sch Med, Univ Colo, 79-83, assoc prof pediat, 81-83, prof med, 83-96, JAMES J WARING ENDOWED PROF, UNIV COLO MED CTR, 96- *Personal Data:* b Rock Island, Ill, Dec, 26, 44; m 69, 88; c 4. *Educ:* Univ Wis-Madison, BS, 67; Univ Minn, Minneapolis, MD, 71. *Honors & Awards:* Bonfils-Stanton Award for Outstanding Contrib Sci Med. *Prof Exp:* From instr to assoc prof internal med, Univ Minn, 74-79; asst dir & div exp med, 79-89, PROF MED & DIR, WEBB-WARING LUNG INST, 89- *Concurrent Pos:* Mem res comt & site vis, Am Lung Asn, NIH; Young Pulmonary investr grant, Nat Heart & Lung Inst, 74-75; Basil O'Connor starter res award, Nat Found March of Dimes, 75-77; estab investr award, Am Heart Asn, 76-81; co-chmn steering comt, Aspen Lung Conf, 80, chmn, 81. *Mem:* AAAS; Am Asn Immunologists; Am Fedn Clin Res; Am Heart Asn; Am Thoracic Soc; Am Soc Clin Invest; Asn Am Physicians. *Res:* Role of phagocytes and oxygen radicals in lung injury and host defense. *Mailing Add:* Webb-Waring Inst Biomed Res Univ Colo Med Ctr 4200 E Ninth Ave Denver CO 80220. *Fax:* 303-315-8541

REPIQUE, ELISEO, CLINICAL CHEMISTRY & TOXICOLOGY. *Current Pos:* CHEMIST, DEPT PATH & LAB MED, CEDARS-SINAI MED CTR, 75- *Personal Data:* b Negros, Occidental, Philippines, 1931. *Educ:* Philippine Union Col, BS, 53, BS, 56; Chicago Med Sch, MS, 73, PhD(clin chem), 74. *Mem:* Am Asn Clin Chem; Nat Acad Clin Biochemists. *Mailing Add:* 4042 Marchena Dr Los Angeles CA 90065

REPJAR, ANDREW G, ELECTRICAL ENGINEERING. *Current Pos:* GROUP LEADER, ANTENNA & MAT METROL, NAT INST STAND & TECHNOL, 75- *Personal Data:* b Nov 14, 41. *Educ:* Ohio State Univ, PhD(elec eng), 70. *Honors & Awards:* Silver Medal, US Dept Com, 89. *Mailing Add:* Antenna Mats & Metrol Group, Nat Inst Stand & Technol 325 Broadway Boulder CO 30303

REPKA, BENJAMIN C, PATENTS, POLYPROPLENE. *Current Pos:* RETIRED. *Personal Data:* b Buffalo, NY, July 5, 27; m 53, Marie Santercole; c Michael X, Mark L, David A & Daniel F. *Educ:* Canisius Col, BS, 49, MS, 52; Purdue Univ, PhD(phys org chem), 57. *Prof Exp:* Chemist, Carborundum Co, 50-53; res chemist, Hercules, Inc, 56-71, sr res chemist, 71-73, res scientist, 73-78, res assoc & proj leader polypropylene, 78-83, mgr patent coord, 83-87, mgr new technol, 87-89. *Concurrent Pos:* Consult polymer processes, Condux, 90- *Mem:* Am Chem Soc; Sigma Xi. *Res:* Polyolefins; organometallics; heterogeneous catalysis; polymerization processes; technology acquisition. *Mailing Add:* 206 N Star Rd Newark DE 19711-2935

REPKO, WAYNE WILLIAM, ELEMENTARY PARTICLE PHYSICS. *Current Pos:* from asst prof to assoc prof, 70-79, PROF THEORET PHYSICS, MICH STATE UNIV, 79- *Personal Data:* b Detroit, Mich, Mar 21, 40; m 66; c 3. *Educ:* Wayne State Univ, BS, 63, PhD(theoret physics), 67. *Prof Exp:* Res assoc theoret physics, Wayne State Univ, 67-68 & Johns Hopkins Univ, 68-70. *Concurrent Pos:* Vis assoc prof, Johns Hopkins Univ, 76- *Mem:* Am Phys Soc. *Res:* Quantum field theory; quantum electrodynamics; elementary particle physics. *Mailing Add:* Dept Physics Mich State Univ East Lansing MI 48823

REPLOGLE, CLYDE R, PHYSIOLOGY, OPERATIONS RESEARCH. *Current Pos:* chief, Environ Med Div, 72-77, Manned Systs Effectiveness Div, 77-79, CHIEF, SPEC PROJ BR, AIR FORCE ARMSTRONG LAB, 79- *Personal Data:* b Detroit, Mich, Nov 13, 35; m 85, Karan Johnson; c Charles R. *Educ:* Mich State Univ, BS, 58, MS, 60, PhD(physiol), 67. *Honors & Awards:* Barchi Prize, 86; Rist Prize, 88. *Prof Exp:* Instr physiol, USAF Inst Technol, 62-64, asst prof bioeng & physiol, 64-68, chief, Environ Physiol Br, 68-72, adj prof bioeng, 68-77. *Concurrent Pos:* Adj prof eng, Air Force Inst Technol, 68-; adj prof biomed sci, Wright State Univ, 79-; fel, Prints Maurits Lab, Hague, Neth. *Res:* Chemical and biological warfare defense analysis; man-machine system, human operator and manned weapon system performance; environmental medicine; all aspects of the impact of chemical and biological warfare environments on Air Force operations; toxic effects of agents and their impact on human performance; casualty analysis; human factor analysis of the impact of protective equipment. *Mailing Add:* 7838 Old Clifton Rd Springfield OH 45502. *E-Mail:* replogle@erinet.com

REPLOGLE, JOHN A(SHER), HYDRAULICS, AGRICULTURAL ENGINEERING. *Current Pos:* res agr engr, USDA, 63-66, res hydraul engr, 66-75, res leader, Water Conserv Lab, 75-90, RES HYDRAUL ENGR & LEAD SCIENTIST IRRIG & WATER QUAL RES, AGR RES SERV, USDA, 90- *Personal Data:* b Charleston, Ill, Jan 13, 34; m 57, Louisa R Roudebush; c Neal K & Brent J. *Educ:* Univ Ill, BS, 56, MS, 58, PhD(civil eng), 64. *Honors & Awards:* James R Croes Medal, Am Soc Civil Engrs, 77; Award Excellence Technol Transfer, Fed Lab Consortium, 91; Hancor Award, Am Soc Agr Engrs, 92. *Prof Exp:* Agr engr, Soil Conserv Serv, USDA, 56; res asst agr eng, Univ Ill, 56-58, instr, 58-63. *Concurrent Pos:* Consult, USAID, India, 82, 83, 86 & 92 Bangladesh, 85 & 87; chmn, Irrig & Drainage Div, Am Soc Civil Engrs, 88-89; news corresp, 91-; consult, UN, 93. *Mem:* AAAS; Am Soc Agr Engrs; Am Soc Civil Engrs. *Res:* Agricultural land drainage, irrigation and hydrology; fluid mechanics; hydraulic structures; water resources planning and development; flow measurement; basic physical science; irrigation hydraulics; irrigation-distribution system operations. *Mailing Add:* US Water Conserv Lab 4331 E Broadway Phoenix AZ 85040. *Fax:* 602-379-4355; *E-Mail:* jreplogl@uswcl.ars.ag.gov

REPLOGLE, LANNY LEE, ORGANIC CHEMISTRY. *Current Pos:* from asst prof to assoc prof, 61-69, PROF CHEM, CALIF STATE UNIV, SAN JOSE, 69- *Personal Data:* b San Bernardino, Calif, Oct 30, 34; m 58; c 2. *Educ:* Univ Calif, Berkeley, BS, 56; Univ Wash, PhD(org chem), 60. *Prof Exp:* Res instr chem, Univ Wash, 60-61. *Concurrent Pos:* NSF grants, San Jose State Col, 62-69; Nat Res Coun sr res associateship, Ames Res Ctr, NASA, 70-71; consult, Paul Masson Vineyards. *Mem:* Am Chem Soc. *Res:* Chemistry of azulene and its derivatives; nonbenzenoid aromatics; heterocyclic analogs of nonbenzenoid aromatic hydrocarbons; wine chemistry. *Mailing Add:* 2954 Kildare Rd Sunol CA 94586-9428

REPLOGLE, ROBERT LEE, CARDIOVASCULAR SURGERY, THORACIC SURGERY. *Current Pos:* CHIEF CARDIAC SURG, MICHAEL REESE HOSP, 79-; CHIEF CARDIAC SURG, COLUMBIA HOSP, 86-; CHIEF CARDIAC SURG, INGALLS HOSP, 89- *Personal Data:* b Ottumwa, Iowa, Sept 30, 31; m 58; c 3. *Educ:* Cornell Col, BS, 56; Harvard Med Sch, MD, 60. *Hon Degrees:* DSc, Cornell Col, 72. *Prof Exp:* Asst resident surg, Peter Bent Brigham Hosp, Boston, Mass, 61-63; res fels, Children's Hosp Med Ctr, Boston & Harvard Med Sch, 63-64; sr resident, Children's Hosp Med Ctr, Boston, 64-65; asst resident, Mass Gen Hosp, Boston, 65-66; sr resident, Children's Hosp Med Ctr, 66, asst, 66-67; asst prof surg, Pritzker Sch Med, Univ Chicago, 67-70, assoc prof surg & chief pediat surg, 70-74, prof surg & chief cardiac surg, 74-79. *Concurrent Pos:* Asst surg, Harvard Med Sch, 66-67; dir cardiac surg, Michael Reese Hosp & Med Ctr, 77- *Mem:* Soc Univ Surg; Am Asn Thoracic Surg; Int Soc Surg; Am Surg Asn. *Res:* Cardiovascular physiology; rheology. *Mailing Add:* 1160 E 56th Chicago IL 60637-1541

REPORTER, MINOCHER C, DEVELOPMENTAL BIOLOGY, MOLECULAR BIOLOGY. *Current Pos:* PROF, DEPT BOT & PLANT PATH, ORE STATE UNIV, 89- *Personal Data:* b Bombay, India, Feb 8, 28; US citizen; m 52, Cleo; c 3. *Educ:* Johns Hopkins Univ, AB, 52; Mass Inst Technol, PhD(food technol), 59. *Prof Exp:* Res asst, Develop Dept, A D Witten Co, Mass, 59; res asst nutrit, Mass Inst Technol, 59; res fel, Geront Br, Nat Heart Inst, 59-62; asst investr develop biol, Dept Embryol, Carnegie Inst, 62-65; staff scientist, Battelle-Charles F Kettering Res Lab, 65-68, investr, 68-86; vis prof, Bot Dept, Miami Univ, Oxford, Ohio, 87-89. *Concurrent Pos:* Adj assoc prof, Antioch Col, 68- & Wright State Univ, 79-; mem, Mantech Environ Serv, Environ Res Lab, US Environ Protection Agency, 89-90; affil, Ecol Planning & Toxicol Inc, 91- *Mem:* AAAS; Am Soc Microbiol; Am Soc Biol Chemists; Am Soc Cell Biol; Am Soc Plant Physiol; Biophys Soc. *Res:* Nitrogen fixation and control of energy supply; differentiation and cellular development; cell physiology; nitrogen fixation in culture; secondary metabolites from cultured cells; new tests for assessment of rhizophere ecology using plants, plant cell cultures and bacteria. *Mailing Add:* 1005 NW Alder Creek Dr Corvallis OR 97330. *Fax:* 541-737-3573; *E-Mail:* reportem@bcc.orst.edu

REPPER, CHARLES JOHN, SOLID STATE PHYSICS. *Current Pos:* LEAD PROJ ENGR, GEN ELEC CO, 72- *Personal Data:* b Philadelphia, Pa, Nov 1, 34. *Educ:* St Joseph's Univ, Pa, BS, 56; Drexel Univ, MS, 65. *Prof Exp:* Physicist, Res Lab, 56-64 & Appl Res Lab, 64-66, res scientist & proj engr, Phys Electronics Dept, Philco Corp, 66-72. *Mem:* Am Phys Soc. *Res:* Photoconductivity; electroluminescent gallium arsenide P-N junctions; thin film metal-oxide structures; solid state photo detectors; metallurgy and measurements of the electrical and optical properties of semiconductors; environmental effects on solid state devices and electro-optical sensors. *Mailing Add:* 7324 N 20th St Philadelphia PA 19138

REPPERGER, DANIEL WILLIAM, ELECTRICAL ENGINEERING, MATHEMATICS. *Current Pos:* Nat Res Coun appointment eng control theory, Aerospace Med Res Lab, Wright Patterson AFB, 73-74, systs analyst elec eng, Systs Res Lab, 74-75, systs analyst elec eng, Aerospace Med Res Lab, 75-94, RES ELEC ENGR, ARMSTRONG LAB, WRIGHT PATTERSON AFB, 94- *Personal Data:* b Charleston, SC, Nov 24, 42; m 68, 88, Frances Sullivan; c Lisa (Cornwell) & Dan III. *Educ:* Rensselaer Polytech Inst, BSEE, 67, MSEE, 68; Purdue Univ, PhD(elec eng), 73, PE, 75. *Honors & Awards:* H Schuck Award, 78; Armstrong Award, 80; F Russ Biomed Award, 89; Affil Coun Award, 92. *Prof Exp:* Res asst elec eng, Rensselaer Polytech Inst, 67-68; teaching instr, Purdue Univ, 68-71, David Ross res fel, 71-73. *Concurrent Pos:* Reviewer tech papers, Inst Elec & Electronics Engrs Trans Automatic Control, 72-, Inst Elec & Electronics Engrs Trans Systs, Man & Cybernet, 74- & Human Factors, 77-; adj prof, Sch Elec Eng, Wright State Univ, 83-; assoc ed, Inst Elec & Electronics Engrs Trans Control Syst Technol; assoc ed, J Intelligent & Fuzzy Systs. *Mem:* Fel Inst Elec & Electronics Engrs; Nat Soc Prof Engrs; Sigma Xi. *Res:* Modern control systems theory; modeling; identification; man-machine systems; numerical algorithms; applications and theoretical aspects of optimal control and estimation theory; human factors engineering; holder of eight patents and 17 Air Force Inventions. *Mailing Add:* 833 Blossom Heath Rd Dayton OH 45419-1102. *Fax:* 937-255-9687

REPPERT, STEVE MARION, CIRCADIAN RHYTHM RESEARCH. *Current Pos:* ASSOC PEDIAT, MASS GEN HOSP, 85- *Personal Data:* b Sioux City, Iowa, Sept 4, 46; m 68, Mary Alice Herman; c 3. *Educ:* Univ Nebr, Omaha, BS, 73, MD, 73. *Hon Degrees:* MA, Harvard Univ, 93. *Honors & Awards:* E Mead Johnson Award for Outstanding Res in Pediat, 89; NIH-NICHD Merit Award, 92. *Prof Exp:* Pediat resident, Mass Gen Hosp, 73-76; clin fel , Harvard Med Sch, 73-76; clin assoc, NIH, 76-79; from instr to prof, Harvard Med Sch, 79-93. *Concurrent Pos:* Res fel, Charles King Trust, Boston, 81-83; prin investr, NIH grants, 81, March Dimes grants 81-88 & estab investr, Am Heart Asn, 85-90; dir, Lab Develop Chronobiol, Mass Gen Hosp, 83. *Mem:* Am Heart Asn; Am Physiol Soc; Am Soc Clin Invest; Endocrine Soc; Soc Neurosci; Soc Pediat Res. *Res:* Neurobiology; circadian rhythms. *Mailing Add:* Chronobiol Lab Harvard Univ Mass Gen Hosp Childrens Serv Boston MA 02114

REPPOND, KERMIT DALE, FOOD TECHNOLOGY, SEAFOOD. *Current Pos:* CHEMIST, KODIAK LAB, NAT MARINE FISHERY SERV, 76- *Personal Data:* b Farmerville, La, Oct 31, 45; m, Sharon Vollmer; c Matthew. *Educ:* Northeast La Univ, BS, 67. *Res:* Development of methods to enhance utilization of various seafood for human consumption. *Mailing Add:* Kodiak Nat Marine Fishery Serv 900 Trident Way Kodiak AK 99615-7401

REPPUCCI, NICHOLAS DICKON, PSYCHOLOGY. *Current Pos:* PROF PSYCHOL, UNIV VA, 76- *Personal Data:* b Boston, Mass, May 1, 41; m 67; c 3. *Educ:* Univ NC, Chapel Hill, BA, 62; Harvard Univ, MA, 64, PhD(clin psychol), 68. *Honors & Awards:* G Stanley Hall lectr, Am Psychol Asn, 84. *Prof Exp:* Lectr & res assoc psychol, Harvard Univ, 67-68; from asst prof to assoc prof psychol, Yale Univ, 68-76. *Concurrent Pos:* Dir community psychol, Psychol Dept, Univ Va, 76-, dir grad studies, 86-, consult, Inst Law, Psychiat & Pub Policy, 78-; chair, Taskforce Psychol & Pub Policy, Am Psychol Assoc, 80-84; mem, Internal Review Comts, NIMH, 80-83 & 87-89; dir Yale Psychol Educ Clin, Yale Univ, 70-73, dir clin psychol, dept psychol, 69-70; dir clin psychol, dept psychol, Univ Va, 76-80; assoc ed, Law & Human Behav, 88-; scholar award psychol, Va Soc Sci Asn, 91. *Mem:* Fel Am Psychol Asn (pres, div 27 community psychol, 86). *Res:* Research children's competencies, child sexual abuse, juvenile delinquency, custody and other psycho-legal issues of children and families; preventive interventions relating to changing human service organizations. *Mailing Add:* Dept Psychol Univ Va 102 Gilmer Hall Charlottesville VA 22903

REPPY, JOHN DAVID, PHYSICS. *Current Pos:* from assoc prof to prof physics, 66-87, JOHN L WETHERILL PROF PHYSICS, CORNELL UNIV, 87- *Personal Data:* b Lakewood, NJ, Feb 16, 31; m 59, Judith Voris; c 3. *Educ:* Univ Conn, BA, 54, MS, 56; Yale Univ, PhD(physics), 61. *Honors & Awards:* Fritz London Award, 81. *Prof Exp:* NSF fel physics, Oxford Univ, 61-62; asst prof, Yale Univ, 62-66. *Concurrent Pos:* Guggenheim fel, 72-73; Fulbright-Hays fel, 78; Guggenheim fel & Sci Res Coun sr res fel, 79-80. *Mem:* Fel Nat Acad Sci; Fel Am Phys Soc; fel AAAS; fel NY Acad Sci. *Res:* Macroscopic quantum properties of superconductors and superfluid helium; cooperative phenomena. *Mailing Add:* Dept Physics Cornell Univ Clark Hall Ithaca NY 14853. *Fax:* 607-255-6428

REQUA, JOSEPH EARL, OPERATING SYSTEMS & NETWORK SOFTWARE, MANAGEMENT OF SOFTWARE DEVELOPMENT. *Current Pos:* Programmer, Lawrence Livermore Nat Lab, 65-81, researcher, 81-83, group leader, Comput Dept, 83-86, USER SYSTS DIV LEADER, LAWRENCE LIVERMORE NAT LAB, 86-, SR STAFF MEM, LIVERMORE COMPUT CTR, 91- *Personal Data:* b Willits, Calif, Oct 17, 38; m 63, Joyce Mainzer; c Gail. *Educ:* Univ Calif, Berkeley, BS, 61, MA, 63; Univ Ill, Urbana, MS, 65. *Res:* Advancement in the state of the art of distributed supercomputer networking technology; architecture; protocols; creating systems; graphic user interfaces; scientific visualization. *Mailing Add:* 563 Brookfield Dr Livermore CA 94550. *Fax:* 510-423-8715; *E-Mail:* jrequa@llnl.gov

REQUARTH, WILLIAM H, SURGERY. *Current Pos:* asst prof, 47-66, prof, 66-86, EMER CLIN PROF SURG, UNIV ILL COL MED, 86- *Personal Data:* b Charlotte, NC, Jan 23, 13; m 77, Connie Harper; c Kurt, Betsy, Jeff, Jay, Tim & Suzanna. *Educ:* James Milliken Univ, BS, 34; Univ Ill, MD, 39, MSc, 40; Am Bd Surg, dipl, 47. *Prof Exp:* Intern, St Luke's Hosp, Chicago, 38-39; residency surg, Cook County Hosp, 39-46. *Concurrent Pos:* Mem attend staff, Macon County Hosp, St Mary's Hosp, Decatur, Ill & Ill Res Hosp. *Mem:* Am Soc Surg Hand; Am Asn Surg Trauma; fel Am Col Surgeons; Soc Surg Alimentary Tract; Cent Surg Asn; Western Surg Asn. *Res:* General surgery; surgery of the hand. *Mailing Add:* 158 W Prairie Ave Decatur IL 62523

REQUE, PAUL GERHARD, MEDICINE. *Current Pos:* ASSOC DIR DERMAT & SYPHIL, LLOYD NOLAND FOUND HOSP, 47- *Personal Data:* b New York, NY, May 28, 07; m 36; c 2. *Educ:* Duke Univ, MD, 34. *Prof Exp:* Assoc dermat & instr internal med, Sch Med, Duke Univ, 40-46; assoc prof dermat, Sch Med, Univ Ala, Birmingham, 46-81. *Concurrent Pos:* Lectr, Univ NC, 40-42; consult, Vet Admin Hosp, 46-52. *Mem:* Soc Invest Dermat; Am Acad Dermat; Nat Asn Chain Drug Stores; AMA. *Res:* Borate absorption through the dermis and mucous membranes; chromatography; drug idiosyncrasy; antibody-antigen reactions; systemic sclerosis. *Mailing Add:* 3850 Galleria Woods Dr Birmingham AL 35244

REQUICHA, ARISTIDES A G, COMPUTER AIDED DESIGN & MANUFACTURING, GEOMETRIC MODELING. *Current Pos:* PROF COMPUT SCI & ELEC ENG, UNIV SOUTHERN CALIF, 86- *Personal Data:* b Monte Estoril, Port, Mar 18, 39; m 70, Shahin A Hakim. *Educ:* Univ Lisbon, EE, 62; Univ Rochester, PhD(elec eng), 70. *Prof Exp:* Lectr physics, Univ Lisbon, 61-63; res scientist, Saclant Res Ctr, NATO, 70-73; res assoc, Univ Rochester, 73-75, sr scientist & assoc dir, Prod Automation Proj, 75-85, dir, 85-86, assoc prof elec eng, 83-86. *Concurrent Pos:* Assoc ed, Asn Comput Mach Trans Graphics, 84-90; area ed, Graphic Models & Image Processing, 89- *Mem:* Inst Elec & Electronics Engrs; Asn Comput Mach; AAAS; Am Asn Artificial Intel; Soc Mfg Engrs; Sigma Xi. *Res:* Programmable automation; computer aided design and manufacturing for electromechanical products; artificial intelligence and computational geometry; spatial reasoning; geometric uncertainty; automatic planning for manufacturing and inspection; object-oriented geometric computation; molecular robotics and nanotechnology. *Mailing Add:* Comput Sci Dept Univ Southern Calif Los Angeles CA 90089-0781. *E-Mail:* requicha@lipari.usc.edu

RERICK, MARK NEWTON, ORGANIC CHEMISTRY, SYSTEMS ANALYSIS. *Current Pos:* from asst prof to assoc prof, 60-68, PROF ORG CHEM, PROVIDENCE COL, 69-, CHMN, DEPT CHEM, 80- *Personal Data:* b Syracuse, NY, Jan 31, 34; m 56, Kay Murray; c Mark D, Cheryl M, Debra A, Kirk A & Paul M. *Educ:* Le Moyne Col, BS, 55; Univ Notre Dame, PhD(chem), 59. *Prof Exp:* Res assoc, Univ Notre Dame, 58-59; res fel, Calif Inst Technol, 59-60. *Mem:* AAAS; Am Chem Soc. *Res:* Reductions of organic compounds with complex and mixed metal hydrides; conformational analysis of mobile cyclohexane systems; systems analysis of complex systems. *Mailing Add:* 181 Angell Ave Cranston RI 02920

RESAU, JAMES HOWARD, CONFOCAL LASER SCAN MICROSCOPY, TISSUE CULTURE. *Current Pos:* res scientist & assoc, 74-75, assoc prof & tenure, 85-92, STAFF SCIENTIST, DEPT PATH, SCH MED, UNIV MD, 92- *Personal Data:* b Baltimore, Md, May 19, 46; m 70; c 2. *Educ:* Western Md Col, BA, 68; Johns Hopkins Univ, cert cytopath, 73; Univ Md, MS, 78, PhD(path), 85. *Prof Exp:* Cytotechnologist assoc, Johns Hopkins Univ, 72-74. *Mem:* Am Soc Cell Biol; Tissue Cult Asn; Am Soc Micros. *Res:* Confocal laser scanning analysis of oncogene products and ligands as they relate to structure function effects in human and other mammalian cells, tissues, and organs with emphasis on carcinogenesis, development, injury and growth mechanisms. *Mailing Add:* ABL-BRP bldg 538 Nat Cancer Inst-FCRDC Univ Md PO Box B Frederick MD 21702-1201

RESCH, GEORGE MICHAEL, PHYSICS, ASTRONOMY. *Current Pos:* CONSULT, 90- *Personal Data:* b Baltimore, Md, Mar 26, 40; m 63; c 1. *Educ:* Univ Md, BS, 63; Fla State Univ, MS, 65, PhD(physics), 74. *Prof Exp:* Res asst physics, Fla State Univ, 63-68; res assoc astron, Clark Lake Radio Observ, 68-71; res asst astron, Univ Md, 71-74; mem tech staff, Jet Propulsion Lab, 74-83, prog mgr, 83-90. *Mem:* Am Inst Physics; Am Astron Soc; Am Geophys Union. *Res:* Instrumentation development and measurement systems with application to geodesy and astronomy. *Mailing Add:* Jet Propulsion Lab M-S 238-700 4800 Oak Grove Dr Pasadena CA 91109. *E-Mail:* gmr@logos.jpl.nasa.gov

RESCH, HELMUTH, FOREST PRODUCTS. *Current Pos:* PROF, UNIV BODENKULTUR, VIENNA, 92- *Personal Data:* b Vienna, Austria, May 22, 33; m 60; c 2. *Educ:* Agr Univ, Vienna, dipl eng, 56; Utah State Univ, MS, 57, PhD(wood technol), 60. *Prof Exp:* Res asst, Utah State Univ, 56-57, US Forest Serv, 57 & J Neils Lumber Co, 58; asst, Agr Univ, Vienna, 58-60; asst & assoc prof wood technol, Univ Calif, Berkeley, 62-70; prof & head dept, Forest Prod Dept, Ore State Univ, Sch Forestry, 70-87, consult, 87-92. *Concurrent Pos:* Dir, Austrian Forest Prod Lab, 92-96. *Mem:* Soc Wood Sci & Technol (pres, 80-81); Forest Prod Res Soc; Int Acad Wood Sci. *Res:* Physical properties of wood, processing of timber into lumber, plywood and other manufactured products. *Mailing Add:* Univ Bodenkultur Gregor Mendelstr 33 Vienna A-1180 Austria. *Fax:* 43-1-79826-2350

RESCH, JOSEPH ANTHONY, NEUROLOGY. *Current Pos:* from assoc prof to prof neurol, Univ Minn, 62-84, asst vpres health sci affairs, 70-77, head dept, 77-82, EMER PROF NEUROL, UNIV MINN, MINNEAPOLIS, 84- *Personal Data:* b Milwaukee, Wis, Apr 29, 14; m 39, Rose Catherine Ritz; c Rose, Frank & Catherine. *Educ:* Univ Wis, BS, 36, MD, 38; Am Bd Psychiat & Neurol, dipl, 49. *Prof Exp:* Rockefeller fel neurol, Univ Minn, 46-48; pvt pract, 48-62. *Mem:* Fel Am Acad Neurol; Am Asn Neuropath; Am Electroencephalog Soc; Am Neurol Asn. *Res:* Cerebrovascular disease; geographic pathology. *Mailing Add:* 900 River Beach Rd The Sea Ranch CA 95497

RESCHER, NICHOLAS, PHILOSOPHY OF SCIENCE, COGNITIVE THEORY. *Current Pos:* prof, 61-70, UNIV PROF PHILOS, UNIV PITTSBURGH, 70- *Personal Data:* b Hagen, Ger, July 15, 28; nat US; m 68, Dorothy Henle; c Mark, Owen, Catherine & Elizabeth. *Educ:* Queens Col NY, BS, 49; Princeton Univ, PhD(philos), 51. *Hon Degrees:* LHD, Loyola Univ, 70, Lehigh Univ, 73; Dr, Univ Cordoba, 93, Univ Konstanz, 94. *Honors & Awards:* Alexander von Humboldt Prize, 83. *Prof Exp:* Instr philos, Princeton Univ, 51-52; res mathematician, Rand Corp, 54-57; assoc prof philos, Lehigh Univ, 57-61. *Concurrent Pos:* Ford Found fel, 59; Guggenheim fel, 70-71; ed-in-chief, Am Philos Quart, 64-94; secy gen, Int Union Hist & Philos Sci, 69-75; hon mem, Corpus Christi Col, Oxford, 78-; pres, Eastern Div, Am Philos Asn, 89-90. *Mem:* Am Philos Asn; Philos Sci Soc. *Res:* Philosophy of science. *Mailing Add:* Dept Philos Univ Pittsburgh Pittsburgh PA 15260

RESCIGNO, ALDO, MATHEMATICAL BIOLOGY, PHARMACOKINETICS. *Current Pos:* ADJ PROF, COL PHARM, UNIV MINN, MINNEAPOLIS, 93- *Personal Data:* b Milan, Italy, Aug 27, 24; US citizen; m 50, Luisa Frisia; c Federico Gauss. *Educ:* Univ Milan, Laurea in Physics, 48. *Prof Exp:* Res asst med physics, Tumor Ctr, Italy, 49-52; asst phys chem, Bracco Indust Chim, 52-55; tech dir nuclear instrumentation, Metalnova SpA, 55-59 & DISI, 59-61; res asst biophys, Donner Lab, Univ Calif, Berkeley, 61-62, lectr med physics, 62-63, asst prof, 63-64; fel phys biochem, Australian Nat Univ, 65-69; assoc prof physiol, Univ Minn, Minneapolis, 69-75; mathematician, Lab Theoret Biol, Nat Cancer Inst, NIH, 75-77; prof physiol, Univ Minn, Minneapolis, 77-79; prof biomath, Univ Witwatersrand, Johannesburg, 80-81; res prin, Sch Med, Yale Univ, New Haven, 82-87; prof pharmacokinetics, Univ Ancona, Italy, 87-88; prof pharmacokinetics, Univ Parma, Italy, 88-93. *Concurrent Pos:* Vis prof, LADSEB, Ctr Nuclear Res, Padova, Italy, 75; Kiiliam Scholar, Univ Calgary, 79; vis scientist, Genentech Inc, San Francisco, 90-93; adj prof, Col Pharm, Univ Minn, 93- *Mem:* Soc Gen Systs Res; Brit Inst Physics; Soc Math Biol; Soc Pharmacokinetics & Biopharmaceut; Am Asn Pharmaceut Scientists. *Res:* Mathematical models of biological system; theory of compartments; drug and tracer kinetics; general system theory; deterministic population dynamics. *Mailing Add:* 14764 Square Lake Trail Stillwater MN 55082-9278. *Fax:* 612-430-9739; *E-Mail:* resci001@maroon.tc.umn.edu

RESCIGNO, THOMAS NICOLA, CHEMICAL PHYSICS. *Current Pos:* staff scientist, 75-79, group leader, 79-85, SR SCIENTIST, LAWRENCE LIVERMORE NAT LAB, 85- *Personal Data:* b New York, NY, Sept 10, 47; m 86, Erie A Mills. *Educ:* Columbia Col, BA, 69; Harvard Univ, MA, 71, PhD(chem physics), 73. *Honors & Awards:* Am Inst Chemists Medal. *Prof Exp:* Res fel, Calif Inst Technol, 73-75. *Concurrent Pos:* Vis scientist, Los Alamos Nat Lab, 87, 91 & 93; guest prin investr, Lawrence Berkeley Nat Lab, 96- *Mem:* Fel Am Phys Soc; Am Chem Soc. *Res:* Theoretical atomic and molecular physics-low energy electron scattering; atomic and molecular photoabsorption; electronic structure of atoms and molecules; manybody theory. *Mailing Add:* Lawrence Livermore Nat Lab PO Box 808 Livermore CA 94550. *Fax:* 510-424-4320; *E-Mail:* tnr@llnl.gov

RESCONICH, EMIL CARL, PLANT VIROLOGY. *Current Pos:* assoc prof, 62-72, chmn dept, 62-72, PROF BIOL, ST FRANCIS COL, PA, 72- *Personal Data:* b Portage, Pa, Oct 17, 23. *Educ:* St Francis Col, Pa, BA, 54; Univ Notre Dame, PhD(biol), 59. *Prof Exp:* NSF fel, Univ Calif, Berkeley, 59-60; asst prof biol, Col Steubenville, 60-62. *Mem:* AAAS; Am Soc Plant Physiol; Bot Soc Am; Am Phytopath Soc; Sigma Xi. *Res:* Physiology of plant virus infection; cell physiology; plant virology. *Mailing Add:* Dept Biol St Francis Col Loretto PA 15940

RESCONICH, SAMUEL, ORGANIC CHEMISTRY. *Current Pos:* From asst prof to assoc prof, 60-70, PROF CHEM, ST FRANCIS COL, PA, 70- *Personal Data:* b Portage, Pa, July 31,33. *Educ:* St Francis Col, Pa, BS, 54; Purdue Univ, PhD(org chem), 61. *Mem:* Am Chem Soc; Sigma Xi; Am Asn Univ Professors. *Res:* Organometallic compounds; organic synthesis of fluorine containing compounds. *Mailing Add:* 1319 Gillespie Ave Portage PA 15946-1529

RESCORLA, ROBERT A, EXPERIMENTAL PSYCHOLOGY. *Current Pos:* chmn dept, 85-88, PROF PSYCHOL, UNIV PA, 81-, JAMES SKINNER PROF SCI, 86-, DEAN, COL ARTS & SCI. *Personal Data:* b Pittsburgh, Pa, May 9, 40; m 92, Shirley Steele; c Eric & Michael. *Educ:* Swarthmore Col, BA, 62; Univ Pa, PhD(psychol), 66. *Hon Degrees:* MA, Yale Univ, 75. *Honors & Awards:* Distinguished Sci Contrib Award, Am Psychol Asn, 86; Warren Medal, Soc Exp Psychologists, 91. *Prof Exp:* From asst prof to prof psychol, Yale Univ, 66-81. *Mem:* Nat Acad Sci; Am Psychol Asn; Psychonomic Soc; Soc Exp Psychologists; AAAS; Am Psychol Soc. *Res:* Elementary learning processes in non-human animals, especially Pavlovian conditioning and instrumental learning. *Mailing Add:* Dept Psychol Univ Pa Philadelphia PA 19104

RESH, VINCENT HARRY, AQUATIC ECOLOGY, WETLAND ECOLOGY. *Current Pos:* from asst prof to assoc prof, 75-84, PROF ENTOM, UNIV CALIF, BERKELEY, 84- *Personal Data:* b Jonathan. *Educ:* Georgetown Univ, BS, 67; Niagara Univ, MS, 69; Univ Louisville, PhD(biol & water resources), 73. *Prof Exp:* Asst prof biol, Ball State Univ, 73-75. *Concurrent Pos:* Ed, Ann Rev Entom, 76-; scholar in residence, Rockefeller Found, Bellabio, Italy, 82; Lady Davis vis prof, Hebrew Univ, Jerusalem, 90; fel, Nat Sci Res Ctr, Lyon, France, 92. *Mem:* NAm Benthological Soc; Entom Soc Am; Int Asn Ecol; Sigma Xi; Int Soc Theoret & Appl Limnol. *Res:* Biological assessment of water quality, life history studies of aquatic insects, management of wetland habitats, ecology of springs and development of ecological theory. *Mailing Add:* Dept Environ Sci Policy & Mgt Univ Calif Berkeley CA 94720

RESHKIN, MARK, GEOMORPHOLOGY, GENERAL ENVIRONMENTAL SCIENCES. *Current Pos:* from asst prof to assoc prof geol, Ind Univ Northwest, 64-71, chmn dept, 68-71, dir div pub & environ affairs, 72-75, assoc prof, 71-77, PROF PUB & ENVIRON AFFAIRS, IND UNIV NORTHWEST, 71-, PROF GEOL, 77-, ASST VICE CHANCELLOR ACAD AFFAIRS, 89- *Personal Data:* b East Orange, NJ, May 31, 33; m 61; c 2. *Educ:* Rutgers Univ, AB, 55; Ind Univ, MA, 58, PhD(geol), 63. *Prof Exp:* Instr geol, Univ Maine, 63-64. *Concurrent Pos:* Sr scientist, Nat Park Serv, 80-82. *Mem:* AAAS; Geol Soc Am; Glaciol Soc; Am Quaternary Asn; Am Pub Admin. *Res:* Geomorphology of northern Rocky Mountains; geomorphology and glacial geology of northern Indiana; environmental geology of northwest Indiana; environmental management; research administration. *Mailing Add:* Dept Geosci Ind Univ Northwest 3400 Broadway Gary IN 46408-1197

RESHOTKO, ELI, AEROSPACE SCIENCES. *Current Pos:* from assoc prof to prof eng, Case Western Res Univ, 64-88, head, Div Fluid Thermal & Aerospace Sci, 70-76, chmn, Dept Mech & Aerospace Eng, 76-79, KENT H SMITH PROF ENG, CASE WESTERN RES UNIV, 88- *Personal Data:* b New York, NY, Nov 18, 30; m 53, Adina Venit; c Deborah, Naomi & Miriam R. *Educ:* Cooper Union, BME, 50; Cornell Univ, MME, 51; Calif Inst Technol, PhD(aeronaut, physics), 60. *Honors & Awards:* Fluid & Plasmadynamics Award, Am Inst Aeronaut & Astronaut, 80 & Dryden Lectureship Res, 94. *Prof Exp:* Aeronaut res scientist, Lewis Lab, Nat Adv Comt Aeronaut, 51-55, head, Fluid Mech Sect, 56-57, head high temperature plasma sect, Lewis Res Ctr, NASA, 60-61, chief, Plasma Physics Br, 61-64. *Concurrent Pos:* Mem res adv comt fluid mech, NASA, 61-64, aeronaut adv comt, 80-87 & chmn, adv subcomt aerodyn, 83-85; mem, Plasma Physics Panel, Physics Study Comt, Nat Acad Sci, 64; Susman vis prof, Israel Inst Technol, 69-70; chmn, US Boundary Layer Transition Study Group, 70-; consult, Arvin/Calspan, Dynamics Technol Inc, Boeing Co, United Technol Res Ctr; US mem, Fluid Dynamics Panel, Adv Group Aerospace Res & Develop, NATO, 81-88; chmn steering comt, Case/NASA-Lewis Inst Computational Mech Propulsion, 85-92; dean, Case Inst Technol, 86-87; mem, Ohio Sci & Eng Roundtable, 91-; mem Univ Space Res Asn/NASA Inst Comput Applns Sci & Eng Sci Coun, 92-95. *Mem:* Nat Acad Eng; fel Am Acad Mech (pres, 86-87); fel Am Soc Mech Engrs; fel Am Inst Aeronaut & Astronaut; fel Am Phys Soc; fel AAAS. *Res:* Boundary layer theory and transition; aerodynamic heating; hydrodynamic stability; magnetohydrodynamics; advanced propulsion and power generation. *Mailing Add:* Case Sch Eng Case Western Res Univ Cleveland OH 44106-7222. *Fax:* 216-368-6445; *E-Mail:* exr3@po.cwru.edu

RESKO, JOHN A, REPRODUCTIVE PHYSIOLOGY. *Current Pos:* from asst prof to assoc prof, 65-77, PROF PHYSIOL, ORE HEALTH SCI UNIV, 77-, CHMN DEPT, 81-; SCIENTIST REPRODUCTIVE PHYSIOL, ORE REGIONAL PRIMATE RES CTR, 71- *Personal Data:* b Patton, Pa, Oct 28, 32; m 62, Magdalen Redmond; c Rebecce E (Welch) & John T. *Educ:* St Charles Sem, AB, 56; Marquette Univ, MS, 60; Univ Ill, PhD(animal sci), 63. *Prof Exp:* USPHS fel steroid biochem, Col Med, Univ Utah, 63-64; asst scientist reproductive physiol, Ore Regional Primate Res Ctr, 64-77. *Concurrent Pos:* Mem, Reproductive Biol Study Sect, 81-85; chmn, Endocrine & Metar Sect, Am Physiol Soc, 91-92. *Mem:* AAAS; Soc Study Reproduction (pres, 88-89); Am Physiol Soc; Endocrine Soc; Soc Neurosci. *Res:* Fetal endocrinology; influence of hormones on behavior; regulation of brain aromatase activity. *Mailing Add:* Dept Physiol & Pharmacol Ore Health Sci Univ Portland OR 97201-3098. *Fax:* 503-494-4352; *E-Mail:* reskj@ohsu.edu

RESLER, E(DWIN) L(OUIS), JR, AERONAUTICAL ENGINEERING. *Current Pos:* assoc prof aerospace & elec eng & appl physics, 56-68, dir grad sch Aerospace Eng, 63-72, PROF AEROSPACE & ELEC ENG & APPL PHYSICS, CORNELL UNIV, 58-, JOSEPH NEWTON PEW, JR PROF ENG, 68- *Personal Data:* b Pittsburgh, Pa, Nov 20, 25; m 48; c 5. *Educ:* Univ Notre Dame, BS, 47; Cornell Univ, PhD(aeronaut eng), 51. *Prof Exp:* Res assoc, Grad Sch Aeronaut Eng, Cornell Univ, 48-51, asst prof, 51-52; assoc res prof, Inst Fluid Dynamics & Appl Math, Univ Md, 52-56. *Concurrent Pos:* Prin physicist, Avco Corp, 63; dir, Sibley Sch Mech & Aerospace Eng, 72-77; resident consult, Pratt & Whitney Aircraft, 80-81; vis prof, Case Western Reserve, Lewis Res Lab, NASA, Cleveland, Ohio, 88-89. *Mem:* Am Phys Soc; Am Inst Aeronaut & Astronaut; Int Acad Astronaut; Sigma Xi; Int Sci Radio Union. *Res:* Gas dynamics; aerodynamics; shock waves; magnetohydrodynamics; ferrohydrodynamics; pollution control; hypersonic engines. *Mailing Add:* 204 Upson Hall Cornell Univ Ithaca NY 14853

RESNICK, CHARLES A, PHARMACOLOGY, TOXICOLOGY. *Current Pos:* PHARMACOLOGIST, FOOD & DRUG ADMIN, 70- *Personal Data:* b New York, NY, July 28, 39; m 63; c 3. *Educ:* Brooklyn Col Pharm, BS, 62; Univ Pittsburgh, PhD(pharmacol), 70. *Mem:* NY Acad Sci; Am Heart Asn. *Res:* Beta adrenoceptor blocking agents; cardiovascular applications and oncogenic potential. *Mailing Add:* 1733 Glastonberry Rd Potomac Rockville MD 20854

RESNICK, JOEL B, SYSTEMS ENGINEERING. *Current Pos:* DEP ASST SECY DEFENSE, RES AFFAIRS, 93- *Personal Data:* b Brooklyn, NY, Jan 24, 35; m 57; c Suzanne, Joshua, Peter, Justin, Adam & Benjamin. *Educ:* City Col New York, BS, 57; Mass Inst Technol, MS, 62. *Prof Exp:* Engr, Lincoln Lab, Mass Inst Technol, 57-70; systs engr & analyst, US Arms Control & Disarmament Agency, 70-72; dir strategic forces off, Off Asst Secy Defense for systs anal, 72-78, dir, Prog Assessment Off, Intel Community Staff, 78-80; div mgr & asst vpres, Sci Applns Inc, 80-91; prof staff, House Armed Serv Comt, 91-93. *Res:* Analysis of national security issues related to planning for the US militiary posture. *Mailing Add:* 10604 Trotters Trail Potomac MD 20854

RESNICK, LAZER, PARTICLE PHYSICS, THEORETICAL PHYSICS. *Current Pos:* asst prof, 67-71, ASSOC PROF PHYSICS, CARLETON UNIV, 71- *Personal Data:* b Montreal, Que, June 25, 38; m 64; c 3. *Educ:* McGill Univ, BSc, 59; Cornell Univ, PhD(theoret physics), 65. *Prof Exp:* Res assoc physics, Brookhaven Nat Lab, 64-65; Nat Res Coun Can fel, Niels Bohr Inst, Copenhagen, Denmark, 65-66 & Tel-Aviv Univ, 66-67. *Mem:* Am Phys Soc; Can Asn Physicists. *Res:* High energy and elementary particle physics; quantum mechanics. *Mailing Add:* Dept Physics Carleton Univ Ottawa ON K1S 5B6 Can

RESNICK, MARTIN I, UROLOGIC ONCOLOGY, URORADIOLOGY. *Current Pos:* PROF & CHMN UROL, SCH MED, CASE WESTERN RESERVE UNIV, 81-, PROF ONCOL, 86- *Personal Data:* b Brooklyn, NY, Jan 12, 43; m 65; c 2. *Educ:* Alfred Univ, BA, 64; Bowman Gray Sch Med, MD, 69; Northwestern Univ, MS, 73. *Honors & Awards:* Gold Cystoscope Award, Am Urol Asn. *Prof Exp:* Instr, 75-77, asst prof, 77-79, assoc prof, urol, Bowman Gray Sch Med, 79-81. *Concurrent Pos:* consult, Organ Systs Coord Ctr Nat Cancer Inst, 83- *Mem:* Am Urol Asn; Am Col Surgeons; Soc Univ Urol; Am Asn Genitourinary Surgeons; Clin Soc Genitourinary Surgeons. *Res:* Studies consist of identification of characterization of urinary macromolecules as they relate to urolithiasis Other areas of imaging modalities. *Mailing Add:* 11100 Euclid Ave Cleveland OH 44106-5046. *Fax:* 216-844-1900; *E-Mail:* mir@po.cwru.edu

RESNICK, OSCAR, physiology, pharmacology, for more information see previous edition

RESNICK, PAUL R, FLUORINE CHEMISTRY. *Current Pos:* from chemist to sr res chemist, E I Du Pont de Nemours & Co, Inc, 62-74, res assoc, 74-85, res fel, 85-88, sr res fel, 88-91, DU PONT FEL, E I DU PONT DE NEMOURS & CO, INC, 91- *Personal Data:* b New York, NY, Apr 7, 34; m 66; c 1. *Educ:* Swarthmore Col, BA, 55; Cornell Univ, PhD(org chem), 61. *Honors & Awards:* Creative Work in Fluorine Chem Award, Am Chem Soc, 95. *Prof Exp:* Fel, Univ Calif, Berkeley, 60-62. *Mem:* Am Chem Soc. *Res:* Fluorinated monomers, such as vinyl ethers and olefins; fluorinated polymers, such as Teflon and Nafcon; amorphous fluoropolymers, such as Teflon AF. *Mailing Add:* Dupont Fluoroprod PO Drawer Z Fayetteville NC 28302-1770

RESNICK, ROBERT, THEORETICAL PHYSICS. *Current Pos:* RETIRED. *Personal Data:* b Baltimore, Md, Jan 11, 23; m 45, Mildred Saltzman; c Trudy, Abby & Regina. *Educ:* Johns Hopkins Univ, AB, 43, PhD(physics), 49. *Honors & Awards:* Exxon Found Award, 53; Oersted Medal, Am Asn Physics Teachers, 75. *Prof Exp:* Physicist, Nat Adv Comt Aeronaut, 44-46; from asst prof to assoc prof physics, Univ Pittsburgh, 49-56; assoc prof, Rensselaer Polytech Inst, 56-57, prof physics, 58-93, Edward P Hamilton distinguished prof sci, 75-93. *Concurrent Pos:* Mem, Comn Col Physics, 60-68; hon res fel, Harvard Univ, 64-65; adv ed, John Wiley & Sons, Inc, 67-90; Fulbright prof, Peru, 71; vis prof, People's Repub China, 81 & 85; adv ed, Macmillan Publ, 90-; coun, Textbook Authors Asn, 90-92. *Mem:* Fel Am Phys Soc; Am Soc Eng Educ; Am Asn Physics Teachers (pres, 88-89); fel AAAS; Sigma Xi; Am Asn Univ Profs. *Res:* Aerodynamics; nuclear and atmospheric physics; instructional materials; educational research and development; relativity and quantum physics; history of physics; author or co-author of 7 different textbooks in relativity, quantum physics and general physics. *Mailing Add:* 23221 L'Ermitage Ctr Boca Raton FL 33433. *E-Mail:* resnir@aol.com

RESNICK, SIDNEY I, MATHEMATICS. *Current Pos:* PROF OPERS RES, CORNELL UNIV, 87- *Personal Data:* b New York, NY, Oct 27, 45; m 69; c 2. *Educ:* Queens Col, NY, BA, 66; Purdue Univ, Lafayette, MS, 68, PhD(math statist), 70. *Honors & Awards:* Lady Davis fel, 82; SERC fel, 86. *Prof Exp:* Lectr probability & statist, Israel Inst Technol, 69-72; asst prof statist, Stanford Univ, 72-77; assoc prof, Colo State Univ, 78-80, prof statist, 81-87. *Concurrent Pos:* Vis prof, Erasmus Univ, 81-82, Sussex Univ, 86-87. *Mem:* Fel Inst Math Statist. *Res:* Probability and stochastic processes; extreme value theory; regular variation; weak convergence; stochastic models. *Mailing Add:* Dept Indust Eng Cornell Univ Rhodes Hall Ithaca NY 14853-0001

RESNICK, SOL DONALD, HYDROLOGY. *Current Pos:* from assoc dir to dir, Water Resources Res Ctr, 66-84, EMER PROF HYDROL & HYDROLOGIST, UNIV ARIZ, 84- *Personal Data:* b Milwaukee, Wis, June 15, 18; m 81, Susan K Golden; c Rachel & Harry. *Educ:* Univ Wis, BS, 41 & 42, MS, 49. *Hon Degrees:* DSc, Univ Ariz, 93. *Prof Exp:* Asst hydrol engr, Tenn Valley Authority, 42-43; instr math, Carson-Newman Col, 43-44; asst prof hydrol, Colo State Univ, 49-52; irrig specialist, Int Coop Admin, India, 52-57. *Concurrent Pos:* Citizen ambassador prog, People to People, China & Tibet, 87; vis scientist, Ben Gurion Univ, Israel, 89, 92; prof engr, Ariz & Colo. *Mem:* Am Soc Agr Eng; Am Soc Civil Engr; Int Comn Irrig & Drainage. *Res:* Irrigation, urban hyrology, water conservation and augmention; water harvesting, seedage and evaporation control and ground water recharge. *Mailing Add:* Water Resources Res Ctr Univ Ariz Tucson AZ 85721. *Fax:* 520-529-6345

RESNIK, FRANK EDWARD, analytical chemistry; deceased, see previous edition for last biography

RESNIK, HARVEY LEWIS PAUL, SUICIDOLOGY. *Current Pos:* MED DIR, HUMAN BEHAV FOUND, 74-; CHIEF EXEC OFFICER, ASSOC MENTAL HEALTH PROF INC, 86-91 & 96- *Personal Data:* b Buffalo, NY, Apr 6, 30; wid; c Rebecca G, Henry S & Jessica R. *Educ:* Univ Buffalo, BA, 51; Columbia Univ, MD, 55; Univ Pa, certs med hypnosis & marriage counseling, 62; Del Valley Group Psychother Inst, cert group ther, 62; Philadelphia Psychoanalysis Inst, cert psychoanalysis, 67; Am Bd Psychiat & Neurol, dipl, 66. *Honors & Awards:* Charles W Burr Res Prize, Philadelphia Gen Hosp, 56; Gold Medal, Am Psychiat Asn, 72. *Prof Exp:* Intern, Philadelphia Gen Hosp, 55, resident, 56; resident, Jackson Mem Hosp, Miami, 59-61; consult, Ment Health Asn Southeastern Pa, 65-67; assoc prof psychiat & assoc chmn dept, Sch Med, State Univ NY Buffalo, 67-68, prof psychiat & dep chmn dept, 68-69; chief ctr studies suicide prev, NIMH, 69-72, chief sect crisis intervention, Suicide & Ment Health Emergencies, 72-74. *Concurrent Pos:* Fel, Univ Pa, 62; fel, Reproductive Biol Res Found, St Louis, 71; clin prof, Sch Med, George Washington Univ, 69-; prof lectr, Sch Med, Johns Hopkins Univ, 69-; ed, Bull Suicidology, Am Psychiat Asn, 69-74; prof, Fed City Col, 71-72; consult, WHO, Am Red Cross, Nat Cancer Inst, Nat Naval Med Ctr, Dept Defense & Pub Defender's Off; clin prof, Sch Med, Uniformed Serv Univ Health Sci, 77-79; spec Nato fel Brussels, Belg, 86; vis prof psychiat, Sch Med & Law, Cath Univ Leuven, Belg, 86. *Mem:* Fel Am Psychiat Asn; fel Am Col Psychiat; Am Acad Psychiat Law. *Res:* Crisis intervention; emergency mental health services; suicide, including prevention programs, diagnosis and management of suicidal and depressed individuals; treatment of sexual dysfunctions and criminal sexual offenders. *Mailing Add:* Air Rights Ctr 7315 Wisconsin Ave No 1300W Bethesda MD 20814-3210. *Fax:* 301-907-8637

RESNIK, ROBERT ALAN, BIOCHEMISTRY. *Current Pos:* RETIRED. *Personal Data:* b New York, NY, Nov 11, 24; m 52. *Educ:* Purdue Univ, BS, 48, MS, 50, PhD(biophys, physiol), 52. *Prof Exp:* NIH fel, Northwestern Univ Ill, 52-53; chief biochemist, Ophthalmic Chem Sect, Nat Inst Neurol Dis & Blindness, NIH, 53-63, chemist, Lab Phys Biol, Nat Inst Arthritis & Metab Dis, 63-68, chief eval scientist biophys sci, Div Res Grants, NIH, 68-70, chief, Res Analysis & Eval Br, 70-71, prog planning off, Nat Eye Inst, 71-73, chief reports & eval br, Nat Heart & Lung Inst, 73-78. *Mem:* AAAS; Am Chem Soc; Am Soc Biol Chemists; Sigma Xi. *Res:* Interactions of metals with proteins; protein chemistry; nucleic acids and proteins; science administration. *Mailing Add:* 5508 Hoover St Bethesda MD 20817-3716

RESNIK, ROBERT KENNETH, INORGANIC CHEMISTRY. *Current Pos:* sr inorg chemist, 65-66, SCIENTIST, RES LABS, J T BAKER CHEM CO, 66- *Personal Data:* b Pleasant Unity, Pa, May 19, 36; m 64. *Educ:* St Vincent Col, BS, 58; Univ Pittsburgh, PhD(inorg chem), 64. *Prof Exp:* Res chemist,

Exxon Res & Eng Co, 64-65. *Mem:* Am Chem Soc; Sigma Xi. *Res:* Coordination and inorganic compounds; agriculture chemicals; industrial inorganic chemicals; properties of antacid chemicals. *Mailing Add:* 1709 Wynnwood Lane N Easton PA 18042

RESNIKOFF, GEORGE JOSEPH, mathematical statistics; deceased, see previous edition for last biography

RESNIKOFF, HOWARD L, MATHEMATICS. *Current Pos:* STAFF MEM, FUTURE WAVE, 95- *Personal Data:* b New York, NY, May 13, 37; m 59; c 3. *Educ:* Mass Inst Technol, BS, 57; Univ Calif, Berkeley, PhD(math), 63. *Prof Exp:* Mathematician, Electrodata Div, Burroughs Corp, 57-58; res scientist, Res Labs, Lockheed Missiles & Space Co, 62-64; mem, Inst Advan Study, 64-66; asst prof math, Rice Univ, 66-68, actg dir, Comput Ctr 71, assoc prof, 68-73, prof, 73-75; chmn, Univ Calif, Irvine, 75-78, prof, 75-80; dir, Div Info Sci & Technol, NSF, 78-80; mem fac, Harvard Univ, 80-88; vpres & dir res, Thinking Mach Corp; pres, Aware, Inc, 88-95. *Concurrent Pos:* NSF fel, Univ Munich, 62-63; partner, R&D Consult Co, Calif, 64- & R&D Press, Calif, 72-77; Alexander von Humboldt Found, US sr scientist award, Univ Muenster, 74-75. *Res:* Automorphic function theory; theory of Jordan algebras; linguistic structure of written language; information retrieval; library automation; history of mathematics. *Mailing Add:* 2130 Moss Ave Cambridge MA 02140

RESO, ANTHONY, PETROLEUM & ECONOMIC GEOLOGY. *Current Pos:* staff res geologist, Tenneco Oil Co, 62-86, GEOL MGR, PEAK PROD CO, 86-, VPRES, 88- *Personal Data:* b London, Eng, Aug 10, 31; nat US. *Educ:* Columbia Univ, AB, 54, MA, 55; Rice Univ, PhD(geol), 60. *Honors & Awards:* Distinguished Serv Award, Am Asn Petrol Geologists, 85; Distinguished Ser Award, Geol Soc Am, 96. *Prof Exp:* Instr geol, Queens Col, NY, 54; asst, Columbia Univ, 54-55; geologist, Atlantic Richfield Corp, 55-56; asst, Univ Cincinnati, 56-57; asst prof geol, Amherst Col, 59-62. *Concurrent Pos:* Res consult, 60-61; Geol Soc Am grant & Am Asn Petrol Geologists grant, 58-59; NSF fel, 59; cur invert paleont, Pratt Mus, Amherst, Mass, 59-62; lectr, Univ Houston, 62-65; mem, Bd Advs, Gulf Univ Res Corp, 67-75, chmn, 68-69; vis prof geol, Rice Univ, Houston, 80; gen chmn, Am Asn Petrol Geologists Nat Conv, 79. *Mem:* Fel Geol Soc Am; fel AAAS; Am Asn Petrol Geologists (treas, 86-88); Paleont Soc; Soc Sedimentary Geol; Sigma Xi. *Res:* Earth history and subdivision of the geological time scale; invertebrate paleontology; world cretaceous stratigraphy; petroleum geology; distribution of economic resources and international trade; economic geology. *Mailing Add:* Peak Prod Co PO Box 130785 Houston TX 77219-0785

RESS, RUDYARD JOSEPH, PHARMACOLOGY. *Current Pos:* SR RES PHARMACOLOGIST, HOECHST-ROUSSEL PHARMACEUT, INC, AM HOECHST CORP, 83- *Personal Data:* b Bronx, NY, Oct 7, 50; m 81. *Educ:* Univ Fla, BS, 74, PhD(physiol), 81. *Prof Exp:* Res fel pharmacol, div cardiol, Hershey Med Ctr, Pa State Univ, 81-83. *Mem:* Am Physiol Soc. *Res:* Cardiovascular research and antihypertensive therapy; new drug development. *Mailing Add:* 16 Tuccamirgan Rd Flemington NJ 08822

RESSLER, CHARLOTTE, AGRICULTURAL & FOOD CHEMISTRY, PHARMACEUTICAL CHEMISTRY. *Current Pos:* prof pharmacol, 74-92, EMER PROF PHARMACOL, UNIV CONN HEALTH CTR, FARMINGTON, 92- *Personal Data:* b West New York, NJ, July 21, 24. *Educ:* NY Univ, BA, 44; Columbia Univ, MA, 46, PhD(org chem), 49. *Prof Exp:* Res assoc biochem, Med Col, Cornell Univ, 49-54, from asst prof to assoc prof, 55-74. *Concurrent Pos:* Am Heart Asn estab investr, Med Col, Cornell Univ, 57-59; assoc mem, Inst Muscle Dis, Inc, 59-63, mem, 63-, head, Div Protein Chem, 59-74; mem, Med Chem Study Sect, NIH, 72-75. *Mem:* AAAS; Am Chem Soc; Am Soc Biol Chemists. *Res:* Peptide hormones; amino acid metabolism; natural and synthetic neurothyrogens; enzyme characterization; amide reactions; organic rearrangements; drug allergy mechanisms, toxins in legumes. *Mailing Add:* Dept Pharmacol Univ Ct Health Ctr Farmington CT 06030-6125. *Fax:* 860-679-3693; *E-Mail:* ressler@sun.uchc.edu

RESSLER, NEIL WILLIAM, ENGINEERING, LASERS. *Current Pos:* Res scientist, Sci Res Staff, Ford Motor Co, 67-71, prin eng chassis, 71-73, supvr, 73-76, dept mgr, 76-78, exec engr, 78-81, chief engr, Climate Control Div, exec dir vehicle oper, 89-94, VPRES ADVAN VEHICLE TECHNOL, FORD MOTOR CO, 94- *Personal Data:* b Columbus, Ohio, June 1, 39; m 81; c 3. *Educ:* Gen Motors Inst, BSME, 62; Univ Mich, MS, 63, PhD(physics), 67. *Mem:* Soc Automotive Engrs. *Res:* Research development and production engineering of automotive climate control systems and heat exchangers. *Mailing Add:* Prod Develop & Technol Ctr Ford Motor Co MD507 PO Box 110 Dearborn MI 48123

RESSLER, NEWTON, BIOPHYSICS. *Current Pos:* from assoc prof to prof, 68-90, EMER PROF BIOCHEM PATH, UNIV ILL MED CTR, 90- *Personal Data:* b Detroit, Mich, Sept 19, 23; m 54; c 2. *Educ:* Univ Mich, BS, 47; Univ Chicago, MS, 49; Wayne State Univ, PhD(biochem), 53. *Prof Exp:* Res biochemist, Wayne County Gen Hosp, 53-65; asst prof biochem, Univ Mich, 65-68. *Mem:* Am Chem Soc; Am Asn Clin Chemists; Biophys Soc; Sigma Xi; Nat Acad Clin Biochem. *Res:* Nature and control of enzymes; multiple enzyme forms and energy transduction. *Mailing Add:* 30 Red Haw St Northbrook IL 60062-3723

REST, DAVID, CHEMICAL ENGINEERING. *Current Pos:* FOOD PROCESSING CONSULT, ARTHUR D LITTLE, INC, 62- *Personal Data:* b Chicago, Ill, Mar 27, 17; m 39; c 2. *Educ:* Armour Inst Technol, BS, 37; Univ Calif, MS, 60. *Prof Exp:* Supt chem prod, G D Searle & Co, 38-47; chief res engr, Armed Forces Qm Food & Container Inst, 47-55, chief, Nuclear Effects Br, 55-58, dir, Food Radiation Preserv Div, 58-62. *Mem:* Am Chem Soc; Health Physics Soc; Inst Food Technol. *Res:* Radiation processing of biological materials; low pressure sublimation of water in food stuffs; process control of food production facilities; chemical and nuclear engineering design; technical and economic evaluation of international food processing enterprises. *Mailing Add:* 3450 N Lakeshore Dr No 2702 Chicago IL 60657-2862

REST, RICHARD FRANKLIN, MICROBIOLOGY. *Current Pos:* assoc prof, 83-90, PROF, DEPT MICROBIOL, HAHNEMANN UNIV SCH MED, PHILADELPHIA, PA, 90- *Personal Data:* b Chicago, Ill. *Educ:* Univ Mass, Amherst, BS, 70; Univ Kans, PhD(microbiol), 74. *Prof Exp:* Fel neutrophil functions, Dept Bact & Immunol, Sch Med, Univ NC, Chapel Hill, 74-77; asst prof phagocyte bact interactions, 77-83, assoc prof microbiol, Sch Med, Health Sci Ctr, Univ Ariz, 83. *Concurrent Pos:* NIH fel, Dept Bact & Immunol, Sch Med, Univ NC, 75-77; Nat Inst Allergy & Infectious Dis grants, 78-94. *Mem:* Am Soc Microbiol. *Res:* Interaction of pathogenic Neisseria with human phagocytes and epithelial cells; biochemical and enzymatic analysis of human leukocyte phagolysosomes. *Mailing Add:* Dept Microbiol & Immunol Hahnemann Univ Sch Med Broad & Vine Sts Philadelphia PA 19102-1178

RESTAINO, ALFRED JOSEPH, PHYSICAL CHEMISTRY, POLYMER CHEMISTRY. *Current Pos:* PRES, CREATIVE ASSETS & CONSULT CORP, 87- *Personal Data:* b Brooklyn, NY, Feb 18, 31; m 53, Rae Sessa; c Stephen, Alfred, Peter, Mario & Lisa. *Educ:* St Francis Col, NY, BS, 52; Polytech Inst Brooklyn, MS, 54, PhD(chem), 55. *Prof Exp:* AEC fel, 54-56; supvr radiation res, Martin Co, 56-58; mgr radiation chem sect, ICI Americas, Inc, 58-68, mgr polymer chem, 68-71, asst dir chem, res dept, 71-74, dir, corp res dept, 75-87. *Concurrent Pos:* Asst prof, St Francis Col, NY, 55-56; adj prof, Drexel Inst Technol, 57; mem Gov Sci Adv Coun, Del, 70-72; mem sci adv comt, AEC, 70-73; prof grad exten, Univ Del, 71-74; exec dir, Gov High Tech Task Force, Delaware, 87-92; mem sci & technol adv comt, Delaware Environ Portection Agency, 89-; expert witness polymer sci, 89- *Mem:* Am Chem Soc; NY Acad Sci; AAAS. *Res:* Organic chemistry; thermoset polymers, water soluble polymers, thermoplastics and photochemistry; novel reactions for synthesis of specialty products including agricultural chemicals; reaction injection molding; composites; advanced materials; over 100 patents and open literature publications. *Mailing Add:* 615 Black Gates Rd Wilmington DE 19803

RESTAINO, FREDERICK A, PHYSICAL PHARMACY, PHARMACEUTICAL DEVELOPMENT. *Current Pos:* RETIRED. *Personal Data:* b Brooklyn, NY, Dec 9, 34; m 58, Camille Giordano; c Frederick J, Deborah Ann & Denise Marie. *Educ:* St Johns Univ, NY, BS, 56; Rutgers Univ, MS, 58; Purdue Univ, PhD(phys pharm), 62. *Prof Exp:* From asst instr to instr org chem, Rutgers Univ, 56-58; unit head aerosol res, Merck Sharp & Dohme, 62-65, unit head sterile prod, 65-70, unit head fluids-topicals, 69-70, unit head tablet & capsules & sr res fel, Res Labs, 70-84, dir pharmaceut develop, 85-95. *Mem:* Am Pharmaceut Asn; Am Asn Pharmaceut Scientists. *Res:* Solubilization; aerosol research; sterile products research and development; fluids-topical development; tablet and capsule research and development; solid dosage form development. *Mailing Add:* 1721 Brittany Dr Res Labs Ambler PA 19002

RESTER, ALFRED CARL, JR, nuclear physics, nuclear nonproliferation, for more information see previous edition

RESTER, DAVID HAMPTON, NUCLEAR PHYSICS. *Current Pos:* MGR ANALYTICAL METHODS, MEAD OFF SYSTS, 79- *Personal Data:* b Bogalusa, La, June 14, 34; m 58. *Educ:* Tulane Univ, BS, 56; Rice Univ, MA, 58, PhD(physics), 60. *Prof Exp:* Asst prof physics, Tulane Univ, 60-63; sr scientist, Ling-Tempco-Vought Inc Res Ctr, 63-71; sr scientist, Advan Technol Ctr, Inc, 71-73; supvr electrophys, 73-79. *Mem:* Am Phys Soc; Soc Info Display. *Res:* Low energy studies of nuclear structure by method of internal conversion electron spectroscopy; study of electron scattering at intermediate energies observing bremsstrahlung production and scattered electrons. *Mailing Add:* 7027 DeLoache Ave Dallas TX 75225

RESTORFF, JAMES BRIAN, SOLID STATE PHYSICS. *Current Pos:* RES PHYSICIST, NAVAL SURFACE WARFARE CTR, 76- *Personal Data:* b Wytheville, Va, June 22, 49; m 73, Kathleen A Leonard; c Cheryl. *Educ:* Univ Md, BS, 71, MS, 75, PhD(physics), 76. *Concurrent Pos:* Adj prof physics, Montgomery Col, Rockville, Md. *Mem:* Am Phys Soc. *Res:* Magnetic materials. *Mailing Add:* 5902 Chestnut Hill Rd College Park MD 20740. *E-Mail:* restorff@oasys.dt.navy.mil

RESTREPO, RODRIGO ALVARO, MATHEMATICS. *Current Pos:* from asst prof to prof, 59-95, EMER PROF MATH, UNIV BC, 95- *Personal Data:* b Medellin, Colombia, Nov 6, 30. *Educ:* Lehigh Univ, BA, 51; Calif Inst Technol, PhD(math), 55. *Prof Exp:* Res fel, Calif Inst Technol, 55-56; lectr, Univ BC, 56-58; vis asst prof, Stanford Univ, 58-59. *Concurrent Pos:* Vis prof, Interam Statist Training Ctr, Chile, 63-64 & COPPE, Fed Univ Rio de Janeiro, 70-71, 72 & 74. *Mem:* Am Math Soc; Math Asn Am; Can Math Cong. *Res:* Game theory; linear programming. *Mailing Add:* Dept Math Univ BC 1984 Mathematics Rd Rm 121 Vancouver BC V6T 1Z2 Can

RESWICK, JAMES BIGELOW, BIOMEDICAL ENGINEERING. *Current Pos:* RETIRED. *Personal Data:* b Ellwood City, Pa, Apr 16, 22; m 73; c 3. *Educ:* Mass Inst Technol, SB, 43, SM, 48, ScD(mech eng), 54. *Hon Degrees:* DEng, Rose Polytech Inst, 68. *Honors & Awards:* Isabel & Leonard Goldenson Award, United Cerebral Palsy Asn, 74. *Prof Exp:* Instr mach design, Mass Inst Technol, 46-50, from asst prof to assoc prof mech eng, 50-59; prof mech eng & dir eng design, Case Inst Technol, 59-70; prof biomed eng & orthopaed, Univ Southern Calif, 70-81; assoc dir, Nat Inst Handicapped Res, US Dept Educ, Washington, DC, 81-83; dir, Va Rehab Res & Develop Eval Unit, Va Med Ctr, Wash, 84-88; assoc dir, Nat Inst Disability & Rehab Res, US Dept Educ, Washington, DC, 88-95. *Concurrent Pos:* NSF sr fel, Imp Col, Univ London, 57-58; mem prosthetics res & develop comt, Nat Acad Sci, 60 & Inst Med, 72; dir, Rehab Eng Ctr, Rancho Los Amigos, 70-80. *Mem:* Inst Med-Nat Acad Sci; Nat Acad Eng; assoc Am Acad Orthop Surgeons; Biomed Eng Soc; fel Inst Elec & Electronics Engrs; Rehab Engr Soc NAm (founding pres). *Res:* Engineering design education; automatic control theory and application; dynamics; product design and development; biomedical engineering; administration of rehabilitation engineering. *Mailing Add:* 1003 Dead Run Dr McLean VA 22101

RETALLACK, GREGORY JOHN, PALEOPEDOLOGY, TERRESTRIAL PALEOECOLOGY. *Current Pos:* asst prof, 81-85, assoc prof, 86-92, PROF GEOL, UNIV ORE, EUGENE, 92- *Personal Data:* b Hobart, Australia, Nov 8, 51; m 81, Diane Alice Johnson; c Nicholas & Jeremy. *Educ:* Macquarie Univ, Australia, BA, 73; Univ New Eng, BSc Hons, 74, PhD(geol), 78. *Honors & Awards:* Stillwell Medal, Geol Soc Australia. *Prof Exp:* Vis asst prof geol, Northern Ill Univ, 77-78; vis scholar biol, Ind Univ, 78-79 & proj co-dir, 79-81. *Mem:* Sigma Xi; Geol Soc Am; Geol Soc Australia; Bot Soc Am; AAAS. *Res:* Paleopedological and paleoecological research into Gondwanan Triassic fossil plants; cretaceous dispersal and rise to dominance of angiosperms; tertiary development of grasslands; evolution of soils through geological time. *Mailing Add:* Dept Geol Univ Ore Eugene OR 97403

RETALLICK, WILLIAM BENNETT, CHEMICAL ENGINEERING. *Current Pos:* CONSULT CHEM ENGR, 80- *Personal Data:* b Yonkers, NY, Jan 16, 25; m 49, Kathryn MacDonald; c Martha. *Educ:* Univ Mich, BSE, 48; Univ Ill, MS, 52, PhD(chem eng), 53. *Prof Exp:* Process engr, Phillips Petrol Co, 48-50 & Consol Coal Co, 53-64; res engr, Houdry Process & Chem Co, 64-71, sr chem engr, 71-74; vpres res & develop, Oxy-Catalyst, Inc, 74-80. *Concurrent Pos:* Develop award, US Dept Energy, NSF. *Mem:* Am Chem Soc; Am Inst Chem Engrs; Sigma Xi; AAAS. *Res:* Pilot scale research in coal; exploratory research on chemicals and catalysts; catalysts and catalytic processes; catalytic combustion; catalytic converters for automobiles. *Mailing Add:* 1432 Johnny's Way West Chester PA 19382. *Fax:* 610-399-1478

RETCOFSKY, HERBERT L, SPECTROSCOPY, COAL SCIENCE. *Current Pos:* Res physicist phys chem, 58-76, chief molecular spectros, Br Analytical Chem Coal, 76-79, MGR, ANALYTICAL CHEM DIV, PITTSBURGH ENERGY TECHNOL CTR, US DEPT ENERGY, 79- *Personal Data:* b Brownsville, Pa, Apr 1, 35; m 61; c 7. *Educ:* Calif State Col, Pa, BS, 57; Univ Pittsburgh, MS, 65. *Concurrent Pos:* US assoc ed, Fuel, 81- *Mem:* Am Chem Soc; Soc Appl Spectros. *Res:* Applications of spectral techniques in coal research. *Mailing Add:* 1155 Locust Ave Pittsburgh PA 15236-3415

RETELLE, JOHN POWERS, JR, AEROSPACE ENGINEERING. *Current Pos:* PRES, PAR GOVT SYSTS CORP, NEW HARTFORD, NY, 93- *Personal Data:* b Flushing, NY, Jan 1, 46; m 75, Joan F Kremer; c 2. *Educ:* US Air Force Acad, BS, 67; Univ Colo, MS, 69, PhD(aerospace eng), 78; Golden Gate Univ, MBA, 71. *Prof Exp:* Flight test engr aerospace eng, Air Force Flight Test Ctr, Edwards AFB, Calif, 69-72 & Fr Flight Test Ctr, Istres, France, 72-73; from instr to asst prof aeronaut, USAF Acad, 73-75, assoc prof aeronaut & dir labs & develop, 79-81; prog mgr sensor simulation, Air Force Human Resources Lab, Williams AFB, Ariz, 82-84; prog mgr, Defense Advan Res Proj Agency, Arlington, Va, 84-88; dir, advan appln, Lockheed Corp, Calabasas, Calif, 88-90; mgr, Advan Comput Labs, Lockheed Missiles & Space Co, Palo Alto, Calif, 90-93. *Mem:* Assoc fel Am Inst Aeronaut & Astronaut; Inst Elec & Electronics Engrs; Am Asn Artificial Intel. *Res:* Wind tunnel experimentation on dynamic stall and unsteady flow separation using laser Doppler techniques and numerical simulation; applications of high performance computing to massive data problems. *Mailing Add:* 3274 Craig Rd Clinton NY 13323. *Fax:* 315-738-8304; *E-Mail:* retellej@partech.com

RETHERFORD, JAMES RONALD, MATHEMATICS. *Current Pos:* from asst prof to assoc prof, 64-70, PROF MATH, LA STATE UNIV, BATON ROUGE, 70-, CHMN, MATH DEPT. *Personal Data:* b Panama City, Fla, Oct 1, 37; m 61. *Educ:* Fla State Univ, BS, 59, MS, 60, PhD(math), 63. *Prof Exp:* Asst prof math, Univ Chattanooga, 60-61; instr, Fla State Univ, 64. *Mem:* Am Math Soc; Math Asn Am. *Res:* Series and operators determined by series in Banach spaces. *Mailing Add:* 509 Castle Kirk Rd Baton Rouge LA 70808

RETHWISCH, DAVID GERARD, HETEROGENEOUS CATALYSTS, MEMBRANE SCIENCE. *Current Pos:* asst prof, Dept Chem & Mats Eng, 85-90, ASSOC PROF CHEM ENG, DEPT CHEM & BIOCHEM ENG, UNIV IOWA, 90- *Personal Data:* b LaCrosse, Wis, Mar 28, 59; m 81; c 4. *Educ:* Univ Iowa, BS, 79; Univ Wis-Madison, PhD(chem eng), 85. *Concurrent Pos:* Consult, Oral B Labs, 85, Rolscreen Inc, 86, Amana Corp, 88-90, Amoco Chem Co, 90-95, Dupont, 91-92, Climax Molybdenum, 95-, Bectin-Dickinson, 96; vis prof, Univ Del, 92. *Mem:* Am Chem Soc; Am Inst Chem Engrs; Sigma Xi; Am Soc Eng Educators. *Res:* Use of photoresponsive polymers as membranes with capability of real time control; enzyme-facilitated transport through liquid membranes; enzyme production of saccharide based polymers. *Mailing Add:* Dept Chem & Biochem Eng Univ Iowa Iowa City IA 52242. *Fax:* 319-335-1415; *E-Mail:* drethwis@icaen.uiowa.edu

RETIEF, DANIEL HUGO, PREVENTIVE DENTISTRY, DENTAL MATERIALS. *Current Pos:* PROF BIOMAT & SR SCIENTIST, INST DENT RES, UNIV ALA, SCH DENT, 77- *Personal Data:* b Winburg, OFS, Repub SAfrica, Apr 25, 22; US citizen; m 52; c 3. *Educ:* Univ Stellenborch, BSc, 42, MSc, 44, DSc, 84; Univ Witwatersrand, BDS, 53, PhD(dent), 75. *Prof Exp:* Prof res & dir res, Dent Res Unit, SAfrican Med Res Coun & Univ Witersrand, 70-76. *Concurrent Pos:* Sr foreign dent scientist fel, Am Asn Dent Res, 75; assessor, Nat Health & Med Res Coun, Commonwealth Australia, 82-84; referee, Med Res Coun Can, 82-84; consult, dent serv, Vet Admin, 83- *Mem:* Int Asn Dent Res; Royal Soc SAfrica; Int Dent Fedn; Europ Orgn Caries Res; Soc Biomat; AAAS; Royal Soc Belgium Dent Med; Acad Dent Mat. *Res:* Polymeric dental resins; acid etch technique; preventive dentistry; effect of flouride and micronutrients on dental caries; dental caries epidemiology. *Mailing Add:* 3624 Bellemeade Way Birmingham AL 35223

RETNAKARAN, ARTHUR, INSECT PHYSIOLOGY, BIOCHEMISTRY. *Current Pos:* RES SCIENTIST, FOREST PEST MGT INST, 68- *Personal Data:* b Trichy, India, Aug 28, 34; m 60; c 2. *Educ:* Univ Madras, MA, 55; Univ Wis, MS, 64, PhD(entom), 67. *Prof Exp:* Lectr zool, Voorhees Col, Vellore, India, 55-58, prof, 58-62; fel, Univ Wis, 67-68. *Concurrent Pos:* Vis prof, Univ Louis Pasteur, Strasbourg, France, 74-75; Fulbright scholar, 62-67; vis scientist, Commonwealth Sci & Industrial Res Orgn, Canberra, Australia, 83-84. *Mem:* Entom Soc Am; Entom Soc Can; AAAS. *Res:* Use of juvenile hormone analogs and moult inhibitors in controlling forest insect pests; insect reproductive physiology; benzoyl ureas for insect control; antijuvenile hormones; chitin synthesis in insects. *Mailing Add:* 50 Ashgrove Ave Sault Ste Marie ON P6A 4X2 Can

RETSEMA, JAMES ALLAN, BIOCHEMISTRY, MICROBIOLOGY. *Current Pos:* RES ADV IMMUNOL & INFECTIOUS DIS, CENT RES, PFIZER INC, 69- *Personal Data:* b Muskegon, Mich, Feb 27, 42; m 69; c 2. *Educ:* Mich State Univ, BS, 64; Univ Iowa, MS, 67, PhD(biochem), 69. *Prof Exp:* Res asst biochem, Univ Iowa, 64-69. *Concurrent Pos:* Fel, McArdle Lab Cancer Res, Univ Wis, 69. *Mem:* Am Soc Microbiol; Am Acad Microbiol. *Res:* Discovery and development of antibacterials and antiprotozoan and their spectrum of activity, mode of action, mechanism of destruction and structural activity relationships. *Mailing Add:* 21 Overlook Rd Gales Ferry CT 06335

RETTALIATA, JOHN THEODORE, MECHANICAL ENGINEERING. *Current Pos:* RETIRED. *Personal Data:* b Baltimore, Md, Aug 18, 11; m 70, Caryl Pucci; c Brian, Stephen & Patricia. *Educ:* Johns Hopkins Univ, BE, 32, DEng, 36. *Hon Degrees:* DEng, Mich Col Mining & Technol, 56 & Rose Polytech Inst, 70; DSc, Valparaiso Univ, 59; LLD, DePaul Univ, 62, 62 & Chicago-Kent Col Law, 69; LHD, Loyola Univ, 70. *Honors & Awards:* Jr Award, Am Soc Mech Engrs, 41, Spec Award, 51. *Prof Exp:* Instr & head dept, Baltimore Col Ctr, Md, 34-35; lab technician, USDA, 35; head calculation div, Allis-Chalmers Co, Wis, 36-44, mgr res & gas turbine develop div, 44-45; prof mech eng & head dept, Ill Inst Technol, 45-48, dean eng, 48-52, vpres, 50-52, pres, Inst, IIT Res Inst & Inst Gas Technol, 52-73; chmn bd, Banco Di Roma, Chicago, 73-87. *Concurrent Pos:* Mem bd vis, Air Univ, 55-58, chmn, 57-58; mem, Nat Aeronaut Space Coun, 59. *Mem:* Fel AAAS; fel Am Soc Mech Engrs. *Res:* Super-Saturated steam; gas turbine engineering; jet engineering; science administration. *Mailing Add:* 8901 S Pleasant Chicago IL 60620

RETTENMEYER, CARL WILLIAM, ENTOMOLOGY, ECOLOGY. *Current Pos:* exec off, biol sci group, 83-85, DIR, CONN STATE MUS NATURAL HIST, 82-; PROF BIOL, UNIV CONN, 71- *Personal Data:* b Meriden, Conn, Feb 10, 31; m 54; c 2. *Educ:* Swarthmore Col, BA, 53; Univ Kans, PhD(entom), 62. *Prof Exp:* From asst prof to assoc prof entom, Kans State Univ, 60-71; head syst & evolutionary biol, Univ Conn, 80-83. *Concurrent Pos:* NSF res grants, 62- & Orgn Trop Studies, 65, 67 & 69. *Mem:* Fel AAAS; Am Asn Mus; Asn Trop Biol; Animal Behav Soc. *Res:* Ecology and behavior of army ants and associated arthropods; taxonomy of Dorylinae; insect behavior, mimicry mutualism; biological photography; Neotropical insects. *Mailing Add:* Univ Conn U-23 Mus Natural Hist Storrs CT 06269-0001

RETTENMIER, CARL WAYNE, MOLECULAR BIOLOGY, PATHOLOGY. *Current Pos:* STAFF MEM, DEPT PATH, CHILDREN'S HOSP, LOS ANGELES. *Personal Data:* b Erie, Pa, Oct 23, 52. *Educ:* Syracuse Univ, BS, 74; Rockefeller Univ, PhD(virol), 79; Cornell Univ, MD, 80. *Prof Exp:* Resident anat path, Lab Path, NIH, 80-82, jr staff pathologist, 82-83; res assoc tumor cell biol, St Jude Children's Res Hosp, 83-84, asst mem tumor cell biol, 84. *Mem:* AAAS; Am Soc Microbiol; Am Assoc Path. *Res:* Oncogene expression; tyrosine-specific protein kinases; mechanisms of cell surface receptor-mediated signal transduction; growth factor biosynthesis. *Mailing Add:* PO Box 27427 Los Angeles CA 90027

RETTORI, OVIDIO, CANCER PHYSIOPATHOLOGY. *Current Pos:* PHYSIOL PROF CANCER PHYSIOPATH, SCH MED, CAISM/UNICAMP, BRAZIL, 87. *Personal Data:* b Parana, Entre Rios, Arg, June 16, 34; m 76, Ana N Vieira-Matos; c Elisa, Andres B & Annelisse. *Educ:* Nat Col Parana, BSc, 51; Univ Buenos Aires, MD, 59. *Honors & Awards:* Augusto Pi-Suner Ann Award Best Physiol Exp Work, Catalan Soc, Caracas, Venezuela, 81. *Prof Exp:* Fel, NIH, 64-68; sr res scientist, Nat Res Coun, Arg, 68-76; assoc prof physiol respiratory & kidney physiol, Sch Med, Univ Buenos Aires, 68-76; physiol prof respiratory & kidney physiol, Sch Med, Univ Oriente Venezuela, 76-86, res coordr, 84-86. *Concurrent Pos:* Postdoctoral, Univ Calif, Los Angeles, 68. *Mem:* Am Physiol Soc. *Res:* Cancer physiopathology; experimental models; detection, identification and inhibition of humoral mediators involved in the remote lethal effects of cancer. *Mailing Add:* Univ Pesq Bioquimicas CAISM/UNICAMP CP 6151 Campinas SP CEP 13081 Brazil. *Fax:* 55-192-39-7580; *E-Mail:* cavalcanti@ccvax.unicamp.br

RETZ, KONRAD CHARLES, NEUROPHARMACOLOGY, NEUROCHEMISTRY. *Current Pos:* ASST PROF PHARMACOL, TEX COL OSTEOP MED, 83- *Personal Data:* b Oelwein, Iowa, Feb 19, 52. *Educ:* Augustana Col, Ill, BA, 74; Univ Iowa, PhD(pharmacol), 79. *Prof Exp:* Dept Pharmacol & Exp Therapeut, 79-81, fel, Dept Neurosci, Sch Med, Johns Hopkins Univ, Baltimore, 81-82, Long Island Res Inst, SUNY, Stony Brook, 82-83. *Mem:* AAAS; Am Chem Soc; Soc Neurosci; NY Acad Sci. *Res:* Mechanisms of analgesia; mode of action of excitatory amino acid neurotransmitters; regulation of energy metabolism in the central nervous system and calcium involvement in neurotransmission; modulation of behavior in autoimmune mice; neurotransmission in aging. *Mailing Add:* Am Osteop Asn 142 E Ontario St Chicago IL 60611-2864

RETZER, KENNETH ALBERT, MATHEMATICS EDUCATION. *Current Pos:* PROF MATH, ABILENE CHRISTIAN UNIV. *Personal Data:* b Jacksonville, Ill, Nov 6, 33; m 53; c 3. *Educ:* Ill Col, AB, 54; Univ Ill, EdM, 57, PhD(math educ), 67. *Prof Exp:* Instr high sch, Ill, 54-58, asst supt, 55-58; from asst prof to prof math, Ill State Univ, 59-, asst head dept, 68-70. *Concurrent Pos:* Partic, NSF Acad Year Inst Math, Univ Ill, 58-59. *Mem:* AAAS; Math Asn Am. *Res:* Effects of teaching logic on verbalization and on transfer of discovered mathematical generalizations; strategies for teaching mathematics. *Mailing Add:* 58 Bay Shore Ct Abilene TX 79602

RETZLOFF, DAVID GEORGE, CATALYSIS, MODELING. *Current Pos:* asst prof, 75-84, ASSOC PROF CHEM ENG, UNIV MO, COLUMBIA, 84- *Personal Data:* b Pittsburgh, Pa, Feb 19, 39; m 71, Debra R Renz; c Lauren B. *Educ:* Univ Pittsburgh, BS, 63, MS, 65, PhD(chem eng), 67. *Prof Exp:* Mem staff, Lab Chem, Technol & Tech High Sch, Delft, Neth, 67-68; res assoc, Univ Colo, 68-69; asst prof chem eng, Kans State Univ, 69-73; res engr, Exxon Res & Eng Co, 73-75. *Mem:* Am Inst Physics; Am Math Soc; Am Chem Soc; Soc Ind & Appl Math. *Res:* Development of catalysts to perform specific chemical transformations; mathematical analysis of models for chemical reactors. *Mailing Add:* 1461 S Mesa Dr Univ Mo W2025EBE Columbia MO 65201. *Fax:* 573-884-4940; *E-Mail:* chender@mizzou1.missouri.edu

REUBEN, JACQUES, POLYMER CHARACTERIZATION. *Current Pos:* RETIRED. *Personal Data:* b Plovdiv, Bulgaria, Mar 17, 36; US citizen; m 63, Rose Levy; c David, Vered & Violet. *Educ:* Technion-Israel Inst Technol, BSc, 61, MSc, 65; Weizmann Inst Sci, PhD(phys chem), 69. *Prof Exp:* Postdoctoral fel, Univ Pa, 69-71, vis lectr biophys, 76-77; res assoc, Weizmann Inst Sci, 71-72, sr scientist, 72-76; assoc prof chem, Univ Houston, 77-80; sr res chemist, Hercules Inc, 80-88, res scientist, 88-94. *Concurrent Pos:* Co-ed, Biol Magnetic Resonance, 76- *Mem:* Am Chem Soc; Am Soc Biochem & Molecular Biol. *Res:* Nuclear magnetic resonance studies of molecules of biological interest, and analysis and description of cellulose derivatives; carbon-13 nuclear magnetic resonance spectroscopy of carbohydrates; interaction of small molecules and ions with biological macromolecules; lanthanide shift reagents. *Mailing Add:* 38 Club Lane Wilmington DE 19810. *Fax:* 302-995-4117

REUBEN, JOHN PHILIP, BIOPHYSICS. *Current Pos:* RETIRED. *Personal Data:* b Seattle, Wash, Mar 12, 30; m 55; c 3. *Educ:* Grinnell Col, BA, 54; Univ Rochester, MS, 56; Univ Fla, PhD(physiol), 59. *Prof Exp:* Res assoc, Col Physicians & Surgeons, Columbia Univ, 59-60, NSF fel, 60-62, from asst prof to prof neurol, 60-81. *Mem:* Biophys Soc; Am Physiol Soc. *Res:* Neurophysiology; neuropharmacology; muscle; molecular studies of synaptic and electrically excitable membranes. *Mailing Add:* RR 2 Box 751 Woodstock VT 05091

REUBEN, RICHARD N, MEDICINE. *Current Pos:* Assoc prof pediat neurol, 54-70, assoc prof, 70-85, PROF CLIN NEUROL, SCH MED, NY UNIV, 85- *Personal Data:* b New York, NY, June 21, 20; m 49; c 3. *Educ:* Columbia Univ, AB, 40, MD, 43. *Mem:* Am Acad Neurol; Child Neurol Soc; Am Acad Pediat. *Res:* Neurological disorders of childhood. *Mailing Add:* NY Univ Sch Med 530 First Ave New York NY 10016-6402

REUBEN, ROBERTA C, PHARMACEUTICAL INDUSTRY. *Current Pos:* PRES, JOHNSTON REUBEN ASSOC, 89- *Personal Data:* b Chicago, Ill, Jan 25, 36; m 55; c 4. *Educ:* Columbia Univ, BA, 69, PhD(biochem), 73. *Prof Exp:* Postdoctoral molecular biol, Roche Inst Molecular Biol, 73-75; asst prof human genetics, Columbia Univ, 75-80; dir molecular biol, Merck & Co, 80-85; vpres molecular biol, Cistron Biotechnol, 85; dir virol, Schering Plough, 86-87, dir bus develop, 87-89. *Mem:* Soc Biol Chemists; AAAS. *Res:* Biochemistry; molecular biology. *Mailing Add:* Johnston Reuben Assoc PO Box 857 Far Hills NJ 07931

REUBER, MELVIN D, PATHOLOGY, MEDICINE. *Current Pos:* CONSULT HUMAN & EXP PATH, 81- *Personal Data:* b Blakeman, Kans, Nov 10, 30. *Educ:* Univ Kans, AB, 52, MD, 58. *Prof Exp:* Intern path, Sch Med, Univ Md, 58-59, resident, 59-61; res fel, Beth Israel Hosp & Harvard Med Sch, 61-62, asst pathologist & asst instr, 62-63; med officer, Lab Path, Nat Cancer Inst, 63-65; from asst prof to assoc prof path, Sch Med, Univ Md, Baltimore City, 65-74; consult human & exp path, 75-97; pathologist, Frederick Cancer Res Ctr, Md, 76-81. *Concurrent Pos:* Med officer, Lab Biol, Nat Cancer Inst, 65-69 & etiol, 69-71. *Mem:* Am Soc Exp Path; Am Asn Cancer Res; Am Asn Path & Bact; Soc Toxicol; Int Acad Path. *Res:* Hepatic carcinogenesis; toxicology. *Mailing Add:* 11014 Swansfield Rd Columbia MD 21044

REUCROFT, PHILIP J, INDUSTRIAL & MANUFACTURING ENGINEERING, POLYMER PHYSICS. *Current Pos:* assoc prof, 69-75, dir, Mat Characterization Facil, 88-94, PROF MAT SCI, UNIV KY, 75- *Personal Data:* b Leeds, Eng, Mar 29, 35; m 61, Sheila Powers; c Lisa M, Miles a & Noel E. *Educ:* Univ London, BSc, 56, PhD(phys chem) & dipl, Imp Col, 59. *Prof Exp:* Fel phys chem, Nat Res Coun Can, 59-61; res chemist, Franklin Inst Res Labs, Pa, 61-63, sr res chemist, 63-65, sr staff chemist, 65-66, actg lab mgr, 66-67, lab mgr, 67-69. *Concurrent Pos:* Consult, Franklin Inst Res Labs, Pa, 69-71; Ashland Oil Found prof, Univ Ky, 70-74, Inst Mining & Minerals Res fel, 78-79; mem adv comt, Am Carbon Soc, 79-85. *Mem:* Fel Am Soc Metals Int; Am Chem Soc; Royal Soc Chem; Am Phys Soc; Am Carbon Soc. *Res:* Solid-gas interactions; adsorption; intermolecular forces; thermodynamics; solid state properties of polymers and molecular solids; conductivity; photoconductivity; molecular diffusion; crystallinity and crystal growth; coal science; heterogeneous catalysts; surface characterization; surface science; CVD films. *Mailing Add:* Dept Chem & Mat Eng Univ Ky Lexington KY 40506-0046. *E-Mail:* reuc@engr.uky.edu

REUCROFT, STEPHEN, PARTICLE PHYSICS. *Current Pos:* MATTHEWS DISTINGUISHED PROF PHYSICS, NORTHEASTERN UNIV, BOSTON, MA, 86- *Personal Data:* b Leeds, Eng, May 17, 43; m 70. *Educ:* Univ Liverpool, BSc, 65, PhD(physics), 69. *Prof Exp:* Demonstr, Univ Liverpool, 65-69; res fel, Europ Orgn Nuclear Res, Switz, 69-71; res assoc, Vanderbilt Univ, 71-73; asst prof res, Vanderbilt Univ, 73-78; staff physicist, Europ Orgn Nuclear Res, Geneva, Switz, 79-86. *Concurrent Pos:* Vis scientist, Europ Orgn Nuclear Res, 71-78, sci assoc, 78; vis physicist, Fermilab, Chicago, 75- & Brookhaven Nat Lab, 76-; staff scientist, Max-Planck Inst, Munich, 77; adj assoc prof, Vanderbilt Univ, 79-; sci assoc, Europ Coun Nuclear Res, Geneva, 78 & group leader, Europ Parliament; adj prof, Northeastern Univ, 84-85, chmn, 88- *Mem:* Fel Inst Physics Eng; Am Phys Soc. *Res:* Fundamental structure and basic interactions of sub-nuclear particles. *Mailing Add:* Dept Physics Northeastern Univ 360 Huntington Ave Boston MA 02115

REUDINK, DOUGLAS O, MATHEMATICS, PHYSICS. *Current Pos:* Mem tech staff, 65-72, head, Satellite Systs Res Dept, 72-79, DIR, RADIO RES LAB, BELL LABS, 79- *Personal Data:* b West Point, Nebr, May 6, 39; m 61. *Educ:* Linfield Col, BA, 61; Ore State Univ, PhD(math), 65. *Mem:* Am Inst Aeronaut & Astronaut; fel Inst Elec & Electronics Engrs. *Res:* Communications; satellite systems; mobile radio; integral transforms; wave propagation. *Mailing Add:* Metro Wave Commun 8700 148th Ave NE Redmond WA 98052

REULAND, DONALD JOHN, FORENSIC CHEMISTRY, BIOANALYTICAL CHEMISTRY. *Current Pos:* asst prof inorg-nuclear chem, 64-68, assoc prof chem, 68-75, PROF CHEM, IND STATE UNIV, TERRE HAUTE, 75- *Personal Data:* b Philadelphia, Pa, May 25, 37; m 60, Alice M Weindel; c Lynne (Mackay) & Gary. *Educ:* St Joseph's Univ, Pa, BS, 59; Carnegie-Mellon Univ, MS, 61, PhD(nuclear-inorg chem), 63. *Prof Exp:* Teaching asst chem, Carnegie-Mellon Univ, 59-61, proj chemist, 61-63; res chemist, Thomas A Edison Res Lab, 63-64. *Concurrent Pos:* Res chemist, Ames Nat Lab, 67. *Mem:* Sigma Xi. *Res:* Study of oxoranadium species as biologically active agents. *Mailing Add:* Dept Chem Ind State Univ Terre Haute IN 47809. *Fax:* 812-237-2232; *E-Mail:* chreul@scifac.indstate.edu

REULAND, ROBERT JOHN, RADIOCHEMISTRY. *Current Pos:* PROF CHEM, LORAS COL, IOWA, 64- *Personal Data:* b Philadelphia, Pa, Feb 9, 35; m 59, Mary E Snider; c Robert C & Elizabeth A (Hentrich). *Educ:* St Joseph's Univ, Philadelphia, BS, 56; Iowa State Univ, MS, 59, PhD(inorg chem), 63. *Prof Exp:* Instr chem, St Joseph's Univ, Philadelphia, 59-60; mem tech staff mat res, Tex Instruments Inc, Dallas, 63-64. *Mem:* Sigma Xi. *Res:* Preparation and structure determination of metal tungsten bronzes. *Mailing Add:* Dept Chem Loras Col 1450 Alta Vista St Dubuque IA 52001-4399

REUNING, RICHARD HENRY, PHARMACOLOGY. *Current Pos:* from asst prof to assoc prof, 70-80, PROF PHARMACEUT, COL PHARM, OHIO STATE UNIV, 80- *Personal Data:* b Wellsville, NY, Jan 3, 41; m 63; c 2. *Educ:* State Univ NY, Buffalo, BS, 63, PhD(pharmaceut), 68. *Honors & Awards:* Lyman Award, Am Asn Cols Pharm, 75. *Prof Exp:* USPHS fel pharmacol, Univ Mo-Kansas City, 68-69. *Mem:* AAAS; Acad Pharmaceut Sci; Am Asn Cols Pharm; Am Soc Pharmacol Exp Therapeut. *Res:* Biological drug transport; biopharmaceutics of digitalis glycosides; pharmacokinetics; assay, metabolism and pharmacokinetics of narcotic antagonists; alterations of membrane permeability. *Mailing Add:* Dept Pharm Col Med Ohio State Univ 500 W 12th Ave Columbus OH 43210-1291

REUPKE, WILLIAM ALBERT, SCIENCE SOFTWARE. *Current Pos:* SR TEST ENGR, GEN SCI CORP/SAIC, 96- *Personal Data:* b Chicago, Ill, Jan 22, 40; m 83; c 2. *Educ:* Northwestern Univ, BA, 61; Ind Univ, MA, 67; Ga Inst Technol, MS, 73, PhD(nuclear eng), 77. *Honors & Awards:* Group Achievement Award, NASA, 85, 91 & 93; Dr Robert H Goddard Hist Essay Award, Nat Space Club, 91. *Prof Exp:* Physicist, NASA Lewis Res Ctr, 63-64; res engr, Lockheed Missiles & Space Co, 67-68; eng physicist, Stanford Linear Accelerator Ctr, 68-71; staff mem, Los Alamos Nat Lab, 77-82; sr engr, Comput Sci Corp, 83-95. *Mem:* AAAS; Am Phys Soc; fel Brit Interplanetary Soc; Am Inst Aeronaut & Astronaut; Am Nuclear Soc; Inst Elec &

Electronics Engrs. *Res:* Scientific spacecraft ground software systems; interstellar transport and communication; nuclear rocket propulsion; space history. *Mailing Add:* Gen Sci Corp 7501 Forbes Blvd Suite 103 Seabrook MD 20706

REUSCH, WILLIAM HENRY, SYNTHETIC ORGANIC CHEMISTRY. *Current Pos:* from asst prof to assoc prof, 58-68, PROF CHEM, MICH STATE UNIV, 68- *Personal Data:* b Carbondale, Ill, Dec 2, 31; m 56; c 3. *Educ:* Univ Mich, BS, 53; Columbia Univ, PhD(chem), 57. *Prof Exp:* NSF fel, Imp Col, Univ London, 57-58. *Concurrent Pos:* NIH spec fel, Stanford Univ, 65-66. *Mem:* Am Chem Soc; Royal Soc Chem. *Res:* Natural products and their rational synthesis; strained ring intermediates. *Mailing Add:* Dept Chem Mich State Univ East Lansing MI 48823

REUSS, LUIS, MEMBRANE TRANSPORT, EPITHELIAL TRANSPORT. *Current Pos:* PROF & CHMN PHYSIOL & BIOPHYS, UNIV TEX MED BR, 86- *Personal Data:* b Santiago, Chile, July 18, 40; US citizen; m, Elsa Bello; c Luis F & Alejandro E. *Educ:* Univ Chile-Santiago, BA, 57, MD, 64. *Prof Exp:* Resident, Dept Internal Med, Univ Chile, Santiago, 64-66, instr pathophysiol, 66-69, assst prof exp sci, 70-72; Fogarty NIH fel, div nephrology, Dept Med, Univ NC, 72-74, Louis G Welt fel, 74-75, asst prof med, 75-76; assoc prof physiol & biophys, Wash Univ Sch Med, 76-80, prof, 80-86. *Concurrent Pos:* Mem physiol study sect, NIH, 80-94. *Mem:* Biophys Soc; Am Physiol Soc; AAAS; NY Acad Sci; Soc Gen Physiologists (pres, 90-91); Asn Chmn Depts Physiol. *Res:* The mechanisms of ion and water transport across epithelial cell membranes and its regulation; cell physiology of cancer cells, with emphasis on multi-drug resistance. *Mailing Add:* Dept Physiol & Biophys Univ Tex Med Br 301 University Blvd Rte F-41 Galveston TX 77555-0641. *Fax:* 409-772-3381; *E-Mail:* reuss@beach.utmb.edu

REUSS, ROBERT L, GEOLOGY. *Current Pos:* Asst prof, 69-75, ASSOC PROF GEOL, TUFTS UNIV, 75- *Personal Data:* b New York, NY, May 31, 42; m 66. *Educ:* Ohio Wesleyan Univ, AB, 64; Univ Mich, Ann Arbor, MS, 67, PhD(geol), 70. *Mem:* Mineral Soc Am; Geol Soc Am; Soc Econ Geologists. *Res:* Igneous and metamorphic petrology; relationship and timing of igneous events, metamorphic reactions and structural deformation. *Mailing Add:* Dept Geol Tufts Univ Medford MA 02155

REUSS, RONALD MERL, HUMAN BIOLOGY, SCIENCE EDUCATION. *Current Pos:* PROF BIOL, STATE UNIV NY BUFFALO, 64-, INSTR ANAT & PHYSIOL & PRE-HEALTH ADV, 78- *Personal Data:* b Buffalo, NY, Jan 29, 33; m 54, 79; c 4. *Educ:* State Univ NY, Albany, BA, 54, MA, 55; State Univ NY, Buffalo, DEd, 70. *Prof Exp:* Sci teacher gen sci & biol, Kenmore Pub Schs, 55-64. *Concurrent Pos:* Sci consult, Carson City Schs, 68 & S-K Sci Co, Tonawanda, NY, 77-80 & Matte Polygraph, Buffalo, NY, 84-88; mem res staff, Lung Tumor Antigens, Roswell Park Inst, NY, 79. *Mem:* Nat Sci Teachers Asn; AAAS. *Res:* Individualized instruction in anatomy and physiology and muscle physiology; polygraph validity. *Mailing Add:* 15 Duffy Dr Tonawanda NY 14150

REUSSER, FRITZ, MOLECULAR BIOLOGY, MICROBIOLOGY. *Current Pos:* RETIRED. *Personal Data:* b Steffisburg, Switz, Dec 19, 28; US citizen; m 53; c 2. *Educ:* Swiss Fed Inst Technol, Dipl, 53, DSc(microbiol), 55. *Prof Exp:* Res asst microbiol, Swiss Fed Inst Technol, 53-55; Nat Res Coun Can fel, Prairie Regional Lab, Nat Res Ctr, Sask, 55-57; res assoc, Res Labs, Upjohn Co, Kalamazoo, 57-71, sr scientist, Res Div, 71-95. *Concurrent Pos:* Mem, adv bd, Pohl Cancer Res Lab, Okla State Univ. *Mem:* Am Chem Soc; Am Soc Microbiol. *Res:* AIDS termination; genetic engineering; antibiotics; mode of action. *Mailing Add:* 6548 Trotwood Kalamazoo MI 49002

REUSSNER, GEORGE HENRY, DENTAL RESEARCH, NUTRITION. *Current Pos:* RETIRED. *Personal Data:* b Bethlehem, Pa, Dec 18, 18; m 50, Margaret Dahm; c Catherine & Charles. *Educ:* Lehigh Univ, BA, 40; Purdue Univ, MS, 50. *Prof Exp:* Chemist, Bethlehem Steel Corp, 40-42 & 46-48; assoc chemist, Gen Foods Corp, 49-54, proj leader biochem, 54-60, from chemist to sr chemist, Tech Ctr, 61-70, res specialist, 70-75, sr res specialist, 75-81, prin scientist, Cent Res, Gen Foods Tech Ctr, 81-84. *Mem:* Am Chem Soc; Am Asn Lab Animal Sci; Am Inst Nutrit; Soc Environ Geochem & Health; Int Asn Dental Res. *Res:* Mineral nutrition; dental health and diet; cereal nutrition. *Mailing Add:* 31 Nostrand Dr Toms River NJ 08757-5645

REUSZER, HERBERT WILLIAM, SOIL MICROBIOLOGY. *Current Pos:* assoc prof, 47-70, EMER PROF AGRON, PURDUE UNIV, 70- *Personal Data:* b Jamestown, Mo, Aug 4, 03; wid; c John H & Margaret (Myers). *Educ:* Univ Mo, BS, 25; Rutgers Univ, MS, 30, PhD(soil microbiol), 32. *Prof Exp:* Res specialist agron, NJ Exp Sta, 26-29, asst soil microbiol, 29-32, instr, 32-33; assoc bacteriologist, Exp Sta, Colo State Col, 33-40; coop agent, Soil Conserv Serv, USDA & Exp Sta, Auburn Univ, 40-47. *Concurrent Pos:* Asst marine bact, Oceanog Inst Woods Hole, 30-31, jr marine bacteriologist, 32-33. *Mem:* Fel AAAS; Am Soc Microbiol; Soil Sci Soc Am; Am Soc Agron; Brit Biochem Soc; Sigma Xi. *Res:* Soil microbiology; origin and nature of soil organic matter; decomposition of cellulose; nonsymbiotic nitrogen fixation; relation of microorganisms to soil physical properties and liberation of plant nutrients in the soil; microbial decomposition of organotoxicants; axenic growth of plants. *Mailing Add:* 10161 River Landing Rd Denton MD 21629

REUTER, GERALD LOUIS, VETERINARY & AGRICULTURAL PHARMACY. *Current Pos:* sect head vet formulations pharmaceut develop, 68-79, res assoc pharmaceut res & develop, 79-88, HEAD, PARENTERAL PROD, PHARMACEUT SCI, WYETH AYERST RES, 88- *Personal Data:* b Providence, RI, Mar 16, 34; m 57, Beverly Sklut; c Merrill W, Rhonda B (Pais) & David P (deceased). *Educ:* RI Col Pharm, BS, 56. *Prof Exp:* Pharmaceut chemist, Hess & Clark Div, Richardson Merrell, Inc, 60-68. *Mem:* Am Pharmaceut Asn. *Res:* Human and veterinary pharmaceutical products, including animal health products and feed medication products; pisicide formulations; liquid and parenteral formulation, research and development. *Mailing Add:* 35 Crescent Dr Plattsburgh NY 12901

REUTER, HARALD, PHARMACOLOGY. *Current Pos:* dean fac med, 83-85, PROF PHARMACOL, UNIV BERN, SWITZ, 69-, CHMN, 72- *Personal Data:* b Dusseldorf, Ger, Mar 25, 34; Swiss citizen; m 60; c 3. *Educ:* Univ Freiburg, Ger, Med, 59; Univ Mainz, Ger, Dr Med, 60. *Honors & Awards:* Award for Outstanding Res, Int Soc Heart Res, 84; Marcel-Benoist Prize, Swiss Govt, 85; Schmiedeberg Medal, Ger Pharmacol Soc, 87; US Cole Award, Biophys Soc, 93. *Prof Exp:* Asst pharmacol, Univ Mainz, Ger, 60-65, privatdozent, 65-69. *Concurrent Pos:* Vis scientist, Mayo Clin, Rochester, Minn, 67-68; vis prof, Yale Univ, Conn, 78-79 & 86, Japan Soc Promotion Sci, 78, Beijing Univ, China, 87 & Stanford Univ, Calif, 92-96. *Mem:* Foreign assoc Nat Acad Sci; Physiol Soc Gt Brit; Am Physiol Soc; Ger Acad Sci; Swiss Acad Med Sci; Ger Soc Pharmacol & Toxicol. *Res:* Regulation and modulation of ion channels, ion transport and receptors in cell membranes; calcium and cell function; growth and differentiation of neurons; synaptic vesicle recycling. *Mailing Add:* Dept Pharmacol Univ Bern Friedbuehlstr 49 Bern CH-3010 Switzerland

REUTER, ROBERT A, MATERIAL SCIENCE, PHYSICAL CHEMISTRY. *Current Pos:* PRES, DYLON INDUSTS INC, 73- *Personal Data:* b Dunkirk, NY, Aug 3, 28; m 56; c 3. *Educ:* St Bonaventure Univ, BS, 49. *Prof Exp:* Exp chemist, Am Locomotive Co, 49-50; engr, Nat Carbon Co, 53-57; group leader nuclear fuel develop, Carbon Prod Div, Union Carbide Corp, 57-63, asst plant mgr, Nuclear Fuel Prod, Union Carbide Corp, Lawrenceburg, Tenn, 63-71, proj mgr, Polycrystalline Graphite Develop, Union Carbide Corp, Parma, Ohio, 71-73. *Mem:* Am Nuclear Soc; Am Ceramic Soc; Am Soc Lubrication Engrs. *Res:* Uranium carbide nuclear fuels; chemical vapor deposition coatings; high temperature materials processing; polycrystalline graphite production; refractory cements; solid state lubricants. *Mailing Add:* 14430 Indian Creek Rd Cleveland OH 44130-1045

REUTER, ROBERT CARL, JR, THEORETICAL & APPLIED MECHANICS. *Current Pos:* mem tech staff, Sandia Nat Labs, 68-79, supvr, Appl Mech Div 1544, 79-91, supvr, Mech Process Eng Div 2484, 91-92, MGR, MFG TECHNOL PROG DEVELOP 2401, SANDIA NAT LABS, 93- *Personal Data:* b Pittsburgh, Pa, Apr 30, 39; m 61; c 3. *Educ:* Univ Ill, BS, 64, MS, 65, PhD(appl mech), 67. *Prof Exp:* Mem tech staff struct mech, Martin Marietta Corp, 67-68. *Mem:* Am Soc Mech Engrs. *Res:* Development and application of the mechanics of composite materials with an emphasis on residual stresses in composites; mechanical and thermomechanical analysis of heterogeneous, orthotropic, wound structures; evaluation of the effects of processing parameters on mechanical states in wound structures; supervise technical staff in numerous areas of applied mechanics; managed technical staff in manufacturing process development and manufacturing technologies program development. *Mailing Add:* 6808 Barber Pl E Albuquerque NM 87109. *Fax:* 505-844-6584; *E-Mail:* rcreute@sandia.gov

REUTER, STEWART R, RADIOLOGY. *Current Pos:* PROF RADIOL & CHMN DEPT, HEALTH SCI CTR, UNIV TEX, SAN ANTONIO, 80- *Personal Data:* b Detroit, Mich, Feb 14, 34; m 66, Marianne Ahfeldt. *Educ:* Ohio Wesleyan Univ, AB, 55; Case Western Res Univ, MD, 59; Am Bd Radiol, dipl, 64; San Francisco Univ, JD, 80. *Prof Exp:* Intern med, Hosp, Univ Calif, 59-60, researcher, 60-63; instr radiol, Stanford Univ, 63-64; Picker res fel, 64-66; from asst prof to assoc prof, Univ Mich, 66-69; assoc prof, Univ Calif, San Diego, 69-72; prof radiol, Univ Mich, Ann Arbor, 72-75; prof radiol & vchmn radiol, Univ Calif, Davis, 76-80. *Mem:* Fel Am Col Radiol; fel Am Hearth Asn; fel Am Col Legal Med (pres, 96-97); Soc Cardiovasc & Interventional Radiol. *Res:* Angiography, particularly visceral circulation and development of techniques to improve visceral angiography; therapeutic anglography. *Mailing Add:* 3923 Morgans Creek San Antonio TX 78230

REUTER, WILHAD, analytical chemistry, for more information see previous edition

REUTER, WILLIAM L(EE), ELECTRICAL ENGINEERING. *Current Pos:* chief engr, 79-82, vpres opers, 82-96, SR ENG PETE LIEN & SONS, INC, 96- *Personal Data:* b Hartford, SDak, July 21, 34; m 59, Loreli M James; c Lee & Lisa. *Educ:* SDak Sch Mines & Technol, BS, 56, MS, 58; Iowa State Univ, PhD(elec eng), 67. *Prof Exp:* From instr to assoc prof elec eng, SDak Sch Mines & Technol, 56-72; mgr res & develop, Dunham Assocs, Inc, 72-79; pres, Rapidata, Inc, 73-79. *Concurrent Pos:* Vpres, Res Specialists Inc, 69-80, bd dir, 70-92; bd dir, SymCom, Inc, 89- *Mem:* Inst Elec & Electronics Engrs; Sigma Xi; Nat Soc Prof Engrs. *Res:* Systems; network theory; numerical methods; computer programming; process control; signal processing. *Mailing Add:* 3402 Fairhaven Rapid City SD 57702. *Fax:* 605-342-6979

REUTHER, THEODORE CARL, JR, METALLURGICAL ENGINEERING, NUCLEAR MATERIALS. *Current Pos:* SR DIR DEVELOP STAFF, OAK RIDGE NAT LAB, 90- *Personal Data:* b Wheeling, WVa, Apr 16, 33; m 55; c 2. *Educ:* Carnegie Inst Technol, BS, 56,

MS, 58; Cath Univ Am, DrEngr, 65. *Prof Exp:* Res metallurgist, US Naval Res Lab, 59-68; metall engr, Div Reactor Develop & Technol, USAEC. 68-75, metal engr, Off Fusion Energy, US Dept Energy, 75-90. *Mem:* Metall Soc; Am Soc Metals. *Res:* Diffusion; crystal growth and defects; refractory metals and alloys; creep; nuclear metallurgy; grain boundary energy and structure; irradiation effects; fusion reactor materials development; transportation systems infrastructure. *Mailing Add:* 11 Clemson Ct Rockville MD 20850

REUTHER, WALTER, HORTICULTURE. *Current Pos:* chmn dept, 56-66, prof, 56-77, EMER PROF HORT, UNIV CALIF, RIVERSIDE, 77- *Personal Data:* b Manganoui, NZ, Sept 21, 11; nat US; m 35; c 2. *Educ:* Univ Fla, BS, 33; Cornell Univ, PhD(plant physiol), 40. *Prof Exp:* Instr res, Univ Fla, 33-36; asst horticulturist, Citrus Exp Sta, 36-37, head, Dept Hort, Univ Fla, 55-56; asst, Cornell Univ, 37-40, asst prof pomol, 40; from assoc horticulturist to prin horticulturist, USDA, 40-55; sr horticulturist in-chg, US Date Garden, Calif, 41-46. *Concurrent Pos:* Mem, Adv Comt Citrus & Subtrop Fruit Res, USDA, 62-63 & hort crops res, 63-69; mem eval comt sr fels, Nat Acad Sci, 64-; mem, Comt Trop Studies; consult to USAID, FAO, UNDP, Rockefeller Found, World Bank & var other govts & pvt insts, 63-; chmn bd, Am Soc Hort Sci, 63-64. *Mem:* AAAS; fel Am Soc Hort Sci (vpres, 61-62, pres, 62-63); Am Soc Plant Physiol; Am Pomol Soc (vpres, 65-66). *Res:* Mineral nutrition of tree fruits; relation of leaf analysis to nutritional status of citrus; water relations and irrigation of tree fruits; toxicity of copper in citrus orchard soils; influence of climate on citrus. *Mailing Add:* 12751 Gateway Park Rd Poway CA 92064

REUWER, JOSEPH FRANCIS, JR, TRIBOLOGY. *Current Pos:* Res chemist, Armstrong World Industs, Inc, 62-65, res supvr, 65-69, sr scientist, 69-90, sr prin scientist, 90-93, CONSULT, ARMSTRONG WORLD INDUSTS, INC, 93- *Personal Data:* b Harrisburg, Pa, May 31, 31; m 58, Mabel Gooding; c Daniel & Edith. *Educ:* Lehigh Univ, BS, 53; Mass Inst Technol, SM, 57; Univ NH, PhD(org chem), 62. *Concurrent Pos:* Adj prof, Franklin & Marshall Col, 64-66. *Mem:* Am Chem Soc. *Res:* Tribology of polymeric surfaces; mechanisms by which wear occurs on organic and organic/inorganic surfaces; effect of multilayer structures on surface wear. *Mailing Add:* 144 N School Lane Lancaster PA 17603-2511

REVANKAR, VITHAL V S, ADVANCED MATERIALS RESEARCH & DEVELOPMENT, CHEMICAL PROVEN RESEARCH & DEVELOPMENT. *Current Pos:* SR RES SCIENTIST, ZEOCAT ENVIRO, 93- *Personal Data:* b Dharwad, India, June 2, 59; m, Smita. *Educ:* Karanataka Univ, BS, 78; Bombay Univ, BSc, 81 PhD(chem eng technol), 87. *Prof Exp:* Qual control technologist, Color-Chem, Thana Ltd, 80; jr res fel, Nat Chem Lab, 81-83, sr res fel, 83-86; fel, Univ Ill, 86-87; res assoc, State Univ NY, Buffalo, 87, res asst prof, 87-93. *Concurrent Pos:* Lectr, State Univ NY, Buffalo, 87-88; vis fel, Univ Karlstruhe, 89; consult, ART, 93- *Mem:* Am Ceramic Soc; Am Inst Chem Engrs; Mat Res Soc. *Res:* Advanced materials especially ceramic fibers, powder, windows, tubes. *Mailing Add:* 18 Tee Ct Buffalo NY 14211-4941

REVAY, ANDREW W, JR, ELECTROMAGNETICS, ENGINEERING EDUCATION. *Current Pos:* assoc prof elec eng, Fla Inst Technol, 67-69, head dept, 71-80, head dept mech eng, 72-78, assoc dean res, 77-80, dean sci & eng, 80-86, PROF ELEC ENG, FLA INST TECHNOL, 69-, VPRES, ACAD AFFAIRS, 86- *Personal Data:* b New Kensington, Pa, Oct 8, 33; wid; c Kenneth & Andrea. *Educ:* Univ Pittsburgh, BS, 55, MS, 56, PhD(elec eng), 63. *Honors & Awards:* Centennial Medal, Inst Elec & Electronics Engrs. *Prof Exp:* Asst prof elec eng, Univ Pittsburgh, 59-64, assoc res prof, 64-67. *Concurrent Pos:* Consult adv bd hardened elec power systs, Nat Acad Sci, 63-70 & Harris Corp, 68-86; prin investr res contracts. *Mem:* Inst Elec & Electronics Engrs; Am Soc Eng Educ; Nat Soc Prof Eng; Sigma Xi. *Res:* Electromagnetic field research and application; lightning and electromagnetic pulse protection. *Mailing Add:* FIT-VP Acad Affairs 150 W University Blvd Melbourne FL 32901-6975

REVEAL, JAMES L, PLANT TAXONOMY, SYSTEMATIC BOTANY. *Current Pos:* Asst prof, 69-74, assoc prof, 74-81, PROF BOT, UNIV MD, COLLEGE PARK, 81- *Personal Data:* b Reno, Nev, Mar 29, 41; m 61, 78; c 3. *Educ:* Utah State Univ, BS, 63, MS, 65; Brigham Young Univ, PhD(bot), 69. *Concurrent Pos:* Res assoc, Smithsonian Inst, 70-; secy-gen, Int Cong Syst & Evoluntionary Biol, 73-85; co-pres, Int Cong Syst & Evolutionary Biol, 86- *Mem:* Am Inst Biol Sci; Bot Soc Am; Am Soc Plant Taxon; Int Asn Plant Taxon; Sigma Xi; fel Linnean Soc. *Res:* Floristic studies in intermountain West, vascular plants of North America, northern Mexico and state of Maryland; monographical studies in Eriogonum and related genera; botanical nomenclature. *Mailing Add:* Dept Bot Univ Md College Park MD 20742-0001

REVEL, JEAN PAUL, CELL BIOLOGY. *Current Pos:* prof, 71-78, ALBERT BILLINGS RUDDOCK PROF BIOL, CALIF INST TECHNOL, 78- *Personal Data:* b Strasbourg, France, Dec 7, 30; nat US; m 57, 86; c 3. *Educ:* Univ Strasbourg, France, BS, 49; Harvard Univ, PhD, 57. *Honors & Awards:* Distinguished Scientist Award, Med Scis Micros Soc Am, 93. *Prof Exp:* Whitney fel anat, Med Col, Cornell Univ, 57-58, res assoc, 58-59; instr, Harvard Med Sch, 61, assoc, 61-63, from asst prof to prof, 63-71. *Concurrent Pos:* Mem, Molecular Biol Study Sect, NIH, 70-74; mem, Develop Biol Panel, NSF, 76-80; mem bd sci adv, Nat Inst Aging,; chair, Sect G, AAAS, 91-92. *Mem:* AAAS; Am Asn Anat; Am Soc Cell Biol (pres, 72); Soc Develop Biol; Microscope Soc Am (pres, 88). *Res:* Correlation between structure and function; ultrastructural cytochemistry; investigation of cell to cell communication; structure of channel proteins by molecular biology and cytology; structure-function relationships; electron microscopy; atomic force microscopy of biological molecules. *Mailing Add:* Div Biol 156-29 Calif Inst Technol Pasadena CA 91125-0001. *Fax:* 626-449-0756; *E-Mail:* revelj@romeo.caltech.edu

REVELANTE, NOELIA, BIOLOGICAL OCEANOGRAPHY, EUTROPHICATION. *Current Pos:* assoc res prof, 78-90, res prof, 90-95, ASSOC EMER PROF, UNIV MAINE, 95- *Personal Data:* b Rovinj, Croatia, Yugoslavia, Jan 15, 42; m 74, Malvern Gilmartin; c Darren G. *Educ:* Univ Zagreb, Yugoslavia, BSc, 66, MSc, 70, PhD, 74. *Prof Exp:* From res asst to sr assoc res scientist, Ctr Marine Res, Inst Rudjer Boskovic, Yugoslavia, 66-75; sr scientist, Australian Inst Marine Sci, 76-78. *Concurrent Pos:* Mem, Int Comn Sci Explor Mediter Sea; Int Atomic Energy fel, 74-75,; Queen's fel, Australia, 84-85. *Mem:* AAAS; Am Soc Limnol & Oceanog; Int Phycol Soc. *Res:* Pico- and nanoplankton ecology and taxonomy; primary and secondary aquatic production; eutrophication; microbiology; microzooplankton. *Mailing Add:* Dept Zool Univ Maine Orono ME 04469

REVELL, JAMES D(EWEY), AIRCRAFT NOISE CONTROL, AERODYNAMICS. *Current Pos:* res develop scientist, 65-75, RES & DEVELOP SCIENTIST ACOUST, LOCKHEED AIRCRAFT CORP, CALIF, 75- *Personal Data:* b Toledo, Ohio, Feb 17, 29; m 55; c 2. *Educ:* Univ Calif, Los Angeles, BS, 52, MS, 58, PhD(eng), 66. *Prof Exp:* Thermodynamicist, Northrup Aircraft, Inc, Calif, 52-54, aerodynamicist, 54-57; sr tech specialist, NAm Aviation, Inc, 57-60; sr specialist dynamics & loads, Norair Div, Northrup Corp, 60-62, mem tech mgt, 62-65. *Mem:* Assoc fel Am Inst Aeronaut & Astronaut; Acoust Soc Am. *Res:* Fluid mechanics; unsteady aerodynamics; acoustics of moving fluids; aerodynamic noise and jet noise theory; turbulence; boundary layer theory; gas dynamics; scattering refraction; aeroelasticity; noise transmission through structures. *Mailing Add:* Lockheed Adv Develop Co Dept 25-22 Bldg 611 Plant 10 1011 Lockheed Way Palmdale CA 93599-0001

REVELLE, CHARLES S, ENVIRONMENTAL SCIENCE, ARMS CONTROL POLICY. *Current Pos:* assoc prof, 70-75, PROF GEOG & ENVIRON ENG, JOHNS HOPKINS UNIV, 75-, COORDR OPERS RES GROUP, 78- *Personal Data:* b Rochester, NY, Mar 26, 38; m 62; c 2. *Educ:* Cornell Univ, BChE, 61, PhD(civil eng), 67. *Prof Exp:* Res assoc, Ctr Environ Qual Mgt, Cornell Univ, 67, asst prof environ systs eng, 67-70. *Concurrent Pos:* Vis asst prof, Johns Hopkins Univ, 68-69; Fulbright award, Erasmus Univ, Rotterdam, Neth, 75. *Mem:* Regional Sci Asn; Inst Mgt Sci; Opers Res Soc Am; Am Geophys Union; AAAS. *Res:* Applications of systems analysis and operations research to environmental and public problems such as water quality and water quanity management, public health systems; modeling of urban and regional problems, especially location systems such as ambulance and fire protectionn; modelling of arms control alternatives. *Mailing Add:* Dept Environ Eng Ames Hall Johns Hopkins Univ 3400 N Charles St Baltimore MD 21218-2608

REVESZ, AKOS GEORGE, SOLID STATE CHEMISTRY. *Current Pos:* CONSULT SOLID STATE & MAT SCI, REVESZ ASSOC, 84- *Personal Data:* b Balassagyarmat, Hungary, July 25, 27; US citizen; m 56, 75; c 1. *Educ:* Budapest Tech Univ, Dipl Ing, 50, Dr Ing, 68. *Prof Exp:* Staff mem thermodyn iron metall, Iron & Metal Res Inst, Budapest, 50; staff mem semiconductors, Tungsram Co, 51-54, dept head, 55-56; staff mem anodic oxide films & solid state capacitors, Philips Co, Neth, 57-59 & growth & properties thin films, RCA Labs, 60-69; mem tech staff, Comsat Labs, 69-72, dept head, 72-74, sr staff scientist, 74-81, sr scientist, 81-84. *Concurrent Pos:* Vis res prof, Howard Univ, Washington, DC, 84-86; vis prof, Univ Leuren, Belg, 88, 91. *Mem:* Fel Am Inst Chemists; Electrochem Soc. *Res:* Semiconductor and solid state devices; oxidation of semiconductors; insulator-semiconductor interfaces; properties of thin oxide films; noncrystalline solids. *Mailing Add:* 7910 Park Overlook Dr Bethesda MD 20817

REVESZ, GEORGE, RADIOLOGY, ELECTRICAL ENGINEERING. *Current Pos:* assoc prof, 66-76, PROF RADIOL, SCH MED, TEMPLE UNIV, 76-; CONSULT, UNIV PA. *Personal Data:* b Budapest, Hungary, July 29, 23; nat US; m 91; c 2. *Educ:* Swiss Fed Inst Technol, MS, 48; Univ Pa, PhD, 64. *Honors & Awards:* Bowen Award, Brit Inst Phys, 54; Stauffer Award, Asn Univ Radiologists, 82. *Prof Exp:* Develop engr, Salford Labs, Gen Elec Co, Eng, 49-52; mem staff res, Brit Rayon Res Asn, 52-54; sr proj engr, 54-57, sect head, 57-59, tech dir, Robertshaw-Fulton Controls Co, 59-61; res sect mgr, Philco Corp, Pa, 61-62, mgr instrumentation, Microelectronics Div, 62-68. *Concurrent Pos:* Adj prof Sch Eng, Temple Univ, 84-91. *Mem:* Asn Univ Radiologists; Am Asn Physicists Med; Optical Soc Am. *Res:* Measuring and improving diagnostic accuracy in medicine; computer analysis of medical images; medical decision making and computers. *Mailing Add:* Dept Diag Imaging Temple Univ Sch Med 3400 N Broad St Philadelphia PA 19140-5104

REVESZ, ZSOLT, COMPUTATIONAL EXPERIMENTS, ENGINEERING ANALYSIS. *Current Pos:* GEN MGR, REVESZ & ASSOCS, SWITZ, 85- *Personal Data:* b Jan 16, 1923; m 88. *Educ:* Voeresmarty Gymnazium, Budapest, BA, 68; Tech Univ Budapest, dipl eng, 74; Century Univ, DSc(eng), 80. *Prof Exp:* Res scientist & assoc prof computer sci, Tech Univ Budapest, 74-75; develop engr, Brown, Boveri & Cie Co, Switz, 75-78; eng analyst & proj mgr, Electrowatt Eng Serv, Switz, 79-89. *Concurrent Pos:* Fac adv, Century Univ, Beverly Hills & Albuquerque, 80-; res scientist & sr asst energy technol, Swiss Fed Inst Technol, 89-91. *Mem:* Am Soc Mech Engrs; Am Nuclear Soc. *Res:* Engineering application in structural mechanics, piping analysis, computational fluid flow-heat transfer and energy systems; developments for analysis algorithms, computer graphics, nuclear and non-nuclear electricity generating devices; author of over 60 publications. *Mailing Add:* Assoc Consult Engrs Revesz & Assocs PO Box 1126 Baden CH-5401 Switzerland. *Fax:* 41-56-4062731

REVETTA, FRANK ALEXANDER, GEOPHYSICS. *Current Pos:* from instr to assoc prof, 62-77, PROF GEOL, STATE UNIV NY COL POTSDAM, 77- *Personal Data:* b Monongahela, Pa, June 18, 28; m 61; c 2. *Educ:* Univ Pittsburgh, BS, 53; Ind Univ, MA, 57; Univ Rochester, PhD(geophys), 70. *Prof Exp:* Geophysicist, Geophys Serv Inc, 57-58; teacher earth sci, Elizabeth-Forward High Sch, 59-62. *Mem:* Am Geophys Union; Nat Asn Geol Teachers. *Res:* Gravity and magnetic surveys; interpretation of magnetic anomalies, seismology with emphasis on regional seismic networks, seismic and electrical methods of prospecting. *Mailing Add:* Geol State Univ NY Col 44 Piierrpont Ave Potsdam NY 13676-2200

REVILLARD, JEAN-PIERRE, IMMUNOPHARMACOLOGY, MUCOSAL IMMUNITY. *Current Pos:* asst prof immunol, 73-81, dean biol, Human Biol Fac, 77-84, COORDR, DEPT IMMUNOL, CLAUDE BERNARD UNIV, LYON, 74-, PROF, 81- *Personal Data:* b Suresnes, France, Jan 12, 38; m 61, Marie L Cuilleret; c Sophie (Kaufman) & Anne. *Educ:* Claude Bernard Univ, Lyon, MD, 64, MSc, 62, cert immunol, 73. *Prof Exp:* Res assoc, immunol, NIH, NY Univ Med Sch, 66-67; asst nephrology, Lyon's Hosp, 68-73. *Concurrent Pos:* Spec adv on PhD biol, Minister Educ, 82-85; dir, Uro-Nephro Transplantation Clin Immunol, Res Unit, NIH & Med Res, Nat Ctr Sci Res, 86-; vpres, Educ Comt Int, Union Immunol Socs, 89- *Mem:* Am Asn Immunologists; Brit Soc Immunol; Transplantation Soc; Europ Dialysis & Transplant Asn. *Res:* Basic and clinical immunology; new treatments with monoclonal antibodies or cytokines, mucosal immunity, B and T lymphocyte activation. *Mailing Add:* Hop E Herriot Pavillon P Cedex 03 Lyon 69437 France. *Fax:* 33-7-2330044

REVIS-WAGNER, CHARLES KENYON, ECOLOGY, BIOLOGY. *Current Pos:* asst prof, 77-81, ASSOC PROF BIOL, CLEMSON UNIV, 81- *Personal Data:* b Cleveland, Ohio, Mar 11, 43; m 66; c 2. *Educ:* Emory Univ, BA, 65; Univ Ga, MS, 68, PhD(zool), 73. *Honors & Awards:* Am Soc Mammalogists Award, 72. *Prof Exp:* Lectr zool, Univ Ga, 70-72; asst prof biol, Southwestern at Memphis, 72-77. *Concurrent Pos:* Consult, Community Develop Task Force, 75-77. *Mem:* Ecol Soc Am; Am Soc Mammalogists; Am Inst Biol Sci; Sigma Xi. *Res:* Bioenergetics of terrestrial populations; microecosystem investigation of population growth. *Mailing Add:* Dept Bio Sci Clemson Univ Clemson SC 29632-0001

REVOILE, SALLY GATES, AUDIOLOGY. *Current Pos:* ASST PROF AUDIOL RES, DEPT HEARING RES, 76-, DIR, CTR AUDITORY & SPEECH SCIS, GALLUDET COL. *Personal Data:* b Pittsburgh, Pa. *Educ:* Univ Md, BA, 62, MA, 65, PhD(hearing sci), 70. *Prof Exp:* Res audiologist, Vet Admin Hosp, Wash, DC, 62-76. *Mem:* Am Speech & Hearing Asn; Acoust Soc Am. *Res:* Use of hearing aids by the hearing impaired. *Mailing Add:* 4112 Culver St Kensington MD 20895

REVTER, JAMES D, AERONAUTICAL ENGINEERING. *Current Pos:* PROJ MGR, PIONEER PARACHUTE CO, CONN. *Honors & Awards:* Aerodyn Decelerator Syst Award, Am Inst Aeronaut & Astronaut, 92. *Mem:* Am Inst Aeronaut & Astronaut. *Mailing Add:* Pioneer Parachute Co 95 Lakewood Circle S Manchester CT 06040-7018

REVZIN, ALVIN MORTON, PHARMACOLOGY, NEUROPHYSIOLOGY. *Current Pos:* RETIRED. *Personal Data:* b Chicago, Ill, Nov 8, 26; m 56. *Educ:* Univ Chicago, SB, 47, SM, 48; Univ Colo, PhD(physiol), 57. *Prof Exp:* Instr physiol, Med Col SC, 48-49; asst, Col Dent, NY Univ, 49-50; asst, Child Res Coun, Denver, Colo, 51-55; med res assoc, Galesburg State Res Hosp, 57-60; pharmacologist, Nat Heart Inst, 60-63; pharmacologist, Civil Aeromed Inst, Fed Aviation Admin, 63- 93. *Concurrent Pos:* Adj prof pharmacol, 63-71; prof pharmacol & psychiat, Univ Okla, 71- *Mem:* Am Soc Pharmacol & Exp Therapeut; Soc Neurosci; Asn Res Vision Ophthal; Bioelectromagnetics Soc. *Res:* Neuropharmacology of psychotomimetic compounds; neurotoxicity of pesticides and environmental pollutants; comparative neurology of the avian brain; bioeffects of nonionizing electromagnetic radiation; vision and performance; vision. *Mailing Add:* 791 S Youngfield Ct Lakewood CO 80228-2812

REVZIN, ARNOLD, MOLECULAR BIOLOGY, BIOPHYSICAL CHEMISTRY. *Current Pos:* asst prof, 75-81, assoc prof, 81-86, PROF BIOCHEM, MICH STATE UNIV, 86-, ASSOC DEAN, COL NAT SCI, 87- *Personal Data:* b Chicago, Ill, Jan 23, 43; m 66; c 2. *Educ:* Univ Mich, Ann Arbor, BSc(chem eng) & BSc (eng math), 64; Univ Wis-Madison, PhD(chem, 69. *Prof Exp:* Res assoc, Enzyme Inst, Univ Wix, 69-70; res fel, polymer dept, Weizmann Inst, Israel, 70-72; res fel, Max Planck Inst Biophys Chem, Germany, 72072; NIH fel & res assoc, Inst Molecular Biol, Univ Ore, Eugene, 73-75. *Concurrent Pos:* Dir, biochem prog, NSF, 84-85. *Mem:* Biophys Soc; Am Soc Biol Chemists. *Res:* Physical and biochemical studies of nucleic acid-protein interations involved in regulating transcription. *Mailing Add:* Dept Biochem Mich State Univ East Lansing MI 48824-1319

REWCASTLE, NEILL BARRY, NEUROPATHOLOGY. *Current Pos:* dir, Dept Histopath, 81-91, NEUROPATHOLOGISTS, FOOTHILLS HOSP, 91-; PROF PATH, UNIV CALGARY, 81-, SPEC ACAD ADV DEAN, FAC MED, 95- *Personal Data:* b Sunderland, Eng, Dec 12, 31; Can citizen; m 58, Eleanor Boyd; c David, Malcolm, Ian & John. *Educ:* St Andrews Univ, MB, ChB, 55; Univ Toronto, MA, 62; FRCP(C) cert gen path, 62, FRCP(C), cert neuropath, 68. *Prof Exp:* Lectr path, Univ Toronto, 64-68, actg head, Div Neuropath, Banting Inst, 65-69, from assoc prof to prof neuropath & head div, Dept Path, 69-81; head dept, Univ Calgary, 81-91. *Concurrent Pos:* Res fel path, Med Res Coun Can, 60-64; Med Res Coun Can & Muscular Dystrophy Asn Can res fels, 64-70; pathologist, Toronto Gen Hosp, 64-81; consult neuropathologist, Off Chief Med Examr, Alta. *Mem:* Am Asn Neuropath; Can Asn Path; Can Asn Neuropath (secy, 65-69, pres, 77-79); Can Med Asn. *Res:* Human nervous system diseases; skeletal muscle diseases; electron microscopy; neurodegenerative disease; neurooncology. *Mailing Add:* Foothill Gen Hosp Dept Histopath 1403 29th St NW Calgary AB T2N 2T9 Can. *Fax:* 403-670-4748; *E-Mail:* barry.rewcastle@crhahealth.ab.ca

REWOLDT, GREGORY, PLASMA PHYSICS. *Current Pos:* res physicist, 75-89, PRIN RES PHYSICIST, PLASMA PHYSICS LAB, PRINCETON UNIV, 89- *Personal Data:* b Ann Arbor, Mich, Apr 21, 48. *Educ:* Calif Inst Technol, BS, 70; Mass Inst Technol, PhD(physics), 74. *Prof Exp:* Physicist, Res Lab Electronics, Mass Inst Technol, 74-75. *Concurrent Pos:* Lectr, dept astrophys sci, Princeton Univ, 79-84, assoc prof, 84-85. *Mem:* Fel Am Phys Soc. *Res:* Theoretical plasma physics, especially drift and trapped particle instabilities, and stellarator MHD computations. *Mailing Add:* Plasma Physics Lab Princeton Univ PO Box 451 Princeton NJ 08543. *Fax:* 609-243-2662; *E-Mail:* rewoldt@theory.pppl.gov

REX, ROBERT WALTER, EXPLORATION GEOLOGY. *Current Pos:* CONSULT, VENTURE CAPITAL & INVEST BANKING, 85- *Personal Data:* b New York, NY; m 52. *Educ:* Harvard Univ, AB, 51; Stanford Univ, MS, 53; Univ Calif, PhD(oceano), 58. *Prof Exp:* Geologist, US Geol Surv, 51-53; oceanogr, US Navy Electronics Lab, 53; geologist, Scripps Inst Oceanog, Univ Calif, San Diego, 54-57; sr res assoc geochem, Chevron Oil Field Res Co, Stand Oil Co, Calif, 58-67; prof geol sci, Univ Calif, Riverside, 67-72; vpres explor, Pac Energy Corp, Hughes Aircraft Co, Marina Del Rey, Calif, 72-73; pres, Repub Geothermal Inc, Santa Fe Springs, 73-83, chmn bd, 83-85. *Concurrent Pos:* Consult, Jet Propulsion Lab, Calif Inst Technol, 63-65; res geologist, Inst Geophys & Planetary Physics, 67-72, asst dir, 71-72; dir, Geothermal Resources Prog, Univ Calif, Riverside, 68-72; res affil, Inst Geophys, Univ Hawaii, 69-; consult, US Bur Reclamation; chmn, Geothermal Adv Bd, Univ Calif, 70-72; mem, President's Panel, Off Sci & Technol, 71-73 & Nat Adv Panel, Hawaii Geothermal Proj, 73-; mem, Tech Adv Comt, Calif Geothermal Resources Bd, 71-; consult, Los Alamos Sci Lab, 71- & Oak Ridge Nat Lab, 72-; dir, Geothermal Resources Coun, 76-86. *Mem:* Geol Soc Am; Am Geophys Union; AAAS; Geochem Soc; Sigma Xi; Mineral Soc Am. *Res:* Exploration and resource assessment of geothermal resources; oil and gas exploration; economic geology; mineral-water interactions; mineralogy of deep sea sediments and atmospheric dust; x-ray powder diffraction; geochemistry of geothermal systems; clays and clay minerals; exploration systems, strategy, economics and technology; energy resource and technology evaluation for venture capital and investment banking. *Mailing Add:* 2780 Casalero Dr La Habra CA 90631

REXER, JOACHIM, METALLURGY. *Current Pos:* CONSULT, NASA SPACE STA FREEDOM, ANALEX CORP, 89- *Personal Data:* b New York, NY, Nov 30, 28; m 62; c 2. *Educ:* Brooklyn Col, BA, 52; Iowa State Univ, MS, 59, PhD(metall), 62. *Honors & Awards:* Recipient of Certs Recognition Creative Develop Tech Innovations, NASA, 82. *Prof Exp:* Jr chemist, Ames Labs, Iowa State Univ, 52-54 & 57, asst metall, 57-62; metallurgist, Parma Tech Ctr, Union Carbide Corp, 62-71, sr res scientist, Carbon Prod Div, 71-82, mgr, Micros Dept, 82-88. *Mem:* Am Soc Metals. *Res:* High temperature reaction kinetics; chemical vapor deposition; free space reactions; vacuum and pressure technology; powder metallurgy; high temperature processing in hydrogen atmospheres. *Mailing Add:* 9269 Highland Dr Brecksville OH 44141

REXFORD, DEAN R, fluorine chemistry; deceased, see previous edition for last biography

REXROAD, CAIRD EUGENE, JR, REPRODUCTIVE PHYSIOLOGY. *Current Pos:* RES PHYSIOLOGIST DAIRY CATTLE, REPRODUCTION LAB, ANIMAL SCI INST, BELTSVILLE AGR RES CTR, MD, 74- *Personal Data:* b Fairmont, WVa, Jan 6, 47; m 68, Doreen R Summers; c Caird III & Leah D. *Educ:* WVa Univ, BS, 68; Univ Wis-Madison, MS, 72, PhD(reproductive physiol & endocrinol), 74. *Mem:* Am Soc Animal Sci; Soc Study Reproduction; Int Embryo Transfer Soc; Int Soc Animal Genetics. *Res:* Endocrine regulation of sperm transport and uterine motility; transfer of genes into farm animals. *Mailing Add:* 2490 Fall Breeze Ct Gambrills MD 21054. *Fax:* 301-504-8414; *E-Mail:* crexroad@asrr.arsusda.gov

REXROAD, CARL BUCKNER, GEOLOGY. *Current Pos:* PALEONTOLOGIST, IND GEOL SURV, 61- *Personal Data:* b Columbus, Ohio, Apr 2, 25; m 51, Edythe Evans; c Carl Evans. *Educ:* Univ Mo, BA, 49, MS, 50; Univ Iowa, PhD(geol), 55. *Honors & Awards:* Pander Soc Medal, 92. *Prof Exp:* Instr geol, La Tech Univ, 50-53; asst prof, Tex Tech Univ, 55-58; assoc prof, Univ Houston, 58-61. *Concurrent Pos:* Adj prof, Ind Univ, 79-; chief, Pander Soc, 85-90; Ill State Geol Surv Res Affil, 57-61; vis prof, Univ Iowa, 67-68. *Mem:* Soc Econ Paleontologists & Mineralogists; Am Asn Petrol Geol; Pander Soc; Paleontological Soc. *Res:* Carboniferous, Silurian and Ordovician conodonts and related stratigraphy; karst and environmental geology. *Mailing Add:* Ind Geol Surv 611 N Walnut Grove Bloomington IN 47405. *Fax:* 812-855-2862; *E-Mail:* crexroad@indiana.edu

REY, CHARLES ALBERT, HIGH INTENSITY ACOUSTICS, ACOUSTIC TRANSDUCER DEVELOPMENT. *Current Pos:* vpres, 78-86, pres Intersonics Inc, 86-94, PRES INTERSONICS TECHNOL, 93- *Personal Data:* b Oklahoma City, Okla, Apr 8, 34; m 60, Toni Stapley; c Kristin, David, Julie, Lynne, Bruce & Michael. *Educ:* Univ Chicago, AB, 56, BS, 57, MS, 59, PhD(physics), 64. *Prof Exp:* Res assoc physics, Enrico Fermi Inst Nuclear Studies, 63-64; physicist, Lawrence Radiation Lab, Univ Calif, 64-70;

asst prof physics, Univ Notre Dame, 70-74; dir res, Interand Corp, 77-78. *Mem:* AAAS; Am Phys Soc; Sigma Xi; Acoust Soc Am. *Res:* Acoustics; materials processing; communications engineering; high energy physics; elementary particle structure; particle detectors; electronics; acoustic levitation; containerless processing; acoustic transduction, opto-acoustics. *Mailing Add:* 1332 Woodland Lane Riverwoods IL 60015. *Fax:* 847-940-8510

REY, WILLIAM K(ENNETH), aerospace engineering; deceased, see previous edition for last biography

REYER, RANDALL WILLIAM, DEVELOPMENTAL BIOLOGY, REGENERATION. *Current Pos:* from assoc prof to prof, 57-87, actg chmn dept, 77-78, EMER PROF ANAT, SCH MED, WVA UNIV, 87- *Personal Data:* b Chicago, Ill, Jan 23, 17; m 43, Carolyn E Murray; c Elizabeth A & Mary L. *Educ:* Cornell Univ, BA, 39, MA, 42; Yale Univ, PhD(zool), 47. *Honors & Awards:* Benedum, Distinguished Scholar Award, Biosci & Med, WVa Univ, 86. *Prof Exp:* Lab asst zool, Yale Univ, 42-46, instr, 47-50; instr biol, Wesleyan Univ, 46-47; asst prof anat, Sch Med, Univ Pittsburgh, 50-57. *Concurrent Pos:* Prin investr res grants, NIH, 51-82. *Mem:* Am Soc Zoologists; Soc Develop Biol; Am Asn Anat; Int Soc Develop Biol; Am Inst Biol Sci; Differentiation Soc. *Res:* Embryonic development and regeneration of the crystalline lens and neural retina in Amphibia; microsurgical, light, electron microscopic and autoradiographic techniques; embryology; microscopic; regeneration. *Mailing Add:* Dept Anat WVa Univ Sch Med 4052 HSN PO Box 9128 Morgantown WV 26506-9128. *Fax:* 304-293-8159

REYERO, CRISTINA, CELL PHYSIOLOGY. *Current Pos:* STAFF MEM, DYNAMICS BIO STIMULATION, 93- *Personal Data:* b Madrid, Spain, Mar 15, 49; Austrian citizen. *Educ:* Complutense Univ, Madrid, Spain, BS, 65, MS, 71, PhD(biochem), 74; Univ Vienna, PhD(biochem), 75. *Prof Exp:* Res assoc, L Boltzmann Inst Leukemia Res, Vienna, Austria, 74-75, Dept Path, Div Immunol, Sch Med, Yale Univ, 77-79 & Dept Dermat, 80, Dept Anat II, Univ Heidelberg, Fed Repub Ger, 81-83; asst prof biochem, Vienna Univ Vet Sci, 75-77; asst prof immunol & cell biol, Dept Biol, Northeastern Univ, 83-88; founder & pres, Intertech Ventures, Ltd, 91-93. *Mem:* Am Soc Cell Biol; Am Asn Immunologists. *Res:* Regulation of cell growth and differentiation induced by low molecular weight products of tumor lymphoid cells. *Mailing Add:* 70 Walnut St Wellesley MA 02181

REYES, ANDRES ARENAS, plant pathology, agricultural microbiology, for more information see previous edition

REYES, PHILIP, NUCLEOTIDE METABOLISM, ENZYMOLOGY. *Current Pos:* from asst prof to assoc prof, 70-83, PROF BIOCHEM, SCH MED, UNIV NMEX, 83- *Personal Data:* b Tulare, Calif, Sept 5, 36; m 62; c 3. *Educ:* Univ Calif, Davis, 58, MS, 59, PhD(biochem), 63. *Prof Exp:* Res fel, McArdle Lab Cancer Res, Univ Wis-Madison, 63-65; USPHS fel enzymol, Scripps Clin & Res Found, 65-67; res assoc, Children's Cancer Res Found, 67-70. *Concurrent Pos:* Nat Adv Environ Health Sci Coun, NIH, 80-83, Cancer Res Manpower Rev Comt, 85-88; Scholar award, Leukemia Soc Am, 70-75. *Mem:* AAAS; Am Asn Cancer Res; Am Soc Biochem & Molecular Biol; Am Soc Trop Med Hyg. *Res:* Molecular basis for the mechanism of action of pyrimidine, purine and folic acid analogs; nucleotide synthesis and metabolism; cancer chemotherapy; biochemistry of malaria parasites. *Mailing Add:* Dept Biochem Univ NMex Sch Med Albuquerque NM 87131-0001

REYES, VICTOR E, PHARMACOLOGY. *Current Pos:* asst prof, ASSOC PROF, MED BR, UNIV TEX, 95- *Personal Data:* b Caracas, Venezuela, May 27, 59; m 82; c Victor Emmanuel, Xavier Enrique & Christopher Daniel. *Educ:* Tex Tech Univ, BS, 80, MS, 82; Univ Tex, PhD(microbiol immunol), 86. *Honors & Awards:* Young Investr Travel Award, Am Digestive Health Asn & Am Gastroenterol Asn. *Prof Exp:* Teaching asst med microbiol, Tex Tech Univ Health Sci Ctr, 80-82; asst immunol, Med Br, Univ Tex, 82-84; McLaughlin fel, 84-86; res assoc, Med Ctr, Univ Mass, 86-89, instr, 89-91, asst prof immunol, 91- *Mem:* Am Asn Immunologists; Hispanic Am Biomed Asn; AAAS; Mucosal Immunol Soc. *Res:* Roles or invariant chains in antigen processing and presentation; antigen presentation mediated by class I MHC molecules; structural characteristics of antigenic peptides; role of the epithelium on the regulation of mucosal immune responses. *Mailing Add:* Dept Pediat Rm 2-300 Univ Tex Med Br 301 University Blvd Galveston TX 77555. *Fax:* 409-772-1761; *E-Mail:* vreyes@pedi.utmb.edu

REYES, ZOILA, ORGANIC CHEMISTRY. *Current Pos:* sr org chemist, 56-86, CONSULT, SRI INT, 86- *Personal Data:* b Bucaramanga, Colombia, July 18, 20. *Educ:* Univ WVa, AB & MS, 45; Johns Hopkins Univ, PhD(org chem), 48. *Prof Exp:* Res chemist, Gen Aniline & Film Corp, 48. *Mem:* AAAS; Am Chem Soc; Sigma Xi; NY Acad Sci. *Res:* Proteins; amino acids; fatty acids and derivatives; heterocyclic compounds; photochemistry; photopolymers; polymer technology; microencapsulation; chemical and radiation induced graft copolymerization; biotechnology. *Mailing Add:* 317 Yale Menlo Park CA 94025-5229

REYES-GUERRA, ANTONIO, DENTAL SURGERY. *Current Pos:* RETIRED. *Personal Data:* b San Salvadore, El Salvador, Aug 4, 16; m 54, Olive I Scott; c Richard B & Alan S. *Educ:* St Josephs Col, BA & BS, 38; Univ El Salvadore, DDS, 43; Univ Pa, DDS, 46. *Prof Exp:* From intern to resident oral surg, Rosales Hosp, 43-44; dir dent pub health, Pub Health Dept, El Salvadore, 44; oral surgeon, Polyclin Hosp, New York, 56-60, Lincoln Hosp, New York, 55-62; ed, J Am Soc Advan Anesthesia in Dent, 73-88. *Mem:* Am Soc Advan Anesthesia in Dent (pres, 70-71); Am Dent Asn; Am Dent Soc Anesthesia; Int Dent Fedn Anesthetists. *Res:* Anesthesiology in dentistry. *Mailing Add:* 50 Winterhill Rd Tuckahoe NY 10707

REYHNER, THEODORE ALISON, FLUID MECHANICS. *Current Pos:* Sr specialist engr, 60-80, PRIN ENGR, BOEING COM AIRPLANE CO, SEATTLE, 80- *Personal Data:* b Paterson, NJ, Nov 17, 40; m 68. *Educ:* Stanford Univ, BS, 62, MS, 63, PhD(eng mech), 67. *Mem:* Assoc fel Am Inst Aeronaut & Astronaut. *Res:* Boundary layer and shock wave-boundary layer interactions computations; three-dimensional transonic potential flow; computational fluid mechanics; numerical analysis. *Mailing Add:* Boening Comm Airplane Group PO Box 3707 Seattle WA 98124-2207

REYHNER, THEODORE O, ENGINEERING. *Current Pos:* actg head dept eng, 57-58, head civil eng, 67-74 & 78, prof, 56-82, chmn div eng, 78-81, EMER PROF CIVIL ENG, CALIF STATE UNIV, CHICO, 82- *Personal Data:* b Paterson, NJ, Apr 19, 15; m 40; c 2. *Educ:* Newark Col Eng, BS, 37; Columbia Univ, AM, 38; NY Univ, PhD(educ admin), 50; Stanford Univ, MS, 63. *Prof Exp:* Struct draftsman, Robins Conveying Belt Co, NY, 37-38; instr math & physics, Newark Col Eng, 40-42; instr physics, Cooper Union, 42-43; instr civil eng, Lehigh Univ, 43-44; engr timber mech div, Forest Prods Lab, US Forest Serv, Wis, 44-46; assoc prof civil eng, Univ NDak, 46-47; assoc prof archit, Sch Archit & Allied Arts, Univ Ore, 47-49; assoc prof civil eng, Univ Denver, 49-53 & Mich Col Mining & Technol, 53-56. *Concurrent Pos:* NSF sci fac fel, 62-63; consult civil eng, 82- *Mem:* Fel Am Soc Civil Engrs; Am Soc Eng Educ; Am Concrete Inst. *Res:* Reinforced concrete; structural engineering; statistical education. *Mailing Add:* 1325 Neal Dow Ave Chico CA 95926

REYNA, LUIS GUILLERMO, FINANCIAL MATHEMATICS, LARGE SCALE COMPUTATIONS. *Current Pos:* RES STAFF MEM, RES DIV, INT BUS MACH CORP WATSON RES CTR, 85- *Personal Data:* b Cordoba, Arg, Apr 6, 56; m 84, Carolina M Dewez; c Sol M & Matias M. *Educ:* Nat Univ Cordoba, Licenciado, 79; Calif Inst Technol, PhD(math), 83. *Prof Exp:* Courant instr appl math, Courant Inst, NY Univ, 82-84; Alexander von Humboldt res fel, Aerodyn Inst, 84-85. *Concurrent Pos:* Vis mem, Nat Ctr Atmospheric Res, 81 & Math Res Ctr, 82; vis prof, Nat Univ Buenos Aires, 89. *Mem:* Soc Indust & Appl Math; Am Finance Asn; Financial Mgt Asn; Int Fedn Nonlinear Analysts. *Res:* Development of efficient numerical algorithms for the solution of problems arising from either physical or financial applications. *Mailing Add:* 88 Laddins Rock Rd Old Greenwich CT 06870. *E-Mail:* reyna@watson.ibm.com

REYNAFARJE, BALTAZAR, BIOENERGENICS, TRANSDUCTION. *Current Pos:* ASST PROF BIOL CHEM, SCH MED, JOHNS HOPKINS UNIV, 75- *Educ:* Univ St Marcos, Lima, Peru, MD, 53. *Res:* Effects of oxidation concentration on energy. *Mailing Add:* 410 Worthington St Marco Island FL 33937

REYNARD, ALAN MARK, PHARMACOLOGY. *Current Pos:* asst prof, 64-68, ASSOC PROF PHARMACOL, SCH MED, STATE UNIV NY BUFFALO, 68- *Personal Data:* b Boston, Mass, Oct 11, 32; m 61; c 2. *Educ:* George Washington Univ, BS, 53; Univ Minn, PhD(biochem), 60. *Prof Exp:* Fel biochem, Univ Wash, 60-62; fel pharmacol, Yale Univ, 62-64. *Res:* Antibiotics; antibiotic-resistance in bacteria complement. *Mailing Add:* Dept Pharmacol 127 Farber Hall SUNY Health Sci Ctr 3435 Main St Buffalo NY 14214-3001

REYNARD, KENNARD ANTHONY, POLYMER CHEMISTRY, INORGANIC CHEMISTRY. *Current Pos:* RETIRED. *Personal Data:* b Philadelphia, Pa, Jan 13, 39; m 66; c 1. *Educ:* St Louis Univ, BS, 60, MS, 64, PhD(chem), 67. *Honors & Awards:* IR-100 Award, Indust Res Mag, 71. *Prof Exp:* Proj engr, USAF, Fla, 66-69; group leader polymer chem, Horizons Res Inc, 69-72, head, Chem Dept, 72-74, mgr contract res & develop, 74-76; tech mgr fluids, emulsions & compounds, Wacker Silicones Corp, 76-78, tech dir, 78-88, dir qual assurance, 88-93. *Mem:* Am Chem Soc; Am Soc Qual Control. *Res:* Synthesis of monomers and polymers polysiloxanes; characterization of polyphosphazenes, inorganic chemistry; elastomers; phosphorus-nitrogen compounds, boron-nitrogen compounds, organo-silicon compounds, organometallic chemistry; waste utilization, electrostatics, inks and toners; research and development in chemistry and physics as related to materials and processes. *Mailing Add:* 2496 Cedarwood Dr Adrian MI 49221-9209

REYNHOUT, JAMES KENNETH, DEVELOPMENTAL BIOLOGY. *Current Pos:* ASST PROF BIOL, OAKLAND UNIV, 78- *Personal Data:* b Mysore City, India, July 6, 42; US citizen; m 63; c 4. *Educ:* Barrington Col, BS, 64; Brown Univ, MS, 68, PhD(develop biol), 71. *Prof Exp:* Res assoc biol, Purdue Univ, 70-73; asst prof biol, Holy Cross Col, 73-75; res scientist, Mich Cancer Found, 76-78. *Mem:* Soc Develop Biol; Am Soc Zoologists; AAAS; Sigma Xi. *Res:* Developmental regulation, especially endocrine mechanisms stimulating meiosis; chromosomal interaction in hybrids; chromosomal proteins in developmental regulation. *Mailing Add:* Biol Dept Bethel Col 3900 Bethel Dr St Paul MN 55112-6979

REYNIK, ROBERT JOHN, MATERIALS SCIENCE & ENGINEERING, RESEARCH & TECHNOLOGY EDUCATION ADMINISTRATION. *Current Pos:* assoc prog dir eng mat, Div Eng, NSF, 70-71, dir eng mat prog, Div Mat Res, 71-74, dir metall prog, 74-84, sect head, Metall Polymers, Ceramics & Electronic Mat, 84-90, head off spec progs mat, 90-94, SR

STAFF SCIENTIST, NSF, 94- *Personal Data:* b Bayonne, NJ, Dec 25, 32; m 59, Walker; c Michael, Christopher, Jonathan, Katherine, Steven & Kevin. *Educ:* Univ Detroit, BS, 56; Univ Cincinnati, MS, 60, PhD(theoret phys chem), 63. *Prof Exp:* Mem tech staff, Bell Tel Labs, Inc, NY, 57-58; res fel appl sci & elec eng, Univ Cincinnati, 58-59, lectr math & elec eng, 59-61; head, Physics Dept, Ohio Col Appl Sci, 61-62; lectr math, Xavier Univ, Ohio, 62-63; fel metall eng, Univ Pa, 63-64; from asst prof to assoc prof, Drexel Univ, 64-70. *Concurrent Pos:* Indust consult, 65-; res grants, NSF, 65-72 & Am Iron & Steel Inst, 67-71; NIH dent training grant, 67-72; chmn, Physics & Chem Mat Comt, Metall Soc, chmn Met Trans A Publ Comt, mem first deleg, People's Rep China, 78 & mem Prog Comt, 80-83; mem Planning Group & prog dir, Electo, Metall & Corrosion Work Group, US-USSR Sci & Technol Int Agreement, 73-; deleg to nat comn on mat policy, NSF liaison rep numerous comt, Nat Acad Sci; comt, Nat Metall Adv Bd, 71-; chmn, interagency mat group, Comt Mat/Off Sci & Technol Policy, 84-; vis prof mat sci & eng, Univ Pa, 82-83; liason rep, mat systs eng sub-panel, Eng Res Bd, Comt Eng & Tech Systs, NSF liaison rep comts, Nat Acad Sci & Nat Mat Adv Bd, 71-; chmn, Long Range Planning Comt, Electronic, Magnetic Photonic Mat Div, Metall Soc, 90-91; mem, sr exec serv, Fed Govt, 85-; Am Inst Mining Metall & Petrol Engrs, Engrs Pulp Policy Coun, Am Asn Eng Soc, 93-; vchmn Joint Comt Indust & Technol, Comt Educ & Human Resources, Fed Coord Coun Sci, Engr & Technol Comt Tech Educ. *Mem:* Am Inst Mining Metall & Petrol Engrs; Metal Soc; Sigma Xi; fel Am Soc Metals Int; Am Chem Soc; Mat Res Soc; AAAS; Am Phys Soc. *Res:* Transport properties of liquid metals; biomaterials; electronic and magnetic behavior of materials; material research and technology education administration. *Mailing Add:* Off Sci & Tech Rm 1270 4201 Wilson Blvd Arlington VA 22230. *Fax:* 703-306-0515; *E-Mail:* rreynik@nsf.gov

REYNOLDS, BRIAN EDGAR, MEDICINAL CHEMISTRY, ORGANIC CHEMISTRY. *Current Pos:* RETIRED. *Personal Data:* b Drogheda, Ireland, Mar 5, 36; m 60; c 2. *Educ:* Queen's Univ, Belfast, 59, PhD(org chem), 62. *Prof Exp:* Res fel chem, Univ Rochester, 62-64; res scientist med chem, McNeil Labs, Inc, 64-93. *Mem:* Am Chem Soc; Royal Soc Chem. *Res:* Synthesis and biosynthesis of natural products; synthesis of organic chemicals for possible use as pharmaceuticals. *Mailing Add:* 285 55th St Avalon NJ 08202

REYNOLDS, BRUCE G, NUCLEAR PHYSICS. *Current Pos:* CHIEF EXEC OFFICER, OMEGA SERV GROUP, 82- *Personal Data:* b Ft Myers, Fla, Jan 16, 37; m 61, Dee Ring; c Bruce Jr & Jennifer. *Educ:* Fla State Univ, BS, 61, PhD(physics), 66. *Prof Exp:* Asst prof physics, Fla State Univ, 66-68; asst prof physics & elec eng, Ohio Univ, 68-71; physicist & staff engr, Martin Marietta Corp, 71-74; physicist, Argonne Nat Lab, 74-80; mem tech staff, Bell Tel Labs, 80-81; prin engr, Stromberg Carlson, 81-82. *Mem:* Am Phys Soc; Am Nuclear Soc; Inst Elec & Electronics Engrs. *Res:* Experimental high energy particle physics; hardware/software design of data analysis systems; electrooptical instrumentation and systems engineering; operations research and economic planning; electromagnetic pulse phenomena and electromagnetic compatibility; analysis of telecommunication systems; hydrology and water resource analysis. *Mailing Add:* 3521 Calgary Mt Dora FL 32757

REYNOLDS, CHARLES ALBERT, CHEMISTRY. *Current Pos:* from asst prof to prof, 47-88, assoc chmn dept, 61-67, EMER PROF CHEM, UNIV KANS, 88- *Personal Data:* b Colorado Springs, Colo, Apr 1, 23; m 53; c 6. *Educ:* Stanford Univ, AB, 44, MA, 46, PhD(analytical chem), 47. *Prof Exp:* Asst instr chem, Stanford Univ, 44-47. *Concurrent Pos:* Mem opers res group, US Army Chem Corps, 51-53; tech dir, Edgewood Arsenal, 67-69. *Mem:* Am Chem Soc. *Res:* Organic functional group analysis; complex ion reactions in non-aqueous solvents; thermochemical methods of analysis. *Mailing Add:* 2209 Hill Ct Lawrence KS 66049

REYNOLDS, CHARLES C, METALLURGY, CERAMICS. *Current Pos:* RETIRED. *Personal Data:* b Webb City, Mo, July 17, 27; m 48; c 3. *Educ:* Mass Inst Technol, SB, 47, SM, 54, PhD(metall), 64. *Prof Exp:* Asst prof metall, Mass Inst Technol, 54-57; asst prof, Thayer Sch, Dartmouth Col, 57-60, asst dean, 57-59; fel, Mass Inst Technol, 60-62; assoc prof mech eng, Worcester Polytech Inst, 62-67, prof, 67-81, George F Fuller prof mech eng, 65-82; adj prof & consult, Dept Indust & Mfg Eng, Univ RI, 82-94. *Mailing Add:* PO Box 597 Jamestown RI 02835

REYNOLDS, CHARLES F, SLEEP, AFFECTIVE DISORDERS. *Current Pos:* ASSOC PROF PS6YCHIAT & NEUROL, UNIV PITTSBURGH, 83-; DIR SLEEP EVAL CTR, WESTERN PSYCHIAT INST & CLIN, 84- *Personal Data:* b 1947. *Educ:* Univ Va, BA, 69; Yale Univ, MD, 73; Am Bd Psychiat & Neurol, dipl, 78. *Honors & Awards:* Marie Eldridge Award, Am Psychiat Asn, 82. *Concurrent Pos:* Dir Geopsychiat Clin Res Unit, Western Psychiat Inst & Clin, 87-; mem Psychopath & Clin Biol Res Rev Comt, NIMH, 83-87; prin investr, NIMH, 83-; res scientist develop award, 80- *Mem:* Psychiat Res Soc; Am Col Psychiatrists. *Res:* Sleep, aging and mental illness; the effects of depression on sexual function in men and on maintenance therapies in late life depression. *Mailing Add:* 3811 OHara St Rm 1135 E Pittsburgh PA 15213-2597

REYNOLDS, CHARLES WILLIAM, HORTICULTURE. *Current Pos:* RETIRED. *Personal Data:* b Ala, Nov 30, 17; m 55; c 1. *Educ:* Univ Ala, AB, 41; Ala Polytech Inst, BS, 47, MS, 49; Univ Md, PhD(hort), 54. *Prof Exp:* Instr hort, Ala Polytech Inst, 49-52, assoc prof, 52-53; from asst prof to assoc prof veg crops, Univ Md, College Park, 54-65, prof hort, 65-82. *Concurrent Pos:* Consult, Guatemala, 75, USSR, 78-79 & People's Repub China, 85. *Mem:* Am Soc Hort Sci. *Res:* Mineral nutrition of cucumbers; effects of supplemental irrigation on yield and quality of vegetable corps; cultural studies with cauliflower; vegetable seed production in the United States. *Mailing Add:* 712 Lee Rd 157 Opelika AL 36801

REYNOLDS, CLAUDE LEWIS, JR, EXPERIMENTAL SOLID STATE PHYSICS, MATERIALS SCIENCE. *Current Pos:* from mem tech staff to distinguished mem tech staff, AT&T Bell Labs, 80-96, DISTINGUISHED MEM TECH STAFF, LUCENT TECHNOL, BELL LABS, 96- *Personal Data:* b Roanoke, Va, Dec 16, 48; m 70, 89, Mary E Derr; c Karen, Brian, Kristin & Jeffrey. *Educ:* Va Mil Inst, BS, 70; Univ Va, MS, 72, PhD(mat sci), 74. *Prof Exp:* Sr scientist, Dept Mat Sci, Univ Va, 74-75; res assoc physics, Univ Ill, Urbana, 75-77; sr proj engr, Union Carbide Corp, 77-80. *Mem:* Am Phys Soc; Am Asn Physics Teachers; Sigma Xi; Inst Elec & Electronics Engrs; Mat Res Soc. *Res:* III-V materials growth and properties; electronic materials; metalorganic chemical vapor deposition; molecular beam epitaxy; semiconductor injection lasers; optoelectronics; heterostructure transistors; quantum wells; properties of materials at low temperatures. *Mailing Add:* Lucent Technol Bell Labs 9999 Hamilton Blvd Breinigsville PA 18031. *Fax:* 610-391-2434; *E-Mail:* steelr@lucent.com

REYNOLDS, DAVID B, BIOMEDICAL ENGINEERING, ARTIFICIAL ORGANS-IMPLANTS. *Current Pos:* ASSOC PROF BIOMED & HUMAN FACTORS ENG, WRIGHT STATE UNIV, 80- *Personal Data:* B July 5, 49; m; c 3. *Educ:* Univ Va, PhD(biomed eng), 78. *Mem:* Biomed Eng Soc; Am Physiol Soc. *Res:* Biofluid mechanics; pulmonary mechanics; artificial urinary sphincter; computer modeling of cardiovascular system. *Mailing Add:* 207 Russ Eng Ctr Wright State Univ Dayton OH 45435-0001

REYNOLDS, DAVID GEORGE, PHYSIOLOGY. *Current Pos:* PROF SURG & DIR RES, DEPT SURG, UNIV S FLA COL MED, 87- *Personal Data:* b South Chicago Heights, Ill, Nov 25, 33; m 87; c 2. *Educ:* Knox Col, Ill, BA, 55; Univ Ill, Urbana, MS, 57; Univ Iowa, PhD(physiol), 63. *Prof Exp:* Med Serv Corps, US Army, 57-77, chief basic sci br, US Army Med Field Serv Sch, Tex, 58-60 & 63-65, actg chief dept gastroenterol, Walter Reed Army Inst Res, 65-68, asst chief, 68-72, dep dir div surg, 72-74, dir div surg, 74-77; from assoc prof to prof surg, Univ Iowa, 77-87, dir, Surg Labs & Res, Hosps & Clins, 77-87. *Concurrent Pos:* Spec lectr, Sch Hosp Admin, Baylor Univ, 63-65. *Mem:* Am Physiol Soc; Soc Exp Biol & Med; Asn Acad Surg; Am Fedn Clin Res; NY Acad Sci; Shock Soc (pres, 86-87). *Res:* Gastrointestinal physiology and pharmacology; endogenous opioids; sphlanchnic blood flow; shock. *Mailing Add:* 110 Bank St Minneapolis MN 55414

REYNOLDS, DAVID STEPHEN, APPLIED STATISTICS, APPLIED MATHEMATICS. *Current Pos:* Dept mgr mfg, 54-60, statist engr, 60-62, statist serv group leader, 63-73, DATA SERV MGR PROD DEVELOP, PROCTER & GAMBLE CO, 73- *Personal Data:* b Cincinnati, Ohio, Nov 12, 32; m 58; c 4. *Educ:* Univ Cincinnati, Mech Engr, 54; Fla State Univ, MS, 65, PhD(statist), 69. *Mem:* Am Statist Asn; Inst Math Statist. *Mailing Add:* 9636 Leebrook Dr Cincinnati OH 45231

REYNOLDS, DON RUPERT, MYCOLOGY. *Current Pos:* CUR & HEAD BOT, 75-, MOLECULAR SYST, NATURAL HIST MUS, LOS ANGELES, 93- *Personal Data:* b Shreveport, La, Aug 22, 38. *Educ:* Tex A&M Univ, BS, 60; La State Univ, MS, 62; Univ Tex, Austin, PhD(bot), 70. *Prof Exp:* Mycologist, Univ Philippines, 63-67. *Concurrent Pos:* Adj prof, Univ Southern Calif, 75. *Mem:* Mycol Soc Am. *Res:* Systematics and evolution ascomycete fungi. *Mailing Add:* 900 Exposition Blvd Los Angeles CA 90007

REYNOLDS, DONALD C, GENERAL PHYSICS, SOLID STATE PHYSICS. *Current Pos:* UNIV RES CTR, WRIGHT STATE UNIV, DAYTON, OHIO, 89- *Personal Data:* b Sioux City, Iowa, July 28, 20. *Educ:* Morningside Col, BS, 43; Univ Iowa, MS, 48. *Honors & Awards:* Photo Voltaic Founders Award, Inst Elec & Electronics Engrs, 85. *Prof Exp:* Mat researcher, Battelle Mem Inst, 48-52; res engr, Aerospace Res Lab, Wright Patterson AFB, 52-75, sr scientist, Avionis Lab, 75-89. *Mem:* Fel Am Phys Soc. *Mailing Add:* 1439 Torrence Dr Springfield OH 45503

REYNOLDS, DONALD KELLY, ELECTRICAL ENGINEERING. *Current Pos:* prof, 59-, EMER PROF ELEC ENG, UNIV WASH. *Personal Data:* b Portland, Ore, Dec 9, 19; m 45; c 3. *Educ:* Stanford Univ, BA, 41, MA, 42; Harvard Univ, PhD(eng sci, appl physics), 48. *Prof Exp:* Res engr, Radio Res Lab, Harvard Univ, 42-45; sr res engr, Stanford Res Inst, 48-53; assoc prof elec eng, Tech Inst Aeronaut, Brazil, 53-56; prof & head dept, Seattle Univ, 56-59. *Concurrent Pos:* Sci attache, US Dept State, Am Embassy, Brazil, 72-74. *Mem:* Fel Inst Elec & Electronics Engrs. *Res:* Electronic circuits; antennas; applied electromagnetic theory. *Mailing Add:* Dept Elec Eng Univ Wash Seattle WA 98195

REYNOLDS, EDWIN CLINTON, MECHANICAL ENGINEERING. *Current Pos:* aerospace engr, Okla City Air Logistics Ctr, Tinker AFB, 65-75, dep chief, Engine Test Br, 75-80, chief, Prod Eng Test Sect, 80-81, BR CHIEF, PROD ENG BR, OKLA CITY AIR LOGISTICS CTR, TINKER AFB, 81- *Personal Data:* b Olney, Ill, Mar 4, 39; m 65, Wanda Faye Wesson; c Courtney Rae & Gregory Clinton. *Educ:* Univ Okla, BSME, 62, MME, 69. *Honors & Awards:* Fed Engr of Yr Award, Nat Soc Prof Engrs, 94. *Prof Exp:* Assoc engr, LTV Aerospace Corp, Dallas, 62-63; propulsion design engr, Gen Dynamics Corp, Ft Worth, 63-64. *Mem:* Nat Soc Prof Engrs; Am Soc Mech Engrs. *Res:* Contributed many technical papers to professional journals and conferences. *Mailing Add:* 6507 NW 96th St Oklahoma City OK 73162-7408

REYNOLDS, ELBERT BRUNNER, JR, MECHANICAL ENGINEERING. *Current Pos:* ASSOC PROF MECH ENG & TECHNOL, TEX TECH UNIV, 64- *Personal Data:* b Bryan, Tex, Sept 17, 24; m 64; c 2. *Educ:* Tex A&M Univ, BS, 47; Pa State Univ, MS, 48; Univ Wis, PhD(mech eng), 57. *Prof Exp:* From instr to asst prof mech eng, Pa State Univ, 48-53; serv engr, E I du Pont de Nemours & Co, 57-61; assoc prof mech eng, Univ Va, 61-64. *Concurrent Pos:* Consult, US Naval Weapons Lab, Va, 63-64; NSF grant, 65-67. *Mem:* Am Soc Mech Engrs; Soc Automotive Engrs. *Res:* Thermodynamics; heat transfer; compressible fluid flow; optical instruments for study of heat transfer and compressbile fluid flow; direct energy conversion. *Mailing Add:* 5437 Eighth Pl Lubbock TX 79416

REYNOLDS, GEORGE THOMAS, BIOPHYSICS, HIGH ENERGY PHYSICS. *Current Pos:* Res physicist, Nat Defense Res Comt, 41-44, from asst prof to assoc prof, 46-58, dir, Ctr Environ Studies, 71-74, PROF PHYSICS, PRINCETON UNIV, 58- *Personal Data:* b Trenton, NJ, May 27, 17; m 44; c 4. *Educ:* Rutgers Univ, BS, 39; Princeton Univ, MA, 42, PhD(physics), 43. *Concurrent Pos:* Guggenheim fel, 55-56; consult radiation detection, blast effects & oceanog, 58-; fel, Churchill Found, Cambridge Univ, 73-74; mem bd trustees, Rutgers Univ, 75-; Sci & Eng Res Coun fel, Oxford Univ, 81-82, Royal Soc Res fel, 85. *Mem:* Fel Am Phys Soc; Am Geophys Union; Biophys Soc; fel AAAS. *Res:* Mass spectroscopy; fluid dynamics; cosmic ray; high energy nuclear physics; image intensification; bioluminescence; x-ray diffraction of biological structures. *Mailing Add:* Dept Physics Princeton Univ PO Box 708 Princeton NJ 08544

REYNOLDS, GEORGE WARREN, METEOROLOGICAL SUPPORT PROGRAMS & SYSTEMS, TORNADO DAMAGE PATTERNS. *Current Pos:* SR SCIENTIST, LATCO, 83- *Personal Data:* b Decatur, Ill, May 10, 16; m 41, Virginia Guernsey; c George W & David L. *Educ:* James Millikin Univ, BA, 39; St Louis Univ, MS, 50; Tex A&M Univ, PhD(meteorol & Oceanog), 62. *Prof Exp:* Res assoc & lectr meteorol, Univ Mich, 56-58; meteorologist, US Army Electronic Proving Ground, 58-62; design engr, Martin-Marietta Corp, 62-63; br chief, Geophys Environ, Us Army Res Off, Europe, 63-65; prof meteorol & oceanog, Utah State Univ, 66-72; mgr. Environ Off, Woodward Clyde Consults, 72-75; supvr, Air Qual Assessment, Tenn Valley Authority, 75-83. *Concurrent Pos:* Vis assoc prof meteorol, Univ Mo, Columbia, 65-66; cert consult meteorologist. *Mem:* Am Meteorol Soc. *Res:* Meteorological applications to practical problems; meteorological measurement systems such as Doppler weather radar, lightning detection systems, automatic weather observing stations, quality assurance; tornado forces; wind shear and thermodynamic stability of the lowest 100 meters of the atmosphere. *Mailing Add:* 5895 S Rock Rose Pl Boise ID 83716. *Fax:* 602-840-9405

REYNOLDS, GEORGE WILLIAM, JR, MATERIALS PHYSICS, CHEMICAL PHYSICS. *Current Pos:* from asst prof to assoc prof sci educ, State Univ NY, Albany, 63-65, assoc prof sci, 65-70, assoc prof physics, 70-83, EMER PROF PHYSICS, STATE UNIV NY, ALBANY, 83- *Personal Data:* b South Glens Falls, NY, Aug 18, 28; m 80, Dorothy Nelbach; c 8. *Educ:* Col Educ, Albany, BS, 53, MS, 58; Ohio State Univ, PhD(physics), 66. *Prof Exp:* Teacher, Del Acad & Cent Sch, 53-56; teacher & chmn sci dept, Fulton High Sch, 56-59; asst prof sci educ, Col Educ, Albany, 59-61; instr physics, Ohio State Univ, 62-63. *Concurrent Pos:* Lectr, Naval Res Off Sch, 61-63 & 69-72; consult, Naval Res Lab, 79-88, small computer sys consult, 84- *Mem:* Am Asn Physics Teachers; Nat Sci Teachers Asn; Am Meteorol Soc; Mat Res Soc; Am Phys Soc. *Res:* Chemical kinetics; ion beam-solid interactions and analysis; design and development of instrumentation; ion beam metallurgy. *Mailing Add:* Reynolds Sci Enterprises 26951 Leport St SE Bonita Springs FL 33923. *E-Mail:* nfn06232@naples.net

REYNOLDS, GLENN MYRON, NUCLEAR PHYSICS. *Current Pos:* staff scientist nuclear physics, 70-84, VPRES, SCI APPLNS INT CORP, 85- *Personal Data:* b Alexandria, Minn, Jan 30, 36; m 58, Joyce Kietzmann; c Bruce, Dale & Carolyn. *Educ:* Univ Minn, BS, 61, PhD(physics), 66. *Prof Exp:* Res assoc nuclear physics, Cyclotron Lab, Univ Mich, 66-68; staff assoc, Gulf Gen Atomic, Inc, 68-70. *Mem:* Am Phys Soc; Am Nuclear Soc. *Res:* Charged particle reactions; gamma ray spectroscopy; fission; neutron spectroscopy; nondestructive testing; radiation effects. *Mailing Add:* 1611 Calle Plumerias Encinitas CA 92024. *E-Mail:* grynolds@cts.com

REYNOLDS, GRAY F, FORESTRY. *Current Pos:* DEP CHIEF, NAT FOREST SYST. *Personal Data:* b Burley, Idaho, Oct 27, 45. *Mailing Add:* Nat Forest Syst Rm 3NW PO Box 96090 Washington DC 20090-6090

REYNOLDS, HARRY AARON, JR, veterinary pathology; deceased, see previous edition for last biography

REYNOLDS, HARRY LINCOLN, SPACECRAFT DESIGN. *Current Pos:* CONSULT, ROCKWELL INT, 94- *Personal Data:* b Portchester, NY, Mar 31, 25; m 50, Katherine Haile; c Patricia & Margaret. *Educ:* Rensselaer Polytech Inst, BS, 47; Univ Rochester, PhD(physics), 51. *Prof Exp:* Sr scientist, Oak Ridge Nat Lab, 51-55; sr scientist & div leader, Lawrence Livermore Nat Lab, 55-64, assoc dir, 65-81; prog dir, NASA, Houston, 65; dep assoc dir, Los Alamos Nat Lab, 81-85; dir advan concepts, Rockwell Int Corp, 85-94. *Concurrent Pos:* Consult, Dept Defense & Dept Energy, 65-85, Oak Ridge Nat Lab, 90-95; mem, Army Sci Bd, 82-88. *Mem:* Fel Am Phys Soc. *Res:* Energetic heavy ion nuclear physics; nuclear reactor studies; nuclear weapon physics; arms control; spacecraft design; strategic defense. *Mailing Add:* 801 Via Somonte Palos Verdes Estates CA 90274

REYNOLDS, HERBERT MCGAUGHEY, BIOMECHANICS, ANTHROPOMETRICS. *Current Pos:* from asst prof to assoc prof, 77-91, PROF, DEPT BIOMECH & DEPT ANTHROP, MICH STATE UNIV, 91- *Personal Data:* b Bryan, Tex, Aug 28, 42; m 88, Shelly Smith; c Stacey, Greg, JR, Justin & Alexis. *Educ:* Southern Methodist Univ, BA, 64, MA, 71, PhD(phys anthrop), 74. *Prof Exp:* Anthropologist, Protection & Survival Lab, Civil Aeromed Inst, Fed Aviation Admin, 69-73, res anthrop, 73; res investr, Univ Mich, 73-74; asst res scientist phys anthrop, Dept Biomed, Hwy Safety Res Inst, 74-77. *Concurrent Pos:* Consult, Biomed Sci Dept, Res Labs, Gen Motors Corp, 75-76, Franklin Inst, Philadelphia, 77-78, Haworth Inc, 79-81, Hoover Universal, 81-85 & Motor Wheel, 85, Johnson Controls, 86-87 & Deere & Co, 91-93. *Mem:* Soc Study Human Biol; Human Biol Coun; Am Soc Biomech; Am Asn Phys Anthropologists; Sigma Xi. *Res:* Three-dimensional systems anthropometry; biomechanics; kinematics; human morphology; osteology; mathematical modeling of the human body; human factors; seated operator posture; ergonomics. *Mailing Add:* Dept Biomech Mich State Univ East Lansing MI 48824-1316. *Fax:* 517-487-2023; *E-Mail:* reynolds@ergo.msu.edu

REYNOLDS, JACK, ELECTRICAL & NUCLEAR ENGINEERING. *Current Pos:* RETIRED. *Personal Data:* b Norman, Okla, Jan 11, 29; m 64, Solveig Stridh; c Ingrid & Frederick. *Educ:* Univ Okla, BSEE, 56, ME, 58; Univ Lund, PhD(physics), 64. *Prof Exp:* Engr, RCA, 56; adv studies scientist, Lockheed Missile Systs Div, 58; instr elec eng, Univ Okla, 56-58, instr & engr, Comput Proj, 59-61, res assoc, Res Inst, 61; consult, Stand Elec A/B, Denmark, 62-63; asst prof, Univ Okla & res assoc, Res Inst, 64-67, proj dir, 65-67; sr mem tech staff, Equip Res & Develop Lab, Tex Instruments Inc, 67-78, semiconductor prog mgr, 78-94. *Concurrent Pos:* NSF res grant, 65-67; sr mem tech staff, Sematech. *Mem:* Inst Elec & Electronics Engrs; Sigma Xi. *Res:* Solid state nuclear particle detectors; measurement of beta spectra; investigation of nonlinear effects in semiconductor devices; microwave integrated circuits; solid state microwave devices and components. *Mailing Add:* Tex Instruments Inc 13500 N Central Expressway PO Box 6015 Dallas TX 75222

REYNOLDS, JACQUELINE ANN, BIOCHEMISTRY, BIOPHYSICS. *Current Pos:* from asst prof to assoc prof biochem, Duke Univ, 69-80, prof physiol, 80-88, prof cell biol, 88-92, EMER PROF, DUKE UNIV, 92- *Personal Data:* b Los Angeles, Calif, Oct 19, 30; c 4. *Educ:* Pac Univ, BS, 51; Univ Wash, PhD(phys chem), 63. *Prof Exp:* Res asst prof microbiol, Wash Univ, 66-69. *Concurrent Pos:* John Simon Guggenheim fel, 77-78. *Mem:* Am Soc Biol Chemists. *Res:* Lipid-proteins interactions; structure of serum lipoproteins and biological membranes; physical chemistry of amphiphiles; active transport. *Mailing Add:* Tarlswood Back Lane Easingwold York Y0G 3B6 England. *E-Mail:* canod@dial.pipex.com

REYNOLDS, JAMES BLAIR, FISHERY SCIENCE. *Current Pos:* LEADER & ASSOC PROF, ALASKA COOP FISH RES UNIT, UNIV ALASKA, FAIRBANKS, 78- *Personal Data:* b Ypsilanti, Mich, Nov 9, 39; m 60; c 6. *Educ:* Utah State Univ, BS, 61; Iowa State Univ, MS, 63, PhD(fishery biol), 66. *Prof Exp:* Fishery biologist, Great Lakes Fishery Lab, US Fish & Wildlife Serv, 66-72; asst leader, Mo Coop Fishery Unit, US Fish & Wildlife Serv & asst prof, Sch Forestry, Fisheries & Wildlife, Univ Mo-Columbia, 72-78. *Mem:* Am Fisheries Soc; NAm Benthological Soc; Am Inst Fishery Res Biol; Sigma Xi. *Res:* Fishery mensuration and dynamics, including effects of exploitation; aquatic habitat alteration; biometrics and sampling methodology. *Mailing Add:* 4627 Harvard Circle Fairbanks AK 99709-3011

REYNOLDS, JAMES HAROLD, ENVIRONMENTAL ENGINEERING. *Current Pos:* VPRES, CONSOER TOWNSEND ENVIRODYNE ENGRS INC, 96- *Personal Data:* b Ogden, Utah, Feb 18, 45; m 67, Chrystine Heward; c Cheri, Tami, Juli, Kimi, Bryan & Niki. *Educ:* Utah State Univ, BS, 70, MS, 72, PhD(environ eng), 74. *Prof Exp:* Res engr, Utah Water Res Lab, 73-74; asst prof environ eng, Utah State Univ, 74-80, head div, 78-80; vpres, Montgomery Watson, 80-96. *Concurrent Pos:* Consult engr & vpres, Middlebrooks & Assoc, 72-80; pres, Intermountain Consults & Planners, 78-80. *Mem:* Water Pollution Control Fedn; Asn Environ Eng Profs; Govt Refuse Collection & Disposal Asn. *Res:* Water and wastewater treatment; biological kinetics; physical chemical waste treatment lagoons; small wastewater treatment systems toxicity. *Mailing Add:* Consoer Townsend Envirodyne Engrs Inc 303 E Wacker Dr Suite 600 Chicago IL 60601

REYNOLDS, JAMES HOWARD, PALEOMAGNETISM & MAGNETOSTRATIGRAPHY, VOLCANOLOGY. *Current Pos:* CONSULT, JR MAGSTRAT LTD, 95- *Personal Data:* b Geneva, NY, Feb 13, 53; m 75, Haidee Wilson; c Elise & Elena. *Educ:* Dartmouth Col, AB, 75, MA, 77, PhD(geol), 87. *Prof Exp:* Environ geologist, WVa Geol Surv, 78-79; lectr geol Colgate Univ, 80-82, instr, 82-83; asst prof, Norwich Univ, 87-92, Western Carolina Univ, 93-97. *Concurrent Pos:* Lectr geol, Fulbright Found Argentina, 89; prin investr, Petrol Res Fund, 91-93 & 94-96; adj prof, Univ Pittsburgh, 96- *Mem:* Geol Soc Am; Am Asn Petrol Geologists; Am Geophys Union. *Res:* Chronostratigraphy of neogene strata in active mountain belts. Information is used to glean the tectonic evolution of foreland basins and is applied to hydrocarbon exploration. *Mailing Add:* JR Magstrat Ltd PO Box 300 Webster NC 28788-0300. *E-Mail:* magstrat1@wcu.campus.mci.net

REYNOLDS, JEFFERSON WAYNE, PHYSICAL CHEMISTRY. *Current Pos:* Res chemist, 51-52 & 54-63, SR RES CHEMIST, TENN EASTMAN CO, EASTMAN KODAK CO, 63- *Personal Data:* b Elizabethton, Tenn, Sept 11, 26; m 54; c 2. *Educ:* ETenn State Col, BS, 50; Ohio State Univ, MS, 54. *Mem:* Am Chem Soc; fel Am Inst Chemists. *Res:* Surface chemistry-surface area and pore structure; transition elements-preparation of heterogeneous catalysts; aliphatic chemistry-evaluation of catalysts in hydrogenations, oxidations, condensations; measurement of design data; thermodynamics. *Mailing Add:* 131 Chandler Rd Fall Branch TN 37656-9738

REYNOLDS, JOHN C, PROGRAMMING LANGUAGE, SEMANTICS. *Current Pos:* PROF COMPUT SCI, CARNEGIE MELLON UNIV, 86- *Personal Data:* b Ill, June 1, 35; m 60, Mary Allen; c Edward A & Matthew C. *Educ:* Purdue Univ, BS, 56; Harvard Univ, AM, 57, PhD(physics), 61. *Honors & Awards:* Annual Prog Systs & Lang Paper Award, Asn Comput Mach, 71. *Prof Exp:* From asst physicist to assoc physicist, Appl Math Div, Argonne Nat Lab, 61-70; prof comput & info sci, Syracuse Univ, 70-86. *Concurrent Pos:* Actg asst prof, Stanford Univ, 65-66; prof lectr, Comt Info Sci, Univ Chicago, 68; mem, Working Group 2.3 Prog Methodology, Int Fedn Info Processing, 69-; sr res assoc, Queen Mary Col, Univ London, 70-71; vis res fel, Univ Edinburgh, 76-77; mem, Working Group Formal Lang Definition, Int Fedn Info Processing, 77-91; researcher, Nat Inst Res Info & Automation, France, 83-84 & Imp Col, London, 94-95. *Mem:* Asn Comput Mach. *Res:* Design of programming languages and languages for specifying program behavior, mathematical tools for defining the semantics of such languages, and methods for proving that programs meet specifications; mathematical semantics; programming methodology. *Mailing Add:* Sch Comput Sci Carnegie Mellon Univ Pittsburgh PA 15213-3890

REYNOLDS, JOHN DICK, PLANT EMBRYOLOGY. *Current Pos:* RETIRED. *Personal Data:* b Darby, Pa, June 6, 21; m 48, Jean Pringle. *Educ:* Temple Univ, BS, 49, MEduc, 51; Univ SC, PhD(biol), 66. *Prof Exp:* Instr biol, Hampden-Sidney Col, 50-51; asst prof, Coker Col, 51-62; instr, Univ SC, 62-65; asst prof, Univ Southern Miss, 65-67; assoc prof biol, Va Commonwealth Univ, 67-87. *Concurrent Pos:* Instr, Univ SC, Lancaster Campus, 59-62. *Mem:* AAAS; Am Biol Sci; Bot Soc Am; Int Soc Plant Morphol; Phytochem Soc. *Res:* Uses of infrared spectrophotometry in plant taxonomy; studies in cytoplasmic male sterility; callose distribution and function in the plant kingdom; effect of toxins on gametophyte development in plants. *Mailing Add:* MCR 61 Box 978 Topping VA 23169

REYNOLDS, JOHN ELLIOTT, III, MARINE MAMMALOGY. *Current Pos:* Asst prof biol, 80-86, assoc prof biol & marine sci, 86-90, PROF BIOL & MARINE SCI, ECKERD COL, 90- *Personal Data:* b Baltimore, Md, Nov 8, 52; m 75, Kristen M O'Conor; c John E. *Educ:* Western Md Col, BA, 74; Univ Miami, MS, 77, PhD(biol oceanog), 80. *Concurrent Pos:* Adj fac prof natural sci, Dept Marine Sci, Univ SFla, 82-; prin investr, res grants, Fla Power & Light Co, 82-, US Marine Mammal Comn, 82-90, Save the Manatee Club, 87-, Fla Dept Educ, 85-90; coordr biol, Eckerd Col, 83-85, marine sci, 83-86, chmn natural sci collegium, Eckerd Col, 86-92; mem, Sci Adv Comt, Save the Manatee Club, 87-; mem, Comt Sci Adv on Marine Mammals, US Marine Mammal Comn, 89-, chair, 90-91; comn chmn, 91- *Mem:* Am Soc Mammalogists; Soc Marine Mammal. *Res:* Marine mammals, especially West Indian manatees and bottlenose dolphins; functional anatomical studies; population assessments; behavioral research; applications of geographic information systems to management of marine mammals and their habitats. *Mailing Add:* Eckerd Col PO Box 12560 St Petersburg FL 33733

REYNOLDS, JOHN HAMILTON, ISOTOPE GEOPHYSICS, COSMOCHEMISTRY. *Current Pos:* from asst prof to prof, 50-61, chmn dept, 84-86, EMER PROF PHYSICS, UNIV CALIF, BERKELEY, 89- *Personal Data:* b Cambridge, Mass, Apr 3, 23; m 75, Ann Burchard; c Amy, Horace M, Brian M, Karen L & Petra C. *Educ:* Harvard Univ, AB, 43; Univ Chicago, SM, 48, PhD(physics), 50. *Hon Degrees:* DSc, Coimbra Univ, Portugal, 87. *Honors & Awards:* John Price Wetherill Medal, Franklin Inst, 65; J Lawrence Smith Medal, Nat Acad Sci, 67; Golden Plate Award, Am Academy Achievement, 68; Except Sci Achievement Medal, NASA, 73; Leonard Medal, Meteoritical Soc, 73. *Prof Exp:* Asst, Electro-Acoustic Lab, Harvard Univ, 41-43; assoc physicist, Argonne Nat Lab, 50. *Concurrent Pos:* Guggenheim fel, Bristol Univ, 56; NSF sr fel, Univ Sao Paulo, 63; Fulbright-Hays res award, Univ Coimbra, Portugal, 71; NSF US-Australia Coop Sci awardee, Univ Western Australia, 78; Guggenheim fel, Los Alamos Sci Lab, 87. *Mem:* Nat Acad Sci; fel Am Phys Soc; fel Geochem Soc; Meteoritical Soc; fel Am Acad Arts & Sci; fel Europ Asn Geochem. *Res:* Mass spectrometry; meteoritics; lunar studies; origin and chronology of solar system; noble gas geochemistry. *Mailing Add:* Dept Physics Univ Calif Berkeley CA 94720-7300. *Fax:* 510-643-8497; *E-Mail:* reynolds@garnet.berkeley.edu

REYNOLDS, JOHN HORACE, AGRONOMY, PLANT PHYSIOLOGY. *Current Pos:* from asst prof to assoc prof agron, 62-78, PROF PLANT & SOIL SCI, UNIV TENN, KNOXVILLE, 78- *Personal Data:* b Darby, Pa, Aug 7, 37; m 63, Marjorie Lavers; c Steven & Mark. *Educ:* Univ Md, BS, 59; Univ Wis, MS, 61, PhD(forage crop physiol), 62. *Prof Exp:* Res asst agron, Univ Wis, 59-62. *Mem:* Am Soc Agron; Soil & Water Conserv Soc; Crop Sci Soc Am; Am Forage & Grassland Coun. *Res:* Forage crop physiology; forage quality analysis; photosynthesis. *Mailing Add:* Dept Plant & Soil Sci Univ Tenn Knoxville TN 37996

REYNOLDS, JOHN HUGHES, IV, PHYSICAL CHEMISTRY, TECHNICAL MANAGEMENT. *Current Pos:* Sr res chemist, R J Reynolds Tobacco Co, 68-76, res group leader, 76-80, mgr biobehav res, 80-90, PRIN SCIENTIST, R J REYNOLDS TOBACCO CO, 90- *Personal Data:* b Rome, Ga, Sept 25, 40; m 63, Lee Smith; c Alison L. *Educ:* Shorter Col, Ga, BA, 62; Clemson Univ, MS, 65, PhD(chem), 68. *Mem:* Sigma Xi; Asn Chemoreception Sci; AAAS. *Res:* Product research and development. *Mailing Add:* 7618 Rolling Oak Ct Clemmons NC 27012-9145

REYNOLDS, JOHN KEITH, WILDLIFE MANAGEMENT. *Current Pos:* CHMN, TORONTO REGION CONSERV AUTHORITY, 81- *Personal Data:* b London, Ont, Sept 29, 19; m 45; c 3. *Educ:* Univ Western Ont, BSc, 49, MSc, 50, PhD, 52. *Prof Exp:* Wildlife biologist, Ont Dept Lands & Forests, 52-54, from asst dist forester to dist forester, 54-63, supvr fisheries, 63-64, chief exec off, Prime Minister's Dept, 64-69, secy cabinet, Off of the Prime Minister, 69-71, dep minister, Prime Minister's Dept, 71-72, dep prov secy resources develop, 72-74, dep minister, Ministry Natural Resources, 74-81. *Concurrent Pos:* Mem adv comt sci policy, comt coordrs Can coun resource & environ ministers, Can forestry adv coun, fac adv bd, Fac Forestry, Univ Toronto & adv coun, Sch Admin Studies, York Univ; mem bd trustees, Can Nat Sportsmen's Fund; pres, J K Reynolds Consult Inc. *Mem:* Wildlife Soc; Can Can Soc Environ Biologists. *Res:* Life history studies on Canadian birds and mammals; management of fur-bearers and big game; administration of natural resources. *Mailing Add:* 5 Castledene Crescent Scarborough ON M1T 1R9 Can

REYNOLDS, JOHN TERRENCE, FLUID MECHANICS, NUCLEAR PHYSICS. *Current Pos:* PHYSICIST, KNOLLS ATOMIC POWER LAB, GEN ELEC CO, 64- *Personal Data:* b Savannah, Ga, Oct 26, 37; m 59; c 4. *Educ:* Rice Univ, BA, 60; Duke Univ, PhD(physics), 64. *Mem:* Am Phys Soc. *Res:* Turbulent fluid flow; neutron cross sections. *Mailing Add:* 25 Walden Glen Ballston Lake NY 12019

REYNOLDS, JOHN THEODORE, BACTERIOLOGY. *Current Pos:* from asst prof to prof bact, 56-74, PROF MICROBIOL, CLARK UNIV, 74- *Personal Data:* b Boston, Mass, Apr 27, 25; m 48; c 1. *Educ:* Boston Col, BS, 51; Univ Mass, MS, 55, PhD(bact), 62. *Prof Exp:* Instr biol, Springfield Col, 52-54; instr bact, Smith Col, 54-56. *Concurrent Pos:* NIH fel marine microbiol, Univ Miami, 63-64; res assoc, Inst Indust & Agr Microbiol, Univ Mass, 65-; Fulbright lectr, Univ Saigon, 66-67; adj prof, Univ Mass, Amherst, 69- *Mem:* Sigma Xi. *Res:* Aquatic bacteriology; microbiological cellulolytic activity; microbial physiology. *Mailing Add:* Dept Biol Clark Univ Worcester MA 01610

REYNOLDS, JOHN WESTON, PEDIATRICS. *Current Pos:* PROF DEPT PEDIAT, ORE HEALTH SCI UNIV, 77- *Personal Data:* b Portland, Ore, Aug 5, 30; m 54. *Educ:* Reed Col, BA, 51; Univ Ore, MD, 56. *Prof Exp:* From intern to resident, Med Sch, Univ Minn, Minneapolis, 56-59, from instr to prof pediat, 61-77. *Concurrent Pos:* NIH spec res fel, Med Sch, Univ Minn, Minneapolis, 59-61; NIH career develop award, 64-74. *Mem:* AAAS; Soc Pediat Res; Endocrine Soc; Am Pediat Soc. *Res:* Pediatric endocrinology; metabolism and nutrition; steroid metabolism in infants and children; neonatal medicine. *Mailing Add:* Dept Pediat Ore Health Sci Univ Portland OR 97201

REYNOLDS, JOHN Z, TECHNICAL MANAGEMENT. *Current Pos:* dir staff, Environ/Corp Planning Res, 69-91, DIR GAS FACIL, PLANNING & RES, CONSUMERS POWER CO, 90- *Personal Data:* b Kansas City, Kans, July 31, 40; m 63; c 2. *Educ:* Kans State Univ, BS, 62; Univ Mich, MS & MPh 64, PhD(environ health), 66. *Prof Exp:* Consult, Resource Develop, James Calvert Consult Engr, 67; engr, Indust Conserv, Commonwealth Assoc Inc, 67-69. *Concurrent Pos:* Tech adv, Edison Elec Inst, 70-80; mem, Lake Michigan Cooling Water Studies Panel, 73-75, Non-Radiation Environ Effects Comt, Am Nat Standards Inst, 75, Michigan Sea Grant External Adv Comt, 76; instr, Jackson Community Col, 77; proj mgr, Electric Power Res Inst, 78-79. *Mem:* AAAS. *Res:* Environmental effects of pumped storage hydroelectric development, cooling systems and water resource development. *Mailing Add:* 1772 Crouch Rd Jackson MI 49201

REYNOLDS, JOSEPH, CHEMICAL ENGINEERING, POLLUTION CONTROL. *Current Pos:* From asst prof to assoc prof, 64-77, chmn dept, 76-83, PROF CHEM ENG, MANHATTAN COL, 77- *Personal Data:* b New York, NY, May 19, 35; m 73, Barbara Geary; c Megan & Marybeth. *Educ:* Cath Univ Am, BA, 57; Rensselaer Polytech Inst, PhD(chem eng), 64. *Concurrent Pos:* Consult, Dept Justice. *Mem:* Am Inst Chem Engrs; Air & Waste Mgt Asn; Am Soc Eng Educ. *Res:* Modelling of air pollution control equipment; electrostatic precipitators; filter bag houses; modelling and design of heat recovery equipment; hazardous waste incineration. *Mailing Add:* 450 E 240th St Bronx NY 10471-1710. *Fax:* 718-796-9812; *E-Mail:* reynolds@manvax.bitnet, reynolds@manvax.cc.mancol.edu

REYNOLDS, JOSEPH MELVIN, PHYSICS. *Current Pos:* from asst prof to prof, La State Univ, Baton Rouge, 50-62, head, Dept Physics & Astron, 62-65, vpres grad studies & res, 65-68, vpres instr & res, 68-81, actg vpres acad affairs, 66-68, vpres acad affairs, 81-85, Boyd prof, 62-85, vpres, 85-, BOYD EMER PROF PHYSICS, LA STATE UNIV, BATON ROUGE, 85- *Personal Data:* b Woodlawn, Tenn, June 16, 24; m 50; c 3. *Educ:* Vanderbilt Univ, BA, 46; Yale Univ, MS, 47, PhD(physics), 50. *Prof Exp:* Instr physics, Conn Col, 48-49. *Concurrent Pos:* Guggenheim fel, Kamerlingh Onnes Lab, Univ Leiden, 58-59; mem, Nat Sci Bd, NSF, 66-78; mem, Navig Studies Bd, Nat Acad Sci, 74-75, chmn, Panel Advan Navig Systs, 78-, Space Sci Bd, Nat Acad Sci, 88-, Gov Bd, Am Inst Physics, 87-; Space Sci Bd, Study "Major Directions of Space Sci", Nat Acad Sci, 84-; task force, Sci Uses Space Sta, NASA, 84-; chmn, PHCE Sci Rev Bd, NASA, 83- *Mem:* Fel Am Phys Soc; fel AAAS; Sigma Xi; Am Inst Aeronaut & Astronaut. *Res:* Low temperature physics; liquid helium; superconductivity in pure metals and alloys; gravitational radiation; magnetic properties of metals; transport effects and nuclear magnetic resonance in metals; gravitational physics. *Mailing Add:* Dept Physics La State Univ Baton Rouge LA 70803

REYNOLDS, JOSHUA PAUL, ZOOLOGY. *Current Pos:* prof biol & dean fac, 64-71, vchancellor acad affairs, 71, ADJ PROF BIOL, UNIV NC, WILMINGTON, 71- *Personal Data:* b High Falls, NC, Oct 17, 06; m 37; c 2. *Educ:* Guilford Col, BS, 28; Univ NC, MS, 29; Johns Hopkins Univ, PhD(zool), 34. *Hon Degrees:* DSc, Univ NC, Wilmington, 85. *Prof Exp:* Instr biol, Guilford Col, 29-31; actg asst prof zool, Univ NC, 32-33; from asst prof to to prof biol, Birmingham-Southern Col, 34-49; prof zool, Fla State Univ, 49-64, from asst dean to dean col arts & sci, 51-64. *Concurrent Pos:* Gen Educ Bd grants, Univ Pa, 40-41 & 48-49. *Mem:* Fel AAAS; Am Soc Zoologists; Genetics Soc Am. *Res:* Genetics and cytology of Sciara; human genetics; chromosome behavior. *Mailing Add:* 8111 Blue Heron Dr E Wilmington NC 28403

REYNOLDS, KEVIN A, BIOSYNTHESIS, ENZYME MECHANISMS. *Current Pos:* ASST PROF BIOCHEM, SCH PHARM, UNIV MD, BALTIMORE, 89- *Personal Data:* b Oxford, Eng, Mar 18, 63. *Educ:* Southampton Univ, BSc, 84, PhD(chem), 87. *Prof Exp:* Res assoc, Dept Chem, Univ Wash, Seattle, 87-89. *Mem:* Am Soc Pharmacog; Am Asn Cols Pharm. *Res:* Elucidation of biosynthetic pathways to antibiotics and other secondary metabolites in microorganisms; investigations of the origins of these pathways and mechanistic studies of the enzymes responsible for catalyzing the individual steps. *Mailing Add:* Univ Md 20 N Pine St Baltimore MD 21201-1142

REYNOLDS, LAWRENCE P, ANGIOGENESIS, METABOLISM. *Current Pos:* from asst prof to assoc prof, 85-94, PROF PHYSIOL, NDAK STATE UNIV, 94-, DIR, CELL BIOL CTR, 90- *Personal Data:* b Winslow, Ariz, May 31, 53; m 76, Lavona K Cleaver; c Shaun & Scott. *Educ:* Ariz State Univ, BS, 77, MS, 80; Iowa State Univ, PhD(reproductive physiol), 83. *Prof Exp:* Fetal nutrit, US Meat Animal Res Ctr, USDA, 83-85. *Concurrent Pos:* Co-investr, NSF-Exp Prog Stimulate Competitive Res, 86-; co-prin investr, NIH-Nat Inst Child Health & Human Develop, USDA, 87- & USDA NRICGP. *Mem:* AAAS; Am Physiol Soc; Am Soc Animal Sci; Soc Study Fertil; Soc Study Reproduction. *Res:* Physiology of pregnancy; normal growth, development and function of uterus and placenta, especially their blood supplies; mechanisms regulating growth and development of uterine and placental vascular beds, and the role of angiogenic factors in these processes. *Mailing Add:* Dept Animal & Range Sci NDak State Univ Fargo ND 58105. *Fax:* 701-237-7590

REYNOLDS, LESLIE BOUSH, JR, PHYSIOLOGY, CLINICAL MEDICINE. *Current Pos:* PROF PHYSIOL & FAMILY PRACT, QUILLEN-DISHNER COL MED, ETENN STATE UNIV, JOHNSON CITY, 77-, ASST DEAN & DIR MED EDUC, 77- *Personal Data:* b Lakeland, Fla, Aug 16, 23; m 47; c 2. *Educ:* Randolph-Macon Col, BS, 49; Ga Inst Technol, MS, 51; Univ SC, PhD(physiol), 61; Northwestern Univ, MD, 66. *Prof Exp:* Engr textile fibers dept, Dacron Res Div, E I du Pont de Nemours & Co, 51-54, group leader analytical res & process control, 54-58; asst physiol, Med Col SC, 58-61; asst prof, Med Sch, Northwestern Univ, Chicago, 61-64, res assoc med, 64-67; actg chmn dept physiol, Univ Tenn Med Units, Memphis, 68-69, assoc prof physiol & med, 67-76; staff mem, Al-Med Pract Corp, Dresden, Tenn, 76-77. *Concurrent Pos:* Dir, Memphis Emphysema Clin, 70-72; pres, Asseverator Enterprises, Inc, 76- *Mem:* Aerospace Med Asn; Am Physiol Soc; Am Chem Soc; Am Thoracic Soc; Am Col Chest Physicians; Am Acad Family Physicians. *Res:* Lung mechanics and reflexes; medical education; chest disease. *Mailing Add:* James Quillen Col Med PO Box 328 Kingsport TN 37662-0924

REYNOLDS, MARION RUDOLPH, JR, MATHEMATICAL STATISTICS. *Current Pos:* asst prof, 72-81, ASSOC PROF STATIST & FORESTRY, VA POLYTECH INST & STATE UNIV, 81- *Personal Data:* b Salem, Va, Nov 1, 45; div; c 2. *Educ:* Va Polytech Inst & State Univ, BS, 68; Stanford Univ, MS, 71, PhD(oper res), 72. *Prof Exp:* Statistician, Hercules, Inc, 68. *Mem:* Am Statist Asn; Opers Res Soc Am; Am Soc Qual Control. *Res:* Sequential analysis; nonparametric statistics; quality control; validation of simulation models; applications of statistics and operations research to forestry. *Mailing Add:* Dept Statist Va Polytech Inst Blacksburg VA 24061-0439

REYNOLDS, MARJORIE LAVERS, NUTRITION. *Current Pos:* RETIRED. *Personal Data:* b Collingwood, Ont, Jan 10, 31; m 63, John; c Steven & Mark. *Educ:* Univ Toronto, BA, 53; Univ Minn, MS, 57; Univ Wis, PhD(nutrit, biochem), 64. *Prof Exp:* Res dietitian, Mayo Clinic, 57-59 & Cleveland Metrop Gen Hosp, 59-60; res asst nutrit, Univ Wis, 60-63; res assoc, Univ Tenn, 63-66; instr nutrit, Ft Sanders Hosp Sch Nursing, 67-76, renal dietitian, Ft Sanders Kidney Ctr, 78-79; instr, State Tech Inst, Knoxville, 82-88. *Mem:* Am Dietetic Asn. *Res:* Human nutrition; obesity; gastric secretion. *Mailing Add:* 7112 Stockton Dr Knoxville TN 37909

REYNOLDS, MICHAEL DAVID, EDUCATION ADMINISTRATION, SCIENCE ADMINISTRATION & ECLIPSE ASTRONOMY. *Current Pos:* EXEC DIR, CHABOT OBSERV & SCI CTR, 91- *Personal Data:* b Jacksonville, Fla, Mar 30, 54; m 73, Debra Thompson; c Aimee & Jeremy. *Educ:* Thomas Edison State Col, BA, 79; Univ NFla, MEd, 83; Univ Fla, PhD(sci ed & astron), 90. *Prof Exp:* Field entomologist, USDA, 79; instr & dept chair physics, Fletcher Sr High Sch, 80-86; lectr & amb space sci, Fla Dept Educ, 86-88; dir astron, Brest Planetarium, Mus Sci & Hist, 88-91. *Concurrent Pos:* Adj prof astron, Univ NFla, 83-91; mem, Space Sci Adv Bd, Nat Sci Teachers Asn, 87-90; consult, Am Col Testing Bd, 90-91; bd mem, Adams Environ Adv Bd, Jacksonville, Fla, 90-91. *Mem:* Am Astron Soc; Nat Sci Teachers Asn. *Res:* Chemistry of photographic emulsions for use in astronomical photography, particularly planetary; meteoritics; planetary and eclipse astronomy, astronomy writer and astronomy education. *Mailing Add:* Chabot Observ & Sci Ctr 10902 Skyline Blvd Oakland CA 94619. *Fax:* 510-530-3499; *E-Mail:* reynolds@ousd.k12.ca.us

REYNOLDS, ORLAND BRUCE, ANIMAL PHYSIOLOGY. *Current Pos:* from asst to prof, 68-88, EMER PROF BIOL, NORTHERN MICH UNIV, 88- *Personal Data:* b Mountain Home, Idaho, Feb 15, 22; m 54, Moira Davison; c Ronald D. *Educ:* Idaho State Col, BS, 44; Boston Univ, AM, 55, PhD(biochem), 60. *Prof Exp:* Fel biol, Harvard Univ, 60-61; instr, Sch Med, Boston Univ, 61-62; asst prof, Middlebury Col, 62-68. *Mem:* AAAS; Am Chem Soc; Sigma Xi; Comt Sci Invest Claims Paranormal. *Res:* Comparative physiology; vision. *Mailing Add:* 225 E Michigan St Marquette MI 49855-3823

REYNOLDS, PETER HERBERT, GEOCHRONOLOGY, GEOPHYSICS. *Current Pos:* from asst prof physics to assoc prof physics & geol, 69-90, prof earth sci & physics, 90-96, PROF & CHAIR EARTH SCI, DALHOUSIE UNIV, 96- *Personal Data:* b Toronto, Ont, Sept 28, 40; m 67; c 2. *Educ:* Univ Toronto, BSc, 63; Univ BC, PhD(geochronology), 67. *Prof Exp:* Nat Res Coun Can fel, Australian Nat Univ, 68-69. *Mem:* Geol Asn Can. *Res:* Applications in economic geology and to tectonic problems. *Mailing Add:* Dept Earth Sci Dalhousie Univ Halifax NS B3H 4H6 Can. *E-Mail:* preynold@is.dal.ca

REYNOLDS, PETER JAMES, STATISTICAL PHYSICS, PHASE TRANSITIONS, QUANTUM MONTE CARLO. *Current Pos:* PROG MGR, PHYSICS DIV, OFF NAVAL RES, 88- *Personal Data:* b New York, NY, Nov 19, 49; m 82, Louise Perini. *Educ:* Univ Calif, Berkeley, AB, 71; Mass Inst Technol, PhD(physics), 79. *Prof Exp:* Asst res prof, Boston Univ, 79-83; staff scientist, Nat Res Comput Chem, Lawrence Berkeley Lab, Univ Calif, 80-81, Mat & Chem Sci Div, 82-88. *Concurrent Pos:* Vis scientist, Fundamental Res Labs, Nippon Elec Co, Japan, 85; res chemist, Dept Chem, Univ Calif, Berkeley, 88; adj assoc prof chem, San Francisco State Univ, 88-91. *Mem:* Fel Am Phys Soc; Sigma Xi; NY Acad Sci; Optical Soc Am; Mat Res Soc. *Res:* Phase transitions in disordered systems, particularly the critical properties of generalized percolation models near their connectivity threshold, and of polymeric systems, especially by renormalization group and Monte Carlo simulation techniques; Quantum Monte Carlo studies of atoms and molecules. *Mailing Add:* 800 N Quincy St Arlington VA 22217. *E-Mail:* pjr@ohm.nrl.navy.mil

REYNOLDS, RAY THOMAS, PLANETARY SCIENCES. *Current Pos:* res scientist, Theoret Studies Br, Space Div, 62-70, chief, 70-79, res scientist, 79-88, ASSOC THEORET & PLANETARY STUDIES BR, SPACE SCI DIV, AMES RES CTR, NASA, 88- *Personal Data:* b Lexington, Ky, Sept 2, 33; m 62, Yolanda Gallegos; c Mark & Daniel. *Educ:* Univ Ky, BS, 54, MS, 60. *Honors & Awards:* Newcombe-Cleveland Award, AAAS, 79; Except Sci Achievement Medal, NASA, 80. *Prof Exp:* Proj scientist, Am Geog Soc, Thule, Greenland, 60-61. *Mem:* Am Astron Soc; fel Am Geophys Union; fel Meteoritical Soc; Am Inst Aeronaut & Astronaut. *Res:* Theoretical studies of the origin, evolution and present state of the solar system with emphasis upon the composition, structure and thermal history of the planets and their satellites. *Mailing Add:* Planetary Systs Br Space Sci Div NASA Ames Res Ctr Moffett Field CA 94035

REYNOLDS, RICHARD ALAN, MATERIALS SCIENCE, SOLID STATE PHYSICS. *Current Pos:* TECH DIR, HUGHES RES LAB, 89- *Personal Data:* b Los Angeles, Calif, Dec 14, 38; m 63; c 2. *Educ:* Stanford Univ, BSc, 60, MSc, 63, PhD(mat sci), 66; Univ Sheffield, MSc, 61. *Prof Exp:* Mem tech staff math physics, Cent Res Labs, Tex Instruments Inc, 65-75; dir, Defense Sci Off, Defense Advan Res Proj Agency, 75-89. *Mem:* Inst Elec & Electronics Engrs Electrochem Soc; Infrared Info Asn; Am Ceramic Soc. *Res:* Electron transport in semiconductors; photoconductive processes in infrared detector materials; materials preparation; processing of semiconductors; compound semiconductors; display technology; high temperature mechanical properties of metals. *Mailing Add:* Hughes Res Lab 3011 Malibu Canyon Rd Malibu CA 90265

REYNOLDS, RICHARD CLYDE, MEDICAL EDUCATION, PHILANTHROPY. *Current Pos:* COURTESY PROF, HEALTH SCI CTR, UNIV FLA, 96- *Personal Data:* b Saugerties, NY, Sept 2, 29; m 54, Mary J Beck; c Karen, Stephanie & Wayne. *Educ:* Rutgers Univ, New Brunswick, BS, 49; Johns Hopkins Univ, MD, 53. *Hon Degrees:* DSc, Hahneman Univ, 89, New York Med Col, 91. *Prof Exp:* From intern to resident med, Johns Hopkins Hosp, 53-55, resident, 57-58, fel med, 58-59; pvt pract, 59-68; assoc prof med, 68-71, asst dean community health, 71-73, prof & chmn dept, community health & family med, Col Med, Univ Fla, 71-78; dean & prof med, Robert Wood Johnson Med Sch, 78-87, sr vpres acad affairs, 84-87, exec vpres, Robert Wood Johnson Found, 88-96. *Mem:* Am Col Physicians; AMA; Am Acad Family Physicians. *Res:* Rural health; problems of health care delivery; evaluation of medical education. *Mailing Add:* Univ Fla Health Sci Ctr Dept Med Civ IM PO Box 100277 Gainesville FL 32610

REYNOLDS, RICHARD TRUMAN, ECOLOGY, ZOOLOGY. *Current Pos:* wildlife biologist res, Bur Land Mgt, 78-79, RES ANIMAL ECOLOGIST, FOREST SERV, ROCKY MOUNTAIN FOREST & RANGE EXP STA, USDA, 79 - *Personal Data:* b Oakland, Calif, Dec 31, 42. *Educ:* Ore State Univ, BS, 70, MS, 75, PhD(wildlife ecol), 79. *Prof Exp:* Res assoc, Dept Fisheries & Wildlife, Ore State Univ, 73-74. *Concurrent Pos:* Consult res, Forest Serv Range & Wildlife Habitat Lab, 74 & Fish & Wildlife Serv, USDA, 75; affil fac, Dept Fisheries & Wildlife Biol, Colo State Univ, 81- *Mem:* Cooper's Ornith Soc; Am Ornith Union; Ecol Soc Am; Raptor Res Found; Asn Field Ornithologists. *Res:* Community and behavioral ecology of vertebrates with an emphasis on the morphological, and ecological underpinnings of their habitat requirements and preferences. *Mailing Add:* Rocky Mountain Forest & Range Exp Sta 240 W Prospect Rd Fort Collins CO 80526-2098

REYNOLDS, ROBERT COLTART, JR, PETROLOGY, GEOCHEMISTRY. *Current Pos:* from asst prof to assoc prof, 60-69, PROF GEOL, DARTMOUTH COL, 69- *Personal Data:* b Scranton, Pa, Oct 4, 27; m 50; c 3. *Educ:* Lafayette Col, BA, 51; Wash Univ, PhD(geol), 55. *Prof Exp:* Sr res engr, Res Ctr, Pan-Am Petrol Corp, 55-60. *Concurrent Pos:* Instr, Benedictine Heights Col, 56-60; expert, US Army Cold Regions Res & Eng Lab, 64-; consult, Oak Ridge Nat Lab, 66. *Mem:* Geochem Soc; fel Geol Soc Am; fel Mineral Soc Am; Clay Minerals Soc. *Res:* Rates and types of chemical weathering and aqueous transport in extreme environments; clay mineralogy and ion exchange processes on clays; computer modeling of the chemistry of aquatic systems. *Mailing Add:* Earth Sci Dartmouth Col Hanover NH 03755

REYNOLDS, ROBERT D, CARDIOVASCULAR CLINICAL RESEARCH. *Current Pos:* MEM STAFF, CLIN RES DEPT, HOECHST MARION ROUSSEL. *Personal Data:* b Butler, Pa, Dec 11, 44. *Educ:* Clarion State, BA, 70; Univ Cincinnati, PhD(physiol), 74. *Mem:* Am Heart Asn; Am Soc Pharmacol & Exp Therapeut. *Mailing Add:* Clin Res Dept Hoechst Marion Roussel 10236 Marion Park Dr Kansas City MO 64137-1405

REYNOLDS, ROBERT DAVID, NUTRITION, BIOLOGICAL CHEMISTRY. *Current Pos:* RES CHEMIST VITAMIN B6 NUTRIT, VITAMIN & MINERAL NUTRIT LAB, HUMAN NUTRIT RES CTR, USDA, 75- *Personal Data:* b Mansfield, Ohio, June 25, 43; m 64; c 2. *Educ:* Ohio State Univ, Columbus, BS, 65; Univ Wis-Madison, PhD(cancer res), 71. *Prof Exp:* Res fel cancer res, Biochem Inst, Univ Freiburg, WGer, 71-72; asst mem cancer res, Fred Hutchinson Cancer Res Ctr, Seattle, 72-73; res assoc vitamin D metabol, Dept Biochem, Univ Wis, 73-75. *Concurrent Pos:* Fel, Damon Runyon Mem Fund for Cancer Res, 71-72; adj prof, Dept Human Nutrit & Food Systs Univ Md, 80-; hon consult, Child's Health Ctr, Warsaw, Poland, 87. *Mem:* AAAS; Am Inst Nutrit; Am Soc Clin Nutrit. *Res:* Energy metabolism at high altitude; nutritional requirements of vitamin B-6. *Mailing Add:* Dept Nutrit & Dietetics Mc 517 Univ Ill 1919 W Taylor St Chicago IL 60612

REYNOLDS, ROBERT EUGENE, PHYSICS. *Current Pos:* From asst prof to assoc prof, 63-79, PROF PHYSICS, REED COL, 79- *Personal Data:* b Dallas, Tex, Nov 25, 34; m 56, 70, Ellen Fahey; c Alison, Daniel & Celia. *Educ:* Univ Tex, BA(math) & BS(physics), 56, MA, 58, PhD(physics), 61. *Concurrent Pos:* Vis prof oceanog, Ore State Univ, 87-92. *Mem:* Am Phys Soc; Am Asn Physics Teachers; Am Geophys Union; Fedn Am Scientists. *Res:* Theoretical physics. *Mailing Add:* Dept Physics Reed Col 3203 SE Woodstock Blvd Portland OR 97202. *Fax:* 503-777-7770; *E-Mail:* reyn@reed.edu

REYNOLDS, ROBERT GENE, MACHINE LEARNING, EVOLUTIONARY COMPUTATION. *Current Pos:* interim chair, 90-92, ASSOC PROF COMPUT SCI, WAYNE STATE UNIV, 88- *Personal Data:* b Apr 28, 47; m 83, Kathy Savatsky; c Lauren S. *Educ:* Univ Mich, BS, 70, MA, 72, MS, 78, PhD(comput sci), 79. *Prof Exp:* Asst prof comput sci, Mich State Univ, 79-83. *Concurrent Pos:* Vis assoc prof anthrop, Univ Mich, 91; assoc ed, Int J Sci & Technol, 87- , Int J Software Eng & Knowledge Eng, (90-, Int J Artificial Intel Tools, 91- *Mem:* Inst Elec & Electronics Engrs Comput Soc; Am Asn Artificial Intel; Asn Comput Mach. *Res:* Artificial intelligence, specifically machine learning with an emphasis on evolutionary learning strategies including cultural algorithms and genetic algorithms; use of machine learning techniques to address problems in software engineering; generating software metrics and software reuse. *Mailing Add:* Dept Comput Sci Wayne State Univ 431 State Hall Detroit MI 48202. *Fax:* 313-577-6868; *E-Mail:* reynolds@cs.wayne.edu

REYNOLDS, ROBERT N, ANESTHESIOLOGY. *Current Pos:* Instr surg anesthesia, 52-54, from asst prof to assoc prof anesthesia, 54-66, PROF ANESTHESIA, SCH MED, TUFTS UNIV, 66- *Personal Data:* b Troy, NY, Feb 26, 22; m 51; c 3. *Educ:* Yale Univ, BS, 44; Albany Med Col, MD, 46. *Concurrent Pos:* Asst anesthesiol, New Eng Med Ctr Hosp, Boston, Mass, 51-53, asst anesthetist, 54-55, anesthetist, 55-67, sr anesthetist, 67-; consult pediat anesthesiol, US Naval Hosp, Chelsea, Mass, 68- *Mem:* AMA; Am Soc Anesthesiol; Am Acad Pediat; Am Soc Pharmacol & Exp Therapeut; Asn Univ Anesthetists; Sigma Xi. *Res:* Respiratory physiology in infants; pediatric anesthesia. *Mailing Add:* 46 Homestead Park Needham MA 02194-1518

REYNOLDS, ROBERT WARE, SOLID STATE PHYSICS. *Current Pos:* MEM TECH STAFF, GEN RES CORP, 76- *Personal Data:* b Kingsport, Tenn, Sept 21, 42; m 65; c 2. *Educ:* Davidson Col, BS, 64; Vanderbilt Univ, PhD(physics), 69. *Prof Exp:* Res scientist, Advan Technol Ctr, Inc, 69-76. *Mem:* Am Phys Soc; Sigma Xi. *Res:* Military systems analysis; high energy laser effects and propagation modeling; electron paramagnetic resonance spectroscopy; infrared detection. *Mailing Add:* Sparta Inc 4901 Corporate Dr NW-102 Huntsville AL 35805

REYNOLDS, ROBERT WILLIAMS, physiology, psychology, for more information see previous edition

REYNOLDS, ROGER SMITH, nuclear engineering, for more information see previous edition

REYNOLDS, ROLLAND C, pathology; deceased, see previous edition for last biography

REYNOLDS, RONALD J, SPACE PHYSICS, ASTRONOMY. *Current Pos:* res assoc & lectr physics, 73-76, from asst scientist to assoc scientist, 76-87, SR SCIENTIST, DEPT PHYSICS, UNIV WIS-MADISON, 87- *Personal Data:* b Chicago Heights, Ill, May 17, 43; m 66; c 2. *Educ:* Univ Ill-Champaign, BS, 65; Univ Wis-Madison, MS, 67, PhD(physics), 71. *Prof Exp:* Res assoc, Nat Acad Sci-Nat Res Coun, Goddard Space Ctr, NASA, 71-73. *Mem:* Am Astron Soc; Am Inst Physics; Int Astron Union. *Res:* Detection and spectroscopic analysis of faint emission lines from the interstellar medium and the earth's upper atmosphere. *Mailing Add:* Dept Astron Univ Wis Madison WI 53706

REYNOLDS, ROSALIE DEAN (SIBERT), ORGANIC CHEMISTRY. *Current Pos:* CONSULT, ACAD PRESS, 73- *Personal Data:* b Jacksonville, Ill, Mar 8, 26; m 48, Joseph F. *Educ:* Ill Col, AB, 47; Univ Wyo, MS, 50, PhD(org chem), 53. *Prof Exp:* Instr chem, Univ Wyo, 52; res assoc, Univ Colo, 53-54; lectr & res assoc, Univ Southern Calif, 54-55; asst prof, Univ Wyo, 55-60; from assoc prof to prof chem, Northern Ill Univ, 60-81. *Mem:* Am Chem Soc; Sigma Xi. *Res:* Theoretical and synthetic organic chemistry. *Mailing Add:* 1852 Perry Ct Sycamore IL 60178-3016

REYNOLDS, SAMUEL D, JR, WELDING CODES & STANDARDS, WRITING WELDING HANDBOOK CHAPTERS. *Current Pos:* CONSULT, 95- *Personal Data:* b Upper Darby, Pa, Dec 19, 31; m 54, 84, Angela Corvelli; c 4. *Educ:* Lehigh Univ, BS, 53. *Prof Exp:* Engr/sr engr, Heat Transfer Div, Westinghouse Elec Corp, 57-68, mgr mat eng, Heat Transfer Div, 68-77, fel engr, Tampa Div, 77-80, lead reactor eng, US Nuclear Regulatory Comn, 80-86, fel engr, PGBU, 86-95. *Concurrent Pos:* Fac mem, Temple Univ Eve Col, 57-62 & Drexel Inst Technol (Univ) Evening Col, 62-68; mem, Filler Metals Comn, Am Welding Soc, 70- & Sect IX, Am Soc Mech Engrs, 80- *Mem:* Fel Am Soc Metals Int; fel Am Welding Soc; Nat Asn Corrosion Engrs; Am Soc Mech Engrs. *Res:* Development of specialized welding procedures for power plant heat exchangers, pressure vessels, steam turbines and electrical generators. *Mailing Add:* 1003 Neely St Oviedo FL 32765

REYNOLDS, SANDRA RAE, CANCER IMMUNOLOGY, PARASITE IMMUNOLOGY. *Current Pos:* assoc res scientist, 93-96, RES ASST PROF DERMAT, NY UNIV MED CTR, 96- *Personal Data:* b Muskegon, Mich. *Educ:* Univ Mich, BS, 67, MS, 84, PhD(epidemiol), 89. *Prof Exp:* Med technologist, Univ Mich Med Ctr, 67-79; res fel, Harvard Sch Pub Health, 89-93, res assoc, 93. *Res:* Application of basic research to clinical problems with a focus on developing vaccines for important diseases; development of a t-cell peptide epitope vaccine for schistosomiasis; development of peptide t-cell assays for monitoring patients in clinical trials for melanoma vaccines; early detection for breast cancer; breast cancer vaccine development. *Mailing Add:* Dept Dermat NY Univ Med Ctr 550 First Ave New York NY 10016

REYNOLDS, TELFER BARKLEY, INTERNAL MEDICINE. *Current Pos:* res fel, 53, from asst prof to prof, 53-78, CLAYTON G LOOSLI PROF MED, SCH MED, UNIV SOUTHERN CALIF, 78- *Personal Data:* b Regina, Sask, July 30, 21; nat US; m 55; c 2. *Educ:* Univ Calif, Los Angeles, AB, 41; Univ Southern Calif, MD, 45; Am Bd Internal Med, dipl, 53. *Hon Degrees:* Dr, Univ Montpellier, 85. *Prof Exp:* Chief resident physician, Los Angeles Co Gen Hosp, 50-51; Giannini res fel med, Hammersmith Hosp, London, Eng, 52. *Mem:* Am Soc Clin Invest; Asn Am Physicians; master Am Col Physicians. *Res:* Liver diseases. *Mailing Add:* Co USC Med Ctr 1200 N State St Los Angeles CA 90033-4525

REYNOLDS, THOMAS ALAN, DEVELOPMENT OF MATERIALS FOR CHEMICAL SEPARATIONS, DEVELOPMENT OF MATERIALS FOR SENSORS & OPTICS. *Current Pos:* DIR RES, CHEM TECHNOLOGIES INC, 95-' PRES, REYTECH INC, 95- *Personal Data:* b Winona, Minn, Dec 18, 59; c 3. *Educ:* Idaho State Univ, BA, 85; Wash State Univ, MS, 89; Ore State Univ, PhD(chem), 92. *Prof Exp:* Sr chemist, Bend Res Inc, 92-95. *Concurrent Pos:* Consult, AER Energy Resources, 95-; prin investr, Dept Energy, 96-, USDA, 96- *Mem:* Mat Res Soc; Am Chem Soc; AAAS; N Am Membrane Soc. *Res:* Initiation and direction of research programs in the development of new materials; membranes and absorbents, modification of carbon surfaces, chemical sensors, conductive materials for batteries and nonlinear optical materials. *Mailing Add:* 61513 Twin Lakes Loop Bend OR 97702-9566. *Fax:* 541-385-0390; *E-Mail:* treynolds@chemica.com

REYNOLDS, THOMAS DE WITT, PSYCHIATRY. *Current Pos:* resident psychiat, 56-57 & 59-61, asst dir behav studies, 61-70, supvry med officer psychiat res, W A White Serv, 70-71, chief, 71-72, CLIN DIR, W A WHITE SERV, ST ELIZABETHS HOSP, WASH, DC, 72- *Personal Data:* b Detroit, Mich, July 25, 29; m 51; c 3. *Educ:* Univ Chicago, BA, 47, MD, 55. *Prof Exp:* Intern med, George Washington Univ Hosp, 55-56. *Concurrent Pos:* Assoc prof, George Washington Univ, 67- *Res:* Mathematical approaches to behavioral time series; stability characteristics of such time series in schizophrenic and other types of psychiatric patients. *Mailing Add:* PO Box 218 Washington Grove MD 20880-0218

REYNOLDS, TOM DAVIDSON, ENVIRONMENTAL ENGINEERING. *Current Pos:* from asst prof to assoc prof, 65-77, PROF CIVIL ENG, TEX A&M UNIV, 77- *Personal Data:* b Gatesville, Tex, Apr 2, 29; m 54; c 2. *Educ:* Tex A&M Univ, BSCE, 50; Univ Tex, MSSE, 61, PhD(civil eng), 63. *Prof Exp:* Proj engr, Lockwood, Andrews & Newnan, Consult Engrs, 50-51 & 53-59; asst prof civil eng, Univ Tex, 64-65. *Mem:* Am Soc Civil Engrs; Am Water Works Asn; Water Pollution Control Fedn. *Res:* Investigations concerning water and waste treatment, particularly industrial waste treatment using biological processes. *Mailing Add:* Dept Civil Eng Tex A&M Univ College Station TX 77843

REYNOLDS, VERNON H, SURGERY, ONCOLOGY. *Current Pos:* Res assoc microbiol & surg, 60-61, asst prof, 62-69, ASSOC PROF SURG, SCH MED, VANDERBILT UNIV, 69- *Personal Data:* b Oak Park, Ill, Dec 31, 26; c 2. *Educ:* Vanderbilt Univ, BA, 52, MD, 55. *Concurrent Pos:* Intern & resident surg, Peter Bent Brigham Hosp, Boston, 55-62; NIH fel exp path, 57-58; Arthur Tracy Cabot teaching fel surg, Harvard Med Sch, 61-62; Am Cancer Soc adv clin fel, 62-65; Markle scholar med sci, 62- *Mem:* Am Col Surgeons; Sigma Xi. *Res:* Carbohydrate chemistry; tumor metabolism; cancer chemotherapy. *Mailing Add:* Vanderbilt Hosp Surg Nashville TN 37232

REYNOLDS, WARREN LIND, INORGANIC CHEMISTRY. *Current Pos:* Asst, Univ Minn, 52-54, lectr anal chem, 54-55, lectr inorg chem, 55-56, from asst prof to assoc prof, 56-67, PROF INORG CHEM, UNIV MINN, MINNEAPOLIS, 67- *Personal Data:* b Gull Lake, Sask, Nov 29, 20; m 46, Rose M Pallone; c Allan J, Lawrence W & Michael L. *Educ:* Univ BC, BA, 49, MA, 50; Univ Minn, PhD, 55. *Concurrent Pos:* NSF sr fel, 62-63; Fulbright-Hays res award, 72-73. *Mem:* Am Chem Soc; Am Phys Soc; Royal Soc Chem. *Res:* Kinetics of electron-transfer and substitution reactions; solvation numbers, labilities and contact shifts of metal ions in non-aqueous solvents; bonding in inorganic species. *Mailing Add:* Dept Chem Univ Minn Minneapolis MN 55455

REYNOLDS, WILLIAM CRAIG, MECHANICAL ENGINEERING. *Current Pos:* from asst prof to assoc prof mech eng, Stanford Univ, 57-66, chmn dept, 72-82, chmn, Inst Energy Studies, 74-82, chmn dept, 89-93, PROF MECH ENG, STANFORD UNIV, 66- *Personal Data:* b Berkeley, Calif, Mar 16, 33; m 53; c 3. *Educ:* Stanford Univ, BS, 54, MS, 55, PhD(mech eng), 57. *Honors & Awards:* G Edwin Burks Award, Am Soc Eng Educ, 72; Fluids Eng Award, Am Soc Mech Engrs, 89. *Prof Exp:* Aeronaut res scientist, NASA-Ames Lab, 55. *Concurrent Pos:* Nuclear engr, Aerojet-Gen Nucleonics Div, Gen Tire & Rubber Co, 57; NSF sr fel, Nat Phys Lab, UK, 64-65; vis prof, Pa State Univ, 72; Fairchild scholar, Calif Inst Technol, 84; co-chmn, Stanford Integrated Mfg Asn, 90-; consult fluid & appl mech; co-chair, Stanford Integrates Mfg Asn, 89-94. *Mem:* Nat Acad Eng; fel Am Soc Mech Engrs; fel Am Phys Soc (secy-treas, 84 & 85); Am Asn Univ Profs; Sigma Xi; Am Soc Eng Educ; Am Inst Aeronaut & Astronaut. *Res:* Blowdown thermodynamics; ignition of metals; non-isothermal heat transfer; zero-g fluid mechanics; turbulent boundary layer flow structure; turbulence-wall interactions; stability of gas films; stability of laminar and turbulent flows; boundary-layer calculation methods; surface-tension-driven flows; organized waves in turbulent shear flows; turbulence computation; unsteady turbulent boundary layers; internal combustion engine cylinder flows; unsteady jets and separating flows; turbulence modeling. *Mailing Add:* Dept Mech Eng Stanford Univ Stanford CA 94305-3030

REYNOLDS, WILLIAM FRANCIS, ALGEBRA. *Current Pos:* from asst prof to prof, 57-70, WALKER PROF MATH, TUFTS UNIV, 70- *Personal Data:* b Boston, Mass, Jan 31, 30; m 62, Pauline Fitzgerald; c Nancy & Jane. *Educ:* Col of the Holy Cross, AB, 50; Harvard Univ, AM, 51, PhD(math), 54. *Prof Exp:* Res fel math, Harvard Univ, 54-55; C L E Moore instr, Mass Inst Technol, 55-57. *Concurrent Pos:* Instr, Col Holy Cross, 54-55; prin investr, NSF grants, Tufts Univ, 65-74. *Mem:* Am Math Soc; Math Asn Am. *Res:* Representation theory of finite groups, especially modular and projective representations with applications to structure of groups. *Mailing Add:* Three Preble Gardens Rd Belmont MA 02178. *Fax:* 617-627-3966; *E-Mail:* reynolds@jade.tufts.edu

REYNOLDS, WILLIAM ROGER, ZEOLITE PETROLOGY. *Current Pos:* asst prof, 68-73, ASSOC PROF GEOL, UNIV MISS, 73- *Personal Data:* b Chicago, Ill, Dec 27, 29; m 56; c 5. *Educ:* Univ Wis, BS, 58; Fla State Univ, MS, 62, PhD(geol), 66. *Prof Exp:* Sr geologist, Pan Am Petrol Corp, 66-68. *Mem:* Soc Econ Paleontologists & Mineralogists; Nat Asn Geol Teachers; Sigma Xi; Clay Minerals Soc; Am Geol Soc. *Res:* Stratigraphy; clay mineralogy; sedimentation. *Mailing Add:* Geol Univ Miss Gen Delivery University MS 38677-9999

REYNOLDS, WILLIAM WALTER, SURFACE COATINGS, PETROLEUM CHEMISTRY. *Current Pos:* CONSULT, 87- *Personal Data:* b Pasadena, Calif, Jan 29, 25; m 53; c William, Robert & Todd. *Educ:* Univ Calif, BS, 48. *Honors & Awards:* Roon Award, 57, 58. *Prof Exp:* Res chemist, Shell Oil Co, 48-55, group leader, 55-60, asst chief res chemist, 60-63, spec analyst, 63-65, mgr prod planning, Petrochem Div, Shell Chem Co, 65-67, mgr mkt res, 67-68, mgr econ coord, Chem Econ Dept, 68-75, mgr chem econ, 75-79, mgr chem stategic studies, 79-81, econ consult, Prod Econ Dept, 81-87. *Concurrent Pos:* Mem adv bd, Corp Planner Roundtable, Duke Univ. *Mem:* Am Chem Soc; Chem Mkt Res Asn. *Res:* Petroleum solvents; surface coatings technology; polymer solutions; antioxidants; high temperature fluids; wear of internal combustion engines; petroleum derived additives; petrochemicals; market planning and decision theory; micro-economics; organizational effectiveness. *Mailing Add:* 23519 Creekview Dr Spring TX 77389

REYNOLDS, WYNETKA ANN KING, EMBRYOLOGY. *Current Pos:* CHANCELLOR, CITY UNIV NEW YORK, 90- *Personal Data:* b Coffeyville, Kans, Nov 3, 37; m 83, Thomas H Kirschbaum; c Rachel R & Rex K. *Educ:* Kans State Teachers Col, BS, 58; Univ Iowa, MS, 60, PhD(zool), 62. *Hon Degrees:* Ten hon degrees (DSc, LHD, PhD). *Honors & Awards:* Prize Award, Cent Asn Obstet & Gynec, 68. *Prof Exp:* Asst prof biol, Ball State Univ, 62-65; from asst prof to prof anat, Univ Ill Med Ctr, 65-79, res prof obstet & gynec, 73-79, assoc vchancellor res & dean, Grad Col, 77-79; prof anat, obstet, gynec & provost, Ohio State Univ, 79-82; chancellor, Calif State Univ, 82-90. *Concurrent Pos:* Mem, biol bd, Grad Record Exam, Am Inst Biol Sci; mem, Comt Nutrit Mother & Presch Children, Nat Acad Sci; mem, Primate Adv Bd, Res Resources, NIH; mem, Int Life Scis Inst Bd, Am Bd Med Specialties, Nat Res Coun Comt, Undergrad Sci Bd. *Mem:* Am Asn Anat; Am Soc Zoologists; Soc Develop Biol; Soc Gynec Invest; Endocrine Soc; Sigma Xi; Perinatal Res Soc. *Res:* Transplantation of endocrine pancreas; calcium metabolism in pregnancy; toxicity of methylmercury for fetus and neonate; nutrition during development of fetus. *Mailing Add:* City Univ New York 535 E 80th St New York NY 10021

REYNOLDS-WARNHOFF, PATRICIA, ORGANIC CHEMISTRY. *Current Pos:* RETIRED. *Personal Data:* b Washington, DC, Feb 26, 33; m 56; c 3. *Educ:* Trinity Col, DC, AB, 54; Mass Inst Technol, SM, 59; Univ Southern Calif, PhD(org chem), 62. *Prof Exp:* Res asst org chem, Nat Heart Inst, 55-57; res assoc org biochem, Univ Western Ont, 62-63, instr, 63-64, sessional lectr org chem, 64-65, asst prof org chem, 65-93. *Res:* Natural product structure determination; mechanisms of epoxide rearrangements; rearrangements of alpha-haloketones; hydride transfer reactions. *Mailing Add:* 259 Windemere Rd London ON N6G 2J7 Can

REYNOSO, GUSTAVO D, MEDICINE, PATHOLOGY. *Current Pos:* CHIEF PATH, WILSON MEM HOSP, 72- *Personal Data:* b Gomez Palacio, Mex, Sept 18, 32; US citizen; m 59; c 4. *Educ:* Ateneo Fuente Univ, Mex, BS, 50; Univ Nuevo Leon, MD, 58. *Prof Exp:* Resident path, St Luke's Hosp, Milwaukee, Wis & Marquette Univ, 61; M K Kellogg Found grant, prof path, Sch Med & dir clin labs, Univ Hosp, Univ Nuevo Leon, 61-65; asst clin prof path, Marquette Univ, Sch Med, 65-68; chief cancer res pathologist, Roswell Park Mem Inst, 68-72. *Concurrent Pos:* Assoc pathologist, St Luke's Hosp, Milwaukee, 65-68; asst prof exp path, State Univ NY Buffalo, 68-72; mem immunol subcomt, Nat Colorectal Cancer Prog, 71- *Mem:* AAAS; Am Soc Clin Pathologists; Col Am Pathologists; Asn Clin Scientists; Am Asn Clin Chemists. *Res:* Cancer immunology; biochemical diagnosis of cancer; hormonal interactions in the cancer patient. *Mailing Add:* 1335 Snippan Ave Stamford CT 06902

REZ, PETER, ELECTRON MICROSCOPY & DIFFRACTION, ELECTRON ENERGY LOSS SPECTROSCOPY. *Current Pos:* asst prof, 85-91, ASSOC PROF PHYSICS & CTR SOLID STATE SCI, ARIZ STATE UNIV, 91- *Educ:* Univ Cambridge, BA, 73, MA, 76; Univ Oxford, PhD, 77. *Honors & Awards:* Corning Award, Microbeam Analysis Soc. *Prof Exp:* Asst specialist, Dept Mat Sci, Univ Calif, Berkeley, 77-78, asst res engr, 81-82; asst specialist, Kevex Corp, 78-81; software mgr, Va Microscopes Ltd, 83-85. *Mem:* Inst Physics (UK); Am Phys Soc; Microbeam Analysis Soc; Microscopy Soc Am. *Res:* Electron scattering at electron microscope energies; electron energy loss spectroscopy in the electron microscope (in particular application of near edge structure to studies of bonding); formation of kidney stones; X-ray & electron scattering theory for radiation treatment planning. *Mailing Add:* Ctr Phys Solid State Sci Ariz State Univ Tempe AZ 85287-0002

REZA, FAZLOLLAH M, ELECTRICAL CIRCUIT THEORY, INFORMATION THEORY. *Current Pos:* ADJ PROF SYSTS & COMMUN, MCGILL UNIV, CAN, 75- & CONCORDIA UNIV, CAN, 79- *Personal Data:* b Resht, Iran, Jan 1, 15; m 45; c 6. *Educ:* Teheran Univ, BS & MS, 38; Columbia Univ, MS, 46; Polytech Inst NY, PhD(elec eng), 50. *Prof Exp:* Mem staff elec eng, Mass Inst Technol, 51-55 & Syracuse Univ, 55-68; ambassador, Univ Paris, 69-74. *Concurrent Pos:* Vis prof, Polytech Zurich, Swiss Fed Inst Technol, 62-63; Univ Colo, Boulder, 62 & 65 & Royal Tech Univ, Copenhagen, 63; pres, Tech Univ Sharif (Aryamehr), Iran, 67-68 & Tehran Univ, 68-69; ambassador Iran to Unesco, Paris, 69-74 & Iran to Can, 74-78; hon prof, Polytech Univ, NY, 75 & McGill Univ, Can, 78; hon mem bd, Atomic Energy Iran, 89. *Mem:* Fel Inst Elec & Electronics Engrs; emer mem Am Math Soc; fel AAAS; NY Acad Sci; Sigma Xi. *Mailing Add:* 5 Sandhurst Ct Ottawa ON K1V 9W9 Can

REZAK, MICHAEL, NEUROANATOMY, NEUROPHYSIOLOGY. *Current Pos:* Assoc anat, 76-77, ASST PROF, DEPT ANAT, MED CTR, UNIV ILL, 77- *Personal Data:* b Bradfeing, Ger, Sept 10, 48; US citizen. *Educ:* Univ Wis, BA, 70; Bradley Univ, MA, 72; Univ Ill, PhD(anat-neuroanat), 76. *Mem:* Soc Neurosci; Asn Res Vision & Ophthal; AAAS; Am Soc Primatologists; Am Psychol Asn. *Res:* Neuroanatomical and neurophysiological organization of the mammalian central nervous system. *Mailing Add:* Glenbrook Hosp Div Neurol 2100 Pfingsten Rd Glenview IL 60025

REZAK, RICHARD, GEOLOGICAL OCEANOGRAPHY. *Current Pos:* from assoc prof to prof, 67-90, VIS PROF OCEANOG, 91-, EMER PROF, TEX A&M UNIV, 91- *Personal Data:* b Syracuse, NY, Apr 26, 20; m 65, Anna L Nesselrode; c Christine. *Educ:* Syracuse Univ, AB, 47, PhD(geol), 57; Wash Univ, AM, 49. *Prof Exp:* Instr geol, St Lawrence Univ, 49-51; geologist, US Geol Surv, 52-58; res geologist, Shell Develop Co, 58-63, res assoc, 63-67. *Concurrent Pos:* Prin investr, US Minerals Mgt Serv, 74-83, mem outer continental shelf adv bd & regional tech working group, Gulf Mex region, 83-93; consult, Espy-Houston, Inc & Racal Decca Surv, Inc, 81-84, Tech Disciplines, Inc, 89-90. *Mem:* Fel Geol Soc Am; Soc Econ Paleont & Mineral; Int Phycol Soc; fel AAAS; Am Asn Petrol Geologists; Int Asn Sedimentol. *Res:* Systematics and environmental significance of fossil algae; contributions of algae to carbonate sediments; carbonate stratigraphy and diagenesis, especially cementation; seismic stratigraphy and salt tectonics. *Mailing Add:* Dept Oceanog Tex A&M Univ College Station TX 77843-3146

REZANKA, IVAN, NUMERICAL METHODS. *Current Pos:* scientist, 74-81, sr scientist, 81-83, MGR, XEROX CORP, 84- *Personal Data:* b Prachatice, Czech, Sept 30, 31; m 59; c 2. *Educ:* Charles Univ, Prague, MS, 54; Czech Inst Technol, PhD(physics), 62. *Honors & Awards:* Czech Acad Sci Award, 62, Prize, 68. *Prof Exp:* Res asst aerodynamics, Res & Testing Inst Aerodynamics, Czech, 54-55; from physicist to sr physicist, Nuclear Res Inst, 55-68; res assoc nuclear physics, Res Inst Physics, Stockholm, 68-69; res assoc & lectr, Heavy Ion Accelerator Lab, Yale Univ, 69-74, asst dir, 71-74. *Concurrent Pos:* Consult, Doll Res, Inc, 74-76. *Mem:* Am Phys Soc. *Res:* Nuclear physics, gamma ray and beta ray spectroscopy; computer hardware and software; activation analysis; medical physics; applied physics, fluid dynamics, continuum mechanics, acoustics; xerography; electrography; ink jet physics. *Mailing Add:* Six Squire Lane Pittsford NY 14534

REZEK, GEOFFREY ROBERT, computer integrated manufacturing, project management, for more information see previous edition

REZNICEK, ANTON ALBERT, PLANT TAXONOMY, PHYTOGEOGRAPHY. *Current Pos:* From asst cur to assoc cur, 78-92, CUR, UNIV MICH, ANN ARBOR, 92- *Personal Data:* b Plochingen, Ger, June 11, 50; Can citizen; m 78, Susan A White. *Educ:* Univ Guelph, BSc, 71; Univ Toronto, MSc, 73, PhD(bot), 78. *Concurrent Pos:* Dir, Matthaei Bot Gardens, Univ Mich, Ann Arbor, 87-89. *Mem:* Am Soc Plant Taxonomists; Int Asn Plant Taxon; Bot Soc Am. *Res:* Systematics of Cyperaceae worldwide, primarily Carex; geography of the North American flora, especially disjunct species; plant migrations, persistence of relict species, and dynamics of plant communities that harbor relict species; floristics of the Great Lakes region; history of botanical exploration. *Mailing Add:* 890 Wickfield Ct Ann Arbor MI 48105. *Fax:* 313-763-0369; *E-Mail:* tony.reznicek@um.cc.umich.edu

REZNICEK, BERNARD WILLIAM, nuclear power, for more information see previous edition

REZNICK, BRUCE ARIE, POLYNOMIALS. *Current Pos:* asst prof, 79-83, assoc prof, 83-89, PROF MATH, UNIV ILL, URBANA-CHAMPAIGN, 89- *Personal Data:* b New York, NY, Feb 3, 53. *Educ:* Calif Inst Technol, BS, 73; Stanford Univ, PhD(math), 76. *Prof Exp:* Asst prof math, Duke Univ, 76-78; NSF fel, Univ Calif, Berkeley, 78-79. *Concurrent Pos:* Putnam Probs Comn, 82-85; Sloan fel, 83-87. *Mem:* Am Math Soc; Math Asn Am; Asn Women Math. *Res:* Algebra and number theory which are susceptible to combinational methods including polynomials, lattice points and inequalities. *Mailing Add:* Math Dept Univ Ill 1409 W Green St Urbana IL 61801

REZNIKOFF, WILLIAM STANTON, MOLECULAR GENETICS. *Current Pos:* from asst prof to assoc prof, 70-78, chair, Dept Biochem, 86-91, PROF BIOCHEM, COL AGR & LIFE SCI, UNIV WIS-MADISON, 78-, EVELYN MERCER PROF BIOCHEM & MOLECULAR BIOL, 85- *Personal Data:* b New York, NY, Apr 29, 41; m 67, Catherine Armstrong; c Sarah, Joseph & Charles. *Educ:* Williams Col, Mass, BA, 63; Johns Hopkins Univ, PhD(biol), 67. *Prof Exp:* Fel bact genetics, Harvard Med Sch, 68-70. *Concurrent Pos:* Nat Inst Gen Med Sci career develop award, 72-77; Harry & Evelyn Steenbock career develop award, Univ Wis, 74-78; bd dirs, Promega, 80-94; consult, Biogen SA, 81. *Mem:* Am Soc Microbiol; Am Soc Biol Chemists. *Res:* Analysis of the structure and function of genetic regulatory regions, promoters, operators, associated with genes in Escherichia coli and its viruses; analysis of bacterial transposable elements. *Mailing Add:* Dept Biochem Univ Wis 420 Henry Mall Madison WI 53706-1569. *Fax:* 608-262-3453

RHAMY, ROBERT KEITH, urology, physiology, for more information see previous edition

RHEAD, WILLIAM JAMES, MEDICAL GENETICS, BIOCHEMICAL GENETICS. *Current Pos:* From asst prof to assoc prof, 79-89, actg dir, 91-92, PROF PEDIAT, UNIV IOWA, 89-, ACTG DIR, DIV MED GENETICS, 94- *Personal Data:* b Paris, France, Feb 20, 46; div; c Paul & Evan. *Educ:* Univ Calif, San Diego, BA, 68, PhD(chem), 74, MD, 74; Yale Univ, MPh, 69. *Honors & Awards:* Noel Raine Award, Soc Study Inborn Errors Metab, 82. *Concurrent Pos:* Fac partic, Inter-Dept PhD Prog Genetics, Univ Iowa, 79-, Human Nutrit, 80-, Neurosci, 84-; pres & bd dirs, Asn Glycogen Storage Dis, 89-94; bd dirs, Soc Inherited Metab Dis, 90-93. *Mem:* Am Soc Human Genetics; AAAS; Soc Study Inborn Errors Metab; Soc Pediat Res; Soc Inherited Metab Disorders; Am Inst Nutrit. *Res:* Enzymatic, molecular and genetic defects causing inherited diseases of fatty acid oxidation, mitochondrial function and energy metabolism in man; riboflavin-responsive fatty acid oxidation disorders; glutathione synthetase deficiency. *Mailing Add:* Dept Pediat Iowa City IA 52242. *Fax:* 319-356-3347; *E-Mail:* william-rhead@uiowa.edu

RHEE, AARON SEUNG-JOON, POLYOLEFIN PRODUCT RESEARCH & DEVELOPMENT, DEVELOPMENT OF POLYOLEFIN POLYMERS FOR GEOMEMBRANE, PIPE, & HOSE TUBING APPLICATIONS. *Current Pos:* sr engr polyolefins res & develop, Union Carbide Corp, 80-84, proj scientist, 84-87, res scientist, 87-92, SR RES SCIENTIST POLYOLEFINS RES & DEVELOP, UNION CARBIDE CORP, 92- *Personal Data:* b Seoul, Korea, Aug 15, 46; US citizen; m, Sarah E Park; c David E, Brian B & Christine A. *Educ:* Seoul Nat Univ, Korea, BS, 69, MS, 72; Univ Caalif, Los Angeles, MS, 77, PhD(heat & masstransfer-solar energy), 80. *Prof Exp:* Instr, Army Capt, Korean Mil Acad, Seoul, 72-75; res engr, Univ Calif, Los Angeles, 75-80. *Mem:* Am Soc Mech Engrs. *Res:* Process research and development for the production of alpha-olefins polymers in a gas-phase fluidized-bed UNIPOL reactors; polyethylenes for geomembranes, pipe, and hose-tubing applications. *Mailing Add:* Union Carbide Corp 1 River Rd Bound Brook NJ 08805. *Fax:* 732-271-5059, 7949

RHEE, CHOON JAI, TOPOLOGY. *Current Pos:* asst prof, 66-71, assoc prof, 71-86, PROF MATH, WAYNE STATE UNIV, 87- *Personal Data:* b Pyungyang, Korea, Sept 13, 35; m 64. *Educ:* Univ of the South, BA, 60; Univ Ga, MA, 62, PhD(math), 65. *Prof Exp:* Asst prof math, Randolph-Macon Woman's Col, 65-66. *Mem:* Am Math Soc; Math Asn Am; Sigma Xi. *Res:* Homotopy functors; point set topology. *Mailing Add:* Wayne State Univ Detroit MI 48202-9861

RHEE, G-YULL, PHYSIOLOGICAL ECOLOGY OF ALGAE. *Current Pos:* From res scientist I to res scientist IV, 71-80, RES SCIENTIST V, CTR LABS & RES, NY DEPT HEALTH, ALBANY, 80- *Personal Data:* b Kyunggi-Do, Korea, Feb 10, 39; US citizen; m 68; c 2. *Educ:* Seoul Nat Univ, BS, 61; Northeastern Univ, Boston, MS, 67; Cornell Univ, Ithaca, NY, PhD(aquatic microbiol), 71. *Concurrent Pos:* Adj assoc prof, Cornell Univ, Ithaca, NY, 80- *Mem:* Am Soc Limnol & Oceanog; Phycol Asn Am; Am Soc Microbiol; AAAS. *Res:* Effects of environmental factors in algae physiology and ecology. *Mailing Add:* 213 Featherwood Ct Schenectady NY 12303

RHEE, HAEWUN, MATHEMATICS. *Current Pos:* assoc prof, 68-72, PROF MATH, STATE UNIV NY COL ONEONTA, 72- *Personal Data:* b Seoul, Korea, Sept 12, 37; m 65; c 2. *Educ:* Johns Hopkins Univ, AB, 60; Univ Mass, Amherst, PhD(math), 68. *Prof Exp:* Instr math, Ohio Wesleyan Univ, 64-65; asst prof, Am Int Col, 67-68. *Mem:* Am Math Soc. *Res:* Partial differential equations. *Mailing Add:* Dept Math State Univ NY Col Fitzelle Bldg Rm 321 Oneonta NY 13820

RHEE, JAY JEA-YONG, CHEMICAL PHYSICS, PHYSICAL CHEMISTRY. *Current Pos:* From asst prof to assoc prof, 68-77, PROF CHEM, UNIV LA VERNE, 77- *Personal Data:* b Seoul, Korea, Oct 3, 37; US citizen; m 63; c 2. *Educ:* Univ La Verne, BA, 62; Univ NMex, MS, 66, PhD(chem), 67. *Concurrent Pos:* Vis assoc prof chem, Univ Calif, Davis, 75; consult, Synthane-Taylore Corp, La Verne, Calif; resident dir, Korea Telecommun Co, Ltd, Bell Tel, Antwerp, Belgium, 79-81. *Mem:* Am Chem Soc; Am Inst Physics; Korean Chem Soc. *Res:* Multiphoton spectroscopy and ODMR applications; laser applications on isotope separations; quantum theory; molecular spectroscopy. *Mailing Add:* 2803 Blossom Lane Apt T Redondo Beach CA 90278-2009

RHEE, MOON-JHONG, PLASMA PHYSICS. *Current Pos:* from asst prof to assoc prof, 70-83, PROF ELEC ENG, UNIV MD, 83- *Personal Data:* b Shinanchoo, Korea, Feb 19, 35; m 66; c 4. *Educ:* Seoul Nat Univ, BS, 58, MS, 60; Cath Univ Am, PhD(appl physics), 70. *Prof Exp:* Instr physics, Seoul Nat Univ, 64-66; res fel appl physics, Cath Univ Am, 66-70. *Concurrent Pos:* Vis prof, Seoul Nat Univ, 77-78 & Nat Univ Rosario, 85; consult, Naval Surface Weapons Ctr, 80- *Mem:* Am Phys Soc; Korean Phys Soc; Inst Elec & Electronics Engrs. *Res:* Collective ion acceleration; generation and measurement of charged particles in plasma focus; microwave generation; pulsed power system; picosecond optoelectronic switching. *Mailing Add:* 14313 Sturtevant Rd Silver Spring MD 20905

RHEE, SEONG KWAN, TRIBOLOGY, NOISE & VIBRATION. *Current Pos:* dir mat & mech, Allied Signal Automotive Tech Ctr, 82-91, vpres res, Allied Signal Friction Mat, 91-93, vpres technol, Allied Signal Braking Systs, 93-96, VPRES FRICTION MAT TECHNOL, ALLIED SIGNAL AUTOMOTIVE ASIA, 96- *Personal Data:* b Mokpo, Korea, Aug 18, 36; US citizen; m 75, Mary Kaye Kromminga; c David, Jonathan, Jennifer & Christina. *Educ:* Chosun Univ, BS, 59; Univ Cincinnati, MS, 62, PhD(mat sci), 66. *Honors & Awards:* James Mueller Award, Am Ceramic Soc, 91. *Prof Exp:* Mem tech staff, Sci Res Inst, Korean Ministry Nat Defense, 59-60; mgr mat technol, Bendix Corp Res Labs, 75-76, dir mat chem, 76-81, dir, Mat Develop Ctr, 81-83. *Concurrent Pos:* Chmn, Int Conf Wear of Mat, 81; chmn, Eng Ceramics Div, Am Ceramics Soc, 89-90. *Mem:* Am Soc Mat; Am Soc Automotive Engrs; fel Am Ceramic Soc; fel Am Inst Chemists. *Res:* Surface energy of solids; oxidation of metals; alloying behavior of metals; composite materials; tribology and friction materials; abrasive ceramics; grain growth in metals and ceramics; hard coatings; automotive sensors; tribology and noise vibration particularly relating to braking systems. *Mailing Add:* 21222 Summerside Lane Northville MI 48167

RHEE, SUE GOO, ENZYMOLOGY. *Current Pos:* postdoctoral fel, NIH, 73-74, vis scientist, 74-75, staff fel, 75-79, sr biochem, 79-88, CHIEF, SECT SIGNAL TRANSDUCTION, LAB BIOCHEM, NAT HEART LUNG BLOOD INST, NIH, 88- *Personal Data:* b Seoul, Korea, July 6, 43; c 2. *Educ:* Seoul Nat Univ, BS, 65; Catholic Univ Am, PhD(org chem), 71. *Prof Exp:* Ordnance Maint Officer, Korean Army, 65-67; teaching asst, Phys Chem Lab, Catholic Univ Am, Wash, DC, 67-68, res asst, 68-71, postdoctoral fel, 71-72; postdoctoral fel, State Univ NY, Binghamton, 72-73. *Mem:* Am Soc Biochem & Molecular Biol; Am Chem Soc. *Res:* Signal transduction. *Mailing Add:* Nat Heart Lung & Blood Inst NIH Bldg 3 Rm 122 Bethesda MD 20892-0001

RHEES, RAYMOND CHARLES, INORGANIC CHEMISTRY, ANALYTICAL CHEMISTRY. *Current Pos:* dir res & develop, 68-70, VPRES RES, PAC ENG & PROD CO NEV, 70- *Personal Data:* b Ogden, Utah, Jan 29, 14; m 38; c 5. *Educ:* Utah State Univ, BS, 40, MS, 44; Iowa State Univ, PhD(light scattering), 51. *Prof Exp:* Chemist, Kalunite Inc, 42-44; instr chem, Utah State Univ, 44-45 & Iowa State Univ, 45-51; sr chemist, Union Carbide Nuclear Corp, 51-52, sect head atomic energy, 52-53, dept head, 53-56; sect head anal chem, Am Potash & Chem Corp, 56-60, sect head boron hydrides, 60-63, sect head tech serv, 63-68. *Mem:* Am Chem Soc; Water Pollution Control Fedn; Electrochem Soc; Air Pollution Control Asn. *Res:* Light scattering; analytical and uranium chemistry; fine particle properties; boron hydrides; chlorates and perchlorates; borates; chemical specialties; electrolytic processes in pollution control. *Mailing Add:* 657 Sixth St Boulder City NV 89005-2941

RHEES, REUBEN WARD, NEUROENDOCRINOLOGY. *Current Pos:* from asst prof to assoc prof zool, 73-84, PROF ZOOL, BRIGHAM YOUNG UNIV, 84- *Personal Data:* b Ogden, Utah, Apr 1, 41; m 63; c 5. *Educ:* Univ Utah, BS, 67; Colo State Univ, PhD(physiol), 71. *Prof Exp:* Res asst physiol, Colo State Univ, 67-70, teaching asst physiol, 70-71; fel anat, Univ Utah, Med Sch, 71-72; asst prof physiol, Weber State Col, 72-73. *Concurrent Pos:* Vis prof, Anatomy, Univ Calif, Los Angeles, Med Sch. *Mem:* Am Physiol Soc. *Res:* Neuroendocrine mechanisms by which hormones exert regulatory and behavioral effects on the central nervous system; interrelationships between the endocrine and nervous systems. *Mailing Add:* Dept Zool Brigham Young Univ 575 WIDB Provo UT 84602

RHEIN, ROBERT ALDEN, INORGANIC CHEMISTRY, POLYMER CHEMISTRY. *Current Pos:* RES CHEMIST, WEAPONS DIV, NAVAL AIR WARFARE CTR, 79- *Personal Data:* b San Francisco, Calif, Aug 18, 33; m 56, Ellen J Emerson; c R Alden, Mark E, Kathleen (Steinley), Dirck N & Jane M. *Educ:* Univ Calif, BS, 55; Univ Pittsburgh, MS, 58; Univ Wash, PhD(chem), 62. *Prof Exp:* Assoc engr, Westinghouse Elec Corp, 55-58; eng designer, Boeing Airplane Co, 58-60; sr engr chem, Jet Propulsion Lab, Calif Inst Technol, 62-79. *Concurrent Pos:* Appointment, Univ Mass, 83-84. *Mem:* Am Chem Soc. *Res:* Ultrasonics in liquid systems; inorganic fluorine chemistry; powdered metals combustion; propellant chemistry; silicon chemistry; elastomers. *Mailing Add:* 424 E Kendall Ave Ridgecrest CA 93555-7642

RHEINBOLDT, WERNER CARL, NUMERICAL ANALYSIS. *Current Pos:* ANDREW W MELLON PROF MATH, UNIV PITTSBURGH, 78- *Personal Data:* b Berlin, Ger, Sept 18, 27; US citizen; m 59; c Michael & Matthew. *Educ:* Heidelberg Univ, dipl, 52; Univ Freiburg, PhD(math), 55. *Honors & Awards:* Sr Alex V Humboldt Award, 88. *Prof Exp:* Mathematician aerodyn, Eng Bur Blume, Ger, 55-56; fel appl math, Inst Fluid Dynamics & Appl Math, Univ Md, 56-57; mathematician numerical anal, Comput Lab, Nat Bur Stand, 57-59; asst prof & dir comput ctr, Syracuse Univ, 59-62; dir comput sci ctr, Univ Md, College Park, 62-65, res assoc prof, Inst Fluid Dynamics & Appl Math, 62-63, res prof, 63-72, res prof comput sci ctr, 68-78, prof, Dept Math, 72-78, dir appl math prog, 74-78. *Concurrent Pos:* Asn Comput Mach rep, Nat Acad Sci-Nat Res Coun, 65-67; ed, J Numerical Anal, Soc Indust & Appl Math, 65-; managing ed, 70-73; consult ed, Acad Press, 67-; vis prof, Soc Math Data Processing, Bonn, Ger, 69; consult, Div Comput Res, NSF, 72-75 & 81-89; mem, Adv Comt, Army Res Off, 74-78, exec comt, 81-84; chmn, Comt Appl Math, Nat Res Coun, 79- 85, mem, Bd Math Sci, 84-90; chmn, Bd Trustees, Soc Indust & Appl Math. *Mem:* Am Math Soc; Soc Indust & Appl Math (vpres, 76, pres, 77-78); fel AAAS. *Res:* Applied and computational mathematics; computer applications. *Mailing Add:* Dept Math & Statist Univ Pittsburgh Pittsburgh PA 15260-0001. *E-Mail:* wcrhein@vms.cis.pitt.edu

RHEINGOLD, ARNOLD L, ORGANOMETALLIC CHEMISTRY, CRYSTALLOGRAPHY. *Current Pos:* vis prof, 81-82, assoc prof, 82-86, PROF, CHEM, UNIV DEL, 86- *Personal Data:* b Chicago, Ill, Oct 6, 40; m 66, Janice Faber; c Margaret & Alison. *Educ:* Case Western Reserve Univ, AB, 62, MS, 63; Univ Md, PhD(inorg chem), 69. *Prof Exp:* Proj mgr organometall chem, Glidden-Durkee Div, SCM Corp, 63-65; res fel, Va Polytech Inst, 69-70; from asst prof to prof chem, State Univ NY Col Plattsburgh, 70-81. *Mem:* AAAS; Am Chem Soc; Am Crystal Asn. *Res:* Transition metal/main group cluster synthesis; synthesis and characterization of main group compounds; preparative electrochemistry; main-group homoatomic ring and chain structures; crystallography. *Mailing Add:* Dept Chem Univ Del Newark DE 19716. *Fax:* 302-831-6335; *E-Mail:* arnrhein@udel.edu

RHEINLANDER, HAROLD F, SURGERY. *Current Pos:* from instr to assoc prof, 49-66, PROF SURG, SCH MED, TUFTS UNIV, 66-, VCHMN, DEPT SURG, 79- *Personal Data:* b Ashland, Maine, June 10, 19; m 42. *Educ:* Univ Maine, BA, 41; Harvard Med Sch, MD, 44; Am Bd Surg, dipl, 52; Am Bd Thoracic Surg, dipl, 62. *Prof Exp:* Asst surg, Harvard Univ, 45-46, John Milton fel, 48-49. *Concurrent Pos:* Intern, Peter Bent Brigham Hosp, 44-45; resident, 45-46; resident, Childrens Hosp, Boston, 48-49; resident, New Eng Ctr Hosp, 49-51; asst surg, 50-52, asst surgeon, 52-58, surgeon & chief thoracic serv, 58-; consult, Boston Vet Admin Hosp, 66- *Mem:* Soc Thoracic Surg; Am Asn Thoracic Surg; Am Soc Artificial Internal Organs; Am Col Chest Physicians; Soc Vasc Surg; Am Col Surg. *Mailing Add:* NE Med Ctr 750 Washington St Boston MA 02111-1854

RHEINS, LAWRENCE A, IMMUNODERMATOTOXICOLOGY. *Current Pos:* GEN MGR, INVITRO LAB TECHNOL, ADV TISSUE SCI, UNIV CALIF, SAN DIEGO. *Personal Data:* b Cincinnati, Ohio, Mar 8, 55; m 77; c 2. *Educ:* Univ Cincinnati, BS, 78, MS, 80, PhD(biol sci), 84. *Prof Exp:* Postdoctoral fel, Dept Dermat, Univ Cincinnati, 84-86, asst prof dermat, 86-88; mgr, Skin Care Lab, Procter & Gamble, 88-90; asst dir clin safety & toxicol, Hill Top Res Inc, 90- *Concurrent Pos:* Dermat Found res grant, 85. *Mem:* Am Asn Immunologists; Soc Investigative Dermat; Soc Pediat Dermat; NY Acad Sci; Soc Cosmetic Chemists; Cosmetic Toiletry & Fragrance Asn. *Res:* Effects of environmental toxicants on the immune cells of the skin, immunodermatotoxicology; mechanism of action of inflammatory mediations of the skin. *Mailing Add:* In Vitro Lab Technol Adv Tissue Sci Univ Calif San Diego 10933 N Torrey Pines Rd La Jolla CA 92037

RHEINS, MELVIN S, MICROBIOLOGY, IMMUNOLOGY. *Current Pos:* RETIRED. *Personal Data:* b Cincinnati, Ohio, May 13, 20; m 48; c 2. *Educ:* Miami Univ, BA & MA, 46; Ohio State Univ, PhD(microbiol), 49. *Prof Exp:* From instr to assoc prof pathogenic microbiol, Ohio State Univ, 49-59, actg chmn, Dept Microbiol, 64-65, chmn, 65-67, prof microbiol, 59-84. *Concurrent Pos:* Spec consult, USPHS, 61-63. *Mem:* Fel Am Acad Microbiol; Am Soc Microbiol; NY Acad Sci; Sigma Xi. *Res:* Pathogenesis and immunology of pulmonary diseases, collagen diseases and ocular infection, diseases and malignancies. *Mailing Add:* 12075 Stockwell Rd Sunbury OH 43074

RHEINSTEIN, JOHN, PHYSICS. *Current Pos:* RETIRED. *Personal Data:* b Gardelegen, Ger, May 23, 30; US citizen; m 56, Mary E Jones; c Bruce, Lilo & Eric. *Educ:* Dartmouth Col, AB, 51; Univ Chicago, MS, 57; Munich Tech Univ, PhD(physics), 61. *Prof Exp:* Lectr physics, Munich Br, Univ Md, 58-60; staff mem syst anal, Mass Inst Technol, 61-66, assoc group leader, 66-69, from asst site mgr to assoc site mgr, 69-73, group leader, Lincoln Lab, 73-90; consult, 90-96. *Mem:* AAAS; Inst Elec & Electronics Engrs. *Res:* Medical physics; electromagnetic theory; reentry physics; systems analysis. *Mailing Add:* Ten Gould Rd Lexington MA 02173-1012. *E-Mail:* john.rheinstein@channel1.com

RHEINSTEIN, PETER HOWARD, PHARMACEUTICAL REGULATION, ADMINISTRATION OF HEALTH CARE DELIVERY. *Current Pos:* dir, Div Drug Advertising & Labeling, US Food & Drug Admin, 74-82, actg dep dir, 83-84, actg dir, Off Drugs, 83-84, dir, Off Drug Stand, 84-90, DIR, MED STAFF, OFF HEALTH AFFAIRS, US FOOD & DRUG ADMIN, 90- *Personal Data:* b Cleveland, Ohio, Sept 7, 43; m 69, Miriam R Weissman; c Jason E. *Educ:* Mich State Univ, BA, 63, MS, 64; Johns Hopkins Univ, MD, 67; Univ Md, JD, 73; Am Bd Family Pract, dipl, 77, cert geriat med, 96. *Honors & Awards:* President's Award, Am Col Legal Med, 85, 86, 89 & 90; Outstanding Serv Award, Drug Info Asn, 90. *Prof Exp:* Med intern, US Pub Health Serv Hosp, San Francisco, 67-68, med resident, Baltimore, 68-70; instr, Univ Md Sch Med, 70-73. *Concurrent Pos:* Med dir extended care facils, CHC Corp, 72-74; adj prof forensic med, George Washington Univ, 74-76; adv on essential drugs, Regional Off Southeast Asia, Manila, WHO, 81-; Food & Drugs Admin deleg to US Pharmacopeial Conv, Inc, 85-90; bd dirs, Drug Info Asn, 82-90; mem bd gov, Am Col Legal Med, 83-92; chmn ann meeting, Drug Info Asn, 91 & 94. *Mem:* Drug Info Asn (pres, 84-85, 88-89); fel Am Col Legal Med (treas, 85-88 & 90-91); fel Am Acad Family Physicians; AMA; Am Bar Asn; Fed Bar Asn. *Res:* Evaluation of medical technologies to determine safety, effectiveness and cost effectiveness; mechanisms by which technologies become known to the professions and to the public and by which they are incorporated into medical practice. *Mailing Add:* 621 Holly Ridge Rd Severna Park MD 21146-3520. *Fax:* 301-443-2446; *E-Mail:* prheinst@bangate.fda.gov

RHEINWALD, JAMES GEORGE, EPITHELIAL CELL BIOLOGY, CELL CULTURE. *Current Pos:* from asst prof to assoc prof physiol, 78-90, ASSOC PROF DERMAT, BRIGHAM & WOMEN'S HOSP, HARVARD MED SCH, BOSTON, 93- *Personal Data:* b Chicago, Ill, June 25, 48; m 68, Krystal Luckhart; c 1. *Educ:* Univ Ill, Urbana, BS & MS, 70; Mass Inst Technol, PhD(cell biol), 75. *Honors & Awards:* Fac Res Award, Am Cancer Soc. *Prof Exp:* Res assoc cell biol, Mass Inst Technol, 76-78; asst scientist tumor biol, Dana-Farber Cancer Inst, 78-83, assoc prof physiol, 83-90; vpres, res & develop, Biosurface Technol, Inc, Cambridge, Mass, 91-93. *Mem:* Tissue Cult Asn; Am Soc Cell Biol; Int Soc Differentiation; Soc Investigative Dermat. *Res:* Growth control and differentiated function in human epithelial tissues and cultured cells; identification and study of tissue and tumor-specific proteins. *Mailing Add:* Brigham & Women's Hosp Thorn 805 75 Francis St Boston MA 02115-6110

RHEMTULLA, AKBAR HUSSEIN, GROUP THEORY, ORDERED STRUCTURES. *Current Pos:* PROF MATH, UNIV ALTA, 68- *Personal Data:* b Zanzibar, Tanzania, June 8, 39; Can citizen; m 67; c 3. *Educ:* Univ Cambridge, PhD(math), 67. *Concurrent Pos:* Vis prof, Univ Sao Paulo, Brazil, 82, Universita dejli Studi, Napoli, Italy, 88; mem bd, Can Math Soc, 85- *Mem:* Am Math Soc; Can Math Soc. *Res:* Author of 50 publications in algebra, mostly in group theory and ordered structures. *Mailing Add:* Univ Alta Edmonton AB T6G 2G1 Can

RHIM, JOHNG SIK, VIROLOGY, MEDICAL SCIENCES. *Current Pos:* virologist, 78-80, SR INVESTR, NAT CANCER INST, 80-; ADJ, PROF, GEORGETOWN UNIV, WASHINGTON, DC, 87- *Personal Data:* b Korea, July 24, 30; US citizen; m 62; c 6. *Educ:* Seoul Nat Univ, BS, 53, MD, 57. *Prof Exp:* Res fel poliovirus, Children's Hosp Res Found, Cincinnati, Ohio, 58-60; res fel reovirus, Baylor Col Med, 60-61; res fel Japanese B encephalitis, Grad Sch Pub Health, Univ Pittsburgh, 61-62; res assoc infant diarrhea, Sch

Med, La State Univ, Costa Rica, 62-64; vis scientist arbovirus, Nat Inst Allergy & Infectious Dis, 64-66; proj dir career res, Microbiol Asn Inc, 66-78. *Concurrent Pos:* Mem bd dirs, Winchester Sch, Silver Spring, Md; mem bd dirs, Soc Biomed Res, Rockville, MD. *Mem:* AAAS; Am Asn Cancer Res; Am Asn Immunologists; Soc Exp Biol & Med; Am Soc Microbiol; AMA; Int Assoc Comp Leukemia Res; Int Soc Prev Oncol. *Res:* In vitro chemical physical and viral cocarcinogenesis; immunoprevention of cancer; mechanism of carcinogenesis; isolation and characterization of oncogenes and tumor suppressor genes; prostate carcinogenesis. *Mailing Add:* Nat Cancer Inst Bldg 567 Rm 182 Frederick MD 21702. *Fax:* 301-496-8479

RHIM, WON-KYU, PHYSICS, PHYSICAL CHEMISTRY. *Current Pos:* res fel chem phys, Dept Chem Eng, 71-73, MEM TECH STAFF PHYSICS, JET PROPULSION LAB, CALIF INST TECHNOL, 73- *Personal Data:* b Seoul, Korea, Oct 20, 37; US citizen; m 64; c 4. *Educ:* Seoul Nat Univ, Korea, BS, 61, MS, 63; Univ NC, Chapel Hill, PhD(physics), 70. *Prof Exp:* Res assoc chem phys, Mass Inst Technol, 69-71. *Mem:* Am Phys Soc. *Res:* Solid state nuclear spin dynamics and spin thermodynamics; study of magnetic interactions in solids; instrumentation for magnetic resonance experiments. *Mailing Add:* 1800 San Pasqual St Pasadena CA 91106

RHINEHART, ROBERT RUSSELL, II, CHEMICAL PROCESS CONTROL PLASMA ETCHING, FLUIDS DYNAMICS. *Current Pos:* asst prof chem eng, 85-, PROF CHEM ENG, TEX TECH UNIV. *Personal Data:* b Neptune, NJ, Jan 19, 46; m 67; c 2. *Educ:* Univ Md, Col Park, BS, 68, MS, 69; NC State Univ, Raleigh, PhD(chem eng), 85. *Honors & Awards:* Schoenborn Award, Am Inst Chem Engrs, 85. *Prof Exp:* Engr, Fibers Tech Ctr, Celanese Corp, 69-72, engr, Celriver Plant, 72-73, sr engr, Fibers Mkt Co, 73-80, area supvr, Celriver Plant, 80-82; teaching asst, Introd Comput Prog, NC State Univ, 82-85. *Concurrent Pos:* Tech chmn, IND-Asn Nonwoven Indust; proj engr coal gasification, Pilot Plant, NC State Univ, 83-85, consult process control, 87-88. *Mem:* Am Inst Chem Engrs; Instrument Soc Am; Am Soc Eng Educ. *Res:* Modeling, optimization, and control of chemical processes of industrial nature; plasma etching and semiconductors. *Mailing Add:* Dept Chem Eng Tex Tech Univ PO Box 43121 Lubbock TX 79409-3121

RHINES, PETER BROOMELL, FLUID DYNAMICS. *Current Pos:* PROF OCEANOG & ATMOSPHERIC SCI, SCH OCEANOG, UNIV WASH, SEATTLE, 84- *Personal Data:* b Hartford, Conn, July, 23, 42; m 68, Linda Mattson; c Andrew. *Educ:* Mass Inst Technol, BSc & MSc, 64; Cambridge Univ, UK, PhD(appl math & theoret physics), 67. *Prof Exp:* Fel oceanog, Dept Meteorol, Mass Inst Technol, 67-68, asst prof, 68-71; res scientist, Cambridge Univ, UK, 71-72; assoc scientist, Woods Hole Oceanog Inst, 72-74, sr scientist, 74-84. *Concurrent Pos:* Vis prof, Nat Ctr Atmospheric Res, 69 & 72, Univ BC, 75, Univ Colo, 76, Calif Inst Tech & Princeton Univ, 78; fel, Christ's Col, Cambridge, UK, 79-80; Guggenheim fel, Dept Appl Math & Theoret Physics, Cambridge Univ, 79-80; Green scholar, Inst Geophys & Planetary Physics, Univ Calif, San Diego, 81; Queen's fel marine sci, Australia, 88. *Mem:* Nat Acad Sci; fel Am Geophys Union. *Res:* Circulation of the oceans, waves, eddies and currents; climate and transport of natural and artificial trace chemicals in the seas. *Mailing Add:* Sch Oceanog W B 10 Univ Wash Seattle WA 98195

RHINESMITH, HERBERT SILAS, organic chemistry; deceased, see previous edition for last biography

RHO, JINNQUE, MICROBIOLOGY. *Current Pos:* asst prof, Univ Bridgeport, 79-82, Yale vis fac fel, 82-83, & 90-91, assoc prof, 85-89, ELIPHALET REMINGTON PROF ENVIRON MICROBIOL, UNIV BRIDGEPORT, 82-, PROF MICROBIOL, BIOL DEPT, 90- *Personal Data:* b Korea, Sept 15, 38; US citizen; m 70, Hong Soon Park; c Mira. *Educ:* Seoul Nat Univ, BS, 61; Clark Univ, MA, 69; Univ Mass, PhD(microbiol), 72. *Prof Exp:* Res asst, Inst Agr & Indust Microbiol, Univ Mass, 68-71, teaching asst soil microbiol, 71-72, fel, Dept Environ Sci, 72-74, sr res assoc, Water Res Ctr, Mass Agr Exp Sta, 74-77, asst prof aquatic microbiol, Dept Environ Sci, 77-79. *Concurrent Pos:* Consult, USDA Forest Service, Conn, New Eng Res Inc, Mass, Protech Inc, Conn, Aquapura Corp, Conn; affil asst prof, Dept Biol, Clark Univ, 77-79; coordr, Olin Corp Environ Sci & Eng Prog, 88-, co-prin investr nitrogen transformation by heterotrophs, Mass Agr Exp Sta; adj prof, Sacred Heart Univ, 91. *Mem:* Am Soc Microbiol; Am Soc Limnol & Oceanog; Sigma Xi. *Res:* Ecology and biochemistry of heterotrophic nitrifying bacteria; copper resistant bacteria in aquatic environments; stabilizer compositions for stabilizing aqueous systems; bioaerosols in indoor environment. *Mailing Add:* 36 Whitney Lane Orange CT 06477. *E-Mail:* jrho@cse.bridgeport.edu

RHO, JOON H, BIOCHEMISTRY. *Current Pos:* assoc prof med & pharm, 75-82, PROF MED & PHARM, SCHS MED & PHARM, UNIV SOUTHERN CALIF, 82- *Personal Data:* b Pyongbuk, Korea, Jan 19, 22; m 47; c 5. *Educ:* Seoul Nat Univ, BS, 50; Duke Univ, MS, 56, PhD(biochem), 58. *Prof Exp:* Asst prof biol, Sung Kyun Kwan Univ, Korea, 53-56, from assoc prof to prof, 57-59; Nat Acad Sci fel, Calif Inst Technol, 59-62, sr scientist, Jet Propulsion Lab, 62-66, tech staff mem, 67-73, sr biologist, Calif Inst Technol, 73-75. *Concurrent Pos:* Prin investr, Apollo Sample Anal Porphyrin Compounds, 71-74; mem bd gov, State Bar Calif; NIH grant awards. *Mem:* Am Chem Soc; AAAS; Int Soc Study Origin Life; Soc Exp Biol Med & Neurosci. *Res:* Neurogenic hypertension; chemical carcinogenesis, metabolism of antihypertentive drugs; fluorometric analyses of biological and biomedicinal compounds. *Mailing Add:* 1555 Hilcrest Ave Pasadena CA 91106

RHOADES, BILLY EUGENE, MATHEMATICS. *Current Pos:* RETIRED. *Personal Data:* b Lima, Ohio, Sept 27, 28; m 49, Mary L Arant; c Raymond S & Mary L (Fern). *Educ:* Ohio Northern Univ, AB, 51; Rutgers Univ, MS, 53; Lehigh Univ, PhD, 58. *Prof Exp:* Asst math, Rutgers Univ, 52-53; from instr to prof, Lafayette Col, 53-65; from assoc prof to prof math, Ind Univ, Bloomington, 65-94. *Concurrent Pos:* Vis prof, Univ Tel-Aviv, Israel, 73; Fulbright fel, Szeged, Hungary, 92. *Mem:* Am Math Soc; Math Asn Am; Nat Coun Teachers Math. *Res:* Transformations in sequence spaces; fixed point theorems. *Mailing Add:* 3128 Coppertree Dr Bloomington IN 47401. *Fax:* 812-855-0046; *E-Mail:* rhoades@ucs.indiana.edu

RHOADES, EVERETT RONALD, INTERNAL MEDICINE, MICROBIOLOGY. *Current Pos:* ASSOC DEAN, OKLA COL MED & COMMUNITY AFFAIRS, 93- *Personal Data:* b Lawton, Okla, Oct 24, 31; m 53; c 5. *Educ:* Univ Okla, MD, 56. *Prof Exp:* Intern, Gorgas Hosp, CZ, 56-57; resident med, Med Ctr, Univ Okla, 57-60, clin asst, 60-61; chief infectious dis, Wilford Hall, USAF Hosp, 61-66; from asst prof med & microbiol to prof med, Med Ctr, Univ Okla, 66-82, chief infectious dis, 68-82; dir, Indian Health Serv, 82-93. *Concurrent Pos:* Consult, Med Ctr, Univ Okla, 63-66, Surgeon Gen, 65-66 & Eastern & Western Okla Tuberc Sanatarium, 66-75; chief infectious dis, Vet Admin Hosp, Oklahoma City, 66-; mem adv coun, Nat Inst Allergy & Infectious Dis; mem health comt, Asn Am Indian Affairs; Markle scholar acad med, 67-72. *Mem:* Am Soc Microbiol; Am Fedn Clin Res; Am Col Physicians; Asn Am Indian Physicians (pres, 75); Infectious Dis Soc Am. *Res:* Various aspects of cryptococcosis, including the effect of antifungal compounds on organisms and humans; host-parasite factors in lower respiratory infections. *Mailing Add:* 1808 Dorchester Dr Oklahoma City OK 73120

RHOADES, HARLAN LEON, PLANT NEMATOLOGY. *Current Pos:* RETIRED. *Personal Data:* b Tuscola, Ill, Mar 7, 28; m 53; c 2. *Educ:* Univ Ill, BS, 52, MS, 57, PhD(plant path), 59. *Prof Exp:* Soil conservationist, Agr Res Serv, USDA, 52-55; asst plant nematologist, Univ Fla, 59-67, assoc prof & assoc nematologist, 67-73, prof nematol & nematologist, 73-90. *Mem:* Soc Nematol. *Res:* Control of plant nematodes attacking vegetables. *Mailing Add:* 106 Crystal View S Sanford FL 32773-4808

RHOADES, JAMES DAVID, SOIL SCIENCE, CLAY MINERALOGY. *Current Pos:* Res soil chemist, 65-74, res leader, 74-88, DIR, US SALINITY LAB, AGR RES SERV, USDA, 89- *Personal Data:* b Tulare, Calif, May 13, 37; m 58; c 3. *Educ:* Univ Calif, Davis, BS, 62, MS, 63; Univ Calif, Riverside, PhD, 66. *Honors & Awards:* Appl Res Award, Soil Sci Soc Am, 89. *Concurrent Pos:* adj prof soil sci, Univ Calif, Riverside. *Mem:* Fel Am Soc Agron; fel Soil Sci Soc Am; Soil & Water Conserv Soc; Int Comn Irrig & Drainage. *Res:* Interactions between salts in waters and soils; assessment of soil salinity; fixation of mineral elements by clay minerals; water quality criteria; use of saline waters for irrigation. *Mailing Add:* 17065 Harlo Heights Dr Riverside CA 92503

RHOADES, JAMES LAWRENCE, ENZYMOLOGY, PROTEIN CHEMISTRY. *Current Pos:* prof, 70-80, chmn dept, 70-92, WILLIAM E REID PROF CHEM, BERRY COL, 80- *Personal Data:* b Mishawaka, Ind, Apr 24, 33; m 58, Nancy Phillips; c Nancy, Mary, Judy & James. *Educ:* Purdue Univ, BS, 55, MS, 57, PhD(chem), 61. *Prof Exp:* From asst prof to assoc prof chem, Northwestern State Col, La, 60-70. *Concurrent Pos:* Vis assoc prof chem, Purdue Univ, 65, 67 & 69; res assoc, Univ Tenn, Memphis, 63, 75, 76, 77, 79 & 84 & Emory Univ, 88. *Mem:* Am Chem Soc; Sigma Xi. *Res:* Chemistry and mechanism of action of enzymes, especially the plant phenolase complex; biosynthesis of coenzyme A; B-protein assay for cancer; liver transglutaminase. *Mailing Add:* Dept Chem 495016 Berry Col Mt Berry GA 30149-5016

RHOADES, LAWRENCE J, PUBLIC HEALTH. *Current Pos:* dep dir, 92-93, DIR, DIV POLICY & EDUC, OFF RES INTEGRITY, US DEPT HEALTH & HUMAN SERVS, 93- *Personal Data:* b Shamokin, Pa, Feb 12, 37. *Educ:* Rockford Col, BA, 67; Mich State Univ, MA, 69, PhD(sociol), 73. *Prof Exp:* H K Corning prof, chmn & dir, Rehab Med, Columbia Univ, 91-92. *Mem:* AAAS; Am Col Physicians; Am Cong Rehab Med; Am Physiol Soc; AMA; Int Rehab Med Asn; NY Acad Sci; Royal Soc Med; Soc Neurosci. *Mailing Add:* Off Res Integrity US Dept Health & Human Servs 5515 Security Lane Suite 700 Rockville MD 20852. *Fax:* 301-443-5351

RHOADES, RICHARD G, CHEMICAL ENGINEERING, MATHEMATICS. *Current Pos:* Res chem engr, Propulsion Lab, US Army Missile Command, 63-66, prog mgr air breathing propulsion, 66-72, dir, Army Rocket Propulsion Technol & Mgt Ctr, 68-70, chief, Adv Res Projs Div, 69, group leader ballistic missile defense propulsion, 70-73, dir propulsion directorate, US Army Missile Res & Develop Command, 73-81, assoc dir technol, 81-88, ASSOC DIR SYSTS, US ARMY MISSILE COMMAND, 89- *Personal Data:* b Northampton, Mass, Aug 15, 38; m 67, Dale Turner; c Lauren, Anna & Jennifer. *Educ:* Rensselaer Polytech Inst, BChE, 60, PhD(chem eng, math), 64; Mass Inst Technol, MS, 77. *Honors & Awards:* Firepower Award, Am Defense Preparedness Asn, 89. *Concurrent Pos:* Adj asst prof, Univ Ala, Huntsville, 65-69. *Mem:* Am Inst Chem Engrs; Sigma Xi. *Res:* Fluid dynamics of packed beds; gas generation and pressurization for missiles; analytical techniques and methodology for propulsion system selection and technology planning; air breathing propulsion system analysis, design and experimentation. *Mailing Add:* 133 Walker Ave Huntsville AL 35801

RHOADES, RODNEY A, PHYSIOLOGY. *Current Pos:* assoc prof, 77-81, PROF PHYSIOL & CHMN DEPT, SCH MED, IND UNIV, 81- *Personal Data:* b Greenville, Ohio, Jan 5, 39; m 61; c 2. *Educ:* Miami Univ, BS, 61, MS, 63; Ohio State Univ, PhD(physiol), 66. *Prof Exp:* NASA fel, Ohio State Univ, 64-66; asst prof appl physiol, Pa State Univ, 66-72, assoc prof biol, 72-75; scientist, NIH, 75-76. *Concurrent Pos:* NIH career develop award, 75-80. *Mem:* AAAS; Am Physiol Soc; Biophys Soc; Am Thoracic Soc; Soc Exp Biol & Med. *Res:* Pulmonary circulation. *Mailing Add:* Dept Physiol & Biophys-MS 374 Ind Univ Sch Med 635 Barnhill Dr Indianapolis IN 46202-5120

RHOADS, ALLEN R, ENZYMOLOGY, CELL BIOLOGY. *Current Pos:* Fel biochem & pharmacol, Howard Univ, 71-72; from asst prof to assoc prof, 72-88, PROF BIOCHEM, COL MED, HOWARD UNIV, 89- *Personal Data:* b Reading, Pa, Dec 19, 41; m 69, Marcia Szczepanek. *Educ:* Kutztown State Univ, BS, 66; Univ Md, PhD(biochem), 71. *Mem:* Am Chem Soc; AAAS; NY Acad Sci; Am Soc Biochem & Molecular Biol. *Res:* Regulation by nucleotides and calcium; structure, function and relationships of purinergic receptors and calmodulin-dependent enzymes in vascular and nervous tissue. *Mailing Add:* Howard Univ Col Med Dept Biochem & Molecular Biol Washington DC 20059. *Fax:* 202-806-5784

RHOADS, DONALD CAVE, ENVIRONMENTAL SENSOR DEVELOPMENT. *Current Pos:* SR SCIENTIST, SCI APPLNS INT CORP, 85- *Personal Data:* b Rockford, Ill, Feb 14, 38; m 59, Christobel Kramer; c Mark & Douglas. *Educ:* Cornell Univ, BA, 60; Univ Iowa, MS, 63; Univ Chicago, PhD(paleo zool), 65. *Hon Degrees:* MS, Yale Univ, 75. *Prof Exp:* From assoc prof to prof geol, Yale Univ, 65-85. *Concurrent Pos:* Adj prof geol, Boston Univ, 88- *Mem:* Sigma Xi. *Res:* Organism-sediment relationships in marine environment; biogenic sedimentary structures in marine sediments; biogenic processes on the seafloor; ecology of low oxygen marine environments; environmental sensor development. *Mailing Add:* 22 Widgeon Rd Falmouth MA 02540. *Fax:* 508-540-7839; *E-Mail:* dcrhoads@aol.com

RHOADS, FREDERICK MILTON, SOIL CHEMISTRY, SOIL PHYSICS. *Current Pos:* asst soil chemist, 66-72, assoc soil chemist, 72-78, PROF SOIL SCI, NFLA RES & EDUC CTR, UNIV FLA, 78- *Personal Data:* b New Site, Miss, Jan 12, 36; m 53, Sue Isbell; c Deborah & Timothy. *Educ:* Miss State Univ, BS, 58, PhD(soil chem), 66; Tex A&M Univ, MS, 63. *Prof Exp:* Soil scientist, Soil Conserv Serv, USDA, 58-61. *Mem:* Soil Sci Soc Am; Am Soc Agron. *Res:* Plant nutrition of field and vegetable crops; irrigation of field and vegetable crops; soil fertility and testing; soil-water. *Mailing Add:* 319 N 11th St Quincy FL 32351

RHOADS, GEORGE GRANT, EPIDEMIOLOGY, INTERNAL MEDICINE. *Current Pos:* ENDOWED PROF PUB HEALTH & DIR, NJ GRAD PROG PUB HEALTH, ROBERT WOOD JOHNSON MED SCH, UNIV MED & DENT NJ, 89- *Personal Data:* b Philadelphia, Pa, Feb 11, 40; m 65, Frances Secker; c Thomas C & James E. *Educ:* Haverford Col, BA, 61; Harvard Univ, MD, 65; Univ Hawaii, MPH, 70. *Prof Exp:* Intern, Univ Pa Hosp, 65-66, resident, 66-68; lt commander, Heart Dis Control Prog, USPHS, 68-70; asst dir, Honolulu Heart Study, 70-71 & 72-74; from assoc to prof pub health, Univ Hawaii, 74-82, chmn, Dept Pub Health Sci, 78-81; chief, Epidemiol Br, Nat Inst Child Health & Human Develop, NIH, 82-89. *Concurrent Pos:* Dir, Div Environ Health, Environ & Occup Health Scis Inst, NJ. *Mem:* AAAS; Soc Epidemiol Res; Int Epidemiol Asn; Am Pub Health Asn; Am Epidemiol Soc. *Res:* Epidemiology of chronic disease; coronary heart disease and stroke in Japanese migrants and their descendants; epidemiology of low birth weight, congenial malformations, pediatric lead poisoning and other problems in maternal and child health. *Mailing Add:* Dept Environ Comm Med 675 Hoes Lane Piscataway MD 08854

RHOADS, JOHN GARRETT, SOFTWARE SYSTEMS, PHYSICAL ANTHROPOLOGY. *Current Pos:* SOFTWARE DESIGN ENGR, HEWLETT-PACKARD CO, 96- *Personal Data:* b Wilmington, Del, Oct 24, 48; m 81, Susan S Bean; c Edith. *Educ:* Harvard Col, AB, 72; Harvard Univ, AM, 74, PhD(biol anthrop), 77. *Prof Exp:* Assoc prof anthrop, Yale Univ, 76-84; eng mgr, Hayden Software, 84-85, Lab Technol Corp, 85-89; consult, Rhoads Systs Inc, 89-96. *Res:* Real time computer monitoring of biomedical data; software quality engineering. *Mailing Add:* 148 Asbury St Hamilton MA 01982. *E-Mail:* john-rhoads@hp.com

RHOADS, JOHN MCFARLANE, psychiatry, for more information see previous edition

RHOADS, JONATHAN EVANS, SURGERY. *Current Pos:* asst instr surg, Sch Med, Univ Pa, 34-35, instr, 35-39, assoc, 39-47, assoc prof, 47-49, J William White prof surg res, 49-50, prof surg, Grad Sch Med, 50-64, prof surg, Sch Med, 51-57, chmn Univ, 56-59, from actg dir to dir, Harrison Dept Surg Res, 44-72, John Rhea Barton prof surg, 59-72, PROF SURG, SCH MED, UNIV PA, 72- *Personal Data:* b Philadelphia, Pa, May 9, 07; m 36, 90; c 6. *Educ:* Haverford Col, BA, 28; Johns Hopkins Univ, MD, 32; Univ Pa, DSc(med), 40. *Hon Degrees:* LLD, Univ Pa, 60, MA, 71; DSc, Haverford Col, 62, Swarthmore Col, 69, Med Col Pa, 74, Hahnemann Med Col, 78, Duke Univ, 79, Georgetown Univ, 79, Med Col Ohio, 85; DLitt, Jefferson Univ, 79; DMedSc, Yale Univ, 90. *Honors & Awards:* Sheen Award, AMA, 80; Ann Nat Award, Am Cancer Soc, 73; Prize, Soc Int Surg, 79; Goldberger Award, AMA; Medal, Nat Cancer Inst, 87; Swanberg Award, Am Med Writers Asn, 87; Medal of the Surgeon Gen of the US, 87; Benjamin Franklin Medal, Am Philos Soc, 88. *Prof Exp:* Intern, Hosp Univ Pa, 32-34, asst chief resident, 34. *Concurrent Pos:* Mem, Franklin Inst, Pa; mem adv coun, Nat Inst Gen Med Sci, 63-67; vpres sci affairs, Inst Med Res, 64-76; mem, US Senate Panel Consults on Conquest of Cancer, 70; mem & chmn, Nat Cancer Adv Bd, 72-79. *Mem:* Am Philos Soc (secy, 63-66, pres, 77-84); Int Fedn Surg Cols (vpres, 72-78, pres, 78-81); Soc Clin Surg (pres, 58-60); Am Surg Asn (pres, 72-73); Am Col Surgeons (pres, 71-72); Royal Col Surgeons Eng; Royal Col Surgeons Edinburg; Royal Col Physicians & Surgeons Can; Polish Asn Surgeons; Asn Surgeons India. *Res:* Nutrition of surgical patients; physiological factors regulating the level of prothrombin; factors affecting adhesion formation; clinical aspects of cancer. *Mailing Add:* Univ Pa Sch Med 3400 Spruce St Philadelphia PA 19104-4220

RHOADS, ROBERT E, NUCLEIC ACID BIOCHEMISTRY, PLANT VIROLOGY. *Current Pos:* asst prof, 73-79, res prof, 84-85, ASSOC PROF BIOCHEM, DEPT BIOCHEM, UNIV KY, 80- *Personal Data:* b San Antonio, Tex, Oct 14, 44; m 66; c 3. *Educ:* Rice Univ, BA, 66; George Washington Univ, PhD(biochem), 71. *Prof Exp:* NIH fel biochem, 66-68 & Roche Inst Molecular Biol, 68-70; fel pharmacol, dept pharmacol, Stanford Univ, 70-72, res assoc, 72-73. *Concurrent Pos:* Assoc prof, Inst Molecular & Cellular Biol, Univ Louis Pasteur, Strasbourg, France, 80-81; guest prof, Inst Biochem, Univ Vienna, Austria, 85. *Mem:* Am Soc Biol Chemists; Am Soc Virol; AAAS. *Res:* The biochemistry of protein synthesis in eukaryotes and the mode of virus gene expression; chestnut blight disease and diseases caused by potyviruses; mRNA structure and function. *Mailing Add:* Dept Biochem & Molecular Biol La State Univ Med Ctr 1501 Kings Hwy PO Box 33932 Shreveport LA 71130-3932

RHOADS, WILLIAM DENHAM, ANALYTICAL CHEMISTRY, METABOLISM. *Current Pos:* PRES, COLO ANALYTICAL, 84- *Personal Data:* b Livingston, Mont, Dec 8, 34; m 59; c 3. *Educ:* Col Pac, BS, 59, MS, 60, PhD(chem), 68. *Prof Exp:* Res assoc anal chem, Allergan Pharmaceut, Calif, 64-66; res asst, Diamond Walnut Growers, Calif, 66-68; sr anal chemist, Abbott Labs, Ill, 68-70; pres & dir res, Analytical Develop Corp, 71-75; sr anal chemist, Ciba-Geigy, NC, 83-84. *Mem:* Am Chem Soc. *Res:* Development of analytical procedures for the pharmaceutical, veterinary, agricultural chemical and food and beverage industries, specializing in gas and high speed liquid chromatography. *Mailing Add:* Col Analytical Res & Develop Corp 4720 Forge Rd Unit 108 Colorado Springs CO 80907-3549

RHODE, EDWARD A, JR, VETERINARY MEDICINE, PHYSIOLOGY. *Current Pos:* from asst prof to assoc prof vet med, 51-64, actg dean, Sch Vet Med, 77-78, assoc dean instr, 71-82, PROF VET MED, UNIV CALIF, DAVIS, 64- , DEAN, SCH VET MED, 82- *Personal Data:* b Amsterdam, NY, July 25, 26; m 55; c 5. *Educ:* Cornell Univ, DVM, 47. *Prof Exp:* Instr vet med, Kans State Col, 48-51. *Concurrent Pos:* USPHS spec fel, 59-60 & 66-67; mem, basic sci coun, Am Heart Asn; actg dir, Vet Med Training Hosp, 68-69. *Mem:* AAAS; Am Vet Med Asn; Am Physiol Soc; Am Soc Vet Physiol & Pharmacol; Am Col Vet Internal Med; Sigma Xi; Asn Am Vet Med Cols. *Res:* Comparative mammalian cardiovascular physiology; veterinary cardiology; clinical medicine. *Mailing Add:* Sch Vet Med Univ Calif Davis CA 95616

RHODE, SOLON LAFAYETTE, III, VIROLOGY, CELL BIOLOGY. *Current Pos:* assoc prof, 84-87, PROF, MED SCH, UNIV NEBR, 87- *Personal Data:* b Reading, Pa, Dec 28, 38; m 65; c 2. *Educ:* Princeton Univ, AB, 60; Thomas Jefferson Univ, MD, 64, PhD(exp path), 68. *Prof Exp:* Fel exp path, Jefferson Med Col, 68-69; med officer, USN, 69-70; assoc investr, Inst Med Res, Bennington, Vt, 70-80, dir, 80-84. *Res:* Virology of parvoviruses and DNA viruses; DNA replication and repair; molecular genetics; cancer. *Mailing Add:* Med Microbiol Univ Nebr 600 42nd St Omaha NE 68198-0001

RHODE, WILLIAM STANLEY, NEUROPHYSIOLOGY. *Current Pos:* Fel neurophysiol, Univ Wis, 69-70, asst dir, 70-72, asst dir & asst prof, 72-77, PROF NEUROPHYSIOL, COMPUT FACIL LAB, UNIV WIS, 83- *Personal Data:* b Chicago, Ill, Nov 4, 41; c 4. *Educ:* Univ Wis, Madison, BS, 63, MS, 64, PhD(elec eng), 70. *Honors & Awards:* Samuel Talbot Award, Inst Elec & Electronics Engrs, 70. *Mem:* Sigma Xi; Asn Res Otolaryngol. *Res:* Auditory neurophysiology; investigation of cochlear mechanics; use of computers and instrumentation in neurophysiology; morphological-physiological correlations in the cochlear nucleus; neural circuits and complex signal processing in the auditory system. *Mailing Add:* Dept Neurophys Univ Wis Med Sch 1300 University Ave Madison WI 53706-1585

RHODEN, RICHARD ALLAN, MAMMALIAN TOXICOLOGY, OCCUPATIONAL HEALTH & SAFETY. *Current Pos:* HEALTH SCIENTIST, AM PETROL INST, 89- *Personal Data:* b Coatesville, Pa, May 8, 30; m 93, Yvonne L Johnson-Mills; c Richard Jr. *Educ:* Lincoln Univ, AB, 51; Drexel Univ, MS, 67, PhD(environ toxicol), 71. *Prof Exp:* Chemist mil procurement, Defense Personnel Support Ctr, 51-56; chemist coatings develop, Naval Air Eng Ctr, 56-62, chemist aerospace safety & health, 62-66, res chemist, Naval Air Develop Ctr, 66-72; environ scientist environ health, Environ Protection Agency, 72-75; res pharmacologist occup health, Nat Inst Occup Safety & Health, NIH, 75-82, health scientist adminr, Nat Cancer Inst, 82-84, exec secy, Safety & Occup Health Study Sect, NIH/DRG, 84-89. *Concurrent Pos:* Lectr, Philadelphia Col Art, 71-72; lectr biol sci, Fed City Col, 73-74; fed exec, Develop Prog, 78-80. *Mem:* Am Chem Soc; Am Conf Govt Indust Hygienists; fel AAAS; Am Indust Hyg Asn; Air & Waste Mgt Asn; Soc Toxicol. *Res:* Inhalation toxicology; occupational and environmental health effects. *Mailing Add:* PO Box 34472 Washington DC 20043-4472. *Fax:* 202-682-8270; *E-Mail:* rhoden@api.org

RHODES, ALLEN FRANKLIN, SUBSEA PRODUCTION EQUIPMENT, DEEP OIL & GAS DRILLING. *Current Pos:* CONSULT, ALLEN F RHODES, BUS ADV & CONSULT ENGR, CONSULT, SILVER FOX ADVISORS, 86- *Personal Data:* b Estherville, Iowa, Oct 3, 24; m 62, Carol Haisler; c James Fleming & Stephen Haisler. *Educ:* Villanova Univ, BSME, 47; Univ Houston, ML, 50. *Honors & Awards:* Robert Henry Thurston Award, Am Soc Mech Engrs, 78, Charles Russ Richards Mem Award, 87; Howard Conley Medal, Am Nat Standard Inst, 80. *Prof Exp:* Asst dir engr admin, Hughes Tool Co, 47-52; pres, McEvoy Co, 52-63; vpres engr & res, Rockwell Mfg Co, 63-70; vpres corp planning & develop, ACF Indust, 71-73; pres & chief exec officer, McEvoy Oilfield Equip Co, 74-79; exec vpres & chief exec officer, Goldrus Marine Drilling, 79-82; pres & chief exec officer, Warren Oilfield Serv, 81-82, Anglo Energy, 83-86 & Gripper Inc, 87-90; vpres & chief finance officer, Hydrotech Syst Inc, 91. *Concurrent Pos:* Chmn, Comt Dept Trans Gas Pipeline Safety Stand, 69-73; dir, Keystone Intl, Triten Corp, 80-, Rawson-Koenig, 86-, Southwest Rees Inst, 89-, Texas Microsyst, 89-92. *Mem:* Nat Acad Eng; fel Inst Mech Engrs, Gr Brit; fel Am Soc Mech Engrs; Soc Petrol Engrs; Am Petrol Inst. *Res:* Pioneer in completion equipment for deep oil and gas wells; methods and equipment for subsea well completion. *Mailing Add:* 5643 Ella Lee Lane Houston TX 77056. *Fax:* 713-626-4413

RHODES, ANDREW JAMES, medical microbiology, public health; deceased, see previous edition for last biography

RHODES, ASHBY MARSHALL, PLANT BREEDING. *Current Pos:* From instr to asst prof, 51-65, assoc prof, 65,79, PROF VEG CROPS, UNIV ILL, URBANA, 79- *Personal Data:* b Hinton, WVa, July 5, 23. *Educ:* WVa Univ, BS, 48; Mich State Col, PhD(farm crops), 51. *Mem:* Am Soc Hort Sci; Am Genetic Asn; Soc Syst Zool; Sigma Xi. *Res:* Breeding of sweet corn, cucurbits and horse radish; taxonomy; economic botany. *Mailing Add:* c/o C T Ripberger 2101 Cherry St NE St Petersburg FL 33704-4645

RHODES, BUCK AUSTIN, RADIOLOGY, PHARMACOLOGY. *Current Pos:* CONSULT. *Personal Data:* b LaUnion, NMex, Aug 30, 35; c 1. *Educ:* NMex State Univ, BS, 58; Johns Hopkins Univ, PhD(radiol sci), 68. *Prof Exp:* From asst prof radiol sci to assoc prof radiol & environ health, Sch Med, Hyg & Pub Health, Johns Hopkins Univ, 66-75; prof pharmacol & radiol, Med Ctr, Univ Kans, 75-76; prof pharm & radiol, Univ NMex, 76-81; vpres sci affairs, Summa Med Corp, Albuquerque, NMex, 81-85; pres, Rhomed, Inc, Albuquerque, NMex, 85- *Mem:* Soc Nuclear Med. *Res:* Development of new radiopharmaceuticals and diagnostic tests for vascular diseases; immuno diagnostics and therapy. *Mailing Add:* 1003 Forrester Albuquerque NM 87102

RHODES, CHARLES KIRKHAM, ATOMIC PHYSICS, LASERS. *Current Pos:* prof, 78-82, res prof physics, 82-87, ALBERT A MICHELSON PROF PHYSICS, UNIV ILL, CHICAGO, 87- *Personal Data:* b NY, June 30, 39; m 64, 76; c 4. *Educ:* Cornell Univ, BEE, 63; Mass Inst Technol, MEE, 65, PhD(physics), 69. *Prof Exp:* Staff specialist, Control Data Corp, NY, 69-70; physicist, Lawrence Livermore Lab, Univ Calif, 70-75; sr physicist, Molecular Physics Ctr, SRI Int, 75-77. *Concurrent Pos:* Lectr appl sci, Univ Calif, Davis, 71-75; mem, Adv Group Electron Devices; comt mem, Joint Coun Quantum Electronics; adj prof elec eng, Stanford Univ. *Mem:* Fel Am Phys Soc; fel Inst Elec & Electronics Engrs; Europ Physics Soc; fel Optical Soc Am; Sigma Xi; fel AAAS. *Res:* X-ray production, femto second lasers, atomic and molecular energy transfer, chemical processes and kinetics, coherent pulse propagation, saturation spectroscopy; nonlinear optics; collisional broadening of spectral lines, and high pressure electron-beam excited ultraviolet and visible lasers. *Mailing Add:* Dept Physics Univ Ill 1919 W Taylor Chicago IL 60612

RHODES, DALLAS D, GEOMORPHOLOGY. *Current Pos:* from asst prof to assoc prof geol, 77-86, chmn dept, 85-87, DIR, FAIRCHILD AERIAL PHOTOG COLLECTION, WHITTIER COL, 81-, CHMN, DEPT GEOL, 90-, PROF, 86-; DIR W M KECK FOUND IMAGE PROCESSING LAB, 90- *Personal Data:* b El Dorado, Kans, Aug 8, 47; m 79, Lisan Ann Rossbacher. *Educ:* Univ Mo-Columbia, BS, 69; Syracuse Univ, MA & PhD(geol), 73. *Prof Exp:* Asst prof geol, Univ Vt, 73-77. *Concurrent Pos:* Consult geologist, NY State Geol Surv, 75-76 & Jet Propulsion Lab, 80-84; resident dir, Denmark's Int Study Prog, 83; vis researcher, Univ Uppsala, Sweden, 84; vis prof geol, Univ Mo, Columbia, 90, 91 & 93, Stanford Univ, 92-93. *Mem:* Am Geophys Union; Geol Soc Am; Sigma Xi; Nat Asn Geol Teachers. *Res:* Detailing relationships of fluvial hydraulic geometry to the river's sedimentology, channel shape, and channel pattern; analysis of hydraulic geometry in terms of a most probable state; tectonic geomorphology of southern California. *Mailing Add:* Dept Geol Whittier Col Whittier CA 90608. *Fax:* 562-693-6117; *E-Mail:* drhodes@whittier.edu

RHODES, DAVID R, ANALYTICAL CHEMISTRY, ELECTROCHEMISTRY. *Current Pos:* Res chemist, Chevron Res Co, 61-71, sr res chemist, 71-74, sr res assoc, 74-87, CONSULT SCIENTIST, CHEVRON RES CO, 87- *Personal Data:* b Wichita, Kans, Oct 22, 36; m 54; c 4. *Educ:* Friends Univ, BA, 57; Univ Ill, MS, 59, PhD(chem), 61. *Mem:* Am Chem Soc; Electrochem Soc. *Res:* Electroanalytical chemistry; pollution analysis; trace analysis; corrosion; fuel cells. *Mailing Add:* 1301 Quarry Ct No 112 Richmond CA 94801-4153

RHODES, DONALD FREDERICK, RADIOISOTOPE APPLICATIONS. *Current Pos:* INDEPENDENT CONSULT, 86- *Personal Data:* b Johnstown, Pa, July 1, 32; m 56. *Educ:* Univ Pittsburgh, BS, 54, MLitt, 56; Pac Western Univ, PhD(physics), 82. *Honors & Awards:* IR-100 Award, 68. *Prof Exp:* Inst elec measuurements, Physics Dept, Univ Pittsburgh, 55-56; engr, Westinghouse Elec Corp, 56-57; radio safety officer, Gulf Res & Develop Co, 68-83, res physicist, 58-86. *Concurrent Pos:* Consult nuclear technol, US Govt, 73-74 & radiotracer tests, Exxon Co, 81-82; accident prev coun, Fed Aviation Admin, 81-85. *Mem:* Am Nuclear Soc; Health Physics Soc; Inst Elec & Electronics Engrs. *Res:* Nuclear instrumentation development, radioactive tracer studies of chemical plant processes and oil well enhanced recovery applications; neutron activation analysis, radiation effects, nuclear well logging, applications of ultrasonics and flexible automation with robotics; early development of on-line data processing hardware; current applications of microcomputers. *Mailing Add:* Univ Pittsburgh Appl Res Ctr 345 William Pitt Way Pittsburgh PA 15238

RHODES, DONALD R(OBERT), MUSICOLOGY. *Current Pos:* UNIV PROF ELEC ENG, NC STATE UNIV, 66- *Personal Data:* b Detroit, Mich, Dec 31, 23; div; c 4. *Educ:* Ohio State Univ, BEE, 45, MSc, 48, PhD(elec eng), 53. *Honors & Awards:* John T Bolljahn Award, Inst Elec & Electronics Engrs, 63; Benjamin G Lamme Medal, Ohio State Univ, 75. *Prof Exp:* Res assoc elec, Ohio State Univ, 44-54; res engr, Cornell Aeronaut Lab, Inc, 54-57; head basic res dept, Radiation, Inc, 57-61, sr scientist, 61-66. *Concurrent Pos:* Instr, Ohio State Univ, 48-52. *Mem:* Fel AAAS; fel Inst Elec & Electronics Engrs. *Res:* Antenna synthesis. *Mailing Add:* Dept Elec Eng NC State Univ Raleigh NC 27695-7911

RHODES, DOUG, GEOLOGY. *Honors & Awards:* William J Stephenson Outstanding Serv Award, Nat Speleol Soc, 91. *Mailing Add:* PO Box 12334 Albuquerque NM 87195-0334

RHODES, E(DWARD), CHEMICAL ENGINEERING. *Current Pos:* from asst prof to assoc prof, 64-74, PROF CHEM ENG, UNIV WATERLOO, 74-, CHMN DEPT, 76- *Personal Data:* b Elland, Eng, Jan 31, 38; m 62; c 3. *Educ:* Univ Manchester, BScTech, 60, MScTech, 61, PhD(chem eng), 64. *Prof Exp:* Asst lectr chem eng, Univ Manchester, 62-64. *Mem:* Brit Inst Chem Engrs; Am Inst Chem Engrs; Can Soc Chem Eng. *Res:* Multiphase flow; mass transfer; boiling; condensation. *Mailing Add:* Dept Chem Tech Univ 1360 Barrington St PO Box 1000 Halifax NS B3J 2X4 Can

RHODES, EDWARD JOSEPH, JR, SOLAR ASTRONOMY, SPACE PHYSICS. *Current Pos:* asst prof, 79-85, ASSOC PROF ASTRON, UNIV SOUTHERN CALIF, 85- *Personal Data:* b San Diego, Calif, June 1, 46; m 72; c 2. *Educ:* Univ Calif, Los Angeles, BS, 68, MA, 71, PhD(astron), 77. *Prof Exp:* Fel researcher, Univ Calif, Los Angeles, 75-77, asst res astronomer, 78-79. *Concurrent Pos:* Scientist, Jet Propulsion Lab, 70-77, sr scientist, 78-83, mem tech staff, 83-; res fel, Dept Physics, Calif Inst Technol, 77-78; adj asst prof astron, Univ Southern Calif, 78-79; mem, Adv Solar Observ Sci Study Team, NASA, 81-83, Solar Beacon Sci Study Team, 81-83, Solar Cycle & Dynamics Sci Working Group, 78-79 & Star Probe Imaging Comt, 79-80. *Mem:* Am Astron Soc; Am Geophys Union; Sigma Xi; Int Astron Union. *Res:* Observational and theoretical research into the internal structure of the sun using the tool of solar oscillations; spatial behavior of the solar wind; operator of the 60-foot solar tower telescope of the Mount Wilson observatory. *Mailing Add:* Dept Astron Univ Southern Calif Mail Code 1342 Los Angeles CA 90089

RHODES, FRANK HAROLD TREVOR, GEOLOGY, PALEONTOLOGY. *Current Pos:* PRES, CORNELL UNIV, 77-, PROF GEOL, 77- *Personal Data:* b Warwickshire, Eng, Oct 29, 26; m 52, Rosa Lillian Carlson; c Jennifer, Catherine, Penelope & Deborah. *Educ:* Univ Birmingham, BSc, 48, PhD, 50, DSc, 63. *Hon Degrees:* LLD, Wooster Col, 76, Nazareth Col Rochester, 79, Skidmore Col, 89, Univ Mich, 90, Clemson Univ, 91, Dartmouth Col, 93; LHD, Colgate Univ, 80, Johns Hopkins Univ, 82, Wagner Col, 82, Hope Col, 82, Resselaer Polytechnic Inst, 82, LeMoyne Col, 84, Pace Univ, 86, Alaska Pac Univ, 87, Hamilton Col, 87, State Univ NY, 92; DSc, Univ Wales, 81, Bucknell Univ, 85, Univ Ill, 86, Reed Col, 88, Elmira Col, 89, Univ Southampton, 89; DLitt, Univ Nev, 82; EdD, Ohio State Univ, 92. *Honors & Awards:* Daniel Pidgeon Fund Award, Geol Soc London, 53; Lyell Fund Award, 57; Gurley lectr, Cornell Univ, 60; Bownocker lectr, Ohio State Univ, 66; Bigsby Medal, 67. *Prof Exp:* Fel & Fulbright scholar, Univ Ill, 50-51; lectr geol, Univ Durham, 51-54; asst prof, Univ Ill, 54-55, assoc prof, 55-56, dir, Wyo Field Sta, 56; prof geol & head dept, Univ Wales, Swansea, 56-68, dean fac sci, 67-68; prof geol & mineral, Univ Mich, Ann Arbor, 68-77, res assoc, Mus Paleont & dean, Col Lit Sci & Arts, 71-74, vpres acad affairs, 74-77. *Concurrent Pos:* Vis prof, Univ Ill, 59; External examinerships, Univ Bristol, 58-61, Univ Belfast, 60-62, Oxford Univ & Univ Reading, 63-65; dir, First Int Field Studies Conf, NSF-Am Geol Inst, 61; ed geol ser, Commonwealth & Int Libr, 62-; mem, Bd Geol Surv Gt Brit, 63-65; mem Australian vchancellor's comt vis, Australian Univs, 64; Brit Coun lectr univs & geol surveys, India, Pakistan, Thailand, Turkey & Iran, 64; NSF sr scientist fel, Ohio State Univ, 65-66; mem geol & geophys comt & subcomt postgrad awards, Nat Environ Res Coun, 65-68; mem curric panel, Coun Educ Geol Sci, 70-71, chmn panel, 71; mem bd trustees, Carnegie Found Advan Teaching, 78-86, vchmn, 83-85, chmn, 85-86; mem, Nat Sci Bd, 87- *Mem:* Geol Soc London; Brit Palaeont Asn (vpres, 63-68); Brit Asn Advan Sci; Geol Soc Am; Paleont Soc; Am Asn Petrol Geologists; Paleontographical Soc; Soc Econ Paleontologists & Mineralogists. *Res:* Stratigraphy; micropaleontology, especially conodonts; evolution; extinction; biogeochemistry; paleoecology; higher education; science and public policy. *Mailing Add:* Cornell Univ 300 Day Hall Ithaca NY 14853

RHODES, IAN BURTON, ELECTRICAL ENGINEERING, APPLIED MATHEMATICS. *Current Pos:* PROF ELEC & COMPUT ENG, UNIV CALIF, SANTA BARBARA, 80- *Personal Data:* b Melbourne, Australia, May 29, 41; m 64; c 2. *Educ:* Melbourne, BE, 63, MEngSc, 65; Stanford Univ, PhD(elec eng), 68. *Prof Exp:* Res engr, Stanford Res Inst, 67; asst prof elec eng, Mass Inst Technol, 68-70; assoc prof eng & appl sci, Wash Univ, 70-76, prof, 76-80. *Mem:* Soc Indust & Appl Math; Inst Elec & Electronics Engrs. *Res:* Decision and control sciences; system theory; control theory; estimation theory; optimization theory. *Mailing Add:* Dept Elec & Comput Eng Univ Calif Santa Barbara CA 93106

RHODES, JACOB LESTER, NUCLEAR PHYSICS. *Current Pos:* from assoc prof to prof, 57-85, emer prof physics, 85-94, CONSULT, LEBANON VALLEY COL, 94- *Personal Data:* b Linville, Va, Jan 13, 22; m 60; c 4. *Educ:* Lebanon Valley Col, BS, 43; Univ Pa, PhD, 58. *Prof Exp:* Asst res physicist, Johns Hopkins Univ, 43-46; asst instr physics, Univ Pa, 46-49, asst res physicist, 49-52; asst prof & chmn dept, Roanoke Col, 52-56. *Mem:* Am Phys Soc; Am Asn Physics Teachers. *Res:* Low energy nuclear physics, electronics; x-ray diffraction. *Mailing Add:* Dept Physics Lebanon Valley Col 1654 Rita Lane Lebanon PA 17042

RHODES, JAMES B, GASTROENTEROLOGY, BIOCHEMISTRY. *Current Pos:* from asst prof to assoc prof med & physiol, 66-79, PROF MED, UNIV KANS MED CTR, KANSAS CITY, 79- *Personal Data:* b Kansas City, Mo, July 22, 28; m 60; c 3. *Educ:* Univ Kans, AB, 54, MD, 58. *Prof Exp:* Intern med & surg, Univ Chicago Hosps, 58-59, resident med, 60-62; asst med, 64-66. *Concurrent Pos:* Fel biochem, Ben May Lab Cancer Res, Univ Chicago, 59-60, trainee gastroenterol, Univ Hosps, 62-64; fel, Chicago Med Sch, 64-66, res assoc biochem, 64-66. *Mem:* AAAS; Am Physiol Soc; AMA; Am Gastroenterol Asn; Am Soc Gastrointestinal Endoscopy; fel Am Col Physicians. *Res:* Clinical gastroenterology; digestive biochemistry; digestion and absorption of the intestinal epithelial cell; physiology. *Mailing Add:* Dept Med Univ Kans Med Ctr Kansas City KS 66103. *Fax:* 913-588-3975

RHODES, JOHN LEWIS, MATHEMATICS. *Current Pos:* from asst prof to assoc prof, 63-70, PROF MATH, UNIV CALIF, BERKELEY, 70- *Personal Data:* b Columbus, Ohio, July 16, 37; m; c 4. *Educ:* Mass Inst Technol, BS, 60, PhD(math), 62. *Prof Exp:* NSF fel, Paris, France, 62-63. *Concurrent Pos:* Vpres, Krohn-Rhodes Res Inst, 64-68; USAF res grant, Univ Calif, Berkeley, 65-68; mem, Inst Advan Study, 66; Alfred P Sloan fel, 67; NSF grants, 63-; ed, J Pure & Appl Algebra, Publ NHolland; ed-in-chief, Int J Algebra & Comput World Sci Publ. *Res:* Algebraic theory of finite state machines, finite and infinite semi groups; finite physics from an algebraic viewpoint; neural nets; context free languages. *Mailing Add:* Dept Math Univ Calif 927 Evans Hall Berkeley CA 94720-3840

RHODES, JOHN RATHBONE, X-RAY EMISSION SPECTROMETRY, AIR & STACK GAS MONITORING. *Current Pos:* mgr applies, 69-82, mgr res & develop, 82-85, VPRES RES & DEVELOP, COLUMBIA SCI INDUST, 85-; CONSULT RADIATION GAUGING & ANALYSIS, 87- *Personal Data:* b Bradford, Eng, Dec, 1934; US citizen; m 61, Elspeth Duncan; c Helen, Duncan, Douglas, Alison & Graham. *Educ:* Cambridge Univ, BA, 58, MA, 66. *Prof Exp:* Sr sci officer, Atomic Energy Res Estab, Harwell, UK, 58-66; res scientist, Tex Nuclear Corp, 66-69. *Concurrent Pos:* Lectr nuclear physics, Postgrad Educ Ctr, UK, 61-64; teacher physics, Reading Tech Col, UK, 62-64; tech adv, Int Atomic Energy Agency, 66-78; prin investr numerous res & develop contracts, 66-80. *Mem:* Am Chem Soc; Am Soc Testing & Mat; Am Soc Nondestructive Testing. *Res:* Radiation thickness gauging; x-ray flourence analysis-portable analyzer development; technology and applications development for in-situ analysis of alloys, geochemical samples; air particulates, hazardous waste; continuous emission and ambient air monitors; technology and instrument development. *Mailing Add:* 8610 Tallwood Dr Austin TX 78759. *Fax:* 512-258-5004

RHODES, JUDITH CAROL, MEDICAL MYCOLOGY, VIRULENCE MECHANISMS. *Current Pos:* asst prof, 82-87, ASSOC PROF MYCOL, DEPT PATH & LAB MED, UNIV CINCINNATI COL MED, 87- *Personal Data:* b Tulsa, Okla, Jan 27, 49. *Educ:* Univ Okla, BS, 71, MS, 73; Univ Calif, Los Angeles, PhD(microbiol & immunol), 80. *Prof Exp:* Fel mycol sect, Lab Clin Invest, Nat Inst Allergy & Infectious Dis, NIH, 80-82. *Concurrent Pos:* Dir, Mycol Lab, Univ Hosp, Univ Cincinnati, 82-97, assoc dir clin microbiol, 85-97, prin investr, Dept Path & Lab Med, Col Med, 84-; sci dir, Microbiol Lab, Health Alliance Greater Cincinnati, 96- *Mem:* Am Soc Microbiol; Mycol Soc Am; Med Mycol Soc Americas; Int Soc Human & Animal Mycol; Am Soc Clin Path; Asn Molecular Path. *Res:* Virulence mechanisms in pathogenic fungi, especially Cryptococcus neoformans and Aspergillus. *Mailing Add:* Dept Path & Lab Med Univ Cincinnati Col Med Cincinnati OH 45267-0529

RHODES, LANDON HARRISON, PLANT PATHOLOGY. *Current Pos:* Asst prof, 76-82, ASSOC PROF PLANT PATH, OHIO STATE UNIV, 82- *Personal Data:* b Alton, Ill, Mar 15, 47; m 70; c 1. *Educ:* Univ Ill, BS, 70, MS, 75, PhD(plant path), 77. *Mem:* Am Phytopath Soc; Mycol Soc Am. *Res:* Forage crop pathology. *Mailing Add:* Dept Plant Path Ohio State Univ 2021 Coffey Rd Columbus OH 43210-1044

RHODES, MITCHELL LEE, PULMONARY DISEASES. *Current Pos:* EXEC SECY, ACCREDITATION COUN CONTINUING MED EDUC, 92- *Personal Data:* b Chicago, Ill, Feb 12, 40; m 63; c 3. *Educ:* Univ Ill, Urbana, BS, 61, Chicago, MD, 65; Lake Forest Grad Sch Mgt, MBA, 91. *Honors & Awards:* Cecile Lehman Mayer Res Award Pulmonary Dis, Am Col Chest Physicians, 74. *Prof Exp:* USPHS trainee pulmonary dis, Univ Chicago, 68-70, instr med, 70; clin instr med, Univ Calif, San Francisco, 71-72; from asst prof to assoc prof med, Col Med, Univ Iowa, 72-76; from assoc prof to prof med, Col Med, Ind Univ, 76-85; assoc dean clin affairs & prof med, Chicago Med Sch, 85-92. *Concurrent Pos:* Chief pulmonary dis, USPHS Hosp, San Francisco, 70-72; NIH pulmonary acad awardee, Nat Heart & Lung Inst, 74-76; gov, Am Col chest Physicians, 79-85, Bd Regents, 90-93. *Mem:* Fel Am Col Physicians; fel Am Col Chest Physicians (treas, 90-); Am Col Physician Execs. *Res:* Use of computer assisted instruction in medical education; correlation of ultrastructural and metabolic changes in lung tissue; continuing medical education. *Mailing Add:* 1730 Seton Rd Northbrook IL 60062-1341

RHODES, RICHARD AYER, II, PHYSICS. *Current Pos:* RETIRED. *Personal Data:* b Hartford, Conn, Feb 13, 22. *Educ:* Bowdoin Col, AB, 43; Yale Univ, MS, 47; Brown Univ, PhD(physics), 61. *Prof Exp:* Instr, Bowdoin Col, 43-44; jr physicist, US Naval Res Lab, 44-45; asst prof, Physics Dept, Univ Conn, 47-62; Univ Fla, 62-66; assoc prof physics, Fla Presby/Eckerd Col, 66-73; vis assoc prof, Physics Dept, Randolf-Macon Col, 85-86; vis prof, Va Milit Inst, 86-87, Physics Edpt, Eckerd Col, 87-94. *Mem:* Am Phys Soc; Acoust Soc Am; Optical Soc Am; AAAS. *Res:* Liquids; ionic collisions. *Mailing Add:* 205 NW Monroe Circle N St Petersburg FL 33702

RHODES, ROBERT ALLEN, PHARMACEUTICAL CHEMISTRY. *Current Pos:* from asst prof to assoc prof, 70-84, PROF CHEM, MID GA COL, 84- *Personal Data:* b Harrisonburg, Va, May 10, 41; m 63, Rose Weaver; c Geoffrey P, Anthony L & Kathryn E. *Educ:* Bridgewater Col, BA, 63; Univ Md, Baltimore, PhD(pharmaceut chem), 68. *Prof Exp:* Asst biochem, Ahmadu Bello Univ, Nigeria, 68-70. *Concurrent Pos:* Fel, Oak Ridge Assoc Univs, 76; fel, GD Searle, 83; res assoc, Ga State Univ, 84-90. *Mem:* AAAS; Am Chem Soc; Sigma Xi. *Res:* Indole and heterocyclic synthesis. *Mailing Add:* 224 Brookwood Dr Dublin GA 31021. *E-Mail:* arhodes@warrior.mgc.peachnet.edu

RHODES, ROBERT SHAW, HEMATOLOGY, OCCUPATIONAL MEDICINE. *Current Pos:* assoc med dir, Gen Motors, 78-82, dir health serv, Hydromatic Div, 82-87, regional med dir, Detroit West, 87-93, DIR HEALTH SERVS, EAST REGION, GEN MOTORS CO, 93-; MEM STAFF, DEPT MED, BYER MEM HOSP. *Personal Data:* b Orangeburg, SC, Mar 3, 36; m 94, Gwendolyn; c Robin, Robert, Candice & Nekole. *Educ:* SC State Col, BS, 58; Meharry Med Col, MD, 62; Univ Mich, MPH, 84. *Prof Exp:* Intern, Hubbard Hosp, Nashville, 62-63; med officer & aviation pathologist, Armed Forces Inst Path Aerospace Br, 67-70; fel hemat, Dept Internal Med, Vanderbilt Univ, 70-72; resident path, Meharry Med Col, 63-67, dir, Hemat & Clin Labs, 72-75, assoc prof internal med & path, 72-78. *Concurrent Pos:* Consult aerospace pathologists, Nat Transp Safety Bd, 67-70; assoc investr clin studies, Vanderbilt Univ Clin Res Ctr, 70-72; proj dir, Nat Heart & Lung Inst Contract, Clin Trials Vaso-occlusive Crisis Treatment, Meharry Med Col, 71-73; mem ad hoc sickle cell contracts rev comt, Nat Heart & Lung Inst, 74-76; consult, Nat Asn Sickle Cell Dis, Nat Educ Proj Sickle Cell Dis, 75-86, Gen Motors, 78- *Mem:* Am Soc Clin Path; Am Col Occup & Environ Med; Am Soc Safety Engrs; Am Nat Med Asn; AMA. *Res:* Miscellaneous studies on the natural history of sickle cell disease and the sickling process and occupational medicine; environmental and preventive medicine. *Mailing Add:* Regional Dir Health Serv Div Med Dir Gen Motors NAO 6225 Sheridan Ave C-318 Williamsville NY 14221

RHODES, RONDELL H, developmental biology, histology; deceased, see previous edition for last biography

RHODES, RUSSELL G, PHYCOLOGY. *Current Pos:* PROF LIFE SCI & HEAD DEPT, SOUTHWEST MO STATE UNIV, 77- *Personal Data:* b St Louis, Mo, Aug 28, 39; m 61; c 1. *Educ:* Univ Mo-Kansas City, BS, 61; Univ Tenn, MS, 63, PhD(bot), 66. *Prof Exp:* Res assoc bot, Univ Tenn, 66; assoc prof bot, Kent State University, 66-77. *Concurrent Pos:* Mem, Ohio Biol Surv, 67. *Mem:* Phycol Soc Am; Brit Phycol Soc; Int Phycol Soc; Sigma Xi. *Res:* Morphogenesis of brown algae; cultivation of acidophilic algae; isolation and cultivation of Chyrsophytan algae. *Mailing Add:* Home Econ Southwest Mo State Univ 901 S National Ave Springfield MO 65804-0027

RHODES, WILLIAM CLIFFORD, THEORETICAL CHEMISTRY, CHEMICAL DYNAMICS. *Current Pos:* Am Cancer Soc fel chem, Fla State Univ, 58-59, from instr to assoc prof, 59-70, exec dir, Inst Molecular Physics, 75-79, dir, 79-80, PROF CHEM, FLA STATE UNIV, 70- *Personal Data:* b Birmingham, Ala, Aug 8, 32; m 57; c 3. *Educ:* Howard Col, AB, 54; Johns Hopkins Univ, PhD(biochem), 58. *Concurrent Pos:* Am Cancer Soc fel, 60-61; NSF sr fel, 64-65; NIH career develop award, 65-70. *Mem:* Sigma Xi. *Res:* Biophysics; quantum chemistry; dynamic aspects of molecular excitation and relaxation processes; selective excitation by laser and conventional light; energy channeling in molecular systems. *Mailing Add:* PO Box 555 Crystal Beach FL 34681-0555

RHODES, WILLIAM HARKER, veterinary medicine, for more information see previous edition

RHODES, WILLIAM HOLMAN, CERAMICS, METALLURGY. *Current Pos:* STAFF MEM, OSRAN-SYLVANIA LABS, 95- *Personal Data:* b Oneonta, NY, Sept 13, 35; m 57; c 2. *Educ:* Alfred Univ, BS, 57; Mass Inst Technol, ScD(ceramics), 65. *Honors & Awards:* Ross Coffin Purdy Award, 83; Hobart M Kraner Award, 83; Leslie H Warner Award, 85. *Prof Exp:*

Trainee, Gen Elec Co, 57-58, engr, 60-62; group leader ceramics, Mat Sci Dept, Avco Systs Div, 65-73; sr staff scientist GTE Labs, Inc, 73-95. *Concurrent Pos:* Co-chair, Panel Ceramics & Ceramic Composites, Nat Acad Sci, 85. *Mem:* Fel Am Ceramic Soc (pres, 88-89); Sigma Xi. *Res:* Physical ceramics, especially mechanical and optical properties, kinetics of densification by sintering and pressure sintering and basic diffusion studies; fabrication of ceramics, composites and metals from powders. *Mailing Add:* Four McKeever Dr Lexington MA 02173

RHODES, WILLIAM TERRILL, ELECTRICAL ENGINEERING, OPTICS. *Current Pos:* from asst prof to assoc prof, 71-80, PROF ELEC ENG, GA INST TECHNOL, 81- *Personal Data:* b Palo Alto, Calif, Apr 14, 43; div; c 3. *Educ:* Stanford Univ, BS, 66, MSEE, 68, PhD(elec eng), 72. *Prof Exp:* Res asst electronics labs, Stanford Univ, 69-71. *Concurrent Pos:* Consult, Naval Res Lab, 74-, Lockheed Electronics, 80- & Aerodyne Res, Inc, 81-; Humboldt res fel, Univ Erlangen, Nurnberg, 76; dir, Optical Soc Am, 84-86; gov, Soc Photo-Optical Instrumentation Engrs, 83-85; ed, Appl Optics, 87-93; chair, Denver Bus Challenge, Dept Elec Comp Eng, Univ Colo, Boulder, 90-91. *Mem:* Fel Soc Photo-Optical Instrumentation Engrs; fel Optical Soc Am; Inst Elec & Electronics Engrs. *Res:* Synthetic aperture optics; image formation; hybrid optical-digital signal processing; numerical and algebraic optical processing; noncoherent optical processing; acousto-optic signal processing; computational vision; morphological image processing. *Mailing Add:* Sch Elec Eng Ga Inst Technol Atlanta GA 30332-0250. *Fax:* 404-894-6285; *E-Mail:* bill.rhodes@ee.gatech.edu

RHODES, YORKE EDWARD, PHYSICAL ORGANIC & ASTROCHEMISTRY. *Current Pos:* asst prof, 65-71, asst dean, 87-89, ASSOC PROF ORG CHEM, NY UNIV, 71-, DIR, SCI & ENG, 88- *Personal Data:* b Elizabeth, NJ, Mar 25, 36; m 75, Mechthilde Weggenmann; c Yorke E III, Christopher A, Timothy A & Matthias R. *Educ:* Univ Del, BS, 57, MS, 59; Univ Ill, PhD(org chem), 64. *Prof Exp:* NIH fel org chem, Yale Univ, 64-65. *Concurrent Pos:* Guest prof, Freiburg Univ, 72-73 & Tech Univ Munich, 77-78; Alexander von Humboldt sr US scientist award, 78; Jet Propulsion Lab, Calif Inst Tech, 80 & 81; assoc prof, Univ Grenoble, France, 87; chair-elect, NY Sect, Am Chem Soc, 97; mem, Nat Minority Affairs Comt, Am Chem Soc, 97- *Mem:* Am Chem Soc; Royal Chem Soc; NY Acad Sci. *Res:* Small ring chemistry; carbonium ion rearrangements; neighboring group participation, especially by alkyl and cyclopropane; solvolysis mechanisms; nonaqueous solvents; stereochemistry and reaction mechanisms; synthesis and reactions of strained polycyclic systems; organic chemistry of the interstellar media prediction and mechanism of formation of new compounds. *Mailing Add:* Dept Chem NY Univ New York NY 10003. *Fax:* 212-260-7905; *E-Mail:* rhodes@is2.nyu.edu

RHODIN, JOHANNES A G, ELECTRON MICROSCOPY, INTRAVITAL RECORDING OF MICROVASCULAR BEDS. *Current Pos:* PROF & CHMN, DEPT ANAT, UNIV SFLA, 79- *Personal Data:* b Lund, Sweden, Sept 30, 22; m 94, Judie Laurent; c Anders & Erik. *Educ:* Karolinska Inst, Stockholm, MD, 50, PhD(anat), 54. *Honors & Awards:* Landis Res Award, Microcirculatory soc, 68. *Prof Exp:* Instr anat, Karolinska Inst, 50-54, asst prof, 54-58; assoc prof, Sch Med, New York Univ, 58-60, prof, 60-64; prof & chmn, Dept Anat, New York Med Col, 64-74, Univ Mich, Ann Arbor, 74-77 & Med Sch, Karolinska Inst, 77-79. *Concurrent Pos:* Mem, Nobel Assembly, Karolinska Inst, Sweden, 77-79. *Mem:* Am Soc Cell Biol; Am Asn Anatomists; Microcirculatory Soc; Europ Soc Microcirculation; Europ Artery Club; hon mem Ital Soc Anat. *Res:* Study of microvascular beds, combining intravital video recordings of rat mesenteric microvessels with subsequent analyses of the same vascular segments in the transmission electron microscope; capillary sprout formation, endothelial cell movements, transformation of fibroblasts into pericytes and ultimately smooth muscle cells of differentiating arterioles, small arteries, venules and veins; beta-amyloid effect on arterioles; Alzheimer's disease. *Mailing Add:* Univ SFla Col Med Dept Anat 12901 N Bruce B Downs Blvd Tampa FL 33612. *Fax:* 813-974-2058; *E-Mail:* jrhodin@golgi.panat.med.usf.edu

RHODIN, THOR NATHANIEL, JR, CHEMICAL PHYSICS. *Current Pos:* assoc prof appl physics, 58-68, PROF APPL PHYSICS & MEM FAC, SCH APPL & ENG PHYSICS, CORNELL UNIV, 68- *Personal Data:* b Buenos Aires, Arg, Dec 9, 20; US citizen; m 48; c 4. *Educ:* Haverford Col, BS, 42; Princeton Univ, AM, 45, PhD(chem physics), 46. *Prof Exp:* Res assoc, Manhattan Proj, Princeton Univ, 42-47; mem staff, Inst Study Metals, Univ Chicago, 47-51; res assoc, Eng Res Lab, E I du Pont de Nemours & Co, 51-58. *Concurrent Pos:* NSF fel, Cambridge Univ, 64-65; vis prof, Mass Inst Technol, Univ Munich & Univ Tokyo; adv ed, Surface Sci J; Humboldt sr scientist Award, WGermany, 85-86. *Mem:* Fel Am Phys Soc; Am Vacuum Soc; Am Chem Soc; Am Asn Univ Profs. *Res:* Physics and chemistry of metal and semiconductor surfaces and interfaces; synchrotron radiation spectroscopy; cluster chemistry; surface extended x-ray absorption fine structures; laser-solid interaction; time resolved surface processes; ion enhanced surface chemistry. *Mailing Add:* Sch Appl & Eng Physics Clark Hall G217 Cornell Univ Ithaca NY 14850

RHODINE, CHARLES NORMAN, ELECTRICAL & BIOLOGICAL ENGINEERING. *Current Pos:* Assoc prof, 59-80, PROF ELEC ENG, UNIV WYO, 80-, ASST HEAD DEPT, 83- *Personal Data:* b Denver, Colo, Jan 10, 31; m 57, Barbara I Sanborn; c Brent N, Craig W & Susan L. *Educ:* Univ Wyo, BS, 57, MS, 59; Purdue Univ, PhD, 73. *Concurrent Pos:* NSF fel, Purdue Univ, 67-69. *Mem:* Inst Elec & Electronics Engrs; Nat Soc Prof Engrs; Sigma Xi. *Res:* Communications and information theory, its application to biological systems; development of computer-aided teaching equipment. *Mailing Add:* Dept Elec Eng Univ Wyo Box 3295 Univ Sta Laramie WY 82070

RHORER, RICHARD L, INDUSTRIAL & MANUFACTURING ENGINEERING. *Current Pos:* CHIEF, FABRICATION TECHNOL DIV, NAT INST STAND & TECHNOL, 95- *Personal Data:* b El Paso, Tex, June 28, 42. *Educ:* Univ NMex, MA, 67. *Prof Exp:* Staff, Los Alamos Nat Lab, 67-95. *Mem:* Am Soc Precision Eng (pres, 96). *Mailing Add:* Nat Inst Stand & Technol Bldg 304 Rm 135 Rte 270 Gaithersburg MD 20899. *E-Mail:* richard.rohrer@nist.gov

RHOTEN, WILLIAM BLOCHER, CELLULAR BIOLOGY. *Current Pos:* PROF & CHAIRPERSON, SCH MED, MARSHALL UNIV, 91- *Personal Data:* b Orange, NJ, Feb 11, 43; m 69, Donna Sawyer; c Justin, Tara & Jeremy. *Educ:* Colo State Univ, BS, 65; Univ Ill, Urbana, MS, 68; Pa State Univ, PhD(anat), 71. *Prof Exp:* Res fel path, Sch Med, Wash Univ, 71-73; instr med, Div Endocrinol & Metab, Sch Med, Univ Ala, 73-74; asst prof anat, Sch Basic Med Sci, Col Med, Univ Ill, Urbana, 74-80; from asst prof, assoc prof Anat, NJ Med Sch, Univ Med & Dent NJ, 80-91. *Concurrent Pos:* Reviewer, Endocrine, Bone & Mineral, Anat Record, NSF, & Sci Endocrinol; head, Histol & Cell Biol Unit, Univ Cape Town, 85-86. *Mem:* Am Asn Anat; Am Soc Cell Biol; AAAS; NY Acad Sci; Micros Soc Am; Asn Anat Cell NB Chairs. *Res:* Cellular biology; gene expression in experimental biology; in situ hybridization; structure-function relationships in the endocrine pancreas; in situ immunodetection; calcium-binding proteins; intracellular calcium. *Mailing Add:* Dept Anat & Cell Biol Marshall Univ Med Sch 1542 Spring Valley Dr Huntington WV 25704-9388. *Fax:* 304-696-7290; *E-Mail:* rhoten@marshall.edu

RHOTON, ALBERT LOREN, JR, NEUROSURGERY. *Current Pos:* prof neurol surg & chief div, 72-79, R D KEENE FAMILY PROF NEUROL SURG & CHMN DEPT, UNIV FLA, 79- *Personal Data:* b Parvin, Ky, Nov 18, 32; m 57, Joyce L Moldenhauer; c Eric L, Albert J, Alice S & Laurel A. *Educ:* Ohio State Univ, BS, 54; Wash Univ, MD, 59. *Honors & Awards:* Billings Bronze Medal, AMA, 69; Jones Award, Am Asn Med Illustr, 69. *Prof Exp:* Fel neurol surg, Sch Med, Wash Univ, 63-65, NIH spec fel neuroanat, 65-66; from instr to asst prof neurol surg, Mayo Found, Univ Minn, 66-72. *Concurrent Pos:* Consult, Gainesville Vet Admin Hosp; NIH travel award, 65; Krayenbuhl lectr & hon guest, Swiss Soc Neurol Surg, 75 & Japanese Neurosurg Soc, 77; vis fac mem & lectr, Harvard Univ, Duke Univ, Johns Hopkins Univ, Univ Pa, Univ Chicago & Univ Calif, San Francisco & Los Angeles; bd gov, Am Col Surgeons, 79-85. *Mem:* Am Asn Neurol Surg (treas, 83-86, vpres, 87, pres elect, 88); Am Col Surgeons; Cong Neurol Surg (vpres, 73-74, pres, 78); Neurosurg Soc Am; Soc Neurol Surg (treas, 76-79, pres, 93); Am Surg Asn; NAm Skull Base Soc, (pres, 93). *Res:* Microneurosurgery; microsurgical anatomy; neuroanatomy of the cranial nerves; microsurgery of cerebrovascular disease; developer of microsurgical instruments. *Mailing Add:* Box 100265 Univ Fla Med Ctr Gainesville FL 32610. *Fax:* 352-392-8413; *E-Mail:* rhoton@neocortex.health.ufl.edu

RHYKERD, CHARLES LOREN, PLANT PHYSIOLOGY, AGRONOMY. *Current Pos:* from asst prof to prof agron, 60-87, ASSOC DIR, INT PROG AGR, PURDUE UNIV, WEST LAFAYETTE, 87- *Personal Data:* b Cameron, Ill, Apr 7, 29; m 54, Eileen McIlrath; c Charles L Jr, Robert L & Linda M. *Educ:* Univ Ill, BS, 51, MS, 52; Purdue Univ, PhD(agron), 57. *Prof Exp:* Asst agron, Univ Ill, 51-52; technician, Producers Seed Co, Ill, 53-54; asst instr agron, Ohio State Univ, 54-55; asst, Purdue Univ, 55-56, instr, 56-57; soil scientist, US Regional Pasture Res Lab, Pa, 57-60. *Concurrent Pos:* US AID consult, Brazil, 65; vis prof, Univ Calif, Davis, 67-68; co-dir, Nat Corn & Sorghum Proj, Brazil, AID contract with Brazilian Ministry of Agr & Purdue Univ, 73-75; mem, Am Forage & Grassland Coun; short-term US AID consult, Portugal, 81, 82 & 84, Africa, 84. *Mem:* Am Soc Agron; Crop Sci Soc Am. *Res:* Physiology of forage crops; soil fertility. *Mailing Add:* IPIA AG AD Bldg Purdue Univ West Lafayette IN 47907-1968. *Fax:* 765-494-9613; *E-Mail:* cls@admin.agad.purdue.edu

RHYNE, A LEONARD, MATHEMATICAL STATISTICS. *Current Pos:* DIR OPERS RES, LORILLARD INC, 80- *Personal Data:* b Charlotte, NC, Dec 19, 34; m 56; c 4. *Educ:* Univ NC, AB, 57; NC State Univ, PhD(math statist), 64. *Prof Exp:* Prof math, Elon Col, 60-62; assoc prof biostatist, Bowman Gray Sch Med, 62-80, dir comput ctr, 65-77. *Mem:* Inst Math Statist; Biomet Soc; Am Statist Asn. *Res:* Applications of computer science and statistical methods in various areas of research. *Mailing Add:* 1837 Runnymeade Rd Winston-Salem NC 27104

RHYNE, JAMES JENNINGS, SOLID STATE PHYSICS, MAGNETISM. *Current Pos:* dir, mu res reactor, 90-96, PROF PHYSICS, UNIV MO, COLUMBIA, 90- *Personal Data:* b Oklahoma City, Okla, Nov 14, 38; m 82, 90, Susan Watson; c Edward & Nancy. *Educ:* Univ Okla, BS, 59; Univ Ill, Urbana, MS, 61; Iowa State Univ, PhD(physics), 65. *Hon Degrees:* Dr, Univ Nancy, France, 95. *Prof Exp:* Res asst physics, Iowa State Univ, 63-65; res physicist, Solid State Div, US Naval Ord Lab, 65-75; physicist, Nat Inst Stands & Technol, 75-90. *Concurrent Pos:* Nat Acad Sci-Nat Res Coun associateship, US Naval Ord Lab, 65-66; adj prof, Am Univ, 75-80, co-ed, Proc Conf Magnetism & Magnetic Mat, 70-75; fac appointee, Nat Inst Stands & Technol, 91- *Mem:* Fel Am Phys Soc; Mat Res Soc. *Res:* Magnetic and transport properties of rare-earth metals and compounds; neutron scattering in magnetic materials. *Mailing Add:* Physics Dept Univ Mo Columbia MO 65211. *Fax:* 573-882-4195; *E-Mail:* jrhyne@showme.missouri.edu

RHYNE, THERESA MARIE, COMPUTER GRAPHICS, SCIENTIFIC VISUALIZATION. *Current Pos:* sr systs analysts comput graphics, Unisys Corp, US Environ Protection Agency Info Ctr, 87-90, tech leader, Sci Visualization Ctr, 90-92, sr sci visualization researcher, Martin Marietta, 93, LEAD SCI VISUALIZATION RESEARCHER, SCI VISUALIZATION

CTR, LOCKHEED MARTIN, US ENVIRON PROTECTION AGENCY, 94- *Personal Data:* b Denver, Colo, Sept 20, 54. *Educ:* Stanford Univ, BS, 76, MS, 77 & 81. *Prof Exp:* Analyst, Ctr Info Technol, Stanford Univ, 81-82, long range planner, 82-83; budget & planning officer, 83-85; comput graphics & univ comput consult, 85-87. *Concurrent Pos:* Instr comput art, NC Mus Art, 88-89 & 93; instr comput art & consult, Meredith Col, 90-91; dir at large, Spec Interest Group Graphics, Asn Comput Mach, 96-98. *Mem:* Asn Comput Mach; Int Cartographic Asn; Inst Elec & Electronics Engrs; AAAS; Air Waste & Mgt Asn; Math Asn Am. *Res:* Exploring how geographic information systems and scientific visualizations tools can be integrated together to assist effective environmental sciences research and policy making. *Mailing Add:* Lockheed Martin Sci Visualization Ctr US Environ Protection Agency 86 Alexander Dr Research Triangle Park NC 27711. *E-Mail:* trhyne@vislab.epa.gov

RHYNE, THOMAS CROWELL, ENVIRONMENTAL CHEMISTRY. *Current Pos:* asst prof, 72-80, prof chem & asst dean, grad sch, 80-88, CHAIR, CHEM DEPT, APPALACHIAN STATE UNIV, 96- *Personal Data:* b Lincolnton, NC, Nov 8, 42; m 65, Billie S Green; c Peter T & Catherine L. *Educ:* Appalachian State Univ, BS, 65, MA, 67; Va Polytech Inst & State Univ, PhD(chem), 71. *Prof Exp:* Res assoc chem, Aerospace Res Labs, Wright-Patterson AFB, Ohio, 71-72. *Concurrent Pos:* Nat Acad Sci-Nat Res Coun fel, 71-72. *Mem:* Am Chem Soc; Am Soc Mass Spectrometry. *Res:* Mass spectrometry; atmospheric chemistry. *Mailing Add:* Chem Dept Appalachian State Univ Boone NC 28608. *E-Mail:* rhynetc@appstate.edu

RHYNE, V(ERNON) THOMAS, ELECTRICAL ENGINEERING, COMPUTER ENGINEERING. *Current Pos:* DIR, ATLAS STANDS LABS, 90- *Personal Data:* b Gulfport, Miss, Feb 18, 42; m 61, Glenda (Pevey); c Amber & Tommy. *Educ:* Miss State Univ, BS, 62; Univ Va, MEE, 64; Ga Inst Technol, PhD(elec eng), 67. *Honors & Awards:* Terman Award, Am Soc Eng Educ, 80; Spensley Horn Jubas & Lubitz, 83- *Prof Exp:* Aerospace technologist data systs, Langley Res Ctr, NASA, 62-65; instr elec eng, Ga Inst Technol, 65-67; from asst prof to prof, Tex A&M Univ, 67-83; dir, Cad Prog, MCC, 84-87. *Concurrent Pos:* Consult, Tex Instruments Inc, Dallas, 68-69 & Elec Power Res Inst, 78-82; Darby & Darby expert witness, 79-92, Dorsey & Whitney, 93- *Mem:* Inst Elec & Electronics Engrs. *Res:* Computer engineering (general); standards for electronic commerce. *Mailing Add:* Atlas Stand Labs 3410 Day Star Cove Austin TX 78746. *Fax:* 512-338-3895

RHYNER, CHARLES R, SOLID STATE PHYSICS, SOLID WASTE MANAGEMENT. *Current Pos:* from asst prof to assoc prof, 68-85, PROF PHYSICS, UNIV WIS-GREEN BAY, 85- *Personal Data:* b Wausau, Wis, Mar 25, 40; m 63; c 4. *Educ:* Univ Wis, BS, 62, MS, 64, PhD(physics), 68. *Prof Exp:* Asst prof physics, Univ Wis-Kenosha, 67-68; physicist, US Naval Radiol Defense Lab, Calif, 68. *Mem:* Am Phys Soc; Sigma Xi; Am Asn Physics Teachers. *Res:* Thermoluminescence; color centers in alkali halides; radiation dosimetry; solid waste management. *Mailing Add:* Dept Physics Univ Wis 2420 Nicolet Dr Green Bay WI 54311-7001

RHYNSBURGER, ROBERT WHITMAN, astronomy, for more information see previous edition

RIAHI, DANIEL NOUROLLAH, GEOPHYSICS, MECHANICAL ENGINEERING. *Current Pos:* vis asst prof, 80-82, asst prof, 82-85, ASSOC PROF MECH, UNIV ILL, URBANA-CHAMPAIGN, 85- *Personal Data:* b Shahrekord, Iran, Oct 30, 43; US citizen; m 84. *Educ:* Tehran Univ, BM, 66; Fla State Univ, MS, 70, PhD(appl math), 74. *Prof Exp:* Teaching asst appl math, Fla State Univ, 70-72, res asst fluid mech, 72-74, postdoctoral fel fluid mech, 74-77; instr math, Winthrop Col, 77-78; sr researcher fluid mech, Univ Calif, Los Angeles, 78-80. *Concurrent Pos:* Consult math, Sch Social Work, Fla State Univ, 70-71; chmn, Appl Math Comt, Winthrop Col, 77-78; eng mech chief ad, Univ Ill, 85-86, eng mech coordr, 85-86; vis scholar, Cambridge Univ, Eng, 86; prin investr, Nat Ctr Supercomput Applns, 90-93 & NSF, 86-91; chmn, Awards Comt, Theory & Appl Mech Dept, Univ Ill, 90-91, Tech Session, Div Fluid Dynamics, Am Phys Soc, 88 & 89; chmn invited speakers, Mid-Western Mech Conf, 91 & tech session organizer, 91; chmn tech sess, Int Cong, CRB awards, 85-86 & 93-94. *Mem:* Soc Indust & Appl Math; Am Phys Soc; assoc fel Am Inst Aeronaut & Astronaut; Am Acad Mech; Sigma Xi. *Res:* Author of over 125 publications including books, chapters and invited papers; fluid mechanics; applied mathematics; heat transfer; magneto hydrodynamics; instability and materials processing. *Mailing Add:* Dept Theoret & Appl Mech Univ Ill 104 S Wright St Urbana IL 61801. *E-Mail:* d__riahi@uiuc.edu

RIAZ, M(AHMOUD), ELECTRICAL ENGINEERING. *Current Pos:* assoc prof, 59-78, PROF ELEC ENG, UNIV MINN, MINNEAPOLIS, 78- *Personal Data:* b Paris, France, Feb 27, 25; nat US; m 64; c 1. *Educ:* Univ Paris, LLB, 44; Univ Cairo, Egypt, BSc, 46; Rensselaer Polytech Inst, MEE, 47; Mass Inst Technol, ScD, 55. *Honors & Awards:* Levy Medal, Franklin Inst, 72. *Prof Exp:* Asst elec eng, Mass Inst Technol, 52-54, from instr to asst prof, 54-59. *Mem:* Inst Elec & Electronics Engrs; Brit Inst Elec Eng; Int Solar Energy Soc. *Res:* Energy conversion and control; electromechanical systems; power systems; solar energy systems. *Mailing Add:* Dept Elec Eng 4-178 Elec Eng Comput Sci Bldg 200 Union St SE Minneapolis MN 55455

RIBAK, CHARLES ERIC, NEUROSCIENCE, NEUROANATOMY. *Current Pos:* from asst prof to assoc prof, 78-90, PROF ANAT, UNIV CALIF, IRVINE, 90- *Personal Data:* b Albany, NY, July 19, 50; m 77, Julia Wendruck; c Marc & William. *Educ:* State Univ NY, Albany, BS, 71; Boston Univ, PhD(neuroanat), 76. *Honors & Awards:* Michael Prize, 87; Jacob Javits Award, Nat Inst Neurol Dis & Stroke, NIH, 90. *Prof Exp:* Assoc res scientist neurosci, City Hope Nat Med Ctr, 75-78. *Concurrent Pos:* Klingenstein fel neurosci. *Mem:* Am Asn Anatomists; Soc Neurosci; fel AAAS; Int Brain Res Orgn. *Res:* Analysis of neurons in normal and epileptic cerebral cortex with the electron microscope; neurocytology of gamma-aminobutyric acid neurons with immunocytochemistry; electron microscopic studies of local circuit neurons in the hippocampus and neocortex. *Mailing Add:* Dept Anat & Neurobiol Univ Calif Irvine CA 92717. *E-Mail:* ceribak@uci.edu

RIBAN, DAVID MICHAEL, SCIENCE EDUCATION. *Current Pos:* ASSOC PROF, DEPT SCI, DAYTONA BEACH COMMUNITY COL, 90- *Personal Data:* b Chicago, Ill, May 10, 36; m 63; c 3. *Educ:* Northern Ill Univ, BSEd, 57; Univ Mich, MA, 60; Purdue Univ, MS, 67, PhD(physics educ), 69. *Prof Exp:* Teacher physics, Luther High Sch South, Chicago, 57-60 & Leyden Sch, Northlake, Ill, 60-67; teaching asst, Purdue Univ, 68-69; assoc prof, Ind Univ Pa, 70-73, prof, 74-91. *Concurrent Pos:* Dir, Intermediate Sci Curric Study Training Prog, Installed User Prog, NSF, 72-73 & Teacher Training Prog, 75-76, dir, Proj Physics Training Prog, 74-75 & 75-76. *Mem:* Nat Asn Res Sci Teaching; Am Asn Physics Teachers; AAAS; Nat Sci Teachers Asn; Nat Educ Asn. *Res:* Science curriculum implementation; learning theory; effects of field work in science in promoting learning; history of the development of scientific ideas. *Mailing Add:* Daytona Beach Community Col Dept Sci Daytona Beach FL 32114

RIBBE, PAUL HUBERT, MINERALOGY. *Current Pos:* assoc prof, 66-72, PROF MINERAL, VA POLYTECH INST & STATE UNIV, 72- *Personal Data:* b Bristol, Conn, Apr 2, 35; m 58; c 3. *Educ:* Wheaton Col, Ill, BS, 56; Univ Wis, MS, 58; Cambridge Univ, PhD(crystallog), 63. *Honors & Awards:* Distinguished Pub Serv Medal Mineral Soc Am, 93; Schlumberger Medal, Mineral Soc Gt Brit & Ireland, 95. *Prof Exp:* Mineralogist, Corning Glass Works, 58-60; NSF fel, Univ Chicago, 63-64; asst prof geol, Univ Calif, Los Angeles, 64-66. *Concurrent Pos:* Ed, Reviews Mineral. *Mem:* Microbeam Anal Soc; fel Mineral Soc Am (vpres, 85-86, pres, 86-). *Res:* Crystal structure analysis and chemistry of rock-forming minerals, particularly feldspars and orthosilicates. *Mailing Add:* Dept Geol Sci Va Polytech Inst & State Univ Blacksburg VA 24061-0420. *E-Mail:* ribbe@vt.edu

RIBBENS, WILLIAM B(ENNETT), ELECTRICAL ENGINEERING. *Current Pos:* res asst, Univ Mich, Ann Arbor, 60-63, res engr, Cooley Elec Lab, 63-65, assoc res engr, 65-67, proj dir, 67-69, ASSOC PROF ELEC & COMPUT ENG, UNIV MICH, ANN ARBOR, 69- *Personal Data:* b Grand Rapids, Mich, May 26, 37; m 72. *Educ:* Univ Mich, Ann Arbor, BSEE, 60, MS, 61, PhD(elec eng), 65. *Prof Exp:* Design engr, Lear Inc, Mich, 60. *Concurrent Pos:* Consult to various industs. *Mem:* Inst Elec & Electronics Engrs; Optical Soc Am. *Res:* Coherent optical data processing and optical metrology; instrumentation. *Mailing Add:* 2424 Londonderry Rd Ann Arbor MI 48104

RIBE, FRED LINDEN, PHYSICS. *Current Pos:* prof, 77-90, EMER PROF NUCLEAR ENG, UNIV WASH, SEATTLE, 90- *Personal Data:* b Laredo, Tex, Aug 14, 24; m 46, Mally G Kemp; c James K, Frederick C, Robert G & Thomas E. *Educ:* Univ Tex, BS, 44; Univ Chicago, SM, 50, PhD(physics), 51. *Prof Exp:* Engr, Eng Res Assocs, Inc, 46-47; asst, Inst Nuclear Studies, Univ Chicago, 47-50; mem staff, Los Alamos Sci Lab, Univ Calif, 51-74, div leader, Controlled Thermonuclear Res Div, 74-77. *Concurrent Pos:* Vis prof, Univ Iowa, 56; Guggenheim fel, Inst Plasma Physics, Munich, Ger, 63-64; adj prof physics, Univ Tex, Austin, 74-76. *Mem:* Fel Am Phys Soc; Am Nuclear Soc. *Res:* Nuclear reactions; fast neutron research; atomic collisions; plasma physics. *Mailing Add:* 1821 Sun Mountain Dr Santa Fe NM 87501

RIBELIN, WILLIAM EUGENE, veterinary pathology, for more information see previous edition

RIBENBOIM, PAULO, MATHEMATICS. *Current Pos:* PROF MATH, QUEEN'S UNIV, ONT, 62- *Personal Data:* b Recife, Brazil, Mar 13, 28; m 51, Huguette Demangelle; c Serge & Eric. *Educ:* Univ Brazil, BS, 48; Univ Sao Paulo, PhD, 57. *Hon Degrees:* Dr, Univ Caen, France. *Honors & Awards:* Polya Award, Math Asn Am, 95. *Prof Exp:* Asst, Cent Brazil Phys Res, 49-50; prof math, Hermon, Army Tech Sch, Brazil, 52-53; res chief, Inst Pure & Appl Math, 57-59; vis assoc prof, Univ Ill, 59-62. *Concurrent Pos:* Vis prof, Northeastern Univ, Boston, 65, Univ Paris, 69-70, Univ Ill, Urbana, 83 & Univ Strasbourg, 91. *Mem:* Fel Royal Soc Can; Am Math Soc; assoc Brazilian Acad Sci; Can Math Soc; Math Soc France; Am Math Soc; Soc Math Suisse; Math Asn Am. *Res:* Algebra; theory of ideals; commutative algebra; algebraic number theory; Fermat's last theorem. *Mailing Add:* Dept Math Queen's Univ Kingston ON K7L 3N6 Can. *Fax:* 613-545-2964

RIBES, LUIS, ALGEBRA. *Current Pos:* asst prof, 70-72, assoc prof, 72-79, PROF MATH, CARLETON UNIV, 79- *Personal Data:* b Madrid, Spain, Sept 12, 40; m 64; c 2. *Educ:* Univ Madrid, Licenciado, 62; Univ Rochester, MA, 65, PhD(math), 67; Univ Madrid, DrCiencias, 69. *Prof Exp:* Asst prof math, Univ Ill, Urbana, 67-68; res assoc & asst prof math, Queen's Univ, 68-70. *Mem:* Am Math Soc; Can Math Cong; Spanish Math Soc. *Res:* Cohomology of groups, discrete and profinite; structure of free profinite and free products of profinite groups; combinational group theory. *Mailing Add:* Dept Math Carleton Univ Ottawa ON K1S 5B6 Can

RIBLET, GORDON POTTER, ELECTRICAL ENGINEERING, PHYSICS. *Current Pos:* RES SCIENTIST ENG, MICROWAVE DEVELOP LABS, INC, 72- *Personal Data:* b Boston, Mass, Dec 12, 43; m 72; c 2. *Educ:* Yale Univ, BS, 65; Univ Pa, MS, 66, PhD(physics), 70. *Prof Exp:* Res scientist physics, Univ Cologne, 70-72. *Concurrent Pos:* Dir, Parametric Indust, 76-80; pres, Fab-Braze Corp, 77- *Mem:* Am Phys Soc; Inst Elec & Electronics Engrs. *Res:* Solid state physics, especially effect of magnetic impurities on superconductivity; microwave technology, especially circuit properties of multiport networks. *Mailing Add:* Microwave Develop Labs 135 Crescent Rd Needham MA 02194

RIBLET, HENRY B, ELECTRICAL ENGINEERING. *Current Pos:* RETIRED. *Personal Data:* b Clayton, NMex, May 20, 11. *Educ:* Friends Univ, AB, 34. *Prof Exp:* Br supvr, Data Control, Appl Physics Lab, Johns Hopkins Univ, 64-76. *Mem:* Fel Inst Elec & Electronics Engrs. *Mailing Add:* Johns Hopkins Univ Appl Physics Lab Johns Hopkins Rd Laurel MD 20810

RIBLET, LESLIE ALFRED, PHARMACOLOGY, PHYSIOLOGY. *Current Pos:* DIR, PRECLIN RES PHARMACEUT, RES & DEVELOP DIV, BRISTOL-MYERS CO. *Personal Data:* b Wayne County, Ohio, Aug 10, 41; m 65; c 1. *Educ:* Ashland Col, BS, 63; Univ Mo-Kansas City, BS, 66, MS, 68; Univ Iowa, PhD(pharmacol), 71. *Prof Exp:* Sr scientist, Mead Johnson Res Ctr, 71-74, sr investr, Mead Johnson Pharmaceut Div, 74-76, sr res assoc pharmacol, 76-79, sect mgr, 79- *Mem:* Soc Neurosci; Sigma Xi; AAAS; Soc Exp Biol Med; NY Acad Sci. *Res:* Central nervous system pharmacology with emphasis on quantitative electroencephalogram correlates of behavioral and neurochemical indices of brain function. *Mailing Add:* Viatech Imaging 158 Main St PO Box 456 Ivoryton CT 06442

RIBLET, ROY JOHNSON, IMMUNOLOGY, GENETICS. *Current Pos:* MEM STAFF, MED BIOL INST. *Personal Data:* b Charlotte, NC, Dec 24, 42; m 64; c 3. *Educ:* Calif Inst Technol, BS, 64; Stanford Univ, PhD(genetics), 71. *Prof Exp:* Fel immunol, Salk Inst, 71-74; res assoc immunogenetics, Inst Cancer Res, 74-75, asst mem, 75-78, assoc mem immunogenetics, 78- *Concurrent Pos:* Fel, Damon Runyon Mem Fund Cancer Res, Inc, 71-73; spec fel, Leukemia Soc Am, 73-75; NIH res grant, 77-84. *Mem:* Genetics Soc Am; AAAS; Am Asn Immunologists. *Res:* Genetic control of the immune response; mouse antibody genetics; mitogen response genetics; antibody structure and function. *Mailing Add:* Med Biol Inst 11077 N Torrey Pines Rd La Jolla CA 92037-1082

RIBNER, HERBERT SPENCER, AEROACOUSTICS, JET NOISE. *Current Pos:* staff scientist aeroacoust, 75-76, DISTINGUISHED RES ASSOC, LANGLEY RES CTR, NASA, 78-; EMER PROF AEROSPACE STUDIES, INST AEROSPACE STUDIES, UNIV TORONTO, 78- *Personal Data:* b Seattle, Wash, Apr 9, 13; m 49, Lelia Byrd; c Carol & David. *Educ:* Calif Inst Technol, BS, 35; Wash Univ, MS, 37, PhD(physics), 39. *Honors & Awards:* Turnbull lectr, Can Aeronaut & Space Inst, 68; Aeroacoust Award, Am Inst Aeronaut & Astronaut, 76, Dryden lectr, 81; Can 125 Commemorative Medal, 93. *Prof Exp:* From physicist to dir lab, Brown Geophys Co, Tex, 39-40; from physicist to head, Stability Anal Sect, Langley Lab, Nat Adv Comt Aeronaut, Va, 40-49, from consult to head boundary layer sects, Lewis Lab, Ohio, 49-54; res assoc, Inst Aerospace Studies, Univ Toronto, 55-56, from asst prof to prof aerospace studies, 56-78. *Concurrent Pos:* Vis prof, Univ Southampton, 60-61; chmn Sonic Boom Panel, Int Civil Aviation Orgn, 70-71; consult, De Havilland Aircraft, Ministry Transp, Can, 70-73 & Gen Elec Co, Cincinnati, 73-75. *Mem:* Fel Am Inst Aeronaut & Astronaut; fel Royal Soc Can; fel Am Phys Soc; fel Acoust Soc Am; fel Can Aeronaut & Space Inst; Can Acoust Asn. *Res:* X-rays; cosmic rays; development of gravity meter; aerodynamics; aeroacoustics; jet noise; sonic boom; acoustics of thunder; propellers; shock-turbulence interaction; author of over 100 technical publications. *Mailing Add:* Inst Aerospace Studies Univ Toronto 4925 Dufferin St Downsview ON M3H 5T6 Can

RICARDI, LEON J, ELECTRICAL ENGINEERING, SYSTEM ANALYSIS & SYNTHESIS. *Current Pos:* CONSULT ENGR, 96- *Personal Data:* b Brockton, Mass, Mar 21, 24; m 47; c 3. *Educ:* Northeastern Univ, BS, 49, MS, 52, PhD(elec eng), 69. *Prof Exp:* Engr, James L Waters, Inc, 49-50, Andrew Alford Consult Eng, 50-51, proj engr, Gabriel Labs, 51-54; staff mem, Mass Inst Technol, 54-55, asst group leader radio frequency components & antennas, 55-57, group leader antenna & commun syst, 57-85, head, Technol Adv Off, Lincoln Labs, 82-85; pres consult engr, Div Electromagnetic Sci, LJR Inc, 85-96. *Concurrent Pos:* Lectr & teacher, Northeastern Univ, 69-80. *Mem:* Fel Inst Elec & Electronics Engrs. *Res:* Design and development of microwave components and antennas for use in ground, air and space communications systems and radars; investigation of electromagnetic wave propagation phenomena; communications systems analysis. *Mailing Add:* 1525 Curtis Ave Manhattan Beach CA 90266

RICCA, PAUL JOSEPH, ANALYTICAL CHEMISTRY. *Current Pos:* PRES, RICCA CHEM CO, 75- *Personal Data:* b Brooklyn, NY, Apr 25, 39; m 61; c 2. *Educ:* Syracuse Univ, AB, 61; Purdue Univ, PhD(analytical chem), 66. *Prof Exp:* Asst, Purdue Univ, 61-65; adv planning analyst, LTV Aerospace Corp, Dallas, 67-68, eng specialist, 68-71, dir labs & vpres, Anderson Labs, Inc, Ft Worth, 71-75. *Mem:* AAAS; Am Chem Soc; Am Ord Asn. *Res:* Electrochemical kinetics and reaction mechanisms; formulation and development of new missile system concepts; production of prepared chemical reagents and testing solutions. *Mailing Add:* 3315 Thorntree Ct Arlington TX 76016-2066

RICCA, VINCENT THOMAS, HYDROLOGY, HYDRAULIC ENGINEERING. *Current Pos:* from asst prof to prof, 63-92, EMER PROF CIVIL ENG, OHIO STATE UNIV, 92- *Personal Data:* b New York, NY, Dec 19, 35; m 57, Carole Sue Halpern; c 3. *Educ:* City Col New York, BS, 62; Purdue Univ, Lafayette, MS, 64, PhD(water resources eng), 66. *Honors & Awards:* Raymond Q Armington Award, Ohio State Univ, 68, Lichtenstien Mem Award, 72. *Prof Exp:* Teaching assoc civil eng, Purdue Univ, Lafayette, 62-63. *Concurrent Pos:* Hydrol & hydraul eng consult, 66- *Mem:* Fel Am Soc Civil Engrs. *Res:* Small watershed hydrology; flood plain management; streamflow simulation computer modeling; groundwater studies; stream surface profiles; acid mine drainage models. *Mailing Add:* 3117 Mountview Rd Columbus OH 43221

RICCI, BENJAMIN, APPLIED PHYSIOLOGY. *Current Pos:* Chmn dept, 71-73, PROF EXERCISE SCI, UNIV MASS, AMHERST, 66- *Personal Data:* b Cranston, RI, Apr 5, 23; m 44; c 3. *Educ:* Springfield Col, BPE, 49, MS, 50, PhD(appl physiol), 58. *Concurrent Pos:* Fulbright fel, Inst Work Physiol, Oslo, Norway, 71 & Inst Human Physics, Rome, Italy, 78. *Mem:* Sigma Xi. *Res:* Adaptation of biochemical, biomechanical, heat regulatory, cardiopulmonary and neuromuscular systems to stress imposed by work or exercise. *Mailing Add:* 615 Bay Rd Amherst MA 01002-3542

RICCI, ENZO, APPLIED PHYSICS, ATOMIC PHYSICS. *Current Pos:* RETIRED. *Personal Data:* b Buenos Aires, Arg, Nov 8, 25; m 57; c 3. *Educ:* Univ Buenos Aires, Lic chem sci, 52, PhD(chem), 54; Univ Tenn, MS, 71. *Prof Exp:* Staff mem nuclear chem res, Arg AEC, 53-61, head activation analysis group nuclear chem res & develop, 61-62; staff mem nuclear chem & physics res & develop, Oak Ridge Nat Lab, 62-80; mgr res & develop enrichment safeguards, Nuclear Div, Union Carbide Corp, 80-89. *Concurrent Pos:* Lab asst, Univ Buenos Aires, 50-57, lab demonstr, 58-59, prof, 61-62; Int Atomic Energy Agency fel, Chalk River Nuclear Labs, Can, 59-61. *Mem:* Fel Am Nuclear Soc; Am Chem Soc; Arg Chem Asn. *Res:* Nuclear methods of analysis; nuclear reaction cross sections; fusion plasma-wall interactions; x-ray and electron spectroscopy. *Mailing Add:* 996 W Outer Dr Oak Ridge TN 37830

RICCI, JOHN ETTORE, PHYSICAL CHEMISTRY. *Current Pos:* From instr to prof, 31-77, EMER PROF CHEM, NY UNIV, 77- *Personal Data:* b New York, NY, Jan 1, 07. *Educ:* NY Univ, BS, 26, MS, 28, PhD(chem), 31. *Concurrent Pos:* Consult, Oak Ridge Nat Lab, 53- *Mem:* Am Chem Soc. *Res:* Phase rule; aqueous solubilities; solid solutions; non-aqueous solvents; ionization constants; hydrogen ion concentration; fused salts. *Mailing Add:* 17 Nolan Ave Yonkers NY 10704

RICCI, JOHN SILVIO, JR, PHYSICAL CHEMISTRY, INORGANIC CHEMISTRY. *Current Pos:* PROF CHEM, UNIV SOUTHERN MAINE, 81- *Personal Data:* b Springfield, Mass, Aug 27, 40. *Educ:* Am Int Col, AB, 62; Columbia Univ, MA, 63; State Univ NY, Stony Brook, PhD(chem), 69. *Prof Exp:* Fel chem, Northwestern Univ, 69-70; prof, Windham Col, 70-77 & Williams Col, 77-81. *Concurrent Pos:* Res collabr, Brookhaven Nat Lab, 71- *Mem:* Am Chem Soc; Am Crystallog Asn. *Res:* Molecular structure determination of transition metal complexes; organo-phosphorus and organo-sulfur compounds. *Mailing Add:* Univ Southern Main Chem Dept 96 Falmouth St Box 9300 Portland ME 04104-9300

RICCIARDI, ROBERT PAUL, GENETIC ENGINEERING, MOLECULAR VIROLOGY. *Current Pos:* ASST PROF CANCER RES, WISTAR INST, 81- *Personal Data:* b Quincy, Mass, June 18, 46; m 83. *Educ:* Boston Univ, BA, 68; Col William & Mary, MA, 73; Univ Ill, Urbana, PhD(cellular & molecular biol), 77. *Prof Exp:* Teacher chem, Lisbon High Sch, NH, 68-69; Am Cancer Soc fel, Brandeis Univ, 77-78, Nat Cancer Inst fel, Sch Med, Harvard Univ, 78-80, Charles A King Trust fel, 80-81; asst prof genetics & microbiol, Univ Penn, 81- *Concurrent Pos:* Consult, Dept Molecular Genetics, Smith Kline & Beckman, 85- , Workshop Oncogenic Human Polyomaviruses, Nat Cancer Inst, 85; vis prof, Sch Med, Univ Ferrara, Italy, 86. *Res:* Investigation of mechanisms that regulate both viral genes and oncogenes. *Mailing Add:* 137 Forge Rd Glen Mills PA 19342

RICCIUTI, FLORENCE CHRISTINE, HUMAN GENETICS. *Current Pos:* PROF BIOL & CHMN, DEPT BIOL, ALBERTUS MAGNUS COL, 75- *Personal Data:* b New Haven, Conn, Aug 29, 44. *Educ:* Albertus Magnus Col, BA, 66; Yale Univ, PhD(biol), 73. *Prof Exp:* Asst res med genetics, Yale Univ Med Sch, 66-68, fel, Dept Human Genetics, 72-75. *Mem:* Sigma Xi. *Res:* Human gene mapping using somatic cell genetics and studying differentiation and X chromosome inactivation in embryonic and adult tissues. *Mailing Add:* 42 Livingston St New Haven CT 06511

RICCOBONO, PAUL XAVIER, DETERGENTS, TEXTILES. *Current Pos:* mgr, Household Prods Res & Develop, 90-93, ASSOC DIR, RES & DEVELOP, BLOCK DRUG CO, 93- *Personal Data:* b New York, NY, Jan 5, 39; div. *Educ:* Brooklyn Col, BS, 59; NY Univ, MS, 63, PhD(org chem), 64. *Prof Exp:* Res chemist, Nat Biscuit Co, 59-60 & E I du Pont de Nemours & Co, Inc, 64-67; sr res chemist, Airco, 67-68; group leader, Cent Res Labs, J P Stevens & Co, Inc, 68-71, mgr, Cent Analysis Dept, 71-73, mgr, 73-77, dir, Mat Res & Eval Dept, 77-81; dir res, Congoleum Corp, 81-84; dept head, Colgate-Palmolive Co, 84-89. *Concurrent Pos:* Assoc res dir, Indust Res Inst. *Mem:* Instrument Soc Am; Am Chem Soc; Am Soc Testing & Mat. *Res:* Resolution of optically active cyclooctatetraene derivatives; photochemistry of maleic anhydride derivatives; preparation and properties of graft copolymers; toxic chemicals legislation; textile chemistry; advanced materials characterization and analysis techniques; utilization of cold plasma and radiation for materials performance modification; detergent formulations; household products consumer research; household product research and development. *Mailing Add:* 72 Dogwood Lane Bedminster NJ 07921

RICE, BARBARA SLYDER, MATHEMATICS. *Current Pos:* ASSOC PROF MATH, ALA AGR & MECH UNIV, 75- *Personal Data:* b Chambersburg, Pa, Dec 19, 37; m 63, Laurence B; c 4. *Educ:* Clark Univ, AB, 59; Univ Va, MA, 61, PhD(math), 65. *Prof Exp:* Res asst math, Univ Va, 61-63; adj prof, Fla Inst Technol, 63-73. *Mem:* Am Math Soc; Math Asn Am. *Res:* Development of more effective teaching processes for use with mathematically inexperienced students. *Mailing Add:* 308 Flemington Rd SE Huntsville AL 35802

RICE, BERNARD, PHYSICAL CHEMISTRY. *Current Pos:* from asst prof to assoc prof, 49-61, PROF CHEM, ST LOUIS UNIV, 61- *Personal Data:* b Milwaukee, Wis, Dec 5, 14. *Educ:* George Washington Univ, BS, 37; Univ Chicago, PhD(chem), 48. *Prof Exp:* Chemist, Nat Bur Stand, 38-42. *Mem:* Am Chem Soc. *Res:* Molecular structure; spectroscopy; theoretical chemistry. *Mailing Add:* 7456 Parkdale Ave St Louis MO 63105

RICE, CHARLES EDWARD, ENGINEERING, AGRICULTURE. *Current Pos:* RES HYDRAULIC ENGR, AGR RES SERV, USDA, 78- *Personal Data:* b Seminole, Okla, Feb 13, 32; m 56; c 2. *Educ:* Okla State Univ, BS, 60, MS, 61; Univ Minn, Minneapolis, PhD(agr eng), 72. *Prof Exp:* Res engr, Agr Res Serv, USDA, 61-66; asst prof, 66-74, assoc prof agr eng, Okla State Univ, 74- *Mem:* Am Soc Agr Engrs; Sigma Xi. *Res:* Open channel hydraulics; hydraulics of conservation structures; overland flow. *Mailing Add:* Rte 5 Box 336 Stillwater OK 74074

RICE, CHARLES MERTON, TECHNICAL MANAGEMENT. *Current Pos:* PRES, RICE INC, 78- *Personal Data:* b Whitmore Lake, Mich, Jan 26, 25; m 47; c 8. *Educ:* Albion Col, AB, 48; Univ Mo-Rolla, MS, 49; Oak Ridge Reactor Sch, MS, 53. *Honors & Awards:* Prod Eng Master Design Award, 63. *Prof Exp:* Assoc prof physics, Oglethorpe Univ, 49-51; physicist, AEC, 51-54; proj supvr, Ford Instrument Co, 54-55; head atomic power eng group, Sargent & Lundy, 55-56; mgr reactor eng dept, Advanced Technol Lab, 56-59; prog mgr, Aerojet Gen Corp, 59-69; pres, Idaho Nuclear Corp, 69-70 & Aerojet Nuclear Co, 70-72; pres & chmn bd, Energy Inc, 72-81; prin, LRS Consult, 81-90. *Mem:* Fel Am Nuclear Soc; Atomic Indust Forum. *Res:* Gas cooled reactor technology, nuclear rocket propulsion and water reactor safety. *Mailing Add:* Rice Inc 355 W 14th St Idaho Falls ID 83402

RICE, CHARLES MOEN, III, ANIMAL RNA VIRUSES. *Current Pos:* from asst prof to assoc prof, 86-96, PROF, SCH MED, WASHINGTON UNIV, 96- *Personal Data:* b Sacramento, Calif, Aug 25, 52. *Educ:* Univ Calif, Davis, BS, 74; Calif Inst Technol, PhD(biochem), 81. *Prof Exp:* Res fel, Calif Inst Technol, 81-84, staff biologist, 85; vis fel, Australian Nat Univ, 85. *Mem:* AAAS; Am Soc Virol; Am Soc Microbiol; Soc Gen Microbiol (Brit); Am Soc Biochem & Molecular Biol. *Res:* Molecular genetics of RNA virus replication, primarily alphaviruses, flaviviruses and Hepatitis C virus. *Mailing Add:* Dept Molecular Microbiol Washington Univ Sch Med Campus Box 8230 660 S Euclid Ave St Louis MO 63110-1093. *Fax:* 314-362-1232

RICE, CLIFFORD PAUL, DATA QUALITY THROUGH DATA MONITORING & RECORDING. *Current Pos:* supvry chemist anal chem, 86-89, RES CHEMIST ENVIRON CHEM, PATUXENT WILDLIFE RES CTR, 89- *Personal Data:* b San Diego, Calif, May 12, 40; m 74; c 3. *Educ:* Wash State Univ, BS, 62; Cornell Univ, PhD(bot & insect biochem), 72. *Prof Exp:* Res assoc environ chem, Syracuse Res Corp, 71-74; instr pesticide chem, Univ RI, 74-77; res assoc environ chem, 76-77; assoc res scientist environ chem, Great Lakes Res Div, Univ Mich, 78-85; res scientist environ chem, Large Lakes Res Sta, US Environ Protection Agency, 86. *Concurrent Pos:* Adv, State NY Environ Comn, NY State Dept Environ Conserv, 78-; chief scientist, Activ of Joint US/USSR expeds to Bering & Pac Ocean, Patuxent Wildlife Res Ctr, 88-; liaison mem, TSCA's Interagency Testing Comt, 89- *Mem:* AAAS; Am Chem Soc. *Res:* Environmental chemistry and effects of organochlorine pollutants; long range atmospheric transport of toxaphenes; microlayer processes involving movement of PCBs in the Great Lakes; congener specific effects and occurrence of PCBs in avian systems. *Mailing Add:* USDA Environ Chem Lab Bldg 007 Rm 213 BARC-West Beltsville MD 20705

RICE, DALE WARREN, MARINE MAMMALOGY. *Current Pos:* WILDLIFE RES BIOLOGIST, NAT MARINE FISHERIES SERV, 58- *Personal Data:* b Grand Haven, Mich, Jan 21, 30. *Educ:* Ind Univ, AB, 52; Univ Fla, MS, 55. *Prof Exp:* Wildlife res biologist, US Fish & Wildlife Serv, 55-58. *Concurrent Pos:* Mem cetacean specialist group, Survival Serv Comn, Int Union Conserv Nature & Natural Resources, 67- *Mem:* Am Soc Mammalogists; Wildlife Soc; Soc Syst Zool; Soc Marine Mammal; Am Ornithologist Union. *Res:* Life history, ecology, population dynamics and systematics of marine mammals, especially baleen whales and sperm whales. *Mailing Add:* Dept Nat Marine Fisheries 7600 Sand Point Way Bldg 4 Seattle WA 98115

RICE, DALE WILSON, PHYSICAL CHEMISTRY. *Current Pos:* TECH DIR, BEAUMAC CO, 88- *Personal Data:* b Jamestown, NY, Nov 21, 32; m 60; c 2. *Educ:* Mass Inst Technol, SB, 54, PhD(polymer chem), 61. *Prof Exp:* Res assoc, Corning Glass Works, 61-75; eng consult, Centorr Assocs, Inc, 75-78, tech dir, 78-81; pres, Delta Labs, 81- *Mem:* AAAS; Am Chem Soc; Am Ceramic Soc; Am Asn Crystal Growth. *Res:* High temperature technology; engineering design; high temperature and vacuum technology. *Mailing Add:* Garland Rd RFD No 1 Barrington NH 03825

RICE, DAVID A, PEDIATRICS. *Current Pos:* ASSOC PROF BIOMED ENG, TULANE UNIV, 81-, GRAD FAC, 83-, ADJ ASSOC PROF PEDIAT, 85-, NEWCOMB FEL, 91- *Educ:* Univ Alaska, Fairbanks, BS, 68; Purdue Univ, MS, 70, PhD(elec eng), 74. *Honors & Awards:* Young Investr Award, NIH, 77. *Prof Exp:* Univ fel, Ohio State Univ, 75-76, fac, Biomed Eng Ctr, 77-81. *Concurrent Pos:* Prin investr, Nat Heart Lung & Blood Inst, NIH, 74-77, 77-80, 83-87, Am Heart Asn, 76-79, NSF, 80-81, 87-88, 88-90, 90-93, Tulane Univ, 82-83, Edward G Schilieder Educ Found, 82-84, S S Kraman, Univ Ky, 84-87 & Brown Found, 92-93, 93-94; qual assurance officer, Dept Vet Physiol & Pharmacol, Ohio State Univ, 79-80. *Mem:* Sr mem Inst Elec & Electronics Engrs; assoc mem Acoust Soc Am; Sigma Xi; AAAS; Int Lung Sounds Asn; Am Soc Eng Educ. *Res:* Contributed numerous articles to professional journal. *Mailing Add:* 1537 Short St New Orleans LA 70118-4011

RICE, DENNIS KEITH, LASER PHYSICS, STRATEGIC PLANNING. *Current Pos:* prin engr, Laser Technol Labs, Northrop Corp, 71-74, dir eng, 74, mgr, Laser Lab, 74-76, prog mgr, 76-78, mgr laser-optical eng, Northrop Corp Res & Technol Ctr, 78-80, asst to gen mgr technol & planning, 80-82, mgr advan systs, 82-85, vpres advan systs, 85-86, vpres & chief scientist, Northrop Electro-Mech Div, 86-89, vpres transition team, Northrop Electronics Systs Div, 89-90, vpres systs eng & planning, 90-91, VPRES PLANNING, NORTHROP GRUMMAN CORP, 91- *Personal Data:* b Newell, WVa, Dec 12, 39; m 70; c 3. *Educ:* Cleveland State Univ, BEE, 64; Univ Southern Calif, MSEE, 66, PhD(elec eng), 69. *Prof Exp:* Staff physicist, Union Carbide, 69-70. *Mem:* Am Mgt Asn; Am Defense Preparedness Asn; Nat Security Indust Asn. *Res:* Optics; thin films; spectroscopy; solid state physics; acoustics. *Mailing Add:* 650 S Scout Trail Anaheim CA 92807

RICE, DOROTHY PECHMAN, HEALTH STATISTICS, MEDICAL ECONOMICS. *Current Pos:* prof-in-residence, 82-94, EMER PROF, DEPT SOCIAL & BEHAV SCIS, SCH NURSING, UNIV CALIF, SAN FRANCISCO, 94- *Personal Data:* b Brooklyn, NY, June 11, 22; m 43, John D; c 3. *Educ:* Univ Wis, BA, 41. *Hon Degrees:* DSc, Col Med & Dent NJ, 79. *Honors & Awards:* Jack C Massey Award, 78; Sedqick Mem Medal, Am Pub Health Asn, 88; Presidential Award for Leadership, Asn Health Servs Res, 88. *Prof Exp:* Pub health analyst health serv res, Div Hosp & Med Facil, USPHS, 60-62; soc sci analyst, Div Res & Statist, Social Security Admin, 62-64; pub health analyst econ, Div Community Health Serv, USPHS, 64-65; chief, Health Ins Res Br, Social Security Admin, 65-72, dep asst commr res & statist, 72-76; dir health statist, Nat Ctr Health Statist, 76-82. *Mem:* Inst Med-Nat Acad Sci; fel Am Statist Asn; fel Am Pub Health Asn; Am Econ Asn; Asn Health Servs Res; Nat Acad Soc Ins. *Res:* The organization, delivery and financing of health services, cost of illness, aging and chronic illness; disability. *Mailing Add:* Dept Social & Behav Sci Univ Calif San Francisco CA 94143-0646. *Fax:* 415-476-1253

RICE, ELROY LEON, ALLELOPATHY, CHEMICAL ECOLOGY. *Current Pos:* From asst prof to prof bot, 48-66, David Ross Boyd prof, 67-81, DAVID ROSS BOYD EMER PROF BOT, UNIV OKLA, 81- *Personal Data:* b Edmond, Okla, Jan 31, 17; m 45; c 2. *Educ:* Cent State Col, Okla, BA, 38; Univ Okla, MS, 42; Univ Chicago, PhD(bot), 47. *Concurrent Pos:* Vis prof biol, Purdue Univ, 62-63. *Mem:* Fel AAAS; Ecol Soc Am; Am Soc Plant Physiol. *Res:* Changes in microclimate, microorganisms, soil factors and allelochemicals during plant succession; writing of scientific monographs in chemical ecology. *Mailing Add:* Dept Bot & Microbiol Univ Okla 770 Van Vleet Oval Norman OK 73019

RICE, EUGENE WARD, SANITARY-PUBLIC HEALTH BACTERIOLOGY, DISINFECTION. *Current Pos:* RES MICROBIOLOGIST, DRINKING WATER RES DIV, US ENVIRON PROTECTION AGENCY, 78- *Personal Data:* b Cincinnati, Ohio, Feb 23, 49; m, Treva K Cox; c Rachel K, Rebecca M & Hannah R. *Educ:* Georgetown Col, BS, 71; Ohio Univ, MS, 74; Univ Cincinnati, PhD(environ microbiol), 89. *Prof Exp:* Teacher, McAuley & Western Hills High Schs, 74-78. *Concurrent Pos:* Mem, Organisms Water Comt & Microbiol Res Comt, Am Water Works Asn, 88-; chair, Joint Task Group, Coliform Bacteria Stand Methods Exam Water & Wastewater, Am Pub Health Asn, 89-; contribr, Global Task Force Cholera Control, WHO, 91-92. *Mem:* Am Soc Microbiol; Am Water Works Asn; Sigma Xi. *Res:* Methods for detection of bacteria in water, survival and disinfection; removal of indicator and pathogenic microorganisms in source water and drinking water. *Mailing Add:* US Environ Protection Agency Cincinnati OH 45268. *Fax:* 513-569-7328; *E-Mail:* rice.gene@epamail.epa.gov

RICE, FRANK J, EMBRYOLOGY. *Current Pos:* from asst prof to assoc prof, 61-79, chmn dept, 70-76, PROF BIOL, FAIRFIELD UNIV, 79- *Personal Data:* b Putnam, Conn, Oct 10, 24; m 52, Kathleen M Ryan; c Marilyn, Andrew, Janet, William, Thomas, Cassie & David. *Educ:* Colo State Univ, BS, 50; Univ Wyo, MS, 51; Univ Mo, PhD(genetics), 56. *Prof Exp:* Mgr beef cattle ranch, San Carlos Apache Tribal Enterprises, Ariz, 53-54; geneticist, USDA, Mont, 56-61. *Res:* Genetics; physiology of reproduction; natural family planning. *Mailing Add:* Dept Biol Fairfield Univ 1073 N Benson Rd Fairfield CT 06430-5171. *Fax:* 203-254-4126; *E-Mail:* fjrice@fair1.fairfield.edu

RICE, JACK MORRIS, GEOLOGY. *Current Pos:* ASST PROF GEOL, UNIV ORE, 77- *Personal Data:* b Salina, Kans, Aug 30, 48; m 75; c 2. *Educ:* Dartmouth Col, AB, 70; Univ Wash, MS, 72, PhD(geol), 75. *Prof Exp:* Gibbs instr, Yale Univ, 75-77. *Mem:* Geol Soc Am; Mineral Soc Am; Am Geophys Union. *Res:* Field, analytical and theoretical studies bearing on the mineralogy and petrology of metamorphic rocks; thermodynamics of rock-forming silicate minerals. *Mailing Add:* Dept Geol Univ Ore Eugene OR 97403

RICE, JAMES K, WATER CHEMISTRY. *Current Pos:* CONSULT ENGR, 76- *Personal Data:* b Pittsburgh, Pa, Mar 12, 23; m 46; c 2. *Educ:* Carnegie Inst Technol, BS, 46, MS, 47. *Honors & Awards:* Award of Merit, Am Soc Testing & Mat, 70. *Prof Exp:* Res engr, Cyrus W Rice & Co, 47-52, sr engr, 52-59, pres, 59-67, pres & gen mgr, Rice Div, NUS Corp, 67-73, sr vpres, 73-76. *Concurrent Pos:* Mem, Coal Slurry Adv Panel, Off Technol Assessment, US Cong, 76-78. *Mem:* Fel Am Soc Testing & Mat; fel Am Inst Chemists; Am Chem Soc; Nat Asn Corrosion Engrs; fel Am Soc Mech Engrs. *Res:* Monitoring of microchemical contaminants in the aquatic environment and in industrial water and waste water; water technology of thermal power systems. *Mailing Add:* 17415 Batchellor's Forest Rd Olney MD 20832-2715

RICE, JAMES KINSEY, CHEMICAL PHYSICS, LASERS. *Current Pos:* STAFF MEM CHEM PHYSICS, SANDIA LABS, 69- *Personal Data:* b Harvey, Ill, June 5, 41; m 63; c 2. *Educ:* Ind Univ, Bloomington, BS, 63; Calif Inst Technol, PhD(chem), 68. *Prof Exp:* Res fel chem, Calif Inst Technol, 68-69. *Mem:* AAAS; Am Chem Soc; Am Phys Soc; Am Soc Mass Spectrom; Sigma Xi. *Res:* Chemical lasers; reaction dynamics; electron beam pumped gas laser. *Mailing Add:* Sandia Natl Labs Org 6600 MS 0726 Albuquerque NM 87185-0726

RICE, JAMES R, GEOPHYSICS, ENGINEERING MECHANICS. *Current Pos:* MCKAY PROF ENG SCI & GEOPHYS, HARVARD UNIV, 81- *Personal Data:* b Frederick, Md, Dec 3, 40; m, Renata Dmowska; c Douglas, Jonathan & Martin Wartak. *Educ:* Lehigh Univ, BS, 62, MSc, 63, PhD, 64. *Hon Degrees:* ScD, Lehigh Univ, 85, Northwestern Univ, 96. *Honors & Awards:* George R Irwin Medal, Am Soc Testing & Mat, 82; William Prager Medal, Soc Eng Sci, 88; Distinguished Serv Award, Am Acad Mech, 92; Francis Birch lectr, Am Geophys Union, 93; Timoshenko Medal, Am Soc Mech Engrs, 94. *Prof Exp:* Fel, Brown Univ, 64-65, from asst prof to prof eng, 65-81, Ballou prof theoret & appl mech, 73-81. *Concurrent Pos:* Mem, Solid State Sci Comt, Comn Phys Sci, Math & Resources, Nat Res Coun, 84-90, Panel on Mat Res Opportunities & Needs, 86-88, Comt Seismol, 92-; corp mem, Woods Hole Oceanog Inst, 89-92. *Mem:* Nat Acad Sci; Nat Acad Eng; fel Am Soc Mech Engrs; fel AAAS; fel Am Geophys Union. *Res:* Fracture mechanics in technology and geophysics; earthquake phenomena. *Mailing Add:* Div Eng & Appl Sci & Dept Earth Planet Sci Harvard Univ 29 Oxford St Cambridge MA 02138

RICE, JAMES THOMAS, SCIENCE & WOOD TECHNOLOGY. *Current Pos:* RETIRED. *Personal Data:* b Birmingham, Ala, Feb 7, 33; m 54, 75; c 4. *Educ:* Auburn Univ, BS, 54; NC State Univ, MS, 60, PhD(wood technol), 64. *Prof Exp:* From instr to asst prof wood technol, NC State Univ, 59-65; assoc prof, Univ Ga, 65-69, assoc prof forest resources, 70-95; mgr wood adhesives develop, Cent Resin Develop Lab, Ga-Pac Corp, 69-70. *Concurrent Pos:* Tech coordr, Adhesive & Sealant Coun, 66-69 & 72-78; chmn, Comt D-14 Adhesives, Am Soc Testing & Mat, 86-90. *Mem:* Am Soc Testing & Mat; Forest Prod Res Soc; Soc Wood Sci & Technol. *Res:* Adhesives and adhesive bonded products, especially those with wood as an adherend. *Mailing Add:* 545 Hawthorne Lane Charlotte NC 28204

RICE, JERRY MERCER, EXPERIMENTAL PATHOLOGY, BIOCHEMISTRY. *Current Pos:* Res scientist, Biol Br, 66-69, head perinatal carcinogenesis sect, Lab Exp Path, 73-80, SR SCIENTIST, LAB EXP PATH, DIV CANCER ETIOLOGY NAT CANCER INST, 69-, CHIEF, LAB COMP CARCINOGENESIS, 81- *Personal Data:* b Washington, DC, Oct 3, 40; m 69, 78, Mary Janocha; c Stacey & Stephen. *Educ:* Wesleyan Univ, BA, 62; Harvard Univ, PhD(biochem), 66. *Honors & Awards:* Outstanding Serv Medal, USPHS, 90. *Concurrent Pos:* Comn officer, USPHS, 66-; consult, George Washington Univ, 91- *Mem:* Sigma Xi; Am Chem Soc; Teratology Soc; Am Asn Cancer Res; Am Soc Microbiol; Am Soc Invest Path. *Res:* Chemical carcinogenesis, especially transplacental carcinogenesis. *Mailing Add:* World Health Orgn IARC 150 Cours Albert Thomas 69372 Lyon Cedar 08 MD 21702-1201. *Fax:* 301-846-5946

RICE, JOHN RISCHARD, APPLIED MATHEMATICS, COMPUTER SCIENCE. *Current Pos:* prof math & comput sci, 64-89, head, 83-96, DISTINGUISHED PROF COMPUT SCI, PURDUE UNIV, 89- *Personal Data:* b Tulsa, Okla, June 6, 34; m 54, Nancy A Bradfield; c Amy L & Jenna M. *Educ:* Okla State Univ, BS, 54, MS, 56; Calif Inst Technol, PhD(math), 59. *Honors & Awards:* George E Forsythe Mem Lectr, 75. *Prof Exp:* Nat Bur Coun-Nat Bur Stand res fel math, Nat Bur Stand, 59-60; sr res mathematician, Gen Motors Res Labs, 60-64. *Concurrent Pos:* Chmn, COSERS Panel on Numerical Computation, 74-78; ed-in-chief, Asn Comput Mach Trans Math Software, 74-; chmn, Signum, 77-79, Comput Res Asn, 91-93; Int Fed Info Processing Working Group 2.5; vpres & trustee, Int Asn Math & Comput Simulation, 92- *Mem:* Nat Acad Sci; Nat Acad Eng; Soc Indust & Appl Math; fel Am Comput Mach; fel AAAS. *Res:* Approximation theory; numerical analysis; mathematical software, computational science supercomputing; author or coauthor of various publications. *Mailing Add:* Dept Comput Sci Purdue Univ West Lafayette IN 47907. *Fax:* 765-494-0739; *E-Mail:* rice@cs.purdue.edu

RICE, JOHN T(HOMAS), mechanical engineering, for more information see previous edition

RICE, KENNER CRALLE, SYNTHETIC ORGANIC CHEMISTRY, MEDICINAL CHEMISTRY. *Current Pos:* CHIEF, SECT DRUG DESIGN & SYNTHESIS, NAT INST DIABETES DIGESTIVE & KIDNEY DIS, 87- *Personal Data:* b Rocky Mount, Va, May 14, 40. *Educ:* Va Mil Inst, BS, 61; Ga Inst Technol, PhD(org chem), 66. *Honors & Awards:* Sato Mem Int Award, 83. *Prof Exp:* Capt, Walter Reed Army Inst Res, Wash, DC, 66-68; NIH fel, Ga Inst Technol, 68-69; sr scientist, Process Res, Ciba Pharmaceut Co, Ciba-Geigy Corp, 69-72; NIH sr staff fel, 72-76, res chemist, Nat Inst Arthritis, Metab & Digestive Dis, 77-86. *Concurrent Pos:* Adj prof pharmacol, dept pharmacol & exp therapeut, Sch Med, Univ Md, Baltimore. *Mem:* Am Chem Soc; Pytochemical Soc Europe; Am Pharmaceut Asn; Soc Neurosci. *Res:* The chemistry of analgesics, their antagonists and other drugs which act on the central nervous system; stereochemistry of drugs in relation to their mechanism of action and receptor interactions; isolation, structural elucidation and synthesis of natural products, especially alkaloids; positron emission tomography in the study of the central nervous system. *Mailing Add:* 9007 Kirkdale Rd Bethesda MD 20817-3331

RICE, MARION MCBURNEY, BACTERIOLOGY, BOTANY. *Current Pos:* RETIRED. *Personal Data:* b Syracuse, NY, Feb 20, 23; m 52; c 2. *Educ:* DePauw Univ, AB, 48, MA, 49; Univ Wis, PhD(bact), 53. *Prof Exp:* Eli Lilly & Co, 41-44, asst, 45 & 49; asst, Ind Univ, 48; asst bact, Univ Wis, 49-50; bacteriologist, Stuart Circle Hosp, Richmond, Va, 53-54; instr biol, Richmond Prof Inst, Col William & Mary, 55-58; asst prof bot & bact, Rockford Col, 58-60 & 63-66; instr biol, Beloit Col, 60; assoc prof bot, Univ Wis, Rock Co Campus, 66-88. *Concurrent Pos:* Asst bact, Univ Wis, 59. *Mem:* Am Soc Microbiol. *Res:* Antibiotics; cytology of streptomyces; phytogeography; botulism. *Mailing Add:* 2514 W Memorial Dr Janesville WI 53545

RICE, MARY ESTHER, INVERTEBRATE ZOOLOGY. *Current Pos:* assoc cur invert zool, Mus Natural Hist, 66-74, scientist-in-chg, Smithsonian Marine Sta, Link Port, 81-89, CUR INVERT ZOOL, MUS NATURAL HIST, SMITHSONIAN INST, 74-, DIR, SMITHSONIAN MARINE STA, LINK PORT, 89- *Personal Data:* b Washington, DC, Aug 3, 26. *Educ:* Drew Univ, AB, 47; Oberlin Col, MA, 49; Univ Wash, PhD(zool), 66. *Prof Exp:* Instr zool, Drew Univ, 49-50; res assoc radiation biol, Col Physicians & Surgeons, Columbia Univ, 50-53; res biologist, NIH, 53-61; teaching asst, Univ Wash, 61-66. *Concurrent Pos:* Mem-at-large, Biol Sci Sect Comt, AAAS. *Mem:* Fel AAAS; Am Inst Biol Sci; Am Soc Zoologists (pres, 79). *Res:* Development, reproductive biology and systematics of marine worms of the phylum Sipuncula; life histories of marine invertebrates. *Mailing Add:* 2307 Oak Dr Ft Pierce FL 34949-1506

RICE, MICHAEL ALAN, MOLLUSCAN AQUACULTURE, COMPARATIVE PHYSIOLOGY OF MARINE INVERTEBRATES. *Current Pos:* MARINE BIOLOGIST, OCEAN ENG DIV, INTERSTATE ELECTRONICS CORP, 77-; ASSOC PROF FISHERIES & AQUALCULT, UNIV RI, 87- *Personal Data:* b San Jose, Calif, Mar 4, 55; m 83, Rufina Delizo; c Maria I. *Educ:* Univ San Francisco, BS, 77; Univ Calif, Irvine, MS, 81, PhD(comp physiol), 87. *Prof Exp:* Res asst, Univ Calif, Irvine, 77-81, 85-87. *Concurrent Pos:* Vol extensionist, US Peace Corps, Philippines, 81-85; res assoc, Int Ctr Marine Resource Develop, 87-; consult, Stellar Sea Farms, Philippines, 91; vis lectr, Marine Biol Lab, 93; sr Fulgright fel, Philippines, 96-97. *Mem:* AAAS; Am Soc Zoologists; Nat Shellfisheries Asn; Am Soc Limnol & Oceanog; World Aquacult Soc; Oceanog Soc. *Res:* Study of factors that influence growth and recruitment of bivalve mollusks; role of dissolved organic material as a nutrition source for marine invertebrates. *Mailing Add:* Dept Fisheries Animal & Vet Sci Univ RI Kingston RI 02881. *Fax:* 401-874-4017; *E-Mail:* rice@uriacc.uri.edu

RICE, MICHAEL JOHN, CONDENSED MATTER PHYSICS, THEORETICAL PHYSICS. *Current Pos:* sr scientist, 74-84, PRIN SCIENTIST, XEROX WEBSTER RES, 84- *Personal Data:* b Cowes, UK, Dec 25, 40; m 65; c 3. *Educ:* Univ London, BSc, 62, PhD(theoret physics), 66. *Prof Exp:* Asst prof physics, Imp Col, Univ London, 65-68; staff physicist, Gen Elec Res & Develop Lab, 68-71; staff mem, Brown Boveri Res Ctr, Switz, 71-74. *Concurrent Pos:* Vis asst prof physics, State Univ NY, Stony Brook, 68; Nordita prof physics, Nordisk Inst Theoret Atomic Physics, Denmark, 78-79; consult, Optical Spectros Prog, Xerox-Ohio State Univ, 78- *Mem:* Fel Am Phys Soc; Am Chem Soc; fel Inst Physics; fel Phys Soc UK; fel Swiss Phys Soc; Sigma Xi. *Res:* Microscopic theory of quantum fluids, metals and alloys, semiconductors, ionic conductors and organic radical-ion solids. *Mailing Add:* 1213 Gerrads Cross Webster NY 14580

RICE, NANCY REED, ONCOGENIC RETROVIRUSES. *Current Pos:* staff, 76-80, sr scientist, 80-83, HEAD, MOLECULAR BIOL RETROVIRUSES SECT, FREDERICK CANCER RES DEVELOP CTR, 83- *Personal Data:* b Chicago, Ill, July 20, 40. *Educ:* Stanford Univ, BA, 61; Harvard Univ, MA, 63, PhD(biol), 69. *Prof Exp:* Fel molecular biol, 68-71, staff mem molecular biol, Carnegie Inst Wash Dept Terrestrial Magnetism, 72-76. *Concurrent Pos:* Mem aging rev comt, Nat Inst Aging, 74-78; mem develop biol panel, NSF, 75. *Mem:* Am Soc Biol Chemists. *Res:* Molecular biology of retroviruses; rel oncogene. *Mailing Add:* Basic Res Prog NCI Frederick Cancer Res Develop Ctr Bldg 560 PO Box B Frederick MD 21702-1201

RICE, NORMAN MOLESWORTH, MATHEMATICS. *Current Pos:* ASSOC PROF MATH, QUEEN'S UNIV, ONT, 65- *Personal Data:* b Ottawa, Ont, Oct 13, 39; m 62; c 2. *Educ:* Queen's Univ, Ont, BS, 62; Calif Inst Technol, PhD(math), 66. *Mem:* Am Math Soc; Math Asn Am; Can Math Cong. *Res:* Functional analysis; vector lattices. *Mailing Add:* Dept Math Queen's Univ Kingston ON K7L 3N6 Can

RICE, PAUL LAVERNE, MEDICAL ENTOMOLOGY. *Current Pos:* RETIRED. *Personal Data:* b Bancroft, Nebr, Dec 28, 06; m 39; c 3. *Educ:* Univ Idaho, BS, 31, MS, 32; Ohio State Univ, PhD(entom), 37. *Hon Degrees:* DSc, Alma Col, Mich, 67. *Prof Exp:* Instr entom & asst entomologist, Univ

Idaho, 31-33; asst entomologist, Univ Del, 36-37; prof biol, Alma Col, 37-42; assoc entomologist & actg head dept, Univ Del, 42-45; prof biol, head dept & dean fac, Alma Col, 45-50; prof biol, Whittier Col, 50-58; assoc dir, Malaria Eradication Training Ctr, AID, Jamaica, 58-62; mem staff grants prog, NIH, 62-64; var pos, Vector-Borne Dis Training, Ctr Dis Control, USPHS, 64-70, contractor, 72-78. *Concurrent Pos:* In chg malaria team, USPHS, Int Coop Admin, Ethiopia, 55-57; consult, 70-72. *Res:* Mosquito borne diseases. *Mailing Add:* 2373 Burnt Creek Rd Decatur GA 30033

RICE, PETER (FRANKLIN), FOREST PATHOLOGY. *Current Pos:* RETIRED. *Personal Data:* b Toronto, Ont, May 18, 39; m 64; c 2. *Educ:* Univ Toronto, BScF, 62, MScF, 64, PhD(forest path), 68. *Prof Exp:* Lectr forest path, Univ Toronto, 66-68; pathologist, Royal Bot Gardens, 68-, asst dir conserv, Univ Lethbridge, coordr, Proj Paradise, Royal Bot Gardens, 93- *Mem:* Can Phytopath Soc; Am Phytopath Soc; Can Inst Forestry. *Res:* Diseases of ornamental plants, especially woody plants. *Mailing Add:* Royal Bot Gardens PO Box 399 Hamilton ON L8N 3H8 Can

RICE, PETER MILTON, OPERATIONS RESEARCH, SOFTWARE SYSTEMS. *Current Pos:* From asst prof to assoc prof, 63-84, asst to dean, 77-82, EMER PROF MATH, UNIV GA, 84- *Personal Data:* b Montclair, NJ, Oct 14, 37; m 62; c 2. *Educ:* St John's Col, MD, AB, 59; Fla State Univ, PhD(math), 63. *Concurrent Pos:* Alexander von Humboldt res fel & Sarah Moss res fel, Univ Bonn, 66-67; Alexander von Humboldt res fel, Inst Math Econ, Univ Bielefeld & Inst Higher Educ, Vienna, 75-76. *Mem:* Math Asn Am. *Res:* Software development for educational testing; artificial intelligence. *Mailing Add:* 386 Milledge Circle Athens GA 30606

RICE, PHILIP A, CHEMICAL ENGINEERING. *Current Pos:* from asst prof to assoc prof, 65-77, chair, Dept Chem Eng & Mat Sci, 85-90, PROF CHEM ENG, SYRACUSE UNIV, 77-, CHAIR, DEPT CHEM ENG & MAT SCI, 95- *Personal Data:* b Ann Arbor, Mich, Aug 3, 36; m 59, Wiley Van Doren; c 3. *Educ:* Univ Mich, BSE, 59, MSE, 60, PhD(chem eng), 63. *Prof Exp:* Chem engr, Analysis Serv, Inc, Va, 63-65. *Concurrent Pos:* Res assoc prof, Upstate Med Ctr, State Univ NY, 70-; prog mgr, Chem, Biochem & Thermal Eng Div, NSF, 84-85. *Mem:* Fel Am Inst Chem Engrs; Am Chem Soc; AAAS; Sigma Xi; Am Asn Univ Professors. *Res:* Transport and metabolism in biological systems; water renovation processes; vacuum spay stripping of dissolved and emulsified organics from water; heat transfer processes involving a change of phase; biokinetics and reactor designs. *Mailing Add:* Dept Chem Eng & Mat Sci Syracuse Univ Syracuse NY 13244

RICE, RICHARD EUGENE, GROUND WATER SYSTEMS, ARTIFICIAL & NATURAL MEMBRANES. *Current Pos:* asst prof chem, 92-95, ASSOC PROF LIBERAL STUDIES, UNIV MONT, 95- *Personal Data:* b Leominster, Mass, June 13, 43. *Educ:* Univ NH, BS, 65; Univ Mich, MS, 67; Univ Mont, MFA, 74; Mich State Univ, PhD(phys chem), 82. *Prof Exp:* Res asst, St Vincent Hosp, Worcester, Mass, 68-72; Int Res & Exchanges Bd fel, Inst Colloid & Water Chem, Ukr Acad Sci, Kiev, USSR, 79-80; Nat Res Coun res assoc, US Army Chem Res & Develop Ctr, 83-84; res scientist, Holcomb Res Inst, Butler Univ, 84-89; vis asst prof chem, phys & astron, Ind Univ NW, 88-90; asst prof multidisciplinary studies, NC State Univ, 90-92. *Mem:* AAAS; Am Chem Soc; Am Geophys Union; Hist Sci Soc. *Res:* Theory of contaminant transport and reaction in ground water systems; theory of ion transport across artificial and natural membranes; history of chemistry in late 19th and early 20th centuries; history of Russian and Soviet chemistry. *Mailing Add:* Liberal Studies Prog Univ Mont Missoula MT 59812-1026. *Fax:* 406-243-4076; *E-Mail:* rerice@lewis.umt.edu

RICE, RICHARD W, ANIMAL NUTRITION, BIOCHEMISTRY. *Current Pos:* PROF ANIMAL SCI, UNIV ARIZ, 75- *Personal Data:* b Ainsworth, Nebr, Aug 10, 31; m 52; c 2. *Educ:* Univ Nebr, BS, 53, MS, 58; Mich State Univ, PhD(animal nutrit), 60. *Prof Exp:* From asst prof to prof animal sci, Univ Wyo, 60-75. *Mem:* Soc Range Mgt; Am Soc Animal Sci; Am Dairy Sci Asn. *Res:* Ruminant nutrition; forage evaluation; factors affecting feed intake; fat metabolism in the ruminant; applied animal ecology. *Mailing Add:* 7865 N Avenida de Carlotta Tucson AZ 85704

RICE, RIP G, OZONE TECHNOLOGIES, CHEMISTRY. *Current Pos:* OZONE CONSULT, 82-; PRES, RICE INT CONSULT ENTERPRISES, 82- *Personal Data:* b New York, NY, Apr 19, 24; m 48, Billie Womack; c David W. *Educ:* George Washington Univ, BS, 47; Univ Md, PhD, 57. *Honors & Awards:* Founders Award, Int Ozone Asn, 79; HM Rosen Mem Award, Int Ozone Asn, 93. *Prof Exp:* Analytical chemist, Nat Bur Stand, DC, 47-50; chemist, US Naval Res Lab, 50-55; org chemist, US Naval Ord Lab, Md, 55-57; res chemist, Gen Dynamics/Convair, Tex, 57-59, staff scientist, Sci Res Lab, 59-60, tech dir adv prod dept, Calif, 60-62; sr chemist, W R Grace & Co, 62-63, res supvr, 63-64, mgr inorg chem res, 64-67, dir contract opers, 67-72; mgt consult-resident rep, 72-77; corp mgr gov relations, Jabcob Eng Group, 71-81, dir, environ systs, Adv Systs Div, 81-82. *Concurrent Pos:* Tech adv, Int Ozone Asn, 74-; ed-in-chief, Ozone Sci & Eng, 85-, Ozone News, 92- *Mem:* Am Chem Soc; Water Pollution Control Fedn; Int Ozone Asn (pres-elect, 79-81, pres, 82-84); Am Water Works Asn; Am Inst Chem Engrs; Water Quality Asn; Int Asn Water Pollution Res; Int Bottled Water Asn; Nat Environ Health Asn; Soc Soft Drink Technol. *Res:* Ozone technology; inorganic, polymer, organic chemistry; environmental sciences. *Mailing Add:* Rip G Rice Inc 1331 Patuxent Dr Ashton MD 20861-9759. *Fax:* 301-774-4493

RICE, ROBERT ARNOT, SCIENCE EDUCATION. *Current Pos:* NAT JR SCI & HUMANITIES JUDGING CHAIR, ACAD APPL SCI, CONCORD, NH, 93- *Personal Data:* b San Francisco, Calif, Apr 4, 11; m, Esther P Roossinck. *Educ:* Univ Calif, BA, 34, MA, 47. *Honors & Awards:* Armed Forces Chem Asn Award, 56; Distinguished Serv Sci Educ, Nat Sci Teachers Asn, 86. *Prof Exp:* Teacher, Geyserville Union High Sch, Calif, 35-40, prin, 40-41; teacher, Berkeley High Sch, 41-61, chmn dept sci, 49-61; supvr sci & math, Berkeley Unified Sch Dist, 61-64, consult, 64-70, dir On Target Sch, 71-73, work experience coordr, 73-75; dir, Northern Calif-Western Nev Jr Sci & Humanities Symp, 62-93. *Concurrent Pos:* pres, Calif Sci Teachers Asn, 49-50, exec dir, 62-90; exec dir, San Francisco Bay Area Sci Fair, 54-59, bd dirs, 60-; mem, Chem Comt, Nat Sci Teacher's Asn, 56-60, adv comt mem, 70; adminr, NSF Summer Insts Sci Teachers, Univ Calif, Berkeley, 57-65; mem, Int Sci Fair Coun, Sci Serv Inc, 59-68; ed, Sic Teacher, 60-61; coordr, Children's Area, US Sci Exhib, Centrury 21 Expos, Seattle, 61; asst to dir, Lawrence Hall Sci, 64-69, coordr pub progs, 69-75, liaison mem, 66-69 & 66-73; bd dirs, Calif Heart Asn, 55-61; chmn, public educ comt, Alameda County Heart Asn, 67-69, bd dirs, 66-71; dir, 18th Int Sci Serv Inc, 59-68; mem adv & res comt, Alameda Co TB & Health Asn, 65-69; coordr, Indust Initiatives Sci & Math Educ, 85-87, dir acad, 87. *Mem:* Nat Sci Teachers Asn (pres, 60-61). *Res:* Author and co-author of several publications. *Mailing Add:* 41 Barcelona Ct Danville CA 94526. *Fax:* 510-642-1055

RICE, ROBERT HAFLING, TOXICOLOGY, CELL BIOLOGY. *Current Pos:* from asst prof to assoc prof, 79-91, PROF TOXICOL, HARVARD SCH PUB HEALTH, 91-; PROF TOXICOL, UNIV CALIF, DAVIS. *Personal Data:* b Birmingham, Ala, Dec 31, 44. *Educ:* Mass Inst Technol, SB, 67; Univ Calif, Berkeley, PhD(molecular biol), 72. *Prof Exp:* Fel, Univ Calif, Davis, 72-75, Mass Inst Technol, 75-79. *Mem:* AAAS; Am Soc Cell Biol; Soc Toxicol. *Res:* Biochemical aspects of differentiation and toxicology of cultivated epithetial cells, with emphasis on mechanisms of cross-linked envelope formation and chronic effects of exposure to xenobiotics in the environment. *Mailing Add:* Dept Environ Toxicol Univ Calif Davis CA 95616-8588. *Fax:* 530-752-3394; *E-Mail:* rhrice@vcdavis.edu

RICE, ROBERT VERNON, BIOCHEMISTRY. *Current Pos:* fel chem physics, sr fel independent res, Carnegie-Mellon Univ, 57-67, prof biol sci & chmn dept, Mellon Inst Sci, 71-77, prof biochem, 67-87, EMER PROF, BIOL & CHEM, CARNEGIE-MELLON UNIV, 87- *Personal Data:* b Barre, Mass, Aug 13, 24; div; c 2. *Educ:* Northeastern Univ, BS, 50; Univ Wis, MS, 52, PhD(biochem), 55. *Prof Exp:* Asst biochem, Univ Wis, 51-54. *Concurrent Pos:* Vis prof, Med Ctr, Univ Calif, San Francisco, 63. *Mem:* AAAS; Am Soc Biol Chem; Am Soc Cell Biol; Biophys Soc; Am Soc Hort Sci. *Res:* Electron microscopy of muscle; physical biochemistry of macromolecules; cell biology; plant tissue culture. *Mailing Add:* 30 Burnham Dr Falmouth MA 02540

RICE, ROY WARREN, CERAMICS, MATERIALS SCIENCE ENGINEERING. *Current Pos:* CONSULT, 94- *Personal Data:* b Seattle, Wash, Aug 31, 34; m 64, Doris Gutzeit; c Colleen S & Craig R. *Educ:* Univ Wash, BS, 57, MS, 62. *Prof Exp:* Res engr, Boeing Co, 57-68; sect head, 68-74, head ceramics br, Naval Res Lab, 74-84; dir mat res, W R Grace, 84-94. *Mem:* Fel Am Ceramic Soc; fel Am Soc Metals. *Res:* Ceramics and ceramic composites, especially the relationships between processing-microstructure and physical, particularly mechanical, properties and failure analysis. *Mailing Add:* 5411 Hopark Dr Alexandria VA 22310. *Fax:* 410-531-4767

RICE, STANLEY ALAN, POLLUTION BIOLOGY, INVERTEBRATE DEVELOPMENT. *Current Pos:* asst prof, 84-87, ASSOC PROF BIOL, UNIV TAMPA, 87- *Personal Data:* b Los Angeles, Calif, Mar 4, 47; m; c 2. *Educ:* Calif State Univ, Long Beach, BS, 73, MS, 75; Univ SFla, PhD(invertebrate zool), 78. *Prof Exp:* Res asst, Calif State Univ, Long Beach, 73-75, Univ SFla, 75-78; fel, Harbor Br Found, 78-80; staff scientist, Mote Marine Lab, 80-84. *Mem:* Am Soc Zoologists; Am Micros Soc; Sigma Xi. *Res:* Invertebrate life histories; polychaete reproduction and development; population genetics; culture of marine invertebrates; pollution biology. *Mailing Add:* Dept Biol Univ Tampa 401 W Kennedy Blvd Tampa FL 33606-1450

RICE, STANLEY DONALD, POLLUTION BIOLOGY, COMPARATIVE PHYSIOLOGY. *Current Pos:* Res physiologist, Nat Marine Fisheries Serv, 71-86, PROG MGR, HABITAT RES ALASKA, DUKE BAY FISHERIES LAB, 87- *Personal Data:* b Vallejo, Calif, Jan 20, 45; m 66; c 1. *Educ:* Chico State Col, BA, 66, MA, 68; Kent State Univ, PhD(physiol), 71. *Concurrent Pos:* Invited contribr, Petrol Marine Environ, Nat Acad Sci; vis researcher, Beaufort Lab, 86, dept zool-physiol& La State Univ, Baton Rouge, 85 & 87. *Mem:* Am Soc Zoologist; Sigma Xi; AAAS. *Res:* Environmental research, lab and field, fish and crabs, oil effects, metabolism, uptake; TBT toxicity, uptake, author of 70 scientific publications; environmental physiology, smoltification, salinity tolerance; Alaskan fish and invertebrates; author of 70 publications. *Mailing Add:* Auke Bay Fisheries Lab 11305 Glacier Hwy Juneau AK 99801

RICE, STEPHEN LANDON, FRICTION & WEAR OF MATERIALS, TRIBODYNAMICS. *Current Pos:* VPROVOST RES, UNIV NEV, LAS VEGAS, 96- *Personal Data:* b Oakland, Calif, Nov 23, 41; m 65, Penny Baum; c Andrew L & Katherine G. *Educ:* Univ Calif, Berkeley, BS, 64, MEng, 69, PhD(mech eng), 72. *Honors & Awards:* Teetor Award, Soc Automative Engrs, 75; Young Fac Award, Dow Chem Co/Am Soc Eng Educ, 75; Fulbright-Hays Award, 78-79. *Prof Exp:* Design engr, Lawrence Berkeley Lab, 64-69; from asst prof to prof mech eng, Univ Conn, 72-83; prof & chair, Dept Mech Eng & Aerospace eng, Cent Fla Univ, 83-88, assoc dean eng & dir res, 88-96. *Concurrent Pos:* Dir, Automation, Robotics, Mfg Lab, Univ Conn, 80- & Design Proj Prog, 73-; prin investr, AFOSR Wear Proj, Univ

Conn, 76-80, Dept Energy Wear Proj, 81-84, CAD/CAM Kinematics Proj, Control Data, 80-82, NSF Wear-Laser Speckle Proj, 86-88 & NASA/KSC Coop Agreement, 89-; ed, DELOS Lab Compendium, Am Soc Eng Educ, 76-82; evaluator, ASME/ABET Mech Eng Prog, 87- Mem: Am Soc Eng Educ; fel Am Soc Mech Engrs. Res: Friction and wear of engineering materials; emphasis on formation and characterization of subsurface triboprocessed zones; dynamic effects in sliding contact; tribotesting. Mailing Add: Univ Nev 4505 Maryland Pkwy Box 451046 Las Vegas NV 89154-1046. Fax: 407-823-5483; E-Mail: rice@ucf1vm.cc.ucf.edu

RICE, STUART ALAN, PHYSICAL CHEMISTRY. Current Pos: from asst prof to prof, Univ Chicago, 57-60, dir, James Franck Inst, 62-68, mem, Comt Math Biol, 68-80, Louis Block prof, 69-77, chmn dept, 71-77, dean, Div Phys Sci, 80-95, FRANK P HIXON DISTINGUISHED SERV PROF CHEM, UNIV CHICAGO & JAMES FRANCK INST, 77- Personal Data: b New York, NY, Jan 6, 32; m 52, Marian R Coopersmith; c Barbara E & Janet A. Educ: Brooklyn Col, BS, 52; Harvard Univ, AM, 54, PhD(chem), 55. Hon Degrees: DSc, Notre Dame Univ & City Univ NY, 82. Honors & Awards: A Cressy Morrison Prize, NY Acad Sci, 55; Award Pure Chem, Am Chem Soc, 62, L H Baekeland Award, 71; Marlowe Medal, Faraday Soc, 63; King Lectr, Johns Hopkins Univ, 63; Falk-Plaut Lectr, Columbia Univ & Reilly Lectr, Univ Notre Dame, 64; Farkas Lectr, Hebrew Univ Jerusalem, 65; Medal of Free Univ Brussels, 66; Venable Lectr, Univ NC, 68; G K Rollefson Lectr, Univ Calif, Berkeley, 68; Louderman Lectr, Wash Univ, 68; Llewellyn John & Harriet Manchester Quantrell Award, 70; W A Noyes Lectr, Univ Tex, 75, A D Little Lectr, Northeastern Univ, 76; Foster Lectr, Univ Buffalo, 76; F T Gucker Lectr, Univ Ind, 76; Liversidge Lectr, Univ Sydney, 78; A R Gordon Distinguished Lectr, Univ Toronto, 78; Peter Debye Award, Am Chem Soc, 85, Hildebrand Award, 86; Baker Lectr, 85-86; Centenary Lectr, Royal Soc Chem, 86-87. Prof Exp: Jr fel, Soc Fels, Harvard Univ, 55-57. Concurrent Pos: Alfred P Sloane fel, 58-62; Guggenheim fel, 60-61; NSF sr fel & vis prof, Free Univ Brussels, 65-66; mem bd dirs, Bull Atomic Sci, 65-; co-ed, Advan Chem Physics, 66-83; vis prof, H C Orsted Inst, Copenhagen Univ, 70-71.. Mem: Nat Acad Sci; AAAS; Am Chem Soc; Am Phys Soc; Chem Soc; Danish Royal Soc; Am Philos Soc; Am Acad Arts & Sci. Res: Statistical theory of matter; transport phenomena in dense media; electronic structure of liquids, solids and molecular crystals; statistical mechanics of simple systems; theory of phase transitions; photochemistry; properties of liquid surfaces and monolayers; optimal control of selectivity of chemical reactions. Mailing Add: 5421 S Greenwood Ave Chicago IL 60615-5103

RICE, THEODORE ROOSEVELT, marine ecology, for more information see previous edition

RICE, THOMAS B, AGRICULTURAL RESEARCH. Current Pos: CONSULT, 95- Personal Data: b Washington, DC, July 18, 46; m 90, Barbara J Long; c Kevin & Jessica. Educ: Amherst Col, BA, 68; Yale Univ, PhD(biol), 73. Prof Exp: Postdoctoral plant tissue cult & genetics, Brookhaven Nat Lab, 73-74; res assoc, Mich State Univ, 74-76; sr res scientist, Cent Res, Pfizer, Inc, Groton, Conn, 76-78, proj leader, 78-80, mgr, 80-81, dir, 81-85; vpres & dir res, DeKalb-Pfizer Genetics, 85-86, exec vpres, dir res & dir, US Prod Opers, 86-90, pres & chief operating officer, 90-93, sr vpres, De Kalb Genetics Corp, 93-95. Concurrent Pos: Adj asst prof bot, Conn Col, 82, adj assoc prof, 84, adj prof, 85. Mem: AAAS; NY Acad Sci; assoc mem Sigma Xi. Res: Genetic transformation of corn; development of herbicide resistant, insect resistant and nutritionally improved corn hybrids. Mailing Add: 64 Twin Lakes Dr Waterford CT 06385. Fax: 815-758-3711

RICE, THOMAS MAURICE, THEORETICAL SOLID-STATE PHYSICS. Current Pos: PROF, FED TECH INST, ZURICH, SWITZ, 81- Personal Data: b Dundalk, Ireland, Jan 26, 39; nat US; m 66, Helen D Spreiter; c Peter, Susan & Margrit. Educ: Univ Col Dublin, Ireland, BSc, 59, MSc, 60; Univ Cambridge, Eng, PhD(physics), 64. Hon Degrees: DSc, Nat Univ Ireland, 89. Prof Exp: Asst lectr physics, Univ Birmingham, 63-64; res assoc physics, Univ Calif, San Diego, 64-66; mem tech staff, Bell Labs, 66-75, res head, Theoret Physics Dept, 75-78, head, Surface Physics Dept, 78-81. Concurrent Pos: Vis lectr physics, Fed Tech Inst, Zurich, Switz, 70-71; prof, Simon Fraser Univ, Burnaby, BC, 74-75; hon mem, Royal Irish Acad, 88. Mem: Nat Acad Sci; Europ Phys Soc; Swiss Phys Soc; fel Am Phys Soc. Mailing Add: Theoretische Phyik ETH-Honggerberg Zurich 8093 Switzerland. Fax: 41-1-633-1115; E-Mail: rice@itp.phys.ethz.ch

RICE, W(ILLIAM) B(OTHWELL), MECHANICAL ENGINEERING. Current Pos: from assoc prof to prof, 50-82, EMER PROF MECH ENG, QUEEN'S UNIV, KINGSTON, ONT, 82- Personal Data: b Montreal, Que, June 10, 18; wid; c 3. Educ: McGill Univ, BEng, 44, MEng, 56; Sir George Williams Univ, BSc, 50; Univ Montreal, DASc, 59. Hon Degrees: LLD, Concordia Univ, 87. Honors & Awards: Gold Medal, Soc Mfg Engrs, 82; Eng Medal, Asn Prof Engrs Ont, 85. Prof Exp: Asst prof mech eng, McGill Univ, 47-50. Concurrent Pos: Distinguished vis prof, Ariz State Univ, 82-83; pres, NAm Mfg Res Inst, Soc Mfg Engrs, 83-84. Mem: Fel Am Soc Mech Engrs; fel Eng Inst Can (pres, 85-86); fel Soc Mfg Engrs; Int Inst Prod Eng Res; fel Can Soc Mech Eng (pres, 80-81). Res: Manufacturing processes, particularly the effect of friction on mechanics of cutting, extrusion and rolling; manufacturing systems for small organizations. Mailing Add: Dept Mech Eng Queen's Univ 149 Liddell Circle Kingston ON K7M 2T5 Can

RICE, WALTER WILBURN, ANALYTICAL CHEMISTRY. Current Pos: RETIRED. Personal Data: b Harrogate, Tenn, Apr 30 18; wid; c Robert Wayne. Educ: Lincoln Mem Univ, BS, 42. Prof Exp: Chemist & lab supvr, DOE, Union Carbide Nuclear Co, 46-83. Mem: AAAS; Am Chem Soc; Am Vacuum Soc; emer mem Am Soc Mass Spectrometry. Res: Mass spectrometry; vacuum technology; gamma ray scintillation. Mailing Add: 121 W Maiden Lane Oak Ridge TN 37830

RICE, WARREN, ENGINEERING. Current Pos: prof eng, 58-89, chmn, Dept Mech Eng, 67-74, EMER PROF ENG, ARIZ STATE UNIV, 89- Personal Data: b Okla, Oct 11, 25; c 3. Educ: Agr & Mech Col, Tex, PhD(mech eng), 58. Prof Exp: Instr mech eng, Tex Tech Col, 49-50; from instr to assoc prof, Agr & Mech Col, Tex, 50-58. Concurrent Pos: NSF grants, 56-57; indust res grants, 58-66 & 67-74. Mem: Am Soc Mech Engrs. Res: Engineering science; fluid mechanics; heat transfer, particularly boundary layer study and devices influenced by boundary layer phenomena. Mailing Add: 2042 E Balboa Dr Tempe AZ 85282

RICE, WENDELL ALFRED, SYMBIOTIC DINITROGEN FIXATION. Current Pos: RES SCIENTIST SOIL MICROBIOL, RES STA, CAN DEPT AGR, 70- Personal Data: b Saskatoon, Sask, Apr 24, 39; m 62; c 3. Educ: Univ Sask, BSA, 63, MSc, 66, PhD(soil microbiol), 70. Concurrent Pos: Soils advh, Barani Agr Res & Develop Proj, Islamabad, Pakistan, 85-87. Mem: Can Soc Soil Sci; Int Soc Soil Sci; Can Soc Microbiologists. Res: Effect of environmental factors on Rhizobium growth and survival, nodulation, and nitrogen fixation; microbial transformations of soil nitrogen. Mailing Add: Soil Sect Res Sta PO Box 29 Beaverlodge AB T0H 0C0 Can

RICE, WILLIAM JAMES, THERMODYNAMICS. Current Pos: RETIRED. Personal Data: b Whallonsburgh, NY, Aug 6, 27. Educ: Worcester Polytech Inst, BS, 47, MS, 48; Princeton Univ, PhD(chem eng), 64. Prof Exp: Instr chem eng, Cath Univ Am, 48-53; from asst prof to prof chem eng, Villanova Univ, 53-91. Concurrent Pos: Vis res prof, Inst Energy Conversion, Univ Del, 77-78, pres, Villanova Univ Sigma Xi (87-88). Mem: Am Inst Chem Engrs; Sigma Xi. Res: Fluid dynamics; transport properties; separation processes; thermodynamics. Mailing Add: PO Box 728 Broomall PA 19008-0728

RICH, ABBY M, ELECTRON MICROSCOPY, LEUKOCYTES. Current Pos: staff info systs develop, 87-90, DIR COMPUT PROG, PRUDENTIAL SECURITIES, 90- Personal Data: b Newark, NJ, Mar 20, 50. Educ: Oberlin Col, BA, 72; Univ NC, PhD(zool), 78. Prof Exp: Asst, Med Ctr, NY Univ, 78-81, res asst, 81-82, res assoc & fel, 82-85, asst prof cell biol, 85-86. Mem: Am Asn Cell Biol; Harvey Soc; NY Acad Sci. Res: Mechanisms of cell activation with an emphasis on stimulus response coupling; leukocytes and other phagocytic cells. Mailing Add: Prudentila Securities One NY Plaza 4th Floor New York NY 10292

RICH, ALEXANDER, MOLECULAR BIOPHYSICS, MOLECULAR BIOLOGY. Current Pos: from assoc prof to prof, 58-74, WILLIAM THOMPSON SEDGWICK PROF BIOPHYS, MASS INST TECHNOL, 74- Personal Data: b Hartford, Conn, Nov 15, 24; m 52; c 4. Educ: Harvard Univ, AB, 47; Harvard Med Sch, MD, 49. Hon Degrees: DSc, Fed Univ Rio de Janeiro, 81, Eidgenossiche Tech Hochschule, Switz, 93, Freie Universitat, Berlin, Ger, 96; PhD, Weizmann Inst Sci, Israel, 92. Honors & Awards: Nat Medal Sci, 95; Skylab Achievement Award, NASA, 74; Theodore von Karmen Award, 76; Pres Award, NY Acad Sci, 77; Jabotinsky Medal, Jabotinsky Found, 80; Lewis S Rosenstiel Award, 83; Linus Pauling Medal, Am Chem Soc, 95; Nat Medal of Sci, 95. Prof Exp: Res fel chem, Calif Inst Technol, 49-54; chief, Sect Phys Chem, NIH, 54-58. Concurrent Pos: Fel, Nat Res Coun, 49-51 & mem gov bd, 85-88; vis scientist, Cavendish Lab, Cambridge, Eng, 55-56; mem, Postdoctoral Fel Bd, NIH, 55-58, mem, Career Award Comt, 64-67; Guggenheim Found fel, 63; mem, Vis Comt, Biol Dept, Yale Univ, 63 & Weizmann Inst Sci, 65-66; mem, Exobiol Comt, Space Sci Bd, Nat Acad Sci, 64-65 & US Nat Comt, Int Orgn Pure & Appl Biophys, 65-67 & 79-83, chmn, Comt USSR & Eastern Europe Exchange Prog, 73-76, mem adv bd, Acad Forum, 75-82, Gov-Univ-Indust Res Round Table, 84-; mem corp, Marine Biol Lab, Woods Hole, 65-77; mem, Lunar & Planetary Missions Bd, NASA, 68-71, biol team, Viking Mars Mission, 69-80 & life sci comt, 70-75; mem biol adv comt, Oak Ridge Nat Lab, 72-76; mem, Int Res & Exchanges Bd, Am Coun Learned Socs, 73-76; mem, Sci Adv Bd, Stanford Synchroton Radiation Proj, 76-80; mem, Nat Sci Bd, 76-82; mem, US-USSR Joint Comn Sci & Technol, Dept State & sr consult, Off Sci & Technol Policy, Exec Off Pres, Washington, DC, 77-81; mem coun, Pugwash Conf Sci & World Affairs, Geneva, Switz, 77-82; mem, Sci Rev Comt, Howard Hughes Med Inst, Miami, Fla, 78-; mem bd dirs, Med Found Boston, Mass, 81-90; chmn, Sci Adv Comt, Dept Molecular Biol, MassGen Hosp, Boston, Mass, 83-87; mem, Nat Adv Bd Physicians Social Responsibility, 83-; mem, Comt USSR & Eastern Europe, Nat Res Coun, Washington, DC, 86-, Nat Adv Comt Pew Scholar Prog, Pew Mem Trust, New Haven, Conn, 86-88. Mem: Nat Acad Sci; sr mem Inst Med-Nat Acad Sci; Biophys Soc; Am Crystallog Asn; fel Am Acad Arts & Sci; fel AAAS; Am Soc Biol Chemists; Am Soc Microbiol; Am Philos Soc; hon mem Japanese Biochem Soc; Am Chem Soc; Europ Molecular Biol Orgn; foreign mem Fr Acad Sci; foreign mem Russ Acad Sci. Res: Molecular structure of biological systems; x-ray crystallography; protein chemistry; nucleic acid chemistry; polymer molecular structure; information transfer in biological systems; mechanism of protein synthesis; origin of life; physical chemistry of nucleotides and polynucleotides; author or coauthor of over 450 publications. Mailing Add: Dept Biol Rm 68-233 Mass Inst Technol 77 Massachusetts Ave Cambridge MA 02139-4307

RICH, ARTHUR GILBERT, PHYSICAL PHARMACY, PHARMACEUTICS. Current Pos: VPRES, SCI, DE LAIRE, INC NY, 88- Personal Data: b Brooklyn, NY, Mar 21, 36; m 64; c 2. Educ: Columbia Univ, BS, 57; Univ Iowa, MS, 59, PhD, 62. Prof Exp: Res chemist, Julius Schmid, Inc, 62-63, proj leader pharmaceut res & develop, 63-65; sr res scientist, Johnson & Johnson, New Brunswick, 65-69; group leader, Ortho Pharmaceut Corp, 69-72; prog mgr, Avon Prods, Inc, Suffern, NY, 72-88. Concurrent Pos: Union Carbide res fel, State Univ Iowa, 57-62; lectr, Ctr Prof Advan, 76-77. Mem: AAAS; Acad Pharmaceut Sci; Am Pharmaceut Asn; NY Acad Sci; fel

Royal Soc Health; Sigma Xi; Soc Cosmetic Chemists. *Res:* Design and development of suitable pharmaceutical and cosmetic vehicles for maximum topical effect of drug and cosmetic agents. *Mailing Add:* 7 Craftwood Dr Spring Valley NY 10977-7204

RICH, AVERY EDMUND, plant pathology; deceased, see previous edition for last biography

RICH, BEN R, aerothermodynamics; deceased, see previous edition for last biography

RICH, CHARLES CLAYTON, GEOLOGY. *Current Pos:* from inst to prof geol, 58-90, dir univ honors prog, 65-69, EMER PROF GEOL, BOWLING GREEN STATE UNIV, 90- *Personal Data:* b Cincinnati, Ohio, Dec 8, 22; m 66; c 2. *Educ:* Wittenberg Univ, AB, 45; Harvard Univ, MA, 50, PhD(geol), 60. *Prof Exp:* Lectr geol, Victoria Univ, NZ, 52-54. *Mem:* Geol Soc Am; Nat Asn Geol Teachers; Am Quaternary Asn. *Res:* Glacial and Pleistocene geology. *Mailing Add:* Dept Geol Bowling Green State Univ Bowling Green OH 43403

RICH, CLAYTON, MEDICINE, ENDOCRINOLOGY. *Current Pos:* EMER PROVOST & REGENTS PROF, UNIV OKLA, 94- *Personal Data:* b New York, NY, May 21, 24; div; c 1. *Educ:* Cornell Univ, MD, 48. *Prof Exp:* Extern path, New York Hosp, Cornell Univ, 48, asst physician, 49-50; intern med, Albany Hosp & Med Col, Union Univ, NY, 48-49, asst resident & asst med, 50-51; asst, Rockefeller Inst & asst physician, Hosp, 53-58, asst prof, Inst & assoc physician, Hosp, 58-60; from asst prof to prof med, Sch Med, Univ Wash, 60-71, assoc dean, 68-71; chief staff, Stanford Univ Hosp, 71-77, dean & vpres med affairs, Stanford Univ, 71-78, Karl & Elizabeth Naumann prof med, 77-78; vis sr scholar, Inst Med-Nat Acad Sci, 79-80; exec dean, Col Med, Okla Univ, Oklahoma City, 80-83, prof med, Col Med & provost & exec officer, 80-92, vpres health sci, 83-92, prof health admin, Col Pub Health, 85-92. *Concurrent Pos:* Chief radioisotope serv, Vet Admin Hosp, 60-70, assoc chief staff, 62-71, chief staff, 68-70; attend physician, Univ & King Co Hosps, Seattle, 62-71. *Mem:* Inst Med-Nat Acad Sci; Am Soc Clin Invest; Endocrine Soc; Am Col Physicians; AMA; Asn Am Physicians. *Res:* Academic administration. *Mailing Add:* 13450 64th Terr NE Kirkland WA 98034

RICH, DANIEL HULBERT, BIO-ORGANIC CHEMISTRY. *Current Pos:* asst prof, 70-75, assoc prof, 75-81, PROF PHARMACEUT CHEM, UNIV WIS-MADISON, 81- *Personal Data:* b Fairmont, Minn, Dec 12, 42; m 64; c 2. *Educ:* Univ Minn, BS, 64; Cornell Univ, PhD(org chem), 68. *Honors & Awards:* H I Romnes Award, 80. *Prof Exp:* Res assoc org chem, Cornell Univ, 68; res chemist, Dow Chem Co, 68-69; fel org chem, Stanford Univ, 69-70. *Concurrent Pos:* NIH fel, 68; mem, Bioorg Natural Prod Study Sect, NIH, 81-; consult, 80- *Mem:* AAAS; Am Chem Soc; Am Pharmaceut Asn. *Res:* Synthesis of peptides and hormones; inhibition of peptide receptors and proteases; characterization, synthesis, and mechanisms of action of peptide natural products. *Mailing Add:* Sch Pharm 425 N Charter St Madison WI 53705-1515

RICH, DANNY CLARK, COLORIMETRY, VISUAL PSYCHOPHYSICS. *Current Pos:* MGR RES, DATACOLOR INT, 84- *Personal Data:* b Payette, Idaho, Apr 23, 51; m, Phyllis Elaine Phillips; c Amanda Kathleen, Brandon Clark & Bryan Charles. *Educ:* Univ Idaho, BS, 73; Va Polytech Inst, MS, 77; Rensselaer Polytech Inst, PhD(chem), 80. *Prof Exp:* Group leader, Coatings Res Ctr, Sherwin-Williams Co, 80-84. *Mem:* Optical Soc Am; Am Asn Physics Teachers; Optical Engr Soc; Soc Photog Scientists & Engrs; Inter-soc Color Coun (secy, 89-92, 92-96). *Res:* Instruments for color measurement; metrology of color measuring instruments; models of pigmented turbid media; models relating instrumental color measurements to visual color measurements. *Mailing Add:* 86 Joni Ave Hamilton Square NJ 08690. *Fax:* 609-895-7461; *E-Mail:* dannyrich@aol.com

RICH, EARL ROBERT, ECOLOGY. *Current Pos:* PRES, RIO PALENQUE RES CORP, 72- *Personal Data:* b Marquette, Mich, Aug 30, 25; m 74, Donna Davidson; c Lars, Lynn (Thompson) & Lee (Askew). *Educ:* Univ Chicago, SB, 49, PhD(zool), 54. *Prof Exp:* NSF fel statist, Univ Calif, 54-55, lectr, 55-56, instr biostatist, 56-57; from asst prof to assoc prof zool, Univ Miami, 57-70, assoc dean, Col Arts & Sci, 68-70, prof biol, 70-85. *Mem:* Ecol Soc Am; AAAS; Am Soc Zool; Soc Wetland Scientists; Sigma Xi. *Res:* Population dynamics and ecology; wetland ecology; man's impact on environment; inshore marine biology. *Mailing Add:* PO Box 249118 Coral Gables FL 33124-9118. *E-Mail:* erich@umiami.edu

RICH, ELLIOT, CIVIL ENGINEERING. *Current Pos:* RETIRED. *Personal Data:* b Brigham City, Utah, May 27, 19; m 43; c 6. *Educ:* Utah State Univ, BS, 43; Univ Utah, MS, 51; Univ Colo, PhD(civil eng), 68. *Prof Exp:* Hydraul engr, US Bur Reclamation, 46-47; instr, Weber Col, 47-50, head eng dept, 50-56; assoc prof, 56-67, head dept civil eng, 67-75, prof civil eng, Utah State Univ, 67-, assoc dean, col eng, 75-85. *Concurrent Pos:* Consult, AEC, 59. *Mem:* Am Soc Eng Educ; Am Soc Civil Engrs (pres, 77-78). *Res:* Structures. *Mailing Add:* 1640 E 1140 N Logan UT 84321

RICH, FREDRICK JAMES, PALYNOLOGY. *Current Pos:* ASSOC PROF GEOL & CHAIR, GA SOUTHERN UNIV, 88- *Personal Data:* m 81, Sharon D Allshouse; c Andrew, Katherine & Thomas. *Educ:* Univ Wis, BS, 73; Pa State Univ, PhD(geol), 79. *Prof Exp:* From asst prof to assoc prof geol & geol eng, SDak Sch Mines & Technol, 79-88. *Concurrent Pos:* Distinguished lectr, Am Asn Petrol Geologists, 82-83; ed, Am Asn Stratigr Palynologists Newslett, 88-91. *Mem:* Sigma Xi; Am Asn Stratigr Palynologists; Paleont Res Inst. *Res:* Palynology, paleoecology and geochronology of Pliocene and Pleistocene coastal plain deposits of Florida, Georgia and South Carolina; earth science teacher education. *Mailing Add:* Dept Geol & Geog Ga Southern Univ PO Box 8149 Statesboro GA 30460

RICH, GEORGE F, BIOMEDICAL ENGINEERING, ANESTHESIOLOGY. *Current Pos:* ASST PROF ANESTHESIOL & BIOMED ENG, UNIV VA, 89- *Personal Data:* b Salt Lake City, Utah, Aug 15, 57. *Educ:* Univ Utah, BS, 79, MD & PhD(biomed eng), 85. *Mem:* Am Soc Anesthesiol; Biomed Eng Soc. *Mailing Add:* Dept Anesthesiol Health Sci Ctr Univ Va PO Box 238 Charlottesville VA 22908

RICH, HARRY LOUIS, SHIP PROTECTION, MARINE SCIENCE. *Current Pos:* RETIRED. *Personal Data:* b New York, NY, Apr 30, 17; m 41; c 2. *Educ:* Brooklyn Col, BA, 39. *Prof Exp:* Jr physicist, David Taylor Naval Ship Res & Develop Ctr, US Navy, 42-43, asst physicist, 43-44, physicist, 44-49, supvr, shock sect, 49-53, shock br, 53-65, coordr, shock res, 66-67, tech dir, oper dive-under, 67-68, head, engr facil div, 70-71, asst to tech dir, 72-74; lectr eng, Mass Inst Technol, 74-89. *Concurrent Pos:* Navy rep, Dept Defense Shock & Vibration Info Ctr, 57-71; US rep, Int Electrotech Comn, 64-74, Int Standards Orgn, 64-; sci adv, S Korean Navy, 71-72; consult, 74- *Mem:* Fel Acoust Soc Am; fel Inst Environ Sci; Soc Naval Architects & Marine Engrs. *Res:* Dynamics of explosions and their effects on mechanical systems and structures; instrumentation for shock and vibration; design of mechanical systems for shock loading and shock simulation. *Mailing Add:* 6765 Brigadoon Dr Bethesda MD 20817

RICH, JIMMY RAY, NEMATICIDES, NEMATODE RESISTANCE IN PLANTS. *Current Pos:* From asst prof to assoc prof, Univ Fla, 76-86, actg dir, Agr Res Ctr, 80-84, asst dir, 84-88, PROF, UNIV FLA, 86- *Personal Data:* b Collins, Ga, Oct 29, 50. *Educ:* Univ Ga, BSA, 72, MS, 73; Univ Calif, Riverside, PhD(plant path), 76. *Honors & Awards:* Distinguished Serv Award, Orgn Trop Am Nematologists. *Concurrent Pos:* Ed-in-chief, Nematropica; pres, Orgn Trop Am Nematologists; consult, Vol in Overseas Coop Assistance. *Mem:* Soc Nematologists; Am Phytopath Soc; Orgn Trop Am Nematologists; Tobacco Dis Coun. *Res:* Nematode management; chemical control, plant resistance and biocontrol; new crops and management procedures. *Mailing Add:* Univ Fla Rte 3 Box 4370 Quincy FL 32351

RICH, JOHN CHARLES, ASTROPHYSICS, LASERS. *Current Pos:* PRES, HUGHES DANBURY OPTICAL SYSTS, INC, 89- *Personal Data:* b Wichita, Kans, Oct 12, 37; m 63, Kathleen; c 3. *Educ:* Harvard Univ, AB, 59, AM, 60, PhD(astron), 67. *Prof Exp:* Physicist, Air Force Weapons Lab, 60-74, div chief, 74-77, comdr, 77-78, prog dir, 78-82; eng dir, Perkin-Elmer Corp, 83-85, gen mgr, 85-89. *Concurrent Pos:* Instr, Univ Va, 69-70. *Mem:* Am Astron Soc; Am Geophys Union; Am Inst Aeronaut & Astronaut; Sigma Xi. *Res:* Atomic and molecular physics; radiative processes; stellar atmospheres; optics. *Mailing Add:* 28 Sharp Hill Rd Ridgefield CT 06877-3735

RICH, JOSEPH ANTHONY, PLASMA PHYSICS. *Current Pos:* RETIRED. *Personal Data:* b Hazardville, Conn, July 23, 16; m 45, Anne Yankus; c Sally A & Patricia A. *Educ:* Harvard Univ, BSc, 38; Brown Univ, MSc, 39; Yale Univ, PhD(physics), 50. *Prof Exp:* Physicist, Cent Res Lab, Monsanto Chem Co, 43-45, sr physicist, 45-47; physicist, Knolls Atomic Power Lab, Gen Elec Co, 49-52 & Electron Physics Dept, Res & Develop Ctr, 52-60, physicist, Gen Physics Lab, Res & Develop Ctr, 60-81. *Mem:* Am Phys Soc; Math Asn Am; sr mem Inst Elec & Electronics Engrs; Sigma Xi. *Res:* Microwave electronics; nuclear physics; high current arcs. *Mailing Add:* 1385 Ruffner Rd Schenectady NY 12309

RICH, JOSEPH WILLIAM, NONEQUILIBRIUM GAS DYNAMICS, CHEMICALLY REACTING FLOWS. *Current Pos:* prof mech eng, 86-96, PROF CHEM PHYSICS, OHIO STATE UNIV, 90-, RALPH W KURTZ PROF, 96- *Personal Data:* b New Orleans, La, Aug 6, 37; m 60, Beatrice Jewell; c Grant & Anne. *Educ:* Carnegie Inst Technol, BS, 59; Univ Va, MAE, 61; Princeton Univ, MA, 63, PhD(aerospace & mech sci), 65. *Prof Exp:* Sci staff, Cornell Aeronaut Lab, 65-72; prin engr, Calspan Corp, 72-82, head physics & chem sect, Arvin/Calspan Adv Technol Ctr, 82-86. *Concurrent Pos:* Vis prof, Dept Mech Eng, Carnegie-Mellon Univ, 85, Fulbright fel, Ecole des Arts et Manufactures, Paris, 88. *Mem:* Am Inst Aeronaut & Astronaut; AAAS; Am Phys Soc. *Res:* Nonequilibrium gas dynamics; molecular energy transfer; development of new gas lasers; developed first electrically-excited supersonic flow carbon monoxide gas laser; isotope separation in vibrationally nonequilibrium gases. *Mailing Add:* 286 W South St Worthington OH 43085. *Fax:* 614-292-3163

RICH, KENNETH C, PEDIATRICS. *Current Pos:* PROF PEDIAT, COL MED, UNIV ILL, 82- *Personal Data:* b Berkeley, Calif, Apr 7, 43; c 2. *Educ:* Tulane Univ, MD, 70. *Mem:* Soc Pediat Res; Am Rheumatism Asn; Clin Immunol Soc; Am Col Pheumatol. *Res:* Pediatric rheumatology and immunology; epidemiologic studies of perinatal HIV infection. *Mailing Add:* Dept Pediat Univ Ill Coll Med 840 S Wood St M/C 856 Chicago IL 60612

RICH, KENNETH EUGENE, SOFTWARE SYSTEMS, MEDICAL INSTRUMENTATION. *Current Pos:* sr comput appl scientist, 81-83, MGR, COMPUTERIZED SYST DEVELOP, CAPINTEC, INC, 83- *Personal Data:* b Alton, Ill, Nov 19, 43; m 68; c 2. *Educ:* Rose-Hulman Inst Technol, BS, 66; Univ Rochester, PhD(biophys), 71. *Prof Exp:* Res assoc biophys & instrumentation, Dept Biochem, Case Western Res Univ, 71-75; staff fel comput instrumentation & molecular biol, Nat Inst Neurologic Commun Dis & Stroke, 76-78; scientist comput instrumentation, Technico Instrument Corp, 78-81. *Concurrent Pos:* USPHS fel, Case Western Res Univ, 71-75. *Mem:* Biophys Soc; Am Chem Soc; Sigma Xi; AAAS; Inst Elec & Electronics Engrs; Soc Photo-Optical Instrumentation Engrs. *Res:* Management of systems group working on ambulatory cardiac function monitor and nuclear medicine department management systems; image processing. *Mailing Add:* 2342 Charros Rd Sandy UT 84092

RICH, LEONARD G, PHYSICS, ELECTRICAL ENGINEERING. *Current Pos:* SCI DIR, GERBER SCI INC, 65-, VPRES RES GERBER SCI PROD, 82-, TECH DIR, 95- *Personal Data:* b New York, NY, Mar 28, 25; m 55, Gloria Solomon; c Donna (Lubchansky). *Educ:* St Lawrence Univ, BS, 45. *Prof Exp:* Res physicist, Crystal Res Labs, Inc, 46-47; pres, Norbert Photo Prod Co, 47-49; asst chief engr electronics, McMurdo Silver Co, 49-50, chief engr, 50-51; proj engr, New London Instrument Co, Inc, 51-53; proj leader res & develop, Andersen Labs, Inc, 53-56; sr proj engr, Roth Lab, 56-65. *Mem:* Inst Elec & Electronics Engrs. *Res:* Electronic physics; ultrasonic delay lines; magnetic memory for signal-to-noise improvement through video integration; signal generators and test instruments for industry; computer-controlled digital and analog graphic output devices; robotic scanners; digital adaptive servos; computer generation of color images; Ink-Jet technology; large areas color sign generators; optical lens generators; eight patents. *Mailing Add:* Gerber Sci Prod 151 Batson Dr Manchester CT 06040

RICH, LINVIL G(ENE), ENVIRONMENTAL ENGINEERING. *Current Pos:* dean eng, 61-72, prof 72-81, alumni prof, 82-87, EMER ALUMNI PROF, ENVIRON SYSTS ENG, CLEMSON UNIV, 87- *Personal Data:* b Pana, Ill, Mar 10, 21; m 44; c 2. *Educ:* Va Polytech Inst, BS, 47, MS, 48, PhD(biochem), 51; Environ Eng Intersoc, dipl. *Honors & Awards:* Hering Medal, Am Soc Civil Engrs, 83. *Prof Exp:* From instr to assoc prof sanit eng, Va Polytech Inst, 48-55; from assoc prof to prof, Ill Inst Technol, 56-61. *Concurrent Pos:* Consult, Environ Protection Agency. *Mem:* Fel Am Soc Civil Engrs; Am Soc Eng Educ; Am Acad Environ Engrs; Asn Environ Eng Prof. *Res:* Environmental engineering. *Mailing Add:* Col Eng Clemson Univ Clemson SC 29632

RICH, MARK, CARBONIFEROUS FORAMINIFERAL BIOSTRATIGRAPHY. *Current Pos:* from assoc prof to prof, 63-90, EMER PROF GEOL, UNIV GA, 90- *Personal Data:* b Chicago, Ill, Feb 1, 32; m 58, Symma Kitover; c Todd, Jon, Jordana, David & Daniel. *Educ:* Univ Calif, Los Angeles, AB, 54; Univ Southern Calif, MA, 56; Univ Ill, PhD(geol), 59. *Prof Exp:* Asst geol, Univ Ill, 57-59; asst prof, Univ NDak, 59-63. *Mem:* Geol Soc Am; Nat Water Well Asn. *Res:* Sedimentary petrology; stratigraphy; micropaleontology; foraminiferal biostratieraphy of carboniferous rocks in southern Appalachians. *Mailing Add:* Dept Geol Univ Ga Athens GA 30602

RICH, MARVIN A, microbiology, virology, for more information see previous edition

RICH, MARVIN R, BIOPHYSICS. *Current Pos:* res asst, Dept Biol, 81-85, RES SCIENTIST, NY UNIV, 85- *Personal Data:* b Bronx, NY, Oct 29, 47. *Educ:* Rensselaer Polytech Inst, BS, 69; NY Univ, MS, 77, PhD(biophys), 81. *Mem:* AAAS; NY Acad Sci; Am Soc Photobiol. *Res:* Use of model membrane systems in the study of lipid peroxidation and free radical mechanisms. *Mailing Add:* NY Univ c/o Prof Ken Goldberg 637 East Bldg 239 Green St New York NY 10003

RICH, MICHAEL, MATHEMATICS. *Current Pos:* STAFF MEM, IAI, 81- *Personal Data:* b Chicago, Ill, July 23, 40; m 63, Beverly; c 4. *Educ:* Roosevelt Univ, BS, 62; Ill Inst Technol, MS, 65, PhD(math), 69. *Prof Exp:* Asst prof math, Ind Univ, 67-69. *Concurrent Pos:* From asst prof to prof math, Temple Univ, 69-85; vis assoc prof, Ben Gurion Univ Negev, 74-75. *Mem:* Am Math Soc; Math Asn Am. *Res:* Ring theory; nonassociative algebras; software systems. *Mailing Add:* 6 Haerez St Ginot Shomron Israel. *Fax:* 972-3-935-5969; *E-Mail:* mrich@malat.iai.co.il

RICH, PETER HAMILTON, LIMNOLOGY. *Current Pos:* asst prof, 72-80, ASSOC PROF ECOL, UNIV CONN, 80- *Personal Data:* b Wellfleet, Mass, Nov 7, 39; div; c 1. *Educ:* Hunter Col, AB, 63; Mich State Univ, MS, 66, PhD, 70. *Prof Exp:* Res assoc biol, Brookhaven Nat Lab, 70-72. *Mem:* AAAS; Ecol Soc Am; Am Soc Limnol & Oceanog; Int Asn Theoret & Appl Limnol. *Res:* Measurement of the functional, community parameters of the aquatic ecosystem, especially benthos; aquatic ecosystem energetics. *Mailing Add:* Ecol U-42 Univ Conn Storrs CT 06269-0002

RICH, RICHARD DOUGLAS, ORGANIC CHEMISTRY. *Current Pos:* res chemist, Loctite Corp, 70-78, res assoc, 78-79, scientist, 79-92, SR DEVELOP SCIENTIST, LOCTITE CORP, 92- *Personal Data:* b Chicago, Ill, Nov 30, 36; m 59, Karen Lloyd; c 2. *Educ:* Rensselaer Polytech Inst, BChE, 58; Univ Md, PhD(org chem), 68. *Prof Exp:* Res chemist, US Naval Ord Lab, Md, 58-68; sr scientist, Bickford Res Labs, Inc, Ensign-Bickford Co, Conn, 68-70. *Concurrent Pos:* Adj prof, Univ Hartford, 69-72. *Mem:* Am Inst Chemists; Am Chem Soc. *Res:* Organic chemistry of explosives; plastic binders for propellants and explosives; anaerobic and cyanoacrylate adhesives. *Mailing Add:* Loctite Corp 1001 Trout Brook Crossing Rocky Hill CT 06067. *E-Mail:* drdickrich@aol.com

RICH, ROBERT PETER, MATHEMATICS, COMPUTER SCIENCES. *Current Pos:* RETIRED. *Personal Data:* b Lowville, NY, Aug 28, 19; wid; c Elaine & David. *Educ:* Hamilton Col, AB, 41; Johns Hopkins Univ, PhD(math), 50. *Prof Exp:* Mathematician, Appl Physics Lab, Johns Hopkins Univ, 50-89, dir, Comput Ctr, 56-89, assoc prof biomed eng, 69-89, oper analyst, 85-89. *Mem:* AAAS; Am Math Soc; Asn Comput Mach; Soc Indust & Appl Math. *Res:* Digital computing. *Mailing Add:* 1109 Schindler Dr Silver Spring MD 20903. *E-Mail:* bobrich@erols.com

RICH, ROBERT REGIER, IMMUNOBIOLOGY. *Current Pos:* from asst prof to assoc prof, 73-78, HEAD, IMMUNOL SECT, BAYLOR COL MED, 77-, PROF MICROBIOL & IMMUNOL & CHIEF CLIN IMMUNOL, 78-, PROF MED, 79-, VPRES & DEAN RES, 90- *Personal Data:* b Newton, Kans, Mar 7, 41; m 74; c 2. *Educ:* Oberlin Col, AB, 62; Univ Kans, MD, 66. *Prof Exp:* Intern, Univ Wash, 66-67, asst resident, 67-68; clin assoc immunol, NIH, 68-71; NIH res fel immunol, Harvard Med Sch, 71-73. *Concurrent Pos:* Asst med, Peter Bent Brigham Hosp, Boston, 72-73; attend physician, Vet Admin Hosp, Houston, 73-; adj asst prof, Grad Sch Biomed Sci, Univ Tex Health Sci Ctr, Houston, 75-79; prog dir, Gen Clin Res Ctr, Methodist Hosp, Houston, 75-77; NIH res career develop award, 75-77; investr, Howard Hughes Med Inst, 77-; mem immunobiol study sect, NIH, 77-81; assoc ed, J Immunol, 78-82 & J Infections Dis, 83-88; adj prof, Grad Sch Biomed Sci, Univ Tex Health Sci Ctr, Houston, 79-; adv ed. J Exp Med, 80-84; Transplantation Biol & Immunol Comt, Nat Inst Allergy & Infections Dis, 82-86, chmn, 84-86; Nat Ctr Grants Subcomt, Arthritis Found, 83-86, chmn, 84-86, Nat Res Comt, 84-, vchmn, 85-86, chmn, 86-89; bd dirs, Am Bd Allergy & Immunol, 88-, chmn, 91-; adv comt, res prog, Nat Mult Sclerosis Soc, 89-; bd gov, Am Med Internal Med, 90- *Mem:* Am Asn Immunologists; Am Asn Pathologists; fel Am Col Physicians; Am Soc Clin Invest; Asn Am Physicians; fel Am Acad Allergy & Immunol; fel Infections Dis Soc Am; Am Clin & Climat Soc; Clin Immunol Soc. *Res:* Major histocompatibility complex and T lymphogne genetics and function in mice and humans. *Mailing Add:* Dept Microbiol & Immunol Baylor Col Med 1 Baylor Plaza M Debakey Ctr M929 Houston TX 77030-3498

RICH, RONALD LEE, PERIODICITY, QUALITATIVE ANALYSIS. *Current Pos:* dean, 79-80, SCHOLAR IN RESIDENCE, BLUFFTON COL, OHIO, 81- *Personal Data:* b Washington, Ill, Mar 29, 27; m 53, Elaine Sommers; c Jonathan, Andrew, Miriam & Mark. *Educ:* Bluffton Col, BS, 48; Univ Chicago, PhD(chem), 53. *Prof Exp:* Instr chem, Bethel Col, Kans, 50-51; mem staff, Los Alamos Sci Lab, 53; assoc prof chem, Bethel Col, Kans, 53-55; chemist, Nat Bur Stand, 55-56; prof chem, Bethel Col, Kans, 56-63 & 64-66, Int Christian Univ, Tokyo, 71-79; res fel, Harvard Univ, 63-64; prof, Int Christian Univ, Tokyo, 66-69; prof chem & chmn div natural sci, Bethel Col, Kans, 69-71; res fel, NC State Univ, 89-90. *Concurrent Pos:* Vis prof chem, Stanford Univ, 74, Univ Ill, 75 & Univ Oregon, 84. *Res:* Correlation of chemical and physical properties with structure; development of non-sulfide qualitative analysis. *Mailing Add:* 112 S Spring St Bluffton OH 45817-1112. *E-Mail:* richr@bluffton.edu

RICH, ROYAL ALLEN, REPRODUCTIVE PHYSIOLOGY. *Current Pos:* RETIRED. *Personal Data:* b North Platte, Nebr, Aug 6, 34; m 56; c 4. *Educ:* Univ Nebr, BS, 57; Utah State Univ, MS, 60, PhD(physiol), 65. *Prof Exp:* Instr zool & physiol, Utah State Univ, 62-64; assoc prof, Univ Northern Colo, 65-73, prof zool, 73-93. *Mem:* Soc Study Reproduction. *Res:* Mammalian physiology; influence of ovarian hormones on uterine biochemistry, especially deciduoma formation in the rat; post-partum involution. *Mailing Add:* Dept Biol Sci Univ Northern Colo Greeley CO 80639-0002

RICH, SAUL, PHYTOPATHOLOGY. *Current Pos:* res assoc, Crop Protection Inst, 47-48, from asst plant pathologist to sr plant pathologist, 48-72, chief dept plant path & bot, 72-83, EMER PLANT PATHOLOGIST, CONN AGR EXP STA, 83- *Personal Data:* b Detroit, Mich, Nov 25, 17; m 46, Helen Felsenfeld; c Deborah & Daniel. *Educ:* Univ Calif, BS, 38, MS, 39; Ore State Col, PhD(plant path), 42. *Prof Exp:* Asst plant pathologist, Univ Wyo, 46. *Mem:* Fel AAAS; fel Am Phytopath Soc (treas, 52-58); Soc Indust Microbiol (pres, 66). *Res:* Air pollution; fungicides; vegetable diseases. *Mailing Add:* 65 Adla Dr Hamden New Haven CT 06514

RICH, SUSAN MARIE SOLLIDAY, MICROBIOLOGY, IMMUNOLOGY. *Current Pos:* from instr to assoc prof, 73-87, PROF MICROBIOL & IMMUNOL, BAYLOR COL MED, 87- *Personal Data:* b Rockford, Ill, June 17, 41; c 1. *Educ:* Beloit Col, Wis, BS, 63; Univ Wis-Madison, MS, 65; Baylor Col Med, PhD(microbiol & immunol), 79. *Prof Exp:* Res technician, Univ Chicago, 66-67; proj specialist, Dept Med Genetics, Univ Wis-Madison, 67-70; res asst, Dept Path, Med Sch, Harvard Univ, 70-73. *Concurrent Pos:* Prin investr, NIH, 80-83, 82-87 & 90-91; mem, Immunobiol Study Sect, Div Res Grants, NIH, 81-85 & Allergy & Clin Immunol Subcomt Allergy Immunol & Transplantation Res Comt, Nat Inst Allergy & Infectious Dis, 88-; co-dir, Med Scientist Training Prog, Baylor Col Med, 90- *Mem:* Am Asn Immunologists. *Res:* Regulation of Ts cell growth and differentiation; regulatory abnormalities in immunologic diseases; author of numerous technical publications. *Mailing Add:* Dept Microbiol & Immunol Baylor Col Med Michael E Debakey Ctr M929B Houston TX 77030-3498

RICH, TERRELL L, cardiovascular physiology; deceased, see previous edition for last biography

RICH, THOMAS HEWITT, PALEOMAMMALOGY, DINOSAUR SYSTEMATICS & PALEOGEOGRAPHY. *Current Pos:* CUR VERT PALEONT, MUS VICTORIA, MELBOURNE, AUSTRALIA, 74- *Personal Data:* b Evanston, Ill, May 30, 41; Australian & US citizen; m 66, Patricia A Vickers; c Leaellyn & Timothy. *Educ:* Univ Calif, Berkeley, AB, 64, MA, 67; Columbia Univ, PhD(geol), 73. *Honors & Awards:* Michael Daley Award, 93; Whitley Award, Royal Zool Soc NSW. *Prof Exp:* Comput programmer, Lawrence Radiation Lab, Univ Calif, 64-67; lab tech, Am Mus Natural Hist, 71-73. *Mem:* Soc Vert Paleont; AAAS; Geol Soc Australia; Australian Mammal Soc. *Res:* Documentation of the origin and evolution of the Australian mammal fauna; documentation of Australian polar dinosaurs and reconstructing their paleoenvironment; new fossil localities. *Mailing Add:* Victoria Mus PO Box 666E Melbourne 3001 Australia. *Fax:* 61-3-9663-3669; *E-Mail:* trich@genoa.mov.vic.gov.au

RICH, TRAVIS DEAN, REPRODUCTIVE PHYSIOLOGY. *Current Pos:* BEEF NUTRITIONIST, MOORMAN MFG CO, RANGE NUTRITIONIST, 89- *Personal Data:* b Ryan, Okla, Oct 5, 40; m 64, Virginia L Vincent; c Russ T & Cory V. *Educ:* Okla State Univ, BS, 62, MS, 67; Purdue Univ, Lafayette, PhD(animal sci), 70. *Prof Exp:* Beef herdsman, Okla State Univ, 62-65, teaching asst animal sci, 65-67; res asst, Purdue Univ, Lafayette, 67-70; asst prof, SDak State Univ, 70-72; researcher beef cattle reprod, Res & Exten Ctr, Tex A&M Univ, 72-73; exten beef cattle specialist, Dept Animal Sci, Okla State Univ, 73-78, assoc prof animal sci & indust, 74-78; chief exec officer, Am Polled Hereford Asn, 79-89. *Mem:* Am Soc Animal Sci; Soc Study Reprod. *Res:* Beef cattle reproduction; endocrinology of postpartum period, puberty and superovulation; genetic improvement of beef cattle; physiology of reproduction. *Mailing Add:* 1406 Narcisco NE Albuquerque NM 87112. *Fax:* 505-323-2025

RICHARD, ALFRED JOSEPH, PHYSICAL CHEMISTRY. *Current Pos:* RETIRED. *Personal Data:* b Gardner, Mass, Mar 30, 28; m 54. *Educ:* Clark Univ, PhD(chem), 58. *Prof Exp:* Asst prof chem, Med Col Va, 58-64, assoc prof, 64-76, prof pharmaceut chem, 76-91. *Mem:* Am Chem Soc. *Res:* Physical properties of proteins; compressibilities of pure liquids. *Mailing Add:* Hwy 65 Prospect VA 23960

RICHARD, BENJAMIN H, STRUCTURAL GEOLOGY, GEOPHYSICS. *Current Pos:* asst prof, 66-70, ASSOC PROF GEOL, WRIGHT STATE UNIV, 70- *Personal Data:* b Phoenixville, Pa, May 6, 29. *Educ:* Va Polytech Inst, BS, 58; Ind Univ, MA, 61, PhD(geol), 66. *Prof Exp:* From instr to asst prof geol, Wittenberg Univ, 62-66. *Mem:* Nat Asn Geol Teachers; Sigma Xi. *Res:* Structural geology and geophysics; use of gravity to locate large pockets of gravel within glacial debris. *Mailing Add:* Dept Geol Sci Wright State Univ Dayton OH 45435

RICHARD, CHRISTOPHER ALAN, neural control of respiration, state-related control of respiration, for more information see previous edition

RICHARD, CLAUDE, BREEDING FOR DISEASE RESISTANCE, ROOT DISEASE. *Current Pos:* RETIRED. *Personal Data:* b Quebec City, Que, Mar 18, 44; m 67; c 2. *Educ:* Laval Univ, BSc, 67, MSc, 69, PhD(phytopath), 73. *Prof Exp:* Prof bot, Laval Univ, 72-73; res scientist agr, Agr Can, 73-96. *Concurrent Pos:* Ed, Phytoprotection, 82-85; asst ed, Can J Plant Path, 87-89, Can J Bot, 89-92. *Mem:* Can Phytopath Soc; Am Phytopath Soc. *Res:* Foliar and root diseases of forage legumes mainly alfalfa; selection of alfalfa for persistance and disease resistance; survey of alfalfa diseases; ice nucleation activity of bacteria and fungi. *Mailing Add:* 1056 Jean-Dumetz Ste-Foy PQ G1W 4K7 Can. *Fax:* 418-648-2402; *E-Mail:* richardc@qcrssf.agr.ca

RICHARD, CLAUDE, plasma physics, optical physics, for more information see previous edition

RICHARD, JEAN-PAUL, EXPERIMENTAL PHYSICS. *Current Pos:* res assoc, 65-68, from asst prof to assoc prof, 68-81, PROF PHYSICS, UNIV MD, COLLEGE PARK, 81- *Personal Data:* b Quebec, Que, June 10, 36; m 63; c 2. *Educ:* Laval Univ, BA, 56, BS, 60; Univ Paris, DSpec(physics), 63, DSc(physics), 65. *Prof Exp:* Res attache physics, Nat Ctr Sci Res, France, 63-65. *Mem:* Am Inst Physics; Can Asn Physicists. *Res:* Gravity; astronomy; relativity; earth physics. *Mailing Add:* Dept Physics & Astron Univ Md College Park MD 20742

RICHARD, JOHN L, MYCOLOGY. *Current Pos:* Microbiologist, Nat Animal Dis Ctr, 63-90, RES LEADER, MYCOTOXIN RES UNIT, NAT CTR AGR UTILIZATION RES, USDA, 90- *Personal Data:* b Melbourne, Iowa, May 19, 38; m, Myrna Alters; c 4. *Educ:* Iowa State Univ, BS, 60, MS, 63, PhD(mycol), 68. *Concurrent Pos:* Chair, US-Japan Natural Resources Panel Toxic Microorganisms. *Mem:* Med Mycol Soc Americas; Am Soc Microbiol; Int Soc Human & Animal Mycol; Asn Off Anal Chemists; Sigma Xi. *Res:* Fluorescent antibody, cultural techniques, transmission and electron microscopy of Dermatophilus congolensis; equine ringworm; mycotoxicoses; effects of mycotoxins on immunity; aerosol-toxins and infectious fungal agents; avian aspergillosis; interactions of toxins with infectious disease; analysis of mycotoxins. *Mailing Add:* Nat Ctr Agr Utilization Res 1815 N University St Peoria IL 61604. *Fax:* 309-681-6686

RICHARD, JOHN P, BIOCHEMISTRY. *Current Pos:* PROF CHEM, STATE UNIV NY, BUFFALO, 93- *Personal Data:* US citizen. *Educ:* Ohio State Univ, BS, 74, PhD(chem), 79. *Prof Exp:* Teaching fel, Brandeis Univ, 79-82; res assoc, Fox Chase Cancer Ctr, 82-84; asst prof chem, Univ Ky, 85-93. *Concurrent Pos:* Res fel, Cambridge Univ, Eng, 84-85. *Mem:* Am Chem Soc; Am Soc Biol Chemists; AAAS. *Res:* Mechanism of enzyme action; mechanism of reaction of small molecules in solution. *Mailing Add:* Dept Chem State Univ NY 633 Natural Sci & Math Bldg Buffalo NY 14260

RICHARD, PATRICK, ELECTRON PHYSICS, ATOMIC PHYSICS. *Current Pos:* PROF PHYSICS, KANS STATE UNIV, 72- *Personal Data:* b Crowley, La, Apr 28, 38; m 60; c 2. *Educ:* Univ Southwestern La, BS, 61; Fla State Univ, PhD(physics), 64. *Prof Exp:* Res asst prof nuclear physics, Univ Wash, 65-68; from asst prof to prof physics, Univ Tex, Austin, 68-72. *Concurrent Pos:* Consult, Columbia Sci Res Inst, 69-71. *Mem:* Am Phys Soc. *Res:* Characteristic x-rays and Auger electons produced in collisions of energetic heavy ions with heavy atoms. *Mailing Add:* Dept Physics Cardwell Hall Kans State Univ Manhattan KS 66506

RICHARD, PIERRE JOSEPH HERVE, PALYNOLOGY, PALEOECOLOGY. *Current Pos:* PROF GEOG, UNIV MONTREAL, 76- *Personal Data:* b Montreal, Can, July 9, 46; m 70. *Educ:* Univ Laval, BS, 67; Univ Paris, DEA, 68; Univ Montpellier, Dr Etat, 76. *Prof Exp:* Prof bot, Univ Que, Chicoutimi, 71-76. *Mem:* Palynology Asn Fr Lang; Bot Asn Can; Can Quaternary Asn; Int Soc Limnol; Can Asn Palynology. *Res:* Pollen analysis of late Pleistocene deposits, mainly in Quebec, for paleobiogeographic reconstruction; pollen morphology and methodology, organic sediments and other microfossils. *Mailing Add:* Dept Geog Univ Montreal PO Box 6128 Montreal PQ H3C 3J7 Can

RICHARD, RALPH MICHAEL, STRUCTURAL ENGINEERING, SOLID MECHANICS. *Current Pos:* assoc prof, 63-65, PROF CIVIL ENG, UNIV ARIZ, 65- *Personal Data:* b South Bend, Ind, Dec 15, 30; m 61; c 3. *Educ:* Univ Notre Dame, BSCE, 52; Wash Univ, MSCE, 56; Purdue Univ, PhD(civil eng), 61. *Prof Exp:* Instr civil eng, Wash Univ, 55-56; engr, McDonnell Aircraft, McDonnell Douglas Corp, 56-58; res asst, Purdue Univ, 59-61; asst prof civil eng, Univ Notre Dame, 61-63. *Concurrent Pos:* Consult, US Dept Defense, 63-65, General Dynamics Corp, 66-72, Kitt Peak Nat Observ, 68-70, City Investing Co, Los Angeles, 72-78, Welton Becket & Assoc, 74-76 & US Ballistics Lab, Md, 78. *Mem:* Am Soc Civil Engrs; Am Acad Mech; Sigma Xi. *Res:* Aseismic design; steel connection design; lightweight high resolution optical structural systems. *Mailing Add:* 4421 E Coronado Dr Tucson AZ 85718-1521

RICHARD, RICHARD RAY, ORBITAL EXPERIMENTS, THERMAL MANAGEMENT. *Current Pos:* RETIRED. *Personal Data:* b Nederland, Tex, Sept 12, 27; m 55; c 2. *Educ:* Univ Tex, BS, 55. *Prof Exp:* Test engr instrumentation, Convair Div, Gen Dynamics Corp, 54-61; sr engr electronics, Brown Eng Co, Ala, 61-63; proj engr instrumentation, Manned Spacecraft Ctr, Johnson Space Ctr, NASA, 63-65, head measurement sect, 65-67, head infrared sect, 67-81, head adv progs, 81-92, exp integration mgr, 85-92. *Mem:* Instrument Soc Am. *Res:* Aircraft flutter prediction instrumentation; noncontacting vibration and measurement techniques; Saturn fuel measurement techniques; angular accelerometer and miscellaneous devices; development of digital sensing techniques; cryogenic refrigeration using molecular adsorption in zeolites for gas storage; raising operating temperature of photonic infrared detectors; granted one patent. *Mailing Add:* 8415 Delwin Houston TX 77034

RICHARD, ROBERT H(ENRY), electronic & systems engineering, for more information see previous edition

RICHARD, TERRY GORDON, ENGINEERING MECHANICS, METALLURGY. *Current Pos:* PROF ENG MECH, UNIV WIS-MADISON, 81- *Personal Data:* b Marshfield, Wis, Feb 25, 45; m 76; c 3. *Educ:* Univ Wis-Madison, BS, 68, MS, 69, PhD(eng mech), 73. *Prof Exp:* Engr, Owen Ayers & Assoc, 66-67 & Naval Weapons Ctr, 68; teaching asst mech, Univ Wis-Madison, 68-72, fel, 73-75; prof eng mech, Ohio State Univ, 75-81. *Concurrent Pos:* Res scientist, Kimberly Clark Corp, 69-70; consult, Battelle Mem Inst-Columbus Div, 76-79, Al Lee Corp, 77-80, Columbia Gas Corp, 79, Joint Implant Surgeons Inc, 79-81 & Sensotec Inc, 79-81. *Mem:* Soc Exp Stress Anal; Soc Adv Eng Educ; Sigma Xi; Am Soc Mech Engrs. *Res:* Photoelasticity, holography, fatigue, fracture mechanics and cryogenic materials characterization. *Mailing Add:* Dept Eng Mech 2316 Eng Hall Univ Wis 1415 Engineering Dr Madison WI 53706-1607

RICHARDS, A(LVIN) M(AURER), STRUCTURAL ENGINEERING. *Current Pos:* from asst prof to prof, 49-83, EMER PROF CIVIL ENG, UNIV AKRON, 83- *Personal Data:* b Akron, Ohio, Sept 24, 26; m 49; c 2. *Educ:* Univ Akron, BSCE, 48; Harvard Univ, MSCE, 49; Univ Cincinnati, PhD(struct), 68. *Prof Exp:* Designer, Barber & Magee, Ohio, 49. *Concurrent Pos:* Consult. *Mem:* Am Soc Civil Engrs. *Res:* Computer applications to structural design and to the instructional process. *Mailing Add:* 4067 Wilshire Circle Sarasota FL 34238

RICHARDS, ADRIAN F, marine science & technology management, for more information see previous edition

RICHARDS, ALBERT GLENN, insect physiology; deceased, see previous edition for last biography

RICHARDS, ALBERT GUSTAV, DENTAL RADIOLOGY, FLORAL RADIOGRAPHY. *Current Pos:* RETIRED. *Personal Data:* b Chicago, Ill, Jan 7, 17; m 42, Marian R Kauffman; c Jean, Kathleen, Susan, Joanne & Nancy. *Educ:* Univ Mich, BS, 40, MS, 43. *Honors & Awards:* Gold Medal, Photog Soc Am, 93. *Prof Exp:* From instr to prof dent, Univ Mich, Ann Arbor, 40-74, Marcus L Ward prof, 74-80. *Concurrent Pos:* Consult, Vet Admin Hosp, Ann Arbor, 54-, Nat Res Coun, 58, dent health proj, Dept HEW, 62- & Comt X-Ray Protection Dent Off, Nat Comn Radiation Protection, 63-; mem, Nat Adv Environ Coun, USPHS, 69-71. *Mem:* Am Dent Asn; Am Acad Dent Radiol; Acad Oral Roentgenol (pres, 62-63). *Res:* Electron microscopy, radiation hygiene and dosimetry in dentistry; radiographic technics for pedodontists and exodontists; erythema; dental and x-ray machine designs; invented dynamic tomography and dental x-ray technique trainer; 3-D x-rays of flowers. *Mailing Add:* 395 Rock Creek Dr Ann Arbor MI 48104

RICHARDS, CHARLES DAVIS, PLANT TAXONOMY. *Current Pos:* from instr to assoc prof, 52-63, PROF BOT, UNIV MAINE, ORONO, 63- *Personal Data:* b Cumberland, Md, May 14, 20; m 43; c 5. *Educ:* Wheaton Col, Ill, BA, 43; Univ Mich, MA, 47, PhD(bot), 52. *Prof Exp:* From instr to asst prof bot, Mich Col Mining & Technol, 47-50; instr, Univ Mich, 51. *Res:* Flora and grasses of Maine; plant ecology of Mt Kathdin; aquatic flowering plants; plant geography; rare and endangered plants. *Mailing Add:* 22 Spencer Orono ME 04473

RICHARDS, CHARLES NORMAN, PHYSICAL ORGANIC CHEMISTRY. *Current Pos:* SR RES CHEMIST, CORN PROD RES, ANHEUSER-BUSCH, INC, 68- *Personal Data:* b Buffalo, NY, Mar 3, 42. *Educ:* Canisius Col, BS, 64; Univ Hawaii, PhD(phys org chem), 68. *Mem:* Am Chem Soc. *Res:* Pyrolysis gas chromatography applied to synthetic and natural polymers; thermodynamic activation parameters in mixed aqueous systems; modified food starches. *Mailing Add:* 12215 Country Manor Lane St Louis MO 63141

RICHARDS, CLYDE RICH, DAIRY HUSBANDRY. *Current Pos:* RETIRED. *Personal Data:* b Paris, Idaho, June 9, 21; m 46, Carrol Maughan; c Russell, Keith & Debra. *Educ:* Utah State Agr Col, BS, 43; Cornell Univ, MS, 49, PhD(dairy husb), 50. *Prof Exp:* Asst animal husb, Cornell Univ, 46-50; lectr animal breeding, Super Sch Agr, Athens, Greece, 50-51; from asst prof to assoc prof animal indust, Univ Del, 51-61; dep asst adminr, USDA, 76-77, prin animal nutritionist, Coop State Res Serv, 61-83, dir, Int Feedstaffs Inst, Agr Res Serv & Utah State Univ, 83-85. *Mem:* AAAS; Am Inst Nutrit; Am Soc Animal Sci; Am Dairy Sci Asn; Sigma Xi. *Res:* Roughage digestibility using indicator techniques; nutrient content of lima bean silage; ketosis in dairy cattle; agricultural research programs at land grant colleges of 1890; research administration. *Mailing Add:* 1772 E 1400 N Logan UT 84341

RICHARDS, DALE OWEN, STATISTICS. *Current Pos:* RETIRED. *Personal Data:* b Morgan, Utah, July 4, 27; m 55; c 3. *Educ:* Utah State Univ, BS, 50; Iowa State Univ, MS, 57, PhD(statist, indust eng), 63. *Prof Exp:* Statistician, Gen Elec Co, 52-55; instr indust eng, Iowa State Univ, 55-59, asst prof, 59-63; from assoc prof to prof statist, Brigham Young Univ, 63-95, chmn dept, 66-69. *Concurrent Pos:* Consult, Am Can Co, 58; opers analyst, USAF contract, Iowa State Univ Standby Unit, 59-70; consult, Nuclear Div, Kaman Aircraft Corp, 60, CEIR, Inc, 65-70 & Andrulus Res Corp, 87-91. *Mem:* Am Statist Asn; Am Soc Qual Control. *Res:* Application of statistical and operations research techniques to industrial situations; SPC and TQM. *Mailing Add:* 3774 N 700 E Provo UT 84604

RICHARDS, EARL FREDERICK, ELECTRICAL ENGINEERING. *Current Pos:* from asst prof to prof, 62-92, EMER PROF ELEC ENG, UNIV MO, ROLLA, 92- *Personal Data:* b Detroit, Mich, Mar 11, 23; m 46, Marjorie Holt; c Dennis & Laura. *Educ:* Wayne State Univ, BS, 51; Mo Sch Mines & Metall, MS, 61; Univ Mo, PhD(elec eng), 71. *Prof Exp:* Engr elec, Electronic Control Corp, 51-52, Pa Salt Mfg Co, 52-54; instr elec, Mo Sch Mines & Metall, 58-61. *Concurrent Pos:* Lectr elec, Univ Detroit, 56-68; res engr, Argonne Nat Lab, 63; consult, Ford Motor Co, 66-67, Emerson Elec Co, 78-80, Magnetic Peripherals, 80, Wanlass Corp, 81, Pub Serv Comn Mo, 82, US Corps Engrs, 83, Asn Mo, 84-85, Fasco Industs, 91, Bussman Fuse, 91 & Black & Decker Corp, 92-93, C R Magnetics, 95, Tempel Steel Co, 96. *Mem:* Sigma Xi; Inst Elec & Electronics Engrs; Nat Soc Prof Engrs; Small Motors Mfrs Asn. *Res:* Linear and non-linear control systems theory; simulation and modelling techniques; digital filtering; power system analysis and stability; electrical machinery; author of over 75 publications in the area of power and control systems. *Mailing Add:* Dept Elec Eng Univ Mo Rolla MO 65401. *Fax:* 573-341-4532

RICHARDS, EDMUND A, PHYSIOLOGY, PHARMACOLOGY. *Current Pos:* PROF PHYSIOL, UNIV NORTHERN COLO, 69- *Personal Data:* b Grand Rapids, Mich, Jan 25, 35; m 56; c 2. *Educ:* Purdue Univ, BS, 57; Univ Ill, MS, 59, PhD(physiol), 65; Univ Stockholm, MD, 67. *Honors & Awards:* Int Pharmacol Award, 75; R A Gregory Award Med Res, 73; William S Merrill Award, 77. *Prof Exp:* Assoc pharmacologist, Eli Lilly & Co, 59-61; res assoc physiol, Univ Ill, 63-65; guest scientist, Karolinska Inst, Sweden, 65-67; assoc prof physiol, Baylor Univ Col Med, 67-69. *Concurrent Pos:* Int lectr, Gt Brit & Scand, 72; Astra Pharmaceut Co, Gen Mills, Inc, WHO, Int Drug Control, Foreign Med Schs & AIDS Int. *Mem:* Am Gastroenterol Soc; Am Physiol Soc; Am Inst Biol Sci; fel Royal Soc; Int Pharmacol Cong; NY Acad Sci; fel Royal Brit Med Soc. *Res:* Gastroenterological research related to pancreatic and gastric secretion and peptic ulceration; the transfer of pharmacological active drugs across the human placental membranes; pharmacology of smooth muscle. *Mailing Add:* Dept Biol Univ Northern Colo 2309 59th Ave Greeley CO 80634-8914

RICHARDS, F PAUL, FISHERY BIOLOGY, IMPACT ASSESSMENT. *Current Pos:* SR PROG DIR, EARTH TECH, 91- *Personal Data:* b Stoneham, Mass, Sept 22, 46; div, Joan; c 2. *Educ:* Univ Mass, Amherst, BS, 68; Univ Mass, Dartmouth, MS, 74. *Prof Exp:* Asst marine fishery biologist, Mass Div Marine Fisheries, 69; fishery biologist, Essex Marine Lab, 69-72; fisheries lab mgr, Environ Sci Div, NUS Corp, 74-76; aquatic ecol prog mgr, Ecol Analysts, Inc, 76-79; supvr, Ecol Sci & Planning Dept, Environ Div, Charles T Main Inc, 79-91. *Concurrent Pos:* Consult, US Army CEngr, 70-71. *Mem:* Am Fisheries Soc; Am Inst Fishery Res Biologists. *Res:* Identification, assessment and mitigation of the impacts of large capital project construction and operation on aquatic ecosystems; changes in distribution, behavior and population dynamics of fishes. *Mailing Add:* Earth Tech 196 Baker Ave Concord MA 01742. *Fax:* 978-371-2468; *E-Mail:* prichards@earthtech.com

RICHARDS, FRANK FREDERICK, BIOCHEMISTRY, MEDICINE. *Current Pos:* assoc prof med & microbiol, 68-74, PROF INTERNAL MED, SCH MED, 74-, DIR, YALE-MACARTHUR CTR MOLECULAR PARASITOL, YALE UNIV, 85- *Personal Data:* b London, Eng, Nov 14, 28; m 58; c 3. *Educ:* Cambridge Univ, BA, 53, MB, BChir, 56, MD, 63. *Prof Exp:* Intern surg, St Mary's Hosp, London, 57-58; intern med, Oxford Univ, 58; resident, Brompton Hosp, 59; sr resident invest med, St Mary's Hosp Med Sch, 59-60, lectr, 60-64; res assoc biochem, Harvard Med Sch, 64-66; assoc med, Mass Gen Hosp, 66-68. *Concurrent Pos:* Res fel biochem, St Mary's Hosp, London, 58-59; Am Heart Asn adv res fel, 64-66; estab investr, Am Heart Asn, 66-71. *Res:* Protein chemistry and molecular biology as applied to parasitology and virology; pulmonary disease. *Mailing Add:* 24 Huntington St New Haven CT 06511-8056

RICHARDS, FREDERIC MIDDLEBROOK, PROTEIN CHEMISTRY. *Current Pos:* from asst prof to prof biochem, 54-91, chmn, Dept Molecular Biophys & Biochem, 63-67 & 69-72, STERLING EMER PROF, 91- *Personal Data:* b New York, NY, Aug 19, 25; m 48, 58, Sarah Wheatland; c Sarah, Ruth (Gray) & George H. *Educ:* Mass Inst Technol, SB, 48; Harvard Univ, PhD, 52. *Hon Degrees:* DSc, Univ New Haven. *Honors & Awards:* Pfizer-Paul Lewis Award Enzyme Chem, 65; Kai Linderstrom-Lang Award, 78; Merck Prize, Am Soc Biochem & Molecular Biol, 88; Stein & Moore Prize, Protein Soc, 88. *Prof Exp:* Res fel phys chem, Harvard Univ, 52-53; dir, Jane Coffin Childs Mem Fund Med Res, 76-91. *Concurrent Pos:* Fel, Nat Res Coun, Carlsberg Lab, Copenhagen, Denmark, 54, NSF, Cambridge Univ, 55 & Guggenheim, 67. *Mem:* Nat Acad Sci; AAAS; Biophys Soc (pres, 72); Am Crystallog Asn; Am Soc Biochem & Molecular Biol (pres, 79). *Res:* Proteins. *Mailing Add:* 69 Andrews Rd Guilford CT 06437-3715

RICHARDS, FREDERICK, II, MEDICAL ONCOLOGY, HEMATOLOGY. *Current Pos:* instr med, 71-73, asst prof, 73-77, ASSOC PROF MED, BOWMAN GRAY SCH MED, 77- *Personal Data:* b Charleston, SC, Aug 28, 38; m 62, Anne I Walters; c Frederick, Laura A & Charles P. *Educ:* Davidson Col, BS, 60; Med Univ SC, MD, 64. *Prof Exp:* Chief internal med, USAF Hosp, Lubbock, Tex, 66-68. *Mem:* Am Soc Clin Oncol; Am Soc Hemat; AMA; fel Am Col Physicians; Am Asn Cancer Res. *Res:* Treatment of malignant disease and hematological conditions. *Mailing Add:* Med Ctr Blvd Winston-Salem NC 27157-1082

RICHARDS, GARY PAUL, VIROLOGY, ANALYTICAL METHODS RESEARCH. *Current Pos:* food inspector, Northeast Inspection Off, US Dept Com, Gloucester, Mass, 75-77, microbiologist, College Park Lab, Md, 77-78, dir, Bio Res & Testing Lab, 78-88, RES MICROBIOLOGIST, CHARLESTON LAB, SC, NAT MARINE FISHERIES SERV, NAT OCEANIC & ATMOSPHERIC ADMIN, US DEPT COM 78- *Personal Data:* b Springfield, Mass, June 4, 50; m 73; c 3. *Educ:* Univ NH, BA, 73. *Prof Exp:* Dir qual control & res, Rockland Shrimp Corp, Maine, 73-75. *Mem:* Am Soc Microbiol; Sigma Xi. *Res:* Human enteric viruses in shellfish including hepatitis A, polio, Norwalk and other viruses of public health significance; extraction and assay of viruses from contaminated shellfish; evaluate cell cultures for virus propagation and assay; development and evaluate molecular biology methods for virus detection. *Mailing Add:* 4391 Cloudmont Dr Hollywood SC 29449-5808

RICHARDS, GEOFFREY NORMAN, WOOD CHEMISTRY. *Current Pos:* RETIRED. *Personal Data:* b Eng, Apr, 3, 27; Australian citizen; m 50; c 3. *Educ:* Birmingham Univ, Eng, BSc, 48, PhD(chem), 51, DSc, 64. *Prof Exp:* Org chemist, Brit Rayon Res Asn, 51-57, sr org chemist, 58-60; dep dir res, AMF Brit Res Lab, 60-64; Nevitt prof chem, James Cook Univ, N Queensland, 65-85, dean fac sci, 71-74; prof & dir, Wood Chem Lab, Univ Mont, 85-96. *Concurrent Pos:* Asst prof biochem, Purdue Univ, 57-58; tech adv, Am Machine & Foundry Co, Europe, 64; vis prof, Univ Miami Med Sch, 69; counr, Australian Inst Nuclear Sci, 72-85; exec secy, Int Carbohydrate Orgn, 78-83. *Mem:* Fel Royal Soc Chem; fel Royal Australian Chem Inst. *Res:* Carbohydrate and polysaccharide chemistry; reaction mechanisms; digestion in ruminants; chemistry of marine mucins; sucrose chemistry and technology; wood chemistry and technology; biomass utilization, especially pyrolysis, gasification and combustion. *Mailing Add:* 400 Pattee Canyon Dr Missoula MT 59803

RICHARDS, GRAYDON EDWARD, SOIL FERTILITY. *Current Pos:* RETIRED. *Personal Data:* b Gilmer Co, WVa, July 2, 33; m 56, Patricia Royster; c Kent & Craig. *Educ:* WVa Univ, BS, 55; Ohio State Univ, MSc, 59, PhD(agron), 61. *Honors & Awards:* Jour Award, Am Soc Agron, 76. *Prof Exp:* Teacher high sch, WVa, 55-57; res asst agron, Ohio State Univ, 57-61; res agronomist, Int Minerals & Chem Corp, 61-67; sr res scientist & proj leader agron, Continental Oil Co, 67-70; regional agronomist, Agr Div, Olin Corp, 70-79; chief agronomist, Smith-Douglass Div, Borden Inc, 80; acct supvr fertilizer, Doane Agr Serv, 80-81; mgr, agr & tech serv, Vistron Corp, 81-83; assoc prof, Univ Ark, Northeast Res Exten Ctr, 84, head, Dept Agr & dir, Southwestern Res & Exten Ctr, Monticello Campus, 84-89; pres, Reeder Auto Parts Inc, 90-95. *Mem:* Am Soc Agron; Soil Sci Soc Am; Am Chem Soc. *Res:* Chemistry of soil potassium and essential micronutrient elements; plant growth regulators; micronutrient nutrition of plants; fertilization for optimum yields; efficient use of phosphatic fertilizer. *Mailing Add:* 914 Ann Dr Marshall MO 65340

RICHARDS, HUGH TAYLOR, NUCLEAR PHYSICS, ION SOURCES. *Current Pos:* res assoc nuclear physics, Univ Wis-Madison, 46-47, from asst prof to prof, 47-52, chmn, Dept Physics, 60-63, 66-69 & 85-88, assoc dean, Col Lett & Sci, 63-66, prof 52-88, EMER PROF, NUCLEAR PHYSICS, UNIV WIS-MADISON, 88- *Personal Data:* b Baca Co, Colo, Nov 7, 18; m 44, Mildred Paddock; c David, Thomas, John, Margaret, Beth & Robert. *Educ:* Park Col, BA, 39; Rice Inst, MA, 40, PhD(physics), 42. *Prof Exp:* Fel physics, Rice Univ, 39-41, asst physics, 41-42, res assoc uranium proj, Off Sci Res & Develop, 42; scientist, Univ Minn, 42-43 & Manhattan Dist, Los Alamos Sci Lab, 43-46. *Mem:* Fel Am Phys Soc; Am Asn Physics Teachers. *Res:* Nuclear scattering cross sections; yields and angular distributions of nuclear reactions; nuclear energy levels and reaction energies; isospin forbidden reactions; negative ion sources. *Mailing Add:* 1902 Arlington Pl Madison WI 53705-4002

RICHARDS, J SCOTT, REHABILITATION MEDICINE. *Current Pos:* from asst prof to assoc prof rehab med, 80-90, dir training med rehab, 85-87, DIR RES, UNIV ALA, BIRMINGHAM, 87-, PROF REHAB MED, 90- *Educ:* Oberlin Col, BA, 68; Univ Mich, MS, 73; Kent State Univ, PhD(psychol), 77. *Prof Exp:* Elem teacher, Detroit Pub Schs, 68-71; res asst, Inst Fisheries Res, 71-73; teaching asst, Kent State Univ, 73-74, psychol intern, 73-77. *Concurrent Pos:* Co-dir, Univ Ala Birmingham-SCI Care Syst & Nat Sci Statist Ctr, 89-; consult, Ctrs Dis Control & Nat Inst Disability & Rehab Res. *Mem:* Am Psychiat Asn. *Res:* Rehabilitation medicine. *Mailing Add:* Univ Ala Med Rehab Res/Training Univ Ala Birmingham State Sch Med 1717 Seventh Ave S Birmingham AL 35294-0001

RICHARDS, JACK LESTER, ORGANIC & PHOTOGRAPHIC CHEMISTRY. *Current Pos:* Sr res chemist, 69-76, tech assoc, 77-81, RES ASSOC, RES LABS, EASTMAN KODAK CO, 81- *Personal Data:* b Apr 29, 40; US citizen; m 64; c 2. *Educ:* Rochester Inst Technol, BS, 65; Univ Rochester, PhD(org chem), 70. *Mem:* Am Chem Soc. *Res:* Synthesis of organic compounds for applications in image formation systems; chemistry of organosulfur and organosulfur-nitrogen compounds; research and development work on color photographic systems; production and quality control of color photographic products; worldwide coordination of complex technical programs. *Mailing Add:* 2259 Latta Rd Rochester NY 14612

RICHARDS, JAMES AUSTIN, JR, PHYSICS. *Current Pos:* RETIRED. *Personal Data:* b Boston, Mass, Apr 15, 16; m 39; c 4. *Educ:* Oberlin Col, BA, 38; Duke Univ, PhD(physics), 42. *Prof Exp:* Instr physics, Bucknell Univ, 42-46; tutor physics & math, Olivet Col, 46-49; asst prof physics, Univ Minn, Duluth, 49-51; res physicist, Am Viscose Corp, 51-55; prof physics, Drexel Inst Technol, 55-65; dean instr, Community Col Philadelphia, 65-68; prof physics, State Univ NY Agr & Tech Col Delhi, 68-82, instrnl developer, 82-85. *Mem:* Soc Friends Kiwanis. *Res:* Atomic physics; nuclear science. *Mailing Add:* Box 162 Treadwell NY 13846

RICHARDS, JAMES FREDERICK, BIOCHEMISTRY. *Current Pos:* from instr to assoc prof, 60-75, PROF BIOCHEM, UNIV BC, 75- *Personal Data:* b Amherst Island, Ont, Mar 15, 27; div; c 3. *Educ:* Queen's Univ, Ont, BA, 49, MA, 52; Univ Western Ont, PhD(biochem), 58. *Prof Exp:* Nat Res Coun Can overseas fel biochem, Glasgow Univ, 59-60. *Mem:* Can Biochem Soc. *Res:* Polyamine metabolism and hormone function. *Mailing Add:* Food Sci Dept Univ BC Vancouver BC V6T 1Z4 Can

RICHARDS, JAMES L, OPERATIONS RESEARCH, COMPUTER SCIENCE. *Current Pos:* Asst prof math & comput sci, 76-81, assoc prof comput sci, 81-83, PROF COMPUT SCI, BEMIDJI STATE UNIV, 83- *Personal Data:* b Kankakee, Ill, Dec 26, 46; m 69; c 2. *Educ:* Ill State Univ, BS, 68; Univ Mo-Rolla, MS, 72, PhD(math), 76. *Mem:* Asn Comput Mach. *Res:* Integer programming, optimization theory and programming languages. *Mailing Add:* Dept Math & Comput Sci Bemidji State Univ Bemidji MN 56601-2699

RICHARDS, JOANNE S, REPRODUCTIVE ENDOCRINOLOGY. *Current Pos:* PROF, DEPT CELL BIOL, BAYLOR COL MED. *Personal Data:* b Exeter, NH, Apr 23, 45. *Educ:* Oberlin Col, BA, 67; Brown Univ, MAT, 68, PhD(physiol chem), 70. *Prof Exp:* Asst prof biol, Univ NDak, 70-71; fel, 71-73, instr, 73-74, asst prof reprod endocrinol, Univ Mich, 74- *Concurrent Pos:* Prin investr, NIH grants, 76-79; Nat Inst Child Health & Human Develop res career develop award, 78; res career develop award, NIH, 78-83. *Mem:* Endocrine Soc; Am Soc Cell Biol; Soc Study Reproduction. *Res:* Mammalian reproductive endocrinology; mechanisms of hormone action; ovarian cell physiology; molecular endocrinology. *Mailing Add:* Dept Cell Biol Baylor Col Med One Baylor Plaza Houston TX 77030-3498

RICHARDS, JOHN HALL, BIOCHEMISTRY. *Current Pos:* from asst prof to assoc prof, 57-70, PROF CHEM, CALIF INST TECHNOL, 70- *Personal Data:* b Berkeley, Calif, Mar 13, 30; m 54, 75; c 4. *Educ:* Univ Calif, BS, 51, PhD, 55; Oxford Univ, BSc, 53. *Honors & Awards:* Lalor Award, 56. *Prof Exp:* Instr chem, Harvard Univ, 55-57. *Concurrent Pos:* Consult, Appl Biosysts, E I du Pont de Nemours & Co. *Mem:* Am Chem Soc; Protein Soc. *Res:* Mechanism of protein function; molecular immunology. *Mailing Add:* Chem & Chem Eng Div 147-75 Calif Inst Technol Pasadena CA 91125

RICHARDS, JOSEPH DUDLEY, INDUSTRIAL CHEMISTRY. *Current Pos:* RETIRED. *Personal Data:* b Hanover, NH, Sept 13, 17; m 40, Audrey Hampton Samuels; c Gale E, Joseph D Jr, Tracey C & William H. *Educ:* Dartmouth Col, AB, 39. *Prof Exp:* Analyst, Duralyo Co, Pa, 39-40 & Weirton Steel Co, WVa, 40-41; spectrogr, Am Steel & Wire Co, Mass, 40-44, US Bur Mines, 44-45 & Nat Bur Stand, Washington, DC, 45; res chemist-in-chg, Instruments Lab, Chem & Pigment Div, SCM Corp, Baltimore, 45-50, res group leader chem pigment, Chem & Pigment Div, 50-57, asst to dir res, Pigments & Color Dept, 57-61, group leader new prod, 61-63, liaison mkt res, 63-66, mgr econ eval, Glidden-Durkee Div, 66-67, mgr new serv, 67-70, mgr com develop, 70-80, mgr spec sales & com develop, Pigments Group, 80-83. *Mem:* Am Chem Soc. *Res:* Emission spectroscopy; electron microscopy; x-ray diffraction; pigment and inorganic chemistry; research planning; chemical marketing. *Mailing Add:* 113 Tenbury Rd Lutherville MD 21093-6338

RICHARDS, KENNETH JULIAN, CHEMICAL METALLURGY, METALLURGICAL ENGINEERING. *Current Pos:* RETIRED. *Personal Data:* b Long Beach, Calif, Nov 29, 32; m 58; c 3. *Educ:* Univ Utah, Salt Lake City, BS, 56, PhD(metall eng), 62. *Prof Exp:* Process eng refining, Union Oil, 56; process eng fractionation, C F Braun, 57; develop eng rare earth separation, US Intel Agency, 57-59; group leader metals & ceramics res, Aerospace Res Labs, 62-67; sr scientist chem metall, Kennecott Copper Corp, 67-70, sect head refining res, 70-72, mgr process metall, 72-74, res dir, Metal Mining Div Res Ctr, 74-84; pres, Tech Div, Kerr-McGee Corp, 84-96. *Concurrent Pos:* Mat consult, Air Force Mat Lab, 65-67, Air Force Ballistics Missile Div, 65-67, & NASA, 65-67. *Mem:* Metall Soc; Am Inst Mining Metall & Petrol Eng; Am Soc Metals; Am Inst Chem Eng; Soc Mining Engrs. *Res:* Extractive metallurgy; process development; technical planning; research management. *Mailing Add:* 3701 Harris Dr Edmond OK 73013

RICHARDS, L(ORENZO) WILLARD, ATMOSPHERIC OPTICS. *Current Pos:* VPRES, SONOMA TECH, INC, 82- *Personal Data:* b Logan, Utah, July 11, 32; m 66, Nancy Cutter; c Michael & Martha. *Educ:* Calif Inst Technol, BS, 54; Harvard Univ, AM, 56, PhD, 60. *Prof Exp:* From instr to asst prof chem, Amherst Col, 59-66; indust res fel, Cabot Corp, 66-68, mem tech staff, 68-74; mem tech staff, Environ Monitoring & Serv Ctr, Rockwell Int, 74-79; sr proj mgr, Meteorol Res, Inc, 79-82. *Concurrent Pos:* USPHS fel, Univ Calif, Berkeley, 64-65; adj prof, Rensselaer Polytech Inst, 71-73. *Mem:* Am Chem Soc; Am Geophy Union; Optical Soc Am; Am Asn Aerosol Res; Air & Waste Mgt Asn. *Res:* Atmospheric chemistry; aerosols; light scattering by particles; multiple scattering of light; gas phase chemical kinetics; atmospheric sciences. *Mailing Add:* 5510 Skylane Blvd Suite 101 Santa Rosa CA 95403. *Fax:* 707-527-9398; *E-Mail:* will@sonomatech.com

RICHARDS, MARK P, BIOCHEMISTRY, PHYSIOLOGY. *Current Pos:* RES ANIMAL SCIENTIST, NONRUMINANT ANIMAL NUTRIT LAB, USDA, 79- *Educ:* Rutgers Univ, PhD(nutrit biochem), 77. *Mailing Add:* Growth Biol Lab USDA Bldg 200 Rm 201 Beltsville MD 20705

RICHARDS, MARVIN SHERRILL, organic chemistry; deceased, see previous edition for last biography

RICHARDS, NOLAN EARLE, DEVELOPMENT & TRANSITIONING, IMPROVED CELL TECHNOLOGY. *Personal Data:* b Kaitaia, NZ, Oct 27, 30; US citizen; m 54, Helen M Mackenzie; c Bruce E & Robin L. *Educ:* Univ Auckland, BSc, 51, MSc 52; Univ NZ, PhD(phys chem), 56. *Prof Exp:* Res fel electrochem, Univ Pa, 54-56; Stanley Elmore fel, Imp Col, London, 56-57; res & develop proj mgr, Reynolds Metals, 57-73, lab mgr, Mgf Technol Lab, 74-93. *Concurrent Pos:* Vis prof aluminum technol, Northern Univ Technol, China, 86, metall, Univ Auckland, 94 & electrochem, Tech Univ Norway, 94. *Mem:* Metall Soc. *Res:* Aluminum production, reduction process modernization, control and optimization of processes, cell design, raw material acquisition and reclamation, thermomechanical processing of alloys, and environmental compliance; development of life cycle analysis. *Mailing Add:* 117 Kingswood Dr Florence AL 35630. *Fax:* 205-766-1813

RICHARDS, NORVAL RICHARD, SOILS. *Current Pos:* RETIRED. *Personal Data:* b Ont, Can, July 2, 16; m 51; c 2. *Educ:* Univ Toronto, BSA, 38; Mich State Univ, MS, 46. *Hon Degrees:* DSc, Laval Univ, 67. *Prof Exp:* Agr res officer soil classification, Agr Res Br, Can, 38-50; prof soils & head dept, Univ Guelph, 50-62, dean, 62-72, prof land resource sci, Ont Agr Col, 72-81. *Concurrent Pos:* Chmn, Can Agr Res Coun, 75- *Mem:* Int Soil Sci Soc; fel Soil Conserv Soc Am; Can Soc Soil Sci (pres, 56); fel Agr Inst Can (pres, 75). *Res:* Soil classification. *Mailing Add:* 59 Green Guelph ON N1H 2H4 Can

RICHARDS, OLIVER CHRISTOPHER, BIOCHEMISTRY. *Current Pos:* from instr to asst prof, 65-72, ASSOC PROF BIOCHEM, COL MED, UNIV UTAH, 72- *Personal Data:* b Jamesburg, NJ, Jan 13, 33; m 63; c 2. *Educ:* Syracuse Univ, BS, 55; Univ Ill, PhD(biochem), 60. *Prof Exp:* NSF fel, Univ Minn, Minneapolis, 62-63; NSF fel, Univ Calif, Los Angeles, 63-64, res assoc, 64-65. *Mem:* Am Soc Biol Chemists. *Res:* Structure, replication and function of extranuclear DNAs in eukaryotes; replication of animal viruses. *Mailing Add:* Molec Biol & Biochem Univ Calif 3205 Biol Sci II Irvine CA 92717-0001

RICHARDS, PAUL BLAND, emergency management, disaster management, for more information see previous edition

RICHARDS, PAUL GRANSTON, SEISMIC WAVE PROPAGATION. *Current Pos:* from asst prof to assoc prof, Columbia Univ, 71-79, chmn dept, 80-83, assoc dir, Lamont-Doherty Geol Observ, 80-83, PROF GEOL SCI, COLUMBIA UNIV, 79-, MELLON PROF, 87- *Personal Data:* b Cirencester, Eng, Mar 31, 43; US citizen; m 68, Jody Porterfield; c Mark & Gillian. *Educ:* Univ Cambridge, BA, 65; Calif Inst Technol, MS, 66, PhD(geophys), 70. *Honors & Awards:* James B Macelwane Award, Am Geophys Union, 77. *Prof Exp:* Asst res geophysicist, Univ Calif, San Diego, 70-71. *Concurrent Pos:* Alfred P Sloan Found fel, 73-74; Am ed, Geophys J, Royal Astron Soc, 73-77; Guggenheim Found fel, 77-78; MacArthur Found fel, 81-86; William C Foster fel, US Arms Control & Disarmament Agency, 84-85, 93-94; pres, Seismol, Am Geol Union, 92-94. *Mem:* Seismol Soc Am; fel Am Geophys Union; Royal Astron Soc; Arms Control Asn; fel AAAS. *Res:* Co-author of 2 volumes text in quantitative seismology; interpretation of seismic signals to infer properties of the earth, and of earthquake and explosion sources; analysis of seismic data on nuclear explosions, and the relationship to nuclear test ban treaty verification. *Mailing Add:* Lamont-Doherty Earth Observ Rte 9W Palisades NY 10964. *E-Mail:* richards@lamont.columbia.edu

RICHARDS, PAUL LINFORD, INFRARED PHYSICS. *Current Pos:* PROF PHYSICS, UNIV CALIF, BERKELEY, 66- *Personal Data:* b Ithaca, NY, June 4, 34; m 65, Audrey Jarratt; c 2. *Educ:* Harvard Univ, AB, 56; Univ Calif, PhD(physics), 60. *Prof Exp:* NSF fel, Royal Soc Mond Lab, Cambridge Univ, 59-60; mem tech staff, Bell Labs, Inc, 60-66. *Concurrent Pos:* Miller Inst fac fel, 70-71, 87-88; Guggenheim fel, Cambridge Univ, 73-74; Alexander von Humboldt sr scientist, Max Planck Inst, Stuttgart, 82; vis prof, Ecole Normale Superieure, Paris, 84 & 95. *Mem:* Nat Acad Sci; Am Phys Soc; fel Am Acad Arts & Sci. *Res:* Astrophysics; low temperature solid state physics; far infrared; superconductivity; magnetic resonance. *Mailing Add:* Dept Physics Univ Calif Berkeley CA 94720-7300

RICHARDS, PETER MICHAEL, hydrogen in solids, kinetics of reactions, for more information see previous edition

RICHARDS, R RONALD, PHYSICAL CHEMISTRY. *Current Pos:* Assoc prof, 64-77, PROF CHEM, GREENVILLE COL, 77- *Personal Data:* b Wenatchee, Wash, Nov 22, 37; m 61; c 3. *Educ:* Seattle Pac Col, BS, 59; Univ Wash, PhD(phys chem), 64. *Concurrent Pos:* Fel, NASA Langley Res Ctr, Old Dom Univ, 71-72; res fel, Argonne Nat Lab, 78-79. *Mem:* Am Chem Soc. *Res:* Thermodynamics; kinetics; analysis. *Mailing Add:* Greenville Col 315 E College Ave Greenville IL 62246-1199

RICHARDS, RICHARD DAVISON, OPHTHALMOLOGY. *Current Pos:* PROF OPHTHAL & HEAD DEPT, SCH MED, UNIV MD, BALTIMORE CITY, 60- *Personal Data:* b Grand Haven, Mich, Mar 10, 27; m 50; c 3. *Educ:* Univ Mich, AB, 48, MD, 51; Univ Iowa, MSc, 57; Am Bd Ophthal, dipl, 58. *Prof Exp:* Asst prof ophthal, Col Med, Univ Iowa, 58-60. *Concurrent Pos:* Attend physician, Vet Admin Hosp, Iowa City, 58-60. *Mem:* AAAS; Asn Res Vision & Ophthal; Am Acad Ophthal & Otolaryngol; fel Am Col Surgeons; Am Ophthal Soc. *Res:* Radiation cataracts. *Mailing Add:* 6553 Diamond Hall Rd Easton MD 21601

RICHARDS, ROBERTA LYNNE, BIOCHEMISTRY, IMMUNOLOGY. *Current Pos:* Res chemist biochem & immunol lipids, Dept Immunol, 74-78, RES CHEMIST BIOCHEM & IMMUNOL LIPIDS, DEPT MEMBRANE BIOCHEM, WALTER REED ARMY INST RES, 78- *Personal Data:* b Salt Lake City, Utah, Apr 20, 45; m 76, James O; c Kathleen & Elena. *Educ:* Bucknell Univ, BS, 67; Purdue Univ, PhD(biochem), 74. *Mem:* AAAS; Am Oil Chemists Soc; Am Chem Soc; Am Asn Immunol. *Res:* Immunology of membrane lipids and liposomal model membranes; receptor functions of lipids; efficacy of liposomes as antigen carriers and adjuvants in vaccines. *Mailing Add:* Dept Membrane Biochem Walter Reed Army Inst Res Washington DC 20307-5100. *Fax:* 202-782-0721; *E-Mail:* dr.__roberts__owens@wrsmtp__ccmail.army.mil

RICHARDS, ROGER T(HOMAS), ACOUSTICS, PHYSICS. *Current Pos:* PHYSICIST, NAVAL UNDERWATER SYST CTR, 87- *Personal Data:* b Akron, Ohio, June 19, 42; m 86, Mary E. *Educ:* Westminster Col, Pa, BS, 64; Ohio Univ, MS, 68; Pa State Univ, PhD(acoust), 80. *Prof Exp:* Assoc engr, Transducer Lab, Gen Dynamics & Electronics, 68-69, engr, Acoust Dept, 69-71; NASA trainee, Pa State Univ, 71-74; staff assoc acoust, Appl Res Lab, 76-80; sr scientist, Bolt, Beranek & Newman, 84-87. *Concurrent Pos:* Consult electro-acoust res, State College, Pa, 73-75; grad asst, Pa State Univ, 74-80. *Mem:* AAAS; Acoust Soc Am; Am Inst Aeronaut & Astronaut; Nat Speleol Soc; Am Cryptographic Asn; NY Acad Sci. *Res:* Acoustic propagation and scattering; design of sonar transducers and arrays; sociological and psychological effects of noise pollution. *Mailing Add:* 169 Payer Lane Mystic CT 06355-1644. *Fax:* 401-841-6401; *E-Mail:* r.richards@npt.nuwc.navy.mil

RICHARDS, THOMAS L, MARINE BIOLOGY, ZOOLOGY. *Current Pos:* PROF BIOL, CALIF POLYTECH STATE UNIV, SAN LUIS OBISPO, 69- *Personal Data:* b Santa Monica, Calif, Feb 2, 42; m 65; c 4. *Educ:* Calif State Univ, Long Beach, BS, 64, MA, 66; Univ Maine, PhD(zool), 69. *Concurrent Pos:* Res assoc, Univ Malaysia, 76-77; res affil, Univ Hawaii Inst Marine Biol, 83-84; actg dir, Trop Agr Progs, Bigham Young Univ, Hawaii, 84-85; sabbatical, Darling Marine Sci Ctr, Univ Maine, 90. *Mem:* Marine Biol Asn UK; Sigma Xi; Am Soc Zool; Western Soc Naturalists. *Res:* Physiological ecology of intertidal invertebrates, adults and larvae, oyster and abalone mariculture; developmental biology of invertebrate meroplankton; fresh water prawn aquaculture; marine environmental education. *Mailing Add:* Biol Sci Calif Polytech State Univ 1 Poly View Dr San Luis Obispo CA 93407-0001

RICHARDS, VICTOR, SURGERY. *Current Pos:* RETIRED. *Personal Data:* b Ft Worth, Tex, June 4, 18; m 41; c 4. *Educ:* Stanford Univ, AB, 35, MD, 39; Am Bd Surg, dipl, 45; Bd Thoracic Surg, dipl, 45. *Honors & Awards:* Gold-Headed Cane lectr, Univ Calif Sch Med, 88. *Prof Exp:* From instr to prof surg, Sch Med, Stanford Univ, 42-59, chmn dept, 55-58, clin prof, 59-91; chief surg, Children's Hosp, 59-90; clin prof surg, Univ Calif, San Francisco, 65-91. *Concurrent Pos:* Commonwealth res fel, Harvard Univ, 50-51; mem spec comt, USPHS, 58-62; ed, Oncol, 68-70; mem surg study sect B, NIH; consult, USPHS, Letterman Gen, Oak Knoll Naval & Travis AFB Hosps. *Mem:* Soc Exp Biol & Med; Sigma Xi; Pan-Pac Surg Asn (vpres, 72-); Am Cancer Soc; Soc Surg Alimentary Tract (vpres, 72-73); Am Surg Soc; Am Thoracic Soc. *Res:* Cancer; cardiovascular surgery; transplantation and preservation of tissues and cells. *Mailing Add:* 1500 Heaven Hill Rd Sonoma CA 95476-3225

RICHARDS, W(ALTER) BRUCE, PHYSICS. *Current Pos:* from asst prof to assoc prof, 67-82, chmn, Physics Dept, 86-90, PROF PHYSICS, OBERLIN COL, 82-, ASSOC DEAN, COL ARTS & SCI, 96- *Personal Data:* b Cortland, Ohio, Jan 29, 41; m 96, Phyllis Gortain; c Michael & Katherine. *Educ:* Oberlin Col, AB, 61; Univ Calif, Berkeley, PhD(physics), 66. *Prof Exp:* Physicist, Lawrence Radiation Lab, 65-66; res assoc & lectr physics, Tufts Univ, 66-67. *Concurrent Pos:* Vis assoc prof physics, Case Western Res Univ, 81-82; NASA summer fac fel, Lewis Res Ctr, 83, 84. *Mem:* Acoust Soc Am; Am Asn Physics Teachers; Am Phys Soc; Sigma Xi. *Res:* Musical acoustics; physics of wind instruments. *Mailing Add:* Cox Admin Bldg Oberlin Col Oberlin OH 44074-1088. *Fax:* 440-775-6662; *E-Mail:* bruce.richards@oberlin.edu

RICHARDS, WILLIAM JOSEPH, ICHTHYOLOGY. *Current Pos:* SR SCIENTIST, SOUTHEAST FISHERIES CTR, 83- *Personal Data:* b Scranton, Pa, Apr 7, 36; m 58, Carol Stoodley; c James L, Joseph D & Robert P. *Educ:* Wesleyan Univ, BA, 58; State Univ NY, MS, 60; Cornell Univ, PhD(vert zool), 63. *Honors & Awards:* Silver Medal, US Dept Com. *Prof Exp:* Fishery biologist, Biol Lab, US Bur Com Fisheries, DC, 63-65, res syst zoologist, 65, Trop Atlantic Biol Lab, 65-71; zoologist & prog mgr, Nat Marine Fisheries Serv, 71-77, dir, Miami Lab, 77-83. *Concurrent Pos:* Mem working group, Food & Agr Orgn UN, 65-; adj asst prof, Inst Marine Sci, Univ Miami, 66-68, adj assoc prof, Rosenstiel Sch Marine & Atmospheric Sci, 68-74, adj prof, 74-; ed, Bull Marine Sci, 74-; sci ed, Nat Marine Fisheries Serv, 83-86. *Mem:* Am Soc Ichthyol & Herpet; Western Soc Naturalists; fel Am Inst Fishery Res Biologists; Sigma Xi. *Res:* Systematics of fishes, especially the study of larval pelagic fishes and the family Triglidae; recruitment mechanisms of fishes; larval fish ecology especially relating to physical oceanography and ocean climate. *Mailing Add:* Southeast Fisheries Ctr 75 Virginia Beach Dr Miami FL 33149. *Fax:* 305-361-4515; *E-Mail:* omnet: w.richards

RICHARDS, WILLIAM REESE, BIOCHEMISTRY, PROTEIN SCIENCE. *Current Pos:* from asst prof to assoc prof, 68-91, PROF CHEM, SIMON FRASER UNIV, 91- *Personal Data:* b Springfield, Mo, June 27, 38; wid; c Jeremy. *Educ:* Univ Calif, Riverside, AB, 61; Univ Calif, Berkeley, PhD(org chem), 66. *Prof Exp:* NIH fel chem dept, St Mary's Hosp Med Sch, Eng, 66-67; fel bact, Univ Calif, Los Angeles, 67-68. *Concurrent Pos:* Sabbatical leave microbiol, Univ Freiburg, WGer, 77-78; res scientist biochem, Univ Bristol, UK, 83-84; sabbatical leave molecular biol, Univ Sheffield, UK, 90. *Mem:* Am Soc Photobiol. *Res:* Biosynthesis of chlorophylls; affinity chromatography, photoaffinity labeling, and kinetic mechanisms of enzymes of chlorophyll synthesis; labeling of membrane proteins; regulation of bacteriochlorophyll synthesis. *Mailing Add:* Inst Molecular Biol & Biochem Simon Fraser Univ Burnaby BC V5A 1S6 Can. *Fax:* 604-291-5583; *E-Mail:* williamr@sfu.ca

RICHARDS, WINSTON ASHTON, MATHEMATICAL STATISTICS. *Current Pos:* ASSOC PROF MATH & STATIST, PA STATE UNIV, CAPITOL COL, 69- *Personal Data:* b Trinidad, WI; m 64, Kathleen Hoolihan; c Ashton, Winston, Marie, Michael, Bridgitte, Mary, Patricia & Edward. *Educ:* Marquette Univ, BS, 59, MS, 61; Univ Western Ont, MA, 66, PhD(math), 71. *Prof Exp:* Instr math, Aquinas Col, 60-61; chmn dept high sch, Mich, 64-65. *Concurrent Pos:* Pa State Univ res grant, 72-73; statist expert, Orgn Am States, 75-, Pa Dept Agr, 89, 90 & 91; consult training govt statisticians, Repub Trinidad, Tobago & eastern Caribbean, 76-81; consult, UN, 79; vis sr lectr, Univ West Indies, Trinidad, 80-81 & 81-82. *Mem:* Int Asn Surv Statisticians; Inst Math Statist; Math Asn Am; Can Math Cong; Am Statist Asn. *Res:* Exact distribution theory; n-dimensional geometry; mathematical modeling; national income; applied statistics. *Mailing Add:* Dept Math Pa State Univ Capitol Col Middletown PA 17057. *Fax:* 717-948-6401

RICHARDSON, ALBERT EDWARD, NUCLEAR FISSION, GAMMA SPECTROMETRY. *Current Pos:* asst prof, NMex State Univ, 55-60, assoc prof, 60-91, EMER ASSOC PROF PHYS CHEM, 91- *Personal Data:* b Lovelock, Nev, Feb 4, 29; m 59, Shirley Dial; c Corinne, Elisabeth, David, Margaret, Anne, John & Stephen. *Educ:* Univ Nev, BS, 50; Iowa State Univ, PhD(phys chem), 56. *Prof Exp:* Asst radiochem, Ames Lab, Iowa State Univ, 50-55. *Concurrent Pos:* Vis prof, Adams State Col, 63; consult, White Sands Missile Range, 65-71, contractor, 73-74, chemist, 81-88, res chemist, 88-92; US AEC fel, Univ Colo, 68-69; vis staff mem, Los Alamos Nat Lab, 75-80 & Sandia Lab, 83. *Mem:* Sigma Xi; Am Chem Soc. *Res:* Nuclear chemistry; activation analysis; hot atom chemistry; neutron radiography. *Mailing Add:* 2457 U 50 Rd Cedaredge CO 81413-4992. *E-Mail:* lovelock@wic.net

RICHARDSON, ALFRED, JR, ORGANIC CHEMISTRY. *Current Pos:* RETIRED. *Personal Data:* b Jersey City, NJ, Feb 18, 32; m 56; c 4. *Educ:* Rutgers Univ, BS, 53; Lehigh Univ, MS, 55, PhD(chem), 58. *Prof Exp:* Asst chem, Lehigh Univ, 53-58; proj leader med chem res, William S Merrell Co, Merrell Dow Pharmaceut Inc, 58-67, sect head org res, 67-71, mgr res info, Merrell-Nat Labs, 71-76, dir com develop, Richardson-Merrell Inc, 76-81, dir sci & com develop, 81-84, assoc dir drug reg, 84-92. *Concurrent Pos:* Lectr eve col, Univ Cincinnati, 66-70. *Mem:* AAAS; Am Chem Soc; Drug Info Asn; Am Inst Chemists; NY Acad Sci. *Res:* Medicinal chemistry; synthetic organic chemistry; interdisciplinary product development; licensing; health care products; regulatory affairs. *Mailing Add:* 6429 Revere Ave Taylor Park OH 45233

RICHARDSON, ALLAN CHARLES BARBOUR, RADIATION HEALTH, NUCLEAR PHYSICS. *Current Pos:* exec secy, Radiol Health Sci Training Comt, Environ Control Admin & Radiol Health Study Sect, US Environ Protection Agency, 69-72, spec asst sci coord & eval, Off Radiation Progs, 72-73, asst standard develop, 73-77, chief, Fed Guide Br, 77-80, chief, Gen Radiation Standards Br, 80-82, chief, Guides & Criteria Br, Off Radiation Progs, 82-90, DEP DIR, CRITERIA & STANDARDS DIV, OFF RADIATION & INDOOR AIR, US ENVIRON PROTECTION AGENCY, 90- *Personal Data:* b Toronto, Ont, July 14, 32; US citizen; m 56, 86, Sara Keeney; c David, Andrew, Michael, Jerome & Eden. *Educ:* Col William & Mary, BS, 54; Univ Md, MS, 58. *Honors & Awards:* Bronze Medals, US Environ Protection Agency, 73, 83 &92. *Prof Exp:* Physicist, Nat Bur Stand, 58-69. *Concurrent Pos:* Consult radiation protection policy, Nuclear Energy Agency, Orgn Econ Coop & Develop, Paris, 79- & Int Atomic Energy Agency, 82-; mem, Int Comn Radiol Protection, 93- *Mem:* Am Nuclear Soc; Health Physics Soc; Am Phys Soc. *Res:* National and international radiation protection policy and standards; fast neutron cross-sections; neutron age measurements. *Mailing Add:* Off Radiation & Indoor Air 6602J Environ Protection Agency 401 M St SW Washington DC 20460. *E-Mail:* richardson.allan@epamail.epa.gov

RICHARDSON, ALLYN (ST CLAIR), ENGINEERING. *Current Pos:* COMPUTILITY PERSONAL COMPUT & SMALL SYSTS SERV. *Personal Data:* b Edmonton, Alta, Nov 16, 18; nat US; wid; c 6. *Educ:* Univ BC, BASc, 41; Harvard Univ, SM, 49. *Prof Exp:* Asst chemist anal & process control, BC Pulp & Paper Co, Can, 41-42; from asst engr to sr engr, Can Dept Nat Health & Welfare, 42-46, dist engr pub health, 46-50; res engr hydraul, Harvard Univ, 50-53, res engr bact aerosol viability study, 53-54, res engr soil stabilization res, 54-55; sr engr, Radar Dept, Raytheon Co, 55-58; asst prof, Civil Eng & Dir, Fluid Network Lab, Tufts Univ, 58-59; proj dir, Instrumentation Res & Develop, United Res, Inc, 59-61 & Trans-Sonics, Inc, 61-65; res proj engr, WHO, 65-67; dir off res progs, Region I, Environ Protection Agency, 67-84. *Concurrent Pos:* Consult & vis prof sanit sci, Cent Univ Venezuela; staff adv res & educ projs, Am Region Hq, Wash, DC; consult, Univ Tehran; chmn, Bd Water Commn, 82- *Mem:* Am Water Works Asn; Inst Elec & Electronics Engrs-Computer Asn. *Res:* Methods for control and improvement of air, water and land environment; environmental needs and standards, especially water hygiene, water pollution control and solid wastes management; application of microcomputers in management of environmental control processes; application of microcomputers in small water supply systems design, expansion and management. *Mailing Add:* Computility Water Dept PO Box 257 West Groton MA 01472

RICHARDSON, ARLAN GILBERT, BIOCHEMISTRY, ORGANIC CHEMISTRY. *Current Pos:* STAFF, AUDIE L MURPHY MEM VET ADMIN HOSP, 90- *Personal Data:* b Beatrice, Nebr, Jan 23, 42; m 66. *Educ:* Peru State Col, BA, 63; Okla State Univ, PhD(biochem), 68. *Prof Exp:* Teaching asst biochem, Okla State Univ, 67-68; asst prof chem, Fort Lewis Col, 68-69; NIH fel biochem, Univ Minn, St Paul, 69-71; asst prof chem, Ill State Univ, 71-75, assoc prof chem & biol Sci, 71-90. *Mem:* AAAS; Am Chem Soc; Am Soc Microbiol; Sigma Xi. *Res:* Bacterial transformation and genetics; protein synthesis, especially the effect of various diets upon polysome profiles and protein synthesis in rat liver. *Mailing Add:* Audie L Murphy Mem Vet Admin Hosp 7400 Merton Mintar Blvd San Antonio TX 78284

RICHARDSON, ARTHUR JEROLD, AGRICULTURAL REMOTE SENSING, GEOGRAPHIC INFORMATION SYSTEMS. *Current Pos:* RETIRED. *Personal Data:* b Aransas Pass, Tex, Mar 16, 38; m 65; c 1. *Educ:* Tex Agr & Indust Col, BA, 65. *Prof Exp:* Mem staff phys sci tech, USDA, 67-68, physicist, 68-93. *Mem:* Am Soc Photogram. *Res:* Agricultural remote sensing; published studies using spectral radiometric measurements of crop and soil conditions in the field, from aircraft, and satellite multispectral sensors. *Mailing Add:* 2407 Trails End Kerrville TX 78028

RICHARDSON, BILLY, RESEARCH ADMINISTRATION. *Current Pos:* INDEPENDENT CONSULT, 93- *Personal Data:* b Channelview, Tex, June 20, 36. *Educ:* Tex A&M Univ, BS, 58, MS, 64, PhD(biol), 67. *Prof Exp:* Res technician, Tex A&M Univ, 58-59, instr floricult, 59-62; chief, Cellular Physiol Br, Environ Sci Div, USAF Sch Aerospace Med, 67-72, dep chief, Environ Sci Div, 72-73, chief, Crew Environ Br, 73-76, dep chief, Crew Technol Div, 76-78, chief, Biomet Div, 78-79, dir spec proj, 79-80, dir, Chem Defense Prog Off, 80-81, chief, Crew Technol Div, 81-82; tech dir, Pentagon, 82-87, prog exec, 87-89, dep asst to secy defense, Chem Matters, 89-93. *Concurrent Pos:* Consult, new fighter aircraft, Can Forces, 77-78. *Mem:* Fel Am Inst Chemists; assoc fel Aerospace Med Asn; Am Inst Biol Sci; Sigma Xi; Am Defense Preparedness Asn. *Res:* Steroid metabolism in plants; mechanism of oxygen toxicity; aerospace physiology; cellular and biochemical effects of environmental stresses; aircrew protection and life support systems; chemical warfare defense; biological warfare defense; chemical arms control; assistance to Russian chemical weapons destruction program. *Mailing Add:* 4611 Kimby Lane Aberdeen MD 21001

RICHARDSON, BOBBIE L, engineering; deceased, see previous edition for last biography

RICHARDSON, CHARLES, PROCESS DEVELOPMENT, TECHNOLOGY TRANSFER. *Current Pos:* DIR PROD & ENG, RIBI IMMUNOCHEM RES, 88- *Personal Data:* b Sewickley, Pa, Sept 6, 51. *Educ:* Carnegie-Mellon Univ, BS, 73; Univ Cincinnati, PhD(biol chem), 78. *Prof Exp:* Asst, Univ Cincinnati, 78-80; asst prof biochem, Univ Wyo, 80-83; vpres protein eng, Syntro Corp, 83-88. *Mem:* Fel Am Inst Chemists; AAAS; Am Chem Soc; Parenteral Drug Asn. *Res:* Scale up and transfer; production of biological immune modulaters for pharmaceutical use; protein design and expression of novel protein polymers. *Mailing Add:* 363 Poplar Lane Florence MT 59833-6834. *Fax:* 406-363-6129

RICHARDSON, CHARLES BONNER, PHYSICS. *Current Pos:* from asst prof to assoc prof, 66-74, PROF PHYSICS, UNIV ARK, FAYETTEVILLE, 74- *Personal Data:* b Dallas, Tex, Jan 18, 30;, 59; c 1. *Educ:* Univ Pittsburgh, BS, 57, PhD(physics), 62. *Prof Exp:* Res asst prof physics, Univ Wash, 62-66. *Concurrent Pos:* Vis scientist, Brookhaven Nat Labs, 83, Naval Res Labs, 87. *Mem:* Am Phys Soc. *Res:* Optics; atmospheric physics. *Mailing Add:* Dept Physics Univ Ark Fayetteville AR 72701-1202

RICHARDSON, CHARLES CLIFTON, BIOCHEMISTRY. *Current Pos:* from asst prof to assoc prof, Harvard Med Sch, 64-69, chmn dept, 78-87, PROF BIOCHEM, HARVARD MED SCH, 69-, EDWARD S WOOD PROF BIOCHEM, 79- *Personal Data:* b Wilson, NC, May 7, 35; m 61, Ute I Hanssum; c Thomas C & Matthew W. *Educ:* Duke Univ, BS, 59, MD, 60. *Hon Degrees:* AM, Harvard Univ, 67. *Honors & Awards:* Am Chem Soc Award in Biol Chem, Eli Lilly & Co, 68; Merit Award, NIH, 86; Merck Award Biochem & Molecular Biol, Am Soc Biochem & Molecular Biol, 96. *Prof Exp:* Intern med, Duke Univ, 60-61; res fel, Dept Biochem, Sch Med, Stanford Univ, 61-63. *Concurrent Pos:* Career Develop Award, NIH, 67-76; consult, physiol chem study sect, NIH, 70-74; assoc ed, Annual Rev Biochem, 72-83, ed, 83; mem, Nat Bd Med Examrs, 73-76, adv comt, nucleic acids & protein synthesis, Am Cancer Soc, 75-78, adv div, Max-Planck-Inst Moleculare Gentik, Berlin, 80-89, vis comt, Boston Biomed Res Found, 85- coun res & clin invest, Am Cancer Soc, 89-92; assoc, Helicon Found, San Diego, Ca, 83; bd dir, US Biochem Corp, Cleveland, 83-; mem sci adv comt, Genetics Inst, Cambridge, Mass, 86-; mem ed bd, J Biol Chem, 68-73, 84-88. *Mem:* Nat Acad Sci; Inst Med-Nat Acad Sci; Am Soc Biol Chemists; fel Am Acad Arts & Sci; Am Chem Soc. *Res:* DNA metabolism. *Mailing Add:* Dept Biol Chem & Molecular Pharmacol Harvard Med Sch 25 Shattuck St Boston MA 02115. *Fax:* 617-432-3362; *E-Mail:* ccr@bcmp.med.harvard.edu

RICHARDSON, CLARENCE ROBERT, PHYSICS. *Current Pos:* RETIRED. *Personal Data:* b Lovelock, Nev, Jan 10, 31; m 55, Donna Ames; c Karen & Jeffrey. *Educ:* Univ Nev, BS, 57; Johns Hopkins Univ, PhD(physics), 63. *Prof Exp:* Jr physicist, Naval Ord Test Sta, Calif, 57; physicist, Appl Physics Lab, Johns Hopkins Univ, 58-59; from asst physicist to assoc physicist, Brookhaven Nat Lab, 63-67; physicist high energy physics prog, Div Res, US AEC, 67-73, physicist nuclear sci prog, 73-75, dept mgr solar inst proj off, US Energy Res & Develop Admin, 75-76, dir prog planning div, 79, phys sci planning specialist, prog planning div, basic energy sci, 76-79, prog mgr medium energy nuclear physics, 79-90, dep dir, Nuclear Physics Div, Dept Energy, 90-94. *Concurrent Pos:* Vis physicist, Europ Lab Particle Physics, Switz, 70-71; co-chmn, Bubble Chamber Working Group, 73-74 & 78-79. *Mem:* Am Phys Soc. *Res:* Elementary particle research using bubble chambers; cta meson and omega hyperon discovery. *Mailing Add:* 337 Mountain Valley Dr Hendersonville NC 28739

RICHARDSON, CLARENCE WADE, HYDROLOGY, CIVIL ENGINEERING. *Current Pos:* Agr engr, Tex Agr Exp Sta, 64-65 & Agr Res Serv, 66-77, agr engr, Sci & Educ Admin-Fed Res, 78-80, res leader, 80-86, LAB DIR, AGR RES SERV, USDA, 86- *Personal Data:* b Temple, Tex, Nov 15, 42; m 64; c 3. *Educ:* Tex A&M Univ, BS, 64, MS, 66; Colo State Univ, PhD(civil eng), 76. *Honors & Awards:* Cert Merit, USDA, 81. *Mem:* Am Soc Agr Engrs; Soil Conserv Soc Am. *Res:* Deterministic hydrologic modeling; stochastic simulation of precipitation patterns; agricultural water quality. *Mailing Add:* USDA Agr Res Serv 808 E Blackland Rd Temple TX 76502-6712

RICHARDSON, CURTIS JOHN, WETLAND ECOLOGY, PLANT ECOLOGY. *Current Pos:* assoc prof, 77-87, prof resource ecol, Sch Forestry & Environ Studies & dep dir, Ecotoxicol Prog, 80-92, PROF ECOL, NICHOLOS SCH ENVIRON, 88-, DIR, WETLAND CTR, DUKE UNIV, 89- *Personal Data:* b Gouverneur, NY, July 27, 44; m 72, Carol; c John & Suzanne. *Educ:* State Univ NY, Cortland, BS, 66; Univ Tenn, PhD(ecol), 72. *Prof Exp:* Asst prof resource ecol, Sch Natural Resources, Univ Mich, 72-77, asst prof plant ecol, Biol Sta, 73. *Concurrent Pos:* Ecologist, AEC, 68; res fel ecol, Ecol Sci Div, Oak Ridge Nat Lab, 70-72. *Mem:* AAAS; Am Inst Biol Sci; Ecol Soc Am; Sigma Xi; Soil Sci Soc Am; Soc Wetland Scientists (pres, 87-88). *Res:* Ecosystem analysis of wetland and forest systems; linkages between terrestrial and aquatic ecosystems with an emphasis on phosphorus chemistry and biogeochemical cycles as influenced by man; plant stress physiology biomarker, and plant ecotoxicology. *Mailing Add:* Duke Wetland Ctr Duke Univ Durham NC 27708. *Fax:* 919-684-8741; *E-Mail:* curtr@env.duke.edu

RICHARDSON, DANIEL RAY, PHYSIOLOGY. *Current Pos:* asst prof, 70-74, ASSOC PROF PHYSIOL & BIOPHYS, SCH MED, UNIV KY, 74- *Personal Data:* b Martinsville, Ind, May 5, 39; m 59; c 2. *Educ:* Ind Univ, Bloomington, BA, 65, Ind Univ, Indianapolis, PhD(physiol), 69. *Prof Exp:* Fel, Univ Calif, San Diego, 69-70. *Mem:* Microcirc Soc; NY Acad Sci; Soc Exp Biol & Med; Am Heart Asn; Am Physiol Soc. *Res:* Studies of peripheral vascular dynamics in man and laboratory animal models. *Mailing Add:* Dept Physiol & Biophys Univ Ky Col Med Lexington KY 40536-0084

RICHARDSON, DAVID LOUIS, ORBITAL MECHANICS, PLANETARY MOTION. *Current Pos:* from asst prof to assoc prof, 77-88, PROF DYNAMICS & ORBITAL MECH, UNIV CINCINNATI, 89- *Personal Data:* b New York, NY, Sept 27, 48; c 2. *Educ:* Ind Univ, AB, 70; Cornell Univ, MS, 72, PhD(space mech), 77. *Prof Exp:* Struct analyst, US Naval Surface Weapons Lab, 73-74; orbital analyst, Comput Sci Corp, 74-77. *Concurrent Pos:* Prin investr, NSF, 78-80, 84-88; res worker, Nat Bur Stand, 80- *Mem:* Am Astron Soc; Int Astron Union; Am Astronaut Soc. *Res:* Planetary motion analysis; orbital dynamics of artificial satellites; application of analytical and semi-analytical methods to the problems of space mechanics; dynamical systems. *Mailing Add:* Dept Aerospace Eng ML No 70 Univ Cincinnati Cincinnati OH 45221-0070

RICHARDSON, DAVID W, CARDIOLOGY. *Current Pos:* RETIRED. *Personal Data:* b Nanking, China, Mar 22, 25; US citizen; m 48, Frances Wingfield; c Donald, Sarah, David & John. *Educ:* Davidson Col, BS, 47; Harvard Med Sch, MD, 51. *Prof Exp:* Intern, Yale-New Haven Med Ctr, 51-52, asst resident, 52-53; from asst resident to resident, Med Col Va, 53-55, NIH fel cardiovasc physiol, 55-56; chief cardiovasc sect & assoc chief staff res, Vet Admin Hosp, 56-62; vis fel cardiovasc dis, Oxford Univ, 62-63; assoc prof med, Med Col Va, 63-67, prof med, 67-95, chmn div cardiol, 72-86, actg chmn dept, 73-74. *Concurrent Pos:* Fel coun clin cardiol, Am Heart Asn; consult, Vet Admin Coop Study Antihypertensive Agents, 62-82; Va Heart Asn Chair cardiovasc res, Med Col Va, 62-71; vis prof, Inst Cardiovasc Res, Univ Milan, 71-72. *Mem:* Am Fedn Clin Res; Am Clin & Climat Asn; Am Soc Clin Invest; fel Am Col Physicians; fel Am Col Cardiol. *Res:* Clinical hypertension and cardiology; prevention of myocardial infarction; neural control of circulation; cardiac arrhythmias. *Mailing Add:* 5501 Queensbury Rd Richmond VA 23226-2121. *Fax:* 804-288-3929; *E-Mail:* dwrichards@ruby.vcu.edu

RICHARDSON, DON ORLAND, ANIMAL SCIENCE, DAIRY SCIENCE. *Current Pos:* asst prof dairy sci, Univ Tenn, 63-67, assoc prof dairying, 67-72, assoc prof, 72-75, PROF ANIMAL SCI, UNIV TENN, KNOXVILLE, 75-, DEAN. *Personal Data:* b Auglaize Co, Ohio, May 12, 34; c 4. *Educ:* Ohio State Univ, BS, 56, MS, 57 & PhD(animal breeding), 61. *Prof Exp:* Asst dairy breeding, Ohio State Univ, 56-58, instr, 60; dairy husbandman, Agr Res Serv, USDA, 58-61, dairy genetist, 61-63. *Mem:* Am Dairy Sci Asn. *Res:* Evaluation of progress resulting from various selection schemes utilized with daity cattle, including an evaluation of correlated responses to single trait selection on milk yield. *Mailing Add:* 7732 Luxmore Dr Knoxville TN 37919-6807

RICHARDSON, DONALD EDWARD, NEUROSURGERY. *Current Pos:* Assoc prof, 64-74, PROF & CHMN DEPT NEUROSURG, TULANE UNIV, SCH MED, 80-; DIR, PAIN TREAT CTR, HOTEL DIEU HOSPITAL, NEW ORLEANS, LA, 78- *Personal Data:* b Vicksburg, Miss, Oct 5, 31; div; c 5. *Educ:* Millsaps Col, BS, 53; Tulane Univ, MD, 57. *Concurrent Pos:* Assoc clin prof neurosurg, La State Univ, Med Ctr, New Orleans, 74-80. *Mem:* AAAS; AMA; Am Asn Neurol Surg; Am Col Surgeons; Int Soc Res Stereonencephalotomy. *Res:* Clinical and research neurosurgery; basic neurophysical research; electrophysiology of the sensory system of spinal cord and brain. *Mailing Add:* Tulane Med Ctr Hosp & Clin 1415 Tulane Ave New Orleans LA 70112-2605

RICHARDSON, EDWARD HENDERSON, JR, OBSTETRICS & GYNECOLOGY. *Current Pos:* RETIRED. *Personal Data:* b Baltimore, Md, Dec 24, 11; m 48; c 3. *Educ:* Princeton Univ, AB, 34; Johns Hopkins Univ, MD, 38; Am Bd Obstet & Gynec, dipl, 47. *Prof Exp:* From instr to asst prof, Sch Med, Johns Hopkins Univ, 43-59, emer prof gynec, 82- *Concurrent Pos:* Consult, Vet Admin Hosp, Baltimore, Md. *Mem:* Fel Am Col Obstet & Gynec. *Res:* Female urology. *Mailing Add:* 304 Northwind Rd Baltimore MD 21204-6728

RICHARDSON, ELISHA ROSCOE, ORTHODONTICS, ANATOMY. *Current Pos:* from asst prof dent radiol to assoc prof orthod, 62-76, prof & dir postgrad educ, 67-85, assoc dean, 77-85, PROF & DEAN, SCH DENT, MEHARRY MED COL, 88- *Personal Data:* b Monroe, La, Aug 15, 31; m 67; c 3. *Educ:* Southern Univ, BS, 51; Meharry Med Col, DDS, 55; Univ Ill, MS, 63; Univ Mich, PhD(Human growth & develop), 88. *Prof Exp:* NIH fel, Univ Ill, 60-62; prof & chmn, dept orthod, Univ Colo, 85-88. *Concurrent Pos:* Prin investr, Nat Inst Child Health & Human Develop, res grant, 65-68; guest lectr, John F Kennedy Ctr Res Educ & Human Develop, 66-68 & George Peabody Col, 66-68; prin investr, Nat Inst Dent Res grant, 68; consult, Vet Admin Hosp, Nashville, Tenn, 68; pres, Craniofacial Biol Group, Int Asn Dent Res, 78-79. *Mem:* Am Dent Asn; Am Asn Orthod; fel Am Col Dentists; Int Asn Dent Res; NY Acad Sci. *Res:* Craniofacial region; maxillary growth; periodontal membrane; uvula and tongue; tooth size and eruption, growth of face and jaws. *Mailing Add:* 5325 Forest Acres Dr Nashville TN 37220

RICHARDSON, ERIC HARVEY, APPLIED OPTICS, ASTRONOMY. *Current Pos:* CONSULT, EHR OPTICAL SYSTS, 91-; ADJ PROF, UNIV VICTORIA, 91- *Personal Data:* b Portland, Ore, Aug 14, 27; Can citizen; m 78. *Educ:* Univ BC, BA, 49, MA, 51; Univ Toronto, PhD(molecular spectros), 59. *Honors & Awards:* N Copernicus Medal, Poland, 73. *Prof Exp:* Res asst, Gen Elec Co, Stanmore Labs, London, 52-53; res asst, Dominion Astrophys Observ, 54-57, res officer, 59-91. *Concurrent Pos:* Optical consult, NASA Lunar Laser Ranging Exp, McDonald Observ, 69, Can-France-Hawaii Telescope Corp, 73-78, Viking Satellite, 81-85 & NASA Astrometric Space Telescope proposal, 85; mem, high resolution camera instrument definition team, large space telescope, NASA, 73-75; co-investr, Space Shuttle, 85- *Mem:* Int Astron Union; Soc Photo-Optical Instrumentation Engrs. *Res:* Optical design of space and ground based telescopes and associated instruments. *Mailing Add:* 1871 Elmhurst Pl Victoria BC V8N 1R1 Can

RICHARDSON, EVERETT V, HYDRAULICS, HYDROLOGY. *Current Pos:* assoc prof civil eng, Colo State Univ, 65-68, adminr, Eng Res Ctr, 68-83, dir, Hydraul Lab, 83-88, prof 68-88, prof-in-charge, Hydraul Prog, 83-88, trans prof, 88-94, EMER PROF CIVIL ENG, COLO STATE UNIV, 94- *Personal Data:* b Scottsbluff, Nebr, Jan 5, 24; m 48, Billie A Kleckner; c Thomas E, Gail L (Frick) & Jerry R. *Educ:* Colo State Univ, BS, 49, MS, 60, PhD(civil eng), 65. *Honors & Awards:* J C Stevens Award, Am Soc Civil Engrs, 61, Hydraul Div Task Comt Excellence Award, 93, Hans Albert Einstein Award, 96. *Prof Exp:* Hydraul engr, Wyo Qual Water Br, US Geol Surv, 49-53 & Iowa Surface Water Br, 53-56, res hydraul engr, Water Resources Div, 56-68. *Concurrent Pos:* Consult, US Bur Pub Rd, 65-, US CEngr, 67-, World Bank Reconstruct & Develop, 70-, Colo Hwy Dept, 74-, US Bur Reclamation, 74- & USAID, 76-, US Transp Safety Bd, 87-88; dir, USAID Prog, Colo State Univ, 74-76, proj dir, Egypt Water Use & Mgt, 77-85 & Eygpt Irrigation Improv & Res Proj, 85-; mem joint workshop on res mgt, Nat Acad Sci/Egypt Nat Acad Sci, 75; mem, Int Comn Irrigation & Drainage, AAAS, NY State Bridge Safety Assurance Task Force, 88-90; sr assoc, Resource Consults Inc, Ft Collins, Colo, 88-94; chmn Task Force Bridge Scour, Am Soc Civil Engrs, 90-96. *Mem:* Am Soc Civil Engrs; Sigma Xi. *Res:* Internal structure of turbulent shear flow; diffusion of waste in natural streams; measurement of fluid flow; erosion and sedimentation, river mechanics, irrigation and water management, scour of bridges. *Mailing Add:* Ayres Assoc PO Box 270460 Ft Collins CO 80527. *Fax:* 970-223-5578

RICHARDSON, F C, BOTANY. *Current Pos:* CHANCELLOR, IND UNIV SE, 96- *Personal Data:* b Whitehaven, Tenn, Sept 22, 36; m 60; c 2. *Educ:* Rust Col, BA, 60; Atlanta Univ, MSc, 64; Univ Calif, Santa Barbara, PhD(bot), 67. *Prof Exp:* Asst prof bot, Ind Univ Northwest, 67-71, assoc prof bot & chmn dept, 71-72, dean arts & sci, 72-84, prof bot, 82; vpres acad affairs, Jackson State Univ, 84-85; vpres acad affairs, Moorhead State Univ, 85-89; pres, Buffalo State Col, 89-96. *Mem:* Am Inst Biol Sci; Bot Soc Am; Int Soc Plant Morphol; Am Asn Higher Educ; Am Asn State Cols & Univ. *Res:* Plant morphology; origin and evolution of the angiosperms using the anatomy and development of the flower, particularly the carpel, as the primary tool; nodal anatomy of elm species in connection with Dutch elm succeptibility in the family. *Mailing Add:* Univ Ind SE 4201 Grant Line Rd New Albany IN 47150

RICHARDSON, FRANCES MARIAN, CHEMICAL & BIOMEDICAL ENGINEERING. *Current Pos:* res assoc, NC State Univ, 51-60, assoc dir, res assoc prof eng res, 60-80, eng oper prog, 80-85, dir, extradept degree progs, Col Eng, 85-89, from assoc prof to prof, 90-92, EMER PROF BIOL & AGR ENG, NC STATE UNIV, 92- *Personal Data:* b Roanoke, Va, May 6, 22. *Educ:* Roanoke Col, BS, 43; Univ Cincinnati, MS, 47. *Prof Exp:* Chemist, E I du Pont de Nemours & Co, 43-45; asst chem, Univ Cincinnati, 45-47; res chemist, Leas & McVitty, Inc, 48-49. *Concurrent Pos:* Vis assoc prof, Case Western Reserve Univ, 67-68. *Mem:* AAAS; Royal Soc Health; Soc Women Engrs; Am Inst Chem Engrs; Sigma Xi; Am Chem Soc. *Res:* Infrared imaging thermography; biomedical engineering; fluid flow; flow visualization. *Mailing Add:* NC State Univ 184 Weaver Labs Raleigh NC 27695-7625. *E-Mail:* billie@richardson@ncsu.edu

RICHARDSON, FREDERICK S, THEORETICAL CHEMISTRY, PHYSICAL CHEMISTRY. *Current Pos:* from asst prof to prof, 69-91, chair, Chem Dept, 83-87 & 92-97, COMMONWEALTH PROF CHEM, UNIV VA, 91- *Personal Data:* b Carlisle, Pa, June 8, 39; m 59, Joan MacMillan; c Julie, Elizabeth, Christine & Jonathan. *Educ:* Dickinson Col, BS, 61; Princeton Univ, MA, 63, PhD(chem), 66. *Prof Exp:* Instr chem, Princeton Univ, 65-66; officer, US Army CEngr, 66-68; fel, Univ Calif, San Diego, 68-69. *Mem:* AAAS; Am Chem Soc; Am Phys Soc. *Res:* Theoretical and experimental aspects of molecular electronic spectroscopy; optical properties of lanthanide ions and complexes; natural and magnetic optical activity in molecules and crystals; coupling of electronic states by molecular vibrations. *Mailing Add:* Dept Chem Univ Va Charlottesville VA 22901. *Fax:* 804-924-3966; *E-Mail:* far@virginia.edu

RICHARDSON, GARY HAIGHT, DAIRY CHEMISTRY, DAIRY MICROBIOLOGY. *Current Pos:* prof diary & food sci, 67-73, prof nutrit & food sci, 73-90, EMER PROF, NUTRIT & FOOD SCI, UTAH STATE UNIV, 89- *Personal Data:* b Grace, Idaho, Nov 30, 31; m 54; c 6. *Educ:* Utah State Agr Col, BS, 53; Univ Wis, PhD(dairy & food industs), 60. *Prof Exp:* Dairy chemist, Res Labs, Swift & Co, Ill, 59-61; res mgr, Dairyland Food Labs, Inc, Wis, 61-63, res dir, 63-67. *Concurrent Pos:* Dairyland Food Labs, Inc grant, 68-; USPHS grant, 69-72; Kellogg fel, Univ Col, Cork, Ireland, 81. *Mem:* Am Dairy Sci Asn; Inst Food Technol; Am Soc Microbiol; Inst Asn Milk, Food & Environ Sanit. *Res:* Dairy cultures; dehydration; accelerated cheese flavor development; enzyme utilization in production of dairy flavors; staphylococcal enterotoxin production in cheese products; prevention of defects in Swiss cheese; assay of milk constitutents. *Mailing Add:* Dept Nutrit & Food Sci Utah State Univ 750 N 1200 E Logan UT 84322-8700

RICHARDSON, GEORGE S, ENDOCRINOLOGY, GYNECOLOGY. *Current Pos:* clin assoc, 59-71, asst prof, 71-74, ASSOC PROF SURG, HARVARD MED SCH, 74- *Personal Data:* b Boston, Mass, Dec 1, 21; m 58; c 3. *Educ:* Harvard Univ, BA, 43, MD, 46. *Hon Degrees:* LHD, Emerson Col, 64. *Prof Exp:* From intern to resident surg, Mass Gen Hosp, 46-55; instr surg, Harvard Med Sch, 54-55; asst, Mass Gen Hosp, 55-59. *Concurrent Pos:* Res fel physiol, Harvard Med Sch, 47-48; NIH res grants, 58-; assoc vis surgeon, Mass Gen Hosp, 64-75, vis surgeon, 76-, gynecologist, 77-; Nat Cancer Inst spec fel, SW Found Res & Educ, 69-71. *Mem:* Am Fertil Soc; Endocrine Soc; Soc Pelvic Surgeons; Am Col Surgeons. *Res:* Steroid hormones in relation to neoplasia; human endometrium. *Mailing Add:* Mass Gen Hosp Boston MA 02114

RICHARDSON, GERALD LAVERNE, CHEMICAL ENGINEERING. *Current Pos:* RETIRED. *Personal Data:* b Ft Morgan, Colo, Sept 21, 28. *Educ:* Univ Colo, BS, 50. *Prof Exp:* Jr engr, Hanford Atomic Prod Div, Gen Elec Co, 50-55, engr, 55-62, sr engr, 62-65; sr develop engr, Pac Northwest Lab, Battelle Mem Inst, 65-69, res assoc, 69-70; prin engr, Westinghouse Hanford Co, 70-79, fel engr, 79-84. *Res:* Separation and purification of radioactive isotopes from irradiated uranium; development of solvent extraction processes and equipment; nuclear fuel cycle waste management. *Mailing Add:* 1109 Pine St Richland WA 99352-2135

RICHARDSON, GRAHAM MCGAVOCK, ORGANIC CHEMISTRY. *Current Pos:* RETIRED. *Personal Data:* b Emory, Va, Jan 10, 12; m 40, Mary Cook; c Janet (Sky), Lisa (Troutman) & Mary. *Educ:* Univ Tenn, BS, 34; Mass Inst Technol, PhD(org chem), 39. *Prof Exp:* Chemist, Acetate Yarn Div, Tenn Eastman Corp, 34-36; instr chem, Franklin Tech Inst, Boston, 38-39; chemist, E I Du Pont de Nemours & Co, Inc, 39-42 & 44-51, supvr, 42-44 & 51-62, specialist textile fibers, dyeing & finishing, 62-76; dir res & develop, Lutex Chem Corp, 76-86. *Mem:* Am Asn Textile Chem & Colorists; Am Asn Textile Technol; Am Soc Testing & Mat. *Res:* Process development of dyes; dyeing; organo sodium compounds; detergents; wetting agents; textile processing and finishing; cosmetics; vinyl polymers; flammability test methods for textile materials. *Mailing Add:* Box 3654 Greenville Wilmington DE 19807

RICHARDSON, GRANT LEE, AGRONOMY. *Current Pos:* RETIRED. *Personal Data:* b Safford, Ariz, June 20, 19; m 43; c 6. *Educ:* Univ Ariz, BS, 47, MS, 48; Ore State Col, PhD(farm crops), 50. *Prof Exp:* Asst prof agron, Purdue Univ, 50-53; assoc prof, 53-57, prof agron, Ariz State Univ, 57-83. *Concurrent Pos:* Team leader, Ariz State Univ-Kufra Agr Team, 73-77; res agron, Wash State Univ, 84-86; res dir, Univ Wyo, 88-89. *Mem:* Crop Sci Soc Am; Am Soc Agron. *Res:* Crop production in arid regions; crop physiology. *Mailing Add:* 1550 N Stapley 134 Mesa AZ 85223

RICHARDSON, HAROLD, MEDICAL MICROBIOLOGY. *Current Pos:* assoc prof, 71-76, PROF MICROBIOL, MED CTR, MCMASTER UNIV, 76-. *Personal Data:* b Ferryhill, Eng, Apr 13, 38; m 60; c 3. *Educ:* Univ Durham, BSc, 59, MB, BS, 62; Univ Newcastle, Eng, MD, 68. *Honors & Awards:* Comdr, Order of St John of Jerusalem, 75. *Prof Exp:* Demonstr bact, Univ Newcastle, Eng, 63-64, lectr, 64-69, sr lectr microbiol, 69-71. *Concurrent Pos:* Consult, United Newcastle Upon Tyne Hosps, 69-71; dir med microbiol, McMaster Univ, 76-. *Mem:* Am Soc Clin Path; Am Soc Microbiol; Path Soc Gt Brit & Ireland. *Res:* Control of colicine production and role of colicinogeny in epidemiology of Escherichia coli infection. *Mailing Add:* Dept Microbiol Rm 2N30 Chedoke-McMaster Hosp Hamilton ON L8N 3Z5 Can

RICHARDSON, HENRY RUSSELL, SEARCH THEORY, STOCHASTIC PROCESSES. *Current Pos:* VPRES, METRON, 88-. *Personal Data:* b Pittsburgh, Pa, July 24, 38; m 60; c 2. *Educ:* Univ Pittsburgh, BS, 60; Brown Univ, MS, 62, PhD(math), 65. *Prof Exp:* Sr vpres, Daniel H Wagner Assoc, 64-85; vpres, Ctr Naval Analysis, 85-87; prof math & oper res, US Naval Acad, 87-88. *Mem:* Oper Res Soc Am; Inst Math Statist. *Res:* Application of probability theory to problems in search for lost objects and in financial portfolio optimization. *Mailing Add:* 5911 Colfax Ave Alexandria VA 22311

RICHARDSON, HERBERT HEATH, MECHANICAL ENGINEERING, TRANSPORTATION. *Current Pos:* dep chancellor & dean eng, Tex A&M Univ Syst, 84-91, dir, Tex Eng Exp Sta, 85-91, chancellor, 91-93, DIR, TEX TRANSP INST, TEX A&M UNIV SYST, ASSOC VICE CHANCELLOR ENG, ASSOC DEAN ENG, REGENTS PROF & DISTINGUISHED PROF ENG, 93-. *Personal Data:* b Lynn, Mass, Sept 24, 30; m 73, Barbara Ellsworth; c 5. *Educ:* Mass Inst Technol, SB & SM, 55, ScD(mech eng), 58. *Honors & Awards:* Moody Award, 70; Centennial Medal, Am Soc Mech Engrs, 80, Rufus Oldenberger Medal, 84; Secy Transp Medal, US Dept Transp, Distinguished Serv Medal. *Prof Exp:* Res engr, Dynamic Anal & Control Lab, Mass Inst Technol, 53-57, proj supvr, 57-58; ord officer, Ballistics Res Lab, US Army, Aberdeen, Md, 58-59; from asst prof to prof mech eng, Mass Inst Technol, 59-70, head, Systs & Design Div, Dept Mech Eng & Dir, Analog-Hybrid Comput Facil, 67-70; chief scientist, US Dept Transp, 70-72; prof, Mass Inst Technol, 72-84, head dept, 74-82, assoc dean, 82-84. *Concurrent Pos:* Sr consult, Foster-Miller Assocs, 58- & dir; mem bd dirs, TenX Corp, TechCom, Inc, & Tex Utilities Co. *Mem:* Nat Acad Eng; Am Soc Mech Educ; NY Acad Sci; fel AAAS; hon mem Am Soc Mech Engrs; Sigma Xi; Inst Elec & Electronics Engrs. *Res:* Dynamic systems; automatic control; lubrication; transportation; fluid mechanics. *Mailing Add:* Dir Tex Transp Inst CE/TTI Bldg Suite 801 Tex A&M Univ Syst College Station TX 77843-3135. *Fax:* 409-845-9356

RICHARDSON, J MARK, STOCHASTIC PROCESSES, MATHEMATICAL ANALYSIS. *Current Pos:* TECH STAFF, HALLIBURTON. *Personal Data:* b Duncan, Okla, Apr 27, 54. *Educ:* Okla State Univ, BS, 75, MS, 77, PhD(elec eng), 80. *Prof Exp:* Res assoc & teaching assoc circuit analysis, Okla State Univ, 75-80; mem tech staff, Sandia Nat Labs. *Concurrent Pos:* Software engr, Halliburton Co, 77; mem tech staff, Sandia Nat Labs, 78. *Mem:* Inst Elec & Electronics Engrs. *Res:* Stochastic integration and its relation to numerical integration; nuclear safety and safeguards at operating nuclear power plants and fuel cycle facilities; signal processing; estimation theory and techniques. *Mailing Add:* 913 W Chestnut Ave Duncan OK 73533-4448

RICHARDSON, J(OHN) STEVEN, PSYCHONEUROPHARMACOLOGY, NEUROCHEMISTRY. *Current Pos:* from asst prof to assoc prof, 76-83, PROF PHARMACOL, UNIV SASK, 83-. *Personal Data:* b London, Ont, Mar 24, 43; m 66, Arleen Kwasniewski; c Rob & Ethan. *Educ:* Univ Toronto, BA, 65; Univ Vt, MA, 68, PhD(psycho-pharmacol), 72. *Prof Exp:* neurochem & histopharmacol, Lab Clin Sci, NIMH, NIH, 71-73. *Concurrent Pos:* Consult, Dannemara State Hosp, NY, 68-71; med consult, Royal Univ Hosp, Saskatoon, 79-; consult, Forensic Psychopharmacol; vis assoc prof, Univ Conn, 81-82; dir, US Neurosci Inc, 93-. *Mem:* Can Col Neuropsychopharmacol; Am Soc Pharmacol & Exp Therapeut; Pharmacol Soc Can; Am Soc Neurochem; Int Soc Neurochem; Soc Neurosci; Can Asn Neurosci. *Res:* Neuropsychopharmacological and neurochemical analysis of brain function utilizing biochemical, histochemical, pharmacological and behavioral methodologies to elucidate the mechanisms whereby the limbic system and the basal ganglia exert homeostatic control over cognitive, emotional, hormonal, cardiovascular and motor activity. *Mailing Add:* Dept Pharmacol Col Med Univ Sask 107 Wiggins Rd Saskatoon SK S7N 5E5 Can. *Fax:* 306-966-6220

RICHARDSON, JAMES ALBERT, PHARMACOLOGY. *Current Pos:* instr physiol & pharmacol, Med Univ SC, 42-47, assoc pharmacol, 48, from asst prof to prof, 49-85, actg chmn dept, 71-72, EMER PROF PHARMACOL, MED UNIV SC, 85-. *Personal Data:* b Schenectady, NY, Jan 27, 15; m 49; c 4. *Educ:* Univ SC, BS, 36; Univ Miss, MS, 40; Univ Tenn, PhD(physiol), 49. *Prof Exp:* Instr pharmacy, Univ Miss, 40-41. *Mem:* AAAS; Am Soc Pharmacol & Exp Therapeut; Soc Exp Biol & Med; Am Fedn Clin Res; Sigma Xi. *Res:* Autonomic drugs; cardiovascular drugs; spinal anesthesia; toxicology of kerosene and decaborane; blood coagulation; catecholamines. *Mailing Add:* 1515 Burning Tree Rd Charleston SC 29412

RICHARDSON, JAMES T(HOMAS), CHEMICAL ENGINEERING. *Current Pos:* assoc prof, 69-70, PROF & CHMN CHEM ENG, UNIV HOUSTON, 70-. *Personal Data:* b Gillingham, Eng, Aug 5, 28; nat US; m 50; c 2. *Educ:* Rice Inst, BA, 50, MA, 54, PhD(physics), 55. *Prof Exp:* Jr chemist, Pan-Am Refining Corp, 50-52; Welch Found fel, Rice Inst, 55-56; res physicist, Humble Oil & Refining Co, 56-65, sr res physicist, Esso Res & Eng Co, 59-64, res specialist, 64-66, res assoc, 66-69. *Mem:* Am Phys Soc; Am Chem Soc; Sigma Xi; Am Inst Chem Engrs. *Res:* Mass and infrared spectroscopy; x-ray and electron diffraction; electron microscopy; adsorption; magnetism; low temperature physics; adiabatic demagnetization; catalysis; defect solid state; electron spin resonance. *Mailing Add:* Chem Eng Dept Univ Houston Houston TX 77204-4792

RICHARDSON, JAMES WYMAN, QUANTUM CHEMISTRY, THEORETICAL CHEMISTRY. *Current Pos:* from instr to assoc prof chem, 57-73, prof 73-95, EMER PROF CHEM, PURDUE UNIV, W LAFAYETTE, 95-. *Personal Data:* b Sioux Falls, SDak, Aug 8, 30; m 52, Eileen M Johnson; c Janilyn, James Jr, Barbara & Gregory. *Educ:* SDak Sch Mines & Technol, BS, 52; Iowa State Col, PhD(chem), 56. *Prof Exp:* Asst, Ames Lab, Iowa State Col, 53-56; res assoc physics, Univ Chicago, 56-57. *Concurrent Pos:* Visitor, Philips Res Labs, Neth, 67-68, Univ Groningen, Neth, 84, Univ Leiden, Neth, 84; assoc ed, J Solid State Chem, 84-. *Mem:* Am Chem Soc; Am Phys Soc; Mats Res Soc. *Res:* Theory of electronic properties of small molecules; transition-metal complex ions, and ionic solids. *Mailing Add:* Dept Chem 1393 Brown Bldg Purdue Univ West Lafayette IN 47907-1393. *Fax:* 765-494-0239

RICHARDSON, JANE S, BIOCHEMISTRY. *Current Pos:* assoc, Dept Anat, Duke Univ, 70-84, med res assoc prof, Depts Biochem & Anat, 84-88, med res assoc prof, 88-91, JAMES B DUKE PROF BIOCHEM, DEPT BIOCHEM, DUKE UNIV, 91-. *Personal Data:* b Teaneck, NJ, Jan 25, 41; m 63; c 2. *Educ:* Swarthmore Col, BA, 62; Harvard Univ, MA, 66, MAT, 66. *Hon Degrees:* DSc, Swarthmore Col, 86. *Honors & Awards:* MacArthur Award. *Prof Exp:* Tech asst, Dept Chem, Mass Inst Technol, 64-69; gen phys scientist, Lab Molecular Biol, Nat Inst Arthritis & Metab Dis, NIH, 69. *Concurrent Pos:* MacArthur Found Inst grant, 85-90; coun mem, Biophys Soc, 85-88, exec bd, 86-88; co-dir, Molecular Graphics & Modeling Shared Resource, Duke Comprehensive Cancer Ctr, 88-; coun mem, Protein Soc, 89-, Nat Ctr Res Resources, NIH, 90-; grantee, Merck, Sharp & Dohme res grant, 88-91; indust consult, Upjohn, Hoffman-LaRoche, Allied Chem, Becton Dickinson, Nutrasweet, Biosym & Tripos. *Mem:* Nat Acad Sci; Biophys Soc; Am Crystallog Asn; Protein Soc; Molecular Graphics Soc. *Res:* Comparison and classification of protein structures; design of new proteins for synthesis; protein crystallography; protein folding; representation of protein structures; conformational details in proteins; interpretation of electron density maps and evaluation of errors; structural information in reciprocal space; internal packing, subunit packing and crystal packing; concerted motions for protein modeling; comparison of nuclear magnetic resonance and x-ray structures; electronic publishing. *Mailing Add:* Dept Biochem Med Ctr Duke Univ PO Box 3711 Durham NC 27710. *Fax:* 919-684-8885; *E-Mail:* jsr@sumabiochem.duke.edu

RICHARDSON, JASPER E, NUCLEAR PHYSICS, PETROLEUM ENGINEERING. *Current Pos:* RETIRED. *Personal Data:* b Memphis, Tenn, Nov 8, 22; m 47, Nellie C Harwell; c Ann H, Janet K, Susan C, Patricia L & Ellen C. *Educ:* Yale Univ, BS, 44; Rice Univ, MA, 48, PhD(physics), 50. *Prof Exp:* Instr physics, Univ Miss, 46-47; asst prof, Auburn Univ, 50-51; physicist, Med Div, Oak Ridge Inst Nuclear Studies, 51-53, Univ Tex MD Anderson Hosp & Tumor Inst, 53-55; res physicist, Bellaire Res Ctr, Shell Develop Co, Tex, 55-69, sr engr, Shell Oil Co, 69-72, staff engr, 72-86. *Mem:* Am Phys Soc; Soc Petrol Engrs. *Res:* Petrophysics; nuclear physics; medical physics; field testing new techniques for tertiary oil recovery. *Mailing Add:* 15015 Parkville Dr Houston TX 77068

RICHARDSON, JAY WILSON, JR, AQUATIC ENTOMOLOGY, AQUATIC ECOLOGY. *Current Pos:* ENTOMOLOGIST, ACAD NAT SCI PHILADELPHIA, 64- *Personal Data:* b Salt Lake City, Utah, Aug 1, 40. *Educ:* Univ Utah, BS, 62, MS, 64. *Prof Exp:* Teaching asst invert zool, Univ Utah, 62-64. *Concurrent Pos:* Biologist, Bur Com Fisheries, 62; asst to dir entom, Stroud Water Res Ctr, Acad Nat Sci Philadelphia, 69-73; entomologist, Coun Environ Qual, Exec Off President, 71-72, Savannah River Plant, E I Du Pont de Nemours & Co, Inc, 71-75 & Nat Comn Water Qual, 74-75; proj mgr environ consult, Dept Limnol, Acad Nat Sci Philadelphia, 75- *Mem:* Sigma Xi; Entom Soc Am; Am Entom Soc; Ecol Soc. *Res:* Taxonomy and ecology of ephemeroptera; trichoptera; environmental pollution, especially fresh water biological monitoring. *Mailing Add:* 873 E Vine St Murray UT 84107

RICHARDSON, JEFFERY HOWARD, PHYSICAL CHEMISTRY. *Current Pos:* chem sci div leader, 88-93, CHEMIST, LAWRENCE LIVERMORE LAB, 74-, PROG DEVELOP, 93- *Personal Data:* b Oakland, Calif, Nov 23, 48; m 78. *Educ:* Calif Inst Technol, BS, 70; Stanford Univ, PhD(chem), 74. *Concurrent Pos:* Consult, Mallinckrodt, 78. *Mem:* Am Chem Soc; Sigma Xi; AAAS. *Res:* Applications of laser spectroscopy to analytical problems; oil shale chemistry; photoelectrochemistry; organic materials; chemical synthesis and processing; high explosives; low density materials. *Mailing Add:* 1466 Oxford Pl Livermore CA 94550-6533. *Fax:* 510-423-4967; *E-Mail:* richardson6@llnl.gov

RICHARDSON, JOEL ALBERT, REACTIVE EXTRUSION, PROCESS DEVELOPMENT. *Current Pos:* sr res engr, 90-91, ASSOC RES ENGR, AMOCO CHEM CO, 91- *Personal Data:* m, Debra L Orley; c Jill & Adam. *Educ:* Ariz State Univ, MS, 73; Univ Tex, Austin, PhD(chem eng), 77. *Prof Exp:* Res engr, Amoco Chem Co, 76-84, staff res engr, 84-88; sr res engr, Amoco Peformance Prods, 88-90. *Mem:* Am Chem Soc; Am Inst Chem Engrs; Soc Of Plastics Engrs. *Res:* Developing new polymer based processes and products. *Mailing Add:* Amoco Chem Co PO Box 3011 Naperville IL 60565. *E-Mail:* jarichardson@amoco.com

RICHARDSON, JOHN L(LOYD), TECHNOLOGY & COMPETITIVE INTELLIGENCE, STRATEGIC PLANNING & NEW BUSINESS DEVELOPMENT. *Current Pos:* PRIN, RICHARDSON CONSULT GROUP, 88- *Personal Data:* b Ventura, Calif, Jan 29, 35; m 57, Thora Ann Bergsteinsson; c David, Eric, Karen, Kristen & Thomas. *Educ:* Stanford Univ, BS, 56, PhD(chem eng), 64. *Prof Exp:* Res & develop engr, Aeronutronic Div, Ford Motor Co, 61-62, sr engr, 62-64; sect supvr, Chem Lab, Res Labs, Philco-Ford Corp, 64-65, mgr, Appl Chem Dept, Appl Res Labs, Aeronutronic Div, Newport Beach, 65-71, Mgr Res & Eng Dept, Liquid Process Prod, 71-74; gen mgr, Recovery Systs, Oxy Metal Industs Corp, 74-78, mgr mkt & proj mgr, Voylite-Plating Systs Div, 78-81; pres & chief exec officer, Seagold Industs Corp, Burnaby, BC, 81-84; pres & chief exec officer, Engenics Inc, Menlo Park, Calif, 84-88. *Mem:* Am Inst Chem Engrs; Soc Competitive Intel Profs. *Res:* Energy and mass transfer in chemically reacting systems; reverse osmosis and ultrafiltration, desalination, water purification, and effluent treatment; the development and growth of technology-based businesses, including the management of product commercializations and turnarounds; design, development and installation of competitive/technology intelligence systems; technology and commercialization assessments. *Mailing Add:* 2356 Branner Dr Menlo Park CA 94025-6304. *Fax:* 650-854-2136; *E-Mail:* jlr@rcgc.com

RICHARDSON, JOHN MARSHALL, PHYSICS, TELECOMMUNICATIONS. *Current Pos:* PRIN STAFF OFFICER, NAT ACAD SCI, NAT RES COUN, 80- *Personal Data:* b Rock Island, Ill, Sept 5, 21; m 44; c 4. *Educ:* Univ Colo, BA, 42; Harvard Univ, MA, 47, PhD(physics), 51. *Honors & Awards:* Gold Medal Award, US Dept Com, 64. *Prof Exp:* Assoc head, Physics Div, Inst Indust Res, Univ Denver, 50-52; physicist, Nat Bur Stand, 52-60, chief, Radio Stand Lab, 60-67, dep dir, Inst Basic Stand, 66-67; dir, Off Stand Rev, US Dept Com, 67-68, actg dir, Off Telecommun, 69-70 & 72-74, dep dir, 70-72, dir, 76-78, chief scientist, Nat Telecommun & Info Admin, 78-80. *Concurrent Pos:* Nat Bur Stand rep, Consult Comt Definition Second, Int Comt Weights & Measures, 61-67; conf chmn, Int Conf Precision Electromagnetic Measurements, 62; chmn UC Comn I, Int Union Radio Sci, 64-67; mem at large, US Nat Comt, 69-72; exec secy, Comt Telecommun, Nat Acad Eng, 68-69; US mem, Panel Comput & Commun, Orgn Econ Coop & Develop, 70-77; vchmn, Working Party Info, Comput & Communs Policy, 77-79; mem Comt Commun & Info Policy, Inst Elec & Electronics Engrs, 80. *Mem:* Fel AAAS; fel Inst Elec & Electronics Engrs; fel Am Phys Soc. *Res:* Gaseous discharges; microwave spectroscopy; microwave physics; atomic time and frequency standards; precision electromagnetic measurements and standards; telecommunications technology, management and policy; science policy. *Mailing Add:* 7116 Armat Dr Bethesda MD 20817-2106

RICHARDSON, JOHN PAUL, MOLECULAR BIOLOGY, GENE EXPRESSION. *Current Pos:* from asst prof to assoc prof, 70-78, PROF CHEM, IND UNIV, BLOOMINGTON, 78- *Personal Data:* b Pittsfield, Mass, June 27, 38; m 66, Lislott Voegelin; c John Jr, Alexandra & Gabriella. *Educ:* Amherst Col, BA, 60; Harvard Univ, PhD(biochem), 66. *Prof Exp:* NIH fel, Inst Biol Physio-Chimique, Paris, 65-67; Am Cancer Soc fel, Inst Molecular Biol, Geneva, Switz, 67-69; res assoc molecular genetics, Univ Wash, 69-70. *Concurrent Pos:* NIH res grant, Ind Univ, Bloomington, 71-; career develop award, NIH, 72-77; pathobiol chem study sect, 75-78, Genetic Basis Dis Rev Comt, 81-85, merit award, 87-97; ed, Gene, 83-95. *Mem:* Am Soc Biochem & Molecular Biol; Am Soc Microbiol; fel AAAS. *Res:* Biosynthesis of RNA in bacteria; mechanism of action of RNA polymerases and termination factors; regulation of gene expression. *Mailing Add:* Dept Chem Ind Univ Bloomington IN 47405. *Fax:* 812-855-8300; *E-Mail:* jrichard@bio.indiana.edu

RICHARDSON, JOHN REGINALD, NUCLEAR PHYSICS. *Current Pos:* assoc prof, 46-52, PROF PHYSICS, UNIV CALIF, LOS ANGELES, 52- *Personal Data:* b Edmonton, Alta, Oct 31, 12; nat US; m 38; c 2. *Educ:* Univ Calif, Los Angeles, AB, 33; Univ Calif, PhD(physics), 37. *Hon Degrees:* DSc, Univ Victoria, Can. *Prof Exp:* Nat Res Coun fel physics, Univ Mich, 37-38; asst prof, Univ Ill, 38-42; physicist, Manhattan Proj, Univ Calif, 42-46. *Concurrent Pos:* Sci liaison officer, Off Naval Res, London, 53-54 & 56-57; mem comt sr reviewers, US AEC, 52-71; dir, Tri Univ Meson Facility, Univ BC, 71-76; vis scientist, 76- *Mem:* Fel Am Phys Soc; Sigma Xi. *Res:* Nucleon-nucleon interaction; nuclear structure; cyclotrons. *Mailing Add:* 2860 Country Dr Apt 227 Fremont CA 94536

RICHARDSON, JONATHAN L, LIMNOLOGY, PLANT ECOLOGY. *Current Pos:* From asst prof to assoc prof, 66-80, PROF BIOL, FRANKLIN & MARSHALL COL, 80- *Personal Data:* b Philadelphia, Pa, May 15, 35; m 63, Alice Elmore; c Catherine W & Mary S. *Educ:* Williams Col, BA, 57; Univ NZ, MA, 60; Duke Univ, PhD(zool), 65. *Concurrent Pos:* NSF res grant, EAfrican lakes & climatic hist, 69-72; US-Australia Coop sci fel, 80-81; interim dir, N Mus, Franklin & Marshall Col, 90-91. *Mem:* AAAS; Int Soc Limnol; Ecol Soc Am; Am Inst Biol Sci; Am Soc Limnol Oceanog; Int Soc Diatom Res. *Res:* Limnology and paleoecology of tropical lakes; ecology of diatoms; plant ecology of disturbed habitats; primary productivity of aquatic ecosystems; stream ecology. *Mailing Add:* 521 State St Lancaster PA 17603. *Fax:* 717-291-4088; *E-Mail:* j__richardson@acad.fandm.edu

RICHARDSON, JOSEPH GERALD, ENGINEERING ADMINISTRATION. *Current Pos:* RETIRED. *Personal Data:* b Gulf, Tex, Oct 28, 23; m 71; c 4. *Educ:* Tex A&M Univ, BS, 47; Mass Inst Technol, MS, 48. *Honors & Awards:* Uren Award, Soc Petrol Engrs, 77, Degolyer Award, 78. *Prof Exp:* Jr res eng, Humble Oil & Refining Co, 48-51, res supvr, 51-64; sect supvr, Exxon Prod Res Co, 64-80, res scientist, 80-82, sr eng scientist, 82-86; consult, 86- *Concurrent Pos:* Adv bd, Exploitech, 87- *Mem:* Hon mem Nat Acad Engrs; hon mem Am Inst Mech Engrs; hon mem Soc Petrol Engrs. *Res:* Basic research on multiphase oil, gas, and water flow in porous rocks; developed standard core analysis procedures; developed theory for capillary inhibitions of water by reservoir rocks. *Mailing Add:* 12434 Wood Thorpe Lane Houston TX 77024

RICHARDSON, KATHLEEN SCHUELLER, ORGANIC CHEMISTRY. *Current Pos:* instr, 75-76, asst prof, 76-80, ASSOC PROF CHEM, CAPITAL UNIV, 80- *Personal Data:* b New York, NY, Sept 28, 38; m 70. *Educ:* Bryn Mawr Col, BA, 60; Radcliffe Col, MA, 62; Harvard Univ, PhD(chem), 66. *Prof Exp:* Res scientist org chem, Bell Tel Labs, 66-68; asst prof, Vassar Col, 68-74; lectr, Ohio State Univ, 74-75. *Mem:* AAAS; Am Chem Soc. *Res:* Cycloaddition reactions. *Mailing Add:* 415 Clinton Heights Ave Columbus OH 43202-1251

RICHARDSON, KEITH ERWIN, PHYSIOLOGICAL CHEMISTRY & TOXICOLOGY. *Current Pos:* RETIRED. *Personal Data:* b Tucson, Ariz, Apr 22, 28; m 52; c 6. *Educ:* Brigham Young Univ, BS, 52, MS, 55; Purdue Univ, PhD(biochem), 58. *Prof Exp:* Asst biochem, Purdue Univ, 55-58; fel agr chem, Mich State Univ, 58-60; from asst prof to assoc prof physiol chem, Ohio State Univ, 60-67, prof physiol chem & vchmn dept, 66-92. *Mem:* AAAS; Am Chem Soc; Am Soc Plant Physiol; Am Soc Biol Chem; Sigma Xi; Am Inst Nutrit. *Res:* Enzymology; primary hyperoxaluria and oxalic acid metabolism; enzyme regulation; intermediate metabolism; metabolic inborn errors of metabolism. *Mailing Add:* 4020 Mountview Rd Columbus OH 43220

RICHARDSON, LAVON PRESTON, MICROBIOLOGY. *Current Pos:* asst prof microbiol, 61-64, co-dir sci teaching ctr, 67, ASSOC PROF MICROBIOL, OKLA STATE UNIV, 65- *Personal Data:* b Ranger, Tex, July 6, 25; m 50; c 2. *Educ:* Tex Christian Univ, AB, 48; NTex State Univ, MA, 49; Okla State Univ, EdD, 58. *Prof Exp:* From instr to asst prof biol, Cent State Univ, Okla, 49-57; from asst prof to asst prof bact, Okla State Univ, 57-59; adminr, DeLeon Munic Hosp, Tex, 59-60; asst prof biol, Tarleton State Col, 60-61. *Concurrent Pos:* Asst dir spec proj, NSF, 66-67; coordr, This Atomic World Prog. *Mem:* Am Soc Microbiol; Nat Asn Biol Teachers; Am Pub Health Asn; Am Inst Biol Sci. *Res:* Colony movement in Bacillus alvei. *Mailing Add:* 1618 Chiquita Ct Stillwater OK 74075

RICHARDSON, LEE S(PENCER), PHYSICAL PROCESS METALLURGY, PROCESS SIMULATION. *Current Pos:* RETIRED. *Personal Data:* b Syracuse, NY, Mar 17, 29; m 56, Joyce Schultz; c Martin & Scott. *Educ:* Mass Inst Technol, SB, 50, SM, 51, ScD(phys metall), 56. *Prof Exp:* Res asst oxidation & nitriding titanium, Mass Inst Technol, 50-51, res asst creep rupture titanium, 53-55; jr metallurgist, Oak Ridge Nat Lab, 51-52; res metallurgist, Westinghouse Elec Corp, 55-56; indust staff mem, Los Alamos Sci Lab, 56-58; res metallurgist, Westinghouse Elec Corp, 58-60, supvry metallurgist, 60-63; mgr ceramics & metall res, Foote Mineral Co, 63-69, dir res & eng, Ferroalloy Div, 69-71, dir res & develop, 72-77; mgr mat sci, EG&G Idaho Inc, 77-80, mgr hot cell opers, 80-83, tech leader plasma processing, 83-86; prof metall eng, Univ Idaho, 86-90. *Mem:* Am Soc Metals; Am Inst Mining, Metall & Petrol Engrs; Sigma Xi. *Res:* High temperature materials; alloy development; ferroalloys; inorganic chemistry of lithium and manganese; computer simulation; materials for energy production and conversion; plasma processing; advanced material processing. *Mailing Add:* 210 N Garfield Moscow ID 83843-3664. *E-Mail:* elenje@turbonet.com

RICHARDSON, LEONARD FREDERICK, MATHEMATICAL ANALYSIS. *Current Pos:* from asst prof to assoc prof, 73-84, PROF MATH, LA STATE UNIV, 85- *Personal Data:* b Brooklyn, NY, Nov 23, 44; m 72; c 2. *Educ:* Yale Univ, BA & MA, 65, PhD(math), 70. *Prof Exp:* Instr math, Yale Univ, 70-71; CLE Moore instr math, Mass Inst Technol, 71-73. *Concurrent Pos:* NSF res grant, 74-84; NSF Int travel grant, 75, 76, 81; vis assoc prof math, Univ Conn, 77-78. *Mem:* Am Math Soc. *Res:* Harmonic analysis on manifolds; projections, measures, distributions and differential operators on nilmanifolds; representation theory. *Mailing Add:* Dept Math Lockett Hall La State Univ Baton Rouge LA 70803

RICHARDSON, MARY FRANCES, INORGANIC CHEMISTRY, CRYSTALLOGRAPHY. *Current Pos:* from asst prof to assoc prof, Brock Univ, 71-81, chmn dept, 79-82, chmn dept, 95-98, PROF CHEM, BROCK UNIV, 81- *Personal Data:* b Barbourville, Ky, Sept 3, 41. *Educ:* Univ Ky, BS, 62, PhD(chem), 67. *Prof Exp:* Contractor, Aerospace Res Labs, Wright-Patterson AFB, 67-71. *Mem:* Am Chem Soc; Am Crystallog Asn; fel Chem Inst Can. *Res:* Crystallographic packing; asymmetric syntheses and stereochemical control of reactions on single crystals; x-ray crystal structures; polymorphism in crystals. *Mailing Add:* Dept Chem Brock Univ St Catharines ON L2S 3A1 Can. *E-Mail:* mrichard@abacus.ac.brocku.ca

RICHARDSON, MICHAEL LEWELLYN, musculoskeletal radiology, for more information see previous edition

RICHARDSON, NEAL A(LLEN), ENGINEERING. *Current Pos:* RETIRED. *Personal Data:* b Casper, Wyo, Mar 14, 26; m 52, Anna M Downing; c Robert L & Neal V. *Educ:* Univ Calif, Los Angeles, BS, 49, MS, 53, PhD(eng), 62. *Prof Exp:* Lectr eng, Univ Calif, Los Angeles, 49-62; mgr, TRW Systs Group, 62-76, mgr coal conversion progs, 76-78, dir advan systs eng, TRW Automotive Electronics Group, TRW Energy Systs Group, 78-86. *Concurrent Pos:* NSF sci fac fel, 61. *Mem:* Soc Automotive Engrs; Sigma Xi. *Res:* Advanced energy conversion processes including electrochemical systems; vehicle power train development and engineering including power plant emissions characterization and control; chemical processes based on coal; new catalytic process to produce high BTU gas; electronic controls and sensors for transportation. *Mailing Add:* 30823 Cartier Dr Rancho Palos Verdes CA 90275

RICHARDSON, PAUL ERNEST, PLANT ANATOMY & PATHOLOGY. *Current Pos:* from asst prof to assoc prof, 68-82, researcher, Okla Agr Exp Sta, 73-82, FROM PROF TO EMER PROF BOT, OKLA STATE UNIV, 82-, RES PROF PLANT PATH, AGR RES STA, 82- *Personal Data:* b Covington, Ky, Dec 29, 34; m 58; c 1. *Educ:* Univ Ky, AB, 57; Univ Cincinnati, MEd, 62, MS, 66, PhD(bot), 68; Univ NC, Chapel Hill, MAT, 63. *Prof Exp:* Teacher, Lloyd Mem High Sch, Ky, 57-59 & Holmes High Sch, 59-62. *Mem:* Bot Soc Am; AAAS; Am Phytopath Soc; Torrey Bot Club; Am Inst Biol Sci; Sigma Xi. *Res:* Structure, especially ultrastructure of pathological and stress states in vascular (crop) plants; comparative structure of flowering plants. *Mailing Add:* 1023 S Western St Okla State Univ Stillwater OK 74074

RICHARDSON, PAUL NOEL, ORGANIC CHEMISTRY. *Current Pos:* Res chemist, 52-57, tech rep, 57-64, consult, 64-65, supvr, 66-70, sr res chemist, Plastic Dept, 71-80, RES ASSOC, POLYMER PROD DEPT, E I DU PONT DE NEMOURS & CO, INC, 80- *Personal Data:* b Minneapolis, Minn, Mar 31, 25; m 46, 84; c 3. *Educ:* Univ Minn, BS, 49, PhD(org chem), 52. *Honors & Awards:* Pres Cup, Soc Plastic Engrs, 72. *Concurrent Pos:* Instr, Univ Del. *Mem:* Am Chem Soc; Soc Plastic Engrs (treas, 70). *Res:* Polymer chemistry; plastics engineering. *Mailing Add:* 11 N Wynwyd Dr Newark DE 19711-7424

RICHARDSON, PETER DAMIAN, BIOMEDICAL ENGINEERING. *Current Pos:* res assoc, 58-60, from asst prof to prof eng, 60-84, PROF ENG & PHYSIOL, BROWN UNIV, 84- *Personal Data:* b West Wickham, Eng, 35. *Educ:* Univ London, BSc, 55, PhD(eng) & DIC, 58; City & Guilds of London Inst, ACGI, 55. *Hon Degrees:* MA, Brown Univ, 65; DSc(eng), Univ London, 74, DSc, 83. *Honors & Awards:* Humbolt Found Award, 76; Prize Med, Jung Found, 87. *Prof Exp:* Demonstr eng, Imp Col, Univ London, 55-58. *Concurrent Pos:* Sci Res Coun Eng sr res fel, 67-68. *Mem:* Fel Am Soc Mech Engrs; Am Soc Eng Educ; Am Soc Artificial Internal Organs; Biomed Eng Soc; Am Instr Med Biol Eng; fel Royal Soc London. *Res:* Heat and mass transfer, fluid dynamics; theory and technology of artificial internal organs; blood flow. *Mailing Add:* Div Eng Box D Brown Univ Providence RI 02912. *E-Mail:* peter_richardson@brown.edu

RICHARDSON, PHILIP LIVERMORE, PHYSICAL OCEANOGRAPHY, MARINE SCIENCE. *Current Pos:* from asst scientist to assoc scientist, 74-89, SR SCIENTIST, WOODS HOLE OCEANOG INST, 89- *Personal Data:* b New York, NY, Oct 31, 40; m 66, Judith Benet; c Arthur & Mary. *Educ:* Univ Calif, Berkeley, BS, 64; Univ RI, MS, 70, PhD(phys oceanog), 74. *Prof Exp:* Lt jr grade, US Coast & Geod Surv, 64-66; asst, Sch Oceanog, Univ RI, 67-69, res asst, 69-73, asst prof, 73-74. *Concurrent Pos:* Vis scientist, Nat Mus Natural Hist, Oceanog Phys Lab, Paris, 78-79, Oceanog Ctr Brittany, Brest, France, 83 & Scripp's Inst Oceanog, La Jolla, 86. *Mem:* AAAS; Am Geophys Union; Am Meteorol Soc. *Res:* General ocean circulation; gulf stream; oceanic eddies; equatorial currents; historical studies. *Mailing Add:* Woods Hole Oceanog Inst Woods Hole MA 02543. *Fax:* 508-457-2181; *E-Mail:* prichardson@whoi.edu

RICHARDSON, RALPH J, SOLID STATE PHYSICS. *Current Pos:* dir, Technol & Innovation Mgt, 80-83, mgr, Tech Diversification, 83-88, TECH DIR, ELECTRONICS AIR PROD & CHEM, SRI INT, 88- *Personal Data:* b Jamestown, NDak, Feb 28, 41; m 64; c 3. *Educ:* Rockhurst Col, AB, 62; St Louis Univ, MS, 64, PhD(physics), 69. *Prof Exp:* Sr Scientist, McDonnell Douglas Res Labs, McDonnell Douglas Corp, 69-81. *Concurrent Pos:* Bd mem, UTI Instrument, Inc. *Mem:* Am Phys Soc. *Res:* Electron spin resonance; combustion; chemical lasers; high purity gases for semiconductor applications. *Mailing Add:* 4976 Meadow Lane Macungie PA 18062

RICHARDSON, RANDALL MILLER, GEOPHYSICS, EARTH SCIENCE. *Current Pos:* asst prof, 78-83, ASSOC PROF GEOSCIENCES, UNIV ARIZ, 83- *Personal Data:* b Santa Monica, Calif, Dec 29, 48; m 77; c 2. *Educ:* Univ Calif, San Diego, BA, 72; Mass Inst Technol, PhD(geophys), 78. *Mem:* Am Geophys Union; Sigma Xi. *Res:* Intraplate deformation and driving mechanism for plate tectonics through observation and finite element modeling of stress; analysis of strain accumulation release at plate boundaries; inverse modeling. *Mailing Add:* Dept Geosci Univ Ariz 1600 E University Blvd Tucson AZ 85721-0001

RICHARDSON, RAYMAN PAUL, SCIENCE EDUCATION. *Current Pos:* from instr to assoc prof, 71-78, PROF PHYS SCI & SCI EDUC, FAIRMONT STATE COL, 78- *Personal Data:* b Piedmont, Mo, May 17, 39; m 66, 92, Amy A Schuster; c Cammie M & Paul E. *Educ:* Cent Methodist Col, AB, 61; Univ Mo, MST, 64; Ohio State Univ, PhD(sci educ), 71. *Prof Exp:* Teacher chem & math, St Clair Pub Schs, 61-64; teacher phys sci, Antilles Sch Syst, 64-67. *Mem:* Nat Sci Teachers Asn. *Res:* Measurement of scientific curiosity and interests of elementary school children. *Mailing Add:* Dept Math & Sci Fairmont State Col 1201 Locust Ave Fairmont WV 26554-2489. *E-Mail:* fsa00162@mail.unnet.edu

RICHARDSON, RICHARD HARVEY, ECOSYSTEM POLICY DEVELOPMENT, CONSERVATION ECONOMIC & ECOSYSTEM ANALYSIS. *Current Pos:* Assoc res scientist, Genetics Found, 64-65, NIH fel zool, 65-67, from lectr to assoc prof, 65-79, PROF ZOOL, UNIV TEX, AUSTIN, 79- *Personal Data:* b Mexia, Tex, Mar 24, 38; m, Patricia Quarles; c Desni L, Russell E & Kaci E. *Educ:* Tex A&M Univ, BS, 59; NC State Univ, MS, 62, PhD(genetics), 65. *Concurrent Pos:* USPHS career develop award, 70-75; on loan, Entom Dept, Univ Hawaii-Manoa; lead chem teacher, Kamemamena Sch, Honolulu, 88-89; certified educr, Holistic Resource Mgt Ctr. *Mem:* Fel AAAS; Am Inst Biol Sci; Soc Range Mgt; Agr Food & Human Values Soc; Am Soc Naturalists. *Res:* Genetics of mating behavior and population structure; chromosomal, behavioral and biochemical changes during the evolution of the genus Drosophila; population genetics and ecology of natural and laboratory populations; genetics, evolutionary biology and biogeography of screwworms, Cochliomyia species; ticks; ecology of native prairies; watershed development in grasslands; remote sensing analysis in rangeland ecology; rural community development; regenerative agriculture. *Mailing Add:* 608 Fairfield Lane Austin TX 78751. *Fax:* 512-471-9651; *E-Mail:* d.richardson@mail.utexas.edu

RICHARDSON, RICHARD LAUREL, ELECTRIC POWER SYSTEM THEORY, ULTRASONICS. *Current Pos:* CONSULT, 93- *Personal Data:* b Chelan, Wash, Aug 12, 26; m 48, Patricia Fenner; c 6. *Educ:* Univ Colo, Boulder, BS, 53; Univ Idaho, MS, 61. *Honors & Awards:* Inst Elec Electronics Engrs Centennial Medal, 84. *Prof Exp:* Tech grad, Gen Elec Co, 53-55, engr, 55-60, mathematician, 60-65; sr res scientist, Pac Northwest Labs, Battelle Mem Inst, 65-80; sr engr, UNC Nuclear Indust Inc, 80-85; prin engr, Westinghouse Hanford Co, 88-90; staff engr, Rockwell Hanf Co & Pac Northwest Labs, Battelle Northwest, 90-93. *Concurrent Pos:* Instr, Columbia Basin Col; lectr, Joint Ctr Grad Study, Richland, Wash; lectr IV, Wash State Univ, Tri Cities. *Mem:* Inst Elec & Electronics Engrs; Sigma Xi. *Res:* Stress wave propagation, thermal diffusion; sphere packing and related molecular models, especially transmission and distribution of electrical energy and industrial control. *Mailing Add:* 4950 Dove Ct West Richland WA 99352

RICHARDSON, ROBERT COLEMAN, LOW TEMPERATURE PHYSICS. *Current Pos:* From asst prof to prof, 67-87, F R NEWMAN PROF PHYSICS, CORNELL UNIV, 87-, DIR LAB ATOMIC & SOLID STATE PHYSICS, 90- *Personal Data:* b Washington, DC, June 26, 37; m 62, Betty McCarthy; c Jennifer & Pamela. *Educ:* Va Polytech Inst, MS, 60; Duke Univ, PhD(physics), 66. *Honors & Awards:* Nobel Prize in Physics, 96; Simon Prize, Brit Phys Soc, 77; Buckley Prize, Am Phys Soc, 81. *Concurrent Pos:* Vis scientist, Bell Lab, 84. *Mem:* Nat Acad Sci; fel Am Phys Soc; fel AAAS; Am Acad Arts & Sci. *Res:* Studies of thermal and magnetic properties of solid and liquid helium at very low temperatures. *Mailing Add:* Dept Physics Clark Hall Cornell Univ Ithaca NY 14853-2501

RICHARDSON, ROBERT ESPLIN, physics, electrical engineering; deceased, see previous edition for last biography

RICHARDSON, ROBERT LLOYD, ELECTRICAL ENGINEERING, NUCLEAR MEDICINE. *Current Pos:* ASSOC PROF RADIOL, STATE UNIV NY HEALTH SCI CTR, 70- *Personal Data:* b Syracuse, NY, Oct 1, 29; m 57, Barbara Vinton; c Eric, Steven, Neil, Kurt, Paul & Scott. *Educ:* Syracuse Univ, BEE, 51, MEE, 56, PhD(elec eng), 61. *Prof Exp:* Res asst elec eng, Syracuse Univ, 51-53, res assoc, 53-56, from instr to asst prof, 56-64; res engr, Syracuse Univ Res Corp, 64-70. *Concurrent Pos:* Lectr, Syracuse Univ, 71-76, adj prof, 76- *Mem:* Inst Elec & Electronics Engrs; Soc Nuclear Med. *Res:* Electronic circuits and electronics applied to medicine. *Mailing Add:* Div Nuclear Med State Univ NY Health Sci Ctr Syracuse NY 13210-2399

RICHARDSON, ROBERT LOUIS, BACTERIOLOGY. *Current Pos:* RETIRED. *Personal Data:* b Lexington, Ky, Mar 19, 22; m 50; c 3. *Educ:* Univ Louisville, DMD, 44; Univ Iowa, MS, 53. *Prof Exp:* Practicing dentist, Ky, 47-48; from instr to asst prof restorative dent, Univ Tex, 48-51; instr periodontia, Col Med, Univ Iowa, 51-52, asst prof microbiol, 53-64, assoc prof microbiol, 64-85. *Mem:* AAAS; Am Soc Microbiol; Int Asn Dent Res. *Res:* In vitro studies of dental caries; microorganisms in the mouth. *Mailing Add:* 321 Melrose Ct Iowa City IA 52246

RICHARDSON, ROBERT WILLIAM, STATISTICAL MECHANICS, NUCLEAR PHYSICS. *Current Pos:* Asst res scientist, Courant Inst Math Sci, 63-65, from asst prof to assoc prof physics, 65-75, chmn dept, 82-85, PROF PHYSICS, NY UNIV, 75- *Personal Data:* b Sydney, Australia, Sept, 5, 35; US citizen; div; c 2. *Educ:* Univ Mich, BS & MA, 58, PhD(physics), 63. *Concurrent Pos:* Consult, Lawrence Berkeley Lab. *Mem:* Am Phys Soc; AAAS; Sigma Xi. *Res:* Many-body problem; nuclear models; low temperature physics; transport theory. *Mailing Add:* 305 E 24th St Apt 10F New York NY 10010-4025

RICHARDSON, RUDY JAMES, NEUROTOXICOLOGY. *Current Pos:* from asst prof to assoc prof, 75-84, actg dir toxicol, 93, PROF TOXICOL, UNIV MICH, 84-, ASSOC PROF NEUROL, 87-, DIR TOXICOL, 94- *Personal Data:* b Winfield, Kans, May 13, 45; m 70, 85; c 3. *Educ:* Wichita State Univ, BS, 67; Harvard Univ, ScM, 73, ScD(physiol-toxicol), 74. *Prof Exp:* NASA trainee chem, State Univ NY, Stony Brook, 67-70; Nat Int Environ Health Sci trainee toxicol, Harvard Univ, 70-74; res biochem neurotoxicol, Med Res Coun, Eng, 74-75. *Concurrent Pos:* Consult, Environ Protection Agency, 76-; mem safe drinking water comt & toxicol subcomt, Nat Acad Sci, 78-79 & 84; vis scientist, Warner-Lambert/Parke-Davis Pharmaceut Res Div, 82-83; invited speaker, Second Int Meeting Cholinesterases, Bled, Yugoslavia & Gordon Conf Toxicol, 84; pres, Neurotoxicol Specialty Sect, Soc Toxicol, 87-88; mem sci adv panel, US Environ Protection Agency, 87-90; consult, Off Technol Assessment, US Cong, 88-90, NIOSH, 90-; vis prof toxicol, Univ Padua, Italy, 91. *Mem:* Am Chem Soc; AAAS; Soc Neurosci; Soc Toxicol; Sigma Xi; Am Soc Neurochem; Int Soc Neurochem. *Res:* Delayed neurotoxicity of organophosphorus compounds; neurotoxic esterase, neuropathy target esterase; models of neurological disease; maintenance and plasticity of neurons; biomembranes; biological functions of glutathione; transport of heavy metals; leukocytes as biomonitors and models of certain neuronal functions; neuroimmunomodulation; connectivity of scientific fields; philosophy of science; development of new methodologies for neurotoxicity assessment. *Mailing Add:* Toxicol Res Lab Sch Pub Health Univ Mich Ann Arbor MI 48109-2029. *Fax:* 313-763-8095; *E-Mail:* rudy.richardson@um.cc.umich.edu

RICHARDSON, STEPHEN GILES, MEDICAL LABORATORY DIAGNOSTIC TEST SYSTEM RESEARCH & DEVELOPMENT. *Current Pos:* group leader, Organon Teknika Corp, 86-89, sect head, 89-90, prog mgr, 90-94, ASSOC DIR, DIAGNOSTIC PROD DEVELOP, ORGANON TEKNIKA CORP, 94- *Personal Data:* b Minneapolis, Minn, Sept 17, 51; m 81, Maureane Hoffman. *Educ:* Wartburg Col, Iowa, BA, 72; Univ Iowa, MS, 74, PhD(org chem), 81. *Prof Exp:* Res assoc, Chem Dept, Duke Univ, 82-84; scientist, Becton Dickinson Res Ctr, 84-86; group leader, Dade-Baxter Diagnostics, 86. *Mem:* Am Chem Soc; Sigma Xi; Am Asn Blood Banks; Am Asn Clin Chem; assoc mem Royal Soc Chem UK. *Res:* Management of the research, development and transfer of reagents and instrument systems to automate clinical coagulation testing, and of other products for clinical laboratories. *Mailing Add:* 5408 Sunny Ridge Dr Durham NC 27705. *Fax:* 919-620-2107; *E-Mail:* mda180@aol.com, s_richardson@otc.akzonobel.nl

RICHARDSON, STEPHEN H, MICROBIOLOGY, BACTERIAL PATHOGENESIS. *Current Pos:* from asst prof to assoc prof, 63-71, PROF MICROBIOL, BOWMAN GRAY SCH MED, 71- *Personal Data:* b Kalamazoo, Mich, June 30, 32; c Kristen, Stephanie, James, Benjamin & Ryan. *Educ:* Univ Calif, Los Angeles, BA, 55; Univ Southern Calif, MS, 59, PhD(bact), 60. *Prof Exp:* Lectr, Univ Southern Calif, 59-61; res assoc, Tobacco Industs Res Comt, 60-61; trainee, Enzyme Inst, Univ Wis, 61-63. *Concurrent Pos:* Mem cholera adv comt, NIH, 69-73, US-Japan Cholera Panel, 69-76; adj prof biol, Wake Forest Univ, 71-; found lectr, Am Soc Microbiol, 71-72; guest scientist, Cholera Res Lab, Bangladesh, 72-73; consult, NIH Infectious Dis Comt, 77-93; pres NC br, Am Soc Microbiol, 77-78; mem, bacteriol/mycology study sect, NIH, 78-82; consult, Int Ctr Diarrheal Dis Res, Bangladesh, 83-, ICDDRB & UNICEF, Columbia, SAm, 84. *Mem:* AAAS; Am Soc Microbiol; Am Soc Trop Med & Hyg; Sigma Xi; Am Acad Microbiol. *Res:* Bacteriology; membrane systems and virulence; mechanisms of microbial pathogenesis; physiology of Vibrio cholerae; enterotoxin-induced diarrheal diseases; genetic mechanisms of host resistance; virulence factors of halophilic vibrios; international health; intracellular enteric pathogens. *Mailing Add:* Dept Microbiol Bowman Gray Sch Med Med Ctr Blvd Winston-Salem NC 27157. *Fax:* 910-716-9928; *E-Mail:* srichard@bgsm.edu

RICHARDSON, SUSAN D, MASS SPECTROMETRY, STRUCTURAL ELUCIDATION. *Current Pos:* Postdoctoral assoc, 89, RES CHEMIST, US ENVIRON PROTECTION AGENCY, 89- *Personal Data:* b Brunswick, Ga, Oct 13, 62; m 84, Andy; c Kelsey. *Educ:* Ga Col, Milledgeville, BS, 84; Emory Univ, Atlanta, PhD(chem), 89. *Mem:* Sigma Xi; Am Soc Mass Spectrometry; Am Chem Soc. *Res:* Mass spectrometric techniques, including low and high resolution EI and CI mass spectrometry and FAB mass spectrometry, to identify chemical pollutants of unknown structure that are found in the environment. *Mailing Add:* 1350 Brittain Estates Dr Watkinsville GA 30677

RICHARDSON, TERRY DAVID, FEEDING POPULATION & PRODUCTION ECOLOGY OF FRESHWATER INVERTEBRATES, MOLLUSCS. *Current Pos:* ASST PROF AQUATIC BIOL & ANIMAL PHYSIOL, UNIV NALA, 91- *Personal Data:* Sept 11, 60; m 81, Donna Box. *Educ:* Univ N Ala, BS, 82; Univ Ala, MS, 86; La State Univ, PhD(zool), 90. *Prof Exp:* Fel, Oak Ridge Assoc Univs, 90-91. *Concurrent Pos:* Res subcontractor, NSF-Exp Prog Stimulate Competitive Res, 92-; res contractor, Tenn Valley Authority, 92- *Mem:* Ecol Soc Am; NAm Benthological Soc. *Res:* Estimation and distribution of invertebrate secondary production in a freshwater wetland; impact of the zebra mussel, Dreissena polymorpha, on native bivalve assemblages in the Tennessee River. *Mailing Add:* Univ NAla Florence AL 35632-0001. *Fax:* 205-760-4329

RICHARDSON, THOMAS, FOOD CHEMISTRY, BIOCHEMISTRY. *Current Pos:* RETIRED. *Personal Data:* b Ft Lupton, Colo, Dec 4, 31; m 54; c 2. *Educ:* Univ Colo, Boulder, BS, 54; Univ Wis-Madison, MS, 56, PhD(biochem), 60. *Prof Exp:* Fel food chem, Univ Calif, Davis, 60-62; from asst prof to assoc prof, Univ Wis-Madison, 62-69, prof food chem, Wis-Madison, 70. *Mem:* Am Chem Soc; Inst Food Technol; Am Dairy Sci Asn. *Res:* Application of insoluble enzymes to food processing, analysis and structure; applied enzymology in general. *Mailing Add:* PO Box 737 Berthoud CO 80513

RICHARDSON, VERLIN HOMER, CHEMISTRY, SCIENCE EDUCATION. *Current Pos:* RETIRED. *Personal Data:* b Gage, Okla, July 5, 30; m 51; c 3. *Educ:* Northwestern State Col, Okla, BS, 52; Phillips Univ, MEd, 57; Okla State Univ, MS, 58; Univ Okla, PhD(sci educ), 69. *Prof Exp:* Teacher, Pub Sch, Okla, 52-56; instr chem, El Dorado Jr Col, Kans, 58-62; assoc prof, Cent State Univ, Okla, 62-76, prof chem, 76-96. *Mem:* Am Chem Soc. *Res:* Inorganic chemistry. *Mailing Add:* 316 Ramblewood Terr Edmond OK 73034-4330

RICHARDSON, WALLACE LLOYD, ORGANIC CHEMISTRY. *Current Pos:* Sr res assoc, Fuels, Asphalts & Spec Prods, 54-69, mgr, Fuel Chem Div, MGR EXPLOR ADDITIVES DIV, PROD RES DEPT, CHEVRON RES CO, STANDARD OIL, CALIF, 84- *Personal Data:* b Santa Barbara, Calif, Sept 16, 27; m 51; c 4. *Educ:* Univ Calif, BS, 51; Mass Inst Technol, PhD(org chem), 54. *Mem:* Am Chem Soc; Sigma Xi. *Res:* Mechanism of combustion chemistry of knock and antiknock reactions; application of surfactants in hydrocarbon systems; wax crystal modification for improvement of low temperature flow. *Mailing Add:* 17761 Grizzly Bear Dr Grass Valley CA 94549

RICHARDSON, WILLIAM C, EDUCATION ADMINISTRATION. *Current Pos:* PRES & CHIEF EXEC OFFICER, KELLOGG FOUND, 95- *Personal Data:* b Passaic, NJ, May 11, 40; c 2. *Educ:* Trinity Col, Hartford, Conn, BA, 62; Univ Chicago, MBA, 64, PhD, 71. *Hon Degrees:* LHD, Thomas Jefferson Univ, Goucher Col, Univ Md, Loyola Col, Washington Col, Johns Hopkins Univ & Pa State Univ, 95. *Prof Exp:* From asst prof to prof health serv, Sch Pub Health & Community Med, Univ Wash, 71-84, dean grad sch & vprovost res, 81-84; exec vpres & provost, Pa State Univ, 84-90, prof family & community med, Milton S Hershey Med Ctr, 84-90; pres, Johns Hopkins Univ, 90-95, prof health & policy mgt, Sch Hyg & Pub Health, 90-95. *Concurrent Pos:* Chmn, Joint Panel Nat Health Care Surv, Nat Res Coun/Inst Med Nat Acad Sci, 89-92. *Mem:* Inst Med-Nat Acad Sci; fel Am Pub Health Asn. *Res:* Financing of health care; author of numerous publications. *Mailing Add:* Kellogg Found 1 Michigan Ave E Battle Creek MI 49017

RICHARDSON, WILLIAM HARRY, organic chemistry, for more information see previous edition

RICHART, F(RANK) E(DWIN), JR, civil engineering; deceased, see previous edition for last biography

RICHART, RALPH M, PATHOLOGY, OBSTETRICS & GYNECOLOGY. *Current Pos:* from asst prof to assoc prof path, 63-69, PROF PATH, COL PHYSICIANS & SURGEONS, COLUMBIA UNIV, 69-; DIR PATH & CYTOL, SLOANE HOSP, PRESBY HOSP, NEW YORK, 63- *Personal Data:* b Wilkes Barre, Pa, Dec 14, 33; c 2. *Educ:* Johns Hopkins Univ, BA, 54; Univ Rochester, MD, 58. *Prof Exp:* Teaching fel path, Harvard Med Sch, 59-60; instr path & obstet & gynec, Med Col Va, 61-63. *Concurrent Pos:* USPHS spec res fel, 61-63, career res develop award, 61-63 & 65-69; asst vis obstetrician & gynecologist, Harlem Hosp, New York, 63; from asst attend pathologist to assoc attend pathologist, Presby Hosp, 63-69, attend pathologist, 69-; consult, Ford Found Pop Off, 69. *Mem:* Am Soc Cytol; Soc Gynec Invest; assoc fel Am Col Obstetricians & Gynecologists; Int Acad Cytol; Am Asn Path & Bact. *Res:* Cervical neoplasia; human reproduction. *Mailing Add:* Dept Path Columbia Univ Col P&S New York NY 10032-3702

RICHARZ, WERNER GUNTER, AERO ACOUSTICS. *Current Pos:* MEM STAFF DEPT MECH & AERONAUT ENG, CARLETON UNIV. *Personal Data:* b Troisdorf, WGer, June 24, 48; Can citizen. *Educ:* Univ Toronto, BASc, 72, MASc, 74, PhD(aero acoust), 78. *Prof Exp:* Asst prof, Inst Space Sci, Univ Toronto, 78- *Mem:* Am Inst Aeronaut & Astronaut; Acoust Soc Am; Can Aeronaut & Space Inst. *Res:* Generation of sound by unsteady flows; stability of shear flows; unsteady aerodynamics. *Mailing Add:* Dept Mech & Aeronaut Eng Carleton Univ Ottawa ON K1S 5B6 Can

RICHASON, BENJAMIN FRANKLIN, JR, REMOTE SENSING, CARTOGRAPHY. *Current Pos:* PROF GEOG, CARROLL COL, 52- *Personal Data:* b Logansport, Ind, July 24, 22. *Educ:* Ind Univ, BA, 48, MA, 49; Univ Nebr, PhD(geog), 60. *Prof Exp:* Instr geog, Morton Jr Col, 49-51. *Concurrent Pos:* Pres, Wis Coun Conserv Educ, 60-61, Nat Coun Geog Educ, 69-70 & Wis Coun Geog Educ, 78-79; ed, Remote Sensing Quart, 78-84 & Remote Sensing Feature, J Geog, 78-83. *Mem:* Asn Am Geographers; Am Soc Photogram. *Res:* Remote sensing using infrared and radar to explore ore bodies and archaeological sites. *Mailing Add:* Dept Geol St Cloud State Univ St Cloud MN 56301-4498

RICHASON, GEORGE R, JR, NUCLEAR CHEMISTRY. *Current Pos:* from asst prof to assoc prof, 47-64, ASSOC HEAD DEPT, UNIV MASS, AMHERST, 61-, PROF CHEM, 66- *Personal Data:* b Turners Falls, Mass, Apr 3, 16; m 40, Frances J. Lipinski; c 1. *Educ:* Univ Mass, BS, 37, MS, 39. *Hon Degrees:* DSC, Univ Mass, 91. *Prof Exp:* Instr high sch, Mass, 39-42 & 46-47. *Mem:* Am Chem Soc; Sigma Xi. *Res:* Radiochemistry. *Mailing Add:* Dept Chem Univ Mass Amherst MA 01003-0035

RICHBERG, CARL GEORGE, FOOD SCIENCE. *Current Pos:* CONSULT, 90- *Personal Data:* b Syracuse, NY, July 10, 28; m 55. *Educ:* Syracuse Univ, BS, 51, MS, 53, PhD(microbiol), 56. *Prof Exp:* Asst indust microbiol, bact & food tech, Syracuse Univ, 51-56, effects of radiation on food, Inst Indust Res, 56; res assoc, Res Ctr, Lever Bros Co, 57-72, develop scientist, 72-90. *Mem:* AAAS; NY Acad Sci; Sigma Xi; Inst Food Technol; Fedn Am Scientists; Am Asn Cereal Chemists. *Res:* Oral microbiology; emulsions and protein chemistry; industrial microbiology; submerged culture methods; germicides; sterilization; dairy science; baking science and technology. *Mailing Add:* 344 Concord St Cresskill NJ 07626-1318

RICHELSON, ELLIOTT, PSYCHOPHARMACOLOGY. *Current Pos:* from asst prof to assoc prof, 75-81, CONSULT MAYO CLIN, MAYO MED SCH, 75- PROF PSYCHIAT & PHARMACOL, 81-, DIR RES, 88- *Personal Data:* b Cambridge, Mass, Apr 3, 43; m 69; c 3. *Educ:* Brandeis Univ, BA, 65; Johns Hopkins Univ, MD, 69; Am Bd Psychiat & Neurol, cert, 76. *Honors & Awards:* A E Bennet Basic Sci Res Award, Soc Biol Psychiat, 77; Daniel H Efron Award, Am Col Neuropsychopharmacol, 86. *Prof Exp:* Asst prof pharmacol & exp therapeut, Sch Med, Johns Hopkins Univ, 72-75. *Concurrent Pos:* Borden res award med, Sch Med, Johns Hopkins Univ, 69, NIMH res scientist develop award, 74; distinguished investr, Mayo Found, 90; asst secy, Soc Biol Psychiat, 90. *Mem:* Fel Am Psychiat Asn; Am Soc Neurochem; Am Soc Pharmacol & Exp Therapeut; Soc Biol Psychiat. *Res:* Psychiatry and pharmacology. *Mailing Add:* Mayo Clin-Jacksonville 4500 San Pablo Rd Jacksonville FL 32224-3899

RICHER, CLAUDE-LISE, MICROSCOPIC ANATOMY, ENDOCRINOLOGY. *Current Pos:* Asst histol, 57-59, from asst prof to assoc prof, 59-80, ASST DEAN FAC MED, UNIV MONTREAL, 69- PROF ANAT, 80- *Personal Data:* b St Hyacinthe, Que, Nov 20, 28. *Educ:* Univ Montreal, BA, 48, MD, 54, MS, 57. *Mem:* Endocrine Soc; Am Asn Anatomists; Can Asn Anat; Can Physiol Soc; Am Chem Soc. *Res:* Neuroendocrinology; magnesium deficiency and its effect on adrenal function. *Mailing Add:* Dept Chem Succ A Centre d'ville Univ Montreal PO 6128 Montreal PQ H3C 3J7 Can

RICHER, HARVEY BRIAN, ASTRONOMY. *Current Pos:* from instr to assoc prof, 70-83, PROF ASTRON, UNIV BC, 83- *Personal Data:* b Montreal, Que, Apr 7, 44; m 72; c 2. *Educ:* McGill Univ, BS, 65; Univ Rochester, MS, 68, PhD(physics, astron), 70. *Prof Exp:* Assoc astron, Univ Rochester, 65-70. *Concurrent Pos:* Vis prof, Univ Uppsala, Sweden, 77-78; vis astron, Can-France Hawaii telescope, 84-85; NSERC Grant Selection Comt, 84-86; Killam sr fac fel, 91- *Mem:* AAAS; Am Astron Soc; Can Astron Soc; Royal Astron Soc. *Res:* Carbon stars; globular culsters. *Mailing Add:* Dept Geophys & Astron Univ BC 1292219 Main Mall Vancouver BC V6T 1Z4 Can

RICHER, JEAN-CLAUDE, organic chemistry, for more information see previous edition

RICHERSON, HAL BATES, ALLERGY, IMMUNOLOGY. *Current Pos:* Resident internal med, Univ Iowa Hosps, 61-64, fel allergy, 64-66, FRP, ASST PROF TO PROF INTERNAL MED & DIR, ALLERGY-IMMUNOL DIV, COL MED, UNIV IOWA, 66- *Personal Data:* b Phoenix, Ariz, Feb 16, 29; wid; c Anne, George, Miriam, Julia & Susan. *Educ:* Univ Ariz, BS, 50; Northwestern Univ, MD, 54. *Concurrent Pos:* Consult, Vet Admin Hosp, Iowa City, 66-; vis lectr, Med Sch, Harvard Univ, 68-69; NIH spec fel immunol, Mass Gen Hosp, 68-69; mem, report rec comt allergy-immunol, Liaison Comt on Grad Med Educ, 80-85; mem, Pulmonary Dis Adv Comt, Nat Heart, Lung & Blood Inst, NIH, 83-87, Gen Clin Res Ctr, Comn Div Res Resources, 89-93; vis res prof, Brompton Hosp, London, Eng, 84. *Mem:* Fel Am Col Physicians; fel Am Acad Allergy; Am Asn Immunol; Am Fedn Clin Res; Am Thoracic Soc. *Res:* Study of the lung as an immunological target organ; animal models of hypersensitivity pneumonitis; pathogenesis of bronchial asthma. *Mailing Add:* Dept Internal Med Univ Iowa Hosps & Clins Iowa City IA 52242

RICHERSON, JIM VERNON, ENTOMOLOGY. *Current Pos:* ASST PROF BIOL, SUL ROSS STATE UNIV, ALPINE, TEX, 79- *Personal Data:* b Bossier City, La, Sept 22, 43; m 65; c 1. *Educ:* Univ Mo-Columbia, BA, 65, MSc, 68; Simon Fraser Univ, PhD(biol sci), 72. *Prof Exp:* Res technician, Biol Control Insects Lab, USDA, 65-68; res assoc entom, Pa State Univ, University Park, 72-76; fel entom, Tex A&M Univ, College Station, 76-79. *Mem:* Entom Soc Am. *Res:* Behavior of insects as it relates to pest management and control programs; host-parasite relationships and sex pheromone biology and behavior; medical-veterinary entomology; aquatic entomology; bio-control of range and weeds. *Mailing Add:* Dept Biol Sul Ross State Univ 400 N Harrison St Alpine TX 79832-0001

RICHERSON, PETER JAMES, LIMNOLOGY, HUMAN ECOLOGY. *Current Pos:* Asst prof, 71-87, dir, Inst Ecol, 83-89, PROF ENVIRON STUDIES, UNIV CALIF, DAVIS, 87- *Personal Data:* b San Mateo, Calif, Oct 11, 43; m 78, Lois Callaghan; c Scott & Kate. *Educ:* Univ Calif, Davis, BS, 65, PhD(zool), 69. *Honors & Awards:* Guggenheim Fel, 84; Stanley Prize, 89. *Concurrent Pos:* Consult, Nat Water Comn, 70-71; co-investr, NSF grants, 72-89. *Mem:* AAAS; Am Soc Limnol & Oceanog; Ecol Soc Am; Soc Human Ecol; Am Soc Naturalists. *Res:* Human ecology; theory of cultural evolution; plankton community ecology, tropical limnology. *Mailing Add:* Div Environ Studies Univ Calif Davis CA 95616. *Fax:* 530-752-3350; *E-Mail:* pjricherson@ucdavis.edu

RICHERT, ANTON STUART, PARTICLE PHYSICS, NUCLEAR PHYSICS. *Current Pos:* SR SCIENTIST, BIO-DYNAMICS RES & DEVELOP CORP, EUGENE, ORE, 86-, SYST ENGR, SUN STUDS INC. *Personal Data:* b Newton, Kans, May 19, 35; m 60; c 2. *Educ:* Caltech, BS, 57; Cornell Univ, PhD(exp physics), 62. *Prof Exp:* Res assoc high energy physics, Cornell Univ, 62-63; asst prof physics, Univ Pa, 63-69; assoc prof physics, Ore State Univ, 69-76; sr systs analyst, Sun Studs-Veneer, Roseburg, Ore, 76-86. *Mem:* Am Phys Soc. *Res:* Photo production and neutral decays of pion resonances; cosmic ray muons; lepton conservation; pion-nucleus interactions. *Mailing Add:* PO Box 74 Winchester OR 97495-0074

RICHERT, NANCY DEMBECK, MOLECULAR BIOLOGY. *Current Pos:* Expert, 78-82, sr staff fel, 82-84, SR INVESTR, NAT CANCER INST, NIH, 84- *Personal Data:* b Pittsburgh, Pa, July 23, 45. *Educ:* Univ Rochester, PhD(microbiol), 73. *Mem:* Sigma Xi; AAAS; Endocrine Soc; Am Soc Cell Biol. *Mailing Add:* 4601 N Park Ave Apt 1702B Chevy Chase MD 20815-4525

RICHES, DAVID WILLIAM HENRY, PEDIATRICS. *Current Pos:* ASST PROF DEPT BIOCHEM, BIOPHYS & GENETICS, HEALTH SCI CTR, UNIV COLO, 85-, ASST PROF, DIIV PULMONARY SCI, DEPT MED, 89- *Personal Data:* b Apr 8, 55; m; c 2. *Educ:* Univ Birmingham, Eng, BSc Hons, 76, PhD(immunol), 79. *Prof Exp:* Res fel, Dept Immunol, Univ Birmingham, Eng, 79-83; res fel, 83-85, staff researcher, Dept Pediat, Nat Jewish Ctr Immunol & Respiratory Med, Denver, 85- *Concurrent Pos:* grants, Biomed Res Support, NJC, Colo Inst Res, R01 CA50107, & SCOR, 85-97; reviewer, J Am Rev Respiratory Dis, J Immunol, Clin Immunol & Immunopath, Immunol, Biochem Pharmacol, Substance & Alcohol Actions/Misuse & Lymphokine Res; grant reviewer, NSF, Vet Admin Career Develop Prog & NIH. *Mem:* Soc Leukocyte Biol; Am Soc Cell Biol. *Res:* Immunology; pediatrics. *Mailing Add:* Dept Pediat & Respiratory Med Nat Jewish Ctr Immunol & Respiratory Med 1400 Jackson St D405 Denver CO 80206-2762

RICHES, WESLEY WILLIAM, CHEMISTRY. *Current Pos:* RETIRED. *Personal Data:* b Mt Pleasant, Mich, Feb 13, 14; m 41; c 2. *Educ:* Cent Mich Univ, AB, 35; Univ Mich, MS, 36, PhD(chem), 41. *Hon Degrees:* ScD, Cent Mich Univ, 63. *Prof Exp:* Res chemist pigments dept, E I Du Pont De Nemours & Co, 41-55, salesman, 55-63, tech serv chemist, 63-64, group suprv, 64-66, mgr, Chem Dyes, 66-79. *Mem:* Am Chem Soc; Tech Asn Pulp & Paper Inst. *Res:* Pigments; surface chemistry. *Mailing Add:* 726 Loveville Rd Hockessin DE 19707-1505

RICHEY, CLARENCE B(ENTLEY), AGRICULTURAL ENGINEERING. *Current Pos:* assoc prof, 70-76, EMER PROF AGR ENG, PURDUE UNIV, 76- *Personal Data:* b Winnipeg, Man, Dec 28, 10; m 36; c 2. *Educ:* Iowa State Univ, BSAE, 33; Purdue Univ, BSME, 39. *Honors & Awards:* Cyrus Hall McCormick Gold Medal, Am Soc Agr Engrs, 77. *Prof Exp:* Time study engr, David Bradley Mfg Works, Ill, 33-36; instr farm power-mach, Purdue Univ, 36-41; asst prof, Ohio State Univ, 41-43; suprv adv develop eng, Elec Wheel Co, Ill, 43-46; proj engr, Harry Ferguson, Inc, Mich, 46-47; res eng, Dearborn Motors Corp, 47-53; suprv tractor & implement div, Ford Motor Co, 53-57, chief res engr, 57-62; chief engr & partner, Five Mfg Co, Ohio, 62-64; chief engr, Fowler Div, Massey-Ferguson Inc, Calif, 64-69, prod mgt engr, Massey-Ferguson Ltd, 70. *Mem:* Am Soc Agr Engrs. *Res:* Farm equipment; field machinery and tractors; biomass energy & gasification. *Mailing Add:* 2217 Delaware Dr West Lafayette IN 47906

RICHEY, HERMAN GLENN, JR, ORGANIC CHEMISTRY. *Current Pos:* from asst prof to assoc prof, Pa State Univ, 59-69, asst head, 83-88, prof, 69-94, EMER PROF CHEM, PA STATE UNIV, 94- *Personal Data:* b Chicago, Ill, May 25, 32; m 62, Jane B Moss; c Susan, Anna & Daniel. *Educ:* Univ Chicago, BA, 52; Harvard Univ, MA, 55, PhD(chem), 59. *Prof Exp:* NSF fel chem, Yale Univ, 58-59. *Concurrent Pos:* Sloan fel, 64-68; John Simon Guggenheim fel, 67-68; consult, Koppers Co, Inc, 63-88, INDSPEC Chem Corp, 89- *Mem:* Am Chem Soc; Royal Soc Chem; Sigma Xi. *Res:* Structures, new reactions, and mechanisms of reactions, particularly of polar, main-group organometallic compounds; organometallic chemistry of polar main group elements. *Mailing Add:* Dept Chem Pa State Univ University Park PA 16802. *Fax:* 814-865-3314; *E-Mail:* hgr@chem.psu.edu

RICHEY, WILLIS DALE, PHYSICAL CHEMISTRY. *Current Pos:* from asst prof to assoc prof, 63-74, Buhl prof, 76-77, PROF CHEM, CHATHAM COL, 74- *Personal Data:* b Bedford, Ohio, July 26, 30; c 1. *Educ:* Hiram Col, BA, 52; Univ Rochester, PhD(chem), 58. *Prof Exp:* Res chemist, Diamond Alkali Co, 57-58; from asst prof to assoc prof chem, Bethany Col, 58-62; vis assoc prof, Colby Col, 62-63. *Concurrent Pos:* Vis scholar, Freer Gallery Art, Smithsonian Inst, 69-70; fac res partic, Pittsburgh Energy Technol Ctr, Dept Energy, 78-79. *Mem:* AAAS; Am Chem Soc; Am Phys Soc; Royal Soc Chem; Int Inst Conserv Hist & Artistic Works; Am Geophys Union; Mineral Soc Am. *Res:* Chemical aspects of the conservation of objects of historic and artistic value; thermodynamics of the conversions of inorganic constituents of coals during liquifaction and gasification processes; corosion of metals. *Mailing Add:* 5023 Bayard St Pittsburgh PA 15213-1901

RICHIE, JOHN PETER, JR, AGING, METABOLIC EPIDEMIOLOGY. *Current Pos:* sr res fel, Div Nutrit & Endocrinol, 87-88, assoc res scientist nutrit biochem, Div Nutrit Carcinogenesis, 88-, RES SCIENTIST, DIV NUTRIT CARCINOGENESIS; ASSOC RES PROF, DEPT EXP PATH, NY MED COL, 88- *Personal Data:* b Holden, Mass, Nov 11, 56; m 89. *Educ:* Worcester Polytech Inst, BS, 78; Univ Louisville, MS, 83, PhD(biochem), 86. *Honors & Awards:* George A Sacher Award, Geront Soc Am, 86. *Prof Exp:* Res assoc toxicol, Dept Pharm & Toxicol, Univ Louisville, 86-87. *Mem:* Sigma Xi; Soc Exp Biol & Med; Am Soc Biochem & Molecular Biol; Oxygen Soc; Geront Soc Am. *Res:* Biochemistry of aging, with emphasis on glutathione and other redox systems; effects of aging and nutrition on host factors which regulate susceptibility of individuals to diseases and toxins; metabolic epidemiology of diseases of aging. *Mailing Add:* Am Health Found One Dana Rd Valhalla NY 10595

RICHLEY, E(DWARD) A(NTHONY), MECHANICAL ENGINEERING, PHYSICS. *Current Pos:* RETIRED. *Personal Data:* b Cleveland, Ohio, Sept 5, 28; m 50; c 2. *Educ:* Cleveland State Univ, BME, 59; Case Western Reserve Univ, MS, 63. *Prof Exp:* Res scientist, Lewis Res Ctr, NASA, 59-62, head, Propulsion Components Sect, 62-68, chief, Ion Physics Br, 68-70, mem dir staff, 70-72, chief off oper analysis & planning, 72-76, chief mgt opers officer, 76-80, dir admin, 80-88. *Mem:* Assoc fel Am Inst Aeronaut & Astronaut. *Res:* Institutional and research and development operations analysis and planning. *Mailing Add:* 4475 Valley Forge Dr Cleveland OH 44126-2826

RICHLIN, JACK, PHYSICAL CHEMISTRY. *Current Pos:* from asst prof to assoc prof, 65-86, PROF PHYS CHEM, MONMOUTH COL, NJ, 86- *Personal Data:* b New York, NY, Jan 17, 33; m 76; c 2. *Educ:* Brooklyn Col, BS, 54; Purdue Univ, MS, 57; Rutgers Univ, PhD(chem), 64. *Prof Exp:* Sr res chemist, Allied Chem Corp, 62-65. *Mem:* Am Chem Soc. *Res:* Polymer physics; computer application to education; solution and surface properties of detergents and surfactants. *Mailing Add:* Dept Chem Monmouth Col West Long Branch NJ 07764

RICHMAN, ALEX, PSYCHIATRY, EPIDEMIOLOGY. *Current Pos:* PRES, ALGOPLUS CONSULT LTD, 94- *Personal Data:* b Winnipeg, Man, Jan 23, 29; m 52; c 4. *Educ:* Univ Man, MD, 53; McGill Univ, dipl psychiat, 57; Johns Hopkins Univ, MPH, 60. *Prof Exp:* Staff asst, Comt Ment Health Serv, Can Ment Health Asn, 56-60; asst prof psychiat, Univ BC, 60; proj dir, Can Royal Comn Health Serv, 62-63; head, Sect Social Psychiat, Univ BC, 63-66; med officer, WHO, Geneva, 66-67; assoc prof epidemiol & dir training prog psychiat epidemiol, Columbia Univ, 67-69; prof psychiat, Mt Sinai Sch Med & chief utilization rev psychiat, Beth Israel Med Ctr, 69-78; prof, Dept Psychiat & Prev Med, Dalhousie Univ, 78-94. *Concurrent Pos:* Nat Ment Health res award, Can Ment Health Asn, 64; assoc prof psychiat, Univ BC, 64-66; consult, WHO, Ministry Health, Jamaica, 64-66; Nat Health Scientist award, 78-82; consult, Southern NB Ment Health Planning Comt, 80-82 & Policy & Planning Unit, Ment Health Br, Ont Ministry of Health, 81- *Mem:* Am Pub Health Asn. *Res:* Social psychiatry; epidemiology; mental disorders; quality assurance; evaluation; planning of mental health services; aviation safety. *Mailing Add:* 502-5675 Spring Garden Rd Halifax NS B3J 1H1 Can. *Fax:* 902-423-5156; *E-Mail:* algoplus@kayhay.com

RICHMAN, DAVID BRUCE, BIOLOGICAL CONTROL, SPIDER TAXONOMY. *Current Pos:* fel, 78-81, asst prof, 83-89, SCI SPECIALIST, NMEX STATE UNIV, 89- *Personal Data:* b Dunkirk, NY, Nov 6, 42; m 77, Lynda Goin; c Julia A & Rebecca L. *Educ:* Univ Ariz, BS, 70, MS, 73; Univ Fla, PhD(invert zool), 77. *Prof Exp:* Fel, Univ Fla, 77-78 & 81-82. *Mem:* Am Inst Biol Sci; Entom Soc Am; Am Arachnological Soc; Int Hymenopterists Soc; Asn Systs Collections. *Res:* Systematics and ethology of jumping spiders; biological control of range weeds; development of arthropod manuals; biological control of insects using natural enemies in cropping systems; arthropod biodiversity. *Mailing Add:* Dept Entom Plant Path & Weed Sci NMex State Univ Las Cruces NM 88003. *Fax:* 505-646-8087; *E-Mail:* nmbugman@taipan.nmsu.edu

RICHMAN, DAVID M(ARTIN), ENERGY SCIENCE & TECHNOLOGY, RESEARCH MANAGEMENT. *Current Pos:* SR STAFF, BDM FEDERAL INC, 92- *Personal Data:* b New York, NY, Mar 13, 32; m 60; Majoryle Lechter; c Michael & Nancy. *Educ:* Columbia Univ, AB, 53, BA, 54, MS, 56. *Prof Exp:* Chem engr, Nuclear Eng Dept, Brookhaven Nat Lab, 55-58; radiation specialist, Div Isotope Develop, US AEC, 58-60, chemist, Div Res, 60-71, chief, Eng Chem & Isotope Prep Br, Div Phys Res, 71-72; head, Indust Appln & Chem Sect, Int Atomic Energy Agency, 72-74; chief, Chem Energy & Geosci Br, ERDA, 74-76, sr prog analyst, Off Asst Admin Solar & Geothermal Energy, 76-77; head, Prog Planning & Implementation Off, Off Asst Secy Conserv & Solar Appln, Dept Energy, 77-78, sr prog analyst, Off Asst Secy Energy Technol, 79-80, actg dir, Res & Tech Assessment Div, 80, staff phys scientist, Off Basic Energy Sci, Energy Res, 80-90, sci adv to dir energy res, 90-92. *Mem:* Am Chem Soc; Am Inst Chem Engrs. *Res:* Isotopic radiation source design; radiation chemistry; research policy and planning; isotope separations, transplutonium element production; separations chemistry; research materials distribution; solar energy; administration of basic research. *Mailing Add:* 8106 Whittier Blvd Bethesda MD 20817-3123. *Fax:* 301-320-5509

RICHMAN, DAVID PAUL, NEUROIMMUNOLOGY, EXPERIMENTAL NEUROPATHOLOGY & NEUROSCIENCE. *Current Pos:* PROF & CHMN, DEPT NEUROL, CTR NEUROSCI, UNIV CALIF, DAVIS, 91- *Personal Data:* b Boston, Mass, June 9, 43; m 69, Carol von Bastion; c Sarah & Jacob. *Educ:* Princeton Univ, AB, 65; Johns Hopkins Univ, MD, 69. *Prof Exp:* Intern & asst resident, Albert Einstein Col Med, 69-71; asst resident neurol, Mass Gen Hosp, 71-73, chief resident, 73-74, clin & res fel, 74-76; from asst prof to prof, Dept Neurol & Comt Immunol & Neuro Biol, Univ Chicago, 76-91, Marjorie & Robert E Straus prof neuro sci, 88-91. *Concurrent Pos:* chmn, Med Avd Bd, Myasthenia Gravis Found; instr neurol, Harvard Univ, 75-76; mem, Aging Rev Comt, Nat Inst Aging, 84-85 & Immunol Sci Study Sect, Diag Related Group, NIH, 86-90. *Mem:* Sigma Xi; Am Acad Neurol; AAAS; Am Asn Immunol; Am Neurol Asn. *Res:* Cellular immunology of neurological diseases and structure and function of acetylcholine receptors; myasthenia gravis and experimental myasthenia; monoclounal anti-acetylcholine receptor antibodies and anti-idiotypic antibodies; chimeric antibodies. *Mailing Add:* Dept Neurol Univ Calif 1515 Newton Ct Davis CA 95616. *E-Mail:* dprichman@ucdavis.edu

RICHMAN, DONALD, electrical engineering; deceased, see previous edition for last biography

RICHMAN, DOUGLAS DANIEL, INFECTIOUS DISEASES, VIROLOGY. *Current Pos:* PROF PATH & MED, UNIV CALIF SAN DIEGO, 76- *Personal Data:* b New York, NY, Feb 15, 43; m 65, Eva Acquino; c Sara & Matthew. *Educ:* Dartmouth Col, AB, 65; Stanford Univ, MD, 70. *Res:* Basic and clinical investigation in the pathogenesis and therapy of infection with human immunodeficiency virus, the cause of AIDS. *Mailing Add:* Dept Path & Med Univ Calif San Diego 9500 Gilman Dr La Jolla CA 92093-0679. *Fax:* 619-552-7445; *E-Mail:* drichman@ucsd.edu

RICHMAN, ISAAC, ELECTROOPTICS, SPECTROSCOPY. *Current Pos:* SPECIALIST & FEL, MCDONNELL DOUGLAS ELECTRONIC SYSTS CO, 66- *Personal Data:* b Havana, Cuba, Apr 3, 32; US citizen; m 60; c 2. *Educ:* Univ Calif, Los Angeles, BA, 54, MA, 58, PhD(physics), 63. *Prof Exp:* Res engr, Elec Div, Nat Cash Register Co, 56-58; mem tech staff crystal physics, Lab Div, Aerospace Corp, 63-66; res physicist, Univ Calif, Los Angeles, 66. *Mem:* Am Phys Soc. *Res:* Research and development in the areas of infrared and visible detection, imaging, radiometry, and spectroscopy; lattice vibration studies; infrared photoconductor studies, spectroscopy of dielectrics. *Mailing Add:* 1842 Port Manleigh Pl Newport Beach CA 92660-6626. *E-Mail:* richman@strasys.mdc.com

RICHMAN, JUSTIN LEWIS, MEDICINE, CARDIOLOGY. *Current Pos:* lectr, Univ, 53-60, from instr to sr instr, 56-58, asst prof, 58-79, ASSOC PROF MED, SCH MED, TUFTS UNIV, 70- *Personal Data:* b Providence, RI, Apr 12, 25; m 57; c 3. *Educ:* Brown Univ, AB, 46; Tufts Univ, MD, 49; Am Bd Internal Med, dipl, 56. *Prof Exp:* Lectr, Harvard Univ, 52-53. *Concurrent Pos:* USPHS fel cardiol, 51-53; physician-in-chg, Dept Med, Boston Dispensary, 56-68, chief electrocardiography lab, 57-68; consult, Mass Heart Asn, 57-60 & NH Heart Asn, 59-; physician-in-chief, Med Clin, New Eng Med Ctr Hosps, 56-68. *Mem:* AAAS; Am Heart Asn; Am Soc Internal Med; fel Am Col Cardiol. *Res:* Clinical cardiology; spatial vectorcardiography and electrocardiography. *Mailing Add:* 25 Boylston St Chestnut Hill MA 02167-1710

RICHMAN, MARC H(ERBERT), METALLURGY, MATERIALS SCIENCE. *Current Pos:* from asst prof to assoc prof, Brown Univ, 63-67, dir, Electron Microscopy Facil, 70-86, PROF ENG, BROWN UNIV, 70-, DIR, UNDERGRAD PROGS ENG, 91- *Personal Data:* b Boston, Mass, Oct 14, 36; m 63, Ann Yoffa. *Educ:* Mass Inst Technol, BS, 57, ScD(metall), 63. *Honors & Awards:* Outstanding Young Faculty Award, Am Soc Eng Educ, 69; Albert Sauveur Award, Am Soc Metals, 69; Freeman Award, Providence Eng Soc, 89; Excellence in Teaching Award, Tech Anal Corp, 92; Engr of Year Award, RI Soc Prof Engrs. *Prof Exp:* Instr metall, Mass Inst Technol, 57-60, res asst, 60-63. *Concurrent Pos:* Instr, Dept Educ, Commonwealth Mass, 58-62; consult engr, 58-; adj staff, Dept Med, Miriam Hosp, Providence, RI, 74-86; bioengr, Dept Orthop, RI Hosp, Providence, 79-93; pres, Marc H Richman, Inc, Consult Engrs, 81- *Mem:* Am Soc Metals; Am Crystallog Asn; Am Inst Mining, Metall & Petrol Engrs; fel Am Inst Chem; Am Ceramic Soc; fel Nat Acad Forensic Engrs. *Res:* Study of phase transformations by optical, electron and field ion microscopy; relation of properties to structure; development of ceramic materials by microstructural design; biomaterials in orthopaedics and cardiovascular systems; forensic engineering. *Mailing Add:* 291 Cole Ave Providence RI 02906-3452. *Fax:* 401-863-1157; *E-Mail:* mrichman@brownvm.brown.edu

RICHMAN, MICHAEL B, CLIMATOLOGY, MULTIVARIATE STATISTICAL TECHNIQUES. *Current Pos:* ASST PROF, SCH METEOROL, UNIV OKLA, 94- *Personal Data:* b Manhasset, NY, May 27, 54; m 77, Carol J Bistline; c Lindsay & Alexander. *Educ:* State Univ NY, BA, 76; Univ Ill, MS, 80; PhD, 94. *Prof Exp:* Prof scientist, Ill State Water Surv, 78-91; res scientist, Coop Inst Mesoscale Meteorol Studies, 90-94.

Concurrent Pos: Prin investr, Nat Oceanic & Atmospheric Admin, 88-90 & 96-, NSF, 90-96 & US Environ Protection Agency, 91-96; assoc ed, J Climate, 89-96; consult, Salt River Proj, 91; lectr, Max Planck Inst Meteorol, Ger, 92. *Mem:* Am Meteorol Soc; Sigma Xi; Am Statist Asn. *Res:* Climatology and multivariate statistical techniques. *Mailing Add:* Dept Meteorol 1310 Sarkeys Energy Ctr 100 E Boyd St Norman OK 73019. *E-Mail:* mrichman@ou.edu

RICHMAN, PAUL G, VACCINES, ALLERGENIC PRODUCTS. *Current Pos:* res chemist, Lab Allergenic Prod, Div Bact Prod, Food & Drug Admin, 79-90, chemist, Vaccine & Allergenic Prod Br, Div Biol Investigational New Drugs, 90-93, actg chief, Bact Vaccines & Allergenic Prod Br, Div Vaccines & Related Prod Applns, Off Vaccines Res & Rev, Ctr Biol Eval & Res, 93-94 CHIEF, BACT VACCINES & ALLERGENIC PROD BR, DIV VACCINES & RELATED PROD APPLICATION, OFF VACCINES RES & REV, CTR BIOL EVAL & RES, FOOD & DRUG ADMIN, 94- *Personal Data:* b New York, NY, Jan 24, 47; m 76, Janet Healy; c Peter & Sarah. *Educ:* City Univ NY, BS, 67; Cornell Univ, PhD(biochem), 75. *Prof Exp:* Res assoc biochem, Dept Biol, Yale Univ, 74-76; staff fel, Lab Biochem, Nat Cancer Inst, 76-79. *Concurrent Pos:* Actg lab chief, Lab Allergenic Prod, Food & Drug Admin, 88-89, actg br chief, Vaccine & Allergenic Prod Br, 92-93. *Mem:* Am Chem Soc. *Res:* Mechanism of enzyme action; protein chemistry; protein structure-function relationships; allergenic extract standardization and assay development. *Mailing Add:* Ctr Biol Eval & Res Off Vaccines & Related Prod Applns WOC-I 1401 Rockville Pike HFM-475 Suite 370N Rockville MD 20852

RICHMAN, ROBERT ALAN, PEDIATRIC ENDOCRINOLOGY, GROWTH. *Current Pos:* PROF PEDIAT & CHIEF, DIV PEDIAT ENDOCRINOL, HEALTH SCI COL, STATE UNIV NY, SYRACUSE, 76- *Personal Data:* b Brooklyn, NY, Nov 21, 40; m 64, Donnaline Schinfeld; c Peter B, Michael S & Tamara J. *Educ:* Brandeis Univ, BA, 62; Queens Col, MA, 63; Upstate Med Ctr, MD, 67. *Prof Exp:* Internship pediat, Boston City Hosp, 67-68; residency, Mt Sinai Hosp, NY, 68-69; NIH fel pediat endocrinol, Univ NC, 69-71; asst prof pediat, Sch Med, Univ Ill, 73-74; NIH special res fel physiol, Sch Med, Vanderbilt Univ, 74-76. *Concurrent Pos:* Pres, SUNY Med Aluni Assoc, 92- *Mem:* Endocrine Soc; Lawson Wilkins Pediat Endocrine Soc; fel Am Acad Pediat; Am Fedn Clin Res; AAAS; Soc Pediat Res. *Res:* Hormonal regulation of growth. *Mailing Add:* State Univ NY Health Sci Ctr 750 E Adams St Syracuse NY 13210. *Fax:* 315-464-7564

RICHMAN, ROBERT MICHAEL, TRANSITION METAL PHOTOCHEMISTRY. *Current Pos:* chmn, Sci dept, 87-96, ASSOC PROF & CHMN, SCI DEPT, MT ST MARY'S COL, 96- *Personal Data:* b Pasadena, Calif, Apr 27, 50; m 76, Linda Dochter. *Educ:* Occidental Col, AB, 71; Univ Ill, Urbana, MS, 72, PhD(inorg chem), 76. *Prof Exp:* NSF fel, Calif Inst Technol, 76-77; asst prof, Carnegie-Mellon Univ, 77-84, asst dept head chem, 84-87. *Mem:* Am Chem Soc. *Res:* Transition metal photochemistry in homogeneous solution aimed at developing new strategies for solar energy conversion. *Mailing Add:* Sci Dept Mt St Mary's Col Emmitsburg MD 21727-7799. *Fax:* 301-447-5755; *E-Mail:* richman@msmary.edu

RICHMAN, ROGER H, METALLURGY & PHYSICAL METALLURGICAL ENGINEERING. *Current Pos:* PRIN & TECH DIR, DAEDALUS ASSOCS, INC, 85- *Personal Data:* b Newark, NJ, May 4, 29; m 53, Beverly Resnick; c Joshua. *Educ:* NMex Inst Mining Technol, BS, 50; Lehigh Univ, PhD, 58. *Prof Exp:* Staff scientist & suprv, Sci Res Staff, Ford Motor Co, 58-75; proj mgr, Elec Power Res Inst, 75-79; gen mgr & vpres, Aptech Eng Serv, 79-84. *Mem:* Fel Am Soc Metals Int; Am Inst Mining Metall & Petrol Engrs; Nat Asn Corrosion Engrs; Mat Res Soc; AAAS; Sigma Xi. *Res:* Development of materials for power-generation technologies; fatigue analysis; phase transition mechanisms; failure analysis. *Mailing Add:* Daedalus Assoc 2134 Old Middlefield Way E Mountain View CA 94043-2404. *Fax:* 650-964-4210

RICHMAN, SUMNER, AQUATIC ECOLOGY. *Current Pos:* From instr biol to assoc prof, 57-70, chmn dept, 77-84 & 88-92, PROF BIOL, LAWRENCE UNIV, 70- *Personal Data:* b Boston, Mass, Dec 15, 29; m 52, Joyce Clements; c Nancy, Robert & Jeffrey. *Educ:* Hartwick Col, AB, 51; Univ Mass, MA, 53; Univ Mich (zool), 57. *Hon Degrees:* MA, Laurence Univ, 94. *Concurrent Pos:* Vis prof marine biol, Tel-Aviv Univ & Marine Lab, Eilat, Israel, 72 & Chesapeake Biol Lab, Univ Md, 74-75, Marine Biol Lab, Woods Hole, 88-89; col accreditation evaluator, N Cent Asn Col & Sec Schs, 72-; Smithsonian Inst Foreign Currency Grant, 72, sea grants, 78-, NSF-ROA grant, 88-89; rev comt, NCent Asn Col & Sec Schs, 93- *Mem:* AAAS; Ecol Soc Am; Am Soc Limnol & Oceanog; Sigma Xi; Int Cong Limnol. *Res:* Energy transformation in aquatic systems; secondary productivity and zooplankton feeding behavior. *Mailing Add:* Dept Biol Lawrence Univ Appleton WI 54912. *E-Mail:* richmans@lawrence.edu

RICHMOND, ARTHUR DEAN, ATMOSPHERIC PHYSICS, UPPER ATMOSPHERIC ELECTRODYNAMICS. *Current Pos:* SCIENTIST, NAT CTR ATMOSPHERIC RES, 83- *Personal Data:* b Long Beach, Calif, Mar 13, 44; m 71; c 2. *Educ:* Univ Calif, Los Angeles, BS, 65, PhD(meteorol), 70. *Prof Exp:* Asst res meteorologist, Univ Calif, Los Angeles, 70-71; Nat Acad Sci resident res assoc, Air Force Cambridge Res Labs, 71-72; res assoc upper atmospheric physics, High Altitude Observ, Nat Ctr Atmospheric Res, 72-76; res assoc, Coop Inst Res Environ Sci, Univ Colo, 76-77; res assoc, Nat Oceanic & Atmospheric Admin, 77-80, space scientist, 80-83. *Concurrent Pos:* Consult, Rand Corp, 66-69; NATO fel sci, Lab Physique de l'Exosphere, Univ Paris, 73-74; assoc prof physics, 89; comt mem, Comt Solar-Terrestrial Res, Nat Res Coun, 82-85, Comt Solar & Space Physics, 93-96; Japan Soc Prom Sci fel, 86; chmn, Div 2, Int Assoc Geomagnetism & Aeronomy, 91-95.

Mem: AAAS; Am Geophys Union; Am Meteorol Soc. *Res:* Upper atmospheric electric fields and currents; geomagnetism; atmospheric dynamics. *Mailing Add:* NCAR High Altitude Observ Boulder CO 80307-3000

RICHMOND, CHARLES WILLIAM, ORGANIC CHEMISTRY. *Current Pos:* assoc prof, 69, PROF CHEM, UNIV N ALA, 69- *Personal Data:* b New Martinsville, WVa, Jan 8, 38; m 66; c 3. *Educ:* David Lipscomb Col, BA, 60; Univ Miss, PhD(org chem), 64. *Prof Exp:* Asst prof chem, David Lipscomb Col, 64-69. *Mem:* Am Chem Soc. *Res:* Preparation of heterocyclic compounds for use as potential drugs. *Mailing Add:* Chem Univ NAla 1 N Alabama Florence AL 35632-0001

RICHMOND, CHESTER ROBERT, RADIOBIOLOGY, RISK ANALYSIS. *Current Pos:* PROF BIOMED SCI, UNIV TENN-OAK RIDGE GRAD SCH BIOMED SCI, 75-, FROM ASSOC DIR BIOMED & ENVIRON SCI TO ASSOC DIR EMER, OAK RIDGE NAT LAB, 74- *Personal Data:* b South Amboy, NJ, May 29, 29; m 52; c 4. *Educ:* NJ State Col, Montclair, BA, 52; Univ NMex, MS, 54, PhD(biol), 58. *Honors & Awards:* E O Lawrence Award, US AEC, 74; G Failla Award & Lectr, Radiation Res Soc, 76; W H Langham Mem Lectr, Univ Ky, 87. *Prof Exp:* Asst physiol, Univ NMex, 54-55; asst, Los Alamos Sci Lab, 55-57, mem staff, 57-68; mem staff, Div Biol & Med, US AEC, 68-71; leader biomed res group, Los Alamos Sci Lab, 71-73, alternate health div leader, 73-74. *Concurrent Pos:* Mem, Nat Coun Radiation Protection & Measurements, 74-; comt 2, Int Comn Radiol Protection, 77-; bd dirs, Nat Coun Radiation Protection & Measurements & Inst Biomed Imaging, Univ Tenn, 88- *Mem:* Fel AAAS; Health Physics Soc; Sigma Xi; Soc Risk Analysis; Radiation Res Soc; NY Acad Sci. *Res:* Water and electrolyte metabolism; comparative metabolism of radionuclides; anthropometry; biological effects of internal emitters; health & environ effects of energy production; radiobiology of actinide elements. *Mailing Add:* 108 Westwind Dr Oak Ridge TN 37830-8618

RICHMOND, GERALD MARTIN, QUATERNARY GEOLOGY. *Current Pos:* SR GEOLOGIST, BR CENT GEN GEOL, US GEOL SURV, 42- *Personal Data:* b Providence, RI, July 30, 14; m 41, 67; c 4. *Educ:* Brown Univ, BA, 36; Harvard Univ, MA, 39; Univ Colo, PhD, 54. *Honors & Awards:* Kirk Bryan Award, Geol Soc Am, 65; Albrecht Penck Medal, Deutsche Quartarvereinigung, 78. *Prof Exp:* Instr geol, Univ Conn, 40; geologist, Spec Eng Div, Panama Canal, 41-42. *Concurrent Pos:* NSF grant, Alps, 60-61; mem qual adv group, US Comn Stratig Nomenclature; mem stratig comn, Int Union Quaternary Res, 77-; mem, US Nat Comt for Int Geol Correlation Prog, 74-78; US working group, Quaternary Glaciation in Northern Hemisphere, 74- *Mem:* AAAS; Int Union Quaternary Res (secy gen, 62-65, pres, 65-69); fel Geol Soc Am; Am Quaternary Asn; Sigma Xi. *Res:* Glacial and surficial geology; quaternary stratigraphy and correlation; fossil soils; geomorphology. *Mailing Add:* 3950 S Hillcrest Dr Denver CO 80237

RICHMOND, ISABELLE LOUISE, NEUROBIOLOGY, NEUROSURGERY. *Current Pos:* ASSOC PROF NEUROSURG, EASTERN VA MED SCH, 84-; CLIN PROF SURG, UNIFORMED SERVS UNIV, 86- *Educ:* Cornell Univ, PhD(neurobiol), 68; Duke Univ, MD, 74. *Concurrent Pos:* Pres, Norfolk Acad Med. *Mem:* Am Asn Neurol Surgeons; fel Am Col Surgeons; AMA. *Res:* Nerve repair; pituitary adenoma. *Mailing Add:* 229 W Bute St No 230 Norfolk VA 23510

RICHMOND, JAMES KENNETH, PHYSICS. *Current Pos:* CONSULT, MINING & INDUST CADRE, 83- *Personal Data:* b Chattanooga, Tenn, June 23, 20; m 44; c 4. *Educ:* Ga Inst Technol, BS, 42; Univ Pittsburgh, MS, 43; MA, 58. *Honors & Awards:* US Dept Interior Award, 59 & 75. *Prof Exp:* Res engr, Westinghouse Elec Corp, 42-44, 47-49; asst nuclear physics, Univ Pa, 46-47; physicist combustion, US Bur Mines, 49-59; res specialist advan propulsion, Sci Res Labs, Boeing Co, 59-69, sr basic res scientist, 69-71; res physicist, US Bur Mines, 71-80, suprvry res physicist, 80-83. *Concurrent Pos:* Instr, Carnegie Inst Technol, 55-59; consult, Comt Fire Res & Fire Res Conf, Nat Acad Sci-Nat Res Coun, 59; vis instr, Community Col, Allegheny Co, PA, 84-87; instr, Bellevue & Edmond's Community Cols, 89- *Mem:* Am Phys Soc; Inst Elec & Electronics Engrs. *Res:* Prevention of fires and explosions in coal mines, oil shale mines and other mines; supervision of group engaged in conducting research on full-scale explosions in experimental mines and the instrumentation thereof. *Mailing Add:* 12553 37th Ave NE Seattle WA 98125

RICHMOND, JAMES M, SYNTHESIS OF NITROGEN BASED SURFACTANTS. *Personal Data:* b Armstrong, Iowa, July 29, 41; m 63, Jeannette McCorkle; c Colin R. *Educ:* Iowa State Univ, BS, 63; Kans State Univ, PhD(org chem), 74. *Prof Exp:* Captain, USMC, 63-69; chemist, Procter & Gamble Co, 74-76; chemist, Armak Co, 76-78, sect head, 78-80, area mgr, Akzo Chem Am, Akzo Am, 80-83, dept head, chem res mgr, Akzo Chemicals, 89-91; dir, Formulations, Sandoz Agro, Inc, 92-97. *Concurrent Pos:* Edm Cationic Surfactants, Org Chem, 90. *Mem:* Am Chem Soc; Am Oil Chemists Soc. *Res:* Process and product development of nitrogen derivatives of natural fats and oils, especially amines, amides, ethoxylates, nitriles and quaternary ammonium salts; author of one book and 14 patents. *Mailing Add:* 1469 Farington Ct Naperville IL 60563-2218. *E-Mail:* richmonj@ix.netcom.com

RICHMOND, JONAS EDWARD, BIOCHEMISTRY. *Current Pos:* assoc biochemist, 63-69, BIOCHEMIST, UNIV CALIF, BERKELEY, 69- *Personal Data:* b Prentiss, Miss, July 17, 29; m 57, Mattie L Humes; c Keith & Gigi. *Educ:* Univ Tenn, BS, 48; Univ Rochester, MS, 50, PhD(biochem, biophys), 53. *Prof Exp:* Res assoc biophys, Univ Rochester, 50-55, instr biophys & biochem, 56-57; estab investr, Am Heart Asn, Harvard Med Sch, 57-63. *Concurrent Pos:* NIH fel, Univ Rochester, 53-55; Commonwealth fel, Oxford Univ, 55-56; mem, Allergy & Immunol A Study Sect, NIH, 65-69, career develop, 65-70, nutrit study sect, Marc Study Sect; consult, US HEW, 66- & NIH, 71, 74; pres, Alameda Co Heart Asn, 74-; vpres, Am Heart Asn Calif affil, chmn, Res Comn. *Mem:* AAAS; Am Chem Soc; Radiation Res Soc; Am Soc Biol Chem; Biophys Soc; Sigma Xi; Am Physiol Soc; Am Soc Cell Biol. *Res:* Chemistry and biochemistry of proteins; protein and amino acid metabolism; transport and membrane function; intermediary metabolism; radiation chemistry; biochemistry and biophysics of growth; molecular biology; cell recognition and differentiation; cell surface chemistry. *Mailing Add:* Dept Nutrit Sci 219 Morgan Hall Univ Calif Berkeley CA 94720

RICHMOND, JONATHAN YOUNG, VIROLOGY, GENETICS. *Current Pos:* DIR, OFF HEALTH & SAFETY, CTR DIS CONTROL, 90- *Personal Data:* b Norwalk, Conn, Feb 10, 41; m 66, Anne Tucker; c Eleanor, Patricia, Jennifer & Katherine. *Educ:* Univ Conn, BA, 62, MS, 64; Hahnemann Med Col, PhD(genetics), 68. *Honors & Awards:* Silver Beaver Award, Bd Sci Affairs, 81; Cert Merit, USDA/Agr Res Serv, 83. *Prof Exp:* NSF-Nat Res Coun fel virol & cytol, US Dept Agr, 67-69, res microbiologist, 69-79, biol safety officer, Plum Island Animal Dis Ctr, 79-83; chief, Safety Opers Sect, Occup Safety & Health Br, Div Safety, NIH, 83-90. *Concurrent Pos:* Safety specialist, Disaster Med Assistance Team, PHHS, 83-88, Acquired Immune Deficiency Syndrome, video tech expert, 88-; dir, Who Collaborating Ctr Appl Biosafety & Training, 90- *Mem:* Am Asn Lab Animal Sci; Am Biol Safety Asn (pres, 86); fel Am Acad Microbiol; Am Soc Microbiol. *Res:* Virus/cell interrelationships; sterilization of biological materials by gamma irridation; development and presentation training programs in: occupational safety and health, biological safety, chemical safety, animal use and care, infectious waste management. *Mailing Add:* Off Health & Safety MS F05 Ctr Dis Control Atlanta GA 30333. *Fax:* 404-639-2294; *E-Mail:* jyr1@cdc.gov

RICHMOND, JULIUS BENJAMIN, MEDICINE, PEDIATRICS. *Current Pos:* prof child psychiat & human develop, Fac Pub Health & Fac Med, Harvard Med Sch, 71-73, prof prev & social med & chmn dept, 71-79, prof health policy, 81-88, dir, Div Health Policy Res & Educ, 83-88, JOHN D MACARTHUR EMER PROF HEALTH POLICY, HARVARD MED SCH, 83- *Personal Data:* b Chicago, Ill, Sept 26, 16; m 85, Rhee Chidekel; c Barry J, M Jean (Glick) & Charles Allen. *Educ:* Univ Ill, BS, 37, MD & MS, 39; Am Bd Pediat, dipl. *Hon Degrees:* DSc Ind Univ, 78, Rush Presby St Luke Med Ctr, 78, Univ Ill, 79, Georgetown Univ, 80, State Univ NY, Syracuse, 86, Univ Ariz, 91; DMS, Med Col Pa, 80; DPS, Nat Col Educ, Evanston, 80; LHD, Tufts Univ, 86. *Honors & Awards:* Gustav Lienhart Award, Inst Med, Nat Acad Sci, 86; Aldrich Award, Am Acad Pediat; Martha May Eliot, Am Pub Health Asn, Sedgwick Medal; Ittleson Award, Am Ortho Psychiat Asn; Howland Award, Am Pediat Soc. *Prof Exp:* Resident, Cook Co Hosp, Chicago, Ill, 46; prof pediat, Col Med, Univ Ill, 46-53; prof & chmn dept, Col Med, State Univ NY Upstate Med Ctr, 53-71. *Concurrent Pos:* Markle Found scholar med sci, 48-53; supt inst juvenile res, Ill State Dept Pub Welfare, 52-53; dir, Proj Headstart, Off Econ Opportunity, 65-; dean med fac, State Univ NY Upstate Med Ctr, 65-71; psychiatrist in chief, Children's Hosp Med Ctr, Boston, 71-77; asst secy for Health & Surgeon Gen, USPHS, HEW, 77-81; adv child health policy, Children's Hosp Med Ctr, 81- *Mem:* Inst Med-Nat Acad Sci; Am Psychiat Asn; Am Pub Health Asn; Soc Pediat Res; Am Pediat Soc; Am Acad Pediat. *Res:* Pediatrics; psychological aspects of pediatrics; child development. *Mailing Add:* 79 Beverly Rd Chestnut Hill MA 02167

RICHMOND, MARTHA ELLIS, BIOCHEMISTRY. *Current Pos:* from asst prof to assoc prof, 75-83, PROF CHEM, SUFFOLK UNIV, 83- *Personal Data:* b Wilmington, Del, Sept 10, 41; m 69; c 2. *Educ:* Wellesley Col, Mass, AB, 62; Tufts Univ, PhD(biochem), 69; Harvard Univ, MPH, 88. *Prof Exp:* Res fel bact & immunol, Harvard Med Sch, 69-70; res assoc med, Sch Med, Tufts Univ, 70-73; lectr, 73-74, asst prof biol, Univ Mass, Boston, 74-75. *Concurrent Pos:* Consult staff scientist, Health Effects Inst, Cambridge, Mass, 89- *Mem:* Sigma Xi; Am Chem Soc. *Res:* Biosynthesis of complex carbohydrates; regulation of complex carbohydrate synthesis in mammalian systems. *Mailing Add:* Dept Chem Suffolk Univ 8 Ashburton Pl Boston MA 02108-2701

RICHMOND, MILO EUGENE, VERTEBRATE ZOOLOGY, REPRODUCTIVE BIOLOGY. *Current Pos:* ASST PROF WILDLIFE SCI, NY STATE COL AGR & LIFE SCI & ASST LEADER NY COOP WILDLIFE RES UNIT, CORNELL UNIV, 68- *Personal Data:* b Cutler, Ill, Aug 29, 39. *Educ:* Southern Ill Univ, Carbondale, BA & BS, 61; Univ Mo-Columbia, MS, 63, PhD(zool), 67. *Prof Exp:* Asst instr zool, Univ Mo-Columbia, 64-67; asst prof biol, ETenn State Univ, 67-68. *Mem:* Am Soc Mammal; Wildlife Soc. *Res:* Ecology and physiology of reproduction of vertebrates; mammalian population dynamics, especially microtine rodents. *Mailing Add:* Dept Natural Resources 112 Fernow Hall Cornell Univ Ithaca NY 14853-3001

RICHMOND, OWEN, MECHANICAL ENGINEERING. *Current Pos:* CORP FEL & DIR, ALCOA TECH CTR, 83- *Personal Data:* b Geneva, Ill, Apr 1, 28. *Educ:* Bradley Univ, BS; Univ Ill, MS; Pa State Univ, PhD(theoret & appl mech). *Honors & Awards:* Appl Mech Award, Am Soc Mech Engrs, Nadai Award; Frary Award Lifetime Tech Achievement, Aluminum Co Am; Doolittle Distinguished Lectr, NC State Univ, 97. *Mem:* Nat Acad Eng. *Mailing Add:* Dir Core Tech Alcoa Tech Ctr 100 Technical Dr Alcoa Center PA 15069

RICHMOND, PATRICIA ANN, DEVELOPMENT OF SPECIALTY PROTEIN & STARCH BASED PRODUCTS. *Current Pos:* Food technologist, A E Staley Mfg Co, 75-77, lab mgr new prod develop, 77-79, group mgr sweetner develop, 79-85, mgr food & indust starch res & develop, Staley Continental Inc, 85-88, DIR FOOD INGREDIENT RES & DEVELOP, A E STALEY MFG CO, 88- *Personal Data:* b Salina, Kans, May 18, 47; m 82. *Educ:* Kans State Univ, BS, 70; Cornell Univ, MS, 72, PhD(food chem), 75. *Mem:* Inst Food Technologists; Am Asn Cereal Chemists. *Res:* Development of specialty protein and starch-based products for the food industry; development of high fructose corn syrup and other corn-based sweetners. *Mailing Add:* A E Staley Mfg Co 2200 E Eldorado Decatur IL 62525

RICHMOND, ROBERT CHAFFEE, RADIOBIOLOGY. *Current Pos:* res asst prof, 79-87, RES ASSOC PROF, NORRIS COTTON CANCER CTR, DARTMOUTH-HITCHCOCK MED CTR, HANOVER, NH, 87- *Personal Data:* b New York, NY, May 3, 43; m 68; c 1. *Educ:* Univ NH, BA, 66; Univ Tex, Austin, MA, 70, PhD(radiation biol), 72. *Prof Exp:* Teacher biol & chem, Chester High Sch, Vt, 66-68; res assoc radiation biol, Univ Kans, Lawrence, 73-75; vis scientist radiation biol, US Army Natick Develop Ctr, 75-77; instr radiol & radiation med, Boston Univ Med Ctr, 77-79. *Concurrent Pos:* Nat Res Coun fel, 75-77. *Mem:* Radiation Res Soc; Sigma Xi; AAAS; NY Acad Sci. *Res:* Chemical and thermal potentiation of cellular sensitivity and mutagenesis to radiation; chemistry and consequences of radiation-induced and antitumor drug-induced damage. *Mailing Add:* 1 Medical Center Dr Dartmouth Hitchcock Med Ctr Hanover NH 03756

RICHMOND, ROBERT H, INVERTEBRATE REPRODUCTIVE & CONSERVATION BIOLOGY, ENVIRONMENTAL BIOLOGY OF TROPICS. *Current Pos:* from asst prof to assoc prof, 86-88, dir, 88-91, PROF MARINE BIOL, UNIV GUAM MARINE LAB, 92- *Personal Data:* b White Plains, NY, May 26, 54; m 93, Cynthia Schubert; c Keana (Avery). *Educ:* Univ Rochester, BS, 76; State Univ NY, MS, 82, PhD(biol sci), 83. *Prof Exp:* Res tech, Dept Radiation Biol & Biophys, Univ Rochester, 75-76; res, Mid Pac Res Lab, 80-82; fel, Smithsonian Trop Res Inst, 84-85, Smithsonian Inst, 85-86. *Concurrent Pos:* Adj grad fac, Dept Zool, Univ Hawaii, Manoa, 90- *Mem:* Am Soc Zoologists; Western Soc Naturalists; Int Soc Reef Studies; Am Soc Molecular Marine Biol & Biotechnol. *Res:* Coral reef biology and ecology; reproductive biology and larval ecology of invertebrates; population biology and population genetics; environmental biology of tropical marine and island communities; evolutionary biology. *Mailing Add:* Marine Lab Univ Guam UOG Sta Mangilao GU 96923. *Fax:* 671-734-6767; *E-Mail:* richmond@uog9.uog.edu

RICHMOND, ROLLIN CHARLES, POPULATION GENETICS, BIOCHEMICAL GENETICS. *Current Pos:* DEAN, COL ARTS & SCI, UNIV SFLA, 90- *Personal Data:* b Nairobi, Kenya, May 31, 44; US citizen; m 75. *Educ:* San Diego State Univ, AB, 66; Rockefeller Univ, PhD(genetics), 71. *Prof Exp:* From asst prof to assoc prof zool, Ind Univ, 70-75; assoc prof genetics, NC State Univ, 76; assoc prof, Ind Univ, 76-81, prof, 81-90. *Concurrent Pos:* Assoc ed, J Soc Study Evolution, 75-77, Genetica, 81- & J Heredity, 81- *Mem:* Sigma Xi; Genetics Soc Am; Soc Study Evolution; Am Soc Naturalists; Ecol Soc Am. *Res:* Population genetics of natural and artificial populations of Drosophila with particular emphasis on the adaptive significance of isozyme variants; behavioral genetics of Drosophila. *Mailing Add:* Col Arts & Sci Univ SFla CPR 107 4202 Fowler Ave Tampa FL 33620-9951

RICHMOND, THOMAS G, ACTIVATION OF C-F BONDS. *Current Pos:* asst prof, 85-91, ASSOC PROF CHEM, UNIV UTAH, 91- *Personal Data:* b Buffalo, NY, Jan 4, 57; m 89. *Educ:* Brown Univ, ScB, 79; Northwestern Univ, PhD(chem), 84. *Prof Exp:* Res fel, Calif Inst Technol, 83-85. *Concurrent Pos:* Camille & Henry Dreyfus new fac fel, Dreyfus Found, 85; NSF presidential young investr, 89; Alfred P Sloan res fel, 91-93. *Mem:* Am Chem Soc. *Res:* Inorganic and organometallic chemistry; activation of C-F bonds; metal based molecular receptors; coordination chemistry and the design of new materials; environmental chemistry. *Mailing Add:* Dept Chem Univ Utah Salt Lake City UT 84112

RICHMOND, WILLIAM D, MECHANICAL ENGINEERING. *Current Pos:* asst lab dir, Battelle Mem Inst, 68-71; dir proj & facil, Pac Northwest Div, 71-79, dir, Hanford Proj, 79-85, DEP DIR, ENG TECHNOL, BATTELLE MEM INST, 85- *Personal Data:* b Denver, Colo, July 19, 25; m 48; c 5. *Educ:* Univ Wis, BSME, 46. *Prof Exp:* Engr, Bur Reclamation, 46-47, & Hanford Atomic Proj Opers, 47, Gen Elec Co, 47-64, proj engr, 47-56, supvr proj engr, 56-59, plant mgr reactor opers, 59-68. *Res:* Nuclear reactors. *Mailing Add:* 1014 Cedar Ave Richland WA 99352

RICHSTONE, DOUGLAS ORANGE, ASTRONOMY, ASTROPHYSICS. *Current Pos:* from asst prof to assoc prof astron, 80-88, chmn, Astron Dept, 85-90, PROF ASTRON, UNIV MICH, 88- *Personal Data:* b Alexandria, Va, Sept 20, 49. *Educ:* Calif Inst Technol, BS, 71; Princeton Univ, PhD(astrophys), 75. *Prof Exp:* Res fel astron, Calif Inst Technol, 74-76; asst prof physics, Univ Pittsburgh, 77-80. *Mem:* Royal Astron Soc; Am Astron Soc; Int Astron Union. *Res:* Quasi-stellar objects; structure of galaxies and clusters of galaxies; stellar dynamics; cosmology. *Mailing Add:* 2150 Overlook St Ann Arbor MI 48103. *Fax:* 313-763-6317; *E-Mail:* dor@astro.lsa.umich.edu

RICHTER, ACHIM, PHYSICS. *Current Pos:* dean fac physics, 94-96, PROF PHYSICS, TECH UNIV DARMSTADT, 74- *Personal Data:* b Dresden, Ger, Sept 21, 40; m 88, Christine Monika Leipert; c Rebecca & Tobias. *Educ:* Univ Heidelberg, dipl, 65, Dr, 67, Habilitation Physics, 71. *Hon Degrees:* D, Chalmers, Univ Sweden, 95; Dr, Univ Ghent, Belg, 96. *Honors & Awards:* Alexander von Humboldt Award, 88; Max Planck Res Prize Physics, Math & Astron, 92. *Prof Exp:* Res assoc, Max Planck Inst Nuclear Physics, 67 & Fla State Univ, 67-68; postdoctoral fel, Argonne Nat Lab, 68-70; docent physics, Univ Heidelberg, 71; assoc prof, Ruhr Univ, 71-74. *Concurrent Pos:* Head, Nuclear Physics Div, Ger Phys Soc, 81-83; head, Sci Coun, Soc Heavy Ion Res, Darmstadt, 94- *Mem:* Ger Phys Soc; Royal Soc SAfrica. *Res:* Contributed numerous articles to professional journals. *Mailing Add:* Telemannweg 17 64287 Darmstadt Germany. *Fax:* 49-6151-164321; *E-Mail:* richter@linac.ikp.physik.th-darmstadt.de

RICHTER, BURTON, PHYSICS. *Current Pos:* Res assoc, Stanford Univ, 56-60, from asst prof to assoc prof, 60-67, tech dir, Stanford Linear Accelerator Ctr, 82-84, PROF PHYSICS, STANFORD UNIV, 67-, PAUL PIGOTT PROF PHYS SCI, 80-, DIR, STANFORD LINEAR ACCELERATOR CTR, 84- *Personal Data:* b Brooklyn, NY, Mar 22, 31; m 60, Laurose Becker; c Elizabeth & Matthew. *Educ:* Mass Inst Technol, BS, 52, PhD(physics), 56. *Honors & Awards:* Nobel Prize in Physics, 76; Loeb Lectr, Harvard Univ, 74; DeShalit Lectr, Weizmann Inst, 75; E O Lawrence Medal, US Dept Energy, 76. *Concurrent Pos:* Consult, Dept Energy, NSF; mem bd dirs, Varian Corp, Litel Instruments. *Mem:* Nat Acad Sci; fel AAAS; fel Am Phys Soc (pres, 94); Europ Phys Soc; fel Am Acad Arts & Sci. *Res:* High energy physics; particle accelerators; colliding beam system; over 300 publications. *Mailing Add:* Stanford Linear Accelerator Ctr Stanford Univ PO Box 4349 Mail Stop 80 Stanford CA 94309. *Fax:* 650-926-4500

RICHTER, DONALD, DATA ANALYSIS, TOTAL QUALITY. *Current Pos:* assoc prof statist, 64-72, dir doctoral off, 74-76, PROF STATIST, GRAD SCH BUS, NY UNIV, 72- *Personal Data:* b Brooklyn, NY, Sept 3, 30; m 67; c 2. *Educ:* Bowdoin Col, AB, 52; Univ NC, PhD(statist), 59. *Prof Exp:* Asst prof statist, Univ Minn, 59-61; mem tech staff, Bell Tel Labs, 61-64. *Mem:* Am Statist Asn; Inst Math Statist; Am Soc Qual Control. *Res:* Statistical methods; statistical software; quality management. *Mailing Add:* Dept Statist Grad Sch Bus NY Univ 44 W Fourth St New York NY 10012. *E-Mail:* drichter@stern.nyu.edu

RICHTER, DOROTHY ANNE, APPLIED, ECONOMIC & ENGINEERING GEOLOGY. *Current Pos:* PRIN & CHIEF EXEC OFFICER, HAGER-RICHTER GEOSCI, INC, 84- *Personal Data:* b New Britain, Conn, June 26, 48. *Educ:* Bates Col, BS, 70; Boston Col, MS, 73; Harvard Univ, 75-80. *Prof Exp:* Staff geologist, dept earth & planetary sci, Mass Inst Technol, 72-76; chief geologist, Rock of Ages Corp, 76-84. *Mem:* Sigma Xi; Geol Soc Am; Am Inst Prof Geologists; Am Soc Testing & Mat. *Res:* Effects of microstructures on physical properties of igneous rocks; geology of dimension stone resources and applications; applications of surface & borehole geophysics to environmental & engineering problems. *Mailing Add:* Hager-Richter Geosci Inc 8 Industrial Way-D10 Salem NH 03079. *Fax:* 603-893-8313; *E-Mail:* dorothy@hager-richter.com

RICHTER, EDWARD EUGENE, ORGANIC CHEMISTRY, INORGANIC CHEMISTRY. *Current Pos:* RETIRED. *Personal Data:* b Hebron, Ill, Oct 22, 19; m 41, Virginia Scheithe; c Edward & Mark. *Educ:* DePauw Univ, BA, 41. *Prof Exp:* Chemist, Jones-Dabney Co, 41-44 & Am-Marietta Co, 46-50; chief chemist, Kay & Ess Co, 50-51; tech dir & spec projs engr, Moran Paint Co, 51-60; tech dir & vpres, Blatz Paint Co Inc, 60-89. *Mem:* Am Chem Soc; Fedn Socs Coatings Technol. *Res:* Protective and decorative industrial type organic coatings. *Mailing Add:* 304 Old Farm Rd Louisville KY 40207-2308

RICHTER, ERWIN (WILLIAM), BIOCHEMISTRY. *Current Pos:* instr phys sci, 63-67, asst prof, 70-72, ASSOC PROF CHEM, UNIV NORTHERN IOWA, 72- *Personal Data:* b Ironwood, Mich, Jan 29, 34. *Educ:* Northern Mich Univ, BS, 56; Univ Northern Iowa, MS, 63; Univ Iowa, PhD(biochem), 70. *Prof Exp:* High sch teacher, Mich, 56-62. *Res:* Particle analysis of atmospheric pollutants; structure of proteins; pesticide residues in fish, pheasants and rabbits in Iowa; science education. *Mailing Add:* Dept Chem Univ Northern Iowa Cedar Falls IA 50614-0001

RICHTER, G PAUL, CHEMICAL EDUCATION. *Current Pos:* Asst prof, 65-69, assoc prof, 69-78, PROF CHEM, WVA WESLEYAN COL, 78- *Personal Data:* b Rahway, NJ, Aug 13, 37; m 61, Marjorie Gilmore; c Karl & Karen. *Educ:* Grinnell Col, BA, 59; Univ Minn, PhD(inorg chem), 68. *Concurrent Pos:* Researcher, Univ Gottingen, WGer, 76-77. *Mem:* AAAS; Am Chem Soc; Nat Speleological Soc; Am Asn Univ Profs. *Res:* Sulfur-nitrogen chemistry; nonmetal compounds; inorganic aquatic chemistry. *Mailing Add:* WVa Wesleyan Col 59 College Ave Buckhannon WV 26201-2995. *Fax:* 304-472-2571

RICHTER, GEORGE NEAL, GASIFICATION. *Current Pos:* sr res chem engr, Montebello Res Lab, 65-80, technologist, 80-83, res mgr, 83-89, RES FEL, TEXACO INC, MONTEBELLO RES LAB, 89-, HON FEL, 93- *Personal Data:* b Denver, Colo, Mar 13, 30; m 60, Carol Bush; c Julie, David, William, Peter & Andrew. *Educ:* Yale Univ, BE, 51; Calif Inst Technol, MS, 52, PhD(chem eng), 57. *Prof Exp:* Res fel, Calif Inst Technol, 57-58, asst prof chem eng, 58-65. *Mem:* Am Inst Chem Engrs. *Res:* Synthesis gas and hydrogen generation by partial oxidation; coal gasification and conversion; alternate energy process development and commercialization; waste gasification and environmental impact measurements; research planning and coordination. *Mailing Add:* 1470 Granada Ave San Marino CA 91108. *Fax:* 562-699-7408

RICHTER, GOETZ WILFRIED, PATHOLOGY, CELL BIOLOGY. *Current Pos:* PROF PATH, UNIV ROCHESTER, 67- *Personal Data:* b Berlin, Ger, Dec 19, 22; nat US; wid; c James, Elizabeth & Marianne. *Educ:* Williams Col, AB, 43; Johns Hopkins Univ, MD, 48; Am Bd Path, dipl, 53. *Prof Exp:* Instr path, Med Col, Cornell Univ, 50-51, res assoc, 51-53, from asst prof to assoc prof, 53-67. *Concurrent Pos:* Ledyard fel, NY Hosp & Cornell Univ, 51-53; Rockefeller Found grant, 56-61; vis investr, Rockefeller Inst, 56-57; ed, Int Rev Exp Path, 60-93; Health Res Coun New York career scientist, 61-67; consult, NIH, 63-67, ad hoc, 68-; ed, Beitraege zur Pathologie, 71-78, Path Res & Pract, 78-90, Am J Path, 65-86. *Mem:* Electron Micros Soc Am; Soc Exp Biol & Med; Am Soc Cell Biol; Int Acad Path; fel AAAS; Sigma Xi; Harvey Soc; Am Soc Invest Path. *Res:* Experimental pathology; cell biology; ferritin and iron metabolism; pathology of heart muscle; lead poisoning. *Mailing Add:* Univ Rochester Dept Path 601 Elmwood Ave Box 626 Rochester NY 14642-0001. *Fax:* 716-273-1027

RICHTER, HAROLD GENE, INORGANIC CHEMISTRY. *Current Pos:* RETIRED. *Personal Data:* b Fontanet, Ind, Mar 5, 25; m 54; c 4. *Educ:* Franklin Col, AB, 47; Mass Inst Technol, MS, 50, PhD(inorg chem), 52. *Prof Exp:* Jr physicist, Argonne Nat Lab, 47-48; instr chem, Univ Ore, 52-54; radiochemist, US Naval Radiol Defense Lab, Calif, 54-55; asst to pres, Nuclear Sci & Eng Corp, Pa, 55-58; chief radiochemist, Res Triangle Inst, 59-71; chemist, off air progs, Environ Protection Agency, 71-89. *Mem:* AAAS; Am Chem Soc; Sigma Xi. *Res:* Radiochemistry of fission products; industrial applications of isotopes; analytical chemistry; biomedical instrumentation; atmospheric chemistry; air pollution control. *Mailing Add:* 8601 Little Creek Farm Rd Chapel Hill NC 27516

RICHTER, HELEN WILKINSON, RADIATION CHEMISTRY, FREE RADICAL REACTIONS. *Current Pos:* asst prof, 84-89, ASSOC PROF DEPT CHEM, UNIV AKRON, 89- *Personal Data:* b Biloxi, Miss; c 1. *Educ:* Woman's Col Ga, BA, 67; Ohio State Univ, MS, 70, PhD(phys chem), 74. *Prof Exp:* Res assoc radiation chem, Brookhaven Nat Lab, Upton, NY, 74-75; res chemist, Radiation Res Labs, 76, sr res chemist, dept chem, Carnegie-Mellon Univ, 76-84. *Concurrent Pos:* Fel, Nat Defense Educ Act Title IV, 67-70; vis res assoc & vis scientist, Radiation Lab, Univ Notre Dame, 76-; Samuel & Emma Winters fel, 80. *Mem:* Am Asn Adv Sci; Am Chem Soc; Soc Free Res. *Res:* Application of physical chemistry and radiation chemistry to the study of biochemical reaction mechanisms; free radical reactions; oxy-radicals of biological interest; iron-catalyzed peroxide decompositions. *Mailing Add:* Dept Chem Univ Akron Akron OH 44325-3601

RICHTER, HERBERT PETER, PHYSICAL CHEMISTRY, POLYMER CHEMISTRY. *Current Pos:* res chemist, 70-79, res coordr, Polymer Chem, 79-86, head, Combustion & Detonation Res Br, 86-92, SR SCIENTIST, RES DEPT, NAVAL WEAPONS CTR, 92- *Personal Data:* b St Paul, Minn, Jan 22, 39; m 62, Patricia Jones; c Deborah & Steven. *Educ:* San Diego State Univ, BA, 65, MS, 67. *Prof Exp:* Teaching asst & res asst, Chem Dept, San Diego State Univ, 66-67; chemist, Electronic Warfare Dept, 67-70. *Concurrent Pos:* Sr fel, Naval Air Warfare Ctr. *Mem:* Am Chem Soc; Sigma Xi. *Res:* Energetic materials; polymer and surface chemistry; physical and mechanical properties of polymers; photochemistry and photophysics; chemiluminescence. *Mailing Add:* 1809 Woodbine Pl Oceanside CA 92054

RICHTER, JOEL EDWARD, INTERNAL MEDICINE, GASTROENTEROLOGY. *Current Pos:* PROF MED DIR CLIN RES, UNIV ALA, BIRMINGHAM, 89- *Personal Data:* b Newport, RI, Oct 23, 49; m 71; c 3. *Educ:* Tex A&M Univ, BS, 70; Univ Tex, Southwestern Med Sch, MD, 75. *Prof Exp:* Intern internal med, US Naval Hosp, Philadelphia, 75-76; resident, Nat Naval Med Ctr, Bethesda, Md, 76-78, fel gastroenterol, 78-80, staff, 80-82; from asst prof to assoc prof gastroenterol, Bowman Gray Med Sch, Winston-Salem, NC, 82-89. *Concurrent Pos:* Staff gastroenterologist, NC Baptist Hosp, Winston-Salem, 82- *Mem:* Am Gastroenterol Asn; fel Am Col Physicians; Am Soc Gastrointestinal Endoscopy; Am Asn Advan Liver Dis; fel Am Col Gastroenterol. *Res:* Gastroesophagal reflux; esophagal motility disorders; non-cardiac chest pain; functional gastrointestinal diseases. *Mailing Add:* Dept Gastroenterol Cleveland Clin 9500 Euclid Ave S40 Cleveland OH 44195

RICHTER, JOHN LEWIS, NUCLEAR PHYSICS. *Current Pos:* group leader, TD-4, 78-81, prog mgr, 82-86, STAFF MEM PHYSICS, LOS ALAMOS SCI LAB, 58- *Personal Data:* b Laredo, Tex, July 26, 33; m 95, Dixie Busey Hanks; c Don A & Alan W. *Educ:* Univ Tex, Austin, BS, 54, MS, 56, PhD(physics), 58. *Concurrent Pos:* Consult study nuclear testing, Jasons, 95. *Mem:* Am Phys Soc. *Res:* Nuclear weapon science. *Mailing Add:* Los Alamos Nat Lab MS B229 PO Box 1663 Los Alamos NM 87545

RICHTER, JUDITH ANNE, NEUROPHARMACOLOGY, NEUROCHEMISTRY. *Current Pos:* from asst prof pharmacol to assoc prof pharmacol & neurobiol, 71-84, PROF PHARMACOL & NEUROBIOL, MED SCH, IND UNIV, INDIANAPOLIS, 84- *Personal Data:* b Wilmington, Del, Mar 4, 42. *Educ:* Univ Colo, BA, 64; Stanford Univ, PhD(pharmacol), 69. *Prof Exp:* Wellcome Trust fel, Cambridge Univ, 69-70 & Inst Psychiat, Univ London, 70-71. *Concurrent Pos:* Vis assoc prof pharmacol, Univ Ariz Health Sci Ctr, Tucson, 83; mem, Biomed Res Rev Comn, Nat Inst Drug Abuse, 83-87. *Mem:* AAAS; Am Soc Neurochem; Int Soc Neurochem; Soc Neurosci; Am Soc Pharmacol Exp Therap; Sigma Xi. *Res:* Neurotransmission and drugs affecting transmitter systems; mechanism of action of barbiturates; weaver mutant mouse. *Mailing Add:* Inst Psychiat Res Ind Univ Med Sch 791 Union Dr Indianapolis IN 46202-4887

RICHTER, MAXWELL, IMMUNOLOGY, PATHOLOGY. *Current Pos:* PROF PATH, UNIV OTTAWA, 72- *Personal Data:* b Montreal, Que, June 11, 33; m 58; c 2. *Educ:* McGill Univ, BSc, 54, PhD(biochem), 58, MD, 64. *Prof Exp:* From asst prof to assoc prof exp med, McGill Univ, 58-72; assoc prof immunol & allergy, 70-72. *Concurrent Pos:* Mem staff, Dept Immunol & Allergy, Royal Victoria Hosp, Montreal, 68-; Med Res Coun scholar immunol, Univ Ottawa Clin, Victoria Hosp, 70- *Mem:* Am Acad Allergy; Am Asn Immunol; NY Acad Sci; Brit Soc Immunol; Can Soc Immunol. *Res:* Immunopathology. *Mailing Add:* Dept Path Fac Med Univ Ottawa 451 Smyth Rd Ottawa ON K1H 8M5 Can

RICHTER, RAYMOND C, GEOLOGY. *Current Pos:* RETIRED. *Personal Data:* b Riverside, Calif, Apr 17, 18; wid; c Lynnae (Evans), Patricia (Lewis) & James. *Educ:* Univ Calif, BA, 40, BS, 42. *Prof Exp:* Supv eng geologist, Calif Dept Water Resources, 46-66, staff geologist, Resources Agency, 66-75; consult geologist, 76-82. *Mem:* Geol Soc Am; Asn Eng Geologists. *Res:* Engineering geology; ground water geology. *Mailing Add:* 2252 Camborne Dr Modesto CA 95356

RICHTER, REINHARD HANS, ORGANIC CHEMISTRY. *Current Pos:* RETIRED. *Personal Data:* b Reinswalde, Ger, Oct 3, 37; m 65. *Educ:* Univ Tuebingen, BS, 60; Stuttgart Tech Univ, MS, 62, PhD(org chem), 65. *Honors & Awards:* Chamberland Award, New Haven Sect, Am Chem Soc, 83. *Prof Exp:* NIH fel, Mellon Inst, 65-68; staff scientist, Donald S Gilmore Res Labs, UpJohn Co, 68-84; mgr chem res, Dow Chem USA, 85-88, res mgr, 88-89, sr res mgr, 89-94. *Mem:* Am Chem Soc; Ger Chem Soc. *Res:* Organic synthesis; heterocycles; isocyanates; nitrile oxides; thermoplastic polyurethanes; polyurethane foams. *Mailing Add:* 1459 Glarus Ct Incline Village NV 89451

RICHTER, ROY, THEORETICAL PHYSICS. *Current Pos:* res fel theoret physics, Gen Motors Res Labs, 82, sr res scientist, 82-85, staff res scientist, 85-93, sect mgr computational physics, 89-96, SR STAFF RES SCIENTIST, GEN MOTORS RES LABS, 93- *Personal Data:* b Brooklyn, NY, Aug 25, 56; c Stefan, Dana & Paul. *Educ:* Rennselaer Polytech Inst, BS(math) & BS(physics), 75; Cornell Univ, MS, 79, PhD(theoret physics), 82. *Prof Exp:* Teaching asst physics, Dept Physics, Cornell Univ, 75-78; res asst theoret physics, Nordic Inst Theoret Atomic Physics, 79-81; teaching fel, Mont State Univ, 81-82. *Mem:* Am Phys Soc. *Res:* Theoretical solid state physics; metals; surfaces; optimization methods. *Mailing Add:* Gen Motors Res Labs 30500 Mound Rd MS 480 106 144 Warren MI 48090-9055. *E-Mail:* rrichter@gmr.com

RICHTER, STEPHEN L(AWRENCE), RADAR ELECTRONIC-COUNTER-COUNTER-MEASURES & SURVEILLANCE SYSTEMS, ALGORITHM DEVELOPMENT. *Current Pos:* sr engr, 71-73, PRIN ENGR, RAYTHEON CO, 73- *Personal Data:* b Brooklyn, NY, Dec 29, 42; m 62, Diane S Sarner; c Isaac S. *Educ:* Columbia Univ, BS, 63, MS, 64, PhD(electromagnetic theory), 67. *Prof Exp:* Res asst elec eng, Columbia Univ, 63-66, preceptor, 66-67, asst prof, 67-68, res scientist, 68; asst prof, City Col New York, 68-71. *Concurrent Pos:* Consult, 64-67 & 70; reviewer, proc, Inst Elec & Electronics Engrs, 68-87. *Mem:* Sr mem Inst Elec & Electronics Engrs; Am Phys Soc; Sigma Xi. *Res:* Systems analysis; adaptive signal processing and discrimination; communication and information theory; radar; electronic-counter-counter-measures; software requirements; optical and image processing; stochastic processes; computer and numerical methods; electromagnetic wave propagation; guided waves and antennas; applied mathematics and physics; system integration and testing; four patents awarded in image processing. *Mailing Add:* 16 Hynes Lane Harvard MA 01451-1917

RICHTER, THOMAS A, CCDS, ELECTRO-OPTICS. *Current Pos:* OWNER, RICHTER ENTERPRISES, 84-; OWNER, TECHNOLINK (AMERICAS), 92- *Personal Data:* b Chicago, Ill, Feb 25, 38; m 93, Cheri Anvel; c Steven A. *Educ:* Univ Wis, Madison, BS(metall eng) & BS(naut sci), 61, MS, 64; Univ Chicago, MBA, 69. *Prof Exp:* Metallurgist, Griffin Wheel Co, 64-67; chief metallurgist, Chicago Rawhide, 68; mgr, Optical Coating Lab, 69-75; dir, Optical Radiation, 76-79; vpres, Exotic Mat, 80; vpres & gen mgr, Magnum Technol, 81-83. *Concurrent Pos:* Consult, Jet Propulsion Lab, 87-88; mem liaison comt, Int Soc Optical Eng Indust Rels, 88-, prog chmn, Aerospace Sensing Symposa, 89-; panelist, Res Adv Bd, Aviation Week, 90-91. *Mem:* Int Soc Optical Eng; Am Astron Soc. *Res:* Optical components and subsystems; imaging; granted three patents. *Mailing Add:* 5579 W City Rd Apt 5N Del Norte CO 81132

RICHTER, WAYNE H, MATHEMATICS. *Current Pos:* ASSOC PROF MATH, UNIV MINN, MINNEAPOLIS, 69- *Personal Data:* b New York, NY, June 7, 36; c 1. *Educ:* Swarthmore Col, AB, 58; Princeton Univ, MA, 60, PhD(math), 63. *Prof Exp:* From instr to asst prof math, Rutgers Univ, 61-69. *Concurrent Pos:* Fac fel, Rutgers Univ, 64-65; NSF res grant, 66-68 & 70-75. *Mem:* Am Math Soc; Asn Symbolic Logic. *Res:* Theory of recursive functions; mathematical logic. *Mailing Add:* Dept Math Univ Minn Minneapolis MN 55455-0100

RICHTERS, ARNIS, EXPERIMENTAL PATHOLOGY. *Current Pos:* From instr to asst prof, 68-75, assoc prof path, 75-91, PROF, SCH MED, UNIV SOUTHERN CALIF, 91- *Personal Data:* b Sauka, Latvia, Sept 23, 28; US citizen; c 1. *Educ:* Univ Ariz, BS, 57, MS, 59; Univ Southern Calif, PhD(exp path), 67. *Concurrent Pos:* Site vis, Breast Cancer Task Force, Nat Cancer Inst, 72; reviewer, Monroe County Cancer & Leukemia Asn, 73- *Mem:* Tissue Cult Asn; Int Acad Path; AAAS; Sigma Xi. *Res:* Correlation of in vivo and in vitro behavior of cancer and the lymphocyte responses in cancer draining lymph nodes; ultrastructure of lymphocyte-target cell interactions; air pollution and health. *Mailing Add:* Dept Pathol Univ S Calif 2011 Zonal Ave Los Angeles CA 90033-1034

RICHTOL, HERBERT H, ANALYTICAL CHEMISTRY, PHOTOCHEMISTRY. *Current Pos:* from asst prof to assoc prof, 61-74, PROF CHEM, RENSSELAER POLYTECH INST, 74-, DEAN, UNDERGRAD COL, 85- *Personal Data:* b New York, NY, Aug 13, 32; m 56, Iris Klar; c Nancy A, Susan G, Elise C & Michael B. *Educ:* St Lawrence Univ, BS, 54; NY Univ, PhD(chem), 61. *Prof Exp:* Instr chem, NY Univ, 60-61. *Mem:* AAAS; Am Chem Soc. *Res:* Photoelectrochemistry; luminescence; liquid crystals. *Mailing Add:* 850 N Randolph St Apt 1906 Arlington VA 22203

RICK, CHARLES MADEIRA, JR, CYTOGENETICS, EVOLUTION. *Current Pos:* instr & jr geneticist, 40-44, asst prof & asst geneticist, 44-49, assoc prof & assoc geneticist, 49-55, dir, Tomato Genetics Stock Ctr, 50-82, PROF VEG CROPS & GENETICIST, UNIV CALIF, DAVIS, EXP STA, 55- *Personal Data:* b Reading, Pa, Apr 30, 15; m 38, Martha Overholts; c Susan C (Baldi) & John W. *Educ:* Pa State Col, BS, 37; Harvard Univ, AM, 38, PhD(genetics), 40. *Honors & Awards:* Vaughan Award, Am Soc Hort Sci, 45; Campbell Award, AAAS, 59; M A Blake Award, Am Soc Hort Sci, 74; Frank N Meyer Medal, Am Genetics Asn, 82; Thomas Roland Medal, 83; Distinguished Econ Botanist, Soc Econ Bot, 87; Genetic & Plant Breeding Award, Nat Coun Com Plant Breeders, 87; Alexander von Humboldt Award, 93. *Prof Exp:* Tech asst, Harvard Univ, 38. *Concurrent Pos:* Guggenheim fel, 49, 51; Rockefeller res fel, 56-57; vis lectr, NC State Col, 56; fac res lectr, Univ Calif, 61; Carnegie vis prof, Univ Hawaii, 63; mem, Galapagos Int Sci Proj, 64; lectr, Univ Sao Paulo, 65; vis scientist, Univ PR, 68; centennial lectr, Ont Agr Col, Univ Guelph, 74; adj prof, Univ Rosario, Argentina, 80, Univ lectr, Cornell Univ, 88. *Mem:* Nat Acad Sci; fel AAAS; Genetics Soc Am; Soc Study Evolution; fel Am Soc Hort Sci; hon fel Indian Soc Genetics & Plant Breeding. *Res:* Natural relationships amongst the tomato, Lycopersicon, species are investigated via cytology, incompatibility, hybrid fertility, and genetic variability, including molecular markers. *Mailing Add:* Dept Veg Crops Univ Calif Davis CA 95616. *Fax:* 530-752-9659

RICK, CHRISTIAN E(DWARD), chemical engineering; deceased, see previous edition for last biography

RICK, PAUL DAVID, MICROBIAL PHYSIOLOGY, BIOCHEMISTRY. *Current Pos:* ASSOC PROF MICROBIOL, UNIFORMED SERV HEALTH SCI UNIV, 83- *Educ:* Univ Minn, PhD(biochem), 71. *Res:* Genetics; biogenesis of microbial membranes. *Mailing Add:* Dept Microbiol Uniformed Serv Health Sci Univ 4301 Jones Bridge Rd Bethesda MD 20814-4799

RICKABY, DAVID A, PULMONARY PHYSIOLOGY, CARDIOVASCULAR PHYSIOLOGY. *Current Pos:* RES PHYSIOLOGIST, VET ADMIN MED CTR, MILWAUKEE, 79- *Educ:* Med Col Wis, PhD(physiol), 79. *Mailing Add:* Dept Physiol Va Med Ctr 5000 W National Ave Res Serv 151 Milwaukee WI 53295-1000

RICKARD, CORWIN LLOYD, SCIENCE ADMINISTRATION, NUCLEAR ENGINEERING. *Current Pos:* EXEC VPRES, SIBIA INC, 83- *Personal Data:* b Medina, Ohio, Sept, 26, 26; m 48; c 2. *Educ:* Univ Rochester, BS, 47, MS, 49; Cornell Univ, PhD(eng, math), 61. *Prof Exp:* Asst eng, Univ Rochester, 47-48, instr, 48-49, asst prof, 49-52; instr, Cornell Univ, 52-54; nuclear engr, Brookhaven Nat Lab, 54-56; res staff mem nuclear eng, Gen Atomic Div, Gen Dynamics Corp, 56-66, vpres, Gulf Gen Atomic Inc, 67-77, exec vpres, Gen Atomic Co, 77-83. *Concurrent Pos:* Consult, Brookhaven Nat Lab, 49, Worthington Corp, NY, 50, Boeing Aircraft Co, Wash, 51, Adv Electronic Res Lab, Gen Elec Co, 53-54. *Mem:* Am Nuclear Soc (vpres, 80-81, pres, 81-82); Am Soc Mech Engrs; AAAS. *Res:* Thermodynamics; gas cooled nuclear reactor core and plant development, design and engineering; nuclear power plant economics and fuel cycles. *Mailing Add:* PO Box 472 Rancho Santa Fe CA 92067-0472

RICKARD, EUGENE CLARK, CAPILLARY ELECTROPHORESIS FOR PEPTIDE MAPPING & CHIRAL ANALYSIS. *Current Pos:* sr chemist, 71-76, res scientist, 77-84, SR RES SCIENTIST, ELI LILLY & CO, 85- *Personal Data:* b Wichita, Kans, Oct 19, 43; m 70; c Mark & Renee. *Educ:* Wichita State Univ, BS, 65, MS, 67; Univ Wis-Madison, PhD(anal chem), 72. *Prof Exp:* Lectr anal chem, Univ Wis-Madison, 70-71. *Concurrent Pos:* Mem, Fel Comt, Anal Div, Am Chem Soc, 90- *Mem:* Am Chem Soc; Sigma Xi. *Res:* Development of analytical methods to determine purity and stability of pharmaceuticals; peptide mapping and chiral separations by capillary electrophoresis. *Mailing Add:* Analytical Develop Eli Lilly & Co Dept MC769 Drop 0724 Indianapolis IN 46285. *Fax:* 317-277-2154

RICKARD, JAMES ALEXANDER, PHYSICS. *Current Pos:* RETIRED. *Personal Data:* b Austin, Tex, July 9, 26; m 52; c 2. *Educ:* Tex A&I Univ, BS & MS, 48; Univ Tex, PhD(physics), 54. *Prof Exp:* Res engr, Houston Res Lab, Humble Oil & Ref Co, 53-62, res mgr, Esso Prod Res Co, Tex, 63-71, sr adv, Exxon Corp, 71-76, planning mgr, Exxon Prod Res Co, 76-84; res mgr, Standard Oil Prod Co, 84-87, vpres, Brit Petrol, 89-90. *Mem:* Am Phys Soc; Marine Technol Soc (pres, 77-78); Am Inst Mining, Metall & Petrol Eng; Soc Naval Architects & Marine Engrs; Sigma Xi. *Res:* Petroleum; ocean engineering. *Mailing Add:* 3837 Del Montee Houston TX 77209

RICKARD, JAMES JOSEPH, ASTRONOMY, COMPUTER SCIENCE. *Current Pos:* solar astronr, Univ Md CLRO, 82-86, SOLAR ENERGY ENG, COMPUT CONSULT. *Personal Data:* b Seattle, Wash, Sept 20, 40; m 63. *Educ:* San Jose State Univ, BA, 62; Univ MD, MS, 65, PhD(astron), 68. *Prof Exp:* Teaching asst astron, Univ Md, 62-64, res asst radio astron, 64-67, res fel, 67-68; res fel astron, Calif Inst Technol-Hale Observ, 68-69; staff astronr, Europ Southern Observ, 69-76; res scientist astron, Univ Iowa, 77-80; partner/owner, Borrego Solar Systs, 80- *Concurrent Pos:* Earth resources consult, Terra Inst, 76- *Mem:* Am Astron Soc; Int Astron Union. *Res:* Galactic structure; physics of the interstellar medium; instrumentation; computer systems design; extragalactic radio sources. *Mailing Add:* 737 San Pablo Rd Borrego Springs CA 92004

RICKARD, JOHN TERRELL, SIGNAL PROCESSING, INFORMATION THEORY. *Current Pos:* sr prin engr, 75-80, SR VPRES, ORINCON CORP, 80- *Personal Data:* b Humboldt, Tenn, Sept 17, 47; m 71, Lois; c Jessica, Marissa & Tyler. *Educ:* Fla Inst Technol, BS, 69, MS, 71; Univ Calif, San Diego, PhD(eng physics), 75. *Prof Exp:* Electronics engr, Harris Corp, Melbourne, Fla, 69-71. *Mem:* Inst Elec & Electronics Engrs. *Res:* Random processes; adaptive signal processing; detection theory. *Mailing Add:* Mitchum Jones & Templeton 530 Main Ave Durango CO 81301

RICKARD, LAWRENCE VROMAN, PALEONTOLOGY, STRATIGRAPHY. *Current Pos:* sr paleontologist, 56-73, assoc paleontologist, 73-77, PRIN PALEONTOLOGIST, MUS & SCI SERV, STATE GEOL SURV, NY, 77- *Personal Data:* b Cobleskill, NY, July 10, 26; m 52; c 5. *Educ:* Cornell Univ, BA, 51, PhD(geol), 55; Univ Rochester, MS, 53. *Prof Exp:* Asst prof geol, St Lawrence Univ, 55-56. *Concurrent Pos:* Mem, Paleont Res Inst. *Mem:* Geol Soc Am; Paleont Soc. *Res:* Stratigraphy and paleontology of the Silurian and Devonian rocks of New York. *Mailing Add:* 1210 Sixth St Kinderhook NY 12106

RICKARD, LEE J, INFRARED ASTRONOMY, RADIO ASTRONOMY. *Current Pos:* ASTROPHYSICIST, NAVAL RES LAB, 87- *Personal Data:* b Miami, Fla, Dec 24, 49; m 72, 86; c 2. *Educ:* Univ Miami, BS, 69; Univ Chicago, MS, 72, PhD(astrophys), 75. *Prof Exp:* Res assoc, Nat Radio Astron Observ, 75-77, asst scientist, 77-79, assoc scientist, 79-80; from asst prof to assoc prof, Dept Physics & Astron, Howard Univ, 84-87. *Concurrent Pos:* Radio astronr, Naval Res Lab, 83-84; res astronr, Sachs/Freeman Assoc, Inc, 84-86; res astronr, Appl Res Corp, 86-87. *Mem:* Am Astron Soc; Int Astron Union. *Res:* Radio spectroscopy, specifically interstellar molecules, molecular constituents of galaxies, interstellar masers and atomic recombination lines; problems of active galactic nuclei; infrared emission from galaxies; image processing and sensor enhancement. *Mailing Add:* Code 7210 Naval Res Lab 4555 Overlook Ave SW Washington DC 20375

RICKARD, WILLIAM HOWARD, JR, BOTANY. *Current Pos:* SR RES SCIENTIST, ECOL DEPT, PAC NORTHWEST LAB, BATTELLE MEM INST, 65- *Personal Data:* b Walsenburg, Colo, May 15, 26; m 53; c 1. *Educ:* Univ Colo, BA, 50, MA, 53; Wash State Univ, PhD(bot), 57. *Prof Exp:* Asst prof bot, N Mex Highlands Univ, 57-60; biol scientist, Hanford Atomic Prod Opers, Gen Elec Co, 60-65. *Mem:* AAAS; Ecol Soc Am; Soc Range Mgt; Northwest Sci Asn; Sigma Xi. *Res:* Plant ecology; fate and behavior of trace elements and radionuclides in terrestrial ecosystems; primary productivity and mineral cycling in shrub steppe ecosystems. *Mailing Add:* 1904 Lassen Ave Richland WA 99352

RICKART, CHARLES EARL, MATHEMATICS. *Current Pos:* from instr to prof, 43-83, chmn dept, 59-65, EMER PROF MATH, YALE UNIV, 83- *Personal Data:* b Osage City, Kans, June 28, 13; m 42, Annabel Erickson; c Mark C, Eric A & Thomas M. *Educ:* Univ Kans, BA, 37, MA, 38; Univ Mich, PhD(math), 41. *Hon Degrees:* MA, Yale Univ, 59. *Prof Exp:* Peirce instr & tutor math, Harvard Univ; 41-43. *Mem:* AAAS; Am Math Soc; Math Asn Am. *Res:* Functional analysis; theory of Banach algebras; function algebras; structuralism and structures. *Mailing Add:* Dept Math Yale Univ New Haven CT 06520

RICKART, ERIC ALLAN, SYSTEMATIC ZOOLOGY, CONSERVATION BIOLOGY. *Current Pos:* cur birds & mammals, 85-91, CUR VERTEBRATES, UTAH MUS NATURAL HIST, UNIV UTAH, 91- *Personal Data:* b New Haven, Conn, Feb, 7, 50; m 91, Shelby Mikkelsen. *Educ:* Univ Kans, BS, 74, MA, 76; Univ Utah, PhD(biol), 82. *Prof Exp:* collections mgr & vis asst prof, Dept Biol Sci, Univ Tex, El Paso, 84-85. *Concurrent Pos:* Adj assoc prof biol, Biol Dept, Univ Utah, 90-; res assoc, Div Mammals, Field Mus Natural Hist, 90- *Mem:* Am Soc Mammalogists; Soc Conserv Biol. *Res:* Community ecology, biogeography, systematics and conservation of mammals (primarily rodents, insectivores and bats); geographic focus on tropical Asia and western United States. *Mailing Add:* 865 Harrison Ave Salt Lake City UT 84105. *Fax:* 801-585-3684; *E-Mail:* rickart@geode.umnh.utah.edu

RICKBORN, BRUCE FREDERICK, ORGANIC CHEMISTRY. *Current Pos:* from asst prof to assoc prof, 62-71, provost, Col Creative Studies, 69-71, PROF CHEM, UNIV CALIF, SANTA BARBARA, 71- *Personal Data:* b New Brunswick, NJ, Feb 23, 35; m 55; c 1. *Educ:* Univ Calif, Riverside, BA, 56; Univ Calif, Los Angeles, PhD(chem), 60. *Prof Exp:* Asst prof chem, Univ Calif, Berkeley, 60-62. *Concurrent Pos:* NSF sr fel, 66-67; Alfred P Sloan fel, 67-69; Fulbright sr lectr, Bogata, Columbia, 70; assoc dean, Col Letters & Sci, Univ Calif, Santa Barbara, 71-73, dean, 73-78. *Mem:* Am Chem Soc; AAAS; Sigma Xi. *Res:* Mechanism and stereochemistry of small ring forming and opening reactions; organometallics; conformational analysis; photochemistry; hydride reduction; strong base induced reactions. *Mailing Add:* 4661 La Espada Dr Santa Barbara CA 93111-1301

RICKELS, KARL, PSYCHIATRY, PSYCHOPHARMACOLOGY. *Current Pos:* PROF PSYCHIAT & PHARMACOL, UNIV PA, 69-, STUART & EMILY MUDD PROF HUMAN BEHAV REPRODUCTION, 77- *Personal Data:* b Wilhelmshaven, Ger, Aug 17, 24; US citizen; m 64; c 3. *Educ:* Univ Munster, MD, 51. *Concurrent Pos:* Dir psychopharmacol res, Univ Pa, 64-; chmn, OTC Sedatives, Tranquilizers and Sleep Aids Rev Panel, Food & Drug Admin, 72-75; chief psychiat, Phildelphia Gen Hosp, 75-77. *Mem:* Fel Acad Psychosom Med; fel Am Soc Clin Pharmacol & Therapeut; fel Am Col Neuropsychopharmacol; fel Am Psychiat Asn; fel Int Col Neuropsychopharmacol. *Res:* Clinical psychopharmacology; evaluation of psychotropic drugs in anxiety, depression and insomnia and tranquilizer dependency; study of the role of non-specific factors in drug and placebo response; assessment of emotional symptoms in various family practice and OB-GYN patients and their response to stress and hormonal treatment, i.e. premenstrual syndrome, in vitro fertilization and teenage pregnancy. *Mailing Add:* Dept Psychiat Univ Pa Col Med Philadelphia PA 19104

RICKENBERG, HOWARD V, DEVELOPMENTAL BIOLOGY. *Current Pos:* CONSULT, IMMUNOTECH SA, MARSEILLE, 90- *Personal Data:* b Nuremberg, Ger, Feb 3, 22; nat US; m 53; c 3. *Educ:* Cornell Univ, BS, 50; Yale Univ, PhD(microbiol), 54. *Prof Exp:* Am Cancer Soc fel, Pasteur Inst, Paris, 54-55 & Nat Inst Med Res, Eng, 55-56; from instr to asst prof microbiol, Univ Wash, 56-60; assoc prof bact, Ind Univ, 61-63; prof bact, 63-66; prof microbiol, Sch Med, Univ Colo, Denver, 66-71; prof biochem, biophys & genetics, 71-88. *Concurrent Pos:* Ida & Cecil Green investigatorship develop biochem, 75-88; prof, Dept Molecular & Cellular Biol, Nat Jewish Ctr Immunol & Respiratory Med, 86-88; Fulbright scholar, Univ Ivory Coast, Abidjan, 88-89. *Mem:* Am Soc Microbiol; Am Soc Biol Chem; Am Soc Cell Biol. *Res:* Gene-enzyme relationships, metabolism and differentiation. *Mailing Add:* Immunotech SA 130 ave de Lattre de Tassigny Marseille 177 F-13276 Cedex 9 France. *Fax:* 334-91-17-27-40

RICKER, NEIL LAWRENCE, CHEMICAL ENGINEERING. *Current Pos:* ASSOC PROF CHEM ENG, UNIV WASH, 78- *Personal Data:* b Stambaugh, Mich, Oct 15, 48; m 71. *Educ:* Univ Mich, Ann Arbor, BS, 70; Univ Calif, Berkeley, MS, 72, PhD(chem eng), 78. *Prof Exp:* Sci systs analyst, Air Prod & Chem, Inc, 72-75. *Mem:* Am Inst Chem Engrs; Am Chem Soc. *Res:* Process dynamics and control; chemical process analysis and conceptual design; wastewater treatment by physical and chemical methods. *Mailing Add:* 1160 20th Ave E Seattle WA 98112

RICKER, RICHARD EDMOND, STRESS CORROSION CRACKING, HYDROGEN EMBRITTLEMENT. *Current Pos:* metallurgist, 86-89, GROUP LEADER, CORROSION GROUP, NAT INST STAND & TECHNOL, 89- *Personal Data:* b Newport News, Va, Feb 26, 52; c Carrie E & Jacob E. *Educ:* NC State Univ, BS, 75, MS, 78; Rensselaer Polytech Inst, PhD(mat eng), 83. *Honors & Awards:* Bronze Medal, US Dept Com, 91. *Prof Exp:* Sr engr, Lynchburg Res Ctr, Babcock & Wilcox Co, 77-79; asst prof mat sci & eng, Univ Notre Dame, 84-86. *Mem:* Am Soc Metals Int; Am Soc Testing & Mat; Electrochem Soc; Metall Soc Am Inst Mech Engrs; Nat Asn Corrosion Engrs; AAAS. *Res:* Corrosion measurement techniques; corrosion behavior of new materials; atmospheric corrosion; mechanisms of environmentally induced fracture and environmentally induced fracture behavior of new materials. *Mailing Add:* 16549 Sioux Lane Gaithersburg MD 20878

RICKER, RICHARD W(ILSON), CERAMICS ENGINEERING. *Current Pos:* RETIRED. *Personal Data:* b Galion, Ohio, Mar 30, 14; m 44; c 5. *Educ:* Alfred Univ, BS, 34; Pa State Col, MS, 50, PhD(ceramics), 52. *Prof Exp:* Mem staff res & develop, Libbey-Owens-Ford Glass Co, 34-48; res assoc, Pa State Col, 48-52; res engr, Alcoa Res Labs, Aluminum Co Am, 52-55, asst chief, Process Metall Div, 55-60; asst dir res, Ferro Corp, 60-66; tech dir ceramics, Harshaw Chem Co, 66-71; ceramic consult, 71- *Concurrent Pos:* Consult refractories & whitewares projs, South Korea, Turkey, Mexico, Columbia, Brazil & Egypt. *Mem:* Fel Am Ceramic Soc; Sigma Xi. *Res:* Phase equilibria; refractories; porcelain enamel; ceramic color pigments; whitewares. *Mailing Add:* 1431 NE 55 St Ft Lauderdale FL 33334

RICKER, WILLIAM EDWIN, BIOLOGY. *Current Pos:* RETIRED. *Personal Data:* b Waterdown, Ont, Aug 11, 08; m 35, Marion T Cardwell; c Karl E, John F, Eric W & Angus C. *Educ:* Univ Toronto, BA, 30, MA, 31, PhD, 36. *Hon Degrees:* DSc, Univ Man, 70; LLD, Dalhousie Univ, 72. *Honors & Awards:* Gold Medal, Prof Inst Pub Serv Can, 66; Flavelle Medal, Royal Soc Can, 70; F E J Fry Medal, Can Soc Zoologists, 83; Officer Order Can, 86. *Prof Exp:* Sci asst, Fisheries Res Bd Can, Nanaimo, 31-38; jr scientist, Int Pac Salmon Fisheries Comn, BC, 38-39; from asst prof to prof zool, Ind Univ, 39-50; ed publ, Fisheries Res Bd Can, Nanaimo, 50-62, biol consult to chmn & staff, 62-63, actg chmn, Ottawa, 63-64, chief scientist, Nanaimo, 64-73; vol contract investr, Pac Biol Sta, Nanaimo, 73-93. *Concurrent Pos:* Dir, Ind Lake & Stream Surv, Ind Dept Conserv, 39-50. *Mem:* Fel Royal Soc Can; fel AAAS; Wildlife Soc; Prof Inst Pub Serv Can; Am Fisheries Soc; Can Soc Zoologists; Am Soc Limnol & Oceanog (pres, 59); Arctic Inst NAm; Can Soc Wildlife & Fishery Biologists; Int Asn Limnol; Sigma Xi. *Res:* Zoology. *Mailing Add:* 3052 Hammond Bay Rd Nanaimo BC V9T 1E2 Can

RICKERT, DAVID A, ENVIRONMENTAL SCIENCES. *Current Pos:* Chemist urban hydrol prog, US Geol Surv, 69-72, res hydrologist, chief, Willamette River Basin Study, 72-75, res hydrologist, chief, Land-Use-River Qual Study, Water Resources Div, 75-77, chief, Ore 208 Assessment, Ore Dept Environ Qual, 77-79, coordr, River Qual Assessment Prog, 79-80, sr staff scientist, 80-82, spec asst to chief hydrologist, 82-85, CHIEF, OFF

WATER QUAL, WATER RESOURCES DIV, US GEOL SURV, 85- *Personal Data:* b Trenton, NJ, Mar 14, 40; m 62; c 3. *Educ:* Rutgers Univ, BS, 62, MS, 65, PhD(environ sci), 69. *Honors & Awards:* W R Boggess Award, Am Water Resources Asn, 74. *Concurrent Pos:* Secy, Water Qual Comn, Int Asn Hydrol Sci, 81-87, vpres, 87- *Mem:* AAAS; Int Asn Hydrological Sci; Am Water Resources Asn (vpres, 82-84, pres, 84). *Res:* Development and implementation of large-scale interdisciplinary programs for land and water-resources assessment; environmental chemistry and biology; applied hydrology; environmental geology; land-use analysis. *Mailing Add:* Off Water Qual US Geol Surv Mail Stop 412 Reston VA 20192

RICKERT, DOUGLAS EDWARD, TOXICOLOGY, PHARMACOLOGY. *Current Pos:* sect head, 87-92, assoc dir, Dept Drug Metab, 93-96, DIR BIOANALYSIS & DRUG METAB, GLAXO WELLCOME INC, 96- *Personal Data:* b Sioux City, Iowa, Jan 27, 46; m 81. *Educ:* Univ Iowa, BS, 68, MS, 72, PhD(pharmacol), 74; Am Bd Toxicol, dipl, 80. *Prof Exp:* Asst prof pharmacol, Mich State Univ, 74-77; analytical biochemist, Chem Indust Inst Toxicol, 77-87. *Concurrent Pos:* Adj assoc prof toxicol Univ NC, 79- *Mem:* AAAS; Soc Toxicol; Am Soc Pharmacol & Exp Therapeut; Am Soc Mass Spectros. *Res:* Biological disposition of foreign compounds and their toxicity. *Mailing Add:* Glaxo Wellcome Inc 5 Moore Dr Research Triangle Park NC 27709. *Fax:* 919-990-5652

RICKERT, NEIL WILLIAM, COMPUTER OPERATING SYSTEMS. *Current Pos:* PROF COMPUT SCI, NORTHERN ILL UNIV, 85- *Personal Data:* b Perth, Australia, June 2, 39; m 65; c 2. *Educ:* Univ Western Australia, BSc, 62; Yale Univ, PhD(math), 65. *Prof Exp:* From instr to asst prof math, Yale Univ, 65-68; assoc prof math, Univ Ill, Chicago Circle, 68-85. *Concurrent Pos:* Mem, Inst Advan Study, 66-67. *Mem:* Am Math Soc; Math Asn Am; Asn Comput Mach; AAAS; Inst Elec & Electronics Engrs. *Res:* Computer operating systems; distributed computer systems, including distributed databases and distributed computational algorithms. *Mailing Add:* Dept Comput Sci Northern Ill Univ De Kalb IL 60115

RICKERT, RUSSELL KENNETH, PHYSICS. *Current Pos:* RETIRED. *Personal Data:* b Chalfont, Pa, Feb 6, 26; m 49; c 3. *Educ:* West Chester State Col, BS, 50; Univ Del, MS, 53; NY Univ, EdD(sci ed), 61. *Prof Exp:* Teacher high sch, Md, 50-52 & Del, 52-55; instr phys sci, Salisbury State Col, 55-56; from asst prof to prof phys sci, West Chester State Col, 56-74, chmn, Dept Sci, 64-68, dean, Sch Sci & Math, 69-79, prof physics, 74-90. *Mem:* AAAS; Am Asn Physics Teachers. *Res:* Physics teaching, especially the development of physical science courses for students who are not science majors; aerospace science education; solar energy research and development. *Mailing Add:* 921 Baylowell Dr West Chester PA 19380

RICKETT, FREDERIC LAWRENCE, ANALYTICAL BIOCHEMISTRY, PROCESS IMPROVEMENT. *Current Pos:* from res assoc to sr res asoc anal biochem, Dept Res & Qual Assurance, Am Tobacco Co, 66-91, supvr leaf servs, 91-93, asst mgr, 93, MGR LEAF SERVS, DEPT RES & QUAL ASSURANCE, AM TOBACCO CO, 94- *Personal Data:* b Woodridge, NJ, Mar 11, 39; m 63, Pamela Miller; c Bretten I, Shana B & Bryce E. *Educ:* Pa State Univ, BS, 61, MS, 63, PhD, 66. *Prof Exp:* Instr biochem, Pa State Univ, 63-66. *Concurrent Pos:* Adj Chem Dept, John Tyler Community Col, 80-82, 94- *Mem:* Am Chem Soc; Sigma Xi. *Res:* Analytical methodology for lipids and other plant constituents, tobacco and tobacco smoke, flavoring agents; pesticide analysis, process development and quality control related to tobacco. *Mailing Add:* 12521 Easy St Chester VA 23831-5114. *Fax:* 804-757-7667

RICKETTS, GARY EUGENE, ANIMAL SCIENCE. *Current Pos:* Livestock exten specialist sheep & beef cattle, 64-86, EXTEN SPECIALIST, SHEEP & EXTEN PROG LEADER, UNIV ILL, URBANA, 86- *Personal Data:* b Willard, Ohio, Aug 2, 35; m 58, Audrey Wheeler; c Dawn, John & Mark. *Educ:* Ohio State Univ, BS, 57, MS, 60, PhD(animal sci), 63. *Honors & Awards:* Am Soc Animal Sci Ext Award, 84. *Mem:* Am Soc Animal Sci; Am Regist Prof Animal Scientists. *Res:* Author of numerous publications. *Mailing Add:* 128 ASL Univ Ill 1207 W Gregory Dr Urbana IL 61801. *Fax:* 217-244-2871

RICKETTS, JOHN ADRIAN, PHYSICAL CHEMISTRY. *Current Pos:* from asst prof to assoc prof, 52-62, dir grad studies, 66-69, PROF CHEM, DEPAUW UNIV, 62- *Personal Data:* b Lakewood, Ohio, Feb 29, 24; m 48; c 2. *Educ:* Ind Univ, BS, 48; Western Reserve Univ, MS, 50, PhD(chem), 53. *Prof Exp:* Lectr, Fenn Col, 51. *Mem:* Am Chem Soc; Royal Soc Chem; Sigma Xi. *Res:* Electrochemistry; thermodynamics, chemical kinetics. *Mailing Add:* 702 Highridge Greencastle IN 46135-1410

RICKEY, FRANK ATKINSON, JR, NUCLEAR PHYSICS. *Current Pos:* asst prof, 68-76 ASSOC PROF NUCLEAR PHYSICS, PURDUE UNIV, LAFAYETTE, 76- *Personal Data:* b Baton Rouge, La, Nov 21, 38; m 62; c 2. *Educ:* La State Univ, Baton Rouge, BS, 60; Fla State Univ, PhD(physics), 66. *Prof Exp:* Res assoc nuclear physics, Los Alamos Sci Lab, 66-68. *Mem:* Am Phys Soc. *Res:* Low energy nuclear physics; charged particle reactions; nuclear structure. *Mailing Add:* 610 Rose St West Lafayette IN 47906

RICKEY, MARTIN EUGENE, nuclear physics, musical acoustics; deceased, see previous edition for last biography

RICKLEFS, ROBERT ERIC, ECOLOGY. *Current Pos:* from asst prof to assoc prof, 68-80, PROF BIOL, UNIV PA, 80- *Personal Data:* b San Francisco, Calif, June 6, 43. *Educ:* Stanford Univ, AB, 63; Univ Pa, PhD(biol), 67. *Prof Exp:* Nat Res Coun vis res assoc, Smithsonian Trop Res Inst, 67-68. *Mem:* Soc Study Evolution; Am Soc Naturalists; Ecol Soc Am; Am Ornithologists Union; Cooper Ornith Soc. *Res:* Evolutionary ecology; development and reproductive biology of birds; population and community ecology. *Mailing Add:* Dept Biol Univ Mo 8001 Natural Bridge Rd St Louis MO 63121-4499

RICKLES, FREDERICK R, HEMATOLOGY. *Current Pos:* DEP ASST DIR, HEMAT DIS BR, CTR DIS CONTROL, 93- *Personal Data:* b Chicago, Ill, Sept 24, 42; m 64, Kathryn Goodman; c Andrew & Jason. *Educ:* Col Med, Univ Ill, MD, 67. *Honors & Awards:* Humanitarian Award, Nat Hemophilia Found, 90. *Prof Exp:* Intern & resident internal med, Univ Rochester-Strong Mem Hosp, 67-70, fel hemat, 70-71; dir, Coagulation Res Lab, Walter Reed Army Inst Res, 71-74; from asst prof to prof med, Univ Conn, 74-93, co-chief, Div Hemat-Oncol, Sch Med, 81-85, chief, 85-93. *Concurrent Pos:* Clin asst prof med, George Washington Univ, 71-74; attend physician, Walter Reed Army Med Ctr, 71-74 & John Dempsey-Univ Conn Hosp, 74-; chief, Hemat Sect, Vet Admin Hosp, Newington, Conn, 74- & Hemat-Oncol Sect, 81-; consult, Artificial Kidney-Chronic Uremia Prog, Nat Inst Arthritis, Metab & Digestive Dis-NIH, 74-78; Vet Admin res grant, 74-; Nat Cancer Inst & Nat Heart, Lung & Blood Inst grants, NIH, 78; med res serv assoc chief staff, Vet Admin Hosp, Newington, Conn, 78-81; grants, Am Heart Asn, 83-86 & Am Cancer Soc, 85-; vpres, NIH/Nat Cancer Inst, Med Sci Affairs, Nat Hemophilia Found, 87-93; prof med & pediat, Emory Univ Sch Med & dir Comp Hemophilia Prog, 93- *Mem:* AAAS; Am Fedn Clin Res; Am Asn Immunologists; Am Soc Hemat; Int Soc Thrombosis & Hemostasis. *Res:* Blood coagulation; cancer; delayed hypersensitivity; endotoxin biochemistry; membrane proteins; role of tissue factor in tumor biology and blood clotting. *Mailing Add:* Ctr Dis Control 1600 Clifton Rd NE Atlanta GA 30333. *Fax:* 404-679-4638; *E-Mail:* frr0@ciddas1.em.cdc.gov

RICKLES, NORMAN HAROLD, ORAL PATHOLOGY. *Current Pos:* RETIRED. *Personal Data:* b Seattle, Wash, May 8, 20; m 50, Eva Simons; c Tamara R (Luria) & Nessa E. *Educ:* Wash Univ, DDS, 47; Univ Calif, MS, 51. *Prof Exp:* Instr dent med, Col Dent, Univ Calif, 47-48, lectr, 48-52, asst clin prof, 52-56; from assoc prof to prof dent, Univ Ore, 56-85, head, Dept Oral Path, 56-76, emer prof dent, Dent Sch, 85-87. *Concurrent Pos:* Fel, Armed Forces Inst Path, 54-56; consult to Surgeon Gen, Madigan Army Hosp, Ft Lewis, Wash, 58-; Fulbright prof, Sch Dent Med, Hebrew Univ, Israel, 66-67; sabbatical vis prof & consult, Guys Hosp, London, 77-78. *Mem:* Am Soc Clin Path; Am Dent Asn; Am Acad Oral Med; Am Acad Oral Path (pres, 62-63); Int Acad Path. *Res:* Dental caries; allergy; methods of teaching dental students; screening tests for dental patients; histochemistry and methods of evaluation of oral disease; fluorescent and immunoperoxidase microscopy; transplantation of dental pulp. *Mailing Add:* 1515 SW Westwood Dr Portland OR 97201

RICKLIN, SAUL, CHEMICAL ENGINEERING. *Current Pos:* RETIRED. *Personal Data:* b New York, NY, Sept 5, 19; m 47, Lois Webster; c 4. *Educ:* Columbia Univ, BS, 39, ChE, 40. *Prof Exp:* Process engr, Metal & Thermit Corp, NJ, 40-46; consult engr, 46-47; asst prof chem, Brown Univ, 47-54; consult engr, Ricklin Res Assocs, 54-59; vpres, Dixon Industs Corp, 59-66, exec vpres, 66-70, pres, 70-77, chmn, 77-81, consult, 81-91. *Concurrent Pos:* Dir, NTN Rulon Industs Co, Ltd, Japan, 66-; vpres, Valflon, SpA, Italy, 71-81; vpres, G D Spencer Co, Ltd, Can, 71-; dir, Entwistle Corp, 76-90, EFD Corp; dir, 82-89. *Mem:* Am Chem Soc; Am Inst Chem Engrs. *Res:* Thermit reactions; aluminothermics; incendiaries; tracer ammunition; ceramic materials; metal organics; fine particle technology; electroplating; metal finishing; corrosion; friction and wear of dry bearings; fluorocarbon plastics. *Mailing Add:* PO Box 91 Bristol RI 02809

RICKMAN, RONALD WAYNE, SOIL CONSERVATION. *Current Pos:* SOIL SCIENTIST, SCI & EDUC ADMIN-AGR RES, USDA, 66- *Personal Data:* b Pomeroy, Wash, June 28, 40; m 63; c 3. *Educ:* Wash State Univ, BS, 63; Univ Calif, Riverside, PhD(soil physics), 66. *Mem:* Am Soc Agron; Am Soc Agr Engrs; Sigma Xi. *Res:* Dryland small grain growth simulation; wheat root growth and water use; water conservation; wheat production. *Mailing Add:* 11036 NW 12th St Apt C Pendleton OR 97801-1276

RICKS, BEVERLY LEE, PHYSIOLOGY, ZOOLOGY. *Current Pos:* asst prof, 65-70, ASSOC PROF BIOL, NORTHEAST LA UNIV, 70- *Personal Data:* b Grand Chenier, La, Oct 10, 28; m 51; c 2. *Educ:* Miss State Univ, BS, 50, PhD(physiol), 69; Miss Col, MS, 53. *Honors & Awards:* OBTA Award, Nat Asn Biol Teachers, 63. *Prof Exp:* Teacher high schs, Miss, 51-65. *Mem:* Nat Asn Biol Teachers; Am Inst Biol Sci; Entom Soc Am. *Res:* Feeding preferences; seasonal changes in stored nutrients; distribution of digestive enzymes in the imported fire ant. *Mailing Add:* Dept Biol Northeast La Univ 700 University Ave Monroe LA 71209-0001

RICKSECKER, RALPH E, CHEMICAL METALLURGY, METALLURGICAL ENGINEERING. *Current Pos:* METALL CONSULT, INT & DOMESTIC, 77- *Personal Data:* b Cleveland, Ohio, Sept 9, 12; m 38, Ruth Ilitt; c Ralph E Jr & Ruth A (Clouse). *Educ:* Western Res Univ, BS, 44, MS, 50. *Prof Exp:* Anal chemist, Chase Brass & Copper Co, Inc, Cleveland, 30-35, asst chief chemist, 34-35, chief chemist, 35-45, process metallurgist, 45-48, chief metallurgist, 48-50, dir metall, 50-77. *Mem:* Am Chem Soc; Am Soc Test & Mat; Soc Automotive Eng; Am Inst Mining, Metall & Petrol Eng; Am Soc Metals. *Res:* Physical metallurgy of copper and copper alloys. *Mailing Add:* 130 E 196th St Euclid OH 44119-1034

RICKTER, DONALD OSCAR, INFORMATION SCIENCE. *Current Pos:* RETIRED. *Personal Data:* b Rio Dell, Calif, May 5, 31; m 59; c 2. *Educ:* Univ Calif, Davis, AB, 52, MS, 55; Mich State Univ, PhD(chem), 64. *Prof Exp:* Instr chem, Santa Ana Col, 57-59; scientist & info mgr, res div, Polaroid Corp, Cambridge, 64-96. *Mem:* Am Chem Soc. *Res:* Photographic chemistry (developers, dyes, novel polymers, restrainers, synthesis); management of information systems; current development in science and technology. *Mailing Add:* 88 Hemlock St Arlington MA 02174-2157

RICORD, LOUIS CHESTER, BIOMEDICAL COMPUTING, INFORMATION SYSTEMS. *Current Pos:* res scientist Biomed Info Systs, 78-83, MGR APPL INFO SYSTS, BATTELLE COLUMBUS LABS, 83- *Personal Data:* b Burbank, Calif, Aug 16, 51. *Educ:* Univ Utah, BS, 73, ME, 75, PhD(med biophys, comput), 78. *Concurrent Pos:* Res assoc, NIH, 74-78; adj asst prof, Ohio State Univ, 80- *Mem:* Inst Elec & Electronics Engrs; Comput Soc; Soc Comput Med; Asn Comput Mach. *Res:* Computer assisted decision making in health sciences; medical data base design and construction; computer applications in laboratory animal toxicology; general information system applications development. *Mailing Add:* 1645 Guilford Rd Columbus OH 43221

RIDDELL, JAMES, mathematics; deceased, see previous edition for last biography

RIDDELL, JOHN EVANS, economic geology, for more information see previous edition

RIDDELL, ROBERT JAMES, JR, THEORETICAL PHYSICS. *Current Pos:* RETIRED. *Personal Data:* b US, June 25, 23; m 50, Kathryn Jane Gamble; c Cynthia (Dunham), Stephen Louis (deceased) & James Duncan. *Educ:* Carnegie Inst Technol, BS, 44; Univ Mich, MS, 47, PhD(physics), 51. *Prof Exp:* From instr to asst prof physics, Univ Calif, 51-55, physicist, Radiation Lab, 55-58; physicist, AEC, 58-60; physicist, Lawrence Berkeley Lab, 60-82. *Mem:* Am Phys Soc. *Res:* High energy physics and strong interactions. *Mailing Add:* 1095 Arlington Blvd El Cerrito CA 94530

RIDDERHOFF, JOHN C, LABORATORY SYSTEMS, PUBLIC HEALTH. *Current Pos:* SCI ADMINR, DIV LAB SYSTS, CTR DIS CONTROL, 93- *Personal Data:* b Quantico, Va, Sept 20, 56. *Educ:* Va Commonwealth Univ, BS, 78; Univ NC, Chapel Hill, MPH, 85, DrPH, 87. *Prof Exp:* Staff, Microbiol Div, Consolidated Lab Syst Va, 79-84; postdoctoral fel, Med Col Va, Am Soc Microbiol, 87-89; dep dir, Del Pub Health Lab, 89-92. *Mem:* Am Soc Microbiol. *Mailing Add:* Div Lab Systs CDC 4770 Buford Hwy MS G25 Atlanta GA 30341

RIDDICK, FRANK ADAMS, JR, ENDOCRINOLOGY. *Current Pos:* CLIN PROF MED, MED SCH, TULANE UNIV, NEW ORLEANS, 77- *Personal Data:* b Memphis, Tenn, June 14, 29; m 52; c 3. *Educ:* Vanderbilt Univ, BA, 51, MD, 54. *Prof Exp:* Instr med, Med Sch, Tulane Univ, New Orleans, 61-65, from clin asst prof to assoc prof, 65-77; from asst med dir to assoc med dir, Ochsner Clin, 68-75, head sect endocrinol & metab dis, Dept Internal Med, 76-85, med dir, 75- *Mem:* Inst Med-Nat Acad Sci; fel Am Col Physicians Execs; Am Fedn Clin Res; AMA; Am Acad Med Dirs; Am Soc Internal Med. *Mailing Add:* Ochsner Clinic 1514 Jefferson Hwy New Orleans LA 70121. *E-Mail:* riddick@ochsner.org

RIDDIFORD, LYNN MOORHEAD, INSECT ENDOCRINOLOGY, DEVELOPMENTAL BIOLOGY. *Current Pos:* assoc prof zool, 73-75, PROF ZOOL, UNIV WASH, 75- *Personal Data:* b Knoxville, Tenn, Oct 18, 36; m 70, James W Truman. *Educ:* Radcliffe Col, AB, 58; Cornell Univ, PhD(develop biol, protein chem), 61. *Prof Exp:* NSF res fel biol, Harvard Univ, 61-63; instr, Wellesley Col, 63-65; res fel, Harvard Univ, 65-66, from asst prof to assoc prof, 66-73. *Concurrent Pos:* NSF res grant, 64-; mem, Trop Med & Parasitol Study Sect, NIH, 74-78, res grant, 75-; res grant, USDA, 78-82, 85-87 & 89-97, panel mem biol stress plants, 79, 89 & 94; mem, Int Comt Symp Comp Endocrinol, 78-93; vis scholar, Stanford Univ, 79-80, Univ Cambridge, 86-87; Guggenheim fel, 79-80; panel mem regulatory biol, NSF, 84-88; mem, Gov Bd, Int Ctr Insect Physiol & Ecol, Nairobi, Kenya, 85-91, vis scientist, 87 & chmn, Prog Comt, 89-91; sr int fel, NIH, 86-87; vis scientist, Commonwealth Sci & Indust Res Orgn, Canberra, Australia, 93-94. *Mem:* Fel AAAS; Am Soc Cell Biol; Soc Comp & Integrative Biol (pres, 91); Soc Develop Biol; Am Soc Biochem & Molecular Biol; fel Entom Soc Am; fel Royal Entom Soc; fel Am Acad Arts & Sci. *Res:* Hormonal control of insect development and behavior; mechanism of hormone action; insect olfaction; pheromones. *Mailing Add:* Dept Zool Univ Wash Box 351800 Seattle WA 98195-1800. *Fax:* 206-543-3041; *E-Mail:* lmr@u.washington.edu

RIDDLE, DAVID, CHEMISTRY, ENVIRONMENTAL CHEMISTRY. *Current Pos:* Res chemist & lectr environ eng, 73-75, ASSOC PROF CHEM, TEX A&M UNIV, 75- *Personal Data:* b Marshall, Tex, Nov 5, 46. *Educ:* ETex Baptist Univ, BS, 68; Tex A&M Univ, PhD(anal chem), 73. *Mem:* Fel Am Inst Chemists. *Mailing Add:* Dept Chem Univ Texas 3900 University Blvd Tyler TX 75799

RIDDLE, DONALD LEE, DEVELOPMENTAL GENETICS, NEMATOLOGY. *Current Pos:* from asst prof to assoc prof, 75-85, PROF BIOL, UNIV MO, COLUMBIA, 85-, DIR MOLECULAR BIOL PROG, 89- *Personal Data:* b Vancouver, Wash, July 26, 45; m 69; c 2. *Educ:* Univ Calif, Davis, BS, 68, Berkeley, PhD(genetics), 71. *Honors & Awards:* Chancellor's Award for Outstanding Fac Res, Univ Mo, 87. *Prof Exp:* NIH trainee genetics, Univ Calif, Berkeley, 69-71, assoc molecular biol, Santa Barbara, 71-72; fel, Jane Coffin Childs Mem Fund, Med Res Coun Lab Molecular Biol, 73-75. *Concurrent Pos:* Prin investr, Res Grants & Contracts, NIH, 77-, NSF, 83-86; dir, Caenorhabditis Genetics Ctr, 79-92; vis prof nemat, Commonwealth Sci & Indust Res Orgn, Australia, 83; mem, Div Res Grants, Genetics Study Sect, NIH, 85-; ed bd, Developmental Genetics, 86-88; assoc ed, J Nematol, 88-90; vis prof, Simon Fraser Univ, BC, Can, 89; honor lectr, Asn Big 8 Univs, 89-90; chmn, Univ Mo Res Bd, 92-94. *Mem:* Genetics Soc Am; Soc Develop Biol; Soc Nematologists; AAAS. *Res:* Genetic analysis of nematode development and behavior using a dispersal stage called the dauer larva as a model system; molecular genetics of TGF-B family ligands and their receptors. *Mailing Add:* Div Biol Sci Tucker Hall Univ Mo Columbia MO 65211. *Fax:* 573-884-9676

RIDDLE, GEORGE HERBERT NEEDHAM, PHYSICS, ELECTRON OPTICS & INFORMATION DISPLAY. *Current Pos:* SR MEM TECH STAFF, DAVID SARNOFF RES CTR, 87- *Personal Data:* b New York, NY, Mar 29, 40; m 65, Elinor Tyne; c Margaret, Adele & George. *Educ:* Princeton Univ, AB, 62; Univ Ill, MS, 64; Cornell Univ, PhD(appl physics), 71. *Prof Exp:* Mem tech staff, RCA Labs, 64-66 & 73-84, sr mem tech staff, 84-87; res physicist, Esso Res & Eng Co, 71-73. *Mem:* Sigma Xi; Soc Info Display. *Res:* Surface physics; electron optics and electron beam instrumentation; video-disc stylus technology; display device technology. *Mailing Add:* 21 Grover Ave Princeton NJ 08540. *Fax:* 609-734-2886; *E-Mail:* lriddle@sarnoff.com

RIDDLE, LAWRENCE H, FUNCTIONAL ANALYSIS. *Current Pos:* asst prof, 89-92, ASSOC PROF MATH, AGNES SCOTT COL, 92- *Personal Data:* b Jenkintown, Pa, Mar 1, 54; m 85. *Educ:* Carnegie-Mellon Univ, BS, 76; Univ Ill, MS, 81, PhD(math), 82. *Prof Exp:* Asst prof math, Emory Univ, 82-89. *Mem:* Am Math Soc; Math Asn Am. *Res:* Functional analysis; math education. *Mailing Add:* Dept Math & Comput Sci Agnes Scott Col Decatur GA 30030-3797

RIDDLE, WAYNE ALLEN, INVERTEBRATE PHYSIOLOGY. *Current Pos:* asst prof, 77-83, ASSOC PROF PHYSIOL, ILL STATE UNIV, 83- *Personal Data:* b Madison, Wis, Nov 3, 45. *Educ:* Utah State Univ, BS, 68; Univ NMex, MS, 73, PhD(biol), 77. *Prof Exp:* Vis asst prof biol, Univ NMex, 76-77. *Mem:* Am Soc Zoologists; Ecol Soc Am. *Res:* Respiratory physiology; cold hardiness; water relations and osmoregulation of terrestrial arthropods and molluscs. *Mailing Add:* Dept Biol Sci Ill State Univ Normal IL 61790-4120

RIDE, SALLY KRISTEN, PHYSICS. *Current Pos:* DIR, CALIF SPACE INST, UNIV CALIF, SAN DIEGO, 89-, PROF PHYSICS, 89- *Personal Data:* b Los Angeles, Calif, May 26, 51; div. *Educ:* Stanford Univ, BA & BS, 73, PhD(physics), 78. *Prof Exp:* Trainee, NASA, 78-79; astronaut, 79-87; sci fel, Stanford Univ, 87-89. *Concurrent Pos:* Mem, Presidential Comn on Space Shuttle, 86. *Res:* Physics. *Mailing Add:* Dept Physics Mail Code 0319 Univ Calif La Jolla CA 92093

RIDENER, FRED LOUIS, JR, ELEMENTARY PARTICLE PHYSICS. *Current Pos:* Asst prof, 77-83, ASSOC PROF PHYSICS, PA STATE UNIV, 83- *Personal Data:* b El Reno, Okla, Sept 19, 44; m 71. *Educ:* NMex State Univ, BS, 68; Iowa State Univ, PhD(physics), 76. *Mem:* Am Phys Soc. *Res:* Elementary particle theory, especially polarization, electroweak form factors and relativistic wave equations; response functions for nonlinear systems. *Mailing Add:* 560 Pleasant View Dr Apollo PA 15613

RIDENHOUR, RICHARD LEWIS, FISH BIOLOGY. *Current Pos:* from asst prof to assoc prof, Humboldt State Univ, 60-70, asst dean acad affairs, 67-69, dean acad planning, 69-81, PROF FISHERIES, HUMBOLDT STATE UNIV, 70-, DEAN, COL NAT RES, 81- *Personal Data:* b Santa Rosa, Calif, July 13, 32; m 54; c 5. *Educ:* Humboldt State Col, BS, 54; Iowa State Col, MS, 55; PhD(fisheries), 58. *Prof Exp:* Aquatic biologist com fisheries, State Fish Comn, Ore, 58-60. *Concurrent Pos:* Consult, Water Develop Proj, Modesto & Turlock Irrig Dist, Int Eng Co, San Francisco. *Mem:* Am Fisheries Soc; Am Inst Fishery Res Biol. *Res:* Biometrics; ecology. *Mailing Add:* 2736 Sunnygrove Ave Arcata CA 95521

RIDENOUR, MARCELLA V, MOTOR DEVELOPMENT. *Current Pos:* PROF MOTOR DEVELOP, TEMPLE UNIV, 74- *Personal Data:* b New Martinsville, WVa, Nov 29, 45; m 73; c 2. *Educ:* Miami Univ, BS, 67; Purdue Univ, MS, 68 & PhD(motor develop), 72. *Mem:* Am Soc Testing & Mat. *Mailing Add:* Dept Phys Educ Temple Univ 1701 N Broad St Philadelphia PA 19122-2504

RIDEOUT, DONALD ERIC, MATHEMATICS. *Current Pos:* asst prof, 70-74, ASSOC PROF MATH, MEM UNIV NFLD, 74-, DEP HEAD MATH, 87- *Personal Data:* b Burlington, Nfld, May 15, 42; m 65; c 2. *Educ:* Mem Univ Nfld, BA, 63, BSc, 64; McGill Univ, PhD(math), 70. *Prof Exp:* Lectr math, McGill Univ, 66-70. *Concurrent Pos:* Nat Res Coun Can fel, 70-72 & 72-74. *Mem:* Math Soc Can. *Res:* Algebraic number theory. *Mailing Add:* Dept Math & Statist Mem Univ Nfld St John's NF A1C 5S7 Can. *Fax:* 709-737-3010; *E-Mail:* drideout@riemann.math.mun.ca

RIDEOUT, JANET LITSTER, CHEMISTRY. *Current Pos:* STAFF MEM, INSPIRE PHARM, 96- *Personal Data:* b Bennington, Vt, Jan 6, 39; m 73, Ralph L Jr. *Educ:* Mt Holyoke Col, AB, 61, MA, 63; State Univ NY Buffalo, PhD(chem), 68. *Prof Exp:* Res chemist, Burroughs Wellcome Co, 68-70, sr res chemist, 70-79, group leader, Exp Ther Dept, 79-83, group leader, 83-88, asst div dir, 88-91, assoc div dir, Org Chem Div, 91-95. *Mem:* Am Chem Soc; NY Acad Sci; fel Am Inst Chemists; AAAS. *Res:* Organic synthesis; heterocyclic compounds; nucleosides; purines; pyrimidines; imidazoles; metabolites; cancer chemotherapy; antiviral chemotherapy. *Mailing Add:* 4222 Emperor Blvd Suite 470 Durham NC 27703

RIDEOUT, SHELDON P, PHYSICAL METALLURGY. *Current Pos:* RETIRED. *Personal Data:* b Toronto, Ohio, Nov 5, 27; m 47; c 6. *Educ:* Mich Technol Univ, BS, 48; Univ Notre Dame, MS, 51. *Prof Exp:* Engr, Ladish Co, Wis, 48-49; staff mem, Tech Metall Lab, Savannah River Plant, E I DuPont de Nemours & Co Inc, 51-63, process supvr, 53-55, sr supvr, 55-63, res supvr, Nuclear Mat Div, 63-78, chief supvr reactor mat tech, Savannah River Lab, 78- *Mem:* Am Soc Metals; Nat Asn Corrosion Engrs. *Res:* Metallurgy of materials for nuclear reactors; stress corrosion of stainless steel and titanium alloys; hydrogen effects in metals. *Mailing Add:* 245 Barnard Ave SE Aiken SC 29801

RIDEOUT, VINCENT C(HARLES), ELECTRICAL ENGINEERING. *Current Pos:* PROF ELEC ENG, UNIV WIS-MADISON, 55- *Personal Data:* b Chinook, Alta, May 22, 24; nat US; m 39; c 4. *Educ:* Univ Alta, BSc, 38; Calif Inst Technol, MS, 40. *Prof Exp:* Mem tech staff elec eng, Bell Tel Labs, Inc, 39-46; asst prof, Univ Wis, 46-49, assoc prof, 49-54; vis prof, Indian Inst Sci, 54-55. *Concurrent Pos:* Vis prof, Univ Colo, 63-64 & Inst Med Physics, Utrecht, Holland, 70-71; mem, Bull Mfrs Engrs Comt. *Mem:* AAAS; fel Inst Elec & Electronics Engrs. *Res:* Control systems; computing, bioengineering, socio-economics. *Mailing Add:* ECE Dept Univ Wis Madison WI 53706

RIDER, AGATHA ANN, PUBLIC HEALTH NUTRITION, FAT SOLUBLE VITAMINS. *Current Pos:* RETIRED. *Personal Data:* b May 13, 19; m 48, Rowland V Rider. *Educ:* Johns Hopkins Univ, MS, 46. *Prof Exp:* asst prof biochem, Sch Hyg & Pub Health, Johns Hopkins Univ, 72-86. *Mem:* Am Chem Soc; Am Inst Nutrit; Sigma Xi; AAAS. *Res:* Vitamin A nutrition; prenatal and postnatal nutrition and development of offspring (rats); lifelong moderate ethanol intake (including prenatal) and longevity in rats; diet and colon cancer; vitamin A deficiency blindness. *Mailing Add:* 5400 Vantage Point Rd No 1111 Columbia MD 21044

RIDER, BENJAMIN FRANKLIN, ANALYTICAL CHEMISTRY. *Current Pos:* RETIRED. *Personal Data:* b Cleveland, Ohio, Dec 4, 21; m 44; c Pamela, Scott & Linda. *Educ:* Mt Union Col, BS, 43; Purdue Univ, MS, 44, PhD(anal chem), 47. *Prof Exp:* Res assoc, Knolls Atomic Power Lab, Gen Elec Co, 47-57, res assoc, Vallecitos Nuclear Ctr, 57-81. *Mem:* Am Chem Soc; fel Am Inst Chem; Am Soc Test & Mat. *Res:* Spectrophotometry; radiochemistry; medical radioisotopes processing; nuclear fuel burnup analysis; fission yields compilation. *Mailing Add:* 4137 Norris Rd Fremont CA 94536-5013

RIDER, DON K(EITH), ORGANIC POLYMER CHEMISTRY, MATERIALS ENGINEERING. *Current Pos:* RETIRED. *Personal Data:* b Rockford, Ill, Feb 12, 18; m 49, Lois Forsberg; c Douglas K, Bruce N & Kenneth A. *Educ:* Univ Mich, BS, 39, MS, 41. *Prof Exp:* Chemist resin develop, Rohm & Haas Co, 41-46, group leader ion exchange develop, 46-47; chemist binder res, Chicopee Mfg Corp Div, Johnson & Johnson, 47-48; chemist, Resins Laminates Develop, AT&T Bell Labs, 48-59, head, Org Mat Res & Develop Dept, 59-75, head, Org Mat Eng Dept, 75-78. *Concurrent Pos:* Mem tech panel, Mat Adv Bd, Nat Acad Sci-Nat Res Coun, 56-57, spec comt adhesive bonded struct components, Bldg Res Adv Bd, 63-65; consult, Archit Plastics Int, 64-66; mem ad hoc comt, Predictive Testing, Nat Acad Sci-Nat Res Coun, 70-72; consult, 78- *Mem:* Am Chem Soc. *Res:* Adhesives, bonded structures and casting resins; laminates; structural plastics; laminated thermoset materials; printed circuits; fibrous reinforcements. *Mailing Add:* 788 Park Shore Dr B24 Naples FL 34103

RIDER, JOSEPH ALFRED, GASTROENTEROLOGY. *Current Pos:* DIR GASTROINTESTINAL RES LAB, FRANKLIN HOSP, 63- *Personal Data:* b Chicago, Ill, Jan 30, 21; m 43; c 2. *Educ:* Univ Chicago, SB, 42, MD, 44, PhD(pharmacol), 51; Am Bd Internal Med, dipl; Am Bd Gastroenterol, dipl. *Prof Exp:* Intern internal med, Presby Hosp, Chicago, 44-45; asst resident med, Univ Tex, 47-49; resident, Univ Chicago, 49-50, instr, 51-52; asst prof, Med Ctr, Univ Calif, San Francisco, 53-59, asst clin prof, 59-66, asst chief gastrointestinal clin, 53-61. *Mem:* Am Soc Pharmacol & Exp Therapeut; Soc Exp Biol & Med; Am Geriat Soc; fel Am Gastroenterol Asn; fel Am Col Physicians. *Res:* Tolerance of organic phosphates in men; hypersensitivity factors in ulcerative colitis; cytology in the diagnosis of gastrointestinal malignancies; gastric secretion and motility; color television endoscopy. *Mailing Add:* 350 Parnassus Ave Suite 900 San Francisco CA 94117-3608

RIDER, PAUL EDWARD, SR, PHYSICAL CHEMISTRY. *Current Pos:* from asst prof to assoc prof, 69-79, asst provost, 82-83, PROF CHEM, UNIV NORTHERN IOWA, 79-, EXEC DIR, IOWA ACAD SCI, 88- *Personal Data:* b Des Moines, Iowa, Nov 22, 40; m 63; c 3. *Educ:* Drake Univ, BA, 62; Iowa State Univ, MS, 64; Kans State Univ, PhD(phys chem), 69. *Prof Exp:* Instr chem, Drake Univ, 64-66; vis prof, Coe Col, 69. *Concurrent Pos:* Consult, Shell Develop Co, Houston. *Mem:* Am Chem Soc; AAAS; Iowa Acad Sci. *Res:* Thermodynamic studies of weak hydrogen bonds; theoretical consideration of polymer solution formation; history and philosophy of science. *Mailing Add:* Dept Chem Univ Northern Iowa Cedar Falls IA 50613

RIDER, RONALD EDWARD, COMPUTER SCIENCE, PHYSICS. *Current Pos:* Res scientist comput sci & physics, Xerox Corp, 72-77, mgr electronic subsyst develop, 77-86, co-mgr, Palo Alto Res Ctr, 86-89, VPRES, CORP ARCHIT, XEROX CORP, 89- *Personal Data:* b Pasadena, Calif, June 11, 45; m 69; c 2. *Educ:* Occidental Col, AB, 67; Wash Univ, AM, 69, PhD(physics), 72. *Res:* Computer systems; word processing; image processing. *Mailing Add:* 3333 Coyote Hill Rd Palo Alto CA 94304-1314

RIDER, ROWLAND VANCE, BIOSTATISTICS. *Current Pos:* From asst prof to assoc prof pub health admin, 50-65, prof pop dynamics, 65-82, EMER PROF POP DYNAMICS, SCH HYG & PUB HEALTH, JOHNS HOPKINS UNIV, 82- *Personal Data:* b Syracuse, NY, Aug 23, 15; m 48, Agatha Ann Siegen Thaler. *Educ:* Amherst Col, AB, 37; Syracuse Univ, MA, 38; Johns Hopkins Univ, ScD(biostatist), 47. *Mem:* AAAS; Pop Asn Am; Am Pub Health Asn; Am Statist Asn; Int Union Sci Study Pop. *Res:* Study prematures, maternal and child health and family planning administration evaluation. *Mailing Add:* 5400 Vantage Point Rd No 1111 Columbia MD 21044

RIDGE, DOUGLAS POLL, PHYSICAL CHEMISTRY. *Current Pos:* From asst prof to assoc prof, 72-85, PROF CHEM, UNIV DEL, 85- *Personal Data:* b Portland, Ore, Nov 9, 44; m 71; c 6. *Educ:* Harvard Col, AB, 68; Calif Inst Technol, PhD(chem), 72. *Mem:* Am Phys Soc; Am Chem Soc. *Res:* Reactive and nonreactive ion molecule interactions in the gas phase; ion cyclotron resonance spectroscopy; gas phase organometallic chemistry. *Mailing Add:* Dept Chem Univ Del Newark DE 19716

RIDGE, JOHN CHARLES, PLEISTOCENE PALEOMAGNETISM, GLACIAL SEDIMENTATION. *Current Pos:* asst prof, 86-91, ASSOC PROF GEOL, TUFTS UNIV, 91- *Personal Data:* b Bethlehem, Pa, Mar 9, 55; m 85, Mary Jo Healy; c Christopher George & Daniel Patrick. *Educ:* Lehigh Univ, BS, 77, MS, 83; Syracuse Univ, PhD(geol), 85. *Prof Exp:* Teaching asst geol, Syracuse Univ, 80-85. *Concurrent Pos:* Geologist, NY State Geol Surv, 80-82, NH State Geol Surv, 86-89 & 92-93. *Mem:* Geol Soc Am; Am Quaternary Asn; Am Geophys Union. *Res:* Paleomagnetism and secular variation of remanent magnetization as recorded in glacial sediments, varve and glacial stratigraphy and glacial processes; genesis of landscapes during interglacial and periglacial intervals; geomorphology. *Mailing Add:* Dept Geol Tufts Univ Medford MA 02155. *Fax:* 617-627-3584

RIDGE, JOHN DREW, APPLIED, ECONOMIC & ENGINEERING GEOLOGY. *Current Pos:* RETIRED. *Personal Data:* b Cincinnati, Ohio, July 3, 09; m 41; c 2. *Educ:* Univ Chicago, SB, 30, SM, 32, PhD(econ geol), 35. *Honors & Awards:* Henry Krumb Lectr, 71; Mineral Econ Award, 72. *Prof Exp:* Res petrographer, Universal-Atlas Cement Co, Ind, 35-36; petrologist, US Nat Park Serv, Washington, DC, 36-37; geologist, Cerro de Pasco Copper Corp, Peru, 37-40 & NJ Zinc Co, 46-47; assoc prof econ geol, Pa State Univ, 47-51, prof mineral econ, 51-64, asst dean col mineral indust, 53-64, prof econ geol & mineral econ, 64-75, head dept mineral econ, 51-75. *Concurrent Pos:* Mem, Earth Sci Div, Nat Res Coun, 67-70 & 68-71; mem panel mineral econ, Nat Acad Sci, 67-79; ed, Graton-Sales Volume, 68-72; Nat Acad Sci exchange scientist in Poland, 69 & 70, Romania, 73, USSR & Yugoslavia, 77; mem comt crit & strategic mat, Nat Mat Adv Bd, 69-71; exchange scientist, NSF, 69 & 73 & Nat Res Coun, 70, 72, 74 & 77; adj prof geol, Univ Fla, 75-80, actg chmn dept, 80-81, vis prof, 80-83. *Mem:* Int Asn Genesis Ore Deposits (pres, 76-80, past pres, 80-84); Soc Econ Geol; Am Soc Mining, Metall & Petrol Engrs; fel Am Mineral Soc; fel Geol Soc Am. *Res:* Geology and geochemistry of metallic ore deposits; chemistry of metasomatism, stable isotopes and ore genesis; politics and economics of mineral exploration and exploitation. *Mailing Add:* 400 Brentwood Rd Charlottesville VA 22901

RIDGEWAY, BILL TOM, PARASITOLOGY, PROTOZOOLOGY. *Current Pos:* assoc prof, 66-71, PROF ZOOL & PARASITOL, EASTERN ILL UNIV, 71- *Personal Data:* b Columbia, Mo, Dec 23, 27; m 52; c 3. *Educ:* Friends Univ, AB, 52; Wichita State Univ, MS, 58; Univ Mo, PhD(zool), 66. *Prof Exp:* From instr to asst prof zool, Southwestern Col, 58-63; res asst parasitol, Univ Mo, 63-66, asst prof invert zool, 66. *Concurrent Pos:* Vis prof, Inland Environ Lab, Univ Md, 74-75; prog officer, Ann Midwest Conf Parasitologists, 81, presiding officer, 85; contract scientist, Ill Dept Conserv, 76-80. *Mem:* Am Soc Parasitol; Am Micros Soc; Am Soc Protozoologists. *Res:* Protozoan ectosymbionts of freshwater invertebrates; helminth and protozoan parasites of wild rodents; systematics of nemotodes. *Mailing Add:* 2614 Fifth St Charleston IL 61920-3011

RIDGWAY, ELLIS BRANSON, PHYSIOLOGY, BIOPHYSICS. *Current Pos:* asst prof, 72-77, ASSOC PROF PHYSIOL, MED COL VA, 77- *Personal Data:* b Philadelphia, Pa, May 14, 39; m 64, 80; c 3. *Educ:* Mass Inst Technol, SB, 63; Univ Ore, PhD(biol), 68. *Prof Exp:* NATO fel, Univ Col, Univ London, 69; USPHS fel, Cambridge Univ, 69-70; USPHS fel, Friday Harbor Labs, Univ Wash, 70-71. *Mem:* AAAS; Soc Gen Physiol; Biophys Soc. *Res:* Role of calcium as an activator in muscle, nerve and synapse; biophysics of muscle contraction and membrane permeability. *Mailing Add:* Dept Physiol Med Col Va Box 551 MCV Sta Richmond VA 23298

RIDGWAY, GEORGE JUNIOR, MICROBIOLOGY, BIOCHEMISTRY. *Current Pos:* RETIRED. *Personal Data:* b Lincoln, Nebr, Aug 26, 22; m 47; c 3. *Educ:* Univ Wash, Seattle, BS, 49, MS, 51, PhD(microbiol), 54. *Prof Exp:* Biochemist, US Bur Com Fisheries, 54-64; asst lab dir, Northeast Fisheries Ctr, Nat Marine Fisheries Serv, Woods Hole, 64-71, dir, Biol Lab, Maine, 71-73, asst ctr dir, 73-75. *Mem:* AAAS; Sigma Xi. *Res:* Comparative immunology, immunogenetics, immunochemistry and biochemical genetics of fishes and other animals as applied to discrimination of natural populations. *Mailing Add:* 142 Bog Hill Rd West Gardiner ME 04345

RIDGWAY, HELEN JANE, BIOCHEMISTRY. *Current Pos:* Chemist, 60-68, res investr biochem, 68-86, CHAIR, CHEM DEPT, WADLEY INSTS MOLECULAR MED, 86- *Personal Data:* b Ft Worth, Tex, Aug 10, 37. *Educ:* NTex State Col, BA, 59; Baylor Univ, MS, 63, PhD(chem), 68. *Concurrent Pos:* Mem coun thrombosis, Am Heart Asn. *Mem:* Am Chem Soc; fel Int Soc Hemat; Am Heart Asn. *Res:* Biochemistry of blood coagulation; leukemia and cancer chemotherapy; platelet function. *Mailing Add:* 9675 Arkansas St Beaumont TX 77707

RIDGWAY, JAMES STRATMAN, POLYMER CHEMISTRY, SYNTHETIC FIBERS. *Current Pos:* CHEM CONSULT, 93- *Personal Data:* b Paintsville, Ky, July 27, 36; m 59, Bernice T Schmitt; c Keith S & Brian C. *Educ:* Univ Louisville, BS, 58, MS, 59, PhD(org chem), 61. *Prof Exp:* Technician, Girdler Co, 57; teaching asst gen chem & qual anal, Univ Louisville, 57-58, res asst org chem, 58-61; res chemist, Chemstrand Res Ctr, Inc, 61-66, sr res chemist, 66-67; sr res chemist, Monsanto Co, 68-69, res specialist, 69-76, sr res specialist, 76-93. *Mem:* Am Chem Soc; fel Am Inst Chemists. *Res:* Polymer structure-property relationships; synthesis of polyamides and copolyamides; synthetic fiber applications for textile and tire cords; melt and solution polycondensation reactions; high modulus organic fibers; fiber flammability, textile colorfastness; anti-soil and stain resistant fibers; carpet fiber properties. *Mailing Add:* 1314 Hound Chase Circle Pensacola FL 32514

RIDGWAY, RICHARD L, ENTOMOLOGY. *Current Pos:* MEM FAC, ENTOM DEPT, TEX A&M UNIV, 80-, USDA, BELTSVILLE, MD, 75- *Personal Data:* b Brownfield, Tex, Nov 9, 35; m 57; c 2. *Educ:* Tex Tech Col, BS, 57; Cornell Univ, MS, 59, PhD(entom), 60. *Honors & Awards:* Geigy Recognition Award, Entom Soc Am, 72. *Prof Exp:* Exten entomologist, Tex A&M Univ, 60-63, res entomologist, Entom Res Div, 63-70, entomologist-in-charge, Cotton Inst, 70-72, entomologist, Univ, 71-72, mem grad fac, 65-75, res leader, 72-75; staff scientist cotton & tobacco insects, Agr Res Serv, USDA, Washington, DC, 75-80. *Mem:* AAAS; Entom Soc Am; Int Orgn Biol Control. *Res:* Methods of application of systematic insecticides; behavior of insecticides in plants and soil; selective insecticides; biological control of insect pests. *Mailing Add:* 2229 Countryside Dr Silver Spring MD 20905

RIDGWAY, ROBERT WORRELL, ORGANIC CHEMISTRY. *Current Pos:* MGR OFF COOP EDUC, AM CHEM SOC, 80- *Personal Data:* b Hampton, Va, July 14, 39; m 60; c 1. *Educ:* Drexel Univ, BS, 66; Univ NH, PhD(org chem), 70. *Prof Exp:* NSF fel & res assoc, Princeton Univ, 69-70; asst prof chem, J C Smith Univ, 70-72; asst prof chem, Rollins Col, 72-75, assoc prof, 75-80. *Mem:* Am Chem Soc; Royal Soc Chem; Sigma Xi. *Res:* Organometallic stereochemistry, especially asymmetric reductions and biologically important systems; synthetic organic chemistry. *Mailing Add:* 909 Laurel St Pocomoke City MD 21702

RIDGWAY, SAM H, ENVIRONMENTAL PHYSIOLOGY. *Current Pos:* SR SCIENTIST, NAVAL OCEAN SYSTS CTR, 80- *Personal Data:* b San Antonio, Tex, June 26, 36; m 64, Jeanette Fuller. *Educ:* Tex A&M Univ, BS, 58, DVM, 60; Cambridge Univ, PhD(neurobiol), 73. *Honors & Awards:* Gilbert Curl Sci Award, Naval Undersea Ctr, 73. *Prof Exp:* Res vet, US Naval Missile Ctr, 62-63, Univ Southern Calif, 63-65 & Univ Calif, Santa Barbara, 65-66; res vet, 66-72, head, Biomed Div, Naval Undersea Ctr, 72-80. *Concurrent Pos:* USN res sponsor, 62- & Univ Calif, Santa Barbara & Inst Environ Stress, 65-; sr res fel, Cambridge Univ, 70-72; sci adv, Marine Mammal Comn, 75-77, chmn, 77-78; coun mem, Inst Lab Animal Resources, Nat Acad Sci-Nat Res Coun, 75-78, mem, Comt Low Frequency Sound & Marine Mammal Hearing; mem res comt, San Diego Zoo, 73-89. *Mem:* NY Acad Sci; AAAS; Am Vet Med Asn; Sigma Xi; Explorers Club; Acoust Soc Am; Int Asn Aquatic Animal Med. *Res:* Marine mammal physiology; dolphin neurobiology; aquatic animal medicine; bioacoustics. *Mailing Add:* NCCOSC/N Rad 49620 Beluga Rd San Diego CA 92152-6266. *Fax:* 619-553-1346; *E-Mail:* ridgway@nosc.mil

RIDGWAY, STUART L, ENERGY CONVERSION. *Current Pos:* CONSULT, 90- *Personal Data:* b Freeport, Ill, July 27, 22; m 63, Frances Himckley; c Paul, John, Alexander, Susan, Ellen & Douglas. *Educ:* Haverford Col, BS, 43; Princeton Univ, PhD(physics), 52. *Prof Exp:* Group leader fire control res, US Naval Res Lab, 43-46; instr physics, Princeton Univ, 50-52, res assoc, 52-53; res assoc, Brookhaven Nat Lab, 53-56; mem sr staff, TRW Inc, 56-62; mem sr tech staff, Gen Tech Corp, 62-66; sr physicist, Princeton Appl Res Corp, 66-73; sr res scientist, R & D Assocs, 73-89; sr mech engr, Pac Int Ctr for High Technol Res, 89-90. *Mem:* Am Phys Soc; Combustion Inst; NY Acad Sci; AAAS. *Res:* Beta decay; high energy physics; heat transfer; combustion dynamics; motor vehicle exhaust control; ocean thermal energy conversion. *Mailing Add:* 537 Ninth St Santa Monica CA 90402. *E-Mail:* 76407.2227@compuserve.com

RIDGWAY, WILLIAM C(OMBS), III, COMPUTING, FUND RAISING SOFTWARE. *Current Pos:* INDEPENDENT CONSULT, 90- *Personal Data:* b Orange, NJ, Apr 28, 36; m, Carol Oko; c 6. *Educ:* Princeton Univ, BSE, 57; NY Univ, BEE, 59; Stanford Univ, PhD(elec eng), 62. *Prof Exp:* Mem tech staff, 57-68, head mil data systs eng dept, 68-70, head ocean data systs dept, 70-72, dir, Par Software & Data Processing Ctr, 72-73, dir, Comput Technol & Prog Develop Ctr, Bell Tel Labs, 73-82; dir, Comput Telecommunications & Eng Info Ctr, 82-85; adminr, Telecommun & Info Systs, Dept Treas, NJ, 85-90; pres, R3 Info Syst, 90- *Concurrent Pos:* Mem resource & technol panel, Comput Sci & Eng Bd, Nat Acad Sci; mem tech staff, AT&T Info Systs, 82-85. *Mem:* Asn Comput Mach; Inst Elec & Electronics Engrs; Sigma Xi. *Res:* Development of advanced computing services; specializing in consulting with charitable organizations on using information management for fund raising. *Mailing Add:* 68 Neck Rd Old Lyme CT 06371

RIDHA, R(AOUF) A, ENGINEERING MECHANICS, STRUCTURAL ENGINEERING. *Current Pos:* mgr tire physics & math, Akron, Ohio, 83-86, mgr tire-vehicle eng technol, Goodyear Tech Ctr, Luxembourg Goodyear Tire & Rubber Co, 86-92, mgr predictive testing dept, 92-95, SR RES & DEVELOP ASSOC, GOODYEAR TECH CTR, AKRON, OHIO, 95- *Personal Data:* b Karbala, Iraq, Aug 10, 39; US citizen; m 73, Dalal Al-Shaiban; c Susan, Jennifer & Jeffrey. *Educ:* Univ Baghdad, BS, 59; Univ Ill, Urbana, MS, 63, PhD(struct), 66; Kent State Univ, MBA, 78. *Prof Exp:* Supv engr struct, Govt Iraq, 59-62; anal specialist, Energy Controls Div, Bendix Corp, 66-73; res assoc, Cent Res Labs, Firestone Tire & Rubber Co, 73-78; head, Eng Mech Sect, Gen Tire & Rubber Co, 78-80, sect head, Physics & Eng Mech Sect, Res Div, 80-83. *Concurrent Pos:* Lectr, Ind Univ, South Bend, 69-73 & Mich State Univ, 70-71; lectr IV, Univ Akron, 77-78; ed, Tire Sci & Technol, 83-94; pres, Tire Soc, 94-96. *Mem:* Soc Eng Sci; assoc fel Am Inst Aeronaut & Astronaut; Tire Soc. *Res:* Engineering mechanics; structural optimization; stability; nonlinear analysis; finite element methods; composite materials; aerospace structures; numerical methods; tire mechanics; tire stresses and deformation; analysis and design of composite structures. *Mailing Add:* Goodyear Tech Ctr PO Box 3531 Akron OH 44309-3531. *Fax:* 330-796-8752; *E-Mail:* usgtrdcb@ibmmail.com

RIDINGS, GUS RAY, RADIOLOGY. *Current Pos:* MEM STAFF, RIDGE RADIOL ONCOL ASN. *Personal Data:* b Arbyrd, Mo, Nov 22, 18; m 41; c 2. *Educ:* Ark State Col, AB, 39; Vanderbilt Univ, MD, 50. *Prof Exp:* Instr radiol, Col Med, Vanderbilt Univ, 55-56; assoc prof, Sch Med, Univ Miss, 56-57; prof, Sch Med, Univ Okla, 57-62; prof, Sch Med, Univ Mo, Columbia, 63-67; clin prof radiother, Univ Tex Southwestern Med Sch Dallas & radiotherapist, St Paul Hosp, 67-71; dir, C J Williams Cancer Treat Ctr, Baptist Mem Hosp, 71-75; dir, Southeast Hosp Radiation Oncol Ctr, 75- *Concurrent Pos:* Consult, Vet Admin Hosp. *Mem:* Soc Nuclear Med; Radiol Soc NAm; Am Asn Cancer Educ; Am Soc Therapeut Radiologists; Sigma Xi. *Res:* Radiation therapy. *Mailing Add:* 18 E Lake Dr Cape Girardeau MO 63701

RIDLEN, SAMUEL FRANKLIN, POULTRY SCIENCE. *Current Pos:* from assoc prof to prof, 58-86, asst head dept animal sci, 78-86, EMER PROF POULTRY, COOP EXTEN SERV, UNIV ILL, URBANA, 86- *Personal Data:* b Marion, Ill, Apr 24, 16; m 46, Helen L Camp; c Judith E, Barbara J & Mark E. *Educ:* Univ Ill, BS, 40; Mich State Univ, MS, 57. *Honors & Awards:* Poultry Sci Asn Exten Award, 65; Super Serv Award, USDA, 82. *Prof Exp:* Instr high sch, Ill, 40-43; asst prof poultry, Exten Div, Univ Ill, 46-53; gen mgr, Honegger Breeder Hatchery, Ill, 53-56; assoc prof poultry, Univ Conn, 57-58. *Mem:* Fel Poultry Sci Asn; World Poultry Sci Asn. *Res:* Poultry management and production economics; effect of different cage densities and protein levels on the performance of laying hens. *Mailing Add:* 1901 Lakeside Dr Urbana IL 61821

RIDLEY, ESTHER JOANNE, plant physiology; deceased, see previous edition for last biography

RIDLEY, PETER TONE, PHYSIOLOGY, PHARMACOLOGY. *Current Pos:* asst dir pharmacol, Allergan Pharmaceut, 67-71, dir pharmacol, 71-75, dep dir res, 75-81, VPRES RES & DEVELOP, ALLERGAN PHARMACEUT, DIV SMITH KLINE & FR LABS, 81- *Personal Data:* b Meriden, Conn, Nov 11, 36; m 59; c 3. *Educ:* Rutgers Univ, BA, 59; Univ Pa, PhD(physiol), 64. *Prof Exp:* Jr pharmacologist, Smith Kline & Fr Labs, 59-60; USPHS fel, Karolinska Inst, Sweden, 64-65; asst prof physiol, George Washington Univ, 65-67. *Mem:* Am Physiol Soc; Am Gastroenterol Asn. *Res:* Physiology and pharmacology of the gastrointestinal tract; central neural control of gastrointestinal function. *Mailing Add:* 865 Sandcastle Corona Del Mar CA 92625

RIDOLFO, ANTHONY SYLVESTER, RHEUMATOLOGY, CLINICAL PHARMACOLOGY. *Current Pos:* RETIRED. *Personal Data:* b Montclair, NJ, Oct 27, 18; m 42; c 2. *Educ:* Rutgers Univ, BS, 40; Ohio State Univ, MS, 42, PhD, 47, MD, 54; Am Bd Internal Med, dipl, 64. *Prof Exp:* Assoc prof pharm, Univ Toledo, 42-44; assoc prof, Ohio State Univ, 47-50; fel cardiol, Marion County Gen Hosp, Indianapolis, Ind, 57-58; from physician to sr physician, Eli Lilly & Co, 58-73, sr clin pharmacologist, 73-86. *Concurrent Pos:* Instr, Sch Med, Ind Univ, Indianapolis, 57-60, from asst to assoc, 60-65, from asst prof to assoc prof, 65-75, clin prof med, 75-79, prof med, 79-; mem bd dirs, Ind Arthritis Found, 61-, pres, 71-72; chmn sect rheumatic dis & anti-inflammatory agent, Am Soc Clin Pharmacol & Therapeut, 74-77; mem, US Pharmacopeia Panel on Analgesics, Sedatives & Anti-Inflammatory Agents; mem, Comt Relationships Pharmaceut Houses, Nat Arthritis Found, 81- *Mem:* Fel Am Col Physicians; Am Fedn Clin Res; Am Rheumatism Asn; AMA; Am Soc Clin Pharmacol & Therapeut. *Mailing Add:* 5207 S State Rd No 421 Zionsville IN 46077

RIE, JOHN E, BIOREMEDIATION, SITE REMEDIATION. *Current Pos:* VPRES TECHNOL, CBRS INC, 95- *Personal Data:* b New York, NY, Aug 26, 44; m 91, Deborah Luby. *Educ:* Univ Vt, BA, 66; Wayne State Univ, PhD(chem), 72. *Prof Exp:* Res chemist photopolymers, Kalle Aktiengesellschaft Div, Hoechst AG, 71-72, prod mgr photoresist, 72-74; sr res chemist photopolymers, Photopolymer Systs, W R Grace & Co, 74-78; group leader, Dynacure Printed Circuit Prod, Thiokol/Dynachem Corp, 78-80; mgr mat sci, PCK Technol Div, Kollmorgen Corp, 80-87. *Concurrent Pos:* Consult & adj lect, Univ New Haven, 96- *Mem:* Am Chem Soc; Sigma Xi. *Mailing Add:* 38 Tunxis Circle Meriden CT 06450-7401

RIEBESELL, JOHN F, PLANT ECOLOGY, POPULATION ECOLOGY. *Current Pos:* asst prof, 77-83, ASSOC PROF BIOL, UNIV MICH, DEARBORN, 83- *Personal Data:* b Oneida, NY, March 18, 48. *Educ:* State Univ NY, Albany, BS, 70, MS, 71; Univ Chicago, PhD(biol), 75. *Prof Exp:* Vis asst prof biol, Col Wooster, 76-77. *Concurrent Pos:* Dir, Adirondack Lab, 76-79 & 90-92. *Mem:* Ecol Soc Am; Sigma Xi; AAAS; Asn Am Geographers. *Res:* Population biology and physiological ecology; photosynthetic adaptations in plants; effects of environmental modification on population densities and community stability; land use planning; biogeography. *Mailing Add:* Dept Natural Sci Univ Mich Dearborn MI 48128. *E-Mail:* jriebese@sb_fl.umd.umich.edu

RIEBMAN, LEON, ELECTRONICS ENGINEERING. *Current Pos:* pres, Am Electronic Labs, Inc, 51-87, CHMN BD & CHIEF EXEC OFFICER, AEL INDUSTS INC, 87- *Personal Data:* b Coatesville, Pa, Apr 22, 20; m 42; c 2. *Educ:* Univ Pa, BSEE, 43, MSEE, 47, PhD(elec eng), 51. *Prof Exp:* Sr engr, Philco Corp, 45-46; res assoc & part-time instr, Univ Pa, 48-51. *Concurrent Pos:* Mem bd eng educ, Univ Pa, 68; dir, Ampal, 70- *Mem:* Fel Inst Elec & Electronics Engrs. *Res:* Electronics, particularly antenna and microwaves; computers. *Mailing Add:* AEL Industs Inc Richardson Rd Box 552 Lansdale PA 19446

RIECHEL, THOMAS LESLIE, ANALYTICAL CHEMISTRY, ELECTROCHEMISTRY. *Current Pos:* asst prof, 78-83, ASSOC PROF CHEM, MIAMI UNIV, 83- *Personal Data:* b Bakersfield, Calif, July 9, 50. *Educ:* Univ Calif, Davis, BS, 72, Riverside, PhD(chem), 76. *Prof Exp:* Res assoc chem, State Univ NY Buffalo, 76-77 & Univ Del, 78. *Mem:* Am Chem Soc; Sigma Xi; Soc Electroanalytical Chem. *Res:* Electrochemical and spectroscopic studies of models for metalloenzymes; ion selective electrodes; chemically modified electrodes; room temperatures molten salt electrolytes. *Mailing Add:* Dept Chem Miami Univ Oxford OH 45056

RIECHERT, SUSAN ELISE, ZOOLOGY. *Current Pos:* From asst prof to assoc prof, 73-82, PROF ZOOL, UNIV TENN, 82- *Personal Data:* b Milwaukee, Wis, Oct 20, 45. *Educ:* Univ Wis-Madison, BA, 67, MS, 70, PhD(zool), 73. *Concurrent Pos:* Assoc cur invert, Univ Wis Zool Mus, 71-77; asst ed, J Arachnology; pres, Am Arachnologist, 84-85; Fogarty Found Fel. *Mem:* Ecol Soc Am; Animal Behav Soc; Sigma Xi; Am Arachnological Asn; Entom Soc Am; AAAS. *Res:* Food-based spacing in spiders; underlying factors responsible for observed patterns of local animal distribution; game playing and interaction strategies in spiders; evolution of social behavior; generalist predator control of pests in agroecosystems. *Mailing Add:* Dept Ecol/Evolutionary Biol Univ Tenn Knoxville TN 37996-1610

RIECK, H(ENRY) G(EORGE), CHEMICAL ENGINEERING. *Current Pos:* SR RES SCIENTIST, PAC NORTHWEST LABS, BATTELLE MEM INST, 65- *Personal Data:* b Eugene, Ore, Aug 30, 22; m 53; c 3. *Educ:* Ore State Col, BS, 43, MS, 44. *Prof Exp:* Engr, Gen Elec Co, 47-65. *Res:* Development and design of equipment used in air sampling (land, marine and aircraft based systems); water sampling (rivers, lakes and ocean based systems); collection and measurement of radionuclides in various sampling regimes; nuclear counting equipment and techniques in nondestructive assay of low level nuclear wastes for transuranic radionuclide content; remote handling equipment and techniques for manipulation of high level radionuclide sources. *Mailing Add:* 1101 Winslow Ave Richland WA 99352

RIECK, JAMES NELSON, POLYMER CHEMISTRY. *Current Pos:* Res chemist, 60-73, group leader polymer chem, 73-81, SECT MGR POLYURETHANE RES, MOBAY CHEM CORP, 81- *Personal Data:* b Wheeling, WVa, Aug 7, 39; c 2. *Educ:* West Liberty State Col, BS, 61; WVa Univ, PhD(org chem), 73. *Mem:* Am Chem Soc. *Res:* Polyurethane textile coatings; polyurethane adhesives; prepolymers; modified isocyanates; bonding agents; rubber adhesive agents. *Mailing Add:* Bayer Corp St Rte 2 New Martinsville WV 26155

RIECK, NORMAN WILBUR, ANATOMY. *Current Pos:* RETIRED. *Personal Data:* b Union City, NJ, Feb 16, 23; m 53; c 1. *Educ:* Hope Col, AB, 53; Univ Mich, MS, 56, PhD(anat), 57. *Prof Exp:* Instr anat, Sch Med, Temple Univ, 57-59 & Sch Med, Univ Mich, 59-62; from assoc prof to prof, Hope Col, 62-86. *Mem:* Am Am Anat; Am Mus Natural Hist; Am Inst Biol Sci. *Res:* Neuroanatomy; stimulation of occipital lobe of monkey. *Mailing Add:* 986 Laketown Dr Holland MI 49423

RIECKE, EDGAR ERIC K, ORGANIC POLYMER CHEMISTRY. *Current Pos:* RES CHEMIST, EASTMAN KODAK CO, 72- *Personal Data:* b Spencer, Iowa, Dec 29, 44; m 66; c 1. *Educ:* Univ SDak, BA, 67; Univ Mo, Kansas City, PhD(chem), 71. *Prof Exp:* Fel chem, Univ Rochester, 72. *Mem:* Am Chem Soc. *Mailing Add:* Eastman Kodak Co 1700 Dewey Ave Rochester NY 14650-1724

RIECKHOFF, KLAUS E, CHEMICAL PHYSICS, SOLID STATE PHYSICS. *Current Pos:* assoc prof, Simon Fraser Univ, 65-66, actg dean sci, 66-67, prof, 66-93, assoc dean grad studies, 73-76, EMER PROF PHYSICS, SIMON FRASER UNIV, 93- *Personal Data:* b Weimar, Ger, Feb 8, 28; Can citizen; m 49, Marianne Neder; c Bernhard A, Claudia A & Cornelia A. *Educ:* Univ BC, BSc, 58, MSc, 59, PhD(physics), 62. *Prof Exp:* Mem res staff physics, Res Lab, IBM Corp, Calif, 62-65. *Concurrent Pos:* Vis scientist, Res Lab, IBM Corp, 67-68 & 76-77; vis prof, Inst Appl Physics, Univ Karlsrhe, 69-70; mem bd govs, Simon Fraser Univ, 78-84, 87-93; vis prof, Univ PR, Mayaguez, 87 & 89, Univ Queensland, Brisbane, Queensland, Australia, 87, Univ Bayreuth, Bayreuth, Ger, 87 & 90. *Mem:* Am Phys Soc; Can Asn Physicists. *Res:* Low temperature solid state; magneto-optics; spin-lattice relaxation; nonlinear optics; multiphoton processes in organic molecules; intermolecular and intramolecular energy transfer; spontaneous and stimulated Brillouin and Raman scattering; molecular luminescence; electrohydrodynamics. *Mailing Add:* Dept Physics Simon Fraser Univ Burnaby BC V5A 1S6 Can. *Fax:* 604-291-3592; *E-Mail:* k_rieckhoff@sfu.ca

RIEDEL, BERNARD EDWARD, PHARMACY. *Current Pos:* RETIRED. *Personal Data:* b Provost, Alta, Sept 25, 19; wid; c Gail L, Dwain E & Barry R. *Educ:* Univ Alta, BSc, 43, MSc, 49; Univ Western Ont, PhD(biochem), 53. *Hon Degrees:* DSc, Univ Alta, 90. *Prof Exp:* Assoc prof pharm, Univ Alta, 46-50, 52-58, prof, 58-62, exec asst to vpres, 62-67; prof pharmaceut sci & dean fac, Univ BC, 67-84, coordr health sci, 77-84. *Concurrent Pos:* Pres bd trustees, BC Cancer Control Agency, 84-85; chmn bd trustees, BC Organ Transplant Soc, 86-89; pres bd dir, BC Lung Asn, 90-92. *Mem:* AAAS; Am Chem Soc; Can Biochem Soc; Pharmacol Soc Can; hon mem Can Pharmaceut Asn. *Res:* Biochemistry; radioisotope technology. *Mailing Add:* 8394 Angus Dr Vancouver BC V6P 5L2 Can

RIEDEL, EBERHARD KARL, STATISTICAL MECHANICS, THEORETICAL SOLID STATE PHYSICS. *Current Pos:* assoc prof, 75-78, PROF PHYSICS, UNIV WASH, 78- *Personal Data:* b Dresden, Ger, Dec 25, 39. *Educ:* Univ Koln, Cologne, Ger, Physics Dipl, 64; Tech Univ Munchen, Munich, Ger, Dr rer nat, 66. *Prof Exp:* Res physicist, Max-Planck Inst Physics, Munich, Ger, 65-68 & Inst V Laue-Langevin, Munich, Ger & Grenoble, France, 69; res assoc physics, Cornell Univ, Ithaca, NY, 69-71; from asst prof to assoc prof physics, Duke Univ, Durham, NC, 71-75. *Concurrent Pos:* Nordita prof, Niels Bohr Inst, Copenhagen, Denmark, 78; vis scientist, Ctr Nuclear Studies, Grenoble, France, 83. *Mem:* Fel Am Phys Soc; Europ Physics Soc. *Res:* Theories of condensed matter, especially phase transitions and critical phenomena. *Mailing Add:* 6828 17th Ave NE Seattle WA 98115

RIEDEL, GERHARDT FREDERICK, PHYTOPLANKTON PHYSIOLOGICAL ECOLOGY, TRACE ELEMENT GEOCHEMISTRY. *Current Pos:* investr, 85-87, SR SCIENTIST, ACAD NATURAL SCI, BENEDICT ESTUARINE RES LAB, 87- *Personal Data:* b Santa Monica, Calif, July 8, 51; m 73; c 2. *Educ:* Humboldt State Univ, BA & BS, 74; Ore State Univ, MS, 78, PhD(oceanog), 83. *Prof Exp:* Fel, Harbor Br Found, 83-85. *Mem:* AAAS; Am Geophys Unions; Am Soc Limnol Oceanog; Phycol Soc Am; Oceanog Soc. *Res:* Trace element and nutrient uptake by marine and estuarine organisms, particularly the effect of chemical forms on uptake; loss and regeneration of trace elements and nutrients involving chemical transformations. *Mailing Add:* Acad Nat Sci Estuarine Res Ctr 10545 Mackall Rd St Leonard MD 20685

RIEDEL, HERBERT HEINZ JOACHIM, UNIVERSAL ALGEBRA. *Current Pos:* INSTR MATH, TRIDENT TECH COL, 92- *Personal Data:* b Galt, Ont, Nov 26, 58; US citizen; m 94, Lisa M; c Frederick W. *Educ:* Univ Pretoria, BSc, 79; Univ Waterloo, MMath, 80, PhD(pure math), 84. *Prof Exp:* Lectr, Bowling Green State Univ, 84-85; asst prof, The Citadel, 85-90. *Mem:* Math Asn Am. *Res:* Undergraduate mathematics education; algebra, calculus, statistics and use of technology. *Mailing Add:* PO Box 21448 Charleston SC 29413. *E-Mail:* zpriedel@trident.jec.sc.us

RIEDEL, RICHARD ANTHONY, dentistry; deceased, see previous edition for last biography

RIEDEL, WILLIAM REX, MICROPALEONTOLOGY. *Current Pos:* RETIRED. *Personal Data:* b South Australia, Sept 5, 27; m 52, 63; c 3. *Educ:* Univ Adelaide, MSc, 52, DSc, 76. *Prof Exp:* Paleontologist, SAustralian Mus, 48-50; res fel, Oceanog Inst, Sweden, 50-51; paleontologist, SAustralian Mus, 54-55; asst res geologist, Scripps Inst Oceanog, Univ Calif, San Diego, 56-62, assoc res geologist, 62-68, res geologist, 68-91. *Concurrent Pos:* With US Geol Surv, 59; chmn, Geol Res Div, Scripps Inst Oceanog, 78-83. *Mem:* Paleont Soc. *Res:* Systematic and stratigraphic investigations of Mesozoic to Quaternary Radiolaria; deep sea sediments; stratigraphy of microscopic fish skeletal debris; information-handling for stratigraphic and paleoenvironmental interpretations. *Mailing Add:* 553 Gravilla Pl La Jolla CA 92037

RIEDER, CONLY LEROY, CELL BIOLOGY, HIGH VOLTAGE ELECTRON MICROSCOPY. *Current Pos:* SR RES SCIENTIST, WADSWORTH CTR, 80-, CHIEF, LAB CELL REGULATION, 94-; PROF, DEPT BIOMED SCI, STATE UNIV NY, ALBANY, 85- *Personal Data:* b Orange, Calif, Nov 2, 50; m 79, Susan Mowogrodzki; c Leila & Rachel. *Educ:* Univ Calif, Irvine, BS, 72; Univ Ore, Eugene, MS, 75, PhD(cell biol), 77. *Prof Exp:* Res fel cell biol, Univ Ore, Eugene, 75-77; res asst zool, Univ Wis-Madison, 77-79, NIH fel pathobiol, 79-80. *Concurrent Pos:* Res scientist VI, Wadsworth Ctr Labs & Res, NY State Dept Health, Albany, 80-; prof biol, State Univ NY, Albany, 80-; adj prof physiol, Albany Med Col, 84- *Mem:* Am Soc Cell Biol; Micros Soc Am. *Res:* Develop and apply video light microscopic, high voltage electron microscopic and immunologic methods to study the mechanisms involved in the movement of cell organelles, especially chromosomes. *Mailing Add:* Wadsworth Ctr Div Molecular Med Albany NY 12201. *Fax:* 518-486-4901; *E-Mail:* rieder@wadsworth.org

RIEDER, RONALD FREDERIC, MEDICINE, HEMATOLOGY. *Current Pos:* from asst prof to assoc prof, 67-76, dir hemat, 76-89, PROF MED, STATE UNIV NY DOWNSTATE MED CTR, 76- *Personal Data:* b New York, NY, July 13, 33; m 64, Daniele Diette; c David & Isabelle. *Educ:* Swarthmore Col, BA, 54; NY Univ, MD, 58; Am Bd Internal Med, dipl & cert med & hemat. *Prof Exp:* Intern, III, NY Univ Med Div, Bellevue Hosp, 58-59, asst resident, 59-60, fel microbiol, NY Univ, 60-61; fel immunol, Pasteur Inst, Paris, 61-62; fel hemat, Sch Med, Johns Hopkins Univ, 62-64; asst resident, III & IV, NY Univ Med Div, 64-65; res assoc, Montefiore Hosp, 65-67. *Concurrent Pos:* Assoc med, Albert Einstein Col Med, 65-67; vis prof lectr, Nuffield Unit Med Genetics, Univ Liverpool, 68; WHO traveling fel, 68; Macy Found fac scholar, 75-76; vis fel, Wolfson Col, Oxford Univ, 75-76. *Mem:* Am Soc Clin Invest; Asn Am Physicians; Am Soc Hemat; fel Am Col Physicians; Am Physiol Soc. *Res:* Abnormal hemoglobins; hemoglobin synthesis; thalassemia. *Mailing Add:* Dept Med State Univ NY Health Sci Ctr Brooklyn NY 11203

RIEDER, RONALD OLRICH, PSYCHIATRIC RESEARCH, PSYCHIATRIC EDUCATION. *Current Pos:* DIR RESIDENCY TRAINING, DEPT PSYCHIAT, COLUMBIA UNIV, 79-, PROF, CLIN PSYCHIAT, 89-, ASSOC CHAIR EDUC, 94- *Personal Data:* b Wyandotte, Mich, Feb 20, 42; m 66, Corinne Holman; c Alyssa & Melanie. *Educ:* Harvard Univ, BA, 64, MD(med), 84. *Prof Exp:* Intern pediat, Johns Hopkins Hosp, 68-69; resident psychiat, Albert Einstein Col Med, 69-71; res assoc psychiat, 71-73, res psychiatrist, Intramural Res, NIMH, 73-79. *Mem:* Am Psychopath Asn; Am Psychiat Asn; Am Asn Psychiat Residency Training; AAAS. *Res:* Genetics and neuroanatomical aspects of schizophrenia. *Mailing Add:* NY State Psychiat Inst 722 W 168th St New York NY 10032-2603. *Fax:* 212-960-2356

RIEDER, SIDNEY VICTOR, BIOCHEMISTRY. *Current Pos:* RETIRED. *Personal Data:* b Philadelphia, Pa, Oct 22, 21; m 49; c 2. *Educ:* Philadelphia Col Pharm, BS, 43; Univ Pa, MS, 48, PhD(biochem), 53. *Prof Exp:* Instr biochem, Univ Pa, 52-53; from inst to asst prof, Sch Med, Yale Univ, 53-61. *Mem:* AAAS. *Res:* Intermediary metabolism of amino sugars; carbohydrates. *Mailing Add:* 118 Rockaway Ave Marblehead MA 01945-2742

RIEDER, WILLIAM G(ARY), MECHANICAL ENGINEERING. *Current Pos:* from asst prof to assoc prof, 70-81, PROF MECH ENG, NDAK STATE UNIV, 81- *Personal Data:* b Williston, NDak, Oct 28, 34; m 62; c 2. *Educ:* NDak State Univ, BSME, 56; Ohio State Univ, MSc, 62; Univ Nebr, Lincoln, PhD(mech eng), 71. *Prof Exp:* Design engr, Atomic Energy Div, Phillips Petrol Co, 56-59; prin mech engr, Battelle Mem Inst, Ohio, 59-65; asst prof mech eng, NDak State Univ, 65-68; consult, Dept Econ Develop, State of Nebr, 68-69. *Mem:* AAAS; Am Soc Mech Engrs; Am Soc Eng Educ. *Res:* Energy conversion; thermal sciences; fluid mechanics; nuclear experiments; vacuum and processing phenomena; writing engineering modeling. *Mailing Add:* 1905 18th St Fargo ND 58103

RIEDERER-HENDERSON, MARY ANN, CELL BIOLOGY. *Current Pos:* CONSULT, 87- *Personal Data:* b Buffalo, NY, July 21, 43; m 67. *Educ:* Daemon Col, BS, 64; Univ Wis-Madison, MS, 66; Univ Ga, PhD(biochem), 71. *Prof Exp:* Instr microbiol, Univ Fla, 71-72; asst prof biol, Rollins Col, Winter Park, Fla, 72-76, assoc prof, 76-77; res asst prof, Sch Med, Univ Wash, 77-87. *Mem:* AAAS; Am Soc Cell Biol. *Res:* Growth factors; collagen biosynthesis; ultrasound and tissues. *Mailing Add:* 1057 Summit Ave E Seattle WA 98102-4432

RIEDERS, FREDRIC, TOXICOLOGY, PHARMACOLOGY. *Current Pos:* PRES, TOXICON ASSOC, LTD, 76- *Personal Data:* b Vienna, Austria, July 9, 22; US citizen. *Educ:* NY Univ, AB, 48, MS, 49; Jefferson Med Col, PhD(pharmacol & toxicol), 51. *Prof Exp:* Prod chemist, Myer's 1890 Soda, Inc, New York, 40-42; qual control chemist, Penetone Corp, NJ, 42-43; jr toxicologist forensic toxicol, Lab Chief Med Examr New York, 46-49; from instr to assoc prof, 51-56, prof pharmacol, Jefferson Med Col, 56-; pres & lab dir, Nat Med Serv, Inc, 70- *Concurrent Pos:* Chief toxicologist forensic toxicol, Off Med Examr, Philadelphia, 56-70; ed bull, Int Asn Forensic Toxicol, 60-63; NIH fel, Jefferson Med Col, 63-68; NIH & Pa Health Dept fels, Off Med Examr, Philadelphia, 67-69; adj prof toxicol, Drexel Univ, 67-69; mem toxicol study sect, NIH, 69-70. *Mem:* Am Acad Forensic Sci; Am Bd Clin Chem; Am Soc Pharmacol & Exp Therapeut; Am Chem Soc; Int Asn Forensic Toxicol. *Res:* Bioanalytical and forensic toxicology; heavy metals; cyanogenetic and interactive mechanisms of toxic actions. *Mailing Add:* Nat Med Serv PO Box 433 Willow Grove PA 19090-0433

RIEDESEL, CARL CLEMENT, pharmacology; deceased, see previous edition for last biography

RIEDESEL, MARVIN LEROY, PHYSIOLOGY. *Current Pos:* from asst prof to assoc prof, 59-71, PROF BIOL, UNIV NMEX, 71- *Personal Data:* b Iowa City, Iowa, Nov 8, 25; m 49; c 1. *Educ:* Cornell Col, BA, 49; Univ Iowa, MS, 53, PhD, 55. *Prof Exp:* Asst, Col Dent, 50-53, fel physiol, Univ Iowa, 53-55; res assoc occup health, Grad Sch Pub Health, Univ Pittsburgh, 55-59. *Mem:* AAAS; Am Physiol Soc; NY Acad Sci; Int Soc Biometeorol; Soc Cryobiol. *Res:* Environmental and comparative physiology; mammalian hibernation; electrolyte metabolism; water balance. *Mailing Add:* Dept Biol Univ NMex Albuquerque NM 87131-1091

RIEDHAMMER, THOMAS M, DRUG DELIVERY. *Current Pos:* PRES, WORLDWIDE PHARMACEUT, BAUSCH & LOMB, 94- *Personal Data:* b Buffalo, NY. *Educ:* State Univ NY, BA, 70, PhD(chem), 75. *Prof Exp:* Sr res chemist, Bausch & Lomb Inc, 75-77, dept mgr, 78-81, dir, 82-84; dir, Paco Res Corp, 84-85, vpres, 85-86, pres, 87-93. *Mem:* Parenteral Drug Asn; Asn Advan Med Inst; Am Chem Soc. *Res:* Products and treatments for disorders and diseases of the anterior segment of the eye; transdermal drug delivery systems; awarded 12 US patents. *Mailing Add:* 8500 Hidden River Pkwy Tampa FL 33637

RIEDINGER, LEO LOUIS, NUCLEAR PHYSICS. *Current Pos:* asst prof, 71-76, ASSOC PROF PHYSICS, UNIV TENN, KNOXVILLE, 71- *Personal Data:* b Brownwood, Tex, Nov 25, 44; m 66; c 1. *Educ:* Thomas More Col, AB, 64; Vanderbilt Univ, PhD(physics), 69. *Prof Exp:* NSF fel, Niels Bohr Inst, Copenhagen Univ, 68-69; res assoc nuclear physics, Univ Notre Dame, 69-71. *Concurrent Pos:* Consult, Oak Ridge Nat Lab, 72-73. *Mem:* Am Phys Soc. *Res:* Low energy nuclear structure; radioactive decay experiments; in-beam coulomb-excitation and heavy-ion reaction experiments. *Mailing Add:* Dept Physics & Astron Univ Tenn Knoxville TN 37996-1200

RIEDL, H RAYMOND, PHYSICS. *Current Pos:* RETIRED. *Personal Data:* b Colorado Springs, Colo, Aug 25, 35; m 59; c 7. *Educ:* Creighton Univ, BS, 57. *Prof Exp:* Physicist, Solid State Br, Naval Surface Warfare Ctr, 57-94, independent res dir, 94. *Mem:* Am Phys Soc. *Res:* Solid state physics; semiconductors; epitaxial films; amorphous films. *Mailing Add:* 10418 Knollwood Dr Hyattsville MD 20783

RIEDL, JOHN ORTH, MATHEMATICAL PEDAGOGY, USES OF COMPUTATION IN MATHEMATICS TEACHING. *Current Pos:* Asst prof, 65-70, from asst dean to assoc dean, 69-87, actg dean, 85-87, ASSOC PROF MATH, OHIO STATE UNIV, 70-, DEAN & DIR, MANSFIELD REGIONAL CAMPUS, 87- *Personal Data:* b Milwaukee, Wis, Dec 9, 37; m 61, Mary L Priestap; c John, Ann, James, Steven & Daniel. *Educ:* Marquette Univ, BS, 58; Univ Notre Dame, South Bend, MS, 60, PhD(math), 63. *Honors & Awards:* Grad Fel, NSF. *Concurrent Pos:* Chmn, comt minicourses, Math Asn Am, 80-87; coord dean, Regional Campuses, Ohio State Univ. *Mem:* Math Asn Am. *Res:* Functional analysis; locally convex topological vector spaces. *Mailing Add:* Ohio State Univ 1680 University Dr Mansfield OH 44906-1547

RIEFFEL, MARC A, OPERATOR ALGEBRAS, GROUP REPRESENTATIONS. *Current Pos:* Lectr, 63-64, from actg asst prof to asst prof, 64-68, assoc prof, 68-73, PROF MATH, UNIV CALIF, BERKELEY, 73- *Personal Data:* b New York, NY, Dec 22, 37; m 59; c 3. *Educ:* Harvard Univ, AB, 59; Columbia Univ, PhD(math), 63. *Mem:* Am Math Soc. *Res:* Functional analysis. *Mailing Add:* Univ Calif Berkeley CA 94720-3840

RIEGEL, GARLAND TAVNER, ENTOMOLOGY. *Current Pos:* from asst prof to prof, 48-78, head dept, 63-76, EMER PROF ZOOL, EASTERN ILL UNIV, 78- *Personal Data:* b Bowling Green, Mo, Aug 26, 14; m 41; c 4. *Educ:* Univ Ill, BS, 38, MS, 40, PhD(entom), 47. *Prof Exp:* Asst entom, Ill Natural Hist Surv, 37-42; fel, Grad Col, Univ Ill, 47-48. *Concurrent Pos:* Distinguished prof, Eastern Ill Univ, 78. *Mem:* AAAS; Entom Soc Am; Soc Syst Zool. *Res:* Classification of Braconidae, Alysiinae and Dacnusinae; insect ecology and morphology. *Mailing Add:* 1133 Fourth St Charleston IL 61920

RIEGEL, ILSE LEERS, CANCER RESEARCH. *Current Pos:* Fel, 52-54, managing ed, Cancer Res, 54-64, SR SCIENTIST, MCARDLE LAB CANCER RES, UNIV WIS-MADISON, 64- *Personal Data:* b Berlin, Germany, June 16, 16; m 40, Reinholdt; c Steven & Kate. *Educ:* Univ Wis, Madison, BA, 41, MA, 49, PhD(endocrinol), 52. *Mem:* Sigma Xi. *Mailing Add:* McArdle Lab Cancer Res Univ Wis Madison WI 53706

RIEGEL, KURT WETHERHOLD, RESEARCH ADMINISTRATION. *Current Pos:* RETIRED. *Personal Data:* b Lexington, Va, Feb 28, 39; m 74; c 3. *Educ:* Johns Hopkins Univ, AB, 61; Univ Md, PhD(astron), 66. *Prof Exp:* Res fel astron, Univ Md, 66; asst prof, Univ Calif, Los Angeles, 66-74; mgr, Energy Conserv Prog, Fed Energy Admin, Dept Energy, 74-75, chief technol & consumer prod energy conserv, 75-77, dir, Consumer Prod Div, 77-95; head, Nat Astron Ctrs, 82-95; dir, Environ Prog Safety & Health, USN, 89-95. *Concurrent Pos:* Consult, Aerospace Corp, 67-70; prof astron, Extens, Univ Calif, Los Angeles, 68-74; consult, Rand Corp, 73-74; vis fel, Univ Leiden, 72-73; dir environ eng & technol, Environ Protection Agency, 80-82. *Mem:* AAAS; Am Phys Soc; Am Astron Soc; Int Astron Union; Int Radio Sci Union. *Res:* Environmental pollution control technology; galactic radio astronomy; interstellar medium; energy technology. *Mailing Add:* Rte 1 Box 225A Glasgow VA 24555

RIEGER, ANNE LLOYD, ORGANIC CHEMISTRY. *Current Pos:* Res assoc chem, 62-68, res assoc biol & med sci, 68-70, 71-74, res assoc chem, 74-77, ASST PROF RES, BROWN UNIV, 77- *Personal Data:* b Philadelphia, Pa, Feb 6, 35; m 57, Philip H Rieger; c Christine. *Educ:* Reed Col, BA, 56; Stanford Univ, MS, 59; Columbia Univ, PhD, 62. *Mem:* Sigma Xi; Am Chem Soc. *Res:* Free radical chemistry and halogenating agents; synthesis of steroids; isolation and indentification of steroids from biological systems; electron transfer intermediates in photosynthetic systems; inorganic free radical reactions. *Mailing Add:* Dept Chem Brown Univ Box H Providence RI 02912

RIEGER, MARTIN MAX, COSMETIC CHEMISTRY. *Current Pos:* CONSULT, 86- *Personal Data:* b Braunschweig, Ger, Apr 12, 20; nat US; m 43; c 2. *Educ:* Univ Ill, BS, 41; Univ Minn, MS, 42; Univ Chicago, PhD(chem), 48. *Honors & Awards:* Cosmetic Indust Buyer & Suppliers Asn Award, 62; Medal Award, Soc Cosmetic Chemists, 74. *Prof Exp:* Chemist, Transparent Package Co, 42-44; instr, DePaul Univ, 47; res chemist, Lever Bros Co, 48-55; sr res assoc, Warner Lambert Co, 55-60, dir toiletries & cosmetics res, 60-71, assoc dir chem-proprietary res, 71-75, dir chem-biol res, 75-77, dir chem res, 77-82, sr res fel, Consumer Prod Div, 77-86, instr, Ctr Prof Advan, 86-95. *Concurrent Pos:* Ed, J Soc Cosmetic Chem, 62-67. *Mem:* Am Chem Soc; Soc Cosmetic Chem (pres, 72-73); Am Inst Chemists. *Res:* Cosmetics; proprietaries; aging; skin; hair; antacids; oral hygiene; cosmetic science with emphasis on safety and sterility; oxidative damage; free radicals. *Mailing Add:* 304 Mountain Way Morris Plains NJ 07950-1910. *E-Mail:* riegerplus@worldnet.att.net

RIEGER, PHILIP HENRI, PHYSICAL CHEMISTRY. *Current Pos:* from instr to assoc prof, 62-77, PROF CHEM, BROWN UNIV, 77- *Personal Data:* b Portland, Ore, June 24, 35; m 57, Anne B Lloyd; c Christine. *Educ:* Reed Col, BA, 56; Columbia Univ, PhD(chem), 62. *Prof Exp:* Instr chem, Columbia Univ, 61-62. *Concurrent Pos:* Vis prof, Univ Adelaide, SAustralia, 70-71, Univ Otago, Dunedin, NZ, 77-78 & Univ Bristol, UK, 91-92. *Mem:* Am Chem Soc; Royal Soc Chem. *Res:* Solution physical chemistry of transition metal coordination and organometallic compounds; electron spin resonance; electrochemistry; mechanisms of reactions initiated by electron transfer. *Mailing Add:* Dept Chem Brown Univ Providence RI 02912. *Fax:* 401-863-2594; *E-Mail:* philip_rieger@brown.edu

RIEGER, SAMUEL, SOIL MORPHOLOGY. *Current Pos:* RETIRED. *Personal Data:* b New York, NY, Sept 29, 21; m 47; c 3. *Educ:* Cornell Univ, BS, 43; Univ Wis, MS, 47; State Col Wash, PhD(soils), 52. *Prof Exp:* Soil surveyor, State Geol & Natural Hist Surv, Wis, 46, 47; soil scientist, US Bur Reclamation, 47-49; asst soils, State Col Wash, 49-52; soil scientist, Soil Conserv Serv, USDA, 52-55, state soil scientist, 55-78. *Mem:* Soil Sci Soc Am; Am Soc Agron; Sigma Xi. *Res:* Soil morphology, genesis, and classification, particularly of arctic and subarctic soils. *Mailing Add:* 5817 NE 181 St Seattle WA 98155

RIEGERT, PAUL WILLIAM, INSECT PHYSIOLOGY. *Current Pos:* RETIRED. *Personal Data:* b Can, Dec 5, 23; m 48; c 4. *Educ:* Univ Sask, BA, 44; Mont State Col, MSc, 48; Univ Ill, PhD(entom, physiol), 54. *Prof Exp:* Agr asst entom, Can Dept Agr, 44-47; lectr entom, Mont State Col, 47-48; entomologist, Entom Sect Res Lab, Can Dept Agr, 48-68; prof biol, Univ Sask, 68-72; head dept, Univ Regina, 72-79, prof, 72-86. *Mem:* Fel Entom Soc Can; Orthopterist Soc; fel Royal Entom Soc London. *Res:* Sensory and behavioral aspects of insect physiology; bioenergetics; history of entomology. *Mailing Add:* 103 Mayfair Crescent Regina SK S4S 5T9 Can

RIEGGER, OTTO K, METALLURGICAL ENGINEERING. *Current Pos:* res engr, 64-67, DIR RES, RES LAB, TECUMSEH PROD CO, 67- *Personal Data:* b Howell, Mich, Dec 11, 35; m 60; c 3. *Educ:* Univ Mich, BSE, 58, MSE, 59, PhD(metall eng), 63. *Prof Exp:* Res engr appl res off, Ford Motor Co, 62-64. *Mem:* Am Soc Metals; Am Foundrymen's Soc; Am Ceramic Soc; Soc Mfg Eng; Soc Die Casting Eng. *Res:* Applied research administration; computer aided product design and simulation; manufacturing engineering and process specification. *Mailing Add:* 5060 Doral Dr Ann Arbor MI 48108-8568

RIEGLE, GAIL DANIEL, ENDOCRINOLOGY, REPRODUCTIVE PHYSIOLOGY. *Current Pos:* From asst prof to assoc prof, 64-76, PROF PHYSIOL, MICH STATE UNIV, 76-, ASSOC DEAN ACAD AFFAIRS, COL OSTEOP MED, 80- *Personal Data:* b De Soto, Iowa, Feb 19, 35; m 60; c 2. *Educ:* Iowa State Univ, BS, 57; Mich State Univ, MS, 60, PhD(physiol), 63. *Concurrent Pos:* Develop of Undergrad & Grad Clin Educ Prog. *Mem:* Geront Soc; Am Physiol Soc; Soc Exp Biol & Med; Sigma Xi. *Res:* Effects of stress and aging on endocrine and reproductive control systems. *Mailing Add:* Col Osteop Med Mich State Univ East Lansing MI 48823

RIEHL, HERBERT, METEOROLOGY. *Current Pos:* RETIRED. *Personal Data:* b Munich, Ger, Mar 30, 15; nat US; m 52; c 2. *Educ:* NY Univ, MS, 42; Univ Chicago, PhD(meteorol), 47. *Honors & Awards:* Losey Award, Am Inst Aeronaut & Astronaut, 60; Andrew G Clark Award, Colo State Univ, 72; Meisinger Award, Am Meteorol Soc, 47, Rossby Award, 79. *Prof Exp:* Instr meteorol, Univ Wash, 41-42; from instr to prof, Univ Chicago, 42-60; prof & head dept, Colo State Univ, 60-72; prof, Free Univ Berlin, 72-76; vis scientist, Nat Ctr Atmospheric Res, 76-79; prof, Coop Inst Res Environ Sci, 79-83. *Concurrent Pos:* Consult, USN & US Weather Bur; consult, Sen, Berlin, 74-75. *Mem:* AAAS; Am Meteorol Soc; Am Geophys Union; Royal Meteorol Soc; Ger Meteorol Soc; Sigma Xi. *Res:* General circulation; jet streams; tropical meteorology; climatology; hydrometeorology. *Mailing Add:* 1200 Humboldt St Apt 1106 Cheesman Towers W Denver CO 80218-2462

RIEHL, JAMES PATRICK, PHYSICAL CHEMISTRY, THEORETICAL CHEMISTRY. *Current Pos:* ASST PROF CHEM, UNIV MO, ST LOUIS, 77- *Personal Data:* b Toms River, NJ, Aug 6, 48; m 72; c 1. *Educ:* Villanova Univ, BS, 70; Purdue Univ, PhD(phys chem), 75. *Prof Exp:* Instr chem, Univ Va, 75-77. *Concurrent Pos:* Res investr, Am Chem Soc Petrol Res Fund, 78-80 & Res Corp, 78. *Mem:* Am Chem Soc. *Res:* Molecular dynamics and structure of condensed phases; molecular spectroscopy; optical activity. *Mailing Add:* Dept Chem Mich Tech Univ Houghton MI 49931-1295

RIEHL, JERRY A, PHYSICS, CHEMISTRY. *Current Pos:* RETIRED. *Personal Data:* b Kalispell, Mont, July 25, 33; m 75; c 7. *Educ:* Seattle Univ, BS, 62; Wash State Univ, PhD(chem), 66. *Prof Exp:* Assoc prof physics, Seattle Univ, 66-74, chmn dept, 71-74; sr res specialist, Boeing Com Airline Co, 74-80; res prof chem, Seattle Univ, 78-80; scientist, Phys Dynamics, 80-83; dean tech educ, S Seattle Community Col, 84-94. *Concurrent Pos:* Res consult, 74- *Mem:* Am Chem Soc; Am Phys Soc; fel Inst Environ Sci; Soc Automotive Engr; Am Soc Testing & Mat. *Res:* Air pollution control; gas-turbine emissions; nuclear analysis. *Mailing Add:* 9315 Fauntleroy Way SW Seattle WA 98136-2620

RIEHL, MARY AGATHA, ORGANIC CHEMISTRY. *Current Pos:* PROF CHEM, COL ST SCHOLASTICA, 45- *Personal Data:* b Raleigh, NDak, Feb 17, 21. *Educ:* Col St Scholastica, BA, 42; Inst Divi Thomae, MS, 45; Cath Univ, PhD(chem), 66. *Concurrent Pos:* NSF sci fac fel, 62-63; NSF res participation grant, Argonne Nat Lab, 69, Ill Inst Technol, 71. *Mem:* AAAS; Am Chem Soc; Am Inst Chem; Sigma Xi. *Res:* Biochemical studies in cancer, especially enzyme systems in cancerous and normal tissue; chromic acid oxidations of organic compounds; EPA laboratory. *Mailing Add:* Col St Scholastica Duluth MN 55811

RIEHLE, ROBERT ARTHUR, JR, UROLITHIASIS, SHOCK WAVE LITHOTRIPSY. *Current Pos:* asst prof urol surg, Med Sch & asst attend surgeon, 81-86, assoc prof urol surg & assoc attend surgeon, 87-90, MED DIR, NEW YORK HOSP, CORNELL UNIV, 90-; MED DIR, ALBANY MEM HOSP, 90- *Personal Data:* b San Diego, Calif, Oct 24, 47; m. *Educ:* Yale Univ, BA, 69; Columbia Univ, MD, 73. *Prof Exp:* Asst prof urol, Wayne State Univ, 80-81. *Concurrent Pos:* Asst ed, Endourology, 86-90. *Mem:* Am Col Surgeons; Am Urol Asn; Am Col Physician Execs; Int Soc Urol; Endourol Soc; AMA. *Res:* Disintegration of kidney stones using extra-corporeal shock wave lithotripsy; use of percutaneous surgery for stone removal and intra-renal surgery; dose response curve analysis of urologic procedures. *Mailing Add:* Blue Shield NENY 187 Wolf Rd Albany NY 12205

RIEHM, CARL RICHARD, ORTHOGONAL REPRESENTATIONS OF FINITE GROUPS. *Current Pos:* chmn dept, 73-79, PROF MATH, MCMASTER UNIV, 73- *Personal Data:* b Kitchener, Ont, May 2, 35; m 58, Elaine S McKinnon; c Derek J & Marc Philip. *Educ:* Univ Toronto, BA, 58; Princeton Univ, PhD(math), 61. *Prof Exp:* From lectr to asst prof math, McGill Univ, 61-63; from asst prof to assoc prof, Univ Notre Dame, 63-73. *Concurrent Pos:* Mem, Inst Advan Study, 66-67; vis prof, Harvard Univ, 67-68. *Mem:* Am Math Soc; Can Math Soc. *Res:* Orthogonal representations of finite groups; arithmetic theory of quadratic forms. *Mailing Add:* Dept Math McMaster Univ Hamilton ON L8S 4K1 Can. *Fax:* 905-522-0935; *E-Mail:* riehm@mcmaster.ca

RIEHM, JOHN P, BIOCHEMISTRY. *Current Pos:* assoc prof, 70-77, PROF BIOL & CHMN DEPT, UNIV WEST FLA, 77- *Personal Data:* b Fergus, Ont, Mar 24, 35; m 63; c 1. *Educ:* Ont Agr Col, BSA, 56; Mich State Univ, PhD(biochem), 62. *Prof Exp:* Fel, Cornell Univ, 62-65; asst prof biochem, Univ Calif, Santa Barbara, 65-70. *Mem:* Am Chem Soc. *Res:* Chemical and physical properties of proteins. *Mailing Add:* Dept Cell & Molecular Biol Univ WFla 1100 Univ Pkwy Pensacola FL 32514

RIEKE, CAROL ANGER, MATHEMATICS, ASTRONOMY. *Current Pos:* RETIRED. *Personal Data:* b Milwaukee, Wis, Jan 17, 08; m 32; c 2. *Educ:* Northwestern Univ, BA, 28, MA, 29; Radcliffe Col, PhD(astron), 32. *Honors & Awards:* Caroline I Wilby Prize. *Prof Exp:* Berliner fel, Radcliffe Col, 32-33, tutor astron, 33-36; instr, Johns Hopkins Univ, 37; asst physics, Univ Chicago, 38-42; computer, Mass Inst Tech, 42-46; instr, Purdue Univ, 47-52; instr math & astron, Thornton Community Col, 57-85. *Concurrent Pos:* Asst, Mass Inst Tech, 33-36, computer, 33-38. *Mem:* Am Astron Soc. *Res:* Spectroscopic parallaxes; astronomical spectroscopy; molecular spectra; airplane propulsion; galactic clusters. *Mailing Add:* 2535 N Avenida San Valle Tucson AZ 85715-3404

RIEKE, GARL KALMAN, ANATOMY, NEUROSCIENCE. *Current Pos:* MEM STAFF, DEPT ANAT SCI, MEHARRY MED COL. *Personal Data:* b Seattle, Wash, June 30, 42. *Educ:* Univ Wash, BS, 65, BS, 66; La State Univ, PhD(anat), 71. *Prof Exp:* Asst prof anat, Hahnemann Med Col & Hosp, 73-78; asst prof anat, Col Med, Tex A&M Univ, 78- *Concurrent Pos:* Fel physiol, Univ Calif, Los Angeles, 71-73. *Mem:* AAAS; Sigma Xi; Soc Neurosci. *Res:* Neuronal interactions; local circuits; homing and magnetic fields. *Mailing Add:* Dept Anat Sci Meharry Med Col 1005 D B Todd Blvd Nashville TN 37208

RIEKE, GEORGE HENRY, ASTRONOMY. *Current Pos:* res assoc, Lunar & Planetary Lab, 70-73, asst prof astron, Steward Observ & Lunar & Planetary Lab, 73-75, assoc prof, 75-80, PROF ASTRON, STEWARD OBSERV & LUNAR & PLANETARY LAB, UNIV ARIZ, 80- *Personal Data:* b Boston, Mass, Jan 5, 43. *Educ:* Oberlin Col, AB, 64; Harvard Univ, MA, 65, PhD(physics), 69. *Prof Exp:* Fel astron, Smithsonian Astrophys Observ, 69-70. *Concurrent Pos:* Alfred P Sloan Found fel, 76-80; prin investr, Space Infrared Telescope Facil; dep dir, Steward Observ. *Res:* Infrared astronomy. *Mailing Add:* 5801 N Paseo Ventoso Tucson AZ 85750

RIEKE, HERMAN HENRY, III, PETROLEUM ENGINEERING, GEOLOGY. *Current Pos:* TECH STAFF, DIRECTORATE GEN MINERAL RESOURCES, JEDDAH, SAUDI ARABIA, 89- *Personal Data:* b Louisville, Ky, June 18, 37; m 64; c 6. *Educ:* Univ Ky, BS, 59; Univ Southern

Calif, MS, 64 & 65, PhD(petrol eng), 70. *Honors & Awards:* Crown Medal, Shah of Iran, 76. *Prof Exp:* Chief geologist, United Minerals, Inc, Los Angeles, 63-64; staff engr, Electro-Osmotics, Inc, Los Angeles, 64-66; lectr petrol eng, Univ Southern Calif, 66-68; res scientist, Res & Develop, Continental Oil Co, Ponca City, 69-71; asst prof petrol eng, Col Mineral & Energy Resources, WVa Univ, 71-81, assoc prof, 76-81; mem tech staff, TRW Inc, 77-81; prod mgr, 81-82, dir explor & geol, Poi Energy, Inc, Cleveland, Ohio, 82-83; sr vpres, Geofax, Inc, Cleveland, Ohio, 84-89; dir, WVa Energy & Environ Res Corp, Inc, Morgantown, WVa, 84-89. *Concurrent Pos:* Eng scientist, Res Eng Exp Sta, WVa Univ, 71-81. *Mem:* Soc Petrol Engrs; Geol Soc Am; Soc Prof Well Log Analysts; Soc Econ Paleont & Mineral; Am Inst Prof Geologists; Int Asn Study Clays. *Res:* Abnormal subsurface pressure detection; reservoir engineering; formation evaluation; compaction of sediments; geothermal energy; evaluation of mineral resources; oil and gas production; microcomputer based expert systems; artificial intelligence; expert witness, oil and gas. *Mailing Add:* 161 Poplar Dr Morgantown WV 26505

RIEKE, JAMES KIRK, PHYSICAL CHEMISTRY. *Current Pos:* res chemist, 54-57, proj leader, 57-62, group leader, 62-65, asst to dir plastics dept lab, 65-70, ASST TO DIR PHYS RES, DOW CHEM USA, 70- *Personal Data:* b Barrington, Ill, Apr 15, 24; m 49; c 3. *Educ:* Univ Ill, BS, 49; Univ Wis, MS, 52, PhD(chem), 54. *Prof Exp:* Asst chem, Univ Wis, 49-54. *Mem:* AAAS; Am Chem Soc; Soc Plastics Eng; Sigma Xi; Soc Rheology. *Res:* Luminescence properties induced in crystals by high energy radiation; physical properties of high polymers; graft copolymers. *Mailing Add:* 4715 Swede Ave Midland MI 48642-3861

RIEKE, MARCIA JEAN, ASTRONOMY. *Current Pos:* Res assoc, Lunar & Planetary Lab, Univ Ariz, 76-78, res assoc infrared astron, 78-79, asst astronr, Steward Observ, 79-83, assoc astronr, 83-84, assoc prof, 84-93, PROF ASTRON & ASTRONR, UNIV ARIZ, 93- *Personal Data:* b Hillsdale, Mich, June 13, 51; div. *Educ:* Mass Inst Technol, SB, 72, PhD(physics), 76. *Honors & Awards:* Van Biesbroeck Prize, 80. *Concurrent Pos:* Counr, Am Astron Soc, 90-92. *Mem:* Sigma Xi; Am Astron Soc. *Res:* Infrared observations of extragalactic objects; development of infrared detectors for astronomical use. *Mailing Add:* 5801 N Paseo Ventoso Tucson AZ 85750

RIEKE, PAUL EUGENE, TURF MANAGEMENT, SOIL SCIENCE. *Current Pos:* From asst prof to assoc prof, 63-72, PROF CROP & SOIL SCI, MICH STATE UNIV, 72- *Personal Data:* b Kankakee, Ill, May 13, 34; m 57; c 2. *Educ:* Univ Ill, BS, 56, MS, 58; Mich State Univ, PhD(soil sci), 63. *Mem:* Sigma Xi; Soil Sci Soc Am; fel Crop Sci Soc Am; Am Soc Agron; Am Soc Hort Sci. *Res:* Physical and chemical properties of soils affecting turf management. *Mailing Add:* Dept Crop & Soil Sci 286 Plant & Soil Sci Mich State Univ East Lansing MI 48824-1325

RIEKE, REUBEN DENNIS, ORGANIC CHEMISTRY. *Current Pos:* Interim chmn & chmn, dept chem, 81-85, PROF CHEM, UNIV NEBR, LINCOLN, 77- *Personal Data:* b Lucan, Minn, Mar 7, 39; m 62, Loretta Hoffeld; c R Dennis Jr & Elizabeth A. *Educ:* Univ Minn, Minneapolis, BCh, 61; Univ Wis-Madison, PhD(org chem), 66. *Prof Exp:* Assoc phys org chem, Univ Calif, Los Angeles, 65-66; from asst prof to prof phys org chem, Univ NC, Chapel Hill, 66-76; prof, NDak State Univ, 76-77. *Concurrent Pos:* NIH res fel, 65-66; participant, Am Chem Soc Course Molecular Orbital Theory, 68-70; fel, Alfred P Sloan Found, 73-77; fel, Alexander von Humboldt Found, 73-74; vis prof, Tech Univ, Munich, 73-74, Prince Univ, 85 & Stanford Univ, 90; mem adv bd, critical rev in surface chem, 88; app, Howard S Wilson Regents Prof Chem, 87. *Mem:* Am Chem Soc; Sigma Xi; fel AAAS. *Res:* Preparation and study of chemistry of activated metals, electrochemical studies of organic and organometallic compounds; development of new synthetic methods using organometallics; preparation and study of organic metals. *Mailing Add:* Dept Chem Univ Nebr Lincoln NE 68588-0304

RIEKELS, JERALD WAYNE, PLANT PHYSIOLOGY, HORTICULTURE. *Current Pos:* Asst prof, 64-68, ASSOC PROF HORT SCI, UNIV GUELPH, 68- *Personal Data:* b Muskegon, Mich, Oct 31, 32; m 58; c 3. *Educ:* Mich State Univ, BS, 59, MS, 60; Univ Calif, Davis, PhD(plant physiol), 64. *Concurrent Pos:* Grants, Nat Res Coun Can, 65-69; Ont Dept Univ Affairs, 69 & Potash Inst Can, 71. *Mem:* Am Soc Hort Sci; Am Soc Plant Physiol; Int Soc Hort Sci; Coun Agr Sci & Technol; Coun Soil Testing & Plant Anal; Sigma Xi. *Res:* Vegetable physiology, culture and production with emphasis on mineral nutrition. *Mailing Add:* Dept Hort Univ Guelph Guelph ON N1G 2W1 Can

RIEL, GORDON KIENZLE, HEALTH PHYSICS. *Current Pos:* Chem engr, 56-59, PHYSICIST, NAVAL ORD LAB, 59- *Personal Data:* b Columbus, Ohio, Oct 26, 34; m 54, Anne L Rutledge; c Gordon W, Valeria L (Kendall) & Cynthia G (Brown). *Educ:* Univ Fla, BChE, 56; Univ Md, MS, 61, PhD, 67. *Concurrent Pos:* Consult, 69- *Mem:* Health Physics Soc; Instrument Soc Am; Nat Soc Prof Engrs; Am Phys Soc. *Res:* Measurement of radiation in the ocean including cosmic rays, natural and artificial radioactive isotopes; neutron spectrometry and personnel dosimetry; radiation monitoring systems for nuclear reactors and environment; computer modeling of radiation fields. *Mailing Add:* NSWCCD Code 682 9500 McArthur Blvd West Bethesda MD 20817-5700. *E-Mail:* griel@oasys.dt.navy.mil

RIEL, RENE ROSAIRE, FOOD SCIENCE. *Current Pos:* FOOD RES CONSULT, 88- *Personal Data:* b Sherrington, Que, Oct 21, 23; m 58, Desrosiers Marguerite; c 3. *Educ:* Univ Montreal, BSA, 47, MSc, 49; Univ Wis, PhD(dairy indust, biochem), 52. *Honors & Awards:* David Prize, 60; Berard Award, 74. *Prof Exp:* Prof dairy chem, Univ Montreal, 52-53; res officer, Chem Div, Sci Serv, 53-59; head chem sect, Dairy Tech Res Inst, Can Dept Agr, 59-62; dir dept food sci, Laval Univ, 62-71, prof food opers, 62-74; food res coordr, Can Dept Agr, 74-83; dir, Saint-Hyacinthe Ctr Food Sci Res, 83-88. *Mem:* Am Dairy Sci Asn; Inst Food Technologists; Can Inst Food Sci & Technol; Chem Inst Can; Fr-Can Asn Advan Sci. *Res:* Protein extraction; texturization; modified fats; freeze-drying. *Mailing Add:* 60 rue Therien Hull PQ J8Y 1J1 Can

RIEMANN, HANS, VETERINARY MEDICINE. *Current Pos:* res fel food microbiol, Univ Calif, Davis, 64-65, from lectr to assoc prof, 65-69, prof pub health, 69-80, chief investr, Field Res & Training Prog, 71-80, chairperson, Dept Epidemiol & Prev Med, 78-88, dir, Master Prev Vet Med Prog, 81-88, PROF, UNIV CALIF, DAVIS, 80- *Personal Data:* b Harte, Denmark, Mar 11, 20; m 43, 65; c 2. *Educ:* Royal Vet & Agr Col, Denmark, DVM, 43; Copenhagen Univ, PhD(microbiol), 63, Am Col Vet Prev Med, dipl. *Honors & Awards:* Dr C O Jensen's Food Microbiol Reward, 53. *Prof Exp:* Pvt pract, 43; vet inspector food, Pub Health Serv, Denmark, 43-45; microbiologist, Tech Lab, Ministry Fisheries, 45-54; chief microbiologist, Danish Meat Res Inst, 54-57 & dir res planning, 60-64; res asst microbiol, Univ Ill, 57-60. *Concurrent Pos:* Lectr, Royal Vet & Agr Col, Denmark, 60-64. *Mem:* Am Vet Med Asn; Am Soc Microbiol; Sigma Xi. *Res:* Veterinary epidemiology and preventive medicine. *Mailing Add:* Dept Pop Health/Reprod Sch Vet Med Univ Calif Davis CA 95616

RIEMANN, JAMES MICHAEL, ORGANIC CHEMISTRY. *Current Pos:* PROF CHEM, PFEIFFER COL, 66-, DIR ACAD COMPUT, 79-, CHMN, DIV NATURAL & HEALTH SCI, 82- *Personal Data:* b Philadelphia, Ill, Oct 14, 40; m 63; c 2. *Educ:* Berea Col, BA, 62; Univ Ohio, PhD(chem), 68. *Concurrent Pos:* Vis prof gen chem, Iowa State Univ, 73-74. *Mem:* Am Chem Soc; Sigma Xi. *Res:* Flash vacuum pyrolysis in synthesis; ozonolysis of aqueous organic mixtures. *Mailing Add:* PO Box 326 Misenheimer NC 28109-0326

RIEMANN, JOHN G, ENTOMOLOGY. *Current Pos:* res entomologist, Man & Animal Br, 62-64, RES ENTOMOLOGIST, METAB & RADIATION LAB, ENTOM RES DIV, USDA, 64-, RES ENTOM, BIO SCI RES LAB, AGR RES LAB. *Personal Data:* b Gladstone, NMex, June 18, 28; m 61. *Educ:* Tex Tech Col, BA, 51; Univ Tex, MA, 54, PhD(zool), 61. *Prof Exp:* Asst prof biol, West Tex State Col, 57-60; vis asst prof zool, Tulane Univ, 61-62. *Mem:* Entom Soc Am; AAAS. *Res:* Radiation biology, cytology and reproductive physiology of insects. *Mailing Add:* 3119 Par St NE Fargo ND 58102

RIEMENSCHNEIDER, ALBERT LOUIS, ELECTRICAL ENGINEERING. *Current Pos:* asst prof, 67-74, assoc prof, 80-82, PROF ELEC ENG, SDAK SCH MINES & TECHNOL, 82-, HEAD DEPT, 83- *Personal Data:* b Cody, Nebr, May 18, 36; wid; c Richard, David & Barbara. *Educ:* SDak Sch Mines & Technol, BSEE, 59, MSEE, 62; Univ Wyo, PhD(elec eng), 69. *Honors & Awards:* Benjamin Dasher Award, Am Soc Eng Educ/Inst Elec & Electronics Engrs, 82; John A Curtis Award, Am Soc Eng Educ, 83. *Prof Exp:* Engr, Sperry Utah Co, 59-60; instr elec eng, Univ Wyo, 62-67; gen mgr, Syncom, Inc, 74-80. *Concurrent Pos:* Res engr, Natural Resources Res Inst, 64-67; consult, Respec Corp, 70-74, Durham Assoc, 80-82 & ALR Eng, 82- *Mem:* Inst Elec & Electronics Engrs; Nat Soc Prof Engrs. *Res:* Control systems; instrumentation; hybrid computations; computer aided design; computer aided instruction; microprocessors; digital control. *Mailing Add:* Elect Eng Dept SDak Sch Mines & Technol 501 E St Joseph St Rapid City SD 57701. *E-Mail:* ariemens@silver.sdsmt.edu

RIEMENSCHNEIDER, PAUL ARTHUR, MEDICINE, DIAGNOSTIC RADIOLOGY. *Current Pos:* PROF RADIOL, STATE UNIV NY, HEALTH SCI CTR, SYRACUSE, 84- *Personal Data:* b Cleveland, Ohio, Apr 17, 20; m 45, Mildred McCarthy; c Barbara A (Updike), Nancy E (Christensen), David A, Paul A, Mary E (Sales) & Sarah B (Kass). *Educ:* Baldwin-Wallace Col, BS, 41; Harvard Univ, MD, 44; Am Bd Radiol, dipl. *Honors & Awards:* Gold Medal, Am Col Radiol, 82; Gold Medal, Am Roentgen Ray Soc, 86; Gold Medal, Radiol Soc NAm, 90. *Prof Exp:* Asst radiol, Harvard Med Sch, 49; from asst prof to assoc prof, Med Col, Syracuse Univ, 50-51; from assoc prof to prof, Col Med, State Univ NY Upstate Med Ctr, 52-65; dir diag radiol, Santa Barbara Cottage Hosp, 64-92. *Concurrent Pos:* Consult, Oak Ridge Inst; mem bd trustees, Am Bd Radiol; vis prof, Univ Malaya, 91-92. *Mem:* Roentgen Ray Soc (pres, 80); Radiol Soc NAm; Am Col Radiol (pres, 75). *Res:* Diagnostic radiology with particular emphasis on cerebral angiography. *Mailing Add:* PO Box 689 Santa Barbara CA 93102

RIEMENSCHNEIDER, ROBERT, ANIMAL SCIENCE & NUTRITION. *Current Pos:* DIR, GRAIN & FEED DIV, US DEPT AGR, 95- *Personal Data:* b Baltimore, Md, Apr 3, 50. *Mailing Add:* US Dept Agr Grain & Feed Div 14th & Independence Ave SW Rm 56035 Washington DC 20250-1000

RIEMENSCHNEIDER, SHERMAN DELBERT, MATHEMATICS. *Current Pos:* Nat Res Coun grant & asst prof, 70-75, assoc prof, 75-82, PROF MATH, UNIV ALTA, 82- *Personal Data:* b Alliance, Ohio, Sept 11, 43; m 67, Rama Schinagle; c Kylee & Brice. *Educ:* Hiram Col, AB, 65; Syracuse Univ, MA, 67, PhD(math), 69. *Prof Exp:* Lectr math, Univ Wash, 69-70. *Concurrent Pos:* Vis scholar, Univ Tex, 76-77; vis assoc prof, Univ SC, 80-81. *Mem:* Math Asn Am; Soc Indust & Appl Math; Can Math Soc (vpres, 87-89, pres, 91-92, past-pres, 92-93); Can Appl Math Soc. *Res:* Interpolation of operators; approximation theory; splines. *Mailing Add:* Dept Math Univ Alta Edmonton AB T6G 2G1 Can. *Fax:* 403-492-6826; *E-Mail:* sriemens@vega.math.ualberta.ca.

RIEMER, DONALD NEIL, AQUATIC BIOLOGY. *Current Pos:* RETIRED. *Personal Data:* b Newark, NJ, Feb 14, 34; m 56, Janet Tepper; c Cathy & Michael. *Educ:* Rutgers Univ, BS, 56, PhD(weed control), 66; Auburn Univ, MS, 60. *Prof Exp:* Fisheries biologist, NJ Div Fish & Game, 61-62; instr aquatic weed sci, Rutgers Univ, New Brunswick, NJ, 62- 66, asst res prof, 66-69, assoc res prof aquatic weed sci, 69-94, chmn, Dept Soil & Crops, 75-82. *Mem:* Soc Aquatic Plant Mgt; Asn Aquatic Vascular Plant Biologists. *Res:* Life histories, ecology and control of aquatic vegetation. *Mailing Add:* 256 Pennington Harburton Rd Pennington NJ 08534

RIEMER, PAUL, ENGINEERING. *Current Pos:* RETIRED. *Personal Data:* b Poland, Mar 20, 24; nat US; m 49; c 3. *Educ:* Univ Sask, BE, 47. *Prof Exp:* From asst prof to prof civil eng, Univ Sask, 50-89. *Mem:* Fel Can Soc Civil Engrs; Eng Inst Can. *Res:* Structural engineering. *Mailing Add:* 34 Cambridge Crescent Saskatoon SK S7H 3P8 Can

RIEMER, ROBERT KIRK, HORMONAL REGULATION, UTERINE PHYSIOLOGY. *Current Pos:* Teaching fel, 82-86, asst res pharmacologist, 86-91, CARDIO- THORACIC SURG DEPT, UNIV CALIF, SAN FRANCISCO, 91- *Personal Data:* c 1. *Educ:* Univ Calif, Santa Barbara, BA, 76; Univ Ark, PhD(pharmacol), 82. *Mem:* Am Soc Pharmacol & Exp Therapeut; AAAS. *Res:* Hormonal regulation of autonomic responses in uterus and myocardium. *Mailing Add:* Cardio-Thoracic Surg Univ Calif PO Box 0118 San Francisco CA 94143-0001

RIEMER, ROBERT LEE, SCIENCE POLICY FOR PHYSICS & ASTRONOMY. *Current Pos:* prog officer, 85-88, SR PROG OFFICER & ASSOC DIR, BD PHYSICS & ASTRON, NAT ACAD SCI-NAT RES COUN, 88- *Personal Data:* b Sheboygan, Wis, June 11, 51; m 80. *Educ:* Univ Wis-Madison, BS, 73; Univ Kans, Lawrence, MS, 78, PhD(physics), 80. *Prof Exp:* Postdoctoral res assoc, High-Energy Physics Group, Univ Kans, Lawrence, 80; proj geophysicist, Gulf Oil Co, 80-85. *Mem:* Am Phys Soc; Sigma Xi; Nat Res Coun. *Res:* Science policy reports in physics and astronomy. *Mailing Add:* 1035 Rynex Dr Alexandria VA 22312-3011. *Fax:* 202-334-2791; *E-Mail:* priemer@nas.edu

RIEMER-RUBENSTEIN, DELILAH, MEDICAL ADMINISTRATION, NEUROPSYCHIATRY. *Current Pos:* RETIRED. *Personal Data:* b Brooklyn, NY, Aug 28, 10; m 37; c 3. *Educ:* Tufts Univ, BS, 31; Med Col Pa, MD, 36. *Honors & Awards:* Bronze Medal, Am Cong Phys Med, 55. *Prof Exp:* Intern, Univ Hosp, Boston, Mass, 36-37; jr physician, Boston Dispensary, 37-47; ward physician, Vet Admin Hosp, Bedford, Mass, 48-53, chief phys med & rehab serv, 53-63; dir, John T Berry Rehab Ctr, Mass Dept Ment Health, 63-79; med dir, Pentucket Chronic Hosp, 79-84; consult, Shaughnessy Rehab Hosp, 84-85. *Concurrent Pos:* Physician in chg, Am Red Blood Donor Ctr, New Eng, Am Red Cross, 42-45; asst, Sch Med, Tufts Univ, 57-63, instr, 63-66; asst physician, Boston Dispensary, Mass, 58-66; fel, Harvard Sch Pub Health. *Mem:* Am Cong Rehab Med; Am Psychiat Asn; Am Asn Ment Deficiency. *Res:* Mental retardation in all its aspects from developmental to results of habilitation and rehabilitation; psychiatry; geriatrics. *Mailing Add:* 250 Hammond Pond Pkwy No 1205 Chestnut Hill MA 02167-1537

RIEMERSMA, H(ENRY), ELECTRICAL ENGINEERING, PHYSICS. *Current Pos:* Intermediate res engr, 58-61, res engr, 61-64, sr engr, 65-70, res prog adminr, 70-75, SR ENGR, RES & DEVELOP CTR, WESTINGHOUSE ELEC CORP, 75- *Personal Data:* b Neth, Nov 30, 28; US citizen; m 56; c 4. *Educ:* Univ Mich, BS, 57; Carnegie Inst Technol, MS, 65. *Res:* Attainment of ultrahigh vacua; superconducting equipment, magnets, transformers, generators; electrical breakdown in various environment. *Mailing Add:* 617 Penny Dr Pittsburgh PA 15235

RIEMKE, RICHARD ALLAN, REACTOR SAFETY ANALYSIS CODES, THERMAL HYDRAULICS. *Current Pos:* CONSULT ENGR, IDAHO NAT ENG LAB, EG&G IDAHO, INC, 80- *Personal Data:* b Vallejo, Calif, Oct 11, 44. *Educ:* Univ Calif, Berkeley, BA, 67, MA, 71, PhD(eng sci), 77. *Prof Exp:* Res fel, Univ Southern Calif, 77-78; res engr, Del Mar Avionics, 79; staff fel, NIH, 80. *Mem:* Am Nuclear Soc; Am Soc Mech Engrs; Biomed Eng Soc; Soc Comput Simulation; Soc Math Biol; Soc Eng Sci. *Res:* Develop, assess and assist users of the reactor safety analysis code RELAP 5; thermal hydraulics, two-phase flow, computational fluid dynamics and software development. *Mailing Add:* Idaho Nat Eng Lab Lockheed Martin Idaho Technol Idaho Falls ID 83415-3880

RIES, EDWARD RICHARD, PETROLEUM GEOLOGY, EXPLORATION GEOLOGY. *Current Pos:* PETROL GEOLOGIST & INT PETROL CONSULT, AFRICA, EUROPE, SINO-SOVIET & SE ASIA, 86- *Personal Data:* b Freeman, SDak, Sept 18, 18; m 49; c Rosemary M (Zellmer) & Victoria E (Jennings). *Educ:* Univ SDak, AB, 41; Univ Okla, MS, 43, PhD(geol), 51. *Prof Exp:* Asst geologist, Geol Surv SDak, 41; geophys interpreter, Robert H Ray, Inc, 42; jr geologist, Carter Oil Co, 43-44, geologist, 44; sr geologist, Standard Vacuum Oil Co, India, 51-53, sr regional geologist, Stand Vacuum Petrol Mataschappij, Indonesia, 53-59, geol adv, 59-62; geol adv, Mobil Petrol Co, Inc, 62-65, staff geologist, Int Div, Mobil Oil Corp, 65-71, sr regional explorationist, Mobil Tech Serv, Inc, 71-73, sr regional explorationist, Mobil Explor & Prod Serv Inc, 73-76, sr geol adv, 76-79, assoc geol adv, 79-82, sr geol consult, Int Petroleum Explor, 82-83 & consult to Mobil Oil Corp, 83-86. *Concurrent Pos:* Vis lectr, Calcutta Univ, 52-53 & NY Univ, 65-70. *Mem:* AAAS; Geol Soc Am; NY Acad Sci; Am Asn Petrol Geologists; Soc Explor Geophysicists. *Res:* Search for and evaluate the petroleum potential of hydrocarbon provenances and their specific prospects by use of applied geological and geophysical techniques; author of numerous proprietary and published domestic and international geological, geophysical, and geochemical reports and professional papers; spectrum covers generation, migration and entrapment of hydrocarbons; evaluation of production and reserves and estimates of future hydrocarbon potential. *Mailing Add:* 6009 Royal Crest Dr Dallas TX 75230-3434

RIES, RICHARD RALPH, OPERATIONS MANAGEMENT, PROGRAM MANAGEMENT. *Current Pos:* SR STAFF ASSOC, INT PROG, NSF, 96. *Personal Data:* b New Ulm, Minn, Nov 16, 35; m 64, Erika; c Stefan & Thomas. *Educ:* St Edward's Univ, BS, 57; Univ Minn, MS, 59, PhD(physics), 63. *Prof Exp:* Res assoc physics, Max Planck Inst Chem, 63-64; instr physics, Harvard Univ, 64-65; asst prog dir, US-Japan Coop Sci Prog, NSF, 65-66, staff assoc int sci activities, Tokyo Liaison Off, 66-70, prof assoc, Off Int Progs, 70-72, regional mgr Europ & Am sect, 72-74, dept head, Off Int Progs, 75-76, dir opers & anal, Sci Tech & Int Affairs, 77-84, exec officer, 84-89, dir, Div Int Progs, 90-92; counr, St & Environ,, Am Embassy Bonn, Ger, 92-96. *Mem:* AAAS; Am Phys Soc. *Res:* Mass spectroscopy; positive ion optics; precise measurement of atomic masses; administration of international cooperative science programs; science policy; allocation of science resources; operations management; planning and evaluation; science diplomacy. *Mailing Add:* 2500 Childs Lane Alexandria VA 22308. *Fax:* 49-228-339-2838

RIES, RONALD EDWARD, GRASS SEEDLING MORPHOLOGY & ANATOMY. *Current Pos:* RANGE SCIENTIST RECLAMATION & SEEDLING ESTAB RES, AGR RES SERV, USDA, 74- *Personal Data:* b Powell, Wyo, Feb 7, 44; m 66, Ann L Taplin; c Ryan E & Rod E. *Educ:* Univ Mont, BS, 66, MS, 68; Univ Wyo, PhD(range mgt), 73. *Honors & Awards:* Outstanding Reclamation Researcher, Am Soc Surface Mining & Reclamation, 84. *Prof Exp:* Teaching & res asst forest grazing, Univ Mont, 66-68; nat resource specialist forestry & range, Bur Land Mgt, 68; res asst arid land ecol, Univ Wyo, 70-73, res assoc, 73-74. *Concurrent Pos:* Chmn, Energy Resources Div, Soil Conserv Soc Am, 86. *Mem:* Soc Range Mgt; Sci Res Soc NAm; Am Soc Surface Mining & Reclamation (pres, 85). *Res:* Principles and techniques important in revegetation of man-caused disturbed areas with emphasis on go-back cropland; effects of water on plant species and community establishment; prairie hay as a seed source for revegetation; grass seedling establishment, morphology and anatomy. *Mailing Add:* Northern Great Plains Res Ctr Box 459 Mandan ND 58554-0459. *Fax:* 701-667-3054

RIES, STANLEY K, HORTICULTURE, PLANT PHYSIOLOGY. *Current Pos:* From asst prof to assoc prof, 53-65, PROF HORT, MICH STATE UNIV, 65- *Personal Data:* b Kenton, Ohio, Sept 6, 27; m 49; c 3. *Educ:* Mich State Col, BS, 50; Cornell Univ, MS, 51, PhD(veg crops), 54. *Honors & Awards:* Golden Key Outstanding Res Award, AAAS. *Concurrent Pos:* Consult, Int Atomic Energy Agency, Vienna, 72-82; coop researcher, Rockefeller Found & Ford Found in Mex, Costa Rica, Turkey, Asia, various chem companies. *Mem:* Fel AAAS; fel Am Soc Hort Sci; Brit Plant Growth Regulation Soc; Am Soc Plant Physiol; Sigma Xi; Plant Growth Regulation Soc. *Res:* Plant growth regulation; isolation; identification and mode of action of new naturally occuring plant growth regulators. *Mailing Add:* A440 Plant & Soil Sci Mich State Univ 288 Plant Sci Bldg East Lansing MI 48824-1325

RIES, STEPHEN MICHAEL, PLANT PATHOLOGY. *Current Pos:* asst prof, 73-80, ASSOC PROF PLANT PATH, UNIV ILL, URBANA, 80- *Personal Data:* b Watertown, SDak, Apr 4, 44; m 66; c 3. *Educ:* SDak State Univ, BS, 66; Mont State Univ, PhD(microbiol), 71. *Prof Exp:* Res assoc plant path, Mont State Univ, 71; res assoc chem, Univ Colo, 71-72; res assoc plant physiol, Univ Calif, Riverside, 72-73. *Mem:* Am Phytopath Soc. *Res:* Identification and control of diseases of fruit crops and the motility and chemotaxis of bacterial pathogens of fruit crops. *Mailing Add:* N 533 Turner Hall Univ Ill 1102 S Goodwin Urbana IL 61801

RIESE, RUSSELL L(LOYD), ELECTRICAL ENGINEERING. *Current Pos:* RETIRED. *Personal Data:* b Kulm, NDak, June 20, 23; m 45; c 1. *Educ:* Univ Wash, BSEE, 46; Okla State Univ, MS, 50, PhD, 55. *Prof Exp:* Res assoc, Phys Sci Lab, NMex State Univ, 46-47, from instr to assoc prof elec eng, 47-56; prof elec & comput eng & chmn depts, Ariz State Univ, 57-61; prof & assoc chmn, Sch Eng, San Fernando Valley State Col, 61-63; assoc dean acad planning, Off of Chancellor, Calif State Cols, 63-67; chief higher educ specialist & head, Sect Acad Plans & Progs, Calif Postsecondary Educ Comn, 67-82. *Concurrent Pos:* Consult, Daley Elec Co, 58-59, Gen Elec Co, 59-61, Western Mgt Consults, 60-63, Marquardt Corp, 61-62, Electronics Assocs Inc, 65- & W N Samarzich & Assocs, 79-81, Higher Educ, 82- *Mem:* Am Soc Eng Educ; Inst Elec & Electronics Engrs; Sigma Xi. *Res:* Network synthesis; reliability; radar; controls; computers; power systems. *Mailing Add:* 4120 Wintercrest Ln Shingle Springs CA 95682

RIESE, WALTER CHARLES RUSTY, PETROLEUM EXPLORATION, GEOCHEMISTRY. *Current Pos:* sr prin geologist, 93-96, CONSULT GEOLOGIST, VASTAR RESOURCES, 96- *Personal Data:* b Newport, RI, June 8, 51; m 73, 84, Trisha L Laura; c Clay Jonathan & Monica Leigh. *Educ:* NMex Tech, BS, 73; Univ NMex, MS, 77, PhD(geol), 80. *Prof Exp:* Asst geologist, Vanguard Explor, 71 & NMex Bur Mines & Mineral Resources, 72-73; geologist, Technol Appln Ctr, Univ NMex, 73-74; proj geologist, Gulf Mineral Resources Co, 74-81; proj geochemist, Anaconda Copper Co, 81-83, admin coordr, Anaconda Minerals, 83-84; sr geologist, Arco Explor, 84-85, area geologist, 85-89, dist geologist, 89-92, area explor mgr Arco Oil & Gas Co, 92-93. *Concurrent Pos:* Res asst, Univ NMex, 79-81; instr, Arapahoe Community Col, 83 & Univ Houston, 85-89; affil fac, Colo State Univ, 85-; adj asst prof, Rice Univ, 85-93, adj assoc prof, 93-; lectr, Calif State Univ, Bakersfield, 89-93. *Mem:* Soc Econ Geologists; Am Inst Professional

Geologists; Asn Explor Geochemists; Am Asn Petrol Geologists; Geol Soc Am; Sigma Xi; Int Asn Cosmochem & Geochem. *Res:* Applied geochemical exploration research in biogeochemistry and geomicrobiology; seismic stratigraphy; scanning electron microscopic alterations studies; geochemical reservoir and formation damage studies. *Mailing Add:* 22003 Castlewind Circle Katy TX 77450. *Fax:* 281-584-3131; *E-Mail:* rriese1@is.arco.com

RIESELBACH, RICHARD EDGAR, INTERNAL MEDICINE, PHYSIOLOGY. *Current Pos:* from instr to assoc prof internal med, 65-73, chmn dept, 73-77, PROF MED, MED SCH, UNIV WIS-MADISON, 73-, CHIEF MED & COORDR ACAD AFFAIRS, MT SINAI MED CTR, 73- *Personal Data:* b Milwaukee, Wis, Dec 5, 33; m 56; c 3. *Educ:* Univ Wis-Madison, BS, 55; Harvard Med Sch, MD, 58. *Prof Exp:* Fel nephrology, Wash Univ, 62-64, instr internal med, Med Sch, 64-65. *Concurrent Pos:* Markle Found scholar, 69. *Mem:* Am Soc Clin Invest; Am Fedn Clin Res; Am Soc Nephrology. *Res:* Renal physiology and pathophysiology. *Mailing Add:* 1022 Hillside Ave Madison WI 53705

RIESEN, AUSTIN HERBERT, physiological psychology; deceased, see previous edition for last biography

RIESEN, JOHN WILLIAM, REPRODUCTIVE PHYSIOLOGY. *Current Pos:* from asst prof to assoc prof animal indust, 70-83, PROF ANIMAL SCI, UNIV CONN, 83- *Personal Data:* b Summit, NJ, Aug 18, 41; m 63; c 2. *Educ:* Univ Mass, BS, 63; Univ Wis, MS, 65, PhD, 68. *Prof Exp:* Fel, Primate Ctr, Univ Wis, 68-70. *Mem:* Am Soc Animal Sci; Soc Study Reproduction; Am Dairy Sci Asn. *Res:* Physiology of the postpartum cow; control of ovulation; physiology and endocrinology of spermatogenesis. *Mailing Add:* Animal Sci U-40 Univ Conn 3636 Horse Barn Storrs Mansfield CT 06269-0002

RIESENFELD, PETER WILLIAM, NUCLEAR SCIENCE. *Current Pos:* RESEARCHER, RI NUCLEAR SCI CTR, 75- *Personal Data:* b Minneapolis, Minn, Sept 6, 45; m 72; c 2. *Educ:* Univ Calif, Berkeley, BS, 67; Princeton Univ, MS, 69, PhD(chem & physics), 71. *Prof Exp:* Res asst, Inst Theoret Physics, Univ Frankfurt, 72-74; instr physics, Ind Univ, Bloomington, 74-75. *Concurrent Pos:* Consult, Res Inst Nuclear Physics, Ger, 72-74. *Mem:* Sigma Xi; Am Phys Soc; AAAS. *Res:* Heavy ion physics, nuclear techniques for chemical analysis. *Mailing Add:* PO Box 232 Saunderstown RI 02874-0232

RIESENFELD, RICHARD F, COMPUTER SCIENCE. *Current Pos:* Asst prof elec eng, Univ Utah, 72-74, asst prof, 74-76, assoc prof, 77-81, dept chair, 81-87, PROF COMPUT SCI, UNIV UTAH, 81- *Personal Data:* b Milwaukee, Wis, Nov 26, 44; m 74, Elaine Cohen; c Samantha & Rebecca. *Educ:* Princeton Univ, AB, 66; Syracuse Univ, MA, 69, PhD(comput sci), 73. *Concurrent Pos:* Consult comput aided design; adj asst prof math, Univ Utah, 74-76, adj prof mech eng, 82- *Mem:* Asn Comput Mach; Soc Indust & Appl Math; Math Asn Am. *Res:* Developing mathematical models for representing geometric shape information in a computer; computer graphics; an experimental computer-aided design/computer-aided manufacturing system. *Mailing Add:* Dept Comput Sci Univ Utah Salt Lake City UT 84112

RIESER, LEONARD M, ATOMIC PHYSICS, NUCLEAR PHYSICS. *Current Pos:* from instr to prof, Dartmouth Col, 52-81, Dept Provost, 59-64, dean fac arts & sci, 64-69 & 71-82, provost, 67-81, vpres, 71-82, Fairchild prof, 81-92, EMER PROF PHYSICS, DARTMOUTH COL, 92- *Personal Data:* b Chicago, Ill, May 18, 22; m 44, Rosemary L; c 4. *Educ:* Univ Chicago, BS, 43; Stanford Univ, PhD(physics), 52. *Prof Exp:* Asst physics, Metall Lab, Univ Chicago, 44 & Los Alamos Sci Lab, 45-46; asst, Stanford Univ, 46-51, res assoc, 51-52. *Concurrent Pos:* Pres, New Eng Conf Grad Educ, 65-66; chmn, AAAS, 74; chmn bd, Bull Atomic Scientists; mem, Fulbright Coun, Int Exchange Scholars, 88; vis scholar, Mac Arthur Found; mem bd trustees, Hampshire Col & Latin Am Scholar Prog Am Univ. *Mem:* AAAS (pres 73-); Interciencia Asn (vpres, 76-, pres, 80-84); Am Phys Soc; Biophys Soc; Am Asn Physics Teachers. *Res:* Reflection of x-rays; x-ray microscopy; proportional counters; experimental nuclear physics; biophysics. *Mailing Add:* Dept Physics Dartmouth Col 6127 Wilder Lab Hanover NH 03755

RIESKE, JOHN SAMUEL, BIOCHEMISTRY. *Current Pos:* RETIRED. *Personal Data:* b Provo, Utah, Sept 25, 23; m 49; c 6. *Educ:* Brigham Young Univ, BA, 49; Univ Utah, PhD(biol chem), 56. *Prof Exp:* Biochemist, US Army Res & Develop Command, 55-60, trainee respiratory enzymes, Inst Enzyme Res, Univ Wis, 60-64; asst prof, Inst Enzyme Res, Univ Wis, 64-66; assoc prof, Ohio State Univ, 66-75, prof physiol chem, 75-85. *Concurrent Pos:* USPHS career develop award, 64-65. *Mem:* AAAS; Am Soc Biol Chemists. *Res:* Structure and function of respiratory enzymes; cholinesterase enzymes; photosynthesis. *Mailing Add:* 6940 Mills Rd Ostrander OH 43061

RIESS, KARLEM, PHYSICS. *Current Pos:* from asst prof to prof, 43-78, EMER PROF PHYSICS, TULANE UNIV, 78- *Personal Data:* b New Orleans, La, Apr 17, 13. *Educ:* Tulane Univ, BS, 33, MS, 35; Brown Univ, PhD(physics), 43. *Prof Exp:* Instr math, Tulane Univ, 33-35, reader, 35-36; prof, high sch, La, 36-42; jr chemist, USN Yard, Philadelphia, 42; instr physics, Brown Univ, 42-43. *Mem:* Am Phys Soc; Am Chem Soc; Am Math Soc; Am Crystallog Asn. *Res:* Electromagnetic waves in a bent pipe of rectangular cross section; biophysics; mathematical physics. *Mailing Add:* 17 Audubon Blvd New Orleans LA 70118

RIESS, RONALD DEAN, MATHEMATICS. *Current Pos:* asst prof, 67-78, ASSOC PROF MATH, VA POLYTECH INST & STATE UNIV, 78- *Personal Data:* b North English, Iowa, Sept 28, 40; m 62; c 1. *Educ:* Iowa State Univ, BS, 63, MS, 65, PhD(numerical anal), 67. *Prof Exp:* Instr math, Iowa State Univ, 66-67. *Res:* Conditioning eigen value problems; numerical analysis of integration. *Mailing Add:* Dept Math Va Polytech Inst & State Univ Blacksburg VA 24061

RIESZ, PETER, PHYSICAL CHEMISTRY, RADIATION BIOLOGY. *Current Pos:* res chemist, 58-81, chief, Radiation Biol Sect, Lab Pathophysiol, 81-83, SR INVESTR, RADIATION BIOL BR, NAT CANCER INST, 83- *Personal Data:* b Vienna, Austria, Oct 2, 26; US citizen; m 53; c 3. *Educ:* Oxford Univ, BA, 46, BSc, 47; Columbia Univ, PhD(phys chem), 53. *Prof Exp:* Res assoc phys chem, Pa State Univ, 53-54; res assoc, Brookhaven Nat Lab, 54-56; res assoc radiation chem, Argonne Nat Lab, 56-58. *Mem:* Am Chem Soc; Radiation Res Soc; Am Soc Photobiol; Oxygen Soc; Int Soc Free Radiacal Res; Europ Soc Sonochemistry. *Res:* Sonochemistry; radiation chemistry; effects of ionizing and ultraviolet radiation on nucleic acids and proteins; electron spin resonance; free radical mechanisms; spin trapping; photochemistry; sonodynamic therapy. *Mailing Add:* Nat Cancer Inst Bldg 10 Rm B3B69 Bethesda MD 20892-1002. *Fax:* 301-480-2238; *E-Mail:* sono@helix.nih.gov

RIETHOF, THOMAS ROBERT, PHYSICAL CHEMISTRY, ELECTROOPTICS. *Current Pos:* Physicist, Aerophys Applns, 56-63, mgr reentry physics, 64-68, mgr sensor systs, 68-80, CONSULT PHYSICIST, SPACE SYSTS DIV, GEN ELEC CO, PHILADELPHIA, 80- *Personal Data:* b Teplice, Czech, July 29, 27; nat US; m 49. *Educ:* Manchester Col, AB, 49; Purdue Univ, MSc, 51, PhD(phys chem), 54. *Mem:* AAAS; Am Chem Soc; Optical Soc Am; Am Inst Aeronaut & Astronaut. *Res:* Electrooptical sensors and experiments; remote sensing, optical and infrared, military and civilian; thermal radiation and its measurement. *Mailing Add:* 4124 Barberry Dr Lafayette Hill PA 19444

RIETVELD, WILLIS JAMES, FOREST PHYSIOLOGY. *Current Pos:* MEM STAFF, FORESTRY SCI LAB, RHINELANDER, WIS, PROG MGR, CTR FOR SEMI-ARID AGRIFORESTRY, UNIV NEBR, 88- *Personal Data:* b Harvey, Ill, Oct 30, 42. *Educ:* Ore State Univ, BS, 65, MS, 67; Univ Ariz, PhD(plant physiol), 74. *Prof Exp:* Res plant physiologist, Rocky Mountain Forest & Range Exp Sta, US Forest Serv, Forestry Sci Lab, Northern Ariz Univ, 66-76; prin plant physiologist, North Cent Forest Exp Sta, Forestry Sci Lab, Southern Ill Univ, 76- *Mem:* Soc Am Foresters; Sigma Xi. *Res:* Physiological quality of tree planting stock and post-planting seedling growth; water relations; allelopathy. *Mailing Add:* 8501 Sandalwood Dr Lincoln NE 68520

RIEWALD, PAUL GORDON, MATERIALS SCIENCE, FIBER SCIENCE & SYSTEMS. *Current Pos:* Res engr mat eng & develop, E I Du Pont de Nemours & Co Inc, 68-74, sr res engr, 74-77, res assoc mat eng & develop, 77-82, sr res assoc, 82-93, RES FEL, E I DU PONT DE NEMOURS & CO, INC, 93- *Personal Data:* b E Grand Rapids, Mich, Aug 31, 41; m 68, Kathryn F (VerMerris); c Scott & Brian. *Educ:* Univ Mich, BS, 63, MS, 64, PhD(metall eng), 68. *Res:* Characterization and study of fibrous materials; industrial applications, research and development of products from fibers including advanced composites; ropes and cables; ballistic armor; fiber reinforced cement/concrete, automotive uses; protective apparel. *Mailing Add:* 1002 Industrial Rd E I Du Pont de Nemours & Co Inc Old Hickory TN 37138

RIFAS, LEONARD, METABOLISM, BONE RESEARCH. *Current Pos:* RES INSTR MED, JEWISH HOSP, SCH MED, WASH UNIV, ST LOUIS, 79- *Personal Data:* b Sept 20, 46; m 69, Geraldine Shapiro; c Joanne A & Stephanie M. *Educ:* Univ Mo, Columbia, AB, 69, MS, 73. *Prof Exp:* Dir, Cell Cult Lab, Dept Biochem, Albert Einstein Col Med, Bronx, NY, 73-79. *Concurrent Pos:* Reviewer, J Calcified Tissue Int, J Bone & Mineral Res, J Cell & Tissue Res, Am J Physiol, J Clin Endocrinol & Metab. *Mem:* Am Soc Cell Biol; AAAS; Am Soc Bone & Mineral Res; NY Acad Sci; Fedn Am Soc Exp Biol; Endocrine Soc. *Res:* Study of bone cell biology including effect of cytokines on bone cell physiology and function; relationship of immune system products on the pathophysiology of osteoporosis; study of metalloproteinase secretion by bone cells under the influence of cytokines; immunological assays; immunology; cell biology; bone cell metabolism. *Mailing Add:* Dept Internal Med Div Bone Wash Univ Sch Med 216 S Kingshiway St Louis MO 63110-1092. *Fax:* 314-454-5325

RIFE, WILLIAM C, ORGANIC CHEMISTRY. *Current Pos:* HEAD, DEPT CHEM, CALIF POLYTECH STATE UNIV, 77- *Personal Data:* b Chicago, Ill, Dec 29, 33; m 62, 70. *Educ:* NCent Col, BA, 56; Univ Ill, PhD(chem), 60. *Prof Exp:* Assoc prof chem, Parsons Col, 60-62; patent chemist, Owens-Ill Glass Co, 62-64; prof chem, NCent Col, 64-72, chmn div humanities, 72-76; fel, Pa State Univ, 76-77. *Mem:* AAAS; Am Chem Soc. *Res:* Organometallic compounds; isobenzofurans. *Mailing Add:* 2795 Johnson Ave San Luis Obispo CA 93401

RIFFEE, WILLIAM HARVEY, PHARMACOLOGY. *Current Pos:* ASST PROF PHARMACOL, UNIV TEX, AUSTIN, 75- *Personal Data:* b Steubenville, Ohio, Feb 17, 44; m 67; c 1. *Educ:* WVa Univ, BS Pharm, 67; Ohio State Univ, PhD(pharmacol), 75. *Prof Exp:* Pharm officer, USPHS, 67-70; teaching & res assoc pharmacol, Col Pharm, Ohio State Univ, 71-75. *Mem:* Am Pharmaceut Asn. *Res:* Investigation of the effects of drugs on the central nervous systems with particular emphasis on neurotransmitter dynamics; the study of the mechanisms responsible for the development of tolerance to and physiological dependence on various drugs of abuse. *Mailing Add:* Col Pharm Rm 2 220BA Univ Tex Austin TX 78712-1199

RIFFER, RICHARD, NATURAL PRODUCTS CHEMISTRY, AIR & WATER POLLUTION. *Current Pos:* CHIEF CHEMIST, CALIF & HAWAIIAN SUGAR CO, 72- *Personal Data:* b Chicago, Ill, Dec 3, 39. *Educ:* Ind Univ, BS, 61; Univ Calif, Berkeley, MS, 63, PhD(agr chem), 67. *Prof Exp:* Asst specialist, natural prod chem, Forest Prod Lab, Univ Calif, Berkeley, 63-69; res chemist, US Forest Serv, 69-72. *Concurrent Pos:* Res chemist, Statewide Air Pollution Res Ctr, Univ Calif, 69-72; exec comt, US Nat Comt Sugar Anal; fac, Cane Sugar Refiners Inst, Nicholls State Univ, Thibodaux, La, 89- *Mem:* Am Chem Soc; Am Asn Sugar Beet Technol; Asn Off Anal Chem; Int Comn Uniform Methods Sugar Anal. *Res:* Structure elucidation of natural products; pyrolysis mechanisms; cellulose biosynthesis; electrokinetic properties of colloids; ion exchange and reverse osmosis; flavor and aroma chemistry; light scattering; polysaccharides; toxicology, cancer and forensic chemistry. *Mailing Add:* 1401 Walnut St Berkeley CA 94709. *Fax:* 510-787-2916

RIFFEY, MERIBETH M, biology, for more information see previous edition

RIFFLE, JERRY WILLIAM, FOREST PATHOLOGY. *Current Pos:* RETIRED. *Personal Data:* b Mishawaka, Ind, Jan 7, 34; m 59; c 6. *Educ:* Mich State Univ, BS, 57, MS, 59; Univ Wis, Madison, PhD(plant path), 62. *Prof Exp:* Res asst forest path, Mich State Univ, 57-58 & Univ Wis, Madison, 58-62; res plant pathologist, USDA Forest Serv, Rocky Mountain Forest & Range Exp Sta, 62-87. *Concurrent Pos:* Plant pathologist, Ace Pest Control, Syracuse, Ind. *Mem:* Am Phytopath Soc; Soc Nematologists; Mycol Soc Am. *Res:* Diseases of trees in plantings and natural stands; mycorrhizae of conifers; forest nematology. *Mailing Add:* RR 4 Syracuse IN 46567

RIFINO, CARL BIAGGIO, PHARMACEUTICAL CHEMISTRY. *Current Pos:* SUPVR PROCESS DEVELOP, ICI AMERICAS, INC, 77- *Personal Data:* b New York, NY, Aug 21, 38; m 64; c 5. *Educ:* Fordham Univ, BS, 59; St John's Univ, NY, MS, 64; Purdue Univ, West Lafayette, PhD(med chem), 68. *Prof Exp:* Res investr, Olin Mathieson & Co, Inc, 67-68; res investr, Squibb-Beech Nut, Inc, 68-71, preformulations sect, Squibb Corp, 71-72, process develop mgr, Topical & Parenteral Trade Prod, Squibb Corp, 72-76; sect chief new prod develop, Morton-Norwich Corp, 76-77. *Concurrent Pos:* Bd dir, Int Soc Pharmaceut Engrs, 82-86. *Mem:* Am Pharmaceut Asn; Acad Pharmaceut Sci; Sigma Xi; Am Mgt Asn; Parenteral Drug Asn; Int Soc Pharmaceut Engrs; Am Asn Pharmaceut Scientists. *Res:* Physical pharmacy, especially suspension technology and dissolution characteristics of solid solutions; scaleup activities in solids and liquids. pharmaceutical science; process validation activities. *Mailing Add:* PO Box 4520 Newark DE 19714-4520

RIFKIN, ARTHUR, PSYCHOPHARMACOLOGY. *Current Pos:* PSYCHIATRIST, HILLSIDE HOSP, DIV LONG ISLAND JEWISH MED CTR, DIR, MEN RETARDATION & DEVELOPMENTALLY DISABLED SERV, GLEN OAKS, NY, 92-; PROF PSYCHIAT, ALBERT EINSTEIN COL MED. *Personal Data:* b New York, NY, Apr 7, 37; m 61, Eva Buschke; c William & Deborah. *Educ:* Columbia Col, BA, 57; State Univ NY Downstate Med Ctr, MD, 61. *Prof Exp:* Staff psychiatrist, Hillside Hosp, 67-69, dir, Aftercare Clin, 69-76; res psychiatrist, NY State Psychiat Inst, 76-79; assoc clin prof psychiat, Col Physicians & Surgeons, 77-79; dir, Div Clin Psychopharmacol Res, Mt Sinai Med Ctr & assoc prof, 79-84, prof psychiat, Mt Sinai Sch Med, 84-88; asst dir psychiat, Queens Hosp Ctr, Jamaica, NY, 88-92. *Concurrent Pos:* Fel psychiat res, State Univ NY Downstate Med Ctr, 67-69. *Mem:* Fel Am Col Neuropsychopharmacol; Collegium Int Neuropsychopharmacologicicum; Am Psychopath Asn; Psychiat Res Soc; fel Am Psychiat Asn. *Res:* Drug treatment of schizophrenia, affective disorders, panic disorders and psychiatric disorders in mentally retarded. *Mailing Add:* Hillside Hosp Glen Oaks NY 11004. *Fax:* 718-343-7739

RIFKIN, BARRY RICHARD, EXPERIMENTAL PATHOLOGY, ORAL MEDICINE. *Current Pos:* ASSOC PROF ORAL MED, PATHOBIOL & ORAL PATH, COL DENT, NY UNIV, 80-, CHMN, DEPT ORAL MED, 80-, ASSOC PROF BIOMED SCI, GRAD FAC, COL ARTS & SCI, 81- *Personal Data:* b Trenton, NJ, Mar 30, 40; div; c 2. *Educ:* Ohio State Univ, BS, 61; Univ Ill, MS, 64; Temple Univ, DDS, 68; Univ Rochester, PhD(path), 74. *Prof Exp:* Assoc prof path & dent res, Med Sch, Univ Rochester, 73-80, assoc pathologist, Strong Mem Hosp, 74-80. *Concurrent Pos:* Prin investr, Pathogenesis of Bone Loss in Peridontal Disease, Nat Inst Dent Res, 76-80. *Mem:* Int Acad Path; Int Asn Dent Res; Am Soc Bone & Mineral Res; Sigma Xi. *Res:* Inflammation and bone resorption; mechanisms of localized bone loss; pathogenesis of bone loss in periodontal disease; vitro structure of bone resorption. *Mailing Add:* Div Basic Sci NY Univ Dent Ctr 345 E 24th St New York NY 10010

RIFKIN, ERIK, PATHOBIOLOGY. *Current Pos:* PRES, RIFKIN & ASSOCS, INC, 79- *Personal Data:* b Brooklyn, NY, Sept 13, 40; m 64; c 2. *Educ:* Rutgers Univ, BA, 64; Univ Hawaii, MS, 67, PhD(zool), 69. *Prof Exp:* Res asst biol, Rutgers Univ, 64-65; res asst, Univ Hawaii, 66-67; Nat Res Coun assoc pathobiol, Naval Med Res Inst, 69-70; dir ecol, Antioch Col, 70-72; consult environ planning, Urban Life Ctr, Columbia, Md, 72-73; dir environ studies prog, New Col, 73-74; dir, Environ Planning/Res Inst, 74-78. *Mem:* Am Inst Biol Sci; AAAS; Am Soc Zoologists; Soc Invert Path. *Res:* Pathobiology of invertebrates, with emphasis on those organisms cultured for aquaculture and/or mariculture systems; surface mining and the environment; environmental policy; analysis and evaluation of the adverse environmental effects caused by coal and nonfuel mining operations. *Mailing Add:* 2901 Boston St, No 314 Baltimore MD 21224

RIFKIND, ARLEEN B, TOXICOLOGY, ENDOCRINOLOGY. *Current Pos:* asst prof pediat, Cornell Univ, 71-75, asst prof med, 71-82, from asst prof to assoc prof pharmacol, 73-82, chmn Gen Fac Coun, 84-86, PROF PHARMACOL & ASSOC PROF MED, MED COL, CORNELL UNIV, 83- *Personal Data:* b New York, NY, June 29, 38; m 61, Robert S; c Amy & Nina. *Educ:* Bryn Mawr Col, BA, 60; NY Univ, MD, 64. *Prof Exp:* Intern med, III & IV Med Div, Bellevue Hosp, 64-65, first year resident, 65; clin assoc endocrine br, Nat Cancer Inst, 65-68; res assoc endocrine pharmacol, Rockefeller Univ, 68-71. *Concurrent Pos:* Staff fel, Nat Inst Child Health & Human Develop, 65-68; USPHS spec fel, Rockefeller Univ, 68-70; USPHS spec fel, 71-72; adj asst prof, Rockefeller Univ, 71-74; prin investr grants, Nat Found, Am Cancer Soc, NY State Health Res Found, Nat Inst Environ Health Sci, 72-; mem, Environ Health Sci Review Comt, Nat Inst Environ Health Sci, 81-83 & 84-85, chmn, 85-; Superfund Basic Res Prog Review Group, 87, 88; mem, Toxicol Study Sect, 89-93; mem, Environ Health & Safety Coun, Am Health Found, 90-94; bd sci counr, Agency Toxic Substances & Dis Registry, USPHS, 92- *Mem:* AAAS; Am Soc Pharmacol & Exp Therapeut; Am Soc Clin Pharmacol; Endocrine Soc; Am Soc Clin Invest; Toxicol Soc. *Res:* Mechanisms of polychlorinated biphenyl and dioxin toxicity; p450 and arachidonic acid metabolism; heme, porphyrin and mixed function oxidase regulation; biochemical pharmacology. *Mailing Add:* Dept Pharmacol Med Col Cornell Univ 1300 York Ave New York NY 10021-4896. *Fax:* 212-746-8835

RIFKIND, BASIL M, LIPID METABOLISM RESEARCH. *Current Pos:* dep chief, Lipid Metab Br, 71-74, proj officer, Lipid Res Clin Prog, 71-80, CHIEF, LIPID METAB-ATHEROGENESIS BR, DIV HEART & VASCULAR DIS, NAT HEART, LUNG & BLOOD INST, 74-, DEP ASSOC DIR, HYPERTENSION, ARTERIOSCLEROSIS & LIPID METAB PROG, 79- *Personal Data:* b Glasgow, Scotland, Sept 17, 34; US citizen; m; c 3. *Educ:* Univ Glasgow, MB, ChB, 57, MD, 72; FRCP(G), 73. *Honors & Awards:* Watson Prize Lectr, Royal Col Physicians & Surgeons, Glasgow, 70. *Prof Exp:* House surgeon, County Hosp, Ormskirk, Eng, 57-58; house physician, Royal Infirmary, Glasgow, Scotland, 58, sr house officer internal med, 59-60, registrar, 60-63, registrar internal med to prof, E M McGirr Univ Dept Med, 63-65, sr registrar, Glasgow Teaching Hosp, 65-71. *Concurrent Pos:* Sr house officer clin path, Crumpsall Hosp, Manchester, Eng, 58-59. *Res:* Hypertension; internal medicine; vascular diseases. *Mailing Add:* 11710 Farmland Dr Rockville MD 20852

RIFKIND, DAVID, INTERNAL MEDICINE, INFECTIOUS DISEASES. *Current Pos:* PROF MICROBIOL & HEAD DEPT, UNIV ARIZ, COL MED, 67-, PROF MED, 71-, HEAD SECT INFECTIOUS DIS, 71- , CLIN PROF, DEPT INT MED SECT INFECTIOUS DIS, 83- *Personal Data:* b Los Angeles, Calif, Mar 11, 29; m 57; c 2. *Educ:* Univ Calif, Los Angeles, AB, 50, PhD(microbiol), 53; Univ Chicago, MD, 57. *Prof Exp:* Res asst, Univ Chicago, 55-57; clin assoc, Nat Inst Allergy & Infectious Dis, 59-61; from instr to asst prof med, Univ Colo Med Ctr, Denver, 62-67, head, Sect Infectious Dis, 66-67. *Concurrent Pos:* Consult, Fitzsimons Gen Hosp, Denver, 64-; attend physician, Vet Admin Hosp, 66- *Mem:* Am Soc Microbiol; Am Fedn Clin Res; Infectious Dis Soc Am. *Res:* Infectious diseases complicating immunosuppressive drug therapy; mechanisms of action of endotoxin; respiratory, viral and mycoplasmal infections; viral latency and activation; antimicrobial drug therapy. *Mailing Add:* PO Box 17568 Munds Park AZ 86017

RIFKIND, JOSEPH MOSES, PHYSICAL BIOCHEMISTRY. *Current Pos:* res chemist, 73-85, CHIEF, SECT MOLECULAR DYNAMICS, NAT INST AGING, 85- *Personal Data:* b New York, NY, Jan 13, 40; m 64; c 4. *Educ:* Yeshiva Univ, BA, 61; Columbia Univ, MA, 62, PhD(phys chem), 66. *Prof Exp:* Res assoc biophys chem, Univ Minn, 65-67; from staff fel to sr staff fel molecular biol, Geront Nat Inst Child Health & Human Develop, 68-73. *Concurrent Pos:* Pegram hon fel, 65-66; NIH fel, 67. *Mem:* AAAS; Am Chem Soc; Biophys Soc; Geront Soc. *Res:* Thermodynamics and kinetics of conformational transitions in polypeptides, proteins and nucleic acids; structure function relationships in proteins and nucleic acids; oxygenation of hemoglobin; interaction between proteins and nucleic acids; regulation of oxygen transport; hemolysis of the erythrocyte; the erythrocyte membrane; membrane fluidity; oxyradicals. *Mailing Add:* Nat Inst Aging 4940 Eastern Ave Baltimore MD 21224

RIFKIND, RICHARD A, MEDICINE, HEMATOLOGY. *Current Pos:* MEM, SLOAN-KETTERING INST & DIR, SLOAN-KETTERING DIV, GRAD SCH MED SCI, CORNELL UNIV, 81-, CHMN, SLOAN-KETTERING INST, 83- *Personal Data:* b New York, NY, Oct 26, 30; m 56; c 2. *Educ:* Yale Univ, BS, 52; Columbia Univ, MD, 55. *Prof Exp:* Intern med, Presby Hosp, New York, 55-56, resident, 56-57 & 60-61; assoc med, Col Physicians & Surgeons, Columbia Univ, 62-63, from asst prof to prof med & human genetics, 63-81. *Concurrent Pos:* Nat Found fel, 59-60; USPHS trainee hemat, 61-62; Guggenheim fel, 65-66. *Mem:* Am Soc Cell Biol; Asn Am Physicians; Am Soc Clin Invest; Electron Micros Soc Am; Am Soc Hemat. *Res:* Developmental biology; molecular biology; hematology. *Mailing Add:* Mem Sloan-Kettering Cancer Ctr 1275 York Ave New York NY 10021-6094

RIGA, ALAN, PHYSICAL CHEMISTRY, MATERIALS SCIENCES. *Current Pos:* SR RES CHEMIST, LUBRIZOL CORP, 60- *Personal Data:* b Cleveland, Ohio, Apr 17, 37. *Educ:* Case Western Res Univ, BA, 60, MS, 62, PhD(chem physics), 67. *Mem:* Fel Soc Plastics Engrs; fel NAm Thermal Anal Soc; Am Soc Testing & Mat; Am Chem Soc. *Mailing Add:* Lubrizol Corp 29400 Lakeland Blvd Wickliffe OH 44092-2298

RIGAMER, ELMORE F, PSYCHIATRY. *Current Pos:* Regional psychiatrist, SAsia, Europ & Soviet Union, US State Dept, Washington, DC, 77-87, dir, Ment Health Servs, 87-88, dep asst secy ment health, 88-91, dep asst secy med affairs, 91-92, DEP ASST SECY STATE & MED DIR, US STATE DEPT, 94-; CLIN PROF PSYCHIAT, SCH MED, GEORGE WASHINGTON UNIV, 90- *Educ:* Spring Hill Col, BS, 62; La State Univ, MD, 66; Harvard Univ, MPA, 93; Am Bd Psychiat & Neurol, dipl. *Prof Exp:* Assoc prof psychiat & pub health, Sch Med, Univ Liberia, 71-73; dir child & adolescent psychiat, Ochsner Clin, New Orleans, La, 73-77. *Concurrent Pos:* Asst med dir, Catherine Mills Psychiat Hosp, Peace Corps, 71-73; consult, La State Dept Ment Health, 73-77, Cath Charities of Archidiocese New Orleans, 73-77, Near E SAsia Coun Int Educ, 77-, Kaiser Permanente Health Maintenance Orgn, 88-92 & Christ Child Soc Archdiocese Wash, 92-; clin assoc prof pediat & child psychiat, Sch Med, Tulane Univ, 75-77; fel, John F Kennedy Sch Govt, Harvard Univ, 92-93. *Mem:* Fel Am Psychiat Asn; Am Col Physician Execs; Am Col Psychiatrists. *Mailing Add:* 4412 Westover Pl NW Washington DC 20016

RIGANATI, JOHN PHILIP, ELECTRICAL ENGINEERING, APPLIED MATHEMATICS. *Current Pos:* DIR COMM COMPUT, SARNOFF CORP. *Personal Data:* b Mt Vernon, NY, Apr 11, 44; m 66; c 3. *Educ:* Rensselaer Polytech Inst, BEE, 65, MEng, 66, PhD(elec eng), 69. *Honors & Awards:* Eng of Yr Award, Rockwell Int, 77. *Prof Exp:* Co-op engr commun systs, Advan Systs Develop Div, IBM Corp, 61-63, co-op engr thin films & CPU design, Res Div, 63-65; engr mini-comput control systs, Syst Sales & Eng, Gen Elec Co, 67; instr elec eng, Rensselaer Polytech Inst, 68-69; mem tech staff pattern recognition, Electronics Res Ctr, Rockwell Int Corp, 69-77, chief scientist identification systs, Collins Commun Switching Systs Div, Com Telecommun Group, 77-80; chief comput syst component div, Nat Bur Stand, 80-85; dir syst res, Supercomputing Res Ctr, 85- *Concurrent Pos:* Lectr, Inst Elec & Electronics Engrs, 75-78; co-ed, J Supercomput, 85- *Mem:* Inst Elec & Electronics Engrs; Pattern Recognition Soc; Sigma Xi; Asn Comput Mach. *Res:* Pattern recognition applied to identification systems and image and speech processing; queueing and statistical sampling theory; distributed computer systems; microfilm information retrieval; digital signal processing; coding and decoding; cryptography; data base design; music theory; high performance computer architecture, operating systems, compilers, languages and performance measures. *Mailing Add:* Sarnoff Corp Corp & Comput Lab 10 Saxon Way Skillman NJ 08558

RIGAS, ANTHONY L, ELECTRICAL ENGINEERING. *Current Pos:* from asst prof to assoc prof, 66-73, PROF ELEC ENG & DIR ENG EDUC, OUTREACH DIV, UNIV IDAHO, 73- *Personal Data:* b Andros, Greece, May 3, 31; US citizen; m 59; c 1. *Educ:* Univ Kans, BSEE, 58, MSEE, 62; Univ Beverly Hills, PhD(eng), 78. *Prof Exp:* Elec engr, US Naval Missile Ctr, Point Mugu, 58-61; teaching fel, Univ Kans, 61-63; sr res engr, Lockheed Missile & Space Div, 63-65, Delmo Victor Co, 65-66. *Concurrent Pos:* Asst prof, Grad Prog, San Jose State Col, 63-65; NASA-Stanford faculty fel, 67; NSF fel, Princeton Univ, 68; US Cong fel, AAAS, 75-76 & Inst Elec & Electronics Engrs; Cong fel, Inst Elec & Electronics Engrs. *Mem:* Am Soc Eng Educ; Simulation Coun; Sigma Xi; fel Inst Elec & Electronics Engrs. *Res:* Missiles and space vehicles guidance and control systems; biological and environmental systems analysis; computer simulation. *Mailing Add:* 4000 Hwy 200 E Sandpoint ID 83864

RIGAS, DEMETRIOS A, BIOCHEMISTRY, BIOPHYSICS. *Current Pos:* From res asst to res assoc biochem, 47-53, from asst prof to prof, 53-86, EMER PROF BIOCHEM, MED SCH, ORE HEALTH SCI UNIV, 86- *Personal Data:* b Andros, Greece, Feb 2, 21; US citizen; m 55; c 2. *Educ:* Univ Eng Sci, Athens, ChE, PhD(phys chem), 41. *Concurrent Pos:* Vis prof, Med Sch, Univ Athens & Democritos Ctr Nuclear Res, 70-71. *Mem:* Sigma Xi; Am Asn Biol Chemists; Biophys Soc; Am Chem Soc; NY Acad Sci. *Res:* Biophysical chemistry of proteins; effects of ionizing radiations on mammalian cells; lymphocyte transformation and function; kinetics of cell proliferation. *Mailing Add:* 6420 SW 90th Ave Portland OR 97223-7219

RIGASSIO, JAMES LOUIS, ENGINEERING. *Current Pos:* asst prof, 58-59, assoc prof, 59-65, PROF INDUST ENG, NEWARK COL ENG, 65-, CHMN DEPT, 69- *Personal Data:* b Union City, NJ, Aug 13, 23; m 59; c 4. *Educ:* Newark Col Eng, BS, 48; Yale Univ, ME, 49. *Prof Exp:* Develop engr, Johnson & Johnson, 49-52, indust engr, Ethicon Inc Div, 52-55, chief engr, 55-58. *Concurrent Pos:* Adj prof, Newark Col Eng, 56-58; grants, Newark Col Eng Res Found, 62-63 & 68-69; consult, NJ Sch Bds Asn, 68- & Nat Asn Advan Colored People, 71- *Mem:* Am Soc Mech Engrs; Am Inst Indust Engrs; Am Soc Eng Educ; Nat Soc Prof Engrs; Indust Rels Res Asn. *Res:* Queuing theory; production process design and control; scheduling theory; work methods; job evaluation. *Mailing Add:* 23 Colony Dr Summit NJ 07901

RIGATTO, HENRIQUE, FETAL & NEWBORN RESPIRATION CONTROL, PEDIATRICS. *Current Pos:* PROF PEDIAT, WOMEN'S HOSP-HEALTH SCI CTR, 80- *Personal Data:* b Porpo Alegre, Brazil, Nov 23, 37. *Educ:* Univ Rio Grande Do Sul, Brazil, MD, 63. *Mem:* Am Fedn Clin Res; Soc Pediat Res; NY Acad Sci. *Mailing Add:* Dept Pediat Reproductive Med & Physiol Univ Man Health Sci Ctr Women's Ctr WR125 735 Notre Dame Ave Winnipeg MB R3E 0L8 Can

RIGAUD, MICHEL JEAN, MATERIALS SCIENCE. *Current Pos:* PROF METALL ENG & CHMN DEPT, POLYTECH SCH, MONTREAL, 76- *Personal Data:* b Paris, France, Oct 22, 39; Can citizen; m 63; c 3. *Educ:* Polytech Sch, Montreal, BApplSc, 63, MApplSc, 64, Dr(metall), 66. *Prof Exp:* Asst prof metall, Polytech Sch, Montreal, 66-71, assoc prof & head dept, 71-74; assoc dir res, Sidbec-Dosco, 74-76. *Concurrent Pos:* Consult, Metall & Mat. *Mem:* Can Metall Soc (treas, 68-); fel Can Inst Mining & Metall (pres, Metall Soc, 76); Am Soc Metals; Am Ceramic Soc. *Res:* Extractive metallurgy; steelmaking; direct reduction; refractories; ceramics. *Mailing Add:* CIREP c/o CRIQ 8475 Christophe Colomb Montreal PQ H2M 2N9 Can

RIGBY, CHARLOTTE EDITH, MICROBIOLOGY, HEALTH SCIENCES. *Current Pos:* RES SCIENTIST VET MICROBIOL, ANIMAL DIS RES INST, 83- *Personal Data:* b Winnipeg, Man, July 9, 40. *Educ:* Univ Man, BSc, 60, MSc, 63; Univ Ottawa, PhD(microbiol), 71; Univ Sask, dipl vet microbiol, 75. *Prof Exp:* Lectr med microbiol, Univ Man, 66-68; res scientist vet microbiol, Inst Animal Sci, Havana, Cuba, 71-73; resident, Univ Sask, 74-75; res scientist vet microbiol, Animal Dis Res Inst, Agr Can, 75-81, Animal Path Lab, 81-83. *Mem:* Am Soc Microbiol; Can Soc Microbiologists. *Res:* Molecular virology of livestock diseases; brucellosis of cattle. *Mailing Add:* 265 Scenic View Close NW Calgary AB T3L 1Y5 Can

RIGBY, DONALD W, PARASITOLOGY. *Current Pos:* RETIRED. *Personal Data:* b Anaheim, Calif, Feb 14, 29; m 50; c 1. *Educ:* La Sierra Col, BA, 50; Walla Walla Col, MA, 56; Loma Linda Univ, PhD(biol, parasitol), 67. *Prof Exp:* Med technologist, USPHS Hosp, Ft Worth, Tex, 53-54; prof parasitol, Walla Walla Col, 58-92. *Mem:* AAAS; Am Soc Parasitol; Am Soc Zool; Sigma Xi. *Res:* General parasitology; host-parasite relationships; invertebrate zoology. *Mailing Add:* 14655 Oak St No 3 Saratoga CA 95070

RIGBY, F LLOYD, AGRICULTURAL CHEMISTRY, BIOCHEMISTRY. *Current Pos:* vpres, 69-79, TECH DIR, JOHN I HAAS, INC, 65-, EXEC VPRES, 80- *Personal Data:* b Calgary, Alta, Nov 10, 18; m 63; c 2. *Educ:* Univ Alta, BSc, 42, MSc, 44; McGill Univ, PhD(agr chem), 48. *Prof Exp:* Sr res chemist, Res Div, Can Breweries, 48-63, dir res, 63-65. *Mem:* Am Soc Brewing Chemists; Master Brewers Asn Am; Brit Inst Brewing; Am Chem Soc. *Res:* Plant biochemistry; fermentation biochemistry; food flavors; development of hop concentration. *Mailing Add:* 6801 Alpine Way Yakima WA 98908

RIGBY, J KEITH, PALEONTOLOGY. *Current Pos:* RETIRED. *Personal Data:* b Fairview, Utah, Oct 8, 26; m 45, Ruth M Krebs; c J Keith Jr, Claudia M (Bosworth) & Jaynanne (Meads). *Educ:* Brigham Young Univ, BS, 48, MS, 49; Columbia Univ, PhD(geol), 52. *Prof Exp:* Geologist, Carter Oil Co, 47-48; geologist, Humble Oil & Refining Co, 52-53; from asst prof to prof geol, Brigham Young Univ, 53-90, actg dean, Grad Sch, 90-91. *Concurrent Pos:* Consult geologist, Union Oil Co Can, 60-74 & Phillips Petrol Co, 75; vis prof, La State Univ, 65; ed, J Paleont, 82-85. *Mem:* Geol Soc Am; Paleont Soc; Am Asn Petrol Geologists; Geol Asn Can; Paleont Asn; Soc Econ Paleont Mineral. *Res:* Carbonate deposition and paleoecology of reefs; Upper Paleozoic paleontology; regional geology of Utah, Nevada and Western Canada; fossil sponges and reefs of the world; paleoecology. *Mailing Add:* 496 E 4380 N Provo UT 84604. *Fax:* 801-378-8143

RIGBY, PAUL HERBERT, MANAGEMENT SCIENCES, APPLIED STATISTICS. *Current Pos:* RETIRED. *Personal Data:* b Humboldt, Ariz, Aug 6, 24; m 54; c 2. *Educ:* Univ Tex, Austin, BBA, 45, MBA, 48, PhD(statist), 52. *Prof Exp:* Sr price economist, Regional Off, Off Price Stabilization, Wash, 51-52; res assoc & asst prof mkt & regional econ, Bur Bus Res, Univ Ala, 52-54; assoc prof statist & dir, Ctr Res Bus & Econ, Ga State Univ, 54-56; prof econ & dir, Ctr Res Bus & Econ, Univ Houston, 56-62; assoc prof mgt & dir, Bus Studies, Ctr Res, Univ Mo, Columbia, 62-64; prof mgt sci & dir, Div Res & Grad Progs, Pa State Univ, University Park, 64-95. *Concurrent Pos:* Fulbright fel, Nat Univ Mex, 62; vpres, Assoc Univs Bus & Econ Res, 66-67, pres, 67-68; consult, Inst Politecnicol Nacional, Mexico City, 81; pres, Centre Community Hosp Corp, 87- *Mem:* Am Statist Asn; Inst Mgt Sci; Am Inst Decision Sci. *Res:* Cost benefit analysis; problem solving and decision making; program analysis and evaluation; managerial economics. *Mailing Add:* 131 Legion Lane State College PA 16801

RIGBY, PERRY G, INTERNAL MEDICINE, HEMATOLOGY. *Current Pos:* dean, 81-85, chancellor, 85-94, PROF MED, LA STATE UNIV, SHREVEPORT, 78-, DIR, HEALTH CARE SYSTS, MED CTR, 94- *Personal Data:* b East Liverpool, Ohio, July 1, 32; m 57, Joan Worthington; c Matthew, Peter, Thomas & Martha. *Educ:* Mt Union Col, BS, 53; Western Reserve Univ, MD, 57. *Hon Degrees:* DSc, Mount Union Col, 76. *Honors & Awards:* Markle Scholar Acad Med, 65. *Prof Exp:* Intern med, Univ Va Hosp, 58, resident, 58-60; clin asst, Boston City Hosp, 61-62; fel hemat, Mass Mem Hosp, 62; from asst prof to assoc prof, Univ Nebr Med Ctr, Omaha, 64-69, prof anat, 69-74, prof hemat, 68-74, prof internal med, 69-78, asst dean curric, 71-72, assoc dean acad affairs, 72-74, prof med educ, chmn dept med & educ admin & dean, Col Med, 74-78. *Concurrent Pos:* Head hemat, Eugene C Eppley Inst, 64-68; Markle scholar acad med, 65. *Mem:* Am Chem Soc; Am Soc Hemat; Am Asn Cancer Res; fel Am Col Physicians; Int Soc Hemat. *Res:* Immunology; cancer biology; RNA metabolism. *Mailing Add:* La State Univ Med Ctr 433 Bolivar St New Orleans LA 70112-2223. *Fax:* 504-568-5588

RIGDEN, JOHN SAXBY, ACOUSTICS. *Current Pos:* assoc prof, 68-74, PROF PHYSICS UNIV MO, ST LOUIS, 74- ; Dir PHYSICS PROG, AM INST PHYSICS, 87- *Personal Data:* b Painesville, Ohio, Jan 10, 34; m 53, Diana Wyllie; c 6. *Educ:* Eastern Nazarene Col, BS, 56; Johns Hopkins Univ, PhD(phys chem), 60. *Hon Degrees:* DSc, Denison Univ, 95. *Prof Exp:* Res fel chem physics, Harvard Univ, 60-61; asst prof physics, Eastern Nazarene Col, 61-64, assoc prof & head dept, 64-67; assoc prof, Middlebury Col, 67-68. *Concurrent Pos:* Res assoc, Harvard Univ, 66-67; Nat Endowment Humanities grant, 70; US rep, Int Sci Exhib, Burma, 70; Fulbright fel, Burma,

71, Uruguay, 75; ed, Am J Physics, 78- *Mem:* Am Phys Soc; Am Asn Physics Teachers; Hist Sci Soc; fel AAAS. *Res:* History and philosophy of science; teaching of science. *Mailing Add:* Amer Inst One Physics Ellipse College Park MD 20740. *Fax:* 301-229-3831; *E-Mail:* jsr@aip.org

RIGDON, ORVILLE WAYNE, ORGANIC CHEMISTRY, PETROLEUM CHEMISTRY. *Current Pos:* SR PROJ CHEMIST, RES & TECH DEPT, TEXACO INC, PORT ARTHUR, 72- *Personal Data:* b Ashland, La, Aug 25, 32; m 55; c 2. *Educ:* Northwestern State Col, La, BS, 58; Univ Va, PhD(org photo oxidation), 66. *Mem:* AAAS; Am Chem Soc. *Res:* Petrochemicals applied research; additives and commodity chemicals. *Mailing Add:* 4618 Fountainhead Dr Houston TX 77066-2635

RIGDON, RAYMOND HARRISON, NEOPLASM, EXPERIMENTAL INFLAMMATION. *Current Pos:* RETIRED. *Personal Data:* Musella, Ga, Jul 30, 05. *Educ:* Emory Univ, MD, 31. *Prof Exp:* Prof Path, Med Br, Univ Tex, Galveston. *Mailing Add:* 373 S Main St Madison GA 30650-1610

RIGDON, ROBERT DAVID, TOPOLOGY. *Current Pos:* asst prof, 75-80, ASSOC PROF MATH, IND UNIV-PURDUE UNIV, INDIANAPOLIS, 80- *Personal Data:* b Louisville, Ky, Dec 11, 42. *Educ:* Princeton Univ, AB, 65; Univ Calif, Berkeley, PhD(math), 70. *Prof Exp:* Asst prof math, Northwestern Univ, 70-72; vis asst prof, Univ Ky, 72-73; lectr, Calif State Univ, Dominguez Hills, 73-75. *Mem:* Sigma Xi; Am Math Soc. *Res:* Obstruction theory in algebraic topology. *Mailing Add:* 2822 Lake Forest Indianapolis IN 46268-1244

RIGERT, JAMES ALOYSIUS, ROCK MECHANICS. *Current Pos:* Asst prof, 73-79, ASSOC PROF GEOPHYS, UNIV NOTRE DAME, 79- *Personal Data:* b Beaverton, Ore, Feb 13, 35. *Educ:* Univ Portland, BS, 57; Cornell Univ, MS, 60; Univ Ill, PhD(physics), 72; Tex A&M Univ, PhD(geophys), 80. *Mem:* AAAS; Am Geophys Union; Geol Soc Am; Sigma Xi. *Res:* Deformation processes in rock; internal deformation, rock strength, and frictional properties of surfaces at high pressures. *Mailing Add:* Dept Civil Eng & Geol Sci Univ Notre Dame Notre Dame IN 46556-0767. *E-Mail:* jrigert@rayleigh.ce.nd.edu

RIGGI, STEPHEN JOSEPH, GENERAL MANAGEMENT. *Current Pos:* PRES & CHIEF EXEC OFFICER, TELOR OPHTHAL PHARMACEUT, INC, 89- *Personal Data:* b Pa, Oct 11, 37; m 57; c 3. *Educ:* Univ Scranton, BS, 59; Univ Tenn, MS, 61, PhD(psysiol), 63. *Prof Exp:* Group leader, Pennwalt Pharmaceut Div, Lederle Labs, 63-74, dir pharmacol, 74-76, dir biol res, 76-81, vpres res & develop, 81-85, exec vpres, 85-86, pres, 86-88. *Mem:* Am Soc Pharmacol & Exp Therapeut; Asn Res Vision & Ophthal. *Res:* Development of pharmaceuticals for treatment of age-related diseases of the eye. *Mailing Add:* 58 Skytop Rd Ipswich MA 01938-1478

RIGGLE, EVERETT C, NUMERICAL ANALYSIS. *Current Pos:* PROF MATH, CALIF STATE UNIV, CHICO, 58-, CHMN DEPT, 73- *Personal Data:* b Spokane, Wash, Aug 4, 32; m 52; c 3. *Educ:* Eastern Wash State Col, AB, 52; Ore State Univ, MS, 58. *Concurrent Pos:* NSF fac fel. *Mem:* Asn Comput Mach; Math Asn Am. *Res:* Gradient methods for the solution of linear systems; Tchcbycheff approximation. *Mailing Add:* Dept Math Calif State Univ Chico CA 95929-1000

RIGGLE, J(OHN) W(EBSTER), CHEMICAL & ELECTRICAL ENGINEERING. *Current Pos:* RETIRED. *Personal Data:* b Painesville, Ohio, Feb 6, 24; wid. *Educ:* Carnegie Inst Technol, BSc, 45; Univ Mich, MS, 46; Univ Del, MSc, 61. *Prof Exp:* Res engr, E I du Pont de Nemours & Co, Inc, Wilmington, 46-64, staff engr, Tenn, 64-69, sr res engr, WVa, 69-73, process engr, Design Div, Del, 73-76, sr develop engr, 76-78, proj coordr, Photo Prod Dept, NY, 78-82. *Mem:* Sigma Xi. *Res:* Fundamental engineering properties of materials; high vacuum fluid dynamics; mass transfer operations; photoelectric analysis; process dynamics; high polymer technology; water gel explosives technology; nitric acid technology; electronic thick film technology. *Mailing Add:* 121 Westminster Dr Dover DE 19904

RIGGLE, JOHN H, MATHEMATICS. *Current Pos:* RETIRED. *Personal Data:* b Avella, Pa, May 28, 26; m 51; c 2. *Educ:* Washington & Jefferson Col, BA, 50; Univ Pittsburgh, MLitt, 52; Cent Mich Univ, MA, 64. *Prof Exp:* Teacher high sch, Pa, 50-64; assoc prof math, California State Col, Pa, 64-91. *Mailing Add:* 623 McGovern Rd Houston PA 15342

RIGGLE, TIMOTHY A, MATHEMATICS. *Current Pos:* assoc prof, 68-76, PROF MATH & GRAD FAC, BALDWIN-WALLACE COL, 76-, PROF & DEPT HEAD, MATH & COMPUT SCI, 84- *Personal Data:* b Coshocton, Ohio, Dec 24, 40; div; c 4. *Educ:* Wittenberg Univ, AB, 62, MEd, 66; Ohio State Univ, PhD(math educ), 68; Case Western Res Univ, MS, 76. *Prof Exp:* Instr math, Lima Campus, Ohio State Univ, 66-68. *Mem:* Math Asn Am; Asn Comput Mach. *Res:* Mathematics education; operations research. *Mailing Add:* Dept Math Baldwin-Wallace Col 275 Eastland Rd Berea OH 44017

RIGGLEMAN, JAMES DALE, HORTICULTURE, PLANT PHYSIOLOGY. *Current Pos:* DIR CORP DEVELOP, STEWART CO, MACON, MO, 93- *Personal Data:* b Washington, DC, Feb 6, 33; m 54, Gloria Carroll; c Robert C & Margaret A (Ackroyd). *Educ:* Univ Md, BS, 55, MS, 61, PhD(hort, plant physiol), 64. *Prof Exp:* Res asst hort, Univ Md, 57-64; res biologist, Plant Res Lab, Asia Pac, E I du Pont de Nemours & Co, Inc, 64-67, sr sales res biologist, 67-72, prod develop mgr, 72-78, prod develop coordr, 78-79, mgr field stas, 79, mgr new prod develop, 79-81, mgr licensing & univ relations, 81-84, mgr licensing, 84-93. *Mem:* Fel Weed Sci Soc Am (pres, 85-86); Sigma Xi; Int Weed Sci Soc; Weed Sci Soc Japan; Southern Weed Sci Soc; Northeastern Weed Sci Soc. *Res:* Experimental insecticides, fungicides and herbicides. *Mailing Add:* PO Box 122 Montchanin DE 19710. *Fax:* 302-658-1749; *E-Mail:* 104202.3663@compuserve.com

RIGGS, ARTHUR DALE, MOLECULAR BIOLOGY. *Current Pos:* SR RES SCIENTIST, CITY OF HOPE MED CTR, 69-, CHMN, BIOL DIV, 81-, DEAN, GRAD PROG, 93- *Personal Data:* b Modesto, Calif, Aug 8, 39; m 60; c 3. *Educ:* Univ Calif, Riverside, AB, 61; Calif Inst Technol, PhD(biochem), 66. *Honors & Awards:* Juv Diabetes Found Res Award, 79. *Prof Exp:* USPHS fel, Salk Inst Biol Studies, Calif, 66-69. *Mem:* AAAS. *Res:* Chromosome structure; gene regulation; X chromosome inactivation; DNA methylation. *Mailing Add:* City Hope Med Ctr 1500 Duarte Rd Duarte CA 91010. *Fax:* 626-358-7703

RIGGS, AUSTEN FOX, II, BIOCHEMISTRY. *Current Pos:* from asst prof to assoc prof zool, 56-65, PROF ZOOL, UNIV TEX, AUSTIN, 65- *Personal Data:* b New York, NY, Nov 11, 24; m 52; c 3. *Educ:* Harvard Univ, AB, 48, AM, 49, PhD, 52. *Prof Exp:* Instr biol, Harvard Univ, 53-56. *Mem:* Sigma Xi. *Res:* Biochemistry of proteins. *Mailing Add:* Dept Zool Univ Tex Austin TX 78712-1064

RIGGS, BYRON LAWRENCE, INTERNAL MEDICINE. *Current Pos:* CONSULT, DIV ENDOCRINOL & METAB, MAYO CLIN & FOUND, 62-, PROG DIR, MAYO GEN CLIN RES CTR, 91- *Personal Data:* b Hot Springs, Ark, Mar 24, 31; m 55, Janet T Brewer; c Byron K & Ann T. *Educ:* Univ Ark, BS, 53, MD, 55; Univ Minn, MS, 62. *Honors & Awards:* Clin Investr Award, Endocrine Soc, 89; Frederic C Bartter Award, Am Soc Bone & Mineral Res, 90. *Prof Exp:* Consult internal med, Mayo Clin, 62; from instr to prof med, Mayo Med Sch, Univ Minn, 62-85, chmn, Div Endocrinol, 74-85. *Concurrent Pos:* Royal Soc Med traveling fel, 73; Purvis & Roberta Tabor prof med res, Mayo Med Sch, 87-; distinguished investr, Mayo Found, 91. *Mem:* Am Fedn Clin Res; Endocrine Soc; Am Col Physicians; Am Soc Clin Invest; Am Soc Bone & Mineral Res (pres, 85-86); Asn Am Physicians; Nat Osteoporosis Found (pres, 90-92); Am Col Endocrinol. *Res:* Clinical investigative studies on osteoporosis and bone cell biology; epidemiologic studies, clinical trials and pathophysiological studies on cause and treatment; bone biology studies include assessment of cellular and molecular effects of sex steroids and effects of growth factors in regulating function of cells of the osteoblast lineage. *Mailing Add:* 432 Tenth Ave SW Rochester MN 55902

RIGGS, CARL DANIEL, ZOOLOGY. *Current Pos:* vpres acad affairs & prof biol, Univ SFla, 71-80, dean, grad sch & coordr Univ res, 80-86, interim dean Col Pub Health, 83-84, DIR, CTR EXCELLENCE MATH, SCI & COMPUT TECHNOL, UNIV SFLA, 86- *Personal Data:* b Indianapolis, Ind, Dec 7, 20; m 54; c 4. *Educ:* Univ Mich, BS, 44, MS, 46, PhD(zool), 53. *Prof Exp:* Asst, Univ Mich, 44-45, fel, 45-47; instr zool, Univ Okla, 48-49, asst prof & actg dir, Okla Biol Surv, 49-54, dir, 54-70, from assoc prof to prof zool, 54-71, dir, Univ Biol Sta, 50-69, cur, Mus Zool, 54-66, dean, Grad Col, 65-71, vpres grad studies, 66-71, actg provost, 70-71. *Concurrent Pos:* Consult, Coun Grad Schs, 65-71 & 80-86. *Mem:* AAAS; Am Fisheries Soc; Am Soc Ichthyologists & Herpetologists; Sigma Xi. *Res:* Taxonomy, natural history and distribution of North American fresh water fishes. *Mailing Add:* Univ SFla SCA 464 Tampa FL 33620. *Fax:* 813-974-3572

RIGGS, CHARLES LATHAN, MATHEMATICS. *Current Pos:* assoc prof, 53-60, prof, 60-89, EMER PROF MATH, TEX TECH UNIV, 89- *Personal Data:* b Bearden, Ark, Aug 13, 23; m 51, Virginia Casterton. *Educ:* Tex Christian Univ, BA, 44; Univ Mich, MA, 45; Univ Ky, PhD(math, statist), 49. *Prof Exp:* Instr math, Univ Ky, 46-49; asst prof, Kent State Univ, 49-51; asst prof, East Tex State Univ, 51-53. *Concurrent Pos:* Consult, NSF/USAID on assignment to India, 67 & 68. *Mem:* Am Math Soc; Math Asn Am; Sigma Xi. *Res:* Mathematical statistics; probability. *Mailing Add:* 3805 61st St Lubbock TX 79413-5205

RIGGS, CHARLES LEE, TEXTILES & DETERGENTS. *Current Pos:* Asst prof & detergency res coordr, 74-79, assoc prof, 79-84, PROF, TEX WOMAN'S UNIV RES INST, 84- *Personal Data:* b Clayton, NMex, Aug 21, 46; m 67; c 2. *Educ:* Southwestern Okla State Univ, BS, 67; Okla State Univ, PhD(chem), 74. *Mem:* Am Chem Soc; Am Asn Textile Chemists & Colorists; Sigma Xi; Am Oil Chemists Soc. *Res:* Interactions between surfactants, alkalis and other detergent components and auxiliaries with textile fibers and finishes. *Mailing Add:* PO Box 425529 Denton TX 76204-5529

RIGGS, DIXON L, HUMAN PHYSIOLOGY. *Current Pos:* RETIRED. *Personal Data:* b St Mary's, WVa, June 25, 24; m 52; c 2. *Educ:* Marietta Col, AB, 49; Univ Mich, MS, 50. *Prof Exp:* Res assoc ecol, Inst Human Biol, Univ Mich, 50; asst prof biol, Simpson Col, 51; assoc prof, Huron Col, 52-58; from assoc prof to emer prof biol, Univ Northern Iowa, 58-87. *Mem:* AAAS; Nat Sci Teachers Asn; Am Soc Mammal. *Res:* Mammalian physiology and ecology; alcohol, particularly the ingestion, metabolism and effects on the body. *Mailing Add:* 139 Hawthorne Ave Waterloo IA 50702

RIGGS, HAMMOND GREENWALD, JR, MICROBIOLOGY. *Current Pos:* FROM ASST PROF TO ASSOC PROF MED MICROBIOL MED SCH, UNIV MO, COLUMBIA, 68- *Personal Data:* b Drumright, Okla, July 30, 31; m 59, Harriet Martin; c Madalyn & Martin. *Educ:* Okla State Univ, BA, 55,

MS, 65; Univ Tex Southwestern Med Sch Dallas, PhD(microbiol), 69. *Honors & Awards:* O B Williams Award, Am Soc Microbiol. *Prof Exp:* Res technician & chemist oil prod anal, Jersey Prod Res Co, Okla, 55-62. *Concurrent Pos:* Univ Mo assoc prof advan fel diag virol, Yale Univ, 69; vis prof, King Faisal Univ Col Med, Damman, Saudi Arabia, 83-84, Univ Autonoma Guadalajara, Mex, 87 & 88, Ross Univ Sch Vet Med, St Kitt's, WI, 88. *Mem:* Am Soc Microbiol. *Res:* Bacterial genetics concerned with regulation of biosynthesis of cell wall and virulence factors; diagnostic medical microbiology. *Mailing Add:* Dept Microbiol Univ Mo Columbia Med Sci One Hospital Dr Columbia MO 65201-5276. *Fax:* 573-882-4287

RIGGS, JAMES W, JR, PHYSICS. *Current Pos:* From instr to asst prof math & physics, La Sierra Univ, 47-53, from assoc prof to prof physics, 53-82, head dept, 59-78, EMER PROF PHYSICS, LA SIERRA UNIV, 82- *Personal Data:* b Houston, Tex, Mar 15, 14; m 40, 76, Rosemarie White; c James D & Charles D. *Educ:* Loma Linda Univ, BA, 47; Tex A&M Univ, MS, 53, PhD(physics), 58. *Concurrent Pos:* Radio meteor res, Am Meteor Soc. *Mem:* Am Asn Physics Teachers; Optical Soc Am; Am Phys Soc. *Res:* Molecular physics and spectroscopy. *Mailing Add:* 759 Sourdough Rd West Point CA 95255

RIGGS, KARL A, JR, ECONOMIC GEOLOGY. *Current Pos:* asst prof, 68-73, ASSOC PROF GEOL, MISS STATE UNIV, 73- *Personal Data:* b Thomasville, Ga, Aug 12, 29; m 52, Patricia A Hartrick; c George H, Kathryn A (Keen) & Linda K. *Educ:* Mich State Univ, BS, 51, MS, 52; Iowa State Univ, PhD(geol), 56. *Prof Exp:* Instr geol, Iowa State Univ, 52-56; sr res geologist, Mobil Field Res Lab, 56-59; consult geol, Tex, 59-66; asst prof, Western Mich Univ, 66-68. *Concurrent Pos:* Consult numerous firms, 52-97. *Mem:* Mineral Soc Am; Soc Sedimentary Geol; fel Geol Soc Am; Am Inst Prof Geologists; Asn Eng Geologists; Am Inst Mining, Metall & Petrol Engrs. *Res:* Rock classification; mineralogy and petrology of serpentinite; carbonates; Pleistocene till and loess, stratigraphy and sedimentation; strategic minerals. *Mailing Add:* Dept Gersci Miss State Univ Mississippi State MS 39762-5857. *Fax:* 601-325-2907

RIGGS, LORRIN ANDREWS, PHYSIOLOGICAL PSYCHOLOGY. *Current Pos:* res assoc, 41-45, from asst prof to prof psychol, 45-68 4, Edgar J Marston prof, 68-77, EMER PROF PSYCHOL, BROWN UNIV, 77- *Personal Data:* b Harput, Turkey, June 11, 12; US citizen; m 37, 94, Caroline B Cressman; c Douglas & Dwight. *Educ:* Dartmouth Col, AB, 33; Clark Univ, AM, 34, PhD(psychol), 36. *Honors & Awards:* Warren Medal, 56; Friedenwald Award, 66; Edgar D. Tillyer Award, Optical Soc Am, 69; Ives Medal, 82; Prentice Medal, Am Acad Optom, 73; Distinguished Sci Contrib Award, Am Psychol Asn, 74; Kenneth Craik Award, St Johns Col, Cambridge Univ, 79. *Prof Exp:* Nat Res Coun fel biol sci, Johnson Found Med Physics, Univ Pa, 36-37; instr psychol, Univ Vt, 37-38 & 39-41; res assoc, Brown Univ, 38-39. *Concurrent Pos:* Assoc ed, J Optical Soc Am, Vision Res & Sensory Processes, 62-71; Guggenheim fel, Cambridge Univ, 71-72; pres, Eastern Psychol Asn, 75-76; William James fel, Am Psychol Soc, 89. *Mem:* Nat Acad Sci; AAAS (vpres, 64); Asn Res Vision & Ophthal (pres, 77); Optical Soc Am; Soc Exp Psychol; Am Acad Arts & Sci; Nat Eye Coun. *Res:* Human vision; vision in animals; electric responses in eye. *Mailing Add:* Kendal-at-Hanover 80 Lyme Rd No 104 Hanover NH 03755

RIGGS, LOUIS WILLIAM, ENGINEERING. *Current Pos:* RETIRED. *Personal Data:* b Pearsau, Tex, June 29, 22; m 46; c 2. *Educ:* Univ Calif, Berkeley, BS, 48. *Honors & Awards:* A P Greensfelder Award, Am Soc Civil Engrs, 67. *Prof Exp:* Civil engr, Div Bay Toll Xing, State Calif, 48-51; proj engr, Tudor Eng Co, 51-61, vpres, 61-63, pres, 63-84, chmn, 84-86, consult, 86-88. *Concurrent Pos:* Chmn, Building Futures Coun, 84-88. *Mem:* Nat Acad Eng; Am Pub Works Asn; Soc Mil Engrs (vpres & pres, 80-82); Am Consult Engrs Coun (vpres, 79-81); Am Soc Civil Engrs. *Res:* Consulting civil engineering; application of physical and engineering principals to the design of bridges, highways and transit structures. *Mailing Add:* 3682 Happy Valley Rd Lafayette CA 94549

RIGGS, OLEN LONNIE, JR, CORROSION, ELECTROCHEMISTRY. *Current Pos:* PRES, OLRAN CORP, 91- *Personal Data:* b Bethany, Okla, Aug 25, 25; m 47, Ann R France; c Debra A & Michael O. *Educ:* Eastern Nazarene Col, BS, 49. *Prof Exp:* Group supvr corrosion sci, Continental Oil Co, 52-68; res dir mat eng, Koch Industs, Inc, 68-69; sr res assoc mat, Getty Oil Co, 69-70; sr staff chemist Electro Chem, Kerr-McGee Corp, 71-91. *Mem:* Electrochem Soc; Nat Asn Corrosion Engrs; fel Am Inst Chemists; NY Acad Sci; Sigma Xi. *Res:* New electrolytic processes based on modern concepts; metal/solution interfaces, especially corrosion process and its control; design of electrolytic cells and their component parts; author of 50 papers and granted 71 US patents and 2 books. *Mailing Add:* Olran Corp PO Box 968 Bethany OK 73008. *Fax:* 405-341-8551

RIGGS, PHILIP SHAEFER, astronomy; deceased, see previous edition for last biography

RIGGS, RICHARD, MATHEMATICS EDUCATION. *Current Pos:* from instr to assoc prof, 64-78, PROF MATH, JERSEY CITY STATE COL, 78- *Personal Data:* b Polo, Ill, Oct 8, 38; m 61; c 1. *Educ:* Knox Col, Ill, AB, 60; Rutgers Univ, MA, 64, EdD(math educ), 68; Stevens Inst Technol, MS, 85. *Prof Exp:* High sch teacher, Mich, 60-61 & Tex, 61-63. *Mem:* Math Asn Am. *Res:* Mathematics education at the secondary and undergraduate level. *Mailing Add:* 3 Gianna Ct Randolph NJ 07869-2816. *E-Mail:* riggs@jcs1.jcstate.edu

RIGGS, ROBERT D, PHYTONEMATOLOGY. *Current Pos:* from asst prof to prof, 58-92, UNIV PROF PLANT PATH, UNIV ARK, FAYETTEVILLE, 92- *Personal Data:* b Pocahontas, Ark, June 15, 32; m 54, Jennie L Willis; c Rebecca D, Deborah D, Robert D Jr & James M. *Educ:* Univ Ark, BSA, 54, MS, 56; NC State Col, PhD(plant path), 58. *Honors & Awards:* USDA Superior Serv Award Sci Res, 94; Outstanding Plant Pathologist Award, Southern Div, Am Phys Soc, 95. *Prof Exp:* Asst plant path, Univ Ark, 54-55; asst, NC State Col, 55-58. *Mem:* Fel Soc Nematologists; Sigma Xi; Am Phytopath Soc; Brazilian Soc Nematologists. *Res:* Plant parasitic nematodes; variability, control and host range; biology and management of cyst and root-knot nematodes on soybean and cotton. *Mailing Add:* Dept Plant Path/217 Plant Sci Univ Ark Fayetteville AR 72701. *E-Mail:* rdriggs@comp.uark.edu

RIGGS, RODERICK D, NUCLEAR PHYSICS. *Current Pos:* PROF PHYSICS, SPRING ARBOR COL, MICH, 89- *Personal Data:* b Racine, Wis, Apr 15, 31; m 55; c 3. *Educ:* Dubuque Univ, BS, 55; Iowa State Univ, MS, 57; Mich State Univ, PhD, 71. *Honors & Awards:* Distinguished Serv Citation, Nat Am Asn Physics Teachers, 80. *Prof Exp:* Instr physics & chem, Jackson Community Col, 58-61, dean men, 61-62, dean students, 62-65, chmn, Dept Physics, 65-69, prof physics & eng & head dept, 69-87, prof physics, 73-89. *Concurrent Pos:* Lectr & consult physics curric, Spring Arbor Col, 65-69, adj prof, 84-89; consult, Sci Assocs, 65-83. *Mem:* Am Asn Physics Teachers. *Res:* Theory and development of training programs in nuclear reactor technology; physics curriculum development; comparative European science education; low energy gamma ray spectroscopy. *Mailing Add:* Dept Nat Sci Spring Arbor Col Spring Arbor MI 49283-9984

RIGGS, SCHULTZ, MATHEMATICS. *Current Pos:* RETIRED. *Personal Data:* b Owensboro, Ky, Feb 10, 41. *Educ:* Univ Ky, BS, 62, MS, 64, PhD(math), 70. *Prof Exp:* Instr math, Western Ky Univ, 67-69; asst prof, Jackson State Col, 71-96. *Mem:* Am Math Soc; Math Asn Am. *Res:* Analysis. *Mailing Add:* 170 E Griffith Apt 301 Jackson MS 39201

RIGGS, STANLEY R, GEOLOGY. *Current Pos:* from asst prof to assoc prof, 67-77, PROF GEOL, E CAROLINA UNIV, 77- *Personal Data:* b Watertown, Wis, May 20, 38; m 60; c 2. *Educ:* Beloit Col, BS, 60; Dartmouth Col, MA, 62; Univ Mont, PhD(geol), 67. *Prof Exp:* Res & explor geologist, Int Minerals & Chem Corp, 62-67. *Mem:* Geol Soc Am; Soc Econ Paleontologists & Mineralogists; Sigma Si. *Res:* Modern nearshore and estuarine sediment studies in the southeastern United States; interpretation of the Atlantic Coastal Plain stratigraphy and sedimentary petrology. *Mailing Add:* Dept Geol ECarolina Univ Greenville NC 27858

RIGGS, STUART, MEDICINE, MICROBIOLOGY. *Current Pos:* from asst prof to assoc prof, 62-69, clin assoc prof 69-84, ASST PROF MICROBIOL, BAYLOR COL MED, 66-, CLIN PROF MED, 84- *Personal Data:* b Port Arthur, Tex, Sept 23, 28; c 3. *Educ:* Rice Inst, 47-49; Univ Tex, MD, 53; Am Bd Internal Med, dipl, 61, cert, 74, cert infectious dis, 72. *Prof Exp:* Intern, Univ Iowa, 53-54, resident internal med, Univ Hosps, 54-57; instr med, Univ Tex, Med Br, Galveston, 59-61; res fel infectious dis, Univ Tex, Southwestern Med Sch, Dallas, 61-62. *Concurrent Pos:* Attend physician, John Sealy Hosp, Galveston, Tex, 59-61 & Parkland Mem Hosp, Dallas, 61-62; attend physician, Ben Taub Gen Hosp, Houston, 62-69; head sect infectious dis med serv & supvr clin microbiol lab, 66-69; consult, Vet Admin Hosp, Houston, 64-66; attend physician internal med, Methodist Hosp, Tex, 67-; attend physician internal med & chief infectious dis, St Luke's Episcopal Hosp, 73-85. *Mem:* AAAS; Am Fedn Clin Res; Am Soc Microbiol; fel Am Col Physicians; AMA. *Res:* Viral respiratory and central nervous system infections; mycoplasma serology; infectious diseases. *Mailing Add:* Kelsey Seybold Clin 1111 Augusta Dr Houston TX 77030

RIGGS, THOMAS ROWLAND, BIOCHEMISTRY, NUTRITION. *Current Pos:* from asst prof to prof, 55-86, EMER PROF BIOL CHEM, UNIV MICH, ANN ARBOR, 86- *Personal Data:* b Dallas, Ore, Oct 30, 21; m 58; c 2. *Educ:* Ore State Col, BS, 44, MS, 45; Tufts Univ, PhD(biochem, nutrit), 50. *Prof Exp:* Instr biochem, Tufts Univ, 49-50, from instr to asst prof biochem & nutrit, Med & Dent Schs, 50-55. *Mem:* Am Soc Biol Chemists; Am Inst Nutrit. *Res:* Amino acid transport, especially as altered by hormones and nutritional factors. *Mailing Add:* 1906 Dunmore Ann Arbor MI 48103

RIGGS, VICTORIA G, ELECTRICAL ENGINEERING, QUALITY SYSTEMS. *Current Pos:* MEM TECH STAFF, AT&T BELL LABS, 82- *Personal Data:* b Feb 14, 56; US citizen. *Educ:* State Univ NY, Binghamton, BS, 82; Rutgers State Univ, MS, 88. *Mem:* Inst Elec & Electronics Engrs; Asn Women Sci; Am Soc Qual Control. *Res:* Lightwave semiconductor research and development and manufacturing. *Mailing Add:* AT&T Bell Labs Rm 14C-406 67 Whippany Rd Whippany NJ 07981. *E-Mail:* vgr@hogpa.ho.att.com

RIGGSBY, ERNEST DUWARD, SCIENCE EDUCATION, SCIENCE WRITING. *Current Pos:* PROF SCI EDUC & PHYS SCI, COLUMBUS COL, 69- *Personal Data:* b Nashville, Tenn, June 12, 25; m 62, Dutchie; c Lyn. *Educ:* Tenn Polytech Inst, BS, 48; George Peabody Col, BA, 55, MA, 56, EdS, 58, EdD, 64. *Honors & Awards:* Gen Aviation Mfg Asn Cert Merit in Aerospace Sci, 75. *Prof Exp:* High sch teacher, 53-54; teacher math & sci, Univ of the South, 54-55; from instr to prof phys sci & sci educ, Troy State Col, 55-67; vis prof sci educ, Auburn Univ, 67-69. *Concurrent Pos:* Mem, Nat Aerospace Educ Adv Comt, 60-; educ consult, Ark Proj, Int Paper Co, 61 & US Steel Corp, 62; guest prof, Fla Inst Technol, 63-68; vis scientist, Ala Acad Sci & NSF Coop High Sch-Col Sci Proj, 64-66; spec consult, Ala Proj, US Off

Educ, 65-66; vis prof, Univ Puerto Rico, 68, Fla Inst Technol, 70-74 & Auburn Univ; vis grad prof, Univ PR, 75-76. *Mem:* Fel AAAS; Nat Asn Res Sci; life mem Nat Sci Teachers Asn; World Aerospace Orgn (vpres). *Res:* Philosophy of science and scientific methodology; programmed instruction for use in science education; science teacher education through newer media; dimensional analysis as applied to teacher education in science; aerospace science. *Mailing Add:* 1709 Ashwood Ct Columbus GA 31904

RIGGSBY, WILLIAM STUART, CANDIDA MOLECULAR BIOLOGY. *Current Pos:* from asst prof to assoc prof, 69-79, PROF MICROBIOL, UNIV TENN, KNOXVILLE, 79-; DIR, TENN GOVERNOR'S SCH SCI, 91- *Personal Data:* b Ashland, Ky, July 25, 36; m 63, Katherine Buxton; c Andrew M, Matthew L & Benjamin C. *Educ:* George Washington Univ, AB, 58, Yale Univ, MS, 60, PhD(molecular biol), 64. *Prof Exp:* USPHS fel nucleic acids, Oak Ridge Nat Lab, 65-68, biochemist, 68-69. *Concurrent Pos:* NIH career develop award, 72-79; vis prof molecular genetics, Univ PR, 81- *Mem:* AAAS; Am Soc Microbiol; Genetics Soc Am; Soc Study Evolution. *Res:* Nucleic acid sequence homology; yeast evolution; control of RNA synthesis in yeast morphogenesis; DNA probes for clinical identification. *Mailing Add:* Dept Microbiol Univ Tenn 1345 Circle Park Knoxville TN 37996-0001. *Fax:* 615-974-4007; *E-Mail:* riggsby@utkvs.utk.edu

RIGHTHAND, VERA FAY, VIROLOGY, MOLECULAR BIOLOGY. *Current Pos:* asst prof, 68-74, ASSOC PROF VIROL, SCH MED, WAYNE STATE UNIV, 74- *Personal Data:* b Pittsfield, Mass, Sept 4, 30. *Educ:* Univ Rochester, BA, 52; Rutgers Univ, PhD(microbiol), 63. *Prof Exp:* Jr biologist, Am Cyanamid Co, 52-55; res asst virol, Rockefeller Inst Med Res, 55-59; from instr to asst prof, State Univ NY, Buffalo, 63-68. *Mem:* AAAS; Am Soc Microbiol; Sigma Xi; Am Soc Virol; fel Am Acad Microbiol. *Res:* Host cell-virus interrelationship; picornaviruses; biochemical replication of viruses; factors influencing cell susceptibility to virus infections; persistent infections by normally cytocidal viruses; molecular basis for viral persistence. *Mailing Add:* Dept Immunol & Microbiol Wayne State Univ Sch Med Detroit MI 48201. *Fax:* 313-577-1155; *E-Mail:* vrightha@med.wayne.edu

RIGHTMIRE, GEORGE PHILIP, PALEO-ANTHROPOLOGY, SKELETAL BIOLOGY. *Current Pos:* Asst prof, State Univ NY, 69-73, chmn dept, 76-78, assoc prof, 73-82, PROF ANTHROP, STATE UNIV NY, BINGHAMTON, 82- *Personal Data:* b Boston, Mass, Sept 15, 42; m 66, Berit Johansson; c Anna & Eric. *Educ:* Harvard Col, AB, 64; Univ Wis, MS, 66, PhD(human biol), 69. *Concurrent Pos:* Nat Inst Gen Med Sci spec res fel, Osteological Res Lab, Univ Stockholm, 73; vis scientist, Archeol Dept, Univ Cape Town, 75-76; assoc ed, Am J Phys Anthrop, 83-88 & 95- & J Human Evol, 86-87 & 94-96; Contrib ed, Quart Rev Archaeol, 87-88, Rev Archaeol, 89- *Mem:* Am Phys Anthrop; Human Biol Asn; Sigma Xi; Soc Syst Zool; fel AAAS. *Res:* Biometric studies of recent human populations in Africa; early humans in Africa and Asia; statistical methods in physical anthropology; hominid paleontology. *Mailing Add:* Dept Anthrop State Univ NY Binghamton NY 13902-6000. *Fax:* 607-777-2477; *E-Mail:* gpright@bingvmb.cc.binghamton.edu

RIGHTMIRE, ROBERT, NUCLEAR CHEMISTRY. *Current Pos:* PRES, SYTRAN ASN, 85- *Personal Data:* b Bedford, Ohio, Sept 28, 31; m 58; c 4. *Educ:* Hiram Col, BA, 53; Carnegie Inst Technol, MS, 56, PhD(chem), 57. *Prof Exp:* Tech specialist & electrochemist, Standard Oil Co, Ohio, 57-61, systs coordr, 61-64, res supvr, 64-69, mgr electrokinetics div, 69-71, petrol prod develop, 71-73, mgr petrol res & develop, 76-81, dir corp res, 81-85. *Concurrent Pos:* Vis prof, Case Western Reserve Univ, 85. *Mem:* Am Chem Soc; Am Petrol Inst. *Res:* Energy conversion; battery research; coal and shale oil conversion process research; biochemistry; photochemistry; photovoltaic materials research; petroleum fuels and lubricants; geochemistry; catalysis research; surface science. *Mailing Add:* 220 Hiram College Dr Northfield OH 44067-2417

RIGHTSEL, WILTON ADAIR, BACTERIOLOGY. *Current Pos:* TECH DIR MICROBIOL, BAPTIST MEM HOSP, MEMPHIS, 66-, CLIN ASSOC PROF MICROBIOL, 76- *Personal Data:* b Terre Haute, Ind, July 21, 21; m 46; c 2. *Educ:* Ind Univ, AB, 42; Ind State Teachers Col, MS, 47; Univ Cincinnati, PhD(bact), 51; Am Bd Med Microbiol, dipl. *Prof Exp:* Med technologist, St Anthonys Hosp, Terre Haute, 46-47; lab asst bact, Univ Cincinnati, 48-51; med bacteriologist, Biol Labs, Chem Corps, Camp Detrick, 51-52; assoc res virologist, Parke, Davis & Co, 52-53, res virologist, 53-58, sr res virologist, 58-61, lab dir virol, 62-63, dir virol, 63-66; assoc prof microbiol, Med Units, Univ Tenn, Memphis, 66- *Mem:* Am Soc Microbiol; Am Soc Clin Path; Tissue Cult Asn; Brit Soc Gen Microbiol; fel Am Acad Microbiol; Signa Xi. *Res:* Medical bacteriology and immunology; tularemia; virology; chemotherapy of virus diseases and neoplasms; tissue culture; application of cell cultures in viruses and cancer. *Mailing Add:* 5886 Brierhedge Ave Memphis TN 38120

RIGLER, A KELLAM, numerical analysis, optics, for more information see previous edition

RIGLER, NEIL EDWARD, ENVIRONMENTAL CHEMISTRY. *Current Pos:* RETIRED. *Personal Data:* b Waco, Tex, Nov 2, 08; m 34; c 2. *Educ:* Trinity Univ, Tex, BS, 30; Univ Tex, MA, 32, PhD(org chem), 35. *Prof Exp:* From asst to instr, Univ Tex, 30-35; agent, Bur Plant Indust, USDA, 35-37; res chemist, E R Squibb & Sons, 37; assoc agronomist, Exp Sta, NC State Col, 37-38; plant physiologist, Exp Sta, Agr & Mech Col, Tex, 38-43; org chemist & group leader antibiotic res, Heyden Chem Corp, 43-53; dir process develop antibiotics, Fine Chem Div, Am Cyanamid Co, 53-55, sr res chemist, Lederle Labs Div, 55-60, head, Anal Develop Dept, 60-73; consult, Havens & Emerson, Inc, 73-82. *Mem:* Fel AAAS; fel Am Inst Chemists; Am Chem Soc; NY Acad Sci. *Res:* Isolation, purification, identification and determination of natural products; analytical and chemical process development; pollution analysis; industrial waste treatment. *Mailing Add:* 1111 Monroe Vlg Jamesburg NJ 08831-1696

RIGNEY, CARL JENNINGS, PHYSICS. *Current Pos:* RETIRED. *Personal Data:* b Port Arthur, Tex, July 28, 25; m 48, Margaret Roth; c Daniel, David, Martin, Robert & Thomas. *Educ:* Univ Louisville, BS, 47; Northwestern Univ, MS, 48, PhD, 51. *Prof Exp:* Asst prof physics, Southern Ill Univ, 50-51; asst prof, Northern Ill Univ, 51-56; prof, Stephen F Austin State Col, 56-57; head dept, Lamar Univ, 57-78, prof physics, 57-92. *Concurrent Pos:* Consult, Gen Elec Co, Ill, 54-55. *Mem:* Am Phys Soc; Am Asn Physics Teachers. *Res:* Measurements for thermal conductivity. *Mailing Add:* 2004A Ann Arbor Ave Austin TX 78704

RIGNEY, DAVID ARTHUR, PHYSICAL METALLURGY, TRIBOLOGY. *Current Pos:* Asst prof mem, 67-75, prof metall eng, 75-88, PROF MAT SCI & ENG, OHIO STATE UNIV, 88-, ASSOC DIR, CTR MAT RES, 89- *Personal Data:* b Waterbury, Conn, Aug 8, 38; m 65, Ann Fairbairn; c Mark D & Heather A. *Educ:* Harvard Univ, AB, 60, SM, 62; Cornell Univ, PhD(mat sci eng), 66. *Prof Exp:* Researcher, Mat Res Lab, Univ Ill, Urbana, 65-66. *Concurrent Pos:* Vis researcher, Cambridge Univ, Eng, 81; deleg, US/China Bilateral meeting, 81, chmn, US/China Wear meeting, 83; guest, USSR Acad Sci, 87; ed, Scripta Metallurgica, 88; guest prof eng, Tohoku Univ, Sendai, Japan, 90; vchmn, Gordon Res Conf Tribol, 98, chair, 2000. *Mem:* Fel Am Soc Metals Int; Am Inst Mining, Metall & Petrol Engr; Mat Res Soc; Sigma Xi. *Res:* Solidification; liquid metals; magnetic resonance; electromigration; friction and wear (materials aspects, deformation, microstructure). *Mailing Add:* Dept Mat Sci & Eng Ohio State Univ Columbus OH 43210-1179. *Fax:* 614-292-1537

RIGNEY, DAVID ROTH, BIOPHYSICS, MOLECULAR BIOLOGY. *Current Pos:* ASST PROF MED, HARVARD MED SCH, 86- *Personal Data:* b Carbondale, Ill, Dec 27, 50. *Educ:* Univ Tex, Austin, BA, 72, PhD(physics), 78. *Prof Exp:* Res scientist biophysics, Inst Cancer Res, 78-80, biophysicist, 81-86; res assoc, Mass Inst Technol, 86- *Concurrent Pos:* NIH trainee, 78-80; assoc dir, Arrhythmia & Bioeng. *Mem:* AAAS; Biophys Soc; Cell Kinetics Soc; Tissue Cult Asn. *Res:* Theoretical biology; cell physiology; biochemical stochastics; biostatistics; cardiovascular physiology; electro-optical instrumentation; bioengineering; animal physiology. *Mailing Add:* Dept Arrhythmia Biomed Eng-Cardiovasc Beth Israel Hosp 330 Brookline Ave Boston MA 02215

RIGNEY, EARNEST DOUGLAS, JR, MATERIALS SCIENCE & ENGINEERING. *Current Pos:* biomed engr, Dept Biomat, 87-89, ASST PROF, DEPT MAT SCI & ENG, UNIV ALA, BIRMINGHAM, 89- *Personal Data:* b Jan 13, 58. *Educ:* Univ Ala, Birmingham, BSME & MS, 85, BME & PhD 89. *Prof Exp:* Engr asst, Biomed Electronics Dept, Univ Ala Hosp, 77-79; jr engr, Ala Power Co, 80-81, generating plant engr, 81-83. *Concurrent Pos:* Consult, Carbomedics Inc, Meadox Med Inc, Richard's Med Inc, Wright Med Technol, Acrco Int Inc, Hughes Missles Elec, Huie Fernamgbuqe & Stewart. *Mem:* Am Soc Metals Int; Biomed Eng Soc; Soc Biomat; Nat Asn Corrosion Engrs; Am Asn Dent Researchers; Acad Dent Mat; Sigma Xi. *Res:* Contributed numerous articles to professional journals. *Mailing Add:* 3845 River Run Trail Birmingham AL 35243

RIGNEY, JAMES ARTHUR, ORGANIC CHEMISTRY, BIOCHEMISTRY. *Current Pos:* RETIRED. *Personal Data:* b Flushing, NY, July 12, 31; m 58; c 4. *Educ:* Fordham Univ, BS, 53; Va Polytech Inst, MS, 59, PhD(org chem), 61. *Prof Exp:* Res chemist, Am Cyanamid Co, 53-57; res chemist, Esso Res Labs, 61-66; sr chemist, Enjay Chem Co, La, 66-67; from asst prof to prof chem, Univ PEI, 67-92, chmn dept, 72-77. *Mem:* Am Chem Soc; NY Acad Sci. *Res:* Organosulfur chemistry; chemistry of marine plants; catalysis. *Mailing Add:* 47 Roper Dr Sherwood PE C1A 6J1 Can

RIGNEY, MARY MARGARET, MEDICAL MICROBIOLOGY. *Current Pos:* RETIRED. *Personal Data:* b Albany, Mo, Nov 10, 26. *Educ:* Northwest Mo State Col, BS, 50; Univ Mo, Columbia, MA, 60, PhD(microbiol), 68. *Prof Exp:* From asst prof to assoc prof, Univ Wis, Oshkosh, 68-78, prof biol, 78- *Mem:* AAAS; Am Soc Microbiol; Sigma Xi. *Res:* Growth characteristics of aeromonas species; isolation and characterization of endotoxins and hemolysins of aeromonas species; pathogenicity of aeromonas species for warm and cold-blooded animals. *Mailing Add:* 833 Guenevere Dr St Louis MO 63011

RIGOR, BENJAMIN MORALES, SR, ANESTHESIOLOGY. *Current Pos:* PROF ANESTHESIOL & CHMN DEPT, SCH MED, UNIV LOUISVILLE, 81- *Personal Data:* b Rizal, Philippines, Oct 13, 36; US citizen; m 61; c 3. *Educ:* Univ Philippines, BS, 57; Univ of the East, Manila, MD, 62; Am Bd Anesthesiol, dipl, 70. *Prof Exp:* Instr pharmacol, Univ of the East Med Sch, 62-63; res assoc, Univ Ky, 65-66, resident anesthesiol, Med Ctr, 66-68, asst prof, 68-69; assoc prof, 69-71, prof anesthesiol & chmn dept, Col Med, NJ, 71-74; prof anesthesiol & chmn dept, Med Sch, Univ Tex, Houston, 74-81, prof & med dir nurse anesthesiol educ, 76-81. *Concurrent Pos:* USPHS grant, Univ Ky, 63; Am Heart Asn grant, 66; chief obstet anesthesia, Naval Hosp, Portsmouth, Va, 71-73; consult anesthesiol, Vet Admin Hosp, East Orange, Newark Beth Israel Med Ctr & St Barnabas Med Ctr, NJ, 71-74; consult, M D Anderson Hosp & Univ Tex Cancer Systs, 74-81; chief anesthesia, Hermann-Univ Hosp, Houston, 74- & Univ Hosp, Louisville 81-

Mem: Am Soc Anesthesiol; Int Anesthesia Res Soc; fel Am Col Anesthesiol; AMA; Acad Anesthesiol. *Res:* Biological transport of non-electrolytes in the blood brain barrier; clinical pharmacology of drugs; fluid and parenteral therapy; clinical anesthesia. *Mailing Add:* Dept Anesthesiol Univ Louisville Sch Med Health Sci Ctr Louisville KY 40292

RIGROD, WILLIAM W, OPTICAL RESONATORS, PHYSICAL OPTICS. *Current Pos:* RETIRED. *Personal Data:* b New York, NY, Mar 29, 13; m 39, Elisabeth Gill. *Educ:* Cooper Union, BS, 34; Cornell Univ, MS, 41; Polytech Univ, DEE, 50. *Prof Exp:* Res scientist, Ignatyev Res Inst, USSR, 34-35, All-Union Electrotech Inst, USSR, 35-39; develop engr, Westinghouse Elec Corp, NJ, 40-51; mem tech staff, Electronics Res Lab, Bell Labs, Inc, 51-77; consult, Los Alamos Sci Lab, 79-88. *Mem:* Sr mem Inst Elec & Electronics Eng; emer mem Sigma Xi; emer mem Optical Soc Am. *Res:* Microwave electronics; physics of electron beams and gaseous discharges; lasers; physical optics. *Mailing Add:* Rte 19 Box 91-T Sunlit Hills Santa Fe NM 87505

RIGSBY, GEORGE PIERCE, GEOLOGY,GLACIOLOGY. *Current Pos:* RETIRED. *Personal Data:* b Wichita Falls, Tex, Nov 19, 15; m 43, 68, Jeanne Brink; c Jeanne (Brink) & David C. *Educ:* Calif Inst Technol, BS, 48, MS, 50, PhD(geol), 53. *Prof Exp:* Res scientist, Snow, Ice & Permafrost Res Estab, CEngrs, US Army, 53-56; res scientist, USN Electronics Lab, 56-59; staff scientist, Arctic Inst NAm, 59-68; assoc prof geol, US Int Univ, Elliott Campus, 68-74; geologist, Geothermal Surv, Inc, 74-85. *Mem:* Geol Soc Am; Am Mineral Soc; Am Geophys Union; Glaciol Soc; Sigma Xi. *Res:* Glaciology; field and laboratory investigation of ice; arctic field research; mineralogy; petrology; petrography; geothermal field research. *Mailing Add:* 1542 Alcala Pl San Diego CA 92111

RIHA, WILLIAM E, JR, FOOD MICROBIOLOGY. *Current Pos:* VPRES RES & DEVELOP, JOSEPH E SEAGRAM & SONS INC, 89- *Personal Data:* b New Brunswick, NJ, Sept 15, 43; m 66, Joan Murphy; c William & Jennifer. *Educ:* Rutgers Univ, New Brunswick, BS, 65, MS, 69, PhD(food sci), 72. *Prof Exp:* Res asst food sci, Rutgers Univ, New Brunswick, 65-72; food scientist, Hunt-Wesson Foods, Inc, 72-74, group leader, 74-76, sect head, 76; dir tech serv, Cadbury North Am, Peter Paul Cadbury, 76-78, mgr food technol, 78-80; with res & tech serv, Pepsico, Inc, 80-83, group mgr, US Prod Develop & dir, Int Prod Develop, 83-89. *Concurrent Pos:* Consult food indust, 68-72. *Mem:* Inst Food Technologists; Sigma Xi. *Res:* Food product development and research; food microbiology. *Mailing Add:* Joseph E Seagram & Sons Inc 103 Corp Park Dr White Plains NY 10604

RIHM, ALEXANDER, JR, SANITARY ENGINEERING. *Current Pos:* CONSULT, 76- *Personal Data:* b New York, NY, May 18, 16; m 40; c 2. *Educ:* NY Univ, BS, 36, MS, 39. *Honors & Awards:* J Smith Griswold Award, Air Pollution Control Asn, 80. *Prof Exp:* Mem field party, Brader Construct Corp, 37-39; dist sanit engr, NY State Dept Health, 39-44, water supply engr, 47-49, water pollution control engr, 49-51, chief radiol health & air sanit sect, 52-57, exec secy air pollution control bd, 57-66, asst comnr health, 66-70; dir, Div Air Resources, NY State Dept Environ Conserv, 70-76. *Concurrent Pos:* Adj prof, Rensselaer Polytech Inst; mem, Nat Air Qual Criteria Adv Comt. *Mem:* Am Pub Health Asn; hon mem Air Pollution Control Asn (pres, 73-74). *Res:* Air pollution control. *Mailing Add:* 28 Euclid Ave Delmar NY 12054

RIJKE, ARIE MARIE, BIOMATERIALS, POLYMER SCIENCE. *Current Pos:* SR SCIENTIST MAT SCI, UNIV VA, 70-, ASST PROF RADIOL MED. *Personal Data:* b Velsen, Neth, Apr 6, 34; US citizen; m 78, Suzanne Dischoff. *Educ:* State Univ Leiden, BS, 56, MS & PhD(phys chem), 61; State Univ NY, MS, 60; Univ Amsterdam, MD, 78. *Prof Exp:* Res officer surface chem, Nat Defense Res Orgn, Neth, 61-64; res officer polymer, Coun Sci & Indust Res, 64-66; lectr chem, Univ Cape Town, 66-67; res assoc polymer physics, Inst Molecular Biophys, Fla State Univ, 67-69; lectr, Univ Witwatersrand, 69-70. *Mem:* Am Chem Soc; Opers Res Soc; AAAS. *Res:* Implant tissue response; development of new biomate rials for soft and hard tissue replacement; dental composites. *Mailing Add:* Dept Radiol Health Sci Ctr Univ Va Box 170 Charlottesville VA 22908. *Fax:* 804-982-5660; *E-Mail:* amra@virginia.edu

RIKANS, LORA ELIZABETH, BIOCHEMICAL PHARMACOLOGY, AGING. *Current Pos:* from asst prof to assoc prof, 77-90, PROF PHARMACOL, UNIV OKLA, 90- *Personal Data:* b Grand Rapids, Mich, Feb 7, 40; m 62, Eric; c Eric Jr & Christopher J. *Educ:* Mich State Univ, BS, 61, MS, 62; Univ Mich, Ann Arbor, PhD(pharmacol), 75. *Honors & Awards:* Tokyo Metrop Inst Geront Oversea Invitation Award, 90. *Prof Exp:* Res assoc nutrit, Mich State Univ, 62-63; clin chemist, St Marys Hosp, Saginaw, Mich, 64-67; res asst pharmacol, Dow Chem Co, Midland, Mich, 67-69; fel, Univ Mich, 70-75, scholar pharmacol, 75-77. *Concurrent Pos:* Prin investr, Nat Inst Aging, 78- & Nat Inst Environ Health Sci, 92-96; Masua hon lectr, 89-90. *Mem:* Am Soc Pharmacol & Exp Therapeut; Sigma Xi; Int Soc Study Xenobiotics; Soc Toxicol. *Res:* Aging modification of drug metabolism; aging modification of drug toxicity; mechanisms of chemically induced toxicity. *Mailing Add:* Dept Pharmacol PO Box 26901 Oklahoma City OK 73190. *Fax:* 405-271-7477; *E-Mail:* lora-rikans@uokhsc.edu

RIKE, PAUL MILLER, CARDIOLOGY, INTERNAL MEDICINE. *Current Pos:* RETIRED. *Personal Data:* b Duquesne, Pa, Feb 6, 13; m 45. *Educ:* Univ Pittsburgh, BS, 36, MD, 38; Thiel Col, DSc, 71. *Prof Exp:* Asst prof med, Sch Med, Univ Pittsburgh, 48-92. *Concurrent Pos:* Active staff, Magee Womens Hosp & Presby Univ Hosp; consult, Western Psychiat Inst & Clin. *Mem:* Am Heart Asn; fel Am Col Physicians; fel Am Col Cardiol; fel Am Col Angiol. *Mailing Add:* 4625 Fifth Ave Pittsburgh PA 15213

RIKER, DONALD KAY, PHARMACEUTICAL RESEARCH & DEVELOPMENT, NEUROPHARMACOLOGY. *Current Pos:* sr res investr, Richardson-Vicks Inc, 82-84, prin res investr, 84-86, asst dir appl clin res, 86-90, assoc dir clin develop, 90-93, RICHARDSON-VICKS/ PROCTER & GAMBLE FEL, 94- *Personal Data:* b New York, NY, Oct 22, 45; m 65, Leigh Bartley; c 2. *Educ:* Univ Kans, BA, 69; Cornell Univ, PhD(neurobiol behav), 77. *Honors & Awards:* US Antarctic Serv Medal, 68. *Prof Exp:* Fel, Rockefeller Univ, 68-70; fel pharmacol, 76-79, res assoc, Yale Univ, 80-82. *Concurrent Pos:* Mem, US Antarctic Res Prog, 68; res health scientist, Vet Admin, 80-81. *Mem:* Soc Neurosci; Sigma Xi; Am Soc Pharmacol & Exp Therapeut; Drug Info Asn; Am Acad Allergy, Asthma & Immunol. *Res:* Pharmaceutical research management; design and execution of clinical programs to evaluate drug safety and efficacy; over-the-counter development of new technology; respiratory drug development; Rx/OTC switch. *Mailing Add:* Procter & Gamble Healthcare 8700 Mason-Montgomery Rd Mason OH 45040. *Fax:* 513-622-1900

RIKER, WALTER FRANKLYN, JR, NEUROPHARMACOLOGY, CLINICAL PHARMACOLOGY. *Current Pos:* Res fel pharmacol, Med Col, Cornell Univ, 41-44, from instr to prof, 44-83, instr med, 45-46, chmn, Pharmacol Dept, 56-83, Revlon prof, 79-86, EMER PROF PHARMACOL, MED COL, CORNELL UNIV, 86- *Personal Data:* b Bronx, NY, Mar 8, 16; m 41, Virginia Jaeger; c Donald Kay, Walter III & Wayne S. *Educ:* Columbia Univ, BS, 39, Cornell Univ, MD, 43. *Hon Degrees:* DSc, Med Col Ohio, 80. *Honors & Awards:* John J Abel Prize, Am Pharmacol Soc, 51; Torald Sollmann Award, Am Soc Pharmacol & Exp Ther, 86; Oscar B Hunter Award in Clin Pharmacol, Am Soc Clin Pharmacol & Ther, 90. *Concurrent Pos:* Traveling fel, Am Physiol Soc Cong Oxford, Eng, 47; assoc ed, J Pharmacol & Exp Therapeut, 50-57; vis prof, Univ Kans, 53-54; mem, Pharmacol Comt, Nat Bd Med Examrs, 56-59; mem, Pharmacol Study Sect, USPHS, 56-59, Pharmacol Training Grant Comt, 58-61, chmn, 61-63; mem, Adv Coun, Nat Inst Gen Med Sci, 63; mem, Toxicol Panel, President's Sci Adv Comt, 65; mem, Pharmacol-Toxicol Rev Comt, NIH, 65-68; mem adv comts, Pharmaceut Mfrs Asn Found, 65-87; vis scientist, Roche Inst Molecular Biol, 71-72, adj mem, 72-75; mem, Adv Coun, Nat Inst Environ Health Sci, 72-75; mem ad drugs, Nat Football League, 73-85; sci adv bd, Sterling Winthrop Res Inst, 73-76; chmn, Sci Adv Comt, Irma T Hirschal Trust, 73-83, mem, Consult Comt, 73-; Sterling Drug vis prof, Cornell Univ Med Col, 79, mem bd overseers, 81-86; dir, Richardson Vicks Inc, 79-85; hon mem med staff, NY Hosp, 80- *Mem:* Fel AAAS; Am Acad Neurol; Am Soc Pharmacol & Exp Therapeut; Sigma Xi; Am Soc Clin Pharmacol & Therapeut; Soc Neurosci; hon fel Am Col Clin Pharmacol. *Res:* Neuromuscular transmission; neuropharmacology; general pharmacology; neuromuscular pharmacology; delineation and reactivities of mammalian motor nerve endings; laboratory and clinical studies of anti-curare drugs, muscle relaxants and myasthenia gravis; neurotoxicity and pharamacologic changes during denervation; drug abuse. *Mailing Add:* Dept Pharmacol Rm A1028 Cornell Univ Med Col 1300 York Ave New York NY 10021

RIKER, WILLIAM KAY, PHARMACOLOGY. *Current Pos:* prof & chmn dept, 69-91, EMER PROF PHARMACOL, MED SCH, ORE HEALTH SCI UNIV, 91- *Personal Data:* b New York, NY, Aug 31, 25; m 47, 83, Leena Mela; c Eleanor, Gainor & Victoria. *Educ:* Columbia Univ, BA, 49; Cornell Univ, MD, 53. *Prof Exp:* Intern, II Med Div, Bellevue Hosp, New York, 53-54; instr pharmacol, Sch Med, Univ Pa, 54-57, assoc, 57-59, asst prof, 59-61; Nat Inst Neurol Dis & Blindness spec fel physiol, Sch Med, Univ Utah, 61-64; assoc prof, Woman's Med Col Pa, 64-68, prof & chmn dept, 68-69. *Concurrent Pos:* Pa Plan scholar, 58-61; field ed neuropharmacol, J Pharmacol & Exp Therapeut, 68-; mem, Pharmaceut Toxicol Prog Comn, 68-72 & Neurol Dis Prog Proj Rev Comt B, 75-79; mem pharmacol-morphol adv comt, Pharmaceut Mfrs Asn Found, 70-85, sci adv coun, 78-92. *Mem:* Am Soc Pharmacol & Exp Therapeut (secy-treas, 78-79, pres, 85-86); Japan Pharmacol Soc; Am Epilepsy Soc. *Res:* Physiology and pharmacology of synaptic transmission. *Mailing Add:* 4326 SW Warrens Way Portland OR 97221-3246

RIKIHISA, YASUKO, RICKETTSIAL DISEASE, IMMUNOLOGY. *Current Pos:* ASSOC PROF PATHOBIOL, COL VET MED, OHIO STATE UNIV, 86- *Educ:* Univ Tokyo, Japan, PhD(pharmacol), 77. *Prof Exp:* Assoc prof pathobiol, Va Polytech Inst & State Univ, 81-86. *Mailing Add:* Dept Vet Biosci Col Vet Med Ohio State Univ 1925 Coffey Rd Columbus OH 43210-1092

RIKOSKI, RICHARD ANTHONY, ELECTRICAL & ELECTRONICS ENGINEERING. *Current Pos:* PRES, TECH ANALYSIS CORP, CHICAGO, 78- *Personal Data:* b Kingston, Pa, Aug 13, 41; div; c 2. *Educ:* Univ Detroit, BEE, 64; Carnegie-Mellon Univ, MSEE, 65, PhD(elec eng, appl space sci), 68; Case Western Reserve Univ, post-doctoral, 71. *Prof Exp:* Solid state engr, Electronic Defense Lab, Int Tel & Tel Corp, NJ, 62, solid state engr, Space Commun Lab, 63; guid engr, AC Electronics Div, Gen Motors Corp, Wis, 64; instr elec eng, Carnegie-Mellon Univ, 67-68; asst prof, Univ Pa, 68-74; assoc prof elec eng, Ill Inst Technol, 74-80. *Concurrent Pos:* Engr, Hazeltine Res, Ill, 69; consult metroliner vehicle dynamics, Ensco Inc, Va, 70; NASA-Am Soc Eng Educ fel, Case Western Reserve Univ, 71; mem educ activ bd, Inst Elec & Electronics Engrs, 79-83; mem Energy Comt, Inst Elec & Electronics Engrs, 84-85; eng consult. *Mem:* Sr mem Inst Elec & Electronics Engrs; Sigma Xi; Nat Fire Protection Asn. *Res:* Plasma physics; magnetohydrodynamics; circuit theory, simulations; thick film; microelectronics; fluid mechanics; energy conversion; product liability; evaluation of new technological concepts; analysis of patent claims; engineering problem solving. *Mailing Add:* PO Box 444 Beverly Shores IN 46301. *Fax:* 773-975-2488; *E-Mail:* rikoski@niia.net

RIKVOLD, PER ARNE, STATISTICAL PHYSICS, COMPUTATIONAL PHYSICS. *Current Pos:* assoc prof, 87-92, PROF PHYSICS, FLA STATE UNIV, 92- *Personal Data:* b Hadsel, Norway, Oct 4, 48; m 93, Paulette A Bond. *Educ:* Univ Oslo, Norway, BSc, 71, MSc, 76; Osaka Univ Foreign Studies, Japan, dipl, 77; Temple Univ, Philadelphia, Pa, PhD(physics), 83. *Prof Exp:* Res fel physics, Japanese Ministry Educ, Kyushu Univ, Fukuoka, Japan, 77-78 & Norweg Res Coun Sci & Humanities, Temple Univ, 81-83; res assoc physics, Univ Oslo, Norway, 78-81; res assoc mech eng, State Univ NY, Stony Brook, 83-85; sr res chemist prod develop indust water treatment, ChemLink Indust & Petrol Chem, Subsid Atlantic Richfield Co, 85-87. *Concurrent Pos:* Vis scientist, Dept Physics, Kyushu Univ, Fukuoka, Japan, 79, Dept Theoret Physics, Univ Geneva, Switz, 81-82, Inst Solid State Physics, Julich, WGer, 82; vis scholar, Ctr Advan Computational Sci, Temple Univ, 86-87; fac assoc, Supercomputer Computations Res Inst & Ctr Mat Res & Technol, Fla State Univ, 87-; vis scientist, Tohwa Inst Sci & Kyushu Univ, Fukuoka, Japan, 91, Kyoto Univ, Japan, 93 & 96, IBM Bergen Sci Ctr, Norway, 87 & 88 & McGill Univ, Montreal, Can, 95- *Mem:* Am Phys Soc; Norweg Phys Soc; Europ Phys Soc; Sigma Xi. *Res:* Computationally oriented, statistical-mechanics based research in materials science and chemical physics; phase transitions in low-dimensional systems and their applications to surface science, electrochemistry, high-temperature superconductors and magnetic materials. *Mailing Add:* Dept Physics Fla State Univ Tallahassee FL 32306-3016. *Fax:* 850-644-0098; *E-Mail:* rikvold@scri.fsu.edu

RILA, CHARLES CLINTON, INORGANIC CHEMISTRY, ORGANIC CHEMISTRY. *Current Pos:* prof chem & head dept, 65-92, chmn div natural sci, 67-79, EMER PROF CHEM, IOWA WESLEYAN COL, 92- *Personal Data:* b Pittsburgh, Pa, Aug 1, 28; m 50; c 2. *Educ:* Col Wooster, BA, 50; Ill Inst Technol, PhD(chem), 55; Univ Evansville, MS, 85. *Prof Exp:* From instr to asst prof chem, Ohio Wesleyan Univ, 55-62; assoc prof, Parsons Col, 62-65. *Concurrent Pos:* Dir, Res & Develop, SAI Corp, 79-81. *Mem:* Am Chem Soc. *Res:* Transition metal complexes; chemical education; computer applications to chemical education. *Mailing Add:* 506 Vine St Mt Pleasant IA 52641

RILES, JAMES BYRUM, ALGEBRA. *Current Pos:* From asst prof to assoc prof, 67-76, PROF MATH, ST LOUIS UNIV, 76- *Personal Data:* b Dexter, Iowa, Feb 16, 38; m 60; c 3. *Educ:* Reed Col, BA, 59; Univ London, PhD(algebra), 67. *Concurrent Pos:* Consult, Col Assistance Prog, St Louis Univ, 70- *Mem:* Am Math Soc; London Math Soc. *Res:* Infinite group theory. *Mailing Add:* St Louis Univ St Louis MO 63103-2007

RILEY, BERNARD JEROME, REGULATION LIAISON & VEHICLE SECURITY. *Current Pos:* RETIRED. *Personal Data:* b Eau Claire, Wis, Feb 15, 28; m 51, Evelyn Crigger; c Timothy J, Maureen A, Michael P, Jeanine M, William T, Kathleen A, Brian P & Mary A. *Educ:* St Mary's Col, Minn, BS, 48; Univ Detroit, MS, 50, MBA, 61. *Prof Exp:* Radioceramicist, Glass Div Res Labs, Pittsburgh Plate Glass Co, 54-55; sr res chemist, Isotope Lab, Res Labs, Gen Motors Tech Ctr, 55-65, sect chief, Mil Vehicles Oper, Detroit Diesel Allison Div, 65-77, staff develop engr, Auto Safety Eng, 77-88. *Mem:* Am Chem Soc; Int Asn Auto-Theft Investr. *Res:* Use of radioactive tracers in solution of research problems, principally in fields of electrochemistry and surface chemistry. *Mailing Add:* 365 Willowtree Lane Rochester Hills MI 48306-4254

RILEY, CARROLL LAVERN, ANTHROPOLOGY & ARCHEOLOGY ETHNOHISTORY. *Current Pos:* from asst prof to prof, Southern Ill Univ, 55-87, dir mus, 72-74, chmn dept, 79-82, EMER DISTINGUISHED PROF, SOUTHERN ILL UNIV, 87-; SR RES ASSOC, MUS NMEX, 90- *Personal Data:* b Summersville, Mo, Apr 18, 23; m 48, Brent R Locke; c Benjamin L, Victoria S (Evans) & Cynthia W. *Educ:* Univ NMex, AB, 48, PhD, 52; Univ Calif, Los Angeles, MA, 50. *Prof Exp:* Instr, Univ Colo, Boulder, 53-54; asst prof, Univ NC, Chapel Hill, 54-55; res assoc, Lab Anthrop, Mus NMex, 87-90. *Concurrent Pos:* Res collabr, Smithsonian Inst, 88-; adj prof, NMex Highlands Univ, 89-; grantee, Soc Sci Res Coun, NIH, Am Philos Soc, Am Coun Learned Socs & Nat Endowment for Humanities. *Res:* Anthropology; archaeology, physical anthropology, linguistics, ethnohistory of greater southwest from first human occupation to early historic times. *Mailing Add:* 1106 Sixth St Las Vegas NV 87701-4311. *E-Mail:* criley@nmhu.campus.mci.net

RILEY, CHARLES MARSHALL, ECONOMIC GEOLOGY. *Current Pos:* RETIRED. *Personal Data:* b Chicago, Ill, Aug 17, 20; m 46; c 4. *Educ:* Univ Chicago, BS, 42; Univ Minn, MS, 48, PhD(geol), 50. *Prof Exp:* Asst geol, Univ Minn, 47-50; asst prof, Univ Nebr, 50-57; res geologist, Exxon Prod Res Co, 57-83; res geologist, Aramco, 83-86. *Mem:* Fel Geol Soc Am; Am Asn Petrol Geol. *Res:* Sedimentary petrography; organic geochemistry; dolomite; petroleum; economic minerals. *Mailing Add:* 11938 Wink Dr Houston TX 77024

RILEY, CLAUDE FRANK, JR, AERONAUTICAL & MECHANICAL ENGINEERING. *Current Pos:* OWNER, RILEY ASSOCS, 84- *Personal Data:* b Milledgeville, Ga, Apr 24, 22; m 47, Dorothy Dixon; c Thomas F, Michael John & Janet Marie. *Educ:* Ga Inst Tech, BS, 43; Univ Mich, MS, 49. *Prof Exp:* Propulsion engr, Bell Aircraft Corp, 46-47; assoc prof, Univ Mich, 47-50; sr operating vpres, Booz, Allen & Hamilton, 50-70; corp & group vpres & mem exec comt, Auerbach Corp Sci & Technol, 70-72, gen mgr, Auerback Asn, Inc, 71-72; vpres & gen mgr, Computing & Software Corp, 72-74; vpres, Tracor, Inc, mem bd dirs, Tracor-Jitco, 74-84; vpres, McLean Group 84-89. *Concurrent Pos:* Mem bd dir, Am Fedn Info Processing Socs; exec off, Ga Mil Col; chmn distinguished lect series, Nat Bd Trade; lectr, Int Telemetry Conf; chmn, Proj Aristotle, Nat Security Indust Asn; chief exec officer, Compdata Inc, 70-72; vpres & mem bd, Comprehensive Health Serv, Inc, 84-, Promana, Inc, 84- & Baheth USA Inc, 89; pres, Riley Assocs, 89- *Mem:* Assoc fel Am Inst Aeronaut & Astronaut; Prof Engrs Soc. *Res:* Aeronautics; propulsion; instrumentation; computer technology; scientific and general management and marketing. *Mailing Add:* 10825 Foxhunt Lane Potomac MD 20854

RILEY, CLYDE, PHYSICAL CHEMISTRY. *Current Pos:* Proj assoc, Univ Wis-Madison, 65-67, asst prof, 67-68, assoc prof, 68-79, PROF CHEM, UNIV ALA, HUNTSVILLE, 79-, CHMN DEPT, 72- *Personal Data:* b Niagara Falls, NY, Feb 19, 39; m 61. *Educ:* Univ Rochester, BS, 60; Fla State Univ, PhD. *Mem:* Am Chem Soc. *Res:* Laser induced chemistry; reactive scattering from crossed molecular beams; pyrolysis decomposition mechanisms by modulated molecular beam velocity; analysis mass spectrometry; electrodeposition in low gravity. *Mailing Add:* Univ Ala Chem Dept Huntsville AL 35899

RILEY, DANNY ARTHUR, ANATOMY. *Current Pos:* MEM STAFF, DEPT ANAT, MED COL WIS. *Personal Data:* b Rhinelander, Wis, Nov 18, 44; m 70; c 1. *Educ:* Univ Wis, BS, 66, PhD(anat), 71. *Prof Exp:* Muscular Dystrophy Asn Am fel, NIH, 72-73; asst prof anat, Univ Calif, San Francisco, 73-. *Mem:* Int Soc Electromyographic Kinesiology; Am Asn Anatomists. *Res:* Skeletal muscle, differentiation of fiber types; regeneration, neural dependence, hormonal dependence as studied histochemically, electronmicroscopically and physiologically. *Mailing Add:* Dept Anat & Cell Biol Med Col Wisc 8701 Watertown Plank Rd Milwaukee WI 53226

RILEY, DAVID, PULMONARY DISEASE. *Current Pos:* From asst prof to assoc prof, 73-87, PROF MED, ROBERT WOOD JOHNSON MED SCH, 87- *Personal Data:* b New York, NY, Sept 6, 42; m; c 2. *Educ:* Univ Md, MD, 68. *Concurrent Pos:* Adj prof physiol & biophys, Robert Wood Johnson Med Sch. *Mem:* Am Thoracic Soc; Am Physiologic Soc; Am Col Chest Physicians; Am Col Physicians. *Res:* Study of mechanism of lung injury with particular emphasis on connective tissue; genetics of interstitial lung disease. *Mailing Add:* Dept Med Rm C-B04 UMDNJ Robert Wood Johnson Med Sch 675 Hoes Lane Piscataway NJ 08854-5635

RILEY, DAVID WAEGAR, RHEOLOGY, MATERIAL SCIENCE ENGINEERING. *Current Pos:* CONSULT, EXTRUSION ENGRS, 81- *Personal Data:* b Winchester, Mass, May 7, 21; div; c 3. *Educ:* Tufts Col, BS, 43; Ohio State Univ, MSc, 49, PhD(chem), 51. *Prof Exp:* Res chemist, Res Ctr, Goodyear Tire & Rubber Co, 43-44 & 46; asst gen chem, Ohio State Univ, 46 & 49-51; res chemist, Polychem Dept, E I du Pont de Nemours & Co, 51-54; res chemist, Silicones Div, Union Carbide Corp, 54-60; sr develop engr, Western Elec Co, 60-67; res adv & group mgr technol, Gen Cable Res Ctr, 67-76; dir plastics eng, Sci Process & Res, 76-78; mat res specialist, Tenneco Chemicals, Inc, 78-81. *Mem:* Fel AAAS; fel Am Inst Chem; Am Chem Soc; fel Soc Plastics Engrs; Inst Elec & Electronics Engrs; fel Am Soc Testing & Mats. *Res:* Polyethylene; silicone polymers; rheology of polyvinyl chloride compounds; thermal stability and extrusion of polymers; computer simulation of extrusion; coefficient of friction of plastics; theory of lubrication of polyvinyl chloride compounds; instruments for polymer melt analysis; molecular structure of polymers related to rheology. *Mailing Add:* Extrusion Eng 858 Princeton Ct Neshanic Station NJ 08853-9686

RILEY, DENNIS PATRICK, BIOINORGANIC CHEMISTRY, ASYMMETRIC CATALYSIS. *Current Pos:* SR SCI FEL & MGR, METALL-MEDIATED CHEM RES, MONSANTO CORP RES, 84- *Personal Data:* b Tiffin, Ohio, Jan 22, 47; m 73, Carole A Clark; c Eric W. *Educ:* Heidelberg Col, BS, 69; Ohio State Univ, PhD(chem), 75. *Prof Exp:* Staff indexer chem, Chem Abstr Serv, 69-71; fel chem, Univ Chicago, 75-76; res chemist, Technol Div, Procter & Gamble Co, 76-84. *Concurrent Pos:* Adj prof, Washington Univ, St Louis, 93- *Mem:* Am Chem Soc; fel AAAS; Sigma Xi; Oxygen Soc. *Res:* Catalytic asymmetric hydrogenations; better catalysts for molecular oxygen activation; synthetic redox enzyme mimetics as human pharmaceuticals. *Mailing Add:* 800 Chancellor Heights Dr Ballwin MO 63011

RILEY, DONALD RAY, COMPUTER GRAPHICS & COMPUTER AIDED DESIGN, INTELLIGENT SYSTEMS. *Current Pos:* From asst prof to assoc prof, 76-88, actg assoc provost, 92-93, PROF MECH ENG, UNIV MINN, 88-, ASSOC VPRES ACAD AFFAIRS & ASSOC PROVOST ACAD COMPUT & INFO TECHNOL, 93- *Personal Data:* b Goshen, Ind, Mar 6, 47; m 68, Jennifer Hoogenboom; c Alyson K & Ian. *Educ:* Purdue Univ, BS, 69, MS, 70, PhD(mech eng), 76. *Honors & Awards:* Ralph R Teetor Educ Award, Soc Automotive Engrs, 85; AT&T Found Excellence Educ Award, Am Soc Eng Educ, 85. *Concurrent Pos:* Dir, Comput Graphics & Comput Aided Design Lab, Productivity Ctr, Univ Minn, 79-91, assoc dir, Productivity Ctr, 87-91; contrib ed, Comput Mech Eng, Am Soc Mech Engrs, 82-88, assoc ed, J Mech & Mach Theory, 84-90; co-founder & vpres, Minn Techno Transfer, Inc, 84-; mem tech adv bd, Aries Technol Inc, 86-92; co-founder & bd dirs, Digital Dent Systs, Inc, 88-; chmn, Comput Eng Div, Am Soc Mech Engrs, 90-91; mem bd dirs, CICNET Inc & MRNET, Inc. *Mem:* Am Soc Mech Engrs; Inst Elec & Electronics Engrs Comput Soc; Asn Comput Mach; Soc Mfg Engrs; Nat Comput Graphics Asn; Am Soc Eng Educ; Inter Univ Commun Coun; Col & Univ Systs Exchange. *Res:* Computer graphics; computer-aided design; computer-aided manufacturing; knowledge-based systems; bioengineering; product development process; information technology. *Mailing Add:* Univ Minn 120 Morrill Hall 100 Church St SE Minneapolis MN 55455. *Fax:* 612-624-3814; *E-Mail:* drriley@mailbox.mail.umn.edu

RILEY, EDGAR FRANCIS, JR, radiobiology; deceased, see previous edition for last biography

RILEY, GENE ALDEN, PHYSIOLOGY. *Current Pos:* assoc prof, 66-72, chmn, Dept Pharmacol, 70-87, PROF PHARMACOL, SCH PHARM, DUQUESNE UNIV, 72- *Personal Data:* b Wheeling, WVa, July 7, 30; m 53, Mona L Clark; c Thomas C, William C & John C. *Educ:* Duquesne Univ, BS, 52; Case Western Res Univ, PhD(pharmacol), 61. *Prof Exp:* From instr to asst prof pharmacol, Western Res Univ, 61-66. *Concurrent Pos:* NIH res grant, 64-69; mem teaching staff, St Francis Hosp, Pittsburgh, 67-87. *Mem:* Am Pharmaceut Asn; Acad Pharmaceut Sci; Am Soc Consult Pharmacists; Nat Asn Retail Druggists. *Res:* Hormonal control of intermediary metabolism; drug mechanisms leading to intracellular variations in adenosine-phosphate. *Mailing Add:* 313 Kingsberry Circle Pittsburgh PA 15234. *Fax:* 412-396-5130

RILEY, HARRIS D, JR, PEDIATRICS, INFECTIOUS DISEASES. *Current Pos:* PROF PEDIAT, SCH MED, VANDERBILT UNIV. *Personal Data:* b Clarksdale, Miss, Nov 12, 25; m 50; c 3. *Educ:* Vanderbilt Univ, BA, 45, MD, 48. *Prof Exp:* Instr pediat, Sch Med, Vanderbilt Univ, 53-57; prof pediat, Univ Okla, 58-75, distinguished prof, 75-91. *Mem:* Soc Pediat Res; Am Acad Pediat; Am Pediat Soc; Infectious Dis Soc Am; Pediat Infectious Dis Soc. *Res:* Infectious diseases, immunology and renal disease. *Mailing Add:* Vanderbilt Childrens Hosp Vanderbilt Univ Med Ctr Nashville TN 37232-8555

RILEY, JAMES A, PHYSICS. *Current Pos:* from asst prof to assoc prof, 69-79, PROF PHYSICS, DRURY COL, 79- *Personal Data:* b Minneapolis, Minn, May 26, 37; m 62; c 2. *Educ:* Univ Minn, BS, 60; Temple Univ, MA, 64; Univ Minn, PhD(physics), 69. *Prof Exp:* Pub sch teacher, Mich, 60-63; instr physics, Mankato State Col, 64-65. *Concurrent Pos:* Res Corp Fredrick Gardner Cottrell grant, 70. *Mem:* Am Asn Physics Teachers; Am Asn Univ Prof. *Res:* Interaction of atomic oxygen with solid surfaces; analysis of causes of failure of carbonated beverage bottles and closures. *Mailing Add:* Dept Physics Drury Col 900 N Benton Springfield MO 65802

RILEY, JAMES DANIEL, PURE MATHEMATICS. *Current Pos:* INSTR, MOORPARK COL, 88- *Personal Data:* b Tuscola, Ill, June 25, 20; m 52, Elaine A Kutschinski; c Dane A & Gregory A. *Educ:* Park Col, AB, 42; Univ Kans, MA, 48, PhD(math), 52. *Prof Exp:* Asst instr math, Park Col, 46; asst, Univ Kans, 46-48; mathematician, Naval Res Lab, 48-49; asst, Univ Md, 49-50; mathematician, Naval Ord Lab, 52-54; asst prof math, Univ Ky, 54-55; asst prof, Iowa State Univ, 55-58; mem tech staff, Space Tech Labs, Inc Div, Thompson Ramo Wooldridge, Inc, 58-61; mem tech staff, Aerospace Corp, 61-66; staff mathematician, Hughes Aircraft Co, Calif, 66-67; sr exec adv, Western Div, McDonnell Douglas Astronautics Co, Huntington Beach, 67-72; sr staff scientist, 72-74; mem tech staff, TRW, Inc, 74-75; lectr math, Univ Kebangsaan, Malaysia, 75-77; mem staff, Abacus Prog Corp, 77-80, Honeywell, Inc, 80-85; mem staff, Lockheed Aircraft Corp, 85-90. *Mem:* Am Math Soc; Soc Indust & Appl Math; Math Asn Am. *Res:* Complex variables; numerical analysis. *Mailing Add:* 6195 Sylvan Dr Simi Valley CA 93063-4754

RILEY, JOHN FRANCIS, CHEMSTRY, PROPELLANTS ORDNANCE. *Current Pos:* PRES, JHON F RILEY, INC, 93- *Personal Data:* b New Bedford, Mass, Mar 23, 27. *Prof Exp:* Consult scientist & sr mgr Labs, Lockheed Missiles & Space Co, 66-93. *Res:* Chemistry; propellant ordnance. *Mailing Add:* 1842 Edgewater Dr Palo Alto CA 94303-3015

RILEY, JOHN PAUL, AGRICULTURAL ENGINEERING. *Current Pos:* res asst, 63-67, assoc prof, 67-71, PROF CIVIL ENG, UTAH STATE UNIV, 71- *Personal Data:* b Celista, BC, June 27, 27; m 52, Dorothy Everton; c David J, Pamela S, Steven P & Heather A. *Educ:* Univ BC, BASc, 50; Utah State Univ, CE, 53, PhD(civil eng), 67. *Honors & Awards:* Gov Medal for Sci & Technol. *Prof Exp:* Res fel civil eng, Utah State Univ, 51-52; asst hydraul engr, Water Rights Br, BC Prov Govt, 52-54; instr agr eng, Ore State Univ, 54-57; dist eng, Water Rights Br, BC Prov Govt, 57-62, proj eng, Water Invests Br, 62-63. *Mem:* Am Soc Civil Engrs; Sigma Xi; Am Soc Eng Educ; fel Am Water Resources Asn; Am Geophys Union. *Res:* Water rights and computer simulation of water resource systems. *Mailing Add:* Hydrol & Water Res Div Logan UT 84322-4110. *Fax:* 435-750-1185

RILEY, JOHN THOMAS, COAL CHEMISTRY, ANALYTICAL INSTRUMENTATION. *Current Pos:* from asst prof to prof, Western Ky Univ, 68-81, actg head dept, 81, dir, Ctr Coal Sci, 85-95, John Robinson prof, 87, MGR, COAL & FUEL CHARACTERIZATION LAB, WESTERN KY UNIV, 81-, MAT CHARACTERIZATION CTR, 95- *Personal Data:* b Bardstown, Ky, Apr 2, 42; m 63, Rita Hayes; c Sheila M & John P. *Educ:* Western Ky Univ, BS, 64; Univ Ky, PhD(inorg & anal chem), 68. *Concurrent Pos:* Consult industs, 70-; prin investr & co-prin investr 45 external grants, 79-96. *Mem:* Am Chem Soc; Sigma Xi; Am Soc Testing & Mat. *Res:* Coal desulfurization, self-heating and quality deterioration of coal and chemistry of micronized coal; determination of major, minor and trace elements in coal, coal ash and coal-derived materials; atomic spectroscopy; materials science. *Mailing Add:* Dept Chem Western Ky Univ Bowling Green KY 42101. *Fax:* 502-745-6293; *E-Mail:* john.riley@wku.edu

RILEY, KENNETH LLOYD, CHEMICAL ENGINEERING. *Current Pos:* Staff engr, 67-80, SR STAFF ENGR, EXXON RES & DEVELOP LABS, EXXON CO, USA, 80- *Personal Data:* b New Orleans, La, Feb 25, 41; m 61; c 2. *Educ:* La State Univ, BS, 63, MS, 65, PhD(chem eng), 67. *Concurrent Pos:* Adj prof chem eng, La State Univ, 78- *Mem:* Am Inst Chem Engrs; Am Chem Soc; Catalysis Soc. *Res:* Heterogeneous catalysis; development of petroleum and petrochemical processing catalysts and processes; catalyst characterization; process modelling; catalyst preparation; catalyst deactivation. *Mailing Add:* 1289 Rodney Dr Baton Rouge LA 70808-5874

RILEY, LEE HUNTER, JR, ORTHOPEDIC SURGERY. *Current Pos:* From instr to assoc prof, 63-73, chmn dept, 79-91, PROF ORTHOP SURG, SCH MED, JOHNS HOPKINS UNIV, 73-, DISTINGUISHED SERV PROF. *Personal Data:* b St Louis, Mo, May 21, 32; m 57, Helen Mutch; c Lee H III & Reed D. *Educ:* Univ Okla, BS, 54, MD, 57. *Concurrent Pos:* Fel orthop surg, Armed Forces Inst Path, 61; consult, Perry Point Vet Admin Hosp, 63- & Loch Raven Vet Admin Hosp, 68-; mem subcomt rehab & related health serv personnel, Nat Res Coun, 67-; orthop surgeon-in-chief, Johns Hopkins Hosp, 79-91. *Mem:* Am Acad Orthop Surg; Am Col Surgeons; Orthop Res Soc; Am Orthop Asn; Asn Acad Surg; Am Surg Asn. *Res:* Intracellular calcification; orthopedic pathology; total joint replacement; cervical spine surgery. *Mailing Add:* Johns Hopkins Univ 607 N Caroline St Baltimore MD 21287-0882

RILEY, MARK ANTHONY, HIGH SPIN STATES IN NUCLEI, GAMMA-RAY SPECTROSCOPY. *Current Pos:* asst prof physics, 91-94, assoc prof, 94-96, PROF PHYSICS, FLA STATE UNIV, 96- *Personal Data:* b Salford, UK, June 10, 59; m 85; c 2. *Educ:* Univ Liverpool, BSc Hons, 81, PhD(nuclear struct), 85. *Prof Exp:* Res assoc nuclear physics, Niels Bohr Inst, 85-87, Oak Ridge Nat Lab & Univ Tenn, 87-88; advan fel, Univ Liverpool, 88-90. *Mem:* Am Phys Soc. *Res:* Effect of rapid rotation upon the unique quantum system of the atomic nucleus using the techniques of gamma-ray spectroscopy. *Mailing Add:* Dept Physics Fla State Univ Tallahassee FL 32306. *Fax:* 850-644-8630; *E-Mail:* mriley@nucott.physics.fsu.edu

RILEY, MATILDA WHITE, AGING, GERONTOLOGY. *Current Pos:* assoc dir, 85-92, SR SOCIAL SCIENTIST, NAT INST AGING, 92- *Personal Data:* b Boston, Mass, Apr 19, 11. *Educ:* Radcliffe Col, AB, 31, MA, 37. *Hon Degrees:* LHD, Rutgers Univ, 83; DSC, Radcliffe Col, 94. *Honors & Awards:* Commonwealth Award Sociol, 84; Distinguished Creative Contrib to Geront Award, Geront Soc Am, 90; Pres US Meritorius Rank Award, 90; Kent Award, 92. *Prof Exp:* Emer prof sociol, Rutgers Univ, Bowdoin Col. *Mem:* Nat Acad Sci; fel Ctr Advan Study Behav Sci; Eastern Sociol Soc (pres); Geront Soc; AAAS; Am Sociol Asn (pres, 86). *Res:* Author of several books on aging. *Mailing Add:* Dept Health & Human Serv NIH Gateway Bldg Rm 525A Bethesda MD 20892. *E-Mail:* Bitnet: i3y@nihcu.gov

RILEY, MICHAEL VERITY, BIOCHEMISTRY, OPHTHALMOLOGY. *Current Pos:* assoc prof, 69-78, PROF BIOMED SCI, EYE RES INST, OAKLAND UNIV, 78- *Personal Data:* b Bradford, Eng, Dec 27, 33; m 63; c 4. *Educ:* Cambridge Univ, BA, 55, MA, 60; Univ Liverpool, PhD(biochem), 61. *Honors & Awards:* Alcon Res Inst Award, 87. *Prof Exp:* USPHS fel, Sch Med, Johns Hopkins Univ, 61-62; sr lectr biochem, Inst Ophthal, Univ London, 62-69. *Concurrent Pos:* Lister travel fel, Royal Col Surgeons Eng, 67; vis prof, Sch Med, Wash Univ, 67-68; NIH career develop award, 71; mem vision res & training comt, Nat Eye Inst, 71-75; vis prof, Welsh Nat Sch Med, Univ Wales, Cardiff, 75. *Mem:* Asn Res Vision & Ophthal; Sigma Xi; NY Acad Sci; Int Soc Eye Res. *Res:* Transport processes and metabolism that relate to control of hydration and transparency of the cornea; other ocular transport and metabolism. *Mailing Add:* Eye Res Inst Oakland Univ Rochester MI 48309-4401

RILEY, MICHAEL WALTERMIER, INDUSTRIAL ENGINEERING, HUMAN FACTORS. *Current Pos:* ASST PROF INDUST ENG, UNIV NEBR, 75- *Personal Data:* b Sedalia, Mo, Feb 11, 46; m 71; c 2. *Educ:* Univ Mo-Rolla, BS, 68; NMex State Univ, MS, 73; Tex Tech Univ, PhD(indust eng), 75. *Honors & Awards:* R R Teetor Award, Soc Automotive Engrs, 77. *Prof Exp:* Field engr oil prod, Shell Oil Co, 68-70; data analyst missile testing, US Army, 70-72; res asst measurement studies, NMex State Univ, 72-73; instr indust eng, Tex Tech Univ, 73-75. *Concurrent Pos:* NSF traineeship, 74-75. *Mem:* Am Inst Indust Engrs; Am Soc Eng Educ; Sigma Xi; Human Factors Soc; Soc Automotive Engrs. *Res:* Applied human factors; applied operations research. *Mailing Add:* 6030 S 72nd St Lincoln NE 68516

RILEY, MONICA, MOLECULAR GENETICS, GENOME EVOLUTION. *Current Pos:* from assoc prof to prof, 66-89, EMER PROF BIOCHEM, STATE UNIV NY STONY BROOK, 89-; SR SCIENTIST, MARINE BIOL LAB, WOODS HOLE, 89- *Personal Data:* b New Orleans, La, Oct 4, 26; div; c 3. *Educ:* Smith Col, BA, 47; Univ Calif, Berkeley, PhD(biochem), 60. *Prof Exp:* Asst prof bact, Univ Calif, Davis, 60-66. *Concurrent Pos:* USPHS fel, Stanford Univ, 61-62; vis scientist, Univ Brussels, 81; chmn, Comt Molecular & Genetic Microbiol Pub & Sci Affairs Bd, Am Soc Microbiol, 84-87; mem, working groups of recombinant DNA adv comt & NIH, 86-88; organizer, conf on rgn bact chromosome, sponsored by NSF & Am Soc Microbiol, 88 & Third Int E Coli Genome Meeting, 94; chmn & orgn, Gordon Conf Pop Biol & Evolution Microorganisms, 89; ed, Bact Chromosome, Am Soc Microbiol, 90; vis prof, Union Paris-Sud, 91 & 93; co-ed, Escherichia Coli & Salmonella Typhimurium, Am Soc Microbiol, 94. *Mem:* Am Soc Microbiol; Sigma Xi. *Res:* Molecular mechanisms of genome evolution in enterobacteria; evolution of proteins and of the bacterial genome is studied by comparative analysis of genetic maps and by analysis of sequences of bacterial proteins. *Mailing Add:* Marine Biol Lab Woods Hole MA 02543. *Fax:* 508-540-6902; *E-Mail:* mriley@hoh.mbl.edu

RILEY, PATRICK EUGENE, electronics engineering, for more information see previous edition

RILEY, PETER JULIAN, EXPERIMENTAL HIGH ENERGY NUCLEAR PHYSICS, EXPERIMENTAL PARTICLE PHYSICS. *Current Pos:* from asst prof to assoc prof, 62-76, PROF PHYSICS, UNIV TEX, AUSTIN, 76- *Personal Data:* b Kamloops, BC, July 6, 33; m 59, Eva Barkhouse; c Joan,

Kenneth, Chris & Michael. *Educ:* Univ BC, BASc, 56, MASc, 58; Univ Alta, PhD(nuclear physics), 62. *Prof Exp:* Res asst, Fla State Univ, 58-59; grad asst, Univ Alta, 59-61. *Concurrent Pos:* Res partic, Oak Ridge Nat Lab, 66; prog dir, Intermediate Energy Nuclear Physics, NSF, Washington, DC, 84-85; chmn, Dept Physics, Univ Tex, 92- *Mem:* Am Phys Soc. *Res:* Nuclear spectroscopy; reactions and scattering; direct nuclear reactions; nucleon-nucleon interactions, with emphasis on elastic and inelastic polarization measurements at medium energies; measurements of rare kaon decays; relativistic heavy ion physics. *Mailing Add:* Dept Physics Univ Tex RLM 5208 Austin TX 78712. *Fax:* 512-471-9637; *E-Mail:* riley@utaphy.ph.utexas.edu

RILEY, REED FARRAR, INDUSTRIAL CHEMISTRY. *Current Pos:* PRES, REED RILEY ASSOC, INC, 92- *Personal Data:* b Chicago, Ill, Aug 5, 27; m 51, 71, Fran; c Kim, Stephen, Kristin, Meredith, David & Alex. *Educ:* Univ Ill, BS, 49; Mich State Univ, PhD(chem), 54; Columbia Univ, JD, 71. *Prof Exp:* Asst prof, Bucknell Univ, 54-57; from asst prof to assoc prof, Polytech Inst Brooklyn, 57-65; eng specialist, Bayside Labs, Gen Tel & Electronics, Inc, 65-68; patent atty, Stand Oil Co, Inc, 71-74, sr patent atty, 74-77 & 86-92, dir tech liaison, 77-85. *Concurrent Pos:* Res Corp grant, 56-57; NSF res grant, 63-65; AEC contract, 63-65; adj prof, NY Inst Technol, 69-71. *Mem:* Sigma Xi. *Res:* Activated carbons; catalysed processes. *Mailing Add:* 2411 N Burling Chicago IL 60614. *Fax:* 773-477-7653; *E-Mail:* Rileyr@delphi.com

RILEY, RICHARD FOWBLE, PHYSIOLOGICAL CHEMISTRY. *Current Pos:* RETIRED. *Personal Data:* b South Pasadena, Calif, Mar 23, 17; wid. *Educ:* Pomona Col, BA, 39; Univ Rochester, PhD(biochem), 42. *Prof Exp:* Asst biochem & pharmacol, Sch Med & Dent, Univ Rochester, 39-42, instr pharmacol, 42-45; fel biochem, Sch Med, Buffalo, 45-47; asst prof pharmacol, Univ Rochester, 47-49; fel clin radiol, Sch Med, Univ Calif, 49-53, fel physiol chem & radiol, 53-55, assoc prof, 55-82. *Concurrent Pos:* Rep from Univ Calif, Los Angeles, to tech info div, AEC, DC. *Mem:* AAAS; Am Chem Soc; Am Soc Pharmacol & Exp Med; Radiation Res Soc; Soc Exp Biol & Med. *Res:* Radiation biology; radioactive pharmaceuticals for nuclear medicine. *Mailing Add:* 24055 Paseo Del Lago Apt 257 Laguna Hills CA 92653-2638

RILEY, RICHARD KING, MECHANICAL ENGINEERING. *Current Pos:* res engr, 78-80, SR RES ENGR, PHILLIPS PETROL CO, 80- *Personal Data:* b Marshalltown, Iowa, June 4, 36; m 61; c 3. *Educ:* State Univ Iowa, BS, 61, MS, 65; Univ Mo-Rolla, PhD(mech eng), 70. *Prof Exp:* Develop engr, Western Elec Corp, 65-66; from instr to asst prof mech eng, Univ Mo-Rolla, 66-76; prin engr, Dravo Corp, 76-78. *Mem:* Am Soc Mech Engrs; Sigma Xi; Soc Automotive Engrs. *Res:* Petroleum fuels and combustion research. *Mailing Add:* 6600 SE Baylor Dr Bartlesville OK 74006

RILEY, RICHARD LORD, MEDICINE. *Current Pos:* from assoc prof to prof med, 50-77, from assoc prof to prof environ med, Sch Hyg & Pub Health, 50-77, EMER PROF MED, JOHNS HOPKINS UNIV, 77-, EMER PROF ENVIRON HEALTH SCI, 77- *Personal Data:* b North Plainfield, NJ, July 10, 11; m 47; c 3. *Educ:* Harvard Univ, BS, 33, MD, 37. *Honors & Awards:* Trudeau Medal, Am Lung Asn, 70. *Prof Exp:* Intern, Chas V Chapin Hosp, Providence, RI, 37-38, St Luke's Hosp, NY, 38-40; asst resident, Chest Serv, Bellevue Hosp, New York, 40-42; researcher, Off Sci Res & Develop, 42-43; from assoc to asst prof med, Columbia Univ, 47-50; assoc prof, Inst Indust Med, NY Univ, 49-50. *Concurrent Pos:* Physiol Res Sect, Sch Aviation Med, USN, Pensacola, Fla, 46; hon prof, Fac Med, Univ Autonoma de Puebla, Mex, 60. *Mem:* Assoc Am Physiol Soc; assoc Am Thoracic Soc (pres, 77-78); assoc Am Soc Clin Invest; assoc Asn Am Physicians; Sigma Xi; hon mem Can Thoracic Soc; hon mem Thoracic Soc UK. *Res:* Respiratory physiology; cardiovascular physiology; airborne infection; environmental control of airborne infection by ultraviolet air disinfection. *Mailing Add:* Petersham MA 01366-0066

RILEY, ROBERT C, BIOCHEMISTRY. *Current Pos:* PRIN ENTOMOLOGIST, COOP STATE RES SERV, USDA, 68- *Personal Data:* b Brooklyn, NY, Aug 14, 28; m 53, Toni A Puccini; c Brian C & Gail R (Dotson). *Educ:* Hobart Col, BA, 51; Clemson Univ, MS, 59; Rutgers Univ, New Brunswick, PhD(entom), 64. *Honors & Awards:* Outstanding Agr Entom Award, Am Registry Prof Entomologists, 83. *Prof Exp:* Qual control & formulation chemist, Geigy Agr Chem Div, Geigy Chem Corp, 51-55; anal chemist, Clemson Univ, 57-59; from res asst to res assoc entom, Rutgers Univ, 59-64, from asst res prof to assoc res prof entom, 64-68. *Concurrent Pos:* Coordr, Integrated Pest Mgt, 74-75. *Mem:* Entom Soc Am; fel AAAS. *Res:* Integrated control of insects and pest management; economic entomology; pesticides; research information and retrieval systems; grant management. *Mailing Add:* 5013 Cedar Lane W Bethesda MD 20814. *E-Mail:* riley@reeusda.gov

RILEY, ROBERT GENE, ANALYTICAL CHEMISTRY. *Current Pos:* res scientist, Battelle Mem Inst, 76-78, sr res scientist, 78-82, mgr, Environ Chem Sect, Earth Sci Dept, 82-87, mgr, Terrestrial Sci Sect, Environ Sci Dept, 87-88, MGR, GEOCHEM SECT, ENVIRON SCI DEPT, PAC NORTHWEST LABS, BATTELLE MEM INST, 88- *Personal Data:* b Oakland, Calif, June 9, 46. *Educ:* Calif State Univ, Hayward, BS, 69; State Univ NY, PhD(org chem), 74. *Prof Exp:* Res assoc agr chem, Wash State Univ, 74-76. *Mem:* Am Chem Soc. *Res:* Transport, fate and effects of energy related contaminants in aquatic, terrestrial and subsurface environments; distribution and fate of anthropogenic pollutants discharged to estuarine water bodies; synthetic, organic and natural products chemistry. *Mailing Add:* Battelle Pacific NW Lab PO Box 999 Richland WA 99352

RILEY, ROBERT LEE, POLYMER CHEMISTRY, ORGANIC CHEMISTRY. *Current Pos:* PRES, SEPARATION SYSTS INT, 86- *Personal Data:* b Iola, Kans, Jan 8, 35; m 58; c 1. *Educ:* Regis Col, Colo, BS, 56. *Honors & Awards:* Indust Res, Inc Award, 72. *Prof Exp:* Chemist, Convair Div, Gen Dynamics Corp, Tex, 57-58, res chemist, Gen Dynamics Sci Res Lab, Calif, 58-62, from staff assoc to staff mem, Gen Atomic Div, Gen Dynamics Corp, 62-67, staff mem, Gulf Gen Atomic, Inc, 67-72, mgr membrane res & develop, Gulf Environ Systs Co, 72-74; dir res & develop dept, fluid systs div, Universal Oil Prod Inc, 74-84; dir, Technol Fluid Systs Div, Allied Signal Corp, 85-86. *Concurrent Pos:* Guest scientist, Max Planck Inst Biophys, 71. *Mem:* AAAS; Am Chem Soc; Nat Water Supply Improv Asn. *Res:* Environmental science and technology; biomedical engineering; membrane research and development for desalination by reverse osmosis; seawater desalination; gas separation processes; membrane transport, structure and separations technology. *Mailing Add:* 5803 Cactus Way La Jolla CA 92037

RILEY, STEPHEN JAMES, PHYSICAL CHEMISTRY. *Current Pos:* chemist, 80-90, SR CHEMIST, ARGONNE NAT LAB, 90- *Personal Data:* b Washington, DC, July 17, 43. *Educ:* Oberlin Col, Ohio, BA, 65; Harvard Univ, MA, 67, PhD(chem), 70. *Prof Exp:* NIH fel chem, Univ Calif, San Diego, 70-72, res asst chem, 72-73; asst prof chem, Yale Univ, 73-80. *Mem:* Am Phys Soc. *Res:* Chemical and physical properties of isolated metal clusters. *Mailing Add:* Chem Div Argonne Nat Lab 9700 S Cass Ave Argonne IL 60439. *Fax:* 630-252-4954; *E-Mail:* riley@anlchm.chm.anl.gov

RILEY, TERRY ZENE, ECOLOGY OF RING-NECKED PHEASANTS, WETLAND ECOLOGY. *Current Pos:* FIELD REPRESENTATIVE, WILDLIFE MGT INST, 94- *Personal Data:* b Onawa, Iowa, July 27, 49; m 94, Nancy L Derey; c Jason & Samantha. *Educ:* Kans State Univ, BS, 76; NMex State Univ, MS, 78; Ohio State Univ, MS, 87 PhD(zool), 89. *Prof Exp:* Wildlife biologist, Forest Serv, USDA, 78-85; Upland wildlife res biologist, Iowa Dept Natural Resources, 89-94. *Mem:* Sigma Xi; Wildlife Soc. *Res:* Determine landscape effects of row-crop agriculture on ring-necked pheasants in Iowa; survival of hen pheasants in winter and day-old pheasant chicks (up to 4 weeks) in summer to determine how landscape changes affect survival. *Mailing Add:* 528 N Seventh St Chariton IA 50049. *Fax:* 515-774-5448

RILEY, THOMAS N, MEDICINAL CHEMISTRY. *Current Pos:* head, 82-90, actg dean, 87-88 & 92-94, PROF MED CHEM, DEPT PHARM SCI, SCH PHARM, AUBURN UNIV, 90- *Personal Data:* b Mishawaka, Ind, Dec 2, 39; m 60, Phyllis; c 2. *Educ:* Univ Ky, BS, 63; Univ Minn, Minneapolis, PhD(med chem), 69. *Prof Exp:* Teaching asst med chem, Col Pharm, Univ Minn, 63-64, res asst, 64-67; PHS trainee, 67-69; from asst prof to prof, Sch Pharm, Univ Miss, 69-82. *Mem:* Am Chem Soc; Sigma Xi. *Res:* Design, synthesis and evaluation of organic medicinal agents in an attempt to elucidate the molecular mechanisms of drug action; medicinal chemistry of drugs affecting the nervous system including analgesics, anticonvulsants, antihistaminics and bronchodilators. *Mailing Add:* Sch Pharm Auburn Univ Auburn AL 36849. *Fax:* 334-844-8331; *E-Mail:* rileytn@mail.auburn.edu

RILEY, WILLIAM F(RANKLIN), ENGINEERING MECHANICS, MECHANICAL ENGINEERING. *Current Pos:* from assoc prof to prof, 66-78, distinguished prof, 78-88, EMER DISTINGUISHED PROF ENG MECH, IOWA STATE UNIV, 88- *Personal Data:* b Allenport, Pa, Mar 1, 25; m 45, Helen E Chilzer; c Carol A (Stasak) & William F II. *Educ:* Carnegie Inst Technol, BS, 51; Ill Inst Technol, MS, 58. *Honors & Awards:* M M Frocht Award, 77. *Prof Exp:* Mech engr, Mesta Mach Co, 51-54; assoc engr, Armour Res Found, 54-58, res engr, 58-61, sr res engr, 61, sect mgr, IIT Res Inst, 61-64, sci adv, 64-66. *Concurrent Pos:* Am consult, US Agency Int Develop Summer Inst Prog, Bihar Inst Technol, Sindri, India, 66, Indian Inst Technol, Kanpur, India, 70. *Mem:* Fel Soc Exp Mech. *Res:* Photoelasticity, especially the solution of three-dimensional and dynamic stress problems. *Mailing Add:* 1518 Meadowlane Ave Ames IA 50010

RILEY, WILLIAM ROBERT, PHYSICS. *Current Pos:* asst physics, Ohio State Univ, 48-50, instr, 51-53, instr in chg demonstrations, 53-59, from asst prof to assoc prof, 59-87, EMER ASSOC PROF PHYSICS, OHIO STATE UNIV, 87- *Personal Data:* b Bellaire, Ohio, July 31, 22; m 49, Mary C Greig; c Norene J (Holmes) & Jonathan H. *Educ:* Hiram Col, AB, 44; Ohio State Univ, BSc, 51, MA, 52, PhD(sci ed, physics), 59. *Prof Exp:* Instr math & physics, Hiram Col, 46-48. *Concurrent Pos:* Consult, Bur Educ Res, Ohio State Univ, 57-58, res found mobile lab, 59-60; dir, In-serv Insts in Physics, NSF-Ohio State Univ, 65-67, 68-73 & 78-82; consult, North Bengal Univ, India, 64; mem, NSF sci liaison staff, New Delhi, India, 67-68; film review ed, Am J Physics, 69-75. *Mem:* Sigma Xi; AAAS; Nat Sci Teachers Asn; Am Asn Physics Teachers. *Res:* Science education. *Mailing Add:* Dept Physics Ohio State Univ 174 W 18th Ave Columbus OH 43210-1106

RILL, RANDOLPH LYNN, PHYSICAL BIOCHEMISTRY. *Current Pos:* from asst prof to assoc prof, 72-83, PROF CHEM, FLA STATE UNIV, TALLAHASSEE, 84- *Personal Data:* b Canton, Ohio, Oct 19, 44; m 66, Louise H Stolarz; c Matthew C, Bryan R, Douglas W & Liane E. *Educ:* Franklin & Marshall Col, BA, 66; Northwestern Univ, Evanston, PhD(phys chem), 71. *Honors & Awards:* Career Develop Award, USPHS, 75. *Prof Exp:* USPHS fel biophys, Dept Biochem & Biophys, Ore State Univ, Corvallis, 70-72. *Concurrent Pos:* Mem, NIH Biomed Study Sect. *Mem:* Biophys Soc; Am Soc Biol Chemists; Am Chem Soc. *Res:* Physical and chemical studies of DNA-protein interactions; DNA drug and small molecule interactions; self-organization of macromolecules; conformational properties of DNA; biological nuclear magnetic resonance. *Mailing Add:* Dept Chem Fla State Univ Tallahassee FL 32306-3006. *E-Mail:* rill@chem.fsu.edu

RILLEMA, JAMES ALAN, ENDOCRINOLOGY, PHYSIOLOGY. *Current Pos:* from asst prof to assoc prof, 71-79, PROF PHYSIOL, SCH MED, WAYNE STATE UNIV, 79- *Personal Data:* b Grand Rapids, Mich, Nov 6, 42; m 68; c 3. *Educ:* Calvin Col, BS, 64; Mich State Univ, MS, 66, PhD(physiol), 68. *Prof Exp:* NIH fel, Emory Univ, 68-70, res assoc physiol, 70-71. *Concurrent Pos:* Fogarty Sr Int Fel, VanLeeuwenholtz Cancer Inst, Amsterdam, Neth, 80-81. *Mem:* AAAS; Endocrine Soc; Am Physiol Soc; Soc Exp Biol & Med; Sigma Xi. *Res:* Hormones, especially mechanism of action. *Mailing Add:* Dept Physiol Sch Med Wayne State Univ 540 E Canfield Detroit MI 48201-1908

RILLING, HANS CHRISTOPHER, biochemistry, for more information see previous edition

RILLINGS, JAMES H, AUTOMATIC CONTROL SYSTEMS, INTELLIGENT CONTROL. *Current Pos:* PRIN RES ENGR, GEN MOTORS RES LABS, 70- *Personal Data:* b Mineola, NY, June 5, 42; m 78. *Educ:* Rensselaer Polytech Inst, BSEE, 64, MSEE, 66, DEng, 68. *Prof Exp:* Instr elec eng, Rensselaer Polytech Inst, 66-68; engr, Electronics Res Ctr, NASA, 68-70. *Mem:* Inst Elec & Electronics Engrs; Soc Automotive Engrs; Sigma Xi. *Res:* Computer applications to automatic control; intelligent systems; systems engineering. *Mailing Add:* 668 Ardmoor Dr Bloomfield Village MI 48301-2414

RILOFF, ELLEN, COMPUTER SCIENCES, ARTIFICIAL INTELLIGENCE. *Current Pos:* ASST PROF, DEPT COMPUT SCI, UNIV UTAH. *Educ:* Carnegie Mellon Univ, BS; Univ Mass, MS & PhD. *Mailing Add:* Dept Comput Sci Univ Utah 3190 MEB Bldg Salt Lake City UT 84112. *E-Mail:* riloff@cs.utah.edu

RIM, KWAN, ENGINEERING MECHANICS, BIOMEDICAL ENGINEERING. *Current Pos:* from asst prof to assoc prof, 60-68, PROF MECH, UNIV IOWA, 68-, CHMN DEPT MECH & HYDRAUL, 72-, ASSOC DEAN ENG, 74-, ADJ PROF MED, DEPT ORTHOP SURG, 70- *Personal Data:* b Korea, Nov 7, 34; m 62; c 3. *Educ:* Tri-State Col, BS, 55; Northwestern Univ, MS, 58, PhD(theoret & appl mech), 60. *Honors & Awards:* Teetor Educ Fund Award, Soc Automotive Eng, 65. *Prof Exp:* Engr, Int Bus Mach Corp, NY, 56. *Concurrent Pos:* Consult, Deere & Co, Ill, 64-66; actg chmn dept mech & hydraul, Univ Iowa, 71-72. *Mem:* Soc Indust & Appl Math; Am Soc Mech Engrs; Am Soc Eng Educ; Sigma Xi. *Res:* Classical mechanics of deformable bodies, such as the theory of elasticity and viscoelasticity; optimal design; biomechanics. *Mailing Add:* 604 Granada Ct Iowa City IA 52246-2914

RIM, YONG SUNG, ORGANIC CHEMISTRY. *Current Pos:* Res chemist, 68-70, res scientist, 70-75, sr res scientist, Oxford Res Ctr, 75-78, sr group leader elastomer res, 78-80, MGR ETHYELENE-PROPYLENE-DIENE MONOMER RES & DEVELOP, UNIROYAL CHEM, UNIROYAL INC, 80- *Personal Data:* b Changryun, Korea, Mar 15, 35; m 59; c 2. *Educ:* Yonsei Univ, Korea, BS, 57; Univ Tex, Austin, PhD(chem), 67. *Mem:* Am Chem Soc. *Res:* Nonbenzenoid aromatic chemistry; free radical chemistry; fire retardant polymer chemistry; elastomer syntheses and evaluation of elastomers. *Mailing Add:* 15286 Sunny Horse Way Centreville VA 22020

RIMAI, DONALD SAUL, SOLID STATE PHYSICS & ADHESION SCIENCE, ELECTROPHOTOGRAPHY. *Current Pos:* sr res scientist, Eastman Kodak, 79-80, assoc scientist, 80-85, sr staff scientist, 85-92, RES ASSOC, EASTMAN KODAK CO, 92- *Personal Data:* b New York City, NY, Oct 17, 49; m 77. *Educ:* Rensselaer Polytech Inst, BS, 71; Univ Chicago, MS, 73, PhD(physics), 77. *Honors & Awards:* Charles Ives Award, Soc Imaging Sci & Technol. *Prof Exp:* Res assoc, Purdue Univ, 77-79. *Mem:* Am Phys Soc; NY Acad Sci; Sigma Xi; Am Chem Soc; Adhesion Soc. *Res:* Particle adhesion; ultrasonic properties; xerography; electrophotography. *Mailing Add:* PO Box 505 Webster NY 14580. *Fax:* 716-253-1542; *E-Mail:* isbaoo@kr25.profs.kodak.com

RIMAI, LAJOS, NONLINEAR OPTICS, SPECTROSCOPY. *Current Pos:* STAFF SCIENTIST, PHYSICS DEPT, FORD MOTOR CO, 54- *Personal Data:* b Budapest, Hungary, Apr 10, 30; US citizen; m 54; c 3. *Educ:* Univ San Paulo, Brazil, EE, 52, BS, 53; Harvard Univ, PhD(appl physcis), 59. *Prof Exp:* Instr elec eng, Inst Aeronaut Technol, San Jose Campus, San Paulo, Brazil, 53-55; scientist physics, Res Div, Raytheon Co, 59-64. *Mem:* Am Phys Soc. *Res:* Spectroscopic probes of molecular interactions, structure and combustion; nonlinear laser spectroscopic diagnostics of combustion; resonance effects in Raman spectroscopy; resonance Raman spectroscopy of biologically active chromophores (visual pigments); laser velocimetry. *Mailing Add:* 632 Ridgewood Ct Ann Arbor MI 48103

RIMBEY, PETER RAYMOND, THEORETICAL SOLID STATE PHYSICS, ELECTROMAGNETICS. *Current Pos:* SR SPECIALIST ENGR, BOEING COM AIRPLANE GROUP, 90-95, 97-, ATT WIRELESS DATA, 96- *Personal Data:* b LaGrande, Ore, Aug 27, 47; c Juliana J. *Educ:* Eastern Ore State Col, BA, 69; Univ Ore, PhD(physics), 74. *Prof Exp:* Res assoc, Ind Univ, 73-74; fel, Ames Lab, Energy Res & Develop Admin, Iowa State Univ, 75-78; fel, Univ Wis-Milwaukee, 78-80; mem staff, Boeing Aerospace, 80-84; physics dept, Eastern Ore State Col, 83-84 & Seattle Univ, 84-90. *Concurrent Pos:* Contract engr & appl math, Vector Res, Seattle; adj prof elect eng, Henry Cogswell Col, Everett, Wash, 96-. *Mem:* Am Phys Soc; Sigma Xi; Am Asn Physics Teachers. *Res:* Many-body theory; condensed matter; optical properties of semiconductors, molecular crystals and metals; photoemission; surface physics; photo-electro-chemistry; excitons and polarons; transport in semiconductors; electro- and thermo-transport; atomic diffusion; applied mathematics; eletromagnetism. *Mailing Add:* 4129 39th Ave SW Seattle WA 98116. *E-Mail:* primbey@woldnet.att.net

RIMES, WILLIAM JOHN, analytical chemistry, for more information see previous edition

RIMLAND, DAVID, INFECTIOUS DISEASES. *Current Pos:* from asst prof to assoc prof, 81-90, PROF MED, INFECTIOUS DIS, SCH MED, EMORY UNIV, 90- *Personal Data:* b Havana, Cuba, Aug 8, 44; US citizen; wid; c 2. *Educ:* Emory Univ, BS, 66 MD, 70; Am Bd Internal Med, dipl & cert infectious dis. *Prof Exp:* Intern & resident internal med, Barnes Hosp, 70-72; epidemic intel serv officer, Ctr Dis Control, 72-74; resident & fel, Emory Univ Affil Hosps, 74-77. *Concurrent Pos:* Staff physician, Vet Admin Med Ctr, Atlanta, 77-90, dir, Human Immunodeficiency Virus Prog, 89-, chief, infectious dis, 90-, dir, Acquired Immune Deficiency Syndrome Res Ctr, 93- *Mem:* Am Soc Microbiol; Am Fedn Clin Res; Infectious Dis Soc Am; Soc Hosp Epidemiologists Am. *Res:* HIV disease; epidemiology of hospital infections. *Mailing Add:* Med Serv Vet Admin Med Ctr 1670 Clairmont Rd Decatur GA 30033. *Fax:* 404-728-7782

RIMM, ALFRED A, GENETICS, STATISTICS. *Current Pos:* PROF BIOSTATIST, MED COL WIS, 66- *Personal Data:* b Atlantic City, NJ, Apr 13, 34; m 58; c 4. *Educ:* Rutgers Univ, BS, 56, MS, 58, PhD(dairy sci), 62. *Prof Exp:* Sr res scientist, Roswell Park Mem Inst, 63-66. *Mem:* Am Statist Asn; Biomet Soc; Am Pub Health Asn. *Res:* Controlled clinical trials; epidemiology studies in obesity and heart disease; public health statistics; teaching biostatistics in medical school; computers for medical research; immunobiology; disease registeries. *Mailing Add:* Case Western Res Univ Sch Med 2119 Abington Rd Cleveland OH 44106-2333

RIMOIN, DAVID (LAWRENCE), MEDICAL GENETICS. *Current Pos:* assoc prof, 70-73, PROF MED & PEDIAT, SCH MED, UNIV CALIF, LOS ANGELES, 73-; CHMN, DEPT PEDIAT, CEDARS SINAI MED CTR, LOS ANGELES, 86- *Personal Data:* b Montreal, Que, Nov 9, 36; m 62, 80, Ann Garbor; c Anne, Michael & Lauren. *Educ:* McGill Univ, BSc, 57, MSc, & MD, CM, 61; Johns Hopkins Univ, PhD(human genetics), 67. *Honors & Awards:* E Mead Johnson Award, 76; Ross Outstanding Young Investr, 76; Colonel Harland Sanders Award, March of Dimes, 97. *Prof Exp:* Asst prof med & pediat, Wash Univ, 67-70; chief med genetics, Harbor Gen Hosp, 70-86. *Concurrent Pos:* Lectr med, Sch Med, Johns Hopkins Univ, 67-71; consult, Orthop Hosp, Los Angeles, 70-, Fairview State Hosp, Costa Mesa, 71- & Cedars-Sinai Med Ctr, Los Angeles, 71- *Mem:* Inst Med; Am Fedn Clin Res (secy-treas, 73-76); Soc Pediat Res; Am Soc Human Genetics; fel Am Col Physicians; Asn Am Physicians; Am Pediat Soc; Am Soc Clin Invest (pres, 84); Am Col Med Genetics (pres, 90-96). *Res:* Dwarfism; birth defects; genetic disorders of the endocrine glands. *Mailing Add:* 8700 Beverly Blvd Los Angeles CA 90048. *E-Mail:* drimoin@mailgate.csmc.edu

RIMROTT, F(RIEDRICH) P(AUL) J(OHANNES), ENGINEERING MECHANICS. *Current Pos:* from asst prof to prof mech eng, 60-93, EMER PROF MECH ENG, UNIV TORONTO, 93- *Personal Data:* b Halle, Ger, Aug 4, 27; m 55, Doreen McConnell; c Karla, Robert, Kira & Elizabeth. *Educ:* Univ Karlsruhe, Dipl Ing, 51; Univ Toronto, MASc, 55; Pa State Univ, PhD(eng mech), 58; Tech Univ Darmstadt, DrIng, 61. *Hon Degrees:* DSc, Victoria Univ, 92, Univ St Petersburg, 96; DEng, Victoria Univ, 92; DrIng, Magdeburg Univ, 97. *Honors & Awards:* Queen's Silver Anniversary Medal, 77; Downing Award, Can Soc Mech Engrs, 96; Alexander von Humboldt Res. *Prof Exp:* Design engr locomotives, Henschel-Werke Kassel, Ger, 51-52; instr mech eng, Univ Toronto, 53-55; from instr to asst prof eng mech, Pa State Univ, 55-60. *Concurrent Pos:* Vis prof, Wien Tech Univ, 69 & 86, Hannover Tech Univ, 70, Ruhr Univ, 71 & Univ Wuppertal, 78 & Hamburg-Harburg Tech Univ, 87, 89, Magdeburg Univ, 92, 93, 94, 95, 96 & 97; pres, 15th Int Cong Theoret & Appl Mech, 80. *Mem:* Fel Can Soc Mech Engrs; fel Eng Inst Can; Sigma Xi; fel Can Aeronaut & Space Inst; fel Am Soc Mech Engrs; fel Inst Mech Engrs. *Res:* Plasticity; creep; fatigue; strain and stress measurement; vibrations; strength of materials; elasticity; machine design; gyrodynamics. *Mailing Add:* Dept Mech & Indust Eng Univ Toronto Toronto ON M5S 3G8 Can. *Fax:* 416-978-7753

RINALDI, LEONARD DANIEL, mathematics; deceased, see previous edition for last biography

RINALDI, PETER L, NUCLEAR MAGNETIC RESONANCE APPLICATIONS & METHOD DEVELOPMENT. *Current Pos:* assoc prof, 87-91, DIR MOLECULAR SPECTROS LAB, UNIV AKRON, 87-, PROF ANALYTICAL CHEM, 91- *Personal Data:* b Brooklyn, NY, Oct 30, 53; m 76, Mary Larkin. *Educ:* Polytech Inst Brooklyn, BS, 74; Univ Ill, Urbana, PhD(org chem), 78. *Prof Exp:* NIH res fel, Fla State Univ, 78-80; asst prof org chem, Case Western Res Univ, 80-83; nuclear magnetic resonance applns chemist & mgr, Field Appl Labs, Varian Assocs, 84-87. *Concurrent Pos:* Nuclear magnetic resonance consult var firms. *Mem:* Am Chem Soc. *Res:* Nuclear magnetic resonance liquid and solid state techniques to study structure, reactivity and dynamics in polymer, organic, inorganic and biochemistry; development of new methods of nuclear magnetic resonance analysis; particular emphasis on nuclear magnetic resonance analysis of polymers. *Mailing Add:* Dept Chem Univ Akron Akron OH 44325-3601. *Fax:* 330-972-7370; *E-Mail:* plr@atlas.chemistry.uakron.edu

RINALDO, CHARLES R, ACQUIRED IMMUNE DEFICIENCY SYNDROME. *Current Pos:* ASSOC PROF PATH, SCH MED, UNIV PITTSBURGH, 85- *Educ:* Univ Utah, PhD(microbiol), 73. *Mailing Add:* Dept Path Univ Pittsburgh Grad Sch Publ Health A416 Crabtree Hall Pittsburgh PA 15261-0001

RINARD, GILBERT ALLEN, PHYSIOLOGY, ENDOCRINOLOGY. *Current Pos:* from instr to asst prof Physiol, 68-76, ASSOC PROF PHYSIOL, EMORY UNIV, SCH MED, 76- *Personal Data:* b Denver, Colo, Dec 16, 39; m 61; c 4. *Educ:* George Fox Col, BA, 61; Ore State Univ, MS, 63; Cornell Univ, PhD(endocrinol), 66. *Prof Exp:* NIH fel pharmacol, Case Western Res Univ, 66-68. *Mem:* Am Physiol Soc. *Res:* Mechanism of action of drugs used in asthma therapy; cyclic nucleotides; smooth muscle; cellular mechanisms of asthma. *Mailing Add:* Dept Physiol Emory Univ 1440 Clifton Rd NE Atlanta GA 30322

RINCHIK, EUGENE M, GENETICS. *Current Pos:* PROF, SARAH LAWRENCE COL, 93- *Personal Data:* b Troy, NY, May 29, 57. *Educ:* Cornell Univ, BS, 79; Duke Univ, PhD(genetics, microbiol & immunol), 83. *Prof Exp:* Sr staff scientist, Biol Div, Oak Ridge Nat Lab, 85-93. *Concurrent Pos:* Adj asst prof, Univ Tenn, 86-93. *Mem:* Genetics Soc Am; AAAS. *Res:* Experimental germ-line mutagenesis and developmental genetics in the mouse; mouse genome analysis. *Mailing Add:* Sarah Lawrence Col One Mead Way Bronxville NY 10708. *Fax:* 914-395-2662; *E-Mail:* erinchik@mail.slc.gov

RIND, DAVID HAROLD, CIRCULATION MODELING, CLIMATE DYNAMICS. *Current Pos:* SPACE SCIENTIST, GODDARD INST SPACE STUDIES, NASA, 81- *Personal Data:* b New York, NY, May 1, 48. *Educ:* City Col, City Univ New York, BS, 69; Columbia Univ, MA, 73, PhD(meteorol & geophysics), 76. *Prof Exp:* Res assoc, Lamont Doherty Geol Observ, 76-81. *Concurrent Pos:* Lectr, Columbia Univ, 78-82, adj asst prof, 82-; consult, Goddard Inst Space Studies, NASA, 79-81. *Mem:* Am Meteorol Soc; Am Geophys Union. *Res:* Climate and upper atmosphere research using computer models of the atmosphere; observations of upper atmosphere parameters and geophysicsal wave propagation. *Mailing Add:* 201 W 70th St New York NY 10023

RINDERER, THOMAS EARL, GENETICS, INSECT BEHAVIOR. *Current Pos:* RES GENETICIST & RES LEADER, BEE BREEDING & STOCK CTR LAB, AGR RES SERV, USDA, 75-, RES LEADER, HONEYBEE BREEDING, GENETICS & PHYSIOL LAB. *Personal Data:* b Dubuque, Iowa, Sept 16, 43; m 67, 80. *Educ:* Loras Col, BS, 66; Ohio State Univ, MSc, 68, PhD(insect path), 75. *Mem:* Entom Soc Am; Bee Res Asn; Soc Invert Path; Am Behav Soc. *Res:* Epigenetics of disease events, including breeding for resistance and susceptibility in insects and understanding the influence of environmental factors; behavior, behavior genetics, and pathogenetics of honey bees; nector foraging and defensive behavior of both European and Africanized honeybees. *Mailing Add:* 657 Magnolia Wood Ave Baton Rouge LA 70808

RINDERKNECHT, HEINRICH, BIOCHEMISTRY, ORGANIC CHEMISTRY. *Current Pos:* RETIRED. *Personal Data:* b Zurich, Switz, Jan 21, 13; US citizen; m 39, Peggy Wark; c H Robin, Margaret, John & Yvonne S. *Educ:* Swiss Fed Inst Technol, MSc, 36; Univ London, PhD(biochem), 39. *Hon Degrees:* DSc, Univ London, 80. *Prof Exp:* Res chemist, Roche Prod, Ltd, Eng, 39-47; assoc dir biochem res, Aligena Co, Switz, 47-49; res fel chem, Calif Inst Technol, 49-54; res dir org chem, Crookes Labs, London, Eng, 54-55; dir res & develop, Calbiochem, Calif, 55-62; sr res fel chem, Calif Inst Technol, 62-70; from assoc prof to prof, Sch Med, Univ Southern Calif, 64-70; chief med biochem, Vet Admin Hosp, Sepulveda, 70-85; prof med, Univ Calif, Los Angeles, 70-85. *Concurrent Pos:* Consult, Cilag A G, Switz, 49-54, Geigy Pharmaceut, 55-57 & Stuart Co, Calif, 59-61; mem ed comt, Int J Pancreatology, 86- *Mem:* AAAS; Am Fedn Clin Res; Brit Biochem Soc; fel Royal Soc Health; NY Acad Sci; Int Asn Pancreatology. *Res:* Development of synthetic analgesics and local anesthetics; synthesis of nucleotides, enzyme substrates and metabolites; ultrarapid method for fluorescent labeling of proteins; role of proteolytic and lysosomal enzymes in acute pancreatitis and cancer of the pancreas; radioimmunoassay of peptide hormones. *Mailing Add:* 1971 Cielito Lane Santa Barbara CA 93105

RINDLER, WOLFGANG, RELATIVITY THEORY, COSMOLOGY. *Current Pos:* prof math, 69-80, PROF PHYSICS, UNIV TEX, DALLAS, 80- *Personal Data:* b Vienna, Austria, May 18, 24; m 59, 77, Linda Veret; c Eric, Cindy & Mitchell. *Educ:* Univ Liverpool, BSc, 45, MSc, 47; Univ London, PhD, 56. *Prof Exp:* Asst lectr pure math, Univ Liverpool, 47-49; lectr math, Univ London, 49-56; from instr to asst prof, Cornell Univ, 56-63; from assoc prof to prof, Southwest Ctr Advan Studies, 63-69. *Concurrent Pos:* NSF fel, Hamburg & King's Col, Univ London, 61-62; Nat Res Coun Italy fel, Univ Rome, 68-69; vis prof, Univ Vienna, 75 & 87; vis fel, Churchill Col, Cambridge, 90. *Mem:* Fel Am Phys Soc; fel Royal Astron Soc; Int Astron Union; Int Soc Gen Relativity & Gravitation. *Res:* Relativity; cosmology; spinors. *Mailing Add:* Dept Physics Univ Tex Dallas Richardson TX 75083-0688. *Fax:* 972-883-2848; *E-Mail:* rindler@utdallas.edu

RINDONE, GUY E(DWARD), GLASS SCIENCE & TECHNOLOGY. *Current Pos:* asst, Pa State Univ, 47-48, from asst prof to prof, 49-81, chmn sect, 69-80, EMER PROF CERAMIC SCI, PA STATE UNIV, UNIVERSITY PARK, 81-; PRES, MAT RES CONSULTS, INC, 81- *Personal Data:* b Buffalo, NY, Aug 11, 22; wid; c Wayne & Gary. *Educ:* Alfred Univ, BS, 43; Pa State Univ, MS, 46, PhD(ceramics), 48. *Honors & Awards:* Forrest Award, Am Ceramic Soc, 63, Founders Award, 84, Toledo Glass Award, 84; Bleininger Award, 88. *Prof Exp:* Glass technologist, Sylvania Elec Prod, Inc, 43-45 & Glass Sci Inc, 45-47. *Concurrent Pos:* Prog chmn, Int Cong Glass, DC, 62; mem coun, Int Comn Glass; mem, Univs Space Res Asn, NASA, 72-87. *Mem:* Fel Am Ceramic Soc (vpres, 77-78); fel Brit Soc Glass Technol. *Res:* Ceramic and glass science; solarization; gas evolution anelasticity, nucleation and crystallization processes and electrochemical behavior of glass; small angle x-ray scattering of glass; relaxation processes; glass strength; fluorescence; microstructure, laser light scattering; nuclear waste encapsulation; optical glass; gradient index glasses. *Mailing Add:* 247 McCormick Ave State College PA 16801. *E-Mail:* rindone@ems.psu.edu

RINE, DAVID C, COMPUTER SCIENCE, INFORMATION SYSTEMS. *Current Pos:* PROF & CHMN COMPUT & INFO SCI, GEORGE MASON UNIV, 85-, PROF COMPUT SCI & INFO & SOFTWARE SYSTS ENG, 91- *Personal Data:* b Bloomington, Ill, Nov 16, 41; m; c 2. *Educ:* Ill State Univ, BS, 60; Okla State Univ, MS, 66; Univ Iowa, PhD(math), 70. *Honors & Awards:* Honor Roll Award, Inst Elec & Electronics Engrs Comput Soc, 77 & 81, Spec Award, 77; Centennial Award, Inst Elec & Electronics Engrs, 84, Pioneer Award, Computer Soc, 88. *Prof Exp:* Database systs consult, 78-82; educ consult, 80-85. *Concurrent Pos:* Consult, govt & indust contracts; software eng consult, 87- *Mem:* Inst Elec & Electronics Engrs; Computer Soc; Am Fedn Info Processing Soc; Int Coun Comput Educ; Asn Comput Mach. *Res:* Database systems; knowledge based systems with an emphasis on logic programming, logic design and software engineering; software engineering; systems analysis; object oriented software development. *Mailing Add:* Dept Comput Sci Software Systs Eng George Mason Univ 4400 Univ Fairfax VA 22030

RINEHART, EDGAR A, MOLECULAR SPECTROSCOPY, LASERS. *Current Pos:* asst prof, 64-67, assoc prof, 67-77, PROF PHYSICS & ASTRON, UNIV WYO, 77- *Personal Data:* b Guthrie, Okla, Oct 16, 28; m 59; c 2. *Educ:* Cent State Col, Okla, BS, 52; Univ Okla, MS, 55, PhD(physics), 61. *Prof Exp:* Asst prof physics, Univ Idaho, 60-61; adj asst prof, Univ Okla, 61-64. *Concurrent Pos:* Consult, Lawrence Livermore Lab, 66- & Martin Marietta Corp, 78-79; Fac res partic, US DOE Oak Ridge Assoc Univ, 87. *Mem:* Am Phys Soc; Am Chem Soc; Soc Appl Spectros; Optical Soc Am; Sigma Xi; Inst Elec & Electronics Engrs. *Res:* Microwave spectroscopy, line widths and intensities; free radicals; laser physics; optics; astronomy. *Mailing Add:* Dept Physics & Astron Univ Wyo PO Box 3905 Laramie WY 82071

RINEHART, FRANK PALMER, BIOPHYSICAL CHEMISTRY. *Current Pos:* from asst prof to assoc prof, 77-87, PROF CHEM, UNIV VI, 88- *Personal Data:* b Washington, DC, Mar 1, 44. *Educ:* Western Md Col, BA, 66; Univ Calif, Berkeley, PhD(chem), 71. *Prof Exp:* Lectr chem, Univ Ife, Nigeria, 71-74; researcher biophys chem, Univ Calif, Davis, 74-77, lectr chem, 77. *Mem:* Am Chem Soc. *Res:* Analysis of repetitive sequences in eucaryotic DNA; design of microcomputer software for chemistry courses. *Mailing Add:* Dept Chem Univ VI No 2 John Brewers Bay Charlotte Amalie VI 00802

RINEHART, JAY KENT, CHEMISTRY. *Current Pos:* Sr res chemist, 67-85, RES ASSOC, PPG INDUSTS, INC, 85- *Personal Data:* b Xenia, Ohio, Apr 13, 40; m 61; c 2. *Educ:* Univ Cincinnati, BS, 62; Univ Minn, Minneapolis, PhD(org chem), 67. *Mem:* Am Chem Soc; AAAS. *Res:* Synthesis of new pesticides; structure-activity correlations as a tool for new pesticide design; carbene chemistry; small ring chemistry; bridged aromatic compounds; organic sulfur chemistry; heterocyclic chemistry; agricultural chemistry; synthesis of isotopically labelled compounds; radiochemistry. *Mailing Add:* Bristol Myers Squib Co PO Box 4000 Princeton NJ 68543-4000

RINEHART, JOHN SARGENT, PHYSICS. *Current Pos:* RETIRED. *Personal Data:* b Kirksville, Mo, Feb 8, 15; m 40; c 2. *Educ:* Northeastern Mo State Teachers Col, BS, 34, AB, 35; Calif Inst Technol, MS, 37; Univ Iowa, PhD(physics), 40. *Honors & Awards:* Presidential Cert Merit. *Prof Exp:* Asst physics, Calif Inst Technol, 35-37; asst, Univ Iowa, 37-40, Kans State Col, 40 & Wayne State Univ, 41-42; assoc physicist, Nat Bur Stand, 42; sect tech aide, Nat Defense Res Comt, 42-45; head physicist & supvr exp range, Res & Develop Div, NMex Sch Mines, 45-48; head terminal ballistics br, US Naval Ord Testing Sta, Inyokern, 49-50, mech br, 50-51 res physicist, 51-55; asst dir astrophys lab, Smithsonian Inst, 55-58; prof mining eng & dir mining res lab, Colo Sch Mines, 58-64; dir res, US Coast & Geod Surv, 64-65; dir sci & eng, Environ Sci Serv Admin, 65-66, sr res fel, Nat Oceanic & Atmospheric Admin, 68-73. *Concurrent Pos:* Adj prof, Univ Colo, Boulder, 68-73. *Mem:* Am Geophys Union. *Res:* Interior, exterior and terminal ballistics; failure of metals under impulsive loading; hypersonics; rock physics; geysers; geothermal areas. *Mailing Add:* Hyperdynamics PO Box 392 Santa Fe NM 87501-0392

RINEHART, KENNETH LLOYD, ORGANIC CHEMISTRY. *Current Pos:* From instr to assoc prof, 54-64, univ scholar, 89-92, PROF ORG CHEM, UNIV ILL, URBANA, 64-, SR UNIV SCHOLAR, 89- *Personal Data:* b Chillicothe, Mo, Mar 17, 29; m 61, Marlyn Joan Whitsitt; c 3. *Educ:* Yale Univ, BS, 50; Univ Calif, PhD(chem), 54. *Honors & Awards:* Squibb Lectr, Rutgers Univ, 61 & 83; Werner Lectr, Univ Kans, 65; A D Little Lectr, Mass Inst Technol, 75; Barnett Lectr, Northeastern Univ, 81; Andrews Lectr, New South Wales, 82; Smith Lectr, Okla State Univ, 83; Res Achievement Award, Am Soc Pharmacog, 89; Karcher lectr, Univ Okla, 91; Marple-Schweitzer Lectr, Northwestern Univ, 90; Herbert C Brown Lectr, Purdue Univ, 90; Karcher Lectr, Univ Okla, 91; Ole Gisvold Mem Lectr, Univ Minn, 95; Guenther Award, Am Chem Soc, 97. *Concurrent Pos:* Fels, Orgn Europ Econ Coop, 60, Guggenheim, 62, Fulbright, 66 & Erskine, 83; assoc, Ctr Advan

Study, Univ Ill, 69-70; distinguished vis lectr, Tex A&M Univ, 80; consult, PharmaMar & NIH. *Mem:* Am Chem Soc; Royal Soc Chem; Am Soc Biol Chem; Am Soc Microbiol; fel AAAS; Am Soc Mass Spectrometry; Am Soc Biochem & Molecular Biol; Chem Soc; Am Soc Pharmacog (vpres, 94-95, pres, 95-96); Am Peptide Soc; Sigma Xi. *Res:* Structure, biosynthesis and synthesis of natural products; antibiotics and marine natural products; mass spectrometry; chemistry of natural products with pharmacological activity. *Mailing Add:* 454 Roger Adams Lab Box 45-5 Univ Ill 600 S Mathews Ave Urbana IL 61801-3792

RINEHART, ROBERT R, GENETICS, RADIATION BIOLOGY. *Current Pos:* RETIRED. *Personal Data:* b Shenandoah, Iowa, Apr 5, 32; m 55; c 3. *Educ:* San Diego State Col, AB, 58; Univ Tex, PhD(zool), 62. *Prof Exp:* USPHS fel genetics, Oak Ridge Nat Lab, 62-63; res assoc, Ind Univ, 63-64; from assoc prof to prof biol, San Diego State Univ, 64-95. *Concurrent Pos:* AEC res grant, 64-; res assoc, State Univ Leiden, Neth, 68-69. *Mem:* AAAS; Genetics Soc Am. *Res:* Radiation induced mutation repair of radiation damage; chromosome mechanics in Drosophila. *Mailing Add:* 6434 Del Cerro Blvd San Diego CA 92120

RINEHART, WALTER ARLEY, ENGINEERING MANAGEMENT, AEROSPACE ENGINEERING. *Current Pos:* Assoc engr thermodyn, McDonnell Douglas Corp, 59, from res asst to res assoc arc heaters, 59-64, res scientist, 64-69, group engr, 69-70, sr group engr gas dynamics, 70-72, sect mgr, 72-77, br chief, 77-86, chief tech engr, 86-90, DIR, MCDONNELL DOUGLAS CORP, 90- *Personal Data:* b Peoria, Ill, June 1, 36; m 59, Carol Vickery; c Vicki & Linda. *Educ:* Univ Mo-Rolla, BS, 59. *Concurrent Pos:* Nat Tech Comt Ground Testing & Simulation, 75-78. *Mem:* Am Inst Aeronaut & Astronaut. *Res:* Technology development with emphasis toward aerodynamics; aerothermodynamics, propulsion, thermal management; vehicle synthesis for future aerospace vehicles. *Mailing Add:* 16232 Lone Cabin Dr Chesterfield MO 63005

RINER, JOHN WILLIAM, MATHEMATICS. *Current Pos:* from asst prof to assoc prof, 59-69, assoc, Systs Res Group, 60-64, PROF MATH, OHIO STATE UNIV, 69-, VCHMN DEPT, 70- *Personal Data:* b Kansas City, Mo, July 29, 24; m 47; c 5. *Educ:* Rockhurst Col, BS, 47; Univ Notre Dame, MS, 49, PhD(math), 53. *Prof Exp:* Instr math, Univ Notre Dame, 49-50 & St Peters Col, 53-56; asst prof, St Louis Univ, 56-59. *Mem:* Am Math Soc. *Res:* Topology; organization theory. *Mailing Add:* 5404 Hollister St Columbus OH 43235

RINES, HOWARD WAYNE, PLANT GENETICS, PLANT BREEDING. *Current Pos:* ADJ ASSOC PROF, DEPT AGRON & PLANT GENETICS, UNIV MINN, ST PAUL, 76- *Personal Data:* b Portland, Ind, Feb 19, 42; m 65; c 3. *Educ:* Purdue Univ, BS, 64, MS, 66; Yale Univ, PhD(genetics), 69. *Prof Exp:* Captain, US Army Reserves, 69-71; asst prof bot & genetics, dept bot, Univ Ga, Athens, 71-76; res geneticist, Agr Res Serv, USDA, 76- *Mem:* Am Soc Agron; Int Asn Plant Tissue Cult. *Res:* Plant genetics; application of genetics, tissue culture, and molecular biology to crop improvement; introgression of useful genes from wild species and other exotic sources into cultivated species by conventional and nonconventional techniques. *Mailing Add:* Agron 411 Univ Minn Borlaug Hall 1991 Upper Buford Circle St Paul MN 55108-6024

RINES, ROBERT HARVEY, ENGINEERING. *Current Pos:* PARTNER, RINES & RINES, 47-, PRES & PROF LAW CHMN, FRANKLIN PIERCE LAW CTR, 73- *Personal Data:* b Boston, Mass, Aug 30, 22; wid, Carol Williamson; c Christopher, Robert Louis & Suzi Kay Ann. *Educ:* Mass Inst Technol, BS, 42; Georgetown Univ, JD, 47; Nat Chiao Tung Univ, PhD, 72; New Eng Col Law, DJ, 74; Notre Dame Col, DSc, 94. *Honors & Awards:* Gordon McKay Lectr, Harvard Univ, 56-58; Inventions Citation Pres Carter & US Dept Com, 80; Medal of Honor, Acad Appl Sci, 89; Nat Inventors Hall of Fame, 94. *Prof Exp:* Asst examr, US Patent Off, 46-47. *Concurrent Pos:* Lectr inventions & innovations, Mass Inst Technol, 62-; mem, Nat Inventors Coun, 63-67 &81-; comt mem, Nat Inventors Hall of Fame, 74- *Mem:* Nat Acad Eng; sr mem Inst Elec & Electronics Engrs; AAAS; fel Int Soc Cryptozool; Acad Appl Sci (pres, 89); Sci Res Soc Am; Sigma Xi. *Res:* Granted patent in radar and sonar field. *Mailing Add:* 81 N State St Concord NH 03301-4329

RING, DENNIS RANDALL, economic entomology, for more information see previous edition

RING, JAMES GEORGE, DATABASE ADMINISTRATION, NUCLEAR MEASUREMENTS. *Current Pos:* prin tech analyst, 82-90, SR SYST ANALYST, COMMONWEALTH EDISON, 91- *Personal Data:* b Chicago, Ill, July 26, 38. *Educ:* Ill Inst Technol, BS, 60, PhD(physics), 66. *Prof Exp:* Res assoc physics, Univ Ill, Urbana, 65-68; vis asst prof, Univ Ill, Chicago Circle, 68-71; res physicist, Packard Instrument Co, 72-74, sr res physicist, lab, 74-82. *Mem:* Am Phys Soc; Sigma Xi. *Res:* Optical properties of color centers in alkali halides; Borrmann effect in germanium and silicon; laser Raman scattering; applied research on radiation detectors; computer assisted spectral analysis. *Mailing Add:* 10626 S Albany Ave Chicago IL 60655-2114

RING, JAMES WALTER, SOLAR ENERGY, INDOOR AIR QUALITY. *Current Pos:* From asst prof to assoc prof, 57-69, chmn dept, 68-80, PROF PHYSICS, HAMILTON COL, 69-, WINSLOW PROF PHYSICS, 75- *Personal Data:* b Worcester, NY, Feb 24, 29; m 59, Elizabeth Muir; c Andrew J. *Educ:* Hamilton Col, AB, 51; Univ Rochester, PhD(physics), 58. *Honors & Awards:* Cert Achievement & Prize for Design, Construct & Testing Solar Classroom, Acad Educ Develop, 80. *Concurrent Pos:* NSF sci fac fel, AERE Harwell, UK, 65-66; attached physicist, Phys Chem Lab, Oxford Univ, UK, 73; vis fel, Princeton Univ, 81; guest reseacher, Tech Univ Denmark, 87; radiation officer, Hamilton Col, 64-84, eng liaison officer, 75-, pres, Am Asn Univ Prof chap, 87-93, chmn dept, 91-92; founding mem, Sigma Xi Chaps, Hamilton Col. *Mem:* Am Phys Soc; Am Asn Physics Teachers. *Res:* Dielectrics; inelastic neutron scattering; H-bonded liquids; vibrational modes; solar energy; energy conservation; passive solar heating; infiltration and ventilation; computer energy management; thermal comfort indoors; solar energy in the Roman Empire; environmental physics. *Mailing Add:* Dept Physics Hamilton Col Clinton NY 13323. *Fax:* 315-859-4696; *E-Mail:* jring@itsmail1.hamilton.edu

RING, JOHN ROBERT, ANATOMY. *Current Pos:* from asst prof to assoc prof, Sch Dent Med, Washington Univ, 47-62, asst dean pre-clin instr & res, 67-72, chmn, Anat Dept, 74-77, prof anat, 62-83, dir admis, 72-83, asst dean biomed sci & chmn dept, 77-83, EMER PROF, SCH DENT MED, WASHINGTON UNIV, 83- *Personal Data:* b Warsaw, Ind, Nov 19, 15; m 48, Lucile Wiley; c 3. *Educ:* Univ Ill, AB, 39; Brown Univ, ScM, 41, PhD(biol), 43. *Prof Exp:* Instr anat, Sch Med, St Louis Univ, 43-47. *Mem:* Am Asn Dent Schs; AAAS; Am Asn Anat; Int Asn Dent Res; Sigma Xi. *Res:* Sex endocrinology; gerontology; histology and histochemistry of endocrine organs and oral tissues. *Mailing Add:* 2041 Reservoir Loop Rd 755 Catalpa Ave Selah WA 98942

RING, MOREY ABRAHAM, INORGANIC CHEMISTRY. *Current Pos:* from asst prof to assoc prof chem, 62-69, PROF CHEM, SAN DIEGO STATE UNIV, 69- *Personal Data:* b Detroit, Mich, Aug 31, 32; m 60; c 4. *Educ:* Univ Calif, Los Angeles, BS, 54; Univ Wash, PhD(chem), 60. *Prof Exp:* Fel chem, Johns Hopkins Univ, 60-61; sr engr, Rocketdyne Div, NAm Aviation, Inc, 61-62. *Mem:* Am Chem Soc. *Res:* Chemistry of group IV compounds, especially silicon hydrides. *Mailing Add:* Dept Chem San Diego State Univ San Diego CA 92182-0002

RING, PAUL JOSEPH, PHYSICS & RADIOLOGICAL SCIENCE. *Current Pos:* ASSOC PROF PHYSICS, UNIV MASS LOWELL, 67- *Personal Data:* b Winthrop, Mass, Dec 1, 28; m 66; c 4. *Educ:* Boston Col, BS, 50; Rensselaer Polytech Inst, MS, 54; Brown Univ, PhD(physics), 63. *Prof Exp:* Scientist physics, Nuclear Magnetics Corp, Perkin-Elmer Corp, 56-57; res asst, Brown Univ, 57-60; consult, Metals & Controls, Inc, Mass, 60-61; res asst, Brown Univ, 61-63; scientist semiconductors, Transitron Electronics Corp, Mass, 63-64; scientist electrooptics, RCA, Mass, 64-67. *Concurrent Pos:* Vis prof, Inst Educ Technol, Univ Surrey, Eng. *Mem:* Health Physics Soc; Sigma Xi. *Res:* Solid state and infrared physics; cathodoluminescence; minerals; nuclear magnetic resonance; education; ultrasonics; dosimeters; spectral measurements of dosimeters. *Mailing Add:* Dept Physics & Appl Sci Univ Mass 1 University Ave Lowell MA 01854

RING, RICHARD ALEXANDER, ENTOMOLOGY. *Current Pos:* from asst prof to assoc prof, 66-88, PROF ENTOM, UNIV VICTORIA, BC, 88- *Personal Data:* b Glasgow, Scotland, Sept 24, 38; m 60; c 2. *Educ:* Glasgow Univ, BSc, 61, PhD(entom), 65. *Prof Exp:* Asst prof zool, Univ BC, 64-65; Nat Res Coun Can fel, Entom Res Inst, Can Dept Agr, 65-66. *Mem:* Soc Cryobiol; Can Soc Zool; Can Entom Soc; Arctic Inst NAm; Entom Soc Am; fel Royal Entom Soc. *Res:* Insect ecology and physiology; extrinsic and intrinsic control of diapause and coldhardiness in insects; intertidal insects; insect biodiversity in the canopy of temperate old-growth rain forests. *Mailing Add:* Dept Biol Univ Victoria Box 1700 Victoria BC V8W 2Y2 Can. *Fax:* 250-721-7120; *E-Mail:* raring@uvic.ca

RING, TERRY WILLIAM, ENVIRONMENTAL SCIENCE. *Current Pos:* PRES, SILVER CREEK OUTFITTERS INC, IDAHO, 80- *Personal Data:* b Lewiston, Idaho, Nov 11, 55. *Educ:* Boise State Univ, BA, 79. *Honors & Awards:* Oak Leaf Award, Nature Conservancy, 93. *Concurrent Pos:* Bd dirs, Idaho Nature Conservancy, 82-, chmn 86-92. *Mem:* Nature Conservancy. *Mailing Add:* PO Box 1096 Sun Valley ID 83353-1096

RINGEISEN, RICHARD DELOSE, MATHEMATICS, GRAPH THEORY & APPLICATIONS. *Current Pos:* DEAN, COL SCI, OLD DOMINION UNIV, NORFOLK, VA, 93- *Personal Data:* b Kokomo, Ind, Mar 18, 44; m 65, Carolyn Byrer; c Heather L & Bradley R. *Educ:* Manchester Col, BS, 66; Mich State Univ, MS, 68, PhD(math), 70. *Prof Exp:* Asst prof math, Colgate Univ, 70-74; from asst prof to assoc prof math, Ind Univ-Purdue Univ, Ft Wayne, 74-79; from asst prof to assoc prof math, Clemson Univ, 79-86, prof & dir grad studies math, 86-88, head math sci, 88-93. *Concurrent Pos:* Vis scientist human eng, Aerospace Med Res Lab, Wright-Patterson AFB, 78-79; sci officer discrete math, Off Naval Res, 85-86; actg dir math sci, Clemson Univ, 86. *Mem:* Am Math Soc; Math Asn Am; Soc Indust & Appl Math; AAAS; Coun Col Arts & Sci. *Res:* Graph theory, with special emphasis in applications, modelling and topological problems; network models for social sciences. *Mailing Add:* ECarolina Univ Greenville NC 27858-4353. *Fax:* 757-683-3034; *E-Mail:* ring@cs.odu.edu

RINGEL, GERHARD, GRAPH THEORY. *Current Pos:* prof, 70-90, EMER PROF MATH, UNIV CALIF, SANTA CRUZ, 90- *Personal Data:* b Kollnbrunn, Austria, Oct 28, 19; Ger citizen; m 45, 66, Isolde Putsky; c Gerhard, Renate (Preuschoft) & Ingrid. *Educ:* Friedrich-Wilhelms Univ, Dr rer nat, 51, Habilitation, 53. *Hon Degrees:* Dr rer pol hc, Univ Fredriciana, 83; Dr rer nat hc, Free Univ Berlin, 94. *Prof Exp:* Lectr math, Friedrich-Wilhelms Univ, Bonn, 53-56, asst prof, 56-60; lectr math,

Johann-Wolfgang-Goethe-Univ, Frankfurt, 57-60; assoc prof, Free Univ Berlin, 60-66, prof math, 66-70, dir II Math Inst, 69-70. *Concurrent Pos:* Vis prof, Univ Calif, Santa Cruz, 67-68. *Mem:* Ger Math Asn; Am Math Soc; Inst Combinatorics Appln Can; Am Lepidopterist Soc. *Res:* Published 75 research articles and 3 books; combinatorics and graph-theory. *Mailing Add:* Univ Calif 1156 High St Santa Cruz CA 95064-0118

RINGEL, SAMUEL MORRIS, CLINICAL PHARMACOLOGY, INFECTIOUS DISEASES. *Current Pos:* PHARMACEUT CONSULT, RINGEL ASSOCS, 85- *Personal Data:* b New York, NY, Nov 29, 24; m 51, Sylvia David; c David, Jonathan & Alan. *Educ:* Hunter Col, BA, 50; Univ Mich, MS, 51; Mich State Univ, PhD(mycol), 56. *Prof Exp:* Jr microbiologist, Hoffmann-La Roche, 51-52; asst mycol, Mich State Univ, 53-56; from assoc plant pathologist to plant pathologist, Agr Mkt Serv, USDA, 56-61; from sr scientist to sr res assoc, Dept Microbiol & Immunol, Warner-Lambert Res Inst, 61-78; from asst dir to assoc dir clin pharmacol, Revlon Health Care Group, 79-84. *Concurrent Pos:* Vis scientist, NJ Acad Sci, 65-67; pres, Theobald Smith Soc, 77-78; consult numerous univs, industs & insts, 78-85. *Mem:* Int Soc Human & Animal Mycoses; Soc Indust Microbiol; Am Soc Clin Pharmacol & Therapeut; Am Soc Microbiol; NY Acad Sci. *Res:* Fungal enzymes; antifungal agents; post-harvest diseases of fruits and vegetables; medical and pharmaceutical microbiology; antibiotics; cardiovascular research. *Mailing Add:* 7202 NW 93rd Ave Tamarac FL 33321

RINGEL, STEVEN ADAM, ELECTRONIC MATERIALS, PHOTOVOCTAICS. *Current Pos:* ASST PROF ELEC ENG, OHIO STATE UNIV, 91- *Personal Data:* b New Brunswick, NJ, July 21, 62; m 85, Karen; c Seth & Brett. *Educ:* Pa State Univ, BS, 84, MS, 86; Ga Inst Technol, PhD(elec eng), 91. *Concurrent Pos:* NSF. *Mem:* Inst Elec & Electronics Engrs; Mat Res Soc; Vacuum Soc. *Res:* Epitaxial growth, characterization and processing of electronic materials and devices; group III-V and IV semiconductors; defects; lattice-mismatched systems; photovoltoics. *Mailing Add:* Ohio State Univ Dept Elec Eng 2015 Neil Ave Columbus OH 43210. *Fax:* 614-292-7596; *E-Mail:* ringel@ee.eng.ohio_state.edu

RINGER, DAVID P, CHEMICAL CARCINOGENESIS, GENE EXPRESSION. *Current Pos:* SECT HEAD, BIOCHEM PHARMACOL, SAMUEL ROBERTS NOBLE FOUND, INC, 75- *Educ:* Wayne State Univ, Detroit, PhD(biochem), 73. *Res:* Carcinogenic metabolism. *Mailing Add:* 812 N Creek Dr Edmond OK 73034

RINGER, LARRY JOEL, STATISTICS. *Current Pos:* from instr to assoc prof, 65-75, res scientist, Data Processing Ctr, 74-76, PROF STATIST & ASST HEAD DEPT, TEX A&M UNIV, 75- *Personal Data:* b Cedar Rapids, Iowa, Sept 24, 37; m 60, Jean Bradley; c Margaret, Michael & Susan. *Educ:* Iowa State Univ, BS, 59, MS, 62; Tex A&M Univ, PhD(statist), 66. *Prof Exp:* Res asst statist, Iowa State Univ, 59-61. *Concurrent Pos:* Assoc res statistician, Tex Transportation Inst, 70-79; Statisical consult, Data Processing Ctr, 81-82. *Mem:* Am Statist Asn; Am Soc Qual Control; Sigma Xi. *Res:* Statistical methods and techniques as applied to problems in engineering and physical sciences; agriculture. *Mailing Add:* Dept Statist Tex A&M Univ College Station TX 77843-3143

RINGER, ROBERT KOSEL, PHYSIOLOGY. *Current Pos:* from asst prof to assoc prof, 57-64, prof physiol, 65-89, PROF AVIAN PHYSIOL, MICH STATE UNIV, 64-, EMER PROF PHYSIOL, 89- *Personal Data:* b Ringoes, NJ, Feb 21, 29; m 51, Joan Harwick; c Kevin James. *Educ:* Rutgers Univ, BS, 50, MS, 52, PhD(physiol), 55. *Honors & Awards:* Founder's Award, Soc Environ Toxicol & Chem, 96. *Prof Exp:* Asst prof avian physiol, Rutgers Univ, 55-57. *Concurrent Pos:* On leave, Unilever Res Lab, Eng, 66-67 & Environ Protection Agency Res Lab, Corvallis, Ore, 84-85. *Mem:* Am Asn Avian Path; fel Poultry Sci Asn (pres, 89-90); World Poultry Sci Asn; Soc Environ Toxicol & Chem. *Res:* Cardiovascular research; endocrinology; environmental toxicology. *Mailing Add:* 9740 SW Bayshore Dr Traverse City MI 49684. *Fax:* 616-947-0613, 352-383-2650

RINGHAM, GARY LEWIS, PHYSIOLOGY, PHARMACOLOGY. *Current Pos:* CLIN RES ASSOC, ABBOTT LABS. *Personal Data:* b Boonville, Ind, Nov 11, 41; m 64; c 2. *Educ:* Butler Univ, BS, 63, MS, 66; Univ Utah, PhD(pharmacol), 71. *Prof Exp:* Fel physiol, Univ Colo Med Ctr, Denver, 71-73; res instr, Univ Utah, 73-76, asst prof physiol, 76- *Res:* Physiology and pharmacology of synaptic transmission; excitation-secretion coupling; impulse origin and conduction. *Mailing Add:* Abbott Labs Bldg J23 1 Abbot Park Rd Abbott Park IL 60064

RINGLE, DAVID ALLAN, PHYSIOLOGY, IMMUNOLOGIC TEST METHODS. *Current Pos:* CONSULT IMMUNOPHYSIOL, 76- *Personal Data:* b Wausau, Wis, Sept 28, 24; m 49, Stata Norton. *Educ:* Univ Wis, BS, 49; Columbia Univ, MA, 52; NY Univ, PhD(cellular physiol), 60. *Prof Exp:* Scientist, Warner-Lambert Pharmaceut Co, NY, 52-53; biologist, Am Cyanamid Co, Conn, 53-54; USPHS fel, Col Physicians & Surgeons, Columbia Univ, 60-62; prin physiologist, Midwest Res Inst, 62-76. *Mem:* Harvey Soc; Am Soc Zoologists; Reticuloendothelial Soc; Sigma Xi. *Res:* Tissue metabolism; reticuloendothelial system function; plasma protein alterations; amphibian yolk; shock; structure and function of cell membranes; cellular immunology; lymphocyte physiology; antilymphocyte serum; immunologic effects of morphine; immunologic detection methods; antibody production. *Mailing Add:* PO Box 8013 Prairie Village KS 66208

RINGLE, JOHN CLAYTON, NUCLEAR ENGINEERING. *Current Pos:* assoc prof, 66-84, reactor adminr, 66-80, ASSOC DEAN GRAD SCH, ORE STATE UNIV, 80-, PROF NUCLEAR ENG, RADIATION CTR, 84- *Personal Data:* b Kokomo, Ind, Aug 28, 35; m 60, Judith A Bollen; c Bonny, Kathleen, Molly & Margaret. *Educ:* Case Inst Technol, BS, 57, MS, 59; Univ Calif, Berkeley, PhD(nuclear eng), 64. *Prof Exp:* Res physicist, Cambridge Res Lab, 63-66. *Concurrent Pos:* Vis scientist, Cadarache Nuclear Lab, France, 75. *Mem:* Am Phys Soc; Am Nuclear Soc; Sigma Xi. *Res:* Environmental effects of nuclear power; high level and low level radioactive waste management. *Mailing Add:* Radiation Ctr A-100 Ore State Univ Corvallis OR 97331. *Fax:* 541-737-3313; *E-Mail:* ringlej@ccmail.orst.edu

RINGLEB, CHRISTINE CHARLOTTE KAROLINE, HEURISTIC ALGORITHMS, TIME SERIES ANALYSIS. *Current Pos:* DIR RES, CQG INC, 86- *Personal Data:* b Burgau, Ger, Oct 5, 48; US citizen; div; c Ada E. *Educ:* Univ Frankfurt, Ger, dipl, 73; Univ Aberdeen, Gt Brit, PhD(ecol), 77. *Prof Exp:* Postdoctoral fel, Univ Aberdeen, 77-79, Univ Bayreuth, Ger, 80-84, Inst Animal Resource Ecol, Univ BC, 84-85. *Mem:* AAAS; Inst Elec & Electronics Engrs; Math Asn Am; Am Statist Asn. *Res:* Refutability of the efficient market hypothesis and of various random walk models of economic time series using non-linear, non-stationary time series analysis, neural net technology, and heuristic and artificial reasoning computer models. *Mailing Add:* 1537 Hwy 133 Carbondale CO 81623-2156. *Fax:* 970-963-2378; *E-Mail:* didi@cqg.com

RINGLEE, ROBERT J, MECHANICS, ELECTRICAL ENGINEERING. *Current Pos:* RETIRED. *Personal Data:* b Sacramento, Calif, Apr 23, 26; m 49, Helen Laura Carleton; c 3. *Educ:* Univ Wash, BS, 46, MS, 48; Rensselaer Polytech Inst, PhD(mech), 64. *Prof Exp:* Engr, Gen Elec Co, 48-55, supvr design, 55-60, sr engr, 60-67, mgr systs reliability, Elec Utility Eng Oper, 67-69; prin engr & dir, Power Technol Inc, 69-86, prin consult, 86-93. *Concurrent Pos:* Mem, Expert Adv Study Comt 38, Int Conf Large Elec Systs, 53-; adj prof, Polytech Inst Brooklyn, 65-66; Atwood Assoc, Int Conf Large High Voltage Elec Systs; pres, Adirondeck Mountain Club, 90-93, actg exec dir, 94. *Mem:* Fel Inst Elec & Electronics Engrs; fel AAAS. *Res:* Systems sciences; vibration, noise; process modelling; system reliability; control theory. *Mailing Add:* Power Technol Inc PO Box 1058 Schenectady NY 12301. *Fax:* 518-374-6760

RINGLER, DANIEL HOWARD, LABORATORY ANIMAL MEDICINE. *Current Pos:* Fel, 67-69, instr, 69-71, asst prof, 71-75, assoc prof, 75-79, PROF LAB ANIMAL MED, UNIV MICH, 79- *Personal Data:* b Oberlin, Ohio, Aug 19, 41; m 63; c 2. *Educ:* Ohio State Univ, DVM, 65; Univ Mich, MS, 69; Am Col Lab Animal Med, dipl, 71. *Honors & Awards:* Griffin Award, Am Asn Lab Animal Sci. *Concurrent Pos:* Consult, Animal Resources Br, Div Res Resources, NIH, 73-; mem, Am Asn Accreditation Lab Animal Care, 74-, Adv Coun, Inst Lab Animal Resource, Nat Res Coun-Nat Nat Acad Sci, 75-78. *Mem:* Am Asn Lab Animal Sci; Am Vet Med Asn. *Res:* Spontaneous diseases of laboratory animals; use of animals in biomedical research; diseases and husbandry of amphibians; pathogenic bacteriology. *Mailing Add:* 3404 E Dobson Pl Ann Arbor MI 48105

RINGLER, NEIL HARRISON, AQUATIC ECOLOGY, FISHERY BIOLOGY. *Current Pos:* from asst prof to prof zool, 75-89, ASSOC CHMN & PROF ENVIRON FOREST & BIOL, COL ENVIRON SCI & FOREST BIOL, STATE UNIV NY, 89- *Personal Data:* b Long Beach, Calif, Nov 12, 45; m 68. *Educ:* Calif State Univ, Long Beach, BA, 67; Ore State Univ, MS, 70; Univ Mich, PhD(fisheries biol), 75. *Prof Exp:* Res asst, Ore Game Comn, Ore State Univ, 68-69; teaching fel ichthyol & aquatic entom, Sch Natural Resources, Univ Mich, 71-74. *Concurrent Pos:* Res biologist, Pac Biol Sta, Nanaimo, BC, 85. *Mem:* Sigma Xi; Am Fisheries Soc; Am Soc Ichthyologists & Herpetologists; Ecol Soc Am; NAm Benthological Soc. *Res:* Foraging tactics and behavior of fishes; salmonid biology; population ecology of fishes and aquatic invertebrates; role of predation in structering aquatic communities; stream ecology; effects of forest practices on streambeds; restoration of perturbed fish communities. *Mailing Add:* 19 Gettman Dr Baldwinsville NY 13027-9491

RINGO, GEORGE ROY, EXPERIMENTAL PHYSICS. *Current Pos:* PHYSICIST, ARGONNE NAT LAB, 48- *Personal Data:* b Minot, NDak, Jan 19, 17; m 41, Miriam Kovner; c Martin, Susan & James. *Educ:* Univ Chicago, BS, 36, PhD(physics), 40. *Prof Exp:* Physicist, US Rubber Co, RI, 41; physicist, Naval Res Lab, DC, 41-48. *Mem:* Am Phys Soc; Sigma Xi; fel Am Phys Soc. *Res:* Neutron physics; ion microscopy. *Mailing Add:* 16 W 220 97th St Hinsdale IL 60521-6898

RINGO, JAMES LEWIS, LEARNING & MEMORY, VISION. *Current Pos:* res fel neurosci, Ctr Brain Res, Univ Rochester, 82-85, asst prof neurosci, 85-87, asst prof, Dept Physiol, 87-91, assoc prof, Dept Physiol, 91-96, ASSOC PROF, DEPT NEUROBIOL & ANAT, UNIV ROCHESTER, 96- *Personal Data:* b La Grange, Ill, May 17, 51; m 81; c 3. *Educ:* Mass Inst Technol, BS, 73; Duke Univ, PhD(physiol), 79. *Prof Exp:* Fulbright fel med physics, Univ Amsterdam, 81-82. *Mem:* AAAS; NY Acad Sci; Neurosci Soc. *Res:* Neurophysiologic description of vision and visual memory; the inter hemispheric transfer of information and the split brain. *Mailing Add:* 99 Westland Ave Rochester NY 14618-1044. *E-Mail:* ringo@cvs.rochester.edu

RINGO, JOHN ALAN, BIOENGINEERING, BIOMEDICAL ENGINEERING. *Current Pos:* from asst prof to assoc prof, 77-83, prof elec eng, 83-, ASSOC DEAN, WASH STATE UNIV. *Personal Data:* b Spokane, Wash, Dec 29, 41; m 64; c 3. *Educ:* Wash State Univ, BS, 64; Univ Wash, MS,

67, PhD(elec eng), 71. *Prof Exp:* Assoc engr, Douglas Aircraft Co, 64; assoc res engr, Boeing Co, 66-67. *Mem:* Sigma Xi. *Res:* Application of engineering principles for understanding the interactive heart-artery systems; specialized instrumentation for measurement in physiological systems; solid state device properties and their application in linear circuit design. *Mailing Add:* Deans Off Wash State Univ Dana Hall No 146 PO Box 642714 Pullman WA 99164-2714

RINGO, JOHN MOYER, BEHAVIORAL GENETICS. *Current Pos:* From asst prof to assoc prof, 74-88, PROF ZOOL, UNIV MAINE, 88- *Personal Data:* b Columbia, Mo, Nov 25, 43; m 69, 90, Ada Zohar; c Kate & Preston. *Educ:* Univ Calif, Berkeley, AB, 69; Univ Calif, Davis, PhD(genetics), 73. *Concurrent Pos:* Assoc ed, Behav Genetics, 78-81, Evolution, 89-91; vis scientist, Brandeis Univ, 82-83; Scheinfeld vis prof, Hebrew Univ, Jerusalem, 89. *Mem:* Behav Genetics Asn; Soc Study Evolution; Genetics Soc Am; Am Soc Naturalists; Sigma Xi. *Res:* Genetic analysis of stereotyped behavior, biological clocks, and reproductive behavior in Drosophilia. *Mailing Add:* Dept Zool Univ Maine Orono ME 04469. *Fax:* 207-581-2537; *E-Mail:* ringo@maine.maine.edu

RINGS, ROY WILSON, ENTOMOLOGY. *Current Pos:* assoc chmn ctr, 61-73, prof entom, 61-77, EMER PROF ENTOM, OHIO STATE UNIV 77- *Personal Data:* b Columbus, Ohio, Aug 15, 16; m 42; c 3. *Educ:* Ohio State Univ, BSc, 38, MSc, 40, PhD(entom), 46. *Prof Exp:* Asst, Ohio Exp Sta, 41-42; specialist in chg, Div Plant Indust, State Dept Agr, 46-47; asst entomologist, 47-53; assoc prof entom, Ohio Agr Exp Sta, 54-61. *Concurrent Pos:* US Army, med entom, 43-46. *Mem:* Entom Soc Am; Am Mosquito Control Asn; fel, AAAS. *Res:* Noctuidae of Ohio. *Mailing Add:* Ohio Agr Res & Develop Ctr Wooster OH 44691

RINGSDORF, WARREN MARSHALL, JR, DENTISTRY, NUTRITION. *Current Pos:* asst prof, 59-64, assoc prof, 64-82, PROF CLIN DENT, UNIV ALA, BIRMINGHAM, 82- *Personal Data:* b Elba, Ala, May 2, 30; m 55; c 2. *Educ:* Asbury Col, BA, 51; Univ Ala, MS, 56; Univ Ala, Birmingham, DMD, 56; Am Bd Oral Med, dipl, 63. *Honors & Awards:* Chicago Dent Soc Res Award, 66 & 68; Honors Achievement Award, Angiol Res Found, Inc, 68. *Prof Exp:* Pvt dent pract, Ala, 58-59. *Concurrent Pos:* Fel, Univ Ala, Birmingham, 60-62; attend oral med, Vet Admin Hosp, Birmingham, Ala, 60-; consult, Hq US Army Infantry Ctr, Ft Benning, Ga, 64-74 & Nutritech Corp, Santa Barbara, 80-; pres, Seven, Inc. *Mem:* Am Dent Asn; Am Acad Oral Med; Acad Orthomolecular Psychiat. *Res:* Role of diet and nutrition in host resistance and susceptibility and its relationship to prevention of disease occurrence and recurrence. *Mailing Add:* 728 Sussex Dr Birmingham AL 35226

RINI, FRANK JOHN, OPHTHALMOLOGY, RADIATION PHYSICS & BIOLOGY. *Current Pos:* STAFF, MANHATTAN EYE, EAR, THROAT HOSP, 87- *Personal Data:* b New York, NY, Feb 18, 52; m 84; c 1. *Educ:* Columbia Univ, BA, 74, MA, 76, MPh, 77, PhD(physics), 78, MD, 82. *Prof Exp:* Res assoc radio physics, Columbia Univ, 76-78; res assoc radiobiol, Lawrence Berkeley Lab, 79; res assoc ocular radio, Eye Inst, Columbia Univ, 81-86. *Concurrent Pos:* Ophthal resident, Eye Inst, Columbia, 83-86. *Mem:* Am Acad Ophthal; Asn Res Vision & Ophthal. *Res:* Effects of different radiation modalities on ocular tissues, particularly the lens. *Mailing Add:* One Wilbur Rd Suffern NY 10901

RINK, GEORGE, BLACK WALNUT GENETICS, ADMINISTRATION. *Current Pos:* DEP DIR, TIMBER LAKE CIVILIAN CONS CAMP, 96- *Personal Data:* b Riga, Latvia, Jan 17, 42; US citizen; m 66; c 3. *Educ:* NY Univ, BA, 63; Univ Tenn, MS, 71, PhD(forest genetics), 74. *Prof Exp:* Asst prof forestry, Stephen F Austin State Univ, 75-80; res geneticist, NCent Forest Exp Sta, USDA Forest Serv, 80-96. *Concurrent Pos:* Adj asst prof, Dept Forestry, Southern Ill Univ, 81-96. *Mem:* Sigma Xi; Soc Am Foresters; Walnut Coun. *Res:* Genetic variation in black walnut, white oak and southern pines; genetic resistance to stress during establishment. *Mailing Add:* Tall Timbers Civilian Cons Camp 59868 E Hwy 224 Estacada OR 97023

RINK, RICHARD DONALD, HUMAN ANATOMY & TOLERANCE, INJURY RECONSTRUCTION. *Current Pos:* From instr to assoc prof, 67-80, PROF ANAT, SCH MED, UNIV LOUISVILLE, 80-, RES PROF SURG ANAT, 81- *Personal Data:* b Chicago, Ill, Mar 29, 41; m 62; c 2. *Educ:* Beloit Col, BA, 63; Tulane Univ, PhD(anat), 67. *Mem:* Asn Advan Auto Med; Am Asn Anatomists; Shock Soc. *Res:* Medicolegal investigation to determine cause of injury, or risk of injury; injury mechanisms. *Mailing Add:* Dept Anat Health Sci Ctr Univ Louisville Sch Med Louisville KY 40292. *Fax:* 502-852-6228

RINKE, RONALD ANTHONY, ENGINEERING GRAPHICS IMAGING SYSTEMS, QUALITY SYSTEMS & MANAGEMENT. *Current Pos:* SR DESIGN ENGR NEW TECHNOL, WESTERN LITHOTECH, 95- *Personal Data:* m 88, Diane Lee Dyer. *Educ:* Univ Mo, BS, 84. *Honors & Awards:* President's Award, Soc Mfg Engrs, 90, Ralph E Cross Outstanding Young Engr, 97. *Prof Exp:* Mfg & appln engr, Andrew Structures Corp, 79-87; automation engr, Zenith Electronics, 87-92; mfg engr, Positronic Industries, 92-93 & Paul Mueller Co, 93-95. *Concurrent Pos:* Consult & lectr, ISO9000 Systs, Soc Mfg Engrs, Am Prod & Inventory Control & SW Mo State Univ, 92- *Mem:* Soc Mfg Engrs; Am Soc Mech Engrs. *Res:* Developed high-speed laser imaging system for the graphics industry. *Mailing Add:* 119 Oak Tree Lane Ozark MO 65721

RINKEMA, LYNN ELLEN, LEUKOTRIENE RESEARCH. *Current Pos:* PHARMACOLOGIST, ELI LILLY & CO, 81- *Educ:* Loyola Univ, MS, 81. *Mailing Add:* Lilly Toxicol Labs PO Box 708 Greenfield IN 46140

RINKER, GEORGE ALBERT, JR, ELECTROMAGNETIC MATTER, SELF-ORGANIZING INFORMATION NETWORKS. *Current Pos:* Fel, 71-73, STAFF MEM PHYSICS, LOS ALAMOS SCI LAB, 73- *Personal Data:* b Lubbock, Tex, Feb 7, 45; c 3. *Educ:* Franklin Col, BA, 67; Univ Calif, Irvine, MA, 70, PhD(physics), 71. *Concurrent Pos:* Vis scientist, Nuclear Energy Res Inst, J lich, WGer, 76-77; vis lectr, Univ Fribourg, Switz, 77, 85. *Mem:* Am Phys Soc. *Res:* Advanced computational methods applied to fundamental problems in many body-quantum-mechanical electromagnetic systems. *Mailing Add:* Dept Physics Colo State Univ Ft Collins CO 80523

RINKER, GEORGE CLARK, ANATOMY. *Current Pos:* assoc prof, 62-70, asst dean sch med, 70-73, PROF ANAT, SCH MED, UNIV SDAK, VERMILLION, 70-, ASSOC DEAN SCH MED, 73- *Personal Data:* b Hamilton, Kans, Apr 8, 22; m 44; c 3. *Educ:* Univ Kans, AB, 46; Univ Mich, MS, 48, PhD(zool), 51. *Prof Exp:* From instr to asst prof anat, Univ Mich, 50-62. *Mem:* Am Asn Anat. *Res:* Comparative mammalian and human gross anatomy. *Mailing Add:* 509 Poplar Ave Vermillion SD 57069

RINKER, ROBERT G(ENE), CHEMICAL ENGINEERING. *Current Pos:* assoc prof, 67-73, chmn dept, 73-78, PROF CHEM ENG, UNIV CALIF, SANTA BARBARA, 73- *Personal Data:* b Vincennes, Ind, Dec 31, 29; m 63; c 3. *Educ:* Rose Polytech Inst, BS, 51; Calif Inst Technol, MS, 55, PhD(chem eng), 59. *Prof Exp:* Res fel, Calif Inst Technol, 59-60, asst prof, 60-67. *Concurrent Pos:* Consult, NAm Instrument Co, 55, Electro Optical Systs, Inc, 60, Dow Chem Co, 64-65, MHD Res, Inc, 65-67, Sci Appln, Inc, 70-87, JRB Assocs, 70-87 & Omnia Res, 85-; fel, Am Inst Chem Engrs. *Mem:* AAAS; Am Inst Chem Engrs; Sigma Xi. *Res:* Chemical kinetics; reactor design; catalysis. *Mailing Add:* Chem Engr Univ Calif Santa Barbara CA 93106

RINNE, JOHN NORMAN, FISHERY BIOLOGY, AQUATIC ECOLOGY. *Current Pos:* FISHERY RES BIOLOGIST, US FOREST SERV, 76- *Personal Data:* b Pawnee City, Nebr, Mar 19, 44; m 66; c 1. *Educ:* Peru State Col, BSE, 66; Ariz State Univ, MS, 69, PhD(zool), 73. *Prof Exp:* Chief field invest res, Ariz State Univ, 72-73; fishery res biologist, EAfrican Community, 73-75; fishery res biologist, US Fish Wildlife Serv, 76. *Concurrent Pos:* Consult, Squawfish Recovery Team, 76-77, Ariz Trout Recovery Team & Gila Trout Recovery Team, 76-; area coordr, Desert Fishes Coun, 77- *Mem:* Am Fisheries Soc; Am Inst Fishery Res Biologists. *Res:* Habitat, biology and distribution of endangered fish in the southwestern United States; fisheries and ecology of desert and tropical resources. *Mailing Add:* 1803 Wakonda St Flagstaff AZ 86004

RINNE, ROBERT W, PLANT PHYSIOLOGY. *Current Pos:* PROF PLANT PHYSIOL, DEPT AGRON, UNIV ILL, URBANA, 64- *Personal Data:* b Hammond, Ind, Jan 6, 32; m 56; c 4. *Educ:* DePauw Univ, BA, 55; Purdue Univ, BS, 57, MS, 59, PhD(plant physiol), 61. *Prof Exp:* Asst plant physiol, Purdue Univ, 57-61; res assoc microbiol, Dartmouth Med Sch, 61-62; NIH fel biochem, Wayne State Univ, 62-64. *Mem:* Am Soc Plant Physiol; Crop Sci Soc Am. *Res:* Metabolism of the developing soybean seed. *Mailing Add:* 1002 E McHenry St Urbana IL 61801

RINNE, VERNON WILMER, DENTISTRY. *Current Pos:* RETIRED. *Personal Data:* b Pawnee City, Nebr, Dec 15, 25; m 48; c 5. *Educ:* Univ Nebr, BS & DDS, 53. *Prof Exp:* From instr to assoc prof oper dent, Univ Nebr-Lincoln, 53-68, chmn, Dept Restorative Dent, 69-72, prof adult restoration, Col Dent, 69-89. *Concurrent Pos:* Consult, USPHS, 60. *Mem:* Am Asn Dent Res. *Res:* Dental materials. *Mailing Add:* RR 9 Lincoln NE 68516

RINSE, JACOBUS, physical chemistry, biochemistry; deceased, see previous edition for last biography

RINZEL, JOHN MATTHEW, APPLIED MATHEMATICS. *Current Pos:* Mathematician, Div Comput Res & Technol, NIH, 68-70 & 73-75, RES MATHEMATICIAN & CHIEF, MATH RES BR, NAT INST DIABETES, DIGESTIVE & KIDNEY DIS, NIH, 75- *Personal Data:* b Milwaukee, Wis, July 18, 44; m 67; c 2. *Educ:* Univ Fla, BS, 67; NY Univ, MS, 68, PhD(math), 73. *Concurrent Pos:* Vis instr, Dept Math, Univ Md, College Park, 75- *Mem:* Soc Indust & Appl Math; Am Math Soc; Soc Neurosci. *Res:* Biomathematics; mathematical models for electrical signaling in biological cells; theoretical neurophysiology; numerical analysis. *Mailing Add:* Bldg 31 Rm 4B-54A Nat Inst Health Math Res Br Bethesda MD 20892-0001

RIO, DONALD C, EUKARYOTIC GENE EXPRESSION. *Current Pos:* FROM ASST PROF TO ASSOC PROF, DEPT BIOL, MASS INST TECHNOL, 87- *Personal Data:* b New Britain, Conn, July 7, 57. *Educ:* Univ Colo, BA, 79; Univ Calif, Berkeley, PhD(biochem), 83. *Honors & Awards:* Presidential Young Investr Award, NSF, 88. *Prof Exp:* Res asst, 79-83, fel biochem, Univ Calif, Berkeley, 84-86. *Concurrent Pos:* Assoc mem, Whitehead Inst Biomed Res, 87- *Mem:* AAAS. *Res:* Regulation of eukaryotic gene expression; transcriptional control mechanisms; eukaryotic transposable elements; differential gene expression during development of the fruit fly, Drosophila melanogaster; RNA transcription and processing. *Mailing Add:* Dept Molecular & Cell Biol Univ Calif Berkeley CA 94720-4759

RIO, MARIA ESTHER, NUTRITIONAL RECOVERY, EVALUATION NUTRITIONAL STATUS. *Current Pos:* Minor positions basic nutrit, Sch Pharm & Biochem, 61-70, from asst prof to assoc prof, 70-85, head, Dept Health Sci, 90-93, coun, 90-94, PROF NUTRIT, SCH PHARM &

BIOCHEM, 85-, VICE HEAD, 93- Personal Data: b Gonzalez Chaves, Buenos Aires, Apr 5, 36; wid; c Maria M & Gabriela G. Educ: Tandil Nat Sch, BS, 54; Univ Buenos Aires, Pharmacyst, 60, Biochemist, 62, Biochemist PhD(nutrit), 69. Hon Degrees: Univ Buenos Aires, Degree with honors, 62. Concurrent Pos: Career investr nutrit, Nat Res Coun, CONICET, 70-; exec secy, Nat Prog Food Res Sci & Technol, 83-86; prin investr, PID-CONICET Proj, 84-, IDRC N Degree , 85-88, SANCOR-CONICET-CERELA Proj, 88-91 & SANCOR-CMN Proj, 90-91; consult, Centro Munic de Nutricion 90-91. Mem: Am Inst Nutrit; Am Soc Clin Nutrit; Int Union Nutrit Sci. Res: Nutritional recovery projects conducted to evaluate proficiency of formulations for nutritional support and recovery; biochemical evaluation of nutritional status: basic and operative research. Mailing Add: Dept Bromatol-Exp Nutrit Univ Buenos Aires Junin 956-2 Piso Buenos Aires 1113 Argentina

RIO, SHELDON T, MATHEMATICS. Current Pos: RETIRED. Personal Data: b Raymond, Mont, May 9, 27; m 50; c 2. Educ: Westmar Col, BA, 50; Mont State Univ, MA, 54; Ore State Univ, PhD(anal), 59. Prof Exp: Chmn, Dept Math, Pac Univ, 55-57; assoc prof, Western Wash State Col, 59-63; chmn dept math, Southern Ore Col, 63-72, prof, 63-89, dir, Sch Sci & Math, 79-89. Concurrent Pos: Prof, Univ Delhi, 67. Mem: Am Math Soc; Math Asn Am; Nat Coun Teachers Math. Res: Analysis; topology. Mailing Add: 570 Taylor St Ashland OR 97520

RIOPEL, JAMES L, PLANT MORPHOLOGY. Current Pos: Asst prof, 60-66, assoc dean grad sch arts & sci, 68-69, ASSOC PROF BIOL, UNIV VA, 66-, DIR MT LAKE BIOL STA, 60- Personal Data: b Kittery, Maine, May 24, 34; m 56; c 3. Educ: Bates Col, AB, 56; Harvard Univ, MS, 58, PhD(biol), 60. Concurrent Pos: NSF Instnl grant, 62-63; Am Cancer Soc Instnl grant, 63-64; NSF grant, 65-67. Mem: Bot Soc Am; Torrey Bot Club; Soc Develop Biol; Int Soc Plant Morphol. Res: Developmental plant anatomy and morphogenesis; regulation on cell differentiation and organ origin and determination. Mailing Add: Dept Biol Univ Va Gilmer Hall 229 Charlottesville VA 22903

RIOPELLE, ARTHUR J, SENSATION & PERCEPTION, BRAIN FUNCTION. Current Pos: Boyd prof, 79-89, EMER BOYD PROF PSYCHOL, LA STATE UNIV, 89- Personal Data: b Thorpe, Wis, Apr 22, 20; m 42; c 3. Educ: Univ Wis-Madison, PhD(psychol), 50. Mem: Am Physiol Soc; Am Psychol Asn. Res: Primate behavior. Mailing Add: Dept Psychol La State Univ La State Univ 9710 Highland Baton Rouge LA 70810-4031

RIORDAN, JAMES F, PROTEIN CHEMISTRY, ENZYMOLOGY. Current Pos: from asst prof to assoc prof, 68-87, PROF BIOCHEM, HARVARD MED SCH, 87- Personal Data: b New Haven, Conn, Feb 6, 34; m 70, Charlotte Hart; c Cynthia, Barbara, James & Michelle. Educ: Fairfield Univ, BS, 55; Fordham Univ, MS, 57, PhD(enzym), 61. Hon Degrees: MA, Harvard Univ, 87. Prof Exp: Instr chem, US Merchant Marine Acad, 57-58 & Fordham Univ, 58-61; res fel biol chem, Harvard Med Sch, 61-64, assoc, 66-68,; res assoc, Brigham & Women's Hosp, 64-65, asst dir, Clin Chem Lab, 66-86, assoc biochemist, 61-, med dir, Clin Chem Lab, 86-95.. Concurrent Pos: Nat Found fels, 62-63 & 64-65; NIH fel, 63-64; ed, J Inorg Biochem, 79-96; exec ed, Analytical Biochem, 79-; mem adv bd, Clin Chem Standards, Nat Bur Standards, 71-74, Med Chem Study Sect, NIH, 74-77, chmn, Bioanalytical & Metallobiochem Study Sect, 79-82, small bus innovation res study sect, 92-; assoc ed, Biochem, 94- Mem: Am Chem Soc; Am Soc Biochem & Molecular Biol; AAAS; Sigma Xi. Res: Chemical modification of proteins; proteolytic enzymes; angiogenesis; zinc metalloenzymes; angiotensin converting enzyme. Mailing Add: Seeley G Mudd Bldg 250 Longwood Ave Boston MA 02115. Fax: 617-566-3137; E-Mail: jriordan@warren.med.harvard.edu

RIORDAN, JOHN RICHARD, BIOCHEMISTRY. Current Pos: INVESTR BIOCHEM, RES INST, HOSP SICK CHILDREN, 73-; PROF, DEPTS BIOCHEM & CLIN BIOCHEM, UNIV TORONTO, 74- Personal Data: b St Stephen, NB, Sept 2, 43; m 70. Educ: Univ Toronto, BSc, 66, PhD(biochem), 70. Prof Exp: Fel, Max Planck Inst Biophys, Frankfurt, 70-73. Concurrent Pos: Can Cystic Fibrosis Found fel, 70; res grants, Med Res Coun Can, 81- & Can Cystic Fibrosis Found, 82- Mem: Can Fedn Biol Soc; Am Soc Biol Chem. Res: Studies of mammalian cell plasma membrane glycoproteins, particularly normal structure, function and aberrations thereof in genetic disease; including cystic fibrosis, disorders of myclimation and cancer. Mailing Add: 109 Madison Ave Toronto ON M5R 2S3 Can

RIORDAN, MICHAEL DAVITT, PETROLEUM CHEMISTRY. Current Pos: RETIRED. Personal Data: b Willimantic, Conn, Oct 21, 21; m 45, Bette Cunningham; c Elizabeth D McDermott. Educ: Col Holy Cross, BS, 43, MS, 44. Prof Exp: Analytical chemist, Texaco Inc, 43-45, chemist, 45-54, proj leader fuels res, 54-57, asst supvr, 57-61, asst supvr process res, 61-67, res supvr chem res, 67-76, staff coordr, 76-79, mgr petrol prod res staff, 79-82. Mem: Am Chem Soc. Res: Petroleum products; petroleum processing; petrochemicals. Mailing Add: PO Box 1755 Anna Maria FL 34216

RIORDON, J(OHN) SPRUCE, COMPUTER SYSTEMS ENGINEERING, COMMUNICATIONS. Current Pos: sessional lectr, Carleton Univ, 67-68, asst prof eng, 68-70, assoc prof syst eng, 70-77, chmn dept syst eng & comput sci, 70-75, chmn, Dept Systs Eng & Comput Sci, 78-81, prof systs eng, 77-81, dean eng, 81-91, VPRES FINANCE & ADMIN, CARLETON UNIV, 91- Personal Data: b Springs, SAfrica, June 28, 36; Can citizen; m 63; c 3. Educ: McGill Univ, BEng, 57, MEng, 61; Univ London, PhD(automatic control eng), 67. Prof Exp: Res officer, Nat Res Coun Can, 57-68. Concurrent Pos: Nat Res Coun Can res grant, 68-; consult, Dept Energy, Mines & Resources, 71-73, Ministry State Urban Affairs, 75-76 & Dept Commun, 80- Mem: Inst Elec & Electronics Engrs; Can Info Processing Soc. Res: Mobile communications; computer networks; distributed databases; modelling and simulation; information systems design; application of digital computers to on-line process control; optimum control of stochastic processes; adaptive control systems; modelling of dynamic systems; information storage and retrieval; management information systems. Mailing Add: 18 Eisenhower Crescent Nepean ON K2J 3Z8 Can

RIOS, PEDRO AGUSTIN, CRYOGENICS. Current Pos: VPRES, GUTIERREZ CO, 87- Personal Data: b Havana, Cuba, Apr 26, 38; US citizen; m 60, Thania Ferrer; c Thania & Agustin. Educ: Mass Inst Technol, BS, 59 & 60, MS, 67, ScD(mech eng), 69. Honors & Awards: IR-100 Award Indust Res & Develop, 80. Prof Exp: Plant engr, Airco Indust Gases, 60-62, asst plant supt, 63-65; res assoc, Mass Inst Technol, 69-70; mech & proj engr, Gen Elec Co, 70-73, mgr, Rotating Mach Unit, 73-77, mgr, Electro-Mech Br, Res & Develop Ctr, 77-87. Mem: Am Soc Mech Engrs; Sigma Xi. Res: Application of cryogenics and superconductivity to rotating electrical machinery, electrical apparatus and magnets; computer aided engineering tools for electromagnetic and electromechanical devices and fluid flow. Mailing Add: 11 Wright Farm Concord MA 01742

RIOUX, CLAUDE, SPACE PHYSICS. Current Pos: res fel, 84-89, RES ASSOC, UNIV LAVAL, 89- Personal Data: b Mont-Joli, Que, June 4, 53; m 76; c 2. Educ: Univ Laval, BAC, 75, MSc, 78, PhD(nuclear physics), 82. Prof Exp: Natural sci & eng res coun fel, Lawrence Berkeley Lab, 82-84. Res: Microgravity and fractal aggregates. Mailing Add: Dept Physics Univ Laval Pavillon Vachon Ste Foy PQ G1K 7P4 Can

RIOUX, ROBERT LESTER, GEOLOGY. Current Pos: RETIRED. Personal Data: b Natick, Mass, June 11, 27; m 58; c 6. Educ: Univ NH, BA, 53; Univ Ill, MS, 55, PhD(geol), 58. Prof Exp: Asst geol, Univ Ill, 54-55; geologist, US Geol Surv, 56-94. Mem: Geol Soc Am; Am Asn Petrol Geologists. Res: Economic geology of mineral fuels and fertilizers; conservation of mineral lands; economic geology of mineral fuels and fertilizaers; conservation of mineral lands. Mailing Add: 2817 Germantown Rd Oakton VA 22124

RIPARBELLI, CARLO, AERONAUTICAL ENGINEERING. Current Pos: RETIRED. Personal Data: b Rome, Italy, Nov 15, 10; nat US; m 58, Ellen J Dennis. Educ: Univ Rome, Italy, DSc(civil eng), 33, DSc(aeronaut eng), 34, libero docente, 40. Prof Exp: Design engr aircraft, S A Caproni, Italy, 35-37, chief designer, 41-43; asst prof aeronaut eng, Univ Rome, 37-41; res assoc, Princeton Univ, 47-48; from asst prof to assoc prof, Cornell Univ, 49-55; design specialist aircraft, Convair Div, Gen Dynamics Corp, 55-59, mem res staff space craft, Gen Atomic Div, 60-65, eng staff specialist, Pomona Div, 65-72; eng consult, 73-85. Concurrent Pos: Designer, Italian Air Ministry, 41-43; consult, Princeton Univ, 49-50, Aeronaut Macchi, Italy, 49-53, Cornell Aeronaut Lab, NY, 51, Bur Ships, USN, 53-55 & Aerospace Corp, Sci Applns Inc, 73-80. Mem: assoc fel Am Inst Aeronaut & Astronaut; Italian Aerotechnol Asn. Res: Dynamics of structures; impact problems; theoretical and experimental stress analysis; design of aircraft and space craft structures. Mailing Add: 4429 Arista Dr San Diego CA 92103

RIPIN, BARRETT HOWARD, PLASMA PHYSICS. Current Pos: RES PHYSICIST, BR HEAD & SCIENTIST, NAVAL RES LAB, 73- Personal Data: b Troy, NY, Oct 27, 42. Educ: Rensselaer Polytech Inst, BS, 64; Univ Md, PhD(physics), 71. Honors & Awards: Appl Sci Award, Sigma Xi, 88. Prof Exp: Res asst plasma physics, Univ Md, 65-70; res assoc controlled thermonuclear res, Princeton Plasma Physics Lab, Princeton Univ, 70-71; asst prof physics, Univ Calif, Los Angeles, 71-73. Concurrent Pos: Assoc ed, Lasers & Particle Beams & Phys Rev E; counr-at-large, Am Phys Soc, 91-94, chmn, Publ Oversight comt, Fusion Energy adv comt, Dept Ener, comt, Div Plasma Physics; adj prof, Dept Physics, Univ Md. Mem: Sr mem Inst Elec & Electronics Engrs; fel Am Phys Soc; AAAS. Res: Experimental investigations of laser-produced plasmas, laser fusion, controlled thermonuclear research and space plasmas; laser light scattering; self-generated magnetic fields; nonlinear wave interactions; hydrodynamic interactions. Mailing Add: 7536 Sebago Rd Bethesda MD 20817-4842. Fax: 202-767-3869; E-Mail: ripin@cfe1.nrl.navy.mil

RIPKA, WILLIAM CHARLES, MOLECULAR MODELING, DRUG DESIGN. Current Pos: RES FEL, MEDJ PROD DEPT, E I DU PONT DE NEMOURS & CO, INC, 65-; VPRES, PHARMACEUT RES, CORVAS, INC, 90- Personal Data: b Los Angeles, Calif, June 2, 39; m 67; c 1. Educ: Calif Inst Technol, BS, 61; Univ Ill, PhD(chem), 66. Mem: Am Chem Soc. Res: Computer graphics and molecular modeling in drug design; organic and pharmaceutical chemistry. Mailing Add: 10819 Red Rock Dr San Diego CA 92131-1836

RIPLEY, DENNIS L(EON), CHEMISTRY, ENGINEERING. Current Pos: MGR PROCESSING & THERMO, BDM, OKLA, 88- Personal Data: b Joplin, Mo, Aug 30, 38; m 58; c 3. Educ: Kans State Univ, BS, 59; Univ Tex, PhD(phys chem), 67. Prof Exp: Chem engr, Dow Chem Co, 59-61 & US Bur Mines, 61-63; from res chemist to mgr planning & econ, Phillips Petrol Co, 66-88. Mem: Am Chem Soc. Res: Synthetic fuels; catalysts and catalytic processes; petroleum processes; fuel stability. Mailing Add: 53411 E 260 Rd Afton OK 74331-6205

RIPLEY, EARLE ALLISON, BIOMETEOROLOGY, AGROMETEOROLOGY. *Current Pos:* micrometeorologist, Matador Proj, 68-74, from assoc prof to prof, Plant Ecol Dept, 74-84, PROF, CROP SCI & PLANT ECOL DEPT, UNIV SASK, 84- *Personal Data:* b Sydney, NS, June 29, 33; m 67, Jean H McCrae; c Stephen H. *Educ:* Dalhousie Univ, BSc, 53; Univ Toronto, MA, 55. *Prof Exp:* Meteorologist, Meteorol Br, Can, 55-60 & Nigerian Meteorol Serv, 60-62; agrometeorologist, EAfrican Agr & Forestry Res Orgn, 62-67. *Mem:* Fel Can Meteorol Soc; fel Royal Meteorol Soc; Am Meteorol Soc. *Res:* Micrometeorology; agricultural meteorology; environmental impact analysis; drought climatology. *Mailing Add:* Dept Crop Sci & Plant Ecol Univ Sask Saskatoon SK S7N 5A8 Can

RIPLEY, LYNN S, MOLECULAR MECHANISMS OF MUTATION. *Current Pos:* from asst prof to assoc prof, 84-94, PROF, DEPT MICROBIOL & MOLECULAR GENETICS, UNIV MED & DENT NJ, NJ MED SCH, 94- *Personal Data:* b Great Lakes, Ill, May 7, 46. *Educ:* Mich State Univ, BS, 68; Univ Ill, Champaign-Urbana, MS, 70, PhD(microbiol), 74. *Prof Exp:* Fel, Microbiol, Univ Ill, 74-77; sr staff fel, Lab Genetics, Nat Inst Environ Health Sci, 77-84. *Concurrent Pos:* Adj asst prof, Dept Microbiol & Immunol, Univ NC, 80-84; prin investr, Am Cancer Soc, NSF, NIH, 84- *Mem:* AAAS; Genetics Soc Am. *Res:* Theoretical and experimental development of theories of how mutations occur with particular emphasis on spontaneous mutation and mutation in evolution and cancer. *Mailing Add:* Univ Med & Dent NJ 185 S Orange Ave Newark NJ 07103-2714

RIPLEY, ROBERT CLARENCE, ANATOMY, CELL BIOLOGY. *Current Pos:* From instr to asst prof of biol med sci, 67-74, asst dean, 74-78, ASSOC DEAN HEALTH CAREERS, BROWN UNIV, 78- *Personal Data:* b Attleboro, Mass, Oct 24, 40. *Educ:* Brown Univ, AB, 62; Univ Calif, Los Angeles, PhD(anat), 66. *Mem:* Am Asn Med Cols. *Res:* Electron microscopy. *Mailing Add:* Brown Univ PO Box 1883 Providence RI 02912

RIPLEY, SIDNEY DILLON, II, ZOOLOGY. *Current Pos:* secy, 64-84, EMER SECY, SMITHSONIAN INST, 84- *Personal Data:* b New York, NY, Sept 20, 13; m 49; c 3. *Educ:* Yale Univ, BA, 36; Harvard Univ, PhD(zool), 43. *Hon Degrees:* MA, Yale Univ, 61; DHL, Marlboro Col, 65 & Williams Col, 72; DSc, George Washington Univ, 66, Cath Univ Am, 68, Univ Md, 70, Cambridge Univ, 74, Brown Univ, 75 & Trinity Col, 77; LLD, Dickinson Col, 67, Hofstra Univ, 68 & Yale Univ, 75; DEng, Stevens Inst Technol, 77, Gallaudet Col, 81, Johns Hopkins Univ, 84 & Harvard Univ, 84. *Honors & Awards:* Gold Medals, NY Zool Soc, 66 & Zool Soc Belg, 70; Tata Mem Lectr, 75; Delacour Medal, Int Coun Bird Preserv, 82; James Smithson Medal, Smithsonian Inst, 84; Arthur A Medal Ornith, Cornell Univ, 84; Onassis Medal, Athens, 84; Presidential Medal of Freedom, 85; Thomas Jefferson Award, Am Soc Interior Decorators; Distinguished Serv Award, Am Asn Mus, 85; Padma Bhushan Award, Govt of India, 86; Charles Reed Bishop Medal, 90. *Prof Exp:* Zool collector, Acad Natural Sci Philadelphia, 36-39; vol asst, Am Mus Natural Hist, NY, 39-40; asst, Harvard Univ, 41-42; asst cur birds, Smithsonian Inst, 42-43; lectr, Yale Univ, 46-49, from asst prof to assoc prof zool, 49-61, prof biol, 61-64. *Concurrent Pos:* From assoc cur to cur, Peabody Mus Natural Hist, Yale Univ, 46-64, dir, 59-64; dir, Pac War Mem, 46-50; deleg, UN Sci Conf Conserv Utilization Resources, 49; Fulbright fel, NE Assam, 50; deleg, Int Union Preserv Nature, Caracas, 52, mem, Exec Bd, 64; Guggenheim fel, Yale Univ & NSF fel, Indonesia, 54; pres, Int Coun Bird Preserv, 58-82, emer pres, 82-; bd trustees, World Wildlife Fund, 62-, Leader exped, Yale Univ & Smithsonian Inst, India & Nepal, 46-47, Nat Geog Soc, Yale Univ & Smithsonian Inst, Nepal, 48-49, Neth New Guinea, 60 & Bhutan & India, 67-77; deleg, UN Sci Conf Conserv Utilization Resources, 49; trustee, White Mem Found; deleg, Stockholm Environ Conf, 72. *Mem:* Nat Acad Sci; fel AAAS; fel Am Ornithologists Union; Soc Study Evolution; Soc Syst Zool; Am Philos Soc; Am Acad Arts Sci; Sigma Xi; fel Am Acad Arts & Lett. *Res:* Speciation and evolution in vertebrate zoology, primarily ornithology. *Mailing Add:* Smithsonian Inst NHB Rm 336 Washington DC 20560. *Fax:* 202-357-1628

RIPLEY, THOMAS H, BIOLOGY. *Current Pos:* RETIRED. *Personal Data:* b Bennington, Vt, Nov 18, 27; m 48; c 3. *Educ:* Va Polytech Inst, BS, 51, PhD, 58; Univ Mass, MS, 54. *Prof Exp:* Wildlife consult res admin, Dept Fish & Game, Mass, 53-56; instr biol, Va Polytech Inst, 56-57; wildlife consult res admin, Dept Fish & Game, Mass, 57; res biologist, Comn Game & Inland Fisheries, Va, 57-58; asst dir, Southeast Forest Exp Sta, asst to dep chief for res & chief range & wildlife res, US Forest Serv, 58-69; dir forestry, fisheries & wildlife develop, 69-78, mgr, Off Natural Resources, Tenn Valley Authority, 79-89. *Mem:* Wildlife Soc; Soc Am Foresters; Am Forestry Asn (pres, 81-82); Am Inst Biol Sci; Int Union Forestry Res Orgn. *Res:* Forest land management; wildlife, range, watershed and timber resources. *Mailing Add:* 721 Whirlaway Circle Knoxville TN 37923-2144

RIPLEY, WILLIAM ELLIS, MARINE RESOURCES DEVELOPMENT. *Current Pos:* dir fisheries develop, Brazil, 65-69, UN fisheries officer, NY, 70-82, CONSULT FISHERIES DEVELOP, UN DEVELOP PROG, 82- *Personal Data:* b Turlock, Calif, Nov 4, 17; m 40; Idamae Jones; c Diane, Randy & Sharon. *Educ:* Univ Wash, BS, 39. *Prof Exp:* Fish biologist, Calif Dept Fish & Game, 40-53, asst & chief, Marine Resources Br, 53-63; chief, tech asst, Nat Marine Fisheries Serv, US Bur Com Fisheries, 63-65. *Concurrent Pos:* Fisheries adv UN Develop Prog, Brazil, Indonesia, Colombia, Malaysia, Sri Lanka, Senegal, E & W Africa, Indian Ocean, Carribbean, Singapore, Hong Kong, Japan, 54-55 & 70-84; spec fisheries adv, US Embassy, Brazil, 68-69. *Mem:* Am Fisheries Soc; Int Fisheries Soc; emer mem Am Inst Fisheries Res Biologists. *Res:* Marine fisheries, shark, sardine, demersal and trawl fisheries; exploration, management and development of marine resources; formulator and administrator of 125 international marine and freshwater fisheries programs for the United Nations and United Nations Development Program. *Mailing Add:* Hacienda Carmel No 221 Carmel CA 93923

RIPLING, E(DWARD) J, METALLURGICAL ENGINEERING. *Current Pos:* PRES & DIR RES, MAT RES LAB, INC, 60- *Personal Data:* b Lewistown, Pa, Feb 25, 21; m 43; c 3. *Educ:* Pa State Univ, BS, 42; Case Inst Technol, MS, 48, PhD(phys metall), 52. *Honors & Awards:* David Ford Mc Farland Award, Penn State Chap, Am Soc Metals, 84. *Prof Exp:* Metallurgist, Westinghouse Elec Co, 43-44 & Copperweld Steel Co, 44-46; asst, Case Inst Technol, 46-52, asst prof & res dir, 52-55; lab dir mech metall, Continental Can Co, Inc, 55-60. *Mem:* Fel Am Soc Metals; Am Inst Mining, Metall & Petrol Engrs. *Res:* Metal forming; mechanical properties of materials. *Mailing Add:* 2051 Cummings Lane Flossmoor IL 60422

RIPMEESTER, JOHN ADRIAN, PHYSICAL CHEMISTRY. *Current Pos:* fel, Nat Res Coun Can, 72-74, from asst res officer to assoc res officer, 74-82, sr res officer chem, 82-90, SR RES OFFICER, STEACIE INST MOLECULAR SCI, NAT RES COUN CAN, 90- *Personal Data:* b Voorburg, Neth, Feb 11, 44; Can citizen; m 67, Mary B Tillett; c Heather A & Wendy L. *Educ:* Univ BC, 65, PhD(chem), 70. *Prof Exp:* Res assoc chem, Univ Ill, Urbana-Champaign, 70-72. *Concurrent Pos:* Vis scientist, Univ BC, 82-83; sect head, Colloid & Clathrate Chem Sect, NRC, 86-90; adj prof, Carleton Univ, 87- *Mem:* Chem Inst Can. *Res:* Molecular motion in solids; nuclear magnetic resonance; supramolecular chemistry. *Mailing Add:* 29 Delong Dr Ottawa ON K1J 7E5 Can

RIPPEN, ALVIN LEONARD, DAIRY SCIENCE. *Current Pos:* RETIRED. *Personal Data:* b Campbell, Nebr, Nov 6, 17; m 43; c 3. *Educ:* Univ Nebr, BSc, 40; Ohio State Univ, MSc, 41. *Prof Exp:* Sales engr, Creamery Package Mfg Co, 45-50; plant supt dairy processing, Kegle Dairy Co, Mich, 50-57; asst prof agr eng, Mich State Univ, 57-64, assoc prof food sci, 64-69, prof, 69-80, exten specialist, 57-80. *Mem:* Am Dairy Sci Asn. *Res:* Dairy products processing; dairy plant engineering. *Mailing Add:* 1511 Birchwood Dr Okemos MI 48864

RIPPEN, THOMAS EDWARD, seafood technology & marketing, for more information see previous edition

RIPPERGER, EUGENE ARMAN, ENGINEERING MECHANICS. *Current Pos:* assoc dir, Eng Mech Res Lab, 52-64, dir, 64-85, prof aerospace eng & eng mech, 52-82, EMER PROF ENG MECH, UNIV TEX, AUSTIN, 82- *Personal Data:* b Stover, Mo, July 7, 14; m 40; c 3. *Educ:* Kans State Col, BS, 39; Univ Tex, MS, 50; Stanford Univ, PhD(eng mech), 52. *Prof Exp:* Asst res engr, Portland Cement Asn, 39-42; asst engr, US War Dept, 42-43; from instr to asst prof, Univ Tex, 46-50; asst, Stanford Univ, 50-52. *Mem:* Fel Am Soc Mech Engrs; Soc Exp Mech; Inst Elec & Electronics Engrs. *Res:* Impact; experimental mechanics; bioengineering. *Mailing Add:* 3700 Highland View Dr Austin TX 78731. *Fax:* 512-471-6539

RIPPIE, EDWARD GRANT, PHARMACEUTICS. *Current Pos:* from asst prof to assoc prof, Univ Minn, Minneapolis, 59-66, head dept, 66-74, dir grad studies, 74-81, head dept, 86-88, PROF PHARMACEUT, UNIV MINN, MINNEAPOLIS, 66- *Personal Data:* b Beloit, Wis, May 29, 31; m 55; c 1. *Educ:* Univ Wis, BS, 53, MS, 56, PhD(pharm), 59. *Honors & Awards:* Ebert Prize, Acad Pharmaceut Sci Am Pharaceut Asn, 82, Advan Indust Pharm Award, 85. *Prof Exp:* Asst pharm, Univ Wis, 56. *Concurrent Pos:* Mem comt rev, US Pharmacopoeia, 70-80. *Mem:* Am Chem Soc; Am Pharmaceut Asn; Am Asn Cols Pharm; fel Acad Pharmaceut Sci; fel Am Inst Chemists; fel AAAS. *Res:* Pharmaceutics; physical chemical behavior of physiologically active chemical species within anisotropic solvents; mechanisms of mass transport within beds of particulate solids; viscoelasticity of pharmaceutical tablets during and after compression. *Mailing Add:* 2 North Mallard Rd North Oaks MN 55127-2572. *Fax:* 612-624-2974

RIPPLE, WILLIAM JOHN, REMOTE SENSING, GEOGRAPHIC INFORMATION SYSTEMS. *Current Pos:* res assoc, 84-88, asst prof, 88-92, ASSOC PROF, DEPT FOREST RESOURCES & DIR, ENVIRON REMOTE SENSING APPLNS LAB, ORE STATE UNIV, 92- *Personal Data:* b Yankton, SDak, Mar 10, 52. *Educ:* SDak State Univ, BS, 74; Univ Idaho, MS, 78; Ore State Univ, PhD(geog), 84. *Honors & Awards:* Presidential Citation for Meritorious Serv, Am Soc Photogram & Remote Sensing, 90. *Prof Exp:* Data analyst, SDak State Planning Bur, 77-81. *Concurrent Pos:* Prin investr, Earth Commercialization Applns Prog, NASA, 88-; assoc ed, Photogram Eng & Remote Sensing J, 88- *Mem:* Am Soc Photogram & Remote Sensing; Soc Am Foresters; Int Asn Landscape Ecol. *Res:* Remote sensing and geographic information systems for the study of forest ecosystems, landscape ecology and wildlife habitat; author and co-author of over 35 technical publications. *Mailing Add:* Dept Forestry 108 Peavy Hall Ore State Univ Corvallis OR 97331

RIPPON, JOHN WILLARD, MEDICAL MYCOLOGY. *Current Pos:* asst prof, 63-69, ASSOC PROF MED, UNIV CHICAGO, 70- *Personal Data:* b Toledo, Ohio, May 19, 32. *Educ:* Univ Toledo, BS, 53; Univ Ill, MS, 57, PhD(microbiol), 59. *Prof Exp:* Res asst biochem, Univ Ill, 57-59; res assoc, Northwestern Univ, 59-60; instr biol, Loyola Univ, Ill, 60-63. *Concurrent Pos:* Res bacteriologist, Vet Admin Hosp, Hines, Ill, 59-60, consult biochemist, 60-62, consult mycologist, 73-; ed-in-chief Mycopathologia, 74- *Mem:* Am Soc Microbiol; Mycol Soc Am; Int Soc Human & Animal Mycol; Sigma Xi. *Res:* Mechanisms of fungal pathogenicity; physiology of dimorphism in pathogenic fungi. *Mailing Add:* RR 1 Box 375 Sawyer MI 49125

RIPPS, HARRIS, PHYSIOLOGY. *Current Pos:* from asst prof to assoc prof ophthal, 59-67, PROF OPHTHAL & PHYSIOL, SCH MED, NY UNIV, 67- *Personal Data:* b New York, NY, Mar 9, 27; m 49; c 3. *Educ:* Columbia Univ, BS, 50, MS, 53, MA, 56, PhD(physiol psychol), 59. *Prof Exp:* Assoc optom, Columbia Univ, 51-56. *Concurrent Pos:* Nat Inst Neurol Dis & Blindness spec fels, 62 & 63; USPHS career develop award, 63- *Mem:* AAAS; Biophys Soc; Harvey Soc; Am Asn Res Vision & Ophthal; NY Acad Sci. *Res:* Visual physiology, especially visual pigments; electrical activity of retina. *Mailing Add:* Dept Ophthal Anat & Cell Biol Univ Ill Col Med 1855 W Taylor St Chicago IL 60612-4319

RIPS, E(RVINE) M(ILTON), ELECTRICAL ENGINEERING. *Current Pos:* RETIRED. *Personal Data:* b Tulsa, Okla, Mar 7, 21; m 48; c 3. *Educ:* Mass Inst Technol, BS, 42; Carnegie Inst Technol, MS, 47. *Prof Exp:* Asst exp historadiography, Sloan-Kettering Inst Cancer Res, 48-50; instr elec eng, Polytech Inst Brooklyn, 50-52; asst chief engr, Cent Transformer Co, Ill, 52-56; chief engr, Hamner Electronics Co, NJ, 56-58; from asst prof to assoc prof, NJ Inst Technol, 58-84. *Concurrent Pos:* Consult, forensic eng, 65- *Mem:* Sr mem Inst Elec & Electronics Engrs. *Res:* Circuit design by digital computers; regulated direct-current power supplies. *Mailing Add:* 26 Gary St Dayton NJ 08810

RIPS, LANCE JEFFREY, COGNITIVE PSYCHOLOGY, COGNITIVE SCIENCE. *Current Pos:* PROF PSYCHOL, NORTHWESTERN UNIV, 93- *Personal Data:* b Omaha, Nebr, Dec 19, 47; m, Julie W Johnson; c Eve. *Educ:* Swarthmore Col, BA, 70; Stanford Univ, PhD(psychol), 74. *Prof Exp:* Prof psychol, Univ Chicago, 74-93. *Mem:* Psychonomics Soc; Am Psychol Soc; Am Psychol Asn; Cognitive Sci Soc. *Res:* Mental processes involved in reasoning, memory for word meanings, and memory for autobiographical episodes. *Mailing Add:* 2029 Sheridan Rd Evanston IL 60208

RIPY, SARA LOUISE, MATHEMATICAL ANALYSIS. *Current Pos:* RETIRED. *Personal Data:* b Lawrenceburg, Ky, July 22, 24. *Educ:* Randolph-Macon Woman's Col, BA, 46; Univ Ky, MA, 49, PhD(math), 57. *Prof Exp:* Instr math, Univ Ky, 46-54 & 56-57, Randolph-Macon Woman's Col, 54-56 & Vassar Col, 57-58; from asst prof to prof math, Agnes Scott Col, 58-89, chmn dept, 70-86. *Res:* Summability theory; analytic continuation. *Mailing Add:* 143 Winnona Dr Decatur GA 30030

RIRIE, DAVID, AGRONOMY. *Current Pos:* RETIRED. *Personal Data:* b Ririe, Idaho, Mar 20, 22; m 46; c 5. *Educ:* Brigham Young Univ, BS, 48; Rutgers Univ, PhD, 51. *Prof Exp:* Agronomist, Sugar Beet Proj, Univ Calif, 51-55; chmn dept agr, Church Col NZ, 55-63; soils & irrig farm adv, 63-80, dir, Monterey Co, Agr Exten Serv, Univ Calif, 81-89. *Concurrent Pos:* Consult, FMC Int, Eastern Europe. *Mem:* Am Soc Agron; Soil Sci Soc Am; Am Soc Hort Sci. *Res:* Nutrition studies with sugar beets; effects of growth regulators on sugar beets; peat land reclamation; vegetable crop culture; cereal crop fertilization. *Mailing Add:* 1061 University Ave Salinas CA 93901

RIS, HANS, CELL BIOLOGY. *Current Pos:* from assoc prof to prof, 49-84, EMER PROF ZOOL, UNIV WIS-MADISON, 84- *Personal Data:* b Bern, Switz, June 15, 14; nat US; m 80, Theron Brown; c Christopher & Anet. *Educ:* Columbia Univ, PhD(cytol), 42. *Honors & Awards:* Distinguished Investr Award, Micros Soc Am, 83; E B Wilson Award, Am Soc Cell Biol, 93. *Prof Exp:* Asst zool, Columbia Univ, 39-40, lectr, 41-42; Seessel fel, Yale Univ, 42; instr biol, Johns Hopkins Univ, 42-44; asst physiol, Rockefeller Inst, 44-47, assoc, 47-49. *Concurrent Pos:* Hon prof life sci, Peking Univ, Beijing, 95. *Mem:* Nat Acad Sci; fel Am Acad Arts & Sci; Am Soc Naturalists; Genetics Soc Am; Am Soc Cell Biol; fel AAAS; Micros Soc Am. *Res:* Chromosome structure and chemistry; physiology of cell nucleus; mitosis; cell ultrastructure; nuclear envelope structure. *Mailing Add:* Dept Zool Univ Wis Madison WI 53706. *Fax:* 608-265-4076; *E-Mail:* hansris@macc.wisc.edu

RISBUD, SUBHASH HANAMANT, GLASS SCIENCE, REFRACTORY MATERIALS. *Current Pos:* ASST PROF CERAMIC ENG, UNIV ILL, URBANA, 79- *Personal Data:* b New Delhi, India, Aug 3, 47; m 74; c 1. *Educ:* Indian Inst Technol, BS, 69; Univ Calif, Berkeley, MS, 71, PhD(ceramic eng), 76. *Honors & Awards:* Ross Coffin Purdy Award, Am Ceramic Soc, 79. *Prof Exp:* Eng assoc mat res, Stanford Univ, 71-73; ceramic engr, GTE-WESGO Corp, Calif, 73-74; asst prof mech eng, Univ Nebr-Lincoln, 76-78; asst prof mat sci & eng, Lehigh Univ, 78-79. *Concurrent Pos:* Prin investr, Mat Res Lab, Univ Ill, Urbana, 79- *Mem:* Am Ceramic Soc; Am Soc Eng Educ. *Res:* Glasses and glass-ceramics: developing the scientific framework for new and unusual glasses in non-oxide ceramic systems, crystallization behavior, microstructure, and properties. *Mailing Add:* 3313 Seabright Av Davis CA 95616

RISBY, EDWARD LOUIS, PARASITOLOGY, CELL BIOLOGY. *Current Pos:* RETIRED. *Personal Data:* b Clarksdale, Miss, Sept 14, 33; m 57; c 3. *Educ:* Lane Col, BS, 56; Southern Ill Univ, Carbondale, MA, 59; Tulane Univ, PhD(parasitol, cell biol), 68. *Prof Exp:* Asst prof biol, Lane Col, 58-61 & Southern Univ, 61-66; asst prof microbiol, Meharry Med Col, 68-78, asst dean grad studies, 71-78; prof & head, Dept Biol Sci, Tenn State Univ, 78-88, dean grad studies & res, 88-95. *Concurrent Pos:* Consult premed prog, United Negro Col Fund, Fisk Univ, 71- & Dillard Univ, 72. *Mem:* Am Soc Parasitol; Soc Protozool; Am Soc Microbiol. *Res:* Comparative study of trypanosomal physiology and pathobiology observed in experimental trypanosomiasis. *Mailing Add:* 3017 Vista Dr Nashville TN 37218

RISBY, TERENCE HUMPHREY, ANALYTICAL CHEMISTRY, ENVIRONMENTAL HEALTH SCIENCES. *Current Pos:* assoc prof, 79-88, dir, Div Environ Chem & Biol, 89-93, PROF ENVIRON HEALTH SCI, JOHNS HOPKINS UNIV, 88-, PROF PATH, 94-, PROF INT HEALTH, 96- *Personal Data:* b Essex, Eng, June 9, 47; m 83, Barbara Morrison; c Lauren Paige. *Educ:* Imp Col, Univ London, DIC, 68, PhD(chem), 70; Royal Inst Chem, MRIC Chem, 75; FRSC, 80. *Prof Exp:* Res fel chem, Univ Madrid, 70-71; res assoc, Univ NC, Chapel Hill, 71-72; asst prof chem, Pa State Univ, 72-78. *Concurrent Pos:* Europ fel, Royal Soc, 70-71; consult, Appl Sci Labs, 74-78, Sci Res Instruments Corp, 75-77. *Mem:* Royal Inst Gt Brit; Am Chem Soc; Soc Appl Spectros; Am Soc Mass Spectros; fel assoc Inst Chem; fel Royal Soc Chem; Sigma Xi; fel Chromatographic Soc; Oxygen Soc. *Res:* Use of thermodynamic models to predict the bioavailability, bioaccumulation and bioactivity of xenobiotics for health effects studies; non-invasive markers of tissue injury. *Mailing Add:* Johns Hopkins Univ 615 N Wolfe St Baltimore MD 21205. *Fax:* 410-955-0027; *E-Mail:* thrisby@welchlink.welch.jhu.edu

RISDON, THOMAS JOSEPH, LUBRICANTS, TRIBOLOGY. *Current Pos:* Res asst, 63-67, sr res asst, 67-70, res assoc, 70-75, sr res assoc, 75-78, SR RES SPECIALIST, CLIMAX MOLYBDENUM CO, AMAX, INC, 78- *Personal Data:* b Detroit, Mich, Sept 22, 39; m 79; c 1. *Educ:* Univ Detroit, BSChE, 62. *Mem:* Am Soc Lubrication Engrs. *Res:* New uses and applications for molybdenum disulfide and other molybdenum compounds as lubricants or lubricant additives. *Mailing Add:* 4871 Dexter-Pinckney Rd Dexter MI 48130

RISEBERG, LESLIE ALLEN, ELECTRONICS, OPTICS. *Current Pos:* mem tech staff, GTE Labs Inc, 72-75, res mgr, 75-81, dir, Lighting Technol Ctr, 81-82, dir, Components Res Lab, 82-85, dir, Elec & Photonics Lab, 85-88, dir, Systs Technol Lab, GTE Labs, Inc, 88-95, VPRES TECHNOL PLANNING, GTE CORP, 95- *Personal Data:* b Malden, Mass, July 23, 43; m 64, Marilyn Oxman; c Jocelyn & Andrew. *Educ:* Harvard Univ, AB, 64; Johns Hopkins Univ, PhD(physics), 68. *Prof Exp:* Mem tech staff, Bell Tel Labs, 68; guest lectr physics, Hebrew Univ Jerusalem, 68-69; mem tech staff corp res & eng, Tex Instruments Inc, 70-72. *Concurrent Pos:* Consult, Raytheon Co, 70- & Lawrence Livermore Lab, 74. *Mem:* Am Phys Soc; Inst Elec & Electronics Engrs; Sigma Xi; Optical Soc Am. *Res:* Quantum electronics; solid state physics; optics; phosphors; solid state devices; lighting technology; materials science; integrated circuits; fiber optics; semiconductor technology; telecommunications, networks, multimedia, computer systems, video. *Mailing Add:* GTE Corp Stamford Forum Stamford CT 06904. *Fax:* 781-466-4116

RISEMAN, EDWARD M, COMPUTER VISION. *Current Pos:* From asst prof to assoc prof, 69-78, chmn, Dept Comput & Info Sci, 81-85, PROF COMPUT & DIR COMPUT VISION LAB, DEPT COMPUT & INFO SCI, UNIV MASS, AMHERST, 78- *Personal Data:* b Washington, DC, Aug 15, 42. *Educ:* Clarkson Col Technol, BS, 64; Cornell Univ, MS, 66, PhD(elec eng), 69. *Concurrent Pos:* Co-prin investr, equip grants, NSF, 77-79, 82-84, Digital Equipment Corp, 77; res grants, NSF, 79-, Army Res Inst, 80-82, Defense Advan Res Proj Agency, 82-87, Air Force Off Sci Res, 83-, Defense Mapping Agency & Off Naval Res, 84-86, Honeywell, 85, Gen Dynamics, 85-86 & Naval Res Lab, 85; consult & inst observer, SRI, Menlo Park, 78; prin investr res grant, Digital Equip Corp, 80-81 & NSF, 84-87. *Mem:* Inst Elec & Electronics Engrs; Asn Comput Mach; Pattern Recognition Soc; Am Asn Artificial Intel. *Res:* Visual perception by machine; development of real-time computers. *Mailing Add:* Comput Sci Dept Grad Res Ctr Univ Mass Amherst MA 01003

RISEN, WILLIAM MAURICE, JR, PHYSICAL CHEMISTRY, INORGANIC CHEMISTRY. *Current Pos:* From instr to assoc prof, 66-75, chmn dept, 72-80, PROF CHEM, BROWN UNIV, 75- *Personal Data:* b St Louis, Mo, July 22, 40; m 64; c 2. *Educ:* Georgetown Univ, ScB, 62; Purdue Univ, PhD(phys chem), 67. *Concurrent Pos:* Consult, NSF; mem, Coun Chem Res; consult, Indust. *Mem:* Am Chem Soc; Am Phys Soc; Am Ceramic Soc. *Res:* Molecular spectroscopy; studies of glasses and polymers; far infrared and laser Raman spectra of ionic polymers and glasses; electron-delocalized materials. *Mailing Add:* Dept Chem Brown Univ Providence RI 02912

RISER, NATHAN WENDELL, INVERTEBRATE ZOOLOGY. *Current Pos:* prof biol, Northeastern Univ, 57-79, dir, Marine Sci Inst, 66-79, prof, 79-85, EMER PROF MARINE BIOL, NORTHEASTERN UNIV, 85- *Personal Data:* b Salt Lake City, Utah, Apr 11, 20; m 43, Jean L Folz; c 3. *Educ:* Univ Ill, AB, 41; Stanford Univ, AM, 47, PhD, 49. *Prof Exp:* Actg instr biol, Stanford Univ, 49; instr zool, Univ Pa, 49-50; from assoc prof to prof biol, Fisk Univ, 50-56; res assoc marine biol, Woods Hole Oceanog Inst, 56-57. *Concurrent Pos:* Vis prof, Univ NH, 50-52 & 53-58; instr, Marine Biol Lab, Woods Hole, 52; res assoc, Woods Hole Oceanog Inst, 57-59; assoc, Mus Comp Zool, Harvard Univ, 57-62. *Mem:* Am Micros Soc. *Res:* Nemertine morphology, systematics; invertebrate systematics, morphology, histology and embryology; soft bodied interstitial fauna of the Northwest Atlantic and New Zealand. *Mailing Add:* Marine Sci Inst East Point Nahant MA 01908-1696. *Fax:* 781-581-6076

RISER, WAYNE H, ORTHOPEDICS, CANINE HIP DYSPLASIA. *Current Pos:* PROF VET PATH, COL VET MED, UNIV FLA, 79- *Personal Data:* b Earlham, Iowa, Aug 29, 09; m 76, Mary A Wirthen Carter. *Educ:* Iowa State Univ, DVM, 32, MS, 45; Univ Bern, Dr med vet, 73. *Hon Degrees:* MA, Univ Pa, 74. *Prof Exp:* Owner, Riser Small Animal Hosp, 36-60; res fel, Armed Forces Inst Path, 60-63; prof path, Univ Pa, 63-79. *Concurrent Pos:* Lectr, Dept Path, Northwestern Univ, 50-63; vis investr, Oxford Univ, Nuffield

Orthop Ctr & Royal Vet Col, 63; consult mil dog prog, Walter Reed Army Inst Res, 69-76; instr orthop path, Univ Pa, 70-79; instr pract mgt, Univ Pa, 70-87, Univ Fla, 79-; vet, Vet Hosp, Wilmington, Del, 72-86; affil staff mem & vet consult, Alfred I DuPont Hosp, 72-86. *Mem:* Am Col Vet Path; Am Animal Hosp Asn (pres, 60); Am Vet Med Asn. *Res:* Canine hip dysplasia; etiology; osteochondritis dessecans chondrocalcinosis in the shoulders of dogs. *Mailing Add:* 1631 NW 19th Circle Gainesville FL 32605

RISHEL, RAYMOND WARREN, MATHEMATICS. *Current Pos:* PROF MATH, UNIV KY, 72- *Personal Data:* b Phillips, Wis, June 27, 30; m 57; c 2. *Educ:* Univ Wis, BS, 52, MS, 53, PhD(math), 59. *Prof Exp:* Instr math, Brown Univ, 59-60; res specialist, Boeing Co, SWash, 60-68; assoc prof math, Wash State Univ, 68-69; mathematician, Bell Tel Labs, 69-72. *Mem:* Soc Indust & Appl Math. *Res:* Optimal control theory; probability. *Mailing Add:* Dept Math Univ Ky Lexington KY 40506-0001

RISHELL, WILLIAM ARTHUR, POULTRY BREEDING. *Current Pos:* res geneticist, 75-76, DIR RES, ARBOR ACRES FARM INC, 76- *Personal Data:* b Lock Haven, Pa, Mar 1, 40; m 60; c 2. *Educ:* Univ Md, BS, 62; Iowa State Univ, MS, 65, PhD(poultry breeding), 68. *Prof Exp:* Geneticist & dir breeding res, Indian River Int, Tex, 67-75. *Mem:* Poultry Sci Asn; World Poultry Sci Asn; Am Genetic Asn. *Res:* Applied poultry breeding and research; statistical analyses of experiments; estimation of genetic parameters. *Mailing Add:* 188 Highwood Dr South Glastonbury CT 06073

RISING, EDWARD JAMES, INDUSTRIAL ENGINEERING. *Current Pos:* RETIRED. *Personal Data:* b Troy, NY, Nov 10, 26; m 49; c 3. *Educ:* Rensselaer Polytech Inst, BME, 50; Syracuse Univ, MME, 53; Univ Iowa, PhD(indust eng), 59. *Prof Exp:* Instr mech eng, Syracuse Univ, 51-54; asst prof, Kans State Univ, 54-56; instr mech & hydraul, Univ Iowa, 56-60; assoc prof indust eng & asst dean, Univ Mass, Amherst, 60-71, prof indust eng & opers res, 71-89. *Concurrent Pos:* Consult, Mo River Div, US Corps Engrs, 58, Educ Testing Serv, NJ, 60, Package Mach Corp, Mass, 60, City of Gardner, 61, Franklin Co Hosp, Greenfield, 64-66, Sprague & Carlton, NH, 66, Paper Serv Corp, Mass, 70 & USPHS, 72; Joseph Lucas vis prof, Univ Birmingham. *Mem:* Am Soc Eng Educ; Am Inst Indust Engrs; Am Hosp Asn; Opers Res Soc Am. *Res:* Hospital systems; engineering education. *Mailing Add:* 72 Sand Hill Rd North Amherst MA 01002

RISING, JAMES DAVID, SYSTEMATIC ZOOLOGY. *Current Pos:* ASSOC PROF ZOOL, UNIV TORONTO, 69- *Personal Data:* b Kansas City, Mo, Aug 10, 42; m 65; c 1. *Educ:* Univ Kans, BA, 64, PhD(zool), 68. *Prof Exp:* Fel, Cornell Univ, 68-69. *Mem:* Am Ornithologists Union; Am Soc Naturalists; Soc Study Evolution; Ecol Soc Am; Soc Syst Zool. *Res:* Biology of birds; distribution, abundance, ecology, systematics, behavior and physiology of birds, especially systematic theory; interpopulational variation of vertebrate animals. *Mailing Add:* Dept Zool Ramsey Wright Labs Univ Toronto Toronto ON M5S 1A1 Can

RISINGER, GERALD E, CHEMISTRY. *Current Pos:* asst prof biochem, 63-71, ASSOC PROF BIOCHEM, LA STATE UNIV, BATON ROUGE, 71- *Personal Data:* b Pekin, Ill, Nov 13, 33; m 53; c 2. *Educ:* Bradley Univ, BS, 55; Iowa State Univ, PhD(org chem), 60. *Prof Exp:* Asst prof org chem, Arlington State Col, 60-62 & La Polytech Inst, 62-63. *Concurrent Pos:* Petrol Res Fund grant, 63-66; USPHS res grant, 64-66. *Mem:* Am Chem Soc; Sigma Xi. *Res:* Bio-organic chemistry; characterization and synthesis of natural products; biogenesis of alkaloids and terpenes; biochemical mechanisms of coenzymatic and enzymatic reactions. *Mailing Add:* 650 Seyburn Ct Baton Rouge LA 70808

RISIUS, MARVIN LEROY, PLANT BREEDING. *Current Pos:* from asst prof to assoc prof, Pa State Univ, University Park, 66-77, prof forage breeding, 77-79, interim head, 94-95, PROF SMALL GRAIN BREEDING, PA STATE UNIV, UNIVERSITY PARK, 79- *Personal Data:* b Buffalo Center, Iowa, July 20, 31; m 59; c 2. *Educ:* Iowa State Univ, BS, 58; Cornell Univ, MS, 62, PhD(plant breeding), 64. *Prof Exp:* Res assoc corn breeding, Cornell Univ, 64-66. *Mem:* Am Soc Agron; Crop Sci Soc Am; Nat Asn Col & Teachers Agr. *Res:* Plant breeding and genetics with small grains. *Mailing Add:* Dept Agron 116 Ag Sci Pa State Univ University Park PA 16802-3504

RISK, MICHAEL JOHN, MARINE ECOLOGY, PALEOECOLOGY. *Current Pos:* ASST PROF GEOL, McMASTER UNIV, 71- *Personal Data:* b Toronto, Ont, Feb 17, 40; m 65; c 2. *Educ:* Univ Toronto, BSc, 62; Univ Western Ont, MSc, 64; Univ Southern Calif, PhD(biol), 71. *Prof Exp:* Staff mem, Dept Geol Sci, Brock Univ. *Mem:* AAAS; Soc Econ Paleontologists & Mineralogists; Geol Asn Can. *Res:* Species diversity and substrate complexity; coral reef diversity; trace fossils; early history of the invertebrate phyla; animal-sediment relationships. *Mailing Add:* Dept Geol Sci McMaster Univ 1280 Main St W Hamilton ON L8S 4L8 Can

RISKIN, JULES, PSYCHIATRY. *Current Pos:* actg dir, 58, assoc dir, 59-76, DIR, MENT RES INST, 76- *Personal Data:* b Oakland, Calif, Aug 25, 26; m 60; c 2. *Educ:* Univ Chicago, PhB, 48, MD, 54. *Prof Exp:* Intern, Col Med, Univ Ill, 54-55; intern psychiat res, Cincinnati Gen Hosp, Ohio, 55-58. *Concurrent Pos:* NIMH res grant co-prin investr, Ment Res Inst, 61-65, prin investr, 66-69. *Mem:* Am Psychiat Asn; AMA. *Res:* Developing a methodology for studying whole family interaction; studying technique and theory of family therapy. *Mailing Add:* 555 Middlefield Rd Palo Alto CA 94301

RISLEY, JOHN MARCUS, ENZYMOLOGY, CARBOHYDRATE CHEMISTRY. *Current Pos:* asst prof, 88-94, ASSOC PROF CHEM, UNIV NC, CHARLOTTE, 94- *Personal Data:* b New Castle, Ind, Nov 28, 52. *Educ:* Ball State Univ, BS, 76; Purdue Univ, PhD(chem), 80. *Prof Exp:* Res assoc, Purdue Univ, 80-85, asst res scientist, 85-86, vis asst prof chem, 87-88. *Concurrent Pos:* Prin investr, Univ NC, Charlotte, 89-; mem, Org Reactions Mechanisms Group, Royal Soc Chem. *Mem:* Am Soc Biochem & Molecular Biol; Am Chem Soc; Royal Soc Chem; Sigma Xi; Soc Physics Students. *Res:* Report and study the oxygen-18 isotope shift in carbon-13 nuclear magnetic resonance that has important applications in biochemistry and organic chemistry; study properties of the glycoconjugate enzyme glycosylasparaginase. *Mailing Add:* Dept Chem Univ NC Charlotte NC 28223. *Fax:* 704-547-3151; *E-Mail:* jmrisley@unccvm.uncc.edu

RISLEY, JOHN STETLER, ATOMIC PHYSICS, PHYSICS EDUCATION RESEARCH. *Current Pos:* from asst prof to assoc prof, 76-84, PROF PHYSICS, NC STATE UNIV, 84- *Personal Data:* b Seattle, Wash, Mar 3, 42; m 65, Dellaine Anderson; c Renelle, James & Steven. *Educ:* Univ Wash, BS, 65, MS, 66, PhD(physics), 73. *Honors & Awards:* Distinguished Serv Award, Am Asn Physics Teachers. *Prof Exp:* Teaching asst & res assoc physics, Univ Wash, 65-75; vis asst prof, Univ Nebr, 76. *Concurrent Pos:* Secy, Int Conf Physics of Electronic & Atomic Collisions, 77-89; mem prog comt electronic & atomic physics, Am Phys Soc, 78-79 & 84-87; column ed, Physics Teacher, 83-88; ed, Physics Acad Software, 87-; co-chmn, Conf Computers in Physics Instr, 88; dir, Acad Software Libr, 88-; mem, Comt Int Sci Affairs, Am Phys Soc, 93-95. *Mem:* Fel Am Phys Soc; Sigma Xi; fel AAAS; Am Asn Physics Teachers. *Res:* Atomic collisions physics; negative ions; autodetaching states; vacuum ultraviolet radiation; synchrotron radiation; density matrix; electron collisions; physics courseware; computers in teaching physics. *Mailing Add:* Dept Physics NC State Univ Raleigh NC 27695-8202. *Fax:* 919-515-2682; *E-Mail:* risley@ncsu.edu

RISLEY, MICHAEL SAMUEL, REPRODUCTIVE BIOLOGY. *Current Pos:* ASSOC PROF BIOL, FORDHAM UNIV, 87- *Personal Data:* b June 30, 48; c Gabrielle (Solomon). *Educ:* Manhattan Col, BS, 70; City Univ New York, PhD(biol), 77. *Prof Exp:* Assoc prof cell biol & histol, Med Col, Cornell Univ, 84-87. *Mem:* Am Soc Cell Biol; Soc Study Reprod. *Res:* Reproductive genetic toxicology; chromosome structure; spermatogenesis. *Mailing Add:* Dept Biol Fordham Univ Fordham Univ Fordham Rd Bronx NY 10458-0001

RISLOVE, DAVID JOEL, ORGANIC CHEMISTRY. *Current Pos:* assoc prof, 68-77, PROF CHEM, WINONA STATE UNIV, 77- *Personal Data:* b Rushford, Minn, Nov 16, 40; m 63, Susan M Schacht; c Kaye & Lori. *Educ:* Winona State Col, BA, 62; NDak State Univ, PhD(chem), 68. *Prof Exp:* Am Petrol Inst res asst, NDak State Univ, 65-68. *Concurrent Pos:* Vis scientist, 3M Co, St Paul, Minn, 83-84, Univ Minn, 76. *Mem:* Am Chem Soc. *Res:* Pyrrole and porphyrin chemistry; synthetic organic chemistry; kinetics and mechanisms of organic reactions; acid-base chemistry in non-aqueous media; polyanilines and N-substituted-2, 4-dinitroaniline compounds. *Mailing Add:* Dept Chem Winona State Univ Winona MN 55987

RISPOLI, FRED JOSEPH, OPERATIONS RESEARCH. *Current Pos:* ASST PROF MATH, DOWLING COL, 86- *Personal Data:* b Brooklyn, NY, Feb 3, 59; m 86, Loretta Tarter; c Loren & Nicholas. *Educ:* Univ Conn, BS, 81; State Univ NY, Stony Brook, PhD(appl math & statist), 90. *Concurrent Pos:* Consult, Arrow Electronics Inc, 90-, NY State Dept Motor Vehicles, 92. *Mem:* Opers Res Soc Am; Math Prog Soc; Soc Indust & Appl Math. *Res:* Theoretical properties related to the efficiency of algorithms that solve problems arising in operations research. *Mailing Add:* Dept Math Dowling Col Oakdale NY 11769. *Fax:* 516-589-6644; *E-Mail:* rispolif@dowling.edu

RISS, WALTER, NEUROANATOMY, PSYCHOLOGY. *Current Pos:* from instr to prof, State Univ NY Downstate Med Ctr, 54-85, asst dean grad studies, 70-73, dir biol psychol, 71-75, EMER PROF ANAT, STATE UNIV NY DOWNSTATE MED CTR, 85- *Personal Data:* b New Britain, Conn, Jan 1, 25; m 51, Barbara A Johnson; c Richard, Elizabeth, Joan & George. *Educ:* Univ Conn, BA, 49; Univ Rochester, PhD(psychol), 53. *Prof Exp:* Res assoc anat, Univ Kans, 52-53, USPHS fel, 53-54. *Concurrent Pos:* Prin founder & ed-in-chief, Brain, Behav & Evolution, 68-86. *Mem:* Am Asn Anatomists; Soc Neurosci. *Res:* Evolution of the nervous system and behavior; brain functions and behavior; testing brain function with use of computers. *Mailing Add:* 3 Addison Lane Greenvale NY 11548

RISSANEN, JORMA JOHANNES, MATHEMATICS, INFORMATION THEORY. *Current Pos:* MEM RES STAFF, INFO THEORY & MATH, IBM RES, 60- *Personal Data:* b Finland, Oct 20, 32; m 57, Riitta Aberg; c Juhani & Natasha. *Educ:* Tech Univ Helsinki, dipl eng, 56, Techn Lic, 60, Techn Dr(control theory, math), 65. *Hon Degrees:* Dr, Tech Univ Tampere, Finland, 92. *Honors & Awards:* R W Hamming Medal, Inst Elec & Electronics Engrs, 93. *Concurrent Pos:* Prof control theory, Linkoping Univ, Sweden, 73-74; coord ed, J Statist Planning & Inference; assoc ed, IMA J Math Control & Infor & J Computational & Appl Math. *Mem:* Fel Inst Elec & Electronics Engrs. *Res:* Information theory; estimation and statistics; probability theory. *Mailing Add:* IBM Res DPE-B2/802 Almaden Res Ctr 650 Harry Rd San Jose CA 95120-6099

RISSE, GUENTER BERNHARD, HISTORY OF MEDICINE. *Current Pos:* PROF & CHMN HIST HEALTH SCI, UNIV CALIF, SAN FRANCISCO, 85- *Personal Data:* b Buenos Aires, Arg, Apr 28, 32; US citizen; m; c 3. *Educ:* Univ Buenos Aires, MD, 58; Univ Chicago, MA, 66, PhD(hist), 71. *Honors & Awards:* William H Welch Medal, Am Asn Hist Med, 88. *Prof Exp:* Asst med, Med Sch, Univ Chicago, 63-67; asst prof hist med, Med Sch, Univ Minn, 69-71; assoc prof hist med, Univ Wis-Madison, 71-76, prof hist med, 76-85, prof health sci, 76-85. *Concurrent Pos:* Am Philos Soc fel, 72, 77 & 82; NIH grant, Univ Wis, 72-74 & 82-83; Univ Calif grant, 87-92. *Mem:* Am Asn Hist Med; Ger Soc Hist Med, Sci & Technol; Hist Sci Soc; Int Acad Hist Med; Brit Soc Social Hist Med. *Res:* History of modern european medicine; history of the hospital, history of epidemics, twentieth century health sciences. *Mailing Add:* 600 Nomega St Apt 8A San Francisco CA 94122

RISSER, ARTHUR CRANE, JR, ORNITHOLOGY. *Current Pos:* asst cur birds, 74-76, cur birds, 76-81, gen cur birds, 81-86, GEN MGR, SAN DIEGO ZOO, 86- *Personal Data:* b Blackwell, Okla, July 8, 38; m 78; c 3. *Educ:* Grinnell Col, BA, 60; Univ Ariz, MS, 63; Univ Calif, Davis, PhD(zool), 70. *Prof Exp:* Mus technician, Smithsonian Inst, US Nat Mus, 63-64; res assoc med ecol, Int Ctr Med Res & Training, Univ Md, 64-65; asst zool, Univ Calif, Davis, 65-67, lab technician, 67-70; asst prof biol, Univ Nev, Reno, 70-74. *Concurrent Pos:* Adj prof zool, San Diego State Univ, 77-; mem, Calif condor recovery team; co-chmn, working group on Calif condor captive reproduction & re-introduction; dir, Int Fedn Conserv Birds, 80- *Mem:* Am Asn Zool Parks & Aquariums; Am Pheasant & Waterfowl Soc; Cooper Ornith Soc; Am Fedn Aviculture; Int Fedn Conserv Birds. *Res:* Avian reproduction. *Mailing Add:* 2901 Spruce St San Diego CA 92104

RISSER, PAUL GILLAN, ECOSYSTEMS. *Current Pos:* VPRES, DEPT RES, UNIV NMEX, PRES, MIAMI UNIV, OXFORD, OH. *Personal Data:* b Blackwell, Okla, Sept 14, 39; m 61; c 4. *Educ:* Grinnell Col, BA, 61; Univ Wis-Madison, MS, 65, PhD(bot & soils), 67. *Prof Exp:* Res asst, Jackson Lab, 61-63; asst prof bot, Univ Okla, Norman, 67-72, assoc prof, 72-77, chmn, Dept Bot & Microbiol & prog dir ecosyst studies, 77-81, prof, 78-81; chief, Ill Natural Hist Surv, 81- *Mem:* Ecol Soc Am (secy, 78-82); Sigma Xi; Brit Ecol Soc; Soc Range Mgt. *Res:* Systems analysis of grassland ecosystems, particularly, dynamics of energy and material storage and transfer; studies of vegetation structure; natural resource planning. *Mailing Add:* 500 E High St Miami Univ Oxford OH 45056-1618

RISSING, JOHN PETER, INFECTIOUS DISEASES. *Current Pos:* from asst prof to assoc prof med, 76-85, CHIEF INFECTIOUS DIS DIV, MED COL GA, 80-, PROF MED 85- *Personal Data:* b Ft Wayne, Ind, Apr 16, 43; m 72, Kathleen; c Brian, Erika, David, Sabrina & Kirstin. *Educ:* Ind Univ, AB, 65; St Louis Univ, MD, 69. *Prof Exp:* Resident med, Ind Univ Med Ctr, 69-72, fel infectious dis, 72-74. *Concurrent Pos:* Chief infectious dis, Vet Admin Hosp, Augusta, 76- *Mem:* Fel Am Col Physicians; fel Infectious Dis Soc Am. *Res:* Pathogenesis and therapy of osteomyelitis; HIV therapy. *Mailing Add:* Dept Med/Infectious Dis Med Col Ga Augusta GA 30901-3130. *Fax:* 706-721-2000

RISSLER, JANE FRANCINA, PLANT PATHOLOGY. *Current Pos:* ASST PROF PLANT PATH, UNIV MD, 78- *Personal Data:* b Martinsburg, WVa, Jan 1, 46. *Educ:* Shepherd Col, BA, 66; WVa Univ, MA, 68; Cornell Univ, PhD(plant path), 77. *Prof Exp:* Fel fungal physiol, Boyce Thompson Inst, 77-78. *Mem:* Am Phytopath Soc. *Res:* Phytopathogenic bacteria; diseases of ornamental plants and turf grass. *Mailing Add:* Six Plateau Pl Greenbelt MD 20770

RISTENBATT, MARLIN P, COMMUNICATION SYSTEMS. *Current Pos:* assoc res engr, 56-61, res engr, 61-65, GROUP LEADER COMMUN, UNIV MICH, ANN ARBOR, 65- *Personal Data:* b Lebanon, Pa, Oct 12, 28; m 57; c 1. *Educ:* Pa State Univ, BS, 52, MS, 54; Univ Mich, PhD(elec eng), 61. *Prof Exp:* Instr elec eng, Pa State Univ, 52-54; sr engr, HRB-Singer, Inc, 54-56. *Mem:* AAAS; sr mem Inst Elec & Electronics Engrs. *Res:* Application of communications theory, decision theory, estimation theory and computer methods to devise and evaluate new communication techniques and systems. *Mailing Add:* Commun & Signal Process Lab Univ Mich Eecs Bldg N Campus Ann Arbor MI 48109

RISTEY, WILLIAM J, TECHNICAL MANAGEMENT. *Current Pos:* ASSOC, MICRO CTR, 96- *Personal Data:* b Cresco, Iowa, Aug 1, 38; m 66, Elizabeth Mitchell; c Catherine (Patterson), John, Sara & Michael. *Educ:* Memphis State Univ, BS, 60; Vanderbilt Univ, PhD(phys chem), 66; Northwestern Univ, MM, 79. *Prof Exp:* Res assoc crystallog, Vanderbilt Univ, 65-66; chemist struct chem, Esso Res & Eng , 66-69; sr scientist polymer physics, Chemplex Co, 69-78; prin scientist mat res, Arco Chem Co, 78-86; res supvr, Hercules Inc, 87-91, consult, 92; sr chemist, Force Industs, 93-96. *Concurrent Pos:* Instr, Dept Mgt, Pa State Univ, Great Valley. *Mem:* Am Chem Soc. *Res:* Material science; quantitative methods; statistics; quality; safety. *Mailing Add:* 605 Hickory Lane Berwyn PA 19312

RISTIC, MIODRAG, VETERINARY MEDICINE. *Current Pos:* PROF VET PATH & HYG, UNIV ILL, URBANA, 60-, PROF VET RES, 65- *Personal Data:* b Serbia, Yugoslavia, May 16, 18; nat US; m 50; c 1. *Educ:* Univ Munich, dipl, 50; Col Vet Med, Ger, Dr Vet Med, 50; Univ Wis, MS, 53; Univ Ill, PhD, 59. *Prof Exp:* Asst prof microbiol, Col Vet Med, Ger, 50-51; proj asst vet sci, Univ Wis, 51-53; from assoc pathologist to pathologist, Univ Fla, 53-60. *Concurrent Pos:* Mem comt anaplasmosis & transmissible dis of swine, US Animal Health Asn; Anglo-Am fel, Europe; mem comt on rickettsia, Bergey's Manual; consult, Agency Int Develop & Rockefeller Found. *Mem:* Soc Immunol; Conf Res Workers Animal Dis; Am Vet Med Asn; Am Soc Trop Med & Hyg; Soc Protozool. *Res:* Infectious diseases of domestic animals, with special emphasis on blood diseases of man and animals. *Mailing Add:* Dept Path Biol Col Vet Med Univ Ill 410 Burkwood Ct W Urbana IL 61801-5937

RISTIC, VELIMIR MIHAILO, PLASMA PHYSICS, ELECTRICAL ENGINEERING. *Current Pos:* from asst prof to assoc prof, 72-80, PROF ELEC ENG, UNIV TORONTO, 80- *Personal Data:* b Skopje, Yugoslavia, Oct 10, 36; m 64, Jelica Conic; c Milica. *Educ:* Univ Belgrade, BS, 60, MS, 64; Stanford Univ, MS, 66, PhD(elec eng), 69. *Prof Exp:* Res asst elec eng, Boris Kidric Inst Nuclear Sci, Belgrade, 61-62; lectr, Univ Belgrade, 62-65; res asst plasma physics, Stanford Univ, 66-68. *Concurrent Pos:* Res assoc, Inst Geomagnetic Sci & lectr, Univ Nis, 62-65; Nat Res Coun Can & Defence Res Bd Can res grants, Univ Toronto, 68-72; Ont Dept Univ Affairs res grant, 69-70. *Mem:* Inst Elec & Electronics Engrs. *Res:* Microwave acoustics; acousto-optic signal processing; wave-wave and wave-particle interactions in acoustics, optics and electromagnetics; real-time signal processing. *Mailing Add:* Dept Elec & Comput Eng Univ Toronto Toronto ON M5S 1A4 Can. *Fax:* 416-485-0032

RISTINEN, ROBERT A, NUCLEAR PHYSICS. *Current Pos:* from asst prof to assoc prof, 66-72, PROF, DEPT PHYSICS, UNIV COLO, 72- *Personal Data:* b Park Rapids, Minn, Apr 2, 34. *Educ:* Univ Minn, BS, 59; Univ Colo, MS, 61, PhD, 62. *Prof Exp:* Res assoc, Brookhaven Nat Lab, 62-64, from asst physicist to assoc physicist, 64-66. *Concurrent Pos:* Vis scientist, TRIUMF Lab, Univ BC, Vancouver, 87-88. *Mem:* Fel Am Phys Soc. *Res:* Nuclear physics; author of 97 publications. *Mailing Add:* Dept Physics Univ Colo CB390 Boulder CO 80309

RISTOW, BRUCE W, PHYSICAL CHEMISTRY. *Current Pos:* from asst prof to assoc prof chem, State Univ NY, Geneseo, 67-72, dean grad studies, 72-75, asst vpres, 75-86, ASSOC VPRES ACAD AFFAIRS, STATE UNIV NY, GENESEO, 86- *Personal Data:* b Chicago, Ill, June 24, 40; m 66; c 3. *Educ:* Northwestern Univ, BA, 62; Cornell Univ, PhD, 66. *Prof Exp:* NIH fel, Yale Univ, 66-67. *Mem:* Am Chem Soc; Sigma Xi. *Res:* Electron spin resonance; electrochemistry. *Mailing Add:* 540 Antlers Dr Rochester NY 14618-2128

RISTROPH, JOHN HEARD, FORECASTING, ECONOMIC ANALYSIS & COMPUTER APPLICATIONS. *Current Pos:* assoc prof, 83-92, PROF ENG MGT, UNIV SOUTHWESTERN LA, 92-, COORD ENG MGT, 93- *Personal Data:* b New Orleans, La, Nov 12, 46; m 69, Margaret Morrison; c Camille M, Elizabeth (Barrett) & Kathryn (Fleurange). *Educ:* La State Univ, BS, 69, MS, 70; Va Polytech Inst & State Univ, PhD(indust eng & opers res), 75. *Prof Exp:* From instr to asst prof indust eng, La State Univ, 73-79; dir econ develop & policy & planning, La Dept Natural Resources, 79-83. *Concurrent Pos:* Lectr, La State Univ & Univ Southwestern La, 79-83; citizen to citizen ambassador opers res & energy, Russia. *Mem:* Inst Indust Engrs; Opers Res Soc Am; Am Soc Eng Educ; Inst Mgt Sci. *Res:* Forecasting, economic analysis, operations management and computer applications; published 48 articles and papers. *Mailing Add:* Dept Eng Mgt Univ SW La Lafayette LA 70504-0400. *E-Mail:* ristroph@usl.edu

RISTVET, BYRON LEO, ENVIRONMENTAL SCIENCES. *Current Pos:* sci adv geol, Air Force Weapons Lab, 73-77, geoscientist, Defense Nuclear Agency, 77-83, S-CUBED DIV, MAXWELL LABS, 83- *Personal Data:* b Tacoma, Wash, Aug 22, 47; m 75. *Educ:* Univ Puget Sound, BS, 69; Northwestern Univ, PhD(geol), 76. *Honors & Awards:* Secy Air Force Res & Develop Award, 75. *Mem:* Geochem Soc; Soc Econ Paleontologists & Mineralogists; Clays & Clay Minerals Soc; Am Mineral Soc. *Res:* Quaternary geology of atolls; reverse weathering reactions and their global implications; explosion effects phenomena on the solid earth; environmental impact analysis. *Mailing Add:* 1505 Soplo Rd SE Albuquerque NM 87123

RITCEY, GORDON M, INORGANIC CHEMISTRY, ORGANIC CHEMISTRY. *Current Pos:* CONSULT, HYDROMETALL & WASTE MGT, 89- *Personal Data:* b Halifax, NS, May 17, 30; m 55; c 1. *Educ:* Dalhousie Univ, BSc, 52; Univ Melbourne, D Appl Sci, 93. *Honors & Awards:* Hydrometall Medal, Chem Inst Can, Alcan Award. *Prof Exp:* Chemist, Radioactivity Div, Mines Br, Dept Energy, Mines & Resources, Can, 52; chief chemist, Eldorado Mining & Refining Co, 52-57, chief chemist res & develop & res chemist, 57, chief chemist, 59-60, head chem res group, 60-67; res scientist & head hydrometall sect, Mineral Sci Div, Dept Energy Mines & Resources, 67-80, res scientist & head, Process Metall Sect, Extrn Metall Labs, Canmet, 80-88. *Concurrent Pos:* Mem, UN & CESO projs, Africa, Egypt & Brazil; lectr & consult. *Mem:* Am Inst Mining, Metall & Petrol Eng; Chem Inst Can; Can Soc Chem Engrs; Can Inst Mining & Metall. *Res:* Solution chemistry relating to hydrometallurgy; recovery and separation of metals from leach solutions resulting from work on solvent extraction has resulted in plants for the recovery of uranium, cobalt, nickel, zirconium and hafnium; rare earth separations; design of tailings treatment. *Mailing Add:* 258 Grandview Rd Nepean ON K2H 8A9 Can

RITCEY, JAMES ALEXANDER, COMMUNICATIONS SYSTEMS, SIGNAL PROCESSING. *Current Pos:* asst prof elec eng, 85-91, assoc prof, 91-95, PROF ELEC ENG, UNIV WASH, 95- *Personal Data:* b Montclair, NJ, June 22, 54; m, Kim Borden; c Allison Anne. *Educ:* Duke Univ, BSE, 76; Syracuse Univ, MSEE, 81; Univ Calif, San Diego, PhD(elec eng), 85. *Prof Exp:* Engr, Gen Elec Co, 76-81. *Mem:* Inst Elec & Electronics Engrs. *Res:* Developing efficient numerical methods for the performance evaluation of signal processing for communications. *Mailing Add:* Univ Wash Box 352500 Seattle WA 98195

RITCH, ROBERT, OPHTHALMOLOGY. *Current Pos:* CHIEF, GLAUCOMA SERV, NY EYE & EAR INFIRMARY, 83- *Personal Data:* b New Haven, Conn, May 14, 44. *Educ:* Harvard Univ, BA, 67; Albert Einstein Univ, MD, 72; Am Bd Ophthal, dipl, 77; Am Bd Laser Surg, dipl,

85. *Honors & Awards:* Honor Award, Am Acad Ophthal, 85; John Roche Mem Lectr, Winthrop Univ Med Ctr, NY, 85; Charimet Kanchararanya Mem Lectr, Fifth Ann Bangkok Ophthal cong, 89; Spec Honoree, Glaucoma Found, 90; Charles H May Mem Lectr, NY Acad Med, 91. *Prof Exp:* Lab instr biol, Rice Univ, Houston, Tex, 67-68; intern, St Vincent's Med Ctr, New York, NY, 72-73; resident, Mt Sinai Sch Med, NY, 73-75, chief resident, 75-76, fel, Head Ophthal Found, 76-77, NIH fel, 77-78, from instr to assoc prof ophthal, 77-82; prof ophthal, NY Med Col, Valhalla, 83- *Concurrent Pos:* Grants, numerous insts, 64-; asst clin ophthal, City Hosp Ctr Elmherst, 76-78, dir, Glaucoma Serv, 78-82; consult ophthal, Vet Admin Hosp, Bronx, NY, 77-82; dir, Glaucoma Clin, Beth Israel Med Ctr, 77-78; rep, Nat Comt Glaucoma Educ, Washington, DC, 78; mem, Med Serv Plan Adv Coun, Mt Sinai, 79-81; actg dir, City Hosp Ctr Elmhurst, 79-81, dir, 81-82; vis prof, Univ Fla, Gainesville, 83, Scheie Eye Inst, Pa, 85 & Health Sci Ctr, State Univ NY, 87; chmn sci adv bd, Glaucoma Found, 84-; mem, Glaucoma Adv Comt, Nat Soc Prevent Blindness, 86-, Glaucoma Screening Comt, 87-; consult ophthal, Manhattan Eye, Ear & Throat Hosp, 88-; mem spec study sect, NIH, 91; bd dirs, Dooley Found & UN Vol Develop Coun, 91- *Mem:* Fel Am Acad Ophthal; fel Am Col Surgeons; fel Int Col Surgeons; fel Am Soc Laser Surg & Med; Ophthalmic Laser Surg Soc (secy-treas, 82-); Am Med Asn; Int Glaucoma Cong; AAAS; Am Soc Cell Biol; Asn Res Vision & Ophthal. *Mailing Add:* Dept Ophthal NY Eye & Ear Infirmary 310 E 14th St New York NY 10003-4201

RITCHEY, JOHN MICHAEL, INORGANIC CHEMISTRY, ORGANOMETALLIC CHEMISTRY. *Current Pos:* asst prof, Ft Lewis Col, 72-73, chmn dept, 73-77, assoc prof, 74-77, PROF CHEM, FT LEWIS COL, 78- *Personal Data:* b Wichita, Kans, Dec 14, 40; m 64; c 1. *Educ:* Univ Colo, PhD(inorganic chem), 68. *Prof Exp:* Clin chemist, Wesley Med Ctr, 62-63; asst prof chem, Furman Univ, 68-70 & Northern Ariz Univ, 70-72. *Concurrent Pos:* Consult, Four Corners Environ Res Inst, 72-, dir, 73-; collabr, Los Alamos Nat Lab, 80-; counr, Coun Undergrad Res, 84-86, 90- *Mem:* AAAS; Am Chem Soc; Sigma Xi. *Res:* Organometallic chemistry, especially heterobimetallic synthesis, zero valent metal cluster compounds; trace metal analysis, especially in natural systems; synthetic inorganic and organic chemistry, especially ligand design. *Mailing Add:* Dept Chem Ft Lewis Col Durango CO 81301-3999

RITCHEY, KENNETH DALE, SOIL FERTILITY. *Current Pos:* res soil scientist, PR, 85-91, RES SOIL SCIENTIST, AGR RES SERV, USDA, WVA, 91- *Personal Data:* b Washington, DC, Oct 24, 44; m 71, Sarah N Medlycott; c Jonathan D & Emily J. *Educ:* Carnegie Inst Technol, BS, 65; Cornell Univ, MS, 67, PhD(agron), 73. *Prof Exp:* Soil fertil specialist int agr progs, Univ Wis, 73-74; res assoc soil fertil, Cornell Univ, 74-78; res specialist & consult soil fertil, IICA Brasilia, Brazil, 79-85. *Mem:* Int Soil Sci Soc; Am Soc Agron; Am Soil Sci Soc; Brazilian Soil Sci Soc; Sigma Xi; Am Chem Soc. *Res:* Nitrogen, magnesium, micronutrient and potassium responses in highly weathered tropical soils; amelioration of subsoil acidity by leaching of calcium sulfate; utilization of coal combustion by-products as soil amendments. *Mailing Add:* USDA Agr Res Serv PO Box 400 Beaver WV 25813

RITCHEY, SANFORD JEWELL, NUTRITION. *Current Pos:* assoc prof, Va Polytech Inst & State Univ, 63-66, head dept nutrit & foods, 66-73, assoc dean, Col Home Econ, 73-80, PROF HUMAN NUTRIT, VA POLYTECH INST & STATE UNIV, 69-, DEAN, COL HUMAN RESOURCES, 80- *Personal Data:* b Columbia, Miss, Feb 6, 30; m 57, Elizabeth Agnew; c Kenneth, Eric & Julia. *Educ:* La State Univ, BS, 51; Univ Ill, MS, 56, PhD(animal nutrit), 57. *Honors & Awards:* Borden Award, 79. *Prof Exp:* Fel biochem, Tex A&M Univ, 57-59; asst prof food & nutrit, 59-63. *Mem:* AAAS; Am Chem Soc; Inst Food Technologists; Am Inst Nutrit. *Res:* Food science; nutritional relationships in growing children. *Mailing Add:* Dept Human Nutrit & Food Va Polytech Inst & State Univ Blacksburg VA 24061

RITCHEY, WILLIAM MICHAEL, PHYSICAL CHEMISTRY. *Current Pos:* assoc prof phys chem, 68-79, ASSOC PROF MACROMOLECULAR SCI, CASE WESTERN RESERVE UNIV, 69-, PROF CHEM & MACROMOLECULAR SCI, 79- *Personal Data:* b Mt Vernon, Ohio, June 2, 25; m 47; c 3. *Educ:* Ohio State Univ, BS, 50, MS, 53, PhD(phys chem), 55. *Prof Exp:* Chemist, Battelle Mem Inst, 52-55; sr res chemist, Res Dept, Standard Oil Co, Ohio, 55-66, group leader, 66-68. *Concurrent Pos:* Asst, Ohio State Univ, 50-54. *Mem:* AAAS; Am Chem Soc; Soc Appl Spectros. *Res:* Applications of nuclear magnetic resonance in the solution and solid state, polymer characterization in structures, motion and morphology; x-ray spectroscopy and differential thermal analysis to petroleum chemistry, polymers and fossil fuels. *Mailing Add:* 851 Hawood Dr South Euclid OH 44121-3403

RITCHIE, ADAM BURKE, THEORETICAL CHEMISTRY. *Current Pos:* STAFF MEM, TEST PROG, LAWRENCE LIVERMORE NAT LAB, 86- *Personal Data:* b Waynesboro, Va, Sept 8, 39; m 61; c 2. *Educ:* Univ Va, BA, 60, MA, 61, PhD(chem), 68. *Prof Exp:* Air Force Off Sci Res fel chem, Harvard Univ, 68-69; Nat Acad Sci-Nat Res Coun-NASA resident res assoc atomic physics, Goddard Space Flight Ctr, 69-71; from asst prof to prof chem, Univ Ala, 71-86. *Mem:* Am Chem Soc. *Res:* Faraday effect; perturbation theory; correlation energies of molecules; atomic and molecular collision processes. *Mailing Add:* 1951 Creek Rd Livermore CA 94550

RITCHIE, ALEXANDER CHARLES, PATHOLOGY. *Current Pos:* head dept, 61-74, prof, 61-89, EMER PROF PATH, UNIV TORONTO, 86- *Personal Data:* b Auckland, NZ, Apr 2, 21; m 56, Susan. *Educ:* Univ NZ, MB, ChB, 44; Oxford Univ, DPhil(path), 50; Royal Col Physicians Can, cert specialist gen path, 55; Am Bd Path, dipl, 56; FRCP(C), 64; FRCPath, 70; FRCP(Australasia), 72. *Honors & Awards:* Centennial Medal, Can, 67, Jubilee Medal, 77. *Prof Exp:* Mem, Brit Empire Cancer Campaign Res Unit, Oxford Univ, 47-49, Walker studentship path; vis fel oncol, Chicago Med Sch, 51-52; lectr path, McGill Univ, 54-55, Douglas res fel, 55-56, asst prof, 55-58, Miranda Fraser assoc prof comp path, 58-61. *Concurrent Pos:* Mem consult panel, Can Tumour Registry, 58-75; pathologist-in-chief, Toronto Gen Hosp, 62-75; consult, Wellesley Hosp, 62-74, Hosp Sick Children, 62-, Women's Col Hosp, 63-74, Ont Cancer Inst, 64-74, Toronto Western Hosp, 75-, Toronto Gen Hosp, 86- & Mt Sinai Hosp, 72-75 & 88-; chief examr lab med, Royal Col Physicians & Surgeons, Can, 73-77; secy, World Asn Soc Path, 75-81, pres, 81-85, pres, World Path Found, 80-84. *Mem:* Am Asn Cancer Res; fel Col Am Path; hon mem Can Asn Path (pres, 67-69); Int Acad Path; hon mem Asn Clin Pathologists; Can Asn Pathologists. *Res:* Oncology; pathology of tumors and cancer; occupational lung disease. *Mailing Add:* 625 Avenue Rd Suite 304 Toronto ON M4V 2K7 Can

RITCHIE, AUSTIN E, AGRICULTURE, AGRICULTURAL EDUCATION. *Current Pos:* RETIRED. *Personal Data:* b Van Wert, Ohio, Feb 3, 18; m 42; c 4. *Educ:* Ohio State Univ, BSc, 46, MSc, 51, PhD(agr educ), 55. *Prof Exp:* Teacher, Gibsonburg High Sch, 47-48 & Hilliard High Sch, 48-50; from instr to assoc prof, Ohio State Univ, 48-62, asst dean & secy agr, 57-63 & 64-65, actg exec dean spec serv, 63-64, prof agr educ, 62-81, asst dean acad affairs agr, 65-81, emer prof agr educ, 81. *Mem:* AAAS. *Res:* Administration college of agriculture and home economics; agriculture curricula; general education and teacher education. *Mailing Add:* 5651 Brickstone Pl Hilliard OH 43026

RITCHIE, BETTY CARAWAY, AUDIOLOGY. *Current Pos:* ASSOC PROF COMMUN SCI & DISORDERS, UNIV WIS, MILWAUKEE, 72-, CHMN DEPT, 82- *Personal Data:* b Dyersburg, Tenn, June 16, 29; m 66, Don; c Claire. *Educ:* La State Univ, BA, 50, MA, 51; Northwestern Univ, PhD(audiol), 64. *Prof Exp:* Speech correctionist, La Pub Schs, 51-53; dir, WTenn Hearing & Speech Ctr, 53-60; asst prof speech & dir, Hearing Eval Ctr, Univ Wis, Milwaukee, 63-70; assoc prof, Southern Ill Univ, 70-72. *Concurrent Pos:* Audiological consult, Interstate Forging Indust, Inc, 78- *Mem:* Am Audiol Soc; Am Speech-Lang-Hearing Asn; Acad Rehab Audiol. *Res:* Effects of compression amplication on speech intelligibility; evaluation of the efficiency of the verbal auditory screening for children; aural rehabilitation for older adults. *Mailing Add:* Dept Commun Sci & Disorders Univ Wis PO Box 413 Milwaukee WI 53201

RITCHIE, CALVIN DONALD, ORGANIC CHEMISTRY. *Current Pos:* prof chem, 61-92, EMER PROF CHEM, STATE UNIV NY, BUFFALO, 92- *Personal Data:* b Arlington, Va, Jan 30, 30; m 52, Elaine Tauzin; c 4. *Educ:* George Washington Univ, BS, 54, PhD(phys org chem), 60. *Honors & Awards:* Schoellkopf Medal, Western NY Sect Am Chem Soc, 70. *Prof Exp:* Org chemist, Food & Drug Admin, 56-60; Welch fel chem, Rice Univ, 60-61. *Concurrent Pos:* Vis scholar, Stanford Univ, 76. *Mem:* Am Chem Soc; Royal Soc Chem. *Res:* Physical organic chemistry, particularly dealing with solvent effects and substituent effects in organic chemistry. *Mailing Add:* 20 Marjorie Trail Ormond Beach FL 32174-8501. *E-Mail:* 75211.721@compuserve.com

RITCHIE, DAVID JOSEPH, INFECTIOUS DISEASES, ANTIBIOTICS. *Current Pos:* instr clin pharm, 89-90, ASST PROF PHARM PRACT, ST LOUIS COL PHARM, 90- *Personal Data:* b St Louis, Mo, Mar 2, 65; m 89, Linda K Byers; c Lauren. *Educ:* Purdue Univ, BS, 88, PharmD, 89. *Prof Exp:* Clin pharm residency, Jewish Hosp St Louis, 89-90. *Mem:* Am Soc Microbiol; Am Col Clin Pharm; Am Soc Hosp Pharmacists; Soc Infectious Dis Pharmacists. *Res:* In vitro microbiology studies; pharmacokinetic analyses; antibiotic studies. *Mailing Add:* St Louis Col Pharm 4588 Parkview Pl St Louis MO 63110-1029. *Fax:* 314-454-5250

RITCHIE, DAVID MALCOLM, PULMONARY PHARMACOLOGY, IMMUNOPHARMACOLOGY. *Current Pos:* scientist, R W Johnson Pharmaceut Res Inst, 78-80, sr scientist, 80-85, prin scientist, 85-91, RES FEL, R W JOHNSON PHARMACEUT RES INST, 91- *Personal Data:* b Woodbury, NJ, Apr 13, 50; m 72, Deborah Jones; c Christopher & Jillian. *Educ:* Rutgers Univ, BA, 72; Hahnemann Med Col, MS, 74, PhD(pharmacol), 76. *Honors & Awards:* Phillip Hoffman Award. *Prof Exp:* Fel pharmacol, Hahnemann Med Col, 74-76; res assoc, Med Col Pa, 76-78. *Mem:* Inflammation Res Asn; Int Soc Immunopharmacol; Am Soc Pharmacol Exp Ther; AAAS; NY Acad Sci. *Res:* Leukotriene and lipoxygenase pathway of arachidonic metabolism as they relate to hypersensitivity disease and inflammation; role of leukotrienes and their management in asthma and inflammatory disease. *Mailing Add:* R W Johnson Pharmaceut Res Inst Rte 202 PO Box 300 Raritan NJ 08869-0602. *Fax:* 908-526-6469; *E-Mail:* ritchie@prius.jnj.com

RITCHIE, GARY ALAN, PHYSIOLOGICAL ECOLOGY. *Current Pos:* environ impact analyst, 73-74, tech planner forestry & raw mat res develop, 74-76, RES PROJ LEADER PLANT PHYSIOL, WEYERHAEUSER CO, 77- *Personal Data:* b Washington, DC, Aug 23, 41. *Educ:* Univ Ga, BS, 64; Univ Wash, MF, 66, PhD(forest ecol), 71. *Prof Exp:* Environ engr, US Army Corps Engrs, 71-73. *Mem:* Sigma Xi; Soc Am Foresters. *Res:* Financial analysis of long and short-term research investments in forestry, forest regeneration, forest management and forest genetics; reforestation and tree seedling production technology. *Mailing Add:* 8026 61 Ave NE Olympia WA 98506-9139

RITCHIE, HARLAN, ANIMAL SCIENCE, NUTRITION. *Current Pos:* Asst instr, 57-64, from asst prof to assoc prof, 64-71, PROF ANIMAL HUSB, MICH STATE UNIV, 71- *Personal Data:* b Albert City, Iowa, Aug 3, 35; m 97, Leah Cox; c William, Donald & Christopher. *Educ:* Iowa State Univ, BS, 57; Mich State Univ, PhD(animal husb), 64. *Honors & Awards:* Exten Award & Indust Serv Award, Am Soc Animal Sci. *Mem:* Am Soc Animal Sci; Sigma Xi; Am Registry Prof Animal Scientists; Coun Agr Sci Technol. *Res:* Trace elements in swine nutrition; beef cattle management. *Mailing Add:* Dept Animal Sci 113 Anthony Mich State Univ East Lansing MI 48823. *Fax:* 517-353-1699

RITCHIE, JAMES CUNNINGHAM, botany, ecology, for more information see previous edition

RITCHIE, JERRY CARLYLE, ECOLOGY. *Current Pos:* SOIL SCIENTIST, HYDROL LAB, USDA, BELTSVILLE, 78- *Personal Data:* b Richfield, NC, Dec 13, 37; m 66, Carole J Atanasoff; c Jarryl B & Karen L. *Educ:* Pfeiffer Col, BA, 60; Univ Tenn, Knoxville, MS, 62; Univ Ga, PhD(bot), 67. *Prof Exp:* Res asst ecol, Oak Ridge Nat Lab, 62; fel plant sci, Southeastern Watershed Res Ctr, Univ Ga, 67-68; botanist, US Sedimentation Lab, Agr Res Serv, USDA, Oxford, Miss, 68-78. *Mem:* Ecol Soc Am; Am Soc Agron. *Res:* Radioecology, limnology, sedimentation; remote sensing. *Mailing Add:* ARS Hydrol Lab BARC-W Bldg 007 Beltsville MD 20705. *Fax:* 301-504-8931; *E-Mail:* jritchie@asrr.arsusda.gov

RITCHIE, JOE T, SOIL PHYSICS, PHYSICAL CHEMISTRY. *Current Pos:* STAFF MEM, INST WATER RES, MICH STATE UNIV. *Personal Data:* b Palestine, Tex, June 2, 37; m 59; c 1. *Educ:* Abilene Christian Col, BS, 59; Tex Tech Col, MS, 61; Iowa State Univ, PhD(soil physics), 64. *Prof Exp:* Lab asst agr, Abilene Christian Col, 57-59; res asst, Tex Agr Exp Sta, 59-61; asst agron, Iowa State Univ, 61-64; physicist, Tex Res Found, 64-66; res soil scientist, Soil & Water Conserv Res Div, Agr Res Serv, USDA, 66- *Concurrent Pos:* Consult, Tex Instruments, Inc, 65. *Mem:* Am Soc Agron; Soil Sci Soc Am; Am Chem Soc; Am Statist Asn; Am Geophys Union; Sigma Xi. *Res:* Application of gas-solid chromatography for analysis of soil gases; measurement of microclimate as related to evapotransportation; soil moisture estimation under row crops. *Mailing Add:* Plant & Soil Sci Bldg Mich State Univ East Lansing MI 48824-1325

RITCHIE, JOSEPH MURDOCH, PHARMACOLOGY, PHYSIOLOGY. *Current Pos:* chmn dept pharmacol, 68-74, dir div biol sci, 75-78, EUGENE HIGGINS PROF PHARMACOL, SCH MED, YALE UNIV, 68- *Personal Data:* b Scotland, June 10, 25; m 51, Brenda Bigland; c Alasdair J & Jocelyn A. *Educ:* Aberdeen Univ, BSc, 44; Univ London, BSc, 49, PhD(physiol), 52, DSc, 60. *Hon Degrees:* MA, Yale Univ, 68; DSc, Aberdeen Univ, 87. *Honors & Awards:* Van Dyke Mem Award, 83. *Prof Exp:* Lectr physiol, Univ London, 49-51; mem staff, Nat Inst Med Res, Eng, 51-56; from asst prof to prof pharmacol, Albert Einstein Col Med, 56-68. *Concurrent Pos:* Overseas fel, Churchill Col, Cambridge Univ, 64-65. *Mem:* Am Soc Pharmacol; Am Physiol Soc; Brit Physiol Soc; fel Royal Soc; Brit Pharmacol Soc. *Res:* Biophysics of muscle and nerve. *Mailing Add:* Dept Pharmacol Sch Med Yale Univ 333 Cedar St New Haven CT 06510

RITCHIE, KIM, BIOCHEMISTRY. *Current Pos:* STAFF MEM, AUX CERAMICS, 80- *Personal Data:* b Korea, Apr 13, 36; US citizen; m 59; c 1. *Educ:* ETenn State Col, BA, 59; Univ Tenn, MS, 61; Ariz State Univ, PhD(chem), 67. *Prof Exp:* Res chemist, Tenn Eastman Co, 61-62; res biochemist, Parke-Davis Co, 62-64; res biochemist, Barrow Neurol Inst, St Joseph's Hosp, Phoenix, Ariz, 64-68; sr chemist, Motorola Inc, 68-76, lab mgr, Process Technol Lab, Semiconductor Res & Develop Lab, Semiconductor Prod Div, 76-80. *Mem:* Electrochem Soc; AAAS; Am Chem Soc; NY Acad Sci. *Res:* Neurochemistry; copper metabolism in central nervous system; organometallic interaction with biopolymers; solid state chemistry; polymer surface chemistry. *Mailing Add:* 409 Lafayette Rd Myrtle Beach SC 29577-4198

RITCHIE, ROBERT OLIVER, MECHANICAL ENGINEERING, FRACTURE MECHANICS. *Current Pos:* assoc prof metall, 81-82, PROF MAT SCI, UNIV CALIF, BERKELEY, 82- *Personal Data:* b Plymouth, Eng, Jan 2, 48; m 91, Haiying Song; c James. *Educ:* Cambridge Univ, BA, 69, MA & PhD(metall, mat sci), 73, ScD, 90. *Honors & Awards:* Most Outstanding Sci Accomplishment Award, Dept Energy, 82, 89; G R Irwin Medal, Am Soc Testing & Mat, 85; C W McGraw Res Award, Am Soc Eng Educ, 87; C H Mathewson Gold Medal, Minerals, Metals, & Mat Soc-Inst Mech Engrs, 85; M A Grossmann Award, Am Soc Metals, 80; Rosenhain Medal, Inst Mat, London, 92; Distinguished Struct Mat Scientist/Engr Award, Minerals, Metals & Mat Soc, 96. *Prof Exp:* Res assoc metall & mat sci, Churchill Col, Cambridge Univ, 72-74; lectr mat sci & eng, Univ Calif, Berkeley, 74-76, res metallurgist mat, Lawrence Berkeley Lab, 76; from asst prof to assoc prof mech eng, Mass Inst Technol, 77-81; dir, Ctr Adv Mat, Lawrence Berkeley Lab, 87-95, dep dir, Mat Sci Div, 90-94, head, Struct Mats Dept, 95. *Concurrent Pos:* Goldsmith's res fel, Churchill Col, Cambridge Univ, 72-74; Miller res fel, Univ Calif, Berkeley, 74-76; hon visit prof, Univ Plymouth, UK, 92-; vpres, Int Cong on Fractive, 93- *Mem:* Fel Am Soc Metals; Am Inst Mining, Metall & Petrol Engrs; fel Brit Inst Mat; Am Soc Testing & Mat; Mat Res Soc. *Res:* Deformation and failure of engineering materials, especially metallurgy, toughness, fatigue and environmentally-assisted failure and wear of metals and alloys; ceramics, intermetallics and composites; metallurgy and physical metallurgical engineering. *Mailing Add:* 590 Grizzly Peak Blvd Berkeley CA 94708-1238. *Fax:* 510-486-4995; *E-Mail:* roritchie@lbl.gov

RITCHIE, ROBERT WELLS, COMPUTER SCIENCE, MATHEMATICS. *Current Pos:* dir, Computer Systs Ctr, Hewlett-Packard Labs, 88-90, DIR, UNIV AFFAIRS, HEWLETT-PACKARD CO, 90- *Personal Data:* b Alameda, Calif, Sept 21, 35; m 57, Audrey Kelly; c Scott & Lynne. *Educ:* Reed Col, BA, 57; Princeton Univ, MA, 59, PhD(math), 61. *Prof Exp:* Instr math, Dartmouth Col, 60-62; from asst prof to assoc prof math, Univ Wash, 62-69, assoc dean grad sch, 66-69, assoc math & comput sci & vprovost acad admin, 69-72, prof comput sci & vprovost & asst vpres acad affairs, 72-76, prof & chmn comput sci, 77-83; mgr, Comput Sci Lab, Palo Alto Res Ctr, 83-88; vpres, Univ Affairs, Xerox Corp, 88. *Concurrent Pos:* Vis scientist, Xerox Palo Alto Res Ctr, 81-82. *Mem:* AAAS; Am Math Soc; Asn Symbolic Logic; Asn Comput Mach; Inst Elec & Electronics Engrs. *Res:* Mathematical logic and linguistics; computability theory; theory of algorithms; complexity theory. *Mailing Add:* 7 Alexis Ct Menlo Park CA 94025

RITCHIE, RUFUS HAYNES, RADIATION PHYSICS. *Current Pos:* Corp fel, 85-90, PHYSICIST, HEALTH PHYSICS DIV, OAK RIDGE NAT LAB, 49-, DISTINGUISHED RES STAFF MEM, 78-, SR CORP FEL, 90- *Personal Data:* b Blue Diamond, Ky, Sept 24, 24; m 44, Dorothy Estes; c Susan R (Austin) & David A. *Educ:* Univ Ky, BS, 47, MS, 49; Univ Tenn, PhD, 59. *Hon Degrees:* Dr Hon Causa, Univ Pais Vasco, 92. *Honors & Awards:* Jesse W Beams Award, Am Phys Soc, 84. *Prof Exp:* Instr physics, Univ Ky, 48-49. *Concurrent Pos:* Vis res prof, Inst Physics, Aarhus Univ, 61-62; adj prof physics, Univ Tenn, 65-, Univ Ky, 68-69; vis prof, NY Univ, 72, Bhaba Atomic Res Ctr, Bombay, India, 73, Inst Physics, Odense Univ, Denmark, 80-81 & Univ Pais Vasco, 89, 91 & 93; sr vis fel, Cavendish Lab, Cambridge Univ, 75-76, Royal Soc guest res fel, 81; overseas fel, Churchill Col, 75-76; bd dir, Pellissippi Int Inc, 87; exec comt, SE Sect, Am Phys Soc, chmn, 93; Iberdrola chair, Univ Pais Vosco, Spain, 95; sr res fel, Jap Soc Prom Sci. *Mem:* AAAS; fel Am Phys Soc; Radiation Res Soc; Bohmische Phys Soc. *Res:* Interaction of radiation with matter; physics of quantum plasmas; collective excitations in condense matter; many-body theory; surface physics; charged particle track structure. *Mailing Add:* Health Sci Res Div Oak Ridge Nat Lab PO Box 2008 Oak Ridge TN 37830-6123. *Fax:* 423-574-6210; *E-Mail:* ekr@ornl.gov

RITCHIE, STEPHEN G, TRANSPORTATION ENGINEERING, ARTIFICIAL INTELLIGENCE. *Current Pos:* from asst prof to assoc prof, 85-93, VCHAIR, DEPT CIVIL ENG, UNIV CALIF, IRVINE, 88-, PROF TRANSP ENG, 93- *Personal Data:* b Melbourne, Australia, Nov 14, 54. *Educ:* Monash Univ, BE, 77, M Eng Sc, 81; Cornell Univ, PhD(civil & environ eng), 83. *Honors & Awards:* NSF Presidential Young Investr Award, 87. *Prof Exp:* Asst prof transp eng, Univ Wash, 83-85. *Concurrent Pos:* Res engr, Inst Transp Studies, Univ Calif, Irvine, 85- *Mem:* Am Soc Civil Engrs; Inst Transp Engrs; Am Asn Artificial Intel; Transp Res Bd. *Res:* Transportation and traffic systems engineering; advanced technology development and application; artificial intelligence. *Mailing Add:* Dept Civil & Environ Eng Univ Calif Irvine CA 92697

RITCHIE, WALLACE PARKS, JR, SURGERY, GASTROINTESTINAL & ENDOCRINE SURGERY. *Current Pos:* prof & chmn, 83-93, STAFF MEM, DEPT SURG, SCH MED, TEMPLE UNIV, PROF SURG, 93-, EXEC DIR, AM BD SURG, 94- *Personal Data:* b St Paul, Minn, Nov 4, 35; m 60; c 3. *Educ:* Yale Univ, BA, 57; Johns Hopkins Univ, MD, 61; Univ Minn, PhD(surg), 71. *Prof Exp:* From intern to resident surg, Yale-New Haven Med Ctr, 61-63; from resident to chief resident, Sch Med, Univ Minn, 64-69, instr, 69-70; chief dept surg gastroenterol, Div Surg, Walter Reed Army Inst Res, 70-73; from asst prof to prof surg, Sch Med, Univ VA, 73-83. *Mem:* Am Fedn Clin Res; Am Gastroenterol Asn; Asn Acad Surg (pres, 76-77); Soc Univ Surgeons; Am Surg Asn. *Res:* Gastric mucosal resistance as a factor in ulcerative disease of the upper gastrointestinal tract. *Mailing Add:* Am Bd Surg Inc 1617 John F Kennedy Blvd Philadelphia PA 19102

RITENOUR, GARY LEE, PLANT PROTECTION, PLANT PHYSIOLOGY. *Current Pos:* assoc prof, 69-74, PROF AGRON, CALIF STATE UNIV, FRESNO, 74- *Personal Data:* b Warsaw, Ind, Oct 5, 38; m 63; c 2. *Educ:* Purdue Univ, West Lafayette, BS, 60; Univ Calif, Davis, MS, 62, PhD(plant physiol), 64. *Prof Exp:* Univ Ill res fel, Univ Ill, Urbana, 64-66 & farm adv agron crops, Agr Exten Serv, Univ Calif, 66-69. *Mem:* Am Soc Agron; Weed Sci Soc Am. *Res:* Use of agricultural chemicals in crop production. *Mailing Add:* Dept Plant Sci Calif State Univ 2415 E San Ramon Fresno CA 93740-8033

RITER, JOHN RANDOLPH, JR, PHYSICAL CHEMISTRY. *Current Pos:* from asst prof to assoc prof, 62-71, PROF CHEM, UNIV DENVER, 71- *Personal Data:* b Denver, Colo, Apr 18, 33; m 55; c 4. *Educ:* Colo Sch Mines, PRE, 56; Univ Wash, PhD(chem), 62. *Prof Exp:* Jr engr, Boeing Co, 56-58, assoc res engr, 58-60; instr chem, Univ Wash, 61-62. *Concurrent Pos:* Assoc Western Univ fac fel physics, Univ Calif, Berkeley, 68; vis prof, Math Inst, Oxford Univ, 71; consult, Colo Pathologists Regional Lab, 76- *Mem:* Am Chem Soc; Am Phys Soc. *Res:* Thermodynamics; high-temperature spectroscopy. *Mailing Add:* 2507 S Kearney St Denver CO 80222-6325

RITER, STEPHEN, ELECTRICAL ENGINEERING, ENVIRONMENTAL SCIENCE. *Current Pos:* prof elec eng & chmn, Dept Comput Sci, 80-89, dean eng & dir, Ctr Environ Resource Mgt, 89-96, PROVOST & ACAD VPRES, UNIV TEX, EL PASO, 96- *Personal Data:* b Providence, RI, Mar 7, 40; m 64; c 2. *Educ:* Rice Univ, BA, 61, BSEE, 62; Univ Houston, MS, 67, PhD(elec eng), 68. *Prof Exp:* From asst prof to prof elec eng, Tex A&M Univ, 68-79, asst dir, Ctr Urban Progs, 72-76, assoc dir, Ctr Energy & Mineral Resources, 76-77, dir, Tex Energy Exten Serv, 77-79. *Concurrent Pos:* Ed, Trans Geosci, Inst Elec & Electronics Engrs, 72; prin investr, res prog image enhancement using artificial intel, Nat Inst Justice, 84-; chmn, El Paso Pub Util Regulatory Bd, 86-90 & El Paso Pub Serv Bd; proj dir, Develop Meteorol Sensor RPVS, US Army, 86- *Mem:* Inst Elec & Electronics Engrs; Marine Technol Soc; Sigma Xi; Technol Transfer Soc; Nat Soc Prof Engrs. *Res:* Environmental resource management. *Mailing Add:* Acad Affairs Univ Tex El Paso TX 79968

RITGER, PAUL DAVID, COMPUTER ANALYSIS OF UNDERWATER SOUND. *Current Pos:* RETIRED. *Personal Data:* b Orange, NJ, Sept 10, 25; wid; c Paul Jr, Robert, Nancy & Suzanne. *Educ:* Holy Cross Col, BS, 45; Univ Pa, MA, 48; NY Univ, PhD(appl math), 56. *Prof Exp:* Instr math, Univ Mass, 48-50; assoc prof, Stevens Inst Tech, 54-68; distinguished mem tech staff, Bell Lab, 68-95. *Mem:* Math Asn Am. *Res:* System engineering in development, implementation, and testing of computerized surveillance information processing systems for fixed and towed arrays of hydrophones for the US Navy. *Mailing Add:* 14 Gunther St Mendham NJ 07945. *E-Mail:* 110100. 315@compuserve.com

RITLAND, RICHARD MARTIN, VERTEBRATE ZOOLOGY, PALEONTOLOGY. *Current Pos:* from assoc prof to prof paleont, 60-80, PROF GEOL, ANDREWS UNIV, 77- *Personal Data:* b Grants Pass, Ore, July 3, 25; m 46; c 5. *Educ:* Walla Walla Col, BA, 46; Ore State Col, MS, 50; Harvard Univ, PhD, 54. *Prof Exp:* From instr to asst prof biol, Atlantic Union Col, 47-52; from instr to asst prof, Loma Linda Univ, 54-60. *Mem:* AAAS; Soc Study Evolution; Soc Vert Paleont; Paleont Soc; Geol Soc Am. *Res:* Tertiary and cretaceous paleo-ecology. *Mailing Add:* PO Box 263 Berrien Springs MI 49103

RITSCHEL, WOLFGANG ADOLF, PHARMACOKINETICS. *Current Pos:* assoc prof, Univ Cincinnati, 69-72, prof biopharmaceut, 72-77, head, Div Pharmaceut & Drug Delivery Systs, 85-95, PROF PHARMACOKINETICS & BIOPHARMACEUT, MED COL, UNIV CINCINNATI, 77-, PROF PHARMACOL, 81- *Personal Data:* b Trautenau, Bohemia, Jan 10, 33; m 91, Ingrid M Wallner; c Alexander & Barbara. *Educ:* Innsbruck Univ, MPharm, 55; Univ Strasbourg, DPharm, 60; Univ Vienna, DPhil, 65; Univ Villarreal, MD, 89. *Honors & Awards:* Theodore Koerner Prize, Pres Repub Austria, 62, Cross Honor Sci & Arts, 75; Hertha Heinemann Mem Prize, Ger Pharmaceut Indust, 65. *Prof Exp:* Chief pharmacist, Girol SA, Zurich, Switz, 58-59; head pharmaceut res, Biochemie AG, Kundl, Austria, 59-61; prof chem & pharmaceut, Notre Dame Col, Dacca, EPakistan, 61-64; head, Dept Pharm, 62-64; head technol pharmaceut res, Siegfried AG Sackingen, Ger, 65-68. *Concurrent Pos:* Vis prof, Med Acad, Krakow, 73 & 77, San Marcos, Lima, 73-, Univ Clermont-Ferrard, 91-92, Univ Madrid, 92; prof, San Marcos Univ, Lima, 73-, Univ Cayetano Heredia, Lima, 79-; fel Grad Sch, Univ Cincinnati, 93; Fulbright Sr Scholar Award, 93-94; prof, Nat Univ Mayor San Marcos, Lima, Peru, 73. *Mem:* Acad Pharmaceut Sci; Am Asn Pharmaceut Scientists; Nat Res Coun; fel Am Col Clin Pharmacol; Roy Acad Spain; Acad Sci Chile; Acad Sci Peru. *Res:* Pathways of absorption of drugs; bioavailability of drugs; development of testing procedures; pharmacokinetics of drugs; clinical pharmacokinetics; geriatrics; chronopharmacokinetics; population pharmacokinetics; high-altitude drug research. *Mailing Add:* Col Pharm Univ Cincinnati Med Ctr Cincinnati OH 45267-0004. *Fax:* 513-558-4372

RITSKO, JOHN JAMES, EXPERIMENTAL SOLID STATE PHYSICS. *Current Pos:* SCIENTIST PHYSICS, XEROX CORP, 74- *Personal Data:* b Pittston, Pa, July 8, 45; m 67; c 2. *Educ:* Mass Inst Technol, BS, 67; Princeton Univ, MS, 69, PhD(physics), 74. *Mem:* Am Phys Soc; Sigma Xi. *Res:* Study of electronic states and elementary excitations of organic and molecular solids by means of high energy inelastic electron scattering and ultraviolet photoemission spectroscopy. *Mailing Add:* IBM TJ Watson Res Ctr Box 218 Yorktown Heights NY 10598

RITSON, DAVID MARK, PHYSICS. *Current Pos:* assoc prof, 64-71, PROF PHYSICS, STANFORD UNIV, 71- *Personal Data:* b London, Eng, Nov 10, 24; m 52; c 4. *Educ:* Oxford Univ, BA, 44, DPhil(physics), 48. *Prof Exp:* Res fel physics, Dublin Inst Advan Studies, Ireland, 48-49; asst & instr, Univ Rochester, 49-52; lectr physics & res physicist, Mass Inst Technol, 52-64. *Res:* Cosmic rays; high energy accelerator physics; particularly properties of fundamental particles. *Mailing Add:* 756 Santa Ynez St Palo Alto CA 94305

RITT, PAUL EDWARD, JR, CHEMISTRY. *Current Pos:* DIR ACAD AFFAIRS, BABSON COL, 86- *Personal Data:* b Baltimore, Md, Mar 3, 28; m 50; c 6. *Educ:* Loyola Col, Md, BS, 50; Georgetown Univ, MS, 52, PhD(chem), 54. *Prof Exp:* Lab asst, Loyola Col, Md, 50; res asst, Harris Res Labs, Inc, 50-52; chemist, Melpar, Inc, Westinghouse Air Brake Co, 52-54; proj chemist, 54-56, chief chemist, 56-57, mgr chem lab, 57-59, mgr phys sci lab, 59-60, dir res, 60-62, vpres res, 62-67; pres, Appl Sci Div & Appl Technol Div, Litton Indusits, 67-68; vpres & dir res, GTE Labs, Inc, 68-86. *Concurrent Pos:* Lectr, Univ Va, 57-59 & Am Univ, 58-; vpres & gen mgr, Training Corp Am, Melpar, Inc, 65-66, pres 66-67. *Mem:* Am Chem Soc; Electrochem Soc; Am Ceramic Soc; Am Inst Chemists; NY Acad Sci; Inst Elec & Electronics Engrs; AAAS; Royal Soc Chemists. *Res:* Organometallic synthesis; rare earth ceramics; solid state phenomenon; thin films; integrated circuits; optical communications; plasma physics; high temperature measurements; space instrumentation; special purpose data processing; electron systems; systems integration; telecommunications; robotry; operations research. *Mailing Add:* 36 Sylvan Lane Weston MA 02193-1028

RITT, ROBERT KING, APPLIED MATHEMATICS. *Current Pos:* chmn dept, 71-76, PROF MATH, ILL STATE UNIV, 71- *Personal Data:* b New York, NY, Dec 30, 24; m 50; c 4. *Educ:* Columbia Univ, AB, 44, PhD(math), 53. *Prof Exp:* Lectr math, Columbia Univ, 46-48; from instr to assoc prof, Univ Mich, 48-62; div mgr, Conductron Corp, 62-68; pres, Ritt Labs, Inc, 68-71. *Mem:* Am Math Soc; Math Asn Am. *Res:* Electromagnetic theory; foundations of statistical mechanics; perturbation theory of symetric operators. *Mailing Add:* 1017 Porter Lane Normal IL 61761

RITTELMEYER, LOUIS FREDERICK, JR, PSYCHIATRY. *Current Pos:* from asst prof to prof psychiat, 66-92, CLIN PROF PSYCHIAT, SCH MED, GEORGETOWN UNIV, 92- *Personal Data:* b Mobile, Ala, Dec 23, 24; m 49; c 8. *Educ:* Spring Hill Col, BS, 45; Med Col Ala, MD, 47. *Prof Exp:* Instr prev med & asst dir, Dept Gen Pract, Col Med, Univ Tenn, 54-55; assoc prof & dir post-grad educ & student health serv, Med Ctr, Univ Miss, 55-59; assoc med dir, Mead Johnson & Co, 59-60, vpres & med dir, 60-63. *Concurrent Pos:* Consult, Surgeon Gen, US Army, 57-65. *Mem:* Fel Am Psychiat Asn; Asn Acad Psychiat. *Res:* Psychiatry in primary care medicine; continuing education. *Mailing Add:* 940 Dead Run Dr McLean VA 22101

RITTENBAUGH, CHERYL K, NUTRITIONAL ANTHROPOLOGY & EPIDEMIOLOGY. *Current Pos:* from instr to asst prof, Dept Anthrop, Univ Ariz, 72-75, res assoc, Dept Family & Community Med, 80-81, adj asst prof, 81-83, from res asst prof to res assoc prof, 83-87, ASSOC PROF, DEPT FAMILY & COMMUNITY MED, UNIV ARIZ, 87- *Personal Data:* b Pittsburgh, Pa, Nov 26, 46. *Educ:* Rice Univ, BA, 68; Univ Calif Los Angeles, MA, 71; Univ Mich Ann Arbor, MPH, 79. *Prof Exp:* Teaching asst Dept Anthrop, Univ Calif Los Angeles, 70-71; asst prof Dept Anthrop, Col Human Med, Mich State Univ, 75-79. *Concurrent Pos:* Numerous grants, var orgn, 71-91; fac grad prog nutrit sci, Univ Ariz, 81-, actg chief, Nutrit Sect, Dept Family & Community Med, 89-90; US rep comt II/4, Nutrit & Anthrop, Int Union Nutrit Sci, 86-90; grant reviewer, NIH, Nat Cancer Inst & NSF. *Mem:* Fel AAAS; Am Anthrop Asn; Am Asn Phys Anthropologists; Am Pub Health Asn; Soc Med Anthrop; Am Inst Nutrit; fel Human Biol Coun. *Res:* Human nutrition and food consumption; epidemiology; diet and cancer; diabetes; obesity; nutritional and medical anthropology; contemporary US, Native Americans, Egypt. *Mailing Add:* Dept Family & Community Med Univ Ariz Tucson AZ 85724-0001

RITTENBERG, MARVIN BARRY, IMMUNOLOGY, MICROBIOLOGY. *Current Pos:* from asst prof to assoc prof med & microbiol, 66-73, PROF MICROBIOL & IMMUNOL, MED SCH, ORE HEALTH SCI UNIV, 73- *Personal Data:* b Los Angeles, Calif, Sept 10, 31; m 54; c 2. *Educ:* Univ Calif, Los Angeles, AB, 54, MA, 57, PhD(microbiol), 61. *Prof Exp:* Inst Microbiol fel, Rutgers Univ, 61-63; NIH fel immunochem, Calif Inst Technol, 63-66. *Concurrent Pos:* Leukemia Soc Am scholar, 67-71; consult diag immunol, United Med Labs, Portland, 68-73; mem exec comt & bd dirs, Ore Comprehensive Cancer Ctr Prog, 72-76; assoc ed, J Immunol, 75-81; consult, Crime Detection Lab Syst, Ore State Police, 75-77, NIH Immunobiol Study Sect, 77-81 & Zymogenetics, Inc, 84-90; vis prof zool, Univ Col London, 72-73 & 80-81; mem, Adv Comt Immunol & Immunother, Am Cancer Soc, 78-82, scholar, 80-81; vis scientist, Imp Cancer Res Fund Labs, London, 87-88. *Mem:* AAAS; Am Asn Immunologists; Am Soc Microbiol; Sigma Xi. *Res:* Development and control of immunological memory through differentiation of B lymphocytes; evolution of molecular recognition by antibodies. *Mailing Add:* Dept Molecular Microbiol & Immunol Ore Health Sci Univ 3181 SW Sam Jackson Park Rd Portland OR 97201-3098. *Fax:* 503-494-6862; *E-Mail:* rittenbg@ohsu.edu

RITTENBERG, SYDNEY CHARLES, bacteriology; deceased, see previous edition for last biography

RITTENBURY, MAX SANFORD, SURGERY, BIOCHEMISTRY. *Current Pos:* from asst prof to assoc prof, 66-72, PROF GEN SURG, MED UNIV SC, 72- *Personal Data:* b Bailey, NC, Dec 16, 28; m 50; c 2. *Educ:* The Citadel, 46-49; Med Col Va, MD, 53. *Prof Exp:* Resident gen surg, Med Col Va, 56-62, from instr to asst prof, 62-66. *Concurrent Pos:* Surg res fel, Med Col Va, 59-62, USPHS res grants, 59-, fel, 60-62, spec fel, 63-64. *Mem:* AAAS; Am Col Surgeons; Soc Surg Alimentary Tract; Am Asn Surg Trauma; Am Fedn Clin Res. *Res:* Disease of the pancreas; immune and enzymatic response of the body to stress and thermal injury; surgical bacteriology. *Mailing Add:* Med Univ Hosp 171 Ashley Ave Charleston SC 29425-0001

RITTENHOUSE, HARRY GEORGE, BIOLOGICAL CHEMISTRY. *Current Pos:* HEAD CANCER DIAG RES, HYBRITECH INC, 91- *Personal Data:* b Spokane, Wash, Oct 19, 42. *Educ:* Univ Puget Sound, BS, 68; Wash State Univ, PhD(biochem), 72. *Prof Exp:* Am Cancer Soc fel biochem, Univ Calif, Los Angeles, 73-74; asst prof biochem, Ment Health Res Inst, Univ Mich, Ann Arbor, 75-78, sr res assoc, 78-79; head, Tumor Makers Res Lab, Abbott Labs, 79-91. *Res:* Isolation and characterization of surface glycoproteins from cultured animal cells. *Mailing Add:* Hybritech Inc 8958 Terman Ct PO Box 269006 San Diego CA 92121. *Fax:* 213-828-6634

RITTENHOUSE, LARRY RONALD, RANGE SCIENCE. *Current Pos:* PROF RANGE SCI, COLO STATE UNIV, 81- *Personal Data:* b Lewellen, Nebr; c 4. *Educ:* Utah State Univ, BS, 62; Univ Nebr, MS, 66, PhD, 69. *Prof Exp:* Asst, Univ Nebr, 64-69; from asst prof to assoc prof, Eastern Ore Agr Res Ctr, 69-74; assoc prof, Tex A&M Res & Exten Ctr, 75-81. *Mem:* Am Soc Animal Sci; Soc Range Mgt. *Mailing Add:* Range Sci Colo State Univ Ft Collins CO 80523-0001

RITTENHOUSE, SUSAN E, LIPID METABOLISM. *Current Pos:* ASSOC PROF BIOCHEM, BIRMINGHAM WOMEN'S HOSP, HARVARD UNIV, 84- *Personal Data:* b New York, NY, Mar 18, 45. *Educ:* Harvard Univ, PhD(biochem), 72. *Prof Exp:* From asst prof to assoc prof biochem, Sch Med, Boston Univ, 76-84. *Mem:* Am Soc Cell Biol; Am Soc Biol Chemists; Sigma Xi; Am Heart Asn; Int Soc Thrombosis & Hematosis. *Mailing Add:* Jefferson Med Col 476 Jefferson Alumni Hall Philadelphia PA 19107-6799

RITTER, A(LFRED), AERODYNAMICS. *Current Pos:* PRES, A RITTER INC, AEROSPACE CONSULTING, 88- *Personal Data:* b Brooklyn, NY, Mar 15, 23; m 47; c 3. *Educ:* Ga Inst Technol, BS, 43, MS, 47; Cornell Univ, PhD(aerodyn), 51. *Prof Exp:* Aerodynamicst, Glenn L Martin Co, 46; asst, Ga Inst Technol, 47-48; aeronaut res engr, Off Naval Res, 51-54; supvr aerophys, Armour Res Found, Ill Inst Technol, 54-58; vpres & dir res, Adv Res Div, Therm Inc, 58-64, pres, Therm Advan Res, Inc NY, 64-68; asst head, Appl Mech Dept, 68-70, asst head, 70-78, head, Aerodyn Res Dept, Calspan Corp, 78-80; dir technol, Calspan Corp, Arnold Eng Develop Ctr, Arnold AFB, 80-86; sr staff, Booz-Allen & Hamilton, 86-88. *Concurrent Pos:* Instr, Eve Div, Ill Inst Technol, 56-58; vis lectr, Cornell Univ, 65; mem Nat Adv Bd, Univ Tenn Space Inst, chmn, 87-90; mem, Int Coun Aeronaut Sci prog comt, Nat Res Coun comt on Earthquake Eng, 84, on Assessment Nat Aerospace Wind Tunnel Facil, 87-88, SDIO Blue Ribbon Panel Rev ARROW Missile Prog, 89; adj prof aerospace eng, Univ Ala, Huntsville, 88- *Mem:* AAAS; fel Am Inst Aeronaut & Astronaut (tech vpres, 81-85); NY Acad Sci; Sigma Xi. *Res:* Shock wave theory; high temperature gas dynamics; transonic aerodynamics; technical management; strategic defense missile systems; aero-optics. *Mailing Add:* 10044 Meredith Lane Huntsville AL 35803

RITTER, DALE FRANKLIN, GEOLOGY, FLUVIAL GEOMORPHOLOGY. *Current Pos:* EXEC DIR, QUATERNARY SCI CTR, DESERT RES INST, RENO, 90- *Personal Data:* b Allentown, Pa, Nov 13, 32; m 53, 62, Esta Lewis; c Duane, Darryl, Glen & Lisa. *Educ:* Franklin & Marshall Col, AB, 55, BS, 59; Princeton Univ, MA, 63, PhD(geol), 64. *Prof Exp:* Asst prof geol, Franklin & Marshall Col, 64-72; prof geol, Southern Ill Univ, Carbondale, 72-90. *Concurrent Pos:* Chmn, Quaternary Geol, Geomorphol Div, Geol Soc Am, 88-89; RIS rep, Int Asn Geomorphol, 91-93. *Mem:* AAAS; fel Geol Soc Am; Sigma Xi. *Res:* Geomorphology and Pleistocene geology specifically in analysis of processes. *Mailing Add:* Quaternary Sci Ctr Desert Res Inst 7010 Dandini Blvd Reno NV 89512. *Fax:* 702-673-7397

RITTER, DONALD LAWRENCE, METALLURGY & MATERIALS SCIENCE. *Current Pos:* CHMN & PRES, NAT ENVIRON POLICY INST, WASHINGTON, 93- *Personal Data:* b New York, NY, Oct 21, 40; m, Edith Duerksen; c Jason & Kristina. *Educ:* Lehigh Univ, BS, 61; Mass Inst Technol, MS, 63, ScD, 66. *Honors & Awards:* Award for Distinguished Pub Serv, Inst Elec & Electronics Engrs, 90. *Prof Exp:* Mem fac, Calif State Polytech Univ, 68-69; contract consult, Gen Dynamics Co, 68-69; mem fac, Dept Metall & Mat Sci, Lehigh Univ, 69-76, from asst to vpres res, 69-76, mgr res prog develop, 76-79; cong mem, Pa, 79-93. *Concurrent Pos:* Sci exchange fel, US Nat Acad Sci-Soviet Acad Sci, Baikov Inst, Moscow, 67-68; chmn, Task Force Tech & Policy, US House Rep; mem, House Comn Security & Coop in Europe, 80-; mem, Polit Sci Vis Comt, Mass Inst Technol, 82-85. *Mem:* Fel Am Inst Chemists; Nat Soc Prof Engrs; Am Soc Metals; Sigma Xi. *Res:* Metallurgical engineering. *Mailing Add:* Nat Environ Policy Inst 1100 17th St NW Suite 330 Washington DC 20036

RITTER, E GENE, SPEECH-LANGUAGE PATHOLOGY. *Current Pos:* ASSOC PROF SPEECH & HEARING CTR, IND UNIV, BLOOMINGTON, 69- *Personal Data:* b N Kansas City, Mo, Apr 2, 28; m 53; c 2. *Educ:* William Jewell Col, AB, 50; Univ Mo, MA, 56, PhD(speech path), 62. *Prof Exp:* Teacher speech & Eng, Lathrop Pub Schs, 51-53; supvr, Lab Schs, Univ Mo, 53-56; instr speech, Univ Hawaii, Hilo, 56-58; clinician speech path, Univ Mo, 58-62; assoc prof speech & hearing clin, Univ Hawaii, 62-69. *Concurrent Pos:* Consult speech path, var hosps, Honolulu, 62-69, Gov of Guam, 67 & Bloomington Hosp & Bloomington Convalescent Ctr, 69-; fel, Mayo Grad Sch Med, 66. *Mem:* Fel Am Speech-Lang-Hearing Asn. *Res:* Diagnosis and treatment of aphasia and apraxia of speech. *Mailing Add:* 511 N Staats Dr Bloomington IN 47408

RITTER, EDMOND JEAN, BIOCHEMISTRY. *Current Pos:* dir biol res, Laser Lab, 65-68, assoc prof, 68-85, biochemist, Div Basic Sci Res, Inst Develop Res, 68-87, EMER PROF RES PEDIAT, CHILDREN'S HOSP RES FOUND, UNIV CINCINNATI, 85- *Personal Data:* b Cleveland, Ohio, Dec 11, 15; m, Alexandra Engel; c 5. *Educ:* Ohio State Univ, BChE, 37; Univ Toledo, MS, 41; Univ Cincinnati, PhD, 70. *Prof Exp:* Chemist & chem engr, Sun Oil Co, 37-43; org res chemist, Sharples Chem, Inc, Pa Salt Mfg Co, 43-49; dir, Cimcool Lab, Cincinnati Milling Mach Co, 49-65. *Mem:* AAAS; Am Chem Soc; Teratology Soc; Soc Develop Biol. *Res:* Protein chemistry; experimental teratology and cytology; mental retardation; developmental biology; relationship of inhibition of DNA and ATP synthesis to death and differentiation of proliferating cells. *Mailing Add:* 432 Evanswood Pl Cincinnati OH 45220. *E-Mail:* rittere@ucbeh.san.uc.edu

RITTER, ENLOE THOMAS, PHYSICS. *Current Pos:* physicist, US Dept Energy, 68-80, dir, Div Nuclear Physics, 80-85, prog mgr, Chicago Opers Off, 86-88, PHYSICIST, DIV HIGH ENERGY PHYSICS, US DEPT ENERGY, 88- *Personal Data:* b Memphis, Tenn, June 21, 39; div. *Educ:* Southwestern at Memphis, BS, 61; Johns Hopkins Univ, PhD(physics), 66. *Prof Exp:* Staff mem, P Div, Los Alamos Sci Lab, 66-68. *Mem:* Am Phys Soc. *Res:* Nuclear science; high energy physics. *Mailing Add:* 6807 Farmbrook Circle Frederick MD 21703. *Fax:* 301-903-2597

RITTER, GARRY LEE, ANALYTICAL CHEMISTRY. *Current Pos:* SR SOFTWARE ENGR, NICOLET INSTRUMENT CORP, 83- *Personal Data:* b Michigan City, Ind, Nov 14, 49; m 71. *Educ:* Wabash Col, BA, 70; Univ NC, PhD(analytical chem), 76. *Prof Exp:* Res assoc, Nat Bur Standards, 76-77; sr scientist, Schering Corp, 77-80; proj mgr, Ciba Geigy Pharmaceut, 83. *Concurrent Pos:* Nat Acad Sci-Nat Res Coun fel, Nat Bur Standards, 76-77. *Mem:* Am Chem Soc; Am Statist Asn. *Res:* Interpretation of chemical data using optimization techniques and robust statistical techniques; numerical solutions to mixture problems; automation of laboratory instrumentation with active control and real time data acquisition and interpretation. *Mailing Add:* Nicolet Instrument Corp 5225 Verona Rd Madison WI 53711-4495

RITTER, GERHARD X, MATHEMATICS & COMPUTER VISION RESEARCH. *Current Pos:* PROF COMPUT SCI & MATH, UNIV FLA, 83-, DIR, CTR COMPUT VISION RES, 87- *Personal Data:* b Bochum, WGer, Oct 27, 36. *Educ:* Univ Wis-Madison, PhD(math), 71. *Mem:* Math Asn Am; Asn Comput Mach; Inst Elec & Electronics Engrs. *Res:* Computer vision research. *Mailing Add:* Computer & Info Sci Dept Univ Fla CSE 322 Gainesville FL 32611

RITTER, HARTIEN SHARP, PHYSICAL CHEMISTRY. *Current Pos:* CONSULT COATINGS, 81- *Personal Data:* b Iola, Kans, Oct 13, 18; m 41, Charlotte Burtnett; c Harriet A (Burd) & Christopher S II. *Educ:* Univ Kans, AB, 41; Univ Akron, MS, 54, PhD, 64. *Prof Exp:* Res chemist, Olin Industs, Ill, 41-46; asst dir res, Calcium Carbonate Co, 46-48; sr res chemist, Chem Div, Pittsburgh Plate Glass Co, 48-59, supvr inorg chem, 60-64; sr supvr inorg chem, Chem Div, PPG Industs, Inc, 64-81. *Mem:* Am Chem Soc; Fedn Socs Plant Technol. *Res:* Colloid chemistry of pigments in paints and related products; application research in protective coatings. *Mailing Add:* 1495 Shanabrook Dr Akron OH 44313-5733

RITTER, HOPE THOMAS MARTIN, JR, PROTOZOOLOGY. *Current Pos:* prof, 66-87, EMER PROF CELLULAR BIOL, UNIV GA, 87- *Personal Data:* b Allentown, Pa, Sept 24, 19; m 46, 70, Linda Blissit; c Hope T M, Robin Ann (Rountree), Pamela Jane (Patton) & Jennifer. *Educ:* Cornell Univ, AB, 43; Lehigh Univ, MS, 47, PhD, 55. *Prof Exp:* Instr zool & gen biol, Lehigh Univ, 48-55, asst prof zool, gen biol & comp physiol, 55-57; res fel, Biol Labs, Harvard Univ, 57-59, lectr biol, 59-61; asst prof, State Univ NY, Buffalo, 61-66. *Concurrent Pos:* Lectr cell div mech, 87- *Mem:* AAAS; Soc Protozoologists; Am Soc Cell Biologists. *Res:* Biology of Cryptocercus and termite protozoa; insect blood cells; tissue culture; anaerobic metabolism. *Mailing Add:* Dept Cellular Biol Univ Ga Biol Sci Bldg Athens GA 30602. *Fax:* 706-542-4271

RITTER, HUBERT AUGUST, OBSTETRICS & GYNECOLOGY. *Current Pos:* PRES EDUC & RES FOUND, AMA, 77- *Personal Data:* b St Louis, Mo, Aug 30, 24; m 49; c 1. *Educ:* Westminster Col, Mo, AB, 45; St Louis Univ, MD, 48. *Honors & Awards:* Robert Schlueter Award, 85. *Prof Exp:* Actg chmn dept obstet & gynec, St Louis Univ, 76-78. *Concurrent Pos:* Trustee, Am Med Asn, 76-; comnr, Nat Joint Pract Comn, 77- & Joint Comn on Accreditation of Hosps, 82-85. *Mem:* Am Fertil Soc; Am Col Surgeons; Am Col Obstet & Gynec; AMA (secy-treas, 82-85). *Res:* Incompetence of uterine cervix. *Mailing Add:* 1035 Bellevue Ave St Louis MO 63117

RITTER, JAMES CARROLL, SPACE EXPERIMENTS, RADIATION EFFECTS IN MICROELECTRONICS. *Current Pos:* res physicist, 62-73, head, Satellite Survivability Sect, 73-83, HEAD, RADIATION EFFECTS BR, US NAVAL RES LAB, 83- *Personal Data:* b Denver, Colo, Apr 12, 35; m 59, Diane Chestnut; c James F, June K, Jonathan C & Brian D. *Educ:* Univ Colo, AB, 57; Purdue Univ, MS, 62. *Prof Exp:* Physicist, Radiation & Nucleonics Lab, Westinghouse Elec Corp, 59-60 & Nat Bur Stand, 61-62. *Mem:* Am Phys Soc; Sigma Xi; AAAS; sr mem Inst Elec & Electronics Engrs. *Res:* Nuclear reactions and spectroscopy; radiation hardening of electronic devices; satellite survivability; space radiation; single event upset; space dosimetry; Combined Release and Radiation Effects Satellite microelectronics experiment; High Temperature Superconductivity Space experiment; microelectronics and photonics test bed. *Mailing Add:* Code 6610 US Naval Res Lab Washington DC 20375-5320. *Fax:* 202-404-8076

RITTER, JOHN EARL, JR, MATERIALS SCIENCE, METALLURGY. *Current Pos:* From asst prof to assoc prof, 65-76, PROF MECH ENG, UNIV MASS, AMHERST, 76- *Personal Data:* b Baton Rouge, La, July 17, 39; m; c 4. *Educ:* Mass Inst Technol, BS, 61, MS, 62; Cornell Univ, PhD(metall), 66. *Mem:* Am Ceramic Soc. *Res:* Mechanical behavior of materials; adhesion between dissimilar materials. *Mailing Add:* Dept Mech Eng Univ Mass Amherst MA 01003

RITTER, JOSEPH JOHN, SYNTHETIC INORGANIC CHEMISTRY. *Current Pos:* RES CHEMIST, NAT BUR STANDARDS, 63- *Personal Data:* US citizen. *Educ:* Siena Col, BS, 60; Univ Hawaii, MS, 63; Univ Md, PhD(inorg chem), 71. *Mem:* Am Chem Soc. *Res:* Reactivity of volatile boranes and silanes; inorganic chemistry of corrosive reactions on ferrous metals; nature of passive films on metals; electrochemistry. *Mailing Add:* 503 Park Ave Mt Airy MD 21771

RITTER, KARLA SCHWENSEN, BIOCHEMISTRY. *Current Pos:* vis prof, 78-79, asst prof, 79-85, ASSOC PROF BIOL & ENTOM, DREXEL UNIV, 85- *Personal Data:* b Detroit, Mich, Oct 30, 50; m 74. *Educ:* Ohio State Univ, BS, 71; Univ Calif, Berkeley, PhD(entom), 76. *Prof Exp:* Res fel,

Harvard Univ, 76-77. *Mem:* Sigma Xi; Entom Soc Am; Am Entom Soc; Soc Invertebrate Path; Am Registry Prof Entomologists. *Res:* Function and metabolism of sterols in insects; physiological and histopathological effects of insect disease. *Mailing Add:* 5870 Timber Ridge Trail Madison WI 53711

RITTER, MARK ALFRED, RADIATION BIOLOGY, RADIATION ONCOLOGY. *Current Pos:* asst prof, 85-94, ASSOC PROF, CLIN CANCER CTR, UNIV WIS, 94- *Personal Data:* b San Francisco, Calif, May 11, 48; m 74. *Educ:* Univ San Francisco, BS, 70; Univ Calif, MS, 72, PhD(nuclear eng), 76; Univ Miami, MD, 84. *Prof Exp:* Res assoc, Sch Pub Health, Harvard Univ, 76-77; asst prof, Univ Pa, 77-82, resident radiation ther, 85. *Mem:* Radiation Res; Am Soc Photobiol; AAAS; Am Soc Therapeut Radiation Oncol; Am Soc Clin Oncol. *Res:* Cell kinetics; radiation oncology. *Mailing Add:* 600 Highland Ave Madison WI 53792

RITTER, NADINE MARIE, ANALYTICAL BIOCHEMISTRY & BIOTECH PRODUCT DEVELOPMENT, QUALITY CONTROL & REGULATORY AFFAIRS. *Current Pos:* SR RES BIOCHEMIST, ABBOTT DIAGNOSTICS, 92- *Personal Data:* b New Orleans, La, June 20, 58; m 80, William J Ward; c Random. *Educ:* Univ Houston-Clear Lake, BS, 84; Rice Univ-Houston, MA, 88, PhD(cell biol), 88. *Prof Exp:* Res asst, Dent Sci Inst, Univ Tex, 78-80, sr res asst, 80-84; grad fel, Dept Molecular Biol & Biochem, Rice Univ, 84-88; postdoctoral fel, Dept Biochem, Dent Br, Univ Tex, 88-92. *Concurrent Pos:* Chem coordr, Houston Mus Natural Sci, 85-89; young investr award, Tex Mineralized Tissue Soc, 89; vol scientist, Sci-By-Mail, Boston Mus Sci, 89-91; sci consult, Childrens Mus Houston, 90-91; pres, Asn Women Sci, Gulfcoast, 90-91, Chicago, 96-97; chair, GLP/CGMP Comt Asn, Biomolecular Resource Facil, 96-97. *Mem:* Sigma Xi; Am Soc Cell Biol; Am Asn Promotion Sci. *Res:* Analytical biochemistry of biotechnical products, laboratory quality control, test method/process validation, regulatory affairs, protein biochemistry, cell biology, technology transfer, biotechnology product development and scale-up, well-characterized biologicals, compliance of research and development facilities. *Mailing Add:* Infectious Dis Diag Dept 9A1 Bldg AP8B 100 Abbott Park Rd Abbott Park IL 60064. *E-Mail:* nadine@ritterward.com

RITTER, PRESTON PECK OTTO, BIOCHEMISTRY. *Current Pos:* asst prof, 70-78, PROF CHEM, EASTERN WASH UNIV, 78- *Personal Data:* b Memphis, Tenn, Mar 29, 41; m 61; c 2. *Educ:* Univ Calif, Berkeley, BS, 63; Univ Wis-Madison, MS, 65, PhD(biochem), 67. *Prof Exp:* Investr biochem, Biol Div, Oak Ridge Nat Lab, 67-69; res asst prof, Col Med, Baylor Univ, 69-70. *Concurrent Pos:* Vis staff, Health Res Lab, Los Alamos Sci Lab, NMex, 75-76. *Mem:* Am Chem Soc; AAAS. *Res:* Absorption and metabolism of antibiotics; protein and nucleic acid biochemistry. *Mailing Add:* Dept Chem & Biochem MS 74 Eastern Wash Univ Cheney WA 99004. *Fax:* 509-359-6973; *E-Mail:* pritter@ewu.edu

RITTER, R(OBERT) BROWN, CHEMICAL ENGINEERING. *Current Pos:* CONSULT ENGR, 89- *Personal Data:* b Winchester, Va, Jan 12, 21; m 45; c 2. *Educ:* Ohio State Univ, BChE & MS, 50. *Honors & Awards:* Am Soc Eng Educ Eng Graphics Convair Award, 59. *Prof Exp:* Chem engr, E I du Pont de Nemours & Co, 50-53; sr chem engr, C F Braun & Co, 53-59 & Chemet Engrs, Inc, 59-62; chief process engr, Aetron Div, Aerojet Gen Corp, 62-67; asst tech dir, Heat Transfer Res, Inc, Alhambra, 67-80; sr tech specialist, Fluor Technol, Inc, Irvine, Calif, 80-87; vpres engr, Spottwood Eng, Inc, Seal Beach, Calif, 87-89. *Concurrent Pos:* Lectr, Long Beach State Univ, 80-81, Calif Poly State Univ, 83-84. *Mem:* Am Inst Chem Engrs. *Res:* Heat transfer, condensation, fouling and rating methods; thermodynamics, chemical process, cryogenics, nuclear waste treatment and disposal; process plant design, process equipment, instrumentation and controls. *Mailing Add:* 595 Old Ranch Rd Seal Beach CA 90740-2836

RITTER, ROGERS C, EXPERIMENTAL GRAVITATIONAL PHYSICS, BIOPHYSICS. *Current Pos:* from asst prof to assoc prof, 61-70, PROF PHYSICS, UNIV VA, 70- *Personal Data:* b Pleasanton, Nebr, Oct 27, 29; m 50; c 3. *Educ:* Univ Nebr, BSc, 52; Univ Tenn, PhD(physics), 61. *Prof Exp:* Inst eng, Oak Ridge Gaseous Diffusion Plant, 52-59, Oak Ridge Inst Nuclear Studies fel physics, Oak Ridge Nat Lab, 59-61. *Concurrent Pos:* Mem, Fundamental Constants Comt, Nat Res Coun-Nat Acad Sci, 79-84 & Panel Basic Standards, Nat Res Coun, 82- *Res:* Fundamental constants; precision measurement; biophysics; urology and cardiovascular medical physics; experimental gravitation. *Mailing Add:* Dept Physics Univ Va 205 McCormick Rd Charlottesville VA 22903

RITTER, WALTER PAUL, NEUROPSYCHOLOGY. *Current Pos:* assoc prof, 71-80, PROF PSYCHOL, LEHMAN COL, 80- *Personal Data:* b Brooklyn, NY, Oct 8, 29; m 56; c 1. *Educ:* City Col New York, BA, 59; Columbia Univ, PhD(psychol), 63. *Prof Exp:* Psychologist, Suffolk County Ment Health Bd, 62-64; supvr clin psychologist, NY Univ Med Ctr, Goldwater Hosp, 64-65; fel neurol, 65-68, from asst prof neurol to vis asst prof anat, Albert Einstein Col Med, 68-74. *Concurrent Pos:* Vis asst prof neurosci, Albert Einstein Col Med, 74- *Mem:* Am Psychol Asn; AAAS; Psychonomic Soc; Int Neuropsychol Soc. *Res:* Electrophysiological correlates of information processing. *Mailing Add:* 750 Kappock St Bronx NY 10463

RITTER, WILLIAM FREDERICK, WATER RESOURCES. *Current Pos:* from asst prof to assoc prof, 71-82, PROF AGR ENG, UNIV DEL, 82-, DEPT CHMN, 92-, PROF CIVIL ENG, 94- *Personal Data:* b Stratford, Ont, Mar 25, 42; m 66; c 2. *Educ:* Univ Guelph, BSA, 65; Univ Toronto, BAS, 66; Iowa State Univ, MS, 68, PhD(agr eng, sanit eng), 71. *Honors & Awards:* Young Engr of Year, Am Soc Agr Eng, Gunloposon; Water Resources Award, New Castle Co; Super Achievement Award, Environ Protection Asn; Outstanding Serv Award, Am Soc Civil Eng. *Prof Exp:* Res assoc agr eng, Iowa State Univ, 66-71. *Concurrent Pos:* Res grants, Hercules, Inc, 72-76, Del Water Resources Ctr, 74-76 & 78-80, 82-87, E I du Pont de Nemours & Co, Inc, 74-75 & 76-77, Univ Del Res Found, 74-75, 208 Prog, Environ Protection Agency, 76-81, Allied Chem Co, 77-78, State of Del, 79-81, 85-, Environ Protection Agency, 80-86, Clean Lakes Prog, Environ Protection Agency, 81-83, USDA, Del, 83-87, 86-89; exec comt, Irrigation & Drainage Div, Am Soc Civil Engrs, 87-92; bd dir, USDA, 89-90 & 92-94, Am Soc Agr Engs, 90-92, US Geol Surv, 90-93, Nat Geog, 92-93 & Environ Protection Agency, 93-; distinguished lectr, Norteast Region, Am Soc Agr Engrs. *Mem:* Am Soc Civil Engrs; fel Am Soc Agr Engrs; Water Environ Fedn; Am Water Works Asn; Can Soc Agr Engrs; Am Soc Eng Educ; Can Water Resources Asn. *Res:* Agricultural waste management; water quality modeling; land disposal of industrial and municipal wastes; irrigation; groundwater pollution and lake eutrophication; non point source pollution. *Mailing Add:* Dept Agr Eng Univ Del Newark DE 19711. *Fax:* 302-831-3651; *E-Mail:* william. ritter@nivs.udel.edu

RITTERMAN, MURRAY B, APPLIED MATHEMATICS. *Current Pos:* ASST PROF MATH, HOFSTRA UNIV, 77- *Personal Data:* b New York, NY, Oct 19, 14; m 44; c 4. *Educ:* NY Univ, PhD(math), 55. *Prof Exp:* Instr math, Long Island Univ, 47-52; engr, Sylvania Elec Prod Inc Div, Gen Tel & Electronics Corp, 52-59, eng specialist, GTE Labs, 59-72; asst prof math, York Col, NY, 72-77. *Mem:* Am Math Soc; Math Asn Am. *Res:* Differential and difference equations; communication and information theory; electron optics. *Mailing Add:* 576 Marion Dr East Meadow NY 11554

RITTERSON, ALBERT L, MEDICAL PARASITOLOGY. *Current Pos:* From instr to asst prof, 52-68, assoc prof, 68-86, EMER PROF MICROBIOL & PARASITOL, SCH MED, UNIV ROCHESTER, 86- *Personal Data:* b New Brunswick, NJ, Mar 13, 24; m 57; c 1. *Educ:* Rutgers Univ, BS, 45, MS, 48; Univ Calif, Los Angeles, PhD(zool), 52. *Concurrent Pos:* China Med Bd fel, Cent Am, 57. *Mem:* AAAS; Am Soc Parasitologists; Am Soc Trop Med & Hyg; Sigma Xi. *Res:* Host parasite relationships; leishmaniasis, trichinosis and malaria in the golden and Chinese hamsters; innate resistance and parasite invasion; microbiology; immunology. *Mailing Add:* 200 Howland Ave Rochester NY 14620

RITTGERS, STANLEY EARLE, FLUID MECHANICS, VASCULAR HEMODYNAMICS RESEARCH. *Current Pos:* assoc prof, 87-92, PROF BIOMED ENG, UNIV AKRON, 92-, DIR, VASCULAR DYNAMICS RES LAB, 87- *Personal Data:* b Des Moines, Iowa, Jan 24, 47; m, Eva; c David & Andrew. *Educ:* State Univ NY, Buffalo, BS, 68; Ohio State Univ, MS, 75, PhD(biomed eng), 78. *Prof Exp:* Res biomed engr & dir, Vascular Res Lab, McGuire Vet Admin Med Ctr, 78-86. *Concurrent Pos:* Grants, A D Williams Fund, Med Col Va, 79-80, Uniqon Indust Inc, 82-83, VA, 82-85, 86-87, Res Challenge Equip Funds, 88-89, Nat Ctr Res Resources, NIH, 92-94; dir, Peripheral Vascular Res Lab, McGuire Vet Admin Med Ctr, 79-86, Inst Biomed Eng Res, Col Eng, Univ Akron, 93-; asst prof surg, Med Col Va, Va Commonwealth Univ, 82-84, affil asst prof surg, 84-86; affil asst prof physiol, Med Col Va, Va Commonwealth Univ, 83-86; from asst prof to assoc prof biomed eng prog, Sch Basic Health Sci, Va Commonwealth Univ, 84-87; consult, Non-Invasive Vascular Lab, Summa Health Syst, Ohio, 87-, adj sci staff, 87-; Vascular Hemodynamics Res Lab, 88-; co-prin investr, Owens B R Acad Challenge, 87-93, Akron City Hosp Found, 88, 91-92, NIH, Nat Inst Aging, 91-92; prin investr, Akron City Hosp Found, 88-89, 88-93, 89, 90, 91-92, 92, 93, Vet Admin Merit Review, 89-91, W L Gore & Assoc, 91-92, Summa Health Syst Found, 94; co-investr, Am Heart Asn, 89-90, 90-91, The Whitaker Found, 93-; assoc ed, J Biomech Eng, 94- *Mem:* Am Soc Eng Educ; Biomed Eng Soc; Am Soc Mech Engrs; NATO fel Advan Studies Inst; Sigma Xi; Asn Advan Med Instrumentation; Soc Vascular Technol; Am Inst Ultrasound Med; Inst Elec & Electronics Engrs Eng Med & Biol Soc. *Res:* Contributions to publications, journals, abstracts and video recordings all over the United States. *Mailing Add:* 5760 Bradford Way Hudson OH 44236

RITTMANN, BRUCE EDWARD, ENVIRONMENTAL BIOTECHNOLOGY, BIOLOGICAL PROCESSES. *Current Pos:* JOHN EVANS PROF, NORTHWESTERN UNIV, 92- *Personal Data:* b St Louis, Mo, Nov 17, 50; m 86, Marylee MacDonald; c 4. *Educ:* Washington Univ, St Louis, BS & MS, 74; Stanford Univ, Phd(environ eng), 79. *Honors & Awards:* Eng Sci Award, Asn Environ Eng Professors, 79 & 93 & CH2M- Hill Award, 89 & Montgomery Award, Acad Achievement Award, Am Water Works Asn, 90; Walter L Huber Res Prize, Am Soc Civil Engrs, 90; ARI Clarke Prize, Nat Water Res Inst, 94. *Prof Exp:* Environ engr, Sverdrup & Parcel & Assocs, Inc, St Louis, MO, 74-75; grad res asst, Stanford Univ, 75-79, scholar & lectr, 79; lectr, San Jose State Univ, 79; from asst prof to prof environ eng, Univ Ill, Urbana-Champaign, 80-92. *Concurrent Pos:* Presidential young investr award, NSF, 84; Xerox fac res award, Col Eng, Univ Ill, Urbana-Champaign, 85; mem adv comt, Crit Eng Systs Div, NSF, 86-90; Univ Scholar, Univ Ill, 87; mem, Comt Simulation Contaminant Transp in Groundwater, Nat Res Coun, Nat Acad Sci, 87-89; bd dirs, Asn Environ Eng Professors, 88-92; editor-in-chief, Biodegradation, 96- *Mem:* Water Pollution Control Fedn; Am Soc Civil Engrs; fel AAAS; Int Asn Water Pollution Res & Control; Asn Environ Eng Professors (vpres, 89-90, pres, 90-91); Am Water Works Asn; Am Soc Microbiol. *Res:* Application of biotechnology for environmental control; use of molecular tools in the study of biological processes; biofilm kinetics, biodegradation of low-concentration and hazardous organic chemicals, and in situ bioremediation of contaminated aquifers. *Mailing Add:* Northwestern Univ Dept Civil Eng 2145 Sheridan Rd Evanston IL 60208-3109. *Fax:* 847-491-4011; *E-Mail:* b_rittmann@nwu.edu

RITTNER, EDMUND SIDNEY, APPLIED PHYSICS, ENERGY CONVERSION. *Current Pos:* CONSULT SCIENTIST, 84- *Personal Data:* b Boston, Mass, May 29, 19; m 42, Marcella Weiner; c Leona. *Educ:* Mass Inst Technol, SB, 39, PhD(chem), 41. *Honors & Awards:* Inst Elec & Electronics Engrs Photovoltaic Founders Award, 85. *Prof Exp:* Little fel chem, Mass Inst Technol, 41-42, res assoc, Div Indust Coop, 42-46; res physicist & sect chief, Philips Labs Div, NAm Philips Co, Inc, 46-62, dir, Dept Physics, 62-69; mgr physics lab, Comsat Labs, 69-81, exec dir phys sci, 81-84. *Mem:* Fel Inst Elec & Electronics Engrs; fel Am Phys Soc. *Res:* Semiconductors; photoconductivity; infrared; thermionic emission; solid state devices; solar cells. *Mailing Add:* 700 New Hampshire Ave Washington DC 20037-2406

RITTS, ROY ELLOT, JR, MICROBIOLOGY, IMMUNOLOGY. *Current Pos:* chmn dept, Mayo Clin, 68-80, prof oncol & head, 80-95, PROF MICROBIOL, MAYO MED SCH, UNIV MINN, 68-, EMER PROF MICROBIOL RES LAB, 80- *Personal Data:* b St Petersburg, Fla, Jan 16, 29. *Educ:* George Washington Univ, AB, 48, MD, 51; Am Bd Microbiol, dipl; Am Bd Med Lab Immunol, dipl. *Honors & Awards:* Wisdom Award Honor, Wisdom Soc, 70; Award Merit, Int Union Immunol Socs, 86. *Prof Exp:* Intern, DC Gen Hosp, 51-52; fel med, Sch Med, George Washington Univ, 52-53, resident, George Washington Univ Hosp, 53-54; res fel, Harvard Med Sch, 54-55; vis investr microbiol & path, Rockefeller Inst, 55-57, res assoc immunol, 57-58; from assoc prof microbiol to prof microbiol & trop med, Sch Med, Georgetown Univ, 58-64, chmn dept microbiol & trop med & prof lectr med, 59-64; dir inst biomed res, educ & res found, AMA, 64-68, dir med res, 66-68. *Concurrent Pos:* Life Ins Med Res Fund fel, 54-57; prof lectr, Sch Med, Univ Chicago, 64-68; mem, Am Bd Microbiol, 65-67; chmn ad hoc sci adv comt, USPHS-Food & Drug Admin, 70-71, consult, 71-; chmn adv comt diag prod, Food & Drug Admin, 72-75; Nat Food & Drug Adv Comt, 75-78; mem carcinogenesis comt, Nat Comt Clin Lab Stand, Nat Cancer Inst, 80-; mem, Am Bd Med Lab Immunol, 76-83 & 88-92; mem bd dirs, Int Assoc Study Lung Cancer, 74-76, secy, 76-78; sect ed, J Immunol, 84-88; mem exp comt immunol, WHO, 84-96; mem Exp Immunol Study Sect, NIH, 85-89. *Mem:* Fel Am Col Physicians; fel Am Clin Sci; fel Royal Soc Health; fel Am Col Chest Physicians; fel Am Acad Microbiol; fel Infectious Dis Soc Am; Am Asn Immunologists; Am Asn Cancer Res; Am Soc Clin Oncol. *Res:* Immunotherapy; tumor immunology. *Mailing Add:* Microbiol Res Lab Mayo Clin Rochester MN 55905. *Fax:* 507-280-0289

RITTSCHOF, DANIEL, BEHAVIORAL ECOLOGY, CHEMICAL ECOLOGY. *Current Pos:* asst prof zool, Marine Studies, 88-90, ASSOC PROF ZOOL & ENVIRON, DUKE UNIV, 91- *Personal Data:* b Morenci, Ariz, Feb 26, 46; m 80; c 2. *Educ:* Univ Mich, BS, 68, MA, 70, PhD, 75. *Prof Exp:* Teaching asst, Univ Mich, 68-74, lectr zool, 74-75; fel, Univ Calif, Riverside, 75-78, res physiologist, Los Angeles, 78-80; marine scientist, Univ Del, 80-88. *Concurrent Pos:* Dir, Grad Studies, Ocean Scientists Prog; vis assoc prof, Hinh Konh Univ Sci & Technol, 95-96; Ray Lankston fel, Manihy Biol Asn, UK, 96. *Mem:* Am Soc Zoologists; Asn Chemoreception Sci; Int Soc Chem Ecol. *Res:* Marine chemical sensing; anti fouling; molecules and mechanisms of chemoattraction of Urosalpinx cinerea; functions of chemical sensing in the integration of resource utilization in marine environments and in the gastropod shell habitat web; chemical camouflaging and inhibition facilitation of chemoresponses, soluble pollutants; teratogenic effects; assays of behavioral toxicity. *Mailing Add:* Marine Lab Duke Univ 135 Pivers Island Rd Beaufort NC 28516. *E-Mail:* dan@metolius.ml.duke.edu

RITVO, EDWARD R, PSYCHIATRY. *Current Pos:* From asst prof to assoc prof, 64-77, PROF IN RESIDENCE PSYCHIAT, SCH MED, UNIV CALIF, LOS ANGELES, 77- *Personal Data:* b Boston, Mass, June 1, 30; m 61; c 4. *Educ:* Harvard Col, BA, 51; Boston Univ, MD, 55. *Res:* Adult and child psychiatry, including psychoanalysis and neurophysiology. *Mailing Add:* Neuropsych Inst 760 Westwood Plaza Los Angeles CA 90024

RITZERT, ROGER WILLIAM, BIOCHEMISTRY. *Current Pos:* SR BIOCHEMIST, TECH CTR, OWENS-ILL INC, 67- *Personal Data:* b Aurora, Ill, Jan 24, 36; m 62; c 3. *Educ:* NCent Col, Ill, BA, 58; Mich State Univ, MS, 61, PhD(biochem), 66. *Prof Exp:* Asst biochem, Mich State Univ, 58-65; res biochemist, Div Biochem & Microbiol, Battelle Mem Inst, 65-67. *Concurrent Pos:* Adj asst prof, Med Col Ohio, Toledo, 71- *Mem:* Am Soc Microbiol; Am Chem Soc; Tissue Cult Asn. *Res:* Biochemistry of plant growth and development; cellular responses responses to toxicants in vitro. *Mailing Add:* 6009 Jeffrey Lane Sylvania OH 43560

RITZ-GOLD, CAROLINE JOYCE, BIOENERGETICS. *Current Pos:* CHIEF SCIENTIST, CTR BIOMOLECULAR STUDIES, 86- *Personal Data:* b Cleveland, Ohio; m 78, Cliff. *Educ:* Calif State Univ, Long Beach, BS, 66, MS, 69; Univ Southern Calif, PhD(biochem), 78. *Prof Exp:* Fel, Cardiovasc Res Inst, Univ Calif, San Francisco, 78-82; NSF vis prof, San Francisco State Univ, 84-86. *Concurrent Pos:* Advan res fel, Am Heart Asn, 80-81. *Mem:* Biophys Soc; Am Phys Soc; Sigma Xi; Protein Soc. *Res:* Use of concepts and methods from condensed matter theory and polymer physics to gain physical insight into mechanisms of free energy transfer, conversion, and storage in proteins and assemblies. *Mailing Add:* Ctr Biomolecular Studies 38451 Timpanogas Fremont CA 94536. *Fax:* 510-791-5185

RITZI, EARL MICHAEL, TUMOR IMMUNOLOGY, RETROVIROLOGY. *Current Pos:* ASSOC PROF VIROL, HEALTH SCI CTR, TEX TECH UNIV, 84- *Personal Data:* b Worcester, Mass, June 4, 46; m 69, Elizabeth A St Pierre; c Christopher M. *Educ:* Univ Mass, BS, 68; Princeton Univ, MA, 70, PhD(virol), 72. *Prof Exp:* Res asst virol, Princeton Univ, 72; res assoc, Worcester Found Exp Biol, 72-75; sr staff assoc virol, Inst Cancer Res, Columbia Univ, 75-77; asst prof virol, Univ Tenn, Ctr Health Sci, 77-82; assoc prof virol, State Okla Organized Res Prog, OCOMS, Tulsa, 82-84. *Concurrent Pos:* Post doctoral fel, Am Cancer Soc, 73-75; chmn, Immunol Sect, Nat Cancer Inst Site Rev Panel, 78-, mem virol sect, 78-; prin investr, Am Cancer Soc Willie Mae Darwin Mem Grant, 78-81 & NIH Cancer Res Grant, 81-86; chairperson, Memphis Am Cancer Soc Fund Raising Camp, 80-; sci fair judge, Am Soc Microbiol, 80-; virol lectr, Miami Int Med Sch Rev, 89- *Mem:* Am Asn Cancer Res; Am Asn Immunologists; Am Soc Microbiol; Sigma Xi. *Res:* Expression of retroviral proteins and human tumor-associated antigens, studied to determine their utility as signals for the presence of solid tumors and to control expression of HIV-1. *Mailing Add:* Dept Microbiol Health Sci Ctr Tex Tech Univ Lubbock TX 79430. *Fax:* 806-743-2334; *E-Mail:* micemr@ttuhsc.edu

RITZMAN, ROBERT L, INORGANIC CHEMISTRY, RADIOCHEMISTRY. *Current Pos:* PRES, RLR CONSULT SERVS, SUNNYVALE, CALIF, 92- *Personal Data:* b Peoria, Ill, Nov 19, 32; m 59, Laura M Bullett; c Donald P. *Educ:* Bradley Univ, BS, 55; Rensselaer Polytech Inst, PhD(phys chem), 61. *Prof Exp:* Sr scientist phys chem, Battelle-Columbus Labs, 59-75; sr scientist, 75-80, vpres, Sci Applns Int Corp, 80-84; tech adv, Elec Power Res Inst, 84-92. *Mem:* Am Chem Soc; fel Am Nuclear Soc. *Res:* Chemical separations; nuclear reactor safety and accident analysis; nuclear radiation effects; fission-product chemistry; fission-gas release; environmental impact analysis; nuclear fuel cycle risk analysis; nuclear reactor severe accident phenomena. *Mailing Add:* 1220-225 Tasman Dr Sunnyvale CA 94089

RITZMAN, THOMAS A, TREATMENT ANXIETY, TREATMENT OBESITY. *Current Pos:* RETIRED. *Personal Data:* b Mayaguez, PR, Feb 18, 14; m 41; c 3. *Educ:* Yale Univ, BA, 36; Harvard Med Sch, MD, 40. *Honors & Awards:* Achievement Award, Am Acad Med Hypnoanal, 88. *Prof Exp:* Pvt pract obstet & gynec, 46-81; pvt pract med hypnoanal, 73. *Mem:* Am Col Obstet & Gynec; Am Acad Med Hypnoanal; NY Acad Sci. *Res:* The use of guided analysis to effect permanent cure of emotion and systemic physical illness. *Mailing Add:* 78860 Via Meloda La Quinta CA 92253

RITZMANN, LEONARD W, INTERNAL MEDICINE, CARDIOLOGY. *Current Pos:* RETIRED. *Personal Data:* b South Bend, Ind, Sept 8, 21; m 42, Dorothy Reese; c Mary, Rebecca (Strom) & Elizabeth (Helms). *Educ:* Valparaiso Univ, AB, 42; Wash Univ, MD, 45; Am Bd Internal Med, dipl. *Prof Exp:* Intern internal med, Barnes Hosp, St Louis, 45-46; asst resident med, Salt Lake Co Gen Hosp, 47-48, fel cardiol, 48-49, chief resident, 49-50; Am Heart Asn fel cardiol, Postgrad Med Sch London, Eng, 50-51; sect chief cardiol, Vet Admin Hosp, Portland, 53-56, chief med, 56-60, sect chief cardiol, 60-70, staff cardiol, 70-90; prof med, Sch Med, Univ Ore, 63-90. *Mem:* Am Heart Asn; Christian Med Soc (pres, 78-80). *Res:* Electrocardiography; vectorcardiography; cardiac arrhythmias; cor pulmonale; coronary heart disease; pacemakers. *Mailing Add:* 4230 SW Sixth Ave Portland OR 97201

RITZMANN, RONALD FRED, PSYCHOPHARMACOLOGY, DRUG ABUSE. *Current Pos:* RES SCIENTIST, ADVAN IMMUNO THERAPEUT. *Personal Data:* b Cicero, Ill, June 16, 43. *Educ:* Northern Ill Univ, BA, 65; MA, 68, PhD(neurosci), 73. *Prof Exp:* Res assoc, Dept Physiol & Biophys, Med Ctr, Univ Ill, 77-78, asst prof physiol, 78-86, assoc fac, Drug & Alcohol Abuse Res & Training Prog, 80-88; res pharmacologist, Westside Vet Admin Med Ctr, 84-88. *Concurrent Pos:* Dir, Behav Pharmacol, Advan Immuno Therapeut, Tustin, Calif. *Mem:* Neurosci Soc; Am Soc Neurochem; Int Soc Biomed Res Alcoholism. *Res:* Neurochemical basis for the development of tolerance and physical dependence on psychoactive drugs with particular interest in the modification of the addictive states by peptides. *Mailing Add:* Advan Immuno Therapeut 122231 Pevero Tustin CA 92680-1106. *Fax:* 818-364-3465

RIVA, JOHN F, BIOSTRATIGRAPHY, TAXONOMY. *Current Pos:* VIS PROF, GEORESOURCES, INRS, UNIV QUE, 95- *Personal Data:* b Digoman (Belluno), Italy, June 17, 29; Can citizen; div; c Patricia G, Elizabeth A & David F. *Educ:* Univ Nev, BA, 50, MSc, 57; Columbia Univ, PhD(geol), 62. *Prof Exp:* Res assoc geol, McGill Univ, 61-63; asst prof, Villanova Univ, 63-66; from asst prof to titular prof, Laval Univ, 66-94. *Concurrent Pos:* Soc Sigma Xi res awards, 64-65, 67 & 70; NSF res grant, 64-67; res assoc, Columbia Univ, 66-68 & 70-71; Nat Res Coun Can yearly grants, 67-94; paleozoic stratig, paleont & tectonics & taxonomy NE & Cent Nev. *Mem:* Sr fel Geol Soc Am; Sigma Xi; Palaeont Asn. *Res:* Ordovician and Silurian graptolites, their taxonomy and biostratigraphy. *Mailing Add:* 1238 Rouville St Ste Foy PQ G1W 3T7 Can. *Fax:* 418-654-2615; *E-Mail:* jriva@gsc.nrcan.gc.ca

RIVA, JOSEPH PETER, JR, GEOLOGY, STRUCTURAL & PETROLEUM GEOLOGY. *Current Pos:* GEOL CONSULT, 66- *Personal Data:* b Chicago, Ill, Oct 31, 35; m 63, Susanne Bozenhardt; c Monica & Michaela. *Educ:* Carleton Col, BA, 57; Univ Wyo, MS, 59. *Honors & Awards:* Reeve & Noyes Acad Prize, Carleton Col; Fel Award, NSF. *Prof Exp:* Geologist, Tenn Gas & Oil Co, 59; consult geologist, G H Otto Co, Chicago, 61-65 & Earth Sci Labs, Ohio, 65-66; geologist, Sci Info Exchange, Smithsonian Inst, 66-67, actg chief earth sci br, 67-69, chief, 69-74; specialist earth sci, Sci Policy Res Div, Cong Res Serv, Libr Cong, Washington, DC, 74-96, asst chief, 85-86. *Concurrent Pos:* Detail, US Geol Surv, 80; mem, Comt Offshore Hydrocarbon Resource Estimation Methodology & Comt Undiscovered Oil & Gas Res, Nat Res Coun Nat Acad Sci. *Mem:* Am Asn Petrol Geologists; Am Inst Prof Geologists; Sigma Xi. *Res:* Petroleum geology; natural gas; underground gas storage; energy policy; world oil and gas resources, and future production; authored over 200 publications and 4 books. *Mailing Add:* 9705 Mill Run Dr Great Falls VA 22066

RIVARD, JEROME G, FLUID MECHANICS. *Personal Data:* b Hudson, Wis, Nov 21, 32; m 55; c Brenda, Robert & Diane. *Educ:* Univ Wis, BSME, 55. *Honors & Awards:* Edward Cole Medal, Soc Automotive Engrs. *Prof Exp:* Dir eng, Bendix, 62-76; chief engr, Ford Motor Co, 76-86. *Mem:* Nat Acad Eng; fel Inst Elec & Electronics Engrs; fel Soc Automotive Engrs. *Res:* Application of electronics to automotive systems. *Mailing Add:* 29401 S Seaway Ct Harrison Township MI 48045

RIVAS, MARIAN LUCY, MEDICAL GENETICS, COMPUTER SYSTEMS. *Current Pos:* ASSOC PROF PEDIAT, UNIV TENN, MEMPHIS. *Personal Data:* b New York, NY, May 6, 43. *Educ:* Marian Col, BS, 64; Ind Univ, MS, 67, PhD(med genetics), 69; Am Bd Med Genetics, cert, 82. *Prof Exp:* Fel med genetics, Dept Med, Johns Hopkins Hosp, 69-71; asst prof biol, Rutgers Univ, Douglas Col, 71-75; assoc prof, Ore Health Sci Univ, 75-82, dir genetic coun, Hemophilia Ctr, 77-79, prof med genetics, 82-; assoc scientist, Neurol Sci Inst, Good Samatitan Hosp, 78- *Concurrent Pos:* Lectr Biol, Marian Col, 66-68; dir, Genetic Counseling Grad Prog, Rutgers Univ, 71-75; adj asst prof med genetics, Ind Univ, 71-75; mem, Mammalian Cell Lines Comt, Nat Inst Gen Med Sci, NIH, 75-76, adv comt, 76-80; consult, Interregional Cytogenetics Register Syst & Nat Mutant Cell Bank, 75-; staff mem, Emmanuel Hosp, Portland, 81-; mem, NIH-Venezuela Comn Huntington's Chorea, 82- *Mem:* Am Soc Human Genetics; Am Epilepsy Soc; NY Acad Sci; Sigma Xi. *Res:* Human gene mapping; genetic aspects of epilepsy; human pedigree and segregation analyses; computer applications in clinical genetics and genetic counseling; population genetics; ethnic distribution of genetic disease. *Mailing Add:* Univ Tenn 711 Jefferson Suite 523 Memphis TN 38105

RIVELA, LOUIS JOHN, GENERAL CHEMISTRY, ANALYTICAL CHEMISTRY. *Current Pos:* From asst prof to assoc prof inorg chem, 77-89, CHMN, DEPT INORG CHEM, WILLIAM PATERSON COL, 69-, PROF, 89- *Personal Data:* b Brooklyn, NY, Feb 24, 42; m 64; c 1. *Educ:* Rutgers Univ, New Brunswick, BS, 63; Univ NC, Chapel Hill, MS, 67, PhD(inorg chem), 70. *Concurrent Pos:* Princeton fac fel, 87. *Mem:* Am Chem Soc; Sigma Xi; Am Inst Chem. *Res:* Synthesis and characterization of coordination compounds containing organophophines. *Mailing Add:* 115 Andover Dr Wayne NJ 07470-2951

RIVELAND, A(RVIN) R(OY), CIVIL ENGINEERING. *Current Pos:* RETIRED. *Personal Data:* b Buxton, NDak, July 29, 23; m 52; c 3. *Educ:* Univ NDak, BS, 45; Univ Nebr, MS, 54. *Prof Exp:* Engr, Lium & Burdick, Engrs, 45-57; from instr to prof civil eng, Univ Nebr, Lincoln, 80-89. *Mem:* Am Soc Civil Engrs; Am Soc Eng Educ; Am Concrete Inst. *Res:* Structures; ultimate strength design in reinfored concrete. *Mailing Add:* 540 Wedgewood Dr Lincoln NE 68510

RIVENSON, ABRAHAM S, PATHOLOGY OF CANCER, CARCINOGENESIS. *Current Pos:* SR PATHOLOGIST, AM HEALTH FOUND, VALHALLA, NY, 77- *Personal Data:* b Roman, Rumania, Nov 22, 26; US citizen; m 49; c Irene. *Educ:* Univ Bucharest, MD, 54. *Concurrent Pos:* Res prof pathol, NY Med Col, Valhalla, NY, 77- *Mem:* NY Acad Med; Am Asn Cancer Res; Europ Asn Cancer Res. *Res:* Experimental pathology; carcinogenesis. *Mailing Add:* Am Health Found Naylor Dana Inst One Dana Rd Valhalla NY 10595-1599. *Fax:* 914-328-4161; *E-Mail:* 013725.1576@compuserve.com

RIVERA, AMERICO, JR, biochemistry, neurochemistry, for more information see previous edition

RIVERA, EVELYN MARGARET, ENDOCRINOLOGY, CANCER. *Current Pos:* from asst prof to assoc prof, 65-72, PROF ZOOL, MICH STATE UNIV, 72- *Personal Data:* b Hollister, Calif, Nov 10, 29; div. *Educ:* Univ Calif, Berkeley, AB, 52, MA, 60, PhD(zool), 63. *Honors & Awards:* UNESCO Award, Int Cell Res Orgn, 65; Res Career Develop Award, NIH, 67-72 & Res Fel Award, 78-79. *Prof Exp:* Am Cancer Soc fel biochem, Nat Inst Res Dairying, Reading, Eng, 63-65. *Concurrent Pos:* Sabbatical leave, Cancer Res Lab, 71-72; mem, Exp Biol Comt, Breast Cancer Task Force, Nat Cancer Inst, 73-76, Carcinogenesis Comt, 76-79, Cancer Cause & Prev Comt, 79-81, Reproductive Endocrinol Comt, 85-87; sabbatical leave, Transplantation Biol Sect, Clin Res Ctr, Harrow, Eng, 78-79; ed, Tissue Cult Asn Report, 86-90; reviewing ed, In Vitro Cellular & Develop Biol, 90-; chairperson student affairs & awards, Soc In Vitro Biol, 93- *Mem:* Fel AAAS; Am Asn Can Res; Soc Exp Biol & Med; Tissue Cult Asn; Brit Soc Endocrinol; Sigma Xi. *Res:* Biology of mammary tumors; hormonal control of mammary development in vivo and in vitro. *Mailing Add:* Dept Zool Mich State Univ East Lansing MI 48824-1115. *Fax:* 202-432-2789; *E-Mail:* riverae@pilot.msu.edu

RIVERA, EZEQUIEL RAMIREZ, ELECTRON MICROSCOPY, ULTRASTRUCTURE. *Current Pos:* from asst prof to assoc prof, 74-85, PROF BIOL SCI, UNIV LOWELL, MASS, 85- *Personal Data:* b Alpine, Tex, Oct 17, 42; m 70, Dorkmai Koonwong; c 1. *Educ:* Sul Ross State Col, Tex, BS, 64; Purdue Univ, MS, 67; Univ Tex, Austin, PhD(biol sci & bot), 73. *Prof Exp:* Res technician bot & plant pathol, Purdue Univ, 66-67; clin lab technician clin chem, US Army, Ft Dix, NJ, 67; asst chief biochem & toxicol, 6th US Army Med Lab, Ft Baker, Calif, 68; chief biochem, 376th Med Lab, US Army Support, Thailand, 69-70; instr bot, Univ Tex, Austin, 72; asst prof biol, Univ Notre Dame, Ind, 73-74. *Concurrent Pos:* Referee, Scanning Electron Micros, 80-, Protoplasma Int J Cell Biol, 82-; guest assoc prof trop med, Mahidol Univ, Bangkok, Thailand, 81; dir biol sci, New Eng Soc Electron Micros, 82, from vpres to pres, 83-84, dir, 85; testing, Univ Lowell Res Found, 83-; referee, Physiol, Cellular & Molecular Biol Comt, NSF, 83-; guest adv med indust, Univ Perpignan, Perpignan, France, 86; pres, Univ Mass-Lowell Club, Sigma Xi, 89-93. *Mem:* Bot Soc Am; Am Soc Plant Physiologists; Micros Soc Am; Sigma Xi. *Res:* Ultrastructure of overwintering and desert plants; cytochemistry of secretory components in marine snails; cytology of schistosome development; plant physiology of carbon 13/carbon 12 fractionation and calcium oxalate; spermatogenesis in snails, fish. *Mailing Add:* Dept Biol Univ Mass Lowell Lowell MA 01854. *Fax:* 978-934-3044

RIVERA, WILLIAM HENRY, ANALYTICAL CHEMISTRY. *Current Pos:* RETIRED. *Personal Data:* b El Paso, Tex, Jan 26, 31; m 58, Margaret Mary Mattingly; c Kathleen Maha (Cook), Julie Ann (Gurule), Amy Susan (Henderson), William Henry Jr & Margaret Ann (Lugo). *Educ:* Univ Louisville, BS, 53, PhD(chem), 62. *Prof Exp:* Nuclear engr, Gen Dynamics/Ft Worth, 56-58; asst chem, Univ Louisville, 58-62; from asst prof to assoc prof chem, Univ Tex, El Paso, 62-80, asst grad dean, 73-76, assoc prof, 85-95; asst to vpres acad affairs, US Naval Acad, 76-80, Chem Dept, 80-85, chmn dept, 81-85. *Concurrent Pos:* Consult, Nuclear Effects Directorate, White Sands Missile Range, NMex, 64- *Mem:* Am Chem Soc; Am Soc Testing & Mat; Sigma Xi. *Res:* Radiation effects on organic materials, radiation induced polymerization; photon and neutron activation analysis; dosimetry; environmental analysis; radiation protection. *Mailing Add:* Chem Dept Univ Tex El Paso TX 79902

RIVERA-CALIMLIM, LEONOR, NEUROPSYCHOPHARMACOLOGY. *Current Pos:* Assoc prof, 76-94, EMER PROF PHARMACOL, DEPT PHARMACOL, SCH MED & DENT, UNIV ROCHESTER, 94- *Educ:* Univ St Tomas, Manila, Phillipines, MD, 53. *Res:* Drugs in Parkinsonism; drugs in psychiatry. *Mailing Add:* 33 Hickering Ridge Rd Rochester NY 14625

RIVERO, JUAN ARTURO, HERPETOLOGY. *Current Pos:* from instr to assoc prof, 43-58, dir inst marine biol & zool garden, 54-63, dir dept biol, Univ, 59-60, actg dean arts & sci, 62-63, dean, 63-66, PROF ZOOL, UNIV PR, MAYAGUEZ, 58- *Personal Data:* b Santurce, PR, Mar 5, 23; m, Eneida Bordallo; c 2. *Educ:* Univ PR, BS, 45; Harvard Univ, MA, 51, PhD(biol), 52. *Honors & Awards:* Distinguished prof, Univ PR, 87- *Prof Exp:* Asst plant physiologist, Inst Trop Agr, PR, 45. *Concurrent Pos:* Assoc, Mus Comp Zool, Harvard Univ, 68; Guggenheim Found fel, 70; temporary investr, Venezuelan Inst Sci Invests; Herpet League fel; distinguished investr, Univ Puerto Rico, 85. *Mem:* AAAS; Asn Island Marine Labs Caribbean (pres, 58-60); corresp mem Soc Venezolana de Ciencias Naturales; PR Acad Arts & Sci; Soc La Salle Ciencias Naturales. *Res:* Currently authoring three books. *Mailing Add:* Dept Biol Univ PR Col Cont Sta Mayaguez PR 00708

RIVERS, DOUGLAS BERNARD, FERMENTATION MICROBIOLOGY, ENVIRONMENTAL BIOREMEDIATION. *Current Pos:* head, Fermentation & Bioprocess Technol Sect, 87-93, MGR, APPL & ENVIRON MICROBIOL GROUP & MGR, BIOTECHNOL PROG, SOUTHERN RES INST, 93- *Personal Data:* b Beatrice, Nebr, May 24, 51; m 83, Diane Shock; c 2. *Educ:* Kans State Univ, BS, 74; Auburn Univ, MS, 76; Univ Ark, PhD(microbiol), 83. *Prof Exp:* Biochemist, Gulf Oil Corp, 76-79, group leader, 79; res assoc, Univ Ark, 79-83, asst prof microbiol, 84; sr microbiologist, Archer Daniels Midland Co, 84-86; sr biotechnologist, Southern Res Inst, 86-87. *Concurrent Pos:* Adj prof, Dept Biology, Univ Ala, Birmingham. *Mem:* Am Soc Microbiol; Soc Indust Microbiol; Am Soc Qual Control. *Res:* Environmental bioremediation; process development through biochemical engineering in foods, specialty chemicals and commodity chemicals; fermentations and separations to produce enzymes, ethanol and monoclonal antibodies; diagonostics based on Enzyme-Linked Immunosorbent Assay technology; technology assessments. *Mailing Add:* 3818 Viceroy Apt 5 Okemos MI 48864. *Fax:* 205-581-2877

RIVERS, JERRY MARGARET, NUTRITION. *Current Pos:* RETIRED. *Personal Data:* b Bogota, Tex, Sept 29, 29. *Educ:* Tex Tech Univ, BS, 51, MS, 58; Pa State Univ, PhD(nutrit, biochem), 61. *Prof Exp:* Dietitian, USPHS, 51-53 & Methodist Hosp, 53-57; from asst prof to emer prof nutrit, Cornell Univ, 62-88; adj res prof, Univ Tex, 88-90. *Concurrent Pos:* Res grants, NIH, 63-, Nutrit Found, 66- & USDA, 78-; fels, Mary Swantz Rose, General Foods, Mead Johnson; adj prof, Univ Tex, 85- *Mem:* Am Dietetic Asn; Am Inst Nutrit; Sigma Xi; Am Home Econ Asn. *Res:* Ascorbic acid metabolism. *Mailing Add:* PO Box 145 610 Braley Hill Rd Brooktondale NY 14817

RIVERS, JESSIE MARKERT, ORGANIC CHEMISTRY, NATURAL PRODUCTS CHEMISTRY. *Current Pos:* SR RES CHEMIST TOBACCO CHEM, R J REYNOLDS TOBACCO CO, 77- *Personal Data:* b Elizabeth City, NC, July 9, 49; m 71. *Educ:* Meredith Col, AB, 71; NC State Univ, PhD(org chem), 78. *Mem:* Am Chem Soc; Sigma Xi. *Res:* Isolation, characterization and synthesis of naturally occurring tobacco constituents; relationship of tobacco chemistry to tobacco utilization. *Mailing Add:* 213 E King St Edenton NC 27932

RIVERS, PAUL MICHAEL, ORGANIC CHEMISTRY, ANALYTICAL CHEMISTRY. *Current Pos:* Sr chemist, 70-71, dir qual control & dir, Anal Dept, 71-84, DIR CORP ENVIRON AFFAIRS, REILLY TAR & CHEM CORP, 84- *Personal Data:* b Schenectady, NY, July 18, 44; m 66; c 2. *Educ:* LeMoyne Col, BS, 66; Univ Notre Dame, Ind, PhD(org chem), 70. *Mem:* Am Chem Soc; Am Soc Testing Mats. *Res:* Gas and liquid chromatographic separation of pyridine derivatives; analytical methods in air and water pollution control; isolation and identification of organic chemicals. *Mailing Add:* 8244 Colt Dr Plainfield IN 46168-9755

RIVERS, WILLIAM J(ONES), FLUID MECHANICS & POWER, HYDRAULICS. *Current Pos:* PROF MECH ENG, CALIF STATE UNIV, NORTHRIDGE, 65-, CHAIR, MECH ENG DEPT, 93- *Personal Data:* b Lakeland, Fla, May 28, 36; div; c 2. *Educ:* Univ Fla, BME, 59; Purdue Univ, MSME, 61, PhD(mech eng), 64; Univ Southern Calif, MSAE, 70. *Honors & Awards:* Ralph R Teetor Award, Soc Automotive Engrs, 70. *Prof Exp:* Sr res engr, Rocketdyne Div, NAm Aviation, Inc, 64-65. *Concurrent Pos:* Res engr, Rocketdyne Div, NAm Aviation, Inc, 65-66; develop engr, Marquardt Corp, 66-67; thermodynamics engr, Lockheed Calif Co, 68-69; NSF fac fel, Univ Southern Calif, 69-70; tech consult, Peerless Pump Co, 71-72. *Mem:* Am Soc Mech Engrs. *Res:* Centrifugal pump performance and axial thrust; fluid power systems; experimental methods. *Mailing Add:* Mech Eng Dept Calif State Univ Northridge CA 91330. *Fax:* 818-677-2140; *E-Mail:* wrivers@csun.edu

RIVES, JOHN EDGAR, SPECTROSCOPY & SPECTROMETRY. *Current Pos:* from asst prof to prof, 63-96, EMER PROF PHYSICS, UNIV GA, 96- *Personal Data:* b Birmingham, Ala, 1933; m 94, Diane B Barret; c Joel M, John D, Paula J, Rebecca J, Stephen D & Patrick C. *Educ:* Auburn Univ, BS, 55; Duke Univ, PhD(physics), 62. *Prof Exp:* Asst prof physics, Univ Ga, 59-60; instr & res assoc, Duke Univ, 61-63. *Concurrent Pos:* Consult, Oak Ridge Nat Lab, 67-68. *Mem:* Fel Am Phys Soc; Am Asn Univ Professors; Sigma Xi. *Res:* Optical properties of solids; laser induced phonon physics; heat transport in magnetic insulators; atmospheric ultraviolet monitoring. *Mailing Add:* Dept Physics & Astron Univ Ga Athens GA 30602. *Fax:* 706-542-2492; *E-Mail:* jerives@nal.physast.uga.edu

RIVEST, BRIAN ROGER, INVERTEBRATE REPRODUCTIVE BIOLOGY, BIOLOGY OF GASTROPODS. *Current Pos:* asst prof, 81-88, ASSOC PROF INVERT ZOOL, ZOOL MARINE BIOL & INTROD BIOL, STATE UNIV NY, CORTLAND, 88- *Personal Data:* b Schenectady, NY, May 16, 50; m 75; c 2. *Educ:* Cornell Univ, BS, 72; Univ NH, MS, 75; Univ Wash, PhD(zool), 81. *Prof Exp:* Actg assoc dir invert zool, Fri Harbor Labs, Univ Wash, 80-81. *Concurrent Pos:* Vis assoc prof, Shoals Marine Lab, Cornell Univ, 82- *Mem:* Am Soc Zoologists; Western Soc Naturalists; AAAS; Am Malacological Union. *Res:* Developmental patterns and reproductive biology of gastropod molluscs, with special interest in extra embryonic sources of nutrition. *Mailing Add:* Biol Dept State Univ NY PO Box 2000 Cortland NY 13045-0900

RIVEST, RONALD L, CRYPTOGRAPHY. *Current Pos:* PROF COMPUT SCI, MASS INST TECHNOL, 74- *Educ:* Yale Univ, BS, 69; Stanford Univ, PhD(comput sci), 74. *Mem:* Nat Acad Eng; Inst Elec & Electronics Engrs; Asn Comput Mach. *Mailing Add:* Mass Inst Technol 545 Technology Sq Rm 324 Cambridge MA 02139

RIVETT, ROBERT WYMAN, BIOCHEMISTRY. *Current Pos:* RETIRED. *Personal Data:* b Omaha, Nebr, Jan 20, 21; m 40, Myra J Bevins; c 3. *Educ:* Univ Nebr, BS, 42, MS, 43; Univ Wis, PhD(biochem), 46. *Prof Exp:* Res microbiologist, Abbott Labs, 46-48, group leader antibiotic develop, 48-57, asst to dir develop, 57-58, mgr develop, 58-59, dir, 59-64, dir, Sci Admin & Serv, 64-71; dir, Corp Qual Assurance Stand & Audits, 71-76, dir, Qual Assurance Agr & Vet Div, 76-77, Sci Prod Div, 77-78, vpres, Alpha Therapeut Corp, Qual Assurance, 78-82; consult, pharmaceut & related fields, 82-88. *Mem:* Am Chem Soc; Am Inst Chem EngrS; Am Soc Qual Control. *Res:* Organic chemistry; nutrition of bacteria; natural products; streptolin; fermentation equipment. *Mailing Add:* 3303 Taos Ct Deming NM 88030-9601

RIVIER, CATHERINE L, REPRODUCTIVE ENDOCRINOLOGY. *Current Pos:* ASSOC RES PROF, CLAYTON FEDN LABS, PEPTIDE BIOL. *Personal Data:* b Vaud, Switzerland, June 21, 43; m 67; c 2. *Educ:* Univ Lausanne, Switzerland, Lic es Sci, 68, PhD, 72. *Prof Exp:* Fel, 72-74, sr res assoc, 74-79, asst res prof, Salk Inst, 79- *Mem:* Endocrine Soc; Am Physiol Soc; Soc Neurosci; Soc Study Reproduction; Res Soc Alcoholism. *Res:* Mechanism of control of prolactin, gonadotropin and adrenocorticotrophic hormone secretion. *Mailing Add:* Salk Inst 10010 Torrey Pine Rd La Jolla CA 92037

RIVIER, JEAN E F, NEUROENDOCRINOLOGY. *Current Pos:* res assoc, Saik Inst, 70-73, from asst prof to assoc prof, 73-83, assoc prof & sr res mem, 84-89, PROF, SAIK INST, 89- *Personal Data:* b Casablanca, Morocco, July 14, 41; US citizen; m 67; c 2. *Educ:* Univ Lausanne, PhD, 68. *Honors & Awards:* Vincent der Vigneaud Award, 90; Signey H Ingbar Distinguished Serv Awrad, Endocrine Soc, 95. *Prof Exp:* Fel, Univ Lausanne, 69; fel, Rice Univ, Houston, Tex, 69-70. *Concurrent Pos:* Bd dir, Ferring Res Inst, Inc. *Mem:* Am Chem Soc; Endocrine Soc; Protein Soc; Am Peptide Soc; Am Soc Biochem & Molecular Biol. *Res:* Neuroendocrinology involved in isolation and analysis of new peptide hormones, their total synthesis and pharmacology; neuroendocrinology involved in isolation and analysis of new peptide hormones and endotoxins, their total synthesis, pharmacology and drug design. *Mailing Add:* Salk Inst 10010 N Torrey Pines Rd La Jolla CA 92037-1002

RIVIER, NICOLAS YVES, GLASS, MANY-BODY THEORY. *Current Pos:* PROF THEORET PHYSICS, UNIV LOUIS PASTEUR, STRASBOURG, 93- *Personal Data:* b Lausanne, Switz, Aug 5, 41; m 71, Lynn McElroy; c Andre, Catherine & Samuel. *Educ:* Univ Lausanne, dipl physics, 65; Cambridge Univ, PhD(physics), 68. *Prof Exp:* Asst prof physics, Univ Calif, Los Angeles, 68-69, lectr, Riverside, 69-70; lectr, Imp Col, 70-86, reader theoret solid state physics, 86-93. *Concurrent Pos:* Vis prof, Univ Fed Da Paraiba, Brazil, 73-77, Univ Provence, France, 79-82, Univ Porto, Port, 82, Univ Lausanne & Geneva, Switz, 85 & Lausanne Univ, 90; vis scientist, Inst Theoret Physics, Univ Calif, Santa Barbara, 83, Los Alamos Nat Lab, 84 & Argonne Nat Lab, 87-90; mem, Fr Phys Soc. *Mem:* Am Phys Soc; Europ Phys Soc; Inst Physics. *Res:* Glass structure and properties; gauge aspects of condensed matter; geometry and topology of disorder; cellular networks, structure and evolution; maximum entropy inference; quasicrystals; grain boundaries. *Mailing Add:* Phys Theoret Lab 3 Rue de L'Universite Strasbourg 67084 France. *Fax:* 33-88-35-81-82

RIVIERE, GEORGE ROBERT, IMMUNOLOGY, DENTISTRY. *Current Pos:* PROF & CHMN DEPT ORAL BIOL, SCH DENT, UNIV MO, KANS CITY, 87- *Personal Data:* b Decatur, Ill, Feb 26, 43; m 71; c 2. *Educ:* Drake Univ, BA, 66; Univ Ill, Chicago Med Ctr, BSD, 66, DDS, 68, MS, 70; Univ Calif, Los Angeles, PhD(immunol), 73. *Prof Exp:* Researcher, Dent Res Inst, USN, 73-75; from asst prof to assoc prof, Univ Calif, Los Angeles, 75-81, prof, Sch Med & Dent, Dent Res Inst, 82-97. *Concurrent Pos:* USPHS fel, Nat Inst Dent Res, 73-75; prin investr, Nat Inst Dent res grant, 76-83 & NIH career res develop award, 77-82. *Mem:* Int Asn Dent Res; Sigma Xi; AAAS; Am Asn Immunologists. *Res:* Transplantation immunology; immunogenetics; regulation of immune responses, especially immunity to enteric microorganisms and role of immunity in development. *Mailing Add:* Dept Pediat Dent Ore Health Sci Univ 611 SW Campus Dr Portland OR 97201-3097

RIVIERE, JIM EDMOND, PHARMACOKINETICS, TOXICOLOGY. *Current Pos:* prof toxicol, 88-92, BURROUGHS WELLCOME DISTINGUISHED PROF VET PHARMACOL, NC STATE UNIV, 92- *Personal Data:* b New Bedford, Mass, Mar 3, 53; m 76; c 3. *Educ:* Boston Col, BS, 76, MS, 76; Purdue Univ, DVM & PhD(pharmacol), 80. *Honors & Awards:* Beecham Award Res Excellence, 86; Ebert Prize, Am Pharmaceut Asn, 91. *Prof Exp:* Assoc pharmacol, Purdue Univ, 80-81; from asst prof to assoc prof, NC State Univ, 81-88. *Concurrent Pos:* Prin investr, NIH, Environ Protection Agency, US Army Med Res & Develop Command & USDA, 84-, expert panelist, Dermal Toxicol Workshops, 88; dir, Cutaneous Pharmacol & Toxicol Ctr, NC State Univ, 88-; ed, J Vet Pharmacol Therapeut, 89-93. *Mem:* Soc Toxicol; Am Vet Med Asn; Am Acad Vet Pharmacol & Therapeut; Sigma Xi; Am Asn Pharmaceut Scientists. *Res:* Dermatopharmacology; cutaneous toxicology; toxicokinetics of drug and chemical percutaneous absorption using invivo and invitro animal models; drug residues; author of six books and 250 manuscripts; granted 4 US patents. *Mailing Add:* Col Vet Med Cutaneous Pharmacol Toxicol Ctr NC State Univ 4700 Hillborough St Raleigh NC 27606. *Fax:* 919-829-4358; *E-Mail:* jim_riviere@ncsu.edu

RIVIN, DONALD, SURFACE CHEMISTRY, ADSORPTION & TEXTILE PROPERTIES. *Current Pos:* chief, Mat Sect, 88-92, group leader mat, 93-95, PRIN SCIENTIST, US ARMY NATICK RD&E CTR, 95- *Personal Data:* b Brooklyn, NY, Oct 5, 34; m 56, Marcia T Siegel; c Nancy, Alissa, Russell & Rachel. *Educ:* Columbia Univ, BA, 55, MA, 57, PhD(chem), 62. *Prof Exp:* Res chemist, Cabot Corp, Billerica, 59-61, group leader org chem, 61-69, sr res assoc, Fine Particle Technol Dept, 69-74, dir, 74-80, corp res fel & dir environ health, 80-88. *Concurrent Pos:* Chmn, Environ Health Asn, 78-81; vchmn, Resource Recovery Coun, 80-84. *Mem:* AAAS; Am Chem Soc; Catalysis Soc; Am Carbon Soc; Sigma Xi. *Res:* Adsorption and reactions on carbon and oxide surfaces; heterogeneous catalysis; organic reaction mechanisms; environmental chemistry; adsorption properties of colloidal and microporous solids; liquid interaction with textiles. *Mailing Add:* US Army Natick RD&E Ctr Natick MA 01760-5019

RIVIN, EVGENY (EUGENE) I, PROBLEM SOLVING, VIBRATION CONTROL. *Current Pos:* PROF MECH ENG, WAYNE STATE UNIV, 81-, DIR, MACH TOOL RES, 85- *Personal Data:* Igor & Natasha. *Educ:* Moscow Mach Tools Inst, Engr, 54, Cand Sci(mach design), 62; USSR Supreme Attefsation Bd, DSc, 71. *Honors & Awards:* Shingo Prize Excellence in Mfg, 91. *Prof Exp:* Sr engr, Moscow Movie Camera Plant, 54-57; sr scientist mach tools, Exp Res Inst, 57-68; head, Lab Vibration Control, Inst Stand, Moscow, 68-75; prin staff engr, Ford Motor Co, 76-81. *Concurrent Pos:* Chmn, Russ Lit Comt, Am Soc Mech Engrs, 84-87; vis prof, Inst Sound & Vibration Res, 87; ed, Vibration Eng J, 87-91; in-house consult, Gen Motors Corp, 88; prin res engr, Ford Motor Co, 94-95; co-prin, Triz Group, 95- *Mem:* Fel Am Soc Mech Engrs; Int Inst Prod Eng Res; Soc Mfg Engrs. *Res:* Methodology for advanced machine components; solving vibration control problems; principles of mechanical design of robots. *Mailing Add:* Wayne State Univ 5050 Anthony Wayne Dr Detroit MI 48202. *Fax:* 313-577-8789; *E-Mail:* rivin@eng.wayne.edu

RIVKIN, ISRAEL, IMMUNOLOGY. *Current Pos:* PRIN SCIENTIST, DEPT INFLAMMATION & ALLERGY, SCHERING CORP, 78- *Personal Data:* b Rochester, NY, Feb 14, 38; m 65; c 4. *Educ:* Yeshiva Univ, BA, 59; NY Univ, MS, 68; Univ Conn, PhD(immunol), 74. *Prof Exp:* Res asst rheumatology, Downtown Med Ctr, State Univ NY, 64-65; res assoc biochem pharmacol, Squibb Inst Med Res, 68-70, sr res investr immunol, 73-78. *Concurrent Pos:* Squibb sabbatical fel, 70. *Mem:* NY Acad Sci; AAAS. *Res:* The study of the effects of drugs on in vitro and in vivo neutrophil and monocycle chemotaxis; design biological systems for testing new anti-inflammatory drugs. *Mailing Add:* 1 Opatut Ct Edison NJ 08817

RIVKIN, MAXCY, CONTROL SYSTEMS, PAPER SCIENCE. *Current Pos:* Group leader tech serv papermaking systs, Kraft Div, Westvaco Corp, 63-70, group leader process systs, Covington Res Ctr, 70-78, dir res, Laurel Res Ctr, 78-87, MGR CORP ENG, WESTVACO CORP, 92-, VPRES, 94- *Personal Data:* b Columbia, SC, Mar 31, 37; m 59, Judith Hirschman; c Victor & Jan. *Educ:* Univ SC, BS, 59. *Prof Exp:* Indust dir, Rigesa Ltd, Valinlos, Sao Paulo,

Brazil, 87-91. *Mem:* Tech Asn Pulp & Paper Indust; Instrument Soc Am; NY Acad Sci; Soc Rheology. *Res:* Development and implementation of experimental or prototype process control systems in the manufacture of pulp and paper and of allied products; development and implementation of systems for the management of research and technology; properties of coated papers. *Mailing Add:* 10028 Century Dr Ellicott City MD 21042

RIVKIN, RICHARD BOB, BIOLOGICAL OCEANOGRAPHY. *Current Pos:* ASSOC PROF, MEM UNIV NFLD. *Personal Data:* b Brooklyn, NY, Nov 17, 49; div; c 3. *Educ:* City Col New York, BS, 72, MS, 75; Univ RI, PhD(biol sci), 79. *Prof Exp:* Assoc res scientist phytoplankton ecol, Johns Hopkins Univ, 78; staff mem, Horn Pt Environ Lab, Univ Md. *Mem:* Am Soc Limnol & Oceanog; Phycol Soc Am; Am Soc Plant Physiologists; Sigma Xi. *Res:* Phytoplankton nutrient physiology and biochemistry; phytoplankton ecology; interactions of water motion and phytoplankton ecology. *Mailing Add:* Ocean Scis Ctr Mem Univ Nfld St John's NF A1C 5S7 Can

RIVLIN, RICHARD S, DRUG-NUTRIENT INTERACTIONS, VITAMIN METABOLISM. *Current Pos:* CHIEF NUTRIT SERV, MEM SLOAN-KETTERING CANCER CTR, 79-; PROF MED, CORNELL UNIV MED COL, 79- *Personal Data:* b Forest Hills, NY, May 15, 34; m 60, 76; c 4. *Educ:* Harvard Univ, AB, 55, MD, 59; Am Bd Internal Med, dipl, 69. *Honors & Awards:* Grace A Goldsmith Lect Award, Am Col Nutrit, 81; Scroll of Appreciation, Am Fedn Aging Res, 85; Virgil Sydenstricker Lectr, Med Col Georgia, 89. *Prof Exp:* Attend physician med serv, Baltimore City Hosps, 64-66; assoc med, Col Physicians & Surgeons, 66-67; from asst prof to assoc prof med, 67-79; chief & asst physician endocrinol, Francis Delafield Hosp, 66-75. *Concurrent Pos:* Lectr clin med, Johns Hopkins Univ Sch Med, 65-66; chief nutrit div, NY Hosp-Cornell Med Ctr, 79-; prin investr, Clin Nutrit Res Unit, 80-; prin investr, Clin Nutrit Res Unit, 80-; ser ed, Contemp Issues Clin Nutrit, 81-; vis prof, Univ Ariz, Tucson, 84 & Wright State Univ, Dayton, Ohio, 85; consult diet, nutrit & cancer, Am Cancer Soc, 85-; mem, Nat Adv Comt Colorectal Cancer, Am Cancer Soc, 85-; mem, Nat Sci Adv Coun, Am Fedn Aging, 85-; mem Black-White Survival Study, NIH Sci Adv Comt, Nat Cancer Inst, 85-; mem coun, Am Soc Clin Nutrit, 89. *Mem:* Am Soc Clin Nutrit; Am Inst Nutrit; Am Soc Clin Invest; Soc Exp Biol & Med; fel Am Col Physicians; Am Physiol Soc. *Res:* Inhibition of flavin biosynthesis by Adriamycin in rat skeletal muscle and mechanisms underlying the differential effects of ethanol on the bio-availability of riboflavin and flavin-adenine dinucleotide; chlorpromazine and quinacrine inhibit flavin-adenine dinucleotide biosynthesis in skeletal muscle and alteration in age-related decline of beta-adrenergic receptor binding in adipocytes during riboflavin deficiency. *Mailing Add:* Mem Sloan-Kettering Cancer Ctr 1275 York Ave New York NY 10021-6094

RIVLIN, RONALD SAMUEL, APPLIED MATHEMATICS. *Current Pos:* centennial univ prof & dir, Ctr Appln Math, 67-80, adj prof, 80-81, EMER PROF, LEHIGH UNIV, 81- *Personal Data:* b London, Eng, May 6, 15; m 48; c 1. *Educ:* Cambridge Univ, BA, 37, MA, 39, ScD(math), 52. *Hon Degrees:* DSc, Univ Ireland & Univ Nottingham, Eng, 80, Tulane Univ, 82, Univ Thessaloniki, 84. *Honors & Awards:* Bingham Medal, Soc Rheology, 58; Panetti Prize, Acad Sci, Turin, 75; Timoshenko Medal, Am Soc Mech Engrs, 87. *Prof Exp:* Res scientist, Res Labs, Gen Elec Co, Ltd, 37-42; sci officer, Ministry Aircraft Prod, Telecommun Res Estab, 42-44; from physicist to supt res, Brit Rubber Producers Res Asn, 44-52; consult, US Naval Res Labs, 52-53; prof appl math, Brown Univ, 53-63, chmn, Div Appl Math, 58-63, L Herbert Ballou Univ prof, 63-67. *Concurrent Pos:* Guest scientist, Nat Bur Stand, 46-47; res scientist, Davy-Faraday Lab, Royal Inst, London, 47-52; vis lectr, Calif Inst Technol, 53; Guggenheim fel, Univ Rome, 61-62; mem mech adv comt, Nat Bur Stand, 65-70; mem, Comt Appln Math, Nat Res Coun, 65-68; vis prof, Univ Paris, 66-67; mem, Nat Comt Theoret & Appl Mech, 72-80, chmn, 76-78; Alexander von Humboldt sr scientist award, 81; fel, Inst Advan Study, Berlin, 84-85; distiguished vis prof, Univ Del, 85-86. *Mem:* Nat Acad Eng; fel Am Acad Arts & Sci; Soc Rheology; fel Am Soc Mech Engrs; hon mem Mexican Soc Rheology; fel Soc Eng Sci; fel Am Phys Soc; fel Acad Mech; hon mem Royal Irish Acad; hon mem Acad Naz d Lincei. *Res:* Finite elasticity; physics of rubber; continuum mechanics of viscoelastic solids and fluids. *Mailing Add:* 1604 Merryweather Dr Bethlehem PA 18015

RIVLIN, THEODORE J, MATHEMATICS. *Current Pos:* MATHEMATICIAN, IBM CORP, 59- *Personal Data:* b Brooklyn, NY, Sept 11, 26. *Educ:* Brooklyn Col, BA, 48; Harvard Univ, MA, 50, PhD(math), 53. *Prof Exp:* Instr math, Johns Hopkins Univ, 52-55; asst, Inst Math Sci, NY Univ, 55-56; sr math analyst, Engine Div, Fairchild Engine & Aircraft Corp, 56-59. *Mem:* Am Math Soc; Soc Indust & Appl Math; Math Asn Am. *Res:* Approximation theory; function theory; numerical analysis. *Mailing Add:* 41 Cowdin Circle Chappaqua NY 10514

RIXON, RAYMOND HARWOOD, LIVER REGENERATION, ENDOCRINOLOGY. *Current Pos:* RETIRED. *Personal Data:* b Vancouver, BC, July 17, 26; m 57; c 4. *Educ:* Univ BC, BA, 48, MA, 50; Univ Western Ont, PhD(physiol), 55. *Prof Exp:* Fel physiol, Fac Med, Univ Western Ont, 55-56; asst res officer, Atomic Energy Can Ltd, 56-62, assoc res officer, 62-68; assoc res officer, Div Biol, Nat Res Coun Can, 68-70, sr res officer, 70-93; info officer, Joseph F Morgan Res Found, 93-96. *Res:* Physiological and biochemical control of cell proliferation (especially liver regeneration) and osteophoresis. *Mailing Add:* 9 Parklane Ct Gloucester ON K1B 3H3 Can

RIZACK, MARTIN A, BIOCHEMISTRY, PHARMACOLOGY & MEDICINE. *Current Pos:* asst physician, Rockefeller Univ, 57-60, assoc prof & assoc physician, 60-65, assoc dean grad studies, 68-74, assoc prof, head lab cellular biochem & pharmacol & physician, 65-90, EMER PROF, ROCKEFELLER UNIV, 90- *Personal Data:* b New York, NY, Nov 19, 26; m 64, 87, Angeline R Mastri; c 5. *Educ:* Columbia Univ, MD, 50; Rockefeller Univ, PhD, 60; Am Bd Internal Med, dipl, 57, recertified, 74. *Prof Exp:* Intern, Cornell Med Div, Bellevue Hosp, 50-51, asst resident physician, 51; asst resident physician, St Luke's Hosp, 53-55, chief resident physician, 55-56, res assoc, 56-57. *Concurrent Pos:* Fel, Rockefeller Univ, 57-60; asst attend physician, St Luke's Hosp, 60-71, assoc attend physician, 71-80, adj sr attend physician, 80-; consult ed, Med Lett, 74- *Mem:* Fel Am Col Physicians; Am Soc Pharmacol & Exp Therapeut; Am Soc Bio chem & Molecular Biol. *Res:* Biochemistry and physiology of hormone action; lipolytic enzymes; biochemical pharmacology. *Mailing Add:* Rockefeller Univ 1230 York Ave New York NY 10021-6399. *Fax:* 201-327-8287; *E-Mail:* rizack@rockvax.rockefeller.edu

RIZKALLA, SAMI H, STRUCTURAL ENGINEERING, BRIDGES. *Current Pos:* from asst prof to assoc prof, 79-88, PROF STRUCT, UNIV MAN, CAN, 88-, DIR STRUCT ENG, RES & DEVELOP FACIL & ASSOC DEAN ENG, 92-, CONSULT ENG STRUCT, 80- *Personal Data:* b Alexandria, Egypt, Feb 5, 45; Can citizen; m 70, Mary Y; c Carolyn R & Natalie R. *Educ:* Alexandria Univ, Egypt, BSc, 65; NC State Univ, MSc, 74, PhD(civil), 76. *Prof Exp:* struct engr, Vibro Cast-in-place, Piles, Egypt, 65-66 & Govt Egypt, 66-68; instr civil, Alexandria Univ, Egypt, 68-71; grad teaching civil, NC State Univ, 71-76; fel civil, Univ Alta, Can, 76-78. *Concurrent Pos:* Consult engr, Gonda, Egypt, F Saleh, USA & Con Force St, Can, 81-84, Penner & Keeler Partners, Reid Crowther, Can Nat, 84-88 & Wardrop Eng, Dillon Eng & ID Eng, 89-; vis prof, NSW, Sydney, Australia, Nagaoka Tech Univ & Yamanashi Univ, Japan, 88; vpres, Prairie Region, Can Soc Civil Eng, 89-91, chmn, Struct Div, 91- *Mem:* Fel Can Soc Civil Engrs; fel Am Concrete Inst; fel Am Soc Civil Engrs; Prestressed Concrete Inst; Japanese Soc Civil Eng; Can Standard Asn. *Res:* Behaviour of reinforced concrete and prestressed concrete structures; laboratory and field testing of structures; durability of concrete; wooden poles for hydro transmission; use of advanced composite material in civil engineering application. *Mailing Add:* 7 Prestwood Pl Winnipeg MB R3T 4Y9 Can. *Fax:* 204-275-3773

RIZKI, TAHIR MIRZA, DEVELOPMENTAL GENETICS, CELL BIOLOGY. *Current Pos:* assoc prof, 61-64, PROF BIOL, UNIV MICH, ANN ARBOR, 64- *Personal Data:* b Hyderabad, India, Jan 8, 24; nat US; m 49; c 3. *Educ:* Osmania Univ, India, BSc, 44; Muslim Univ, MSc, 46; Columbia Univ, PhD(zool), 53. *Prof Exp:* Demonstr zool, Muslim Univ, 45-46, lectr, 46-48; asst, Columbia Univ, 51-52; Cramer res fel genetics, Dartmouth Col, 52-54; Am Cancer Soc fel, Yale Univ, 54-56; from asst prof to assoc prof biol, Reed Col, 56-61. *Mem:* AAAS; Am Soc Zoologists; Am Soc Naturalists; Sigma Xi; Soc Invert Path. *Res:* Developmental genetics of Drosophila; biology of hemocytes and melanotic tumors in Drosophila; parasitoids of Drosophila; cell death. *Mailing Add:* 1230 Ardmoor Ave Ann Arbor MI 48103

RIZZA, PAUL FREDERICK, CARTOGRAPHY. *Current Pos:* asst prof geog, Slippery Rock Univ, 72-75, chmn geog & cartog, 72-78, assoc prof, 75-78, actg dean, Sch Social & Behav Sci, 78-80, PROF & CHMN GEOG & ENVIRON STUDIES DEPT, SLIPPERY ROCK UNIV, 81- *Personal Data:* b New Britain, Conn, Dec 15, 38; m 79; c 3. *Educ:* Cent Conn State Col, BS, 65, MS, 68; Univ Ga, PhD(geog), 73. *Prof Exp:* Teacher geog & hist, Haddam Sch, Conn, 65-67; teacher world human geog, Univ Ga, 68-70. *Concurrent Pos:* Sr Fulbright scholar, Coun Int Exchange Scholars, Finland, 76; vis prof, Helsinki Sch Econ, Finland, 81. *Mem:* Asn Am Geogr; Am Cong Surv & Mapping; Am Geog Soc; NAm Cartog Info Soc. *Res:* Rural land use in the United States and Scandinavia; thematic cartography. *Mailing Add:* Dept Geog & Environ Studies Slippery Rock Univ Slippery Rock PA 16057

RIZZI, GEORGE PETER, ORGANIC CHEMISTRY. *Current Pos:* RES CHEMIST, MIAMI VALLEY LABS, PROCTER & GAMBLE CO, 64- *Personal Data:* b Middletown, Conn, Sept 25, 37; m 59; c 2. *Educ:* Worcester Polytech Inst, BS, 59, MS, 61, PhD(org chem), 63. *Prof Exp:* Res assoc chem, Stanford Univ, 63-64. *Mem:* Am Chem Soc; Sigma Xi. *Res:* Organic synthesis; natural products; flavors; organic reactions involved in biochemical processes. *Mailing Add:* 542 Blossom Hill Lane Cincinnati OH 45224-1406

RIZZO, DONALD CHARLES, ENTOMOLOGY, PARASITOLOGY. *Current Pos:* from asst prof to assoc prof, 74-94, HEAD, BIOL DEPT, MARYGROVE COL, 74-, CHMN, DIV NAT SCI & MATH, 75-, PROF BIOL, 95- *Personal Data:* b Boston, Mass, June 10, 45. *Educ:* Boston State Col, AB, 68; Cornell Univ, MS, 70, PhD(entom), 73. *Prof Exp:* Res asst insect path, Cornell Univ, 68-73; instr biol, Siena Heights Col, 73-74. *Concurrent Pos:* Dir, Minority Inst Sci Improv Prog, NSF, inst grants, 84-85, spec proj grants, 85-87; vis prof, Univ Mich Med Sch, Post Baccalaureate Pre Med Scholar Prog, 91, 92, 93, 94, 95 & 96. *Mem:* Nat Sci Teachers Asn; Am Asn Univ Prof; Nat Geog Soc; Am Inst Biol Sci. *Res:* Fungal pathogens of medically and economically important insects, especially dipterans. *Mailing Add:* Dept Biol Marygrove Col 8425 W McNichols Rd Detroit MI 48221. *Fax:* 313-864-6670

RIZZO, PETER JACOB, PLANT PHYSIOLOGY, CELL BIOLOGY. *Current Pos:* from lectr to asst prof, 75-82, ASSOC PROF CELL BIOL, TEXAS A&M UNIV, 82- *Personal Data:* b Gary, Ind, Dec 10, 40; m; c 2. *Educ:* Ind Univ, AB, 67, MA, 68; Univ Mich, PhD(plant physiol), 72. *Prof Exp:* Res assoc plant physiol, Purdue Univ, 72-75. *Concurrent Pos:* NIH fel,

72. *Mem:* Soc Protozoologists; AAAS; Sigma Xi; Soc Cell Biol. *Res:* Histone occurance in lower eukaryotes; histone-like proteins in dinoflagellates; evolution of nucleosomes. *Mailing Add:* Biol Dept Tex A&M Univ College Station TX 77843

RIZZO, THOMAS GERARD, PHENOMENOLOGY OF NEW PHYSICS BEYOND THE STANDARD MODEL. *Current Pos:* STAFF PHYSICIST, SLAC, 94- *Personal Data:* b New York, NY, June 22, 55; m 85, JoAnne L Hewett. *Educ:* Fordham Univ, BS, 74; Columbia Univ, MA, 75; Univ Rochester, PhD(physics), 78. *Prof Exp:* Res assoc, Physics Dept, Brookhaven Nat Lab, 79-81; asst prof & assoc physicist, Ames Lab, Iowa State Univ, 81-83, assoc prof physics & physicist, 83-87, prof physics & sr physicist, 87-92. *Concurrent Pos:* Vis scientist, Technion, 86, Univ Tex-Austin, 87, Triumf, 87 & HEP Div, Argonne Nat Lab, 91-93; vis prof, Univ Wis-Madison, 89-91. *Mem:* Am Phys Soc; AAAS; Europ Phys Soc. *Res:* Phenomenological implications of new physics scenarios; how low energy experiments can be used to distinguish between various schemes; superstring-inspired E6 models; fourth generation particles; exone particles; new particle production at future colliders; new gauge bosons. *Mailing Add:* Theory Group MS81 SLAC Stanford Univ Stanford CA 94309. *Fax:* 650-926-2525; *E-Mail:* rizzo@slacvx.slac.stanford.edu

RIZZOLI-MALANOTTE, PAOLA, MODELING OF OCEAN GENERAL CIRCULATION, DATA ASSIMILIATION METHODS. *Current Pos:* from asst prof to assoc prof, 81-90, PROF PHYS OCEANOG, MASS INST TECHNOL, 90- *Personal Data:* b Lomoo, Italy, Apr 18, 46; m 87, Peter Stone. *Educ:* Univ Padua, Italy, PhD(physics), 68; Univ Calif, San Diego, PhD(oceanog), 78. *Prof Exp:* Scientist, Nat Res Coun Italy, 71-81; fel, Scripps Inst Oceanog, 78-80. *Concurrent Pos:* Vis scientist, Woods Hole Oceanog Inst, 87-88; consult, Columbia Univ, 90- & Univs Space Res Asn, 93- *Mem:* Am Phys Soc; Am Geophys Union; Am Meteorol Soc; Oceanog Soc; Europ Geophys Soc. *Res:* Numerical modeling of the ocean general circulation; data assimilation methods; coherent structures and nonlinear waves in the atmosphere and the ocean. *Mailing Add:* 75 Cambridge Pkwy Cambridge MA 02142. *Fax:* 617-253-4464; *E-Mail:* Omnet: p.rizzouli

RIZZUTO, ANTHONY B, microbiology, biochemistry, for more information see previous edition

ROACH, ARCHIBALD WILSON KILBOURNE, BOTANY. *Current Pos:* From asst prof to assoc prof, 50-57, prof bot, 57-77, PROF BIOL SCI, NTEX STATE UNIV, 77- *Personal Data:* b Omaha, Nebr, Sept 15, 20; m 42; c 3. *Educ:* Univ Colo, BA, 46, MA, 48; Ore State Univ, PhD, 51. *Concurrent Pos:* Mem, Int Bur Plant Taxon & Nomenclature. *Mem:* Ecol Soc Am. *Res:* Phytosociology; southwestern aquatic actinomycetes. *Mailing Add:* 2319 Fowler Dr Denton TX 76201

ROACH, DAVID MICHAEL, OCEANOGRAPHY. *Current Pos:* PROF PHYSICS, CALIF POLYTECH STATE UNIV, SAN LUIS OBISPO, 66- *Personal Data:* b Detroit Lakes, Minn, Oct 10, 39; m 61; c 2. *Educ:* SDak Sch Mines & Technol, BS, 61, MS, 63; Ore State Univ, PhD(oceanog), 74. *Prof Exp:* Instr physics, SDak Sch Mines & Technol, 63-64; asst prof, Wis State Univ-Whitewater, 64-66. *Res:* Determination of refractive index distributions of oceanic particulates. *Mailing Add:* Physics Calif Polytech State Univ 1 Polyview Dr San Luis Obispo CA 93407-0001

ROACH, DON, ANALYTICAL CHEMISTRY. *Current Pos:* assoc prof, 69-80, PROF CHEM & CHMN DEPT, MIAMI-DADE COMMUNITY COL, 80- *Personal Data:* b Bono, Ark, Dec 10, 36; m 57; c 1. *Educ:* Ark State Univ, BS, 59; Univ Ark, Fayetteville, MS, 63; Univ Mo-Columbia, PhD(anal biochem), 70. *Honors & Awards:* William Henry Hatch Fel. *Prof Exp:* Technician, Univ Ark, Fayetteville, 63-64; asst prof chem, Miami-Dade Jr Col, 64-67; chemist, Exp Sta Chem Labs, Univ Mo-Columbia, 67-68. *Concurrent Pos:* Consult. *Mem:* Am Chem Soc. *Res:* Gas-liquid chromatography of biologically important compounds. *Mailing Add:* 12190 SW 93 Ave Miami FL 33176-5002

ROACH, DONALD VINCENT, PHYSICAL CHEMISTRY. *Current Pos:* asst prof, 65-72, ASSOC PROF CHEM, UNIV MO-ROLLA, 72- *Personal Data:* b Oak Grove, Mo, Jan 18, 32. *Educ:* Univ Mo, BS, 54, PhD(phys chem), 62. *Prof Exp:* Res assoc, Univ Calif, Berkeley, 62-63 & Univ Mo-Columbia, 63-64; res chemist, US Naval Weapons Lab, 64-65. *Mem:* Am Chem Soc. *Res:* Gas-solid surface interactions; adsorption of gases on solids; exchange of energy between gases and solids. *Mailing Add:* 1117 Duane Ave Univ Mo Rolla MO 65401

ROACH, J ROBERT, ORGANIC CHEMISTRY, FOOD CHEMISTRY. *Current Pos:* RETIRED. *Personal Data:* b Stockton, Ill, Nov 24, 13; m 50, Marilyn Cooney; c Steven F, Barbara (Carroll) & Patricia M. *Educ:* Iowa State Col, BS, 36; Purdue Univ, PhD(org chem), 42. *Prof Exp:* Pittsburgh Plate Glass Co fel, Northwestern Univ, 41-43; proj leader org chem, Gen Mills, Inc, 43-50, sect leader, Food Develop Dept, 50-56, dept head, 56-61, dir food develop activity, 61-69, vpres & dir res & develop food group, 69-77. *Mem:* Am Chem Soc; Am Asn Cereal Chemists; Inst Food Technologists. *Res:* Food development; convenience foods. *Mailing Add:* 24 Luverne Minneapolis MN 55419

ROACH, JOHN FAUNCE, RADIOLOGY. *Current Pos:* RETIRED. *Personal Data:* b Boston, Mass, July 21, 12; m 39; c 1. *Educ:* Harvard Univ, AB, 35, MD, 39. *Prof Exp:* From asst prof to assoc prof radiol, Johns Hopkins Univ, Sch Med, 47-50; chmn dept, 50-77, prof radiol, Albany Med Col, 50-91; consult, NY State Educ Dept, 81-91. *Concurrent Pos:* Consult, Vet Admin Hosp, Albany; mem, Pub Health Coun, State Health Dept, NY; trustee & pres, Am Bd Radiol; pres, Am Bd Med Specialties; exec secy, NY State Bd for Med, 77-81. *Mem:* Radiol Soc NAm; Am Roentgen Ray Soc (past pres); fel Am Col Radiol. *Mailing Add:* Albany Med Ctr Hosp Albany NY 12204-1502

ROACH, MARGOT RUTH, BIOPHYSICS, BIOENGINEERING. *Current Pos:* from asst prof to assoc prof biophys, Univ Western Ont, 65-71, from asst prof to assoc prof med, 65-78, chmn dept, 70-78, PROF BIOPHYS, UNIV WESTERN ONT, 71-, PROF MED, 78- *Personal Data:* b Moncton, NB, Dec 24, 34; m 94, Franklyn St Aubyn House. *Educ:* Univ NB, BSc, 55; McGill Univ, MD, CM, 59; Univ Western Ont, 60-62, PhD(biophys), 63; FRCP(C), 65. *Hon Degrees:* DSc, Univ New Brunswick, 81. *Honors & Awards:* Ciba Found Award, 59. *Prof Exp:* Jr intern, Victoria Hosp, London, Ont, 59-60; Med Res Coun Can fel, Univ Western Ont, 60-62, Ont Heart Found fel cardiol, Victoria Hosp, 62-63; asst resident med, 63-64; asst resident, Toronto Gen Hosp, Ont, 64-65. *Concurrent Pos:* Young investr's award, Am Col Cardiol, 63; Med Res Coun Can fel, Nuffield Inst Med Res, Oxford, Eng, 65-67; Med Res Coun Can scholar biophys & med, Univ Western Ont, 67-70; mem active teaching staff med, Victoria Hosp, 67-72; res grants, Med Res Coun Can, 68-70 & 71-, Ont Heart Found, 68-, Can Tuberc Assn, 69-70, Ont Thoracic Soc, 71- & Picker Found, 71-73; Can rep, Adv Group Aeronaut Res & Develop, NATO, 69-71; mem comt on scholar, Med Res Coun Can, 71-72; res consult, Westminster Hosp, 71-73; mem adv comt biophys, Nat Res Coun, 71-78; consult, Univ Hosp, 72-; assoc ed, Can J Physiol Pharmacol, 73-79; Commonwealth vis scientist appl math & theoret physics, Cambridge, 75; mem, Bioeng Comt, Med Res Coun, 93-96. *Mem:* Can Physiol Soc; Can Cardiovasc Soc; Can Soc Clin Invest; Can Biophys Soc. *Res:* Hemodynamics; elastic properties of tissues; effects of vibration on tissues; arterial elasticity; atherosclerosis; the role of hemodynamic factors in localized arterial disease, such as poststenotic dilatation, atheroscierosis, brain aneurysms, dissecting aneurysms; angioplasy. *Mailing Add:* Dept Med Biophys Univ Western Ont London ON N6A 5C1 Can. *E-Mail:* mroach@irus.rri.uwo.ca

ROACH, PETER JOHN, GLYCOGEN METABOLISM, MECHANISMS OF HORMONE ACTION. *Current Pos:* from asst prof to assoc prof, 79-85, PROF BIOCHEM, SCH MED, IND UNIV, 85- *Personal Data:* b Rangeworthy, UK, June 8, 48; m 75. *Educ:* Univ Glasgow, BSc, 69, PhD(biochem), 72. *Prof Exp:* Fel, Univ Calif, Los Angeles, 72-74, Univ Va, 74-75, Univ Pisa, Italy, 75-77; instr pharmacol, Univ Va, 77-79. *Mem:* Am Soc Biol Chem. *Res:* Mechanisms by which hormones regulate enzyme activity, with the main focus on covalent phosphorylation in the control of glycogen metabolism. *Mailing Add:* Dept Biochem Sch Med Ind Univ 635 Barnhill Dr Indianapolis IN 46202-5122

ROACH, ROBIN RUTHERFORD, CONSUMER SCIENCE & EDUCATION. *Current Pos:* asst prof, 94-96, ASSOC PROF, DEPT CONSUMER SCI & EDUC, UNIV MEMPHIS, 96-; DIR, AM DIETETIC ASN DIDACTIC PROG DIETETICS, 84- *Educ:* Memphis State Univ, BS, 76; Tulane Univ, MPH, 80; Vanderbilt Univ, EdD(sci educ), 89. *Honors & Awards:* New Researchers Award, Am Dietetic Asn, 93. *Prof Exp:* Nutritionist, N Memphis Community Health Clin, Tenn, 77-78; clin nutritionist, Children's Hosp, New Orleans, 78-81; instr, Dept Home Econs, Memphis State Univ, 81-89, asst prof, 89-94; asst prof clin nutrit, Col Grad Health Scis, Univ Tenn, 88-89. *Concurrent Pos:* Dietetic intern, Univ Ark Med Ctr, 77; nutrit fel, Univ Tenn Child Develop Ctr, 82; grantee, Memphis State Univ, 85-86, Am Dietetic Asn, 90 & 93, Univ Memphis, 96; mem res, coun, Col Educ, 85-88; adj asst prof clin nutrit, Col Grad Health Sci, Univ Tenn, Memphis, 88-89; mem nutrit comt, Am Heart Asn, 89-91; chmn, Col Educ Task Force Home Econs Mission, Dept Consumer Sci Educ, Univ Memphis, 91; Fulbright grantee, US Info Agency & Coun Int Exchange Scholars, 95. *Mem:* Am Dietetic Asn. *Res:* Authored several professional publications. *Mailing Add:* Dept Consumer Sci & Educ Univ Memphis Memphis TN 38152. *Fax:* 901-678-5324; *E-Mail:* roach.robin@coe.memphis.edu

ROACH, WILLIAM KENNEY, ENTOMOLOGY. *Current Pos:* SPECIALIST-IN-CHARGE, PLANT PEST CONTROL SECT, OHIO DEPT AGR, 72- *Personal Data:* b Cincinnati, Ohio, Feb 2, 42; m 64; c 2. *Educ:* St Louis Univ, BS, 64; Ohio State Univ, PhD(entom), 71. *Prof Exp:* Surv entomologist, Ohio State Univ, 69-70. *Mem:* Entom Soc Am. *Res:* Taxonomy of Empidid flies. *Mailing Add:* 373 Aylesbury Dr Westerville OH 43082

ROACHE, LEWIE CALVIN, ZOOLOGY. *Current Pos:* From instr to assoc prof, SC State Col, 47-69, from actg head to head dept, 56-69, chmn dept natural sci, 69-77, PROF BIOL, SC STATE COL, 69-, DEAN, SCH ARTS & SCI, 77- *Personal Data:* b Dalzell, SC, Oct 31, 25; m 59. *Educ:* SC State Col, BS, 47, MS, 54; Cath Univ, PhD(zool), 60. *Mem:* AAAS; Ecol Soc Am; Nat Inst Sci. *Res:* Systematics of the freshwater Cyclopoid Copepods. *Mailing Add:* 516 Willow Rd NE Orangeburg SC 29115

ROADMAN, CHARLES H, II, GYNECOLOGY & OBSTETRICS. *Current Pos:* USAF, 68-, clin lab officer, Wilford Hall Med Ctr, Lackland AFB, 68-69, internship & residency, Keeslere Med Ctr, Keesler AFB, 73-77, staff obstetrician, chief obstets & gynec, chief surg serv, chief hosp servs, 401st Tactical Hosp, Torrejon Air Base, Spain, 77-80, SURGEON GEN, USAF,

HQ, BOLLING AFB, 96- *Educ:* Washington & Lee Univ, BS, 67; Emory Univ, MD, 73; Am Bd Obstet & Gynec, dipl. *Mailing Add:* Off Air Force Surgeon Gen Med Inquiries & Info 110 Luke Ave Rm 400 Bolling AFB Washington DC 20332-7050

ROADS, JOHN OWEN, METEOROLOGY, CLIMATOLOGY. *Current Pos:* NSF fel, 72-77, ASST RES METEOROLOGIST, SCRIPPS INST OCEANOG, UNIV CALIF, SAN DIEGO, 77- *Personal Data:* b Boulder, Colo, Jan 20, 50. *Educ:* Univ Colo, BA, 72; Mass Inst Technol, PhD(meteorol), 77. *Prof Exp:* Res asst, Nat Ctr Atmospheric Res, 70-72. *Concurrent Pos:* Res asst, Mass Inst Technol, 75-77. *Mem:* Am Meteorol Soc. *Res:* Numerical modelling; dynamic meteorology; climate modelling. *Mailing Add:* Scripps Inst Oceanog Univ Calif San Diego La Jolla CA 92093-0224

ROADSTRUM, WILLIAM H(ENRY), ENGINEERING, ENGINEERING ECONOMICS. *Current Pos:* from adj prof to prof, 63-80, EMER PROF ELEC ENG, WORCESTER POLYTECH INST, 80- *Personal Data:* b Chicago, Ill, June 22, 15; m 43; c 2. *Educ:* Lehigh Univ, BS, 38; Carnegie Inst Technol, MS, 48, PhD(elec eng), 55. *Prof Exp:* Elec engr, US Bur Mines, Pa, 39-41, 45-47; asst prof electronics, US Naval Postgrad Sch, 48-50, 52-53; systs engr, Adv Electronics Ctr, Gen Elec Co, NY, 55-57, mgr missile systs eng, Light Mil Dept, 57-59, mgr detection & surveillance eng, 59-60, mgr info storage & retrieval, Adv Tech Labs, 60-63. *Concurrent Pos:* Consult, eng practices & eng mgt, William H Roadstrum Inc, 64- *Mem:* Sigma Xi; sr mem Inst Elec & Electronics Engrs. *Res:* Systems engineering; engineering economy; management theory and techniques in engineering and development projects; education and development of engineers. *Mailing Add:* 9 Juniper Lane Holden MA 01520

ROALES, ROBERT R, ENVIRONMENTAL TOXICOLOGY, ENVIRONMENTAL PHYSIOLOGY. *Current Pos:* from asst prof to assoc prof anat & physiol, Natural Sci Dept, Ind Univ, Kokomo, 74-87, coordr allied health sci, 87-91, chmn, Dept Biol & Phys Sci, 87-96, actg dean arts & sci, 90, CHAIR, DIV ALLIED HEALTH SCI, IND UNIV, KOKOMO, 92-, ASST DEAN, SCH ALLIED HEALTH SCI, SCH MED, 92-, CHAIR, DEPT NATURAL, INFO & MATH SCI, 96- *Personal Data:* b New York, NY, July 17, 44; m 69, Francoise Galland; c Nicole. *Educ:* Iona Col, BS, 66; NY Univ, MS, 69, PhD(biol), 73. *Honors & Awards:* Founder's Award, NY Univ, 74. *Prof Exp:* Lectr biol, Bor Manhattan Community Col, 69-70; teaching fel biol, NY Univ, 70-73, asst res scientist, 73-74. *Concurrent Pos:* Consult, T F H Publ, 73; adj asst prof biol, LaGuardia Community Col & NY Univ, 73-74. *Mem:* AAAS; Am Fisheries Soc; Am Inst Biol Sci; NY Acad Sci; Sigma Xi; Nat Asn Adv Health Professions. *Res:* Establishment of tolerance limits of fish and fish embryos to various heavy metals and organic phosphorous pesticides; effects of these compounds on inhibiting the immune systems of fish as evidenced by decreased antibody levels when exposed to viral and bacterial antigens; effects of heavy metal pollutants on lipid content of fish. *Mailing Add:* Dept Natural, Info & Math Sci 2300 S Washington St PO Box 9003 Kokomo IN 46904-9003. *Fax:* 765-455-9528; *E-Mail:* rroales@iukfs1.iuk.indiana.edu

ROALSVIG, JAN PER, NUCLEAR PHYSICS, HIGH ENERGY PHYSICS. *Current Pos:* PROF PHYSICS, STATE UNIV NY, BUFFALO, 62- *Personal Data:* b Stavanger, Norway, Mar 23, 28; m 54; c 5. *Educ:* Univ Oslo, BSc, 52, MSc, 55; Norweg Inst Pedag, BEd, 53; Univ Sask, PhD(physics), 59. *Prof Exp:* Asst prof physics, St John's Univ, NY, 59-62. *Concurrent Pos:* Res prof, Chalmers Univ Technol, Sweden, 69-70, Univ BC, Can, 79; docent, Norweg Tech Univ, 72-73. *Mem:* Am Phys Soc; Am Asn Physics Teachers; Can Asn Physicists; Norweg Phys Soc. *Res:* Pair-production; absolute beta-counting; photo-alpha and photo-neutron reactions; nuclear spectroscopy; gamma ray detectors; hyperfragments. *Mailing Add:* Dept Physics/Rm 259 Fronczak Hall SUNY Buffalo-N Campus Buffalo NY 14260-0001

ROAN, VERNON P, MECHANICAL ENGINEERING, AEROSPACE ENGINEERING. *Current Pos:* assoc prof mech eng, 71-73, grad coordr, 85-90, PROF MECH ENG, UNIV FLA, 73-, DIR, CTR ADVAN STUDIES ENG, 89- *Personal Data:* b Ft Myers, Fla, Nov 19, 35; c 2. *Educ:* Univ Fla, BS, 58, MS, 59; Univ Ill, PhD(aeronaut & mech eng), 66. *Honors & Awards:* Nat Winner Urban Vehicle Design, Student Competition Relevant Eng, 72, Nat Winner Era II Wind Systs Design, 77, Nat Winner Energy Efficient Vehicle Design, 79; Ralph R Tector Award, Soc Automotive Engrs, 75. *Prof Exp:* Sr design eng, Pratt & Whitney. *Concurrent Pos:* Consult, E I du Pont de Nemours & Co, Inc, 73-83, Jet Propulsion Lab, 80-86, Pratt & Whitney Aircraft, 85-, Georgetown Univ, 87-; chmn, Subcomt Univ Activities Elec & Hybrid Elec Vehicles, Inst Elec & Electronics Engrs, 77-; mem staff, Brunel Univ, Uxbridge, Eng, 79-80. *Mem:* Soc Automotive Engrs; Sigma Xi; Am Soc Mech Engrs; Am Inst Aeronaut & Astronaut; Am Soc Eng Educ. *Res:* Gasdynamics; propulsion systems; wind systems; electric and hybrid electric vehicles; development of first hybrid electric bus in US; alternative fuels; fuel cell power systems. *Mailing Add:* Dept Mech Eng Univ Fla Gainesville FL 32611

ROANE, CURTIS WOODARD, PLANT PATHOLOGY. *Current Pos:* From asst plant pathologist to assoc plant pathologist, Exp Sta, Va Polytech Inst & State Univ, 47-68, from assoc prof to prof, 48-86, EMER PROF PLANT PATH, VA POLYTECH INST & STATE UNIV, 86- *Personal Data:* b Norfolk, Va, Apr 19, 21; m 47, Martha A Kotila; c E Lee & Martha (Vanbusmirk). *Educ:* Va Polytech Inst, BS, 43, MS, 44; Univ Minn, PhD(plant path), 53. *Concurrent Pos:* Assoc ed, Phytopathology, 69-71, Plant Dis Reporter, 78-81; chmn, Southern Small Grain Worker's Conf, 70-72, Eastern Wheat Workers Conf, 78-81; chmn, NAm Barley Res Workers, 81-84; pres, Potomac Div, Am Phytopath Soc. *Mem:* Sigma Xi; fel Am Phytopath Soc. *Res:* Fungi on grasses; history of plant pathology in Virginia. *Mailing Add:* 607 Lucas Dr Blacksburg VA 24060

ROANE, MARTHA KOTILA, mycology, taxonomic botany; deceased, see previous edition for last biography

ROANE, PHILIP RANSOM, JR, VIROLOGY, IMMUNOLOGY. *Current Pos:* asst prof, 72-77, ASSOC PROF MICROBIOL, HOWARD UNIV, 78- *Personal Data:* b Baltimore, Md, Nov 20, 27. *Educ:* Morgan State Col, BS, 52; Johns Hopkins Univ, MS, 60; Univ Md, PhD, 70. *Prof Exp:* Asst microbiol, Sch Med, Johns Hopkins Univ, 60-64; virologist, Microbiol Assocs, Inc, 64-72, dir qual control, 67-72. *Concurrent Pos:* Mem, Virol Study Sect, NIH, 76-80, Viral & Rickettsial Rev Subcomt, 79-; consult, Hem Res Inc, Rockville Md, 81- *Mem:* AAAS; Am Soc Microbiol; Am Asn Immunologists. *Res:* Biophysical and immunological properties of viruses; biochemistry of tumor and transformed cells induced by a common virus. *Mailing Add:* Dept Microbiol Howard Univ 520 W St NW Washington DC 20001-2337

ROANTREE, ROBERT JOSEPH, medical microbiology; deceased, see previous edition for last biography

ROARK, BRUCE (ARCHIBALD), PLANT PHYSIOLOGY, PLANT BREEDING. *Current Pos:* JTPA PLANNER, S DELTA PLANNING & DEVELOP DIST, 84- *Personal Data:* b New York, NY, Jan 19, 20; m 46, 77; c 7. *Educ:* Univ Western Australia, BSc, 49 & 50; Univ Adelaide, PhD, 56. *Prof Exp:* Plant physiologist, Sci & Educ Admin, Agr Res, USDA, Mayaguez, PR, 56-58 & Miss, 58-70, supvry plant physiologist, 70-79; plant breeder, Northrup King Seed Co, 81-83. *Mem:* Am Soc Plant Physiologists; Am Soc Agron; Crop Sci Soc Am; Sigma Xi. *Res:* Water relations; stress resistance genotype and environment interactions; upland cotton; plant breeding. *Mailing Add:* 1304 Newport Pl Greenville MS 38701-8320

ROARK, JAMES L, ORGANIC CHEMISTRY, CHEMISTRY EDUCATION. *Current Pos:* From asst prof to assoc prof chem, 69-75, PROF & CHMN CHEM DEPT, KEARNEY STATE COL, 76- *Personal Data:* b Kansas City, Mo, Mar 27, 43; m 67; c 2. *Educ:* Nebr Wesleyan Univ, BA, 65; Tex Christian Univ, PhD(chem), 69. *Concurrent Pos:* Robert Welch res fel, Tex Christian Univ, 67-69; NSF fel, Tufts Univ, 71; dir water analysis lab, Kearney State Col, 72-76, proj dir water qual study, 73-75, high ability high sch students, 74-77, sec chem teachers, 77-; vis prof, Univ Va, 81-82. *Mem:* Am Chem Soc; Nat Sci Teachers Asn; Sigma Xi. *Res:* Non-traditional methods of instruction; computer based methods of instruction; chemistry curriculums for secondary education; natural products chemistry. *Mailing Add:* 824 W 27th St Kearney NE 68847-4359

ROARK, TERRY P, ASTRONOMY, ASTROPHYSICS. *Current Pos:* pres, 87-92, PROF PHYSICS & ASTRON, UNIV WYO, 97- *Personal Data:* b Okeene, Okla, June 11, 38; m 63; c 1. *Educ:* Oklahoma City Univ, BA, 60; Rensselaer Polytech Inst, MS, 62, PhD(astron), 66. *Prof Exp:* Asst prof astron, Ohio State Univ, 66-76, prof, 76, asst provost curric, 77-79, assoc provost instr, 79-83; prof physics & vpres student affairs, Kent State, 83-87. *Concurrent Pos:* Comnr, Western Interstate Comn Higher Educ, 87-97. *Mem:* Am Astron Soc; Int Astron Union; Astron Soc Pac; Sigma Xi. *Res:* Observational and theoretical investigation of the solid interstellar medium, binary and white dwarf stars. *Mailing Add:* 1752 Edward Dr Laramie WY 82072

ROATH, WILLIAM WESLEY, PLANT BREEDING. *Current Pos:* RES AGRONOMIST, AGR RES SERV, USDA, 85- *Personal Data:* b Torrington, Wyo, Dec 7, 34; m 55, Mary C Phillips; c Paul D, William W Jr, Patricia L, Craig E, David B, Michelle G & Beverly R. *Educ:* Mont State Univ, BS, 57, PhD(genetics), 69. *Prof Exp:* Res agronomist, Dekalb Agr Res, Inc, 71; res geneticist, Agr Res Serv, USDA, 78-82; agronomist, Zamare Proj, Zambia, 82-84. *Mem:* Am Soc Agron; Crop Sci Soc Am. *Res:* Germ plasm (oilseeds and new crop) evaluation and enhancement. *Mailing Add:* 506 Easy Box St Apt 472 West Union IA 52175. *Fax:* 515-294-4880; *E-Mail:* wwroath@iastate.edu

ROB, CHARLES G, SURGERY. *Current Pos:* PROF SURG, E CAROLINA SCH MED, GREENVILLE, NC, 78- *Personal Data:* b Weybridge, Eng, May 4, 13; nat US; m 41; c 4. *Educ:* Cambridge Univ, MA, 34, MB, BCh, 37, MCh, 41, MD, 60; FRCS, 39. *Hon Degrees:* MCh, Trinity Col, Dublin, 61. *Prof Exp:* Reader surg, Univ London, 46-50, prof, 50-60; prof surg & chmn dept, Sch Med, Univ Rochester, 60-78. *Concurrent Pos:* Consult, Brit Army, Royal Nat Orthop Hosp, London; mem court examr, Royal Col Surgeons. *Mem:* Asn Surg Gt Brit & Ireland (hon secy); Royal Soc Med; Int Soc Cardiovasc Surg (pres, 61); hon fel Venezuelan Surg Soc. *Mailing Add:* 4982 Sentinel St Bethesda MD 20816

ROBARGE, WAYNE, SOIL SCIENCE, ANALYTICAL CHEMISTRY. *Current Pos:* RES SCIENTIST & FAC, DEPT SOIL SCI, NC STATE UNIV, 77- *Personal Data:* b NJ, 1947. *Educ:* Cornell Univ, BS, 69, MS, 71; Univ Wis, PhD(soil chem), 75. *Mem:* Am Chem Soc; Soil Sci Soc Am. *Mailing Add:* Dept Soil Sci NC State Univ PO Box 7619 Raleigh NC 27695

ROBAUGH, DAVID ALLAN, HIGH TEMPERATURE REACTION MECHANISMS, KINETICS. *Current Pos:* ASSOC CHEMIST, MIDWEST RES INST, KANSAS CITY, MO, 85- *Personal Data:* b Uniontown, Pa, Mar 28, 54. *Educ:* Calif State Univ, BS, 76; WVa Univ, PhD(phys chem), 81. *Prof Exp:* Res fel, Chem Kinetics Div, Nat Bur Standards, 81-85. *Mem:* Am Chem Soc. *Res:* Kinetics and mechanisms of high-temperature organic reactions via very low-pressure pyrolysis and shock tube experiments. *Mailing Add:* Midwest Res Inst 425 Volker Blvd Kansas City MO 64110-2241

ROBB, ERNEST WILLARD, ORGANIC CHEMISTRY. *Current Pos:* assoc prof, 65-75, PROF ORG CHEM, STEVENS INST TECHNOL, 75- *Personal Data:* b Dodge City, Kans, Sept 4, 31; m 60; c 3. *Educ:* Kans State Univ, BS, 52; Harvard Univ, MS, 54, PhD(chem), 56. *Prof Exp:* Fels, Iowa State Col, 56-57, Mass Inst Technol, 57-58 & Harvard Univ, 58-59; res chemist, Fritzsche Bros, Inc, 59-60; res scientist, Philip Morris Inc, 60-63, sr scientist, 63-65. *Mem:* AAAS; Am Chem Soc. *Res:* Mechanism of organic reactions; organic stereochemistry. *Mailing Add:* Dept Chem Stevens Inst Technol Castle Pt Sta Hoboken NJ 07030-5991

ROBB, JAMES ARTHUR, PATHOLOGY, VIROLOGY. *Current Pos:* staff pathologist, 90-93, ASSOC DIR LABS & DIR ANATOMIC & MOLECULAR PATH, CEDARS MED CTR, MIAMI, 93- *Personal Data:* b Pueblo, Colo, Nov 13, 38; m 62; c 4. *Educ:* Univ Colo, Boulder, BA, 60; Univ Colo, Denver, MD, 65; Am Bd Anat Path, dipl, Am Bd Dermatopath, dipl; Am Bd Cytopath, dipl; Am Bd Clin Path, dipl. *Honors & Awards:* Pathologist of the Year, San Diego Co Soc Pathologists, 89. *Prof Exp:* Intern anat path, Yale Med Ctr, 65-66, resident, 66-68; res assoc molecular virol, Nat Inst Arthritis & Metab Dis, 68-71; from asst to assoc prof path, Univ Calif, San Diego, 71-78; vchmn & staff pathologist, Green Hosp Scripps Clin, La Jolla, Calif, 78-90. *Concurrent Pos:* Adj prof path, Sch Med, Univ Calif, 78-90; fel Col Am Pathol. *Mem:* AAAS; Am Soc Cell Biol; Am Soc Microbiol; Am Asn Pathologists; Am Soc Clin Pathologists; AMA; Int Acad Pathol; Int Acad Cytol. *Res:* Molecular biology of latent human viruses; study of the animal virus-mammalian cell interactions resulting in various human diseases; detection of antigens in formalin-fixed, paraffin-embedded human tissues. *Mailing Add:* Path Dept Columbia Cedars Med Ctr 1400 NW 12th Ave Miami FL 33136

ROBB, RICHARD A, MEDICAL IMAGING, COMPUTED TOMOGRAPHY. *Current Pos:* DIR, RES COMPUT FACIL, MAYO FOUND, 72-, PROF BIOPHYSICS, GRAD SCH MED, 84- *Personal Data:* b Price, Utah, Dec 2, 42. *Educ:* Univ Utah, BA, 65, MS, 68, PhD(comput sci), 71. *Concurrent Pos:* Prin investr & staff consult, Res Comput Facil, Mayo Found, 76- *Mem:* Am Physiol Soc; Biomed Eng Soc; AAAS; Asn Advan Technol Biomed Sci; Sigma Xi. *Res:* Computurized processing, display and analysis of biomedical imagery; x-ray computed tomography; three dimensional image display. *Mailing Add:* Dept Physiol & Biophys Mayo Clinic & Found 200 First St SW Rochester MN 55905

ROBB, RICHARD JOHN, MOLECULAR IMMUNOLOGY, LYMPHOKINES. *Current Pos:* DIR MOLECULAR BIOL, BIOMIRA USA, INC, 95- *Personal Data:* b Detroit, Mich, Nov 1, 50; m 71; c 2. *Educ:* Mich State Univ, BS, 72; Harvard Univ, PhD(biochem & molecular biol), 78. *Prof Exp:* Jane Coffin Child mem Fund fel, Uppsala Univ, Sweden, 78-79 & Darthmouth Univ, 79-80; res assoc, Dartmouth Univ, 80-81; prin scientist, E I Du Pont de Nemours Co, Inc, 81-84, res leader, 84-86, group leader, Cent Res & Develop Dept, 86-88, res fel, Med Prod Dept, 88-90, res fel, Inflammatory Dis, Dupont Merck Pharmaceuticals, 91-93; dir molecular biol, Oncotherapeut, Inc, 93-95. *Concurrent Pos:* Assoc ed, J Immunol, 85-89; adj assoc prof, Univ Pa, 85-89. *Mem:* Am Asn Immunologists. *Res:* Mechanistic action of lymphokines; purification and molecular characterization of lymphokines and their receptors; signal transduction and differentiation events following lymphokine-receptor interaction; cancer vaccine development; tlymphocyte signal transduction. *Mailing Add:* Biomira USA Inc 1002 Eastpark Blvd Cranbury NJ 08512. *Fax:* 609-655-1755

ROBB, THOMAS WILBERN, RUMINANT NUTRITION, FORAGE EVALUATION. *Current Pos:* int tech serv rep, 85-89, proj mgt, 89-96, BUS MGR, PITMAN-MOORE, 96- *Personal Data:* b Marshall, Mo, Apr 25, 53; c 2. *Educ:* Cent Mo State Univ, BS, 73; Univ Mo, Columbia, MS, 75; Univ Ky, PhD(animal sci), 80. *Prof Exp:* Asst prof animal sci, NC State Univ, 81-84, NE Brazil, 81-83; res assoc, Va Tech Univ, 84-85. *Mem:* Am Soc Animal Sci; Am Registry Prof Animal Scientists. *Res:* Ruminant nutrition research, primarily forages in northeast Brazil, meat producing sheep and goats and with dairy goats. *Mailing Add:* Mallinckrodt Vet 421 Hawley St Mundelein IL 60060

ROBB, WALTER L(EE), CHEMICAL ENGINEERING. *Current Pos:* PRES, VANTAGE MGT INC, SCHENECTADY, NY, 93- *Personal Data:* b Harrisburg, Pa, Apr 25, 28; m 54, Anne Gruver; c Richard A, Steven J & Lindsey S. *Educ:* Pa State Col, BS, 48; Univ Ill, MS, 49, PhD(chem eng), 51. *Hon Degrees:* DSc, Worcester Polytech Inst; DEng Milwaukee Sch Eng. *Honors & Awards:* Pioneer Award, Imaging Div, Nat Elec Mfg Asn; Nat Medal Technol, 93. *Prof Exp:* Engr, Knolls Atomic Power Lab, Gen Elec Co, 51-56, res engineer, Res Lab, 56-62, mgr chem process sect, 62-66, mgr res & develop, Silicone Prod Dept, 66-68, mgr med develper, Schenectady, 68-71, gen mgr silicone prod dept, Waterford, 71-73, gen mgr chem & metall div, 73, sr vpres & group exec, Med Systs Group, 73-86, sr vpres corp res & develop, 86-93. *Concurrent Pos:* Coun, Nat Acad Eng; adv coun, Critical Technol Inst; chmn, NEO Path Inc; bd dir, Cree Res, Celgene & Marguette Med Systs. *Mem:* Nat Acad Eng; Am Inst Chem Engrs. *Res:* Permeable membranes; diagnostic imaging equipment. *Mailing Add:* 1358 Ruffner Rd Schenectady NY 12309-2506. *Fax:* 518-782-0030

ROBBAT, ALBERT, JR, ELECTROCHEMISTRY, CHROMATOGRAPHY. *Current Pos:* ASSOC PROF CHEM, TUFTS UNIV, 80- *Personal Data:* b Boston, Mass, Apr 11, 54; m; c 2. *Educ:* Univ Mass, Boston, BA, 76; Pa State Univ, PhD(chem), 80. *Concurrent Pos:* Res assoc anal chem, US Dept Energy, Pittsburgh, 81-82; prin investr, Anal Div. *Mem:* Am Chem Soc; Electrochem Soc. *Res:* Development of GC-MS for on-site detection of organic compounds; Electroreactivity and affinity of biologically important species: iron, sulfur, molybdenum proteins, and condensed thiophenes; application of radio frequency, static and magnetic fields in chromatography. *Mailing Add:* Dept Chem Tufts Univ Medford MA 02155-5555

ROBBERS, JAMES EARL, PHARMACOGNOSY. *Current Pos:* from asst prof to assoc prof, 66-75, PROF PHARMACOG, PURDUE UNIV, W LAFAYETTE, 75- *Personal Data:* b Everett, Wash, Oct 18, 34; m 57, Diann Blankenburg. *Educ:* Wash State Univ, BS & BPhar, 57, MS, 61; Univ Wash, PhD(pharmacog), 64. *Honors & Awards:* Edwin Leigh Newcomb Award, 63; Hon Mem, Asn Francaise pour l'Enseignement et la Recherche en Pharmacognosie. *Prof Exp:* Asst prof pharmacog, Univ Houston, 64-66. *Concurrent Pos:* Ed, J Nat Prod, 84-93. *Mem:* Hon mem Am Soc Pharmacog. *Res:* Isolation, physiology, biosynthesis, genetics and molecular control of fungal metabolites. *Mailing Add:* Sch Pharm & Pharmacol Sci Purdue Univ West Lafayette IN 47907-1333. *Fax:* 765-494-1414; *E-Mail:* jrobbers@pharmacy.purdue.edu

ROBBERSON, DONALD LEWIS, GENE STRUCTURE, GENE TRANSPOSITION. *Current Pos:* asst biologist, 73-83, CHIEF, SECT MOLECULAR GENETICS, UNIV TEX, SYST CANCER CTR, MD ANDERSON HOSP & TUMOR INST, 83-, PROF GENETICS & GENETICIST, 84- *Personal Data:* b Shawnee, Okla, Sept 10, 41; div; c 3. *Educ:* Okla Baptist Univ, BS, 63; Calif Inst Technol, PhD(biophys), 71. *Prof Exp:* Res fel mitochondrial DNA replication, dept path, Stanford Univ Med Ctr, 71-72; res fel polyoma virus genetics, Imp Cancer Res Fund, 72-73. *Concurrent Pos:* Mem, molecular biol study sect, NIH, 80- *Mem:* Am Soc Cell Biol; Am Soc Biol Chemists. *Res:* Structure and replication of mitochondrial DNA sequences in normal and malignat animal cells; electron microscopy of nucleic acids; recombinant DNA techniques. *Mailing Add:* Dept Genetics Univ Tex MD Anderson Cancer Ctr 1515 Holcombe Blvd Houston TX 77030-2603. *Fax:* 713-794-4295

ROBBIN, JOEL W, MATHEMATICS. *Current Pos:* asst prof, 67-73, PROF MATH, UNIV WIS-MADISON, 73- *Personal Data:* b Chicago, Ill, May 28, 41; m 66. *Educ:* Univ Ill, BS, 62; Princeton Univ, MA, 64, PhD(math), 65. *Prof Exp:* Instr math, Princeton Univ, 65-67. *Mem:* Am Math Soc; Asn Symbolic Logic. *Res:* Logic; differential equations. *Mailing Add:* Dept Math Univ Wis 480 Lincoln Dr Madison WI 53706-1313

ROBBINS, ALLEN BISHOP, PHYSICS. *Current Pos:* from instr to assoc prof, 56-68, chmn dept, 79-95, PROF PHYSICS, RUTGERS UNIV, NEW BRUNSWICK, 68- *Personal Data:* b New Brunswick, NJ, Mar 31, 30; m 79, Alice Ayrs; c Catherine, Marilyn, Carol & Melanie. *Educ:* Rutgers Univ, BSc, 52; Yale Univ, MS, 53, PhD(physics), 56. *Concurrent Pos:* Imp Chem Industs res fel, Univ Birmingham, 57-58, lectr, 60-61. *Mem:* AAAS; fel Am Phys Soc; Am Asn Physics Teachers. *Res:* Nuclear physics. *Mailing Add:* 14 Claire Dr Bridgewater NJ 08807-1808

ROBBINS, APRIL RUTH, BIOCHEMICAL GENETICS, CELL BIOLOGY. *Current Pos:* SR INVESTR, NAT INST DIABETES, DIGESTIVE & KIDNEY DIS, NIH, 83- *Educ:* Brown Univ, PhD(biochem genetics), 74. *Mailing Add:* Lab Cell Biochem & Biol NIH Bldg 8 Rm 303 Bethesda MD 20892

ROBBINS, CHANDLER SEYMOUR, ORNITHOLOGY. *Current Pos:* WILDLIFE RES BIOLOGIST, BIOL RESOURCES DIV, US GEOL SURV, 96- *Personal Data:* b Belmont, Mass, July 17, 18; m 48, Eleanor G Cooley; c Jane, Stuart, George & Nancy. *Educ:* Harvard Univ, AB, 40; George Washington Univ, MA, 50. *Hon Degrees:* ScD, Univ Md, 95. *Honors & Awards:* Arthur A Allen Award, 79; Paul Bartsch Award, 79; Ludlow Griscom Award, 84; Eugene Eisenmann Award, 87; Chuck Yeager Award, 90. *Prof Exp:* Chief sect, US Fish & Wildlife Serv, 61-76, wildlife biologist, Migratory Non-Game Bird Studies, 45-96. *Concurrent Pos:* Ed, Md Birdlife, 47-; mem, Int Bird Census Comt; secy, Int Bird Ringing Comt, 71-87; tech ed, Audubon Field Notes, 52-70 & Am Birds, 71-74 & 79-89. *Mem:* Fel Am Ornith Union; Wilson Ornith Soc; Cooper Ornith Soc; Am Meteorol Soc; Asn Field Ornithologists. *Res:* Distribution, migration, abundance and habitat requirements of North American birds; monitoring of bird population levels; analysis of records of banded birds; breeding bird atlas methodology; field identification of birds. *Mailing Add:* Patuxent Wildlife Res Ctr Laurel MD 20708-4015. *Fax:* 301-497-5624

ROBBINS, CLARENCE RALPH, COSMETIC CHEMISTRY, ORGANIC CHEMISTRY. *Current Pos:* sect head, Colgate Palmolive Co, 66-72, sect head toiletries, 72-74, sr sect head hair & soap prod, 74-77, sr res assoc skin & hair res, 77-81, sr scientist hair res, 81-86, res fel, 86-91, distinguished fel, Hair Res, 91-94, VPRES ADVAN TECHNOL, COLGATE PALMOLIVE CO, 94- *Personal Data:* b Point Marion, Pa, Aug 25, 38; m 71, Marjorie G Johnson; c Laura J & Mark J. *Educ:* WVa Wesleyan Col, BS, 60; Purdue Univ, PhD(org chem), 64. *Honors & Awards:* Lit Award, Soc Cosmetic Chemists, 83; Maison de Navarre Medal Award, 89. *Prof Exp:* Res chemist hair res, 64-66. *Concurrent Pos:* Asst prof dermal pharmacol, Farleigh Dickinson Univ, 83-84; ed, J Soc Cosmetic Chemists, 87-92. *Mem:* Soc Cosmetic Chemists; Am Oil Chemists Soc. *Res:* Chemical and physical properties of human hair and skin, especially physical property changes of hair and skin to toiletry and surfactant treatments and to other environmental influences. *Mailing Add:* Colgate Palmolive Co 909 River Rd Piscataway NJ 08854

ROBBINS, D(ELMAR) HURLEY, COMPUTER AIDED ENGINEERING. *Current Pos:* MGR, RES & DEVELOP MATH MODELING, 88- *Personal Data:* b Elmira, NY, Dec 5, 37; m 68, Renate Knochenhauer; c Andrew W. *Educ:* Univ Mich, BSE(eng mech) & BSE(math), 60, MSE, 61, PhD(eng mech), 65. *Honors & Awards:* Metrop Life Award, Nat Safety Coun, 70. *Prof Exp:* Asst prof eng mech, Ohio State Univ, 65-67; res scientist, Hwy Safety Res Inst, Univ Mich, Ann Arbor, 67-88. *Mem:* Am Soc Mech Engrs; Soc Automotive Engrs; Sigma Xi. *Res:* Theory of shells; mechanical properties of engineering and biological materials; analytical and experimental simulation of automotive crash impact; acoustics of musical instruments. *Mailing Add:* 1469 Biggers Dr Rochester Hills MI 48309-1611

ROBBINS, DAVID ALVIN, BANACH MODULES, BANACH BUNDLES. *Current Pos:* From asst prof to assoc prof, Trinity Col, 72-84, chmn dept, 78-84 & 88-90, spec asst to pres, 88-90, PROF MATH, TRINITY COL, 84-, SEABURY PROF MATH & NATURAL PHILOS, 95, CHMN DEPT, 96- *Personal Data:* b May 11, 47. *Educ:* Dartmouth Col, AB, 67; Bucknell Univ, MA, 68; Duke Univ, MA, 70, PhD(math), 72; Rensselaer Polytech Inst, MS, 83. *Concurrent Pos:* Ace fel academ adin, 87-88. *Mem:* Am Math Soc; Math Asn Am. *Res:* Fields and bundles of Banach spaces; banach modules. *Mailing Add:* Dept Math Trinity Col Hartford CT 06106

ROBBINS, DAVID O, VISUAL NEUROSCIENCE. *Current Pos:* asst prof, 73-78, ASSOC PROF, DEPT PSYCHOL, OHIO WESLEYAN UNIV, 78- *Personal Data:* b Bryn Mawr, Pa, July 1, 43; m 71; c 2. *Educ:* Lycoming Col, BA, 65; Univ Del, MA, 68, PhD(physiol psychol), 70. *Prof Exp:* Fel vision, Eye Res Found, 69-70, prin investr, Dept Physiol, 70-73, dir res, 72-73. *Concurrent Pos:* Prin investr contracts, US Army Res & Develop Command, 70- *Mem:* Asn Res Vision & Ophthal; Sigma Xi; Am Psychol Soc; Soc Neurosci. *Res:* Electrophysiological bases of color vision with emphasis on single cell receptive field organization to color and movement in reptiles; adverse effects of intense, coherent (laser) light on retinal physiology and function in rhesus monkeys. *Mailing Add:* Dept Psychol Ohio Wesleyan Univ Delaware OH 43015-2398. *Fax:* 614-368-3299; *E-Mail:* dorobbins@cc.owu.edu

ROBBINS, DICK LAMSON, MEDICINE, IMMUNOLOGY. *Current Pos:* from asst prof to assoc prof, 76-88, PROF MED, DEPT INTERNAL MED, DIV RHEUMATOL, ALLERGY & CLIN IMMUNOL, UNIV CALIF, SCH MED, DAVIS, 88-, PROF MED, VET ADMIN NORTHERN CALIF HEALTH CARE SYSTS, 94- *Personal Data:* b Boston, Mass, May 13, 41; c 3. *Educ:* Lawrence Univ, BA, 63; Univ Vt Col Med, MD, 67. *Prof Exp:* Internship, Good Samaritan Hosp, Phoenix, 67-68; residency internal med, Univ Ore Med Sch, Portland, 68-71; active duty, Dept Med, US Naval Hosp, Balboa Park, San Diego, 71-73, co-dir, 72-73; res fel rheumatol, Scripps Clin & Res Found, La Jolla, 73-76. *Concurrent Pos:* Res fel, NIH, 74-76; prog chair, Soc Fels, Scripps Clin & Res Found, 74-75, pres, 75-76; Earle C Anthony award, 76-77; consult varco, 76-80; prin investr, 77-94. *Mem:* Fel Am Rheumatism Asn; Am Soc Zool; AAAS; Int Soc Develop & Comp Immunol; fel Am Col Rheumatol; Am Med Asn. *Res:* Immunology; rheumatology; author of 55 publications and 1 book. *Mailing Add:* Div Rheumatol & Immunol 110 TB 192 Univ Calif Davis CA 95616

ROBBINS, DONALD EUGENE, PHYSICS. *Current Pos:* RETIRED. *Personal Data:* b San Saba, Tex, July 4, 37; m 56; c 3. *Educ:* Tex Christian Univ, BA, 60; Univ Houston, PhD(physics), 69. *Prof Exp:* Nuclear engr, Gen Dynamics, Ft Worth, 60-62; sr nuclear engr, Ling Temco Vought, Dallas, 62-63; physicist, Johnson Space Ctr, NASA, 63-96. *Concurrent Pos:* Lectr, San Jacinto Col, Tex, 69-70, Univ Houston, 72-78. *Mem:* Am Phys Soc. *Res:* Atmospheric physics; catalytic attack of minor species on stratospheric ozone; institute measurements of ozone and other stratospheric species; measurement of vacuum ultraviolet photoabsorption cross section for gases of interest to atmospheric physics. *Mailing Add:* 1902 Orchard Glen Ct Houston TX 77062-4785

ROBBINS, EDITH SCHULTZ, ELECTRON MICROSCOPY, CELL TURNOVER. *Current Pos:* Instr, 68-71, from asst prof to assoc prof, 72-80, PROF BIOL, MANHATTAN COMMUNITY COL, CITY UNIV NEW YOR, 81- *Personal Data:* b Galveston, Tex, July 4, 41; m 66, Peter L; c George M. *Educ:* Barnard Col, AB, 62; NY Univ, MS, 65, PhD(biol), 70. *Concurrent Pos:* Adj instr, New York Univ Sch Med, 70-72, adj asst prof, 72-75, adj assoc prof, 75- *Mem:* Am Soc Cell Biol; AAAS; Sigma Xi; NY Acad Sci; Micros Soc Am. *Res:* Studies on epithelial polarity; examination of cells with various electron microscopy techniques including freeze-fracture and scanning; trypanosome structure/function correlations; cellular morphometry of bronchi; cell cycling studies using immunocytochemistry. *Mailing Add:* Dept Cell Biol New York Univ Sch Med 550 First Ave MSR 629 New York NY 10016-6402. *Fax:* 212-263-8139

ROBBINS, ELEANORA IBERALL, BIOGEOLOGY, PALEOECOLOGY. *Current Pos:* Vol, US Peace Corps Geol Surv, Tanzania, 64-66, GEOLOGIST, US GEOL SURV, 67- *Personal Data:* b Washington, DC, July 20, 42; m 72, C Brian. *Educ:* Ohio State Univ, BS, 64; Univ Ariz, MS, 72; Pa State Univ, PhD(geosci), 82. *Concurrent Pos:* Mem bd, Am Asn Stratig Palynologists, 89-91. *Mem:* Am Soc Surface Mining Reclamation; Am Asn Stratig Palynologists; Asn Women Geoscientists; Soc Wetland Scientists. *Res:* Acid mine drainage microbiology, relationship between coal, petroleum, and ore deposits; publications on organic tissues, microorganisms and minerals in Precambrian iron formation, in Mn nodules, and in carbonaceous gold deposits. *Mailing Add:* US Geol Surv Nat Ctr MS 956 Reston VA 20192. *Fax:* 703-648-6419; *E-Mail:* nrobbins@.usgs.gov

ROBBINS, ERNEST ALECK, BIOCHEMISTRY. *Current Pos:* RETIRED. *Personal Data:* b Boy River, Minn, Mar 26, 26; m 46; c 6. *Educ:* Univ Minn, BChem, 51, PhD(biochem), 57. *Prof Exp:* Eng aide, State Hwy Dept, Minn, 49-51; asst, Univ Minn, 51-56; res chemist, Rohm and Haas Co, Pa, 56-71; head food biochem, Anheuser-Busch, Inc, 71-75, assoc dir yeast prod res, 75-92. *Mem:* Am Chem Soc; Am Asn Cereal Chem; Inst Food Technol; Sigma Xi. *Res:* Production, properties and utilization of enzymes from microorganisms; development of food and fermentation products. *Mailing Add:* 7880 Oak Lawn Pl Cedar Hill MO 63016-2550

ROBBINS, FREDERICK CHAPMAN, PEDIATRICS. *Current Pos:* UNIV PROF, CASE WESTERN RESERVE UNIV, 80- & EMER DEAN, SCH MED, 80- *Personal Data:* b Auburn, Ala, Aug 25, 16; m 48, Alice Northrop; c Alice C & Louise (Enders). *Educ:* Univ Mo, BA, 36, BS, 38; Harvard Med Sch, MD, 40; Am Bd Pediat, dipl, 51. *Hon Degrees:* DSc, John Carroll Univ, 55, Univ Mo, 58; LLD, Univ NMex, 68; DSc, Univ NC, 79, Tufts Univ, 83, Med Col Ohio, 83, Albert Einstein Col Med, 84, Med Col Wis, 84; DMedSc, Med Col Pa, 84; LLD, Univ Ala, Birmingham, 85. *Honors & Awards:* Nobel Prize in Physiol & Med, 54; First Mead Johnson Award, 53; Award for Distinguished Achievement Modern Med, 63; Med Mutual Hon Award, 69. *Prof Exp:* Resident bact, Children's Hosp, 40-41, intern med, 41-42, asst resident, 46-47, resident, 47-48; Nat Res Coun fel virus dis, Children's Hosp, Boston, 48-50; instr & assoc pediat, Harvard Med Sch, 50-52; prof pediat, Sch Med, Case Western Reserve Univ, 50-80, dean, Sch Med, 66-80, prof community health, 73-80; pres, Inst Med-Nat Acad Sci, 81-85. *Concurrent Pos:* Asst, Children's Med Serv, Mass Gen Hosp, Boston, 50-52; dir, Dept Pediat & Contagious Dis, Cleveland Metrop Gen Hosp, 52-66; consult, Communicable Dis Ctr, USPHS, Ga, 54-60 & adv comt, Bur Biologics, Food & Drug Admin, 84- *Mem:* Nat Acad Sci; Am Philos Soc; Am Pediat Soc (pres, 73-74); emer mem Ad Soc Clin Invest; Soc Exp Biol & Med; Soc Pediat Res (pres, 61-62); Am Acad Arts & Sci; emer mem Am Acad Pediat; fel AAAS; hon mem Asn Am Physicians. *Res:* Recognition and epidemiology of Q fever; immunology of mumps; tissue culture-poliomyelitis virus. *Mailing Add:* Dept Epidemiol & Biostatist Case Western Res Univ Sch Med Cleveland OH 44106

ROBBINS, GORDON DANIEL, ELECTROCHEMISTRY. *Current Pos:* DIR ANALYSIS SERV, MARTIN MARIETTA ENERGY SYST, 93- *Personal Data:* b Rocky Mount, NC, Feb 8, 40; m 67; c 2. *Educ:* Univ NC, BS, 62; Princeton Univ, MA, 64, PhD(electrochem), 66. *Prof Exp:* Fulbright fel, Molten Salts, Tech Univ Norway, 66-67; res chemist, Oak Ridge Nat Lab, 67-72, dir, Off Prof Univ Rels, 72-77, dir, Info Div, 78-93. *Mem:* Am Soc Info Sci. *Res:* Aqueous electrochemistry; thermodynamics, transport properties, electrochemistry and electrical conductivity of molten salts. *Mailing Add:* 41 Riverview Dr Oak Ridge TN 37830

ROBBINS, HERBERT ELLIS, MATHEMATICAL STATISTICS. *Current Pos:* NJ PROF MATH STATIST, RUTGERS UNIV, 86- *Personal Data:* b New Castle, Pa, Jan 12, 15; m 42, 66, Carol Hallett; c Mary, David, Emily, Marcia & Mark. *Educ:* Harvard Univ, AB, 35, AM, 36, PhD(math), 38. *Hon Degrees:* ScD, Purdue Univ, 74. *Honors & Awards:* Wald Lectr, 69; Neyman Lectr, 82; Patten Lect, Ind Univ, 88; Hitchcock Lectr, Univ Calif, 89; Fisher Lectr, 93. *Prof Exp:* Instr & tutor math, Harvard Univ, 36-38; asst, Inst Advan Study, 38-39; instr, NY Univ, 39-42; assoc prof math statist, Univ NC, 46-49, prof, 50-53; prof, Columbia Univ, 53-85. *Concurrent Pos:* Guggenheim fel, 52-53 & 75-76; vis prof, Univ Minn, 65 & Purdue Univ, 65; prof, Univ Mich, 67-68. *Mem:* Nat Acad Sci; fel Inst Math Statist (pres, 65-66); Am Acad Arts & Sci. *Res:* Mathematical statistics, especially sequential experimentation; theory of probability; numerous articles to professional publications. *Mailing Add:* Dept Statist Rutgers Univ New Brunswick NJ 08903. *Fax:* 732-932-3428

ROBBINS, JACKIE WAYNE DARMON, AGRICULTURAL ENGINEERING, DRIP IRRIGATION. *Current Pos:* prof agr eng & head dept, 71-87, PROF CIVIL ENG, LA TECH UNIV, 87- *Personal Data:* b Spartanburg, SC, Feb 6, 40; m 63, Betty Wright; c Jay & Robin. *Educ:* Clemson Univ, BS, 61, MS, 65; NC State Univ, PhD(biol & agr eng), 70. *Prof Exp:* E C McArthur fel, Clemson Univ, 62-63; asst prof agr eng, La State Univ, 63-65; res asst, NC State Univ, 65-68, res assoc biol & agr eng, 68-70; assoc prof agr eng, Univ Mo, 70-71. *Concurrent Pos:* NSF grant & vis prof, Univ Hawaii, 77-78; consult, dept tech serv, Repub SAfrica, 79, Water Res Comn, 81 & Comn Int du Genic Rural, 86; owner, Robbins Asn, Irrigation-Mart; pres, La Blueberry Asn Inc. *Mem:* Am Soc Agr Engrs; Am Soc Eng Educ; Sigma Xi; Irrigation Asn; Nat Soc Prof Engrs. *Res:* Agricultural waste and waste water management; soil and water conservation; groundwater hydrology; irrigation. *Mailing Add:* 3303 McDonald Ave Ruston LA 71270. *Fax:* 318-255-7572

ROBBINS, JACOB, ENDOCRINOLOGY, MEDICAL RESEARCH. *Current Pos:* res scientist, Nat Inst Diabetes, Digestive & Kidney Dis, 54-62, chief, Clin Endocrinal Br, 61-91, chief, Genetic & Biochem Br, 91-95, EMER SCIENTIST, NAT INST DIABETES, DIGESTIVE & KIDNEY DIS, 95- *Personal Data:* b Yonkers, NY, Sept 1, 22; m 49, Jean Adams; c Alice E, Susan L & Mark S. *Educ:* Cornell Univ, AB, 44, MD, 47; Am Bd Internal Med, dipl. *Honors & Awards:* Van Meter Award, Am Thyroid Asn, 55, Distinguished Serv Award, 83; Meritorious Serv Medal, USPHS, 71; Distinguished Serv Award, Endocrine Soc, 95. *Prof Exp:* Intern med, NY Hosp, 47-48; res, Mem Hosp, 48-50; instr, Med Col, Cornell Univ, 50-54. *Concurrent Pos:* Res fel, Sloan-Kettering Inst Cancer Res, 50-53, asst, 53-54, clin asst, Mem Ctr, 51-53, asst attend physician, 53-54; vis scientist, Calsberg Lab, Copenhagen, Denmark, 59-60; ed-in-chief, Endocrinol, 68-72. *Mem:* AAAS; Endocrine Soc; Am Physiol Soc; Am Thyroid Asn (pres, 74-75); Asn Am Physicians; Europ Thyroid Asn; hon mem Japan Endocrine Soc; hon mem Ital Endocrine Soc. *Res:* Thyroid physiology; biochemistry and disease. *Mailing Add:* 7203 Bradley Blvd Bethesda MD 20817

ROBBINS, JAMES CLIFFORD, LIPID SYNTHESIS, ATHEROSCLEROSIS. *Current Pos:* RES FEL, MERCK & CO, INC, 84- *Educ:* Univ Mich, PhD(biochem), 73. *Mailing Add:* 974 Ridge Rd Monmouth Junction NJ 08852. *Fax:* 732-594-6645

ROBBINS, JAY HOWARD, CELL BIOLOGY, MEDICINE. *Current Pos:* res assoc, NIMH, 63-65, SR INVESTR, NAT CANCER INST, 65- *Personal Data:* b New York, NY, Feb 10, 34; m 61, Joan Raff; c Jonathan, Jeffrey & Joshua. *Educ:* Harvard Univ, AB, 56; Columbia Univ, MD, 60. *Prof Exp:* Intern, Mt Sinai Hosp, NY, 60-61, asst resident, 61-62, fel med, 63. *Mem:* Am Fedn Med Res; Soc Invest Dermat; Soc Neurosci. *Res:* DNA repair and carcinogenesis; cell growth and differentiation; study of effect of DNA-damaging agents on cultured cells from patients with degenerative neurological disease and/or with cancer. *Mailing Add:* 8209 Gainsborough Ct W Potomac MD 20854. *Fax:* 301-496-5370

ROBBINS, JOHN ALAN, LIMNOLOGY, OCEANOGRAPHY & RADIOCHEMISTRY. *Current Pos:* adj prof, Sch Natural Resources, 84-90, SR RES SCIENTIST, ENVIRON RES LAB, UNIV MICH, 90-, ADJ PROF, SCH PUB HEALTH, 90- *Personal Data:* b Syracuse, NY, Jan 19, 38; m 66; c 2. *Educ:* Swarthmore Col, BA, 59; Univ Rochester, PhD(nuclear physics), 67. *Honors & Awards:* RPI Sci Award, 55; Bausch & Lomb Sci Achievement Award, 55. *Prof Exp:* Res assoc nuclear physics, Univ Rochester, 68-69; res assoc air chem, Dept Atmospheric Sci, Univ Mich, Ann Arbor, 69-70; asst res physicist, Great Lakes Res Div, Univ Mich, Ann Arbor, 70-73, assoc res physicist, 73-76, sr res scientist limnol, 76-80; physicist, Great Lakes Environ Res Lab, Nat Oceanic & Atmospheric Admin, Ann Arbor, Mich, 80-; vis prof, Univ Constance, Ger, 89. *Concurrent Pos:* Co-founder & consult, Environ Res Group, Inc, Ann Arbor, 70-78; consult, Wildlife Supply Co, Saginaw, Mich, 74- & Radiol & Environ Res Div, Argonne Nat Lab, Ill, 78-; guest ed, Chem Geol, 84. *Mem:* Am Soc Limnol & Oceanog; Int Asn Great Lakes; Sigma Xi; Soc Int Limnol. *Res:* Physics and chemistry of lakes; radiolimnology and sediment geochronology; radiotracer studies of animal-sediment interactions; mathematical modeling of limnological processes. *Mailing Add:* Environ Res Lab 2205 Commonwealth Blvd Ann Arbor MI 48105

ROBBINS, JOHN B, HUMAN DEVELOPMENT. *Current Pos:* CHIEF, LAB DEVELOP & MOLECULAR IMMUNITY, NAT INST CHILD HEALTH & HUMAN DEVELOP, NIH, 83- *Personal Data:* b Brooklyn, NY, Dec 1, 32. *Educ:* New York Univ, BA, 56, MD, 59. *Hon Degrees:* MD, Univ Goteborg, Sweden, 76. *Honors & Awards:* E Mead Johnson Award, Am Acad Pediat, 75; Henry Bale Mem Lectr, Nat Inst Biol Stand & Control, 79; Erwin Neter Mem Lectr, Univ Buffalo, 84; Henry L Barnett Lectr, Albert Einstein Col Med, 85; Maxwell Finland Lectr, Infectious Dis Soc Am, 89; Louis Weinstein Lectr, Tufts Univ, 89. *Prof Exp:* Student investr, NY Univ, Col Med, 57-59; intern/resident, Children's Med Serv, Mass Gen Hosp, Boston, 59-60; res fel, Dept Pediat, Univ Fla, 61-64; asst prof pediat & microbiol, Univ Fla, Gainesville, 64-67; guest scientist, Dept Chem Immunol, Weizmann Inst Sci, Rehovot, Israel, 65-66; from asst prof to assoc prof pediat, Albert Einstein Col Med, 67-70; clin dir, Nat Inst Child Health & Human Develop, NIH, 70-72, chief, Develop Immunol Br, 71-74; dir, Div Bact Prod, Bur Biologics, Food & Drug Admin, 74-83. *Concurrent Pos:* Assoc mem, Armed Forces Epidemiol Bd, 70; assoc ed, J Immunol, 74; consult, WHO, Nat Inst Vaccines & Sera & Shanghai Inst Vaccines & Sera, Beijing, People's Repub China, Dept Pub Health & Inst Prev Med, Nat Taiwan Univ. *Mem:* Nat Acad Sci; Inst Med-Nat Acad Sci; Soc Infectious Dis; Am Soc Clin Invest; Asn Am Physicians; Am Asn Immunologists; fel Am Acad Microbiol; Soc Pediat Res. *Res:* Vaccines. *Mailing Add:* NIH Nat Inst Child Health & Human Develop Lab Develop & Molecular Immunity Bldg 6 Rm 424 Bethesda MD 20892

ROBBINS, JOHN EDWARD, BIOCHEMISTRY. *Current Pos:* RETIRED. *Personal Data:* b Chamberlin, SDak, Apr 2, 35; m 58; c 1. *Educ:* Carroll Col, Mont, BA, 58; Mont State Univ, MS, 61, PhD(chem), 63. *Prof Exp:* NIH fel, Univ Ore, 63-66; asst prof, Mont State Univ, 67-70, assoc prof chem, 70-77, assoc prof biochem, 77- *Mem:* AAAS; Am Chem Soc; Sigma Xi. *Res:* Subunit structure of enzymes as related to their functional roles in enzyme functions of catalysis and control. *Mailing Add:* 206 South Eighth Mont State Univ Bozeman MT 59715

ROBBINS, KAY ANN, COMPUTER SCIENCE. *Current Pos:* PROF, DEPT MATH, UNIV TEX, SAN ANTONIO, 76- *Educ:* Mass Inst Technol, BS, 71 PhD(appl math), 75. *Mem:* Am Phys Soc; Am Geophys Union; Inst Elec & Electronics Engrs. *Res:* Computer science. *Mailing Add:* Div Comput Sci Univ Tex 6900 N Loop 1604 W San Antonio TX 78249

ROBBINS, KEITH CRANSTON, MICROBIOLOGY. *Current Pos:* RETIRED. *Personal Data:* b Berwyn, Ill, Feb 3, 44; m 67, Barbara A Byrne; c Christine A, Nancy E & Elizabeth E. *Educ:* Ind Univ, BA, 67; Am Univ, MS, 72; George Washington Univ, PhD, 77. *Prof Exp:* Staff scientist, Hazelton Labs, Vienna Va, 72-80; cancer expert, Nat Cancer Inst, Bethesda, 80-85; sect chief, Nat Inst Dent Res, Bethesda, 88-96, lab chief, 92-96. *Concurrent Pos:* Invited lectr, Australian Biochem Soc, Am Heart Asn, Nat Geriat Soc, Am Soc Biochem & Molecular Biol, Arg Cong Cancer, Frontiers Clin Dent, Am Soc Microbiol, Mich Cancer Found, Cells Growth & Cancer, Upjohn Pharms, Pfizer Pharms, Sterling Drug, Nova Pharms, Cor Therapeuts, Pfizer Inc & numerous univs. *Mem:* AAAS. *Res:* Discovery of gene specifying platelet-derived growth factor; discovered a number of oncogenes; granted 2 US patents. *Mailing Add:* 11713 Bluesmoke Trail Reston VA 22091

ROBBINS, KELLY ROY, STATISTICS, BIOCHEMISTRY. *Current Pos:* assoc prof, 79-89, PROF & HEAD NUTRIT, UNIV TENN, KNOXVILLE, 89- *Educ:* Univ Ill, PhD(nutrit), 79. *Concurrent Pos:* Light, nutrition and other environmental influences on growth and reproduction of poultry and swine. *Mem:* Am Soc Animal Sci; Poultry Sci Asn; Am Inst Nutrit. *Mailing Add:* Dept Animal Sci 206 Brehm Hall Univ Tenn PO Box 1071 Knoxville TN 37901-1071

ROBBINS, KENNETH CARL, BIOCHEMISTRY. *Current Pos:* prof, 70-87, EMER PROF MED & PATH, PRITZKER SCH MED, UNIV CHICAGO, 87-; RES PROF, NORTHWESTERN UNIV, 88- *Personal Data:* b Chicago, Ill, Sept 1, 17; m 46; c 2. *Educ:* Univ Ill, BS, 39, MS, 40, PhD(biol chem), 44. *Honors & Awards:* Elwood A Sharp Lect Award, Sch Med, Wayne State Univ, 71; Prix Servier Medal & Prize, Fifth Int Congress Fibrinolysis, Malmo, Sweden, 80. *Prof Exp:* Instr biol chem, Univ Ill, 44-47; asst prof dept path, Western Reserve Univ Sch Med, 47-51; head protein sect, Biochem Res Dept, Res Labs, Armour & Co, 51-56, sect head, Biochem Dept, Cent Labs, Res Div, 56-58; dir biochem res & develop dept, Michael Reese Res Found, 58-73, sci dir, 73-84. *Concurrent Pos:* Mem hemat study sect, Div Res Grants, NIH, 71-75 & 78-82; chmn, Gordon Conf Hemostasis, 75; mem, Blood Diseases and Resources Adv Comt, Nat Heart, Lung & Blood Inst, NIH, 76-80; co-chmn, Subcomt on Fibrinolysis, Int Comt on Thrombosis & Hemostasis, 77-80, chmn, 80-82; mem, Int Comt Thrombosis & Hemostasis, 80-86. *Mem:* Soc Exp Biol & Med; Am Chem Soc; Am Asn Immunol; Am Soc Biol Chem; Am Soc Hemat; Int Soc Thrombosis & Hemostasis. *Res:* Blood coagulation and fibrinolysis; animal proteins and enzymes. *Mailing Add:* Oncol Div Northwestern Univ Med Sch 6101 N Sheridan Rd E 36C Chicago IL 60660-2801

ROBBINS, LANNY ARNOLD, CHEMICAL ENGINEERING. *Current Pos:* Chem engr, Dow Chem Co, 66-67, res engr, 67-70, sr pilot plant engr, 70-72, res specialist, 72-73, sr res specialist, 73-76, assoc scientist, 76-79, sr assoc scientist, 79-83, res scientist, 83-88, sr res scientist, 88-97, RES FEL, DOW CHEM CO, 97- *Personal Data:* b Wahoo, Nebr, Apr 3, 40; m 62, Connie Polich; c James & Debra. *Educ:* Iowa State Univ, BS, 61, MS, 63, PhD(chem eng), 66. *Concurrent Pos:* Adj prof, Mich State Univ, 82. *Mem:* Am Inst Chem Engrs. *Res:* Commercial separations and purification processes, with emphasis on melt crystallization, liquid-liquid extraction, packed tower strippers, absorbers and distillation; miniplant design and operation; pressure swing absorption, distillation process control and optimization. *Mailing Add:* 4101 Old Pine Trail Midland MI 48642-8892

ROBBINS, LEONARD GILBERT, GENETICS, MOLECULAR BIOLOGY. *Current Pos:* from asst prof to assoc prof, 72-82, PROF ZOOL, MICH STATE UNIV, 83-, PROF, GENETICS DEPT EVOLUTIONARY BIOL, UNIV SIENA, ITALY, 97- *Personal Data:* b Brooklyn, NY, Aug 10, 45; m 83, Ellen E Swanson; c Daniel C & Rachel V. *Educ:* Brooklyn Col, BS, 65; Univ Wash, PhD(genetics), 70. *Prof Exp:* NIH trainee zool, Univ Tex, Austin, 70-72. *Concurrent Pos:* NIH-Fogarty sr int fel, Madrid, Spain, 80-81, Bari, Italy, 91-92; mem, NSF-BRI panel, 92- *Mem:* Genetics Soc Am; Fedn Am Scientist. *Res:* Formal and molecular genetics of higher organisms; maternal and zygotic gene action; genetic regulation of chromosome behavior in Drosophila; molecular and functional organization of ribosomal RNA genes. *Mailing Add:* Genetics Prog S308 Molecular Biol Addn Mich State Univ East Lansing MI 48824-1312. *Fax:* 517-353-1926; *E-Mail:* 21675mgr@msu.edu

ROBBINS, MARION LERON, HORTICULTURE, PLANT BREEDING. *Current Pos:* Resident dir, Sweet Potato Res Sta, 84-88, RESIDENT DIR, CALHOUN RES STA, CLEMSON UNIV, 88- *Personal Data:* b Chesnee, SC, Aug 18, 41; m 65, 96, Jeanette Rogers; c Jack, Rona B, Jeff & Kyle. *Educ:* Clemson Univ, BS, 64; La State Univ, MS, 66; Univ Md, PhD(hort breeding), 68. *Prof Exp:* Asst prof hort, Iowa State Univ, 68-72; from assoc prof to prof, Clemson Univ, 72-84. *Concurrent Pos:* Consult on veg prod & tea; ed, J Veg Crop Prod. *Mem:* Am Soc Hort Sci; Int Soc Hort Sci; Res Ctr Adminr Soc; Asn Soil Agr Scientists; Interam Soc Hort Sci; Sigma Xi. *Res:* Vegetable production research; breeding and physiology; influence of cultural practices on yield and quality of vegetables; tea as a crop for the United States; okra research and development. *Mailing Add:* Calhoun Res Sta PO Box 539 Calhoun LA 71225. *Fax:* 318-644-7244; *E-Mail:* rrobbins@agctr.lsu.edu

ROBBINS, MARK OWEN, NON-EQUILIBRIUM PHASE TRANSITIONS, DYNAMICS IN DISORDERED SYSTEMS. *Current Pos:* from asst prof to assoc prof, 86-92, PROF PHYSICS, DEPT PHYSICS & ASTRON, JOHNS HOPKINS UNIV, 92- *Personal Data:* b Indianapolis, Ind, Nov 7, 55; m 93, Patricia M McGuiggan. *Educ:* Harvard Univ, BA, 77, MA, 77; Cambridge Univ, cert, 78; Univ Calif, Berkeley, PhD(physics), 83. *Prof Exp:* Fel, Corp Res Sci Lab, Exxon Res & Eng Co, 83-85. *Concurrent Pos:* Pres young investr, NSF, 86-91; fel, Sloan Found, 87-88; consult, Exxon Res & Eng Co, 86-; vis assoc prof, Univ Calif, Santa Barbara, 89, Univ Minn, 91. *Mem:* Am Phys Soc; Mat Res Soc. *Res:* Theoretical studies of dissipation, dynamics and phase transitions in non-equilibrium systems; shear-melting of solids; interface motion in random media, friction, adhesion and spreading. *Mailing Add:* Dept Physics & Astron Johns Hopkins Univ Baltimore MD 21218. *Fax:* 410-516-7239; *E-Mail:* mr@pha.jhu.edu

ROBBINS, MURRAY, INORGANIC CHEMISTRY. *Current Pos:* MEM TECH STAFF, BELL TEL LABS, INC, 67- *Personal Data:* b Brooklyn, NY, Mar 9, 31; m 54; c 1. *Educ:* Brooklyn Col, BS, 53, MA, 54; Polytech Inst Brooklyn, PhD(inorg chem), 62. *Prof Exp:* Res chemist, Columbia Univ Mineral Beneficiation Labs, 53-54; instr inorg chem, Polytech Inst Brooklyn, 60-62; res chemist, David Sarnoff Res Labs, Radio Corp Am, 62-67. *Mem:* Am Chem Soc; Am Phys Soc; Sigma Xi. *Res:* Synthesis and properties of solid state materials and crystal growth. *Mailing Add:* 110 Kent Dr Berkeley Heights NJ 07922-2332

ROBBINS, NAOMI BOGRAD, STATISTICS, RELIABILITY. *Current Pos:* MEM TECH STAFF, BELL LABS, 60- *Personal Data:* b Paterson, NJ, May 8, 37; m 62; c 2. *Educ:* Bryn Mawr Col, AB, 58; Cornell Univ, MA, 62; Columbia Univ, PhD(math statist), 71. *Mem:* Am Statist Asn; Sigma Xi. *Mailing Add:* 11 Christine Ct Wayne NJ 07470

ROBBINS, NORMAN, NEUROPHYSIOLOGY, ENVIRONMENT. *Current Pos:* from asst prof to assoc prof anat, 70-84, prof develop genetics & anat, 84-89, PROF NEUROSCI, SCH MED, CASE WESTERN UNIV, 89-, DIR, CTR ENVIRON, 93-, CO-DIR. *Personal Data:* b Brooklyn, NY, Apr 15, 35; m 68; c 2. *Educ:* Columbia Col, AB, 55; Harvard Univ, MD, 59; Rockefeller Univ, PhD(biol), 66. *Prof Exp:* Intern med, 2nd Div, Bellevue Hosp, 59-60; jr asst resident med, Peter Bent Brigham Hosp, 60-61; fel neurobiol, Rockefeller Univ, 61-66; res assoc neurophysiol, Spinal Cord Div, Nat Inst Neurol Dis & Blindness, 66-69; vis scientist, Kyoto Prefectural Univ Med, 69-70. *Mem:* AAAS; Soc Neurosci; Am Pub Health Asn. *Res:* Neurobiology; physiology of development, plasticity and aging of the neuromuscular junction. *Mailing Add:* Dept Neurosci Sch Med Case Western Res Univ 2119 Abinlton Rd Cleveland OH 44106-2333

ROBBINS, PAUL EDWARD, ORGANIC CHEMISTRY. *Current Pos:* assoc prof, 66-75, prof, 75-86, EMER PROF CHEM, ARMSTRONG STATE COL, 86- *Personal Data:* b Camden, NJ, Apr 4, 28; m 54; c 3. *Educ:* Univ Pa, BS, 52; Ga Inst Technol, PhD(chem), 56. *Prof Exp:* Res chemist, E I du Pont de Nemours & Co, 56-60; assoc prof textile chem, Clemson Univ, 60-66. *Mem:* Am Chem Soc; AAAS; Sigma Xi. *Res:* Catalytic hydrogenation; physical and synthetic organic chemistry; polymer chemistry and rheology; textile chemistry; films. *Mailing Add:* 14 Keystone Dr Savannah GA 31406-5727

ROBBINS, PHILLIPS WESLEY, CELL SURFACE PROTEINS & CARBOHYDRATES. *Current Pos:* from asst prof to prof, 59-77, AM CANCER SOC PROF BIOCHEM, MASS INST TECHNOL, 77- *Personal Data:* b Barre, Mass, Aug 10, 30; m 53; c 2. *Educ:* DePauw Univ, AB, 52; Univ Ill, PhD(biochem), 55. *Honors & Awards:* Eli Lilly Award Biol Chem, 66. *Prof Exp:* Res assoc, Mass Gen Hosp, 55-57; asst prof, Rockefeller Inst, 57-59. *Mem:* Nat Acad Sci; Am Soc Biochem & Molecular Biol; Am Soc Microbiol; Sigma Xi. *Res:* Sulfate activation; synthesis of complex polysaccharides; cell-virus relationships. *Mailing Add:* Dept Biol Ctr Cancer Res Mass Inst Technol Cambridge MA 02139. *Fax:* 617-258-8315; *E-Mail:* robbinsp@mit,edu

ROBBINS, R(OGER) W(ELLINGTON), ELECTRICAL ENGINEERING. *Current Pos:* RETIRED. *Personal Data:* b Belmont, Mass, July 25, 20; m 46; c 2. *Educ:* Univ Wis, BS, 42. *Prof Exp:* Elec draftsman, Jackson & Moreland, Mass, 42-43; field engr, Submarine Signal Co, 43, supvr tech div, Equip Dept, 43-45, asst admin engr, 45-46; res engr, Operadio Mfg Co, 46-51, proj engr, 51-53; mgr govt contracts div, Dukane Corp, 53-65, tech dir, spec prod div, 65-70, eng mgr, 70-86. *Mem:* AAAS; Inst Elec & Electronics Engrs; Ultrasonic Indust Asn (pres, 75-77). *Res:* Devices which require the use of moving mechanical parts in conjunction with electrical circuits; optics; ultrasonics. *Mailing Add:* Park Manor Bldg F 700 W Fabyan Pkwy Apt 1117F Batavia IL 60510

ROBBINS, RALPH COMPTON, NUTRITION, PHYSIOLOGY. *Current Pos:* asst prof nutrit, 59-66, ASSOC PROF NUTRIT, INST FOOD & AGR SCI, UNIV FLA, 66- *Personal Data:* b Spurrier, Tenn, Feb 7, 21; m 51. *Educ:* Tenn Technol Univ, BS, 52; Iowa State Univ, MS, 55; Univ Ill, PhD(nutrit), 58. *Prof Exp:* Res fel nutrit & biochem, Med Col SC, 58-59. *Mem:* Am Chem Soc. *Res:* Effectiveness in the diet of naturally occurring blood cell antiadhesive compounds against certain types of circulating dysfunction. *Mailing Add:* 1410 NW 28th St Gainesville FL 32605

ROBBINS, RALPH ROBERT, ASTROPHYSICS. *Current Pos:* asst prof 68-72, ASSOC PROF ASTRON, UNIV TEX, AUSTIN, 72. *Personal Data:* b Wichita, Kans, Sept 2, 38. *Educ:* Yale Univ, BA, 60; Univ Calif, Berkeley, PhD(astron), 66. *Prof Exp:* McDonald Observ fel, Univ Tex, Austin, 66-67; asst prof physics, Univ Houston, 67-68. *Concurrent Pos:* Prin investr, NSF grant, Univ Tex Austin, 70-72; sci educ consult, AID. *Mem:* Am Astron Soc; Int Astron Union; fel Royal Astron Soc; Am Asn Physics Teachers. *Res:* Theoretical and observational astrophysics of gas nebulae and Seyfert galaxies; radiative transfer; atomic and plasma physics. *Mailing Add:* Dept Astron Univ Tex Austin TX 78712

ROBBINS, RICHARD J, UNDERGROUND EXCAVATION SYSTEMS. *Current Pos:* VCHMN, ATLAS COPCO ROBBINS, ING. *Personal Data:* m 66; c 2. *Educ:* Mich Technol Univ, BS, 56. *Honors & Awards:* Daniel C Jackling Award & lectr, Am Inst Mining Engrs, 84. *Prof Exp:* US CEngrs, Eng Res & Develop Labs, Ft Belvoire, VA, 56-58. *Concurrent Pos:* US deleg, Int Tunneling Asn, 75-76. *Mem:* Nat Acad Eng. *Res:* Underground excavation systems. *Mailing Add:* 1325 Fourth Ave Suite 1930 Seattle WA 98101-2509

ROBBINS, ROBERT JOHN, COMPUTER SCIENCE, DATABASE SYSTEMS & THEORY MANAGEMENT. *Current Pos:* VPRES INFO TECH, FRED HUTCHINSON CANCER RES CTR, SEATTLE, WASH, 95- *Personal Data:* b Niles, Mich, May 10, 44; m 84, Coreen A Kelly; c Alexandra K. *Educ:* Stanford Univ, AB, 66; Mich State Univ, BS, 73, MS, 74, PhD(zool), 77. *Prof Exp:* Instr genetics, Mich State UNiv, 76-77; from asst prof to assoc prof, 77-87; staff assoc, NSF, 87-89, prog dir, 90-93; prog mgr bioinfo infrastruct, US Dept Energy, 93-95. *Concurrent Pos:* Fel, Univ Calif, Davis, 78-79; assoc prof med info & comput sci, Johns Hopkins Univ, Baltimore, 91-, dir, Appl Res Lab, William H Welch Med Libr, Sch Med, 91- *Mem:* Am Inst Biol Sci; Am Soc Microbiol; Genetics Soc Am; Inst Elec & Electronics Engrs Comput Soc; Asn Comput Mach. *Res:* Computer applications in biology; general genetics; database systems & theory; development at computer systems for the management and analysis of biological information. *Mailing Add:* 21454 NE 143rd St Woodinville WA 98072. *Fax:* 301-903-8521; *E-Mail:* robbins@er.doe.gov

ROBBINS, ROBERT KANNER, BUTTERFLY EVOLUTION. *Current Pos:* ASSOC CUR, DEPT ENTOM, RES ENTOMOLOGIST, SMITHSONIAN INST, 83- *Personal Data:* b New York, NY, Oct 26, 47. *Educ:* Brown Univ, AB, 69; Tufts Univ, PhD(biol), 78. *Prof Exp:* Fel biol, Smithsonian Trop Res Inst, 78-79; fel biol, US Nat Mus, 81-82. *Concurrent Pos:* Exec coun, Lepidopterists' Soc. *Mem:* Soc Study Evolution; Soc Am Naturalists; AAAS; Lepidopterists' Soc; Soc Syst Zool. *Res:* Inferring butterfly phynology; using phylogenies to study the evolution of butterfly predator avoidance mechanisms, foodplant use, courtship/mating behavior, biogeography and species diversity; hereditability of behavior; statistical estimation of demographic parameters from field data; systematics of lepidoptera. *Mailing Add:* Entomol NHB Stop 127 Smithsonian Inst Washington DC 20560

ROBBINS, ROBERT RAYMOND, BOTANY, ULTRASTRUCTURE. *Current Pos:* MEM STAFF, IDAHO STATE UNIV. *Personal Data:* b Des Moines, Iowa, May 28, 46. *Educ:* Iowa State Univ, BS, 68; Univ Ill, Urbana, MS, 73. PhD(bot), 77. *Prof Exp:* Instr human anat, US Army Med Field Serv Sch, San Antonio, Tex, 69-71; lectr bot, Univ Ill, Urbana, 76, fel, 76-77; asst prof bot, Univ Wis-Milwaukee, 77. *Mem:* AAAS; Bot Soc Am; Am Bryol & Lichenological Soc; Am Inst Biol Sci; Am Fern Soc. *Res:* Ultrastructure of plant reproductive cells, especially bryophyte and lower vascular plant spermatogenesis; ragweed pollen development. *Mailing Add:* 1052 Stone Valley Sandy UT 84094-7325

ROBBINS, ROGER ALAN, PHOTORESIST PROCESS DEVELOPMENT, THERMAL CONTACT PHYSICS. *Current Pos:* sect head, 73-85, SR MEM TECH STAFF, SILICON PROCESS DEVELOP CTR, TEX INSTRUMENTS, 86- *Personal Data:* m 68, Anne E Broussard; c Stanley B & Janet L. *Educ:* Tex A&M Univ, BS, 66; Tex Tech Univ, MS, 69, PhD(physics), 73. *Prof Exp:* Mgr res & develop optical litho, Nikon Precision, 85-86. *Mem:* Am Phys Soc; Am Vacuum Soc. *Res:* Develop less than or equal to 0.25 micrometer optical patterning capability for semiconductor IC manufacturing; develop equipment for electron cyclotron resonance plasma etching; develop electron beam lithography tools for photomask generation and far sub-micron direct write applications in semiconductor industry. *Mailing Add:* 210 Willow Circle Allen TX 75002. *Fax:* 972-995-1916; *E-Mail:* robbins@spdc.ti.com

ROBBINS, STANLEY L, PATHOLOGY. *Current Pos:* VIS PROF PATH, HARVARD UNIV SCH MED, 80- *Personal Data:* b Portland, Maine, Feb 27, 15; m 40, Eleanor Peskin; c Janet, Jonathan & Jeffrey. *Educ:* Mass Inst Technol, BS, 36; Tufts Univ, MD, 40. *Honors & Awards:* Distinguished Path, Int Acad Path, 92; Gold Headed Cane, Am Asn Path, 93. *Prof Exp:* From instr to prof path, Boston Univ Sch Med, 41-72, chmn dept, 72-80. *Concurrent Pos:* Vis prof, Univ Glasgow, 60 & Hebrew Univ, Israel, 75; consult, Framingham Union Hosp, 65-80 & Vet Admin Hosp, Roxbury, Mass, 70-80; dir, Mallory Inst Path, 70-76; assoc ed, Human Path, 75- *Mem:* Am Asn Pathologists; Int Acad Path; AAAS; Am Soc Exp Path. *Res:* Pathology. *Mailing Add:* Dept Path Brigham & Womens Hosp 75 Francis St Cambridge MA 02115

ROBBINS, WAYNE BRIAN, ANALYTICAL CHEMISTRY. *Current Pos:* MGR, S D WARREN CO, 85- *Personal Data:* b Dayton, Ohio, Oct 12, 51; m 72; c 3. *Educ:* Univ Cincinnati, BS, 75, MS, 77, PhD(analytical chem), 78. *Prof Exp:* Asst prof chem, Utah State Univ, 78-79; res scientist, Union Camp Corp, 79-85. *Concurrent Pos:* Adj prof, Dept Chem Eng, Univ Maine, Orono, Maine. *Mem:* Am Chem Soc; Soc Appl Spectros; Tech Asn Pulp & Paper Indust. *Res:* Process development for pulp and paper. *Mailing Add:* Inst Paper Sci & Tech 500 Tenth St NW Atlanta GA 30318-5714

ROBBINS, WILLIAM PERRY, ELECTRICAL ENGINEERING. *Current Pos:* asst prof, 69-75, ASSOC PROF ELEC ENG, UNIV MINN, MINNEAPOLIS, 75- *Personal Data:* b Atlanta, Ga, May 29, 41; m 65. *Educ:* Mass Inst Technol, BSEE, 63, MSEE & Elec Engr, 65; Univ Wash, PhD(elec eng), 71. *Prof Exp:* Res engr, Boeing Co, 65-69. *Mem:* Am Inst Physics; Inst Elec & Electronics Engrs; Sigma Xi. *Res:* Acoustic surface wave properties and devices; active circuit design. *Mailing Add:* Dept Elec Eng Univ Minn Minneapolis MN 55455

ROBBLEE, ALEXANDER (ROBINSON), POULTRY NUTRITION. *Current Pos:* from asst prof to prof, 48-84, EMER PROF POULTRY NUTRIT, UNIV ALTA, 84- *Personal Data:* b Calgary, Alta, Jan 21, 19; m 44, Margaret I; c James A, Douglas N, Elizabeth J & Nancy M. *Educ:* Univ Alta, BSc, 44, MSc, 46; Univ Wis, PhD(poultry biochem), 48. *Honors & Awards:* Golden Award, Can Feed Indust Asn. *Prof Exp:* Govt agr fieldman, Dept Agr, Alta, 40-44; instr poultry nutrit, Univ Alta, 45-46 & Univ Wis, 47-48. *Concurrent Pos:* McCalla res prof, Univ Alta. *Mem:* Fel Poultry Sci Asn; fel Agr Inst Can; Worlds' Poultry Sci Asn; Can Soc Nutrit Sci. *Res:* Studies of B-vitamins (riboflavin, B12, biotin, pyridoxine) and investigation of the nutritive value of rapeseed and canola meals for poultry. *Mailing Add:* Dept Animal Sci Univ Alta Edmonton AB T6G 2P5 Can

ROBE, THURLOW RICHARD, ENGINEERING MECHANICS. *Current Pos:* instr civil eng, 60-63, dean, 80-86, EMER DEAN, COL ENG & TECHNOL, OHIO UNIV, 96- *Personal Data:* b Petersburg, Ohio, Jan 25, 34; m 55, Eleanora; c Julia, Kevin, Stephen & Edward. *Educ:* Ohio Univ, BSCE, 55, MS, 62; Stanford Univ, PhD(eng), 66. *Prof Exp:* Engr, Lamp Div, Gen Elec Co, Ohio, 55, Locomotive & Car Equip Dept, Pa, 55-56, Flight Propulsion Lab, Ohio, 59-60; from asst prof to prof eng mech, Univ Ky, 65-80, assoc dean, Col Eng, 76-80. *Concurrent Pos:* Eng consult, Westinghouse Air Brake Co, 67-69, Int Bus Mach Corp, 69-70 & QED Assocs, 75-83; fel, Am Coun Educ, 70-71; innovation ctr authority, Ohio Univ, 83-; bd dirs, Accreditation Bd Eng & Technol, 88-91; bd govs, Edison Mats Tech Ctr. *Mem:* Am Soc Mech Engrs; Am Soc Eng Educ; Nat Soc Prof Engrs. *Res:* Engineering mechanics with emphasis on analysis of dynamical systems. *Mailing Add:* Rm 378 Stocker Ctr Ohio Univ Athens OH 45710. *Fax:* 740-593-0659; *E-Mail:* robe@bobcat.ent.ohiou.edu

ROBEL, GREGORY FRANK, CONTROL THEORY, FUNCTIONAL ANALYSIS. *Current Pos:* SR SPECIALIST ENGR, BOEING CO, SEATTLE, WASH, 86- *Personal Data:* b Yakima Wash, May 5, 55. *Educ:* Harvey Mudd Col, BS, 77; Univ Mich, Ann Arbor, PhD(math), 82. *Prof Exp:* Asst prof math, Iowa State Univ, Ames, 82-86. *Concurrent Pos:* Lectr, Cogswell Col North, Kirkland, Wash, 87- *Mem:* Am Inst Aeronaut & Astronaut; Am Math Soc; Inst Elec and Electronics Engrs; Soc Indust & Appl Math. *Res:* Functional analysis and operator theory, and their applications to the engineering disciplines of control systems and signal processing. *Mailing Add:* Boeing M/S 7L-2S PO Box 3707 Seattle WA 98124-2207

ROBEL, ROBERT JOSEPH, APPLIED ECOLOGY, FISH & WILDLIFE SCIENCE. *Current Pos:* asst prof zool, 61-66, assoc prof biol, 66-71, PROF ENVIRON BIOL, KANS STATE UNIV, 71- *Personal Data:* b Lansing, Mich, May 21, 33; m 60, Anice Blanc. *Educ:* Mich State Univ, BS, 56; Univ Idaho, MS, 58; Utah State Univ, PhD(ecol), 61. *Prof Exp:* Biologist aide, Idaho Fish & Game Dept, 57-58. *Concurrent Pos:* Aquatic biologist, Bear River Club Co, 58-61; Sr Fulbright res fel, Nature Conserv, 67-68; governor's sci adv, 69-80; chmn, Gov Energy & Natural Resources Coun; proj leader, US Congress Off Technol Assessment; distinguished vis lectr, numerous countries. *Mem:* Fel AAAS; Wildlife Soc; Ecol Soc Am; Am Soc Mammal; Animal Behav Soc; Sigma Xi; Brit Ecol Soc; Am Ornithologists Union; Am Inst Biol Sci. *Res:* Animal ecology with emphasis on avian population dynamics, comparative avian behavior, avian dispersal and movement patterns and avian bioenergetics; natural resources management; energy and environmental considerations, environmental assessments. *Mailing Add:* Div Biol Ackert Hall Kans State Univ Manhattan KS 66506-4901. *Fax:* 785-532-6653

ROBEL, STEPHEN B(ERNARD), MECHANICAL ENGINEERING. *Current Pos:* Instr math & physics, 48-49, from asst prof to assoc prof, 50-77, PROF MECH ENG, SEATTLE UNIV, 77- *Personal Data:* b Selah, Wash, Jan 29, 23; m 54; c 5. *Educ:* Seattle Univ, BS, 48; Univ Notre Dame, MS, 51. *Mem:* Am Soc Mech Engrs; Am Soc Eng Educ; Am Soc Artificial Internal Organs. *Res:* Thermodynamics; heat transfer; applied mechanics; cardiovascular research. *Mailing Add:* 1104 17th Ave Seattle WA 98112

ROBENS, JANE FLORENCE, VETERINARY MEDICINE, TOXICOLOGY. *Current Pos:* PROG OFFICER FOOD SAFETY & HEALTH, AGR RES SERV, USDA, 81- *Personal Data:* b Utica, NY, July 23, 31. *Educ:* Cornell Univ, DVM, 55; Am Bd Vet Toxicol, dipl. *Prof Exp:* Vet clinician, Ambassador Animal Hosp, 58-61; vet med officer, US Food & Drug Admin, 64-65, res vet, Div Toxicol Eval, 65-68; asst dir drug regulatory affairs, Hoffmann-La Roche Inc, 68-75; toxicologist, Cancer Bioassay Prog, Tracor Jitco Inc, 75-79; chief, Animal Feed Safety Br, Food & Drug Admin, 79-80. *Concurrent Pos:* Assoc ed, Toxicol & Appl Pharmacol, 78- *Mem:* Am Vet Med Asn; Womens Vet Med Asn; Am Asn Lab Animal Sci; Soc Toxicol; Am Col Vet Toxicol. *Res:* Evaluation of the safety and efficacy of drugs used in veterinary medicine; teratological and carcinogenic potential of pesticides, drugs and other chemicals. *Mailing Add:* 5713 Lone Oak Dr Bethesda MD 20814

ROBERDS, RICHARD MACK, INTERDISCIPLINARY SCIENCE, INNOVATIVE SCIENCE-EDUCATION PROCESSES. *Current Pos:* PROF INTEGRATED SCI & TECHNOL, JAMES MADISON UNIV, 93-, DIR, INTEGRATED SCI & TECHNOL PROG, 95- *Personal Data:* b Lawrence, Kans, June 22, 34; m 58, M Marchena Lanyon; c Michael Richard, Catherine Marcy & Wendy Marilana. *Educ:* Univ Kans, AB, 56, MA, 63; Air Force Inst Technol, PhD(nuclear eng), 75. *Prof Exp:* Br chief, Exp Physics Br, Air Force Weapons Lab, Kirtland, AFB, 75-77, chief, Reconnaissance & Weapon Delivery Div, Air Force Avionics Lab, Wright-Patterson AFB, Ohio, 77-80; dept head & assoc prof eng technol, Clemson Univ, 80-84; dean, Sch Eng Technol & Eng, Univ Tenn, Martin, 84-86, assoc dean, Space Inst, 86-91, actg dean, 89-91, prof eng sci, 91-93. *Concurrent Pos:* Mem, Advan Propulsion Systs Tech Comt, Am Inst Aeronaut & Astronaut, 95- *Mem:* Assoc fel Am Inst Aeronaut & Astronaut; Am Phys Soc; Am Soc Eng Educ; Am Nuclear Soc; Sigma Xi. *Res:* Radiation protection engineering and health physics. *Mailing Add:* 820 Mockingbird Dr Harrisonburg VA 22801. *Fax:* 540-568-2761; *E-Mail:* roberdrm@jmu.edu

ROBERGE, ANDRE, ATMOSPHERIC PHYSICS. *Current Pos:* PROD MGR, SCI-TECH INSTRUMENTS, CAN. *Honors & Awards:* Luigi Provasoli Award, Phylogical Soc Am, 94. *Mailing Add:* Sci Tech Instruments 1526 Fletcher Rd Saskatoon SK S7M 5M1 Can

ROBERGE, ANDREE GROLEAU, BIOCHEMISTRY. *Current Pos:* fel, Med Res Coun Can, 70-71, prof neurochem, Labs Neurobiol, Fac Med, 71-89, PROF, NUTRIT HUMAINE DEPT, LAVAL UNIV, 91- *Personal Data:* b Quebec, Que, Aug 5, 38; m 60; c 4. *Educ:* Laval Univ, BSc, 60, DSc(biochem), 69. *Prof Exp:* Med Res Coun Can fel, McGill Univ, 69-70; exec dir & sci dir, Inst Armand-Frappier, Que Univ, 89-91. *Concurrent Pos:* Med Res Coun Can grants, 71-76 & scholar, 73-78. *Mem:* AAAS; Can Biochem Soc; Am Soc Neurochem; Brit Biochem Soc; Soc Neurosci. *Res:* Catecholaminergic and serotoninergic metabolisms related to locomotor activity to stressfull situation and to nutrition and drugs inhibiting or activating these metabolisms. *Mailing Add:* Dept Nutrit Humaine Laval Univ FSAA Quebec PQ G1K 7P4 Can

ROBERGE, FERNAND ADRIEN, BIOMEDICAL ENGINEERING, CARDIOLOGY. *Current Pos:* from asst prof to prof physiol, Fac Med, 65-78, dir biomed eng, Inst Ecole Polytech, 78-88, PROF BIOMED ENG, UNIV MONTREAL, 78-, DIR, RES GROUP BIOMED MODELING, 88-, ASSOC DEAN GRAD STUDIES, 96- *Personal Data:* b Thetford Mines, Que, June 11, 35; m 58; c 4. *Educ:* Polytech Sch Montreal, BAS & Engr, 59, MScA, 60; McGill Univ, PhD(control eng, biomed eng), 64. *Honors & Awards:* D W Ambridge Award, 64; Rousseau Award, Asn Can-France Advan Sci, 86; Leon Lortie Award, 87. *Prof Exp:* Develop engr numerical control, Sperry Gyroscope Co, Montreal, 60-61. *Concurrent Pos:* Mem, Res Group Neurol Sci, Med Res Coun Can, Univ Montreal, 67-75; mem, Sci Coun Can, 71-74; mem, Grant Comt Biomed Eng, Med Res Coun Can, 71-76; mem, Sci Comt, Can Heart Found, 74-77; mem, Killam Prog Can Coun, 74-77; mem, Elec Eng Comt, Nat Sci Eng Res Coun, Can, 81-83, chmn, 85-88. *Mem:* Fel Inst Elec & Electronics Engrs; Can Physiol Soc; Can Med & Biol Eng Soc (vpres, 74-76); Int Fedn Med Electronics & Biol Eng; Biomed Eng Soc; fel Royal Soc Can; fel Am Inst Med & Biol Eng. *Res:* Membrane biophysics; cardiovascular regulation and control, cardiac arrhythmias; assessment of medical technologies. *Mailing Add:* Inst de Genie Biomed Univ Montreal PO Box 6128 Sta A Montreal PQ H3C 3J7 Can. *Fax:* 514-343-6112; *E-Mail:* roberge@igb.umontreal.ca

ROBERGE, JAMES KERR, ELECTRICAL ENGINEERING. *Current Pos:* From asst prof to assoc prof, 67-76, PROF ELEC ENG, MASS INST TECHNOL, 76- *Personal Data:* b Jersey City, NJ, June 13, 38; m 61; c 2. *Educ:* Mass Inst Technol, SB, 60, SM, 62, ScD(elec eng), 66. *Concurrent Pos:* Consult, 60- *Mem:* Inst Elec & Electronics Engrs; Sigma Xi. *Res:* Electronic circuit design, particularly low power, high performance designs for difficult environments; control system design. *Mailing Add:* Dept Elec Eng Mass Inst Technol 77 Massachusettes Ave Cambridge MA 02139

ROBERGE, MARCIEN ROMEO, microbiology, for more information see previous edition

ROBERSON, BOB SANDERS, HOST PARASITE RELATIONSHIPS, IMMUNE REACTIONS. *Current Pos:* PROF MICROBIOL (IMMUNOL), UNIV MD, 64- *Personal Data:* b Smithfield, NC, Oct 3, 29; m 57, Charlotte Jones; c Paul B & Bob S Jr. *Educ:* Univ NC, Chapel Hill, BA, 51, PhD(bact & immunol), 60. *Prof Exp:* Asst prof med microbiol, Cornell Univ Med Col, 61-64. *Mem:* Am Asn Immunologists; Am Soc Microbiol; Am Fisheries Soc; Sigma Xi; AAAS; NY Acad Sci. *Res:* Immunology of host-parasite relationships, mechanisms of virulence, modifications of normal immune responses induced by exogenous substances; flow cytometric evaluation of activities of immune cells from normal and compromised fish. *Mailing Add:* Dept Microbiol Univ Md College Park MD 20742-4451. *Fax:* 301-314-9489; *E-Mail:* br11@umail.umd.edu

ROBERSON, EDWARD LEE, VETERINARY ANTHELMINTICS. *Current Pos:* res assoc path & parasitol, 67-70, from instr to assoc prof, 70-82, PROF PARASITOL, COL VET MED, UNIV GA, 82- *Personal Data:* b Tarboro, NC, June 10, 35; m 60; c 2. *Educ:* Duke Univ, AB, 57, MAT, 65; Univ Ga, DVM, 61, PhD(parasitol), 72. *Prof Exp:* Teacher, Raleigh Pub Schs, NC, 63-66; NSF fel parasitol, NC State Univ, 66-67. *Mem:* Am Soc Parasitologists; Am Asn Vet Parasitologists (vpres, 77-79, pres, 79-81); Am Vet Med Asn; World Asn Advan Vet Parasitol. *Res:* Lactogenic and prenatal transmission and chemotheraphy of veterinary helminths. *Mailing Add:* 190 Sunny Brook Dr Athens GA 30605

ROBERSON, HERMAN ELLIS, GEOLOGY, MINERALOGY. *Current Pos:* From instr to assoc prof, 59-74, PROF GEOL & ENVIRON STUDIES, STATE UNIV NY BINGHAMTON, 74- *Personal Data:* b Texarkana, Tex, Apr 27, 34; m 62; c 1. *Educ:* Univ Tex, BS, 55, MA, 57; Univ Ill, PhD(geol), 59. *Mem:* AAAS; Mineral Soc Am; Soc Econ Paleont & Mineral; Mineral Soc Gt Brit. *Res:* Clay mineralogy; sedimentation. *Mailing Add:* Geol Dept State Univ NY PO Box 6000 Binghamton NY 13902-6000

ROBERSON, JOHN A(RTHUR), HYDRAULIC ENGINEERING. *Current Pos:* RETIRED. *Personal Data:* b Woodland, Wash, June 4, 25; m 47; c 3. *Educ:* Wash State Univ, BS, 48; Univ Wis, MS, 50; Univ Iowa, PhD, 61. *Prof Exp:* Asst hydraul engr, Wash State Univ, 50-54; physicist hydrodyn res, US Naval Mine Defense Lab, 55-56; asst prof civil eng, Wash State Univ, 56-59, assoc prof, 59-66; assoc prof, Seato Grad Sch Eng, Bangkok, 63-65; prof civil eng, Wash State Univ, 66-88, assoc dean res & grad studies, Col Eng, 81-83. *Concurrent Pos:* Faculty dept civil & environ eng. *Mem:* Am Soc Civil Engrs; Am Soc Eng Educ; Int Asn Hydraulic Res; Sigma Xi. *Res:* Fluid mechanics and hydraulics; author of two books. *Mailing Add:* NW 405 Orion Dr Pullman WA 99163

ROBERSON, NATHAN RUSSELL, NUCLEAR PHYSICS. *Current Pos:* dep dir, 88-92, DIR, TRIANGLE UNIVS NUCLEAR LAB, 92- *Personal Data:* b Robersonville, NC, Dec 13, 30; m 54, Ruth Haislip; c David W, Michael T & Mary (Russell). *Educ:* Univ NC, BS, 54, MS, 55; Johns Hopkins Univ, PhD(nuclear physics), 60. *Prof Exp:* Jr instr physics, Johns Hopkins Univ, 55-60; res assoc, Princeton Univ, 60-63; from asst prof to assoc prof, 63-74, prof physics, Duke Univ, 74- *Concurrent Pos:* Mem bd dirs, Triangle Univs Comput Ctr, 75-80 & LAMPF Users Group, 92-; mem, Network Steering Comt, Dept Energy, 86-89, Nuclear Phys Panel Computer, 88- *Mem:* Fel Am Phys Soc. *Res:* Nuclear spectroscopy; few-nucleon reactions with polarized targets; use of electronic computers for data acquisition; studies of symmetry violating interactions. *Mailing Add:* Dept Physics Box 90308 Duke Univ Durham NC 27708

ROBERSON, ROBERT H, POULTRY NUTRITION, BIOCHEMISTRY. *Current Pos:* RETIRED. *Personal Data:* b Tuckerman, Ark, July 3, 28; m 51; c 6. *Educ:* Okla State Univ, BS, 51; Univ Ark, MS, 56; Mich State Univ, PhD(poultry nutrit, biochem), 59. *Prof Exp:* From asst prof to prof poultry nutrit, NMex State Univ, 59-91. *Mem:* Poultry Sci Asn; Am Inst Nutrit; World Poultry Sci Asn. *Res:* Mineral-zinc, calcium, protein and amino acids. *Mailing Add:* 720 Watson Lane Las Cruces NM 88005

ROBERSON, WARD BRYCE, PLANT PHYSIOLOGY. *Current Pos:* From asst prof to assoc prof, 66-78, PROF BIOL, HARDING UNIV, 78- *Personal Data:* b Hamilton, Ala, Jan 17, 39; m 68; c 1. *Educ:* Harding Col, BA, 61; Utah State Univ, MS, 64, PhD(plant physiol), 67. *Mem:* AAAS. *Res:* Membrane permeability; plant water relations. *Mailing Add:* Dept Biol Harding Univ 900 E Center Ave Searcy AR 72149-0001

ROBERT, KEARNY QUINN, JR, PHYSICS, ENGINEERING. *Current Pos:* RES PHYSICIST, USDA SOUTHERN REGIONAL RES CTR, 77- *Personal Data:* b Liberty, Tex, June 12, 43; m 68; c 3. *Educ:* Tulane Univ, BA, 65, BS, 65, PhD(physics), 70. *Prof Exp:* Asst physics, Tulane Univ, 66-70; res physicist, Gulf South Res Inst, 70-76. *Concurrent Pos:* Lectr physics, St Mary's Dominican Col, 66; res consult, Physics Dept, Tulane Univ, 72-76, adj asst prof, Sch Eng, 76- *Mem:* Am Phys Soc; Am Asn Physics Teachers; Health Physics Soc; Am Soc Nondestructive Testing; Sigma Xi. *Res:* Environmental health sciences; radiological health and health physics; industrial hygiene; medical diagnostics; nondestructive testing; computer simulation; textile engineering; dust control; nuclear physics. *Mailing Add:* 4501 S Tonti St New Orleans LA 70125

ROBERT, SUZANNE, ANIMAL STRESS, STRAY VOLTAGE. *Current Pos:* postdoctoral fel, 86-87, RES SCIENTIST SWINE ETHOLOGY, RES AGR & AGR FOOD CAN, LENNOXVILLE, 87- *Personal Data:* b Montreal, Que, Can, Feb 18, 57; m 83; c 2. *Educ:* Univ Montreal, DVM, 79; Univ Claude Bernard, Lyon, France, DEA, 80. *Prof Exp:* Postdoctoral fel swine ethology, Univ Montreal, Fac Vet Med, 83-86. *Concurrent Pos:* Pres, Lennoxville Res Sta Animal Care Comt, 87; mem, Comn Agr Biol CPAQ, 89. *Mem:* Can Soc Animal Sci; Int Soc Appl Ethology. *Res:* Effects of stray voltage on the welfare, health and productivity of pigs; effects of feed restriction and develop alternative feeding practices that allow to achieve a high standard of animal performance and health while addressing animal welfare concern over confinement rearing; segregated early weaning, behavior and welfare of sows and piglets. *Mailing Add:* Res Agr & Agr Food Can 2000 Rd 108 E PO Box 90 Lennoxville PQ J1M 1Z3 Can. *Fax:* 819-564-5507; *E-Mail:* roberts@em.agr.ca

ROBERT, TIMOTHY ALBERT, SCIENTIFIC DIRECTOR OF FORENSIC URINE DRUG TESTING LABORATORY, DIRECTOR OF CLINICAL LABORATORY PERFORMING ANALYSIS OF PSYCOACTIVE DRUGS. *Current Pos:* VPRES FORENSIC TOXICOL, NAT PSYCHOPHARMACOL LAB, 88- *Personal Data:* b Detroit, Mich, Aug 24, 48. *Educ:* Univ Mich, BS, 71; La State Univ, MS, 77; ETenn State Univ, PhD (biomed sci & pharmacol), 79. *Prof Exp:* Asst prof pharmacol, Quillen Dishner Col Med, Johnson City, Tenn, 79-84; asst prof pharmacol & biochem, Ross Univ Sch Med, Dominican, Wis, 84-86; assoc dir toxicol, Roche Biomed Labs, NJ, 86-87; dir chem & toxicol, Int Clin Labs, Nashville, Tenn, 87-88. *Concurrent Pos:* Inspector, Nat Lab Cert Prog, 92- *Mem:* Am Soc Pharmacol & Exp Therapeut; Soc Toxicol. *Res:* Methods of analysis for drugs of abuse and new psychopharmacological agents, methods are generally based on GOL and or GOC/MS techniques. *Mailing Add:* Nat Psychopharmacol Labs 9320 Park W Blvd Knoxville TN 37923-4331

ROBERTO, FRANCISCO FIGUEROA, ENVIRONMENTAL MICROBIOLOGY, MICROBIAL PHYLOGENY. *Current Pos:* sr scientist, 88-92, tech leader, 91-94, sci specialist, 92-96, GROUP LEADER, IDAHO NAT ENG LAB, 94- *Personal Data:* b Clarkston, Wash, Apr 11, 58. *Educ:* Univ Calif, Davis, BS, 80, Riverside, PhD(biochem), 85. *Prof Exp:* Lab asst, Dept Biochem & Biophys, Univ Calif, Davis, 78-80, res asst, Dept Biochem, Riverside, 80-84, fel, Dept Plant Path, 84-86. *Concurrent Pos:* Adj fac molecular biol, Dept Biol Sci, Idaho State Univ, 90-; affil fac, Dept Microbiol, Molecular Biol & Biochem, Univ Idaho, 93-; consult sci, 96- *Mem:* Am Soc Microbiol; Soc Gen Microbiol. *Res:* Genetics and phylogeny of acidophilic bacteria; expression of methane monoxygenase; biomaterials; bioadhesives. *Mailing Add:* Indust Biotechnol Idaho Nat Eng Lab PO Box 1625 Idaho Falls ID 83415-2203. *Fax:* 208-526-0828; *E-Mail:* ffr@inel.gov

ROBERTO, JAMES BLAIR, PARTICLE SOLID INTERACTIONS. *Current Pos:* Group leader, 80-84, sect leader, 86-90, RES STAFF MEM, SOLID STATE DIV, OAK RIDGE NAT LAB, 74-, DIV DIR, 90- *Personal Data:* b Portland, Me, Sept 4, 46; m 70; c 2. *Educ:* Mass Inst Technol, SB, 68; Cornell Univ, MS, 69, PhD (appl physics), 74. *Concurrent Pos:* vis scientist, Kernforschungsanlage, Juelich, Fed Rep Ger, 77, 78; co-ed, Plasma Surface Interactions in Controlled Fusion Devices, 82; co-chmn, V Int Conf on Plasma Surface Interactions in Controlled Fusion Devices, 82; vis scientist, Max-Planck-Institut für Plasmaphysik, Garching Fed Rep Ger, 83; co-ed, Advanced Photon & Particle Techniques for the Characterization of Defects in Solids, 85; Gen co-chmn, 1986 fall meeting Mat Res Soc, 86; co-chmn, sematech workshop on advanced ion implantation technol, 87; co-ed, Ion Beam Processing of Adv Electronic Mat, 89; co-chmn, Wash Mat Forum, 91; mem, Solid State Sci Comt, Nat Res Coun, 93- *Mem:* Mat Res Soc (vpres, 89, 1st vpres, 90, pres, 91); Am Phys Soc; AAAS. *Res:* Interaction of particle beams with materials including ion-solid interactions; ion implantation, plasma-surface interactions; fusion materials research. *Mailing Add:* 520 Old Tavern Circle Knoxville TN 37922

ROBERTS, A(LBERT) S(IDNEY), JR, MECHANICAL & NUCLEAR ENGINEERING, THERMAL PHYSICS. *Current Pos:* from asst prof to assoc prof thermal eng, chmn & grad prog dir, Thermal Eng Group, 65-72, assoc dean eng, 74-77, PROF MECH ENG, OLD DOM UNIV, 72- *Personal Data:* b Washington, NC, Sept 16, 35; m 57, Llew Bowers; c Leigh, Sidney, Llewellyn & Amanda. *Educ:* NC State Univ, BS, 57, PhD(nuclear eng, plasma physics), 65; Univ Pittsburgh, MS. *Prof Exp:* Assoc engr, Bettis Atomic Power Lab, Westinghouse Elec Corp, 57-60; res asst exp plasma physics, Plasma Physics Lab, NC State Univ, 61-65. *Concurrent Pos:* Consult, NASA, 66-80; guest res engr, AB Atomenergi, Studsvik, Sweden, 68-69; guest lectr, Nat Acad Sci, Roumania, 68; prin investr, Old Dom Univ Res Found, 70- *Mem:* Sigma Xi; Am Soc Eng Educ; fel Am Soc Mech Engrs; Am Soc Heating, Refrig & Air-Conditioning Engrs. *Res:* Heat transfer; physical gas dynamics; plasma energy conversion methods; nuclear power reactors; solar energy conversion; building heating, ventilating and air-conditioning; energy systems; thermodynamics and fluid mechanics. *Mailing Add:* 5437 Glenhaven Crescent Norfolk VA 23508. *Fax:* 757-683-5344; *E-Mail:* roberts@mem.odu.edu

ROBERTS, A WAYNE, MATHEMATICS. *Current Pos:* PROF MATH, MACALESTER COL, 65- *Personal Data:* b Chicago, Ill, Aug 29, 34; m 56; c 3. *Educ:* Ill Inst Technol, BS, 56; Univ Wis, MS, 58, PhD(math), 65. *Prof Exp:* Instr math, Morton Jr Col, 58-62; teaching asst, Univ Wis-Madison, 62-65. *Mem:* Math Asn Am. *Res:* Mathematical analysis; convex functions; optimization theory. *Mailing Add:* Dept Math Macalester Col St Paul MN 55105-1899

ROBERTS, ALFRED NATHAN, HORTICULTURE. *Current Pos:* Asst, 39-41, from instr to assoc prof, 41-57, prof, 57-80, EMER PROF HORT, ORE STATE UNIV, 80- *Personal Data:* b Welsh, La, Nov 6, 17; m 39; c 3. *Educ:* Ore State Univ, BS, 39, MS, 41; Mich State Univ, PhD(hort), 53. *Honors & Awards:* Alex Laurie Award, Am Soc Hort Sci, 65, Stark Award, 68, Colman Award, 72, J H Gourley Medal, 77. *Mem:* Fel Am Soc Hort Sci; Int Plant Propagator's Soc; Int Hort Soc; Scand Soc Plant Physiol. *Res:* Ornamental plant physiology, growth and development; bulb crop physiology; root regeneration physiology. *Mailing Add:* 3107 NW Firwood Pl Corvallis OR 97330

ROBERTS, ANITA BAUER, GROWTH FACTORS. *Current Pos:* SR SCIENTIST, LAB CHEMOPREV, NIH, NAT CANCER INST, 76-, DEP DIR, 90- *Personal Data:* b Pittsburgh, Pa, Mar 4, 42; m 64, Robert; c Gregory & Karl. *Educ:* Oberlin Col, BA, 64; Univ Wis-Madison, PhD(biochem), 68. *Prof Exp:* Fel, Dept Pharmacol, Harvard Med Sch, 68-69; asst prof biochem, Dept Chem, Ind Univ, 73-75. *Concurrent Pos:* Ed, Molecular Endocrinol; assoc ed, J Biol Chem. *Mem:* Am Soc Biol Chemists; Am Asn Cancer res; Endocrinol Soc; Wound Healing Soc (pres elect). *Res:* Study of peptide growth factors, particularly transforming growth factors, and their role in control of both normal and neoplastic cellular physiology. *Mailing Add:* Lab Chemoprev NIH Nat Cancer Inst Bldg 41 Rm C629 Bethesda MD 20892-5055

ROBERTS, ARTHUR, NEUTRINO ASTRONOMY, PHYSICS INSTRUMENTATION. *Current Pos:* RETIRED. *Personal Data:* b New York, NY, July 6, 12; m 35, Janice Banner; c Richard & Judith A. *Educ:* City Col NY, BS, 31; Columbia Univ, MA, 33; NY Univ, PhD(physics), 36. *Honors & Awards:* Pres Cert Merit, 48. *Prof Exp:* Res assoc physics, Mass Inst Technol, 37-42, group leader, Radiation Lab, 42-45; assoc prof physics, Univ Iowa, 46-50; from assoc prof to prof, Univ Rochester, 50-60; sr physicist, Argonne Nat Lab, 60-67; sr physicist, Fermi Nat Lab, 67-79; vis prof physics, Univ Hawaii, 80-82, consult, 82-85. *Concurrent Pos:* Physicist, London Br, Off Naval Res, 53-54; vis physicist, CERN, Geneva, 61-62; Harwell Lab, Didcot, Eng, 65, Rutherford Lab, Eng, 73-74; adj prof, Univ Chicago, 70-73. *Mem:* Am Physics Soc; Comput Music Asn; Sigma Xi. *Res:* Radioactivity; use of radioisotopes in medicine; nuclear physics; microwave spectroscopy; high energy physics; cosmic rays and neutrino astronomy. *Mailing Add:* 15 176 Rochdale Circle Lombard IL 60148

ROBERTS, AUDREY NADINE, immunology, virology, for more information see previous edition

ROBERTS, BRADLEY LEE, INTERMEDIATE ENERGY PARTICLE PHYSICS. *Current Pos:* from asst prof to assoc prof, 77-89, assoc chmn, Physics Dept, 89-92, PROF PHYSICS, BOSTON UNIV, 89- *Personal Data:* b Bristol, Va, Aug 11, 46; m 91, Karen Ellis; c John E. *Educ:* Univ Va, BS, 68; Col William & Mary, MS, 70, PhD(physics), 74. *Prof Exp:* Res assoc medium energy nuclear physics, Sci Res Coun, Rutherford Lab, Chilton, Eng, 74-76 & Lab Nuclear Sci, Mass Inst Technol, 76-77. *Concurrent Pos:* Guest asst physicist, Brookhaven Nat Lab, 76-83; res affil, Lab Nuclear Sci, Mass Inst Technol, 78-; co-prin investr, NSF grant, Photo Nuclear & Fundamental Particle Physics; guest assoc physicist, Brookhaven Nat Lab, 83-; mem, prog comt, Brookhaven Nat Lab AGS, 88-91, chmn, User's Exec Comt, 89-91. *Mem:* Fel Am Phys Soc; Sigma Xi. *Res:* Intermediate energy nuclear and particle physics; exotic atoms; muon physics; kaon physics; hyperon physics; weak decays and CP violation. *Mailing Add:* Dept Physics 590 Commonwealth Ave Boston MA 02215. *Fax:* 617-353-9393; *E-Mail:* roberts@buphyc.bu.edu

ROBERTS, BRUCE R, PLANT PHYSIOLOGY. *Current Pos:* CONSULT, 89- *Personal Data:* b Leonia, NJ, May 19, 33; m 56; c 2. *Educ:* Gettysburg Col, AB, 56; Duke Univ, MF, 60, PhD(plant physiol), 63. *Honors & Awards:* Res Award, Int Soc Arboricult, 75, Authors Citation, 81. *Prof Exp:* Res plant physiologist, Nursery Crops Res Lab, USDA, 63-89. *Concurrent Pos:* Adj prof, Ohio Wesleyan Univ. *Mem:* Am Soc Plant Physiol; Sigma Xi; Am Soc Hort Sci; hon life mem Int Soc Arboricult. *Res:* Plant and tree physiology; water relations; physiological response to plant stress. *Mailing Add:* Dept Bot Ohio Wesleyan Univ Delaware OH 43015

ROBERTS, BRYAN WILSON, ORGANIC CHEMISTRY. *Current Pos:* asst prof, 67-70, assoc prof, 70-81, asst chmn dept chem, 73-77, PROF CHEM, UNIV PA, 81-, CHMN DEPT, 81- *Personal Data:* b Pinehurst, NC, Feb 12, 38; m 60; c 2. *Educ:* Univ NC, BS, 60; Stanford Univ, PhD(org chem), 64. *Prof Exp:* Nat Acad Sci-Nat Res Coun fel, Calif Inst Technol, 63-64; asst prof chem, Univ Southern Calif, 64-67. *Mem:* Am Chem Soc; Royal Soc Chem. *Res:* Synthetic organic chemistry; synthesis of natural products and of molecular systems of theoretical interest. *Mailing Add:* Dept Chem D5 Univ Pa Philadelphia PA 19104-6323

ROBERTS, C SHELDON, MATERIALS SCIENCE & ENGINEERING. *Current Pos:* CONSULT MAT & PROCESSES, 63- *Personal Data:* b Rupert, Vt, Oct 27, 26; m 50, Patricia Wiseman; c David M, Steven H & Wayne E. *Educ:* Rensselaer Polytech Inst, BMetE, 48; Mass Inst Technol, SM, 49, ScD(metall), 52. *Hon Degrees:* DEng, Rensselaer Polytech Inst, 88. *Honors & Awards:* Alfred Noble Award, 54. *Prof Exp:* Res metallurgist, Dow Chem Co, Mich, 51-56; mem sr staff, Semiconductor Lab, Beckman Instrument Corp, Calif, 56-57; head mat res & develop, Fairchild Semiconductor Corp, 57-61; head mat, Amelco Semiconductor Div, Teledyne, Inc, 61-63. *Concurrent Pos:* Pres, Timelapse Inc, 71-74; trustee, Rensselaer Polytech Inst, 72-88 & Am Soc Metals, 84-87. *Mem:* Am Soc Mat Int; Electrochem Soc; Mat Res Soc; Inst Elec & Electronics Engrs; Sigma Xi; Soc Air Safety Investrs; Mineral Metal & Mat Soc. *Res:* Deformation and fracture of metals; materials processing technology; magnesium and its alloys; semiconductor materials development; material processing technology; behavior of solid state electronic devices; failure analysis of engineering materials. *Mailing Add:* 2725 NW Starview Dr Bend OR 97701

ROBERTS, CARLYLE JONES, health physics, for more information see previous edition

ROBERTS, CATHERINE HARRISON, protein chemistry, physical biochemistry, for more information see previous edition

ROBERTS, CHARLES A, JR, THEORETICAL PHYSICS. *Current Pos:* chmn dept, 56-70, prof, 56-94, EMER PROF PHYSICS, CALIF STATE UNIV, LONG BEACH, 94- *Personal Data:* b Changsha, China, Oct 21, 25; US citizen; m; c 5. *Educ:* Univ Calif, Los Angeles, BS, 49; Univ Southern Calif, MS, 51; Univ Md, PhD(physics), 56. *Prof Exp:* Physicist, Physics Naval Res Lab, Wash, DC, 52-53. *Concurrent Pos:* Res Corp grant theoret physics, 58-60; NSF grant, 62-64; NSF fel, Brussels, 64-65; consult, Naval Ord Lab, Calif, Douglas Aircraft Co & Aeroneutronics; sr Fulbright award, Dept State, 74- *Mem:* Am Phys Soc. *Res:* Nonequilibrium statistical mechanics applied to the field of plasma physics; equilibrium statistical mechanics; interaction of electromagnetic waves with plasmas; elastic surface waves in solids. *Mailing Add:* 2247 Ohio Ave Signal Hill CA 90806

ROBERTS, CHARLES BROCKWAY, INORGANIC CHEMISTRY, ANALYTICAL CHEMISTRY. *Current Pos:* RETIRED. *Personal Data:* b Kansas City, Mo, July 31, 18; m 46; c 3. *Educ:* Univ Alta, BSc, 40; Univ Ark, MS, 50; Univ Ill, PhD(anal chem), 56. *Prof Exp:* Explosives chemist, Kankakee Ord Works, US Civil Serv, 41-43; chemist, Ethyl Corp, 43-46; teacher & prin pub schs, Ark, 47-53; asst analytical chem, Univ Ill, 53-56; analytical chemist, Dow Chem Co, 56-59, analytical specialist, 59-63, sr res chemist, 63-72, sr res specialist, 72-79, quality control supvr, 79-82. *Mem:* Am Chem Soc; Sigma Xi. *Res:* Analytical methods development. *Mailing Add:* 713 Columbia Rd Midland MI 48640-3430

ROBERTS, CHARLES SHELDON, SOFTWARE ENGINEERING, OPERATING SYSTEMS. *Current Pos:* Mgr, Syst Archit Lab, Hewlett-Packard Co, Cupertino, Calif, 88-90, mgr, Univ Res Grants, 90-92, PRIN LAB SCIENTIST & MGR, WINTEL SYSTS DEPT, HEWLETT-PACKARD LABS, PALO ALTO, CALIF, 92- *Personal Data:* b Newark, NJ, Sept 25, 37; m 59, Wendy Shadlen; c Lauren (Gold) & Tamara G. *Educ:* Carnegie-Mellon Univ, BS, 59; Mass Inst Technol, PhD(physics), 63. *Prof Exp:* Mem tech staff, AT&T Bell Labs, 63-68, head, Comput Technol Dept, 68-70, Info Processing Res Dept, 70-73, Interactive Comput Systs Res Dept, 73-82 & Advan Systs Dept, 82-88. *Mem:* Am Phys Soc; Asn Comput Mach; Inst Elec & Electronics Engrs; Sigma Xi. *Res:* Computer operating systems and software; database management; software and system architecture; theory of molecular scattering; theory of plasmas; physics of The Van Allen belts and the earth's magnetosphere; experiments aboard earth satellites to measure particles and electromagnetic waves. *Mailing Add:* 210 Manresa Ct Los Altos CA 94022-4623. *Fax:* 650-857-5172; *E-Mail:* csrob@hplabs.hp.com

ROBERTS, CLARENCE RICHARD, HORTICULTURE, PLANT PHYSIOLOGY. *Current Pos:* RETIRED. *Personal Data:* b Cushing, Okla, May 4, 26; m 51, Twilla Teel; c Elaine, Susan (Keller), Gayla (Burns) & Donna (Powell). *Educ:* Okla State Univ, BS, 49, MS, 51; Tex A&M Univ, PhD(hort), 64. *Prof Exp:* Asst co agt, Okla State Univ, 50-54; exten horticulturist, Kans State Univ, 54-67; exten horticulturist, Univ Ky, 67-93. *Concurrent Pos:* Indonesia training teachers, 89. *Mem:* Am Soc Hort Sci. *Res:* Nutrition of vegetable crops; post harvest physiology studies; development of vegetable production systems. *Mailing Add:* 2315 Clear Creek Rd Nicholasville KY 40356

ROBERTS, CYNTHIA J, BIOMEDICAL ENGINEERING. *Current Pos:* ASST PROF BIOMED ENG & SURG, OHIO STATE UNIV, 89- *Personal Data:* b Chicago, Ill, Nov 22, 58. *Educ:* Univ Iowa, BS, 79; Ohio State Univ, MS, 86, PhD(biomed eng), 89. *Mem:* Inst Elec & Electronics Engrs Lasers & Electro Optics Soc; Biomed Eng Soc; Sigma Xi; Asn Res Vision & Opthalmol; Int Soc Optical Eng. *Mailing Add:* 1661 Moreland Dr Columbus OH 43220-3115

ROBERTS, DANIEL ALTMAN, plant virology, teaching, for more information see previous edition

ROBERTS, DAVID CRAIG, CHEMICAL INFORMATION SCIENCE, CHEMOMETRICS. *Current Pos:* systs scientist & mem tech staff, Mitre Corp, 85-, LEAD SCIENTIST, MITRETEK SYSTS, 96- *Personal Data:* b Madison, Wis, Feb 21, 48; m 79, Laura Abbott; c Molly & Rebecca. *Educ:* Univ Wis, BA, 70; Mass Inst Technol, PhD(org chem), 75. *Prof Exp:* Res fel org chem, Univ Calif, Los Angeles, 75-77; asst prof chem, Rutgers Univ, 77-83; assoc prof chem, Fordham Univ, 83-85. *Concurrent Pos:* Prin investr, Petrol Res Fund grant, 78-80 & NIH grant, 83-85. *Mem:* Am Chem Soc. *Res:* Environmental management; chemical estimation and modeling methods; information science; structure-activity relationships; computational chemistry. *Mailing Add:* Mitretek Systs MS-Z-420 7525 Colshire Dr McLean VA 22102-7400. *Fax:* 703-610-1561; *E-Mail:* droberts@mitretek.org

ROBERTS, DAVID DUNCAN, CARBOHYDRATE BIOCHEMISTRY, CELL ADHESION. *Current Pos:* staff fel, Nat Inst Diabetes & Digestive & Kidney Dis, NIH, 84-86, sr staff fel, 86-87, res chemist, 87-88, CHIEF BIOCHEM PATH SECT, NAT CANCER INST, NIH, 88- *Personal Data:* b Indiana, Pa, July 1, 54; m 93, Nancy S Templeton; c Benjamin & James. *Educ:* Mass Inst Tech, BS, 76; Univ Mich, PhD(biochem), 83. *Prof Exp:* Postdoctoral scholar, Univ Mich, 83-84. *Mem:* Am Soc Biochem & Molecular Biol; Soc Glycobiol; AAAS. *Res:* Role of thrombospondin in cell adhesion and migration and tumor metastasis; biochemistry of cell surface carbohydrates and their function in adhesion and host-pathogen interactions. *Mailing Add:* Lab Path Bldg 10 Rm 2A33 10 Ctr MSC 1500 NIH Bethesda MD 20892. *E-Mail:* droberts@helix.nih.gov

ROBERTS, DAVID HALL, RADIO ASTRONOMY, THEORETICAL ASTROPHYSICS. *Current Pos:* from asst prof to prof, 80-89, WILLIAM R KENAN JR PROF ASTROPHYS, BRANDEIS UNIV, 92- *Personal Data:* b Washington, DC, Feb 4, 47; m 74, Mary Fedarko; c Rebecca, Matthew & Kathryn. *Educ:* Amherst Col, AB, 69; Stanford Univ, PhD(physics), 73. *Honors & Awards:* Group Achievement Award, NASA, 88. *Prof Exp:* Res assoc physics, Univ Ill, Urbana, 73-75; res physicist, Univ Calif, San Diego, 75-78; res scientist, Res Lab Electronics, Mass Inst Technol, 78-79. *Concurrent Pos:* Vis scientist, Res Lab Electronics, Mass Inst Technol, 79-82, Ctr Space Res, 82-87; vis assoc radio astron, Calif Inst Technol, 87-88; consult, Jet Propulsion Lab, 87-88. *Mem:* Am Phys Soc; Am Astron Soc; Sigma Xi; Int Astron Union; Int Union Radio Sci. *Res:* Non-thermal phenomena in galactic and extragalactic objects; radio astronomy; very-long baseline interferometry; pulsars, quasars, radio sources; radio astronomy from space. *Mailing Add:* Dept Physics Brandeis Univ Waltham MA 02254. *Fax:* 781-736-2915; *E-Mail:* dhr@vlbi.astro.brandeis.edu

ROBERTS, DAVID WILFRED ALAN, PLANT PHYSIOLOGY, BIOCHEMISTRY. *Current Pos:* RETIRED. *Personal Data:* b Yeadon, Eng, Sept 21, 21; m 60, Gilmour; c Mary C Goodsell. *Educ:* Univ Toronto, BA, 42, PhD(plant physiol), 48. *Prof Exp:* Res assoc, Nat Cancer Inst Can, Toronto, 48-49; plant physiologist, Res Sta, Can Dept Agr, 49-87. *Mem:* Am Soc Plant Physiol. *Res:* Genetics of cold resistance of wheat and traits that correlate with cold hardiness; cold resistance. *Mailing Add:* 2129 18th Ave S Lethbridge AB T1K 1C7 Can

ROBERTS, DEAN WINN, JR, IMMUNOLOGY, TOXICOLOGY. *Current Pos:* RES SCIENTIST, NAT CTR TOXICOL RES, 77- *Personal Data:* b Jan 9, 45; c 3. *Educ:* Hahnemann Med Col, PhD(microbiol, immunol), 77. *Honors & Awards:* FDA Comnr Spec Citation, 86. *Prof Exp:* Res scientist, Univ Ark Med Sci, 79- *Concurrent Pos:* Rosenstadt vis prof, fac pharm, Univ Toronto, 88. *Mem:* Am Asn Immunologists; Soc Toxicol. *Res:* Immunotoxicology; immunochemical detection of carcinogen-DNA adducts and drug-protein adducts. *Mailing Add:* Nat Ctr Toxicol Res Jefferson AR 72079

ROBERTS, DEWAYNE, BIOCHEMICAL PHARMACOLOGY. *Current Pos:* RETIRED. *Personal Data:* b Okla, Sept 7, 27; m 51; c 3. *Educ:* Okla State Univ, BS; Wash Univ, PhD. *Prof Exp:* Res scientist, Roswell Park Mem Inst, 57-62; asst chief biochem pharmacol, Children's Cancer Res Found, Boston, 62-68; mem, Dept Preclin & Clin Pharmacol, St Jude Children's Res Hosp, 68-88. *Concurrent Pos:* Res assoc, Grad Dept Biochem, Brandeis Univ, 62-65, Harvard Med Sch, 62-68; adj prof biol, Northeastern Univ, 66-67; assoc prof pharmacol, Univ Tenn, Memphis, 68-88. *Mem:* Am Asn Cancer Res; Am Soc Pharmacol & Exp Therapeut; Am Fedn Clin Res; Sigma Xi. *Res:* Biochemistry of nucleic acid precursors and the effect of drugs on their biosyntheses in relation to cancer chemotherapy; molecular basis of acquired resistance to oncolytic drugs. *Mailing Add:* 6193 Ivanhoe Rd Bartlett TN 38134-5927

ROBERTS, DONALD DUANE, PHYSICAL ORGANIC CHEMISTRY. *Current Pos:* assoc prof, 63-74, PROF CHEM, LA TECH UNIV, 74- *Personal Data:* b Jamestown, NDak, Feb 18, 29; m 52; c 5. *Educ:* Jamestown Col, BS, 50; Loyola Univ, MS, 57, PhD(org chem), 62. *Prof Exp:* Res chemist, Sherwin Williams Co, 52-54; group leader polymer chem, Borg-Warner Corp, 54-58; asst proj chemist, Am Oil Co, 58-60; res assoc org chem, Plastics Div, Allied Chem Corp, 62-63. *Concurrent Pos:* Res Corp grant, 64-65; Petrol Res Fund grant, 66-68; NSF grant, 69-71. *Mem:* Am Chem Soc; Sigma Xi. *Res:* Cyclopropylcarbinyl system; solvent effects; medium size rings; linear free energy relationships; solvent effects in solvolysis reactions. *Mailing Add:* 2301 Cypress Springs Ave Ruston LA 71270

ROBERTS, DONALD RAY, medical entomology, population dynamics, for more information see previous edition

ROBERTS, DONALD RAY, PLANT PHYSIOLOGY, WEED SCIENCE. *Current Pos:* RETIRED. *Personal Data:* b Trenton, Tenn, Dec 21, 29; m 57; c 3. *Educ:* Univ Tenn, BSA, 52, MS, 59; Auburn Univ, PhD(bot), 66. *Prof Exp:* Instr agron, Univ Tenn, 57-59; asst bot, Auburn Univ, 60-63; plant physiologist, Southeastern Forest Exp Sta, US Forest Serv, 63- *Mem:* Am Soc Plant Physiologists; Soc Am Foresters. *Res:* Lightwood induction research; herbicide physiology, especially metabolism of atrazine; biosynthesis of oleoresin in slash pine and physiology of pine oleoresin extraction. *Mailing Add:* 306 SW 123rd St Newberry FL 32669

ROBERTS, DONALD WILSON, INSECT PATHOLOGY. *Current Pos:* asst entomologist, 65-69, assoc insect pathologist, 70-73, INSECT PATHOLOGIST, BOYCE THOMPSON INST PLANT RES, 74-, COORDR, INSECT PATH RESOURCE CTR, 79- *Personal Data:* b Phoenix, Ariz, Jan 20, 33; m 59, Mae A Strand; c Marc D & Sara J. *Educ:* Brigham Young Univ, BS, 57; Iowa State Univ, MS, 59; Univ Calif, Berkeley, PhD(entom), 64. *Honors & Awards:* L O Howard Distinguished Achievement Award, Entom Soc Am, 89. *Prof Exp:* NSF fel, Swiss Fed Inst Technol, 64-65. *Concurrent Pos:* USPHS res grants, 66-76; consult, WHO, 74-78, res grants, 75-84; USDA res grants, 76-; exchange scientist, US-India, 78; consult, Brazil gov, 78-82; US Nat Acad Sci-Nat Res Coun, 76-77, US Agency Int Develop grants, 81-92; Fulbright sr res scholar, Australia, 85. *Mem:* AAAS; Entom Soc Am; Am Soc Microbiol; Mycol Soc Am; Soc Invert Path (vpres, 86-88, pres, 88-90); Soc Entom Brazil. *Res:* Insect mycoses including molecular biology of mechanisms used by fungi to overcome insects; toxins produced by insect-infecting fungi; pathogens of mosquito larvae; pox-like viruses of insects; integration of pathogens into pest management programs in developing nations. *Mailing Add:* Boyce Thompson Inst Tower Rd Ithaca NY 14853-1801. *Fax:* 607-254-1242; *E-Mail:* dwr2@cornell.edu

ROBERTS, DORIS EMMA, PUBLIC HEALTH NURSING. *Current Pos:* RETIRED. *Personal Data:* b Toledo, Ohio, Dec 28, 15. *Educ:* Peter Bent Brigham Sch Nursing, dipl nursing, 38; Geneva Col, BS, 44; Univ Minn, MPH, 58; Univ NC, PhD, 67. *Honors & Awards:* Meritorious Serv Award, NIH & USPHS, 71; Sedgwick Mem Award, Am Pub Health Asn, 79. *Prof Exp:* Staff nurse, Vis Nurse Asn, New Haven, 38-40; sr nurse, Neighborhood House, Millburn, NJ, 42-45; supvr tuberc, Baltimore Co Dept Health, Towson, Md, 45-46; tuberc consult, Md State Dept Health, 46-50; consult & chief nurse tuberc prog, USPHS, 50-57, consult, Div Nursing, 58-63; chief, Nursing Pract Br, Health Resources Admin, HEW, 66-75, consult nursing, 75-83. *Concurrent Pos:* Comt officer, USPHS, 45-75; adj prof pub health nursing, Univ NC, Chapel Hill, 75-89; consult, WHO, 61-83; consult prof health prof training prog, US Vet Admin, 83-89. *Mem:* Inst Med-Nat Acad Sci; fel Am Pub Health Asn; hon mem Am Acad Nursing. *Res:* Evaluation of health services effectiveness based on quality and outcome measures. *Mailing Add:* 9707 Old Georgetown Rd Apt 1112 Bethesda MD 20814

ROBERTS, DURWARD THOMAS, JR, organic polymer chemistry, for more information see previous edition

ROBERTS, EARL JOHN, CHEMISTRY. *Current Pos:* jr chemist, Southern Utilization Res Br, USDA, 42-44, from asst chemist to chemist, 44-62, res chemist, Southern Res & Develop Div, 62-72, SR CHEMIST, CANE SUGAR REFINING RES PROJ, SCI & EDUC ADMIN-AGR RES, USDA, 72- *Personal Data:* b Magee, Miss, May 14, 13; m 44; c 2. *Educ:* Miss Col, BA, 39; La State Univ, MS, 42. *Prof Exp:* High sch teacher, Miss, 39-40; analyst, Miss Testing Lab, 40-41; asst chem, La State Univ, 41-42. *Concurrent Pos:* Teaching fel, Tulane Univ, 48- *Res:* Organic chemistry of the by-products of the sugar industry; composition of sugar cane juice; structure of modified cellulose; identification and determination of minor constituents in refined cane sugar. *Mailing Add:* 6748 Orleans Ave New Orleans LA 70124

ROBERTS, EDGAR D, VETERINARY PATHOLOGY. *Current Pos:* AT DELTA REGIONAL PRIMATE CTR, 88- *Personal Data:* b Odessa, Tex, Mar 23, 31; m 50; c 2. *Educ:* Colo State Univ, BS, 57, DVM, 59; Iowa State Univ, MS, 62, PhD(vet path), 65. *Prof Exp:* Res asst vet path, Vet Med Res Inst, 59-62; pathologist, Nat Animal Dis Lab, 62-63; asst prof vet path, Iowa State Univ, 63-65; vet pathologist, Rockefeller Found, 65-69; head animal health, Int Ctr Trop Agr, Colombia, 69-71; prof vet path & head dept, Sch Vet Med, La State Univ, Baton Rouge, 71-88. *Mem:* Am Vet Med Asn; Am Col Vet Path; Int Acad Path. *Res:* Pathogenesis of nutritional and infectious diseases of the swine and equine species; naturally occurring diseases of the tropics. *Mailing Add:* Tulane Regional Primate Ctr 18703 Three Rivers Rd Covington LA 70433

ROBERTS, ESTHER PEARL, PSYCHIATRY. *Current Pos:* MED DIR, MENT HEALTH SERVS, US DEPT STATE. *Personal Data:* b Nashville, Tenn, Nov 11, 42. *Educ:* Fisk Univ, BA, 64; Meharry Med Col, MD, 68; Columbia Univ, MPH, 74. *Concurrent Pos:* Assoc prof, HH Sci Ctr, Univ Tenn; asst prof, Columbia Med Sch, NY. *Mem:* Am Psychiat Asn; Am Col Psychiatrist. *Res:* Consultation techniques; indigenous mental health therapists in East and West Africa; minority psychiatrists as clinicians/administrators. *Mailing Add:* 2401 E St NW Washington DC 20522-0101. *Fax:* 202-663-1840

ROBERTS, EUGENE, BIOCHEMISTRY. *Current Pos:* chmn, Dept Biochem, 54-68, chmn, Div Neurosci, 68-83, DIR, DEPT NEUROBIOCHEM, BECKMAN RES INST CITY HOPE, DUARTE, CALIF, 83-; RES PROF NEUROL, SCH MED, UNIV SOUTHERN CALIF, 85- *Personal Data:* b Krasnodar, Russia, Jan 19, 20; US citizen; m 77; c 3. *Educ:* Wayne State Univ, BS, 40; Univ Mich, MS, 41, PhD(biochem), 43. *Hon Degrees:* Laurea Dr, Univ Florence. *Honors & Awards:* Distinguished Serv Award, Wayne State Univ, 66; Distinguished Scientist Award, Beckman Res Inst City Hope, 83; Louis & Bert Freedman Found Award Res Biochem, NY Acad Sci, 86. *Prof Exp:* Asst head, Uranium Compounds Res, Inhalation Sect, Univ Rochester, 43-46; res assoc, Barnard Free Skin & Cancer Hosp & Sch Med, Washington Univ, St Louis, Mo, 46-54. *Concurrent Pos:* Mem, Comt Brain Sci, Div Med Sci, Nat Res Coun, Nat Acad Sci, 66-70; mem, Neurol B Study Sect, Div Res Grants, NIH, Bethesda, Md, 67-69; mem, Coun Int Soc Neurochem, 69-73 & Bd Sci Counrs, Nat Inst Neurol Dis & Stroke, NIH, Bethesda, Md, 69-73; adj prof biochem & neurol, Sch Med, Univ Southern Calif, 70-; mem, USA Nat Comt, Int Brain Res Orgn, Nat Res Coun, Nat Acad Sci, Washington, DC, 76-79; fel, Ctr Advan Study Behav Sci, Stanford, Calif, 78; mem bd trustees, Calif Found Biochem Res, La Jolla Calif, 79-, chmn, 81-82; mem bd sci counselors, Nat Inst Neurol & Commun Dis & Stroke, 80-84; adj sr scientist, Hal B Wallis Res Facil, Eisenhower Med Ctr, Rancho Mirage, Calif, 89-91. *Mem:* Nat Acad Sci; Am Asn Cancer Res; Am Chem Soc; Am Inst Chemists; Am Soc Biol Chemists; Am Soc Neurochem (pres, 71-72); Am Soc Pharmacol & Exp Therapeut; fel NY Acad Sci; Int Soc Neurochem; Sigma Xi; Soc Exp Biol & Med; Soc Neurosci; World Fedn Neurol. *Res:* Neurochemistry; biochemistry of cancer; comparative biochemistry; general metabolism. *Mailing Add:* Dept Neurobiochem Beckman Res Inst City Hope Duarte CA 91010. *Fax:* 626-357-1929

ROBERTS, FLOYD EDWARD, JR, ORGANIC CHEMISTRY. *Current Pos:* Chemist, Merck & Co, Inc, 62-64, sr chemist, 64-69, res fel, 69-79, SR RES FEL, MERCK SHARPE & DOHME RES LABS, 79- *Personal Data:* b Philadelphia, Pa, Dec 2, 34; m 56; c 3. *Educ:* Franklin Col, AB, 56; Pa State Univ, MS, 58; Purdue Univ, PhD(org chem), 63. *Mem:* Am Chem Soc. *Res:* Steroids and other medicinals; antibiotics; natural product isolation. *Mailing Add:* 220 Valley Rd Princeton NJ 08540-3473

ROBERTS, FRANCIS DONALD, DENTAL PRODUCTS, NONWOVEN FABRICS. *Current Pos:* PRES, PERIODONTIX, INC, 93- *Personal Data:* b Utica, NY, Jan 18, 38; m 64, Nancy Crowder; c Christine M, Susan M, Karen E & Katherine A. *Educ:* Utica Col, BA, 59; Cornell Univ, PhD(org chem), 64. *Prof Exp:* Res chemist, Colgate-Palmolive Co, New York, 64-66, sect head, 66-70, tech coordr toilet articles, Pharmaceut Div, 70-72, asst mgr oral res, 72-73, dir purchasing raw mat, 73-76, dir res & develop, 76-81, vpres res & develop, 81-86, vpres technol & planning, Kendall Co Div, 86-89; pres & chief exec officer, Spectra Sci Inc, 89-92; pres, F D Roberts & Assoc, 92-93. *Mem:* Am Chem Soc. *Res:* Synthesis of new organo-sulfur compounds; condensed aromatics; oral research, especially treatment of caries and periodontal disease; nonwoven fabrics, acrylic and rubber based pressure sensitive adhesives; medical devices, surgical dressings, urological products; anti-embolism compression therapy; intravenous therapy; specialty dyes; polymers; medical devices and drugs. *Mailing Add:* Two Bridle Path Circle Dover MA 02030-2400

ROBERTS, FRANKLIN LEWIS, CYTOLOGY, GENETICS. *Current Pos:* from asst prof to assoc prof, 64-74, Coe Fund res grant, 65-66, chmn dept, 75-81, PROF ZOOL, UNIV MAINE, ORONO, 74- *Personal Data:* b Waterboro, Maine, Feb 21, 34; wid; c 5. *Educ:* Univ Maine, BS, 57; NC State Univ, PhD(genetics), 64. *Prof Exp:* Instr sci, Gorham State Teachers Col, 58-59; instr zool, NC State Univ, 59-64. *Concurrent Pos:* NSF res grant, 66-69 & City Hope Med Ctr, Duarte, Calif, 68, Tilapice aquacult, Haiti, 80- *Mem:* Am Soc Nat; AAAS; Am Soc Ichthyol & Herpet; Genetics Soc Am. *Res:* Cytotaxonomy and cytogenetics of cold blooded vertebrates, particularly fishes; cell culture of cold blooded vertebrate tissues; genetics of parthenogenesis. *Mailing Add:* Dept Zool Murray Hall Univ Maine Orono ME 04469-0001

ROBERTS, FRED STEPHEN, DISCRETE MATHEMATICS, MATHEMATICAL MODELING. *Current Pos:* assoc prof, Rutgers Univ, 72-76, actg dir, Rutgers Ctr Oper Res, 82-83, assoc dir, Ctr Dir Math & Theoret Comput Sci, 89-92, actg dir, 91-93, PROF MATH, RUTGERS UNIV, 76- *Personal Data:* b New York, NY, June 19, 43; m 72, Helen Marcus; c Sarah & David. *Educ:* Dartmouth Col, AB, 64; Stanford Univ, MS, 67, PhD(math), 68. *Prof Exp:* NIH traineeship math psychol, Univ Pa, 68; mathematician, Rand Corp, 68-72. *Concurrent Pos:* Daniel Webster Nat Scholar, 61-64; Woodrow Wilson fel, 64-65; mem, Inst Advan Study, Princeton, 71-72; prin investr, NSF awards, 72-79, 83-; vis prof oper res, Cornell Univ, 79-80; sci research awards, Air Force, 79-83, 85-; Alexander von Humboldt fel, 84; vis, AT&T Bell Labs, 86-88; consult, Rand Corp, Orgn Econ Coop & Develop, Contruct Eng Res Lab, Inst Gas Technol; Robert G Stone vis prof, Northeastern Univ, 90-; prin investr, Off Naval Res Grants, 93- *Mem:* Am Math Soc; Math Asn Am; Soc Indust & Appl Math (secy, 77-81, vpres, 84-87); Oper Res Soc Am; Soc Math Psychol; Consortium Math & Applns; Soc Inst Math Sci (secy, 87-92). *Res:* Mathematical models in the social, biological and environmental sciences and of problems of communications and transportation; combinatorial mathematics and graph theory; theory of measurement; operations research; utility, decision-making, and social choice. *Mailing Add:* Dept Math Rutgers Univ New Brunswick NJ 08903-2101. *Fax:* 732-932-5530; *E-Mail:* froberts@dimacs.rutgers.edu

ROBERTS, FREDDY LEE, CIVIL ENGINEERING. *Current Pos:* T L JAMES PROF, LA TECH UNIV, 90- *Personal Data:* b Dermott, Ark, Dec 29, 41; m 64, Judy Smith; c Susan & Sarabeth. *Educ:* Univ Ark, Fayetteville, BSCE, 64, MSCE, 66; Univ Tex, Austin, PhD(civil eng), 70. *Prof Exp:* Soils engr, Grubbs Consult Engrs Inc, Ark, 65; res engr, Univ Ark, Fayetteville, 64-66; consult piles, Hudson, Matlock, Dawkins & Panak Res Engrs, 66-67; res engr & teaching asst hwy roughness, Univ Tex, Austin, 66-69, vis assoc prof, 75-78, res engr, 81-83; from asst prof to assoc prof civil eng, Clemson Univ, 69-75; vis assoc prof, Univ Tex, Austin, 75-78; chief engr, Austin Res Engrs Inc, 78-81; res engr, Univ Tex, Austin, 81-83; assoc prof civil eng, Tex A&M Univ, 83-85; prof civil eng, Auburn Univ 86-90; dir, Nat Ctr Asphalt Technol, 86-90. *Concurrent Pos:* Mem, Transp Res Bd, Nat Acad Sci-Nat Res Coun; mat & design consult, Rauhut Eng, Austin, 81-95. *Mem:* Am Soc Civil Engrs; Asn Asphalt Paving Technol. *Res:* Pavement material evaluation and use in design; asphalt and recycled mixture design; development of infrastructure engineering and management systems; development of pavement thickness design procedures; evaluation of stripping test methods; construction of asphalt pavements; evaluation of pavement performance. *Mailing Add:* Civil Eng Prog Latech Univ PO Box 10348 Ruston LA 71272-0001. *Fax:* 318-257-2562

ROBERTS, GEORGE A(DAM), METALLURGY. *Current Pos:* RETIRED. *Personal Data:* b Uniontown, Pa, Feb 18, 19; m 71; c 3. *Educ:* Carnegie Inst Technol, BSc, 39, MSc, 41, DSc, 42. *Prof Exp:* Res metallurgist, Vanadium-Alloys Steel Co, 41-45, chief metallurgist, 45-53, vpres, 53-61, pres, Vasco Metals Corp, Pa, 61-66; pres, Teledyne, Inc, 66-90, from vchmn to chmn, 90-93. *Mem:* Nat Acad Eng; fel Am Soc Metals (vpres, 53, pres, 54); Soc Mfg Eng; Am Chem Soc; fel Am Inst Mining, Metall & Petrol Engrs. *Res:* Metallurgy of tool steels; heat treatment of hardenable steels; powder metallurgy of ferrous alloys; mechanical properties of steels. *Mailing Add:* 7848 Croydon Ave Los Angeles CA 90174

ROBERTS, GEORGE E(DWARD), SYSTEMS ANALYSIS. *Current Pos:* RETIRED. *Personal Data:* b Portsmouth, Eng, Sept 25, 26; m 50; c 1. *Educ:* Portsmouth Naval Col Eng, BSc, 45. *Prof Exp:* Apprentice elec eng, Portsmouth Dockyard, Brit Admiralty, 42-47, design draftsman, 47-51; design draftsman, Can Vickers Ltd, 51-52; elec engr, Tech Prods Dept, RCA Victor Co, Ltd, 52-56 & Defense Dept, 56-58, sr mem sci staff, Res Labs, 58-66; mem tech staff, Gen Res Corp, 66-74; systs analyst, Litton Mellonics, 74-76; mem prof staff, Geodynamics Corp. 76-80, mgr, 80-89. *Res:* Probability and statistics; antennas; mathematical analysis. *Mailing Add:* 494 Gibralter Dr Anacortes WA 98221

ROBERTS, GEORGE P, POLYMER CHEMISTRY. *Current Pos:* Res scientist, Corp Res Ctr, Uniroyal Inc, NJ, 64-69, group leader acrylonitrile-butadiene-styrene res, Chem Div, Conn, 69-74, mgr polymer appl res, Corp Res & Develop, 74-84, dir new technol, 84-86, tech dir, Uniroyal Chem Co, 86-91, bus mgr trilene liquid polymers, 91-96, TECH DIR PLASTIC ADDITIVES, UNIROYAL CHEM CO, 97- *Personal Data:* b Barton, Vt, Dec 25, 37; m 59, Barbara DeMar; c Kent D, Deirdre, Dawn & Thomas P. *Educ:* Univ Vt, BS, 59; Northwestern Univ, PhD(phys chem), 64. *Mem:* Am Chem Soc; Soc Plastics Engrs. *Res:* Polymer characterization; relationship of properties of polymers to morphology and molecular structure; stabilization and property modification through the use of additives, process development and polymer applications. *Mailing Add:* World Hq Uniroyal Chem Co Benson Rd Middlebury CT 06749. *Fax:* 203-573-2525

ROBERTS, GEORGE W(ILLARD), CHEMICAL REACTION ENGINEERING, HETEROGENEOUS CATALYSIS. *Current Pos:* dept head, 89-94, PROF CHEM ENG, NC STATE UNIV, 89- *Personal Data:* b Bridgeport, Conn, Aug 9, 38; m 63, Mary Perdriau; c Claire I & William T. *Educ:* Cornell Univ, BChE, 61; Mass Inst Technol, ScD, 65. *Prof Exp:* Instr heat transfer, Mass Inst Technol, 63; chem engr, Rohm & Haas Co, 65-67, projs supvr, 68-69; assoc prof chem eng, Wash Univ, 69-71; mgr chem & chem eng, Engelhard Industs Div, Engelhard Minerals & Chem Corp, 72-77; dir, Corp Res & Develop Dept, Air Prod & Chem, Inc, 77-81, gen mgr, Com Develop Div, Process Systs Group, 81-89. *Mem:* Am Chem Soc; Am Inst Chem Engrs; emer mem Indust Res Inst. *Res:* Applying the principles of chemical reaction engineering, reaction kinetics and hetergereous catalysis to problems in pollution; prevention and alternate fuels; research management; commercial development; research management; commercial development. *Mailing Add:* 1610 St Mary's St Raleigh NC 27608-2219. *Fax:* 919-515-3465; *E-Mail:* roberts@che.ncsu.edu

ROBERTS, GLENN DALE, CLINICAL MICROBIOLOGY, CLINICAL MYCOLOGY & MYCOBACTERIOLOGY. *Current Pos:* instr microbiol & lab med, 72-77, from asst prof to assoc prof, 77-86, PROF MICROBIOL & LAB MED, MAYO MED SCH, 87- *Personal Data:* b Gilmer, Tex, Apr 9, 43; m 73, Kathleen L Brackin; c Michael G, Heather M & Megan L. *Educ:* NTex State Univ, BS, 67; Univ Okla, MS, 69, PhD(med mycol), 71; Am Bd Med Microbiol, cert, 79. *Prof Exp:* Fel clin mycol, Col Med, Univ Ky, 71-72. *Concurrent Pos:* Consult, Mayo Clin & Mayo Found, 72- *Mem:* Med Mycol Soc of the Americas; Int Soc Human & Animal Mycol; Am Soc Clin Path; Am Soc Microbiol; Am Thoracic Soc; fel Am Acad Microbiol. *Res:* Diagnostic and clinical mycobacteriology and mycology; mycotic serology. *Mailing Add:* Div Clin Microbiol Mayo Clin Rochester MN 55905. *E-Mail:* Roberts.glenn@mayo.edu

ROBERTS, HAROLD R, INTERNAL MEDICINE, HEMATOLOGY. *Current Pos:* Instr path, 60-62, assoc prof path & med, 62-70, chief, Div Hemat, Dept Med, 68-77, PROF PATH & MED, UNIV NC, SCH MED, CHAPEL HILL, 70- *Personal Data:* b Four Oaks, NC, Jan 4, 30; m 58; c 2. *Educ:* Univ NC, BS, 52, MD, 55. *Res:* Blood coagulation; hemorrhage; thrombosis. *Mailing Add:* Med Hematol 5 Univ NC Med Sch Chapel Hill NC 27599. *Fax:* 919-966-7639, 966-6923

ROBERTS, HARRY HEIL, MARINE GEOLOGY, SEDIMENTOLOGY. *Current Pos:* Asst prof geol res, 69-74, assoc prof, 74-78, PROF MARINE SCI, COASTAL STUDIES INST, LA STATE UNIV, BATON ROUGE, 78-, DIR, COASTAL STUDIES INST, 87- *Personal Data:* b Huntington, WVa, Feb 2, 40; m 63, Mary S Hamb; c Andrew. *Educ:* Marshall Univ, BS, 62; La State Univ, Baton Rouge, MS, 66, PhD(geol), 69. *Honors & Awards:* I A Leverson Award, Am Asn Petrol Geologists, 92. *Mem:* Soc Econ Paleontologists & Mineralogists; Am Asn Petrol Geologists; Coastal Soc; Int Asn Sedimentol. *Res:* Sedimentology associated with reef and deltaic environments; dynamics and ecology of reefs; marine geology of shelves and slopes; geology and sedimentology of natural oil seeps of continental slope Gulf of Mexico. *Mailing Add:* Oceanog La State Univ Baton Rouge LA 70803-0001. *Fax:* 504-388-2520

ROBERTS, HARRY VIVIAN, STATISTICS. *Current Pos:* from instr to assoc prof, 49-59, prof statist, 59-93, EMER PROF STATIST & QUAL MGT, UNIV CHICAGO, 93- *Personal Data:* b Peoria, Ill, May 1, 23; m 43; c 2. *Educ:* Univ Chicago, BA, 43, MBA, 47, PhD(bus), 55. *Prof Exp:* Mkt res analyst, McCann-Erickson, Inc, 46-49. *Concurrent Pos:* Assoc ed, Am Statistician News, 53-73 & J Am Statist Asn, 76-; Ford Found fel, 59-60. *Mem:* AAAS; Am Econ Asn; fel Am Statist Asn; Inst Math Statist; Royal Statist Soc. *Res:* Statistical theory and applications, especially interactive data analysis and quality management; statistical decision theory and applications, especially to medical diagnosis and treatment. *Mailing Add:* Grad Sch Bus Univ Chicago 1101 E 58th St Chicago IL 60637

ROBERTS, HOWARD C(REIGHTON), engineering; deceased, see previous edition for last biography

ROBERTS, IRVING, GENETIC ENGINEERING. *Current Pos:* RES PROF, DEPT MICROBIOL & IMMUNOL, MED COL VA, 82- *Personal Data:* b Brooklyn, NY, Jan 9, 15; m 38, 66; c 2. *Educ:* City Col New York, BS, 34; Columbia Univ, MS, 35, PhD(phys chem), 37. *Prof Exp:* Asst chem, Columbia Univ, 35-39; chem engr, Weiss & Downs Inc, NY, 39-43; group leader, Manhattan Proj, 43-45; div engr, Process Div, Res & Develop Dept, Elliott Co, 45-50; consult, 50-56; dir planning, Reynolds Metals Co, 56-61, vpres, 61-78; consult engr, 78-82. *Mem:* Am Chem Soc; Am Inst Chem Engrs; Am Soc Mech Engrs. *Res:* Long-range planning and economic evaluation; the aluminum industry; oxygen and other low temperature plants; new chemical processes; development of DNA shuttle plasmids for anaerobic bacteria. *Mailing Add:* 9007 Woodsorrel Dr Richmond VA 23229

ROBERTS, J(ASPER) KENT, ENGINEERING. *Current Pos:* RETIRED. *Personal Data:* b Ryan, Okla, Jan 15, 22; m 43; c 2. *Educ:* Univ Okla, BSCE, 47; Univ Mo, MSCE, 50. *Prof Exp:* From instr to assoc prof civil eng, Univ Mo, Rolla, 47-57, prof, 57-85, asst dean eng, 70-80. *Mem:* Am Soc Civil Engrs; Nat Soc Prof Engrs; Am Soc Eng Educ. *Mailing Add:* 906 Murry Lane Rolla MO 65401

ROBERTS, J T ADRIAN, MECHANICAL PROPERTIES, CORROSION. *Current Pos:* mgr mat sci & technol, 85-87, Dep Dir Res, 87-89, DIR LAB PROGS, BATTELLE PAC NORTHWEST LABS, 89- *Personal Data:* b Northwich, Cheshire, Eng, May 21, 44; US citizen; m 65; c 2. *Educ:* Manchester Univ, UK, BSc, 65, MSc, 66, PhD(metall), 68. *Prof Exp:* Group leader ceramic properties, Argonne Nat Lab, 68-74; sr prog mgr fuels & mat, nuclear power div, Elec Power & Res Inst, 74-85. *Concurrent Pos:* Vis assoc prof mat sci, Cornell Univ, 79; vis lectr mat sci, Univ Calif, Berkeley, 80-85 & Stanford Univ, 81-85; trustee, Am Ceramic Soc, 82-85; exec comt mem, mat sci & technol div, Am Nuclear Soc, 83-90, chmn, 89-90. *Mem:* Fel Am Ceramic Soc (vpres, 86-87); fel Am Nuclear Soc; Am Inst Metall Eng. *Res:* Materials science in support of energy production; ceramic and metal structural behavior for use in nuclear reactors (LWR, LMFBR) and advanced systems (fusion, MHD and batteries); environmental restoration and waste management. *Mailing Add:* 2001 Harris Ave Richland WA 99352

ROBERTS, JAMES ALLEN, UROLOGY. *Current Pos:* res assoc, 67-72, res scientist, 72-78, SR RES SCIENTIST & HEAD, UROL, TULANE REGIONAL PRIMATE CTR, 78-; PROF & ASSOC CHMN, RES, TULANE UNIV SCH MED, 87- *Personal Data:* b Beach, NDak, May 31, 34; m 86, Hilda Peachy; c Jennifer, Mary & Thomas. *Educ:* Univ Chicago, BS, 55, MD, 59. *Honors & Awards:* Original Res Award, Southern Med Asn, 90. *Prof Exp:* Asst prof, Tulane Univ Sch Med, 67-71; assoc prof urol, 71-75. *Concurrent Pos:* Fogarty sr int fel, 84; mem, Surg Anesthesiol & Trauma Study Sect, Div Res Grants, NIH. *Mem:* Sigma Xi; Am Urol Asn; Soc Univ Urologists; Urodynamics Soc. *Res:* Ureteral and renal physiology and studies on etiology of vesicoureteral reflux; urinary tract infection and the pathophysiology of pyelonephritis, etiology of renal damage from bacterial infection; clinical studies of urinary tract infection. *Mailing Add:* Dept Urol Tulane Regional Primate Ctr 18703 Three Rivers Rd Covington LA 70433. *Fax:* 504-893-1352; *E-Mail:* jr@tpc.tulane.edu

ROBERTS, JAMES ARNOLD, TELECOMMUNICATIONS ENGINEERING & RESEARCH, NATIONAL DEFENSE DATA PROCESSING SYSTEMS. *Current Pos:* PROF & CHAIR ELEC ENG & COMPUT SCI, UNIV KANS, 90- *Personal Data:* b Vandalia, Ill, Mar 11, 44; m 65, Carol Helton; c J Michael & Sally A. *Educ:* Univ Kans, BS, 66; Mass Inst Technol, MS, 68; Santa Clara Univ, PhD(elec eng), 79. *Prof Exp:* Mem tech staff, RCA, 66-69 & ESL Inc, 69-75; sect head, ESL Inc, Subsid TRW, 75-78, dept mgr, 78-80, lab mgr, 80-83, prog mgr, TRW Inc, 83-87, mgr, TRW Denver Opers, 87-90. *Concurrent Pos:* Lectr elec eng & comput sci, Santa Clara Univ, 78-83; prin investr, Ctr Res Inc, 90-, trustee, 91-; consult, Nellcor Inc, 91, AeroComm Inc, 92; dir, Kantronics Inc, 91-; mem, Kans Elec Utilities Res Prog Tech Comt, 91- *Mem:* Inst Elec & Electronics Engrs; Am Soc Eng Educ; Nat Elec Eng Dept Heads Asn. *Res:* Statistical communication theory, information theory, indoor wireless communication systems, spread-spectrum communications and telecommunication networks. *Mailing Add:* Univ Kans 415 Snow Hall Lawrence KS 66045. *Fax:* 785-864-4971; *E-Mail:* jroberts@eecs.ukans.edu

ROBERTS, JAMES C, JR, PATHOLOGY. *Current Pos:* PATHOLOGIST & DIR RES, LITTLE CO MARY HOSP, 60-, DIR, CETACEAN RES LAB, 62- *Personal Data:* b New York, NY, Feb 13, 26; m 49; c 4. *Educ:* Wesleyan Univ, AB, 45; Univ Rochester, MD, 49. *Prof Exp:* Asst path, Wash Univ, 49-51; instr, Univ Pittsburgh, 53-55, asst prof, 55-58; pathologist & dir med educ, ETenn Baptist Hosp, 58-60. *Concurrent Pos:* Hartford fel, Arteriosclerosis Res, 55-58; prin investr, Res Grants, 57-; consult, Los Angeles County Harbor Hosp, 62-; co-chmn conf comp arteriosclerosis, Nat Heart Inst, Calif, 64-65; Nuffield traveling fel, Zool Soc London, 65. *Mem:* Am Heart Asn; Am Soc Mammal; AMA; Am Asn Path & Bact; fel Col Am Path. *Res:* Immunopathology; arteriosclerosis; comparative arteriosclerosis and morphology. *Mailing Add:* 15 Portuguese Bend Rd Rolling Hills CA 90274-5072

ROBERTS, JAMES E, CIVIL ENGINEERING. *Current Pos:* Mgr, Bridges Design Sect, Calif Dept Transp, 68-72, chief, Eng Equip Div, 76-81, proj dir, 81-85, chief bridge design engr, 85-87, chief bridge eng, 87-93, dept dir eng serv, 93-94, DIR ENG SERV DEPT & CHIEF STRUCT ENG, CALIF DEPT TRANSP, 94- *Personal Data:* b Jameson, Mich, Nov 24, 30. *Educ:* Univ Calif, Berkeley, BS, 53; Univ Southern Calif, MS, 66. *Honors & Awards:* Construct Mgt Award, Am Soc Civil Engrs, 96. *Mem:* Nat Acad Eng; fel Am Soc Civil Eng; Am Concrete Inst; Am Welding Soc; Am Asn State Hwy & Transp Officials. *Mailing Add:* Eng Serv Dept Calif Dept Transp PO Box 942874 Sacramento CA 94274. *Fax:* 916-227-8251; *E-Mail:* jroberts@trmx2.dot.ca.gov

ROBERTS, JAMES ERNEST, SR, economic entomology; deceased, see previous edition for last biography

ROBERTS, JAMES HERBERT, experimental nuclear physics; deceased, see previous edition for last biography

ROBERTS, JAMES LEWIS, BIOCHEMISTRY, MOLECULAR BIOLOGY. *Current Pos:* MEM STAFF, DEPT BIOCHEM, COL PHYSICIANS & SURGEONS, COLUMBIA UNIV, 79- *Personal Data:* b Lima, Peru, Oct 23, 51; US citizen; m. *Educ:* Colo State Univ, BS, 73; Univ Ore, PhD(chem), 78. *Honors & Awards:* Golden Lamport Award, Excellence Basic Sci. *Prof Exp:* Res technician biochem, Colo State Univ, 70-73; teaching asst, Univ Ore, 73-74; fel biochem, Univ Calif, 78-79. *Mem:* AAAS; Am Chem Soc; Soc Neurosci; Int Neuroendocrine Soc. *Res:* Biosynthesis and regulation of the adrenocorticotropin-endorphin precursor; recombinant DNA cloning of pituitary and brain adrenocorticotropin-endorphin; glucocorticoid and thyroid hormone regulation of gene expression; gene structure. *Mailing Add:* Neurobiol A14-44 Mt Sinai Med Ctr One Gustave Levy Pl New York NY 10029-6504. *Fax:* 212-996-9785

ROBERTS, JAMES M, OBSTETRICS & GYNECOLOGY. *Current Pos:* AT DEPT RES, MAGEE WOMEN'S RES INST. *Personal Data:* b Taylor, Mich, Mar 22, 41. *Educ:* Univ Mich, MD, 66; Am Bd Obstet & Gynec, cert fetal & maternal med. *Honors & Awards:* Gordon Jimenssen Lectr, Univ Okla, 90. *Prof Exp:* Resident obstet & gynec, Univ Mich Hosp, 67-71; postdoctoral res fel, Cardiovasc Res Inst, Univ Calif, San Francisco, 73-75, from asst prof to assoc prof, Dept Obstet & Gynec & Reproductive Sci, 75-84, assoc staff mem, 80-84, sr staff mem, Cardiovasc Res Inst & prof, Obstet & Gynec & Reproductive Sci, 84- *Concurrent Pos:* NIH res grants, 78-93; NIH res career develop awards, 79-84; perinatal consult, Marin Gen Hosp, 83-; mem coun, Perinatal Res Soc, 84-87, Comt Treat Hypertension During Pregnancy, NIH & 5 Yr Plan Comt, Nat Inst Child Health & Human Develop, 89; chmn, Fetal Mat Med Network, Nat Inst Child Health & Human Develop, 91-; prof fac mem, Molecular Med Prog, Univ Calif, San Francisco, 91- *Mem:* Am Fedn Clin Res; Am Col Obstet & Gynec; Soc Gynec Invest; Endocrine Soc; Neurosci Soc; Soc Perinatal Obstetricians; Perinatal Res Soc (pres-elect, 90); NY Acad Sci; Am Soc Pharmacol & Exp Therapeut; Am Gynec & Obstet Soc. *Res:* Modulation of adrenergic response and receptors by steroid hormones; role of endothelial injury in preclampsia; author of more than 100 technical publications. *Mailing Add:* Dept Res Magee Women's Res Inst Rm 610 204 Craft Ave Pittsburgh PA 15213. *Fax:* 412-647-1133

ROBERTS, JAMES RICHARD, PHYSICS. *Current Pos:* PHYSICIST, NAT BUR STAND, 64- *Personal Data:* b Flint, Mich, July 1, 37; m 60; c 3. *Educ:* Univ Mich, BS, 59, MS, 61, PHD(physics), 64. *Concurrent Pos:* Nat Bur Stand training grant & vis scientist, Aarbus Univ, Denmark, 70-71, Los Alamos Nat Lab, Wroclaw, Poland. *Mem:* Am Inst Physics. *Res:* Plasma spectroscopy; experimental determination of atomic transition probabilities; stark broadening parameters and other atomic parameters of ionized plasmas. *Mailing Add:* 17927 Wheatridge Dr Germantown MD 20874

ROBERTS, JANE CAROLYN, PHYSIOLOGY, HIBERNATION. *Current Pos:* asst prof, 72-79, ASSOC PROF, DEPT BIOL, CREIGHTON UNIV, 79- *Personal Data:* b Malden, Mass, Nov 14, 32. *Educ:* Univ Mass, Amherst, BS, 54; Univ Calif, Los Angeles, MA, 56, Univ Calif, Santa Barbara, PhD(biol & physiol), 71. *Prof Exp:* Grad res physiologist, Med Ctr, Univ Calif, Los Angeles, 57-63, asst specialist physiol, 63-64, asst res physiologist, 64-67; assoc specialist, Dept Ergonomics & Phys Educ, Univ Calif, Santa Barbara, 67-71; res worker, Dept Ophthal Res, Columbia Univ, 71-72. *Mem:* Am Physiol Soc; Am Soc Zoologists; Soc Exp Biol & Med; Sigma Xi. *Res:* Metabolic and biochemical changes in hibernation and temperature acclimation. *Mailing Add:* Dept Biol Creighton Univ Omaha NE 68178. *Fax:* 402-280-5595; *E-Mail:* robertsj@creighton.edu

ROBERTS, JAY, PHARMACOLOGY. *Current Pos:* PROF PHARMACOL & CHMN DEPT, MED COL PA, 70- *Personal Data:* b New York, NY, July 15, 27; m 50; c 2. *Educ:* Long Island Univ, BS, 49; Cornell Univ, PhD(pharmacol), 53. *Prof Exp:* Instr physiol, Hunter Col, 53; res fel pharmacol, Med Col, Cornell Univ, 53-54, from instr to assoc prof, 54-66; prof, Univ Pittsburgh, 66-70. *Concurrent Pos:* Asst ed, Biol Abstr, 56-72; Lederle fac award, 57-60; mem study sect pharmacol, USPHS, 66-72; mem, Geriat Adv Panel, US Pharmocopeia, 80-90; sr investr award, SE Heart Asn; pres, Midatlantic Pharmacol Soc, 89-92. *Mem:* AAAS; Am Soc Pharmacol & Exp Therapeut; fel Am Col Cardiol; Soc Exp Biol & Med; Cardiac Muscle Soc (secy-treas, 65-67, pres, 67-69); Geront Soc Am. *Res:* Neuromuscular and cardiovascular pharmacology; aging. *Mailing Add:* Dept Pharmacol Suite 750 Allegheny Univ Health Ctr EPPI 3200 Henry Ave Philadelphia PA 19129-1137. *Fax:* 215-843-1515

ROBERTS, JEFFREY WARREN, MOLECULAR BIOLOGY, BIOCHEMISTRY. *Current Pos:* asst prof, 74-80, assoc prof biochem, 80-85 PROF, BIOCHEM CORNELL UNIV, 86- *Personal Data:* b Flint, Mich, Feb 16, 44; m 68; c 2. *Educ:* Univ Tex, BA, 64; Harvard Univ, PhD(biophys), 70. *Prof Exp:* NSF fel, Lab Molecular Biol, Med Res Ctr, 70-71; jr fel, Harvard Soc Fels, 71-73. *Res:* Regulation of gene expression, especially mechanism of lysogenic induction and the mechanism of positive control in the life cycle of bacteriophage lambda. *Mailing Add:* Biochem Molecular & Cell Biol Cornell Univ 349 Biotech Bldg Ithaca NY 14853

ROBERTS, JERRY ALLAN, APPLIED MATHEMATICS. *Current Pos:* RETIRED. *Personal Data:* b Landis, NC, July 31, 31; m 55; c 4. *Educ:* NC State Univ, BEngPhys, 58, MS, 60, PhD(appl math), 64. *Prof Exp:* Res asst, NC State Univ, 57-63, instr, 63-65; from asst prof to assoc prof math, Davidson Col, 65-93. *Mem:* Math Asn Am; Soc Indust & Appl Math; Asn Comput Mach. *Res:* Use of numerical analysis and digital computers to obtain approximate solutions of boundary-value problems arising from problems in fracture mechanics; experimental statistics. *Mailing Add:* 157 Surfside Lane Mooresville NC 28115

ROBERTS, JOEL LAURENCE, MATHEMATICS. *Current Pos:* from asst prof to assoc prof, 72-80, PROF MATH, UNIV MINN, MINNEAPOLIS, 80- *Personal Data:* b Denver, Colo, Sept 5, 40; m 64; c 3. *Educ:* Mass Inst Technol, BS, 63; Harvard Univ, MA, 64, PhD(math), 69. *Prof Exp:* Asst prof math, Purdue Univ, Lafayette, 68-72. *Concurrent Pos:* Vis lectr, Nat Univ Mex, 69; NSF res grant, Purdue Univ, Lafayette, 70-72, Univ Minn, 72-; vis scholar, Univ Calif, Berkeley, 79; vis prof, Nat Univ Mex, 87. *Mem:* Am Math Soc. *Res:* Algebraic geometry; properties of algebraic varieties in projective spaces; intersection theory and enumerative geometry; commutative algebra. *Mailing Add:* Sch Math Univ Minn Minneapolis MN 55455-0487

ROBERTS, JOHN D, ORGANIC CHEMISTRY NUCLEAR MAGNETIC RESONANCE SPECTROSCOPY. *Current Pos:* prof org chem, Calif Inst Technol, 53-72, chmn, Div Chem & Chem Eng, 63-68, actg chmn, 72-73, inst prof chem, 72-78, vpres, provost & dean fac, 80-83, EMER INST PROF CHEM & LECTR, CALIF INST TECHNOL, 88- *Personal Data:* b Los Angeles, Calif, June 8, 18; m 42; c Anne C, Donald W, John P & Allen W. *Educ:* Univ Calif, Los Angeles, BA, 41, PhD(chem), 44. *Hon Degrees:* Dr rer nat, Univ Munich, 62; DrSci, Temple Univ, 64, Univ Notre Dame, 93, Univ Wales, 93. *Honors & Awards:* Pure Chem Award, Am Chem Soc, 54, Roger Adams Award, 67, James Flack Norris Award, 79; Harrison Howe Award, 57; Nichols Medal, 71; Tolman Medal, 75; Linus Pauling Award, 80; Richards Medal, 82; Willard Gibbs Gold Medal, 83; Priestley Medal, 87; Madison Marshall Award, 89; Robert A Welch Award, 90; Nat Medal Sci, 90; Seaborg Medal, 91; Achievement in Magnetic Resonance, 91; Arthur C Cope Award, 94. *Prof Exp:* Instr chem, Univ Calif, Los Angeles, 44-45; Nat Res Coun fel, Harvard Univ, 45-46, instr, 46; from instr to assoc prof, Mass Inst Technol, 46-53. *Concurrent Pos:* Consult, E I Du Pont de Nemours & Co, 49- & Union Carbide, 49-62; Guggenheim fel, 52-53 & 55; lectureships and professorships at var cols & univs, US & abroad, 56-; mem, Adv Panel Chem, NSF, 57-60, chmn, 59-60, mem, Adv Comt Math, Phys & Eng Sci, 61-64, chmn, 62-64, mem, Adv Comt Math & Phys Sci, 64-66; mem, Chem Adv Panel, Off Sci Res, Air Force, 59-61; dir & consult ed, W A Benjamin, Inc, 60-67; chmn, Chem Sect, Nat Acad Sci, 68-71, chmn, Class I, 76-79, coun, 80-83; trustee, L B Leakey Found, 83-92; mem bd dirs, Huntington Med Res Inst, 84-, treas, 89-93. *Mem:* Nat Acad Sci; Am Philos Soc; AAAS; Am Chem Soc; Am Acad Arts & Sci; Sigma Xi. *Res:* Small-ring organic compounds; relation between structure and reactivity; nuclear magnetic resonance spectroscopy of nitrogen and carbon; applications of nuclear magnetic resonance spectroscopy to organic chemistry, biology and medicine. *Mailing Add:* Div Chem & Chem Eng Mail Code 164-30 Calif Inst Technol Pasadena CA 91125

ROBERTS, JOHN EDWIN, CHEMISTRY. *Current Pos:* RETIRED. *Personal Data:* b Laconia, NH, Mar 6, 20; m 44; c 2. *Educ:* Univ NH, BS, 42, MS, 44; Cornell Univ, PhD(inorg chem), 47. *Prof Exp:* Asst chem, Univ NH, 42-44 & Cornell Univ, 44-46; from asst prof to prof chem, Univ Mass, Amherst, 46-83. *Concurrent Pos:* Fel fluorine chem, Univ Wash, 58-59; vis prof, Univ Cairo, 61-62; sabbatical, Anal Inst, Univ Vienna, 71. *Mem:* Am Chem Soc. *Res:* Molar refraction; indium fluoride systems; rare earth chemistry; fluorides of less familiar elements; the system indium trifluoride-water and the tendency of indium to form fluoanions; peroxydisulfuryldifluoride; fluorosulfonates; trifluoracetates; microchemistry and chemical microscopy; chemistry of art and archaeology; thermal analytical methods. *Mailing Add:* 12 W Diane Dr Keene NH 03431-2633

ROBERTS, JOHN ENGLAND, PHYSICS. *Current Pos:* RETIRED. *Personal Data:* b Los Angeles, Calif, Dec 27, 22; m 57; c 2. *Educ:* Univ Calif, BS, 44, PhD(chem), 50. *Prof Exp:* Tech asst chem, Univ Calif, 43-44, jr scientist, Manhattan Dist, 44-46, asst, Dept Chem, 46-50, physicist, Lawrence Radiation Lab, 50-70; chmn, Dept Sci & Math, Parks Col, St Louis Univ, 70- *Concurrent Pos:* Lectr physics, St Mary's Col, Calif, 67-70. *Mem:* Am Phys Soc; Am Asn Physics Teachers. *Res:* Physics and mathematics. *Mailing Add:* Dept Sci & Math Parks Col St Louis Univ Falling Springs Rd Cahokia IL 62206-1998

ROBERTS, JOHN FREDRICK, ZOOLOGY, CELL BIOLOGY. *Current Pos:* from asst prof to assoc prof, 65-74, PROF ZOOL, NC STATE UNIV, 74- *Personal Data:* b Gallup, NMex, Oct 12, 28; m 51; c 4. *Educ:* Univ Ariz, BS, 56, PhD(zool), 64. *Prof Exp:* Asst prof biol, NMex Highlands Univ, 61-65. *Concurrent Pos:* USPHS res grants, 64-65 & 69-72. *Mem:* Sigma Xi; Soc Protozool; Am Soc Cell Biol. *Res:* Mitochondrial nucleic acids; morphogenesis; trypanosomes. *Mailing Add:* Dept Zool NC State Univ Box 7617 Raleigh NC 27695-0001

ROBERTS, JOHN HENDERSON, mathematics, for more information see previous edition

ROBERTS, JOHN LEWIS, COMPARATIVE PHYSIOLOGY. *Current Pos:* from instr to assoc prof physiol, 52-69, PROF PHYSIOL, UNIV MASS, AMHERST, 70- *Personal Data:* b Waukesha, Wis, May 23, 22; m 50; c 2. *Educ:* Univ Wis, BS, 47, MS, 48; Univ Calif, Los Angeles, PhD, 53. *Prof Exp:* Asst zool, Univ Wis, 47-48 & Univ Calif, Los Angeles, 48-51. *Concurrent Pos:* With zool inst & mus, Univ Kiel, 59-60; USPHS spec fel, 66-67; guest lectr, Dept Zool, Univ Bristol, 66-67; sr res assoc, Nat Res Coun-Nat Oceanog & Atmospheric Admin, La Jolla, Calif, 73-75; panelist, NSF, 77-80; vis prof zool, Univ Hawaii, Manoa, Honolulu, 80; vis investr, Physiol Res Lab, Scripps Inst Oceanog, La Jolla, Calif, 84. *Mem:* Fel AAAS; Soc Gen Physiol; Am Fisheries Soc; Am Soc Zool (secy, 76-79); Sigma Xi. *Res:* Physiological adaptations of poikilotherms; respiratory and cardiac physiology of fish; neural control of respiration and swimming in fish. *Mailing Add:* Dept Biol Univ Mass Amherst MA 01003

ROBERTS, JOSEPH BUFFINGTON, MATHEMATICS. *Current Pos:* from instr to assoc prof, 52-70, PROF MATH, REED COL, 70- *Personal Data:* b Albany, NY, Sept 9, 23; m 44; c 3. *Educ:* Case Inst Technol, BS, 44; Univ Colo, MA, 50; Univ Minn, PhD(math), 55. *Prof Exp:* Jr scientist radiochem, Manhattan Proj, Univ Calif, 45-46; asst math biol, Univ Chicago, 46-48; instr chem & math, Univ Wyo, 48-49; asst math, Univ Minn, 50-52. *Concurrent Pos:* Vis asst prof, Wesleyan Univ, 56-57; NSF res grant, 58-67; res assoc, Univ London, 62-63; Agency Int Develop vis prof, Univ Col, Dar es Salaam, 65-67; vis prof, Dalhousie Univ, 69-70; consult, Bonneville Power Admin, 58-61. *Mem:* Am Math Soc; Math Asn Am; Fedn Am Sci; Indian Math Soc; London Math Soc. *Res:* Number theory; summability; orthogonal functions. *Mailing Add:* Dept Math Reed Col Portland OR 97202-8199

ROBERTS, JOSEPH LINTON, PHYSICAL CHEMISTRY, BIOCHEMISTRY. *Current Pos:* from asst prof to assoc prof, 66-74, PROF CHEM, MARSHALL UNIV, 74- *Personal Data:* b Atlanta, Ga, Nov 13, 29; m 53; c 3. *Educ:* Oglethorpe Univ, BS, 53; Univ SDak, MA, 55; Univ Cincinnati, PhD(theoret chem), 64. *Prof Exp:* Res asst systs analytical, Biostatist Dept, Kettering Lab, Col Med, Univ Cincinnati, 59, res asst analytical chem, Dept Toxicol, 59-61; res chemist, Dept Med Res, Vet Hosp, Cincinnati, 61-66; asst prof biochem & exp med, Col Med, Univ Cincinnati, 65-66. *Mem:* Am Chem Soc. *Res:* Chemistry of fire suppression; computer modeling of fire suppression systems; models for effect of solvent or reactions. *Mailing Add:* Dept Chem Marshall Univ 400 Hal Greer Blvd Huntington WV 25755-0001

ROBERTS, JULIAN LEE, JR, ANALYTICAL CHEMISTRY. *Current Pos:* from asst prof to assoc prof chem, 64-73, PROF CHEM, UNIV REDLANDS, 73- *Personal Data:* b Columbia, Mo, June 15, 35; m 65. *Educ:* Univ Southern Calif, BA, 57; Northwestern Univ, PhD(analytical chem), 62. *Prof Exp:* Instr chem, Univ Redlands, 61-63; res chemist & vis lectr, Univ Calif, Riverside, 63-64. *Concurrent Pos:* NSF sci fac fel, Calif Inst Technol, 68-69; vis scientist, Lab Org & Analytical Electrochem, Ctr Nuclear Studies, Grenoble, France, 75-76. *Mem:* AAAS; Am Chem Soc; NY Acad Sci. *Res:* Structural and electroanalytical chemistry; mechanisms of electrochemical reactions; electrochemistry of dissolved gases and coordination compounds. *Mailing Add:* Dept Chem Univ Redlands 955 N Grove St Redlands CA 92373-0999

ROBERTS, KENNETH DAVID, BIOCHEMISTRY, ENDOCRINOLOGY. *Current Pos:* RETIRED. *Personal Data:* b Montreal, Que, Nov 20, 31; m 60, Norma Lydon; c Kathryn A. *Educ:* George Williams Col, BSc, 55; McGill Univ, PhD(biochem), 60. *Prof Exp:* Chemist, Charles E Frosst & Co, 49-55; Jane C Childs Mem Fund fel, Univ Basel, 61-63; asst prof biochem, Columbia Univ, 63-69; from assoc prof to prof biochem, Univ Montreal, 69-96. *Concurrent Pos:* Corresp ed, Steroids, 63-89; consult, Endocrine Lab, Maisonneuve Hosp, Montreal, 69-, mem grants comt, Med Res Coun Can, 71-89; sci officer, Found Res, Que, 89- *Mem:* AAAS; NY Acad Sci; Can Fertility Soc; Endocrine Soc; Can Biochem Soc; Can Fertil & Andrology Soc (pres, 89-90). *Res:* Biochemistry of steroids and steroid conjugates; reproduction; biochemistry of sperm capacitation and acrosome reaction enzymes of mammalian spermatozoa. *Mailing Add:* 2084 de la Regence St Bruno de Montarville PQ J3V 4B6 Can. *Fax:* 514-252-3569

ROBERTS, LARRY SPURGEON, ZOOLOGY, PARASITOLOGY. *Current Pos:* ADJ PROF BIOL, UNIV MIAMI, 90- *Personal Data:* b Texon, Tex, June 30, 35; m 62; c 4. *Educ:* Southern Methodist Univ, BSc, 56; Univ Ill, MSc, 58; Johns Hopkins Univ, ScD(parasitol), 61. *Prof Exp:* Henry Baldwin Ward Medal, Am Soc Parasitol, 71. *Prof Exp:* USPHS-NIH trainee, McGill Univ, 61-62; trainee, Univ Mass, Amherst, 62-63, from asst prof zool to prof 62-79; prof & chairperson, Tex Tech Univ, Lubbock, 79-84, prof biol sci, 84-90. *Concurrent Pos:* USPHS-NIH spec fel, Johns Hopkins Univ, 69-70; adj prof biol sci, Fla Int Univ, 89-93. *Mem:* Am Soc Parasitol (vpres, 85, 96); Soc Protozoologists; Am Soc Trop Med Hyg; Am Micros Soc (vpres, 75); Crustacean Soc; Int Soc Reef Studies; Am Acad Underwater Sci. *Res:* Developmental biochemistry of helminth parasites, especially cestodes; regulation of carbohydrate and energy metabolism in cestodes; systematics and morphology of parasitic copepods. *Mailing Add:* 27700 SW 164th Ave Homestead FL 33031. *E-Mail:* lroberts@umiami.ir.miami.edu

ROBERTS, LAWRENCE G, DATA COMMUNICATIONS, PACKET SWITCHING. *Current Pos:* PRES, ATM SYSTS, 93- *Personal Data:* b Norwalk, Conn, Dec 21, 37; c 2. *Educ:* Mass Inst Technol, BS, 59, MS, 60, PhD(elec eng), 63. *Honors & Awards:* L M Erickson Award Commun Res, 81; W Wallace McDowell Award, Inst Elec & Electronics Engrs, 92; Harry Goode Mem Award, Int Fedn Info Processing. *Prof Exp:* Mem staff, Lincoln Lab, Mass Inst Technol, 63-67; dir, Info Process Techniques Defense Advan Res Projs Agency, 67-73; pres, Telenet Commun Corp, 73-79, GTE Telenet Corp, 80-82 & GTE Subscriber Network, 80-82; chmn, Net Express, Inc, 82-93. *Concurrent Pos:* Pres, DHL Corp, 82-83. *Mem:* Nat Acad Eng; Inst Elec & Electronics Engrs; Sigma Xi; Asn Comput Mach. *Res:* ATM switch design; cells-in-frames protocol and switch design; dramatically reducing the internet congestion with explicit rate flow control. *Mailing Add:* 170 Sunrise Dr Woodside CA 94062

ROBERTS, LEE KNIGHT, DERMATOLOGY, PHOTOBIOLOGY. *Current Pos:* sr prin scientist, 89-92, ASSOC RES FEL, SCHERING-PLOUGH INC, 92- *Personal Data:* b Salt Lake City, Utah, Sept 9, 49; m 69, Dawn Leonard; c Chelsey & Joshua. *Educ:* Univ Utah, BS, 72, PhD(anat), 80. *Prof Exp:* Postdoctoral fel immunol, Univ NMex, 80-82; from instr to asst prof immunol & dermat, Univ Utah Sch Med, 82-89. *Mem:* Soc Investigative Dermat; Am Asn Immunologists; AAAS; Am Soc Photobiol. *Res:* Photoimmunology and photodermatology; first to clone tumor-antigen-specific suppressor T-cells from uvb-exposed mice; demonstrating common tumor antigens being shared by uvb-induced tumors and uvb-exposed skin; demostated sunscreen lotions prevent immune suppression induced by solar simulated ultraviolet energy. *Mailing Add:* Advan Prod Res Schering-Plough Inc 3030 Jackson Ave Memphis TN 38151. *Fax:* 901-320-5526; *E-Mail:* 103731.3360@compuserve.com, lee.roberts@spcorp.com

ROBERTS, LEIGH M, PSYCHIATRY. *Current Pos:* resident, Univ Hosps, 53-56, clin instr, Sch Med, 56-58, from asst prof to assoc prof, 59-71, actg chmn dept, 72-75, PROF PSYCHIAT, SCH MED, UNIV WIS-MADISON, 71- *Personal Data:* b Jacksonville, Ill, June 9, 25; m 46; c 4. *Educ:* Univ Ill,

BS, 45, MD, 47. *Prof Exp:* Intern med, St Francis Hosp, Peoria, Ill, 47-48; pvt pract, 48-50. *Concurrent Pos:* Staff psychiatrist, Mendota State Hosp, Madison, 56-58, consult, 60-; consult, Wis Child Ctr, Sparta, 56-58, Cent State Hosp, 62-70 & State Ment Health Planning, 63-; mem spec rev bd, Wis Div Corrections, 63-; mem bd, Methodist Hosp, Madison, 65- & Goodwill Industs, 71- *Mem:* AAAS; fel Am Psychiat Asn; AMA. *Res:* Community psychiatry; psychiatry and law. *Mailing Add:* 722A Sauk Ridge Tr Madison WI 53705-1157

ROBERTS, LEONARD, APPLIED MATHEMATICS, AERODYNAMICS. *Current Pos:* DIR AERONAUT & FLIGHT SYSTS, AMES RES CTR, NASA, 70-; MEM STAFF, DEPT ASTRONAUT ENG, STANFORD UNIV. *Personal Data:* b Prestatyn, North Wales, UK, Sept 27, 29; US citizen; m 55; c 2. *Educ:* Univ Manchester, BSc, 52, MSc, 54, PhD, 55. *Prof Exp:* Res assoc, Mass Inst Technol, 55-57; aerospace res engr theoret, Mech Div, Langley Res Ctr, NASA, 57-59, head, Math Physics Br, Dynamic Loads Div, 59-66, dir, Mission Anal Div, NASA Hq, 66-69; Stanford Sloan fel, 69-70. *Concurrent Pos:* Consult prof aeronaut & astronaut, Stanford Univ, 75- *Mem:* Am Inst Aeronaut & Astronaut; Am Helicopter Soc. *Res:* Aerodynamics; flight dynamics; guidance and control; aeronautical vehicles; aviation systems; research using wind tunnels, simulators and experimental aircraft; management of aeronautical research and development. *Mailing Add:* Aeronaut & Astronaut Eng Durano Durand Bldg R277 269 Stanford Univ Stanford CA 94305

ROBERTS, LEONIDAS HOWARD, PHYSICAL SCIENCES, ASTRONOMY. *Current Pos:* RETIRED. *Personal Data:* b Garard's Ft, Pa, Feb 27, 21; m 45; c 2. *Educ:* Waynesburg Col, BS, 48; WVa Univ, MS, 49; Univ Fla, PhD(appl math), 58. *Prof Exp:* From instr to asst prof phys sci, Univ Fla, 49-61, assoc prof phys sci & astron, 61-71, prof, 71-91. *Mem:* Am Astron Soc. *Res:* Astronomy. *Mailing Add:* 1506 NW 36 Way Gainesville FL 32605

ROBERTS, LESLIE GORDON, MATHEMATICS. *Current Pos:* From asst prof to assoc prof, 68-83, PROF MATH, QUEEN'S UNIV, ONT, 83- *Personal Data:* b Flin Flon, Man, Aug 16, 41; m 67. *Educ:* Univ Man, BSc, 63; Harvard Univ, PhD(math), 68. *Mem:* Am Math Soc; Can Math Cong. *Res:* Algebraic K-theory; algebraic geometry. *Mailing Add:* Dept Math & Statist Queen's Univ Kingston ON K7L 3N6 Can

ROBERTS, LORIN WATSON, PLANT PHYSIOLOGY, PLANT TISSUE CULTURE VASCULAR DIFFERENTIATION. *Current Pos:* from asst prof to prof bot, 57-91, EMER PROF BOT, UNIV IDAHO, 91- *Personal Data:* b Clarksdale, Mo, June 28, 23; m 67, Florence R Greathouse; c Michael Hamlin, Daniel Hamlin & Margaret S. *Educ:* Univ Mo, AB, 48, MA, 50, PhD(bot), 52. *Honors & Awards:* Chevalier de l'Ordre du Merite Agricole, France, 61. *Prof Exp:* Asst bot, Univ Mo, 49-52; from asst prof to assoc prof biol, Agnes Scott Col, 52-57. *Concurrent Pos:* Vis asst prof, Emory Univ, 52-55; pres, Bot Sect, Int Cong Histochem & Cytochem, Paris, 60; Fulbright res prof, Kyoto Univ, 67-68; vis prof, Bot Inst, Univ Bari, 68; Maria Moors Cabot res fel, Harvard Univ, 74; Fulbright vis lectr, NEastern Hill Univ, Shillong, Mcghalaya, India, 77; Fulbright sr scholar & vis fel, Australian Nat Univ, Canberra, 80; fel, Univ London, 84; vis fel, Alexander von Humboldt, Australian Nat Univ, 92. *Mem:* Fel AAAS; Bot Soc Am; Am Soc Plant Physiol; Int Asn Plant Tissue Cult; Sigma Xi; Am Inst Biol Serv. *Res:* Physiology of vascular differentiation; physiological action of plant hormones. *Mailing Add:* 920 Mabelle Ave Moscow ID 83843-3834

ROBERTS, LOUIS DOUGLAS, SOLID STATE PHYSICS, THEORETICAL PHYSICS. *Current Pos:* PROF PHYSICS, UNIV NC, CHAPEL HILL, 68- *Personal Data:* b Charleston, SC, Jan 27, 18; m 42, Marjorie Lawson; c Joyce Carol (Heck). *Educ:* Howard Col, AB, 38; Columbia Univ, PhD(phys chem), 41. *Prof Exp:* Nat Res Coun fel, Cornell Univ, 41-42; res physicist, Gen Elec Co, NY, 42-46; physicist, Oak Ridge Nat Lab, 46-68. *Concurrent Pos:* Vchair, Southeastern Sect, Am Phys Soc, 54-55, chmn, 55-56; Fulbright fel & Guggenheim fel, Oxford Univ, 58-59; prof, Univ Tenn, 63-68. *Mem:* Fel Am Phys Soc. *Res:* Semiconductors; vacuum tube design and ion optics; neutron diffusion theory and measurement; low temperature physics; low energy nuclear and solid state physics; high pressure physics; electron many-body studies. *Mailing Add:* 1116 Sourwood Circle Chapel Hill NC 27514

ROBERTS, LOUIS REED, CHEMICAL ENGINEERING. *Current Pos:* RETIRED. *Personal Data:* b Wray, Colo, July 8, 23; m 48; c 3. *Educ:* Univ Colo, BS, 49; Rice Univ, MA, 51; Univ Tex, PhD(chem eng), 63. *Prof Exp:* Jr chemist, Gulf Oil Corp, 51-53, chemist, 53-56; chem engr, Southwest Res Inst, 56-58; sr chem engr, Union Tex Petrol Div, Allied Chem Corp, 62-63, engr, Cent Res Lab, 63-70, res chem engr, Chem Res Lab, 70-76; div dir, State Tex, 76-93. *Mem:* Fel Am Inst Chem Engrs. *Res:* Vapor-liquid equilibria of hydrocarbon fixed-gas systems; high temperature chemistry; petrochemical and polymer processes. *Mailing Add:* 8611 Honeysuckle Austin TX 78759

ROBERTS, LOUIS W, PHYSICS. *Current Pos:* RETIRED. *Personal Data:* b Jamestown, NY, Sept 1, 13; m 38, Mercedes; c Louis M & Lawrence E. *Educ:* Fisk Univ, AB, 35; Univ Mich, MS, 37. *Hon Degrees:* LLD, Fisk Univ, 85. *Prof Exp:* Teaching asst physics & math, Fisk Univ, 35-36; instr, St Augustine's Col, 37-40, assoc prof physics 41-43; asst prof, Howard Univ, 43-44; sr engr, Sylvania Elec Prod, Inc, 44-46, sect head tubes, 46-47, mgr tube develop, 47-50; pres, dir & founder, Microwave Assocs, 50-51, vpres, 51-55; eng specialist, Bomac Labs, Inc Div, Varian Inc, 55-59; vpres, dir & founder, Metcom Inc, 59-67; consult optics & microwaves, Electronic Res Ctr, NASA, 67, chief, Microwave Lab, 67-68; chief, Optics & Microwave Lab, 68-70; from dep dir to dir technol, US Dept Transp, 70-77, dir energy & environ, 77-79, dep dir, 79, dir data systs & technol, 80-82, dir off admin, 82-83, assoc dir off opers eng, 83-84, actg dep dir, 84, actg dir, 84-85, dir transp systs ctr, 85-89. *Concurrent Pos:* Res assoc, Stand Oil NJ, 35-36; prof, A&T State Univ, NC, 41-43; instr, US Signal Corps Sch, 42; prof, Shaw Univ, 42-43 & Army Specialized Training Prog, Wash, DC, 43-44; staff mem, Res Lab Electronics, Mass Inst Technol, 50-51; pres, Elcon Lab, Inc, Metcom Inc & consult, Addison-Wesley Press, 63-67; mem, US-Japan Natural Resources Comt, US Dept Interior, 69-78, adv group aerospace res & develop, Nato, 73-79; mem bd trustees, Univ Hosp, Boston Univ, 73-; vis engr & lectr, Mass Inst Technol, 79-80. *Mem:* AAAS; fel Inst Elec & Electronics Engrs; Am Phys Soc; Am Math Soc; Am Inst Aeronaut & Astronaut. *Res:* Microwave and optical techniques and components; plasma research and solid state component and circuit development; all aspects of transportation and logistics, including applications of artificial intelligence. *Mailing Add:* Five Michael Rd Wakefield MA 01880

ROBERTS, LYMAN JACKSON, CLINICAL PHARMACOLOGY. *Current Pos:* PROF PHARMACOL & MED, VANDERBILT UNIV, 76- *Educ:* Univ Iowa, MD, 69. *Res:* Prostaglandin research; internal medicine. *Mailing Add:* Dept Pharmacol Vanderbilt Univ Sch Med 21st Ave S & Garland Nashville TN 37232-0001

ROBERTS, MALCOLM JOHN, METALLURGY. *Current Pos:* res engr, Bethlehem Steel Corp, 67-71, supvr, 71-79, sect mgr, 79-82, div mgr, 82-84, assoc dir res, 84-85, dir res, 85-96, VPRES TECH & CHIEF TECH OFFICER, BETHLEHEM STEEL CORP, 96- *Personal Data:* b Widnes, UK, Nov 8, 42; m 64, Margaret I Turner; c Kathryn, Christopher & Jillian. *Educ:* Univ Liverpool, Eng, BEng, 63, PhD, 66. *Prof Exp:* Res assoc, Cornell Univ, 66-67. *Mem:* Am Inst Mech Engrs; Am Soc Metals; Am Iron & Steel Inst; Indust Res Inst. *Res:* Metals. *Mailing Add:* Bethlehem Steel Corp 1170 Eighth Ave Bethlehem PA 18016-7699

ROBERTS, MARTIN, BIOCHEMISTRY. *Current Pos:* CONSULT, ROBERTS ENTERPRISES, 85- *Personal Data:* b Brooklyn, NY, May 8, 20; m 49; c 4. *Educ:* City Col New York, BS, 42; Brooklyn Col, MA, 47; Univ Southern Calif, PhD(biochem), 51. *Prof Exp:* Res org chem, Schwarz Labs, Inc, 43-47; sr clin res biochemist, Don Baxter, Inc, 51-66; mgt & med dir, Artificial Kidney Supply Div, Sweden Freezer Mfg Co, Seattle, 66-71; dir clin invest, 71-74, vpres mkt, CCI Life Systs Inc, Van Nuys, 74-76; vpres, 76-80, dir & med & regulatory affairs, Redy Labs, Organon Teknika, 80-85. *Mem:* Am Soc Artificial Internal Organs; Int Soc Artificial Internal Orgns; Am Soc Nephrology; Int Cong Nephrology. *Res:* Nucleic acid derivatives; parenteral and nutritional solutions, peritoneal and hemodialysis. *Mailing Add:* 16022 Parthenia St Sepulveda CA 91343-4806

ROBERTS, MARY FEDARKO, BIOCHEMISTRY, PHYSICAL CHEMISTRY. *Current Pos:* assoc prof, 87-91, PROF CHEM, BOSTON COL, 91- *Personal Data:* b Pittsburgh, Pa, July 11, 47; m 74; c 1. *Educ:* Bryn Mawr Col, AB, 69; Stanford Univ, PhD(chem), 74. *Prof Exp:* Res assoc biochem, Univ Ill, Urbana-Champaign, 74-75; NIH trainee biol, Univ Calif, San Diego, 75-77, NIH fel chem, 77-78; asst prof chem, Mass Inst Technol, 78-86. *Mem:* Am Chem Soc. *Mailing Add:* Dept Chem Merkert Chem Ctr 2609 Beacon St Chestnut Hill MA 02167. *Fax:* 617-552-2705

ROBERTS, MERVIN FRANCIS, ANIMAL BEHAVIOR, ICHTHYOLOGY. *Current Pos:* MGR RES & DEVELOP, WIDGET CO OLD LYME, 68- *Personal Data:* b New York, NY, June 7, 22; m 49, Edith Foster; c Edith, Martha, Nancy & Neel. *Educ:* Alfred Univ, BS, 47. *Prof Exp:* Sr inspector, NY Port Authority, 47-56; lab mgr, De Lackner Helicopters, NY, 56-58 & Irco Corp, 58-59; assoc ed, McGraw Hill Publ Co, 59-60; ed supvr, Anco Tech Writing Serv, 60-61; mgr res & develop, T F H Publ, Inc, 61-67, asst to pres res & develop, 67-68. *Concurrent Pos:* Fish behav consult, Northeast Utilities Serv Corp, 70-; mem, Govr's Coun Marine Resources, Conn, 70-73, chmn, 71, shellfish commr, 82-; consult, Salmonoid Aquacult, 85-, Tilapia Aquacult, Diocese Alleppey, Kerala, India, 87- *Mem:* Am Fisheries Soc; Am Littoral Soc; Estuarine Res Soc. *Res:* Photography of high speed animal movements; small animal maintenance; fish culture; tidemarsh ecosystems; author or coauthor of over 30 publications on care of caged animals and on tidemarsh life. *Mailing Add:* Duck River Lane Old Lyme CT 06371

ROBERTS, MICHAEL FOSTER, CARDIOVASCULAR PHYSIOLOGY, RECEPTOR PHYSIOLOGY. *Current Pos:* from asst prof to assoc prof, 81-90, PROF BIOL, LINFIELD COL, 90- *Personal Data:* b Guatemala, Aug 8, 43; US citizen; m 66; c 2. *Educ:* Univ Calif, Berkeley, BA, 66; Univ Wis-Madison, MA, 68, PhD(zool), 72. *Prof Exp:* Asst fel & asst prof epidemiol, John B Pierce Found Lab, Yale Univ, 72-81. *Concurrent Pos:* Prin investr, NIH, 82-85 & Am Heart Asn, 85-86. *Mem:* AAAS; Sigma Xi; Am Physiol Soc. *Res:* Peripheral circulation and temperature regulation; contractile mechanisms in peripheral blood vessels; influence temperature has on the process of transmitter release, uptake, degradation and receptor binding. *Mailing Add:* Dept Biol Linfield Col McMinnville OR 97128. *E-Mail:* mrobert@linfield.edu

ROBERTS, MORTON SPITZ, RADIO ASTRONOMY, GALAXIES. *Current Pos:* scientist, 64-78, from asst dir to dir, 69-84, SR SCIENTIST, NAT RADIO ASTRON OBSERV, 78- *Personal Data:* b New York, NY, Nov 5, 26; m 51, Josephine Taylor; c Elizabeth (Mason). *Educ:* Pomona Col, BA, 48; Calif Inst Technol, MS, 50; Univ Calif, PhD(astron), 58. *Hon Degrees:* DSc, Pomona Col, 79. *Prof Exp:* Asst prof physics, Occidental Col,

49-52; physicist underwater ord, US Naval Ord Testing Sta, 52-53; jr res astronr, Univ Calif, 57-58, NSF fel, 58-59, lectr astron & asst res astronr, Radio Astron Lab, 59-60; lectr astron & res assoc, Observ, Harvard Univ, 60-64. *Concurrent Pos:* Vis prof, Univ Calif, Berkeley, 68, State Univ NY, Stony Brook, 68, Inst Theoret Astron, Cambridge, 72, 86-87 & Univ Groningen, 72; Sigma Xi nat lectr, 70-71; assoc ed, Astron J, 77-79. *Mem:* Nat Acad Sci; Int Union Radio Sci; Am Astron Soc (vpres, 71-72); Int Astron Union (vpres, 88-94, treas, 92-97). *Res:* Galaxies; galactic structure; interstellar and extragalactic matter. *Mailing Add:* Nat Radio Astron Observ 520 Edgemont Rd Charlottesville VA 22903-2475. *Fax:* 804-296-0278; *E-Mail:* mroberts@nrao.edu

ROBERTS, NORMAN HAILSTONE, APPLIED STATISTICS. *Current Pos:* RETIRED. *Personal Data:* b Seattle, Wash, Mar 3, 22; div; c 3. *Educ:* Univ Wash, BS, 46, PhD(physics), 57. *Prof Exp:* Asst physicist, Appl Physics Lab, Univ Wash, 55, instr mech eng, 56-57, from assoc physicist to physicist, Appl Physics Lab, 57-65, actg assoc prof mech eng, 66-68, assoc prof, 68-92. *Concurrent Pos:* Consult, Nuclear Regulatory Comn, 74- *Mem:* AAAS; NY Acad Sci; Syst Safety Soc. *Res:* Electron energy loss; ferroelectricity; statistics, reliability and systems analysis, fault tree analysis; physics of the oceans. *Mailing Add:* 2316 N 128th St Seattle WA 98133

ROBERTS, P ELAINE, HORMONAL REGULATION OF INSECT REPRODUCTION & GENE EXPRESSION. *Current Pos:* from asst prof to assoc prof cell biol & insect physiol, 86-91, PROF ENTOM, COLO STATE UNIV, 91- *Personal Data:* b Mt Clements, Mich, Feb 18, 44. *Educ:* Western Mich Univ, BA, 67; Univ Ill, PhD(cell biol), 76. *Prof Exp:* Res asst, Western Mich Univ, 67-70; postdoctoral fel, Dept Molecular Med, Mayo Clin, 76-78 & Queen's Univ, Ont, 78-79. *Concurrent Pos:* NIH grant, 83; NSF grant, 87; vis scientist, USDA, 87, Challenge grant, 93-; Colo Agr Exp Sta grant, 88; actg assoc dean agr sci, Colo State Univ, 93-94. *Mem:* Entom Soc Am; AAAS; Sigma Xi; Asn Women Sci. *Res:* Mechanism by which juvenile hormone regulates gene expression in insects. *Mailing Add:* Dept Entom Colo State Univ Ft Collins CO 80523. *E-Mail:* eroberts@lamar.colostate.edu

ROBERTS, PAUL ALFRED, genetics, for more information see previous edition

ROBERTS, PAUL HARRY, MAGNETOHYDRODYNAMICS. *Current Pos:* PROF MATH & PROF GEOPHYS SCI, UNIV CALIF, LOS ANGELES, 86- *Personal Data:* b Aberystwyth, Wales, UK, Sept 9, 29; m 89. *Educ:* Cambridge Univ, Eng, BA, 51, MA & PhD(math), 54, ScD, 67. *Prof Exp:* Res assoc, Univ Chicago, 54-55; sci officer, Awre, Aldermaston, Eng, 55-56; ICI res fel, Univ Durham, Eng, 56-59, lectr physics, 59-61; assoc prof astron, Univ Chicago, 61-63; prof math, Univ Newcastle upon Tyne, UK, 63-85. *Mem:* Fel Royal Soc London. *Res:* Magnetohydrodynamics and applications to earth's core; fluid mechanics, including two phase flow and superfluid mechanics. *Mailing Add:* Math Dept Univ Calif Los Angeles 6556 Math Scis Box 951555 Los Angeles CA 90095-1555

ROBERTS, PAUL OSBORNE, JR, TRANSPORTATION MANAGEMENT. *Current Pos:* VPRES, SCI APPLN INT CORP, MCLEAN, VA, 95-, HEAD TRASP CONSULT DIV, 95- *Personal Data:* b Memphis, Tenn, Mar 6, 33; m 57, Mary J Smalley; c Becky, Scott & Lee. *Educ:* Tex A&M Univ, BS, 55; Mass Inst Technol, SM, 57; Northwestern Univ, PhD(transp eng), 65. *Prof Exp:* Engr in chg, Electronic Computer Ctr, Michael Baker, Jr, Inc, Pa, 57-60; asst prof civil eng, Mass Inst Technol, 60-66; lectr transp, Econ Dept, Harvard Univ, 66-69, assoc prof transp & logistics, Bus Sch, 69-72; prof transp eng & sr lectr, Sloan Sch Mgt, Mass Inst Technol, 72-76, prof civil eng & dir, Ctr Transp Studies, 76-80; prin, Transp Consult Div, Booz Allen & Hamilton, Inc, 80-83; pres, Transmode Consult, Inc, 83-95. *Concurrent Pos:* Mem, Hwy Res Bd, Nat Acad Sci-Nat Res Coun. *Mem:* Opers Res Soc Am; Inst Traffic Engrs; Sigma Xi; Transp Res Forum. *Res:* Economic and engineering analysis of transportation systems, particularly as related to economic development; engineering project analyses; decision theory; business logistics; industry location; urban growth; trucking; intermodal transportation; transportation and logistics research. *Mailing Add:* 3301 39th St NW Washington DC 20016

ROBERTS, PAUL V, CIVIL & ENVIRONMENTAL ENGINEERING. *Current Pos:* from adj prof to assoc prof, 76-84, assoc dept chmn, 85-90, PROF ENVIRON ENG, DEPT CIVIL ENG, STANFORD UNIV, 84-, C L PECK PROF ENG, 89- *Educ:* Princeton Univ, BS, 60; Cornell Univ, PhD(chem eng), 66; Stanford Univ, MS, 71. *Honors & Awards:* Res Achievement Award, Am Water Works Asn, 83, 85-87 & 91. *Prof Exp:* Process engr, Chevron Res Co, 66-68; res engr, Stanford Res Inst, 68-71; sr res scientist & group leader process eng, Swiss Fed Inst Water Supply & Water Pollution Control, Dubendorf, Switz, 72, head, Eng Dept, 73-76. *Concurrent Pos:* Bd dir, Asn Environ Eng Prof, 81-84. *Mem:* Nat Acad Eng. *Res:* Chemical process and environmental engineering with emphasis on trace contaminants, water reuse, unit operations of water treatment and advanced waste treatment; transfer of volatile organic pollutants to the atmosphere; tranformations and fates of trace contaminants in the ground-water environment; hazardous waste remediation; sorption and mass transfer phenomena; principal investigator on 25 sponsored projects at Stanford since 1976. *Mailing Add:* Dept Civil Eng Stanford Univ Stanford CA 94305

ROBERTS, PETER MORSE, SEISMOLOGY, ULTRASONICS. *Current Pos:* fel geoeng, 89-92, sr geophysicist consult, 92-97, PROJ GEOPHYSICIST, LOS ALAMOS NAT LAB, 97- *Personal Data:* b Pottstown, Pa, Sept 14, 55; m 85, Jule A Collins; c Alexander C & Natasha E. *Educ:* Mass Inst Technol, BS, 79, PhD(geophys), 89. *Prof Exp:* Tech asst, Seismic Instrument Lab, Mass Inst Technol, 79-82, res asst earth, atmospheric & planetary sci, 82-85; res fel geol sci, Univ Southern Calif, 85-89. *Mem:* Am Geophys Union; Seismol Soc Am. *Res:* Teleseismic waveform modeling used to determine crustal structure beneath volcanic systems; operating and designing equipment systems for recording seismic and ultrasonic data; laboratory ultrasonics experimentation for materials testing and formation damage reduction in oil wells. *Mailing Add:* Los Alamos Nat Lab EES-4 Mail Stop D443 Los Alamos NM 87545. *Fax:* 505-667-8487; *E-Mail:* roberts@natasha.lanl.gov

ROBERTS, R MICHAEL, REPRODUCTION, MOLECULAR BIOLOGY. *Current Pos:* F McKenzie distinguished prof reproductive biol, 88-96, PROF ANIMAL SCI & BIOCHEM, UNIV MO, COLUMBIA, 85-, CHAIR, VET PATHOBIOL, 95-, CUR PROF, 96- *Educ:* Oxford Univ, PhD(plant biochem), 65. *Honors & Awards:* Res Award, Soc Study Reproduction, 90; Sydney A Asdell Lectr, Cornell Univ, 90; USDA Distinguished Scientist, 92; Arnoraso Lectr, Soc Study Fertil, 94; Milstein Award, Int Soc Interferon & Cytokine Res, 95; Alexander von Humbolt Award Agr, 96. *Prof Exp:* Res assoc & asst prof, Dept Biol, State Univ NY, 65-68; sr res fel, UK Atomic Energy Authority, 68-69; from asst prof to prof biochem, Univ Fla, 70-85. *Concurrent Pos:* USPHS Res Career Develop Award, 72-77; fel, WHO, 77; sr fel, NATO, 77; mem, Biochem Panel, NSF, 84-87 & Reproductive Biol Study Sect, NIH, 87-91; NIH Reproductive Biol Study Sect, 87-91; Merit Award, NIH, 90- *Mem:* Nat Acad Sci. *Mailing Add:* Biochem Molecular Biol J245 Jhmhc Univ Fla Gainesville FL 32611

ROBERTS, RALPH, PHYSICAL CHEMISTRY, CHEMICAL KINETICS. *Current Pos:* PRES, ROBERTS CONSULTS, INC, 84- *Personal Data:* b Bridgeton, NJ, May 31, 15; m 39; c 2. *Educ:* Cath Univ Am, BS, 36, MS, 38, PhD(phys chem), 40. *Prof Exp:* Chemist, US Naval Eng Exp Sta, 40-46, sci adminr phys chem, Off Naval Res, 46-55, sci liaison officer, London, 55-56, res coordr, 56-58, head, Propulsion Chem Br, 58-60, dir power prog, 60-74; mem tech staff, Mitre Corp, 75-84. *Concurrent Pos:* Guest chemist, Brookhaven Nat Lab, 51; vis scientist, Yale Univ, 71-72. *Mem:* Am Chem Soc; fel AAAS; Combustion Inst. *Res:* Chemical propulsion; energy conversion systems; electrochemical power sources. *Mailing Add:* 3308 Camalier Dr Chevy Chase MD 20815

ROBERTS, RALPH JACKSON, GEOLOGY. *Current Pos:* GEOL CONSULT, 81- *Personal Data:* b Rosalia, Wash, Jan 31, 11; wid; c Michael, Steven (deceased) & Kim. *Educ:* Univ Wash, BS, 35, MS, 37; Yale Univ, PhD, 49. *Honors & Awards:* Distinguished Serv Award, Dept Interior, 83; Mining man of year, Am Inst Mining Eng, 91. *Prof Exp:* Geologist, US Geol Surv, 39-42, Cent Am, 42-45 & Nev-Utah, 45-71, tech adv econ geol, Saudi Arabia, 72-78, Nev, 78-80. *Concurrent Pos:* Ralph J Roberts Ctr Res Econ Geol Univ Nev, Reno Nev, 95. *Mem:* Geol Soc Am; Soc Econ Geologists; Am Inst Mining Eng. *Res:* Economic and structural geology of Nevada; geology of Cordilleran fold-belt; volcanogenic ore deposits in Arabian Shield; economic geology, western United States and Central America. *Mailing Add:* 6229A North Pkwy Tacoma WA 98407

ROBERTS, REGINALD FRANCIS, PHYSICAL CHEMISTRY. *Current Pos:* PVT REGIST PATENT AGENT. *Personal Data:* b Baton Rouge, La, Feb 14, 23; m 72, Alidale Pine. *Educ:* La State Univ, AB, 42, BS, 47, MS, 50. *Prof Exp:* From asst res chemist to sr res chemist, Kaiser Aluminum & Chem Corp, 50-58, sr develop chemist, 59-63; sr res chemist, Dow Chem Co, Plaquemine, 64-84, proj leader tech & patent liaison, 84-86. *Res:* Chemical kinetics; reaction mechanisms; physical organic chemistry; structural theory; effect of structure on reactivity; relationship between physical properties and molecular structure; thermodynamics. *Mailing Add:* PO Box 515 Baton Rouge LA 70821. *Fax:* 504-389-9770

ROBERTS, RICHARD, MECHANICAL ENGINEERING. *Current Pos:* From asst prof to assoc prof, 64-77, PROF MECH ENG, LEHIGH UNIV, 77- *Personal Data:* b Atlantic City, NJ, Feb 16, 38; m 60; c 3. *Educ:* Drexel Univ, BS, 61; Lehigh Univ, MS, 62, PhD(mech eng), 64. *Honors & Awards:* Spraragen Award, Am Welding Soc, 72. *Mem:* Am Soc Mech Engrs; Am Soc Testing & Mat; Am Soc Eng Educ; Am Welding Soc; Am Soc Metals. *Res:* Fracture mechanics; material behavior; experimental stress analysis. *Mailing Add:* 317 Bierys Bridge Rd Bethlehem PA 18017

ROBERTS, RICHARD B, INFECTIOUS DISEASES. *Current Pos:* PROF MED, MED COL, CORNELL UNIV, 70- *Personal Data:* b New Haven, Conn, Feb 26, 33. *Educ:* Temple Univ, MD, 59. *Mailing Add:* Dept Med Med Col Cornell Univ Rm F441 1300 York Ave New York NY 10021-4805

ROBERTS, RICHARD CALVIN, APPLIED MATHEMATICS. *Current Pos:* RETIRED. *Personal Data:* b Akron, Ohio, May 26, 25; m 49; c 1. *Educ:* Kenyon Col, AB, 46; Brown Univ, ScM, 46, PhD(appl math), 49. *Prof Exp:* Asst appl math, Brown Univ, 46-48, res assoc, 48-50; fel, Univ Md, 50-51; mathematician, US Naval Ord Lab, 51-66, chief, Math Dept, 60-66; div chmn, Univ Md, Baltimore Co, 66-74, dean, Div Math & Physics, 74-78, chmn, Dept Math & Comput Sci, 82-85, prof, 78-92, emer prof math, 92. *Mem:* Am Math Soc; Math Asn Am; Am Comput Mach. *Res:* Fluid dynamics; numerical methods; finite differences. *Mailing Add:* 5170 Phanton Ct Columbia MD 21044-1318

ROBERTS, RICHARD HARRIS, MEDICAL ENTOMOLOGY, VETERINARY ENTOMOLOGY. *Current Pos:* RES ASSOC, FLA STATE COL ARTHOPODS, 88- *Personal Data:* b Buffalo, NY, Oct 24, 24; m 54, 86, Fontaine; c Jonathan, Michael & David. *Educ:* Univ Buffalo, BA, 50, MA, 52; Univ Wis, PhD(med & vet entom), 56. *Prof Exp:* Asst invert zool, Univ Buffalo, 50-52; vet entom, Univ Wis, 52-56; res entomologist, Sci & Educ Admin-Fed Res, USDA, 56-84. *Concurrent Pos:* Adj assoc prof entom, Miss State Univ, 65-75; adj prof entom, Univ Fla, 76- *Mem:* Entom Soc Am; Am Mosquito Control Asn; Am Soc Trop Med & Hyg. *Res:* Livestock-affecting insects, especially biology, control and taxonomy of Tabanidae and the vectors of bovine anaplasmosis; pesticide development on mosquitoes, houseflies, stableflies, ticks and chiggers. *Mailing Add:* 2241 NW 49th Terr Gainesville FL 32605

ROBERTS, RICHARD JOHN, MOLECULAR BIOLOGY. *Current Pos:* sr staff investr, Cold Spring Harbor Lab, 72-86, asst dir res, 86-92, DIR RES, NEW ENG BIOLAB, 92- *Personal Data:* b Derby, Eng, Sept 6, 43; m 65, 86, Jean Tagliabue; c Alison, Andrew, Christopher & Amanda. *Educ:* Sheffield Univ, BSc, 65, PhD(org chem), 68. *Hon Degrees:* MD, Univ Uppsala, Sweden, 92; Bath Univ, 94; DS, Sheffield Univ, 94, Derby Univ, 95. *Honors & Awards:* Nobel Prize Physiol or Med, 93; Bourke Lectr, Boston Univ, 94; Dakin Lectr, Adelphi Univ, 94; Golden Plate Award, Am Acad Achievement, 94; Ada Doisy Lectr, Univ Ill, 96; William Ferdinand Mem Lectr, Sheffield Univ, 97. *Prof Exp:* Fel chem, Sheffield Univ, 68-69; fel biochem, Harvard Univ, 69-70, res assoc, 71-72. *Concurrent Pos:* Consult, New Eng Biolabs, 75- & Genex Corp, 78-; John Simon Guggenheim fel, 79-80; Miller prof, Univ Calif, Berkeley, 91; Wei Lun vis prof, Chinese Univ, 96; vis prof, Univ Bath, Eng, 96- *Mem:* Am Chem Soc; NY Acad Sci; Am Soc Microbiol; Fedn Am Soc Exp Biol; fel Royal Soc; Am Soc Biol Chem; AAAS; foreign fel Nat Acad Med Sci; fel Am Soc Arts & Scis. *Res:* Restriction endonucleases and their application for DNA sequence analysis and genetic engineering; computational molecular biology; DNA methylases. *Mailing Add:* New England Biolabs 32 Tozer Rd Beverly MA 01915. *Fax:* 978-921-1527; *E-Mail:* roberts@neb.com

ROBERTS, RICHARD NORMAN, ANALYTICAL CHEMISTRY. *Current Pos:* environ chem, 90-96, ADJ PROF CHEM & RES ASSOC, STATE UNIV NY, OSWEGO, 96- *Personal Data:* b Lockport, NY, Sept 3, 30; m 61, Nancy Roloff; c Barbara (Gallagher) & Eric. *Educ:* Univ Buffalo, BA, 57, MA, 59, PhD(biochem), 62. *Prof Exp:* Fel biochem, Rutgers Univ, 62-64; res assoc, Cornell Univ, 64-65; res biochemist, Gen Elec Co, Syracuse, 65-69, anal chemist, 69-90. *Mem:* AAAS; Am Chem Soc; Sigma Xi. *Res:* Intermediary metabolism; metabolic pathways; products of microbial metabolism on synthetic and natural substrates; related organo-analytical techniques, especially gas chromatography and infrared spectrophotometry; gas chromatographic identification of micro-organisms; environment analysis. *Mailing Add:* 7212 Fiddler Bay Lane Chincoteague VA 23336

ROBERTS, RICHARD W, ORGANIC CHEMISTRY, PULP & PAPER CHEMISTRY. *Current Pos:* RETIRED. *Personal Data:* b Milwaukee, Wis, Dec 9, 21; m 43, Barbara Zimmerman; c Jack & Diane. *Educ:* Marquette Univ, BS, 43; Lawrence Univ, MS, 49, PhD, 51. *Prof Exp:* Instr chem, Marquette Univ, 47; res chemist, Int Paper Co, 51-52 & Marathon Corp, 52-63; res supvr & comput mgr, Wausau Paper Mills Co, 63-85. *Mem:* Am Chem Soc; Tech Asn Pulp & Paper Indust; Am Soc Qual Control. *Res:* Computer process control; pulp bleaching; product development; statistical techniques. *Mailing Add:* 845 Everest Dr Rothschild WI 54474-1020

ROBERTS, ROBERT ABRAM, MATHEMATICS. *Current Pos:* chmn dept, 72-77, PROF MATH, WASH & LEE UNIV, 72- *Personal Data:* b Iowa City, Iowa, Oct 28, 23; m 49; c 3. *Educ:* WVa Wesleyan Col, BS, 45; Univ WVa, MS, 48; Univ Mich, PhD, 54. *Prof Exp:* Asst prof math, Univ WVa, 52-53; asst prof, Univ Miami, 53-58; sr mathematician, Bettis Plant, Westinghouse Elec Corp, Pa, 58-59; assoc prof math, Ohio Wesleyan Univ, 59-61; from assoc prof to prof, Denison Univ, 61-72. *Concurrent Pos:* NSF fel, 65-66. *Mem:* AAAS; Am Math Soc; Math Asn Am; Soc Indust & Appl Math; Sigma Xi. *Res:* Mathematical physics; atomic structure; numerical analysis; computing machinery; educational use of machines. *Mailing Add:* Rte 5 Box 126 Lexington VA 24450

ROBERTS, ROBERT RUSSELL, MICROBIOLOGY, IMMUNOLOGY. *Current Pos:* RETIRED. *Personal Data:* b Fitchburg, Mass, Mar 4, 31; m 53; c 3. *Educ:* Brigham Young Univ, BS, 70, MS, 72, PhD(microbiol), 75. *Prof Exp:* Microbiologist, Hawaiian Sugar Planters Asn, 76-93. *Mem:* AAAS; Am Soc Microbiol; Am Chem Soc. *Res:* Biomass energy; immunology; microbial and yeast genetics; industrial fermentations; general applied microbiology; wastewater treatment. *Mailing Add:* 92-1545 Aliinui Dr Apt C Kapolei HI 96707-2226

ROBERTS, ROBERT WILLIAM, CHEMICAL ENGINEERING, POLYMER ENGINEERING. *Current Pos:* RETIRED. *Personal Data:* b Riverside, Ill, July 24, 23; m 46, Marilyn Helen Schrimper; c Lynn E, William A & Robert F. *Educ:* Wash Univ, St Louis, BSChE, 48; Univ Iowa, MS, 60, PhD(chem eng), 62. *Prof Exp:* Develop engr, Aluminum Ore Co, 48, prod engr, 49-51; foreman extrusion, Cryovac Div, W R Grace & Co, 51-52, plant engr, 52-57, tech dir, Western Div, 57-59; group supvr process res, Allegany Ballistics Lab, Hercules, Inc, 62-64; dir res & develop, Cadillac Plastics & Chem Co, 64-66; from assoc prof to prof, Univ Akron, 66-77, head dept, 70-77, Robert Iredell prof chem eng & res assoc, Inst Polymer Sci, 77-88. *Concurrent Pos:* Dean, Plastics Eng Prog, Algerian Inst Petrol, 79-80. *Mem:* Fel Am Inst Chem Engrs. *Res:* Process design and economics; plastic processing; thermodynamics; research administration. *Mailing Add:* 2352 Chatham Rd Akron OH 44313. *Fax:* 330-972-7257; *E-Mail:* rwroberts@uakron.edu

ROBERTS, RONALD C, PHYSICAL BIOCHEMISTRY. *Current Pos:* RES BIOCHEMIST, MARSHFIELD MED FOUND, 66- *Personal Data:* b Meadville, Pa, Jan 28, 36; m 60, 85; c 2. *Educ:* Pa State Univ, BS, 57; Univ Minn, PhD(biochem), 64. *Prof Exp:* Res asst biochem, Univ Minn, 57-64, NIH fel & res assoc, 64-66. *Concurrent Pos:* Adj assoc prof chem, Univ Wis-Stevens Pt, 78-83; adj prof, Biol Dept, Univ Wis-Oshkosh, 80-82; vis scientist, Ctr Res & Develop Life Sci, E I Du Pont, Wilmington, Del, 83-84. *Mem:* Am Chem Soc; Am Soc Biochemists & Molecular Biol; AAAS; Sigma Xi; Am Diabetes Asn. *Res:* Physical and chemical characterization of proteins, particularly blood serum proteins; chemical and immunological studies on the antigens of hypersensitivity pneumonitis. *Mailing Add:* 950 Cushing Pl 950 Cushing Pl Plainfield NJ 07062-2202

ROBERTS, RONALD FREDERICK, SURFACE CHEMISTRY. *Current Pos:* MEM TECH STAFF RES, BELL LABS, 71- *Personal Data:* b Brooklyn, NY, Mar 26, 44; m 66; c 2. *Educ:* St John's Univ, BS, 65; Long Island Univ, MS, 67; NY Univ, PhD(phys chem), 72. *Mem:* AAAS; Am Chem Soc; Soc Appl Spectroscopy. *Res:* Electron spectroscopic investigation of the adsorption of chemical species onto inorganic surfaces as related to corrosion inhibition, and the chemical modification of polymer surfaces as related to adhesion and other phenomena. *Mailing Add:* Lucent Tech Rm D Lab 9333S John Young Pkwy Orlando FL 32819-8698

ROBERTS, RONNIE SPENCER, CHEMICAL ENGINEERING, BIOCHEMICAL ENGINEERING. *Current Pos:* asst prof, 76-81, ASSOC PROF CHEM ENG, GA INST TECHNOL, 81- *Personal Data:* b Pascagoula, Miss, June 5, 43; m 72; c 1. *Educ:* Univ Miss, BSChE, 66; Univ Tenn, Knoxville, MS, 72, PhD(chem eng), 76. *Prof Exp:* Tech serv engr, Monsanto Co, 66-69. *Concurrent Pos:* Consult, Milliken & Co, 77-78, Stake Technol Ltd, 80-83, FTI, 89- *Mem:* Am Inst Chem Engrs; Am Soc Eng Educ; AAAS. *Res:* Vigorous stationary phase fermentation; microbial processes; reactor design; solvent delignification of biomass. *Mailing Add:* Sch Chem Eng Ga Inst Technol Atlanta GA 30332-0100

ROBERTS, ROYSTON MURPHY, organic chemistry; deceased, see previous edition for last biography

ROBERTS, SHARON K, HEALTH EDUCATION & ADMINISTRATION. *Current Pos:* chmn, Dept Clin Sci, 83-87, PROF MED TECHNOLOGIST, CALIF STATE UNIV, 73- *Personal Data:* b Dec 4, 41; m, Dean Sheehy. *Educ:* Calif State Univ, San Jose, BA, 63; Cent Mich Univ, MA, 76; Tex A&M Univ, PhD(allied health educ & admin), 85. *Honors & Awards:* Joseph P Klein Award, Am Soc Med Technol, 89. *Concurrent Pos:* Deleg, Am Soc Med Technol, 86-90, Int Asn Med Lab Technologists, 86, 90, 92 & 94; consult ed, Clin Lab Sci, 87-89; chair, Calif Coalition Clin Lab Profs, 88-89; med technologist, 89-; contact, Legis Activist Liaison, Am Soc Med Technol; Fulbright fel, Clin Lab Sci Prog, Iceland, 95. *Mem:* Am Soc Clin Lab Sci; Am Soc Clin Pathologists. *Res:* Author of numerous publications. *Mailing Add:* Dept Biol Sci Calif State Univ Bakersfield CA 93309. *Fax:* 805-664-2132; *E-Mail:* skroberts@csubak.edu

ROBERTS, SHEPHERD, COMPARATIVE PHYSIOLOGY. *Current Pos:* from asst prof to assoc prof, 61-75, PROF BIOL, TEMPLE UNIV, 75- *Personal Data:* b Princeton, NJ, Mar 15, 32; m 55; c 4. *Educ:* Princeton Univ, AB, 54, MA, 57, PhD(biol), 59. *Prof Exp:* Instr biol, Princeton Univ, 59-61. *Concurrent Pos:* Prin investr, Bermuda Biol Sta, Off Naval Res, 59-60. *Mem:* AAAS; Animal Behav Soc; Int Soc Chromobiol. *Res:* Biological chronometry; diurnal rhythmic activities in animals. *Mailing Add:* Dept Biol Temple Univ Broad & Montgomery Philadelphia PA 19122

ROBERTS, SIDNEY, ENDOCRINOLOGY, NEUROCHEMISTRY. *Current Pos:* from asst prof to assoc prof, 48-57, PROF BIOL CHEM, SCH MED, UNIV CALIF, LOS ANGELES, 57- *Personal Data:* b Boston, Mass, Mar 11, 18; m 43, Clara Szego. *Educ:* Mass Inst Technol, SB, 39; Univ Minn, MS, 42, PhD(biochem), 43. *Honors & Awards:* Ciba Award, Endocrine Soc, 53. *Prof Exp:* Instr physiol, Sch Med, Univ Minn, 43-44; instr, Sch Med, George Washington Univ, 44-45; res assoc, Worcester Found Exp Biol, 45-47; asst prof physiol chem, Sch Med, Yale Univ, 47-48. *Concurrent Pos:* Guggenheim fel, Univ London, 57-58; consult, Vet Admin Hosp, Long Beach, Calif, 51-55, NSF, 55-59, Vet Admin Hosp, Los Angeles, 58-62, Los Angeles Co Heart Asn, 58-60, 62-63 & NIH, 60-63; exec comn, Am Chem Soc, 56-59; ed, Brain Res, Neurochem Res, Am J Physiol & Proc Soc Exp Biol & Med; chair, academic senate, Univ Calif, Los Angeles, 89-90. *Mem:* AAAS; Endocrine Soc (vpres, 68-69); Am Soc Biol Chemists; Am Soc Neurochem; Am Physiol Soc; Am Chem Soc; Soc Neurosci; Biochem Soc Gt Brit; Int Soc Neurochem; Sigma Xi. *Res:* Regulation and role of protein synthesis and protein phosphorylations in endocrine and neural function. *Mailing Add:* Dept Biol Chem Sch Med Univ Calif Los Angeles CA 90024. *Fax:* 310-459-7587; *E-Mail:* sr@ucla.edu

ROBERTS, STEPHEN D, COMPUTER SCIENCE, COMPUTER SIMULATION. *Current Pos:* PROF INDUST ENG & HEAD DEPT, NC STATE UNIV, 90- *Personal Data:* b Warsaw, Ind, Sept 3, 42. *Educ:* Purdue Univ, BS, 65, MS, 66, PhD(indust eng), 68. *Prof Exp:* From assoc prof to prof indust eng, Purdue Univ, 72-90. *Concurrent Pos:* From assoc prof to prof internal med, Sch Med, Ind Univ, 72-90; head health systs, Regenstrief Inst, 74-90. *Mem:* Asn Comput Mach; Inst Mgt Sci; Inst Indust Engrs. *Mailing Add:* Dept Indust Eng NC State Univ Box 7906 Raleigh NC 27695-7906

ROBERTS, STEPHEN WINSTON, SYSTEMS DESIGN & SYSTEMS SCIENCE. *Current Pos:* PRES, DATA DESIGN GROUP, LA JOLLA, CALIF, 85- *Personal Data:* b Chicago, Ill, May 4, 41; m 65, Edda Fuhr; c Mark. *Educ:* San Diego State Univ, BS, 72, MS, 74; Duke Univ PhD(plant ecol), 78. *Prof Exp:* Res asst, Dept Biol, San Diego State Univ, 72-74; teaching & res asst, Dept Forestry, Duke Univ, 74-77; adj prof biol, San Diego State Univ, Calif & res prof, Systs Ecol Res Group, 78-84; assoc prof, Fac Ciencias Biol, Pontificia Univ Catolica Chile, Santiago, 84-85. *Concurrent Pos:* Grad fel, Duke Univ, 74-77; Res Award, Duke Univ, 76 & 77; co-prin investr, NSF grant, 77-81 & 81-84; environ consult, Chambers Consults & Planners, Stanton, Calif, 78-84; prin investr, US Dept Agr Grant, 81-84; researcher, photosynthesis in tropical plants, Orgn Tropical Studies Res Sta, Costa Rica, 84-85; Coop Res Projs, USDA Forest Serv, Riverside Fire Lab, 89- *Mem:* AAAS; Ecol Soc Am; Sigma Xi. *Res:* Ecophysiology research in plants, primarily gas exchange and water relations; measuring instruments associated with ecophysiology research; author of various publications. *Mailing Add:* Data Design Group PO Box 3318 La Jolla CA 92038

ROBERTS, THEODORE S, neurosurgery, for more information see previous edition

ROBERTS, THOMAS D, electrophysics, for more information see previous edition

ROBERTS, THOMAS DAVID, ORGANIC CHEMISTRY, POLYMER CHEMISTRY. *Current Pos:* chemist, 79-84, sr chem, 84-89, PRIN CHEMIST, TEX EASTMAN CO, 89- *Personal Data:* b Quanah, Tex, July 11, 38; m 57; c 3. *Educ:* Abilene Christian Col, BS, 59; Ohio State Univ, PhD(chem), 67. *Prof Exp:* Res chemist, Explor Group, Pittsburgh Plate Glass Co, Ohio, 59-62; from asst prof to assoc prof chem, Univ Ark, Fayetteville, 67-77, prof, 77-79. *Concurrent Pos:* Petrol Res Fund grant, 67-69, 71-73 & 75-79; Res Corp grant, 69; vis assoc prof, Univ Fla, 73. *Res:* Synthesis of strained small ring and pseudo-aromatic compounds; new polymers; new synthetic reactions. *Mailing Add:* Res Labs Tex Eastman Co Longview TX 75607

ROBERTS, THOMAS GEORGE, LASERS, PLASMA PHYSICS. *Current Pos:* OWNER & RES SCIENTIST, TECHNOCO, HUNTSVILLE, ALA, 85- *Personal Data:* b Ft Smith, Ark, Apr 27, 29; m 58, Alica A Harbin; c Marcia (Dale), Lawrence D & Regina (Carter). *Educ:* Univ Ga, BS, 56, MS, 57; NC State Univ, PhD(physics), 67. *Prof Exp:* Instr physics, Univ Ga, 56-57; physicist, Army Rocket & Guided Missile Agency, 57-62 & US Army Missile Command, 62-85; staff scientist, Phys Dynamics, Inc, 86-89. *Concurrent Pos:* Consult, Ballistic Missile Defense Technol Ctr & Southeastern Inst Technol, 75-85, SAIC, Celtic Res & BDM, 85- *Mem:* Am Phys Soc; fel Optical Soc Am; sr mem Inst Elec & Electronics Engrs. *Res:* Behavior of very intense relativistic electron beams in plasmas; effects of short duration pulses of high energy on materials; high power laser technology where the active medium is a plasma or aerodynamic gases; the physics of high energy particle beams. *Mailing Add:* 1780 Joe Quick Rd New Market AL 35761

ROBERTS, THOMAS GLASDIR, micropaleontology, stratigraphy, for more information see previous edition

ROBERTS, THOMAS L, IMMUNOLOGY, MEDICAL SCIENCES. *Current Pos:* RETIRED. *Personal Data:* b Key West, Fla, Apr 17, 32; c 3. *Educ:* Talladega Col, AB, 57; Trinity Univ, Tex, MS, 61; Clark Univ, PhD(microbiol, biochem), 65, PhD(pub admin), 77. *Prof Exp:* Res asst physiol, Med Br, Univ Tex, Galveston, 57-58; microbiologist, USAF Sch Aerospace Med, 58-63; from asst prof to prof biol, Worcester State Col, 65-69, chmn dept biol, 72-76, prof biol, 69-88, educ dir, Nuclear Med Technol Prog, Mass Med Sch, 76-88. *Concurrent Pos:* Res assoc, Clark Univ, 65-67, res affiliate, 67-68; trustee, Rehab Ctr Worcester County, Inc, 75-81, pres, 77-81. *Mem:* Fel Sigma Xi; AAAS; NY Acad Sci; Am Soc Microbiol; fel Am Inst Chemists. *Res:* Immunochemistry related to learning under physical stresses. *Mailing Add:* 321 Catherine St Key West FL 33040-7504

ROBERTS, THOMAS M, direct & inverse scattering, electromagnetics, for more information see previous edition

ROBERTS, VERNE LOUIS, BIOMECHANICS, MECHANICAL ENGINEERING. *Current Pos:* ADJ PROF, DEPT MECH ENG, DUKE UNIV, 73-, DIR, INST PROD SAFETY, 79- *Personal Data:* b Kansas City, Mo, Aug 11, 39; m 57; c 3. *Educ:* Univ Kans, BS, 60; Univ Ill, MS, 61, PhD(eng mech), 64. *Honors & Awards:* Res Award, Am Soc Testing & Mat, 66. *Prof Exp:* From asst prof to assoc prof eng mech, Wayne State Univ, 63-66, assoc prof neurosurg, 66; head dept biomech, Univ Mich, Ann Arbor, 66-73. *Concurrent Pos:* Assoc urol, Wayne State Univ, 64-66, fac res fel, 65; consult, Vet Admin, 64-66; mem engrs Joint Coun Comt Interaction Eng with Med & Biol, 65-66; co-ed in chief, J Biomech, 67-; mem, Comt Head Protection, Unified Space Appln Mission Stand Inst, 68-; mem, Adv Comt, Stapp Car Crash Conf, 68-; dir, Nat Driving Ctr, 73-78. *Mem:* Am Soc Mech Engrs; Am Soc Safety Engrs; Syst Safety Soc; Am Soc Biomech; Europ Soc Biomech; Soc Automotive Engrs. *Res:* Biomechanics of trauma; safe product design. *Mailing Add:* 7 Surf Ct Wilmington NC 28405

ROBERTS, W(ILLIAM) NEIL, METALLURGY. *Current Pos:* RETIRED. *Personal Data:* b Prince Albert, Sask, May 27, 31; m 58; c 1. *Educ:* Univ Sask, BA, 52, Hons, 53, MA, 54; Univ Leeds, PhD(metall), 61. *Prof Exp:* Patent examr, Can Govt Patent & Copyright Off, 55-56; sci officer, Can Dept Mines & Tech Surv, Can Dept Energy, Mines & Resources, 57-58, res scientist, Metal Physics Sect, 61-72, head metal physics sect, Phys Metall Res Labs, 71-91. *Mem:* Am Soc Metals; Am Inst Mining, Metall & Petrol Engrs; Am Soc Testing & Mat. *Res:* Development of improved sutures for microsurgery; evaluation of steels for line pipe; transmission electron microscopy of austenitic steels and chromium molybdenum steels for fuel conversion; transmission electron microscopy of dual phase steels for automotive applications. *Mailing Add:* 74 Rothwell Dr Ottawa ON K1J 7G6 Can

ROBERTS, WALDEN KAY, MICROBIOLOGY, BIOCHEMISTRY. *Current Pos:* PROF MICROBIOL, MED SCH, UNIV COLO, DENVER, 76- *Personal Data:* b Independence, Mo, July 1, 34; m 66; c 3. *Educ:* Iowa State Univ, BS, 56; Univ Calif, Berkeley, PhD(biochem), 60. *Prof Exp:* NSF fel, Univ Newcastle, Eng, 60-62; asst prof molecular biol, Univ Calif, Berkeley, 62-67. *Mem:* Am Soc Biol Chem. *Res:* Antifungal proteins from plants; cell-specific toxins; interferon. *Mailing Add:* Dept Microbiol & Immunol Univ Colo Health Sci Ctr 4200 E Ninth Ave Denver CO 80262-0001. *Fax:* 303-270-6785

ROBERTS, WALTER HERBERT B, ANATOMY. *Current Pos:* EMER PROF ANAT, LOMA LINDA UNIV, 56- *Personal Data:* b Field, BC, Jan 24, 15; US citizen; c 3. *Educ:* Loma Linda Univ, MD, 39. *Prof Exp:* Med dir, Rest Haven Hosp, Sidney, BC, 40-53. *Mem:* Am Asn Anatomists. *Res:* Gross anatomy. *Mailing Add:* Dept Pathol & Human Anat Loma Linda Univ Stewart St Loma Linda CA 92350

ROBERTS, WARREN WILCOX, NEUROSCIENCES. *Current Pos:* from assoc prof to prof, 62-89, EMER PROF PSYCHOL, UNIV MINN, MINNEAPOLIS, 89- *Personal Data:* b Lincoln, Nebr, Oct 22, 26; m 67, Eunice Kyllo; c Benjamin T & Jeremy C. *Educ:* Stanford Univ, BA, 48, MA, 53; Yale Univ, PhD(psychol), 56. *Prof Exp:* Fel psychol, Yale Univ, 56-57; asst res anatomist, Univ Calif, Los Angeles, 57-59; asst prof psychol, Syracuse Univ, 59-62. *Mem:* Soc Neurosci. *Res:* Brain mechanisms of motivation; thermoregulation. *Mailing Add:* N218 Elliott Hall Univ Minn Minneapolis MN 55455

ROBERTS, WILLARD LEWIS, nutritional biochemistry, for more information see previous edition

ROBERTS, WILLIAM C, PATHOLOGY. *Current Pos:* MEM STAFF, PATH BR, NIH. *Mailing Add:* Baylor Cardiovascular Inst, Baylor Univ Med Ctr 3500 Gaston Ave 4th Floor Roberts Bldg Dallas TX 75246

ROBERTS, WILLIAM JOHN, CHEMISTRY, FIBER TECHNOLOGY. *Current Pos:* RETIRED. *Personal Data:* b Philadelphia, Pa, June 5, 18; m 48, Eleanor Kennedy; c 2. *Educ:* Univ Pa, AB, 42, MS, 44, PhD(org chem), 47. *Prof Exp:* Asst chemist, United Gas Improv Co, Pa, 36-41, res chemist, 41-44, asst to mgr, 44-45; asst to dir, Pa Indust Chem Corp, 46-47, from asst dir res to dir res, 48-57; dir res, Summit Res Labs, Celanese Corp, 57-64, vpres & tech dir, Celanese Fibers Co, 65-74; vpres & tech dir, Fiber Div, FMC Corp, 74-76; consult, 76-86. *Concurrent Pos:* Asst instr, Univ Pa, 42-44. *Mem:* Am Chem Soc. *Res:* Organic synthesis; hydrocarbons; polymerization; isomerization; pyrolysis and petrochemicals; polymers; plastics; fibers, especially man-made fibers; oxygenated chemicals; research management. *Mailing Add:* 65 Peachcroft Rd Bernardsville NJ 07924

ROBERTS, WILLIAM KENNETH, RUMINANT NUTRITION. *Current Pos:* NUTRIT CONSULT, NUTRIT-LAB SERV INC, 68- *Personal Data:* b Provo, Utah, Dec 10, 28; m 56, Joan Wharton; c Jeffrey, Tamera (Auther) & Julie (Pancrazi). *Educ:* Calif State Polytech Col, BS, 52; Wash State Univ, MS, 57, PhD(animal nutrit), 59. *Prof Exp:* Res asst animal sci, Wash State Univ, 55-59; fel nutrit & biochem, Grad Sch Pub Health, Univ Pittsburgh, 59-60; from asst prof to assoc prof, animal nutrit, Univ Man, 60-66; res specialist, Kern Co Land Co, Calif, 66-68. *Concurrent Pos:* Nat Res Coun Can res grants, 61-66. *Mem:* Am Soc Animal Sci; Sigma Xi; AAAS. *Res:* Ruminant nutrition concerning fat deposition and volatile fatty acid metabolism; vitamin A utilization; the role of potassium in ruminant nutrition. *Mailing Add:* Nutrit-Lab Servs Inc Box 26626 Phoenix AZ 85068-6626

ROBERTS, WILLIAM WOODRUFF, JR, APPLIED MATHEMATICS, ASTRONOMY. *Current Pos:* From asst prof to assoc prof, 69-82, PROF APPL MATH, UNIV VA, 82- *Personal Data:* b Huntington, WVa, Oct 8, 42; m 67; c 2. *Educ:* Mass Inst Technol, SB, 64, PhD(appl math), 69. *Concurrent Pos:* Consult, Du Pont, 86-, Union Carbide Corp, 81; vis scientist, Inst Hautes Etudes Scientifiques, Bures-sur-Yvette, France, 74, Kapteyn Astron Inst, Univ Groningen, Neth, 74, Huygens Lab, Univ Leiden, Neth, 75, Int Bus Mach, T J Watson Res Ctr, Yorktown Heights, NY, 80, Inst Comput Appln Sci & Eng, NASA Langley Res Ctr, Hampton, Va, 80-81, Nat Radio Astron Observ, Va, 88; Nordita guest prof, Stockholms Observ, Saltsjobaden, Sweden, 74-75; mem, Va Inst Theoretical Astron. *Mem:* Am Astron Soc; Soc Indust & Appl Math; Int Astron Union; Sigma Xi; Am Inst Aeronaut & Astronaut. *Res:* Fluid mechanics; dynamics of galaxies of gas and stars; shock waves; star formation; nonlinear wave motion; computational mathematics; computational fluid dynamics; rarefied gas dynamics. *Mailing Add:* 309 Westminster Rd Charlottesville VA 22901-2257

ROBERTSEN, JOHN ALAN, MEDICAL MICROBIOLOGY, ENVIRONMENTAL AND BIOHAZARD CONTROL. *Current Pos:* VPRES & CHIEF OPERATING OFFICER, EXTENSOR CORP, 73- *Personal Data:* b Kenosha, Wis, June 21, 26; m 57; c Steven Anthony & Christine Marie. *Educ:* Univ Wis, BS, 52, MS, 56, PhD(med microbiol), 58. *Prof Exp:* Chief, Microbiol Sect, Leprosy Res, USPHS Hosp, Carville, La, 58-62; leader, Infectious Diseases Group, Pitman-Moore Div, Dow Chem Co, 62-65, leader, microbiol group, Biohazards Dept, Dow Chem Co, 65-69; dir microbiol, St Francis Hosp & Thornton-Haymond Labs, Indianapolis, 69-71; dir tech mkt, Kallestad Labs, Inc, Minneapolis, 71-73. *Concurrent Pos:* Former US contrib ed, Int J Leprosy; founder & pres, Robertsen Biomed Consults; prin, Robertsen & Assocs Mgt Consults; consult, Zinpro Corp, Sci Int Res, Inc & others. *Mem:* AAAS; Int Leprosy Asn; Am Asn Contamination Control; Am Soc Trop Med & Hyg; Am Asn Lab Animal Sci; Am Soc Performance Improv; Am Radio Relay League; Nat Disaster Med Syst. *Res:* Immunodiagnostics; host-parasite relationships in tropical diseases, especially leprosy; control and containment of biological hazards; hospital environmental control; time allocation, behavior and task analyses of persons in health-care-related and administrative or professional positions; work measurement methodology at the managerial level; 8 patent disclosures; food processing industry sanitation. *Mailing Add:* 17273 Hampton Ct Minnetonka MN 55345-2517. *E-Mail:* ka00sc@n0bsn.ampr.org

ROBERTSHAW, JOSEPH EARL, SYSTEMS ANALYSIS, ENERGY MANAGEMENT. *Current Pos:* Assoc prof, 61-72, PROF PHYSICS, PROVIDENCE COL, 72- *Personal Data:* b Providence, RI, Apr 19, 34. *Educ:* Providence Col, BS, 56; Mass Inst Technol, MS, 58, PhD(physics), 61. *Concurrent Pos:* Vis prof systs eng, Ga Inst Technol, 70-71; consult, GTE Labs, Waltham, Mass, 81-82. *Mem:* Am Phys Soc; Nat Asn Physics Teachers; Inst Elec & Electronics Engrs; Asn Energy Eng; Am Soc Eng Educ. *Res:* Systems analysis and engineering; systems approach to problem solving in engineering designs; socio-technical fields; energy management; factory productivity improvement; control theory; optimization. *Mailing Add:* Dept Physics Eng Systs Providence Col Providence RI 02918

ROBERTS-MARCUS, HELEN MIRIAM, BIOSTATISTICS. *Current Pos:* from asst prof to assoc prof, 72-80, PROF MATH, MONTCLAIR STATE UNIV, 80- *Personal Data:* b Panama City, Panama, June 22, 43; US citizen. *Educ:* City Col New York, BS, 64; Johns Hopkins Univ, PhD(biostatist), 70. *Prof Exp:* Asst prof statist, Univ Calif, Riverside, 70-72. *Concurrent Pos:* Consult, Pac State Hosp, Pomona, Calif, 70-72, Loma Linda Univ Hosp, Calif, 70-72, Hosp Res Assoc, Fanwood, NJ, 77-79 & Boyle-Midway, Cranford, NJ, 81-; vis assoc prof, Oper Res & Indust Eng, Cornell Univ, 79-80. *Mem:* Am Statist Asn; Math Asn Am; Soc Indust Appl Math. *Res:* Stochastic models in biology; mathematical genetics. *Mailing Add:* Dept Math Comput Sci Richardson Hall Rm 204 Montclair State Univ Valley Rd Upper Montclair NJ 07043

ROBERTSON, A(LEXANDER) F(RANCIS), MECHANICAL ENGINEERING. *Current Pos:* RETIRED. *Personal Data:* b Vancouver, BC, Aug 31, 12; nat US; m 46, Beatric Fleenor; c Alan, Catherine & Colin. *Educ:* Univ Wis, BS, 35, MS, 38, PhD(mech eng), 40. *Honors & Awards:* Gold Medal Award, US Dept Com, 75; Edward Bennett Rosa Award, Nat Bur Standards, 78; Charles P Dudly Award, Am Soc Testing Mat, 86; Kawagoe Gold Medal Award, Int Asn Fire Safety Sci. *Prof Exp:* Engr, Fairbanks, Morse & Co, Wis, 35-37, res engr, 40-41; engr, US Naval Ord Lab, DC, 41-46 & Manhattan Dist, Chicago, 46; res engr, Battelle Mem Inst, 46-47; res assoc, Inst Textile Technol, 47-50; chief, Fire Res Sect, Nat Bur Stand, 50-68, tech asst dir, Inst Appl Technol, 68-70, tech asst chief, Fire Technol Div, 70-73, sr scientist, 73-85, guest worker, Ctr Fire Res, 85-96. *Concurrent Pos:* NAm ed, Fire & Mat, 76-85. *Mem:* Am Phys Soc; Combustion Inst; AAAS. *Res:* Diesel and gaseous combustion; heat transfer; electromechanical transducers; problems relating to unwanted fires; national and international fire standards. *Mailing Add:* 4228 Butterworth Pl NW Washington DC 20016-4532

ROBERTSON, ABEL ALFRED LAZZARINI, JR, paleo pathology, for more information see previous edition

ROBERTSON, ALAN ROBERT, COLORIMETRY, COLOR SCIENCE. *Current Pos:* res officer physics, 65-91, dir mech stand, 91-95, dir chem mech & radiation stand, 95-96, DIR, CHEM MECH STAND, NAT RES COUN CAN, 96- *Personal Data:* b Wakefield, Eng, Sept 3, 40; m 64, Margaret H Burrows; c Mark & Keith. *Educ:* Univ London, BSc, 62, PhD(physics), 65. *Concurrent Pos:* Assoc ed, Color Res & Appln, 78-; pres, Can Nat Comt, Int Comn Illum, 84-92; pres, Int Color Asn, 90-93; chmn, NAm Metrol Collab, 95-97; vpres, Int Comm Illum, 95- *Mem:* Can Soc Color (pres, 79-81); Inter-Soc Color Coun; Optical Soc Am; Int Color Asn (vpres, 86-89, pres, 90-93). *Res:* Colour-difference evaluation, colour measurment, spectrophotometry, colour rendering, reflectance standards; colour order systems. *Mailing Add:* Nat Res Coun Montreal Rd Ottawa ON K1A 0R6 Can. *E-Mail:* alan.robertson@nrc.ca

ROBERTSON, ALEX F, PEDIATRICS, BIOCHEMISTRY. *Current Pos:* chmn dept, 71-81, PROF PEDIAT, MED COL GA, 71- *Personal Data:* b Staunton, Va, Dec 5, 32. *Educ:* Univ Va, BA, 53, MD, 57; Univ Mich, MA, 62. *Prof Exp:* From instr to asst prof pediat, Univ Mich, 63-65; from asst prof to assoc prof, Ohio State Univ, 65-71, dir div neonatology, 65-71. *Mem:* Soc Pediat Res; Am Pediat Soc; Am Acad Pediat; Sigma Xi; AOA. *Res:* Neonatology; bilirubin-albumin binding in neonates. *Mailing Add:* 4228 Butterworth Pl Washington DC 20016

ROBERTSON, ANDREW, AQUATIC ECOLOGY. *Current Pos:* fishery biologist, IFYGL Proj Off, Nat Oceanic & Atmospheric Admin, 71-74, head biol chem group, Great Lakes Environ Res Lab, 74-81, dep dir, Off Marine Pollution Assessment, 81-82, dir, Nat Marine Pollution Prog Off, 82-86, chief, Ocean Assessments Div, 86-92, CHIEF, COASTAL MONITORING & BIOEFFECTS ASSESSMENT DIV, NAT OCEANIC & ATMOSPHERIC ADMIN, 92- *Personal Data:* b Port Huron, Mich, Sept 15, 36; m 65, Mary Johnson; c Andrew VII & Jan C. *Educ:* Univ Toledo, BS, 58; Univ Mich, MA, 61, PhD(zool), 64. *Prof Exp:* Asst res limnologist, Univ Mich, Ann Arbor, 64-67, assoc res limnologist, 67-68; assoc prof zool, Univ Okla, 68-71. *Mem:* Am Soc Limnol & Oceanog; Ecol Soc Am; Crustacean Soc; Int Asn Great Lakes Res; Estuarine Res Fedn. *Res:* Great Lakes ecology; systematics and distribution of calanoid copepods; modeling of Great Lakes ecosystems; marine pollution. *Mailing Add:* NOAA/NOS N/ORCA2 Sta 10110SSMC4 1305 East West Hwy Silver Spring MD 20910. *Fax:* 301-443-8933; *E-Mail:* Omnet: a.robertson

ROBERTSON, BALDWIN, MEMBRANE BIOPHYSICS, STATISTICAL MECHANICS. *Current Pos:* res assoc, Nat Bur Stand, 66-68, physicist, 68-89, PHYSICIST, NAT INST STANDARDS & TECHNOL, 89- *Personal Data:* b Los Angeles, Calif, Sept 26, 34; m 62; c 3. *Educ:* Stanford Univ, BS, 56, MS, 57, PhD(physics), 65. *Prof Exp:* Instr & res assoc, Cornell Univ, 64-66. *Mem:* Am Phys Soc. *Res:* Nonequilibrium statistical mechanics; experimental and theoretical biophysics and chemical relaxation kinetics, membrane enzymes. *Mailing Add:* Biotechnol Div Nat Inst Standards & Technol Gaithersburg MD 20899. *E-Mail:* baldwin@nist.gov

ROBERTSON, BEVERLY ELLIS, CRYSTALLOGRAPHY, MOLECULAR BIOLOGY. *Current Pos:* from asst prof to assoc prof 69-76, PROF PHYSICS, UNIV REGINA, 76- *Personal Data:* b Fredericton, NB, Feb 5, 39; m 58, Elaine Pickard; c Scott & Kelly (Gaetz). *Educ:* Univ NB, BSc, 61; McMaster Univ, MSc, 65, PhD(physics), 67. *Prof Exp:* Assoc chem, Cornell Univ, 67-69. *Concurrent Pos:* Vis prof, Univ Stuttgart, 76-77; mem, Sci Coun Can, 78-84; adj prof, Univ Sask, 90- *Mem:* Am Crystallog Asn; Am Chem Soc; Health Physics Soc; Can Asn Physicists (pres, 96-97). *Res:* Crystal structure determination; deformation densities; crystallographic software. *Mailing Add:* Dept Physics Univ Regina Regina SK S4S 0A2 Can. *Fax:* 306-585-4894; *E-Mail:* robertsb@leroy.cc.uregina.ca, bush.info@eagle.wbm.ca

ROBERTSON, BOBBY KEN, PHYSICAL CHEMISTRY. *Current Pos:* Asst prof, 65-74, ASSOC PROF PHYS CHEM, UNIV MO, ROLLA, 74-, DEAN STUDENTS, 78- *Personal Data:* b Reed, Okla, June 20, 38. *Educ:* WTex State Univ, BA, 60; Tex A&M Univ, PhD, 65. *Mem:* Am Chem Soc; Am Crystallog Asn. *Res:* Interpretation of molecular structure by use of x-ray crystallography. *Mailing Add:* Dept Chem Univ Mo PO Box 249 Rolla MO 65401

ROBERTSON, CHARLES WILLIAM, JR, PHYSICS. *Current Pos:* RES ASSOC, E I DU PONT DE NEMOURS & CO, INC, 73- *Personal Data:* b Memphis, Tenn, Mar 2, 43; m 89. *Educ:* Southwestern at Memphis, BS, 65; Fla State Univ, PhD(physics), 69. *Prof Exp:* Res assoc physics, Kans State Univ, 70-73. *Mem:* Optical Soc Am; Sigma Xi. *Res:* Application of optical and spectroscopic techniques to the measurement of material properties in the infrared, visible and ultraviolet. *Mailing Add:* PO Box 154 Wilmington DE 19732-0154

ROBERTSON, CLYDE HENRY, ENTOMOLOGY. *Current Pos:* RETIRED. *Personal Data:* b Heath Springs, SC, Aug 8, 29; m 51; c 2. *Educ:* Wofford Col, BS, 50; Duke Univ, MA, 52, PhD(zool), 55. *Prof Exp:* From asst prof to prof biol, Pfeiffer Col, 56-90, head dept, 56-74, chmn, Div Natural Sci, 74-90, emer prof biol, 90-92. *Res:* Vertebrate morphology; development and metamorphosis of insectan respiratory systems. *Mailing Add:* 105 Old Salisbury Rd Richfield NC 28137

ROBERTSON, DALE NORMAN, organic chemistry, for more information see previous edition

ROBERTSON, DAVID, AUTONOMIC DISORDERS, SPARE MEDICINE & PHYSIOLOGY. *Current Pos:* from asst prof to assoc prof, 78-86, PROF MED & PHARM, VANDERBILT UNIV, 86- *Personal Data:* b Dickson Co, Tenn, May 23, 47; m 76; c 1. *Educ:* Vanderbilt Univ, BA, 69, MD, 73. *Prof Exp:* Instr med, Johns Hopkins Hosp, 77-78. *Concurrent Pos:* Teaching & res scholar award, Am Col Physicians, 78-81 & res career develop award, 81-86; vis prof, Dept Molecular Endocrinol, All-Union Cardiol Res Ctr, Moscow, USSR, 84 & Dept Anat & Embryol, Univ Col London, UK, 85; Scholar, Burroughs Wellcome, 86-91; dir, Clin Res Ctr, Vanderbilt Univ, 87- & Ctr Space Physiol & Med, 89-; William N Creasy Vis Prof Clin Pharm, 90. *Mem:* Am Soc Clin Invest; Aerospace Med Asn; Am Fedn Clin Res. *Res:* How the brain controls the heart and blood pressure; acute blood pressure disturbances and chronic acquired or genetic deficiency and carried out. *Mailing Add:* Dept Med Pharm & Neurol Vanderbilt Univ Sch Med AA 3328 MCN Nashville TN 37232-2195

ROBERTSON, DAVID C, ATMOSPHERIC CHEMISTRY, THEORETICAL PHYSICS. *Current Pos:* PRIN SCIENTIST, SPECTRAL SCI INC. *Personal Data:* b Scotia, Calif, Nov 13, 42; m 67; c 1. *Educ:* Stanford Univ BS, 66; Univ Calif, Santa Barbara, PhD(theoret physics), 70. *Mem:* Am Phys Soc; Am Meteorol Soc. *Res:* IR spectroscopy; atmospheric radiative transport. *Mailing Add:* Spectral Sci Inc 99 S Bedford St No 7 Burlington MA 01803

ROBERTSON, DAVID G C, METALLURGY & EXTRACTIVE METALLURGICAL ENGINEERING, RESEARCH ADMINISTRATION. *Current Pos:* DIR, CTR PYRO METALL, PROF METALL, UNIV MO, ROLLA, 85- *Personal Data:* b Dublin, Ireland, Dec 29, 41; m 70; c 2. *Educ:* Imp Col, London, UK, BSc, 63; Univ NSW, Sydney, Australia, PhD(metall), 68. *Prof Exp:* Lectr metall, Imp Col, 69-82, reader metall, 82-85. *Concurrent Pos:* Consult, var co, 69-; dir, Generic Mineral Technol Ctr Pyrometall, 85-. *Mem:* Metall Soc. *Res:* Metallurgy and extractive metallurgical engineering. *Mailing Add:* 216 Fulton Hall Univ Mo 1870 Miner Circle Rolla MO 65409-0249. *Fax:* 573-341-4739

ROBERTSON, DAVID MURRAY, NEUROPATHOLOGY, PATHOLOGY. *Current Pos:* RETIRED. *Personal Data:* b Melville, Sask, May 4, 32; m 56; c 3. *Educ:* Queen's Univ, Ont, MD, CM, 55, MSc, 60; Royal Col Physicians, cert, 60, fel neuropath, 68; Am Bd Path, cert anatomic path & neuropath, 77. *Prof Exp:* From asst prof to prof path, Queen's Univ, Ont, 62-96, head dept, 79-87. *Concurrent Pos:* Neuropathologist, Kingston Gen Hosp, 62-, chief pathologist, 79-87. *Mem:* Am Asn Neuropath; Can Asn Path; Can Asn Neuropath; Int Acad Path. *Res:* Nutritional diseases of nervous system; diabetic neuropathy; cerebrovascular disease. *Mailing Add:* Richardson Lab Dept Path Queen's Univ Kingston ON K7L 3N6 Can

ROBERTSON, DAVID WAYNE, MEDICINAL CHEMISTRY, CANCER DRUG DISCOVERY. *Current Pos:* vpres chem, 91-92, vpres res, 92-93, VPRES DISCOVERY RES, LIGAND PHARMACEUT, INC, 93- *Personal Data:* b Dumas, Tex, July 30, 55. *Educ:* Stephen F Austin State Univ, BS, 77; Univ Ill, MS, 78, PhD(org chem), 81. *Prof Exp:* Sr scientist, Eli Lilly & Co, 81-89, dir cent nervous syst res, 89-91. *Concurrent Pos:* Adj prof, China Pharmaceut Univ & Nanjing Univ, 93- *Mem:* Am Chem Soc; AAAS; NY Acad Sci; Am Heart Asn; Am Soc Pharmacol & Exp Therapeut; Soc Neurosci. *Res:* Setting research strategy; using the dramatically enhanced understanding of the steroid hormone receptor super family and their functions at the molecular level to design new medicines for treatment of cancer. *Mailing Add:* Ligand Pharmaceut 10255 Sci Center Dr San Diego CA 92121-3016. *Fax:* 619-625-4521

ROBERTSON, DONALD, MECHANICAL ENGINEERING. *Current Pos:* RETIRED. *Personal Data:* b Baltimore, Md, Nov 29, 10; m 55; c 1. *Educ:* Cornell Univ, ME, 32. *Prof Exp:* Foreman copper furnace, Am Smelting & Refining Co, 33-36; eng specification writer, Leeds & Northrup Co, 36-37, engr, 37-45, head, Pyrometer Sect, 45-55, chief res & develop, Pyromet Group, 55-62, head, Temperature Measurements Sect, Res & Develop Ctr, 62-68, mgr stand prod eng, Sensor Div, 68-69, mgr develop & eng, 69-73; temperature measurement expert, 73-76; independent temperature consult, 76. *Res:* Temperature primary elements. *Mailing Add:* 77 Middle Rd Apt 366 Bryn Mawr PA 19010

ROBERTSON, DONALD CLAUS, BIOCHEMISTRY, MICROBIOLOGY. *Current Pos:* PROF & DEPT HEAD, UNIV ID, 92- *Personal Data:* b Rockford, Ill, Mar 5, 40; m 62; c 2. *Educ:* Univ Dubuque, BS, 62; Iowa State Univ, PhD(biochem), 67. *Prof Exp:* Chemist, Nat Animal Dis Lab, Ames, Iowa, 62-67; res assoc biochem, Mich State Univ, 67-70; from asst prof to prof microbiol, Univ Kans, 70-92, prof,. *Concurrent Pos:* NIH trainee, 67-70; mem bact & mycol study sect, NIH, 79-83; hon lectr, Mid-Am State Univs Asn, 81-82. *Mem:* Am Soc Microbiol; AAAS; Sigma Xi; Am Asn Univ Professors; Am Acad Microbiol; Am Soc Biochem Molecular Biol. *Res:* Microbial physiology; protein chemistry; biochemistry of host-parasite relationships. *Mailing Add:* Dept Microbiol, Molecular Biol & Biochem Univ Idaho Moscow ID 83844-3052. *Fax:* 208-885-6518; *E-Mail:* dcr@oidaho.edu

ROBERTSON, DONALD EDWIN, MOLECULAR DESIGN, PROCESS DEVELOPMENT. *Current Pos:* TECH CONSULT, 86- *Personal Data:* b Edmonton, Alta, Jan 8, 29; nat US; m 52; c 1. *Educ:* Univ Alta, BSc, 51; Univ Utah, PhD(chem), 59. *Prof Exp:* Res org chemist, US Gypsum Co, 60-62; res org chemist, Interchem Corp, 62-65; res org chemist, Com Solvents Corp & Int Minerals & Chem Corp, 65-86. *Mem:* Am Chem Soc; Chem Inst Can; fel Am Inst Chemists. *Res:* Design and synthesis of bioactive compounds; synthesis of natural products; carbohydrate and polymer chemistry; process and product development; technical writing. *Mailing Add:* 5235 E Greenbriar Dr Apt 6 Terre Haute IN 47802-4451

ROBERTSON, DONALD HUBERT, ANALYTICAL CHEMISTRY. *Current Pos:* RESEARCHER, NATICK LABS, US ARMY, 62- *Personal Data:* b Monmouth, Maine, June 6, 34. *Educ:* Bates Col, BS, 56; Univ Glasgow, PhD(chem), 73. *Prof Exp:* Researcher, Gen Foods Corp Res Ctr, 56-57, Natick Labs, US Army, 57-59 & Gen Foods Corp Res Ctr, 59-62. *Mem:* AAAS; Am Chem Soc; Pattern Recognition Soc. *Res:* Chromatography; mass spectrometry; computer processing as related to natural products, especially foodstuffs. *Mailing Add:* S&TD US Army Natick Lab Natick MA 01760-5020

ROBERTSON, DONALD SAGE, MAIZE GENETICS. *Current Pos:* from asst prof to prof, 57-91, chmn dept, 75-80, EMER PROF GENETICS, IOWA STATE UNIV, 91- *Personal Data:* b Oakland, Calif, June 27, 21; m 52, Roxana Sidensol; c Mark T, William P & Martha L (Alexander). *Educ:* Stanford Univ, AB, 47; Calif Inst Technol, PhD, 51. *Honors & Awards:* Gov Sci Medal, Iowa, 84. *Prof Exp:* Head dept sci, Biola Bible Col, 51-57. *Mem:* Genetics Soc Am; Sigma Xi. *Res:* Genetic control of mutation in maize; discoverer of the mutator transposable element system of maize. *Mailing Add:* Dept Zool & Genetics Iowa State Univ Ames IA 50011-4198

ROBERTSON, DOUGLAS REED, ANATOMY, ENDOCRINOLOGY. *Current Pos:* assoc prof, 70-76, PROF ANAT, STATE UNIV NY UPSTATE MED CTR, 76- *Personal Data:* b Buffalo, NY, Sept 11, 38; m 67, Judith Pesany; c 2. *Educ:* Univ Buffalo, BA, 61; State Univ NY Buffalo, MA, 63; State Univ NY Upstate Med Ctr, PhD(anat), 66. *Prof Exp:* Asst prof anat, Col Med, Univ Fla, 66-70. *Concurrent Pos:* NIH res grant, Inst Arthritis, Metab & Digestive Dis, 67-70; NSF grant, Div Biol & Med Sci, 82-85. *Mem:* Am Asn Anatomists; Am Soc Cell Biol; Am Soc Zoologists; Sigma Xi. *Res:* Secretory mechanisms of the ultimobranchial body; endocrinology and physiology of the hormones, calcitonin and parathormone in amphibians; annual and diurnal rhythms of calcitonin secretion and plasma calcium; enzyme immunoassay for frog calcitonin; immunohistochemistry of calcitonin; autonomic nervous system. *Mailing Add:* Dept Anat & Cell Biol State Univ NY Health Sci Ctr Syracuse NY 13210. *E-Mail:* robertsd@vax.cs.hscsyr.edu

ROBERTSON, DOUGLAS SCOTT, GEOPHYSICS, ASTRONOMY. *Current Pos:* GEODESIST, NAT GEODETIC SURV, NAT OCEAN SURV, NAT OCEANIC & ATMOSPHERIC ADMIN, 77- *Personal Data:* b Three Rivers, Mich, Dec 29, 45; m 72; c 1. *Educ:* Principia Col, BS, 68; Mass Inst Technol, PhD(geophys), 75. *Prof Exp:* Mem tech staff, Comput Sci Corp, 75-77. *Mem:* Am Geophys Union; Am Astron Soc; AAAS; Int Astron Union. *Res:* Use of very-long-baseline radio interferometry to study polar motion, earth rotation, precession, nutation, earth tides, tectonic crustal deformations and astrometry. *Mailing Add:* 2952 Sand Dollar Ct Longmont CO 80503

ROBERTSON, DOUGLAS WELBY, ELECTRONICS. *Current Pos:* CONSULT, 80- *Personal Data:* b Crawford, Ga, June 13, 24; m 49, Martha L Gardner; c Donald B, Charles J & Carol (McDermott). *Educ:* Ga Inst Technol, BS, 51, MS, 57. *Prof Exp:* Electronic technician, US Civil Serv, 42-44 & 46-47; res asst eng exp sta, Ga Inst Technol, 50-53, res engr, 53-57; mem tech staff, ITT Labs, Int Tel & Tel Corp, 57-59; res engr, Ga Inst Technol, 59-62, head, Commun Br, 62-72, chief, Commun Div, 72-75, dir, Electronics Technol Lab, Eng Exp Sta, 75-80. *Mem:* AAAS; sr mem Inst Elec & Electronics Engrs; Acoust Soc Am. *Res:* Voice intelligibility; speech communication systems; electromagnetic compatibility; piezoelectric crystals and oscillators; antennas; electronic measurements; solid state components; radar systems; research management. *Mailing Add:* 2937 Henderson Rd Tucker GA 30084

ROBERTSON, EDWARD L, THEORY OF COMPUTATION, COMPUTIONAL COMPLEXITY. *Current Pos:* assoc prof, 78-84, PROF COMPUT SCI, IND UNIV, 84- *Personal Data:* b St Paul, Minn, July 16, 44; m 69; c 2. *Educ:* Calif Inst Technol, BS, 66; Univ Wis, MS, 68, PhD(comput sci), 70. *Prof Exp:* Asst prof comput sci, Univ Wis, 70-71; res fel, Univ Ghana, Africa, 71-72; asst prof, Univ Waterloo, 72-74, Pa State Univ, 74-78. *Concurrent Pos:* Ed, Info Technol for Develop, 85-; vchmn, Comn Informatics in Develop, Int Fedn Info Processing, 85- *Mem:* Asn Comput Mach; Inst Elec & Electronics Engrs; Soc Indust & Appl Math. *Res:* Theory of computation and computational complexity; design and analysis of algorithms; software engineering; computers in economic development; database systems. *Mailing Add:* Dept Comput Sci Ind Univ Lindley Hall Bloomington IN 47405

ROBERTSON, EUGENE CORLEY, PHYSICAL PROPERTIES OF ROCKS. *Current Pos:* RETIRED. *Personal Data:* b Tucumcari, NMex, Apr 9, 15; m 72, Sheila O'Flaherty; c James G & Andrew W. *Educ:* Univ Ill, BS, 36; Harvard Univ, MA, 48, PhD(geol), 52. *Honors & Awards:* Meritorius Serv Award, US Geol Surv, 81. *Prof Exp:* Mining geologist, Anaconda Co, 36-42; geophysicist, US Geol Surv, 49-90. *Mem:* Am Inst Mining, Metall & Petrol Eng; Am Geophys Union; Geol Soc Am; Mineral Soc Am. *Res:* Deformation of rocks; experimental geology; strength, elastic and thermal properties of rocks; fault characteristics in the earth and applications to overthrust faulting and earthquake prediction. *Mailing Add:* US Geol Surv 955 Nat Ctr Reston VA 20192. *Fax:* 703-648-6717; *E-Mail:* ecrobert@usgs.gov

ROBERTSON, G PHILIP, ECOSYSTEM DYNAMICS, SOIL MICROBIOLOGY. *Current Pos:* asst prof, 85-90, ASSOC PROF, CROP & SOIL SCI DEPT, W K KELLOGG BIOL STA, MICH STATE UNIV, 90- *Personal Data:* b Houston, Tex, Oct 12, 53. *Educ:* Hampshire Col, Amherst, BA, 76; Ind Univ, Bloomington, PhD(biol), 80. *Prof Exp:* Andrew H Mellon Found postdoctoral fel, 80-81. *Concurrent Pos:* Ed, Plant & Soil, 84-89 & Ecol & Ecol Monogr, 88-91. *Mem:* Ecol Soc Am; Soil Sci Soc Am; AAAS. *Res:* Ecosystem ecology; nutrient dynamics in disturbed terrestrial communities, including agricultural; nitrogen fluxes; spatial dynamics; microbial transformations in soil. *Mailing Add:* Kellogg Biol Sta Mich State Univ 3700 E Gull Lake Dr Hickory Corners MI 49060

ROBERTSON, GEORGE GORDON, ANATOMY. *Current Pos:* prof, 52-80, chmn dept, 61-80, EMER PROF ANAT, UNIV TENN COL MED, 80- *Personal Data:* b St John, NB, Jan 30, 16; nat; m 46, Margaret Mason; c George Gordon III, William Don. *Educ:* Acadia Univ, BSc, 36, BA, 37; Yale Univ, PhD(zool), 41. *Prof Exp:* Asst biol, Yale Univ, 38-41; fel anat, Sch Med, Univ Ga, 41-42; instr anat, La State Univ, 42-43; from instr to assoc prof, Baylor Univ Col Med, 43-52. *Concurrent Pos:* Vis assoc prof anat, Col Basic Med Sci, Univ Tenn, Memphis, 48 & 51. *Mem:* Am Asn Anatomists. *Res:* Developmental genetics; ovarian transplantation; human embryology; experimental teratology. *Mailing Add:* 5800 Old Providence Rd Apt 3303 Charlotte NC 28226

ROBERTSON, GEORGE HARCOURT, BIOCHEMICAL ENGINEERING. *Current Pos:* RES CHEM ENGR AGR & FOOD ENG, WESTERN REGIONAL RES LAB, SCI & EDUC ADMIN-AGR RES, USDA, 69- *Personal Data:* b Evergreen Park, Ill, Jan 30, 43; m 67, Susan Templeton; c Margaret H & George S. *Educ:* Univ Ill, Urbana, BS, 65; Univ Calif, Berkeley, PhD(chem eng), 70. *Mem:* Inst Food Technologists; Am Inst Chem Engrs; Am Chem Soc. *Res:* Textile (wool) and food (sweetcorn) process modifications to reduce energy use, waste or pollutant generation; ethylalcohol fuels separation and generation; chemicals from plant tissue culture. *Mailing Add:* 36 Meese Circle USDA 800 Buchanan St Danville CA 94526-5315. *Fax:* 510-559-5777

ROBERTSON, GEORGE LEVEN, ANIMAL SCIENCE. *Current Pos:* RETIRED. *Personal Data:* b Alexandria, La, Feb 7, 21; m 43; c 3. *Educ:* La State Univ, BS, 41; Tex A&M Univ, MS, 47; Univ Wis, PhD(animal husb, genetics), 51. *Prof Exp:* Asst animal husb, Tex A&M Univ, 41-42, instr, 46-48, from asst prof to assoc prof, 48-55; prof animal sci & head dept, 55-77; exec dir, La State Univ, Baton Rouge, 77-92. *Mem:* Fel AAAS; Am Soc Animal Sci; Sigma Xi. *Res:* Physiology of reproduction in farm animals. *Mailing Add:* 7017 Perkins Rd Baton Rouge LA 70808

ROBERTSON, H THOMAS, II, RESPIRATORY PHYSIOLOGY, ANIMAL PHYSIOLOGY. *Current Pos:* PROF MED, UNIV HOSP, UNIV WASH, 82- *Personal Data:* b Abilene, Tex; m 70, Christine Johnston; c Dana & Marla. *Educ:* Harvard Univ, MD, 68. *Honors & Awards:* Res Career Develop Award, NIH. *Concurrent Pos:* Dir, Educ Med, Swed Hosp, Seattle. *Mem:* Fel Am Col Physicians; Am Physiol Soc; Am Thoracic Soc. *Res:* Respiratory physiology; pulmonay gas exchange, pulmonary circulation, human exercise physiology. *Mailing Add:* Dept Med Univ Hosp Pulmonary Med Box 356522 Univ Wash Seattle WA 98195-6522. *Fax:* 206-685-8673; *E-Mail:* tomorolt@u.washington.edu

ROBERTSON, HARRY S(TROUD), PLASMA PHYSICS, STATISTICAL MECHANICS. *Current Pos:* from asst prof to prof, 49-87, chmn dept, 52-62, 72-74, EMER PROF PHYSICS, UNIV MIAMI, FLA, 87- *Personal Data:* b Montgomery, Ala, Sept 26, 21; m 43, Mary F Adamo; c 3. *Educ:* Univ NC, BS, 42; Johns Hopkins Univ, PhD(physics), 49. *Prof Exp:* Radio engr, US Naval Res Lab, 42-46; asst physics, Johns Hopkins Univ, 47-49. *Concurrent Pos:* Vis lectr, Johns Hopkins Univ, 56-57; consult, Oak Ridge Nat Lab, 58-69 & Princeton Plasma Physics Lab, 61; vis prof, Univ Edinburgh, 71. *Mem:* Am Phys Soc; Sigma Xi. *Res:* Plasma transport properties; plasma stability and oscillations; cesium plasmas; moving striations; statistical thermodynamics; chaos; author of one book. *Mailing Add:* Dept Physics Univ Miami Univ Sta Box 248046 Coral Gables FL 33124. *Fax:* 305-284-4222; *E-Mail:* robertson@phyvax.ir.miami.edu

ROBERTSON, HUGH ELBURN, biochemistry, microbiology, for more information see previous edition

ROBERTSON, HUGH MERETH, GENETICS OF TRANSPOSONS. *Current Pos:* asst prof, 87-93, ASSOC PROF, DEPT ENTOM, UNIV ILL, 93- *Personal Data:* b Johannesburg, SAfrica, Dec 19, 55; m 94, Christina Nordholm. *Educ:* Univ Witwatersrand, SAfrica, BSc, Hons, 78, PhD(zool), 82. *Prof Exp:* Guyer fel zool, Univ Wis-Madison, 82-84, lectr, 85, proj assoc genetics, 85-87. *Mem:* Soc Study Evolution; Animal Behav Soc; Genetics Soc Am; AAAS; Entom Soc Am. *Res:* Olfactory receptors; genetics of transposable elements. *Mailing Add:* Dept Entom Univ Ill 505 S Goodwin Urbana IL 61801. *Fax:* 217-244-3499; *E-Mail:* hughrobe@uiuc.edu

ROBERTSON, IAN NICOL, STRUCTURAL ENGINEERING. *Current Pos:* ASST PROF STRUCTURAL ENG, UNIV HAWAII, MANOA, 92- *Personal Data:* b Johannesburg, SAfrica, May 25, 57; m 85, Rene Rademan; c Jessica A & Michael H. *Educ:* Univ Witwatersrand, SAfrica, BSc, 78; Rice Univ, MS, 83, PhD(civil eng), 90. *Prof Exp:* Proj engr, Ove Arup & Partners, SAfrica, 81-82 & 85; proj mgr, Walter P Moore & Assoc, Houston, 89-92. *Mem:* Am Soc Civil Engrs; Am Concrete Inst; Prestressed-Precast Concrete Inst. *Res:* Experimental and analytical research into the behavior of reinforced and prestressed concrete structures subjected to seismic loads. *Mailing Add:* 2125 Kakela Pl Honolulu HI 96822. *Fax:* 808-956-5014; *E-Mail:* ianr@manoa.eng.hawaii.edu

ROBERTSON, J(OHN) A(RCHIBALD) L(AW), MATERIALS SCIENCE, NUCLEAR SAFETY. *Current Pos:* CONSULT, 85- *Personal Data:* b Dundee, Scotland, July 4, 25; Can citizen; m 54, Betty-Jean Moffatt; c Clare D (Kortner), Ean S & Fiona H (Hogan). *Educ:* Cambridge Univ, BA, 50, MA, 53. *Honors & Awards:* W B Lewis Medal, Can Nuclear Asn, 87; W J Kroll Zirconium Medal, 93. *Prof Exp:* Sci officer metall, Atomic Energy Res Estab, UK Atomic Energy Authority, 50-55, sect leader, 55-57; res officer, Chalk River Nuclear Labs, Atomic Energy Can Ltd, 57-63, head, Reactor Mat Br, 63-70, dir, Fuels & Mat Div, 70-75, asst to vpres & gen mgr, Chalk River Nuclear Labs, 75-82, dir program planning, 82-85. *Concurrent Pos:* Co-ed, J Nuclear Mat, 67-71. *Mem:* Fel Royal Soc Can; Can Acad Sci. *Res:* Research and development programs for nuclear reactor systems; irradiation effects in nuclear fuels; nuclear safety and waste management. *Mailing Add:* 1 Kelvin Crescent PO Box 2047 Deep River ON K0J 1P0 Can

ROBERTSON, JACK M, MATHEMATICS. *Current Pos:* asst prof, 64-70, assoc prof, 70-77, PROF MATH, WASH STATE UNIV, 77- *Personal Data:* b Clovis, NMex, Sept 26, 37; m 57; c 3. *Educ:* Eastern NMex Univ, BS, 59; Univ Utah, MS, 61, PhD(math), 64. *Prof Exp:* Teaching asst math, Univ Utah, 59-64. *Concurrent Pos:* Assoc dir, NSF Summer Inst Sec Teachers, Wash State, 66-67, dir, 68-69. *Mem:* Am Math Soc; Math Asn Am. *Res:* Topology; analysis; mathematics education. *Mailing Add:* Dept Math Wash State Univ Pullman WA 99164-3113

ROBERTSON, JACQUELINE LEE, INSECT PHYSIOLOGY, INSECT TOXICOLOGY. *Current Pos:* POSTDOCTORAL, UNIV CALIF, DAVIS, 97- *Personal Data:* b Petaluma, Calif, July 9, 47; m 70, Joseph A. *Educ:* Univ Calif, Berkeley, BA, 69, PhD(entom), 73. *Honors & Awards:* Outstanding Scientist, Int Union Forestry Related Orgn, 86. *Prof Exp:* Res entomologist, Pac SW Forest & Range Exp Sta, Insect Biochem & Genetics Proj, Forest Serv, Berkeley, Calif, 79-97. *Concurrent Pos:* Teaching asst, Univ Calif, Berkeley, 70-72, res asst, 72-73; ed, J Econ Entom, 82- *Mem:* Entom Soc Can; Entom Soc Am; AAAS; Am Soc Zoologists. *Res:* Influence of population genetics and biochemical markers on host-insect interactions; toxicology of insecticides to forest insect pests; toxicological biostatistics; interactions of phytophagous insects and their hosts in the context of population genetics and biochemical diversity. *Mailing Add:* Dept Entom Burgess Hall Univ Calif Davis CA 95616. *Fax:* 707-762-1124

ROBERTSON, JAMES ALDRED, CHEMISTRY, FRUIT QUALITY. *Current Pos:* RETIRED. *Personal Data:* b Knoxville, Tenn, July 13, 31; m 54; c 2. *Educ:* Univ Tenn, BS, 53, MS, 57; Ohio State Univ, PhD(dairy technol), 62. *Prof Exp:* Chemist, M&R Dietetic Labs, Inc, 62-63; res chemist, Southern Utilization Res & Develop Div, Agr Res Serv, USDA, New Orleans, La, 63-69, res leader, Richard B Russell Agr Res Ctr, Athens, Ga, 69-93. *Mem:* Inst Food Technol. *Res:* Purification and specificity of lipase in milk; distribution of fatty acids in blood lipids; toxic fungal metabolites; composition, flavor and oxidative stability of sunflower seed and oil; methods of analysis of sunflower seed; field and storage damage of soybeans and sunflower; extending shelf life and reducing postharvest loss of fruits; postharvest factors influencing quality of stone fruit. *Mailing Add:* 180 Mockingbird Circle Athens GA 30605

ROBERTSON, JAMES ALEXANDER, SOIL FERTILITY, SOIL MANAGEMENT. *Current Pos:* Assoc prof soil sci, Univ Alta, 55-71, chair, 89-94, prof, 71-97, EMER PROF SOIL SCI, UNIV ALTA, 97- *Personal Data:* b Basswood, Man, Apr 15, 31; m 57, Margaret; c Brian & Diane. *Educ:* Univ Man, BSA, 53, MSc, 55; Purdue Univ, PhD, 63. *Concurrent Pos:* Mem, Alta Inst Agrology. *Mem:* Fel Can Soc Soil Sci (secy-treas, 58-60, pres, 72-73); Am Soc Agron; Sigma Xi. *Res:* Phosphorus sorption by Alberta soils; plant uptake of phosphorus from various soil horizons; methods of measuring phosphorus availability; soil management on long-term Breton plots; potassium status of Alberta soils. *Mailing Add:* Dept Renewable Resources Univ Alta 442 Earth Sci Bldg Edmonton AB T6G 2E3 Can

ROBERTSON, JAMES BYRON, MATHEMATICS. *Current Pos:* from asst prof to assoc prof, 66-77, PROF MATH, UNIV CALIF, SANTA BARBARA, 77- *Personal Data:* b Spiceland, Ind, Mar 29, 37; m 61; c 2. *Educ:* Mass Inst Technol, SB, 59; Ind Univ, PhD(math), 64. *Prof Exp:* From instr to asst prof math, Cornell Univ, 63-66. *Concurrent Pos:* NSF grant, 70-73; Fulbright lectr, Tbilisi, USSR, 77. *Mem:* Am Math Soc; Math Asn Am. *Res:* Ergodic theory; prediction theory. *Mailing Add:* 131 Carlo Dr Goleta CA 93117-2050

ROBERTSON, JAMES DAVID, anatomy; deceased, see previous edition for last biography

ROBERTSON, JAMES DOUGLAS, SEISMIC INTERPRETATION. *Current Pos:* Sr res geophysicist, Arco, 75-79, res dir geophys, 79-83, dep gen mgr geol res, 83-85, offshore mgr, Geophys Div, 85-86, explor staff mgr, 86-89, vpres geosci opers, 89-90, vpres explor opers, 90-95, VPRES EXPLOR, ARCO, 95- *Personal Data:* b New Rochelle, NY, Feb 15, 48; m 75, Stella Miller; c Douglas & Paul. *Educ:* Princeton Univ, BSE, 70; Univ Wis, MS, 72, PhD(geophys), 75. *Concurrent Pos:* Vis lectr, Dept Geosci, Univ Tex, Dallas, 80-84; lectr, continuing educ, Soc Explor Geophysicists, 83-85. *Mem:* Soc Explor Geophysicists (1st vpres, 91-92, pres, 94-95); Am Asn Petrol Geologists; Am Geophys Union; Soc Petrol Engrs. *Res:* Petroleum exploration and development. *Mailing Add:* Arco Int Oil & Gas Co PAI-331 2300 W Plano Pkwy Plano TX 75075

ROBERTSON, JAMES MCDONALD, OCCUPATIONAL EPIDEMIOLOGY, ENVIRONMENTAL EPIDEMIOLOGY. *Current Pos:* asst prof, 71-75, ASSOC PROF EPIDEMIOL, UNIV WESTERN ONT, 75- *Personal Data:* b Edinburgh, Scotland, Feb 27, 40; Can citizen; m 76, Judith A Warner; c Stacy, Wendy, Theodore & Andra. *Educ:* Univ Toronto, DVM, 61; Univ Pa, MSc, 66. *Prof Exp:* Res fel epidemiol, Res Coun Can, 62-65; from asst prof to assoc prof, Univ Sask, 66-71. *Concurrent Pos:* Int cancer fel epidemiol, Harvard Sch Pub Health, 71-72; sessional lectr, Univ Sask, 72-78; assoc prof epidemiol, Fac Grad Studies, Univ Western Ont, 73-, actg dir, Lab Animal Serv, 82, assoc mem, Health Care Res Unit, 86-89, dir, Occup Health & Safety Resource Ctr, 86-; consult, Environ Health Asn Carbon Black Indust, 74- & Can Portland Cement Asn, 88- *Mem:* AAAS; Am Col Epidemiol; Soc Epidemiol Res; Can Vet Med Asn. *Res:* Morbidity and mortality studies in the carbon black industry; antioxidant vitamins in cataract prevention; environmental effects on reproduction. *Mailing Add:* 829 Hickory Rd London ON N6H 2V3 Can. *Fax:* 519-661-3934; *E-Mail:* ohsman@uwoadmin.uwo.ca

ROBERTSON, JAMES MAGRUDER, ECONOMIC GEOLOGY. *Current Pos:* GEOGOLIST, WIS GEOL SURVEY, 92- *Personal Data:* b Port Clinton, Ohio, Sept 24, 43; m 70. *Educ:* Carleton Col, BA, 65; Univ Mich, Ann Arbor, MS, 68, PhD(econ geol), 72. *Prof Exp:* Asst prof geol, Mich Technol Univ, 72-74; mining geologist, NMex Bur Mines & Mineral Resources, 74-86, sr econ geologist, 86-88, assoc dir, 88-92. *Mem:* Geochem Soc; Sigma Xi; Geol Soc Am; Soc Econ Geol. *Res:* Evaluating the geology, petrology and mineral resource potential of the Precambrian rocks of New Mexico. *Mailing Add:* Wis Geol Survey 3817 Mineral Point Rd Madison WI 53705

ROBERTSON, JAMES SYDNOR, MEDICAL PHYSICS, NUCLEAR MEDICINE & GENERAL PHYSIOLOGY. *Current Pos:* RETIRED. *Personal Data:* b Richmond, Va, Nov 27, 20; m 44, Ruth Henrici; c Kathleen, John & Marion. *Educ:* Univ Minn, BS, 43, MB, 44, MD, 45; Univ Calif, PhD(physiol), 49. *Prof Exp:* From asst physiologist to assoc physiologist, Univ Calif, 46-50; biophysicist & asst physician, Brookhaven Nat Lab, 50-51, head med physics div & physician, 51-74; consult nuclear med, Mayo Clin, 75-84; dir, Human Health Div, US Dept Energy, 84-94. *Mem:* AAAS; Am Physiol Soc; Radiation Res Soc; Soc Nuclear Med; Health Physics Soc; Am Math Soc. *Res:* Electrolyte metabolism, neutron capture therapy; tracer theory; radiation dosimetry; positron emission tomography. *Mailing Add:* 18909 Tributary Lane Gaithersburg MD 20879-3409. *Fax:* 301-540-1579; *E-Mail:* jisir@aol.com

ROBERTSON, JAMES THOMAS, NEUROSURGERY. *Current Pos:* from instr to assoc prof neurosurg, 64-73, PROG DIR, PROF & CHMN, DEPT NEUROSURG, COL MED, UNIV TENN, 73-, ACTG CHAIR & PROF ANAT & NEUROBIOL, 89- *Personal Data:* b McComb, Miss, Apr 5, 31; m 52, Valerie Brower; c 6. *Educ:* Univ Tenn, Memphis, MD, 54; Am Bd Neurol Surg, cert, 62. *Prof Exp:* Teaching fel surg, Harvard Med Sch, 59-60; chief neurosurg, USAF, Travis AFB, 60-63. *Concurrent Pos:* Chief neurosurg, Regional Med Ctr, Memphis, Vet Admin Med Ctr; consult, Methodist Hosp, Memphis, LeBonheur Children's Hosp, St Joseph's Hosp, Calif Med Facil, 60-63, Jackson-Madison Co Hosp, Tenn & Semmes-Murphey Clin, 77-; vis prof var univs, 74-86; deleg, Cong Neurol Surgeons, AMA, 75-80; mem, Exec Comt, Am Med Asn Stroke Coun, 79-, chmn, Sci Prog, 83-86, deleg, 85-87, vchmn, 91; mem, Tech Rev Comt Stroke, NIH, 81; chmn, Cerebral Vasc Sect, Am Asn Neurol Surgeons, 82, mem, Exec Comt, 84; mem, Cardiovasc Comt, Am Col Surgeons, 85-88, bd goov, 87-, adv coun vasc surg, 88-91. *Mem:* Cong Neurol Surg (treas, 69-74, pres, 74-75); Am Asn Neurol Surgeons (treas, 86-89, vpres, 89-90, pres-elect, 90-91, pres, 91-92); fel Am Col Surgeons; Asn Acad Surg; Soc Univ Neurosurg (pres, 65); Am Acad Neurol Surg (treas, 81-83, secy, 83-86, pres-elect, 87, pres, 88); AMA. *Res:* Profound hypothermia; work with prostaglandins and the vasospasm phenomenon; platelet activity in experimental subarachnoid hemorrhage; pathogenesis and treatment of stoke; studies on cerebral vasospasm; author or co-author of 112 publications and one book. *Mailing Add:* 847 Monroe Rm 427 Memphis TN 38163. *Fax:* 901-448-8468

ROBERTSON, JANET PAWEL, RADIATION DAMAGE IN MATERIALS, REACTOR STRUCTURAL MATERIALS. *Current Pos:* Grad res asst, 84-91, RES STAFF MEM, OAK RIDGE NAT LAB, 91- *Personal Data:* b Oak Ridge, Tenn, Dec 24, 62; m 96, J Lee. *Educ:* Univ Tenn, BS, 85, MS, 87; Vanderbilt Univ, PhD(eng), 91. *Mem:* Am Soc Metals Int; Sigma Xi; Mat Res Soc. *Res:* Radiation damage in materials; development of fusion reactor structural materials; design of neutron irradiation experiments. *Mailing Add:* PO Box 2008 Mail Stop 6376 Oak Ridge TN 37831-6376. *E-Mail:* robertsonjp@ornl.gov

ROBERTSON, JEROLD C, PHYSICAL ORGANIC CHEMISTRY. *Current Pos:* From instr to asst prof, 61-74, ASSOC PROF ORG CHEM, COLO STATE UNIV, 74- *Personal Data:* b Provo, Utah, Mar 20, 33; m 53; c 3. *Educ:* Brigham Young Univ, BS, 58, PhD(org chem), 62. *Concurrent Pos:* Assoc chmn, Chem Dept, Colo State Univ, 73- *Res:* Mechanisms of organic reactions, specifically aromatic electrophic substitution, Baeyer-Villiger oxidation and Schmidt reaction with olefins; molecular orbital calculations on chemisorption of small molecules on metal surfaces. *Mailing Add:* 125 Fairway Lane Ft Collins CO 80525

ROBERTSON, JERRY EARL, ORGANIC CHEMISTRY, MEDICINAL CHEMISTRY. *Current Pos:* sr chemist, Riker Labs, Inc, 63-64; supvr synthetic med res, Cent Res Labs, 64-67, mgr, Synthetic Med Res Sect, 67-70, dir tech planning and coord, 70-71, dir, Chem Res Dept, 71-73, mgr, Surg Prod Dept, 74-75, gen mgr, Surg Prod Div, 75-79, div vpres surg, 79-80. *Personal Data:* b Detroit, Mich, Oct 25, 32; m 55; c 3. *Educ:* Miami Univ, BS, 54; Univ Mich, MS, 56, PhD(org chem), 59. *Prof Exp:* Sr chemist, Lakeside Labs, Colgate-Palmolive Co, Wis, 59-60, group leader cardiovasc med chem, 60-61, sect chief, 61-63. *Mem:* Am Chem Soc. *Res:* Medicinal chemistry of cardiovascular and psychopharmacologic agents. *Mailing Add:* 10 Partridge Lane St Paul MN 55127-6308

ROBERTSON, JERRY L(EWIS), PROCESS MODELING-OPTIMIZATION. *Current Pos:* Chem engr, Esso Res & Eng Co, 55-65, sr engr, 65-69, eng assoc, 69-71, sect head, 71-74, mgr process & systs eng, Centrifuge Enrichment, Exxon Nuclear Co, Inc, 74-78, sr eng assoc, 78-82, ENG ADV, EXXON RES & ENG CO, 82- *Personal Data:* b Tulsa, Okla, Oct 25, 33; m 56; c 2. *Educ:* Okla State Univ, BS, 55; Northwestern Univ, PhD(chem eng), 62. *Concurrent Pos:* Chmn, Heat Transfer & Energy Conversion Div, 86. *Mem:* Am Inst Chem Engrs; Am Chem Soc; AAAS; Am Petroleum Inst; NY Acad Sci. *Res:* Mass transfer in porous media; process design and economic optimization; plant start up; liquified natural gas processing; uranium enrichment; energy conservation/efficiency. *Mailing Add:* 20 Westwind Sand Springs OK 74063

ROBERTSON, JOHN CONNELL, ANIMAL NUTRITION. *Current Pos:* Area livestock specialist, Univ Ky, 60-63, state exten livestock specialist, 63-66, prof 66-97, ASSOC DEAN COL AGR, UNIV KY, 69-, EMER PROF ANIMAL SCI, 97- *Personal Data:* b Carrollton, Ky, Nov 24, 31; m 56; c 4. *Educ:* Univ Ky, BS, 53, MS, 57, PhD(animal nutrit), 60. *Mem:* Am Soc Animal Sci. *Res:* Interrelationships of certain minerals, mainly calcium, phosphorous, zinc, and amino acids. *Mailing Add:* 116 Eastin Rd Lexington KY 40505

ROBERTSON, JOHN DAVID, RADIOANALYTICAL CHEMISTRY, ION BEAM ANALYSIS. *Current Pos:* ASST PROF CHEM, UNIV KY, 89-, FAC ASSOC, CTR APPL ENERGY RES, 91-; CHIEF SCIENTIST, ELEMENT ANALYSIS CORP, TALLAHASSEE, FLA, 93- *Personal Data:* b Poplar Bluff, Mo, Aug 5, 60; m 83, Lois I Moffitt; c James D, Kirsten L & Timothy E. *Educ:* Univ Mo, BS, 82; Univ Md, PhD(chem), 86. *Prof Exp:* Fel, Lawrence Berkeley Lab, 87-89. *Concurrent Pos:* Lectr, Univ Calif, Berkeley, 87-89. *Mem:* Am Chem Soc; Am Phys Soc. *Res:* Development and application of surface and trace element ion-beam analysis techniques; applications include fuel science and clean fuels, trace elements in neurological disorders and thin-films and thin-film devices. *Mailing Add:* Dept Chem Univ Ky Lexington KY 40506-0055. *Fax:* 606-323-1069; *E-Mail:* jdrobson@pop.uky.edu

ROBERTSON, JOHN HARVEY, PROCESS CONTROL, MICROBIOLOGY. *Current Pos:* res microbiologist, Upjohn Co, 68-78, bioeng, 78-81, sr res microbiologist, 81-90, sr microbiologist, 90-91, TECH CONSULT, UPJOHN CO, 91- *Personal Data:* b Cheyenne, Wyo, Dec 6, 41; m 66; c Denice N & Andrea L. *Educ:* Univ Wyo, BS, 68. *Prof Exp:* Design draftsman, Dynaelectron Corp, 63 & Wyott Mfg, Wyo, 64-65; design engr & draftsman, State Wyo Engrs Off, 65-66. *Mem:* Qual Assurance Acad; Inst Environ Sci; AAAS; Parenteral Drug Asn. *Res:* Development of microbiological assay methods for new product candidates or products; development of new sterilization and process methods for production; particulate control (clean room technology). *Mailing Add:* Pharmacia & Upjohn Inc 7171 Portage Rd Kalamazoo MI 49001

ROBERTSON, JOSEPH HENRY, RANGE CONSERVATION. *Current Pos:* from assoc prof to prof agron & range mgt, 47-67, chmn dept, 52-64, range ecologist, 51-71, head Div Plant Sci, 59-65, prof range sci, 67-71, actg assoc dir, Agr Exp Sta, 75, actg assoc dean, Col Agr, 76, EMER PROF RANGE SCI, UNIV NEV, RENO, 71- *Personal Data:* b Carrington, NDak, Jan 10, 06; m 33, Yerda Mason; c 5. *Educ:* Nebr State Teachers Col, Peru, AB, 28; Univ Nebr, MS, 32, PhD(bot), 39. *Honors & Awards:* Frederic Renner Award, 77. *Prof Exp:* Teacher, pub schs, Nebr, 25-27 & Idaho, 28-30; instr biol, plant anat, bot & zool, Wis State Teachers Col, River Falls, 32-35; asst instr plant ecol, Univ Nebr, 36-39; jr range examr, Range Res, US Forest Serv, 40-42, forest ecologist, Range Exp Sta, 42-47. *Concurrent Pos:* Lectr range mgt & chief of party, WVa Univ-USAID contract team & head, Dept Range Mgt, Egerton Col, Kenya, 65-67; consult watershed revegetation, Develop & Resources Corp, Khorramabad, Iran, 71-73; prin investr native shrub proj, Foresta Inst Ocean & Mountain Studies, 74-76, mem bd dirs, 75-79; leader, watershed veg surv, Nev Div Forestry, 76 & agr collection, Arch, Nev Univ, 78; consult, Desert Res Inst, Univ Nev, 80 & Res Mgt Co, 81. *Mem:* Soc Range Mgt. *Res:* Artificial revegetation of range land; ecology of sagebrush-grass zone; domestication of native shrubs. *Mailing Add:* 920 Evans Ave Reno NV 89512-2805

ROBERTSON, KENNETH RAY, TAXONOMIC BOTANY. *Current Pos:* from asst scientist to assoc scientist, 76-84, SCIENTIST, ILL NAT HIST SURV, 84-, CUR HERBARIUM, 76- *Personal Data:* b Detroit, Mich, July 26, 41; c 1. *Educ:* Univ Kans, BS, 64, MA, 66; Wash Univ, PhD(bot), 71. *Prof Exp:* Teaching asst bot & biol, Univ Kans, 64-66; instr biol, Forest Park Community Col, 69-70; asst cur, Arnold Arboretum, Harvard Univ, 71-76. *Mem:* Am Soc Plant Taxonomists; New Eng Bot Club. *Res:* Classification and evolution of the Rosaceae; fruits and seeds, especially form, structure and dispersal; systematics of Jacquemontia (Convolvulaceae); flora of the southeastern United States. *Mailing Add:* 607 E Peabody Dr Champaign IL 61820

ROBERTSON, LESLIE EARL, STRUCTURAL ENGINEERING. *Current Pos:* DIR DESIGN & CONSTRUCT, LESLIE ROBERTSON ASSOC, 58- *Personal Data:* b Los Angeles, Calif, Feb 12, 28; m 82; c 4. *Educ:* Univ Calif, Berkeley, BS, 52. *Hon Degrees:* DSc, Univ Western Ont, 83; DEng, Rensselaer Polytech Inst, 86, Lehigh Univ, 90. *Honors & Awards:* Raymond C Reese Res Prize, Am Soc Civil Engrs, 71, State -of-the-Art Award, 88; Richard J Carrol lectr, Johns Hopkins Univ, 85; Inst Honor, Am Inst Archit, 89; John F Palmer Award, 91; Prof Gengo Matsui Prize, 93. *Prof Exp:* Struct engr, Kaiser Engrs, Oakland, Calif, 52-54, John A Blume, San Francisco, 54-57 & Raymond Int Co, NY, 57-58. *Concurrent Pos:* Chmn comt risks & liabilities, Kinetic Energies Resource Coun, 75-; chair, Coun Tall Bldgs & Urban Habitat; steering comt, Int Coun Wind Eng; mem, Cornell Eng Col Coun; invited lectr, various nat & int univs. *Mem:* Nat Acad Eng; fel Am Soc Civil Engrs; Am Concrete Inst; Am Soc Testing & Mat; Am Soc Concrete Construction; Int Asn Bridge & Struct Eng; fel NY Acad Sci; Am Inst Archit; Univs Coun Consult Engrs. *Res:* Author of over 300 technical papers. *Mailing Add:* 211 E 46th St New York NY 10017-2989

ROBERTSON, LYLE PURMAL, NUCLEAR PHYSICS, INTERMEDIATE ENERGY PHYSICS. *Current Pos:* assoc prof physics, 66-72, PROF PHYSICS, UNIV VICTORIA, BC, 72- *Personal Data:* b Vancouver, BC, Aug 15, 33; m 55; c 2. *Educ:* Univ BC, BA, 55, MA, 58, PhD(nuclear physics), 63. *Prof Exp:* Res officer reactor physics, Atomic Energy Can Ltd, 57-60; Nat

Res Coun Can overseas fel, 63-65; sr res officer nuclear physics, Rutherford High Energy Lab, Eng, 65-66. *Concurrent Pos:* Royal Soc Can Rutherford Mem fel, 63-64. *Mem:* Can Asn Physicists; Am Phys Soc. *Res:* Intermediate energy nuclear and particle physics, associated with triumf; nucleon-nucleon interaction at intermediate energy. *Mailing Add:* Dept Physics & Astron Univ Victoria Box 3055 Victoria BC V8W 3P6 Can

ROBERTSON, LYNN SHELBY, JR, soil science; deceased, see previous edition for last biography

ROBERTSON, MALCOLM SLINGSBY, MATHEMATICS. *Current Pos:* prof, 66-72, EMER PROF MATH, UNIV DEL, 72- *Personal Data:* b Brantford, Ont, July 18, 06; US citizen; m 34; c 2. *Educ:* Univ Toronto, BA, 29, MA, 30; Princeton Univ, PhD(math), 34. *Prof Exp:* Nat Res Coun fel, Univ Chicago, 34-35; instr math, Yale Univ, 35-37; from instr to prof math, Rutgers Univ, 37-66. *Mem:* Math Asn Am; Am Math Soc; Sigma Xi. *Res:* Theory of functions of complex variable; conformal mapping; univalent functions; multivalent and typically real functions. *Mailing Add:* 107 29-18th St Dawson Creek BC V1G 4N5 Can

ROBERTSON, MERTON M, EXPERIMENTAL PHYSICS, OPTICAL SIGNATORES OF MISSILE REENTRIES. *Current Pos:* RETIRED. *Personal Data:* b Scobey, Mont, Aug 16, 24; m 57, Geneva J Baum; c Mark D. *Educ:* Univ Mont, BA, 51; Univ Wis, MS, 56, PhD(physics), 60. *Prof Exp:* Proj assoc physics, Univ Wis, 60-61; mem tech staff, Sandia Lab, AEC, Dept Energy, 61-66, tech div supvr, 66-72, proj leader, 72-92, sr mem tech staff, 89-92. *Concurrent Pos:* Fulbright fel, Neth, 51-52; sci comdr, Airborn Solar Eclipse Exped, Sandia Lab, Arg, 66. *Mem:* Am Phys Soc. *Res:* Optical spectroscopy and instrumentation; interferometry; hyperfine structure; nuclear moments of radioactive atoms; optical studies of missile reentries; solar physics; plasma physics; high speed radiometry, photography and photometry; fiber optics; opto electronics. *Mailing Add:* 6608 Natalie NE Albuquerque NM 87110-1312

ROBERTSON, NAT CLIFTON, PHYSICAL CHEMISTRY, RESEARCH MANAGEMENT. *Current Pos:* RETIRED. *Personal Data:* b Atlanta, Ga, July 23, 19; m 46, Elizabeth Peck; c Henry, Amanda & Paul. *Educ:* Emory Univ, AB, 39; Princeton Univ, PhD(phys chem), 42. *Hon Degrees:* ScD, Emory Univ, 70. *Prof Exp:* Asst chem, Princeton Univ, 40-41; res assoc, Nat Defense Res Comt, 42-43; res chemist, Stand Oil Develop Co, 43-47; group leader, Celanese Corp Am, 47-51; dir petrochem dept, Nat Res Corp, 51-55; vpres & dir res, Escambia Chem Corp, 55-58; vpres res & develop, Spencer Chem Co & Spencer Chem Div, Gulf Oil Corp, 58-66; vpres res, Air Prod & Chem, Inc, 66-69, sr vpres & dir, 69-77; dir & sci adv, Marion Labs, Inc, 77-89; dir, C H Kline & Co, 77-86. *Mem:* Fel AAAS. *Res:* Kinetics of gas reactions; catalysis; physical methods of separation; free radicals. *Mailing Add:* 156 Philip Dr Princeton NJ 08540

ROBERTSON, NEIL, MATHEMATICS. *Current Pos:* PROF MATH, OHIO STATE UNIV. *Honors & Awards:* Delbert Ray Fulkerson, Am Math Soc, 94. *Mailing Add:* Math Dept Ohio State Univ 231 W 18th Ave Columbus OH 43210-1174

ROBERTSON, PHILIP ALAN, PLANT ECOLOGY. *Current Pos:* asst prof bot, 70-77, ASSOC PROF BOT, SOUTHERN ILL UNIV, CARBONDALE, 77- *Personal Data:* b Sept 9, 38; US citizen; m 67; c 2. *Educ:* Colo State Univ, BS, 62, MS, 64, PhD(plant ecol), 68. *Prof Exp:* Instr range sci, Colo State Univ, 67-68; asst prof biol, State Univ NY Col Oneonta, 68-70. *Mem:* Ecol Soc Am; AAAS; Am Inst Biol Sci; Soc Range Mgt. *Res:* Analysis of structure and function of terrestrial plant communities. *Mailing Add:* Plant Biol Dept Southern Ill Univ Carbondale IL 62901-6509

ROBERTSON, RALEIGH JOHN, ORNITHOLOGY. *Current Pos:* DIR, BIOL STA, QUEENS UNIV, 72-, PROF BIOL, 83- *Personal Data:* b Reinbeck, Iowa, Nov 8, 42; m 66; c Laurel & Tedd. *Educ:* Grinnell Col, BA, 65; Univ Iowa, MSc, 67; Yale Univ, PhD(ecol), 71. *Mem:* Am Ornithologists Union; Ecol Soc Am; Can Soc Zoologists. *Res:* Behavioral ecology of reproduction in birds including mating systems, sexual selection, parental investment and competition. *Mailing Add:* Biol Dept Queens Univ Kingston ON K7L 3N6 Can

ROBERTSON, RANDAL MCGAVOCK, physics; deceased, see previous edition for last biography

ROBERTSON, RAYMOND E(LIOT), ORGANIC CHEMISTRY, PETROLEUM CHEMISTRY. *Current Pos:* res chemist phys & org chem, 76-83, SR RES SCIENTIST & MGR EXPLOR & NEW PROD DIV, WESTERN RES INST, UNIV WYOMING RES CORP, 83- *Personal Data:* b St Louis, Mo, Aug 17, 40; m 77; c 1. *Educ:* Cent Mo State Col, BS, 62; Colo State Univ, MS, 71; Univ Wyo, PhD(chem), 76. *Prof Exp:* Res chemist org synthesis, Tretolite Co, Petrolite Corp, Webster Groves, Mo, 63-69; instr chem, Eastern Wyo Col, 75-76. *Mem:* Am Chem Soc. *Res:* Micellar catalysis; petroleum recovery and demulsification chemistry; asphalt chemistry and relationships between asphalt physical and chemical properties; acyloin condensation chemistry. *Mailing Add:* Western Res Inst 365 N Ninth St Laramie WY 82070. *Fax:* 307-721-2300

ROBERTSON, RICHARD EARL, MATERIALS SCIENCE & ENGINEERING. *Current Pos:* PROF MAT SCI & ENG, UNIV MICH, 86-, DIR, MACROMOLECULAR SCI & ENG CTR, 95- *Personal Data:* b Long Beach, Calif, Nov 12, 33; m 55, 74, Patricia L Richmond; c Christopher E & Jill K. *Educ:* Occidental Col, BA, 55; Calif Inst Technol, PhD(chem), 60. *Prof Exp:* NSF fel, Wash Univ, 59-60; phys chemist, Gen Elec Res & Develop Ctr, 60-70; staff scientist, Ford Motor Co, 70-86. *Mem:* AAAS; fel Am Phys Soc; Am Chem Soc; Sigma Xi. *Res:* Mechanical properties and structure of polymers; adhesion; structure and properties of polymers; fabrication, behavior and failure analysis of fiber composites. *Mailing Add:* Dept Mat Sci & Eng Univ Mich 2300 Hayward St Ann Arbor MI 48109-2136. *Fax:* 313-763-4788; *E-Mail:* rer@umich.edu

ROBERTSON, RICHARD THOMAS, NEUROBIOLOGY. *Current Pos:* ASST ASSOC PROF ANAT & BIOL SCI, UNIV CALIF IRVINE, 76- *Personal Data:* b Spokane, Wash, July 25, 45. *Educ:* Wash State Univ, BS, 67; Univ Calif, Irvine, MS, 68, PhD(biol sci), 72. *Prof Exp:* Res assoc neuroanat, Univ Oslo, 71-72; res scientist neurobiol, Fels Res Inst, 72-76. *Concurrent Pos:* Adj mem, Psychol Dept, Antioch Col, 73-76. *Mem:* Soc Neurosci; Am Asn Anatomists; Psychonomic Soc. *Res:* Neuroanatomical and neurophysiological studies of nonspecific sensory systems of the brainstem, thalamus and cerebral cortex. *Mailing Add:* Dept Anat & Neurobiol Univ Calif Irvine Col Med Irvine CA 92717

ROBERTSON, ROBERT, MALACOLOGY. *Current Pos:* Asst cur mollusks, Acad Natural Sci Philadelphia, 60-65, assoc cur mollusks, 65-76, chmn malacol, 69-72, cur malacol, 76-88, HON CUR MALACOL, ACAD NATURAL SCI PHILADELPHIA, 88- *Personal Data:* b Suffolk, Eng, Nov 14, 34; c 1. *Educ:* Stanford Univ, AB, 56; Harvard Univ, PhD(biol), 60. *Concurrent Pos:* Secy, Inst Malacol, 65-70, pres-elect, 70-73, pres, 73-74, co-ed-in-chief, Malacologia, 73-88. *Mem:* Fel AAAS; Am Malacol Union (pres, 83-84); Marine Biol Asn UK; Malacol Soc Japan; Australia Soc Malacol; Asian Soc Malacol. *Res:* Marine gastropods; systematics; larvae; anatomy; life histories; ecology, especially foods and reproduction of gastropods; paleontology; marine zoogeography. *Mailing Add:* Acad Natural Sci Philadelphia Dept Malacol 1900 Benjamin Franklin Pkwy Philadelphia PA 19103-1195

ROBERTSON, ROBERT GRAHAM HAMISH, NEUTRINO PHYSICS. *Current Pos:* PROF PHYSICS, UNIV WASH, 94- *Personal Data:* b Ottawa, Ont, Oct 3, 43; m 80, Peggy Dyer; c Ian. *Educ:* Oxford Univ, BA, 65; McMaster Univ, PhD(nuclear physics), 71. *Honors & Awards:* Bonner Prize, Am Phys Soc, 97. *Prof Exp:* Res assoc, Cyclotron Lab, Mich State Univ, 71-72, asst prof nuclear physics, 72-73; from asst prof to prof physics, 73-83; staff mem, Los Alamos Nat Lab, 81-88, fel, 88-94. *Concurrent Pos:* Res assoc, Princeton Univ, 75-76; Alfred P Sloan fel, 76-78; vis scientist, Chalk River Nuclear Labs, 79, Argonne Nat Lab, 80. *Mem:* Brit Inst Physics; Can Asn Physicists; fel Am Phys Soc. *Res:* Weak interactions; atomic beam magnetic resonance; nuclear astrophysics; isobaric multiplets; nuclei far from stability; neutrino mass; solar neutrinos. *Mailing Add:* Dept Physics Univ Wash Box 351560 Seattle WA 98195. *E-Mail:* rghr@u.washington.edu

ROBERTSON, ROBERT JAMES, EXERCISE PHYSIOLOGY. *Current Pos:* ASSOC PROF & DIR, HUMAN ENERGY RES LAB, DEPT HEALTH & PHYS EDUC, UNIV PITTSBURGH, 76- *Personal Data:* b Hazleton, Pa, Oct 7, 43; m 67; c 1. *Educ:* West Chester State Col, BS, 66; Univ Pittsburgh, MA, 67, PhD(health & phys educ), 73. *Prof Exp:* Asst dir, Phys Fitness Res Lab, Univ Health Ctr, 71-73; asst prof & dir, Phys Fitness Res Lab, Dept Health Educ, Nebr Ctr Health Educ, Univ Nebr, 73-76. *Concurrent Pos:* Coordr, Health & Phys Educ Prog, Univ Pittsburgh. *Mem:* Am Alliance Health Phys Educ & Recreation; Am Heart Asn; Am Col Sports Med. *Res:* Physiological and perceptual correlates of exercise stress; exercise as a therapeutic modality in coronary heart disease; energy cost of load carriage; effect of red blood cell reinfusion and bicarbonate ingestion on physical working capacity; carbohydrate metabolism. *Mailing Add:* 128 Dupont Circle Pittsburgh PA 15243-1317

ROBERTSON, ROBERT L, ENTOMOLOGY. *Current Pos:* assoc prof, 60-69, exten prof, 69-84, EMER PROF ENTOM, NC STATE UNIV, 84- *Personal Data:* b Blountsville, Ala, July 20, 25; m 65, Ruth Farmer; c Karen P (Ferrell). *Educ:* Auburn Univ, BS, 50, MS, 54. *Prof Exp:* Asst county agr agent, Auburn Univ, 50-52, res asst entom, 52-54, asst prof, 54-57; entomologist, Am Cyanamid Co, 57-58; exten entomologist, Univ Ga, 58-60. *Concurrent Pos:* Exec dir, Turfgrass Coun NC, 84-89, Inc, Ciba-Turf & Ornamentals; consult, Dow Chem USA, Am Agr Serv, Inc, Ciba-Turf & Ornamentals, 89. *Mem:* Entom Soc Am; Int Turfgrass Asn. *Res:* Insects of economic importance on tobacco, cotton, peanuts, ornamentals and turf; turf plant growth regulators. *Mailing Add:* 409 Holly Circle Cary NC 27511

ROBERTSON, ROSS ELMORE, PHYSICAL CHEMISTRY, ORGANIC CHEMISTRY. *Current Pos:* prof chem, 69-81, AOSTRA res prof, 80-82, EMER PROF CHEM, UNIV CALGARY, 81- *Personal Data:* b Kennetcook, NS, Oct 5, 15; m 45; c 4. *Educ:* Mt Allison Univ, BSc, 41, MSc, 42; McGill Univ, PhD(chem), 44. *Prof Exp:* From mem staff to prin res officer, Nat Res Coun Can, 44-69. *Mem:* Am Chem Soc; fel Chem Inst Can; fel Royal Soc Can; Royal Soc Chem. *Res:* Detailed mechanisms of solvolysis; solvent isotope effects in kinetics and equilibria; secondary deuterium isotope effects; water-oil emulsions; water purification. *Mailing Add:* 7227 Oak Crescent Calgary AB T3B 2C7 Can

ROBERTSON, SCOTT HARRISON, PLASMA PHYSICS. *Current Pos:* asst res physicist, 75-80, ASSOC RES PHYSICIST PLASMA PHYSICS, UNIV CALIF, IRVINE, 80- *Personal Data:* b Washington, DC, Nov 6, 45; m 73. *Educ:* Cornell Univ, BS, 68, PhD(appl physics), 72. *Prof Exp:* Sr res assoc plasma physics, Columbia Univ, 72-74. *Mem:* Am Phys Soc; AAAS; Inst Elec & Electronics Engrs. *Res:* Experimental investigations of the propagation of intense ion and electron beams, and their interaction with magnetically confined target plasma, particularly heating, focusing, and microwave emission due to collective processes. *Mailing Add:* Astro-Geophys/Campus Box 391 Univ Colo Boulder CO 80309

ROBERTSON, STELLA M, MONOCLONAL ANTIBODIES, IMMUNE REGULATION. *Current Pos:* ASST DIR THERAPEUT RES, ALCON LABS INC, 81- *Educ:* Johns Hopkins Univ, PhD(biol), 78. *Mailing Add:* Dept Res & Deevelop Alcon Labs Inc 6201 S Freeway Med Ctr R2-41 Ft Worth TX 76134. *Fax:* 817-551-4584

ROBERTSON, T(HOMAS) M(ILLS), ELECTRICAL ENGINEERING. *Current Pos:* PRES T M ROBERTSON INC, 86- *Personal Data:* b Tallula, Ill, Oct 1, 22; m 43, Anna Holacher; c Cheryl & Nancy. *Educ:* Univ Ill, BS, 43. *Prof Exp:* Electronic engr, Farnsworth TV & Radio, 46-47 & Kellex Corp, 47-48; sect leader labs, Vitro Corp Am, 48-53, group leader, 53-54, asst dept head, 54-57, dept head, 57-69, dept head, Vitro Labs Div, Automation Industs Inc, 69-76, dir customer rels, 76-80, vpres, Vitro Corp, 80-86. *Concurrent Pos:* Chmn anti-submarine warfare adv comt, Nat Security Indust Asn. *Mem:* Sr mem Inst Elec & Electronics Engrs; Nat Soc Prof Engrs. *Res:* Ordnance equipment; weapons and systems for undersea warfare. *Mailing Add:* 11404 Rouem Dr Potomac MD 20854

ROBERTSON, THOMAS N, MATHEMATICS. *Current Pos:* RETIRED. *Personal Data:* b St Andrews, Scotland, Oct 22, 31; US citizen; m 58; c 2. *Educ:* Univ St Andrews, BSc, 53; Col Aeronaut, MSc, 55; Univ Southern Calif, MA, 60. *Prof Exp:* Aerodynamicist, Eng Elec Co, 55-57; from instr to assoc prof math, Occidental Col, 60-79, chmn dept, 69-75 & 78-83, prof math, 79-92. *Concurrent Pos:* Danforth teacher grant, 63-64; Fulbright lectr, Turkey, 73-74. *Mem:* Math Asn Am. *Res:* Supersonic aerodynamics; numerical analysis. *Mailing Add:* 22 Yankee Point Dr Carmel Highlands CA 93923

ROBERTSON, TIM, MATHEMATICAL STATISTICS. *Current Pos:* from asst prof to assoc prof statist, 65-74, PROF STATIST, UNIV IOWA, 74- *Personal Data:* b Denver, Colo, Oct 4, 37; m 59, Joan Slater; c Kelly, Jana, Doug & Mike. *Educ:* Univ Mo, BA, 59, MA, 61, PhD(statist), 66. *Prof Exp:* Asst prof math, Cornell Col, 61-63. *Concurrent Pos:* Vis prof, Univ NC, 74-75 & Univ Calif, Davis, 83-84; Eugene Lukacs Distinguished vis prof, Bowling Green State Univ, 91-92. *Mem:* Fel Inst Math Statist; fel Am Statist Asn; Math Asn Am; Int Statist Inst. *Res:* Mathematical statistics with particular interests in the theory and applications of order restricted estimates, hypothesis tests and related problems. *Mailing Add:* Dept Statist & Actuarial Sci Univ Iowa Iowa City IA 52242. *Fax:* 319-335-3017; *E-Mail:* troberts@stat.uiowa.edu

ROBERTSON, W(ILLIAM) D(ONALD), materials science; deceased, see previous edition for last biography

ROBERTSON, WALTER VOLLEY, VERTEBRATE ZOOLOGY. *Current Pos:* from asst prof to assoc prof, 64-73, PROF BIOL & ADMIN ASST, STEPHEN F AUSTIN STATE UNIV, 73- *Personal Data:* b Malakoff, Tex, Apr 6, 31; m 57; c 5. *Educ:* Stephen F Austin State Col, BS, 51; Tex A&M Univ, MS, 59, PhD(zool), 64. *Prof Exp:* Instr zool, Tex A&M Univ, 60-64. *Mem:* Am Soc Zoologists. *Res:* Comparative vertebrate anatomy, osteology of North American clupeid fishes and brain morphology of rodents. *Mailing Add:* Dept Biol Stephen F Austin State Univ 1936 North St Nacogdoches TX 75961-3410

ROBERTSON, WILBERT JOSEPH, JR, INORGANIC CHEMISTRY. *Current Pos:* sr staff engr, Nuclear Div, 67-70, RES PROJ CHEMIST, TECH DIV, KERR-McGEE CORP, 70- *Personal Data:* b Washington, DC, Mar 28, 28; m 55; c 4. *Educ:* George Washington Univ, BS, 50; Univ Wis, PhD(inorg chem), 55. *Prof Exp:* Chemist, Uranium Div, Mallinckrodt Chem Works, 55-60, res supvr uranium processing, 60-66, chemist, Opers Div, 66-67. *Mem:* Am Chem Soc; Am Nuclear Soc; Sigma Xi. *Res:* Hydrometallurgy; solvent extraction; mineral processing and purification; extractive metallurgy. *Mailing Add:* 7320 Hammond Ave Kerr-McGee Corp Oklahoma City OK 73132-5716

ROBERTSON, WILLIAM, IV, RESEARCH ADMINISTRATION. *Current Pos:* PROG DIR, ANDREW W MELLON FOUND, 79- *Personal Data:* b Glen Ridge, NJ, Sept 12, 43; m 70, Alicia Sorenson; c Paige & William. *Educ:* Parsons Col, BS, 66; Sam Houston State Univ, MA, 69. *Prof Exp:* Tutor biol, Parsons Col, 66-67; res technician biochem, Med Ctr, NY Univ, 67-68; sci secy, Comt Water Qual Criteria, Nat Acad Sci, 71-72, staff officer, Environ Studies Bd, 72-73, tech asst, Comn Natural Resources, 73-78, exec secy, Int Environ Progs Comt, 74-78. *Mem:* Am Soc Limnol & Oceanog; Ecol Soc Am. *Res:* Research administration. *Mailing Add:* Andrew W Mellon Found 140 E 62nd St New York NY 10021

ROBERTSON, WILLIAM O, PEDIATRICS, MEDICAL ADMINISTRATION. *Current Pos:* from asst dean to assoc dean, 63-72, assoc prof, 63-72, PROF PEDIAT, SCH MED, UNIV WASH, 72- *Personal Data:* b New York, NY, Nov 24, 25; m 52; c 5. *Educ:* Univ Rochester, BA, 46, MD, 49. *Prof Exp:* From instr to assoc prof pediat, Col Med, Ohio State Univ, 56-63, asst dean, 62-63. *Concurrent Pos:* Consult, US Army Madigen Hosp, 64-72. *Mem:* AAAS; Am Med Writers' Asn; Am Asn Poison Control Ctr (treas, 63-64). *Res:* Medical malpractice and risk management; nutrition; accidental poisoning; education. *Mailing Add:* Children's Hosp-Med Ctr PO Box 5371 Seattle WA 98105-0371

ROBERTSON, WILLIAM VAN BOGAERT, BIOCHEMISTRY, NUTRITION. *Current Pos:* RETIRED. *Personal Data:* b New York, NY, Sept 15, 14; m 41, 68, Maria E Tejera; c William Jr, Wilhelmina L & Jose R. *Educ:* Stevens Inst Technol, ME, 34; Univ Freiburg, PhD(chem), 37. *Prof Exp:* Res chemist, Mass Gen Hosp, Boston, 38-41; res fel, Nat Cancer Inst, 41-44; res assoc, Univ Chicago, 44-45; asst prof exp med, Univ Vt, 45-48, assoc prof biochem & exp med, 48-52, prof biochem, 52-61; from assoc prof to emer prof biochem, Stanford Univ, 61-87. *Concurrent Pos:* Dir res & educ, Children's Hosp, Stanford, 62-79; vis prof biochem, Univ del Valle, Cali, Colombia, 67-68 & Univ Saigon, Viet-Nam, 74; consult nutrit, Nat Inst Child Health & Human Develop, Bethesda, Md, 78; prog mgr human nutrit, NSF, 79-81, prog dir metab biol, 81-87. *Mem:* Fel AAAS; Am Chem Soc; Sigma Xi; Am Soc Biol Chemists; Am Soc Clin Nutrit. *Res:* Biochemistry of connective tissue metabolism of collagen and glycosaminoglycans; nutritional biochemistry; actions of vitamin C. *Mailing Add:* 10580 Hidden Mesa Pl Monterey CA 93940-6627

ROBERTS-PICHETTE, PATRICIA RUTH, ECOLOGY. *Current Pos:* sr prog officer, Multilateral Br, 79-82, SR POLICY ANALYST, AMERICAS BR, CEDA, 89- *Personal Data:* b Hamilton, NZ, Dec 22, 30; m 67; c 2. *Educ:* Univ NZ, BSc, 53, MSc, 54; Duke Univ, PhD, 57. *Prof Exp:* Asst prof biol, Pfeiffer Col, 57-58; from asst prof to assoc prof, Univ NB, 58-67; consult & pvt researcher, 67-73; exec secy, Man & Biosphere Prog Can, liaison & coord directorate, Environ Can, 73-79; dep secy to JAC, CGIAR, Rome, Italy, 82-89. *Concurrent Pos:* Consult, Dept Natural Resources, Prov NB, 66-68 & Dept Agr, 68-71, Can Dept Forestry, 68 & Environ Can, 71-72. *Mem:* AAAS; Ecol Soc Am; Can Bot Asn. *Res:* Community ecology; vegetation and floras of specific regions; plant succession and distribution; pollution biology. *Mailing Add:* 430 Besserer St Ottawa ON K1N 6C1 Can

ROBERTSTAD, GORDON WESLEY, BACTERIOLOGY. *Current Pos:* dir health related prog, 75-81, prof microbiol, 68-88, EMER PROF, UNIV TEX, EL PASO, 88- *Personal Data:* b Madison, Wis, Sept 29, 23; m 48; c 4. *Educ:* Univ Wis, BS, 49, MS, 51; Colo State Univ, PhD(bact), 59. *Prof Exp:* Instr bact, Univ Wyo, 49-50; proj asst, Univ Wis, 51-52; instr bact, Univ Wyo, 52-57, asst prof, 57-59, assoc prof microbiol, 59-64; prof bact & head dept, SDak State Univ, 64-68. *Concurrent Pos:* NIH fel, Commun Dis Ctr, Atlanta, Ga, 62-63. *Mem:* Fel Am Acad Microbiol; Am Soc Allied Health Professions; Sigma Xi; Mycol Soc Am; Int Soc Human & Animal Mycol. *Res:* Antigenic studies of Vibrio fetus; taxonomy of microaerophilic Actionomycetes; epidemiology of dermatophytic and systemic fungi; aeromycology. *Mailing Add:* 120 Coupland Ct El Paso TX 79922

ROBERTUS, JON DAVID, X-RAY CRYSTALLOGRAPHY OF PROTEINS, DRUG DESIGN. *Current Pos:* PROF BIOCHEM, UNIV TEX, 74- *Personal Data:* b Minneapolis, Minn, Mar 1, 45; m 71; c 3. *Educ:* Univ Minn, BA, 67; Univ Calif, San Diego, PhD(biol), 72. *Prof Exp:* Postdoctoral fel, Lab Molecular Biol, MRC, 72-74. *Mem:* Am Crystallog Asn; Protein Soc; AAAS; Am Soc Biochem & Molecular Biol. *Res:* Elucidating structure and mode of actions of proteins of biomedical importance; structure based drug design, X-ray diffraction and protein engineering. *Mailing Add:* Chem & Biochem Dept Univ Tex Austin TX 78712. *Fax:* 512-471-8696; *E-Mail:* jrobertus@mail.utexas.edu

ROBEY, FRANK A, INFLAMMATION, PEPTIDE SYNTHESIS. *Current Pos:* CHIEF, PEPTIDE & IMMUNOCHEM UNIT, NAT INST DENT RES, NIH, BETHESDA, MD, 86- *Personal Data:* b June 15, 50; m 77, Pamela Gehron; c Jillian & Chuck. *Educ:* Boston Col, BS, 72; Cath Univ, PhD(phys chem), 77. *Prof Exp:* Res chemist, Molecular Pharmacol Lab, Div Biochem & Biophys, Ctr Drugs & Biologics, Food & Drug Admin, 79-86. *Concurrent Pos:* Adj assoc prof, George Washington Univ Med Ctr; fac fel, Barnett Inst Mat Sci, Northeastern Univ. *Mem:* Am Peptide Soc; Am Chem Soc; Am Soc Biochem & Molecular Biol. *Res:* Synthetic vaccines, inflammation. *Mailing Add:* NIDR NIH Bldg 30 Rm 211 9000 Rockville Pike Bethesda MD 20892-0001

ROBEY, PAMELA GEHRON, BONE CELL BIOCHEMISTRY, CELL BIOLOGY. *Current Pos:* Sr staff fel, 83-87, BIOLOGIST, NAT INST DENT HEALTH, NIH, 87- *Personal Data:* b Oct 31, 52; m; c 2. *Educ:* Cath Univ Am, PhD(biol), 79. *Mem:* Am Soc Bone & Mineral Res; Am Soc Biochem & Molecular Biol; Am Soc Cell Biol. *Res:* Matrix protein biochemistry. *Mailing Add:* Bone Res Br Bldg 30 Rm 106 NIDR NIH 9000 Rockville Pike Bethesda MD 20892-0001. *Fax:* 301-480-2880

ROBEY, ROGER LEWIS, SYNTHETIC ORGANIC CHEMISTRY. *Current Pos:* SR ORG CHEMIST, ELI LILLY & CO, 74- *Personal Data:* b Fairmont, WVa, June 18, 46; m 68; c 2. *Educ:* Marietta Col, BS, 68; Princeton Univ, MS, 71, PhD(org chem), 72. *Prof Exp:* Assoc, Ohio State Univ, 72-74. *Mem:* Am Chem Soc. *Res:* Organic synthesis; synthesis of heterocycles. *Mailing Add:* 4831 Brentridge Pkwy Greenwood IN 46143-9368

ROBIE, NORMAN WILLIAM, PHARMACOLOGY. *Current Pos:* asst prof, 77-79, ASSOC PROF PHARMACOL, LA STATE UNIV MED CTR, 79- *Personal Data:* b Washington, DC, Jan 21, 42. *Educ:* Auburn Univ, BS, 64, MS, 69; Med Univ SC, PhD(pharmacol), 72. *Prof Exp:* Fel clin pharmacol, Sch Med, Emory Univ, 72-75; asst prof pharmacol, Univ Tex Health Sci Ctr, San Antonio, 75-77. *Mem:* Am Soc Pharmacol & Exp Therapeut. *Res:* Autonomic cardiovascular pharmacology. *Mailing Add:* Dept Pharmacol La State Univ Med Ctr 1901 Perdido St New Orleans LA 70112

ROBILLARD, GEOFFREY, CHEMICAL ENGINEERING. *Current Pos:* RETIRED. *Personal Data:* b Niagara Falls, NY, Feb 25, 23; m 63; c 2. *Educ:* Mass Inst Technol, BS, 44, MS, 47. *Prof Exp:* Chemist, Carbide & Carbon Chem Co Div, Union Carbide Corp, 47-52; res engr, Calif Inst Technol, 52-53, sect chief, 53-59, div chief, 59-63, dep proj mgr, 63-68, mgr, Eng Mech Div, 68-73, dep asst lab dir, 73-76, asst lab dir planning & rev, 76-78, asst lab dir for energy & technol appln, Jet Propulsion Lab, 78-85, asst lab dir for eng & review, 85-88. *Mem:* Am Inst Aeronaut & Astronaut; Sigma Xi. *Res:* Propulsion; structures; materials; system design and development; Ranger, Mariner & Voyager projects; energy, safety, reliability and quality assurance. *Mailing Add:* PO Box 842 Bodega Bay CA 94923

ROBILLARD, PAUL D, HYDROLOGY & WATER RESOURCES. *Current Pos:* ASSOC PROF AGR & BIOENG, PA STATE UNIV, 87- *Personal Data:* b Leominster, Mass, July 5, 46. *Educ:* Univ Notre Dame, BS, 68, MS, 75; Cornell Univ, PhD(agr eng), 86. *Honors & Awards:* Gunlogson Award, Am Soc Agr Engrs, 95. *Prof Exp:* Civil engr, Peace Corps, 68-70; teacher, Ward Law Sch, 71-72; res officer, Canberra, Australia, 76-77; res assoc, Cornell Univ, 77-86. *Concurrent Pos:* Fulbright scholar, Coun Int Exchange Scholars, 96. *Mem:* Am Soc Agr Engrs; Am Soc Civil Engrs; Am Water Resources. *Mailing Add:* Dept Civil Eng Pa State Univ 226 Agr Eng Bldg University Park PA 16802. *Fax:* 814-863-1031; *E-Mail:* pdr1@psu.edu

ROBILLIARD, GORDON ALLAN, MARINE ECOLOGY, RESOURCE DAMAGE ASSESSMENT METHODOLOGY. *Current Pos:* SR CONSULT & VPRES, ENTRIX INC, 85- *Personal Data:* b Victoria, BC, May 19, 43; m 72; c 2. *Educ:* Univ Victoria, BSc, 65; Univ Wash, MS, 67, PhD(zool), 71. *Prof Exp:* Sr aquatic ecologist, Woodward-Clyde Consults, 71-85. *Concurrent Pos:* Mem comt on appl ecol theory to environ problems, Nat Acad Comn Life Sci, 84-86. *Mem:* Ecol Soc Am; Sigma Xi. *Res:* Ecology and feeding habits of opisthobranch molluscs; ecological consequences of predation by fish and large motile invertebrates in marine benthic communities; polar marine ecology; methods to evaluate the value of natural resources damaged by man's activities. *Mailing Add:* 3214 Kirby Lane Walnut Creek CA 94598-3910

ROBIN, ALLEN MAURICE, PROJECT MANAGEMENT. *Current Pos:* RETIRED. *Personal Data:* b Chicago, Ill, Jul 10, 34; m 60; c 2. *Educ:* Univ Ill, BS, 57; Univ Southern Calif, MS, 66. *Prof Exp:* Sr chem engr, VELSICOL Chem Corp, 56-62; sr thermo engr, Gen Dynamics Corp, Pomona, Calif, 62-65; sr chem engr, res chem engr, sr res chem engr & technologist, Montebello Res Lab, Texaco Inc, 65-83, res mgr, 65-96. *Mem:* Am Inst Chem Eng. *Res:* Oil/coal/core gasification; high temperature desulfurization/ filtration of fuel gas; waste gasification liquefaction. *Mailing Add:* Texaco Inc 329 N Durfee Ave South El Monte CA 91733

ROBIN, BURTON HOWARD, ORGANIC CHEMISTRY. *Current Pos:* RETIRED. *Personal Data:* b Chicago, Ill, Mar 19, 26; m 47, 87; c 3. *Educ:* Roosevelt Univ, BS, 48; Univ Chicago, MS, 49. *Prof Exp:* Res chemist, Corn Prod Co, 49-51; res chemist, Swift & Co, 51-57; res chemist, Visking Corp, 58-59; res chemist, Nalco Chem Co, 59-63; chmn, Dept Phys Sci, Kennedy-King Col, 69-74, from assoc prof to prof chem, 63-93. *Mem:* AAAS; Am Chem Soc; Sigma Xi. *Res:* Coagulants; surfactants; corrosion and rust inhibitors; flotation agents; vinyl polymers; emulsion polymerization; fats and fatty acids and derivatives; qualitative analysis; physical science. *Mailing Add:* 5648 S Harper Chicago IL 60637

ROBIN, EUGENE DEBS, PHYSIOLOGY, RISK & BENEFIT ANALYSIS. *Current Pos:* prof med & physiol, Sch Med, Stanford Univ, 70-88, actg chmn, Dept Med, 71-73, actg chmn & curric & acad consult, Dept Physiol, 80-88, EMER PROF MED & PHYSIOL, SCH MED, STANFORD UNIV, 88- *Personal Data:* b Detroit, Mich, Aug 23, 19; m, Jane Nobel; c Anna (Lundstrom) & Donald. *Educ:* George Washington Univ, SB, 46, SM, 47, MD, 51. *Prof Exp:* Res fel med, Harvard Med Sch, 52-53; sr asst resident med serv, Peter Bent Brigham Hosp, Boston, 53-54; asst med, Harvard Med Sch, 54-55, instr, 55-58, assoc, 58-59; from assoc prof to prof, Sch Med, Univ Pittsburgh, 59-70. *Concurrent Pos:* Asst, Peter Bent Brigham Hosp, 52-53; chief med resident, 54-55, jr assoc, 55-57, assoc, 57-59, assoc dir, Cardiovasc Training Prog, 58-59; chmn pulmonary adv comt, Nat Heart & Lung Inst, 71-74; consult, Issues Med Ethics, India. *Mem:* Am Physiol Soc; Am Soc Clin Invest; Am Thoracic Soc (pres, 70-71); Am Col Physicians. *Res:* Clinical physiology; intracellular acid-base metabolism; intracellular gas exchange; comparative physiology and biochemistry; medical risk benefit analysis. *Mailing Add:* PO Box 1185 Trinidad CA 95570

ROBIN, MICHAEL, SYNTHETIC ORGANIC CHEMISTRY, TRAINING SCIENTIST & ENGINEERS. *Current Pos:* TECH TRAINING CONSULT (SCIENTIST & ENGRS), ROBIN ASSOC, SCOTCH PLAINS, NJ, 91- *Personal Data:* b New York, NY, May 17, 19; m 43, Beatrice Janoer; c Tina E & Alan L. *Educ:* City Col New York, BS, 40; NY Univ, ChE, 44; Brooklyn Col, MS, 50. *Prof Exp:* Sr org chemist org & pharmaceut res & develop, Nepera Chem Co, Inc, NY, 46-51; res & develop chemist metallic soap, Nuodex Prod Co, Inc, NJ, 51-53; chief chemist org & pharmaceut, Simpson Labs, Simpson Coal & Chem Co, 53-56; group leader chem org res & develop, Catalin Corp Div, 56-68, mgr chem prod div lab, 68-73, plant mgr fine chem dept, 73-74, mgr, Mfg Servs, Ashland Chem Co, Ashland Oil & Refining Co, 74-76; tech dir, Ctr Prof Advan, East Brunswick, NJ, 77-86, vpres tech dir & dir inplant training worldwide, 86-91. *Mem:* AAAS; Am Chem Soc; Am Inst Chem; Soc Plastics Eng; NY Acad Sci; Am Inst Chem Engrs. *Res:* Fine organic and pharmaceutical product and process research and development; organic synthesis; antioxidants and stabilizers for organic materials. *Mailing Add:* 1508 Ashbrook Dr Scotch Plains NJ 07076

ROBINETT, RICHARD W, SPIN-POLARIZATION PHENOMENOLOGY, COLLIDER PHENOMENOLOGY. *Current Pos:* ASSOC PROF PHYSICS, PA STATE UNIV, 86- *Personal Data:* b Bayamon, PR, Oct 2, 53; m 84, Sarah Q Malone; c Katherine & James. *Educ:* Univ Minn, BA, 75, PhD(physics), 81. *Prof Exp:* Res assoc, Univ Wis-Madison, 81-83, Univ Mass, Amherst, 83-86. *Concurrent Pos:* Vis res scientist, Argonne Nat Labs, 94-95. *Mem:* Am Phys Soc; Am Asn Physics Teachers. *Mailing Add:* Dept Physics Pa State Univ University Park PA 16802. *E-Mail:* rick@phys. psu.edu

ROBINETTE, HILLARY, JR, CHEMISTRY. *Current Pos:* PRES, ROBINETTE RES LABS, INC, 52- *Personal Data:* b Wilmington, Del, Jan 27, 13; m 34; c 2. *Educ:* Temple Univ, AB, 34. *Prof Exp:* Res chemist, Rohm and Haas Co, Pa, 33-39; pres, W H & F Jordon Jr Co, 39-41; mem res staff, Com Solvents Corp, Ind, 41-42; mgr mkt develop, Publicker Industs, Inc, Pa, 45-48; res dir, Amalgamated Chem Corp, 48-52. *Mem:* AAAS; Am Asn Textile Chem & Colorists; Am Soc Testing & Mat; fel Am Inst Chemists. *Res:* Organic chemistry; textile chemicals. *Mailing Add:* 10333 Campana Dr Sun City AZ 85351-1098

ROBINETTE, MARTIN SMITH, AUDIOLOGY. *Current Pos:* assoc prof audiol, 74-80, ASSOC PROF COMMUN, UNIV UTAH, 80- *Personal Data:* b Sacramento, Calif, Sept 18, 39; m 65; c 3. *Educ:* Univ Utah, BS, 65, MS, 67; Wayne State Univ, PhD(audiol), 70. *Prof Exp:* Asst prof audiol, Univ Wyo, 70-74. *Mem:* Acoust Soc Am; Int Soc Audiol; Am Speech & Hearing Asn. *Res:* Lateralization of sound image from intensity cues; binaural detection ability at large interaural intensity differences; test for functional hearing loss; diplacusis. *Mailing Add:* 2519 E River Rd NE Rochester MN 55906

ROBINOVITCH, MURRAY R, ORAL BIOLOGY, EXPERIMENTAL PATHOLOGY & PERIODONTOLOGY. *Current Pos:* From instr to assoc prof, 66-75, actg chmn, Dept Oral Biol, 74-76, MEM, CTR RES ORAL BIOL, UNIV WASH, 71-, PROF ORAL BIOL, 75-, CHMN DEPT, 82-, ADJ PROF, DEPT PERIODONT, 82- *Personal Data:* b Brandon, Man, Jan 17, 39; m 64. *Educ:* Univ Minn, BS, 59, DDS, 61; Univ Wash, PhD(salivary gland protein synthesis), 67, cert periodont, 81. *Mem:* Am Soc Cell Biol; Am Dent Asn; Int Asn Dent Res; Am Asn Oral Biologists; Am Acad Periodont. *Res:* Protein synthesis in salivary and other exocrine glands; secretion and the secretory product; anti-HIV-1 activity of secretions. *Mailing Add:* 12514 42nd Ave NE Seattle WA 98125. *Fax:* 206-685-3162

ROBINOW, CARL FRANZ, MICROBIOLOGY. *Current Pos:* from assoc prof to prof, 49-91, EMER PROF MICROBIOL & IMMUNOL, UNIV WESTERN ONT, 91- *Personal Data:* b Hamburg, Ger, Apr 10, 09; m 38; c 2. *Educ:* Univ Hamburg, MD, 35. *Prof Exp:* Researcher, Copenhagen, Denmark, 35-37, St Bartholomew's Hosp, London, 37-40 & Strangeways Lab, Cambridge Univ, 40-47; vis lectr, US univs, 47-49. *Mem:* Am Soc Microbiol; Bot Soc Am; fel Royal Soc Can. *Res:* Cytology of bacteria and fungi. *Mailing Add:* Health Sci Ctr Dept Microbiol & Immunol Univ Western Ontario London ON N6A 5C1 Can

ROBINOW, MEINHARD, NUTRITION, PEDIATRICS. *Current Pos:* prof, 79-81, clin prof, 81-87, EMER CLIN PROF PEDIAT, SCH MED, WRIGHT STATE UNIV, 82- *Personal Data:* b Hamburg, Ger, May 19, 09; US citizen; m 44; c 3. *Educ:* Hamburg, Ger, MD, 35. *Prof Exp:* Asst prof pediat, Med Col, Augusta, Ga, 38-39 & 42-43; dir phys growth, Fels Res Inst, 39-42; prof pediat, Sch Med, Univ Va, 75-79. *Concurrent Pos:* From 1st lieutenant to Major, US Army Med Corps, 43-46. *Mem:* Am Acad Pediat; Am Pediat Soc; Am Soc Human Genetics; Am Nutrit Inst; AAAS; AMA. *Res:* Dysmorphology and genetics - delineation of new malformation syndromes; nutritional anthropometry. *Mailing Add:* 1735 Chapel St Wright State Univ PO Box 927 Dayton OH 45404-1815

ROBINOWITZ, CAROLYN BAUER, EDUCATION, CHILD & ADOLESCENT PSYCHIATRY. *Current Pos:* PROF, SCH MED, GEORGETOWN UNIV, 95- *Personal Data:* b Brooklyn, NY, July 15, 38; m 62, Max; c Mark & David. *Educ:* Wellesley Col, AB, 59; Wash Univ Sch Med, MD, 64. *Honors & Awards:* Bowis Award, Am Col Psychiatrists, 94. *Prof Exp:* Training specialist, Div Manpower & Training Progs, NIMH, 68-69, chief, Physician Training Sect, 69-70; chief, Child Psychiat Ambulatory Serv, Univ Miami Sch Med, 70-72; dir educ, Dept Psychiat Behav Sci, George Washington Univ Med Ctr, 72-74, training prog dir, Psychiatrist as a Teacher Proj, 75-76; dir, Off Educ, Am Pshchiat Asn, 76-87, dept med dir, 76-86, sr dep med dir, 86-95. *Concurrent Pos:* Ment health career develop award, NIMH, 66-70; coordr, Child Psychiat Training, Nat Ctr Ment Health Serv Training & Res, St Elizabeth's Hosp, 69-70; dir, Pediat-Psychiat Liason Prog, Univ Miami Sch Med, 70-72; dir psychiat, Mailman Ctr Child Develop, 70-72 & chief child psychiat training & coord med sch educ, Dept Psychiat, 70-72; proj dir, Comm Ment Health Ctr,

Jackson Mem Hosp, Univ Miami, 72; consult field fac, Goddard Col, 73-75; training prog dir, Educ Develop Psychiat Educr Proj, 77-84; training proj dir, Curric Develop Geriat Psychiat Proj, 82-83; prin investr, Alcohol & Drug Abuse Educ Proj, Nat Inst Drug Abuse-Nat Inst Alcohol Abuse & Alcoholism, 85-87; training prog dir, Human Immunodefiency Virus/Acquired Immuno Deficiency Syndrome Educ Proj, 86-; prin investr, State-Univ Collaboration Proj, 89-94. *Mem:* Fel Am Psychiat Asn; fel Am Col Psychiatrists; Group Advan Psychiat (pres, 89-91); Am Bd Psychiat & Neurol (vpres, 85, secy, 84, pres, 86). *Mailing Add:* Assoc Dean Students Sch Med Georgetown Univ 3900 Reservoir Rd NW Washington DC 20007. *Fax:* 202-682-0432

ROBINS, CHARLES RICHARD, ICHTHYOLOGY. *Current Pos:* from asst prof to prof, 56-69, chmn dept marine sci, 61-63, MAYTAG PROF MARINE BIOL, SCH MARINE & ATMOSPHERIC SCI, UNIV MIAMI, 69-, CUR FISHES, 66-, PROF ICHTHYOLOGY, 74-, CHMN, DIV BIOL & LIVING RESOURCES, 78-, ACTG DEAN, ROSENTIEL SCH MARINE & ATMOSPHERIC SCI, 81- *Personal Data:* b Harrisburg, Pa, Nov 25, 28; m 65; c 3. *Educ:* Cornell Univ, BA, 50, PhD(ichthyol), 54. *Prof Exp:* Asst gen zool, Cornell Univ, 50-51, ichthyol & taxon, 51-54. *Concurrent Pos:* Res assoc, Cornell Univ, 52; ed, Bull Marine Sci & Gulf & Caribbean, 61-62; mem panel syst biol, NSF, 66-69; proj & prog rev comn, Marine Lab, Duke Univ, 68-70; comt inshore & estuarine pollution, Hoover Found, 69; mem ecol adv comt, Environ Protection Agency, 75-78. *Mem:* AAAS; Am Soc Ichthyologists & Herpetologists (vpres, 64 & pres-elect, 82); Am Soc Syst Zool; Am Soc Zool; Am Inst Fishery Res Biol. *Res:* Taxonomy, morphology, ecology and behavior of fishes. *Mailing Add:* 448 N 1500 Rd Lawrence KS 66049-9190

ROBINS, ELI, psychiatry, neurology; deceased, see previous edition for last biography

ROBINS, JACK, PHYSICAL CHEMISTRY, POLYMER CHEMISTRY. *Current Pos:* RETIRED. *Personal Data:* b Roselle, NJ, Feb 17, 19; m 49, Lottie Levin; c Arthur & Larraine. *Educ:* City Col New York, BS, 40; Univ Buffalo, MA, 48; Polytech Inst Brooklyn, PhD(phys chem), 59. *Prof Exp:* Chemist, Vandium Corp Am, 44-48; chemist, Am Electrometal Corp, 48-49; chemist, Bd Transport, NY, 49-54; chemist, Wilmot & Cassidy, Inc, 55-56; res chemist, ICI Am, Inc, 59-75; res chemist, Atlas Powder Co, 75-82, consult, 82-84. *Mem:* Am Chem Soc. *Res:* Analytical chemistry; inorganic solutions; gas chromatography; thermodynamics and material properties; microcomputers, software, hardware and interfacing with instruments; scientific programmer. *Mailing Add:* 139-B Cistus Plaza Cranbury NJ 08512

ROBINS, JANIS, POLYMER CHEMISTRY, CATALYSIS. *Current Pos:* PRES, CATALYTIC CROSSLINK, INC, 90- *Personal Data:* b Riga, Latvia, Aug 3, 25; nat US; m 51; c Baiba, Daina, Laila & Zaiga. *Educ:* Univ Wash, Seattle, BS, 52, PhD(chem), 57. *Hon Degrees:* Dr Chem, Latian Acad Sci, 96. *Honors & Awards:* Award of Sci, Merit, Am Foundrymen's Soc, 91. *Prof Exp:* Anal chemist, Wash Farmers Coop, 52, State Dept Agr, Wash, 52-53; anal chemist, Am-Marietta Co, 54, res chemist, 55-57; res chemist, Minn Mining & Mfg Co, 57-65; res assoc, Archer Daniels Midland Co, 65-67, Ashland Chem Co, 67-72; sr res specialist, 3M Co, 72-80, div scientist, 80-90. *Concurrent Pos:* Asst prof chem, Macalester Col, 60-65. *Mem:* Am Chem Soc; Am Foundrymens Soc; Adhesion Soc; Chem Soc Latvia. *Res:* Physical organic chemistry; polymer synthesis; metal ion catalysis; polyurethane, furan, epoxy and phenolic resin technology; foundry binder technology; adhesives technology. *Mailing Add:* Catalytic Crosslink Inc 11 Ludlow Ave St Paul MN 55108-1914. *Fax:* 612-736-2264

ROBINS, MORRIS JOSEPH, BIO-ORGANIC CHEMISTRY, NUCLEIC ACID COMPONENTS-ANALOGUES. *Current Pos:* prof, 87-89, J REX GOATES PROF CHEM, BRIGHAM YOUNG UNIV, 89- *Personal Data:* b Nephi, Utah, Sept 28, 39; m 60, 73, Jackie A Robinson; c Dayne M, Diane, Douglas W, Debra, Dale C. Mark K, Janetta A & Tiffany A. *Educ:* Univ Utah, BA, 61; Ariz State Univ, PhD(org chem), 65. *Prof Exp:* Cancer res scientist biochem, Roswell Park Mem Inst, 65-66; res assoc org chem, Univ Utah, 66-69; from asst prof to prof chem, Univ Alta, 69-86. *Concurrent Pos:* Mem adv comt chemother & hemat, Am Cancer Soc, 77-80; vis prof med chem, Univ Utah, 81-82; mem grant panel, Nat Cancer Inst Can, 83-86; adj prof chem, Univ Alta, 87-88; adj prof med microbiol & immunol, 88-; mem, AIDS & Related Res Study Sect 4, NIH, 95- *Mem:* Am Chem Soc; Am Asn Cancer Res; Int Soc Antiviral Res; Int Soc Nucleic Acids Chem. *Res:* Chemistry of nucleic acid components, nucleoside analogues and related biomolecules; transformations of natural product nucleosides, mechanism-based enzyme inhibitors, anticancer and antiviral agents. *Mailing Add:* Chem Biochem Dept Brigham Young Univ Provo UT 84602-5700. *Fax:* 801-378-5474

ROBINS, NORMAN ALAN, CHEMICAL ENGINEERING, MATHEMATICS. *Current Pos:* PRES, NORMAN A ROBINS CONSULT, 91- *Personal Data:* b Chicago, Ill, Nov 19, 34; m 56; c 2. *Educ:* Mass Inst Technol, BS, 56, MS, 56; Ill Inst Technol, PhD, 72. *Prof Exp:* Metallurgist, Inland Steel Co, 56-60, res metallurgist, 60-62, asst mgr, Res Dept, 62-67, assoc mgr, 67-72, dir process res, 72-77, vpres res, 77-84, vpres technol assessment, 84-86, vpres tech assessment & strategic planning, 86-87, vpres strategic planning, 87-91. *Mem:* Am Inst Mining, Metall & Petrol Engrs; Am Inst Chem Engrs; Math Asn Am. *Res:* Process research and computer process control. *Mailing Add:* Norman A Robins Consult 1507 E 53rd St Suite 115 Chicago IL 60615. *Fax:* 312-697-5165; *E-Mail:* narconsult@.com

ROBINS, RICHARD DEAN, ORGANIC CHEMISTRY. *Current Pos:* RES CHEMIST, LUBRIZOL CORP, 69- *Personal Data:* b North Manchester, Ind, Nov 19, 42; m 69. *Educ:* Manchester Col, BA, 64; Ohio State Univ, MS, 66, PhD(org chem), 68. *Mem:* Am Chem Soc. *Res:* Physical organic and polymer chemistry. *Mailing Add:* 29400 Lakeland Blvd Wickliffe OH 44092

ROBINSON, ALBERT DEAN, GENETICS, MYCOLOGY. *Current Pos:* from asst prof to assoc prof genetics, 68-80, assoc prof, 80-83, PROF BIOL, STATE UNIV NY COL POTSDAM, 83- *Personal Data:* b Sherman Mills, Maine, Mar 28, 39; m 61; c 2. *Educ:* Univ Maine, BA, 61; Johns Hopkins Univ, MAT, 62; Univ Iowa, PhD(bot), 68. *Prof Exp:* Teacher high sch, Nyack, NY, 62-65. *Concurrent Pos:* Dept chmn, State Univ NY Col Potsdam, 86. *Mem:* Am Genetics Asn; Am Inst Biol Sci; Am Soc Human Genetics; Nat Asn Biol Teachers; Sigma Xi. *Res:* meiosis in chives. *Mailing Add:* Dept Biol Potsdam Col State Univ NY Potsdam NY 13676

ROBINSON, ALFRED GREEN, PETROLEUM CHEMISTRY. *Current Pos:* chemist, Tenn Eastman Co Div, 55-58, chemist, Tex Eastman Co Div, 58-73, develop assoc, 73-74, head develop div, 74-77, dir res div, 77-84, dir res & develop 84-89, VPRES, RES & DEVELOP, TEX EASTMAN CO, EASTMAN KODAK CO, 89- *Personal Data:* b Thomasville, Ga, Feb 19, 28; m 51; c 4. *Educ:* Emory Univ, AB, 49, MS, 51, PhD(chem), 55. *Prof Exp:* Chemist, Hercules Powder Co, 51-52. *Mem:* Am Chem Soc. *Res:* Chemical properties of aliphatic carbonyl compounds; synthesis of polymers by condensation polymerization. *Mailing Add:* 501 Terrace Dr Longview TX 75601-3826

ROBINSON, ALIX IDA, CELLULAR DIFFERENTIATION, NUCLEIC ACID STRUCTURE. *Current Pos:* instr anat, State Univ NY, Health Sci Ctr, 66-68, res assoc, 68-71, asst prof, 71-75, ASSOC PROF MICROBIOL, STATE UNIV NY, HEALTH SCI CTR, 75- *Personal Data:* b Ft Worth, Tex, Oct 26, 37; div. *Educ:* Univ Tex, Austin, BA, 59, PhD(zool), 64. *Prof Exp:* Res assoc bot, Univ Ill, Urbana, 64; NIH fel path, Med Sch Univ Gothenburg, Sweden, 64-65; instr zool, Univ Ill, Urbana, 65-66. *Concurrent Pos:* Career develop award, NIH, 68-73; prin investr, NIH grant, 73-76, NSF grants, 81-88; Blinker fel acad admin, State Univ NY, 89. *Mem:* Am Soc Cell Biol; Soc Develop Biol; Am Soc Microbiol. *Res:* Role of asymmetric cell division in cellular differentiation including the source of polar development and the role of microtubules in nuclear migration during fern spore germination. *Mailing Add:* Dept Microbiol State Univ NY Health Sci Ctr 750 E Adams St Syracuse NY 13210-2306. *Fax:* 315-464-4417; *E-Mail:* robinsoa@vax.cs.hscsyr.edu

ROBINSON, ALLAN RICHARD, PHYSICAL OCEANOGRAPHY. *Current Pos:* ASSOC PHYS OCEANOGR WOODS HOLE OCEANOG INST, 60- *Personal Data:* b Lynn, Mass, Oct 17, 32; m 55; c 3. *Educ:* Harvard Univ, BA, 54, MA, 56, PhD(physics), 59. *Prof Exp:* NSF fel meteorol & oceanog, Cambridge Univ, 59-60; from asst prof to assoc prof, 60-68, dir, Ctr Earth & Planetary Physics, 72-75, GORDON McKAY PROF GEOPHYS FLUID DYNAMICS & MEM CTR EARTH & PLANETARY PHYSICS, HARVARD UNIV, 68-, CHMN, COMT OCEANOG, 72- *Concurrent Pos:* Co-chmn, Mid-Ocean Dynamics Exp I Sci Coun, NSF, 71-74; Guggenheim fel, Cambridge Univ, Eng, 72-73; Co-ed-in-chief, Dynamics of Atmospheres & Oceans, 76- *Mem:* Fel Am Acad Arts & Sci. *Res:* Oceanography; dynamics of oceanic motions and geophysical fluid dynamics. *Mailing Add:* Div Eng & Appl Sci Rm 1000 Harvard Univ Pierce Hall Cambridge MA 02138

ROBINSON, ARIN FOREST, NEMATODE BEHAVIOR, NEMATODE PHYSIOLOGY. *Personal Data:* b Carlsbad, NMex, Apr 5, 47. *Educ:* Sul Ross State Univ, BS, 72; Tex Tech Univ, MS, 79, PhD(biol), 83. *Honors & Awards:* Distinguished Serv Award, Org Nematologists Trop Am. *Prof Exp:* Zoologist GS-11, USDA Agr Res Serv, 82-85, GS-12, 85-88, GM-13, 88-92, res zoologist GM-14, 92-97. *Mem:* Orgn Nematologists Trop Am; Soc Nematologists; Europ Soc Nematologists; Int Soc Chem Ecol. *Res:* 44 biology of chemotaxis, phototaxis, and thermotaxis in various nematode species, the geographical distributions of several plant parasitic species; use of attractants and nematophagous fungi to manage nematode pests; nematode resistance in cotton. *Mailing Add:* USDA Agr Res Serv Rte 5 Box 805 College Station TX 77840. *Fax:* 409-260-9470; *E-Mail:* forestr@acs.tamu.edu

ROBINSON, ARTHUR, PEDIATRICS, GENETICS. *Current Pos:* Assoc prof pediat & biophys, Univ Colo, Denver, 64-66, prof pediat, biophys & genetics, 66-86, chmn biophys & genetics, 67-74, EMER PROF PEDIAT, BIOCHEM, BIOPHYS & GENETICS, UNIV COLO, DENVER, 86- *Personal Data:* b New York, NY, Jan 12, 14; m 52, Mary Cane; c Jeffrey & Linda. *Educ:* Columbia Univ, AB, 34; Univ Chicago, MD, 38. *Honors & Awards:* Bonfils-Stanton Found Award, 86. *Concurrent Pos:* Sr fel, Eleanor Roosevelt Inst, 73-; dir prof serv, Nat Jewish Hosp & Res Ctr, 75-83; sr staff, Nat Jewish Ctr Immunol & Respiratory Med, 75- *Mem:* Am Pediat Soc; Am Acad Pediat; Am Soc Human Genetics. *Res:* Cytogenetics, clinical genetics. *Mailing Add:* Nat Jewish Ctr Immun Resp Med 1400 Jackson St Rm G219 Denver CO 80206-2761

ROBINSON, ARTHUR B, MOLECULAR BIOLOGY OF AGING, PROTEIN CHEMISTRY. *Current Pos:* PRES & RES PROF, ORE INST SCI & MED, 81- *Personal Data:* b Chicago, Ill, Mar 24, 42; wid; c Zachary, Noah, Arynne, Joshua, Bethany & Matthew. *Educ:* Calif Inst Technol, BS, 63; Univ Calif, San Diego, PhD(chem), 67. *Prof Exp:* Asst prof chem, Biol Dept, Univ Calif, San Diego, 68-73; res prof, Linus Pauling Inst, 73-79, vpres, 73-75, pres, 75-78. *Res:* Molecular biology of aging; nutrition and preventive medicine; protein chemistry; civil defense engineering; nutrition and analytical biomedical instrumentation. *Mailing Add:* Ore Inst Sci & Med 2251 Dick George Rd Cave Junction OR 97523

ROBINSON, ARTHUR R(ICHARD), STRUCTURAL MECHANICS. *Current Pos:* from assoc prof to prof, 60-93, EMER PROF CIVIL ENG, UNIV ILL, URBANA, 93- *Personal Data:* b Brooklyn, NY, Oct 28, 29. *Educ:* Cooper Union, BCE, 51; Univ Ill, MS, 53, PhD(civil eng), 56. *Honors & Awards:* Moisseiff Award, 70; Walter L Huber Civil Eng Res Award, Am Soc Civil Engrs, 69. *Prof Exp:* Res assoc mech & mat, Univ Minn, 55-57, asst prof, 57-58, asst prof aeronaut eng, 58-60. *Mem:* Am Soc Civil Engrs; Am Soc Mech Engrs. *Res:* Numerical methods; stress waves in solids; analysis of structural systems; earthquake engineering. *Mailing Add:* 2129 Newmark Civil Eng Lab 205 N Mathews Ave Urbana IL 61801. *Fax:* 217-333-9464

ROBINSON, ARTHUR ROBIN, AGRICULTURAL CHEMISTRY, ENDOCRINOLOGY. *Current Pos:* PROF CHEM & HEAD CHEM & SOIL SCI DEPT, NS AGR COL 75- *Personal Data:* b Montreal, Que, May 26, 43; m 68; c 4. *Educ:* McGill Univ, BSc, 67, MSc, 70, PhD(agr chem), 75. *Concurrent Pos:* Proj leader res, NS Dept Agr & Mkt, 76-88, Can NS Livestock Feed Initiative Agreement, 87- *Res:* Animal reproduction with particular reference to hormones and plant estrogens; the application of sewage sludge to agricultural land; determination of lead and other metal ion content of Eastern Canada maple products; cervical mucus peroxidase and heat detection in dairy cattle; effect of Omega three fatty acids in poultry. *Mailing Add:* PO Box 550 Truro NS B2N 5E3 Can

ROBINSON, ARTHUR S, TECHNICAL MANAGEMENT. *Current Pos:* PRES, SYSTS TECHNOL DEVELOP CORP, 80- *Personal Data:* b New York, NY, Sept 26, 25; m; c 6. *Educ:* Columbia Univ, BS, 48; NY Univ, MS, 51; Columbia Univ, DSc, 57. *Mem:* Fel Inst Elec & Electronics Engrs. *Mailing Add:* 11125 Glade Dr Reston VA 22091

ROBINSON, BEATRICE LETTERMAN, PHYCOLOGY. *Current Pos:* from adj asst prof to asst prof, 68-80, assoc acad dean, 80-82, ASSOC PROF, LE MOYNE COL, 82-, DEPT CHAIR, 91- *Personal Data:* b Bloomsburg, Pa, June 6, 41; m 63, Edsel; c Scott C & Mark S. *Educ:* Bloomsburg State Col, BS, 63; Syracuse Univ, PhD(bot), 68. *Prof Exp:* Adj asst prof, Syracuse Univ, 68-75. *Mem:* Am Soc Microbiol; Phycol Soc Am; Asn Women Sci. *Res:* Development in blue-green algae, specifically, photomorphogenesis in Nostoc. *Mailing Add:* Dept Biol Le Moyne Col Le Moyne Heights Syracuse NY 13214. *Fax:* 315-445-4540

ROBINSON, BEROL (LEE), NUCLEAR PHYSICS, SCIENCE EDUCATION. *Current Pos:* RETIRED. *Personal Data:* b Highland Park, Mich, June 25, 24; m 48, Shirley Richie; c David A, Judith D & Joanne K. *Educ:* Harvard Univ, AB, 48; Johns Hopkins Univ, PhD(physics), 53. *Honors & Awards:* Physics Instrnl Lab Equip Prize, Am Asn Physics Teachers, 65. *Prof Exp:* Asst prof physics, Univ Ark, 52-56; asst prof, Western Res Univ, 60-67; assoc prof, Case Western Res Univ, 67-71; prog specialist, Univ Sci Educ, UNESCO, 71-84, consult, 85-90. *Concurrent Pos:* Res fel, Israel AEC, 61-62; vis prof, Rensselaer Polytech Inst, 64; asst to dir, Educ Res Ctr, Mass Inst Technol, 69-71; dir educ component, US Metric Study, 70-71; mem adv comt educ, Europ Phys Soc, 75-80; assoc mem, Int Comn Physics Educ, Int Union Pure & Appl Physics, 74-80. *Mem:* AAAS; Am Phys Soc; Am Asn Physics Teachers; Sigma Xi; Am Asn Univ Professors; Europ Phys Soc. *Res:* Nuclear and x-ray spectroscopy; Mossbauer effect; physics laboratory instruction equipment; science education; international science administration. *Mailing Add:* 1 rue du General Gouraud Meudon 92190 France. *E-Mail:* 101556.1577@compuserve.com

ROBINSON, BRIAN HOWARD, BIOCHEMISTRY, GENETICS. *Current Pos:* SCIENTIST BIOCHEM & GENETICS, RES INST, HOSP SICK CHILDREN, TORONTO, 73- *Personal Data:* b Derby, UK, Sept 24, 44. *Educ:* Bristol Univ, BSc, 65, PhD(biochem), 68. *Prof Exp:* Can Med Res Coun fel biochem, 68-70; lectr, Univ Sheffield, 70-73. *Concurrent Pos:* Prof, Dept Pediat, Univ Toronto, 73-, Dept Biochem, 74-; Can Med Res Coun grants, 75-80. *Mem:* Brit Biochem Soc; Can Biochem Soc. *Res:* Mitochondrial metabolite transport; keto acid dehydrogenases; hereditary disorders of metabolism leading to lactic acidosis and keto acidosis; branched-chain amino acid metabolism; mitochondrial respiratory chain; mitochondrial DNA. *Mailing Add:* Hosp Sick Children 555 University Ave Toronto ON M5G 1X8 Can

ROBINSON, BRUCE B, SCIENCE POLICY. *Current Pos:* dep dir, Off Naval Res, 84-87, dir res progs, 87-93, dep dir sci & technol, 93-95, ASSOC TECH DIR, SCI & TECHNOL PROGS, OFF NAVAL RES, 95- *Personal Data:* b Chester, Pa, Oct 13, 33; m 60, Dorothy Ross; c Douglas R & Christopher S. *Educ:* Drexel Inst, 56; Princeton Univ, MA, 58, PhD(plasma transp properties), 61. *Honors & Awards:* Presidential Meritorious Exec Rank Award, 89. *Prof Exp:* Res asst gen relativity, Yerkes Observ, Univ Chicago, 61; res asst plasma stability, Univ Calif, San Diego, 61-63; mem tech staff atomic physics & solid state plasmas, RCA Labs, 63-75; asst dir prog strategies, US Energy Res & Develop Admin, 75-77; dir technol implementation & policy integration, US Dept Energy, 77-81; sr adv to vpres res, Exxon Res & Develop Corp, 81-84. *Concurrent Pos:* Exec dir, Tech Adv Bd, US Dept Com, 73-75; US rep, Int Energy Agency, Govt Exper Grp Technol Transfer, Paris, 78-81; mem, Int Team Rev Res & Develop Prog, Ministry Econs & Finance, 79. *Mem:* Inst Elec & Electronics Engrs; Am Phys Soc; Oceanog Soc. *Res:* Relativistic cosmology; plasma transport theory; atomic collision theory; plasma stability theory; solid-state device physics; energy research and development planning; research administration. *Mailing Add:* 3437 N Emerson St Arlington VA 22207. *E-Mail:* robinsb@onrhq.onr.navy.mil

ROBINSON, C PAUL, LASERS, CHEMICAL PHYSICS. *Current Pos:* MEM STAFF, SANDIA NAT LABS, 90-, PRES & LAB DIR, 95- *Personal Data:* b Detroit, Mich, Oct 9, 41; m 92, Barbara Thomas; c Paula & Colin. *Educ:* Christian Bros Col, BS, 63; Fla State Univ, Tallahassee, PhD(physics), 67. *Hon Degrees:* PhD, Christian Bros Univ, 89. *Prof Exp:* Chief test operator nuclear reactor tests, Nev, Los Alamos Nat Lab, 67-70, res physicist, Advan Concepts Group, NMex, 70-71, alt group leader chem laser res & develop, 71-73, proj dir laser isotope separation, 73-76, appl photochem div leader, 76-80, assoc dir, 80-85; sr vpres, Ebasco Corp, 85-88; ambassador, US Nuclear Testing Talks, Geneva, Switz, 88-90. *Concurrent Pos:* Chmn, Policy Comt, Stratcom Adv Group. *Mem:* Am Phys Soc; AAAS; Am Nuclear Soc. *Res:* Laser isotope separation research including work on uranium enrichment, laser spectroscopy, laser induced chemistry and tunable lasers; weapons physics; arms control issues. *Mailing Add:* Sandia Nat Lab MS 0101 Albuquerque NM 87185. *Fax:* 505-844-1120; *E-Mail:* cprobin@sandia.gov

ROBINSON, CAMPBELL WILLIAM, CHEMICAL ENGINEERING, BIOTECHNOLOGY. *Current Pos:* from asst prof to assoc prof, 71-81, PROF CHEM ENG, UNIV WATERLOO, 81-, PROF BIOL, 91-, DIR, BIOTECHNOL RES CTR, 91- *Personal Data:* b Edmonton, Alta, June 22, 33; c 3. *Educ:* Univ BC, BASc, 61; Univ Calif, Berkeley, PhD(chem eng), 71. *Honors & Awards:* J W T Spinks lectr, Univ Sask, 91. *Prof Exp:* Process engr, Gulf Oil Can Ltd, 57-62, process unit supt, 62-64, sr process engr, 64-65, tech serv supvr, 65-66. *Concurrent Pos:* Vis prof, Univ Calif, Berkeley, 78-79; assoc ed, Can J Chem Eng, 80-84; co-ed, Comprehensive Biotechnol, vol 4, 85; vis prof, EPF, Lausanne, Switz, 85-86; ed, Can J Chem Eng, 89-; vis prof, Univ BC, 92-93. *Mem:* Can Soc Chem Eng; Chem Inst Can; Am Chem Soc. *Res:* Mass transfer; biochemical engineering, fermentation and waste treatment process design. *Mailing Add:* Dept Chem Eng Univer Waterloo 200 University Ave W Waterloo ON N2L 3G1 Can. *Fax:* 519-746-4979; *E-Mail:* robinson@cape.uwaterloo.ca

ROBINSON, CASEY PERRY, PHARMACOLOGY. *Current Pos:* assoc prof pharmacol, Col Med, 71-80, from asst prof to assoc prof pharmacodynamics, Col Pharm, 71-81, PROF PHARMACOL, COL MED, UNIV OKLA, 81-, PROF PHARMACODYNAMICS, COL PHARM, 81- *Personal Data:* b Idabel, Okla, Oct 10, 32; m 55, Eunice Vanda Bettes; c Cheryl (Bumpus), Kent A & Brian L. *Educ:* Univ Okla, BS, 54, MS, 67; Vanderbilt Univ, PhD(pharmacol), 70. *Prof Exp:* Sr sci investr pharmacol, Am Heart Asn, Med Sch, Univ Calif, Los Angeles, 70-71. *Concurrent Pos:* Co-prin investr, NSF grant, 74-76; prin investr, EPA grant, 77-80, DOD grant, 85-88, 90-95. *Mem:* AAAS; Soc Exp Biol & Med; Am Soc Pharmacol & Exp Therapeut; Soc Toxicol; NY Acad Sci. *Res:* Effects of toxins on cardiovascular responses; neuroeffector mechanisms of blood vessels. *Mailing Add:* Col Pharm Health Sci Ctr Univ Okla PO Box 26901 Oklahoma City OK 73190. *Fax:* 405-271-7477; *E-Mail:* casey_robinson@uokhsc.edu

ROBINSON, CECIL HOWARD, ORGANIC CHEMISTRY, PHARMACOLOGY. *Current Pos:* from asst prof to assoc prof, 63-77, PROF PHARMACOL, JOHNS HOPKINS UNIV, SCH MED, 77- *Personal Data:* b London, Eng, Nov 5, 28; m 56, Sallie Conley; c Susan, John, Lucy & Cynthia. *Educ:* Univ London, BSc, 50, PhD(chem), 54. *Prof Exp:* NSF fel, Wayne State Univ, 54-55; chemist, Glaxo Labs Ltd, 55-56; from chemist to sr chemist, Schering Corp, 56-63. *Mem:* AAAS; Am Chem Soc; Royal Soc Chem; Am Soc Pharmacol & Exp Therapeut. *Res:* Synthetic steroids; enzyme inhibitors; design and synthesis of chemotherapeutic agents; enzyme mechanism; biochemistry. *Mailing Add:* Dept Pharmacol Johns Hopkins Univ Sch Med 720 Rutland Ave Baltimore MD 21205

ROBINSON, CHARLES ALBERT, ORGANIC CHEMISTRY. *Current Pos:* RETIRED. *Personal Data:* b Newton, Mass, July 22, 21; m 54; c 1. *Educ:* Brown Univ, ScB, 43; Mass Inst Technol, PhD(org chem), 50. *Prof Exp:* Develop res chemist, Merck & Co, 43-47; asst chem, Mass Inst Technol, 47-50; res chemist, Arnold, Hoffman & Co, 50-53, res sect leader, 53-57, mem staff develop dept, 57-59, sect leader tech serv, 59-63; sr res scientist, Wyeth Labs, Inc, 63-70, asst to dir, Biol & Chem Develop Div, 70-77, assoc dir chem develop, Res & Develop Dept, 77-81. *Mem:* Am Chem Soc. *Res:* Synthesis of organic compounds; process development; pharmaceuticals. *Mailing Add:* 31 Lonsdale Lane Kennett Square PA 19348

ROBINSON, CHARLES C(ANFIELD), COLLOIDAL SCIENCE, PHOTOCONDUCTIVITY. *Current Pos:* TECH SPECIALIST & PROJ MGR, XEROX CORP, 77- *Personal Data:* b East Orange, NJ, Oct 30, 32; m 61; c 2. *Educ:* Miami Univ, BS, 55; Mass Inst Technol, BS, 55, MS, 57, EE, 59, PhD(elec eng), 60. *Prof Exp:* Asst prof elec eng, Mass Inst Technol, 61-62; sr physicist, Res Ctr, Am Optical Corp, 62-77. *Mem:* Inst Elec & Electronics Engrs; Optical Soc Am. *Res:* Colloidal systems photoconductivity; optical properties of materials; xerographic instrumentation; optical thin films; rare earth studies in glass; magneto-optical effects. *Mailing Add:* Xerox Corp Phillips Rd Webster NY 14580

ROBINSON, CHARLES DEE, ANALYSIS & FUNCTIONAL ANALYSIS. *Current Pos:* chmn, Div Sci, Hardin-Simmons Univ, 69-80, dir, Instnl Res, 80-91, Info Systs, 84-91, PROF MATH & HEAD DEPT, HARDIN-SIMMONS UNIV, 68- *Personal Data:* b Dallas, Tex, July 16, 32; m 54, Clydene Rush. *Educ:* Hardin-Simmons Univ, BA, 56; Univ Tex-Austin, MA, 61, PhD(math), 64; St Johns Col, Santa Fe, MA, 82. *Prof Exp:* Instr math, Hardin-Simmons Univ, 56-59; asst prof, Ariz State Univ, 64-65; assoc prof, Univ Miss, 65-68. *Concurrent Pos:* Dir student sci training projs math, NSF, 67-68, 70-71 & 74-80; pres, Tex Asn Acad Adminrs Math Scis, 88-89; dir, secy & treas, Tex Sect, Math Asn Am, 90- *Mem:* Am Math Soc; Math Asn Am. *Res:* Functional analysis; computational mathematics. *Mailing Add:* 850 Vista Lane Abilene TX 79601

ROBINSON, CHARLES J, REHABILITATION ENGINEERING. *Current Pos:* PROF, DEPT REHAB SCI & TECHNOL, DEPT ELEC ENG, DEPT ORTHOPAEDIC SURG, 92-; BIOMED ENG & NEUROPHYSIOLOGIST, VET ADMIN HOSP, PITTSBURGH, 92- *Personal Data:* b Wheeling, WVa, July 16, 47; m 69, Rosemary Arbogast; c Patrick, Kathleen, Elizabeth, Brian & Megan. *Educ:* Col Steubenville, BS, 69; Ohio State Univ, MS, 71, Wash Univ, DSc, 79. *Honors & Awards:* Purrinje Medal, Czech Soc Med & Biol Sci. *Prof Exp:* Mem tech staff, Bell Tel Labs, Columbus, Ohio, 69-74; assoc anesthesiol, Yale Univ, 79-81; Biomed Engr, Rehab Res & Develop Ctr, Vet Admin Hines Hosp, 81-92, assoc dir, 83-92; prof, Dept Neurol, Stritch Sch Med, Loyola Univ, 89-92. *Concurrent Pos:* Adj asst prof, Physiol Dept, Stritch Sch Med, Loyola Univ, 82-89; assoc dir, Rehab Res & Develop Ctr, Vet Admin Hines Hosp, 83-92, prog dir rehab neurosci, 84-92; prin investr, merit rev, US Dept Vet Affairs, 83-; assoc ed, Inst Elec & Electronics Engrs Trans Biomed Eng, 87-90, dir, 93-94; vis lectr, Bioeng Prog, Univ Ill, Chicago, 90-91. *Mem:* Fel Inst Elec & Electronics Engrs; Inst Elec & Electronics Engrs Eng Med & Biol Soc (vpres 88 & 89, pres 90 & 91); Rehab Eng Soc NAm; Soc Neurosci; fel Am Inst Med & Biol Engrs. *Res:* Rehabilitative neuroscience with a particular emphasis on spinal cord injury; micturition dysfunction; lower limb spasticity and motor control following spinal cord injury; postural stability, falls and balance in the elderly and in computers. *Mailing Add:* Univ Pittsburgh Dept Rehab Sci & Technol 5034 Forbes Tower Pittsburgh PA 15260. *E-Mail:* c.robinson@ieee.org

ROBINSON, CHARLES NELSON, ORGANIC CHEMISTRY. *Current Pos:* assoc prof, 61-66, PROF CHEM, MEMPHIS STATE UNIV, 66- *Personal Data:* b Fayetteville, Tenn, Nov 18, 28. *Educ:* Maryville Col, BS, 49; Univ Tenn, MS, 51, PhD(org chem), 53. *Prof Exp:* Asst, Univ Tenn, 49-50; asst chemist org res, Oak Ridge Nat Lab, 52; fel & asst, Univ Ill, 53-54; from asst prof to assoc prof chem, La Polytech Inst, 56-61. *Mem:* Am Chem Soc; Sigma Xi. *Res:* Structure proof and synthesis of alkaloids and related compounds; organophosphorus chemistry; retinoid chemistry. *Mailing Add:* 547 Wild Cherry Cove Memphis TN 38117

ROBINSON, CLARK, MATHEMATICAL ANALYSIS. *Current Pos:* from asst prof to assoc prof, 69-78, chmn dept, 85-87, PROF MATH, NORTHWESTERN UNIV, 78- *Personal Data:* b Seattle, Wash, Dec 29, 43; m 66. *Educ:* Univ Wash, BS, 66; Univ Calif, Berkeley, PhD(math), 69. *Prof Exp:* Vis prof math, Inst Pure & Appl Math, Rio de Janeiro, Brazil, 70-71. *Mem:* Am Math Soc; Math Asn Am; Soc Indust & Appl Math. *Res:* Differential dynamical systems; global analysis. *Mailing Add:* Northwestern Univ Evanston IL 60208-2730

ROBINSON, CLARK SHOVE, JR, PHYSICS, NUCLEAR PHYSICS. *Current Pos:* RETIRED. *Personal Data:* b Reading, Mass, May 13, 17; m 42, Rachel; c Clark S III & Christine (Franquemont). *Educ:* Mass Inst Technol, SB, 38, PhD(physics), 42. *Prof Exp:* Res assoc radiation lab, Mass Inst Technol, 41-43; res asst prof physics, Univ Ill, Urbana, 46-51, res assoc prof, 51-55, prof, 55-76; translr & ed, Soviet J Nuclear Physics, 76-91. *Concurrent Pos:* Adj prof physics, Mont State Univ, Bozeman, 76-91. *Mem:* Am Phys Soc. *Res:* X-ray study of glass structure; crystal growth in tungsten wire; microwave and other vacuum tubes; development of betatrons; nuclear physics; mesons; Russian translation; radio communication; electronics. *Mailing Add:* 14540 Pony Creek Rd Bozeman MT 59715

ROBINSON, CURTIS, PLANT PHYSIOLOGY. *Current Pos:* ASSOC PROF BIOL, EDINBORO STATE COL, 73- *Personal Data:* b Wilmington, NC, May 12, 34; m 68; c 3. *Educ:* Morgan State Col, BS, 60; Howard Univ, MS, 68; Univ Md, PhD(bot), 73. *Prof Exp:* Teacher sci & math, Lincoln High Sch, Leland, NC, 60-61 & Williston Sr High Sch, Wilmington, 61-62; res biologist, Radiation Biol Lab, Smithsonian Inst, 62-69; res technician immunol, Microbiol Assocs, 65-67. *Mem:* Am Soc Plant Physiologists. *Res:* Studies of light, hormonal, and mineral interactions in etiolated mung bean seedlings. *Mailing Add:* Dept Biol/Health Servs Edinboro Univ Pa 219 Meadville St Edinboro PA 16444-0001

ROBINSON, D(ENIS) M(ORRELL), engineering; deceased, see previous edition for last biography

ROBINSON, DANIEL ALFRED, ALGEBRA. *Current Pos:* From asst prof to assoc prof math, 59-76, PROF MATH, GA INST TECHNOL, 76- *Personal Data:* b Schenectady, NY, Apr 9, 32; m 58; c 3. *Educ:* NY State Teachers Col Albany, BA, 53; Rensselaer Polytech Inst, MS, 54; Univ Wis-Madison, PhD(math), 64. *Mem:* Am Math Soc; Sigma Xi. *Res:* General algebraic structures; loop theory. *Mailing Add:* Sch Math Ga Inst Technol Atlanta GA 30332-0160

ROBINSON, DANIEL OWEN, SOIL SCIENCE. *Current Pos:* assoc prof agron & head dept agr, 50-55, prof agron & dir div agr, 55-70, PROF AGR, ARIZ STATE UNIV, 70- *Personal Data:* b Colonia Dublan, Mex, Jan 28, 18; m 42; c 6. *Educ:* Brigham Young Univ, AB, 42; Univ Ariz, MS, 47; Ohio State Univ, PhD(soil physics), 49. *Prof Exp:* Instr agron, Ohio State Univ, 49-50. *Mem:* AAAS; Soil Sci Soc Am; Am Soc Agron; Sigma Xi. *Res:* Soils; soil physics; plant nutrition. *Mailing Add:* PO Box 484 Thatcher AZ 85552

ROBINSON, DAVID, PLASMA PHYSICS. *Current Pos:* assoc prof, 68-70, chmn dept, 68-86, PROF PHYSICS, DRAKE UNIV, 70- *Personal Data:* b Larne, Ireland, Jan 13, 29; US citizen; m 59, Ellen Mannion; c 4. *Educ:* Queen's Univ, Belfast, BSc, 51, MSc, 53; Univ Western Ont, PhD(physics), 57. *Prof Exp:* Asst lectr physics, Queen's Univ, Belfast, 52-54; res assoc, Univ Western Ont, 54-58; res assoc, Univ Southern Calif, 58-60, asst prof elec eng, 60-64; assoc prof physics, Univ Windsor, 64-68. *Concurrent Pos:* Consult, Northrop Space Labs, 62-64, Electro-Optical Systems, Calif, 65. *Mem:* Am Asn Physics Teachers. *Res:* Molecular spectroscopy; plasmas in hypersonic flow; diagnostic techniques in high-current plasmas and plasma accelerators for space applications. *Mailing Add:* Dept Physics Drake Univ 2507 Univiversity Ave Des Moines IA 50311-4505

ROBINSON, DAVID ADAIR, NEUROPHYSIOLOGY. *Current Pos:* from instr to assoc prof med, 61-70, from asst prof to assoc prof elec eng, 63-75, assoc prof biomed eng, 70-75, assoc prof ophthal, 71-75, PROF OPHTHAL & PROF BIOMED ENG, SCH MED, JOHNS HOPKINS UNIV, 75- *Personal Data:* b Boston, Mass, Dec 9, 25; m 80. *Educ:* Brown Univ, BA, 47; Johns Hopkins Univ, MSc, 56, DrEng(elec eng), 59. *Prof Exp:* From proj engr to vpres res, Airpax Electronics, Inc, Md, 51-56, Fla, 58-61. *Concurrent Pos:* Consult visual sci study sect, Div Res Grants, NIH, 66-70, consult eng in biol & med training comt, 71-73; consult comt vision, Nat Res Ctr, Nat Acad Sci, 77-81 & consult planning comt, Nat Eye Inst, NIH, 76 & 81; NIH res grant, Sch Med, Johns Hopkins Univ, 69- *Mem:* Asn Res Vision & Ophthal; Soc Neurosci. *Res:* Neurophysiology of the eye movement control system. *Mailing Add:* Dept Ophthal Johns Hopkins Univ Sch Med 720 Rutland Ave Baltimore MD 21205

ROBINSON, DAVID ALTON, CLIMATOLOGY, SNOW & ICE. *Current Pos:* PROF GEOG, RUTGERS UNIV, 88-, CHMN, DEPT GEOG, 96-; NJ STATE CLIMATOLOGIST, 91- *Personal Data:* b Hackensack, NJ, May 13, 55; m 83, V Keating Johnson; c Douglas & Andrew. *Educ:* Dickinson Col, BS, 77; Columbia Univ, MS, 81, MPhil, 81, PhD(geol), 84. *Prof Exp:* Assoc res scientist, Lamont-Doherty Earth Observ, Columbia Univ, 84-88. *Concurrent Pos:* Mem, Int Satellite Land Surface Climate Proj Data Preserv Comt, NASA, 84, First Int Satellite Cloud Climate Proj Reg Exp Res Team, 86-89; prin or co-prin investr, 20 res grants, NSF, NASA, Nat Oceanic & Atmospheric Admin, Dept Energy, USAF Off Sci Res, 84-; adj prof, Col New Rochelle, 84-87, Bergen Community Col, 86- 88; vis prof, Univ NC, Asheville, 88; mem, Global Energy & Water Cycle Exp, Nat Res Coun, 93-; chair, Climate Speciality Group, Asn Am Geographers & Polar Meterol & Oceanog Comt, Amn Meteorol Soc. *Mem:* Am Meteorol Soc; Asn Am Geographers; Am Geophys Union; Am Asn State Climatologists; Int Asn Hydrol Sci. *Res:* Climate and climate change; state and regional issues, hemispheric and regional snow cover dynamics and surface albedo; collection and archiving of climatic data. *Mailing Add:* Dept Geog Rutgers Univ New Brunswick NJ 08903

ROBINSON, DAVID BANCROFT, PSYCHIATRY. *Current Pos:* from asst prof to assoc prof psychiat, State Univ NY Upstate Med Ctr, 58-68, actg chmn dept psychiat, 64-68 & 77-78, dir, Adult Psychiat In-Patient Unit, 69-81, prof psychiat, 68-85, consult-liaison psychiat, 81-85 EMER PROF PSYCHIAT, STATE UNIV NY UPSTATE MED CTR, 85- *Personal Data:* b Bellefonte, Pa, Feb 4, 24; m 45, Louise Neff; c Margaret L (Manring), Claire R (Howard), David D, Deborah (Swift) & Eleanor R (Wilcox). *Educ:* Pa State Univ, BS, 44; Univ Pa, MD, 49; Univ Minn, MS, 57. *Honors & Awards:* Silver Award, Psychiat Asn, 67. *Prof Exp:* Intern, Geisinger Mem Hosp Foss Clin, Danville, Pa, 49-50, resident med, 50-51; staff psychiatrist, Rochester State Hosp, Minn, 55-56; instr psychiat, Mayo Clin, Mayo Grad Sch Med, Univ Minn, 57-58. *Concurrent Pos:* Fel med, Mayo Found, Sch Med, Univ Minn, 52-55; sr psychiatrist, Syracuse Vet Admin Hosp & Crouse-Irving Mem Hosp, Syracuse, 58-61; coordr, Psychiat State Hosp Residents, NY State Dept Ment Hyg, 61-64; coordr, Grad Training Prof, Dept Psychiat, State Univ NY Upstate Med Ctr, 61-64; attend psychiatrist, Crouse-Irving Mem Hosp, Syracuse, 61-71 & Syracuse Vet Admin Hosp, 61-; proj dir, NIMH Training Grants, State Univ NY Upstate Med Ctr, 64-68, pres, Med Col Assembly, 71-73. *Mem:* Fel Am Psychiat Asn. *Res:* Psychotherapy; psychosomatic medicine; determinants of deviant behavior and psychosis; methods of teaching psychotherapy. *Mailing Add:* 2870 W Lake Rd Skaneateles NY 13152

ROBINSON, DAVID LEE, NEUROPHYSIOLOGY. *Current Pos:* res physiologist, 78-88, CHIEF, SECT VISUAL BEHAV, LAB SENSORIMOTOR RES, NAT EYE INST, 88- *Personal Data:* b St Louis, Mo, May 2, 43; div; c 2. *Educ:* Springfield Col, BS, 65; Wake Forest Univ, MS, 68; Univ Rochester, PhD(neurosci), 72. *Prof Exp:* Fel neurophysiol, Lab Neurobiol, NIMH, 71-74; res physiologist, Neurobiol Dept, Armed Forces Radiobiol Res Inst, 74-78. *Concurrent Pos:* Fel psychiat, NIMH, 73-74, guest scientist, Lab Neurobiol, 74-78. *Mem:* Soc Neurosci; Asn Res Vision & Ophthal. *Res:* Neural control of visual attention; influence of eye movements on the visual system; neural control of pulvinar head movements. *Mailing Add:* Lab Sensorimotor Res Nat Eye Inst 49/2A50 Bethesda MD 20892. *Fax:* 301-402-0511

ROBINSON, DAVID MASON, CELL BIOLOGY, CRYOBIOLOGY. *Current Pos:* expert consult, NIH, 80-83, sr sci adv, 83-86, dep chief biol, 81-89, assoc dir sci prog, Div Heart & Vascular Dis, Nat Heart, Lung & Blood Inst, 88-93, DIR, VASCULAR RES PROG, NIH, 93-; PROF LECTR LIB STUDIES, GEORGETOWN UNIV, 89- *Personal Data:* b Eccles, Eng, July 7, 32; m 65; c 2. *Educ:* Durham Univ, BSc, 55, PhD(zool), 58. *Prof Exp:* Sect head entom, Cotton Res Sta, Uganda, 59-61; res officer, Hope Dept Zool, Oxford Univ, 61-63; mem sci staff, Med Res Coun Radiobiol Res Unit, Atomic Energy Res Estab, Eng, 63-66; prin sci officer & head cell biol, Microbiol Res Estab, Eng, 66-69; asst res dir, Blood Res Lab, Am Red Cross, 69-74; prof biol, Georgetown Univ, 74-80, adj prof anat & cell biol, 81-89. *Mem:* Soc Cryobiol (secy, 75-76); Biophys Soc; Brit Asn Cancer Res; Am Soc Cell Biol; Brit Soc Low Temperature Biol (treas, 68). *Res:* Functional role of water in living systems; nature and repair of freezing injury in mammalian cells; nature and role of animal cell surface macromolecules. *Mailing Add:* Nat Heart Lung-Blood Inst NIH 2 Rockledge Ctr MSC 7956 Bethesda MD 20892-7956

ROBINSON, DAVID NELSON, APPLIED MECHANICS, RHEOLOGY. *Current Pos:* RESIDENT RES ASSOC, NASA, LERE, 82- *Personal Data:* b Malden, Mass, July 14, 33. *Educ:* Northeastern Univ, BSci, 61; Brown Univ, MSci, 63, PhD(appl mech), 66. *Prof Exp:* Prof appl mech, Dept Theoret & Appl Mech, Cornell Univ, 66-74; res staff mem appl mech, Oak Ridge Nat Lab, 74-82; PROF CIVIL ENG, UNIV AKRON, 82- *Concurrent Pos:* Consult appl mech, Int Bus Mach Corp, 68-72. *Mem:* Am Soc Mech Eng; Am Soc Civil Eng; Sigma Xi. *Res:* Constitutive equations for materials at elevated temperature; mechanics of composite materials; plasticity; viscoplasticity. *Mailing Add:* Dept Civil Eng Univ Akron Akron OH 44325-3905. *E-Mail:* dnr@uakron.edu

ROBINSON, DAVID WEAVER, SURGERY. *Current Pos:* Instr anat, 35-36, from instr to assoc prof surg, 41-54, chmn, Sect Plastic Surg, 46-72, prof surg, 54-78, DISTINGUISHED PROF SURG, COL HEALTH SCI, UNIV KANS, KANSAS CITY, 74- *Personal Data:* b Kansas City, Mo, Nov 15, 14; m 40; c 4. *Educ:* Univ Kans, AB, 35, MS, 47; Univ Pa, MD, 38; Am Bd Plastic Surg, dipl. *Concurrent Pos:* VChancellor clin affairs-actg exec vchancellor, Am Bd Plastic Surg, 61-67, chmn, 67. *Mem:* Am Soc Plastic & Reconstruct Surg (pres, 66-67); Am Surg Asn (2nd vpres, 65-66); Am Asn Plastic Surg; Am Col Surgeons; Sigma Xi. *Mailing Add:* 5516 Groveland Ave Baltimore MD 21215-4244

ROBINSON, DAVID ZAV, OPTICS. *Current Pos:* RETIRED. *Personal Data:* b Montreal, Que, Sept 29, 27; nat US; m 54, Nan Senior; c Marc & Eric. *Educ:* Harvard Univ, AB, 46, AM, 47, PhD(chem physics), 50. *Prof Exp:* Physicist, Baird-Atomic, Inc, 49-52, asst dir res, 52-59; sci liaison officer, US Off Naval Res, London, Eng, 59-60; asst dir res, Baird-Atomic, Inc, 60-61; tech asst, Off Sci & Technol, Exec Off of President, Wash, DC, 61-62, tech specialist, 62-67; vpres acad affairs, NY Univ, 67-70; vpres, Carnegie Corp New York, 70-80, exec vpres, 80-88; exec dir, Carnegie Comm Sci, Technol & Govt, 88-97. *Concurrent Pos:* US del, Int Comn Optics, 59-63, chmn, 61-63; mem, Comt Physics & Soc, Am Inst Physics, 67-70; consult, President's Sci Adv Comt, 67-74; mem, NY State Energy Res & Develop Auth, 71-76; consult, NSF, 71-74 & Nat Acad Sci, 73-; bd trustees, City Univ NY, 76-81, NC Sch Sci & Math, 79-, Santa Fe Inst, 89- *Mem:* Optical Soc Am; AAAS. *Res:* Optics; government and science. *Mailing Add:* 675 Greenwich St No 5B New York NY 10014. *Fax:* 212-675-5870

ROBINSON, DEAN WENTWORTH, CHEMICAL LASERS, SPECTROSCOPY. *Current Pos:* From asst prof to assoc prof, 55-66, chmn dept, 76-83, PROF CHEM, JOHNS HOPKINS UNIV, 66- *Personal Data:* b Boston, Mass, July 22, 29; m 83, MaryEllen McMahon; c Dean Jr, Amy & Jonas. *Educ:* Univ NH, BS, 51, MS, 52; Mass Inst Technol, PhD(infra-red spectros), 55. *Concurrent Pos:* Fulbright res grant & Guggenheim fel, 66-67; vis prof, Univ Lille, 91. *Mem:* Am Chem Soc; fel AAAS. *Res:* Far infrared and low temperature spectroscopy; electronic spectra of small molecules; non-linear optical properties of materials; far infrared chemically-pumped lasers. *Mailing Add:* Dept Chem Johns Hopkins Univ Baltimore MD 21218-2680. *Fax:* 410-516-8420

ROBINSON, DEREK JOHN SCOTT, ALGEBRA. *Current Pos:* from asst prof to assoc prof, 68-74, PROF MATH, UNIV ILL, URBANA, 74- *Personal Data:* b Montrose, Scotland, Sept 25, 38; m; c 3. *Educ:* Univ Edinburgh, BSc, 60; Cambridge Univ, PhD(math), 63. *Honors & Awards:* Sir Edmund Whitaker Mem Prize, Edinburgh Math Soc, 71; Alexander von Humboldt Prize, 79. *Prof Exp:* Lectr math, Queen Mary Col, Univ London, 65-68. *Mem:* Am Math Soc. *Res:* Theory of groups; homological algebra. *Mailing Add:* Dept Math 332 Univ Ill Urbana IL 61801

ROBINSON, DONALD ALONZO, ORGANIC CHEMISTRY. *Current Pos:* PRES, BRENTWOOD ASSOCS, INC, 83- *Personal Data:* b Joliet, Ill, Aug 4, 20; m 49, Mary K Wiegel; c Laurance, Carol, Bruce, Gordon, Joan & John. *Educ:* Iowa State Col, BS, 42; Univ Wis, PhD(org chem), 48. *Prof Exp:* Res chemist, Naugatuck Chem Div, US Rubber Co, 42-46; res chemist, Mallinckrodt Chem Works, Mallinckrodt, Inc, 48-51, mfg improvement suprv, 51-56, asst to opers mgr, 56-62, mkt res mgr, 62-65, asst dir com develop, 65-68, asst to pres, St Louis, 68-72, asst to vchmn, 72-79, asst to pres, 79-82. *Mem:* Am Chem Soc; Chem Mkt Res Asn. *Res:* Halogenation of amines; catalytic dehydrogenation; claisen condensations. *Mailing Add:* 2301 St Clair Ave Brentwood MO 63144. *Fax:* 314-962-8045

ROBINSON, DONALD KEITH, PARTICLE PHYSICS. *Current Pos:* assoc prof, 66-71, PROF HIGH ENERGY PHYSICS, CASE WESTERN RES UNIV, 71- *Personal Data:* b Truro, NS, Aug 29, 32; m 65. *Educ:* Dalhousie Univ, BSc, 54, MSc, 56; Oxford Univ, DPhil(physics), 60. *Prof Exp:* Res assoc high energy physics, Brookhaven Nat Lab, 60-62; from asst physicist to assoc physicist, 62-66. *Mem:* Am Phys Soc. *Res:* High energy particle interactions in bubble chambers; resonance production and decay; exchange processes; counter experiments; K-meson interactions; anti-proton interactions; radiative production and decay of hyperons. *Mailing Add:* Dept Physics Case Western Reserve Univ 10900 Euclid Ave Cleveland OH 44106-7079

ROBINSON, DONALD NELLIS, ORGANIC CHEMISTRY, POLYMER CHEMISTRY. *Current Pos:* sr res chemist, 69-92, STAFF CHEMIST, PENNWALT CO & ELF ATOCHEM NAM, 92- *Personal Data:* b New Brunswick, NJ, Nov 21, 33; m 60, Joan Lundy; c Charles & Jonathan. *Educ:* Cornell Univ, AB, 55; Univ Minn, PhD(org chem), 59. *Prof Exp:* Res chemist elastomers dept, E I du Pont de Nemours & Co, Del, 59-64, develop chemist, Ky, 64-67; asst prof chem, Ky Southern Col, 67-69, actg chmn dept, 68-69. *Mem:* Am Chem Soc. *Res:* Thermoplastics (synthesis, blends, physical evaluation); elastomers; indoles. *Mailing Add:* 316 Colonial Ave Collegeville PA 19426-2538

ROBINSON, DONALD STETSON, pharmacology, medicine, for more information see previous edition

ROBINSON, DONALD W(ALLACE), JR, MECHANICAL & AEROSPACE ENGINEERING. *Current Pos:* CONSULT, 87- *Personal Data:* b Minocqua, Wis, Sept 28, 21; m 47; c 4. *Educ:* Northeastern Univ, BS, 47; Rensselaer Polytech Inst, MS, 68. *Prof Exp:* Aerodynamicist, Chance Vought Aircraft, 47-50; aerodynamicist, Kaman Aircraft Corp, 50-52, flight test engr, 52-53, chief test & develop, 53-56, proj engr, 56-58, proj mgr res & develop, 58-60, chief res engr, 60-69, dir res & develop, 69-76, vpres eng, 76-78, vpres planning & mkt, Kaman Aerospace Corp, 78-87. *Mem:* Am Inst Aeronaut & Astronaut; Am Helicopter Soc; Sigma Xi. *Res:* Fluid mechanics; vibrations; systems analysis; statistical forecasting; management sciences. *Mailing Add:* 43 Tamara Circle Avon CT 06001

ROBINSON, DONALD WILFORD, MATHEMATICS. *Current Pos:* From asst prof to assoc prof, 56-62, PROF MATH, BRIGHAM YOUNG UNIV, 62- *Personal Data:* b Salt Lake City, Utah, Feb 29, 28; m 52, Helen R Sorensen; c Diane, Allen C, Karen, Janette, Marilyn, Lynae & David W. *Educ:* Univ Utah, BS, 48, MA, 52; Case Western Res Univ, PhD(math), 56. *Honors & Awards:* Cert Meritorious Serv, Mathematical Asn, 95. *Concurrent Pos:* NSF fac sr res fel, Calif Inst Technol, 62-63; vis prof, Naval Postgrad Sch, 69-70; Fulbright-Hays lectureship, Univ Carabobo, Valencia, Venezuela, 76-77; vis prof, Rijksuniversigteit Gent, Ghent, Belig, 86. *Mem:* Am Math Soc; Math Asn Am; Sigma Xi; Soc Indust Appl Math. *Res:* Linear algebra and matrix theory. *Mailing Add:* Brigham Young Univ 312 TMCB Provo UT 84602. *E-Mail:* robinson@math.byu.edu

ROBINSON, DOUGLAS WALTER, ANALYTICAL CHEMISTRY. *Current Pos:* SR CHEMIST, JOHNSON MATTHEY, WAYNE, 88- *Personal Data:* b Niagara Falls, NY, Oct 22, 34; m 63; c 2. *Educ:* Hamilton Col, AB, 56; Cornell Univ, MS, 59; Univ RI, PhD(anal chem), 64. *Prof Exp:* Chemist, Cadet Chem Corp, 58-59; chemist, Hooker Chem Corp, 59-61; res chemist, E I du Pont de Nemours & Co, 64-66; proj leader, Pennwalt Corp, King of Prussia, 66-87. *Mem:* Soc Appl Spectros; Am Chem Soc. *Res:* Mass spectroscopy; gas chromatography. *Mailing Add:* 401 Riverview Ave Swarthmore PA 19081

ROBINSON, E ARTHUR, JR, ERGODIC THEORY, DYNAMICAL SYSTEMS. *Current Pos:* asst prof, 86-90, chain, 93-97 ASSOC PROF MATH, GEORGE WASHINGTON UNIV, 90- *Educ:* Tufts Univ, BS, 77; Univ Md, MA, 81, PhD(math), 83. *Prof Exp:* Mem math, Math Sci Res Inst, 83-84; lectr math, Univ Pa, 84-86. *Concurrent Pos:* Prin investr, NSF, 85-96; mem math, Inst Advan Study, Princeton Univ, 86-87. *Mem:* Am Math Soc. *Res:* Spectral multiplicity in ergodic theory; theory of extensions and the theory of joinings; ergodic theory and topological dynamics of tilings. *Mailing Add:* Dept Math George Washington Univ Washington DC 20052. *Fax:* 202-994-6760; *E-Mail:* robinson@math.gwu.edu

ROBINSON, EDWARD J, PHYSICS. *Current Pos:* from asst prof to assoc prof, 65-81, PROF PHYSICS, NY UNIV, 82- *Personal Data:* b New York, NY, June 16, 36; m 59; c 2. *Educ:* Queens Col, NY, BS, 57; NY Univ, PhD(physics), 64. *Prof Exp:* Substitute in physics, Queens Col, NY, 58-59; lectr, City Col New York, 59-61; instr, NY Univ, 61-63; res assoc, Joint Inst Lab Astrophys, Nat Bur Stand & Univ Colo, 64-65. *Mem:* Am Phys Soc. *Res:* Theoretical atomic physics, including atomic structure, scattering, and the interaction of laser radiation with atoms; surface physics. *Mailing Add:* Univ Dept Physics NY Univ Four Washington Pl New York NY 10003

ROBINSON, EDWARD LEE, ACCIDENT RECONSTRUCTION-APPLIED PHYSICS, NUCLEAR PHYSICS. *Current Pos:* RETIRED. *Personal Data:* b Clanton, Ala, Nov 6, 33; m 54, 90, Linda Moon; c Edward L Jr, James A & Paul D. *Educ:* Samford Univ, AB, 54; Purdue Univ, MS, 58, PhD(physics), 62. *Prof Exp:* From asst prof to prof, Samford Univ, 61-67, head dept, 61-67, dir, Cyclotron Lab; dir, Radiation Biol Lab, Univ Ala, Birmingham, 67-80, from assoc prof to prof physics, 67-91, adj prof, criminal justice/forensic sci, 85-91. *Concurrent Pos:* Consult, Hayes Int Corp, 63-68, Accident Reconstruction & Applied Physics Problems. *Mem:* AAAS; Am Phys Soc; Am Asn Physics Teachers; Soc Automotive Eng; Nat Asn Prof Accident Reconstruction Specialist. *Res:* Nuclear spectroscopy; applied physics; vehicular accident analysis and reconstruction; discoverer/co-discoverer six new radioisotopes. *Mailing Add:* 233 Oakmont Rd Univ Ala Birmingham AL 35244-3264

ROBINSON, EDWARD LEWIS, ASTRONOMY. *Current Pos:* from asst prof to assoc prof, 74-85, PROF ASTRON, UNIV TEX, AUSTIN, 85- *Personal Data:* b Pittsburgh, Pa, Aug 29, 45; m; c 1. *Educ:* Univ Ariz, BA, 69; Univ Tex, Austin, PhD(astron), 73. *Prof Exp:* Astronomer, Lick Observ, Univ Calif, Santa Cruz, 73-74. *Concurrent Pos:* Alfred P Sloan Found fel, 78-80. *Mem:* Am Astron Soc; Int Astron Union. *Res:* Observational astrophysics, especially white dwarfs, neutron stars and black holes; interacting binary stars; accretion. *Mailing Add:* Dept Astron Univ Tex 26th & Speedway C-1400 Austin TX 78712

ROBINSON, EDWIN HOLLIS, NUTRITION, FISHERIES. *Current Pos:* FISHERY BIOLOGIST, DELTA RES & EXTEN CTR, MISS STATE UNIV. *Personal Data:* b Florence, Ala, Dec 16, 42; m 65; c 2. *Educ:* Samford Univ, BS, 69; Auburn Univ, MS, 72, PhD(nutrit), 77. *Prof Exp:* Res assoc biochem, Miss State Univ, 77-81; asst prof wildlife & fisheries sci, Tex A&M Univ, 81- *Mem:* Am Inst Nutrit; Am Fisheries Soc; Sigma Xi. *Res:* Nutritional requirements of various aquatic animals. *Mailing Add:* Delta Br Exp Sta Miss State Univ PO Box 197 Stoneville MS 38776-0197. *Fax:* 601-686-7336

ROBINSON, EDWIN JAMES, JR, PARASITOLOGY. *Current Pos:* RETIRED. *Personal Data:* b Wilkes-Barre, Pa, Feb 7, 16; m 48; c 6. *Educ:* Dartmouth Univ, AB, 39; NY Univ, MS, 41, PhD(biol), 49. *Prof Exp:* Asst biol, NY Univ, 39-48; instr parasitol med col, Cornell Univ, 48-51; sr asst scientist, USPHS, 51-54; from asst prof to assoc prof biol, Kenyon Col, 54-60, prof, 60; prof biol, Macalester Col, 63-84. *Mem:* AAAS; Am Micros Soc; Am Soc Parasitol; Soc Protozool; Sigma Xi. *Res:* Ecology and life cycles of trematodes and filarial nematodes. *Mailing Add:* 5928 Halifax Ave S Edina MN 55424-1941

ROBINSON, EDWIN S, GEOPHYSICS, GEOLOGY. *Current Pos:* assoc prof, 67-72, PROF GEOPHYS, VA POLYTECH INST & STATE UNIV, 72- *Personal Data:* b Saginaw, Mich, Apr 29, 35; m 62; c 2. *Educ:* Univ Mich, BS, 57, MS, 59; Univ Wis, PhD(geophys, geol), 64. *Prof Exp:* Res asst geophys, Willow Run Labs, Univ Mich, 56-57; asst geophysicist, Arctic Inst NAm, 57-58; res asst geophys, Willow Run Labs, Univ Mich, 58-59; proj assoc geophys & polar res ctr, Univ Wis, 59-64; asst prof geophys, Univ Utah, 64-67. *Mem:* Am Geophys Union; Soc Explor Geophys; Glaciol Soc; fel Geol Soc Am. *Res:* Studies of seismic waves; exploration seismology in Antarctica; regional gravity and magnetic surveys interaction of earth tides and ocean tides; characteristics of seismic waves from nuclear explosions. *Mailing Add:* Dept Geol Sci Va Polytech Inst PO Box 0420 Blacksburg VA 24063-0001

ROBINSON, ENDERS ANTHONY, MATHEMATICAL PHYSICS. *Current Pos:* McMANN PROF GEOPHYS, UNIV TULSA, 83- *Personal Data:* b Boston, Mass, Mar 18, 30. *Educ:* Mass Inst Technol, SB, 50, SM, 52, PhD(geophys), 54. *Honors & Awards:* Donald G Fink Prize, Inst Elec & Electronics Engrs, 84; Soc Explor Geophys Medal, 69-; Conrad Schlumberger Award, Europ Asn Explor Geophysicists, 67. *Prof Exp:* Geophysicist, Gulf Oil Corp, 54-55; instr math, Mass Inst Technol, 55-56; petrol economist, Exxon Corp, 56-57; asst prof statist, Mich State Univ, 58; assoc prof math, Univ Wis, 58-62; dep prof statist, Uppsala Univ, Sweden, 60-64; vpres & dir, Geosci Inc, 64-65; vpres & dir, Digicon Inc, 65-70; pres, Robinson Res, 70-82; vis prof mech, Cornell Univ, 81-82. *Concurrent Pos:* TRW distinguished lectr, Univ Southern Calif, 80; vis fel, Int Bus Mach Sci Ctr, Rome, Italy, 83. *Mem:* Nat Acad Eng; Soc Explor Geophys; Europ Asn Explor Geophysicists. *Res:* History of science and engineering; popular scientific exposition; seismic wave propagation; signal analysis and digital signal processing; imaging systems and technology; digital spectral analysis and statistical time series analysis; electrical engineering systems and noise analysis; classical mathematical physics and partial differential equations; probability theory and mathematical statistics. *Mailing Add:* Dept Geosci Univ Tulsa Tulsa OK 74104-3189

ROBINSON, FARREL RICHARD, VETERINARY PATHOLOGY, TOXICOLOGY. *Current Pos:* RETIRED. *Personal Data:* b Wellington, Kans, Mar 23, 27; m 49, Mimi Hathaway; c 4. *Educ:* Kans State Univ, BS, 50, BS, DVM & MS, 58; Tex A&M Univ, PhD(vet path), 65, Am Bd Vet Toxicol, dipl; Am Col Vet Pathol, dipl. *Prof Exp:* Res vet, Aerospace Med Res Lab, Wright-Patterson AFB, USAF, 58-62; chief pat br, 64-68, mem staff, Armed Forces Inst Path, 68-71, chief vet path, 72-74, registrar, Am Registries Vet & Comp Path, 72-74; prof toxicol-path, Purdue Univ, 74-93, dir, Animal Dis Diag Lab, 78-85, chief toxicol serv, Animal Dis Diag Lab, 85-93, interim head, Dept Vet Pathobiol, 86-88. *Concurrent Pos:* Vpres, Am Bd Vet Toxicol, 71-73, pres, 76-79; head, Int Ref Ctr Comp Oncol, WHO, 72-74, collab, Tumors Eye, 72-74. *Mem:* Am Vet Med Asn; Am Col Vet Path; Soc Toxicol; Am Bd Vet Toxicol; Am Asn Vet Lab Diag (vpres, 86, pres, 87). *Res:* Pathology of the respiratory system; pathology of laboratory animals; oxygen toxicity; beryllium toxicity; pathology of toxicologic diseases; oncology. *Mailing Add:* 201 W 600 N West Lafayette IN 47906-9727

ROBINSON, FRANK ERNEST, AGRONOMY, IRRIGATION. *Current Pos:* RETIRED. *Personal Data:* b Oaklyn, NJ, Oct 29, 30; m 83; c 5. *Educ:* Rutgers Univ, BS, 52; Purdue Univ, PhD(soil physics), 58. *Prof Exp:* Asst, Purdue Univ, 55-58; assoc agronomist exp sta, Hawaiian Sugar Planters Asn, 58-64; from asst water scientist to water scientist, Dept Land, Air & Water Resources, Univ Calif, 64-92. *Concurrent Pos:* Mem, Int Comn Irrig & Drainage. *Mem:* Int Soc Soil Sci; Am Soil Sci Soc; Am Soc Agr Eng; Am Geophys Union; Am Soc Agron; Am Soc Hort Sci; hon mem Irrig Asn. *Res:* Irrigation management and salinity control; nitrate mobility, soil drainage, sprinkler and drip irrigation of vegetable crops; growth of plants with geothermal water. *Mailing Add:* 986 Nichols Rd El Centro CA 92243

ROBINSON, GENE CONRAD, ORGANIC CHEMISTRY. *Current Pos:* res chemist & res assoc, 54-73, SUPVR, ETHYL CORP, 73- *Personal Data:* b Hurricane, La, July 31, 28; m 59; c 2. *Educ:* Univ Chicago, PhB, 47, MS, 49; Univ Ill, PhD(org chem), 52. *Prof Exp:* Res chemist, Univ Calif, Los Angeles, 52-54. *Mem:* Am Chem Soc; Oceanog Soc; Int Oceanog Found. *Res:* Physical organic chemistry; organometallic chemistry. *Mailing Add:* 1064 N Leighton Dr Baton Rouge LA 70806-1835

ROBINSON, GENE E, SOCIAL INSECT BIOLOGY, HONEY BEE BIOLOGY. *Current Pos:* asst prof entom, 89-94, ASSOC PROF ENTOM & NEUROSCI, UNIV ILL, 94- *Personal Data:* b Buffalo, NY, Jan 9, 55. *Educ:* Cornell Univ, BS, 77, MS, 82, PhD(entom), 86. *Honors & Awards:* Charles D Michener Lectr, Univ Kans, Lawrence, 97. *Prof Exp:* NSF postdoctoral fel environ biol, 89. *Concurrent Pos:* Thomas A Murphy univ scholar, Univ Ill, 93-96, Beckman assoc, Ctr Advan Studies, 95-96; Fulbright scholar, Hebrew Univ, Jerusalem, 95-96. *Mem:* Fel AAAS; Animal Behav Soc; Entom Soc Am; Sigma Xi; Int Union Study Social Insects; Soc Neurosci; Int Soc Neuroethology. *Res:* Endocrine, neural and genetic mechanisms of social behavior; division of labor among bees in a colony. *Mailing Add:* Dept Entom & Neurosci Univ Ill 505 S Goodwin Ave Urbana IL 61801-3795. *Fax:* 217-244-3499; *E-Mail:* generobi@uiuc.edu

ROBINSON, GEORGE DAVID, ATMOSPHERIC PHYSICS. *Current Pos:* RES FEL ATMOSPHERIC PHYSICS, CTR ENVIRON & MAN, INC, 68- *Personal Data:* b Leeds, Eng, June 8, 13; m 48; c 2. *Educ:* Leeds Univ, BSc, 33, PhD(physics), 36. *Honors & Awards:* Buchan Prize, Royal Meteorol Soc, 52. *Prof Exp:* Res asst chem, Leeds Univ, 35-36; tech officer, UK Meteorol Off, 37-44; sci officer atmospheric physics, Kew Observ, Eng, 46-57; dep dir, UK Meteorol Off, 57-68. *Mem:* Fel Brit Inst Physics; hon mem Royal Meteorol Soc (pres, 65-67); fel Am Meteorol Soc. *Res:* Radiative transfer in the earth's atmosphere; predictability of weather and climate; artificial modification of climate. *Mailing Add:* 676 Fern St West Hartford CT 06107

ROBINSON, GEORGE EDWARD, JR, physiology; deceased, see previous edition for last biography

ROBINSON, GEORGE H(ENRY), METALLURGY. *Current Pos:* RETIRED. *Personal Data:* b Detroit, Mich, June 27, 24; m 50; c 7. *Educ:* Univ Detroit, BChE, 49; Carnegie Inst Technol, BS, 50. *Prof Exp:* Asst metall res, Res Labs, Gen Motors, 46-49, jr engr, 50-51, res metallurgist, 51-53, sr res metallurgist, 53-56, supvr ferrous metall res, 56-62, asst head, Metall Eng Dept, 62-71, head, Emmissions Res Dept, 71-73, head, Metall Dept, 73-88. *Mem:* Fel Am Soc Metals; Am Soc Automotive Engrs; Am Inst Mining & Metall Engrs; Am Foundrymens Soc. *Res:* Friction, wear and fatigue behavior of metals; physical metallurgy. *Mailing Add:* 9000 E Jefferson Apt 26-7 Detroit MI 48214

ROBINSON, GEORGE WALLER, ANALYTICAL CHEMISTRY, BIOCHEMISTRY. *Current Pos:* assoc prof, 88-94, PROF CHEM, SOUTHERN COL TECHNOL, 94- *Personal Data:* b Winchester, Ky, Mar 29, 41; m 78, Linda C Hodges; c David & Rebecca. *Educ:* Centre Col Ky, BA, 63; Duke Univ, PhD(biochem), 68. *Prof Exp:* Res assoc protein chem, Rockefeller Univ, 67-70; asst prof biochem, Univ Ky, 70-77; assoc prof chem, Centre Col Ky, 78-81; asst prof chem, Southern Tech Inst, 84-88. *Concurrent Pos:* Vis asst prof, Ga Inst Technol, 81-83, res assoc, 83-84. *Mem:* Am Chem Soc; Sigma Xi. *Res:* Structure-function relationships in proteins and enzymes; electrochemical detectors for high performance liquid chromatography, amino acid analysis, polysaccharide analysis. *Mailing Add:* 2886 Cherokee St Kennesaw GA 30144-2800

ROBINSON, GEORGE WILSE, UNDERSTANDING WATER, COMP CHEMISTRY. *Current Pos:* ROBERT A WELCH PROF CHEM & PROF PHYS, TEX TECH UNIV, 76- *Personal Data:* b Kansas City, Mo, July 27, 24; m 50, Ellen Johnson. *Educ:* Ga Inst Technol, BS, 47, MS, 49; Univ Iowa, PhD(chem), 52. *Honors & Awards:* Alexander von Humboldt Award, 84. *Prof Exp:* Asst phys chem, Univ Iowa, 50-52; fel, Univ Rochester, 52-54; asst prof, Johns Hopkins Univ, 54-59; from assoc prof chem to prof phys chem, Calif Inst Technol, 59-75. *Concurrent Pos:* Prof phys chem & chmn dept, Univ Melbourne, Australia, 75-76. *Mem:* fel Am Phys Soc. *Res:* Ultrafast molecular processes; computational studies of water and aqueous solutions; theory of activated chemical reactions; electron/proton hydration dynamics; solvent effects on chemical reactions. *Mailing Add:* Tex Tech Univ Box 41061 Lubbock TX 79409-1061. *Fax:* 806-742-3590

ROBINSON, GERALD GARLAND, ZOOLOGY, PHYSIOLOGY. *Current Pos:* From instr to assoc prof, 60-77, PROF BIOL SCI, UNIV SFLA, 77- *Personal Data:* b St Louis Co, Minn, May 8, 33; m 60; c 2. *Educ:* Univ Minn, BS, 55, PhD(zool), 60. *Mem:* Am Soc Pharmacog. *Mailing Add:* Dept Biol Sci Univ SFla Lif 136 4202 Fowler Ave Tampa FL 33620-9951

ROBINSON, GERSHON DUVALL, GEOLOGY. *Current Pos:* RETIRED. *Personal Data:* b Tulsa, Okla, Apr 2, 18; m 76, Valerie Rhoda Brown; c Scott, Toby, Henri, James, Neil & Alex. *Educ:* Northwestern Univ, BS, 39; Univ Calif, MA, 41. *Honors & Awards:* Meritorious Serv Award, Dept Interior, 82. *Prof Exp:* Asst geol, Univ Calif, 39-41; petrol geologist, Tide Water Assoc Oil Co, Tex, 41-42; geologist field geol, Alaska, US Geol Surv, 42-45, in charge volcano invests, 45-48, asst chief gen geol br, Colo, 48-51, actg chief, 51-52, field geologist, Mont, 52-60, chief, Northern Rocky Mt Br, 60-64, res geologist, Rocky Mt Environ Geol Br, Colo, 64-72, res geologist, Geol Div, 72-84. *Concurrent Pos:* Consult, Res & Develop Bd, 47-50, Earth Sci Adv Comt, NSF, 76-80; assoc ed, Geol Soc Am, 67-74; chmn, Fed Development Environ Adv Panel, Dept Interior, 78-84; consult, 84- *Mem:* Fel Mineral Soc Am; Soc Econ Geol; fel Geol Soc Am. *Res:* Ore deposits; volcanology; structural geology; geology applied to urban problems; disposal of radioactive waste. *Mailing Add:* 2830 Somass Dr Victoria BC V8R 1R8 Can

ROBINSON, GERTRUDE EDITH, MATHEMATICS EDUCATION. *Current Pos:* RETIRED. *Personal Data:* b Peoria, Ill, Apr 28, 23. *Educ:* Ill State Univ, BS, 45; Univ Wis-Madison, MS, 51, PhD(math educ), 64. *Prof Exp:* Teacher high sch, Ill, 45-57 & Wis, 57-60; asst prof, Univ Ga, 63-69, assoc prof math, 69-77; examiner, Educ Testing Serv, Princeton, NJ, 77-84, sr examiner, 84-87. *Concurrent Pos:* Consult, Ga Educ TV & Ga State Dept Educ, 64-77; Training Teacher Trainers Proj fel, NY Univ, 70-71. *Mem:* Math Asn Am; Nat Coun Teachers Math. *Res:* Diagnostic testing in mathematics for elementary school children; improving spatial ability of girls. *Mailing Add:* 102 Macon Ave Asheville NC 28801

ROBINSON, GILBERT C(HASE), ceramics engineering; deceased, see previous edition for last biography

ROBINSON, GLEN MOORE, III, PHYSICAL CHEMISTRY. *Current Pos:* SR RES SPECIALIST, IMATION CORP, 96- *Personal Data:* b El Dorado, Ark, July 23, 43; m 67, Oree Hoefeld; c Mark O & Luke I. *Educ:* La Polytech Inst, BS, 65; Tulane Univ, La, PhD(phys chem), 70. *Honors & Awards:* Harlan Vergin Award, 3M Co, 74; Heinrich Hertz Award, Inst Electronic & RadioEngrs, 85. *Prof Exp:* Chemist, E I du Pont de Nemours & Co, Inc, 66; sr chemist, 3M Co, 69-76, sr res specialist, 3M Consumer & prof video & audio, 76-96. *Concurrent Pos:* Assoc prof, Bethel Col, 72. *Mem:* Am Chem Soc; Optical Soc Am; Sigma Xi. *Res:* Magnetic tape; ceramics; surface chemistry; molecular spectroscopy; natural and magnetically induced optical activity; applied statistics; computerization of laboratory instruments; computer analysis of micrographs, optical and electron; interferometry; quantum chemistry. *Mailing Add:* Imation Corp 3M Ctr Bldg 236-1N-05 St Paul MN 55144-1000. *Fax:* 612-736-7685; *E-Mail:* gmrobinson@imation.com

ROBINSON, GLENN HUGH, SOILS, LAND USE PLANNING. *Current Pos:* CONSULT SOILS & LAND USE PLANNING, 80- *Personal Data:* b Rosedale, Ind, May 20, 12; m 76; c 3. *Educ:* Purdue Univ, BS, 38, MS, 40; Univ Wis, PhD(soils), 50. *Prof Exp:* Asst agron, Purdue Univ, 38-42; assoc soil surveyor, US Forest Serv, 42-43, assoc soil surveyor, Bur Plant Indust, Soils & Agr Eng, USDA, NC, 43-46 & Wis, 46-51, soil correlator, 51-54, sr soil correlator, Soil Conserv Serv, 54-61; sr soil scientist, Food & Agr Orgn, UN, Brit Guiana, 61-64, sr soil scientist & proj mgr, West Medani, Sudan, 64-69, Land Develop Dept, Thailand, 69-73 & Indonesia, 73-75; sr scientist, econ res sect, USDA, Saudi Arabia, 76-80. *Concurrent Pos:* Consult, Food & Agr Orgn, Malawi, 65, Sudan, 70, Calif, 81 & Jordan, 83. *Mem:* Am Soc Agron; Soil Sci Soc Am; Sigma Xi; Int Soc Soil Sci. *Res:* Soil and land classification, mapping and utilization; agriculture development in new areas; classification and evaluation of soils for Wetland Rice; soil properties in relation to cotton production. *Mailing Add:* RR 1 Box 210A Carbon IN 47837

ROBINSON, GORDON HEATH, HUMAN FACTORS ENGINEERING. *Current Pos:* RETIRED. *Personal Data:* b Detroit, Mich, Oct 23, 31. *Educ:* Wayne State Univ, BS, 54; Univ Mich, Ann Arbor, MS, 55, PhD(instrumentation, eng, psychol), 62. *Prof Exp:* Asst res engr & lectr, Dept Indust Eng & Opers Res, Univ Calif, Berkeley, 61-66; from asst prof to assoc prof indust eng, 66-75, prof indust eng, Univ Wis-Madison, 75- *Mem:* Am Psychol Asn; Am Asn Univ Professors; Human Factors Soc; Brit Ergonomics Res Soc. *Res:* Human performance models; accident causation; sociotechnical systems; quality of working life. *Mailing Add:* 560 Noe St San Francisco CA 94114-2528

ROBINSON, GUNER SUZEK, ELECTRICAL ENGINEERING. *Current Pos:* RETIRED. *Personal Data:* b Nazilli, Turkey, Feb 5, 37; US citizen; div; c 2. *Educ:* Istanbul Tech Univ, BS, 60, MS, 61; Polytech Inst Brooklyn, PhD(elec eng), 66. *Prof Exp:* Asst prof elec eng, Middle East Tech Univ, Ankara, Turkey, 66-68; mem tech staff, Comsat Labs, Commun Satellite Corp, 68-73; res scientist image processing, Image Processing Inst, Univ Southern Calif, 73-76; mem res & tech staff, Northrop Corp, 76-77, mgr, Signal Processing Lab, Northrop Res & Technol Ctr, 77-84, dir, Advan Technol Lab, Electro-Mech Div, 84-89, mgr irnd & technol planning, 89-95. *Concurrent Pos:* Consult, Re-transfer Technol to Turkey, UN Develop Prog, Turkey, 77-78 & 81. *Mem:* Inst Elec & Electronics Engrs; Soc Photo Instrumentation Engrs; Am Asn Artificial Intel; Am Defense Preparedness Asn; Asn Comput Mach; Am Asn Univ Women. *Res:* Education in electrical engineering and computer science; digital signal processing; image signal processing, compression and transmission; applications of image processing to military problems and industrial automation. *Mailing Add:* 27146 Travis Lane Palos Verdes Peninsula CA 90274

ROBINSON, HAROLD ERNEST, BOTANY, ENTOMOLOGY. *Current Pos:* CUR BOT, SMITHSONIAN INST, 62- *Personal Data:* b Syracuse, NY, May 22, 32. *Educ:* Ohio Univ, BS, 55; Univ Tenn, MA, 57; Duke Univ, PhD(bot), 60. *Prof Exp:* Asst prof biol, Wofford Col, 60-61. *Mem:* Bot Soc Am; Am Soc Plant Taxon; Am Bryol & Lichenological Soc; Sigma Xi. *Res:* Bryophytes of Latin American and India; Asteraceae; Dolichopodidae. *Mailing Add:* Dept Bot Nn6 Stop 160 Smithsonian Inst Washington DC 20560

ROBINSON, HOWARD ADDISON, ATOMIC SPECTROSCOPY, PHYSICS OF GLASS. *Current Pos:* RETIRED. *Personal Data:* b Rotterdam, NY, July 30, 09; m 35; c 3. *Educ:* Mass Inst Technol, SB, 30, PhD(physics), 35. *Prof Exp:* Chief physicist, Armstrong Cork Co, 36-51; first secy, US Embassy Paris, US Dept State, 51-57; chmn & prof, Dept Physics, Adelphi Univ, 57-74. *Concurrent Pos:* Attache, US Embassy Stockholm, US Dept State, 47-48; ed, Soviet J Optical Technol, 64- *Mem:* Fel Am Phys Soc; Optical Soc Am. *Res:* Atomic spectroscopy; physics of glass. *Mailing Add:* Four Walnut St Gloucester MA 01930

ROBINSON, HUGH GETTYS, PRECISION MEASUREMENT & ATOMIC PHYSICS, ATOMIC CLOCKS & QUANTUM OPTICS. *Current Pos:* assoc prof, 64-70, PROF PHYSICS, DUKE UNIV, 70- *Personal Data:* b New Orleans, La, Oct 30, 28. *Educ:* Emory Univ, AB, 50; Duke Univ, PhD(physics), 54. *Prof Exp:* Res assoc physics, Duke Univ, 54-55; res assoc, Univ Md, 55-56; res assoc, Univ Wash, Seattle, 56-57; instr, Yale Univ, 57-58, asst prof, 58-63; lectr, Harvard Univ, 63-64. *Mem:* Fel AAAS; fel Am Phys Soc; Sigma Xi. *Res:* Atomic physics; precision measurements in atomic and molecular physics, including fundamental constants; design and construction of appropriate apparatus; atomic clock; diode laser use and control. *Mailing Add:* 2057 Grayden Ct Superior CO 80027-8221

ROBINSON, J(AMES) MICHAEL, ORGANIC & MEDICINAL CHEMISTRY, ENERGY & FUELS. *Current Pos:* from asst prof to prof chem, 76-94, Ashbel Smith prof, 94-96, ELLEN & BILL NOEL DISTINGUISHED PROF ENERGY RES, UNIV TEX PERMIAN BASIN, 96- *Personal Data:* b Shreveport, La, Oct 13, 43; m 70, 82, Mary A Dudley; c James W, William M, Christopher A, John M & Jennifer L. *Educ:* La Tech Univ, BS, 67, MS, 69; La State Univ, Baton Rouge, PhD(org chem), 73. *Prof Exp:* Res assoc med chem, Purdue Univ, 73-74, NIH res fel, 74-75; res assoc org chem, Tulane Univ, 75-76. *Concurrent Pos:* Consult, steel foundarys and precious metals extraction. *Mem:* Am Chem Soc; Coun Undergrad Res. *Res:* Organic, medicinal and analytical chemistry of enamines, imines, pyridines and thiazyls; biomass to liquid fuels, energy research; mechanisms and drug design. *Mailing Add:* Dept Chem Univ Tex Permian Basin Odessa TX 79762. *Fax:* 915-552-2236; *E-Mail:* robinson_m@utpb.edu

ROBINSON, JACK LANDY, ANALYTICAL CHEMISTRY. *Current Pos:* From asst prof to assoc prof, 66-77, PROF CHEM, SE STATE UNIV, 77-, DIR, INST RES & PLANNING & DIR ASSESSMENT, 90-, ASST VPRES ACAD AFFAIRS & GRAD DEAN, 95- *Personal Data:* b Durant, Okla, Jan 6, 40; div; c Jeffrey, Jonathan (deceased) & Justin. *Educ:* Southeastern State Col, BA, 62; Univ Okla, PhD(chem), 66. *Concurrent Pos:* NIH. *Mem:* Am Chem Soc. *Res:* Analysis of polycyclic aromatic hydrocarbons and microbes by chromatographic methods; analysis of oxalic acid in body fluids; chromatography of polymeric adsorbents. *Mailing Add:* PO Box 238 Mead OK 73449-0238. *Fax:* 580-920-7474

ROBINSON, JAMES LAWRENCE, BIOCHEMISTRY, NUTRITION. *Current Pos:* from asst prof to assoc prof biochem, 76-85, PROF BIOCHEM, UNIV ILL, URBANA, 85- *Personal Data:* b Boston, Mass, Feb 23, 42; m 63, Janet Thorpe; c Mark, Majorie & J Glen. *Educ:* Univ Redlands, BS, 64; Univ Calif, Los Angeles, PhD(biochem), 68. *Honors & Awards:* Nutrit Res Award, 81. *Prof Exp:* Teaching asst anal chem & biochem, Univ Calif, Los Angeles, 65-66; NIH res fel, Inst Cancer Res, Philadelphia, 68-70. *Concurrent Pos:* Mem nutrit sci fac, Univ Ill, 72; researcher, Nutrit Res Ctr, Meudon, France, 78-79, Biochem Dept, Univ Nijmegen, Neth, 87-88, Elizabeth Macarthur Agric Inst, Camden, Australia, 93-94. *Mem:* Am Soc Biol Chemists; Am Dairy Sci Asn; Am Inst Nutrit. *Res:* Enzyme mechanisms; metabolic regulation; specific interests in biochemistry, nutrition and physiology associated with bovine inherited disorders (deficiency of uridine monophosphate synthase, citrullinemia, and factor XI deficiency). *Mailing Add:* 132 Animal Sci Lab Univ Ill 1207 W Gregory Dr Urbana IL 61801-3838. *Fax:* 217-333-8804; *E-Mail:* jlrobins@uiuc.edu

ROBINSON, JAMES MCOMBER, clinical biochemistry, for more information see previous edition

ROBINSON, JAMES VANCE, ENTOMOLOGY. *Current Pos:* EXTEN ENTOMOLOGIST, TEX AGR EXTEN SERV, 75- *Personal Data:* b Corsicana, Tex, July 27, 43; m 62; c 3. *Educ:* Tex A&M Univ, BS, 67, MS, 71; Miss State Univ, PhD(entom), 75. *Prof Exp:* Surv entomologist, Miss Agr & Forestry Exp Sta, 71-75. *Mem:* Entom Soc Am. *Mailing Add:* Dept Biol Univ Tex Box 19498 Uta Sta Arlington TX 76019

ROBINSON, JAMES WILLIAM, ELECTRICAL ENGINEERING. *Current Pos:* from asst prof to assoc prof, 66-80, PROF ENG, PA STATE UNIV, 80- *Personal Data:* b Syracuse, NY, Apr 4, 38; m 64; c 4. *Educ:* Univ Mich, Ann Arbor, BSE, 59, MSE, 61, PhD(elec eng), 65. *Prof Exp:* Res asst elec eng, Univ Mich, Ann Arbor, 64-65, res engr, 65-66. *Mem:* Inst Elec & Electronics Engrs; Am Soc Eng Educ. *Res:* Electron and ion beams; beam-surface interactions; electrical discharges. *Mailing Add:* Dept Elec Eng Pa State Univ University Park PA 16802

ROBINSON, JAMES WILLIAM, ANALYTICAL CHEMISTRY, ENVIRONMENTAL INSRUMENIAL SCIENCE. *Current Pos:* assoc prof chem, 64-66, asst dir, Environ Inst, 71-86, PROF CHEM LA STATE UNIV, BATON ROUGE, 66- *Personal Data:* b Kidderminster, Eng, July 12, 23; nat US; m 46, Winifred G Nixon; c James W, Linda W & Sandra J S. *Educ:* Univ Birmingham, BSc, 49, PhD(anal chem), 52, DSc, 77. *Prof Exp:* Sr sci officer, Brit Civil Serv, 52-55; res assoc, La State Univ, 55-56; sr chemist res labs, Esso Stand Oil Co, 56-63; tech adv, Ethyl Corp, 63-64. *Concurrent Pos:* Ed, Spectros Letters, Environ Sci & Health & CRC Handbook Spectros; asst ed, Anal Chimica Acta & Appl Spectros Reviews; Guggenheim fel, 74; chmn, Analy Gordon Conf, 74. *Mem:* Am Chem Soc; Chem Soc; Soc Appl Spectros; fel Royal Chem Soc; Am Inst Chem. *Res:* Speciation analysis of trace metals; atomic absorption inductively coupled plasma emission; molecular spectroscopy; light structure; air quality control; air pollution analysis; acid rain. *Mailing Add:* Dept Chem 440 Chopping Hall La State Univ Baton Rouge LA 70803. *Fax:* 504-388-3458; *E-Mail:* jwrobinson@chemgate.chem.lsu.edu

ROBINSON, JEROME DAVID, CHEMICAL ENGINEERING. *Current Pos:* DIR ENG & TECHNOL, AM CYANAMID CO, 68- *Personal Data:* b Stamford, Conn, Jan 30, 41; m 64; c 2. *Educ:* City Univ New York, BChE, 63; Univ Del, MChE, 66, PhD(chem eng), 68. *Prof Exp:* Res & develop chem engr, E I du Pont de Nemours & Co, 63-64; instr chem eng, Univ Del, 67. *Concurrent Pos:* Adj prof, Newark Col Eng, 69-70. *Mem:* Am Inst Chem Engrs. *Res:* Chemical and environmental process and systems design, analysis and control. *Mailing Add:* Am Cyanamid Co One Campus Dr Parsippany NJ 07054

ROBINSON, JERRY ALLEN, REPRODUCTIVE PHYSIOLOGY, ENDOCRINOLOGY. *Current Pos:* HEALTH SCIENTIST ADMINR, NAT INST ENVIRON HEALTH SCI, RES TRIANGLE PARK, NC, 87-, CHIEF, ORGANS & SYSTS TOXICOL BR, 93- *Personal Data:* b Danville, Ill, Dec 18, 39; m 69, Sharon A Meisner; c Carrie J & Kevin T. *Educ:* Wabash Col, BA, 63; Univ Cincinnati, MS, 66, PhD(zool), 70. *Prof Exp:* Trainee, Wis Regional Primate Res Ctr, Univ Wis-Madison, 70-72, res assoc, 72-73, asst scientist, 73-78, assoc scientist, 78-86; grants assoc, NIH, Bethesda, Md, 86-87. *Concurrent Pos:* Asst dir, Inst Aging, Univ Wis-Madison, 82-84; asst ed, Biol Reproduction, Soc Study Reproduction, 85-86. *Mem:* Am Soc Primatologists; Soc Study Reproduction; Am Soc Zool; Endocrine Soc; Sigma Xi. *Res:* Steroid hormone secretion, metabolism and mechanism of action; reproductive and developmental toxicology. *Mailing Add:* 5112 Hogans Way Clayton NC 27520. *Fax:* 919-541-2843

ROBINSON, JOHN, BACTERIOLOGY, AGRICULTURE. *Current Pos:* from assoc prof to prof microbiol & immunol, 65-87, EMER PROF, UNIV WESTERN ONT, 87- *Personal Data:* b Vancouver, BC, Apr 25, 22; m 46, Jessica Coburn; c Barbara E, Douglas F, Margaret E & Frances A. *Educ:* Univ BC, BSA, 44; McGill Univ, MSc, 45, PhD(bact), 50. *Honors & Awards:* Can Silver Jubilee Medal, 77. *Prof Exp:* Res officer, Nat Res Coun Can, 46-48 & 49-50; res officer, Can Dept Agr, 50-56; bacteriologist, HEW, 56-65. *Mem:* Can Soc Microbiol (secy-treas, 59-61, 72-74, first vpres, 76-77, pres, 77-78). *Res:* Production of antibiotics by fungi; metabolism of halophilic bacteria; isolation and characterization of toxins produced by Staphylococcus aureus; mode of action of lysis of specific bacteria by the predaceous bacterium Bdellovibrio; Bdellovibrio and the ecology of polluted water. *Mailing Add:* J&J Robinson Christmas Tree Farm RR3 Mouth of Keswick NB E0H 1N0 Can

ROBINSON, JOHN MITCHELL, LEUKOCYTE ACTIVATION, ENDOCYTOSIS. *Current Pos:* ASSOC PROF PATH, HARVARD MED SCH, 86- *Educ:* Vanderbilt Univ, PhD(biol), 76. *Mailing Add:* Dept Cell Biol Neurobiol & Anat Ohio State Univ 4072 Graves Hall 333 W Tenth Ave Columbus OH 43210-1239. *Fax:* 614-292-7659

ROBINSON, JOHN MURRELL, ELECTRONIC & MAGNETIC PROPERTIES OF SOLIDS. *Current Pos:* asst prof, 73-78, ASSOC PROF PHYSICS, IND UNIV-PURDUE UNIV, 78-, CHMN DEPT, 79- *Personal Data:* b Lecompte, La, Mar 26, 45. *Educ:* La State Univ, BS, 67; Fla State Univ, MS, 70, PhD(physics), 72. *Prof Exp:* Tech asst, Univ Munich, 70-71; res assoc, Fla State Univ, 72-73. *Mem:* Am Phys Soc; Am Asn Physics Teachers. *Res:* Theoretical models of electronic and magnetic properties of rare earth and actinide materials, particularly mixed valence materials. *Mailing Add:* Dept Physics Ind Univ-Purdue Univ 2101 Coliseum Blvd E Ft Wayne IN 46805

ROBINSON, JOHN PAUL, COMMUNICATION ENGINEERING. *Current Pos:* from asst prof to assoc prof, 65-72, PROF ENG, UNIV IOWA, 72-, ASSOC DEAN. *Personal Data:* b Providence, RI, Jan 1, 39; m 60; c 3. *Educ:* Iowa State Univ, BSEE, 60; Princeton Univ, MSE, 62, PhD(elec eng), 66. *Prof Exp:* Mem tech staff, RCA Labs, 60-62 & IBM Labs, NY, 63-65. *Mem:* Inst Elec & Electronics Engrs; Sigma Xi. *Res:* Digital systems; switching theory; codes for error detection and correction; reliable systems; communication systems. *Mailing Add:* 5408 EB Dept EE Univ Iowa Iowa City IA 52242

ROBINSON, JOHN PRICE, MICROBIOLOGY. *Current Pos:* RETIRED. *Personal Data:* b Charlotte, Tenn, Dec 1, 27; m 60; c 2. *Educ:* Univ Tenn, BS, 54; Vanderbilt Univ, PhD(microbiol), 61. *Prof Exp:* From instr to assoc prof microbiol, Sch Med, Vanderbilt Univ, 61-91. *Concurrent Pos:* USPHS sci res grants, 64-65 & NSF, 66-67. *Mem:* Electron Micros Soc; Am Soc Microbiol. *Res:* Mechanism of antibody-antigen complex formation; biochemical approach and visualization in the electron microscopy. *Mailing Add:* 906 Estes Rd Nashville TN 37215

ROBINSON, JOSEPH DOUGLASS, MEMBRANE TRANSPORT, NEUROSCIENCE. *Current Pos:* from asst prof to assoc prof pharmacol, 64-72, PROF PHARMACOL, STATE UNIV NY HEALTH SCI CTR, 72- *Personal Data:* b Asheville, NC, Nov 28, 34; m 58, Carol Smith; c Karin A & Lisa J. *Educ:* Yale Univ, MD, 59. *Honors & Awards:* Javits Neurosci Investr Award, 86. *Prof Exp:* Intern med, Stanford Univ Hosp, 59-60; res assoc neurochem, NIH, 60-62; fel pharmacol, Sch Med, Yale Univ, 62-64. *Concurrent Pos:* NSF sr fel pharmacol, Cambridge Univ, 71-72; mem pharmacol study sect, NIH, 80-84. *Mem:* AAAS; Am Soc Pharmacol & Exp Therapeut; Biophys Soc; Philos Sci Asn; Hist Sci Soc. *Res:* Membrane structure, permeability and transport; neuroscience; history and philosophy of science. *Mailing Add:* Dept Pharmacol State Univ NY Health Sci Ctr Syracuse NY 13210. *Fax:* 315-464-8014

ROBINSON, JOSEPH EDWARD, PETROLEUM EXPLORATION. *Current Pos:* prof, 76-91, EMER PROF GEOL, SYRACUSE UNIV, 91- *Personal Data:* b Regina, Sask, June 25, 25; div; c 3. *Educ:* McGill Univ, BEng, 50, MSc, 51; Univ Alberta, PhD(geol), 68. *Prof Exp:* Geophysist, Imp Oil Ltd, 51-66; sr geologist, Union Oil Can, 68-76. *Concurrent Pos:* Vis indust assoc, Kans Geol Surv, 70-72; vis prof, Syracuse Univ, 74; asst ed, Int Asn Math Geol, 76-80; prin investr, US Dept Energy, 79-81; geol consult, J E Robinson & Assoc, 76- *Mem:* Soc Explor Geophysists; Am Asn Petrol Geologists; Can Soc Petrol Geologists; Int Asn Math Geol; Soc Independent Prof Earth Scientists. *Res:* Geologic data base construction; management and computer applications in exploration for petroleum, natural gas and other economic minerals; environmental geology and geophysics. *Mailing Add:* Dept Geol Heroy Geol Lab Syracuse Univ Syracuse NY 13244-1070

ROBINSON, JOSEPH ROBERT, PHARMACEUTICS. *Current Pos:* From asst prof to assoc prof, 66-74, PROF PHARM, UNIV WIS-MADISON, 74- *Personal Data:* b New York, NY, Feb 16, 39; m 59, Bonna Hatfield; c James C, Nancy L & Daniel G. *Educ:* Columbia Univ, BS, 61, MS, 63; Univ Wis, PhD(pharm), 66. *Hon Degrees:* DSc, Royal Danish Sch Pharm, Denmark, 89. *Honors & Awards:* Ebert Prize & Res Achievement Award, APhA Found; Janot Medal; Founders Award, Controlled Release Soc; Res Achievement Award, Am Asn Pharmaceut Scientists; Higuchi Medal, Am Pharmaceut Asn; Warster Award, Am Asn Pharmaceut Scientists. *Concurrent Pos:* Vis prof, Johann Goethe Univ, Frankfurt, WGer, 89, ETH, Zurich, Switz, 91. *Mem:* Am Pharmaceut Asn; Am Chem Soc; fel Acad Pharmaceut Sci; fel AAAS; NY Acad Sci; Controlled Release Soc; fel Am Asn Pharmaceut Scientists. *Res:* Biopharmaceutics; ophthalmic pharmacology; mechanisms of drug transport and activity in the eye; controlled drug delivery. *Mailing Add:* Sch Pharm Univ Wis Madison WI 53706. *Fax:* 608-262-4054; *E-Mail:* jrr@pharmacy.wisc.edu

ROBINSON, KENNETH ROBERT, ORGANIC CHEMISTRY. *Current Pos:* RETIRED. *Personal Data:* b Akron, Ohio, Nov 17, 21; m 47; c 4. *Educ:* Ohio Northern Univ, BA, 43; Purdue Univ, MS, 46; Mich State Univ, PhD(chem), 50. *Prof Exp:* Res chemist, E I du Pont de Nemours & Co, 50-55; sr chemist, Koppers Co, Inc, 55-61; res chemist, Maumee Chem Co, 61-63; group leader, Ashland Oil, Inc, 64-71, res assoc res & develop dept, 71-74, mgr govt contracts, 74, mgr cent coding control, 74-87. *Res:* Petroleum chemistry; hydrocarbon oxidation; ozonation; custom chemical synthesis; coal; coal tar chemicals; aromatic chemicals; cellulose and viscose chemistry; synthetic monomer and polymer chemistry; research planning; fuel science; computer sciences. *Mailing Add:* 800 Mission Hills Lane Columbus OH 43235

ROBINSON, KENT, BIOLOGY, SCIENCE EDUCATION. *Current Pos:* RETIRED. *Personal Data:* b Reese, NC, June 22, 24; m 48; c 2. *Educ:* Appalachian State Teachers Col, BS, 50, MA, 52; Ohio State Univ, PhD(sci educ, biol), 66. *Prof Exp:* Teacher pub schs, NC, 50-56; prof biol, Appalachian State Univ, 56-90. *Res:* Botany. *Mailing Add:* 214 Woodland Dr Boone NC 28607

ROBINSON, LAWRENCE BAYLOR, PHYSICS. *Current Pos:* lectr, 57-60, from assoc prof to prof eng, 60-74, asst dean, Sch Eng & Appl Sci, 69-74, PROF ENG & APPL SCI, UNIV CALIF, LOS ANGELES, 74- *Personal Data:* b Tappahannock, Va, Sept 14, 19; m 56; c 3. *Educ:* Va Union Univ, BS, 39; Harvard Univ, MA, 41; PhD(chem physics), 46. *Prof Exp:* Instr math & physics, Va Union Univ, 41-42; teacher math, USSignal Corps Schs, Md, 42; tester radio parts, Victor Div, Radio Corp Am, NJ, 43; asst prof chem & physics, Va Union Univ, 44; asst prof physics, Howard Univ, 46-47, instr phys sci, 47-48, assoc prof physics, 48-51; res physicist, Atomic Energy Res Div, US Naval Res Lab, 53-54; asst prof physics, Brooklyn Col, 54-56; mem tech staff, Space Tech Labs, Inc Div, Thompson Ramo Wooldridge, Inc, 56-60. *Concurrent Pos:* NSF fel, 66-67; guest prof, Aachen Tech Univ, 66-67. *Mem:* Am Phys Soc; Am Asn Physics Teachers. *Res:* Zeta potentials of solutions of electrolytes; surface tension of electrolytes; neutron physics; reactor theory; collision between electrons and atoms; interatomic forces and collisions; magnetic properties of solids; nonequilibrium thermodynamics. *Mailing Add:* Chem Eng 5405 Boelter Univ Calif Los Angeles 405 Hilgard Ave Los Angeles CA 90095-1752

ROBINSON, LEON, FUEL TECHNOLOGY, CORROSION MITIGATION. *Current Pos:* CHEMIST & ENGR, TEX EASTERN CORP, 79-; CORROSION ENGR, TEPPCO, 95- *Personal Data:* b Pontotoc, Miss. *Educ:* Miss State Univ, BS, 65; Univ Calif, PhD(phys org chem), 69. *Prof Exp:* Res chemist, Occidental Petrol Res Lab, 70-75, M N Kellogg Res Lab, 75-79. *Concurrent Pos:* Lectr, Petex Sch, Petex Univ Tex, 84-; comt chmn, Nat Asn Corrosion Engrs, 90-93; mem, Effects of Oxygenates upon Elastomers Comt, Am Petrol Inst. *Mem:* Am Chem Soc; Nat Asn Corrosion Engrs. *Res:* Conversion of coal, shale oil, syntheses gas to liquid and gaseous fuel; mitigation of internal pipe and vessel corrosion by microbiological agents; external protection of structures from corrosion. *Mailing Add:* 651 S Commerce Dr Seymour IN 47274

ROBINSON, LEWIS HOWE, AIR QUALITY MODELING, COMPUTER ALGEBRA SYSTEMS. *Current Pos:* RETIRED. *Personal Data:* b Cody, Wyo, Sept 11, 30; wid. *Educ:* San Jose State Col, BA, 52; Univ Calif, Berkeley, MA, 59. *Prof Exp:* Meteorologist, Pac Southwest Forest & Range Exp Sta, US Forest Serv, 57-60; meteorologist, Pac Gas & Elec Co, 61-66; meteorologist, WeatherMeasure Corp, 66; meteorologist, Aerojet-Gen Corp Div, Gen Tire & Rubber Co, 66-67; pres, Robinson Assocs, 68-71; air pollution meteorologist, 72-73, sr air pollution meteorologist, 73-76, chief res & planning sect, 76-79, dir planning div, Bay Area Air Quality Mgt Dist, 79-87. *Mem:* Am Meteorol Soc; Math Asn Am; Asn Comput Mach; Am Math Soc. *Res:* Air pollution; atmospheric transport and diffusion; statistical prediction. *Mailing Add:* 1100 Gough St, Apt 14A San Francisco CA 94109. *E-Mail:* frgpzia@prodigy.com

ROBINSON, LLOYD BURDETTE, ELECTRONIC INSTRUMENTATION, ASTRONOMY. *Current Pos:* RES PHYSICIST & ASTRONR INSTRUMENTATION & ASTRON, LICK OBSERV, UNIV CALIF, SANTA CRUZ, 69- *Personal Data:* b Gravelburg, Sask, Aug 28, 29; US citizen; m; c 2. *Educ:* Univ Sask, BA, 53, MA, 54; Univ BC, PhD(physics), 57. *Prof Exp:* Res officer electronics, Atomic Energy Can Ltd, 57-62; electronics engr, Lawrence Radiation Lab, Univ Calif, 62-69. *Concurrent Pos:* NSF grants astron, 71- *Mem:* Soc Photo-Optical Instrumentation Engrs; Int Astron Union; Am Astron Soc; Astron Soc Pac. *Res:* Development of electronic and optical instruments for observational optical astronomy; use of small computers as an aid in control and data acquisition; development of low light level sensors. *Mailing Add:* Lick Observ NS-2 Univ Calif Santa Cruz CA 95064

ROBINSON, M JOHN, NUCLEAR ENGINEERING. *Current Pos:* nuclear engr, 72-77, proj mgr, 77-78, partner, 79-91, SR PARTNER, BLACK & VEATCH ENGRS-ARCHITECTS, 91- *Personal Data:* b Monroe, Mich, June 19, 38; m 60; c 4. *Educ:* Univ Mich, BS, 60, MS, 62, PhD(nuclear eng), 65. *Prof Exp:* Res asst nuclear eng, Univ Mich, 60-63, asst res engr, 63-64, res assoc nuclear eng, 64-65, lectr, 65-69; assoc prof nuclear eng, Kans State Univ, 69-72. *Concurrent Pos:* Inst Sci & Technol res fel, 65-66; Int Atomic Energy Agency tech asst expert, heat transfer adv Govt Brazil, 70-71. *Mem:* Am Nuclear Soc. *Res:* Fluid flow and heat transfer; nuclear power systems; reactor physics; shielding; fuel management; radiological effects. *Mailing Add:* Black & Veatch Engrs Power Div 11401 Lamar Overland Park KS 66211

ROBINSON, MARGARET CHISOLM, BIOLOGY. *Current Pos:* prof biol, Savannah State Col, 66-69, head Biol Dept, 69-80, dept chmn Natural Sci, 71-80, actg dean, 80-81, DEAN, SCH SCI & TECH, SAVANNAH STATE COL, 81- *Personal Data:* b Savannah, Ga, Oct 31, 30; m 52; c 2. *Educ:* Savannah State Col, BS, 52; Univ Mich, MS, 55; Wash Univ, PhD(plant physiol), 69. *Prof Exp:* Teacher natural sci, Jefferson County Training High Sch, 52-54; instr biol, Ft Valley State Col, 57-59; teaching fel molecular biol, Wash Univ, 65-66. *Concurrent Pos:* Consult, Sol C Johnson High Sch, 73-77 & 84-88, Herschel V Jenkins High Sch, 75-76, Frank W Spencer Elementary 74 & Richard Arnold High Sch, 76. *Mem:* Am Soc Cell Biol; Am Asn Plant Physiologists; Am Coun Educ; Nat Tech Asn; AAAS; Am Inst Biol Sci. *Res:* Inherited changes in Euglena gracilis induced by ultracentrifugation; antibiotics; antihistamines; micronutrients dificiencies. *Mailing Add:* 4317 Whatley Ave Savannah GA 31404

ROBINSON, MARK TABOR, RADIATION EFFECTS, COMPUTATIONAL PHYSICS. *Current Pos:* RETIRED. *Personal Data:* b Oak Park, Ill, June 23, 26; m 47, Margaret E Dohr; c Susan K & Mark D. *Educ:* Univ Ill, BS, 46; Okla State Univ, MS, 49, PhD(chem), 51. *Prof Exp:* Instr chem, Okla State Univ, 47-49, res assoc, 49-51; res staff mem, Solid State Div, Oak Ridge Nat Lab, 51-96. *Concurrent Pos:* Vis scientist, Metall Div, Atomic Energy Res Estab, Eng, 64-65, Inst Solid State Res, Nuclear Res Estab, Ger, 71-72 & Max-Planck Inst for Plasma Physics, Ger, 83; western hemisphere regional ed, Radiation Effects, 80-84. *Mem:* Am Chem Soc; fel Am Phys Soc. *Res:* Theory of radiation effects in solids; atomic collisions in solids; digital computer applications. *Mailing Add:* 112 Miramar Circle Oak Ridge TN 37830

ROBINSON, MARTIN ALVIN, INORGANIC CHEMISTRY. *Current Pos:* RETIRED. *Personal Data:* b New York, NY, Sept 12, 30; m 56; c 3. *Educ:* NY Univ, BA, 52; Univ Buffalo, MS, 54; Ohio State Univ, PhD(inorg chem), 61. *Prof Exp:* Sr chemist, Battelle Mem Inst, 56-61; group supvr inorg res & develop, Olin Corp, 61-69; dept mgr indust fine chem, J T Baker Chem Co, NJ, 69-71; mgr res & develop, Specialty Chem Div, Allied Chem Corp, 72-85, dir, Buffalo Res Lab, 85- *Concurrent Pos:* Asst prof, Southern Conn State Col, 62-69. *Mem:* Am Chem Soc; Sigma Xi; fel Am Inst Chemists. *Res:* Catalysis; transition metal complexes. *Mailing Add:* 167 Wood Acre Dr East Amherst NY 14051-1758

ROBINSON, MERTON ARNOLD, SCIENTIFIC INSTRUMENTATION, ANALYTICAL CHEMISTRY. *Current Pos:* RETIRED. *Personal Data:* b Los Angeles, Calif, Sept 13, 25; m 49, Glenna Abernathy; c Gail, James & Donald. *Educ:* Univ Calif, Los Angeles, BS, 49. *Prof Exp:* Head anal lab, Riker Labs, Inc, 49-53 & Carnation Res Lab, 53-59; mgr prod assurance, Beckman Instruments, Inc, Anaheim, 59-83; mgr regulatory affairs, Sensormedics Corp, Anaheim, 83-87. *Res:* Optical instruments for satellites; gas chromatography for trace contaminant analysis. *Mailing Add:* 1041 Brookwood Dr La Habra CA 90631. *E-Mail:* 75574.331@compuserve.com

ROBINSON, MICHAEL HILL, ZOOLOGY. *Current Pos:* biologist, Tropical Res Inst, 66-84, asst dir, 80, actg dir, 80-81, dep dir, 81-84, DIR NAT ZOOL PARK, SMITHSONIAN INST, 84- *Personal Data:* b Preston, Eng, Jan 7, 29; US citizen; m 55. *Educ:* Univ Wales, BSc, 63; Oxford Univ, Dphil, 66. *Prof Exp:* Teacher sci, UK Sec Schs, 63-70. *Concurrent Pos:* Vis lectr, Univ Pa, 69; reader biol, New Univ Ulster, 71; adj prof zool, Univ Miami, Coral Gables, 81-; dir, Am Arachnological Soc, 82-; guest lectr, Univ Papua, New Guinea, 74. *Mem:* fel Royal Entom Soc London; fel Zool Soc UK; Asn Study Animal Behav. *Res:* Tropical ecology, and behavior of predators; anti-predator adaptations; courtship and mating behavior in invertebrates (insects and spiders); evolutionary implications of behavior; author of two books and over 150 articles and papers. *Mailing Add:* Nat Zool Park Smithsonian Inst Washington DC 20008-2598

ROBINSON, MICHAEL K, ALLERGIC HYPERSENSITIVITY, TUMOR IMMUNOLOGY. *Current Pos:* STAFF SCIENTIST, GROUP LEADER, SECT HEAD & PRIN SCIENTIST, PROCTER & GAMBLE CO, 85- *Personal Data:* b Toledo, Ohio, Jan 4, 51; m 76, Kathleen Nolan; c Meghann K, Kristen E, John M, Sarah M & Gregory J. *Educ:* Univ Notre Dame, BSc, 73, MSc, 75; State Univ NY, PhD(microbiol), 79. *Prof Exp:* Sr immunologist, Dept Immunochem Res, Evanston Hosp, 82-85. *Concurrent Pos:* Consult, Immunotoxicol Working Group, Task Force Environ Cancer, Heart & Lung Dis, 88-89 & Chem Indust Inst Toxicol, 89. *Mem:* Am Asn Immunologists; AAAS; Am Soc Cancer Res; Soc Investigative Dermat. *Res:* Immune mechanisms in cancer and hypersensitivity; recently working on immunology of skin and respiratory hypersensitivity supporting both product safety and drug development activities. *Mailing Add:* Procter & Gamble Co Miami Valley Labs Cincinnati OH 45253-8707. *Fax:* 513-627-0400; *E-Mail:* robinson.mk@pg.com

ROBINSON, MICHAEL R, AERONAUTICAL ENGINEERING. *Current Pos:* Dir, X-31 Prog, 86-94, prog dir, Advan Aircraft Progs, 91-94, DIR BUS DEVELOP, BOEING N AM, CALIF. *Personal Data:* m, Linda F Braun; c Tara, Jena & Brent. *Educ:* Univ Wash, BS, 66. *Honors & Awards:* DGLR Team Award, 96; Aircraft Design Award, Am Inst Aeronaut & Astronaut, 94. *Concurrent Pos:* Mem bd dirs, Am Inst Aeronaut & Astronaut, chmn, Aircraft Design Comt, 81. *Mem:* Fel Am Inst Aeronaut & Astronaut. *Res:* X-31 enhanced maneuverability fighter demonstrator. *Mailing Add:* Boeing NAm 2201 Seal Beach PO Box 3644 Seal Beach CA 90740-7644

ROBINSON, MYRON, AIR POLLUTION, ENVIRONMENTAL SCIENCE. *Current Pos:* ADJ PROF, LONG ISLAND UNIV, 82- *Personal Data:* b Bronx, NY, Mar 4, 28; m 63, Esther Stencel; c Michael, Miriam, Jonathan & Devorah. *Educ:* City Col New York, BS, 49; NY Univ, MS, 58; Cooper Union, PhD(physics), 75. *Prof Exp:* Physicist, Nat Bur Stand, 50-53, US Army Biol Warfare Labs, 54-56; electronic scientist, US Navy Appl Sci Lab, 53-54 & 56-58; asst dir res, Res-Cottrell, Inc, 58-68; aerosol physicist, Health & Safety Lab, US AEC, NY, 68-75; vis prof, Hebrew Univ, Jerusalem, 75-76; prin sci assoc, Dart Indust, 78-80; prof, Queensborough Community Col, 81-82; safety & health mgr, Defense Logistics Agency, 87-95. *Concurrent Pos:* Consult air pollution control, Res-Cottrell, Inc, Precipitair Pollution Control, Seversky Electronatom, Environ Protect Agency, Energy Res Co, FluiDyne Eng Corp, Israel Environ Protection Agency, Argonne & Brookhaven Nat Labs, India Ministry Energy, Kerr-McGee Corp, UN Indust Develop Agency, 68-; adj prof, Cooper Union, 70-75; vis lectr, Univ Western Ont, 70-71 & Nehru, Madras & Madurai Univs, 76, Israel Inst Technol, 76, Univ Wash & Univ Wis, 80; Fulbright-Hayes fel, 75. *Mem:* Inst Elec & Electronics Engrs; Air Pollution Control Asn; Electrostatic Soc Am (pres, 71-73). *Res:* Particulate air pollution control mechanisms, particularly the extension of electrostatic precipitation to untried areas of application; aerosol technology in industrial hazard evaluation. *Mailing Add:* 73-32 136th St Flushing NY 11367-2827. *Fax:* 718-851-8471

ROBINSON, MYRTLE TONNE, ORGANIC CHEMISTRY. *Current Pos:* Lab mgr, 69-74, LAB DIR, LINDAU CHEM, INC, 74- *Personal Data:* b Cincinnati, Ohio, Jan 12, 29; m 51; c 3. *Educ:* Berea Col, BA, 50; Purdue Univ, MS, 52. *Mailing Add:* Lindau Chem Inc 731 Rosewood Dr Columbia SC 29201

ROBINSON, NEAL CLARK, MITOCHONDRIAL ELECTRON TRANSPORT, MEMBRANE PROTEIN COMPLEXES. *Current Pos:* from asst prof to assoc prof, 77-89, PROF BIOCHEM, UNIV TEX HEALTH SCI CTR, 89- *Personal Data:* b Seattle, Wash, March 6, 42; m 68, LeAnn K Peterson; c Karin C & Amy C. *Educ:* Univ Wash, BS, 64, PhD(biochem), 71. *Prof Exp:* Res assoc & fel, Duke Univ, 71-74; res assoc, Univ Ore, 74-75; lectr biochem, Univ Calif, Davis, 75-77. *Mem:* Biophys Soc; Am Chem Soc; Sigma Xi; Am Soc Biochem & Molecular Biol. *Res:* Protein-phospholipid and protein-detergent interactions with solubilized membrane protein complexes isolated from the inner mitochondrial membrane, especially cytochrome c oxidase and cardiolipm. *Mailing Add:* Dept Biochem Univ Tex Health Sci Ctr 7703 Floyd Curl Dr San Antonio TX 78284-7760

ROBINSON, NORMAN EDWARD, PULMONARY PATHOPHYSIOLOGY. *Current Pos:* assoc prof, 72-78, PROF PHYSIOL & LARGE ANIMAL MED, MICH STATE UNIV, 78-, MATILDA R WILSON PROF LARGE ANIMAL CLIN SERV, 88- *Personal Data:* b Tadley, Eng, Oct 12, 42; m 67; c 2. *Educ:* Univ London, Eng, BVetMed, 65; Univ Calif, Davis, PhD(physiol), 72. *Prof Exp:* Pvt pract vet surg, Eng, 65-66; intern large animal med, Univ Pa, 66-67; assoc vet med, Univ Calif, Davis, 67-70. *Concurrent Pos:* Prin investr, develop collateral ventilation, 75-82 & model bronchial hyperactivity, 81- *Mem:* Am Physiol Soc; Am Thoracic Soc; Am Vet Med Asn. *Res:* Pathophysiology of lung disease in the large domestic mammals, particularly chronic airway disease in the horse and pneumonia in cattle; species variations in collateral ventilation. *Mailing Add:* Dept Large Animal Clin Sci Mich State Univ G-321 Vet Med Ctr East Lansing MI 48824-1314. *Fax:* 517-336-1042

ROBINSON, PAUL RONALD, inorganic chemistry, coordination chemistry, for more information see previous edition

ROBINSON, PETER, PALEONTOLOGY, GEOLOGY. *Current Pos:* cur mus, 61-71, asst prof, 61-71, PROF NATURAL HIST, UNIV COLO, BOULDER, 71-, CUR GEOL, - *Personal Data:* b New York, NY, July 19, 32; m 54, 84; c 2. *Educ:* Yale Univ, BS, 54, MS, 58, PhD(geol), 60. *Prof Exp:* Instr geol, Harpur Col, 55-57; res assoc paleont, Yale Peabody Mus, 60-61. *Concurrent Pos:* NSF grants Eocene Insectivora res, 60-61 & co-recipient for salvage archaeol, Aswan Reservoir, Sudan, 64-67; res assoc, Carnegie Mus Natural Hist, 66-; Smithsonian grant paleont res, Tunisia, 67-81; dir, Colo Paleont Exped to Tunisia, 67-87. *Mem:* AAAS; Soc Vert Paleont; Australian Soc Mammal; Paleont Soc. *Res:* Vertebrate paleontology, especially fossil mammals. *Mailing Add:* Univ Colo Mus Box 315 Boulder CO 80309-0315

ROBINSON, PETER, STRUCTURAL GEOLOGY, PETROLOGY. *Current Pos:* from instr to asst prof, 62-69, assoc prof, 69-76, PROF GEOL, UNIV MASS, AMHERST, 76- *Personal Data:* b Hanover, NH, July 9, 32; m 57, 90, Suzanne A McEnroe; c Christopher, Harold & Alexandra. *Educ:* Dartmouth Col, AB, 54; Univ Otago, NZ, MSc, 58; Harvard Univ, PhD(geol), 63. *Prof Exp:* Raw mat engr, Columbia Iron Mining Co, US Steel Corp, 56-58. *Concurrent Pos:* Lectr, Petrologists Club, Carnegie Inst Geophys Lab, 65; vis scientist, Am Geol Inst, Maine & Dalhousie Univs, 66; NSF res grants, 66-94 & joint res grants with H W Jaffe, 66-74 & with J M Rhodes, 80-86; mem exped, Metamorphic Rocks, Chatham Island, NZ Plateau, 68; subsurface mapping, Northfield Mountain Pumped Storage Hydroelec Proj, 68-70; geol consult, Metrop Dist Comt, Boston, 72-80; co-compiler, US Geol Surv bedrock geol map of Mass, 75-83, DNAG Continent-Ocean Transect E-1 Adirondacks-Georges Bank, 82-86; partic, compiler, field trip leader, Int Geol Correlations Prog, Caledonide Orogen Proj, US, Scand, Can, Gt Brit, 79-84; fel, Norwegian Res Coun Sci & Humanities, Troudeim Univ, Norway, 90, Lund Univ, Swed, 93. *Mem:* Fel Geol Soc Am; fel Mineral Soc Am (vpres, 89-90, pres, 90-91); Am Geophys Union; Mineral Asn Can; Am Alpine Club; fel Japan Soc Prom Sci. *Res:* Structural geology, stratigraphy and tectonic settings of metamorphic rocks in New England, New Zealand and Norway; metamorphic mineral facies; crystal chemistry and exsolution in amphiboles and pyroxenes. *Mailing Add:* Geol Univ Mass Amherst MA 01003-0002. *Fax:* 413-545-1200; *E-Mail:* probinson@eclogite.geo.umass.edu

ROBINSON, PETER JOHN, CLIMATOLOGY, ATMOSPHERIC RADIATION. *Current Pos:* From asst prof to assoc prof, 71-91, PROF CLIMAT, UNIV NC, CHAPEL HILL, 91- *Personal Data:* b Kinston, UK, July 4, 44; m 68; c 2. *Educ:* Univ London, BSc, 65, MPhil, 68; McMaster Univ, PhD(climat), 72. *Concurrent Pos:* Asst dir, Nat Climate Prog Off, Nat Oceanic & Atmospheric Admin, 80-82; dir, NC Climate Prog, 82- *Mem:* Am Meteorol Soc; Am Asn State Climatologists (secy-treas, 79-80). *Res:* Techniques and benefits of using climate data and information in solution of operational planning problems of commercial enterprises; studies of social impacts of climatic change. *Mailing Add:* Dept Geog Univ NC Chapel Hill NC 27599-3220. *Fax:* 919-962-1537; *E-Mail:* robinson@geog.unc.edu

ROBINSON, PRESS L, PHYSICAL CHEMISTRY. *Current Pos:* from asst prof to assoc prof, 63-68, PROF PHYS CHEM, SOUTHERN UNIV, BATON ROUGE, 68- *Personal Data:* b Florence, SC, Aug 2, 37; m 64; c 2. *Educ:* Morehouse Col, BS, 59; Howard Univ, MS, 62, PhD(phys chem), 63. *Prof Exp:* Chemist, NIH, 61. *Concurrent Pos:* Res grants, 64-68. *Mem:* Am Chem Soc; Sigma Xi. *Res:* Molten salt chemistry; explosive metal forming of liquid alloys. *Mailing Add:* Box 10155 Baton Rouge LA 70813

ROBINSON, RALPH M(YER), CHEMICAL ENGINEERING, ORGANIC CHEMISTRY. *Current Pos:* RETIRED. *Personal Data:* b Terre Haute, Ind, Aug 17, 26; m 56, Georgia M Levin; c Aron & Stephen. *Educ:* Univ Ill, BS, 49; Univ Mich, MSE, 50. *Prof Exp:* Chem engr res & develop, Argonne Nat Labs, 51-53; chem engr, Abbott Labs, 53-60, group leader develop, High Pressure Lab, 60-62, mgr, Eng Develop Dept, 62-68, opers mgr oral & topicals prod, Pharmaceut Mfg Div, 68-87, pharmaceut consult, 87-92. *Mem:* Am Chem Soc; Sigma Xi; fel Am Inst Chem Engrs. *Res:* Administration and evaluation of research and development; economic and financial analysis; process development in fermentation, pharmaceutical and chemical areas. *Mailing Add:* 705 Colville Pl Waukegan IL 60087

ROBINSON, RAPHAEL MITCHEL, mathematics; deceased, see previous edition for last biography

ROBINSON, RAYMOND FRANCIS, GEOLOGY. *Current Pos:* RETIRED. *Personal Data:* b Albany, Ore, Sept 25, 14; m, Jeanne E Sitler; c Phoebe, Carola, Adele, Deborah R, Raymond H G, Lorna A, Paula E, Cynthia A & Kathryn E. *Educ:* Union Col, NY, BSc, 36; McGill Univ, MSc, 38. *Prof Exp:* Eng asst, NY State Dept Pub Works, Utica, 39-40; underground sampler, Anaconda Copper Mining Co, Butte, Mont, 41-43, asst mining engr, 43-45; resident geologist & engr, Am Smelting & Refining Co & Fed Mining & Smelting Co, Wallace, Idaho, 45-47; chief geologist, Sunshine Mining Co, Kellogg, Idaho, 47-53; actg dist supvr, Tucson Off Surv, US Geol Surv, 53; sr explor geologist, Bear Creek Mining Co, 53-56, supv geologists, 56-58, sr explor geologist, Develop Div, 58-64; field geologist, Phelps Dodge Corp, Douglas, Ariz, 64-65; dist mgr, Northwest Explor Div Duval Corp, 65-69, & Holt McPhar, 69-71; consult geol eng, Raymond F Robinson, Inc, Reno, Nev, 71-90; consult mining & explor geologist, 71-94 & 97. *Mem:* Am Inst Mining, Metall & Petrol Engrs; Soc Econ Geologists; Asn Explor Geologists; Am Inst Prof Geologists. *Res:* Metal exploration, evaluation and development; surface and underground; regional to specific mining properties; surface and underground; all phases of reconnaissance, detailed examination, evaluation and development; planning, administration and field execution; world-wide operation; exploration and development of two personally owned gold mining properties in Nevada and Idaho. *Mailing Add:* 180 W Laramie Dr Reno NV 89511

ROBINSON, REX JULIAN, analytical chemistry, for more information see previous edition

ROBINSON, RICHARD ALAN, NUCLEAR ENGINEERING, MECHANICAL ENGINEERING. *Current Pos:* Res scientist nuclear technol, 67-78, dept mgr nuclear waste isolation, proj mgt div, 78-90, PROG MGR, ENVIRON TECHNOL, BATTELLE COLUMBUS LABS, 90- *Personal Data:* b Monroe, Mich, Oct 4, 42; c 1. *Educ:* Univ Mich, BSE, 64, MSE, 66. *Mem:* Am Nuclear Soc. *Res:* Nuclear technology; advanced nuclear fuel development; experimental reactor engineering; PWR and BWR LOCA analysis and experimental studies; nuclear material shipping and transportation; nuclear waste disposal and isolation. *Mailing Add:* Battelle Div Strategics Environ Health & Safety Mgt 505 King Ave Columbus OH 43201-2693

ROBINSON, RICHARD C(LARK), CHEMICAL ENGINEERING, PETROLEUM PROCESSING & FUEL TECHNOLOGY. *Current Pos:* SR RES ENGR, CHEVRON RES CO, 74- *Personal Data:* b Seattle, Wash, Nov 4, 37; m 60, Judith A Olts; c Anne, Jennifer & Beth. *Educ:* Univ Wash, BS, 59; Univ Wis-Madison, MS, 61, PhD(chem eng), 65. *Prof Exp:* Res engr, Chevron Res Co, Stand Oil Co, Calif, 65-70, sr res engr, 70-72; asst prof, Colo Sch Mines, 72-74. *Mem:* Am Inst Chem Engrs; Am Chem Soc; Sigma Xi. *Res:* Diffusion in compressed fluids; diffusion coefficient correlation by corresponding states; chemical reaction kinetics; catalytic reforming of naphtha; hydrofining of oils; fluidized catalytic cracking; coking; recycling plastics by coking. *Mailing Add:* Chevron Res Co 100 Chevron Way Richmond CA 94801-2021

ROBINSON, RICHARD CARLETON, JR, RISK & RELIABILITY, CUMPUTER SCIENCES. *Current Pos:* SR OPERS RES ANALYST, US NUCLEAR REGULATORY COMN, WASH, DC, 77- *Personal Data:* b Walton, NY, Aug 29, 27; m 49, Emily Worth; c Barbara, Richard, Ginger & Deborah. *Educ:* Alfred Univ, BA, 50; Kent State Univ, MA, 52; Am Univ, ABD(math statist), 70. *Prof Exp:* Physicist, Argonne Nat Lab, 52-53 & Savannah River Lab, E I du Pont de Nemours & Co, 53-57; analyst, Opers Res Off, Johns Hopkins Univ, 58-61; sr opers res analyst, Res Analysis Corp, Va, 61-72 & Gen Res Corp, Va, 72-75; sr opers res analyst, Ketron Inc, Va, 75-77. *Concurrent Pos:* Prin investr, Res Analysis Corp, 66-72. *Mem:* Am Asn Physics Teachers; Opers Res Soc Am. *Res:* Nuclear reactors and exponential assemblies; electronic instrumentation design for nondestructive testing; programming and systems analysis; computer simulation and gaining; mathematical modeling, applied probability; nuclear safeguards; probabilistic risk analysis of nuclear power plants. *Mailing Add:* 4013 Cleveland St Kensington MD 20895-3806. *Fax:* 301-492-3892

ROBINSON, RICHARD WARREN, HORTICULTURE. *Current Pos:* PROF HORT SCI, NY STATE AGR EXP STA, 61- *Personal Data:* b Los Angeles, Calif, Apr 14, 30; m 63, Inge; c Susan & Sandra. *Educ:* Univ Calif, Davis, BS, 52, MS, 53; Cornell Univ, PhD(veg crops), 62. *Mem:* Am Soc Hort Sci. *Res:* Vegetable breeding, genetics and physiology. *Mailing Add:* Agr Exp Sta Dept Hort Sci Cornell Univ Geneva NY 14456. *Fax:* 315-787-2216; *E-Mail:* rwr1@cornell.edu

ROBINSON, ROBERT EARL, SYNTHETIC ORGANIC CHEMISTRY, ORGANOMETALLIC CHEMISTRY. *Current Pos:* exec vpres & dir, 67-87, PRES, LINDAU CHEM INC, 87- *Personal Data:* b Covington, Ky, Aug 3, 27; m 51, Myrtle Tonne; c Linda, Carol (Cranford) & Timothy. *Educ:* Berea Col, BA, 49; Purdue Univ, MS, 51, PhD, 53. *Prof Exp:* Proj leader, Nat Distillers & Chem Corp, 53-64; group leader, Stauffer Chem Co, 64-66; synthetic res & develop, Cardinal Chem Co, 66-67. *Concurrent Pos:* Consult synthetic organic & organometallic chemistry. *Mem:* Am Chem Soc; fel Am Inst Chemists; NY Acad Sci; AAAS. *Res:* Organometallic compounds; transition metal catalysts; synthetic resins; resin additives; epoxy curing agents; alkali metals; pharmaceutical intermediates; quaternary ammonium compounds. *Mailing Add:* Lindau Chem Inc 731 Rosewood Dr Columbia SC 29201. *Fax:* 803-256-3639

ROBINSON, ROBERT EUGENE, ANALYTICAL CHEMISTRY. *Current Pos:* CONSULT, 94- *Personal Data:* b Provo, Utah, Jan 9, 27; m 51, Thomasina Martin; c Robert E. *Educ:* Univ Okla, BS, 49, MS, 52; Univ Mich, PhD(chem), 59. *Prof Exp:* Chemist asphalt prod develop, Kerr-McGee Oil Co, 49-50; chemist oil prod develop, Sun Oil Co, 52-54; res chemist, Shell Develop Co, 58-69, sr res chemist, 69-75, staff res chemist, 75-90; staff chemist, Valco Instruments Co, 91-92; dir, Gas Chromatography Lab, Triton Anal Co, 92-93. *Concurrent Pos:* Vis res fel, Dept Chem, Leeds, UK, 90-91. *Mem:* Am Chem Soc. *Res:* Raman, infrared and molecular spectroscopy; Raman spectra of fluorocarbon derivatives; catalytic process research and development; separation sciences; gas and supercritical chromatography. *Mailing Add:* 11631 Jaycreek Houston TX 77070-2812

ROBINSON, ROBERT G, PUBLIC HEALTH, MINORITY HEALTH. *Current Pos:* ASSOC DIR PROG DEVELOP, OFF SMOKING & HEALTH, CTRS DIS CONTROL & PREV, 93-; ACTG ASSOC DIR PROG DEVELOP; NAT CTR CHRONIC DIS PREV & HEALTH PROM, ACTG ASSOC DIR MINORITY HEALTH. *Personal Data:* b New York, NY, Aug 11, 43. *Educ:* Adelphi Univ, MSW, 69; Univ Calif, Berkeley, MPH, 77, DPH, 83. *Prof Exp:* Cancer control sci fel, Nat Cancer Inst, 85-88; res assoc dir community planning & develop, Foxchase Cancer Ctr, 88-93. *Mem:* Am Pub Health Asn. *Res:* Develop and evaluate interventions and policies that impart the health status of minority and/or underserved communities; community development and matters pertaining to diversity and inclusivity. *Mailing Add:* Ctrs Dis Control & Prev 1600 Clifton Rd NE D-39 Atlanta GA 30333. *Fax:* 404-639-7039; *E-Mail:* rgro@cdc.gov

ROBINSON, ROBERT GEORGE, CHEMICAL ENGINEERING. *Current Pos:* RES LEADER, HOFFMAN-LAROCHE, INC, 92- *Personal Data:* b Beacon, NY, Aug 13, 37; m 60, Bonnie J Galloway; c Patrick, Rachel, Robert & Samuel. *Educ:* Clarkson Tech Univ, BChE, 58, MChE, 60; Pa State Univ, PhD(chem eng), 64. *Prof Exp:* Scientist, Upjohn Co, 64-77, sr scientist, 77-80, res mgr, 80-84, assoc dir, chem process res & develop, 84-90, assoc dir, chem prod, 90-92. *Concurrent Pos:* Chmn, Food, Pharmaceut & Bioeng Div, Am Inst Chem Engrs, 87-88. *Mem:* Am Inst Chem Engrs; Am Chem Soc; AAAS. *Res:* Controlled cycling mass transfer; countercurrent crystallization; separation and purification; hazard evaluation. *Mailing Add:* 2220 Timberlane Dr Florence SC 29506. *Fax:* 803-629-4128

ROBINSON, ROBERT GEORGE, AGRONOMY, NEW & ALTERNATIVE CROPS. *Current Pos:* asst, 42-47, from asst prof to assoc prof, 48-73, prof, 73-86, EMER PROF AGRON, UNIV MINN, ST PAUL, 86- *Personal Data:* b Minneapolis, Minn, Jan 26, 20. *Educ:* Iowa State Univ, BS, 41; Univ Minn, MS, 46, PhD(agron, soils), 48. *Prof Exp:* Teacher high sch, Iowa, 41-42. *Mem:* Am Soc Agron; Weed Sci Soc Am; Sigma Xi; Soc Econ Bot; Crop Sci Soc Am. *Res:* Field crop production; new and special field crops; farm management. *Mailing Add:* Dept Agron Univ Minn St Paul MN 55108

ROBINSON, ROBERT GEORGE, PHARMACY, RESEARCH ADMINISTRATION. *Current Pos:* PROF & HEAD DEPT PSYCHIAT, UNIV IOWA COL MED, 90- *Personal Data:* b Pittsburgh, Pa, May 21, 45; m, Gretchen Smith; c Christopher & Johnathan. *Educ:* Cornell Univ, BS, 67, MD, 71. *Prof Exp:* Med intern, Montefiore Hosp & Albert Einstein Med Ctr, 71-72; asst psychiatrist & resident, Cornell Univ Med Ctr, 72-73; res assoc, NIMH, 73-75; housestaff fel, Johns Hopkins Univ Sch Med, 75-77, chief resident, 77, from asst prof to prof, 77-90. *Concurrent Pos:* Asst resident, Johns Hopkins Hosp, 75-77; Maudsley exchange resident, Johns Hopkins Hosp & Maudsley Hosp, 76; Mellon fel, Johns Hopkins Univ Sch Med, 77; res scientist, NIMH, 79-90; clin asst prof, Univ Md Sch Med, 83-90; chmn, Behav Neurosci Res Rev Comt, 91-93; mem, Stroke Coun, Am Heart Asn. *Mem:* Soc Neurosci; fel Am Psychiat Asn; Psychiat Res Soc; fel Am Heart Asn; Royal Col Psychologists; Am Col Neuropsychopharmacol. *Res:* Mood disorders associated with brain injury; animal models of affective disorders; mechanism and mood manifestations of brain asymmetry. *Mailing Add:* 200 Hawkins Dr No 2887JPP Iowa City IA 52242-1057. *Fax:* 319-356-2587

ROBINSON, ROBERT L(OUIS), JR, CHEMICAL ENGINEERING. *Current Pos:* from asst prof to assoc prof chem eng, 65-72, REGENTS PROF CHEM ENG, OKLA STATE UNIV, 84- *Personal Data:* b Muskogee, Okla, June 14, 37; m 58. *Educ:* Okla State Univ, BS, 59, MS, 62, PhD(chem eng), 64. *Prof Exp:* Sr res engr, Pan Am Petrol Corp, Okla, 64-65. *Mem:* Am Inst Chem Engrs; Am Chem Soc; Am Soc Eng Educ; Soc Petrol Engrs. *Res:* Thermodynamic and transport properties. *Mailing Add:* 1514 Fairway Dr Stillwater OK 74074

ROBINSON, ROBERT LEO, PHARMACOLOGY. *Current Pos:* RETIRED. *Personal Data:* b Kansas City, Mo, Mar 14, 26; m 55; c 2. *Educ:* Univ Kans, MA, 54, PhD(physiol), 58. *Prof Exp:* From instr to prof pharmacol, Med Ctr, WVa Univ, 59-87. *Mem:* Am Soc Pharmacol & Exp Therapeut. *Res:* Adrenal medullary physiology; pharmacology of autonomic drugs. *Mailing Add:* 1126 Valley View Ave Morgantown WV 26505

ROBINSON, ROBERT W, COMPUTER SCIENCE. *Current Pos:* PROF & HEAD DEPT COMPUT SCI, UNIV GA, 84- *Personal Data:* b Atlanta, Ga, Nov 23, 41. *Educ:* Dartmouth Col, AB & AM, 63; Cornell Univ, PhD(math), 66. *Prof Exp:* Prof math, Southern Ill Univ, 82-84. *Mem:* Asn Comput Mach; Inst Elec & Electronics Engrs; Am Math Soc; Australian Math Soc. *Mailing Add:* Dept Computer Sci Univ Ga 415 Boyd Grad Studies Bldg Athens GA 30602-7404

ROBINSON, ROSCOE ROSS, INTERNAL MEDICINE, NEPHROLOGY. *Current Pos:* NEPHROLOGIST, VANDERBILT UNIV. *Personal Data:* b Oklahoma City, Okla, Aug 21, 29; m 52; c 2. *Educ:* Cent State Univ, BS, 49; Univ Okla, MD, 54; Am Bd Internal Med, dipl, 62. *Prof Exp:* Intern med, Duke Univ, 54-55, asst resident, 55-56; Am Heart Asn res fel, Columbia-Presby Med Ctr, 56-57; instr, Duke Univ, 57-58, assoc, 60-62, from asst prof to assoc prof, 62-69, dir Div Nepthrol, 62-80, prof med, 69-, chief, Div Nephrology, 80- *Concurrent Pos:* Chief resident, Vet Admin Hosp, Durham, NC, 57-58, clin investr, 60-62, attend physician, 62-; sr investr, NC Heart Asn, 62-; mem exec comt, Coun Kidney & Cardiovasc Dis, Am Heart Asn; nat consult internal med, USAF Surgeon Gen; mem sci adv bd, Nat Kidney Found; ed, Kidney Int. *Mem:* Am Physiol Soc; Am Clin & Climat Asn; Europ Dialysis & Transplant Soc; Am Soc Clin Invest; Am Soc Artificial Internal Organs. *Res:* Renal disease and physiology. *Mailing Add:* Dept Med Vanderbilt Univ Med Ctr D 3300 Med Ctr N Nashville TN 37232-0001

ROBINSON, ROSS UTLEY, ANALYTICAL BIOCHEMISTRY. *Current Pos:* PRES, CARDINAL ASSOCS, 85- *Personal Data:* b Minneapolis, Minn, July 30, 28; m 53, Barbara Brown; c Brian, Emily, Judith, Ross S, Rachel & John. *Educ:* Colgate Univ, BA, 49; Wesleyan Univ, MA, 51; Mass Inst Technol, MS, 53. *Prof Exp:* Phys chemist, Abbott Labs, 53-58, sci instrumentation group leader, 58-62, sect mgr, 62-67, res & develop coordr, 67-69, advan technol mgr, 69-71, prod planning & develop, 71-73, dir contract res & develop, 73-75, dir advan systs res, 75-79, assoc dir, Corp Res & Develop, Boehringer Mannheim Corp, 80-81; vpres, Res & Develop, ICL Sci, 81-84; pres & chief exec officer, Mesa Diagnostics, 84-85; exec vpres, Los Alamos Diagnostics, 85-89. *Mem:* AAAS; Am Chem Soc; Sigma Xi. *Res:* Physical, analytical and medical instrumentation; technological forecasting. *Mailing Add:* 2393 Botulph Rd Santa Fe NM 87505. *Fax:* 505-473-5637; *E-Mail:* cardinal@cardinal.sf.com

ROBINSON, RUSSELL LEE, NUCLEAR PHYSICS. *Current Pos:* SCI DIR, HOLIFIELD HEAVY ION RES FACIL, 83- *Personal Data:* b Louisville, Ky, July 30, 31; m 53; c 3. *Educ:* Univ Louisville, BA, 53; Ind Univ, MS, 55, PhD(physics), 58. *Prof Exp:* Asst physics, Ind Univ, 53-58; physicist, Oak Ridge Nat Lab, 58-83. *Mem:* Fel Am Phys Soc. *Res:* Gamma-ray spectroscopy; heavy-ion induced reactions. *Mailing Add:* 134 Newell Lane Oak Ridge TN 37830

ROBINSON, STEPHEN MICHAEL, MATHEMATICAL PROGRAMMING. *Current Pos:* asst dir, Math Res Ctr, Univ Wis-Madison, 71-74, from asst prof to assoc prof comput sci, 72-75, assoc prof, 75-79, PROF INDUST ENG & COMPUT SCI, UNIV WIS-MADISON, 79- *Personal Data:* b Columbus, Ohio, Apr 12, 42; m 68, Chong-Suk Han; c Diana M & James A. *Educ:* Univ Wis-Madison, BA, 62, PhD(computer sci), 71; NY Univ, MS, 63. *Hon Degrees:* Dr, Univ Zurich, Switz, 96. *Prof Exp:* Mem staff, Comput & Numerical Anal Div, Sandia Corp, 62; instr math, US Mil Acad, 68-69. *Concurrent Pos:* Assoc ed, Opers Res, 74-86, Math Opers Res, 75-80, Math Opers forschung & Statist, 77-83; assoc ed, Math Prog, 86-91, ed, Math Opers Res, 81-86, adv ed, Math Opers Res, 87-; mem coun, Opers Res Soc Am, 91-94; mem-at-large coun, Math Prog Soc, 91-94. *Mem:* Math Prog Soc; Inst Indust Engrs; Soc Indust & Appl Math; Inst Oper Res & Mgt Sci. *Res:* Quantitative methods in managerial economics; mathematical programming, especially stochastic programming; decision methods under uncertainty. *Mailing Add:* Dept Indust Eng 1513 University Ave Madison WI 53706-1572. *Fax:* 608-262-8454; *E-Mail:* smr@cs.wisc.edu

ROBINSON, STEWART MARSHALL, MATHEMATICS. *Current Pos:* ADJ ASSOC PROF, CASE-WESTERN RES UNIV, 95- *Personal Data:* b Schenectady, NY, Jan 7, 34; m 60; c 3. *Educ:* Union Col, BS, 55; Duke Univ, PhD(math), 59. *Prof Exp:* Asst prof math, Univ RI, 59-61; asst prof, Smith Col, 61-64; asst prof, Union Col, NY, 64-66, assoc prof, 66-68; assoc prof math, Cleveland State Univ, 68-94. *Mem:* Am Math Soc; Math Asn Am. *Res:* Partial differential equations; topology. *Mailing Add:* 3334 Berkeley Ave Cleveland Heights OH 44118. *E-Mail:* robinson@math.csuohio.edu

ROBINSON, SUSAN ESTES, NEUROPHARMACOLOGY. *Current Pos:* from asst prof to assoc prof pharmacol, 81-95, ASSOC PROF PATH, DEPT PATH, MED COL, VA COMMONWEALTH UNIV, 91-, PROF PHARMACOL, DEPT PHARMACOL & TOXICOL, 95- *Personal Data:* b Radford, Va, Apr 26, 50; m 81, Robert Gillespie; c William B & James C. *Educ:* Vanderbilt Univ, BA, 72, PhD(pharmacol), 76. *Honors & Awards:* Lyndon Baines Johnson Res Award, Am Heart Asn, 80. *Prof Exp:* Staff fel, Lab Preclin Pharmacol, NIMH, 76-79; asst prof, dept med pharmacol & toxicol, Tex A&M Univ, 79-81. *Mem:* AAAS; Am Soc Pharmacol & Exp Therapeut; Soc Neurosci; Am Soc Neurochem; Col Problems Drug Dependence; Neurobehav Teratology Soc. *Res:* Interactions between neurotransmitters in the nervous system and the physiological relevance of the interactions. *Mailing Add:* Dept Pharmacol & Toxicol Med Col Va PO Box 980613 Richmond VA 23298-0613. *Fax:* 804-828-2117; *E-Mail:* serobinson@gems.vcu.edu

ROBINSON, TERENCE LEE, POMOLOGY, CULTURAL SYSTEMS & PHYSIOLOGY. *Current Pos:* asst prof, 84-90, ASSOC PROF POMOL, NY STATE AGR EXP STA, CORNELL UNIV, 90- *Personal Data:* b El Paso, Tex, June 29, 55; m 76; c 6. *Educ:* Brigham Young Univ, BS, 78; Wash State Univ, MS, 82, PhD(hort), 84. *Prof Exp:* Res asst hort, Wash State Univ, 78-84. *Mem:* Am Soc Hort Sci. *Res:* Environmental and cultural limitations of yield in tree fruits; development of orchard production systems that integrate cultivar, soil, climatic, economic and cultural factors to maximize returns. *Mailing Add:* 724 White Springs Dr Geneva NY 14456

ROBINSON, TERRANCE EARL, PHYSIOLOGICAL PSYCHOLOGY, NEUROSCIENCE. *Current Pos:* from asst prof to assoc prof, 78-89, PROF PSYCHOL, UNIV MICH, ANN ARBOR, 89- *Personal Data:* b Rochester, NY, May 22, 49. *Educ:* Univ Lethbridge, BA, 72; Univ Sask, MA, 74; Univ Western Ont, PhD(psychol), 78. *Honors & Awards:* Res Career Develop Award, Nat Inst Neurol & Commun Dis & Stroke. *Prof Exp:* Lectr psychol, Univ Western Ont, 76-77; fel psychobiol, Univ Calif, Irvine, 77-78. *Mem:* Fel AAAS; Soc Neurosci; fel Am Psychol Asn; NY Acad Sci; Am Col Neuropsychopharmacol. *Res:* Neuropsychopharmacology; brain-behavior relations; neuroplasticity. *Mailing Add:* Biophys Prog Univ Mich E Hall 525 E University Ann Arbor MI 48109

ROBINSON, THOMAS B, CIVIL ENGINEERING, ENVIRONMENTAL ENGINEERING. *Current Pos:* RETIRED. *Personal Data:* b Kansas City, Mo, Feb 28, 17. *Educ:* Kans Univ, BS, 39; Columbia Univ, MS, 40. *Prof Exp:* Proj mgr & proj engr, Black & Veatch, 40-56, exec partner, 56-65, asst managing partner, 65-73, managing partner, 73-83. *Mem:* Nat Acad Eng; Am Waterworks Asn; Water Pollution Control Fedn; Nat Soc Prof Engrs; Am Soc Civil Engrs. *Mailing Add:* 6401 Norwood Shawnee Mission MO 66208

ROBINSON, THOMAS JOHN, MATHEMATICS. *Current Pos:* from asst prof to assoc prof, 63-72, PROF MATH, UNIV NDAK, 72- *Personal Data:* b Volga, Iowa, May 7, 35; m 59, Sandra Erickson; c Timothy & Paul. *Educ:* Luther Col, BA, 56; Iowa State Univ, MS, 58, PhD(math), 63. *Prof Exp:* Instr math, Univ NDak, 58-60 & Iowa State Univ, 60-63. *Concurrent Pos:* Fel, Sch Behav Studies, Univ NDak, 71-72. *Mem:* Am Math Soc; Math Asn Am; Sigma Xi. *Res:* Topology; algebra. *Mailing Add:* 2521 Cherry St Grand Forks ND 58201-7449. *E-Mail:* robinson@rsi.cc.und.nodak.edu

ROBINSON, TREVOR, BIOCHEMISTRY. *Current Pos:* from asst prof to assoc prof chem, Univ Mass, Amherst, 61-66, assoc prof, 66-82, prof, 82-92, EMER PROF BIOCHEM, UNIV MASS, AMHERST, 92- *Personal Data:* b Springfield, Mass, Feb 20, 29; m 52, Laura Barme; c June, Heather & Mark. *Educ:* Harvard Univ, AB, 50, AM, 51; Univ Mass, MS, 53; Cornell Univ, PhD(biochem), 56. *Prof Exp:* Res assoc bact & bot, Syracuse Univ, 56-60. *Mem:* Am Soc Plant Physiol; Phytochem Soc NAm; AAAS; Am Soc Pharmacognosy; Sigma Xi; Early Am Industs Asn. *Res:* Plant biochemistry; alkaloids; tannins; history of science. *Mailing Add:* Dept Biochem Univ Mass Amherst MA 01003. *Fax:* 413-545-3291; *E-Mail:* robinson@biochem.umass.edu

ROBINSON, WILBUR EUGENE, CHEMISTRY, FUEL SCIENCE. *Current Pos:* RETIRED. *Personal Data:* b Viola, Kans, Aug 27, 19; m 42; c 2. *Educ:* Sterling Col, BA, 41. *Prof Exp:* Teacher high sch, 41-42; chemist, US Bur Mines, Nev, 42-44, supvry chemist, Wyo, 47-64; sect supvr, Laramie Energy Technol Ctr, US Dept Energy, 64-80. *Mem:* Am Chem Soc; Sigma Xi. *Res:* Constitution and properties of oil-shale kerogen. *Mailing Add:* 1516 Sheridan Laramie WY 82070

ROBINSON, WILLIAM COURTNEY, JR, METALLURGY, CHEMICAL ENGINEERING. *Current Pos:* group leader, 70-85, PLANT MGR, KEMET ELECTRONICS, 85- *Personal Data:* b Weatherford, Tex, July 4, 37; m 64; c 2. *Educ:* Univ Tex, BS, 59; Iowa State Univ, PhD(metall), 64. *Prof Exp:* Jr chem engr, Humble Oil & Refining Co, 59; asst, Ames Lab, 60-64; metallurgist, Oak Ridge Nat Lab, 64-69; sr res scientist, Lockheed-Calif Co, 69-70. *Mem:* Am Soc Metals. *Res:* Vapor deposition of refractory metals; corrosion and adhesive bonding problems on aircraft; high temperature sinterins and powder metallurgical fabrication; anodization; capacitor manufacture. *Mailing Add:* 115 Wood Creek Rd Mauldin SC 29662

ROBINSON, WILLIAM EDWARD, AQUATIC TOXICOLOGY, INORGANIC BIOCHEMISTRY. *Current Pos:* ASSOC PROF, UNIV MASS, BOSTON, 92- *Personal Data:* b Nashua, NH, Dec 27, 48; m 93, Susan S Gibson. *Educ:* Boston Univ, AB, 70; Northeastern Univ, MS, 77, PhD(biol), 81. *Prof Exp:* Instr, Histol Tech, Northeastern Univ, 77, res fel, Dept Biol & Marine Sci Inst, 77-81, instr, Quant Fluorescense Micros, 81; fel, Chem Dept, Brandeis Univ, 81-83; vis investr, Egerton Res Lab, New Eng Aquarium, 81-83, assoc scientist, 83-88, radiation safety officer, 83-92, sr scientist, 88-92. *Concurrent Pos:* Numerous grants from many orgns, 78-97; adj res assoc, Marine Sci & Maritime Studies Ctr, Northeastern Univ, 83-, Chem Dept, Brandeis Univ, 85-88; adj asst prof, Boston Col, 92; co-chair tech adv comt, US Environ Protection Agency, Nat Estuarine Prog, Mass Bays Prog, 93- *Mem:* Soc Integrative & Comp Biol; AAAS; Am Micros Soc; Nat Shellfish Asn; Soc Environ Toxicol & Chem. *Res:* Metal uptake, transport and detoxification in bivalve molluscs; function of vanadium and tunichrome in ascidians; feeding and digestion in bivalve molluscs-adult and larval; chlorophyll breakdown and utilization by invertebrates; effects of turbidity on invertebrate feeding and digestion; molluscan energetics; malacology; numerous publications. *Mailing Add:* Environ Coastal & Ocean Sci Prog Univ Mass-Boston 100 Morrissey Blvd Boston MA 02125-3393. *Fax:* 617-287-7474; *E-Mail:* robinsonw@umbsky.cc.umb.edu

ROBINSON, WILLIAM H, ENTOMOLOGY. *Current Pos:* Asst prof, 70-80, ASSOC PROF ENTOM, VA POLYTECH INST & STATE UNIV, 80- *Personal Data:* b Philadelphia, Pa, Feb 15, 43; m 64; c 3. *Educ:* Kent State Univ, BA, 64, MA, 66; Iowa State Univ, PhD(entom), 70. *Mem:* Entom Soc Am; Entom Soc Can; Am Entom Soc. *Res:* Biology and immature stages of Phoridae; Diptera biology and taxonomy; insects associated with thermal water. *Mailing Add:* Dept Entom Va Polytech Inst & State Univ PO Box 0319 Blacksburg VA 24063-0001

ROBINSON, WILLIAM JAMES, DENDROCHRONOLOGY. *Current Pos:* From res asst to assoc prof, Univ Ariz, 63-76, asst lab, 72-81, dir lab, 82-86, PROF DENDROCHRONOLOGY, LAB TREE-RING RES, UNIV ARIZ, 76- *Personal Data:* b Erie, Pa, Feb 19, 29; m 57; c 2. *Educ:* Univ Ariz, BA, 57, MA, 59, PhD(anthrop), 67. *Mem:* Soc Am Archaeol; Am Quaternary Asn; Tree-Ring Soc. *Res:* Application of special techniques of dendrochronology to archaeology, especially the non-chronological aspect which views the material as an artifact, and reconstruction of past environments. *Mailing Add:* 2314 E Lind Rd Tucson AZ 85718

ROBINSON, WILLIAM KIRLEY, PHYSICS. *Current Pos:* assoc prof, 59-71, prof physics, 71-80, HENRY PRIEST PROF PHYSICS, ST LAWRENCE UNIV, 80- *Personal Data:* b Syracuse, NY, Apr 1, 25; m 50; c 4. *Educ:* Univ Mo, BS, 45; Carnegie Inst Technol, MS, 54, PhD(physics), 59. *Prof Exp:* Instr math, Brevard Col, 48-51. *Mem:* Am Phys Soc; Am Asn Physics Teachers. *Res:* Nuclear measurements; astronomy. *Mailing Add:* 19 College St Canton NY 13617

ROBINSON, WILLIAM LAUGHLIN, WILDLIFE ECOLOGY. *Current Pos:* asst prof, 64-69, PROF BIOL, NORTHERN MICH UNIV, 69- *Personal Data:* b Ironwood, Mich, Mar 29, 33; m 59; c 2. *Educ:* Mich State Univ, BS, 54; Univ Maine, MS, 59; Univ Toronto, PhD(zool, ecol), 63. *Prof Exp:* Asst leader, Maine Coop Wildlife Res Unit, Maine, 63; asst prof biol, Middlebury Col, 63-64. *Concurrent Pos:* NSF res grants, 66-69; sci fac fel, San Diego State Col, 71-72; US Forest Serv res contracts, 72-79; Nat Audubon Soc res grant, 73-75; US Fish & Wildlife Serv contracts, 78-81; Ruffed Grouse Soc res grant, 82-91; Earthwatch grants, 85-91. *Mem:* Sigma Xi; Wildlife Soc; Am Soc Mammal. *Res:* Winter shelter requirements, social behavior and populations of white-tailed deer; homing behavior of meadow mice; ecology of spruce grouse; ecology of wolves; ecology of woodcock; ecology of loons. *Mailing Add:* 410 E Crescent St Marquette MI 49855-3621

ROBINSON, WILLIAM ROBERT, CHEMICAL EDUCATION. *Current Pos:* from asst prof to prof, 67-94, PROF CHEM & SCI EDUC, PURDUE UNIV, LAFAYETTE, 94- *Personal Data:* b Longview, Tex, May 30, 39; m 62; c 3. *Educ:* Tex Technol Col, BS, 61, MS, 62; Mass Inst Technol, PhD(chem), 66. *Prof Exp:* NSF fel, Univ Sheffield, 66-67. *Concurrent Pos:* Adj assoc prof, Dept Earth & Space Sci, State Univ NY Stony Brook, 73; proj seraphim fel, Inst Chem Educ, Univ-Wis Madison, 92-93. *Mem:* AAAS; Am Chem Soc; Nat Asn Res Sci Teaching; Sigma Xi. *Res:* Origins of misconceptions in chemistry. *Mailing Add:* Dept Chem Purdue Univ 1393 Brown West Lafayette IN 47907. *Fax:* 765-494-0239; *E-Mail:* wrrobin@purdue.edu

ROBINSON, WILLIAM SIDNEY, INTERNAL MEDICINE, MOLECULAR BIOLOGY. *Current Pos:* from asst prof to assoc prof, 67-76, PROF MED, DIV INFECTIOUS DIS, SCH MED, STANFORD UNIV, 76- *Personal Data:* b Bloomington, Ind, Nov 24, 33; m 65. *Educ:* Ind Univ, AB, 56; Univ Chicago, MS & MD, 60. *Prof Exp:* Intern internal med, Columbia-Presby Med Ctr, NY, 60-61, jr asst resident, 61-62; sr asst resident, Univ Chicago Hosps, 62-63, resident, 63-64; NIH spec fel, Univ Calif, Berkeley, 64-65, asst prof molecular biol & res biologist, Virus Lab, 65-67. *Concurrent Pos:* Res fel biochem, Argonne Cancer Res Hosp & Univ Chicago, 62-64; mem cancer res training comt, NIH, 71- *Mem:* AAAS; Am Soc Microbiol; Am Soc Clin Invest. *Res:* Biochemistry of virus infection and replication; malignant transformation of cells by tumor viruses; nucleic acid metabolism; infectious diseases. *Mailing Add:* Dept Med Div Infectious Dis Stanford Univ Sch Med Stanford CA 94305-9991

ROBINSON-WHITE, AUDREY JEAN, ANESTHESIOLOGY, VASCULAR CELL PHYSIOLOGY. *Personal Data:* b Houston, Tex, June 14, 43; m 87; c 1. *Educ:* Spelman Col, AB, 65; Boston Col, MS, 75; Boston Univ, PhD(cell biol), 80. *Honors & Awards:* Res Award, Shiley Biomed, 87. *Prof Exp:* Postdoctoral fel, Nat Heart, Lung & Blood Inst, NIH, 80-82, Pratt fel, Nat Inst Gen Med Sci, 82-84; res asst prof, Dept Anesthesiol, Uniformed Serv Univ Health Sci, Bethesda, Md, 84-91, staff mem, Dept Physiol, 84-91. *Concurrent Pos:* Nat Res Serv Award, NIH, 80-82, First Award, 87-91, small instrumentation grant, 89; prin investr, Competitive Award, Uniformed Serv Univ Health Sci, 85-88. *Mem:* AAAS; Am Physiol Soc; Am Soc Pharmacol & Exp Therapeut; NY Acad Sci. *Res:* Biochemistry of the vascular endothelial cell which includes a study of the uptake and metabolism of biogenic amines by endothelial cells from different species and vascular regions; study of the action of three classes of anesthetics on endothelial cell biochemistry, signal transduction systems, and function. *Mailing Add:* 4987 Battery Lane Bethesda MD 20814. *Fax:* 301-656-5739

ROBINTON, ELIZABETH DOROTHY, MICROBIOLOGY, PUBLIC HEALTH. *Current Pos:* from instr to asst prof bact, Smith Col, 44-56, assoc prof bact & pub health, 56-62, prof microbiol & pub health, 62-65, prof biol sci, 65-73, chmn dept, 66-69, EMER PROF BIOL SCI, SMITH COL, 73- *Personal Data:* b Woburn, Mass, June 27, 10. *Educ:* Columbia Univ, BS, 38; Smith Col, MA, 42; Yale Univ, PhD(pub health), 50. *Prof Exp:* Microbiologist, Div Labs, State Dept Health, Conn, 31-42; instr bact, Woman's Col NC, 42-43; instr, Goucher Col, 43-44. *Concurrent Pos:* WHO fel, 65; ed-in-chief, Health Lab Sci, 66-74; chmn, lab sect, Am Pub Health Asn. *Mem:* Med Mycol Soc Americas; Conf State & Prov Pub Health Lab Dirs; Am Soc Microbiol; fel Am Pub Health Asn; fel Am Acad Microbiol; Sigma Xi. *Res:* Environmental and public health microbiology; medical mycology. *Mailing Add:* 235 Walker St No 242 Lenox MA 01240-2709

ROBISHAW, JANET D, PHARMACOLOGY, PHYSIOLOGY. *Current Pos:* MEM STAFF, WEIS CTR RES, GEISINGER CLIN, 86- *Personal Data:* b Midland, Mich, June 18, 56; m. *Educ:* Cent Mich Univ, BS, 79; Pa State Univ, PhD(physiol), 83. *Prof Exp:* Teaching asst, Pa State Univ, 79-81; NIH postdoctoral fel pharmacol, Health Sci Ctr, Univ Tex, 83-86. *Concurrent Pos:* Lectr, Dept Pharmacol, Wash Univ, Case Western Univ & Univ Pa, 86, Dept Neurobiol, Columbia Univ & Dept Physiol, Pa State Univ, 87, Am Heart Asn, 88 & Dept Pharmacol, Mayo Clin, 89; ad hoc mem, Biochem Study Sect, Am Cancer Soc, 87-90; ad hoc reviewer, Nat Heart, Lung & Blood Inst, NIH. *Mem:* Am Soc Biochem & Molecular Biol. *Res:* Author of 23 technical publications. *Mailing Add:* Weis Ctr Res Geisinger Clin 100 N Academy St Danville PA 17822-2614

ROBISON, D(ELBERT) E(ARL), mechanical engineering; deceased, see previous edition for last biography

ROBISON, GEORGE ALAN, BIOCHEMICAL PHARMACOLOGY, ENDOCRINOLOGY. *Current Pos:* PROF PHARMACOL & CHMN DEPT, UNIV TEX MED SCH HOUSTON, 72- *Personal Data:* b Lethbridge, Alta, Nov 4, 34; m 56; c 2. *Educ:* Univ Alta, BSc, 57; Tulane Univ, MS, 60, PhD(pharmacol), 62. *Honors & Awards:* J Murray Luck Award, Nat Acad Sci, 79. *Prof Exp:* Res fel pharmacol, Sch Med, Western Reserve Univ, 62-63; res assoc physiol, Sch Med, Vanderbilt Univ, 63-64, instr physiol & pharmacol, 64-66, asst prof pharmacol, 66-69, assoc prof pharmacol & physiol, 69-72. *Concurrent Pos:* Investr, Howard Hughes Med Inst, 70-72; co-ed, Advances Cyclic Nucleotide Res, 72- *Mem:* Am Chem Soc; Am Soc Pharmacol & Exp Therapeut; Endocrine Soc; NY Acad Sci; Soc Neurosci. *Res:* Biochemical basis of hormone action; biochemical basis of animal behavior. *Mailing Add:* 1445 Lakeside Estates Dr #3004 Houston TX 77042-2253. *Fax:* 713-792-5911

ROBISON, HENRY WELBORN, ICHTHYOLOGY, ZOOLOGY. *Current Pos:* from assoc prof to prof biol, 71-86, dean sci & technol, 87-90, PROF BIOL, SOUTHERN ARK UNIV, 91- *Personal Data:* b Albany, Ga, Mar 24, 45; m 66, Catherine Davis; c Patrick H & Lindsay M. *Educ:* Ark State Univ, BS, 67, MS, 68; Okla State Univ, PhD(zool), 71. *Prof Exp:* Res asst fish social behav, Okla State Univ, 70-71; asst prof zool, Southern Ill Univ, Carbondale, 71. *Concurrent Pos:* Ark Wildlife Conservationist, 78; pres, Ark Acad Sci, 80-81; hon prof, Southern Ark Univ, 81. *Mem:* Am Soc Ichthyologists & Herpetologists; Sigma Xi. *Res:* Taxonomy; ecology and behavior of cyprinid and perciform fishes; fishes of Arkansas; evolution of reproductive behavior in fishes; cray fishes of Arkansas; biodiversity of Arkansas. *Mailing Add:* Dept Biol Southern Ark Univ Box 9354 Magnolia AR 71753-5000. *Fax:* 870-235-5005; *E-Mail:* hwrobison@saymag.edu

ROBISON, LAREN R, PLANT GENETICS, WEED SCIENCE. *Current Pos:* prof agron & hort & chmn dept, 71-82, ASSOC DEAN, COL BIOL & AGR SCI, BRIGHAM YOUNG UNIV, 82-, DIR, BENSON AGR FOOD INST. *Personal Data:* b Georgetown, Idaho, Mar 25, 31; m 55; c 6. *Educ:* Brigham Young Univ, BS, 57, MS, 58; Univ Minn, PhD(plant genetics), 62. *Prof Exp:* Res leader new crops, Univ Nebr, Lincoln, 62-65, res leader exten weed control, vchmn & exten leader, Agron Dept, 65-71. *Mem:* Am Soc Agron; Crop Sci Soc Am; Weed Sci Soc Am; Sigma Xi; Coun Agr Sci & Technol. *Res:* Plant and soil relationships; new and potential crops breeding; weed control methods, including herbicides used, dissipation and crop tolerance; international agriculture development. *Mailing Add:* Dept Agron Brigham Young Univ 275 Widb Provo UT 84602-1049

ROBISON, NORMAN GLENN, GENETICS, AGRONOMY. *Current Pos:* Sorghum breeder, 65-85, TROP MAIZE RES DIR, DE KALB GENETICS CORP, 85- *Personal Data:* b Littlefield, Tex, Oct 5, 38; m 63, Mary Correll; c Molly A, Susan W & Andrew G. *Educ:* Tex Tech Col, BS, 61; Univ Nebr, MS, 63, PhD(agron), 67. *Mem:* Am Soc Agron. *Res:* Direct tropical maize breeding programs worldwide. *Mailing Add:* 110 Thornbrook De Kalb IL 60115-2315

ROBISON, ODIS WAYNE, GENETICS, REPRODUCTIVE PHYSIOLOGY. *Current Pos:* From asst prof to assoc prof, 59-74, PROF ANIMAL SCI & GENETICS, NC STATE UNIV, 74- *Personal Data:* b Lawton, Okla, Aug 23, 34; m 56, Ruth A Knight; c Debra, Russell & Carol. *Educ:* Okla State Univ, BS, 55; Univ Wis, MS, 57, PhD(genetics, animal husb), 59. *Honors & Awards:* Rockefeller Prentice Mem Award, Am Soc Animal Sci; Serv Award, Nat Swine Improv Fedn. *Concurrent Pos:* NSF travel grant, NATO Conf, 62 & 68; mem, AID Mission to Peru; lectr several foreign countries; sect ed, J Animal Sci; dir, Nat Swine Improv Fedn; ed, J Animal Sci Appl Sect; Fulbright Scholar. *Mem:* AAAS; fel Am Soc Animal Sci; Biomet Soc; Sigma Xi; Am Genetic Asn. *Res:* Genetic control of developmental and physiological processes; formulation of selection schemes and breeding systems for efficient manipulation of populations; interaction of genetics and maternal influence on developing processes. *Mailing Add:* 226 Polk Hall NC State Univ Box 7621 Raleigh NC 27695-7621. *Fax:* 919-515-7780; *E-Mail:* owrob@unity.ncsu.edu

ROBISON, RICHARD ASHBY, GEOLOGY, PALEONTOLOGY. *Current Pos:* HEDBERG PROF GEOL, UNIV KANS, 74- *Personal Data:* b Fillmore, Utah, Jan 10, 33; m 53, Joleen Ashman; c Richard, Valerie & Mark. *Educ:* Brigham Young Univ, BS, 57, MS, 58; Univ Tex, PhD(geol), 62. *Prof Exp:* Geologist, US Geol Surv, 59-60; asst prof geol, Univ Utah, 62-66; assoc cur invert paleont, Smithsonian Inst, 66-67; from assoc prof to prof geol, Univ Utah, 67-74. *Mem:* Int Paleont Asn; Palaeont Asn London; fel Geol Soc Am; Paleont Soc. *Res:* Paleontology, particularly Cambrian trilobites and biostratigraphy. *Mailing Add:* Dept Geol Univ Kans Lawrence KS 66045-0001

ROBISON, WENDALL C(LOYD), ELECTRICAL ENGINEERING. *Current Pos:* from instr to assoc prof elec eng, 49-71, PROF ELEC ENG, UNIV NEBR, LINCOLN, 71- *Personal Data:* b Des Moines, Iowa, July 31, 23; m 47; c 3. *Educ:* Iowa State Univ, BSc, 47, MSc, 48, PhD(elec eng), 57. *Prof Exp:* Engr, Gen Elec Co, 48-49. *Mem:* AAAS; Am Soc Eng Educ; Inst Elec & Electronics Engrs. *Res:* Electric network theory including both linear and nonlinear networks; system theory. *Mailing Add:* 510 S 46th St Lincoln NE 68510

ROBISON, WILBUR GERALD, JR, CELL BIOLOGY, EXPERIMENTAL PATHOLOGY. *Current Pos:* sr staff fel, 72-76, geneticist & cell biologist, lab vision res, 76-82, chief sect exp anat, 82-85, CHIEF, SECT PATHOPHYSIOL, NAT EYE INST, 85- *Personal Data:* b Cheyenne, Wyo, Dec 27, 33; m 57, Lucia Panuncio; c Sylvia L (Aamodt), Stanley J, Nancy K (Jackson) & Lydia J (Gettys). *Educ:* Brigham Young Univ, AB, 58, MA, 61; Univ Calif, Berkeley, PhD(genetics), 65. *Honors & Awards:* Spec Achievement Award, Nat Eye Inst, NIH; hon mem Argentine Med Asn. *Prof Exp:* Res geneticist, Univ Calif, Berkeley, 63-65; res fel anat, Harvard Med Sch, 65-66; asst prof biol, Univ Va, 66-72. *Concurrent Pos:* US Air Force Off Sci Res-Nat Acad Sci res fel, 65-66. *Mem:* Am Soc Cell Biol; Asn Res Vision & Ophthal; Sigma Xi. *Res:* Experimental pathology of the eye; ultrastructural and functional interrelationships between the pigment epithelium and the visual cells of the retina; prevention of visual complications of diabetes using inhibitors of aldose reductase; vitamin A, vitamin E, and aging pigments. *Mailing Add:* 1306 Gresham Rd Silver Spring MD 20904-1436. *Fax:* 301-402-1570; *E-Mail:* robisong@box-r.nih.gov

ROBISON, WILLIAM LEWIS, ECOLOGY, RADIOBIOLOGY. *Current Pos:* SR RES SCIENTIST ENVIRON SCI, UNIV CALIF, LAWRENCE LIVERMORE LAB, 65- *Personal Data:* b Grinnell, Iowa, June 18, 38; m 59; c 3. *Educ:* Cornell Col, AB, 56; Univ Calif, Berkeley, MS, 62, PhD(biophysics), 66. *Mem:* AAAS; Health Physics Soc; Nat Coun Radiation Protection & Measurement. *Res:* Environmental science; radionuclide and stable element transport and fate; radiation biology; uptake, retention, dose assessment to populations via food chains. *Mailing Add:* 774 Canterbury Ave Livermore CA 94550

ROBITAILLE, HENRY ARTHUR, DIRECTOR, SCIENCE & TECHNOLOGY. *Current Pos:* DIR SCI & TECHNOL, EPCOT CTR, 81- *Personal Data:* b Washington, DC, Sept 2, 43; m 68, Phyllis Jean; c Renee, Michael & Jennifer. *Educ:* Univ Md, BS, 66; Mich State Univ, MS, 67, PhD(hort), 70. *Honors & Awards:* Cert of Appreciation, USDA, 87; Tribute of Appreciation, US Environ Protection Agency, 88. *Prof Exp:* Prof hort, Okla State Univ, 70-72, Purdue Univ, 72-81. *Concurrent Pos:* Vpres indust, Am Soc Hort Soc; prof, Univ Vicosa, Brazil, 73-75; plant physiologist, USAID, Brazil, 73-75; adj prof, Univ Ariz & Univ Fla, 81-; adv bd, Valencia Community Col, 83- *Mem:* Am Soc Hort Sci; Sigma Xi; AAAS. *Res:* Administer a department doing research and engineering in many areas related to both agriculture and oceanography-marine biology; special expertise in science communications and technical pavilion support. *Mailing Add:* Epcot Ctr PO Box 10000 Lake Buena Vista FL 32830. *Fax:* 407-560-7227

ROBKIN, MAURICE, NUCLEAR ENGINEERING, HEALTH PHYSICS. *Current Pos:* assoc prof, 67-79, prof nuclear eng, 79-94, prof environ health, 81-97, STAFF MEM, DEPT ENVIRON HEALTH, UNIV WASH, 97- *Personal Data:* b New York, NY, Apr 25, 31; m 62, Anne L Hawkins; c 3. *Educ:* Calif Inst Technol, BS, 53; Oak Ridge Sch Reactor Technol, dipl, 54; Mass Inst Technol, PhD(nuclear eng), 61. *Prof Exp:* Physicist, Bettis Atomic Power Lab, Westinghouse Elec Co, 54-56 & Valecitos Atomic Lab, Gen Elec Co, 61-67. *Concurrent Pos:* Vis scientist, Cambridge Univ, 76; consult indust nuclear eng & health physics. *Mem:* Am Nuclear Soc; Health Physics Soc. *Res:* Health physics; environmental radioactivity. *Mailing Add:* Dept Environ Health PO Box 357234 Univ Wash Seattle WA 98195. *Fax:* 206-543-8123; *E-Mail:* robkin@u.washington.edu

ROBL, HERMANN R, THEORETICAL PHYSICS. *Current Pos:* RETIRED. *Personal Data:* b Vienna, Austria, Aug 7, 19; nat US; m 42; c 1. *Educ:* Univ Vienna, PhD, 48; Dr habil, 52. *Honors & Awards:* Korner Award, 54. *Prof Exp:* Asst, Inst Theoret Physics, Vienna, 48-52, asst prof, 52-55; asst, Phys Sci Div, Off Ord Res, 55-56, assoc dir, Physics Div, 56-57, dir, 57-62; dep chief scientist, US Army Res Off, 62-73, chief scientist, 75-85. *Concurrent Pos:* From vis asst prof to vis assoc prof, Duke Univ, 59-65, adj prof, 66-; Army Res Off-Durham res & study proj scholar, 65. *Mem:* Am Phys Soc. *Res:* Quantum optics and mechanics. *Mailing Add:* 2215 Elmwood Ave Durham NC 27707

ROBLE, RAYMOND G, IONOSPHERIC & ATMOSPHERIC DYNAMICS. *Current Pos:* SR SCIENTIST, HIGH ALTITUDE OBSERV, NAT CTR ATMOSPHERIC RES. *Personal Data:* b Wyandotte, Mich, Mar 14, 35. *Educ:* Univ Mich, BSE, 57, MS, 61, PhD(aeronomy), 69. *Mem:* Fel Am Geophys Union. *Mailing Add:* Nat Ctr Atmospheric Res Box 3000 Boulder CO 80307. *Fax:* 303-497-1589; *E-Mail:* roble@ncar.ucar.edu

ROBLES, LAURA JEANNE, BIOLOGY OF PHOTORECEPTORS. *Current Pos:* PROF BIOL, CALIF STATE UNIV, 75- *Educ:* Univ Calif, PhD(biol), 75. *Res:* Electron microscopy; vitamin A cycling. *Mailing Add:* Dept Biol Calif State Univ 1000 E Victoria St Dominguez Hills Carson CA 90747-0005. *Fax:* 310-532-2537

ROBLIN, JOHN M, ECONOMIC ANALYSIS, STRATEGIC PLANNING. *Personal Data:* b Sagada, Philippines, Feb 20, 31; m 66; c Christopher, Keith & Maria. *Educ:* Princeton Univ, BS, 53; Mass Inst Technol, MS, 55; Case Univ, PhD(chem eng), 62. *Honors & Awards:* F C Zeisberg Award, Am Inst Chem Engrs, 53; Regional Tech Award, Am Iron & Steel Inst, 65. *Prof Exp:* Chmn coal & coal chem res, Repub Steel Corp, 63-65, head new prod res, 65-74, mgr, Process & Mat Pkg, 74-78, dir, Res & Develop, 78-81, dir, Strategic Planning, 81-85; dir corp planning, LTV Steel Corp, 85-87; dir eng res, Univ NC, Charlotte, 87-89. *Concurrent Pos:* Affil, Sr Consult Network, 86- *Mem:* Am Iron & Steel Inst; Am Soc Eng Educ; Sigma Xi; Am Inst Chem Engrs. *Res:* Process analysis and development, especially in natural resources, metallurgical industries, coal and coke; management of technology; technology transfer; intellectual capital. *Mailing Add:* PO Box 247 Univ NC Davidson NC 28036. *Fax:* 704-547-3183

ROBOCK, ALAN, CLIMATE DYNAMICS, CLIMATOLOGICAL DATA ANALYSIS. *Current Pos:* from asst prof to assoc prof, 77-96, PROF, DEPT METEOROL, UNIV MD, 96- *Personal Data:* b Boston, Mass, Sept 7, 49; m 90. *Educ:* Univ Wis-Madison, BA, 70; Mass Inst Technol, SM, 74, PhD(meteorol), 77. *Prof Exp:* Vol meteorol, US Peace Corps, Philippines, 70-72. *Mem:* Am Meteorol Soc; AAAS; Am Geophys Union; Fedn Am Scientists. *Res:* Numerical modeling of the climate system; causes of climate change, especially volcanic eruptions, carbon dioxide and natural variability; snow and ice-albedo feedback; climatological data analysis-surface temperature and snow cover; nuclear winter; soil moisture. *Mailing Add:* Dept Meteorol Univ Md College Park MD 20742. *E-Mail:* alan@atmos.umd.edu

ROBOLD, ALICE ILENE, MATHEMATICS, TEACHER EDUCATION. *Current Pos:* Asst prof math, 64-69, assoc prof, 69-76, PROF MATH SCI, BALL STATE UNIV, 76- *Personal Data:* b Daleville, Ind, Feb 7, 28; m 55, Virgil G; c Edward L. *Educ:* Ball State Univ, BS, 55, MA, 60, EdD, 65. *Prof Exp:* Substitute elem sch teacher, Am Elem Sch, Augsburg, Ger, 55-56. *Concurrent Pos:* Ed, Ind Math Teacher (J). *Mem:* Nat Coun Teachers Math; Sch Sci & Math Asn. *Res:* Background of college instructors of mathematics for prospective elementary school teachers. *Mailing Add:* Dept Math Sci Ball State Univ Muncie IN 47306

ROBOZ, JOHN, ANALYTICAL BIOCHEMISTRY, CHEMOTHERAPY. *Current Pos:* res assoc prof clin chem, 69-74, assoc prof, 74-81, PROF NEOPLASTIC DIS, MT SINAI SCH MED, 81- *Personal Data:* b Budapest, Hungary, Oct 14, 31; US citizen; m 61; c 2. *Educ:* Eotvos Lorand, Budapest, BS, 55; NY Univ, MS, 60, PhD(phys chem), 62. *Prof Exp:* Sr engr, Gen Tel & Electronics Res Labs, NY, 57-63; group leader gas analysis res, Cent Res Labs, Air Reduction Co, 63-69. *Mem:* Am Chem Soc; Am Soc Mass Spectrometry; Am Asn Cancer Res; NY Acad Sci; Fedn Am Soc Exp Biol. *Res:* Identification and quantification of antineoplastic agents and metabolites in body fluids and tissues; biological markers of cancer; biochemical diagnosis of opportunistic infections; mass spectrometry, high performance liquid chromatography and other instrumental techniques in clinical chemistry. *Mailing Add:* Dept Neoplastic Dis Mt Sinai Sch Med 11 E 100th St New York NY 10029-6504. *Fax:* 212-860-7186

ROBROCK, RICHARD BARKER, II, INTELLIGENT NETWORK SYSTEMS, NETWORK SERVICES. *Current Pos:* Mem tech staff, Bell Labs, 67-69, supvr, 69-79, dept head, 79-83, dir, 83-84, asst vpres, Bell Commun Res, 84-96, VPRES, BELL COMMUN RES, 96- *Personal Data:* b Cleveland, Ohio, Dec 29, 41; m 70, Ellen Herits; c Kristin & Karl. *Educ:* Case Inst Technol, BS, 63, MS, 65, PhD(elec eng), 67. *Mem:* Fel Inst Elec & Electronics Engrs; AAAS; Sigma Xi. *Res:* Intelligent network software systems for telecommunications networks; real-time fault-tolerant data bases; telecommunications services; programming languages for rapid service creation. *Mailing Add:* Six Timothy Lane Bedminster NJ 07921

ROBSON, ANTHONY EMERSON, EXPERIMENTAL PLASMA PHYSICS. *Current Pos:* head, exp plasma physics br, 72-89, SR SCIENTIST, CONTROLLED FUSION RES & APPLN, NAVAL RES LAB, WASHINGTON, DC, 89- *Personal Data:* b London, Eng, March 29, 32; US citizen. *Educ:* Oxford Univ, BA, 52, MA, 56, DPhil, 56. *Prof Exp:* Sci officer, UK Atomic Energy Authority, Harwell & Culham Labs, 56-66; res scientist, Univ Tex, Austin, 66-72. *Concurrent Pos:* Vis scientist, Imp Col Sci & Technol, London, UK, 85-86. *Mem:* Fel Am Phys Soc. *Res:* Arc discharges; plasma solid interaction; mirror machines; collisionless shock waves; turbulent plasma heating; high magnetic field generation; homopolar generators; relativistic electron beams; high density Z-pinches; fusion reactor studies. *Mailing Add:* 2683 Centennial Ct Alexandria VA 22311

ROBSON, DONALD, NUCLEAR & PARTICLE PHYSICS. *Current Pos:* Res assoc nuclear physics, Fla State Univ, 63-64, from asst prof to assoc prof, 64-67, chairperson, 85-91, PROF PHYSICS, FLA STATE UNIV, 67-, ROBERT O LAWTON DISTINGUISHED PROF, 90- *Personal Data:* b Leeds, Eng, Mar 19, 37; m 60, 71, Martha Breitenlohner; c 3. *Educ:* Univ Melbourne, BSc, 59, MSc, 61, PhD(nuclear physics), 63. *Honors & Awards:* Tom W Bonner Prize, Am Phys Soc, 72. *Concurrent Pos:* Fulbright scholar, 63-64; A P Sloan fel, 66-72; vis prof, Princeton Univ, 71-72, Univ Munchen, WGer, 76-77; Alexander von Humboldt sr scientist award, 76-77; chmn bd trustees, Southeastern Univ Res Asn, 96- *Mem:* Fel Am Phys Soc. *Res:* Theoretical nuclear and particle physics. *Mailing Add:* Dept Physics Fla State Univ Tallahassee FL 32306. *Fax:* 850-644-8630; *E-Mail:* robson@scri.fsu.edu

ROBSON, DOUGLAS SHERMAN, BIOMETRICS. *Current Pos:* Biometrician, Cornell Univ, 49-53, res assoc plant breeding, 54-55, from asst prof to assoc prof, 55-62, prof, 62-87, EMER PROF PLANT BREEDING & BIOMET, CORNELL UNIV, 87- *Personal Data:* b St John, NDak, July 30, 25; m 49, Chitra Vithayasai; c Parry, Suzanne & Rick. *Educ:* Iowa State Col, BS, 49; Cornell Univ, MS, 51, PhD(statist), 55. *Concurrent Pos:* NIH career develop award, Cornell Univ, 62-72; pres, Eastern NAm Region Biomet Soc, 70; consult, 87- *Mem:* Fel Am Statist Asn; fel Am Inst Fishery Res Scientists; Biomet Soc; Statist Soc Can; Int Environmetrics Soc. *Res:* Biological statsitics; sampling theory and applications. *Mailing Add:* 150 MacLaren St PH6 Ottawa ON K2P 0L2 Can. *Fax:* 613-234-3553; *E-Mail:* ac003@freenet.carleton.ca

ROBSON, HARRY EDWIN, PHYSICAL CHEMISTRY. *Current Pos:* CONSULT, LA STATE UNIV, 86- *Personal Data:* b Kans, July 19, 27; m 50; c 3. *Educ:* Univ Kans, BS, 49, PhD(chem), 59. *Prof Exp:* Res chemist, Esso Res Labs, Humble Oil & Refining Co, 57-72, res assoc, Exxon Res & Develop Labs, 72-78, sr res assoc, 78-86. *Res:* Petroleum process catalysts; inorganic synthesis. *Mailing Add:* 3131 Congress Blvd Baton Rouge LA 70808-3139

ROBSON, JOHN HOWARD, POLYMER CHEMISTRY, ORGANIC CHEMISTRY. *Current Pos:* Proj chemist, Union Carbide Corp, 66-77, mgr tech recruiting & mgr tech & managerial educ, 77-80, res scientist, 80-82, technol mgr & group leader, res & develop, 82-93, SR RES SCIENTIST, UNION CARBIDE CORP, 93- *Personal Data:* b East Liberty, Ohio, July 26, 40; m 61; c 2. *Educ:* Ohio Northern Univ, BS, 62; Ohio State Univ, PhD(org chem), 67. *Mem:* Am Chem Soc. *Res:* Development of intermediates and application technology for flexible, high-resiliency and rigid polyurethane foams; chemical process innovation and development; process and project research and development for ethylene oxide, ethylene glycol and formulated products; application support for polyester ethylene glycol. *Mailing Add:* Union Carbide Tech Cent 770-456 PO Box 8361 South Charleston WV 25303-0361

ROBSON, JOHN MICHAEL, NUCLEAR PHYSICS. *Current Pos:* prof, 69-85, EMER PROF PHYSICS, MCGILL UNIV, 85- *Personal Data:* b London, Eng, Mar 26, 20; m 50, Nora Summerhays; c Michael, Lisa & Peter. *Educ:* Cambridge Univ, BA, 42, MA, 46, ScD, 63. *Honors & Awards:* Gold Medal, Can Asn Physicists, 78. *Prof Exp:* Physicist, Radar Res & Develop Estab, Eng, 42-45, Atomic Energy Res Estab, 45-50 & Atomic Energy Can, Ltd, 50-60; prof physics, Univ Ottawa, 60-69; prof physics, Sultan Qaboos Univ, Oman, 86-88. *Mem:* Fel Am Phys Soc; Royal Soc Can; Can Asn Physicists (past pres). *Res:* Radioactive decay of the neutron; inelastic scattering of fast neutrons; shielding of nuclear reactors; ultra cold neutrons; applied mechanics. *Mailing Add:* Dept Physics McGill Univ 3600 Univ St Montreal PQ H3A 2T8 Can

ROBSON, JOHN ROBERT KEITH, nutrition, public health, for more information see previous edition

ROBSON, JOHN WILLIAM, PHYSICS. *Current Pos:* from asst prof to prof, 54-83, EMER PROF PHYSICS, UNIV ARIZ, 83- *Personal Data:* b Coshocton, Ohio, Sept 6, 23; m 48, Bargie Compton; c David & Peggy (Jorgensen). *Educ:* Oberlin Col, BA, 49; Case Inst Technol, MS, 52, PhD(physics), 54. *Prof Exp:* Asst physics, Case Inst Technol, 49-51, instr, 51-54. *Mem:* Am Asn Physics Teachers; Sigma Xi. *Res:* Low energy nuclear physics; applied optics and acoustics. *Mailing Add:* 5671 E Whittier St Tucson AZ 85711

ROBSON, RICHARD MORRIS, BIOCHEMISTRY, ANIMAL SCIENCE. *Current Pos:* assoc prof, 72-77, PROF BIOCHEM & ANIMAL SCI, IOWA STATE UNIV, 77- *Personal Data:* b Atlantic, Iowa, Dec 9, 41; c Kristi, Jeff, Samuel & Anya. *Educ:* Iowa State Univ, BS, 64, MS, 66, PhD(biochem), 69. *Honors & Awards:* Distinguished Res Award, Am Meat Sci Asn, 84; Meat Res Award, Am Soc Animal Sci, 85. *Prof Exp:* NIH fel biochem, Iowa State Univ, 65-69; asst prof biochem animal sci, Univ Ill, 69-72. *Concurrent Pos:* Masua hon res lectr, 84-85; vis sci award, WGer Cancer Res Ctr, 86-87. *Mem:* AAAS; Am Heart Asn; Am Soc Animal Sci; Sigma Xi; Am Soc Cell Biol; Am Soc Biochem & Molecular Biol. *Res:* Biochemistry of muscle tissue with emphasis on the chemistry, structure, molecular biology and function of the myofibrillar/cytoskeletal proteins. *Mailing Add:* Molecular Biol Bldg Iowa State Univ Ames IA 50011

ROBSON, RONALD D, pharmacology, for more information see previous edition

ROBUSTO, C CARL, MATHEMATICS, PHYSICS. *Current Pos:* Assoc prof, 46-56, acad vpres, Queens, 78-80, PROF MATH & PHYSICS, ST JOHN'S UNIV, NY, 56-, EXEC VPRES, 80- *Personal Data:* b Bridgeport, Conn, Nov 29, 16; m 44; c 2. *Educ:* St John's Univ, NY, BS, 39; Columbia Univ, MA, 46; NY Univ, MS, 50; Fordham Univ, PhD, 54. *Concurrent Pos:* Dean jr col, St John's Univ, 62-67, dean gen studies, 68-71; acad vpres, Staten Island & dean, Notre Dame Col, 71-78. *Mailing Add:* 171 97th St Brooklyn NY 11209

ROBY, MARK SINCLAIR, BIOABSORBABLE MATERIALS. *Current Pos:* dir mat develop, US Surg Corp, 92-93, sr dir mat res & develop, 93-95, sr dir mat res & develop & suture mfg, 95-96, SR DIR ADVAN MAT, US SURG CORP, 97- *Personal Data:* b Beltsville, Md, Oct 15, 50; m, Joan Marie Bogues; c Janet & Chris. *Educ:* Univ Conn, BA, 73, PhD(polymer chem), 77; Nasson Col, MBA, 87. *Prof Exp:* Res chemist, Am Cyanamid Co, 77-79, proj leader, 80-81, tech serv mgr, Cyro, Subsid Am Cyanamid Co, 82-85, prod supt, 85-87, bus mgr, 88-90, NE regional sales mgr, 91-92. *Concurrent Pos:* Adj prof, Univ Conn, 97- *Mem:* Am Chem Soc; Soc Plastics Engrs; Bio/Environ Degradable Polymer Soc; AAAS. *Mailing Add:* 11 Grace Lane Killingworth CT 06419

ROBYT, JOHN F, BIOCHEMISTRY. *Current Pos:* res assoc, 64-67, asst prof, 67-73, assoc prof, 73-83, PROF BIOCHEM, IOWA STATE UNIV, 83- *Personal Data:* b Moline, Ill, Feb 17, 35; m 58; c 2. *Educ:* St Louis Univ, BS, 58; Iowa State Univ, PhD(biochem), 62. *Prof Exp:* Asst prof biochem, La State Univ, 62-63; NIH fel, Lister Inst Prev Med, London, Eng, 63-64. *Concurrent Pos:* Consult, E I du Pont de Nemours & Co, 70- *Mem:* Am Soc Biol Chemists; Am Chem Soc. *Res:* Study of the mechanisms of carbohydrase action, the mode of substrate binding, the sequence of catalytic events, the types of groups involved, especially with the polysaccharide synthesizing and degrading enzymes; study of the mechanisms of polysaccharide synthesizing and degrading enzymes; chemical modification of carbohydrates to form new products, especially from starch and sucrose, and for inhibitors of carbohydrate enzymes. *Mailing Add:* Dept Biochem Iowa State Univ Ames IA 50011-0061

ROCCI, MARIO LOUIS, JR, PHARMACOKINETICS, BIOANALYTICAL CHEMISTRY. *Current Pos:* DIR PHARMACEUT RES, ONEIDA RES SERV INC, 88- *Personal Data:* b Utica, NY, Nov 6, 52. *Educ:* Syracuse Univ NY, Buffalo, BS, 76 PhD(pharmaceut), 81. *Prof Exp:* Asst prof pharm & dir, Pharmacokinetics Res Lab, Philadelphia Col Pharm & Sci, 80-83; res assoc prof med & head lab investigative med, Div Clin Pharmacol, Dept Med, Jefferson Med Col, 83-88. *Concurrent Pos:* Consult,

Muck Sharp & Dome Res Lab, 85-88, Nat Asn Clin Res, 85-; clin assoc prof pharm, Philadelphia Col Pharm & Sci, 86- *Mem:* Sigma Xi; fel Am Col Clin Pharmacol; Am Asn Pharmaceut Scientist; Am Soc Clin Pharmacol & Therapeut; Am Fedn Clin Res. *Res:* Evaluating the clinical pharmacokinetics and pharmacodynamics of established as well as investigational drugs; author of over 150 manuscripts, book chapters and abstracts. *Mailing Add:* 27 The Hills Dr Utica NY 13501-5513

ROCCO, GREGORY GABRIEL, RADIOCHEMISTRY. *Current Pos:* RETIRED. *Personal Data:* b Lawrence, Mass, Sept 16, 26; m 50; c 3. *Educ:* Boston Univ, BA, 49; Univ Mich, MS, 50. *Prof Exp:* Radiochemist, Tracerlab, Inc, 49-63; staff chemist, Wentworth Inst, 63-66; mgr radiochem, New Eng Nuclear Corp, North Billercia, Mass, 66-72, mgr Nuclides & Sources Div, 72-81; site mgr, Dupont NEN Prod, 81-85. *Res:* Development of radiochemical procedures for the separation and decontamination of reactor and cyclotron produced isotopes; development of the use of isotopes for medicine, industry and research. *Mailing Add:* 1149 Hillsborough Mile Apt 602 N Hillsboro Beach FL 33062

ROCEK, JAN, PHYSICAL ORGANIC CHEMISTRY. *Current Pos:* dean, Grad Sch, Univ Ill, Chicago, 70-79, actg head dept, 80-81, head, 81-93, PROF CHEM, UNIV ILL, CHICAGO, 66-, VCHANCELLOR RES & DEAN GRAD COL, 93- *Personal Data:* b Prague, Czech, Mar 24, 24; US citizen; m 47; c 2. *Educ:* Prague Tech Univ, ChemE, 49, PhD(chem), 53. *Prof Exp:* Chemist, Inst Chem, Czech Acad Sci, Prague, 53-60; res fel chem, Harvard Univ, 60-62; from assoc prof to prof, Cath Univ, 62-66. *Concurrent Pos:* Actg dean, Grad Sch, Univ Ill, 69-70; vis scholar, Stanford Univ & Univ Cambridge, Eng, 79-80. *Mem:* Am Chem Soc; Sigma Xi. *Res:* Mechanisms of oxidation reactions. *Mailing Add:* 2636 Laurel Lane Wilmette IL 60091

ROCHAIX, JEAN-DAVID, MOLECULAR BIOLOGY. *Current Pos:* PROF, DEPT MOLECULAR BIOL, UNIV GENEVA. *Honors & Awards:* Gilbert Morgan Smith Medal, Nat Acad Sci, 91. *Mailing Add:* Dept Molecular Biol Univ Geneva Geneva Switzerland

ROCHBERG, RICHARD HOWARD, MATHEMATICS. *Current Pos:* from asst prof to assoc prof, 70-81, PROF MATH, WASH UNIV, 81- *Personal Data:* b Baltimore, Md, May 15, 43; m 68; c 2. *Educ:* Princeton Univ, AB, 64; Harvard Univ, MA, 66, PhD(math), 70. *Prof Exp:* Res assoc, Inst Future, 69-70. *Concurrent Pos:* Sr vis fel, Univ Col, London, 78-79. *Mem:* Am Math Soc. *Res:* Function theory, spaces of analytic functions, operator theory. *Mailing Add:* Dept Math Wash Univ St Louis MO 63130

ROCHE, ALEXANDER F, CHILD GROWTH, ANTHROPOMETRICS. *Current Pos:* prof obstet & gynec, 77-90, PROF PEDIAT, WRIGHT STATE UNIV, 77-, UNIV PROF & PROF COM HEALTH, 90- *Personal Data:* b Melbourne, Australia, Oct 17, 21; m 45, Eileen French; c Peter J, Stephen J & Margaret A. *Educ:* Univ Melbourne, MB, BS, 46, PhD(anat), 54, DSc(child growth), 66, MD, 69; FRACP, 80. *Prof Exp:* Intern med, St Vincent's Hosp, Melbourne, 46-48, asst to outpatients surgeon, 48-50; lectr anat, Univ Melbourne, 50-52, sr lectr, 52-62, reader, 62-68; chmn dept growth genetics, 68-71, chief sect phys growth & genetics, Sect Fels Longitudinal Study & Families, Sect Measurement Growth & Maturity, Fels Res Inst, Ohio, 71-77. *Concurrent Pos:* Demonstr, Univ Melbourne, 48-50; Smith-Mundt & Fulbright fels, 52-53; teaching fel, Western Res Univ, 52-53; Rockefeller traveling grant, 52-; 06349390xxxyal Children's Hosp, Melbourne, 67-68, Children's Med Ctr, Dayton, Ohio, 69-, Hamilton Co Diag Clin Ment Retarded, 69-, Univ Cincinnati Affil Prog Ment Retarded, 69-, USAF, Pan-Am Health Orgn, WHO, Inst Nutrit Cent Am & Panama, Nat Health & Nutrit Exam Surv, 71- & Nat Pituitary Agency, 72-; vis prof, Ohio State Univ, 76, Univ Md, 78; mem, Pediat Adv Sub-comt, Food & Drug Admin, 78; fels prof pediat, fels prof obstet & gynecol, Wright State Univ Sch Med; consult, Nat Health & Nutrit Exam Serv, Dept Health & Human Serv, 71; ed-in-chief, J Human Ecol, 93- *Mem:* Am Asn Phys Anthrop; Soc Res Child Develop; Soc Study Human Biol; Anat Soc Gt Brit & Ireland; fel Human Biol Coun. *Mailing Add:* Div Human Biol 1005 Xenia Ave Yellow Springs OH 45387-1695. *Fax:* 937-767-6922; *E-Mail:* aroche@desire.wright.edu

ROCHE, BEN F, JR, RANGE MANAGEMENT. *Current Pos:* RETIRED. *Personal Data:* b Winona, Miss, Feb 2, 24; m 50; c 2. *Educ:* Univ Calif, Davis, BS, 51; Wash State Univ, MS, 60; Univ Idaho, PhD(range ecol), 65. *Prof Exp:* Co exten agent land develop, Wash State Univ, 51-54, veg mgt, 54-57, weed specialist, 58-65, asst prof range ecol, 65-66, assoc prof, 66-71, prof range ecol, 71- *Concurrent Pos:* Coordr res, Colockum Multiple Use Res Ctr, 66- *Mem:* Weed Sci Soc Am; Soc Range Mgt. *Res:* Ecology of secondary succession as created by man's disorder of the primary, particularly the exotic species that seem preadapted to the site. *Mailing Add:* Dept Natural Res Sci Wash State Univ Pullman WA 99164-6410

ROCHE, EDWARD BROWNING, MEDICINAL CHEMISTRY, DRUG DESIGN. *Current Pos:* asst prof, Univ Nebr Med Ctr, Omaha, 66-71, asst dean, 80-83, ASSOC PROF PHARM SCI, COL PHARM, UNIV NEBR MED CTR, OMAHA, 71-, ASSOC DEAN, ACAD AFFAIRS, 83- *Personal Data:* b Stamford, Conn, Apr 29, 38; m 76, Victoria Frisbie; c Janet R (Coe) & Beverly A. *Educ:* Butler Univ, BS, 61, MS, 63; Ohio State Univ, PhD(med chem), 66. *Mem:* AAAS; Am Pharmaceut Asn; Acad Pharmaceut Sci; Am Chem Soc; Sigma Xi; Am Asn Pharm Sci. *Res:* Design of compounds for analgesic drug-receptor interaction studies; synthetic organic medicinal chemistry; the application of physical organic chemistry to the study of mechanism of biological activity; science education; educational administration. *Mailing Add:* Col Pharm Univ Nebr Med Ctr 600 S 42nd St Omaha NE 68198-6000. *Fax:* 402-559-5060; *E-Mail:* eroche@unmc.edu

ROCHE, EDWARD TOWNE, INVERTEBRATE ZOOLOGY, HISTOLOGY. *Current Pos:* from asst prof to prof, 59-86, EMER PROF BIOL SCI, CALIF STATE POLYTECH UNIV, 86- *Personal Data:* b Buenos Aires, Arg, Mar 8, 25; nat US; m 52, Catherine M Patitucy; c David Edward, Laurie Anne & Edward Lawrence. *Educ:* San Diego State Col, AB, 48; Univ Southern Calif, MS, 52, PhD(zool), 57. *Prof Exp:* Asst & assoc, Univ Southern Calif, 53-57; instr life sci, Compton Jr Col, 57-59. *Mem:* Sigma Xi. *Res:* Histology; parasitology; biological education; venomous fishes. *Mailing Add:* Dept Biol Sci Calif State Polytech Univ Pomona CA 91768-4016

ROCHE, GEORGE WILLIAM, FORENSIC SCIENCE. *Current Pos:* assoc prof, 69-71, PROF DEPT CRIMINAL JUSTICE, CALIF STATE UNIV, SACRAMENTO, 71- *Personal Data:* b San Francisco, Calif, May 27, 21; m 54, Janet Hubbard; c Stephen & Sandra. *Educ:* Univ Calif, Berkeley, AB, 42; Univ Minn, Minneapolis, MS, 52. *Prof Exp:* Crime lab analyst, Bur Criminal Apprehension, State Minn, 46-54, lab dir, 54-62; criminalist, Dept Justice, State Calif, 62-64, supvy criminalist, 64-69. *Mem:* Am Acad Forensic Sci; Am Chem Soc; Soc Appl Spectros; Am Soc Criminol; Inst Asn Identification. *Res:* Recognition, individualization and evaluation of physical evidence by application of the natural sciences to law-science matters. *Mailing Add:* 7233 Milford St Sacramento CA 95822

ROCHE, JAMES NORMAN, chemistry, for more information see previous edition

ROCHE, LIDIA ALICIA, NUCLEAR WASTE DISPOSAL & CHEMICAL SAFETY ONCOLOGY, NUCLEAR MATERIALS PROCESSES. *Current Pos:* tech asst to exec dir opers, 41, RES ANALYST, US NUCLEAR REGULATORY COMN, 78-, PROG MGR, 86-, SR SECT CHIEF CHEM SAFETY, NUCLEAR FUEL CYCLE FACIL. *Personal Data:* b Havana, Cuba, May 9, 39; m 61; c 3. *Educ:* The Am Univ, BS, 69, PhD(phys chem), 75. *Prof Exp:* Res technician biomed, Georgetown Univ, 63-69; chemist, Gillette Res Inst, 70-72, res chemist, 75-78. *Mem:* Am Chem Soc. *Res:* Medical uses of radio isotopes; fuel production through waste management and disposal. *Mailing Add:* 623 Warfield Dr Rockville MD 20850-1921

ROCHE, RODNEY SYLVESTER, BIOPHYSICAL CHEMISTRY, POLYMER CHEMISTRY. *Current Pos:* from asst prof to prof chem, 65-78, PROF BIOCHEM & CHEM, UNIV CALGARY, 87-, ASSOC DEAN RES, FAC GRAD STUDIES, 89- *Personal Data:* b Oxford, Eng, July 9, 34; div; c 3. *Educ:* Univ Glasgow, BSc, 57, PhD(polymer chem), 65. *Prof Exp:* Sci officer, Chem Div, UK Atomic Energy Authority Exp Reactor Estab, Scotland, 57-61; asst lectr chem, Univ Glasgow, 62-65. *Concurrent Pos:* Vis scientist, Weizmann Inst Sci, 71-72, 76 & 80. *Mem:* AAAS; Am Chem Soc; Chem Soc; fel Royal Soc Chem; fel Chem Inst Can; Sigma Xi; NY Acad Sci. *Res:* Physical chemistry of macromolecules; conformational studies of polypeptides and proteins; calcium binding proteins; calmodulin; protein engineering and the protein folding problem. *Mailing Add:* Dept Biol Sci Univ Calgary 2500 Univ Dr NW Calgary AB T2N 1N4 Can

ROCHE, THOMAS EDWARD, BIOCHEMISTRY. *Current Pos:* from asst prof to assoc prof, 74-82, PROF BIOCHEM, KANS STATE UNIV, 82-, HEAD DEPT, 90- *Personal Data:* b Denver, Colo, Feb 17, 44; m 66; c 2. *Educ:* Regis Col, Colo, BS, 66; Wash State Univ, PhD(chem), 70. *Prof Exp:* NIH res fel, Clayton Found Biochem Inst, Univ Tex, Austin, 70-72, res assoc, 72-74. *Mem:* Am Chem Soc; Fedn Am Socs Exp Biol; AAAS. *Res:* Structure and function of 2-ketoacid dehydrogenase complexes; regulation of mammalian pyruvate dehydrogenase complex by enzymatic interconversion; cellular organization. *Mailing Add:* Dept Biochem Willard Hall Kans State Univ Manhattan KS 66506-3702. *Fax:* 785-532-7278

ROCHE, THOMAS STEPHEN, INORGANIC CHEMISTRY, PHYSICAL & SEMICONDUCTOR PROCESS CHEMISTRY. *Current Pos:* SR STAFF ENGR, MOTOROLA INC, 89- *Personal Data:* b New York, NY, Apr 9, 46; m 70; c 2. *Educ:* Manhattan Col, BS, 67; State Univ NY, Buffalo, PhD(inorganic chem), 72. *Prof Exp:* Res assoc inorganic chem, Wayne State Univ, 72-73; res assoc organometallic chem, Univ Chicago, 73-75; res chemist, Pullman Kellogg Res & Develop Lab, 75-80; res assoc, Olin Chem, 80-89. *Mem:* Am Chem Soc; Electrochem Soc. *Res:* Inorganic and organometallic chemistry; reaction mechanisms; catalysis; new process research; semiconductor process development and research. *Mailing Add:* 8602 E Cheryl Dr Scottsdale AZ 85258-1415

ROCHEFORT, JOHN S, ELECTRICAL ENGINEERING. *Current Pos:* res assoc elec eng, 49-52, from asst prof to assoc prof commun, 52-62, actg chmn dept elec eng, 72-73, chmn, 77-82, PROF ELEC ENG, NORTHEASTERN UNIV, 62, PROF COMP ENG, 82-, DIR ELECTRONIC, RES LAB, 87- *Personal Data:* b Boston, Mass, June 15, 24; m 52; c 5. *Educ:* Northeastern Univ, BS, 48; Mass Inst Technol, SM, 51. *Prof Exp:* Asst, Servomech Lab, Mass Inst Technol, 48-49, staff engr, 49. *Concurrent Pos:* Vis prof elec eng, Univ Alaska, 74-75; vis engr, Air Force Geophys Lab, Bedford, Mass, 82-83. *Mem:* Am Soc Eng Educ; sr mem Inst Elec & Electronics Engrs. *Res:* Analysis and instrumentation in information theory, networks and radio telemetry; development of airborne instrumentation and radio telemetry systems for high altitude balloons, sounding rockets, shuttle and orbital vehicles; systems incorporating microprocessor control to change experiment in flight as function of experimental data received. *Mailing Add:* 17 High Plain St Sharon MA 02067-1042

ROCHEFORT, JOSEPH GUY, BIOCHEMISTRY, ENDOCRINOLOGY. *Current Pos:* PRES, PHARMEDICAL CONSULTS INC, 88- *Personal Data:* b Astorville, Ont, July 5, 29; m 54; c 2. *Educ:* Laurentian Univ, BA, 51; McGill Univ, BSc, 54, MSc, 56, PhD(biochem), 58. *Prof Exp:* Biochemist, Regional Labs, Dept Health & Welfare, NB, 54-55; Nat Mutiple Sclerosis Soc fel, 58-60; sr scientist, Dept Pharmacol, Abbott Labs, 60-65 & Dept Biochem, 66-69, asst dir, Dept Clin Pharmacol, 69-76, dir dept Clin Res, Can, 76-83; res projects coordinator, Sanofi Recherche, Montpellier, France, 83-87. *Concurrent Pos:* Lectr, Concordia Univ, 64-79. *Mem:* Endocrine Soc; Can Physiol Soc; Can Fertil Soc; Am Fertil Soc; Can Soc Clin Invest; Soc Toxicol Can. *Res:* Anterior pituitary-adrenocorticotrophic hormone distribution and release; adrenal responses to stress; bioassay of synthetic and natural steroid hormones; adrenal steriodogenesis; biochemistry of inflammation; bioavailability; pharmacokinetics; clinical investigation of new drugs. *Mailing Add:* 3450 King Edward Ave Montreal PQ H4B 2C3 Can

ROCHELLE, LORI GATZY, cell culture of primary cells - epithelia, electron paramagnetic resonance spectroscopy of biological samples, for more information see previous edition

ROCHELLE, ROBERT W(HITE), ELECTRICAL ENGINEERING. *Current Pos:* RETIRED. *Personal Data:* b Nashville, Tenn, June 23, 23; m 49; c 4. *Educ:* Univ Tenn, BS, 47; Yale Univ, ME, 49; Univ Md, PhD(elec eng), 63. *Honors & Awards:* Medaille du CNES, France, 65. *Prof Exp:* Electronic scientist, US Naval Res Lab, 49-55, head, Magnetic Amplifier Sect, 55-58; br head, Flight Data Systs Br, Goddard Space Flight Ctr, NASA, 58-71, assoc chief, Commun & Navig Div, 71-73; prof elec eng, Univ Tenn, 73-89; dir, res & develop, Empruve, Inc, 89-91. *Concurrent Pos:* Lectr, Univ Md, 57-59. *Mem:* AAAS; fel Inst Elec & Electronics Engrs; Am Soc Eng Educ; Sigma Xi. *Res:* Application of microcomputers in space and industrial instrumentation. *Mailing Add:* 4042 Kingston Pike Knoxville TN 37919

ROCHESTER, DUDLEY FORTESCUE, PULMONOLOGY, RESPIRATORY MUSCLE PHYSIOLOGY. *Current Pos:* PROF MED & HEAD PULMONARY DIV, DEPT INTERNAL MED, SCH MED, UNIV VA, 76- *Personal Data:* b Bennington, Vt, May 21, 28; m 50; c 2. *Educ:* Columbia Univ, AB, 50; Columbia Univ, MD, 55. *Prof Exp:* Instr med, Col Physicians & Surgeons, Columbia Univ, 62-63, assoc, 63-65, from asst prof to assoc prof, 65-76. *Concurrent Pos:* Physician, Univ Va Hosp, 76- *Mem:* Fel Am Col Physicians; fel Am Col Chest Physicians; Am Physiol Soc; Am Thoracic Soc; Am Fedn Clin Res. *Res:* Function of respiratory muscles and diaphragm with regard to strength, endurance and susceptibility to fatigue in normal humans and patients with chronic pulmonary disease. *Mailing Add:* Dept Med Univ Va 103 Shawnee Ct Charlottesville VA 22901. *Fax:* 804-924-9682

ROCHESTER, EUGENE WALLACE, AGRICULTURAL ENGINEERING. *Personal Data:* b Greenville, SC, July 15, 43; m 68; c 2. *Educ:* Clemson Univ, BS, 65; NC State Univ, MS, 68, PhD(biol & agr eng), 70. *Prof Exp:* Assoc prof agr eng, Auburn Univ, 70-97. *Concurrent Pos:* Consult, Irrig Syst Design, 78-; William Howard Smith fac fel award, Sch Agr & Agr Exp Sta, Auburn Univ, 76. *Mem:* Am Soc Agr Engrs; Irrig Asn. *Res:* Field crop irrigation, especially machinery types, energy requirements and systems for irregular fields; landscape and golf course irrigation design. *Mailing Add:* 625 Jennifer Dr Auburn AL 36830. *E-Mail:* groch@eng.auburn.edu

ROCHESTER, MICHAEL GRANT, GEOPHYSICS, ASTRONOMY. *Current Pos:* assoc prof, Mem Univ Nfld, 67-70, prof physics, 70, prof earth sci, 82, UNIV RES PROF, MEM UNIV NFLD, 86- *Personal Data:* b Toronto, Ont, Nov 22, 32; m 58, Elizabeth Manser; c Susan, Fiona & John. *Educ:* Univ Toronto, BA, 54, MA, 56; Univ Utah, PhD(physics), 59. *Honors & Awards:* Tuzo Wilson medal, Can Geophysical Union, 86. *Prof Exp:* Lectr physics, Univ Toronto, 59-60, asst prof, 60-61; from asst prof to assoc prof, Univ Waterloo, 61-67. *Concurrent Pos:* Mem, Working Group Physical Processes in Earth's Interior, Int Geodynamics Proj, 71-79, Comn Rotation of Earth, Int Astron Union, 73- & Can Subcomt Geodynamics, 74-80; vis prof, York Univ, 74-75, 82-83, Univ Queensland, 77 & McGill Univ, 90-95, St Louis Univ, 97-; mem, Can Nat Comt Int Union Geodesy & Geophys, 74-75, 84-88, Nat Sci Eng Res Coun Earth Sci Grant Selection Comt, 79-82; mem, Bd Dir Lithoprobe Proj, 87-91. *Mem:* AAAS; Am Geophys Union; Can Asn Physicists; Royal Astron Soc; Can Geophys Union; Sigma Xi; fel Royal Soc Can. *Res:* Rotation of the earth; earth tides; dynamics of the earth's core; geomagnetism; planetary physics; free oscillations. *Mailing Add:* Dept Earth Sci Mem Univ Nfld St John's NF A1B 3X5 Can. *Fax:* 709-737-2589; *E-Mail:* mrochest@morgan.ucs.mun.ca

ROCHLIN, PHILLIP, CHEMISTRY, SOUND RECORDINGS. *Current Pos:* RETIRED. *Personal Data:* b New York, NY, Mar 24, 23; div; c Jennifer L & Kevin L. *Educ:* City Col New York, BS, 43; NY Univ, MS, 49; Rutgers Univ, MLS, 60. *Prof Exp:* Analytical chemist, var cos, 43-49; res chemist, Picatinny Arsenal, NJ, 50-63; sci analyst, Nat Referral Ctr Sci & Technol, Libr Cong, DC, 63; supvry chemist & mgr tech libr, Naval Propellant Plant, Indian Head, 63-68; chief accessions & indexing br, Nat Hwy Safety Inst Doc Ctr, 68-69; supvry chemist & dir, Tech Info Div, Naval Ord Sta, Indian Head, 69-84, chemist & tech info specialist, Environ & Energy Off, 79-84; exec dir, Asn Recorded Sound Collections, 85-94. *Concurrent Pos:* Adj instr library Sci, Charles Co Community Col, 73-79. *Mem:* Emer mem Am Chem Soc; hon mem Asn Recorded Sound Collections. *Res:* Explosives and propellants; information storage and retrieval; missiles and rockets. *Mailing Add:* 11200 Lockwood Dr Apt 1805 Silver Spring MD 20901

ROCHLIN, ROBERT SUMNER, NUCLEAR PHYSICS, ARMS CONTROL. *Current Pos:* RETIRED. *Personal Data:* b Yonkers, NY, June 25, 22; m 50, Janet Stemerman; c David & Linda. *Educ:* Cornell Univ, BEE, 44, PhD(physics), 52. *Prof Exp:* Radio engr, US Naval Res Lab, 44-45; physicist, Gen Elec Co, 51-63; mem staff, US Arms Control & Disarmament Agency, 63-96, chief scientist, 82-96. *Concurrent Pos:* Mem US del, US-Soviet Strategic Arms Limitation Talks, Vienna, Austria, 70 & Nuclear Fuel Cycle Eval, 78-80. *Res:* Arms control; negotiations, research and policy formulation. *Mailing Add:* 2709 Ross Rd Chevy Chase MD 20815

RO-CHOI, TAE SUK, BIOCHEMISTRY, PHARMACOLOGY. *Current Pos:* Teaching asst, 62-67, from instr to asst prof, 67-72, RES ASSOC PROF PHARMACOL, BAYLOR COL MED, 72- *Personal Data:* b Seoul, Korea, May 8, 37; m 67, Yong Chun; c Ho Gene & Shin John. *Educ:* Soo Do Med Col, Korea, MD, 62; Baylor Col Med, MS, 64, PhD(pharmacol), 68. *Concurrent Pos:* On leave, Baylor Col Med, 78- *Mem:* AAAS; Sigma Xi; Am Soc Pharmacol & Exp Therapeut; Am Asn Cancer Res; Am Soc Biochem & Molecular Biol. *Res:* Nuclear RNA of cancer and normal cells; primary sequence of nuclear low molecular weight RNA; nuclear and nucleolar RNA transcription and control mechanism of gene expression; ribonucleoprotein complex and their functions; discovery of Trimethyl RC G Cap structures of low molecular weight nuclear RNA (sn RNA) and their functions. *Mailing Add:* 4147 Martinshire Houston TX 77025. *Fax:* 713-667-1417; *E-Mail:* tsrochoi@neosoft.com

ROCHON, PAUL LEO, OPTICAL PROPERTIES OF POLYMERS, LIGHT SCATTERING. *Current Pos:* HEAD & PROF PHYSICS, ROYAL MIL COL CAN, 88- *Personal Data:* b Hawkesbury, Ont, May 27, 49; m 85; c Martha, Isaac & Nathan. *Educ:* Univ Ottawa, BSc, 72, PhD(physics), 76. *Concurrent Pos:* Prof engr, Asn Prof Engrs, 82- *Res:* Investigation into the properties of erasable optical recording polymer films; establish the mechanisms and the parameters in order to design and fabricate films with desired properties. *Mailing Add:* Physics Dept Royal Mil Col Kingston ON K7K 5L0 Can. *Fax:* 613-541-6040; *E-Mail:* rochon@rmc.ca

ROCHOW, EUGENE GEORGE, CHEMISTRY. *Current Pos:* from assoc prof to prof, 48-70, EMER PROF INORG CHEM, HARVARD UNIV, 70- *Personal Data:* b Newark, NJ, Oct 4, 09; m 35, 52, Helen L Smith; c 3. *Educ:* Cornell Univ, BChem, 31, PhD(chem), 35. *Hon Degrees:* MA, Harvard Univ, 48; Dr rer nat, Brunswick Tech Univ, 66, Dresden Tech Univ, 82. *Honors & Awards:* Baekeland Medal, 49; Matiello Award, 58; Perkin Medal, 62; Kipping Award, 65; Norris Award, Am Chem Soc, 74; Stock Prize, German Chem Soc, 83; Wacker Silicon Prize, 92. *Prof Exp:* Res chemist, Haloworks Corp, NJ, 31-32; asst chem, Cornell Univ, 32-35; chemist, Res Lab, Gen Elec Co, 35-48. *Concurrent Pos:* Mem, Nat Res Coun, 48. *Mem:* AAAS; Am Chem Soc; Am Inst Chemists; French Soc Indust Chemists; Int Acad Law & Sci. *Res:* Organosilicon chemistry and silicones; inorganic chemistry. *Mailing Add:* Myerlee Manor 107 1499 Brandywine Circle Ft Myers FL 33919-6764

ROCHOW, THEODORE GEORGE, CHEMICAL MICROSCOPY, RESINOGRAPHY. *Current Pos:* assoc prof, 69-74, EMER ASSOC PROF TEXTILE TECHNOL, NC STATE UNIV, RALEIGH, 74- *Personal Data:* b Newark, NJ, July 8, 07; m 58, Elizabeth Cook; c Theodore F. *Educ:* Cornell Univ, BChem, 29, PhD(chem), 34. *Honors & Awards:* Templin Award, Am Soc Testing & Mat, 73. *Prof Exp:* Group leader micros, Am Cyanamid Co, 34-55, projs mgr chem, 55-56, res fel, 56-69. *Mem:* Fel Am Chem Soc; fel Am Soc Testing & Mat; Electron Micros Soc Am; Optical Soc Am; Am Inst Physics. *Res:* Chemical microscopy; resinography. *Mailing Add:* Wedgwood Apts No 33 704 Smallwood Dr Raleigh NC 27605-1346

ROCHOW, WILLIAM FRANTZ, PLANT PATHOLOGY, PLANT VIROLOGY. *Current Pos:* RETIRED. *Personal Data:* b Lancaster, Pa, Mar 12, 27; m 53, Janet Seymour; c Linda (Hartman) & Peter. *Educ:* Franklin & Marshall Col, BS, 50; Cornell Univ, PhD(plant path), 54. *Honors & Awards:* Superior Serv Award, USDA, 66; Ruth Allen Award, Am Phytopath Soc, 75. *Prof Exp:* Asst plant path, Cornell Univ, 50-54; from asst prof to prof plant path, Cornell Univ, 55-87. *Concurrent Pos:* Nat Found fel, Univ Calif, 54-55; plant pathologist, USDA, 55-86. *Mem:* Fel AAAS; fel Am Phytopath Soc; Am Inst Biol Sci; Am Soc Virol. *Res:* Plant virology, especially virus-vector relationships; luteoviruses. *Mailing Add:* 48 Woodcrest Ave Ithaca NY 14850

ROCK, BARRETT NELSON, PLANT ANATOMY. *Current Pos:* Asst prof, 72-78, ASSOC PROF BIOL, ALFRED UNIV, 78- *Personal Data:* b Warren, Ohio, Sept 8, 42; m 67; c 2. *Educ:* Univ Vt, BA, 66; Univ Md, MS, 70, PhD(bot), 72. *Concurrent Pos:* Field Botanist, Columbia Gas Corp, Ohio, 78-; sabbatical leave, Dept Bot, Univ Calif, Davis, 80. *Mem:* Bot Soc Am; Int Asn Wood Anatomists. *Res:* Anatomical study of vegetative plant tissue, including wood, leaves, and stem tips; megaphytic members of the Asteraceae (compositae); remote sensed vegetation data. *Mailing Add:* Dept Nat Resources Univ NH James Hall Durham NH 03824

ROCK, CHET A, WATER POLLUTION, WATER QUALITY. *Current Pos:* asst chmn, 84, ASSOC PROF ENVIRON ENG, DEPT CIVIL ENG, UNIV MAINE, 85- *Personal Data:* b Vancouver, Wash, Dec 8, 44; m. *Educ:* Wash State Univ, BS, 68; Stanford Univ, MS, 71; Univ Wash, PhD(environ eng), 74. *Prof Exp:* Sanitary eng, Environ Sanitation Prog, USPHS, 68-70; sanitary eng, Lake Restoration Sect, Water Quality Div, Dept Ecol, State Wash, 74-76 & Indust Waste Div, 76-79, asst prof, 79-84. *Mem:* Am Soc Civil Engrs (pres, Maine Sect, 85-86); Water Pollution Control Fedn; Asn Environ Eng Prof; Int Peat Soc; NAm Lake Mgt Soc. *Res:* Onsite wastewater treatment; treatment of industrial wastes; ecological effects of wastewater; restoration of eutrophic lakes; constructed welands. *Mailing Add:* Dept Civil Eng Univ Maine 5711 Boardman Hall Orono ME 04469-5711

ROCK, ELIZABETH JANE, PHYSICAL CHEMISTRY. *Current Pos:* lectr, Wellesley Col, 59-61, from assoc prof to prof, 61-70, chmn dept, 67-70, dir sci ctr, 73-75 & 76-78, Arthur J & Nellie Z Cohen prof chem, 70-92, EMER PROF CHEM, WELLESLEY COL, 92- *Personal Data:* b Plattsburgh, NY, Dec 14, 24. *Educ:* Col Mt St Vincent, BS, 46; Smith Col, MA, 48; Pa State Col, PhD(chem), 51. *Prof Exp:* Asst, Cryogenic Lab, Pa State Col, 48-51, res assoc, Solid State Lab, 51-52; instr chem, Vassar Col, 52-55; from assoc prof to prof textiles, Univ Tenn, 55-59. *Concurrent Pos:* Textile chemist, Exp Sta, Univ Tenn, 55-59; NSF sci fac fel thermochem, Oxford Univ, 66-67; extramural assoc, NIH, 79; vis res prof, Tufts Univ, 81-82. *Mem:* Am Chem Soc. *Res:* Physical chemistry of conservation of stone in monuments; infrared laser induced reactions. *Mailing Add:* 32 Linden St Wellesley MA 02181-5809. *Fax:* 781-283-3642; *E-Mail:* erock@wellesley.edu

ROCK, GAIL ANN, TRANSFUSION MEDICINE, BLEEDING DISORDERS. *Current Pos:* ASST PROF MED, UNIV OTTAWA; CHIEF, DIV HEMAT OTTAWA CIVIC. *Personal Data:* b Winnipeg, Man, Oct 20, 40; m 66; c Jennifer & Christine. *Educ:* St Patricks Col, BSc, 62; Univ Ottawa, PhD(biochem), 66, MD, 72; FRCP(C). *Prof Exp:* Fel biophys, Nat Res Coun Can, 65-67; fel biochem, Univ Ottawa, 68-69; med intern, Ottawa Gen Hosp, 72-73, physician emergency med, 73-74; med dir, Can Red Cross Blood Transfusion Serv, Ottawa, 72-88. *Concurrent Pos:* Adj prof, Dept Biochem, 77-, Dept Lab Med, 78-, clin assoc prof, Dept Med, 86-; prin investr of more than twenty-five grants contracts from var study groups & health & welfare found in Can & Am, 77-88; consult, Dept Med & Lab Med, Univ Ottawa, 78-; mem, Matching Grants Rev Comt & Prog Site Review Comt, Am Red Cross, 83, Subcomt Factor Eight & von Willebrand Factor, Int Soc Thrombosis & Hemostatis, Prog Comt, Haemonetics Res Inst, 81-84, 86 & 87, Ad Hoc Comt, Estab World Asn Apheresis, 85, fractionator, supplier & user working group, Can Red Cross, Planning Prog Comt, First Meeting Int Soc Apheresis, 86, Subcomt Transfusion Med, Am Soc Hemat, 87-; chmn, estab investr award, initial rev group, Am Red Cross, 84-88, Sci Prog Comt, Second Int Meeting, 86-88, Sci Prog Comt Ann Meeting, Am Asn Blood Banks, 85-95; invited consult, blood transfusion prog, Cuba, & Int Red Cross, Brazil, 84; chmn, Can Apheresis Group. *Mem:* World Apheresis Asn (pres, 88-90); Am Asn Blood Banks; Am Soc Apheresis; Can Apheresis Study Group; Inst Asn Study Obesity; Can Hemat Soc (secy-treas). *Res:* Biochemistry of factor VIII and other blood clotting factors and their interaction with platelets; improving yields of fractionated coagulation products; optimization of platelet storage conditions; toxicology of plasticizers in blood products; role of vascular endothelium in hemostasis and thrombosis and apheresis applications. *Mailing Add:* 270 Sandridge Rd Ottawa ON K1L 5A2 Can

ROCK, GEORGE CALVERT, entomology; deceased, see previous edition for last biography

ROCK, MICHAEL KEITH, NEUROSCIENCE. *Current Pos:* DEPT PHYSICAL THERAPY, MAINLAND CITY HOSP, 91- *Personal Data:* b Milwaukee, Wis, Aug 26, 51; m 78. *Educ:* Univ Dallas, BA, 73; Univ Tex Med Br, Galveston, PhD(physiol), 77. *Prof Exp:* Res assoc neurophysiol, Sch Med, Washington Univ, 77-79 & Univ Va, 79-80; assoc mem neurophysiol, Marine Biomed Inst, 80-81; from asst prof to assoc prof, Sch Allied Health Sci, Univ Tex Med Br Galveston, 81-91. *Concurrent Pos:* Adj mem, Marine Biomed Inst, 81-91. *Mem:* Sigma Xi; Soc Neurosci. *Res:* Neurophysiology of simple nervous systems. *Mailing Add:* 304 Desert Willow Ct League City TX 77573

ROCK, PAUL BERNARD, PHYSIOLOGY, MEDICINE. *Current Pos:* INVESTR, ALTITUDE RES DIV, US ARMY RES INST ENVIRON MED, 90- *Personal Data:* b Kansas City, Mo, Dec 15, 45. *Educ:* Univ Colo, BA, 69, MA, 72, PhD(biol), 80; Chicago Col Ostheo Med, MD, 80. *Prof Exp:* Investr, US Army Res Inst Environ Med, 81-87; med resident, Fitzsimons Army Med Ctr, 87-90. *Mem:* Sigma Xi; Am Soc Mammalogists; Am Col Physicians. *Res:* Investigation of environmental medical problems and physiology with an emphasis in medical problems in high terrestrial altitude. *Mailing Add:* 65 Glen Rd Apt N-4 Brookline MA 02146

ROCK, PETER ALFRED, CHEMICAL THERMODYNAMICS, ENVIRONMENTAL CHEMISTRY. *Current Pos:* From asst prof to assoc prof, 64-75, chmn dept, 80-85, PROF CHEM, UNIV CALIF, DAVIS, 75-, DEAN, DIV MATH & PHYS SCI, 95- *Personal Data:* b New Haven, Conn, Sept 29, 39; m 59, M Elaine Rousseleau; c Michael, Deborah & Lisa. *Educ:* Boston Univ, AB, 61; Univ Calif, Berkeley, PhD(chem), 64. *Concurrent Pos:* Nat Inst Neurol Dis & Stroke fel, Ind Univ, 70-71; consult, Dorland Med Dictionaries & World Book Encycl; mem adv group, CAL/EPA Base Closure; prin investr, US Dept Energy Kearney Found. *Mem:* AAAS; Am Chem Soc; Sigma Xi; NY Acad Sci; Nat Fire Protection Asn. *Res:* Environmental chemistry and geochemistry; Inst degradation of alkyl nalides in ground waters removal of hazardous metal ions from waste water streams, biomineralization; author of several chemistry texts. *Mailing Add:* Letters & Sci Deans Off Univ Calif Davis CA 95616. *Fax:* 530-754-9057; *E-Mail:* rock@miles.ucdavis.edu

ROCKAFELLAR, RALPH TYRRELL, MATHEMATICS. *Current Pos:* from asst prof to assoc prof, 66-73, PROF MATH & ADJ PROF COMPUT SCI, UNIV WASH, 73- *Personal Data:* b Milwaukee, Wis, Feb 10, 35; m 64; c 3. *Educ:* Harvard Univ, AB, 57, PhD(math), 63. *Honors & Awards:* Dantzig Prize, 82. *Prof Exp:* Teaching fel math, Harvard Univ, 60-62; mem res staff, Mass Inst Technol, 62-63; asst prof, Univ Tex, 63-65; vis asst prof, Princeton Univ, 65-66. *Concurrent Pos:* Univ Tex res grant, Math Inst, Copenhagen, 64; Air Force Off Sci Res grants, Princeton Univ, 66 & Univ Wash, 66-68. *Mem:* Soc Indust & Appl Math. *Res:* Optimization; variational analysis; convexity. *Mailing Add:* Dept Math Univ Wash-GN-50 Seattle WA 98195

ROCKAWAY, JOHN D, JR, GEOLOGICAL ENGINEERING. *Current Pos:* from asst prof to assoc prof, 68-76, chmn dept, 81-87, PROF GEOL ENG, UNIV MO-ROLLA, 76-, CHMN DEPT, 92- *Personal Data:* b Cincinnati, Ohio, Mar 7, 38; m 62, Linda Newberry; c John, Tom, Kent & Elizabeth. *Educ:* Colo Sch Mines, BS, 61; Purdue Univ, MSE, 63, PhD(civil eng), 68. *Prof Exp:* Instr geol, Purdue Univ, 65-68. *Mem:* Asn Eng Geol; Am Inst Mining, Metall & Petrol Engrs; Int Asn Eng Geologists; Geol Soc Am. *Res:* Geotechnical studies of the physical and engineering properties of earth materials; the impact of land-use and development upon the geological environment. *Mailing Add:* Dept Geol Eng Univ Mo Rolla MO 65401

ROCKCASTLE, VERNE NORTON, ECOLOGY. *Current Pos:* from assoc prof to prof, Cornell Univ, 59-86, EMER PROF SCI & ENVIRON EDUC, 86- *Personal Data:* b Rochester, NY, Jan 1, 20; m 43; c 2. *Educ:* Syracuse Univ, AB, 42; Mass Inst Technol, SM, 44; Cornell Univ, PhD, 55. *Honors & Awards:* Carleton Award, Nat Sci Teachers Asn, 90. *Prof Exp:* Instr meteorol, Mass Inst Technol, 43-44; from asst prof biol to assoc prof biol, State Univ NY, Brockport, 47-56. *Mem:* Am Nature Study Soc (pres, 65); fel AAAS. *Res:* Elementary science education; concept development in science. *Mailing Add:* Dept Educ Cornell Univ 117 Kennedy Ithaca NY 14853

ROCKE, DAVID M, ROBUST STATISTICS, QUALITY CONTROL. *Current Pos:* assoc prof, 80-86, PROF GRAD SCH MGT, UNIV CALIF, DAVIS, 86- *Personal Data:* b Chicago, Ill, June 4, 46; m 71, Carrie Clausen; c Emily & Miriam. *Educ:* Shimer Col, AB, 66; Univ Ill, Chicago, MA, 68, PhD(math), 72. *Honors & Awards:* Youden Prize, 82 & Shewell Award, Chem Div, Am Soc Qual Control, 86; Interlab Testing Award, Am Statist Asn, 85. *Prof Exp:* Vis lectr math, Univ Ill, Chicago, 72-74; univ prof bus admin, Col Bus & Pub Serv, Goveners State Univ, 74-80. *Mem:* Math Asn Am; Am Math Soc; Am Statist Asn; AAAS; Inst Math Statist; Royal Statist Soc; Am Soc Qual Control; Soc Indust & Appl Math. *Res:* Robust statistical methods; quality control and improvement; statistical computing; statistics and public policy. *Mailing Add:* 3200 Cutter Pl Davis CA 95616. *Fax:* 530-752-2924; *E-Mail:* dmrocke@ucdavis.edu

ROCKETT, JOHN A, FLUID MECHANICS. *Current Pos:* CONSULT, 86- *Personal Data:* b Philadelphia, Pa, Aug 6, 22; m 56, Abby Burgess; c Angus & Katharine. *Educ:* Mass Inst Technol, BS, 44; Brown Univ, MS, 51; Harvard Univ, PhD(appl physics), 57. *Honors & Awards:* Silver Medal, Dept Commerce, 77; Harry Bigglestone Award, Soc Fire Protection Engrs, 89. *Prof Exp:* Res engr, Nat Adv Comt Aeronaut, 47-49; res engr, Dept Aeronaut, Mass Inst Technol, 50-53; res engr, United Aircraft Corp res proj, Harvard Univ, 53-57; chief fuel cell technol, United Aircraft Corp, 57-65; dir basic res, Factory Mutual Eng Corp, Mass, 65-68; spec asst to dir, Inst Appl Technol, 68, chief, Off Fire Res & Safety, 68-72, chief fire physics res, 73-80, sr scientist, Ctr Fire Res, Nat Bur Stand, 81-86. *Concurrent Pos:* Vis prof, Tokyo Sci Univ, 82, 84, vis fel, Nat Bldg Technol Ctr, Sydney, 87; vis scientist, VTT, Espoo Helsinki, Finland, 91; adj prof fire protection eng, Univ Md, 94- *Mem:* Soc Fire Protection Engrs; Int Asn Fire Safety Sci. *Res:* Hydrodynamics; combustion and flames; mass-heat transfer; fire behavior; computer modeling of building fires. *Mailing Add:* 4701 Alton Pl NW Washington DC 20016-2041. *Fax:* 202-966-3906; *E-Mail:* 70214.1520@compuserve.com

ROCKETT, THOMAS JOHN, NEW PRODUCTS, CERAMICS. *Current Pos:* assoc prof, 72-78, PROF MAT & CHEM ENG, UNIV RI, 78- *Personal Data:* b Medford, Mass, June 4, 34; m 64, Sarah Hough; c Matthew T, Andrew F & Daniel P. *Educ:* Tufts Univ, BS, 56; Boston Col, MS, 58; Ohio State Univ, PhD(mineral eng), 63. *Prof Exp:* Res mineralogist, Ohio State Univ, 59-61; res ceramist, Wright-Patterson AFB, 61-65; sr res ceramist, Monsanto Res Co, Mass, 65-67, scientist, New Enterprises Div, Monsanto Corp, 67-72. *Concurrent Pos:* NSF fel, 63; lectr, Univ Dayton, 63-65 & Boston Col, 65-71; chmn, Univ RI, 81-87; consult. *Mem:* Mineral Soc Am; Am Ceramic Soc; Am Chem Soc; Am Soc Metals. *Res:* High temperature phase equilibria; composite materials; water/polymer interactions; glass systems and phase separation in glasses; ceramic composites; concept engineering; new product design and development; laser-glass interactions; polymer stability. *Mailing Add:* Dept Chem Eng Univ RI Kingston RI 02881-0805. *Fax:* 401-782-1180; *E-Mail:* rockett@egr.uri.edu

ROCKETTE, HOWARD EARL, JR, BIOSTATISTICS. *Current Pos:* DIR OPERS RES, INST INT NATURAL FAMILY PLANNING, 85- *Personal Data:* b Baltimore, Md, Feb 6, 44; m 68; c 3. *Educ:* Franklin & Marshall Col, BA, 65; Pa State Univ, MA & PhD(statist), 72. *Prof Exp:* prof biostatist, Univ Pittsburgh, 83- *Concurrent Pos:* Dir, Statist Unit, Otititis Media Res Ctr, 81-, co-dir, Statist Ctr, Nat Surg Adjuvant Breast Proj, 82- *Mem:* Am Statist Asn; Biomet Soc; Inst Math Statist; Am Pub Health Asn; Soc Occup & Environ Health. *Res:* Development of methodological techniques and the evaluation and collection of data in the fields of biology, medicine and health, particularly in the areas of clinical trial evluation and occupational health. *Mailing Add:* Sch Pub Health Ill Pub Health Bldg Rm 318-C Univ Pittsburgh Pittsburgh PA 15261

ROCKEY, JOHN HENRY, OPHTHALMOLOGY, IMMUNOCHEMISTRY. *Current Pos:* asst prof microbiol, 62-69, assoc med, 66-70, from asst prof to assoc prof ophthal, 69-73, PROF OPHTHAL, SCH MED, UNIV PA, 73- *Personal Data:* b Madison, Wis, Feb 2, 31. *Educ:* Univ Wis, BS, 52, MD, 55; Univ Pa, PhD(molecular biol), 68. *Honors & Awards:* William J Bleckwenn Award, 55. *Prof Exp:* Intern, Hosp Univ Pa, 55-56; asst resident path, Cornell Med Sch-New York Hosp, 58-59; res assoc & asst physician, Rockefeller Inst Hosp, 59-62. *Concurrent Pos:* Prin investr, USPHS-NIH grants, 62-75; mem grad group molecular biol, Univ Pa, 69-, mem grad group path, 71- & mem grad group immunol, 72-; mem sci staff med res coun molecular pharmacol unit, Med Sch, Cambridge Univ, 70; co-investr, NSF grant, 70-72. *Mem:* Am Asn Immunol. *Res:* Reaginic antibodies; primary structural studies of visual pigments; multiple molecular forms of antibodies. *Mailing Add:* Myrin Circle Scheie Eye Inst 51 N 39th St Philadelphia PA 19104-2689

ROCKHILL, THERON D, MATHEMATICS. *Current Pos:* from asst prof to assoc prof, 62-72, chmn dept, 77-81, PROF MATH, STATE UNIV COL BROCKPORT, 72- *Personal Data:* b Malone, NY, Feb 9, 37; m 58; c 2. *Educ:* Houghton Col, BA, 59; Syracuse Univ, MS, 62; State Univ NY Buffalo, EdD(math & educ), 69. *Prof Exp:* Teacher math, Newfield Cent Sch, 59-61. *Concurrent Pos:* Res assoc, Ctr Res Col Instr Sci & Math, Fla State Univ, 71; pres, Asn Math Teachers NY, 85-86; NSF sci fac fel. *Mem:* Am Math Soc; Math Asn Am; Nat Coun Teachers Math; Soc Indust & Appl Math. *Res:* Numerical analysis and the use of computers in teaching mathematics; author of one book. *Mailing Add:* 15 Sherwood Dr Brockport NY 14420-1437

ROCKHOLD, ROBIN WILLIAM, HYPERTENSION, NEUROPHARMACOLOGY. *Current Pos:* asst prof, 83-88, ASSOC PROF PHARMACOL, DEPT PHARMACOL & TOXICOL, UNIV MISS MED CTR, 88- *Personal Data:* b Dayton, Ohio, Sept 29, 51; m 78; c 1. *Educ:* Kenyon Col, AB; Univ Tenn, PhD(pharmacol), 78. *Prof Exp:* Res fel pharmacol, Pharmacol Inst Univ Heidelberg, WGermany, 78-79; res fel physiol, dept physiol & biophysics, Univ Tenn Ctr Health Sci, 79-82, asst prof, 82-83. *Mem:* Am Heart Asn; Soc Neurosci; Am Soc Pharmacol & Exp Therapeut. *Res:* Regulation of circulatory homeostasis by the central nervous system in normal and pathophysiological conditions such as hypertension; role of neuropeptides and amino acids in specific hypothalamic nuclei. *Mailing Add:* Dept Pharmacol & Toxicol Univ Ms Med Ctr 2500 N State St Jackson MS 39216-4505. *Fax:* 601-984-1637; *E-Mail:* rwrock@fiono.umsmed.edu

ROCKLAND, LOUIS B, AGRICULTURAL CHEMISTRY, FOOD SCIENCE. *Current Pos:* prof & chmn, Dept Food Sci & Nutrit, 80-83, dir, Food Sci Res Ctr, 83-88, EMER DIR, FOOD SCI RES CTR, CHAPMAN COL, 88-; PRES, FOODTECH RES & DEVELOP, 88- *Personal Data:* b NY, July 14, 19; m 43; c 3. *Educ:* Univ Calif, Los Angeles, BA, 40, MA, 47, PhD(phys & biol sci, chem), 48. *Honors & Awards:* Special Award, Inst Food Technologists, 83. *Prof Exp:* Asst chem, Univ Calif, Los Angeles, 40-47, res assoc filter paper chromatog, 49-50; res chemist, Fruit & Veg Chem Lab, Western Utilization Res & Develop Div, Agr Res Serv, USDA, Calif, 49-70, res chemist, Western Regional Res Ctr, 70-80. *Concurrent Pos:* Chmn, Second Int Symp Properties of Water, Osaka, Japan, 78. *Mem:* Fel AAAS; Am Chem Soc; fel Inst Food Technologists; Am Soc Biol Chemists; Am Asn Cereal Chemists. *Res:* Chemical, biological and physical properties of dry legume seeds; chemical properties of amino acids and proteins; methods for filter paper, thin layer and gas chromatography; citrus fruits and walnuts; lemon oil; moisture sorption; water activity-stability relationships in foods and natural products; food product developement. *Mailing Add:* 2306 Boxwood Pl Tustin CA 92680-8352. *Fax:* 714-524-1195

ROCKLIN, ALBERT LOUIS, physical chemistry, industrial chemistry; deceased, see previous edition for last biography

ROCKLIN, ISADORE J, rocklinizing, electronic discharge machining; deceased, see previous edition for last biography

ROCKLIN, ROSS E, LYMPHOKINES, IMMUNO REGULATION. *Current Pos:* SR ASSOC DIR, CLIN RES, BOEHRINGER INGELHEIM CORP, 89- *Educ:* Howard Univ, MD, 66. *Prof Exp:* Chief, Div Allergy, New Eng Med Ctr Hosp, 78-89; prof med allergy, Sch Med, Tufts Univ, 82-89. *Mailing Add:* Astra USA Inc 50 Otis St Westborough MA 01581. *Fax:* 203-798-5442

ROCKLIN, ROY DAVID, ELECTROANALYTICAL CHEMISTRY, ION CHROMATOGRAPHY. *Current Pos:* Res chemist, 80-82, SR CHEMIST, MKT APPLNS, DIONEX CORP, 82- *Personal Data:* b San Francisco, Calif, Aug 3, 53. *Educ:* Univ Calif, Santa Cruz, AB, 75; Univ NC, Chapel Hill, PhD(analytical chem), 80. *Mem:* Am Chem Soc. *Res:* Ion chromatography; electrochemical detectors for liquid and ion chromatography; electroanalytical instrumentation. *Mailing Add:* Dionex Corp PO Box 3603 Sunnyvale CA 94088-3603

ROCKMORE, RONALD MARSHALL, THEORETICAL MEDIUM ENERGY PHYSICS. *Current Pos:* assoc prof, 63-79, PROF PHYSICS, RUTGERS UNIV, 79- *Personal Data:* b New York, NY, Aug 10, 30; m 60; c 2. *Educ:* Brooklyn Col, BS, 51; Columbia Univ, PhD(physics), 57. *Prof Exp:* Asst physics, Columbia Univ, 52-55; NSF fel, 57-58; res assoc, Brookhaven Nat Lab, 58-60; asst prof, Brandeis Univ, 60-63. *Concurrent Pos:* Mem, Inst Advan Study, 57-58; vis lectr, Univ Minn, 58; consult, Repub Aviation Corp, 59-60, Rand Corp, 61-72 & Inst Defense Anal, 62-64; vis physicist, Brookhaven Nat Lab, 64 & 71; visitor, Neils Bohr Inst, Copenhagen, Denmark, 66 & Stanford Linear Accelerator Ctr, 67; vis staff mem, Los Alamos Sci Lab, 67, 72-75 & 88, Argonne Nat Lab, 67 & Ctr Theoret Physics, Trieste, 68; vis mem staff, Theoret Physics Inst, Univ Alta, 72-84; vis theorist, SIN, Villigen, 78; Rutgers Univ fac fel, Imp Col, Univ London, 68-69; Rutgers FASP fel, State Univ NY, Stony Brook, 78 & 88; vis theorist, Saclay, Rutgers FASP fel, 88, Gif-sur-Yvette, 79, 81, 82, 83, 84, 85, 87 & 88. *Mem:* Fel Am Phys Soc. *Res:* Field theory; pion physics; many-body problem; strong and weak interactions; medium-energy physics. *Mailing Add:* Dept Physics Rutgers Univ Piscataway NJ 08855. *E-Mail:* rock@physics.rutgers.edu

ROCKOFF, MAXINE LIEBERMAN, MATHEMATICS. *Current Pos:* CO-FOUNDER, CLARK ROCKOFF & ASSOC, 90- *Personal Data:* b Gary, Ind, July 15, 38; m 56; c 3. *Educ:* George Washington Univ, BS, 58; Univ Pa, MA, 60, PhD(math), 64. *Prof Exp:* Programmer, Univ Pa, 58-60, res fel physiol, 60-61; mathematician, Comput Lab, Nat Bur Stand, 61-64; res assoc, Comput Sci Ctr & Inst Fluid Dynamics, Univ Md, 64-65; res assoc epidemiol & pub health, Yale Univ, 65-68; asst prof, Appl Math, Comput & Biomed Comput Lab, Washington Univ, 68-71; health scientist adminr, Nat Ctr Health Serv Res, 71-75, prog analyst, Off Planning, Eval & Legis, 75-76, health scientist adminr, Nat Ctr Health Serv Res, 76-78, prog analyst, Off Planning & Eval, Dept Energy, 78-79; vpres planning & res, Corp Pub Broadcasting, 79-80; mgr mkt technol, Merrill Lynch, Peirce, Fenner & Smith, 80-90. *Concurrent Pos:* Mem, Panel Impact Comput, Math Curric, Comt Undergrad Prog Math, 71-72; mem bd trustees, Soc Indust & Appl Math, 76-78, chmn bd, 78; mem, Biotechnol Resources Adv Comt, NIH, 78-81. *Mem:* AAAS; Asn Comput Mach; Soc Indust & Appl Math. *Res:* Development of mathematical models for physiological systems; numerical analysis; analysis of health care systems; application of technology and manpower innovations in health care delivery; evaluation of public programs; application of emerging electronic technologies to financial services delivery. *Mailing Add:* Clark Rockoff & Assoc 75 Livingston St Brooklyn NY 11201

ROCKOFF, SEYMOUR DAVID, RADIOLOGY. *Current Pos:* chmn dept, 71-77, PROF RADIOL, GEORGE WASHINGTON UNIV MED CTR, 71-, HEAD SECT CHEST RADIOL, 77- *Personal Data:* b Utica, NY, July 21, 31; c 3. *Educ:* Syracuse Univ, AB, 51; Albany Med Col, MD, 55; Univ Pa, MSc, 61. *Prof Exp:* Staff radiologist, Clin Ctr, NIH, 61-65; from asst prof to assoc prof radiol, Sch Med, Yale Univ, 65-68; assoc prof, Mallinckrodt Inst Radiol, Sch Med, Wash Univ, 68-71. *Concurrent Pos:* Asst attend radiologist, Yale-New Haven Med Ctr, Conn, 65-68; ed-in-chief, Investigative Radiol, 66-76, emer ed-in-chief, 76-; asst radiologist, Barnes & Allied Hosps, St Louis, Mo; consult radiologist, Homer G Phillips Hosp, St Louis & Vet Admin Hosp, 69-71, NIH, Nat Naval Med Ctr, Bethesda, Md & Washington Vet Admin Hosp, DC, 73-, immunodiagnosis, Nat Cancer Inst, NIH, Bethesda, Md, 77 & asbestosis res, 83-; exec dir, Soc Thoracic Radiol, 83- *Mem:* Fel Am Col Radiol; Am Fedn Clin Res; Asn Univ Radiol; AMA; Radiol Soc NAm; Soc Thoracic Radiol (pres, 83-84). *Res:* Contrast media toxicity; image analysis of radiographs; asbestosis imaging. *Mailing Add:* Dept Radiol George Washington Univ Med Ctr 901 23rd St NW Washington DC 20037-2377

ROCKOWER, EDWARD BRANDT, physics, operations research, for more information see previous edition

ROCKS, LAWRENCE, CHEMISTRY. *Current Pos:* Asst prof, 58-72, ASSOC PROF CHEM, C W POST COL, LONG ISLAND UNIV, 58- *Personal Data:* b New York, NY, Aug 27, 33. *Educ:* Queens Col, NY, BS, 55; Purdue Univ, MS, 57; Vienna Tech Univ, Dr Tech, 64. *Mem:* Am Chem Soc. *Mailing Add:* 29 Seville Lane Stony Brook NY 11790-3329

ROCKSTAD, HOWARD KENT, SOLID STATE PHYSICS. *Current Pos:* sr res scientist, 81-86, SR SYSTS ENGR, JET PROPULSION LAB, ATLANTIC RICHFIELD CO, 87- *Personal Data:* b Ada, Minn, Aug 5, 35. *Educ:* St Olaf Col, BA, 57; Univ Ill, Urbana, MS, 59, PhD(physics), 63. *Prof Exp:* Res physicist, Corning Glass Works, NY, 63-70; res physicist, Energy Conversion Devices, Inc, 71-73; sr proj engr, Micro-Bit Div, Control Data Corp, 74-80. *Concurrent Pos:* Lectr, Elmira Col, 67. *Mem:* Am Phys Soc; Inst Elec & Electronics Engrs. *Res:* Physics of electron-beam-accessed metal-oxide-semiconductor memories; metal-oxide-semiconductor charge storage; semiconductor device physics; high-electric-field transport; physics of amorphous semiconductors; optical and electronic properties of semiconductors and insulators; color centers; thermoelectricity; microprobe analysis; silicon micromachining. *Mailing Add:* 1227 Tierra Dr Thousand Oaks CA 91362

ROCKSTEIN, MORRIS, PHYSIOLOGY, GERONTOLOGY. *Current Pos:* EMER PROF PHYSIOL & BIOL, SCH MED, UNIV MIAMI, 81- *Personal Data:* b Toronto, Ont, Jan 8, 16; nat US; wid; c 2. *Educ:* Brooklyn Col, BA, 38; Columbia Univ, MA, 41; Univ Minn, PhD(insect physiol & biochem), 48; Oak Ridge Inst Nuclear Studies, cert, 49. *Prof Exp:* Asst entom, Univ Minn, 41-42; fel nat sci, Nat Res Coun, 46-48; from asst prof to assoc prof zoophysiol, Wash State Univ, 48-53; from asst prof to assoc prof physiol, Sch Med, NY Univ, 53-61; prof physiol & biophys, Univ Miami, 61-81, chmn dept, Sch Med, 67-71, prof nursing, 81-82; pres, Cortisol Med Res, Inc, 83-85. *Concurrent Pos:* Nat Res Coun fel in natural sci, 46-48; instr, Marine Biol Lab, Woods Hole, 54-60, trustee, 62-65, trustee emer, 65-; mem sci coun, Geront Res Found, 60-63; adv, Nat Inst Aging, 61; consult, Am Pub Health Asn, 61-74; adv study sect trop med, NIH, 62-66; abstractor, Excerpta Medica & Chem Abstr; ed, Biol Sci Bannerstone Lectr Ser Geriat & Geront, 64-72; adj prof radiol, Univ Miami Sch Med, 71-73; ed biol sci, Acad Press, 72-; vpres, Int Asn Prolong Human Lifespan; mem sci adv coun, Am Comt, Weizmann Inst, 74-88. *Mem:* Fel AAAS; fel Entom Soc Am; Sigma Xi; Am Gen Physiol; fel Geront Soc (pres, 65-66); Am Physiol Soc; Sigma Xi; Am Soc Zoologists. *Res:* Insect physiology and enzymology; biochemistry of flight; physiology of aging; radiobiology; marine biology; biochemical changes in muscle and nerve tissue (as the two systems which truly age) with age. *Mailing Add:* 600 Biltmore Way Apt 805 Coral Gables FL 33134-7531

ROCKSTROH, TODD JAY, HIGH POWER SOLID STATE LASERS. *Current Pos:* mfg engr, 86-88, proj engr, 88-90, STAFF ENGR, GEN ELEC AIRCRAFT ENGINES, 91- *Personal Data:* b Terre Haute, Ind, Sept 1, 56; m 80; c 2. *Educ:* Purdue Univ, BS, 78, MS, 80; Univ Ill, PhD(mech eng), 86. *Prof Exp:* Mem tech staff, Bell Labs, 80-83. *Mem:* Laser Inst Am; Optical Soc

Am. *Res:* High power (industrial) solid state lasers, primarily slab-base crystal resonator optimization; non-conventional optical design and high power fiber optic transmission. *Mailing Add:* Q20 1 Neumann Way Cincinnati OH 45215-1988

ROCKWELL, DAVID ALAN, OPTICAL PHYSICS. *Current Pos:* head, Laser Physics Sect, Laser Div, Hughes Aircraft Co, 75-81, sr staff physicist, Hughes Res Labs, 81-85, head, Advan Laser Sources Dept, 85-95, spec assignment, Mfg Technol Ctr, Delco Electronics, 95-97, SR SCIENTIST, HUGHES SPACE & COMMUN CO, 97- *Personal Data:* b Chicago, Ill, Nov 11, 45; m 86; c 1. *Educ:* Univ Ill, Urbana, BS, 67; Mass Inst Technol, PhD(physics), 73. *Prof Exp:* Res assoc laser mat, Physics Dept, Univ Southern Calif, 73-75. *Mem:* Am Phys Soc; Inst Elec & Electronics Engrs Laser & Elec & Optics Soc; Optical Soc Am. *Res:* Research and development of solid state laser devices; nonlinear and electrooptic devices; high energy laser sources; phase-conjugate lasers. *Mailing Add:* Hughes Space & Commun Co Bldg 54 MS 5320 PO Box 92919 Los Angeles CA 90009

ROCKWELL, DONALD O, FLUID MECHANICS. *Current Pos:* PAUL B REINHOLD PROF MECH ENG, LEHIGH UNIV, 76- *Personal Data:* b Canton, Pa, Oct 2, 42; m 72. *Educ:* Bucknell Univ, BS, 64; Lehigh Univ, MS, 65, PhD(mech eng), 68. *Prof Exp:* NSF trainee mech eng, Lehigh Univ, 64-67; group leader fluid syst, Harry Diamond Labs, 68-70; asst prof mech eng, Lehigh Univ, 70-72, assoc prof, 72-74; guest prof & Von Humboldt fel, Univ Karlsruhe, Ger, 74-75. *Concurrent Pos:* Dir, Volkswagen Found Prog, Univ Karlsruhe & Lehigh Univ, 77-94; several res grants, Lehigh Univ, 80-94; overseas fel, Churchill Col, Cambridge Univ, 81; consult fluid induced vibration & noise generation, var firms in US, Ger, France, Austria & Switz. *Mem:* Fel Am Phys Soc; Am Inst Aeronaut & Astronaut; Am Soc Mech Engrs; Ger Soc Air & Space Travel. *Res:* Unsteady fluid mechanics. *Mailing Add:* Dept Mech Eng Lehigh Univ Packard Lab Bldg 19 Bethlehem PA 18015. *Fax:* 215-758-4041

ROCKWELL, JULIUS, JR, RIPARIAN DESIGN & CONSTRUCTION & RESTORATION, ENVIRONMENTAL MANAGEMENT. *Current Pos:* ADJ PROF BIOL, ALASKA PAC UNIV, 79- *Personal Data:* b Taunton, Mass, July 25, 18; m 64; c 5. *Educ:* Univ Mich, BS, 40; Univ Wash, PhD(fisheries), 56. *Honors & Awards:* Superior Performance Award, Bur Com Fisheries, 62. *Prof Exp:* Sci asst, Int Pac Halibut Fisheries Comn, 46; from jr res asst to res assoc, Fisheries Res Inst, Univ Wash, 46-54; fisheries res biologist & proj leader, Biol Lab Seattle, Bur Com Fisheries, US Fish & Wildlife Serv, 54-59, chief, Fish Counting Prog, 59-62, chief, Oceanog Instrumentation Unit, Wash, DC, 62-67, spec asst, Br Marine Fisheries, 67-70; staff fishery biologist, Alaska Pipeline Off & Off Special Proj, Bur Land Mgt, US Dept Interior, Anchorage, 70-82. *Concurrent Pos:* Consult riparian restoration speleology. *Mem:* AAAS; Am Fisheries Soc; Am Inst Fishery Res Biologists; Marine Technol Soc; fel Nat Speleology Soc; Soc Ecol Restoration & Mgt. *Res:* Developing methods for riparian habitat protection, evaluation and restoration; data handling and processing systems; operations research; statistical analysis; cave exploration, conservation and management. *Mailing Add:* 2944 Emory St Anchorage AK 99508-4466

ROCKWELL, KENNETH H, ZOOLOGY. *Current Pos:* From instr to assoc prof, 60-72, chmn dept, 69-74, & 79-86, PROF BIOL, JUNIATA COL, 72- *Personal Data:* b Huntington, Pa, Jan 27, 36; m 58; c 3. *Educ:* Juniata Col, BS, 57; Brown Univ, MS, 60; Pa State Univ, PhD(zool), 67. *Concurrent Pos:* Vis scholar, Stanford Univ, 74-75 & Univ Calif, Davis, 87. *Mem:* AAAS; Am Inst Biol Sci. *Res:* Histology of endocrine organs; physiology of altitude exposure. *Mailing Add:* Dept Biol Juniata Col 1700 Moore St Huntingdon PA 16652-2119

ROCKWELL, ROBERT FRANKLIN, POPULATION GENETICS, POPULATION ECOLOGY. *Current Pos:* from asst prof to assoc prof, 76-85, PROF BIOL, CITY COL NEW YORK, 86- *Personal Data:* b Dayton, Ohio, Dec 19, 46. *Educ:* Wright State Univ, BS, 69, MS, 71; Queen's Univ, Ont, PhD(biol), 75. *Prof Exp:* Fel, City Univ New York, 75-76. *Concurrent Pos:* Res assoc, Am Mus Natural Hist, NY, 86- *Mem:* Genetic Soc Am; Soc Study Evolution; Biomet Soc; Behav Genetics Soc; Am Soc Genetics; Sigma Xi. *Res:* Genetic structure of natural populations; biostatistical methods; population biology of migratory waterfowl; fitness estimation in natural populations. *Mailing Add:* Dept Biol City Col Convent Ave at 138th St New York NY 10031

ROCKWELL, ROBERT LAWRENCE, VISCOUS & VISCOELASTIC EFFECTS. *Current Pos:* CHIEF SCIENTIST, EER SYSTS, RIDGECREST, CALIF, 90- *Personal Data:* b Portsmouth, NH, Nov 18, 35; m 60, Sheila K; c Kurt, Bruce & Jennifer. *Educ:* Univ Calif, Berkeley, AB, 59; Stanford Univ, MS, 64, PhD(aeronaut & astronaut), 70. *Prof Exp:* Physicist, Naval Weapons Ctr, China Lake, 58-70, aeronaut engr, 70-90; elec eng, Calif State Univ, Northridge, 80-90. *Concurrent Pos:* Lectr mech eng, Univ Southern Calif, 72-74. *Res:* Nonlinear modeling of arterial blood flow, with emphasis on viscous and viscoelastic effects. *Mailing Add:* 1000 E Skylark Ave Ridgecrest CA 93555-8145

ROCKWELL, SARA CAMPBELL, RADIATION BIOLOGY, EXPERIMENTAL CANCER THERAPY. *Current Pos:* from asst prof to assoc prof, 74-84, PROF THERAPEUT RADIOL, SCH MED, YALE UNIV, 84-, PROF, YALE COMPREHENSIVE CANCER CTR, 89-, DIR, OFF SCI AFFAIRS, SCH MED, 96- *Personal Data:* b Somerset, Pa, Sept 8, 43; c Rebecca (Musier) & Karen R. *Educ:* Pa State Univ, BS, 65; Stanford Univ, PhD(biophys), 71. *Hon Degrees:* MA, Yale Univ, 90. *Prof Exp:* Res fel radiol, Sch Med, Stanford Univ, 71, 72, 74; res fel, Institut de Recherche Radiobiologie Clinique, Institut Gustave Roussy, 73. *Concurrent Pos:* Prin investr, NIH grants & Am Cancer Soc grants, 79-; mem, Exp Therapeut Study Sect, Div Res Grants, NIH, 82-86, Yale Comprehensive Cancer Ctr, 83-, vis comt, Dept Med, Brookhaven Nat Lab, 87-91, Sci Adv Comt Prev Diag, & Ther, 90-91; counr, Radiation Res Soc, 85-88. *Mem:* Radiation Res Soc; Cell Kinetics Soc (pres, 82-83, vpres, 81-82); Am Soc Therapeut Radiol & Oncol; Am Asn Cancer Res; Bioelectromagnetics Soc; Women Cancer Res. *Res:* Biology of solid cancers and the development and testing of new agents and regimens which may improve the treatment of these malignancies. *Mailing Add:* Dept Therapeut Radiol Yale Sch Med Room No 225 HRT PO Box 208040 New Haven CT 06520-8040. *Fax:* 203-737-1771; *E-Mail:* sara.rockwell@yale.edu

ROCKWELL, THEODORE, ENERGY SYSTEMS, ENVIRONMENTAL SCIENCES. *Current Pos:* prin officer & dir, 64-87, DIR, MPR ASSOCS, INC, WASH, DC, 87- *Personal Data:* b Chicago, Ill, June 26, 22; m 47, Mary Compton; c Robert, Teed, Larry & Juanita. *Educ:* Princeton Univ, BSE, 43, MS, 45. *Hon Degrees:* ScD, Tri-State Univ, 60. *Honors & Awards:* AEC Distinguished Serv Medal & Navy Distinguished Civilian Serv Medal, 60; Lifetime Contribution Award, Am Nuclear Soc. *Prof Exp:* Engr, Electromagnetic Separation Plant, Manhattan Proj, Oak Ridge, Tenn, 44-45; head shield eng group, Oak Ridge Nat Lab, 45-49; nuclear engr naval reactors, AEC & nuclear propulsion, Bur Ships, 49-53, dir nuclear technol div, 53-54, tech dir, 54-64. *Concurrent Pos:* Chmn nat shield eng group, AEC, 48-49; mem reactor safety panel, & chmn, Reactor Safety Task Force, Atomic Indust forum, 66-68; mem adv group, NIH, 66; mem adv comt, Dept Chem Eng, Princeton Univ, 67-72; res assoc, Wash Ctr Foreign Policy Res, Johns Hopkins Univ, 65-67, consult, Joint Cong Comt Atomic Energy, 67. *Mem:* AAAS; Sigma Xi; Am Soc Psych Res; Parapsychol Asn; Soc Sci Explor. *Res:* Criteria, procedures and facilities for safe operation of naval and central station nuclear power plants; societal and environmental impact of energy production and use. *Mailing Add:* 3403 Woolsey Dr Chevy Chase MD 20815-3924. *Fax:* 301-652-0534; *E-Mail:* tedrock@cpcug.org

ROCKWELL, THOMAS H, industrial engineering, for more information see previous edition

ROCKWOOD, STEPHEN DELL, LASERS. *Current Pos:* EXEC VPRES, SCI APPLN INT CORP, 87- *Personal Data:* b Ft Scott, Kans, Apr 8, 43; m 64; c 2. *Educ:* Grinnell Col, BA, 65; Calif Inst Technol, MS, 67, PhD(physics), 69. *Prof Exp:* Res officer laser develop, Air Force Weapons Lab, 70-72; staff mem laser develop, Los Alamos Nat Lab, 72-75, group leader tunable lasers, 75-80, dep assoc dir, 80-86, assoc dir inertial fusion, 86-87. *Concurrent Pos:* Adj prof, Inst Modern Optics, Univ NMex; vpres, Advan Technol Assocs; dir, Los Alamos Laser Fusion Prog; consult problems in laser develop & indust applns. *Mem:* Am Phys Soc. *Res:* Development of tunable ir lasers for isotope separation; sulfur, boron, carbon and silicon isotopes. *Mailing Add:* 10260 Campus Point Dr MS-C5 San Diego CA 92121

ROCKWOOD, WILLIAM PHILIP, PSYCHO-PHARMACOLOGY OF DRUGS & ALCOHOL, PHYSIOLOGY. *Current Pos:* From instr to assoc prof, 61-76, chmn, Biol Dept, 87-93, PROF BIOL, RUSSELL SAGE COL, 76- *Personal Data:* b Albany, NY, Dec 7, 30; m 53; c 5. *Educ:* Boston Col, BS, 57; Syracuse Univ, MS, 59; NY Univ, PhD(endocrine physiol), 68. *Concurrent Pos:* Expert witness, alcoholism court trials; dir, Chem Dependency Prog & Addiction Training Inst, Sage Col. *Mem:* AAAS; Sigma Xi; NY Acad Sci. *Res:* Pateral effects of alcohol on newborn children. *Mailing Add:* 15 Milner Ave Albany NY 12203

ROCO, MIHAIL CONSTANTIN, MULTIPHASE PROCESSES & PARTICLE TECHNOLOGY, SCIENCE EDUCATION & MANAGEMENT. *Current Pos:* PROF MECH ENG, UNIV KY, 81-; PROG DIR, NSF, 90- *Personal Data:* b Bucharest, Romania, Nov 2, 47; US citizen; m 86, Ecaterina; c Constance-Amanda M & Charles M. *Educ:* Polytech Inst, Bucharest, Dipl, 70, PhD(fluid dynamics), 76. *Honors & Awards:* Carl Duisberg Award, Carl Duisberg Soc, Ger, 79. *Concurrent Pos:* Vis prof, Univ Paderborn, Ger, 79, Univ Sask, Can, 80, Tohoku Univ, Japan, 89, Cal Inst Technol, Pasadena, 89; prin investr, NSF, 81-89, Dept Energy, IBM, Dresser & Worthington Pump, 81-93; consult, Conoco, IBM, Warman Australia, Codelco Chile, Dresser, NASA, NSF, Organization Am States, Dept Energy, ITT, Can, 81-93; lectr postgrad eng, Japan, Chile, Fla, Ga & Australia, 82-93; assoc tech ed, J Fluids Eng, NY, 85-89; prof multiphase flow, Johns Hopkins Univ, 93- *Mem:* Fel Am Soc Mech Engrs; Am Inst Chem Engrs; Soc Rheology; NY Acad Sci. *Res:* Multiphase flow; hydrotransport of solids through pipes; electro-imaging; slurry pumps; erosion wear; author of two books and 100 research articles. *Mailing Add:* Eng Dept Rm 525 NSF 1401 Wilson Blvd Arlington VA 22230

ROD, DAVID LAWRENCE, MATHEMATICS. *Current Pos:* From asst prof to assoc prof, 66-82, PROF MATH, UNIV CALGARY, 82- *Personal Data:* b Gardner, Mass, Apr 23, 38; m 66. *Educ:* Mass Inst Technol, BS, 60; Univ Wis-Madison, MS, 62, PhD(math), 71. *Mem:* Am Math Soc. *Res:* Hamiltonian systems of differential equations and dynamical systems theory. *Mailing Add:* Univ Calgary Calgary AB T2N 1N4 Can

RODABAUGH, DAVID JOSEPH, ALGEBRA, COMPUTER SCIENCE. *Current Pos:* CONSULT, 93- *Personal Data:* b Kansas City, Mo, Jan 14, 38; m 59; c 3. *Educ:* Univ Chicago, SB, 59, SM, 60; Ill Inst Technol, PhD(math), 63. *Prof Exp:* Instr math, Ill Inst Technol, 62-63; asst prof, Vanderbilt Univ, 63-65; from asst prof to assoc prof, Univ Mo, Columbia, 65-78, prof math,

78-81; mathematician, Lockheed Corp, Calif, 81-93. *Concurrent Pos:* Consult, NASA, 65-66; NSF grant, Univ Mo, Columbia, 67-68; prof, Calif State Univ, Northridge; staff scientist & engr, Lockheed Corp, 81- *Mem:* Asn Comput Mach; Inst Elec & Electronics Engrs; Soc Indust & Appl Math; Sigma Xi. *Mailing Add:* 2760 Bitternut Circle Simi Valley CA 93065

RODAHL, KAARE, WORK PHYSIOLOGY. *Current Pos:* RETIRED. *Personal Data:* Rodal, Norway, Aug 17, 17; nat US; m 46, Joan Hunter; c Anton & Kari. *Educ:* Univ Oslo, Norway, MD, 48, DSc, 50, MD, 57. *Honors & Awards:* Knight, Royal Norweg Order of St Olav, 88. *Prof Exp:* Spec consult, US Dept Air Force, 49, chief, Dept Physiol, Arctic Aeromed Lab, Ladd AFB, Alaska, 50-52, dir res, 54-57; asst prof physiol, Univ Oslo, 52-54; dir res, Lankenau Hosp, 57-65; dir, Inst Work Physiol, 65-87; prof physiol, Norweg Col Phys Educ, 66-87. *Concurrent Pos:* Hon mem staff & fac, Command & Gen Staff Col, US Army, 60. *Mem:* Am Physiol Soc. *Res:* Environmental physiology and medicine; work physiology; metabolism nutrition; vitamins; author of numerous scientific publications. *Mailing Add:* Maaltrostveien 40 Oslo 0390 Norway

RODAN, GIDEON ALFRED, CELL BIOLOGY. *Current Pos:* exec dir bone biol & osteoporosis, 85-96, RES VPRES, MERCK SHARP DOHME RES LABS, 96- *Personal Data:* b Rumania, June 14, 34; m 72, Sevgi Boke; c Aylin & Elan. *Educ:* Hebrew Univ, Hadassah, MD, 64; Weizmann Inst Sci, PhD(chem), 70. *Honors & Awards:* Neuman Award, 93; Pioneer Award, Nat Osteoporosis Foun, 96. *Prof Exp:* From asst prof to prof oral biol, Univ Conn, 70-85, head, 78-85. *Concurrent Pos:* Adj prof path, Univ Pa. *Mem:* Am Soc Bone & Mineral Res (pres, 88); Am Soc Cell Biol; Endocrine Soc; Bone & Mineral Soc. *Res:* Cell biology of hard tissues; hormonal control of growth and differentiation in bone-derived cells; osteoporosis. *Mailing Add:* Merck Sharp & Dohme West Point PA 19486. *Fax:* 215-652-4328; *E-Mail:* rodan@merck.com

RODARTE, JOSEPH ROBERT, PULMONARY PHYSIOLOGY, PATHOPHYSIOLOGY. *Current Pos:* CHIEF, PULMONARY & CRITICAL CARE MED, BAYLOR COL MED. *Personal Data:* b Temple, Tex, Apr 1, 38; c Bettina Rodarte. *Educ:* Harvard Univ, MD, 64. *Prof Exp:* Prof med, Mayo Med Sch, 81-88. *Mem:* Am Col Chest Physicians; Am Thoracic Soc; Am Physiol Soc; Am Fedn Clin Res; Biomed Eng Soc; Am Inst Med & Biol Eng. *Mailing Add:* Baylor Col Med Smith Tower Suite 1225 6550 Fannin Houston TX 77030-2720. *Fax:* 713-790-3648

RODBARD, DAVID, MEDICINE, BIOPHYSICS. *Current Pos:* clin assoc med res, NIH, 66-69, sr investr, 69-78, sect head med res, Biophys Endocrinol Sect, Endocrinol & Reproduction Res Br, Nat Inst Child Health & Human Develop, 79-90, DIR, DIV COMPUT TECH, NAT INST CHILD HEALTH & HUMAN DEVELOP, 90- *Personal Data:* b Chicago, Ill, July 6, 41; m 77. *Educ:* Univ Buffalo, BA, 60; Western Reserve Univ, MD, 64. *Honors & Awards:* Young Investr Award, Clin Radioassay Soc, 79; Ayerst Award, Endocrine Soc, 81. *Prof Exp:* Intern med, King Co Hosp, Seattle, 64-65; resident, Hahnemann Hosp, Philadelphia, 65-66. *Concurrent Pos:* Consult, Int Atomic Energy Agency, 70- & WHO, 74-; assoc ed, Am J Physiol, 76- *Mem:* Endocrine Soc; Am Physiol Soc; Am Soc Biol Chemists; Biomet Soc; Am Soc Clin Invest. *Res:* Endocrinology; physiology; biomathematics; biochemistry; radio immunoassay; physical-chemistry of proteins; neurotransmitters. *Mailing Add:* 10113 Bentcross Dr Rockville MD 20854

RODBELL, DONALD S, physics; deceased, see previous edition for last biography

RODBELL, MARTIN, BIOCHEMISTRY. *Current Pos:* RETIRED. *Personal Data:* b Baltimore, Md, Dec 1, 25; m 40, Barbara C Ledermann; c 4. *Educ:* Johns Hopkins Univ, BA, 49; Univ Wash, PhD(biochem), 54. *Hon Degrees:* Dr, Montpellier Univ, France, 92, Univ Geneva, Switz & Va Commonwealth Univ, 96. *Honors & Awards:* Nobel Prize in Physiol/Med, 94; Jacobaeus Award, Acta Scand Soc, Norway, 73; Gairdner Int Award, 84; Sci Merit Award, Nat Inst Arthritis, Diabetes, Digestive & Kidney Dis, 85; Lounsbery Award, Nat Acad Sci, 87; Shueler Distinguished Lectr, Tulane Univ, 91; Louis Harris Distinguished Lectr, Va Med Col, 93; Nelson Leonard Distinguished Lectr, Univ Ill, 96; Steelman Distinguished Lectr, Univ NC, 96. *Prof Exp:* Res assoc biochem, Univ Ill, 54-56; biochemist, Nat Heart Inst, 56-62 & Nat Inst Arthritis & Metab Dis, 61-70, chief, Lab Nutrit & Endocrinol, 62-85; sci dir, Nat Inst Environ Health Sci, 85-89, chief, Sect Signal Transduction, 89- *Concurrent Pos:* NIH fel, Univ Brussels & Leiden Univ, 60-61; prof & dir, Inst Biochem Clin, Univ Geneva, Switz, 67-68, vis prof, 81-83; adj prof physiol, Univ Med Ctr, Georgetown Univ, 70-83, Dept Biochem, Univ NC, Chapel Hill, 87-, Dept Cell Biol, Duke, 89-, Dept Pharmacol, Va Col Med, 93- *Mem:* Nat Acad Sci; AAAS; Am Soc Biol Chemists; Am Acad Arts & Sci; Japanese Biochem Soc; Europ Asn Study Diabetes; Hungarian Acad Sci; Am Acad Achievement; Belg Royal Soc Med; Sigma Xi. *Res:* Lipoprotein structure and metabolism; fat transport and mechanism of blood triglyceride uptake; hormonal effects on metabolism and glucose transport in isolated adipocytes; structure/function relationships in peptide hormones; mode of action of hormones at the cellular and membrane level; mode of actions of hormones and GTP-regulatory proteins; isolation and characterization of GTP-binding proteins involved in signal transduction; structure of glucose transporters; receptor characterization and isolation; role of cytoskeletal network in signal transduction; role of endosomes in cellular signalling. *Mailing Add:* 306 Elliott Rd Chapel Hill NC 27514. *Fax:* 919-541-7879; *E-Mail:* rodbell@niehs.nih.gov

RODDA, BRUCE EDWARD, CLINICAL TRIALS. *Current Pos:* VPRES RES ADMIN, SCHERING-PLOUGH RES INST, 94- *Personal Data:* b Schenectady, NY, June 21, 42; m 62, 89; c 1. *Educ:* Alfred Univ, BA, 65; Tulane Univ, MS, 67, PhD(biostatist), 69; Fairleigh Dickinson Univ, MBA, 82. *Prof Exp:* Res scientist med statist, Eli Lilly & Co, 69-76; sr dir, Bards Int, Merck & Co, Rahway, NJ, 76-87; vpres, Bristol Myers Squibb Pharm Res Inst, Princeton, NJ, 87-94. *Concurrent Pos:* Asst prof pharmacol, Ind Univ, Med Ctr, 72-76; guest investr, Rockefeller Univ, 77-78; asst prof community med, Univ Ill, 79-90. *Mem:* Am Statist Asn; Drug Info Asn; Int Biomet Soc; Soc Clin Trials; Royal Statist Soc; Sigma Xi. *Res:* Pharmacokinetic modeling; application of novel statistical approaches in clinical research; clinical trial methodology. *Mailing Add:* 46 Charles Rd Bernardsville NJ 07924

RODDA, ERROL DAVID, AGRICULTURAL & STRUCTURAL ENGINEERING. *Current Pos:* assoc prof, 68-75, PROF AGR ENG & FOOD ENG, UNIV ILL, URBANA-CHAMPAIGN, 75- *Personal Data:* b Platteville, Wis, June 3, 28; m 55; c 2. *Educ:* Univ Ill, Urbana, BS, 51, MSCE, 60, MS, 64; Purdue Univ, PhD(agr eng), 65. *Prof Exp:* Engr, Caterpillar Tractor Co, Ill, 51-58; res assoc agr eng, Univ Ill, Urbana-Champaign, 58-62; asst prof, Univ Calif, Davis, 64-68. *Concurrent Pos:* USAID-Univ Ill adv agr eng, Uttar Pradesh Agr Univ, India, 68-70. *Mem:* Am Soc Agr Engrs; Am Soc Eng Educ; AAAS. *Res:* Grain processing and storage; agricultural structures; engineering systems design; food engineering; fuel alcohol. *Mailing Add:* 3317 Stonybrook Dr Champaign IL 61821-5231

RODDA, PETER ULISSE, GEOLOGY. *Current Pos:* CUR, DEPTS INVERT ZOOL & GEOL, CALIF ACAD SCI, 71- *Personal Data:* b Albuquerque, NMex, Nov 18, 29; div. *Educ:* Univ Calif, Los Angeles, AB, 52, PhD(geol), 60. *Prof Exp:* Asst geol, Univ Calif, Los Angeles, 54-57, instr, 57; lectr geol, Univ Tex, Austin, 63-66, assoc prof, 67-71, res scientist, Bur Econ Geol, 58-71. *Mem:* Geol Soc Am; Paleont Soc; Am Asn Petrol Geol; AAAS; Soc Econ Paleont Mineral. *Res:* Stratigraphy and invertebrate paleontology of the Cretaceous and Cenozoic; evolutionary history of the gastropoda; Mesozoic and Cenozoic geology of California. *Mailing Add:* Dept Geol Calif Acad Sci Golden Gate Park CA 94118

RODDEN, JOHN JAMES, AERONAUTICAL & ASTRONAUTICAL ENGINEERING. *Current Pos:* PRIN ENGR SPACE SYSTS, LORAL, 94- *Personal Data:* m 57, Irene Churongy; c John Jay, Timothy Charles & James F. *Educ:* Univ Calif, BS, 55, MS, 56; Stanford Univ, PhD(eng mech), 64. *Prof Exp:* Assoc engr, Lockheed Missiles & Space Co, 56-94, consult engr, 94. *Concurrent Pos:* Instr, San Jose State Univ, 90-91. *Mem:* Fel Am Inst Aeronaut & Astronaut; Sigma Xi. *Mailing Add:* 2071 Robinhood Los Altos CA 94024

RODDICK, JAMES ARCHIBALD, GEOLOGY, COAST PLUTONIC COMPLEX & CIRCUM-PACIFIC PLUTONIC TERRANCE. *Current Pos:* Geologist, 90-96, EMER GEOLOGIST, DEPT NAT RESOURCES, GEOL SURV, CAN, 96- *Personal Data:* b New Westminster, BC, Feb 23, 25; m 63, Asaka Furuya; c Naomi & Kimio. *Educ:* Univ BC, BASc, 48; Calif Inst Technol, MS, 50; Univ Wash, PhD, 55. *Mem:* Fel Geol Soc Am; fel Geol Asn Can; Can Inst Mining & Metall. *Res:* Cordilleran geology; granitic rocks; circum-pacific plutonic terrances. *Mailing Add:* Dept Natural Resources Can Geol Surv Can 605 Robson St Vancouver BC V6B 5J3 Can. *Fax:* 604-666-1124; *E-Mail:* jroddick@gsc.nrcan.gc.ca

RODDICK, JOHN WILLIAM, JR, obstetrics & gynecology, for more information see previous edition

RODDIS, WINIFRED MARY KIM, COMPUTER-AIDED DESIGN, STRUCTURAL DESIGN. *Current Pos:* asst prof, 88-95, ASSOC PROF CIVIL ENG, DEPT CIVIL ENG, UNIV KANS, 95- *Educ:* Mass Inst Technol, BS, 77, MS, 87, PhD(civil eng), 89. *Prof Exp:* Struct engr, Stone & Webster Eng Corp, 77-81, Souza & Truf Eng, 81-84 & A G Lichtenstein Engrs, 86. *Mem:* Am Soc Civil Engrs; Am Soc Eng Educ; Am Asn Artificial Intel; Soc Women Engrs; Sigma Xi; Am Concrete Inst. *Res:* Expert systems; knowledge based systems; artificial intelligence; structural design; infrastructure maintenance; nondestructive evaluation; bridge fatigue; engineering ethics. *Mailing Add:* Dept Civil & Environ Eng Univ Kans 2008 Learned Lawrence KS 66045-2225

RODDY, DAVID JOHN, GEOLOGY, GEOPHYSICS. *Current Pos:* GEOLOGIST, US GEOL SURV, 66- *Personal Data:* b Springfield, Ohio, May 27, 32; c 3. *Educ:* Miami Univ, AB, 55, MS, 57; Calif Inst Technol, PhD(physics, geol), 66. *Prof Exp:* Instr geol, Miami Univ, 54-57; geologist, Jet Propulsion Lab, Calif Inst Technol, 60-64. *Concurrent Pos:* Geologist, Calif Oil Co, 55; instr, USAF Inst Technol, 66. *Mem:* Geol Soc Am; Am Geophys Union; Mineral Soc Am; Sigma Xi. *Res:* Large-scale impact cratering mechanics related to the earth and planets; shock metamorphic studies of very high pressure shock wave deformed natural materials. *Mailing Add:* One Suzette Lane Flagstaff AZ 86001

RODDY, MARTIN THOMAS, CELL BIOLOGY, TERATOLOGY & RISK ASSESSMENT. *Current Pos:* SECT HEAD, HUMAN SAFETY, PROCTER & GAMBLE INC, 88- *Personal Data:* b Washington, DC, Dec 17, 46; wid. *Educ:* St Ambrose Col, BS, 69; Cath Univ Am, MS, 72, PhD(cell biol), 75; Am Bd Toxicol, dipl 80, 85 & 90. *Prof Exp:* Instr human anat, Cath Univ Am, 73-75; med rev officer, Gillette Med Eval Lab, 75-81, sr toxicologist, 81-88. *Mem:* Sigma Xi; AAAS; Am Soc Cell Biol; Tissue Cult Asn Am; Am Col Toxicol. *Res:* Skin and ocular irritation. *Mailing Add:* Procter & Gamble 11050 York Rd Hunt Valley MD 21030. *Fax:* 410-785-5078

RODE, DANIEL LEON, SOLID STATE PHYSICS, PLASMA PHYSICS. *Current Pos:* PROF, WASH UNIV, 80- *Personal Data:* b Delphos, Ohio, Aug 10, 42; m 76, Helene L Kantor; c Matthew S & Meredith S. *Educ:* Univ Dayton, BS, 64; Case Western Res Univ, MS, 66, PhD(appl physics), 68. *Prof Exp:* Mem tech staff semiconductor microwave devices, Bell Tel Labs, 68-70, supvr semiconductor mat, 70-80. *Concurrent Pos:* Fel, Max-Planck Inst, 77. *Mem:* Am Phys Soc; AAAS; Inst Elec & Electronics Engrs; Sigma Xi. *Res:* Electron theory of crystals; band structure of solids; semiconductor crystal growth; thermonuclear plasmas; optoelectronics; electronics. *Mailing Add:* Campus Box 1127 Wash Univ St Louis MO 63130. *Fax:* 314-935-4842

RODE, JONATHAN PACE, ELECTRICAL ENGINEERING, INFRARED IMAGING. *Current Pos:* MEM TECH STAFF INFRARED, ROCKWELL INT SCI CTR, 76- *Personal Data:* b Worcester Mass, Oct 2, 48; m 69. *Educ:* Univ Ore, BA, 70, PhD(physics), 76. *Mem:* Am Phys Soc. *Res:* Development of high performance; two-dimensional arrays of infrared detectors and their incorporation into infrared imaging systems. *Mailing Add:* Rockwell Sci Ctr 1049 Camino Dos Rios Thousand Oaks CA 91360

RODEBACK, GEORGE WAYNE, PHYSICS. *Current Pos:* ASSOC PROF PHYSICS, NAVAL POSTGRAD SCH, 60- *Personal Data:* b Soda Springs, Idaho, Aug 12, 21; m 57; c 2. *Educ:* Univ Idaho, BS, 43; Univ Ill, MS, 47, PhD(physics), 51. *Prof Exp:* Mem staff radiation lab, Mass Inst Technol, 42-45; from res engr to sr tech specialist, Atomics Int Div, NAm Aviation Inc, 51-60. *Mem:* Am Phys Soc; Am Asn Physics Teachers; Sigma Xi. *Res:* Nuclear and reactor physics; analytical mechanics. *Mailing Add:* 1088 Indian Village Rd Pebble Beach CA 93953

RODELL, CHARLES FRANKLIN, POPULATION GENETICS. *Current Pos:* asst prof, 79-81, ASSOC PROF BIOL, COL ST BENEDICT, ST JOHN'S UNIV, 82- *Personal Data:* b La Crosse, Wis, Aug 1, 42; m 67; c 1. *Educ:* Univ Wis, BS, 65; Univ Minn, MS, 67, PhD(genetics), 72. *Prof Exp:* Fel systs ecol, Natural Resource Ecol Lab, Colo State Univ, 72-74; asst prof biol, Vanderbilt Univ, 74-80. *Mem:* AAAS; Genetics Soc Am; Soc Study Evolution; Sigma Xi. *Res:* Development and analysis of life history parameters and demographic patterns on the genetic structure of populations. *Mailing Add:* Genetics 250 Biol Sci Ctr Univ Minn St Paul 1445 Gortner Ave St Paul MN 55108-1095

RODEMEYER, STEPHEN A, PHYSICAL ORGANIC CHEMISTRY. *Current Pos:* from asst prof to assoc prof, 67-74, chmn dept, 71-77, PROF CHEM, CALIF STATE UNIV, FRESNO, 74- *Personal Data:* b Freeport, Ill, Oct 2, 40; m 65; c 2. *Educ:* Col St Thomas, BS, 62; Univ Calif, Berkeley, PhD(chem), 66. *Prof Exp:* NSF res assoc chem, Radiation Lab, Univ Notre Dame, 66-67. *Mem:* Am Chem Soc. *Res:* Kinetics and mechanism; radiation and photochemistry. *Mailing Add:* Calif St Univ Chem Dept 2555 E San Ramon Ave M/S 70 Fresno CA 93740

RODEMS, JAMES D, ELECTRICAL ENGINEERING, ELECTRONICS. *Current Pos:* PRES, JDR SYST CORP, 78- *Personal Data:* b Springfield, Ill, Apr 30, 26; m 47; c 3. *Educ:* Univ Louisville, BEE, 47; Univ Ill, MS, 50. *Prof Exp:* Test engr, Gen Elec Co, 47-48; asst elec eng, Univ Ill, 48-50; instr, Ohio State Univ, 50-51; control systs engr, Bell Aircraft Corp, 51-53; res assoc, Radar & Control Systs, Univ Ill, 53-57; res engr, Radar & Control Systs, Defense Systs Lab, Syracuse Univ Res Corp, 57-78, dir, 61-78. *Concurrent Pos:* Consult, USN Dept, 62- *Mem:* Inst Elec & Electronics Engrs. *Res:* Radar systems; detection; tracking; fire control; feedback; control systems; hybrid real time analog-digital control; maintenance and test engineering; production and process control engineering. *Mailing Add:* JDR Systs Corp 512 Jamesville Ave Syracuse NY 13210

RODEN, GUNNAR IVO, PHYSICAL OCEANOGRAPHY, CLIMATOLOGY. *Current Pos:* res assoc phys oceanog, Univ Wash, 66-68, sr res assoc, 68-82, prin res assoc, 82-91, RES PROF PHYS OCEANOG, UNIV WASH, 91- *Personal Data:* b Tallinn, Estonia, Dec 27, 28; m 58, Ingegerd; c Christopher-Yngve, Lennart & Einar. *Educ:* Univ Calif, Los Angeles, MS, 56. *Prof Exp:* Res oceanographer, Univ Calif, San Diego, 56-64, asst specialist oceanog, 65-66. *Concurrent Pos:* Tech rev consult, Transis Bd, Am Geophys Union, 65-96; assoc ed, Am Geophys Union, 87-90. *Mem:* Am Geophys Union; Am Meteorol Soc; Sigma Xi. *Res:* Oceanic fronts; meso-scale and large-scale thermohaline structure and circulation; flow over topography; remote sensing of the ocean environment; regional oceanography; sea level and climatic change. *Mailing Add:* Sch Oceanog Box 357940 Univ Wash Seattle WA 98195-7940. *Fax:* 206-616-9289; *E-Mail:* ginoden@u.washington.edu

RODEN, MARTIN STEVEN, TELECOMMUNICATIONS, SIGNAL PROCESSING. *Current Pos:* PROF & CHAIR ELEC ENG, CALIF STATE UNIV, LOS ANGELES, 68- *Personal Data:* b Aug 14, 42. *Educ:* Polytech Univ, BSEE, 63, MSEE, 65; Kensington Univ, PhD(elec eng), 82. *Prof Exp:* Staff engr, Bell Tel Labs, 63-68. *Concurrent Pos:* Consult, Hughes Aircraft Co, 77-85, Los Angeles Unified Sch Dist, 85-, Magnavox Advan Prod, 90-; fel, Inst Advan Eng, 78; sr course instr, Learning Tree, 84-89. *Mem:* Inst Elec & Electronics Engrs; Am Soc Eng Edu. *Res:* Textbook author of 15 major texts in telecommunications and electronics; adaptive signal processing. *Mailing Add:* 5659 Halifax Rd Arcadia CA 91007. *Fax:* 213-343-4555; *E-Mail:* mroden@calstatela.edu

RODENBERGER, CHARLES ALVARD, ENGINEERING, FORENSIC ENGINEERING. *Current Pos:* RETIRED. *Personal Data:* b Muskogee, Okla, Sept 11, 26; m 49, Molcie L Halsell; c Kathryn S (Wilcox) & Charles M. *Educ:* Okla State Univ, BS, 48; Southern Methodist Univ, MS, 59; Univ Tex, Austin, PhD(aerospace eng), 68. *Prof Exp:* Jr petrol engr, Amoco Prod Co, 48-51; chief engr, McGregor Bros, Inc, 53-54; petrol engr, Gen Crude Oil Co, 54; sr design engr aircraft struct, Gen Dynamics/FW, 54-60; Halliburton prof eng, Tex A&M Univ, 66-78, asst dean, Col Eng, 77-80, prof, 60-82, emer prof aerospace eng, 82; consult, Gen Dynamics/FW, 82-91. *Concurrent Pos:* Consult, Gen Motors Defense Res Labs, 65-66, Meiller Res, Inc, 66-82 & Southwest Res Inst, 67; expert witness, McMahon, Smart, Surovilc, Suttle, Bohrman & Cobb, 83-85, Mullen, Mac Innes, Redding & Grove, 87-88, Glandon, Erwin, Scarborough, Baker, Choate & Arnot, 87-88, Webb, Stokes & Sparks, 93-; nat pres, JETS Inc, 78-80, Tex State coordr, 75-82, chmn, Adv Comt, 88-89. *Mem:* Am Inst Aeronaut & Astronaut; Am Soc Eng Educ; Sigma Xi; Am Soc Mech Engrs; Nat Soc Prof Engrs (vpres, 80 & 81). *Res:* Design engineering productivity; engineering innovation; oil spill containment; bioengineering orthotic devices; hypervelocity devices; composite structures; problem definition in systems engineering; granted 2 patents. *Mailing Add:* 8377 FM 2228 Baird TX 79504-4813. *E-Mail:* crodenberg@aol.com

RODENHUIS, DAVID ROY, AVIATION WEATHER. *Current Pos:* dir, Climate Anal Ctr, 85-95, meteorologist, Off Meteorol, 96, DIR, AVIATION WEATHER CTR, NAT WEATHER SERV, 96- *Personal Data:* b Michigan City, Ind, Oct 5, 36; m 58; c 2. *Educ:* Univ Calif, Berkeley, BS, 59; Pa State Univ, BS, 60; Univ Wash, PhD(atmospheric sci), 67. *Prof Exp:* From asst prof to assoc prof fluid dynamics & appl math, Univ Md, College Park, 72-76, assoc prof meteorol, 76-85. *Concurrent Pos:* Exec scientist, US Comt Global Atmospheric Res Prog, Nat Acad Sci, 72; sci officer, World Meteorol Orgn, 75-; US-USSR exchange scientist, 80. *Mem:* Am Geophys Union; Am Meteorol Soc. *Res:* Tropical meteorology; convection models; dynamic climate models; aviation applications; climate applications. *Mailing Add:* 102 E 29th St Kansas City MO 64108. *Fax:* 816-426-3453; *E-Mail:* david.rodenhuis@noaa.gov

RODERICK, GEORGE KARLSSON, POPULATION BIOLOGY, POPULATION GENETICS. *Current Pos:* ASST RESEARCHER, UNIV HAWAII, MANOA, 94- *Personal Data:* b Bar Harbor, Maine, Mar 9, 59; m 92, Rosemary Gillespie. *Educ:* Dartmouth Col, AB, 81; Univ Calif, Berkeley, PhD(zool), 87. *Prof Exp:* Instr, Univ Calif, Berkeley, 87; fac res assoc, Univ Md, College Park, 88-89, asst prof, 90-93. *Concurrent Pos:* Mem, Grad Fac Entom, Univ Hawaii, 94-, Grad Fac Ecol, Evolution & Conserv Biol, 94-, grad fac zool, 95- *Mem:* Entom Soc Am; Ecol Soc Am; Soc Study Evolution; Am Soc Naturalists. *Res:* Genetic structure of insect populations; insect/plant interactions. *Mailing Add:* 3050 Maile Way Gilmore 409 Honolulu HI 96822. *Fax:* 808-956-9608; *E-Mail:* roderick@hawaii.edu

RODERICK, GILBERT LEROY, SOIL ENGINEERING. *Current Pos:* asst prof, 68-70, ASSOC PROF CIVIL ENG, UNIV WIS-MILWAUKEE, 70- *Personal Data:* b Waukon, Iowa, Aug 18, 33; m 62. *Educ:* Iowa State Univ, BS, 60, MS, 63, PhD(soil eng), 65. *Prof Exp:* Engr, US Bur Reclamation, 60-61; res assoc soil eng, Iowa Eng Exp Sta, Iowa State Univ, 63-65; asst prof, Univ RI, 65-68. *Concurrent Pos:* Mem, Hwy Res Bd, Nat Acad Sci-Nat Res Coun. *Mem:* Am Soc Civil Engrs. *Res:* Soil stabilization with chemicals; physicochemical properties of soils by x-ray diffraction and adsorption isotherm studies; frost action in soils; ground water flow; lake bottom sediments; disposal of dredging spoil. *Mailing Add:* 4326 N Ardmore Ave Milwaukee WI 53211

RODERICK, THOMAS HUSTON, GENETICS. *Current Pos:* from assoc staff scientist to sr staff scientist, 59-73, SR STAFF SCIENTIST, JACKSON LAB, 75- *Personal Data:* b Grand Rapids, Mich, May 10, 30; m 58; c Margarethe & George. *Educ:* Univ Mich, AB, 52, BS, 53; Univ Calif, Berkeley, PhD(genetics), 59. *Prof Exp:* Asst psychol, Univ Calif, 55-58. *Concurrent Pos:* Lectr, Univ Maine, 65-; vis lectr, Univ Calif, Berkeley, 68; staff, Ctr Human Genetics, 69-, pres bd dirs, 74-77, 89-; adj prof, Univ RI, 70-73; geneticist, Energy Res & Develop Admin, 73-75. *Mem:* AAAS; Am Soc Human Genetics. *Res:* Mammalian genetics; chromosomal inversions; genetics of aging. *Mailing Add:* Jackson Lab 600 Main St Bar Harbor ME 04609-1500. *E-Mail:* thr@jax.org

RODERICK, WILLIAM RODNEY, ORGANIC CHEMISTRY, MEDICINAL CHEMISTRY. *Current Pos:* asst prof natural sci, 72-73, assoc prof natural sci & chem, 73-85, PROF NATURAL SCI & CHEM, ROOSEVELT UNIV, 85-, ASSOC DEAN ACAD AFFAIRS, ALBERT A ROBIN CAMPUS, 92- *Personal Data:* b Chicago, Ill, Aug 6, 33; m 65, Dorothy Paetel. *Educ:* Northwestern Univ, BS, 54; Univ Chicago, SM, 55, PhD(chem), 57. *Prof Exp:* Res fel chem, Harvard Univ, 57-58; asst prof, Univ Fla, 58-62; sr res chemist, Abbott Labs, 62-70, assoc res fel, 70-71. *Mem:* Am Chem Soc; AAAS; Sigma Xi. *Res:* Structural and synthetic organic chemistry; synthesis of antiviral agents. *Mailing Add:* 15193 W Redwood Lane Libertyville IL 60048-1447. *Fax:* 847-619-7294

RODERMEL, STEVEN ROBERT, PHOTOSYNTHESIS, CLOROPLAST MOLECULAR BIOL. *Current Pos:* ASST PROF BOT, IOWA STATE UNIV, 90- *Personal Data:* b Cheyenne, Wyo, Aug 11, 50. *Educ:* Yale Univ, BA, 72; Univ Wyo, MS, 76; Harvard Univ, PhD(cell & develop biol), 87. *Prof Exp:* Lectr, Harvard Univ, 86-90. *Mem:* Am Soc Plant Physiologists; AAAS. *Res:* Analysis of nuclear-cytoplasmic interactions by investigating variegation mutants of Arabidopsis and photosynthetic antisense mutants of tobacco. *Mailing Add:* Dept Bot Iowa State Univ Ames IA 50011-2010. *Fax:* 515-294-1337; *E-Mail:* s1srr@isuvax.bitnet

RODERUCK, CHARLOTTE ELIZABETH, NUTRITION. *Current Pos:* RETIRED. *Personal Data:* b Walkersville, Md, Dec 2, 19. *Educ:* Univ Pittsburgh, BS, 40; State Col Wash, MS, 42; Univ Iowa, PhD(biochem), 49. *Honors & Awards:* Garst Mem Award, UNA-USA, 88. *Prof Exp:* Res chemist, Children's Fund Lab, Mich, 42-46; from asst prof to prof nutrition, Iowa State Univ, 48-73, asst dean grad col, 71-73, assoc dean col home econ, 73-77, Mary B Welch Distinguished prof home econ, 72-88, dir, World Food Inst, 77-88. *Concurrent Pos:* Vis prof, Univ Baroda, 64-66. *Mem:* Soc Exp Biol & Med; Am Chem Soc; Am Inst Nutrit; Sigma Xi; Soc Nutrit Educ; Am Home Econ Asn. *Res:* Nutrition education; nutritional status; intermediary metabolism. *Mailing Add:* 228 Parkridge Circle Ames IA 50014-3645

RODEWALD, LYNN B, ORGANIC CHEMISTRY. *Current Pos:* ASST PROF CHEM, TOWSON STATE UNIV, 75- *Personal Data:* b Norcatur, Kans, Nov 15, 39; m 63; c 2. *Educ:* Whittier Col, BA, 61; Iowa State Univ, PhD(org chem), 64. *Prof Exp:* NIH fel chem, Princeton Univ, 64-65; asst prof, Univ Tex, Austin, 65-72; vis asst prof, Univ Okla, 72-75. *Concurrent Pos:* Petrol Res fund grant, 65-66. *Mem:* Am Chem Soc; Sigma Xi. *Res:* Organic reaction mechanisms; electroorganic chemistry; small ring chemistry. *Mailing Add:* 8215 Rider Ave Baltimore MD 21204

RODEWALD, PAUL GERHARD, JR, CATALYSIS. *Current Pos:* Res chemist, Cent Res Div Lab, Mobil Oil Corp, 63-66, sr res chemist, 66-78, assoc, 76-91, RES ASSOC, CENT RES DIV LAB, MOBIL OIL CORP, 91- *Personal Data:* b Pittsburgh, Pa, May 15, 36; m 58; c 4. *Educ:* Haverford Col, BA, 58; Pa State Univ, PhD(organosilicon chem), 62. *Mem:* Am Chem Soc; Am Chem Soc Petrol Chem. *Res:* Organosilicon chemistry; electrophilic aromatic substitution; organic synthesis; catalysis. *Mailing Add:* 4 Merritt Lane Rocky Hill NJ 08553-1006

RODEWALD, RICHARD DAVID, CELL BIOLOGY. *Current Pos:* ASST PROF BIOL, UNIV VA, 73- *Personal Data:* b Nyack, NY, Mar 20, 44; m 69. *Educ:* Harvard Univ, BA, 66; Univ Pa, PhD(biochem), 70. *Prof Exp:* NSF fel, 70; fel biol, Univ Calif, San Diego, 70-71; fel path, Harvard Med Sch, 71-73. *Concurrent Pos:* Instr physiol, Marine Biol Lab, Woods Hole, 74. *Mem:* Am Soc Cell Biol; AAAS. *Res:* Selective transport of immunoglobulins across the small intestine; glomerular permeability to macromolecules. *Mailing Add:* Dept Biol Univ Va 229 Gilmer Hall Charlottesville VA 22903. *Fax:* 804-982-5626

RODEY, GLENN EUGENE, HUMAN HISTOCOMPATIBILITY, TRANSPLANTATION IMMUNOLOGY. *Current Pos:* PROF PATH & LAB MED, SCH MED, EMORY UNIV, 87- *Personal Data:* b Mansfield, Ohio, Mar 25, 36; m 58, Missy Crawford; c Geoffrey, Gregory, Kristin & Keith. *Educ:* Ohio Univ, BS, 57; Ohio State Univ, MD, 61. *Prof Exp:* Fel immunol, Univ Minn, 67-69; dir histocompatibility, Milwaukee Blood Ctr, 70-74; assoc prof path & med, Med Col, Wis, 74-76; assoc prof, Sch Med, Washington Univ, Mo, 76-81, prof med & path, 81-87. *Concurrent Pos:* Mem, Transplantation Immunol Comt, Nat Inst Allergy & Infectious Dis, NIH, 74-78; managing ed, Human Immunol, 79-84; mem, Transplantation Comt, Am Nat Red Cross, 79-87; vpres, Histocompatibility Comt, UNOS, 97- *Mem:* Am Soc Histocompatibility & Immunogenetics; Am Asn Immunologists; Am Soc Hemat; Cent Soc Clin Res; Transplantation Soc; Am Asn Clin Histocompatibility Testing (pres, 82-83). *Res:* Structure and function of human histocompatibility locus antigens, genetic complex and gene products; mechanisms of HLA alloimunization and techniques to detect donor-specific BOR T cell alloimmunization. *Mailing Add:* Emory Univ Hosp Rm F-147 Emory Univ Sch Med 1364 Clifton Rd NE Atlanta GA 30322. *Fax:* 404-712-4717; *E-Mail:* grodey@emory.edu

RODGERS, ALAN SHORTRIDGE, PHYSICAL CHEMISTRY. *Current Pos:* assoc prof, 67-96, EMER ASSOC PROF, TEX A&M UNIV, 96-; VIS PROF CHEM, EMORY UNIV, 97- *Personal Data:* b St Louis, Mo, Oct 23, 31; m 94, Ann Jones; c 5. *Educ:* Princeton Univ, AB, 53; Univ Colo, PhD(phys chem), 60. *Prof Exp:* Sr chemist, Minn Mining & Mfg Co, 60-65; phys chemist, Stanford Res Inst, 65-67. *Mem:* Am Chem Soc. *Res:* Chemical kinetics; free radical thermochemistry; structure and bond dissociation energy. *Mailing Add:* 742 Highland Forest Rd Cleveland GA 30528

RODGERS, AUBREY, PHYSICS, MATHEMATICS. *Current Pos:* RETIRED. *Personal Data:* b Lexington, Miss, June 11, 29; m 55; c 3. *Educ:* Miss Col, BS, 57; Rensselaer Polytech Inst, dipl, 67; Univ Calif, Los Angeles, dipl 68. *Prof Exp:* Physicist electronics, Naval Coastal Syst Lab, Fla, 57-60; physicist, mech, US Army Missile Comand, Ala, 60-62, gen, 62-64, physicist res, 64-85. *Res:* Investigates revolutionary concepts and techniques of gyroscopic instrumention used in Army inertial guidance, stabilization and navigation systems. *Mailing Add:* 216 Creek Trail Madison AL 35758-8514

RODGERS, BILLY RUSSELL, hydrocarbon fuels & coal conversion, hazardous & radioactive waste technology, for more information see previous edition

RODGERS, BRADLEY MORELAND, PEDIATRIC SURGERY. *Current Pos:* PROF SURG & PEDIAT & CHIEF, DIV PEDIAT SURG, MED SCH, UNIV VA, 81-, CHIEF CHILDREN'S SURG, UNIV VA HOSP, 81- *Personal Data:* b Montclair, NJ, Jan 16, 42; m 69; c 2. *Educ:* Dartmouth Col, BA, 63; Dartmouth Med Sch, BS, 64; Johns Hopkins Univ, MD, 66. *Prof Exp:* Asst prof surg & pediat, Med Ctr, Univ Fla, 74-76, assoc prof, 76-78, prof & assoc chief, Div Pediat Surg, 78-81. *Mem:* Am Col Surgeons; Asn Acad Surg; Am Acad Pediat; Am Surg Asn; Am Pediat Surg AQsn; Soc Clin Surg. *Res:* Neonatal gastric physiology. *Mailing Add:* Univ Va Med Ctr Box 181 Charlottesville VA 22908

RODGERS, CHARLES H, PHYSIOLOGICAL PSYCHOLOGY. *Current Pos:* assoc grant, 81-82 DIR, UROL & MANPOWER PROG, NAT INST DIABETES, DIGESTIVE & KIDNEY DIS, NIH, 82- *Personal Data:* b Sept 5, 32; US citizen; m 66; c 3. *Educ:* Los Angeles State Col Arts & Sci, BA, 58, MS, 61; Claremont Grad Sch, PhD(psychol), 66. *Prof Exp:* Nat Inst Child Health & Human Develop fel physiol & neuroendocrinol, Stanford Univ, Sch Med, 66-68; asst prof psychol, physiol & pharmacol, Iowa State Univ, 68-70; asst prof psychol, physiol & pharmacol, Univ Ill, Col Med, 70-72, assoc prof, 72-81. *Concurrent Pos:* Nat Inst Child Health & Human Develop grant, Iowa State Univ & Univ Ill Col Med, 68-71; Vet Admin grant, West Side Vet Admin Hosp, Chicago, 70-73, psychologist, 70-74; consult, Cook County Hosp, Ill, 74-81. *Mem:* Am Physiol Soc; Endocrine Soc. *Res:* Reproductive physiology in the male and female. *Mailing Add:* 45 Center Dr Bldg 45 Rm 6As 19J Bethesda MD 20892-0001

RODGERS, DAVID W, GEOLOGY. *Current Pos:* ASSOC PROF & CHAIR, DEPT GEOL, IDAHO STATE UNIV, 95- *Personal Data:* b Cleveland, Ohio, July 7, 59. *Educ:* Carleton Col, BA, 81; Stanford Univ, PhD(geol), 97. *Concurrent Pos:* Fulbright scholar, 94. *Mem:* Geol Soc Am; Am Geophys Union; Sigma Xi. *Mailing Add:* Dept Geol Idaho State Univ Pocatello ID 83209-8072. *Fax:* 208-236-4414; *E-Mail:* rodgdavi@isu.edu

RODGERS, EARL GILBERT, AGRONOMY, WEED SCIENCE. *Current Pos:* from instr to assoc prof, 47-59, grad coordr agron, 69-81, PROF AGRON, UNIV FLA, 59-, COORDR AGRON TEACHING, 65- *Personal Data:* b Trenton, Fla, Jan 27, 21; m 43; c 2. *Educ:* Univ Fla, BS, 43, MS, 49; Iowa State Univ, PhD(plant physiol), 51. *Prof Exp:* Asst county agent, Wauchula, Fla, 46-47. *Concurrent Pos:* Consult, USAF, Eglin AFB, Fla, 57. *Mem:* Fel Weed Sci Soc Am (pres, 73); fel Am Soc Agron. *Res:* Crop production; weed science. *Mailing Add:* 611 S W 16th Pl Gainesville FL 32601

RODGERS, FRANK GERALD, PATHOGENIC MECHANISMS, MICROBIAL ULTRA STRUCTURE. *Current Pos:* from asst prof to assoc prof, 85-92, FULL PROF MICROBIOL, UNIV NH, 92-, DIR MCNAIR PROG, 93- *Personal Data:* b Belfast, NIreland, UK, Oct 5, 46; US citizen; m 70, Christine Adams; c Vikki L & Paula J. *Educ:* Univ Surrey, Eng, BSc, 69, PhD(virol & electron micros), 77; Inst Biol, London, Eng, MIBiol, 77. *Prof Exp:* Basic microbiologist virol & electron micros, Pub Health Lab Serv, Virus Ref Lab, London, 69-74, sr microbiologist, 74-75; sr microbiologist, Clin Microbiol, Pub Health Lab Serv, Nottingham, Eng, 75-83, prin microbiologist, 83-85. *Concurrent Pos:* Assoc lectr, Univ Surrey, Eng, 71-75, Trent Polytech, Eng, 78-85; med sci teacher, Med Sch, Univ Nottingham, Eng, 78-85; spec prof, Fac Sci, Univ Nottingham, Eng, 78-85; sect ed, Manual Clin Microbiol, 5th ed, Am Soc Microbiol; bd dirs, Northeast Asn Clin Microbiol & Infectious Dis, 86-91, pres, 89-90; ed, J Clin Microbiol, 91- *Mem:* Fel Royal Micros Soc Eng; Soc Gen Microbiol Eng; Inst Biol Eng; Asn Clin Pathologists Eng; Am Soc Microbiol; AAAS; Sigma Xi. *Res:* Mechanisms by which intracellular infectious agents initiate disease at the cellular and molecular levels; pathogenic mechanisms in legionellosis and listeriosis and Campylobacter infections; ultrastructure of infectious agents and their response to antimicrobials; genetic regulation of virulence; growth characteristics and detection methods for Legionella pneumophila and Listeria monocytogenes; role of toxins in the pathogenicity of Campylobacter jejuni; transfer of genetic material and its role in virulence for Legionella and Campylobacter; role of cytokines in the regulation of disease; animal and cellular models of infection and chemotherapy. *Mailing Add:* Dept Microbiol Univ NH Spaulding Hall Durham NH 03824-4724. *Fax:* 603-862-2359

RODGERS, GLEN ERNEST, INORGANIC CHEMISTRY. *Current Pos:* asst prof, 75-81, ASSOC PROF CHEM, ALLEGHENY COL, 81- *Personal Data:* b Farmington, Maine, Dec 27, 44; m 66; c 3. *Educ:* Tufts Univ, BS, 66; Cornell Univ, PhD(chem), 71. *Prof Exp:* Asst prof chem, Muskingum Col, 70-75. *Concurrent Pos:* Vis prof chem, Univ Cincinnati, 77 & Boston Univ, 78; NSF fac develop fel, Univ BC, 81-82. *Mem:* Am Chem Soc. *Res:* Infrared analysis of the interaction between amino acids and heavy metal cations; synthesis and characterization of metal complexes of homoanular ferrocene derivatives; topics in chemical education and interdisciplinary studies. *Mailing Add:* Dept Chem Allegheny Col Meadville PA 16335-3902

RODGERS, IMOGENE SEVIN, OCCUPATIONAL HEALTH, ENVIRONMENTAL HEALTH. *Current Pos:* PRES CWP ASSOC, 93- *Personal Data:* b Rochester, Pa, Nov 13, 45; m 82, James; c Kimberly. *Educ:* Univ Pittsburgh, BS, 67; Duquesne Univ PhD(pharmaceut chem), 75; Johns Hopkins Univ, MS, 94. *Prof Exp:* Res asst, Univ Pittsburgh, 68-71; radiation safety asst, Duquesne Univ, 71-75; res assoc, Allegheny Gen Hosp, 75-76; chemist & sect chief, Nat Inst Occup Safety & Health, 76-80; health scientist, US Dept Labor, Occup Safety & Health Admin, 80-89; sci coordr, US Environ Protection Agency, 89-93. *Concurrent Pos:* Mem sub comt nickel, Int Union Pure & Appl Chem, 76-79; mem, Chem Eval Comt, Nat Toxicol Prog, Nat Inst Environ Health Sci, 80-89, Working Comt, Dept Health & Human Serv, Ann Report Carcinogens, 85-89. *Mem:* Soc Risk Assesment; Am Pub Health Asn; NY Acad Sci. *Res:* Evaluation of animal toxicology and human health data for the assesment of human health risks from occupational or environmental exposure to chemicals especially carcinogens. *Mailing Add:* 114 Garth Terr Gaithersburg MD 20879

RODGERS, JAMES EARL, MEDICAL PHYSICS. *Current Pos:* asst prof, 81-86, DIR, RADIATION PHYSICS DIV, DEPT RADIATION MED, GEORGETOWN UNIV HOSP, 80-, ASSOC PROF RADIATION MED, SCH MED, GEORGETOWN UNIV, 87-, DIR, RADIATION SCI DEPT, 90- *Personal Data:* b Los Angeles, Calif, Aug 19, 43; m 82, Imogene Sevin;

c 2. *Educ:* Calif State Univ, Long Beach, BS, 66; Univ Calif, Riverside, PhD(physics), 72; Am Bd Radiol, cert therapeut radiol physics, 83. *Prof Exp:* Res physicist, Naval Weapons Ctr-Corona, 67-68; res assoc theoret physics, State Univ NY, Albany, 72-76; asst prof therapeut radiol, Tufts Univ Sch Med, radiation oncol res fel & spec & sci staff, 76-80. *Mem:* Am Phys Soc; Am Col Radiol; Health Physics Soc; Am Asn Phys Med; Am Col Med Physics; Am Soc Therapeut Radiol & Oncol. *Res:* Computer applications in radiation physics and dosimetry; Monte Carlo simulation of radiation energy deposition; digital image processing in radiation therapy; algorithms for 30 dose distribution calculation. *Mailing Add:* 2302 Eagle Rock Pl Silver Spring MD 20906. *Fax:* 301-784-3323; *E-Mail:* jr@gamma.rip.georgetown.edu

RODGERS, JAMES EDWARD, PHYSICAL ORGANIC CHEMISTRY. *Current Pos:* assoc prof, 75-78, PROF CHEM, AZUSA PAC COL, 78- *Personal Data:* b Boise, Idaho, Jan 13, 38; m 58; c 2. *Educ:* Westmont Col, BA, 60; Univ Calif, Berkeley, PhD(chem), 64. *Prof Exp:* Res asst chem, Univ Calif, Berkeley, 60-64; from instr to asst prof, North Park Col, 64-66; from asst prof to assoc prof, Bethel Col, 66-73; vis prof, Westmont Col, 73-74; prof, Bethel Col, 74-75. *Concurrent Pos:* NSF res grant, North Park Col, 65-66. *Mem:* Am Chem Soc; Royal Soc Chem; Royal Inst Chem; Sigma Xi. *Res:* Organic synthesis; photochemistry of allylic systems; reaction mechanisms of the saturated carbon; free radical chemistry. *Mailing Add:* 552 W Comstock Glendora CA 91740-2404

RODGERS, JAMES FOSTER, ECONOMICS. *Current Pos:* res assoc, Ctr Health Policy Res, AMA, Chicago, 79-80, res dir, 80-82, asst to dep exec vpres, 82-85, DIR, AMA, CTR HEALTH POLICY RES, 85- *Personal Data:* b Columbus, Ga, Jan 15, 51; m 75, Cynthia L Bathurst. *Educ:* Univ Ala, Tuscaloosa, BA, 73; Univ Iowa, PhD, 80. *Prof Exp:* Fed intern, Off Res & Statist, Soc Security Admin, Washington, 76-77. *Concurrent Pos:* Hohenberg felm Mfrs Asn & NSF, 78. *Mem:* Am Econ Asn; Am Soc Asn Execs; Am Statist Asn. *Res:* Economics of medical care. *Mailing Add:* Health Policy 515 N State St Chicago IL 60610. *Fax:* 312-464-5849

RODGERS, JOHN, FIELD GEOLOGY. *Current Pos:* from instr to prof, 46-62, Silliman prof, 62-85, EMER SILLIMAN PROF GEOL, YALE UNIV, 85- *Personal Data:* b Albany, NY, July 11, 14. *Educ:* Cornell Univ, BA, 36, MS, 37; Yale Univ, PhD(geol), 44. *Honors & Awards:* Medal of Freedom, US Army, 47; Penrose Medal, Geol Soc Am, 81; Gaudry Prize, Geol Soc France, 87; Fourmanier Medal, Royal Acad Sci, Fine Arts Letts Belg, 87. *Prof Exp:* Asst geol, Cornell Univ, 35-36, instr, 36-37; field geologist, US Geol Surv, 40-46. *Concurrent Pos:* Asst ed, Am J Sci, 48-54, ed, 54-; secy, Comn Stratig, Int Geol Cong, 52-60; sr fel, NSF, France, 59-60; vis lectr, Col France, 60; comnr, Conn Geol & Natural Hist Surv, 60-71; Nat Acad Sci exchange scholar, USSR, 67; Guggenheim fel, Australia, 73-74; vpres, Societe Geologique de France, 60. *Mem:* Nat Acad Sci; AAAS; Geol Soc Am (pres, 70); Am Asn Petrol Geologists; Am Geophys Union; Am Philos Soc. *Res:* Field geology in deformed sedimentary rocks; stratigraphy and structural geology of Appalachian Mountains; comparative anatomy of mountain ranges. *Mailing Add:* Yale Univ Dept Geol PO Box 208109 New Haven CT 06520-8109. *Fax:* 203-432-5668; *E-Mail:* ajs@milne.geology.yale.edu

RODGERS, JOHN BARCLAY, JR, INTERNAL MEDICINE, GASTROENTEROLOGY. *Current Pos:* from asst prof to assoc prof med, 66-74, PROF MED, ALBANY MED COL, 74-, CHIEF SECT GASTROENTEROL, 81- *Personal Data:* b Cleveland, Ohio, Jan 5, 33; m 55; c 3. *Educ:* Denison Univ, BA, 55; Harvard Med Sch, MD, 59. *Prof Exp:* Clin & res fel gastroenterol, Mass Gen Hosp, 64-66. *Mem:* Am Fedn Clin Res; Am Gastrointestinal Asn; Am Asn Study Liver Dis; Am Soc Clin Invest. *Res:* Small bowel function and lipid absorption; factors influencing sterol absorption. *Mailing Add:* Dept Med Albany Med Col 43 New Scotland Ave Albany NY 12208

RODGERS, JOHN H, JR, ECOTOXICOLOGY, CONSTRUCTED WETLANDS. *Current Pos:* assoc dir, Biol Field Sta, Univ Miss, 89-90, dir, 90-95, dir, Ctr Water & Wetland Resources, 93-95, ADJ RES PROF, RES INST PHARMACEUT SCI, UNIV MISS, 89-, PROF, DEPT BIOL, 89-, DIR, ECOTOXICOL PROG, 95- *Personal Data:* b Dillon, SC, Feb 1, 50; m 69, Martha Robeson; c Daniel Joseph & Frank Clifford. *Educ:* Clemson Univ, BS, 72, MS, 74; Va Polytech Inst & State Univ, PhD(bot & aquatic ecol), 77. *Prof Exp:* Res assoc, Biol Dept, Va Polytech Inst & State Univ, 77-78; asst prof, Dept Environ Sci, E Tenn State Univ, 78-79; res scientist II, Inst Appl Sci, Univ NTex, 79-81, asst prof, 82-85, assoc prof, Biol Sci Dept, 85-89. *Concurrent Pos:* Assoc, dir, Inst Appl Sci, Univ NTex, 82-88, dir, Water Res Field Sta, 87-89; consult aquatic toxicologist, US Environ Protection Agency, 89-, NIH, 89-; bd dirs Soc Environ Toxicol & Chem, 95-; assoc ed, J Toxicol & Environ Health, 97- *Mem:* Soc Environ Toxicol & Chem; Aquatic Plant Mgt Soc; AAAS. *Res:* The fate and effects of materials in both aquatic and terrestrial ecosystems with emphasis on innovative approaches to accurately characterize and mitigate impacts. *Mailing Add:* Dept Biol Univ Miss University MS 38677. *Fax:* 601-232-5144; *E-Mail:* byjhr@olemiss.edu

RODGERS, JOHN JAMES, LUBRICATION ENGINEERING, RESEARCH ENGINEERING. *Current Pos:* RETIRED. *Personal Data:* b Glasgow, Scotland, Mar 31, 30; US citizen; m 53, Lila; c 1. *Educ:* Wayne State Univ, BS, 52, MS, 53. *Honors & Awards:* Henry Ford Mem Award, Soc Automotive Engrs, 61. *Prof Exp:* Res engr, Res Labs, Gen Motors Corp, 52-59, sr res engr, 59-81, staff res engr, 81-89; consult, 89-91. *Mem:* Soc Automotive Engrs; Am Soc Lubrication Engrs. *Res:* Friction in lubricated sliding systems, primarily clutch plate systems in automatic transmissions and controlled-slip rear axles; lubricant-seal compatibility engine oils. *Mailing Add:* 5925 Whitfield Dr Troy MI 48098-5101

RODGERS, LAWRENCE RODNEY, INTERNAL MEDICINE. *Current Pos:* asst prof, 49-72, ASSOC PROF CLIN MED, BAYLOR COL MED, 57-, UNIV TEX MED SCH HOUSTON, 72- *Personal Data:* b Clovis, NMex, Mar 9, 20; m 43, Ivy Piper; c Elizabeth, Larry (deceased) & George. *Educ:* WTex State Col, BS, 40; Univ Tex, MD, 43; Am Bd Internal Med, dipl, 57, cert, 74. *Prof Exp:* Intern, Philadelphia Gen Hosp, Pa, 43-44, resident internal med, 46-49. *Concurrent Pos:* Attend physician, Hermann Hosp, 49-66, chmn dept med, 66-71; assoc internist, Univ Tex M D Anderson Hosp & Tumor Inst, 49-, adj prof clin med. *Mem:* AMA; master Am Col Physicians; fel Royal Soc Health; Am Soc Internal Med. *Res:* Internal medicine; inheritable disorders. *Mailing Add:* 5508 Briar Dr Houston TX 77056

RODGERS, MICHAEL A J, PHOTOCHEMISTRY. *Current Pos:* OHIO EMINENT SCHOLAR & PROF CHEM, BOWLING GREEN STATE UNIV, 88- *Personal Data:* b Chesterfield, Eng, Oct 10, 36. *Educ:* Univ Manchester, Eng, MSc, 64, PhD(chem), 66. *Prof Exp:* Fel, Lawrence Berkeley Lab, 66-67; sr res assoc, Univ Manchester, Eng, 68-69, lectr chem, 69-76; res coordr, Ctr Fast Kinetics Res, Univ Tex, Austin, 76-88. *Mem:* Am Chem Soc; Am Soc Photobiol; Am Phys Soc. *Res:* Nature and properties of unstable, short-lived reaction intermediates in chemistry; application of time-resolved techniques in chemistry and biology. *Mailing Add:* Ctr Photochemical Scis Bowling Green State Univ Bowling Green OH 43403-0002

RODGERS, NELSON EARL, MICROBIOLOGY, BIOCHEMISTRY. *Current Pos:* CONSULT MICROBIOL & BIOCHEM, 76- *Personal Data:* b Fredonia, Pa, May 18, 15; m 37; c 1. *Educ:* Allegheny Col, AB, 37; Univ Wis, AM, 40, PhD(bact), 42. *Honors & Awards:* Indust Achievement Award, Inst Food Technologists, 67. *Prof Exp:* Asst biol, Univ Wis, 37-42; chief bacteriologist, Western Condensing Co, 42-46, res mgr, 46-56, assoc dir res, Foremost Dairies, Inc, Calif, 56-64; res assoc, Pillsbury Co, 64-76. *Concurrent Pos:* Bacteriologist, Natural Hist Surv Wis, 38-39; Nutrit Coun, Am Feed Mfrs Asn, 51-54; ed bd, Appl Microbiol, 53-56; AAAS fel, 67. *Mem:* AAAS; Am Soc Microbiol; Am Chem Soc. *Res:* Industrial fermentations; vitamin synthesis by microorganisms; unidentified growth factors in animal nutrition; biochemistry of milk and whey products; microbial polysaccharides; cereal products. *Mailing Add:* 4262 Circle Dr Wayzata MN 55391-3624

RODGERS, RICHARD MICHAEL, BIOCHEMISTRY, IMMUNODIAGNOSIS. *Current Pos:* group leader, 78-81, group leader, Syntex Med Diag, 81-85, GROUP LEADER, SYVA MICROBIOL RES & DEVELOP, SYVA CO, 85- *Personal Data:* b Scranton, Pa, Nov 12, 45; m 94, Judy Passanante. *Educ:* Univ Scranton, BS, 67; Columbia Univ, PhD(biochem), 71. *Prof Exp:* Fel virol, Div Infectious Dis, Stanford Univ, 71-73; sr chemist biochem, Syva Res Inst, 73-78. *Mem:* AAAS; Am Chem Soc; Sigma Xi. *Res:* Mechanism of enzyme action; use of enzymes in immunoassays; protein purification; fluorescence immunoassays; immunodiagnosis of infectious diseases. *Mailing Add:* 557 Irven Ct Palo Alto CA 94306-3952. *Fax:* 408-239-2197

RODGERS, ROBERT STANLEIGH, ANALYTICAL CHEMISTRY. *Current Pos:* MEM STAFF, PRINCETON APPL RES, EG&G, INC, 79- *Personal Data:* b Kew Gardens, NY, Jan 5, 45; m 75; c 2. *Educ:* Polytech Inst Brooklyn, BS & MS, 66; Clarkson Col Technol, PhD(chem), 71. *Prof Exp:* Res asst chem, Calif Inst Technol, 70-72; asst prof, Mich State Univ, 72-73; asst prof chem, Lehigh Univ, 73-79. *Mem:* Am Chem Soc; Electrochem Soc. *Res:* Electrode kinetics; laboratory microprocessors. *Mailing Add:* EG&G Princeton Appl Res PO Box 2565 Princeton NJ 08543-2565

RODGERS, SHERIDAN JOSEPH, ANALYTICAL CHEMISTRY, ENVIRONMENTAL HEALTH. *Current Pos:* Res chemist, 52-60, SECT HEAD ANALYTICAL CHEM, MSA RES CORP, 60- *Personal Data:* b Ellwood City, Pa, Mar 26, 29; m 50, Marilyn Fosnaught; c Alexis (Vahanian), Sheridan Jr, Jill (Maddox) & Scott. *Educ:* Geneva Col, BS, 54. *Mem:* Am Nuclear Soc; Am Soc Test & Mat; Am Indust Hyg Asn. *Res:* Aerosol generation and sampling; air pollution monitoring; measurement and control of dust and toxic fumes in underground mines and vehicular tunnels; development and testing of protective clothing; monitoring and control of workplace health and safety hazards. *Mailing Add:* James Dr Ellwood City PA 16117

RODGMAN, ALAN, ORGANIC CHEMISTRY. *Current Pos:* CONSULT, 87- *Personal Data:* b Aberdare, Wales, Feb 7, 24; nat US; m 47, Doris Curley; c Eric, Paul & Mark. *Educ:* Univ Toronto, BA, 49, MA, 51, PhD(org chem), 53. *Prof Exp:* Res asst, Banting & Best, Dept Med Res, Toronto, 47-53, res assoc, 53-54; sr res chemist, R J Reynolds Tobacco Co, 54-65, head, Natural Prod Chem Sect, 65-72 & 74-75, actg mgr chem res, 73, mgr anal res, 75-76, dir res, 76-80, dir fund res, 80-87. *Concurrent Pos:* Vchmn, Tobacco Sci, 65-67; mem, Nat Cancer Inst Tobacco Working Group, 76-77 & Tech Study Group, Cigarette Safety Act, 84-87; adj prof, Wolfe Univ, Toronto. *Mem:* Am Chem Soc; NY Acad Sci; Chem Inst Can. *Res:* Composition of tobacco smoke; tobacco smoke and health. *Mailing Add:* 2828 Birchwood Dr Winston-Salem NC 27103-3410

RODIA, JACOB STEPHEN, BIO-ORGANIC CHEMISTRY. *Current Pos:* assoc prof, 63-70, PROF CHEM, ST JOSEPH'S COL, IND, 70-, CHMN DEPT CHEM, 81- *Personal Data:* b Chicago, Ill, Apr 7, 23; m 49; c 5. *Educ:* Loyola Univ, Ill, BS, 47; Univ Ill, MS, 48, PhD(org chem), 52. *Prof Exp:* Res chemist, Int Minerals & Chem Corp, Ill, 52-54; assoc prof org chem, Drake Univ, 54-56; res chemist, Westinghouse Labs, 56-60 & 3M Res Labs, 60-63. *Mem:* Am Chem Soc. *Res:* Polymer chemistry; synthesis, mechanism of formation, properties and reactions of new organic and polymeric materials. *Mailing Add:* 1170 Carnaby East Bloomington IN 47401-8730

RODIECK, ROBERT WILLIAM, VISION. *Current Pos:* BISHOP PROF, UNIV WASH, 78- *Personal Data:* b Highland Falls, NY, Apr 17, 37; m 61. *Educ:* Mass Inst Technol, BS, 58, MS, 61; Univ Sydney, PhD(physiol), 65. *Prof Exp:* Lectr physiol, Univ Sydney, 62-67, sr lectr, 67-72, reader physiol, 72-78. *Mem:* Neurosci Soc. *Res:* Neurophysiology; retinal neurophysiology. *Mailing Add:* 5721 Eighth Ave NE Seattle WA 98105

RODIER, ROBERT W, AERONAUTICAL ENGINEERING. *Current Pos:* CHIEF, PARACHUTE ENG BR, US ARMY, NATICK, MASS. *Honors & Awards:* Aerodyn Decelerator Syst Award, Am Inst Aeronaut & Astronaut, 94. *Mailing Add:* Natick Res Develop & Eng Ctr STRNC-UAP Kansas St Natick MA 01760

RODIG, OSCAR RUDOLF, enzyme chemistry, biosynthesis; deceased, see previous edition for last biography

RODIN, ALVIN E, PATHOLOGY, MEDICAL EDUCATION. *Current Pos:* prof & chmn postgrad med & continuing educ, 75-92, EMER PROF PATH, SCH MED, WRIGHT STATE UNIV, 92- *Personal Data:* b Winnipeg, Man, Mar 25, 26; m 51, 74; c 4. *Educ:* Univ Man, MD, 50, MSc, 59; FRCP(C), 59. *Prof Exp:* Teaching fel path, Queen's Univ, Ont, 56-57; res assoc, Univ Man, 57-59; assoc dir, Royal Alexandra Hosp, Edmonton, Alta, 59-60; dir, Misericordia Hosp, 61-63; from asst prof to prof, Med Br, Univ Tex, Galveston, 63-75. *Concurrent Pos:* Consult pathologist, Med-Surg Res Inst, Univ Alta, 59-63. *Mem:* Fel Col Am Path; fel Royal Col Med (Can.); Am Osler Soc; Int Acad Path; fel Royal Soc Med. *Res:* Mercury nephrotoxicity; relationship of pineal to tumor growth; ultrastructure of pineal; radiation induced tumors; congenital heart disease; perinatal disease; medical education; medical history; medical humanism. *Mailing Add:* 4440 Pavlov Ave San Diego CA 92122-3712

RODIN, BURTON, MATHEMATICS. *Current Pos:* from asst prof to assoc prof math, 66-72, chmn dept, 77-81, PROF MATH, UNIV CALIF, SAN DIEGO, 72- *Personal Data:* b St Louis, Mo, June 19, 33; m 62; c 2. *Educ:* Univ Calif, Los Angeles, BA, 55, PhD(math), 61; Univ Chicago, MS, 58. *Prof Exp:* Asst prof math, Harvard Univ, 61-63, Univ Minn, 63-64, Univ Calif, San Diego, 64-65 & Stanford Univ, 65-66. *Mem:* Am Math Soc. *Res:* Complex analysis. *Mailing Add:* Univ Calif San Diego 0112 9500 Gilman Dr La Jolla CA 92093-0112

RODIN, ERVIN Y, APPLIED MATHEMATICS. *Current Pos:* assoc prof, 66-77, PROF APPL MATH, WASH UNIV, 77- *Personal Data:* b Budapest, Hungary, Jan 17, 32; US citizen; m 56, Sarah Leibovitz; c Daphna, Eytan & Allen. *Educ:* Univ Tex, Austin, BA, 60, PhD(math), 64. *Prof Exp:* Spec instr math, Univ Tex, Austin, 60-64; sr mathematician, Wyle Labs, 64-66. *Concurrent Pos:* Organizer & Ed Proceedings, Symp Apollo Appln, 65; mem, Adv Comt Data Processing Systs Antiballistic Missile Defense, Nat Acad Sci, 68-71 & Adv Bd, RETA Consult Environ Engrs, 71-; organizer & gen chmn, Symp Eng Sci in Biomed, 69; chmn, Aleph Found, 71-; organizer & gen chmn, Int Meeting Pollution, Eng & Sci Solutions, Israel, 72; organizer & dir, Appl Finite Element Technol in RR Indust, 75; ed-in-chief, Int J Comput & Math with Appln, Int Series Monographs on Modern Appl Math & Comput Sci, Int J Math Modelling & Appl Math Lett; pres, Inst Appl Sci, Inc. *Mem:* AAAS; Am Math Soc; Math Asn Am; Soc Indust & Appl Math; Soc Eng Sci; Int Asn Math Modeling; Am Inst Aeronaut & Astronaut. *Res:* Applied mathematics, particularly applications of artificial intelligence to differential game theory, to population studies and to transportation problems; nonlinear partial differential and similar equations. *Mailing Add:* Washington Univ Campus Box 1040 One Brookings Dr St Louis MO 63130-4899. *Fax:* 314-935-6121; *E-Mail:* rodin@rodin.wustl.edu

RODIN, JUDITH, PSYCHIATRY. *Current Pos:* PRES, UNIV PA, 94-, PROF PSYCHOL SCH ARTS & SCI, 94-, PROF MED & PSYCHIAT, SCH MED, 94- *Personal Data:* b Philadelphia, Pa, Sept 9, 44; m 78; c 1. *Educ:* Univ Pa, Philadelphia, AB, 66; Columbia Univ, PhD(psychol), 70. *Hon Degrees:* LHD, Univ New Haven, 94, Med Col Pa & Hahnemann Univ, 95; LLD, Lafayette Col, 96. *Honors & Awards:* Katherine D McCormick Distinguished Lectr, Stanford Univ, 82; Katz-Newcomb Lectr, Univ Mich, 84; Distinguished Creative Contrib Award, Gerontol Soc Am, 87; Robert E Miller Lectr, Univ Pittsburgh, 87; Bishop Robert F Joyce Lectr, Univ Vt, 89; Esther & Isadore Kesten Mem Lectr, Univ Southern Calif, 91; 33rd Annl Golden Plate Award, Am Acad Achievement, 94; Woman of inspiration Award, Am Anorexia Bulimia Asn, 95; Glass Ceiling Award, Am Red Cross, 95. *Prof Exp:* Asst prof psychol, NY Univ, 70-72; from asst prof to prof psychol, Yale Univ, 72-83, dir grad studies, 82-89, Philip R Allen prof psychol, 84-94, Prof Med & Psychiat, 85-94, chair, Dept Psychol, 89-91, dean, Grad Sch Arts & Sci, 91-92, provost, 92-94. *Concurrent Pos:* NSF fel, Univ Calif, Irvine, 71; prin investr, NSF, 73-75 & 77-82, NIH, 81-86, 84-89 & 90-94, MacArthur Found, 83-88 & 89-93; mem, Comn Pvt & Pub Needs, Cong Subcomt, 74-75, Comt Substance Abuse & Habitual Behav, Nat Acad Sci, 76-82, Bd Sci Affairs, Am Psychol Asn, 79-82 & Clin Appln & Prev Adv Comt, Nat Heart, Lung & Blood Inst, 80-84; chair, Fogarty Ctr Task Force Res Obesity, NIH, 76-78 & John D & Catherine T MacArthur Found, 83-; assoc ed, Personality & Social Psychol Bull, 76-79, chief ed, Appetite, 79-92; vchair, Panel Health & Behav, Inst Med, 79; dir, Health Psychol Training Prog, Yale Univ, 82-89; John Simon Guggenheim Found fel, 86-87; pres designate, Univ Pa, 94- *Mem:* Inst Med-Nat Acad Sci; fel Am Psychol Asn; fel Acad Behav Med Res; fel AAAS; NY Acad Sci; Sigma Xi; fel Am Acad Arts & Sci; fel Soc Behav Med (pres, 90-91); Soc Exp Social Psychol (secy-treas, 78-80); Am Psychosomatic Soc; Am Philos Soc. *Res:* Health-promoting and health-damaging bahavior; author of numerous publications in medical journals. *Mailing Add:* Univ Pa Off Pres 100 Col Hall Philadelphia PA 09104-6380. *Fax:* 215-898-9659

RODIN, MARTHA KINSCHER, ANATOMY, NEUROPHYSIOLOGY. *Current Pos:* From instr to asst prof, 67-73, ASSOC PROF ANAT, COL MED, WAYNE STATE UNIV, 73- *Personal Data:* b New York, NY, May 18, 29; m 51; c 3. *Educ:* Wagner Col, BS, 52; Wayne State Univ, MS, 65, PhD(anat), 67. *Honors & Awards:* Sigma Xi Res Award, 67. *Concurrent Pos:* Anat consult & assoc psychiat, Lafayette Clin, 72- *Mem:* AAAS; Am Asn Anat. *Res:* Autonomic nerve endings; mechanisms of convulsive disorders; fluorescent mapping of catacholamines in brain. *Mailing Add:* Three Mountainwood Lane Sandy UT 84092

RODINE, ROBERT HENRY, APPLIED MATHEMATICS, PROBABILITY. *Current Pos:* ASSOC PROF MATH, NORTHERN ILL UNIV, 68- *Personal Data:* b West Pittston, Pa, Nov 9, 29; m 53; c 3. *Educ:* Mansfield State Col, BSEd, 52; Purdue Univ, MS, 57, PhD, 64. *Prof Exp:* Chemist, Westinghouse Elec Corp, 52-55; instr math & statist, Purdue Univ, 57-64; asst prof statist, State Univ NY Buffalo, 64-68. *Mem:* Int Asn Math Modeling; Inst Math Statist. *Res:* Applied probability; applications of probability to the natural sciences and engineering. *Mailing Add:* 1315 S Second St DeKalb IL 60115

RODINI, BENJAMIN THOMAS, JR, COMPOSITE MATERIALS. *Current Pos:* struct eng, Space Struct Div, 79-86, staff eng mat eng, 86-88, MGR, MAT ANALYSIS & DEVELOP, GEN ELEC, 88- *Personal Data:* b Philadelphia, Pa, Feb 26, 47; m 75; c 2. *Educ:* Drexel Univ, BS, 70, MS, 72, PhD(appl mech), 75. *Prof Exp:* Sr struct engr, Ft Worth Div, Gen Dynamics, 75-79. *Concurrent Pos:* Adj prof, Drexel Univ, 75. *Res:* Characterization, development, analysis and design of advanced composite structures (polymer and metal matrix). *Mailing Add:* 1610 Lynnewood Dr Havertown PA 19083

RODKEY, FREDERICK LEE, BIOCHEMISTRY. *Current Pos:* RETIRED. *Personal Data:* b Limon, Colo, Apr 13, 19; m 43; c 2. *Educ:* Whitworth Col, BS, 42; Univ Idaho, MS, 43; Harvard Univ, PhD(biol chem), 48. *Prof Exp:* Asst, Univ Idaho, 42-43; tutor biochem sci, Harvard Univ, 44-48, assoc, 49-51, asst prof, 51-58; chemist, US Naval Med Res Inst, 58-79. *Concurrent Pos:* Instr biochem, Harvard Univ, 47-50; consult, New Eng Deaconess Hosp, 48-58. *Mem:* Am Chem Soc; Am Soc Biol Chem; Am Asn Clin Chem. *Res:* Biological oxidation reduction; enzymology; clinical chemistry. *Mailing Add:* 106 Heron Point #106 Chestertown MD 21620-1672

RODKEY, LEO SCOTT, IMMUNOLOGY. *Current Pos:* PROF PATH, UNIV TEX MED SCH, HOUSTON, 82- *Personal Data:* b Topeka, Kans, Jan 18, 41; m 63, Dixie Croft; c Travis L. *Educ:* Univ Kans, BA, 64, PhD(microbiol), 68. *Prof Exp:* NIH fel immunochem, Col Med, Univ Ill, 68-70; from asst prof to assoc prof, Kans State Univ, 70-82. *Concurrent Pos:* Mem, Basel Inst Immunol, 77-78; NIH res career develop award; dir, Bioprocessing Res Ctr, Univ Tex Health Sci Ctr, Houston, 88-90. *Mem:* AAAS; Am Asn Immunologists; Am Asn Pathologists; NY Acad Sci; Am Soc Microbiol. *Res:* Immunohematology; autoantiidiotypic regulation of immune processes; immunopathology; catalytic antibodies. *Mailing Add:* Dept Path Lab Med Univ Tex Health Sci Ctr PO Box 20708 Houston TX 77225-0708. *Fax:* 713-500-0730

RODKIEWICZ, CZESLAW MATEUSZ, FLUID MECHANICS. *Current Pos:* from asst prof to prof, 58-84, EMER PROF, DEPT MECH ENG, UNIV ALTA, 84- *Personal Data:* b Turka, Poland. *Educ:* Polish Univ Col, London, dipl ing, 50; Univ Ill, MSc, 62; Case Inst Technol, PhD(mech eng), 67. *Prof Exp:* Res engr trans-sonic wind tunnel, Eng Elec Co, 52-54; tech asst mech eng, Dowty Equip Ltd, Can, 54-55; lectr, Ryerson Inst Technol, Toronto, 55-58. *Mem:* Fel Am Soc Mech Engrs; Can Soc Mech Engrs; Sigma Xi; sr mem Am Inst Aeronaut & Astronaut. *Res:* Fluid mechanics and heat transfer, especially hypersonic flight, lubrication, blood flow and ice formations. *Mailing Add:* Dept Mech Eng Univ Alta Edmonton AB T6G 2G7 Can. *Fax:* 403-492-2200; *E-Mail:* cmn@frodo.mece.ualberta.ca

RODMAN, CHARLES WILLIAM, ENVIRONMENTAL NOISE, ACOUSTIC INSTRUMENTATION. *Current Pos:* RETIRED. *Personal Data:* b Delaware, Ohio, Mar 27, 28; m 48, Glenna L Mountz; c Leslie L. *Educ:* Ohio State Univ, BSc, 71. *Honors & Awards:* Wallace Waterfall Award, Am Soc Testing & Mat, Award of Merit. *Prof Exp:* Res technician mech eng, Battelle Mem Inst, 51-59, prin res engr acoust, 59-86, sr noise adv, Energy Systs Div, 86-91. *Concurrent Pos:* Chair, Comt E-33, Comt Stand, Am Soc Testing & Mat; consult, community noise characterization & noise control technol. *Mem:* Acoust Soc Am; Am Soc Testing & Mat. *Res:* Community noise; environmental noise; architectural acoustics; machinery noise control; dynamics instrumentation and analysis. *Mailing Add:* 4710 Canterbury Circle Delaware OH 43015

RODMAN, HARVEY MEYER, ENDOCRINOLOGY, DIABETES. *Current Pos:* Asst prof, 72-80, ASSOC PROF MED, SCH MED, CASE WESTERN RES UNIV, 80-, RES FEL & DIR, CLIN RES CTR, 72- *Personal Data:* b New York, NY, Sept, 8, 40. *Educ:* Columbia Col, BA, 62; Univ Chicago, MD, 66. *Mem:* Am Diabetes Asn; Endocrine Soc; Am Fedn Clin Res. *Res:* Immunology of diabetes; diabetes in pregnancy; secondary causes of diabetes. *Mailing Add:* 2053 Staunton Rd Cleveland OH 44118

RODMAN, JAMES ERIC, ADMINISTER REVIEW & GRANTS PROGRAM FOR SYSTEMATIC & POPULATION BIOLOGY RESEARCH, CONDUCT RESEARCH IN MOLECULAR EVOLUTION & PHYLOGENETICS OF FLOWERING PLANTS. *Current Pos:* PROG DIR SYSTBIOL, NSF, 83- *Personal Data:* b Austin, Tex, Oct 2, 45. *Educ:*

Mich State Univ, BS, 67; Harvard Univ, MA, 69, PhD(biol), 73. *Prof Exp:* Asst cur bot, Harvard Univ, 72-73; from asst prof to assoc prof biol, Yale Univ, 73-83. *Res:* Phylogenetic relationships of mustard oil producing plants using data from gene sequencing and from morphological analysis and their ecological interactions with insects. *Mailing Add:* 1630 C Beekman Pl NW Washington DC 20009

RODMAN, JAMES PURCELL, ASTRONOMICAL INSTRUMENTATION. *Current Pos:* Instr, Dept Physics & Math, Mt Union Col, 51-59, assoc prof physics & astron, 62-65, chmn dept, 63-74, dir, Comput Ctr, 66-74 & 77, prof appl physics & astrophys, 66-92, dir tech eng, Radio Sta WRMU-FM, 70-76 chmn dept, 77-85 & 89-94, DIR, CLARKE OBSERV, MT UNION COL, 51-, STAFF ASTRONOMER, 92- *Personal Data:* b Alliance, Ohio, Nov 11, 26; m 50, Margaret J Kinsey; c William J, Jeffrey K, David L & Gretchen. *Educ:* Mt Union Col, BS, 49; Wash Univ, MA, 51; Yale Univ, PhD(astrophys), 63. *Concurrent Pos:* From vpres to pres, Alliance Tool Co, 51-58; physicist, Alliance Ware Inc, 51-55, corp secy, 54-55, Alliance Mach Co, 57-72; res assoc, Dept Astron, Yale Univ, 62-68; chief engr, Rodman Res, 66-; dir, Mt Union Bank, 67-71; trustee, Western Res Acad, 70-91; dir United Nat Bank & Trust Co, 71-96; vis fel, Yale Univ, 82. *Mem:* Am Phys Soc; Am Astron Soc; fel Royal Astron Soc; Am Optical Soc; fel AAAS; Astron Soc Pac; Am Asn Physics Teachers; Am Inst Physics; Sigma Xi. *Res:* Observational astrophysics of unstable stellar atmospheres; astrophysical-physical instrumentation design; x-ray and beta-spectroscopy. *Mailing Add:* Dept Physics & Astron Mt Union Col 1972 Clark Ave Alliance OH 44601

RODMAN, MORTON JOSEPH, pharmacology, for more information see previous edition

RODMAN, NATHANIEL FULFORD, JR, PATHOLOGY. *Current Pos:* chmn dept, 74-89, PROF PATH, MED CTR, WVA UNIV, 74- *Personal Data:* b Norfolk, Va, July 24, 26; m 51, 70; c 4. *Educ:* Princeton Univ, AB, 47; Univ Pa, MD, 51. *Prof Exp:* Intern, Lankenau Hosp, Philadelphia, 51-52; fel & resident path, Sch Med, Univ NC, Chapel Hill, 52-53 & 55-58, from instr to assoc prof, 58-70; prof, Col Med, Univ Iowa, 70-74. *Concurrent Pos:* Nat Heart & Lung Inst res career develop award, 67-70; mem coun thrombosis, Am Heart Asn. *Mem:* AAAS; Electron Micros Soc Am; AMA; Int Acad Path; Soc Exp Biol & Med; Sigma Xi. *Res:* Ultrastructural aspects of problems in thrombosis and atherosclerosis; cytopathology and surgical pathology. *Mailing Add:* Dept Path WVa Univ Med Ctr Morgantown WV 26506-9203. *Fax:* 304-293-2901

RODMAN, TOBY C, CHROMOSOME STRUCTURES, IMMUNOLOGY. *Current Pos:* from instr to assoc prof anat, 69-83, PROF CELL BIOL & ANAT, MED COL CORNELL UNIV, 83- *Personal Data:* b Philadelphia, Pa, May 30, 18; m 43, Leroy; c John & Laurence. *Educ:* Philadelphia Col Pharm & Sci, BSc, 37; NY Univ, MS, 61, PhD(biol), 64. *Prof Exp:* USPHS fel, Columbia Univ, 64-67, res assoc biol sci, 67-69. *Concurrent Pos:* Vis assoc prof, Rockefeller Univ, 76-77, adj assoc prof, 77-83, adj prof, 83- *Mem:* AAAS; Am Soc Cell Biol; Am Asn Anat; Soc Study Reproduction. *Res:* Molecular organization of mammalian gametes and fertilized eggs; immunology of sperm; role of natural antibodies in AIDS. *Mailing Add:* Dept Anat Cornell Univ Med Col New York NY 10021

RODNEY, DAVID ROSS, HORTICULTURE. *Current Pos:* from assoc horticulturist to horticulturist, Exp Sta, 57-83, EMER PROF PLANT SCI, UNIV ARIZ, 83- *Personal Data:* b Jane, Mo, May 15, 19; m 42, Helen Singer; c James D, Steven R & Douglas E. *Educ:* Univ Mo, BS, 40; Ohio State Univ, MSc, 46, PhD(hort), 50. *Prof Exp:* Asst prof pomol, State Univ NY Col Agr, Cornell, 48-53; asst horticulturist, Citrus Exp Sta, Univ Calif, 53-57. *Mem:* Am Soc Hort Sci. *Res:* Citrus rootstocks; tree physiology; plant nutrition. *Mailing Add:* 2025 Cotton Tail Ave Yuma AZ 85364

RODNEY, EARNEST ABRAM, METEOROLOGY, MATHEMATICS. *Current Pos:* RETIRED. *Personal Data:* b Scranton, Pa, Mar 30, 17; m 43; c 2. *Educ:* East Stroudsburg State Col, Pa, BS, 40. *Prof Exp:* Meteorologist, Com US Weather Bur, Wash, DC, 45-46; air traffic control meteorol, USAF, 46, meteorologist, Pope Field, NC, 46-48; meteorologist, Com US Weather Bur, Jacksonville, Fla, 48-49; prin asst, Asheville, NC, 49-51, prin asst, Greensboro, NC, 51-56; meteorologist hurricane res & radiomarine, Nat Weather Serv, Wash, DC, 56-61, meteorologist in chg, Com Nat Ocean & Atmospheric Admin, Fletcher, 61-79. *Concurrent Pos:* Teacher math & sci, Pender County Bd Educ, Burgaw, NC, 40-42; meteorologist & opers officer, USAF 42-45. *Mem:* Am Meteorol Soc. *Res:* Hurricane research and quantitative precipitation research; operational field. *Mailing Add:* 28 Westridge Dr Asheville NC 28803

RODNEY, WILLIAM STANLEY, NUCLEAR PHYSICS, ASTROPHYSICS. *Current Pos:* Physics Dept, 87-92, ADJ PROF, GEORGETOWN UNIV, 92- *Personal Data:* b Scranton, Pa, Dec 20, 26; m 49; c 4. *Educ:* Univ Scranton, BS, 49; Cath Univ, MS, 52, PhD, 55. *Prof Exp:* Physicist optics, Nat Bur Stand, 49-56; Guggenheim fel, Royal Inst Technol, Sweden, 56-57; physicist optics, Nat Bur Stand, 57-58; physicist, Off Sci Res, USAF, 58-62; prog dir, Nuclear Physics Prog, NSF, 62-87. *Concurrent Pos:* Lectr, Cath Univ, 53; vis prof, Calif Inst Technol, 73-74; adj prof, Georgetown Univ, Wash, DC, 81, Frederick Community Col; Fulbright sr scholar, 83 & 89. *Mem:* Fel AAAS; fel Am Phys Soc; fel Optical Soc Am. *Res:* Nuclear astrophysics. *Mailing Add:* 99135 Gable Ridge Terr Rockville MD 20850

RODNICK, KENNETH JOSEPH, ENERGY METABOLISIM OF MUSCLE, THERMAL BIOLOGY OF FISHES. *Current Pos:* ASST PROF PHYSIOL, IDAHO STATE UNIV, 93- *Personal Data:* b Los Angeles, Calif, Dec 12, 57; m 87, Cheryl E Cady. *Educ:* Univ Calif, Davis, BS, 79; Ore State Univ, MS, 83; Stanford Univ, PhD(physiol), 89. *Prof Exp:* Fel, Wash Univ Sch Med, 89-91; res assoc, Univ Maine, 91-93. *Mem:* Am Psysiol Soc; Am Diabetes Asn. *Res:* Biochemical adaptations of striated muscle to changes in activity patterns and reductions in environmental temperature. *Mailing Add:* Dept Biol Sci Idaho State Univ PO Box 8007 Pocatello ID 83209-8007. *Fax:* 208-236-4570; *E-Mail:* rodnkenn@isu.edu

RODNING, CHARLES BERNARD, FLEXIBLE ENDOSCOPY. *Current Pos:* from asst prof to assoc prof, 81-92, actg chmn, 88-89, PROF, DEPTS SURG & ANAT, COL MED, UNIV SALA, 93-, VCHMN, 89- *Personal Data:* b Pipestone, Minn, Aug 4, 43; m 68, Mary E Lipke; c Christopher B, Soren P & Kai J. *Educ:* Gustavus Adolphus Col, BS, 65; Univ Rochester, MD, 70; Univ Minn, PhD(anat), 79. *Honors & Awards:* Bacaner Basic Sci Award, Minn Med Found, 79; Physicians Recognition Award, AMA. *Prof Exp:* Comdr med corps, US Naval Regional Med Ctr, Okinawa, Japan, 79-81. *Concurrent Pos:* Mem SW Oncol Group, 88- *Mem:* Asn Acad Surg; Am Col Surgeons; Am Asn Surg Trauma; Soc Am Gastrointestinal Endoscopic Surgeons; Soc Univ Surgeons; Int Col Surgeons. *Res:* Gastrointestinal immunology and transplantation; flexible fiberoptic endoscopy; medical and surgical history; medical humanities. *Mailing Add:* 2451 Fillingim St Mobile AL 36617

RODOLFO, KELVIN S, MARINE GEOLOGY, VOLCANOLOGY. *Current Pos:* asst prof, 66-70, ASSOC PROF GEOL SCI, UNIV ILL, CHICAGO, 70- *Personal Data:* b Manila, Philippines, Dec 20, 36; US citizen; m 73; c 2. *Educ:* Univ Philippines, BS, 58; Univ Southern Calif, MS, 64, PhD, 67. *Prof Exp:* Geologist, San Jose Oil Co, 59-60; asst, Univ Southern Calif, 61-64, res assoc, 64-66. *Concurrent Pos:* Geologist, Tidewater Oil Co, 62-63; geol oceanogr, Int Indian Ocean Exped, 64; oceanogr, Environ Sci Serv Admin Res Vessel Oceanogr Global Cruise, 67; lithologist, Leg 16, Deep Sea Drilling Proj, 71, Leg 26, 72 & Leg 59, 78, Leg 126, Ocean Drilling Prog, 89; NSF res grants 67, 69, 70, 71, 78, 85 & 88; Danforth Found Assoc, 80-86; sr scientist, Philippine Inst Volcanology & Seismology, 82- *Mem:* Fel AAAS; fel Geol Soc Am; Soc Econ Paleont & Mineral; Am Geophys Union. *Res:* Regional tectonics of Southeast Asia; deep-sea sedimentology; volcanology; volcaniclastic sedimentology. *Mailing Add:* Dept Geol Univ Ill 845 W Taylor St Chicago IL 60607-7057

RODRICK, GARY EUGENE, PARASITOLOGY, SEAFOOD PROCESSING IRRADIATION & DEPURATION. *Current Pos:* Assoc prof, 87-91, PROF DEPT FOOD SCI, UNIV FLA, 91- *Personal Data:* b McPherson, Kans, Oct 5, 43; m, Lynn Bailey; c Michael, Jeffrey & Gene. *Educ:* Kans State Col, Pittsburg, BA, 66, MS, 67; Univ Okla, PhD(zool), 71. *Prof Exp:* NIH fel parasitol, Univ Mass, Amherst, 71-73; res assoc pathobiol, Lehigh Univ, 73-75; asst prof biol, Dodge City Col, 75-78; from asst prof to assoc prof comp med, Col Pub Health, Univ SFla, 82-87, vchmn dept comp med & assoc prof, Col Med, 82-87. *Mem:* Sigma Xi; Am Microbiol Soc; Inst Food Technologists. *Res:* Public health aspects of edible shellfish and fish; seafood processing; schistosomiasis. *Mailing Add:* Food Sci Univ Fla PO Box 110370 Gainesville FL 32611-0370

RODRICK, MARY LOFY, IMMUNOREGULATION, THERMAL INJURY. *Current Pos:* ASST PROF IMMUNOL, HARVARD MED SCH, 82- *Educ:* Univ Calif, Berkeley, PhD(immunol), 81. *Mailing Add:* Dept Surg Brigham & Womens Hosp Harvard Med Sch 75 Francis St Boston MA 02115-6195. *Fax:* 617-734-8353

RODRICKS, JOSEPH VICTOR, RISK ASSESSMENT. *Current Pos:* PRIN, ENVIRON CORP, 82- *Personal Data:* b Brockton, Mass, Feb 25, 38; m 75; c 2. *Educ:* Mass Inst Technol, BS, 60; Univ Md, PhD(biochem), 68; Am Bd Toxicol, dipl, 81. *Prof Exp:* Res chemist, Food & Drug Admin, 65-69; fel chem, Univ Calif, Berkeley, 69-70; chief, Biochem Br, Food & Drug Admin, 70-72, assoc dir, Div Toxicol, 73-77, dep assoc comnr sci, 78-80; vpres & dir life sci, Clement Assocs, 80-82; assoc prof chem, Univ Md, 65- *Concurrent Pos:* Mem, Comt Toxicol, Nat Acad Sci-Nat Res Coun, 78-82 & Comt Risk Assessment, 81-83. *Mem:* Acad Toxicol Sci; Soc Risk Analysis; Am Col Toxicol; Am Chem Soc. *Res:* Review and evaluation for toxicity and exposure data for purposes of estimating the risk to public health associated with exposures to environmental pollutants, occupational hazards, food additives, pesticides, industrial chemicals and natural toxins. *Mailing Add:* Environ Corp 4350 N Fairfax Arlington VA 22203

RODRIGO, RUSSELL GODFREY, HETEROCYCLIC SYNTHESIS, ANIONIC REARRANGEMENTS & CYCLISATIONS. *Current Pos:* assoc prof, 73-77, PROF CHEM, WILFRID LAURIER UNIV, CAN, 77-, CHMN DEPT, 87- *Personal Data:* Can citizen. *Educ:* Univ Ceylon, Sri Lanka, BSc Hons, 58; Univ Nottingham, Eng, PhD(chem), 63. *Prof Exp:* Asst prof chem, Univ Ceylon, Sri Lanka, 63-67; postdoctoral res asst, Univ Waterloo, Can, 68-69; asst prof, Waterloo Lutheran Univ, Can, 69-76. *Concurrent Pos:* Adj prof, Univ Waterloo, 77-; vis prof, Univ Auckland, NZ, 78. *Mem:* Can Inst Chem. *Res:* Development of novel synthetic pathways to benzylisoquinoline, indole, acridone alkaloids and Aspergillus mycotoxins; syntheses using isobenzofurans and o-benzoquinones as reactive intermediates and leading to lignans, anthracyclinones and aromatic antibiotics; Diels-Alder reactions. *Mailing Add:* Dept Chem Wilfrid Laurier Univ 75 Univ Ave W Waterloo ON N2L 3C5 Can. *E-Mail:* rrodrigo@machl.wlu.ca

RODRIGUE, GEORGE PIERRE, ELECTRICAL ENGINEERING. *Current Pos:* prof, 68-77, REGENTS PROF ELEC ENG, GA INST TECHNOL, 77- *Personal Data:* b Paincourtville, La, June 19, 31; m 55; c 6. *Educ:* La State Univ, BS, 52, MS, 54; Harvard Univ, PhD(appl physics), 58. *Prof Exp:* Sr staff engr, Sperry-Rand Corp, 58-61, res consult, 61-68. *Concurrent Pos:* Consult, Sperry-Rand Corp, 68-72, US Army Missle Command, 70-73, Airtron, Inc, 76-82, Los Alamos Sci Lab, 81-85; bd dir, Electromagnetic Sci Inc, 69-73. *Mem:* Fel Inst Elec & Electronics Engrs (vpres, 82-83). *Res:* Ferrites; application of ferrites to microwave devices; microwave acoustic phenomena and devices; near field antenna measurements. *Mailing Add:* 1090 Kingston Dr Atlanta GA 30342

RODRIGUES, ANIL NOEL, MOTION CONTROL. *Current Pos:* DEVELOP ENGR, WELD TOOLING CORP, 78-, VPRES ENG, 82- *Personal Data:* b Bombay, India, Dec 11, 42. *Educ:* Univ Poona, India, BME, 62; Cornell Univ, MM, 64, PhD(mach design), 70. *Prof Exp:* Design engr, Gen Mold & Mach Corp, 64-65; develop engr, Garvey Corp, 71-73, E I DuPont, 73-74, Ronson Corp, 74-78. *Mem:* Soc Manufact Engrs. *Mailing Add:* 3001 W Carson St Pittsburgh PA 15204

RODRIGUES, MERLYN M, OPHTHALMIC PATHOLOGY, CELL BIOLOGY. *Current Pos:* DIR EYE PATH, LAB EYE PATH, UNIV MD, BALTIMORE, 87- *Personal Data:* b Lucknow, India, Aug 24, 38; US citizen; m 67; c 1. *Educ:* Agra Univ, BS, 55; Madras Univ, India, MD, 59; New Delhi Univ, India, MS, 64; George Washington Univ, PhD(path), 71. *Honors & Awards:* Hon Award, Am Acad Ophthal, 84; Sr Sci Investr, Res Prevent Blindness, 88. *Prof Exp:* Dir path serv, Eye Path, Wills Eye Hosp, 71-76; sect chief Clin Eye Path, Eye Res, Nat Eye Inst, NIH, 77-87. *Concurrent Pos:* Chmn, Anat & Path Prog Comt, Asn Res Vision & Opthal, 84-85; mem, Rev Comt, Fight for Sight, 86-88. *Mem:* Am Asn Pathologists; Int Soc Eye Res; Electron Micros Soc Am; Am Acad Opthal; Int Acad Eye Path. *Res:* Characterization of histopathologic changes in corneal genetic diseases; retinoblastoma; retinal degenerations; glaucoma; ocular infections. *Mailing Add:* Ophthalmic Univ Md Sch Med 665 W Baltimore St Baltimore MD 21201-1559

RODRIGUEZ, ANDRES F, PHYSICS EDUCATION. *Current Pos:* from asst prof to prof physics, Univ Pac, 64-86, chmn, Dept Physics, 74-80, prof physics & eng-physics, 86-97, EMER PROF, UNIV PAC, 97- *Personal Data:* b Havana, Cuba, July 20, 29; US citizen; m 56; c 3. *Educ:* Univ Havana, Dr Sci(phys chem), 55. *Prof Exp:* Instr, Havana Univ, Cuba, 55-58, asst prof physics, 58-61; lectr physics, Univ PR, Humacao Regional Col, 63-64. *Concurrent Pos:* Orgn Am States scholar, Inst Physics, Bariloche, Arg, 60, Nat Univ, Mex, 61-63; res assoc, Spec Training Div, Oak Ridge Assoc Univs, Tenn, 67; consult, Int Latin Am Prog, Oak Ridge Assoc Univs, 67-70; expert physics, UNESCO, Univ Antioquia, Colombia, 71-73; sr Fulbright lectr, Colombia SAm, 73 & 74. *Mem:* Am Soc Eng Educ; Am Asn Physics Teachers; Am Phys Soc. *Res:* Physics education; applied physics; engineering physics. *Mailing Add:* Dept Physics Univ Pac 3601 Pacific Ave Stockton CA 95211

RODRIGUEZ, ARGELIA VELEZ, MATHEMATICS, PHYSICS. *Current Pos:* prog dir, Minority Inst Sci Improv Fund, 80-84, SR SCI EDUC PROG OFFICER, MINORITY SCI & ENG IMPROV PROG, US DEPT EDUC, 84- *Personal Data:* b Havana, Cuba, Nov 23, 36; US citizen; m 54; c 2. *Educ:* Univ Havana, BSc, 54, PhD(math), 60. *Prof Exp:* Asst prof math, Marianao Inst, Cuba, 58-61; asst prof math & physics & head dept, Tex Col, 62-64; from asst prof to prof, Bishop Col, 64-79, chair, Div Nat & Math Sci, 75-78; prog mgr, Minority Inst Sci Improv Prog, NSF, 79-80, dir, 80. *Concurrent Pos:* Lectr mod math, NSF In-Serv Inst Sec Teachers, Bishop Col, 65-67; fel comput assisted instruct, Tex Christian Univ, 67-68; dir & coordr, US Off Educ Proj Elem Math Teachers & Teacher Trainers, 70-73; NSF Coop Col Sch Sci Prog Jr High Sch Teachers Math, 72-73; dir & coordr, NSF Math Instrnl Improv Implementation Prog for High Sch Teachers, Dallas Independent Sch Dist, 73-76; liaison officer, Argonne Nat Lab, 74-79. *Mem:* AAAS; Am Math Soc; Nat Coun Teachers Math; Math Asn Am. *Res:* Classical analysis; solutions of partial differential equations; teaching strategies in mathematics and curriculum development for disadvantaged college students; author of numerous publications. *Mailing Add:* US Dept Educret Blvd 600 Independence Ave SW Washington DC 20202-5329

RODRIGUEZ, AUGUSTO, RESEARCH SCIENCE. *Current Pos:* ASSOC PROF POLYMER & PEROXIDE CHEM, CLARK ATLANTA UNIV, 88- *Personal Data:* b New York, NY, Oct 5, 54; m 76; c 2. *Educ:* Univ PR, BS, 76, PhD(chem), 80. *Prof Exp:* Fel org chem, Emory Univ, 80-82; res chemist polymer chem, E I DuPont de Nemours, 82-85; sr res scientist cellulose chem, Kimberly Clark Corp, 85-88. *Concurrent Pos:* Fel, NIH, 80. *Mem:* Am Chem Soc. *Res:* Polysaccharides; use natures polymers to produce thermoplastic materials, superabsorbent products and consumer goods; peroxides, heterocyclic polymers. *Mailing Add:* Dept Chem Atlanta Univ PO Box 365 Atlanta GA 30314-4381

RODRIGUEZ, CARLOS EDUARDO, COMPUTER SCIENCE. *Current Pos:* asst prof, 68-73, ASSOC PROF COMPUT SCI, ETEX STATE UNIV, 73- *Personal Data:* b San Antonio, Tex, Apr 23, 41. *Educ:* Univ Tex, BS, 62, PhD(chem), 66. *Prof Exp:* Res assoc, Univ Tex, 66-68; staff asst comput animated films, Adv Coun Col Chem, 67-68. *Concurrent Pos:* Coun Libr Resources fel, 74-75. *Mem:* Asn Comput Mach; Asn Develop Comput Based Instrnl Systs. *Res:* Computer-assisted instruction; computer science curriculum development. *Mailing Add:* Dept Comput Sci Tex A&M Univ Commerce TX 75428

RODRIGUEZ, CHARLES F, ANALYTICAL CHEMISTRY, EVIRONMENTAL SCIENCE. *Current Pos:* CONSULT, 83- *Personal Data:* b San Antonio, Tex, July 1, 38; m 62, Karen L Vargo; c Miguel, Felipe, Carlos & Gregorio. *Educ:* St Mary's Univ, Tex, BS, 61. *Prof Exp:* Asst chemist, 61-64, res chemist, 64-74, sr res chemist, Southwest Res Inst, 74-83. *Mem:* Am Chem Soc (treas, 68, chmn, 70); Sigma Xi. *Res:* Analytical characterization of petroleum distillate fuels; development of analytical methods for applications in energy; development of analytical methods for environmental; characterization of water, wastewater, soil, air pollutants. *Mailing Add:* 5905 Deer Horn Dr San Antonio TX 78238-2607. *Fax:* 210-225-4415

RODRIGUEZ, DENNIS MILTON, MATHEMATICS. *Current Pos:* Asst prof, 69-76, ASSOC PROF MATH, UNIV HOUSTON DOWNTOWN COL, 76- *Personal Data:* b Tampa, Fla, July 21, 43; m 70. *Educ:* Univ SFla, BA, 65; Univ Calif, Riverside, MA, 66, PhD(math), 69. *Mem:* Math Asn Am. *Res:* Probability theory; stochastic processes. *Mailing Add:* Univ Houston-Downtown 1 Main St Houston TX 77002

RODRIGUEZ, ELOY, PHYTOCHEMISTRY, ENVIRONMENTAL TOXICOLOGY. *Current Pos:* JAMES A PERKINS CHAIR ENVIRON BIOL, CORNELL UNIV, 94- *Personal Data:* b Edinburg, Tex, Jan 7, 47; m, Helena Viramontes; c Pilar & Francisco. *Educ:* Univ Tex, Austin, BA, 69, PhD(phytochem & plant biol), 75. *Honors & Awards:* Rosser-Rivera Lectr, Univ Calif, Riverside & Los Angeles, 85; Martin de la Cruz Medallion, 92. *Prof Exp:* Fel, Univ BC, 75-76; prof develop & cell biol, Univ Calif, Irvine, 76-94. *Concurrent Pos:* Mem, Phytochem Sec, Am Bot Gardens. *Mem:* Fel AAAS. *Res:* Comparative phytochemistry and cell biology of biologically active isoprenoids, sulfur polyacetylenes (dithiins) and cyclic petides in tissue and cell cultures from higher plants; environmental dermatoxicology of immunotoxins and photosensitizers from natural and man-made sources; zoopharmacognacy; plant-vertebrate interaction. *Mailing Add:* Div Biol Sci Bailey Hortorium/Plant Biol Biotech 259 Cornell Univ Ithaca NY 14853. *Fax:* 714-725-3048; *E-Mail:* erodrigu@darwin.bio.uci.edu

RODRIGUEZ, EUGENE, IMMUNOLOGY. *Current Pos:* RETIRED. *Personal Data:* b New York, NY, Mar 26, 33; m 58, 84; c 4. *Educ:* Queen's Col, NY, BS, 54; Johns Hopkins Univ, ScM, 59, ScD(microbiol), 66. *Prof Exp:* Instr microbiol, Med Sch, Johns Hopkins Univ, 66-67; mem field staff, Rockefeller Found, 67-70; immunologist, Div Exp Path, Dept Lab Med, St John's Mercy Med Ctr, 70-91. *Concurrent Pos:* Vis prof, Mahidol Univ, Bangkok, Thailand, 67-69. *Res:* Mechanism of antigen-antibody reactions; biological consequences of antigen-antibody reactions such as immediate and delayed hypersensitivity and complement fixation; immunopath of glomerular diseases. *Mailing Add:* 3322 Colard Lane PO Box 913 Lyons CO 80540-0913

RODRIGUEZ, FEDERICO ANGEL, NATURAL GAS VEHICLES TECHNOLOGY, APPLICATION OF THE NEUTRON ACTIVATION ANALYSIS. *Current Pos:* DIR, METALL INVEST CTR, 88- *Personal Data:* b Monterrey, Nuevo Leon, Mex, Aug 30, 36. *Educ:* Inst Technol & Super Studies, BS, 59; Univ Mich, MS, 62; Univ Tex, PhD(mech eng), 70. *Prof Exp:* Mgr liquid metall, Hylsa, SAm, 69-77, iron & steel develop, 77-79, proj mgr, Alfa Indust, SAm, 79-82; dir, Altertek, 94. *Concurrent Pos:* Prof physics & math, Inst Technol & Super Studies, 62-66; prof physics, Univ Autonoma, 71-, dir, Nuclear Eng Prog, 74-84. *Mem:* Mex Nat Syst Researchers. *Res:* Application of natural gas in vehicular motor engines; application of neutron activation analysis in the study of materials; mechanical effects on bones using cobalt-60 source for sterilization. *Mailing Add:* Via Aremula 312 Colonia Fuentes Del Valle Garza Garcia Nuevo Leon 66220 Mexico. *Fax:* 8-378-6688

RODRIGUEZ, FERDINAND, CHEMICAL ENGINEERING, POLYMER SCIENCE. *Current Pos:* from asst prof to assoc prof 58-71, PROF CHEM ENG, CORNELL UNIV, 71- *Personal Data:* b Cleveland, Ohio, July 8, 28; m 51, Ethel Koster; c Holly & Lida. *Educ:* Case Inst Technol, BS, 50, MS, 54; Cornell Univ, PhD(chem eng), 58. *Honors & Awards:* Hisp Engr Nat Achievement Award, 91. *Prof Exp:* Develop engr, Ferro Chem Corp, Ohio, 50-54. *Concurrent Pos:* Consult, Union Carbide Corp, 60-69. *Mem:* Am Chem Soc; fel Am Inst Chem Engrs; Soc Hisp Prof Engrs; Soc Plastics Engrs. *Res:* Formation, fabrication and evaluation of polymeric materials. *Mailing Add:* Sch Chem Eng Olin Hall Cornell Univ Ithaca NY 14853. *Fax:* 607-255-9166; *E-Mail:* fr@cheme.cornell.edu

RODRIGUEZ, GILBERTO, BIOLOGICAL OCEANOGRAPHY, ECOLOGY OF ESTUARIES. *Current Pos:* investr, 67-95, head, ctr ecol, 81-83, EMER INVESTR BIOL, VENEZUELAN INST SCI RES, 95- *Personal Data:* b Caracas, Venezuela, May 12, 29; m 59, Selua Diaz; c 6. *Educ:* Cent Univ Venezuela, BSc, 55; Univ Miami, MSc, 57; Univ Wales, PhD(zool), 70. *Prof Exp:* Investr marine biol, Univ of the Orient, 59-60; assoc prof biol, Cent Univ Venezuela, 67-77. *Concurrent Pos:* Mem, Venezuelan Coun Agr Res, 67-68; consult, Venezuelan Inst Petrol Technol, 91-95. *Mem:* Brit Soc Exp Biol; Crustacean Soc. *Res:* Ecology of estuaries; taxonomy of freshwater crabs; environmental impact of oil industry; marine sciences. *Mailing Add:* Venezuelan Inst Sci Res PO Box 21827 Caracas Venezuela. *Fax:* 58-2-504-1088; *E-Mail:* grodrigu@oikos.ivic.ve

RODRIGUEZ, HAROLD VERNON, CHEMICAL ENGINEERING. *Current Pos:* assoc prof chem eng, 69-71, dir div eng, 71-76, DEAN, COL ENG, UNIV SALA, 76- *Personal Data:* b New Orleans, La, Aug 30, 32; m 56; c 4. *Educ:* La State Univ, BS, 54, MS, 58, PhD(chem eng), 62. *Prof Exp:* Engr trainee, Natural Gas Dept, Magnolia Petrol Co, 54-55; instr chem eng,

La State Univ, 60-61; sr res technologist, Mobil Oil Corp, 61-69. *Mem:* Am Inst Chem Engrs; Sigma Xi; Am Soc Eng Educ; Soc Am Military Engrs; Nat Soc Prof Engrs. *Res:* Application of heat to underground formations for oil recovery. *Mailing Add:* 2006 Nanadina Ct Univ SAla Mobile AL 36693-0002

RODRIGUEZ, JACINTO, high-voltage & high power electrical testing, for more information see previous edition

RODRIGUEZ, JOAQUIN, GEOLOGY. *Current Pos:* Lectr, 59-62, from instr to assoc prof, 62-79, PROF GEOL, HUNTER COL, 79- *Personal Data:* b New York, NY, Jan 9, 34; m 66, Patricia A Wagstaff. *Educ:* Hunter Col, BA, 55; Ohio State Univ, MSc, 57; Ind Univ, PhD(geol), 60. *Concurrent Pos:* Comt Examr, Grad Record Exam Geol, 86-91; eval panels, Grad Fel Earth Sci, NSF, 86-92, Instrumentation & Lab Improv, 91. *Mem:* AAAS; fel Geol Soc Am; Paleont Soc; Nat Asn Geol Teachers; Int Paleont Asn; Soc Sedimentary Geol. *Res:* Invertebrate paleontology; paleoecology; palichnology; Devonian-Mississippian brachiopods; biostratigraphy; microcomputer applications to geology. *Mailing Add:* Dept Geol & Geog City Univ NY Hunter Col 695 Park Ave New York NY 10021-5024. *Fax:* 212-772-5268

RODRIGUEZ, JORGE LUIS, SEED PRODUCTION, CROP PRODUCTION & MANAGEMENT. *Current Pos:* res asst sugarcane breeding, Gurabo Substa, Univ PR, 63-69 & 77-86, asst to dean, Mayaguez, 86-87, dean & dir, Col Agr, 88-90, ASSOC PLANT BREEDER, GURABO SUBSTA, UNIV PR, 90- *Personal Data:* b Yauco, PR, June 6, 40. *Educ:* Univ PR, Mayaguez, BS, 62; La State Univ, Baton Rouge, MS, 67; Univ Ark, Fayetteville, PhD(agron), 82. *Prof Exp:* Div agronomist, sugarcane prod, C Brewer PR Inc, 62-63; asst field mgr, Sugar Corp PR, 74-76. *Concurrent Pos:* Agr consult, Sugar Corp PR, 82-, mem, Biomass Comt, 87-; sugarcane consult, Hacienda La Caharta, El Salvador, 85- *Mem:* Caribbean Food Crops Soc. *Res:* New sugarcane varieties adapted to mechanization, high sucrose content or fermentable solids resistant to diseases mainly rust and smut, and with desirable agronomic characters. *Mailing Add:* Agr Exp Sta PO Box 306 Gurabo PR 00658

RODRIGUEZ, JOSE ENRIQUE, VIROLOGY. *Current Pos:* asst prof, 68-74, ASSOC PROF MICROBIOL, UNIV IOWA, 74- *Personal Data:* b San Juan, PR, Oct 16, 33; m 61; c 2. *Educ:* Yale Univ, BS, 55; Univ Pa, PhD(microbiol), 63. *Prof Exp:* Res asst virol, Children's Hosp, Philadelphia, 63-65; NIH fel, Inst Virol, Univ Wurzburg, 65-68. *Mem:* Am Soc Microbiol; Sigma Xi. *Res:* Interferons. *Mailing Add:* 1117 Downey Dr Iowa City IA 52240-6033

RODRIGUEZ, JOSE RAUL, EPIDEMIOLOGY OF AGING, NUTRITIONAL ANTI-OXIDANT RESEARCH. *Current Pos:* PROF GERONT, LAFAYETTE UNIV, 89-; RES-PROF GERONT, CARIBBEAN CTR ADVAN STUDIES, 91- & ALLIANCE THEOL SEM, NYAC, NY, 94- *Personal Data:* b Santurce, PR, Feb 11, 59; m 92, Raquel Pagan; c Dharma R. *Educ:* Univ PR, BS, 79, MPH, 86; UCETEC, MD, 83; Fordham Univ, PhD(ment health res), 93. *Prof Exp:* Biosocial res, Consultores en Salud Mental Inc, 86-87; prof sociol & psychol, City Univ NY, 88-91. *Concurrent Pos:* Vol lectr, Latin Am Sexually Transmitted Dis Ctr, 87- *Mem:* Am Pub Health Asn; Am Sociol Asn; NY Acad Sci. *Res:* Nutritional research with antioxidant agents; use of antioxidant vitamins for the treatment and prevention of hypercholesterolemia and cancer; epidemiological mental health research with the elderly. *Mailing Add:* PO Box 14551 Santurce PR 00916. *Fax:* 787-721-7187

RODRIGUEZ, JUAN GUADALUPE, ENTOMOLOGY, ACAROLOGY. *Current Pos:* from asst entomologist to assoc entomologist, 49-59, assoc prof, 59-61, PROF ENTOM, UNIV KY, 61- *Personal Data:* b Espanola, NMex, Dec 23, 20; m 48, Lorraine Ditzler; c Carmen, Teresa, Carla & Rosa. *Educ:* NMex State Univ, BS, 43; Ohio State Univ, MS, 46, PhD(entom), 49. *Honors & Awards:* Outstanding Award Acarology, Am Reg Prof Entom, 84; J E Russart Mem Award, Entom Soc Am, 86. *Prof Exp:* Asst, Ohio State Univ, 46-47, Exp Sta, 48-49. *Concurrent Pos:* Ed, Insect & Mite Nutrit, 72 & Recent Advances Acarol, 79; gov bd, Entom Soc Am, 85-88; chair, centennial comt, Entom Soc Am, 87-89; exec secy, Ky Acad Sci; bd dir, Ky Sci & Technol Coun. *Mem:* Fel AAAS; Am Inst Biol Sci; Entom Soc Can; Sigma Xi; Acarol Soc Am; Entom Soc Am; Nat Agr Adv Serv. *Res:* Axenic culture of arthropods; insect/mite nutrition; insect pest management; host-plant resistance to insects/mites; nutritional ecology of arthropods. *Mailing Add:* Dept Entom Univ Ky Lexington KY 40546-0091

RODRIGUEZ, LORRAINE DITZLER, MICROBIOLOGY, TOXICOLOGY. *Current Pos:* CONSULT, 89- *Personal Data:* b Ava, Ill, July 4, 20; m 48; c 4. *Educ:* Southern Ill Norm Univ, BEduc, 43; Ohio State Univ, MS, 44; Univ Ky, PhD(microbiol), 73. *Prof Exp:* Asst nutritionist, Ohio Agr Res & Develop Ctr, 44-49; fel, Dept Entom, Univ Ky, 73-74; consult, 74-79; extension specialist, Dept Entom, Univ Ky, 79-89. *Mem:* Am Chem Soc; Soc Environ Toxicol & Chem. *Res:* Acaricide resistance; relation of fungi to acarines; biodegradation of pesticides; pesticide impact assessment. *Mailing Add:* 1550 Beacon Hill Rd Lexington KY 40504

RODRIGUEZ, LUIS F, NUCLEAR & HAZARDOUS WASTE TREATMENT, MEDICAL DEVICES MANUFACTURING. *Current Pos:* DIR ENG, MEDTRONIC, INC, 89- *Personal Data:* b Arecibo, PR, Dec 30, 47; US citizen; m 72; c 2. *Educ:* Univ Puerto Rico, BS, 68; Univ Cincinnati, MS, 70, PhD(chem & nuclear eng), 72, Univ Santa Clara, MBA, 82. *Prof Exp:* Sr engr, Monsanto Res Corp, 73-74; sr engr, Gen Elec Co, Wilmington, NC, 74-78; Prod mgr, San Jose, Calif, 78-88; dir eng, Permutit Co, Zurn Ind, 88-89. *Mem:* Am Nuclear Soc; Am Inst Chem Engrs; Am Soc Qual Control. *Res:* Interested in hazardous waste treatment, water treatment and management of nuclear waste. *Mailing Add:* Medtronic PO Box 8687 Humacao PR 00792

RODRIGUEZ, ROCIO DEL PILAR, PHYTOPATHOLOGY. *Current Pos:* instr biol, Univ PR, 72-73, instr plant path, 79-83, asst prof, 88-94, assoc dir, Dept Crop Protection, 96-97, PROF PLANT PATH, UNIV PR, 95- *Personal Data:* b Rio Piedras, PR. *Educ:* Univ PR, BSc, 67, MSc, 72; Pa State Univ, PhD(plant path), 88. *Concurrent Pos:* Consult plant dis, Agr Exp Sta, 81-, prin investr & co-leader, 82-; chairperson, Thesis Comt, Univ PR, 89-; adv, Org Agr Proj, 91-92. *Mem:* Am Phytopath Soc. *Res:* Chemical control of fungal and bacterial diseases of beans, cowpeas, pigeon peas, citron, vegetables and coffee; host-parasite relations of knot disease of citron and root-rot of alfalfa; screened for resistance to coffee rust and pigeon pea foliar diseases; etiology of plant diseases. *Mailing Add:* Dept Plant Protection Col Agr Sci Univ PR Box 5000 Mayaquez PR 00709-5000

RODRIGUEZ, SERGIO, CONDENSED MATTER THEORY. *Current Pos:* assoc prof, 62-64, PROF PHYSICS, PURDUE UNIV, LAFAYETTE, 64- *Personal Data:* b Lautaro, Chile, Dec 12, 30; m 59, Caridad R Floro; c Cecilia R & Katrin M. *Educ:* Univ Calif, Berkeley, AB, 55, MA, 56, PhD, 58. *Honors & Awards:* Alexander von Humboldt Sr US Scientist Award, Alexander von Humboldt Stiftung, Bonn, Fed Repub Ger, 74. *Prof Exp:* Asst prof physics, Univ Wash, 58-59; res asst prof, Univ Ill, 59-60; asst prof, Purdue Univ, 60-61; asst prof elec eng, Princeton Univ, 61-62. *Concurrent Pos:* Consult, Ford Motor Co, Mich, 59-65, Argonne Nat Lab, 60-70, Int Bus Mach Corp, 67; fel, John Simon Guggenheim Mem, 67-68. *Mem:* Fel Am Phys Soc. *Res:* Solid state theory; statistical mechanics. *Mailing Add:* Dept Physics Purdue Univ West Lafayette IN 47907-1396. *Fax:* 765-494-0706; *E-Mail:* srf@physics. purdue.edu

RODRIGUEZ-ARIAS, JORGE H, AGRICULTURAL ENGINEERING. *Current Pos:* RETIRED. *Personal Data:* b Ponce, PR, Apr 24, 15; m 48, Carmen T Quinones-Sepulveda; c Jorge H, Jamie O & Nelson R. *Educ:* Univ PR, Mayaguez, BS, 36; Tex A&M Univ, BS, 45; Kans State Univ, MS, 47; Mich State Univ, PhD, 56. *Hon Degrees:* Dr, Univ PR, Mayaguez, 86. *Prof Exp:* Instr voc agr, PR Reconstruction Admin, Aibonito, 37-42; instr hort, Univ PR, Mayaguez, 37-43, from asst prof to prof agr eng, 47-77, dir, 48-77. *Mem:* Fel Am Soc Agr Engrs; Am Soc Eng Educ; Inst Food Technologists; fel Instnl Agr Engrs. *Res:* Agricultural engineering; horticulture; desorption isotherms and drying rates of shelled corn in the temperature range of 40 to 140 degrees f. *Mailing Add:* Univ PR Fac Residences 3-B PO Box 5158 College Sta Mayaguez PR 00681-5158

RODRIGUEZ-ITURBE, IGNACIO, CIVIL ENGINEERING. *Current Pos:* HEAD CHAIR & R P GREGORY PROF CIVIL ENG, TEX A&M UNIV, 93- *Personal Data:* b Caracas, Venezuela, Mar 8, 42. *Educ:* Univ Zulia, CE, 63; Calif Inst Technol, MS; Colo State Univ, PhD(eng), 67. *Mailing Add:* Civil Eng Dept Tex A&M Univ Rm 221 CETTI Tower College Station TX 77843

RODRIGUEZ-PARADA, JOSE MANUEL, POLYMER LIQUID CRYSTALS, POLYMERIC SURFACES & THIN FILMS. *Current Pos:* RES STAFF POLYMER SCI, DU PONT CENT RES & DEVELOP, 88- *Personal Data:* b Orense, Spain, May 4, 53; Venezuelan citizen; m 78, Yumally Sindoni; c Manuel. *Educ:* Universidad Metropolitana, Caracas, BS, 75; Case Western Res Univ, MS, 83, PhD(polymer sci), 86. *Prof Exp:* Instr polymer chem, Universidad Metropolitana, Caracas, Venezuela, 75-78; postdoctoral fel polymer sci, Max-Planck-Inst Fur Polymer Forschung, Mainz, Ger, 87-88. *Mem:* Am Chem Soc. *Res:* Polymer synthesis and characterization; cationic ring-opening polymerization; liquid crystalline polymers; amphiphilic polymers; polymeric surfaces and thin films; fluoropolymers. *Mailing Add:* Du Pont Cent Res & Develop Exp Sta PO Box 80328 Wilmington DE 19880-0328

RODRIGUEZ-SIERRA, JORGE F, NEUROENDOCRINOLOGY, NEUROSCIENCE. *Current Pos:* asst prof, 78-82, assoc prof, 82-89, PROF ANAT, MED CTR, UNIV NEBR, 89-, ADJ PROF PSYCHOL, 90- *Personal Data:* b Havana, Cuba, Sept 18, 45; m 85, Evonne Condon; c Marina, Jorge & Carlos. *Educ:* Calif State Col, Los Angeles, BA, 70; Calif State Univ, Los Angeles, MA, 72; Rutgers Univ, PhD(psychobiol), 76. *Prof Exp:* Fel neuroendocrinol, Wis Regional Primate Ctr, 76-77. *Concurrent Pos:* Fel anat, Med Ctr, Univ Nebr, 78; asst prof, Dept Psychol, Univ Nebr, Omaha, 79-82, assoc prof, 82-89; vis scientist, NIMH, 85, prof, 89- *Mem:* Endocrine Soc; Soc Neurosci; Soc Study Reproduction; Int Soc Neuroendocrinol; Cajal Club; Soc Exp Biol Med; Am Asn Anat. *Res:* Control of pituitary gland hormonal release by the brain; control of neural development by hormones; development of contraceptives; role of prostaglandins in behavior and pituitary function; neuroendocrinology of behavior; breast cancer. *Mailing Add:* Dept Cell Biol & Anat Univ Nebr Med Ctr Omaha NE 68198-6395. *Fax:* 402-559-7328; *E-Mail:* jrodrigu@mail.unmc.edu

RODWELL, JOHN DENNIS, MOLECULAR IMMUNOLOGY, MONOCLONAL ANTIBODIES. *Current Pos:* sr scientist, Cytogen Corp, 81-82, group leader, 82-84, dir chem res, vpres, Discovery Res, 87-89, VPRES, RES & DEVELOP, CYTOGEN CORP, 89- *Personal Data:* b Boston, Mass, Oct 9, 46; m 71; c 2. *Educ:* Univ Mass, Amherst, BA, 68; Lowell Tech Inst, MS, 71; Univ Calif, Los Angeles, PhD(biochem), 76. *Prof Exp:* Fel, Univ Pa Sch Med, 76-80, res asst prof microbiol, 80-81. *Concurrent*

Pos: Adj asst prof microbiol, Univ Pa Sch Med, 81-89, adj assoc prof, 89- *Mem:* Am Asn Immunologists; Am Chem Soc; AAAS. *Res:* Applications of monoclonal antibodies in in vivo diagnosis and therapy. *Mailing Add:* Cytogen Corp 307 Col Rd E CN 5309 Princeton NJ 08540-5309

RODWELL, VICTOR WILLIAM, BIOCHEMISTRY. *Current Pos:* assoc prof, 65-71, PROF BIOCHEM, PURDUE UNIV, WEST LAFAYETTE, 72- *Personal Data:* b London, Eng, Sept 10, 29; US citizen; m 52; c 4. *Educ:* Wilson Teachers Col, BS, 51; George Washington Univ, MS, 52; Univ Kans, PhD(biochem), 56. *Prof Exp:* USPHS fel biochem, Univ Calif, Berkeley, 56-58; asst prof, Med Ctr, Univ San Francisco, 58-65. *Mem:* Am Soc Biochem & Molecular Biol. *Res:* Regulation of 3-hydroxy-3-methylglutaryl-coenzyme A reductase and cholesterol biosynthesis. *Mailing Add:* Dept Biochem Purdue Univ West Lafayette IN 47907-1153. *Fax:* 765-494-7897

ROE, ARNOLD, engineering, for more information see previous edition

ROE, BENSON BERTHEAU, CARDIO-THORACIC SURGERY, CARDIOPULMONARY PHYSIOLOGY. *Current Pos:* asst clin prof, Sch Med, Univ Calif, 52-59, chief cardiac surg, 58-76, assoc prof, 59-68, prof surg, 65-89, chief thoracic & cardiac surg, 66, co-chief cardiothoractic surg, 77-87, EMER PROF SURG, SCH MED, UNIV CALIF, SAN FRANCISCO, 89- *Personal Data:* b Los Angeles, Calif, July 7, 18; m 45, Jane St John; c David B & Virginia. *Educ:* Univ Calif, AB, 39; Harvard Univ, MD, 43; Am Bd Surg, dipl; Am Bd Thoracic Surg, dipl. *Honors & Awards:* Silver Medal, Am Heart Asn. *Prof Exp:* Intern surg, Mass Gen Hosp, 43-44, from asst resident to resident, 46-50. *Concurrent Pos:* Nat Res Coun fel, Harvard Med Sch, 47-48; Moseley traveling fel, Univ Edinburgh, 51; vis thoracic surgeon, Vet Admin Hosp, Ft Miley; chief cardiothorasic surg, St Luke's Hosp, 52-58; vis surgeon, San Francisco Gen Hosp; chief cardiothorasic surg, St Josephs Hosp, 53-58; dir & chmn, Am Bd Thoracic Surg; vis prof, univs in US, Poland, Spain, England, Nigeria; sr mem, Cardiovasc Inst, Sch Med, Univ Calif, San Francisco, 58- *Mem:* Soc Vascular Surg (vpres); Soc Univ Surg; Am Asn Thoracic Surg; fel Am Col Surg; Am Surg Asn; Soc Thoracic Surgeons (vpres & pres, 72-73); hon mem Polish Surg Asn. *Res:* Cardiopulmonary physiology; author 173 articles including 2 textbooks, 18 textbook chapters, 1 Presidential Address. *Mailing Add:* Div Cardiothoracic Surg S 593 Univ Calif Sch Med San Francisco CA 94143-0118. *Fax:* 415-476-9678, 449-1354

ROE, BRUCE ALLAN, BIOCHEMISTRY, MOLECULAR BIOLOGY. *Current Pos:* PROF CHEM, UNIV OKLA, 81-, ADJ PROF, BIOCHEM & MOLECULAR BIOL, HEALTH SCI CTR. *Personal Data:* b New York, NY, Jan 01, 42; m 63; c 2. *Educ:* Hope Col, BA, 63; Western Mich Univ, MA, 67, PhD(chem), 70. *Prof Exp:* Teacher chem & physics, Marshall Pub Sch, Mich, 63-68; grad teaching fel chem & biochem, Western Mich Univ, 68-70; postdoctoral res fel biochem, State Univ NY, Stony Brook, 70-73; from asst prof to assoc prof chem, Kent State Univ, 73-81. *Concurrent Pos:* NIH fel, State Univ NY, Stony Brook, 71-72; NIH res grants, Kent State Univ, 74-81, Univ Okla, 81-, NIH res career develop fel, 76-81; res assoc prof, Col Med, Northeastern Ohio Univ, 77-81; Sabbatical res assoc, Med Res Coun, Cambridge, Eng, 78-79; sabbatical res, Med Res Coun, Cambridge, Eng, 90. *Mem:* AAAS; Am Soc Biol Chemists. *Res:* The role of modified nucleotides in mammalian transfer ribonucleic acids; structure of mammalian transfer ribonucleic acids; structure of mammalian oncogenes and transfer ribonucleic acid genes; structure and function of tumor transfer ribonucleic acids. *Mailing Add:* Dept Chem & Biochem Univ Ok 620 Parrington Oval Rm 208 Norman OK 73019. *Fax:* 405-325-6111

ROE, BYRON PAUL, ELEMENTARY PARTICLE PHYSICS. *Current Pos:* From instr to assoc prof, 59-69, PROF PHYSICS, UNIV MICH, ANN ARBOR, 69- *Personal Data:* b St Louis, Mo, Apr 4, 34; m 61, Alice S Krauss; c Kenneth & Diana. *Educ:* Wash Univ, AB, 54; Cornell Univ, PhD, 59. *Concurrent Pos:* Brit sci res fel, 79-80; vis scientist, CERN, 67-68 & 89-90; guest scientist, SSC, 91-92. *Mem:* Fel Am Phys Soc. *Res:* High energy physics; fundamental particles; weak interactions. *Mailing Add:* Dept Physics Univ Mich Ann Arbor MI 48109. *Fax:* 313-936-1817; *E-Mail:* byron.roe@umich.edu

ROE, DAVID CHRISTOPHER, NUCLEAR MAGNETIC RESONANCE. *Current Pos:* RES ASSOC, E I DU PONT DE NEMOURS & CO, 79- *Personal Data:* b Toronto, Ont, July 9, 48; m 97, Karen M Bloch. *Educ:* McGill Univ, BSc, 69; Univ Calif, Santa Barbara, PhD(chem), 74. *Prof Exp:* Teaching fel chem, Univ BC, 75-79. *Mem:* Am Chem Soc; Am Phys Soc; AAAS. *Res:* Nuclear magnetic resonance studies of slow exchange phenomena followed by magnetization transfer; gas phase nuclear magnetic resonance for studying heterogeneous catalysis. *Mailing Add:* Cent Res & Develop Du Pont Exp Sta PO Box 80328 Wilmington DE 19880-0328. *Fax:* 302-695-9799; *E-Mail:* roe@peyto.es.dupont.com

ROE, DAVID KELMER, electrochemistry, analytical chemistry, for more information see previous edition

ROE, GLENN DANA, GEOCHEMISTRY. *Current Pos:* sr res geologist, 64-71, supvr, Geochem Sect, 71-73, dir, 73-78, DIR MINERALS & GEOCHEM SECTS, ATLANTIC RICHFIELD CO, 78- *Personal Data:* b Danbury, Conn, Mar 5, 31; m 53; c 2. *Educ:* Tex Christian Univ, BA, 59, MA, 61; Mass Inst Technol, PhD(geochem), 65. *Prof Exp:* Asst astron, Mass Inst Technol, 62-63, asst geol, 63, asst geochronology, 63-64. *Mem:* Am Asn Petrol Geologists. *Res:* Isotopic study of earth mantle rocks, origin and age; geochemical study of sedimentary rocks and their correlation. *Mailing Add:* 7746 El Santo Lane Dallas TX 75248

ROE, JAMES MAURICE, JR, computer support & analysis, for more information see previous edition

ROE, PAMELA, ZOOLOGY. *Current Pos:* PROF BIOL SCI, CALIF STATE UNIV, STANISLAUS, 71- *Personal Data:* b San Angelo, Tex, Oct 18, 42. *Educ:* Univ Tex, Austin, BA, 65; Univ Wash, MS, 67, PhD(zool), 71. *Mem:* AAAS; Ecol Soc Am; Am Soc Zoologists; Am Soc Naturalists. *Res:* Marine invertebrate natural history and ecology; invertebrate zoology. *Mailing Add:* Dept Biol Sci Calif State Univ Stanislaus Turlock CA 95382

ROE, PETER HUGH O'NEIL, GRAPH THEORETIC SYSTEMS MODELLING & DESIGN, COMPUTER NETWORK DEVELOPMENT. *Current Pos:* Lectr math, Univ Waterloo, 60, lectr elec eng, 60-63, asst prof, 63-64, asst prof design & elec eng, 65, assoc prof, 65-69, assoc dean, eng, 77, 78 & 80-86, PROF SYSTS DESIGN, UNIV WATERLOO, 69- *Personal Data:* b Birmingham, Eng, May 18, 34; m 58; c 2. *Educ:* Univ Toronto, BASc, 59; Univ Waterloo, MSc, 60, PhD(elec eng), 63 , Univ Technol, Compeigne, France, Dipl, 76. *Concurrent Pos:* Vis asst prof, Thayer Sch Eng, Dartmouth Col, 63-64; consult, Inst Design, Univ Waterloo, 65-; vis assoc prof, NS Tech Col, 68-69; vis prof, Technol Univ Compiegne & Advan Sch Eng Marseilles, France, 74-75. *Mem:* Inst Elec & Electronics Engrs. *Res:* Systems theory (modelling and simulation), bond graphic, graph theory, matroids; computer operating systems, local area networks, theory of engineering design. *Mailing Add:* Dept Systs Design Univ Waterloo Waterloo ON N2L 3G1 Can

ROE, PHILIP LAWRENCE, COMPUTER ALGORITHMS FOR PREDICTING COMPLEX FLUID FLOW, AIRCRAFT DESIGN. *Current Pos:* PROF AEROSPACE ENG, UNIV MICH, 90- *Personal Data:* b Derby, UK, May 4, 38; m 68, Christine S Coley; c Natasha & Gerard. *Educ:* Cambnridge Univ, BA, 62. *Honors & Awards:* Group Achievement Award, NASA, 92. *Prof Exp:* Sci officer, Royal Aircraft Estab, 62-84; prof computational fluid dynamics, Cranfield Inst Technol, 84-90. *Concurrent Pos:* Consult, Inst Comput Appln Sci & Eng, NASA, 93-; adv ed, J Computational Physics, 95- *Mem:* Am Inst Aeronaut & Astronaut. *Res:* Foundations of algorithm design for fluid flow problems, based on close discrete mimicry of physical processes. *Mailing Add:* 7918 Mason Lane Whitmore Lake MI 48189

ROE, RYONG-JOON, POLYMER SCIENCE, PHYSICAL CHEMISTRY. *Current Pos:* assoc prof, 75-80, PROF MAT SCI & METALL ENG, UNIV CINCINNATI, 80- *Personal Data:* b Pyongyang, Korea, Mar 22, 29; US citizen; m 61; c 3. *Educ:* Seoul Nat Univ, BS, 52, MS, 55; Univ Manchester, PhD(polymer chem), 57. *Prof Exp:* Res chemist, Arthur D Little Res Inst, Inveresk, Scotland, 57-60; res assoc polymer chem, Duke Univ, 60-63; res chemist, E I du Pont de Nemours & Co, Inc, 63-68; mem tech staff, Bell Labs, Inc, 68-75. *Concurrent Pos:* Vis scholar, Centre Recherche Macromolecule, Strasbourg, France, 83-84; vis scholar, Max Plack Inst Breeding Polymer Res, Mainz, Ger, 92; dir, Polymer Res Ctr, Univ Cincinnati, 92-95. *Mem:* Fel Am Phys Soc; Am Chem Soc. *Res:* Physics and chemistry of polymers; thermodynamics of polymers; surface properties of polymers; application of x-ray diffraction to study of polymers; small-angle x-ray scattering; computer simulation of polymers. *Mailing Add:* Univ Cincinnati Mail Location 12 Cincinnati OH 45221-0012. *Fax:* 513-556-2569; *E-Mail:* r.j.roe@uc.edu

ROE, WILLIAM P(RICE), METALLURGY. *Current Pos:* RETIRED. *Personal Data:* b Dover, Del, Aug 25, 23; m 43; c 2. *Educ:* Vanderbilt Univ, AB, 47, MS, 48, PhD(metall, inorg chem), 52. *Prof Exp:* Process develop chemist, Carbide & Carbon Chems Co Div, Union Carbide Corp, 48-49; res metallurgist, Titanium Div, Nat Lead Co, 51-56; sr metallurgist, Southern Res Inst, 56-57; sect leader, Cent Res Labs, 57-60, res supt, 60-63, mgr, 63-69, dir, 69-74, vpres, Asarco, Inc, 74-86; dir, Int Lead Zinc Res Orgn, 72-86. *Concurrent Pos:* Chmn, Int Lead Res Orgn, 83-85; mem, comt vis, Sch Eng, Vanderbilt Univ, 84-; dir, ASA Ltd, 81- *Mem:* Am Soc Metals; Am Inst Mining, Metall & Petrol Engrs; Sigma Xi. *Res:* Metallurgy of nonferrous metals. *Mailing Add:* 320 San Juan Dr Ponte Vedra Beach FL 32082-1818

ROEBBER, JOHN LEONARD, PHYSICAL CHEMISTRY. *Current Pos:* asst prof, 64-70, ASSOC PROF CHEM, NORTHEASTERN UNIV, 70-, EXEC OFFICER, 76- *Personal Data:* b Bonne Terre, Mo, Mar 23, 31; m 55; c 3. *Educ:* Wash Univ, AB, 53; Univ Calif, PhD(chem), 57. *Prof Exp:* Sr chemist, Res Ctr, Texaco, Inc, NY, 57-64. *Mem:* Am Chem Soc. *Res:* Photochemistry; reaction kinetics; free radicals; infrared and ultraviolet spectroscopy; low temperature chemistry. *Mailing Add:* 77 Old Post Rd East Walpole MA 02032-1417

ROEBUCK, ISAAC FIELD, PETROLEUM ENGINEERING. *Current Pos:* PRES, ROEBUCK ASSOCS, INC, 88- *Personal Data:* b Graham, Tex, Sept 6, 30; m 57; c 1. *Educ:* Univ Tex, BS, 53, MS, 55. *Prof Exp:* From instr to asst prof petrol eng, Univ Tex, 54-57; petrol reservoir eng, Core Lab, Inc, 57-58; sr reservoir engr, 58-59, supv petrol engr, 59-61, asst mgr eng, 61-70; vpres & gen mgr, Eng Numerics Corp, 71-73; mgr educ serv, Core Labs, Inc, 74-78; pres, Roebuck-Walton, Inc, 79-88. *Concurrent Pos:* Chmn continuing educ, Soc Petrol Engrs, 84-85; adj prof geol sci, Southern Methodist Univ, 82- *Mem:* Soc Petrol Engrs; Am Asn Petrol Geologists; AAAS; Soc Independent Prof Engrs. *Res:* Flow through porous media; improved oil recovery; computer science; petroleum economics and risk analysis. *Mailing Add:* 6960 Joyce Way Dallas TX 75225

ROECKER, ROBERT MAAR, VERTEBRATE ZOOLOGY. *Current Pos:* RETIRED. *Personal Data:* b US, Nov 30, 22; m 58. *Educ:* Cornell Univ, BS, 47, MS, 48, PhD(zool), 51. *Prof Exp:* Biologist, NY State Dept Conserv, 50-62; assoc prof, 70-77, prof biol, State Univ NY Col Geneseo, 70-85. *Mem:* Am Soc Mammal; Wildlife Soc; Am Soc Ichthyologists & Herpetologists. *Res:* Life history of gray squirrel; life history and management work on New York waters; mammalogy; ichthyology; herpetology; wildlife and natural resource conservation; vertebrate taxonomy. *Mailing Add:* 4309 Reservoir Rd Geneseo NY 14454

ROEDDER, EDWIN WOODS, GEOCHEMISTRY. *Current Pos:* ASSOC, DEPT EARTH & PLANETARY SCI, HARVARD UNIV, 87- *Personal Data:* b Monsey, NY, July 30, 19; wid, Kathleen Rea; c Spencer & Lucy A. *Educ:* Lehigh Univ, BA, 41; Columbia Univ, AM, 47, PhD(geol), 50. *Hon Degrees:* DSc, Lehigh Univ, 76. *Honors & Awards:* Except Sci Achievement Medal, NASA, 73; Werner Medal, German Mineral Asn, 85; Roebling Medal, Mineral Soc Am, 86; Penrose Medal, Soc Econ Geologists, 88; H C Sorby Medal, 93. *Prof Exp:* Res engr, Bethlehem Steel Co, Pa, 41-46; asst geol, Columbia Univ, 46-49; from asst prof to assoc prof mineral, Univ Utah, 50-55; chief, Solid State Group, Geochemical & Petrol Br, US Geol Surv, 55-60, staff geologist, 60-62, geologist, 62-87. *Concurrent Pos:* Mem, Comt Geochemical Res, NSF, 54-55. *Mem:* Nat Acad Sci; Soc Econ Geol; Mineral Soc Am (vpres, 81-82, pres, 82-83); Am Geophys Union; Geochem Soc (pres, 76-77). *Res:* Ore deposition; fluid inclusions in minerals; studies of lunar materials; nuclear waste storage problems; volcanology. *Mailing Add:* Dept Earth & Planetary Sci Harvard Univ Cambridge MA 02138. *Fax:* 617-495-8839

ROEDEL, GEORGE FREDERICK, POLYMER CHEMISTRY. *Current Pos:* RETIRED. *Personal Data:* b Saginaw, Mich, July 1, 16; m 42; c 3. *Educ:* Valparaiso Univ, BS, 38; Purdue Univ, MS, 40, PhD(agr chem), 42. *Prof Exp:* Asst, Purdue Univ, 42; assoc, Res Lab, Gen Elec Co, 43-50; vpres, Tewes-Roedel Plastics Corp, 50-55; prod engr, Chem Mat Dept, 55-56, mgr chem & insulation, AC Motor & Generator Lab, 56-60, specialist silicone resin chem, Silicone Prod Dept, Gen Elec Co, 60-83. *Concurrent Pos:* Assoc prof, Carroll Col, Wis, 50-55. *Mem:* Am Chem Soc. *Res:* Composition and properties of oils and fats; methyl silicone resins; silicone rubber; copolymerization of vinyl silicon compounds; boron chemistry; suspension polymerization of chlorotrifluoroethylene; research and development on silicone resins. *Mailing Add:* 2178 Apple Tree Lane Schenectady NY 12309-4739

ROEDER, BEVERLY LOUISE, CALCIUM & PHOSPHORUS METABOLISM IN RUMINANTS, RUMINANT ACID-BASE BALANCE. *Current Pos:* ASSOC PROF ANIMAL SCI & UNIV VET, BRIGHAM YOUNG UNIV, 90- *Personal Data:* b Newark, Ohio, June 24, 56; m, Karl W Sant; c Jessica A. *Educ:* Wittenberg, Univ, BA, 78; Ohio State Univ, DVM, 82; Kans State Univ, MS, 86; Pa State Univ, PhD(vet sci), 90. *Prof Exp:* Res technician cancer chemother, Battelle Mem Inst, 76-79; assoc vet, Village Vet Clin, 82-84; food animal med resident & clin instr, Kans State Univ, 84-86; res asst, Pa State Univ, 86-90. *Concurrent Pos:* Prin investr bovine metab dis, Brigham Young Univ, 90- *Mem:* Am Vet Med Asn; Am Asn Bovine Practrs; Am Asn Small Ruminant Practrs; NAm Vet Technician Asn; Conf Res, Workers Animal Dis. *Res:* Bovine metabolic disorders using acid-base balance, calcium and phosphorous metabolism, renal function and osmolality of body fluids to prevent and/or detect these abnormalities; investigations of food animal infectious diseases. *Mailing Add:* Dept Animal Sci 386 WIDB Brigham Young Univ Provo UT 84602. *Fax:* 801-378-4211; *E-Mail:* beverly_roeder@byu.edu

ROEDER, CHARLES WILLIAM, STEEL STRUCTURES, SEISMIC DESIGN. *Current Pos:* PROF CIVIL ENG, UNIV WASH, 77- *Personal Data:* b Hershey, Pa, Oct 12, 42; m 69, Nancy L Newman; c Michael T. *Educ:* Univ Colo, Boulder, BS, 69; Univ Ill, Urbana, MS, 71; Univ Calif, Berkeley, PhD(civil eng), 77. *Honors & Awards:* J James Croes Medal, Am Soc Civil Engrs, 79, Raymond C Reese Prize, 84. *Prof Exp:* Struct engr, J Ray McDermott, Inc, 71-74; res asst, Univ Calif, 74-77. *Concurrent Pos:* Prin investr, NSF, Nat Acad Sci, & Am Inst Steel Construct, 77-; chmn, tech comts, Am Soc Civil Engrs, 83-96 & Comt Steel Bridges, Transp Res Bd, 90- *Mem:* Am Soc Civil Engrs; Earthquake Eng Res Inst; Am Inst Steel Construct; Am Welding Soc. *Res:* Structural engineering; seismic behavior of steel structures; thermal movements in bridges; behavior of bridge bearings; heat straightening and curving of steel; inelastic behavior of steel structures; seismic rehabilitation. *Mailing Add:* Univ Wash 233 B More Hall FX-10 Seattle WA 98195

ROEDER, DAVID WILLIAM, PURE MATHEMATICS. *Current Pos:* from asst prof to assoc prof, 70-85, chmn dept, 75-85, PROF MATH, COLO COL, 85- *Personal Data:* b Philadelphia, Pa, June 19, 39; m 66; c 2. *Educ:* Univ NMex, BS, 60; Univ Calif, Berkeley, MA, 62, Univ Calif, Santa Barbara, PhD(math), 68. *Prof Exp:* John Wesley Young Res Instr Math, Dartmouth Col, 68-70. *Mem:* Am Math Soc; Math Asn Am. *Res:* Duality theory of locally compact groups and topological groups; number theory and quadratic forms. *Mailing Add:* Colo Col 14 E Cache La Poudre Colorado Springs CO 80903-3294

ROEDER, EDWARD A, SOLID STATE PHYSICS. *Current Pos:* Asst prof, 67-74, ASSOC PROF PHYSICS, MORAVIAN COL, 74- *Personal Data:* b Sellersville, Pa, Apr 25, 39. *Educ:* Lafayette Col, BS, 61; Lehigh Univ, MS, 63, PhD(physics), 67. *Mem:* Am Asn Physics Teachers. *Res:* Transport number measurements in silver chloride at high temperatures. *Mailing Add:* Dept Physics Moravian Col Main St & Elizabeth Ave Bethlehem PA 18018

ROEDER, LOIS M, PEDIATRICS. *Current Pos:* ASSOC PROF PEDIAT, DEPT PEDIAT, SCH PHARM & SCH MED, UNIV MD, 73- *Personal Data:* b 1932. *Educ:* Johns Hopkins Univ, ScD, 71. *Mem:* Am Soc Neurochemistry; Am Inst Nutrit. *Res:* Metabolic aspects of brain development; etiology of sudden infant death syndrome. *Mailing Add:* 116 Forest Ave Baltimore MD 21228. *Fax:* 410-706-0020

ROEDER, MARTIN, PHYSIOLOGY, BIOCHEMISTRY. *Current Pos:* from asst dean to actg dean arts & sci, 66-74, from assoc prof to prof, 64-95, EMER PROF BIOL SCI, FLA STATE UNIV, 95- *Personal Data:* b Long Branch, NJ, Aug 19, 25; m 57, Rachel Haralson; c Renee (Benjamin) & Karl M. *Educ:* Queens Col, NY, BS, 48; Univ NMex, MS, 51; Univ NC, PhD(zool), 54. *Prof Exp:* Asst biol, Univ NMex, 49-51; US Am Educ Coalition fel, Univ NC, 51-53, asst zool, 53-54; asst prof chem, Woman's Col NC, 54-56, biol, 56-59, assoc prof, 59-64. *Concurrent Pos:* Vpres finance & admin, Fla State Univ, 90-91. *Mem:* Fel AAAS; Am Soc Zoologists; Soc Gen Physiol; Asn Southeastern Biologists; Sigma Xi. *Res:* Cellular physiology; enzyme induction; gene-enzyme relationships; respiratory activity of tumor cells; mineral nutrition; bioluminescence and evolutionary significance of bioluminescence. *Mailing Add:* Dept Biol Sci Fla State Univ Tallahassee FL 32306-2043

ROEDER, PETER LUDWIG, geochemistry, petrology, for more information see previous edition

ROEDER, ROBERT CHARLES, ULTRAVIOLET IRRADIANCE, OZONE. *Current Pos:* PROF PHYSICS, SOUTHWESTERN UNIV, 83- *Personal Data:* b Stratford, Ont, Oct 7, 37; US citizen; m 61, Dagmar Katterfeld; c Robert Jr & Thomas. *Educ:* McMaster Univ, BSc, 59; MSc, 60; Univ Ill, PhD(astrophys), 63. *Prof Exp:* Instr astron, Univ Ill, 62-63; asst prof physics, Queens Univ, 63-64; from asst prof to prof astron, Univ Toronto, 64-83. *Concurrent Pos:* Consult, Kitt Peak Nat Observ, 71-72; vis prof physics, Univ Tex, Austin, 79-80. *Mem:* Am Asn Physics Teachers; Am Astron Soc; Am Phys Soc; Am Geophys Union. *Res:* Measurement program to monitor solar ultraviolet irradiance at this location and compare to theoretical predictions. *Mailing Add:* Southwestern Univ Georgetown TX 78627. *Fax:* 512-863-5788; *E-Mail:* roeder@southwestern.edu

ROEDER, ROBERT GAYLE, NUCLEIC ACID BIOCHEMISTRY. *Current Pos:* prof, 82-85, HEAD, LAB BIOCHEM & MOLECULAR BIOL, ROCKEFELLER UNIV, 82-, ARNOLD O & MABEL S BECKMAN PROF, 85- *Personal Data:* b Boonville, Ind, June 3, 42; m 90; c 2. *Educ:* Wabash Col, Ind, BA, 64; Univ Ill, Urbana, MS, 65; Univ Wash, Seattle, PhD(biochem), 69. *Hon Degrees:* DSc, Wabash Col, 90. *Honors & Awards:* Eli Lilly Award Biol Chem, Am Chem Soc, 77; US Steel Found Award Molecular Biol, Nat Acad Sci, 86; Harvey Soc Lectr, 88; Lewis S Rosentiel Award, 95; Passano Award, 95. *Prof Exp:* Pre-doctoral fel, US Pub Health Serv, 65-69; from asst prof to prof biol chem, Sch Med, Wash Univ, 71-82, prof genetics, 78-82, James S McDonnell prof biochem genetics, 79-82. *Concurrent Pos:* Gilbert Scholar, Wabash Col, 60-64; fel, Am Cancer Soc, Carnegie Inst Wash, 69-71; NIH res career develop award, 73-78; mem, Molecular Biol Study Sect, NIH, 75; James S McDonnell prof biochem genetics, 79-82, Arnold & Mabel Beckman prof biochem & molecular biol, 85-; chairperson, Gordon Res Conf Nucleic Acids, 82; consult, Am Cancer Soc, 83-86; outstanding investr award, Nat Cancer Inst, 86- *Mem:* Nat Acad Sci; Am Soc Biol Chemists; Am Soc Microbiologists; AAAS; Am Chem Soc; fel NY Acad Sci; Harvey Soc; fel Am Acad Microbiol; fel Am Acad Arts & Sci; fel NY Acad Sci; Am Soc Biochem & Molecular Biol; Am Soc Virol; Soc Develop Biol; Protein Soc. *Res:* Regulation of gene expression during cellular growth, differentiation, and transformation; isolation and mechanistic analysis of cellular and viral factors involved in transcriptional control; role of cellular and viral-coded transcriptional activators in HIV replication and pathogenesis. *Mailing Add:* Rockefeller Univ 1230 York Ave New York NY 10021-6399

ROEDER, STEPHEN BERNHARD WALTER, NUCLEAR MAGNETIC RESONANCE, SCIENTIFIC INSTRUMENTATION. *Current Pos:* from asst prof to assoc prof, San Diego State Univ, 68-74, chmn dept, 75-78, chmn dept chem, 79-86, dir, MLA Prog, 86-87 & 89-90, chmn, Dept Physics, 91-94, PROF PHYSICS & CHEM, SAN DIEGO STATE UNIV, 74-, CHMN DEPT CHEM, 95- *Personal Data:* b Dover, NJ, Aug 26, 39; m 69, Phoebe Barber; c Adrienne & Roland. *Educ:* Dartmouth Col, BA, 61; Univ Wis, PhD(chem), 65. *Prof Exp:* Mem tech staff, Bell Labs, Inc, 65-66; instr physics, Univ Ore, 66-68. *Concurrent Pos:* Fel chem, Univ Ore, 66-68; vis prof, Univ BC, 74-75 & Tex A&M Univ, 82; vis staff mem, Los Alamos Sci Lab, 74-91; consult, Lovelace Med Found, 86-88. *Mem:* AAAS; Am Chem Soc; Am Phys Soc; Sigma Xi. *Res:* Pulsed nuclear magnetic resonance; instrumentation; magnetoencephalography. *Mailing Add:* Dept Physics San Diego State Univ San Diego CA 92182-1030. *Fax:* 619-594-4634; *E-Mail:* sroeder@sciences.sdsu.edu

ROEDERER, JUAN GUALTERIO, SPACE PHYSICS, PSYCHOACOUSTICS. *Current Pos:* dir, Geophys Inst, 77-86, prof, 86-93, EMER PROF, UNIV ALASKA, 93- *Personal Data:* b Trieste, Italy, Sept 2, 29; US citizen; m 52, Beatriz Cougnet; c Ernesto, Irene, Silvia & Mario. *Educ:* Univ Buenos Aires, DSc(physics), 52. *Prof Exp:* Teaching asst physics, Univ Buenos Aires, 52-53; res asst high energy physics, Max Planck Inst, 53-55; prof physics, Univ Buenos Aires, 56-67; prof, Univ Denver, 67-77. *Concurrent Pos:* Vis staff mem, Dept Energy, Los Alamos Sci Lab, 68-86; pres, Sci Comn Solar Terrestrial Physics, Int Coun Sci Unions, 86-90; mem, polar res bd, Nat Acad Sci, 80-84, atmosphere sci & climate bd, 83-85; chmn, US Arctic Res Comn, 87-91. *Mem:* Fel Am Geophys Union; Arg Geophys Soc; Acoustical Soc Am; Int Asn Geomag & Aeronomy (pres, 75-79); fel AAAS; Acad Sci Agr; assoc fel Third World Acad Sci. *Res:* Physics of the Magnetosphere, particularly radiation belts, diffusion of trapped particles; psychoacoustics; perception of musical sounds; science policy. *Mailing Add:* 105 Concordia Dr Fairbanks AK 99709-3029. *Fax:* 907-474-5517

ROEDERER, MARIO, GENETICS, IMMUNOLOGY. *Current Pos:* FEL GENETICS, STANFORD UNIV, 88- *Personal Data:* b Buenos Aires, Arg, Apr 30, 63; US citizen. *Educ:* Harvey Mudd Col, BS, 83; Carnegie-Mellon Univ, PhD(biol sci), 88. *Prof Exp:* Res asst, Carnegie-Mellon Univ, 83-88. *Concurrent Pos:* Spec fel, Leukemia Soc Am, Inc, 91- *Mem:* Am Soc Cell Biol; AAAS; Sigma Xi. *Res:* Regulation of mammalian gene expression by inflammatory cytokines and intracellular thiols, especially that of the human immunodeficiency virus; advanced flow cytometric tools for measurement of gene expression during development, especially in the immune system. *Mailing Add:* 1531 Todd St Mountain View CA 94040

ROEGER, ANTON, III, TECHNICAL MANAGEMENT, FUEL TECHNOLOGY & CHEMICAL ENGINEERING. *Current Pos:* RETIRED. *Personal Data:* b Philadelphia, Pa, Oct 19, 35; m 67, Helene Mercier; c 2. *Educ:* Lehigh Univ, BS, 57; Pa State Univ, MS, 59; Univ Va, DSc(chem eng), 63. *Prof Exp:* Res engr, Indust Chem Div, Res & Develop Lab, Shell Chem Co, Deer Park, 62-71; sr engr, Tex Eastern Transmission Corp, 71-77, res adv, 77-78, coordr, Res & Technol Div, 78-80, tech mgr, Synfuels Div, 80-84, tech mgr, Res & Bus Develop Div, 84-86, prog mgr energy utilization, 86-89, tech mgr, Corp Environ Div, 89. *Mem:* Am Inst Chem Engrs; Sigma Xi. *Res:* Synthetic gaseous and liquid fuels; chemicals; two phase flow; radiation chemistry; process research and development; cogeneration of steam and electricity. *Mailing Add:* 4618 Shatner Dr Houston TX 77066-2658

ROEHL, PERRY OWEN, PETROLEUM GEOLOGY. *Current Pos:* Herndon distinguished prof, 81-93, EMER HERNDON DISTINGUISHED PROF GEOL, TRINITY UNIV, SAN ANTONIO, TEX, 93- *Personal Data:* b Detroit, Mich, Jan 2, 25; m 52, Mary Holderness; c Eric, Roger, Diana & Kurt. *Educ:* Ohio State Univ, BS, 50; Stanford Univ, MS, 52; Univ Wis, PhD(geol), 55. *Prof Exp:* Exploitation engr, Shell Oil Co, 55-57, from prod geologist to sr prod geologist, 57-62, sr prod geologist, Shell Oil Co Can, Ltd, 62, res geologist, Shell Develop Co, 62-66; res assoc, Union Oil Co Calif, 66-75; consult, 75-81. *Concurrent Pos:* Chmn carbonate adv comt, Am Petrol Inst, 70-75; Esso vis distinguished lectr, Earth Resources Found, Australia, 86. *Mem:* Fel Geol Soc Am; Am Asn Petrol Geol; Soc Econ Paleont & Mineral; Am Inst Prof Geol; Sigma Xi; Soc Independent Prof Earth Scientists (vpres, 95-97, pres, 97-). *Res:* Carbonate geology, recent sedimentation; petroleum geology; paleoecology; sedimentary petrography; petrophysics; invertebrate paleontology; stratigraphy; marine geology; geological engineering; geophysical transfer technology. *Mailing Add:* 410 Ridge Bluff San Antonio TX 78216. *Fax:* 210-496-3940

ROEHRIG, FREDERICK KARL, PHYSICAL METALLURGY, METALLURGICAL ENGINEERING. *Current Pos:* VPRES, GELLES LABS, INC, 87- *Personal Data:* b Peoria, Ill, June 25, 42; m 67. *Educ:* Bradley Univ, BS, 65; Univ Ill, MS, 67; Ohio State Univ, PhD(metall eng), 76. *Prof Exp:* Res metallurgist, Battelle-Columbus Lab, 67-72; res assoc metallurgy, Owens-Corning Fiberglas Tech Ctr, 76-87. *Mem:* Sigma Xi; Am Soc Metals; Am Inst Mining, Metall & Petrol Eng; Am Powder Metall Inst; Nat Soc Prof Eng. *Res:* Physical metallurgy of high temperature alloys, particularly powder metallurgy; failure analysis of ferrous-non-ferrous alloy systems; field-freezing and electrotransport; patents. *Mailing Add:* 4800 Hayden Blvd Columbus OH 43221

ROEHRIG, GERALD RALPH, ORGANIC & PHYSICAL CHEMISTRY, ENVIRONMENTAL SCIENCE. *Current Pos:* PRES, ROEHRIG & ASSOCS, INC, 93-; SR SCIENTIST, BPF, INC, 93- *Personal Data:* b Aurora, Ill, Nov 2, 41; m 63; c 3. *Educ:* Aurora Col, BS, 63; Univ Ky, MS, 65; Ind Univ, PhD(org chem), 70. *Prof Exp:* Asst prof chem, Aurora Col, 65-75, prof, 75-79; from asst prof to assoc prof, Oral Roberts Univ, 79-87; chief chemist, Calabrian Chems, 87-89; dir sci & technol & sr res scientist, Itex Enterprises, 89-91; mgr, Dallas Lab, Scientech Inc, 92-93; tech specialist, EG&G SSC, 93-95. *Concurrent Pos:* Chmn, Dept Chem, Aurora Col, 70-79, chmn, Div Natural Sci, 74-79, res dir, Res Corp, 76-79; educ consult, Argonne Nat Lab, 71-77; consult, Process Systs Div, John Zink Co, 80-82. *Mem:* Fel Am Inst Chemists; Am Chem Soc; Am Soc Qual Control. *Res:* Chemical and environmental areas; environmental quality assusance. *Mailing Add:* 2306 Stonebrook Circle Carrollton TX 75007-5726

ROEHRIG, JIMMY RICHARD, COLLIDING BEAM PHYSICS. *Current Pos:* RES ASSOC, STANFORD LINEAR ACCELERATOR CTR, 78- *Personal Data:* b Yokohama, Japan, Oct 12, 49. *Educ:* Univ Chicago, BA, 71, PhD(physics), 77. *Prof Exp:* Res assoc, Univ Chicago, 77-78. *Mailing Add:* 28 Roosevelt Circle Palo Alto CA 94306

ROEHRIG, JOHN T, MICROBIOLOGY, INFECTIOUS DISEASES. *Current Pos:* staff fel, Div Vector-Borne Infectious Dis, Ctr Dis Control & Prev, 80-81, res microbiologist, 81-84, SUPVRY RES MICROBIOLOGIST, DIV VECTOR-BORNE INFECTIOUS DIS, CTR DIS CONTROL & PREV, 84-, CHIEF, IMMUNOCHEM BR/SECT, 85-, ARBOVIRUS DIS BR, 94- *Educ:* Univ Ill, Urbana, BS, 73; Univ Mo, Columbia, PhD(microbiol), 77. *Prof Exp:* NIH trainee, Washington Univ Sch Med, St Louis, 78-79. *Concurrent Pos:* Affil fac mem, Dept Microbiol, Colo State Univ, 81-; grantee, US Army, 87-90, NATO, 87-90 & WHO, 89-91. *Mem:* AAAS; Am Soc Virol; Am Soc Microbiol; Sigma Xi; Protein Soc; Am Peptide Soc; Am Soc Trop Med & Hyg. *Res:* Immunology of infectious diseases; virology; published over 65 articles. *Mailing Add:* Nat Ctr Infectious Dis Ctr Dis Control Div Vector-Borne Infectious Dis PO Box 2087 Ft Collins CO 80522-2087. *E-Mail:* jtr1@cidvbil.em.cdc.gov

ROEHRIG, KARLA LOUISE, BIOCHEMISTRY & CELL BIOLOGY, NUTRITION. *Current Pos:* Res asst nutrit biochem, Inst Nutrit, Ohio State Univ, 67-71 & Dept Food Sci & Nutrit, 71-75, asst prof, 78-83, ASSOC PROF NUTRIT BIOCHEM, DEPT FOOD SCI & NUTRIT, OHIO STATE UNIV, 83- *Personal Data:* b Sycamore, Ill, Aug 18, 46; m 67. *Educ:* Univ Ill, BS, 67; Ohio State Univ, PhD(phys chem), 77. *Prof Exp:* res assoc biochem, Sch Med, Ind Univ, 77-78. *Concurrent Pos:* Showalter fel, Dept Biochem, Sch Med, Ind Univ, 77-78; bd mem, Columbus Zool Asn; vis scientist, Dundee Sch Med, Scotland, 80; vis prof, Army Med Serv Corps, Ger, 91; dir res comt, Cent Ohio Diabetes Asn, 96- *Mem:* Am Diabetes Asn; Am Heart Asn; Am Soc Biochem & Molecular Biol; Sigma Xi (pres, 90-91); Am Soc Nutrit Sci. *Res:* Metabolic regulation, especially dietary and hormonal control of enzymes involved in carbohydrate and lipid metabolism; mechanisms of insulin action; enzyme control mechanisms; cytokine regulation of lipogenesis. *Mailing Add:* Dept Food Sci & Nutrit 2121 Fyffe Rd Columbus OH 43210. *E-Mail:* roehrig.1@osu.edu

ROEL, LAWRENCE EDMUND, NEUROCHEMISTRY, NEUROPHARMACOLOGY. *Current Pos:* OPHTHALMOLOGIST, 94- *Personal Data:* b Brooklyn, NY, Aug 19, 49. *Educ:* Princeton Univ, AB, 71; Mass Inst Technol, PhD(nutrit biochem), 76. *Prof Exp:* Fel neurosci, Univ Calif, San Diego, 76-78; asst prof anat, Med Sch, Northwestern Univ, 78-81; med internship, Montefiore Hosp, 85-86; pvt group pract, Spartanburg, SC, 89-94. *Mem:* Soc Neuroscience; Am Chem Soc; NY Acad Sci; Sigma Xi; Am Acad Ophthal. *Res:* Regulation of protein synthesis in neurons and glia; effects of neurotransmitter release; neuronal recognition and synaptogenesis. *Mailing Add:* 735 E Main St Spartanburg SC 29302

ROELFS, ALAN PAUL, PLANT PATHOLOGY. *Current Pos:* Plant pathologist, Coop Rust Lab, Plant Protection Div, Agr Res Serv, USDA, 65-69, res plant pathologist, Cereal Rust Lab, Plant Protection Progs, Animal & Plant Health Inspection Serv, 69-75, SUPVRY RES PLANT PATHOLOGIST, CEREAL RUST LAB, AGR RES SERV, USDA, 75- *Personal Data:* b Stockton, Kans, Nov 18, 36; m 83, LuAnne B Martell; c Ravi P, David A, Judith L (Bertram), Lorene M (Finch) & Rekha L. *Educ:* Kans State Univ, BS, 59, MS, 64; Univ Minn, St Paul, PhD(plant path), 70. *Concurrent Pos:* Prof, Univ Minn. *Mem:* Fel Am Phytopathol Soc; AAAS; Int Asn Aeriobiol; US Fedn Culture Collections; Int Soc Plant Path; hon mem Can Phytopathol Soc. *Res:* Cereal rust epidemiology and physiological race distribution; resistance to the cereal rusts. *Mailing Add:* Cereal Rust Lab Univ Minn St Paul MN 55108

ROELLIG, HAROLD FREDERICK, PALEONTOLOGY. *Current Pos:* RETIRED. *Personal Data:* b Detroit, Mich, Apr 23, 30; m 59; c 4. *Educ:* Concordia Col, Mo, BA, 54; Concordia Sem, dipl theol, 57; Columbia Univ, PhD(geol), 67. *Prof Exp:* Campus chaplain, Lutheran Church, Mo Synod, 60-69; chmn, Earth Sci Dept, Adelphi Univ, 78-81, assoc prof geol, 69-83. *Mem:* Paleont Soc; Soc Vert Paleont; Sigma Xi. *Res:* Philosophical and theological interpretation of evolutionary phenomena; evolution and paleoecological interpretation of marine faunas. *Mailing Add:* 14520 Ferns Corner Rd Monmouth OR 97361-9707

ROELLIG, LEONARD OSCAR, POSITRON ANNIHILATION, SURFACE & ATOMIC PHYSICS. *Current Pos:* vchancellor acad affairs, 78-83, prof physics, 78-96, EMER PROF PHYSICS, CITY COL NEW YORK, 97- *Personal Data:* b Detroit, Mich, May 17, 27; m 52, Pauline Cowdin; c Thomas Leonard, Mark Douglas & Paul David. *Educ:* Univ Mich, AB, 50, MS, 55, PhD(physics), 59. *Prof Exp:* Asst, Univ Mich, 53-58; from asst prof to prof physics, Wayne State Univ, 58-78, dean acad admin, 71-72, assoc provost physics, 72-76. *Concurrent Pos:* Consult, High Energy Physics Div, Argonne Nat Lab, 59-62, Space Tech Lab, 62-63 & Gen Motors Res Lab, 69-71; dir sci res prog, Inner City High Sch Students, 67-71; vis prof, Univ Col, Univ London, 68-69 & Tata Inst Fundamental Res, Bombay, India, 73; pres, Cent Solar Energy Res Corp, 77; physicist, Paul Scherrer Inst, Villigen, Switz, 91-92. *Mem:* Am Phys Soc; NY Acad Sci. *Res:* Solid state studies using position and positronium beams, materials research; atomic physics. *Mailing Add:* 4520 Sioux Dr Boulder CO 80303. *E-Mail:* loroellig@aol.com

ROELOF, EDMOND C, SPACE PHYSICS. *Current Pos:* PRIN PROF STAFF, APPL PHYSICS LAB, JOHNS HOPKINS UNIV, 74- *Personal Data:* b Evanston, Ill, Oct 2, 37. *Educ:* Univ Calif, Los Angeles, AB, 59; Univ Calif, Berkeley, PhD(physics), 66. *Prof Exp:* staff, Boeing Sci Lab, 64-67; Nat Acad Sci-NASA postdoctoral res assoc, Goddard Space Flight Ctr, NASA, Greenbelt, Md, 67-69; asst prof physics, Univ NH, 69-74. *Mem:* Am Geophys Union. *Mailing Add:* Appl Physics Lab Johns Hopkins Univ Johns Hopkins Rd Laurel MD 20723-6099. *Fax:* 301-953-6670; *E-Mail:* edmond.roelof@jhuapl.edu

ROELOFS, LYLE D, MATHEMATICS. *Current Pos:* PROF & CHAIR PHYSICS, HAVERFORD COL, 82- *Personal Data:* b Grand Rapids, Mich, Dec 19, 53; m 75, Lauren Mulder; c Christopher D & Brian A. *Educ:* Calvin Col, BS, 75; Univ Md, MS, 78, PhD(physics), 80. *Prof Exp:* Fel, Brown Univ, 80-82. *Concurrent Pos:* Alexander von Humboldt Found fel, Ger, 85. *Mem:* Am Phys Soc; Am Vacuum Soc; Coun Undergrad Res. *Res:* Surface reconstruction and other phenomena associated with metallic surfaces; studied via total energy calculations and computer simulation. *Mailing Add:* One Featherbed Lane Haverford PA 19041. *Fax:* 610-896-4904; *E-Mail:* lroelofs@haverford.edu

ROELOFS, TERRY DEAN, FISHERIES. *Current Pos:* Asst prof, 71-74, assoc prof, 74-78, PROF FISHERIES, HUMBOLDT STATE UNIV, 78- *Personal Data:* b Manistique, Mich, Nov 3, 42. *Educ:* Mich State Univ, BS, 65; Univ Wash, MS, 67; Ore State Univ, PhD(fisheries), 71. *Mem:* AAAS; Am Fisheries Soc; Am Soc Limnol & Oceanog. *Res:* Water pollution biology; fisheries ecology and limnology; anadromous salmonid ecology and management techniques designed to increase the natural production of these fishes through habitat rehabilitation and enhancement. *Mailing Add:* Fisheries Humboldt State Univ 1 Harps St Arcata CA 95521-8299

ROELOFS, THOMAS HARWOOD, electrical engineering; deceased, see previous edition for last biography

ROELOFS, WENDELL L, INSECT COMMUNICATIONS SYSTEM. *Current Pos:* from asst prof to prof, 65-78, LIBERTY HYDE BAILEY PROF INSECT BIOCHEM, NY STATE AGR EXP STA, DEPT ENTOMOL, CORNELL UNIV, 78-, CHMN DEPT, 91- *Personal Data:* b Orange City, Iowa, July 26, 38; m 89, Donna Gray; c Brenda J, Caryn J, Jeffrey L & Kevin J. *Educ:* Cent Col, Iowa, BA, 60; Ind Univ, Bloomington, PhD(org chem), 64; Mass Inst Technol, Cambridge, 65. *Hon Degrees:* DSc, Cent Col, 85, Hobart & William Smith Cols, 88, Ind Univ, 88, Univ Lund, Sweden, 89, Free Univ Brussels, Belg, 89. *Honors & Awards:* J Everett Bussart Award, Entomol Soc Am, 73; Alexander von Humboldt Award, 77; Am Boyce Mem Lectr, Univ Calif, Riverside; Wolf Prize, 82; Nat Medal Science, 83; Silver Medal, Int Soc Chem Ecol, 90. *Prof Exp:* Fel, NIH, 62-64. *Concurrent Pos:* Deleg insect control, People's Repub China, 76; mem, Comt Biol Pest Species, Nat Res Coun, 76; US-USSR Sci Exchange Conf, Tashent, USSA; sci lectr, Univ Md, 85. *Mem:* Nat Acad Sci; fel AAAS; fel Entomol Soc Am; Am Chem Soc; Sigma Xi; Am Acad Arts & Sci. *Res:* The insect communication system; insect monitoring and control programs; author of over 250 scientific journals; defining sex pheromone blends that are biosynthesized and genetically controlled by female moths. *Mailing Add:* Dept Entomol NY State Agri Exp Sta Geneva NY 14456. *Fax:* 315-787-2326; *E-Mail:* wlr1@cornell.edu

ROELS, OSWALD A, BIOCHEMISTRY, MARINE BIOLOGY. *Current Pos:* RETIRED. *Personal Data:* b Temse, Belg, Sept 16, 21; US citizen; m 50, Dorothy M Broadhurst; c Margaret A. *Educ:* Cath Univ Louvain, BS, 40, MS, 42, PhD(org chem), 44. *Prof Exp:* Head agr biochem dept, Nat Inst Agron Res Belg Congo, 45-49; tech officer, org chem res dept, Imp Chem Industs, Eng, 49-53; dir, Produits Chimiques des Flandres, Belg, 53-55; head nutrit biochem div, Inst Sci Res Cent Africa, Belg Congo, 55-60; assoc prof nutrit biochem, Columbia Univ, 60-65, sr res assoc, Lamont-Doherty Geol Observ, 65-76, assoc chmn marine biol prog, 67-69, chmn, 69-75; prof marine studies, Univ Tex, 76-80; chmn, Maritek Corp, 80-92. *Concurrent Pos:* Consult, Sorbonne Univ, 57 & Vanderbilt Univ, 59; mem, Int Conf Biochem Probs Lipids; prof biol & biochem, Univ Inst Oceanog, City Col New York, 69-76, vis prof, 76-80; adj prof, Rockefeller Univ, 69-76; chmn, UN Indust Develop Orgn-Food & Agr Orgn exp group mkt on fish protein concentrate, Morocco, 69; vis res prof, Laval Univ, Que, 71-79. *Mem:* AAAS; Am Soc Biol Chem; Am Soc Limnol & Oceanog; Inst Environ Sci; Marine Technol Soc. *Res:* N-transfer in aquatic food chains; artificial upwelling, mariculture; effluent aquaculture. *Mailing Add:* 4345 Rosecliff Dr Charlotte NC 28277

ROEMER, ELIZABETH, ASTROMETRY, SOLAR SYSTEM ASTRONOMY. *Current Pos:* assoc prof, 66-69, PROF ASTRONR, DEPT ASTRON & LUNAR & PLANETARY LAB, UNIV ARIZ, 69-, ASTRONOMER, STEWARD OBSERV, 80- *Personal Data:* b Oakland, Calif, Sept 4, 29. *Educ:* Univ Calif, BA, 50, PhD, 55. *Honors & Awards:* Dorothea Klumpke Roberts Prize, 50; Donohoe lectr, Astron Soc Pac, 62; Benjamin Apthorp Gould Prize, Nat Acad Sci, 71. *Prof Exp:* Asst astron, Univ Calif, 50-52, lab technician, Lick Observ, 54-55, res astronr, 55-56; res assoc, Yerkes Observ, Univ Chicago, 56; astronr, Flagstaff Sta, US Naval Observ, 57-66, actg dir, 65. *Concurrent Pos:* Partic, Prog Vis Profs Astron, Am Astron Soc & NSF, 60-75; chmn, Working Group Comets, Comn 20 Pos & Motions Minor Planets, Comets & Satellites, Int Astron Union, 64-79 & 85-88, vpres, 79-82, pres, Comn 20, 82-85, vpres, 73-76 & 85-88, pres, Comn 6 Astron Telegrams, 76-79 & 88-91; comt man at large, Sect D, AAAS, 66-69 & 75-78, coun mem, 66-69 & 72-73; mem coun, Am Astron Soc, 67-70 & Comet Medal Comt, Astron Soc Pac, 68-74; mem, Panel Planetary Astron, Nat Acad Sci, 67; chmn comt, Dept Planetary Sci, Univ Ariz, 72-73; vchmn, Div Dynamical Astron, Am Astron Sci, 73, chmn, 74; mem, Space Sci Rev Panel Associateship Prog, Off Sci Personnel, Nat Res Coun, 73-75, chmn, 75; mem, Subcomt Space Telescope, Space Sci Steering Comt, NASA, 77-78. *Mem:* Fel AAAS; Am Astron Soc; Am Geophys Union; Astron Soc Pac; Sigma Xi; Int Astron Union. *Res:* Comets and minor planets; astrometry and practical astronomy; computation of orbits; astrometric and astrophysical investigations of comets, minor planets and satellites; dynamical astronomy. *Mailing Add:* Lunar & Planetary Lab Space Sci Bldg Univ Ariz Tucson AZ 85721-0092

ROEMER, LOUIS EDWARD, ELECTRICAL ENGINEERING, PHYSICS. *Current Pos:* head, Elec Eng Dept, 89-96, ENTERGY PROF ELEC ENG, LA TECH UNIV, 96- *Personal Data:* b Washington, DC, July 5, 34; m 58; c 3. *Educ:* Univ Del, BS, 55, MS, 63, PhD(appl sci), 67. *Prof Exp:* Assoc engr, Sperry Gyroscope Co, Sperry Rand Corp, 60-63; from instr to asst prof elec eng, Univ Del, 63-68; prof elec eng, Univ Akron, 68-89. *Mem:* Inst Elec & Electronics Engrs; Sigma Xi. *Res:* Wave propagation in plasma; time domain reflectometry; digital signal processing; Bayesian analysis. *Mailing Add:* Elec Eng Dept La Tech Univ Ruston LA 71212. *Fax:* 318-257-4922; *E-Mail:* roemer@engr.latech.edu

ROEMER, MILTON IRWIN, MEDICAL CARE SYSTEMS. *Current Pos:* PROF PUB HEALTH, UNIV CALIF, LOS ANGELES, 62- *Personal Data:* b Paterson, NJ, Mar 24, 16; m 39, Ruth J Rosenbaum; c John E & Beth M. *Educ:* Cornell Univ, BA, 36, MA, 39; NY Univ, MD, 40; Univ Mich, MPH, 43. *Honors & Awards:* Henry E Sigerist lectr, Yale Univ, 80; Sedgwick Medalist, Am Pub Health Asn, 83; Stubenbord Prof, Cornell, 84; Rosenstadt Prof, Univ Toronto, 88. *Prof Exp:* Med officer venereal dis, NJ State Dept Health, 41-42; med officer med care, USPHS, 43-49; assoc prof pub health, Yale Univ, 49-51; sect chief social med, WHO, Geneva, 51-53; dir bur med care, Sask Dept Health, 53-56; prof admin med, Cornell Univ, 57-61. *Concurrent Pos:* World Health Orgn, USAID. *Mem:* Inst Med-Nat Acad Sci; Am Pub Health Asn. *Res:* Organization of medical care; health insurance; rural health; international health care systems; health manpower. *Mailing Add:* Sch Pub Health Univ Calif Los Angeles CA 90024. *Fax:* 310-825-8440

ROEMER, RICHARD ARTHUR, NEUROSCIENCE, COMPUTER SCIENCE. *Current Pos:* med res scientist, 75-80, assoc prof, Dept Psychiat, 81-85, PROF, DEPT PSYCHIAT & NEUROL, TEMPLE UNIV, 85- *Personal Data:* b Minneapolis, Minn, Sept 12, 39; m 72; c 6. *Educ:* Calif State Univ, Northbridge, BA, 68; Univ Calif, Irvine, PhD(psychobiol), 73; Univ Bellgrade, DMS, 84. *Prof Exp:* Sr eng aide digital comput, Litton Data Systs, 62-64; comput specialist reentry systs, Gen Elec Co, 64-66; sr elec engr digital comput, Calif State Univ, Northridge, 66-67; analyst mgt systs, Syst Develop Corp, 67-69; comput syst consult, Enki Res Inst, 69-73; res asst & res assoc, Univ Calif, Irvine, 69-73; res fel psychol, Harvard Univ, 73-75. *Concurrent Pos:* Analyst mgt systs, 69; clin asst prof, Dept Psychiat, Temple Univ, 75-77, res assoc prof, 77-81, assoc prof, 81-85; lectr psychol, Univ Pa & Rutgers Univ, 77-; sr Fulbright scholar, 81, 83 & 84. *Mem:* Soc Neurosci; Inst Elec & Electronics Engrs; Nat Asn On-Line Comput Psychol; Soc Systs, Man & Cybernet; Soc Eng Med & Biol; Am Psychopath Asn; Soc Biol Psychiat. *Res:* Assessment of neuropsychological and neuropharmacological relationships in mentally ill patients; development of multivariate statistical applications in neurobiology. *Mailing Add:* Dept Psychiat Temple Univ Sch Med 4200 & Monument Ave Philadelphia PA 19151

ROENIGK, WILLIAM J, VETERINARY RADIOLOGY. *Current Pos:* PROF VET RADIOL & HEAD DEPT, COL VET MED, TEX A&M UNIV, 75- *Personal Data:* b Cleveland, Ohio, Jan 26, 29; m 53; c 4. *Educ:* Ohio State Univ, DVM, 54; Baylor Univ, MSc, 58; Am Col Vet Radiol, ACVR, 66. *Prof Exp:* From asst prof to prof vet radiol, Vet Clin, Ohio State Univ, 58-67; assoc prof comp radiol & lab animal med, Col Med & dir, Div Vet Med, Children's Hosp Res Found, Univ Cincinnati, 67-72; prof vet radiol, NY State Vet Col, Cornell Univ, 72-75. *Concurrent Pos:* NIH grant, 62-65; consult, five major co. *Mem:* Am Vet Med Asn; Am Col Vet Radiol (pres, 70); Educ Vet Radiol Sci (pres, 66); Radiol Soc NAm; Am Vet Radiol Soc. *Res:* Diagnostic radiology; radiation therapy; nuclear medicine. *Mailing Add:* 1212 Merry Oaks Dr College Station TX 77840-2609

ROEPE, PAUL DAVID, BIOLOGICAL MEMBRANE TRANSPORT, VIBRATIONAL SPECTROSCOPY. *Current Pos:* ASST PROF PHARMACOL, CORNELL UNIV MED COL, 90- *Personal Data:* b Suffern, NY, June 20, 60; m 90. *Educ:* Boston Univ, BA, 82, MA & PhD(chem & math), 87. *Honors & Awards:* Young Investr Award, Biophys Soc, 88. *Prof Exp:* Mem molecular biol, Roche Inst Molecular Biol, Nutley, NJ, 87-89; res assoc, Molecular Biol Inst, Univ Calif, Los Angeles, 89-90; asst mem pharmacol, Mem Sloan-Kettering Cancer Ctr, 90- *Concurrent Pos:* Sackler scholar, Raymond & Beverly Sackler Found, 90. *Mem:* AAAS; Biophys Soc; NY Acad Sci. *Res:* Molecular level studies of chemotherapeutic drug transport in normal and tumor cells. *Mailing Add:* Mem Sloan-Kettering Cancer Ctr 1275 York Ave New York NY 10021-6007

ROEPER, RICHARD ALLEN, MYCOLOGY-SYMBIOSIS OF WOOD-BORING BEETLES & THEIR MUTUALISTIC FUNGI. *Current Pos:* PROF BIOL, ALMA COL, 72- *Personal Data:* b Evanston, Ill, July 13, 38; m 86, Karen T Bracey; c Carleen, Christopher & Eben. *Educ:* Lawrence Col, BA, 60; Miami Univ, Ohio, MAT, 66; Ore State Univ, PhD(bot-mycol), 72. *Prof Exp:* Teacher biol, East Leyden High Sch, 61-63 & Niles Community High Sch, 63-68. *Mem:* Mycol Soc Am; Entom Soc Am; Sigma Xi. *Res:* Systematics and ecology of mutualistic fungi associated with wood-boring ambrosia beetles (Coleoptera: Scolytidae); physiology of these fungi and studies of the biology (behavior and life histories) of the beetles. *Mailing Add:* Dept Biol Alma Col 614 W Superior St Alma MI 48801-1599. *Fax:* 517-463-7277

ROEPKE, HARLAN HUGH, SEDIMENTARY PETROLOGY, ENVIRONMENTAL GEOLOGY. *Current Pos:* from asst prof to assoc prof, 65-77, PROF GEOL, BALL STATE UNIV, 77- *Personal Data:* b Rochester, Minn, Nov 14, 30; m 58, Judith Bole; c Janet & Douglas. *Educ:* Univ Minn, Minneapolis, BA, 53, MS, 58; Univ Tex, Austin, PhD(geol), 70; Purdue Univ, MS, 76. *Prof Exp:* Res asst geol, Minn Geol Surv, 56-58; geologist, Paleont & Stratig Br, US Geol Surv, 58-60, Alaskan Br, summer 60. *Concurrent Pos:* Geol consult, 72- *Mem:* Geol Soc Am; Soc Econ Paleont & Mineral; Sigma Xi; Nat Asn Geol Teachers; Soc Econ Paleont & Mineral. *Res:* Petrology of carbonate rocks; x-ray florescence study of Indiana chert. *Mailing Add:* Geol Dept Ball State Univ 4806 University Ave Muncie IN 47304-3521. *Fax:* 765-285-1624; *E-Mail:* 00hhroepke@bsuvc.bsu.edu

ROER, ROBERT DAVID, BIOMINERALIZATION. *Current Pos:* From asst prof to assoc prof, 79-90, PROF BIOL SCI, UNIV NC, WILMINGTON, 90- *Personal Data:* b New York, NY, Oct 15, 52; m 76, Majorie Smith; c Sara. *Educ:* Brown Univ, ScB, 74; Duke Univ, PhD(zool), 79. *Mem:* Am Physiol Soc; Am Soc Zoologists; Crustacean Soc; Sigma Xi. *Res:* Mechanisms of membrane transport in relation to osmoregulation and in relation to biomineralization; mineral nucleation in crustacean cuticle; fluid dynamics in relation to bone physiology. *Mailing Add:* Dept Biol Sci Univ NC Wilmington 601 S College Rd Wilmington NC 28403-3297. *E-Mail:* roer@uncwil.edu

ROERIG, DAVID L, PULMONARY-DRUG UPTAKE, NARCOTIC ANALGESICS. *Current Pos:* TOXICOL-RES HEALTH SCIENTIST, WOOD VET ADMIN MED CTR, 72-; ASST PROF ANESTHESIOL, DEPT ANESTHESIOL & PHARMACOL, MED COL WIS, 74- *Educ:* Kans State Univ, PhD(biochem), 70. *Res:* Drug metabolism and distribution. *Mailing Add:* Res Health Sci Zablocki Vet Admin Med Ctr Milwaukee WI 53295-9999

ROERIG, SANDRA CHARLENE, OPIATES ACTION, MECHANISMS TO ANALGESIA. *Current Pos:* ASSOC PROF, LA STATE UNIV. *Educ:* Med Col Wis, MA, 76. *Prof Exp:* Res assoc pharmacol, Med Col Wis, 76-88. *Mailing Add:* Dept Pharmacol La State Univ Med Ctr 1501 Kings Hwy Shreveport LA 71130-3932. *Fax:* 318-675-7857

ROESCH, WILLIAM CARL, PHYSICS. *Current Pos:* RETIRED. *Personal Data:* b Saginaw, Mich, Nov 11, 23; m 46; c 3. *Educ:* Miami Univ, Ohio, AB, 45; Calif Inst Technol, PhD(physics), 49. *Prof Exp:* Mgr, Radiol Physics, Gen Elec Co, 49-64; mgr radiol physics, Battelle-Northwest, 65, sr res assoc, 66-70, staff scientist, 70-85. *Concurrent Pos:* Mem, Panel Reassessment on Atomic Bomb Dosimetry, Nat Acad Sci, 82-87 & Biol Effects Ionozing Radiation-4 Comt, 85-88; chmn, Sci Comt No 80 Radiabiol Skin, Nat Coun Radiation Protection & Measurements, 83-90. *Mem:* Am Phys Soc; Radiation Res Soc; Health Phys Soc; Am Asn Physicists Med. *Res:* Radiological physics; instrumentation and dosimetry methods for alpha, beta and gamma rays and neutrons; physics of radiobiology and radiation protection. *Mailing Add:* 1646 Butternut Ave Richland WA 99352

ROESEL, CATHERINE ELIZABETH, IMMUNOLOGY. *Current Pos:* from instr to assoc prof, 51-76, PROF CELL & MOLECULAR BIOL, MED COL GA, 76- *Personal Data:* b Augusta, Ga, Feb 6, 20. *Educ:* Vanderbilt Univ, BA, 41; Wash Univ, PhD(bact), 51. *Prof Exp:* Fel, Carnegie Inst, 50-51. *Mem:* AAAS; Am Soc Microbiol; Asn Am Med Cols. *Res:* Antibody formation; Rubella virus; tissue culture. *Mailing Add:* 2722 Cherry Lane Augusta GA 30909

ROESER, ROSS JOSEPH, AUDIOLOGY. *Current Pos:* DIR, CALLIER CTR, UNIV TEX, DALLAS, 72- *Personal Data:* b Louisville, Ky, Nov 14, 42; m 63; c 3. *Educ:* Western Ill Univ, BS, 66; Northern Ill Univ, MA, 67; Fla State Univ, PhD(audiol), 72. *Concurrent Pos:* Clin assoc prof otolaryngol, Med Sch, Univ Tex Southwestern, 73-; prof grad prog, Univ Tex, Dallas, 73-; Health Educ & Welfare grants, cent auditory processing children, 77-79 & tactile aids, 80-82; NASA grant, Hearing Aid Malfunction Detection Unit. *Mem:* Fel Am Speech & Hearing Asn; Am Auditory Soc (secy-treas, 73-); fel Soc Ear, Nose & Throat Advan Children. *Res:* Central auditory processing in children, tactile aids and other audiology related areas. *Mailing Add:* 1921 Marydale Rd Dallas TX 75208

ROESIJADI, GURITNO, COMPARATIVE PHYSIOLOGY, AQUATIC TOXICOLOGY. *Current Pos:* PROF TOXICOL, CHESAPEAKE BIOL LAB, CTR ENVIRON & ESTUARINE STUDIES, UNIV MD, 86- *Personal Data:* b Tokyo, Japan, Apr 4, 48; US citizen; m 70; c 3. *Educ:* Univ Wash, BS, 70; Humboldt State Univ, MS, 73; Tex A&M Univ, PhD(biol), 76. *Prof Exp:* Res scientist, Battelle Northwest Labs, 76-80, sr res scientist, 80-84; assoc prof biol, Dept Biol, Pa State Univ, 84-86. *Concurrent Pos:* US ed, Marine Environ Res, 80-86, ed, 86-93; mem tech adv comt, Nat Oceanic & Atmospheric Admin Coastal Oceans Prog. *Mem:* AAAS; Am Soc Zoologists; Sigma Xi; Soc Environ Toxicol & Chem; Soc Toxicol. *Res:* Adaptive mechanisms to environmental conditions; physiological, biochemical and molecular mechanisms for the regulation of metals in aquatic animals. *Mailing Add:* Univ Md Box 38 Solomons MD 20688. *Fax:* 410-326-7290; *E-Mail:* groes@cbl.umd.edu

ROESING, TIMOTHY GEORGE, VIROLOGY, VACCINES. *Current Pos:* mgr biol qual control tech serv, 86-87, mgr bact vaccines & blood prod, Recombivax, 88-90, MGR DIPLOID CELL VACCINES, MERCK PHARMACEUT MFG DIV, 91- *Personal Data:* b Abington, Pa, May 14, 47; m 69; c 2. *Educ:* Univ Md, BS, 69; Hahnemann Med Col, MS, 73, PhD(microbiol & immunol), 76. *Prof Exp:* Sr res scientist microbiol, Smith Kline Diag Div, Smith Kline Corp, 76-77; sr proj develop biologist microbiol, Merck Sharp & Dohme Div, Merck & Co, 77-82, sr proj microbiologist, 82-85. *Concurrent Pos:* Fel, Smith Kline Diag, 76-77. *Mem:* Am Soc Microbiol; Tissue Cult Asn. *Res:* Virus-cell interactions with coxsackieviruses; role of coxsackieviruses in heart disease and pancreatitis; enzyme linked immunoassays and fluorescent immunoassays for human viruses. *Mailing Add:* Merck Pharmaceut Mfg Div 28T-105 West Point PA 19486

ROESKE, ROGER WILLIAM, BIO-ORGANIC CHEMISTRY. *Current Pos:* from asst prof to assoc prof, 62-66, PROF BIOCHEM, SCH MED, IND UNIV, 77- *Personal Data:* b Valders, Wis, July 30, 27; m 55; c 2. *Educ:* Univ Wis, BA, 48; Univ Ill, PhD(org chem), 51. *Prof Exp:* Merck fel, Swiss Fed Inst Tech, 51-52; res assoc biochem, Med Col, Cornell Univ, 52-55; sr chemist, Eli Lilly & Co, Ind, 55-61. *Concurrent Pos:* Res Career Develop Award, USPHS, 62-71. *Mem:* AAAS; Am Chem Soc. *Res:* Mechanism of enzyme action; synthesis of peptides; membrane-active peptides. *Mailing Add:* Dept Biochem Ind Univ Sch Med Indianapolis IN 46202-5122

ROESLER, FREDERICK LEWIS, ATOMIC PHYSICS, OPTICAL SPECTROSCOPY. *Current Pos:* from asst prof to assoc prof, 64-70, PROF PHYSICS, UNIV WIS-MADISON, 70- *Personal Data:* b Milwaukee, Wis, Feb 26, 34; m 57, 68, Beatrix; c 5. *Educ:* St Olaf Col, BA, 56; Univ Wis, MS, 58, PhD(physics), 62. *Honors & Awards:* von Humboldt Found Sr US Scientist Award, 75; Group Achievement Award, NASA, 81. *Prof Exp:* Res assoc physics, Univ Wis, 62-63; NSF fel, Lab Aime-Cotton, France, 63-64. *Concurrent Pos:* Consult, Los Alamos Sci Lab, 65-69 & Argonne Nat Lab, 77-; mem comt line spectra of elements, Nat Acad Sci-Nat Res Coun, 67-72; vis assoc prof physics, Univ Ariz, 70; vis prof physics, Univ Munich, 76; sr res assoc, Nat Acad Sci, Nat Res Coun, Space Flight Ctr, 82-83; NSF Prog dir aeronomy, 91-92; actg head, Upper Atmosphere Res Sect, NSF, 91. *Mem:* Am Geophys Union. *Res:* Interference spectroscopy; astronomy; aeronomy; astrophysics. *Mailing Add:* Dept Physics B305 Sterling Hall Univ Wis Madison WI 53706

ROESLER, JOSEPH FRANK, ENVIRONMENTAL ENGINEERING, PHYSICAL CHEMISTRY. *Current Pos:* SUPT LABS, METRO WATER, NASHVILLE, 90- *Personal Data:* b Chicago, Ill, Dec 15, 30; m 61; c 2. *Educ:* Roosevelt Univ, BS, 54; Okla State Univ, MS, 61; Univ Cincinnati, MS, 70. *Honors & Awards:* Water & Waste Water Div Award, Instrument Soc Am, 81, Kermit Kischer Award, 83. *Prof Exp:* Res chemist, Ill Inst Technol, 56-59, Okla State Univ, 60-61 & Rauland Corp, 61-62; res chemist, Div Air Pollution, USPHS, 62-67; sanit engr & mgr instrumentation & automation of waste syst, Nat Environ Res Ctr, 67-78, regional liaison officer, US Environ Protection Agency, 78-82, environ engr, Off Res & Develop, 78-88, chief, sampling & field measurements, 82-88; pres, Cincinnati Engrs Inc, 88-90. *Concurrent Pos:* Dir, Water & Waste Water Indust Div, Instrument Soc Am, 86- *Mem:* Instrument Soc Am; Water Pollution Control Fedn; Am Soc Civil Engrs; Sigma Xi (pres, 86). *Res:* Mathematical modeling of advanced waste water treatment processes; environmental health engineering; aerosols and chemical instrumentation pertaining to air pollution; kinetics and photoemissive surfaces; instrumentation for water quality; automation of wastewater treatment plants. *Mailing Add:* 5630 Valley View Rd Brentwood TN 37027-4687

ROESMER, JOSEF, RADIOCHEMISTRY, REACTOR COOLANT CHEMISTRY. *Current Pos:* sr scientist, Astronuclear Lab, 64-71, fel scientist, Nuclear Energy Systs, 71-91, CONSULT CHEMIST, WESTINGHOUSE ELEC CORP, 92- *Personal Data:* b Konigsberg, Germany, Aug 29, 28; m 59, Alice Clarke; c Christopher J. *Educ:* Univ Mainz, BS, 52, MS, 55; Clark Univ, PhD(nuclear chem), 64. *Prof Exp:* Adv scientist, Nuclear Sci & Eng Corp, 60-64. *Mem:* NY Acad Sci; Am Chem Soc. *Res:* Nuclear reactions; activation and prompt-gamma activation analyses; ultra-low background counting; high-temperature solution chemistry; minimization of formation, activation and transport of corrosion products in nuclear reactor coolants to reduce occupational radiation exposure of workers; decontamination and decommissioning of PWR components; analysis and treatment of radioactive waste. *Mailing Add:* 969 Holly Lynne Dr Pittsburgh PA 15236

ROESNER, LARRY A, RESEARCH ADMINISTRATION. *Current Pos:* assoc, 75-83, vpres, 83-88, TECH DIR, WATER RESOURCES & ENVIRON SCI S REGION, CAMP DRESSER & MCKEE INC, 83-, SR VPRES, 88- *Educ:* Valparaiso Univ, Ind, BS, 63; Colo State Univ, MS, 65; Univ Wash, PhD(sanit eng), 69. *Honors & Awards:* Walter L Huber, Civil Eng Res Prize, 75. *Prof Exp:* Grad res asst, Colo State Univ, 63-65 & Univ Wash, 65-67; prin engr, Water Resources Engrs, Inc, 68-75. *Concurrent Pos:* Chmn, Eng Found Conf, 88; vchmn, Non-Point Sources Pollution Comt, Water Pollution Control Fedn; mem, Comt Wastewater Mgt Coastal Urban Areas, Nat Res Coun. *Mem:* Nat Acad Eng; fel Am Soc Civil Engrs; Am Water Resources Asn; Water Pollution Control Fedn; Am Inst Hydrol; Nat Soc Prof Engrs. *Res:* Author of various publications. *Mailing Add:* Camp Dresser & McKee 2301 Maitland Ctr Pkwy Suite 300 Maitland FL 32751. *Fax:* 407-875-1161

ROESS, WILLIAM B, GENETICS, MOLECULAR BIOLOGY. *Current Pos:* From asst prof to assoc prof, 66-74, chmn, Collegium, 76-86, actg provost, 79, PROF BIOL, COLLEGIUM NATURAL SCI, ECKERD COL, 75- *Personal Data:* b Evanston, Ill, Sept 8, 38; m 57; c 4. *Educ:* Blackburn Col, BA, 61; Fla State Univ, PhD(genetics), 66. *Concurrent Pos:* NIH spec fel, Oak Ridge Nat Labs, 71. *Mem:* AAAS; Sigma Xi. *Res:* Mechanisms and genetic control of amino acid transport in human tissue culture cells; genetic control of membrane synthesis; carcinogenesis in human tissue culture cells. *Mailing Add:* Dept Natural Sci Eckerd Col PO Box 12560 St Petersburg FL 33733-2560

ROESSET, JOSE M, STRUCTURAL DYNAMICS, EARTHQUAKE ENGINEERING. *Current Pos:* prof, Univ Tex, Austin, 78-83, Paul D & Betty Robertson Meek Centinnial prof, 83-90, Robert B Trull chair eng, 90-97, JOE KING CHAIR ENG, UNIV TEX, AUSTIN, 97-; WOFFORD CAIN CHAIR ENG, TEX A&M UNIV, 97-, DIR, OFFSHORE TECHNOL RES CTR, 97- *Educ:* Escuela especial de Ingenieros de Caminos, Civil Engr 59; Mass Inst Technol, Drs, 64. *Prof Exp:* Design engr, Agroman Empresa Constructora, & asst engr, 54- 59-; from asst prof to prof, Mass Inst Technol, 64-78. *Mem:* Nat Acad Eng; fel Am Soc Civil Engrs. *Res:* Non-linear wave propagation; soil amplification; soil-structure interaction and offshore structures. *Mailing Add:* Offshore Technol & Res Ctr 1200 Mariner Dr College Station TX 77843

ROESSLER, CHARLES ERVIN, RADIATION PROTECTION & ENVIRONMENTAL RADIATION, OCCUPATIONAL HEALTH. *Current Pos:* asst prof radiation biophys, 67-72, from asst prof to prof, 72-93, EMER PROF ENVIRON ENG, UNIV FLA, 93- *Personal Data:* b Elysian, Minn, May 1, 34; m 56, Genevieve Schleret; c Teresa, Cynthia, Mary (Wakhuk), Francis, Kathleen (Foster), Jean (Boothby) & Anne (Hall). *Educ:* Mankato State Col, AB, 55; Univ Rochester, MS, 56; Univ Pittsburgh, MPH, 59; Univ Fla, PhD(environ eng), 67; Am Bd Health Physics, cert, 61. *Prof Exp:* Health physicist, Nuclear Power Dept, Res Div, Curtiss-Wright Corp, 56-58; radiol physicist, Fla State Bd Health, 59-65. *Concurrent Pos:* Consult natural radioactivity to phosphate indust; lectr, radiation emergency planning. *Mem:* AAAS; fel Health Physics Soc; Am Indust Hyg Asn; Am Conf Govt Indust Hygienists; Conf Radiation Control Prog Dirs. *Res:* Environmental radiation, particularly naturally occurring radioactivity; environmental and indoor radon. *Mailing Add:* RR 1 Box 139H Elysian MN 56028-0139. *Fax:* 507-362-4513

ROESSLER, DAVID MARTYN, PHYSICS, LASER PROCESSING. *Current Pos:* STAFF RES SCIENTIST, SPECTROSCOPY, GEN MOTORS RES & DEVELOP CTR, 70- *Personal Data:* b London, Eng, Apr 29, 40; m 83, Linda J Beare; c Elizabeth R & Sarah L. *Educ:* Univ London, BSc, 61, PhD(physics), 66. *Prof Exp:* Fel, Univ Calif, Santa Barbara, 66-68; mem, Tech Staff Spectros, Bell Labs, 68-70. *Concurrent Pos:* Fac mem, Physics Dept, Wayne State Univ, 86-, Lawrence Technol Univ Mich, 90-; consult & invited speaker on laser mat processing, optical properties mat. *Mem:* Brit Inst Physics; Sigma Xi; Optical Soc Am; Int Solar Energy Soc; Laser Inst Am; Soc Photo-optical Instrumentation Engrs; Am Inst Physics. *Res:* Optical Properties of solids and aerosols; reflection; luminescence; photoacoustic spectroscopy; laser processing of materials; solar energy materials; author of numerous publications. *Mailing Add:* MC 480-106-224 Gen Motors Res & Develop Ctr 30500 Mound Rd Warren MI 48090-9055. *Fax:* 810-986-3091

ROESSLER, MARTIN A, FISH BIOLOGY. *Current Pos:* PROG DIR, TROP BIOINDUST DEVELOP CO, 73- *Personal Data:* b Hempstead, NY, Apr 7, 39. *Educ:* Univ Miami, BS, 61, MS, 64, PhD(marine sci), 67. *Prof Exp:* Instr fisheries biol, Inst Marine Sci, Univ Miami, 66-69, from asst prof to assoc prof, Rosenstiel Sch Marine & Atmospheric Sci, 69-73. *Mem:* Am Fisheries Soc; Am Soc Ichthyologists & Herpetologists; Am Soc Limnol & Oceanog. *Res:* Ecology of estuaries in Florida; biology of pink shrimp Penaeus duorarum; ecology of fishes; power plant siting and environmental effects of coastal zone development. *Mailing Add:* 7821 SW 114th St Miami FL 33156

ROESSLER, ROBERT L, PSYCHIATRY. *Current Pos:* PROF PSYCHIAT, BAYLOR COL MED, 63- *Personal Data:* b Neillsville, Wis, Sept 2, 21; m 46; c 3. *Educ:* Univ Wis, PhB, 42; Columbia Univ, MD, 45; Am Bd Psychiat & Neurol, dipl, 51. *Prof Exp:* Intern, Englewood Hosp, NJ, 45-46; resident psychiat, Vet Admin Hosp, Madison, Wis, 46-48; resident, Strong Mem Hosp, Rochester, NY, 48-49; instr, Sch Med, Univ Rochester, 49-50; from asst prof to prof, Sch Med, Univ Wis, 50-63, from actg chmn dept to chmn dept, 56-61, dir psychiat inst, 60-61. *Concurrent Pos:* Consult, US Info Agency, 59-61 & Vet Admin Hosp, Madison, 59-61. *Mem:* AAAS; fel Am Psychiat Asn; Am Psychosom Soc; Soc Psychophysiol Res; NY Acad Sci. *Res:* Psychophysiology; psychosomatic medicine. *Mailing Add:* 2502 Underwood St Houston TX 77030

ROESSMANN, UROS, NEUROPATHOLOGY. *Current Pos:* from instr to asst prof, 65-82, PROF INST PATH, CASE WESTERN RES UNIV, 82- *Personal Data:* b Vevce, Slovenia, Sept 9, 25; US citizen; m 57, Ljudmila Lekan; c Anita, Michael, Cathy & Peter. *Educ:* Ohio State Univ, BSc, 51; Case Western Res Univ, MD, 57. *Prof Exp:* Intern med, Michael Reese Hosp, 57-58; resident neurol, Univ Hosps Cleveland, 58-59; resident anat path, Inst Path, Western Res Univ, 59-60; resident neuropath, 61-62; resident anat path, Cleveland Clin, 60-61; captain & asst pathologist, Neuropath Br, Armed Forces Inst Path, 62-64; res assoc, Ment Health Res Inst, Univ Mich, 64-65. *Concurrent Pos:* Consult, Vet Admin Hosp, 74-, Mt Sinai Hosp, 77-; vis prof, Univ Liubljana, Slovernia. *Mem:* An Asn Neuropathologists. *Res:* Morphological aspects of central nervous system pathology; growth and development of the central nervous system; skeletal muscle response to stimulation. *Mailing Add:* Inst Path 0587614xxern Res Univ 11100 Euclid Ave Cleveland OH 44106-2333. *Fax:* 216-844-1810

ROEST, ARYAN INGOMAR, VERTEBRATE ZOOLOGY, TAXONOMY. *Current Pos:* RETIRED. *Personal Data:* b Chicago, Ill, June 13, 25; m 50, Colette Pouteau; c 4. *Educ:* Univ Va, BS, 45; Ore State Col, BS, 48, MS, 49, PhD(zool), 54. *Prof Exp:* Asst, Ore State Col, 49; instr biol & math, Cent Ore Col, 52-55; prof biol, Calif Polytech State Univ, San Luis Obispo, 55-90. *Mem:* Am Soc Mammal; Soc Marine Mammal. *Res:* Vertebrate field zoology, including mammals, birds, reptiles and amphibians; systematic studies of sea otter, red fox, kit fox & kangaroo rat; mammal studies. *Mailing Add:* 1197 Tenth St Los Osos CA 93402

ROETH, FREDERICK WARREN, WEED SCIENCE, CROP PRODUCTION. *Current Pos:* from asst prof to assoc prof, 75-83, PROF AGRON, UNIV NEBR, LINCOLN, 83- *Personal Data:* b Houston, Ohio, Aug 21, 41; m 68, Carol Logemann; c Alicia, Bradley & Cari. *Educ:* Ohio State Univ, BS, 64; Univ Nebr, Lincoln, MS, 67, PhD(agron), 70. *Prof Exp:* Res asst weed sci, Univ Nebr, Lincoln, 64-69; asst prof, Purdue Univ, W Lafayette, 69-75. *Concurrent Pos:* Vis botanist, Univ Calif, Davis, 84-85. *Mem:* AAAS; Weed Sci Soc Am; Am Soc Agron; Coun Agr Sci & Technol; Sigma Xi. *Res:* Weed biology and control in agronomic crops, herbicide dissipation. *Mailing Add:* Box 66 S Cent Ctr Clay Center NE 68933. *Fax:* 402-762-4422

ROETHEL, DAVID ALBERT HILL, SCIENCE ADMINISTRATION, SCIENCE COMMUNICATIONS. *Current Pos:* PRES, PEACHTREE PROM CONSULT, 91- *Personal Data:* b Milwaukee, Wis, Feb 17, 26; m 53; c 2. *Educ:* Marquette Univ, BS, 50, MS, 52; Oak Ridge Sch Reactor Technol, cert, 53. *Honors & Awards:* Nat Serv Award, Nat Registry Clin Chem, 72. *Prof Exp:* Tech specialist, AEC, 52-57; asst to exec secy & mgr, Prof Rel Off, Am Chem Soc, 57-72; exec dir, Nat Registry Clin Chem, 67-72, Am Asn Clin Chem, 68-70; Am Orthotic & Prosthetic Asn, Am Acad Orthotists & Prosthetists, Am Bd Cert Orthotics & Prosthesis, 72-76; exec dir, Nat Cert Comn Chem & Chem Eng, Am Inst Chemists, 77-90. *Concurrent Pos:* Mem, Gov Md Comn Sci Develop, 69; secy-gen, Seventh Int Cong Orthotics & Prosthetics, 75-76, Second World Congress, 75-77; secy-treas, Comn Profs in Sci & Technol, 79-82, comnr, 77-96; dir, Coun Eng & Sci Soc Execs, 82-86; ed, Chemist, 77-; dir, Am Inst Chem, China-US scientific exchange, 85-90, trustee, 82-90. *Mem:* Am Inst Chemists (secy-treas, 79-82, vpres, 90-91); Am Chem Soc; Coun Eng & Sci Soc Execs; Comn Prof Sci & Technol. *Res:* Matters of professional interest to chemist and chemical engineers, such as ethics, economic patterns in compensation, pensions, professional liability insurance and legislative and regulatory concerns which affect the profession. *Mailing Add:* 13218 Bregman Rd Silver Spring MD 20904-3441. *Fax:* 301-384-8666

ROETLING, PAUL G, PHYSICS, OPTICS. *Current Pos:* prin scientist, Xerox Corp, 68-70, mgr optics res area, 70-74, mgr image processing area, 74-78, res fel, 78-96, SR FEL, XEROX CORP, 91- *Personal Data:* b Buffalo, NY, Sept 12, 33; m 60, Janet Jack. *Educ:* Univ Buffalo, BA, 55, PhD(physics), 60. *Prof Exp:* Consult, Cornell Aeronaut Lab, 59-60, physicist, 60-63, sect head optics, 63-68. *Concurrent Pos:* Hon mem, Rochester Sect, Optical Soc Am. *Mem:* Am Phys Soc; fel Optical Soc Am; Inst Elec & Electronics Engrs; fel Soc Photographic Scientists & Engrs. *Res:* Optical image formation and image processing. *Mailing Add:* 1646 Shallow Creek Trail Webster NY 14580

ROETMAN, ERNEST LEVANE, APPLIED MATHEMATICS, ANALYTICAL MECHANICS. *Current Pos:* prof engr, Boeing Comput Serv, 80-81, syst engr, Boeing Mil Airplane Co, mgr electromagnetics anal, Boeing Airplane Co, 86-89, mgr computational mechanics, 89-92, CHIEF ENGR AERODYNAMICS, BOEING DEFENSE & SPACE GROUP, 92- *Personal Data:* b Chandler, Minn, Sept 18, 36; m 85, Rachel Allison; c 2. *Educ:* Univ Minn, BA, 57; Ore State Univ, PhD(math & mech eng), 63. *Prof Exp:* Asst math, Aachen Tech Univ, 63; tech specialist, Bell Tel Labs, 63-65; asst prof, Stevens Inst Technol, 65-68; assoc prof math, Univ Mo, Columbia, 68-75, prof, 75-80. *Concurrent Pos:* Guest prof, Aachen Tech Univ, 75-76; von Humboldt fel, 76; guest prof, Ore State Univ, 79-80. *Mem:* Soc Indust & Appl Math; Am Inst Aeronaut & Astronaut. *Res:* Biofluid mechanics; partial differential equations; irregular boundary value problems; numerical analysis; computational fluid dynamics. *Mailing Add:* 3016 67th Ave SE Mercer Island WA 98040

ROFFLER-TARLOV, SUZANNE K, NEUROCHEMISTRY, NEUROGENETICS. *Current Pos:* From asst prof to assoc prof, 80-97, PROF NEUROSCI, SCH MED, TUFTS UNIV, 97- *Personal Data:* b Missoula, Mont, Apr 19, 38. *Educ:* Univ Chicago, PhD(biopsychol), 68. *Mailing Add:* Dept Neurosci Tufts Univ Sch Med 136 Harrison Ave Boston MA 02111

ROFFMAN, STEVEN, BIOCHEMICAL PHARMACOLOGY. *Current Pos:* res assoc, Columbia Univ, 75-78, assoc, 78-79, asst prof pharmacol, 79-81, RES ASSOC MED, COL PHYSICIANS & SURGEONS, COLUMBIA UNIV, 81- *Personal Data:* b New York, NY, Apr 29, 44. *Educ:* Queens Col, NY, BA, 65; New York Univ, MS, 68, PhD(biochem), 74. *Prof Exp:* Fel biochem, Albert Einstein Col Med, NY, 73-75. *Concurrent Pos:* Info syst mgr, Dept Allergy & Infectious Dis, Roosevelt/St Luke's Hosp Ctr, 87- *Mem:* AAAS. *Res:* Role of prokolytic enzymes in the pathophysiology of inflammation and carcinogenesis; role of vasoactive peptides released in inflammatory disease of lung and skin. *Mailing Add:* Dept Allergy & Infectious Dis Roosevelt/St Luke's Hosp Ctr 428 W 59th St New York NY 10019

ROFFWARG, HOWARD PHILIP, SLEEP-WAKE PHYSIOLOGY, SLEEP DISORDERS. *Current Pos:* PROF PSYCHIAT, UNIV TEX, HEALTH SCI CTR, DALLAS, 77- *Personal Data:* b New York, NY, June 9, 32; m 55; c 2. *Educ:* Columbia Univ, AB, 54, MD, 58. *Honors & Awards:* Pioneer in Sleep Res, Asn Psychophysiol Study Sleep, 77; Nathaniel Kleitman Prize, Asn Sleep Dis Ctr, 81. *Prof Exp:* Res assoc, Mt Sinai Hosp, 61-62; instr psychiat, Columbia Univ, 62-66; from asst prof to assoc prof psychiat, Albert Einstein Col Med, 66-77; dir res, Dept Psychiat & Dir, Sleep Res Lab, 77-93. *Concurrent Pos:* NIMH career res scientist awards & res proj grants, 62-76; dir sleep EEG lab, NY State Psychiat Inst, 62-66, asst attend psychiatrist, 63-66; adj attend psychiatrist, Montefiore Hosp & Med Ctr, 66-71, assoc attend psychiatrist, 71-77; ed-in-chief, Sleep Rev Brain Info Serv, 74-75; mem, Clin Projs Res Rev Comt, NIMH, 76-80; chmn, comt diag classification, Asn Sleep Dis Ctr, 76-79, continuing chair, 76-; consult dir, Sleep & Wake Dis Ctr, Dept Psychiat, Presby Hosp-Univ Tex Health Sci Ctr, Dallas, 82- *Mem:* Sleep Res Soc (vpres, 80-87, pres, 85-87); fel Am Psychiat Asn; fel Am Col Psychiatrists; Am Sleep Dis Asn (pres elect & pres, 88-90). *Res:* Physiology and psychophysiology of sleep and sleep disorders; clinical psychiatry. *Mailing Add:* Dept Psych Univ Miss Med Ctr 2500 N State St Jackson MS 39216-4505

ROGALLO, FRANCIS MELVIN, MECHANICAL & AERONAUTICAL ENGINEERING. *Current Pos:* MEM STAFF KITTY HAWK KITES, NAGS HEAD, NC. *Personal Data:* b Sanger, Calif, Jan 27, 12; m 39, Gertrude Sugden; c Marie, Robert, Carol & Frances. *Prof Exp:* Mem staff, NASA, Hampton, Va, 36-70. *Res:* Patents for Flexible Wing, Corner Kite, others; aerodynamics and wind tunnels. *Mailing Add:* 91 Osprey Lane Kitty Hawk NC 27949-3839

ROGALSKI-WILK, ADRIENNE ALICE, CELL MEMBRANE CYTOSKELETON INTERACTIONS. *Current Pos:* asst prof, 85-91, ASSOC PROF CELL BIOL, DEPT ANAT & CELL BIOL, UNIV ILL, CHICAGO, 91- *Personal Data:* b Chicago, Ill, Aug 2, 53; m 91, Edward Wilk. *Educ:* Univ Chicago, BA, 75; Univ Ill, PhD(cell biol), 81. *Prof Exp:* Fel Nat Res Serv Award cell biol, Univ Calif, San Diego, 81-83, NIH fel, 83-85. *Concurrent Pos:* Prin investr, NIH grant, Dept Anat & Cell Biol, Univ Ill, Chicago, 86-, PEW scholar biomed sci, 87-93. *Mem:* Am Soc Cell Biol; AAAS; NY Acad Sci. *Res:* Molecular cell biology of membrane-cytoskeleton interactions; characterization of novel plasma membrane; actin linker systems in nonerythroid vertebrate cells. *Mailing Add:* Dept Anat & Cell Biol Univ Ill 808 S Wood St Rm 578 Chicago IL 60612-7308. *Fax:* 312-413-0354

ROGAN, ELEANOR GROENIGER, BIOCHEMISTRY. *Current Pos:* res assoc, 73-76, from asst prof to assoc prof, 76-90, TENURE PROF CHEM CARCINOGENESIS, EPPLEY INST & DEPT PHARM SCI, MED CTR, UNIV NEBR, 90- *Personal Data:* b Cincinnati, Ohio, Nov 25, 42; div; c 1. *Educ:* Mt Holyoke Col, AB, 63; Johns Hopkins Univ, PhD(biochem), 68. *Prof Exp:* Lectr biol sci, Goucher Col, 68-69; fel biochem, Univ Tenn, 69-71, res assoc cancer res, 71-73. *Mem:* Am Asn Cancer Res; AAAS; Am Soc Biochem & Molecular Biol. *Res:* Mechanism of carcinogenesis by polycyclic aromatic hydrocarbons and estrogens; nuclear monooxygenase enzyme activities especially those catalyzing activation of carcinogens; oncogenic mutations derived from depurinating DNA adducts of hydrocarbons and estrogens. *Mailing Add:* Eppley Inst Univ Nebr Med Ctr 600 S 42nd St Omaha NE 68198-6805. *Fax:* 402-559-8068; *E-Mail:* egrogan@unmc.edu

ROGAN, JOHN B, ORGANIC CHEMISTRY, POLYMER CHEMISTRY. *Current Pos:* res chemist, 66-69, group leader, Res & Develop Dept, 69-73, RES ASSOC, RES & DEVELOP DEPT, AMOCO CHEM CORP, 73- *Personal Data:* b Kansas City, Kans, Sept 3, 30; m 66. *Educ:* Univ Wyo, BS, 52; Univ Calif, Berkeley, PhD(chem), 55. *Prof Exp:* Res chemist, Elastomer Chem Dept, E I du Pont de Nemours & Co, 55-59; res assoc org chem, Univ Wyo, 59; asst prof chem, Colo State Univ, 59-62; assoc prof, Univ Nev, Reno, 62-66. *Concurrent Pos:* Res grants, NSF, 60-62, Am Chem Soc Petrol Res Fund, 64-66 & Desert Res Inst, Univ Nev, 66. *Mem:* AAAS; Am Chem Soc; Am Inst Chem Eng. *Res:* Polymer synthesis; property-structure relationships. *Mailing Add:* 5611 Mosaic Dr Holiday FL 34690

ROGAN, WALTER J, PUBLIC HEALTH & EPIDEMIOLOGY. *Current Pos:* Med officer, 78-86, chief, Epidemiol Br, 86-91, ASSOC DIR, DIV BIOMET & RISK ASSESSMENT, NAT INST ENVIRON HEALTH SCI, NIH, 91- *Personal Data:* b Bridgeport, Pa, May 27, 49. *Educ:* LaSalle Univ, BA, 71; Univ Calif, Berkeley, MPH, 75, San Francisco, MD, 75. *Concurrent Pos:* Adj assoc prof, Sch Pub Health, Univ NC, 88- *Mem:* Am Epidemiol Soc; Soc Pediat Res; AAAS; Soc Epidemiol Res; Am Col Prev Med. *Res:* Effects of perinatal exposure to toxic chemicals on childhood growth and development. *Mailing Add:* Nat Inst Environ Health Sci MDA3-02 PO Box 12233 Research Triangle Park NC 27709-2233

ROGATZ, PETER, PUBLIC HEALTH. *Current Pos:* LECTR, SCH PUB HEALTH, COLUMBIA UNIV, 58-; PROF CLIN COMMUNITY MED, SCH MED, STATE UNIV NY, STONY BROOK, 68- *Personal Data:* b New York, NY, Aug 5, 26; m 49, Marjorie Plaut; c William & Peggy. *Educ:* Columbia Univ, BA, 46, MPH, 56; Cornell Univ, MD, 49. *Honors & Awards:* Dean Conley Award, Am Col Hosp Adminrs, 75. *Prof Exp:* Dir study home care prog, Hosp Coun Greater New York, 53-55; Commonwealth Fund fel, Columbia Univ, 55-56; assoc med dir, Health Ins Plan Greater New York, 56-57; med adminr, East Nassau Med Group, 57-58; assoc dir hosp & health agency study, Fedn Jewish Philanthropies NY, 58-59; dep dir, Montefiore Hosp, New York, 60-63; dir, Long Island Jewish Hosp, 64-68; dir univ hosp, State Univ NY, Stony Brook, 68-71, co-dir grad prog health care admin, 69-71; sr vpres, Blue Cross & Blue Shield Greater New York, 71-76; pres & co-founder, RMR Health & Hosp Mgt Consults, Inc, 76-84; vpres med affairs, Vis Nurse Serv, NY, 84-91. *Concurrent Pos:* Dir, Study Home Care Progs, Hosp Coun Greater New York, 53-55; Commonwealth Fund fel, Columbia Univ, 55-56; assoc med dir, Health Ins Plan Greater New York, 56-57; med adminr, ENassau Med Group, 57-58; assoc dir, Hosp & Health Agency Study, Fedn Jewish Philanthropies New York, 58-59; lectr, Sch Pub Health, Columbia Univ, 58- *Mem:* Fel Am Col Physicians; fel Am Col Hosp Adminr; fel Am Col Prev Med; fel Am Pub Health Asn; Asn Teachers Prev Med. *Res:* Medical care organization and delivery of health services; community health planning; medical care administration. *Mailing Add:* 76 Oakdale Lane Roslyn Heights NY 11577-1535. *Fax:* 516-621-4906

ROGAWSKI, MICHAEL ANDREW, NEUROLOGY, NEUROSCIENCE. *Current Pos:* ASST PROF NEUROL, SCH MED, JOHNS HOPKINS UNIV, 86-; CHIEF, NEURONAL EXCITABILITY SECT, NAT INST NEUROL DIS & STROKE, NIH, 90- *Personal Data:* b Los Angeles, Calif, April 8, 52; c 2. *Educ:* Amherst Col, BA, 74; Sch Med, Yale Univ, MD & PhD(pharmacol), 80. *Honors & Awards:* Epilepsy Res Award, Am Soc Pharmacol Exp Therapeut, 94. *Prof Exp:* Med staff fel, Lab Neurophysiol, Nat Inst Neurol Dis & Stroke, NIH, 81-86. *Concurrent Pos:* Resident & fel neurol, Johns Hopkins Hosp, 82-85; active staff clin ctr, NIH, 87-; mem, Neuropharmacol & Neurochem Rev Comt, NIMH. *Mem:* Sigma Xi; Soc Neurosci; Am Soc Pharmacol & Exp Therapeut; Am Acad Neurol; Am Epilepsy Asn. *Res:* Cellular neurophysiology and neuropharmacology; anticonvulsant drugs. *Mailing Add:* Neuronal Excitability Sect NINDS NIH Bldg 10 Rm 5C SN-250 10 Center Dr MSC 1408 Bethesda MD 20892. *Fax:* 301-402-6788; *E-Mail:* rogawski@nih.gov

ROGER, WILLIAM ALEXANDER, ELECTRONICS, COMPUTER SCIENCES. *Current Pos:* DEFENSE SCIENTIST ELECTRONICS & SIGNAL PROCESSING, DEFENSE RES ESTAB ATLANTIC, 77- *Personal Data:* b Toronto, Ont, Apr 6, 47; m 69; c 2. *Educ:* Univ Toronto, BASc, 68, MSc, 70; Univ Alta, PhD(physics), 74. *Prof Exp:* Killam fel physics, Dalhousie Univ, 74-77. *Res:* Design and fabrication of electronic instruments for the armed forces; signal processing and analysis of oceanographic acoustic data. *Mailing Add:* Defense Res Estab Atlantic 9 Grove St PO Box 1012 Dartmouth NS B2Y 3Z7 Can

ROGERS, ADRIANNE ELLEFSON, EXPERIMENTAL PATHOLOGY. *Current Pos:* PROF & ASSOC CHMN PATH, BOSTON UNIV SCH MED, 84- *Personal Data:* b Aberdeen, Wash, Feb 18, 33; m 54; c 3. *Educ:* Radcliffe Col, AB, 54; Harvard Med Sch, MD, 58. *Prof Exp:* Intern med, Beth Israel Hosp, Boston, 58-59; res fel path, Boston City Hosp & Harvard Med Sch, 60-62; USPHS res fel, Mallory Inst Path, 62-64, res fel, 64-65; res assoc, Mass Inst Technol, 66-72, sr res scientist nutrit & food sci, 72-85. *Concurrent Pos:* Asst, Harvard Med Sch, 64-67, instr, 68-73; sr resident path, Peter Bent Brigham Hosp, Boston, Mass, 76-77, clin fel, 77-78. *Mem:* Am Asn Cancer Res; Am Soc Exp Path; Am Inst Nutrit. *Res:* Interaction between diet and chemical carcinogenesis; nutritional liver disease, including fatty liver and cirrhosis; toxicity. *Mailing Add:* Dept Path & Lab Med Boston Univ Sch Med 80 E Concord St Boston MA 02118-2394

ROGERS, ALAN BARDE, CHEMISTRY. *Current Pos:* RETIRED. *Personal Data:* b Sergeant Bluff, Iowa, Nov 8, 18; m 41, Ruth Bell; c Steven B, Linda A (Wilson) & James R. *Educ:* Iowa State Col, BSc, 42. *Prof Exp:* Res chemist, Armour & Co, 41-42, chem process develop, 45-48, chem mkt develop, 48-53, head dairy, poultry & specialty prods res, 53-60, assoc tech dir, Food Res Div, 60-64, asst dir, 64-67, asst dir res, 67-80. *Mem:* Poultry Sci Asn; Inst Food Technologists. *Res:* Poultry; frozen foods; dehydrated and dairy products. *Mailing Add:* 7090 E Mescal St Scottsdale AZ 85254-6118

ROGERS, ALAN ERNEST EXEL, RADIO ASTRONOMY. *Current Pos:* ASST DIR, HAYSTACK OBSERV, MASS INST TECHNOL, 67- *Personal Data:* b Harare, Zimbabwe, Oct 3, 41; US citizen; m 68, Louise Holland; c Heather & David. *Educ:* Univ Col Rhodesia & Nyasaland, BSc, 62; Mass Inst Technol, SM, 64, PhD(elec eng), 67. *Honors & Awards:* Rumford Medal, Am Acad Arts & Sci, 71. *Mem:* AAAS; Inst Elec & Electronics Engrs; Am Astron Soc; fel Am Geophys Union; Am Cong Surv & Mapping. *Res:* Emission and absorption of microwave radiation by interstellar hydroxl radical; radar mapping of Venus; very long baseline interferometry; radiometric instrumentation. *Mailing Add:* Haystack Observ Westford MA 01886. *E-Mail:* aeer@newton.haystack.edu

ROGERS, ALVIN LEE, MEDICAL MYCOLOGY, MEDICAL MICROBIOLOGY. *Current Pos:* from instr to prof, 65-94, EMER PROF MED MYCOL, MICH STATE UNIV, 94- *Personal Data:* b Houston, Tex, Jan 18, 29. *Educ:* Southeastern State Univ, BS, 48; Mich State Univ, PhD(med mycol, mycol), 67. *Honors & Awards:* Bessey Res Award, 64. *Prof Exp:* Teacher high sch, Tex, 48-59; instr biol, comp anat & microbiol, Bay City Jr Col, 59; instr biol bot, zool & microbiol, Port Huron Jr Col, 59-61. *Concurrent Pos:* Res assoc, Belo Horizonte Vet Sch, Brazil, 60, Bot Inst Sao Paulo, Brazil, 61 & Nat Univ Colombia, 68; co-dir, Mycol Sect Health Ctr & Animal Diag Lab, Mich State Univ, 77- *Mem:* Int Soc Human & Animal Mycol; Med Mycol Soc Am; Am Soc Microbiol; Mycol Soc Am; Soc Gen Microbiol; Sigma Xi; Med Mycol Soc Am. *Res:* Medical mycology; pathogenicity of fungi pathogenic in humans and animals and medical products produced by these fungi; adherance of Candida albicans to biological surfaces; development of animal models with mycoses for use in antifungal treatment, specifically within liposomes. *Mailing Add:* 1208 Georgetown Dr Safety Harbor FL 34695

ROGERS, BRUCE G(EORGE), CIVIL ENGINEERING. *Current Pos:* RETIRED. *Personal Data:* b Houston, Tex, Feb 20, 25. *Educ:* Univ Houston, BS, 57; Univ Ill, MS, 58, PhD(civil eng), 61. *Prof Exp:* Engr geophys, Robert H Ray Co, Tex, 47-52; engr asst, Tex Hwy Dept, 53-54, sr draftsman, 54-56, assoc design engr, 56; consult civil eng, Turner & Collie, 56-57; teaching asst theoret & appl mech, Univ Ill, 57-59, instr, 59-61; from asst prof to prof civil eng, Lamar Univ, 61-93. *Res:* Civil engineering. *Mailing Add:* Pro Peten Calle Central Flores Peten Itza Guatemala

ROGERS, CHARLES C, ELECTRICAL ENGINEERING. *Current Pos:* from asst prof to prof elec eng, 61-70, chmn dept, 65-70, PROF PHYSICS & ELEC ENG & CHMN DIV, 72-, Rose-Hulman Inst Technol. *Personal Data:* b Crawfordsville, Ind, Jan 27, 31; m 54; c 3. *Educ:* Purdue Univ, BSEE, 53, MSEE, 57, PhD(elec eng), 60. *Prof Exp:* Res asst elec eng, Mass Inst Technol, 55; supt elec power, Crawfordsville Elec Light & Power Co, Ind, 56; teaching asst elec eng, Purdue Univ, 56-57, instr, 57-60; res engr electromagnetics, Collins Radio Co, 60-61. *Concurrent Pos:* Mem adv bd, Aerospace Res Appl Ctr, Indiana Univ, 65-; pvt consult engr. *Mem:* Inst Elec & Electronics Engrs; Am Soc Eng Educ. *Res:* Electromagnetic theory. *Mailing Add:* 9500 Old Ft Harrison Ave Terre Haute IN 47803

ROGERS, CHARLES EDWIN, PHYSICAL CHEMISTRY, MEMBRANE MATERIALS. *Current Pos:* PROF MACROMOLECULAR SCI, CASE WESTERN RESERVE UNIV, 65-; CO-DIR, INTERUNIV & EPIC CTR ADHESIVES, SEALANTS & COATINGS, CASE WESTERN RES UNIV, 89- *Personal Data:* b Rochester, NY, Dec 29, 29; m 54, Barbara J DePuy; c Gregory N, Linda F (Zeigler) & Diana (Powell). *Educ:* Univ Syracuse, BS, 54; Univ Syracuse & State Univ NY, PhD(phys chem), 57. *Prof Exp:* Goodyear res fel & res assoc chem, Princeton Univ, 57-59; mem tech staff polymer chem, Bell Labs, 59-65. *Concurrent Pos:* Chmn comt, Consortium Univs Estab Overseas Educ Insts, 74-79; SRC sr vis fel, Imp Col, London, 71; assoc dir, Ctr Adhesives, Sealants & Coatings, 84-89. *Mem:* Am Chem Soc; Am Phys Soc; Adhesion Soc; NAm Membrane Soc. *Res:* Polymer science; solubility and diffusion in polymers; kinetics and mechanism of polymerization; polymer rheology and properties; polymer degradation; environmental effects on polymers; membrane separation processes and materials; adhesion and adhesives, sealants and coatings; surface science and technology. *Mailing Add:* Dept Macromolecular Sci Case Western Reserve Univ Cleveland OH 44106-7202. *Fax:* 216-368-4202; *E-Mail:* cer@po.cwru.edu

ROGERS, CHARLES GRAHAM, BIOCHEMISTRY, MICROBIOLOGY. *Current Pos:* RETIRED. *Personal Data:* b Summerside, PEI, Mar 13, 29; m 61; c 1. *Educ:* McGill Univ, BSc, 52, MSc, 54; Univ Wis, PhD(microbiol), 63. *Prof Exp:* chemist, Dept Nat Health & Welfare, Can, 54-65, res scientist, 65-92. *Mem:* Am Soc Microbiol; Can Biochem Soc; Sigma Xi; Nutrit Soc Can; Can Inst Food Sci & Technol. *Res:* Dietary stress in relation to lipid composition and metabolism in rat liver tissue and cardiac muscle cells in tissue culture; enzymes of lipid metabolism in cultured heart cells. *Mailing Add:* 41 Okanagan Dr Nepean ON K2H 7E9 Can

ROGERS, CHARLIE ELLIC, ENTOMOLOGY. *Current Pos:* supvr res entomologist & res leader, Conserv & Prod Res Ctr, 80-83, LAB DIR, INSECT BIOL & POP MGT RES LAB, AGR RES SERV, USDA, TIFTON, GA, 83- *Personal Data:* b Booneville, Ark, Aug 13, 38; m 71, Donna C Ray; c Christian E & Cheryl E. *Educ:* Northern Ariz Univ, BS, 64; Univ Ky, MS, 67; Okla State Univ, PhD(entom), 70. *Honors & Awards:* Prof Excellence Award, Am Agr Econ Soc, 79. *Prof Exp:* Teacher biol & social studies, Dysart Pub Schs, Ariz, 64-65; res assoc entom, Okla State Univ, 70-71; asst prof, Agr Exp Sta, Tex A&M Univ, 71-75; res entomologist, Southwestern Great Plains Res Ctr, Sci & Educ Admin-Fed Res, USDA, 75-80. *Concurrent Pos:* Ed, Biol Control, 90- *Mem:* Entom Soc Am; Sigma Xi. *Res:* Biology, ecology and control of insect pests of sunflower and guar; biological control of agricultural pests; insect migration; biology second pathogenicty of parasitic nematodes attacking lepidoptera pests. *Mailing Add:* USDA/ARS-Insect Biol & Pop Mgt Res Lab PO Box 748 Tifton GA 31793. *Fax:* 912-387-2321; *E-Mail:* crogers@tifton.cpes.peachnet.edu

ROGERS, DAVID ELLIOTT, internal medicine, infectious diseases; deceased, see previous edition for last biography

ROGERS, DAVID FREEMAN, FLUID DYNAMICS, AEROSPACE ENGINEERING. *Current Pos:* from asst to assoc prof, US Naval Acad, 64-73, off naval res prof, 71-73, dir cad/ig, 75-85, PROF AEROSPACE ENG, US NAVAL ACAD, 74- *Personal Data:* b Theresa, NY, Sept 3, 37. *Educ:* Rensselaer Polytech Inst, BAeroE, 59, MSAE, 60, PhD(aeronaut, astronaut), 67. *Prof Exp:* Res assoc aeronaut eng, Rensselaer Polytech Inst, 62-64. *Concurrent Pos:* Sr consult, Cadcom, Inc, 70-; hon res fel, Univ Col London, 77-78; vis prof, Univ New Southwales, 80; vis prof, Univ New S Wales Sydney, Australia, 82; Fujitsu fel Royal Melbourne, Inst Tech, Melbourne, Australia, 87. *Mem:* Am Inst Aeronaut & Astronaut; Soc Naval Archit & Marine Engrs; Asn Comput Mach. *Res:* Computer graphics; computer aided manufacturing; curve and surface description; compressible boundary layers; aerodynamics of nonrigid airfoils; computer aided design and interactive graphics; numerical methods; nonlinear two point asymptotic boundary value problems; flight dynamics. *Mailing Add:* Dept Aerospace Eng US Naval Acad Annapolis MD 21402-5042

ROGERS, DAVID PETER, MARINE METEOROLOGY, AIR POLLUTION. *Current Pos:* asst res meteorologist, 88-89, ASSOC RES OCEANOGR, SCRIPPS INST OCEANOG, 89- *Personal Data:* b Barri, Wales, Mar 20, 57; m 82; c 2. *Educ:* Univ E Anglia, UK, BSc, 80; Univ Southampton, PhD(oceanog), 83. *Prof Exp:* From asst res prof to assoc res prof boundary layer meteorol, Desert Res Inst, 83-87; from asst res prof to assoc prof physics, Univ Nev, Reno, 85-87 & 87-88. *Mem:* Fel Royal Meteorol Soc; Am Meteorol Soc; AAAS. *Res:* Observational and numerical studies of the marine atmospheric boundary layer and problems of long range transport of pollutants. *Mailing Add:* Scripps Inst Oceanog La Jolla CA 92093-0230

ROGERS, DAVID T, JR, ECOLOGY. *Current Pos:* RETIRED. *Personal Data:* b Foley, Ala, Apr 10, 35; m 58; c Paul & Nancy. *Educ:* Huntington Col, AB, 58; Univ Ga, MS, 63, PhD(bird migration), 65. *Prof Exp:* Teacher, Marbury High Sch, 59-61 & Southern Union Jr Col, 61-62; from asst prof to prof biol, Univ Ala, Tuscaloosa, 65-94; bird cur, Ala Mus Natural Hist, 89-94. *Concurrent Pos:* US Dept Interior grant, 70-71; NSF grant, 71; US Corps Eng grant, 72-73. *Mem:* Am Field Ornithologists; Am Ornithologists Union; Wilson Ornith Soc. *Res:* Ornithology, especially population and community aspects; bird migration in Latin America. *Mailing Add:* 2708 Firethorn Dr Tuscaloosa AL 35404-5141

ROGERS, DAVID WILLIAM OLIVER, RADIATION DOSIMETRY, MONTE CARLO TRANSPORT. *Current Pos:* RES OFFICER RADIATION DOSIMETRY, NAT RES COUN CAN, 73-, HEAD, IONIZING RADIATION STAND, 85- *Personal Data:* b Toronto, Ont, Aug 11, 45; m 92, Joanna Cygler; c Brenda, Karine, Adam & Mark. *Educ:* Univ Toronto, BSc, 68, MSc, 69, PhD(physics), 72. *Honors & Awards:* Sylvia Fedoruk Prize, 89; Farrington Daniels Award, 91; Landauer lectr, 93. *Prof Exp:* Res assoc, Oxford Nuclear Physics Lab, UK, 72-73. *Concurrent Pos:* Chmn, Med & Biol Physics Div, Can Asn Physicists, 83-84; adj prof physics, Carleton Univ, 86-; assoc ed, Med Physics, 87-; mem, Int Comn Radiation Units & Measurements, Comt Absorbed Dose Stand, CCEMR1(1) Int Bur Weights & Measurements & Radiation Ther Comt, Am Asn Physicists, 88- *Mem:* Can Asn Physicists; Health Physics Soc; Am Asn Physicists Med; Can Radiation Protection Asn; Can Orgn Med Physicists. *Res:* Radiation dosimetry for medical and radiation protection purposes; development and use of coupled electron-photon transport; Monte Carlo codes for medical physics applications; national primary standards for radiation measurement; health physics. *Mailing Add:* Nat Res Coun Can Inst Nat Measurement Stand Montreal Rd Ottawa ON K1A 0R6 Can. *Fax:* 613-952-9865; *E-Mail:* dave@irs.phy.nrc.ca

ROGERS, DEXTER, BIOCHEMISTRY. *Current Pos:* CONSULT PROD DEVELOP, 80- *Personal Data:* b Kyoto, Japan, Dec 14, 21; m 45; c 4. *Educ:* Univ Mich, BS, 44, MS, 46; Ore State Univ, PhD(biochem), 54. *Prof Exp:* Res chemist, Western Condensing Co, Appleton, Wis, 45-51; NSF fel, Stanford Univ, 54-55; instr biochem, Univ Mich, 55-58; instr & res assoc chem, Univ Ore, 58-60; asst prof food & nutrit, Utah State Univ, 60-62, chem, 62-65; asst prof, Univ Mont, 65-66; USPHS spec fel, Ore State Univ, 66-68; prof, State Univ NY Col Cortland, 68-69; lectr, Portland State Univ, 69-70; prof & chmn dept, William Paterson Col NJ, 70-75; prof chem, Bloomfield Col, 75-77; applns & develop chemist, KONTES, 77-79. *Mem:* AAAS; Am Chem Soc; Am Soc Microbiol. *Res:* Biochemistry of microorganisms; sugar transport mechanisms. *Mailing Add:* 108 Pico Ct Meadowbrook Village Mays Landing NJ 08330

ROGERS, DONALD B, SOLID STATE INORGANIC CHEMISTRY. *Current Pos:* RETIRED. *Personal Data:* b Moulton, Ala, Mar 2, 36; m 57; c 4. *Educ:* Vanderbilt Univ, BA, 58; Mass Inst Tech, PhD(inorg chem), 62. *Prof Exp:* Res scientist, Lincoln Lab, Mass Inst Tech, 62-65 & E I DuPont de Nemours, 65-69; res scientist, E I Du Pont de Nemours, 65-69, res supvr, Ctr Res, 69-72, res mgr, Photo Prods, 72-75, lab dir, DuPont Deutschland, 75-78, dir mkt, Printing Systs, 78-82, dir res & develop, Textile Fibers, 82-84, Dir Res & Develop Electronics, 84-94. *Mem:* Indust Res Inst. *Res:* Ceramics and polymers photosensitive coatings; film casting and coating; microelectronic packaging and interconnection; OPTO electronics. *Mailing Add:* 429 Village Dr Daphne AL 36526

ROGERS, DONALD EUGENE, FISH BIOLOGY. *Current Pos:* Fishery biologist, 60-68, mem fac fisheries, 69-77, RES ASSOC PROF FISHERIES, FISHERIES RES INST, UNIV WASH, 77- *Personal Data:* b Los Angeles, Calif, Aug 27, 32; m 55; c 2. *Educ:* Calif State Polytech, San Luis Obispo, BS, 58; Univ Wash, MS, 61, PhD(fisheries), 67. *Mem:* Am Inst Fishery Res Biologists; Am Fisheries Soc; Sigma Xi. *Res:* Fish population dynamics; biology of sockeye salmon. *Mailing Add:* Univ Wash Fisheries Box 357980 Seattle WA 98195-7980

ROGERS, DONALD RICHARD, INORGANIC CHEMISTRY. *Current Pos:* Res chemist, 61-64, group leader chem, 64-65 & 68-71, sr res specialist, 72-79, FEL NUCLEAR OPERS DEPT, MOUND LAB, MONSANTO RES CORP, MIAMISBURG, 79- *Personal Data:* b Richmond, Ky, Apr 27, 32; m 61. *Educ:* Univ Ky, BS, 59, MS, 61, PhD(chem), 68. *Mem:* AAAS; Am Chem Soc; Sigma Xi. *Res:* Coordination chemistry of lanthanide and actinide elements; solvent extraction equilibria; radioisotopic fuels; environmental chemistry of plutonium; nuclear safeguards; uranium and plutonium measurement methods. *Mailing Add:* 975 Fernshire Dr Centerville OH 45459

ROGERS, DONALD WARREN, PHYSICAL CHEMISTRY, ANALYTICAL CHEMISTRY. *Current Pos:* from asst prof to assoc prof, 65-71, PROF CHEM, LONG ISLAND UNIV, 71- *Personal Data:* b Hackensack, NJ, Sept 10, 32; m 56; c 2. *Educ:* Princeton Univ, BA, 54; Wesleyan Univ, MA, 56; NC Univ, PhD(chem, math), 60. *Prof Exp:* Asst prof chem, Robert Col, Istanbul, 60-63 & Long Island Univ, 63-64; master teacher chem & physics, Am Madrid, Spain, 64-65. *Concurrent Pos:* NIH res grants, 71-73, 74-77, 77 & 81-, Cottrell res grant, 83-85 & PRF res grants, 85-87, 88-89 & 89-91; vis prof chem, Univ Ga, 76-77 & Barnard Col, 80-81. *Mem:* Am Chem Soc. *Res:* Enthalpies of hydrogenation; thermochemistry; molecular structure; enthalpimetry; solution theory. *Mailing Add:* Dept Chem Long Island Univ Brooklyn NY 11201

ROGERS, DOUGLAS HERBERT, OPTICS, METAL PHYSICS. *Current Pos:* from asst prof to prof, 54-83, EMER PROF PHYSICS, ROYAL MIL COL CAN, 83- *Personal Data:* b Wolfville, NS, June 2, 26; m 51, Beverley Huntington; c 3. *Educ:* Dalhousie Univ, BSc, 47, MSc, 49; Mass Inst Technol, PhD(physics), 53. *Prof Exp:* Fel low temperature & solid state physics, Nat Res Coun, Can, 52-54. *Mem:* Optical Soc Am; Am Phys Soc; Am Asn Physics Teachers; Can Asn Physicists. *Res:* Attenuation of ultra sound; dislocations; acoustic emission; liquid crystals; holographic interferometry. *Mailing Add:* RR 1 C17 Bowen Island BC V0N 1G0 Can

ROGERS, EDWIN HENRY, COMPUTER SCIENCES, SYSTEMS DESIGN. *Current Pos:* PROF COMPUT SCI & MATH, RENSSELAER POLYTECH INST, 65- *Personal Data:* b Newton, Mass, Nov 5, 36; m 60, Joan B Grant; c 3. *Educ:* Carnegie-Mellon Univ, BS, 58, MS, 60, PhD(math), 62. *Prof Exp:* Res technician, Woods Hole Oceanog Inst, 56-58; teaching asst & instr math, Carnegie Inst Technol, 58-62; Leverhulme vis fel, Univ Strathclyde, 62-63; US Army, 63-65. *Concurrent Pos:* Managing ed, Siam News, Soc Indust & Appl Math, 75-82; vis res prof, Univ Waterloo, 76-77; vis scientist, Gen Electric Res & Develop Ctr, 83. *Mem:* AAAS; Inst Elec & Electronics Engrs Comput Soc; Soc Indust & Appl Math; Asn Comput Mach; Inst Elec & Electronics Engrs. *Res:* Wafer scale systems; yield analysis and fault tolerance; parallel algorithms; nonlinear and multiparameter eigen problems; computer-integrated education; computer supported collaborative system design. *Mailing Add:* Dept Comput Sci Rensselaer Polytech Inst Troy NY 12180-3590. *E-Mail:* rogere@rpi.edu

ROGERS, EMERY HERMAN, PHYSICS. *Current Pos:* gen mgr, 67-75, gen mgr, Anal Instrument Group, Hewlett-Packard Co, 75-79, EXEC DIR, HEWLETT-PACKARD CO FOUND, 79- *Personal Data:* b Los Angeles, Calif, Mar 31, 21; c 3. *Educ:* Stanford Univ, AB, 43, PhD(physics), 51. *Prof Exp:* Asst physics, Stanford Univ, 42-43; physicist, US Naval Res Lab, 43-45; engr nuclear magnetic resonance, Varian Assocs, 49-53, mgr instrument field eng, 53-60, vpres & mgr instrument div, 60-63, vpres instrument group, 63-67. *Mem:* AAAS; Am Phys Soc; Instrument Soc Am; Sci Apparatus Makers Asn. *Res:* Nuclear magnetic resonance; electron paramagnetic resonance; magnetism; analytical instrumentation. *Mailing Add:* 218 Lowell Ave Palo Alto CA 94301

ROGERS, EUGENE J, PHYSICAL MEDICINE & REHABILITATION. *Current Pos:* PROF & CHMN REHAB MED, CHICAGO MED SCH, FINCH UNIV HEALTH SCI, 73- *Personal Data:* b Vienna, Austria, June 13, 21; US citizen; m 52, Joyce M Lighter; c Jay A & Robert J. *Educ:* City Col NY, BS, 43; Chicago Med Sch, BM, 46, MD, 47. *Honors & Awards:* Bronze Medal, Am Cong Rehab Med, 74. *Prof Exp:* Dir instr & asst prof rehab med, State Univ NY, Brooklyn, 60-73. *Concurrent Pos:* Consult, Div Rehab Med, State Educ Dept NY, 63-73, Nara Tripton Adv Bd, 97; secy & dir, Micro Therapeut Inc, 70-72; hon consult rehab med, NY City Police Dept, 70-73. *Mem:* Am Col Physicians; Am Acad Phys Med & Rehab; AMA. *Res:* Diurnal pain variations; fractures and aphasia in strokes; vascular disease or local vascular lesion; fibro myalgia or myofascial pain; tension headaches and fibrositis; medical curriculum changes to meet current needs of society. *Mailing Add:* 1110 N Lake Shore Dr No 13 S Chicago IL 60611

ROGERS, FRANCES ARLENE, protozoology & vertebrate zoology, anatomy; deceased, see previous edition for last biography

ROGERS, FRED BAKER, PREVENTIVE MEDICINE, FAMILY PRACTICE. *Current Pos:* Rotating intern, Univ Hosp, Temple Univ, 48-49, chief resident med, 53-54, USPHS fel, Univ, 54-55, from asst prof to prof, Prev Med, Sch Med, 56-90, chmn, Dept Family Pract & Community Health, 70-77, EMER PROF, PREV MED, SCH MED, TEMPLE UNIV, 90- *Personal Data:* b Trenton, NJ, Aug 25, 26. *Educ:* Temple Univ, MD, 48; Univ Pa, MS, 54; Columbia Univ, MPH, 57; Am Bd Prev Med, dipl, 57. *Concurrent Pos:* Lectr epidemiol, Sch Pub Health, Columbia Univ, 57-68; lectr pub health, Sch Nursing, Univ Pa, 64-67; consult med, US Naval Hosp, Philadelphia, 64-73; hon mem, Royal Soc Med, London, Eng, 90. *Mem:* AMA; fel Am Col Physicians; Am Osler Soc. *Res:* Epidemiology; immunization; history of medicine. *Mailing Add:* 333 W State St Apt 6K Trenton NJ 08618-5749

ROGERS, GERALD STANLEY, MATHEMATICAL STATISTICS. *Current Pos:* from assoc prof to prof, 65-95, EMER PROF MATH, NMEX STATE UNIV, 95- *Personal Data:* b Reading, Pa, Feb 29, 28. *Educ:* Muhlenberg Col, BS, 48; Univ Wash, MA, 51; Univ Iowa, PhD(math), 58. *Prof Exp:* Instr, Lafayette Col, 54-55; asst prof math, Univ Ariz, 58-65. *Mem:* Am Math Soc; Math Asn Am; Am Statist Asn; Inst Math Statist. *Res:* Statistical distribution theory. *Mailing Add:* Dept Math Sci NMex State Univ Las Cruces NM 88003

ROGERS, GIFFORD EUGENE, regional development, irrigation & drainage design, for more information see previous edition

ROGERS, H(ARRY) C(ARTON), JR, PHYSICAL & MECHANICAL METALLURGY, METALWORKING. *Current Pos:* RETIRED. *Personal Data:* b Patchogue, NY, Oct 3, 23; m 47; c 3. *Educ:* Cornell Univ, AB, 47; Rensselaer Polytech Inst, PhD(metall), 56. *Honors & Awards:* McKay-Helm Award, Am Welding Soc, 76 & Adams Mem Award. *Prof Exp:* Res metallurgist, Gen Elec Co, 48-69; prof, Drexel Univ, 69-84, head, Dept Mat Eng, 87-90, A W Grosvenor prof mat Eng, 84-91. *Concurrent Pos:* Vis res scientist, Melbourne Res Labs, BHP Steel Co, Australia, 81 & Mat & Mech Res Ctr, Army, Watertown, Mass, 83; vis prof, Monash Univ, Australia, 81. *Mem:* Fel Am Soc Metals; Am Welding Soc; Am Inst Mining, Metall & Petrol Engrs; fel Am Inst Chemists. *Res:* Materials processing; mechanical behavior and fracture of solids; hydrogen embrittlement of metals; high pressure processing of metals; material behavior under high rates of loading. *Mailing Add:* 784 Congestoga Rd Berwyn PA 19312

ROGERS, HARTLEY, JR, COMPUTABILITY, PROBLEM-SOLVING. *Current Pos:* vis lectr, Mas Inst Technol, 55-56, from asst prof to assoc prof, 56-64, chmn fac, 71-73, assoc provost, 74-80, PROF MATH, MASS INST TECHNOL, 64- *Personal Data:* b Buffalo, NY, July 6, 26; m 54, Adrianne Ellefson; c Hartley, Campbell & Caroline. *Educ:* Yale Univ, AB, 46, MS, 50; Princeton Univ, PhD(math), 52; Cambridge Univ, MA, 68. *Honors & Awards:* Ford Award, Math Asn Am. *Prof Exp:* Asst instr math, Princeton Univ, 50-52; Benjamin Pierce instr, Harvard Univ, 52-55. *Concurrent Pos:* Guggenheim fel, 60-61; vis fel, Clare Hall, Cambridge Univ & NSF sr fel, 67-68; ed, Annals Math Logic, 69-86, J Comput & Syst Sci, 69- & J Symbolic Logic, 63-67; trustee, Buckingham, Browne & Nichols Sch, 75-81 & Kingsley Trust Assoc, 76-78; consult, NSF, 80-; sr assoc, Eliot House, Harvard Univ, 80-; vis scholar, Harvard Univ, 80-81. *Mem:* Am Math Soc; Math Asn Am; Asn Symbolic Logic (vpres, 64-67). *Res:* Mathematical logic and complexity theory; probability and statistics; random and pseudo-random digits; teaching of multivariable calculus. *Mailing Add:* Mass Inst Technol 77 Massachusetts Ave Rm 2-249 Cambridge MA 02139

ROGERS, HARVEY WILBUR, INCINERATION RESEARCH, INFECTIOUS WASTE MANAGEMENT. *Current Pos:* ENVIRON ENGR, CHEM DEMILITARIZATION, CTR DIS CONTROL & PREV, 92- *Personal Data:* b Annapolis, Md, Feb 20, 45; m 70, Patricia Powell; c Michelle & John. *Educ:* WVa Univ, BS, 67, MS, 68. *Prof Exp:* Sanit engr, Off Solid Waste Mgt Prog, USPHS, 68-71, chief systs sect, 71-73; sanit engr, Off Solid Waste Mgt Prog, US Environ Protect Agency, 73-74; environ engr, Div Res Serv, NIH, 74-80, chief, Environ Systs Sect, 80-85, chief, Pollution Control Sect, 85-86, chief, Environ Protect Br, Div Safety, 86-89; environ eng, Incineration Specialist, Agency Toxic Substances Dis Registry, 89-92. *Concurrent Pos:* Lectv univ prof, 75-; adv, Nat Acad Sci, 82-83, WHO, Hosp Waste Mgt, 84-, US Environ Protect Agency, 85-86 & NSF, 88; guest fac, Am Soc Hosp Engrs, 85-88. *Mem:* Air & Waste Mgt Asn; Am Soc Mech Engrs. *Res:* Author of several articles on special waste management; hazardous chemical waste management and incineration technology. *Mailing Add:* Ctr Dis Control & Prev MS F29 1600 Clifton Rd NE Atlanta GA 30333

ROGERS, HOWARD GARDNER, physics, chemistry; deceased, see previous edition for last biography

ROGERS, HOWARD H, ELECTROCHEMISTRY, COMPUTER PROGRAMMING. *Current Pos:* SCIENTIST, HUGHES ELECTRONICS CO, 73- *Personal Data:* b New York, Dec 26, 26; m 78, Maureen Dohn; c Lynne, Mark D & Susan (Reece). *Educ:* Univ Ill, BS, 49; Mass Inst Technol, PhD(inorg chem), 53. *Honors & Awards:* Hyland Patent Award, Hughes Aircraft Co, 87. *Prof Exp:* Res asst chem, Mass Inst Technol, 51-52; from res chemist to res group leader inorg chem, Res Div, Allis-Chalmers Mfg Co, 52-61; from res specialist to sr tech specialist, Res Div, Rocketdyne Div, NAm Rockwell Corp, 61-70; chief res scientist, Martek Instruments, Inc, 70-73. *Mem:* Am Chem Soc; Electrochem Soc; Sigma Xi. *Res:* Batteries, especially nickel-hydrogen; electrochemistry; electronics; fluorine chemistry; high temperature chemistry; advanced wastewater treatment; chemical instrumentation; battery (computer) modelling; programming. *Mailing Add:* 18361 Van Ness Ave Torrance CA 90504

ROGERS, HOWARD TOPPING, SOIL SCIENCE, AGRONOMY. *Current Pos:* head dept, 51-66, prof, 66-76, EMER PROF AGRON & SOILS, AUBURN UNIV, 76- *Personal Data:* b Savedge, Va, July 22, 08; m 37; c 1. *Educ:* Va Polytech Inst, BS, 30; Mich State Col, MS, 36; Iowa State Col, PhD(soil fertility), 42. *Prof Exp:* Instr high schs, Va, 30-34; asst soil surv, Mich State Col, 35; asst soil technologist, Exp Sta, Va Polytech Inst, 36-41; assoc soil chemist, Ala Polytech Inst, 42-46; agronomist & chief, Soil & Fertilizer Res Br, Tenn Valley Authority, 47-51. *Concurrent Pos:* Consult, Tenn Valley Authority, 80. *Mem:* Soil Sci Soc Am; fel Am Soc Agron; Sigma Xi. *Res:* Exo-enzyme systems of plant roots and availability of organic phosphorus to plants; soil and water conservation; effect of lime on physico-chemical properties of soils and crop yields; boron requirements of legumes and boron fixation in soils; summary and analysis of data on crop response to phosphates; agri-chemicals; new fertilizer practices. *Mailing Add:* 260 Fontaine Dr Auburn AL 36830

ROGERS, HOWELL WADE, MEDICAL MICROBIOLOGY, VIROLOGY. *Current Pos:* asst prof, 72-83, ASSOC PROF MICROBIOL & IMMUNOL, IND UNIV SCH MED EVANSVILLE CTR, 83- *Personal Data:* b Ripley, Miss, Nov 26, 43; m 63; c 3. *Educ:* Univ Miss, BA, 65, MS, 67; Univ Okla, PhD(med microbiol), 70. *Prof Exp:* Instr microbiol, Med Ctr, Univ Miss, 70-72, actg asst prof, 72. *Mem:* AAAS; Am Soc Microbiol; Sigma Xi. *Res:* Viral enzymes; Herpes virus immunology; cell-mediated immunity to Herpes simplex virus. *Mailing Add:* Ind Univ Sch Med-Evansville 8600 Univ Blvd Evansville IN 47712

ROGERS, HUGO H, JR, GLOBAL CHANGE, PLANT PHYSIOLOGY. *Current Pos:* PLANT PHYSIOLOGIST, AGR RES SERV, USDA, 76- *Personal Data:* b Atmore, Ala, Aug 2, 47; m 70, Crystal Harmon; c Hannah Star & Hiram Harmon. *Educ:* Auburn Univ, BS, 69, MS, 71; Univ NC, Chapel Hill, PhD(air pollution), 75. *Prof Exp:* Environ engr air pollution & veg, Res Triangle Inst, 75-76. *Concurrent Pos:* Res assoc air pollutant uptake by veg, NC State Univ, 75-76, from asst to assoc prof bot, 76-84; adj assoc prof, Dept Environ Sci & Eng, Sch Pub Health, Univ NC, Chapel Hill, 78-; adj prof, Dept Agron & Soils, Sch Forestry, Auburn Univ, 84-; adj prof, Dept Bot, Duke Univ, 94- *Mem:* Air Pollution Control Asn; Am Soc Plant Physiologists; Am Soc Agr Eng; fel Am Agron Soc; Crop Sci Soc Am; Soil Sci Soc Am; fel AAAS. *Res:* Interaction of vegetation with atmospheric chemicals, especially plant gas exchange and effects of air pollutants on plants; carbon dioxide and field studies; design of research equipment for such work; global environmental change. *Mailing Add:* USDA-Agr Res Serv Nat Soil Dynamics Lab PO Box 3439 Auburn AL 36831-3439. *E-Mail:* hrogers@acesag.auburn.edu

ROGERS, JACK DAVID, MYCOLOGY, PLANT PATHOLOGY. *Current Pos:* Asst prof forestry & asst plant pathologist, Wash State Univ, 63-68, assoc prof plant path, 68-72, PROF PLANT PATH, WASH STATE UNIV, 72-, CHMN, DEPT PLANT PATH, 86- *Personal Data:* b Point Pleasant, WVa, Sept 3, 37; m 58, Belle C Spencer; c 2. *Educ:* Davis & Elkins Col, BS, 60; Duke Univ, MF, 60; Univ Wis, PhD(plant path), 63. *Mem:* Mycol Soc Am (vpres, 75-76, pres-elect, 76-77, pres, 77-78); Am Phytopath Soc; Bot Soc Am; Brit Mycol Soc. *Res:* Forest pathology; botany; cytology; genetics; evolution of Ascomycetes. *Mailing Add:* Dept Plant Path Wash State Univ Pullman WA 99164-6430. *Fax:* 509-335-9581; *E-Mail:* rogers@wsu.edu

ROGERS, JACK WYNDALL, JR, TOPOLOGY. *Current Pos:* assoc prof, 73-76, PROF MATH, AUBURN UNIV, 76- *Personal Data:* b Austin, Tex, Jan 13, 43; m 62; c 2. *Educ:* Univ Tex, BA, 63, MS, 65, PhD(math), 66. *Prof Exp:* From asst prof to assoc prof math, Emory Univ, 66-73. *Mem:* Am Math Soc; Math Asn Am. *Mailing Add:* Auburn Univ Auburn AL 36849-5310

ROGERS, JAMES ALBERT, PHARMACEUTICS, PHYSICAL PHARMACY. *Current Pos:* asst prof, 69-74, assoc prof pharm, 74-88, PROF, UNIV ALTA, 88- *Personal Data:* b Sault Ste Marie, Ont, July 4, 40; m 66, Louise Harding; c Jacelyn & Bradley. *Educ:* Univ Toronto, BS, 63, MS, 66; Univ Strathclyde, Scotland, PhD(pharmaceut technol), 69. *Prof Exp:* Pharmacist, Tamblyn Drug Co, Ltd, 63. *Mem:* Asn Faculties Pharm Can; Am Pharmaceut Asn; Am Asn Pharmaceut Scientists; Controlled Release Soc. *Res:* Dosage form design and formulation of drug delivery systems; drug-biomembrane interactions; partition coefficient basis of quantitative structure activity relationships; liposome approaches to drug dissolution, drug stability and oral drug delivery. *Mailing Add:* Fac Pharm & Pharmaceut Sci Univ Alta Edmonton AB T6G 2N8 Can. *Fax:* 403-492-1217; *E-Mail:* jrogers@pharmacy.ualberta.ca

ROGERS, JAMES EDWIN, GROUND WATER HYDROLOGY, GEOLOGIC MAPPING. *Current Pos:* GEO-HYDROL CONSULT, 85- *Personal Data:* b Waco, Tex, Feb 24, 29; m 57, Margaret A Bruchmann; c James F Rogers. *Educ:* Univ Tex, BS, 55, MA, 61. *Prof Exp:* Supv hydrologist, US Geol Surv, Alexandria, LA, 56-85. *Mem:* Fel Geol Soc Am; Nat Groundwater Asn. *Res:* Ground-water flow through fine-grained deposits; movement of contaminants in the subsurface. *Mailing Add:* 4008 Innis Dr Alexandria LA 71303

ROGERS, JAMES JOSEPH, HYDROLOGY, SYSTEM MODELING. *Current Pos:* COMPUT PROG ANALYST, PAC NORTHWEST RES STA, 83- *Personal Data:* b Salem, NJ, Oct 30, 42; m 65; c 3. *Educ:* Utah State Univ, BS, 64; Univ Ariz, MS, 71, PhD(hydrol), 73. *Prof Exp:* Forester mgt, Apache Nat Forest, 65-71; forester watershed, Rocky Mountain Forest & Range Exp Sta, 71-72, hydrologist, 72-74, hydrologist watershed, 76-83. *Mem:* Sigma Xi; Am Geophys Union. *Res:* Development of computer systems for understanding and predicting effects of land management activities on resource outputs and productivity of southwestern forest ecosystems. *Mailing Add:* 5921 Sunset St Juneau AK 99801

ROGERS, JAMES SAMUEL, AGRICULTURAL ENGINEERING, SOIL PHYSICS. *Current Pos:* AGR ENGR AGR RES SERV, USDA, 83-, ASSOC PROF AGR ENG, LA STATE UNIV, 83- *Personal Data:* b Cassville, Ga, Aug 20, 34; m 56, 89, Sarah Smith; c Pamela & Lora. *Educ:* Univ Ga, BSAE, 55, MS, 62; Univ Ill, Urbana, PhD(soil physics), 69. *Prof Exp:* Agr engr, Agr Res Serv, USDA, Univ Ga, 57-64 & Univ Ill, 64-68; agr engr sci & educ admin-agr, USDA, Univ Fla, 68-83, asst prof agr eng, 77-83. *Mem:* Am Soc Agr Engrs; Am Soc Agron; Soil Sci Soc Am; Soil Conserv Soc Am. *Res:* Water management in wet soils to include drainage, irrigation, water quality, climate modification and more efficient use of water in agriculture. *Mailing Add:* Dept Biol Sci Univ New Orleans New Orleans LA 70122. *Fax:* 504-388-4883; *E-Mail:* srogers@gumbo.age.lsu.edu

ROGERS, JAMES STEWART, EXPERIMENTAL SOLID STATE PHYSICS. *Current Pos:* RETIRED. *Personal Data:* b Santa Maria, Calif, Apr 5, 32; Can citizen; m 56; c 4. *Educ:* Univ Sask, BEng, 54; Univ Alta, MSc, 62, PhD(physics), 64. *Prof Exp:* Fel, Commonwealth Sci & Indust Res Orgn, Australia, 64-66; assoc prof physics, Univ Alta, 68-94. *Mem:* Australian Inst Physics. *Res:* Electron tunneling into superconductors and ferromagnetic materials. *Mailing Add:* Box 8006 Edson AB T7E 1W2 Can

ROGERS, JAMES TED, JR, MATHEMATICS. *Current Pos:* From asst prof to assoc prof, 68-77, PROF MATH, TULANE UNIV, 77- *Personal Data:* b Statesville, NC, July 26, 42; m 66; c 2. *Educ:* Univ NC, Chapel Hill, BS, 64; Univ Calif, Riverside, MA, 66, PhD(math), 68. *Mem:* AAAS; Am Math Soc. *Res:* Point set topology. *Mailing Add:* Tulane Univ New Orleans LA 70118-5698

ROGERS, JAMES TERENCE, (JR), HEAT TRANSFER, NUCLEAR REACTOR SAFETY. *Current Pos:* PROF MECH ENG, CARLETON UNIV, 70- *Personal Data:* b Montreal, Que, Nov 19, 26; m 57, Sharon L Little; c Allison L, Kelly A, Patrick T & Christopher K. *Educ:* McGill Univ, BEng, 48, MEng, 50, PhD(mech eng), 53. *Honors & Awards:* Robert W Angus Medal, Eng Inst Can, 64; J W Stachiewicz Medal, Can Soc Mech Eng, 91; W B Lewis Medal, Can Nuclear Asn, 93. *Prof Exp:* Res engr, Can Dept Mines & Tech Surv, 50-51; asst prof mech eng, Royal Mil Col Can, 53-55; engr & design specialist, Nuclear Div, Canadair Ltd, 55-59; res engr, Gen Atomic Div, Gen Dynamics Corp, 59-60; tech counsr, Atomic Power Dept, Can Gen Elec, 60-70. *Concurrent Pos:* Mem assoc comt heat transfer, Nat Res Coun Can, 66-71; Can deleg, Assembly Int Heat Transfer Conf, 67-82, secy, 74-78; mem, Eng Inst Can Coun, 68-70; mem sci coun, Int Ctr Heat & Mass Transfer, Yugoslavia, 68; consult many orgns, 70-; mem comt energy sci policies, Sci Coun Can, 76-79, Can Nat Comt Heat Transfer, 79-84. *Mem:* Am Soc Mech Engrs; Can Nuclear Soc; fel Can Soc Mech Eng; fel Eng Inst Can. *Res:* Thermohydraulics and heat transfer in nuclear reactors; nuclear reactor safety; combined-purpose use of nuclear reactors. *Mailing Add:* Mech & Aerospace Eng Carleton Univ Ottawa ON K1S 5B6 Can. *Fax:* 613-788-5715

ROGERS, JAMES VIRGIL, JR, radiology, for more information see previous edition

ROGERS, JANET, ORGANIC & POLYMER CHEMISTRY. *Current Pos:* ORG CHEMIST, EDINBORO UNIV PA, 90- *Personal Data:* b St Louis, Mo, 1961. *Educ:* Monmouth Col, BS, 83; Washington Univ, St Louis, MS, 85, PhD(chem), 89. *Prof Exp:* Asst res fel, Chem Dept, Tex Christian Univ, 89. *Mem:* Am Chem Soc; Am Inst Chemists. *Mailing Add:* Edinboro Univ Pa Chem Dept Edinboro PA 16444

ROGERS, JERRY DALE, PHYSICAL CHEMISTRY. *Current Pos:* STAFF RES SCIENTIST, GEN MOTORS RES LABS, 82-, SECT MGR, RES & DEVELOP CTR, 92- *Personal Data:* b Nebo, WVa, Mar 27, 54. *Educ:* WVa Univ, BS, 76; Univ Fla, PhD(chem), 80. *Prof Exp:* Nat Res Coun fel, Goddard Space Flight Ctr, NASA, 80-82,. *Mem:* Coblentz Soc; Am Chem Soc; Am Geophys Union; Sigma Xi; Am Foundrymen's Soc. *Res:* Infrared spectroscopy; atmospheric chemistry and physics; urban air pollution and global changes; chlorofluorocarbons; environmentally conscious manufacturing; casting technologies; paintshop technologies. *Mailing Add:* Health & Environ Dept Gen Motors Res & Develop Ctr Warren MI 48090-9055. *Fax:* 810-986-1910; *E-Mail:* jrogers@cmsa.gmr.com

ROGERS, JESSE WALLACE, PHYSICAL CHEMISTRY. *Current Pos:* From asst prof to assoc prof, 67-77, chmn dept, 69-78, actg vpres acad affairs, 78-80, PROF CHEM, MIDWEST UNIV, 77-, PRES ACAD AFFAIRS, 80- *Personal Data:* b Littlefield, Tex, June 8, 41; m 62; c 1. *Educ:* Univ Tex, Arlington, BS, 63; Tex Christian Univ, PhD(phys chem), 68. *Mem:* Am Chem Soc. *Res:* Electrochemical kinetics. *Mailing Add:* Midwestern State Univ 3410 Taft Blvd Wichita Falls TX 76308-2095

ROGERS, JOHN ERNEST, MICROBIOLOGY, BIOCHEMISTRY. *Current Pos:* RES SCIENTIST MICROBIOL, ENVIRON PROTECTION AGENCY, ATHENS, GA, 85- *Personal Data:* b Ames, Iowa, May 15, 47; c 1. *Educ:* Univ Ill, BS, 69; Wash State Univ, PhD(biochem), 74. *Prof Exp:* NIH fel, Nat Inst Environ Health Sci, 75; res scientist microbiol, Pac Northwest Labs, Battelle Mem Inst, 77-85. *Mem:* Am Soc Microbiol. *Res:* Microbiology of fates and effects of trace metals, radionuclides and organic pollutants in the environment. *Mailing Add:* 4191 Madura Rd Gulf Breeze FL 32561-3544

ROGERS, JOHN GILBERT, JR, WILDLIFE ECOLOGY. *Current Pos:* wildlife biologist, US Fish & Wildlife Serv, 69-78, staff biologist, 78-92, regional dir, Div Wildlife Res, 92-95, DEP DIR, US FISH & WILDLIFE SERV, 95-, ACTG DIR, 96- *Personal Data:* b New York, NY, Sept 13, 41; m 68; c 2. *Educ:* Cornell Univ, BS, 63; NMex State Univ, MS, 66; NC State Univ, PhD(wildlife ecol), 71. *Prof Exp:* Wildlife specialist, NC Agr Exten Serv, 66-67. *Mem:* Am Soc Mammalogists; Ecol Soc Am; Wildlife Soc. *Res:* The chemical senses in animal depredations control. *Mailing Add:* US Fish & Wildlife 1849 C St NW Washington DC 20240

ROGERS, JOHN JAMES WILLIAM, GEOLOGY. *Current Pos:* W R KENAN, JR PROF GEOL, UNIV NC, CHAPEL HILL, 75- *Personal Data:* b Chicago, Ill, June 27, 30; m 56, Barbara Bongard; c 2. *Educ:* Calif Inst Technol, BS, 52, PhD(geol), 55; Univ Minn, MS, 52. *Prof Exp:* From instr to prof geol, Rice Univ, 54-74, chmn dept, 71-74. *Mem:* Am Asn Petrol Geologists; Geol Soc Am; Soc Econ Paleont & Mineral; Geophys Union; hon fel Geol Soc Africa; Geol Soc India. *Res:* Evolution of continents. *Mailing Add:* Dept Geol CB No 3315 Univ NC Chapel Hill NC 27599-3315. *Fax:* 919-966-4519; *E-Mail:* jrogers@email.unc.edu

ROGERS, KENNETH CANNICOTT, PHYSICS. *Current Pos:* from asst prof to assoc prof, 57-64, head, Dept Physics, 68-72, actg provost & dean fac, 72, pres, 72-87, PROF PHYSICS, STEVENS INST TECHNOL, 64-, EMER PRES, 87- *Personal Data:* b Teaneck, NJ, Mar 21, 29; m 56; c 3. *Educ:* St Lawrence Univ, BS, 50; Columbia Univ, MA, 52, PhD(physics), 56. *Hon Degrees:* DSc, St Lawrence Univ, 83; MEng, Stevens Inst Technol, 64, DEng, 87, LHD, St Lawrence Univ, 83. *Prof Exp:* Res assoc, Lab Nuclear Studies, Cornell Univ, 55-57. *Concurrent Pos:* Vis prof, City Col New York, 65-66; consult, Stanford Res Inst, 59-62, Grumman Aircraft Eng Corp, 62-63 & Vitro Labs, 62-72; comnr, US Nuclear Regulatory Comn, 87- *Mem:* Fel Royal Soc Arts; sr mem Inst Elec & Electronics Engrs; NY Acad Sci; Newcomen Soc; Sigma Xi; fel AAAS. *Res:* Plasma, particle accelerator and high energy particle physics; physical electronics. *Mailing Add:* 6202 Perthshire Ct Bethesda MD 20817

ROGERS, KENNETH D, PREVENTIVE MEDICINE. *Current Pos:* From asst prof to assoc prof maternal child health, Grad Sch Pub Health, 52-60, PROF COMMUNITY MED, SCH MED, UNIV PITTSBURGH, 60-, CHMN, 80- *Personal Data:* b Cincinnati, Ohio, May 23, 21. *Educ:* DePauw Univ, AB, 42; Univ Cincinnati, MD, 45; Univ Pittsburgh, MPH, 52. *Res:* Public health; pediatrics. *Mailing Add:* Children's Hosp 3705 Fifth Ave Pittsburgh PA 15213

ROGERS, KENNETH SCIPIO, BIOCHEMISTRY. *Current Pos:* from asst prof to prof, 64-91, EMER PROF BIOCHEM, MED COL VA, VA COMMONWEALTH UNIV, 91- *Personal Data:* b Lafayette, Ind, Oct 8, 35; m 90, Chafica Hindi; c 2. *Educ:* Purdue Univ, BSA, 57, MS, 59, PhD(biochem), 62. *Prof Exp:* USPHS fel, Sch Med, Johns Hopkins Univ, 61-64. *Concurrent Pos:* Vis prof pharmacol & nutrit, Univ SC Sch Med, 88-91; vis scholar, Purdue Univ, 91- *Mem:* AAAS; Am Soc Biol Chem; Soc Exp Biol & Med; Sigma Xi; Int Soc Quantum Biol; Am Inst Nutrit. *Res:* Physical biochemistry; mechanisms of enzyme inhibition and glutamate dehydrogenase; molecular interactions of hydrophobic cations and anions with mitochondria, DNA and proteins; experimental diabetes, hepatocyte, phosphate and vitamin B6 metabolism; cholesterol metabolism and HMG-CoA reductase. *Mailing Add:* Med Col Va 3786W2505 Chalmers IN 47929. *E-Mail:* rogers@purdue.edu

ROGERS, LEE EDWARD, ECOLOGY, ENTOMOLOGY. *Current Pos:* ACAD COORDR, BIOL SCI PROG, WASH STATE UNIV, 95- *Personal Data:* b Haxtun, Colo, Sept 12, 37; m 58, Maxine Lockhart; c Cheryl, Denise & Deanne. *Educ:* Univ Nebr, BS, 67, MS, 69; Univ Wyo, PhD(entom), 72. *Prof Exp:* Teaching asst biol, Univ Nebr, Omaha, 66-69, instr, 69; staff scientist ecol, Pac Northwest Lab, Battelle Mem Inst, 72-95, mgr terrestrial ecol, 88-95. *Concurrent Pos:* Lectr, Wash State Univ, 77-86, adj prof, 86- *Mem:* Entom Soc Am. *Res:* Ecology of semi-arid regions; insect ecology; bioenergetics; effects of electric fields on the environment; ecorisk analysis. *Mailing Add:* Dept Biol Sci Wash State Univ 100 Sprout Rd Richland WA 99352

ROGERS, LEWIS HENRY, ANALYTICAL CHEMISTRY. *Current Pos:* RETIRED. *Personal Data:* b DeFuniak Springs, Fla, Oct 1, 10; m 34, Lucile Ellenberg; c Mary F (Hunt) & James L. *Educ:* Univ Fla, BS, 32, MS, 34; Cornell Univ, PhD(chem), 41. *Prof Exp:* Spectrochem analyst, Exp Sta, Univ Fla, 34-39, from assoc chemist to chemist, 39-48; res chemist, Carbide Nuclear Co Div, Union Carbide Corp, 48-52; leader, Analytical Div, Kraftco Res Lab, 52-54; sr chemist, Air Pollution Found, 54-58; from assoc dir to dir, West Orange Lab, Automation Industs, Inc, NJ, 58-69; dir corp res & develop, Automation Industs, Inc, Calif, 69-71; exec vpres, Air Pollution Control Asn, 71-78; chief scientist, Environ Sci & Engr, 78. *Mem:* AAAS; Am Chem Soc; hon mem Air Pollution Control Asn. *Res:* Society administration; spectrochemistry; soil and nuclear chemistry; photochemistry; trace elements in agriculture; air pollution; high temperature reactions; research management. *Mailing Add:* 2803 NW 83 St Gainesville FL 32606. *Fax:* 352-333-6631

ROGERS, LLOYD SLOAN, SURGERY. *Current Pos:* from asst prof to assoc prof surg, State Univ NY Health Sci Ctr, 53-65, actg chmn dept, 67-70, head div gen surg, Univ Hosp, 67-77, vchmn, dept surg, 78-84, PROF SURG COL MED, STATE UNIV NY HEALTH SCI CTR, 65- *Personal Data:* b Waukegan, Ill, Apr 23, 14. *Educ:* Trinity Col, Conn, BS, 36; Univ Rochester, MD, 41; Am Bd Surg, dipl, 51. *Prof Exp:* Instr chem, Trinity Col, Conn, 36-37; intern surg, Strong Mem Hosp, Rochester, NY, 41-42; asst resident surgeon & resident, Strong Mem & Genesee Hosps, 46-50; asst chief surg serv, Crile Vet Admin Hosp, Cleveland, Ohio, 51-53. *Concurrent Pos:* Chief surgeon, Vet Admin Hosp, 53-81; attend surgeon, Univ Hosp, State Univ NY Health Sci Ctr, 54-; attend surgeon, Crouse-Mem Hosp, 58-; chmn surg adjuvant cancer chemother infusion study group, Vet Admin, 61-80, nat partic surg consult comt, 65-69, mem surg res prog comt, 65-69; mem surg study sect, NIH, 62-67; consult, St Joseph, 66- *Mem:* Am Soc Colon & Rectal Surgeons; Am Col Surg; Soc Surg Alimentary Tract; Cent Surg Asn; Asn Vet Admin Surgeons (pres, 67); Int Soc Surg. *Res:* Cancer surgery, research and chemotherapy; hyperbaric medicine; gastrointestinal physiology and surgery. *Mailing Add:* Dept Surg State Univ NY Health Sci Ctr 750 E Adams St Syracuse NY 13210

ROGERS, LOCKHART BURGESS, analytical chemistry; deceased, see previous edition for last biography

ROGERS, LORENE LANE, BIOCHEMISTRY. *Current Pos:* Eli Lilly & Co fel, Univ Tex, Austin, 49-50, res scientist, Clayton Found Biochem Inst, 50-64, exec asst, 51-57, asst dir, 57-64, assoc dean grad sch, 64-71, vpres univ, 71-74, pres ad interim, 74-75, prof nutrit, 62-79, pres univ, 75-79, EMER PRES, UNIV TEX, AUSTIN, 79- *Personal Data:* b Prosper, Tex, Apr 3, 14; wid. *Educ:* NTex State Col, BA, 34; Univ Tex, MA, 46, PhD(chem), 48. *Hon Degrees:* DSc, Oakland Univ, 72; LLD, Austin Col, 77. *Prof Exp:* Instr high sch, Tex, 34-35; asst, Clayton Found Biochem Inst, Univ Tex, 46-47; prof chem, Sam Houston State Col, 47-49. *Mem:* AAAS; Am Chem Soc; Am Inst Nutrit; fel Am Inst Chem. *Res:* Synthesis of hydantoins; metabolic interrelationships of vitamins and amino acids; metabolic patterns; alcoholism; mental retardation; congenital malformations. *Mailing Add:* 4 Nob Hill Circle Austin TX 78746

ROGERS, LYNN LEROY, ETHOLOGY, ECOLOGY. *Current Pos:* DIR, WILDLIFE RES INST, 93- *Personal Data:* b Grand Rapids, Mich, Apr 9, 39; m 79, Donna Glass; c 4. *Educ:* Mich State Univ, BS, 68; Univ Minn, MS, 70, PhD(ecol), 77. *Honors & Awards:* Anna M Jackson Award, Am Soc Mammalogists, 74; US Forest Serv Qual Res Award, 88. *Prof Exp:* Res asst black bears, Bell Mus Natural Hist, Univ Minn, 68-72; dir, Wildlife Res Inst, 72-76; wildlife res biologist, NCent Forest Exp Sta, Forest Serv, USDA, 76-93. *Concurrent Pos:* Adj prof, Univ Wis, Stevens Point, 91-93. *Mem:* Wildlife Soc; Am Soc Mammalogists; Soc Am Foresters. *Res:* Determining habitat use, food habits, social behavior, travels, physiology and population dynamics of black bears, white-tailed deer and moose in the upper midwest; ecological values of white pines in Minnesota. *Mailing Add:* Wildlife Res Inst 145 W Conan St Ely MN 55731. *Fax:* 218-365-4461

ROGERS, MARION ALAN, GEOCHEMISTRY, PETROLEUM GEOLOGY. *Current Pos:* res supvr petrol geochem, Exxon Prod Res Co, 73-78, sr supvr geologist, Lafayette Prod Dist, Exxon Co, 78-80, dist geologist, Cent Dist, SE Explor Div, New Orleans, 80-81, DIV MGR, RESERVOIR EVAL DIV, EXXON PROD RES CO, 81- *Personal Data:* b Columbus, Ind, Nov 4, 36; div; c 4. *Educ:* Earlham Col, AB, 58; Univ Minn, MS, 62, PhD(geol), 65. *Prof Exp:* Res geologist, Exxon Prod Res Co, Tex, 65-68; res specialist, Serv & Res Labs, Imp Oil, Ltd, Alta, 68-72. *Mem:* Fel Geol Soc Am; Am Asn Petrol Geologists; Am Chem Soc; Geochem Soc; Can Soc Petrol Geologists. *Res:* Petroleum geochemistry; light hydrocarbons; carbon isotopes; biodegradation and water-washing; deasphalting; reservoir bitumens and asphalts; sulfur in oils. *Mailing Add:* 23 Golden Sunset Circle The Woodlands TX 77381-4156

ROGERS, MARK CHARLES, CARDIOPULMONARY RESUSCITATION, CEREBRAL HYPOXIA. *Current Pos:* SR VPRES & CHIEF TECH OFFICER CORP DEVELOP & TECHNOL, PERKIN-ELMER CORP, 96- *Educ:* State Univ NY, MD, 69; Univ Pa, MBA. *Prof Exp:* Vchancellor health affairs, Med Ctr, Duke Univ, exec dir & chief exec officer, Duke Hosp & Health Network; dir, Pediat Intensive Care Unit, Med Sch, Johns Hopkins Univ, 77-96, prof pediat, 80-96, prof & chmn, Dept Anesthesiol & Critical Care Med, 80-96. *Concurrent Pos:* Fulbright scholar, Yugoslavia, 89. *Mem:* Inst Med-Nat Acad Sci. *Res:* Technological developments, particularly in molecular biology; DNA sequencing; polymerase chain reaction; protein analysis; author of numerous publications. *Mailing Add:* 50 Danbury Rd Wilton CT 06897. *Fax:* 919-684-8921

ROGERS, MARLIN NORBERT, FLORICULTURE. *Current Pos:* From assoc prof to prof, 60-87, EMER PROF HORT, UNIV MO-COLUMBIA, 87- *Personal Data:* b Mexico, Mo, Dec 18, 23; m 56; c 2. *Educ:* Univ Mo, BS, 48, MS, 51; Cornell Univ, PhD(plant path), 56. *Concurrent Pos:* Vis prof, Univ Fla, Gainesville, 81-82. *Mem:* Fel Am Soc Hort Sci. *Res:* Plant growth regulators; physiological responses of herbaceous ornamentals to environment; diseases of ornamental plants. *Mailing Add:* 1322 Weaver Dr Columbia MO 65203

ROGERS, MARTHA F, PUBLIC HEALTH & EPIDEMIOLOGY. *Current Pos:* Med epidemiologist, 83-89, CHIEF, EPIDEMIOL BR, DIV HIV/AIDS, CTR DIS CONTROL & PREV, 89- *Personal Data:* b Commerce, Ga, May 16, 51. *Educ:* Med Col Ga, MD, 76. *Mem:* Sigma Xi; Am Acad Pediat. *Mailing Add:* MSE45 Ctr Dis Control & Prev Atlanta GA 30333. *Fax:* 404-639-6118; *E-Mail:* meri@cidhiv.em.cdc.gov

ROGERS, MICHAEL EUGENE, MEDICINAL CHEMISTRY, BIOORGANIC CHEMISTRY. *Current Pos:* staff fel, NIH, 72-75, exec secy, Div Res Grants, Bioorg & Natural Prod Chem Study Sect, 80-88, prog adminr, Nat Inst Gen Med Sci, 88-96, DIR PHARMACOL, PHYSIOL & BIOL CHEM, NAT INST GEN MED SCI, NIH, 96- *Personal Data:* b Columbus, Ga, Oct 2, 45; m 85, Debra Sue McCoy; c Cassandra, Anna & Ethan. *Educ:* Berry Col, BS, 67; Univ Miss, PhD(med chem), 72. *Prof Exp:* Asst prof pharmaceut chem, Va Commonwealth Univ, 75-80. *Res:* Research grants, training grants and fellowships in biochemistry, bioorganic and bioinorganic chemistry, synthetic organic chemistry, pharmacology, anesthesiology and trauma and burn injury. *Mailing Add:* Nat Inst Gen Med Sci NIH Bethesda MD 20892-6200. *Fax:* 301-480-2802; *E-Mail:* rogersm@gm1.nigms.nih.gov

ROGERS, MORRIS RALPH, INDUSTRIAL MICROBIOLOGY, DISINFECTANTS. *Current Pos:* CONSULT, 89- *Personal Data:* b Poughkeepsie, NY, Feb 28, 24; m 54, Delbert Anna Wiener; c Stephen P & Nancy (Welch). *Educ:* Syracuse Univ, BS, 50; Hofstra Univ, MA, 52. *Honors & Awards:* Award, US Dept Army Natick Labs, 58, Tech Dirs Gold Pin Award, 88; Charles Porter Award, Soc Indust Microbiol, 75; Col Rohland A Isker Award, 87. *Prof Exp:* Bacteriologist, Nat Dairy Res Labs, Inc, NY, 50-52; microbiologist, Appl Microbiol Group, Pioneering Res Div, Sci & Adv Technol Lab, US Dept Army Natick Labs, 52-70, res microbiologist, Environ Protection Group, 70-83, chief, Mat Protection Br, 83-89. *Concurrent Pos:* Gov bd, Am Inst Biol Sci, 72-75. *Mem:* Fel Soc Indust Microbiol (vpres, 68, pres, 69); Sigma Xi; Am Soc Microbiol; Am Inst Biol Sci. *Res:* Germicides and fungicides, including inter-disciplinary microbiological and chemical problems; interaction of fungicides with base materials; synergism; effects of microorganisms and insects on prevention of deterioration of materials; biodegradable detergents; biodegration of organic compounds; biodegradation of petroleum products; water purification; sanitation systems; registration of disinfectants/fungicides with Environmental Protection Agency. *Mailing Add:* 47 Hadley Rd Framingham MA 01701

ROGERS, NELSON K, industrial & marine engineering, for more information see previous edition

ROGERS, OWEN MAURICE, GENETICS, PLANT BREEDING. *Current Pos:* Asst prof hort, Univ NH, 59-65, assoc prof plant sci, 65-72, actg chmn dept, 78-79, chmn dept, 79-90, PROF PLANT BIOL, UNIV NH, 72- *Personal Data:* b Worcester, Mass, July 4, 30; m 56; c 2. *Educ:* Univ Mass, BVA, 52; Cornell Univ, MS, 54; Pa State Univ, PhD(genetics, plant breeding), 59. *Mem:* Am Soc Hort Sci; Genetics Soc Am; Sigma Xi. *Res:* Genetics and plant breeding of Syringa and Pelargonium. *Mailing Add:* Dept Plant Biol Univ NH 125 Technology Dr Durham NH 03824-4724

ROGERS, PALMER, JR, BIOCHEMISTRY, MICROBIOLOGY. *Current Pos:* assoc prof, 63-68, PROF MICROBIOL, UNIV MINN, MINNEAPOLIS, 68- *Personal Data:* b New York, NY, Sept 7, 27; m 51, 81, Donna Bernick; c David B, Ethan W, Seth P & Meredith. *Educ:* Johns Hopkins Univ, PhD(biol), 57. *Prof Exp:* Am Cancer Soc fel biochem, Biol Div, Oak Ridge Nat Lab, 57-59; asst prof agr biochem, Ohio State Univ, 59-63. *Concurrent Pos:* NIH spec fel, Max Planck Inst Med Res, Heidelberg, Ger, 72-73; consult, Div Energy Biosci, Dept Energy, 80-81; prog mgr, Alcohol Fuels Competitive Grant, USDA, 90. *Mem:* AAAS; Am Soc Microbiol; Am Soc Biol Chemists; Soc Indust Microbiol. *Res:* Mechanisms of biosynthesis of enzymes in bacteria; regulation of bacterial protein and enzyme synthesis in Escherichia coli and Clostridium acetobutylicum; regulation of solvent production in clostridium acetobutylicum. *Mailing Add:* Dept Microbiol Univ Minn Box 196 Mayo Mem Bldg 420 Delaware St SE Minneapolis MN 55455-0374. *Fax:* 612-626-0623

ROGERS, PETER H, PHYSICS. *Current Pos:* prof, 83-93, FRANK H NEELY PROF, SCH MECH ENG, GA INST TECHNOL, ATLANTA, 94- *Personal Data:* b New York, NY, Jan 8, 45; m 66, Alice Levenson; c Edward, David & Leanne. *Educ:* Mass Inst Technol, SB, 65; Brown Univ, PhD(physics), 70. *Honors & Awards:* A B Wood Award & Prize, Inst Acoust, 79; Biennial Award, Acoust Soc Am, 80. *Prof Exp:* res physicist acoust, Naval Res Lab, Off Naval Res, Washington, DC, 69-75, supvry res physicist, Underwater Sound Res Div, sci officer, 81-83. *Mem:* Fel Acoust Soc Am. *Res:* Nonlinear acoustics; acoustic radiation theory; acoustic measurement theory; marine bioacoustics; shallow water acoustics; structural acoustics. *Mailing Add:* 205 Colewood Way Atlanta GA 30328. *Fax:* 404-894-7790

ROGERS, PHIL H, ELECTRICAL ENGINEERING. *Current Pos:* RETIRED. *Personal Data:* b McKinney, Tex, Apr 13, 24; m 46, Josephine Hodges; c 4. *Educ:* Univ Tex, BS, 44, MS, 47; Univ Mich, PhD, 56. *Prof Exp:* Design engr, Westinghouse Elec Co, 47-48; instr elec eng, Univ Mich, 48-53, assoc res engr, Eng Res Inst, 53-55, asst prof elec eng, 55-56; prof, Univ Ariz, 56-59; asst dir res, Collins Radio Co, Iowa, 59-62; dir prog software develop, Collins Radioc, 63-67; mgr comput systs, Electronic Systs Software, 67-76, dir, 76-80, vpres, 80-90. *Mem:* Inst Elec & Electronics Engrs; Sigma Xi. *Res:* Circuit theory; computer, computer systems and programming systems design; electronic systems embedded software development. *Mailing Add:* 7230 Cliffbrook Dallas TX 75240

ROGERS, PHILIP VIRGILIUS, ENDOCRINOLOGY, EMBRYOLOGY. *Current Pos:* from assoc prof to prof, 47-72, chmn dept, 60-72, EMER PROF BIOL, HAMILTON COL, 72- *Personal Data:* b Utica, NY, Feb 7, 07; m 32; c 3. *Educ:* Hamilton Col, AB, 30, MA, 34; Yale Univ, PhD(anat), 37. *Prof Exp:* Asst biol, Hamilton Col, 32-34; lab asst anat, Sch Med, Yale Univ, 34-37; from instr to asst prof biol, Hamilton Col, 37-45; fel, Johns Hopkins Univ, 45-46. *Concurrent Pos:* Ford Found fel & res assoc, Stanford Univ, 53-54; trustee, Kirkland Col, 69- *Mem:* AAAS; Soc Endocrinol; assoc Am Soc Zool; Am Asn Anat; Sigma Xi. *Res:* Electrical potential changes during the reproductive cycle; comparative studies of the adrenal gland; effect of sulfa drugs on reproduction. *Mailing Add:* 99 Brookside Dr Apt 237 Clinton NY 13323

ROGERS, QUINTON RAY, NUTRITION, BIOCHEMISTRY. *Current Pos:* from asst prof to assoc prof, 66-74, PROF PHYSIOL CHEM, SCH VET MED, UNIV CALIF, DAVIS, 74- *Personal Data:* b Palco, Kans, Nov 24, 36; m 56, Deana Dykstra; c Katrina L (Asay), Terrill D, Tamara G (Ouellette), Kevin A, Wendell E & Pamela D (Landes). *Educ:* Univ Idaho, BS, 58; Univ Wis, MS, 60, PhD(biochem), 63. *Prof Exp:* Res assoc with Dr A E Harper, Mass Inst Technol, 62-63, instr nutrit, 63-64, asst prof physiol chem 64-66. *Mem:* AAAS; Am Inst Nutrit; Am Physiol Soc; Sigma Xi; Am Acad Vet Nutrit; Soc Neurosci. *Res:* Amino acid nutrition and metabolism; feline nutrition; food intake regulation. *Mailing Add:* Dept Molecular Bio Sci Univ Cal-Davis Sch Vet Med Davis CA 95616-8741. *Fax:* 530-752-4698

ROGERS, RALPH LOUCKS, INDUSTRIAL ORGANIC CHEMISTRY. *Current Pos:* RETIRED. *Personal Data:* b Wilkensburg, Pa, Feb 2, 22; m 47, Louise Bierly; c Thomas E, Richard L, James M & Susan I. *Educ:* Juniata Col, BS, 46; Univ Pa, MS, 48, PhD(org chem), 56; Del County Community Col, AAS, 86. *Prof Exp:* From assoc chemist to res chemist, Atlantic Ref Co, 51-69, sr res chemist, 69-83; co-ad instr, Del Co Community Col, 86-91. *Res:* Unnatural amino acids; effects of ionizing radiation on chemicals; physical testing of polymers; multi-component vapor liquid equilbrium; liquid-liquid distribution coefficients; accelerating rate calormetry. *Mailing Add:* 22 Ridgeway Ave Norwood PA 19074

ROGERS, RAYMOND N, EXPLOSIVES CHEMISTRY, EXPLOSIVES ACCIDENT INVESTIGATIONS. *Current Pos:* RETIRED. *Personal Data:* b Albuquerque, NMex, July 21, 27; m 86, Joan L Schindler; c R Scott (deceased) & Amy M (Canzona). *Educ:* Univ Ariz, BS, 48, MS, 51. *Prof Exp:* Chemist, Infilco, Inc, Ariz, 51-52; staff mem anal, Los Alamos Sci Lab, Univ Calif, 52-63, sect leader anal & stability, 63-64, alternate group leader, 64-74, group leader explosives res, 74-81. *Concurrent Pos:* Consult, Petrol Technol Corp, 72- & Hercules, Inc; lab fel, Los Alamos Nat Lab, 81- *Res:* Isotope dilution methods as applied to agricultural chemical problems; analytical chemistry, physical chemistry and thermal stability of organic high explosives, polymers and adhesives; analysis of archeological samples. *Mailing Add:* 1961 Cumbres Patio Los Alamos NM 87544. *E-Mail:* rnrogers@rt66.com

ROGERS, RICHARD BREWER, AGRICULTURAL CHEMISTRY. *Current Pos:* sr res chemist org chem, Mich, 73-77, res specialist, Dow Chem Co, 77-91, DIR GLOBAL FORMULATIONS & ENVIRON CHEM, DOW ELANCO, 91- *Personal Data:* b Paris, Tex, Oct 20, 44; m 66; c 2. *Educ:* Tulane Univ, BS, 66; Univ Wis, MS, 68; Univ Ala, PhD(org chem), 72. *Prof Exp:* Fel, Ind Univ, 71-73. *Mem:* Am Chem Soc. *Res:* Heterocyclic chemistry; specifically biologically active derivatives of pyridine and fused pyridines, naphtheridine, quinazoline and benzo thiophene. *Mailing Add:* Dow Elanco 1957 Camargue Dr Zionsville IN 46077-9054

ROGERS, RICHARD C, NEUROSCIENCE, AUTONOMIC NERVOUS SYSTEM. *Current Pos:* PROF PHYSIOL, COL MED, OHIO STATE UNIV, 86- *Personal Data:* b Burbank, Calif, June 29, 53; m 75; c 1. *Educ:* Univ Calif, Los Angeles, BA, 74, PhD(neurosci), 79. *Prof Exp:* Fel gastroenterol, Ctr Ulcer Res & Educ, 79-80; asst prof physiol, Sch Med, Northwestern Univ, 80- *Concurrent Pos:* Vis scientist, Dept Physiol, Sch Med, Fukuoka Univ, Japan, 80; prin investr, NIH, 81- *Mem:* Soc Neurosci. *Res:* Central neural elaboration of the autonomic nervous system; physiological and anatomical details of visceral afferent control over ingestive behavior, gastrointestinal function and neuroendocrine function. *Mailing Add:* Dept Physiol Col Med Ohio State Univ Graves Hall 333 W Tenth Ave Columbus OH 43210-1238

ROGERS, ROBERT LARRY, BIOCHEMISTRY, AGRONOMY. *Current Pos:* From asst prof to assoc prof, 67-74, supt, Northeast Res Sta, 74-96, PROF PLANT PHYSIOL, PLANT PATH DEPT, LA STATE UNIV, BATON ROUGE, 80-, VCHANCELLOR RES & DIR, LA AGR EXP STA, 96- *Personal Data:* b Lawrence Co, Miss, Feb 10, 42; m 64; c 2. *Educ:* Miss State Univ, BS, 64; Auburn Univ, PhD(plant physiol, biochem), 68. *Mem:* Am Chem Soc; Am Soc Plant Physiol; Weed Sci Soc Am; Am Soc Agron. *Res:* Chemical weed control in agronomic crops; metabolism and mode of action of herbicides; management of agricultural research. *Mailing Add:* La Agr Exp Sta La State Univ PO Box 25055 Baton Rouge LA 70894-5055

ROGERS, ROBERT M, PULMONARY MEDICINE. *Current Pos:* PROF MED & ANESTHESIOL & CHIEF PULMONARY MED, UNIV PITTSBURGH MED SCH, 80- *Educ:* Univ Pa, MD, 60. *Mailing Add:* Pulmonary Allergy & Critical Care Med Dept Med Univ Pittsburgh Sch Med 440 Scaife Hall 3550 Terrace St Pittsburgh PA 15261-0001. *Fax:* 412-648-9203

ROGERS, ROBERT N, SOLID STATE PHYSICS, ACADEMIC ADMINISTRATION. *Current Pos:* CHAIR, DEPT PHYSICS & ASTRON, SAN FRANCISCO UNIV. *Personal Data:* b San Francisco, Calif, Nov 4, 33; m 55; c 4. *Educ:* Stanford Univ, BS, 56, PhD(physics), 62. *Prof Exp:* Res assoc appl sci, Yale Univ, 65-66; asst prof physics, Wesleyan Univ, 60-67; from assoc prof to prof, Univ Colo, Boulder, 67-76, spec asst to pres, 73-75; assoc dean grad sch & coordr res, Univ Colo, Denver, 76- *Concurrent Pos:* Consult, Sandia Lab, 65-66, 67-70, tech staff mem 66-67; admin fel, Am Coun Educ, 73-74. *Mem:* AAAS; Am Phys Soc; Am Asn Physics Teachers. *Res:* Magnetic interactions in solids; paramagnetic resonance in solids and liquids; optical pumping; ion implantation. *Mailing Add:* Dept Physics & Astron San Francisco State Univ 1600 Holloway St San Francisco CA 94132

ROGERS, ROBERT WAYNE, ANIMAL SCIENCE, MEAT & MUSCLE FOOD SCIENCE. *Current Pos:* from asst prof to assoc prof, 64-74, PROF MEAT SCI, MISS STATE UNIV, 74- *Personal Data:* b Russellville, Ky, Aug 6, 38; m 61, Mary Demas; c 3. *Educ:* Univ Ky, BS, 60, MS, 62, PhD(animal sci), 64. *Prof Exp:* Instr, Univ Ky, 63-64. *Concurrent Pos:* Lectr, USDA Meat Inspection Training Ctr, 80-81; dir, Miss State Univ & USDA Meat Grading Training Sch, 81-86; dir tech serv, Southern Belle Foods Inc, 85. *Mem:* Am Soc Animal Sci; Am Meat Sci Asn; Inst Food Technol. *Res:* Curing and processing of pork and beef; methods of extending shelf-life of fresh meats; beef tenderness; efficient production of meat; live animal and carcass evaluation methods. *Mailing Add:* Animal Sci Miss State Univ PO Box 5228 Mississippi State MS 39762-5228

ROGERS, ROBIN DON, X-RAY CRYSTALLOGRAPHY, SOLVENT EXTRACTION OF METAL IONS. *Current Pos:* Asst prof, 82-87, ASSOC PROF CHEM, NORTHERN ILL UNIV, 87- *Personal Data:* b Ft Lauderdale, Fla, Mar 4, 57; m 79, Lillian McWhorten; c William D & Kristin. *Educ:* Univ Ala, BS, 78, PhD(inorg chem), 82. *Concurrent Pos:* Chmn, Rock River Sect, Am Chem Soc, 84-86. *Mem:* Am Chem Soc; Am Crystallog Soc; Sigma Xi. *Res:* Exploration of the synthetic and structural chemistry of the f-elements; f-element separations; dissolved metal ion separations; radio chemistry; environmental inorganic chemistry. *Mailing Add:* Dept Chem Univ Ala Tuscaloosa AL 35487. *Fax:* 815-753-4802; *E-Mail:* t40rdr1@niu

ROGERS, RODDY, CIVIL & GEOTECHNICAL ENGINEERING. *Current Pos:* proj mgr, 85-90, SR ENGR CIVIL ENG SECT SYST ENG, CITY UTILITIES, SPRINGFIELD, 90- *Personal Data:* b Springfield, Mo. *Educ:* Univ Mo, BSCE, 81, MSCE, 83, MSEMgt, 90. *Honors & Awards:* Young Engr Award, Nat Soc Prof Engrs, 91. *Prof Exp:* Asst & staff engr, Dames & Moore Consult Firm, Phoenix, 83-85. *Concurrent Pos:* Teaching asst soil mech, Univ Mo, 81-83, res asst, Soil Mech Lab, 82-83. *Mem:* Nat Soc Prof Engrs; Am Soc Civil Engrs. *Res:* Contributed articles to professional journals. *Mailing Add:* 2241 E Powell St Springfield MO 65804-4692

ROGERS, RODDY R, meteorology, for more information see previous edition

ROGERS, RODNEY ALBERT, BIOLOGY. *Current Pos:* From asst prof to assoc prof, 55-65, chmn dept, 66-92, PROF BIOL, DRAKE UNIV, 65-. *Personal Data:* b Lucas, Iowa, Aug 24, 26; m 56, Frances Ritchey; c Robert & William. *Educ:* Drake Univ, BA, 49, MA, 51; Univ Iowa, PhD(zool), 55. *Concurrent Pos:* Assoc prog dir, NSF, 67-68. *Mem:* AAAS; Am Soc Parasitol; Soc Protozool; Am Soc Trop Med & Hyg; Am Soc Zool. *Res:* Parasitology, especially helminthology; cytology; immunology; microbiology. *Mailing Add:* 4203 40th St Des Moines IA 50310

ROGERS, ROY STEELE, III, ORAL MEDICINE, ORAL IMMUNOLOGY. *Current Pos:* NIH res fel, Mayo Grad Sch Med, 72-73, from instr to assoc prof dermat, Mayo Med Sch, 73-83, assoc dean student affairs 82-84, assoc dean acad affairs, 84-88, PROF DERMAT, MAYO MED SCH, 83-, DEAN, SCH HEALTH-RELATED SCI, 91- *Personal Data:* b Hillsboro, Ohio, Mar 3, 40; m 64, Susan Hudson; c Roy S IV & Katherine H. *Educ:* Denison Univ, BA, 62; Ohio State Univ, MD, 66; Univ Minn, MS, 74. *Prof Exp:* Resident, Duke Univ Med Ctr, 69-71. *Mem:* Am Acad Dermat; Am Dermat Soc Allergy & Immunol; Am Dermat Asn; Soc Invest Dermat; Asn Schs Allied Health Professions. *Res:* Oral medicine, oral immunopathology, immunology, infectious diseases, dermatopathology and immunobullous diseases. *Mailing Add:* Dept Dermat Mayo Clin Rochester MN 55905-0001. *Fax:* 507-284-2072

ROGERS, SAMUEL JOHN, BIOCHEMISTRY. *Current Pos:* asst prof, 66-71, ASSOC PROF BIOCHEM, MONT STATE UNIV, 71- *Personal Data:* b Florence, Ariz, Nov 5, 34; m 61; c 2. *Educ:* Univ Calif, Davis, BS, 56, DVM, 58; Univ Calif, Berkeley, PhD(biochem), 64. *Prof Exp:* Fel chem, Univ Ore, 64-66. *Mem:* Am Chem Soc. *Res:* Chemical modification of the ribiosome; dye-sensitized photooxidation mechanism of action; environmental mutagenesis, metal in mutagenesis. *Mailing Add:* Dept Chem Mont State Univ Bozeman MT 59717-0001

ROGERS, SCOTT ORLAND, MOLECULAR TAXONOMY & PHYLOGENETICS, ANCIENT DNA-EVOLUTION-PLANTS-FUNGI. *Current Pos:* asst prof, 89-93, ASSOC PROF MOLECULAR BIOL, COL ENVIRON SCI & FORESTRY, STATE UNIV NY, 93- *Personal Data:* b Portland, Ore, Oct 8, 53; m 79, Mary A Strong; c Elizabeth C & Benjamin S. *Educ:* Univ Ore, BS, 75, MS, 80; Univ Wash, PhD(molecular biol), 87. *Prof Exp:* Res asst, Ore State Univ, 81-82; teaching asst cellular & molecular biol, Univ Wash, Seattle, 82-83, fel, 83-86, res asst, 86-87, res assoc, 87-89. *Mem:* Sigma Xi; AAAS; Mycol Soc Am; Nat Geog Soc. *Res:* Molecular taxonomy, phylogenetics (evolution) of fungi and plants; development of DNA methods for herbarium, fresh, mummified, fossil and field-collected tissues; transformation of plants for disease resistance. *Mailing Add:* EFB State Univ NY 1 Forestry Dr Syracuse NY 13210. *Fax:* 315-470-6934; *E-Mail:* sorogers@mailbox.syr.edu

ROGERS, SENTA S(TEPHANIE), environmental health, for more information see previous edition

ROGERS, SPENCER LEE, physical anthropology, ethnology, for more information see previous edition

ROGERS, STEARNS WALTER, BIO & ORGANIC CHEMISTRY, SCIENCE EDUCATION. *Current Pos:* assoc prof chem, 76-86, PROF CHEM, MCNEESE STATE UNIV, 86-, ASST DEPT HEAD, 92- *Personal Data:* b Alva, Okla, July 28, 34; m 55, Billie C Parker; c Billie D & Jack E. *Educ:* Northwestern State Col, BS, 56; Okla State Univ, PhD(biochem), 61. *Prof Exp:* Prof chem, Northwestern State Col, Okla, 61-76, dept head, 70-76. *Concurrent Pos:* Chem consult, Olin Indust. *Mem:* Am Chem Soc; Am Inst Chemists; Nat Sci Teachers Asn. *Res:* Utilization of amino acid analogs in the synthesis of bacterial proteins; synthesis of mannans in Pseudonomas auregenosia; topic sporulation in Bacillus cereus organization; interaction of blood platlets with basement membrane and insoluble collagen; chemical modification of basement membranes. *Mailing Add:* McNeese State Univ Dept Chem 4100 Ryan St Lake Charles LA 70609

ROGERS, STEFFEN HAROLD, CELL BIOLOGY, PARASITOLOGY. *Current Pos:* DEAN ARTS & SCI, UNIV RI, 92- *Personal Data:* b Madison, Wis, Apr 17, 41; m 64. *Educ:* Ga Southern Col, BS, 65; Vanderbilt Univ, PhD(biol), 68. *Prof Exp:* NIH training grant, Sch Pub Health & Hyg, Johns Hopkins Univ, 68-70; from asst prof to assoc prof, Univ Tulsa, 70-85, assoc dean, 81-90, actg dean, 90, prof zool, 85-92. *Res:* Cellular biology. *Mailing Add:* Off Dean Arts & Sci Univ RI Kingston RI 02881

ROGERS, SUZANNE M DETHIER, PLANT CELL CULTURE, PLANT PROPAGATION AND PHYSIOLOGY. *Current Pos:* ASST PROF GRAD FAC, DEPT BIOSCI, SALEM-TEIKYO UNIV, 95- *Educ:* Cornell Univ, BS, 77; Ohio State Univ, MS, 80; Univ Ill, PhD(agron), 87. *Prof Exp:* Res assoc, Dept Surg, Ohio State Univ, 78-80; res asst, Dept Agron, Univ Ill, 82-87; asst prof, Dept Hort, Tex A&M Univ, 87-95, fac mem plant physiol & plant biotechnol, 87-95. *Mem:* Soc Invitrobiol; AAAS; Am Soc Hort Sci; Am Soc Plant Physiologists; Int Soc Hort Sci; Cactus & Succulent Soc Am. *Res:* Plant tissue culture development and plant physiology; development of in vitro techniques for propagation and genetic transformation of wetland plants; characterization of foreign gene expression; clone multiplication of difficult-to-propagate and or rare plants; establishment of embryo rescue systems which promote normal morphogenesis resulting in the development of rare hybrids. *Mailing Add:* Dept Biosci Salem Teikyo Univ Salem WV 26426. *Fax:* 304-782-5579; *E-Mail:* rogers@salem.wvnet.edu

ROGERS, TERENCE ARTHUR, physiology, for more information see previous edition

ROGERS, THOMAS F, PHYSICS, ELECTRONICS. *Current Pos:* BD DIR, CHIEF SCIENTIST & ENGR, INT RADIO SATELLITE CORP, 90-; CHMN & BD DIR, LUNACORP, 90- *Personal Data:* b Providence, RI, Aug 11, 23; m 46, Estelle E Hunt; c Clare, Judith & Hope. *Educ:* Providence Col, BSc, 45; Boston Univ, AM, 49. *Honors & Awards:* Space Pioneer Award, Nat Space Soc. *Prof Exp:* Res assoc, Radio Res Lab, Harvard Univ, 44-45; TV proj engr, Bell & Howell Co, 45-46; electronic scientist, Air Force Cambridge Res Ctr, Mass, 46-54, supvry physicist, 54-59; assoc head radio physics div, Lincoln Lab, Mass Inst Technol, 59-63, head commun div & mem steering comt, 63-64; asst dir defense res & eng, Off Secy Defense, US Dept Defense, 64-65, dep dir, 65-67; dir urban technol & res, US Dept Housing & Urban Develop, 67-69; vpres urban affairs, Mitre Corp, 69-72; dir, US Cong Space Study, 82-84. *Concurrent Pos:* Assoc group leader, Lincoln Lab, Mass Inst Technol, 51-53; mem & later panel chmn, Commun Comt, Dept Navy Polaris Command, 60-64; mem, President's Sci Adv Comt Commun Satellite, 61-63, Commun Satellite Panel, Inst Defense Anal, 61-63, Dept Defense-NASA Tech Comt Commun Satellite, 61-64, US Nat Comt, UN Conf Appl Sci & Technol to Lesser Developed Nations, 63, Aeronaut & Astronaut Coord Bd, 65-67, Space Appln Bd, Nat Res Coun, 74-85, Regional Emergency Med Commun Comt, Nat Acad Sci, 76-79 & Voice of AM Adv Comt, Nat Res Coun, 84-88; chmn, NASA Space & Terrestrial Appl Adv Comt, Space Progs Adv Coun, 71-74; chmn, Sophron Found, 80-; founder, Space Phoenix Prog & dir, External Tanks Corp, 86-; chmn, Aerospace Res & Develop Policy Comt, Inst Elec & Electronics Engrs, 91-; pres, Space Transp Asn, 92- *Mem:* Fel Inst Elec & Electronics Engrs; Am Phys Soc; Am Geophys Union; Sigma Xi; Brit Inst Physics. *Res:* Research, development and engineering in electronics; communications; command control; intelligence; reconnaissance; radio wave propagation; electronic memory devices; ultrasonics; molecular physics; housing; city planning and administration; space policy. *Mailing Add:* 7404 Colshire Dr McLean VA 22102

ROGERS, THOMAS HARDIN, hazardous waste site characterization, earthquake hazard evaluation, for more information see previous edition

ROGERS, VERN CHILD, NUCLEAR PHYSICS, NUCLEAR ENGINEERING. *Current Pos:* PRES RES & DEVELOP, ROGERS & ASSOCS ENG CORP, 80- *Personal Data:* b Salt Lake City, Utah, Aug 28, 41; m 62; c 6. *Educ:* Univ Utah, BS & MS, 65; Mass Inst Technol, PhD(nuclear eng), 69. *Prof Exp:* Nuclear engr reactor physics, Argonne Nat Lab, 68-69; assoc prof chem eng & physics, Brigham Young Univ, 69-73; vis assoc prof nuclear eng, Lowell Technol Inst, 70-71; mgr res & develop, IRT Corp, 73-76; vpres res & develop, Ford, Bacon & Davis Utah, Inc, 76-80. *Concurrent Pos:* Adj prof nuclear eng, Univ Utah, 73-; consult to indust & govt or radiation, transp, health effects and disposal. *Mem:* Am Nuclear Soc; Am Phys Soc; Am Chem Soc; Am Health Physics Soc; Am Econ Asn. *Res:* Management of products related to nuclear fuel cycle and decontamination of nuclear facilities; low energy nuclear physics; radiation pathway and risk analysis; resource economic analysis. *Mailing Add:* 747 W 3500 S Bountiful UT 84010. *Fax:* 801-262-1527

ROGERS, WAID, SURGERY. *Current Pos:* from asst prof to assoc prof, 67-74, PROF SURG, UNIV TEX HEALTH SCI CTR, 74; CHIEF SURG, AUDIE MURPHY VET ADMIN HOSP, 73- *Personal Data:* b New York, NY, Sept 7, 27; m 51; c 3. *Educ:* Yale Univ, BA, 50; Cornell Univ, MD, 57; Univ Minn, MS, 66, PhD(surg & oncol), 67. *Prof Exp:* Instr surg, Univ Minn, 67. *Concurrent Pos:* NIH spec fel, 63-; consult gen surg, San Antonio State Tuberc Hosp, 70- *Mem:* Sigma Xi; Am Soc Transplant Surgeons; Am Col Angiol; Transplantation Soc; AAAS. *Res:* Tumor blood flow; transplantation; parenteral nutrition. *Mailing Add:* 923 Serenade San Antonio TX 78213-1336

ROGERS, WALTER RUSSELL, NEUROENDOCRINOLOGY OF CIRCADIAN RHYTHMS, NEUROTOXICOLOGY. *Current Pos:* actg mgr, Sect, 83-89, staff scientist, dept bioeng, 86-89, SR RES PSYCHOLOGIST, BEHAV SCI SECT, DEPT BIOENG, SOUTHWEST RES INST, SAN ANTONIO, TEX, 74-, MGR BIOSCI, 89- *Personal Data:* b Newark, NJ, Aug 11, 45; m 67; c 2. *Educ:* Col Wooster, BA, 67; Univ Iowa, MA, 70, PhD(psychol), 72; Am Bd Toxicol, dipl, 88. *Prof Exp:* Res fel psychobiol, Univ Calif, Irvine, 71-72; asst prof psychol, Univ Northern Iowa, 72-74. *Concurrent Pos:* Adj assoc scientist, dept med & physiol, 80-85, adj scientist, Dept Med & Physiol, Southwest Found Biomed Res, 85- *Mem:* AAAS; Am Primatological Soc; Bioelectromagnetics Soc; Sigma Xi; Soc Toxicol; Behav Toxicol Soc; Int Neurotoxicol Soc. *Res:* Nonhuman primates as models for biomedical research where behavior is a variable; health effects of cigarette smoking, exercise and stress; behavioral toxicology of combustion products and electromagnetic fields; neurobehavioral toxicology; electromagnetic field bioeffects. *Mailing Add:* 6220 Culebra Rd Southwest Res Inst PO Drawer 28510 San Antonio TX 78228-0510. *Fax:* 210-684-6147; *E-Mail:* wrogevs@swri.edu

ROGERS, WILLIAM ALAN, PHYSICS. *Current Pos:* ADJ PROF PHYSICS, SAN ANTONIO COL, 81- *Personal Data:* b Trenton, NJ, Feb 22, 21; m 47; c 4. *Educ:* Oberlin Col, AB, 47; Univ NMex, MS, 51; Univ Pittsburgh, PhD(physics), 58. *Prof Exp:* Res physicist, Res Lab, Westinghouse Elec Corp, 51-60; from assoc prof to prof physics, Thiel Col, 60-66; prof physics, Univ Petrol & Minerals, Dhahran, Saudi Arabia, 66-80, chmn dept, 66-70 & 71-74; mem fac, Dept Physics, Trinity Univ, 80-81. *Concurrent Pos:* Vis fel, Sch Eng & Appl Sci, Princeton Univ, 75-76. *Mem:* Am Asn Physics Teachers. *Res:* Atomic physics; microwave discharge and plasmas; undergraduate teaching. *Mailing Add:* 7422 Saddlewood Ave San Antonio TX 78238

ROGERS, WILLIAM EDWIN, ZOOLOGY, PARASITOLOGY. *Current Pos:* assoc prof, 70-77, PROF BIOL, SHIPPENSBURG STATE COL, 77- *Personal Data:* b Carlisle, Pa, Apr 5, 36; m 60; c 3. *Educ:* Dickinson Col, BS, 58; Pa State Univ, MS, 61; Univ Minn, PhD(zool), 69. *Prof Exp:* Asst prof biol, Shippensburg State Col, 64-65; asst prof, Lycoming Col, 65-70. *Mem:* Soc Protozool; Am Soc Parasitol. *Res:* Morphogenesis and ultrastructure of trypanosomatids found in muscoid flies. *Mailing Add:* Dept Biol Shippensburg Univ N Prince St Shippensburg PA 17257-2210

ROGERS, WILLIAM IRVINE, RESEARCH MANAGEMENT DEVELOPMENT. *Current Pos:* pres, 84-92, FOUNDER, CHADWICK ROGERS, INC, 84- *Personal Data:* b Brooklyn, NY, Dec 10, 27; m 54, Ruthanne Chadwick; c Geoffrey C & Christopher S. *Educ:* Adelphi Col, BA, 49; Univ Vt, MS, 52; Univ Iowa, PhD(biochem), 56. *Prof Exp:* Assoc technologist, Res Ctr, Gen Foods Corp, 56-59, proj leader, 59; consult biochem & sect leader, Life Sci Div, 59-70; sr staff mem, Org Develop Sect, Arthur D Little, Inc, 69-84. *Concurrent Pos:* Vis lectr, Boston Univ & Brandeis Univ, 86-94. *Res:* Application of organic, analytical and physical chemistry to the problems of biochemistry and the physiological disposition and mechanisms of action of drugs; isolation and characterization of natural products; nutrition; organization and management development at interfaces of technical and other operations in academic, industrial and governmental agencies. *Mailing Add:* 67 Turkey Shore Rd Ipswich MA 01938-2333

ROGERS, WILLIAM LESLIE, MEDICAL PHYSICS, NUCLEAR MEDICAL IMAGING. *Current Pos:* res assoc, Dept Internal Med, Univ Mich, 70-73, asst prof, 73-80, assoc res scientist, 80-84, res scientist, 84-87, assoc prof & res scientist, 87-89, PROF & RES SCIENTIST, DEPT INTERNAL MED, UNIV MICH, 89- *Personal Data:* b Boston, Mass, Mar 27, 34; m 62, Ann; c 3. *Educ:* Ohio Wesleyan Univ, AB, 55; Case Western Res, MS, 61, PhD(physics), 67. *Prof Exp:* Engr, Hughes Aircraft Co, 55-58; instr physics, Univ Wyo, 61-62; fel, Case Western Res, 67-68; staff engr, Bendix Aerospace Systs, 68-70. *Concurrent Pos:* Lectr, Dept Physics, Univ Mich, 80-84; assoc ed, Inst Elec & Electronics Engrs, Trans-Med Imaging, 86-92; mem, Radiol & Nuclear Med Study Sect, NIH. *Mem:* Soc Nuclear Med; Sigma Xi; Inst Elec & Electronics Engrs. *Res:* Improved nuclear medicine imaging techniques and instrumentation; develop and test new methods of three-dimensional image reconstruction. *Mailing Add:* Dept Biol Med Eng 1425 Cambridge Rd Ann Arbor MI 48104

ROGERS, WILMER ALEXANDER, FISH PATHOLOGY, FISHERIES MANAGEMENT. *Current Pos:* from instr to assoc prof, 64-77, PROF FISHERIES, AUBURN UNIV, 77- *Personal Data:* b Mt Dora, Fla, Aug 17, 33; m 61; c 4. *Educ:* Univ Southern Miss, BS, 58; Auburn Univ, MS, 60, PhD(fish mgt), 67. *Prof Exp:* Biologist aide, Miss Game & Fish Comn, 57-58; fishery biologist, Ala Dept Conserv, 60-62, US Fish & Wildlife Serv, 62-64. *Concurrent Pos:* Leader, Southeastern Coop Fish Dis Proj, 68-; ed, Southeastern Game and Fish Proc, 74-77; ed, J Aquatic Animal Health, 88- *Mem:* Am Fisheries Soc (pres, Southern Div, 77-78 & Fish Health Sect, 86-87); Am Soc Parasitol; Wildlife Dis Asn; Am Micros Soc. *Res:* General parasites and diseases of fish, especially taxonomy of monogenea; intensive culture of fish; fish immunology. *Mailing Add:* Dept Fisheries Auburn Univ Auburn AL 36849-3501

ROGERSON, ALLEN COLLINGWOOD, MICROBIAL PHYSIOLOGY & GENETICS, MOLECULAR BIOLOGY & EVOLUTION. *Current Pos:* assoc prof, 79-83, chmn dept, 79-86, PROF BIOL, ST LAWRENCE UNIV, 83- *Personal Data:* b Stoke-on-Trent, Eng, Dec 9, 40; US citizen; m 60, Phoebe Northrop; c Peter A & Michael C. *Educ:* Haverford Col, BA, 64; Dartmouth Col, PhD(molecular biol), 69. *Prof Exp:* NIH fel molecular biol, Albert Einstein Med Ctr, Philadelphia, Pa, 68-70; asst prof biol, Bryn Mawr Col, 70-76; res assoc & head, Biol Nitrogen Fixation Group, Div Agr, Fort Valley State Col, Ga, 76-79. *Concurrent Pos:* NIH grant, 71-74; vis res prof, Univ Copenhagen, Denmark, 73-74, Univ Dundee, Scotland, 77 & Univ Rochester, 86-87. *Mem:* AAAS; Am Soc Microbiol; Sigma Xi; Soc Molecular Biol & Evolution. *Res:* Chromosome structure and evolution; bacterial conjugation regulation of molecular synthesis and growth in microorganisms; computer applications. *Mailing Add:* Biol Dept St Lawrence Univ 748 Court St Canton NY 13617-1169. *Fax:* 315-379-5804; *E-Mail:* arog@slomos

ROGERSON, ASA BENJAMIN, PLANT PHYSIOLOGY, AGRONOMY. *Current Pos:* REGIONAL MGR RES & DEVELOP, UNIROYAL CHEM, 70- *Personal Data:* b Williamston, NC, Oct 24, 39; m 65; c 2. *Educ:* NC State Univ, BS, 62; Va Polytech Inst, MS, 65, PhD(plant physiol), 68. *Prof Exp:* Asst prof crop sci, NC State Univ, 68-70. *Mem:* Weed Sci Soc Am. *Res:* Agricultural chemical products involving tobacco, soybeans, cotton, fruits, ornamentals and growth regulants. *Mailing Add:* Uniroyal Chem Co 807 Spring Forest Rd Suite 1600 Raleigh NC 27609

ROGERSON, JOHN BERNARD, JR, ASTROPHYSICS. *Current Pos:* from res assoc & lectr to assoc prof, 56-67, PROF ASTRON, PRINCETON UNIV, 67- *Personal Data:* b Cleveland, Ohio, Sept 3, 22; m 43; c 3. *Educ:* Case Univ, BS, 51; Princeton Univ, PhD(astron), 54. *Prof Exp:* Carnegie fel astron, Mt Wilson Observ, 54-56. *Mem:* Am Astron Soc; Int Astron Union. *Res:* Solar atmosphere; photoelectric spectrophotometry; high altitude astronomy with balloon and satellite borne telescopes and equipment. *Mailing Add:* 277 Moore St Princeton NJ 08540

ROGERSON, PETER FREEMAN, ANALYTICAL CHEMISTRY. *Current Pos:* ANALYTICAL CHEMIST, NAT WATER QUAL LAB, US GEOL SURV, 86- *Personal Data:* b Stoke-on-Trent, Eng, Mar 12, 44; US citizen; m 66; c 2. *Educ:* Univ Vt, BS, 66; Univ NC, Chapel Hill, PhD(analytical chem), 71. *Prof Exp:* Res assoc, Cornell Univ, 70-71; res chemist, Environ Res Lab, Environ Protection Agency, 71-86. *Mem:* Am Soc Mass Spectrometry; Am Chem Soc; AAAS. *Res:* Analytical chemistry as applied to pollution control research. *Mailing Add:* US Geol Surv 5293 Ward Rd Arvada CO 80002-1932

ROGERSON, ROBERT JAMES, GLACIER MASS BALANCE, QUATERNARY HISTORY. *Current Pos:* PROF, DEPT GEOG, UNIV LETHBRIDGE, 88- *Personal Data:* b Lancaster, Eng, July 4, 43; Can citizen; m 68; c 2. *Educ:* Liverpool Univ, BA, 65; McGill Univ, MSc, 67; Macquarie Univ, Australia, PhD(earth sci), 79. *Prof Exp:* Sci officer, Glaciology Div, Inland Waters Br, Ottawa, 67-69; lectr, Mem Univ Nfld, 69-72, from asst prof to assoc prof, 72-86, prof & head geog dept, 86-88. *Concurrent Pos:* Consult, Westfield Minerals, 79 & Ice Eng, 81-82; secy coun, Sch Grad Studies Mem Univ, 85-86; asst dir, Labrador Inst Northern Studies, 85-88. *Mem:* Int Glaciol Soc; Geol Asn Can(pres, Nfld sect, 86-87); Sigma Xi (secy, 87-); Asn Am Geographers; Brit Geomorphol Res Group; Can Asn Geographers. *Res:* Mass-balance and dynamics of cirque glaciers in Torngat Mountains of Labrador and the Yoho region of Canadian Rockies; glacial geology and quaternary history of Labrador, Newfoundland and the Arctic. *Mailing Add:* Dept Geog Univ Lethbridge 4401 University Dr Lethbridge AB T1K 3M4 Can

ROGERSON, THOMAS DEAN, ORGANIC CHEMISTRY, AGRICULTURAL CHEMISTRY. *Current Pos:* Sr chemist, 74-81, mgr, 81-90, PATENT DEPT, ROHM & HAAS CO, 90- *Personal Data:* b Salt Lake City, Utah, Oct 31, 46; m 68, Katherine Kasula; c Anne & Emily. *Educ:* Mich State Univ, BS, 68; Cornell Univ, MS, 71, PhD(org chem), 74; Temple Univ, JD, 94. *Concurrent Pos:* NIH fel, Dept Entom & Limnol, Cornell Univ, 73-74. *Res:* Synthesis and structure-activity relationships of biologically-active compounds; terpenes, alkaloids and toxins; pesticide metabolism and residue analysis; pesticide registration; agricultural chemicals patent. *Mailing Add:* 136 Britany Dr Chalfont PA 18914

ROGGE, THOMAS RAY, ENGINEERING MECHANICS, APPLIED MATHEMATICS. *Current Pos:* from asst prof to assoc prof eng mech, 65-76, PROF AEROSPACE ENG & ENG MECH, IOWA STATE UNIV, 76- *Personal Data:* b Oelwein, Iowa, Oct 29, 35; m 60; c 3. *Educ:* Iowa State Univ, BS, 58, MS, 61, PhD(appl math), 64. *Prof Exp:* Asst prof math, Univ Ariz, 64-65. *Mem:* Soc Indust & Appl Math; Soc Eng Sci. *Res:* Elastic wave propagation in bounded media; finite element analysis; blood flow in human arterial system. *Mailing Add:* Dept Aerospace Eng & Eng Mech Iowa State Univ 2019 Black Eng Bldg Ames IA 50011

ROGGENKAMP, PAUL LEONARD, REACTOR PHYSICS, NUCLEAR ENGINEERING. *Current Pos:* SELF EMPLOYED, 88- *Personal Data:* b Jefferson Co, Ky, May 3, 27; m 50; c 5. *Educ:* Louisville Univ, BA, 49; Univ Ind, MS, 51, PhD(physics), 53. *Prof Exp:* Res physicist, 52-57, sr supvr, 57-59, sr physicist 59-61, chief supvr, 61-64, res mgr, 64-85, sr consult, E I du Pont de Nemours & Co Inc, Aiken, SC, 85-87. *Mem:* Am Phys Soc; fel Am Nuclear Soc. *Res:* Beta decay; operational planning; reactor engineering. *Mailing Add:* 1418 Socastee Dr North Augusta SC 29841

ROGIC, MILORAD MIHAILO, ORGANIC CHEMISTRY, COMPUTATIONAL CHEMISTRY. *Current Pos:* RETIRED. *Personal Data:* b Belgrade, Yugoslavia, July 23, 31; US citizen; m 56, Zora F Markovic; c Aleksandra, George & Maria. *Educ:* Univ Belgrade, BS, 56, PhD(org chem), 61. *Prof Exp:* Asst prof chem, Univ Belgrade, 58-61; res assoc, Worcester Found Exp Biol, 61-62, Univ Notre Dame, 62-64 & Univ Sask, 65-66; asst prof, Purdue Univ, 66-69; res group leader, Allied Corp, 69-77, res supvr, 77-80, sr res assoc org chem, 80-86; res mgr, Mallinckrodt Med Inc, 86-89, assoc res dir org chem, 89-94. *Mem:* Am Chem Soc. *Res:* New organic reactions; organic reaction mechanism; metal catalyzed oxidants; chemistry of clinical reagents; organic chemistry of sulfur dioxide; organoborane chemistry; stereochemistry and conformational analysis; electrophilic additions; nitrogen containing organic compounds; x-ray contrast media agents; technetium based radiopharmaceuticals; molecular modeling; computational chemistry; pharmaceutical chemistry. *Mailing Add:* 15 Vanessa Dr St Louis MO 63131

ROGLER, JOHN CHARLES, ANIMAL NUTRITION. *Current Pos:* Res asst, 51-53 & 55-57, from asst prof to assoc prof, 57-66, PROF ANIMAL NUTRIT, PURDUE UNIV, WEST LAFAYETTE, 66- *Personal Data:* b Providence, RI, Sept 21, 27; m 51; c 2. *Educ:* Univ RI, BS, 51; Purdue Univ, MS, 53, PhD(poultry nutrit), 58. *Honors & Awards:* Am Feed Indust Assoc Nutrit Res Award, 85. *Mem:* Fel AAAS; Am Inst Nutrit; fel Poultry Sci Asn; Soc Exp Biol & Med. *Res:* Study requirements, interactions and biochemical functions of nutrients. *Mailing Add:* 195 Blueberry Lane West Lafayette IN 47906-4811

ROGLER, LLOYD HENRY, ISSUES OF MINORITY MENTAL HEALTH, PSYCHIATRIC DIAGNOSIS. *Current Pos:* ALBERT SCHWEITZER UNIV PROF, FORDHAM UNIV, 74- *Personal Data:* b San Juan, PR, July 21, 30; m 86, Susan Shapiro; c Lloyd C & Lynn. *Educ:* Univ Iowa, BS, 51, MA, 52, PhD(sociol), 57. *Hon Degrees:* LHD, John Jay Col Criminal Justice. *Honors & Awards:* Acad Excellence Award, Nat Coalition Hisp Ment Health & Human Serv Org. *Prof Exp:* Asst prof sociol, Univ PR, 57-60; vis prof behav scis, 71-72; lectr sociol, Yale Univ, 60-62, from asst prof to assoc prof, 62-68, assoc chmn, Latin Am Studies, 64-65; prof, Case Western Res Univ, 68-74. *Concurrent Pos:* Consult, Nat Adv Ment Health Coun, NIMH, 72-76; Ida Beam distinguished vis prof, Univ Iowa, 80; consult, Mayor's Comm Sci & Technol, New York City, 84-86, Comm Hispanic Concerns 85-87; vis prof sociol, Yale Univ, 90-91; vis prof psychiat, Albert Einstein Col Med, 90-91 & NY Univ Bellevue Med Ctr, 92-93. *Mem:* Am Sociol Asn; Fel Am Psychol Asn; Am Psychiat Asn. *Res:* Drafting of major theoretical statements integrating the research literature on issues having to do with culturally sensitive research, acculturation of immigrants, pathways to mental health care and cultural influence on psychiatric diagnosis. *Mailing Add:* 9 Round Hill Rd Dobbs Ferry NY 10522. *Fax:* 718-817-5779; *E-Mail:* rogler@murray.fordham.edu

ROGNLIE, DALE MURRAY, MATHEMATICS. *Current Pos:* assoc prof, 69-77, PROF MATH, SDAK SCH MINES & TECHNOL, 77- *Personal Data:* b Grand Forks, NDak, July 12, 33; m 55; c 4. *Educ:* Concordia Col, Moorhead, Minn, BA, 55; Univ NDak, MS, 58; Iowa State Univ, PhD, 69. *Prof Exp:* Instr math, Univ NDak, 56-60; res engr, Boeing Co, Wash, 60-66, supvr math group, 66. *Concurrent Pos:* Eve lectr, Seattle Univ, 61 & Pac Lutheran Univ, 61-63. *Mem:* Soc Indust & Appl Math; Sigma Xi; Math Asn Am. *Res:* Special functions; integral transforms; numerical analysis. *Mailing Add:* 284 Westberry Ct N Rapid City SD 57702-2771

ROGNLIEN, THOMAS DALE, PLASMA PHYSICS, IONOSPHERIC PHYSICS. *Current Pos:* PHYSICIST PLASMA PHYSICS, LAWRENCE LIVERMORE LAB, 75- *Personal Data:* b June 2, 45; US citizen; m 71, Judith L Roberts; c Gretchen E. *Educ:* Univ Minn, BEE, 67; Stanford Univ, MS, 69, PhD(elec eng), 73. *Prof Exp:* Res assoc ionospheric plasma physics, Nat Oceanic & Atmospheric Admin, 72-74; res assoc plasma physics, Univ Colo, 74-75. *Concurrent Pos:* Nat Res Coun fel, 72-74. *Mem:* Am Phys Soc; AAAS. *Res:* Linear and nonlinear waves in plasmas; real space and velocity space transport of particles in plasmas via analytic and computational models; application to fusion and plasma processing. *Mailing Add:* Lawrence Livermore Lab MS L-630 PO Box 808 Livermore CA 94550. *E-Mail:* rognlien1@llnl.gov

ROGOFF, GERALD LEE, PLASMA PHYSICS. *Current Pos:* PRIN MEM TECH STAFF, GTE LABS, INC, 82- *Personal Data:* b New Haven, Conn, June 7, 39; m 62. *Educ:* Yale Univ, BA, 61; Mass Inst Technol, PhD(physics), 69. *Prof Exp:* Res asst physics, Mass Inst Technol, 61-66; sr scientist, 69-78, fel scientist, Res & Develop Ctr, Westinghouse Elec Corp, 78-82. *Concurrent Pos:* Lectr, Carnegie-Mellon Univ, 73-75; assoc ed, Inst Elec & Electronics Engrs Trans Plasma Sci, 85-90. *Mem:* AAAS; Am Phys Soc; Sigma Xi; Inst Elec & Electronics Engrs. *Res:* Physics of electrical discharges in gases; gaseous electronics; optical diagnostics of ionized gases. *Mailing Add:* PO Box 2973 Framingham MA 01701-0411

ROGOFF, WILLIAM MILTON, VETERINARY ENTOMOLOGY. *Current Pos:* RETIRED. *Personal Data:* b New York, NY, Mar 15, 16; m 47, Esther Petersen; c Barbara L & James D. *Educ:* Univ Conn, BS, 37; Cornell Univ, PhD(insect morphol), 43. *Honors & Awards:* Outstanding Award, Am Registry Prof Entomologists, 82, Outstanding Award Med & Vet Entom, 82. *Prof Exp:* Entomologist, US Navy, 43-46; assoc, Exp Sta, Univ Calif, Riverside, 46-47; asst prof entom & zool & asst entomologist, Exp Sta, SDak State Univ, 47-49, assoc prof & assoc entomologist, 49-53, prof & entomologist, 53-62; res entomologist, Agr Res Serv, USDA, Ore, 62-68, res leader western insects affecting man & animals, Fresno, Calif, 68-78, res entomologist & prof entom, 78-80, emer prof entom, Livestock Insect Res Unit, Agr Res Serv, Univ Nebr, USDA, 80-83; assoc, Exp Sta, Univ Calif, Davis, 84-92. *Concurrent Pos:* Fulbright res scholar, Commonwealth Sci & Indust Res Orgn, Australia, 55-56. *Mem:* Fel AAAS; Entom Soc Am; Am Mosquito Control Asn. *Res:* Insect morphology and behavior; pheromones; veterinary entomology; systemic insecticides in livestock; insect vectors of disease organisms. *Mailing Add:* 908 Hacienda Ave Davis CA 95616-0131

ROGOL, ALAN DAVID, PEDIATRICS, ENDOCRINOLOGY. *Current Pos:* from asst prof to assoc prof pediat, 75-84, asst prof pharmacol, 77-87, PROF PEDIAT, SCH MED, UNIV VA, 84-, PROF PHARMACOL, 87- *Personal Data:* b New Haven, Conn, March 9, 41; m 68, Joanne Schoderbek; c Ian & Babette. *Educ:* Mass Inst Technol, BS, 63; Duke Univ, PhD(physiol), 70, MD, 70. *Prof Exp:* Intern pediat, Johns Hopkins Hosp, 70-71, resident, 71-72 & 74-75; fel endocrinol, NIH, 72-74. *Concurrent Pos:* Co-dir, Blue Ridge Poison Control Ctr, 81-87. *Mem:* Am Acad Pediat; Am Fedn Clin Res; Endocrinol Soc; Soc Pediat Res; Sigma Xi; fel Am Col Sports Med. *Res:* Neuroendocrinology; mechanism of growth hormone secretion mechanism of insulin action; mechanism of insulin action; endocrinology of endurance training. *Mailing Add:* 685 Explorers Rd Charlottesville VA 22901-8441

ROGOLSKY, MARVIN, MICROBIOLOGY. *Current Pos:* assoc prof biol & med, 77-80, PROF BASIC LIFE SCI, UNIV MO, KANSAS CITY, 80- *Personal Data:* b Passaic, NJ, Apr 17, 39; m 90, Barbara Jacobson; c Jonathan, Vered & Abagail. *Educ:* Rutgers Univ, BA, 60; Northwestern Univ, MS, 62; Syracuse Univ, PhD(microbiol), 65. *Prof Exp:* Asst biol, Northwestern Univ, 60-62; NIH fel microbiol, Scripps Clin & Res Found, 65-67; from instr to assoc prof microbiol, Col Med, Univ Utah, 67-76. *Concurrent Pos:* Gen Res Support Fund grant & Am Cancer Soc inst grant, 67-68; NIH res grants, 68-71, 72-75 & 76-79; Gen Res Support Fund grant, Univ Utah, 71-72; Weldon Springs Endowment Fund grants, 80-85; Sarah Morrison bequest basic res internal med grant, 85-87, fac research grant, 89-91. *Mem:* Am Soc Microbiol; fel Am Acad Microbiol. *Res:* Genetic regulation of bacterial sporulation; genetic mapping and gene transfer in Staphylococcus aureus; genetic control of staphylococcal exfoliative toxin production; staphylococcal plasmids. *Mailing Add:* Med Sch Univ Mo Kansas City MO 64108

ROGOSA, GEORGE LEON, PHYSICS. *Current Pos:* RETIRED. *Personal Data:* b Lynn, Mass, Jan 16, 24; m 50. *Educ:* Johns Hopkins Univ, AB, 44, PhD(physics), 49. *Honors & Awards:* Arthur S Flemming Award, 63. *Prof Exp:* From jr instr to asst prof physics, Johns Hopkins Univ, 44-49; from asst prof to assoc prof physics, Fla State Univ, 49-56; physicist, Eng Develop Br, Div Reactor Develop, USAEC, 56-57, Physics & Math Br, 57-73, asst dir nuclear sci, Div Phys Res, 73-75; asst dir nuclear sci, Div Phys Res, US Energy Res & Develop Admin, US Dept Energy, 75-77, dir, Div Nuclear Physics, 77-79. *Concurrent Pos:* Adj prof physics, Duke Univ, 80- *Mem:* Am Phys Soc. *Res:* Transuranic x-ray spectra; anamalous transmission of x-rays in Laue diffraction; x-ray absorption edges; technical administration of atomic and nuclear physics research programs. *Mailing Add:* 5 Berwick Ct Durham NC 27707. *Fax:* 919-660-2525

ROGOWSKI, ROBERT STEPHEN, PHYSICAL CHEMISTRY, MOLECULAR SPECTROSCOPY. *Current Pos:* SR RES SCIENTIST, NASA LANGLEY RES CTR, 68- *Personal Data:* b Batavia, NY, Oct 7, 38; m 58; c 3. *Educ:* Canisius Col, BS, 60; Mich State Univ, PhD(phys chem), 68. *Concurrent Pos:* Adj prof chem, Christopher Newport Col, 69-79. *Mem:* AAAS; Am Chem Soc. *Res:* Metrology, optics, optical fiber sensors and properties of composite materials such as graphite/epoxy. *Mailing Add:* 109 Wicomico Turnpike Yorktown VA 23693-2614

ROGUSKA-KYTS, JADWIGA, INTERNAL MEDICINE, NEPHROLOGY. *Current Pos:* Intern, Northwestern Univ, 58-59, resident, 59-63, NIH fel, 64-66, asst prof, 70-74, ASSOC PROF MED, NORTHWESTERN UNIV, MED SCH, CHICAGO, 74- *Personal Data:* b Warsaw, Poland, May 11, 32; m 60. *Educ:* Univ Poznan, Poland, MA, 52; Poznan Med Sch, MD, 58. *Concurrent Pos:* Attend physician, Cook County Hosp, Chicago, 64-68, Passavant Mem Hosp, 66-, Med Sch, Northwestern Univ, Chicago, 66- & Vet Admin Res Hosp, 70-; assoc chief div med, Northwestern Mem Hosp, Chicago. *Mem:* AAAS; Am Fedn Clin Res; Am Soc Nephrology; Am Heart Asn; fel Am Col Physicians. *Res:* Hypertension; renal pressor system; uremia. *Mailing Add:* 707 N Fairbanks Ct Chicago IL 60611-3042

ROHA, MAX EUGENE, ORGANIC CHEMISTRY. *Current Pos:* INNOVATIVE SOLUTIONS, DR MAX ROHA ASSOCS, BRECKSVILLE, OH, 84- *Personal Data:* b Meadville, Pa, Apr 14, 23; m 46; c 3. *Educ:* Allegheny Col, BS, 44; Harvard Univ, AM, 47, PhD, 49. *Prof Exp:* Sr tech man, 49-59, mgr plastics res, 60-62, dir sci liaison, 62-78, dir explor new prods, 78-81, dir new spec polymers & chem, res & develop, Res Ctr, B F Goodrich Co, 81-84. *Concurrent Pos:* Res, Case Western Reserve Univ, 84-, Univ Akron, 90- *Mem:* Am Chem Soc. *Res:* Polymers; plastics; research and development planning; project evaluation and conceptualization. *Mailing Add:* 8205 Parkview Rd Brecksville OH 44141-2917

ROHACH, ALFRED F(RANKLIN), NUCLEAR ENGINEERING. *Current Pos:* From asst prof to assoc prof, 63-79, PROF NUCLEAR ENG, IOWA STATE UNIV, 79- *Personal Data:* b Toledo, Iowa, Jan 30, 34; m 61; c 4. *Educ:* Iowa State Univ, BS, 59, MS, 61, PhD(nuclear eng), 63. *Concurrent Pos:* AEC fel, 64-66; fac improvement leave, Southern Calif Edison Co, 77-78. *Mem:* Am Nuclear Soc. *Res:* Radiation shielding; numerical analysis in nuclear reactor theory; nuclear power economics; nuclear fuel management. *Mailing Add:* 2120 Stevenson Dr Ames IA 50010

ROHAN, PAUL E(DWARD), NUCLEAR ENGINEERING, SOFTWARE DEVELOPMENT. *Current Pos:* SR CONSULT, 90- *Personal Data:* b Evergreen Park, Ill, May 5, 43; m 70. *Educ:* Univ Detroit, BS, 65; Univ Ill, Urbana, MS, 66, PhD(nuclear eng), 70. *Prof Exp:* Sr staff physicist, Combustion Eng, Inc, 70-72, supvr nuclear eng, 72-74, sect mgr, 74-77, task area mgr physics, 77-79, mgr computer analysis, 79-90. *Mem:* Sigma Xi; Am Nuclear Soc. *Res:* Computational methods for nuclear reactor analyses; reactor physics; numerical analysis. *Mailing Add:* 76 Overlook Dr Windsor CT 06095-2657

ROHATGI, PRADEEP KUMAR, MATERIALS SCIENCE, MATERIALS ENGINEERING & MATERIALS POLICY. *Current Pos:* PROF MAT, COL ENG, UNIV WIS-MILWAUKEE, 85-, FORD BRIGGS & STRATTON CHAIR PROF, 90-, WIS DISTINGUISHED PROF, 96- *Personal Data:* b Kanpur, India, Feb 18, 43; m 68, Kalpana Devaraj; c 2. *Educ:* Banaras Hindu Univ, India, BS, 61; Mass Inst Technol, MS, 63, DSc, 64. *Honors & Awards:* Indranil Award, Mining & Mettal Soc India, 78; Gold Medal Technnol Future, Indian Res Ctr, 81; Distinguished Engr Award, Asn Engrs India, 84; World Intellectual Property Orgn Award, 86. *Prof Exp:* Res Metallurgist, Int Nickel Co, 64-68; res engr mat, Homer Res Lab, Bethelehem Steel, 69-72; prof mat sci, Indian Inst Sci, Bangalore, India, 72-77; dir, Coun Sci & Indust Res, India, 77-85. *Concurrent Pos:* Vis prof, Indian Inst Technol, New Dehli, 82-83 & San Jose Univ, 83, Mass Inst Technol, 86-90. *Mem:* Fel Am Soc Metals; Am Inst Metall Engrs; Am Foundrymen Soc; fel AAAS; fel Third World Acad Sci. *Res:* Dendritic solidification of solutions; synthesis of cast metal ceramic composites and characterization of their mechanical, physical and tribological properties; structure and properties of natural fibers and synthesis of composites using these fibers; alloy development; granted 13 US patents, two Indian patents and two British patents. *Mailing Add:* Dept Mat Univ Wis PO Box 784 Milwaukee WI 53201

ROHATGI, UPENDRA SINGH, MECHANICAL ENGINEERING, FLUID FLOW & HEAT & MASS TRANSFER IN SYSTEMS. *Current Pos:* MECH ENGR & GROUP LEADER THERMOHYDRAUL REACTORS, BROOKHAVEN NAT LAB, 75- *Personal Data:* b Kanpur, India, Mar 3, 49; m 75, Charu; c Ruchi & Udai (Singh). *Educ:* Indian Inst Technol, Kanpur,

BTech, 70; Case Western Res Univ, MS, 72, PhD(fluid & thermal sci), 75. *Honors & Awards:* Recognition Award, Am Soc Mech Enngrs. *Concurrent Pos:* Engr aircraft fuel pumps, TRW Inc, Cleveland, 74 & Chandler-Evans, 81; consult, UN Deveop Prog, Defence Nuclear Facil Safety Bd; vis prof, Indian Inst Technol; adj prof, Cooper Union, NY & State Univ NY, Stony Brook; assoc tech ed, Am Soc Mech Engrs, J Fluids Eng. *Mem:* Am Soc Mech Engrs; Sci Res Soc NAm; Am Nuclear Soc. *Res:* Multi-phase flow; thermohydraulic of reactors; reactor safety turbomachinery. *Mailing Add:* 32 Robinhood Lane East Setauket NY 11733. *Fax:* 516-282-7650

ROHATGI, VIJAY, MATHEMATICAL STATISTICS & PROBABILITY, FINANCE & INVESTMENTS. *Current Pos:* assoc prof, 72-73, chmn, Dept Math & Statist, 83-85, PROF MATH, BOWLING GREEN STATE UNIV, 73-; PRES, V R CONSULT CO, INC, 96- *Personal Data:* b Delhi, India, Feb 1, 39; m 71, Bina Parab; c Sameer. *Educ:* Univ Delhi, BSc, 58, MA, 60; Univ Alta, MS, 64; Mich State Univ, PhD(math statist), 67. *Prof Exp:* From asst prof to assoc prof math, Cath Univ Am, 67-72. *Concurrent Pos:* Vis prof, Ohio State Univ, 79-80; investment analyst & consult, 87- *Mem:* Am Statist Asn; Int Statist Inst; Inst Math Statist. *Res:* Statistical inference; probability limit laws; order statistics; finance and investments. *Mailing Add:* Dept Math Bowling Green State Univ Bowling Green OH 43403. *Fax:* 419-372-6092, 703-404-2767; *E-Mail:* vrohatg@andy.bgsu.edu

ROHDE, CHARLES RAYMOND, PLANT BREEDING. *Current Pos:* RETIRED. *Personal Data:* b Glasgow, Mont, Sept 3, 22; m 45, Edith B Emmert; c James Michael, Charles Richard, Linda Ann, David Alan & Beth Ann. *Educ:* Mont State Col, BS, 47; Univ Minn, PhD(plant genetics), 53. *Prof Exp:* Asst prof agron & small grain breeder, Univ Wyo, 50-51; assoc prof, Ore State Univ, 52-70, wheat breeder, Pendleton Exp Sta, 52-76, 70-76, prof agron, 70-76; prof agron, Columbia Basin Agr Res Ctr, 76-87, emer prof, 87- *Mem:* Am Soc Agron. *Res:* Wheat breeding and genetics. *Mailing Add:* 2230 SW Ladow Pendleton OR 97801

ROHDE, FLORENCE VIRGINIA, ENGINEERING MATHEMATICS, ACTUARIAL MATHEMATICS. *Current Pos:* prof, 66-83, EMER PROF MATH, MISS STATE UNIV 83- *Personal Data:* b Davenport, Iowa, May 15, 18. *Educ:* Univ Northern Iowa, AB, 39; Univ Rochester, MM, 40; Miami Univ, AM, 45; Univ Ky, PhD(math), 50. *Prof Exp:* Teacher pub schs, Iowa, 40-42; instr music & math, Miami Univ, 42-45; asst math, Ohio State Univ, 45-46; instr math & astron, Univ Ky, 46-50; from instr to assoc prof math & astron, Univ Fla, 50-57; prof math, Univ Chattanooga, 57-66. *Concurrent Pos:* Mathematician, Naval Res Lab, 53, US Naval Weapons Lab, 56 & 57 & Tenn Valley Authority, 59-62. *Mem:* Soc Indust & Appl Math; Am Math Soc; Math Asn Am. *Res:* Engineering and actuarial mathematics; numerical analysis; number theory. *Mailing Add:* Box 5172 Mississippi State MS 39762-5172

ROHDE, RICHARD ALLEN, PLANT PATHOLOGY. *Current Pos:* from asst prof to assoc prof, 59-68, head dept, 68-81, PROF PLANT PATH, UNIV MASS, AMHERST, 68-, ASSOC DEAN, FOOD & NAT RESOURCES & ASSOC DIR, MASS AGR EXP STA, 84- *Personal Data:* b Peekskill, NY, Sept 28, 29; m 55; c 4. *Educ:* Drew Univ, AB, 51; Univ Md, MS, 56, PhD(plant path), 58. *Prof Exp:* Asst plant path, Univ Md, 58-59. *Concurrent Pos:* Vis scientist, Rothamsted Exp Sta, Eng, 67; vis prof, Univ Ariz, 74; nematologist, Coop State Res Serv, USDA, 81. *Mem:* AAAS; Am Phytopathological Soc; Soc Nematol. *Res:* Ecology and physiology of plant parasitic nematodes; plant diseases caused by nematodes. *Mailing Add:* 18 Butterhill Rd Amherst MA 01002

ROHDE, RICHARD WHITNEY, MATERIALS SCIENCE, TRIBOLOGY. *Current Pos:* Staff mem, Shock Wave Physics Div, Sandia Nat Lab, 67-69, supvr, Phys & Mech Metall Div, 69-82, mgr, Mat Dept, 83-90, mgr, Environ Health & Safety Dept, 90-92, DEP DIR ENVIRON SAFETY & HEALTH, SANDIA LABS, 67- *Personal Data:* b Salt Lake City, Utah, Dec 23, 40; m 61; c 5. *Educ:* Univ Utah, BS, 63, PhD(metall), 67. *Concurrent Pos:* Ed, Am Soc Mech Engrs Trans, J Eng Mat & Technol, 87- *Mem:* Metall Soc; Am Inst Mining, Metall & Petrol Engrs; Am Soc Metals; Am Soc Testing & Mat; Am Soc Mech Engrs. *Res:* Dislocation dynamics in shock loaded materials; shock loading equation of state; phase transformation in metals; dislocation dynamics; stress corrosion cracking; friction, lubrication and wear; inleastic deformation modeling. *Mailing Add:* Sandia Lab PO Box 5800 MS 1050 Albuquerque NM 87185-1050

ROHDE, STEVE MARK, APPLIED MATHEMATICS, TRIBOLOGY. *Current Pos:* Res scientist appl math, Gen Motors Res Labs, 70-79, head systs eng activ, Proj Trilby, 85-88, MGR, SYSTS ANALYSIS & INFO MGT DEPT, GEN MOTORS SYSTS ENERGY CTR, GEN MOTORS RES LABS, 88- *Personal Data:* b Newark, NJ, May 18, 46; m; c 2. *Educ:* NJ Inst Technol, BS, 67; Lehigh Univ, MS, 69, PhD(math), 70. *Honors & Awards:* Henry Hess Award, Am Soc Mech Engrs, 73; Harry Kummer Mem Award, Am Soc Testing & Mat, 76; Burt L Newkirk Tribology Award, Am Soc Mech Engrs, 77; Clifford Steadman Award, Inst Mech Engrs, 84. *Mem:* Fel Am Soc Mech Engrs; Soc Automotive Engrs. *Res:* Advanced vehicle systems; tribology; computer aided engineering; control of mechanical systems. *Mailing Add:* 3369 Pontiac Trail Ann Arbor MI 48105

ROHDE, SUZANNE LOUISE, THIN FILMS, VACUUM SCIENCE. *Current Pos:* ASST PROF MECH ENG, UNIV NEBR-LINCOLN, 92- *Personal Data:* b Denver, Colo, Feb 13, 63; m 85, John R. *Educ:* Iowa State Univ, BS, 85; Northwestern Univ, MS, 88, PhD(mat sci & eng), 91. *Honors & Awards:* Natl Young Investr, NSF. *Prof Exp:* Eng technician, Spangler Lab, Iowa State Univ, 85-86; res asst eng, Dept Mat Sci & Eng, Northwestern Univ, 86-89; dir res, Biophotonics, Inc, Milwaukee, 89-91. *Concurrent Pos:* Res scientist, Birl Indust Res Lab, Evanston, 89-91. *Mem:* Mat Res Soc; Am Vacuum Soc; Am Soc Metals; Metall Soc; Am Asn Eng Educr. *Res:* Thin film deposition equipment and processes; sputter deposition and molecular beam epitaxy based processes; characterization of thin film couples by stem, tem, xtem, auger, edax and x-ray. *Mailing Add:* Univ Nebr-Lincoln Dept Mech Eng 104N Walter Scott Eng Ctr Lincoln NE 68588-0656. *Fax:* 402-472-1465; *E-Mail:* srohde@unlinfo.unl.edu

ROHEIM, PAUL SAMUEL, PHYSIOLOGY, MEDICINE. *Current Pos:* PROF PHYSIOL, MED & PATH, LA STATE UNIV MED CTR, 77- *Personal Data:* b Kiskunhalas, Hungary, July 11, 25; US citizen; m 57; c 1. *Educ:* Med Sch Budapest, MD, 51. *Prof Exp:* Demonstr physiol, Med Sch Budapest, 47-51, asst prof, 51-56; res assoc, Hahnemann Med Col, 57-58; instr med, Albert Einstein Col Med, 58-62, assoc in med, 62-63, from asst prof physiol to prof physiol & med, 63-77. *Concurrent Pos:* Intern, Univ Budapest Clins, 51-52; NIH fel, Albert Einstein Col Med, 58-62, New York Health Res Coun career scientist award, 68-73; estab investr, Am Heart Asn, 63-68, mem coun on arteriosclerosis. *Mem:* Am Physiol Soc; Fedn Am Socs Exp Biol; Hungarian Physiol Soc. *Res:* Lipid and lipoprotein metabolism; arteriosclerosis. *Mailing Add:* Dept Phyiol La State Univ Med Ctr 1542 Tulane Ave New Orleans LA 70112

ROHL, ARTHUR N, MINERALOGY. *Current Pos:* PRIN, ARTHUR ROHL ASSOCS INC, 85- *Personal Data:* b Brooklyn, NY, May 11, 30. *Educ:* Columbia Univ, BS, 58, MA, 60, PhD(geol), 72. *Prof Exp:* Asst prof environ & occup med, Mt Sinai Sch Med, 69-85. *Concurrent Pos:* Expert, New York Bd Educ, 72-85, US Environ Protection Agency & Occup Safety & Health Admin, 73-88, Repub Ireland, 74-85, Govt Bermuda & Nat Inst Occup Safety & Health, 75-86; consult, Philadelphia Bd Educ, 74-89. *Mem:* Sigma Xi; AAAS; Mineral Soc Am. *Res:* Identification and quantification of asbestos minerals in tissue specimens, water, air and in bulk samples; characterization of mineral dusts which cause disease, such as talc, quartz and asbestos. *Mailing Add:* Box 455 Durham PA 18039

ROHLF, F JAMES, BIOMETRY, POPULATION BIOLOGY. *Current Pos:* assoc prof biol, 69-72, chmn, Dept Ecol & Evolution, 75-80 & 90-91, PROF BIOL, STATE UNIV NY STONY BROOK, 72- *Personal Data:* b Blythe, Calif, Oct 24, 36; m 59, Patricia R Loustclet; c Kathryn M & Karen M. *Educ:* San Diego State Col, BS, 58; Univ Kans, PhD(entom), 62. *Prof Exp:* Asst prof biol, Univ Calif, Santa Barbara, 62-65; assoc prof statist biol, Univ Kans, 65-69. *Concurrent Pos:* Statist consult, NY Pub Serv Comn, 75-, IBM, 77-, US Environ Protection Agency, 78-80 & Appl Biomath Inc, 84-; vis scientist, IBM, Yorktown Heights, NY, 76-77 & 80-81. *Mem:* Biomet Soc; Asn Comput Mach; Soc Syst Zool; Classification Soc. *Res:* Applications of multivariate analysis, cluster and factor analysis to systematics, morphometrics, and population biology. *Mailing Add:* 3 Heritage Lane Setauket NY 11733. *E-Mail:* jim.rohlf@sunysb.edu

ROHLF, MARVIN EUGUENE, ANIMAL FEED PRODUCTION, BEEF CATTLE NUTRITION. *Current Pos:* RETIRED. *Personal Data:* b Ida Grove, Iowa, Mar 10, 27; m 54, Barbara Murphy; c Scott, Craig, Steve, Tim & Paul. *Educ:* Iowa State Univ, BS, 50, MS, 54. *Prof Exp:* Asst nutritionist, Golden Sun Feeds Inc, 54-56, nutritionist, 56-70, vpres, Res & Develop, Golden Sun Feeds Div United Brands, 70-80, sr vpres, 80-92. *Concurrent Pos:* Chmn, Iowa Feed & Nutrit Serv, 60-61; chmn various comt, Nat Feed Ingredient Asn, 76-81, asst chmn bd, 80-81, chmn bd, 81-82; bd gov, Advan Regist Prof Animal Scientists. *Mem:* Am Soc Animal Sci; Am Soc Poultry Sci; Am Soc Dairy Sci; Advan Regist Prof Animal Scientists. *Res:* Nutritonal conduction with swine of all ages; beef cattle, dairy beef and cage layers. *Mailing Add:* 12895 Hwy 327 Spirit Lake IA 51360. *Fax:* 407-779-3956; *E-Mail:* mrohlf@digital.net

ROHLFING, DUANE L, BIOCHEMISTRY, EVOLUTION. *Current Pos:* from asst prof to assoc prof, 68-76, PROF BIOL, UNIV SC, 76- *Personal Data:* b Cape Girardeau, Mo, Nov 18, 33; m 56; c 4. *Educ:* Drury Col, BS, 55; Fla State Univ, MS, 60, PhD(biochem), 64. *Prof Exp:* Nat Acad Sci res assoc enzyme models, Ames Res Ctr, NASA, Calif, 64-66; Med Found Boston sr res fel enzymes, Mass Inst Technol, 66-68. *Mem:* AAAS; Am Chem Soc; Am Soc Biol Chem; Int Soc Study Origins Life. *Res:* Molecular and cellular evolution; polyamino acids; protocells; catalysis. *Mailing Add:* Dept Biol Univ SC Columbia SC 29208-0001

ROHLFING, STEPHEN ROY, MICROBIOLOGY, INFECTIOUS DISEASES. *Current Pos:* SR SPECIALIST CLIN RES, SURG DIV 3M CO, 91- *Personal Data:* b Toledo, Ohio, July 25, 36; m 59, Janet; c Valerie & Curt. *Educ:* Bowling Green State Univ, BS, 58; Miami Univ, MS, 60; Western Res Univ, PhD(microbiol), 65. *Prof Exp:* Assoc microbiol, Chicago Med Sch, 65-66, asst prof, 66-70; from instr to asst prof pharmacog, Col Pharm, Univ Minn, Minneapolis, 70-80, assoc prof pharmacol, 80-90. *Concurrent Pos:* Sr scientist, Riker Res Labs, Minn Mining & Mfg Co, 70-72, res specialist, Riker Labs, Inc, 72-75, supvr microbiol, 75-78, proj leader, Antiinfective Drug Res, 78-85,; sr res specialist, 85-90. *Mem:* Can Soc Microbiol; Am Soc Microbiol; Brit Soc Antimicrobial Chemother; Europ Soc Clin Microbiol. *Res:* Gene-enzyme relationships; molecular characteristics of lymphomas; anti-infective research and development; asepsis and surgical wound infection; sterilization. *Mailing Add:* 1081 Cedarwood Dr Woodbury MN 55125. *Fax:* 612-736-7329

ROHM, C E TAPIE, JR, INFORMATION MANAGEMENT, INFORMATION STRATEGIES & PLANNING. *Current Pos:* asst prof mgt & comput, 79-81, PROF INFO MGT, CALIF STATE UNIV, SAN BERNARDINO, 83- *Personal Data:* b Long Beach, Calif, June 2, 47; m 72, Karen; c 8. *Educ:* Brigham Young Univ, BS, 73, MA, 74; Ohio Univ, PhD(psychol, commun & mgt), 77. *Prof Exp:* Asst to dean, Ohio Univ, 77-79; assoc prof bus & comput, Whittier Col, 81-83. *Concurrent Pos:* Corp treas, Ohio Univ Med Assocs, Inc, 78-79; vis prof, Univ Dar es Salaam, 88-89; Fulbright sr scholar, 88-89; ed-in-chief, J Int Info Mgt, 90-93, 91- *Mem:* Int Info Mgt Asn (pres, 86-91); AAAS; Acad Mgt; Asn Comput Mach. *Res:* Focus on decision-making within individuals to increase productivity; international issues for developing countries in information management. *Mailing Add:* Dept Info & Decision Sci Calif State Univ San Bernardino CA 92407. *Fax:* 909-880-5994

ROHMAN, MICHAEL, THORACIC & TRAUMA SURGERY. *Current Pos:* PROF SURG, NY MED COL, 70-; CHIEF CARDIOTHORACIC SURG, LINCOLN MED & MENT HEALTH CTR, 79- *Personal Data:* b New York, NY, Nov 21, 25; m 48, Joelyn L Iser; c Lisa & Debra. *Educ:* Boston Univ, MD, 50. *Prof Exp:* From intern to chief resident surg, Mass Mem Hosp, 50-55; asst & chief resident thoracic surg, Bronx Munic Hosp Ctr, 55-58; from instr to asst prof cardio-thoracic surg, Albert Einstein Col Med, 58-69, from asst clin prof to assoc clin prof, 69-70. *Concurrent Pos:* Nat Tuberc Asn fel, Albert Einstein Col Med, 57-59; consult cardio-thoracic surg, Northern Westchester Hosp, Yonkers Gen Hosp, United Hosp & Montrose Vet Admin Hosp, 66-79; dir surg, Westchester County Med Ctr, 64-79. *Mem:* Am Col Chest Physicians; Am Heart Asn; fel Am Col Surg; Soc Thoracic Surg; Am Asn Surg Trauma. *Res:* Small arterial anastamoses; pulmonary hemodynamics, particularly bronchial artery circulation. *Mailing Add:* Dept Surg Lincoln Med & Ment Health Ctr 234 E 149th St Bronx NY 10451. *Fax:* 718-579-4620

ROHN, REUBEN D, TEACHING MEDICAL STUDENTS & RESIDENTS, RESEARCH ON PUBERTY TRACE ELEMENTS & OSTEOPOROSIS. *Current Pos:* coordr pediat clerkship, 77-90, DIR ADOLESCENT MED & PEDIAT ENDOCRINOL, CHILDRENS HOSP KINGS DAUGHTERS, 76-; PROF PEDIAT, EASTERN VA MED SCH, 89- *Personal Data:* b Israel, Apr 12, 45; US citizen; m 71, Judith Semel; c Karen. *Educ:* Brooklyn Col, BA, 67; NY Med Col, MD, 71; Am Bd Pediat, cert pediat, 76, cert pediat endocrinol, 80, cert adolescent med, 94. *Prof Exp:* From asst prof to assoc prof, Eastern Va Med Sch, 76-89. *Concurrent Pos:* Mem, Norfolk Sch Health Coun, 77-93; mem, Comt Youth & Adolescent, Va Chap, Am Acad Pediat, 78-; adj prof chem, Old Dominion Univ, 84- *Mem:* Lawson Wilkins Pediat Endocrine Soc; Soc Adolescent Med; fel Am Acad Pediat; Sigma Xi. *Res:* Objectification of pubertal maturation scales; trace element metabolism in diabetes and other endocrinopathies; osteoporosis in multiply handicapped children. *Mailing Add:* 601 Childrens Lane Norfolk VA 23507. *Fax:* 757-668-9761; *E-Mail:* rrohn@chkd.1evms.edu

ROHN, ROBERT JONES, MEDICINE, HEMATOLOGY-ONCOLOGY. *Current Pos:* from instr to asst prof med, 50-55, assoc med & coordr cancer educ, 55-68, prof med, 68-74, cancer coordr, 68-85, Bruce Kenneth Wiseman prof med,74-85, DISTINGUISHED EMER PROF MED, IND UNIV, INDIANAPOLIS, 85- *Personal Data:* b Lima, Ohio, June 16, 18; m 42; c 4. *Educ:* DePauw Univ, AB, 40; Ohio State Univ, MD, 43. *Prof Exp:* Intern, Ohio State Univ Hosp, 43-44, resident internal med, 44-46, resident hemat, 48-50. *Concurrent Pos:* Consult, Vet Admin & Army Hosps, 52-85; chmn, Nonprofit Div, Soc Retired Exec, 88- *Mem:* Am Soc Hemat; Reticuloendothelial Soc; fel Am Col Physicians; Am Fedn Clin Res; Int Soc Hemat. *Res:* Cytological and clinical hematology. *Mailing Add:* 7334 A King George Dr Indianapolis IN 46260

ROHNER, THOMAS JOHN, UROLOGY. *Current Pos:* from asst prof to assoc prof, 70-75, PROF SURG, MILTON S HERSHEY MED CTR, PA STATE UNIV, 75-, CHIEF DIV UROL, 70- *Personal Data:* b Trenton, NJ, Jan 1, 36; c 2. *Educ:* Yale Univ, BA, 57; Univ Pa, MD, 61. *Prof Exp:* Resident gen surg, Hosp, Univ Pa, 62-64, resident urol, 64-67; USPHS spec fel, Dept Pharm, Sch Med, 69-70. *Concurrent Pos:* Consult urol, Vet Admin Hosp, Lebanon, Pa, 70- & Elizabethtown Hosp Children & Youth, Pa, 70- *Mem:* Am Urol Asn; Am Col Surgeons; Soc Pediat Urol; Asn Acad Surg. *Res:* In vitro contractile mechanisms of bladder and ureteral smooth muscle. *Mailing Add:* M S Hershey Med Ctr Pa State Univ Box 820 Hershey PA 17033

ROHOLT, OLIVER A, JR, IMMUNOLOGY. *Current Pos:* RETIRED. *Personal Data:* b Preston, Idaho, May 30, 16; m 44; c 2. *Educ:* Univ Mont, BA, 39; Univ Calif, PhD(biochem), 53. *Prof Exp:* Asst, Utah State Agr Col, 40-41; asst, Univ Calif, 47-50; instr, State Col Wash, 50-56; sr cancer res scientist, Roswell Park Mem Inst, 56-63, assoc cancer res scientist, 63-65, prin cancer res scientist, 65-79, cancer res scientist vi, 79-83, actg dept chmn, molecular immunol, Roswell Park Mem Inst, 80-82. *Concurrent Pos:* Assoc res prof, Roswell Park Div, Grad Sch, State Univ NY Buffalo, 66-83; mem grad fac, Niagara Univ, 68-83. *Mem:* Am Chem Soc; Am Soc Biochem & Molecular Biol; Sigma Xi. *Mailing Add:* 2233 E Behrend Dr Apt 78 Phoenix AZ 85024-1853

ROHOVSKY, MICHAEL WILLIAM, PATHOLOGY. *Current Pos:* VPRES RES & DEVELOP, JOHNSON & JOHNSON PROF INC, 94- *Personal Data:* b Youngstown, Ohio, Feb 26, 37; m 65, Karen Andreas; c Paul & Stephanie. *Educ:* Ohio State Univ, DVM, 60, MSc, 65, PhD(vet path), 67. *Prof Exp:* NIH fel vet path, Ohio State Univ, 62-67, asst prof, 67-69; dir path labs, Merrell Nat Labs, 69-72; dir path, Arthur D Little Inc, 72-77; vpres res & develop, Pittman-Moore Inc, 77-81; dir, Med Affairs & Orthop Res & Develop, Johnson & Johnson Products Inc, 81-86, vpres res & develop, Johnson & Johnson Inc, 86-93. *Concurrent Pos:* Adj asst prof path, Sch Med Univ Cincinnati, 69-72; indust rep, FDA Adv Panel, Gen, Med & Personal Use, 86- *Mem:* NY Acad Sci; fel Am Col Vet Pharmacol & Therapeut; Int Acad Path; Am Col Vet Pathologists; AAAS; Am Vet Med Asn. *Res:* Infectious diseases of animals; neoplastic diseases; antiviral therapy; toxicology and drug safety; medical devices development; orthopaedic and neurosurgical devices. *Mailing Add:* Johnson & Johnson Prof Inc 325 Paramount Dr Raynham MA 02767

ROHR, DAVID M, TAXONOMY, BIOGEOGRAPHY. *Current Pos:* from asst prof to assoc prof, 80-89, PROF GEOL, SUL ROSS STATE UNIV, 89-, CHMN, 92- *Personal Data:* b Portsmouth, Va, Sept 9, 47; m 94, Elizabeth Measures. *Educ:* Col William & Mary, BS, 69; Ore State Univ, PhD(geol), 77. *Prof Exp:* Asst prof geol, Univ Ore, 77-79 & Univ Wash, 79-80. *Mem:* Paleont Soc; fel Geol Soc Am; Paleont Res Inst; Soc Econ Paleontologists & Mineralogists; Int Paleont Asn. *Res:* Lower Paleozoic (Ordovician through Lower Devonian) gastropods; paleoecology; lower Paleozoic stratigraphy. *Mailing Add:* Dept Geol Sul Ross State Univ, Box C-147 Alpine TX 79832. *Fax:* 915-837-8692; *E-Mail:* drohr@sul-ross-1.sulross.edu

ROHR, ROBERT CHARLES, PHYSICS. *Current Pos:* RETIRED. *Personal Data:* b Leonia, NJ, Feb 27, 22; m 46; c 3. *Educ:* Guilford Col, BS, 43; Univ Wis, MS, 47; Univ Tenn, PhD(physics), 55. *Prof Exp:* Physicist, Union Carbide Nuclear Co, div, Union Carbide Corp, 47-53; physicist, Gen Elec Co, 55-59, mgr cold water assembly, 59-66, mgr cold water assembly/adv test reactor, 66-72, mgr chem & radiol controls navy training support, 72-74, sr proj engr, Prototype Opers & Eng, 74-77, mgr Reactor Eng Oper Ship & Prototype Testing, Knolls Atomic Power Lab, Gen Elec Co, 77-87; adj prof, nuclear eng physics dept, RPI, 89-93. *Mem:* Am Phys Soc; Am Nuclear Soc. *Res:* Critical assembly experiments; beta ray spectroscopy; radiation and particle detectors. *Mailing Add:* 615 Gordon Rd Schenectady NY 12306

ROHRBACH, KENNETH G, PLANT PATHOLOGY. *Current Pos:* assoc plant pathologist, 73-77, plant pathologist, 78-85, ASST DIR, HAWAII INST TROP AGR & HUMAN RESOURCES, UNIV HAWAII, MANOA, 85- *Personal Data:* b Ashland, Ohio, Oct 16, 40; m 62; c 3. *Educ:* Ohio State Univ, BS, 62; Univ Idaho, MS, 64; Colo State Univ, PhD(plant path), 67. *Prof Exp:* Res asst plant dis, Univ Idaho, 62-64 & Colo State Univ, 64-67; plant pathologist, Dole Co, 67-70 & Pineapple Res Inst, 70-73. *Mem:* Am Phytopath Soc. *Res:* Diseases of tropical crops. *Mailing Add:* Hawaii Inst Trop Agr & Human Resources Univ Hawaii-Manoa 3050 Maile Way Honolulu HI 96822

ROHRBACH, MICHAEL STEVEN, pulmonary research, biochemistry; deceased, see previous edition for last biography

ROHRBACH, ROGER P(HILLIP), AGRICULTURAL ENGINEERING. *Current Pos:* From asst prof to assoc prof, 68-78, PROF BIOL & AGR ENG, AGR EXP STA, NC STATE UNIV, 78- *Personal Data:* b Canton, Ohio, Oct 12, 42; m 65; c 3. *Educ:* Ohio State Univ, PhD(agr eng), 68. *Honors & Awards:* FMC Corp Young Designer Award, Am Soc Agr Engrs, 81. *Mem:* Am Soc Agr Engrs. *Res:* Fruit production mechanization; blueberries and grapes; irradiation processes applied to agriculture; process engineering in agriculture. *Mailing Add:* Dept Biol & Agr Eng NC State Univ Raleigh NC 27695-7625

ROHRER, DOUGLAS C, X-RAY CRYSTALLOGRAPHY. *Current Pos:* res assoc, 73-74, res scientist cyrstallog, 74-78, ASSOC RES SCIENTIST, MOLECULAR BIOPHYS DEPT, MED FOUND BUFFALO, 78- *Personal Data:* b Cleveland, Ohio, Dec 24, 42; m 66; c 2. *Educ:* Western Reserve Univ, BA, 66; Case Western Reserve Univ, PhD(chem), 70. *Prof Exp:* Res assoc crystallog, Crystallog Dept, Univ Pittsburgh, 70-73. *Concurrent Pos:* Vis prof, Sch Pharm, Oregon State Univ, 79. *Mem:* Am Chem Soc; Am Crystallog Asn; Am Inst Physics. *Mailing Add:* Upjohn Co 7247-677-131 301 Henrietta St Kalamazoo MI 49007-4940

ROHRER, HEINRICH, PHYSICS. *Current Pos:* MGR, PHYSICS DEPT, IBM ZURICH RES LAB, 86- *Personal Data:* b Buschs, Switz, JUNE 6, 33. *Educ:* Swiss Inst Technol, Dipl, 55, PhD(physics), 60. *Hon Degrees:* DSc, Rutgers Univ, 87; Marseille Univ, 88; Madrid Univ, 88, Tsukuba Univ, 94. *Honors & Awards:* Nobel Prize in Physics, 86; King Faisal Int Prize Sci, 84; Cresson Medal, Franklin Inst, 87; Nat Inventors Hall Fame, 94. *Prof Exp:* Res asst, Swiss Inst Technol, Zurich, Switz, 60-61; fel, Rutgers Univ, 61-63. *Concurrent Pos:* Vis scholar, Univ Calif, Santa Barbara, 74-75; IBM fel, 86; bd dirs, Swiss Fed Inst Technol, 93. *Mem:* Foriegn assoc Nat Acad Sci; fel & hon mem Royal Microscopical Soc; hon mem Swiss Asn Eng & Archit; hon mem Swiss Phys Soc; hon mem Swiss Acad Tech Scis. *Mailing Add:* IBM Zurich Res Lab Saemerstr Four 8803 Rueschlikon Zurich Switzerland

ROHRER, JAMES WILLIAM, CELLULAR IMMUNOLOGY, IMMUNE REGULATION. *Current Pos:* ASSOC PROF MICROBIOL & IMMUNOL, COL MED, UNIV S ALA, 85- *Educ:* Univ Kans, PhD(microbiol), 75. *Mailing Add:* Dept Microbiol & Immunol Col Med Univ S Ala LMB Bldg Mobile AL 36688-0002. *Fax:* 334-460-7931

ROHRER, ROBERT HARRY, PHYSICS. *Current Pos:* From instr to asst prof eng, 40-51, from asst prof to assoc prof physics, 51-61, assoc prof radiol, 56-62, chmn dept physics, 63-69, PROF PHYSICS, EMORY UNIV, 61-, PROF RADIOL, SCH MED, 62- *Personal Data:* b Philadelphia, Pa, Sept 20, 18; m 42; c 4. *Educ:* Emory Univ, BS, 39, MS, 42; Duke Univ, PhD(physics), 54. *Mem:* Am Phys Soc; Health Physics Soc; Soc Nuclear Med (vpres, 71-72); Am Asn Physicists Med; Am Asn Physics Teachers; Sigma Xi. *Res:* Nuclear radiation spectroscopy; radiation dosimetry; low energy neutron spectroscopy. *Mailing Add:* 642 Deerwood Lane Stone Mountain GA 30087-5330

ROHRER, RONALD A, ELECTRICAL ENGINEERING, COMPUTER ENGINEERING. *Current Pos:* prof elec eng, Carnegie-Mellon Univ, 74-75, prof, 85-89, dir, Ctr Excellence Comput-Aided Design, 89-92, HOWARD M WILKOFF UNIV PROF ELEC & COMPUT ENG & DIR, CTR COMPUT AIDED DESIGN, CARNEGIE-MELLON UNIV, 90- *Personal Data:* b Aug 19, 39; m, Casey Jones; c Sigrid, Gunther & Max. *Educ:* Mass Inst Technol, BS, 60; Univ Calif, Berkeley, MS, 61, PhD (elec eng), 63. *Honors & Awards:* Frederick Emmons Terman Award, Am Soc Elec Eng, 78; Circuit & Systs Soc Award, Inst Elec & Electronics Engrs, 90. *Prof Exp:* Asst prof elec eng, Univ Ill, Urbana, 63-65; asst prof appl anal, State Univ NY, Stony Brook, 65-66; from asst prof to assoc prof elec eng & comput sci, Univ Calif Berkeley, 66-72; prof & chmn, Dept Elec Eng, Univ Maine, 77-79, Southern Methodist Univ, 79-80; prof & chmn, Dept Elec Eng & Comput Sci, Univ Colo, Colorado Springs, 80-81. *Concurrent Pos:* Assoc ed, Inst Elec & Electronics Engrs Trans Circuit Theory, 66-69 & Computer-Aided Design, Trans Circuits & Systs, 81-84; mem tech staff & sect mgr, Fairchild Res & Develop, Palo Alto, Calif, 68-70; prog chmn, Int Conf Circuit Theory, Inst Elec & Electronics Engrs, 69, Long-Range Planning Comt, 69-70, chmn, Circuit Theory Group Computer-Aided Design Subcomt, 70-71; mgr, Elect Eng Anal Progs, Softech Inc, Waltham, Mass, 71-72; Alexander von Humboldt prize, 72; vis lectr, Univ Colo, Boulder, 76-77; prin investr, NSF grant, Univ Maine, 77-79, Southern Methodist Univ, 80-81, Carnegie-Mellon Univ, 88-90 & Semiconductor Res Corp grant, 90; co-prin investr, Elec Power Res Inst, 77-80; mem, Rev Eng & Eng Technol Studies Comt, Am Soc Eng Educ, 78-80; staff scientist, Indust Electronics Design Lab, Gen Elec Co, 81, prog mgr, Integrated Circuit Design Automation, Microelectronics Ctr, 82, dir, Electronic Prod Mkt, 82-83; dir & gen mgr micro electronics group, Sci Calculations Inc, 83-85; mem bd dirs, Integrated Silicon Systs Inc, 90-, Perform Signal Integrity, 92- *Mem:* Nat Acad Eng; fel Inst Elec & Electronics Engrs; Inst Elec & Electronics Engrs Circuits & Systs Soc (pres elect, 86, pres, 87). *Res:* Efficient and accurate electronic circuit and system simulation; efficient and accurate electronic circuit and system simulation. *Mailing Add:* Dept Elec & Comput Eng Carnegie Mellon Univ Pittsburgh PA 15213-3890. *Fax:* 412-268-3204; *E-Mail:* rohrer@gauss.ece.cmu.edu

ROHRER, WESLEY M, JR, MECHANICAL ENGINEERING, THERMODYNAMICS. *Current Pos:* Instr eng, Johnstown Ctr, 47-49, from instr to asst prof, 49-55, ASSOC PROF MECH ENG, UNIV PITTSBURGH, 55- *Personal Data:* b Johntown, Pa, Sept 12, 21; m 43; c 3. *Educ:* Univ Pittsburgh, BS, 47; Mass Inst Technol, SM, 61. *Concurrent Pos:* Consult, IBM Corp, 61-63, Adv Bd Hardened Elec Systs, Nat Acad Sci, 64-67 & World Bank, 80; vpres eng & natural sci, Univ Sci Ctr, Inc, 68-71, eng consult, 71-; vpres, Hosp Utility Mgt, Inc, 80-81. *Mem:* Combustion Inst (treas, 64-82); Am Soc Eng Educ; AAAS; Sigma Xi. *Res:* Radiative heat transfer; air pollution abatement; combustion; two-phase flow; boiling heat transfer; efficient energy utilization. *Mailing Add:* 220 Summit Dr Pittsburgh PA 15238-2922

ROHRIG, IGNATIUS A, METALLURGY. *Current Pos:* CONSULT METALL APPLN, 75- *Personal Data:* b Detroit, Mich, Jan 10, 10. *Educ:* Univ Detroit, BSMetE, 33. *Prof Exp:* Metall engr, Detroit Edison, 33-59, asst supvr, Eng Lab, 40-53, asst div head mat eng dept, 59-75. *Concurrent Pos:* Instr metall, Detroit Tech, 47-50; chmn comt, Am Soc Mech Eng, sub-comts, 62-75, Am Soc Testing & Mat. *Mem:* Fel Am Soc Testing & Mat; fel Am Soc Metals. *Res:* Twenty publications in the field of applications of metals at elevated temperatures. *Mailing Add:* 15131 Newburgh Rd No 3 Livonia MI 48154

ROHRINGER, ROLAND, PLANT PATHOLOGY. *Current Pos:* RETIRED. *Personal Data:* b Nurnberg, Ger, Aug 12, 29; nat Can; m 58; c 2. *Educ:* Univ Göttingen, PhD(agr), 56. *Prof Exp:* Fel plant path, Univ Göttingen, 56, res asst, 58-59; res asst biochem, Univ Wis, 56-58; res officer agr, Pesticide Res Inst, Can Dept Agr, 59, head, Cereal Rust Sect, 63-73, head cereal dis sect, 74-91. *Mem:* Phytochem Soc NAm. *Res:* Physiology of parasitism in plants; molecular biology of cereal rust diseases. *Mailing Add:* Univ Goettingen Schlaggenweg 3I 35094 Goettingen Germany. *E-Mail:* rrohrin@gwdg.de

ROHRL, HELMUT, MATHEMATICS. *Current Pos:* chmn dept, 68-71, PROF MATH, UNIV CALIF, SAN DIEGO, 64- *Personal Data:* b Straubing, Ger, Mar 22, 27. *Educ:* Univ Munich, DSc(math), 49, Habilitation, 53. *Prof Exp:* Asst prof math, Univ Wurzburg, 49-51; asst prof, Univ Munich, 51-53, 54-55, docent, 55-58; res assoc, Univ Chicago, 58-59; from assoc prof to prof, Univ Minn, 59-64; vis prof, Harvard Univ, 62-63. *Concurrent Pos:* Asst prof, Univ Munster, 53-54; vis prof, Princeton Univ, 67-68, Univ Munich, 72-73 & Univ Nagoya, 76. *Mem:* Am Math Soc; Ger Math Asn. *Res:* Pure mathematics. *Mailing Add:* 9322 La Jolla Farms Rd La Jolla CA 92037-1125

ROHRLICH, FRITZ, FOUNDATIONS OF PHYSICS, PHILOSOPHY OF SCIENCE. *Current Pos:* prof, 63-91, EMER PROF PHYSICS, SYRACUSE UNIV, 91- *Personal Data:* b Vienna, Austria, May 12, 21; nat US; m 94, Phyllis; c Emily & Paul. *Educ:* Inst Technol, Israel, ChemE, 43; Harvard Univ, MA, 47, PhD(physics), 48. *Hon Degrees:* DSc, Univ Graz, Austria, 96. *Honors & Awards:* Fulbright Lectr, US Dept State, Cent Europ, 74. *Prof Exp:* Mem staff, Inst Adv Study, 48-49; res assoc physics, Nuclear Studies Lab, Cornell Univ, 49-51; lectr, Princeton Univ, 51-53; from assoc prof to prof, Univ Iowa, 53-63. *Concurrent Pos:* Vis prof, Johns Hopkins Univ, 58-59, Tel-Aviv Univ, 67, Univ Warsaw, 77, Acad Sci Bulgaria, 78, Univ Calif, Irvine, 81 & Stanford Univ, 81; consult, Nat Bur Stand, 58-61. *Mem:* NY Acad Sci; fel Am Phys Soc; Fedn Am Sci; Philos Sci Asn. *Res:* Quantum field theory; quantum electrodynamics; relativistic particle dynamics; classical charged particles; philosophy of science. *Mailing Add:* Dept Physics Syracuse Univ Syracuse NY 13244-1130. *E-Mail:* rohrlich@syr.edu

ROHRMANN, CHARLES A(LBERT), INDUSTRIAL CHEMICALS, NUCLEAR FUEL PROCESSING. *Current Pos:* RETIRED. *Personal Data:* b Pendleton, Ore, Dec 17, 11; m 39, Elva Ann Chamblin; c Charles A Jr, George F, Vicki L & Joanne E. *Educ:* Ore State Univ, BS, 34; Ohio State Univ, PhD(chem eng), 39. *Honors & Awards:* I R 100 Award, Am Inst Chem Engrs, 71, R & D 100 Award, 84 & 91. *Prof Exp:* Res chem engr, Grasselli Chem Dept, E I Du Pont de Nemours & Co, Ohio, 39-43; plant process supvr, Pa, 43-48; chem engr, Gen Elec Co, 48-64; sr res assoc, Battelle Northwest, Wash, 65-68, consult, Chem & Metall Div, 68-70, staff engr, Chem Tech Dept, 70-77, resident consult, 77-83, tech specialist, Pac Northwest Labs, Battelle Mem Inst, 83-95. *Mem:* Am Chem Soc; fel Am Inst Chem Engrs. *Res:* Heavy inorganic and organic chemicals; sulfur-nitrogen chemicals; applications in the atomic energy industry; production recovery and applications of nuclear energy by-products and special radioisotopes; air pollution control; biomass conversion. *Mailing Add:* 4707 W Seventh Ave Kennewick WA 99336-4142

ROHRS, HAROLD CLARK, CELL PHYSIOLOGY. *Current Pos:* Asst prof, 66-72, assoc prof, 72-79, PROF ZOOL, DREW UNIV, 79- *Personal Data:* b Alexandria, Ky, Sept 23, 40; m 62; c 2. *Educ:* Transylvania Col, AB, 61; Univ Ky, PhD(physiol), 66. *Concurrent Pos:* Vis res prof, Univ Oslo, 73-74. *Mem:* Am Physiol Soc; Am Soc Zoologists. *Res:* Transport-process in blood and bone marrow cells. *Mailing Add:* Dept Biol Drew Univ 36 Madison Ave Madison NJ 07940

ROHRSCHNEIDER, LARRY RAY, VIROLOGY, ONCOLOGY. *Current Pos:* asst mem tumor virol, 76-80, ASSOC MEM TUMOR VIROL, FRED HUTCHINSON CANCER RES CTR, 81- *Personal Data:* b Minneapolis, Minn, Oct 2, 44; m 71; c 2. *Educ:* Univ Wis, BS, 67; Univ Wis, PhD(oncol), 73. *Prof Exp:* Res fel, Nat Cancer Inst, NIH, 73-76. *Concurrent Pos:* Res grant, HEW, USPHS, 77-; res asst prof microbiol, Univ Wash, 78- *Mem:* AAAS; Sigma Xi; Am Soc Cell Biol. *Res:* Investigation of the mechanism of transformation by avian RNA tumor virus; biochemistry of transforming proteins and expression of tumor specific cell surface antigens. *Mailing Add:* Dept Cell Biol Fred Hutchinson Cancer Res Ctr 1124 Columbia St Rm B2-152 Seattle WA 98104-2092. *Fax:* 206-667-5216

ROHSENOW, WARREN M(AX), HEAT TRANSFER. *Current Pos:* from asst prof to assoc prof, 45-56, prof, 56-86, EMER PROF MECH ENG, MASS INST TECHNOL, 86- *Personal Data:* b Chicago, Ill, Feb 12, 21; m 46; c John, Brian, Damaris, Sandra & Anne. *Educ:* Northwestern Univ, BS, 41; Yale Univ, MEng, 43, DEng(heat power), 44. *Honors & Awards:* Gold Medal, Am Soc Mech Engrs, 51, Jr Award, 52; Yale Eng Asn Award, 52; Heat Transfer Div Mem Award, Am Soc Mech Engrs, 67, Max Jakob Mem Award, 71. *Prof Exp:* Lab asst mech eng, Yale Univ, 41-43, instr, 43-44. *Concurrent Pos:* Consult engr, 46-; dir & co-founder, Dynatech Corp, 57-95 & Thermal Proc Syst, 88-94. *Mem:* Fel Nat Acad Eng; hon mem Am Soc Mech Engrs; fel Am Acad Arts & Sci. *Res:* Gas turbines; heat transfer; thermodynamics. *Mailing Add:* 32 Carroll St Falmouth ME 04105

ROHWEDDER, WILLIAM KENNETH, MASS SPECTROMETRY. *Current Pos:* RETIRED. *Personal Data:* b Williston Park, NY, June 15, 32. *Educ:* Lehigh Univ, BS, 54, MS, 57, PhD(chem), 60. *Prof Exp:* Sr engr, Bendix Corp, 60-61; chemist, Northern Regional Res Lab, Agr Res Serv, USDA, 62-92. *Mem:* Am Chem Soc; Am Oil Chemists Soc; Am Soc Mass Spectrometry. *Res:* Mass spectrometry of natural and isotopically labeled blood lipids, chemical derivatives from oilseeds and other natural products. *Mailing Add:* 3900 N Stable Ct Apt 205 Peoria IL 61614-6950

ROHWEDER, DWAYNE A, AGRONOMY. *Current Pos:* prof forage crops & exten agronomist, 63-87, EMER PROF FORAGE CROPS, EXTEN DIV, UNIV WIS-MADISON, 88-; CONSULT, 88- *Personal Data:* b Marshalltown, Iowa, Aug 12, 26; m 48, Wilma J Slot; c Thomas M & Mary J (Vinic). *Educ:* Iowa State Univ, BS, 48, MS, 56, PhD(crop prod & soil mgt), 63. *Honors & Awards:* Distinguished Grasslander Award, Am Forage & Grassland Coun, 94. *Prof Exp:* Co exten dir, Exten Div, Iowa State Univ, 48-54, area exten agronomist, 55-59, exten agronomist, 59-63. *Concurrent Pos:* Agronomist & chief of party, Univ Wis-USAID univ develop contract, Univ Rio Grande do Sul, Brazil, 67-69; agr enten educr, Am Soc Agron, 79; prof agronomist, 88- *Mem:* Am Forage & Grassland Coun; fel Am Soc Agron; fel Crop Sci Soc; Soil Conserv Soc Am. *Res:* Forage crop production; forage quality and evaluation. *Mailing Add:* 26425 S Ribbonwood Sun Lakes AZ 85248

ROHWER, ROBERT G, CEREAL CHEMISTRY, CORN & OTHER GRAINS. *Current Pos:* CONSULT, GRAIN PROD & MKT, 86- *Personal Data:* b Ft Calhoun, Nebr, Nov 20, 20; m 43, Barbara T Richards; c Robert G, Heidi (Hoart), Rebeca (Jagnore) & Richard J. *Educ:* Univ Nebr, BS, 43. *Prof Exp:* Chemist, Am Cyanamid Co, 43-48; plant supt, KrimKo Corp,

48-49; supr sweetner res, Clinton Corn Processing Co, Stand Brands, Inc, 49-59; res chemist, Grain Processing Corp, 59-62, sales mgr, 62-66, vpres, 66-78, sr vpres & dir mkt, 78-86. *Concurrent Pos:* Bd dirs, Starch Round Table, 85- *Mem:* Am Chem Soc; Tech Asn Pulp & Paper Indust; Inst Food Technol; Am Asn Cereal Chem. *Res:* Corn wet milling; starch, sugars and syrups; ion exchange. *Mailing Add:* PO Box 4122 Jackson WY 83001-4122. *Fax:* 307-733-4660

ROHY, DAVID ALAN, SOLID STATE PHYSICS. *Current Pos:* mgr applied sci, 81-87, MGR PROCESS DEVELOP & DIR PROD DEVELOP, SOLAR TURBINE INC, CATERPILLAR, 87- *Personal Data:* b Santa Barbara, Calif, July 30, 40; m 64; c 3. *Educ:* Univ Calif, Santa Barbara, BA, 62; Cornell Univ, PhD(physics), 68. *Prof Exp:* Physicist instrumentation, Lawrence Livermore Labs, Univ Calif, 67-70; res engr instrumentation & energy storage, Solar Turbines, 70-76, prog mgr, energy storage, hydrogen & instrumentation Int Harvester, 76-80. *Mem:* Am Phys Soc; Am Defense Prepardness Asn. *Res:* Development of waste heat recovery; thermal energy storage and thermal energy conversion systems using metal hydrides; hydrogen energy systems; instrumentation for gas turbine engines, particularly gas and solid temperature measurement; development of gas turbine engines. *Mailing Add:* 8639 Warmwell Dr San Diego CA 92119

ROIA, FRANK COSTA, JR, ECONOMIC BOTANY, MICROBIOLOGY. *Current Pos:* Assoc prof, 67-77, PROF BIOL, PHILA COL PHARM & SCI, 77- *Personal Data:* b New Bedford, Mass, June 5, 36; m 60; c 3. *Educ:* Mass Col Pharm, BS, 58, MS, 60, PhD(biol sci), 67. *Honors & Awards:* Award, Soc Cosmetic Chem, 67. *Mem:* Soc Cosmetic Chem; Sigma Xi; Am Soc Microbiol. *Res:* Antimicrobial activity of plants; microbial flora and its relationship to dandruff. *Mailing Add:* Dept Biol Sci Philadelphia Col Pharm & Sci 675 S 43rd St Philadelphia PA 19104-4441

ROISTACHER, SEYMOUR LESTER, DENTISTRY. *Current Pos:* ATTEND DENTIST, QUEENS HOSP CTR, 60-, DIR DENT, 64-; PROF DENT MED, STATE UNIV NY, STONY BROOK, 70- *Personal Data:* b New York, NY, May 21, 22; m 46; c 3. *Educ:* City Col NY, BS, 41; NY Univ, DDS, 44. *Concurrent Pos:* Mem, Sect Oral Surg, Anesthesia & Hosp Dent, Am Asn Dent Schs, 68-, chmn, Coun Hosp Dent Serv, 69-, vpres, Coun Hosp, 70- *Mem:* Fel Am Col Dent; Am Asn Hosp Dent; fel Int Col Dent. *Res:* Myofascial pain in the facial areas. *Mailing Add:* Dept Dent Med Queens Hosp Ctr 82-68 164th St Jamaica NY 11432

ROITBERG, BERNARD DAVID, EVOLUTION OF OVIPOSITION-RELATED BEHAVIORS, EFFECTS OF BEHAVIOR ON POPULATION DYNAMICS. *Current Pos:* from asst prof to assoc prof biol, 82-93, PROF POP BIOL, SIMON FRASER UNIV, 93- *Personal Data:* b Windsor, Ont, June 24, 53; m 77, Carol A Hubbard; c Gabriela. *Educ:* Simon Fraser Univ, BSc, 75; Univ BC, MSc, 77; Univ Mass, PhD(entom), 82. *Honors & Awards:* Hewitt Award, Entom Soc Can, 90. *Prof Exp:* Res assoc entom, Univ Mass, 81-82. *Concurrent Pos:* Assoc ed, Entom Soc Can, 88-; guest prof, Univ Kiel, Ger, 93. *Mem:* Entom Soc Can; Entom Soc Am; Animal Behav Soc; Behav Ecol Soc; Brit Ecol Soc. *Res:* Interface between behavior and population biology; develop models to predict how insects respond to changing environments as well as higher level effects using life history theory. *Mailing Add:* Dept Biosci Simon Fraser Univ Burnaby BC V5A 1S6 Can. *Fax:* 604-291-3496; *E-Mail:* roitberg@sfu.ca

ROITMAN, JAMES NATHANIEL, ORGANIC CHEMISTRY. *Current Pos:* RES CHEMIST, WESTERN REGIONAL LAB, USDA, 69- *Personal Data:* b Providence, RI, June 29, 41; m 72, Esther Thommen; c Thomas B. *Educ:* Brown Univ, BA, 63; Univ Calif, PhD(org chem), 69. *Mem:* Am Chem Soc; NY Acad Sci; Am Soc Pharmacog. *Res:* Isolation, characterization, and synthesis of naturally occurring compounds possessing biological activity; pyrrolizidine alkaloids; flavones; antifungal metabolites from microorganisms. *Mailing Add:* Western Regional Res Ctr USDA Albany CA 94710. *Fax:* 510-559-5777

ROITMAN, JUDY, TOPOLOGY, BOOLEAN ALGEBRA. *Current Pos:* from asst prof to assoc prof, 78-86, PROF MATH, UNIV KANS, 86- *Personal Data:* b New York, NY, Nov 12, 45; m 78, Stanley Lombardo; c Ben. *Educ:* Sarah Lawrence Col, BA, 66; Univ Calif, Berkeley, MA, 72, PhD(math), 74. *Prof Exp:* Asst prof math, Wellesley Col, 74-77; mem, Inst Advan Study, 77. *Mem:* Am Math Soc; Asn Symbolic Logic; Asn Women Math; Nat Coun Teachers Math; Math Asn Am. *Res:* Applications of set theory to topology and Boolean algebra; consistency results. *Mailing Add:* Dept Math Univ Kans Lawrence KS 66045

ROITMAN, PETER, ELECTRONICS, SOLID STATE PHYSICS. *Current Pos:* NAT RES COUN FEL PHYSICS, NAT BUR STANDARDS, 76- *Personal Data:* b Boston, Mass, Aug 30, 49. *Educ:* Dartmouth Col, BA, 72; Princeton Univ, PhD(elec eng), 76. *Mem:* Am Phys Soc; Am Vacuum Soc; Inst Elec & Electronics Engrs; Sigma Xi. *Mailing Add:* Nat Inst Stand & Technol Bldg 225-Rm B310 Washington DC 20234

ROIZMAN, BERNARD, VIROLOGY, MOLECULAR BIOLOGY OF HERPES VIRUSES. *Current Pos:* from assoc prof to prof microbiol, Univ Chicago, 65-70, prof microbiol & biophys, 70-81, Joseph Regenstein prof, 81-83, JOSEPH REGENSTEIN DISTINGUISHED SERV PROF VIROL, DEPT MOLECULAR GENETICS & CELL BIOL, BIOCHEM & MOLECULAR BIOL, UNIV CHICAGO, 84- *Personal Data:* b Chisinau, Romania, Apr 17, 29; nat US; m 50, Betty Cohen; c Arthur F & Niels B. *Educ:* Temple Univ, BA, 52, MS, 54; Johns Hopkins Univ, ScD, 56. *Hon Degrees:* LHD, Governors State Univ, Ill, 84; MD, Univ Ferrara, Italy, 91. *Honors & Awards:* Esther Langer Award Achievement Cancer Res, 74; Centennial Medal, Inst Pasteur, Paris, France, 87; ICN Int Prize Virol, ICN Found, 88. *Prof Exp:* Instr microbiol, Sch Med & Sch Hyg & Pub Health, Johns Hopkins Univ, 56-57, res assoc, 57-58, asst prof, 58-65. *Concurrent Pos:* Lederle med fac award, 60; Am Cancer Soc scholar, Pasteur Inst, France, 61-62; USPHS career develop award, 63-65; Am Cancer Soc fac res assoc award, 66-71; mem develop res working group, Spec Virus Cancer Prog, Nat Cancer Inst, 67-71, consult, 67-73; Int Agency Res Against Cancer traveling fel, Karolinska Inst, Sweden, 70; mem steering coun, Human Cell Biol Prog, NSF, 71-74; chmn herpesvirus study group, Int Comn Taxon of Viruses, 71-; consult, Nat Sci Fedn, 72-74; lectr, Am Found Microbiol, 74-75; mem bd sci consult, Sloan Kettering Inst, NY, 75-81; mem, Task Force Virol, Nat Inst Allergy & Infectious Dis, 76-77; mem, Study Sect Virol & Res Grants Rev Bd, NIH, 76-80; mem, bd trustees, Goodwin Inst Cancer Res, 77-; chmn sci adv bd, Teikeo Showa Univ Ctr, Tampa Bay Inst Biomed Res, 83-, chmn bd dirs, 91-; mem, Briefing Panel on Prev & Treatment of Viral Dis, Off Pres Sci Adv, 86; ed-in-chief, Infectious Agents & Dis, 91-96. *Mem:* Nat Acad Sci; fel Am Acad Arts & Sci; fel Am Acad Microbiol; Am Soc Microbiol; fel Japanese Soc Prom Sci; Am Soc Virol; Am Soc Biochem & Molecular Biol. *Res:* Molecular biology of herpes simplex viruses. *Mailing Add:* Univ Chicago 910 E 58th St Chicago IL 60637. *Fax:* 773-702-1631; *E-Mail:* bernard@kovler.uchicago.edu

ROJAHN, JOHANNES, PSYCHOPATHOLOGY IN MENTAL RETARDATION. *Current Pos:* assoc prof, 87-95, PROF PSYCHOL & PSYCHIAT, OHIO STATE UNIV, 95- *Personal Data:* b Vienna, Austria, May 23, 48; m 75, Hermi Troglauer; c Helene & Rudolf. *Educ:* Univ Vienna, Austria, PhD(psychol), 76. *Prof Exp:* Res fel, Fulbright-Hayes, 76; asst prof psychol, Univ Marburg, Ger, 79-84; Univ Pittsburgh, 84-87. *Concurrent Pos:* Assoc ed, Res & Develop Disabilities, 80-; acad unit dir, Nisonges Ctr, Univ Affil Prog, 87-; assoc ed, Am J Ment Retardation, 95- *Mem:* Am Asn Mental Retardation; Am Psychol Asn. *Res:* Behavior disorders and psychopathology in mental retardation; affect in mental retardation. *Mailing Add:* 1581 Dodd Dr Columbus OH 43210. *Fax:* 614-292-3727; *E-Mail:* rojahn.1@osu.edu

ROJAS, RICHARD RAIMOND, underwater acoustics, signal processing, for more information see previous edition

ROJIANI, KAMAL B, STRUCTURAL RELIABILITY. *Current Pos:* ASST PROF STRUCT, DEPT CIVIL ENG, VA POLYTECH INST & STATE UNIV, 78- *Personal Data:* b Bombay, India, Oct 22, 48; Pakistan citizen. *Educ:* Univ Karachi, BE, 71; Univ Ill, Urbana, MS, 73, PhD(civil eng), 77. *Prof Exp:* Comput programmer, Dept Finance, State Ill, 74; teaching & res asst, Dept Civil Eng Univ Ill, 73-77. *Concurrent Pos:* Struct engr, Bechtel Power Corp, 80; co- prin investr, US Dept Interior, Bur Surface Mines, 80-82; prin investr, Res Initiation Grant, NSF, 81-83; mem, Comt Load Resistance Factor Design, Am Soc Civil Engrs, 82- *Mem:* Am Soc Civil Engrs. *Res:* Application of probabilistic concepts to the solution of civil engineering problems, and specifically in the area of structural reliability. *Mailing Add:* 201 Craig Dr Blacksburg VA 24060

ROJO, ALFONSO, ICHTHYOLOGY. *Current Pos:* from assoc prof to prof, 70-97, EMER PROF ICHTHYOL, ST MARY'S UNIV, NS, 97- *Personal Data:* b Burgos, Spain, Jan 22, 21; Can citizen; m 56; c 3. *Educ:* Univ Valladolid, BSc & BA, 43; Univ Madrid, MSc, 53, PhD(ichthyol), 56. *Prof Exp:* Biologist, Spanish Dept Fisheries, 54-58; asst scientist, Fisheries Res Bd Can, 58-61; from asst prof to assoc prof, comp anat & ichthyol, St Mary's Univ, NS, 61-68; assoc prof expert fisheries & oceanog, Food & Agr Orgn, UN, 68-70. *Concurrent Pos:* Sci adv for Spain, Int Comn Northwest Atlantic Fisheries, 54-58; sci adv for Can, Int Comn Great Lakes, 58-61. *Mem:* Am Fisheries Soc; Can Soc Zool; Soc Syst Zool. *Res:* Problems of systematics at the species level in relation to larval forms of commerical fishes; study of a possibility of linking sciences and humanities through bioethics. *Mailing Add:* Dept Biol St Mary's Univ Robie St Halifax NS B3H 3C3 Can

ROJSTACZER, STUART ALAN, HYDROGEOLOGY, ENGINEERING GEOLOGY & GEOLOGIC HAZARDS. *Current Pos:* asst prof geol, 90-96, ASSOC PROF GEOL, ENVIRON & ENG, DUKE UNIV, 96- *Personal Data:* b Milwaukee, Wis, July 19, 56; m 79, Hollis Welstein; c Claire. *Educ:* Univ Wis, BS, 77; Univ Ill, MS, 81; Stanford Univ, PhD(earth sci), 88. *Honors & Awards:* Young Investr Award, NSF, 94. *Prof Exp:* Res hydrologist, US Geol Surv, 84-90. *Concurrent Pos:* Vis prof, Stanford Univ, 92, Venice Int Univ, 97; assoc ed, Geol, 93-97, Water Resources Res, 94-96; dir, Ctr Hydrol Sci, Duke Univ, 95-; mem, Comt Earth Gravity from Space, Nat Res Coun, 96-97. *Mem:* Am Geophys Union; Geol Soc Am. *Res:* Extend the understanding of the role of fluids in geologic processes and human induced earth science hazards; development of theoretical models and the collection of field data in novel settings using new field methods. *Mailing Add:* Duke Univ 106 Old Chem Box 90230 Durham NC 27708-0230. *Fax:* 919-684-5833; *E-Mail:* stuart@duke.edu

ROKACH, JOSHUA, LEUKOTRIENES, PROSTAGLANDINS. *Current Pos:* PROF CHEM, FLA INST TECHNOL, 89-, DIR, CLAUDE PEPPER INST AGING & THERAPEUT RES, 89- *Personal Data:* b Cairo, Egypt, Sept 17, 35; Can citizen. *Educ:* Hebrew Univ, MSC, 62; Weizmann Inst Sci, Israel, PhD, 64. *Honors & Awards:* Prix Urgel Archambault, 86; John LaBatt Ltd Award, Can Soc Chem, 88; Xerox Lectr, 88; Chinese Acad Sci Taiwan Award, 88; Prix Paul Ehrlich, Paris, France, 90. *Prof Exp:* Fel, Weizmann Inst Sci, 64-65; Max-Planck Inst, 65-66; sr res chemist, Merck Frosst Labs, Merck Frosst Can Inc, 66-74, group leader, 74-77, sr res fel, 77-79, dir med chem,

79-81, exec dir res, 81-88, distinguished sr scientist, 88-89. *Concurrent Pos:* Ed, Prostaglandins and J Lipid Mediators. *Mem:* Am Chem Soc; Chem Inst Can; Asn Res Vision & Ophthal. *Res:* Novel approach to degenerative diseases (eg cardiovascular, alzheimer, etc); study of free radical production in diseases; synthesis of isoprostanes and the development of methods to measure them in vivo; synthesis and biosynthesis of lipoxygenase products. *Mailing Add:* Claude Pepper Inst 150 W University Blvd Melbourne FL 32901-6988. *Fax:* 407-952-1818; *E-Mail:* jrokach@fit.edu

ROKEACH, LUIS ALBERTO, AUTOIMMUNE DISEASE. *Current Pos:* assoc res scientist, 86-87, RES SCIENTIST, AGOURON INST, LA JOLLA, CALIF, 87- *Personal Data:* b Buenos Aires, Arg, Nov 1, 51; m 73; c 2. *Educ:* Hebrew Univ Jerusalem, Israel, BS, 74; Univ Libre de Bruxelles, Belg, MS, 81, PhD(molecular biol), 84. *Prof Exp:* Res asst, Dept Clin Path, Clin Olivos, Buenos Aires, Arg, 77-80; postdoctoral res assoc, Dept Biol, San Diego State Univ, 84-86. *Concurrent Pos:* Prin investr, Agouron Inst, La Jolla, Calif, 90- *Mem:* Sigma Xi. *Res:* Role of autoantigens in autoimmune disease; cellular function of autoantigens. *Mailing Add:* Dept Biochem Univ Montreal CP 6128 Succ Centre Ville Montreal PQ H3C 3J7 Can. *Fax:* 514-343-6069

ROKITA, MARY ANNE, ENVIRONMENTAL & HYPERBARIC PHYSIOLOGY. *Current Pos:* ASST PROF PHYSIOL, STATE UNIV NY, BUFFALO, 76- *Educ:* State Univ NY, Buffalo, PhD(biol), 73. *Res:* Aerospace physiology. *Mailing Add:* Dept Physiol 124 Sherman Hall State Univ NY Buffalo Buffalo NY 14214-3078. *Fax:* 716-829-2344

ROKNI, MOHAMMAD ALI, chaotic dynamics, for more information see previous edition

ROKOP, DONALD J, SPECIFIC ISOTOPE IONIZATION ENHANCEMENT, MEASUREMENT OF ATOM ABUNDANCES OF ISOTOPES. *Current Pos:* STAFF SCIENTIST, LOS ALAMOS NAT LAB, 78- *Personal Data:* b Aurora, Ill, May 15, 39; m 64; c 3. *Educ:* Lake Forest Col, BA, 61. *Honors & Awards:* Award of Excellence, Dept Energy, 85; Antarctic Serv Medal, US Congress & NSF, 86. *Prof Exp:* Sci assoc, Argonne Nat Lab, 61-78. *Concurrent Pos:* Group leader anal mass spectrometry, Argonne Nat Lab, 68-78; founder & co-chair Isotope Ratio Measurements Comt, Am Soc Mass Spectrometry, 80-83; sect leader mass spectrometry, Los Alamos Nat Lab, 86-88, asst group leader, 88-89, tech coordr mass spectrometry develop, 89-; organizer, A O Nier Symposium Inorg Mass Spectrometry, 91. *Mem:* AAAS. *Res:* Thermal ionization and electron bombardment analytical mass spectrometric techniques for application to problems in nuclear physics, chemistry, geology, geophysics, and atmospheric dynamics; determining low abundance isotopes. *Mailing Add:* 1705 Los Pueblos St Los Alamos NM 87544

ROKOSKE, THOMAS LEO, SOLID STATE PHYSICS. *Current Pos:* from instr to asst prof, 64-67 & 71-74, ASSOC PROF PHYSICS, APPALACHIAN STATE UNIV, 74- *Personal Data:* b Danville, Ill, Feb 25, 39; m 61; c 3. *Educ:* Loyola Univ, La, BS, 61; Fla State Univ, MS, 63; Auburn Univ, PhD(physics), 73. *Prof Exp:* Instr physics, Fla State Univ, 64. *Concurrent Pos:* Vchmn, NC Adv Coun Metrication, 74-75, chmn, 75-76; dir, Indust Metric Educ Conf, 74-75. *Mem:* Am Phys Soc; Am Asn Physics Teachers. *Res:* Electrical conduction in thin films. *Mailing Add:* Dept Physics Appalachian State Univ Boone NC 28608

ROLAND, ALEX, HISTORY OF TECHNOLOGY. *Current Pos:* assoc prof, 81-87, PROF MIL HIST & HIST TECHNOL, DUKE UNIV, 87-, CHAIR, DEPT HIST, 96- *Personal Data:* b Providence, RI, Apr 7, 44; m 79, Elizabeth Sullivan; c Michael K, Christopher S & Daniel H. *Educ:* US Naval Acad, BS, 66; Univ Hawaii, MA, 70; Duke Univ, PhD(hist), 74. *Prof Exp:* Historian, NASA, 73-81. *Concurrent Pos:* Harold K Johnson vis prof mil hist, US Army War Col; vis fel, Dibner Inst, 94-95. *Mem:* Soc Hist Technol (secy, 84-); Soc Mil Hist; Hist Sci Soc. *Res:* History of technology and war in the West from earliest times to the present, with specialization in aerospace history. *Mailing Add:* Dept Hist Duke Univ Durham NC 27708. *Fax:* 919-681-7670; *E-Mail:* aroland@acpub.duke.edu

ROLAND, CHARLES GORDON, HISTORY OF MEDICINE, COMMUNICATION SCIENCE. *Current Pos:* JASON A HANNAH PROF HIST MED, MCMASTER UNIV, 77- *Personal Data:* b Winnipeg, Man, Jan 25, 33; m 53, 79, Connie Rankin; c John, Christopher, David & Kathleen. *Educ:* Univ Man, BSc & MD, 58. *Honors & Awards:* Jason Hannah Medal, Royal Soc Can, 94. *Prof Exp:* Physician pvt pract, 59-64; sr ed jour, AMA, 64-69; prof biomed commun & chmn dept & assoc prof hist med, Mayo Med Sch & Mayo Found, 69-77. *Concurrent Pos:* Sid W Richardson vis prof med humanities, Med Br, Univ Tex, Galveston, 84. *Mem:* Am Med Writers Asn (pres, 69-70); Am Asn Hist Med (secy-treas, 76-79); Am Osler Soc (secy-treas, 75-85, pres, 86-87); Can Soc Hist Med (pres, 93-95); Int Soc Hist Med. *Res:* Variety of investigations into the sociology and history of scientific communication; history of medicine in the nineteenth century; health and medical care in Axis prisoner of war camps during World War II. *Mailing Add:* 3N10-HSC McMaster Univ Hamilton ON L8N 3Z5 Can. *E-Mail:* rolandc@fhs.mcmaster.ca

ROLAND, DAVID ALFRED, SR, NUTRITIONAL BIOCHEMISTRY. *Current Pos:* ALUMNI PROF POULTRY NUTRIT, AUBURN UNIV, 76- *Personal Data:* b Cochran, Ga, Jan 2, 43; m 65; c 2. *Educ:* Univ Ga, BS, 66, PhD(nutrit), 70. *Honors & Awards:* Research Award, Poultry Sci Asn, 73 & Egg Sci Award, 74. *Prof Exp:* Res asst nutrit, Univ Ga, 66-67; assoc prof mgt & poultry & asst poultry scientist, Univ Fla, 70-76. *Mem:* AAAS; Poultry Sci Asn; World Poultry Sci Asn. *Res:* Mineral metabolism; egg shell quality; poultry management; lipid metabolism; reproductive physiology. *Mailing Add:* Dept Poultry Sci Auburn Univ Auburn AL 36849-3501

ROLAND, DENNIS MICHAEL, PHARMACEUTICAL CHEMISTRY, MEDICINAL CHEMISTRY. *Current Pos:* sr scientist, Ciba/Geigy Corp, 79-84, sr res scientist, 84-89, mgr, Pharmaceut Div, 89-91, dir, 92-93, EXEC DIR INFLAMMATION & OSTEOARTHRITIS CHEM, CIBA PHARMACEUT, 94- *Personal Data:* b New Castle, Ind, July 16, 49; m 71, Deborah; c Timothy & Jeffrey. *Educ:* Ball State Univ, BS, 71; Univ Vt, PhD(org chem), 77. *Prof Exp:* Fel org synthesis, Colo State Univ, 77-79. *Concurrent Pos:* Nat Res Serv Award, NIH, 77-79. *Mem:* Am Chem Soc; NY Acad Sci; Inflammation Res Asn. *Res:* Design and synthesis of new biologically active molecules for use as theraputic agents. *Mailing Add:* Ciba Geigy Pharm Div Res 106 556 Morris Ave Summit NJ 07901-1330. *Fax:* 908-277-2405

ROLA-PLESZCZYNSKI, MAREK, IMMUNOLOGY. *Current Pos:* from asst prof to assoc prof, 76-85, RES SCHOLAR IMMUNOL, FAC MED, UNIV SHERBROOKE, 81-, PROF, 85- *Personal Data:* b Fermo, Italy, Aug 9, 47; Can citizen; m 71; c 2. *Educ:* Séminaire de Sherbrooke, BA, 66; Univ Sherbrooke, Que, MD, 70; Nat Bd Med Examr, dipl med, 71; FRCP(C), 78. *Honors & Awards:* Frosst Medal, Frosst Co & Univ Sherbrooke, 71. *Prof Exp:* Res fel immunol, Sch Med, Georgetown Univ, 73-75 & Harvard Med Sch, 75-76. *Concurrent Pos:* Chmn, Exam Comt Clin Immunol, Royal Col Physicians, Canada, 84- *Mem:* Am Asn Immunologists; Soc Pediat Res; Can Immunol Soc; Can Soc Clin Invest. *Res:* Discovery and characterization of a distinct subset of human peripheral blood lymphocytes; modulation of cytotoxic and immunoregulatory activities of lymphocytes by leukotrienes, neuropeptides and hormones; immunopathology of pulmonary diseases. *Mailing Add:* Immunol Div Dept Pediat Ctr Hosp Univ Sherbrooke 3001 12 E Ave Nord Sherbrooke PQ J1H 5N4 Can. *Fax:* 819-564-5215

ROLD, JOHN W, GEOLOGY, GEOLOGIC HAZARDS. *Current Pos:* GEOL CONSULT & EXPERT WITNESS, 92- *Personal Data:* b Kirkman, Iowa, May 23, 27; m 56, Phyllis Kamber; c Marc, Becky, Cindy & Gregory. *Educ:* Univ Colo, Boulder, AB, 48, MS, 50. *Honors & Awards:* Distinguished Pub Serv Award, Am Asn Petrol Geologists, 84-; Serv Award, Am Inst Prof Geologists, John T Galey Award Pub Serv, 96. *Prof Exp:* Field geologist, Magnolia Petrol, (Mobil Oil), 48; dist geologist, Chevron Oil, 50-69 & Mont-Dakotas Dist, Billings, 65-69; area geologist, La Gulf Coast, New Orleans, 53-55, Denver Basin Colo, 55-58; dist staff geologist, Colo, Nebr & Kans, 58-63, & Plains dist, Eastern Colo, Nebr & Kans, 63-65; state geologist & dir, Colo Surv, 69-92. *Concurrent Pos:* Crew geophysicist, various Rocky Mt provinces & Williston Basin, Wyo, Utah, Mont & N & SDak, 51-52; chmn, Geo Soc Am, 80; mem bd gov, Am Geol Inst, 80-81; comt chmn, Nat Res Coun, 82-83, Nat Acad Sci, 82-83. *Mem:* Am Asn Petrol Geol; Geol Soc Am; Am Inst Prof Geologists (pres, 81); hon mem Asn Am State Geologist. *Res:* Cause and timing of geologic hazards and mitigation of geologic constraints to development. *Mailing Add:* 2534 S Balsam St Lakewood CO 80227

ROLDAN, LUIS GONZALEZ, CRYSTALLOGRAPHY, TECHNICAL LAB ASSESSMENT. *Current Pos:* DIR, LGR MICRORES, 86- *Personal Data:* b Garafia, Tenerifee Spain, Aug 8, 25; m 61, Carmen; c Jose, Luis, Mary & Carlos. *Educ:* Univ Sevilla, Lic Chem, 50, DSc, 57. *Prof Exp:* Adj prof exp physics, Univ Sevilla, Spain, 53-57; from res physicist to sr res physicist, Brit Rayon Res Asn, Manchester, Eng, 57-61; sr res chemist, Cent Res Lab, Allied Chem Corp, 61-63, from scientist to sr scientist, 63-68; res assoc & head, Phys Chem Sect, J P Stevens & Co, Inc, Greenville, SC, 68-76, mgr, Physics & Micros Dept, Tech Ctr, 76-86. *Concurrent Pos:* Vis prof, Univ Beira Interior, Covilha, Portugal, 87; adj prof, NC State Univ, Raleigh, NC, 88-94; tech expert, Nat Vol Lab Accreditation Prog, Nat Inst Stand & Technol, 88-93; prof catedratico, Univ Beira Interior, Portugal, 93- *Mem:* Fiber Soc; Am Chem Soc; Am Crystallog Asn; Royal Span Soc Phys & Chem. *Res:* Structure of organic compounds, macromolecules and polymers by x-ray diffraction techniques; morphology of these compounds by electron microscopy; relationship of structure and morphology with physical properties; metallography; ceramics structure; fiber physics and textiles: research and development. *Mailing Add:* 124 Becky Don Dr Greer SC 29651-1213. *E-Mail:* lroldan@ubistaf.ubi.pt

ROLETT, ELLIS LAWRENCE, INTERNAL MEDICINE, CARDIOLOGY. *Current Pos:* PROF MED, DARTMOUTH MED SCH, 77-; CHIEF CARDIOL, DARTMOUTH-HITCHCOCK MED CTR, 77- *Personal Data:* b New York, NY, July 10, 30; m 56; c 3. *Educ:* Yale Univ, BS, 52; Harvard Univ, MD, 55. *Prof Exp:* Intern med, Mass Gen Hosp, Boston, 55-56; asst resident, New York Hosp, 56-57; resident, Mass Gen Hosp, 59-60, clin fel cardiol, 60-61; asst med, Peter Bent Brigham Hosp, 61-63; from asst prof to prof, Univ NC, Chapel Hill, 63-74; prof med, Univ Calif, Los Angeles, 74-77. *Concurrent Pos:* Am Heart Asn res fel, 61-63; res grant, USPHS, 64-77, career develop award, 67-72; Lederle med fac award, 65-67; chief cardiol, Vet Admin Wadsworth Hosp Ctr, 74-77; mem, Merit Rev Bd Cardiovasc Studies, Vet Admin, chmn, 76-79. *Mem:* AAAS; Am Col Cardiol; Am Physiol Soc. *Res:* Cardiodynamics; influence of catecholamines on cardiac muscle function; contractile behavior of isolated myocytes. *Mailing Add:* Dept Cardiol Dartmouth Hitchcock Med Ctr One Med Ctr Dr Lebanon NH 03756. *Fax:* 603-650-6327

ROLF, HOWARD LEROY, MATHEMATICS. *Current Pos:* chmn dept, 71-97, PROF MATH, BAYLOR UNIV, 64- *Personal Data:* b Laverne, Okla, Nov 25, 28; m 61, Anita Ward; c James, Jennifer, Stephanie & Rhonda. *Educ:* Okla Baptist Univ, BS, 51; Vanderbilt Univ, MA, 53, PhD(math), 56. *Prof Exp:* Instr math, Vanderbilt Univ, 54-56; asst prof, Baylor Univ, 56-57; assoc prof, Georgetown Univ, 57-59; asst prof & dir comput cent, Vanderbilt Univ, 59-64. *Concurrent Pos:* Vis assoc, Calif Inst Technol, 67-68. *Mem:* Am Math Soc; Math Asn Am. *Res:* Lattice theory; abstract algebra. *Mailing Add:* Dept Math Baylor Univ Waco TX 76798-7328. *Fax:* 254-755-3569; *E-Mail:* howard_rolf@baylor.edu

ROLF, RICHARD L(AWRENCE), STRUCTURAL MECHANICS, STRUCTURAL ENGINEERING. *Current Pos:* res engr, Eng Design Div, Res Labs, Aluminum Co Am, 60-75, sr engr, 75-81, staff engr, Eng Properties & Design Div, 81-83, tech specialist, Prod Eng Div, 83-86, sr tech specialist, Prod Eng Div, 86-87, Prod Design & Mech Div, 87-90, TECH CONSULT, PROD DESIGN & MECH DIV, ALCOA LABS, ALUMINUM CO AM, 90- *Personal Data:* b Milwaukee, Wis, Nov 4, 35; m 61, June F Plesko; c Ann M. *Educ:* Marquette Univ, BS, 58; Univ Ill, Urbana, MS, 60. *Honors & Awards:* J James R Croes Medal, Am Soc Civil Engrs, 66. *Prof Exp:* Res asst civil eng, Univ Ill, Urbana, 58-60. *Mem:* Sigma Xi; Am Acad Mech; Am Soc Civil Engrs. *Res:* Design analysis and testing of various structural members; development of design rules for aluminum, brittle materials and composites; damage evolution in materials. *Mailing Add:* 226 Laura Dr New Kensington PA 15068. *E-Mail:* rolf_rl@alcoa.com

ROLFE, GARY LAVELLE, ECOLOGY, BIOLOGY. *Current Pos:* dir, Metals Task Force, 71-77, from asst prof to assoc prof forest ecol, 72-80, PROF & HEAD, DEPT FORESTRY, UNIV ILL, 80-, HEAD, DEPT NRES, 95- *Personal Data:* b Paducah, Ky, Sept 5, 46; div; c Terry E & Cory. *Educ:* Univ Ill, BS, 68, MS, 69, PhD(ecol), 72. *Concurrent Pos:* Asst dir, Ill Agr Exp Sta, 76-80, interim assoc dir, 92-96. *Mem:* Ecol Soc Am; Soil Sci Soc Am; Soc Am Foresters. *Res:* Ecology of Illinois bottomland forests and private woodland management for multiple values. *Mailing Add:* Dept NRES Univ Ill W-503 Turner Hall Urbana IL 61801

ROLFE, RIAL DEWITT, ANAEROBIC BACTERIOLOGY. *Current Pos:* asst prof, 81-86, ASSOC PROF, DEPT MICROBIOL, TEX TECH UNIV HEALTH SCI CTR, 86-, ASSOC CHMN, 89- *Personal Data:* b St Louis, Mo, Feb 25, 52; c 2. *Educ:* Univ Mo, Columbia, BA, 74, MS, 76, PhD(microbiol), 78. *Prof Exp:* Teaching fel, Sch Med, Univ Calif, Los Angeles, 78-79; dir, Infectious Dis Sect Res Lab, Wadsworth Va Med Ctr, Los Angeles, 79-81. *Concurrent Pos:* Adj asst prof, Sch Med, Univ Calif, Los Angeles, 79-81. *Mem:* Am Soc Microbiol; AAAS; Soc Intestinal Microbial Ecol & Dis. *Res:* Anaerobic bacteria in health and disease. *Mailing Add:* Dept Microbiol Tex Tech Health Sci Ctr PO Box 4569 Lubbock TX 79430

ROLFE, STANLEY THEODORE, FRACTURE MECHANICS. *Current Pos:* Ross H Forney prof, 69-89, A P LEARNED PROF CIVIL ENG, UNIV KANS, 89-, CHMN DEPT, 75- *Personal Data:* b Chicago, Ill, July 7, 34; m 56, Phyllis Williams; c David, Pam & Kathy. *Educ:* Univ Ill, Urbana, BS, 56, MS, 58, PhD(civil eng), 62. *Honors & Awards:* Sam Tour Award, Am Soc Testing & Mat, 71; Henry E Gould Award, Univ Kans, 72 & 73, Irvin E Youngman Res Award, 85; Atom Award, Am Welding Soc, 74; T R Higgins lectr, Am Inst Steel, 80. *Prof Exp:* Res assoc civil eng, Univ Ill, Urbana, 56-62; sect suprv & div chief, US Steel Appl Res Lab, 62-69. *Concurrent Pos:* Chmn, Metall Studies Panel, Nat Acad Sci, 68-71; chmn low cycle fatigue comt, Pressure Vessel Res Coun, 68-70. *Mem:* Nat Acad Eng; Am Soc Mech Engrs; Soc Exp Stress Anal; Am Soc Eng Educ; Am Soc Testing & Mat; Am Soc Civil Engrs. *Res:* Fracture mechanics; failure analysis; fatigue and fracture of structural materials as related to design; experimental stress analysis. *Mailing Add:* Dept Civil & Environ Eng Univ Kans Lawrence KS 66045. *Fax:* 785-864-3199; *E-Mail:* rolfe@kuhub.cc.ukans.edu

ROLKE, WOLFGANG A, STATISTICAL CONSULTING, APPLICATION OF STATISTICS IN HIGH ENERGY PHYSICS. *Current Pos:* DIR, STATIST CONSULT LAB, 94-; ASSOC PROF, UNIV PR, 96- *Personal Data:* b Siegsdorf, Ger, June 2, 61; m 89, Linda Rodriguez. *Educ:* Univ Ulm, BA, 85; Univ Southern Calif, MS, 87, MS, 89, PhD(appl math), 92. *Prof Exp:* Lectr, Santa Monica Col, 88-92. *Mem:* Am Math Soc; Am Math Asn. *Res:* Application of modern statistical tools to data from high energy physics data, specifically to data from fermi national accelerator laboratory experiments E687/831. *Mailing Add:* Univ PR PO Box 5959 College Sta Mayaguez PR 00681. *Fax:* 787-832-4680; *E-Mail:* w_rolke@rumac.upr.clu.edu

ROLL, BARBARA HONEYMAN HEATH, PHYSICAL ANTHROPOLOGY. *Current Pos:* RES ASSOC, DEPT ANTHROP, UNIV PA, 75- *Personal Data:* b Portland, Ore, Apr 4, 10; m 77. *Educ:* Smith Col, BA, 32. *Hon Degrees:* LHD, Smith Col, 89. *Prof Exp:* Res assoc & exec dir, Constitution Lab, Col Physicians & Surgeons, NY, 48-53; instr phys anthrop, Monterey Peninsula Col, 66-74. *Mem:* Fel AAAS; Am Asn Phys Anthrop; fel Am Anthrop Asn; Brit Soc Study Human Biol; Int Asn Human Biol. *Res:* Child development; somatotype methodology and interpretation of somatotype data. *Mailing Add:* 26030 Rotunda Dr Carmel CA 93923

ROLL, DAVID BYRON, MEDICINAL CHEMISTRY. *Current Pos:* assoc prof, 67-76, PROF MED CHEM, COL PHARM, UNIV UTAH, 76-, ASSOC DEAN ACAD AFFAIRS, 77- *Personal Data:* b Miles City, Mont, Mar 16, 40; m 70; c 2. *Educ:* Univ Mont, BS, 62; Univ Wash, PhD(med chem), 66. *Prof Exp:* Res chemist, Pharmaceut Res Lab, Dept HEW, 66-67. *Mem:* Am Pharmaceut Asn. *Res:* Nuclear magnetic resonance and its applications to stereochemical and biochemical problems; medicinal chemistry. *Mailing Add:* 4548 Wallace Lane Salt Lake City UT 84117-4630

ROLL, DAVID E, STRUCTURE & FUNCTION OF TOPOISOMERASES, REGULATION OF TOPOISOMERASES BY PHOSPHORYLATION. *Current Pos:* PROF BIOCHEM, ROBERTS WESLEYAN COL, 78- *Personal Data:* b Baltimore, Md, June 4, 48; m 76, Margaret M; c Mark, Carolyn, Stephen, Christopher & Michael. *Educ:* Harding Col, Searcy, Ark, BS, 70; Univ Ill, MS, 72, PhD(biochem), 76. *Prof Exp:* Res assoc biochem, Univ Pittsburgh Med Sch, 76-78. *Concurrent Pos:* Vis asst prof, Baylor Col Med, Houston, 79, 82 & 83, fel/sabbatical, 85-86; vis asst prof, Dept Biol, Univ Rochester, 84, vis prof, Path Dept, 89; vis prof, Dept Microbiol, Immunol, Univ Rochester, 93; vis scientist, Dept Protein Chem, Lederle-Praxis Biol, Rochester, NY, 94; chmn-elect, Rochester Sect, Am Chem Soc. *Mem:* Am Chem Soc; Fedn Am Scientists; Sigma Xi; Nat Asn Adv Health Prof; Am Sci Affil. *Res:* Structure and function of topoisomerase enzymes and their regulation by phosphorylation; type I topoisomerase has been isolated and purified from Novikoff ascites cells; this topoisomerase has been activated by protein phosphorylation using purified serine Kinase enzymes. *Mailing Add:* Roberts Wesleyan Col 2301 Westside Dr Rochester NY 14624. *Fax:* 716-594-6482; *E-Mail:* rolld@roberts.edu

ROLL, FREDERIC, STRUCTURAL ENGINEERING, REINFORCED & PRESTRESSED CONCRETE. *Current Pos:* from assoc prof to prof, 57-86, EMER PROF CIVIL ENG, UNIV PA, 86- *Personal Data:* b New York, NY, Sept 10, 21; m 50, Christine Opolos. *Educ:* City Col New York, BCE, 44; Columbia Univ, MS, 49, PhD(civil eng), 57. *Hon Degrees:* MA, Univ Pa, 71. *Honors & Awards:* Cert Appreciation, Am Soc Civil Engrs, 66, State-of-the-Art of Civil Eng Award, 74, Outstanding Serv Award, 75, Raymond Reese Res Award, 76, Struct Engr of the Year Award, 87; Cert Appreciation, Am Concrete Inst, 90. *Prof Exp:* Civil engr, W S Briggs, NY, 50; stress analyst, Chance Vought Aircraft Corp, Conn, 44; civil engr, Andrews & Clarke, NY, 44-45; asst civil eng, Columbia Univ, 45-46, instr, 46-50, assoc, 50-57. *Concurrent Pos:* NSF fel, Eng & Port, 63-64, grant, 66-; mem res staff, Cement & Concrete Asn, 70-71; eng consult, 57-; pres, Delaware Valley Chap, Am Concrete Inst, 76; pres, Philadelphia Sect, Am Soc Civil Engrs, 81-82. *Mem:* Fel Am Concrete Inst; Am Soc Civil Engrs; Am Soc Testing & Mat; Soc Exp Stress Anal; Sigma Xi; Prestressed Concrete Inst. *Res:* Creep of plain concrete; shear and diagonal tension in reinforced concrete beams and slabs; structural model analysis; structural and materials testing; reinforced and prestressed concrete; fiber reinforced plastic structural systems. *Mailing Add:* Dept Systs Univ Pa Philadelphia PA 19104

ROLL, JAMES ROBERT, CONCEPTUAL DESIGN MODELING, SYSTEMS DESIGN. *Current Pos:* Sr res engr, Gen Motors Res Labs, 83-86, staff res engr, 86-88, sect head conceptual design, Systs Eng Ctr, 88-91, mgr systs eng methods, GPC, 91-93, MGR DIMENSIONAL MGT APPLNS, MIDSIZE CAR DIV, GEN MOTORS, 94- *Personal Data:* b Chilton, Wis, Aug 31, 58; m 88; c 2. *Educ:* Univ Wis, Madison, BS, 80, MS, 81, PhD(mech eng), 84. *Mem:* Soc Automotive Eng; assoc mem Am Soc Mech Engrs; Sigma Xi; Nat Coun Systs Eng. *Res:* Design techniques and software to assist in the conceptual design of automotive vehicles including mechanisms, powertrains, optimization, trade off analysis techniques and advanced reliability techniques; developing engineering process to be used to design all vehicles at midsize car division. *Mailing Add:* 1305 Baldwin Ann Arbor MI 48104-3623

ROLL, PAUL M, BIOCHEMISTRY. *Current Pos:* RETIRED. *Educ:* Stanford Univ, PhD(biochem), 46. *Prof Exp:* Assoc, Sloan Kettering, NY, 46-54; prof biochem, Med Col Wis, 54-76. *Mem:* AAAS; Biochem Soc; Am Chem Soc; Am Soc biochem & Molecular Biol. *Mailing Add:* N 21 W 24113 Dorchester Dr 17 E Pewaukee WI 53072-4691

ROLL, PETER GUY, PHYSICS. *Current Pos:* VPRES INFO SERV, NORTHWESTERN UNIV, EVANSTON, IL, 84- *Personal Data:* b Detroit, Mich, Apr 13, 33; m 55; c 3. *Educ:* Yale Univ, BS, 54, MS, 58, PhD(physics), 60. *Prof Exp:* Jr scientist nuclear reactor design, Westinghouse Atomic Power Div, 54-56; res asst physics, Yale Univ, 56-58, instr, 59-60; from instr to asst prof, Princeton Univ, 60-65; staff physicist, Comn Col Physics, Univ Mich, 65-66; spec asst to vpres acad admin, 71-84, ASSOC PROF PHYSICS, UNIV MINN, MINNEAPOLIS, 66- *Mem:* AAAS; Am Asn Physics Teachers; Am Comput Mach. *Res:* Low energy nuclear physics; gravity experiments; cosmic background radiation measurements; musical acoustics. *Mailing Add:* 3118 Isabella St Evanston IL 60201

ROLLAND, ALAIN (PIERRE), GENE DELIVERY, ADVANCED & CONTROLLED DRUG DELIVERY. *Current Pos:* dir gene delivery, 93-96, VPRES GENE DELIVERY SCI, GENEMEDICINE, INC, 96- *Personal Data:* b Landivisiau, France, Oct 26, 59; m 81, Corine Lhuissier; c Gabriel, Alix & Benjamin. *Educ:* Rennes Univ, France, Dr, 81, dipl, 83, PhD(pharmaceut sci), 87. *Prof Exp:* Scientist, Ciba-Geigy Pharm, Eng, 87-88; head, Formulation Res Group, Galderma Int, France, 88-93. *Concurrent Pos:* Instr pharmaceut chem, Rennes Univ, 77-80, lectr spec educ hosp pharm, 85-86; prin investr, Small Bus Innovation Res Prog, 95-97. *Mem:* Controlled Release Soc; Am Asn Pharmaceut Scientists; Am Chem Soc. *Res:* Non-viral gene delivery; design, synthesis, formulation and characterization of synthetic gene delivery systems for efficient and safe in vivo gene transfer to defined biological targets; creating and developing novel gene delivery technologies that enable new product opportunities for genes as pharmaceuticals. *Mailing Add:* 8301 New Trails Dr Woodlands TX 77381-4248. *Fax:* 281-364-0858; *E-Mail:* rollaa@genemedicine.com

ROLLAND, WILLIAM WOODY, NUCLEAR PHYSICS. *Current Pos:* PRES, ROLLAND MGT SYST, 83- *Personal Data:* b Asheville, NC, June 8, 31; m 50; c 4. *Educ:* King Col, BA, 53; Duke Univ, PhD, 63. *Prof Exp:* Instr math, King Col, 55-56, assoc prof physics, 59-68; assoc prof comput sci & dir comput ctr, St Andrews Presby Col, 68-83. *Mem:* Am Asn Physics Teachers. *Res:* Nuclear spectroscopy, particularly direct nuclear interactions; studies of variable stars, both eclipsing and intrinsic variables. *Mailing Add:* Maple Dr Laurinburg NC 28352

ROLLASON, GRACE SAUNDERS, EMBRYOLOGY. *Current Pos:* RETIRED. *Personal Data:* b New York, NY, Sept 14, 19; m 44; c 2. *Educ:* Hunter Col, AB, 40; NY Univ, MS, 42, PhD(exp embryol), 48. *Prof Exp:* Asst, Harvard Univ, 44-45; assoc, Amherst Col, 46-47; res assoc, Univ Mass, Amherst, 47-56, from instr to assoc prof zool, 56-85. *Concurrent Pos:* Hunter Col scholar, Woods Hole Marine Biol Lab. *Res:* Mammalian and amphibian embryology. *Mailing Add:* 34 Red Gate Lane Amherst MA 01002-1819

ROLLASON, HERBERT DUNCAN, HISTOLOGY. *Current Pos:* from asst prof to prof, 48-84, asst dean, 65-71, assoc dean, Col Arts & Sci, 72-73, assoc chmn dept, 76-84, EMER PROF ZOOL, UNIV MASS, AMHERST, 84- *Personal Data:* b Beverly, Mass, Mar 20, 17; m 44; c 2. *Educ:* Middlebury Col, AB, 39; Williams Col, AM, 41; Harvard Univ, MA, 43, PhD(biol), 49. *Prof Exp:* Instr anat, L I Col Med, 45-46; instr biol, Amherst Col, 46-48. *Mem:* AAAS; Am Soc Zool; Am Inst Biol Sci. *Res:* Kidney histology and cytology; compensatory hypertrophy; cellular ultrastructure. *Mailing Add:* 34 Red Gate Lane Amherst MA 01002-1819

ROLLE, F ROBERT, ANALYTICAL CHEMISTRY. *Current Pos:* res chemist, Johnson & Johnson, 67-68, group leader, 68-71, asst mgr, 71-75, mgr anal chem, 75-79, asst dir, Cent Lab, 79-80, from asst dir to dir, Tech & Adv Serv, 80-84, RES FEL, CHICOPEE DIV, JOHNSON & JOHNSON, 84- *Personal Data:* b Jamaica, NY, May 21, 39; m 74; c 1. *Educ:* Pratt Inst, BS, 61; Purdue Univ, MS, 65, PhD(phys org chem), 66. *Honors & Awards:* P B Hofmann Res Scientist Award, 73. *Prof Exp:* Res fel kinetics, Univ London, 66-67. *Mem:* The Chem Soc; Am Chem Soc. *Res:* Analytical aspects of nonwoven fabrics; operating room gowns. *Mailing Add:* 1 Lafayette Rd W Princeton NJ 08540-2428

ROLLEFSON, AIMAR ANDRE, NUCLEAR STRUCTURE, PHYSICS. *Current Pos:* assoc prof, 75-80, PROF PHYSICS, UNIV ARK LITTLE ROCK, 80-, DEPT CHAIR PHYSICS & ASTRON, 89- *Personal Data:* b Houston, Tex, Apr 26, 40; m 64, Louise Garay; c 3. *Educ:* Rice Univ, Ba, 60, MA, 62, PhD(physics), 64. *Prof Exp:* Postdoctoral res assoc physics, Univ Pittsburgh, 64-66; postdoctoral res assoc physics, Univ Notre Dame, 66-68, asst prof, 68-75. *Concurrent Pos:* Vis prof, Univ Notre Dame, 80-81. *Mem:* Am Phys Soc; Am Asn Physics Teachers; Sigma Xi. *Res:* Experimental nuclear physics precision energy measurements using a broad-range magnetic spectrograph; study of nuclear reactions of astrophysical importance. *Mailing Add:* Physics & Astron Dept Univ Ark-Little Rock 2801 S University Little Rock AR 72204-3275. *Fax:* 501-569-3314; *E-Mail:* aarollefson@ualr.edu

ROLLEFSON, RAGNAR, PHYSICS. *Current Pos:* Asst, physics 27-30, from instr to assoc prof, 30-46, chmn dept, 47-51, 52-56 & 57-61, prof, 46-76, EMER PROF PHYSICS, UNIV WIS-MADISON, 76- *Personal Data:* b Chicago, Ill, Aug 23, 06; m 36; c 4. *Educ:* Univ Wis, BA, 26, MA, 27, PhD(physics), 30. *Concurrent Pos:* Mem staff, Radiation Lab, Mass Inst Technol, 42-46; chief scientist, Naval Res Lab, Boston, Mass, 46; mem staff, Proj Charles, Mass Inst Technol, 51, Lincoln Lab, 51-52; tech capabilities panel, Off Defense Mobilization, 54-55; chief scientist, US Army, 56-57; actg dir lab, Midwestern Univs Res Asn, 57-60; dir int sci affairs, Dept State, Washington, DC, 62-64. *Mem:* Fel Am Phys Soc. *Res:* Continuous spectrum of mercury vapor; radar; infrared dispersion of gases. *Mailing Add:* Dept Physics Univ Wis 475 N Charter St Madison WI 53706

ROLLEFSON, ROBERT JOHN, LOW TEMPERATURE PHYSICS, SURFACE PHYSICS. *Current Pos:* from asst prof to assoc prof, 73-86, PROF PHYSICS, WESLEYAN UNIV, 86- *Personal Data:* b Madison, Wis, Sept 9, 41; m 65, Virginia Markel; c Matt & Tuney. *Educ:* Univ Wis, BA, 63; Cornell Univ, PhD(physics), 70. *Prof Exp:* Res assoc physics, Univ Wash, 70-73. *Mem:* Am Phys Soc; Sigma Xi. *Res:* Properties of absorbed monolayer gas films; use of nuclear magnetic resonance spectroscopy to study the phases existing at various densities and dynamics of phase changes; investigations of the effects of surface structure on film properties. *Mailing Add:* Dept Physics Wesleyan Univ Middletown CT 06457. *E-Mail:* rrollefson@eagle.wesleyan.edu

ROLLER, DUANE HENRY DUBOSE, bibliography of the history of science, history of physics; deceased, see previous edition for last biography

ROLLER, MICHAEL HARRIS, ANIMAL PHYSIOLOGY. *Current Pos:* RETIRED. *Personal Data:* b Soldier, Kans, Apr 20, 22; m 44; c 3. *Educ:* Kans State Univ, BS & DVM, 50, PhD(physiol), 66; Baylor Univ, cert biophys, 63. *Prof Exp:* Private practice, 50-61; Nat Defense Educ Act fel, 61-64; instr surg & med, Col Vet Med, Kans State Univ, 64, instr physiol, 65-66; USPHS res fel, 64-65; assoc prof, 66-73, prof entom & zool, 73-79, prof vet sci, SDak State Univ, 79-86. *Concurrent Pos:* Moorman res grant zool, 68-69. *Mem:* Am Vet Med Asn; Sigma Xi. *Res:* Ammonia intoxication in cattle, sheep and rabbits, especially blood and tissue changes and reproductive performance. *Mailing Add:* 1011 Forest St Brookings SD 57006

ROLLER, PETER PAUL, PEPTIDE SYNTHESIS, ANTI-TUMOR DRUG DEVELOPMENT. *Current Pos:* RES CHEMIST, NAT CANCER INST, NIH, 72- *Personal Data:* b Debrecen, Hungary, Nov 16, 40; US citizen; m 67; c 3. *Educ:* Univ BC, BSc, 63, MSc, 65; Stanford Univ, PhD(org chem), 69. *Prof Exp:* NIH fel, Univ Hawaii, 70 & Univ Va, 71-72. *Mem:* Am Chem Soc; AAAS; Protein Soc. *Res:* Design and chemical synthesis of peptides, drugs, growth factors, antitumor and antiviral agents; conformational analysis of proteins; spectroscopic analysis of peptides, carcinogens, natural products and hormones; mass spectrometry applications. *Mailing Add:* Lab Medicinal Chem NIH Bldg 37 Rm 5C-02 9000 Rockville Pike Bethesda MD 20892-4255

ROLLER, WARREN L(EON), AGRICULTURAL ENGINEERING. *Current Pos:* from instr to asst prof, Ohio Agr Exp Sta, 55-63, assoc prof, 63-68, assoc chmn dept, 68-81, chmn dept, 81-87, coord prog develop, 87-88, PROF AGR ENG, OHIO AGR RES & DEVELOP, 68-, ASSOC CHMN DEPT, 88- *Personal Data:* b Logansport, Ind, May 31, 29; m 51; c 5. *Educ:* Purdue Univ, BS, 51, MS, 55, PhD(agr eng), 61. *Honors & Awards:* Jour Award, Am Soc Agr Engrs, 64, 70, 78 & 84, Nat Award, 75. *Prof Exp:* Res fel agr eng, Purdue Univ, 53-54; jr agr engr, Agr Res Serv, USDA, 54-55. *Concurrent Pos:* Nat Acad Sci-Nat Res Coun sr vis scientist, US Army Res Inst Environ Med, 67- *Mem:* Sigma Xi; Am Soc Agr Engrs. *Res:* Automatic feeding systems for animal production; environmental control for animal production; effect of thermal environment upon animal reproduction; energy efficiencies in agricultural production systems; biomass production for fuel. *Mailing Add:* 873 Ashwood Dr Wooster OH 44691

ROLLESTON, FRANCIS STOPFORD, BIOCHEMISTRY. *Current Pos:* asst dir grants prog, Med Res Coun Can, 75-77, dir, SP Prog, 77-83, dir pub affairs, 83-86, dir sci eval, 86-93, DIR INNOVATION TEAMS, MED RES COUN CAN, 93- *Personal Data:* b Montreal, Que, June 1, 40; m 64, Susan Harrison; c Andrew, Stephen & Gavin. *Educ:* Queen's Univ, Ont, BSc, 62; Oxford Univ, DPhil(biochem), 66. *Prof Exp:* Fel physiol, Univ Chicago, 66-67, res assoc biochem, 67-68; asst prof, Banting & Best Dept Med Res, Univ Toronto, 68-75. *Concurrent Pos:* Med Res Coun Can oper grants, 68-75. *Mem:* Can Bioethics Soc. *Res:* Operation of peer review processes; guidelines for ethical research involving human subjects and animals. *Mailing Add:* Med Res Coun Fifth Floor 1600 Scott St Ottawa ON K1A 0W9 Can. *Fax:* 613-954-6653; *E-Mail:* frollest@hpb.hwc.ca

ROLLEY, ROBERT EWELL, WILDLIFE POPULATION ECOLOGY, ECOLOGY OF UNGULATES & CARNIVORES. *Current Pos:* WILDLIFE POPULATION ECOLOGIST, BUR RES, WIS DEPT NAT RESOURCES, 92- *Personal Data:* b Whittier, Calif, Apr 23, 55. *Educ:* Univ Calif, Davis, BS, 77; Univ Wis-Madison, MS, 79; Okla State Univ, PhD(wildlife ecol), 83. *Prof Exp:* Res asst, Univ Wis, 77-79, Okla Coop Wildlife Res Unit, 79-82; teaching asst gen biol, Okla State Univ, 82-83; wildlife res biologist, Div Fish & Wildlife, Ind Dept Nat Resources, 83-92. *Mem:* Wildlife Soc; Soc Conserv Biologists; Am Soc Mammalogists. *Res:* Study of the dynamics of mammalian and avian populations, including the determination of long-term trends in population size, the factors that affect population size, and the effectiveness of survey techniques for monitoring population size and composition. *Mailing Add:* 4411 Oak Ct Madison WI 53716. *Fax:* 608-221-6353; *E-Mail:* roller@dnrmai.dnr.wisc.gov

ROLLIN, BERNARD ELLIOT, ANIMAL CONSCIOUSNESS & PAIN, FARM & LABORATORY ANIMAL WELFARE. *Current Pos:* From asst prof to assoc prof philos, 69-79, PROF PHILOS, PHYSIOL & BIOPHYS, COLO STATE UNIV, 80-,DIR BIOETHICAL PLANNING, 80- *Personal Data:* b New York, NY, Feb 18, 43; m 64, Linda M Schieber; c Michael D. *Educ:* City Col NY, BA, 64; Columbia Univ, PhD(philos), 72. *Honors & Awards:* Waco F Childers Award, Am Humane Asn, 82; C W Hume lectr, Univ London, 83; Gustavus Meyers Award, 93; Brownlee Award, Animal Welfare Found Can, 95. *Concurrent Pos:* Consult, US Cong, Australian Parliament, Can Govt, US Govt, United Airlines,ILAR, NIH, USDA, SAfrica Govt & Holland Govt, 80- *Res:* Ethics of animal research; veterinary ethics; ethics of genetic engineering of animals; social ethics pertaining to animal welfare; animal consciousness; animal pain; ethics of science; care and use of laboratory animals; farm animal welfare. *Mailing Add:* Dept Philos Colo State Univ Ft Collins CO 80523. *Fax:* 970-491-4900

ROLLINGER, CHARLES N(ICHOLAS), COMPUTER SYSTEMS, TECHNICAL MANAGEMENT. *Current Pos:* RETIRED. *Personal Data:* b Chicago Heights, Ill, Aug 5, 34; m 57, June Kennedy; c 5. *Educ:* Univ Detroit, BME, 57; Northwestern Univ, MS, 59, PhD(mech eng), 61. *Prof Exp:* Res engr, Roy C Ingersoll Res Ctr, Borg-Warner Corp, 60-61; from instr to asst prof math, USAF Acad, 61-63; res engr, Frank J Seiler Res Lab, Off Aerospace Res, USAF, 64; sr res engr, Res Labs, Whirlpool Corp, 64-66, corp mgr eng & sci comput, 66-68, dir comput sci & technol, 68-72, dir eng res, 72-74; dir comput serv, Berrien Co Govt, 75-94. *Concurrent Pos:* Consult, R C Ingersoll Res Ctr, Borg-Wagner Corp, 61-64; lectr, Univ Denver, 64; sr lectr, Mich State Univ, 64-66; lectr, Univ Notre Dame, 66, adj asst prof mgt, 78-82; adj assoc prof indust eng, Univ Mich, 70-71. *Mem:* Am Soc Mech Engrs. *Res:* Information systems design; management science. *Mailing Add:* 867 Tucker Dr St Joseph MI 49085. *Fax:* 616-429-8020

ROLLINO, JOHN, PHYSICAL CHEMISTRY. *Current Pos:* VIS PROF PHYSICS, RUTGERS-NEWARK STATE UNIV, 95- *Personal Data:* b Brooklyn, NY, Oct 11, 44; m 70; c 2. *Educ:* St Francis Col, NY, BS, 66; Mass Inst Technol, PhD(chem), 69. *Prof Exp:* Asst prof chem & physics, St Francis Col, NY, 69-84; prof chem & physics, Upsala Col, 84-95. *Concurrent Pos:* Consult, PIC Corp, Orange, NJ. *Mem:* Am Chem Soc; Am Inst Physics; Am Asn Physics Teachers. *Res:* Low temperature thermodynamics; solid state charge transfer complexes. *Mailing Add:* 45 Wells Ct Bloomfield NJ 07003

ROLLINS, HAROLD BERT, INVERTEBRATE PALEONTOLOGY, PALEOECOLOGY & PALEOCLIMATOLOGY. *Current Pos:* from asst prof to assoc prof earth sci, 69-78, PROF GEOL & ANTHROP, UNIV PITTSBURGH, 78- *Personal Data:* b Hamilton, NY, Feb 1, 39; m 60, Judith L Crane; c Steven. *Educ:* Colgate Univ, BA, 60; Univ Wis-Madison, MA, 63; Columbia Univ, PhD(geol, invert paleont), 67. *Prof Exp:* NSF-Great Lakes Col Asn teaching intern earth sci & biol, Antioch Col, 67-68, asst prof, 68-69. *Concurrent Pos:* Res assoc, Am Mus Natural Hist, NY & Carnegie Mus, Pa; Latin Am Studies Prog, Univ Pittsburgh. *Mem:* Paleont Soc; Soc Syst Zool; Geol Soc Am; Brit Paleont Asn; Sigma Xi; Paleont Res Inst. *Res:* Phylogeny and functional morphology of Paleozoic Gastropoda; Devonian paleontology and stratigraphy; Paleozoic Monoplacophora; Pennsylvanian peleoecology; coastal geology; geoarchaeology; biomonitoring aquatic systems. *Mailing Add:* Dept Geol Univ Pittsburgh Pittsburgh PA 15260-0001. *Fax:* 412-624-3914; *E-Mail:* snail@vms.cis.pitt.edu

ROLLINS, HOWARD A, JR, HORTICULTURE. *Current Pos:* RETIRED. *Personal Data:* b Dover, NH, July 12, 27; m 52; c 4. *Educ:* Univ Conn, BS, 50; Univ NH, MS, 51; Ohio State Univ, PhD, 54. *Prof Exp:* Assoc prof hort, Winchester Fruit Res Lab, Va Polytech Inst & State Univ, 54-56, prof, 56-67, prof & head dept, 67-70, staff, 85-92; prof hort & chmn dept, Ohio State Univ & Ohio Agr Res & Develop Ctr, 70-85. *Mem:* Am Soc Hort Sci. *Res:* Winter hardiness of apple; apple production, harvest efficiency and tree fruit culture. *Mailing Add:* 1290 Cherry Valley Rd Laconia NH 03246-7800

ROLLINS, ORVILLE WOODROW, INORGANIC CHEMISTRY, ANALYTICAL CHEMISTRY. *Current Pos:* from asst prof to prof, 51-97, EMER PROF CHEM, US NAVAL ACAD, 97- *Personal Data:* b Sybial, WVa, Dec 4, 23; m 47; c 1. *Educ:* Univ WVa, MS, 50; Georgetown Univ, PhD(chem), 66. *Prof Exp:* Instr & asst prof chem, Moravian Col Men, 49-51. *Concurrent Pos:* Consult, Chem Div, Air Force Off Sci Res. *Mem:* Am Chem Soc. *Res:* Isopoly and heteropoly molybdates and tungstates; analytical methods. *Mailing Add:* 730 Sportsman Neck Rd Queenstown MD 21658

ROLLINS, REED CLARK, BOTANY, GENETICS. *Current Pos:* assoc prof bot, 48-54, chmn inst res plant morphol, 55-66, inst plant sci, 65-69, dir Gray Herbarium, 48-78, supvr, Bussey Inst, 67-78, chmn admin comt, Farlow Libr & Herbarium, 74-78, Asa Gray prof syst bot, 54-82, EMER PROF SYST BOT, HARVARD UNIV, 82- *Personal Data:* b Lyman, Wyo, Dec 7, 11; m 39, 78; c 2. *Educ:* Univ Wyo, AB, 33; State Col Wash, SM, 36; Harvard Univ, PhD(bot), 41. *Honors & Awards:* Centenary Medal, French Bot Soc, 54; Cert of Merit, Bot Soc Am, 60; Congress Medal, XI Int Bot Cong, Seattle, 69, XII Int Bot Cong, Leningrad, 75; Gold Seal, Nat Coun State Garden Clubs, 81; Asa Gray Award, Am Soc Plant Taxonomists, 87; 25th Anniversary Medal, Orgn Trop Studies, 88. *Prof Exp:* From instr to assoc prof biol, Stanford Univ, 40-48. *Concurrent Pos:* Asst cur, Dudley Herbarium, Stanford Univ, 40-41, cur, 41-48; assoc geneticist, Guayule Res Proj, USDA, 43-45, geneticist, Div Rubber Plant Invests, 47-48; prin geneticist, Stanford Res Inst, 46-47; ed-in-chief, Rhodora, 50-61; pres, Orgn Trop Studies, Inc, 64-65. *Mem:* Nat Acad Sci; Am Acad Arts & Sci; Am Soc Nat (vpres, 60, pres, 66); Genetics Soc Am; Int Asn Plant Taxon (vpres, 50-54, pres, 54-59). *Res:* Cytology and systematics of the Cruciferae; cytogenetics of the guayule rubber plant and related species of Parthenium. *Mailing Add:* Gray Herbarium Harvard Univ 22 Divinity Ave Cambridge MA 02138

ROLLINS, ROGER WILLIAM, NON-LINEAR DYNAMICS & CHAOS, EXPERIMENTAL SOLID STATE PHYSICS. *Current Pos:* From asst prof to assoc prof, 66-78, PROF PHYSICS, OHIO UNIV, 78-, ASSOC DEAN, COL ARTS & SCIS, 97- *Personal Data:* b Columbia City, Ind, Jan 23, 39; m 61, Betty L Kenner; c Neil A & Alan W. *Educ:* Purdue Univ, BS, 61; Cornell Univ, PhD(appl physics), 67. *Concurrent Pos:* Vis scientist, Inst Exp Nuclear Physics, Univ Karlsruhe, Ger, 72-73. *Mem:* AAAS; Am Phys Soc; Am Asn Physics Teachers. *Res:* Computer simulation and graphics; non-linear systems; superconductivity-hysteresis effects in type II superconductors; deterministic chaos; controlling chaotic systems. *Mailing Add:* Dept Physics Ohio Univ Athens OH 45701. *E-Mail:* rollins@chaos.phy.ohiou.edu

ROLLINS, RONALD ROY, PHYSICAL CHEMISTRY, EXPLOSIVES. *Current Pos:* TEACHING PHYS SCI & CHEM, BRIGHAM YOUNG UNIV-HAWAII, 92- *Personal Data:* b Tooele, Utah, Oct 2, 30; m 92, Patricia Tracy. *Educ:* Univ Utah, BS, 59, PhD(metall), 62. *Prof Exp:* Staff mem direct energy conversion, Vallecitos Atomic Lab, Gen Elec Co, Calif, 62-64; from asst prof to assoc prof theory high explosives, Univ Mo-Rolla, 64-79; chmn, Mineral Processing Eng Dept, WVa Univ, 81-84, prof explosives/mining, 79-92. *Concurrent Pos:* Sr investr, Rock Mech & Explosives Res Ctr, 64-79. *Res:* Hot wire initiation of secondary explosives; factors that sensitize primary and secondary explosives; theory of high explosives; shaped charge explosive effects; high pressure water jets; underground methane explosions; explosive blast casting. *Mailing Add:* PO Box 1967 Brigham Young Univ-Hawaii Laie HI 96762-1294

ROLLINS, WADE CUTHBERT, BIOLOGY. *Current Pos:* Asst, 45-48, instr & jr animal husbandryman, 48-50, asst prof & asst animal husbandryman, 50-56, assoc prof & assoc animal husbandryman, 56-64, prof & geneticist, 64-78, EMER PROF ANIMAL SCI, UNIV CALIF, DAVIS, 78- *Personal Data:* b Jersey City, NJ, Feb 12, 12; m 41; c 1. *Educ:* Univ Calif, AB, 33, MA, 35, PhD(genetics), 48. *Mem:* Biomet Soc; Am Soc Animal Sci. *Res:* Application of genetics to livestock breeding; population genetics. *Mailing Add:* 442 University Ave Davis CA 95616

ROLLINS-CROSS, ETHEL, MATERIAL SHAPING, PATENTS. *Current Pos:* Staff, Patent Exam Group 1100, Patent & Trademark Off, 73-90, Supvry Patent Examr Exam Group 3400, 91-95, dep dir, Group 1100 & 2900, 96, DIR, GROUP 3200, PATENT & TRADEMARK OFF, 96- *Personal Data:* m, Garfield; c Nia & Garfield IV. *Educ:* Norfold State Univ, BS, 71. *Concurrent Pos:* Sr prog mgr, Off Human Capacity Develop, Off Res, USAID. *Res:* Article manufacturing and tools; intellectual property rights issues in government sponsored research in foreign countries. *Mailing Add:* Dir Off Patent Exam Group 3200 Patent & Trademark Off CP2-10A12 Washington DC 20231

ROLLMAN, GARY BERNARD, EXPERIMENTAL PSYCHOLOGY, PAIN. *Current Pos:* PROF PSYCHOL, UNIV WESTERN ONT, 69- *Personal Data:* b New York, NY, Nov 9, 41; m 67, Barbara Marks; c 2. *Educ:* Univ Rochester, BA, 62; Univ Penn, MA, 63, PhD(psychol), 67. *Prof Exp:* Fel, Princeton Univ, 67-69. *Concurrent Pos:* Vis lectr psychol, Princeton Univ, 68-69; prin investr res grants, Natural Sci & Eng, Res Coun Can, 69-; vis scholar psychol, Univ Stockholm, 75-76; vis prof psychol, Univ St Andrews, Scotland, 82-83; mem, People to People Pain Specialists Deleg, People's Repub China, 84; steering comt, London Pain Interest Group, 85-90; exec comt, Can Pain Soc, 85-90, chmn, nominating comt, 86-88, chmn, local arrangements comt, 89-90, sci prog comt, 86-88 & 89-90; mem, task force special pain problems related women, Int Asn Study Pain, 90-; res, Int Asn Study Pain, 93-, sci adv comt, Fac Dent, Univ NC, 95- *Mem:* Int Asn Study Pain; Can Pain Soc; Int Soc Psychophysics; Am Psychol Asn; fel Can Psychol Asn; Psychonomic Soc; fel Am Psychol Soc. *Res:* Pain measurement in laboratory and clinical settings; human experimental psychology, sensation and perception, particularly involving the somatosensory system, psychophysics. *Mailing Add:* Dept Psychol Univ Western Ont London ON N6A 5C2 Can. *E-Mail:* rollman@uwo.ca

ROLLMANN, LOUIS DEANE, INORGANIC CHEMISTRY, PETROLEUM. *Current Pos:* from res chemist to sr res chemist, Mobil Res & Develop Corp, 68-75, assoc chem & prof leader, 75-77, res assoc, 77-80, group mgr, 80-85, mgr, Enhanced & Heavy Oil Recovery, 85-91, RES SCIENTIST, MOBIL RES & DEVELOP CORP, 91- *Personal Data:* b Kingman, Kans, Apr 26, 39; m 67; c 3. *Educ:* Univ Kans, BA, 60, PhD(inorg chem), 67. *Prof Exp:* NIH fel phys chem, Calif Inst Technol, 67-68. *Mem:* Am Chem Soc; Soc Petrol Eng. *Res:* Zeolite synthesis; catalysis; metals in petroleum; petroleum processing; petroleum production; enhanced and heavy oil recovery; petroleum recovery; research management. *Mailing Add:* 211 S Washington Ave Moorestown NJ 08057-3517

ROLLO, FRANK DAVID, physics, medicine, for more information see previous edition

ROLLO, IAN MCINTOSH, PHARMACOLOGY, MICROBIOLOGY. *Current Pos:* RETIRED. *Personal Data:* b Aberdeen, Scotland, May 28, 26; m 49; c 1. *Educ:* Aberdeen Univ, BSc, 45; Univ Man, PhD(pharmacol), 68. *Prof Exp:* Exp officer chem, Ministry of Food, Brit Civil Serv, 46-48; asst chemother, Sch Trop Med, Univ Liverpool, 48-49; res scientist, Wellcome Labs Trop Med, London, 49-58; res scientist, Distillers Co, Ltd, 58-61; prof pharmacol, Fac Med, Univ Man, 61-91. *Mem:* Am Soc Pharmacol & Exp Therapeut; Pharmacol Soc Can; Am Soc Trop Med & Hyg. *Res:* Chemosensitivity testing of human tumors; optimizing production of single-cell suspensions and increasing cloning efficiency in the culture of clonogenic tumor cells. *Mailing Add:* Dept Pharmacol & Therapeut Univ Manitoba Med Fac 770 Bannatyne Ave Winnipeg MB R3E 0W3 Can

ROLLOSSON, GEORGE WILLIAM, physics, for more information see previous edition

ROLLS, BARBARA J, FOOD INTAKE BEHAVIOR & EATING DISORDERS, OBESITY. *Current Pos:* Jean Phillips Shibley prof behav health, 92-94, GUTHRIE CHAIR NUTRIT & PROF NUTRIT, PA STATE UNIV, 94- *Personal Data:* b Washington, DC, Jan 5, 45; c Melissa May & Juliet Helen. *Educ:* Univ Pa, BA, 66; Univ Oxford, Eng, MA(physiol) & PhD(physiol), 70. *Honors & Awards:* Hoffman-LaRoche Lectr in Nutrit to Can, 94; Lederle Award in Human Nutrit, Am Inst Nutrit, 95; Lydia J Roberts Mem Lectr, Univ Chicago, 95; Beaudette-Thompson Lectr, Rutgers Univ, 97. *Prof Exp:* Mary Somerville res fel, Somerville Col, Oxford Univ, 69-72, IBM res fel, 72-74, sr res scientist, 74-84; from assoc prof to prof psychiat, Johns Hopkins Univ, 84-92. *Concurrent Pos:* Jr res fel, Wolfson Col, Univ Oxford, 74-75, E P Abraham res fel, Green Col, 79-82, fel nutrit, 83-84; consult, 83-; mem, Nat Task Force Prev & Treatment Obesity, Nat Inst Diabetes & Digestive & Kidney Dis, 94- *Mem:* NAm Asn Study Obesity (vpres, 94-95, pres elect, 95-96, pres, 96-97); Soc Study Ingestive Behavior (pres elect, 90-91, pres, 91-92); Am Soc Clin Nutrit; Am Inst Nutrit. *Res:* Psychological and physiological controls of food intake and food selection in normal weight and obese humans and in patients with eating disorders; peripheral and central physiological controls of thirst and drinking in humans; aging and the controls of food and fluid intake. *Mailing Add:* Nutrit Dept 226 Henderson Bldg Pa State Univ University Park PA 16802-6501

ROLLWITZ, WILLIAM LLOYD, magnetic resonance, electronic instrumentation; deceased, see previous edition for last biography

ROLNICK, WILLIAM BARNETT, PHYSICS & ACOUSTICS, MATHEMATICS. *Current Pos:* asst prof, 66-70, assoc prof, 71-80, PROF PHYSICS, WAYNE STATE UNIV, 81- *Personal Data:* b Brooklyn, NY, Aug 20, 36; m 62, Ellen Levy; c Stefan & Aaron. *Educ:* Brooklyn Col, BS, 56; Columbia Univ, AM, 60, PhD(physics), 63. *Prof Exp:* Asst prof physics, US Merchant Marine Acad, 63-64; res assoc, Case Inst Technol, 64-66. *Concurrent Pos:* Dir, Res Careers Minority Scholars, Wayne State Univ; Dept Energy res grant, 79-90; res consult, Physics Dept, Univ Mich, 79-89. *Mem:* Am Asn Physics Teachers; Am Phys Soc; Sigma Xi. *Res:* Elementary particle theory; scattering theory; electromagnetic theory; quantum electrodynamics; tachyons. *Mailing Add:* Dept Physics Wayne State Univ Detroit MI 48202. *Fax:* 313-577-3932; *E-Mail:* wrolnick@hal.physics.wayne.edu

ROLOFF, MARSTON VAL, TOXICOLOGY, GENERAL PHYSIOLOGY. *Current Pos:* Sr scientist, Monsanto Co, 78-81, sr res group leader, 81-86, consult, Inhalation Toxicol, 86-90, sr inhalation toxicol consult, 90-95, REGULATORY COMPLIANCE MGR, MONSANTO CO, 96- *Personal Data:* b Charles City, Iowa, June 28, 43; m 69, Gail A Penrod; c Jason & Joshua. *Educ:* Cedarville Col, BS, 65; Nebr Univ, MS, 68; Iowa State Univ, PhD(physiol & pharmacol), 74. *Concurrent Pos:* Cmndg officer, 4th Med Battalion, USMC, 92-94. *Mem:* Am Indust Health Coun; Soc Toxicol; Sigma Xi; Am Physiol Soc; Christian Educators Soc; Am Indust Hyg Asn; Soc Toxicol & Environ Toxicol & Chem. *Res:* Aerosol research; risk assessment on human exposure from toxicology data. *Mailing Add:* 2 El Caballos St Charles MO 63304. *Fax:* 314-537-6134

ROLOFSON, GEORGE LAWRENCE, TOXICOLOGY, ENTOMOLOGY. *Current Pos:* CONSULT TOXICOL & REGULATORY AFFAIRS, 79-; MGR, FED GOVT RELS, CIBA GEIGY CORP. *Personal Data:* b Lincoln, Nebr, July 16, 38. *Educ:* Univ Nebr, BSc, 61, MSc, 64; Va Polytech Inst, PhD(entom & toxicol), 68. *Prof Exp:* Staff specialist insecticide develop, Ciba-Geigy Corp, 68-70, group leader plant protectants, 70-72, toxicologist, 72-75, sr toxicologist, 75-78, mgr toxicol, 78-79. *Mem:* Entom Soc Am. *Res:* Toxicology required for Federal Insecticide, Fungicide and Rodenticide Act and Toxic Substance Control Act. *Mailing Add:* 3908 Buncombe Dr Greensboro NC 27407

ROLSTON, CHARLES HOPKINS, INDUSTRIAL ORGANIC CHEMISTRY. *Current Pos:* res chem, Eastern Lab, Gibbstown, 56-72, sr res chemist, Exp Sta, 72-81, SR CHEMIST, JACKSON LAB, E I DU PONT DE NEMOURS & CO, INC, 81- *Personal Data:* b Harrisonburg, Va, July 25, 27; m 53; c 3. *Educ:* Hampden-Sydney Col, BS, 48; Univ Md, MS, 53. *Prof Exp:* Res org chemist, Westvaco Chlorine-Alkali Div, Food Mach & Chem Corp, 52-54. *Mem:* Am Chem Soc; AAAS; Sigma Xi. *Res:* Synthetic organic chemistry; developmental research on organic intermediates; application of catalytic processes. *Mailing Add:* 24 Budd Blvd Woodbury NJ 08096-3332

ROLSTON, DENNIS EUGENE, SOIL PHYSICS. *Current Pos:* Lab technician, Univ Calif, Davis, 68-70, from asst prof toassoc prof, 70-81, assoc dean, 81-86, PROF SOILS, UNIV CALIF, DAVIS, 81-, DIR, CTR ECOL HEALTH RES, 90- *Personal Data:* b Burke, SDak, June 20, 43; m 69, Mata S Clinger; c Jennifer C & Kathryn M. *Educ:* SDak State Univ, BS, 65; Iowa State Univ, MS, 67; Univ Calif, Davis, PhD(soils), 70. *Mem:* Am Soc Agron; fel Soil Sci Soc Am; Int Soc Soil Sci; Am Geophys Union. *Res:* Water movement in soils; diffusion and displacement of ions and gas in soil; denitrification; contaminant transport in soil. *Mailing Add:* Soil Sci Univ Calif Davis CA 95616-5200. *Fax:* 530-752-1552; *E-Mail:* derolston@ucdavis.edu

ROLSTON, KENNETH VIJAYKUMAR ISSAC, INFECTIOUS DISEASES. *Current Pos:* instr med, 83-84, ASST PROF MED, UNIV TEX MD ANDERSON HOSP & TUMOR INST, 84- *Personal Data:* b Etah, India, Apr 23, 51; US citizen; m 84; c 1. *Educ:* Christian Med Col, India, MB & BS, 72. *Prof Exp:* Intern, Christian Med Col, India, 73-74; Physician, Luteran World Relief Team Cambodia & Vietnam, 74-75; resident internal med, Franklin Square Hosp, Baltimore, 76-78, chief resident, 78-79; staff physician internal med, N Charles Gen Hosp, Baltimore, 79-81; fel infectious dis, Hahnemann Univ, 81-83. *Concurrent Pos:* Co-investr, Nat Inst Allergy & Infectious Dis, 86- & various comp grants, 86- *Mem:* Am Col Physicians; Am Soc Microbiol; Am Venereal Dis Asn; Asn Gnotobiotics; Am Fed Clin Res; AMA; Infectious Dis Soc Am. *Res:* Evaluation of newer antimicrobial agents in-vitro and clinically in immuno suppressed patients; management of infectious complications in AIDS patients; the recognition and description of new infectious agents in AIDS patients. *Mailing Add:* 1515 Holcombe Blvd Houston TX 77030

ROLSTON, LAWRENCE H, ENTOMOLOGY. *Current Pos:* PROF ENTOM, LA STATE UNIV, BATON ROUGE, 68- *Personal Data:* b Parkersburg, WVa, Apr 14, 22; m 41; c 4. *Educ:* Marietta Col, AB, 49; Ohio State Univ, MS, 50, PhD, 55. *Prof Exp:* Jr entomologist & cur, Entom Mus, Univ Ark, 52-55; asst prof entom, Exp Sta, Ohio State Univ, 55-58; from assoc prof to prof, Univ Ark, 58-66, mem exp sta, 58-66; entom specialist, Tex A&M Univ, 66-68. *Res:* Truck insects; agricultural entomology; taxonomy of pentatomidae. *Mailing Add:* Dept Entom La State Univ 410 Life Sci Bldg Baton Rouge LA 70803-0001

ROLWING, RAYMOND H, MATHEMATICS. *Current Pos:* from instr to asst prof, 58-70, asst dean, McMicken Col Arts & Sci, 68-71, ASSOC PROF MATH, UNIV CINCINNATI, 70- *Personal Data:* b Toledo, Ohio, Mar 22, 31; m 56; c 4. *Educ:* Christian Bros Col, BS, 55; Univ Notre Dame, MS, 58; Univ Cincinnati, PhD(math), 63. *Prof Exp:* Instr math, Christian Bros Col, Tenn, 58-60. *Concurrent Pos:* Dir acad year in-serv summer inst sec teachers math & sci, NSF, 65-73; dir leadership develop proj, NSF, 73-75. *Mem:* Am Math Soc; Math Asn Am; Nat Coun Teachers Math. *Res:* Ordinary differential equations; existence and uniqueness theorems; quadratic nonlinear integral equations; calculus of variations; isoperimetric problems; econometrics; learning theories in mathematics; history of mathematics. *Mailing Add:* Dept Math Sci Univ Cincinnati Cincinnati OH 45221-0002

ROM, ROY CURT, HORTICULTURE, POMOLOGY. *Current Pos:* PROF HORT, UNIV ARK, FAYETTEVILLE, 58- *Personal Data:* b Milwaukee, Wis, Jan 29, 22; m 50; c 4. *Educ:* Univ Wis-Madison, BS, 48, PhD(hort soils), 58. *Honors & Awards:* Marshall Wilder Medal, Am Pomol Soc, 85. *Prof Exp:* Asst hort, Univ Wis-Madison, 54-58. *Concurrent Pos:* Consult, Corp Farms, 70- & USAID prog; vis scientist, Nat Acad Sci, Poland & Czech, 75; sabbatical study, France, 79, Yugoslavia, 83. *Mem:* Am Pomol Soc (secy, 80); Int Dwarf Fruit Tree Asn; fel Am Soc Hort Sci. *Res:* Nutrition, physiology, pruning and cultural practices in fruit production; weed control; breeding of apples and peaches; rootstock growth and development. *Mailing Add:* 3098 Roms Orchard Dr Fayetteville AR 72703

ROMACK, FRANK ELDON, cardiovascular diseases, animal physiology; deceased, see previous edition for last biography

ROMAGNANI, SERGIO, internal medicine, for more information see previous edition

ROMAGNOLI, ROBERT JOSEPH, MAGNETO-OPTICS, SURFACE PLASMA WAVES. *Current Pos:* from asst prof to prof, 60-96, chmn, Dept Physics & Astron, 93-96, EMER PROF PHYSICS, CALIF STATE UNIV, NORTHRIDGE, 96- *Personal Data:* b Chicago, Ill, Aug 16, 31. *Educ:* Ill Inst Technol, BS, 53, MS, 54, PhD(physics), 57. *Prof Exp:* Instr physics, Ill Inst Technol, 57-59; lectr, El Camino Col, 59-60. *Concurrent Pos:* Consult to indust. *Mem:* Am Phys Soc; Am Asn Physics Teachers. *Res:* Electromagnetic radiation; optical propagation; photovoltaic devices; electron optics; electromagnetic surface plasma waves; nonlinear magneto-optics. *Mailing Add:* Dept Physics & Astron Calif State Univ Northridge CA 91330-8268

ROMAN, ANN, VIROLOGY, MOLECULAR GENETICS. *Current Pos:* from asst prof to assoc prof microbiol & immunol, 75-88, PROF MICROBIOL & IMMUNOL, SCH MED, IND UNIV, 88- *Personal Data:* b Tampa, Fla, Sept 8, 45; m 74; c 1. *Educ:* Reed Col, BA, 67; Univ Calif, San Diego, PhD(biol), 73. *Concurrent Pos:* Vis scientist, dept virol, Weizmann Inst, Israel, 82-83; chmn elect, DNA viruses div, Am Soc Microbiol, 86-87, chmn, 87-88; mem, Cancer Biol & Immunol Contract Rev Comt, 88- *Mem:* AAAS; Am Soc Microbiol; Am Soc Virol. *Res:* Association of human papillomavirus DNA with benign and malignant lesions; interaction of human papillomavirus with keratinocytes; factor determining the intracellular fate of viral DNA. *Mailing Add:* Microbiol Dept MS 244 Ind Univ Sch Med 635 Barnhill Dr Indianapolis IN 46202-5120

ROMAN, BERNARD JOHN, PHYSICS. *Current Pos:* MEM STAFF, MICROWAVE SEMICONDUCTOR CORP. *Personal Data:* b Kingston, Pa, June 26, 40; m 65; c 3. *Educ:* Carnegie-Mellon Univ, BSc, 62; Northwestern Univ, PhD(physics), 69. *Prof Exp:* Jr engr electronics, Radio Corp Am, 61, 62 & 63; mem staff magnetic devices, Bell Labs, 69- *Mem:* Am Phys Soc. *Res:* Fabrication techniques for magnetic domain (bubble) devices. *Mailing Add:* Motorola Aprdl 3501 Ed Bluestein Blvd MS:K-10 Austin TX 78762

ROMAN, GUSTAVO CAMPOS, NEUROEPIDEMIOLOGY. *Current Pos:* PROF NEUROL, TEX TECH UNIV SCH MED; STAFF MEM, LUBBOCK GEN HOSP. *Personal Data:* b Bogota, Columbia, Sept 7, 46; US citizen; m 72; c 2. *Educ:* Col Emmanuel d'Alzon, BA, 64; Nat Univ Columbia, MD, 71; Am Bd Psychiat & Neurol, dipl neurol, 83. *Prof Exp:* Neurol resident, Med Ctr Hosp, Univ Vt, Col Med, 75-77, chief resident, 77-78, spec fel neurol, 78-79; asst prof, Dept Internal Med, Nat Univ Columbia & San Juan de Rios Univ Hosp, 80-81, Univ El Rosario Sch Med & San Jose Univ Hosp, 82-83; from asst prof to prof, Dept Med & Surg Neurol, Health Sci Ctr Sch Med, Tex Tech Univ, 83-88, actg chmn dept, 85-88; chief, Neuroepidemiol Br, Nat Inst Neurol Dis & Stroke, NIH, Bethesda, Md, 89- *Concurrent Pos:* Asst instr neuroanat, Dept Anat, Nat Univ Columbia, 72-73, asst prof neurol, 80-81; asst prof, Univ El Rosario Sch Med & San Jose Univ Hosp, Bogota, 82-83; staff neurologist, Vet Admin Outpatient Clin, Lubbock, Tex, 83-85; prof staff mem, Lubbock Gen Hosp, 83-89; founding dir, Ctr Sleep Dis, Lubbock Gen Hosp & Tex Tech Univ, 85-88; dir, Electromyography Lab, Dept Med & Surg Neurol, 85-88. *Mem:* Fel Am Acad Neurol; NY Acad Sci; fel Am Col Physicians; Am EEG Soc; Soc Neurosci; AAAS; fel Royal Soc Trop Med & Hyg; Royal Soc Med. *Res:* Neurology; sleep disorders. *Mailing Add:* 108 Village Circle San Antonio TX 78232

ROMAN, JESSE, PLANT NEMATOLOGY. *Current Pos:* Asst nematologist, 56-73, nematologist & head, Dept Entom & Nematol, 73-77, tech asst to dir, Agr Exp Sta, 77-89, EMER PROF ENTOM & NEMATOL, UNIV PR, RIO PIEDRAS, 89- *Personal Data:* b Cabo Rojo, PR, June 18, 31; m 56; c 1. *Educ:* Univ PR, BS, 56; Auburn Univ, MS, 59; NC State Univ, PhD(nematol), 68. *Mem:* Soc Nematol; Orgn Trop Am Nematol (pres, 71); Caribbean Food Crop Soc; Am Soc Agr Sci (pres, 74). *Res:* Taxonomy; morphology; cytology; biology; population dynamics; reproduction and control of plant parasitic nematodes. *Mailing Add:* Three Hortencia No 242 Round Hill Trugillo Alto PR 00976

ROMAN, LAURA M, MOLECULAR BIOLOGY, NEUROSCIENCES. *Current Pos:* ASST PROF BIOL, SCH MED, YALE UNIV, 91- *Personal Data:* b Chicago, Ill, Aug, 14, 55. *Educ:* Smith Col, BA, 77; Yale Univ, PhD(cell biol), 83. *Prof Exp:* Postdoctoral fel, Europ Molecular Biol Lab, 83-86 & Howard Hughes Med Inst, Univ Tex Southwestern, 86-91. *Mem:* Sigma Xi; Am Soc Cell Biol; AAAS; Fedn Am Soc Exp Biol. *Res:* Effect of retinouic acid on the migration and differentiation of murine neural crest cells. *Mailing Add:* Dept Physiol Johns Hopkins Univ Sch Med 725 N Wolfe St Baltimore MD 21205-2185. *Fax:* 203-785-4951

ROMAN, NANCY GRACE, ASTRONOMY. *Current Pos:* CHIEF SCIENTIST, ASTRON DATA CTR, GODDARD SPACE FLIGHT CTR, HUGHES STX, 80- *Personal Data:* b Nashville, Tenn, May 16, 25. *Educ:* Swarthmore Col, BA, 46; Univ Chicago, PhD(astron), 49. *Hon Degrees:* DSc, Russell Sage Col, 66; Hood Col, 69; Bates Col, 71 & Swarthmore Col, 76. *Honors & Awards:* Fed Woman's Award, 62; Except Sci Achievement Award, NASA, 69 & Outstanding Sci Leadership Award, 78; William Randolf Lovelace II Award, Am Astronaut Soc, 80. *Prof Exp:* Asst astron & astrophys, Univ Chicago, 46-48, res assoc, 49-52, instr, 52-54, asst prof, 54-55; astronr, Radio Astron Br, US Naval Res Lab, 55-56, head, Microwave Spectros Sect, 56-57, consult, 58-59; head observational astron prog, NASA Hq, 59-60, chief astron & astrophys progs, 60-61, chief astron & solar physics, 61-63, chief astron, 63-72, chief astron & relativity, 72-79, space telescope prog scientist, 80; consult, 79-90, McDonnell Space Systs Div, 89-95. *Concurrent Pos:* Trustee, Russel Sage Col, 73-78 & Swarthmore Col, 80-84; consult, ORI, 80-88; staff, McDonnell Space Systs Div, 89- *Mem:* Int Astron Union; fel Am Astronaut Soc; Am Astron Soc; fel AAAS; Astron Soc Pac. *Res:* Spectral classification; stellar motions; photoelectric photometry; space research; astronomy data. *Mailing Add:* 4620 N Park Ave Apt 306W Chevy Chase MD 20815. *Fax:* 301-286-1771

ROMAN, PAUL, THEORETICAL PHYSICS, MATHEMATICAL PHYSICS. *Current Pos:* DEAN GRAD STUDIES & RES, STATE UNIV NY PLATTSBURGH, 78- *Personal Data:* b Budapest, Hungary, Aug 20, 25; nat US; m 47, 62; c 4. *Educ:* Eotvos Lorand Univ, MSc, 47, PhD(physics), 48; Hungarian Acad Sci, DSc, 56. *Prof Exp:* Asst lectr physics, E-tv-s Lorand Univ, Budapest, 47-48, lectr, 48-50, sr lectr, 50-51, sr res worker, 54-56; dept chmn, Tech Pedag Col, Budapest, 51-52; res fel, Moscow State Univ, 52-53; dept chmn, Agr Univ, Budapest, 53-54; lectr, Univ Manchester, 57-61; assoc prof physics, Boston Univ, 60-62, prof, 62-78. *Concurrent Pos:* Vis prof, Mex, 72, 74, 75 & 77 & Max Planck Inst, 76, 78, 80 & 82; assoc ed, J Math Physics, 78-81. *Mem:* Fel Am Phys Soc; Am Asn Physics Teachers; Int Asn Math Physicists; Nat Coun Univ Res Adminrs; Soc Res Admin. *Res:* Theory of elementary particles and quantum field theory; mathematical physics; science education and research administration. *Mailing Add:* 230 W Highland Ave Philadelphia PA 19118

ROMAN, RICHARD J, ROLE OF KIDNEY IN HYPERTENSION. *Current Pos:* From asst prof to assoc prof, 81-90, PROF PHYSIOL, MED COL WIS, 90- *Personal Data:* b Dec 19, 51; m 76; c 2. *Educ:* Univ Tenn, PhD(pharmacol), 77. *Mem:* Am Physiol Soc; Am Soc Nephrology. *Res:* Renal physiology; hypertension; renal microcirculation. *Mailing Add:* Dept Physiol Med Col Wis 8701 Watertown Plank Rd Milwaukee WI 53226-4801. *Fax:* 414-257-8570

ROMAN, STANFORD A, JR, EDUCATION ADMINISTRATION, MEDICINE. *Current Pos:* DEAN & PROF, CITY UNIV NEW YORK MED SCH, 90- *Personal Data:* b New York, NY, Nov 19, 42; div; c 2. *Educ:* Dartmouth Col, AB, 64; Columbia Univ, MD, 68; Univ Mich, MPH, 75. *Prof Exp:* Assoc dir ambulatory care, Harlem Hosp Ctr, 72-73; dir clin serv, Healthco Inc, 73-74; asst prof med, Sch Med, Univ NC, 73-74; dir ambulatory care, Boston City Hosp, 74-78; asst prof med & sociomed sci, Sch Med, Boston Univ, 74-78, asst dean, 75-78; med dir, DC Gen Hosp, 78-81; assoc dean, Dartmouth Med Sch, 81-86; dep dean, 86-87; dean & vpres acad affairs, Mosehoabe Sch Med, 87-89; sr vpres med & prof affil, NY Hosp Corp, 89-90. *Concurrent Pos:* Lectr, Sch Pub Health, Harvard Univ, 77-78; prin investr, Boston Comprehensive Sickle Cell Ctr, 75-78; proj dir, Southeast Washington, DC Primary Care Network, 78-91; bd mem, Nat Bd Med Engrs, 88-92; grant rev comt, Nat Health Prom & Dis Prev Ctr, 88-; nat adv group, Assessory Charge Med Educ, 89-; comn mem, NY State Coun Grad Med Educ, 91- *Mailing Add:* City Univ NY Med Sch Sci Bldg 138th St & Convent Ave Rm J909 New York NY 10031

ROMANI, ROGER JOSEPH, PLANT PHYSIOLOGY, CELLULAR SENESCENCE. *Current Pos:* Asst, Univ Calif, Los Angeles, 51-55, asst food scientist, 57-59, lectr pomol, 70-74, prof pomol, 74-93, ASSOC POMOLOGIST, UNIV CALIF, DAVIS, 59-, EMER PROF POMOL, 93- *Personal Data:* b Sacramento, Calif, Dec 17, 19; m 59, Ann Gallichotie; c 4. *Educ:* Univ Calif, BS, 51, PhD(plant physiol, biochem), 55. *Hon Degrees:* Dr, Nat Polytech Inst, Toulouse, France. *Concurrent Pos:* Mem food irradiation adv comt, AEC-Am Inst Biol Sci, 61-63; chmn, Gorden Res Conf Postharvest Physiol, 82. *Mem:* AAAS; Am Soc Plant Physiol; Am Soc Hort Sci. *Res:* Cellular aspects of maturation and senescence; radiation biochemistry; mitochondrial physiology. *Mailing Add:* 227 Russel Blvd Davis CA 95616

ROMANI, ROGER WILLIAM, THEORETICAL PHYSICS, ASTROPHYSICS. *Current Pos:* ASST PROF PHYSICS, STANFORD UNIV, 91- *Educ:* Princeton Univ, AB, 83; Calif Inst Technol, PhD(physics), 87. *Prof Exp:* Res assoc, Astron Dept, Univ Calif, Berkeley, 87-89 & Inst Advan Study, 89-91. *Concurrent Pos:* Corning fel, Inst Advan Study, 89-90; Sloan Found fel, 92-96; Cottrell scholar fel, 94-; vchair, Hobby-Eberly Telescope Bd. *Mem:* Am Astron Soc; Int Astron Union. *Mailing Add:* Dept Physics Stanford Univ Varian Bldg Stanford CA 94305-4060. *Fax:* 650-723-9389; *E-Mail:* rwr@astro.stanford.edu

ROMANKIW, LUBOMYR TARAS, MATERIALS ENGINEERING, ELECTROCHEMISTRY. *Current Pos:* Mem res staff electrochem, Thomas J Watson Res Ctr, 62-63, mgr, Magnetic Mat Group, Components Div, 63-64, mem res staff mat & processes, 65-68, mgr, Magnetic Mat & Devices, 68-78, consult, IBM E Fishkill Develop Lab & Mfg, 78-80, MGR MAT & PROCESS STUDIES, THOMAS J WATSON RES CTR, IBM CORP, 81- *Personal Data:* b Zhowkwa, Ukraine, Apr 17, 31; Can citizen. *Educ:* Univ Alta, BSc, 55; Mass Inst Technol, MSc & PhD(metall), 62. *Concurrent Pos:* Instr, Mass Inst Technol, 59-61. *Mem:* Electrochem Soc (secy-tres, 79-80); Am Electroplaters Soc; Inst Elec & Electronics Engrs; Sigma Xi. *Res:* Magnetic thin films; deposition of thin films; dielectrics; magnetic device design; material selection and fabrication; electrodeposition; magnetic materials; electronic and magnetic device fabrication; chemical engineering; metallurgy. *Mailing Add:* IBM Corp Res Old Orchard Rd Armonk NY 10504

ROMANKO, RICHARD ROBERT, PLANT PATHOLOGY. *Current Pos:* EXT AGRONOMIST, IDACES, 84. *Personal Data:* b Cortland, NY, Dec 18, 25; m 54; c 3. *Educ:* Univ NH, BS, 53; Univ Del, MS, 55; La State Univ, PhD(plant path), 57. *Prof Exp:* Asst fruit fungicides, Univ Del, 53-55; asst plant pathologist, Exp Sta, Univ Idaho, 57-65, assoc plant pathologist, 65-84. *Concurrent Pos:* Sabbatical leave, Univ Calif, Davis, 67-68; mem, Western Alfalfa Improvement Conf. *Mem:* AAAS; Potato Asn Am; Am Phytopath Soc; Sigma Xi. *Res:* Physiology of parasitism; microbial genetics; hop diseases; verticillium diseases; alfalfa management; hop breeding; verticillium physiology. *Mailing Add:* Parma Res & Ext Ctr 29603 Univ Idaho Lane Parma ID 83660

ROMANO, ALBERT, MATHEMATICAL STATISTICS. *Current Pos:* assoc prof, 63-78, PROF MATH, SAN DIEGO STATE UNIV, 78- *Personal Data:* b New York, NY, Feb 2, 27. *Educ:* Brooklyn Col, BA, 50; Wash Univ, St Louis, MA, 54; Va Polytech Univ, PhD, 61. *Prof Exp:* Asst prof math, Ariz State Univ, 58-60; staff statistician, Semiconductor Prod Div, Motorola Inc, 60-63; NSF res assoc, Nat Bur Stand, 62-63. *Mem:* AAAS; Am Math Soc; Am Statist Soc; Inst Math Statist. *Res:* Evolution and population genetics; statistical models. *Mailing Add:* 5697 Amaro Dr San Diego CA 92124

ROMANO, ANTONIO HAROLD, MICROBIOLOGY. *Current Pos:* head microbiol sect, 74-84, dean, Col Liberal Arts & Scis, 92-95, PROF BIOL, UNIV CONN, STORRS, 71- *Personal Data:* b Penns Grove, NJ, Mar 6, 29; m 53, Marjorie J Backus; c Stephen, James & Charles. *Educ:* Rutgers Univ, BS, 49, PhD(microbiol), 52. *Prof Exp:* Assoc microbiologist, Ortho Res Found Div, Johnson & Johnson, 52-54; instr microbial biochem, Rutgers Univ, 54-56; from sr asst scientist to sr scientist, Taft Sanit Eng Ctr, USPHS, Ohio, 56-59; from assoc prof to prof bact, Univ Cincinnati, 59-71. *Concurrent Pos:* NSF sr fel, Univ Leicester, 67-68; vis fel, Cambridge Univ, 79; prog dir cell biol, NSF, 84-85. *Mem:* AAAS; Am Soc Microbiol. *Res:* Microbial physiology and biochemistry; sugar uptake and metabolism in microorganisms. *Mailing Add:* Dept Molecular Biol-Univ Conn U-125 75 N Eagleville Rd Storrs CT 06269. *Fax:* 860-486-4331; *E-Mail:* romano@uconnvm.uconn.edu

ROMANO, PAULA JOSEPHINE, IMMUNOLOGY, MICROBIOLOGY. *Current Pos:* DIR, HISTOCOMPATIBILITY LAB, MILTON S HERSHEY MED CTR, 81- *Personal Data:* b Rochester, NY, Mar 19, 40. *Educ:* Cath Univ Am, AB, 61; Duke Univ, PhD(microbiol, immunol), 74. *Prof Exp:* USPHS fel immunol, Nat Cancer Inst, 75-76; instr, Georgetown Univ, 76-79; dir, Histocompatibility Lab, Found Blood Res, 79-81. *Mem:* Am Soc Histocompatibility & Immunogenetics; Am Soc Microbiol; AAAS; Transplantation Soc. *Res:* Understanding of mechanisms of cellular immune reactions; role of histocompatibility cell surface antigens in disease processes. *Mailing Add:* HLA Labs 500 University Dr Hershey PA 17033

ROMANO, SALVATORE JAMES, ANALYTICAL CHEMISTRY. *Current Pos:* VPRES CORP QUAL ANALYSIS, JOHNSON & JOHNSON INC, 84- *Personal Data:* b Highland Park, NJ, June 2, 41; m 63; c 2. *Educ:* Mt St Mary's Col, BS, 63; Rutgers Univ, PhD(analytical chem), 68. *Prof Exp:* Res chemist, Colgate-Palmolive Res Lab, 68-71; prin scientist & supvr, Ethicon Inc, 71-74, mgr, 74-78, assoc dir res, 78-79; vpres res & develop, Devro Inc, 79-82; dir qual anal, Ortho Pharm, 81-84. *Mem:* Am Chem Soc; Sigma Xi; Am Soc Qual Control. *Res:* Chemical separations, particularly optical isomer separations; high pressure liquid chromatography; pharmaceutical and biotechnical quality control; quality assurance. *Mailing Add:* 1595 Kearney Dr North Brunswick NJ 08902-3012

ROMANOFF, ELIJAH BRAVMAN, PHYSIOLOGY. *Current Pos:* CONSULT. *Personal Data:* b Clinton, Mass, Feb 15, 13; m 42. *Educ:* Worcester Polytech Inst, BS, 34, MS, 36; Tufts Univ, PhD, 52. *Prof Exp:* Jr chemist, Commonwealth Mass, 35-38; jr chemist, Worcester State Hosp, 38-40, asst chemist, 40-41, dir lab, 46-47; res assoc, Worcester Found Exp Biol, 47-60, scientist, 60-62, assoc dir training prog physiol reproduction, 62-68, sr scientist, 62-69; prog dir metab biol, NSF, 69- *Concurrent Pos:* Chemist, Texol Chem Works, 38-41; instr, Univ Exten, State Dept Educ, Mass, 38-42; vis prof, Med Sch, Univ PR, 57-60; lectr, Brown Univ, 65-69. *Mem:* AAAS; Am Physiol Soc; NY Acad Sci; Brit Soc Endocrinol. *Res:* Steroid metabolism; reproduction. *Mailing Add:* 70 Prospect St Shrewsbury MA 01545-2045

ROMANOVICZ, DWIGHT KEITH, CELL BIOLOGY, ENZYME CYTOCHEMISTRY. *Current Pos:* asst prof, 78-82, ASSOC PROF BIOL, WGA COL, 82- *Personal Data:* b Newport News, Va, Sept 1, 48. *Educ:* Dickinson Col, BS, 70; Univ NC, Chapel Hill, PhD(bot), 75. *Prof Exp:* Res assoc cytochem, Dent Res Ctr, Sch Dent, Univ NC, 75-78. *Mem:* Am Soc Cell Biol; Electromicro Soc Am; Am Soc Plant Physiol; Phycological Soc Am. *Res:* Cytochemical localization of plant carbonic anhydrase; ultrastructural investigation of cell wall formation in algae; identification and distribution of scaled algae. *Mailing Add:* Dept Biol WGa Col 1601 Maple St Carrollton GA 30118-0001. *Fax:* 706-836-6720

ROMANOVSKY, ANDREJ ALEXANDROVICH, THERMOPHYSIOLOGY, PATHOPHYSIOLOGY. *Current Pos:* ASSOC SCIENTIST & DIR, THERMOREG LAB, LEGACY RES, HOLLADAY PARK MED CTR, 94- *Personal Data:* b Leningrad, USSR, Apr 9, 61; Belarus citizen. *Educ:* First Leningrad Med Inst, MD, 84; Inst Physiol, Minsk, PhD(physiol), 89. *Prof Exp:* Clin trainee, Inst Exp Med, St Petersburg, Russia, 84-86; jr res scientist, Inst Physiol, Minsk, Belarus, 89-90, res scientist, 90-91, sr res scientist, 91-94. *Concurrent Pos:* Vis scientist, Univ Med Sch, Pecs, Hungary, 88 & 90; postdoctoral res assoc & instr, Dept Physiol, Univ Tenn, 91-94; vis prof, Univ Kanazawa Med Sch, Japan, 94; J F Perkins Jr Mem fel, Am Physiol Soc, 94; sr res scientist, Inst Physiol, Minsk, 94- *Mem:* Soc Neurosci; Am Physiol Soc; Int Entotoxin Soc; Belarusian Physiol Soc. *Res:* Investigation of the mechanisms of body temperature control in health and disease. *Mailing Add:* Thermoreg Lab Legacy Res Holladay Park Med Ctr 1225 Second Ave Portland OR 97208. *Fax:* 503-413-4942; *E-Mail:* romanovs@ohsu.edu, aromanov@lhs.org

ROMANOW, LOUISE ROZAK, VECTOR-PLANT VIRUS RELATIONSHIPS, PLANT RESISTANCE. *Personal Data:* b Boston, Mass, July 15, 50; m 82, William H Swallow. *Educ:* Univ Mass, Amherst, BS, 76; NC State Univ, MS, 80, PhD(entom), 84. *Prof Exp:* Teaching asst ecol, Dept Zool, NC State Univ, 76-77, res asst, Dept Entom, 77-84; ed prog develop, NC Exten Serv, 81-82; vis fel, Inst Hort Plant Breeding, Neth, 84-85. *Mem:* Entom Soc Am; Am Phytopath Soc. *Res:* Relationship of aphid vectors to nonpersistently transmitted viruses and their plant hosts; effects of plant resistance to vector and virus epidemiology; modeling virus epidemiology based on vector movement and characteristics. *Mailing Add:* 1010 Reedy Creek Rd Cary NC 21513. *E-Mail:* iromanow@mindspring.com

ROMANOWICZ, BARBARA ANNA, SEISMOLOGY, GEODYNAMICS. *Current Pos:* PROF GEOPHYS & DIR, SEISMOL LAB, UNIV CALIF, BERKELEY, 91- *Personal Data:* b Suresnes, France, Apr 5, 50; m 79, Mark J Jonikas; c Martin Jonikas & Magdalena Jonikas. *Educ:* France Ministry Educ, agregation, 73; Harvard Univ, MS, 75; Univ Paris, doctorat, astron, 75, doctorat D'etat geophys, 79. *Honors & Awards:* Medaille D'Argent, Nat Ctr Sci Res, France, 92. *Prof Exp:* Sr researcher, Nat Ctr Sci Res, 78-86, dir, Geoscope Prog, 81-90, dir res, 86-90. *Mem:* Fel Am Geophys Union; Seismol Soc Am. *Res:* Global seismology: study of Earth's deep internal structure using normal mode and surface wave data; relation to geodynamics; study of earthquake source processses and scaling properties; deep structures in regions such as Tibet. *Mailing Add:* Univ Calif 475 McCone Hall Berkeley CA 94720

ROMANOWSKI, CHRISTOPHER ANDREW, ALUMINUM ALLOY PROCESSING. *Current Pos:* VPRES TECHNOL, FATA HUNTER INC, 95- *Personal Data:* b London, Eng, July 23, 53. *Educ:* Univ Surrey, Eng, BS Hons, 75, PhD (metall), 81. *Prof Exp:* Res assoc mat eng, Drexel Univ, 79-80, asst prof, 80-82; res engr, Pechiney/Howmet, 82-83; tech mgr, Alumax, 83-84; mgr res & develop, Hunter Eng, 84-86, tech dir, 86-88, sales mgr, 88-95. *Concurrent Pos:* Consult, Alcoa Tech Ctr, 79-82. *Mem:* Metall Soc; Am Soc Metals; Inst Metallurgists. *Res:* Melting, degassing, filtration, continuous strip casting, rolling and annealing of aluminum alloys; development and application of strip cast and powder metallurgy aluminum alloys; design and engineering of aluminum plants. *Mailing Add:* Fata Hunter Inc PO Box 5677 Riverside CA 92517. *Fax:* 909-653-5260

ROMANOWSKI, ROBERT DAVID, BIOCHEMISTRY. *Current Pos:* STAFF MEM, LIVESTOCK POULTRY SCI INST, 88- *Personal Data:* b Chicago, Ill, Oct 4, 31; m 51, 74; c 7. *Educ:* SDak State Univ, BS, 56, MS, 57; Purdue Univ, PhD(biochem), 61. *Prof Exp:* Asst, Purdue Univ, 57-61; asst prof vet biochem, Vet Res Lab, Mont State Univ, 61-66; res chemist, Beltsville Parasitol Lab, USDA, 66-72, res chemist, Animal Parasitol Inst, Nat Agr Res Ctr, 72-88. *Mem:* Am Soc Parasitol. *Res:* Disease resistance of plants; urinary calculi; biochemistry, enzymology and immunology of nematodes; separation and isolation of antigens from nematodes. *Mailing Add:* 703 Northwest Dr Silver Spring MD 20901

ROMANOWSKI, THOMAS ANDREW, experimental high energy physics, for more information see previous edition

ROMANS, JAMES BOND, PHYSICAL CHEMISTRY. *Current Pos:* RETIRED. *Personal Data:* b Monroe, Iowa, Jan 24, 14; m 39, Dorothy Rose; c James R, William R & Larry D. *Educ:* Cent Col, Iowa, BA, 35. *Prof Exp:* Teacher sci, Beaver Consol Sch, Iowa, 36-38; chemist oils & fuels, Nat Bur Stand, 38-46; chemist phys & surface chem, Naval Res Lab, Dept Navy, 46-80; consult, fire suppressive fluids, chem agent protection & fire extinguishants, 80-88. *Mem:* Am Chem Soc; Sigma Xi; AAAS. *Res:* Surface analysis; wettability of surfaces; lubricants; dielectric liquids; friction and wear; fatigue resistance of reinforced plastics in water; desensitization of explosives; frictional electrification of polymers; gas adsorption properties of charcoal; fire suppressive fluids; chemical agent protection; powder-type fire extinguishing agents. *Mailing Add:* 9111 Louis Ave Silver Spring MD 20910

ROMANS, JOHN RICHARD, ANIMAL SCIENCE, BIOCHEMISTRY. *Current Pos:* MEM STAFF, ANIMAL SCI DEPT, SDAK STATE UNIV. *Personal Data:* b Montevideo, Minn, Mar 4, 33; m 56; c 4. *Educ:* Iowa State Univ, BS, 55; SDak State Univ, MS, 64, PhD(animal sci), 67. *Prof Exp:* Asst mgr agr serv dept, John Morrell & Co, 55-56, hog buyer, 58-62; res asst meat & animal sci, SDak State Univ, 62-67; asst prof animal sci, Univ Ill, Urbana, 67-73, assoc prof, 73- *Mem:* Am Soc Animal Sci; Am Meat Sci Asn; Inst Food Technol. *Res:* Increase efficiency of high-quality nutritious food production via meat animals. *Mailing Add:* Dept Animal Range Sci SDak State Univ PO Box 2170 Brookings SD 57007

ROMANS, ROBERT CHARLES, BOTANY. *Current Pos:* asst prof, 69-75, ASSOC PROF BIOL, BOWLING GREEN STATE UNIV, 75- *Personal Data:* b Hawthorne, Wis, Oct 12, 37; m 63; c 1. *Educ:* Univ Wis-Superior, BS, 65, MST, 66; Ariz State Univ, PhD(bot), 69. *Prof Exp:* Asst biol, Univ Wis-Superior, 65-66. *Concurrent Pos:* Ohio Biol Surv grant, 71-72. *Mem:* Bot Soc Am; Am Asn Stratig Palynologists; Int Soc Plant Morphologists. *Res:* Palynology; paleobotany; plant anatomy and morphology. *Mailing Add:* Dept Biol Sci Bowling Green State Univ 1001 E Wooster St Bowling Green OH 43403-0001

ROMANS, ROBERT GORDON, protein chemistry, for more information see previous edition

ROMANS-HESS, ALICE YVONNE, BIOPHYSICAL CHEMISTRY. *Current Pos:* res scientist biochem, Kimberly-Clark Corp, 77-81, prod develop scientist, 81-85, sr res scientist advan prod develop, 85-89, assoc res fel, 89-97, RES FEL, KIMBERLY-CLARK CORP, 97- *Personal Data:* b Wayne, WVa, June 27, 47; m, Gregory J Hess. *Educ:* Marshall Univ, BS, 69; Duke Univ, PhD(biophys chem), 74. *Prof Exp:* Instr biochem, Med Ctr, Univ Ala, 74-77. *Mem:* Am Chem Soc; Biophys Soc; Sigma Xi. *Res:* Biological membranes and protein-lipid interactions; plasma lipoproteins; physical chemistry of biological macromolecules; absorbency; superabsorbents; product development; creativity; visioning. *Mailing Add:* Kimberly-Clark Corp PO Box 999 Neenah WI 54957-0999

ROMANSKY, MONROE JAMES, INTERNAL MEDICINE. *Current Pos:* assoc prof, Sch Med, George Washington Univ, 46-57, chief, Univ Med Div, DC Gen Hosp, 50-69, prof med, 57-91, EMER PROF, SCH MED, GEORGE WASHINGTON UNIV, 91- *Personal Data:* b Hartford, Conn, Mar 16, 11; m 43, Evelyn M Lackman; c Stephen H, Gerald H, Michael A & Richard C. *Educ:* Univ Maine, AB, 33; Univ Rochester, MD, 37. *Prof Exp:* Intern med, Strong Mem Hosp, NY, 37-38, asst resident, 38-39, chief resident, 40-41; Gleason res fel, Univ Rochester, 39-40, instr med, Off Sci Res & Develop Proj, 41-42. *Concurrent Pos:* Consult, USPHS, 46-72, Walter Reed Army Hosp & Cent Off, US Vet Admin, 46-78, Clin Ctr, NIH, 53-72 & Wash Hosp Ctr, 58-78. *Mem:* Am Fedn Clin Res; Soc Med Consults Armed Forces; Soc Exp Biol & Med; Am Soc Microbiol; Infectious Dis Soc Am; AMA; Am Col Physicians. *Res:* Infectious diseases; chemotherapy and antibiotics; immunology; nutrition in obesity. *Mailing Add:* 5600 Wisconsin Ave Chevy Chase MD 20815

ROMARY, JOHN KIRK, PHYSICAL CHEMISTRY. *Current Pos:* prof chem & chmn dept, 68-94, EMER PROF CHEM, UNIV WIS, WHITEWATER, 94- *Personal Data:* b Topeka, Kans, July 26, 34; div; c David, Douglas & Dana. *Educ:* Washburn Univ, BS, 56; Kans State Univ, PhD(phys chem), 61. *Prof Exp:* Asst prof phys chem, Univ Nev, 61-63; from asst prof to assoc prof, Washburn Univ, 63-67; asst prog dir, NSF, 67-68. *Concurrent Pos:* Mem, Gov Comn Educ, State Wis, 69-70. *Mem:* Am Chem Soc; Royal Soc Chem; Am Inst Chemists; NY Acad Sci; Sigma Xi. *Res:* Polarographic, potentiometric, thermodynamic and calorimetric studies of coordination compound formation; synthesis of pyridyl polyamine ligands; development of computer programs for analysis of coordination data. *Mailing Add:* Dept Chem Univ Wis 800 W Main St Whitewater WI 53190

ROMBACH, HANS DIETER, SOFTWARE MEASUREMENT, DEVELOPMENT PROCESS MODELING. *Current Pos:* vis asst prof, 84-86, ASST PROF SOFTWARE ENG, COMPUTER SCI DEPT, UNIV MD, COLLEGE PARK, 86-, ASST PROF SOFTWARE ENG, UMIACS, 86- *Personal Data:* b Herbolzheim, Ger, June 6, 53; m 78; c 2. *Educ:* Univ Karlsvuhe, Ger, MS, 78; Univ Kaiserslautern, Ger, PhD(computer sci), 84. *Prof Exp:* Res scientist, Nuclear Res Ctr, Karlsvuhe, Ger, 78-79; res assoc software eng, Computer Sci Dept, Univ Kaiserslautern, Ger, 79-84. *Concurrent Pos:* Prin investr, SEL NASA/Goddard, Md, 86-, NSF, Wash, DC, 90-; vis researcher, Software Eng Inst, Carnegie Mellon Univ, 87-88; consult, Inst Defense Anal, Fairfax Va & Europ projs, 88-, Northrop Corp, Calif, 89-; lectr, DEC Ger, 89-; NSF presidential young investr award res/teaching software eng, 90. *Mem:* Asn Comput Mach; Inst Elec & Electronics Engrs Computer Soc. *Res:* Formalization of software processes; integration of software measurement; exploration of effective mechanisms for learning and reuse of all kinds of software related experience. *Mailing Add:* Fb Infor Univ Kaiserlautern Postfach 3049 67653 Kaiserslautern Germany

ROMBACH, LOUIS, ORGANIC CHEMISTRY. *Current Pos:* RETIRED. *Personal Data:* b Cincinnati, Ohio, Apr 4, 26. *Educ:* Xavier Univ, BS, 48, MS, 49; Univ Cincinnati, PhD(org chem), 53; Temple Univ, JD, 69. *Prof Exp:* Res scientist & atty, E I DuPont de Nemours, 53-91. *Mem:* Am Chem Soc; fel Am Inst Chemists. *Mailing Add:* 201 N Pembrey Dr Wilmington DE 19803-2005

ROMBEAU, JOHN LEE, OTHER MEDICAL & HEALTH SCIENCES, COLON-RECTAL SURGERY, TREATMENT OF CROHNS DISEASE. *Current Pos:* asst prof, 79-86, SUREGON, HOSP UNIV PA, 79-; ASSOC PROF SURG, 86- *Personal Data:* b Los Angeles, Calif, May 8, 39; m 70; c 2. *Educ:* La Sierra Col, Calif, BA, 62; Loma Linda Univ, MD, 67. *Honors & Awards:* Vol Achievement Award, Crohn's & Colitis Found, 92. *Prof Exp:* Asst prof surg, Univ Calif, Davis, 77-79. *Concurrent Pos:* Doctor surg & nutrit, Martinez Vet Admin Med Ctr, Calif, 77-79; doctor surg & nutrit support, Philadelphia Vet Admin Med Ctr, 79-; ed-in-chief, J Am Soc Parenteral & Enteral Nutrit. *Mem:* Fel Am Col Surgeons; Am Soc Clin Nutrit; Am Soc Parenteral & Enteral Nutrit (vpres, 86, pres, 88); Asn Acad Surg; Soc Surg Alimentary Tract; Am Soc Colon & Rectal Surg; Am Inst Nutrit; Soc Univ Surgeons. *Mailing Add:* Dept Surg Silverstein Pav 4th Hosp Univ Pa 3400 Spruce St Philadelphia PA 19104-4274. *Fax:* 215-349-5070

ROMBERGER, JOHN ALBERT, PLANT PHYSIOLOGY, PLANT ANATOMY. *Current Pos:* RETIRED. *Personal Data:* b Northumberland Co, Pa, Dec 25, 25; m 51, Margery Davis; c Ann I (Meyer) & Daniel D. *Educ:* Swarthmore Col, BA, 51; Pa State Univ, MS, 53; Univ Mich, PhD(bot), 58. *Prof Exp:* Res fel plant physiol, Calif Inst Technol, 58-59; plant physiologist, US Forest Serv, 59-82. *Concurrent Pos:* Vis scholar, Univ Silesia, Poland, 81, 83; independent scholar-writer, 82- *Mem:* Am Soc Plant Physiol; Bot Soc Am; fel AAAS; Soc Hist Technol. *Res:* Tree physiology; growth and development in woody plants; developmental biology; morphogenesis; wood anatomy; morphogenesis and development in higher organisms. *Mailing Add:* 320 Tenn Ave Elizabethville PA 17023-9640

ROMBERGER, KARL ARTHUR, ANALYTICAL CHEMISTRY, PHYSICAL CHEMISTRY. *Current Pos:* RES ASSOC, CABOT CORP, 79- *Personal Data:* b Orwin, Pa, Sept 13, 34; m 58; c 4. *Educ:* Lebanon Valley Col, BS, 56; Pa State Univ, PhD(analytical chem), 67. *Prof Exp:* Res chemist, Oak Ridge Nat Lab, 64-70; group leader chem, Kawecki-Berylco Industs, 70-79. *Mem:* AAAS; Am Chem Soc; Sigma Xi. *Res:* Tantalum and columbium extraction, purification and metallurgy. *Mailing Add:* 100 Martin Ave Gilbertsville PA 19525

ROMBERGER, SAMUEL B, GEOCHEMISTRY, ECONOMIC GEOLOGY. *Current Pos:* MEM FAC, COLO SCH MINES, 75- *Personal Data:* b Harrisburg, Pa, June 12, 39; m 66; c 1. *Educ:* Pa State Univ, BS, 62, PhD(geochem), 68. *Prof Exp:* Asst prof geol, Mich State Univ, 66-69 & Univ Wis-Madison, 69-75. *Concurrent Pos:* Assoc prof geol, Off Water Resources grants, 66-69. *Mem:* Mineral Soc Am; Soc Econ Geologists; Geol Soc Am; Sigma Xi. Mineral Asn Can. *Res:* Determination of the nature, particularly the chemistry, of the processes responsible for the formation of metallic, and uranium ore deposits. *Mailing Add:* Chem Colo Sch Mines 1500 Illinois St Golden CO 80401-1887

ROME, DORIS SPECTOR, cytology, pathology, for more information see previous edition

ROME, JAMES ALAN, PLASMA PHYSICS, COMPUTER GRAPHICS. *Current Pos:* PHYSICIST, FUSION ENERGY DIV, OAK RIDGE NAT LAB, 71-; PRES, SCI ENDEAVORS CORP, KINGSTON, TENN, 84- *Personal Data:* b New York, NY, Oct 12, 42. *Educ:* Mass Inst Technol, SB, 65, SM, 67, ScD, 71. *Prof Exp:* Instr elec eng, Mass Inst Technol, 67-71. *Concurrent Pos:* Assoc ed, Physics Fluids, 79-82. *Mem:* Fel Phys Soc; Inst Elec & Electronics Engrs. *Res:* Particle containment in magnetic fusion devices; optimization of magnetic configurations; theory of neutral beam heating of tokamaks; security of unix computer systems. *Mailing Add:* 22 Mona Lane Oak Ridge TN 37830

ROME, LEONARD H, BIOCHEMISTRY, NEUROSCIENCES. *Current Pos:* from asst prof to assoc prof, 79-88, PROF BIOL CHEM, SCH MED, UNIV CALIF, LOS ANGELES, 88-, VCHMN, BIOL CHEM, 89- *Personal Data:* b Youngstown, Ohio, Feb 2, 49; m 77; c 2. *Educ:* Univ Mich, BS, 72, MS, 73, PhD(biol chem), 75. *Prof Exp:* Staff fel, NIH, 75-79. *Mem:* Am Soc Biochem & Molecular Biol; Am Soc Cell Biol; Am Soc Neurochemistry; AAAS. *Res:* Myelination in the central nervous system utilizing primary cultures of oligodendroglial cells; structure & function of vaults, novel ribonucleoprotein found in cytoplasm; macromolecular transport-organelle biogenesis. *Mailing Add:* Dept Biol Chem 33-257 CHS Sch Med Univ Calif Los Angeles Los Angeles CA 90024-1737. *Fax:* 310-206-5272

ROME, MARTIN, PHYSICAL CHEMISTRY. *Current Pos:* vpres & gen mgr, EMR DIV, 68-71, VPRES & GEN MGR, EMR PHOTOELEC, WESTON INSTRUMENTS, INC, 71- *Personal Data:* b New York, NY, June 20, 25; m 50; c 2. *Educ:* Brooklyn Col, AB, 47; Columbia Univ, AM, 49; Polytech Inst Brooklyn, PhD(phys chem), 51. *Prof Exp:* Sr engr, Electronic Tube Div, Westinghouse Elec Corp, 51-55; chief engr, Photosensitive Tube Div, Machlett Labs, Inc, 55-63; dir res & develop, Electro-Mech Res, Inc, 63-68. *Mem:* AAAS; Optical Soc Am; Inst Elec & Electronics Engrs. *Res:* Photoelectric television camera tubes; semiconductor photoemissive and photoconducting layers; vacuum technology; x-ray image intensifying devices; ultraviolet and visible image converter and intensifier tubes; multiplier phototubes. *Mailing Add:* 55 Linwood Circle Princeton NJ 08540

ROMEO, JOHN THOMAS, PLANT CHEMISTRY, CHEMICAL ECOLOGY. *Current Pos:* asst prof, Univ SFla, 77-79, assoc prof, 80-88, grad dir, 91-92, PROF BIOL, UNIV SFLA, TAMPA, 88-, CHMN, 92- *Personal Data:* b Plattsburgh, NY, July 4, 40; m 66; c 1. *Educ:* Hamilton Col, AB, 62; Univ Idaho, MS, 70; Univ Tex, Austin, PhD(bot), 73. *Prof Exp:* Teacher biol, East Syracuse-Minoa High Sch, 66-69; res assoc phytochem, Inst Biomed Res, Univ Tex, 73; chemist, Tex Air Control Bd, 74; asst prof biol, Oakland Univ, 74-77. *Concurrent Pos:* NSF res grant, 80-86; vis res scientist, Kew Gardens, Eng, 86-87; hon res fel, Birkbeck Col, Univ London, 86-87; ed-in-chief, Recent Advan Phytochem, 94-; co-ed, J Chem Ecol, 97- *Mem:* Sigma Xi; Phytochem Soc NAm (treas, 78-82, pres, 87-88); Int Soc Chem Ecol (secy, 90-); Latin Am Bot Soc. *Res:* Non-protein amino acids, and alkaloids of tropical legumes, application to taxonomic and ecological problems. *Mailing Add:* Dept Biol Univ SFla Lif 136 Tampa FL 33620. *Fax:* 813-974-3263; *E-Mail:* romeo@chuma.cas.usf.edu

ROMEO, TONY, MICROBIOLOGY. *Current Pos:* ASSOC PROF, DEPT MICROBIOL & IMMUNOL, UNIV NTEX HEALTH SCI CTR, FT WORTH, 89- *Personal Data:* b Batesville, Ark, Dec 20, 56; m 83, Lori A Dinello. *Educ:* Univ Fla, BS, 79, MS, 81, PhD(microbiol), 86. *Prof Exp:* Fel, Dept Biochem, Mich State Univ, 86-89. *Concurrent Pos:* Adj assoc prof, Dept Biochem & Molecular Biol, Univ NTex Health Sci Ctr, Ft Worth, 89- *Mem:* Am Soc Microbiol; Am Soc Biochem & Molecular Biol; AAAS; RNA Soc. *Res:* Biochemical, macromolecular and cellular processes that are unique to the stationary phase in bacteria; study of glycogen biosynthesis genes of Escherichia coli as a model system to identify novel regulatory factors; author of 25 technical publications. *Mailing Add:* Dept Microbiol Univ NTex Health Sci Ctr Ft Worth 3500 Camp Bowie Blvd Ft Worth TX 76107. *Fax:* 817-735-2118

ROMER, ALFRED, PHYSICS, SCIENCE EDUCATION. *Current Pos:* from assoc prof to prof, 46-73, EMER PROF PHYSICS, ST LAWRENCE UNIV, 73- *Personal Data:* b Pleasantville, NY, Aug 9, 06; m 33, Emily G Korstad; c Henry F, Anne R & William S. *Educ:* Williams Col, BA, 28; Calif Inst Technol, PhD(physics), 35. *Hon Degrees:* ScD, St Lawrence Univ, 79. *Prof Exp:* Asst chem, Williams Col, 28-29; from asst prof to prof physics, Whittier Col, 33-43; assoc prof, Vassar Col, 43-46. *Concurrent Pos:* Fel, Harvard Univ, 40-41; vis fel, Princeton Univ, 55-56; actg ed, Am J Physics, 62; vis staff mem, Educ Serv Inc, 62-63; consult, AID & Univ Grants Comn, India, 64 & 65; vis prof hist, Univ Calif, Santa Barbara, 75. *Mem:* Fel AAAS; fel Am Phys Soc; Hist Sci Soc; Soc Hist Technol; Am Asn Physics Teachers (secy, 66-70). *Res:* History of physics; history of technology. *Mailing Add:* Dept Physics St Lawrence Univ Canton NY 13617. *Fax:* 315-379-7421; *E-Mail:* arom@ccmaillink.stlawu.edu

ROMER, ROBERT HORTON, LOW TEMPERATURE PHYSICS. *Current Pos:* From instr to assoc prof, 55-66, PROF PHYSICS, AMHERST COL, 66- *Personal Data:* b Chicago, Ill, Apr 15, 31; m 94, Betty Sternberg; c Evan, David & Theodore. *Educ:* Amherst Col, BA, 52; Princeton Univ, PhD(physics), 55. *Concurrent Pos:* Res assoc, Duke Univ, 58-59; vis physicist, Brookhaven Nat Lab, 63-; NSF fel, Univ Grenoble, 64-65; vis prof, Voorhees Col, 69-70; assoc ed, Am J Physics, 68-74, bk rev ed, 82-88, ed , 88- *Mem:* Fel AAAS; fel Am Phys Soc; Am Asn Physics Teachers. *Res:* Nuclear magnetic resonance; environmental physics; energy statistics; physics for non-scientists. *Mailing Add:* Dept Physics Amherst Col Amherst MA 01002

ROMERO, ALEJANDRO F, emissions research, internal combustion engines, for more information see previous edition

ROMERO, JACOB B, CHEMICAL & NUCLEAR ENGINEERING. *Current Pos:* mem fac, 72-80, NATURAL SCI INSTR, EVERGREEN STATE COL, 80- *Personal Data:* b Las Vegas, NMex, July 10, 32; m 61; c 2. *Educ:* Univ NMex, BS, 54; Univ Wash, MS, 57, PhD(chem eng), 59. *Prof Exp:* Res specialist, Aerospace Group, Boeing Co, Wash, 59-66; assoc prof chem & nuclear eng, Univ Idaho, 66-69; specialist engr aerospace group, Boeing Co, Wash, 69-72. *Mem:* Sigma Xi. *Res:* Fluid flow in fluidized beds; analysis of advanced nuclear reactor concepts; cryogenic fluid storage using superinsulations; transient behavior of heat pipes; lasers. *Mailing Add:* 2101 Beverly Beach Dr NW Olympia WA 98502-3429

ROMERO, JUAN CARLOS, ANIMAL PHYSIOLOGY, COMPUTER SCIENCE. *Current Pos:* assoc consult nephrol, 73-76, from asst prof to assoc prof physiol & med, 74-80, PROF PHYSIOL, MAYO SCH MED, MAYO FOUND, 81-, DIR HYPERTENSION RES LAB, 82- *Personal Data:* b Mendoza, Arg, Sept, 15, 37; US citizen; m 63; c 2. *Educ:* San Jose Col, Mendoza, Arg, BS, 55; Univ Mendoza, MD, 64. *Honors & Awards:* Sibley-Hoobler lectr, Univ Mich, 85. *Prof Exp:* Res asst physiol, Inst Path Physiol, Mendoza, 62-66; res assoc physiol, Univ Mich, 68-73. *Concurrent Pos:* Exec secy, Pan Am Coun High Blood Pressure, 76-78; estab investr, Am Heart Asn, 76-81, mem, med adv bd, Coun High Blood Pressure, 77-; mem, grant rev comt, Nat Heart, Lung & Blood Inst, NIH, 81-85; mem, extramural adv bd, dept physiol, Univ Mich, 84-; mem, adv bd rev res projs submitted to NASA, Am Inst Biol Sci, 84-85. *Mem:* Am Heart Asn; Am Fedn Clin Res; Am Inst Biol Sci; Am Physiol Soc; Am Soc Nephrology; Int Soc Hypertension. *Res:* Mechanisms by which the kidney can produce high blood pressure; identification of the hormones that control renal circulation and excretion of salt; manner in which renal circulation is altered; relationship between renal circulation and the function of the kidney to control salt equilibrium. *Mailing Add:* Dept Physiol & Biophys Mayo Med Sch Mayo Clin 200 First St SW Guggenheim Bldg Rochester MN 55905-0001. *Fax:* 507-284-8566

ROMERO-SIERRA, CESAR AURELIO, ANATOMY. *Current Pos:* assoc prof, 67-76, PROF ANAT, QUEEN'S UNIV, ONT, 76- *Personal Data:* b Madrid, Spain, Nov 29, 31; Can citizen; c 5. *Educ:* Univ Granada, BA & BSc, 49, MD, 59; Univ Zaragoza, MD, 60, DSc, 61. *Prof Exp:* Intern dermat, Univ Granada, 59; asst prof anat, Univ Zaragoza, 59-61; Swed Ministry Foreign Affairs fel, 61-62; scholar, Swed Inst, 62; NIH fel, Univ Calif, Los Angeles, 64-65; asst prof anat, Univ Ottawa, 65-67. *Concurrent Pos:* Researcher, Nat Health & Welfare, Ont, 68. *Mem:* AAAS; Am Soc Cell Biol; Can Asn Lab Animal Sci; Can Fedn Biol Socs; Pan-Am Asn Anat. *Res:* Interaction of electromagnetic fields with living organisms; a modeling of neural behavior; biomedical instrumentation. *Mailing Add:* Dept Anat Queen's Univ Kingston ON K7L 3N6 Can

ROMESBERG, FLOYD EUGENE, CHEMICAL ENGINEERING, PHYSICAL CHEMISTRY. *Current Pos:* MGR RES & DEVELOP AUTOMOBILE INTERIORS, JOHNSTOWN DIV, FINDLAY INDUSTS, 87- *Personal Data:* b Garrett, Pa, Jan 31, 27; div; c Beverly Ann, Cynthia Ann & Floyd Eric. *Educ:* Pa State Univ, BS, 49; Bucknell Univ, MS, 50; Univ Cincinnati, PhD(phys chem), 53. *Prof Exp:* Chemist, Dow Chem Co, 53-56, proj leader fibers, 56-59, group leader, 59-63, lab dir films, 63-65, asst to tech dir films res & develop, 65-78, assoc scientist foams & films prod develop, 78-86. *Mem:* Am Chem Soc. *Res:* Technology support of manufacturing and research and development for the industrial polymeric films, including polyethylene, polystyrene, saran, copolymer and multilayer and for the consumer products, including Handiwrap and Saranwrap films and Ziploc bags; product development for cellular foams, heat transfer studies, long range product development for films, foam and composites. *Mailing Add:* 9039 Mt Vernon Rd St Louisville OH 43071. *Fax:* 740-967-3147

ROMEY, WILLIAM DOWDEN, GEOLOGY, SCIENCE EDUCATION. *Current Pos:* chmn dept geol & geog, St Lawrence Univ, 71-76, prof geol, 71-93, prof & chmn geog, 83-93, EMER PROF GEOG & GEOL, ST LAWRENCE UNIV, 93- *Personal Data:* b Richmond, Ind, Oct 26, 30; m 55, Lucretia Leonard; c Catherine, Gretchen & William L. *Educ:* Ind Univ, AB, 52; Univ Calif, Berkeley, PhD(geol), 62. *Prof Exp:* From asst prof to assoc prof geol & sci teaching, Syracuse Univ, 62-69, exec dir, Earth Sci Educ Prog, 69-72. *Concurrent Pos:* Consult, Earth Sci Curriculum Proj, 63-72; vis geol scientist, Am Geol Inst, 64-72 & NY State Educ Dept, 65-69; NSF sci fac fel, Univ Oslo Geol Mus, 67-68; earth sci consult, Compton's Encycl, 71; assoc ed, Geol Soc Am Bulletin, 79-84 & J Geol Educ, 80- *Mem:* Fel AAAS; Fel Geol Soc Am; Nat Asn Geol Teachers (vpres, 71-72, pres, 72-73); Asn Am Geographers; Am Geophys Union; Can Asn Geographers. *Res:* Igneous and metamorphic petrology; structural, Precambrian and general field geology; humanistic learning theory and human potential; regional geography; volcanology and natural hazards. *Mailing Add:* PO Box 294 East Orleans MA 02643. *Fax:* 508-255-2301

ROMICK, GERALD J, AERONOMY. *Current Pos:* SR RES SCIENTIST, APPL PHYSICS LAB, JOHNS HOPKINS UNIV, 90- *Personal Data:* b Ennis, Tex, Jan 26, 32; m 54, Marcia Rosten; c Joan, Jay, Carl, Mark, Claire & Michael. *Educ:* Univ Alaska, BS, 52, PhD(geophys), 64; Univ Calif, Los Angeles, MS, 54. *Prof Exp:* Spectroscopist, US Naval Ord Lab, Calif, 54-56; res asst auroral studies, Geophys Inst, Univ Alaska, 56-58, asst geophysicist, 58-64, from asst prof to prof, 64-82, emer prof geophys, 84; sr res consult, KIA Consults, 82-88; aeronomy prog dir, NSF, 88-90. *Concurrent Pos:* Consult, Lockheed Missiles & Space Co, 66-67 & Appl Physics Lab, Johns Hopkins Univ, 86-88. *Mem:* Am Geophys Union; Int Asn Geomag & Aeronomy. *Res:* Physics of the upper atmosphere; studies of the excitation of the constituents by energetic particle, solar radiation and chemical processes. *Mailing Add:* Johns Hopkins Rd Laurel MD 20723. *E-Mail:* gerald.romick@jhuapl.edu

ROMIG, ALTON DALE, JR, ELECTRON MICROSCOPY. *Current Pos:* ASSOC PROF METALL, NMEX INST MINING & TECHNOL, 81- *Personal Data:* b Bethlehem, Pa, Oct 6, 53. *Educ:* Lehigh Univ, BS, 75, MS, 77, PhD(metall & mat sci), 79. *Honors & Awards:* Castaing Award, Microbeam Anal Soc, 79; Burton Medal, Electron Micros Soc, 88. *Prof Exp:* Mem tech staff, AT&T Technol Inc, Sandia Nat Labs, 79- *Concurrent Pos:* Key reader, Metall Transactions, 80-; lectr, Lehigh Univ, 78-; supvr phys metall, AT&T Technol Inc, Sandia Nat Labs, 88- *Mem:* Am Inst Mining Metall & Petrol Engrs; Am Soc Metals; Microbeam Anal Soc (treas); Electron Micros Soc Am; Sigma Xi; Mat Res Soc. *Res:* Diffusion controlled phase transformations and phase equilibrium in multicomponent metallic alloy systems theoretically and by several experimental techniques including analytical electron microscopy. *Mailing Add:* 4923 Calle De Lune NE Albuquerque NM 87111-2916

ROMIG, PHILLIP RICHARDSON, EXPLORATION, SITE CHARACTERIZATION. *Current Pos:* res assoc earthquake seismol, Colo Sch Mines, 69-74, from asst prof to assoc prof, 74-82, dir, Inst Resource & Environ Geosci, 90-93, PROF, COLO SCH MINES, 82-, DEPT HEAD, 83- *Personal Data:* b Dennison, Ohio, July 24, 38; m 62, Jane E Curfman; c Phillip R & Timothy S. *Educ:* Univ Notre Dame, BS, 60; Colo Sch Mines, MS, 67, PhD(geophys), 69. *Prof Exp:* Syst engr, A C Electronics Div, Gen Motors Corp, 63-64. *Concurrent Pos:* Sr geophysicist, Westinghouse Geores Lab, 69-74; staff seismologist, E D'Appolonia Consult Engrs, 75-80; consult, Sandia Nat Labs, 80-81; distinguished lectr, Soc Explor Geophysicists, 94. *Mem:* Seismol Soc Am; Am Geophys Union; Inst Elec & Electronics Engrs; Soc Explor Geophysicists (vpres, 92-93); Earthquake Eng Res Inst. *Res:* Engineering geophysics and evaluation of seismic hazards, groundwater exploration and toxic waste mapping. *Mailing Add:* Colo Sch Mines-Geophys Golden CO 80401. *Fax:* 303-273-3478; *E-Mail:* promig@mines.edu

ROMIG, ROBERT P, CHEMICAL ENGINEERING. *Current Pos:* Assoc prof, 64-, PROF CHEM ENG, SAN JOSE STATE UNIV. *Personal Data:* b Eugene, Ore, May 1, 36; m 65; c 2. *Educ:* Ore State Univ, BS, 59, MS, 61; Carnegie Inst Technol, PhD(chem eng, fluid flow), 64. *Mem:* Am Inst Chem Engrs; Am Comput Mach. *Res:* Applied mathematics; computer simulation of chemical processes. *Mailing Add:* Dept Chem Eng San Jose State Univ 1 Washington Sq San Jose CA 95192-0082

ROMIG, ROBERT WILLIAM MCCLELLAND, PLANT PATHOLOGY. *Current Pos:* dir, wheat res, 78-79, GENETICIST & WHEAT PROJ LEADER, NORTHRUP KING & CO, 69-, VPRES RES, 79- *Personal Data:* b Cornwall, Ont, July 17, 29; m 52; c 2. *Educ:* Drew Univ, BA, 53; Purdue Univ, MS, 55, PhD(plant path), 57. *Prof Exp:* Asst geneticist, Agr Prog, Rockefeller Found, Colombia, 57-59, assoc geneticist, Chile, 59-62; res plant pathologist, USDA, Univ Minn, St Paul, 62-69. *Mem:* AAAS; Am Phytopathological Soc; Am Soc Agron. *Res:* Small grains; disease resistance; epidemiology; wheat breeding. *Mailing Add:* 8024 Telegraph Rd Minneapolis MN 55438

ROMIG, WILLIAM D(AVIS), CIVIL ENGINEERING, WATER RESOURCES. *Current Pos:* CONSULT, 72- *Personal Data:* b Victor, Iowa, Aug 19, 14; m 39; c 2. *Educ:* Univ Colo, BS, 36. *Prof Exp:* Levelman, US Bur Reclamation, Colo, 36, jr hydraul engr, State Water Conserv Bd, Colo, 37-41; from jr engr to engr, US Bur Reclamation, Colo, 41-45, Washington, DC, 45-53, planning engr, US Foreign Opers, Costa Rica, 53-55 & Washington, DC, 55-63; water resources engr, Near East & SAsia, USAID, Washington, DC, 63-72. *Concurrent Pos:* Mem, Int Comn Irrig & Drainage. *Mem:* Am Soc Civil Engrs. *Res:* Hydrology; multi-purpose water projects, including municipal water and groundwater; agricultural water management. *Mailing Add:* 100 Inca Pkwy Boulder CO 80303

ROMIG, WILLIAM ROBERT, BACTERIOLOGY. *Current Pos:* From instr to asst prof, 57-70, prof, 70-, EMER PROF BACT, UNIV CALIF, LOS ANGELES. *Personal Data:* b Hope, Ark, Mar 4, 26; m 58; c 1. *Educ:* Southwestern State Col, BA, 48; Univ Okla, MS, 54; Univ Tex, PhD(bact), 57. *Mem:* Am Soc Microbiol; Brit Soc Gen Microbiol. *Res:* Bacteriophage; radiation effects on bacteria; bacterial genetics and endospore formation; transformation. *Mailing Add:* 12024 Stanwood Dr Los Angeles CA 90066

ROMINGER, JAMES MCDONALD, SYSTEMATIC BOTANY. *Current Pos:* assoc prof bot, 63-74, prof biol, Northern Ariz Univ, 74-89, cur, Deaver Herbarium, 63-89, EMER PROF BOT, NORTHERN ARIZ UNIV, 90- *Personal Data:* b Charleston, Ill, May 19, 28; m 52; c 3. *Educ:* Eastern Ill Univ, BS, 50; Univ NMex, MS, 55; Univ Ill, PhD(bot), 59. *Prof Exp:* Asst biol, Univ NMex, 50-52; instr, Univ Jacksonville, 55-56; asst bot, Univ Ill, 56-59; instr biol, Black Hills State Col, 59-61; asst prof, Western State Col Colo, 61-63; ranger-naturalist, Grand Teton Nat Park, 63. *Concurrent Pos:* Range technician, Yellowstone Nat Park, 74 & 81. *Mem:* Sigma Xi. *Res:* Agrostology; vascular flora of northern Arizona, especially grass flora; genus Setaria in North America. *Mailing Add:* 1679 W Stevanna Way Flagstaff AZ 86001

ROMINGER, RICHARD, AGRICULTURE, PLANT BREEDING. *Current Pos:* DEP SECY, USDA. *Personal Data:* b Woodland, Calif, July 1, 27; m 95, Evelyne Rowe; c Rick, Charlie, Ruth & Bruce. *Educ:* Univ Calif, Davis, BS, 49. *Prof Exp:* Secy, Calif Dept Food & Agric. *Mailing Add:* USDA Rm 202-BA Whitten Bldg 1400 Independence Ave SW Washington DC 20250

ROMNEY, A KIMBALL, QUANTITIVE & COGNITIVE ANTHROPOLOGY. *Current Pos:* prof, 68-95, RES PROF ANTHROP, UNIV CALIF, IRVINE, 95- *Personal Data:* b Rexbury, Idaho, Aug 15, 25. *Educ:* Brigham Young Univ, BA, 47, MA, 48; Harvard Univ, PhD(anthrop), 56. *Prof Exp:* Asst prof, Univ Chicago, 55-56; asst prof, Stanford Univ, 57-60, assoc prof, 60-66; prof anthrop, Harvard Univ, 66-68. *Concurrent Pos:* Fel, Ctr Advan Study Behav Sci, Stanford Univ, 56-57. *Mem:* Nat Acad Sci; fel Am Acad Arts & Sci. *Mailing Add:* Dept Anthrop Univ Calif Irvine CA 92697. *Fax:* 714-824-4717; *E-Mail:* akromney@uci.edu

ROMNEY, CARL FREDRICK, SEISMOLOGY. *Current Pos:* VPRES, SCI APPLN INT CORP, 85-; PRIN SCIENTIST, CTR MONITORING RES. *Personal Data:* b Salt Lake City, Utah, June 5, 24; m 46, Barbara Doughty; c Kim & Carolyn. *Educ:* Calif Inst Technol, BS, 45; Univ Calif, PhD(geophys), 56. *Honors & Awards:* President's Award for Distinguished Civilian Serv; Presidential Rank Meritorious Exec for Res & Develop, 80. *Prof Exp:* Asst seismol, Univ Calif, 47-49; from seismologist to chief seismologist, Beers & Heroy, 49-54, consult, 54-55; supvry geophysicist, Air Force Off Atomic Energy, 55-58, asst tech dir, Air Force Tech Applns Ctr, 58-73; dep dir, Defense Advan Res Proj Agency, 73-75, dir, Nuclear Monitoring Res Off, 75-79, dep dir res, 79-83, dir, Ctr Seismic Studies, 83-91. *Concurrent Pos:* Mem panel seismic improv, Off Spec Asst to Pres for Sci & Tech, 59; mem US deleg, Negotiations for Threshold Nuclear Test Ban Treaty Limiting Peaceful Nuclear Explosions, Moscow, 74-75; comprehensive nuclear test ban negotiations, Geneva, 77-78. *Mem:* Soc Explor Geophys; Seismol Soc Am; Am Geophys Union. *Res:* Explosion seismology; seismic detection methods and instruments; seismicity; differences between earthquake and explosion signals. *Mailing Add:* 4105 Sulgrave Dr Alexandria VA 22309. *Fax:* 703-243-8950; *E-Mail:* romney@seismo.css.gov

ROMNEY, EVAN M, PLANT NUTRITION, SOILS. *Current Pos:* ELEMENT MGR, NEV APPL ECOL GROUP, US DEPT ENERGY, 72- *Personal Data:* b Duncan, Ariz, Jan 13, 25; m 48; c 4. *Educ:* Brigham Young Univ, BS, 50; Rutgers Univ, PhD(soils), 53. *Prof Exp:* Asst res soil scientist, Atomic Energy Proj, Univ Calif, Los Angeles, 53-60, assoc res soil scientist, 60-65, res soil scientist, Lab Biomed & Environ Sci, 66-, assoc dir, 79- *Mem:* Soil Sci Soc Am; Am Soc Agron. *Res:* Cycling of radioactive materials in plants and soils; trace elements in plants and soils; soil chemistry of rare earth elements; fate and persistence of radioactive fallout in natural environment. *Mailing Add:* 2502 E Leonora St Mesa AZ 85213

ROMNEY, SEYMOUR L, GYNECOLOGY, ONCOLOGY. *Current Pos:* prof & chair obstet & gynec, 57-72, DIR GYNEC CANCER RES, ALBERT EINSTEIN COL MED, 72- *Personal Data:* b New York, NY, June 8, 17; m 45; c 3. *Educ:* Johns Hopkins Univ, AB, 38; NY Univ, MD, 42. *Prof Exp:* Resident gynecologist, Free Hosp Women, 49; resident obstetrician, Boston Lying-in-Hosp, 50; instr gynec & obstet, Harvard Med Sch, 50-51, assoc, 52-56. *Concurrent Pos:* Consult, Nat Cancer Inst, WHO, Planned Parenthood-World Pop, NY State Family Planning Asn & Ari* Res Comn. *Mem:* AAAS; Am Gynec & Obstet Soc; Soc Gynec Invest; Am Soc Clin Cancer Res; NY Acad Sci; NY Acad Med. *Res:* Human reproduction; population and fertility regulation; medical education; nutrition and female genital tract malignancy; cancer prevention. *Mailing Add:* Albert Einstein Col Med Ullmann Bldg Rm 109 1300 Morris Park Ave Bronx NY 10461

ROMO, WILLIAM JOSEPH, PHYSICS. *Current Pos:* from asst prof to assoc prof, 70-84, PROF PHYSICS, CARLETON UNIV, 84- *Personal Data:* b Oregon City, Ore, Jan 17, 34; m 67; c 1. *Educ:* Univ Ore, 60, MS, 61; Univ Wis-Madison, PhD(theoret physics), 67. *Prof Exp:* Res assoc theoret physics, Univ Wis-Madison, 67-68 & Physics Div, Argonne Nat Lab, 68-70. *Mem:* Am Phys Soc; Can Asn Physicists; Sigma Xi. *Res:* Nuclear reaction theory; continuum shell model; resonances; nuclear structure. *Mailing Add:* Dept Physics Carleton Univ 663 Chapman Blvd Ottawa ON K1G 1T5 Can

ROMOSER, WILLIAM SHERBURNE, ENTOMOLOGY. *Current Pos:* from asst prof to assoc prof entom, 65-76, PROF ZOOL, OHIO UNIV, 76-, DIR, OHIO UNIV TROP DIS INST, 89- *Personal Data:* b Columbus, Ohio, Oct 18, 40; m 64, 73, Margaret A Meeker; c Anne, Regan & Kelley. *Educ:* Ohio State Univ, BSc, 62, PhD(entom), 64. *Prof Exp:* Res assoc entom, Ohio State Univ, 65. *Concurrent Pos:* Resident res assoc, Nat Res Coun, US Army Med Res Inst Infectious Dis, Ft Detrick, 84-85. *Mem:* Soc Vector Ecol; Entom Soc Am; Am Mosquito Control Asn; Am Soc Trop Med & Hyg. *Res:* Alimentary morphology and physiology of blood-feeding insects, particularly mosquitoes; development and metamorphosis of insects, particularly mosquitoes; arboviruses; medical entomology. *Mailing Add:* Dept Biol Sci Ohio Univ Athens OH 45701

ROMRELL, LYNN JOHN, REPRODUCTIVE BIOLOGY, HUMAN ANATOMY. *Current Pos:* from asst prof to assoc prof, 79-87, PROF ANAT & CELL BIOL & ASSOC DEAN EDUC, UNIV FLA COL MED, 87-; EXEC DIR, FLA STATE ANAT BD, 83- *Personal Data:* b Idaho Falls, Idaho, Oct 20, 44; m 80, Deanne Barlow; c Janet, David J, Jaime, Robert L, W Devin & Jacob B. *Educ:* Idaho State Univ, BS, 67; Utah State Univ, PhD(zool), 71. *Prof Exp:* NIH res fel anat, Harvard Med Sch, 71-73, instr anat & mem lab human reproduction & reproductive biol, 73-75. *Mem:* Sigma Xi; Soc Study Reproduction; Am Asn Anat; Am Soc Cell Biol; Am Asn Clin Anatomists. *Res:* Reproductive biology; cytology; cell biology; ultrastructure and function of isolated cells; genetic, biochemical and physiological factors which influence sperm development. *Mailing Add:* Dept Anat & Cell Biol Univ Fla Col Med Gainesville FL 32610. *Fax:* 904-392-3940; *E-Mail:* lynn@dean.med.ufl.edu

ROMSDAHL, MARVIN MAGNUS, SURGERY, BIOLOGY. *Current Pos:* from asst prof to assoc prof, 67-75, PROF SURG, M D ANDERSON HOSP & TUMOR INST, UNIV TEX, 75- *Personal Data:* b Havti, SDak, Apr 2, 30; m 58, 83, Virginia L McElvany; c Christine A & Laura M. *Educ:* Univ SDak, AB, 52, BS, 54; Univ Ill, MD, 56; Univ Tex, PhD(biomed sci), 68. *Honors & Awards:* Mead Johnson Award, Am Col Surg, 66-69. *Prof Exp:* Intern, Res & Educ Hosps, Univ Ill, 56-57; resident surg, Vet Admin Hosp, Hines, Ill, 57-58; clin assoc, Surg Br, Nat Cancer Inst, 58-60; resident, Res & Educ Hosps, Univ Ill, 60-63, instr, 63-64. *Concurrent Pos:* USPHS trainee, Univ Ill, 63-64; univ fel, Univ Tex, 64-67; assoc dir sci opers, Nat Large Bowel Cancer Proj, Houston, 77-79. *Mem:* AMA; Am Asn Cancer Res; Am Col Surg; Soc Surg Alimentary Tract; Am Radium Soc. *Res:* Management and surgical treatment of cancer; dissemination of cancer and metastases in experimental systems; immunology of human solid tumors; management of breast, colon and rectal cancers; sarcomas, bone and soft tissue. *Mailing Add:* 4530 Verone Bellaire TX 77401-5514. *Fax:* 713-792-0722

ROMSOS, DALE RICHARD, NUTRITION. *Current Pos:* from asst prof to assoc prof, 71-79, PROF NUTRIT, MICH STATE UNIV, 79- *Personal Data:* b Rice Lake, Wis, Nov 19, 41; m; c 1. *Educ:* Univ Wis, BS, 64; Iowa State Univ, PhD(nutrit), 70. *Honors & Awards:* Mead Johnson Res Award, Am Inst Nutrit. *Prof Exp:* Fel, Univ Ill, Urbana, 70-71. *Concurrent Pos:* NIH res career develop award. *Mem:* Brit Nutrit Soc; Soc Exp Biol & Med; Am Inst Nutrit; NY Acad Sci; Inst Food Technologists. *Res:* Lipid and carbohydrate metabolism; obesity; cardiovascular disease. *Mailing Add:* Dept Food Sci & Human Nutrit Mich State Univ 106 GM Trout Bldg East Lansing MI 48824-1224. *Fax:* 517-353-8963

ROMUALDI, JAMES P, civil engineering; deceased, see previous edition for last biography

RONA, DONNA C, coastal engineering, environmental engineering, for more information see previous edition

RONA, GEORGE, pathology; deceased, see previous edition for last biography

RONA, MEHMET, ELECTRICAL ENGINEERING. *Current Pos:* sr staff, 79-89, DIR PHYSICS, ARTHUR D LITTLE, INC, 89- *Personal Data:* b Adana, Turkey, Oct 18, 39; m 68; c 2. *Educ:* Robert Col, Istanbul, Turkey, BSc, 61; Princeton Univ, PhD(elec eng & physics), 66; Middle E Tech Univ, Dozent, 74. *Prof Exp:* Asst prof physics, Robert Col, 68-69; from asst prof to assoc prof physics, Middle E Tech Univ, 69-79. *Mem:* Am Phys Soc; Europ Phys Soc; Am Math Asn. *Res:* Physics of reduced dimensions; electron-phonon interactions; superconductivity. *Mailing Add:* Arthur D Little Inc 25 Acorn Park Boston MA 02140-2390

RONA, PETER ARNOLD, MARINE GEOLOGY, GEOPHYSICS. *Current Pos:* PROF MARINE GEOL & GEOPHYS, DEPT GEO SCI INST MARINE & COSTAL SCI, RUTGERS UNIV, 94- *Personal Data:* b Trenton, NJ, Aug 17, 34; m 74, Donna Cook; c Jessica. *Educ:* Brown Univ, AB, 56; Yale Univ, MS, 57, PhD(marine geol, geophys), 67. *Honors & Awards:* Bruce Heezen Mem lectr, NY Acad Sci, 85; US Dept Com Gold Medal, 87; Francis P Shepard Medal for Excellence Marine Geol, 86. *Prof Exp:* Explor geologist, Stand Oil Co, NJ, 57-59; res asst Hudson Labs, Columbia Univ, 60-61, marine geologist, 61-67, res assoc marine geol & geophys & prin investr, Ocean Bottom Studies, 67-69; sr geophysicist & chief scientist, Nat Oceanic & Atmospheric Admin, Trans-Atlantic Geotraverse, Atlantic Oceanog & Meteorol Labs, 69-80, prin investr, Metallogenesis Proj, 75-80, prin investr, Marine Minerals Proj, 80-84, sr res geophysicist & prin investr, Vents Prog, 84-94. *Concurrent Pos:* Consult sea floor resources, UN, 70-; adj prof, Univ Miami, 74-; mem, Vis Comt Geol Sci, Brown Univ, 74-77; trustee, Mus Sci, Miami, Fla, 74-, gov & vpres, 77-, chmn, 79-80 & trustee, Int Oceanog Found, 81-; assoc ed, Geol Soc Am, 75-82; mem, Sierra Club Adv Comt, Ocean Environ, 75-80; mem, Nat Oceanic & Atmospheric Admin, Marine Minerals Task Force, 76-84, Penrose Medal Comt, Geol Soc Am, 81-; chmn, Metallogenesis Panel, Manganese Proj, Int Geol Correlation Prog, 76-85, chmn, NATO Advan Res Inst, 80-83; tech expert sea floor resources, US Dept State, 77, adv, Tectonic Map NAm Proj, 81-85; adj prof, Fla Int Univ, 78-79; distinguished lectr, Am Asn Petrol Geologists, 83-84; mem, Vents Prog Coun, Nat Oceanic & Atmospheric Admin, 84-; assoc ed, Am Geophys Union, 88-92; lectr, Distinguished Lect Colloquium, Univ Colo, 91; mem, US-Japan Coop Prog Nat Resources Panel Submersible Res. *Mem:* Fel Geol Soc Am; Am Geophys Union; Soc Explor Geophysicists; fel AAAS; Am Asn Petrol Geologists; Soc Econ Geologists; Acoust Soc Am; Sigma Xi. *Res:* Structure and development of continental margins and ocean basins; marine environment, marine energy and mineral resources; author or coauthor of over 250 publications. *Mailing Add:* Dept Geo Sci Inst Marine & Costal Sci Rutgers Univ PO Box 231 New Brunswick NJ 08903-0231

RONALD, ALLAN ROSS, INFECTIOUS DISEASES, MICROBIOLOGY. *Current Pos:* from asst prof to assoc prof microbiol & internal med, Univ Man, 68-77, prof med microbiol & head dept, 77-85, prof internal med, 85-86, head, Dept Internal Med, 85-90, DISTINGUISHED PROF, UNIV MAN, 86-, ASSOC DEAN RES, 93- *Personal Data:* b Portage la Prairie, Man, Aug 24, 38; m 62; c 3. *Educ:* Univ Man, BSc & MD, 61; FRCP(C), 67; Am Bd Microbiol, dipl, 70. *Honors & Awards:* Thomas Parran Award, Am Venereal Dis Soc, 91; Officer, Order Can, 94. *Prof Exp:* Fel infectious dis, Univ Wash, 65-67, fel microbiol, 67-68; physician-in-chief, Health Sci Ctr, Winnipeg, 85-90. *Concurrent Pos:* Head infectious dis, St Boniface Hosp, 91-95. *Mem:* Fel Am Col Physicians; Infectious Dis Soc Am; Can Soc Clin Invest; Am Soc Clin Invest; Asn Am Physicians; Int Soc Infectious Dis. *Res:* Pathogenesis of recurrent urinary infection; antimicrobial susceptibility testing and resistance; chancroid, and hemophilus ducreyi; international health; AIDS. *Mailing Add:* Sect Infectious Dis St Boniface Hosp 409 Tache Ave Winnipeg MB R2H 2A6 Can

RONALD, BRUCE PENDER, ORGANIC CHEMISTRY. *Current Pos:* Asst prof, 68-77, ASSOC PROF CHEM, IDAHO STATE UNIV, 77- *Personal Data:* b Chicago, Ill, Nov 22, 39; m 67. *Educ:* Portland State Col, BS, 62; Univ Wash, PhD(chem), 68. *Mem:* Am Chem Soc; Royal Soc Chem. *Res:* Carbonium ion reactions; stereochemistry of reactions in asymmetric environments; chemical kinetic applications of nuclear magnetic resonance spectrometry. *Mailing Add:* Dept Chem Idaho State Univ Box 8365 Pocatello ID 83209-8365

RONALD, KEITH, ZOOLOGY. *Current Pos:* prof zool & head dept, 64-71, DEAN COL BIOL SCI, UNIV GUELPH, 71- *Personal Data:* b Llandaff, Wales, Aug 24, 28; m 54; c 1. *Educ:* McGill Univ, BSc, 53, MSc, 56, PhD(parasitol), 58. *Honors & Awards:* Fry Medal Res, Can Soc Zoologists, 81. *Prof Exp:* Marine pathologist, Que Dept Fisheries, 54-58, sr biologist & actg dir, 58; prof parasitol, Ont Agr Col, 58-62; sr scientist, Fisheries Res Bd Can, 62-64. *Concurrent Pos:* Pres & chmn, Huntsman Marine Lab, 67-73; mem Nat Res Coun Grants Comt (Animal), 70-72; mem adv bd, Atlantic Regional Lab, Nat Res Coun, 70-72; mem, Fisheries Res Bd Can, 72-77; chmn, Sci Adv Comt, World Wildlife Fund, Can, 72-76; chmn seal group, Int Union Conserv Nature & Natural Resources, 77- *Mem:* Can Soc Zool (pres, 72); fel Royal Geog Soc; fel Inst Biol; Sigma Xi. *Mailing Add:* 70 Lyon Ave Guelph ON N1H 5C8 Can

RONALD, ROBERT CHARLES, ORGANIC CHEMISTRY. *Current Pos:* ASST PROF CHEM, WASH STATE UNIV, 74- *Personal Data:* b Blue Island, Ill, Apr 22, 44. *Educ:* Portland State Col, BS, 66; Stanford Univ, PhD(org chem), 70. *Prof Exp:* Vis prof chem, Univ Sao Paulo, 70-72; sr res chemist & sect mgr chem, Syva Res Inst, Calif, 72-74. *Concurrent Pos:* Nat Acad Sci overseas fel, 70-72. *Mem:* Am Chem Soc. *Res:* Synthetic organic chemistry; structure and synthesis of natural products and other biologically significant molecules; development of new methods and reagents for synthetic purposes. *Mailing Add:* Dept Chem Wash State Univ Pullman WA 99164-4630

RONAN, MICHAEL THOMAS, ELEMENTARY PARTICLE PHYSICS. *Current Pos:* RES ASSOC EXP HIGH ENERGY PHYSICS, LAWRENCE BERKELEY LAB, 76- *Personal Data:* b Fall River, Mass, Jan 15, 49; m 76; c 2. *Educ:* Southeastern Mass Univ, BS, 70; Northeastern Univ, MS, 73, PhD(physics), 76. *Mem:* Am Phys Soc. *Mailing Add:* Lawrence Berkeley Lab B50B-5239 Univ Calif Berkeley CA 94720

RONCA, LUCIANO BRUNO, RADAR GEOLOGY, GROUND WATER. *Current Pos:* assoc prof, 70-74, PROF GEOL, WAYNE STATE UNIV, 74- *Personal Data:* b Trieste, Italy, Apr 26, 35; US citizen; m 58, 89; c 3. *Educ:* Univ Kans, MS, 59, PhD(geol), 63. *Honors & Awards:* Mt Ronca Antarctica Award, 66. *Prof Exp:* Res assoc geochem, Univ Kans, 63-64; res scientist, Air Force Cambridge Res Labs, 64-67; scientist, Boeing Sci Res Labs, 67-70. *Concurrent Pos:* Vis scientist, Lunar Sci Inst, Houston, Vernadsky Inst Acad Sci, USSR, Univ Bern, Switz, Observ de Paris, France; exchange scientist, Acad Sci USSR-USA, 76, 79-81 & 84-85. *Mem:* AAAS; fel Geol Soc Am; Am Geophys Union; Am Polar Soc. *Res:* Thermoluminescence; radiation damage in geological material; lunar and planetary geology; geostatistics; radar interpretation; ground water. *Mailing Add:* Dept Geol Wayne State Univ 201 Old Main Detroit MI 48202-3940

RONCADORI, RONALD WAYNE, PLANT PATHOLOGY. *Current Pos:* from asst prof to assoc prof 66-80, PROF PLANT PATH, UNIV GA, 80- *Personal Data:* b Centerville, Pa, Nov 19, 35; m 59; c 3. *Educ:* Waynesburg Col, BS, 57; Univ WVa, MS, 59, PhD(plant path), 62. *Prof Exp:* Plant pathologist, US Forest Serv, 62-66. *Mem:* Am Phytopath Soc. *Res:* General plant pathology, especially tree diseases; mycorrhizae; study of shade tree and woody ornamentals diseases with emphasis on dogwood anthracose. *Mailing Add:* Dept Plant Path Univ Ga 1180 E Broad St Athens GA 30601-3040

RONCO, FRANK, JR, FOREST MANAGEMENT. *Current Pos:* CONSULT, 87- *Personal Data:* b Pueblo, Colo, Sept 23, 26; m 48; c 2. *Educ:* Colo State Univ, BS, 51, MS, 60; Duke Univ, DF, 68. *Prof Exp:* Admin forester, Rocky Mountain Forest & Range Exp Sta, US Forest Serv, USDA, 51-56, res forester, 57-86. *Mem:* Soc Am Foresters; Sigma Xi. *Res:* Artificial regeneration and silviculture of Rocky Mountain conifers; tree physiology. *Mailing Add:* 1500 Edgewood St Flagstaff AZ 86004

RONDESTVEDT, CHRISTIAN SCRIVER, JR, INDUSTRIAL ORGANIC CHEMISTRY. *Current Pos:* RETIRED. *Personal Data:* b Minneapolis, Minn, July 13, 23; m 44; c Karen & Nancy. *Educ:* Univ Minn, BS, 43; Northwestern Univ, PhD(org chem), 48. *Prof Exp:* Instr chem, Univ Mich, 47-52, asst prof, 52-56; Guggenheim fel, Univ Munich, 56-57; res chemist, E I Du Pont De Nemours & Co, 57-63, sr res chemist, 63-68, res assoc, 68-85, consult, 85-88. *Concurrent Pos:* Consult, US Rubber Co, 52-56; assoc prof, Univ Del, 60-61; counr, Am Chem Soc, 68-87. *Mem:* Am Chem Soc. *Res:* New low-cost synthesis of industrial organic chemicals, especially acid chlorides, amines, and halogenated compounds; mechanisms of organic reactions; organic sulfur compounds; olefins; free radicals; organic fluorine compounds; organometallic chemistry; polysaccharides. *Mailing Add:* 217 Waverly Rd Wilmington DE 19803-3134

RONEL, SAMUEL HANAN, BIOMEDICAL ENGINEERING. *Current Pos:* VCHMN BD, INTEFERON SCI, INC, 80- *Personal Data:* b Metz, France. *Educ:* Israel Inst Technol, BSc, 64, MSc, 66, DSc(polymers), 69. *Prof Exp:* Asst prof, Israel Inst Technol, 66-69; NIH fel, Clarkson Col Technol, 69-70; res chemist, Hydron Labs, Nat Patent Develop Corp, 70-71; group leader biomat, Hydro Med Sci, Inc, 71-74, dir res & develop, 74-75; vpres res & develop, Nat Patent Develop Corp, 75- *Mem:* Am Chem Soc; Soc Biomat; Int Soc Interferon Res; NY Acad Sci. *Res:* Biocompatible synthetic materials useful for implantation; non-thrombogenic materials for use in the vascular system; prosthetic devices; production and clinical testing of interferon-drug release clinics. *Mailing Add:* Interferon Sci Inc 783 Jersey Ave New Brunswick NJ 08901

RONEY, ROBERT K(ENNETH), ELECTRICAL ENGINEERING, SPACE SYSTEMS. *Current Pos:* RETIRED. *Personal Data:* b Newton, Iowa, Aug 5, 22; m 51, Alice L Mann; c Stephen P & Karen M Dahl. *Educ:* Univ Mo, BS, 44; Calif Inst Technol, MS, 47, PhD(elec eng), 50. *Prof Exp:* Mgr systs anal, Hughes Aircraft Co, 50-60, tech dir res & develop labs, 60-61, from assoc mgr to mgr, Space Systs Div, 61-70, asst group exec, Space & Commun Group, 70, vpres, 73-85, sr vpres, 85-88. *Concurrent Pos:* Mem, US Dept Transp Com Space Transp Adv Comt, 84-87. *Mem:* Nat Acad Eng; fel Inst Elec & Electronics Engrs. *Res:* Dynamic systems analysis and feedback control. *Mailing Add:* 1105 Georgina Ave Santa Monica CA 90402

RONGSTAD, ORRIN JAMES, WILDLIFE ECOLOGY. *Current Pos:* asst prof & wildlife exten specialist, 67-71, assoc prof, 71-78, PROF WILDLIFE ECOL, UNIV WIS-MADISON, 78- *Personal Data:* b Northfield, Wis, Apr 22, 31; m 62; c 3. *Educ:* Univ Minn, BS, 59; Univ Wis, Madison, MS, 63, PhD(wildlife ecol & zool), 65. *Prof Exp:* Fel mammal res, Univ Minn, 65-67. *Mem:* Am Soc Mammal; Wildlife Soc. *Res:* Mammalian ecology, especially hares, rabbits and deer. *Mailing Add:* 1527 Middleton St Middleton WI 53562

RONIS, MAX LEE, OTOLARYNGOLOGY. *Current Pos:* DIR OTORHINOL, ST CHRISTOPHER'S HOSP CHILDREN, 69- *Personal Data:* b May 8, 30; US citizen; m 54; c 3. *Educ:* Muhlenberg Col, BS, 52; Temple Univ, MD & MS, 56. *Prof Exp:* prof otorhinol & chmn dept, Health Sci Ctr, Temple Univ, 69- *Mem:* Am Otol Soc; Am Acad Ophthal & Otolaryngol; Am Laryngol, Rhinology & Otol Soc. *Res:* Anatomy and pathophysiology of diseases of the cochlea-vestibular apparatus. *Mailing Add:* 2106 Spruce St Philadelphia PA 19103-6504

RONKIN, R(APHAEL) R(OOSER), PHYSIOLOGY. *Current Pos:* RETIRED. *Personal Data:* b Los Angeles, Calif, July 8, 19; m 49; c 2. *Educ:* Stanford Univ, AB, 39; Univ Calif, MA, 41, PhD(zool), 49. *Prof Exp:* Biol sci, Univ Del, 49-67; sci liaison staff, New Delhi, 67-69, sci educ prog, 63-64 & 69-70, Int Progs, Nat Sci Found, 70-85. *Concurrent Pos:* Merck sr fel & guest investr, Biol Inst, Carlsberg Found, Denmark, 57-58; mem corp, Marine Biol Lab, Woods Hole. *Mem:* Fel AAAS; Soc Gen Physiol; Sigma Xi; Am Inst Biol Sci. *Res:* International cooperation in science and engineering; science education; cell biology. *Mailing Add:* 3212 McKinley St NW Washington DC 20015-1635. *E-Mail:* rronkin@cpcug.org

RONN, AVIGDOR MEIR, CHEMICAL PHYSICS, MEDICAL PHYSICS. *Current Pos:* assoc prof chem, 73-76, Broeklundian prof, 87-91, PROF CHEM, BROOKLYN COL, CITY UNIV NY, 76-; SR RES SCIENTIST, DEPT OTOLARYNGOL, LONG ISLAND JEWISH MED CTR & ALBERT EINSTEIN MED COL, 92- *Personal Data:* b Tel-Aviv, Israel, Nov 17, 38; US & Israeli citizen; m 63, Linda A Tenney; c David & Karin. *Educ:* Univ Calif, Berkeley, BSc, 63; Harvard Univ, AM, 64, PhD(phys chem), 66. *Prof Exp:* Res chemist, Nat Bur Stand, 66-68; from asst prof to assoc prof phys chem, Polytech Inst Brooklyn, 68-72. *Concurrent Pos:* Vis prof, Tel-Aviv Univ Israel, 71-72, Univ Sao Paulo, 73; Alfred P Sloan fel, 68-70 & 71-73; consult to several cos, 76-; vpres & gen mgr, LIC Indust, Inc, 79-81; Fulbright sr scholar, 83-84; exec dir, Appl Sci Inst, City Univ NY, 87-91, dir, Laser Inst, 87- *Mem:* AAAS; Am Phys Soc; Am Chem Soc; Int Soc Optical Eng; Sigma Xi; Israel Chem Soc; Am Soc Laser Surg & Med. *Res:* Double resonance and energy transfer in rotational and vibrational spectra; infrared lasers; relaxation phenomena in gas lasers; laser catalyzed chemical reactions and laser induced isotope separation; laser induced photodynamic therapy; granted 5 US patents. *Mailing Add:* 27A Bond St Great Neck NY 11021-2046

RONNINGEN, REGINALD MARTIN, NUCLEAR PHYSICS. *Current Pos:* res asst prof physics, 78-81, SPECIALIST, MICH STATE UNIV, EAST LANSING, 81- *Personal Data:* b Frederic, Wis, Aug 19, 47. *Educ:* Univ Wis-River Falls, BS, 69; Vanderbilt Univ, PhD(physics), 75. *Prof Exp:* Res assoc physics, Vanderbilt Univ & Oak Ridge Nat Lab, 74-77; res assoc physics, Max-Planck für Kernphysik, Heidelberg, 77-78. *Mem:* Sigma Xi; Am Phys Soc. *Res:* In-beam gamma ray spectroscopy, light and heavy ion Coulomb excitation, in elastic scattering. *Mailing Add:* Cyclotron Lab Mich State Univ East Lansing MI 48824

RONNINGEN, THOMAS SPOONER, AGRONOMY, CROP BREEDING. *Current Pos:* RETIRED. *Personal Data:* b Hammond, Wis, Oct 3, 18; m 45; c 3. *Educ:* Univ Wis, River Falls, BS, 39; Univ Wis, Madison, MS, 47, PhD(agron), 49. *Prof Exp:* Teacher high sch, Ind, 39-41; chemist, E I du Pont de Nemours & Co, Ind, 41-43; asst agron, Univ Wis, 46-49; from asst prof to assoc prof, Univ Md, 49-56; prin agronomist, Northeast State Agr Exp Stas, USDA, 56-63, asst to adminstr, 63-65, asst adminstr, 65-73, assoc adminr, Coop State Res Serv, 73-77, assoc dep dir coop res, Sci & Educ Admin, 77-79, dir-at-large, 79-84. *Concurrent Pos:* Partic, Fed Exec Inst, Va, 70; dir, Turkish Exec Mgt Seminar, 70-71. *Mem:* Fel AAAS; fel Am Soc Agron; Am Inst Biol Sci. *Res:* Forage breeding and management; microclimatology. *Mailing Add:* 1919 Blackbriar St Silver Spring MD 20903

RONY, PETER R(OLAND), PHYSICAL CHEMISTRY, CHEMICAL ENGINEERING. *Current Pos:* assoc prof, 71-76, PROF CHEM ENG, VA POLYTECH INST & STATE UNIV, 76- *Personal Data:* b Paris, France, June 29, 39; US citizen; m 61, Myriam; c 5. *Educ:* Calif Inst Technol, BS, 60; Univ Calif, Berkeley, PhD(chem eng), 65. *Honors & Awards:* Delos-Tektronix Award, 84. *Prof Exp:* Res specialist, Monsanto Co, 65-70; sr res engr, Exxon Res & Develop Co, 70-71. *Concurrent Pos:* Dreyfus Found Teacher-Scholar grant, 74; ed, Inst Elec & Electronics Engrs Micro, Inst Elec & Electronics Engrs Comput Soc, 83-84. *Mem:* Am Inst Chem Engrs; Am Soc Eng Educ. *Res:* Microcomputers; process instrumentation; chemical microengineering; process controls; engineering education laboratories; hardware systems. *Mailing Add:* 1501 Highland Circle Blacksburg VA 24060-5668. *Fax:* 540-231-5022; *E-Mail:* rony@utvm1.cc.vt.edu

RONZIO, ROBERT A, BIOCHEMISTRY, NUTRITION. *Current Pos:* PROF & CHAIR BASIC MED SCI, BASTYR COL NATURAL HEALTH SCI, 80-; DIR EDUC SERV, GREAT SMOKIES DIAG LAB. *Personal Data:* b Boulder, Colo, Jan 24, 38. *Educ:* Reed Col, BA, 60; Univ Calif, Berkeley, PhD(biochem), 66. *Prof Exp:* NIH fel biochem, Med Sch, Tufts Univ, 65-67; Am Cancer Soc fel, Univ Wash, 67-69; asst prof biochem, Mich State Univ, 69-74, assoc prof, 74-77. *Concurrent Pos:* USPHS res career develop award, 72-77; resource fac prof, Evergreen State Col, 80-86; consult, Diagnos-Techs, Inc, Kent, Wash, 90- *Mem:* Am Chem Soc; fel Am Inst Chemists; Sigma Xi. *Res:* Formation and function of mammalian cell membranes; clinical nutrition. *Mailing Add:* Biotics Res PO Box 36888 Houston TX 77236

ROOBOL, NORMAN R, ORGANIC CHEMISTRY, MATERIALS SCIENCE. *Current Pos:* CONSULT, INDUST PAINTING, 89- *Personal Data:* b Grand Rapids, Mich, Aug 19, 34; m 55; c 4. *Educ:* Calvin Col, BS, 58; Mich State Univ, PhD(org chem), 62. *Prof Exp:* Chemist, Shell Develop Co, 62-65; asst prof org chem, Gen Motors Inst, 65-68, assoc prof mat sci, 68-71, prof mat sci, 71-89. *Concurrent Pos:* Consult coatings appln, 79-; Rodes prof, Russelsheim, WGer; Dow fel. *Mem:* Am Inst Chemists; Soc Mfg Engrs; Soc Automotive Engrs. *Res:* paints and coatings application processes. *Mailing Add:* 507 Haddington Lane Peachtree City GA 30269

ROOD, JOSEPH LLOYD, PHYSICS. *Current Pos:* RETIRED. *Personal Data:* b May 2, 22; m 49; c 4. *Educ:* Univ Calif, AB, 43, MA, 47, PhD(physics), 48. *Prof Exp:* Asst physics, Univ Calif, 43-48; from instr to assoc prof, Univ San Francisco, 48-56; head mat physics lab, Bausch & Lomb, Inc, 56-67; prof physics, Univ Lethbridge, 67-87. *Mem:* AAAS; Am Phys Soc; Optical Soc Am; Am Ceramic Soc; Am Asn Physics Teachers. *Res:* Optical and solid state properties of materials, especially glass and other ceramics. *Mailing Add:* Box 1569 Ft MacLeod AB T0L 0Z0 Can

ROOD, ROBERT THOMAS, ASTROPHYSICS. *Current Pos:* from asst prof to assoc prof, 73-91, PROF ASTRON, UNIV VA, 91- *Personal Data:* b Raleigh, NC, Mar 30, 42; m 78; c 2. *Educ:* NC State Univ, BS, 64; Mass Inst Technol, PhD(physics), 69. *Prof Exp:* Res assoc physics, Mass Inst Technol, 69-71; res fel, Kellogg Lab, Calif Inst Technol, 71-73. *Mem:* AAAS; Am Astron Soc; Int Astron Union; Royal Astron Soc; Soc Sci Explor. *Res:* Stellar interiors; radio astronomy; search for extraterrestrial intelligence. *Mailing Add:* Dept Astron Univ Va Charlottesville VA 22903-3818. *E-Mail:* rtr@virginia.edu

ROODMAN, STANFORD TRENT, IMMUNOLOGY, BIOCHEMISTRY. *Current Pos:* asst prof biochem, St Louis Univ, 70-74, asst prof, 74-85, ASSOC PROF PATH, MED SCH, ST LOUIS UNIV, 85- & DIR, GRAD PROG PATH, 78- *Personal Data:* b St Louis, Mo, Sept 17, 39; m 61, Estelle Knight; c Aaron & Allison. *Educ:* Purdue Univ, BS, 61; Univ Mich, PhD(biochem), 68. *Prof Exp:* NIH Fel, Univ Calif, San Diego, 68-70. *Concurrent Pos:* Vis asst prof, Med Sch, Wash Univ, 81-82, Howard Hughes fel, Selection Comt Immunol, 88-92; consult, Vet Admin, 84-86, Sigma Chem, 90-92; vis scientist, Nat Cancer Inst, Frederick, Md, 91-92. *Mem:* AAAS; Am Asn Immunologists; Int Asn Anal Cytometry. *Res:* AIDS cellular immunology; pathology; characterization and role of growth factors in growth control of retroperitoneal fibromatosis cells from SRV-2 infected macaques with AIDS as an animal model for Kaposi's Sarcoma in human AIDS; flow cytometry. *Mailing Add:* Dept Path St Louis Univ Med Sch St Louis MO 63104-1028. *Fax:* 314-268-5132; *E-Mail:* roodmast@sluvca.slu.edu

ROOF, BETTY SAMS, INTERNAL MEDICINE, ENDOCRINOLOGY METABOLISM. *Current Pos:* assoc prof, 74-80, asst dean student progress, 89-92, PROF MED, MED UNIV SC, 80- *Personal Data:* b Columbia, SC, Apr 13, 26; div; c 4. *Educ:* Univ SC, BS, 44; Duke Univ, MD, 49. *Honors & Awards:* Pres Award, Am Col Obstet-Gynec, 75. *Prof Exp:* Vol vis investr, Rockefeller Inst, NY, 49-50; from intern to asst resident med, Presby Hosp, NY, 50-53; vis fel, Col Physicians & Surgeons, Columbia Univ, 53-55; clin & res fel, Mass Gen Hosp, Boston, 55-56; asst, Rockefeller Inst, 56-57; res fel, Mass Gen Hosp, 57-59; asst res physician, Cancer Res Inst, Univ Calif, San Francisco, 62-63, assoc res physician, 67-71, lectr med, Dept Med & assoc res physician, Cancer Res Inst, 71-74, assoc clin prof med, Dept Med, 74. *Mem:* Endocrine Soc; Int Endocrine Soc; Am Soc Bone & Mineral Res; Am Asn Cancer Res; fel Am Col Physicians; Am Fedn Clin Res. *Res:* Parathyroid hormone produced by non-endocrine tumors; metabolic bone disease; post-menopausal osteoporosis; breast cancer therapy with hormone; hyperparathyroidism. *Mailing Add:* Med Univ SC 171 Ashley Ave Charleston SC 29425-0001

ROOF, JACK GLYNDON, PHYSICAL CHEMISTRY. *Current Pos:* INSTR CHEM, GALVESTON COL, 70- *Personal Data:* b Cleburne, Tex, June 17, 13; m 41; c 3. *Educ:* Univ Calif, Los Angeles, BA, 34, MA, 35; Univ Wis, PhD(phys chem), 38. *Prof Exp:* From instr to asst prof chem, Ore State Col, 38-46; sr chemist, Shell Develop Co, 46-63, res assoc, 63-70. *Concurrent Pos:* Chemist, Nat Defense Res Comt, Northwestern Univ, 42-45; consult, Univ Calif, 46; mem, Joint Task Force One, Bikini, 46. *Mailing Add:* 2017 46th St Galveston TX 77550

ROOF, RAYMOND BRADLEY, JR, CRYSTALLOGRAPHY. *Current Pos:* RETIRED. *Personal Data:* b Battle Creek, Mich, Mar 3, 29; m 51, Shirley J Knoll; c Steven K & Michael B. *Educ:* Univ Mich, BS(chem eng) & BS(metall eng), 51, MS, 52, PhD(mineral, crystallog), 55. *Prof Exp:* Sr engr, Atomic Power Div, Westinghouse Elec Corp, 55-57; crystallogr, Los Alamos Sci Lab, 57-92. *Concurrent Pos:* Vis lectr, Univ Western Australia, 70; adj prof, Univ NMex, 71-72; mem, Joint Comt on Powder Diffraction Stands, 75- *Mem:* Am Crystallog Asn; Sigma Xi. *Res:* Crystallographic structure analysis; powder patterns; computer programming; metallurgical identifications; synthetic minerals. *Mailing Add:* 2700 Vista Grande NW No 102 Albuquerque NM 87120

ROOK, HARRY LORENZ, ANALYTICAL CHEMISTRY. *Current Pos:* res chemist, 69-75, sect chief neutron activation anal, 75-78, CHIEF GAS & PARTICULATE SCI DIV, CTR ANALYTICAL CHEM, NAT BUR STANDARDS, 78- *Personal Data:* b Middletown, Conn, May 31, 40; m 63; c 4. *Educ:* Worcester Polytech Inst, BS, 62, MS, 67; Tex A&M Univ, PhD(analytical chem), 69. *Prof Exp:* Analytical chemist, Monsanto Res Corp, 62-65. *Concurrent Pos:* Sci consult to subcomt on environ & atmosphere, Comt Sci & Technol, US House of Representatives, 75; chmn radioactivity, Off Water Data Coord, 75-; chmn, D-22.03, Am Soc Testing & Mat. *Mem:* Am Chem Soc; Sigma Xi; Am Soc Testing & Mat. *Res:* Analytical methodology using nuclear techniques; studies into proper methods of sampling, storage and preservation of analytical samples; environmental analysis. *Mailing Add:* 312 E Main St Middletown MD 21769

ROOKE, ALLEN DRISCOLL, JR, CIVIL ENGINEERING. *Current Pos:* PARTNER, F B ROOKE & SONS, TEX, 64-; SR ENGR, SCI & TECH CORP, MISS, 84- *Personal Data:* b San Antonio, Tex, Oct 5, 24; m 49, Betty R Whitson; c Victoria L (Lewis) & Cornelia R. *Educ:* Tex A&M Univ, BSCE, 57; Miss State Univ, MSCE, 80. *Prof Exp:* Res civil engr, US Army CEngrs, Miss, 58-83. *Concurrent Pos:* Bd dirs, First Nat Bank, Woodsboro, 85- *Mem:* Res Officers Asn US; Soc Am Mil Engrs. *Res:* Civil engineering. *Mailing Add:* 400 First St Woodsboro TX 78393

ROOKS, CORNELIA B, LIPID CHEMISTRY. *Current Pos:* Biologist, 80-87, BR CHIEF CLIN CHEM, TOXICOL & HEMAT, FOOD & DRUG ADMIN, 91- *Personal Data:* b Richmond, Va, Apr 12, 46. *Educ:* Tenn State Univ, BS, 67; Col Notre Dame, MA, 93. *Mem:* Am Asn Clin Chem. *Mailing Add:* Div Clin Lab Devices FDA 2098 Gaither Rd Rockville MD 20850. *Fax:* 301-594-5941

ROOKS, WENDELL HOFMA, II, PHARMACOLOGY. *Current Pos:* RETIRED. *Personal Data:* b Ann Arbor, Mich, Oct 2, 31; m 55; c 5. *Educ:* Calvin Col, AB, 53; Univ Mich, MS, 54. *Prof Exp:* Staff scientist, Worcester Found Exp Biol, Shrewsbury, Mass, 56-64; asst dept head bioassay, Inst Hormone Biol, Syntex Corp, 64-65, head dept bioassay, 65-80, asst dir inst biol sci, Res Div, 73-86, head sci info dept, 87-92. *Mem:* Am Soc Pharmacol & Exp Therapeut. *Res:* Steroid and prostaglandin bioassay; anti-inflammatory, analgesic and immuno-suppressive pharmacology; reproductive physiology; acne vulgaris. *Mailing Add:* 686 Teresi Lane Los Altos CA 94024

ROOM, ROBIN GERALD WALDEN, ALCOHOL & DRUG EPIDEMIOLOGY, ALCOHOL SOCIAL SCIENCE. *Current Pos:* vpres res & develop, CHIEF SCIENTIST RES, ALCOHOL RES FOUND, TORONTO, 90- *Personal Data:* b Sidney, NSW, Australia, Dec 28, 39; m 87; c 3. *Educ:* Princeton Univ, AB, 60; Univ Calif, Berkeley, MA, 62, MA, 67, PhD(sociol), 78. *Prof Exp:* Res assoc, Drinking Practices Study, Ment Res Inst, 65-69; res scientist, Social Res Group, Western Off, George Washington Univ, 69-71; lectr & prin admin analyst behav sci, Sch Pub Health, Univ Calif, Berkeley, 72-82, sci dir alcohol epidemiol, Social Res Group, 77-81, adj prof social & admin health sci, Sch Pub Health, 82-91; dir & sr scientist alcohol epidemiol, Alcohol Res Group & Inst Epidemiol & Behav Med, Med Res Inst San Francisco, 81-90. *Concurrent Pos:* Chair, Drinking & Drugs Div, Soc Study Social Probs, 75-77; prin investr & sci dir, Nat Alcohol Res Ctr grant, 77-91; panel mem, Nat Acad Sci-Inst Med, 78-82 & 86-87; chair & mem, Alcohol Abuse Prev Rev Comt, Nat Inst Alcohol Abuse & Alcoholism, 79-82; mem & adv, Expert Rev Panel on Drug Dependence & Alcohol Probs, WHO, 79-91. *Mailing Add:* Addiction Res Found 33 Russell St Toronto ON M5S 2S1 Can

ROON, ROBERT JACK, BIOCHEMISTRY, MICROBIOLOGY. *Current Pos:* asst prof, 71-77, ASSOC PROF BIOCHEM, UNIV MINN, MINNEAPOLIS, 77- *Personal Data:* b Grand Rapids, Mich, Nov 3, 43; m 66; c 1. *Educ:* Calvin Col, BS, 65; Univ Mich, Ann Arbor, MS, 67, PhD(biochem), 69. *Prof Exp:* Teaching asst biochem, Univ Mich, Ann Arbor, 65-69; Am Cancer Soc fel, Univ Calif, Berkeley, 70-71. *Concurrent Pos:* NSF fel, Univ Calif, Berkeley, 78. *Res:* Regulation of nitrogen metabolism in saccharomyces mechanism of amino acid transport in saccharomyces; biochemistry of protein secretion in saccharomyces. *Mailing Add:* Dept Biochem 4-225 Millard Hall Univ Minn Sch Med 435 Delaware St SE Minneapolis MN 55455-0347

ROONEY, JAMES ARTHUR, PHYSICS. *Current Pos:* MEM STAFF, JET PROPULSION LAB, PASADENA, CALIF. *Personal Data:* b Springfield, Vt, Sept 15, 43; m 67; c 1. *Educ:* Clark Univ, Mass, BA, 65; Univ Vt, MS, 67, PhD(physics), 70. *Prof Exp:* Res assoc physics, Univ Vt, 71-72; asst prof physics, Univ Maine, 72-76, assoc prof, 76- *Mem:* Am Asn Advan Med Instrumentation; Am Inst Ultrasound Med; Acoust Soc Am; AAAS. *Res:* Biomedical ultrasonics concerning biological effects of ultrasound on membranes and enzymes as well as applications of sound and ultrasound to dispersal of cell aggregates; blood pressure measurements and coagulation studies. *Mailing Add:* Jet Propulsion Lab 4800 Oak Grove Dr Pasadena CA 91109

ROONEY, LAWRENCE FREDERICK, ECONOMIC GEOLOGY. *Current Pos:* GEOLOGIST, US GEOL SURV, 75- *Personal Data:* b Conrad, Mont, Nov 21, 26; m 56; c 3. *Educ:* Univ Mont, BA, 48, MA, 50; Ind Univ, PhD(geol), 56. *Prof Exp:* Jr geologist, Mobil Oil Can, 56-58; asst prof geol, Univ Tex, 58-59; geologist, Humble Oil & Refining Co, 60-62 & Ind Geol Surv, 62-70; prof geol, Flathead Valley Community Col, 70-75. *Mem:* Geol Soc Am. *Res:* Geology of industrial minerals. *Mailing Add:* PO Box 4522 Whitefish MT 59937

ROONEY, LLOYD WILLIAM, FOOD SCIENCE. *Current Pos:* from asst prof to assoc prof cereal chem, 65-77, PROF FOOD SCI NUTRIT, TEX A&M UNIV, 77- *Personal Data:* b Atwood, Kans, July 17, 39; m 63, Maxine T Barenberg; c Bill, Tammy & Marcille. *Educ:* Kans State Univ, BS, 61, PhD(cereal chem), 66. *Prof Exp:* Res asst grain sci, Kans State Univ, 63-65. *Mem:* Fel Int Asn Cereal Sci & Technol; fel Am Asn Cereal Chemists; Inst Food Technologists; Am Chem Soc; Am Soc Agron. *Res:* Research program on determination of physical, chemical, nutritional and processing properties of cereal grains, especially sorghum, maize and wheat, involving close cooperation with plant breeders to use genetic material for cereal improvement; snack food and tortilla research. *Mailing Add:* Cereal Qual Lab Soil & Crop Sci Tex A&M Univ College Station TX 77843-0100. *Fax:* 409-845-0456

ROONEY, PAUL GEORGE, MATHEMATICS. *Current Pos:* from asst prof to prof, 55-91, EMER PROF MATH, UNIV TORONTO, 91- *Personal Data:* b New York, NY, July 14, 25; Can citizen; m 50; c 5. *Educ:* Univ Alta, BSc, 49; Calif Inst Technol, PhD(math), 52. *Prof Exp:* Lectr, Univ Alta, 52-54, asst prof math, 54-55. *Concurrent Pos:* Ed-in-chief, Can J Math, 71-75. *Mem:* Am Math Soc; Math Asn Am; Can Math Soc (vpres, 79-81, pres, 81-83); fel Royal Soc Can. *Res:* Functional analysis. *Mailing Add:* Dept Math Univ Toronto Toronto ON M5S 1A1 Can. *E-Mail:* rooney@math.toronto.ca

ROONEY, SEAMUS AUGUSTINE, LIPID BIOCHEMISTRY, LUNG BIOCHEMISTRY. *Current Pos:* res assoc, Yale Univ, 72-77, sr res assoc, 77-81, sr res scientist, 81-90, RES PROF PEDIAT, DEPT PEDIAT, SCH MED, YALE UNIV, 90- *Personal Data:* b Cork, Ireland, Dec 19, 43; US citizen; m 68, Patricia Scully; c 3. *Educ:* Nat Univ, Ireland, BSc, 64, MSc, 66; Dublin Univ, PhD(biochem), 69, ScD(biochem), 90. *Prof Exp:* Fel lipid chem, Dept Microbiol, Univ Pa, 69-72. *Mem:* Am Soc Biochem & Molecular Biol; Soc Pediat Res; AAAS; Am Thoracic Soc; Am Physiol Soc; Am Soc Cell Biol. *Res:* Hormonal control of pulmonary surfactant production during fetal development; regulation of surfactant secretion; purinoceptor signalling mechanisms; fatty-acid synthase gene regulation; cell biology, molecular biology; pharmacology. *Mailing Add:* Dept Pediat Sch med Yale Univ 333 Cedar St PO Box 208064 New Haven CT 06520-8064. *Fax:* 203-785-7194; *E-Mail:* seamus.rooney@yale.edu

ROONEY, THOMAS PETER, GEOLOGY. *Current Pos:* RETIRED. *Personal Data:* b New York, NY, June 29, 32; m 65, Ashley Schuler; c Siabban & Stephan. *Educ:* City Col New York, BS, 59; Columbia Univ, MA, 62, PhD(geol), 65. *Prof Exp:* Chief, Geophys & Earth Gravity Brand Sci Div, Philips Lab, 66-93. *Mem:* Geol Soc Am; Am Geophys Union; Mineral Soc Am. *Res:* Satellite altimetry; remote sensing; rock deformation; earth's gravity field. *Mailing Add:* 20 Hancock Lexington MA 02173

ROONEY, VICTOR MARTIN, ELECTRONICS ENGINEERING. *Current Pos:* From instr to assoc prof, 70-78, PROF ELECTRONIC ENG, UNIV DAYTON, 78- *Personal Data:* b Paris, Ill, Oct 9, 37; m 60; c 1. *Educ:* Univ Dayton, BEE, 65; Ohio State Univ, MSc, 70. *Concurrent Pos:* Bioeng consult, Miami Valley Hosp, 73-86; ad hoc visitor, Engrs Coun Prof, 73-81; regist eng, State Ohio. *Mem:* Inst Elec & Electronics Engrs. *Res:* Microprocessors; programmable logic controllers-bioengineering; analysis of linear circuits; author of one textbook and co-author of 3. *Mailing Add:* Dept Electronic Eng Technol Dayton Univ 300 College Park Dayton OH 45469. *Fax:* 937-229-3433

ROOP, RICHARD ALLAN, TECHNICAL SERVICE ADMINISTRATION, FOOD REGULATIONS. *Current Pos:* RES QUAL ASSURANCE DIR, TYSON FOODS INC, 93- *Personal Data:* b Decatur, Ind, Jan 5, 55; m 74; c 3. *Educ:* Purdue Univ, BS, 77, PhD(food sci), 81. *Prof Exp:* Group leader, Cent Soya Co, Inc, 81-85; sci dir, Holly Farms Foods, Inc, 85-93. *Mem:* Inst Food Technologists; Sigma Xi. *Res:* Develoment and improvement of products for the frozen food business; quality assurance; technical service; microbiology; production; process engineering. *Mailing Add:* 2210 Oaklawn Dr Springdale AK 72762

ROOP, ROBERT DICKINSON, BIOLOGY, ECOLOGY. *Current Pos:* STAFF, JONES TECHNOL INC. *Personal Data:* b Plainfield, NJ, Sept 23, 49; m 81, Edna Southerland; c Jay L & Sarah M. *Educ:* Hiram Col, BA, 71; State Univ NY Stony Brook, MA, 75. *Prof Exp:* Staff ecologist, Inst Ecol, 74-76; res assoc, Oak Ridge Nat Lab, 76-89; proj dir, Labat-Anderson Inc, 89- *Mem:* AAAS; Am Inst Biol Sci; Ecol Soc Am; Water Environ Fedn; Nat Asn Environ Prof. *Res:* Environmental impact assessment and auditing; waste management; risk assessment; quality criteria for aquatic sediments; environemental aspects of international development. *Mailing Add:* Jones Technol Inc 4425 Forbes Blvd Lanham MD 20706-4338. *Fax:* 301-731-9779; *E-Mail:* roop@delphi.com

ROOP, ROBERT KENNETH, SYNTHETIC FIBERS. *Current Pos:* res engr, Can, 90, SR ENGR, E I DU PONT DE NEMOURS & CO, INC, 90- *Personal Data:* b Pittsburgh, Pa, Apr 27, 63. *Educ:* WVa Univ, BS, 85; Tex A&M Univ, PhD(chem eng), 89. *Prof Exp:* Instr, Tex A&M Univ, 86, fel, 89. *Res:* Polymer engineering of synthetic fibers, modifying polymer and fiber properties to improve the performance automotive upholstery and carpet flood covering; supercritical extraction of hazardous organic compounds from soil and water; validated technique using toxicological assays. *Mailing Add:* 4003 Lyme Ct Greenville NC 27834

ROORDA, JOHN, CIVIL ENGINEERING, APPLIED MECHANICS. *Current Pos:* from asst prof to assoc prof, 66-74, PROF CIVIL ENG, UNIV WATERLOO, 74- *Personal Data:* b Tzummarum, Neth, June 22, 39; Can citizen; m 62; c 4. *Educ:* Univ Waterloo, BASc, 62; Univ London, PhD(struct eng), 65. *Prof Exp:* Fel, civil eng, Northwestern Univ, 65-66. *Concurrent Pos:* Sr vis fel, Sci Res Coun, Eng, 68; vis prof, Cranfield Inst Technol, Eng, 71 & Univ Col, London, 74 & 78. *Res:* Structural analysis; stability of structures; dynamic response of structures; vibration problems; theory of elasticity. *Mailing Add:* Dept Civil Eng Univ Waterloo Waterloo ON N2L 3G1 Can

ROOS, ALBERT, PHYSIOLOGY. *Current Pos:* Fel cardiol, 46-47, from instr to asst prof physiol, 47-54, assoc prof physiol & surg, 54-61, assoc prof physiol, 61-70, PROF PHYSIOL & BIOPHYS, SCH MED, WASH UNIV, 70-, RES PROF ANESTHESIOL, 61- *Personal Data:* b Leyden, Neth, Nov 22, 14; nat US; m 46; c 2. *Educ:* State Univ Groningen, MD, 40. *Mem:* AAAS; Am Physiol Soc. *Res:* Physiology of respiration; membrane transport. *Mailing Add:* Dept Cell Biol & Physiol Sch Med Wash Univ 660 S Euclid Ave St Louis MO 63110-1093. *Fax:* 314-362-7463

ROOS, C(HARLES) WILLIAM, CHEMICAL ENGINEERING, BIOCHEMICAL ENGINEERING. *Current Pos:* ASSOC PROF, CHEM ENG, AUBURN UNIV, 83- *Personal Data:* b Cairo, Ill, July 2, 27; m 50; c 3. *Educ:* Wash Univ, BS, 48, MS, 49, DSc(chem eng), 51. *Prof Exp:* Asst chem eng, Wash Univ, 50-51; res chem eng, Monsanto Co, 51-56, group leader chem eng res, 56-59, sect leader, 59-63, technologist, 63-66, mgr res & develop pioneering res, 66-68, mgr petrol additives res, 68-70, dir technol planning & eval, 70-75, gen mgr, New Enterprise Div, 75-77, dir, Corp Res Labs, 77-79, dir, Technol Admin, 79-82. *Concurrent Pos:* Lectr, Wash Univ, 51- & St Louis Univ, 59- *Mem:* Am Inst Chem Engrs; Nat Soc Prof Engrs; Am Chem Soc; Sigma Xi. *Res:* Catalysis; biochemistry; chemical process development; reaction kinetics; research project evaluation; resource allocation; computer aided design; separations. *Mailing Add:* 915 Cherokee Rd Auburn AL 36830

ROOS, CHARLES EDWIN, ELEMENTARY PARTICLE PHYSICS, ENVIRONMENTAL SCIENCES. *Current Pos:* from assoc prof to prof physics, 59-89, PROF RADIOL SCI, MED SCH, VANDERBILT UNIV, 84-, EMER PROF PHYSICS, 89- *Personal Data:* b Chicago, Ill, Apr 23, 27; m 52, Anne Friedrich; c Margit, Alice, Charles D & Carlton. *Educ:* Univ Tex, BS, 48; Johns Hopkins Univ, PhD(physics), 53. *Prof Exp:* Assoc res staff, Johns Hopkins Univ, 53; from instr to asst prof physics, Univ Calif, Riverside, 54-59. *Concurrent Pos:* Res fel, Calif Inst Technol, 56-67; guest physicist, Brookhaven Nat Lab, CERN, Fermi lab; chmn, Nat Recovery Technol, 83-; prof radiol sci, Vanderbilt Univ Med Sch, 84; treas & dir, Cryomagnetic, Inc, 66-69; dir, Am Magnetics, Inc, 69-85. *Mem:* Fel Am Phys Soc; NY Acad Sci; Sigma Xi. *Res:* Auger transitions; dibaryons, studies of charm and beauty guards, neutrino actrophysics (deep underwater muon and neutrino detection); nonferrons metal sorting-processing of municipal solid waste; photo mesonic reactions; superconductivity; hyperon magnetic moments; medical and health physics; over 150 publications and holder of 16 patents. *Mailing Add:* 2507 Ridgewood Dr Nashville TN 37215. *Fax:* 615-734-6410

ROOS, FREDERICK WILLIAM, AEROSPACE ENGINEERING, FLUID DYNAMICS. *Current Pos:* Prin scientist, Flight Sci Dept, McDonnell Douglas Res Labs, 68-93, SR PRIN TECH SPECIALIST, ADVAN FLIGHT TECHNOL, MCDONNELL DOUGLAS AEROSPACE-E, 93- *Personal Data:* b Sault Ste Marie, Mich, June 4, 40; m 63, Kathryn R Wagner. *Educ:* Univ Mich, BSE, 63, MSE, 65, PhD(aerospace eng), 68. *Concurrent Pos:* Adj prof aviation, Parks Col, 84-85, St Louis Community Col, 89-91 & Cent Mo State Univ, 97-; mem, Fluid Dynamics Tech Comt, Am Inst Aeronaut & Astronaut, 92-96. *Mem:* Am Inst Aeronaut & Astronaut; Am Phys Soc. *Res:* High-lift-system flow physics and high-alpha vortex-dominated flows; turbulent-shear-layer structure and control; unsteady separated flows associated with aircraft buffeting. *Mailing Add:* 11311 Clayton Rd St Louis MO 63131

ROOS, HENRY, microscopic anatomy, physiology, for more information see previous edition

ROOS, JOHN FRANCIS, FISHERIES MANAGEMENT. *Current Pos:* VPRES, PAC SEAFOOD PROCESSORS ASN, 88- *Personal Data:* b Seattle, Wash, Jan 18, 32; m 56; c 3. *Educ:* Univ Wash, BS, 55. *Prof Exp:* Proj leader chignik sockeye salmon studies, Fisheries Res Inst, Univ Wash, 55-60; chief biologist, Int Pac Salmon Fisheries Comn, 68-71, asst dir, 71-82, dir, 82-85. *Mem:* Am Fisheries Soc; Am Inst Fishery Res Biologists. *Mailing Add:* 5516 SW 128th St Mukilteo WA 98275

ROOS, LEO, PHYSICAL ORGANIC CHEMISTRY, PHOTOCHEMISTRY. *Current Pos:* dir new imaging systs, Xidex Corp, 76-84, TECH DIR, DYNACHEM CORP, 84- *Personal Data:* b Amsterdam, Neth, Nov 10, 37; US citizen; m 61; c 3. *Educ:* City Col New York, BS, 61; Univ Cincinnati, PhD(phys org chem), 65. *Prof Exp:* Res chemist, Photoproducts Dept, E I du Pont de Nemours & Co, Inc, 65-71, sr res chemist, 71-76. *Concurrent Pos:* Tech dir, Exxon Epid Div, 84; consult, coating technol, Photopolymer Mft. *Mem:* AAAS; Am Chem Soc; Soc Photog Sci & Eng. *Res:* Photopolymerization; homogeneous catalysis, specifically reaction of cobalt carbonyls with olefins; low energy visible light catalyzed; photopolymer reactions; adhesion between metal substrates and polymer under extreme conditions; electroless plating; catalytic reactions; coating Rheology pertaining to coating large scale planar devices. *Mailing Add:* 6 Hillcrest Dr 227 Freight St New Fairfield CT 06812-4112

ROOS, PHILIP G, NUCLEAR PHYSICS, NUCLEAR REACTIONS. *Current Pos:* from asst prof to assoc prof nuclear physics, 67-75, PROF PHYSICS & ASTRON, UNIV MD, COLLEGE PARK, 75- *Personal Data:* b Wauseon, Ohio, May 16, 38; m 63, Patricia; c Kirsten. *Educ:* Ohio Wesleyan Univ, BA, 60; Mass Inst Technol, PhD(physics), 64. *Prof Exp:* Vis asst prof physics, Univ Md, 64-65; AEC fel nuclear physics, Oak Ridge Nat Lab, 65-67. *Concurrent Pos:* Vis scientist, Inst Nuclear Physics, Orsay, France, 73-74; vis prof, Cyclotron Lab, Ind Univ, Bloomington, Ind, 82-83. *Mem:* Fel Nuclear Physics Div Am Phys Soc. *Res:* Study of nuclear reactions and nuclear structure using particle accelerators. *Mailing Add:* Dept Physics Univ Md College Park MD 20742. *Fax:* 301-314-9525

ROOS, RAYMOND PHILIP, NEUROLOGY, VIROLOGY. *Current Pos:* MEM STAFF, DEPT NEUROL, MED CLINS, UNIV CHICAGO, 78- *Personal Data:* b Brooklyn, NY, Apr 5, 44; m 67; c 1. *Educ:* Columbia Col, BA, 64; State Univ NY Downstate Med Ctr, MD, 68. *Prof Exp:* Intern med, State Univ NY, Kings County Hosp, Brooklyn, 68-69; staff assoc spec chronic dis study sect, Nat Inst Neurol Dis & Stroke, 69-71; resident neurol, Johns

Hopkins Univ, 71-74, instr neurol & NIH fel neurovirol, 74-78. *Concurrent Pos:* Consult neurol, Moore Genetics Clin, Johns Hopkins Univ, 75. *Mem:* Am Acad Neurol. *Res:* Relationship of virus infections, especially defective, slow or unconventional infections to neurological degenerative diseases; virological etiology to certain neurological heritable diseases. *Mailing Add:* Univ Chicago Hosp 5841 Maryland Ave Chicago IL 60637

ROOS, THOMAS BLOOM, ENDOCRINOLOGY, SOFTWARE SYSTEMS. *Current Pos:* from instr to prof zool, 60-71, chmn dept, 69-70, 78-83, PROF BIOL, DARTMOUTH COL, 71- *Personal Data:* b Peoria, Ill, Mar 19, 30; m 53; c 2. *Educ:* Harvard Univ, AB, 51; Univ Wis, MS, 53, PhD(zool), 60. *Hon Degrees:* AM, Dartmouth, 71. *Prof Exp:* Instr zool, Univ Wis, 60. *Concurrent Pos:* USPHS spec fel, 66-67; mem comn undergrad educ biol sci, NSF, 66-70; hon res fel, Univ Col, London, 74-75; Fulbright fel, 88-89; Fulbright fel, Bhabha Atomic Res Ctr (BASC), CCMB, IICB, Univ Delhi, India, 88-89. *Mem:* AAAS; Am Soc Zool. *Res:* Phylogenetic and ontogenetic development and genetic control of hormonal secretory function and responsivity; theoretical biology; use of computers in biology and teaching of biology; automation of data collection and analysis; invention, master scan interpretive densitometer; biochemistry. *Mailing Add:* Dept Biol Sci Dartmouth Col Hanover NH 03755. *E-Mail:* thomas.b.roos@dartmouth.edu

ROOSA, ROBERT ANDREW, MEDICAL MICROBIOLOGY, GENETICS. *Current Pos:* res assoc, Wistar Inst Anat & Biol, 60-64, assoc prof, 64-93, dep dir sci serv, 69-74, sci adminr, 75-93, cur mus, 69-96, EMER PROF, WISTAR INST ANAT & BIOL, 94- *Personal Data:* b Manila, Philippines, June 18, 25; US citizen; m 89, JoAnne Younkins; c R Andrew, James A & Alane A. *Educ:* Univ Conn, BA, 50; Univ Pa, PhD(med microbiol), 57. *Prof Exp:* Res asst, Sch Med, Yale Univ, 50-52; fel, Nat Cancer Inst, 57-60. *Concurrent Pos:* Eleanor Roosevelt Int Cancer Res fel, Med Res Coun Exp Virus Res Unit, Univ Glasgow, 67-68; ed, Info Newslett Somatic Cell Genetics, 69-73. *Mem:* AAAS; Nat Coun Univ Res Admin; Soc Res Admin; Tissue Cult Asn; Am Asn Cancer Res; Radiation Res Soc; Am Assoc Lab Animal Sci; Am Soc Microbiol. *Res:* Nuclear cytology; cancer chemotherapy; mechanisms of drug resistance; nutritional requirements of cells in culture; somatic cell genetics; tumor transplantation; role of the thymus in immunobiology; slow virus diseases of mammals. *Mailing Add:* Wistar Inst Anat & Biol 36th & Spruce Sts Philadelphia PA 19104. *Fax:* 215-898-3995

ROOSENRAAD, CRIS THOMAS, MATHEMATICS. *Current Pos:* DEAN STUDENTS & LECTR, CARLETON COL, 83- *Personal Data:* b Lansing, Mich, July 28, 41; m 64; c 1. *Educ:* Univ Mich, BSc, 63, MSc, 64; Univ Wis, PhD(math), 69. *Prof Exp:* Asst prof math, Williams Col, 69-75, assoc dean & lectr, 75-83. *Mem:* Am Math Soc; Math Asn Am. *Res:* Orthogonal polynomials; special functions. *Mailing Add:* 407 Prairie Northfield MN 55057-2360

ROOT, ALLEN WILLIAM, PEDIATRIC ENDOCRINOLOGY. *Current Pos:* prof pediat & head sect pediat endocrinol, 73-96, PROF BIOCHEM & MOLECULAR BIOL, COL MED, UNIV SFLA, 86- *Personal Data:* b Philadelphia, Pa, Sept 24, 33; m 58; c 3. *Educ:* Dartmouth Col, AB, 55; Harvard Univ, MD, 58; Am Bd Pediat, dipl, 64, 86 & 93, dipl endocrinol, 78, 86 & 93. *Prof Exp:* Intern, Strong Mem Hosp, Rochester, NY, 58-60; resident pediat, Hosp Univ Pa, Philadelphia, 60-62; fel pediat endocrinol, Children's Hosp Philadelphia, 62-65; assoc physician pediat, Sch Med, Univ Pa, 64-66, asst prof, 66-69; from assoc prof to prof, Sch Med, Temple Univ, 69-73; dir univ serv, All Children's Hosp, St Petersburg, 73-89. *Concurrent Pos:* Asst physician endocrinol, Children's Hosp Philadelphia, 65-66; USPHS career develop award, 68-69; chmn, Div Pediat, Albert Einstein Med Ctr, Philadelphia, 69-73; consult ed, J Pediat, 73-81 & J Adolescent Health Care, 79-; mem med adv bd, Nat Pituitary Agency, 74-89. *Mem:* Endocrine Soc; AAAS; Am Pediat Soc; Am Acad Pediat; Soc Pediat Res; Lawson Wilkins Pediat Endocrinol Soc (pres, 88-89). *Res:* Investigation of factors which regulate function of the hypothalamic-pituitary unit and the mechanisms of pubertal maturation. *Mailing Add:* Div Pediat Endocrinol All Children's Hosp 801 Sixth St S St Petersburg FL 33731. *Fax:* 813-892-4219

ROOT, CHARLES ARTHUR, INORGANIC CHEMISTRY. *Current Pos:* From instr to assoc prof, 65-82, PROF CHEM, BUCKNELL UNIV, 82- *Personal Data:* b Rochester, NY, Aug 25, 38; m 63, Martha James; c David E & Stephen C. *Educ:* Ohio Wesleyan Univ, BA, 60; Ohio State Univ, MSc, 62, PhD(chem), 65. *Concurrent Pos:* NSF fac fel, Calif Inst Technol, 71-72, vis assoc prof, 79-80; res fel, Univ Wis, 90-91, vis prof, 96-97. *Mem:* AAAS; Am Chem Soc; Sigma Xi. *Res:* Thermal and photochemistry of vanadium complexes; complexes of oxazolidines. *Mailing Add:* Dept Chem Bucknell Univ Lewisburg PA 17837. *Fax:* 717-524-1739; *E-Mail:* croot@bucknell.edu

ROOT, DAVID HARLEY, MATHEMATICS, ENERGY RESOURCES. *Current Pos:* RETIRED. *Personal Data:* b Columbus, Ohio, Oct 10, 37; m 67; c 2. *Educ:* Mass Inst Technol, BS, 59; Univ Wash, PhD(math), 68. *Prof Exp:* Asst prof math & statist, Purdue Univ, 68-74; mathematician, US Geol Surv, 74-97. *Mem:* AAAS. *Res:* Study of the methods of estimation of the remnants of fossil fuels and of the potentials of various non-fossil fuel energy resources. *Mailing Add:* 5198 Winfield Rd Fairfax VA 22030

ROOT, ELIZABETH JEAN, electron microscopy, neuroscience, for more information see previous edition

ROOT, HARLAN D, GENERAL SURGERY. *Current Pos:* assoc prof, 66-67, ASST CHMN, UNIV TEX HEALTH SCI CTR, SAN ANTONIO, 66-; PROF SURG, 67- *Personal Data:* b Riders Mills, NY, Feb 16, 26; m 53, Catherine Frildride; c 4. *Educ:* Cornell Univ, AB, 50, MD, 53; Univ Minn, PhD(surg); 61, Am Bd Surg, dipl, 61. *Prof Exp:* Univ fel, Univ Minn, 54-60, Nat Cancer Soc fel, 55-59, Am Cancer Soc fel, 59-61, instr surg, Med Sch, 60-66, instr surg, Med Sch, 61, asst prof, 61-66; assoc dir surg, Ancker Hosp, St Paul, Minn. *Concurrent Pos:* Consult, San Antonio State Chest Hosp, 66-, Audie L Murphy Mem Vet Admin Hosp, San Antonio, 73-; surg test comt, Nat Bd Med Examiners, 77-; dist comt applicants, 77- & comt trauma, Am Col Surg, 77-80; gov, Am Col Surgeons, 89-95. *Mem:* AMA; fel Am Col Surgeons; Soc Univ Surgeons; Am Asn Surg Trauma (pres, 88-89); Am Surg Asn; Int Soc Cardiovasc Surg. *Res:* Peripheral vascular surgery and trauma issues. *Mailing Add:* Dept Surg 7703 Floyd Curl Dr San Antonio TX 78284

ROOT, JOHN WALTER, physical chemistry, radiochemistry, for more information see previous edition

ROOT, MARY AVERY, PHARMACOLOGY. *Current Pos:* RETIRED. *Personal Data:* b Hartford, Conn, Oct 28, 18. *Educ:* Oberlin Col, AB, 40; Radcliffe Col, MA, 49, PhD, 50. *Prof Exp:* Pharmacologist, Res Labs, Eli Lilly & Co, 50-63, res assoc, 63-85. *Mem:* Endocrine Soc; Am Soc Pharmacol & Exp Therapeut; Soc Exp Biol & Med; Am Diabetes Asn; NY Acad Sci. *Res:* Carbohydrate metabolism; insulin, diabetes. *Mailing Add:* 4425 N Emerson Ave Indianapolis IN 46226

ROOT, PAUL JOHN, OIL & GAS RESERVOIR ENGINEERING, NATURAL GAS ENGINEERING. *Current Pos:* PRES, PETROL & GEOL ENG, INC, 77- *Personal Data:* b Pittsburgh, Pa, Apr 1, 29; m 56; c 4. *Educ:* Pa State Univ, Bs, 52, MS, 54; Univ Tex, Austin, PhD(petrol eng), 61. *Prof Exp:* Engr, Consolidated Gas Supply Corp, 53-55; instr petrol eng, Pa State Univ, 55-56; asst prof, Univ Tex, Austin, 56-61; res engr, Gulf Res & Develop Co, 61-65; assoc prof petrol eng, Univ Okla, 65-70, prof, 73-75; tech dir, Natural Gas Surv, Fed Energy Regulatory Comn, 70-73; dir, Educ Progs, H Zinder & Assocs, 75-77. *Concurrent Pos:* Lectr, Carnegie-Mellon Univ, 64-65; res engr, Bur Bus & Econ Res, 68-69; consult engr, Fed Energy Regulatory Comn, 73-74; res fel, Off Sci & Pub Policy, 74-75; energy consult, Fed Energy Admin, 78-79 & Pertamina, Indonesian Nat Oil Co. 82-83. *Mem:* Soc Petrol Engrs.; Am Soc Eng Educ; AAAS. *Res:* Natural gas engineering and operations; reservoir engineering; enhanced oil recovery; energy supplies and utilization. *Mailing Add:* 1839 Rolling Hills Norman OK 73072-6707

ROOT, RICHARD BRUCE, ECOLOGY. *Current Pos:* from asst prof to assoc prof, 64-79, PROF ECOL, CORNELL UNIV, 79- *Personal Data:* b Dearborn, Mich, Sept 7, 36; div; c 2. *Educ:* Univ Mich, BS, 58; Univ Calif, Berkeley, PhD(zool), 64. *Honors & Awards:* Howell Award, Cooper Ornith Soc, 63. *Prof Exp:* Assoc zool, Univ Calif, Berkeley, 61-62. *Concurrent Pos:* Mem field staff, Rockefeller Found, Colombia, 70-71; vis prof, Univ Valle, Colombia, 70-71; ed, Ecol & Ecol Monogr, 71-73; res assoc, Mus Vert Zool, Univ Calif, Berkeley, 75; bd dir, Orgn Trop Studies, 76-; vis scientist, Oxford Univ, 83. *Mem:* Ecol Soc Am (vpres, 79-80, pres, 85-86); Asn Trop Biol; Brit Ecol Soc; Am Ornith Union; Entom Soc Am. *Res:* Comparative ecology of insects; adaptive syndromes of birds and insects; plant/herbivore interactions; differences in the structure of natural and agricultural ecosystems; functional classifications. *Mailing Add:* Sect Ecol & Systematics Cornell Univ E 145 Corson Bldg Ithaca NY 14853-0001

ROOT, RICHARD KAY, INTERNAL MEDICINE, INFECTIOUS DISEASES. *Current Pos:* VCHMN, DEPT MED, SCH MED & CHIEF MED SERV, HARBORVIEW MED CTR, 91- *Educ:* Johns Hopkins Univ, MD, 63. *Prof Exp:* Prof med & chmn dept, Univ Calif, San Francisco, 85-91. *Mailing Add:* Harborview Med Ctr 325 Ninth Ave Box 359782 Seattle WA 98104-2499

ROOT, SAMUEL I, GEOLOGY. *Current Pos:* COL WOOSTER, 83- *Personal Data:* b Winnipeg, Man, Mar 1, 30; m 52, Esther Saltzman; c 3. *Educ:* Univ Man, BSc, 52, MSc, 56; Ohio State Univ, PhD(geol), 58. *Prof Exp:* Geologist, Seaboard Oil Co, Can, 52-53; sr geologist, Int Petrol Co Ltd, Colombia, Peru, 57-63; staff geologist, Pa State Geol Surv, 63-65; chief field geologist, 66-78; mem staff, Esso Prospeccao Ltd, Brazil, 78-82. *Concurrent Pos:* Consult, World Bank; Keck grant, 90-94, Hughes grant, 89-93 & NSF grant, 90; prin res fel, Am Chem Soc, 95-96; bd mem, Ohio Lew Lev Radioactive Fac Develop Auth. *Mem:* Geol Soc Am; Am Asn Petrol Geologists; Soc Econ Geologists. *Res:* Areal and structural geology; stratigraphy; nonmetallic mineral deposits. *Mailing Add:* Dept Geol Col Wooster Wooster OH 44691

ROOT, WILLIAM L(UCAS), ENGINEERING. *Current Pos:* prof, 61-87, EMER PROF AEROSPACE ENG, ELEC ENG & COMPUT SCI, UNIV MICH, ANN ARBOR, 88- *Personal Data:* b Des Moines, Iowa, Oct 6, 19; m 40; c 2. *Educ:* Mass Inst Technol, PhD(math), 52. *Honors & Awards:* Com Con Conf Bd Career Achievement Award, 87; Shannon lectr, Info Theory Soc, Inst Elec & Electronics Engrs, 86. *Prof Exp:* Instr math, Mass Inst Technol, 47-51, mem staff, Instrumentation Lab, 51-52 & Lincoln Lab, 52-56, asst leader, Systs Res Group, 57-59, leader anal group, 59-61. *Concurrent Pos:* Vis lectr, Harvard Univ, 58-59; vis prof, Math Res Ctr, Univ Wis, 63-64, Univ Calif, Berkeley, 66-67, Mich State Univ, 66 & 68; NSF sr fel & vis fel, Clare Hall, Univ Cambridge, 70; mem, Army Sci Bd, 79-83. *Mem:* Fel Inst Elec & Electronics Engrs; Am Math Soc. *Res:* Stochastic processes, statistical theory of communications and general system theory; system modelling and identification; estimation and detection theory; information theory. *Mailing Add:* Dept Aerospace Eng Univ Mich Ann Arbor MI 48109-0001

ROOTARE, HILLAR MUIDAR, DENTAL MATERIALS, SURFACE CHEMISTRY. *Current Pos:* RES SCIENTIST, MICROMERITICS INSTRUMENT CORP, 78- *Personal Data:* b Tallinn, Estonia, Apr 26, 28; US citizen; m 59; c 6. *Educ:* Wagner Col, BS, 52; Univ Mich, PhD(dent mat & pharmaceut chem), 73. *Prof Exp:* Chemist & res assoc, Bone Char Res Proj, Inc, Nat Bur Stand, 57-63; dir, Mat Technol Lab, Am Instrument Co, Inc, div Travenol Labs, 63-66; NIH trainee & res asst, Univ Mich, Ann Arbor, 66-73; dir tech res, L D Caulk Co, div Dentsply Int Inc, 73-75; sr res assoc, Dept Dent Mat, Sch Dent, Univ Mich, Ann Arbor, 75-77. *Mem:* Int Asn Dent Res; Am Chem Soc; Am Soc Metals; Fine Particle Soc; Sigma Xi. *Res:* Physical and surface chemistry applied to use of hydroxyapatite as synthetic bone, in characterizing of surfaces, compaction and sintering of powders to reproduce the porous structures of bone for possible use as implants; design and construction of microprocessor controlled instrumentation for automatic measurements and analysis of pore size distributions of porous materials. *Mailing Add:* Qual Assurance/Control Advan Composite Mats 1525 S Buncombe Rd Greer SC 29651-9208

ROOT-BERNSTEIN, ROBERT SCOTT, BIOLOGY, IMMUNOLOGY. *Current Pos:* asst prof natural sci, 88-90, assoc prof, 90-96, PROF, DEPT PHYSIOL, MICH STATE UNIV, 96- *Personal Data:* b Washington, DC, Aug 7, 53; m 78, Michele; c Meredith & Brian. *Educ:* Princeton Univ, AB, 75, PhD(hist sci), 80. *Honors & Awards:* MacArthur Prize, J&CD MacArthur Found, 81; Witebsky Mem Lectr, Univ Buffalo, 93. *Prof Exp:* Fel theoret biol, Salk Inst Biol Studies, 81-83, res assoc, 83-84; res assoc neurobiochem, Vet Admin Hosp, Brentwood, Calif, 85-87. *Concurrent Pos:* Mem adv bd, J Theoret Biol, 84-91; vis assoc prof sci & art, Univ Calif, Los Angeles, 87; consult, Calif Mus Sci & Indust, 87-88; Biolark, Inc, 88-89; Res Div, Parke-Davis Pharmaceut, 90-91; Chiron Corp, 92- AMOCO chem, 92- & Acquired Immune Deficiency Syndrome Found, Sci Bd, Rome, Italy, 93-; mem bd dirs, Impression 5 Sci Mus, 89-90; contrib ed, Sciences, 89-91. *Res:* Theoretical and experimental investigation of autoimmunity and AIDS; theory and applications of molecular complementarity; peptide, neurotransmitter and drug interactions; historical and philosophical studies of discovery process; research management; popular science writing; use of arts by scientists. *Mailing Add:* Dept Physiol Mich State Univ East Lansing MI 48824. *Fax:* 517-355-5125

ROOTENBERG, JACOB, electrical engineering; deceased, see previous edition for last biography

ROOTHAAN, CLEMENS CAREL JOHANNES, PHYSICS. *Current Pos:* res assoc, Univ Chicago, 49-50, from instr to prof, 50-58, prof commun & info sci, 65-68, dir, comput ctr, 62-68, Louis Block prof physics & chem, 68-88, EMER PROF PHYSICS & CHEM, UNIV CHICAGO, 88-; SR SCIENTIST, HEWLETT-PACKARD LABS, PALO ALTO, CALIF, 92- *Personal Data:* b Nymegen, Neth, Aug 29, 18; US citizen; m 50, Judith Cosin; c Karen S, John P E, Peter F, Charles M V & Elizabeth S. *Educ:* Inst Technol, Delft, MS, 45; Univ Chicago, PhD(physics), 50. *Prof Exp:* Instr, Cath Univ Am, 47-49. *Concurrent Pos:* Guggenheim fel, Cambridge Univ, 57; consult, Argonne Nat Lab, 58-66, Lockheed Missiles & Space Co, 60-65, Union Carbide Corp, 65- & IBM Corp, 65-; guest professorships, Ohio State, Columbus, Ohio, 76, Tech Univ, Lyngby, Denmark, 83, & Univ Del, 87-88. *Mem:* Fel Am Phys Soc; Int Acad Quantum Chem; corresp mem, Royal Dutch Acad Sci. *Res:* Theory of atomic and molecular structure; application of digital computers to scientific problems; computer architecture. *Mailing Add:* Hewlett Packard Labs 1501 Page Mill Rd Palo Alto CA 94304-1126. *Fax:* 773-324-6856; *E-Mail:* roothaan@hplabs.hp.com

ROOTMAN, JACK, OPHTHALMOLOGY, PATHOLOGY. *Current Pos:* from asst prof to assoc prof, 76-84, PROF OPHTHAL & PATH, UNIV BC, 85-, CHMN, 90- *Personal Data:* b Calgary, Alta, June 22, 44; m 65, Jenny Puterman; c Russel M, Kathryn A & Daniel B. *Educ:* Univ Alta, Can, MD, 68. *Prof Exp:* Res ophthal, Univ Alta, 73, clin asst prof ophthal & path, 73-75. *Concurrent Pos:* Fel, Med Res Coun, 77-78; grantee, Vancouver Found & BC Cancer Found, 78, McLean Fund, 79, BC Health Care Res Found, 79-81, 83-85, 87-89 & 92, BC Med Serv Found, 82-83, Med Res Coun, 82-88; chmn, Ocular & Orb Tumor Group, BC Cancer Agency, 80-; consult pathologist, Vancouver Gen Hosp, 89 & Can Ref Ctr Cancer Path, Ottawa, 89. *Mem:* Royal Col Physicians & Surgeons; Am Acad Opthal; fel Royal Col Surgeons; fel Can Cancer Soc; Int Orbit Soc; Int Soc Eye Res; Am Asn Ophthal Path; Can Med Asn; Am Asn Ophthalmic Pathologists; Royal Col Pathologists. *Res:* Contributed articles to professional journals. *Mailing Add:* Dept Ophthal Univ BC 2550 Willow St Vancouver BC V5Z 3N9 Can

ROOTS, BETTY IDA, ZOOLOGY, NEUROBIOLOGY. *Current Pos:* from assoc prof to prof, 69-93, chmn, 84-93, EMER PROF ZOOL, UNIV TORONTO, 93- *Personal Data:* b South Croydon, Eng. *Educ:* Univ Col, Univ London, BSc, 49, dipl educ, 50, PhD(zool), 53, DSc, 81. *Prof Exp:* Asst lectr biol, Royal Free Hosp Sch Med, Univ London, 53-59; vis asst prof physiol, Univ Ill, Urbana, 59-61; asst lectr biol, Royal Free Hosp Sch Med, Univ London, 61-62, lectr anat, Univ Col, 62-66; vis scientist physiol, Univ Ill, Urbana, 66-67; res neuroscientist, Univ Calif, San Diego, 68-69. *Concurrent Pos:* Rose Sidgwick mem fel, Univ Ill, Urbana, 59-60. *Mem:* Am Soc Neurochem; Am Oil Chem Soc; Soc Neurosci; Can Soc Zool; Int Soc Develop Neurosci; Int Soc Neurochem. *Res:* Structural and chemical changes in nervous system in relation to environmental factors; cell isolation techniques; structure and function of glial cells. *Mailing Add:* Dept Zool Univ Toronto 25 Harbord St Toronto ON M5S 3G5 Can. *Fax:* 416-978-8532

ROOTS, ERNEST FREDERICK, GEOLOGY, SOCIETY-ENVIRONMENT-RESOURCES RELATIONSHIPS. *Current Pos:* sci adv, 73-89, EMER SCI ADV, DEPT ENVIRON, 89- *Personal Data:* b Salmon Arm, BC, July 5, 23; m 55, June Blomfield; c Charles, Frances, Hannah, Jane & Robin. *Educ:* Univ BC, MASc, 47; Princeton Univ, PhD(geol), 49. *Hon Degrees:* DSc, Univ Victoria, 83. *Honors & Awards:* Queen Elizabeth II Polar Medal, UK, 56 & 86; Patron's Medal, Royal Geog Soc, 65; Massey Medal, Royal Can Geog Soc, 79; Officer of Order, Can, 87; Gold Medal, Prof Inst Pub Serv CAn, 89. *Prof Exp:* Surveyor, Nat Parks Serv, Can, 41-42; asst, Geol Surv Can, 43-44, tech officer, 45-47, geologist, 48-49; asst prof geol, Princeton Univ, 52-54; geologist, Geol Surv Can, 55-58, coordr, Polar Contineal Shelf Proj, 58-72; sr adv, Dept Energy Mines & Resources, 72-73. *Concurrent Pos:* Sr Geologist, Norweg-Brit-Swed Antarctic Exped, 49-52, 54-55; polar res bd, US Nat Acad Sci, 69-82; pres, Int Comn Snow & Ice, 79-84; mem coun, Comt Arctique, 80-; co-chmn, Can-USSR coop Arctic Sci, 84-91; gov & chmn res comt, Arctic Inst NAm, 80-86; pres, Int Arctic Sci Comt, 90-93; chmn, Can Environ ResCoun, 86-91 & UNESCO/MAB Northern Scis Network, 92-; co-chmn, Sci Rev Group High-Level Nuclear Waste Disposal, 90- *Mem:* Geol Soc Am; Am Geophys Union; Glaciol Soc; Arctic Inst NAm; fel Royal Soc Can. *Res:* Tectonics and mineral deposits of Canadian cordillera; geology of Antarctica and the Himalayas; environmental policy; climate change of polar regions; international arctic science policies; societal responses to resources. *Mailing Add:* Sci Adv Emer Dept Environ 351 St Joseph Blvd Pl Vincent Massey Bldg 6th Floor Ottawa ON K1A 0H3 Can. *Fax:* 819-997-5813

ROOVERS, JACQUES E, POLYMER CHEMISTRY, PHYSICAL CHEMISTRY. *Current Pos:* assoc res officer, 67-77, group leader, 90-97, SR RES OFFICER POLYMER CHEM, NAT RES COUN CAN, 77- *Personal Data:* b Deurne, Belg, June 3, 37; m 63, Nicole Vancamp; c 3. *Educ:* Cath Univ Louvain, BSc, 59, PhD(polymer chem), 62. *Prof Exp:* Nat Res Coun Can fel, 63-64; assoc pharmacol, Cath Univ Louvain, 65-66. *Concurrent Pos:* Adj prof, Dept Chem, Univ Athens, Greece, 90- *Mem:* Am Chem Soc; Can High Polymer Forum (secy, 77). *Mailing Add:* 21 Wren Rd Gloucester ON K1J 7H5 Can. *Fax:* 613-991-2384; *E-Mail:* jacques.roovers@nrc.ca

ROOZEN, KENNETH JAMES, GENETICS, MOLECULAR BIOLOGY. *Current Pos:* from asst prof to assoc prof, Univ Ala, Birmingham, 81-87, vchmn, Dept Microbiol, 77-81, dean & co-dir, Grad Sch, 81-88, chmn, 84-87, asst vpres health affairs, 86-88, exec asst to pres, 88-89, vpres univ affairs, 89-90, vpres res & univ affairs, 90-93, PROF, UNIV ALA, BIRMINGHAM, 88-, EXEC VPRES, 93- *Personal Data:* b Milwaukee, Wis, Jan 17, 43; m 81, Sandra Giles; c Karla, Kevin & Kristin. *Educ:* Lakeland Col, BS, 66; Univ SDak, MA, 68; Univ Tenn, Oak Ridge, PhD(microbial genetics), 71. *Prof Exp:* NIH fel pediat, Med Sch, Wash Univ, 71-74. *Concurrent Pos:* Policy fel, Robert Wood Johnson-Nat Acad Sci Health, 83-84. *Mem:* AAAS; Am Soc Microbiol; Sigma Xi; Am Soc Cell Biologists. *Res:* Mammalian cell genetics and biochemistry, specifically mutant isolation, correction of genetic defects, gene mapping and nucleic acid metabolism. *Mailing Add:* Exec VPres Univ Ala-Birmingham 701 S 20th St AB 1064 Birmingham AL 35294-0110. *Fax:* 205-934-1221

ROPER, CLYDE FORREST EUGENE, BIOLOGICAL OCEANOGRAPHY, SYSTEMATICS. *Current Pos:* assoc cur, 66-72, supvr mollusks, 68-70, chair, Dept Invertebrate Zool, 80-85, CUR, SMITHSONIAN INST, MUS NATURAL HIST, 72- *Personal Data:* b Ipswich, Mass, Oct 1, 37; m 58, Ingrid Braunohler; c Erik C & Christopher T. *Educ:* Transylvania Col, AB, 59; Univ Miami, Fla, MS, 62, PhD(marine sci), 67. *Prof Exp:* Sr res asst oceanog, Inst Marine Sci, Univ Miami, 64-66. *Concurrent Pos:* Prin investr, numerous res grants ecol, systs & behav squids & octopuses, 67-; adj lectr, George Washington Univ, 68-; adj prof, Rosenthal Sch Marine & Atmospheric Scis, Univ Miami, Fla, 68-; bd dirs, Inst Malacol, 71-; mem grad comts, Mem Univ, Nfld, 74, Harvard Univ, 74, Univ Md, 78, William & Mary, 81, 92 & 94, Univ Miami, 82, Duke Univ, 83, Univ NSW, Australia, 89, Univ Melbourne, Australia, 90 & 93; consult, Food & Agr Orgn, Fisheries Resources Div, Rome, 75-; affil grad fac, Dept Oceanog, Univ Hawaii, 75-76; founding mem, Cephaloped Int Adv Coun, 81, co-chmn, 81-83, coun mem, 81-86, int workshop coordr, 87-88; fel Comn, Smithsonian Marine Sta, Ft Pierce, Fla, 81-; Nat Mus Natural Hist rep, Am Inst Biol Sci Coun, 88-91. *Mem:* Cephalopod Int Adv Coun; Australian Malacol Soc; Am Malacol Union (pres, 78-80); Marine Biol Asn UK; Inst Malacol (pres, 75-78); Sigma Xi. *Res:* Systematics, distribution, behavior and ecology of recent Cephalopoda (squid, octopus, cuttlefish) of the world, particularly oceanic and tropical forms; phylogenetic relationship of families and orders; functional anatomy of bioluminescent organs, skin structures, color; fisheries resource utilization of cephalopods; author of over 100 papers and books, editor 3 books. *Mailing Add:* Nat Mus Natural Hist Smithsonian Inst Invert Zool - Rm E517 Washington DC 20560. *Fax:* 202-357-2343

ROPER, GERALD C, PHYSICAL CHEMISTRY. *Current Pos:* RETIRED. *Personal Data:* b Tewksbury, Mass, Dec 18, 33; m 57; c 3. *Educ:* Univ Boston, AB, 56, PhD (phys chem), 66. *Prof Exp:* From asst prof to assoc prof phys chem, Dickinson Col, 62-74, prof chem, 74-95, chmn dept, 71-95. *Mem:* Am Chem Soc. *Res:* Inorganic synthesis; transition metal chemistry. *Mailing Add:* 870 Pleasant Valley Rd Biglerville PA 17307

ROPER, L(EON) DAVID, THEORETICAL PARTICLE PHYSICS, BIOPHYSICS. *Current Pos:* from asst prof to assoc prof, Va Polytech Inst & State Univ, 67-74, actg head dept, 77-78, head, 90-95, PROF PHYSICS, VA POLYTECH INST & STATE UNIV, 74- *Personal Data:* b Shattuck, Okla, Dec 13, 35; m 94, Jeanne Baril; c Tamra Dawn (Oliver) & Truda G. *Educ:* Okla Baptist Univ, AB, 58; Mass Inst Technol, PhD(pion-nucleon interaction), 63. *Prof Exp:* Asst, Mass Inst Technol, 58-63; fel, Lawrence

Radiation Lab, Univ Calif, 63-65; asst prof physics, Ky Southern Col, 65-67. *Concurrent Pos:* Instr, Eastern Nazarene Col, 62-63; mem staff, KEK Nat Lab High Energy Physics, Japan, 80-81 & Europ Orgn Nuclear Res. *Mem:* Fel Am Phys Soc. *Res:* Particle scattering phenomenology; nonrenewable resource depletion; computational physics. *Mailing Add:* Dept Physics Va Polytech Inst & State Univ Blacksburg VA 24061-0435. *E-Mail:* roperld@vt.edu

ROPER, MARYANN, cancer research, for more information see previous edition

ROPER, PAUL JAMES, STRUCTURAL GEOLOGY, GEOLOGICAL CONSULTING FOR OIL & GAS. *Current Pos:* TRAINING SPECIALIST III, UNIV TEX, AUSTIN, 96- *Personal Data:* b Detroit, Mich, June 29, 39; div. *Educ:* Univ Mich, Ann Arbor, BS, 62; Univ Nebr, Lincoln, MS, 64; Univ NC, Chapel Hill, PhD(geol), 70. *Prof Exp:* From instr to asst prof geol, Lafayette Col, 69-76; lectr, Univ Wis, Oshkosh, 76-77; assoc prof, Univ SW La, 77-78; prod geologist, Superior Oil Co, 78-80; explor geologist, Ramco Explor, 80-81; pres, Aalpha Explor Co, 81-83; explor geologist, Celeron Oil & Gas Co, 83-85; geol consult, 85-96. *Concurrent Pos:* Explor geologist, Cypress Petrol Co, 78; consult, explor geol; lectr & trainer, oil & gas explor, zeolite indust. *Mem:* Geol Soc Am; Am Geophys Union; Am Geol Inst; Am Asn Petrol Geologists; Earthquake Eng Res Inst. *Res:* Geology and tectonics of Brevard zone, Southern Appalachian Mountains, Motagua fault zone and Sierra de las Minas Mountains, Guatemala; proposed theory of plastic plate tectonics; post-Jurassic tectomism in eastern North America; exploration for oil & gas; zeolites to solve environmental problems. *Mailing Add:* 23014 Grand Rapids Spring TX 77373

ROPER, ROBERT, ELASTOMERS. *Current Pos:* RETIRED. *Personal Data:* b Vienna, Austria, Jan 1, 28; US citizen; m 58, Rhoda Buchler; c Amy (Lyons) & Lisa (Summers). *Educ:* City Col New York, BS, 51; NY Univ, PhD(org chem), 57. *Prof Exp:* Chemist, Esso Res & Eng Co, 57-60, sr chemist, 60-65, res assoc surface coatings, rubbers, adhesives & sealants, 65-78, res assoc info analysts, Exxon Res & Eng Co, 78-93. *Mem:* Am Chem Soc. *Res:* Development of polymers for elastomers, sealants and coatings; effect of polymer structure on properties; polymer synthesis; information retrieval and analysis; patent and technical literature. *Mailing Add:* 22 Oakland Pl Summit NJ 07901

ROPER, ROBERT GEORGE, ATMOSPHERIC TURBULENCE. *Current Pos:* assoc prof to prof aerospace eng, 69-76, prof aerospace eng & geophys sci, 77-80, PROF ATMOSPHERIC SCI, GA INST TECHNOL, 80- *Personal Data:* b Adelaide, Australia, Apr 30, 33; m 58, Claire F Henderson; c Paul (deceased), Geoffrey, David & Carolyn. *Educ:* Univ Adelaide, BSc, 57 & 58, PhD(physics), 63. *Prof Exp:* Demonstr physics, Univ Adelaide, 58, Radio Res Bd grant & res officer upper atmosphere, 62-63; Nat Acad Sci-Nat Res Coun resident res assoc, NASA, Goddard Space Flight Ctr, Md, 64-65; assoc prof aerospace eng, Ga Inst Technol, 65-66; sr res scientist, Australian Defence Sci Serv, 66-69. *Concurrent Pos:* Pres, Int Comt Meteorol Upper Atmosphere, Int Asn Meteorol & Atmospheric Physics, 79-87; Middle Atmosphere Prog Steering Comt, Int Coun Sci Unions, 82-89; co-chmn, Global Meteor Observations Systs, Int Astron Union, Int Union Geod & Geophys, 82- *Mem:* Am Geophys Union; Am Meteorol Soc; fel Australian Inst Physics; Int Asn Geomagnetism & Aeronomy; fel Royal Meteorol Soc. *Res:* Interpretation of upper atmosphere radar data, particular emphasis on measurement of winds and turbulence; radar scattering processes. *Mailing Add:* Sch Earth & Atmospheric Sci Ga Inst Technol Atlanta GA 30332-0340. *Fax:* 404-894-5638; *E-Mail:* roper@eas.gatech.edu

ROPER, STEPHEN DAVID, SENSORY NEUROBIOLOGY, NEUROPLASTICITY. *Current Pos:* PROF ANAT & NEUROBIOL, COLO STATE UNIV, 85- *Personal Data:* b Rock Island, Ill, May 30, 45; m 85; c 2. *Educ:* Harvard Col, BA, 67; Univ Col, London, PhD(physiol), 70. *Prof Exp:* Fel neurobiol, Harvard Med Sch, 70-73; asst prof anat, Med Sch, Univ Colo, 73-79, asst prof physiol, 76-79, assoc prof anat & physiol, 79-85, prof anat & physiol, 85- *Concurrent Pos:* Fulbright fel, 67-69; instr neurobiol, Harvard Med Sch, 71-73; NIH res career develop award; consult, NIH Site Visit Teams, 77-; mem, NIH Neurobiol Study Sect, 81-86; chmn, Dept Anat & Neurobiol, Colo State Univ, 85-90; counr, Asn Chem Reception Sci, 88-91. *Mem:* Am Asn Anat; Soc Neurosci; Am Physiol Soc. *Res:* Chemosensory transduction mechanisms in taste; development and maintenance of synaptic connections in the vertebrate, focusing on trophic interactions between neurons and their targets and upon the regeneration of neural connections after damage. *Mailing Add:* Physiol & Biophys Sch Med Univ Miami PO Box 016430 R430 Miami FL 33101

ROPER, WILLIAM L, MEDICINE. *Current Pos:* DEAN & PROF HEALTH POLICY & ADMNIN, SCH PUB HEALTH, UNIV NC, 97- *Personal Data:* b Birmingham, Ala, July 6, 48; m, Maryann Jedziniak; c William L Jr. *Educ:* Univ Ala, BS, 70, MD, 74, MPH, 81. *Honors & Awards:* President's Award, Asn Health Servs Res, 89; Award Excellence, Nat Asn Health Data Orgn, 91. *Prof Exp:* Resident pediat, Med Ctr, Univ Colo, Denver, 74-77; health officer, Jefferson Co Dept Health, Birmingham, Ala, 77-83; spec asst to pres health policy, White House, Washington, DC, 83-86; adminr, Health Care Financing Admin, Washington, DC, 86-89; dep asst to pres, domestic policy & dir, White House Off Policy Develop, White House, 89-93; pres, Prudential Ctr Health Care Res, Atlanta, Ga, 93-95; sr vpres, Prudential Healthcare, 94-97. *Concurrent Pos:* Community fel, Dept Health & Hosps, City & County, Denver, Colo, 75-76; asst state health officer, Ala Dept Pub Health, Birmingham, 81-83; White House fel, 82-83; dir, Ctrs Dis Control, Atlanta, Ga, 90-93; adminr, Agency Toxic Substances & Dis Registry, Atlanta, Ga, 90-93. *Mem:* Inst Med-Nat Acad Sci; AMA; Am Acad Pediat; Am Pub Health Asn; fel Asn Health Servs Res. *Res:* Author or co-author of over 25 publications. *Mailing Add:* 170 Rosenau Hall Campus Box 7400 Univ NC Chapel Hill NC 27599-7400

ROPP, GUS ANDERSON, organic chemistry; deceased, see previous edition for last biography

ROPP, RICHARD C, SOLID STATE CHEMISTRY. *Current Pos:* EXPERT WITNESS, 86- *Personal Data:* b Detroit, Mich, Mar 26, 27; m 52; c 4. *Educ:* Franklin Col, AB, 50; Purdue Univ, West Lafayette, MS, 52; Rutgers Univ, Newark, PhD(phys chem), 71. *Prof Exp:* Adv develop engr, Sylvania Elec Prod, Pa, 52-63; mgr luminescence, Westinghouse Elec, NJ, 63-71; pres, Luminescence Technol, 71-73; res specialist chem, Rutgers Univ, Newark, 71-81; consult, Allied Chem Corp, 72-73; staff scientist solid state chem, 73-77; dir technol, 78-79, vpres, Petrex Corp, 80-83; vpres, Enhanced Oil Recovery, Can, 84-87; environ consult, 87-88. *Concurrent Pos:* Vpres, Int Superconductor, New York, 89-90. *Mem:* Am Chem Soc; Am Inst Chemists; AAAS; fel Royal Soc Chem; Mat Res Soc; Am Ceramics Soc. *Res:* Luminescent materials; laser hosts; phosphate glass; nuclear waste encapsulation; petroleum recovery; published three books on glass, phosphors and lamps. *Mailing Add:* 138 Mountain Ave Warren NJ 07059. *Fax:* 908-604-8565

ROPP, WALTER SHADE, CHEMISTRY OF ROSINS TERPENES & PEROXIDES, SYNTHETIC POLYMERS & CELLULOSIC POLYMERS. *Current Pos:* CONSULT, 88- *Personal Data:* b Lakeland, Fla, Oct 15, 22; m 49, Carolyn H; c James B, Donald C & Patricia A (Parker). *Educ:* Fla Southern Col, BS, 43; Pa State Col, MS, 44, PhD, 48. *Prof Exp:* Asst, Pa State Col, 43-44 & 45-47; res chemist, Exp Sta, Hercules Inc, 47-52, res supvr, 52-55, sr tech rep, 56-57, sr res chemist, Coatings Div, Res Ctr, 58-61, supvr coatings develop, Polymers Dept, 61-65, sr res chemist, Mat Res Div, 66-68, res assoc, 68-79, sr res assoc, Mat Sci Div, 79-88. *Concurrent Pos:* Instr, Pa State Col, 46-47. *Mem:* Am Chem Soc. *Res:* Plastics, elastomers, organic coatings and water soluble polymers; structure property relationships of polymers; preparation, properties and use of peroxides, terpenes and surface active agents. *Mailing Add:* 440 S Gulfview Blvd No 1503 N Clearwater Beach FL 33515-2518

ROQUEMORE, LEROY, mathematical modelling, computer simulation; deceased, see previous edition for last biography

ROQUES, ALBAN JOSEPH, MATHEMATICAL ANALYSIS. *Current Pos:* instr, 71-72 & 74-76, asst prof math & comput sci, 76-79, assoc prof, 79-85, PROF MATH, LA STATE UNIV, EUNICE, 85-, COORDR DATA PROCESSING, 81- *Personal Data:* b Paulina, La, Feb 3, 41; m 66; c 2. *Educ:* Nicholls State Univ, BS, 63; La State Univ, MS, 65, PhD(math), 74. *Prof Exp:* Math analyst comput sci, Space Div, Chrysler Corp, 65-68; instr math, Southeastern La Univ, 68-69. *Mem:* Math Asn Am. *Res:* Evolution equations in general Banach spaces. *Mailing Add:* 1471 W Elm St Eunice LA 70535

ROQUITTE, BIMAL C, PHYSICAL CHEMISTRY. *Current Pos:* ASSOC PROF PHYS CHEM, UNIV MINN, MORRIS, 66- *Personal Data:* b Calcutta, India, Sept 29, 31; m 61; c 2. *Educ:* Univ Calcutta, BSc, 52, MSc, 55; Univ Rochester, PhD(phys chem), 61. *Prof Exp:* Res assoc chem, Res Found, Ohio State Univ, 61-62; vis fel phys chem, Mellon Inst, 62; fel, Nat Res Coun Can, 62-64 & Mellon Inst, 64-66. *Mem:* Am Chem Soc. *Res:* Unimolecular decomposition of cyclobutane carboxaldehyde; photochemistry of bicyclic hydrocarbons; energy transfer in cyclopentanone both in the gas and solid phase; flash photolysis of hydrocarbon in the far ultraviolet. *Mailing Add:* Math & Sci Univ Minn Morris MN 56267-2134

RORABACHER, DAVID BRUCE, ANALYTICAL CHEMISTRY, INORGANIC CHEMISTRY. *Current Pos:* PROF ANALYTICAL CHEM, WAYNE STATE UNIV, 63- *Personal Data:* b Ypsilanti, Mich, June 8, 35; m 58, Beverly Joan Brown; c Karin, John, Karl & Joanne. *Educ:* Univ Mich, BS, 57; Purdue Univ, PhD(anal chem), 63. *Prof Exp:* Res engr, Ford Motor Co, 57-59. *Concurrent Pos:* NIH fel, Max Planck Inst Phys Chem, 64-65; assoc dean, Wayne State Univ, 84-85. *Mem:* Am Chem Soc. *Res:* Kinetics and mechanisms of coordination reactions and electron transfer reactions; nonaqueous solvation effects; macrocyclic ligand complexes. *Mailing Add:* Dept Chem Wayne State Univ Detroit MI 48202

RORABAUGH, DONALD T, MATERIALS SCIENCE ENGINEERING. *Current Pos:* Proj engr armament res & develop, US Army, 68-78, team leader, 78-84, sr proj engr, 84-87, PROJ MGR ARMAMENT RES & DEVELOP, US ARMY, 87- *Personal Data:* b Phoenixville, Pa, Sept 8, 44; m; Joan L Hoff; c Dennis. *Educ:* Drexel Inst Technol, Philadelphia, Pa, BS, 67, MS, 69; Fla Inst Technol, MS, 86, MBA, 89. *Concurrent Pos:* Asst instr, Drexel Inst Technol, 67-69. *Mem:* Am Soc Metals; Am Inst Mining & Metall Eng; NY Acad Sci; Res Soc NAm; Am Defense Preparedness Asn; Fed Bus Asn. *Res:* Coordinate the efforts of government and industry on research and development efforts aimed at improving armor and anti-armor munitions; munitions; author of over 100 publications; granted three patents. *Mailing Add:* 43 Ridge Rd Budd Lake NJ 07828

RORER, DAVID COOKE, NUCLEAR ENGINEERING, RESEARCH DIRECTION. *Current Pos:* DEP DIV MGR, REACTOR DIV, BROOKHAVEN NAT LAB, 80- *Personal Data:* b Darby, Pa, Oct 25, 37; m 61; Margo Drakou; c Eva, Kathryn & James. *Educ:* Mass Inst Technol, BS, 59; Univ Ill, MS, 61; Duke Univ, PhD(physics), 64. *Prof Exp:* Assoc physicist, Brookhaven Nat Lab, 65-72; reactor engr nuclear eng, Long Island Lighting Co, 72-75. *Concurrent Pos:* Adj prof, Polytech Inst NY, 76-84. *Mem:* Am Phys Soc; Am Nuclear Soc. *Res:* Neutron physics; nuclear cryogenics. *Mailing Add:* 10 Pine Path Port Jefferson NY 11777

RORIG, KURT JOACHIM, MEDICINAL CHEMISTRY, PHARMACOLOGY. *Current Pos:* PRES, CHEMI-DELPHIC CONSULT, 86-; ADJ PROF MED CHEM, UNIV ILL, CHICAGO, 89- *Personal Data:* b Bremerhaven, Ger, Dec 1, 20; US citizen; m 49; c James, Elizabeth & Miriam. *Educ:* Univ Chicago, BS, 42; Carleton Col, MA, 44; Univ Wis, PhD(chem), 47. *Prof Exp:* Chemist, J Seagram & Sons, 42-43; res chemist, G D Searle & Co, 47-60, asst dir, 60-74, assoc dir chem res, 74-79, sect head cardiovasc & renal res, 74-86. *Concurrent Pos:* Lectr, Loyola Univ Chicago, 50-60 & 87-88; adj prof med chem, Univ Ill, Chicago, 88-91. *Mem:* AAAS; Am Chem Soc; NY Acad Sci; Am Soc Pharmacol & Exp Therapeut. *Res:* Cardiovascular and psychotropic drugs; aldol condensations; synthesis of aliphatic disulfonic acids, pyrimidines, imidazoles, oxazolines, steroids and steroid analogs; drug toxicology. *Mailing Add:* 337 Hager Lane Glenview IL 60025

RORK, EUGENE WALLACE, SPACE SURVEILLANCE, ELECTRO OPTICS. *Current Pos:* mem staff, 75-96, CONSULT, LINCOLN LAB, MASS INST TECHNOL, 96- *Personal Data:* b Beatrice, Nebr, Mar 22, 40; m 93, Cynthia Hill; c Jennifer, Megan, Catherine & Wesley. *Educ:* Ohio State Univ, BS, 62, MS, 65, PhD(physics), 71. *Prof Exp:* Vis res assoc & lectr physics, Dept Physics, Ohio State Univ, 71-73; physicist, USAF Avionics Lab, 73-75. *Res:* Ground-based electro optical sensor systems and techniques for detection of artificial satellites in space from reflected sunlight at night and in daytime; photoelectronic imaging devices; computer-controlled telescopes; atmospheric optical phenomena; Mossbauer-effect spectroscopy of gadolinium and dysprosium nuclei. *Mailing Add:* Lincoln Lab 244 Wood St Lexington MA 02173. *Fax:* 781-981-0991; *E-Mail:* rork@ll.mit.edu

RORK, GERALD STEPHEN, PHARMACEUTICAL CHEMISTRY. *Current Pos:* PHARMACEUT CONSULT, 94- *Personal Data:* b Horton, Kans, Feb 12, 47; m 69; c 3. *Educ:* Univ Kans, BS, 69, MS, 73, PhD(pharmaceut chem), 74. *Prof Exp:* Jr chemist, Cook Paint & Varnish Co, 69-71; sr res scientist pharmaceut res & develop, Wyeth labs, Inc, 74-80; Riker Labs Inc, 78-81; assoc dir pharmaceut chem, Interx Res Corp, 81-94. *Mem:* Am Chem Soc; Am Asn Pharmaceut Scientists. *Res:* Improvement of drug bioavailability and dosage from stability; physical organic chemistry; mechanisms of elimination reactions and nucleophilic addition reactions involving slow proton transfer steps; design and development of drug delivery systems. *Mailing Add:* 1213 No 1100 Rd Lawrence KS 66047

RORKE, LUCY BALIAN, NEUROPATHOLOGY. *Current Pos:* PROF PATH, SCH MED, UNIV PA, 73-, CLIN PROF NEUROL, 79- *Personal Data:* b St Paul, Minn, June 22, 29; m 60, Robert R. *Educ:* Univ Minn, BA, 51, MA, 52, BS, 55, MD, 57. *Prof Exp:* Intern med, Philadelphia Gen Hosp, 57-58, resident physician path, 58-61, NIH fels neuropath, 61-62 & neonatal brain path, 63-69, asst neuropathologist & pediat pathologist, 62-68, chief neuropathologist, 68-69, chmn, Dept Anat Path, 69-73, pres med staff, 73-75, chmn, Dept Path, 73-77. *Concurrent Pos:* Consult neuropathologist, Wyeth Res Labs, 62-87; Wistar Inst Anat & Biol, 67-93 & Inst Merieux, Lyons, France, 69-70; neuropathologist, Children's Hosp Philadelphia, 65-, pres med staff, 86-88; forensic ceuropathologist, Off Med Examr, Philadelphia, 77-; interim pathologist-in-chief, Children's Hosp, Philadelphia, 96- *Mem:* Am Asn Neuropath (pres, 81-82); Am Neurol Asn; Am Acad Neurol; Col Am Path. *Res:* Pediatric neuropathology specifically brain tumors and hypoxic Ischemic injury; forensic neuropathology. *Mailing Add:* Dept Path Children's Hosp Philadelphia 324 S 34th St Philadelphia PA 19104-4301

RORRES, CHRIS, MATHEMATICS. *Current Pos:* From asst prof to assoc prof, 70-87, PROF MATH, DREXEL UNIV, 87- *Personal Data:* b Philadelphia, Pa, Jan 2, 41; m 81, Billie Pananes. *Educ:* Drexel Univ, BS, 63; NY Univ, MS, 65, PhD(math), 69. *Mem:* AAAS; Sigma Xi; Soc Indust & Appl Math; Am Math Soc; Math Asn Am. *Res:* Population dynamics; harvesting of renewable resources; solar energy; acoustic scattering. *Mailing Add:* Dept Math & Comput Sci Drexel Univ Philadelphia PA 19104. *E-Mail:* crorres@mes.drexel.edu

RORSTAD, OTTO PEDER, ENDOCRINOLOGY. *Current Pos:* from asst prof to assoc prof, 80-88, PROF MED, UNIV CALGARY, 88- *Personal Data:* b Alesund, Norway, Mar 26, 47; Can citizen; m 74; c 2. *Educ:* Univ BC, BSc, 69, MD, 72; McGill Univ, PhD(exp med), 80. *Prof Exp:* Instr med, Harvard Univ, 79-80. *Concurrent Pos:* Head, Div Endocrinol & Metab, Dept Med, Univ Calgary, 90-; assoc ed, Clin & Investigative Med, 90- *Mem:* Endocrine Soc; Royal Col Physicians & Surgeons Can; Can Soc Clin Invest; Can Soc Endocrinol & Metab; Can Hypertension Soc. *Res:* Regulation of the vasculature by neurotransmitters and hormones with particular reference to vasoactive intestinal peptide; vascular receptor for vasoactive intestinal peptide and the mechanism of action of vasoactive intestinal peptide in normal and hypertensive models. *Mailing Add:* Health Sci Ctr 3330 Hospital Dr NW Calgary AB T2N 4N1 Can

ROS, HERMAN H, physiological modeling & control, medical devices & systems, for more information see previous edition

ROSA, CASIMIR JOSEPH, oxidation, diffusion; deceased, see previous edition for last biography

ROSA, EUGENE JOHN, CHEMICAL PHYSICS. *Current Pos:* PRES & GEN MGR, NYAD INC, 88- *Personal Data:* b Sacramento, Calif, May 25, 37; m 59. *Educ:* Univ Calif, Berkeley, BS, 59; Univ Wash, PhD(chem), 64. *Prof Exp:* Chemist, Shell Develop Co, 64-67, supvr appl physics, 67-72; gen mgr, Veekay Ltd, 72-78; vpres & gen mgr, Ondyne Inc, 78-88. *Res:* Development of analytical and process control instrumentation; development, manufacture and sales of process instrumentation. *Mailing Add:* 913 Tarvan East Dr Martinez CA 94553

ROSA, NESTOR, PLANT PHYSIOLOGY, BIOCHEMISTRY. *Current Pos:* RETIRED. *Personal Data:* b Myrnam, Alta, Jan 15, 36; m 57; c 4. *Educ:* Univ Alta, BSc, 58, MSc, 60; Dalhousie Univ, PhD(biol), 66. *Prof Exp:* Horticulturist, Can Dept Agr, 60-63, plant physiologist, Res Br, Res Sta, 66-95. *Mem:* Can Soc Plant Physiol; Am Soc Plant Physiol; Am Soc Agron; Phytochemistry Soc NAm. *Res:* Physiological and biochemical studies related to growth and development and chemical changes in Nicotiana tabacum and other plants. *Mailing Add:* 5 Charles St Simcoe ON N3Y 1Z5 Can

ROSA, RICHARD JOHN, MAGNETOHYDRODYNAMICS. *Current Pos:* PROF MECH ENG, MONT STATE UNIV, 75- *Personal Data:* b Detroit, Mich, Mar 19, 27; m 50; c 3. *Educ:* Cornell Univ, BEP, 53, PhD(eng physics), 56. *Honors & Awards:* Wiley Award for Res; Faraday Mem Award, Int Liaison Group Magnetohydrodynamics; Rosa-Kantrowitz Award, Magnetohydrodynamics Indust Forum. *Prof Exp:* Res assoc, Cornell Univ, 55-56; prin res scientist, Avco-Everett Res Lab Div, Avco Corp, 56-71, chief scientist, MHD Generator Proj, 71-75. *Concurrent Pos:* Vis lectr, Stanford Univ, 66; magnetohydrodyn ed, J Adv Energy Conversion; vis prof, Univ Sydney, Australia, 78, Tokyo Inst Technol, Japan, 81; coordr, US/Japan Coop Res in Magnetohydrodynamics, 82-86. *Mem:* AAAS; sr mem Inst Elec & Electronics Engrs; sr mem Am Inst Aeronaut & Astronaut; Am Soc Mech Eng. *Res:* Applied physics; magnetohydrodynamics, particularly the development of magnetohydrodynamic generators for large-scale production of electric power from chemical or nuclear fission heat sources. *Mailing Add:* 7900 Bridger Canyon Rd Bozeman MT 59715-8634

ROSALSKY, ANDREW, PROBABILITY LIMIT THEOREMS, REAL & BANACH SPACE VALUED RANDOM VARIABLES. *Current Pos:* from asst prof to assoc prof, 78-90, PROF STATIST, UNIV FLA, 90- *Personal Data:* b New York, NY, July 27, 48; m 82, Mercedes Carrau; c Rachel Natasha. *Educ:* Ind Univ, AB, 70, AM, 72; Rutgers Univ, PhD(statist), 78. *Prof Exp:* Vis asst prof math, Ind Univ, 77-78. *Mem:* Inst Math Statist; Am Math Soc. *Res:* Proving strong and weak probability limit theorems for sums of real and Banach space valued random variables which can have a variety of different dependence structures. *Mailing Add:* Dept Statist Univ Fla Griffin-Floyd Hall Gainesville FL 32611-8545. *Fax:* 352-392-5175; *E-Mail:* rosalsky@stat.ufl.edu

ROSAN, ALAN MARK, CATALYSIS. *Current Pos:* ASSOC PROF CHEM, DREW UNIV, 86- *Personal Data:* b Buffalo, NY, Oct 6, 48; m 69; c 2. *Educ:* Earlham Col, BS, 70; Brandeis Univ, PhD(chem), 75. *Prof Exp:* Fel chem, Yale Univ, 75-77; sr res chemist, Corp Res & Technol, Allied Signal, 77-86. *Mem:* Am Chem Soc; Catalysis Soc; Sigma Xi; NY Acad Sci; AAAS; Int Union Pure & Appl Chem; Planetary Soc. *Res:* Applied and exploratory organometallic chemistry with application to catalysis, photochemistry, reaction mechanism, and organic synthesis. *Mailing Add:* Dept Chem Drew Univ Madison NJ 07940. *Fax:* 973-408-3572; *E-Mail:* arosan@drew.drew.edu

ROSAN, BURTON, ORAL MICROBIOLOGY, PERIDONTICS. *Current Pos:* res assoc microbiol, Univ Pa, 59-62, from asst prof to assoc prof, 63-75, actg chair, 77-78, prof, 75-96, EMER PROF MICROBIOL, SCH DENT MED, UNIV PA, 96- *Personal Data:* b New York, Aug 18, 28; m 51, Helen Mescon; c Rhea, Felice & Jonathan. *Educ:* City Col New York, BS, 50; Univ Pa, DDS, 57, MSc, 62. *Prof Exp:* NIH fel, 57-59. *Concurrent Pos:* Prin investr, NIDR grants, NIH, 59-; clin asst periodont, Albert Einstein Med Ctr, 62-65, attend periodont, 65-76; vis assoc prof, State Univ NY Downstate Med Ctr, 71-72; vis scientist, Nat Inst Dent Res, Sydney, Australia, 75, 80, Royal Col Surgeons, Downe, Eng, 85; ed consult, J Dent Res. *Mem:* AAAS; Int Asn Dent Res; Am Soc Microbiol; NY Acad Sci; Sigma Xi; fel Am Acad Microbiol. *Res:* Structure and biological activities of bacterial surfaces with particular reference to their role in attachment to tissues. *Mailing Add:* Sch Dent Med Univ Pa 4001 Spruce St Philadelphia PA 19104. *E-Mail:* rosan@biochem.dental.upenn.edu

ROSANO, HENRI LOUIS, CHEMISTRY. *Current Pos:* PROF CHEM, CITY COL NEW YORK, 62- *Personal Data:* b Nice, France, Feb 29, 24; US citizen; m 53; c 3. *Educ:* Sorbonne Univ, Lic es phys sc, 46, Dr Sc Eng, 51. *Honors & Awards:* Prize, Fatty Acid Mat Inst Paris, 51; Prize, Soc Cosmetic Chem, 73. *Prof Exp:* Fel, Columbia Univ, 54-55; sr res assoc, Lever Brothers Co, NJ, 55-59; res assoc mineral eng, Columbia Univ, 59-62. *Mem:* Am Chem Soc; Sigma Xi. *Res:* Surface and colloid chemistry. *Mailing Add:* 848 Woodland Ave Oradell NJ 07649-1432

ROSANO, THOMAS GERARD, CLINICAL CHEMISTRY, BIOCHEMISTRY. *Current Pos:* ASSOC PROF PUB HEALTH SCI, STATE UNIV NY, ALBANY, 85- *Personal Data:* b Albany, NY, Oct 22, 48; m 70; c 1. *Educ:* State Univ NY Albany, BS, 70; Albany Med Col, PhD(biochem), 75. *Prof Exp:* Fel clin chem, Dept Lab Med, Univ Wash, 74-76. *Concurrent Pos:* Assoc prof biochem & path, 76-89, prof path & lab med, Albany Med Col, 90-; assoc dir Clin Chem, Albany Med Ctr, 76-86, dir Clin Chem & head lab med, 86- *Mem:* Am Asn Clin Chem; Acad Clin Lab Physicians & Scientists; NY Acad Sci. *Res:* Development of new methodology and techniques in the area of clinical biochemistry clinical toxicology; chromatography; radioimmunoassay; enzymology; endocrine testing; metabolism of cyclosporine; tumor marker testing. *Mailing Add:* Div Lab Med Albany Med Ctr 47 New Scotland Ave Albany NY 12208-3412

ROSAR, MADELEINE E, MATHEMATICS, PHYSICS. *Current Pos:* RES ASSOC, PHILLIP LAB, 78- *Personal Data:* b Alface, France, July 15, 55. *Educ:* Fordham Univ, BS, 77, MS, 80. *Mem:* Am Phys Soc. *Mailing Add:* 98 Somerset Dr Suffern NY 10901-6903

ROSATI, ROBERT LOUIS, MEDICINAL CHEMISTRY. *Current Pos:* res chemist, 70-80, sr res investr, Med Res Lab, 80-87, PRIN RES INVESTR, PFIZER INC, 87- *Personal Data:* b Providence, RI, Mar 3, 42; m 66; c 2. *Educ:* Providence Col, BS, 64; Mass Inst Technol, PhD(org chem), 69. *Prof Exp:* NIH fel chem, Harvard Univ, 69. *Mem:* Am Chem Soc. *Mailing Add:* 71 Deans Mill Rd Stonington CT 06378-9719

ROSATO, FRANK JOSEPH, APPLIED PHYSICS. *Current Pos:* RETIRED. *Personal Data:* b Somerville, Mass, Feb 28, 25; m 50; c 5. *Educ:* Northeastern Univ, BS, 47; Tufts Univ, MS, 49; Harvard Univ, SM, 50, PhD(appl physics), 53. *Prof Exp:* Engr electronics, Polaroid Corp, Mass, 48-49; mathematician, Snow & Schule, Inc, 50; tech dir, GTE Sylvania Inc, Gen Tel & Electronics Corp, 53-73, chief scientist, 73-89. *Concurrent Pos:* Teaching fel, Tufts Univ, 48-49; fel, Harvard Univ, 53; vis lectr, Lowell Univ, 56-61; consult, Inst Naval Studies, 61-65 & Inst Defense Anal, 62; dir naval commun, USN, 64-69. *Mem:* Acoust Soc Am; Am Asn Physics Teachers; sr mem Inst Elec & Electronics Engrs. *Res:* Communication satellite systems; defense communication systems; electronic countermeasures; electromechanical transducers; electroacoustics. *Mailing Add:* 12 Blueberry Lane Lexington MA 02173

ROSAZZA, JOHN N, PHARMACOGNOSY, BIO-ORGANIC CHEMISTRY. *Current Pos:* from asst prof to assoc prof pharmacog, Univ Iowa, 69-73, assoc prof pharm, 73-77, head med chem, Natural Prod Div, Col Pharm, 77-85, PROF PHARM, UNIV IOWA, 77-, HEAD MED CHEM, NATURAL PROD DIV, COL PHARM, 89-, DIR, CTR BIOCATALYSIS & BIOPROCESSING. *Personal Data:* b Torrington, Conn, Dec 25, 40; m 62, Trudi Spaeth; c Paul, Mark & David. *Educ:* Univ Conn, BS, 62, MS, 66, PhD(org pharmacog), 68. *Honors & Awards:* Res Achievement Award in Natural Prod, Am Pharmaceut Assoc, Acad Pharmaceut Sci; Paul Dawson Biotechnol Award, Am Asn Clin Pharmacol. *Prof Exp:* NIH trainee natural prod res, Univ Conn, 65-68; fel pharmaceut biochem, Univ Wis, 68-69. *Mem:* Am Chem Soc; Am Soc Microbiologists; Am Soc Pharmacog; Am Soc Biol Chemist; Soc Indust Microbiol. *Res:* Microbial and enzymatic transformations of organic compounds including natural products, agricultural chemicals, antibiotics, alkaloids, terpenes; microbiology, enzymology, microbial chemistry and biochemistry; all aspects of biocatalysis. *Mailing Add:* Ctr Biocatalysis & Bioprocessing Univ Iowa Oakdale Res Pk 2501 Crosspark Rd Iowa City IA 52242-5006. *Fax:* 319-335-4901

ROSBERG, DAVID WILLIAM, PLANT PATHOLOGY. *Current Pos:* RETIRED. *Personal Data:* b Superior, Wis, Jan 3, 19; m; c 2. *Educ:* St Olaf Col, BS, 40; Ohio State Univ, MS, 47, PhD(plant path), 49. *Prof Exp:* Asst bot & plant path, Ohio State Univ, 46-47, res found, 48-49; from asst prof to prof plant path, Tex A&M Univ, 49-60, prof plant physiol, path & head dept plant sci, 60-74, prof plant path, 74-81, emer prof, 81- *Concurrent Pos:* Mem, President's Cabinet Comt on Environ, Subcomt on Pesticides, Task Group on Training Objectives & Stand as Resource Contact, 71- *Mem:* Fel AAAS; Am Phytopath Soc. *Mailing Add:* 11630 S H 30 College Station TX 77845

ROSBOROUGH, JOHN PAUL, ANIMAL PHYSIOLOGY. *Current Pos:* ADJ PROF PHYSIOL, DENT BR, UNIV TEX HEALTH SCI CTR, 86- *Personal Data:* b Chicago, Ill, June 23, 30; m 54; c 3. *Educ:* Univ Ill, Urbana, BS, 51, MS, 53, BS, 54, DVM, 56, PhD(vet med sci), 69. *Prof Exp:* Res asst physiol, Univ Ill, Urbana, 61-64; NIH fel biophys, Baylor Col Med, 69-70, from asst prof to assoc prof physiol, 71-87. *Mem:* Am Physiol Soc; Am Soc Vet Physiol & Pharmacol. *Res:* Cardiopulmonary resuscitation. *Mailing Add:* 7910 Mobud Dr Houston TX 77036-6402

ROSCHER, DAVID MOORE, PHOTOCHEMISTRY, PHYSICAL ORGANIC CHEMISTRY. *Current Pos:* SCI INSTR, ALEXANDRIA CITY SCH DIST, 75- *Personal Data:* b Mt Vernon, NY, Mar 28, 37; m 64, Nina Matheny. *Educ:* Rutgers Univ, BS, 59; Purdue Univ, PhD(org chem), 66. *Prof Exp:* Robert A Welch fel, Univ Tex, 65-67; res chemist, Celanese Res Co, 67-70; sci instr, Matawan High Sch, 70-75. *Mem:* AAAS; Am Chem Soc; Nat Sci Teachers Asn. *Res:* Gas-phase photochemical processes; photochemical polymerization and solvolysis reactions. *Mailing Add:* 10400 Hunter Ridge Dr Oakton VA 22124. *Fax:* 703-938-2844; *E-Mail:* dmroscher@aol.com

ROSCHER, NINA MATHENY, PHYSICAL ORGANIC CHEMISTRY. *Current Pos:* dir acad admin, Am Univ, 74-76, assoc prof chem, 74-79, assoc dean grad affairs & res, 76-79, vprovost acad serv, 79-85, dean fac affairs, 81-85, PROF CHEM, AM UNIV, 79-, DEPT CHAIR CHEM, 91- *Personal Data:* b Uniontown, Pa, Dec 8, 38; m 64. *Educ:* Univ Del, BS, 60; Purdue Univ, PhD, 64. *Honors & Awards:* Dreyfus Found Award, Am Chem Soc, 96. *Prof Exp:* Eli Lilly fel & instr chem, Purdue Univ, 64-65; instr, Univ Tex, 65-67; sr staff chemist, Coca-Cola Export Corp, 68; asst prof chem, Douglass Col, Rutgers Univ, 68-74, asst dean col, 71-74. *Concurrent Pos:* Mem, Sci Manpower Comn, 79-84, pres, 81-82; bd dir, Am Inst Chemists, 81-86. *Mem:* Am Chem Soc; fel Am Inst Chemists; NY Acad Sci; Soc Appl Spectros; fel AAAS. *Res:* Reaction mechanisms in organic chemistry, particularly in inorganic ion, free radical and light catalysis; structures of organic molecules. *Mailing Add:* Dept Chem Am Univ 4400 Mass Ave NW Washington DC 20016-8016. *Fax:* 202-885-1752; *E-Mail:* nrosche@american.edu

ROSCHLAU, WALTER HANS ERNEST, PHARMACOLOGY. *Current Pos:* sr res asst pharmacol, Connaught Med Res Labs, Univ Toronto, 60-62, res assoc, 62-66, assoc prof, Fac Med, 66-69, prof, 69-89, EMER PROF PHARMACOL, FAC MED, UNIV TORONTO, 89- *Personal Data:* b Sonneberg, Ger, Feb 14, 24; Can citizen; m 51; c 1. *Educ:* Univ Heidelberg, MD, 51. *Prof Exp:* Res asst exp med, W P Caven Mem Res Found, Toronto, Ont, 51-55; res asst, Gardiner Med Res Found, 55-60. *Res:* Blood coagulation; fibrinolytic enzymes; clinical pharmacology. *Mailing Add:* Dept Pharmacol Fac Med Univ Toronto 1 Kings College Circle Toronto ON M5S 1A8 Can

ROSCOE, CHARLES WILLIAM, molecular pharmacology, for more information see previous edition

ROSCOE, HENRY GEORGE, BIOCHEMISTRY, SCIENCE ADMINISTRATION. *Current Pos:* RETIRED. *Personal Data:* b Bridgeport, Conn, Nov 24, 30; m 55; c 3. *Educ:* Columbia Univ, AB, 52; Cornell Univ, PhD(biochem), 60. *Prof Exp:* Sr res biochemist, Lederle Labs, 60-72; assoc, NIH, 72-73, health scientist adminr, Grants Assoc Offi, 73-74 & Nat Inst Neurol & Commun Disorders & Stroke, 74-79, chief, referral br, Div Res Grants, 79-94. *Concurrent Pos:* Exec secy, Res Rev Comt B, Nat Heart, Lung & Blood Inst, 79-94. *Res:* Lipid biochemistry and cardiovascular biochemistry. *Mailing Add:* 33 Edgewood Dr Lexington VA 24450-9121

ROSCOE, JOHN MINER, CHEMICAL KINETICS, GAS PHASE PHOTOCHEMISTRY. *Current Pos:* from asst prof to assoc prof, 70-85, PROF CHEM, ACADIA UNIV, 85- *Personal Data:* b Halifax, NS, Dec 31, 43; m 68; c 2. *Educ:* Acadia Univ, BSc, 65, MSc, 66; McGill Univ, PhD(chem), 70. *Prof Exp:* Fel, Appl Physics Lab, Johns Hopkins Univ, 69-70. *Concurrent Pos:* Distinguished vis scientist, Nat Resources Coun, Ottawa, Can, 83-84; consult, Sohio; vis prof, Univ Waterloo, Ont, Can, 96-97. *Mem:* Chem Inst Can; Royal Soc Chem; InterAm Photochemistry Soc. *Res:* Chemical kinetics of reactions of atoms, molecules, free radicals and excited molecules in the gas phase; kinetic modelling; gas phase photochemistry. *Mailing Add:* PO Box 878 Wolfville NS B0P 1X0 Can

ROSCOE, JOHN STANLEY, JR, PHYSICAL INORGANIC CHEMISTRY. *Current Pos:* SR PARTNER, J S ROSCOE ASSOCS, 72- *Personal Data:* b Dakota Co, Minn, Oct 12, 22; m 46; c 6. *Educ:* Univ Chicago, PhB, 47, MS, 51; St Louis Univ, PhD(chem), 54. *Prof Exp:* Res assoc, St Louis Univ, 52-53; mem staff, Res Dept, Mathieson Chem Corp, 53-59, mem staff, Energy Div, Olin Mathieson Chem Corp, 59-61, res assoc, Chem Div, 61-68; dir res, Quantum Inc, 68-71. *Mem:* Fel AAAS; fel Am Inst Chemists; Am Chem Soc. *Res:* Synthetic and physical chemistry of the hydrides of aluminum and boron; organometallics; compounds of phosphorus, nitrogen and sulfur; high performance epoxy, urethane and polyimide coatings; urethane and silicone elastomers; glass reinforced plastics. *Mailing Add:* 267 Lanyon Dr Cheshire CT 06410-3128

ROSE, ARTHUR L, NEUROLOGY, PEDIATRICS. *Current Pos:* assoc prof, 75-80, DIR, DIV PEDIAT NEROL, HEALTH SCI CTR, STATE UNIV NY, BROOKLYN, 75-, PROF NEUROL, 80- *Personal Data:* b Cracow, Poland, July 21, 32; US citizen; c 2. *Educ:* Univ Bristol, MB ChB, 57; Royal Col Physicians & Surgeons, dipl child health, 59; Am Bd Pediat, dipl, 63; Am Bd Psychiat & Neurol, dipl & cert neurol, 69, cert child neurol, 73. *Prof Exp:* Res fel pediat, Med Sch, Harvard Univ, 61-63; instr neuropath, Col Physicians & Surgeons, Columbia Univ, 66-67; from asst prof to assoc prof neurol & pediat, Albert Einstein Col Med, 67-75. *Concurrent Pos:* Fel behav & neurol sci, Albert Einstein Col Med, 67-69, Nat Inst Neurol Dis & Stroke fels, 69-77; assoc attend neurologist, Bronx Munic Hosp & Montefiore Hosp, 67-; assoc attend neurologist & pediatrician, Albert Einstein Col Hosp, 67-75; attend neurologist, Kings Co Hosp & State Univ Hosp; vediat neurol consult, Long Island Col Hosp. *Mem:* Am Acad Neurol; Child Neurol Soc; Soc Pediat Res; Asn Res Nervous & Ment Dis; Prof Child Neurol. *Res:* Investigation of neurotoxic substances on the development of the nervous system. *Mailing Add:* Dept Neurol Health Sci Ctr State Univ NY Brooklyn Brooklyn NY 11203

ROSE, ARTHUR WILLIAM, APPLIED GEOCHEMISTRY, ORE DEPOSITS. *Current Pos:* from asst prof to assoc prof, Pa State Univ, 67-75, prof, 75-96, dir, Mineral Conserv Sect, 78-85, EMER PROF GEOCHEM, PA STATE UNIV, 75- *Personal Data:* b Bellefonte, Pa, Aug 8, 31; m 71, Marjorie McCraken; c Theresa, Bruce & Edith. *Educ:* Antioch Col, BS, 53; Calif Inst Technol, MS, 55, PhD(geol & geochem), 58. *Prof Exp:* From geologist to sr geologist mineral explor, Bear Creek Mining Co, Kennecott Copper Co, 57-64; mining geologist geol mapping, Div Mines & Minerals, State of Alaska, 64-67. *Concurrent Pos:* Mem, Nat Comt Geochem, Nat Res Coun, 78-81, mem, Bd Energy & Mineral Resources, 84-86. *Mem:* Asn Explor Geochemists (pres, 80-81); Geochem Soc; Soc Econ Geologist (vpres, 89); Geol Soc Am; Soc Mining Engrs. *Res:* Environmental geochemistry; geochemical exploration; geology and geochemistry of metallic ore deposits; economics of mineral resources; geochemistry of sedimentary rocks. *Mailing Add:* Dept Geosci Pa State Univ 218 Deike Bldg University Park PA 16802. *Fax:* 814-863-2001; *E-Mail:* rose@ems.psu.edu

ROSE, BIRGIT, CELL PHYSIOLOGY, MEMBRANE CHANNELS. *Current Pos:* res asst prof, 71-77, res assoc prof, 77-78, RES PROF PHYSIOL & BIOPHYS, MED SCH, UNIV MIAMI, 89- *Personal Data:* b Tegernsee, WGer, Aug 21, 43; m 71. *Educ:* Univ Munich, PhD(natural sci), 70. *Prof Exp:* Lab technician, Med Sch, Stanford Univ, 62-63; lab technician, Stanford Res Inst, 63-64; from res asst to res assoc physiol, Columbia Univ, 67-71. *Mem:*

AAAS; Biophys Soc; Soc Gen Physiol; Am Soc Cell Biol. *Res:* Intercellular communication, its basis of mechanism and role in differentiation; role of calcium in membrane physiology; membrane structure; membrane channels. *Mailing Add:* Marine Biol Lab Woods Hole MA 02543. Fax: 305-547-5931

ROSE, CARL MARTIN, JR, PHYSICS. *Current Pos:* mem staff, 74-78, SUPVR, BELL LABS, 78- *Personal Data:* b Macon, Ga, Aug 31, 36; m 60; c 2. *Educ:* Yale Univ, BS, 58; Univ Chicago, SM, 62; PhD(physics), 67. *Prof Exp:* Res assoc physics, Duke Univ, 66-67, asst prof, 67-74. *Mem:* Am Phys Soc; Asn Comput Mach; Inst Elec & Electronics Engrs. *Res:* Electron beam lithography; real-time computing; pattern recognition; numerical computing techniques. *Mailing Add:* 44 Plymouth Dr Berkeley Heights NJ 07922

ROSE, CHARLES BUCKLEY, ORGANIC CHEMISTRY. *Current Pos:* Asst prof chem, 66-73, ASSOC PROF CHEM, UNIV NEV, RENO, 73- *Personal Data:* b Washington, DC, Feb 8, 38; m 61; c Donal B, Xanne C & Erik J. *Educ:* Brigham Young Univ, BS, 60; Harvard Univ, AM, 63, PhD(org chem), 66. *Mem:* Am Chem Soc; Chem Soc; fel Am Inst Chemists; Sigma Xi. *Res:* Structure elucidation of natural products; development of new synthetic methods; model systems of physiologically active compounds. *Mailing Add:* Dept Chem Univ Nev Reno NV 89557

ROSE, DAVID, PHYSICS. *Current Pos:* RETIRED. *Personal Data:* b Chicago, Ill, Nov 13, 21; m 44; c 2. *Educ:* Univ NDak, BS, 42; Carnegie Inst Technol, DSc, 52. *Prof Exp:* Control chemist, Chicago Sanit Dist, 42; jr physicist, Metall Lab, Chicago, 44; jr engr, Manhattan Engrs, Tenn, 44-45; jr scientist, Los Alamos Sci Lab, Univ Calif, 45-46, asst engr, 46; asst res physicist, Carnegie Inst Technol, 47-52; assoc physicist, Argonne Nat Lab, 52-56; physicist, Gen Atomic Div, Gen Dynamics Corp, 56-66; consult engr, United Engrs & Constructors, 66-67; sr nuclear engr, Argonne Nat Lab, 67- *Res:* Nuclear physics; power reactors; reactor safety. *Mailing Add:* Argonne Nat Lab 9700 S Cass Ave Argonne IL 60439

ROSE, DONALD CLAYTON, MATHEMATICS. *Current Pos:* PROF MATH, UNIV S FLA, 77- *Personal Data:* b Clearmont, Mo, Apr 30, 20; m 42; c 5. *Educ:* Transylvania Col, AB, 45; Univ Ky, MA, 48, PhD(math), 54. *Prof Exp:* Instr astron & math, Univ Ky, 45-54; from assoc prof to prof, Univ SFla, 60-75, chmn dept, 61-75; prof math, Hillsborough Community Col, 75-77. *Mem:* Am Math Soc; Math Asn Am. *Mailing Add:* 951 Malcolm Blvd PO Box 61 Rutherford College NC 28671

ROSE, EARL FORREST, PATHOLOGY. *Current Pos:* PROF PATH, COL MED, UNIV IOWA, 68- *Personal Data:* b Isabel, SDak, Sept 23, 26; m 51; c 6. *Educ:* Yankton Col, BA, 49; Univ SDak, BSM, 51; Univ Nebr, MD, 53; Southern Methodist Univ, LLB, 67. *Prof Exp:* Resident path, Med Ctr, Baylor Univ, 56-58; resident DePaul Hosp, St Louis, 58-60; fel forensic path, Med Col Va, 61, lectr forensic path, 61-63; prof path, Univ Tex Southwestern Med Sch, Dallas, 63-68. *Concurrent Pos:* Dep chief med examr, Commonwealth Va, 61-63; mem, Dallas Co Med Examrs, 63-68; lectr, Col Law, Univ Iowa, 71. *Mem:* Fel Col Am Pathologists; fel Am Clin Pathologists; Am Acad Forensic Sci; AMA. *Res:* Forensic pathology; surgical and autopsy pathology; application of pathology to law. *Mailing Add:* Col Med Dept Path Iowa City IA 52242

ROSE, EVAN ANDREW, ELECTRON-BEAM PHYSICS. *Current Pos:* STAFF SCIENTIST, LOS ALAMOS NAT LAB, 86- *Personal Data:* b Englewood, NJ, May 20, 50. *Educ:* Dartmouth Col, AB, 72; Cambridge Univ, Math Tripos, 73; Cornell Univ, MS, 76; Univ Wis-Madison, PhD(physics), 82. *Prof Exp:* Res scientist, McDonnell Douglas Res Labs, 82-86. *Mem:* Am Phys Soc. *Res:* Electron beam propagation; electron-beam pumped excimer lasers; flash radiography; drift waves in toroidal plasmas. *Mailing Add:* Rte 4 Box 17C Santa Fe NM 87501

ROSE, FRANCIS L, ZOOLOGY. *Current Pos:* PROF BIOL, SW TEX STATE UNIV, 92- *Personal Data:* b Augusta, Ga, Dec 20, 35; m 55; c 4. *Educ:* Univ Ga, BS, 60, MS, 62; Tulane Univ, PhD, 65. *Prof Exp:* NIH fel, Fla State Mus, 65-66; asst prof, Tex Tech Univ, 66-74, prof biol, 74-92. *Concurrent Pos:* Am Philos Soc grant, 65-66. *Mem:* Am Soc Ichthyologists & Herpetologists. *Res:* Anatomy, ecology, behavior and systematics. *Mailing Add:* Dept Biol SW Tex State Univ San Marcos TX 78666-4602

ROSE, FRANK EDWARD, solid state physics, for more information see previous edition

ROSE, GENE FUERST, MATHEMATICS, COMPUTER SCIENCE. *Current Pos:* RETIRED. *Personal Data:* b Erie, Pa, Mar 15, 18; m 40; c 1. *Educ:* Case Inst Technol, BS, 38; Univ Wis, MA, 47, PhD(math), 52. *Prof Exp:* Chemist, Copperweld Corp, Ohio & Pa, 40-42; res engr, Res Labs, Westinghouse Elec Corp, 42-45; res assoc, Allegany Ballistics Lab, George Washington Univ, 45; asst & actg instr math, Univ Wis, 45-52; mem staff, Sandia Corp, 52-55; mem tech staff, Space Tech Labs Inc, Thompson Ramo Wooldridge, Inc, 55-60; sr scientist, Syst Develop Corp, Calif, 60-68; prof math & info sci, Case Western Reserve Univ, 68-77; prof, dept comput sci, Calif State Univ, Fullerton, 77-85. *Concurrent Pos:* Guest prof, Munich Tech Univ, 66-67; guest lectr, Imp Col Sci & Technol, Univ London, 66; Alexander von Humboldt Found grant, Gesfur Math und Datenverarbeitung MBH Bonn, 72-73. *Mem:* Am Math Soc; Math Asn Am; Asn Symbolic Logic. *Res:* Recursive function theory; foundations of mathematics; formal language theory; mathematical machine theory; relational data bases. *Mailing Add:* 1565 Sherwood Village Circle Placentia CA 92670-3105

ROSE, GEORGE DAVID, PROTEIN FOLDING. *Current Pos:* PROF, DEPT BIOPHYS & BIOPHYS CHEM, JOHNS HOPKINS UNIV, 94- *Personal Data:* b Chicago, Ill, Aug 28, 39; c 2. *Educ:* Bard Col, BS, 63; Ore State Univ, MS, 72, PhD(biochem & biophys), 76. *Honors & Awards:* Hinkle Award & Lect, Pa State Univ, 85. *Prof Exp:* Asst prof chem, Univ Del, 77-80; distinguished prof biochem, Pa State Univ, 80-91; prof biochem, Univ NC, Chapel Hill, 91-92; alumni endowed prof biochem & molecular biophys, Wash Univ, 92-94. *Concurrent Pos:* Res career develop award, NIH, 80-85; mem, Bd Ed Adv, Biopolymers, 87-; exec ed, Proteins, Struct, Function & Genetics, 89-90; sci adv bd, Nature Biotechnol, 92- *Mem:* Am Soc Biochem & Molecular Biol; Biophys Soc; Am Chem Soc; AAAS; Protein Soc (secy/treas, 93-); NY Acad Sci. *Res:* Structure, function, self-assembly and dynamics of macromolecules of biological interest, particularly proteins. *Mailing Add:* Dept Biophys & Biophys Chem Johns Hopkins Univ 725 Wolfe St Baltimore MD 21205. Fax: 410-614-3971

ROSE, GORDON WILSON, EPIDEMIOLOGY, CLINICAL MICROBIOLOGY. *Current Pos:* from asst prof to assoc prof, 57-80, PROF BACT, HISTOL & CHEM, WAYNE STATE UNIV, 80- *Personal Data:* b Elmira, NY, Apr 25, 24; m 51; c 3. *Educ:* Wayne State Univ, AB, 50; Univ Detroit, MS, 54; Univ Mich, PhD(epidemiol sci), 65. *Prof Exp:* Asst chem, Wayne State Univ, 47-48, chem, gross anat & histol, Dept Mortuary Sci, 50-54, instr bact, histol & chem, 54-56; spec instr bact, Univ Detroit, 56-57. *Concurrent Pos:* Spec instr, Providence Hosp, Detroit, 57-58; assoc dir dept mortuary sci, Wayne State Univ, 57-65, spec instr, Sch Med, 65; asst dir dept, Deaconess Hosp, 65-66. *Mem:* Am Asn Bioanalysts; Am Soc Clin Pathologists; Am Pub Health Asn; Am Soc Microbiol; Sigma Xi. *Res:* Clinical and post-mortem microbiology; histopathogenesis of infectious diseases; hospital epidemiology. *Mailing Add:* 1205 Devonshire Rd Grosse Pointe Park MI 48230-1155

ROSE, HAROLD WAYNE, ELECTRONICS ENGINEERING, COMPUTER SCIENCE. *Current Pos:* RES SCIENTIST, DEPT PHYSICS, DUKE UNIV. *Personal Data:* b Telluride, Colo, Jan 11, 40; m 64; c 4. *Educ:* Univ Colo, Boulder, BS, 62, MS, 64; Ohio State Univ, PhD(elec eng), 72. *Prof Exp:* Res engr, Air Force Systs Command, Wright-Patterson AFB, 66-71, electronics engr, Avionics Lab, 71- *Mem:* Optical Soc Am; Am Inst Physics. *Res:* Holography; holographic optical elements; coherent optics; lasers; missile guidance techniques; electro-optical trackers; laser trackers. *Mailing Add:* 9 Willowspring Pl Chapel Hill NC 27514

ROSE, HARVEY ARNOLD, FLUID DYNAMICS. *Current Pos:* fel, 77-79, MEM STAFF, LOS ALAMOS NAT LAB, 79- *Personal Data:* b New York, NY, Nov 9, 47. *Educ:* City Col New York, BS, 68; Harvard Univ, MA, 69, PhD(physics), 75. *Prof Exp:* Health serv officer radiol health, USPHS, 70-72; fel fluid turbulence, Nat Ctr Atmospheric Res, 75-76; vis scientist turbulence res, Observ Nice, France, 76-77. *Mem:* Sigma Xi. *Res:* Calculate properties of turbulence, using methods of quantum field theory in high temperature plasmas and in fluids. *Mailing Add:* 3095 Arizona Ave Los Alamos NM 87544

ROSE, HERBERT G, MEDICINE. *Current Pos:* ASSOC CHIEF STAFF, RES & DEVELOP, BRONX VET ADMIN MED CTR, 74- *Personal Data:* b Chicago, Ill, Feb 21, 30. *Educ:* Univ Ill, MD, 54. *Mem:* Am Heart Asn; Am Soc Clin Nutrit; Am Fedn Clin Res. *Res:* Metabolic diseases; lipo protein metabolism. *Mailing Add:* Vet Admin Hosp Bronx NY 10468

ROSE, IRA MARVIN, ORGANIC CHEMISTRY, ANALYTICAL CHEMISTRY. *Current Pos:* RETIRED. *Personal Data:* b Brooklyn, NY, Feb 22, 21; m 54, Naomi Cohen; c Robert. *Educ:* Brooklyn Col, BA, 41; Columbia Univ, AM, 49, PhD(org chem), 52. *Prof Exp:* Analytical chemist, Wallerstein Labs, NY, 41-42; analytical chemist, War Dept, Edgewood Arsenal, Md, 42-44, org chemist, Chem Corps, 46-47; sr org chemist, US Vitamin Corp, NY, 52-58; group leader res & develop indust org chem, Nopco Chem Co, 58-71 & Nopco Div, 71-74; sr res assoc, Process Chem Div, Diamond Shamrock Chem Co, Morristown, 74-82. *Concurrent Pos:* Consult, 82- *Mem:* Am Chem Soc. *Res:* Fine chemical synthesis; industrial organic synthesis, research, product and process development and general analytical chemistry; synthesis, research, development and analysis of chemical warfare agents. *Mailing Add:* 55 Greenwood Dr Millburn NJ 07041

ROSE, IRWIN ALLAN, BIOCHEMISTRY. *Current Pos:* SR MEM, BIOCHEM DIV, INST CANCER RES, FOX CHASE CANCER CTR, 63- *Personal Data:* b Brooklyn, NY, July 16, 26; m 55; c 4. *Educ:* Univ Chicago, BS, 49, PhD(biochem), 52. *Prof Exp:* Fel, Dept Med, Western Res Univ, 52-53 & Dept Pharmacol, NY Univ, 53-54; from instr to assoc prof, Dept Biochem, Sch Med, Yale Univ, 54-63. *Concurrent Pos:* Affil phys biochem, Grad Sch, Univ Pa, 63-70, univ prof, 63-76; Guggenheim fel, Univ Oxford & Hebrew Univ, 72; merit award, NIH, 88-98. *Mem:* Nat Acad Sci; AAAS; Am Chem Soc; Am Soc Biol Chemists; Am Acad Arts & Sci. *Res:* Mechanisms of transfer enzyme; protein degradation; regulation of metabolism; author of numerous publications. *Mailing Add:* Inst Cancer Res 7701 Burholme Ave Philadelphia PA 19111. Fax: 215-728-2412; E-Mail: ia_rose@fcc.edu

ROSE, ISRAEL HAROLD, MATHEMATICS. *Current Pos:* chmn dept, 68-72 & 80-82, prof math, 68-82, EMER PROF & RES PROF, LEHMAN COL, 83- *Personal Data:* b New Britain, Conn, May 17, 17; m 61, Susan Ann Lazarus; c Steven, Dora & Eric. *Educ:* Brooklyn Col, AB, 38, AM, 41; Harvard Univ, PhD(math), 51. *Prof Exp:* Tutor & instr math, Brooklyn Col, 38-41; instr, Pa State Univ, 42-46; from asst prof to assoc prof, Univ Mass, 48-60; from assoc prof to prof math, Hunter Col, 60-68, chmn dept, 66-68. *Concurrent Pos:* Vis asst prof, Mt Holyoke Col, 51-52, vis assoc prof, 54-55 & 58-59; fel, Ford Found, 52-53. *Mem:* Am Math Soc. *Res:* Abstract algebra. *Mailing Add:* 18 Floral Dr Hastings On Hudson NY 10706

ROSE, JAMES A, REGULATION OF VIRUS MACROMELECULAR SYNTHESIS. *Current Pos:* CHIEF MOLECULAR STRUCT SECT, LAB BIOL VIRUSES, NAT INST ALLERGY & INFECTIOUS DIS, NIH, 72- *Educ:* Harvard Univ, MD, 56. *Mailing Add:* Molecular Struct Sect LVD Nat Inst Allergy & Infectious Dis NIH 8512 Hunter Creek Trail Potomac MD 20854-2561

ROSE, JAMES C, PERIONATAL ENDOCRINOLOGY. *Current Pos:* ASSOC PROF PHYSIOL & PHARMACOL, BOWMAN GRAY SCH MED, 82-, ASSOC PROF OBSTET, 83- *Educ:* Med Col Va, PhD(physiol), 74. *Mailing Add:* Dept Physiol Pharmacol & Obstet/Gynec Bowman Gray Sch Med Winston-Salem NC 27157. *Fax:* 919-716-4204

ROSE, JAMES DAVID, NEUROSCIENCE, BIOPSYCHOLOGY. *Current Pos:* assoc prof, 76-80, PROF PSYCHOL, UNIV WYO, 80- *Personal Data:* b Ann Arbor, Mich, Mar 31, 42; m 66; c 2. *Educ:* Cent Mich Univ, BS, 64; Ind Univ, PhD(psychol), 70. *Prof Exp:* Fel, Sch Med, Emory Univ, 69-71; asst prof psychol, Dartmouth Col, 71-74; asst prof neurophysiol & anat, Sch Med, Emory Univ, 74-76. *Concurrent Pos:* Prin investr, NIH res grants, 72- *Mem:* Soc Neurosci; Am Asn Anatomists; Soc Psychoneuroendocrinol. *Res:* Neurological bases of behavior; neurophysiology; neuroanatomy. *Mailing Add:* Dept Psychol Univ Wyo PO Box 3295 Laramie WY 82071-3295

ROSE, JAMES STEPHENSON, ORGANIC CHEMISTRY. *Current Pos:* SR RES CHEMIST, UPJOHN CO, 64- *Personal Data:* b Halifax, NS, Can, July 9, 26. *Educ:* Dalhousie Univ, BSc, 48, MSc, 50; Yale Univ, PhD(chem), 55. *Prof Exp:* Asst prof chem, NS Tech Univ, 54-55; sr res chemist, Olin-Mathieson Chem Corp, 55-62; sr res chemist, Naval Res Estab, NS, 62-64. *Res:* Organic reaction mechanisms; synthetic organic chemistry; structure-spectra correlation of organic compounds. *Mailing Add:* 1820 Durham Rd Guilford CT 06437

ROSE, JAMES TURNER, AERONAUTICAL ENGINEERING. *Current Pos:* AEROSPACE CONSULT, 92- *Personal Data:* b Louisburg, NC, Sept 21, 35; m, Daniele Raymond; c James T & Katharine S. *Educ:* NC State Univ, BS, 57. *Honors & Awards:* Lindberg Award Mgt Leadership, Am Inst Aeronaut & Astronaut, 83, Aerospace Contrib to Soc Award, 93; Exceptional Serv Medal, NASA, 90; Laurels Award, Aviation Week, 90. *Prof Exp:* Prog systs mgr, McDonnell Douglas Astronaut Co, St Louis, 64-69, mgr shuttle opers & implementation, 69-72, mgr shuttle support, 72-74, mgr space processing progs, 76-83, dir electrophoresis opers in space, 83-86; aero res engr, NASA, Va, 57-59, proj engr, 59-64, dir space shuttle eng, Washington, 74-76, asst adminr commun progs, 87-91. *Mailing Add:* 3440 Sunset Ridge Dr Merritt Island FL 32953-8636

ROSE, JOHN CHARLES, PHYSIOLOGY. *Current Pos:* From instr to asst prof med, 54-58, assoc prof physiol & biophys, 58-60, chmn dept biophys, 59-63, dean, Sch Med, 63-73 & 78-79, PROF PHYSIOL & BIOPHYS, SCH MED, GEORGETOWN UNIV, 60-, PROF MED, 73- *Personal Data:* b New York, NY, Dec 13, 24; m 48; c 5. *Educ:* Fordham Univ, BS, 46; Georgetown Univ, MD, 50. *Hon Degrees:* ScD, Georgetown Univ; LLD, Mt St Mary's Col. *Concurrent Pos:* Estab investr, Am Heart Asn, 54-57, coordr med educ, 57-58; med ed, Am Family Physician, 62-88; vchancellor, Med Ctr, 84-87. *Mem:* Am Physiol Soc; Biophys Soc; Soc Exp Biol & Med; Am Col Physicians; Am Fedn Clin Res. *Res:* Cardiovascular physiology; medical education. *Mailing Add:* Georgetown Univ Sch Med 3900 Reservoir Rd NW Washington DC 20007

ROSE, JOHN CREIGHTON, GEOPHYSICS. *Current Pos:* assoc geophysicist, Univ Hawaii, 64-68, prof geosci, 68-74, prof, 74-87, geophysicist, 76-87, EMER PROF GEOPHYS, UNIV HAWAII, 87- *Personal Data:* b Milwaukee, Wis, July 27, 22; div; c 4. *Educ:* Univ Wis, BS, 48, MS, 50, PhD(geol), 55. *Prof Exp:* Res assoc, Woods Hole Oceanog Inst, 50-55; from instr to asst prof geol & geophys, Univ Wis, 55-64. *Concurrent Pos:* Consult, Aero Div, Minneapolis-Honeywell Regulator Co. *Mem:* Am Geophys Union; Europ Asn Explor Geophys. *Res:* International pendulum gravity reference standard; absolute gravity measurements by pulse recycling and laser interferometer; geodesy; explosion seismology; marine gravity. *Mailing Add:* Dept Geol & Geophys Marine Ctr Univ Hawaii-Manoa 2500 Campus Rd Honolulu HI 96822. *Fax:* 808-848-5451

ROSE, JOSEPH LAWRENCE, MECHANICS, MECHANICAL ENGINEERING. *Current Pos:* instr mech eng, 65-69, from asst prof to prof, 70-91, PAUL MORROW PROF ENG, DREXEL UNIV, 91- *Personal Data:* b Philadelphia, Pa, July 5, 42; m 63; c 3. *Educ:* Drexel Inst Technol, BSME, 65, MS, 67; Drexel Univ, PhD(appl mech), 70. *Prof Exp:* Engr, Hale Fire Pump Co, 61-62 & SKF Industs, Inc, 63-64. *Mem:* Am Soc Mech Engrs; Soc Exp Stress Analysis; Am Soc Nondestruct Test; Am Soc Testing & Mat; Acoust Soc Am; Sigma Xi. *Res:* Nondestructive testing; experimental mechanics; stress analysis; wave propagation; composite materials; biomechanics. *Mailing Add:* Dept Eng Sci & Mech Pa State Univ 114 Hallowell Bldg University Park PA 16802

ROSE, KATHLEEN MARY, nucleic acid synthesis, enzymology, for more information see previous edition

ROSE, KENNETH, MICROELECTRONICS, CRYOELECTRONICS. *Current Pos:* assoc prof elec eng, 65-71, PROF ELEC ENG, RENSSELAER POLYTECH INST, 71- *Personal Data:* b Bloomington, Ind, Apr 21, 35; m 59; c 2. *Educ:* Univ Ill, BS, 55, MS, 57, PhD(elec eng), 61. *Prof Exp:* Physicist, Gen Elec Res Lab, 61-65. *Concurrent Pos:* mem, Ctr Advan Interconnect Sci & Technol. *Mem:* AAAS; Inst Elec & Electronics Engrs; Mat Res Soc. *Res:* Very-large-scale integration fabrication, design and testing; yield enhancement; thin film insulators; semiconductors; superconductors; interconnects; CAD tools; cryoelectronics, superconductors and yield enhancement. *Mailing Add:* Elec Comput & Systs Eng Dept Rensselaer Polytech Inst Troy NY 12180-3590. *Fax:* 518-276-8761; *E-Mail:* krose@unix.cie.rpi.edu

ROSE, KENNETH ALAN, COMPUTER MODELING OF ECOLOGICAL SYSTEMS. *Current Pos:* RES SCIENTIST, OAK RIDGE NAT LAB, 87- *Personal Data:* b Oceanside, NY, Dec 27, 57. *Educ:* State Univ NY, Albany, BS, 79; Univ Wash, MS, 81, PhD(fisheries), 85. *Prof Exp:* Res assoc, Univ Wash, 79-83; staff scientist, Martin Marietta Environ Systs, 83-87. *Concurrent Pos:* Adj fac, Univ Tenn, 94- *Mem:* Am Fisheries Soc; Int Soc Ecol Modelling; AAAS; Int Environmetrics Soc. *Res:* Construct and analyze computer models of ecological populations, communities and ecosystems, and their responses to disturbances such as habitat loss, toxicant stress and harvest. *Mailing Add:* Environ Sci Div Oak Ridge Nat Lab PO Box 2008 Oak Ridge TN 37831-6036

ROSE, KENNETH DAVID, MAMMALIAN EVOLUTION. *Current Pos:* from asst prof to assoc prof, 80-90, PROF ANAT, SCH MED, JOHNS HOPKINS UNIV, 90- *Personal Data:* b Newark, NJ, June 21, 49; m 81, Jennie J Neumann; c Caitlin & Chelsea. *Educ:* Yale Univ, BS, 72; Harvard Univ, MA, 74; Univ Mich, PhD(geol & paleont), 79. *Prof Exp:* Fel paleobiol, Smithsonian Nat Mus Natural Hist, 79-80. *Concurrent Pos:* Res collab, 81-89, Dept Paleobiol, Smithsonian Nat Mus Natural Hist, res assoc, 89-; co-ed, J Vert Paleont, 87-90; res assoc, Carnegie Mus Natural Hist, 90- *Mem:* Soc Vert Paleont; Paleont Soc; Am Soc Mammalogists; Soc Syst Zool; Sigma Xi; Am Asn Phys Anthrop; Soc Study Mammalian Evolution. *Res:* Early Cenozoic mammals, with emphasis on systematics and evolution, functional anatomy of the teeth and skeleton, biostratigraphy and biochronology (use of fossil mammals for stratigraphic correlation and determination of relative age of strata), and species diversity. *Mailing Add:* Dept Cell Biol & Anat Sch Med Johns Hopkins Univ Baltimore MD 21205. *Fax:* 410-955-4129; *E-Mail:* kdrose@welchlink.welch.jhu.edu

ROSE, KENNETH E(UGENE), metallurgy, corrosion; deceased, see previous edition for last biography

ROSE, MICHAEL ROBERTSON, GERONTOLOGY. *Current Pos:* assoc prof, 87-90, PROF BIOL, UNIV CALIF IRVINE, 90- *Personal Data:* b Iserlohn, Ger, July 25, 55; Can citizen; m 76, 85, 93, Della Gilmurray; c 1. *Educ:* Queen's Univ, BSc, 75, MSc, 76; Univ, Sussex, PhD, 79. *Honors & Awards:* Pres Prize, Am Soc Naturalists. *Prof Exp:* NATO Sci fel, Univ Wis, Madison, 79-81; from asst prof to assoc prof biol, Dalhousie Univ, 81-88. *Concurrent Pos:* Univ res fel, Dalhousie Univ, 81-88. *Mem:* AAAS; Genetics Soc Am; Soc Study Evolution. *Res:* Drosophila life-history evolution, including fitness-components and senescence; evolution with antagonistic pleiotropy; evolution of sex; human evolution. *Mailing Add:* Dept Ecol & Evolutionary Biol Univ Calif Irvine CA 92717-0001. *Fax:* 714-725-2181; *E-Mail:* mrrose@uci.edu

ROSE, MITCHELL, GAS PHASE PHOTOCHEMISTRY, X-RAY FLUORESCENCE. *Current Pos:* res adv, Master Builders Co, 81-85, PRES, TECH INNOVATIONS, DIV MARTIN MARIETTA CORP, 85- *Personal Data:* b Cleveland, Ohio, Mar 10, 51; m 74; c 5. *Educ:* Maimonides Col, BA, 75; Cleveland State Univ, MS, 77; Case Western Univ, PhD(chem), 79. *Prof Exp:* Anal lab mgr, Mogul Corp, Div Dexter Corp, 79-81. *Res:* Gas phase reaction kinetics; x-ray diffraction, and x-ray fluorescence spectroscopy; computer interfacing for laboratories. *Mailing Add:* 6718 Cottonwood Knoll St West Bloomfield MI 48322

ROSE, NICHOLAS JOHN, MATHEMATICS. *Current Pos:* head dept, 68-77, prof math, 68-89, EMER PROF MATH, NC STATE UNIV, 89- *Personal Data:* b Ossining, NY, Apr 21, 24; m 46; c 4. *Educ:* Stevens Inst Technol, ME, 44; NY Univ, MS, 49, PhD(math), 56. *Prof Exp:* From instr to prof math, Stevens Inst Technol, 46-68, head dept, 60-68, consult, 48-54. *Concurrent Pos:* Consult, Bell Tel Labs, Inc, 54-60. *Mem:* Am Math Soc; Math Asn Am; Soc Indust & Appl Math. *Res:* Differential equations; matrix theory. *Mailing Add:* NC State Univ Box 8205 Raleigh NC 27695-8205

ROSE, NOEL RICHARD, MICROBIOLOGY, IMMUNOLOGY. *Current Pos:* prof & dept chmn, Immunol & Infectious Dis Sch Hyg & Pub Health, 81-93, PROF MED, PROF PATH & DIR IMMUNOL, SCH MED, JOHNS HOPKINS UNIV, 93-, PROF MOLECULAR MICROBIIOL & IMMUNOL, SCH HYG & PUB HEALTH, 93- *Personal Data:* b Stamford, Conn, Dec 3, 27; m 51, Deborah Harber; c Alison, David, Bethany & Jonathan. *Educ:* Yale Univ, BS, 48; Univ Pa, AM, 49, PhD(microbiol), 51; State Univ NY Buffalo, MD, 64; Am Bd Microbiol, dipl; Am Bd Path, dipl; Am Bd Lab Immunol, dipl. *Hon Degrees:* Dr, Univ Calgiari, Italy, 90, Univ Sassari, Italy, 92. *Honors & Awards:* Abbott Award, Am Soc Microbiol; Erwin Neter Mem lectr; Morris F Shaffer Alumni lectr, Tulane Univ; Stuart Mudd Mem lectr, Am Soc Microbiol; Sidney C Werner lectr, Columbia Univ. *Prof Exp:* From instr to assoc prof bact & immunol, State Univ NY Buffalo, 51-66, prof microbiol, Sch Med, 66-73; prof immunol & microbiol & chmn dept, Sch Med, Wayne State Univ, 73-81. *Concurrent Pos:* Consult, Niagara Sanatorium, NY, 53-56 & Edward J Meyer Mem Hosp, Buffalo, 56-73, Vet Admin Hosp, Oak Park, Mich & Sinai Hosp, Detroit, 73-81; from assoc dir to dir, Erie Co Lab, 64-70; asst prof med, State Univ NY Buffalo, 64-73, dir, Ctr Immunol, 70-73; dir, Collab Ctr Autoimmune Dis, WHO, 66-; Wellcome vis prof, Univ SFla; Charles Culpepper vis prof, Univ Nebr, Omaha. *Mem:* Fel Am Pub Health Asn; Tissue Cult Asn; fel Am Acad Allergy; fel Col Am Path; fel Am Acad Microbiol; Am Asn Immunologist; Clin Immunol Soc; Soc Exp Biol & Med; hon mem Austrian Soc Allergy & Clin Immunol. *Res:* Autoimmunity; cellular immunology; clinical immunology; immunopathology; immunotoxicology. *Mailing Add:* 4000 N Charles St Baltimore MD 21218-1756

ROSE, NORMAN CARL, ORGANIC CHEMISTRY. *Current Pos:* from assoc prof to prof, 66-78, ASST DEAN, COL LIB ARTS & SCI, PORTLAND STATE UNIV, 78- *Personal Data:* b Seattle, Wash, Mar 15, 29; m 54, Myra N Rosenthal; c Mark, Bruce, Paul & Nancy. *Educ:* Univ Calif, BS, 50; Univ Kans, PhD(chem), 57. *Prof Exp:* From asst prof to assoc prof chem, Tex A&M Univ, 56-66. *Mem:* Am Chem Soc. *Res:* Learning theories. *Mailing Add:* 15677 NW Clubhouse Dr Portland OR 97229-8724. *Fax:* 503-725-3693

ROSE, PETER HENRY, PHYSICS. *Current Pos:* PRES, KRYTEK CORP, MASS. *Personal Data:* b Lincoln, Eng, Jan 16, 25; m 52; c 2. *Educ:* Univ London, BSc, 45, PhD(physics), 55. *Honors & Awards:* Nat Med of Technol, 96. *Prof Exp:* Sci officer, Nat Gas Turbine Estab, 45-47; asst lectr physics, Univ Leicester, 47-48; res assoc, Mass Inst Technol, 51-52, physicist, Proj Lincoln, 52-53; lectr, Birmingham Univ, 55-56; vpres & dir res, High Voltage Eng Corp, 56-70; pres, Ion Physics Corp, 70-71; pres, Extrion Corp, 71-75; gen mgr, Varian Extrion Div, Varian Assocs, 75-77; pres, Nova Assoc, Inc, 78-80; pres, Ion Implantation Div, Eaton Corp, 80- *Mem:* Fel Am Phys Soc; fel Brit Inst Physics. *Res:* Low energy nuclear physics; accelerators; theoretical and experimental ion optics; plasma and atomic physics as related to the accelerator; ion implantation. *Mailing Add:* 85 Phillips Ave Rockport MA 01966

ROSE, PETER R, PETROLEUM GEOLOGY, STRATIGRAPHY. *Current Pos:* PRES, TEL EXPLOR, 80- *Personal Data:* b Austin, Tex, July 3, 35; m 56, 78; c 3. *Educ:* Univ Tex, BS, 57, MA, 59, PhD(geol), 68. *Prof Exp:* Geologist, Shell Oil Co, 59-66; asst prof geol, State Univ NY Stony Brook, 68-69; staff geologist, Shell Oil Co, 69-73; chief Br Oil & Gas Resources, US Geol Surv, 73-76; chief geol, Energy Reserves Group, Inc, 76-80. *Concurrent Pos:* Vis prof geol, Univ Tex, Austin, 83; distinguished lectr, Am Asn Petrol Geologists, 85; distinguished vis prof geol, Kans State Univ, 88-89. *Mem:* Am Asn Petrol Geologists; fel Geol Soc Am; Soc Econ Paleontologists & Mineralogists; AAAS; Am Inst Prof Geologists; Soc Independent Earth Scientists. *Res:* Petrology and paleoecology of carbonate rocks; carbonate reservoir rocks; analysis of petroleum basins; petroleum resource prediction; exploration risk and uncertainty. *Mailing Add:* 711 W 14th St Austin TX 78701

ROSE, PHILIP I, PHYSICAL CHEMISTRY. *Current Pos:* RETIRED. *Personal Data:* b New York, NY, Apr 3, 39; m 59; c 2. *Educ:* Univ Ariz, BS, 60; Purdue Univ, PhD(phys chem), 64. *Prof Exp:* Sr res chemist, Res Labs, Eastman Kodak Co, 64-73; res assoc, 73-92. *Mem:* Am Chem Soc; Sigma Xi. *Res:* Molecular characterization and physical chemistry of biopolymers. *Mailing Add:* 125 Summit Dr Rochester NY 14620. *E-Mail:* pirose@naz.edu

ROSE, RAYMOND EDWARD, AERODYNAMICS, MATHEMATICS. *Current Pos:* RETIRED. *Personal Data:* b Canton, Ohio, July 17, 26; div; c 4. *Educ:* Univ Kans, BSAE, 51; Univ Minn, MSAE, 56, PhD(aerodyn), 66. *Honors & Awards:* Space Ship Earth Award, NASA, 80. *Prof Exp:* From jr engr to scientist aerodyn, Rosemount Aero Labs, Univ Minn, 51-59, scientist, 59-62, res fel, Univ Minn, 62-66; prin res scientist to proj staff engr & supvr, Aerodyn, Fluid Mech & Control Sci Sect, Res Dept, Systs & Res Ctr, Honeywell, Inc, Minneapolis, Minn, 66-76; NASA Hq, Washington, DC, prog mgr aerodyn & active controls, Aircraft Energy Efficiency Prog Off, 76-79, prog mgr, Gen Aviation, Subsonic Aircraft Technol Off, 79-84, mgr gen aviation & computer aerodyn & coordr, technol transfer control, Aerodyn Div, Off Aeronaut & Space Technol, 84-94. *Concurrent Pos:* Consult, EDO Corp, NY, 62, Pioneer Parachute Co, 65 & Pillsbury Co, Minn, 65; adj prof, Math Dept, Southeastern Univ, Washington, DC, 81-; indust specialist, NASA Spec Assignment, Capitol Goods & Prod Mat Div, Off Export Admin, Int Trade Admin, US Dept Com, Washington, DC, 83-84; speaker & presenter aerospace sci & math, child educator's workshops & student groups. *Mem:* Am Inst Aeronaut & Astronaut. *Res:* Shock swallowing and control concepts for air data sensing; jet-flap aerodynamics; natural laminar flow for general aviation aircraft viscous drag reduction; general aviation crash dynamics (structural design for occupant survivability); single pilot instrument flight rules operations (pilot workload reduction); general aviation aircraft design for stall/spin reduction/elimination. *Mailing Add:* 800 Fourth St SW No S424 Washington DC 20024

ROSE, RAYMOND WESLEY, JR, MOLECULAR GENETICS. *Current Pos:* Asst prof, 70-77, ASSOC PROF BIOL, BEAVER COL, 77-, CHMN DEPT, 74- *Personal Data:* b Cleveland, Ohio, July 5, 41; m 65; c 2. *Educ:* Bucknell Univ, BS, 63, MS, 65; Temple Univ, PhD(biol), 70. *Mem:* Genetics Soc Am; AAAS; Am Soc Zoologists. *Res:* Genetic control of protein synthesis and nucleic acid synthesis in Drosophila; protein and nucleic acid synthesis during early development in Xenopus; effect of environmental pollutants on mammalian development. *Mailing Add:* 725 Crescent Ave Glenside PA 19038

ROSE, RICHARD CARROL, PHYSIOLOGY. *Current Pos:* PROF DEPT PHYSIOL & BIOPHYS, FINCH UNIV HEALTH SCI/CHICAGO MED SCH, ILL, 90- *Personal Data:* b Minneapolis, Minn, Jan 2, 40. *Educ:* Augsburg Col, 65; Mich State Univ, MS, 67, PhD(physiol), 69. *Prof Exp:* USPHS fel, Sch Med, Univ Pittsburgh, 70-71; from asst prof to prof physiol & surg, Milton S Hershey Med Ctr, Pa State Univ, 71-88, mem staff, Dept Surg; prof & chmn, Dept Physiol, Univ ND, AK, 88-90. *Concurrent Pos:* Sr int fel, Fogarty Int Ctr, Univ Otago Med Sch, Dunedin, NZ, 80. *Mem:* Am Physiol Soc; Am Gastroenterol Asn; Biophys Soc; Sigma Xi. *Res:* Vitamin absorption/metabolism; antioxidant metabolism; ascorbic acid glutathione, uric acid tyrosine; ocular physiology of antioxidants. *Mailing Add:* Dept Physiol & Biophys Univ Health Sci/Chicago Med Sch 3333 Green Bay Rd North Chicago IL 60064-3095

ROSE, ROBERT LEON, GEOLOGY. *Current Pos:* from asst prof to prof, 59-72, prof, 72-84, EMER PROF GEOL, SAN JOSE STATE UNIV, 84- *Personal Data:* b San Francisco, Calif, Sept 3, 20; m 42; c 3. *Educ:* Univ Calif, AB, 48, MA, 49, PhD(geol), 57. *Prof Exp:* Geologist, Shell Oil Co, 49-53; assoc geol, Univ Calif, 53-56; actg asst prof geol, Stanford Univ, 56-57; asst econ geologist, Nev Bur Mines, 57-59. *Concurrent Pos:* Consult, Chevron Resources, 73-79. *Mem:* Geol Soc Am; Mineral Soc Am. *Res:* Petrology and petrography of igneous and metamorphic rocks; geology of California and the Franciscan Formation. *Mailing Add:* 1080 Los Viboras Rd Hollister CA 95023

ROSE, ROBERT M(ICHAEL), PHYSICAL METALLURGY, SOLID STATE PHYSICS. *Current Pos:* Ford Found fel eng, 61-63, from asst prof to assoc prof metall, 61-72, PROF MAT SCI & ENG, MASS INST TECHNOL, 72- *Personal Data:* b New York, NY, Apr 15, 37; m 61; c 3. *Educ:* Mass Inst Technol, SB, 58, ScD(phys metall), 61. *Honors & Awards:* Bradley Stoughton Award, Am Soc Metals, 68; Kappa Delta Award, Am Acad Orthop Surgeons, 73. *Concurrent Pos:* Prof, Mat Sci & Eng, Harvard Med Sch-MIT Div Health Sci & Technol, 78-88; mem, Comt Space Biol & Med, Nat Res Coun, Nat Acad Sci, 84-87; adj prof, Sch Vet Med, Tufts Univ, 93- *Mem:* AAAS; Am Phys Soc; Am Inst Mining, Metall & Petrol Engrs; Am Soc Metals; Orthop Res Soc; NY Acad Sci. *Res:* Electrical, magnetic, mechanical and thermodynamic properties of metals at cryogenic and high temperatures; theoretical and practical solid state physics; statistical thermodynamics; surgical implant materials; mammalian bone. *Mailing Add:* Mat Sci Mass Inst Technol 77 Massachusetts Ave Cambridge MA 02139-4307

ROSE, SETH DAVID, DNA PHOTOCHEMISTRY, BIO-ORGANIC CHEMISTRY. *Current Pos:* from asst prof to assoc prof, 76-90, PROF CHEM, ARIZ STATE UNIV, 91- *Personal Data:* b Dayton, Ohio, Nov 11, 48. *Educ:* Univ Calif, Berkeley, BS, 70; Univ Calif, San Diego, PhD(chem), 74. *Prof Exp:* NIH fel biophys, Johns Hopkins Univ, 74-76. *Mem:* Am Chem Soc; Am Soc Photobiol. *Res:* Nucleic acid photochemistry; physical organic chemistry. *Mailing Add:* Dept Chem Ariz State Univ Tempe AZ 85287-1604

ROSE, STUART ALAN, ANALYTICAL CHEMISTRY. *Current Pos:* res chemist, Cent Res Div, 69-73, dept head-group leader, Lederle Labs Div, 73-76, asst to dir qual control, 76-77, mgr, Pearl River Qual Control, 77-81, DIR PHARMACEUT CONTROL, LEDERLE LABS DIV, AM CYANAMID CO, PEARL RIVER, 81- *Personal Data:* b Dayton, Ohio, Sept 17, 42; m 65; c 2. *Educ:* Univ Cincinnati, BA, 64; Wayne State Univ, PhD(analytical chem), 69. *Prof Exp:* Finished prod chemist, Wm S Merrell Div, Richardson-Merrell, Inc, 64-66. *Mem:* Am Chem Soc; Water Pollution Control Fedn. *Res:* General analytical problem solving; technical management. *Mailing Add:* 27601 Tres Vistas Mission Viejo CA 92692

ROSE, TIMOTHY LAURENCE, PHOTOELECTROCHEMISTRY, THIN FILMS. *Current Pos:* sr scientist, 78-83, GROUP LEADER, EIC LABS, INC, 84- *Personal Data:* b Cleveland, Ohio, July 6, 41; m 63; c 3. *Educ:* Haverford Col, BA, 63; Yale Univ, MS, 64, PhD(phys chem), 67. *Prof Exp:* NATO fel physics, Univ Freiburg, 68; from asst prof to assoc prof chem, Tex A&M Univ, 69-78; Nat Res Coun sr res assoc, Air Force Geophys Lab, 76-78. *Mem:* AAAS; Am Chem Soc; Am Phys Soc; Am Vacuum Soc; Electrochem Soc; Mat Res Soc. *Res:* Gas phase methylene reactions and chemical activation; molecular and ion beam photodissociation processes; photochemical and photovoltaic solar energy conversion; electrical and optical properties of thin films; photochemical deposition; photoelectrochemistry on semiconductors; chemical sensors. *Mailing Add:* 238 Manley Rd Milton VT 05468-3551

ROSE, VINCENT C(ELMER), POLLUTION PREVENTION, WATER PURIFICATION & SUPPLY. *Current Pos:* asst prof chem eng, Univ RI, 63-67, from asst prof to assoc prof, 67-82, assoc dean, Grad Sch, 71-95, PROF NUCLEAR & OCEAN ENG, UNIV RI, 83-, DEPT CHAIR CHEM ENG, 95- *Personal Data:* b Fall River, Mass, July 31, 30; m 59; c 3. Alberta Therrien; c James V, William F & David M. *Educ:* Univ RI, BS, 52, MS, 58; Univ Mo, PhD(chem eng), 64. *Prof Exp:* Pilot plant supvr, Lindsay Chem Co, 54-56. *Mem:* Am Inst Chem Engrs; Am Soc Eng Educ; Sigma Xi. *Res:* Plant siting; pollution prevention; water purification and supply; energy planning. *Mailing Add:* DEPT CHEM ENG Univ RI Kingston RI 02881. *Fax:* 401-792-1180; *E-Mail:* rose@egr.uri.edu

ROSE, WALTER DEANE, TRANSPORT PHENOMENA IN POROUS MEDIAS, CAPILLARITY. *Current Pos:* CHIEF SCIENTIST & PRIN CONSULT, ILLINI TECHNOLOGISTS INT, 86. *Personal Data:* b Liberty, Ind, Jan 10, 20; m 39, Edith Madelene Schroder; c Rachel (Phillips), W D Jr,

John G, Bonnie Z, Dean M, James A, Edith E & Rose S. *Educ:* Univ Chicago, BS, 44. *Prof Exp:* Chemist geochem & petrol eng, Stand Oil NJ, 45-47; engr petrol eng, Gulf Res, 48-50; lectr petrol eng, Univ Tex, 50-52; scientist petrol eng, Continental, 52-54; prof petrol eng, Univ Ill, 56-68; prof civil eng, Technion, Israel, 68; prof petrol eng, Mid E Tech Univ, Turkey, 68-69; prof mech eng, Purdue Univ, 69-70; dean appl sci, Abadan Inst Technol, Iran, 71-73; prof petrol eng, Univ Ibadan, Nigeria, 73-75, NMex Tech, 75-77 & Univ Wyo, 78-79; scientist gas technol, Inst Gas Technol, 80-82; prof mech eng, Calif State Univ, Long Beach, 84-86. *Concurrent Pos:* Asst dir, Tex Petrol Res Comt, Austin, 50-51; lectr, Wintershall AG, Kassel, 59-60, CFP, Paris, 60, DEA, Hamburg, 61, Brit Nat Oil Corp, London, 76, BMPP, Melbourne, 90, Santos, Adelaide, 90, Chevron, Brisbane, 91, Univ NSW, Sydney, 91, Woodside, Perth, 91; sci adv, French Petrol Inst, Paris, 62-63; lectr, Petroleos Mexicanos, Mexico City, 65; consult, UNESCO, Pakistan, 70; vis prof, Univ Dacca, 70; vis fel, Commonwealth Sci & Indust Res Orgn, Canberra, Australia, 89; vis lectr, Inst Porous Flow, Langfang (Beijing), Peoples Repub China, 90; res adv, Petro NRS, Kuala Lymper, 91-96. *Mem:* Soc Petrol Engrs. *Res:* Flow of fluids through porous media, including theoretical and experimental investigations of coupled transport processes, and of the action of capillary forces that control the distributions of interstitial fluids. *Mailing Add:* Illini Technologists Int PO Box 2430 Sta A Champaign IL 61825-2430. *Fax:* 217-359-9289; *E-Mail:* swdrose@prairienet.org

ROSE, WAYNE BURL, PHYSICAL CHEMISTRY, PHARMACY. *Current Pos:* MGR CHEM RES, ANIMAL HEALTH DIV, MOBAY, 74- *Personal Data:* b Lamar, Colo, Dec 23, 32; m 56; c 4. *Educ:* Adams State Col, BA, 55, MEd, 57; Kans State Univ, MS, 61, PhD(phys chem), 64. *Prof Exp:* Assoc chemist, Midwest Res Inst, 63-66; res chemist, Chemagro Corp, 66-68, sr res chemist, 68-69, mgr formulations res, 69-74. *Mem:* Sigma Xi; Royal Soc Chem; Am Chem Soc. *Res:* Oxygen fluoride and nitrogen fluoride chemistry; metal ligand complexes in deuterium oxide; histamine heparin interactions in aqueous solutions; surface chemistry; kinetics of decomposition; preparation of pharmaceutical products and their registration; analytical methods and packaging. *Mailing Add:* 421 E Hawley St Mundelein IL 60060

ROSE, WILLIAM DAKE, petroleum geology, for more information see previous edition

ROSE, WILLIAM INGERSOLL, VOLCANOLOGY. *Current Pos:* from asst prof to prof, 70-96, head, Dept Geol Eng, Geol & Geophys, 90-96, CHAIR, DEPT GEOL ENG & SCI, MICH TECHNOL UNIV, 96- *Personal Data:* b Detroit, Mich, Oct 4, 44; m 67, Alexandrine G Rust; c Christopher McKennon & Jason Gerard. *Educ:* Dartmouth Col, AB, 66, PhD(geol), 70. *Prof Exp:* Res asst geol, Dartmouth Col, 66-68; res asst geochronol, Univ Ariz, 68-69; res asst geol, Dartmouth Col, 69-70. *Concurrent Pos:* NSF grants, Guatemala, El Salvador & Nicaragua, 70-72, Guatemalan volcanoes, 73-74 & 78-80, volcanic ash, 75-77 & 90-91, Toba Tuff, 82-85 & volcanic gases, 85-87, 87-89 & 90-91, satellites & eruption clouds, 87-89, 90-92, 91-94; vis scientist, Nat Ctr Atmospheric Res, 77-78, Cascade Volcano observ, US Geol Surv, 81- & Los Alamos Nat Lab, 85-86. *Mem:* AAAS; Int Asn Volcanology & Chem Earth's Interior; Am Geophys Union; fel Geol Soc. *Res:* Volcanic gas geochemistry; volcanic domes; active Central American volcanoes; volcanic ash; volcanic hazards; volcano/atmosphere interactions. *Mailing Add:* Dept Geol Eng & Sci Mich Technol Univ Houghton MI 49931. *Fax:* 906-487-3371; *E-Mail:* raman@mtu.edu

ROSE, WILLIAM K, ASTROPHYSICS. *Current Pos:* PROF ASTROPHYS, UNIV MD, 76- *Personal Data:* b Ossining, NY, Aug 10, 35; m 61, Sheila Tuchman; c Kenneth, Edward & Cindy. *Educ:* Columbia Col, AB, 57; Columbia Univ, PhD(physics), 63. *Prof Exp:* Res staff astrophys, Princeton Univ, 63-67; asst prof, Mass Inst Technol, 67-70, assoc prof, 71. *Mem:* Am Astron Soc; Am Asn Univ Professors; Int Astron Union. *Res:* Stellar evolution; extragalactic astrophysics; radio astronomy; physical processes in stars; cosmology. *Mailing Add:* Dept Astron Univ Md College Park MD 20742. *E-Mail:* wrose@astro.umd.edu

ROSEBERRY, JOHN L, WILDLIFE RESEARCH. *Current Pos:* Res asst zool, Southern Ill Univ, 58-60, researcher zool, 61-84, assoc scientist, 84-89, SR SCIENTIST, COOP WILDLIFE RES LAB, SOUTHERN ILL UNIV, 89- *Personal Data:* b Riverton, Ill, Sept 24, 36. *Educ:* Univ Ill, Urbana, BS, 58; Southern Ill Univ, MA, 61. *Concurrent Pos:* Consult controlled deer hunt, Crab Orchard Nat Wildlife Refuge, 66, 78-; biol adv deer permit task force, Ill Dept Conserv, 77 & 78; Deer Tech Adv Comt, 80- *Mem:* Wildlife Soc; Sigma Xi. *Res:* Vertebrate ecology and population dynamics, especially regulation, exploitation, computer simulation, habitat inventory and analysis; published 2 books. *Mailing Add:* Coop Wildlife Res Lab Southern Ill Univ Carbondale IL 62901. *E-Mail:* jrose@siu.edu

ROSEBERY, DEAN ARLO, FISHERIES. *Current Pos:* prof sci, 52-72, prof & head div sci, 70-85, EMER PROF BIOL & EMER HEAD DIV SCI, NORTHEAST MO STATE UNIV, 85- *Personal Data:* b Stahl, Mo, Sept 23, 19; m 43, Amy Ayres; c J Frank & Margaret E. *Educ:* Northeast Mo State Teachers Col, BS, 41; Va Polytech Inst, PhD(zool), 50. *Prof Exp:* Instr biol, Va Polytech Inst, 46-48; asst chief fish div, State Comn Game & Inland Fisheries, Va, 48-52. *Concurrent Pos:* Fel, Mo Acad Sci. *Mem:* Fel AAAS; Am Fisheries Soc; Wildlife Soc; Am Soc Limnol & Oceanog; Nat Asn Acad Sci (pres, 84-85); Nat Geog Soc; Nat Sci Teachers Asn. *Res:* Freshwater fish management; fisheries biology. *Mailing Add:* 1208 E Illinois St Kirksville MO 63501

ROSEBOOM, EUGENE HOLLOWAY, JR, NUCLEAR WASTE DISPOSAL, EXPERIMENTAL PETROLOGY. *Current Pos:* geologist, Washington, DC, Geol Surv, 59-74, asst chief geologist, Eastern Region, 74-79, prog coordr nuclear waste disposal, Geol Div, 80-84, chief, Off Regional Geol, 84-88, DIR STAFF, GEOL SURV, 89- *Personal Data:* b Columbus, Ohio, Sept 21, 26; m 58; c 4. *Educ:* Ohio State Univ, BS, 49, MS, 51; Harvard Univ, PhD(geol), 58. *Prof Exp:* Res fel, Geophys Lab, Carnegie Inst, 56-59. *Mem:* Mineral Soc Am; Soc Econ Geol. *Res:* Phase equilibria among arsenides, sulfides, silicates; geologic applications; theory of phase equilibria diagrams. *Mailing Add:* US Geol Surv Stop 106 Reston VA 22092

ROSECRANS, JOHN A, PHARMACOLOGY. *Current Pos:* trainee, Yale Univ, from asst prof to assoc prof, 67-78, PROF PHARMACOL, MED COL VA, 78- *Personal Data:* b Brooklyn, NY, July 30, 35; m 58; c 3. *Educ:* St John's Univ, BS, 57; Univ RI, MS, 60, PhD(pharmacol), 63. *Prof Exp:* NIMH fel, Univ Mich, Ann Arbor, 63-64; res asst prof pharmacol, Univ Pittsburgh, 64-65. *Mem:* AAAS; Am Soc Pharmacol & Exp Therapeut; Soc Neurosci. *Res:* Behavioral and biochemical basis of drug dependence. *Mailing Add:* Dept Pharmacol Va Commonwealth Univ MCV Sta PO Box 613 Richmond VA 23298-0613

ROSEGAY, AVERY, TRITIUM LABELING, ORGANIC RADIOCHEMISTRY. *Current Pos:* SR RES FEL, MERCK, SHARP & DOHME RES LABS, RAHWAY, 60- *Personal Data:* b New York, NY, Sept 3, 29. *Educ:* Columbia Univ, BS, 50, MS, 53; NY Univ, PhD (org chem), 60. *Mem:* Am Chem Soc; Int Isotope Soc. *Res:* Synthesis of tritium-labeled compounds; hydrogen-tritium exchange reactions. *Mailing Add:* Merck Res Labs PO Box 2000 Rahway NJ 07065-0900

ROSEHART, ROBERT GEORGE, CHEMICAL ENGINEERING. *Current Pos:* coordr, Chem Eng Group, 70-77, dean, Univ Schs, 77-84, PRES, LAKEHEAD UNIV, 84- *Personal Data:* b Owen Sound, Ont, July 29, 43; m 67, Rita Purvis; c Robert, William & Karen. *Educ:* Univ Waterloo, BASc, 67, MASc, 68, PhD(chem eng), 70. *Prof Exp:* Fluids & heat transfer engr, Atomic Energy Can, 66 & Can Gen Elec, 67. *Concurrent Pos:* Consult, Atomic Energy Can, 67-84; Ont Forestry Coun, 84-; chmn, Ont Adv Comt Resource Dependent Communities, 85-86; Thunder Bay Wafer Bd Study, Govt Ont, 86-87; Ont Premiers Coun, 86-94; chmn, Ont Forest Resources Inventory Comt, 87-88; Ont chief, NAN Land Negotiation, 91- *Res:* Environmental engineering; heat transfer; two-phase flow; water treatment processes; northern development. *Mailing Add:* Lakehead Univ Thunder Bay ON P7B 5E1 Can. *Fax:* 807-343-8075

ROSELAND, CRAIG R, INSECT CHEMICAL ECOLOGY. *Current Pos:* asst prof, 85-91, ASSOC PROF ENTOM, NDAK STATE UNIV, 91- *Personal Data:* b Long Beach, Calif, Oct 15, 49; m 87, Janet Maxwell; c Katrina & Miranda. *Educ:* Univ Calif, Irvine, BS, 72, PhD(insect develop), 76. *Prof Exp:* Res assoc, Univ Wash, 76-81; res assoc, Tree Fruit Res Sta, Wash State Univ, 81-82; res assoc, Kans State Univ, 83-85. *Concurrent Pos:* NIH fel, 77-79. *Mem:* Entom Soc Am; AAAS. *Res:* Analyze the control of synthesis of catecholamines destined for the insect cuticle; investigate the insect attractants that are found in sunflower; study chemical defenses of sunflower against coleopteran pests. *Mailing Add:* Dept Entom NDak State Univ Main Campus Fargo ND 58105. *Fax:* 701-237-8551

ROSELLE, DAVID PAUL, MATHEMATICS. *Current Pos:* PRES, UNIV DEL, 90- *Personal Data:* b Vandergrift, Pa, May 30, 39; m 67, Louise Dowling; c Arthur & Cynthia. *Educ:* West Chester State Col, BS, 61; Duke Univ, PhD(number theory), 65. *Prof Exp:* Asst prof math, Univ Md, 65-68; from assoc prof to prof, La State Univ, Baton Rouge, 68-74; prof math, Va Polytech Inst & State Univ, 74-79, dean grad sch, 79-81, dean res & grad studies, 81-83, univ provost, 83-87; pres, Univ Ky, 87-90. *Concurrent Pos:* Chief investr, NSF grants, 66-71 & 73-75; Nat Res Coun Can fel, 68; assoc ed, Am Math Monthly, 73-75. *Mem:* Am Math Soc; Math Asn Am (secy, 75-); Nat Coun Teachers Math. *Res:* Combinatorial analysis; number theory. *Mailing Add:* Pres Off Univ Del Newark DE 19716-0001

ROSELLI, CHARLES EUGENE, NEUROENDOCRINOLOGY, REPRODUCTIVE BIOLOGY. *Current Pos:* from instr to asst prof, 83-90, COLLAB SCIENTIST, DEPT REPRODUCTIVE BIOL, ORE REGIONAL PRIMATE RES CTR, ORE HEALTH SCI UNIV, 85-, ASSOC PROF PHYSIOL, 90- *Personal Data:* b Harrisburg, Pa, Dec 26, 52; m 89; c 1. *Educ:* Franklin & Marshall Col, BA, 74; Hahnemann Univ, PhD(physiol), 81. *Honors & Awards:* Young Investr Award, Soc Study Reproduction, 83. *Prof Exp:* Postdoctoral assoc reprod physiol, Ore Regional Primate Res Ctr, 81-83. *Concurrent Pos:* Prin investr, Nat Inst Child Health & Human Develop, 87-92, Nat Sci Found, 95- *Mem:* Am Physiol Soc; Endocrine Soc; Soc Neurosci; Soc Study Reproduction. *Res:* Cellular mechanisms of androgen action in brain; effects of androgens on neuropeptide content and neurotransmitter receptor concentrations relative to neuroendocrine functions. *Mailing Add:* Dept Physiol & Pharm L-334 Ore Health Sci Univ 3181 SW Sam Jackson Park Rd Portland OR 97201-3098. *Fax:* 503-494-4352; *E-Mail:* rosellic@ohsu.edu

ROSELLI, ROBERT J, LUNG FLUID & SOLUTE EXCHANGE. *Current Pos:* PROF, BIOMED ENG, VANDERBILT UNIV, 85- *Personal Data:* b Jan 21, 47; m 70, Kathleen Cote; c Joseph, Peter & Michael. *Educ:* Univ Calif, Berkeley, PhD(eng sci), 75. *Mem:* Biomed Eng Soc; Am Physiol Soc; Microcirculatory Soc. *Res:* Cardiovascular system; biomechanics; lasers in prostate surgery; non-invasive detection of transcapillary macromolecular transport. *Mailing Add:* Dept Chem & Biomed Eng Box 36 Sta B Vanderbilt Univ Nashville TN 37232-0001. *E-Mail:* roselli@vuse.vanderbilt.edu

ROSEMAN, ARNOLD S(AUL), GOOD MANUFACTURING PRACTICES & SANITATION INSTRUCTION, DEVELOPMENT OF TOTAL QUALITY MANAGEMENT & HACCP PROGRAMS & EDUCATION. *Current Pos:* PRES, QUAL CONSULT INC, WAYNE, PA, 85-; SR RES ASSOC, DEPT FOOD SCI, BERKS CAMPUS, PA STATE UNIV, READING, 89- *Personal Data:* b Boston, Mass, 1930; m 55, Joan L Lipman; c David J & Ann L. *Educ:* Northeastern Univ, BS, 52; Univ Mass, MS, 54, PhD(food technol), 56. *Prof Exp:* Biochemist rice, Southern Regional Lab, Agr Res Serv, USDA, 56-60; sr scientist, Res & Develop Div, Kraft Co, 60-68; res mgr meats, Res & Develop Dept, John Morrell & Co, 68-74; dir res & develop food technol, CFS Continental, Inc, Chicago, 74-82; vpres, Food Beverages, Jerrico Inc, Lexington, KY, 82-85; dir res, Develop QC & QA, Horace W Longacre, Inc, Franconia, PA, 86-88. *Concurrent Pos:* Fel Am Inst Chem; secy-treas Iowa Sect, Inst Food Technologists, 69-72, chair, 72-74, counr Chicago Sect, 65-69 & 76-81, chmn Food Serv Div, 76-78. *Mem:* Inst Food Technologists; Am Chem Soc; Am Asn Cereal Chemists; Am Soc Qual Control; Int Asn Milk Food & Environ Sanitarians. *Res:* Food and menu product and process development and improvement, especially institutional items and poultry products; organoleptic evaluation of foods; utilization of products by food service; effects of processing and storage on the chemical, physical and organoleptic properties; research management; management and policy; food law and regulatory compliance; various publications and patents. *Mailing Add:* 39 Militia Hill Dr Wayne PA 19087

ROSEMAN, JOSEPH JACOB, MATHEMATICS. *Current Pos:* sr lectr, 74-79, ASSOC PROF, TEL AVIV UNIV, 79- *Personal Data:* b Brooklyn, NY, Nov 11, 35. *Educ:* Mass Inst Technol, BS, 57; Polytech Inst Brooklyn, MS, 61; NY Univ, PhD(math), 65. *Prof Exp:* Chem engr, Gen Elec Co, 57-59; asst prof math, Univ Wis-Madison, 65-67; assoc prof, Polytech Inst Brooklyn, 67-74. *Mem:* Am Math Soc; Math Asn Am; Soc Natural Philos; Soc Indust & Appl Math. *Res:* Mathematical elasticity; fluid dynamics; applied mathematics. *Mailing Add:* Tel Aviv Univ Sch Math Sci Tel Aviv Israel. *Fax:* 972-3-640-9357; *E-Mail:* roseman@math.tau.ac.il

ROSEMAN, SAUL, BIOCHEMISTRY. *Current Pos:* chmn dept biol & dir, McCollum-Pratt Inst, 69-73 & 88-90, prof biol, 65-75, RALPH S O'CONNOR PROF CHAIR BIOL, JOHNS HOPKINS UNIV, 75- *Personal Data:* b New York, NY, Mar 9, 21; m 41, Martha Ozrowitz; c Mark A, Dorinda A & Cynthia B. *Educ:* City Col New York, BS, 41; Univ Wis, MS, 44, PhD(biochem, org chem), 47. *Hon Degrees:* DM, Univ Lund, Sweden, 84. *Honors & Awards:* T Duckett Jones Mem Award, Helen Hay Whitney Found, 73; Rosenstiel Award, Brandeis Univ, 74; Gairdner Found Int Award, 81; Townsend Harris Medal, City Col NY, 87; Merit Award, NIH, 87; John A Lynch Lectr in Life Scis, Univ Notre Dame, 89; Van Niel Lectr, Stanford Univ, 92; Karl Meyer Award, Soc Glycobiol, 93. *Prof Exp:* Res assoc biochem & pediat, Univ Chicago, 48-51, asst prof, 51-53; res assoc, Rackham Arthritis Res Unit, Univ Mich Hosp, 53-54, from asst prof to prof biol chem, 54-65. *Concurrent Pos:* Sci counr, Nat Cancer Inst, 72-80. *Mem:* Nat Acad Sci; Am Acad Arts & Sci; Am Chem Soc; Am Soc Biol Chemists; hon mem Biochem Soc Japan; Am Soc Microbiol; AAAS; Biophys Soc; Am Asn Univ Prof; fel Am Acad Microbiol. *Res:* Chemistry and metabolism of complex carbohydrates; polysaccharides; glycoproteins; glycolipids. *Mailing Add:* Dept Biol Johns Hopkins Univ Charles & 34th Sts Baltimore MD 21218. *Fax:* 410-516-5213

ROSEMAN, THEODORE JONAS, PHARMACEUTICAL CHEMISTRY. *Current Pos:* res scientist, 67-80, SR SCIENTIST PHARM, UPJOHN CO, 80-; VPRES, BAXTER HEALTHCARE CORP, DEERFIELD, ILL. *Personal Data:* b Chicago, Ill, Aug 2, 41; m 63; c 2. *Educ:* Univ Ill, BS, 63; Univ Mich, MS, 65, PhD(pharmaceut chem), 67. *Prof Exp:* Pharmacist, Westridge Med Ctr, 63; teaching asst pharm, Univ Mich, 63-64. *Concurrent Pos:* Past pres, Control Release Soc; adj prof, Philadelphia Col Pharm; ed, Controlled Release Soc Newsletter. *Mem:* Am Pharmaceut Asn; Am Chem Soc; Control Release Soc; Parenteral Drug Asn; Am Soc Hosp Pharmacists; fel Am Asn Pharmaceut Scientists. *Res:* Physical-chemical properties of therapeutic agents; controlled release delivery systems; package-product interactions; drug release mechanisms; product research and development. *Mailing Add:* 16 Nottingham Dr Lincolnshire IL 60069

ROSEMARK, PETER JAY, RADIATION THERAPY PHYSICS. *Current Pos:* RADIATION PHYSICIST, DEPT RADIATION THER, CEDARS-SINAI MED CTR, 77- *Personal Data:* b Los Angeles, Calif, July 28, 55. *Educ:* Mass Inst Technol, Cambridge, ScB, 77; Univ Calif, Los Angeles, MSc, 79, PhD(med physics), 82; Am Bd Radiol, cert therapeut radiol physics, 84. *Concurrent Pos:* Vis lectr, dept radiation oncol, Univ Calif, Los Angeles, 82-; consult physicist, radiation ther serv, Wadsworth Vet Admin, 84- *Mem:* Am Asn Physicists Med; Hosp Physicists Asn; Am Col Radiol; Am Soc Therapeut Radiol & Oncol. *Res:* Dose distribution, calculation and reporting of radioactive implants and other radiation therapy physics problems. *Mailing Add:* Dept Radiation Ther Cedars-Sinai Comprehensive Cancer Ctr 8700 Beverly Blvd Los Angeles CA 90048-0750

ROSEMBERG, EUGENIA, REPRODUCTIVE ENDOCRINOLOGY, PHARMACOLOGY OF REPRODUCTION. *Current Pos:* RES DIR, MED RES INST WORCESTER INC, MASS, 62-; PROF MED, UNIV MASS MED SCH, WORCESTER, MASS, 71- *Personal Data:* b Buenos Aires, Arg. *Educ:* Nat Lyceum Women, Buenos Aires, BS, 36; Univ Buenos Aires, MD, 44. *Prof Exp:* Instr, dept anat, Univ Buenos Aires Med Sch, 40-46, instr pediat, 46-48, res fel, Johns Hopkins Univ Med Sch, endocrinol dept, 48-50, staff mem, Worcester Found Exp Biol, Mass, 53-62; mem med staff, Worcester City Hosp, 55-85, pediat, Univ Hosp, Univ Md, 70-72; dir med res, Worcester City Hosp, Mass, 73-85. *Concurrent Pos:* Assoc pediat & res asst, pediat dept, Univ Hosp, Univ Buenos Aires, 43-48; vis scientist, Univ Montevideo Med Sch, Uruguay, 50; res fel, Pub Health Serv, NIH, Nat Inst Arthritis & Metab Dis, Endocrinol Sect, Bethesda, Md, 51-53; res fel, Med Res Inst & Hosp, Okla, 53; Nat Health, 65-85, Nat Inst Child Health & Human Develop, 69-82. *Mem:* Hon mem Arg Steril; corresp mem Fertil Soc Peru; Am Soc Androl; Am Fertil Soc; fel AAAS; Am Heart Asn. *Res:* Immunological and biological properties of glycoprotein hormones; study of the hypothalamic-pituitary-ovarian and testicular axis as it relates to female and male infertility. *Mailing Add:* 44 Elm St Worcester MA 01609

ROSEMOND, GEORGE P, SURGERY. *Current Pos:* RETIRED. *Personal Data:* b Hillsboro, NC, Aug 23, 10; m 37; c 1. *Educ:* Univ NC, BS, 32; Temple Univ, MD, 34, MS, 39; Am Bd Surg, dipl, 42; Am Bd Thoracic Surg, dipl, 60. *Prof Exp:* From instr to assoc prof surg, Sch Med, Temple Univ, 39-47, clin prof, 47-50, prof clin surg, 50-60, co-chmn, Dept Surg, 60-63, chmn, Div Surg, 63-73, prof surg & chmn dept, 63-73, emer prof surg, Sch Med, 79. *Concurrent Pos:* Mem adv comt & consult physician, Wilkes-Barre Vet Admin Hosp. *Mem:* Am Asn Thoracic Surg; Am Col Chest Physicians; Am Surg Asn; fel Am Col Surg; Am Cancer Soc (pres, 74). *Res:* Cancer, especially cancer of the breast. *Mailing Add:* 825 Olde Hickory Rd Lancaster PA 17601

ROSEN, ALAN, SPACE PHYSICS, BIOMEDICAL ENGINEERING. *Current Pos:* DIR RES, MACH CONSCIOUSNESS INC, 92- *Personal Data:* b Tel Aviv, Israel, Aug 19, 27; nat US; m 56, 85, Alla; c Allana. *Educ:* Univ Southern Calif, BA, 51, MA, 54, PhD(nuclear physics), 58. *Prof Exp:* Asst, Univ Southern Calif, 51-55; lectr physics, 55-58; geophysicist, Space Tech Lab, Inc, Thompson Ramo Wooldridge, Inc, 58-68; dir, Space Sci Lab, TRW Systs Group, 68-92. *Mem:* Am Phys Soc; Am Asn Physics Teachers; Am Geophys Union; Am Inst Aeronaut & Astronaut; Sigma Xi. *Res:* Computer engineerring; artificial intelligent robotic controllers. *Mailing Add:* 1917 Clark Lane-B Redondo Beach CA 90278

ROSEN, ARTHUR LEONARD, BIOPHYSICS, APPLIED MATHEMATICS. *Current Pos:* PVT CONSULT, 89- *Personal Data:* b Chicago, Ill, Apr 30, 34; m 56; c 2. *Educ:* Roosevelt Univ, BS, 57; Univ Chicago, MS, 64, PhD(physics), 71. *Prof Exp:* Res assoc, Dept Cardiovasc Res, Michael Reese Hosp, Chicago, 55-58, res assoc, Dept Surg Res, 60-64; asst dir dept surg res, Hektoen Inst Med Res, 64-78; res assoc, Univ Chicago, 81-83, asst prof, Dept Surg, 83-89; res assoc, Dept Surg, Michael Reese Hosp Chicago, 78-89. *Concurrent Pos:* Asst prof biophys, Dept Surg, Col Med, Univ Ill, 67-78; asst prof bioeng, Univ Ill, 80-81. *Mem:* Am Phys Soc; Biophys Soc; Soc Rheology; Inst Elec & Electronics Engrs; Am Asn Physicists in Med. *Res:* Red blood cell substitutes; control of erythropoiesis. *Mailing Add:* 2323 Schiller Ave Wilmette IL 60091-2329

ROSEN, ARTHUR ZELIG, PHYSICS. *Current Pos:* from instr to assoc prof, 53-64, PROF PHYSICS, CALIF POLYTECH STATE UNIV, SAN LUIS OBISPO, 64- *Personal Data:* b Oil City, Pa, Feb 5, 20; m 41. *Educ:* Univ Calif, BA, 41, PhD(physics), 52. *Prof Exp:* Engr, Permanente Shipyards, 41-42; jr physicist radiation lab, Univ Calif, 42-45, asst physics, 46-51; engr, Berkeley Sci Co, 46; lectr physics, Santa Barbara Col, 51-53. *Concurrent Pos:* NSF sci fac fel, 59. *Mem:* Am Phys Soc; Am Asn Physics Teachers. *Res:* Mass spectrograph development; cosmic ray studies at sea level and mountain altitudes; experimental nuclear physics; environmental radioactivity. *Mailing Add:* Dept Physics Calif Polytech State Univ San Luis Obispo CA 93407

ROSEN, BARRY PHILIP, BIOCHEMISTRY. *Current Pos:* ASSOC PROF BIOCHEM, SCH MED, UNIV MD, BALTIMORE, 71- *Personal Data:* b Hartford, Conn, June 18, 44. *Educ:* Trinity Col, BS, 65; Univ Conn, MS, 68, PhD(biochem), 69. *Prof Exp:* USPHS fel, Cornell Univ, 69-71. *Mem:* Am Soc Microbiol; Am Soc Biol Chemists. *Res:* Structure and function of biological membranes; energy transduction and active transport in microorganisms. *Mailing Add:* Dept Biochem & Molecular Biol Wayne State Univ Sch Med Scott Hall 540 E Canfield Ave Detroit MI 48201-1908. *E-Mail:* brosen@waynest1.bitnet

ROSEN, BERNARD, PLASMA PHYSICS. *Current Pos:* from asst prof to assoc prof physics, 60-73, PROF PHYSICS, STEVENS INST TECHNOL, 73- *Personal Data:* b New York, NY, June 6, 30; m 62; c 2. *Educ:* NY Univ, AB, 50, PhD(physics), 59. *Prof Exp:* Engr, Fed Tel & Radio Co, 51-52 & Bendix Aviation Co, 52-53; instr physics, NY Univ, 55-58; engr, Radio Corp Am, 58-60. *Concurrent Pos:* Consult, Plasma Physics Lab, Princeton Univ, 72-75. *Mem:* Am Phys Soc. *Res:* Computational plasma physics. *Mailing Add:* 934 Red Rd Teaneck NJ 07666

ROSEN, BRUCE IRWIN, ORGANIC CHEMISTRY. *Current Pos:* SR RES SCIENTIST, ORG CHEM, AMOCO CHEM, 84- *Personal Data:* b Chicago, Ill, July 8, 52. *Educ:* Northwestern Univ, BA, 74; Univ Southern Calif, PhD(org chem), 77. *Prof Exp:* Sr res chemist org chem, 3M Co, 77-79; res specialist, org chem, UOP Inc, 79-84. *Mem:* Am Chem Soc; AAAS. *Res:* Synthetic organic chemistry, organometallic chemistry (heterogeneous and homogeneous catalysis) and polymer chemistry. *Mailing Add:* Amoco Chem PO Box 3011 Naperville IL 60566-0400

ROSEN, C(HARLES) A(BRAHAM), ROBOTICS, MACHINE VISION. *Current Pos:* CONSULT, RICOH RES, 90-; DIR, TDG AEROSPACE CORP; DIR, ELEC VEHICLE SYSTS, INC. *Personal Data:* b Toronto, Ont, Dec 7, 17; nat US; m 41, Blanche Jacobson; c Hal, Steven, Naomi & Sema. *Educ:* Cooper Union, BEE, 40; McGill Univ, MEng, 50; Syracuse Univ, PhD(elec eng), 56. *Honors & Awards:* Taylor Award, Inst Elec & Electronics Engrs, 75. *Prof Exp:* Sr examr, Brit Air Comn, NY, 40-43; proj engr, Fairchild

Aircraft, Ltd, Can, 43-47; co-owner, Electrolabs Regist, 47-50; consult engr, Gen Elec Co, 50-57; mgr, Appl Physics Lab, SRI Int, 57-70, Artificial Intel Group, Info Sci Lab, 70-78, consult, 78- *Concurrent Pos:* Co-founder & pres, Machine Intel Co, 78-80, chmn, 80-87; dir, Ridge Vineyards Co, 62-86, Microbot Co, 80-81; Packet Tech Co, 80-89, Cochlea Co, 81-, Telebit Co, 83-89, Picodyne Co, 86-89; mem, Adv Comt Tech Innov, Nat Acad Sci, 72-77; mem, Oversight Comt, Nat Bur Stand, 75-78, Comt Army Robotics & Artificial Intel, Nat Res Coun, 81-83, 86-87, Space Syst & Tech Adv Comt, NASA, 86-90, Rehab Res Adv Comt, Vet Admin, 89-, US Army STAR Comt, Nat Res Coun, 89-93; mem, Space Syst & Tech Adv Comt, NASA, 86-89. *Mem:* Am Phys Soc; Sigma Xi; fel Inst Elec & Electronics Engrs; sr mem Soc Mfg Engrs; fel Am Asn Artificial Intel. *Res:* Learning machines; pattern recognition; artificial intelligence; electron-beam-activated micromachining processes; ferroelectric and piezoelectric devices; programmable automation; robotics. *Mailing Add:* 139 Tuscaloosa Ave Atherton CA 94027. *E-Mail:* rosen@ai.sri.com

ROSEN, CAROL ZWICK, ENGINEERING PHYSICS, MATERIAL SCIENCE ENGINEERING. *Current Pos:* MAT SCIENTIST, THEMOMOETRICS INC, 93- *Personal Data:* b New York, NY; m 62, Bernard; c Richard J & Rachel E. *Educ:* Brooklyn Col, BS, 53; NY Univ, MS, 55; Stevens Inst Technol, PhD(physics), 65. *Prof Exp:* Res assoc, HE & nuclear magnetic resonance, IBM Watson Lab, Columbia Univ, 65-67; res assoc, Stevens Inst Technol, 67-70; index ed, Am Inst Physics, 70-74; asst prof physics, York Col, NY, 74-75; staff physicist, Am Phys Soc, 75-76; scientist non-woven web technol, Johnson & Johnson Co, 76-79; proj mgr superconductivity, Airco Superconductors, 79-80; scientist microelectronics, Advan Technol Syst Inc Div, Austin Co, 80-83; eng specialist, GEC-Marconi Electronic Systs Corp, 84-93. *Concurrent Pos:* Adj prof physics, Queens Col, NY, 75-; instr chem, Barnard Col; instr physics, NY Univ, Fairleigh Dickinson Univ, Hunter Col & York Col-City Univ NY. *Mem:* Am Phys Soc; NY Acad Sci; Am Inst Metall Eng; Am Electroplating Soc; Sigma Xi; Soc Women Engrs (vpres, 73-74 & pres, 74-75). *Res:* Fabrication of superconducting wire and braid; ferroic ceramics and monocrystals designed for electronic applications and materials processing for their production; fabrication and production of magnetic oxides for electronic devices; research and product development of piezoelectric transducers including mathematical modeling of mechanical-electrical-thermal properties along with measurements of the material properties of novel and existing piezoelectrics. *Mailing Add:* 934 Red Rd Teaneck NJ 07666. *Fax:* 732-287-8847

ROSEN, DANIEL R, GENETICS, MOLECULAR BIOLOGY. *Current Pos:* RES SCIENTIST IV, DEPT HEALTH, WADSWORTH CTR, NY STATE, 94- *Personal Data:* US citizen. *Educ:* Univ Rochester, BA, 80; Brandeis Univ, PhD(molecular genetics), 89. *Prof Exp:* Postdoctoral fel, Dana-Farber Cancer Inst, 87-91; res fel, Mass Gen Hosp, 91-94. *Mem:* Am Soc Human Genetics; Am Acad Neurol. *Res:* Mapping identification and isolation of genes causing human neuromuscular diseases. *Mailing Add:* Wadsworth Ctr Empire State Plaza Albany NY 12201-0509. *Fax:* 518-474-7992

ROSEN, DAVID, MATHEMATICS. *Current Pos:* from instr to prof, 52-87, EMER PROF MATH, SWARTHMORE COL, 87- *Personal Data:* b New Haven, Conn, Jan 26, 21; m 46, Gloria Uhlmann; c Carl, Ralph, Paul & Michael. *Educ:* NY Univ, AB, 42; Univ Pa, AM, 49, PhD(math), 52. *Honors & Awards:* Fulbright-Hays lectr, Ireland, 71-72. *Prof Exp:* Asst instr math, Univ Pa, 49-52. *Concurrent Pos:* NSF fac fel, 61-62. *Mem:* Am Math Soc; Math Asn Am; Sigma Xi. *Res:* Automorphic functions; continued fractions. *Mailing Add:* Dept Math Swarthmore Col Swarthmore PA 19081. *E-Mail:* drosen1@swarthmore.edu

ROSEN, DAVID A, ophthalmology, for more information see previous edition

ROSEN, DIANNE L, viroids, for more information see previous edition

ROSEN, EDWARD M(ARSHALL), CHEMICAL ENGINEERING, PROCESS SIMULATION. *Current Pos:* CONSULT, EMR TECHNOL GROUP, 94- *Personal Data:* b Chicago, Ill, Jan 28, 30; m 65; c Howard & Sheila. *Educ:* Ill Inst Technol, BS, 51, MS, 53; Univ Ill, PhD(chem eng), 59. *Prof Exp:* sr sci fel chem eng, Monsanto Co, 59-93. *Concurrent Pos:* Monsanto acad leave chem eng, Stanford Univ, 62-63; lectr, Univ Mo, 72; affil prof, Wash Univ, 74; secy, Cache Corp, 84-85; chmn, Computing & Systs Technol Div, Am Inst Chem Engrs, 85. *Mem:* Am Inst Chem Engrs. *Res:* Process simulation and design. *Mailing Add:* EMR Technol Group 13022 Musket Ct St Louis MO 63167. *Fax:* 314-275-7758; *E-Mail:* 73141.3376@compuserve.com

ROSEN, FRED SAUL, IMMUNOLOGY. *Current Pos:* SR ASSOC MED, CHILDREN'S HOSP, BOSTON, 68-; JAMES L GAMBLE PROF PEDIAT, HARVARD MED SCH, 72-; PRES, CTR BLOOD RES INC, 87- *Personal Data:* b Newark, NJ, May 26, 30. *Educ:* Lafayette Col, AB, 51; Western Res Univ, MD, 55. *Hon Degrees:* MA, Harvard Univ, 70; DSc, Lafayette Col, 78. *Honors & Awards:* E Mead Johnson Award Pediat Res, Am Acad Pediat, 70; Fourth Annual Award Excellence Clin Res, Gen Clin Res Ctr Prog, 92; Jeffrey Modell Found Lifetime Achievement Award, 96. *Prof Exp:* Intern path, Children's Hosp, Boston, 55-56, jr asst resident med, 56-59, sr asst resident, 59-60, res fel, 60-62, asst, 62-63, assoc, 63-68, chief, Immunol Div, 68-85. *Concurrent Pos:* USPHS res officer, Lab Chem Pharmacol, Nat Cancer Inst, NIH, 57-59; teaching fel pediat, Harvard Med Sch, 59-60, res fel, 60-62, instr, 62-63, assoc, 64-65, from asst prof to assoc prof, 66-72; fel, John Simon Guggenheim Mem Found, 74; vis prof, Dept Immunol, Royal Postgrad Med Sch, Univ London, Eng, 74-75; chmn, Sci Adv Comt, Ctr Blood Res, Boston, 76-87; prog dir, Clin Res Ctr, Children's Hosp, Boston, 77-91; chmn, Comt Disadvantaged Scientists, Am Asn Immunologists, 78, Publ Comt, 86-92, Nominating Comt, 87, chmn, Publ Comt, 90-92, Finance Comt, 93; assoc ed, J Clin Invest, 85-87; mem, Med Adv Comt, Immune Deficiency Found, 86-; chmn, Expert Sci Comt Immunodeficiency, WHO, 88; ed, Immunodefiency Rev, 88-; vis prof pediat, Sch Med, Washington Univ, St Louis, Mo, 90-; adj prof, Dept Vet Pathobiol, Sch Vet Med, Purdue Univ, 91-96. *Mem:* Inst Med-Nat Acad Sci; emer mem Am Soc Clin Invest; Am Pediat Soc; Am Asn Immunologists; Asn Am Physicians; emer mem Soc Pediat Res; hon mem Austrian Soc Allergol & Immunol; Am Soc Hemat; Am Acad Arts & Sci. *Res:* Author of various publications. *Mailing Add:* Ctr Blood Res Inc 800 Huntington Ave Boston MA 02115

ROSEN, GERALD HARRIS, DIRAC EQUATION MASS & FEYNMAN PATH SUMMATION. *Current Pos:* prof physics, 66-73, M Russell Wehr prof, 73-90, EMER M RUSSELL WEHR PROF PHYSICS & ATMOSPHERIC SCI, DREXEL UNIV, 90- *Personal Data:* b Mt Vernon, NY, Aug 10, 33; m 63, Sarah L Sweet; c Lawrence A & Karlyn P. *Educ:* Princeton Univ, BSE, 55, MA, 56, PhD(physics), 58. *Prof Exp:* Res assoc Dept Aeronaut Eng, Princeton Univ, 58-59; NSF fel, Inst Theoret Physics, Stockholm, Sweden, 59-60; prin scientist, Martin-Marietta Aerospace Div, 60-63; consult basic & appl res, Southwest Res Inst, 63-66. *Concurrent Pos:* Mem tech staff, Weapons Systs Eval Div, The Pentagon, 60; grantee, NSF, NASA, NIH; Guggenheim & Whiton prizes. *Mem:* Fel AAAS; fel Am Phys Soc; Soc Math Biol; Am Math Soc. *Res:* Theories of relativistic quantum and classical fields; theories of compressible, viscous and combustible fluid flows; turbulence phenomena; nonlinear reaction and transport processes; space-charge-limited currents; biomathematics; nonlinear partial differential equations. *Mailing Add:* 415 Charles Lane Wynnewood PA 19096-1604

ROSEN, GERALD M, FREE RADICAL BIOLOGY. *Current Pos:* Assoc prof, 78-85, PROF PHARMACOL, DUKE UNIV MED SCH, 85- *Educ:* Clarkson Col Technol, PhD(chem), 69; Duke Univ Law Sch, JD, 79. *Mailing Add:* Dept Pharmaceut Sci Univ Md Sch Pharm 20 N Pine St Baltimore MD 21201-1142. *Fax:* 410-706-7184

ROSEN, HAROLD A, ASTRONAUTICS. *Current Pos:* RETIRED. *Personal Data:* b New Orleans, La, Mar 20, 26. *Educ:* Tulane Univ, BE, 47; Calif Inst Technol, ME, 48, PhD, 51. *Hon Degrees:* DSc, Tulane Univ, 75. *Honors & Awards:* Commun Award, Am Inst Aeronaut & Astronaut, 68; Mervin J Kelly Award, Inst Elec & Electronics Engrs, 72; Alexander Graham Bell Medal, 82; L M Ericsson Int Prize, Sweden, 76; Lloyd V Berkner Award, Am Astronaut Soc, 76; Nat Medal Technol, Pres of US, 85; C & C Found Prize, Tokyo, 85; Charles Stark Draper Prize, Nat Acad Eng, 95. *Prof Exp:* Vpres eng & mgr, Commun Systs Div, Space & Commun Group, Hughes Aircraft Co, 56-75, vpres, 75-93. *Concurrent Pos:* Astronaut engr, Nat Space Coun, 64. *Mem:* Nat Acad Eng; fel Am Inst Aeronaut & Astronaut; fel Inst Elec & Electronics Engrs. *Res:* Conceived spin stabilized synchronous communication satellite; development of advanced communication and satellite systems. *Mailing Add:* Hughes Aircraft Co Bldg S64 Mail Sta A402 Airport Sta PO Box 92919 Los Angeles CA 90009

ROSEN, HARRY MARK, MEDICAL ADMINISTRATION. *Current Pos:* from asst prof to assoc prof, 73-80, PROF, MT SINAI SCH MED, 80-, VCHMN, DEPT HEALTH CARE MGT, 79- *Personal Data:* b Philadelphia, Pa, Mar 19, 46. *Educ:* Univ Pa, BS, 68; Columbia Univ, MS, 70; Cornell Univ, PhD, 76. *Prof Exp:* Dir hosp students, New York City Health Serv Admin, 72-73. *Mem:* Am Pub Health Asn; Am Hosp Asn; Am Col Hosp Adminr. *Res:* Evaluation of health care services; quantitative methods in health care management; the quality assurance function. *Mailing Add:* Dept Mgt CUNY Bernard Baruch 17 Lexington Ave Box F1831 New York NY 10010

ROSEN, HENRY, INFECTIOUS DISEASES, MICROBIAL BIOCHEMISTRY. *Current Pos:* fel infectious dis, 74-77, from asst prof to assoc prof, 77-91, PROF MED, UNIV WASH, 91-, ASSOC CHAIR, DEPT MED, 93- *Personal Data:* b Bad Reichenhall, Ger, Nov 26, 46; US citizen; m 79; c Lindsay M & Suzanne E. *Educ:* Yale Col, AB, 68; Univ Rochester, MD, 72. *Prof Exp:* Intern internal med, Univ Wash Affil Hosp, 72-73, resident, 73-74. *Concurrent Pos:* Consult, NIH, 81-85. *Mem:* Fel Infectious Dis Soc Am; Am Fedn Clin Res; Am Col Physicians; Am Soc Clin Invest. *Res:* Understanding the contribution of neutrophils, a subpopulation of circulating white blood cells, towards protecting host organisms from infections. *Mailing Add:* Dept Med RG-20 Univ Wash Seattle WA 98195

ROSEN, HOWARD, DNA REPAIR, GENETIC RECOMBINATION. *Current Pos:* PROF BIOL, CALIF STATE UNIV, LOS ANGELES, 70- *Personal Data:* b Chicago, Ill, July 25, 39; m 64, Constance J Primack; c Diane B & Robert D. *Educ:* Univ Calif, Los Angeles, BS, 61, MS, 65, PhD(bot sci), 68. *Prof Exp:* Fel, Dept Human Genetics, Univ Mich, 69-70. *Concurrent Pos:* Res assoc, Carnegie-Mellon Univ, 72; vis prof zool, Duke Univ, 88-89. *Res:* Mechanism of repair of ultraviolet induced damage in chlamydomonas reinhardtii; mechanism of uniparental inheritance of chloroplast DNA in chlamydomonas reinhardtii. *Mailing Add:* Dept Biol & Microbiol Calif State Univ 5151 State University Dr Los Angeles CA 90032-8000

ROSEN, HOWARD NEAL, CHEMICAL ENGINEERING, WOOD TECHNOLOGY. *Current Pos:* res chem engr, NCent Forest Exp Sta, 70-77, proj leader wood utilization, 77-85, STAFF FOREST PROD & HARVESTING RES, USDA, 85- *Personal Data:* b Takoma Park, Md, June

25, 42; m 69, Anita Slutsky; c Shira & Arie. *Educ:* Univ Md, BS, 64; Northwestern Univ, MS, 66, PhD(chem eng), 69. *Prof Exp:* Develop engr petrol res, Shell Develop Co, 69-70. *Concurrent Pos:* Adj asst prof, Forestry Dept, Southern Ill Univ, 71-84. *Mem:* Am Inst Chem Engrs; Forest Prod Soc; Soc Wood Sci & Technol; Int Union Forest Res Orgn; Hardwood Res Coun. *Res:* Drying, energy conservation, wood utilization, treated wood products, wood physics, recycling & administration. *Mailing Add:* USDA Forest Serv Forest Prod & Harvesting Res PO Box 96090 Washington DC 20090-6090

ROSEN, IRVING, POLYMER CHEMISTRY. *Current Pos:* RETIRED. *Personal Data:* b New York, NY, Apr 3, 24; m 48; c 2. *Educ:* Brooklyn Col, BA, 47; Ind Univ, MS, 49, PhD(chem), 51. *Prof Exp:* Res phys chemist, Reaction Motors, Inc, 51-52; sr chemist, Diamond Alkali Co, 52-55, res group leader polymer & radiation chem, 55-66, sr group leader polymer chem, 66-67; res supvr, Standard Oil Co, Ohio, 67-84, asv to dir res, 81-85. *Mem:* Am Chem Soc; Soc Plastics Engrs. *Res:* Free radical and ionic polymerization; thermoplastic and thermoset polymers; structure-property relations; monomer synthesis; catalysis; chemicals; synfuels. *Mailing Add:* 2657 Green Rd Cleveland OH 44122-1564

ROSEN, IRWIN GARY, NUMERICAL ANALYSIS, CONTROL THEORY. *Current Pos:* ASST PROF MATH, BOWDOIN COL, 80- *Personal Data:* b Long Beach, NY, Feb 19, 54. *Educ:* Brown Univ, ScB, 75, ScM, 76, PhD(appl math), 80. *Concurrent Pos:* Vis scientist, Inst Comput Appln Sci & Eng, 81, consult, 81- *Mem:* Am Math Soc; Soc Indust & Appl Math. *Res:* Numerical approximation methods for the solution of parameter identification and optimal control problems for distributed parameter systems. *Mailing Add:* Dept Math Univ Southern Calif Los Angeles CA 90089

ROSEN, JAMES CARL, CLINICAL PSYCHOLOGY. *Current Pos:* Asst prof, Univ Vt, 76-82, assoc prof, 82-90, dir clin psychol prog, 84-92, PROF PSYCHOL, UNIV VT, 90- *Personal Data:* b Los Angeles, Calif, July 30, 49; m 76; c 2. *Educ:* Univ Calif, Berkeley, BA, 71; Univ Nev, PhD(psych), 76. *Res:* Eating disorders; body image; obesity. *Mailing Add:* Dept Psychol Univ Vt Dewey Hall Burlington VT 05405. *E-Mail:* j_rosen@dewey.uvm.edu

ROSEN, JAMES MARTIN, PHYSICS. *Current Pos:* from asst prof to assoc prof, 68-78, PROF PHYSICS, UNIV WYO, 78- *Personal Data:* b Waseca, Minn, Mar 9, 39; m 67, Mary Johnson; c Greta & Kristin. *Educ:* Univ Minn, BS, 61, MS, 63, PhD(physics), 67. *Prof Exp:* Res assoc, Univ Minn, 67-68. *Mem:* Am Geophys Union; Optical Soc Am. *Res:* Stratospheric constituents; atmospheric research, especially aerosols, ozone & water vapor; atmospheric electricity. *Mailing Add:* Dept Physics & Astron Univ Wyo Laramie WY 82071

ROSEN, JEFFREY KENNETH, DATA PROCESSING. *Current Pos:* PROJ COORD, MED CTR INFOR TECHNOL, 89- *Personal Data:* b Middletown, NY, Dec 27, 41; m 70; c 2. *Educ:* Dartmouth Col, BA, 63; Brown Univ, MA & PhD(physiol), 72. *Prof Exp:* Teacher gen sci, Middletown Bd Educ, NY, 66-68; partner biol consult, L M Kraft Assocs, Goshen, NY, 68-69; asst prof physiol, Univ Dar es Salaam, Tanzania, 72-74; res investr & admin asst to dir, Animal Physiol & Husb, Amphibian Facil, 74-77, sr procedures analyst, data processing, Med Serv Plan Off, 78-80, programmer & Analyst, Hosp Data Systs Ctr, 80-89. *Concurrent Pos:* Fel, Brown Univ, 72. *Mem:* Am Asn Lab Animal Sci; AAAS. *Mailing Add:* 2129 Newport Rd Ann Arbor MI 48103

ROSEN, JEFFREY MARK, BIOCHEMISTRY, ENDOCRINOLOGY. *Current Pos:* from asst prof to assoc prof, 73-82, PROF CELL BIOL, BAYLOR COL MED, 82- *Personal Data:* b New York, NY, Jan 5, 45; m 70; Madeline M Hoffer; c Jennifer D & Rosen. *Educ:* Williams Col, BA, 66; State Univ NY Buffalo, PhD(biochem), 71. *Prof Exp:* Res assoc obstet & gynec, Sch Med, Vanderbilt Univ, 72-73. *Concurrent Pos:* NIH career develop award, 75-80; mem molecular cytol study sect, NIH, 79-83; vis scientist, Imperial Cancer Res Fund, London, 87-88; Am Cancer Soc Scholar grant, 87-88; mem, Am Chem Soc Sci Adv Comt biochem & chem carcinogenesis, 87-; exec ed, Nucleic Acids Res. *Mem:* AAAS; Am Chem Soc; Endocrine Soc; Am Soc Microbiol; Develop Biol Soc; Am Soc Biol Chemists; Am Soc Cell Biol. *Res:* Mechanism of steroid and peptide hormone action; hormonal regulation of mammary gland growth and differentiation; hormonal regulation of breast cancer. *Mailing Add:* Dept Cell Biol Baylor Col Med One Baylor Plaza Houston TX 77030-3498. *Fax:* 713-798-8012; *E-Mail:* jrosen@mbcer.bcm.tmc.edu

ROSEN, JOHN FRIESNER, biochemistry, metabolism, for more information see previous edition

ROSEN, JOSEPH DAVID, FOOD CHEMISTRY, PESTICIDE CHEMISTRY. *Current Pos:* from asst res prof to assoc res prof food sci, 65-74, res prof, 74-88, RES PROF II FOOD SCI, RUTGERS UNIV, NEW BRUNSWICK, 88- *Personal Data:* b New York, NY, Feb 26, 35; m 62; c 4. *Educ:* City Col New York, BS, 56; Rutgers Univ, PhD(org chem), 63. *Prof Exp:* Res chemist, E I du Pont de Nemours & Co, Inc, 63-65. *Concurrent Pos:* Sci adv, Food & Drug Admin, 74-78, 81-87; adv bd, J Agr & Food Chem, 76-78; vis prof pesticide chem, Univ Calif, Berkeley, 78-79; co ed, J Food Safety, 78- 89; NJ Pesticide Rev Comt, 87-; dir, Grad Prog Food Sci, 94- *Mem:* Am Chem Soc; Am Soc Mass Spectromony; Inst Food Technologists. *Res:* Analysis of pesticides, mycotoxins, and industrial chemicals in food by mass spectrometry; metabolism of xenobiotics; photochemistry of pesticides. *Mailing Add:* Dept Food Sci Cook Col Rutgers Univ New Brunswick NJ 08903. *E-Mail:* jrosen@aesop.rutgers.edu

ROSEN, JUDAH BEN, COMPUTER SCIENCE, SCIENTIFIC COMPUTING. *Current Pos:* head dept, 71-80, PROF COMPUT SCI, UNIV MINN, 71- *Personal Data:* b Philadelphia, Pa, May 5, 22; div; c Susan & Lynn. *Educ:* Johns Hopkins Univ, BS, 43; Columbia Univ, PhD(appl math), 52. *Prof Exp:* Jr engr, Gen Elec Co, 43-44; develop engr, Manhattan Proj, 44-47; develop engr, Brookhaven Nat Lab, 47-48; res assoc, Princeton Univ, 52-54; head, Appl Math Dept, Shell Develop Co, 55-62; vis prof comput sci, Stanford Univ, 62-64; prof & chmn dept, Univ Wis-Madison, 65-71, prof, Math Res Ctr, 64-71. *Concurrent Pos:* Consult, Argonne Nat Labs, 76-; prin investr, NSF res grants, 79-85, 95- & Air Force Off Sci Res, 87-94; Lady Davis vis prof, Technion, Israel, 80; invited lectr, Chinese Acad Sci Peking, 80 & 96; fel, Minn Supercomput Inst, 85; adj res prof, Comput Sci & Eng Dept, Univ Calif, San Diego, 92-; sr fel, San Diego Supercomput Ctr, 93. *Mem:* Soc Indust & Appl Math; Asn Comput Mach; Math Prog Soc. *Res:* Computer algorithms and software for nonlinear programming and large-scale optimization problems; algorithms for parallel supercomputers; computation of molecular structure by energy minimization, algorithms for structured approximation in signal processing. *Mailing Add:* 10305 N 28th Ave Plymouth MN 55441. *E-Mail:* jbrosen@cs.ucsd.edu

ROSEN, KENNETH M, AEROSPACE ENGINEERING. *Current Pos:* Dir eng prog, dir design & eng mgr, Blackhawk Helicopters, chief propulsion, VPRES DEVELOP ENG & ADVAN PROG, SIKORSKY AIRCRAFT, 89- *Personal Data:* b New York, NY, May 18, 40. *Educ:* City Univ NY,BA, 62; Rennsalear Polytech Univ, MSME, 65, PhD(mech eng), 70. *Honors & Awards:* Alexander Klemien Award & Notable Achievement Aeronaut, 94. *Concurrent Pos:* mem, NASA/Am Asn Engrs Aeronaut Comt, NASA Roadcraft Comt. *Mem:* Nat Acad Eng; fel Royal Aeronaut Soc; fel Am Helicopter Asn. *Mailing Add:* 6900 Main St MS333A5 PO Box 9729 Stratford CT 06497. *Fax:* 203-386-4403; *E-Mail:* krosen@sikorsky.com

ROSEN, LEON, EPIDEMIOLOGY. *Current Pos:* VIS SCIENTIST, INST PASTEUR, PARIS, FRANCE, 94- *Personal Data:* b Los Angeles, Calif, Oct 4, 26; m 52; c 3. *Educ:* Univ Calif, AB, 45, MD, 48, MPH, 50; Johns Hopkins Univ, DrPH, 53. *Honors & Awards:* Laveran Medal, Societe de Pathologie Exotique; Ashford Medal, Am Soc Trop Med & Hyg. *Prof Exp:* Intern, Gorgas Hosp, Panama, CZ, 48-49; med dir & head, Pac Res Sect, Nat Inst Allergy & Infectious Dis, Univ Hawaii, 50-78, dir, Pac Res Univ, Res Corp, 78-80, dir abrovirus prog, Pac Biomed Res Ctr, 80-94. *Mem:* Am Epidemiol Soc; Am Soc Trop Med & Hyg; Royal Soc Trop Med & Hyg. *Res:* Virology; arthropod-borne viruses; nematode infections; medical entomology. *Mailing Add:* Les Giraults St Fargeau 89170 France

ROSEN, LEONARD CRAIG, ENVIRONMENTAL PHYSICS, ENERGY CONVERSION. *Current Pos:* FAC, DEPT PHYSICS, DIABLO VALLEY COL, 95- *Personal Data:* b New York, NY, Apr 14, 36; div; c Kim R Kulp. *Educ:* Cornell Univ, AB, 57; Columbia Univ, MBA, 59, MA, 64, PhD(physics), 68. *Prof Exp:* Asst prof physics & astron, Dartmouth Col, 69-76; mem staff, Lawrence Livermore Nat Lab, Univ Calif, 76-91. *Concurrent Pos:* Consult, Lawrence Livermore Lab, Univ Calif, 68-76 & Arthur D Little, Inc, 75-76; lectr, San Jose State Univ, 78-79, Univ Calif, Davis, 82-87, San Francisco State Univ, 90-92, Diablo Valley Col, 92-95 & St Marys Col, Calif, 94-95. *Mem:* Am Phys Soc. *Res:* Nucleosynthesis; mathematical models of air pollution; development of energy conversion systems; laser interactions in the atmosphere; radiative transport models. *Mailing Add:* 460 N Civic Dr No 207 Walnut Creek CA 94596. *Fax:* 510-430-7916; *E-Mail:* lrosen@viking.edu

ROSEN, LOUIS, PHYSICS. *Current Pos:* mem staff, Los Alamos Sci Lab, 44-46, alt group leader cyclotron group, 46-49, group leader, Nuclear Plate Lab, 49-65, alt div leader, 62-65, div leader, 65-85, dir, Los Alamos Meson Physics Fac, 65-85, sr fel, 85-90, EMER SR FEL, LOS ALAMOS SCI LAB, 90- *Personal Data:* b New York, NY, June 10, 18; m 41, Mary Terry; c Terry L. *Educ:* Univ Ala, BA, 39, MS, 41; Pa State Univ, PhD(physics), 44. *Hon Degrees:* DSc, Univ NMex, 79, Univ Colo, 88. *Honors & Awards:* Fel E O Lawrence Award, 63; Golden Plate Award, Nat Acad Achievement, 64. *Prof Exp:* Asst physics, Univ Ala, 39-40, instr, 40-41; from asst to instr, Pa State Univ, 41-44. *Concurrent Pos:* Guggenheim fel, 59-60; mem nuclear sci panel & chmn subpanel accelerators; mem, Gov Comt Tech Excellence in NMex, 70-80; sesquicentennial hon prof, Univ Ala, 81. *Mem:* Fel AAAS; fel Am Phys Soc. *Res:* High hydrostatic pressures; x-ray; cosmic rays; nuclear physics; particle accelerators; nuclear and particle physics; accelerators; cancer treatment. *Mailing Add:* Los Alamos Nat Lab PO Box 1663 Los Alamos NM 87545. *Fax:* 505-665-6435

ROSEN, MARC ALLEN, ENERGY, THERMODYNAMICS & HEAT TRANSFER. *Current Pos:* dir, Sch Aerospace Eng, 92-94, PROF MECH ENG, RYERSON POLYTECH UNIV, 86-, CHAIR MECH ENG, 94- *Personal Data:* b Toronto, Ont, July 23, 58. *Educ:* Univ Toronto, BASc, 81, MASc, 83, PhD(mech eng), 87. *Prof Exp:* Res & teaching asst mech eng, Univ Toronto, 81-83; res assoc energy, Inst Hydrogen Systs, 83-86. *Concurrent Pos:* Res assoc, Argonne Nat Lab, 87; adv, Dynawatt Energy Res Corp, 88-; adj prof, Dept Mech Eng, Univ Western Ont, London, Can; assoc ed, Energy-The Int J. *Mem:* Am Soc Mech Engrs; fel Can Soc Mech Eng. *Res:* Thermodynamics and heat transfer especially second law analysis; energy systems analysis; thermal energy storage and solar energy; computer-aided process simulation; cogeneration; district heating and cooling; environmental impact of energy utilization. *Mailing Add:* Dept Mech Eng Ryerson Polytech Univ Toronto ON M5B 2K3 Can. *Fax:* 416-979-5265; *E-Mail:* mrosen@acs.ryerson.ca

ROSEN, MARK DAVID A, CONDENSED MATTER PHYSICS. *Current Pos:* STAFF SCIENTIST, NORTHRUP GRUMMAN CORP, 85- *Personal Data:* b Philadelphia, Pa, Oct 9, 46; m 82, Carol L Katz; c Josh & Sam. *Educ:* Drexel Univ, BS, 69; Harvard Univ, MS, 72, PhD(appl physics), 77. *Prof Exp:* Res fel, Physics Dept, Havard Univ, 77-80; res physicist, Shell Develop Company, 80-85. *Mem:* Int Elec & Electronics Engrs; Am Asn Phys Teachers. *Mailing Add:* 61 Grouse Lane Woodbridge CT 06525

ROSEN, MARVIN, organic chemistry, polymer chemistry, for more information see previous edition

ROSEN, MICHAEL IRA, MATHEMATICS, NUMBER THEORY. *Current Pos:* From instr to assoc prof math, 62-73, PROF MATH, BROWN UNIV, 73- *Personal Data:* b Brooklyn, NY, Mar 7, 38; m 60; c 1. *Educ:* Brandeis Univ, BA, 59; Princeton Univ, PhD(math), 63. *Concurrent Pos:* NSF res grants, 63-78 & 80-88; Off Naval Res fel, 65-66. *Mem:* Am Math Soc; Math Asn Am. *Res:* Algebraic numbers, algebraic functions, arithmetic algebraic geometry, cohomology of groups; Drinfeld modules, the Hilbert class field, formal groups, and special values of L-functions; class number identities and generalizations. *Mailing Add:* 184 Chace Ave Providence RI 02906

ROSEN, MILTON JACQUES, SURFACTANTS, SURFACE CHEMISTRY. *Current Pos:* tutor, Brooklyn Col, 46-50, from instr to assoc prof, 50-66, PROF CHEM, BROOKLYN COL CITY UNIV NEW YORK, 66-, DIR, SURFACTANT RES INST, 87- *Personal Data:* b Brooklyn, NY, Feb 11, 20; m 48, Ellen Doree; c Leslie S, David S & Craig S. *Educ:* City Col New York, BS, 39; Univ Md, MS, 41; Polytech Inst Brooklyn, PhD(org chem), 49. *Honors & Awards:* Plenary lectr, World Surfactants Cong, Munich, 84. *Prof Exp:* Chemist, Jewish Hosp, Brooklyn, 40-42, Glyco Prod Co, 42-44 & Publicker Com Alcohol Co, Pa, 44. *Concurrent Pos:* Fel, Lenox Hill Hosp, 41; chem consult to indust & US govt, 46-; vis prof, Hebrew Univ, Israel, 58-59, 64-65, 71-72 & 80; grants, City Univ New York, 62-64 & 85-89, NSF, 63-71 & 79-90, Pilot Chem Co Calif, 76-78, Yamada Sci Found, Japan, 79, Lever Bros, Res Eng, 87-88, Dow Chem Co, 88-91, Rhone-Poulene, 93- & NSF, 94-; NIH spec fel, 64-65; assoc ed, J Am Oil Chemists Soc, 81-, ed comn, J Dispersion Sci & Technol, 83-, adv bd, J Colloid Interface Sci, 90-92; consult, Chinese Univ Develop Proj Two, US Nat Acad Sci, 86. *Mem:* Am Chem Soc; Am Oil Chem Soc. *Res:* Surface active agents--correlations between structure and properties, utilization, synthesis, analysis; reactions at interfaces. *Mailing Add:* Surfactant Res Inst Brooklyn Col City Univ New York Brooklyn NY 11210. *Fax:* 718-951-4438

ROSEN, MILTON W(ILLIAM), PROPULSION GUIDANCE & CONTROL. *Current Pos:* STUDY LEADER, INST LEARNING RETIREMENT, AM UNIV, 87- *Personal Data:* b Philadelphia, Pa, July 25, 15; m 48, Josephine S Haar; c Nanoy, Deborah & Janet. *Educ:* Univ Pa, BS, 37. *Honors & Awards:* James H Wyld Award for Propulsion, Am Inst Aeronaut & Astronaut, 54. *Prof Exp:* Radio engr guided missiles, Naval Res Lab, 40-45, head rocket sect, Rocket-Sonde Br, 47-52, head, Rocket Develop Br, 53-55, tech dir, Proj Vanguard, 55-58; chief, Rocket Vehicle Develop, NASA, 58-60, dep dir, Off Launch Vehicle Prog, 60-61, dir, Launch Vehicles & Propulsion, Off Manned Space Flight, 61-63, sr scientist, Off Dept Defense & Interagency Affairs, 63-72, dep assoc, Admin Space Sci, 72-74; exec secy, Space Sci Bd, 74-78, Comt Impacts Stratospheric Change, 78-80, exec secy, Comt Underground Coal Mine Safety, 80-83, exec dir, Space Appl Bd, NAS, 83-85. *Concurrent Pos:* Physicist, Liquid Rocket Sect, Jet Propulsim Lab, Calif Inst Technol, 46-47. *Mem:* Fel Am Inst Aeronaut & Astronaut. *Res:* Radio and radar systems for control of guided missiles; ceramic liners for rocket combustion chambers; Viking high-altitude sounding rocket; conception of Vanguard earth satellite vehicle. *Mailing Add:* 5610 Alta Vista Rd Bethesda MD 20817

ROSEN, MORDECAI DAVID, PLASMA PHYSICS, LASER-PLASMA INTERACTIONS. *Current Pos:* after proj mgr shiva physics, 78-82, staff physicist plasma physics & laser fusion target design, 76-84, assoc div leader, laser target design, 84-90, DIV LEADER, LASER TARGET DESIGN, UNIV CALIF, LAWRENCE LIVERMORE LAB, 90- *Personal Data:* b Brooklyn, NY, Nov 23, 51; m 73, Rena C Brickman; c Michael M, Gabriella S & Raphael C. *Educ:* Hebrew Univ, Jerusalem, BSc, 72; Princeton Univ, PhD(astrophys), 76. *Honors & Awards:* "Top 100 Innovators" Sci Dig, 85; Excellence in Plasma Physics Award, Am Phys Soc, 90. *Prof Exp:* From res asst to res assoc, Plasma Physics Lab, Princeton Univ, 72-76. *Concurrent Pos:* Lectr, Dept Appl Sci, Univ Calif, Davis. *Mem:* Fel Am Phys Soc; Soc Photo-Optical Instrumentation Engrs. *Res:* Laser fusion target design; laser-plasma interactions; magnetohydrodynamic stability of tokamaks, shock waves in plasmas; radiation transport; suprathermal electron transport; physics of high energy density; x-ray laser design. *Mailing Add:* L-472 Lawrence Livermore Lab Livermore CA 94550. *Fax:* 510-423-9969; *E-Mail:* rosen2@llnl.gov

ROSEN, MORTIMER GILBERT, obstetrics & gynecology; deceased, see previous edition for last biography

ROSEN, NATHAN, theoretical physics; deceased, see previous edition for last biography

ROSEN, PAUL, PHYSICS, ELECTRONICS. *Current Pos:* res assoc, 58-70, affil biophys, 70-77, SR RES ASSOC, ROCKEFELLER UNIV, 77- *Personal Data:* b New York, NY, Apr 2, 28; m 51; c 4. *Educ:* City Col New York, BS, 53; NY Univ, MS, 66. *Prof Exp:* Res physicist, Patterson Moos Div, Universal Coil Winding Mach, Inc, 53-56; res engr, Fairchild Camera & Instrument Corp, 56-58. *Concurrent Pos:* Instr, Brooklyn Polytech Inst, 62-71; mem adj fac, Fairleigh Dickinson Univ, 71- *Mem:* AAAS; Am Phys Soc; Sigma Xi. *Res:* Biomedical instrumentation; electro-optics; analytical chemistry instrumentation; digital computer interfacing and programming. *Mailing Add:* Dept Elec Rockefeller Univ 1230 York Ave New York NY 10021

ROSEN, PERRY, ORGANIC CHEMISTRY. *Current Pos:* sr chemist, 62-70, res fel, 70-72, group chief, 72-76, sect chief, 76-80, assoc dir, 80-83, DIR, HOFFMANN-LA ROCHE, INC, 83- *Personal Data:* b Bronx, NY, Oct 2, 30; m 60; c 1. *Educ:* City Col New York, BS, 53; Columbia Univ, MS & PhD(chem), 60. *Prof Exp:* Fel, Columbia Univ, 61-62. *Concurrent Pos:* Vis prof chem, Mass Inst Technol, 72- *Mem:* Am Chem Soc; NY Acad Sci; Am Inst Chemists; Int Soc Immunopharmacol; Int Union Pure & Appl Chem; AAAS. *Res:* Synthetic organic chemistry; development of new chemical reactions; development of new drugs primarily in the allergy/inflammation and cardiovascular areas. *Mailing Add:* 26 Sunset Dr North Caldwell NJ 07006

ROSEN, PETER, EMERGENCY MEDICINE. *Current Pos:* ASST DIR, DEPT EMERGENCY MED, UNIV CALIF, SAN DIEGO, MED CTR, 89-, DIR EDUC, 89-, DIR EMERGENCY MED RESIDENCY PROG, 91-, PROF CLIN MED & SURG, SCH MED, 93- *Personal Data:* b Brooklyn, NY, Aug 3, 35; m 59, Ann H; c Henry, Monte, Curt & Ted. *Educ:* Univ Chicago, BA, 55; Wash Univ, St Louis, MD, 60. *Honors & Awards:* Physicians Recognition Award, AMA, 69; Am Hosp Asn Award, AMA, 73; cert Appreciation, Am Col Emergency Physicians, 77, James D Mills Outstanding Contrib Emergency Med Award, 84, Outstanding Contrib Educ Award, 94; Outstanding Leadership Contrib Acad Emergency Med Award, Soc Acad Emergency Med, 90; Outstanding Contrib Emergency Med, Can Asn Emergency Med, 94. *Prof Exp:* Intern, Univ Chicago Hosp & Clins, 60-61, assoc prof, Div Emergency Med, 71-73, prof, 73-77; resident, Highlands Co Hosp, Oakland, 61-65; dir, Div Emergency Med, Denver City Health & Hosps, 77-86 & 87-89. *Concurrent Pos:* Attend physician, Hot Springs Mem Hosp, Wyo, Worland Co Hosp & Basin-Graybull Hosp, 68-71, Univ Chicago Hosps & Clins, 71-77; dir, Emergency Med Residency Prog, Univ Chicago Hosps & Clins, 71-77, Denver Gen Hosp, St Anthony Hosp Syst & St Joseph Hosp, 77-78; emergency med adv, State Colo, 77-85; clin prof, Div Emergency Med, Ore Health Sci, Univ Portland, 78-89; prof, Div Emergency Med, Dept Surg, Health Sci Ctr, Univ Colo, 84-89; dept mgr med affairs, Denver Dept Health & Hosps, 86-87; med dir life flight air med serv, San Diego Med Ctr, Univ Calif, 89-91, mem hosp staff, Tri-City Med Ctr, Oceanside, Calif, 89-, base hosp physician & adj prof med & surg, 89-, chair, Med Ethics Comt, 90- *Mem:* Inst Med-Nat Acad Sci; Am Burn Asn; Am Col Emergency Physicians (pres, 81-82); Am Trauma Soc; Acad Emergency Med; fel Am Col Surgeons. *Res:* Emergency medicine; author and co-author of over 200 publications. *Mailing Add:* Univ Calif 200 W Arbor Dr San Diego CA 92103-8676

ROSEN, RICHARD DAVID, CLIMATE DYNAMICS, GENERAL CIRCULATION. *Current Pos:* sr staff scientist & group mgr, 82-89, PRIN SCIENTIST, BASIC RES, ATMOSPHERIC & ENVIRON RES, INC, 89-, VPRES, 89- *Personal Data:* b Brooklyn, NY, Feb 23, 48; m 73, Michele Litvin. *Educ:* Mass Inst Technol, SB, 70, SM, 70, PhD(meteorol), 74. *Prof Exp:* Staff scientist, Environ Res & Technol, Inc, 74-82. *Concurrent Pos:* Sr lectr, Dept Earth, Atmospheric & Planetary Sci, Mass Inst Technol, 74-; mem, Comt Earth Sci, Nat Acad Sci, 82-84 & Spec Study Groups, Int Asn Geodesy, 83- & Comt Southern Hemisphere, Am Meteorol Soc, 91-94; ed, Am Meteorol Soc Journals, Monthly Weather Rev, 86-87 & J Climate, 88-89; comnr sci & technol activ, Am Meterol Soc, 96- *Mem:* Fel Am Meteorol Soc; Am Geophys Union; Oceanog Soc. *Res:* Interannual variability of general circulation of the atmosphere; atmospheric excitation of earth rotation and polar motion; ability of climate models to simulate circulation; atmospheric branch of global hydrological cycle. *Mailing Add:* Atmospheric & Environ Res Inc 840 Memorial Dr Cambridge MA 02139-3794. *E-Mail:* rdrosen@aer.com

ROSEN, ROBERT, mathematical biology, for more information see previous edition

ROSEN, ROBERT T, NUTRITION, ANALYTICAL CHEMISTRY. *Current Pos:* ASSOC DIR, CTR ADVAN FOOD TECHNOL, 93- *Personal Data:* b NH. *Res:* Nutrition; analytical chemistry. *Mailing Add:* Keats Rd PO Box 293 Pottersville NJ 07979-0293

ROSEN, SAMUEL, MICROBIOLOGY. *Current Pos:* PROF MICROBIOL, OHIO STATE UNIV, 61- *Personal Data:* b New York, NY, Apr 14, 23; m 54, Mindla Weinrich; c Paul & Grant. *Educ:* Brooklyn Col, BA, 48; Univ Ill, MS, 49; Mich State Univ, PhD(microbiol), 53. *Prof Exp:* Technician microbiol, Pyridium Corp, 49-50; res assoc, Mich State Univ, 52-61; prof microbiol, Ohio State Univ, 61-95. *Concurrent Pos:* Consult, Battelle Mem Inst, 62-, Procter & Gamble Co, 70-, Dent Res Inst, Great Lakes, 70, Southern Ill Univ, 72- & Nat Inst Dent Res, 75-; NIH career develop award, Ohio State Univ, 67-72. *Mem:* Int Asn Dent Res; Am Asn Dent Schs; Gnotobiotics Asn; Sigma Xi. *Res:* Experimental dental caries; experimental periodontal disease; microbial taxonomy; infection control. *Mailing Add:* 3625 Ridgewood Dr Hilliard OH 43026

ROSEN, SAUL W, INTERNAL MEDICINE, ENDOCRINOLOGY. *Current Pos:* sr investr, Clin Endocrinol Br, Nat Inst Arthritis, Metab & Digestive Dis, 61-84, dep dir, 84-90, ACTG DIR, CLIN CTR, NIH, 90-94. *Personal Data:* b Boston, Mass, July 29, 28; m 89, Deborah Kieffer; c 3. *Educ:* Harvard Univ, AB, 47; Northwestern Univ, PhD(chem), 55; Harvard Med Sch, MD, 56; Am Bd Internal Med, cert, 63, dipl endocrinol, 65. *Prof Exp:* From intern med to asst resident, Univ Calif Med Ctr, San Francisco, 56-58; clin assoc, Nat Inst Arthritis & Metab Dis, 58-60; sr resident med, Med Ctr, Univ Calif, 60-61. *Mem:* Am Chem Soc; Am Fedn Clin Res; fel Am Col Physicians; Endocrine Soc; Sigma Xi; Asn Am Physicians. *Res:* Clinical endocrinology; ectopic tumor gonadotropins. *Mailing Add:* 7401 Westlake Terr Apt 1104 Bethesda MD 20817

ROSEN, SEYMOUR, KIDNEY DISEASE. *Current Pos:* ASSOC PROF PATH, SCH MED, HARVARD UNIV, 73- *Personal Data:* b Chicago, Ill, Aug 21, 35; m 63; c 2. *Educ:* Univ Ill, MD, 59. *Prof Exp:* Assoc pathologist, 74-82, dir, surg path, Beth Israel Hosp, 82- *Mem:* Fedn Am Soc Exp Biol; Int Acad Pathologists. *Mailing Add:* Dept Path Beth Israel Hosp 330 Brookline Boston MA 02215-5491. *Fax:* 617-278-7120

ROSEN, SIDNEY, HISTORY OF SCIENCE. *Current Pos:* assoc prof sci educ, 58-60, from assoc prof to prof phys sci, 60-82, EMER PROF ASTRON, UNIV ILL, URBANA, 82- *Personal Data:* b Boston, Mass, June 5, 16; m 44, Dorothy Schack; c 1. *Educ:* Univ Mass, AB, 39; Harvard Univ, MAT, 52, PhD(phys sci), 55. *Honors & Awards:* Clara Ingram Judson Mem Award, 70. *Prof Exp:* From instr to asst prof phys sci, Brandeis Univ, 53-58. *Concurrent Pos:* Consult, Comnr Educ, Mass, 57-58 & Am Humanities Sem, 58; vis lectr, Harvard Univ, 58; spec sci consult, Ford Found, Colombia, SAm, 63-64 & 66; Fulbright fel, UK, 63; consult, Encycl Britannica Films, Inc, 64- *Mem:* Fel AAAS; Nat Asn Res Sci Teaching; Hist Sci Soc; Nat Sci Teachers Asn; Am Asn Physics Teachers. *Res:* History of learning; problems of science teaching. *Mailing Add:* Dept Astron Univ Ill 1011 W Springfield Urbana IL 61801-3072. *Fax:* 217-244-7638

ROSEN, SIMON PETER, PHYSICS. *Current Pos:* DEAN SCI, UNIV TEX, ARLINGTON, 90- *Personal Data:* b London, Eng, Aug 4, 33; m 58, 87; c 4. *Educ:* Oxford Univ, BA, 54, PhD(physics), 57. *Prof Exp:* Res assoc physics, Washington Univ, 57-59; scientist, Midwestern Univ Res Asn, 59-61; NATO fel, Oxford Univ, 61-62; from asst prof to prof physics, Purdue Univ, 62-83; staff mem, Los Alamos Nat Lab, 83-90. *Concurrent Pos:* Tutorial fel, Univ Sussex, 69; sr theoret physicist, High Energy Physics Prog, Div Phys Res, US Energy Res & Develop Admin, Washington, DC, 75-77; prog assoc theoret physics, NSF, 81- *Mem:* Fel Am Phys Soc. *Res:* Symmetry theories of elementary particles; theory of weak interactions; high energy physics. *Mailing Add:* Col Sci Univ Tex Arlington TX 76019

ROSEN, SOL, metallurgy, for more information see previous edition

ROSEN, STEPHEN, SCIENTIFIC CAREER TRANSITIONS. *Current Pos:* CHMN, SCI & TECHNOL ADV BD & DIR SCI CAREER TRANSITIONS, CELIA PAUL ASSOCS, INC, NY, 88- *Personal Data:* b New York, NY, May 3, 34; m 84; c 2. *Educ:* Queens Col, NY, BS, 55; Bryn Mawr Col, MA, 58; Adelphi Univ, PhD(physics), 66. *Prof Exp:* Physicist, Int Bus Mach Corp, 58-60; asst prof physics, State Univ NY Maritime Col, 60-67; res adv, Gen Res Labs, NJ, 67-69; mem prof staff, Hudson Inst, 69-70; dir res, Mkt & Planning Group, Inc, 72-84; mem staff technol investments, R S Enrlich & Co, 84-88. *Concurrent Pos:* Sr engr & scientist, Ford Instrument Co Div, Sperry Rand Corp, 63; res assoc, Astrophys Inst, Paris & Nuclear Studies Ctr, Saclay, France, 68; consult, Xerox Corp, Gen Tel & Electronics Corp & Carnegie Corp, 70-; consult, NSF, 73-74 & Fed Energy Admin, 74-75. *Mem:* AAAS; Am Phys Soc; Am Astron Soc; NY Acad Sci. *Res:* Beta and gamma ray spectroscopy; nuclear reactors; radiation effects; operational tactics; high energy interactions; origin and astrophysics of cosmic rays; technological and social forecasting; long-range planning; market planning for high-technology products and services; electronic and print journalism; technology investments; science-careers management and outplacement. *Mailing Add:* 35 W 81st St Apt 1D New York NY 10024-6045. *Fax:* 212-397-1022

ROSEN, STEPHEN L(OUIS), POLYMER SCIENCE & ENGINEERING. *Current Pos:* PROF CHEM ENG & CHMN DEPT, UNIV MO, ROLLA, 90- *Personal Data:* b New York, NY, Nov 25, 37. *Educ:* Cornell Univ, BChE, 60, PhD(chem eng), 64; Princeton Univ, MS, 61. *Prof Exp:* From asst prof to prof chem eng, Carnegie-Mellon Univ, 64-81; prof chem eng, Univ Toledo, 81-90, chmn chem eng, 81-89. *Mem:* Am Chem Soc; Am Inst Chem Engrs; Soc Plastics Engrs. *Res:* Polymeric materials; rheology; polymerization. *Mailing Add:* Dept Chem Eng Univ Mo Rolla MO 65401-0249. *Fax:* 573-341-6033; *E-Mail:* slr@shuttle.cc.umr.edu

ROSEN, STEVEN DAVID, CELL BIOLOGY. *Current Pos:* ASST PROF CELL BIOL, DEPT ANAT, UNIV CALIF, SAN FRANCISCO, 76- *Personal Data:* b New York, NY, Oct 20, 43. *Educ:* Univ Calif, Berkeley, AB, 66; Cornell Univ, PhD(neurobiol), 72. *Prof Exp:* Fel cell biol, Dept Psychiat, Sch Med, Univ Calif, San Diego, 72-76. *Concurrent Pos:* Am Cancer Soc fel, Dept Psychiat, Univ Calif, San Diego, 72-74. *Mem:* AAAS; Am Soc Cell Biol. *Res:* Molecular basis of specific cell adhesion in cellular slime molds and higher systems. *Mailing Add:* Dept Anat Univ Calif San Francisco San Francisco CA 94143-0452. *Fax:* 415-476-4845

ROSEN, STEVEN TERRY, ONCOLOGY, HEMATOLOGY. *Current Pos:* GENEVIEVE TEUTON PROF, MED SCH, NORTHWESTERN UNIV, 89-, DIR CANCER CTR, 89- *Personal Data:* b Brooklyn, NY, Feb 18, 52; m 76; c 2. *Educ:* Northwestern Univ, BM, 72, MD, 76. *Concurrent Pos:* Dir clin progs, Northwestern Mem Hosp, 89-; ed chief, J Northwestern Univ Cancer Ctr, 89- & Contemp Oncol, 90-; chmn, Exhibs/Indust Comt, Am Soc Clin Oncol. *Mem:* Am Asn Cancer Res; AAAS; Am Col Physicians; AMA; Am Soc Clin Oncol; Am Soc Hemat; Cent Soc Clin Res. *Res:* Cutaneous T-cell lymphomas; biology of lung cancer; biologic therapies; hormone receptors. *Mailing Add:* 303 E Chicago Ave Chicago IL 60611-3008

ROSEN, WILLIAM EDWARD, ORGANIC CHEMISTRY, MICROBIOLOGY. *Current Pos:* exec vpres, 68-89, PRES, SUTTON LABS, DIV GAF CHEM CORP, 89- *Personal Data:* b New York, NY, Jan 29, 27; m 53; c 5. *Educ:* NY Univ, BA, 48; Harvard Univ, MA, 50, PhD(chem), 52. *Prof Exp:* Fel, Univ Southern Calif, 52 & Yale Univ, 52-53; sr res chemist, Ciba Pharmaceut Prod, Inc, 53-64; vpres res, Cambridge Res, Inc, 64-68. *Concurrent Pos:* Adj prof, Rutgers Univ. *Mem:* Am Chem Soc; Soc Cosmetic Chem. *Res:* Cosmetic preservation; pharmaceuticals and fine chemicals; process research and development; organic synthesis; steroids; alkaloids. *Mailing Add:* 86 Canoe Brook Pkwy Summit NJ 07901-1435

ROSEN, WILLIAM G, MATHEMATICS. *Current Pos:* RETIRED. *Personal Data:* b Portsmouth, NH, May 13, 21; m 47, 75; c 2. *Educ:* Univ Ill, MS, 47, PhD(math), 54. *Prof Exp:* Instr math, Univ Md, 54-56, asst prof, 56-61; from asst prog dir to assoc prog dir sci educ, NSF, 61-64; staff assoc sci develop, 64-66, spec asst to dir, 66-70, prog dir, Mod Analytical & Probability Prog, 70-79, head, Math Sci Sect, 79-83; dep exec dir, US-Israel Binat Res Found, 83-86; consult, Bd Math Sci, Nat Acad Sci, 86-89; dep exec dir, US-Israel Binat Sci Found, 89-95. *Res:* Science administration. *Mailing Add:* 4000 Tunlaw Rd NW No 621 Washington DC 20007. *Fax:* 972-2-633-287; *E-Mail:* wgr@vms.bujliac.il

ROSEN, WILLIAM M, CHEMISTRY. *Current Pos:* from asst prof to assoc prof, 70-82, PROF CHEM, UNIV RI, 82- *Personal Data:* b Lynn, Mass, Dec 27, 41; m 64; c 2. *Educ:* Univ Calif, Los Angeles, BS, 63; Univ Calif, Riverside, PhD(chem), 67. *Prof Exp:* Teaching asst chem, Univ Calif, Riverside, 63-65; res assoc, 65-66, assoc, 66-67; res assoc, Ohio State Univ, 67-69; asst prof, Purdue Univ, 69-70. *Concurrent Pos:* NIH fel, 67-69; assoc res chemist, Scripps Inst oceanog, 76-77. *Mem:* Am Chem Soc; Chem Soc; Am Inst Chem; AAAS. *Res:* Synthesis of interesting organic and inorganic chemical systems. *Mailing Add:* Dept Chem Univ RI Kingston RI 02881-0809

ROSENAU, JOHN (RUDOLPH), AGRICULTURAL & FOOD ENGINEERING. *Current Pos:* ASSOC PROF FOOD ENG, UNIV MASS, AMHERST, 73-, HEAD DEPT, 85- *Personal Data:* b Sheboygan, Wis, Feb 25, 43; m 65; c 2. *Educ:* Univ Wis-Madison, BS, 65, BSME, 66; Mich State Univ, PhD(agr eng), 70. *Prof Exp:* Asst prof food sci & industs, Univ Minn, St Paul, 70-73. *Mem:* Am Soc Agr Engrs; Inst Food Technol; Sigma Xi. *Res:* Utilization of protein components; new systems for cheese production, soy protein utilization. *Mailing Add:* 127 Columbia Dr Amherst MA 01002

ROSENAU, WERNER, PATHOLOGY, IMMUNOLOGY. *Current Pos:* From asst prof to assoc prof, 61-72, PROF PATH, UNIV CALIF, SAN FRANCISCO, 72- *Personal Data:* b June 28, 29; US citizen. *Educ:* Univ Calif, San Francisco, MD, 56. *Mem:* Am Soc Exp Path; AAAS. *Mailing Add:* Dept Path M-590 Univ Calif San Francisco Sch Med 505 Parnassus Ave San Francisco CA 94143-0102

ROSENAU, WILLIAM ALLISON, plant nutrition; deceased, see previous edition for last biography

ROSENBAUM, DAVID MARK, RISK ANALYSIS, SYSTEMS ANALYSIS. *Current Pos:* PRES, TECH ANALYSIS CORP, 81- & RISK ANALYSIS CORP, 87- *Personal Data:* b Boston, Mass, Feb 11, 35; m 64, Karen Smith; c Benjamin & Shoshana. *Educ:* Brown Univ, ScB, 56; Rensselaer Polytech Inst, MS, 58; Brandeis Univ, PhD(physics), 64. *Prof Exp:* Mem staff, Mitre Corp, 60-64; asst res prof physics, Boston Univ, 64-65; mem staff, Inst Defense Anal, 65-67; expert commun & network analysis, Off Emergency Planning, Exec Off Pres, 67-68; assoc prof elec eng, Polytech Inst Brooklyn, 68-69; sr staff mem, Mitre Corp, 70-72; asst dir anal & asst dir admin, systs & computerization, Off Nat Narcotics Intel, US Dept Justice, 72-73; consult, US AEC, 73-74; consult, Perm Subcomt Invests, US Senate, 74; sr staff mem, Mitre Corp, 74-76; consult to the comptroller gen, US Gen Accounting Off, 76-79; dep asst adminr, Radiation Progs, US Environ Protection Agency, 79-81. *Concurrent Pos:* Consult, Off Emergency Planning, Exec Off Pres, 68-69; pres, Network Anal Corp, 68-70; mem, BD, Beta Instrument Corp, 68-72; chmn, Eng Found Conf Vulnerability Urban Areas Subversive Disruption, 72; consult, Perm Subcomt Invests, US Sen, 74-; pres, Tech Anal Corp, Risk Anal Corp & Brillian Nite Software. *Mem:* Am Phys Soc; sr mem Inst Elec & Electronics Engrs. *Res:* Plasma physics; history of guerilla warfare; network analysis; elementary particles and mathematical foundations of quantum mechanics; energy and environmental policy studies; nuclear safeguards; nuclear proliferation; epidemiology; statistics. *Mailing Add:* 4620 Dittmar Rd Arlington VA 22207. *E-Mail:* dmrose@pobox.com

ROSENBAUM, EUGENE JOSEPH, PHYSICAL CHEMISTRY. *Current Pos:* prof chem, 58-72, EMER PROF CHEM, DREXEL UNIV, 72- *Personal Data:* b New York, NY, July 22, 07; m 32; c 2. *Educ:* Univ Chicago, SB, 29, PhD(chem), 33. *Prof Exp:* Instr chem, Univ Chicago, 31-40; Lalor Found fel,

Harvard Univ, 40-41; res chemist, Sun Oil Co, 41-58. *Mem:* AAAS; Am Chem Soc; Am Soc Testing & Mat; Soc Appl Spectros (pres, 52). *Res:* Applied spectroscopy; Raman spectra and molecular structure. *Mailing Add:* 11 Martins Run Apt B-105 Media PA 19063-1059

ROSENBAUM, FRED J(EROME), electrical engineering, microwave engineering; deceased, see previous edition for last biography

ROSENBAUM, H(ERMAN) S(OLOMON), METALLURGY. *Current Pos:* RETIRED. *Personal Data:* b Philadelphia, Pa, Oct 24, 32; m 53; c 3. *Educ:* Univ Pa, BS, 53, MS, 56; Rensselaer Polytech Inst, PhD(metall), 59. *Honors & Awards:* IR-100, 65 & 83. *Prof Exp:* Lab asst, Sam Tour & Co, 52 & Franklin Inst, 53-56; metallurgist, Res Lab, Gen Elec Co,, 56-64, mgr mat struct & properties, Nucleonics Lab, Vallecitos Nuclear Ctr, 64-76, prin engr & prog mgr, 76-78, sr prog mgr, nuclear energy eng div, 78-95. *Mem:* Am Soc Metals; Am Inst Mining, Metall & Petrol Engrs; Am Nuclear Soc. *Res:* Crystal imperfections; precipitation kinetics in solids; radiation damage; microstructures and properties of irradiated materials; physical metallurgy. *Mailing Add:* 917 Kensington Dr Fremont CA 94539

ROSENBAUM, HAROLD DENNIS, MEDICINE. *Current Pos:* RETIRED. *Personal Data:* b Fairplay, Ky, Aug 17, 21; m 70, Doris Fooks; c Robin, Harold Jr, Nancy, Paula, Stanley & Anthony. *Educ:* Berea Col, AB, 41; Harvard Univ, MD, 44. *Prof Exp:* Instr med, Univ Colo, Sch Med, 47-48; res fel pediat & radiol, Harvard Med Sch & Children's Med Ctr, Boston, 52; radiologist, John Graves Ford Hosp, Georgetown, Ky, 53-60; prof diag radiol & chmn dept, Univ Ky, Med Ctr, 60-93. *Concurrent Pos:* Radiologist, Clark Co Hosp, Winchester, Ky, 53-55, Eastern State Hosp, Lexington, 54-60, Woodford Co Mem Hosp, Versailles, 55-60 & Proj Hope, Corinto, Nicaragua, 66-93; consult cardiorentgenologist, St Joseph's Hosp, Lexington, Ky, 53-93; US Dept HEW grant, Univ Ky, 70-93; CARE-Medico prof, Honduras, 71-93. *Mem:* Emer mem Am Roentgen Ray Soc; emer mem Radiol Soc NAm; emer mem AMA; emer mem Am Heart Asn; emer mem Am Col Radiol. *Res:* Congenital heart disease; radiology; medical and radiological education and clinical service. *Mailing Add:* Univ Ky Med Ctr Lexington KY 40506

ROSENBAUM, IRA JOEL, PHYSICS. *Current Pos:* PHYSICIST, WHITE OAK LAB, NAVAL SURFACE WEAPONS CTR, 66- *Personal Data:* b New York, NY, June 5, 41; c 2. *Educ:* Queen's Col, NY, BS, 62; Am Univ, MS, 67, PhD(physics), 71. *Prof Exp:* Physicist, Nat Bur Standards, 64-66. *Mem:* Am Phys Soc; Acoust Soc Am. *Res:* Acoustic properties of liquid metals at high pressures. *Mailing Add:* 3714 Woodbine St Chevy Chase MD 20815

ROSENBAUM, JOEL L, CELL & MOLECULAR BIOLOGY. *Current Pos:* from asst prof to assoc prof, 68-79, PROF BIOL, YALE UNIV, 79- *Personal Data:* b Massena, NY, Oct 4, 33; c 3. *Educ:* Syracuse Univ, BS, 55, MS, 59, PhD(biol), 63; St Lawrence Univ, MSc, 57. *Honors & Awards:* Newcomb-Cleveland Award, AAAS, 68. *Prof Exp:* Fel, Univ Chicago, 63-68. *Mem:* Am Soc Cell Biol. *Res:* Cell and molecular biology of microtibiles; control of flagellan growth in chlamydenonas. *Mailing Add:* Dept Biol PO Box 208103 Yale Univ 310 Kline Biol Tower New Haven CT 06520-8403. *Fax:* 203-432-5059

ROSENBAUM, JOSEPH HANS, PHYSICS. *Current Pos:* PHYSICIST, SHELL DEVELOP CO, 56- *Personal Data:* b Hannover, Ger, July 1, 25; nat US; m 59; c 1. *Educ:* Lowell Technol Inst, BS, 47; Clark Univ, PhD(chem), 50. *Prof Exp:* Phys chemist, US Naval Ord Lab, 50-53; asst prof textile chem, Lowell Technol Inst, 53-54; phys chemist, US Naval Ord Lab, 54-56. *Mem:* Am Chem Soc; Am Asn Textile Chemists & Colorists; Acoust Soc Am; Am Geophys Union; Soc Explor Geophys. *Res:* Elastic waves; thermodynamics; hydrodynamics; electrochemistry; applied mathematics. *Mailing Add:* 1308 Castle Court Blvd Houston TX 77006-5702

ROSENBAUM, MANUEL, GRANT ADMINISTRATION. *Current Pos:* RETIRED. *Personal Data:* b Detroit, Mich, Sept 13, 29; m 55, Regine Gilbert; c Michael, Harold & Andrew. *Educ:* Univ Mich, BS, 51, MS, 53, PhD(bact), 56. *Prof Exp:* Asst microbiol, Univ Mich, 53-55; instr med col, Cornell Univ, 56-58; res assoc, Wistar Inst Anat & Biol, Univ Pa, 58-60; chief microbiologist, Wayne Co Gen Hosp, Mich, 60-63; res microbiologist, Parke, Davis & Co, 64-71; res assoc, Child Res Ctr, Mich, 71-76; grant & contract adminr, Mich Cancer Found, 76-82 & Wayne State Univ, 82-83; support analyst, Chrysler Corp, 84-96. *Mem:* AAAS; Am Asn Artificial Intel. *Res:* Protein synthesis in development of bacteriophage; nucleic acid metabolism in normal and virus-infected animal cells; viral oncogenesis. *Mailing Add:* 24111 Stratford Oak Park MI 48237-1927. *E-Mail:* 74620.3151@compuserve.com

ROSENBAUM, MARCOS, mathematical physics, for more information see previous edition

ROSENBAUM, PETER ANDREW, HUMAN GENETIC EPIDEMIOLOGY & HERPETOLOGY. *Current Pos:* asst prof, 85-91, ASSOC PROF, BIOL DEPT, STATE UNIV NY, OSWEGO, 91- *Personal Data:* b New York, NY, Sept 11, 52; m, Robin Edelstein; c Samantha & Sophia. *Educ:* Tulane Univ, BS, 74, MS, 76, PhD(biol), 81. *Prof Exp:* Res asst, Delta Regional Primate Res Ctr, Tulane Univ, 73-75, teaching asst, Biol Dept, 75-78, instr, 78-79; res assoc, Dept Med, La State Univ Med Ctr, 80-83, instr, Dept Biometry, Genetics & Med, 83-84; asst prof, 84-85. *Concurrent Pos:* Adj instr, Univ Col, Tulane Univ, 77-85; educ & field consult, Odenheimer Aquarium, New Orleans, 78-81; res assoc, Audubon Zool Gardens, New Orleans, 84-85; field assoc, Burnet Park Zoo, NY, 87- *Mem:* AAAS; Am Inst Biol Sci; Am Soc Zoologists; Am Soc Human Genetics; Am Soc Ichthyologists & Herpetologists; Animal Behav Soc; Int Genetic Epidemol Soc; Sigma Xi; Soc Study Amphibians & Reptiles; Soc Conserv Biol. *Res:* Human genetics, genetics epidemiology and the application of genetic methodologies to conservation, in zoo populations and in the management of rare and endangered species; natural history and evolution; author of several publications. *Mailing Add:* Biol Dept State Univ NY Oswego NY 13126. *Fax:* 315-341-5346; *E-Mail:* par@oswego.edu

ROSENBAUM, ROBERT ABRAHAM, MATHEMATICS. *Current Pos:* prof math, 53-85, univ prof, 77-85, EMER UNIV PROF MATH & SCI, WESLEYAN UNIV, 85- *Personal Data:* b New Haven, Conn, Nov 14, 15; m 42; c Robert J, Joseph G & David W. *Educ:* Yale Univ, BA, 36, PhD(math), 47. *Hon Degrees:* MA, Wesleyan Univ, 54, LHD, 81; LHD, St Josephs Col, Conn, 70; ScD, Conn State UNiv, 93. *Honors & Awards:* Baldwin Medal, 85; Transylvania Medal, 92. *Prof Exp:* From instr to prof math, Reed Col, 40-53. *Concurrent Pos:* NSF fel, Math Inst, Oxford Univ, 58-59; vis scholar, Univ Calif, Berkeley, 62; dean sci, Wesleyan Univ, 63-65, provost, 65-67, acad vpres, 67-69, actg pres, 69-70, chancellor, 70-73; ed, Math Asn Am, 66-68; vis prof, Univ Mass, 73-74, Col St Thomas & St Paul Minn, 83; pres, Conn Acad Educ, Math, Sci & Technol, 91- *Mem:* Fel AAAS; Am Math Soc; Math Asn Am (2nd vpres, 61-62). *Res:* Classical analysis; geometry; subadditive functions. *Mailing Add:* Wesleyan Univ Middletown CT 06457. *Fax:* 860-685-2741; *E-Mail:* rrosenbaum@wesleyan.edu

ROSENBAUM, THOMAS FELIX, CORRELATED SYSTEMS, LOW TEMPERATURE PHYSICS. *Current Pos:* asst prof, 83-86, assoc prof, 86-90, PROF PHYSICS, UNIV CHICAGO, 90-, DIR, JAMES FRANK INST, UNIV CHICAGO, 95- *Personal Data:* b New York, NY, Feb 20, 55; m 87, Katherine T Faber; c Daniel & Michael. *Educ:* Harvard Col, AB, 77, Princeton Univ, MA, 79, PhD(physics), 82. *Honors & Awards:* William L McMillan Award, (Univ Ill & Am Phys Soc, 86). *Prof Exp:* Researcher, AT&T Bell Labs, 79-82. *Concurrent Pos:* Vis scientist, Watson Res Ctr, IBM, 82-83; Alfred P Sloan res fel, Sloan Found, 84; Presidential young investr award, NSF, 84; dir, Mat Res Lab, NSF, 91-94; dir, NSF Mat Ctr Res Experience Undergrad, Univ Chicago, 94-; mem, Prog Comt, Sci & Technol Ctr, NSF, 94- *Mem:* Fel Am Phys Soc; AAAS. *Res:* Ultra low temperature studies of quantum phase transitions; transport, thermodynamic and scattering measurements of disordered electronic and magnetic materials; correlated systems including oxides, sulfides and exotic superconductors; local magnetometry of vortex dynamics. *Mailing Add:* James Franck Inst Univ Chicago 5640 S Ellis Ave Chicago IL 60637. *E-Mail:* t-rosenbaum@uchicago.edu

ROSENBERG, AARON E(DWARD), SIGNAL PROCESSING, PATTERN RECOGNITION. *Current Pos:* Mem tech staff, AT&T Bell Labs, 64-96, PRIN TECH STAFF MEM, AT&T LABS, 96- *Personal Data:* b Malden, Mass, Apr 9, 37; m 61, Judith Fishman; c Samuel, Jonathan & Daniel. *Educ:* Mass Inst Technol, SB & SM, 60; Univ Pa, PhD(elec eng), 64. *Honors & Awards:* Senior Award, Acoust, Speech & Signal Processing Soc, Inst Elec & Electronics Engrs, 86. *Mem:* Fel Inst Elec & Electronics Engrs; fel Acoust Soc Am. *Res:* Speech signal processing and pattern recognition; automatic speech; speaker recognition. *Mailing Add:* AT&T Labs 600 Mountain Ave Rm 2d-531 New Providence NJ 07974. *E-Mail:* aer@research.att.com

ROSENBERG, ABRAHAM, DEVELOPMENTAL NEUROCHEMISTRY, NEURAL SECOND MESSENGER SIGNALLING. *Current Pos:* PROF PSYCHIAT, EMORY UNIV SCH MED, ATLANTA, 96- *Personal Data:* b New York, NY, Aug 12, 24; m 48; c 2. *Educ:* Univ Ill, BS, 47; Polytech Inst Brooklyn, MS, 52; Columbia Univ, PhD(biochem), 56. *Honors & Awards:* James A Shannon Dirs Award. *Prof Exp:* Jr biochemist, Jewish Hosp Brooklyn, 47; res asst, 48-49; supvr clin chem, 49-51; res biochemist, 51-53; res assoc biochem, Columbia Univ, 57-61, asst prof, 61-68; from assoc prof to prof biol chem, Col Med, Pa State Univ, Hershey Med Ctr, 68-82; prof & chmn, Dept Biochem & Biophys, Loyola Univ Med Ctr, 83-88; prof psychiat, NY Univ, 88-90; prof psychiat, Univ Calif, Los Angeles, 89-96. *Concurrent Pos:* USPHS fel, 56; NY Heart Asn res fel, 57-58, sr fel, 59-61; Health Res Coun New York career investr, 61-66; Fulbright prof & res scholar, 74; master res, NIH & Med Res, France, 75; vis prof, Univ Heidelberg, 90; res dir, AyurCore, Inc, 96- *Mem:* Am Soc Biol Chemists; AAAS; Am Soc Neurochem; fel Am Inst Chemists; Sigma Xi. *Res:* Fat-soluble vitamin; analysis, absorption, transport and conversion of provitamin; structure and isolation of complex glycolipids of nervous tissues; lipids in photosynthesis; neurochemistry; synaptic structure-function; cell surface enzymes; nerve development; agonist-induced metabotropic second messenger signalling; glycosphingolipid biology; lysosphinaolipids as neuroregulators. *Mailing Add:* Emory Univ Sch Med Ga Ment Health Inst 1256 Briarcliff Rd Atlanta GA 30306-2694. *Fax:* 404-206-5061; *E-Mail:* arose@emory.edu

ROSENBERG, ALBERTO, PHARMACEUTICS. *Current Pos:* VPRES CLIN RES, WALLACE LABS, DIV CARTER-WALLACE INC, NJ, 87- *Personal Data:* b Arg, Aug 13, 37; m 64; c 2. *Educ:* Nat Col Mariano Moreno, Buenos Aires, 55; Univ Buenos Aires, MD, 62; Univ Southern Calif, Los Angeles, MS, 73. *Prof Exp:* Pvt pract, Buenos Aires, 62-63; pharmacologist, Riker Labs, Northridge, Calif, 63-67; res fel, Orange Co Med Ctr, Santa Ana, Calif, 67-69; res assoc, Vet Admin Ctr, Los Angeles, 69-70; assoc dir clin res dept, Stuart Pharm Div, ICI Am, Inc, Del, 70-78; dir investigational drugs, 78-81; vpres, 81-85; exec dir clin res dept, Wyeth Labs, Pa, 85-86. *Concurrent Pos:* Res assoc gastrointestinal lab, Mt Sinai Hosp, 66-68; consult gastroenterol, Riker Labs, 67-69; res fel, Am Heart Asn, 67-69, advan res fel,

69-70. *Mem:* Am Drug Info Asn; AMA; Am Pharm Asn; Am Soc Clin Pharmacol & Therapeut; Am Heart Asn; Am Fen Clin Res; Am Physiol Soc; Am Gastroenterol Asn; NY Acad Sci; Epilepsy Found. *Res:* Pharmaceutics; hypertension; pharmacology; physiology. *Mailing Add:* Dept Clin Res Wallace Labs Half-Acre Rd Cranbury NJ 08512-0181

ROSENBERG, ALBURT M, biophysics, for more information see previous edition

ROSENBERG, ALEX, mathematics, for more information see previous edition

ROSENBERG, ALEXANDER F, ANALYTICAL CHEMISTRY. *Current Pos:* sr engr, Aircraft Nuclear Propulsion Dept-Nuclear Mat & Propulsion Opers, 59-63, prin chemist, 63-68, chemist, Major Appliance Labs, Major Appliance Bus Group, 68-71, mgr chem analysis, Major Appliance Labs, 71-79, mgr chem analysis, Appl Sci & Technol Lab, 79-82, MGR CHEM ANALYSIS & PROCESS, TECHNOL DEVELOP & APPLNS LAB, MAJOR APPLIANCE BUS GROUP, GEN ELEC CO, 82- *Personal Data:* b Frankfurt am Main, Mar 8, 27; nat US; m 54; c 3. *Educ:* City Col New York, BS, 51; Duke Univ, AM, 53, PhD(chem), 55. *Prof Exp:* Asst, Duke Univ, 51-54; res chemist, Shell Oil Co, 54-59. *Concurrent Pos:* Instr, Univ Houston, 55-59. *Mem:* Chem Soc. *Res:* Development of analytical methods; gas chromatography; mass spectrometry; thermal analysis. *Mailing Add:* 10712 Sunderland Pl Louisville KY 40243

ROSENBERG, ALLAN (HERBERT), PHYSICAL CHEMISTRY. *Current Pos:* SR RES INVESTR, BRISTOL-MYERS CORP, 69- *Personal Data:* b Brooklyn, NY, Dec 18, 38; m 62; c 3. *Educ:* City Col NY, BS, 59; Yale Univ, MS, 62, PhD(chem), 64. *Prof Exp:* Res chemist, Allied Chem Corp, 64-69. *Mem:* AAAS; Am Chem Soc; Am Pharmaceut Asn; Royal Soc Chem. *Res:* Kinetics of drug decomposition; foam stabilization; wetting and adsorption phenomena with respect to human skin; dissolution and absorption of drugs. *Mailing Add:* 129 Irving Ave South Orange NJ 07079-2308

ROSENBERG, ANDREAS, PROTEIN CHEMISTRY. *Current Pos:* PROF PATH, BIOCHEM & BIOPHYS, MED CTR, UNIV MINN, 64- *Personal Data:* b Tartu, Astomia, Nov 3, 24. *Educ:* Univ Upsala, Sweden, PhD(biochem), 60. *Mailing Add:* Lab Med Path Univ Minn Mayo Mem Bldg 420 Delaware St SE Minneapolis MN 55455-0374

ROSENBERG, ARNOLD LEONARD, APPLIED GRAPH THEORY, PARALLEL ALGORITHMS & ARCHITECTURES. *Current Pos:* assoc chair comput sci, 93-96, DISTINGUISHED UNIV PROF COMPUT SCI, UNIV MASS, 86- *Personal Data:* b Boston, Mass, Feb 11, 41; m 64, Susan Pinciss; c Paul & Rachel. *Educ:* Harvard Col, AB, 62; Harvard Univ, AM, 63, PhD(appl math), 66. *Honors & Awards:* Cert Appreciation, Inst Elec & Electronics Engrs Comput Soc, 86. *Prof Exp:* Res staff mem, T J Watson Res Ctr, IBM Corp, 65-81; prof comput sci, Duke Univ, 81-86. *Concurrent Pos:* Vis asst prof, Polytech Inst Brooklyn, 67-69; adj assoc prof math, NY Univ, 70-73, adj prof comput sci, 80-81; vis lectr, Yale Univ, 78-79; vis prof comput sci, Univ Toronto, 79-80; ed-in-chief, Theory Comput Systs; actg chair comput sci, Univ Mass, 92; Lady Davis vis prof, Technion, 94. *Mem:* Asn Comput Mach; Soc Indust & Appl Math; Sigma Xi; fel Inst Elec & Electronics Engrs; fel Asn Comput Mach. *Res:* Graph-theoretic and combinatorial models of computational structures and phenomena; parallel architectures and algorithms; communication networks. *Mailing Add:* Dept Comput Sci Univ Mass Amherst MA 01003. *Fax:* 413-545-1249; *E-Mail:* rsnbrg@cs.umass.edu

ROSENBERG, ARNOLD MORRY, CONSTRUCTION CHEMICALS & MATERIALS. *Current Pos:* res mgr, Construction Prod Div, 69-71, res dir, 71-74, RES MGR, RES DIV, W R GRACE & CO, 74- *Personal Data:* b Boston, Mass, Mar 18, 34; m 55; c 3. *Educ:* Boston Univ, AB, 55; Purdue Univ, PhD(phys chem), 60. *Honors & Awards:* IR-100 Award, Indust Res Mag, 80. *Prof Exp:* Chemist, Dewey & Almy Div, W R Grace & Co, 60-62, group leader, Construct Prod Div, 63-66; sr supvr, Polaroid Corp, 66-69. *Mem:* Am Soc Testing & Mat; Am Concrete Inst; Am Chem Soc; Nat Asn Corrosion Engrs; Transp Res Bd. *Res:* Product development in concrete admixtures, fire proof coatings, insulation, roofing and corrosion control; author or coauthor of 40 publications. *Mailing Add:* 11836 Goya Dr Potomac MD 20854-3307

ROSENBERG, BARBARA HATCH, BIOLOGICAL & CHEMICAL WEAPONS CONTROL. *Current Pos:* ADJ PROF ENVIRON SCI, STATE UNIV NY, PURCHASE, NY. *Personal Data:* b New York, NY; m. *Educ:* Cornell Univ, BA, 50, PhD(biochem), 62; Columbia Univ, MA, 57. *Prof Exp:* Res asst mem, Sloan-Kettering Inst Cancer Res, 62-64, assoc, 64-69, assoc mem, 69-89; assoc prof biochem, Col Med Sci, Cornell Univ, 71-85. *Concurrent Pos:* Am Cancer Soc grant, Inst Sci Res in Cancer, France, 71, 79 & 85; coun mem & proj dir, Fedn Am Scientists, 91- *Mem:* Am Soc Biochem & Molecular Biol; Fedn Am Scientists. *Res:* Genetic action of environmental carcinogens; DNA replication; arms control; public health. *Mailing Add:* Div Nat Sci State Univ NY Col, Purchase Purchase NY 10577. *Fax:* 914-251-6635

ROSENBERG, CHARLES E, HISTORY OF MEDICINE & BEHAVIORAL SCIENCE. *Current Pos:* from asst prof to assoc prof, 63-68, chmn dept, 74-75 & 79-83, PROF, DEPT HIST, UNIV PA, 68-, CHAIR, DEPT HIST & SOCIOL SCI, 91- *Personal Data:* b Nov 11, 36, US citizen; m 80, Drew G Faust; c Leah & Jessica. *Educ:* Univ Wis, BA, 56; Columbia Univ, MA, 57, PhD, 61. *Hon Degrees:* LHD, Univ Wis, 97. *Honors & Awards:* William H Welch Medal, Am Asn Hist Med, 69; Fielding H Garrison lectr, Am Asn Hist Med, 82; Benjamin Rush lectr, Am Psychiat Asn, 88; Sarton Medal. *Prof Exp:* lectr, 61-62, res asst prof, Dept Hist & Hist Sci, Univ Wis, 62-63. *Concurrent Pos:* Fel, Johns Hopkins Univ, Inst Hist Med, 60-61; Guggenheim fel, 65-66 & 88-90; NIH Res Grant, 64-70; sr fel, Nat Endow Humanities, 72-73; mem coun, Hist Sci Soc, 72-75; Hist Life Sci Study Sect, NIH, 72-75; Rockefeller Humanities fel, 76-77; fel, Inst for Advan Study, 79-80; Hist & Philos of Sci Panel, NSF, 81-82; Hist Sci Soc lectr, 82; fel, Ctr Adv Study in Behav Sci, 83-84. *Mem:* Nat Acad Sci; Inst Med-Nat Acad Sci; Am Acad Arts & Sci; Am Asn Hist Med (vpres & pres-elect, 90-); Soc Social Hist Med (vpres, 80 & pres, 81); Orgn Am Historians; Am Antique Soc; Am Asn Hist Med (vpres, 90-92, pres, 92-94). *Res:* History of American medicine and its role in society; author of numerous books and articles. *Mailing Add:* Univ Pa Dept Hist & Soc Sci 3440 Market St Philadelphia PA 19104-3325. *E-Mail:* crosenbe@sas.upenn.edu

ROSENBERG, DAN YALE, PHYTOPATHOLOGY. *Current Pos:* AGR CONSULT SPECIALIZING/REGULATORY AGR, 88- *Personal Data:* b Stockton, Calif, Jan 8, 22; m 54; c 1. *Educ:* Col Pac, AB, 49; Univ Calif, Davis, MS, 52. *Prof Exp:* Jr plant pathologist, Bur Plant Path, Calif Dept Food & Agr, 52-55, asst plant pathologist, 55-59, plant pathologist, 59-63, prog supvr dis detection, 63-72, chief exclusion & detection, 72-76, chief nursery & seed serv, 76-82, spec asst, Div Plant Indust, 82-87. *Concurrent Pos:* Lectr, Univ Calif Exten, Int Training & Educ, Univ Calif, Davis. *Mem:* Am Phytopath Soc; Int Orgn Citrus Virol; Am Soc Forestry. *Res:* Seed-borne plant diseases; regulatory plant pathology involving detection of new or rarely occurring plant diseases to California; regulatory agricultural pests including plant pathology, entomology, weeds occurring in nurseries; vertebrates; seed law enforcement; certification programs for fruit trees, citrus, avocado, and so on; gene resource conservation; recombinant DNA (biotechnology); phytosanitary issues for agricultural exports and imports. *Mailing Add:* Agr Consult 2328 Swarthmore Dr Sacramento CA 95825

ROSENBERG, DAVID MICHAEL, FRESH WATERS, BIOMONITORING. *Current Pos:* RES SCIENTIST, FRESHWATER INST, CAN DEPT FISHERIES & OCEANS, 71- *Personal Data:* b Edmonton, Alta, Aug 24, 43; m 65, Trudy Kline; c Bettina & Lee. *Educ:* Univ Alta, BSc, 65, PhD(entom), 73. *Concurrent Pos:* Adj prof entom, Univ Man, 78- *Mem:* NAm Benthological Soc (pres, 86-87); Entom Soc Can. *Res:* Environmental assessment using benthic macrovertebrates; environmental effects of reservoirs and water diversions; ecology of Chironomidae; aquatic insects of freshwater wetlands; biomonitoring using benthic macroinvertebrates. *Mailing Add:* Dept Fisheries & Oceans Freshwater Inst 501 University Crescent Winnipeg MB R3T 2N6 Can

ROSENBERG, DENNIS MELVILLE LEO, thoracic surgery, cardiovascular surgery; deceased, see previous edition for last biography

ROSENBERG, EDITH E, PULMONARY PHYSIOLOGY. *Current Pos:* ASSOC PROF PHYSIOL, COL MED, HOWARD UNIV, 68 - *Personal Data:* b Berlin, Ger, Jan 24, 28; Can citizen; div. *Educ:* Univ Toronto, MA, 52; Univ Pa, PhD(physiol), 59. *Prof Exp:* Asst biophys, Univ Western Ont, 52-55; asst instr physiol, Sch Med, Univ Pa, 56-57; asst prof, Med Sch, Univ Montreal, 59-63; asst prof exp surg & lectr physiol, McGill Univ, 63-68. *Concurrent Pos:* Univ res fel physiol, Sch Med, Univ Pa, 59; PI on grants, Nat Res Coun Can, Univ Montreal, 60-63 & McGill Univ, 64-68, Wash Heart Asn, 70-71; asst instr, Sch Med, Hebrew Univ, Israel, 54-55; NIH grant, 72-75. *Mem:* Am Physiol Soc; Biophys Soc; Can Physiol Soc; NY Acad Sci; Am Thoracic Soc. *Res:* Respiration and circulation, particularly pulmonary circulation and Va/Q distribution; alveolar-arterial tension differences; pulmonary surfactant; pulmonary diffusing capacity; effect of hyperbaric oxygen; lung elasticity. *Mailing Add:* Dept Physiol & Biophys Howard Univ Col Med Washington DC 20059

ROSENBERG, EDWARD, SYNTHESIS OF MODIFIED SILICON FOR WATER PURIFICATION, NUCLEAR MAGNETIC RESONANCE SPECTROSCOPY. *Current Pos:* PROF CHEM, UNIV MONT, 93- *Personal Data:* b Brooklyn, NY, Sept 20, 43; m 79, Tring Valencich; c David, Jennifer, Anira & Levai. *Educ:* City Col NY, BS, 66; Cornell Univ, PhD(inorg chem), 70. *Prof Exp:* prof chem, Calif State Univ, Northridge, 76-93. *Concurrent Pos:* Consult, Purity Systs Inc, 91- *Mem:* Am Chem Soc; Sigma Xi. *Res:* Mechanisms of small organic molecules with polymetallic, transition metal complexes. *Mailing Add:* Dept Chem Univ Mont Missoula MT 59812. *Fax:* 406-243-4227

ROSENBERG, ELI IRA, ELEMENTARY PARTICLE PHYSICS. *Current Pos:* from asst prof to assoc prof, 79-87, PROF PHYSICS, IOWA STATE UNIV, 87- *Personal Data:* b Brooklyn, NY, Feb 19, 43; m 69, Wendy J Harrod; c Evan. *Educ:* City Col New York, BS, 64; Univ Ill, Urbana, MS, 66, PhD(physics), 71. *Honors & Awards:* US Dept Energy Jr Investr, 79-80. *Prof Exp:* Fel physics, Enrico Fermi Inst, Univ Chicago, 71-72, res assoc, 72, instr, 72-74, asst prof, 74-79. *Concurrent Pos:* assoc physicist, Ames Lab, US Dept Energy, physicist, 81-87, sr physicist, 87-93, prog dir high energy physics, 88-93. *Mem:* AAAS; Sigma Xi; Am Phys Soc. *Res:* Experimental high energy physics; study of asymptotic behavior of scattering processes with counter techniques; direct production of leptons in hadron interactions; electron-positron annihilation; applications of microprocessors to experiments. *Mailing Add:* Dept Physics Iowa State Univ Ames IA 50011. *E-Mail:* redmount@iastate.edu

ROSENBERG, FRED A, MICROBIOLOGY. *Current Pos:* from asst prof to assoc prof, 61-77, PROF MICROBIOL, NORTHEASTERN UNIV, 77- *Personal Data:* b Berlin, Germany, Mar 19, 32; nat US; m 57, Liane Balter; c Alysa Gail. *Educ:* NY Univ, AB, 53; Rutgers Univ, PhD(sanit), 60. *Honors & Awards:* Korean Soc Food Sci & Technol Award, 92. *Prof Exp:* Asst bact, Univ Fla, 54-57; asst sanit, Rutgers Univ, 57-60; res assoc physiol aspects water qual, Grad Sch Pub Health, Univ Pittsburgh, 60-61. *Concurrent Pos:* Books ed, J Col Sci Teaching, 83-; vis prof, Inst Microbiol, Univ Hannover, WGer, 85, 87-88, 91, 92 & 94-95; lectr, Korean Soc Food Sci & Technol, 92. *Mem:* Fel Am Pub Health Asn; Am Soc Microbiol; fel Am Acad Microbiol; Biodeterioration Soc Eng; Soc Indust Microbiol. *Res:* Microbiology of bottled water; marine and freshwater microbiology. *Mailing Add:* Dept Biol Northeastern Univ Boston MA 02115. *Fax:* 617-373-3724; *E-Mail:* frosenberg@lynx.neu.edu

ROSENBERG, GARY, MALACOLOGY, SYSTEMATICS. *Current Pos:* ASST CUR, ACAD NATURAL SCI PHILADELPHIA, 89-, ASSOC CHAIR MALACOL, 91- *Personal Data:* b New Rochelle, NY, Oct 16, 59; m 93, Phyllis E Paston. *Educ:* Princeton Univ, AB, 81; Harvard Univ, PhD(biol), 89. *Concurrent Pos:* Asst adj prof, geol & biol, Univ Pa, 92- *Mem:* AAAS; Am Malacol Union; Geol Soc Am; Sigma Xi. *Res:* Evolution, biogeography and phylogenetic systematics of mollusks, particularly prosobranch gastropods; integrating information from comparative anatomy, allozyme electrophoresis; DNA sequencing and the fossil record. *Mailing Add:* Acad Natural Sci 1900 Benjamin Franklin Pkwy Philadelphia PA 19103. *Fax:* 215-299-1170; *E-Mail:* rosenberg@say.acnatsci.org

ROSENBERG, GARY DAVID, BIOMINERALIZATION. *Current Pos:* asst prof, 79-83, ASSOC PROF GEOL & PALEONT, IND-PURDUE UNIV, 83- *Personal Data:* b Milwaukee, Wis, Aug 2, 44. *Educ:* Univ Wis, BS, 66; Univ Calif, Los Angeles, PhD(geol), 72. *Prof Exp:* Sr res assoc, Geophys Dept, Univ Newcastle-upon-Tyne, Eng, 72-76; res assoc orthop surg, Med Sch, Wash Univ, St Louis, 76-78; vis asst prof geol, Mich State Univ, 78-79. *Mem:* Paleont Soc; UK Paleont Asn; AAAS; Am Malacol Union; Paleont Res Inst; Geol Soc Am. *Res:* Structural and compositional growth patterns in skeletons of living and fossil organisms; paleoecological, medical, geophysical and environmental implications; history of geologic thought and art history. *Mailing Add:* Dept Geol Ind-Purdue Univ 723 W Michigan Indianapolis IN 46202-5132

ROSENBERG, GILBERT MORTIMER, GERIATRIC MEDICINE, LONG TERM CARE. *Current Pos:* MED DIR & MEM, DEPT GERIAT & CONTINUING CARE MED, ST MARY'S LAKE HOSP, KINGSTON, ONT, 80- *Personal Data:* b Montreal, Que, Oct 26, 22; m 47, Ethel Hershman; c Steven & Sheila. *Educ:* McGill Univ, BSc, 42, MDCM, 49, MSc & dipl internal med, 56. *Prof Exp:* Med dir & physician-in-chief, Maimonides Hosp & Home Aged, Montreal, Que, 56-77; prof med & dir, Fanning Ctr, Univ Calgary, 77-80; prof med geriat, Queen's Univ, Kingston, Ont, 80-92. *Concurrent Pos:* Chmn, med adv bd, Can Geriat Res Soc, 86-90. *Mem:* Geront Soc Am (vpres, 77-78); Can Asn Geront (pres, 77-81); Am Col Physicians; Royal Soc Med; Royal Col Physicians & Surgeons Can; Am Geriat Soc; Am Col Chest Physicians. *Res:* Involvement of long-term care patients in medical undergraduate teaching; calcium metabolism in older women. *Mailing Add:* 604-185 Ontario Kingston ON K7L 2Y7 Can. *Fax:* 613-544-6947

ROSENBERG, HARRY, BIOCHEMISTRY, IMMUNOLOGY. *Current Pos:* PHARMACIST, LINCOLN GEN HOSP, 74- *Personal Data:* b Feb 14, 40; Can citizen; m 64; c 2. *Educ:* Univ Toronto, BSc, 61; Univ Mich, BS & PharmD, 68, MS, 70, PhD(pharmacog), 72. *Prof Exp:* Res asst pharmacog, Col Pharm, Univ Mich, 65-69; asst prof, Univ Pittsburgh, 71-72; assoc prof, 72-80, PROF BIOMED CHEM, UNIV NEBR MED CTR, 80- *Concurrent Pos:* Chmn, Dept Pharmaceut Sci, Campbell Univ. *Mem:* Am Asn Cols Pharm; Am Pharmaceut Asn; AAAS; Sigma Xi; Am Asn Col Pharm; Am Asn Pharmaceut Scientists. *Res:* Altered drug metabolism in diabetic state; synthesis and screening of antiarrythmic agents; enzymatic and non-enzymatic glucosylation of biological macromolecules. *Mailing Add:* 6218 Sunnyhills Pl Alta Loma CA 91737

ROSENBERG, HENRY, MALIGNANT HYPERTHERMIA, ANESTHESIOLOGY. *Current Pos:* PROF & CHMN DEPT ANESTHESIOL, HAHNEMANN UNIV, 81- *Personal Data:* b New York, NY, Sept 26, 41; m, Henrietta Kothes; c Felice, Jill & Sondra. *Educ:* Albert Einstein Col Med, MD, 67. *Prof Exp:* Staff mem, Univ Pa Hosp, 74-81. *Mem:* Am Soc Anesthesiologists; AAAS; NY Acad Sci; Am Soc Pharmacol & Exp Therapeut; Malignant Hyperthermia Asn. *Res:* Malignant hyperthermia, neuromuscular pharmacology. *Mailing Add:* Dept Anesthesiol Allegheny Univ Health Sci Allegheny Univ Hosp 230 N Broad St Philadelphia PA 19102-1178

ROSENBERG, HENRY MARK, RADIOLOGY, PERIODONTOLOGY. *Current Pos:* From res asst to res assoc dent, Univ Ill Med Ctr, 54-57, asst prof mat med & therapeut, 58-59, from asst prof to assoc prof radiol, 59-65, assoc head dept, 63-65, actg head dept, 65-67, PROF RADIOL, COL DENT, UNIV ILL MED CTR, 66-, HEAD DEPT, 67- *Personal Data:* b Chicago, Ill, Jan 29, 14; m 39; c 1. *Educ:* Northwestern Univ, DDS, 36. *Concurrent Pos:* Consult, Ill State Psychiat Inst, 60- & div biol & med res, Argonne Nat Lab, 61-; co-prin investr, Nat Inst Dent Res, 62-65. *Mem:* Fel Am Col Dent; Am Dent Asn; Am Acad Periodont; Int Asn Dent Res; Am Acad Dent Radiol; Sigma Xi. *Res:* Aging of bone in human masticatory apparatus; dosimetry in radiology. *Mailing Add:* 763 La Crosse Ave Wilmette IL 60091-2072

ROSENBERG, HERBERT IRVING, VERTEBRATE MORPHOLOGY. *Current Pos:* asst prof vert zool, 69-73, asst dean fac arts & sci, 71-74, ASSOC PROF VERT ZOOL, UNIV CALGARY, 73- *Personal Data:* b Brooklyn, NY, Oct 2, 39; m 77, Eva Zador; c Paul, Robin, Sandra & Monica. *Educ:* City Col New York, BS, 61; State Univ NY, Buffalo, PhD(biol), 68. *Prof Exp:* Fel insect behav, Cornell Univ, 67-69. *Concurrent Pos:* Vis assoc prof zool, Univ Mich, 75-76 & Tel Aviv Univ, 82-83 & 90; vis fel, Murdoch Univ, 94. *Mem:* Am Soc Zoologists. *Res:* Comparative anatomy and histology of vertebrate organ systems. *Mailing Add:* Dept Biol Sci Univ Calgary Calgary AB T2N 1N4 Can. *Fax:* 403-289-9311; *E-Mail:* rosenber@acs.ucalgary.ca

ROSENBERG, HERMAN, MATHEMATICS. *Current Pos:* assoc prof, 60-61, chmn dept, 76-82, PROF MATH, JERSEY CITY STATE COL, 61-, COORDR GRAD STUDIES MATH, 66- *Personal Data:* b Jersey City, NJ, Aug 27, 20. *Educ:* NY Univ, BA, 39, MA, 48, PhD(math), 55. *Prof Exp:* Instr math, Jersey City Pub Sch Syst, 40-60. *Concurrent Pos:* Assoc dir, Esso-Educ Found, Math Inst, NY Univ, 59-60; NSF lectr, Math Inst, Montclair State Col, 63- & Rutgers Univ, 70- *Mem:* Math Asn Am. *Res:* The impact of modern mathematics on trigonometry; modern applications of exponential and logarithmic functions; alternative structures for trigonometry and geometry. *Mailing Add:* Dept Math Jersey City State Col Jersey City NJ 07305-1597

ROSENBERG, HOWARD ALAN, PHARMACEUTICAL PRODUCT DEVELOPMENT, DOSAGE FORM DESIGN. *Current Pos:* mgr prod develop, Zeneca Pharmaceut, 81-87, asst dir pharmaceut develop, 87-90, dir pharmaceut develop, 90-95, VPRES, COM PLANNING, ZENECA PHARMACEUT, 95- *Personal Data:* b Boston, Mass, Mar 6, 47; m 70, Janis Miller; c Lisa & Stacey. *Educ:* Mass Col Pharm & Allied Health Sci, BS, 70; State Univ NY, Buffalo, PhD(pharmaceut), 75. *Prof Exp:* Sr pharmaceut chemist, SmithKline Corp, 74-78, sr investr, 78-79; supvr formulation develop, ICI Pharmaceut, Div ICI Am, 79-81. *Concurrent Pos:* Adj prof, Sch Pharm, Purdue Univ, 89- *Mem:* Am Asn Pharmaceut Scientists; Am Pharmaceut Asn; Controlled Release Soc; Parenteral Drug Asn; Am Soc Hosp Pharmacists; Sigma Xi. *Res:* Design and implementation of pharmaceutical research and development activities including dosage form design and development, drug delivery development, pharmaceutical process optimization and biopharmaceutical principles. *Mailing Add:* 1800 Concord Pike Wilmington DE 19850-5437. *Fax:* 302-886-5375

ROSENBERG, HOWARD C, NEUROPHARMACOLOGY, DRUG ABUSE. *Current Pos:* from asst prof to assoc prof, 77-89, PROF PHARMACOL, MED COL OHIO, 90- *Personal Data:* b Atlantic City, NJ, Apr 17, 47; m 69; c 2. *Educ:* Ithaca Col, BA, 69; Cornell Univ, PhD(pharmacol), 75, MD, 76. *Prof Exp:* Fel pharmacol, Med Col, Cornell Univ, 76-77. *Concurrent Pos:* Assoc dean, Grad Sch, Med Col Ohio. *Mem:* Am Soc Pharmacol & Exp Therapeut; Soc Neurosci; Sigma Xi; AAAS. *Res:* Mechanisms for drug tolerance and dependence; effects of chronically administered benzodiazepines; anticonvulsant drugs; neurotransmitter receptors. *Mailing Add:* Dept Pharmacol & Therapeut Med Col Ohio PO Box 10008 Toledo OH 43699-0008

ROSENBERG, IRA EDWARD, PHOTOCHEMISTRY, PHYSICAL ORGANIC CHEMISTRY. *Current Pos:* prin res scientist, 70-76, sect head, 76-78, MGR ADVAN INSTRUMENTATION, CLAIROL INC, 78- *Personal Data:* b New York, NY, Sept 25, 41; m 83; c 2. *Educ:* Hunter Col, BA, 63; Univ Md, College Park, MS, 66; George Washington Univ, PhD(org chem), 70. *Prof Exp:* Res fel photchem, Mich State Univ, 69-70. *Mem:* Am Chem Soc; Soc Cosmetic Chemists; Sigma Xi. *Mailing Add:* Bristol Myers Squibb Co Bldg 105 Rm 2482 New Brunswick NJ 08903-0191

ROSENBERG, IRWIN HAROLD, GASTROENTEROLOGY, NUTRITION. *Current Pos:* PROF PHYSIOL, NUTRIT & MED, TUFTS UNIV, 86-, DIR, JEAN MAYER USDA HUMAN NUTRIT RES CTR AGING & DEAN NUTRIT SCI. *Personal Data:* b Madison, Wis, Jan 6, 35; m 64; c 2. *Educ:* Univ Wis-Madison, BS, 56; Harvard Univ, MD, 59. *Honors & Awards:* Grace Goldsmith Award, Am Col Nutrit; Robert H Herman Mem Award, Am Soc Clin Nutrit; Jonathan B Rhoads Award, Am Soc Parenteral & Enteral Nutrit; W O Atwater Mem Lectr, USDA, 94; Bristol Myers Squibb Mead Johnson Award for Distinguished Achievement, 96. *Prof Exp:* Instr med, Harvard Med Sch, 65, assoc med, 67; res assoc, Thorndike Mem Lab, Boston City Hosp, 67; vis scientist, Dept Biophys, Weizmann Inst Sci, Israel, 68-69; asst prof med, Harvard Med Sch, 69-70; assoc prof med, Univ Chicago, 70, chief, sect gastroenterol, 71-86, prof med, 75-86, dir, Clin Nutrit Res Ctr, 79-86. *Concurrent Pos:* NIH career develop award, 68-74; Josiah Macy fac scholar award, 74; chmn, Food Drug Admin Panel OTC Vitamin, Mineral & Hematinics Consult Nutrit Prog, US Govt, 75-; mem, Training Grants Study Sect, Gen Med Study Sect, 76-; chmn, Food & Nutrit Bd, Nat Res Coun, Nat Acad Sci. *Mem:* Inst Med-Nat Acad Sci; Am Soc Clin Invest; Am Soc Clin Nutrit; Am Gastroenterol Asn. *Res:* Intestinal absorption and malabsorption; human nutrition with emphasis on metabolic and nutritional aspects of aging; relationship of folate status and blood homocysteine and vascular disease to redefine the diet-heart hypothesis; author of over 200 publications. *Mailing Add:* USDA Human Nutrit Res Ctr Aging Tufts Univ 711 Washington St Boston MA 02111-1525. *Fax:* 617-556-3295

ROSENBERG, ISADORE NATHAN, MEDICINE. *Current Pos:* from asst prof to assoc prof, 54-71, PROF, DEPT MED, SCH MED, BOSTON UNIV, 71- *Personal Data:* b Boston, Mass, May 19, 19; m 54; c 2. *Educ:* Harvard Univ, AB, 40, MD, 43. *Honors & Awards:* Van Meter Prize, Am Goiter Soc, 51; Ciba Award, Endocrine Soc, 54. *Prof Exp:* Intern med, Boston City Hosp, 44, asst res & resident, 47-49; asst, Med Sch, Tufts Col, 49-51, instr, 51-54

Concurrent Pos: Asst med, Boston Univ, 49; res assoc, New Eng Ctr Hosp, 49-54; physician-in-chg endocrine unit, 5th & 6th Med Servs, Boston City Hosp, 54-72, physician-in-chief, 6th Med Serv, 63-72; chief med, Framingham Union Hosp, 72- *Mem:* Am Soc Clin Invest; Endocrine Soc; AMA; Am Thyroid Asn; NY Acad Sci. *Res:* Chemical and metabolic studies of thyroid, pituitary and adrenal. *Mailing Add:* Metrowest MC 115 Lincoln St Framingham MA 01701-6327

ROSENBERG, IVO GEORGE, MATHEMATICS. *Current Pos:* ASSOC MEM, CTR MATH RES, UNIV MONTREAL, 71-, PROF MATH, 83- *Personal Data:* b Brno, Czech, Dec 13, 34; m 66; c 2. *Educ:* Purkyne Univ, Brno, MSc, 58, CandSc, 65, Dr rer nat(math), 66; Brno Tech Univ, Habil Dozent, 66. *Prof Exp:* From lectr to dozent math, Brno Tech Univ, 58-66; from lectr to sr lectr, Univ Khartoum, 66-68; assoc prof, Univ Sask, 68-71. *Res:* Universal algebra. *Mailing Add:* Ctr Math Res Univ Montreal 6128 Succ A Montreal PQ H3C 3J7 Can. *Fax:* 514-343-5700; *E-Mail:* rosenb@ere.umontreal.ca

ROSENBERG, JEROME LAIB, BIOPHYSICAL CHEMISTRY. *Current Pos:* from asst prof to prof chem, Univ Pittsburgh, 53-69, chmn dept biophys & microbiol, 69-71, prof molecular biol, 69-76, dean, Fac Arts & Sci, 69-86, vprovost, 78-89, chmn dept biol sci, 89-90, chmn dept commun, 91, prof chem & biol sci, 76-91, DIR JEWISH STUDIES PROG, UNIV PITTSBURGH, 91-, RES INTEGRITY OFFICER, 92- *Personal Data:* b Harrisburg, Pa, June 20, 21; m 46, Shoshana Gabriel; c Jonathan & Judith. *Educ:* Dickinson Col, AB, 41; Columbia Univ, MA, 44, PhD(phys chem), 48. *Prof Exp:* Lectr chem, Columbia Univ, 42-44, res scientist, SAM Labs, 44-46, instr chem, Univ, 46-48; AEC fel, Univ Chicago, 48-50, res assoc, 50-53. *Concurrent Pos:* NSF sr fel, 62-63. *Mem:* Am Chem Soc; AAAS; Sigma Xi. *Res:* Photochemistry; photosynthesis; luminescence; molecular spectroscopy. *Mailing Add:* Univ Pittsburgh 802 Cathedral of Learning Pittsburgh PA 15260. *Fax:* 412-624-4384; *E-Mail:* jrosenb@vms.cis.pitt.edu

ROSENBERG, JERRY C, SURGERY, TRANSPLANTATION IMMUNOLOGY. *Current Pos:* assoc prof, 68-72, PROF SURG, SCH MED, WAYNE STATE UNIV, 72-; VPRES SURG SERV, HUTZEL HOSP. *Personal Data:* b New York, NY, Apr 23, 29; m 55; c 2. *Educ:* Wagner Col, BS, 50; Chicago Med Sch, MD, 54; Univ Minn, Minneapolis, PhD(surg), 63; Mich State Univ, MBA. *Prof Exp:* Fulbright fel, Univ Vienna, 55-56; univ fel, Univ Minn, Minneapolis, 60-61; asst chief surg, USPHS Hosp, Staten Island, 61-63; instr, Univ Ky, 64-65; adj asst prof pharm, Univ Toledo, 67-68; dir surg, Maumee Valley Hosp, 65-68. *Concurrent Pos:* Consult, Vet Admin Hosp, 68-; chief surg, Hutzel Hosp. *Mem:* Transplantation Soc; Am Asn Hist Med; Am Soc Artificial Internal Organs; Soc Univ Surg; Soc Surg Oncol. *Res:* Mechanisms of immune damage to transplanted organs; biochemical and physiological responses to shock and trauma; breast & thoracic oncology; oncology. *Mailing Add:* Dept Surg 8544 Huntington Rd Huntington Woods MI 48070-1644

ROSENBERG, JONATHAN MICAH, OPERATOR ALGEBRAS, GROUP REPRESENTATIONS. *Current Pos:* assoc prof, 81-85, PROF MATH, UNIV MD, 85- *Personal Data:* b Chicago, Ill, Dec 30, 51; m 90, Jeanne Sauber; c Arieh & Liora. *Educ:* Harvard Univ, AB, 72; Math Tripos Part III, Univ Calif, Berkeley, PhD(math), 76. *Prof Exp:* Asst prof math, Univ Pa, 77-81. *Concurrent Pos:* Sloan fel, 81-84; Ed Proc Am Math Soc, 88-92; Ed K-Theory, 96- *Mem:* Am Math Soc; Math Asn Am. *Res:* Relations between operator algebras and geometry and topology; unitary representation theory of Lie groups; K-theory; index theory. *Mailing Add:* Dept Math Univ Md College Park MD 20742. *E-Mail:* jmr@math.umd.edu

ROSENBERG, JOSEPH, ORGANIC CHEMISTRY. *Current Pos:* RETIRED. *Personal Data:* b New York, NY, Sept 8, 26; m 48; c 3. *Educ:* City Col New York, BS, 48; Kans State Univ, MS, 49; Wayne State Univ, PhD(org chem), 51. *Prof Exp:* Polymer chemist, Gen Elec Co, 51-60; head org chem dept, Tracerlab, Inc, 60-62, mgr Tracerlab Tech Prod Div, Lab Electronics, Inc, Mass, 62-69; group vpres, Int Chem & Nuclear Corp, 70-71; pres, Interex Corp, 71-89. *Mem:* Am Chem Soc. *Res:* Synthetic organic chemistry; pyrolysis of esters; monomer synthesis; polymer chemistry; epoxy resins; polyurethanes; polyesters; addition and condensation polymers; acrylonitrile copolymers; synthesis of radiochemicals. *Mailing Add:* 46 Maugus Hill Rd Wellesley MA 02181

ROSENBERG, LAWSON LAWRENCE, PHYSIOLOGICAL CHEMISTRY. *Current Pos:* jr res biochemist, Univ Calif, Berkeley, 53-56, asst res biochemist, 56-65, from assoc prof to prof physiol, 65-88, prof molecular & cellular biol, 88-92, EMER PROF MOLECULAR & CELLULAR BIOL, UNIV CALIF, BERKELEY, 92- *Personal Data:* b Hagerstown, Md, Apr 3, 20. *Educ:* Johns Hopkins Univ, AB, 40, PhD, 51. *Prof Exp:* Asst physiol chem, Sch Med, Johns Hopkins Univ, 51-52, instr pediat, 52-53. *Mem:* Am Soc Biol Chemists; Endocrine Soc; Am Thyroid Asn. *Res:* Binding of metalloporphyrins to protein; enzymes; pituitary hormones and target organ relationships. *Mailing Add:* 1000 Green St San Francisco CA 94133

ROSENBERG, LEON EMANUEL, GENETICS. *Current Pos:* pres, 91-97, SR VPRES SCI AFFAIRS, BRISTOL-MYERS SQUIBB CO, 97- *Personal Data:* b Madison, Wis, Mar 3, 33; m 79, Diane Drobnis; c Robert, Diana, David & Alexa. *Educ:* Univ Wis, BA, 54, MD, 57. *Hon Degrees:* DSc, Univ Wis, 89, Mt Sinai Sch Med, NY, 92. *Honors & Awards:* Borden Award, Am Acad Pediat, 73; Ellis Island Medal Honor, Nat Ethnic Coalition Orgns, 93. *Prof Exp:* From intern to resident med, Columbia-Presby Hosp, 57-59; clin assoc metab, Nat Cancer Inst, 59-61, sr invest, 61-62 & 63-65; resident med, Yale-New Haven Hosp, 62-63; from asst prof to prof human genetics, med & pediat, Sch Med, Yale Univ, 65-84, dean, 84-91. *Concurrent Pos:* John Hartford Found grant, 65-68; NIH res grant, 65-81; Nat Inst Arthritis & Metab Dis res career develop award, 65-70; Guggenheim fel, 72; mem coun, Inst Med-Nat Acad Sci; bd trustees, Yale-New Haven Hosp. *Mem:* Nat Acad Sci; Inst Med-Nat Acad Sci; Am Fedn Clin Res; Am Soc Human Genetics; Am Soc Clin Invest; Am Asn Med Clins; fel AAAS; fel Am Acad Arts & Sci; Asn Am Physicians. *Res:* Medical genetics; membrane function; biogenesis of mitochondrial enzymes; inherited disorders of amino acid metabolism; mechanism of vitamin transport and coenzyme synthesis. *Mailing Add:* Bristol-Myers Squibb Co PO Box 4000 Princeton NJ 08543-4000. *Fax:* 609-252-6700; *E-Mail:* rosenberg_leon_e@msmail.bms.com

ROSENBERG, LEON T, IMMUNOLOGY. *Current Pos:* from asst prof to prof, 61-92, EMER PROF MICROBIOL & IMMUNOL, 93- *Personal Data:* b New York, NY, Feb 11, 28; m 50; c 2. *Educ:* City Col New York, BSc, 46; Ohio State Univ, MSc, 48; NY Univ, PhD(biol), 58. *Prof Exp:* Res bacteriologist, Bellevue Hosp, 53-55; res assoc immunol, Bronx Hosp, 55-59. *Concurrent Pos:* NIH fel immunol, Stanford Univ, 59-60, Giannini Found fel, 60-61; Eleanor Roosevelt fel, Int Union Against Cancer, Karolinska Inst, Stockholm, 69-70; vis prof, La Trobe Univ, Melbourne, Australia, 86-87. *Mem:* AAAS; Am Asn Immunologists; Am Soc Microbiol. *Res:* Biological functions of antibody and complement; microbiology. *Mailing Add:* Dept Microbiol & Immunol Stanford Univ Stanford CA 94305. *E-Mail:* rosenberg@leldud.stanford.edu

ROSENBERG, LEONARD, PHYSICS. *Current Pos:* from asst prof to assoc prof, 63-70, PROF PHYSICS, NY UNIV, 70- *Personal Data:* b New York, NY, Mar 11, 31. *Educ:* City Col New York, BS, 52; NY Univ, MS, 54, PhD(physics), 59. *Prof Exp:* Assoc res scientist, NY Univ, 59-61 & Univ Pa, 61-63. *Mem:* Am Phys Soc. *Res:* Scattering theory; low-energy atomic and nuclear physics. *Mailing Add:* Dept Physics NY Univ Four Washington Pl New York NY 10003

ROSENBERG, MARK L, PUBLIC HEALTH, INJURY CONTROL & VIOLENCE PREVENTION. *Current Pos:* DIR, NAT CTR INJURY PREV & CONTROL, CTR DIS CONTROL & PREV. *Personal Data:* b Montclair, NJ, July 30, 45; m 76, Jill Dimond; c Julie D & Benjamin D. *Educ:* Harvard Univ, BA, 67, MD & MPP, 72. *Honors & Awards:* Surgeon General's Exemplary Medal; Outstanding Serv Medals, USPHS. *Prof Exp:* Resident internal med, Mass Gen Hosp; resident psychiat, Boston Beth Israel Hosp; resident prev med, Ctr Dis Control & Prev; fac mem, Morehouse Med Sch, Emory Med Sch, Emory Pub Health & Harvard Sch Pub Health. *Concurrent Pos:* Mem bd dirs, Nat Safety Coun; consult, WHO. *Mem:* Inst Med-Nat Acad Sci; Am Found Suicide Prev; Am Pub Health Asn. *Res:* Injury control and violence prevention; authored more than 110 publications. *Mailing Add:* Nat Ctr Injury Prev & Control 4770 Buford Hwy NE K02 Atlanta GA 30341-3724. *Fax:* 770-488-4422; *E-Mail:* mlr@cdc.gov

ROSENBERG, MARTIN, GENE REGULATION. *Current Pos:* DIR MOLECULAR GENETICS, SMITHKLINE & FRENCH LABS, 82-, VPRES BIOPHARMACEUT, RES & DEVELOP, 85- *Personal Data:* b Bridgeport, Conn, Feb 10, 46. *Educ:* Purdue Univ, PhD(biochem), 70. *Honors & Awards:* Arthur S Fleming Award, 82. *Concurrent Pos:* Adj prof, Depts Human Genetics & Microbiol, Univ Pa, biol sci, State Univ NY & biochem, UMD, NJ. *Mem:* Am Soc Biol Chemists; Am Microbiol Soc. *Mailing Add:* UE0428 Smith Kline Beecham Pharmaceut 709 Swedeland Rd PO Box 1539 King of Prussia PA 19406-0939. *Fax:* 215-270-7768

ROSENBERG, MARVIN J, BIOLOGY, MOLECULAR GENETICS. *Current Pos:* assoc prof, 68-74, chmn, Dept Biol Sci, 76-88, PROF BIOL, CALIF STATE UNIV, FULLERTON, 74-, ASSOC DEAN, SCH NATURAL SCI & MATH, 88- *Personal Data:* b New York, NY, Aug 27, 31; m 54; c 2. *Educ:* City Col New York, BS, 52; Cornell Univ, MS, 54; Columbia Univ, PhD(molecular biol), 67. *Prof Exp:* Teacher sec sch, NY, 54-60; asst prof biol, State Univ NY, Stony Brook, 60-68. *Concurrent Pos:* State of NY Res Found grant in aid, 67-69. *Mem:* AAAS; Genetics Soc Am; Bot Soc Am. *Res:* Chromosome structure; radiomimetic effects on chromosome breakage and reunion; density gradient studies of DNA replication after treatment with thymidine analogs; exogenous DNA uptake by tumor cells. *Mailing Add:* 474 Dover Circle Brea CA 92621

ROSENBERG, MURRAY DAVID, DATABASE MANAGEMENT. *Current Pos:* facil leader, 77-81, SECT LEADER TECH INFO, PHILIP MORRIS USA, 81- *Personal Data:* b Philadelphia, Pa, Feb 9, 40; m 63; c 2. *Educ:* Temple Univ, BA, 64, MBA, 71. *Prof Exp:* Res chemist synthetic org chem, Hoffmann-LaRoche Inc, 64-67; med chemist, Smith Kline Corp, 67-69; info scientist, Inst Sci Info, 69-70, sr info scientist, 70-72; systs & stand coordr equal control & info systs, Dutch Boys Paint Div, NL Industs, 72-73, mgr qual assurance & systs develop, 73-75; dir res info systs & mkt, Randex Corp, 75-77. *Concurrent Pos:* Mem bd, Doc Abstr, Inc, 84-85, pres, 86-87; mem, Va Sect ACS Publ Comt, 88-; chmn, Legislative Issues Comt, 88-; mem Exec Comt, Indust Tech Info Mgrs Group, 87- *Mem:* Am Chem Soc; Am Inst Chemists; Am Soc Info Sci; NY Acad Sci; Sigma Xi; Indust Tech Info Mgrs' Group. *Res:* Synthetic organic chemistry in the pharmaceutical industry; scientific and technical information storage and retrieval systems. *Mailing Add:* Scherer Hall Va Commonwealth Univ 923 W Franklin St PO Box 843059 Richmond VA 23284-3059

ROSENBERG, NORMAN J, MICROMETEOROLOGY, CLIMATOLOGY. *Current Pos:* MGR, INTEGRATED EARTH STUDIES, BATTELLE/PAC NORTHWEST LABS. *Personal Data:* b Brooklyn, NY, Feb 22, 30; m 50, Sarah Zacher; c Daniel & Alyssa. *Educ:* Mich State Univ, BS, 51; Okla State Univ, MS, 58; Rutgers Univ, PhD(soil physics), 61. *Honors & Awards:* Centennial Medal, Nat Oceanic & Atmospheric Admin, 70; Award Outstanding Achievement Biometeorol, Am Meteorol Soc, 78. *Prof Exp:* Soil scientist, Israel Soil Conserv Serv, 53-55 & Israel Water Authority, 55-57; res asst soil physics, Okla State Univ, 57-58; from asst prof to assoc prof, Univ Nebr, Lincoln, 61-67, prof agr climat, 67-87, leader agr meteorol sect, Inst Agr & Natural Resources, 74-87, dir, ctr Agr Meteorol & Climat, 79-87, prof agr meteorol, George Holmes, 81-87, emer prof, 87; sr fel & dir Climate Resource Prog, Resources for Future, Washington, DC, 87-92. *Concurrent Pos:* Consult, Nat Oceanic & Atmospheric Admin, 62-, Great Western Sugar Co, 64-68, Water Resources Res Inst, US Dept Interior, 65- & US AID; vis prof, Israel Inst Technol, 68; NATO sr fel sci, 68; NSF grant, 71-; NASA grant, 72-; mem, comt atmospheric sci, Nat Res Coun, 75-78, bd atmospheric sci & climate, 82-85; mem, comt atmospheric sci, Oak Ridge Assoc Univ, 80-87, Sandia Nat Labs, 90; trustee, Nat Insts Global Environ Change, 92- *Mem:* Fel AAAS; fel Am Meteorol Soc; fel Am Soc Agron. *Res:* Microclimatology; ground level micrometeorology; evapotranspiration and windbreak influences on crop growth and development; global carbon dioxide balance and its interaction with plant growth; remote sensing of evapotranspiration in large regions; impact of drought on social, political and physical environment, development of strategies to cope with extended drought; impacts of climatic change; integrated assessment of global change impacts. *Mailing Add:* Integrated Earth Studies Pac NW Lab 910 D St SW Suite 900 Washington DC 20024-2115. *Fax:* 202-646-5233; *E-Mail:* nj__rosenberg@ccmail.pnl.gov

ROSENBERG, PAUL, NAVIGATION, PHOTOGRAMMETRY. *Current Pos:* PRES, PAUL ROSENBERG ASSOCS, 45- *Personal Data:* b New York, NY, Mar 31, 10; m 43, Marjorie S Hillson; c Gale R (Gross). *Educ:* Columbia Univ, AB, 30, AM, 33, PhD, 41. *Honors & Awards:* Abrams Grand Award, Am Soc Photogram, 55; Cogswell Award, US Defense Dept, 86. *Prof Exp:* Chemist, Hawthorne Paint & Varnish Corp, NJ, 30-33; asst physics, Columbia Univ, 34-39; instr, Hunter Col, 39-41; res assoc, Mass Inst Technol, 41, mem staff, Radiation Lab, 41-45. *Concurrent Pos:* Lectr, Columbia Univ, 40-41; mem, Maritime Res Adv Panel, Nat Acad Sci-Nat Res Coun, 59-60, chmn, Navig & Traffic Control Panel, Space Appln Study, 68 & Cartog & Mapping Panel, Comt Remote Sensing Progs, Earth Resources Surv, 73-77; chmn, Nat Conf Clear Air Turbulence, 66; mem, Navig Adv Comt, NASA, 69-70; mem bd dirs, Ctr Environ & Man, 76-85; gen chmn, Joint Conf, Radio Tech Comn Aeronaut, Radio Tech Comn Marine & Inst Navig; mem bd dir, Universal High Technol Corp, 81-85. *Mem:* Nat Acad Eng; fel AAAS (vpres, 66-69); Am Inst Navig (pres, 50-51); fel Inst Elec & Electronics Engrs; NY Acad Sci; fel Am Inst Chemists; fel Explorers Club. *Res:* Molecular beams; kinetic theory of gases; geometric and physical optics; ultrasonics; radar; navigation of land, marine, air and space vehicles; industrial electronics; photogrammetry; space technology; earth satellites; aeronautics; electrophotography; remote sensing. *Mailing Add:* 53 Fernwood Rd Larchmont NY 10538

ROSENBERG, PHILIP, TOXINOLOGY, NEUROCHEMISTRY. *Current Pos:* asst dean grad studies, 71-75, 86-87, chmn sect pharmacol & toxicol, 68-88, PROF PHARMACOL, SCH PHARM, UNIV CONN, 68-, HEAD, DEPT PHARMACEUT SCI, 94- *Personal Data:* b Philadelphia, Pa, July 28, 31; m 56, Sybil Stepman; c Stuart O, Gail L & Rachelle. *Educ:* Temple Univ, BS, 53; Univ Kans, MS, 55; Jefferson Med Col, PhD(pharmacol), 57. *Honors & Awards:* Redi Award, Int Soc Toxinol, 82. *Prof Exp:* Instr pharmacol, Jefferson Med Col, 57-58; res asst neurol & biochem, Col Physicians & Surgeons, Columbia Univ, 58-62, res assoc, 63, asst prof neurol, 63-68. *Concurrent Pos:* USPHS spec fel, Nat Inst Neurol Dis & Blindness, 60-62 & career develop award, 64-68; ed, Toxicon, 70-91; WHO spec consult & vis prof, Sch Med, Tel Aviv Univ, 74-75; Javits neurosci investr award, Nat Inst Neurol Dis & Stroke, NIH, 87-95. *Mem:* Am Pharmaceut Asn; fel Acad Pharmaceut Sci; Am Soc Pharmacol; Int Soc Toxinol (pres, 88-91); Am Soc Neurochem; Soc Toxicol; Am Chem Soc. *Res:* Pharmacodynamics of drugs affecting the nervous system; actions of phospholipases; venom action on biological tissue; membranal permeability; actions of organophosphorus anticholinesterases; toxins and enzymes on membrane organization and asymmetry. *Mailing Add:* Dept Pharmaceut Sci Univ Conn Sch Pharm Storrs CT 06269. *Fax:* 860-486-4998; *E-Mail:* prosen@uconnvm.uconn.edu

ROSENBERG, REINHARDT M, MECHANICS. *Current Pos:* prof eng mech, 58-64, Miller res prof, 64-76, prof, 76-82, EMER PROF ENG MECH, UNIV CALIF, BERKELEY, 82- *Personal Data:* b Tubingen, Ger, Dec 17, 12; nat US; m 37; c 1. *Educ:* Univ Pittsburgh, BS, 41; Purdue Univ, MS, 47. *Hon Degrees:* Dr, Univ Besancon, 62. *Prof Exp:* Engr, Flutter Group, Bell Aircraft Co, 42-44; design specialist, Consol Vultee Aircraft Corp, 44-46; from instr to asst prof aeronaut eng, Purdue Univ, 46-48; assoc prof, Univ Wash, 48-51; design specialist, Boeing Airplane Co, 51-53; prof appl mech, Univ Toledo, 53-58. *Concurrent Pos:* Guggenheim fel, Fulbright fel, 60; ed, Int J Nonlinear Mech & J Franklin Inst. *Res:* Nonlinear oscillations; vibration theory; biomechanics; dynamics; applied mathematics; theoretical and applied mechanics. *Mailing Add:* PO Box 678 Diablo CA 94528

ROSENBERG, RICHARD CARL, MECHANICAL ENGINEERING, MATERIAL SCIENCE. *Current Pos:* Res engr, Gen Motors Res Labs, 67-75, sr res engr, 75-80, staff res engr, 80-85, sr staff res engr, 85-90, SECT HEAD, SPECIF & VALIDATION, GEN MOTORS SYSTS ENG CTR, 90- *Personal Data:* b Chicago, Ill, Mar 14, 43; m 69; c 3. *Educ:* Gen Motors Inst, BS, 66; Rensselaer Polytech Inst, MS, 67. *Mem:* Am Soc Mech Engrs; Soc Automotive Engrs. *Res:* Friction and wear mechanisms, especially bearing alloy development, rolling element bearings, lubricant additive effects and engine friction; vehicle systems engineering. *Mailing Add:* Gen Motors Syst Eng 30200 Mound Rd Warren MI 48092

ROSENBERG, RICHARD MARTIN, INORGANIC CHEMISTRY, RESEARCH ADMINISTRATION. *Current Pos:* Retired. *Personal Data:* b New York, NY, Jan 13, 33; m 55; c 3. *Educ:* Brooklyn Col, BS, 54; Pa State Univ PhD(chem), 59. *Prof Exp:* Res chemist, Cent Res Dept, E I du Pont de Nemours & Co, Inc, 59-69 & Electrochem Dept, 69-70, res supvr, 70-75, res mgr, 75-80, prod mkt mgr, 80-81, prod mkt & planning mgr, 81-83, technical & planning mgr, 83-85, task force mgr, electronic mat div, 85-86, dir res electronics, Electronics Dept, 86-88, dir, planning & new bus develop, 88, vpres & gen mgr electronic mat, 89-91. *Mem:* Am Chem Soc; fel Am Ceramic Soc. *Res:* Solid state materials; hybrid microelectronics. *Mailing Add:* 611 Ogden Ave Swarthmore PA 19081-1599

ROSENBERG, RICHARD STUART, SOCIAL ISSUES. *Current Pos:* ASSOC PROF COMPUT SCI, UNIV BC, 86- *Personal Data:* b Toronto, Ont, Aug 12, 39; m 78; c 3. *Educ:* Univ Toronto, BASc, 61, MASc, 64; Univ Mich, PhD(comput sci), 67. *Prof Exp:* Lab instr physics, Univ Toronto, 61-62; res asst elec eng, 62; asst in res eng, Univ Mich, 62-65, asst math, 65-68, asst prof comput sci, 67-68; from asst prof to assoc prof, Univ BC, 68-84; dir, Comput Sci Div, Dept Math, Statist & Comput Sci, Dalhousie Univ, 84-86. *Mem:* Am Asn Artificial Intel; Asn Comput Mach; Can Soc Computational Studies Intel (pres, 76-78); Comput Prof Soc. *Res:* Artificial intelligence, natural language understanding by computer; dialogue; reference problems; question-answering systems; bibliographic information; retrieval; computers and society; privacy work; free speech, censorship, access; internet social issues. *Mailing Add:* Dept Comput Sci Univ BC Vancouver BC V6T 1Z4 Can. *Fax:* 604-822-5485; *E-Mail:* rosen@cs.ubc.ca

ROSENBERG, ROBERT, VISION. *Current Pos:* Chmn, 71-87, MEM FAC, DEPT VISION SCI, COL OPTOM, STATE UNIV NY, 71- *Personal Data:* b Brooklyn, NY, Jan 3, 30; m 56; c 2. *Educ:* Columbia Univ, BS, 51, MS, 52, State Univ NY, OD, 73. *Concurrent Pos:* Mem, 280 Comt, Am Nat Stand Inst. *Mem:* Fel Am Acad Optom; Optom Soc Am; Am Optom Asn. *Res:* Optics; low vision. *Mailing Add:* Dept Vision Sci State Univ NY Col Optomet New York NY 10010

ROSENBERG, ROBERT CHARLES, BIOINORGANIC CHEMISTRY, ELECTRON PARAMAGNETIC RESONANCE SPECTROSCOPY. *Current Pos:* Asst prof, 77-82, ASSOC PROF CHEM, HOWARD UNIV, 83- *Personal Data:* b New York, NY, Apr 25, 45. *Educ:* Columbia Univ, BA, 67; Calif Inst Technol, PhD(bioinorg chem), 73. *Mem:* Am Chem Soc; Am Soc Biochem & Molecular Biol; Protein Soc. *Res:* Enzyme structure and mechanism. *Mailing Add:* Dept Chem Howard Univ Washington DC 20059. *E-Mail:* rcr@scs.howard.edu

ROSENBERG, ROBERT D, THROMBOSIS, ATHEROSCLEROSIS. *Current Pos:* PROF BIOCHEM, MASS INST TECHNOL, 81-, PROF BIOL. *Educ:* Mass Inst Technol, PhD(biophys), 69. *Prof Exp:* prof med, Harvard Med Sch, 70-81. *Mailing Add:* Ma Inst Tech Bldg 68-480 77 Massachusetts Ave Cambridge MA 02139-4307

ROSENBERG, ROBERT MELVIN, PHYSICAL BIOCHEMISTRY. *Current Pos:* from asst prof to assoc prof chem, 56-67, chmn dept, 61-62, 66-67 & 79-81, assoc dean, Lawrence & Downer Cols, 68-75, PROF CHEM, LAWRENCE UNIV, 67- *Personal Data:* b Hartford, Conn, Mar 9, 26; m 51; c 4. *Educ:* Trinity Col, Conn, BS, 47; Northwestern Univ, PhD(chem), 51. *Prof Exp:* Res assoc chem, Cath Univ Am, 50-51; asst dermat, Harvard Univ, 51-53; asst prof chem, Wesleyan Univ, 53-56. *Concurrent Pos:* NSF sci fac fel, Oxford Univ, 62-63; Am Chem Soc vis scientist, 63-74; resident dir, Assoc Cols Midwest Argonne Sem Prog, Argonne Nat Lab, 67-68; res assoc chem, Univ Wis-Madison, 75-76 & 81-82; res dir, Oak Ridge Sci Semester, 88; res assoc, Oak Ridge Nat Lab, 88-89. *Mem:* AAAS; Am Chem Soc; Royal Soc Chem. *Res:* Physical chemistry of proteins. *Mailing Add:* Dept Chem Lawrence Univ Appleton WI 54912-0599

ROSENBERG, RONALD C(ARL), SYSTEM DYNAMICS, COMPUTER-AIDED ENGINEERING. *Current Pos:* assoc prof, 69-73, PROF MECH ENG, MICH STATE UNIV, 73-, CHAIRPERSON, MECH ENG, 91- *Personal Data:* b Philadelphia, Pa, Dec 15, 37; m 59; c 4. *Educ:* Mass Inst Technol, BSc & MSc, 60, PhD(mech eng), 65. *Honors & Awards:* Teetor Award, Soc Automotive Engrs, 88. *Prof Exp:* Asst prof mech eng, Mass Inst Technol, 66-69. *Concurrent Pos:* Pres & consult, Rosencode Assoc, Inc. *Mem:* Fel Am Soc Mech Engrs; Inst Elec & Electronics Engrs; Soc Comput Simulation; Am Soc Eng Educ. *Res:* Dynamic system modeling and behavior; computer-aided design; software development. *Mailing Add:* Dept Mech Eng Mich State Univ A231 Eng Bldg East Lansing MI 48824-1226

ROSENBERG, SANDERS DAVID, FUELS SCIENCE, HIGH TEMPERATURE MATERIALS. *Current Pos:* PRES, IN-SPACE PROPULSION, 82- *Personal Data:* b New York, NY, Dec 21, 26; m 46, Rita Strauss; c Nathan & Robert. *Educ:* Middlebury Col, AB, 48; Iowa State Univ, PhD(org chem), 52. *Prof Exp:* Sr chemist & group leader org res dept, Rahway Res Lab, Metal & Thermal Corp, NJ, 53-58; prin chemist & mgr fuels & combustion res dept, Chem Prod Div, Aerojet Gen Corp, 58-68, mgr fuels & combustion res, 68-70, mgr chem processing & mat, Aerojet Liquid Rocket Co, 70-73; chief scientist, Aerojet Propulsion Div, Gencorp, Aerojet, 58-93. *Mem:* Assoc fel Am Inst Aeronaut & Astronaut. *Res:* Development of high energy liquid propellants; research on nature of combustion in chemical rocket engines, development of materials for advanced propulsion applications, and development and production of liquid rocket engine systems; extraterrestrial resources utilization; chemical vapor deposition. *Mailing Add:* 628 Commons Dr Sacramento CA 95825. *Fax:* 916-927-6629

ROSENBERG, SAUL ALLEN, INTERNAL MEDICINE, ONCOLOGY. *Current Pos:* from asst prof to assoc prof med & radiol, Sch Med, Stanford Univ, 61-70, chief, Div Oncol, 65-94, Maureen Lyles D'Ambrogio prof med & radiol, 85-94, assoc dean clin prog planning & develop, 89-94, PROF, SCH MED, STANFORD UNIV, 70-, EMER PROF MED & RADIATION ONCOL, 95- *Personal Data:* b Cleveland, Ohio, Aug 2, 27; c 2. *Educ:* Western Reserve Univ, BS, 48, MD, 53; Am Bd Internal Med, dipl. *Honors & Awards:* William Lister Rogers Award, 77; Walter Albion Hewlett Award, 83; David Karnofsky Medal, Am Soc Clin Oncol, 84; Jan Waldenstrom Medal, Swed Acad Oncol, 84; C Chester Stock Award, Mem Sloan Kettering Inst, 90; San Salvatore Found Prize, 96. *Prof Exp:* Spec fel, Med Neoplasia, Mem Ctr Cancer & Allied Dis, NY, 57-58. *Concurrent Pos:* Chief resident physician, Peter Bent Brigham Hosp, Boston, 60-61; chief med serv, Stanford Univ Hosp, 69-71; Eleanor Roosevelt int fel, Am Cancer Soc, 71-72; chmn, Comt Med Oncol, Am Bd Internal Med, 78-80; assoc ed, J Clin Oncol, 82-85; K P Stephen Chang vis prof, Univ Hong Kong, 86. *Mem:* Inst Med-Nat Acad Sci; master Am Col Physicians; Radiation Res Soc; Am Asn Cancer Res; Am Soc Therapeut Radiol & Oncol; Am Fedn Clin Res; Asn Am Physicians; Am Soc Clin Oncol. *Res:* Clinical investigation of malignant lymphomas; cancer chemotherapy. *Mailing Add:* Div Oncol M211 Mail Code 5306 Stanford Univ Med Ctr Palo Alto CA 94305-5306

ROSENBERG, SAUL H, epidemiology, for more information see previous edition

ROSENBERG, SAUL HOWARD, PEPTIDE CHEMISTRY, ORGANIC CHEMISTRY. *Current Pos:* SR GROUP LEADER, ABBOTT LABS, 84- *Personal Data:* b Boston, Mass, Feb 20, 57; m 81. *Educ:* Mass Inst Technol, BS, 79; Univ Calif, PhD(org chem), 84. *Mem:* Am Chem Soc; Sigma Xi. *Res:* Development of novel peptide structures as antihypertensive agents; preparation of new peptide surrogate and the examination of the fate of peptide related compound in vivo. *Mailing Add:* 15 Lighthouse Lane Grayslake IL 60030-2638

ROSENBERG, STEVEN A, CANCER RESEARCH. *Current Pos:* clin assoc, Immunol Br, 70-72, CHIEF SURG, NAT CANCER INST, NIH, 74-; PROF SURG, UNIFORMED SERV UNIV HEALTH SCI, 79-; PROF SURG, SCH MED & HEALTH SCI, GEORGE WASHINGTON UNIV, 88- *Personal Data:* b New York, NY, Aug 2, 40; c 3. *Educ:* Johns Hopkins Univ, BA, 61, MD, 64; Harvard Univ, PhD(biophys), 68. *Hon Degrees:* Dr, Ben Gurion Univ, Israel, 86. *Honors & Awards:* Armand Hammer Cancer Prize, 85 & 88; Friedrich Sasse Prize, Ger, 86; Nils Alwell Prize, Stockholm, Sweden, 87; Griffuel Prize Res, Fr Asn Res Cancer, 88; Milken Family Found Cancer Award, 88; Sheen Award, Am Col Surgeons, 91; Karnofsky Prize, Am Soc Clin Oncol, 91; Golden Plate Award, Am Acad Achievement, 92; G Burroughs Mider Lectr Award, NIH, 92; Int Chiron Award Biomed Res & Training, 92; Claude Jacquillat Award, 93; Rienhoff Award, 93; Johig Wayne Award, Soc Surg Oncol, 96. *Prof Exp:* Intern surg, Peter Bent Brigham Hosp, 63-64; resident, 68-69 & 72-74; res fel immunol, Harvard Med Sch, 69-70. *Concurrent Pos:* USPHS, 70-72; mem, Immunother Prog Sci Rev Group, Nat Cancer Inst, 71-78, US-USSR Coop Cancer Immunother Prog, 74-79 & Comt Surg Educ, Soc Univ Surgeons, 79-81; assoc ed, J Nat Cancer Inst, 74-80; consult surg oncol, Peter Bent Brigham Hosp, 74-; consult to dir clin affairs, MD Anderson Hosp & Tumor Inst, 79-85; mem, Comt Clin Res, Soc Surg Oncol, 80-83, Comt Govt Relations Surg Oncol, 80-, Prog Comt, Am Soc Clin Oncol, 83-84; assoc ed, J Immunol, 82-85; mem bd dirs, Am Soc Clin Oncol, 83-86; assoc, Gannett Ctr Media Studies, Columbia Univ, NY, 86-; corresp, Comt Human Rights, Nat Acad Sci, 87-; ed-in-chief, J Immunother, 90-95; ed, Cancer J Sci Am, 95. *Mem:* Inst Med-Nat Acad Sci; Halsted Soc; Am Asn Immunologists; Am Asn Cancer Res; Am Surg Asn; Soc Univ Surgeons; Soc Surg Oncol; Transplantation Soc; Am Col Surgeons; Am Soc Clin Oncol. *Mailing Add:* NIH Surg Br NCI Bldg 10 Rm 2B42 10 Center Dr MSC 1502 Bethesda MD 20892-1502

ROSENBERG, STEVEN LOREN, MICROBIOLOGY. *Current Pos:* CONSULT, 88- *Personal Data:* b Oakland, Calif, Sept 27, 41; m 68, Emiko A Yamamoto. *Educ:* Univ Calif, Berkeley, AB, 63, PhD(bact), 70. *Prof Exp:* Fel bact, Univ Mass, Amherst, 70-71, NIH fel, 71-72; microbiologist, Phys Chem Lab, Gen Elec Res & Develop Ctr, 72-76; mem staff, Lawrence Berkeley Lab, Univ Calif, 76-81; sr microbiologist, SRI Int, 81-86; sr microbiologist, Biosys, 86-87. *Mem:* Am Chem Soc; Mycol Soc Am; Am Soc Microbiol. *Res:* Experimental study of bacterial evolution; enzymology of lignocellulose degradation; production of fuels and chemicals from cellulosic materials by fermentation; biodegradation of xanthan gum and other oil field chemicals; microbial enhanced oil recovery; commercial cultivation of wild mushrooms. *Mailing Add:* 5555 Greenridge Rd Castro Valley CA 94552

ROSENBERG, STUART A, INTERNAL MEDICINE, RHEUMATOLOGY. *Current Pos:* STAFF PHYSICIAN, OCHSNER CLIN, NEW ORLEANS, 85- *Personal Data:* b Petersburg, Va, Aug 22, 47; m 73; c 2. *Educ:* Univ Va, MD, 73. *Prof Exp:* Asst prof med, Univ Va, 80-85. *Mem:* Am Col Physicians; Am Asn Immunologists; Am Fedn Clin Res; Am Rheumatism Asn. *Mailing Add:* Ochsner Clin 1514 Jefferson Hwy New Orleans LA 70121-2483

ROSENBERG, SUSAN MARY, MOLECULAR MECHANISMS OF MUTATION & GENETIC RECOMBINATION, PHAGE LAMBDA IN VITRO PACKAGING. *Current Pos:* asst prof, 91-96, ASSOC PROF BIOCHEM, FAC MED, UNIV ALTA, 96- *Personal Data:* b Massapequa, NY, Dec 2, 58. *Educ:* State Univ NY, Postdam, BA, 80; Univ Ore, MS, 81, PhD(molecular genetics), 86. *Honors & Awards:* William E Rawls Prize, Eli Lilly/Nat Cancer Inst, Can, 95; Young Scientist Award, Genetics Soc Can, 96. *Prof Exp:* Vis scientist fel, Fr Asn Cancer Res, Inst Jaques Monod, Univ Paris, 87-88, ARC fel, 90; NIH fel, 88-91. *Concurrent Pos:* Res assoc, Univ Oregon, Inst Molecular Biol, 87; fel, Dept Biochem, Univ Utah Med Sch, 88-89, Dept Genetics, Univ Alta, 90-91; vis scientist, Lab Chromosome Biol, Nat Cancer Inst, Frederick Cancer Res Facil, 91; res scientist, Molecular Oncol Prog, Cross Cancer Inst, 91-94; adj prof genetics, Univ Alberta Fac Sci, 92-94, Dept Biol Sci, 94-, adj prof, Fac Med, 94-; Alta Heritage Med Scholar, Alta Heritage Found Med Res, 92-97. *Mem:* Genetics Soc Am; Am Soc Microbiol; AAAS; Can Genetics Soc; Can Soc Biochem & Molecular Cell Biol. *Res:* Improved packaging of phage lambda DNA invitro, important for molecular cloning; molecular mechanisms of genetics: genetic recombination, genome plasticity, heredity, mutation, adaptive mutation, mismatch repair, genetic and genomic instability, phage lambda, escherichia coli, genomic instability in cancer and development. *Mailing Add:* Dept Biochem 4-74 Med Sci Bldg Univ Alta Edmonton AB T6G 2H7 Can. *Fax:* 403-492-0886; *E-Mail:* susan_rosenberg@darwin.biochem.ualberta.ca

ROSENBERG, THEODORE JAY, SPACE PHYSICS. *Current Pos:* from res asst prof to assoc prof, 71-75, res prof, Inst Fluid Dynamics & Appl Math, 75-76, RES PROF, INST PHYS SCI & TECHNOL, UNIV MD, COLLEGE PARK, 76- *Personal Data:* b New York, NY, May 24, 37; m 60, Gabriele Schickler; c Kenneth & Eric. *Educ:* City Col New York, BEE, 60; Univ Calif, Berkeley, PhD(physics), 65. *Prof Exp:* Royal Norweg Coun Sci & Indust Res grant, Univ Bergen, 65-66; res assoc & lectr space sci, Rice Univ, 66-68. *Concurrent Pos:* Royal Norweg Coun Sci & Indust Res fel, Norweg Inst Cosmic Physics, 75-76. *Mem:* Am Geophys Union. *Res:* Magnetosphere and ionosphere of earth; experimental investigations of magnetospheric plasma and wave-particle interaction processes including studies of the aurora, radiowave propagation, magnetic substorms, and the ionospheric effects of particle energy deposition. *Mailing Add:* Inst Phys Sci & Technol Univ Md College Park MD 20742-2431. *Fax:* 301-314-9363

ROSENBERG, WARREN L, ANIMAL PHYSIOLOGY, CYTOLOGY. *Current Pos:* asst prof, 83-87, chair, Dept Biol, 92-94, ASSOC PROF PHYSIOL, IONA COL, 87-, DEAN, SCH ARTS & SCI, 94- *Personal Data:* b Brooklyn, NY, Nov 30, 54; m 80; c 3. *Educ:* City Univ New York, BA, 76; New York Univ, MS, 79, PhD(biol), 82. *Prof Exp:* Fel physiol & biophys, Mt Sinai Sch Med, New York, 82-83. *Concurrent Pos:* Lectr, Iona Col, 81-83; biol photogr, Biol Photo Serv, 81-; res assoc, Cellular Biol Lab, New York Univ, 82- *Mem:* AAAS; NY Acad Sci; Am Soc Cell Biol. *Res:* Role of renal glomerulus in the initiation and maintenance of hypertension; morphology and function of the glomerular filtration barrier. *Mailing Add:* 715 North Ave New Rochelle NY 10801-1890. *Fax:* 914-633-2240; *E-Mail:* wrosenberg@iona.edu

ROSENBERG, ZEDA F, VIROLOGY. *Current Pos:* Asst dir prev res, 87-95, SR SCIENTIST, ADULT PREV RES, NAT INST ALLERGY & INFECTIOUS DIS, NIH, 95- *Personal Data:* b Brooklyn, NY, Dec 27, 53. *Educ:* Rutgers Univ, BA, 74, MS, 76; Harvard Univ, ScD(virol), 80. *Mailing Add:* NIAID Div AIDS Solar Bldg 6003 Executive Blvd Bethesda MD 20892. *Fax:* 301-402-3684; *E-Mail:* zrir@nih.gov

ROSENBERGER, ALBERT THOMAS, OPTICAL PHYSICS, NONLINEAR DYNAMICS. *Current Pos:* ASSOC PROF PHYSICS, UNIV ALA, HUNTSVILLE, 89- *Personal Data:* b Butte, Mont, Jan 27, 50. *Educ:* Whitman Col, BA, 71; Univ Chicago, MS, 72; Univ Ill, Champaign-Urbana, PhD(physics), 79. *Prof Exp:* Vis asst prof physics, Drexel Univ, 79-80; asst prof physics, Western Ill Univ, 80-82; lectr & res assoc, Univ Tex, Austin, 82-85; asst prof physics, Southern Methodist Univ, 85-89. *Concurrent Pos:* Consult, Battelle Columbus Labs, 76-79. *Mem:* Am Phys Soc; Am Asn Physics Teachers; Optical Soc Am; Inst Elec & Electronics Engrs. *Res:* Optical physics and nonlinear dynamical phenomena in optical system including optical bistability and instability; coherent transient effects especially supperradiance and effects of losses in optical resonator. *Mailing Add:* Dept Physics Okla State Univ Stillwater OK 74078-3072

ROSENBERGER, ALFRED L, PRIMATOLOGY. *Current Pos:* ASST PROF, DEPT ANTHROP, UNIV ILL, CHICAGO, 81- *Personal Data:* b New York, NY, Nov 30, 49; m 79. *Educ:* City Col New York, BA, 72; City Univ New York, PhD(anthrop), 79. *Prof Exp:* Lectr & fel, Dept Anat Sci, State Univ NY Stony Brook, 79-81. *Concurrent Pos:* Fulbright fel, Brazil, 82-83. *Mem:* Am Asn Phys Anthropologists; Am Asn Primatologists; Int Soc Primatology; Soc Syst Zool; Soc Vert Paleont. *Res:* Primate evolution, particularly evolution and adaptation of South and Central American monkeys and higher primates as a whole. *Mailing Add:* 9406 Pin Oak Dr Silver Spring MD 20912

ROSENBERGER, DAVID A, PLANT PATHOLOGY. *Current Pos:* Asst prof, 77-84, ASSOC PROF, HUDSON VALLEY LAB, CORNELL UNIV, NY, 84-, SUPT, 90- *Personal Data:* b Quakertown, Pa, Sept 14, 47; m 73, Carol J Freeman; c Sara, Matthew & Nathan. *Educ:* Goshen Col, BS, 69; Mich State Univ, PhD(plant path), 77. *Mem:* AAAS; Am Phytopath Soc; Coun Agr Sci & Technol. *Res:* Plant pathology; phytopathology; agricultural science. *Mailing Add:* Cornell Univ Hudson Valley Lab PO Box 727 Highland NY 12528

ROSENBERGER, FRANZ, CHEMICAL PHYSICS, THERMAL PHYSICS. *Current Pos:* PROF PHYSICS & DIR, CTR MICROGRAVITY & MAT RES, UNIV ALA, HUNTSVILLE, 86- *Personal Data:* b Salzburg, Austria, May 31, 33; m 59, Renate Suesseubach; c Uta, Bernd & Till. *Educ:* Stuttgart Univ, MS, 64; Univ Utah, PhD, 69. *Prof Exp:* Res scientist, 69-70, asst res prof, 70-73, asst prof, 73- 78, assoc prof, 78-81, prof physics, 81-86, dir crystal growth lab, Univ Utah, 66-86. *Concurrent Pos:* Adj prof mat sci & eng, Univ Utah, 81-88. *Mem:* Am Asn Crystal Growth; Am Phys Soc. *Res:* Mass and heat transfer phenomena in crystal growth and materials processing; thermodynamics and kinetics of phase transitions; mass spectroscopy of high temperature vapors; fluid dynamics. *Mailing Add:* 171 Stoneway Trail Madison AL 35758-8543. *Fax:* 205-895-6791

ROSENBERGER, JOHN KNOX, ANIMAL VIROLOGY, AVIAN PATHOLOGY. *Current Pos:* from asst prof to assoc prof, 72-81, PROF VIROL & IMMUNOL, COL AGR SCI, UNIV DEL, 81-, CHAIRPERSON, DEPT ANIMAL SCI & AGR BIOCHEM, 78- *Personal Data:* b Wilmington, Del, Dec 8, 42; m 64; c 2. *Educ:* Univ Del, BS, 64, MS, 66; Univ Wis-Madison, PhD(virol, immunol), 72. *Prof Exp:* Virologist, US Army Biol Labs, 67-69. *Mem:* Wildlife Dis Asn; Am Soc Microbiol; assoc Am Asn Avian Pathologists; AAAS; Sigma Xi. *Res:* Viral arthritis; virus induced immuno suppression; characterization of avian respiratory agents. *Mailing Add:* Dept Animal Sci & Agr Biochem Univ Del Newark DE 19717-0001

ROSENBERRY, TERRONE LEE, BIOCHEMISTRY, NEUROCHEMISTRY. *Current Pos:* assoc prof, 79-85, PROF PHARMACOL, CASE WESTERN RES UNIV, 85- *Personal Data:* b Ft Wayne, Ind, Mar 16, 43; m 65; c 2. *Educ:* Oberlin Col, AB, 65; Univ Ore, PhD(biochem), 69. *Prof Exp:* Res assoc neurol, Columbia Univ, 69-72, asst prof, 72-79. *Concurrent Pos:* Prin investr, NSF grant, 72-, NIH grant, 73- & Muscular Dystrophy Asn grant, 79-; Jacob Javits Neurosci Investr, NIH, 89- *Mem:* Am Chem Soc; Am Soc Biol Chem. *Res:* Membrane proteins; acetylcholinesterase structure and function; glycosylphosphatidylinositol anchors in membranes. *Mailing Add:* Dept Pharmacol Mayo Clin 4500 San Pablo Rd Jacksonville FL 32224-3899. *Fax:* 216-368-3395

ROSENBLATT, CHARLES STEVEN, LIGHT SCATTERING & OPTICS, LIQUID CRYSTALS. *Current Pos:* assoc prof, 87-92, PROF PHYSICS & MACROMOLECULAR SCI, CASE WESTERN RESERVE UNIV, 92- *Personal Data:* b Brooklyn, NY, Aug, 23, 52; m, Miriam Werlin; c 2. *Educ:* Mass Inst Technol, SB, 74; Harvard Univ, PhD, 78. *Prof Exp:* Res fel physics, Lawrence Berkeley Lab, Univ Calif, 78-80; res staff physics, Francis Bitter Nat Magnet Lab, Mass Inst Technol, 80-87. *Mem:* Fel Am Phys Soc; Sigma Xi; Int liquid Crystal Soc. *Res:* Optical, magnetic, and mechanical studies of liquid crystals, liquids, and colloids; phase transitions; light scattering from small biological organisms. *Mailing Add:* Dept Physics Case Western Reserve Univ Cleveland OH 44106. *Fax:* 216-368-4671; *E-Mail:* cxr@po.cwry.edu

ROSENBLATT, DANIEL BERNARD, EARTHQUAKE STATISTICS, GEODESY. *Current Pos:* GEODESIST, NIED, JAPAN, 91- *Personal Data:* b Bloomington, Ind, Apr 28, 56. *Educ:* Univ Calif, Berkeley, BA, 77; Stanford Univ, MA, 78; Univ Calif, Los Angeles, PhD(geophys), 89. *Prof Exp:* Programmer, US Geol Surv, 79-80. *Concurrent Pos:* Nat Res Coun grant, 91-93; Nat Res Coun fel, Pasadena, Ca, 92. *Mem:* Am Geophys Union; Am Inst Physics; Japan Seismologist Soc; Japan Geodetic Soc. *Res:* Mathematical statistics; modeling of seismic risk; geodetic studies of fault movement; nonlinear science, investigation of the behavior of nonlinear and delay differential equations. *Mailing Add:* PO Box 2066 La Jolla CA 92038

ROSENBLATT, DAVID, MATHEMATICAL STATISTICS. *Current Pos:* RES CONSULT, 68- *Personal Data:* b New York, NY, Sept 5, 19; m 50, Joan E Raup. *Educ:* City Col New York, BS, 40. *Prof Exp:* Assoc statistician, Off Price Admin, DC, 41-44; sr economist, Div Statist Stand, US Bur Budget, 44-47, 48-49; asst prof econ, Carnegie Inst Technol, 49-51; consult, 51-53; assoc prof statist, Am Univ, 53-55; prin investr, Off Naval Res, 53-57; res consult, Industs, 55-61; consult, Info Tech Div, Nat Bur Stand, 61-63, mathematician, 63-67. *Concurrent Pos:* Littauer fel, Harvard Univ, 47-48; statist consult, Div Statist Standards, US Bur Budget, 49-53; consult, George Washington Univ, 55, 59-61, 68-; adj prof math & statist, Am Univ, 59-61. *Mem:* Fel AAAS; Am Math Soc; fel Am Statist Asn. *Res:* Applied stochastic processes; theory of graphs and theory of relations; mathematical theory of organizations and complex systems; design of statistical information systems; history of mathematical and symbolic methods in resource and social sciences; relation and Boolean algebraic methods; biological structures and relations. *Mailing Add:* 2939 Van Ness St NW Washington DC 20008

ROSENBLATT, DAVID HIRSCH, CHEMICAL PROPERTY ESTIMATION, ENVIRONMENTAL RISK ASSESSMENT FOR CHEMICALS. *Current Pos:* INDEPENDENT CONSULT & ENVIRON SCIENTIST, ARGONNE NAT LAB, ILL, 90- *Personal Data:* b Trenton, NJ, July 24, 27; m 49, Jaclyn Rivkin; c Jonathan, Aaron & Daniel. *Educ:* Johns Hopkins Univ, BA, 46; Univ Conn, PhD(chem), 50. *Prof Exp:* Res & develop chemist, Baltimore Paint & Color Works, 50-51; chemist, Chem Warfare Labs, US Dept Army, 51-56; org chemist, Johns Hopkins Univ, 56-57; chemist, Chem Res & Develop Labs, US Dept Army, 57-63, chief decontamination res sect, Chem Lab, Edgewood Arsenal, 63-72, res chemist, Health Effects Res Div, US Army Biomed Res & Develop Lab, Ft Detrick, Md, 72-89. *Concurrent Pos:* Instr eve col, Johns Hopkins Univ, 57-70. *Mem:* AAAS; Am Chem Soc; Sigma Xi; Soc Environ Toxicol Chem. *Res:* Nucleophilic displacements; mechanisms of oxidation of amines and other organics in aqueous solution; halogens and halogen oxides; decomposition and complexing of toxic chemical agents; specific analytical methods; risk assessment of environmental pollutants; chemistry and applications of chlorine dioxide; estimation of physico-chemical properties of environmental pollutants. *Mailing Add:* 3316 Old Forest Rd Baltimore MD 21208-3101

ROSENBLATT, DAVID SIDNEY, BIOCHEMICAL GENETICS, PEDIATRICS. *Current Pos:* asst prof, McGill Univ, 75-80, assoc prof, Ctr Human Genetics, 80, assoc prof pediat, 80-87, PROF MED, PEDIAT, CTR HUMAN GENETICS, DIR, DEPT MED, DIV MED GENETICS, MCGILL UNIV & MONTREAL GENERAL & ROYAL VICTORIA HOSPS, 87-, AUX PROF BIOL, 78-, PROF, DEPT HUMAN GENETICS, 93- *Personal Data:* b Montreal, Que, July 14, 46; m 69, Linda Chernin; c Jacalyn & Dana. *Educ:* McGill Univ, BSc, 68, MDCM, 70. *Honors & Awards:* Prix d'excellence for Res into Dis of Children, 86; Aaron Graham lectr, Children's Hosp Los Angeles, 95. *Prof Exp:* Intern pediat med, Montreal Children's Hosp, 70-71; clin & res fel pediat & genetics, Mass Gen Hosp, Harvard Med Sch, 71-73; fel biol, Mass Inst Technol, 73-74; asst resident pediat, Children's Hosp Med Ctr, Harvard Med Sch, 74-75. *Concurrent Pos:* Prin investr, Med Res Coun Can, Genetics Group, McGill Univ, 75-; mem, Genetics Comt, Med Res Coun Can, 78-81, 87-91 & 95, Clin-Scientist Comt, 95-97; vchmn, Res Comt, McGill Univ, Montreal Children's Hosp Res Inst, 80-84; vpres res, Royal Victoria Hosp, 93-96. *Mem:* Am Soc Human Genetics; Can Soc Clin Invest (secy-treas, 87-90, pres, 95); Soc Pediat Res; Can Col Med Genetics; Soc Inherited Metab Disorders (pres, 96-97). *Res:* Inborn errors of folate metabolism in cultured human cells; methotrexate metabolism; inborn errors of cobalamin metabolism. *Mailing Add:* Div Med Genetics Dept Med McGill Univ 687 Pine Ave H5-63 Montreal PQ H3A 1A1 Can. *Fax:* 514-843-1712; *E-Mail:* mc74@musica.mcgill.ca

ROSENBLATT, GERD MATTHEW, PHYSICAL CHEMISTRY, HIGH-TEMPERATURE CHEMISTRY. *Current Pos:* dep dir, 85-89, SR CHEMIST, LAWRENCE BERKELEY LAB, UNIV CALIF, 89- *Personal Data:* b Leipzig, Ger, July 6, 33; US citizen; m 90, Susan F Barnett; c Rachel & Paul. *Educ:* Swarthmore Col, BA, 55; Princeton Univ, PhD(phys chem), 60. *Hon Degrees:* Dr, Vrije Univ Brussel, 89. *Prof Exp:* Chemist, Inorg Mat Res Div, Lawrence Radiation Lab, Univ Calif, 60-63; from asst prof to prof chem, Pa State Univ, Univ Park, 63-81; assoc div leader, Chem-Mat Sci Div, Los Alamos Nat Lab, 81-82, chem div leader, 82-85. *Concurrent Pos:* Lectr, Univ Calif, Berkeley, 62-63; guest scientist & consult, Inorg Mat Res Div, Lawrence Berkeley Lab, Univ Calif, 68-84; mem, Comt High Temperature Sci & Technol, Nat Acad Sci-Nat Res Coun, 70-79 & 84-85, chmn, 77-79 & 84-85, chmn, Workshop High Temperature Sci, Nat Acad-Res Coun-NSF, 79, Panel Solid-State Sci, Acad-Coun, 81-82, Numerical Data Adv Bd, 84-90, chmn, 86-90, & mem Res Briefing Panel Ceramics & Ceramic Compos, 85; vchmn, Gordon Res Conf High Temperature Chem, 72, chmn, 74; vis prof, Vrije Univ & fel, Solvay Inst, Univ Libre Burssels, Belg, 73; mem rev comt, Chem Eng Div, Argonne Nat Lab, 74-80, chmn, 77 & 78, rev comn, High Temperature Mat Lab, Oak Ridge Nat Lab, 78-81; consult, Hooker Chem Co, 76-78, Xerox Corp, 77-78, Los Alamos Sci Lab, 78 & 96-, Aerospace Corp, 79-85 & Solar Energy Res Inst, 80-81; ed, Progress in Solid State Chem, 77-; mem, adv rev bd, Joint Army-Navy-Air Force Thermochem Tables, 77-84; US nat rep, Comn High Temperature Mat & Solid State Chem, Int Union Pure & Appl Chem, 78-85, assoc mem, 85-91, secy, 91-95, chmn, 96-97, mem, US Nat Comt, 86-92; vis fel, Southhampton Univ, & King's Col, Cambridge, 80; adj prof chem, Univ NMex, 81-85; mem, rev comt, Chem Sci Progs, Lawrence Berkeley Lab, 84 & chmn, rev comt, Chem & Mat Sci Dept, Lawrence Livermore Nat Lab, 85-87; mem, adv bd, Sandia Nat Lab, Livermore & Lockheed Missiles & Space Co, 85-89; mem, external rev comt, Chem Div, Los Alamos Nat Lab, 85 & external adv comt, Ctr Mat Sci, 85-94, chmn, 88-94; mem, Basic Energy Sci Lab Prog Panel, Dept Energy, 85-89, Nat Lab Task Force, Indust Res Inst, 87-89; mem, US Nat Comt Data Sci & Technol, 86-92; mem, rev team, Comt Army Chem Stockpile Disposal Prog, Nat Res Coun, Nat Acad Sci, 89-90, Solid State Sci Comt, 88-91, Sci & Tech Info Bd, 90; chmn, Western Regional Mat Sci & Eng Meeting, Nat Res Coun, 90. *Mem:* Am Phys Soc; Am Chem Soc; fel AAAS. *Res:* Spatially resolved and high sensitivity Raman spectroscopic characterization of materials and surface adsorbates; properties and behavior of high-temperature materials and high-temperature gases; thermodynamics; dynamics of gas-surface reactions and of crystal evaporation. *Mailing Add:* 1177 Miller Ave Berkeley CA 94708. *Fax:* 510-486-4114; *E-Mail:* grosenblatt@lbl.gov

ROSENBLATT, JOAN RAUP, MATHEMATICAL STATISTICS. *Current Pos:* dep dir, 78-93, dir, Comput & Appl Math Lab, 93-95, GUEST RESEARCHER, STATIST ENG DIV, NAT INST STAND & TECHNOL, 96- *Personal Data:* b New York, NY, Apr 15, 26; m 50, David. *Educ:* Columbia Univ, AB, 46; Univ NC, PhD(statist), 56. *Honors & Awards:* Fed Woman's Award, 71; Gold Medal, Dept Com, 76; Founders Award, Am Statist Asn, 91. *Prof Exp:* Statist analyst, US Bur Budget, 48; asst statist, Univ NC, 53-54; mathematician, Nat Bur Stand, 55-69, chief statist eng lab, 69-78. *Concurrent Pos:* Statist chair, Sect U, AAAS, 82, secy, 87-91; mem, Comt Appl & Theoret Statist, Nat Res Coun, 85-88. *Mem:* Fel AAAS; Am Math Soc; Int Statist Inst; fel Am Statist Asn (vpres, 81-83); fel Inst Math Statist; Bernoulli Soc. *Res:* Nonparametric statistical theory; applications of statistical techniques in physical and engineering sciences; reliability of complex systems. *Mailing Add:* Nat Inst Stand & Technol Bldg 820 Rm 363 Gaithersburg MD 20899-0001. *E-Mail:* jrr@cam.nist.gov

ROSENBLATT, JUDAH ISSER, BIOMETRICS, BIOSTATISTICS. *Current Pos:* dir acad comput & biostatist, 82-84, PROF PREV MED & COMMUNITY HEALTH, UNIV TEX MED BR, 82-, DIR, BIOMATH, 84- *Personal Data:* b Baltimore, Md, Feb 12, 31; m 56, Lisa Herzfeld; c Daniel. *Educ:* Johns Hopkins Univ, BA, 51; Columbia Univ, PhD, 59. *Prof Exp:* Asst prof math & statist, Purdue Univ, 56-60; assoc prof math, Univ NMex, 60-68, dir math comput lab, 67-68; prof math, Case Western Res Univ, 68-76, prof biomet, 79-92. *Concurrent Pos:* Staff mem, Shriners Burns Inst, 88-NMex, 60-68, Gen Elec Co, 77- *Mem:* Fel Am Statist Asn; fel Inst Math Statist. *Res:* Stochastic processes, numerical analysis, mathematical modelling and analysis. *Mailing Add:* 28 Lakeview Dr Galveston TX 77551. *Fax:* 409-770-6825; *E-Mail:* judab.rosenblatt@utmb.edu

ROSENBLATT, KARIN ANN, CANCER EPIDEMIOLOGY, EPIDEMIOLOGIC METHODS. *Current Pos:* ASST PROF COMMUNITY HEALTH, UNIV ILL, 91- *Personal Data:* b Chicago, Ill, Apr 22, 54. *Educ:* Univ Calif, Santa Cruz, BA, 75; Univ Mich, MPH, 77; Johns Hopkins Univ, PhD(epidemiol), 88. *Prof Exp:* Fel, Univ Wash, 87-89; staff scientist, Fred Hutchinson Cancer Res Ctr, 89-91. *Mem:* Am Col Epidemiol; Soc Epidemiol Res; Am Pub Health Asn; Int Genetic Epidemiol Soc. *Res:* Etiology of male breast cancer, ovarian cancer and endometrial cancer. *Mailing Add:* 120 Huff Hall Univ Ill 1206 S Fourth St Champaign IL 61820. *Fax:* 217-333-2766; *E-Mail:* krosenbl@uiuc.edu

ROSENBLATT, MICHAEL, ENDOCRINOLOGY, BIOCHEMISTRY. *Current Pos:* SR VPRES ACAD AFFAIRS, BETH ISRAEL DEACONESS MED CTR, HARVARD UNIV, CHIEF BONE & MINERAL METAB, FAC DEAN ACAD PROG, ROBERT H EBERT PROF MOLECULAR MED. *Personal Data:* b Lund, Sweden, Nov, 27, 47; m 69; c 2. *Educ:* Columbia Col, AB, 69; Harvard Med Sch, MD, 73. *Honors & Awards:* Fuller Albright Award, Am Soc Bone & Mineral Res, 86; Vincent du Vigneaud Award, Chem & Biol of Reptides. *Prof Exp:* From instr to asst prof med, Harvard Med Sch, Mass Gen Hosp, 76-85; vpres biol res & molecular biol, Merck Sharp & Dohme Res Labs, Merck & Co, Inc, 84-89, sr vpres res, 89- *Concurrent Pos:* Chief, Endocrine Unit, Mass Gen Hosp, 81-84, consult med, 84-; lectr med, Sch Med, Harvard Univ, 85-; adj prof, Sch Med, Univ Pa, 88- *Mem:* Endocrine Soc; Am Soc Bone & Mineral Res; Am Soc Biochem & Molecular Biol; Am Soc Clin Invest; Asn Am Physicians. *Res:* Interaction of parathyroid hormone with receptors; peptide hormone isolation of receptors molecular biology of parathyroid hormone secretion tumor-secreted hypercalcemia factor (paralthyroid hormone-related protein). *Mailing Add:* Div Bone & Mineral Metab Harvard Inst Med Beth Israel Deaconess Med Ctr 330 Brookline Ave DA 944 Boston MA 02215

ROSENBLATT, MURRAY, STOCHASTIC PROCESSES, NON-PARAMETRIC METHODS. *Current Pos:* PROF MATH, UNIV CALIF, SAN DIEGO, 64- *Personal Data:* b New York, NY, Sept 7, 26; m 49, Adylin Lipson; c Karin & Daniel. *Educ:* City Col New York, BS, 46; Cornell Univ, MS, 47, PhD(math), 49. *Prof Exp:* Res assoc math, Cornell Univ, 49-50; from instr to asst prof statist, Univ Chicago, 50-55; assoc prof math, Ind Univ, 56-59; prof appl math, Brown Univ, 59-64. *Concurrent Pos:* Off Naval Res grant, 49-50; Guggenheim fels, 65-66, 71-72; fel, Univ Col London, 66, 72 & Australian Nat Univ, 76; overseas fel, Churchill Col, 79. *Mem:* Nat Acad Sci; Am Math Soc; fel Inst Math Statist; fel AAAS; Int Statist Inst. *Res:* Probability theory; stochastic processes; time series analysis; turbulence. *Mailing Add:* Dept Math Univ Calif San Diego La Jolla CA 92093. *Fax:* 619-534-5273; *E-Mail:* mrosenblatt@ucsd.edu

ROSENBLATT, RICHARD HEINRICH, ZOOLOGY. *Current Pos:* asst res zoologist, Inst, 58-65, from asst prof to assoc prof, 65-73, PROF MARINE BIOL, SCRIPPS INST OCEANOG, PROF, GRAD DEPT & RES ZOOLOGIST, SCI SUPPORT DIV, UNIV CALIF, 73-, VCHMN DEPT, 70-, CUR MARINE VERT, 58-, CHMN, GRAD DEPT, 80- *Personal Data:* b Kansas City, Mo, Dec 21, 30; m 52; c 2. *Educ:* Univ Calif, Los Angeles, AB, 53, MA, 54, PhD, 59. *Prof Exp:* Asst zool, Univ Calif, Los Angeles, 53-56. *Mem:* AAAS; Soc Syst Zool; Am Soc Ichthyol & Herpet; Soc Study Evolution; Am Soc Zool; Sigma Xi. *Res:* Systematics, evolution, ecology and zoogeography of fishes. *Mailing Add:* 5160 Middleton Rd San Diego CA 92109-1520

ROSENBLATT, ROGER ALAN, FAMILY MEDICINE, PUBLIC HEALTH. *Current Pos:* Intern, Affil Hosp, Univ Wash, 71-72, resident, 72-74, from clin instr to assoc prof, Sch Med, 74-85, PROF & VCHMN, DEPT FAMILY MED, SCH MED, UNIV WASH, 85-, MEM GRAD FAC, 85- *Personal Data:* b Denver, Colo Aug 8, 45; m; c 2. *Educ:* Harvard Univ, BA, 67, MD & MPH, 71; Am Bd Family Pract, dipl, 74. *Honors & Awards:* Res Award, Am Rural Health Asn, 85; Hames Res Award, Soc Teachers Family Med, 96. *Concurrent Pos:* Sr surg, USPHS, 74-77; regional med consult, Nat Health Serv Corps, 74-76, dir, 76-77; consult, dir, USPHS Hosp, 74-76, Bur Community Health Servs Recruitment Br, 76, Bur Community Health Servs & Bar Health Manpower, 78, Asst secy Teachers Family Med, 79, Pres Off Sci, Technol & Pol, 80, State Alaska, 81, Nat Rural Healthcare, 83-85, Colo Trust, 90-92, Kans Health Found, 93-; prin investr, USPHS, 77-83, NIH, 83-84 & NSF, 83-85; adj asst prof, Sch Pub Health, 78-81, adj assoc prof, 81-85; chmn, USPHS, 76, Soc Teachers Family Med Task Force, 78-79; med staff mem, Univ Wash Hosp, Seattle, 78-; vis lectr, Ben-Gurion Univ Negev, Israel, 79, Royal Australian Col Gen Practitioners, 84 & Univ Queensland, Australia, 87; consult, USDA, 79-80, HEW, 79, Off Sci & Technol, 80, State Alaska, 81 & Nat Rural Health Care Asn, 83-85; lead witness, Oversight Hearings Nat Health Servs Corps, 80; mem, bd dirs, Am Rural Health Asn, 80; asst, Western Interstate Comn Higher Educ, 81-82; vis prof, Univ Aukland, NZ, 83-84, Univ Calgary, 88, Univ Wales, 92-93 & Mahidol Univ, Thailand, 95; co-founder & mem, Citizens Qual Pub Schs & Parents Educ Union Seattle, 89-; mem, Am Deleg Panam Conf Med Educ, Costa Rica, 91. *Mem:* Inst Med-Nat Acad Sci; Am Acad Family Pysicians; Am Pub Health Asn; Soc Teachers Family Med; Nat Rural Health Asn; Int Soc Technol Assessment Health Care; Asn Health Servs Res; NAm Primary Care Res Group; Int Ctr Family Med. *Res:* Public health; policy-related research on delivery of health services to rural and underserved populations; health work force issues; population control issues and effect on social environment. *Mailing Add:* Dept Family Med Box 354795 Univ Wash Seattle WA 98195-4795. *Fax:* 206-685-0610; *E-Mail:* roger_rosenblatt@fammed.washington.edu

ROSENBLITH, WALTER ALTER, BIOPHYSICS, SENSORY COMMUNICATION. *Current Pos:* from assoc prof to prof commun biophys, Mass Inst Technol, 51-84, staff mem res lab electronics, 51-69, chmn fac, 67-69, from assoc provost to provost, 69-80, inst prof, 75-84, EMER INST PROF, MASS INST TECHNOL, 84- *Personal Data:* b Vienna, Austria, Sept 21, 13; nat US; m 41, Judy Olcott Francis; c Sandra Y & Ronald F. *Educ:* Univ Bordeaux, ing radiotelegraphiste, 36; Ecole Superieure d'Elec, Paris, ing radioelectricien, 37. *Hon Degrees:* ScD, Univ Pa, 76 & SDak Sch Mines & Technol, 80; Dr, Fed Univ Rio de Janeiro, 76; ScD, Brandeis Univ, 88, Univ Miami, 92. *Honors & Awards:* Weizmann lectr, Weizmann Inst Sci, Israel, 62. *Prof Exp:* Res engr, France, 37-39; res asst physics, NY Univ, 39-40; from asst prof to assoc prof, SDak Sch Mines, 43-47 & actg head dept physics; res fel, Psychoacoust Lab, Harvard Univ, 47-51. *Concurrent Pos:* Lectr otol, Harvard Med Sch & Mass Eye & Ear Infirmary, 57-; inaugural lectr, Tata Inst Fundamental Res, Bombay, 62; mem sci adv bd, USAF, 61-62; consult, Life Sci Panel, Pres Sci Adv Comt, 61-66; consult, WHO, 64-65; chmn comt electronic comput in life sci, Nat Acad Sci/Nat Res Coun, 60-64, mem brain sci comt, 65-68, chmn, 66-67; mem cent coun exec comt, Int Brain Res Orgn, 60-68, hon treas, 62-67; mem coun, Int Union Pure & Appl Biophys, 61-69 & pres comn biophys commun & control processes, 64-69; mem bd med, Nat Acad Sci, 67-70; mem, Pres Comn Urban Housing, 67-68, Selection Comt John & Alice Tyler Prize Environ Achievement, 73- & Coun Foreign Rels, 83-92; chmn sci adv coun, Callier Ctr Commun Disorders, 68-85; mem bd gov, Weizmann Inst Sci, 73-86; dir, Kaiser Industs, 68-76; mem adv comt dir, NIH, 70-74; mem comt on scholarly commun, People's Repub China, 77-86; mem, Bd Foreign Scholar, 78-81, chmn, 80-81; co-chmn comt for study on saccharin & food safety policy, Nat Res Coun-Inst Med, 78-79; mem bd trustees, Brandeis Univ, 79-; chmn res comt, Health Effects Inst, 81-89, mem bd, 89-96; mem, Adv Panel Int Educ Exchange, US Info Agency, 82-86; vpres, Int Coun Sci Unions, 84-88; chmn, int adv panel of Chinese Univ Develop Project, 86-91; consult, Carnegie Corp New York, 86-91. *Mem:* Nat Acad Sci (foreign secy, 82-86); Nat Acad Eng; Inst Med-Nat Acad Sci; Inst Elec & Electronics Engrs; Biophys Soc; AAAS; Am Acad Arts & Sci; Acoust Soc Am; World Acad Arts & Sci; Foreign Asn Eng Acad Japan. *Res:* Electrical activity of the nervous system and brain function; sensory communication; science and technology in the university and society. *Mailing Add:* Mass Inst Technol Rm E51-211 Cambridge MA 02139

ROSENBLOOM, ALFRED A, JR, OPTOMETRY. *Current Pos:* Instr neural physiol, Ill Col Optom, 46-48, dir contact lens & subnorm vision clins, 47-48, lectr, 49-54, dean, 55-72, PRES, ILL COL OPTOM, 72-, PROF OPTOM, 77- *Personal Data:* b Pittsburgh, Pa, Apr 5, 21; m; c 2. *Educ:* Pa State Col, BA, 42; Ill Col Optom, OD, 48; Univ Chicago, MA, 53. *Hon Degrees:* DOS, Ill Col Optom, 54. *Concurrent Pos:* Am Optom Found fel, 52-54; reading clinician & res assoc, Dept Educ, Univ Chicago, 53-54; consult, Chicago Lighthouse for Blind, 55-; chmn adv res coun, Am Optom Found, 69-76; lectr, Brit Optical Asn, 70; mem, Optom Exten Prog; mem optom rev comt, Bur Health Prof Educ & Manpower, US Dept Health, Educ & Welfare, Region III; mem state contract task force, Am Optom Found. *Mem:* AAAS; fel Am Acad Optom; Am Optom Asn; Nat Soc Study Educ; Asn Schs & Cols Optom. *Res:* Visual problems of children and youth and the partially sighted; reading problems. *Mailing Add:* 910 N Lake Shore Dr Chicago IL 60611

ROSENBLOOM, ARLAN LEE, PEDIATRICS, ENDOCRINOLOGY. *Current Pos:* from asst prof to prof pediat endocrinol, Col Med, 68-96, dir clin res ctr, Univ Fla, 74-80, EMER DISTINGUISHED SERV PROF, COL MED, UNIV FLA, 96-; ASST MED DIR, CHILDRENS MED SERVS DIST, 93- *Personal Data:* b Milwaukee, Wis, Apr 15, 34; m 58, Edith K Peterson; c Eric David, Maliah Jo, Disa Lynn & Harris Phillip. *Educ:* Univ Wis-Madison, BA, 55, MD, 58. *Prof Exp:* Intern, Los Angeles County Gen Hosp, 58-59; resident, Ventura County Hosp, Calif, 59-60; physician & chief, Medico Hosp, Kratie, Cambodia, 60-61, med officer, Medico, Inc, Pahang, Malaysia, 61-62; resident pediat, Univ Wis-Madison, 62-63, chief resident, 64-65; tech adv epidemiol, Commun Dis Ctr, USPHS, 66-68. *Concurrent Pos:* USPHS training grants pediat & endocrinol, Univ Wis-Madison, 63-64, 65-66. *Mem:* Am Diabetes Asn; Am Acad Pediat; Pediat Endocrine Soc; Soc Pediat Res; Endocrine Soc; Am Pediat Soc; fel Am Col Epidemiol. *Res:* Natural history of diabetes mellitus, including acute and long term complications; growth hormone receptor deficiency in Ecuador; clinical genetic and metabolic studies. *Mailing Add:* Children's Med Serv Ctr 1701 SW 16th Ave Gainesville FL 32608. *Fax:* 352-334-1325; *E-Mail:* arlan.peds@mail.health.ufl.edu

ROSENBLOOM, JOEL, BIOCHEMISTRY, BIOPHYSICS. *Current Pos:* Asst prof biochem & med, Sch Med, 65-71, assoc prof biochem, Sch Dent Med, 71-74, PROF EMBRYOL & HISTOL & CHMN DEPT, SCH DENT MED, UNIV PA, 74-, ASSOC DEAN RES, 85- *Personal Data:* b Denver, Colo, July 18, 35; m 58, Joan; c 2. *Educ:* Harvard Univ, AB, 57; Univ Pa, MD, 62, PhD(biochem), 65. *Concurrent Pos:* Biochemist, Clin Res Ctr, Philadelphia Gen Hosp, 65-73; dir, Ctr Oral Health Res, 78- *Mem:* AAAS; NY Acad Sci; Am Chem Soc; Biophys Soc; Am Soc Biol Chemists. *Res:* Structure of macromolecules; ultracentrifugation; structure and biosynthesis of macromolecules, particularly collagen and elastin; molecular biology. *Mailing Add:* Dept Anat & Histol Univ Pa Sch Dent Med Philadelphia PA 19104-6002. *Fax:* 215-573-2324

ROSENBLUM, ANNETTE TANNENHOLZ, SCIENCE POLICY, CHEMICAL SCIENCES. *Current Pos:* staff writer chem sci, News Serv, Am Chem Soc, Washington, DC, 72-74, asst for res & coordr govt affairs, 74-79, asst to dir, Dept Pub Affairs, 79-84, MGR, OFF SCI POLICY ANALYSIS, AM CHEM SOC, WASHINGTON, DC, 84- *Personal Data:* b Brooklyn, NY, Oct 3, 42; m 66; c 2. *Educ:* Queens Col, BS, 64; Univ Rochester, MS, 67; Ohio State Univ, PhD(org chem), 71. *Prof Exp:* Teaching asst chem, Univ Rochester, 64-66; teaching asst, Ohio State Univ, 66-67, res asst, 67-71.

Concurrent Pos: NY State Col teaching fel, Univ Rochester, 64-66; res chemist, Naval Ord Lab, Dept Navy, 72; interim co-adminr govt affairs, Dept Chem & Pub Affairs, Am Chem Soc, 77-78. *Mem:* AAAS; Am Chem Soc. *Res:* Science policy; legislation; federal regulations; chemical safety and health; environmental improvement. *Mailing Add:* 12008 Trailridge Dr Rockville MD 20854

ROSENBLUM, BRUCE, PHYSICS. *Current Pos:* dep provost, Stevenson Col, 68-73, assoc dir, Ctr Innovation & Entrepreneural Develop, 78-83, PROF PHYSICS, UNIV CALIF, SANTA CRUZ, 66-, CHMN DEPT, 66-70, 89- *Personal Data:* b New York, NY, May 20, 26; m 82; c 3. *Educ:* NY Univ, BS, 49; Columbia Univ, PhD(physics), 59. *Prof Exp:* Res physicist, Dept Physics, Univ Calif, Berkeley, 57-58; mem tech staff, Radio Corp Am Labs, 58-65, head, Gen Res Group, 65-66. *Concurrent Pos:* VPres, Rev & Critique, 80-; consult. *Mem:* Am Phys Soc; Am Asn Physics Teachers; AAAS. *Res:* Molecular physics; microwave spectroscopy; plasmas and transport in semiconductors; superconductivity; biophysics; fundamentals of quantum mechanics. *Mailing Add:* Dept Physics Univ Calif Santa Cruz CA 95064

ROSENBLUM, CHARLES, PHYSICAL CHEMISTRY. *Current Pos:* RETIRED. *Personal Data:* b Brooklyn, NY, Sept 19, 05; m 33; c 1. *Educ:* Univ Rochester, BS, 27; Univ Minn, PhD(phys chem), 31. *Honors & Awards:* Levy Medal, Franklin Inst, 40. *Prof Exp:* Asst chem, Univ Minn, 27-30, assoc, 31-35; fel, Comn Relief Belg Educ Found Louvain, 35-37; instr chem, Princeton Univ, 37-41; sr chemist, Merck & Co, Inc, 41-42; sect head, Kellex Corp, NY, 44; sect head, Merck & Co Inc, 46-50, head, Radioactivity Lab, 50-65, sr investr & dir, 65-70; vis sr res biochemist, Princeton Univ, 70-90. *Mem:* Fel AAAS; Am Chem Soc; Soc Exp Biol & Med; fel Am Inst Chemists; Belg Am Educ Found. *Res:* Photochemistry; radiochemistry; radioactive indicators; activation analysis; adsorption; physical methods of analysis; structure of precipitates; stability of pharmaceuticals. *Mailing Add:* Pennswood Village Rte 413 Newtown PA 18940

ROSENBLUM, DANIEL MARK, QUEUEING THEORY. *Current Pos:* Asst prof quant studies, 87-94, MICROCOMPUTER ANALYST, RUTGERS UNIV FAC MGT, 94- *Personal Data:* b Brooklyn, NY, Oct 11, 52; m 90; c 2. *Educ:* Oberlin Col, BA, 74; Carnegie Mellon Univ, PhD(pub policy anal), 87. *Mem:* Math Asn Am; Inst Opers Res & Mgt Sci. *Res:* Microeconomics theory of queueing; queues as non-pecuniary mediators between market demand and market capacity for a service; market mechanisms for allocation of waiting time among customers. *Mailing Add:* Rutgers Univ Fac Mgt 180 University Ave Newark NJ 07102-1897. *E-Mail:* dmr@newark.rutgers.edu

ROSENBLUM, EUGENE DAVID, MICROBIOLOGY, GENETICS. *Current Pos:* from asst prof to assoc prof, 53-74, dir microbiol grad prog, 72-86, prof, 53-, EMER PROF MICROBIOL, HEALTH SCI CTR, UNIV TEX, DALLAS. *Personal Data:* b Brooklyn, NY, Oct 13, 20; m 56; c 2. *Educ:* Brooklyn Col, BA, 41; Univ Wis, MS, 48, PhD(bact), 50. *Prof Exp:* Bacteriologist, Biol Lab, Cold Spring Harbor, 50-52; res assoc microbiol, May Inst Med Res, Cincinnati, 52-53. *Mem:* AAAS; Am Soc Microbiol; Sigma Xi. *Res:* Genetics of pathogenic bacteria; antibiotic resistance; extrachromosomal inheritance; bacteriophage. *Mailing Add:* 4166 Goodfellow Dr Dallas TX 75229

ROSENBLUM, HAROLD, ELECTRONICS ENGINEERING. *Current Pos:* RETIRED. *Personal Data:* b Paterson, NJ, Mar 30, 18; m 41, Hannah Wrubel; c Lawrence J, Susan (Shevitz) & Ira. *Educ:* Cooper Union, BChE, 43; NY Univ, MEE, 51. *Prof Exp:* Head, Radar Systs Sect, NY Naval Shipyard, 47-54; head, Flight Trainers Br, Naval Training Systs Ctr, 54-57, Air Tactics Br, 57-60, Strike-Air Defense Systs Trainers Div, 60-65 & Aerospace Systs Trainers Dept, 65-67, asst tech dir eng, 67-69, dep dir eng, 69-74; dir tech sales, Appl Devices Corp, Kissimmee, Fla, 77-78; sr staff consult, Link Simulation Systs Div, Singer Co, Silver Spring, Md, 80-87; mgt eng consult, 74-92. *Mem:* Sr mem Inst Elec & Electronics Engrs; NY Acad Sci; Sigma Xi. *Res:* Training devices, research techniques and instructional technology for simulation of air, surface underwater and land warfare weapon systems. *Mailing Add:* 1325 Classic Dr Longwood FL 32779-5816

ROSENBLUM, HOWARD EDWIN, COMMUNICATIONS ENGINEERING, ACOUSTICS. *Current Pos:* RETIRED. *Personal Data:* b Brooklyn, NY, Apr 28, 28; m 50; c 4. *Educ:* City Col New York, BS, 50. *Honors & Awards:* Except Civilian Serv Award, Nat Security Agency, 72. *Prof Exp:* Chief proj engr commun systs, Sanders Assocs, 61-62; div chief res & develop secure speech systs, Nat Security Agency, Ft George Meade, 63-71, asst dir res & develop, 71-73, asst dep dir res & eng, 73-74, dep dir, 74-78, dep dir commun security, 78-83, vpres & gen mgr, Unisys Defense Systs, 83-90. *Concurrent Pos:* Consult, Defense Sci Bd, 76-77; mem, Mil Commun Electronics Bd & Defense Telecommun Coun, 78- *Mem:* AAAS; Armed Forces Commun-Electronics Asn. *Res:* Cryptography; speech compression and digitalization; microelectronics; computer and information science. *Mailing Add:* 1809 Franwall Ave Silver Spring MD 20902

ROSENBLUM, IRWIN YALE, INSULIN-GROWTH FACTOR. *Current Pos:* ASSOC DIR TOXICOL, DRUG SAFETY & METAB, SCHERING PLOUGH RES INST, 94- *Personal Data:* b Youngstown, Ohio, Nov 26, 42; m 78; c 1. *Educ:* Pa State Univ, BS, 64; Univ Wis, PhD(biochem), 69. *Prof Exp:* Res fel, Univ Hawaii, 69-70; joint res assoc, Med Ctr & Univ Ariz, 75-76; sr res scientist, Miami Valley Labs, Proctor & Gamble Co, 71-78; asst prof toxicol, Albany Med Col, Union Univ, 78-81; res dir, Large Primate Div, White Sands Res Ctr, 81; assoc prof pharmacol & toxicol, Philadelphia Col Pharm & Sci, 82-87; scientist, Warner-Lambert, 87-94. *Concurrent Pos:* Dir clin chem, Int Ctr Environ Safety, 78-80; adj prof, Park Col, 79-81; consult, Coulston Int Corp, 81; adj prof, Drexel Univ, 85. *Mem:* Soc Toxicol; Am Soc Primatologists; Am Diabetes Asn; Int Primatol Soc; Sigma Xi. *Res:* Identification and characterization of insulin and insulin-like growth factor receptors in early preimplantation embryos; chemical-induced genotoxicity in male germ cells. *Mailing Add:* 9 Winding Way Andover NJ 07821-2598

ROSENBLUM, LEONARD ALLEN, PRIMATOLOGY, PSYCHOBIOLOGY. *Current Pos:* from instr to assoc prof, 61-72, PROF PSYCHIAT, STATE UNIV NY DOWNSTATE MED CTR, 72- *Personal Data:* b Brooklyn, NY, May 18, 36; m 56; c 2. *Educ:* Brooklyn Col, BA, 56, MA, 58; Univ Wis-Madison, PhD, 61. *Prof Exp:* Res asst psychol, Brooklyn Col, 56-58; res asst psychol, Univ Wis, 58-61, teaching fel, 61. *Concurrent Pos:* NIMH career develop award, 64-71; reviewer small grants, NIMH, 74-77, basic behavioral sci, 78-82. *Mem:* fel Am Psychol Asn; Am Soc Primatol; Int Acad Sex Res; Int Primatol Soc; Int Soc Develop Psychobiol (pres, 80); Sigma Xi. *Res:* Mother-infant relations and effects of early experience on development in primates; sexual behavior and its development and control. *Mailing Add:* Dept Psychiat State Univ NY Health Sci Col Med 450 Clarkson Ave Brooklyn NY 11203-2012. *Fax:* 718-270-3887

ROSENBLUM, MARTIN JACOB, COMPUTER SCIENCE, APPLIED MATHEMATICS. *Current Pos:* MEM STAFF INFO SYSTS, WESTERN ELEC CO, 80- *Personal Data:* b Stamford, Conn, Dec 6, 28; m 55; c 2. *Educ:* Yale Univ, BA, 50, MA, 51; State Univ NY Stony Brook, MS, 75; Stevens Inst Technol, MS, 81. *Prof Exp:* Asst physics, Yale Univ, 54-59, res assoc, 59-61; from assoc physicist to physicist, Brookhaven Nat Lab, 61-75; mem tech staff, Bell Labs, 75-80. *Concurrent Pos:* Ford fel, Europ Orgn Nuclear Res, Switz, 63-64. *Mem:* AAAS; Asn Comput Mach; Inst Elec & Electronics Engrs. *Res:* Computer sciences; communication science; digital systems; data analysis. *Mailing Add:* 70 Great Hills Rd Short Hills NJ 07078

ROSENBLUM, MARVIN, MATHEMATICS. *Current Pos:* from asst prof to assoc prof, 55-65, chmn dept, 69-72, prof math, 65-78, COMMONWEALTH PROF MATH, UNIV VA, 78- *Personal Data:* b Brooklyn, NY, June 30, 26; m 59; c 5. *Educ:* Univ Calif, BS, 49, MA, 51, PhD(math), 55. *Prof Exp:* Actg instr math, Univ Calif, 54-55. *Concurrent Pos:* Mem, Inst Advan Study, 59-60. *Mem:* Am Math Soc; Math Asn Am; Soc Indust & Appl Math. *Res:* Hilbert space; harmonic analysis. *Mailing Add:* Kerchof Hall Univ Va Charlottesville VA 22903-3199

ROSENBLUM, MYRON, ORGANIC CHEMISTRY. *Current Pos:* from asst prof to assoc prof, 58-66, PROF CHEM, BRANDEIS UNIV, 66- *Personal Data:* b New York, NY, Oct 20, 25; m 58. *Educ:* Columbia Univ, AB, 49; Harvard Univ, AM, 50, PhD(chem), 54. *Prof Exp:* Res assoc, Columbia Univ, 53-55; asst prof chem, Ill Inst Technol, 55-58. *Concurrent Pos:* Guggenheim fel, 65-66; vis prof, Israel Inst Technol, 66. *Mem:* Am Chem Soc; Royal Soc Chem. *Res:* Organometallic chemistry of the transition elements; reaction mechanisms; synthesis. *Mailing Add:* Dept Chem Brandeis Univ Waltham MA 02154-2700

ROSENBLUM, ROBERT, COMPUTER & INFORMATION SCIENCE. *Current Pos:* SOFTWARE RESEARCHER, METROLIGHT STUDIOS, LOS ANGELES, 90- *Educ:* Univ Ill, BS, 87; Ohio State Univ, MS, 90. *Mailing Add:* MetroLight Studios 5724 W Third St Suite 400 Los Angeles CA 90036-3078

ROSENBLUM, SAM, GEOCHEMISTRY. *Current Pos:* CONSULT GEOL, 81- *Personal Data:* b New York, NY, Jan 25, 23; m 47; c 2. *Educ:* City Col New York, BS, 49; Stanford Univ, MS, 51. *Prof Exp:* Geologist, US Bur Reclamation, 51; geologist, Br Mineral Deposits, 52-57, Br Foreign Geol, Taiwan, 57-61, Geochem Census Unit, 61-63, Br Mil Geol, 63-65, Br Foreign Geol, Bolivia, 65-67, Off Int Geol, Liberia, 67-72, mineralogist, Br Explor Res, US Geol Surv, 72-80. *Mem:* Geol Soc Am; Mineral Soc Am; Int Asn Geochem & Cosmochem; Soc Environ Geochem & Health; Asn Explor Geochemists. *Res:* Mineralogy; petrography; geochemistry; economic and exploration geology; rare-earth element mineralogy; application of geochemistry to health studies. *Mailing Add:* 12165 W Ohio Pl Lakewood CO 80228

ROSENBLUM, STEPHEN SAUL, SEMICONDUCTOR EQUIPMENT MANUFACTURING, PLASMA PROCESSING. *Current Pos:* SR SCIENTIST, ADVAN ENERGY INDUSTS, INC, 95- *Personal Data:* b Brooklyn, NY, Sept 26, 42; m 72, Ellen McLaughlin; c Andrew & Leah. *Educ:* Columbia Univ, AB, 63; Univ Calif, Berkeley, PhD(chem), 69. *Prof Exp:* Res fel physics, Calif Inst Technol, 69-70; guest lectr, Freie Univ, Berlin, 70-72; vis staff mem, Hahn-Meitner Inst, Berlin, 72-74; postdoctoral fel cryogenics, Los Alamos Sci Lab, 74-77; staff scientist physics, Lawrence Berkeley Lab, 77-85; sr engr, Varian Assocs, 85-91; sr res scientist appl electronics, Kobe Steel USA, Inc, 91-95. *Mem:* Am Phys Soc; Am Chem Soc; fel Am Inst Chemists; Am Vacuum Soc. *Res:* Development of equipment for commercial thin film manufacturing using plasma processing, principally the power supplies and applicators. *Mailing Add:* 212 Santa Rita Ave Palo Alto CA 94301

ROSENBLUM, WILLIAM I, NEUROPATHOLOGY. *Current Pos:* PROF PATH & CHMN, DIV NEUROPATH, MED COL VA, 69-, VCHMN, DEPT PATH, 79- *Personal Data:* b New York, NY, July 6, 35; m 58; c 3. *Educ:* Swarthmore Col, BA, 57; NY Univ, MD, 61. *Prof Exp:* USPHS fel path

& neuropath & intern & resident path, Sch Med, NY Univ, 61-66; assoc prof neuropath, Northwestern Univ, 68-69. *Concurrent Pos:* Res assoc, Nat Inst Neurol & Commun Disorders & Stroke & assoc pathologist, Clin Ctr, NIH, 66-68; asst pathologist, Passavant Mem Hosp, Chicago, 68-69; consult neuropath, Evanston Hosp, 68-69; mem exec comt, Coun on Stroke, Am Heart Asn. *Mem:* Am Asn Path & Bact; Am Asn Neuropath; Am Soc Exp Path; Am Physiol Soc; Microcirc Soc; Sigma Xi. *Res:* Cerebral circulation in health and disease. *Mailing Add:* Dept Pathol & Neuropath Med Col Va Va Commonwealth Univ 305 Tarrytown Dr Richmond VA 23229-7322

ROSENBLUM, WILLIAM M, PHYSICS, OPTOMETRY. *Current Pos:* PROF PHYSICS & OPTOM, UNIV ALA, BIRMINGHAM, 70- *Personal Data:* US citizen. *Educ:* Univ Miami, BS, 58; Fla State Univ, MS, 60; Tufts Univ, PhD(physics), 67. *Prof Exp:* Asst, Fla State Univ, 58-60; instr physics, Univ Miami, 60-62 & Tufts Univ, 62-66; sr scientist, Phys Optics Dept, Tech Opers, Inc, 66-68, Optical Eng Dept, Polaroid Corp, Mass, 68-69 & NASA Electronics Res Ctr, 69-70. *Concurrent Pos:* Instr, Harvard Exten Serv, 67-68 & Northeastern Univ, 69-70. *Mem:* Am Phys Soc; Optical Soc Am. *Res:* Optical design and fabrication; growth of protein crystals in a microgravity environment. *Mailing Add:* Dept Optom Univ Ala Med Ctr Birmingham AL 35294

ROSENBLUTH, JACK, NEUROCYTOLOGY, MYELIN DEFICIENCY DISEASES. *Current Pos:* assoc prof, 66-71, PROF PHYSIOL, SCH MED, NY UNIV, 71- *Personal Data:* b New York, NY, Nov 8, 30; m 60; c 3. *Educ:* Columbia Univ, AB, 52; NY Univ, MD, 56. *Honors & Awards:* Javits Neurosci Invest Award, 85. *Prof Exp:* Intern & asst resident med, Bellevue Hosp, New York, 56-58; Nat Found fel, Nat Inst Neurol Dis & Blindness, 58-59, sr asst surgeon, 59-61; USPHS spec fel, Med Ctr, Univ Calif, San Francisco, 61-62; instr anat, Harvard Med Sch, 62-63; asst prof, Albert Einstein Col Med, 63-66. *Concurrent Pos:* Mem, Neurol Study Sect B, NIH, 79-; vis prof, Univ London, 81-82; mem, Sci Peer Rev Comt A, Nat Mult Sclerosis Soc, 90- *Mem:* AAAS; Am Asn Anatomists; Soc Neurosci; Am Soc Cell Biol. *Res:* Neurobiology, neuroglial interactions, demyelination, remyelination, glial transplantation. *Mailing Add:* Dept Physiol & Neurosci Sch Med NY Univ 400 E 34th St RR714 New York NY 10016. *Fax:* 212-263-7191

ROSENBLUTH, MARSHALL N, THEORETICAL PHYSICS. *Current Pos:* prof, 87-93, EMER PROF PHYSICS, UNIV CALIF, SAN DIEGO, 93-; SCIENTIST, ITERUS SAN DIEGO JOINT WORK SITE, 97. *Personal Data:* b Albany, NY, Feb 5, 27; m 51; c 2. *Educ:* Harvard Univ, BS, 45; Univ Chicago, PhD, 49. *Honors & Awards:* Nat Medal of Sci, 97. *Prof Exp:* Instr physics, Stanford Univ, 49-50; mem staff, Los Alamos Sci Lab, Univ Calif, 50-56; sr res adv, Gen Dynamics Corp, 56-60; prof physics, Univ Calif, San Diego, 60-67; vis prof astrophys sci, Sch Natural Sci, Inst Advan Study, Princeton Univ, 67-80, vis res physicist, Plasma Physics Lab, 67-80; fac mem, Inst Fusion Studies, Univ Tex, 80-87. *Concurrent Pos:* Fac mem, Dept Physics, Princeton Univ. *Mem:* Nat Acad Sci; fel Am Phys Soc. *Res:* Physics of plasmas. *Mailing Add:* Dept Physics 0319 Univ Calif 9500 Gillman Dr La Jolla CA 92093. *Fax:* 619-542-8602

ROSENBLUTH, SIDNEY ALAN, PHARMACY. *Current Pos:* PROF & DEAN, SCH PHARM, WVA UNIV, 81- *Personal Data:* b Deport, Tex, Nov 20, 33; m 62; c 2. *Educ:* Univ Okla, BS, 55; Univ Tex, MS, 62, PhD(pharm), 66. *Prof Exp:* Pharmacist, Swindle Pharm, Tex, 55-56; hosp pharm resident, Med Ctr Pharm Serv, Univ Ark, 60-61; exchange pharmacist, Univ Hosp Pharm, Copenhagen, 61-62; res assoc, Drug-Plastic Res & Toxicol Lab, Univ Tex, 62-66; res fel, Univ Bath, 66; from asst prof to assoc prof pharmaceut, Col Pharm, Univ Tenn, Memphis, 66-71, prof, 71-75, asst dean clin affairs & chief clin pharm, 73-75, asst dean student affairs, 75-79, assoc dean, 79-81. *Concurrent Pos:* Mead Johnson Labs res grant pharm, 68-69; NIMH res grant & prin investr, 71-73, 76-79, 78-82; Am Cancer Soc, Tenn Div & Regional Med Prog, res grant & prin investr, 73-75; Vet Admin, training grant & prin investr, 74-78; NIMH, training grant & prin investr, 74-78; NIH Bur Health Manpower Educ, res grant & prin investr, 75-78; training grant & prin investr, NIMH, 76-80 & 78-82 & Dept Educ, 80-83. *Mem:* AAAS; Am Acad Pharmaceut Sci; Tissue Cult Asn; NY Acad Sci. *Res:* Use of tissue cultures in investigations of pharmacological and toxicological actions of drugs and chemicals; development and evaluation of new roles and education units for pharmacists in health care delivery. *Mailing Add:* 141 Poplar Dr Morgantown WV 26505-2540

ROSENBROCK, HOWARD H, ENGINEERING. *Current Pos:* EMER PROF, DEPT ELEC ENG & ELECTRONICS, INST SCI & TECHNOL UNIV MANCHESTER, ENG. *Personal Data:* b Dec 16, 20; m 50, Cathryn J Press; c Philip A, Jennifer E & Gina M. *Educ:* Univ Col London, BSc, 41; London Univ, DSc, 63. *Hon Degrees:* DSc, Univ Salford, 87. *Honors & Awards:* Moulton Medal, Inst Chem Engrs, 57; Heaviside Premium, Inst Elec Engrs, 67; Sir Harold Hartley Medal, Inst MC, 70; Control Systs Sci & Eng Award, Inst Elec & Electronics Engrs, 82; Rufus Oldenburger Medal, Am Soc Mech Engrs, 94 110. *Prof Exp:* Res mgr, CJB. *Mem:* Fel Inst Elec Engrs; fel Inst Chem Engrs; fel Royal Soc. *Res:* Theory and application of control; social implications of science and technology. *Mailing Add:* Univ Manchester Control Systs Ctr PO Box 88 Manchester M6O IQD England

ROSENBROOK, WILLIAM, JR, ORGANIC CHEMISTRY. *Current Pos:* sr res chemist, Dept Biochem Res, Abbott Labs, 65-70, Dept Microbiol Chem, 70-74, Dept Chem Res, 74-82, RES INVESTR, ANTI-INFECTIVE DIV, ABBOTT LABS, 82- *Personal Data:* b Omaha, Nebr, Mar 28, 38; m 69, Jeannette Miller; c William W & Edward. *Educ:* Univ Omaha, BA, 60; Mont State Univ, PhD(org chem), 64. *Prof Exp:* Fel, Univ Calif, Berkeley, 64-65. *Mem:* AAAS; Am Chem Soc; Sigma Xi. *Res:* Synthesis of antibiotics and anti-viral agents. *Mailing Add:* Anti-Infective Res Div Dept 47D Abbott Labs Abbott Park IL 60064

ROSENBURG, DALE WEAVER, ORGANIC CHEMISTRY. *Current Pos:* RETIRED. *Personal Data:* b Hannibal, Mo, Dec 2, 27; m 54; c 3. *Educ:* Culver-Stockton Col, AB, 50; Univ Mo, AM, 51, PhD(org chem), 58. *Prof Exp:* Jr chemist, Merck & Co, Inc, NJ, 51-55, chemist, Pa, 58-60, sr chemist & sect leader process develop org chem, Va, 60-64, sect leader process res org chem, NJ, 64-66; from asst prof to prof chem, NW MO State Univ, 66-86. *Mem:* Am Chem Soc; Sigma Xi. *Res:* Process research and development in the synthesis and manufacture of organic compounds of biological interest. *Mailing Add:* Carley Brook Honesdale PA 18431

ROSENCRANS, STEVEN I, MATHEMATICS. *Current Pos:* from asst prof to assoc prof, 65-75, PROF MATH, TULANE UNIV, 75- *Personal Data:* b Brooklyn, NY, Mar 13, 38; m 67, Nancy Marshall; c William, Louie, Timothy, Margaret & Robert. *Educ:* Mass Inst Technol, SB, 60, PhD(math), 64. *Prof Exp:* Instr math, Mass Inst Technol, 64-65. *Concurrent Pos:* Vis assoc prof, Univ NMex, 71-72. *Res:* Mathematical physics; partial differential equations; stochastic processes. *Mailing Add:* Tulane Univ New Orleans LA 70118-5698. *E-Mail:* sir@tulmath.math.tulane.edu

ROSENCWAIG, ALLAN, PHYSICS. *Current Pos:* PRES, THERMA-WAVE INC, 82- *Personal Data:* b Poland, Jan 1, 41; US citizen. *Educ:* Univ Toronto, BASc, 63, MA, 65, PhD(physics), 69. *Prof Exp:* Mem tech staff solid state res, Bell Labs, 69-76; sr scientist, Gilford Instrument Labs, 76-77; physicist, Lawrence Livermore Labs, 77-82. *Concurrent Pos:* Ed, J Photoacoust. *Mem:* Am Chem Soc; Am Optical Soc; Am Phys Soc. *Res:* Thermal-wave imaging; photoacoustics. *Mailing Add:* 3304 Deer Hollow Dr Danville CA 94506-6044

ROSENDAHL, BRUCE RAY, CONTINENTAL RIFTS, ANALYSIS SEISMIC DATA STRUCTURE & STRATIGRAPHY. *Current Pos:* DIR, PROJ PROBE, GEOPHYS, INC, 82-,WEEKS PROF GEOPHYS, ROSENSTEIL SCH MARINE & ATMOSPHERIC SCI, UNIV MIAMI, 89-, DEAN, 89- *Personal Data:* b Jamestown, NY, Dec 28, 46; m 69; c 2. *Educ:* Univ Hawaii, BS, 70, MS, 72; Univ Calif, San Diego, PhD(earth sci), 76. *Prof Exp:* Postodctoral fel geophys, Scripps Inst Oceanog, 76; from asst prof to prof geophys, Dept Geol, Duke Univ, 76-89. *Concurrent Pos:* Consult, World Bank, Maj Petrol Cos, 76-; adv, Nat Geol Mag, 87-89, PBS Nova TV Spec, 88-89 & Time-Life Bks, 88-89; vpres & chief operating officer, Int Oceanog Found, 89-; tech ed, Sea Frontiers Mag, 89-; dean, Rosentiel Sch Marine & Atmospheric Sci, Univ Miami, 89-; bd dirs, Cono-Sur, Inc, 89-; bd gov, Joint Oceanog Insts, 89-; bd contributors, Miami Herald, 90- *Mem:* Joint Oceanog Insts; Am Geophys Union; Am Asn Petrol Geologists. *Res:* Rifted plate margins and continental rifting using exploration seismic methods; authored more than 100 scientific publications on subjects like Tectono-Stratigraphy, seismic models, and the geometry of rifting; continental rifts and paleo-rift margins-project Probe. *Mailing Add:* Marine Sci Univ Miami PO Box 248106 Miami FL 33124-8106

ROSENDAHL, GOTTFRIED R, OPTICAL SYSTEMS & LENS DESIGN. *Current Pos:* RETIRED. *Personal Data:* b Borna, Ger, Mar 25, 11; nat US; m 39; c 4. *Educ:* Dresden Tech, Dipl Eng, 35, Dr Eng, 38; Johns Hopkins Univ, MA, 36. *Prof Exp:* Res asst, Dresden Tech, 38-40; head optics lab, E Leitz, Inc, Ger, 40-42, sr scientist, Peenemuende, Ger, 43-46; head optics lab, E Leitz, Inc, 46-53; consult physics, Air Defense Command, Holloman AFB, NMex, 53-54; tech dir, E Leitz, Inc, NY, 54-57; sr scientist, Ball Bros Res Corp, Colo, 58-60, Gen Elec Co, 60-62, Fed Lab, Int Tel & Tel Corp, 63-64 & Link Group, Gen Precision, Inc, NY, 64-67; res physicist, Naval Training Equip Ctr, 67-78. *Concurrent Pos:* Lectr, Univ Pa, 61-62, Exten Ctr, Purdue Univ, 63-64, State Univ NY Binghamton, 66-67 & Univ Cent Fla, 79, 80 & 87. *Mem:* Fel Optical Soc Am. *Res:* Physical and geometrical optics; optical systems and instruments; photometry and radiometry; metrology. *Mailing Add:* 2079 Penguin Ct Oviedo FL 32765

ROSENDORFF, CLIVE, CARDIOLOGY. *Current Pos:* Alexander B Gutman prof in residence, 90-91, PROF MED & ASSOC CHMN, MT SINAI SCH MED, 91-; CHIEF MED SERV, VET ADMIN MED CTR, BRONX, 91- *Personal Data:* b Bloemfontein, SAfrica, Mar 28, 38. *Educ:* Univ Witwatersrand, SAfrica, BSc Hons, 58, MB BCh, 62, MD, 77, DSc, 84; Univ London, PhD, 69. *Prof Exp:* Lectr & consult physician, St Thomas Hosp Med Sch, 65-69; sir Otto Beit prof, chmn, Dept Physiol & sr physician, Dept Med, Univ Witwatersrand, 70-91, dean, Med Sch, 87-89. *Concurrent Pos:* Vis prof med & cardiol, Sch Med, Yale Univ, 69-70, Cardiovasc Res Inst, Univ Calif, San Francisco, 77-78 & Hosp Lariboisiere, Paris, 90. *Mem:* Fel Am Col Physicians; fel Am Col Cardiol; fel Royal Soc; fel Royal Col Physicians. *Res:* Hypertension; role of adrenergic receptors in the regulation of arterial blood pressure; abnormalities in hypertension; receptor-effector coupling mechanisms in vascular smooth muscle cells; pharmacologic management of high blood pressure. *Mailing Add:* Mt Sinai Sch Med Dept Med Box 9000 1 Gustave L Levy Pl New York NY 10029. *Fax:* 718-579-1635; *E-Mail:* rosendorff.clive@bronx.va.gov

ROSENE, WALTER, JR, WILDLIFE ECOLOGY, WILDLIFE MANAGEMENT. *Current Pos:* CONSULT WILDLIFE MGT, 69- *Personal Data:* b Ogden, Iowa, May 15, 12; m 37, Kathryn Giles; c 2. *Educ:* Iowa State Univ, BS, 34; Auburn Univ, MS, 37. *Prof Exp:* Game technician, Iowa State Planning Bd, 34-35; technician, Ala State Conserv Comn, 38; proj biologist, Soil Conserv Serv, USDA, 38-39, area biologist, 39-40, conservationist, 40-46; biologist, US Fish & Wildlife Serv, 46-69. *Concurrent Pos:* Spec writing proj, NAm Wildlife Found, 64-70; vis prof, Miss State Univ, 78. *Mem:* Wildlife Soc. *Res:* Ecology and population dynamics of the bobwhite quail and mourning dove in the southeast; evaluation of introduced plants in wildlife management; evaluation of effects of insecticides on wildlife. *Mailing Add:* 127 Oak Circle Gadsden AL 35901

ROSENFELD, ARTHUR H, NUCLEAR PHYSICS. *Current Pos:* from asst prof to prof, 57-94, actg chmn, Dept Comput Sci, 67-68, EMER PROF PHYSICS, UNIV CALIF, BERKELEY, 94-; SR ADV TO ASST SECY ENERGY EFFICIENCY & RENEWABLE ENERGY, DEPT ENERGY, 94- *Personal Data:* b Birmingham, Ala, June 22, 26; m 55; c 3. *Educ:* Va Polytech Univ, BS, 44; Univ Chicago, PhD(physics), 54. *Hon Degrees:* DSc, Univ Durham, Eng, 83. *Honors & Awards:* Leo Szilard Award, Am Phys Soc, 86; Sadi Carnot Award Energy Conserv, 93; Star of Energy Efficiency Award, 95. *Prof Exp:* Res assoc, Inst Nuclear Studies, Univ Chicago, 54-55; res assoc, Lawrence Berkeley Lab, 55-64, dir, Particle Data Group, 64-75, leader, Particle Physics Res Group A, 71-73, leader, Energy-Efficient Bldgs Res Prog, 75-86, dir, Ctr Bldg Sci, 86-94. *Concurrent Pos:* Mem comt uses comput, Nat Acad Sci-Nat Res Coun, 62-65 & statist data panel, Physics Surv Comt, 70-72; mem panel univ comput facil, NSF, 63-66, chmn, 65-66, chief investr, Univ Comput Facil Grant, 70-72; assoc ed, J Comput Physics, 64-73, Energy & Buildings, 79- & Energy, The Int J, 88-; mem subpanel B, High Energy Physics Adv Panel, AEC, 67-69; mem, Physics Info Comt, Am Inst Physics, 69-71; mem, Energy Comt, Fedn Am Scientists, 77-; vis prof, Col France, Paris, 78; co-founder, Am Coun Energy Efficient Economy, 79, chmn, 81-83, pres, 84-90, bd mem, 90-94; founder & actg dir, Calif Inst Energy Efficiency, Univ Calif, 88-90, res bd mem, 90-94; bd dirs, Int Inst Energy Conserv, 92-94; co-chair, Subcomt Construct & Bldg, Civilian Indust Technol Comt, Nat Sci & Technol Coun, 94- *Mem:* Fel Am Phys Soc; Fedn Am Scientists. *Res:* Physics of elementary particles; use of digital computers to process data; energy policy and utilization; author of 345 scientific papers. *Mailing Add:* US Dept Energy 1000 Independence Ave SW EE-1 Washington DC 20585

ROSENFELD, AZRIEL, COMPUTER VISION, IMAGE PROCESSING. *Current Pos:* RES PROF, UNIV MD, COLLEGE PARK, 64-, DIR, CTR AUTOMATION RES, 83- *Personal Data:* b New York, NY, Feb 19, 31; m 59, Eve Hertzberg; c Elie, David & Tova. *Educ:* Yeshiva Univ, BA, 50, MHL, 53, MS, 54, DHL, 55; Columbia Univ, MA, 51, PhD(math), 57. *Hon Degrees:* DTech, Linkoping Univ, Sweden, 80, Dulu Univ, Finland, 94. *Honors & Awards:* Piore Award, Inst Elec & Electronics Engrs, 85; Pres Award, Math Vision Asn, 87; Fu Award, Int Asn Pattern Recognition, 88; Boode Award, Inst Elec & Electronics Engrs Comput Soc, Wiener Award. *Prof Exp:* Physicist, Fairchild Controls Corp, 54-56; engr, Ford Instrument Co, 56-59; mgr res, Budd Electronics Inc, 59-64. *Concurrent Pos:* Vis asst prof, Grad Sch Math, Yeshiva Univ, 58-63; pres, Asn Orthodox Jewish Scientists, 63-65; pres, IM Tech Inc, 75-92; dir, Mach Vision Asn, 85-88. *Mem:* Math Asn Am; fel Inst Elec & Electronics Engrs; fel Int Asn Comput Mach; fel Int Asn Pattern Recognition (pres, 80-84); fel Am Asn Artificial Intel. *Res:* Computer processing of pictorial information. *Mailing Add:* 847 Loxford Terr Silver Spring MD 20901-1132

ROSENFELD, CARL, EXPERIMENTAL HIGH ENERGY PHYSICS. *Current Pos:* ASSOC PROF, UNIV SC, 86- *Personal Data:* b Baltimore, Md, Dec 25, 44. *Educ:* Mass Inst Technol, BS, 66; Calif Inst Technol, PhD(physic), 77. *Honors & Awards:* Outstanding Jr Investr, Dept Energy, 86. *Prof Exp:* Res assoc, Univ Rochester, 77-81, sr res assoc, 81-84; asst prof, res, La State Univ, 84-85. *Mem:* Am Phys Soc. *Res:* Elementary particles; electron positron annihilation at high energy. *Mailing Add:* Dept Physics Univ SC Columbia SC 29208. *Fax:* 803-777-3065; *E-Mail:* carl@scuche.psc.scarolina.edu

ROSENFELD, CHARLES RICHARD, NEONATAL-PERINATAL MEDICINE, DEVELOPMENTAL BIOLOGY. *Current Pos:* from asst prof to GEORGE L MACGREGOR PROF PEDIAT, UNIV TEX SOUTHWESTERN MED SCH, 73- *Personal Data:* b Atlanta, Ga, Aug 25, 41; m 71, Ann Marie Anderson; c Evan L, Scott B & Jason A. *Educ:* Emory Univ, MD, 66. *Prof Exp:* Intern, Yale-New Haven Hosp, 66-67; from resident to chief resident, Albert Einstein Col Med, 67-71; postdoctoral fel, Sch Med, Univ Colo, 71-73. *Concurrent Pos:* Assoc ed, Early Human Develop & J Soc Gynec Invest. *Mem:* Soc Pediat Res; Am Pediat Soc; Am Physiol Soc; Endocrine Soc; Soc Perinatal Res; Soc Gynec Invest. *Res:* Cardiovascular adaptation in pregnancy and in the fetus and neonate specifically, ontogeny of smooth muscle proteins and receptors. *Mailing Add:* Dept Pediat Univ Tex Southwestern Med Ctr 5323 Harry Hines Blvd Dallas TX 75235

ROSENFELD, DANIEL DAVID, PETROLEUM CHEMISTRY. *Personal Data:* b Brooklyn, NY, May 7, 33; m 57; c 2. *Educ:* Brooklyn Col, BS, 55; Univ Pa, MS, 57, PhD(org chem), 61. *Prof Exp:* Res chemist, Esso Res & Eng Co, 60-66, sr res chemist, 66-71, res assoc, 71-88, head aromatics tech serv, 72-79, head, Aromatics Lab, Exxon Chem Co, 79-88. *Mem:* Am Chem Soc. *Res:* Synthesis of solid rocket propellants; reactions in aprotic solvents; synthesis and screening of agricultural pesticides; process development; ketone solvents; hydotreating desulphurization studies; catalyst evaluations; zeolite adsorption. *Mailing Add:* Exxon Chem Co PO Box 4900 Baytown TX 77522-4900

ROSENFELD, GEORGE, MEDICAL RESEARCH, ENDOCRINOLOGY. *Current Pos:* BIOMED CONSULT, 64- *Personal Data:* b Cambridge, Mass, Nov 6, 19; m 59, Ida Ray Herman. *Educ:* Mass Inst Technol, BS, 40, MS, 41; Geogetown Univ, PhD(biochem), 52. *Honors & Awards:* Res Commendation, US Navy, 56. *Prof Exp:* Asst chemist, Mass State Dept Pub Health, 41-43; asst toxicologist, Med Res Div, US War Dept, 42; mem staff, Med Sch, Cornell Univ, 43-46; officer-in-chg, Navy Chem Warfare Sch, Calif, 46-50 & Naval Med Res Inst, 50-57; assoc res physiologist, Univ Calif, Berkeley, 57-60, res biochemist, 60-63. *Mem:* Endocrine Soc; Am Physiol Soc; Sigma Xi; fel AAAS. *Res:* Stress physiology; endocrinopathy; acute and chronic alcoholism; neurohormones; radiation medicine. *Mailing Add:* 50 Vista Del Mar Ct Oakland CA 94611

ROSENFELD, ISADORE, MEDICINE. *Current Pos:* clin asst prof, 64-71, CLIN PROF MED, CORNELL UNIV COL MED, 79-; ATTEND PHYSICIAN, NY HOSP, 78- *Personal Data:* b Montreal, Que, Sept 7, 26; US citizen; m 56, Camilla Master; c Arthur, Stephen, Hildi (Silbert) & Herbert. *Educ:* McGill Univ, BSc, 47, MD & CM, 51; FRCPS(C). *Honors & Awards:* Grand Ufficiale Italian Order of Merit, 93. *Prof Exp:* Attend physician, Mem Hosp, 78-. *Concurrent Pos:* Hatch Cummings vis prof med, Methodist Hosp, Baylor Col Med, 82; mem, Bd Visitors, Sch Med, Univ Calif, Davis, 82; chmn, Found Biomed Res; fel Coun Epidemiol, Am Heart Asn. *Mem:* Fel Am Col Physicians; fel Am Col Chest Physicians; fel Am Col Cardiol; NY Acad Sci. *Res:* Clinical cardiology, author of various medical publications. *Mailing Add:* 125 E 72nd St New York NY 10021

ROSENFELD, JACK LEE, COMPUTER SCIENCE, TECHNICAL EDITING. *Current Pos:* Res staff mem comput sci, T J Watson Res Ctr, 61-89, ASSOC ED, IBM J RES & DEVELOP, IBM CORP, 89- *Personal Data:* b Pittsburgh, Pa, June 6, 35; m 69, Annelise Kjaer; c Helen & Erik. *Educ:* Mass Inst Technol, SB & SM, 57, ScD(elec eng), 61. *Honors & Awards:* Silver Core, Int Fedn Info Processing, 77. *Concurrent Pos:* Adj prof, Columbia Univ, 65-72. *Mem:* Int Fedn Info Processing; Inst Elec & Electronics Engrs. *Res:* Computer architecture; parallel processing; distributed systems. *Mailing Add:* IBM J Res & Develop PO Box 218 Yorktown Heights NY 10598-0218. *Fax:* 914-945-2018; *E-Mail:* rosenj@watson.ibm.com

ROSENFELD, JEROLD CHARLES, ORGANIC CHEMISTRY, POLYMER CHEMISTRY. *Current Pos:* SR RES CHEMIST, OCCIDENTAL PETROL CORP, GRAND ISLAND, 70- *Personal Data:* b New Haven, Conn, Apr 13, 43; m 67, Jane Berol; c Joanna E & Andrew E. *Educ:* Clark Univ, BA, 65; Yale Univ, PhD(chem), 70. *Mem:* Am Chem Soc. *Res:* Preparation of non-burning and high temperature plastics. *Mailing Add:* 18 Willow Green Dr Amherst NY 14228-3420

ROSENFELD, JOHN L, GEOLOGY. *Current Pos:* from asst prof to prof, 57-91, EMER PROF GEOL, UNIV CALIF, LOS ANGELES, 91- *Personal Data:* b Portland, Ore, July 14, 20; m 43, Juanita Baker; c Susan J & John L Jr. *Educ:* Dartmouth Col, AB, 42; Harvard Univ, AM, 49, PhD(geol), 54. *Prof Exp:* Asst prof geol, Mo Sch Mines, 49-55; vis asst prof, Wesleyan Univ, 55-57. *Concurrent Pos:* Comn, Conn Geol & Natural Hist Surv, 55-57; Guggenheim fel, 63; res assoc, Harvard Univ, 63-64 & 71-72. *Mem:* AAAS; fel Geol Soc Am; fel Mineral Soc Am; Am Geophys Union. *Res:* Structure, petrology and stratigraphy of metamorphic rocks in western New England; application of physical and chemical properties of minerals to petrology; structural petrology; solid inclusion piezothermometry; tectonometamorphic rates; schistosity. *Mailing Add:* 2401 Arbutus Dr Los Angeles CA 90049-1208. *Fax:* 310-825-2779; *E-Mail:* ibenavw@mvs.oac.ucla.edu

ROSENFELD, LEONARD M, PHYSIOLOGY, BIOCHEMISTRY. *Current Pos:* Instr physiol, Jefferson Med Col, 64-68, physiol coordr, Sch Nursing, Col Allied Health Sci, 74-75, Jefferson Med Col, 75-80, coordr, Struct & Function Course Anat & Physiol, 77-79, ASST PROF PHYSIOL, JEFFERSON MED COL, THOMAS JEFFERSON UNIV, 68-, CLIN PROF, COL ALLIED HEALTH SCI, 84- *Personal Data:* b Philadelphia, Pa, June 28, 38; m 62; c 3. *Educ:* Univ Pa, AB, 59; Jefferson Med Col, PhD(physiol), 64. *Concurrent Pos:* Vis lectr, Pa State Univ, Ogontz Campus, 69-71, vis prof, 71-74. *Mem:* AAAS; Soc Exp Biol & Med; Am Physiol Soc; Sigma Xi. *Res:* Medical/science education; history of medicine; electrolyte interactions in metabolic systems; factors influencing the phosphatase enzyme system; environmental biology; biological effects of air pollution; acute biochemical changes following myocardial infarction; intestinal integrity; alteration in intestinal blood flow; malnutrition. *Mailing Add:* Dept Physiol Jefferson Med Col 1025 Walnut St Philadelphia PA 19107-5001

ROSENFELD, LOUIS, BIOCHEMISTRY, CLINICAL CHEMISTRY. *Current Pos:* asst prof, 61-67, dir chem, Univ Hosp, 61-73, ASSOC PROF CLIN PATH, MED CTR, NY UNIV, 67-, DIR SPEC CHEM, UNIV HOSP, 73- *Personal Data:* b Brooklyn, NY, Apr 8, 25. *Educ:* City Col New York, BS, 46; Ohio State Univ, MS, 48, PhD(physiol chem), 52. *Prof Exp:* Asst instr physiol chem, Ohio State Univ, 52; res assoc biochem, Univ Va, 52-53; biochemist, Wayne Co Gen Hosp, 54-56 & Beth-El Hosp, 56-61. *Concurrent Pos:* Instr sci, Rutgers Univ, Newark, 57-63. *Mem:* Fel AAAS; Asn Clin Sci; Nat Acad Clin Biochem; Am Asn Clin Chem. *Res:* Fibrinogen; plasma coagulation; heparin; electrophoresis; protein analysis, glycosaminoglycans, thyroid hormones; history of chemistry and medicine. *Mailing Add:* 1417 E 52nd St Brooklyn NY 11234

ROSENFELD, MARTIN HERBERT, MICROBIOLOGY, CLINICAL BIOCHEMISTRY. *Current Pos:* assoc prof, 70-74, chmn Div Diag Progs, 70-77, PROF MED TECHNOL, SCH ALLIED HEALTH PROF, STATE UNIV NY, STONY BROOK, 74-, CHMN DEPT MED TECHNOL, 70-, ASST DEAN GRAD PROGS, 73- *Personal Data:* b Rockaway Beach, NY, May 30, 26; m 52; c 2. *Educ:* Brooklyn Col, BA, 50; St John's Univ, MS, 62, PhD(microbiol), 72. *Prof Exp:* Supvr labs, A Angrist, 50-55 & Horace Harding Hosp, 55-60; lab adminr, Montefiore-Morrisania Hosp Affil, 63-70. *Concurrent Pos:* Mem & chmn nat comt instnl orgn, Asn Schs Allied Health Prof, 71-74; mem bd adv, NY City Dept Lab Supvrs, 79-83; med technologist, Am Soc Clin Pathologists, 52-; clin lab scientist, Nat Cert Agency Med Lab Personnel, 79-; consult med technol educ, Marshall Univ, WVa, 85- *Mem:* Am Am Soc Clin Chem; NY Acad Sci; Am Soc Microbiol; Am Asn Bioanalysts; Am Inst Biol Sci; fel Nat Acad Clin Biochem; fel Asn Clin Scientists. *Res:* Detection of microorganisms and quantitative assay of blood constituents by automated chemiluminescent technique; ratios and analysis of lipids by infra-red spectroscopy. *Mailing Add:* Div Med Technol State Univ NY Health Sci Col Med Stony Brook NY 11794-0001

ROSENFELD, MELVIN, MATHEMATICS. *Current Pos:* from lectr to asst prof, 64-70, ASSOC PROF MATH, UNIV CALIF, SANTA BARBARA, 70- *Personal Data:* b New York, NY, Apr 19, 34; m 57; c 1. *Educ:* Univ Calif, Los Angeles, BA, 56, MA, 62, PhD(math), 63. *Prof Exp:* Lectr math, Univ Calif, Los Angeles, 63-64. *Concurrent Pos:* NSF grant, 66-67. *Mem:* Am Math Soc; Math Asn Am. *Res:* Functional analysis. *Mailing Add:* 401 Yankee Farm Rd Santa Barbara CA 93109-1054

ROSENFELD, MELVIN ARTHUR, sedimentology, academic administration, for more information see previous edition

ROSENFELD, MICHAEL G, MEDICINE. *Current Pos:* postdoctoral fel, 71-72, from asst prof to prof biol, 72-83, PROF, DEPT MED, SCH MED, UNIV CALIF, 83- *Educ:* Johns Hopkins Univ, BA, 62; Univ Rochester, MD, 66. *Honors & Awards:* Ernst Oppenheimer Award, 83. *Prof Exp:* Intern resident, Sch Med, Washington Univ, 66-71. *Concurrent Pos:* Postdoctoral fel, Nat Cancer Inst, NIH, 68-70; investr, Howard Hughes Med Inst, 85-; adj prof, Salk Inst, 85-, Scripps Res Inst, 96- *Mem:* Nat Acad Sci; Am Acad Arts & Sci. *Res:* Sensory and motor neurons; Ames dwarfism; over 150 published articles. *Mailing Add:* Dept Medicine Sch Med Univ Calif San Diego M-013 La Jolla CA 92093. *Fax:* 619-534-8180; *E-Mail:* mrosenfeld@ucsd.edu

ROSENFELD, NORMAN SAMUEL, MATHEMATICS. *Current Pos:* assoc prof, 68-79, deal col, 80-94, PROF MATH, YESHIVA UNIV, 79-, DEAN COL, 80- *Personal Data:* b New York, NY, July 21, 34; m 78, Barbara Goodman; c Shoshana, Jennie & Joseph. *Educ:* Yeshiva Univ, BA, 54; Syracuse Univ, MA, 56; Yale Univ, PhD(math), 59. *Prof Exp:* Res asst, Yale Univ, 57-58; lectr, City Col New York, 58-59; asst res scientist, Courant Inst Math Sci, NY Univ, 59-61; from asst prof to assoc prof, NY Univ, 61-68. *Concurrent Pos:* Vis asst prof, Belfer Grad Sch Sci, Yeshiva Univ, 60-61. *Mem:* Am Math Soc; Math Asn Am. *Res:* Functional analysis. *Mailing Add:* Dept Math Yeshiva Univ 500 W 185th St New York NY 10033-3299. *E-Mail:* rosenfel@yu1.yu.edu

ROSENFELD, ROBERT L, APPLIED MECHANICS, COMPUTER SCIENCE. *Current Pos:* PROG MGR, DEFENSE ADVAN RES PROG, 85- *Personal Data:* b New York, NY, Aug 6, 37; m 59; c 2. *Educ:* Mass Inst Technol, SB, 59; Calif Inst Technol, PhD(appl mech), 62. *Prof Exp:* Engr, Components Div, IBM Corp, 62-64; mem tech staff, RCA Labs, 64-69; mgr applns dept, Appl Logic Corp, 69-70; staff analyst, Computer Servs Dept, Consumers Power Co, 70-74, reliability & performance adminr elec prod, 74-81, nuclear planning adminr nuclear opers, 81-84; prin eng, Tech Analysis Corp, 84- 85. *Mem:* Am Soc Mech Engrs; Inst Elec & Electronics Engrs; Asn Comput Mach. *Mailing Add:* Advan Res Proj Agency 3701 N Fairfax Dr Arlington VA 22203

ROSENFELD, ROBERT SAMSON, BIOCHEMISTRY. *Current Pos:* PROF BIOCHEM, ALBERT EINSTEIN COL MED, 72- *Personal Data:* b Richmond, Va, June 24, 21; m 44; c 3. *Educ:* Univ Pittsburgh, PhD(chem), 50. *Prof Exp:* Asst prof biochem, Sloan-Kettering Div, Med Col, Cornell Univ, 50-63; INVESTR, INST STEROID RES, MONTEFIORE HOSP & MED CTR, 63- *Concurrent Pos:* Asst, Sloan-Kettering Inst Cancer Res, 50-56, assoc mem, 56-63. *Mem:* Am Chem Soc; Endocrine Soc; Am Heart Asn. *Res:* Steroid chemistry. *Mailing Add:* 5956 Kirkwall Ct Dublin OH 43017-9001

ROSENFELD, RON GERSHON, ENDOCRINOLOGY, BIOLOGY. *Current Pos:* CHAIR, PEDIAT DEPT, SCH MED, ORE UNIV, 94- *Personal Data:* b Brooklyn, NY, June 22, 46; m 68; c 2. *Educ:* Columbia Col, 68; Stanford Univ, MD, 73. *Prof Exp:* Resident pediat, Stanford Univ Med Ctr, 73-76; from asst prof to prof, Stanford Univ, 77-94. *Mem:* Am Diabetes Asn; AAAS. *Res:* Growth factors and receptors in normal and malignant cells. *Mailing Add:* Dept Pediat Ore Health Sci Univ Sch Med 3181 Sam Jackson Park Rd Portland OR 97201-3011

ROSENFELD, SHELDON, PHYSIOLOGY. *Current Pos:* RETIRED. *Personal Data:* b New York, NY, Dec 28, 21; m 53; c 4. *Educ:* Middlesex Sch Vet Med, DVM, 45; Brooklyn Col, BA, 48; Univ Calif, MS, 55; Univ Southern Calif, PhD(physiol), 64. *Prof Exp:* Asst med, Med Col, Cornell Univ, 46-48; res assoc aviation med, Sch Med, Univ Southern Calif, 48-50, instr & res assoc physiol, 50-53, asst prof, 50-53; sr res assoc, Cedars Sinai Med Res Inst, Mt Sinai Hosp, 53-86. *Mem:* Am Physiol Soc; Am Heart Asn; Soc Exp Biol & Med; Int Soc Nephrology; Am Soc Nephrology. *Res:* Renal physiology; hypertension. *Mailing Add:* 2819 Hutton Dr Beverly Hills CA 90210

ROSENFELD, STEPHEN I, ALLERGY, IMMUNOLOGY. *Current Pos:* from asst prof to assoc prof, 72-87, PROF MED, SCH MED, UNIV ROCHESTER, 87- *Personal Data:* b New York, NY, May 8, 39; m 60; c 2. Elise Golub; c Scott & David. *Educ:* Univ Rochester, BA, 59, MD, 63. *Prof Exp:* Instr med, Sch Med, Boston Univ, 70-72. *Mem:* Fel Am Acad Allergy; Am Fedn Clin Res; fel Am Col Rheumatology; Am Asn Immunol; Clin Immunol Soc. *Res:* Biological functions and genetics of the human complement system; clinical immunology; Fc receptors. *Mailing Add:* Box 695 Med Ctr Univ Rochester 601 Elmwood Ave Rochester NY 14642. *Fax:* 716-273-1070

ROSENFELD, STUART MICHAEL, SYNTHETIC CHEMISTRY. *Current Pos:* asst prof, 82-88, ASSOC PROF CHEM, SMITH COL, 88- *Personal Data:* b New Haven, Conn, Jan 28, 48. *Educ:* Colby Col, BA, 69; Brown Univ, PhD(org chem), 73. *Prof Exp:* Fel chem, Dept Chem, Brandeis Univ, 72-73 & Dyson Perrins Lab, Oxford Univ, 73-74; asst prof, Dept Chem, Univ RI, 75-77 & Univ Mass, 77-78; asst prof chem, Brandeis Univ, 78-79 & Wellesley Col, 79-82. *Mem:* Am Chem Soc; Sigma Xi. *Res:* observation and study of transient intermediates formed during chemical reactions; synthesis and structural studies of spirocyclopropyl compounds, beta-keto acids and strained aromatic compounds. *Mailing Add:* Dept Chem Smith Col Northampton MA 01063

ROSENFIELD, ALAN R(OBERT), FRACTURE MECHANICS. *Current Pos:* PRES, ROSENFIELD & ROSENFIELD, 94- *Personal Data:* b Chelsea, Mass, Sept 7, 31; m 60, Margaret A Young; c Ann B & Joel W. *Educ:* Mass Inst Technol, SB, 53, SM, 55, ScD, 59. *Prof Exp:* Metallurgist, Mass Inst Technol, 59-61; fel metall, Univ Liverpool, 61-62; res leader, Battelle Mem Inst, 62-94. *Concurrent Pos:* Consult, Open Univ, 74-85. *Mem:* Fel Am Soc Metals Int. *Res:* Fracture mechanics; advanced techniques to measure strength and toughness; relations between strength and microstructure; physical metallurgy; experimental and analytical studies of fracture resistance of engineering materials, principally steels and ceramics. *Mailing Add:* 1650 Ridgeway Pl Columbus OH 43212

ROSENFIELD, ALLAN, OBSTETRICS & GYNECOLOGY, FAMILY PLANNING. *Current Pos:* DEAN & JOSEPH R DELAMAR PROF PUB HEALTH PROF OBSTET & GYNEC, 86- *Personal Data:* b Cambridge, Mass; m, Clare Stein; c Paul A & Jill E. *Educ:* Harvard Col, BA, 55; Columbia Univ, MD, 59. *Honors & Awards:* Royal Order of White Elephant, Thailand. *Prof Exp:* Dir Hosp Serv, USAF, Osan, Korea, 61-62; Hamilton Air Force Hosp, 62-63; sr registrar dept obstet & gynecol, Univ Lagos Med Sch, Nigeria, 66-67; repr & med adv, PopCouncil, Ministry Pub Health, Thailand, 67-73; assoc dir, Tech Assistance Div, & dir, Maternal & Child Health/Family Planning Prog, Pop Council New York, 73-75; prof obstet-gynec & pub health & dir, Ctr Pop & Family Health & head, Div Pop & Family Health, Columbia Univ Sch Pub Health, 75-88. *Concurrent Pos:* Ed bds, Studies in Family Planning, 74-80, Pop Reports, 78-, Int J Gynecol & Obstet, 78-, Family Planning Perspectives, 80-, Contraceptive Technol Update, 80-; dir, div ambulatory care, dept obstet & gynecol, Columbia Presby Med Ctr, 77-86; actg chmn dept obstet & gynecol & actg dir obstet & gynecol serv, Presby Hosp, Columbia Univ, 83-85; consult, Am Pub Health Asn, World Bank, UN Fund Pop Activ, USAID, WHO, Health & Human Serv, Nat Inst Child Health & Human Develop, NY State Dept Health, New York City Dept Health; sect ed, Family Planning, Current Opinion in Obstet & Gynecol, 88-90. *Mem:* Nat Acad Sci-Inst Med; fel Am Col Obstet & Gynecol; fel Am Pub Health Asn; fel Am Fertility Soc; Asn Reproductive Health Prof; Pop Asn Am; Asn Teachers Maternal & Child Health; New York Acad Med. *Res:* Population studies; contraception; women reproductive health; domestic health policy; international health. *Mailing Add:* Sch Pub Health Columbia Univ 600 W 168th St New York NY 10032

ROSENFIELD, ARTHUR TED, DIAGNOSTIC RADIOLOGY, URINARY TRACT IMAGING. *Current Pos:* from asst prof to assoc prof, 75-83, PROF DIAG RADIOL, SCH MED, YALE UNIV, 83-, PROF UROL, 87- *Personal Data:* b Waterbury, Ct, Dec 7, 42; m 68, Nancy; c 3. *Educ:* Brandeis Univ, BA, 64; NY Univ, MD, 68; Am Bd Radiol, dipl, 74. *Hon Degrees:* MA, Yale Univ, 84. *Prof Exp:* Intern med, Montefiore Hosp, Pittsburgh, 68-69; surgeon, USPHS, Baltimore, 69-70, sr surgeon, 70-71; resident, Beth Israel Hosp, Boston, 71-73, chief resident, 73-74; instr radiol, Mass Gen Hosp, 74-75. *Concurrent Pos:* Instr med, Univ Pittsburgh, 68-69; clin fel, Harvard Med Sch, 71-74. *Mem:* Radiol Soc NAm; Am Roentgen Ray Soc; fel Soc Uroradiol; Am Col Radiol; sr mem Am Inst Ultrasound Med; Asn Univ Radiologists; Sigma Xi; Am Urol Asn. *Res:* Evaluation of urinary tract disease by imaging techniques, particularly sectional imaging; author of 150 publications; computed tomography. *Mailing Add:* Yale Univ Sch Med Dept Diag Radiol 333 Cedar St New Haven CT 06510

ROSENFIELD, DANIEL, PUBLIC HEALTH. *Current Pos:* dir sci affairs, M&M/Mars, 79-92, CORP DIR SCI AFFAIRS, MARS INC, 93- *Personal Data:* b Philadelphia, Pa, Jan 3, 32; m 71. *Educ:* Univ Mass, BS, 53; Rutgers Univ, MS, 55, PhD(food sci, biochem), 59. *Prof Exp:* Dir quality control & res, Engelhorn Meat Packing Co, 59-60; sr food technologist, Gen Foods Tech Ctr, 60-62, Off Tech Coop & Res, USAID, 65-67; group leader food proteins & plant physiol, Union Carbide Res Inst, 62-65, 67-68; dep dir nutrit & agribus group, USDA, 68-71, dir nutrit & tech serv, staff, Food & Nutrit Serv, 71-73; dir nutrit affairs, Miles Labs, Inc, 73-79. *Concurrent Pos:* US deleg workshop food, US Nat Acad Sci-Indonesian Inst Sci, 68; mem new foods panel, White House Conf Food, Nutrit & Health, 69; partic workshop prepare guidelines nat prog food enrichment & fortification, Pan Am Health Orgn, 73; mem, World Soy Protein Conf, 73 & Xth Int Cong Nutrit, 75; adj prof nutrit, Sch Med, Ind Univ, 78- *Mem:* AAAS; Inst Food Technologists; Am Chem Soc; Am Inst Nutrit. *Res:* Relationship of diets to physical well being including oral health; technology of fortification and fabrication of new foods; availability of food nutrients effectiveness of dietary supplements. *Mailing Add:* Mars Inc 6885 Elm St McLean VA 22101-3883

ROSENFIELD, JOAN E, ATMOSPHERIC RADIATIVE TRANSFER, STRATOSPHERIC CLIMATE STUDIES. *Current Pos:* sci programmer & analyst, Sigma Data Serv, 77-89, sr res scientist, Univ Space Res Asn, 89-93, SR SCIENTIST, APPL RES CORP, NASA GODDARD SPACE FLIGHT CTR, 94- *Personal Data:* b Boston, Mass, Aug 12, 39. *Educ:* Brandeis Univ, AB, 61; Univ Minn, Minneapolis, PhD(phys chem), 69. *Prof Exp:* Res asst chem, Children's Cancer Res Found, Boston, 61-62; res specialist phys chem, Univ Minn, Minneapolis, 69-71; teaching fel, 71-72; staff fel physics, Nat Inst Arthritis, Metab & Digestive Dis, 73-77. *Concurrent Pos:* Eastman Kodak sci award, 68. *Mem:* Am Meteorol Soc; Am Geophys Union. *Res:* Radiation in troposphere-stratosphere climate models; theoretical chemistry; electronic structure of molecules; Atmospheric remote sensing. *Mailing Add:* 7101 Ora Glen Ct Greenbelt MD 20770

ROSENFIELD, RICHARD ERNEST, HEMATOLOGY, IMMUNOLOGY. *Current Pos:* Resident hemat, Mt Sinai Hosp, 47-48, res asst, 48-51, clin asst, Outpatient Dept, Med Div, Hemat Clin, 48-53, res asst med, Blood Bank, 51-53, from asst to assoc hematologist, 53-61, dir, Blood Bank, 57-80, prof med, Mt Sinai Sch Med, 66-71, prof path, 72-85, prof med, 79-85, ATTEND HEMATOLOGIST, MT SINAI HOSP, 61-, EMER DIR, DEPT BLOOD BANK & CLIN MICROS, 81-, EMER PROF MED, MT SINAI SCH MED, 85- *Personal Data:* b Pittsburgh, Pa, Apr 7, 15; m 44; c 2. *Educ:* Univ Pittsburgh, BS, 36, MD, 40. *Honors & Awards:* Landsteiner Award, Am Asn Blood Banks; Philip Levine Award, Am Soc Clin Pathologists, 75. *Concurrent Pos:* Asst physician, Willard Parker Hosp, New York, 50-56; NIH res fel ABO erythroblastosis, Mt Sinai Hosp, New York, 59-70, NIH blood bank dirs training fel, 62-77, NIH contract hepatitis, New York & Boston, 72-73; ed-in-chief, Transfusion, Am Asn Blood Banks, 67-71. *Mem:* NY Acad Sci; Am Soc Clin Pathologists; Int Soc Hemat; Int Soc Blood Transfusion; Am Asn Immunologists. *Res:* Study, largely immunochemical, of human blood types and the clinical significance of allogeneic immune responses. *Mailing Add:* Mt Sinai Med Ctr Box 1079 1176 Fifth Ave New York NY 10029-6503. Fax: 212-996-1029

ROSENFIELD, ROBERT LEE, PEDIATRIC ENDOCRINOLOGY. *Current Pos:* from asst prof to assoc prof, 68-78, PROF PEDIAT & MED SCH, UNIV CHICAGO, 78- *Personal Data:* b Robinson, Ill, Dec 16, 34; m; c Tom M, Ben R & Saul R. *Educ:* Northwestern Univ, Evanston, BA, 56; Northwestern Univ, Chicago, MD, 60. *Prof Exp:* Intern, Philadelphia Gen Hosp, 60-61; resident pediat, Children's Hosp Philadelphia, 61-63; instr, Med Sch, Univ Pa, 65-68. *Concurrent Pos:* USPHS trainee, Children's Hosp Philadelphia, 65-68; Forgarty Sr Int fel, 77-78. *Mem:* Endocrine Soc; Soc Pediat Res; Am Pediat Soc; Soc Gynec Invest; Lawson Wilkins Pediat Endocrine Soc. *Res:* Androgen physiology; reproductive endocrinology; growth disorders. *Mailing Add:* Dept Pediat Med Sch Univ Chicago 5841 Maryland Ave Chicago IL 60637-1463

ROSENGREEN, THEODORE E, HAZARDOUS & TOXIC WASTE DISPOSAL, ENERGY RESOURCE DEVELOPMENT & ANALYSIS. *Current Pos;* RETIRED. *Personal Data:* b Tooele, Utah, Feb 19, 37; m; c 4. *Educ:* Univ Wash, BS, 62, MS, 65; Ohio State Univ, PhD(geol), 70. *Prof Exp:* Explor geologist, Humble Oil Refining Co, 65-67; sr geologist, assoc Dames & Moore, 70-85; geol consult, 85-87. *Mem:* Fel Geol Soc Am. *Res:* Quaternary geology, nuclear and thermal power plant siting studies, environmental impact studies of energy resource developments; investigation of hazardous and toxic waste disposal. *Mailing Add:* 4412 143rd Ave SE Bellevue WA 98006

ROSENGREN, JACK WHITEHEAD, PHYSICS. *Current Pos:* asst assoc dir at large, 90-93, LAB ASSOC, LAWRENCE LIVERMORE NAT LAB, 94- *Personal Data:* b Chula Vista, Calif, Oct 2, 26; m 49, Patricia Dorking; c Paul G & Margaret (Graham). *Educ:* Univ Calif, Berkeley, AB, 48, PhD(physics), 52. *Prof Exp:* Physicist, Radiation Lab, Univ Calif, 48-52; from instr to asst prof physics, Mass Inst Technol, 52-55; head, Reactor Physics Sect, Missile Systs Div, Lockheed Aircraft Corp, 55-57; staff physicist, Aeronutronic Systs, Inc, Ford Motor Co, 57; physicist, Lawrence Livermore Lab, Univ Calif, 57-63, head, Large Weapons Physics Div, 63-64, assoc dir nuclear design, 64-68 & spec projs, 68-72; dep dir sci & technol, Defense Nuclear Agency, 72-74; sr physicist, R&D Assocs, 74-90. *Concurrent Pos:* Mem, Polaris Re-entry Body Coord Comt, 58-60; mem Mark 11 re-entry vehicle joint working group, USAF, 60-63, penetration prog panel, Ballistic Systs Div, 62-64 & ballistic missile re-entry systs consult group, 66-68; mem sci adv comt, Defense Intel Agency, 65-71; mem sci adv panel, US Army, 66-68, consult, 68-70; assoc ed, J Defense Res, 67-70; mem defense sci bd, Nuclear Test Detection Task Force, 67-72; mem Bethe Panel, Foreign Weapons Eval Group, 67-72; mem comt sr reviewers, AEC, 69-72 & Energy Res & Develop Admin, 76-77; consult, Tech Eval Panel (classification), Dept Energy, 77-83. *Mem:* Am Phys Soc; AAAS; Sigma Xi. *Res:* Experimental nuclear physics; nuclear weapon design; nuclear weapon effects; nuclear weapon security; nuclear materials safeguards; nuclear weapon requirements studies; nuclear test ban verification; arms control studies. *Mailing Add:* Lawrence Livermore Nat Lab L-160 Univ Calif PO Box 808 Livermore CA 94550

ROSENGREN, JOHN, FRESHWATER BIOLOGY. *Current Pos:* RETIRED. *Personal Data:* b Wooster, Ohio, Sept 29, 28; m 55, Beverly K; c Eric, Karl & Paul. *Educ:* Col Wooster, BA, 49; Columbia Univ, MA, 55, EdD, 58. *Prof Exp:* Instr biol, Am Univ Beirut, 49-53; instr, High Sch, 55-58; assoc prof, William Patterson Col NJ, 59-63, prof biol, 64-96. *Mem:* AAAS; Nat Sci Teachers Asn; Nat Asn Biol Teachers. *Res:* Freshwater Porifera. *Mailing Add:* 332 Eastside Ave Ridgewood NJ 07450-5331

ROSENHAN, A KIRK, FIRE PROTECTION. *Current Pos:* ENGR, 85- *Personal Data:* b Jefferson City, Mo, May 3, 40; div; c Katharyn. *Educ:* Univ Mo, Columbia, BS, 62; Miss State Univ, MS, 65. *Prof Exp:* Engr, Eastman Kodak Co, 62-63; instr mech eng, Miss State Univ, 63-68, bus, 70-72 & indust eng, 74-85; grad asst mech eng, Okla State Univ, 68-69; engr, Int Asn Fire Chiefs, 69-70; head fire sci, Vo-Tec, Racine, Wis, 72-74. *Concurrent Pos:* Fire coordr, Oktibbeha County, Miss, 88-; mem, Safety Comt, Am Soc Mech Engrs; mem, 1901 Comt, Nat Fire Protection Asn. *Mem:* Soc Fire Protection Engrs; Am Soc Mech Engrs; Int Asn Arson Investigators; Inst Fire Safety; Inst Fire Engrs. *Res:* Fluid dynamics in fire equipment and appliances. *Mailing Add:* Drawer KJ Mississippi State MS 39762

ROSENHEIM, D(ONALD) E(DWIN), ELECTRICAL ENGINEERING. *Current Pos:* RETIRED. *Personal Data:* b New York, NY, Mar 23, 26; m 58; c 2. *Educ:* Polytech Inst Brooklyn, BS, 49; Columbia Univ, MS, 57. *Prof Exp:* Develop engr, Servo Corp Am, 49-51; engr, Develop Labs, IBM Corp, 51-53, res staff mem, Thomas J Watson Res Ctr, 53-60, mgr circuits & systs, 60-63, mgr solid state electronics, 63-66, dir appl res, 66-72, asst IBM dir res, 72-73, dir, San Jose Res Lab, 73-83, asst dir, IBM Almaden Res Ctr, 83-92. *Concurrent Pos:* Lectr, City Col NY, 55-56 & Columbia Univ, 57-58. *Mem:* Fel Inst Elec & Electronics Engrs. *Res:* Digital systems and technology, especially solid state materials, devices and circuits for logic, storage and input/output applications in data processing systems. *Mailing Add:* 128 Smith Creek Dr Los Gatos CA 95030

ROSENHOLTZ, IRA N, TOPOLOGY. *Current Pos:* ASST PROF MATH, UNIV WYO, 73- *Personal Data:* b New York, NY, May 14, 45; c 2. *Educ:* Brandeis Univ, BA, 67; Univ Wis, MA & PhD(math), 72. *Prof Exp:* Asst prof math, Grinnell Col, Iowa, 72-73. *Concurrent Pos:* NDEA Title IV fel, Univ Wis, 71-72. *Mem:* Math Asn Am; Am Math Soc. *Res:* Continua; fixed point problems; remetrization. *Mailing Add:* Eastern Ill Univ Charleston IL 61920

ROSENKILDE, CARL EDWARD, FLUID DYNAMICS, NONLINEAR WAVE PROPAGATION. *Current Pos:* PRIN SCIENTIST, C R SCI, 93- *Personal Data:* b Yakima, Wash, Mar 16, 37. *Educ:* Wash State Univ, BS, 59; Univ Chicago, MS, 60, PhD(physics), 66. *Prof Exp:* Fel physics, Argonne Nat Lab, 66-68; asst prof math, NY Univ, 68-70; asst prof physics, 70-76; assoc prof physics, Kans State Univ, 76-79; physicist, Lawrence Livermore Nat Lab, 79-93. *Concurrent Pos:* Vis scientist, Lawrence Livermore Lab, 77-78, partic guest, 93-97. *Mem:* AAAS; Am Astron Soc; Am Phys Soc; Soc Indust & Appl Math; Am Geophys Union; Acoust Soc Am. *Res:* Fluid dynamics; nonlinear wave propagation in complex media. *Mailing Add:* 2604 Crater Rd Livermore CA 94550-6603. Fax: 510-449-8984; E-Mail: rosnklde@aimnet.com

ROSENKOETTER, GERALD EDWIN, CONSTRUCTION, CIVIL ENGINEERING. *Current Pos:* exec vpres, Sverdrup Corp, 85-88, VCHMN, SVERDRUP CORP, 88-; PARTNER, 3 SVERDRUP PARTNERSHIPS, 77-; PRES, 88- *Personal Data:* b St Louis, Mar 16, 27; m 49, June Beekman; c Claudia, Ruth & Carole L. *Educ:* Washington Univ, St Louis, BSCE, 51; Sever Inst Technol, MSCE, 57. *Prof Exp:* Sr struct engr, Sverdrup & Parcel, Inc, St Louis, 51-56, proj engr, 56-60, engr mgr, Denver, 60-62; proj mgr, Sverdrup & Parcel & Assocs, St Louis, 62-69, chief engr, 69-74, vpres, 74-80; pres, SPCM, Inc, 80-85. *Concurrent Pos:* Dir, Conserv & Sch Arts, St Louis, 89-92. *Mem:* Am Soc Chem Engrs. *Res:* Construction. *Mailing Add:* 42 Ballas Ct St Louis MO 63131

ROSENKRANTZ, BARBARA G, HISTORY OF SCIENCE. *Current Pos:* Assoc prof, Harvard Univ, 73-75, prof hist sci, 75-93, chmn dept, 84-89, EMER PROF HIST SCI, HARVARD UNIV, 93- *Personal Data:* b New York, NY, Jan 11, 23. *Educ:* Radcliff Col, AB, 44; Clark Univ, PhD, 70. *Mem:* Fel Inst Med-Nat Acad Sci; Am Hist Asn; Hist Sci Soc; Am Asn Hist Sci; fel Am Acad Arts & Sci. *Res:* Author of numerous publications. *Mailing Add:* Hist Sci Dept Sci Ctr 235 Harvard Univ Cambridge MA 02138

ROSENKRANTZ, DANIEL J, DATABASE SYSTEMS, ALGORITHMS. *Current Pos:* PROF COMPUT SCI, STATE UNIV NY, ALBANY, 77-, DEPT CHAIR, 93- *Personal Data:* b Brooklyn, NY, Mar 5, 43; m 69, Carole Jaffee; c Holly, Sherry, Jody & Andrew. *Educ:* Columbia Univ, BS, 63, MS, 64 & PhD(elec eng), 67. *Prof Exp:* Info scientist, Bell Tel Labs, 66-67; Gen Elec Res & Develop Ctr, 67-77. *Concurrent Pos:* Area ed, Formal Lang & Models of Comput, J Asn for Comput Mach, 81-86; prin comput scientist, Phoenix Data Syst, 83-85; ed chief, J Asn for Comput Mach, 86-91. *Mem:* fel Asn Comput Mach; Inst Elec & Electronics Engrs Comput Soc; Europ Asn Theoret Comput. *Res:* Database systems; algorithms; fault-tolerant computing; computer-aided design; complexity theory; compiler design theory; automata theory; software engineering. *Mailing Add:* Comput Sci Dept State Univ NY 1400 Washington Ave Albany NY 12222. Fax: 518-442-3560; E-Mail: djr@cs.albany.edu

ROSENKRANTZ, JACOB ALVIN, MEDICINE, HOSPITAL ADMINISTRATION. *Current Pos:* RETIRED. *Personal Data:* b New York, NY, Feb 12, 14; m 36; c 4. *Educ:* City Col New York, BS, 33; Columbia Univ, MA, 34, MD, 38. *Prof Exp:* Res asst, Columbia Univ, 41-42, 46; chief outpatient serv, Bronx Vet Admin Hosp, 47-49, asst chief prof servs, 49-52, attend, Med Serv, 52; chief prof servs, Vet Admin Hosp, East Orange, NJ, 52-56; adminr, Southern Div, Albert Einstein Med Ctr, 56-59; exec dir, Newark Beth Israel Hosp, 59-68; chief, Outpatient Clin, Vet Admin, 71-82. *Concurrent Pos:* Fel, Postgrad Med Sch, NY Univ, 41-46 & 48, asst physician, 41-, instr, 54-; clin assoc prof community & prev med & exec dir & assoc dean hosp admin, New York Med Col Flower & Fifth Ave Hosps, 68-71. *Mem:* Fel Am Geriat Soc; fel Am Pub Health Asn; fel Am Col Physicians; fel Am Col Prev Med; fel Am Col Healthcare Execs; Sigma Xi; fel Royal Soc Health; fel NY Acad Sci. *Res:* Hypertension; galactose and glucose tolerance; arteriosclerosis; infectious mononucleosis; bilateral nephrectomy in rats; potassium and electrocardiograms; thyroid diseases; benign paroxysmal peritonitis; Paget's disease; puerperal sepsis. *Mailing Add:* 5367 A Privet Pl Delray Beach FL 33484

ROSENKRANTZ, MARCY ELLEN, COMPUTATIONAL CHEMISTRY. *Current Pos:* ASSOC DIR SUPERCOMPUT TECHNOL, CORNELL THEORY CTR, CORNELL UNIV, 94- *Personal Data:* b New York, NY, June 15, 48; m 79, Daniel D Konowalow. *Educ:* Harpur Col, BA, 69; State

Univ NY, Binghamton, MA, 76, PhD(theoret chem), 84. *Prof Exp:* Teacher chem, Binghamton City Schs, 69-80; res assoc physics, Harvard Smithsonian Ctr Astrophys, 84-85; resident res assoc chem, Nat Res Coun, 85-86; adj asst prof chem, State Univ NY, Binghamton, 86-87; res scientist chem, Univ Dayton Res Inst, 87-93. *Mem:* Am Chem Soc; Am Phys Soc; Sigma Xi. *Res:* Electronic structure calculations on systems which promise to possess high energy density; dispersion energies and polarizabilities of small molecules; algorithms and tools for computational chemistry on super computers. *Mailing Add:* Eng & Theory Ctr Bldg Cornell Univ Ithaca NY 14853. *Fax:* 607-254-8888; *E-Mail:* marcyr@tc.cornell.edu

ROSENKRANZ, EUGEN EMIL, PLANT PATHOLOGY. *Current Pos:* RES PLANT PATHOLOGIST, AGR RES STA, USDA, 64- *Personal Data:* b Wilno, Poland, July 9, 31; US citizen. *Educ:* Univ Wis, BS, 56, MS, 57, PhD(plant path), 61. *Prof Exp:* Fel microbial genetics, Univ Wis, 61-62, res assoc plant path, 63-64. *Concurrent Pos:* Adj prof plant path, Miss State Univ, 71-86. *Mem:* Am Phytopath Soc. *Res:* Diseases of maize caused by viruses and mycoplasma-like organisms; insect transmission of mycoplasma-like organisms and viruses affecting corn and other gramineaceous plants. *Mailing Add:* 55 Ridge Dr Starkville MS 39759

ROSENKRANZ, HERBERT S, CANCER RESEARCH, RISK ASSESSMENT. *Current Pos:* PROF & CHMN, DEPT ENVIRON & OCCUP HEALTH, UNIV PITTSBURGH, 90- *Personal Data:* b Vienna, Austria, Sept 27, 33; US citizen; m 59; c 8. *Educ:* City Col New York, BS, 54; Cornell Univ, PhD(biochem), 59. *Prof Exp:* Res assoc biochem, Univ Pa, 60-61; from asst prof to prof microbiol, Col Physicians & Surgeons, Columbia Univ, 61-76; prof microbiol & chmn, dept microbiol, NY Med Col, 76-81; prof & chmn, Dept Environ Health Sci & prof biochem, pediat, oncol & radiol, Case Western Res Univ, 81-90. *Concurrent Pos:* Nat Cancer Inst fel, Sloan-Kettering Inst, 59-60; res career develop award, NIH, 65-75; vis prof, Hebrew Univ, Med Sch, Jerusalem, 71-72; Int Comn for Protection Against Environ Mutagens & Carcinogens, 77-; del, Fifth Soviet-Am Symp Environ Mutagenesis & Carcinogenesis, 78; chmn DNA panel, Gene & Toxicol Prog, Environ Protection Agency, 79-; scientific review panel health effects, 80-; guest investr, Nat Coun Res Ctr Japan, 80 & Toxicol Study Sect, NIH, 84. *Mem:* Soc Toxicol; Am Asn Cancer Res; Am Chem Soc; Am Soc Biol Chemists; Am Soc Microbiol; AAAS; Environ Mutagen Soc; Genetic Soc Am; Sigma Xi. *Res:* Chemistry and biology of nucleic acids; biochemical basis of mutagenicity and carcinogenicity; causes and prevention of cancer; risk assessment. *Mailing Add:* Dept Environ & Occup Health Univ Pittsburgh 260 Kappa Dr Pittsburgh PA 15238. *Fax:* 412-624-1289

ROSENKRANZ, PHILIP WILLIAM, REMOTE SENSING. *Current Pos:* res assoc, 73-89, PRIN RES SCIENTIST, MASS INST TECHNOL, 89- *Personal Data:* b Buffalo, NY, Oct 30, 45. *Educ:* Mass Inst Technol, SB, 67, SM, 68, PhD(elec eng), 71. *Prof Exp:* Resident res assoc, Jet Propulsion Lab, Calif Inst Technol, 71-73. *Concurrent Pos:* Mem, comt F, Int Union Radio Sci. *Mem:* AAAS; Am Geophys Union; Inst Elec & Electronics Engrs; Int Union Radio Sci. *Res:* Remote sensing of earth; radio astronomy. *Mailing Add:* Mass Inst Technol Cambridge MA 02139

ROSENLICHT, MAXWELL, MATHEMATICS. *Current Pos:* PROF MATH, UNIV CALIF, BERKELEY, 59- *Personal Data:* b Brooklyn, NY, Apr 15, 24; m 53; c 3. *Educ:* Columbia Univ, AB, 47; Harvard Univ, PhD(math), 50. *Honors & Awards:* Cole Prize, Am Math Soc, 60. *Prof Exp:* Nat Res Coun fel, Univ Chicago & Princeton Univ, 50-52; from asst prof to assoc prof math, Northwestern Univ, 52-59. *Concurrent Pos:* Fulbright fel, Univ Rome, 54-55; Guggenheim fel, 57-58; mem, Inst Advan Sci Studies, France, 62-63. *Mem:* Am Math Soc. *Res:* Algebraic groups; differential algebra. *Mailing Add:* PO Box 584 Homewood CA 96141

ROSENMAN, IRWIN DAVID, ORGANIC CHEMISTRY, TRANSPORTATION. *Current Pos:* RETIRED. *Personal Data:* b Brooklyn, NY, Apr 9, 23; m 50, Hilda Keer; c Michael, Stephen & Scott. *Educ:* Univ Pa, BA, 45; Univ Conn, MS, 48, PhD(biochem), 51. *Prof Exp:* Asst instr anal chem, Univ Conn, 48-50; chemist, Ames Aromatics, Inc, 51-53; chemist & pres, Ames Labs, Inc, 53-85. *Mem:* Sigma Xi; Am Chem Soc. *Res:* Organic synthesis of aliphatic and aromatic amines, oximes and other nitrogen containing compounds; antiskinning agents; electrophoresis; antioxidants and additives for paint and inks; amines; transportation consultant (hazardous materials). *Mailing Add:* Consults Ames Labs Box 3024 Milford CT 06460-0824

ROSENMAN, RAY HAROLD, MEDICINE. *Current Pos:* ASSOC CHIEF DEPT MED, MT ZION HOSP & MED CTR, SAN FRANCISCO, CALIF, 51-; DIR CARDIOVASC RES, STANFORD RES INST, SRI INT, MENLO PARK, CALIF, 78- *Personal Data:* b Akron, Ohio, Nov 17, 20; m 45, 78; c 2. *Educ:* Univ Mich, AB, 41, MD, 44. *Prof Exp:* Intern, Michael Reese Hosp, Chicago, 44-45; resident path, Wayne Co Gen Hosp, Eloise, Mich, 45-46; resident internal med & cardiovasc dis, Michael Reese Hosp, 48-50. *Concurrent Pos:* Fel Coun Epidemiol, Am Heart Asn; consult, Sch Aerospace Med, San Antonio, Brooks AFB, USAF, 74-79; mem, Nat Task Force Epidemiol of Heart Dis, Nat Heart, Lung & Blood Inst, 78; Am Heart Asn fel, 59-60, assoc chief, Harold Brunn Inst, Mt Zion Hosp & Med Ctr, San Francisco, Calif, 51-78; mem study sect, Behav Med, NIH, 81-; mem adv bd coun, High Blood Pressure Res, Am Heart Asn, 66- & expert adv coun, Health Econ, Basel, 81-; trustee, Am Inst Stress, Yonkers, NY, 81-; co-chmn, Int Symp Psychophysiol Risk Factors, Carlsbad, Czech, 81; mem rev panel, Coronary-Prone Behav, Jacksonville, Fla & Workshop, Cholesterol & Non-Cardiovasc Mortality, Nat Heart, Lung & Blood Inst, Bethesda, Md, 81-; guest lectr, Australia, 74, 78 & 80; guest lectr, Klinik Hohenreid, Munich, Ger & Ciba Symp, Stratford, Eng, 78, Charing Cross Hosp, London, Eng, 79, Ciba Symp, Montsoult, France, Netherlands Inst Adv Study Humanities & Social Sci, Amsterdam, Holland, conf, Coronary-Prone Behav, Univ Freiburg, Ger & Univ SFla, Tampa, 80, conf, Psychol Factors Before & After Myocardial Infarction, Europ Soc Cardiol, Nice, France, Ger Conf, Coronary-Prone Behav, Altenberg, Ger & Switzerland, Univ Hosps, Basel, Zurich, Bern, Geneva & Lausanne, 81. *Mem:* Am Col Cardiol; Am Soc Clin Invest; Am Soc Internal Med; Am Physiol Soc. *Res:* Lipid metabolism; pathogenesis of coronary heart disease; hypertension and the predictive role of risk factors; role of Type-A behavior pattern in coronary heart disease. *Mailing Add:* 2200 Pacific Ave San Francisco CA 94115

ROSENMANN, EDWARD A, enzymology, protein chemistry, for more information see previous edition

ROSENMAYER, CHARLES THOMAS, ELECTRONIC & FIBER OPTIC CABLING MATERIALS. *Current Pos:* LEAD TECHNOLOGIST, W L GORE & ASSOCS, 91- *Personal Data:* b St Louis, Mo, Aug 3, 60; m 86, Donna Davis; c Luke & Allison. *Educ:* Univ Mo, Rolla, BS, 82; Rice Univ, MS & PhD(mat sci), 89. *Prof Exp:* Engr, Hughes Tool Co, 82-86; res asst, Rice Univ, 86-89; staff engr, IBM, 89-91. *Mem:* Int Electronics Packaging Soc. *Res:* Reliability (fatigue life) of electronic and fiber optic cabling materials. *Mailing Add:* 1431 Grover Rd Eau Claire WI 54701-5632. *Fax:* 512-276-7614; *E-Mail:* 73321.2656@compuserve.com

ROSENOW, EDWARD CARL, JR, MEDICINE. *Current Pos:* exec vpres, 60-77, EMER EXEC VPRES, AM COL PHYSICIANS, 77- *Personal Data:* b Chicago, Ill, Apr 7, 09; m 31; c 2. *Educ:* Carleton Col, BA, 31; Harvard Med Sch, MD, 35; Univ Minn, MSc, 39; Am Bd Internal Med, dipl, 46; FRCP, 68. *Hon Degrees:* DSc, Carleton Col, 67 & MacMurray Col, 73. *Honors & Awards:* Stengel Award, Am Col Physicians, 76. *Prof Exp:* Exec dir, Los Angeles Co Med Asn, 57-59. *Concurrent Pos:* Clin prof, Sch Med, Univ Pa, 60-66, emer clin prof, 66-; trustee, Carleton Col, 68-; dir med educ, Grad Hosp, Philadelphia, 71-78. *Mem:* Int Soc Internal Med (pres elect, 78-); Am Clin & Climat Asn; Am Fedn Clin Res; hon fel Am Col Chest Physicians; Am Med Writers Asn (pres, 65). *Res:* Postgraduate education; medical administration. *Mailing Add:* 3300 Darby Rd C-103 Haverford PA 19041

ROSENQUIST, BRUCE DAVID, VETERINARY VIROLOGY. *Current Pos:* RETIRED. *Personal Data:* b Chicago, Ill, June 19, 34; m 56; c 2. *Educ:* Iowa State Univ, DVM, 58; Univ Mo-Columbia, PhD(microbiol), 68. *Prof Exp:* Staff, USPHS, Atlanta, Ga & Haddonfield, NJ, 58-60; vet, Morton Grove Animal Hosp, Ill, 60-61 & Depster Animal Clin, Skokie, Ill, 61-64; res assoc vet microbiol, Sch Vet Med, Univ Mo, Columbia, 64-68, Space Sci Res Ctr, 65-66, from asst prof to prof, vet microbiol, 68-92. *Concurrent Pos:* NIH fel, 66-68; mem working team for bovine & equine picornaviruses, WHO-Food & Agr Orgn Prog Comp Virol, 73- *Mem:* Conf Res Workers Animal Dis; Am Vet Med Asn; Int Soc Interferon Res; Am Col Vet Microbiol; Am Soc Virology. *Res:* Bovine viral respiratory disease; interferon; bovine rhinoviruses; nutrition and bovine viral disease. *Mailing Add:* HC1 Box 1140 Isabella MO 65676

ROSENQUIST, EDWARD P, ORGANIC CHEMISTRY, PHYSICAL CHEMISTRY. *Current Pos:* Res chemist, Shell Oil Co, Ill, 65-69, chemist, Head Off Mfg Res, NY, 69-70, sr engr, Mkt Lubricants, Tex, 70-73, supvr staff, Shell Develop Co, Wood River, Ill & Houston, Tex, 73-78, mgr res recruitment, 78-80, mgr res & develop coord, Oil Prods, Shell Oil Co, 80-83, sr staff res engr, 83-85, MGR, SHELL DEVELOP CO, HOUSTON, TEX, 85- *Personal Data:* b Dayton, Ohio, Feb 28, 38; m 64, Kaye Ingle; c 3. *Educ:* Denison Univ, BS, 60; Purdue Univ, PhD(org chem), 65. *Mem:* Am Chem Soc. *Res:* Organic synthesis; lubricants and detergents research. *Mailing Add:* 5614 Bermuda Dunes Lane Houston TX 77069-2735

ROSENQUIST, GLENN CARL, MEDICINE. *Current Pos:* DIR RES, CHILDREN'S HOSP, NAT MED CTR, 80- *Personal Data:* b Lincoln, Nebr, Aug 29, 31; m 53; c 6. *Educ:* Univ Nebr, BA, 53, MD, 57. *Prof Exp:* USPHS fel embryol, Carnegie Inst Washington, 63-65; fel pediat cardiol, Johns Hopkins Univ, 65-67, asst prof pediat, 67-71, assoc prof, 71-76; prof pediat & chmn, Col Med, Univ Nebr, 76-80; PROF CHILD HEALTH & DEVELOP, GEORGE WASHINGTON UNIV, 80- *Concurrent Pos:* Prof path, Johns Hopkins Univ, 72-76; mem, Human Embryol & Develop Study Sect, 75-79. *Mem:* Am Asn Anatomists; Soc Develop Biol; Teratol Soc; Am Col Cardiol; Am Acad Pediat. *Res:* Early development of organ systems in the chick embryo; embryology of the heart and lung; pathology of congenital heart disease. *Mailing Add:* George Wash Univ Children's Hosp Nat Med Ctr 111 Michigan Ave Washington DC 20010

ROSENQUIST, GRACE LINK, PEPTIDES PURIFICATION & ASSAY, TYROSINE SULFATION. *Current Pos:* lectr, 75-80, PROF ANIMAL PHYSIOL, UNIV CALIF, DAVIS, 80- *Personal Data:* b Los Angeles, Calif; m 60, John; c Kerstin & Marta. *Educ:* Willamette Univ, BA, 54; Univ Wis-Madison, MS, 58, PhD(zool), 61. *Prof Exp:* Fel, Calif Inst Technol, 61-64; USPHS fel, Sch Med, Wash Univ, 64-66; instr med microbiol, Sch Med, Stanford Univ, 66-68, res assoc, 68-70, res assoc med & microbiol, 70-74. *Concurrent Pos:* Vis scientist, Inst Animal Physiol, Cambridge, UK, 72-73, Ctr Ulcer Res & Educ, Los Angeles, 74-75; vis scientist, Nat Inst Med Res, London, 81-82. *Mem:* AAAS; Am Asn Immunol. *Res:* Function and structure of cholecystokinin; evolution of gastrointestinal hormones; radioimmunoassay of gastrin, cholecystokinin; peptide purification; enzymatic sulfation of tyrosine in peptides and proteins; sequence requirements for tyrosine sulfation. *Mailing Add:* Dept Neurobiol Physiol & Behav Univ Calif Davis Davis CA 95616. *Fax:* 530-752-5582; *E-Mail:* glrosenquist@ucdavis.edu

ROSENQUIST, THOMAS H, CARDIOVASCULAR DEVELOPMENT, SMOOTH MUSCLE CELL DIFFERENTIATION. *Current Pos:* PROF & CHMN, DEPT CELL BIOL & ANAT, UNIV NEBR, 91- *Personal Data:* b Dubuque, Iowa, Feb 16, 42; m 78, Dianne King; c Frank, Gunnar & Kevin. *Educ:* Univ Dubuque, BS, 64; La State Univ, PhD(anat), 69. *Prof Exp:* Instr, Univ Southern Calif Col Med, 69-70, asst prof, 70-73; from assoc prof to prof, Med Col Ga, 73-91. *Mem:* Fedn Am Socs Exp Biol; Sigma Xi. *Res:* Differentiation of vascular smooth muscle cells; developmental heterogeneity of vascular smooth muscle cells and the impact of the embryonic origin of vascular smooth muscle upon the distribution of atherosclerosis. *Mailing Add:* Dept Cell Biol/Anat Univ Nebr 600 S 42nd St Omaha NE 68198-6395. *Fax:* 402-559-7328

ROSENSHEIN, JOSEPH SAMUEL, HYDROLOGY, GEOHYDROLOGY. *Current Pos:* PVT CONSULT, 94- *Personal Data:* b Kimball, WVa, Apr 19, 29; m 51, Helene Silverman; c Leonard O, Richard A & Susan B. *Educ:* Univ Conn, BA, 52; Johns Hopkins Univ, MA, 53; Univ Ill, Urbana, PhD(geol), 67. *Honors & Awards:* Meritorious Serv Award, Dept Interior, 86, Distinguished Serv Award, 96; Distinguished Serv Award, Hydrogeol Div, Geol Soc Am, 94; Am Inst Hydrol Founders Award, 96. *Prof Exp:* Geologist, Ind Dist, US Geol Surv, 53-63, subdist chief, RI & NY Dist, 64-66, RI & Cent New Eng Dist, 66-67 & Tampa Subdist, Fla Dist, 67-75, chief Kans Dist, 75-87, dep asst chief hydrol, prog coord & tech support & installation restoration prog coord, Water Resources Div, 87-94, act chief, off ground water, 91-92. *Concurrent Pos:* sr vpres Am Inst Hydrol, 90-94; pres, US Chapt Int Asn Hydrogeologists, 92-96; chmn, Hydrogeol Div, Geol Soc Am, 90; copres Org Comt Second USA/USSR Joint Cont Environ Hydrology & Hydrogeol, Washington, DC, 93. *Mem:* Am Geophys Union; fel Geol Soc Am; Int Asn Hydrogeologists; Am Inst Hydrol. *Res:* Hydrology of aquifer systems; estuarine hydrology; hazard wastes contamination aquifer systems; subsurface storage of wastes; hydraulic characteristics and modeling of aquifer systems; remote sensing of the environment. *Mailing Add:* Virginia Beach VA 23456-7308. *Fax:* 757-416-1018

ROSENSHINE, MATTHEW, OPERATIONS RESEARCH, MATHEMATICS. *Current Pos:* prof, 68-92, EMER PROF INDUST ENG, PA STATE UNIV, 92- *Personal Data:* b New York, NY; m; c 2. *Educ:* Columbia Univ, AB, 52, MA, 53; Univ Ill, MS, 56; State Univ NY, Buffalo, PhD(opers res), 66. *Prof Exp:* Engr aerodyn, Bell Aircraft Corp, 53-56; instr, Univ Ala, Huntsville, 57; prin math, Aeronaut Lab, Cornell Univ, 58-68. *Concurrent Pos:* Instr, Univ Buffalo, 53-55 & NMex State Univ, 58; lectr, State Univ NY, Buffalo, 66-68; consult, Aeronaut Lab, Cornell Univ, 69-70, Xerox Corp, 72, Fed Energy Admin, 73-76 & Fed RR Admin, 78-80. *Mem:* Opers Res Soc Am; Inst Mgt Sci. *Res:* Queueing theory and control applied to large scale systems, especially air traffic and railroads. *Mailing Add:* 207 Hammond Bldg Pa State Univ University Park PA 16802

ROSENSON, LAWRENCE, ELEMENTARY PARTICLE PHYSICS, EXPERIMENTAL PHYSICS. *Current Pos:* from instr to assoc prof, 58-67, PROF PHYSICS, MASS INST TECHNOL, 67- *Personal Data:* b Brooklyn, NY, May 20, 31; m 63; c 2. *Educ:* Univ Chicago, AB, 50, MS, 53, PhD(physics), 56. *Prof Exp:* Res assoc physics, Univ Chicago, 56-58. *Mem:* Fel Am Phys Soc. *Res:* Experimental elementary particle physics; particle spectroscopy; weak and strong interactions. *Mailing Add:* Nuclear Sci Lab Bldg 24-520 Mass Inst Technol 77 Mass Ave Cambridge MA 02139

ROSENSPIRE, ALLEN JAY, MOLECULAR BIOLOGY. *Current Pos:* SCIENTIST, KARMANOS CANCER INST, DETROIT, 95- *Personal Data:* b New York, NY, May 25, 49; m 77; c 2. *Educ:* State Univ NY, Stony Brook, BS, 70; State Univ NY, Buffalo, PhD(biophys sci), 78. *Prof Exp:* Res fel, dept microbiol, State Univ NY, Buffalo, 78-79; res fel lab immunobiol, Sloan-Kettering Inst Cancer Res, 79-82, res assoc, 83-85; sr res scientist, Bio Magnetech Corp, Ny, 86; asst prof immunol & biophys, Dept Biol, Wayne State Univ, Detroit, 86-87, assoc, Dept Immunol & Microbiol, 87-95. *Concurrent Pos:* Consult, Bio Magnetech Corp, Ny, 86-; scientist, Mich Cancer Found, 94-95; adj asst prof, Sch Med, Wayne State Univ, Detroit, 96- *Mem:* Am Asn Immunologists; Sigma Xi. *Res:* Molecular biology of membrane receptors and the mechanisms of receptor mediated cell activation in the lymphocyte; the application of magnetic substrates in cell separation and immuno-assay techniques. *Mailing Add:* Karmanos Cancer Inst 110 E Warren Detroit MI 48201

ROSENSTARK, SOL(OMON), ELECTRICAL ENGINEERING. *Current Pos:* PROF ELEC & COMPUT ENG, NJ INST TECHNOL, 68- *Personal Data:* b Poland, May 13, 36; US citizen; m 60; c 2. *Educ:* City Col New York, BEE, 58; NY Univ, MEE, 61, PhD(elec eng), 66. *Prof Exp:* Jr engr, Polarod Electronics Corp, 58-59; assoc develop engr, Norden Labs, Div United Aircraft Corp, 59-61; lectr, City Col New York, 61-63; teaching fel, NY Univ, 64-65, res asst, 65-66; mem tech staff, Bell Tel Labs, 66-68. *Mem:* Inst Elec & Electronics Engrs; Sigma Xi. *Res:* Communication theory; electronics; microprocessors. *Mailing Add:* 17 Whitman St West Orange NJ 07052-2027

ROSENSTEEL, GEORGE T, THEORETICAL PHYSICS, NUCLEAR STRUCTURE. *Current Pos:* from asst prof to assoc prof, 78-84, chmn, Dept Physics, 85-91, PROF PHYSICS, TULANE UNIV, 84- *Personal Data:* b Baltimore, Md, Sept 30, 47. *Educ:* Univ Toronto, BS, 73; MS, 74, PhD, 75. *Prof Exp:* Nat Res Coun Can postdoc fel, McMaster Univ, 76-78; asst prof math, Ariz State Univ, 81-82. *Concurrent Pos:* Vis prof, La State Univ, 85, Yale Univ, 86; Brit Sci & Eng Univ Coun vis fel, Univ Sussex, 86; NSF grant, 79-; NSF fel, 85-87, 87-90; vis prof, Nat Inst Nuclear Theory, Univ Wash, 92. *Mem:* Am Phys Soc; Am Math Soc; Sigma Xi; Am Asn Univ Prof; Am Asn Physics Teachers. *Res:* Theoretical nuclear physics; mathematical physics; applied mathematics; author of 100 publications. *Mailing Add:* Tulane Univ Dept Physics New Orleans LA 70118

ROSENSTEIN, A(LLEN) B, ENGINEERING. *Current Pos:* lectr eng, 46-58, PROF ENG & APPL SCI, UNIV CALIF, LOS ANGELES, 58- *Personal Data:* b Baltimore, Md, Aug 25, 20; m; c 3. *Educ:* Univ Ariz, BS, 40; Univ Calif, Los Angeles, MS, 50, PhD, 58. *Prof Exp:* Elec engr, Convair Div, Gen Dynamics Corp, 40-41; sr elec engr, Lockheed Aircraft Corp, 41-42; chief plant engr, Utility Appliance Co, 42-44. *Concurrent Pos:* Consult, Atomic Energy Comn, US Air Force, US Corps Eng, Douglas Aircraft Co, Beckman Instruments & Marquardt Aircraft Co, 46-; chmn bd, Inet, Inc, 47-53, consult engr, 54-; dir, Pioneer Magnetics, Inc, Int Transformer Co, Inc & Foreign Resource Serv. *Mem:* AAAS; Am Soc Eng Educ; Inst Elec & Electronics Engrs; NY Acad Sci; Sigma Xi. *Res:* Magnetic amplifiers; ferromagnetic systems; automatic controls; system design; engineering organization; education; computer aided design; educational planning. *Mailing Add:* 314 S Rockingham Los Angeles CA 90049-3638

ROSENSTEIN, ALAN HERBERT, metallurgy, for more information see previous edition

ROSENSTEIN, BARRY SHELDON, PHOTOBIOLOGY, RADIATION BIOLOGY. *Current Pos:* ASSOC PROF RADIOL MED, BROWN UNIV, 86- *Personal Data:* b Roanoke, Va, June 17, 51; m 73; c 2. *Educ:* Univ Rochester, BA, 73, MS, 76, PhD(radiation biol), 78. *Prof Exp:* Res fel, Brookhaven Nat Lab, 78-80; asst prof radiol, Univ Tex Health Sci Ctr, Dallas, 80-86. *Mem:* AAAS; Am Inst Biol Sci; Am Soc Photobiol; Environ Mutagen Soc; Sigma Xi; Radiation Res Soc. *Res:* Induction and repair of DNA damages induced by solar ultra-violet radiation. *Mailing Add:* Dept Radiation Ther City Univ NY Mt Sinai Sch Med One Gustave Levy Plaza New York NY 10029-6504

ROSENSTEIN, GEORGE MORRIS, JR, MATHEMATICS, HISTORY OF MATHEMATICS. *Current Pos:* from asst prof to assoc prof, Franklin & Marshall Col, 67-80, assoc dean acad affairs, 94-95, interim pres, 95-96, PROF MATH, FRANKLIN & MARSHALL COL, 80-, ASSOC VPRES ACAD AFFAIRS, 96- *Personal Data:* b Philadelphia, Pa, Feb 27, 37; m 59, Harriet McGovran; c Beth. *Educ:* Oberlin Col, AB, 59; Duke Univ, MA, 62, PhD(math), 63. *Prof Exp:* Asst prof math, Western Res Univ, 63-67. *Concurrent Pos:* Chief reader, Advan Placement Exam, 88-91; assoc dean Acad Affairs, Franklin & Marshall Col, 94-95. *Mem:* Math Asn Am; Am Math Soc; Hist Sci Soc; Sigma Xi; Nat Coun Teachers Math. *Res:* History of 19th Century mathematics, focusing on the evolution of calculus; point-set topology; metric topology. *Mailing Add:* Franklin & Marshall Col Box 3003 Lancaster PA 17604-3003. *Fax:* 717-399-4455; *E-Mail:* g_rosenstein@acad.fandm.edu

ROSENSTEIN, JOSEPH GEOFFREY, MATHEMATICAL LOGIC, MATHEMATICS EDUCATION. *Current Pos:* from asst prof to assoc prof, 69-79, vchmn dept & dir, Undergrad Prog, 81-85, PROF MATH, RUTGERS UNIV, NEW BRUNSWICK, 79- *Personal Data:* b London, Eng, Feb 8, 41; US citizen; m 69, Judith; c Mira, Ariela, Dalia, Neshama & Nessa. *Educ:* Columbia Univ, BA, 61; Cornell Univ, PhD(math logic), 66. *Prof Exp:* Instr & res assoc math, Cornell Univ, 66; asst prof math, Univ Minn, Minneapolis, 66-69. *Concurrent Pos:* Mem Sch Math, Inst Advan Study, 76, 77; dir, NJ Math Coalition, 91- *Mem:* Am Math Soc; Math Asn Am; Asn Symbolic Logic; Nat Coun Teachers; Nat Coun Supervisors Math. *Res:* Recursion theory; model theory; linear orderings. *Mailing Add:* 223 S Third Ave Highland Park NJ 08904. *E-Mail:* joer@math.rutgers.edu

ROSENSTEIN, LAURENCE S, toxicology, carcinogenesis; deceased, see previous edition for last biography

ROSENSTEIN, MARVIN, RADIATION DOSIMETRY, RADIATION PROTECTION. *Current Pos:* dir, Off Health Physics, 82-95, STAFF FEL, CTR DEVICES & RADIOL HEALTH, FOOD & DRUG ADMIN, 95- *Personal Data:* b Baltimore, Md, Sept 5, 39. *Educ:* Univ Md, BSChemE, 61, PhD(nuclear eng), 71; Rensselaer Polytech Inst, MS, 66. *Prof Exp:* Prog coordr anal qual control serv, Div Radiol Health, Northeast Radiol Health Lab, Mass, 62; chief radiation exposure intel sect, Stand & Intel Br, Nat Ctr Radiol Health, Md, 67; mem, US Am Stands Inst, 68-69; guest worker, Ctr Radiation Res, Nat Bur Stand, 69-74; fac res assoc, Lab Polymers & Radiation Sci, Dept Clin Eng, Univ Md, 71-74; dep chief, Radiation Measurements & Calibration Br, Div Electronic Prods, Bur Radio Health, Rockville, 71, spec asst to dir, 72, dep dir, 73, dep dir, 73, sr sci adv, 79; asst clin prof radiol, Sch Med & Sci, George Washington Univ, 77-90; dep assoc comnr, Policy Coord Off, Food & Drug Admin, Rockville, 78. *Mem:* Nat Coun Radiation Protection & Measurements; Health Physics Soc; Sigma Xi. *Res:* Patent for radiation dosimeter; absorbed dose from medical xrays; radiation risk estimate; dosimetry for epidemiological studies; absorbed dose to the public from radiation emergencies; electron depth dose and dosimetry; radiochemistry; radioactivity in food; environmental health; radiological health. *Mailing Add:* Food & Drug Admin 16071 Industrial Dr MD MS2-6 Gaithersburg MD 20877. *Fax:* 301-827-3775; *E-Mail:* mxr@fdadr.cdrh.fda.gov

ROSENSTEIN, ROBERT, PHARMACOLOGY. *Current Pos:* from instr to asst prof, 65-77, ASSOC PROF PHARMACOL, DARTMOUTH MED SCH, 77-, PHARMACOLOGIST, RES SERV, VET ADMIN CTR, 65- *Personal Data:* b New York, NY, Aug 7, 33; m 65; c 2. *Educ:* Columbia Univ, BS, 55, MS, 57; Univ Utah, PhD(pharmacol), 62. *Prof Exp:* Teaching asst biol, Col Pharm, Columbia Univ, 55-57; res asst pharmacol, Col Med, Univ Utah, 57-58; res instr, Sch Med, Univ Okla, 62-65, asst res prof, 65. *Concurrent Pos:* Res pharmacologist, Civil Aeromed Res Inst, Fed Aviation Agency, 62-65.

Mem: AAAS; Am Physiol Soc; Am Soc Pharmacol & Exp Therapeut; Soc Neurosci. *Res:* Respiratory pharmacology and physiology; actions of drugs upon brain stem; blood platelet pharmacology; pathology. *Mailing Add:* 8741 E Aloe Dr Apache Junction AZ 85219

ROSENSTEIN, ROBERT WILLIAM, INFECTIOUS DISEASES, ANTIGEN BIOCHEMISTRY. *Current Pos:* mgr, 82-88, TECH DIR, INDUST RES & DEVELOP, BECTON DICKINSON ADVAN DIAG, 88- *Personal Data:* b New York, NY, Mar 26, 44; m 66; c 2. *Educ:* Univ Wis, BS, 64; Yale Univ, PhD(biochem), 69. *Prof Exp:* Group mgr, Diag Res & Develop, Ortho Diag, 78-79; assoc investr immunol, Howard Hughes Med Inst, 79-82. *Mem:* Am Chem Soc; Am Soc Microbiologists; Am Asn Immunologists. *Res:* Rapid diagnostics for infectious diseases and hormones. *Mailing Add:* Becton Dickinson Microbiol Syst 39 Loveton Circle Sparks MD 21152

ROSENSTEIN, SHELDON WILLIAM, ORTHODONTICS. *Current Pos:* PROF ORTHOD, DENT SCH, NORTHWESTERN UNIV, 74- *Personal Data:* b Chicago, Ill, Oct 16, 27; m 55; c 3. *Educ:* Northwestern Univ, DDS, 51, MSD, 55. *Prof Exp:* Attend orthodontist, Children's Mem Hosp, Chicago, 55-74. *Concurrent Pos:* Prof orthod, Sch Med, St Louis Univ, 69-74. *Mem:* Sigma Xi. *Res:* Growth and development of orthodontics; clinical cleft lip and palate. *Mailing Add:* Northwestern Univ Dent Sch 4801 W Peterson Ave Chicago IL 60646

ROSENSTOCK, HERBERT BERNHARD, SOLID STATE PHYSICS, STATISTICAL PHYSICS. *Current Pos:* INDEPENDENT CONSULT, 87- *Personal Data:* b Vienna, Austria, Dec 5, 24; nat US; m 50; c James A, Walter H & Linda (Urgohart). *Educ:* Clemson Univ, BS, 44; Univ NC, MS, 50, PhD(physics), 52. *Prof Exp:* Theoretical physicist, US Naval Res Lab, 51-80; res physicist, Sachs & Freeman Assocs, Landover, Md, 80-87. *Concurrent Pos:* Res contract adv, Off Naval Res, 65-66; vis prof, Univ Utah, 70-71. *Mem:* AAAS; fel Am Phys Soc; Sigma Xi; Fedn Am Sci. *Res:* Solid state theory, especially lattice dynamics, energy transfer, color centers, multiphonon absorption, amorphous solids and dislocations; atmospheric physics and light propagation; probability theory; heat conduction; radiation damage to electronic devices; applied mathematics. *Mailing Add:* 5715 Janice Lane Temple Hills MD 20748

ROSENSTOCK, LINDA, OCCUPATIONAL & ENVIRONMENTAL HEALTH. *Current Pos:* Med resident, Univ Wash, Seattle, 77-80, chief resident, Primary Care Internal Med, 79-80, prev med resident, 80-82, actg asst prof, Dept Med, 82-83, from asst prof to assoc prof, 83-93, from adj prof to assoc prof, Dept Environ Health, 83-93, MEM GRAD SCH FAC, UNIV WASH, SEATTLE, 85-, PROF, DEPT MED & DEPT ENVIRON HEALTH, 93-; DIR, NAT INST OCCUP SAFETY & HEALTH, WASHINGTON, DC, 94- *Personal Data:* b New York, NY, Dec 20, 50. *Educ:* Brandeis Univ, AB, 71; Johns Hopkins Univ, MD, 77, MPH, 77; Am Bd Internal Med, dipl, 80; Am Bd Prev Med, dipl, 82. *Concurrent Pos:* Robert Wood Johnson clin scholar, Univ Wash, Seattle, 80-82, actg instr, Dept Med, 80-82, lectr, Dept Environ Health, 82-83, dir, Occup & Environ Med Prog, Dept Med, 82-94, dir, Occup & Environ Med Prog, Dept Environ Health, 86-94, dir, Occup & Environ Med Residency/Fel Training Prog, Depts Environ Health & Med, 86-94, dir, Occup Med Educ Prog, Northwest Occup Health & Safety Educ Resource Ctr, 86-94; dir, Occup & Environ Med Clin, Harborview Med Ctr, Seattle, 81-87, actg sect head gen internal med, 92-94; Henry H Kaiser Family Found fac scholar, 84-89; mem, Comt Fire Toxicol, Nat Acad Sci, 85-86, Comt Role Physician Occup/Environ Med, Inst Med, 87-88, NIH Study Sect, Safety & Occup Health, 88-92; consult, Nat Inst Occup Health, Stockholm, Sweden, 90 & Pan Am Health Orgn, Working Group Pesticides, 91-92; assoc ed, Int J Occup Med & Toxicol, 91- *Mem:* Inst Med-Nat Acad Sci; fel Am Col Physicians; Am Col Occup Med; Am Thoracic Soc; Soc Gen Internal Med; Am Pub Health Asn. *Res:* Author of numerous publications. *Mailing Add:* Nat Inst Occup Safety & Health Humphrey Bldg Rm 715H 200 Independence Ave SW Washington DC 20201

ROSENSTOCK, PAUL DANIEL, ORGANIC CHEMISTRY. *Current Pos:* PRIN CONSULT, CREATIVE REGULATORY SOLUTIONS, BENSALEM, PA, 95-, PRIN CHEMIST, ROUX ASSOC, WEST DEPT, FORD, NJ, 96- *Personal Data:* b Brooklyn, NY, Apr 1, 35; m 56; c 2. *Educ:* Polytech Inst Brooklyn, BS, 56; Pa State Univ, PhD(chem), 60. *Prof Exp:* Chemist, Ethyl Corp, Mich, 60; med chemist, Nat Drug Co, Pa, 63-64; chemist, Rohm & Haas Co, 64-67, group leader, Plant Trouble-Shooting Lab, 67-70, head, Chem Process Develop Lab, 70-74, mgr, Process Develop Dept, 74-81, mgr develop & environ control, Rohn Haas Del Valley, Inc, 81-87, mgr regulatory affairs, 88-90; vpres, BCM Engrs, Inc, 90-92; dir regulatory affairs, Suvar Co, NJ, 93-95. *Concurrent Pos:* Mem, bd examiners, Hazard Control Mgr Cert Bd, 85-89. *Mem:* Water Pollution Control Asn; Air Pollution & Waste Mgt Asn; Am Inst Indust Hyg Asn. *Res:* Process development and design; predominantly on polymers and extrusion; environmental sciences; sanitary and environmental engineering. *Mailing Add:* 3598 Neshaminy Valley Dr Bensalem PA 19020-1109

ROSENSTRAUS, MAURICE JAY, BIOLOGY. *Current Pos:* GROUP LEADER, ROCHE MOLECULAR SYST, BRANCHBURG, NJ, 93- *Personal Data:* b Brooklyn, NY, Mar 13, 51; m 77, Paula Selkow; c David. *Educ:* Rensselaer Polytech Inst, BS, 72; Columbia Univ, PhD(biol), 77. *Prof Exp:* Fel develop genetics, Princeton Univ, 76-78; asst prof biol, Rutgers Univ, New Brunswick, 78-85; sr res scientist, Enzo Biochem, NY, 85-89; prin res scientist, Cytogen Corp, Princeton, 89-93. *Mem:* AAAS; Genetics Soc Am; Sigma Xi. *Res:* Nucleic acid amplification based tests for the diagnosis of infectious and genetic diseases. *Mailing Add:* 40 Smith Rd Somerset NJ 08873

ROSENSTREICH, DAVID LEON, CELLULAR IMMUNOLOGY, ALLERGY. *Current Pos:* PROF, DEPT MED, ALBERT EINSTEIN COL MED, 80-, DIR, DIV ALLERGY & IMMUNOL, 81- *Personal Data:* b New York, NY, Nov 16, 42; m 65, Victoria Abokrek; c Jonathan, Peter & Rebecca. *Educ:* City Col NY, BS, 63; NY Univ, MD, 67. *Prof Exp:* Clin assoc, Nat Inst Allergy & Infectious Dis, 69-72; sr investr, Nat Inst Dent Res, 72-79. *Concurrent Pos:* Vis assoc prof, Rockefeller Univ, 78-79. *Mem:* Am Asn Immunologists; Am Soc Clin Invest; Am Fedn Clin Res; Am Acad Allergy; Am Asn Physicians. *Res:* Regulation of immunity; etiology of allergic and inflammatory diseases. *Mailing Add:* Dept Med Albert Einstein Col Med 1300 Morris Park Ave Bronx NY 10461. *Fax:* 718-430-8573; *E-Mail:* rosenstr@aecom.yu.edu

ROSENSWEIG, JACOB, THORACIC SURGERY, CARDIOVASCULAR SURGERY. *Current Pos:* CHAPMAN PROF VASCULAR RES & DIR, CHAPMAN VASCULAR LAB, SOUTHERN COL OPTOM, MEMPHIS, 84- *Personal Data:* b Montreal, Que, Dec 1, 30; m 52; c 3. *Educ:* McGill Univ, BSc, 51, MD, CM, 55, PhD(exp surg), 60. *Prof Exp:* Fel cardio-thoracic surg, Jewish Gen Hosp, Montreal, 61-62, jr asst, 62-66, assoc surgeon, 66-71, dir clin teaching unit surg, 69-71; assoc prof surg, Sch Med, Univ Conn, 71-74; clin assoc prof surg, Med Sch, Univ Tenn, Memphis, 74-77; clin assoc prof surg, Univ Ark Health Sci, 77-84. *Concurrent Pos:* Clin fel cardiac surg, Royal Victoria Hosp, 61-63; consult thoracic surg, Mt Sinai Hosp, Ste Agathe, Que, 62-71 & thoracic & cardiovasc surg, Maimonides Hosp, Montreal, 66-71; Que Heart Found grant, Jewish Gen Hosp, Montreal, 63-70; Med Res Coun Can grant, Lady Davis Inst Med Res, Montreal, 67-73, head surg div, Exp Surg, 67-68, sr investr, 68-71; vis consult, Nat Heart Inst, Md, 68; lectr surg, McGill Univ, 70; chief surg, Mt Sinai Hosp, Hartford, Conn, 71-74; consult cardiovasc surg, Vet Admin Hosp, Newington, Conn, 72-74; mem staff, Baptist Mem, St Joseph & Methodist Hosps, Memphis, 74-, St Francis Hosp, Memphis, 76-, chmn, Cardiovasc Surg & Thoracic Surg, 81-82; mem coun thrombosis & fel coun cardiovasc surg, Am Heart Asn. *Mem:* Am Col Surgeons; Am Asn Thoracic Surg; Soc Thoracic Surg; fel Am Col Cardiol. *Res:* Circulatory and pulmonary support systems; transplantation, specifically role of platelets in rejection; cerebrovascular and occular vascular disease. *Mailing Add:* Rosensweig Clin 3960 Knight Arnold Rd No 202 Memphis TN 38118-3008

ROSENSWEIG, NORTON S, GASTROENTEROLOGY, CLINICAL NUTRITION. *Current Pos:* from asst prof to assoc prof clin med, 69-78, ASSOC CLIN PROF MED, COL PHYSICIANS & SURGEONS, COLUMBIA UNIV, 79- *Personal Data:* b Brooklyn, NY, Aug 1, 35; m 63; c 3. *Educ:* Princeton Univ, AB, 57; NY Univ, MD, 61. *Prof Exp:* Instr med, Sch Med, Johns Hopkins, 66-69; res internist, US Army Med Res & Nutrit Lab, 66-69; asst prof med, Sch Med, Colo Univ, 67-69; assoc prof med, Med Sch, Cornell Univ, 78-79. *Concurrent Pos:* Dir clin GI, St Luke's Hosp, 69-78; attend physician, St Luke's-Roosevelt Hosp Ctr, 69-78, 79-; prin investr, NIH & US Army Res Grants, 70-75; gov, Am Col Gastroenterol, 78-80; chief gastroenterol & nutrit, N Shore Univ Hosp, 78-79. *Mem:* Am Gastroenterol Asn; Am Soc Clin Nutrit; Am Fedn Clin Res; Am Col Physicians; Am Col Gastroenterol; Am Asn Study Liver Dis. *Res:* Difference between blacks and whites in the incidence of lactase dificiency; series of papers on dietary, vitamin and hormone regulation of human intestinal enzymes; non-cardiac chest pain. *Mailing Add:* Two E 84th St New York NY 10028

ROSENSWEIG, RONALD E(LLIS), CHEMICAL ENGINEERING, FLUID MECHANICS. *Current Pos:* BLAISE PASCAL PROF PHYSICS, UNIV PIERRE & MARIE CURIE, FRANCE, 96- *Personal Data:* b Hamilton, Ohio, Nov 8, 32; m 54, Ruth E (Cohen); c Scott E, Beth E & Perry E. *Educ:* Univ Cincinnati, ChE, 55; Mass Inst Technol, SM, 56, ScD(chem eng), 59. *Honors & Awards:* IR-100 Awards, 65, 68, 70 & 72; Alpha Chi Sigma Award, Am Inst Chem Engrs, 85; Dr Ronald E Rosensweig Res Award named in honor, Ferrofluidics Corp. *Prof Exp:* Asst prof chem eng, Mass Inst Technol, 59-62; sect chief, Avco Corp, Mass, 62-69; founding pres & tech dir, 69-72, chmn, treas & tech dir, 72-73, mem bd dirs, Ferrofluidics Corp, 69-83; res assoc, Corp Res Labs, Exxon Res & Eng Co, 73-76, sr res assoc, 76-85, sci adv, 85-95. *Concurrent Pos:* Indust consult, Nat Res Corp, Linde, Dynatech, 59-62; vis prof chem eng, Univ Minn, 80, vis prof physics, Univ Chicago, 90; steering comt chmn, ICMF, 77-92, mem, 92-; Myerhoff vis prof, Weizmann Inst Sci, Israel, 96. *Mem:* Nat Acad Eng; Am Inst Chem Engrs; Am Phys Soc. *Res:* Magnetic fluids; turbulent mixing; fluidized beds; ferrohydrodynamics. *Mailing Add:* 34 Gloucester Rd Summit NJ 07901. *Fax:* 908-730-3042; *E-Mail:* rerosen@erenj.com

ROSENTHAL, ALEX, ORGANIC CHEMISTRY. *Current Pos:* RETIRED. *Personal Data:* b Scollard, Alta, Oct 16, 14; m 47, Bess Sidorsky; c Arthur, Paula, Eve & Valerie. *Educ:* Univ Alta, BSc, 43, BEd, 47, MSc, 49; Ohio State Univ, PhD(chem), 52. *Prof Exp:* Teacher pub sch, Can, 34-37; prin & teacher high sch, 38-41, 44-46; instr, War Vet Sch, 46-47; fel, Univ Utah, 52-53; from asst prof to prof chem, Univ BC, 53-79. *Concurrent Pos:* Vis prof, Cambridge Univ, 63-64; Killam sr res fel, 75-76; vis scientist, Salk Inst, Sloan Kettering Inst, 75-76. *Mem:* Am Chem Soc; fel Chem Inst Can. *Res:* Photoamidation studies; branched-chain sugar nucleosides; glycosyl amino acids; synthesis of analogs of nucleoside antibiotics. *Mailing Add:* 744 W 53rd Ave Vancouver BC V6P 1K4 Can

ROSENTHAL, ALLAN LAWRENCE, OPHTHAMOLOGY, CLINCAL RESEARCH. *Current Pos:* VPRES CLIN RES, DIV PHARMACEUT, ALLERGAN INC, 91- *Personal Data:* b Montreal, Que, Feb 16, 48; m 71, Patti Salerno; c 2. *Educ:* McGill Univ, BS, 69; Fla State Univ, MS, 72; State Univ NY Upstate Med Ctr, PhD(microbiol), 75. *Prof Exp:* Fel, Brookhaven Nat Lab, 75-78; asst prof biol, Tex Christian Univ, 78-80; scientist, Alcon Labs, Inc, 80-91. *Mailing Add:* Allergan Inc 2525 Dupont PO Box 19534 Irvine CA 92623-9534. *Fax:* 714-246-6756; *E-Mail:* rosenthal_allan@allergan.com

ROSENTHAL, ARNOLD JOSEPH, DESIGN OF EXPERIMENTS, STATISTICAL ANALYSIS OF DATA. *Current Pos:* vpres, Exec Sci Inst, 55-87, PARTNER, ESI ASSOCS, WHIPPANY, NJ, 87- *Personal Data:* b New York, NY, July 9, 22; m 47, Dorothy Shaw; c 4. *Educ:* Polytech Inst Brooklyn, PhD, 58. *Prof Exp:* Sr res chemist, Celanese Corp, Cumberland, Md, 41-44, 47, sr res assoc, Celanese Res Co, Summit, NJ, 47-82. *Concurrent Pos:* Ed, Qual Control & Appl Statist, 56-87 & Opers Res & Mgt Sci, 61-87; staff, Res Inst Scientists Emer, Drew Univ, Madison, NJ, 83- *Mem:* Am Chem Soc; Opers Res Soc Am; Am Soc Qual Control; Am Statist Asn. *Res:* Synthetic fibers; mechanisms of chemical reactions; physical chemistry of polymers; statistical design and analysis of experiments; operations research. *Mailing Add:* Eight Ford Hill Rd Whippany NJ 07981

ROSENTHAL, ARTHUR FREDERICK, BIOCHEMISTRY. *Current Pos:* DIR BIOCHEM, REN LABS. *Personal Data:* b Brooklyn, NY, Aug 3, 31; m 67; c 3. *Educ:* Antioch Col, BS, 54; Harvard Univ, AM, 56, PhD(biochem), 60; Am Bd Clin Chem, dipl, 74. *Prof Exp:* Fel chem, Univ Birmingham, 61-62 & Auburn Univ, 62; chief biochem, Long Island Jewish-Hillside Med Ctr, 62-72; assoc prof path, State Univ NY, Stony Brook, 72- *Concurrent Pos:* Prin investr, NIH Proj Grant, 63-; adj prof biochem, PhD Prog Biochem, City Univ New York, 74-; adj prof, City Univ NY; exten assoc prof, Univ Puerto Rico, 76- *Mem:* Am Chem Soc; The Chem Soc; Am Asn Clin Chemists; Am Soc Biol Chemists. *Res:* Phospholipid chemistry and biochemistry; synthetic organophosphorus chemistry; lipid chemistry and metabolism; clinical chemistry; protein modification. *Mailing Add:* E5RD Specialty Labs 830 NW 57th Ct Ft Lauderdale FL 33309

ROSENTHAL, DAN G, TITANIUM ALLOYS,METAL MATRIX COMPOSITES. *Current Pos:* SR DEVELOP ENGR, ALLIED SIGNAL AEROSPACE, 77- *Personal Data:* b Bucharest, Romania, May 8, 39; US citizen; m, Gabriela Micsumescu; c Andy. *Educ:* Polytech Inst, Bucharest, Romania, MS, 57; Polytech Inst, NY, MS, 82; Polytech Univ, Bucharest, PhD(mat sci-environ), 94. *Mem:* Am Soc Metals Int. *Res:* Studies and applications of alpha-2 titanium aluminide alloys; titanium aluminide composites. *Mailing Add:* 19 Great Oak Rd Shelton CT 06484-5210

ROSENTHAL, DONALD, ANALYTICAL CHEMISTRY, PHYSICAL CHEMISTRY. *Current Pos:* assoc prof, 61-66, exec officer, Dept Chem, 81-88, prof, 66-91, EMER PROF CHEM, CLARKSON UNIV, 91- *Personal Data:* b Princeton, NJ, July 16, 26; m 55; c 4. *Educ:* Princeton Univ, AB, 49; Columbia Univ, AM, 50, PhD(chem), 55. *Prof Exp:* Instr chem, Columbia Univ, 54-55 & Univ Minn, 55-56; from instr to asst prof, Univ Chicago, 56-61. *Concurrent Pos:* Sr res assoc, Brandeis Univ, 70-71; ed, Comput Chem Educ Newslett, 81-88; mem, comt comput chem educ, Div Chem Educ, Am Chem Soc. *Mem:* AAAS; Am Chem Soc; NY Acad Sci. *Res:* Solution chemistry; equilibria, acidity and kinetics in aqueous and non-aqueous solutions; potentiometry and spectrophotometry; instrumental methods of analysis; chromatography; computer simulation. *Mailing Add:* Dept Chem Clarkson Univ Potsdam NY 13699-5810

ROSENTHAL, ERIC THOMAS, DEVELOPMENTAL BIOLOGY, MARINE BIOLOGY. *Current Pos:* ASST PROF, PAC BIOMED RES CTR, UNIV HAWAII, 87- *Educ:* Wesleyan Univ, BA, 76; Harvard Univ, PhD(cell & develop biol), 83. *Res:* Molecular biology of development in marine invertebrates with particular focus on MRNA metabolism and translation. *Mailing Add:* Dept Biol Sci Calif State Univ Hayward CA 94542. *Fax:* 808-599-4817; *E-Mail:* ericr@uhunix.uhcc.hawaii.edu

ROSENTHAL, F(ELIX), MECHANICS. *Current Pos:* PRES, SIGNAL SEPARATION TECHNOL, 93- *Personal Data:* b Munich, Ger, Feb 6, 25; nat US; m, Mildrid Nyhamar; c Linda, Fred & Andy. *Educ:* Ill Inst Technol, BS, 47, MS, 48, PhD(appl mech), 52. *Prof Exp:* Instr, Ill Inst Technol, 47-50, res engr, Armour Res Found, 48-54; proj engr & head, Math Sect, Res Ctr, Clevite Corp, 54-58; staff scientist, Raytheon Co, 58-61; adv engr, Fed Systs Div, IBM Corp, 61-68; vpres res & develop, Oceanog, Inc, 68-69; independent consult mech design, underwater acoust & signal processing, 69-71; head appl mech br, Naval Res Lab, 71-78, res mech eng, 78-92. *Mem:* Am Soc Mech Engrs; Fedn Am Sci; sr mem Inst Elec & Electronics Engrs; World Federalist Asn. *Res:* Applied mechanics; elasticity, dynamics; acoustics; active cancellation of noise and vibration; piezoelectric transducers; wave propagation; oceanography; acoustic and seismic signal processing; theory & application of noise cancelling; structural dynamics; fluid mechanics; underwater engineering; underwater acoustics. *Mailing Add:* 4020 Iva Lane Annandale VA 22003. *Fax:* 703-978-4973; *E-Mail:* sigsep@ix.netcom.com

ROSENTHAL, FRED, NEUROPHYSIOLOGY. *Current Pos:* ASSOC RES PHYSIOLOGIST, CARDIOVASC RES INST, MED SCH, UNIV CALIF, SAN FRANCISCO, 70- *Personal Data:* b Breslau, Ger, Feb 26, 31; US citizen; m 57; c 2. *Educ:* Univ Calif, Berkeley, BA, 52, PhD(psychol), 56; Stanford Univ, MD, 60. *Prof Exp:* Res physiologist, Univ Calif, Berkeley, 60-62; fel neurophysiol, Univ Wash, 62-64; asst prof, New York Med Col, Flower & Fifth Ave Hosps, 64-69, assoc prof, 69-70. *Mem:* Am Physiol Soc; Biophys Soc. *Res:* Description of the extracellular electric field around cortical pyramidal tract neurons; effects of radiation on brain function; relations between somatic motor systems and cardiovascular changes. *Mailing Add:* 825 Van Ness Ave 405 San Francisco CA 94109-7837

ROSENTHAL, GERALD A, PLANT BIOCHEMISTRY, CHEMICAL ECOLOGY. *Current Pos:* from asst prof to assoc prof, 73-80, PROF BIOL, UNIV KY, 80- *Personal Data:* b New York, NY, Jan 9, 39; m 60; c 3. *Educ:* Syracuse Univ, BS, 62; Duke Univ, MF, 63, PhD(plant physiol, biochem), 66. *Prof Exp:* NIH fel biochem, Med Col, Cornell Univ, 66-69; asst prof biol, Case Western Reserve Univ, 69-72. *Concurrent Pos:* NIH grant, 70-73, 74-78, 79-82 & 82-87; NSF grants, 73-75, 76-79, 80-83 & 89-93; Lady Davis prof agr entom, Hebrew Univ Jerusalem, 79; Fulbright-Hays res scholar, Univ Louis Pasteur, 85. *Mem:* Int Soc Chem Ecol. *Res:* Plant amino acid metabolism and enzymology; biochemistry of plant-insect interaction; chemical-ecology. *Mailing Add:* Dept Biol Sci Univ Ky 500 S Limestone St Lexington KY 40506-0001

ROSENTHAL, GERSON MAX, JR, ECOLOGY, ZOOLOGY. *Current Pos:* Ford fel, Univ Chicago, 54, instr nat sci, 54-56, from asst prof to assoc prof, 59-76, prof biol, social sci & geog, 76-89, EMER PROF BIOL, UNIV CHICAGO, 87- *Personal Data:* b Pittsfield, Mass, Mar 13, 22; m 54, Marcia White; c Jonathan M. *Educ:* Dartmouth Col, AB, 43; Univ Calif, MS, 51, PhD(zool), 54. *Honors & Awards:* Quantrell Award, 63. *Prof Exp:* Asst zool, Univ Chicago, 46-48; asst, Univ Calif, 49-51, assoc, 52-53. *Concurrent Pos:* Consult ecol, Oak Ridge Inst Nuclear Res, 63-76; vis scientist, Argonnne Nat Lab, 69-70, consult ecol, 70-74. *Mem:* AAAS; Ecol Soc Am; Am Inst Biol Sci. *Res:* Physiological ecology; energetics of ecosystems; radioecology; biogeography; relationship of organisms to microclimates; animal populations. *Mailing Add:* 17 Gates-Blake Hall Univ Chicago 5845 S Ellis Ave Chicago IL 60637

ROSENTHAL, HAROLD LESLIE, BIOCHEMISTRY, NEUROSCIENCES. *Current Pos:* from asst prof to assoc prof, 58-64, chmn dept, 58-74, prof, 65-87, EMER PROF MED SCI, SCH DENT, WASHINGTON UNIV, 87- *Personal Data:* b Elizabeth, NJ, Mar 26, 22; m 47, Rose Schwartz; c Jenifer A & Pamela S. *Educ:* Univ NMex, BSc, 44; Rutgers Univ, PhD(biochem), 51. *Prof Exp:* Res biochemist, Rutgers Univ, 49-51; res biochemist, Philadelphia Gen Hosp, 51; instr med, Tulane Univ, 51-53; chief biochem, Rochester Gen Hosp, 53-58. *Concurrent Pos:* Res assoc, Minerva Found Med Res, Helsinki, Finland, 66; Nat Acad Sci exchange scientist, Inst Nutrit, Budapest, Hungary, 73-74. *Mem:* Am Chem Soc; Am Inst Nutrit; Am Soc Biol Chemists; fel AAAS; Sigma Xi. *Res:* Intermediary metabolism; vitamins and radioactive isotopes; neurochemistry; brain research. *Mailing Add:* 7541 Teasdale University City MO 63130

ROSENTHAL, HENRY BERNARD, NUCLEAR SAFETY ENGINEERING, RISK ASSESSMENT. *Current Pos:* RETIRED. *Personal Data:* b Philadelphia, Pa, Dec 31, 17; m 45, Frances Joyce Lipman; c Lynne M (DeLuca) & David M. *Educ:* Trenton State Col, BS, 40; Rutgers Univ, MS, 51. *Prof Exp:* Group leader, critical nuclear exps, ANP Dept, Gen Elec Co, 51-56; supvr, critical reactor exps, Nuclear Div, Martin Marietta, 57-68, mgr, nuclear survivability, Orlando Div, 68-75; sr nuclear safety engr, US Dept Energy, 76-84. *Concurrent Pos:* Self-employed consult nuclear safety, 84- *Mem:* Am Nuclear Soc; AAAS; Am Soc Safety Engrs; sr mem Syst Safety Soc; Soc Risk Analysis; Sigma Xi. *Res:* Safety analysis review, appraisal and risk assessment systems; missile system survivability and hardness to nuclear weapons effects; developmental experimental radiation, nuclear criticality and nuclear reactor physics. *Mailing Add:* 107 Water Oak Dr Sanford FL 32773

ROSENTHAL, HOWARD, CHEMICAL ENGINEERING. *Current Pos:* RETIRED. *Personal Data:* b Brooklyn, NY, Sept 15, 24; m 51, Arlene Weinstein; c Andrea & Iden. *Educ:* City Col New York, BChE, 44; NY Univ, MChE, 49. *Prof Exp:* Res engr, Sunray Elec Co, 46-47; asst chem eng, NY Univ, 48-49; mem tech staff, RCA Labs, 49-59, indust hyg & safety engr, RCA Corp, 59-63, sr tech adminr, 63-66, mgr tech admin, 66-68, adminr staff serv, Res & Eng, 68-70, dir, 70-72, staff vpres eng, 72-86. *Mem:* Inst Elec & Electronics Engrs. *Res:* Engineering management. *Mailing Add:* 3600 Conshohocken Ave Philadelphia PA 19131

ROSENTHAL, IRA MAURICE, PEDIATRICS, PEDIATRIC ENDOCRINOLOGY. *Current Pos:* From asst prof to prof, 53-90, head dept, 74-82, EMER PROF PEDIAT, ABRAHAM LINCOLN SCH MED, UNIV ILL COL MED, 90- *Personal Data:* b New York, NY, June 11, 20; wid; c Anne (Glist) & Judith. *Educ:* Univ Ind, AB, 40, MD, 43. *Concurrent Pos:* Clin prof pediat, Univ Chicago. *Mem:* Soc Pediat Res; Endocrine Soc; Am Acad Pediat; Am Fedn Clin Res; Am Pediat Soc; Sigma Xi. *Res:* Pediatric endocrinology and metabolism; sexual differentiation abnormalities; catecholamine metabolism. *Mailing Add:* Dept Pediat Univ Chicago 5841 S Maryland Ave Mail Code 5053 Chicago IL 60637. *Fax:* 773-702-0443

ROSENTHAL, J WILLIAM, OPHTHALMOLOGY, SURGERY. *Current Pos:* From instr to assoc clin prof, 52-71, CLIN PROF OPHTHAL, MED SCH, TULANE UNIV, 71- *Personal Data:* b New Orleans, La, Oct 30, 22; m 45, Harriet Stern; c Paul & Susan. *Educ:* Tulane Univ, BS, 43, MD, 45; Univ Pa, MSc, 52, DSc, 62; Am Bd Ophthal, dipl, 54. *Honors & Awards:* Serv Award, Am Acad Ophthal, 85, Honor Award, 90. *Concurrent Pos:* Sr ophthal surg, Touro Infirmary & Eye, Ear, Nose & Throat Hosp, 52-; chief ophthal, Smithsoman Inst; cur, Am Acad Ophthal Found Mus. *Mem:* Fr Ophthal Soc; fel Am Col Surgeons; Am Acad Ophthal & Otolaryngol; fel Royal Soc Med; fel Int Col Surgeons; Am Col Surgeons; Am Col Surgeons. *Res:* Tularemia; pterygia; glaucoma with brachydactyly and spherophakia; trachoma; accident prone children; microsurgery; history of spectacles. *Mailing Add:* 3322 St Claude Ave New Orleans LA 70117

ROSENTHAL, JEFFREY, PHOTOELECTROCHEMISTRY. *Current Pos:* from asst prof to assoc prof, 82-90, PROF ANALYTICAL CHEM, UNIV WIS, RIVER FALLS, 90- *Personal Data:* b El Paso, Tex, Sept 18, 53; m 75; c 3. *Educ:* Univ Minn, Duluth, BS, 75; Purdue Univ, PhD(anal chem), 80. *Prof Exp:* Asst prof, Oakland Univ, 80-82. *Mem:* Am Chem Soc. *Res:* Semiconductor photoelectrochemistry; design of instrumentation (optimized for transient measurements); computer controlled instrumentation and chemical software in CTT. *Mailing Add:* Dept Chem Univ Wis River Falls WI 54022

ROSENTHAL, JOHN WILLIAM, MODEL THEORY, DECIDABILITY THEORY. *Current Pos:* from asst prof to assoc prof, 71-84, PROF MATH, ITHACA COL, 84- *Personal Data:* b New York, NY, Sept 6, 40; m 68, Heather A Levine; c Marc A & Joshua. *Educ:* Mass Inst Technol, BS, 65, PhD(math), 68. *Prof Exp:* Asst prof math, State Univ NY Stony Brook, 68-71, NSF res contract, 69-71. *Concurrent Pos:* Vis assoc prof, Mich State Univ, 77-78; vis lectr, Univ Sydney, Australia, 78; vis res prof, Mich State Univ, 84-85; visitor, Hebrew Univ, 85; vis prof, Cornell Univ, 92-93. *Mem:* Math Asn Am; Am Math Soc; Asn Symbolic Logic. *Res:* Mathematical logic; model theory; decidability theory; constructive algebra; computational complexity; algebraically closed fields; asymptotic methods in combinatorics. *Mailing Add:* Dept Math & Comput Sci Ithaca Col Ithaca NY 14853-5901

ROSENTHAL, JUDITH WOLDER, SCIENCE FOR LIMITED ENGLISH PROFICIENT STUDENTS. *Current Pos:* PROF BIOL, KEAN COL NJ, 74- *Personal Data:* b New York, NY, May 12, 45; c 1. *Educ:* Brown Univ, BA, 67, PhD(physiol chem), 71; Kean Col, MA, 95. *Prof Exp:* Fel, Univ Toronto, 71-72 & McMaster Univ, 72-73. *Mem:* AAAS; Nat Asn Bilingual Educ; Teachers Eng Speakers Other Lang. *Res:* Science for limited English proficient students; bilingual higher education; science, technology and society. *Mailing Add:* Dept Biol Kean Col NJ Union NJ 07083

ROSENTHAL, KEN STEVEN, HERPES SIMPLEX VIRUS VIRULENCE MECHANISMS, GLYCOPROTEIN PROCESSING. *Current Pos:* from asst prof to assoc prof, 79-91, PROF MICROBIOL & IMMUNOL, NORTHEASTERN OHIO UNIV COL MED, 91- *Personal Data:* b Brooklyn, NY, July 23, 51; m 75, Judith E Lindner; c Joshua A & Rachel B. *Educ:* Univ Del, BS, 73; Univ Ill, Urbana, MS, 76, PhD(biochem), 77. *Prof Exp:* Res asst, Univ Ill, 73-77; res fel, Harvard Med Sch, 77-79. *Concurrent Pos:* Grad fac, Kent State Univ, 79-; consult, Merz & Co Inc, 83-90; adj assoc prof, Akron Univ, 84-; vis prof, Dept Biochem, Case Western Reserve Univ Med Sch, 92-93; co-auth & ed, Med Microbiol, 94, Ace Microb/Immunol. *Mem:* Am Soc Microbiol; AAAS; Am Soc Biochem & Molecular Biol; Sigma Xi; NY Acad Sci. *Res:* The study of herpes simplex virus glycoproteins and their role in infection and immunity; antiviral drugs including tromantadine, amantadine and D609; virology; heteroconjugate antiviral vaccines. *Mailing Add:* 4209 SR 44 PO Box 95 Rootstown OH 44272. *Fax:* 440-325-2524

ROSENTHAL, KENNETH LEE, CELL MEDIATED IMMUNITY, VIROLOGY. *Current Pos:* asst prof, 81-86, ASSOC PROF IMMUNOL, MCMASTER UNIV, CAN, 86- *Personal Data:* b Chicago, Ill, Nov 29, 50; m 77; c 2. *Educ:* Univ Ill, Urbana, BSc, 72, MSc, 74; McMaster Univ, Can, PhD(med sci), 78. *Prof Exp:* Fel immunol, Scripps Clin Res Found, Calif, 78-80 & Univ Zurich, Switz, 80-81. *Concurrent Pos:* Damon Runyon Fel, Walter Winchell Cancer Found, 78 & Swiss Nat Sci Found, 80; scholar, Med Res Coun Can, 82-87. *Mem:* Am Asn Immunologists; Can Soc Immunol; Am Soc Microbiol; Am Soc Virol. *Res:* Generation, specificity and role of anti-viral cytotoxic T lymphocytes; acquired immunodeficiency syndrome (AIDS); virus-lymphocyte interactions. *Mailing Add:* Dept Path McMaster Univ Health Sci Ctr 1200 Main St W HSC 3N26 Hamilton ON L8N 3Z5 Can. *Fax:* 416-522-6750

ROSENTHAL, LEE, ELECTRICAL & SYSTEMS ENGINEERING. *Current Pos:* assoc prof, 72-80, PROF, FAIRLEIGH DICKINSON UNIV, 80- *Personal Data:* b Brooklyn, NY, Nov 28, 37. *Educ:* Polytech Inst Brooklyn, BEE, 58, PhD(elec eng), 67; Calif Inst Technol, MS, 59. *Prof Exp:* Engr, Hughes Aircraft Co, 58-59; lectr elec eng, City Col New York, 62-66; asst prof, Stevens Inst Technol, 66-70, Hofstra Univ, 70-72. *Res:* Linear integrated circuits; process control; technology and the arts; technology and society. *Mailing Add:* Dept Eng Technol Fairleigh Dickinson Univ Teaneck NJ 07666

ROSENTHAL, LEONARD JASON, VIROLOGY, MOLECULAR BIOLOGY. *Current Pos:* asst prof microbiol, 75-82, ASSOC PROF MICROBIOL & PEDIAT, GEORGETOWN UNIV SCH MED & DENT, 82- *Personal Data:* b Boston, Mass, June 23, 42; m 76; c 2. *Educ:* Univ Vt, BA, 64; Southern Ill Univ, MA, 66; Kans State Univ, PhD(bact), 69. *Prof Exp:* Res fel, Harvard Med Sch, 69-71, instr, 72-73; Europ Molecular Biol Orgn fel, Univ Geneva, 73-74 & Leukemia Soc Am Spec fel, NIH, 74-75. *Concurrent Pos:* Mem, sci adv bd, Int Biotechnol, Inc; mem, Vincent L Lombardi Cancer Ctr, 75-; panelist, Res Initiation & Support Prog, NIH, 75-76, reviewer, 80-81; contract reviewer, Nat Inst Child Health & Human Develop, 79-81; Leukemia Soc Am Scholar, 80-85; sci adv bd, Int Biotechnol, Inc, 83-87; mem special study sect, Nat Heart, Lung, & Blood Inst, 88; hon prof virol, Wuhan Univ, 88-, hon prof microbiol, Jinan Univ, 88- *Mem:* Am Soc Microbiol; Sigma Xi; Am Soc Virol. *Res:* Determining the association of human herpes viruses with cancer; author of numerous books, chapters, and papers. *Mailing Add:* 302 Currier Dr Rockville MD 20850-2927

ROSENTHAL, LOIS C, PHYSICAL CHEMISTRY. *Current Pos:* asst prof, 77-84, ASSOC PROF CHEM, UNIV SANTA CLARA, 84- *Personal Data:* b Boston, Mass, Mar 20, 46; c 3. *Educ:* Simmons Col, BS, 68; Univ Calif, Berkeley, PhD(chem), 75. *Prof Exp:* Instr chem, Diablo Valley Col, 75-77. *Mem:* Am Chem Soc. *Res:* Molecular motion in fluids; infrared and Raman spectroscopy. *Mailing Add:* 49 Pearl Ave Winthrop MA 02152

ROSENTHAL, LOUIS AARON, ELECTRONICS ENGINEERING. *Current Pos:* from assoc prof to prof, 44-81, EMER PROF ELEC ENG, RUTGERS UNIV, NEW BRUNSWICK, 81- *Personal Data:* b New York, NY, Aug 16, 22; wid; c 3. *Educ:* City Col New York, BEE, 43; Polytech Inst Brooklyn, MEE, 47. *Prof Exp:* Elec engr, Star Elec Motor Co, NJ, 43; instr elec eng, Lehigh Univ, 44. *Concurrent Pos:* Consult, US Naval Surface Weapons Ctr, 46-, Union Carbide Corp, 50-86 & var chemcorps. *Mem:* Sr mem Inst Elec & Electronics Engrs; Sigma Xi; Electrostatic Soc Am. *Res:* Corona discharge processing; static electricity hazards and control; electroexplosive devices. *Mailing Add:* 384B Stirling Dr Cranbury NJ 08512-3922

ROSENTHAL, MICHAEL DAVID, SOLID STATE PHYSICS. *Current Pos:* chief, Int Nuclear Affairs Div, 86-95, CHIEF, NUCLEAR SAFEGUARDS & TECHNOL DIV, US ARM CONTROL & DISARMAMENT AGENCY, 95- *Personal Data:* b Brooklyn, NY, Dec 30, 43; m 81; c 2. *Educ:* Wesleyan Univ, BA, 65; Cornell Univ, PhD(physics), 72. *Prof Exp:* Res assoc sci policy, Prog Sci, Technol & Soc, Cornell Univ, 71-73; instr physics, Dept Physics, Rutgers Univ, 73-74; asst prof physics, Swarthmore Col, 74-77; phys sci officer, Non Proliferation Bur, US Arms Control & Disarmament Agency, 77-81; sr officer, Int Atomic Energy Agency, 81-86. *Concurrent Pos:* Vis scientist, Cornell Univ, 74; consult math policy res, 76-77. *Mem:* Sigma Xi; AAAS; Fedn Am Scientists. *Res:* International safeguards and nuclear non-proliferation issues related to the nuclear non-proliferation treaty; nuclear cooperation; regional arms control. *Mailing Add:* 8809 Gallant Green Dr McLean VA 22102. *Fax:* 202-736-4336; *E-Mail:* rosentmi@alda.gov

ROSENTHAL, MICHAEL R, INORGANIC CHEMISTRY, ENVIRONMENTAL SCIENCES. *Current Pos:* DEP SECY, MD HIGHER EDUC COMN, 96. *Personal Data:* b Youngstown, Ohio, Dec 2, 39; m 63, Linda Gabler; c Heidi, Erika & Nicolas. *Educ:* Case Western Res Univ, AB, 61; Univ Ill, MS, 63, PhD(chem), 65. *Prof Exp:* From asst prof to assoc prof, Bard Col, 65-73, prof chem, 73-84, assoc dean acad affairs, 80-84; vpres acad affairs & dean, St Mary's Col Md, 84-89, prof chem, 84-89; provost & dean fac, prof chem, Southwestern Univ, 89-96. *Mem:* AAAS; Am Chem Soc; Royal Soc Chem. *Res:* Coordination chemistry; water chemistry in the natural environment; water pollution. *Mailing Add:* 107 Mansion Dr Annapolis MD 21403. *Fax:* 410-974-3513; *E-Mail:* mrosenth@mhec.state.md.us

ROSENTHAL, MILTON FREDERICK, MINERALS & CHEMICALS. *Current Pos:* EMER DIR, SALOMON INC & FERRO CORP. *Personal Data:* b New York, NY, Nov 24, 13; m 43, Frieda Bojar; c Ann (Mitro). *Educ:* City Col NY, BA, 32; Columbia Univ, LLB, 35. *Prof Exp:* Res asst, NY State Law Rev Comn, 35-37; law secy, Fed Judge William Bondy, 37-40; assoc atty, Leve, Hecht & Hadfield, 40-42; secy & treas, Hugo Stinnes Corp, 46-48, exec vpres & treas, 48-49, pres, dir & chief exec officer, 49-64; pres, dir & chief exec officer, Minerals & Chems Philipp Corp, 64-67; pres, dir & chief, oper officer, Englehard Minerals & Chem Corp, 67-71, chmn, pres, chief exec officer & dir, 71-81. *Mailing Add:* 450 Woodlands Rd Harrison NY 10528-1220

ROSENTHAL, MIRIAM DICK, LIPID METABOLISM, CELL BIOLOGY. *Current Pos:* ASSOC PROF BIOCHEM, EASTERN VA MED SCH, 77- *Educ:* Brandeis Univ, PhD(develop biol), 74. *Mailing Add:* Dept Biochem Med Sch Eastern Va PO Box 1980 Norfolk VA 23501-1980. *Fax:* 757-623-4864

ROSENTHAL, MURRAY WILFORD, NUCLEAR ENGINEERING. *Current Pos:* CONSULT, 94- *Personal Data:* b Greenville, Miss, Feb 25, 26; m 49, Miriam Teplit; c Elaine & Douglas. *Educ:* La State Univ, BS, 49; Mass Inst Technol, PhD(chem eng), 53. *Honors & Awards:* Distinguished Career Award, Fusion Power Assocs, 93. *Prof Exp:* Develop engr, Oak Ridge Nat Lab, 53-55, lectr, Oak Ridge Sch Reactor Technol, 55-56, leader, Reactor Anal Group, 55-59, group leader, Anal Advan Reactor Div, 59-61, proj engr, Pebble Bld Reactor Exp, 61-63, head, Long Range Planning sect, 63-65, dir planning & eval, 65, dir, Molten Salt Reactor Prog, 66-73, actg dep lab dir, 73-74, assoc lab dir, Advan Energy Systs, 74-81, dep dir, 89-93. *Concurrent Pos:* Vis prof, Mass Inst Technol, 61; tech asst to asst gen mgr reactors, Atomic Energy Comn, 65-66; US deleg, Panel Utilization Thorium in Power Reactors, Int Atomic Energy Agency, Vienna, 65, Manila Conf Probs & Prospects of Nuclear Power Appln Develop Countries, 66 & Int Conf on Nuclear Energy, Geneva, 71; dir, Am Nuclear Soc, 70-73; adv panel fusion energy, Energy Res & Prod Subcomt, Comt Space Sci & Technol, US House Rep, 81-86; adv ed, Eng Sci & Technol News, 80-82; magnetic fusion adv comt, 82-84, Japan-US Magnetic Fusion Coor Comt, 82-88, US-USSR Joint Fusion Power Coor Comt, 85-88; mem adv panel, Off Technol Assessment Magnetic Fusion Res & Demonstration, 86-88. *Mem:* Nat Acad Eng; fel Am Nuclear Soc; Sigma Xi; AAAS. *Res:* Energy research and development. *Mailing Add:* 124 Carnegie Dr Oak Ridge TN 37830

ROSENTHAL, MURRAY WILLIAM, PHARMACEUTICAL CHEMISTRY. *Current Pos:* CONSULT, PHARMACEUT INDUST, 83- *Personal Data:* b Stamford, Conn, Aug 15, 18; m 47; c 2. *Educ:* Pa State Univ, BS, 41, MS, 42. *Prof Exp:* Chemist, Philadelphia Qm Depot, 42-43 & Edcan Labs, 46-48; asst res dir, McKesson-Robbins, 48-51; from asst res dir to res dir, Block Drug Co, Inc, 51-62, vpres res & develop, 62-83. *Concurrent Pos:* Dir, Therapeut Res Found. *Mem:* AAAS; Am Chem Soc; Am Pharmaceut Asn. *Res:* Development of proprietary pharmaceuticals and toiletries. *Mailing Add:* 688B Old Nassau Rd Jamesburg NJ 08831-1696

ROSENTHAL, MYRON, BRAIN METABOLISM, ELECTROPHYSIOLOGY. *Current Pos:* PROF NEUROL & PHYSIOL BIOPHYS, SCH MED, UNIV MIAMI, 77- *Educ:* Duke Univ, PhD(physiol & pharmacol), 69. *Mailing Add:* Dept Neurol & Physiol/Biophys Sch Med Univ Miami PO Box 016960 Miami FL 33101

ROSENTHAL, NATHAN RAYMOND, BIOCHEMISTRY, PHARMACOLOGY. *Current Pos:* RETIRED. *Personal Data:* b Washington, DC, Oct 29, 25; m 55, Marjorie Broder; c Joanne C (Levine), Stuart B, Barbara S (Ritter) & Amy L (Goldstein). *Educ:* Georgetown Univ, BS, 49, MS, 51, PhD(biochem), 57. *Honors & Awards:* Meritorious Achievement Award, US Dept Army, 57. *Prof Exp:* Chemist, NIH, 51-54; biochemist, Walter Reed Army Inst Res, 54-58; chemist, Bur Drugs, Food & Drug Admin, 58-90. *Concurrent Pos:* Chem consult. *Mem:* Am Chem Soc; Asn Off Anal Chem; Sigma Xi. *Res:* Biochemistry of endocrine glands and their regulation and metabolism; biological activity of organophosphorous pesticides; manufacturing controls on radiopharmaceutical, antineoplastic, cardio-renal, psychopharmacologic, new drugs and investigational new drugs. *Mailing Add:* 18708 Bloomfield Rd Olney MD 20832-1308

ROSENTHAL, NORMAN E, PSYCHIATRY. *Current Pos:* CHIEF, SECT ENVIRON PSYCHIAT, CLIN PSYCHOBIOL BR, NIMH, 79- *Personal Data:* m 74, Leora Rosen; c Joshua. *Educ:* Univ Witwatersrand, Johannesburg, MD. *Honors & Awards:* Anna Monika Found Prize, 91. *Prof Exp:* Intern, Johannesburg Gen Hosp; From resident to chief resident psychiat, NY State Psychiat Inst, Columbia Presby Med Ctr, 76-79. *Mem:* Soc Light Ther & Biol Rhythms (pres). *Res:* Mood disorders and biological rhythms; effects of seasons on mood and behavior and the antidepressant effects of light; author of numerous articles. *Mailing Add:* 11110 Stephalee Lane Rockville MD 20852

ROSENTHAL, PETER (MICHAEL), MATHEMATICS. *Current Pos:* from asst prof to assoc prof, 67-76, PROF MATH, UNIV TORONTO, 76- *Personal Data:* b New York, NY, June 1, 41; m 60, 85; c 5. *Educ:* Queens Col, NY, BS, 62; Univ Mich, Ann Arbor, MA, 63, PhD(math), 67. *Prof Exp:* Instr math, Univ Toledo, 66-67. *Mem:* Am Math Soc; Can Math Soc. *Res:* Operators on Hilbert and Banach spaces. *Mailing Add:* Dept Math Univ Toronto Toronto ON M5S 1A1 Can. *E-Mail:* rosent@math.toronto.ca

ROSENTHAL, RICHARD ALAN, MECHANICAL & OPTICAL ENGINEERING. *Current Pos:* CONSULT, 96- *Personal Data:* b Newark, NJ, Aug 29, 36; div; c 2. *Educ:* Mass Inst Technol, BSME, 58, MSME, 59; Worcester Polytech Inst, MBA, 87. *Prof Exp:* Mem tech staff, Bell Tel Labs, Inc, 59-64; sr engr, Itek Corp, 64-65; staff engr, 65-68; sr optical engr, Polaroid Corp, 68-71, work mgr, 71-79, tech mgr, Instrumentation & Electronics Eng Div, 79-91, tech mgr graphics imaging, 91-96. *Mem:* Sr mem Am Soc Mech Engrs. *Res:* Electrooptical and electromechanical instruments and instrumentation systems. *Mailing Add:* 5 Bacon St Winchester MA 01890

ROSENTHAL, ROBERT, PSYCHOLOGY, SOCIAL & CLINICALLY METHODOLOGICAL. *Current Pos:* lectr clin psychol, 62-67, chmn, Dept Psychol, 92-95, PROF SOCIAL PSYCHOL, HARVARD UNIV, MASS, 67-, EDGAR PIERCE PROF PSYCHOL, 95- *Personal Data:* b Giessen, Ger, Mar 2, 33; US citizen; m 51, MaryLu Clayton; c Roberta, David C & Virginia. *Educ:* Univ Calif, Los Angeles, AB, 53, PhD(clin psychol), 56. *Honors & Awards:* Co-recipient, Behav Sci Res Prize, AAAS, 60 & 93; Cattell Awards, Soc Exp Social Psychol, 67 & 95, Campbell Award, 88, Monograph Award, 96, Distinguished Scientist Award, 96. *Prof Exp:* Lectr, Univ Southern Calif, 56-57; from asst prof to assoc prof & coordr clin training, Univ NDak, 57-62. *Concurrent Pos:* Actg instr, Univ Calif, Los Angeles, 57; vis assoc prof, Ohio State Univ, 60-61; lectr, Boston Univ, 65-66; sr Fulbright scholar, 72; Guggenheim fel, 73-74; fel, Ctr Advan Study Behav Sci, 88-89. *Mem:* Fel AAAS; fel Am Psychol Soc; Soc Exp Social Psychol; Sigma Xi; fel Am Psychol Asn; fel Soc Pers Soc Psychol. *Res:* Interpersonal expectancy effects; nonverbal communication; research methods; data analysis including contrast analysis and meta-analysis. *Mailing Add:* Harvard Univ 33 Kirkland St Cambridge MA 02138-2044

ROSENTHAL, RUDOLPH, ORGANIC CHEMISTRY. *Current Pos:* RETIRED. *Personal Data:* b Atlantic City, NJ, Mar 24, 23; m 60; c 2. *Educ:* Temple Univ, AB, 44, MA, 48; Univ Southern Calif, PhD(chem), 51. *Prof Exp:* Res chemist, Allied Chem Corp, 51-61; sr res chemist, Glenolden, Atlantic Richfield Co, Newton Sq, 61-81, sr res chemist, 81. *Mem:* Am Chem Soc. *Res:* Olefin oxides; catalytic oxidation; nitration of olefins; isocyanates. *Mailing Add:* Apt 822 777 W Germantown Pike Plymouth Meeting PA 19462-1022

ROSENTHAL, SAUL HASKELL, PSYCHIATRY. *Current Pos:* PRIV PRACT, 73- *Personal Data:* b Brooklyn, NY, Nov 14, 36; m 80, Cynthia Storrie; c Jonathan, David & Sadie. *Educ:* Harvard Univ, BA, 58, Harvard Med Sch, MD, 62; Am Bd Psychiat & Neurol, dipl, 69. *Prof Exp:* Intern med, Boston City Hosp, Harvard Med Sch, 62-63, resident psychiat, Mass Ment Health Ctr, 63-66; psychiatrist, USAF, 66-68; asst prof, Univ Tex, 68-69, coordr residency training, 68-72, assoc prof psychiat, Univ Tex, Med Sch, San Antonio, 69-73. *Concurrent Pos:* Assoc clin prof psychiat, Univ Tex Med Sch, San Antonio, 73- *Mem:* Fel Am Psychiat Asn; AMA. *Res:* Depression; electrosleep. *Mailing Add:* Oak Hills Med Bldg 7711 Louis Pasteur Dr San Antonio TX 78229-3419

ROSENTHAL, SOL ROY, pathology, immunology; deceased, see previous edition for last biography

ROSENTHAL, STANLEY ARTHUR, MEDICAL MYCOLOGY, MICROBIOLOGY. *Current Pos:* from asst microbiol to asst prof dermat, 52-71, ASSOC PROF EXP DERMAT, MED CTR, NY UNIV, 61- *Personal Data:* b Paterson, NJ, July 9, 26; m 48; c 2. *Educ:* Rutgers Univ, BS, 48; Univ Maine, MS, 50; Pa State Col, PhD(bact), 52. *Prof Exp:* USPHS spec fel, Prince Leopold Inst Trop Med, Antwerp, Belg, 60-61. *Mem:* Am Soc Microbiol; Med Mycol Soc Am; Int Soc Human & Animal Mycol. *Res:* Dermatophytosis; transmission of ringworm; identification of fungi. *Mailing Add:* Dept Dermat NY Univ Med Sch 550 First Ave New York NY 10016

ROSENTHAL, STANLEY LAWRENCE, METEOROLOGY. *Current Pos:* RETIRED. *Personal Data:* b Brooklyn, NY, Dec 6, 29; m 53; c 3. *Educ:* Fla State Univ, MS, 53, PhD(meteorol), 58. *Honors & Awards:* Gold Medal, Dept Com, 70. *Prof Exp:* Instr meteorol, Fla State Univ, 57-58; mem staff, Los Alamos Sci Lab, 58-59; asst prof meteorol, Fla State Univ, 59-60; mem staff, Nat Oceanic & Atmospheric Admin, 60-75, chief, Modeling Group, 75-78, dir, Nat Hurricane Res Lab, 78-79, dep dir, Atlantic Oceanog & Meteorol Lab, 79-93. *Concurrent Pos:* Adj prof, Univ Miami; chmn, Oceans & Atmospheres Sect, Fla Acad Sci, 78-79; mem coun, Am Meteorol Soc, 81-83, comt on hurricanes & trop meteorol, 81-84, chmn, 83-84. *Mem:* Fel AAAS; fel Am Meteorol Soc. *Res:* Application of dynamic meteorology ot the tropical portions of the atmosphere; application of numerical weather prediction techniques to the tropics; dynamics and numerical simulation of hurricanes. *Mailing Add:* 13301 SW 99th Pl Miami FL 33176. *E-Mail:* stanrosent@aol.com

ROSENTHAL, THEODORE BERNARD, microscopic anatomy, physiology, for more information see previous edition

ROSENTHAL, WILLIAM S, GASTROENTEROLOGY, PHYSIOLOGY. *Current Pos:* from asst prof to assoc prof med, 61-69, PROF MED & CHIEF SECT, NY MED COL, 69-, RES PROF PHYSIOL, 73- *Personal Data:* b New York, NY, June 21, 25; m 54; c 2. *Educ:* Univ Minn, BA, 46; State Univ NY, 50. *Prof Exp:* Intern, Michael Reese Hosp, Chicago, 50-51; resident med, Vet Admin Hosp, Brooklyn, 51-52 & 53-55; res asst liver dis, Postgrad Med Sch, Univ London, 55-56; res asst gastroenterol, Mt Sinai Hosp, NY, 57-61. *Concurrent Pos:* Chief sect gastroenterol, Westchester County Med Ctr, NY Med Col, 77-96, training prog med. *Mem:* Am Gastroenterol Asn; Am Asn Study Liver Dis; Am Col Physicians; Am Col Gastroenterol (pres, 77-78); Am Soc Human Genetics; Am Physiol Soc. *Res:* Clinical and laboratory investigation of the pathological physiology of gastrointestinal and liver disease. *Mailing Add:* Dept Med/Div Gastroenterol NY Med Col Munger Pavilion Rm 206 Valhalla NY 10595. *Fax:* 914-993-4317

ROSENTHALE, MARVIN E, PHARMACOLOGY. *Current Pos:* vpres, 93-, PRES, ALLERGAN/LIGAND JOINT VENTURE. *Personal Data:* b Philadelphia, Pa, Dec 13, 33; m 59; c 2. *Educ:* Philadelphia Col Pharm & Sci, BSc, 56, MSc, 57; Hahnemann Med Col, PhD(pharmacol), 60. *Prof Exp:* Pharmacologist, Lawall & Harrison Res & Control Labs, 51-60; pharmacologist, Wyeth Labs, Inc, 60-69, mgr immunoinflammatory pharmacol, 69-77; dir, Div Pharmacol, Ortho Pharmaceut Corp, 77-79, dir, Div biol Res, 79-82, vpres drug discovery worldwide, 89-93, group dir drug discovery, 82- *Concurrent Pos:* Vis assoc prof, Hahnemann Med Col, 63-; instr, Univ Pa, 64-67; adj prof, Philadelphia Col Pharm & Sci, 65- *Mem:* Am Soc Pharmacol & Exp Therapeut; Soc Exp Biol & Med; Am Rheumatism Asn. *Res:* Inflammation and allergy, particularly autoimmune diseases; cardiovascular and renal pharmacology; retinolds. *Mailing Add:* 14 Burnings Tree Rd Newport Beach CA 92660

ROSENTRATER, C RAY, MATHEMATICS, COMPUTER SCIENCE. *Current Pos:* from asst prof to assoc prof, 80-91, PROF MATH, DEPT MATH & COMPUT SCI, WESTMONT COL, 91- *Personal Data:* b Upland, Calif, Nov 4, 52. *Educ:* Ind Univ, MA, 75, MA, 78, PhD(math), 80; Univ Toronto, MS, 88. *Prof Exp:* Instr, Houghton Col, 75-76. *Concurrent Pos:* Fulbright scholar, Francisco Morazan Nat Pedagogical Univ, Honduras, 95-96. *Mem:* Math Asn Am; Am Math Soc; Asn Christians Math Soc. *Mailing Add:* Dept Math & Comput Sci Westmont Col 955 La Paz Rd Santa Barbara CA 93108-1099. *Fax:* 805-565-6122; *E-Mail:* rosentr@westmont.edu

ROSENWALD, GARY W, CHEMICAL ENGINEERING, PETROLEUM ENGINEERING. *Current Pos:* chem engr, Waste Mgt Div, 87-90, CHEM ENGR, RICHLAND OPERS OFF, US DEPT ENERGY, 87-, SAFETY OFF, TANK WASTE STORAGE, TANK WASTE REMEDIATION SYST, 91- *Personal Data:* b Manhattan, Kans, Jan 10, 41; m 65, Elizabeth L Young; c Joanmarie (Marks), Gary Jr, Julianne & Vicki. *Educ:* Univ Kans, BS, 64; Kans State Univ, MS, 66; Univ Kans, PhD(chem eng), 72. *Prof Exp:* High sch teacher math, Dickinson Co Community High Sch, 64-66; res engr petrol prod, Cities Serv Co, 70-73, sr res engr, 73-83; assoc prof petrol eng, Univ Wyo, 83-86. *Mem:* Am Nuclear Soc; Am Chem Soc; Am Inst Chem Engrs. *Res:* Petroleum production, especially oil recovery by thermal and chemical flooding methods, reservoir performance and numerical simulation; environmental engineering; radioactive and mixed waste management. *Mailing Add:* 129 MacArthur St Richland WA 99352. *Fax:* 509-376-2002

ROSENWASSER, LANNY JEFFERY, MEDICINE. *Current Pos:* ASSOC PROF MED, SCH MED, TUFTS UNIV, 79- *Educ:* New York Univ, MD, 72. *Mailing Add:* Immunol Nat Jewish Ctr 1400 Jackson St Denver CO 80206-2761. *Fax:* 303-398-1806

ROSENZWEIG, CARL, QUANTUM CHROMODYNAMICS. *Current Pos:* from asst prof to assoc prof, 76-86, PROF PHYSICS, SYRACUSE UNIV, 86- *Personal Data:* b Brooklyn, NY, June 10, 46; m 76; c 3. *Educ:* Polytechnic Univ, BS, 67, MS, 67; Harvard Univ, PhD(physics), 72. *Prof Exp:* Res assoc, Univ Calif, 72-73, Weizman Inst Sci, 73-74 & Univ Calif, 74-75; res asst prof, Univ Pittsburg, 75-76. *Concurrent Pos:* Vis scientist, Inst Theoret Physics, 88 & Hebrew Univ, 94. *Mem:* Am Phys Soc; Am Asn Physics Teachers. *Res:* Elementary particle physics. *Mailing Add:* Dept Physics Syracuse Univ Syracuse NY 13244-1130. *E-Mail:* rosez@suhep.phy.syr.edu

ROSENZWEIG, DAVID YATES, INTERNAL MEDICINE, PULMONARY DISEASE. *Current Pos:* from instr to asst prof, 62-72, ASSOC PROF MED, MED COL WIS, 72- *Personal Data:* b Detroit, Mich, June 9, 33; m 58; c 5. *Educ:* Wayne State Univ, BS, 54, MD, 57. *Prof Exp:* Intern, Sinai Hosp, Detroit, 57-58; resident internal med, Vet Admin Hosp, Denver, 58-60; fel pulmonary dis, Univ Colo, 60-62. *Concurrent Pos:* Consult, Vet Admin Hosp, Wood, Wis, 66-; fel pulmonary physiol, Postgrad Med Sch, Univ London, 67-68. *Mem:* Am Thoracic Soc; Am Fedn Clin Res; Int Union Against Tuberculosis; fel Am Col Physicians; Am Physiol Soc; fel Am Col Chest Physicians. *Res:* Pulmonary disease and physiology; distribution of pulmonary ventilation and perfusion; exercise physiology; mycobacterial infections. *Mailing Add:* Med Col Wis Clin Froedtert Mem Lutheran Hosp 9200 W Wisconsin Ave Milwaukee WI 53226

ROSENZWEIG, MARK RICHARD, NEUROSCIENCES, BIOLOGICAL PSYCHOLOGY. *Current Pos:* from asst prof to assoc prof, Univ Calif, Berkeley, 50-60, res prof, Miller Inst Basic Res in Sci, 58-59 & 65-66, prof, 60-92, EMER PROF PSYCHOL, UNIV CALIF, BERKELEY, 92-, PROF GRAD STUDIES, 94- *Personal Data:* b Rochester, NY, Sept 12, 22; m 47, Janine S Chappat; c Anne J, Suzanne J & Philip M. *Educ:* Univ Rochester, BA, 43, MA, 44; Harvard Univ, PhD(psychol), 49. *Hon Degrees:* Dr, Univ Rene Descartes, Sorbonne, 80. *Honors & Awards:* Distinguished Sci Contrib Award, Am Psychol Asn. *Prof Exp:* Res assoc, Psycho-Acoust Lab, Harvard Univ, 49-51. *Concurrent Pos:* Fulbright res fel & Soc Sci Res Coun fel, Paris, 60-61; ed, Ann Rev Psychol, 68-94; Am Psychol Asn rep, Int Union Psychol Sci, 70-72; vis prof, Univ Paris, 73- 74, mem exec comt, 72-96; rep div physiol & comp psychol, Coun Am Psychol Sci, 83-86; chmn US Nat Comt, Int Union Psychol Sci, Nat Acad Sci-Nat Res Coun, 85-88, mem, 89-96. *Mem:* Nat Acad Sci; fel Am Psychol Asn; Int Brain Res Orgn; Am Physiol Soc; Soc Neurosci; Soc Francaise Psychol; Int Union Psychol Sci (pres, 88-92); fel, Am Psychol Soc. *Res:* Neuroscience and behavior; neural processes in learning and memory; history of psychology; neurochemistry of stages of memory formation; international psychological science; effects of enriched experience on brain and behavior. *Mailing Add:* 470 Michigan Ave Berkeley CA 94707-1738. *Fax:* 510-642-5293; *E-Mail:* memory@garnet.berkeley.edu

ROSENZWEIG, MICHAEL LEO, POPULATION ECOLOGY, MAMMALOGY. *Current Pos:* dept head, 75-76, PROF ECOL & EVOLUTIONARY BIOL, UNIV ARIZ, 75- *Personal Data:* b Philadelphia, Pa, June 25, 41; m 61, Carole Citron; c Ephron, Juli & Abby (Daniel). *Educ:* Univ Pa, AB, 62, PhD(zool), 66. *Honors & Awards:* 30th Paul L Errington Mem Lectr, Iowa State Univ, 94; Dennis Chitty Lectr, Univ BC, 95-96. *Prof Exp:* Asst prof biol, Bucknell Univ, 65-69 & State Univ NY, Albany, 69-71; assoc prof, Univ NMex, 71-75. *Concurrent Pos:* Assoc ed, Paleobiol, 83-86; ed-in-chief, Evolutionary Ecol, 86-; chair, Res Support Liaison Comt Ecol, Evolution Syst, 86-88 & Div Ecol, Am Soc Zoologists, 85-86; Rudi Lemberg Travelling fel, Australian Acad Sci, 88-89; Jock Marshall fel, Monash Univ, Melbourne, Australia, 89; Brittingham fel, Univ Wis, 90-91; distinguished vis prof, Univ Miami, 96-97; distinguished lectr, Mountain Res Ctr, Mont State Univ, 97; distinguished vis scholar, Univ Umea, Sweden, 97. *Mem:* Ecol Soc Am; Soc Study Evolution (vpres, 88-89); Am Soc Naturalists; Japanese Soc Pop Ecol; Am Soc Zoologists; Brit Ecol Soc. *Res:* Biodiversity; evolutionary ecology; community ecology of mammals; habitat selection. *Mailing Add:* Dept Ecol & Evolutionary Biol Univ Ariz Tucson AZ 85721. *Fax:* 520-621-9190; *E-Mail:* scarab@ccit.arizona.edu

ROSENZWEIG, NORMAN, PSYCHIATRY, EDUCATION & RESEARCH ADMINISTRATION. *Current Pos:* from asst prof to assoc prof, 62-73, PROF PSYCHIAT, WAYNE STATE UNIV, 73-; ASSOC PROF PSYCHIAT, MICH STATE UNIV, 72- *Personal Data:* b New York, NY, Feb 28, 24; m 45, Carol Treleaven; c Elizabeth A. *Educ:* Univ Chicago, MB, 47, MD, 48; Univ Mich, MS, 54; Am Bd Psychiat & Neurol, dipl, 54. *Honors & Awards:* Rush Gold Medal Award, Am Psychiat Asn; Presidential Award, Puerto Rico Med Asn, 81; Warren Williams Speaker's Award, Assembly of Am Psychiat Asn, 86. *Prof Exp:* From instr to asst prof psychiat, Dept Psychiat, Med Sch, Univ Mich, 53-61; interim chmn, Mich State Univ, 87-90. *Concurrent Pos:* Dir joint res proj, Univ Mich & Ypsilanti State Hosp, 57-59; chmn dept, Sinai Hosp, Detroit, 61-90; interim chmn, Dept Psychiat, Wayne State Univ, 87-90. *Mem:* NY Acad Sci; fel Am Col Psychiat; AMA; fel Am Psychiat Asn; AAAS; hon mem Royal Australia New Zealand Col Psychiat; hon mem Indian Psychiat Soc. *Res:* Schizophrenia; mind-brain relationships; perceptual integration and isolation; psychological consequences of physical illness; social attitudes; primary preventive intervention to reduce untoward outcomes in teen-age pregnancy. *Mailing Add:* 26211 Central Park Blvd Ste Southfield MI 48076-4164

ROSENZWEIG, WALTER, PHYSICS. *Current Pos:* RETIRED. *Personal Data:* b Vienna, Austria, Sept 23, 27; US citizen; m 49; c 3. *Educ:* Rutgers Univ, BS, 50; Univ Rochester, MS, 52; Columbia Univ, PhD(physics), 60. *Prof Exp:* Assoc health physicist, Brookhaven Nat Lab, 51-53; res physicist, Radiol Res Lab, Columbia Univ, 53-60; mem tech staff semiconductor physics, AT&T Bell Labs, 60-72, supvr semiconductor memories, 72-85, supvr prod support, 85-89. *Mem:* Radiation Res Soc; Inst Elec & Electronics Engrs. *Res:* Radiation dosimetry; radiation damage to semiconductors and devices; semiconductor memory design, large scale integrated circuit design; semiconductor device physics. *Mailing Add:* 8431 Glen View Ct Orlando FL 32819

ROSENZWEIG, WILLIAM DAVID, MICROBIOL ECOLOGY, ENVIRONMENTAL MICROBIOLOGY. *Current Pos:* ASST PROF MICROBIOL, WEST CHESTER UNIV, 87- *Personal Data:* b New York, NY, Feb 6, 46. *Educ:* St John's Univ, BS, 69; Long Island Univ, MS, 71; NY Univ, PhD(biol), 78. *Honors & Awards:* Gladys Mateyko Award, NY Univ, 77. *Prof Exp:* Instr microbiol, NY Univ, 74-78; res fel microbiol, Rutgers Univ, 78-80; asst prof microbiol, Drexel Univ, 80-87. *Mem:* Am Soc Microbiol; Sigma Xi; Am Water Works Asn. *Res:* Environmental biology; ecology and physiology of nematode-trapping fungi; microbiological quality of potable water. *Mailing Add:* Dept Biol West Chester Univ West Chester PA 19383

ROSES, ALLEN DAVID, NEUROLOGY, MOLECULAR GENETICS. *Current Pos:* chief resident, Duke Univ Med Ctr, 70-71; instr med, 70-73, from asst prof to assoc prof med, Div Neurol, 73-79, CHIEF, DIV NEUROL, DEPT MED, DUKE UNIV MED CTR, 77-, PROF NEUROL, 79-, PROF NEUROBIOL, 89-, JEFFERSON-PILOT CORP PROF NEUROBIOL & NEUROL, 90- *Personal Data:* b Paterson, NJ, Feb 21, 43. *Educ:* Univ Pittsburgh, BS, 63; Univ Pa, MD, 67; Am Bd Psychiat & Neurol, dipl, 73. *Honors & Awards:* Leadership & Excellence Alzheimer's Dis Award, Nat Inst Aging, 88; Rita Hayward Gala Award, Alzheimer's Asn, 94; Potamkin Prize, 94; George H Bishop Lectr, Washington Univ, St Louis, 96; Parke-David Prize, 96; Alois Alzheimer Award, 96. *Prof Exp:* Med intern, Hosp Univ Pa, 67-68; resident neurol, NY Neurol Inst, 68-70. *Concurrent Pos:* Vis fel neurophysiol, Col Physician & Surgeons Columbia Univ, 70; Nat Mult Sclerosis Soc fel, Lab Neurochem, Div Neurol, Duke Univ Med Ctr, 71-73, Lab Virol, Div Pediat Neurol, 71-73; attend physician neurol & pediat neurol, Duke Univ Med Ctr, 73-, Durham Vets Admin Med Ctr, 73-; consult neurol, Cherry Hosp, NC, 73-76; dir, Duke Neuromuscular Res Clin, Duke Univ Med Ctr, 74-, Neurosci Study Prog, Sch Med, 75-85, asst prof biochem, 77-89, investr, Howard Hughes Med Inst, 77-81, dir, Duke Muscular Dystrophy Asn Clin, 79-, Joseph & Kathleen Bryan Alzheimer's Dis Res Ctr, 85- & Ctr Human Genetics, 96-; trustee, Am Neurol Asn, 82-84; sci advr, Cyprus Inst Neurol & Genetics, 90-; nat vpres, Muscular Dystrophy Asn Nat Hq, 94- *Mem:* Inst Med-Nat Acad Sci; hon foreign mem Asn Brit Neurologists; corresp mem Int Acad Biomed & Drug Res; fel Am Acad Neurol; Am Neurol Asn; Am Soc Clin Res; NY Acad Sci; Am Chem Soc; Am Soc Human Genetics; Am Soc Biol Chemists. *Res:* Molecular genetics and mechanics of human neurological disease expression, particularly Alzeheimer's disease, myotonic muscular dystrophy, Duchenne muscular dystrophy, motor neuron diseases, Huntington's disease; biochemistry of cellular systems with special reference to neurological and neurogenetic diseases. *Mailing Add:* Div Neurol Duke Univ Med Ctr Box 2900 Durham NC 27710

ROSEVEAR, JOHN WILLIAM, BIOCHEMISTRY. *Current Pos:* PRES, BIO-METRIC SYSTS, INC, 79- *Personal Data:* b Glenns Ferry, Idaho, Feb 19, 27; m 49; c 4. *Educ:* Ore State Col, BS, 49; Northwestern Univ, MD, 53; Univ Utah, PhD(biochem), 58. *Prof Exp:* Intern, Evanston Hosp Asn, 54; asst to staff, Sect Biochem, Mayo Clin, 58-59, consult, 59-69; assoc prof, Div Health Comput Sci, Univ Minn, Minneapolis, 69-71; med dir & dir clin chem, Kallestad Labs Inc, 71-74, dir labs, 74-75, vpres labs, 75-76, vpres sci affairs, 76-79. *Concurrent Pos:* Clin assoc prof, Univ Minn, Minneapolis, 71- *Mem:* AAAS; Am Chem Soc; AMA. *Res:* Carbohydrate groups of proteins; diabetes mellitus; biochemical monitoring of patients; chromatographic analyses of organic acids; cancer detection tests; radioimmunoassay systems. *Mailing Add:* Camas Diag Co 1313 Fifth St SE No 219 Minneapolis MN 55414-4504

ROSHAL, JAY YEHUDIE, GENETICS. *Current Pos:* from instr to assoc prof, Univ Minn, 58-63, chmn div sci & math, 62-64, prof, 63-84, EMER PROF BOT, UNIV MINN, MORRIS, 84- *Personal Data:* b Chicago, Ill, Aug 27, 22; m 89, Hertha Googe. *Educ:* Univ Chicago, PhB, 48, SB, 49, SM, 50, PhD(bot), 53. *Prof Exp:* Instr bot, Oberlin Col, 53-55; res assoc, Ben May Lab, Univ Chicago, 55-56; asst prof bot, Eastern Ill Univ, 57-58. *Concurrent Pos:* Mem secretariat, Space Sci Bd, Nat Acad Sci, 62-63; lectr, Univ Tex, 65-66; hon res assoc, Harvard Univ, 68-69; vpres, Genderm Corp, 84-90; consult, Genderm Corp, 90-92. *Mem:* Mycol Soc Am; Am Soc Plant Physiol. *Res:* Mycology; physiology; microbial genetics. *Mailing Add:* 2124 N Monroe St Arlington VA 22207

ROSHKO, ALEXANA, ANALYTICAL ELECTRON SPECTROSCOPY, ELECTRON MICROSCOPY. *Current Pos:* MAT SCIENTIST, NAT INST STAND & TECHNOL, 88- *Personal Data:* US citizen. *Educ:* Mass Inst Technol, SB, 81, PhD(ceramics sci), 87; Postdoctoral, Mass Inst Technol, 87-88. *Mem:* Mat Res Soc; Am Ceramic Soc; Electron Micros Soc Am. *Res:* Structure-property relationships in electronic and magnetic ceramics; microstructure, grain boundary chemistry; point defect chemistry and diffusion, surface, grain boundary and bulk, in these materials and how they affect material behavior. *Mailing Add:* Nat Inst Stand & Technol MC 815-04 325 Broadway Boulder CO 80303

ROSHKO, ANATOL, TURBULENT SHEER FLOW. *Current Pos:* res fel, Calif Inst Technol, 52-55, from asst prof to prof, 55-85, actg dir, Grad Aeronaut Labs, 85-87, THEODORE VON KARMEN PROF AERONAUT, CALIF INST TECHNOL, 85- *Personal Data:* b Bellevue, Alta, July 15, 23; nat US; m 57; c 2. *Educ:* Univ Alta, BSc, 45; Calif Inst Technol, MS, 47, PhD(aeronaut), 52. *Honors & Awards:* Dryden Res lectr, Am Inst Aeronaut & Astronaut, 76; Dynamics Prize, Am Phys Soc, 87. *Prof Exp:* Instr math, Univ Alta, 45-46, lectr eng, 49-50. *Concurrent Pos:* Sci liaison officer, Off Naval Res, London, 61-62; consult, McDonnell Douglas Corp, 54-90 & Rocketdyne Corp Div, Rockwell Int, 84-90; founding dir, Wind Eng Res Inc, 70; mem, Aeronaut & Space Eng Bd. *Mem:* Nat Acad Eng; fel AAAS; fel Am Inst Aeronaut & Astronaut; Am Phys Soc; fel Can Aeronaut & Space Inst. *Res:* Gas dynamics; separated flow; turbulence; transonic and supersonic aerodynamics. *Mailing Add:* Calif Inst Technol Mail Sta 105-50 1201 E California Blvd Pasadena CA 91125

ROSHWALB, IRVING, statistics; deceased, see previous edition for last biography

ROSI, DAVID, BIOLOGY, MUTASYNTHESIS. *Current Pos:* from asst res biologist to res biologist, Sterling Winthrop Res Inst, 60-70, group leader, 66-89, sr res investr, 89-94 SR RES BIOLOGIST, STERLING WINTHROP RES INST, 70- *Personal Data:* b Utica, NY, Apr 22, 32; m 56; c 4. *Educ:* Utica Col, BS, 54; Univ NH, MS, 56. *Prof Exp:* Jr bacteriologist & jr sanit chemist, Div Labs & Res Water Pollution, NY State Dept Health, 56-58, sanit chemist, 58-60. *Mem:* Am Soc Microbiol; Sigma Xi; AAAS. *Res:* Microbial conversion, isolation and characterization of synthetic organic compounds of pharmaceutical interest; in vivo and in vitro drug metabolism studies; new antibiotics via mutagenesis; natural products; pharmacokinetics. *Mailing Add:* 2 Boncroft Dr East Greenbush NY 12061-2004

ROSI, FRED, ELECTRONIC MATERIALS. *Current Pos:* RES PROF, DEPT MAT SCI, SCH ENG & APPL SCI, UNIV VA, CHARLOTTESVILLE, 78- *Personal Data:* b Jan 13, 21. *Educ:* Yale Univ, BE, 42, ME, 47, MS, 48, PhD(physics), 49. *Honors & Awards:* David Saonoff Medal in Sci. *Prof Exp:* Engr specialist, Sylvania Elec Prod, 49-54; mem tech staff, RCA Labs, dir, Mat Res Lab, vpres, Mat & Device Res, 54-72; dir, Res & Develop, Am Can Co, 73-75; gen dir, Res & Develop, Reynolds Metals Co, 75-78. *Concurrent Pos:* Consult, Cent Intel Agency, 72-73, 80, NASA, 79-81, Energy Conversion Devices, 83-, Gen Elec Co, 84-; mem Awards Comt, Am Inst Mettall Engrs, 58-67; mem, Res Adv Comt, NASA, 60-65; adv comt, Dept Physics, Univ Ky, 68-71; comt elec Mat Devices, Nat Acad Sci, 70-71; adv bd, Gould Incorp, 79-83. *Mem:* AAAS; fel Am Phys Soc; fel Am Inst Metall Engr; Sigma Xi. *Res:* Author of numerous articles in various publications. *Mailing Add:* 2 Ramsbury Ct Richmond VA 23233

ROSIER, RONALD CROSBY, MATHEMATICS. *Current Pos:* ASST PROF MATH, GEORGETOWN UNIV, 70- *Personal Data:* b Baltimore, Md, Jan 23, 43; m 65; c 3. *Educ:* Boston Col, AB, 65; Univ Md, PhD(math), 70. *Mem:* Math Asn Am; Am Math Soc. *Res:* Functional analysis. *Mailing Add:* CBMS 1529 18th St Washington DC 20036

ROSIN, ROBERT FISHER, SOFTWARE ARCHITECTURE OF INFORMATION SYSTEMS. *Current Pos:* VPRES & PRIN ARCHITECT, ENHANCED SERV PROVIDERS, INC, SHREWSBURY, NJ, 89- *Personal Data:* b Chicago, Ill, Mar 19, 36; m 63, Rosalie Lite; c 2. *Educ:* Mass Inst Technol, BS, 57; Univ Mich, MS, 60, PhD(commun sci), 64. *Prof Exp:* From asst prof to assoc prof eng & appl sci, Yale Univ, 64-68; assoc prof comput sci & vchmn dept, State Univ NY Buffalo, 68-70, prof, 70-74; prof comput sci, Iowa State Univ, 74-76; mem tech staff, Bell Labs, Holmdel, NJ, 76-78, consult, 78-83; consulting mem tech staff, Syntex, Inc, Eatontown, NJ, 83-86; dist mgr, Bell Commun Res, Red Bank, NJ, 86-89. *Concurrent Pos:* Nat Sci Found res grant, 70-72; NATO res grant, 72-73; vis prof, Univ Aarhus, 72-74. *Mem:* Asn Comput Mach; Inst Elec & Electronics Engrs Comput Soc. *Res:* Software and communication systems; software system architecture; realization of computer systems via software, hardware and firmware. *Mailing Add:* Enhanced Serv Providers Inc 39 Avenue of the Common Shrewsbury NJ 07702. *E-Mail:* rosin%espi@bcr.cc.bellcore.com

ROSING, WAYNE C, FUNGAL ULTRASTRUCTURE. *Current Pos:* asst prof, 80-84, ASSOC PROF BIOL, MIDDLE TENN STATE UNIV, 84- *Personal Data:* b Kenosha, Wis, Oct 6, 47. *Educ:* Univ Wis-Madison, BS, 69; Univ Tex, Austin, PhD(bot & mycol), 75. *Prof Exp:* Asst prof, George Peabody Col, 76-80. *Mem:* Mycol Soc Am; Sigma Xi; Bot Soc Am. *Res:* Ultrastructural studies of fungi; ascomycete spore formation. *Mailing Add:* 1221 Charlton Dr Antioch TN 37013-1360

ROSINGER, EVA L J, ENVIRONMENTAL POLICY, INTERNATIONAL ENVIRONMENTAL AFFAIRS. *Current Pos:* DEP DIR ENVIRON ORGN ECON COOP & DEVELOPMENT, PARIS, 94- *Personal Data:* b July 21, 41; Can citizen; m 69, Herbert E. *Educ:* Tech Univ, Prague, MSc, 63, PhD(chem), 68. *Prof Exp:* Researcher indust res, 67-68; fel chem eng, Univ Toronto, 68-70; res librarian tech info, Tech Univ, Aachen, Ger, 71-72; res officer environ comput modelling, Atomic Energy Can Ltd, 73-79, head, Systs Assessment Sect, 79-84, sci asst dir, Waste Mgt Div, 80-84, head, Environ & Safety Assessment Br, 85-86, exec asst to pres, 86-87, dir Waste Mgt Concept Rev, 87-90; dir gen, Can Coun Ministers Environ, 90-94. *Concurrent Pos:* Vpres, Radioactive Waste Mgt Comt, Orgn Econ Coop & Develop/Nuclear Energy Agency, Paris; bd dir, Can Mem Eng Found,; adv coun, Univ Waterloo. *Mem:* Can Nuclear Soc (pres, 89-90); Women Sci & Eng. *Res:* Environmental policies; evaluation and analysis of environmental systems; scientific and organizational strategies related to international environmental issues, documenting options and providing scientific advice. *Mailing Add:* Orgn Econ Coop & Develop 2 rue Andre Pascal 75775 Paris Cedex 16 France. *Fax:* 33-1-24-78-76; *E-Mail:* eva.rosinger@oecd.org

ROSINGER, HERBERT EUGENE, nuclear power reactor safety, small reactor technology, for more information see previous edition

ROSINSKI, JAN, ATMOSPHERIC CHEMISTRY. *Current Pos:* RETIRED. *Personal Data:* b Warsaw, Poland, Feb 10, 17; nat US; wid; c Maciej C. *Educ:* Warsaw Inst Technol, dipl, 49; Univ Warsaw, PhD, Dr habil, 80; Univ Bologna, Libera Docenza, 70. *Prof Exp:* Res chemist, Brit Celanese, Ltd, 48-51; chief chemist, Poray, Inc, Ill, 51-52; sr engr, IIT Res Inst, 52-62; scientist, Nat Ctr Atmospheric Res, 62-89. *Res:* Fine particles; radiochemistry; colloids; geochemistry, atmospheric chemistry and physics; ice nucleation in marine, mixed marine-continental and continental air masses; chemistry of ice-forming and cloud condensation nuclei. *Mailing Add:* 590 Ord Dr Boulder CO 80303-4732

ROSINSKI, JOANNE, PLANT PHYSIOLOGY & CELL BIOLOGY. *Current Pos:* from asst prof to assoc prof, 80-91, PROF BIOL, SWEET BRIAR COL, 91- *Personal Data:* b Milwaukee, Wis. *Educ:* Marquette Univ, BS, 66; State Univ NY, Buffalo, PhD(biol), 70. *Prof Exp:* Res fel, Harvard Univ, 71-73; asst prof biol, Williams Col, 73-78; res assoc, Brookhaven Nat Lab, 78-80. *Concurrent Pos:* NIH fel, Harvard Univ, 71-73. *Mem:* Bot Soc Am; Am Inst Biol Sci. *Res:* Chloroplast development; plant tissue culture; scanning electron microscopy. *Mailing Add:* Biol Dept Sweet Briar Col Sweet Briar VA 24595-1056

ROSINSKI, MICHAEL A, AUTOMOTIVE PROTOTYPE BODY SHEETMETAL DEVELOPMENT. *Current Pos:* SR PROJ ENGR, NISSAN RES & DEVELOP, 2000-. *Personal Data:* b Detroit, Mich, Oct 7, 62; m 91. *Educ:* Oakland Univ, BSE, 85, MSME, 88. *Prof Exp:* Sr mfg engr, Prototype Develop, Gen Motors, 85-89. *Mem:* Am Soc Mech Engrs; Am Welding Soc. *Res:* Automotive prototype sheetmetal development; reducing development cycle; developing alternative sheetmetal development methods and strategies and implementing these ideas on future car models. *Mailing Add:* 6842 Ellinwood White Lake MI 48383

ROSKA, FRED JAMES, DIELECTRICS, ELECTROSTATICS. *Current Pos:* SPECIALIST, MINN MINING & MFG CO, 81- *Personal Data:* b Sheboygan, Wis, May 7, 54. *Educ:* Univ Wis, BS, 76, PhD(chem), 81. *Res:* High field dielectric properties of polymers; structure-property relationships in semi-crystalline polymers; electrostatic processes; electrical coronas. *Mailing Add:* 1724 Lamplite Ct 3M Ctr St Paul MN 55125

ROSKAM, JAN, AEROSPACE ENGINEERING. *Current Pos:* PRES, DESIGN ANAL & RES CORP, 90- *Personal Data:* b The Hague, Neth, Feb 22, 30; US citizen; m 56, Tiny. *Educ:* Delft Technol Univ, MS, 54; Univ Wash, PhD(aeronaut, astronaut), 65. *Prof Exp:* Asst chief designer, Aviolanda Aircraft Co, Neth, 54-56; aerodyn engr, Cessna Aircraft Co, 57-59; sr group engr, Boeing Co, 59-67; from assoc prof to Ackers prof aerospace eng, Univ Kans, 67-90, chmn dept, 72-76. *Concurrent Pos:* Pres, Design Anal & Res Corp. *Mem:* Assoc fel Am Inst Aeronaut & Astronaut; Royal Aeronaut Soc; Neth Royal Inst Engrs; Sigma Xi; fel Soc Automotive Engrs. *Res:* Airplane stability, control and design; effects of aeroelasticity on stability, control and design; automatic flight controls. *Mailing Add:* Dar Corp 120 E Ninth St Suite 2 Lawrence KS 66044. *Fax:* 785-832-0524

ROSKAMP, GORDON KEITH, WEED SCIENCE, AGRONOMY. *Current Pos:* asst prof agron, 75-81, ASSOC PROF AGR, WESTERN ILL UNIV, 81- *Personal Data:* b Quincy, Ill, July 4, 50; m 74; c 2. *Educ:* Western Ill Univ, BS, 71; Univ Mo-Columbia, MS, 73, PhD(agron), 75. *Prof Exp:* Res asst weed sci, Western Ill Univ, 70-71 & Univ Mo-Columbia, 71-75. *Concurrent Pos:* Grants from var chem co, Ill Soybean Operating Bd & Nat Crop Ins Asn. *Mem:* Weed Sci Soc Am; Am Soc Agron. *Res:* Weed control, especially in corn, soybeans and pastures; hail damage to corn; control of multiflora rose; herbicide damage to soybeans. *Mailing Add:* Dept Agr Western Ill Univ 900 W Adams St Macomb IL 61455-1396

ROSKES, GERALD J, APPLIED MATHEMATICS. *Current Pos:* ASSOC PROF MATH, QUEENS COL, CITY UNIV NY, 70- *Personal Data:* b Edgewood, Md, June 27, 43. *Educ:* Mass Inst Technol, BS, 65, PhD(math), 70. *Prof Exp:* Mem tech staff, Bell Tel Labs, 69-70. *Mem:* Am Math Soc; Soc Indust & Appl Math; Math Asn Am. *Res:* Nonlinear wave theory; singular perturbation theory. *Mailing Add:* Dept Math Queens Col Flushing NY 11367

ROSKIES, ETHEL, HEALTH PSYCHOLOGY, BEHAVIORAL MEDICINE. *Current Pos:* PROF PSYCHOL, UNIV MONTREAL, CAN, 80- *Personal Data:* b Montreal, Can, Nov 27, 33; m 53, 81; c 2. *Educ:* McGill Univ, Can, BA, 54, MA, 61; Univ Montreal, MA, 63, PhD(psychol), 69. *Prof Exp:* Staff psychologist, Montreal Childrens Hosp, 66-68, lectr psychol, 68-69, asst prof psychol, 69-74, assoc prof psychol, 74-80. *Concurrent Pos:* Vis scholar, Univ Calif, Berkeley, 77-78, Inst Soc Res, Mich, 85-86, MRC-ESRC Soc & Appl Psychol Unit, Univ Sheffield, UK, 86-; res assoc, Behavior Therapy Serv, Montreal Gen Hosp, 76-77; prin invest, Montreal Type A Intervention Proj, 82-85. *Mem:* Fel Can Psychol Asn; Am Psychol Asn; fel Soc Behav Med; fel Am Inst Stress; Can Register Health Serv Providers; Assoc Adv Behav Ther. *Res:* Management of work stress; behavioral interventions to reduce illness risk. *Mailing Add:* Dept Psychol Univ Montreal PO Box 6128 Br A Sta S River Montreal PQ H3C 3J7 Can

ROSKIES, RALPH ZVI, ELEMENTARY PARTICLE PHYSICS. *Current Pos:* SCI DIR, PITTSBURGH SUPERCOMPUT CTR, 86- *Personal Data:* b Montreal, Que, Nov 24, 40; m 63; c 3. *Educ:* McGill Univ, BSc, 61; Princeton Univ, MA, 63, PhD(math), 66. *Prof Exp:* Instr physics, Yale Univ, 65-67; I Meyer Segals fel, Weizmann Inst, 67-68; asst prof, Yale Univ, 68-72; assoc prof, 72-78, PROF PHYSICS, UNIV PITTSBURGH, 79- *Concurrent Pos:* Yale jr fac fel, Stanford Linear Accelerator Ctr, 71-72; Alfred P Sloan fel, 73-77. *Mem:* Am Phys Soc; Inst Elec & Electronics Engrs. *Res:* High energy theoretical physics; quantum electrodynamics; Yang-Mills fields; lattice field theory; high performance computing. *Mailing Add:* Dept Physics Univ Pittsburgh Pittsburgh PA 15260. *Fax:* 412-268-5832; *E-Mail:* roskies@psc.edu

ROSKOS, ROLAND R, PHYSICAL CHEMISTRY. *Current Pos:* Asst prof, 66-69, assoc prof, 69-76, PROF CHEM, UNIV WIS-LA CROSSE, 76- *Personal Data:* b Arcadia, Wis, July 9, 40; m 66; c 2. *Educ:* Wis State Univ, La Crosse, BS, 62; Iowa State Univ, MS, 64, PhD(phys chem), 66. *Concurrent Pos:* Consult, Gunderson Clin, Ltd, La Crosse, Wis, 67- *Mem:* Am Chem Soc; Sigma Xi. *Res:* Chemical and medical instrumentation; physical and chemical properties as related to structure; applications and theory of lasers; isotope effects. *Mailing Add:* 1220 Seiler Lane La Crosse WI 54601-6072

ROSKOSKI, JOANN PEARL, ECOLOGY, MICROBIOLOGY. *Current Pos:* mgr spec projs, 89-91, prog dir ecol, 91-92, ACTG DEPT DIV DIR ENVIRON BIOL, NSF, 92- *Personal Data:* b Paterson, NJ, June 18, 47; m 79, Michael T Koterba; c Nathan & Zachary. *Educ:* Rutgers Univ, BA, 69, MS, 72; Yale Univ, PhD(forest ecol), 77. *Prof Exp:* Res asst microbiol, E R Squibb Corp, 69-71; Rockefeller found fel, Res Inst Biotic Resources, 77-80; mem fac, Plant Sci Dept, Univ Ariz, 80-83; assoc soil scientist, Niftal Proj, Univ Hawaii, 83-85, assoc dir, 85-88; prog officer, Nat Res Coun, 88-89. *Mem:* Ecol Soc Am; Sigma Xi; Int Soc Trop Ecol. *Res:* Nutrient cycling in tropical ecosystems, especially the role of nitrogen fixation in tropical agroecosystems; agroforestry; nitrogen fixation in agriculture. *Mailing Add:* NSF Div Environ Biol 4201 Wilson Blvd Rm 635 Arlington VA 22230. *Fax:* 703-306-0367; *E-Mail:* jroskosk@nsf.gov

ROSKOSKI, ROBERT, JR, BIOCHEMISTRY. *Current Pos:* PROF & HEAD, BIOCHEM DEPT, LA STATE UNIV MED CTR, 79-, FRED G BRAZDA PROF BIOCHEM & MOLECULAR BIOL, 91- *Personal Data:* b Elyria, Ohio, Dec 10, 39; m 74, Laura Martinsek. *Educ:* Bowling Green State Univ, BS, 61; Univ Chicago, MD, 64, PhD(biochem), 68. *Prof Exp:* USPHS fel biochem, Univ Chicago, 64-66; sr investr, Sch Aerospace Med, USAF, 67-69; USPHS spec fel, Rockefeller Univ, 69-72; from asst prof to assoc prof biochem, Univ Iowa, 72-79. *Concurrent Pos:* Mem, Biochem Test Comt, Nat Bd Med Examnrs, 81-84; mem, Sci Rev Panel, Vet Affairs Admin, 92-95. *Mem:* Am Chem Soc; NY Acad Sci; Am Soc Neurochem; Am Soc Biol Chemists; Soc Neurosci; Am Soc Pharmacol & Exp Therapeut; Int Soc Neurochem; Asn Med & Grad Depts Biochem (secy, 94-96, pres, 97). *Res:* Enzymology of Ras farnesyltransferase; fluorescence properties of proteins; protein prenylation; cancer chemotherapy; signal transduction; ras oncogene; published numerous articles. *Mailing Add:* Dept Biochem Med Ctr La State Univ Florida Ave PO Box 129 New Orleans LA 70119-2799. *Fax:* 504-619-8775; *E-Mail:* biocrr@lsumc.edu

ROSLER, LAWRENCE, COMPUTER SCIENCES. *Current Pos:* DIR, COMPUT LANG LAB, HEWLETT PACKARD, PALO ALTO, CALIF, 87- *Personal Data:* b Brooklyn, NY, Feb 20, 34; m 65; c 2. *Educ:* Cornell Univ, BA, 53; Yale Univ, MS, 54, PhD(physics), 58. *Prof Exp:* Jr physicist, Cornell Aeronaut Labs, 53, jr mathematician, 54; mem tech staff, AT&T Bell Labs, Murray Hill, 57-67, supvr comput graphics systs group, 67-76, head, lang eng dept, 76-87. *Mem:* AAAS; Sigma Xi; Asn Comput Mach; Am Phys Soc. *Res:* Man-machine graphical interaction; small-computer systems; computer languages. *Mailing Add:* Hewlett-Packard Co 1501 Page Mill Rd No 10-14 Palo Alto CA 94304-1126

ROSLER, RICHARD S(TEPHEN), CHEMICAL ENGINEERING. *Current Pos:* SR MEM TECH STAFF, APPLIED MAT, INC, 88- *Personal Data:* b Spokane, Wash, Jan 29, 37; m 61, Connie Park; c Pam, Jeff, Greg & Amy. *Educ:* Gonzaga Univ, BS, 59; Northwestern Univ, PhD(chem eng), 62. *Prof Exp:* Sr aerothermo engr, United Aircraft Corp, 62-64; from asst prof to assoc prof chem eng, Gonzaga Univ, 64-68; process engr, Shell Develop Co, Calif, 68-69; dir res & develop, Applied Mat, Inc, 69-77; mgr semiconductor mat res, Motorola, Inc, 77-79; corp dir res & develop, Advan Semiconductor Mat Am, 79-86; mgr process eng, Spectrum CVD, Subsid Motorola, Inc, 86-88. *Mem:* Am Vacuum Soc; Electrochem Soc. *Res:* Technical management of development of equipment and processes on low pressure chemical vapor deposition reactors and plasma reactors for the processing of semiconductor wafers for the semiconductor industry. *Mailing Add:* 7500 E McCormick Pkwy No 78 Scottsdale AZ 85258. *E-Mail:* dick_rosler@amat.com

ROSLINSKI, LAWRENCE MICHAEL, TOXICOLOGY, ENVIRONMENTAL HEALTH. *Current Pos:* INDUST TOXICOLOGIST, FORD MOTOR CO, 73- *Personal Data:* b Detroit, Mich, May 28, 42; m 64; c 3. *Educ:* Univ Mich, BS, 64; Wayne State Univ, MS, 66, PhD(pharmacol, physiol), 68. *Prof Exp:* Indust hygienist, Indust Bur Indust Hyg, Detroit, Mich, 64; fel toxicol, Sch Pub Health, Univ Mich, 68-69; prof assoc, Nat Acad Sci, 69-72; toxicologist, Environ Protection Agency, 72-73. *Concurrent Pos:* Comnr, Toxic Substances Control Comn, State Mich, 79- *Mem:* AAAS; Am Indust Hyg Asn; Am Bd Indust Hyg; Soc Toxicol; Am Bd Toxicol. *Res:* Pharmacology; industrial hygiene; physiology; biochemistry; toxicology. *Mailing Add:* 46770 Betty HL Plymouth MI 48170

ROSLYCKY, EUGENE BOHDAN, MICROBIOLOGY. *Current Pos:* RETIRED. *Personal Data:* b Tovste, Ukraine, May 8, 27; Can citizen; wid; c 2. *Educ:* Univ Man, BSc, 53, MSc, 55; Univ Wis-Madison, PhD(microbiol), 60. *Prof Exp:* Asst microbiol, Univ Man, 53-55; asst bact, Univ Wis-Madison, 55-59; res scientist microbiol, Res Ctr, Agr Can, 59-92. *Concurrent Pos:* Hon lectr, Fac Med & Dent, Univ Western Ont, 65-, lectr, dept russ studies, 71-74; chmn, Int Subcomt Agrobacterium & Rhizobium, Int Asn Microbiol Socs, 74-83. *Mem:* Can Soc Microbiol; Am Soc Microbiol; Soc Gen Microbiol; Ukrainian Free Acad Sci; Shevchenko Sci Soc. *Res:* Characterization of bacteriophages; bacteriocins; serological reactions; herbicides in relation to microbes; rhizobia, agrobacteria & azotobacter mutations; herbicide residues. *Mailing Add:* 195 Tarbart Terr London ON N6H 3B3 Can

ROSMAN, HOWARD, PHYSICAL CHEMISTRY. *Current Pos:* from instr to assoc prof chem, 56-72, chmn dept, 67-75 & 77- 80, prof chem, 72-93, ADJ PROF, HOFSTRA UNIV, 93- *Personal Data:* b New York, NY, July 17, 29; m 52; c 2. *Educ:* State Univ NY, BA, 51, MA, 52; Columbia Univ, PhD(chem), 58. *Prof Exp:* Asst chem, Columbia Univ, 52-56. *Concurrent Pos:* Lectr gen studies sch, Columbia Univ, 57-60. *Mem:* Am Chem Soc; AAAS; Sigma Xi. *Res:* Photochemistry of luminescent species. *Mailing Add:* 193 Dogwood Rd Valley Stream NY 11580. *E-Mail:* chmhzr@hofstra.edu

ROSNER, ANTHONY LEOPOLD, ENZYMOLOGY, ENDOCRINOLOGY. *Current Pos:* DIR RES & EDUC, FOUND CHIROPRACTIC EDUC & RES, 92-; CONSULT, CTR ALTERNATIVE MED RES, HARVARD UNIV, 96- *Personal Data:* b Greensboro, NC, Nov 13, 43; m 66, Ruth Marks; c Rachael. *Educ:* Haverford Col, BS, 66; Harvard Univ, PhD(med sci), 72. *Prof Exp:* Teaching fel biochem, Harvard Univ, 69-72; fel molecular biol, Nat Inst Neurol Dis & Stroke, NIH, 72-73; staff fel, 73-74; res fel endocrinol, Med Sch, Tufts Univ, 74-75; res fel, 75-77, res assoc, 75-81, instr path, 81-83, tech dir, Clin Chem Lab, Beth Israel Hosp, Boston, 81-83; instr path, Harvard Med Sch, 81-83; tech dir, New England Path Serv, 83-86; dept admin, Dept Chem, Brandeis Univ, 86-91; res grants dir, Neonatology Children's Hosp, 91-92. *Concurrent Pos:* Fel, Nat Inst Gen Med Sci, 72; res assoc biol chem, Harvard Med Sch, 78-81; dir, Estrogen Receptor Assay Lab & tech dir, Clinical Chem Lab, Beth Israel Hosp, Boston, 81-83; consult, New Eng Path Serv, 86-96; bd dirs, New Eng Chap Am Chem Soc, 90-; Andelot fel, Harvard Univ; sect ed, J Neuromuscular Skeletal Syst. *Mem:* AAAS; Am Chem Soc; Am Pub Health Asn; Am Soc Cell Biol; Soc Res Admin; Am Asn Clin Chemists. *Res:* Kinetics and control mechanisms attendant upon the binding of steroid hormones to receptor proteins in target tissues, comprised of either normal or cancerous cells; research designs and outcomes in alternative medicine. *Mailing Add:* 1443 Beacon St Apt 201 Brookline MA 02146-4707. *Fax:* 703-276-8178

ROSNER, CARL H, ELECTRICAL ENGINEERING. *Current Pos:* CHMN BD, INTER MAGNETICS GEN CORP, 80-, PRES, 84- *Personal Data:* b Hamburg, Ger, Apr 4, 29. *Prof Exp:* Res assoc, Upsala Univ & Royal Inst Tech; staff scientist, Gen Elec Res & Develop Ctr, 55-67; mgr, Gen Elec Superconductive Prod. *Concurrent Pos:* Pres, Technol Develop Corp, Can, 80-83. *Mem:* Nat Acad Eng; Inst Elec & Electronics Engrs; Am Phys Soc; AAAS; Am Mgt Asn. *Res:* Published many articles on superconductive and electronic devices; granted 7 US patents. *Mailing Add:* Intermagnetics Gen Corp PO Box 461 Latham NY 12110-0461

ROSNER, DANIEL E(DWIN), CHEMICAL ENGINEERING, MECHANICAL ENGINEERING. *Current Pos:* assoc prof, 69-74, PROF CHEM ENG & APPL SCI, YALE UNIV, 74- *Personal Data:* b New York, NY, Oct 30, 33; m 58; c 2. *Educ:* City Col New York, BME, 55; Princeton Univ, MA, 57, PhD(aero eng), 61. *Hon Degrees:* MA, Yale Univ, 74. *Prof Exp:* Head interface kinetics & transport group, AeroChem Res Labs, Inc, 58-69. *Concurrent Pos:* Vis prof mech eng, Polytech Inst Brooklyn, 64-67; consult, Gen Elec Corp, Exxon & AeroChem Res Labs; fel, Guggenheim, jet propulsion, Barcelow Univ, 55-57, Gen Elec Co, 57; consult, Gen Elec Corp, SCM chemicals, Babcock & Wilcox, AVCO-Lycoming-Textron, Vortec & Shell; chmn, chem eng dept, Yale Univ, 84-87. *Mem:* Am Soc Eng Educ; Am Inst Chem Engrs; Am Inst Aeronaut & Astronaut; Sigma Xi; Combustion Inst; Am Chem Soc. *Res:* Energy and mass transfer in chemically reacting flow systems; experimental and theoretical studies in heterogeneous chemical kinetics; combustion; aerosol deposition, nucleation, growth, dispersion and coagulation; transport phenomena in materials processing; transport processes in chemically reacting flow systems; aeronautical engineering. *Mailing Add:* Dept Chem Eng Yale Univ PO Box 2159 New Haven CT 06520-2159

ROSNER, FRED, HEMATOLOGY, MEDICAL ETHICS. *Current Pos:* dir, Div Hemat, 70-78, dir, Dept Med, Queens Hosp Ctr, Long Island Med Ctr, 78-93, DIR, DEPT MED, MT SINAI SERV, QUEENS HOSP CTR, 93-; PROF MED, MT SINAI SCH MED, 93- *Personal Data:* b Berlin, Germany, Oct 3, 35; m 59, Saranne Eskolsky; c 4. *Educ:* Yeshiva Univ, BA, 55; Albert Einstein Col Med, MD, 59; Am Col Physicians, FACP(internal med), 70. *Prof Exp:* Asst dir, Div Hemat, Maimonides Med Ctr, 65-70. *Concurrent Pos:* Lectr, State Univ NY, Brooklyn, 72-; vis mem, Albert Einstein Col Med, Bronx NY, 75-; prof med, State Univ NY, Stony Brook, 78-89, consult, Univ Hosp, 81-; consult, Med Res Coun Can, 81-; prof med, Albert Einstein Col Med, 89-93. *Mem:* Am Soc Hemat; AMA; Am Soc Clin Oncol; Am Assoc Hist Med. *Res:* Internal medicine and hematology; medical education and medical ethics; medical history and Jewish medicine. *Mailing Add:* 82-68 164th St Jamaica NY 11432. *Fax:* 718-883-6124

ROSNER, JONATHAN LINCOLN, PHYSICS. *Current Pos:* PROF PHYSICS, UNIV CHICAGO, 82- *Personal Data:* b New York, NY, July 23, 41; m 65, Joy E Fox; c Hannah & Benjamin. *Educ:* Swarthmore Col, AB, 62; Princeton Univ, MA, 63, PhD(physics), 65. *Prof Exp:* Res asst prof physics, Univ Wash, 65-67; vis lectr, Tel-Aviv Univ, 67-69; from asst prof to prof, Univ Minn, Minneapolis, 69-82. *Concurrent Pos:* Consult, Argonne Nat Lab, 71-74, Fermi Nat Accelerator Lab, 75-78 & Brookhaven Nat Lab, 79-82; translr, Am Inst Physics, 71-73 & 78-92; Alfred P Sloan res fel, Univ Minn, Minneapolis, Europ Orgn Nuclear Res, Geneva & Stanford Linear Accelerator Ctr, 71-73; mem, Inst Advan Study, 72, 76-77, 88-89; vis res assoc, Calif Inst Technol, 70, 72 & 75; mem, High Energy Physics adv panel, 75, 87-91, subpanel on new facil, 77 & subpanel on long range planning, 81; mem bd trustees, Aspen Ctr Physics, 78-; mem natural sci & eng grant selection comt, High Energy Physics, Can, 80-82; mem exec comt, Div Particles & Fields, Am Phys Soc, 84-87; prog comt, Cornell Electron Storage Ring, 86-88; Stanford Linear Accelerator Ctr, 95- *Mem:* Fel Am Phys Soc. *Res:* Theoretical and elementary particle physics. *Mailing Add:* Enrico Fermi Inst Univ Chicago 5640 S Ellis Ave Chicago IL 60637

ROSNER, JUDAH LEON, MOLECULAR BIOLOGY. *Current Pos:* Biologist, NIH, 67, scientist, 67-70, staff fel, 70-74, RES BIOLOGIST, NIH, 74- *Personal Data:* b New York, NY, Oct 18, 39; div; c 1. *Educ:* Columbia Col, BA, 60; Yale Univ, MS, 64, PhD(biol), 67. *Mem:* Am Soc Microbiol; AAAS. *Res:* Molecular biology and genetics of bacteria, bacterial viruses and transposable genetic elements; antibiotic-resistance mechanisms; outer membrane protein regulation, aspirin effects. *Mailing Add:* NIH Bldg 5 Rm 333 Bethesda MD 20892

ROSNER, MARSHA R, CELL GROWTH. *Current Pos:* assoc prof, 87-94, PROF, BEN MAY INST PHARMACOL & PHYSIOL SCI, UNIV CHICAGO, 94- *Personal Data:* b Springfield, Mass, Nov 8, 50; m 71, Robert; c Daniela K & Nicole E. *Educ:* Mass Inst Technol, PhD(biochem), 78. *Prof Exp:* Asst prof toxicol, Mass Inst Technol, 82-86, Assoc Prof, 86-87. *Concurrent Pos:* Chair, Cancer Biol Comt, Univ Chicago. *Mem:* Am Soc Biol Chemists; Am Soc Cellular Biol; Am Cancer Soc; Am Soc Microbiol. *Res:* Study of mechanisms by which cells signal, particularly in response to growth factors and tumor promoters. *Mailing Add:* 4950 S Greenwood Chicago IL 60615

ROSNER, ROBERT, PLASMA ASTROPHYSICS, SOLAR PHYSICS. *Current Pos:* PROF ASTRON, UNIV CHICAGO, 87-, CHMN, DEPT ASTRON & ASTROPHYS, 91- *Personal Data:* b Garmisch-Partenkirchen, WGer, June 26, 47; US citizen; m 71, Marsha Rich; c Daniela K & Nicole E. *Educ:* Brandeis Univ, BA, 69; Harvard Univ, PhD(physics), 75. *Prof Exp:* From instr to assoc prof astron, Harvard Univ, 77-86. *Concurrent Pos:* Woodrow Wilson Found fel, 69; res fel solar x-ray astron, Harvard Col Observ, 76-78. *Mem:* Fel Am Phys Soc; Int Astron Union; Am Astron Soc; Soc Indust & Appl Math; Am Geophys Union. *Res:* Solar and stellar x-ray astronomy; plasma heating, transport processes, diagnostics; astrophysical magnetic field generation and diffusion; fluid dynamics. *Mailing Add:* Enrico Fermi Inst Univ Chicago 5640 S Ellis Ave Chicago IL 60637. *E-Mail:* rrosner@oddjob.uchicago.edu

ROSNER, SHELDON DAVID, PHYSICS. *Current Pos:* ASST PROF PHYSICS & NAT RES COUN CAN GRANT, UNIV WESTERN ONT, 71- *Personal Data:* b Toronto, Ont, Feb 19, 41; m 67; c 2. *Educ:* Univ Toronto, BSc, 62; Harvard Univ, AM, 63, PhD(physics), 68. *Prof Exp:* Nat Res Coun Can fel, Clarendon Lab, Oxford Univ, 69-71. *Concurrent Pos:* Vis fel, Univ Colo, 78-79. *Mem:* Am Phys Soc; Can Asn Physicists. *Res:* Atomic physics; optical pumping; atomic and molecular beams; precise resonance measurements of atomic and molecular structure of fundamental interest. *Mailing Add:* Dept Physics Univ Western Ont London ON N6A 3K7 Can. *Fax:* 519-661-2033

ROSNER, WILLIAM, ENDOCRINOLOGY. *Current Pos:* Instr med, Columbia Univ, 67-69, assoc, 69-70, asst clin prof med, 70-72, asst prof, 72-73, assoc prof, 73-82, PROF MED, COL PHYSICIANS & SURGEONS, COLUMBIA UNIV, 82- *Personal Data:* b Brooklyn, NY, Jan 7, 33. *Educ:* Univ Wis, BA, 54; Albert Einstein Col Med, MD, 61. *Concurrent Pos:* Asst attend physician, Roosevelt Hosp, 67-79, assoc attend physician, 69-72, attend physician & dir, Div Endocrinol, 72- *Mem:* Fel Am Col Physicians; Am Fedn Clin Res; Am Soc Biol Chemists; Am Soc Clin Invest; Endocrine Soc. *Res:* Steroid hormones, including the steroids secreted by the adrenal cortex, the ovaries, and the testis, their transport in plasma and the specific plasma proteins to which they are bound. *Mailing Add:* Div Encodrinol Roosevelt Hosp 428 W 59th St New York NY 10019-1192

ROSOFF, BETTY, ENDOCRINOLOGY. *Current Pos:* from asst prof to prof, 74-86, EMER PROF BIOL, STERN COL, YESHIVA UNIV, 86- *Personal Data:* b New York, NY, May 28, 20; m 42; c 1. *Educ:* Hunter Col, BA, 42, MA, 60; City Univ New York, PhD(biol), 66. *Prof Exp:* Res chemist, Nat Aniline Div, Allied Chem Corp, NY, 43-48; res assoc cancer, Montefiore Hosp, Bronx, 52-62; instr biol, Bronx Community Col, 64-65; lectr, Hunter Col, 65-67; assoc prof, Paterson State Col, 67-68. *Concurrent Pos:* Lectr physiol, Hunter Col, 61-64, adj prof, 68-75; mem working cadre, Nat Prostatic Cancer Proj, 74-79; vis investr, Am Mus Natural Hist, 81-82. *Mem:* AAAS; NY Acad Sci; Am Physiol Soc; Sigma Xi. *Res:* Zinc and trace metal metabolism; zinc and prostatic pathology; gonadotrophic control of prostate; thymus gland in development; radioactive isotope decontamination. *Mailing Add:* 280 Ninth Ave Apt 17H New York NY 10001-5702

ROSOFF, MORTON, PHYSICAL CHEMISTRY, SURFACE CHEMISTRY. *Current Pos:* PROF, PHYS PHARMACY, ARNOLD & MARIE SCHWARTZ COL PHARMACEUT SCI, LONG ISLAND UNIV, 84- *Personal Data:* b Brooklyn, NY, Feb 19, 22. *Educ:* Brooklyn Col, BA, 42, MA, 49; Duke Univ, PhD(chem), 55. *Prof Exp:* Res assoc & lectr colloid chem, Columbia Univ, 52-54; adj asst prof biophys chem, Sloan Kettering Inst Cancer Res, 54-58; sr scientist, IBM Watson Labs, NY, 60-64; sr scientist surface chem, Columbia Univ, 64-68, assoc prof phys chem & chmn dept, Col Pharmaceut Sci, 68-76; group leader phys pharm, USV Pharmaceut Corp, 76-84. *Concurrent Pos:* Adj prof, City Univ New York, 56-75; sr scientist, Lever Bros Inc, NJ, 59-60; consult, Vet Admin Hosp, East Orange, NJ, 64, Dr Madaus Inc, WGer, 65-68, Am Stand & Testing, NY, 66-69 & Carter Wallace Inc, NJ, 69-74, Pennelt Inc, Pa, 85-86. *Mem:* Am Chem Soc; AAAS. *Res:* Physical chemistry of biological macromolecules; surface chemistry of biological macromolecules, microemulsions; metastable colloidal systems; physical pharmacy. *Mailing Add:* 15 Wellesley Ave Yonkers NY 10705-3841

ROSOLOWSKI, JOSEPH HENRY, PHYSICAL PROPERTIES OF CERAMICS. *Current Pos:* PHYSICIST, CORP RES & DEVELOP CTR, GEN ELEC CO, 60- *Personal Data:* b Fall River, Mass, May 18, 30; m 52; c 2. *Educ:* Rensselaer Polytech Inst, BS, 52, PhD(solid state physics), 61. *Honors & Awards:* Ross Coffin Purdy Award, Am Ceramic Soc, 76. *Prof Exp:* Assoc physicist, Res & Develop Ctr, Vitro Corp Am, 52-54. *Concurrent Pos:* AEC exchange scientist, Poland, 62-63. *Mem:* Am Phys Soc; Am Ceramic Soc; Sigma Xi. *Res:* Diffusion in solids; physical properties of ceramics; radiation effects in metals; technical management. *Mailing Add:* 1435 Myron St Schenectady NY 12309

ROSOMOFF, HUBERT LAWRENCE, MEDICINE. *Current Pos:* prof neurol surg & chmn dept, Sch Med, 71-94, MED DIR, COMPREHENSIVE PAIN CTR, UNIV MIAMI, 78-, PROF & EMER CHMN, SCH MED. *Personal Data:* b Philadelphia, Pa, Apr 11, 27; m 50; c 2. *Educ:* Univ Pa, AB, 48; Hahnemann Med Col, MD, 52; Columbia Univ, DMedSci, 60. *Honors & Awards:* Jeremiah Fix Award, 82; Am Acad Neur Surg Award, 56; Presidential Award, Southern Pain Soc, 90; Distinguished Serv Award, Am Pain Soc, 91. *Prof Exp:* Intern, Hahnemann Hosp, Pa, 52-53; asst resident surgeon, Presby Hosp, New York, 53-54, asst resident neurosurgeon, 54-55; asst resident neurosurgeon, Neurol Inst, New York, 57-58, resident neurosurgeon, 58-59; from asst prof to assoc prof neurol surg, Sch Med, Univ Pittsburgh, 59-66; prof & chmn dept, Albert Einstein Col Med & chief hosp, 66-71. *Concurrent Pos:* Neurosurgeon, Presby Hosp & chief neurosurg, Vet Admin Hosp, Pittsburgh, 59-66; chief neurol surg, Bronx Munic Hosp Ctr & chief, Montefiore Hosp & Med Ctr, 66-71; chief neurosurg sect, Vet Admin Hosp, Miami, 71-; chmn dept neurosurg, Jackson Mem Hosp, Miami, 71-; chief, pain & rehab servs, SShore Med Hosp & Med Ctr, 85- *Mem:* AMA; Am Col Surg; Cong Neurol Surg; Soc Neurol Surg; Am Acad Pain Med; Soc Neurosci; Am Asn Neurosurg; Am Pain Soc. *Res:* Neurological surgery; physiology; hypothermia; transplantation; pain. *Mailing Add:* Univ Miami Comprehensive Pain & Rehab Ctr 600 Alton Rd Miami Beach FL 33139

ROSOWSKY, ANDRE, ORGANIC CHEMISTRY, MEDICINAL CHEMISTRY. *Current Pos:* assoc biol chem, 64-78, prin assoc pharmacol, 78-87, ASSOC PROF, BIOL CHEM & MOLECULAR PHARMACOL, HARVARD MED SCH, 87- *Personal Data:* b Lille, France, Mar 3, 36; US citizen; m 62, Erlene Cohen; c David, Lisa & Jessica. *Educ:* Univ Calif, Berkeley, BS, 57; Univ Rochester, PhD(org chem), 61. *Prof Exp:* NSF res fel, Harvard Univ, 61-62; res assoc path, Children's Cancer Res Found & Children's Hosp Med Ctr, Dana-Farber Cancer Inst, 62-74. *Concurrent Pos:* Adj assoc prof med chem, Northeastern Univ, 76-82, adj prof, 82- *Mem:* Am Chem Soc; Am Asn Cancer Res. *Res:* Design and synthesis of new biologically active compounds, especially nitrogen heterocycles; medicinal chemistry. *Mailing Add:* Div Cancer Pharmacol Dana-Farber Cancer Inst 44 Binney St Boston MA 02115-6084

ROSS, ALAN, BIOSTATISTICS. *Current Pos:* assoc prof, 64-67, chmn dept, 67-81, PROF BIOSTAT, SCH HYG & PUB HEALTH, JOHNS HOPKINS UNIV, 67- *Personal Data:* b Hamilton, Ohio, Aug 25, 26; m 50; c 3. *Educ:* Brown Univ, AB, 50; Iowa State Univ, MS, 52, PhD(statist), 60. *Prof Exp:* Res assoc biostatist, Sch Pub Health, Univ Pittsburgh, 54-56; from asst prof to assoc prof behav sci, Sch Med, Univ Ky, 56-64. *Concurrent Pos:* Prin investr, Med Comput Planning grant, HEW, 62-63; chief biostatist consult, Off Aviation Med, Fed Aviation Admin, 66-70; statist adv, Int Collab Study Med Care, WHO, 66-73; prog dir, Biostatist Training grant, Nat Inst Gen Med Sci, 66-76 & Pub Health Statist Training grant, HEW, 69-74; chief statistician, Afghan Demog Study, USAID proj, 71-76; statist adv, Precursors of Learning Disability, Kennedy Inst, Johns Hopkins, 76-87; statist adv, Chagasic Infection & Myocardiopathy, WHO, Venezuela, 77-; vis prof, Univ Adelaide, Australia, 82, Univ Nairobi, Kenya, 87 & Univ Padua, Italy, 90, 92. *Mem:* Fel Am Statist Asn; Biomet Soc; Int Asn Surv Statisticians; Am Pub Health Asn. *Res:* Sampling theory and methods. *Mailing Add:* Dept Biostatist Johns Hopkins Univ Baltimore MD 21205. *Fax:* 301-955-0958

ROSS, ALBERTA BARKLEY, CHEMISTRY, INFORMATION SCIENCE. *Current Pos:* supvr, 64-71, consult, 71-72, SUPVR, RADIATION CHEM DATA CTR, UNIV NOTRE DAME, 72- *Personal Data:* b Moores Hill, Ind, July 26, 28; m 56, Joseph H; c Mary A, Joseph H Jr, Robert B & Kathleen R. *Educ:* Purdue Univ, BS, 48; Wash Univ, BS, 51; Univ Md, PhD(chem), 57. *Prof Exp:* Tech librn, Monsanto Chem Co, 48-53; res assoc, Univ Mich, 57-58. *Mem:* Am Chem Soc; Inter-Am Photochem Soc; Europ Photochem Asn; Sigma Xi. *Res:* Radiation chemistry; chemical kinetics; data compilation; chemical literature. *Mailing Add:* 1438 E Monroe St South Bend IN 46615-1006

ROSS, ALEXANDER, ORGANIC CHEMISTRY, ENVIRONMENTAL PROTECTION. *Current Pos:* TECH DIR, RADTECH INT, 93- *Personal Data:* b St Louis, Mo, Feb 7, 20; m 47, Dorothy Cantor; c Sara C. *Educ:* Wayne Univ, BS, 42; Univ Mich, MS, 50, PhD(org chem), 53. *Prof Exp:* Control chemist, Swift & Co, 42; instr chem, Univ Mich, 51; res chemist, Ethyl Corp, 52-55, asst res supvr, 55; sr res chemist, Olin-Mathieson Chem Corp, Conn, 56-57, sect chief, 57-59; head org res, Metal & Thermit Corp, 59-61, Europ tech mgr, M&T Chem Inc, Switz, 61-63, mgr org chem res & develop, NJ, 63-64, mgr chem res & develop, 64-65, dir res, 65-68, tech dir, 68-74; dir res & develop, Spencer Kellogg Div, Textron Inc, 74-76, vpres res & develop, 77-86; sr scientist res & develop, Environ Protection Agency, 91-93. *Concurrent Pos:* Consult & lectr, 86-91. *Mem:* AAAS; Am Chem Soc; Soc Plastics Engrs; Asn Res Dirs; NY Acad Sci. *Res:* Mechanism of antiknock action; organic phosphorus and agricultural chemistry; stereochemistry of carbocyclic systems; organohydrazine compounds; organometallics; stabilizers for polymers; organotin biocides; urethane chemicals; metal treatment; ceramics; polymers; catalysts; resins for coatings, inks, adhesives; urethanes, polyesters. *Mailing Add:* 400 N Cherry St Falls Church VA 22046

ROSS, ALONZO HARVEY, GROWTH FACTOR RECEPTORS, DIFFERENTIATION. *Current Pos:* SR SCIENTIST, WORCESTER FOUND EXP BIOL, 88- *Personal Data:* b Louisville, Ky, Sept 25, 50; m 74. *Educ:* Cornell Univ, BA, 72; Stanford Univ, PhD(chem), 77. *Honors & Awards:* Schweisguth Prize, Int Soc Pediat Oncol, 89. *Prof Exp:* Res assoc, Wistar Inst, 81-84, asst prof, 85-88. *Concurrent Pos:* Asst prof, Dept Neurol, Univ Pa Sch Med, 86-88; assoc prof, Dept Biochem, Univ Mass Med Col, 89- *Mem:* Am Asn Cancer Res; Am Asn Immunologists; Am Chem Soc; Am Soc Neurochem; Int Soc Differentiation; Soc Neurosci. *Res:* Developed the first anti-phosphotyrosine antibodies; study the structure of the nerve growth factor receptor and differentiation of neural tumor cells. *Mailing Add:* Worcester Found 222 Maple Ave Shrewsbury MA 01545. *E-Mail:* ross@sci.wfeb.edu

ROSS, ALTA CATHARINE, VITAMIN METABOLISM, ATHEROSCLEROSIS. *Current Pos:* from asst prof to assoc prof, 78-88, PROF BIOCHEM, MED COL PA, 88-, DIR DIV NUTRIT. *Personal Data:* b Santa Monica, Calif, Jan 19, 47; m 69. *Educ:* Univ Calif, Davis, BS, 70; Cornell Univ, MNS, 72, PhD(biochem), 76. *Honors & Awards:* Mead Johnson Award, Am Inst Nutrit, 86. *Prof Exp:* Staff & res assoc med, Columbia Univ, 76-78. *Concurrent Pos:* Coun fel, Am Heart Asn, 81- *Mem:* AAAS; Sigma Xi; Am Inst Nutrit; Am Heart Asn; Am Soc Cell Biol. *Res:* Vitamin A transport and metabolism; lipoprotein metabolism; hepatic retinoid metabolism; nutrition and immune function. *Mailing Add:* Pa State Univ 126 S Henderson Bldg University Park PA 16802-6504. *Fax:* 215-843-8849

ROSS, ARTHUR LEONARD, DESIGN REVIEW & FAILURE PREVENTION. *Current Pos:* CONSULT ENG, 91- *Personal Data:* b New York, NY, Mar 9, 24; m 48, Amy J Cohan; c Bradley & Anne. *Educ:* NY Univ, BAeE, 48, MAeE, 50, EngScD(aeronaut eng), 54. *Prof Exp:* Consult engr struct anal methods, Aircraft Nuclear Propulsion Dept, Gen Elec Co, 54-61, mgr S5G struct eval, Knolls Atomic Power Lab, 61-66, staff engr struct mech, Re-entry Systs Div, 66-91. *Concurrent Pos:* Chmn, Reliablity, Stress Anal & Failure Prev Comt, Am Soc Mech Engrs, 78-82, chmn, Philadelphia Sect, 82-83, chmn, Design Eng Div, 85-86; mem, Structures Tech Comn, Am Inst Aeronaut & Astronaut. *Mem:* Fel Am Soc Mech Engrs; Am Acad Mech; Sigma Xi; Am Inst Aeronaut & Astronaut. *Res:* Research and development of mechanical stress analysis, shock and vibration, hypervelocity impact, thermal stress, pressure vessels and composite materials; consultation and design reviews for failure prevention and mechanical design support. *Mailing Add:* Consult Eng 122 Maple Ave Bala Cynwyd PA 19004

ROSS, BERNARD, MECHANICAL & STRUCTURAL ENGINEERING. *Current Pos:* sr mem staff & exec, Failure Analysis Assocs, 70-78, pres, 78-82, chmn bd, 78-89, EMER CHMN BD, FAILURE ANALYSIS ASSOCS, 89- *Personal Data:* b Montreal, Que, Nov 10, 34; US citizen; m 68, Shelley Spencer; c Jonathan & Jennifer. *Educ:* Cornell Univ, BME, 57; Stanford Univ, MSc, 59, PhD(aeronaut eng), 65; Nat Sch Advan Aeronaut Studies, France, dipl aeronaut eng, 60; Univ Edinburgh, dipl eng mech, 61; Cornell Univ, cert advan eng study, 88. *Prof Exp:* Assoc engr, Marquardt Aircraft Co, 57-58; res asst aeronaut eng, Stanford Univ, 60-64, res assoc, 64-65; eng physicist, Stanford Res Inst, 65-70. *Concurrent Pos:* Consult, Failure Anal Assocs, 68-70; vis lectr, Univ Santa Clara, 70-78; distinguished lect speaker, Am Inst Aeronaut & Astronaut, 90-91; consult prof, Stanford Univ, 91-; pres Int Soc Law, Technol & Ins, Vienna, 96. *Mem:* AAAS; Am Soc Mech Engrs; Am Inst Aeronaut & Astronaut; Sigma Xi; Nat Soc Prof Engrs; Soc Automotive Engrs. *Res:* Experimental and theoretical research in the buckling of thin shell structures and the penetration of solids by projectiles; structural and mechanical analysis of failures; fracture mechanics; design analysis. *Mailing Add:* PO Box 3015 Menlo Park CA 94025. *Fax:* 650-328-2995; *E-Mail:* kng_fruk@faol.com

ROSS, BRADLEY ALFRED, COMPUTER SIMULATION & MODELING. *Current Pos:* SR ENGR, MONSANTO CO, 79- *Personal Data:* b Brooklyn, NY, June 5, 52. *Educ:* Univ Pa, BS, 74, MS, 76, PhD(chem eng), 79. *Mem:* Am Inst Chem Engrs; Sigma Xi. *Res:* Computer programs to aid in design, maintenance and operation of chemical plants, with emphasis on steady-state simulation. *Mailing Add:* 705 General Scott Rd King of Prussia PA 19406-1578

ROSS, BRUCE BRIAN, DYNAMIC METEOROLOGY. *Current Pos:* Physicist meteorol, Geophys Fluid Dynamics Lab, 71-89, ASST DIR, NAT OCEANIC & ATMOSPHERIC ADMIN, 89- *Personal Data:* b Bryn Mawr, Pa, June 30, 44; m 68, Keyo Smith; c Erika & Brian. *Educ:* Brown Univ, ScB, 66; Princeton Univ, MA, 68, PhD(aerospace eng), 71. *Concurrent Pos:* NSF grad fel, 66-70. *Mem:* Am Meteorol Soc; AAAS. *Res:* Mesoscale meteorology; numerical modeling of generation and maintenance of severe storm systems. *Mailing Add:* Geophys Fluid Dynamics Lab NOAA/Princeton Univ PO Box 308 Princeton NJ 08542. *E-Mail:* br@gfdl.gov

ROSS, CHARLES ALEXANDER, GEOLOGY, STRATIGRAPHY PALEOBIOLOGY. *Current Pos:* CONSULT, GEO BIO STRAT, 92-; RES ASSOC, DEPT GEOL, WESTERN WASH UNIV, 92- *Personal Data:* b Champaign, Ill, Apr 16, 33; m 59, June P Phillips. *Educ:* Univ Colo, BA, 54; Yale Univ, MS, 58, PhD(geol), 59. *Prof Exp:* Res assoc, Yale Univ, 59-60; from asst geologist to assoc geologist, Ill State Geol Surv, 60-64; from asst prof to prof geol, Western Wash Univ, 64-82, chmn dept, 77-82; staff geologist to sr staff geologist, Stratigraphic Sci, Gulf Oil Explor Prod Co, 82-83, dir, Stratigraphic Sci, 83-85; sr biostratigrapher, Chevron USA, 85-92. *Concurrent Pos:* NSF res grants late Paleozoic fusulinaceans, 64-68; consult petrol explor, Geol Surv Can, 75; mem, Int Subcomn Permian Stratig, 75-88; corresp mem, Int Subcomt Carboniferous Stratig, 73- & Int Subcomt Ordovician Stratig, 88- *Mem:* Fel AAAS; fel Geol Soc Am; hon mem Soc Sedimentary Geol; Am Asn Petrol Geol; Soc Study Evolution; Cushman Found Foraminiferal Res (pres, 81-82, 90-91). *Res:* Biostratigraphy and paleontology, including foraminiferal faunas; paleoclimatology; paleoecology; recent large calcareous Foraminifera; paleobiogeography; sequence stratigraphy, global correlations; accreted terranes of late Paleozoic origins. *Mailing Add:* GeoBioStrat 600 Highland Dr Bellingham WA 98225-6410

ROSS, CHARLES BURTON, COMPUTER SCIENCES. *Current Pos:* asst prof, 71-80, ASSOC PROF COMPUT SCI, WRIGHT STATE UNIV, 80- *Personal Data:* b Rochester, NY, July 23, 34; m 62; c 2. *Educ:* Villanova Univ, BS, 57; Purdue Univ, Lafayette, MS, 63, PhD(physics), 69. *Prof Exp:* AEC fel, Los Alamos Sci Lab, 69-71. *Mem:* Asn Comput Mach. *Res:* Digital design. *Mailing Add:* Dept Comput Sci Wright State Univ 303 Russ Engr Ctr 3640 Colonel Glenn Dayton OH 45435-0002

ROSS, CLAY CAMPBELL, JR, MATHEMATICS. *Current Pos:* assoc prof, 73-81, dir acad comput, 77-81, PROF MATH & CONSULT, FAC COMPUT, UNIV SOUTH, 81- *Personal Data:* b Lexington, Ky, June 17, 36; m 64. *Educ:* Univ Ky, BS, 59; Univ NC, MA, 61, PhD(math), 64. *Prof Exp:* From asst prof to assoc prof math, Emory Univ, 67-73. *Concurrent Pos:* Vis prof math, Univ Mo, Rolla, 79-80. *Mem:* Math Asn Am; Soc Indust & Appl Math; Asn Comput Mach; Sigma Xi. *Res:* Singular differential equations and systems. *Mailing Add:* Dept Math Univ South 735 University Ave Sewanee TN 37383-1000

ROSS, CLEON WALTER, PLANT PHYSIOLOGY, PLANT BIOCHEMISTRY. *Current Pos:* From asst prof to assoc prof, 60-70, PROF BOT & PLANT PATH, COLO STATE UNIV, 70- *Personal Data:* b Driggs, Idaho, May 27, 34; m 56; c 3. *Educ:* Brigham Young Univ, BS, 56; Utah State Univ, MS, 59, PhD(plant physiol), 61. *Mem:* Am Soc Plant Physiol. *Res:* Mechanisms of hormone-induced plant growth. *Mailing Add:* Dept Biol Colo State Univ Ft Collins CO 80523-0001

ROSS, DAVID A, GEOLOGICAL OCEANOGRAPHY. *Current Pos:* from asst scientist to assoc scientist, Woods Hole Oceanog Inst, 67-78, dir, Marine Policy & Ocean Mgt Prog, 78-85, chmn, Dept Geol & Geophys, 85-90, SR SCIENTIST, WOODS HOLE OCEANOG INST, 78- *Personal Data:* b New York, NY, Aug 8, 36. *Educ:* City Col New York, BS, 58; Univ Kans, MS, 60; Univ Calif, San Diego, PhD(oceanog), 65. *Prof Exp:* Res asst geol, Univ Kans, 58-60; res oceanogr, Scripps Inst Oceanog, Calif, 60-65. *Concurrent Pos:* Instr, Mass Inst Technol, 71-78 & Fletcher Sch Law & Diplomacy, Tufts Univ, 71-78; mem exec bd, Law of the Sea Inst, 74-80; Ocean Affairs Adv Comn, Dept of State, 75-80, Sea Grant Coordr, 77-93; mem, Ocean Policy Comt, Nat Acad Sci, 77-82, Ocean Studies Bd, 85-91; consult, 90- *Mem:* Fel AAAS; fel Geol Soc Am; Am Geophys Union. *Res:* Black Sea, Mediterranean Sea, Red Sea and Persian Gulf; geology and geophysics of marginal seas; uses of the ocean marine affairs. *Mailing Add:* Woods Hole Oceanog Inst Falmouth MA 02543. *E-Mail:* dross@whoi.edu

ROSS, DAVID SAMUEL, PHYSICAL ORGANIC CHEMISTRY. *Current Pos:* PHYS ORG CHEMIST, SRI INT, 64- *Personal Data:* b Los Angeles, Calif, Dec 5, 37; m 66; c 1. *Educ:* Univ Calif, Los Angeles BS, 59; Univ Wash, PhD(org chem), 64. *Mem:* Am Chem Soc. *Res:* Chemical reaction kinetics; thermochemistry and mechanism gas and solution phases; acid-base catalysis; coal dissolution and liquefaction; chemistry related to synthetic fuels; fundamental studies in aromatic nitration and oxidation. *Mailing Add:* SRI Int P5269 Menlo Park CA 94025

ROSS, DAVID STANLEY, AGRICULTURAL ENGINEERING, BIOLOGICAL ENGINEERING. *Current Pos:* asst prof, 73-78, ASSOC PROF AGR ENG, UNIV MD, 78- *Personal Data:* b DuBois, Pa, Apr 16, 47; m 95, Deborah Marie Watrous; c 2. *Educ:* Pa State Univ, BS, 69, MS, 71, PhD(agr eng), 73. *Honors & Awards:* Blue Ribbon Awards, Am Soc Agr Engrs, 77, 78, 79, 80, 83 & 96. *Prof Exp:* Res asst agr eng, Pa State Univ, 69-71, NSF trainee, 71-72. *Concurrent Pos:* Assoc ed, Am Soc Agr Eng, 73-; 1977 & 1978 Yearbk Agr Comt, USDA, 76-78. *Mem:* Am Soc Agr Engrs; Irrigation Asn; Coun Agr Sci & Technol. *Res:* Extension education programs in nursery and greenhouse structures, environment and equipment;

equipment for turf, fruit and vegetable producers; trickle irrigation; energy conservation; post harvest cooling and handling of fruits and vegetables. *Mailing Add:* Biol Resources Eng Dept Univ Md College Park MD 20742-5711

ROSS, DAVID WARD, THEORETICAL PHYSICS. *Current Pos:* univ fel, Univ Tex, Austin, 66-67, asst prof physics, 66-70, res scientist, 66-74, asst dir, 74-91, ASSOC DIR THEORET PROG, FUSION RES CTR, UNIV TEX, AUSTIN, 91- *Personal Data:* b Detroit, Mich, Aug 11, 37; m 59, Sara E Schumacher; c Michael D & Andrew W. *Educ:* Univ Mich, BS, 59; Harvard Univ, AM, 60, PhD(physics), 64. *Prof Exp:* Res assoc physics, Univ Ill, Urbana, 64-66. *Concurrent Pos:* Mem, Inst Advan Study, Princeton Univ, 70-71; asst dir, Inst Fusion Studies, Univ Tex, Austin, 80-83. *Mem:* AAAS; fel Am Phys Soc. *Res:* Linear and nonlinear stability theory, radio frequency heating, and thermal transport of fusion plasmas. *Mailing Add:* 6705 Lexington Rd Austin TX 78757-4370. *Fax:* 512-471-6715; *E-Mail:* ross@peaches.ph.utexas.edu

ROSS, DENNIS KENT, THEORETICAL PHYSICS. *Current Pos:* From instr to assoc prof, 68-79, PROF PHYSICS, IOWA STATE UNIV, 79- *Personal Data:* b Hebron, Nebr, May 4, 42; m 66; c 1. *Educ:* Calif Inst Technol, BS, 64; Stanford Univ, PhD(physics), 68. *Mem:* Am Phys Soc; Int Astron Union. *Res:* Radar reflection test of general relativity; absorption in high energy photo production; large angle multiple scattering; magnetic monopoles; scalar-tensor theory of gravitation; charge quantization; Weyl geometry and quantum electrodynamics; gauge supersymmetry; fiber bundles and supergravity; holonomy groups and spontaneous symmetry breaking. *Mailing Add:* Dept Physics Iowa State Univ Ames IA 50011

ROSS, DONALD CLARENCE, GEOLOGY. *Current Pos:* RETIRED. *Personal Data:* b Buffalo, NY, Mar 15, 24; m 48; c 3. *Educ:* Univ Iowa, BA, 48, MS, 49; Univ Calif, Los Angeles, PhD(geol), 52. *Prof Exp:* Asst, Univ Iowa, 48-49; geologist, State Geol Surv, Iowa, 49; asst, Univ Calif, Los Angeles, 49-52; geologist, US Geol Surv, 52-89. *Res:* Igneous and metamorphic petrology; granitic rocks of the White and Inyo Mountains, California; granitic basement of the San Andreas fault region, Coast and Tranverse Ranges; tectonic framework, Southern Sierra Nevada, California. *Mailing Add:* 301 Barclay Ct Palo Alto CA 94306

ROSS, DONALD EDWARD, MECHANICAL ENGINEERING. *Current Pos:* ENG EXEC, JAROS BAUM & BOLLES, NY, 71-, SR PARTNER, 77- *Personal Data:* b New York, NY, May 2, 30; m 54, Jeanne E McKessy; c Susan, Christopher & Carolyn. *Educ:* Columbia Univ, BA, 52, BS, 53; NY Univ, MBA, 60. *Prof Exp:* Engr, Carrier Corp, New York City, 55-70; vpres, Dynadata, 70-71. *Mem:* Nat Acad Eng; Am Soc Mech Eng; Nat Soc Prof Engrs; fel Am Soc Heating Refrigerating & Air Conditioning Engrs; Am Consult Engrs Coun; Nat Bur Eng Regist. *Res:* Mechanical engineering. *Mailing Add:* Jaros Baum & Bolles 345 Park Ave New York NY 10154-0004

ROSS, DONALD JOSEPH, NUTRITIONAL BIOCHEMISTRY. *Current Pos:* from instr to prof, Fairfield Univ, 50-64, chmn dept, 60-70, 77-80, Decamp prof, 79-85, PROF BIOL, FAIRFIELD UNIV, 85- *Personal Data:* b Brooklyn, NY, Mar 26, 28; m 51, Christine D Laforet; c Donald J Jr, Christine M (Earls) & Edmund C. *Educ:* Fordham Univ, BS, 49, PhD(physiol), 56; Boston Col, MS, 50. *Prof Exp:* Asst biol, Boston Col, 49-50. *Concurrent Pos:* Dir biochem lab, St Vincent's Hosp, Bridgeport, Conn, 57-59, consult, 59-90; consult, MK Labs, Fairfield, 60-85, USV Labs, 78. *Mem:* AAAS; NY Acad Sci; fel Am Inst Chem; Am Inst Biol; Sigma Xi. *Res:* Biochemistry of insect metamorphosis; invertebrate physiology; cardiac enzymology; enzyme induction of cardiac and vascular atherosclerotic lesions. *Mailing Add:* 473 Wormwood Rd Fairfield CT 06430. *Fax:* 203-254-4253; *E-Mail:* djross@fair1.fairfield.edu

ROSS, DONALD K(ENNETH), ELECTRICAL & INDUSTRIAL ENGINEERING. *Current Pos:* pres, 62-90, CHMN BD, ROSS & BARUZZINI, 90- *Personal Data:* b St Louis, Mo, Apr 15, 25; m 51, Peggy Grosberg; c Pamela T. *Educ:* Univ Minn, BSEE, 46; Mass Inst Technol, MSEE, 48; Wash Univ, DSc(indust eng), 60. *Honors & Awards:* Outstanding Achievement Award, Inst Elec & Electronics Engrs Indust Appln Soc, 89. *Prof Exp:* Asst, Mass Inst Technol, 46-48. *Concurrent Pos:* Prof assoc, Bldg Res Adv Bd, Nat Acad Sci, 70-85. *Mem:* Fel Inst Elec & Electronics Engrs; fel Am Consult Engrs Coun; Sigma Xi. *Res:* Effects of illumination on task performance; interaction of lighting and HVAC (heating, ventilating and air conditioning) systems. *Mailing Add:* 9 Crosswinds Dr St Louis MO 63132-4303

ROSS, DONALD MORRIS, industrial hygiene, for more information see previous edition

ROSS, DORIS LAUNE, BIOCHEMISTRY. *Current Pos:* Med technologist, 47-54, sect head chem, Clin Labs, 54-56, chief med technologist & teaching supvr, 56-64, clin biochemist, Hermann Hosp & prof clin lab sci, Med Sch, Univ Tex Health Sci Ctr, 67-77, PROF PATH & LAB MED & ASSOC DEAN SCH ALLIED HEALTH SCI, MED SCH, UNIV TEX, 77- *Personal Data:* b Thorndale, Tex, Apr 20, 26. *Educ:* Tex Woman's Univ, BS, 47; Baylor Univ, MS, 58; Univ Tex, PhD(biochem), 67. *Concurrent Pos:* Chief med technologist, Care Medico, Algeria, 62. *Mem:* Am Soc Med Technol; Am Assn Clin Chemists; fel Am Acad Clin Biochem; fel Am Soc Allied Health Professions. *Res:* Clinical chemistry; clinical laboratory methodology; protein structure; immunoglobulins. *Mailing Add:* Univ Tex Sch Allied Health Sci PO Box 20708 Houston TX 77225-0708

ROSS, DOUGLAS TAYLOR, STRUCTURED ANALYSIS & DESIGN, COMPUTER-AIDED DESIGN. *Current Pos:* RETIRED. *Personal Data:* b Canton, China, Dec 21, 29; US citizen; m 51; c 3. *Educ:* Oberlin Col, AB, 51; Mass Inst Technol, SM, 54. *Honors & Awards:* Joseph Marie Jaquard Mem Award, Numerical Control Soc, 75; Distinguished Contrib Award, Soc Mfg Engrs, 80. *Prof Exp:* Head comput applns group, Mass Inst Technol Elec Syst Lab, 52-69; pres, Softech, Inc, 69-75, chmn, 75-89, emer chmn, 89-94. *Concurrent Pos:* Lectr, Dept Elec Eng, Mass Inst Technol, 60-69, Dept Elec Eng & Comput Sci, 83-; mem, working group 23 prog methods, Int Fedn Info Processing, working group algol NATO Software Eng Conf Garmisch & Rome, 68 & 69, var comts, Asn Comput Mach, syst lang & discrete mfg; SofTech prin investr, Air Force AFCAM & ICAM projs, 74-77; gen chmn, Specif Reliable Software Conf, Inst Elec & Electronics Engrs, 79, Inst Comput & Sci Technol eval panel, Nat Res Coun, 81-83; chmn bd, SofTech Microsysts, Inc, 79-81; trustee & dir, Charles Babbage Inst, 84-; dir, Cognition, Inc, 85-89. *Mem:* Asn Comput Mach; AAAS; Sigma Xi. *Res:* Created and directed development APT system for automatic programming of numerically controlled machine tools, now an international standard; created first software engineering language and software production tools. *Mailing Add:* 33 Dawes Rd Lexington MA 02173

ROSS, EDWARD WILLIAM, JR, MATHEMATICS, APPLIED MATHEMATICS. *Current Pos:* RETIRED. *Personal Data:* b Jackson Heights, NY, July 3, 25; m 55; c 5. *Educ:* Webb Inst Naval Archit, BSc, 45; Brown Univ, ScM, 49, PhD(appl math), 54. *Prof Exp:* Fel, Exp Towing Tank, Stevens Inst Technol, 46-47; res engr, 51-52; mathematician, US Army Res Agency, Watertown Arsenal, 55-68; staff mathematician, Natick Res & Develop Command, US Army, 68-93; res prof, Dept Math Sci, Worcester Polytech Inst, 85-93. *Concurrent Pos:* Secy Army res & study fel, 60-61. *Res:* Plasticity; elasticity; thin shell theory; differential equations; asymptotic theory; mechanical vibrations; biological statistics. *Mailing Add:* 152 Barton Dr Sudbury MA 01776

ROSS, ELDON WAYNE, forest pathology, for more information see previous edition

ROSS, ELLIOTT M, BIOLOGICAL SIGNAL TRANSDUCTION, RECEPTORS. *Current Pos:* assoc prof, 81, PROF PHARMACOL, UNIV TEX SOUTHWESTERN MED CTR, 85- *Personal Data:* b Stockton, Calif, Jan 16, 49; m 73; c 1. *Educ:* Univ Calif, Davis, BSc, 70; Cornell Univ, PhD(biochem), 75. *Prof Exp:* Postdoctoral fel pharmacol, Univ Va, 75-78; asst prof biochem & pharmacol, 78-81. *Concurrent Pos:* Mem, Pharmacol Sci Rev Comt, Nat Inst Gen Med Sci, 89-92. *Mem:* Am Chem Soc; Am Soc Biochem & Molecular Biol; Am Peptide Soc; Am Soc Pharmacol & Exp Therapeut. *Res:* Regulation of membrane-bound enzymes and receptors; GTP-binding regulatory proteins, G proteins, and G protein- coupled receptors; receptor-mimetic peptides. *Mailing Add:* Dept Pharmacol Univ Tex Southwestern Med Ctr 5323 Harry Hines Blvd Dallas TX 75235-9041. *Fax:* 214-648-2994; *E-Mail:* ross@utsw.swmed.edu

ROSS, ERNEST, POULTRY NUTRITION. *Current Pos:* RETIRED. *Personal Data:* b New York, NY, Dec 23, 20; m 49; c 4. *Educ:* Ohio State Univ, PhD(poultry nutrit), 55. *Prof Exp:* Asst poultry nutrit, Ohio State Univ, 51-55; from asst poultry scientist to assoc poultry scientist, Univ Hawaii, 57-65, poultry scientist, 65-92. *Concurrent Pos:* Consult, UCC Training Proj, Kampot, Cambodia. *Mem:* Poultry Sci Asn; World Poultry Sci Asn. *Res:* Physiological aspects of nutrition; tropical feedstuffs; environmental housing; management. *Mailing Add:* 225 Hermosa Ave No 105 Long Beach CA 90802

ROSS, FRED MICHAEL, INDUSTRIAL DIAMOND PROCESSING, DIAMOND RECLAMATION. *Current Pos:* CHMN BD DIRS, ROBONARD, INC, 80- *Personal Data:* b New York, NY, Aug 26, 21; m 54, Nee Kilar; c Robin, Bonnie & Richard. *Educ:* Mich Technol Univ, BS, 43. *Honors & Awards:* Silver Medal, Bd Control, Mich Technol Univ, 78. *Prof Exp:* Sr gas analyst, Pure Oil Co, 43-44; electronics technician's mate radar, US Navy, 44-45; chem engr, Multiplate Glass Corp, 45-51; chief chemist, Diamond Dust Co, Inc, 52-80, pres & chief exec officer, 54-80. *Concurrent Pos:* Dir, Indust Diamond Asn Am, 77-78; consult org chem. *Mem:* Fel Am Inst Chemists. *Res:* Industrial diamond process for the manufacture of Ovate diamonds for use in petroleum bits & geological core drills; processes for the reclamation of diamonds from industrial diamond-bearing waste materials. *Mailing Add:* 10325 Crosswind Rd Boca Raton FL 33498. *Fax:* 561-483-7198; *E-Mail:* 72274.764@compuserve.com

ROSS, FREDERICK KEITH, STRUCTURAL CHEMISTRY, CRYSTALLOGRAPHY. *Current Pos:* SR RES SCIENTIST, UNIV MO, 79- *Personal Data:* b Red Oak, Iowa, Nov 11, 42; m 64. *Educ:* Western Wash State Col, AB, 64; Univ Ill, Urbana, MS, 66, PhD(chem), 69. *Prof Exp:* Res assoc chem, Brookhaven Nat Lab, 69-71, State Univ NY Buffalo, 71-72; asst prof, Va Polytech Inst & State Univ, 72-79. *Mem:* Am Chem Soc; The Chem Soc; Am Crystallog Asn. *Res:* X-ray, neutron and gamma-ray diffraction; electronic distributions in solids by diffraction methods; diffraction physics of materials; low temperature x-ray and neutron diffraction. *Mailing Add:* Res Reactor Univ Mo Columbia MO 65211. *Fax:* 573-882-3443; *E-Mail:* ross@reactor.murr.missouri.edu

ROSS, GERALD FRED, ELECTRONICS. *Current Pos:* pres, 81-96, CHMN & CHIEF EXEC OFFICER, ANRO ENG, INC, SARASOTA, FLA, 96- *Personal Data:* b New York, NY, Dec 14, 30; m 53; c 3. *Educ:* City Col New York, BEE, 52; Polytech Univ, MEE, 55, PhD(electronics), 63. *Prof Exp:* Res asst microwave receivers, Univ Mich, 52-53; sr staff engr, W L Maxson Corp,

NY, 54-58; res sect head phased array radar, Sperry Gyroscope Co, NY, 58-65, mem res staff microwaves, Sperry Rand Res Ctr, 65-68, mgr, Sensory & EM Systs Dept, Sperry Res Ctr, Sudbury, 68-81. *Concurrent Pos:* Bd fels, Polytech Univ. *Mem:* Nat Acad Eng; Sigma Xi; Fel Inst Elec & Electronics Engrs. *Res:* Transient behavior studies related to microwave devices and high resolution radar systems; subnanosecond pulse technology and impulse radar. *Mailing Add:* Anro Eng Inc 1800 Second St Suite 878 Sarasota FL 34236

ROSS, GILBERT STUART, neurology, for more information see previous edition

ROSS, GORDON, PHYSIOLOGY, INTERNAL MEDICINE. *Current Pos:* from asst to assoc res pharmacologist, 63-66, from asst prof to assoc prof physiol & med, 66-72, PROF PHYSIOL & MED, SCH MED, UNIV CALIF, LOS ANGELES, 72- *Personal Data:* b London, Eng, Sept 24, 30; m 54; c 2. *Educ:* Univ London, BSc, 51, MB, BS, 54. *Prof Exp:* Demonstr pharmacol, St Bartholomew's Hosp, London, 51-55; house physician & surgeon, St Mary Abbot's Hosp, 55-56; med registr, Mayday Hosp, 58-60 & King's Col Hosp, 60-63. *Mem:* Am Fedn Clin Res; Am Physiol Soc; Sigma Xi. *Res:* Coronary circulation; adrenergic mechanisms. *Mailing Add:* Dept Physiol Sch Med Univ Calif Los Angeles Los Angeles CA 90024

ROSS, HARLEY HARRIS, RADIO ANALYTICAL CHEMISTRY, CHEMICAL INSTRUMENTATION. *Current Pos:* RETIRED. *Personal Data:* b Chicago, Ill, Apr 18, 35; m 59, 82; c 4. *Educ:* Univ Ill, Urbana, BS, 57; Wayne State Univ, MS, 58, PhD(radiochem), 60. *Honors & Awards:* IR-100 Award, 67. *Prof Exp:* Scientist, Spec Training Div, Oak Ridge Inst Nuclear Studies, 60-63, chemist, Oak Ridge Nat Lab, 63-66, asst group leader nuclear & radiochem, 66-72, group leader anal instrumentation, 72-85, head spec radiochem res, 85-97. *Concurrent Pos:* Prof, Univ Tenn, 85-90. *Mem:* Sigma Xi. *Res:* Analytical applications of radioisotopes; liquid scintillator technology; organic luminescent properties; analytical instrumentation; radioisotope energy conversion; atomic and molecular spectroscopy; spectroscopic instrumentation. *Mailing Add:* 106 Albion Rd Oak Ridge TN 37830-7871

ROSS, HOWARD PERSING, GEOPHYSICS, ECONOMIC GEOLOGY. *Current Pos:* sect head apply geophys, Earth Sci Lab, Res Inst, 77-94, RES PROF & SR GEOPHYSICIST, ENERGY & GEOSCI INST, UNIV UTAH, 95- *Personal Data:* b Stockbridge, Mass, Oct 26, 35; m 58, Barbara Lewis; c Steven D, Krista S & Kimber A. *Educ:* Univ NH, BA, 57; Pa State Univ, MS, 63, PhD(geophys), 65. *Honors & Awards:* Patent Disclosure Award, Dept Defense, 67. *Prof Exp:* Comput, United Geophys Corp, Calif, 58-60; res gen phys scientist, Air Force Cambridge Res Lab, Mass, 65-67; sr res geophysicist, Explor Serv Div, Kennecott Explor, Inc, 67-77. *Concurrent Pos:* Investr, Apollo Appln Prog, NASA, 66-67; mem peer rev panels, nuclear waste isolation, 79-87; proj mgr & sr geophysicist, Geophys Consult, 80- *Mem:* Am Geophys Union; Soc Explor Geophys; Europ Asn Geoscientists & Engrs; Am Asn Petrol Geologists; Geothermal Resource Coun. *Res:* Potential field methods; research geophysics; mathematical models of geologic and geophysical processes; remote sensing; porphyry copper geology; geoelectric studies; mineral exploration; geothermal research; nuclear waste isolations studies; granted a patent disclosure award for the Dept of Defense. *Mailing Add:* 7089 S Pinecone St Salt Lake City UT 84121. *Fax:* 801-585-3540

ROSS, HUGH COURTNEY, ELECTRICAL ENGINEERING, HIGH VOLTAGE CONTROL. *Current Pos:* PRES & GEN MGR, ROSS ENG CORP, CAMPBELL, 64-; CHIEF ENGR, HV CONSULT LT, SARATOGA, CALIF, 64- *Personal Data:* b Turlock, Calif, Dec 31, 23; m 50, 84, Patricia Anne Malroy; c John Clare, James Gordon & Robert William. *Educ:* Stanford Univ, BSEE, 50. *Prof Exp:* Instr, San Benito High Sch & Jr Col, 50-51; chief engr, Vacuum Power Switches, Jennings Radio Mfg Corp, San Jose, Calif, 51-62; ITT jennings, 62-64, chief engr, HV Consult, Saratoga, Calif, 64- *Concurrent Pos:* Chmn, Santa Clara Valley Subsection Inst Elec & Electronics Engrs, 60-61. *Mem:* Fel Inst Elec & Electronics Engrs; Am Vacuum Soc; Am Soc Metals. *Res:* High voltage devices; major development in high power vacuum relays; vacuum switches; vacuum circuit breakers; high voltage voltmeters; digital and analog; high voltage control wide band HV and measurement; author of many articles for Institute of Electrical and Electronic Engineers transactions and other technical journals; HV control measurement and safety. *Mailing Add:* Ross Eng Corp 540 Westchester Dr Campbell CA 95008

ROSS, IAN KENNETH, MYCOLOGY, CELL BIOLOGY. *Current Pos:* from asst prof to assoc prof, 64-73, vchmn dept 86-87, PROF BIOL, UNIV CALIF, SANTA BARBARA, 73- *Personal Data:* b London, Eng, May 22, 30; m 56, Muriel E Mayhew; c Karen & Keith. *Educ:* George Washington Univ, BS, 52, MS, 53; McGill Univ, PhD(bot), 57. *Prof Exp:* Lectr bot, McGill Univ, 57; res assoc mycol, Univ Wis, 57-58; from instr to asst prof bot, Yale Univ, 58-64. *Concurrent Pos:* Sect ed, Can J Microbiol, 88-90; BP venture res fel, 88-92; sect ed, Mycol Res. *Mem:* AAAS; Mycol Soc Am; Am Soc Cell Biol; Am Soc Microbiol. *Res:* Biochemistry and molecular biology of differentiation and development of filamentous fungi; transduction of light reception into morphogenetic and genetic changes; molecular basis of aging. *Mailing Add:* Dept Molecular Cell & Develop Biol Univ Calif Santa Barbara Santa Barbara CA 93106. *Fax:* 805-893-4724; *E-Mail:* ross@lifesci.lscf.ucsb. edu

ROSS, IAN M(UNRO), ELECTRICAL ENGINEERING. *Current Pos:* Mem tech staff, AT&T Bell Labs, 52-59, dir, Semiconductor Lab, Murray Hill, NJ, 59-62, dir, Semiconductor Device & Electron Tube Lab, Allentown, Pa, 62-64, managing dir, Bellcomm, Inc, 64-68, pres, 68-71, exec dir, Network Planning Div, Bell Labs, 71-73, vpres, Network Planning & Customer Serv, 73-76, exec vpres, 76-79, pres, 79-91, PRES EMER, AT&T BELL LABS, 91- *Personal Data:* b Southport, Eng, Aug 15, 27; nat US; m 55; c 3. *Educ:* Cambridge Univ, BA, 48, MA & PhD(elec eng), 52. *Honors & Awards:* Morris N Liebermann Mem Prize Award, Inst Radio Engrs, 63; Indust Res Inst Medal, 87; Inst Elec & Electronics Engrs Founders Medal, 88. *Concurrent Pos:* Mem bd dirs, Sandia Nat Lab, BF Goodrich Co & Thomas & Betts Corp. *Mem:* Nat Acad Sci; Nat Acad Eng; fel Inst Elec & Electronics Engrs; fel Am Acad Arts & Sci. *Res:* Systems engineering and development. *Mailing Add:* AT&T Bell Labs 100 Crawfords Corner Rd Rm 1L323 Holmdel NJ 07733. *Fax:* 732-949-5353; *E-Mail:* imr@mhwpa.lucent.com

ROSS, IRA JOSEPH, AGRICULTURAL ENGINEERING. *Current Pos:* assoc prof, 67-70, PROF AGR ENG, UNIV KY, 70- *Personal Data:* b Live Oak, Fla, Apr 8, 33; m 55; c 3. *Educ:* Univ Fla, BAgE, 55; Purdue Univ, MS, 57, PhD, 60. *Prof Exp:* Asst, Purdue Univ, 55-56, instr & asst in agr eng, 56-59; asst prof agr eng & asst agr engr, Univ Fla, 59-65, assoc prof & assoc agr engr, 65-67. *Res:* Electric power and processing. *Mailing Add:* Dept Agr Eng Univ Ky Lexington KY 40506-0001

ROSS, IRVINE E, ELECTRICAL ENGINEERING. *Current Pos:* RETIRED. *Personal Data:* b Needham, Mass, Sept 28, 08. *Educ:* Mass Inst Technol, SB, 30 & SM, 31. *Prof Exp:* Eng mgr, Gen Elec, 48-68. *Mem:* Fel Inst Elec & Electronics Engrs. *Mailing Add:* 4627 North Dr Ft Wayne IN 46815

ROSS, JAMES NEIL, JR, CARDIOVASCULAR PHYSIOLOGY, VETERINARY CARDIOLOGY. *Current Pos:* PROF & CHMN, DEPT MED, SCH VET MED, TUFTS UNIV, 81- *Personal Data:* b Akron, Ohio, Dec 18, 40; m 64; c 3. *Educ:* Ohio State Univ, DVM, 65, MSc, 67; Baylor Col Med, PhD(physiol), 72; Am Col Vet Internal Med, dipl, 73 & 74; Am Col Vet Emergency & Critical Care, dipl, 90. *Prof Exp:* Res asst, dept vet physiol & pharm, Ohio State Univ, 61-65, res assoc vet cardiol, 65-67, lectr clin cardiol, 65-67; from instr to asst prof, Dept Surg & Physiol, Baylor Col Med, 67-74, asst dir vivarium, 67-69, asst chief exp surg, Taub Labs Mech Circulatory Support, 70-74; assoc prof physiol, Med Col Ohio, 74-81. *Concurrent Pos:* Consult, Vet Admin Hosp, Houston, 70-73; mem, Coun Clin Cardiol, Am Heart Asn; mem adv bd vet specialties & coun educ, Am Vet Med Asn, 89- *Mem:* Acad Vet Cardiol (pres, 73-75); Am Soc Artificial Internal Organs; Am Vet Med Asn; Am Col Vet Internal Med; Am Physiol Soc. *Res:* Hemodynamics; circulatory assist-replacement devices and techniques; biomaterials for blood interfacing; cardiovascular models; congenital heart disease; veterinary cardiology; cardiovascular surgery. *Mailing Add:* Dept Med Sch Vet Med Tufts Univ 200 Westboro Rd North Grafton MA 01536-1895

ROSS, JAMES WILLIAM, JR, ANALYTICAL CHEMISTRY, PHYSICAL CHEMISTRY. *Current Pos:* VPRES & DIR RES, ORION RES INC, 62- *Personal Data:* b Ft Lewis, Wash, June 23, 28; m 50, Etta Brucker; c Eve L, Andrew J & Edward P. *Educ:* Univ Calif, Berkeley, BA, 51; Univ Wis-Madison, PhD(chem), 57. *Prof Exp:* Chemist, Tidewater Assoc Oil Co, 51-53; instr chem, Univ Wis, 53-54; asst prof chem, Mass Inst Technol, 57-62. *Concurrent Pos:* Dir bd, Orion Res Inc, 62-; A D Williams distinguished vis scholar, Med Col Va, Va Commonwealth Univ, 72-73. *Mem:* Am Chem Soc; Am Electrochem Soc; fel AAAS. *Res:* Ion selective electrodes; theory, modes of fabrication and application to chemical and medical analysis; electrochemistry; numerous US patents. *Mailing Add:* PO Box 96 Chestnut Hill MA 02167

ROSS, JEFFREY, MOLECULAR BIOLOGY. *Current Pos:* asst prof, 74-78, ASSOC PROF, MCARDLE LAB CANCER RES, UNIV WIS-MADISON, 78- *Personal Data:* b St Louis, Mo, Feb 25, 43; m 68; c 2. *Educ:* Princeton Univ, BA, 65; Wash Univ, MD, 69. *Prof Exp:* Intern med, Cedars-Sinai Med Ctr, Los Angeles, Calif, 69-70; res assoc, NIH, 70-74. *Res:* Mechanism of synthesis of messenger RNA in eukaryotes with emphasis on the characterization of a precursor of globin messenger RNA; role of heme in development of authentic erythroid cells and of cultured erythroleukemic, Friend cells; mRNA synthesis and stability in the thalassemias. *Mailing Add:* Oncol Univ Wis Med Sch 450 N Randall Ave Madison WI 53706-1506

ROSS, JEFFREY ALAN, CHEMICAL CARCINOGENESIS, MUTAGENESIS. *Current Pos:* Nat Res Coun fel, 85-86, RES BIOLOGIST, US ENVIRON PROTECTION AGENCY, 86- *Personal Data:* b Thayer, Mo, Oct 19, 55; m 77, Lisa L Pnazek; c Trillian E, Jennifer A & Marissa K. *Educ:* Univ Tex, Dallas, BS, 77, PhD(biol), 82. *Prof Exp:* Fel, Univ Tex Syst Cancer Ctr, 82-85. *Mem:* Am Asn Cancer Res; AAAS; Asn Biomolecular Resource Facil; NY Acad Sci; Genotoxicity & Environ Mutagenesis Soc. *Res:* Investigations of the mechanisms of action of environmental chemical carcinogens; formation, removal and molecular consequences of carcinogen-DNA adducts. *Mailing Add:* US Environ Protection Agency MD-68 Research Triangle Park NC 27711. *E-Mail:* ross.jeffrey@epamail. epa.gov

ROSS, JOHN, PHYSICAL CHEMISTRY. *Current Pos:* chmn dept, 83-89, PROF CHEM, STANFORD UNIV, 80-, CAMILLE & HENRY DREYFUS PROF, 85- *Personal Data:* b Vienna, Austria, Oct 2, 26; nat US; m 50; c 2. *Educ:* Queens Col, NY, BS, 48; Mass Inst Technol, PhD, 51. *Hon Degrees:*

Weizmann Inst Sci, 84; Queens Col, State Univ NY, 87; Univ Bordeaux, France, 87. *Honors & Awards:* Irving Langmuir Award, Am Chem Soc. *Prof Exp:* Res assoc phys chem, Mass Inst Technol, 50-52; res fel, Yale Univ, 52-53; from asst prof to prof chem, Brown Univ, 53-66; prof & chmn dept, Mass Inst Technol, 66-71, Frederick George Keyes prof chem, 71-80, chmn fac, 75-77. *Concurrent Pos:* Fel, NSF, 52-53, Guggenheim Found, 59-60 & Sloan Found, 60-64; vis Van der Waals prof, Univ Amsterdam, 66; mem bd govs, Weizmann Inst Sci, 71-; chmn fac, Mass Inst Technol, 75-77. *Mem:* Nat Acad Sci; Am Chem Soc; fel Am Phys Soc; fel Am Acad Arts & Sci; fel AAAS. *Res:* Chemical instabilities; oscillatory reactions; thermodynamics of systems far from equilibrium; efficiency of thermal, chemical, and biological engines; chemical computers. *Mailing Add:* Dept Chem Stanford Univ Stanford CA 94305

ROSS, JOHN, JR, MEDICINE, CARDIOLOGY. *Current Pos:* PROF MED & DIR CARDIOVASC DIV, SCH MED, UNIV CALIF, SAN DIEGO, 68- *Personal Data:* b New York, NY, Dec 1, 28; m 58; c 3. *Educ:* Dartmouth Col, AB, 51; Cornell Univ, MD, 55. *Prof Exp:* Clin assoc & sr investr, Nat Heart Inst, 56-60; asst resident, Columbia-Presby Med Ctr, 60-61 & Med Col, Cornell Univ, 61-62; attend physician & chief sect cardiovasc diag, Cardiol Br, Nat Heart Inst, 62-68. *Concurrent Pos:* Consult, Nat Conf Cardiovasc Dis, 63; mem cardiol adv comt, Nat Heart & Lung Inst, 74- *Mem:* Am Physiol Soc; fel Am Col Cardiol (vpres, 72-73); Am Soc Clin Invest; fel Am Col Physicians; Asn Am Physicians. *Res:* Cardiovascular research; cardiac catheterization techniques; mechanics of cardiac contraction; physiology of coronary circulation. *Mailing Add:* Dept Med 0613B Univ Calif San Diego 9500 Gilman Dr La Jolla CA 92093-0613. *Fax:* 619-534-1626

ROSS, JOHN B(YE), ELECTRICAL ENGINEERING. *Current Pos:* Sr physicist, 67-80, RES ASSOC, EASTMAN KODAK CO, 80- *Personal Data:* b St Louis, Mo, June 14, 39; m 72, Carol; c 2. *Educ:* Pa State Univ, BS, 61, MS, 63, PhD(elec eng), 67. *Mem:* Inst Elec & Electronics Engrs. *Res:* Applications of instrumentation and computers to analysis of the quality of film emulsion systems. *Mailing Add:* 2 Pinehill Dr Pittsford NY 14534

ROSS, JOHN BRANDON ALEXANDER, BIOCHEMISTRY. *Current Pos:* asst prof, Dept Biochem, 82-86, ASSOC PROF, MT SINAI SCH MED, 87- *Personal Data:* b Suffern, NY, Feb 18, 47. *Educ:* Antioch Col, BA, 70; Univ Wash, PhD(biochem), 76. *Prof Exp:* Res assoc, Dept Chem, Univ Wash, 76-78; assoc res scientist, dept biol, Johns Hopkins Univ, 78-80; sr res fel, Dept Lab Med, Sch Med, Univ Wash, 80-82. *Mem:* Sigma Xi; Am Chem Soc; Am Soc Photobiol; Biophys Soc; Optical Soc Am. *Res:* Time resolved luminescence of biomolecules; structure of polypetides and proteins in solution; lipid, protein, and steroid interactions; luminescence assay in medicine. *Mailing Add:* Dept Biochem Mt Sinai Sch Med One Gustave L Levy Pl New York NY 10029. *Fax:* 212-996-7214

ROSS, JOHN PAUL, plant pathology, for more information see previous edition

ROSS, JOSEPH C, INTERNAL MEDICINE, PULMONARY DISEASES. *Current Pos:* PROF MED, VANDERBILT UNIV, 81-, ASSOC VCHANCELLOR HEALTH AFFAIRS, 82- *Personal Data:* b Tompkinsville, Ky, June 16, 27; m 52, Isabelle Nevins; c Laura A (Abney), Sharon L (Shaub), Jennifer J (Goodman), Mary M (Hearn) & Jeff A. *Educ:* Univ Ky, BS, 50; Vanderbilt Univ, MD, 54; Am Bd Internal Med, dipl & cert pulmonary dis. *Prof Exp:* Intern med, Vanderbilt Univ Hosp, 54-55; resident, Duke Univ Hosp, 55-57, USPHS fel, 57-58; from instr to prof, Sch Med, Ind Univ, 58-70; prof med & chmn dept, Med Univ SC, 70-80. *Concurrent Pos:* Mem, President's Nat Adv Panel on Heart Dis, 72, Vet Admin Merit Rev Bd Respiration, 72-76, Cardiovasc Study Sect, Nat Heart Inst, 66-70, Comt Respiratory Physiol, Nat Acad Sci 66-67, Prog Proj Comt, NIH, 71-75; mem, Pulmonary Subspecialty Bd, 72-78, Am Bd Internal Med, 72-81, Adv Coun, Nat Heart, Lung & Blood Inst, NIH, 81-85. *Mem:* Asn Am Physicians; Am Soc Clin Invest; Am Physiol Soc; Am Col Physicians; Am Col Cardiol; Am Col Chest Physicians (pres, 78). *Res:* Pulmonary physiology, diffusion, function tests and capillary bed; emphysema. *Mailing Add:* D-3300 Med Ctr N Vanderbilt Univ Nashville TN 37232. *Fax:* 615-343-5390

ROSS, JOSEPH HANSBRO, ORGANIC CHEMISTRY. *Current Pos:* from asst prof to assoc prof, 63-94, from asst chmn to chmn dept, 67-73, EMER ASSOC PROF CHEM, IND UNIV, SOUTH BEND, 94- *Personal Data:* b Houston, Tex, May 24, 25; m 56; c 4. *Educ:* Rice Inst, BS, 46; Univ Tex, MA, 48; Univ Md, PhD(chem), 57. *Prof Exp:* Res assoc & fel chem, Univ Mich, 57-58; res chemist, Stamford Labs, Am Cyanamid Co, 58-63. *Mem:* Am Chem Soc; AAAS; Royal Soc Chem; Sigma Xi. *Res:* Reaction mechanisms; amine oxidations and condensations; nitrogen heterocycles; chromatography and solvent interactions; dyes. *Mailing Add:* Ind Univ 1700 Mishawaka Ave PO Box 7111 South Bend IN 46634

ROSS, JUNE ROSA PITT, MARINE SCIENCES, PALEOBIOGEOGRAPHY. *Current Pos:* res assoc, Western Wash Univ, 65-67, assoc prof, 67-70, chair, 89-90, PROF BIOL, WESTERN WASH UNIV, 70- *Personal Data:* b Taree, NSW, Australia, 31; m 59. *Educ:* Univ Sydney, BSc, 53, PhD(geol), 59, DSc, 74. *Prof Exp:* Res fel, Yale Univ, 57-60; res assoc, Univ Ill, 60-65. *Concurrent Pos:* NSF res grants, 60-71; pres, Fac Sen, Western Wash Univ, 84-85; conf host, Int Bryozool Asn, 86. *Mem:* Soc Study Evolution; Marine Biol Asn UK; Int Bryozool Asn (pres, 93-95); Australian Marine Sci Asn; Micro Soc Am; Paleont Soc (treas, 87-93); Paleont Asn. *Res:* Ectoprocta; evolution biogeography and ecology; evolution of marine invertebrates and marine communities. *Mailing Add:* Dept Biol Western Wash Univ Bellingham WA 98225-9160

ROSS, KEITH ALAN, THIN FILMS, MICROELECTRONICS. *Current Pos:* PROCESS ENGR, AM MICROSYSTS, INC, 96- *Personal Data:* b Sturgis, SDak, Dec 19, 52; m 87, June Glover; c Samantha & Kelsi. *Educ:* SDak Sch Mines & Technol, BS, 75, MS, 77, PhD(elec eng), 83. *Prof Exp:* Assoc eng, IBM, 77-79; instr, SDak Sch Mines & Technol, 82-83, asst prof, 83-90, assoc prof teaching, 90-96. *Mem:* Am Vacuum Soc. *Res:* Deposition and characterization of semiconducting and conducting films. *Mailing Add:* Am Microsysts, Inc 2300 Buckskin Rd Pocatello ID 83201. *Fax:* 208-234-6795; *E-Mail:* kross@poci.amis.com

ROSS, KENNETH ALLEN, MATHEMATICS. *Current Pos:* assoc prof, 64-70, PROF MATH, UNIV ORE, 70- *Personal Data:* b Chicago, Ill, Jan 21, 36; m 86, Ruth Madsen; c Laurel & Emily. *Educ:* Univ Utah, BS, 56; Univ Wash, Seattle, MS, 58, PhD(math), 60. *Prof Exp:* Res instr math, Univ Wash, 60-61; asst prof, Univ Rochester, 61-64. *Concurrent Pos:* Vis asst prof, Yale Univ, 64-65; Alfred P Sloan Found fel, 67-70; vis prof, Univ BC, 80-81. *Mem:* Am Math Soc; Math Asn Am (secy, 84-89; assoc secy, 90-93; pres, 95-96). *Res:* Abstract harmonic analysis over topological groups. *Mailing Add:* Dept Math Univ Ore Eugene OR 97403-1222. *E-Mail:* ross@math.uoregon.edu

ROSS, LAWRENCE JAMES, PHYSICAL ORGANIC CHEMISTRY. *Current Pos:* RETIRED. *Personal Data:* b Brooklyn, NY, Sept 4, 29; m 59; c 3. *Educ:* Fordham Univ, BS, 50; Rutgers Univ, PhD(chem), 61. *Prof Exp:* Chemist, Nat Starch & Chem Corp, 50-55, supvr control methods lab, 55-57; from res chemist to sr res chemist, Am Cyanamid Agr Ctr, 60-75, group leader, 75-78, mgr formulations, 78-83, sr formulations coordr, 83-87. *Mem:* Am Chem Soc; fel Am Inst Chem. *Res:* Preparation and characterization of starch derivatives; mechanism of organic reactions; preparation of sulfonamides; preparation of brighteners of the styryl benzoxazole type; organic intermediates; process development; agricultural chemicals. *Mailing Add:* 1789 Woodfield Rd Martinsville NJ 08836-9637

ROSS, LAWRENCE JOHN, ELECTRICAL ENGINEERING. *Personal Data:* b New York, NY, Jan 17, 42; m 65, Carol M Wood; c Catherine M, Sharon M, Patricia A & James L. *Educ:* Manhattan Col, BSEE, 63. *Prof Exp:* elec engr, Lewis Res Ctr, NASA, 63-78, dir launch vehicles, 78-80, dir space flight syst, 80-87, dep dir, 87-90, dir, 90-95. *Concurrent Pos:* Bd govs, Nat Space Club, 90; bd dirs, Greater Cleveland Growth Asn, 91. *Mem:* Nat Space Club; Am Inst Aeronaut & Astronaut. *Res:* Electrical engineering; aeronautics and astronautics. *Mailing Add:* 31028 Walker Rd Bay Village OH 44140

ROSS, LEONARD LESTER, ANATOMY, NEUROBIOLOGY. *Current Pos:* prof anat & chmn dept, 73-90, EXEC VPRES, ANNENBERG DEAN & CHIEF ACAD OFFICER, MED COL PA, 90- *Personal Data:* b New York, NY, Sept 11, 27; m 51; c 2. *Educ:* NY Univ, AB, 46, MS, 49, PhD(anat), 54. *Honors & Awards:* Linback Award; Founders Award. *Prof Exp:* Res assoc, NY Univ, 49-52; asst prof anat, Med Col Ala, 52-57; from assoc prof to prof, Med Col, Cornell Univ, 57-73. *Concurrent Pos:* NIH fel, Cambridge Univ, 67-68. *Mem:* Electron Micros Soc Am; Histochem Soc; Am Asn Anatomists; Am Soc Cell Biol; Soc Neurosci; Col Physicians. *Res:* Nervous system; electron microscopy; histochemistry; biogenic amines; psychoneuroimmunology. *Mailing Add:* Allegheny Univ Health Sci MS490 Broad & Vine Sts Philadelphia PA 19102. *Fax:* 215-842-4074

ROSS, LOUIS, MATHEMATICS, STATISTICS. *Current Pos:* assoc prof, 46-77, EMER PROF MATH, UNIV AKRON, 77- *Personal Data:* b Akron, Ohio, Mar 24, 12; m 42; c 1. *Educ:* Univ Akron, BA, 34, BS, 35, MAEd, 39; Western Res Univ, PhD(statist), 55. *Prof Exp:* Teacher pub sch, Ohio, 35-41. *Concurrent Pos:* Dir Ohio-Ky-Tenn region, US Metric Asn, Inc, 72- *Mem:* Math Asn Am; Am Statist Asn; fel Am Soc Qual Control; Sigma Xi. *Res:* Quality control and reliability; impact of metrication on education, business, and industry in the US. *Mailing Add:* 271 Lake Pointe Dr Akron OH 44333-1791

ROSS, LYNNE FISCHER, ENZYMATIC MODIFICATION OF FOOD PROTEINS. *Current Pos:* RES CHEMIST, AGR RES SERV SOUTHERN REGIONAL RES CTR, USDA, 83- *Personal Data:* b New Orleans, La, Sept 14, 44. *Educ:* La State Univ, Baton Rouge, 66; Univ Tenn Med Ctr, Memphis, MS, 70; La State Univ Med Ctr, New Orleans, PhD(clin biochem), 80. *Prof Exp:* Med technologist, Clin Chem Lab, Oschner Found Hosp, New Orleans, 66-68; supvr, Clin Chem Lab, City Memphis Hosp, 68-70; asst prof clin chem, Dept Med Technol CAHP, Temple Univ, Philadelphia, 70-75; lab dir, Laser Res Found, New Orleans, 81-83. *Mem:* Am Soc Advan Sci; Am Chem Soc; Am Soc Microbiol; Am Oil Chemists Soc; Am Soc Plant Physiologists; Plant Growth Regulatory Soc Am. *Res:* The isolation of enzymes and characterization of enzymes as well as other protein-ligand interactions in severak physiological systems both in plants and mammals. *Mailing Add:* PO Box 6130 Destin FL 32541-6130

ROSS, MALCOLM, MINERALOGY & PETROLOGY, HEALTH EFFECTS OF MINERAL DUSTS. *Current Pos:* MINERALOGIST, US GEOL SURV, 54-59 & 61- *Personal Data:* b Washington, DC, Aug 22, 29; m 56, Daphne Riska; c Christopher A & Alexander M. *Educ:* Utah State Univ, BS, 51; Univ Md, MS, 59; Harvard Univ, PhD(geol), 62. *Honors & Awards:* Distinguished Serv Award, US Dept Interior, 86; Distinguished Pub Serv Award, Mineral Soc Am, 90. *Mem:* AAAS; fel Mineral Soc Am (treas, 76-80, pres, 91); fel Geol Soc Am; Am Geophys Union; Mineral Asn Can. *Res:* Mineralogy, petrology and crystallography of rock-forming silicates; subsolidus phase changes in silicates; pyroxene and amphibole geothermometry; relationships between human health and exposure to mineral particulates; mineralogy and petrology of alkalic rocks; material effects of acid rain. *Mailing Add:* US Geol Surv Nat Ctr 955 Reston VA 22092. *Fax:* 703-648-6032; *E-Mail:* mross@macsmac.er.usgs.gov

ROSS, MALCOLM S F, chromatography, medicinal chemistry, for more information see previous edition

ROSS, MARC CHRISTOPHER, ELECTRON PARTICLE ACCELERATORS, PARTICLE BEAM INSTRUMENTATION. *Current Pos:* Res asst, 82-84, ENG PHYSICIST, STANFORD LINEAR ACCELERATOR CTR, 84- *Personal Data:* b Ithaca, NY, Feb 22, 53; m 77, Sarah Good; c Max & Zachery. *Educ:* Univ Ill, BS, 77; Northwestern Univ, PhD(physics), 82. *Honors & Awards:* US Particle Accelerator Sch Prize, 93. *Mem:* Am Phys Soc. *Res:* Linear collider research and development; particle beam instrumentation; large accelerator control systems; laser and microwave based particle accelerator devices. *Mailing Add:* Stanford Linear Accelerator Ctr MS 66 Stanford CA 94309. *Fax:* 650-926-4928; *E-Mail:* mcrec@slac.stanford.edu

ROSS, MARC HANSEN, THEORETICAL PHYSICS. *Current Pos:* dir Residential Col, 74-77, PROF PHYSICS, UNIV MICH, ANN ARBOR, 63-; SR SCIENTIST, ARGONNE NAT LAB, 84- *Personal Data:* b Baltimore, Md, Dec 24, 28; m 49; c 3. *Educ:* Queens Col, NY, BS, 48; Univ Wis, PhD, 52. *Prof Exp:* NSF fel, Cornell Univ, 52-53; assoc physicist, Brookhaven Nat Lab, 53-55; from asst prof to prof physics, Ind Univ, 55-63. *Concurrent Pos:* NSF fel, Univ Rome, 60-61. *Mem:* Am Phys Soc. *Res:* Physics of energy use; environmental physics. *Mailing Add:* Dept Physics Univ Mich Ann Arbor MI 48109

ROSS, MARVIN, HIGH PRESSURE PHYSICS. *Current Pos:* div leader condensed matter physics, 87-93, PHYS CHEMIST, LAWRENCE LIVERMORE NAT LAB, 63-, LAB ASSOC, 93- *Personal Data:* b Brooklyn, NY, June 27, 31; m 58; c Mark & Steven. *Educ:* Brooklyn Col, BS, 55; Pa State Univ, PhD(chem), 60. *Prof Exp:* Res assoc, Univ Calif, Berkeley, 60-63. *Concurrent Pos:* Ed-in-chief, High Pressure Res, 82-93. *Mem:* Fel Am Phys Soc. *Res:* Theoretical studies of condensed media at high pressures and temperatures; applications of shock waves to high pressure and high temperature research. *Mailing Add:* Lawrence Livermore Lab L-299 Box 808 Univ Calif Livermore CA 94550. *Fax:* 510-422-2851

ROSS, MARVIN FRANKLIN, CLIFFORD ALGEBRAS & LIE ALBEBRAS. *Current Pos:* ASST PROF PHYSICS, UNIV PAC, 84- *Personal Data:* b Sacramento, Calif, Sept 27, 51. *Educ:* Univ Calif, San Cruz, BA, 72; Univ Calif, Davis, MA, 74, PhD(physics), 80. *Prof Exp:* Lectr physics, Univ Calif, Davis, 79-84. *Mem:* Am Phys Soc; Sigma Xi. *Res:* Clifford algebras and relativistic quantum mechanics and elementary particles; cluster-bethe-lattice calculation of the density of states of amorphous silicon. *Mailing Add:* 1620 Morgan Lane Redondo Beach CA 90278

ROSS, MARY HARVEY, CYTOGENETICS, BEHAVIOR. *Current Pos:* from instr to assoc prof, 59-80, PROF ENTOM, VA POLYTECH INST & STATE UNIV, 80- *Personal Data:* b Albany, NY, Apr 1, 25; m 47; c Mary J, Robert & Nancy. *Educ:* Cornell Univ, BA, 45, MA, 47, PhD(paleont), 50. *Prof Exp:* Biologist, Oak Ridge Nat Lab, 51. *Concurrent Pos:* NSF grants, 71-73 & 80-83; Naval Facil Eng Command grant, 74; Off Naval Res grant, 77-86; adj assoc prof, NC State Univ, 77-79; mem orgn comt, Genetics Sect, XV Int Cong Entom; counr, Am Genetics Asn, 77-80. *Mem:* Am Genetic Asn (secy, 80-82, pres, 84); Entom Soc Am; Genetics Soc Am; Sigma Xi; Genetics Soc Can; fel Royal Entom Soc London. *Res:* Genetics, cytogenetics and behavior of the cockroach. *Mailing Add:* Dept Entom Va Polytech Inst & State Univ Blacksburg VA 24061

ROSS, MERRILL ARTHUR, JR, WEED SCIENCE. *Current Pos:* asst prof bot, 65-69, assoc prof plant physiol, 69-75, ASSOC PROF BOT & PLANT PATH, PURDUE UNIV, WEST LAFAYETTE, 75-, EXTEN WEED SPECIALIST, 65- *Personal Data:* b Montrose, Colo, June 2, 35; m 55, 73; c 5. *Educ:* Colo State Univ, BS, 57, MS, 59, PhD(plant physiol), 65. *Prof Exp:* Instr bot & plant path & jr plant physiologist, Colo State Univ, 59-65. *Mem:* Weed Sci Soc Am. *Res:* Weed control; agronomy; botany; control of Johnson grass, Canada thistle and other perennial weeds in Indiana crop production systems. *Mailing Add:* Dept Bot Purdue Univ West Lafayette IN 47907-1968

ROSS, MICHAEL H, ANATOMY, CELL BIOLOGY. *Current Pos:* prof path & dir, 71-77, CHMN DEPT ANAT, SCH MED, UNIV FLA, 77- *Personal Data:* b Jamaica, NY, Oct 23, 30; m 58; c 3. *Educ:* Franklin & Marshall Col, BS, 51; NY Univ, MS, 59, PhD(biol), 60. *Prof Exp:* From instr to assoc prof anat, Sch Med, NY Univ, 60-71. *Concurrent Pos:* Chmn, Fla State Anat Bd, 71-; assoc ed, Am J Anat, 70-73 & Anat Record, 75- *Mem:* Am Asn Anatomists; Am Soc Cell Biol; Pan-Am Asn Anat; Soc Study Reprod; hon mem Bolivian Soc Anat. *Res:* Cell biology; tissue development; testicular function and developmental changes. *Mailing Add:* Dept Anat & Cell Biol Univ Fla Univ Fla J Hillis Miller Health Ctr 1600 SW Archer Rd PO Box 100235 Gainesville FL 32610-0235. *Fax:* 904-392-3305

ROSS, MICHAEL RALPH, AQUATIC ECOLOGY, FISH BIOLOGY. *Current Pos:* Asst prof, 75-80, ASSOC PROF FISHERIES BIOL, UNIV MASS, 80- *Personal Data:* b Middletown, Ohio, Apr 19, 47; m 70; c 2. *Educ:* Miami Univ, BS, 69; Ohio State Univ, MS, 71, PhD(zool), 75. *Concurrent Pos:* Vis asst prof, Itasca Biol Sta, 79-81. *Mem:* Sigma Xi; Am Soc Ichthyologists & Herpetologists; Ecol Soc; AAAS; Am Fisheries Soc. *Res:* Behavior, mating systems, life history and population dynamics of fishes. *Mailing Add:* Dept Forestry & Wildlife Holdsworth Hall Univ Mass Amherst MA 01003

ROSS, MONTE, COMMUNICATIONS. *Current Pos:* mgr laser technol, 66-74, prog mgr, 74-81, dir, Laser Commun Systs, 81-87, PRES, LASER DATA TECHNOL, MCDONNELL DOUGLAS ASTRONAUT, CO, 87- *Personal Data:* b Chicago, Ill, May 26, 32; m 57; c 3. *Educ:* Univ Ill, BSEE, 53; Northwestern Univ, MSEE, 62. *Honors & Awards:* Technol Award, Am Inst Aeronaut & Astronaut; McDonnell Douglas Fel Award, 85. *Prof Exp:* Elec engr, Chance-Vought Corp, 53-54 & Corps of Engrs, 54-56; electronic engr, Motorola, Inc, 56-57; sr engr, Hallicrafters Co, 57-59, group mgr electronics res & develop, 59-61, from assoc dir res to dir res, 61-66. *Concurrent Pos:* Adv ed, Laser Focus Mag, 66-70; tech ed, Laser Appln Ser, Acad Press, 70-; reviewer of grants, Nat Sci Found, 75-; affil prof, Wash Univ. *Mem:* Fel Inst Elec & Electronics Engrs; Am Inst Aeronaut & Astronaut. *Res:* Laser communications systems; fiber optic systems; space communications; laser research and development, especially communications and guidance; diode laser systems. *Mailing Add:* 19 Beaver Dr St Louis MO 63141

ROSS, MYRON JAY, ELECTRICAL ENGINEERING. *Current Pos:* ENG DEPT MGR, TELECOMMUN SYSTS, GTE GOVT SYSTS, 74- *Personal Data:* b Winthrop, Mass, June 10, 42; m 68; c 2. *Educ:* Northeastern Univ, BS, 64, MS, 66, PhD(elec eng), 70. *Honors & Awards:* NASA Commendation, Apollo Prog; Centennial Medal, Inst Elec & Electronics Engrs, 84. *Prof Exp:* Staff engr, Proj Apollo, Draper Lab, Mass Inst Technol, 63-66; test dir test & eval, Mat Testing Directorate, Aberdeen Proving Ground, Md, 70-72; advan res & develop engr secure voice systs, GTE Sylvania, Needham, Mass, 72-74; eng specialist commun systs, CNR, Inc, Newton Mass, 74. *Concurrent Pos:* NASA trainee fel, 66-69; lectr elec eng, Northeastern Univ, 68-70; NDEA fel, 70; assoc prof & lectr mgt sci, George Washington Univ, 71-72; lectr comput sci, Boston Univ, 78; lectr digital switching, Univ Calif, Los Angeles & Univ Md, 78- *Mem:* Inst Elec & Electronics Engrs; Sigma Xi. *Res:* Telecommunications switching systems; data communication systems; integrated digital voice and data switching; secure voice systems; military communications networks. *Mailing Add:* 43 Condor Rd Sharon MA 02067-2948

ROSS, PHILIP, ECOLOGY. *Current Pos:* RETIRED. *Personal Data:* b Newton, Mass, Nov 2, 26; m 52, Jane McElroy; c John F & James G. *Educ:* Brown Univ, AB, 49; Univ Mass, MS, 51; Harvard Univ, PhD(plant ecol & geog), 58, MPH, 68. *Prof Exp:* Fulbright res scholar trop agr, Imperial Col, 57-58; botanist, Mil Geol Br, US Geol Surv, DC, 58-62; asst chief training grants sect, Nat Inst Dent Res, NIH, 62-63, chief, Res Grants Sect, 63-65, asst head, Spec Int Progs Sect, Off Int Res, 65-68; pres, Int Sugar Res Found, Inc, 68-70; exec secy, Comt Effects of Herbicides in Vietnam, 70-74, exec secy, Bd Agr & Renewable Resources, Nat Acad Sci-Nat Res Coun, 74-86. *Concurrent Pos:* Prof lectr, Am Univ, 59-65. *Mem:* Explorers Club. *Res:* Plant ecology and geography; vegetation mapping; microclimate; human ecology; science administration; agriculture. *Mailing Add:* 9108 Seven Locks Rd Bethesda MD 20817

ROSS, PHILIP NORMAN, JR, ELECTROCHEMISTRY, CATALYSIS. *Current Pos:* assoc div dir, 88-90, actg sci div adv light source, 91-93, PRIN INVESTR ELECTROCHEM, LAWRENCE BERKELEY LAB, UNIV CALIF, BERKELEY, 78- *Personal Data:* b Washington, DC, Oct 31, 43; m 92, Meredith Montgomery; c Sara & Sean. *Educ:* Yale Univ, BS, 65, PhD(eng, appl sci), 72; Univ Del, MS, 69. *Prof Exp:* Proj engr chem eng, Explor Develop Div, Procter & Gamble Corp, 66-69; sr res assoc electrochem, Pratt & Whitney Aircraft & Power Systs Div, United Technol Corp, 72-76, sr scientist, United Technol Res Ctr, 76-78. *Concurrent Pos:* Detailee to US Dept Energy, Off Basic Energy Sci, Div Mat Sci, 87-88. *Mem:* Am Chem Soc; Am Vacuum Soc; Electrochem Soc. *Res:* Electrochemical energy conversion and storage systems (fuel cells and batteries); electrodeposition of metals and semiconductors; electrochemical remediation of hazardous and/or toxic waste. *Mailing Add:* Mat & Chem Sci Div Lawrence Berkeley Lab Berkeley CA 94720. *Fax:* 510-486-5530; *E-Mail:* pnross@lbl.gov

ROSS, PHILIPPE EDWARD, AQUATIC TOXICOLOGY, CONTAMINATED SEDIMENT HAZARD ASSESSMENT. *Current Pos:* PROF & HEAD DEPT BIOL, THE CITADEL, 91- *Personal Data:* b Bangor, Maine, Oct 22, 49; m 72, Linda Yas; c Kie Zuraw. *Educ:* McGill Univ, BSc, 72, MSc, 75; Univ Waterloo, PhD(biol), 80. *Prof Exp:* Aquatic ecologist Beak Consults, Ltd, 79-80; asst prof, Univ Montreal, 80-85; assoc aquatic toxicologist, Ill Natural Hist Surv, 85-91. *Concurrent Pos:* Univ res fel, Nat Sci & Eng Res Coun, Can, 80-85; assoc prof, Univ Ill, Urbana-Champaign, 85-91; sr environ adv, US Environ Protection Agency, 88-92; prof, Clemson Univ & Med Univ SC, 93-; sci coordr, Nat Indicator Study, 93-94; mem, Tech Adv Comt, Coastal Oceans Prog, Nat Oceanic & Atmospheric Admin, 93-; sr guest scientist, NATO, 94, 95 & 96. *Mem:* AAAS; Soc Environ Toxicol & Chem; Am Soc Limnol & Oceanog; Int Limnol Soc; Phycol Soc Am; Aquatic Ecosyst Health & Mgt Soc (secy, 92-). *Res:* Assessment and remediation of contaminated bottom sediments; effects of pollution on tidal creeks, marshes and estuaries; appropriate technology for developing countries; seafood safety. *Mailing Add:* Dept Biol The Citadel 171 Moultrie St Charleston SC 29409. *Fax:* 803-953-7084; *E-Mail:* rossp@citadel.edu

ROSS, REUBEN JAMES, JR, PALEONTOLOGY, STRATIGRAPHY SEDIMENTATION. *Current Pos:* ADJ PROF GEOL, COLO SCH MINES, 80- *Personal Data:* b New York, NY, July 1, 18; m 42; c 4. *Educ:* Princeton Univ, AB, 40; Yale Univ, MS, 46, PhD(geol), 48. *Prof Exp:* Field asst, Newfoundland Geol Surv, 38; asst prof geol, Wesleyan Univ, 48-52; geologist, Paleont & Stratig Br, US Geol Surv, 52-80. *Concurrent Pos:* Chmn subcomn Ordovician Stratigraphy, Int Union Geol Sci, 74- *Mem:* Paleont Soc; Geol Soc Am; Am Asn Petrol Geologists; Brit Palaeontograph Soc; Soc Econ Paleont & Mineral. *Res:* Invertebrate paleontology and Ordovician stratigraphy of Basin Ranges. *Mailing Add:* 5255 Ridge Trail Bow Mar Littleton CO 80123

ROSS, RICHARD FRANCIS, VETERINARY MICROBIOLOGY. *Current Pos:* from instr to asst prof vet path, Iowa State Univ, 62-65, assoc prof, 66-72, distinguished prof, 82, prof-in-chg, 85-90, assoc dir & assoc dean, 90-92, interim dean, 92-93, PROF VET MICROBIOL, IOWA STATE UNIV, 72-, DEAN, 93- *Personal Data:* b Washington, Iowa, Apr 30, 35; m 57, Karen M Paulsen; c Scott & Susan. *Educ:* Iowa State Univ, DVM, 59, MS, 60, PhD(vet microbiol), 65; Am Col Vet Microbiol, dipl, 67. *Honors & Awards:* Howard Dunne Mem lectr, Am Asn Swine Pract, 84, Howard Dunne Mem Award, 88; USDA Secy of Agr Award Personal & Prof Accomplishment, 96. *Prof Exp:* Res assoc vet microbiol, Iowa State Univ, 59-61; operating mgr, Vet Labs, Inc, Iowa, 61-62. *Concurrent Pos:* NIH fel, Rocky Mt Lab, Nat Inst Allergy & Infectious Dis, Mont, 65-66; vis prof, Tierarztl Hochschule, Hanover & sr fel Humboldt Found, WGer, 75-76; vchair bd gov, Am Col Vet Microbiologists, 74-75; Adv Bd Agr, (secy 96-97); chair, Int Orgn Mycopiasmology, 90-92. *Mem:* Am Vet Med Asn; Conf Res Workers Animal Dis (pres, 90); Am Soc Microbiol; Int Orgn Mycoplasmology; Am Col Vet Microbiologists (secy-treas, 77-83); AAAS; Asn Am Vet Med Col (pres, 96-97). *Res:* Investigations on pneumonia in swine due to mycoplasma hypneumoniae and haemophilus pleuropneumoniae; agalactia in swine caused by coliform mastitis; arthritis in swine. *Mailing Add:* Col Vet Med Iowa State Univ Ames IA 50011

ROSS, RICHARD HENRY, DAIRY SCIENCE. *Current Pos:* RETIRED. *Personal Data:* b Centre Hall, Pa, Sept 19, 16; m 43; c 3. *Educ:* Pa State Univ, BS, 38, PhD(dairy), 47; WVa Univ, MS, 40. *Prof Exp:* Asst dairy, WVa Univ, 38-40 & Pa State Univ, 40-42; from assoc prof to prof dairy husb, Univ Idaho, 47-53, head dept dairy sci, 60-70, prof dairy sci, 53-78. *Concurrent Pos:* Exten dairyman, Univ Idaho, 74-78. *Mem:* Am Soc Animal Sci; Am Dairy Sci Asn. *Res:* Dairy cattle nutrition and management; pasture. *Mailing Add:* 617 N Eisenhower St Moscow ID 83843

ROSS, RICHARD HENRY, JR, ENVIRONMENTAL DATA FOR PESTICIDE REGISTRATION, PESTICIDE RISK ASSESSMENTS. *Current Pos:* field res rep, Agr Div, Ciba-Geigy Corp, 73-76, sr field res rep, 76-81, sr field res rep II, 81-85, sr environ specialist II, 85-88, MGR ENVIRON & CONTRACT STUDIES, AGR DIV, CIBA-GEIGY CORP, 88-93, DIR BIOCHEM RESOURCES, 93- *Personal Data:* b Bellefonte, Pa, June 5, 46; m 80, Elaine Grevenstuk; c Diedre M & David E. *Educ:* Univ Idaho, Moscow, BS, 68; Mich State Univ, East Lansing, MS, 70, PhD(entom & insect biochem), 72. *Prof Exp:* Postdoctoral insect aging, Argonne Nat Lab, Ill, 72-73. *Mem:* Entom Soc Am; Soc Environ Toxicol & Chem; Am Soc Testing & Mat. *Res:* Environmental and crop tolerance data to support registrations agricultural chemicals; author of various publications. *Mailing Add:* 5424 Bunch Rd Summerfield NC 27358

ROSS, RICHARD STARR, CARDIOLOGY. *Current Pos:* From instr to assoc prof, 54-65, dean med fac & vpres med, 75-90, PROF MED, SCH MED, JOHNS HOPKINS UNIV, 65-, EMER DEAN, 90- *Personal Data:* b Richmond, Ind, Jan 18, 24; m 50, Elizabeth McCracken; c Deborah, Margaret & Richard. *Educ:* Harvard Med Sch, MD, 47. *Concurrent Pos:* Consult, Nat Heart & Lung Inst, 61-78, training grant comt, 71 & adv coun, 74; chmn cardiovasc study sect, NIH, 66; mem bd dirs, Waverly Press, Merck & Co, Johns Hopkins Hosp, Francis Scott Key Med Ctr. *Mem:* Inst Med-Nat Acad Sci; Am Soc Clin Invest; Asn Am Physicians; Am Physiol Soc; master Am Col Physicians; Am Fedn Clin Res. *Res:* Cardiology utilizing physiological and radiological techniques. *Mailing Add:* Johns Hopkins Univ Sch Med 1830 E Monument St Baltimore MD 21205. *Fax:* 410-955-1561

ROSS, ROBERT ANDERSON, SURFACE CHEMISTRY, APPLIED CHEMISTRY. *Current Pos:* RETIRED. *Personal Data:* b Auchinleck, Scotland, Sept 6, 31; m 58; c 3. *Educ:* Univ Glasgow, BS, 54, PhD(phys chem), 58; Univ Strathclyde, ARCST, 54, DSc, 78. *Prof Exp:* Res engr, Marconi's Res Labs, Chelmsford, Eng, 57-59; asst res mgr, Joseph Crosfields Ltd, Warrington, 59-60; lectr inorg chem, Univ Strathclyde, 60-64; head, Dept Chem, Col Technol, Univ Belfast, 64-69; dean sci, Lakehead Univ, 70-75, prof chem, 69-81; dir corp res, Domtar Inc, Montreal, 81-90; adj prof chem, Queens Univ, Kingston, 90-92. *Concurrent Pos:* Grants, Nat Res Coun Can, Dept Energy, Imp Oil Ltd, Ont Dept Environ & Int Nickel Co Ltd. *Mem:* Royal Soc Chem; Can Inst Chem; Can Soc Chem Eng. *Res:* Heterogeneous catalysis and adsorption; technological and combustion chemistry; air and water pollution studies. *Mailing Add:* 9 King Pitt Rd Kingston ON K7L 4V1 Can

ROSS, ROBERT EDGAR, FOOD SCIENCE. *Current Pos:* VPRES, RES & DEVELOP, PEPPERIDGE FARM, 90- *Personal Data:* b Trenton, NJ, Aug 25, 48; m 79, Nancy Handloser; c Jillian & Allison. *Educ:* Rutgers Univ, BS, 70; Univ Mass, MS, 72, PhD(food sci), 73. *Prof Exp:* Res asst prof develop, PepsiCo, Inc, 68; food technologist, Prod Develop, Hunt-Wesson Foods, Inc, 73-74; sr food technologist, 74-75; group leader, 75-77; mgr corp new prod, Nabisco Brands, Inc, 78-79, asst dir, 79-81, assoc dir, 81-82, group dir, Corp Food Res, 81-82, group dir, Baked Goods Res & Develop, 82-84, sr dir, Biscuit Res & Develop, Nabisco Brands, 85-86, dir tech serv, 87-89; vpres, Gum & Confectionery Res & Develop, Warner-Lambert Co, 86-87; vpres, Res & Develop Qual Assurance Oper, Estee Corp, 89-90. *Concurrent Pos:* George H Cook scholar, Rutgers. *Mem:* Inst Food Technologists; Sigma Xi. *Res:* New product development and brand maintenance; technical evaluation of new business opportunities, joint ventures and technology licensing; operations support; quality assurance. *Mailing Add:* 102 Coventry Lane Trumbull CT 06611. *Fax:* 203-846-7369

ROSS, ROBERT EDWARD, ORGANIC CHEMISTRY, PHOTOGRAPHIC SCIENCE. *Current Pos:* RETIRED. *Personal Data:* b Rochester, NY, Nov 19, 37; m 59, Patricia A O'Keefe. *Educ:* St John Fisher Col, BS, 61; Princeton Univ, MA, 63, PhD(org chem), 66. *Prof Exp:* Sr res chemist, Eastman Kodak Co, 66-71, res assoc, 71-92. *Mem:* Am Chem Soc; AAAS; Royal Soc Chem. *Res:* Organic synthesis of heterocyclic compounds, photographic couplers and redox materials; evaluation of photographically useful fragments in a film format; precipitation; sensitization of photo-sensitive silver halide crystals for practical imaging systems. *Mailing Add:* 2587 Browncroft Blvd Rochester NY 14625

ROSS, ROBERT GORDON, PHYTOPATHOLOGY. *Current Pos:* RETIRED. *Personal Data:* b Oxford, NS, July 14, 22; m 52, Doris Waterbury; c Donald & Lynn. *Educ:* McGill Univ, BSc, 49, MSc, 54; Univ Western Ont, PhD(bot), 56. *Prof Exp:* Res officer & plant pathologist, Agr Can, Kentville, NS, 49-76, asst dir res sta, 76-85. *Mem:* Am Phytopath Soc; Can Phytopath Soc (pres, 75-76). *Res:* Tree fruit diseases. *Mailing Add:* Group Box 579 RR 2 Wolfville NS B0P 1X0 Can

ROSS, ROBERT TALMAN, BIOPHYSICAL CHEMISTRY. *Current Pos:* assoc prof biophys, 70-75, assoc prof, 75-81, PROF BIOCHEM, OHIO STATE UNIV, 81- *Personal Data:* b San Diego, Calif, Oct 10, 40; m 62, Donna Baldwin; c R Andrew, David & Marian. *Educ:* Calif Inst Technol, BS, 62; Univ Calif, Berkeley, PhD(chem), 66. *Prof Exp:* Lectr chem, Univ Calif, Berkeley, 66-67; asst prof, Am Univ Beirut, 67-70. *Concurrent Pos:* Chemist, Lawrence Berkeley Lab, Univ Calif, 66-67; dir, Beirut Study Ctr, Univ Calif, 69-70 & Biophys Prog, Ohio State Univ, 81-89; vis scholar, Univ Calif, Berkeley, 83-84; intern, Marion Merrell Dow Res Inst, Cincinnati, 92. *Mem:* Biophys Soc; Am Chem Soc. *Res:* Thermodynamics, statistical mechanics and kinetics of biological systems; photosynthesis; fluorescence spectroscopy; data analysis; molecular modeling. *Mailing Add:* Dept Biochem Ohio State Univ 484 W 12th Ave Columbus OH 43210-1292. *Fax:* 614-292-6773; *E-Mail:* rtr+@osu.edu

ROSS, RODERICK ALEXANDER, APPLIED MATHEMATICS. *Current Pos:* From lectr appl math to assoc prof math, 57-85, PROF MATH, UNIV TORONTO, 85- *Personal Data:* b Ottawa, Ont, June 27, 26. *Educ:* Univ Toronto, PhD(math), 58. *Res:* Wave propagation; differential equations. *Mailing Add:* Dept Math Univ Toronto Toronto ON M5S 1A1 Can

ROSS, RONALD RICKARD, PARTICLE ASTROPHYSICS. *Current Pos:* Res physicist, Lawrence Radiation Lab & lectr physics, 61-63, asst prof, 63-67, assoc prof, 67-72, prof, 72-94, FAC SR SCIENTIST, LAWRENCE BERKELEY LAB, 63-, EMER PROF PHYSICS, UNIV CALIF, BERKELEY, 94- *Personal Data:* b Minneapolis, Minn, July 11, 31; m 52, Adeleen Tarr; c Kristine, Susan & Linda. *Educ:* Univ Calif, Berkeley, BA, 56, PhD(physics), 61. *Honors & Awards:* IBM Fel, 57. *Concurrent Pos:* Vis prof, Inst High Energy Physics, Univ Heidelberg, 66-67. *Mem:* AAAS; Am Phys Soc; Am Asn Physics Teachers. *Res:* Electron-positron interactions; fundamental interactions of particles; search for dark matter. *Mailing Add:* Dept Physics Univ Calif Berkeley CA 94720. *E-Mail:* rrross@lbl.gov

ROSS, RUSSELL, EXPERIMENTAL PATHOLOGY, CELL BIOLOGY. *Current Pos:* from asst prof to assoc prof, Sch Med, Univ Wash, 62-69, assoc dean sci affairs, 71-78, chmn, Path, 82-94, PROF PATH, SCH MED, UNIV WASH, 69-, ADJ PROF BIOCHEM, 78-, DIR CTR VASCULAR BIOL, 90- *Personal Data:* b St Augustine, Fla, May 25, 29; m 56, Jean Teller; c Valerie R & Douglas T. *Educ:* Cornell Univ, AB, 51; Columbia Univ, DDS, 55; Univ Wash, PhD(exp path), 62. *Hon Degrees:* DSc, Med Col Pa, 87. *Honors & Awards:* Gordon Wilson Medal, Am Clin & Climatol Asn, 81; Int Recognition Award, Heart Res Found, 86; Nat Res Achievement Award, Am Heart Asn, 90; Rous-Whipple Award, Am Asn Pathologists, 92. *Prof Exp:* Intern, Presby Hosp, NY, 55-56; staff mem in chg, Oral Surg Sect, USPHS Hosp, Seattle, 56-58. *Concurrent Pos:* NIH career develop res award, 62-67; Guggenheim fel, 66-67; vis fel, Clare Hall, Cambridge Univ, 66-68; mem cell biol study sect B, NIH, 66-69, mem, Molecular Biol Study Sect, 69-71, chmn, 74-76; mem adv coun, Nat Heart, Lung & Blood Inst, 78-81; res comt, Am Heart Asn, 83; mem, Nat Res Adv Bd & Cleveland Clin Fedn; dir, Ctr Vascular Biol, Univ Wash Sch Med, 90. *Mem:* Inst Med-Nat Acad Sci; Histochem Soc; Electron Micros Soc Am; Am Soc Exp Pathologists; Am Asn Pathologists; hon mem Harvey Soc; AAAS; Am Soc Cell Biol; fel Am Acad Arts & Sci. *Res:* Wound healing; connective tissue; inflammation and atherosclerosis; autoradiography and biochemical analyses; cell and molecular biology of growth factors; growth regulatory molecules; cell-cell interactions and signalling. *Mailing Add:* Dept Path Univ Wash Sch Med Box 357470 Seattle WA 98195-7470. *Fax:* 206-685-3018; *E-Mail:* rross@u.washington.edu

ROSS, SAM JONES, JR, SOIL MORPHOLOGY. *Current Pos:* RETIRED. *Personal Data:* b Tompkinsville, Ky, July 4, 31; m 56; c 3. *Educ:* Western Ky State Col, BS, 58; Univ Ky, MS, 61; Purdue Univ, PhD(soil), 73. *Prof Exp:* Asst soils, Univ Ky, 59-61; soil scientist, Va Polytech Inst, 61 & Soil Surv Lab, 62-68; instr soils, Purdue Univ, 68-73; soil scientist, Soil Surv Invest Lab, 73-75, Nat Soil Surv Lab, 75-85. *Mem:* Am Soc Agron; Soil Sci Soc Am. *Res:* Field hydraulic conductivity work and soil physical work in laboratory. *Mailing Add:* 20116 A St Eagle NE 68347

ROSS, SHEPLEY LITTLEFIELD, MATHEMATICS. *Current Pos:* from instr to assoc prof, 55-70, PROF MATH, UNIV NH, 70- *Personal Data:* b Sanford, Maine, Nov 5, 27; m 54; c 4. *Educ:* Univ Boston, AB, 49, AM, 50, PhD(math), 53. *Prof Exp:* Lectr math, Univ Boston, 50-53; instr, Northeastern Univ, 53-54 & Univ Boston, 54-55. *Mem:* Am Math Soc; Math Asn Am. *Res:* Ordinary differential equations. *Mailing Add:* Cate Rd Barrington NH 03825

ROSS, SIDNEY, PHYSICS, RESEARCH ADMINISTRATION. *Current Pos:* STAFF TECH ADV, GOVT SYSTS DIV ENG, RCA CORP, 77- *Personal Data:* b Philadelphia, Pa, May 12, 26; m 48; c 3. *Educ:* Pa State Univ, BS, 48; Univ Pa, MS, 53; Temple Univ, PhD(physics), 61. *Prof Exp:* Physicist interior ballistics res, Pitman-Dunn Labs, US Dept Army, 48-50, weapon systs res, 51-52, chief interior ballistics br, 53-54, ballistics div, 55-56, tech asst dir labs group, 57, asst dir physics res lab, 58-66, dir appl sci lab, 66-68, tech dir, Frankford Arsenal, 68-77. *Mem:* Am Phys Soc; Sigma Xi; Am Chem Soc. *Res:* Plasma physics; magnetohydrodynamics; hyperballistic propulsion and impact systems; advanced weapon systems; solid state physics; lasers; defense sciences and engineering. *Mailing Add:* 6811 Kindred St Philadelphia PA 19149-2220

ROSS, SIDNEY DAVID, CHEMISTRY. *Current Pos:* dir org res, 46-56, res assoc, 56-71, dir corp res & develop, 71-85, Sprague fel, Sprague Elec Co, 85-89, CONSULT, 90- *Personal Data:* b Lynn, Mass, Jan 31, 18; m 42; c 1. *Educ:* Harvard Univ, AB, 39, PhD(org chem), 44; Boston Univ, MA, 40. *Prof Exp:* Asst chem, Boston Univ, 39-40; asst chem, Harvard Univ, 40-41, res assoc, Naval Ord Res Coun, 41-45, Comt Med Res, 45 & Pittsburgh Plate Glass Co fel, 46. *Mem:* Am Chem Soc; Electrochem Soc; The Chem Soc. *Res:* Mechanism of organic reactions; polymerization; kinetics; dielectrics; synthetic organic chemistry. *Mailing Add:* 30 Colonial Ave Williamstown MA 01267-2547

ROSS, STANLEY ELIJAH, ORGANIC FIBER POLYMER, TEXTILES. *Current Pos:* mgr fiber finishes, Emery Div, Quantum Chem Corp, 84, mgr fiber finishes, 84-93, CONSULT, ORG PRODS DIV, HENKEL CORP, 94- *Personal Data:* b Paterson, NJ, Nov 27, 22; m 61, Estelle Schiffer; c Barbara. *Educ:* Rutgers Univ, BS, 43; NY Univ, MS, 49. *Prof Exp:* Res chemist, Cent Res Lab, Celanese Corp Am, 47-52 & Allied Chem Corp, 52-59; head polymer dept, J P Stevens & Co, Inc, 60-65, head process develop dept, 65-67, res assoc, Explor Tech, 67-75, prod develop mgr, 71-74, mgr nonwoven tech, 75-79, mgr fiber technol, Res & Develop Div, 79-84. *Mem:* Am Chem Soc; Fiber Soc (vpres, 74, pres, 75); NY Acad Sci. *Res:* Polymers, fibers and textiles and their characterizations; mechanical behavior; thermoanalysis; extrusion and orientation of thermoplastics; crystallinity behavior; carbonization and pyrolysis of cellulose; development of nonwoven textile structures; cotton dust and its measurement, frictional meas, fiber finish development; fiber lubricants. *Mailing Add:* 201 Bloomfield Lane Greer SC 29650-3808

ROSS, STEPHEN T, MEDICINAL CHEMISTRY. *Current Pos:* assoc sr investr, 61-74, SR INVESTR, SMITH KLINE & FRENCH LABS, 74- *Personal Data:* b Chicago, Ill, Mar 21, 31; m 52; c 2. *Educ:* Univ Ill, BS, 53; Rutgers Univ, MS, 60, PhD(org chem), 61. *Prof Exp:* Chemist, Johnson & Johnson, 55-59. *Mem:* Am Chem Soc; AAAS; NY Acad Sci. *Res:* Structure and activity relationships; synthetic heterocyclic chemistry; organo-analytical chemistry; organophosphorus chemistry; infrared and nuclear magnetic resonance spectroscopy; mass spectrometry; high-performance liquid and gas chromatography. *Mailing Add:* 718 Old State Rd Berwyn PA 19312-1441

ROSS, STEPHEN THOMAS, ICHTHYOLOGY, FISH BIOLOGY. *Current Pos:* from asst prof to assoc prof, 74-83, PROF BIOL, UNIV SOUTHERN MISS, 84- *Personal Data:* b Hollywood, Calif, Nov 9, 44; m 69; c 1. *Educ:* Univ Calif, Los Angeles, BA, 67, Calif State Univ, Fullerton, MA, 70; Univ SFla, PhD(biol), 74. *Prof Exp:* Teaching asst biol, Calif State Univ, Fullerton, 67-69; teaching asst, Univ SFla, 70-71, instr, 72. *Concurrent Pos:* Vis res prof, Univ Okla Biol Sta, 81-82; vis scholar, Dept Wildlife Fisheries Biol, Univ Calif, Davis, 91- *Mem:* Am Soc Ichthyologists & Herpetologists; Am Fisheries Soc; Soc Study Evolution; Soc Systematic Zool; Ecol Soc Am. *Res:* Ecological and evolutionary relationships of fishes. *Mailing Add:* Dept Biol SS Box 5018 Univ Southern Miss Hattiesburg MS 39406-5018

ROSS, STUART THOM, MECHANICAL METALLURGY, MATERIALS SCIENCE. *Current Pos:* VPRES & TECH DIR, ITT MEYER INDUSTS, 76- *Personal Data:* b Green Bay, Wis, July 6, 23; m 49; c 2. *Educ:* Purdue Univ, BSMetE, 47, MSMetE, 49, PhD(metall), 50. *Prof Exp:* Asst chief metallurgist, Harrison Radiator Div, Gen Motors Corp, 50-52; head metall res, Eng Div, Chrysler Corp, 52-59; chief mat engr, Aeronutronic Div, Ford Motor Corp, 59-61; vpres eng & res, Brooks & Perkins, Inc, 61-65; dir eng & develop, Wolverine Tube Div, Universal Oil Prod, 65-69; vpres & tech dir, Crucible Specialty Metals Div, Colt Industs, 69-74 & Int Mill Serv, IU Int, 74-76. *Mem:* Sigma Xi; fel Am Soc Metals; Am Inst Metall Engrs; Am Nuclear Soc; Brit Iron & Steel Inst. *Res:* Hot isostatic compaction; preallocated powders; shapes/cavities; mechanical metallurgy of steel; fracture toughness; failure analysis and causation. *Mailing Add:* 2247 Hallquist Rd Red Wing MN 55066-3957

ROSS, SYDNEY, COLLOID CHEMISTRY. *Current Pos:* from assoc prof to prof, 48-80, EMER PROF COLLOID SCI, RENSSELAER POLYTECH INST, 80- *Personal Data:* b Glasgow, Scotland, July 6, 15. *Educ:* McGill Univ, BSc, 36; Univ Ill, PhD(chem), 40. *Prof Exp:* Instr chem, Monmouth Col, 40-41; res assoc & fel chem, Stanford Univ, 41-45; assoc prof phys chem, Univ Ala, 45-46; sr chemist, Oak Ridge Nat Lab, Tenn, 46-48. *Concurrent Pos:* Mem adv bd, Gordon Res Conf, 54; vis prof, Univ Strathclyde, Scotland, 75-78. *Mem:* Am Chem Soc; Royal Soc Chem. *Res:* Foams and antifoams; electrokinetic phenomena; dispersions and emulsions; adsorption of gases by solids. *Mailing Add:* 2194 Tibbits Ave Rensselaer Polytech Inst Troy NY 12180

ROSS, THEODORE WILLIAM, GEOLOGY. *Current Pos:* Instr, 66-67, chmn dept, 67-70, ASST PROF GEOL, LAWRENCE UNIV, 70-, CHMN DEPT, 74- *Personal Data:* b Oak Park, Ill, May 9, 35; m 62; c 2. *Educ:* Ind Univ, BS, 57, MA, 62; Wash State Univ, PhD(geol), 69. *Mem:* Soc Econ Geol; Nat Asn Geol Teachers; Geol Soc Am. *Res:* Economic geology of metals; determination of pre-Pleistocene bedrock topography of Wisconsin. *Mailing Add:* Dept Geol Lawrence Univ PO Box 599 Appleton WI 54912

ROSS, THOMAS EDWARD, WATER PROBLEMS. *Current Pos:* PROF & CHAIR GEOG, PEMBROKE STATE UNIV, 69- *Personal Data:* b Bud, WVa, Apr 25, 42; m 64; c Candace M & Laura (King). *Educ:* Marshall Univ, BA, 68, MS, 69; Univ Tenn, PhD(geog), 77. *Concurrent Pos:* Consult, Off Econ Develop, Pembroke State Univ, 87-92; bd dirs, Am Indian Specialty Group, Asn Am Geographers, 87-91; distinguished prof, Pembroke State Univ, 89. *Mem:* Asn Am Geogr. *Res:* Environmental issues; groundwater pollution and water supplies in southeastern United States; environmental impacts upon economic development. *Mailing Add:* Geog & Geol Pembroke State Univ 1 University Dr Pembroke NC 28372

ROSS, TIMOTHY JACK, STRUCTURAL ENGINEERING, COMPUTATIONAL SOFTWARE. *Current Pos:* ASSOC PROF STRUCT, UNIV NMEX, 87- *Personal Data:* b Spokane, Wash, Feb 17, 49; m 81; c 4. *Educ:* Wash State Univ, BS, 71; Rice Univ, MS, 73; Stanford Univ, PhD(struct eng), 83. *Prof Exp:* Vulnerability engr, Defense Intel Agency, 73-78; res engr, Air Force Weapons Lab, 78-86. *Concurrent Pos:* Adv, Res Assoc Prog, Nat Res Coun, 84-86; dir & pres, IntelliSys Corp, 86-88. *Mem:* Am Soc Civil Engrs; Int Fuzzy Systs Asn; Am Soc Eng Educ; NAm Fuzzy Info Processing Soc; Soc Exp Mech. *Res:* Exploratory and experimental studies of microfracture in brittle materials; fuzzy logic and expert systems; dynamics of space structures; probability theory; risk assessment. *Mailing Add:* Dept Civil Eng Univ NMex Albuquerque NM 87131. *Fax:* 505-277-1988; *E-Mail:* ross@cedar.unm.edu

ROSS, WILLIAM D(ANIEL), light scattering, for more information see previous edition

ROSS, WILLIAM DONALD, psychoanalysis; deceased, see previous edition for last biography

ROSS, WILLIAM J(OHN), ELECTRICAL ENGINEERING. *Current Pos:* RETIRED. *Personal Data:* b Auckland, NZ, June 11, 30; m 59; c 1. *Educ:* Univ Auckland, BSc, 51, MSc, 53, PhD(physics), 55. *Prof Exp:* Res asst, Ionosphere Res Lab, Pa State Univ, University Park, 55-56; from asst prof to assoc prof elec eng, 56-63, prof, 63-91, head dept, 71-79. *Mem:* Am Geophys Union; Inst Elec & Electronics Engrs; Am Soc Eng Educ. *Res:* Ionospheric radio propagation; ionospheric theory. *Mailing Add:* 257 S Osmond St State College PA 16801

ROSS, WILLIAM MAX, PLANT BREEDING, CROP PRODUCTION. *Current Pos:* RETIRED. *Personal Data:* b Farmington, Ill, Mar 20, 25; m 52; c 5. *Educ:* Univ Ill, BS, 48, MS, 49, PhD(agron), 52. *Prof Exp:* Res asst agron, Univ Ill, 49-51, Kans State Univ, 51-52; res agronomist & res geneticist, Ft Hays Exp Sta, Kans, 52-69, res geneticist & prof, USDA, Dept Agron, Univ Nebr, Lincoln, 69-85. *Concurrent Pos:* Assoc ed, Crop Sci, 80-82. *Mem:* Fel Am Soc Agron; Crop Sci Soc Am. *Res:* Production, breeding and genetics of sorghum; population improvement for yield, grain quality and insect resistance. *Mailing Add:* Rte 13 Lincoln NE 68527

ROSSA, ROBERT FRANK, ALGEBRA. *Current Pos:* from asst prof to assoc prof, 69-84, PROF COMPUT SCI & MATH, ARK STATE UNIV, 84- *Personal Data:* b Kankakee, Ill, Aug 17, 42; m 69; c 1. *Educ:* Univ Okla, BA, 63, MA, 66, PhD(math), 71. *Prof Exp:* Asst math, Univ Okla, 63-69. *Mem:* Am Math Soc; Asn Comput Mach; Inst Elec & Electronics Engrs; Math Asn Am. *Res:* Ring theory; radicals. *Mailing Add:* PO Box 151 State University AR 72467-0151

ROSSALL, RICHARD EDWARD, INTERNAL MEDICINE, CARDIOLOGY. *Current Pos:* RETIRED. *Personal Data:* b Lytham St Annes, Eng, Jan 11, 26; Can citizen; m 52; c 2. *Educ:* Univ Leeds, BSc, 47, MB, ChB, 50, MD, 58; MRCP, 52; FRCP(C), 58; FRCP, 73. *Prof Exp:* House physician internal med, Gen Infirmary, Leeds, Eng, 50, Postgrad Med Sch, Univ London, 50-51 & Brompton Hosp, London, 51; asst chest physician, Bromley & Farnboro, Kent, 51-52; registr, Hull & East Riding Hosp Bd, 54, Gen Infirmary, Leeds, 54-55, sr registr, 55-57; from instr to prof, Univ Hosp, 57-71, from asst dean to assoc dean, 69-78, internal med, Univ Alta, dir, Div Cardiol, 69-97. *Concurrent Pos:* Consult cardiologist, Edmonton Gen, Royal Alexandra & Misericordia Hosps, 57- & Dept Vet Affairs, 70; fel coun clin cardiol, Am Heart Asn. *Mem:* Fel Am Col Cardiol; Can Soc Clin Invest; fel Am Col Physicians; Can Cardiovasc Soc (pres, 80-82). *Res:* Pulmonary lymphatic and blood circulation in health and disease. *Mailing Add:* 8331 Saskatchewan Dr Edmonton AB T6G 2A7 Can

ROSSAN, RICHARD NORMAN, PARASITOLOGY. *Current Pos:* PRIN INVESTR, US ARMY CONTRACT, 90- *Personal Data:* b Chicago, Ill, May 15, 28; m 66; c Alexandra. *Educ:* Univ Ill, BS, 49, MS, 51; Rutgers Univ, PhD(zool), 59. *Prof Exp:* Mem staff, Naval Med Res Inst, 52-56; res training assoc, Howard Univ, 59-60; res assoc, Inst Med Res, Christ Hosp, 60-63; asst prof biol & res parasitologist, Nat Ctr for Primate Biol, Univ Calif, Davis, 63-69; mem prof staff, Gorgas Mem Lab, 69-90, actg chief, Div Parasitol,

87-90, actg dir, 89-90. *Concurrent Pos:* WHO traveling fel, 65. *Mem:* AAAS; Am Soc Parasitol; Am Soc Trop Med & Hyg; Sigma Xi. *Res:* Biology, chemotherapy and immunity of avian and primate malarias; serum changes and immunity associated with visceral leishmaniasis; evaluation of experimental antimalarial drugs in monkey models. *Mailing Add:* PSC 2 Box 2209 APO AA 34002

ROSSANO, AUGUST THOMAS, ENVIRONMENTAL ENGINEERING, AIR QUALITY & INDUSTRIAL HYGIENE. *Current Pos:* prof, 63-81, EMER PROF CIVIL ENG, AIR RESOURCE PROG, UNIV WASH, 81- *Personal Data:* b New York, NY, Feb 1, 16; m 44, Margo Chrisney; c August III, Marilyn, Pamela, Jeannine, Renee, Christopher & Stephen. *Educ:* Mass Inst Technol, BS, 38; Harvard Univ, SM, 41, ScD(air sanit), 54; Am Bd Indust Hyg, dipl, 58; Am Acad Environ Engr, dipl. *Honors & Awards:* Spec Serv Award, USPHS, 58. *Prof Exp:* Res asst civil eng, Univ Ill, 39-40; sanit engr, USPHS, 41-62; vis prof environ health eng, Calif Inst Technol, 60-63. *Concurrent Pos:* Vis prof, Calif Inst Technol, 60-63; consult, WHO, World Bank, 26 foreign govts, US govt & var pvt corps, 60- *Mem:* Am Pub Health Asn; Am Indust Hyg Asn; Air Pollution Control Asn; Am Acad Environ Engrs; Sigma Xi. *Res:* Industrial hygiene engineering; radioactive fallout; air quality network design and supervision; air pollution source testing; air pollution control technology. *Mailing Add:* 10901-176 Circle NE Apt No 4702 Redmond WA 98052

ROSSANT, JANET, MAMMALIAN DEVELOPMENT. *Current Pos:* asst prof, 85-88, PROF DEPT MED GENETICS, UNIV TORONTO, 88-; SR SCIENTIST, MT SINAI HOSP, 85- *Personal Data:* b Chatham, UK, July 13, 50; m 75; c 2. *Educ:* Oxford Univ, BA, 72; Cambridge Univ, PhD(embryol), 76. *Prof Exp:* Vis prof, Dept Immunol, Univ Alta, 77; from asst prof to assoc prof biol, Brock Univ, 77-85. *Concurrent Pos:* Asst prof, Dept Path, McMaster Univ, 81-85; E W R Steacie Fel, 83. *Mem:* Brit Soc Develop Biol; Can Soc Cell Biol; Am Soc Cell Biol; fel Royal Soc Can. *Res:* Early mammalian development, using micromanipulative and molecular genetic approaches to studying early differentiation; teratocarcinoma differentation. *Mailing Add:* Mt Sinai Hosp Samuel Lunenfeld Res Inst 600 University Ave Toronto ON M5G 1X5 Can

ROSSBACHER, LISA ANN, PLANETARY GEOLOGY, SCIENCE WRITING. *Current Pos:* res assoc, 79-93, PROF GEOL, VPRES & DEAN ACAD AFFAIRS, WHITTIER COL, 93- *Personal Data:* b Fredericksburg, Va, Oct 10, 52; m 79, Dallas D Rhodes. *Educ:* Dickinson Col, BS, 75; State Univ NY Binghamton, MA, 78; Princeton Univ, MA, 79, PhD(geol), 83. *Prof Exp:* Instr geol, Dickinson Col, 76-77; from asst prof to assoc prof, Calif State Polytech Univ, 84-91, assoc vpres acad affairs, 87-93, prof 91-93. *Concurrent Pos:* Consult, Repub Geothermal Inc, 79-81; vis researcher, Univ Uppsala, Sweden, 84. *Mem:* AAAS; Asn Women Geoscientists; Asn Earth Sci Ed; Geol Soc Am; Sigma Xi. *Res:* Geomorphology of planetary surfaces, especially solutional landforms (karst and thermokarst) on Earth and Mars; writing on careers in geology and space exploration. *Mailing Add:* Dean Acad Affairs Dickinson Col PO Box 1773 Carlisle PA 17013. *Fax:* 562-698-4067

ROSSBY, HANS THOMAS, PHYSICAL OCEANOGRAPHY. *Current Pos:* PROF OCEANOG, UNIV RI, 75- *Personal Data:* b Boston, Mass, June 8, 37; m 62; c Stan & Bjorn. *Educ:* Royal Inst Technol, Sweden, BS, 62; Mass Inst Technol, PhD(oceanog), 66. *Honors & Awards:* Bigelow Gold Medal, Woods Hole Oceanog Isnt. *Prof Exp:* Res asst mech, Physics Dept, Royal Inst Technol, Sweden, 60-62; res asst geophys, Mass Inst Technol, 62-66, res assoc oceanog, 66-68; from asst prof to assoc prof geophys, Yale Univ, 68-75. *Mem:* Sigma Xi; fel Am Meteorol Soc; fel Am Geophys Union; Oceanog Soc. *Res:* Structure and variability of ocean currents; Gulf stream; North Atlantic current; oceanic microstructure. *Mailing Add:* Dept Oceanog Univ RI South Ferry Rd Narragansett RI 02882. *E-Mail:* tom@rafor.gso.uri.edu

ROSSE, CORNELIUS, ANATOMY, IMMUNOLOGY. *Current Pos:* from asst prof to assoc prof biol struct, 67-75, PROF BIOL STRUCT, SCH MED, UNIV WASH, 75-, CHMN BIOL STRUCT, 81- *Personal Data:* b Csorna, Hungary, Jan 13, 38. *Educ:* Bristol Univ, MB, ChB, 64, MD, 74. *Prof Exp:* House surgeon, United Hosps, Bristol Univ, 64-65, demonstr anat, Univ, 65-67. *Mem:* Exp Hemat Soc; Am Asn Anatomists; Anat Soc Gt Brit & Ireland; Sigma Xi. *Res:* Experimental hematology; problems relating to hemopoietic stem cell and to the role of the bone marrow in producing potentially immunocompetent cells. *Mailing Add:* Dept Biol Struct Univ Wash Sch Med G515 Health Sci SM 20 Seattle WA 98195-0001. *Fax:* 206-543-1524

ROSSE, WENDELL FRANKLYN, MEDICINE, IMMUNOLOGY. *Current Pos:* from asst prof to assoc prof, Duke Univ, 66-72, assoc prof immunol, 70-74, chief immuno-hemat, 71-76, PROF MED, MED CTR, DUKE UNIV, 72-, PROF IMMUNOL, 74-, DIR BLOOD BANK, 71-, CHIEF HEMAT-MED ONCOL, 76- *Personal Data:* b Sidney, Nebr, June 5, 33; m 59; c 4. *Educ:* Univ Omaha, AB, 53; Univ Nebr, MS, 56; Univ Chicago, MD, 58. *Prof Exp:* NIH clin assoc, Nat Cancer Inst, 60-63; vis res fel, Univ London, Med Sch, 63-64; sr investr med, Nat Cancer Inst, 64-66. *Mem:* Am Soc Hemat; Am Asn Physics; Am Soc Clin Invest; Am Fedn Clin Res. *Res:* Immune hemolytic anemia and thrombocytopenia; complement-dependent mechanisms of hemolysis. *Mailing Add:* 0563 Blue Zone Hemet Oncol Duke Univ Med Ctr Box 3934 Durham NC 27710

ROSSEN, JOEL N(ORMAN), PROPULSION SYSTEMS DEVELOPMENT, PROGRAM MANAGEMENT. *Current Pos:* RETIRED. *Personal Data:* b Detroit, Mich, June 22, 27; m 52, Barbara Cohan; c Jonathan, David & Rebecca. *Educ:* Mass Inst Technol, BS, 48, MS, 49. *Prof Exp:* Res engr adhesives, Div Indust Coop, Mass Inst Technol, 49-50; chem engr, Tracerlab, Inc, 50-51; chem engr, Atlantic Res Corp, 51-56, proj engr, 56-57, head, Rocket Ballistics Group, 57-58, asst dir, Solid Propellant Div, 58-60, dir, 60-62; asst mgr, Solid Rocket Br, United Tech Ctr, United Aircraft Corp, 62-64, tech asst, Opers Dept, 64, asst chief engr solid rockets, 64-65, asst prod develop mgr, 65-66, mgr, Advan Technol Br, 66-67, ICM progs, 67-71, FMB Propulsion Progs, 71-73, Ballistic Missile Progs, 73-78 & Solid Rocket Progs, Chem Syst Div, United Technologies Corp, 78-84; tech & mgt consult, J N Roseen, Inc, 84-89. *Mem:* Am Chem Soc; Am Inst Aeronaut & Astronaut; Am Inst Chem Engrs. *Res:* Solid and hybrid rocket propulsion technology development and design; systems development; solid rocket propulsion systems management. *Mailing Add:* 62 Bay Tree Lane Los Altos CA 94022-4601. *E-Mail:* jnormr@prodigy.com

ROSSEN, ROGER DOWNEY, IMMUNOLOGY, INTERNAL MEDICINE. *Current Pos:* from instr to assoc prof, 67-73, PROF MICROBIOL, IMMUNOL & MED, BAYLOR COL MED, 73; CHIEF CLIN IMMUNOL, VET ADMIN HOSP, 72- *Personal Data:* b Cleveland, Ohio, June 4, 35; m 61; c 3. *Educ:* Yale Univ, BA, 57; Western Reserve Univ, MD, 61. *Prof Exp:* From intern to asst resident internal med, Columbia-Presby Hosp, N Y, 61-63, sr resident internal med, 66-67; from clin assoc to clin investr, Lab Clin Invest, Nat Inst Allergy & Infectious Dis, 63-66. *Concurrent Pos:* Nat Inst Allergy & Infectious Dis spec res fel, Baylor Col Med, 67-68; mem adv comt transplantation & immunol, Nat Inst Allergy & Infectious Dis, 70-74; grants, Vet Admin, Dept Health & Human Servs & NIH. *Mem:* Am Asn Immunologists; Am Soc Microbiol; Soc Exp Biol & Med; Am Soc Pathologists. *Res:* Regulation of antibody formation, especially the regulatory influences of the monocyte in B cell differentiation; investigation of monocyte abnormalities in AIDS and related diseases. *Mailing Add:* Dept Microbiol & Immunol Baylor Col Med Houston TX 77030. *Fax:* 713-790-9141, 794-7580; *E-Mail:* rrossen@bcm.tmc.edu

ROSSETTI, LOUIS MICHAEL, SPEECH PATHOLOGY, DEVELOPMENTAL PSYCHOLOGY. *Current Pos:* CHMN COMMUN DISORDERS, UNIV WIS, OSHKOSH, 87- *Personal Data:* b Chicago, Ill, Aug 20, 48; m 72; c 1. *Educ:* Northern Mich Univ, BS, 70, MA, 72; Southern Ill Univ, PhD(speech path), 78. *Prof Exp:* Chief speech pathologist, Children's Develop Ctr, 72-74; res asst, Southern Ill Univ, 74-76; from asst prof to assoc prof speech path, Northwest Mo State Univ, 84-87. *Concurrent Pos:* Lectr & consult, Kirksville Col Osteop Med, 77-; diag consult, Kirksville Diag Ctr, 77- & Head Start Prog Mo, 78; assoc ed, Mo Speech & Hearing Asn J, 78-; res consult, Knoxville Vet Admin Hosp, 78- *Mem:* Am Speech & Hearing Asn. *Res:* Clinical application of distinctive feature theory; infant screening, especially high risk infants. *Mailing Add:* Dept Commun Univ Wis 800 Algoma Blvd Oshkosh WI 54901-3551

ROSSETTOS, JOHN N(ICHOLAS), SOLID MECHANICS, APPLIED MATHEMATICS. *Current Pos:* assoc prof mech & appl math, 69-77, PROF MECH ENG, NORTHEASTERN UNIV, 77- *Personal Data:* b Nisyros, Greece, Mar 11, 32; US citizen; m 63, Elizabeth Puraka; c Nicholas, Linda. *Educ:* Mass Inst Technol, BS & MS, 56; Harvard Univ, MA, 60, PhD(solid mech), 64. *Prof Exp:* Staff engr, Mass Inst Technol, 54-56; res engr, United Aircraft Res Ctr, 56-57; sr engr, Allied Res, Inc & Am Sci & Eng, Inc, 57-59; res scientist appl mech, Langley Res Ctr, NASA, 64-66; sr staff scientist, Mech & Comput, Avco Corp, 66-69. *Concurrent Pos:* Lectr, Univ Va, 64-66; adj prof, Boston Univ, 67-69; vis assoc prof, Mass Inst Technol, 70; NASA res grant, Northeastern Univ, 71-; consult mech, Textron Defense Systs, 81-; hon res assoc struct mech, Harvard Univ, 79-80; vis scientist, Army Mat Technol Lab, 86-87. *Mem:* Am Acad Mech; assoc fel Am Inst Aeronaut & Astronaut; fel Am Soc Mech Engrs. *Res:* Mechanics of damage in composites; composite joints; application of finite element method and computers in engineering science; vibration and buckling of structural components. *Mailing Add:* Dept Mech Eng Northeastern Univ Boston MA 02115. *Fax:* 617-373-2921

ROSSI, ANTHONY MICHAEL, PLANT-INSECT INTERACTIONS, POPULATION & COMMUNITY LEVEL INTERACTIONS. *Current Pos:* RES FEL, DEPT BIOL, UNIV SFLA, 91- *Personal Data:* b Ft Wayne, Ind, Feb 28, 61. *Educ:* Univ Mo, St Louis, BA, 85, MS, 86; Fla State Univ, PhD(biol sci), 91. *Concurrent Pos:* Adj prof, Dept Chem, Hillsborough Community Col, 92- *Mem:* Entom Soc Am; Ecol Soc Am; Nature Conservancy. *Res:* Population dynamics of herbivorous insects, including chemical, genetic and natural enemy effects on herbivorous insects. *Mailing Add:* Dept Biol Univ S Fla Tampa FL 33620

ROSSI, EDWARD P, ORAL PATHOLOGY, DENTISTRY. *Current Pos:* from instr to asst prof, 64-71, ASSOC PROF ORAL PATH & CHMN DEPT, SCH DENT & ASST PROF, SCH MED, CASE WESTERN RES UNIV, 71- *Personal Data:* b Cleveland, Ohio, Jan 28, 34; div; c 1. *Educ:* Kent State Univ, BA, 57; Western Reserve Univ, DDS, 62, MS, 65. *Prof Exp:* Intern, Crile Vet Admin Hosp, 62-63. *Concurrent Pos:* Am Cancer Soc clin fel, 65-66, advan clin fel, 66-69; consult, Cleveland Vet Admin Hosp; mem fel awards comt, Am Fund Dent Educ. *Mem:* Am Dent Asn; Am Acad Oral Path; Am Asn Cancer Educ; Int Acad Path. *Res:* Teaching oral pathology; oral pathology diagnostic laboratory; programmed instruction in dental education. *Mailing Add:* Sch Dent 10900 Euclid Ave Case Western Res Univ Cleveland OH 44106-4905

ROSSI, ENNIO CLAUDIO, MEDICINE. *Current Pos:* assoc prof, 66-72, PROF MED, SCH MED, NORTHWESTERN UNIV, CHICAGO, 72- *Personal Data:* b Madison, Wis, Apr 3, 31; m 57; c 2. *Educ:* Univ Wis, BA, 51, MD, 54; Am Bd Internal Med, dipl, 64. *Prof Exp:* Intern, Ohio State Univ, 54-55; Fulbright scholar, Univ Rome, 55-56; resident med, Univ Wis, 58-61, res fel hemat, 61-63; from instr to asst prof, Marquette Univ, 63-66. *Mem:* Am Fedn Clin Res; Am Soc Hemat. *Res:* Hematology; platelet metabolism and function; abnormal hemoglobins. *Mailing Add:* Dept Med Sch Med Northwestern Univ 303 E Chicago Ave Chicago IL 60611-3072

ROSSI, GEORGE VICTOR, PHARMACOLOGY. *Current Pos:* assoc prof, Philadelphia Col Pharm & Sci, 55-61, dir, Dept Biol Sci, 65-81, dir, Dept Pharmacol & Toxicol, PROF PHARMACOL, PHILADELPHIA COL PHARM & SCI, 77- *Personal Data:* b Ardmore, Pa, Mar 8, 29; m 56; c 1. *Educ:* Philadelphia Col Pharm & Sci, BSc, 51, MSc, 52; Purdue Univ, Lafayette, PhD(pharmacol), 54. *Prof Exp:* Res assoc pharmacol, Nat Drug Co, 54-55. *Concurrent Pos:* Lindback Found Award, 81. *Mem:* AAAS; Am Soc Pharmacol & Exp Therapeut; Am Pharmaceut Asn; fel Acad Pharmaceut Sci; NY Acad Sci. *Res:* Cardiovascular pharmacology; antihypertensive, antiarrhythmic and antianginal drug mechanisms; histamine receptor mechanisms; gastric secretory mechanisms. *Mailing Add:* Dept Pharmacol Philadelphia Col Pharm & Sci 600 S 43rd St Philadelphia PA 19104

ROSSI, GIUSEPPE, MATERIALS SCIENCE ENGINEERING. *Current Pos:* SR RES ENGR, FORD RES LAB, FORD MOTOR CO, 89- *Personal Data:* b Parma, Italy, Oct 27, 55. *Educ:* Univ Parma, Italy, Laurea, 78; Univ Calif, San Diego, MS, 81, PhD(physics), 83. *Prof Exp:* Researcher, Physics Dept, Univ Calif, Berkeley, 83, Santa Barbara, 83-84; Mat Dept, 86-88; researcher, Cavendish Lab, Univ Cambridge, UK, 84-86; res scientist, Elsag SpA, Italy, 88-89. *Mem:* Am Phys Soc. *Res:* Theoretical and computational methods for systems involving many degrees of freedom, including kinetic aggregational phenomena, complex polymeric materials and systems. *Mailing Add:* Ford Motor Co MD 3198 Sci Res Lab PO Box 2053 Dearborn MI 48121-2053. *E-Mail:* rossi@scilab.srl.ford.com

ROSSI, HARALD HERMAN, RADIATION BIOPHYSICS. *Current Pos:* res scientist radiol physics, 46-60, from asst prof to prof, 49-87, PROF RADIOL, COL PHYSICIANS & SURGEONS, COLUMBIA UNIV, 87-, EMER PROF & CONSULT. *Personal Data:* b Vienna, Austria, Sept 3, 17; US citizen; m 46, Ruth M Gregg; c Gerald C, Gwendolyn C (Gladstone) & Harriet D (Furey). *Educ:* Johns Hopkins Univ, PhD(physics), 42. *Honors & Awards:* Shonka Award, Shonka Mem Found, 72; Edith Quimby Mem Lect, 82; Wright Langham Lect, 83; 8th Lauriston Taylor Lectr, Nat Comt Radiol Protection, 84; L H Gray Medal, Int Comt Radiol Units, 85; Distinguished Scientist Award, Health Phys Soc, 87; Landauer Mem Lect, 88. *Prof Exp:* Instr physics, Johns Hopkins Univ, 40-45. *Concurrent Pos:* Res physicist, Nat Bur Stand, 45; physicist & radiation protection officer, Presby Hosp, 54-60; mem, Nat Coun Radiation Protection, 54-, bd dirs, 71-76; chmn, Health Comnrs, Tech Adv Comn Radiation, NY, 58-83; dir Dept Energy, contract radiation physics, biophysics & radiation biol, 60-87; mem, Int Comn Radiation Units, 59-, chmn liaison comt, 75-77; chmn radiation study sect, NIH, 62-67; consult, Off Radiation Control, NY, 63-83; consult, Defense Atomic Support Agency, Armed Forces Radiol Res Inst, 65-70; consult, Brookhaven Nat Lab, 65-80; consult & chmn adv comn radiation aspects SST, Fed Aviation Agency, 68-74; chmn rev comn biol & med res, Argonne Nat Lab, 71-76; consult med use nuclear powered pacemakers, AEC, 71-75; mem, Comt Biol Effects of Iionizing Radiations, Nat Res Coun, 76-82; chmn, Int Comt Radiol Protection/Int Comt Radiol Units joint task group on radiation protection quantities, 80-86. *Mem:* Radiation Res Soc (pres, 74); Am Radium Soc; Radiol Soc NAm; Am Col Radiol; Sigma Xi. *Res:* Radiation dosimetry; radiobiology; radiation protection; biophysics. *Mailing Add:* 105 Larchdale Ave Upper Nyack NY 10960

ROSSI, HUGO, MATHEMATICS. *Current Pos:* DEAN, COL SCI, UNIV UTAH, 87- *Personal Data:* b 1935. *Educ:* City Col, NY, BS, 56; Mass Inst Technol, MS, 57 & Phd(math), 60. *Prof Exp:* Teaching asst, Mass Inst Technol, 57-58; asst prof, Princeton Univ, 60-63; assoc prof, Brandeis Univ, 63-66, prof, 66; assoc ed, Transactions of Am Math Soc, 73-78. *Concurrent Pos:* Ed, Pac J Math, 80-85 & Univ Lect Series, Am Math Soc, 87-; mem, comt sci policy, Am Math Soc, 83-85; vis, Inst Advan Study, Princeton, 83-84; mem, comt status prof, 85-87; Gardner fel, 83; asst prof, Univ Calif, Berkeley, 60. *Res:* Complex analysis. *Mailing Add:* Math Dept Univ Utah Salt Lake City UT 84112

ROSSI, JOHN JOSEPH, MOLECULAR GENETICS. *Current Pos:* RES SCIENTIST & DIR, DEPT MOLECULAR BIOL, BECKMAN RES INST, CITY OF HOPE, 80- *Personal Data:* b Washington, DC, July 8, 46; m 69; c 4. *Educ:* Univ NH, BA, 69; Univ Conn, MS, 71, PhD(genetics), 76. *Prof Exp:* Res assoc, Div Biol & Med, Brown Univ, 76-80. *Concurrent Pos:* Adj prof, Dept Biochem & Dept Microbiol & Molecular Genetics, Univ Med Sch-Loma Linda, Calif. *Mem:* Am Soc Microbiol; AAAS; RNA Soc; Genetics Soc Am; Am Soc Chem & Molecular Biol. *Res:* Mechanisms of gene regulation in prokaryotic and simple eukaryotic systems; messenger RNA splicing; RNA processing; ribozyme inhibition of acquired immune deficiency syndrome viral function. *Mailing Add:* Div Biol Beckman Res Inst City of Hope Duarte CA 91010-3011. *Fax:* 626-301-8271; *E-Mail:* jrossi@smtplick.coh.org

ROSSI, JOSEPH STEPHEN, HEALTH PSYCHOLOGY-BEHAVIORAL MEDICINE, QUANTITATIVE-PSYCHOMETRIC METHODS. *Current Pos:* actg dir, Perception Lab Univ RI, 82-83, res fel, 84-85, from asst prof to assoc prof, 85-95, DIR RES, CANCER PREV RES CTR, UNIV RI, 92-, PROF PSYCHOL, 95- *Personal Data:* b Feb 22, 1951; m 81, Susan R Finkle. *Educ:* RI Col, BA, 75; Univ RI, MA, 79, PhD(psychol), 84. *Prof Exp:* Instr psychol, Univ RI, 78-81, RI Col, 78-82. *Concurrent Pos:* Prin investr, Nat Cancer Inst, 89-91, RI Sun Smart Proj, 91-; consult, NIH, 89, Ctr Dis Control, 91-, Nat Cancer Inst, 92-, Am Cancer Soc, 93- & Am Heart Asn, 93-; adj assoc prof, Roger Williams Cancer Ctr, 91-; vis instr psychol, Conn Col, 92. *Mem:* AAAS; Am Asn Appl & Prev Psychol; Am Psychol Asn; Am Pub Health Asn; Psychometric Soc; Soc Behav Med. *Res:* Research on behavior change for health promotion and disease prevention across a wide range of problems, including smoking cessation, sun exposure, exercise, diet, weight control, alcohol, cocaine, HIV risk reduction, diabetes, radon gas, and psychotherapy; psychometric measurement and instrument development, data analysis, and the development of expert computer systems for health promotion and disease prevention. *Mailing Add:* Cancer Prev Res Ctr Univ RI Kingston RI 02881-0808. *Fax:* 401-792-5562; *E-Mail:* kzpl0l@uriacc.uri.edu

ROSSI, MIRIAM, CRYSTALLOGRAPHY. *Current Pos:* asst prof, 82-89, ASSOC PROF CHEM, VASSAR COL, 89- *Personal Data:* b Asti, Italy, Mar 8, 52; US citizen; m 93, Francesco Caruso; c Alessio. *Educ:* Hunter Col, BA, 74; Johns Hopkins Univ, MA, 76, PhD(chem), 79. *Honors & Awards:* Mid-Hudson Am Chem Soc Res Award, 93. *Prof Exp:* Res asst, Fox Chase Cancer Ctr, 78-82. *Mem:* Am Chem Soc; Am Crystallog Asn. *Res:* Study of anti-carcinogenic molecules using x-ray crystallographic techniques. *Mailing Add:* Vassar Col Box 484 Poughkeepsie NY 12601. *Fax:* 914-437-5732; *E-Mail:* rossi@vassar.edu

ROSSI, NICHOLAS PETER, CARDIOVASCULAR SURGERY. *Current Pos:* from asst prof to assoc prof, 64-72, PROF SURG, UNIV IOWA, 72- *Personal Data:* b Philadelphia, Pa, July 17, 27; m 57; c 4. *Educ:* Univ Pa, 51; Hahnemann Med Col, MD, 55. *Prof Exp:* Instr surg, Univ Iowa, 60-61, assoc, 61-62; instr, Univ Ky, 63-64. *Concurrent Pos:* Fel cardiovasc surg, Univ Ky, 63-64; consult, Oakdale State Sanatorium, 64- *Mem:* AAAS; Am Col Cardiol; AMA; Am Col Surg; Am Col Chest Physicians. *Mailing Add:* Dept Surg Univ Iowa CTS 200 Hawkins Dr Iowa City IA 52242-1009

ROSSI, ROBERT DANIEL, ORGANIC CHEMISTRY. *Current Pos:* proj supvr, 80-83, res assoc, 84-88, TECH DIR, INDUST STARCH RES & DEVELOP, NAT STARCH & CHEM CORP, 88- *Personal Data:* b Philadelphia, Pa, Nov 4, 50; m 77. *Educ:* Philadelphia Col Pharm & Sci, BS, 72; Temple Univ, PhD(chem), 78. *Prof Exp:* Sr chemist, Borg-Warner Chem, 77-80. *Mem:* Am Chem Soc; Soc Advan Mat Process Eng; Int Soc Hybrid Microelectronics; Inst Elec & Electronics Engrs. *Res:* Preparation of unique monomers and their respective homo- and copolymers; chemistry of organophosphorus compounds; conducting polymers; high temperature polymers, polymers for electronic applications; polyimide chemistry. *Mailing Add:* One Maplewood Dr Levittown PA 19506-1016

ROSSIER, ALAIN B, PHYSICAL MEDICINE, REHABILITATION. *Current Pos:* CONSULT, PARAPLEGIC CTR, UNIV ORTHOP CLIN BALGRIST, ZURICH, SWITZ, 86- *Personal Data:* b Lausanne, Switz, Nov 29, 30; wid. *Honors & Awards:* Soc Medal, Int Med Soc Paraplegia, 87; Life Time Achieve Award, Am Spinal Injury Asn, 96. *Prof Exp:* Asst chief, Univ Hosp Geneva & chief, Paraplegic Ctr, Beau-Sejour Hosp, Univ Hosp Geneva, 64-73; chief, Spinal Cord Injury Serv, Vet Admin Med Ctr & prof spinal cord rehab, Harvard Med Sch, 73-84; chief, Paraplegic Ctr, Univ Orthop Clin Balgrist, Zurich, Switz, 86-89; prof paraplegiology, Med Univ Urich, Switz, 86-89. *Concurrent Pos:* Fel, Spinal Cord Injury Serv, Vet Admin Hosp, Long Beach, Calif & Swiss Acad Med Sci, 62-63; consult neurosurg & orthop surg, Children's Hosp Med Ctr, 73-, Spinal Cord Injury, Braintree Hosp & Mass Rehab Hosp; assoc staff mem, New Eng Med Ctr Hosp, Boston; lectr, Harvard Med Sch, 94; adj prof, Spinal Cord Rehab, Tufts Univ, Boston, 94. *Mem:* Int Med Soc Paraplegia; Am Asn Neurol Surg; Am Urol Asn; Am Cong Rehab Med; Int Continence Soc; Am Acad Orthop Surg. *Res:* Spinal cord regeneration, heterotopic bone ossification; urodynamic problems in neurogenic bladder; deep venous thrombosis; spinal fusion; wheelchair bioengineering. *Mailing Add:* 32 Quai Gustave Ador Geneva 1207 Switzerland

ROSSIGNOL, PHILIPPE ALBERT, MEDICAL ENTOMOLOGY. *Current Pos:* Res fel, 78-81, RES ASSOC MED ENTOM, DEPT TROP PUB HEALTH, SCH PUB HEALTH, HARVARD UNIV, 81- *Personal Data:* b Sherbrooke, Que, Jan 15, 50; m 82. *Educ:* Univ Ottawa, BSc, 71; Univ Toronto, MSc, 75, PhD(parasitol), 78. *Mem:* AAAS; Am Soc Trop Med & Hyg; Royal Soc Trop Med & Hyg. *Res:* Physiology of salivatim, oogenesis and parasite transmission of mosquitoes. *Mailing Add:* Dept Entom Ore State Univ 2046 Cordley Hall Corvallis OR 97331-2907

ROSSIN, A DAVID, NUCLEAR ENGINEERING. *Current Pos:* PRES, ROSSIN & ASSOC, LOS ALTOS HILLS, CALIF, 87- *Personal Data:* b Cleveland, Ohio, May 5, 31; m 66, Sandra Howells; c Laura (VanZandt) & Elizabeth. *Educ:* Cornell Univ, BE, 54; Mass Inst Technol, MS, 55; Northwestern Univ, MBA, 63; Case Western Reserve Univ, PhD(metall), 66. *Prof Exp:* Sr scientist metall, Argonne Nat Lab, 55-72; syst nuclear res engr, Commonwealth Edison Co, 72-78, dir res, 78-81; dir, Nuclear Safety Anal Ctr, Elec Power Res Inst, 81-86; asst sec nuclear energy, US Dept Energy, 86-87. *Concurrent Pos:* Fel, Adlai Stevenson Inst, 67-68; affil scholar, Ctr Int Security & Arms Control, Stanford Univ. *Mem:* Am Nuclear Soc (pres, 92-93); Am Soc Testing & Mat; AAAS. *Res:* Reliability of nuclear reactor piping and pressure vessels; radiation embrittlement of reactor materials; nuclear reactor safety systems; nuclear waste disposal and spent fuel management; nuclear nonproliferation policy; history of 1976-77 decision of US to stop reprocessing of spent nuclear reactor fuel. *Mailing Add:* 24129 Hillview Dr Los Altos Hills CA 94024. *Fax:* 650-941-7849

ROSSIN, P(ETER) C(HARLES), PHYSICAL METALLURGY. *Current Pos:* asst vpres prod, Crucible Steel Co Am, 65-67, CHMN, CHIEF EXEC OFFICER & PRES, DYNAMET INC, 67- *Personal Data:* b New York, NY, Sept 29, 23; m 46; c 2. *Educ:* Lehigh Univ, BS, 48; Yale Univ, MS, 50. *Prof Exp:* Res metallurgist, Remington Arms Co, 48-51; res assoc, Gen Elec Co, 51-55; from gen mgr refractomet div to works mgr, Titusville Plant, Universal-Cyclops Steel Corp, 55-64; vpres opers, Fansteel Metall Corp, 64-65. *Mem:* Am Soc Metals. *Res:* Metallurgical processes associated with reactive and refractory metals. *Mailing Add:* Dynamet Inc 195 Museum Rd Washington PA 15301

ROSSING, THOMAS D(EAN), PHYSICS, ACOUSTICS. *Current Pos:* PROF PHYSICS, NORTHERN ILL UNIV, 71- *Personal Data:* b Madison, SDak, Mar 27, 29; m 52; c 5. *Educ:* Luther Col, BA, 50; Iowa State Univ, MS, 52, PhD(physics), 54. *Honors & Awards:* Silver Medal Musical Acoust Soc Am, 92. *Prof Exp:* Physicist, Univac Div, Sperry Rand Corp, 54-57; prof physics, St Olaf Col, 57-71. *Mem:* Am Phys Soc; Am Asn Physics Teachers; fel Acoust Soc Am; Sigma Xi; fel AAAS; Acoustic Soc France. *Res:* Magnetic materials and devices; ferromagnetic resonance; surface effects in fusion reactors; ultrasonic dispersion in gases; musical acoustics. *Mailing Add:* Dept Physics Northern Ill Univ DeKalb IL 60115. *E-Mail:* rossing@physics.niu.edu

ROSSINGTON, DAVID RALPH, PHYSICAL CHEMISTRY. *Current Pos:* from asst prof to prof, NY State Col Ceramics, Alfred Univ, 60-95, prof phys chem, 69-95, head, Div Ceramic Eng & Sci, 76-79 & 82-84, dean, Sch Eng, 84-91, EMER PROF PHYS CHEM, NY STATE COL CERAMICS, ALFRED UNIV, 95- *Personal Data:* b London, Eng, July 13, 32; US citizen; m 55, Angela; c 4. *Educ:* Bristol Univ, BSc, 53, PhD(chem), 56. *Prof Exp:* Res fel phys chem, State Univ NY Col Ceramics, Alfred Univ, 56-58; tech officer paints div, Imp Chem Industs, Eng, 58-60. *Concurrent Pos:* Fulbright traveling fels, 56 & 58. *Mem:* Am Chem Soc; fel Am Ceramic Soc; Nat Inst Ceramic Engrs; Am Soc Eng Educ. *Res:* Surface chemistry; catalysis; adsorption phenomena; chemistry of cement hydration; nuclear waste encapsulation. *Mailing Add:* Sch Ceramic Eng Sci NY State Col Ceramics Alfred Univ Alfred NY 14802. *Fax:* 607-871-2392

ROSSINI, FREDERICK ANTHONY, TECHNOLOGY & SOCIAL FORECASTING, INTERDISCIPLINARY RESEARCH PROCESSES. *Current Pos:* vprovost & prof info systs & systs eng, 89-91, provost & exec vpres acad affairs, 93-96, PROF SYST ENG & PUBLIC POLICY, GEORGE MASON UNIV, 96- *Personal Data:* b Washington, DC, Sept 20, 39; c Anthony J, Laura M & Jon D. *Educ:* Spring Hill Col, BS, 62; Univ Calif, Berkeley, PhD(physics), 68. *Prof Exp:* Actg asst prof physics, Univ Calif, Berkeley, 68, NIMH postdoctoral fel philos, 69-71; Nat Acad Sci res assoc, NASA-Ames Res Ctr, 71-72; from asst prof to prof technol & sci policy, Ga Inst Technol, 72-89, dir, Technol Policy & Assessment Ctr, 81-89, assoc dir, Off Interdisciplinary Progs, 83-85, dir, 85-89; consult, 92. *Concurrent Pos:* Assoc ed, Technol Forecastng & Social Change, 80-90; ed-in-chief, Impact Assessment Bull, 81-84. *Mem:* Int Asn Impact Assessment (treas, 81-88); Sigma Xi; sr mem Inst Elec & Electronics Engrs; AAAS. *Res:* Impact assessment. *Mailing Add:* 1237 Euclid Ave NE Atlanta GA 30307. *Fax:* 404-688-1299; *E-Mail:* frossini@gmu.edu

ROSSIO, JEFFREY L, IMMUNOLOGY, MICROBIOLOGY. *Current Pos:* scientist, 81-85, SR SCIENTIST, NAT CANCER INST, 85-; ASSOC PROF, HOOD COL, 86- *Personal Data:* b Cleveland, Ohio, May 22, 47; m 72, Susan Dunlop; c Sara & Jonathan. *Educ:* Univ Mich, BS, 69; Ohio State Univ, MS, 71, PhD(microbiol), 73. *Prof Exp:* Instr biochem, Univ Tex Med Br, 76-78; asst prof immunol, Wright State Univ, 78-81. *Mem:* Sigma Xi; Am Soc Microbiol. *Res:* AIDS pathogenesis, vaccine development, anti-HIV immune response; immune regulation; immunotherapy. *Mailing Add:* AIDS Vaccine Prog Bldg 535 Nat Cancer Inst Fcrf PO Box B Frederick MD 21701. *Fax:* 301-846-5588; *E-Mail:* rossio@ncifcrf.gov

ROSSITER, BRYANT WILLIAM, ORGANIC CHEMISTRY, ENVIRONMENTAL SCIENCE. *Current Pos:* RETIRED. *Personal Data:* b Ogden, Utah, Mar 10, 31; m 51, Betty Anderson; c Bryant E, Mark W, Diane (Vincent), Steven K, Linda, Karen (Munton), Matthew J & Gregory T. *Educ:* Univ Utah, BA, 54, PhD(org chem), 57. *Honors & Awards:* Will Judy Lect Award, Juniata Col, 78. *Prof Exp:* Res assoc, Eastman Kodax Co, 57-69, assoc head, 69-70, dir chem div, Res Labs, 70-84, dir sci & technol develop, Res Labs, 84-86; pres, Viratek Inc, Costa Mesa, Calif, 86-88; sr vpres, ICN Pharmaceut, 88-90; pres & chief exec officer, Wrecon Indust Inc, 91-96. *Concurrent Pos:* Mem, US Nat Comt, Int Union Pure & Appl Chem, 73-81, finance comt, 75-79, chmn, 77-80; mem bd trustees, Eastman Dent Ctr, 74-, chmn, 82-85 & Eyring Res Inst, 78-79; chmn, Chemrawn comt, 74-86, Int Conf Chem & World Food Supplies, Manila, Philippines, 82; mem, US Nat Acad Adv Comt, Int Coun Sci Unions, 81-; mem, res adv comt, Agency Int Develop, 82-, chmn, 89-92; sr ed, John Wiley & Sons; ed, Phys Methods Chem; mem & fel lectr award, Am Inst Chemists, 88; chmn bd, Nuclear Acid Res Inst, 87-89. *Mem:* Am Chem Soc; Sigma Xi; fel Am Inst Chem; NY Acad Sci; fel AAAS. *Res:* Chemistry of photographic processes; mechanisms of organic reactions; research management; photochemical processes, chemical instrumentation; drug research and development; biological waste reclamation and environmental conservancy. *Mailing Add:* 25662 Dillon Rd Laguna Hills CA 92653. *E-Mail:* bwr@ni.net

ROSSITTO, CONRAD, POLYMER & ORGANIC CHEMISTRY. *Current Pos:* sr res chemist, USM Chem Co, 60-68, mgr polymer synthesis group, 68-70, sr tech adv, 70-73, sr res chemist, USM Corp, 73-78, group leader, Bostic Div, 78-85, lab mgr, 85-88, DIR TECH DEVELOP, EMHART CORP, 88-, CONSULT. *Personal Data:* b Siracusa, Italy, Sept 4, 26; m 53; c 3. *Educ:* Univ Palermo, Dr(chem), 51. *Prof Exp:* Res chemist, BB Chem Co, 54-59. *Mem:* Am Chem Soc; Adhesion Soc; Soc Mfg Engrs; Tech Asn Pulp & Paper Indust. *Res:* Synthesis of polymers to be used in adhesives and coatings. *Mailing Add:* 128 Farrwood Dr Bradford MA 01835-8433

ROSSKY, PETER JACOB, LIQUID STATE THEORY. *Current Pos:* from asst prof to prof chem, 79-90, WATT CENTENNIAL PROF, UNIV TEX, AUSTIN, 90- *Personal Data:* b Philadelphia, Pa, Apr 15, 50; div; c 1. *Educ:* Cornell Univ, BA, 71; Harvard Univ, MA, 72, PhD(chem physics), 78. *Honors & Awards:* Presidential Young Investr Award, NSF, 84. *Prof Exp:* Fel, State Univ NY, Stony Brook, 77-79. *Concurrent Pos:* Alfred P Sloan Found fel, 82; Res Career Develop Award, NIH, 83; Camille & Henry Dreyfus Teacher-Scholar grant, 84. *Mem:* Am Chem Soc; fel Am Phys Soc. *Res:* Theoretical chemistry; statistical mechanics of solution structure and dynamics; aqueous systems; solvent effects in biochemical systems; quantum effects in liquids. *Mailing Add:* Dept Chem & Biochem Univ Tex Austin TX 78712-1167. *Fax:* 512-471-1624

ROSSMAN, AMY YARNELL, mycology, systematics, for more information see previous edition

ROSSMAN, DOUGLAS ATHON, SYSTEMATIC HERPETOLOGY. *Current Pos:* from asst prof to assoc prof zool, 63-67, assoc prof zool & physiol & assoc cur, Mus Zool, 67-76, ADJ PROF ZOOL & PHYSIOL, LA STATE UNIV, 76-, CUR REPTILES, MUS NATURAL SCI, 76- *Personal Data:* b Waukesha, Wis, July 4, 36; m 57, 90, Sharon C Johnson; c Charles E & Kathleen M. *Educ:* Southern Ill Univ, BA, 58; Univ Fla, PhD(zool), 61. *Prof Exp:* Instr zool, Univ NC, 61-63. *Concurrent Pos:* Res grants, Am Philos Soc, 63, NSF, 65-67; dir, Mus Nat Sci, 84-86. *Mem:* Herpetologists League; Am Soc Ichthyol & Herpet; Soc Study Amphibians & Reptiles. *Res:* Taxonomy and evolution of colubrid snake subfamily Natricinae (garter snakes); taxonomy of other colubrid snakes, especially Neotropical; snake osteology. *Mailing Add:* 1796 Stafford Dr Baton Rouge LA 70810. *Fax:* 504-388-3075

ROSSMAN, GEORGE ROBERT, MINERALOGY, INORGANIC CHEMISTRY. *Current Pos:* From instr to assoc prof, 71-83, PROF MINERAL, CALIF INST TECHNOL, 83- *Personal Data:* b LaCrosse, Wis, Aug 3, 44; m, Jeri. *Educ:* Wis State Univ, BS, 66; Calif Inst Technol, PhD(chem), 71. *Mem:* Fel Mineral Soc Am; Am Geophys Union. *Res:* Physical and chemical properties of minerals and related synthetic materials; color; spectroscopy; radiation effects; role of trace water. *Mailing Add:* Geol & Planetary Sci 170-25 Calif Inst Technol 1201 E California Pasadena CA 91125-0001

ROSSMAN, ISADORE, GERIATRICS. *Current Pos:* From assoc prof to prof, 70-84, EMER PROF COMMUNITY HEALTH, ALBERT EINSTEIN COL MED, 84-; MED DIR DEPT HOME CARE & EXTENDED SERV, MONTEFIORE HOSP, BRONX, NY, 54- *Personal Data:* b Elizabeth, NJ, Mar 29, 13; m 43; c 1. *Educ:* Univ Wis, BA, 33; Univ Chicago, PhD(anat), 37, MD, 42. *Honors & Awards:* Coggins Award, 79; Jos Freeman Award, Geront Soc Am, 81, Leavitt Award, 87. *Concurrent Pos:* Ed, Clin Geriat, 71, 79 & 86. *Mem:* NY Acad Med; Gerontol Soc Am. *Res:* Mortality studies; patterns of medical care. *Mailing Add:* 50 W 96 St 111 E 210th St New York NY 10025

ROSSMAN, TOBY GALE, GENETIC TOXICOLOGY. *Current Pos:* Assoc res scientist, 71-73, from asst prof to assoc prof, 73-85, PROF ENVIRON MED, SCH MED, NY UNIV, 85- *Personal Data:* b Weehawken, NJ, June 3, 42; m 90. *Educ:* Washington Sq Col, AB, 64; NY Univ, PhD(microbiol), 68. *Concurrent Pos:* NIH trainee, Med Ctr, NY Univ, 69-71. *Mem:* AAAS; Am Soc Microbiol; Asn Women Sci; Environ Mutagen Soc. *Res:* DNA repair and mutagenesis; genetic toxicology; environmental carcinogenesis. *Mailing Add:* Dept Environ Med Ny Univ Sch Med 550 First Ave New York NY 10016-6481

ROSSMANN, MICHAEL G, CRYSTALLOGRAPHY. *Current Pos:* from assoc prof to prof biol, 64-67, prof biol sci, 67-78, PROF BIOCHEM, PURDUE UNIV, 75-, HANLEY DISTINGUISHED PROF BIOL SCI, 78- *Personal Data:* b Frankfurt, Ger, July 30, 30; m 54, Audrey Pearson; c Alice, Martin & Heather. *Educ:* Univ London, BSc, 50, hons, 51, MSc, 53; Univ Glasgow, PhD(chem), 56. *Hon Degrees:* PhD, Univ Uppsala, 83, Univ Strasbourg, 84, Vrije Univ Brussel, 90, Univ Glasgow, 93, Univ York, 94. *Honors & Awards:* Keilin Lectr, Biochem, Brit Biochem Soc, 83; Fankuchen Award, Am Crystallog Asn, 86; Gairdner Found Int Award, 87; Merck Award, Am Soc Biochem & Molecular Biol, 89; Computerworld Smithsonian Award in Med, 90; Stein & Moore Award, Protein Soc, 94; Ewald Prize, Int Union Crystallog, 96. *Prof Exp:* Asst lectr physics, Univ Strathclyde, 52-56; Fulbright traveling fel chem, Univ Minn, Minneapolis, 56-58; res worker, MRC Lab Molecular Biol, Eng, 58-64. *Mem:* Nat Acad Sci; Am Chem Soc; Am Soc Biochem & Molecular Biol; Biophys Soc; Brit Inst Physics; Am Crystallog Asn; fel Am Acad Arts & Sci; foreign fel Indian Nat Sci Acad; foreign mem Royal Soc London. *Res:* Determination of the structure of biological macromolecules, particularly proteins and viruses, by means of x-ray crystallography. *Mailing Add:* Dept Biol Sci Purdue Univ West Lafayette IN 47907. *E-Mail:* mgr@indiana.biol.purdue.edu

ROSSMILLER, GEORGE EDDIE, AGRICULTURE, ECONOMICS. *Personal Data:* b Great Falls, Mont, June 8, 35; wid; c David W & Diane J. *Educ:* Mont State Univ, BS, 56, MS, 62; Mich State Univ, PhD, 65. *Honors & Awards:* Distinguished Policy Contrib, Am Agr Econ Asn, 92. *Prof Exp:* Res assoc, Mich State Univ, ELansing, 65-66, from asst prof to prof agr econ, 72-80; asst adminr int trade policy, Foreign Agr Serv, USDA, Wash, 79-81, dir planning & anal, 81-85; sr fel & dir, Nat Ctr Food & Agr Policy, Resources Future, 86-92; chief situation & policy studies serv, Food & Agr Orgn, UN, Rome, 92-97. *Concurrent Pos:* Exec dir, Int Policy Coun Agr & Trade, 88-92. *Mem:* Am Agr Econ Asn. *Res:* Agricultural economy; trade policy. *Mailing Add:* The Conifers Kennerleigh Devon Exit 4RS England

ROSSMILLER, JOHN DAVID, BIOCHEMISTRY. *Current Pos:* Chmn dept, Wright State Univ, 80-88, asst prof biol sci, 65-71, interim dean, Col Sci & Eng, 84-86, ASSOC PROF BIOL SCI, WRIGHT STATE UNIV, 71- *Personal Data:* b Elkhorn, Wis, Mar 12, 35; m 57. *Educ:* Univ Wis, BS, 56, MS, 62; PhD(biochem), 65. *Mem:* AAAS. *Res:* Biochemical physiological mechanisms of regulation. *Mailing Add:* 2431 Pine Knott Dr Dayton OH 45431

ROSSMOORE, HAROLD W, BACTERIOLOGY. *Current Pos:* From instr to assoc prof, 54-68, PROF BIOL, WAYNE STATE UNIV, 68- *Personal Data:* b New York, NY, June 15, 25; m 46; c 4. *Educ:* Univ Mich, BS, 49, MS, 51, PhD(bact), 55. *Concurrent Pos:* Fulbright & NSF fels, 64-65; consult. *Mem:* AAAS; Soc Indust Microbiol; Am Soc Microbiol; Soc Invert Path; fel Royal Soc Health. *Res:* Environmental microbiology, especially detection and control of deterioration water and oil systems; mechanisms of infection and resistance, especially in insects. *Mailing Add:* 4341 Fox Pointe Dr West Bloomfield MI 48323

ROSSNAGEL, BRIAN GORDON, PLANT BREEDING, AGRONOMY. *Current Pos:* FEED GRAIN BREEDER BARLEY & OAT, CROP DEVELOP CTR, UNIV SASK, 77- *Personal Data:* b Gladstone, Man, May 19, 52. *Educ:* Univ Man, BSAgr, 73, PhD(plant breeding, agron), 78. *Mem:* Agr Inst Can; Can Soc Agron; Am Soc Agron; Crop Sci Soc Am. *Res:* Breeding and development of genotypes and agronomic practices for the optimum production of barley and oat in Saskatchewan; specializing in the development of hulless barley culture. *Mailing Add:* Crop Develop Ctr Univ Sask 51 Campus Dr Saskatoon SK S7N 5A8 Can

ROSSNER, LAWRENCE FRANKLIN, ASTROPHYSICS. *Current Pos:* DIR COMPUT CTR, EPA ENVIRON RES LAB, NARRAGANSETT, RI, 75- *Personal Data:* b St Louis, Mo, Dec 17, 38; m 60; c 3. *Educ:* Univ Chicago, SB, 60, SM, 61, PhD(astrophys & astron), 66. *Prof Exp:* Res assoc astron, Columbia Univ, 66-68; asst prof physics, Brown Univ, 68-75. *Mem:* Am Astron Soc. *Res:* Application of fluid dynamics to problems of astrophysical interest, particularly galactic structure. *Mailing Add:* 16 ZA Emeline St Providence RI 02906

ROSSO, PEDRO, PERINATAL BIOLOGY. *Current Pos:* adj asst prof nutrit, 72-73, ASST PROF PEDIAT, INST HUMAN NUTRIT, COLUMBIA UNIV, 73- *Personal Data:* b Genoa, Italy, Aug 27, 41; Chilean citizen; m 67; c 3. *Educ:* Cath Univ Chile, BS, 62; Univ Chile, MD, 66. *Prof Exp:* Intern & resident pediat, Univ Chile, 66-69; fel growth & develop, Dept Pediat, Col Med, Cornell Univ, 70-72. *Concurrent Pos:* Consult, Regional Grad Appl Nutrit Course, Seameo Proj, Djakarta, Indonesia, 72 & Nutrit Prog, Univ PR, 75; NIH career develop award, 75. *Mem:* Soc Pediat Res; Am Inst Nutrit; Am Soc Clin Nutrit; Harvey Soc. *Res:* Control of prenatal growth and the influence of maternal nutrition on fetal growth and development. *Mailing Add:* Ctr Med Res Fac Med Cath Univ Casilla 114-D Santiago Chile. *Fax:* 56-2-632-1924

ROSSOL, FREDERICK CARL, MAGNETISM. *Current Pos:* RETIRED. *Personal Data:* b New York, NY, Feb 6, 33; m 54; c 1. *Educ:* Univ Calif, Berkeley, BSEE, 59; NY Univ, MEE, 61; Harvard Univ, MA, 63, PhD(appl physics), 66. *Prof Exp:* Mem tech staff, Bell Labs, Inc, 59-90. *Mem:* Inst Elec & Electronics Engrs; Am Phys Soc; Sigma Xi. *Res:* Magnetic properties of materials. *Mailing Add:* 4106 Spring Brook Dr Edison NJ 08820

ROSSOMANDO, EDWARD FREDERICK, ENZYMOLOGY, DIAGNOSTICS. *Current Pos:* from asst prof to assoc prof, 72-83, PROF BIOCHEM, DEPT BIOSTRUCT & FUNCTION, UNIV CONN HEALTH CTR, 83-; DIR, INST ORAL BIOL, 83- *Personal Data:* b New York, NY, Feb 26, 39; m 65; c 2. *Educ:* Univ Pa Sch Dental Med, DDS, 64; Rockefeller Univ, PhD(biomed sci), 69. *Prof Exp:* Res assoc, Nat Inst Dental Res, NIH, Bethesda, Md, 68-70; special fel, Brandeis Univ, Waltham, Mass, 70-72. *Concurrent Pos:* Vis scientist, Dept Biochem & Biophysics, Univ Pa, 78-79; Dept Med Biochem, Rockefeller Univ, 86, Lab Biochem, Nat Inst Med Res, London, Eng, 86. *Mem:* Am Soc Biochem & Molecular Biol; Am Chem Soc; Am Soc Cell Biol; Am Soc Dental Res. *Res:* Biochemical changes in body fluids associated with diseases; development of immunological methods; studies on cytokines; application to periodontal diseases; enzymatic control of morphogenesis; development of high performance liquid chromatography methods for enzymatic studies; analysis of semerotic units in biomolecules; application to dictyostelium discoideum. *Mailing Add:* Dept Biostruct & Function Univ Conn Health Ctr Farmington CT 06030-0001. *Fax:* 860-679-2910

ROSSON, H(AROLD) F(RANK), CHEMICAL ENGINEERING. *Current Pos:* From asst prof to assoc prof chem eng, 57-66, chmn dept chem & petrol eng, 64-70, PROF CHEM ENG, UNIV KANS, 66- *Personal Data:* b San Antonio, Tex, Apr 4, 29; m 51; c 3. *Educ:* Rice Inst Technol, BS, 49, PhD, 58. *Mem:* Am Chem Soc; Am Inst Chem Engrs. *Res:* Rate processes. *Mailing Add:* Dept Chem & Petrol Eng Univ Kans 4006 Learned Hall Lawrence KS 66045-0501

ROSSON, REINHARDT ARTHUR, BIOTECHNOLOGY & TECHNOLOGY TRANSFER, MICROBIOLOGY & MOLECULAR BIOLOGY. *Current Pos:* DIR, RES DIAG & BIOSCI, 91-; DIR, TECHNOL TRANSFER, 96- *Personal Data:* b Santa Monica, Calif, Oct 5, 49; m 96, LuAnn L Sheldon; c Sara L. *Educ:* Univ Calif, Los Angeles, AB, 71, PhD(microbiol), 78. *Prof Exp:* Res biologist, Scripps Inst Oceanog, 78-81; asst prof marine microbiol, Dept Marine Studies, Marine Sci Inst, Univ Tex, Austin, 81- *Mem:* AAAS; Am Soc Microbiol. *Res:* Homologous and heterologous gene expression in support of fermentation process development programs; bioluminescent biosensors for the rapid detection of chemicals and compounds; new technology assessment, technology transfer, and licensing. *Mailing Add:* 1035 S Seventh St Manitowoc WI 54220. *Fax:* 920-684-5519; *E-Mail:* rrosson@biotechnicalresources.com

ROSSOTTI, CHARLES OSSOLA, COMPUTER ENGINEERING. *Current Pos:* PRES, AM MGT SYSTS INC, VA, 70-, CHIEF EXEC OFFICER, 81-, CHMN BD, 89- *Personal Data:* b New York, NY, Jan 17, 41; m 63, Barbara J Margulies; c Allegra J & Edward C. *Educ:* Georgetown Univ, AB, 62; Harvard Univ, MBA, 74. *Prof Exp:* Mgt consult, Boston Consult Group, 64-65; prin dep asst secy, Off Syst Anal, Dept Defense, Washington, 65-70, Defense Off Syst Anal, 69-70. *Concurrent Pos:* Bd dirs, Index Tech Inc, Sovran Bank, Caterair Int, Nations Bank Va & Georgetown Univ, 69-77 & 92- *Res:* Computers. *Mailing Add:* 3314 N St NW Washington DC 20007

ROSSOW, PETER WILLIAM, CELL CYCLE REGULATION, HORMONE ACTION. *Current Pos:* PRES, BOFFIN RESOURCES, 88- *Personal Data:* b Los Angeles, Calif, Dec 10, 48. *Educ:* Mass Inst Technol, SB, 71; Harvard Univ, PhD(microbiol & molecular genetics), 76. *Prof Exp:* Fel pharmacol, Med Sch, Harvard Univ, 75-79; res assoc, Sidney Farber Cancer Inst, 79-80; assoc staff scientist, Jackson Lab, 80-84; res assoc prof, Univ Paris, France, 84-86; staff scientist, Inst Med Res, San Jose, Calif, 86-87. *Concurrent Pos:* Coop prof zool, Univ Maine, Orono, 81- *Mem:* Am Soc Cell Biol; AAAS; NY Acad Sci. *Res:* Hormonal regulation of normal cell growth and the earliest events in the acquisition of the malignant phenotype in model cell culture systems. *Mailing Add:* 224 Hollister Ave Rutherford NJ 07070

ROSSOW, VERNON J, AERONAUTICS & ASTRONAUTIC ENGINEERING. *Current Pos:* Res scientist, 49-70, SR SCIENTIST, AMES RES CTR, NASA, MOFFETT FIELD, 70- *Personal Data:* b Danbury, Iowa, July 22, 26; m 48, Ruth E Hartwell; c Ellen, Elise, Matthew & Heidi. *Educ:* Iowa State Col, BS, 47; Univ Mich, MS, 49; Swiss Fed Inst Technol, DrTechSci, 57. *Concurrent Pos:* Nat res counc fel, 51-52; mem res adv comt fluid mech, NASA, 63-69. *Mem:* Am Helicopter Soc; Am Geophys Union; assoc fel Am Inst Aeronaut & Astronaut; Am Meteorol Soc. *Res:* Aerodynamics; author of over 70 research papers in fluid mechanics and granted three patents. *Mailing Add:* NASA Ames Res Ctr Mail Stop N247-2 Moffett Field CA 94035-1000

ROST, ERNEST STEPHAN, nuclear physics; deceased, see previous edition for last biography

ROST, THOMAS LOWELL, STRUCTURE & DEVELOPMENT OF ROOTS. *Current Pos:* From asst prof to prof, 72-88, fac asst chancellor, 81-82, chmn, Sect Plant Biol, 94-96, PROF BOT, UNIV CALIF, DAVIS, 83-, ASSOC DEAN, DIV BIOL SCI, 96- *Personal Data:* b St Paul, Minn, Dec 28, 41; m 63, Ann M Ruhland; c Christopher, Timothy & Jacquelyn. *Educ:* St John's Univ, BS, 63; Mankato State Univ, MA, 65; Iowa State Univ, PhD(bot), 71. *Concurrent Pos:* Co-ed, Mech & Control Cell Div, 77; vis fel, Australia Nat Univ, Canberra, 79-80; consult, Food & Agr Org, Univ Uruguay, 79; vis prof, Univ Wroclaw, Wroclaw, Poland, 88, Fac Sci, Univ Uruguay, 89, Univ Exeter, UK, 93. *Mem:* Sigma Xi; Bot Soc Am; Am Inst Biol Sci; Soc Exp Biol. *Res:* The cell cycle in root meristems and the effects of stress factors on structure and development; structure and development of root meristems. *Mailing Add:* Sect Plant Biol Univ Calif Davis CA 95616-8537

ROST, WILLIAM JOSEPH, ORGANIC CHEMISTRY, PHARMACOLOGY. *Current Pos:* RETIRED. *Personal Data:* b Fargo, NDak, Dec 8, 26; m 51; c 3. *Educ:* Univ Minn, BS, 48, PhD(pharmaceut chem), 52. *Prof Exp:* From asst prof to prof pharmaceut chem, Univ Mo-Kansas City, 52-89. *Mem:* Am Chem Soc; Am Pharmaceut Asn. *Res:* Synthesis of chemicals that have possible medicinal activity. *Mailing Add:* 709 W 115th Terr Kansas City MO 64114-5597

ROSTAMIAN, ROUBEN, APPLIED MATHEMATICS. *Current Pos:* assoc prof, 85-87, PROF MATH, UNIV MD, 87-, CHMN, 94- *Personal Data:* b Tehran, Iran, Oct 27, 49. *Educ:* Arya-Mehr Univ, Tehran, BS, 72; Brown Univ, PhD(appl math), 78. *Prof Exp:* Asst prof, Purdue Univ, 77-81; asst prof math, Pa State Univ, 81-83, assoc prof, 83-85; prog dir, NSF, 91-93. *Res:* Qualitative study of solutions of degenerate parabolic equations; asymptotic behavior of solutions in large time; linear and nonlinear elasticity, existence of solutions for problems with internal constraints. *Mailing Add:* Dept Math Univ MD Baltimore MD 21228

ROSTENBACH, ROYAL E(DWIN), CHEMISTRY, ENGINEERING. *Current Pos:* CONSULT, 89- *Personal Data:* b Buffalo, Iowa, Sept 20, 12; m 40. *Educ:* St Ambrose Col, BS, 35; Univ Iowa, MS, 37, PhD(chem, eng), 39. *Prof Exp:* Asst chem, Cath Univ, 35-36; sanit eng, Univ Iowa, 37-39; consult engr, Clark, Stewart & Wood Co, 39-40; chem & pub health engr, USPHS, 40-42; engr, Chem Div, US War Prod Bd, 42-43; chief, Copolymer Br, Off Rubber Reserve, Reconstruct Finance Corp, 43-53; sr engr & specialist, Hanford Atomic Prod Oper, Gen Elec Co, 53-59; sr proj engr, Bendix Aviation Corp, 59-60; res dir, Mast Develop Co, 60-61; prog dir, Div Eng, NSF, 62-88. *Mem:* Am Chem Soc; fel Am Inst Chem; Am Inst Chem Engrs; Water Environ Fedn; Am Nuclear Soc; Health Physics Soc. *Res:* Chemical, environmental, energy and nuclear engineering. *Mailing Add:* 6111 Wiscasset Rd Bethesda MD 20816-2119

ROSTOKER, GORDON, SPACE PHYSICS. *Current Pos:* from asst prof physics to assoc prof, 68-79, PROF PHYSICS, UNIV ALTA, 79-, DIR, INST EARTH & PLANETARY PHYSICS, 85- *Personal Data:* b Toronto, Ont, July 15, 40; m 66; c 3. *Educ:* Univ Toronto, BSc, 62, MA, 63; Univ BC, PhD(geophys), 66. *Honors & Awards:* E W R Steacie Prize, 79. *Prof Exp:* Nat Res Coun Can fel space physics, Royal Inst Technol, Sweden, 66-68. *Concurrent Pos:* Int Union Geod & Geophys appointee, Steering Comt, Int Magnetospheric Study, 73-79; mem grant selection comt space & astron, Nat Res Coun Can, 73-76, chmn, 75-76, mem assoc comt space res, 75-80; Nat Res Coun Can travel fel, 74; ed, Can J Phys, 80-86; McCalla prof, Univ Alberta, 83-84; chmn steering comt, Scostep, Solar-Terr Energy Prog, 88-; mem, Nat Sci Eng Res Coun Can Phys & Astron Comt, 88- & Grant Selection Comt Sci Publ, 88- *Mem:* Am Geophys Union; Can Asn Physicist. *Res:* Study of the solar-terrestrial interaction, with emphasis on the investigation of magnetospheric substorms and magnetosphere-ionosphere coupling using magnetometer arrays and satellite data. *Mailing Add:* Dept Physics Univ Alta Edmonton AB T6G 2M7 Can

ROSTOKER, NORMAN, PHYSICS. *Current Pos:* PROF PHYSICS, UNIV CALIF, IRVINE, 73- *Personal Data:* b Toronto, Ont, Aug 16, 25; m 48; c 2. *Educ:* Univ Toronto, BASc, 46, MA, 47; Carnegie Inst Technol, DSc(physics of solids), 50. *Prof Exp:* Res physicist, Carnegie Inst Technol, 48-53, Armour Res Found, 53-56 & Gen Atomic Div, Gen Dynamics Corp, 56-62; prof physics, Univ Calif, San Diego, 62-65; res physicist, Gen Atomic Div, Gen Dynamics Corp, 65-67; IBM prof eng, Cornell Univ, 67-73, chmn, Dept Appl Physics, 67-70. *Mem:* Fel Am Phys Soc. *Res:* Band theory; design of fission reactors; plasma physics; controlled thermonuclear research; intense electron beams. *Mailing Add:* Dept Physics Univ Calif Irvine CA 92697

ROSTOKER, WILLIAM, metallurgy, biomaterials; deceased, see previous edition for last biography

ROSTOW, WALT WHITMAN, ECONOMICS. *Current Pos:* REX G BAKER JR PROF POLIT ECON, DEPTS ECON & HIST, UNIV TEX. *Personal Data:* b New York, NY, Oct 7, 16; m 47, Elspeth V Davies; c Peter V & Ann (Larner). *Educ:* Yale Univ, BA, 36, PhD, 40. *Honors & Awards:* Outstanding Work in Soc Scis Award, Asn Am Pubis, 90. *Prof Exp:* Instr econ, Columbia Univ, 40-41; asst chief, Ger-Austrian Econ Div, Dept State, 45-46, coun, 61-66; Harmsworth prof Am hist, Oxford Univ, Eng, 46-47; asst to exec secy, Econ Comn Europe, 47-49; Pitt prof Am hist, Cambridge Univ, Eng, 49-50; prof econ hist, Mass Inst Technol, 50-60; staff, Ctr Inst Studies, 51-60; dep spec asst to Pres nat security affairs, 61, spec asst to Pres, 66-69; US rep ambassador, Inter-Am Comt Alliance for Progress, 64-66. *Mem:* Am Acad Arts & Scis; Am Philos Soc. *Res:* Author of numerous publications. *Mailing Add:* 1 Wildwind Pt Austin TX 78746-2434

ROSWELL, DAVID FREDERICK, CHEMISTRY. *Current Pos:* From asst prof to assoc prof, 68-74, PROF CHEM, LOYOLA COL, MD, 74-, DEAN, COL ARTS & SCI, 80- *Personal Data:* b Evansville, Ind, Dec 5, 42; m 65; c 2. *Educ:* Johns Hopkins Univ, AB, 64, PhD(chem), 68; Loyola Col, MBA, 85. *Honors & Awards:* Md Chemist Award, 86. *Concurrent Pos:* Cottrell Res Corp grant, Loyola Col, 69-70; res scientist, Johns Hopkins Univ, 71- *Mem:* Am Chem Soc; Am Inst Chem. *Res:* Chemiluminescence; photochemistry; biochemistry. *Mailing Add:* Dean Arts & Sci Col Arts & Sci Loyola Col Baltimore MD 21210

ROSZEL, JEFFIE FISHER, CYTOPATHOLOGY, VETERINARY PATHOLOGY. *Current Pos:* RETIRED. *Personal Data:* b Amarillo, Tex, Apr 5, 26; m 49; c 1. *Educ:* Univ Pa, VMD, 63; Okla State Univ, PhD(comp path), 75. *Prof Exp:* NIH fel, Hahnemann Med Col & Hosp, 63-65; from instr to asst prof path, Sch Vet Med, Univ Pa, 65-70; vis prof, Okla State Univ, 71-72, from asst prof to prof path, Col Vet Med, 72-92. *Concurrent Pos:* Res assoc, Hahnemann Med Col & Hosp, 66-68; lectr path, Philadelphia Col Pharm & Sci, 68-70; mem vet med rev comt, Bur Health Manpower Educ, NIH, 72 & co-prin investr, Registry Canine & Feline Neoplasms, 72-78. *Mem:* Am Soc Cytol; Vet Cancer Soc. *Res:* Comparative cytopathology of neoplasms. *Mailing Add:* Dept Anat & Pharmacol 250 Vet Med Bldg Okla State Univ Stillwater OK 74078-2007

ROSZKOWSKI, ADOLPH PETER, PHARMACOLOGY. *Current Pos:* RETIRED. *Personal Data:* b Chicago, Ill, July 27, 28; m 51, Delores Rose Kay; c 4. *Educ:* DePaul Univ, BS, 51, MS, 54; Loyola Univ, PhD(pharmacol), 56. *Honors & Awards:* Johnson Medal Award, 65. *Prof Exp:* Mem staff, Dept Pharmacol, G D Searle & Co, 52-53; asst dir biol res, McNeil Labs, Inc, Div Johnson & Johnson, 57-66; head pharmacol, Kendall Res Ctr, Ill, 66-67; dir dept pharmacol & asst dir inst clin med, Syntex Corp, 67-77, vpres, 81-87, dir, Inst Exp Pharmacol, 77-89. *Concurrent Pos:* McNeil fel, Univ Pa, 56-57; instr, Sch Med, Temple Univ, 57-64; lectr, Sch Med, Stanford Univ, 75-79. *Mem:* AAAS; Am Soc Pharmacol & Exp Therapeut; Am Soc Clin Pharmacol & Therapeut; Soc Toxicol. *Res:* Psychopharmacology; autonomic pharmacology; gastrointestinal pharmacology. *Mailing Add:* 15060 Sobey Rd Saratoga CA 95070-6237

ROTA, GIAN-CARLO, MATHEMATICS. *Current Pos:* prof math, 67-74, PROF APPL MATH & PHILOS, MASS INST TECHNOL, 74- *Personal Data:* b Italy, Apr 27, 32; nat US; div. *Educ:* Princeton Univ, BA, 53; Yale Univ, MA, 54, PhD(math), 56. *Hon Degrees:* DSc, Univ Strasbourg, France, 84; Univ L'Aquild, Italy, 90. *Honors & Awards:* Hedrick Lectr, Am Math Asn, 67; Taft Lectr, Univ Cincinnati, 71; Hardy Lectr, London Math Soc, 73; Steele Prize, Am Math Soc, 89. *Prof Exp:* Fel, Courant Inst Math Sci, NY Univ, 56-57; Benjamin Pierce instr math, Harvard Univ, 57-59; from asst prof to assoc prof, Mass Inst Technol, 59-65; prof, Rockefeller Univ, 65-67. *Concurrent Pos:* Sloan fel, 62-64; consult, Los Alamos Nat Lab, 63-71, Rand Corp, 64-71; mem comt math adv, Off Naval Res, 63-67; ed-in-chief, Advan in Math, 68-; vis prof, Univ Colo, 69-80; ed, Studies Appl Math, 70-, J Math Anal & Applns; Andre Aisenstadt vis prof, Univ Montreal, 71; fel, Los Alamos Sci Lab, 71-; chmn, Math Sect, AAAS, 88. *Mem:* Nat Acad Sci; Am Math Soc; fel Academia Argentina de Ciencias; Soc Indust & Appl Math (vpres, 75); fel Inst Math Statist; fel AAAS; fel Am Acad Arts & Sci. *Res:* Combinatorial theory; probability; phenomenology. *Mailing Add:* 1105 Massachusetts Ave Apt 8F Cambridge MA 02138-5217. *Fax:* 617-547-4882; *E-Mail:* rota@math.mit.edu

ROTAR, PETER P, CROP BREEDING, CYTOGENETICS. *Current Pos:* RETIRED. *Personal Data:* b Omaha, Nebr, June 9, 29; m 56; c 4. *Educ:* Washington State Univ, BSc, 54, MSc, 57; Univ Nebr, PhD(agron), 60. *Prof Exp:* Asst prof biol, Salve Regina Col, 60-62; asst prof agron & asst agronomist, Univ Hawaii, 62-72, prof agron & agronomist, 72-, chmn, Dept Agron & Soil Sci, 76-85. *Concurrent Pos:* Vis prof, Univ Fla, Gainesville, 83; consult & agr expert, UN, 84 & 85. *Mem:* Crop Sci Soc Am; Am Soc Agron; Bot Soc Am; Sigma Xi. *Res:* Cytology; cytogenetics of tropical legumes and grasses used for forage and pasture; taxonomy of grasses; crop management. *Mailing Add:* 2314 Sleater-Kinney SE Lacey WA 98503

ROTARIU, GEORGE JULIAN, INSTRUMENTATION APPLICATION OF ISOTOPES TO INDUSTRY, COBALT SIXTY IRRADIATOR DESIGN. *Current Pos:* CONSULT, 84- *Personal Data:* b Los Angeles, Calif, Aug 24, 17; m 48, Janet McAuley; c Mark, Ann & William. *Educ:* Univ Chicago, BS, 39, MS, 40; Univ Ill, PhD(chem), 50. *Prof Exp:* Asst chem & pharmacol, Univ Chicago, 41-45; res chemist, Lever Bros Co, 45-46; instr phys sci, Univ Chicago, 46-48; asst phys chem, Univ Ill, 48-50; res assoc, Univ Calif, 50-52; asst prof phys chem, Loyola Univ, Ill, 52-55; dir inland testing labs & nuclear eng, Cook Elec Co, 55-57; dir, Nuclear Tech & Phys Chem, Booz-Allen Appl Res Inc, Ill, 57-62; chief, Anal & Appl Br, Div Isotopes Develop, US Atomic Energy Comn, 62-64, Chief Systs Eng Sect, Radiation Appl Br, 64-66, prog mgr, Process Radiation Staff, 66-72, Radiation Applications Br, Div Applications Technol, US Atomic Energy Comn, 72-73, prog mgr instrumentation, Div Biomed & Environ Res, US Energy Res & Develop Admin, 73-76, environ progs, Div Technol Assessments, 76- 82, environ protection scientist, Off Nuclear Safety, Off Environ Safety & Health, Dept Energy, 82-84. *Concurrent Pos:* US Rep Int Atomic Energy Agency Conf, Warsaw, Poland & panel, Cracow, Poland, 65 & Munich, 69; Comn Europ Communities Conf, Brussels, Belg, 71; sci consult, Inst Atomic Physics, Bucharest, Romania, 92; nuclear expert, Int Atomic Energy Agency Mission Romania, 93. *Mem:* Am Chem Soc; Am Nuclear Soc; Sigma Xi. *Res:* Nuclear radiation testing; nuclear radiation effects on materials; high altitude environments; environmental testing; lubricants; films and coatings; radioisotope applications in industry and; environmental assessments for magnetohydrodynamics, enhanced gas recovery, enhanced oil recovery and oil shale technologies; health physics appraisal of Department of Energy laboratories, and regulatory aspects; radiobioassay criteria; evaluation of nuclear public information/safety activities of Department of Energy facilities and of selected nuclear industry; design of megacurie cobalt-60 irradiators. *Mailing Add:* 4609 Woodfield Rd Bethesda MD 20814. *Fax:* 301-493-8442

ROTBLAT, JOSEPH, PHYSICS. *Current Pos:* lectr & sr lectr, Dept Physics, Univ London, 40-49, dir res, Nuclear Physics, 45-49, prof physics, St Bartholomew's Hosp Med Col, 50-76, EMER PROF, UNIV LONDON, 76- *Personal Data:* b Warsaw, Poland, Nov, 4, 08. *Hon Degrees:* Several from foreign univs. *Honors & Awards:* Nobel Peace Prize, 95; Albert Einstein Peace Prize, 92; Knight Comdr Order Merit, Ger Govt. *Prof Exp:* Res fel, Radiol Lab, Sci Soc Warsaw, 33-39; asst dir, Atomic Physics Inst, Free Univ, Poland, 37-39; Oliver Lodge fel, Univ Liverpool, 39-40. *Mem:* Fel Royal Soc; foreign hon mem Am Acad Sci; AAAS; foreign mem Czechoslovak Acad Sci; Polish Acad Sci; Brit Inst Radiol. *Mailing Add:* 8 Asmara Rd London NW2 3ST England

ROTELLA, FRANK, INORGANIC CHEMISTRY. *Current Pos:* Appointee, Sci Div, 78-81, INORG CHEM TECHNICIAN, IPNS DIV, ARGONNE NAT LAB, 81- *Personal Data:* b Chicago, Ill, June 2, 49. *Educ:* Univ Chicago, Loyola, BS, 72; Univ Ill, Chicago, MS, 74; State Univ NY, Buffalo, PhD(chem), 79. *Mem:* Am Chem Soc; Am Chem Asn; AAAS. *Mailing Add:* CMB Div Bldg 202 Argonne Nat Lab Argonne IL 60439

ROTELLO, VINCENT M, GENERAL CHEMISTRY, ORGANIC CHEMISTRY. *Current Pos:* ASST PROF, DEPT CHEM, UNIV MASS, AMHERST, 93- *Personal Data:* b Chicago, Ill, Nov 2, 64. *Educ:* Ill Inst Technol, BS, 85; Yale Univ, PhD(chem), 90. *Concurrent Pos:* NSF postdoctoral fel, Mass Inst Technol, 90-93; Cottrell scholar, Res Corp, 96. *Mem:* Am Chem Soc; AAAS; Electrochem Soc. *Mailing Add:* Dept Chem Univ Mass Amherst MA 01003. *Fax:* 413-545-4490; *E-Mail:* rotello@cisco.chem.umass.edu

ROTEM, CHAVA EVE, CARDIOLOGY, EXPERIMENTAL MEDICINE. *Current Pos:* RETIRED. *Personal Data:* b Jan 15, 28; wid; c 2. *Educ:* Univ Lausanne, cert bact, 50, MD, 52; MRCP(Edin), 58, MRCP(L), 58, FRCP(C), 68. *Prof Exp:* House officer pediat, Kantonsspital, Zurich, Switz, 52-53; sr house surgeon, Leicester Chest Unit, UK, 54-55, med registr, Leicester Isolation Hosp & Chest Unit, 55-59, sr med registr cardiol, Cardiac Invest Ctr, 59-60; consult physician, Scottish Mission Hosp, Nazareth, 60-61; cardiologist, NIH Surv Ischeamic & Hypertensive Heart Dis, Rambam Govt Hosp, Haifa, Israel, 62-63; res fel cardiol, Stanford Univ, 63-64; cardiologist, St Paul's Hosp, Vancouver, BC, 64-65; cardiologist, Shaughnessy Hosp, Vancouver, BC, 65-68, head, Div Cardiol, 78-82, In Chg Intensive Coronary Care Univ & Cardiac Catheterization Lab, 68-89; pvt pract, 93-96. *Concurrent Pos:* Physician, Rothschild Hadassa Munic Hosp, Haifa, 62-63. *Mem:* Can Cardiovasc Soc; Soc Microcirc; Israel Soc Cardiol; NY Acad Sci; fel Am Col Cardiol; NAm Soc Pacing & Electrophysiol. *Res:* Investigative cardiology; hydrodynamics of the great blood vessels, especially clinical applications; clinical investigation of new cardiac drugs. *Mailing Add:* Richmond Cardiol Suite 750 6091 Gilbert Rd Richmond BC B7C 5L9 Can

ROTENBERG, A DANIEL, MEDICAL PHYSICS. *Current Pos:* VPRES TECHNOL & DEVELOP, TEAMWORK ENTERPRISES, 91- *Personal Data:* b Toronto, Ont, July 21, 34; m 62; c 4. *Educ:* Univ Toronto, PhD(med biophys), 62. *Prof Exp:* Biophysicist, Montreal Gen Hosp, 63-66, physicist, 66-69; lectr therapeut radiol, Sch Med, McGill Univ, 69-71; head dept biomed physics & physicist, Jewish Gen Hosp, 69-77; asst prof diag radiol, Sch Med, McGill Univ, 70-77; dir res & develop, Coinamatic Inc, Montreal, 77-89. *Concurrent Pos:* Consult, Jewish Gen Hosp, 66-69, Queen Elizabeth Hosp, 68-, St Mary's Hosp, 68-, Reedy Mem Hosp, 69- & Etobicoke Gen Hosp, 72-; assoc scientist, Royal Victoria Hosp, 70- & Northwestern Gen Hosp, 74-; vpres, Beique, Rotenberg & Radford Inc, 66-80; dir, BRRCM Inc, 80- *Mem:* Soc Nuclear Med; Can Asn Physicists (secy-treas, 66-69); Asn Advan Med Instrumentation. *Res:* Hospital physics and instrumentation; microprocessor developments; laser photocoagulation; diagnostic radiology. *Mailing Add:* 54 Elmridge Dr Toronto ON M6B 1A4 Can

ROTENBERG, DON HARRIS, POLYMER CHEMISTRY, OPTICAL PLASTICS & COATINGS. *Current Pos:* PROCESS ENG MGR, SOLA OPTICAL, 96- *Personal Data:* b Portland, Ore, Mar 31, 34; m 58, Barbara Ress; c Laura & Debra. *Educ:* Univ Ore, BA, 55; Harvard Univ, AM, 56; Cornell Univ, PhD(org chem), 60. *Prof Exp:* Res chemist, Enjay Chem Intermediate Div, 60-67, sr res chemist, Enjay Polymer Lab, Esso Res & Eng Co, 67-71; mgr polymer sci & eng, Am Optical Co, 71-75, dir polymer res & develop, 75-78, dir, Mat Sci & Process Lab, 78-80, vpres, 80-85, vpres & gen mgr, Tech Div, Precision Prods, 85-88; tech dir, Coburn Optical Industs, 88-92; vpres res & develop, Neolens, Inc, 94-96. *Concurrent Pos:* Consult, Plastics Technol Assocs, 92- *Mem:* Am Chem Soc; Radtech; Sigma Xi; Soc Plastics Engrs. *Res:* Optical plastics, optical and abrasion resistant coatings, photochromic materials; polyethylene-propylene, butyl and chlorobutyl elastomers; engineering plastics; polyurethanes; chemical and polymer synthesis, analysis, characterization and physical properties; product and process development; contact, ophthalmic, and precision optical lenses and processes. *Mailing Add:* 4507 E 108th St S Tulsa OK 74137-6850. *Fax:* 305-651-5092

ROTENBERG, KEITH SAUL, PHARMACOKINETICS, BIOPHARMACEUTICS. *Current Pos:* SR DIR CORP LICENSING, SEARLE PHARMACEUT, 96- *Personal Data:* b San Francisco, Calif, Oct 10, 50; m 76; c 2. *Educ:* Univ Calif, Berkeley, BA, 72; Univ Md, PhD (pharmacokinetics & biopharmaceut), 77. *Prof Exp:* Reviewer & tech supvr, Div Bioavailability & Bioequivalence, Food & Drug Admin, 77-80; sect head biopharmaceut, Pennwalt Pharmaceut, 80-84, div dir sci info & regulatory affairs, 84-88; sr dir regulatory affairs, Lorex Pharmaceut, 88-96. *Mem:* Am Pharmaceut Asn; Acad Am Pharmaceut Asn; AAAS; Am Chem Soc. *Res:* Pharmacokinetics of nicotine in animals and man; pharmacokinetics and bioavailability of drugs in man; in vivo-in vitro correlations; formulation factors which affect a drugs bioavailability and in vitro dissolution. *Mailing Add:* Searle Pharmaceut 5200 Old Orchard Rd Skokie IL 60077-2900. *Fax:* 847-967-2097; *E-Mail:* ksrote@searle.monsanto.com

ROTENBERG, MANUEL, ATOMIC PHYSICS, BIOPHYSICS. *Current Pos:* RETIRED. *Personal Data:* b Toronto, Ont, Mar 12, 30; nat US; m 52; c 2. *Educ:* Mass Inst Technol, SB, 52, PhD(physics), 55. *Prof Exp:* Staff mem, Los Alamos Sci Lab, 55-57; instr physics, Princeton Univ, 57-58, staff mem, Proj Matterhorn, 58; asst prof physics, Univ Chicago & Inst Comput Res, 50-61; asst prof physics, Univ Calif, San Diego, 61-65, asst dir inst radiation physics & aerodyn, 65-67, assoc prof, 67-70, assoc dean grad studies & res, 71-75, dean grad studies & res, 75-83, chair, Dept Elec & Comput Eng, 88-93, prof appl physics, 70-92. *Concurrent Pos:* Co-ed, Methods Computational Physics, 63-77; founding co-ed, J Computational Physics, 64. *Mem:* Fel Am Phys Soc; Sigma Xi; AAAS. *Res:* Atomic theory; scattering theory; numerical techniques; population theory; cell kinetics. *Mailing Add:* Dept Elec & Comput Eng Univ Calif San Diego La Jolla CA 92093-0407

ROTENBERRY, JOHN THOMAS, AVIAN ECOLOGY, POPULATION & COMMUNITY ECOLOGY. *Current Pos:* DIR, NATURAL RESERVE SYST, UNIV CALIF-RIVERSIDE, 90- *Personal Data:* b Roanoke, Va. *Educ:* Univ Tex, Austin, BA, 69; Ore State Univ, MS, 74, PhD(ecol), 78. *Prof Exp:* Res assoc, Dept Biol, Univ NMex, 78-80; assoc prof, dept Biol Sci, Bowling Green State Univ, 80-90. *Mem:* Ecol Soc Am; Am Ornithologists Union; Am Soc Naturalists; Sigma Xi; Cooper Ornith Soc; Asn Field Ornithologists. *Res:* Animal-environment relationships, particularly their influence on population dynamics and community structure. *Mailing Add:* Dept Biol Univ Calif Riverside CA 92521

ROTERMUND, ALBERT J, JR, CELL BIOLOGY, CELL PHYSIOLOGY. *Current Pos:* asst prof, 70-76, ASSOC PROF BIOL, LOYOLA UNIV, CHICAGO, 77- *Personal Data:* b St Louis, Mo, June 20, 40; m 68, Carol Willson; c Mary, Thomas & Elisa. *Educ:* St Louis Univ, BS, 62, MS, 66; State Univ NY Buffalo, PhD(biol), 69. *Prof Exp:* NIH fel, Brookhaven Nat Lab, 68-70. *Mem:* Am Soc Zool; Sigma Xi; AAAS. *Res:* Cellular physiology and biochemistry; hibernation. *Mailing Add:* 407 E Burr Oak Dr Arlington Heights IL 60004-2125

ROTH, ALLAN CHARLES, SURGICAL RESEARCH. *Current Pos:* res asst prof & dir plastic surg res labs, 86-93, RES ASSOC PROF & DIR PLASTIC SURG RES LABS, DEPT SURG, DIV PLASTIC SURG, UNIV SOUTHERN ILL, SCH MED, 93- *Personal Data:* b St Joseph, Mo, Dec 23, 46; m 68, Penelope Grantham; c Sean & Heidi. *Educ:* Iowa State Univ, BS, 69, MS, 74, PhD(zool), 77. *Prof Exp:* Design engr, Oceans Syst & Los Angeles Div, Rockwell Int, 69-72; res assoc, Dept Physiol & Biophysics, Univ Wash Sch Med, 77-80; asst prof, Div Biomed Eng, Univ Va, Sch Eng & Appl Sci, 80-86. *Concurrent Pos:* Vis prof, Tech Univ, Munich, Ger, 90, Inst Environ Med, Univ Pa, 91, Microsurg Res Ctr, Eastern Va Med Sch, 91. *Mem:* Sigma Xi; Biomed Eng Soc; Inst Elec & Electronics Engrs. *Res:* Zoology (physiology). *Mailing Add:* Dept Surg Southern Ill Univ Sch Med 747 N Rutledge PO Box 19230 Springfield IL 62794-9230. *Fax:* 217-524-2588

ROTH, ARIEL A, BIOLOGICAL OCEANOGRAPHY, PALEONTOLOGY. *Current Pos:* chmn, Dept Biol, 63-73, PROF BIOL, LOMA LINDA UNIV, 63-, DIR, GEOSCI RES INST, 80- *Personal Data:* b Geneva, Switz, July 16, 27; nat US; m 52, Lenore Hardt; c Lawrence & John. *Educ:* Pac Union Col, BA, 48; Univ Mich, MS, 49, PhD(zool), 55. *Prof Exp:* From instr to assoc prof biol, Pac Union Col, 50-57; res assoc, Loma Linda Univ, 57-58; from assoc prof to prof biol & chmn dept, Andrews Univ, 58-63. *Concurrent Pos:* Mem, Geosci Res Inst, 73-; ed, Origins. *Mem:* Sigma Xi; Geol Soc Am; Soc Econ Paleontologists & Mineralogists; Am Asn Petrol Geologists. *Res:* Factors affecting rate of coral growth; parasitology; schistosomiasis; invertebrate zoology; coral reef development; identification of coral reefs; history and philosophy of science. *Mailing Add:* Geosci Res Inst Loma Linda Univ Loma Linda CA 92354. *Fax:* 909-824-4314

ROTH, ARTHUR JASON, MATHEMATICAL STATISTICS AS APPLIED TO DRUG STUDIES. *Current Pos:* MEM STAFF, G D SEARLE CORP, 88- *Personal Data:* b Brooklyn, NY, Oct 8, 49; m 72, Tammie B Davis; c Mark, Noah & Ari. *Educ:* Cornell Univ, BA, 71; Univ Minn, PhD(statist), 75. *Honors & Awards:* Best Presentation, Am Statist Asn, 92. *Prof Exp:* Asst prof statist, Carnegie-Mellon Univ, 75-77; asst prof math, Syracuse Univ, 77-80; mem staff, Ciba-Geigy Corp, 80-88. *Mem:* Inst Math Statist; Am Statist Asn. *Res:* Carcinogenecity testing, categorical data analysis, survival analysis, robust test for trend; group testing, particularly Bayesian and sequential aspects; sequential analysis; nonparametric statistics; ranking and selection problems; multiplicity adjustments. *Mailing Add:* 4155 Suffield Ct Skokie IL 60076. *Fax:* 847-982-4701; *E-Mail:* rotha@skcls.monsanto.com

ROTH, BARBARA, ORGANIC CHEMISTRY. *Current Pos:* RETIRED. *Personal Data:* b Milwaukee, Wis, June 9, 16. *Educ:* Beloit Col, BS, 37; Northwestern Univ, MS, 39, PhD(org chem), 41. *Prof Exp:* Lab asst, Northwestern Univ, 38-41; res chemist, Calco Chem Div, Am Cyanamid Co, 41-51; group leader keratin res, Toni Div, Gillette Co, 51-55; sr res chemist, Wellcome Res Labs, NY, 55-71, group leader, Burroughs Wellcome Co Inc, Res Triangle Park Inc, 71-86; adj prof, Chem Dept, Univ NC, Chapel Hill, 87-93. *Concurrent Pos:* Instr, Lake Forest Col, 40-41; adj prof, Sch Pharm, Univ NC, 71-86. *Mem:* Fel AAAS; Am Chem Soc; NY Acad Sci. *Res:* Pyrimidine and medicinal chemistry; synthetic organic chemistry. *Mailing Add:* 347 Carolina Meadows Villa Chapel Hill NC 27514

ROTH, BEN G, MATHEMATICS. *Current Pos:* From asst prof to assoc prof, 69-79, PROF MATH, UNIV WYO, 79- *Personal Data:* b Bloomington, Ill, Oct 5, 42; m 83; c 4. *Educ:* Occidental Col, AB, 64; Dartmouth Col, AM, 66, PhD(math), 69. *Mem:* Am Math Soc; Math Asn Am. *Res:* Spaces of continuous and differentiable functions; spaces of distributions; rigidity. *Mailing Add:* Dept Math Univ Wyo Laramie WY 82071-3036

ROTH, BENJAMIN, ELEMENTARY PARTICLE PHYSICS. *Current Pos:* from assoc prof to prof, 62-76, EMER PROF PHYSICS, BROOKLYN COL, 76- *Personal Data:* b New York, NY, Feb 6, 09; m 41; c 1. *Educ:* City Col New York, BS, 29; Columbia Univ, MA, 31; Polytech Inst Brooklyn, BEE, 47; Cornell Univ, PhD(physics), 51. *Prof Exp:* Instr physics, Univ Conn, 51-56; from asst prof to assoc prof, Okla State Univ, 57-61. *Mem:* Am Phys Soc. *Res:* Elementary particle physics. *Mailing Add:* 950 E 14th St Brooklyn NY 11230

ROTH, BERNARD, MECHANICAL ENGINEERING. *Current Pos:* from asst prof to assoc prof, 62-71, PROF MECH ENG, STANFORD UNIV, 71- *Personal Data:* b New York, NY, May 28, 33; m 55, Ruth Ochs; c Steven H & Elliot M. *Educ:* City Col New York, BS, 56; Columbia Univ, MS, 58, PhD(mech eng), 62. *Honors & Awards:* Melville Medal, Am Soc Mech Engrs, 67, Machine Design Award, 84; Joseph F Engleberger Award, 86. *Prof Exp:* Lectr mech eng, City Col New York, 56-58. *Concurrent Pos:* Consult, Atlantic Design Co, 57, Columbia Univ, 62-64, Int Bus Mach Corp, 64-67, Univ Neger, Israel, 73 & AEC, France, 76; prin investr, NSF Grants, 63-; vis prof, Technol Univ Delft, 68-69, Kanpur, India, 77, Shanghai, China, 79, Bangalore, India, 84 & Univ Paris, 91-92. *Mem:* Am Soc Mech Engrs; Int Fedn Theory Mach & Mechanisms (pres, 81-84). *Res:* Robotics; interpersonal relations; kinematics; numerical methods, especially computer aided design; machine design, especially analytical techniques. *Mailing Add:* Dept Mech Eng Stanford Univ Stanford CA 94305

ROTH, BRADLEY JOHN, BIOELECTRIC & BIOMAGNETIC PHENOMENA. *Current Pos:* STAFF MEM, DEPT PHYSICS & ASTRON, VANDERBILT UNIV, 96- *Personal Data:* b Clinton, Iowa, Aug 15, 60; m 85, Shirley S Oyog; c Stephanie A & Katherine J. *Educ:* Univ Kans, Lawrence, BS, 82; Vanderbilt Univ, MS, 85, PhD(physics), 87. *Prof Exp:* Res assoc, Living State Physics Group, Dept Physics & Astron, Vanderbilt Univ, 87-88; from staff fel to sr staff fel, Mech Eng Sect, Biomed Eng & Instrumentation Prog, NIH, 88-96. *Concurrent Pos:* Res fel, Am Heart Asn, Tenn, 87-88. *Mem:* Am Phys Soc. *Res:* Biomagnetism; magnetic stimulation; cardiac electrophysiology; EEG analysis; mathematical modeling; computer simulation. *Mailing Add:* Dept Physics & Astron Vanderbilt Univ Box 1807 Sta B Nashville TN 37235. *Fax:* 301-496-6608; *E-Mail:* roth@helix.nih.gov

ROTH, CHARLES, APPLIED MATHEMATICS, THEORETICAL PHYSICS. *Current Pos:* from asst prof to assoc prof, 65-83, PROF MATH, MCGILL UNIV, 83- *Personal Data:* b Huncovce, Czech, Dec 25, 39; Can citizen; m 63; c 2. *Educ:* McGill Univ, BSc, 61, MSc, 62; Hebrew Univ, Israel, PhD(theoret physics), 65. *Prof Exp:* Lectr math & physics, Hebrew Univ, Israel, 63-65. *Mem:* Can Math Cong. *Res:* Applications of group representations and irreducible tensorial sets to atomic and nuclear spectroscopy. *Mailing Add:* Dept Math & Statist McGill Univ Burnside Hall 805 Sherbrooke St W Rm 1005 Montreal PQ H3A 2K6 Can

ROTH, CHARLES BARRON, SOIL CHEMISTRY, MINERALOGY. *Current Pos:* Res assoc, 68-70, from asst prof to assoc prof, 70-85, PROF SOIL CHEM & MINERAL, PURDUE UNIV, 85- *Personal Data:* b Columbia, Mo, Apr 27, 42; m 64, Roberta J Smith; c Bethany L & Christopher B. *Educ:* Univ Mo, BS, 63, MS, 65; Univ Wis, PhD(soil sci), 69. *Concurrent Pos:* Vis assoc prof, Tex A&M Univ, 78-79; vis prof & consult, Univ Nebr, Lincoln, 90; Oak Ridge Inst Sci & Educ fel, US Environ Protection Agency, Athens, Ga, 95. *Mem:* Am Soc Agron; Int Asn Study Clays; Soil Sci Soc Am; Int Soc Soil Sci; Mineral Soc Am; Clay Mineral Soc. *Res:* Physical and chemical effects of iron, aluminum and silica sesquioxides on the physicochemical properties of soils and clays; redox reactions of iron in clay mineral structures; prediction of soil erosion from reclaimed minelands; infrared analysis of water and organic compound interaction with soils and clays. *Mailing Add:* Dept Agron Purdue Univ West Lafayette IN 47907-1150. *Fax:* 765-496-2926; *E-Mail:* roth@dept.agry.purdue.edu

ROTH, DONALD ALFRED, MEDICINE, NEPHROLOGY. *Current Pos:* RETIRED. *Personal Data:* b Slinger, Wis, July 31, 18; m 51, Marie Mercury; c Catherine, Charles, Joanne & Nancy. *Educ:* Univ Wis, PhD(chem), 44; Marquette Univ, MD, 52; Am Bd Internal Med, dipl, 63; Am Bd Nephrol, dipl, 76. *Prof Exp:* Asst chem, Univ Wis, 41-44, instr, 46-48; chief renal sect, Wood Vet Admin Hosp, 58-86; from instr to assoc prof med, Med Col Wis, 61-86, clin prof, 86-90, emer clin prof, 90-92. *Mem:* AMA; Am Diabetes Asn; Am Fedn Clin Res; Am Heart Asn; fel Am Col Physicians; Am Soc Nephrology; Int Soc Nephrology. *Res:* Renal disease; hemodialysis; hypertension, including retinal photography and ultrastructure of kidney. *Mailing Add:* 1620 Revere Dr Brookfield WI 53045

ROTH, ELDON SHERWOOD, GEOMORPHOLOGY. *Current Pos:* ASSOC PROF PHYSICS & DIR ENVIRON SCI, CTR EXCELLANCE EDUC, NORTHERN ARIZ UNIV, 69- *Personal Data:* b St Paul, Minn, Nov 7, 29; m 56. *Educ:* Univ Calif, Los Angeles, BA, 53; Univ Southern Calif, MS, 59, PhD(higher educ), 69. *Prof Exp:* Instr geol & chem, Barstow Col, 60-69. *Mem:* Geol Soc Am; Nat Asn Geol Teachers. *Res:* Local and regional geomorphology; delineation of geomorphic regions by quantitative means; adaptation of computer methods to geomorphic research; energy resources and utilization. *Mailing Add:* 822 Grand Canyon Ave Flagstaff AZ 86001

ROTH, GEORGE STANLEY, GERONTOLOGY, ENDOCRINOLOGY. *Current Pos:* staff fel, Geront Res Ctr, 72-76, RES BIOCHEMIST GERONT, NAT INST AGING, NIH, 76-, CHIEF, MOLECULAR PHYSIOL & GENETICS SECT, 84- *Personal Data:* b Honolulu, Hawaii, Aug 5, 46; m 72; c 2. *Educ:* Villanova Univ, BS, 68; Temple Univ, PhD(microbiol), 71. *Honors & Awards:* Ann Res Award, Am Aging Asn, 81; Sandoz Prize for Geront Res, 89; Third Age Award, Int Asn Geront, 89. *Prof Exp:* Asst microbiol, Sch Med, Temple Univ, 68-71; fel, biochem, Fels Res Inst, 71-72. *Concurrent Pos:* Res consult, George Washington Univ, 77-81; co-ed, Chem Rubber Co Press, 77-; ed, Neurobiol Aging, 80-85; exchange scientist, Nat Acad Sci, 77-80; Alpha Omega Alpha prof, Univ PR, 86; Sigma Chi Scholar in residence, Miami Univ, 89. *Mem:* Fel Geront Soc. *Res:* Effect of aging on hormone action; molecular mechanisms of aging. *Mailing Add:* Nat Inst Aging Hopkins Bayview Med Ctr Baltimore MD 21224. *Fax:* 410-558-8323

ROTH, GERALD J, MEDICINE. *Current Pos:* assoc prof, 84-89, PROF MED, UNIV WASH, SEATTLE, 89-; CHIEF, HEMAT SECT, SEATTLE VET ADMIN CTR, 84- *Personal Data:* b Winona, Minn, Apr 26, 41; c 5. *Educ:* Harvard Col, AB, 63; Harvard Med Sch, MD, 67; Am Bd Internal Med, dipl, 72, dipl hemat, 82. *Prof Exp:* Intern med, Univ Utah Hosp, 67-68, clin fel hemat, 70-71; resident med, Univ Wash Hosp, 68-70; res investr, US Army Med Res Lab, Ft Knox, Ky, 71-74; res fel hemat, Sch Med, Wash Univ, 74-76; from asst prof to assoc prof med, Sch Med, Univ Conn, 76-84. *Concurrent Pos:* Staff physician, Univ Conn Health Ctr, Farmington, 76-84; estab investr, Am Heart Asn, 81-86; mem ad hoc hematol study sect, NIH, 87, 88, 89 & 90, subcomt hemostasis, Am Soc Hemat, 84-87, Vascular Biol Burart Subcomt, Study Sect, Am Heart Asn, 90-93, subcomt on thrombosis, mem & chmn, 90-93, Vet Admin Med Res Serv, Am Soc Hemat, 91-94. *Mem:* Am Fedn Clin Res; Am Soc Hemat; Am Soc Biol Chemists; Am Heart Asn; Am Soc Clin Invest; AAAS; Int Soc Thrombosis & Hemostasis. *Res:* Internal medicine. *Mailing Add:* Dept Med Seattle Vet Admin Med Ctr 111 Med 1660 S Columbian Way Seattle WA 98108-1597. *Fax:* 206-764-2689

ROTH, HAROLD, SOLID STATE PHYSICS. *Current Pos:* DIR, PHILIPS LAB GEOPHYS DIRECTORATE, 93- *Personal Data:* b Wilkes-Barre, Pa, Jan 26, 31; m 52; c 3. *Educ:* Mass Inst Technol, BS, 52; Univ Pa, MS, 54, PhD(physics), 59. *Prof Exp:* Asst physics, Univ Pa, 53-54; res assoc, Gen Atomic Div, Gen Dynamics Corp, Calif, 56-59, staff scientist, 59; staff scientist, Raytheon Res Div, Mass, 59-63, prin scientist, 63-65; chief adv res br, Electronics Res Ctr, NASA, 65-68, chief electronic components lab, 68-70; dir res & advan develop, 70-73; dir res & eng, Electronics Div, Allen-Bradley Co, 73-81; dir, solid state sci directorate, Rome Air Develop Ctr, Hanscom AFB, Mass, 81-93. *Concurrent Pos:* Mem adv subcomt electrophys, NASA, 68-70; chmn, task force automotive solid state electronics, Soc Automotive Engrs & indust adv comt, Milwaukee Sch Eng. *Mem:* Am Phys Soc; Sigma Xi; Inst Elec & Electronics Engrs; Am Inst Physics. *Res:* Semiconductors; galvanomagnetic effects; radiation damage; electrical properties of junctions; passive electronic components; photonics. *Mailing Add:* 60 Mackintosh Ave Needham MA 02192-1238

ROTH, HAROLD PHILMORE, GASTROENTEROLOGY, EPIDEMIOLOGY. *Current Pos:* RETIRED. *Personal Data:* b Cleveland, Ohio, Aug 2, 15; m 52, Kelly C Rabinovitch; c Edward H & Anita A. *Educ:* Western Res Univ, BA, 36, MD, 39; Harvard Univ, MS, 67. *Honors & Awards:* Spec Recognition Award, Am Gastroenterol Asn, 84. *Prof Exp:* Intern, Cincinnati Gen Hosp, 39-40; house officer, Fifth Med Serv, Boston City Hosp, 40-42; asst resident med, Barnes Hosp, St Louis, Mo, 42-43; from clin instr to sr clin instr med, Case Western Res Univ, 49-55, from asst prof to assoc prof, 55-74, assoc prof community health, 71-74; assoc dir digestive dis & nutrit, NIH, 74-83, dir, 83-85, dir, Epidemiol & Data Syst Prog, Nat Inst Diabetes, Digestive & Kidney Dis, 85-91. *Concurrent Pos:* Asst med, Washington Univ, 42-43; chief, Gastroenterol Sect, Vet Admin Hosp, 47-74, dir, Gastroenterol Training Prog, Univ Hosps & Vet Admin, 63-74; asst physician, Out-Patient Dept, Univ Hosps, Cleveland, 49-69, assoc physician, Dept Med, 69-74; USPHS spec fel, Sch Pub Health, Harvard Univ, 66-67; mem, Digestive Dis Comt, USPHS, 74-; mem, Nat Comn Digestive Dis, 76-78 & Nat Digestive Dis Adv Bd, 80- *Mem:* Am Gastroenterol Asn; fel Am Col Physicians; Am Asn Study Liver Dis; Soc Clin Trials (pres, 78-80); Ctr Soc Clin Res. *Res:* Composition of bile and formation of gallstones; patient care, factors influencing patients' cooperation with medical regimens; clinical epidemiology of digestive diseases; esophageal spasm; peptic ulcer; gallstones; improving the medical record in the light of new technologies including the computer work with the committees of the Institute of Medicine and presentations to and through the Medical Records Institute. *Mailing Add:* 10319 Gary Rd Potomac MD 20854. *Fax:* 301-496-2830

ROTH, HEINZ DIETER, PHYSICAL ORGANIC CHEMISTRY. *Current Pos:* PROF CHEM, RUTGERS UNIV, 88- *Personal Data:* b Rheinhausen, Ger, Oct 25, 36; m 64; c 2. *Educ:* Univ Karlsruhe, BS, 58; Univ Cologne, MS, 62, Dr rer nat, 65. *Prof Exp:* Fel org chem, Yale Univ, 65-67; mem tech staff org chem, Bell Labs, 67-88. *Mem:* Am Chem Soc; Ger Chem Soc. *Res:* Reactivity and structure of carbenes, radicals and radical ions; photochemistry; chemically induced magnetic polarization; nuclear magnetic resonance; electron paramagnetic resonance. *Mailing Add:* Chem Rutgers Univ New Brunswick NJ 08903

ROTH, HOWARD, FOOD CHEMISTRY. *Current Pos:* CONSULT, 83-; DIR RES & DEVELOP, R F SCHIFFMANN ASSOC INC, 83- *Personal Data:* b New York, NY, Oct 11, 25; m 43, Judith M Gibberman; c Sally A & Daniel J. *Educ:* City Col New York, BS, 53. *Prof Exp:* Sr proj mgr, DCA Industs Inc, 53-75, assoc dir res & develop, Cent Res Lab, 75-77, dir Corp Res Ctr, 77-83. *Concurrent Pos:* Co-chair & tech dir, Microwave Concepts Inc, Yonkers, NY. *Mem:* Am Chem Soc; Am Oil Chem Soc; Int Microwave Power Inst (treas); Am Asn Cereal Chem. *Res:* Chemistry and physics of fats, oils and cereals; confectionary and bakery products; microwave applications; food product and machine development. *Mailing Add:* 206 Devoe Ave Yonkers NY 10705. *E-Mail:* rothh@aol.com

ROTH, IVAN LAMBERT, MICROBIOLOGY, ELECTRON MICROSCOPY. *Current Pos:* from assoc prof to prof, 66-93, EMER PROF MICROBIOL, UNIV GA, 93- *Personal Data:* b Nixon, Tex, Feb 21, 28; m 51, Charlotte Ulbrich; c Janet R (Clute) & Marc W. *Educ:* Tex Lutheran Col, BA, 50; Univ Tex, MA, 56; Baylor Univ, PhD(microbiol), 63. *Prof Exp:* Anal chemist, Texaco Inc, Tex, 51-54; instr biol, Univ Houston, 58-62; asst prof microbiol, Med Ctr, Univ Ala, 62-66. *Mem:* AAAS; Am Soc Microbiol; Micros Soc Am. *Res:* Ultrastructure of animal tissue infected with bacteria; bacterial virulence, avirulence and pathogenesis in animals; ultrastructure of microbial cells; ultrastructure of bacterial capsules and slime; scanning electron microscopy of slime molds (myxomycetes). *Mailing Add:* Dept Microbiol Univ Ga 821 Bio Sci Athens GA 30602. *Fax:* 706-542-2674

ROTH, J(OHN) REECE, INDUSTRIAL PLASMA ENGINEERING, FUSION ENERGY. *Current Pos:* PROF ELEC ENG, UNIV TENN, KNOXVILLE, 78- *Personal Data:* b Washington, Pa, Sept 19, 37; m 72, Helen M DeCrane; c John A & Nancy A. *Educ:* Mass Inst Technol, SB, 59; Cornell Univ, PhD(eng physics), 63. *Prof Exp:* Aerospace res scientist, Phys Sci Div, Lewis Res Ctr, NASA, 63-78. *Concurrent Pos:* Assoc ed, Trans Plasma Sci, Inst Elec & Electronics Engrs, 73-88; prin investr, Off Naval Res, Air Force Off Sci Res, Army Res Off & Tenn Valley Authority contracts, 80-95; mem, Comt Advan Fusion Power, Nat Acad Sci-Nat Res Coun, 87-88; hon prof, Univ Electronic Sci & Technol China, Chenpu, Sichuan Prov, Peoples Rebub of China, 92; mem, Admin Comt, Inst Elec & Electronics Engrs Nuclear & Plasma Sci Soc, 92-; distinguished lectr, Inst Elec & Electronics Engrs, 93-96. *Mem:* AAAS; Am Nuclear Soc; fel Inst Elec & Electronics Engrs; Am Phys Soc; assoc fel Am Inst Aeronaut & Astronaut; Am Soc Eng Educ; Am Vacuum Soc; Archaeol Inst Am; Sigma Xi. *Res:* High temperature plasma science related to controlled fusion; plasma cloaking of military radar targets; public policy issues in fusion energy; industrial plasma engineering; space applications of fusion energy; ball lightning; applications of atmospheric glow discharges to industrial plasma processing. *Mailing Add:* Dept Elec Eng Univ Tenn 409 Ferris Hall Knoxville TN 37996-2100. *Fax:* 423-974-5492; *E-Mail:* jrr@utk.edu

ROTH, JACK A, MOLECULAR BIOLOGY OF CANCER, ONCOGENES. *Current Pos:* PROF & CHMN, DEPT THORACIC SURG, UNIV TEX M D ANDERSON CANCER CTR, 86- *Personal Data:* b LaPorte, Ind, Jan 29, 45; c 2. *Educ:* Cornell Univ, Ithaca, BA, 67; Johns Hopkins Univ, MD, 71; Am Bd Surg, cert, 81; Am Bd Thoracic Surg, cert, 83. *Concurrent Pos:* Bud S Johnson chair & prof tumor biol, Univ Tex M D Anderson Cancer Ctr; NIH res grant, 87; mem, Esophageal Cancer Strategy Group, Nat Cancer Inst, NIH, 89 & prog comt, Am Soc Clin Oncol, 89-90; chmn, Task Force Acad Surg Oncol Specialties, Soc Surg Oncol, 90; Spec Achievement Award, US Dept Health & Human Serv, 81. *Mem:* Am Asn Cancer Res; Am Asn Immunologists; Am Asn Thoracic Surg; Am Surg Asn; NY Acad Sci. *Res:* Identifying the molecular events critical to the genesis and progression of thoracic cancers; developing technology for modifying expression of cancer genes for therapeutic application. *Mailing Add:* M D Anderson Cancer Ctr Univ Tex 1515 Holcombe Blvd Box 109 Houston TX 77030-4009. *Fax:* 713-794-4901

ROTH, JAMES, ENGINEERING. *Current Pos:* staff, 74-92, PRES & CHIEF EXEC OFFICER, GEN RES CORP, 92. *Personal Data:* b 1936. *Prof Exp:* Staff, Goodyear Aerospace, 59-65 & KMS Tech Ctr, 69-74. *Mailing Add:* Gen Res Corp 1900 Gallows Rd Vienna VA 22182-3865

ROTH, JAMES A, VETERINARY MICROBIOLOGY. *Current Pos:* from instr to assoc prof vet microbiol & prev med, 77-86, chmn, Interdept Prog Immunobiol, 84-87, PROF VET MICROBIOL & PREV MED, COL VET MED, IOWA STATE UNIV, 86-, PROF-IN-CHG, CTR IMMUNITY ENHANCEMENT DOMESTIC ANIMALS, 87- *Personal Data:* b Grinnell, Iowa, Mar 1, 51; m; c 3. *Educ:* Iowa State Univ, DVM, 75, MS, 79, PhD(vet microbiol), 81. *Honors & Awards:* Beecham Award, 86. *Prof Exp:* Vet, Belle Plaine, Iowa, 75-77. *Concurrent Pos:* Prin investr, Nat Cancer Inst, NIH, 89-84; interim chmn, Dept Vet Microbiol & Prev Med, Iowa State Univ, 90-91 & Dept Microbiol, Immunol & Prev Med, 91-; mem bd gov, Am Col Vet Microbiologists, 90-93; prog dir, Nat Inst Allergy & Infectious Dis, NIH, 90-95; proj dir, Agr Res Serv, USDA, 90-91; chmn, Sci Adv Bd, Biotechnol Res & Develop Corp, 91-; mem bd gov, Am Col Vet Microbiologists, 90-91. *Mem:* Am Vet Med Asn; Am Soc Microbiol; Am Asn Immunologists; Am Asn Vet Immunologists (pres, 89); Am Soc Animal Sci; Soc Leukocyte Biol; Am Col Vet Microbiologists. *Res:* Veterinary immunology; author of numerous technical publications; awarded one US patent. *Mailing Add:* Dept Vet Microbiol & Immunol & Prev Med Iowa State Univ Ames IA 50011-2010. *Fax:* 515-294-8500

ROTH, JAMES FRANK, PHYSICAL CHEMISTRY. *Current Pos:* RETIRED. *Personal Data:* b Rahway, NJ, Dec 7, 25; m 50; c 3. *Educ:* WVa Univ, BA, 47; Univ Md, PhD(chem), 52. *Honors & Awards:* E V Murphree Award in Indust & Eng Chem, Am Chem Soc, 76 & Award Indust Chem, 91; R J Kokes Award, Johns Hopkins Univ, 77; Perkin Medal, Soc Chem Indust, 88; Chem Pioneer Award, Am Inst Chem, 86. *Prof Exp:* Sr res chemist, Franklin Inst, 51-54; res chemist, Lehigh Paints & Chem Inc, 54-56 & Cent Res Lab, Gen Aniline & Film Corp, 56-59; mgr, Chem Br, Franklin Inst, 59-60; mgr catalysis res, Cent Res Dept, Monsanto Co, 60-69, mgr catalysis res, 69-73, dir catalysis res, 73-76, dir process sci, Corp Res Labs, 76-80; corp chief scientist, Air Prod & Chemicals, Inc, 80-90. *Mem:* Nat Acad Eng; Catalysis Soc NAm; Am Chem Soc. *Res:* Heterogeneous and homogeneous catalysis. *Mailing Add:* 5440 Eagles Point Circle 205 Sarasota FL 34231. *Fax:* 941-921-5832

ROTH, JAMES LUTHER AUMONT, GASTROENTEROLOGY. *Current Pos:* resident physician, Univ Hosp, 48-49, from instr to assoc gastroenterol, Div Grad Med, 50-54, asst prof physiol, 53-66, from asst prof to prof, 54-68, prof clin gastroenterol, 59-68, chief, Gastroenterol Serv & dir, Inst Gastroenterol, Presby-Univ Pa Med Ctr, 65-86, prof clin med, 68-86, EMER PROF, SCH MED, UNIV PA, 86- *Personal Data:* b Milwaukee, Wis, Mar 8, 17; m 38, 83, Mary A Burns; c Kristina, Lisa & Stephen. *Educ:* Carthage Col, BA, 38, Univ Ill, MA, 39; Northwestern Univ, MD, 44, PhD(physiol), 45; Am Bd Internal Med, dipl, 54; Am Bd Gastroenterol, dipl, 55. *Hon Degrees:* DSc, Carthage Col, 57; MSc, Univ Pa, 71. *Honors & Awards:* Bronze Medal, AMA, Sigma Xi Prize, Joseph Capps Award, Inst Med, Chicago, 44; Order of Christopher Columbus, Govt Dominican Repub, 69; Clin Achievement Award, Am Col Gastroenterologists, 89. *Prof Exp:* Instr physiol, Med Sch Northwestern Univ, 42-44; intern med, Mass Gen Hosp, 44-45; resident physician, Grad Hosp, Philadelphia, 45-46. *Concurrent Pos:* Res fel med, Grad Hosp, Philadelphia, 49-50; dir, Gastrointestinal Res Lab, Grad Hosp, 50-66, chief, Gastrointestinal Clin, 58-66; spec consult, Off Surgeon Gen, US Army, 48-49; mem adv comt rev, US Pharmacopeia XV, 50-60, 70-; exchange prof, Med Sch, Pontif Univ Javeriana, 60, prof extraordinary, 60-; dir grad div gastroenterol, Univ Pa, 61-69; consult, subcomt digestive syst, AMA, 62-64; mem drug efficacy panel, Food & Drug Admin, 66-68; consult, USN, Bethesda & Philadelphia Navy Hosps, 67-; mem bd dirs & chmn prog comt, Digestive Dis Found, 69-72; assoc ed, Bockus' Gastroenterol, ed, 4th ed; sr consult, Presby-Univ PA Med Ctr, 86-; James I A Roth vis prof, Presby Med Ctr, 91. *Mem:* AMA; Am Gastroenterol Asn; fel Am Col Physicians; Pan-Am Med Asn; Bockus Int Soc Gastroenterol (secy-gen, 58-67, vpres, 67-71, pres elect, 71-73, pres, 73-75); Am Col Gastroenterol (vpres, 81-82); hon mem Gastroenterol Socs of Venezuela, Colombia, Dominican Repub, Fla. *Res:* Intermediary metabolism of phenylalanine; caffeine potentiation of gastric secretion; caffeine gastric analysis; cold environment metabolic balances; penetration and hemorrhage in peptic ulcer; pancreatitis; hepatic coma; hazards of anti-cholinergic drugs; salicylate erosion and ulceration; ulcerative colitis. *Mailing Add:* 567 Hickory Lane Berwyn PA 19312

ROTH, JAY SANFORD, BIOCHEMISTRY. *Current Pos:* RETIRED. *Personal Data:* b New York, NY, June 10, 19; c 4. *Educ:* City Col New York, BS, 40; Cornell Univ, MS, 41; Purdue Univ, PhD(org chem), 44. *Prof Exp:* Asst, Purdue Univ, 41-44; asst prof chem, Univ Idaho, 44-47 & Rutgers Univ, 47-50; from asst prof to assoc prof biochem, Hahnemann Med Col, 50-60; prof biochem, Univ Conn, 60-92. *Concurrent Pos:* Brit-Am Cancer Res fel, Strangeways Res Lab, Cambridge, England, 53-54; assoc, Marine Biol Lab, Woods Hole; Nat Cancer Inst career fel, 62-; assoc ed, Cancer Res, 71-76. *Mem:* AAAS; Am Soc Biol Chem; Am Chem Soc; Am Asn Cancer Res. *Res:* Nucleic acids and nucleases in relation to cell division; control mechanisms in cancer; deoxynucleotide metabolism in growth; virus tumor biochemistry. *Mailing Add:* PO Box 692 Woods Hole MA 02543

ROTH, JEROME A, ORGANIC CHEMISTRY. *Current Pos:* from asst prof to assoc prof, 68-78, PROF CHEM, NORTHERN MICH UNIV, 78- *Personal Data:* b Springfield, Ill, Aug 13, 40; m 64; c 2. *Educ:* Loyola Univ, Ill, BS, 62; Ill Inst Technol, PhD(org chem), 66. *Prof Exp:* Assoc catalysis chem, Northwestern Univ, 66-67, instr org chem, 67-68. *Concurrent Pos:* Am Chem Soc res grant, 68-71; vis prof, Univ Cincinnati, 78-79. *Mem:* Am Chem Soc; Org Reactions Catalysis Soc. *Res:* Organic chemical synthesis; mechanisms; transition-metal organic chemical compounds; heterogeneous and homogeneous catalysis. *Mailing Add:* Dept Chem Northern Mich Univ Marquette MI 49855

ROTH, JEROME ALLAN, BIOCHEMISTRY, NEUROPHARMACOLOGY. *Current Pos:* from asst prof to assoc prof, 76-85, PROF, DEPT PHARMACOL & TOXICOL, STATE UNIV NY, BUFFALO, 85- *Personal Data:* b New York, NY, Aug 20, 43; m 85, Patricia R Kowal; c Rachel, Evan, Chrissy & Lyndsey. *Educ:* State Univ NY Col New Paltz, BS, 65; Cornell Univ, MNS, 67, PhD(biochem), 71. *Prof Exp:* Res assoc biochem, Vanderbilt Univ, 71-72; res assoc to asst prof anesthesiol, Sch Med, Yale Univ, 72-76. *Mem:* Int Soc Neurochem; Am Soc Pharmacol & Exp Therapeut; Am Soc Neurochem; Soc Neurosci. *Res:* Post-translational modification of proteins; mechanism of melatonin action; cellular mechanisms regulating manganose effect on cell differentation and toxicity. *Mailing Add:* Dept Pharmacol & Toxicol State Univ NY Buffalo NY 14214. *Fax:* 716-829-8201

ROTH, JESSE, GERIATRICS, ENDOCRINOLOGY. *Current Pos:* RAYMOND & ANNA LUBLIN PROF MED, SCH MED, JOHNS HOPKINS UNIV, DIR, DIV GERIAT MED & GERONT, JOHNS HOPKINS CTR AGING, 91- *Personal Data:* b New York, NY, Aug 5, 34; m 59, Susan Laufer; c Alisa, Alex & Alana. *Educ:* Columbia Univ, BA, 55; Albert Einstein Col Med, MD, 59. *Hon Degrees:* Dr, Univ Uppsala, 80, Univ Rome, 89. *Honors & Awards:* Eli Lilly Award, Am Diabetes Asn, 74, Renold Award, 93; Ernst Oppenheimer Mem Award, Endocrine Soc, 74; Spec Achievement Award, US Dept Health, Educ & Welfare, David Rumbough Mem Award, Juvenile Diabetes Found, 77; Regents' lectr, Univ Calif, 77; G Burroughs Mider Lectr, NIH, 78; Diaz Cristobal Prize, Int Diabetes Fedn, 79; Gairdner Found Ann Award, 80; A Cressy Morrison Award, NY Acad Sci, 80; Joslin Medal, New Eng Diabetes Asn, 81; Hazen Prize, Mt Sinai Sch Med, City Univ, 79; Banting Medal, Am Diabetes Asn, 82; Koch Award, Endocrine Soc, 85; Harvey Lectr, 82. *Prof Exp:* From intern to asst resident, Barnes Hosp, Wash Univ, 59-61; Am Diabetes Asn res fel, Radioisotope Serv, Vet Hosp, Bronx, NY, 61-63; clin assoc, NIH, 63-65, sr investr, 65-66, chief diabetes sect, Clin Endocrinol Br, 66-74, chief diabetes br, Nat Inst Arthritis, Metab & Digestive Dis, 74-83, dir, Div Intramural Res, Nat Inst Diabetes & Digestive & Kidney Dis, 83-91. *Concurrent Pos:* Sr fel, Brookdale Found; sci adv & gov, Weizmann Inst Sci, Israel; ed-in-chief, Diabetes & Metab Reviews; asst surgeon gen, USPHS, 85-91. *Mem:* Endocrine Soc; Am Diabetes Asn; Am Soc Clin Invest (pres, 78-80); Asn Am Physicians; Am Geriat Soc; Geront Soc Am; Am Acad Arts & Sci. *Res:* Genetic basis of late onset diseases; new treatments for diabetes, obesity, aging and their complications. *Mailing Add:* Johns Hopkins Bayview Med Ctr JHAAC 5-B-73 5502 Hopkins Bayview Circle Baltimore MD 21224. *Fax:* 410-550-2116

ROTH, JOHN AUSTIN, CHEMICAL ENGINEERING, ENVIRONMENTAL ENGINEERING. *Current Pos:* from asst prof to prof chem eng, Vanderbilt Univ, 62-74, from asst dean to assoc dean, Sch Eng, 68-72, chmn, Chem Fluid & Thermal Sci Div, 71-75, dir, Ctr Environ Qual Mgt, 74-80, PROF CHEM & ENVIRON ENG, VANDERBILT UNIV, 71- *Personal Data:* b Louisville, Ky, May 14, 34; m 59, Burns; c Suzan & John Jr. *Educ:* Univ Louisville, BChE, 56, MChE, 57, PhD(chem eng), 61. *Prof Exp:* Teaching asst chem eng, Univ Louisville, 56-59. *Concurrent Pos:* Year-in-indust partic, 76-68, Savannah River Lab, E I du Pont de Nemours & Co, Inc, Del, 66; comnr, Ky Bur Environ Protection, 77-78; chmn bd & vpres, Chem & Environ Serv, Inc, 86-; exec dir, Int Chem Oxidation Asn. *Mem:* Water Pollution Control Fedn; Am Inst Chem Engrs; Am Chem Soc; Nat Soc Prof Engrs. *Res:* Water and waste water treatment by ozonation; carbon adsorption; chemical engineering kinetics; mass transfer processes; hazardous materials; mixing processes. *Mailing Add:* Vanderbilt Univ P O Box 1574 Sta B Nashville TN 37235. *Fax:* 615-343-7951; *E-Mail:* jar@vuse.vanderbilt.edu

ROTH, JOHN L, JR, ANGIOSPERM EVOLUTION, PALYNOLOGY. *Current Pos:* BILINGUAL SCI TEACHER, HOLYOKE HIGH SCH, 87-; ADJ PROF BIOL, AM INT COL, SPRINGFIELD, MA, 91- *Personal Data:* b Trenton, NJ, July 5, 49; m 73, Delona Risner; c David, Daniel & Bethany. *Educ:* Brigham Young Univ, BS, 73, MS, 75; Ind Univ, MA, 79, PhD(bot), 81. *Prof Exp:* Vis lectr bot, Ind Univ, 80; res assoc bot, Univ Mass, Amherst, 81-87. *Mem:* Bot Soc Am; Am Soc Plant Taxonomists; Int Org Paleobot; AAAS. *Res:* Angiosperm evolution, systematics, paleobotany and palynology; foliar epidermal anatomy of Magnoliales, Laurales and various Jurassic-Eocene plants; palynology of primitive monocotyledohs living and fossil; paleoecology, foliar physiognomy, depositional selection of plant remains. *Mailing Add:* Holyoke High Sch 500 Beech St Holyoke MA 01040

ROTH, JOHN PAUL, COMPUTER SCIENCE, MATHEMATICS. *Current Pos:* CONSULT, 90- *Personal Data:* b Detroit, Mich, Dec 16, 22; div, Dorothy; c 2. *Educ:* Univ Detroit, BME, 46; Univ Mich, MS, 48, PhD(math), 54. *Honors & Awards:* NASA Award. *Prof Exp:* Instr math, Wayne State Univ, 46-47; res assoc appl math, Univ Mich, 47-53; Pierce instr math, Univ Calif, 53-55; staff mathematician, Inst Adv Study, 55-56; mem res staff, Thomas J Watson Res Ctr, IBM Corp, 56-90. *Concurrent Pos:* Res engr, Continental Aviation & Eng Corp, 46-47; consult, Shell Develop Co, 54-55; adj prof, City Univ New York, 81-82. *Mem:* Am Math Soc; Soc Indust & Appl Math; fel Inst Elec & Electronics Engrs. *Res:* Mathematical computer design; combinatorial topology, especially conceptual and practical use in the solution of physical problems. *Mailing Add:* 25-1 Woods Brooke Circle Ossining NY 10562

ROTH, JOHN R, SALMONELLA BACTERIA. *Current Pos:* chmn, Dept Biol, 89-93, PROF MICROBIOL, UNIV UTAH, 76-, DISTINGUISHED PROF BIOL. *Personal Data:* b Winona, Minn, Mar 14, 39; m 61; c 2. *Educ:* Harvard Univ, BA, 61; Johns Hopkins Univ, PhD, 65. *Honors & Awards:* Rosenblatt Prize, 90. *Prof Exp:* NIH fel, 65-67; from asst prof to prof, Univ Calif, Berkeley, 67-75. *Concurrent Pos:* Mem, Genetics Study Sect, NIH, 72-76, Microbiol Physiol & Genetics Study Sect, 83-87; Guggenheim fel, Col Spring Harbor Lab, 74-75; coordr, Grad Prog Molecular Biol, Univ Utah, 75-88. *Mem:* Nat Acad Sci; Genetics Soc Am; Am Soc Microbiol. *Res:* Genetic analysis of the Salmonella typhimurium bacterium; histidine-purine biosynthesis; chromosomal rearrangements; anaerobic metabolism. *Mailing Add:* Univ Utah 205 Life Sci Salt Lake City UT 84112. *Fax:* 801-585-6207; *E-Mail:* roth@bioscience.utah.edu

ROTH, JONATHAN NICHOLAS, PLANT PATHOLOGY, MARINE BIOLOGY. *Current Pos:* From asst prof to assoc prof, 62-70, PROF BIOL, GOSHEN COL, 70-, CHMN, DEPT BIOL, 80- *Personal Data:* b Albany, Ore, Mar 2, 38; m 59; c 3. *Educ:* Goshen Col, AB, 59; Ore State Univ, PhD(plant path), 62. *Concurrent Pos:* NIH fel, Inst Marine Sci, Miami, Fla, 64-65. *Mem:* Am Inst Biol Sci. *Res:* Phytopathology, mycology; marine algae; invertebrate zoology; development of temperature-independent substitute for agar-agar as a microbiological medium gelling agent. *Mailing Add:* Dept Biol Goshen Col 1700 S Main St Goshen IN 46526-4724

ROTH, KARL SEBASTIAN, BIOCHEMICAL GENETICS, PEDIATRIC METABOLISM. *Current Pos:* PROF PEDIAT, BIOCHEM & MOLECULAR BIOPHYS, MED COL VA, VA COMMONWEALTH UNIV, 81- *Personal Data:* b New York, NY, Mar 3, 41; m 84, Lydia C Noland; c Christopher G, Marcus A, Colin C & Alexander K. *Educ:* Univ Rochester, AB, 63; City Univ NY, MA, 65; Wake Forest Univ, MD, 69. *Prof Exp:* Asst prof pediat, Univ Pa, Sch Med, 76-81. *Concurrent Pos:* consult, State Newborn Screening Prog, Commonwealth Va, 82-; chair, Div Genetics, Endocrinol & Metab, Med Col Va, Va Commonwealth Univ, 82- *Mem:* Fel Am Pediat Soc; Am Soc Pediat Res; fel Fedn Am Socs Exp Biol; fel NY Acad Sci; fel Am Soc Clin Nutrit; fel Soc Inherited Metab Dis. *Res:* Study of the relationship between diabetes mellitus and heme metabolism in the nervous system. *Mailing Add:* Va Commonwealth Univ Med Col Va Box 239 MCV Sta Richmond VA 23298. *Fax:* 804-371-6455; *E-Mail:* ksroth@gems.vcu.edu

ROTH, LAURA MAURER, SOLID STATE PHYSICS. *Current Pos:* res prof sci & math, 73-77, PROF PHYSICS, STATE UNIV NY, ALBANY, 77- *Personal Data:* b Flushing, NY, Oct 11, 30; m 52; c 2. *Educ:* Swarthmore Col, BA, 52; Radcliffe Col, MA, 53, PhD(physics), 57. *Prof Exp:* Staff physicist, Lincoln Lab, Mass Inst Technol, 56-62; prof physics, Tufts Univ, 62-67; physicist, Res & Develop Ctr, Gen Elec Co, 67-72; Abby Rockefeller Mauze vis prof physics, Mass Inst Technol, 72-73. *Concurrent Pos:* Consult, Lincoln Lab, Mass Inst Technol, 62-67. *Mem:* Fel Am Phys Soc; Sigma Xi. *Res:* Band structure of solids; Bloch electrons in magnetic fields; magnetooptics; magnetism; liquid and amorphous metals. *Mailing Add:* 1270 Ruffner Rd Schenectady NY 12309-4601

ROTH, LAWRENCE MAX, PATHOLOGY, ELECTRON MICROSCOPY. *Current Pos:* assoc prof, 71-75, PROF PATH & DIR SURG PATH DIV, SCH MED, IND UNIV, INDIANAPOLIS, 75- *Personal Data:* b McAlester, Okla, June 25, 36; m 65; c 2. *Educ:* Vanderbilt Univ, BA, 57; Harvard Med Sch, MD, 60; Am Bd Path, dipl & cert anat path, 66, cert clin path, 68, cert dermatopath, 74. *Prof Exp:* Intern, Univ Ill Res & Educ Hosps, Chicago, 60-61; resident anat path, Barnes Hosp, St Louis, Mo, 61-63, resident surg path, 63-64; resident clin path, Univ Calif Med Ctr, San Francisco, 67-68; from asst prof to assoc prof path, Sch Med, Tulane Univ, 68-71. *Concurrent Pos:* Nat Inst Gen Med Sci sr res trainee, Hormone Lab, Karolinska Inst, Stockholm, Sweden, 64-65; asst path, Sch Med, Wash Univ, 61-64; series ed, Contemporary Issues Surg Pathol. *Mem:* Am Asn Path; Am Soc Clin Path; US & Can Acad Path Inc; Int Soc Gynec Pathologists; Arthur Purdy Stout Soc Surg Pathologists. *Res:* Gynecological and endocrine pathology; steroid chemistry; electron microscopy; ovarian tumors. *Mailing Add:* Dept Path Ind Univ Sch Med 550 N University Blvd UH 3465 Indianapolis IN 46202-5280

ROTH, LAWRENCE O(RVAL), AGRICULTURAL ENGINEERING. *Current Pos:* From instr to prof, 51-88, EMER PROF AGR ENG, OKLA STATE UNIV, 88- *Personal Data:* b Hillsboro, Wis, June 7, 28; m 54; c 2. *Educ:* Univ Wis, BS, 49 & 51; Okla State Univ, MS, 56, PhD(eng), 65. *Concurrent Pos:* Ford Found residency eng pract fel, 67-68. *Mem:* Am Soc Agr Eng; Am Soc Eng Educ; Weed Sci Soc Am; Nat Soc Prof Engrs. *Res:* Farm power and machinery; machine design and development for drift control of pesticides and mechanization of horticultural crop production. *Mailing Add:* 901 W Eskridge Stillwater OK 74075

ROTH, LEWIS FRANKLIN, FOREST PATHOLOGY, MYCOLOGY. *Current Pos:* from instr to assoc prof, 40-57, prof, 57-79, EMER PROF BOT & PLANT PATH, ORE STATE UNIV, 79-, CONSULT. *Personal Data:* b Poplar, Mont, Apr 12, 14; m 45, Evelyn Swaim; c Kathleen & Sara. *Educ:* Miami Univ, BA, 36; Univ Wis, PhD(plant path), 40. *Prof Exp:* Asst plant path, Univ Wis, 36-38. *Concurrent Pos:* Sci aide, Forest Prod Lab, US Forest Serv, 40, collab, 58- *Mem:* Fel Am Phytopath Soc; Mycol Soc Am; Soc Am Foresters. *Res:* Epidemiology; life history and control of forest diseases; root diseases; dwarf mistletoe; pine needle blight; aquatic fungi. *Mailing Add:* 4798 Becker Circle Albany OR 97321

ROTH, LINWOOD EVANS, CELL BIOLOGY, ELECTRON MICROSCOPY. *Current Pos:* vchancellor grad studies & res, 76-84, PROF CELL BIOL, UNIV TENN, KNOXVILLE, 76- *Personal Data:* b Ft Wayne, Ind, Mar 8, 29; m 49; c 2. *Educ:* Univ Ind, AB, 50; Northwestern Univ, MS, 55; Univ Chicago, PhD(zool), 57. *Prof Exp:* Electron microscopist, Med Sch, Univ Ind, 50-52; sr res technician, Div Biol & Med Res, Argonne Nat Lab, 52- 54, asst scientist, 54-60; from assoc prof to prof biochem & biophys, Iowa State Univ, 60-67, asst dean grad col, 62-67; prof biol & dir, div biol, Kans State Univ, 67-76. *Concurrent Pos:* Ed, Europ J Cell Biol, 74-; dir, Hungarian Exchange Prog, 84-; adv bd, Int Review Cytol. *Mem:* AAAS; Am Soc Cell Biol; Sigma Xi; Am Sci Affil; Electron Micros Soc Am. *Res:* Cell biology; analytical electron microscopy; nitrogen fixation in legumes; aluminum toxicity. *Mailing Add:* 507 Cherokee Blvd Knoxville TN 37919. *Fax:* 423-974-3100

ROTH, MARIE M, ORGANIC & GENERAL CHEMISTRY. *Current Pos:* RETIRED. *Personal Data:* b Boston, Mass, Apr 30, 26; m 51, Donald A; c Catherine, Charles, Joanne & Nancy. *Educ:* Mt Holyoke Col, BA, 45, MA, 47; Univ Wis, PhD(org chem), 52. *Prof Exp:* Res librn, Pittsburgh Plate Glass Co, 51-52; abstractor, Chem Abstr, 52-59; lectr, Univ Wis Ctr Syst, Waukesha County, 71 & 73, lectr gen chem, Washington County, 72-79, 86; lectr, Marquette Univ, 81-82, res assoc, 82-84. *Concurrent Pos:* Adj asst prof, Univ Wis-Milwaukee, 81. *Mem:* Am Chem Soc. *Res:* Heterocyclic compounds and synthesis of antimalarials; synthesis of steroid intermediates; trace solubility studies. *Mailing Add:* 1620 Revere Dr Brookfield WI 53045-2315. *E-Mail:* mmroth@omnifest.uwm.edu

ROTH, MARK A, OBJECT-ORIENTED DATABASES. *Current Pos:* from asst prof to assoc prof comput sci, Dept Elec & Comput Eng, Sch Eng, 83-93, DIR PLANS & OPERS, AIR FORCE INST TECHNOL, 93- *Personal Data:* b Elgin, Ill, Aug 12, 57; m 80, Cheryl E Pfaff; c David, Gary & Julie. *Educ:* Ill Inst Technol, BS, 78; Air Force Inst Technol, MS, 79; Univ Tex Austin, PhD(computer sci), 86. *Prof Exp:* Simulation systs developer, Computer Sci Div, Data Automation Directorate, Hq Air Univ, 80-83. *Mem:* Asn Comput Mach; Inst Elec & Electronics Engrs Comput Soc; Air Force Asn; Mil Opers Res Soc. *Res:* Database management systems; applications for non-traditional databases; computer-simulated wargames; integration of programming languages, software engineering, computer graphics and data base systems. *Mailing Add:* USS Trat Com/J673 901 S AC Blvd Suite 2B10 Offutt AFB NE 68113. *E-Mail:* mroth@afit.af.mil

ROTH, MICHAEL WILLIAM, APPLIED PHYSICS, NEURAL NETWORKS. *Current Pos:* sr physicist, 77-88, PRIN STAFF PHYSICIST, APPL PHYSICS LAB, JOHNS HOPKINS UNIV, 88- *Personal Data:* b Davenport, Iowa, June 30, 52; m 73. *Educ:* MacMurray Col, BA, 71; Univ Ill, Urbana, MS, 72, PhD(physics), 75. *Prof Exp:* Res assoc, Fermi Nat Accelerator Lab, 75-77. *Concurrent Pos:* Proj mgr, Appl Physics Lab, Johns Hopkins Univ, 80-83, sect supvr & proj dir, 81-83, lead eng, 83-86, mem, Adv Tech Subcomt Prog Rev Bd, 86-88, prin investr, 89-; Stuart S Janney fel, Johns Hopkins Univ, 87; tech expert, Technol Initiative Game, Naval War Col, 88; mem, Adv Bd Fels & Profs, Johns Hopkins Univ, 89-90, chair, 90-91; assoc ed, Trans Neural Networks, Inst Elec & Electronics Engrs, 89-90, ed-in-chief, 91-; mem, Neural Networks Coun Exec Comt, Inst Elec & Electronics Engrs, 91-; co-chair, Conf on Appln Artificial Neural Networks, Soc Photo-Optical Instrumentation Eng, 91. *Mem:* Am Asn Artificial Intelligence; Inst Elec & Electronics Engrs; Sigma Xi; Int Neural Network Soc; Soc Photo-Optical Instrumentation Eng. *Res:* Neural networks; systems analysis. *Mailing Add:* Appl Physics Lab Johns Hopkins Univ Johns Hopkins Rd Laurel MD 20707

ROTH, NILES, PHYSIOLOGICAL OPTICS, OPTOMETRY. *Current Pos:* RETIRED. *Personal Data:* b New York, NY, Sept 27, 25; m 52; c 3. *Educ:* Univ Calif, Berkeley, BS, 55, MOpt, 56, PhD(physiol optics), 61. *Prof Exp:* Asst res biophysicist, Univ Calif, Los Angeles, 61-69; from assoc prof to prof physiol optics, Col Optom, Pac Univ, 69-92. *Concurrent Pos:* Res grants, USPHS, 61-65, Am Cancer Soc, 66-67; consult, Long Beach Vet Admin Hosp, 61-69. *Mem:* AAAS; Am Optom Asn; Optical Soc Am; fel Am Acad Optom; Sigma Xi. *Res:* Factors affecting resting ocular refractive state and pupil size; psychophysical and photometric aspects of vision testing. *Mailing Add:* 2113 15th Ave Forest Grove OR 97116-2809

ROTH, NORMAN GILBERT, TECHNICAL MANAGEMENT. *Current Pos:* CONSULT, 91- *Personal Data:* b Chicago, Ill, Dec 11, 24; m 50; c 6. *Educ:* Univ Chicago, BS, 47; Univ Ill, MS, 49, PhD(bact), 51. *Prof Exp:* Bacteriologist, Ft Detrick, Md, 51-57; sr res bacteriologist, Whirlpool Corp, 57-60, dir life support, 60-73, waste mgt, 73-77, res & eng spec projs, 77-88, res & eng tech support, 88-91. *Res:* Aerospace life support, Gemini, Apollo, Skylab, Shuttle, Space Station; food, waste, water, sanitation management systems; microbial deterioration; appliance sanitation; psychrophilic bacteria; bacterial spores. *Mailing Add:* 1801 Briarcliff St Joseph MI 49085

ROTH, PAUL FREDERICK, COMPUTER SIMULATION LANGUAGES & APPLICATIONS. *Current Pos:* PRES PMR INC CONSULTS, 91- *Personal Data:* b Pittsburgh, Pa, Feb 9, 32. *Educ:* Univ Pittsburgh, BS, 53; Univ Pa, MS, 65. *Prof Exp:* Electronics engr, Bell Aircraft Corp, 53-54; develop engr, Goodyear Aircraft Corp, 55-57; mem sr staff engr, Bendix Corp, 57-60; advan systs engr, Gen Elec Co, 60-66; sr tech staff, Burroughs Corp, 66-72; comput scientist, Nat Bur Standards, US Dept Com, 72-79, chief, Div Comput, 80-82; oper res analyst, US Dept Energy, 79-80; assoc prof comput sci, Va Polytech Inst & State Univ, 82-87; assoc prof, Sarasota Eng Ctr, Univ SFla, 87-91. *Concurrent Pos:* Adj lectr comput sci, Villanova Univ, 65-68; adj prof, Univ Md, 75-77 & Va Polytech Inst & State Univ, 75-80; consult, Nat Acad Sci, 81-82. *Mem:* Asn Comput Mach. *Res:* Applications of simulation and modeling to network and computer performance evaluation; computer models for teaching computer science systems topics; computer simulation models of transportation systems. *Mailing Add:* PO Box 3104 Sarasota FL 34230

ROTH, PETER HANS, MICROPALEONTOLOGY, MARINE GEOLOGY. *Current Pos:* assoc prof, 75-82, PROF GEOL & GEOPHYS, UNIV UTAH, 82- *Personal Data:* b Zurich, Switz, June 25, 42; m 88, Ljubica M Nesovic; c Martin M, Stephanie A, Anna S & Barbara Y. *Educ:* Swiss Fed Inst Technol, Zurich, dipl, 65, PhD(geol), 71. *Honors & Awards:* Kern Prize, Swiss Fed Inst Technol, 70. *Prof Exp:* Asst res geologist, Scripps Inst Oceanog, 71-75. *Concurrent Pos:* Mem, Nat Acad Sci-Acad Sci USSR Exchange, 87; Fulbright Sr Scholar, Egypt, 95-96. *Mem:* Am Geophys Union; Oceanog Soc; Swiss Geol Soc; Am Asn Petrol Geologists. *Res:* Biostratigraphy, paleoecology and preservation of calcareous nannofossil; early diagenesis of deep-sea carbonates; paleoceanography. *Mailing Add:* Dept Geol & Geophys Univ Utah Salt Lake City UT 84112. *E-Mail:* phroth@mines.utah.edu

ROTH, RAYMOND EDWARD, STATISTICS. *Current Pos:* Archibald Granville Bush prof math, 68-84, EMER PROF MATH, ROLLINS COL, 84- *Personal Data:* b Rochester, NY, Oct 29, 18; wid; c Mary E (Bush), Patricia (Fischer), Katherine (McCullough), Jean & Joan (Harrington). *Educ:* St Bonaventure Univ, BS, 40, MS, 42; Rochester Univ, PhD(statist), 63. *Prof Exp:* Consult, Gen Elec Co, 43-46; res assoc, Univ Notre Dame, 46-47; asst prof physics, Univ Dayton, 47-49; physicist, Wright-Patterson Air Force Base, 49-50; res assoc, Atomic Energy Proj, Med Sch, Rochester Univ, 53-57; assoc prof math & head dept, St Bonaventure Univ, 58-63, prof & chmn dept, 63-66; prof statist & dir, Comput Ctr, Col Geneseo, State Univ NY, 66-68. *Concurrent Pos:* Vis staff, Med Sch & Math Dept, Univ Okla, 62-63; consult, Civil Aeromed Res Inst, Fed Aviation Agency, Oklahoma City, 62-63 & Med Div, Oak Ridge Inst Nuclear Studies, 64-65. *Mem:* Sigma Xi. *Res:* Flash burn effects; quantal response in a Latin square design of experiment; models. *Mailing Add:* 1261 Tippicanoe Trial Maitland FL 32751

ROTH, RENE ROMAIN, ANIMAL PHYSIOLOGY, HISTORY & PHILOSOPHY OF BIOLOGY. *Current Pos:* from asst prof to assoc prof, 78-93, EMER PROF ZOOL, UNIV WESTERN ONT, 93- *Personal Data:* b Timisoara, Romania, Feb 24, 28; Can citizen; m 61, Hanna Peysack; c Ramon, Roma & Rosana. *Educ:* Univ Cluj, MSc, 50; Univ Alta, PhD(comp endocrinol), 69. *Prof Exp:* Lectr bact, Inst Vet Med, Bucharest, Romania, 50-52; lectr zool & parasitol, Inst Vet Med, Arad, 52-56; res fel endocrinol, Univ Timisoara Hosp, 56-60 & Sch Med, Hebrew Univ, Israel, 60-62. *Concurrent Pos:* Hon lectr, Hist Med & Sci, Univ Western Ont, 85-89; mem exec comt, Can Soc Theoret Biol, 85-92. *Mem:* Hist Sci Soc; Can Soc Hist Philos Sci; NY Acad Sci; Int Soc Hist Philos Sociol Sci; Can Soc Endocrinol & Metab; Can Soc Theoret Biol. *Res:* Influence of light and temperature on gonad activity and nutrition in the red-back vole; effect of protein intake levels on reproduction and dietary self-selection in rats; theoretical biology; history of biology; comparative physiology of growth and nutrition. *Mailing Add:* Dept Zool Univ Western Ont London ON N6A 5B7 Can. *Fax:* 519-661-2014

ROTH, RICHARD FRANCIS, PHYSICS. *Current Pos:* RETIRED. *Personal Data:* b St Louis, Mo, Jan 18, 38; m 63; c 3. *Educ:* Rockhurst Col, BS, 59; Princeton Univ, MA, 61, PhD(physics), 64. *Prof Exp:* Fel physics, Princeton Univ, 63-64, res assoc, 64-65, instr, 65-66; staff physicist, Comn Col Physics, Univ Mich, 66-69; assoc prof physics & astron, Eastern Mich Univ, 69-93. *Mem:* Am Phys Soc; Am Asn Physics Teachers. *Res:* Experimental elementary particle physics; use of computers. *Mailing Add:* 2300 W Alameda Santa Fe NM 87501

ROTH, RICHARD LEWIS, SYMMETRY GROUPS. *Current Pos:* from asst prof to assoc prof, 63-86, PROF MATH, UNIV COLO, BOULDER, 67- *Personal Data:* b New York, NY, Feb 24, 36. *Educ:* Harvard Univ, BA, 58; Univ Calif, Berkeley, MA, 60, PhD(math), 63. *Concurrent Pos:* Regional specialist, NSF, Cent Am, 65-66; Fulbright lectr, Colombia, 69; vis scholar, Univ Ariz, 79-80, Univ Wash, 91-92. *Mem:* Am Math Soc; Math Asn Am. *Res:* Symmetry groups, patterns, tilings, weavings and color symmetry. *Mailing Add:* Dept Math Univ Colo Campus Box 395 Boulder CO 80309-0395

ROTH, ROBERT ANDREW, JR, BIOCHEMICAL PHARMACOLOGY, TOXICOLOGY. *Current Pos:* from asst prof to assoc prof , 82-87, PROF PHARMACOL & TOXICOL, MICH STATE UNIV, EAST LANSING, 87- *Personal Data:* b McKeesport, Pa, Aug 15, 46; div; c 2. *Educ:* Duke Univ, BA, 68; Johns Hopkins Univ, PhD(biochem toxicol), 75; Am Bd Toxicol, dipl. *Prof Exp:* Toxicol test specialist, US Army Environ Hyg Agency, 69-71; res fel pulmonary pharmacol, Dept Anesthesiol, Yale Univ, 75-77. *Mem:* Am Soc Pharmacol Exp & Therapeut; Soc Toxicol. *Res:* Removal and metabolism of drugs and hormones by lung; pulmonary toxicology; effect of carbon monoxide and of hypoxic hypoxia on hepatic drug metabolism; role of platelets and neutrophils in toxic responses; hepatic toxicology. *Mailing Add:* Dept Pharmacol & Toxicol Mich State Univ B346 Life Sci East Lansing MI 48824-0001

ROTH, ROBERT EARL, SCIENCE EDUCATION, NATURAL RESOURCES. *Current Pos:* from asst prof to assoc prof, Ohio State Univ, 69-78, chmn dept, 72-85, asst dir/sch secy, 83-89, sr coordr, Int Affairs, 85-89, actg dir, 93-94, PROF NATURAL RESOURCES, ENVIRON MGT EDUC, SCH NAT RES, OHIO STATE UNIV, 79-, ASSOC DIR, 95- *Personal Data:* b Wauseon, Ohio, Mar 30, 37; m 59, Carol S Yackee; c Robin E & Bruce R. *Educ:* Ohio State Univ, BS, 59 & 61, MS, 60; Univ Wis, PhD(environ educ), 69. *Honors & Awards:* Publ Prize, J Environ Educ, 73; Walter E Jeske Award, NAm Asn Environ Educ, 88. *Prof Exp:* Teacher & conserv educ supvr, Ethical Cult Schs, 61-63; teacher & naturalist, Edwin Gould Found for Children, 63-65; instr outdoor teacher educ, Northern Ill Univ, 65-67; res asst environ educ, Wis Res & Develop Ctr for Cognitive Learning, 67-69. *Concurrent Pos:* Res assoc, Educ Resources Info Ctr Environ Educ, 70-74; from assoc prof to prof, Ohio Agr Res & Develop Ctr & Fac Sci & Math Educ; vis scholar, Midwest Univ Consortium Int Affairs, Univ Develop Proj, Indonesia, 88; prin investr, US AID Natural Resource Mgt Proj, Environ Educ, Dominican Repub, 81-88. *Mem:* NAm Asn Environ Educ (pres elect, 75-76, pres, 76-77); Nat Sci Teachers Asn; Conserv Educ Asn. *Res:* Concept development and attitude formation in environmental management; curriculum development; program modeling and interpretive skill development and evaluation; information analysis in environmental education; program and international environmental education development. *Mailing Add:* 570 Morning St Worthington OH 43085. *Fax:* 614-292-7432

ROTH, ROBERT EARL, RADIOLOGY. *Current Pos:* from asst prof to assoc prof, 55-59, prof radiol & chmn dept, 59-69, PROF RADIATION ONCOL & CHMN DEPT, UNIV ALA, MED COL, BIRMINGHAM, 69- *Personal Data:* b Springfield, Ill, Mar 3, 25; m 48; c 5. *Educ:* Univ Ill, BS, 47, MD, 49. *Prof Exp:* Intern, St Louis Co Hosp, Clayton, Mo, 49-50; resident, US Naval Hosp, San Diego, Calif, US Vet Admin Hosp, Nashville, Tenn & Vanderbilt Univ Hosp, 50-54; asst chief radiol, US Vet Admin Hosp, 54-55. *Concurrent Pos:* Actg chief radiol, Vet Admin Hosp, Birmingham, Ala; consult, Vet Admin Hosps, Birmingham & Tuskegee, Ala. *Mem:* AAAS; fel Am Col Radiol; Soc Nuclear Med; Radiol Soc NAm; NY Acad Sci. *Res:* Radiation therapy. *Mailing Add:* Norwood Clin 1528 N 26th St Birmingham AL 35234-1911

ROTH, ROBERT HENRY, JR, NEUROPHARMACOLOGY. *Current Pos:* From instr to asst prof, 66-69, assoc prof pharmacol, 69-77, PROF PSYCHIAT & PHARMACOL, YALE UNIV, 77- *Personal Data:* b Hackensack, NJ, Sept 18, 39; m 63; c 2. *Educ:* Univ Conn, BS, 61; Yale Univ, PhD(pharmacol), 65. *Concurrent Pos:* Nat Inst Gen Med Sci fel physiol, Karolinska Inst, Sweden, 65-66; USPHS res grants, 66-72. *Mem:* Am Soc Pharmacol & Exp Therapeut. *Res:* Neuropharmacology and neurochemistry, especially related to central nervous system depressants and sleep; monoamines and chemical transmission in the nervous system; endogenous factors in control of neurohumors in the nervous system. *Mailing Add:* Dept Pharmacol Yale Univ Sch Med 333 Cedar St New Haven CT 06510-3219. *Fax:* 203-785-7670

ROTH, ROBERT MARK, BIOLOGY, GENETICS. *Current Pos:* from asst prof to assoc prof, 68-76, chmn dept, 78-93, PROF BIOL, ILL INST TECHNOL, 76-, EXEC CHMN, 93- *Personal Data:* b Brooklyn, NY, Apr 9, 43; m 64; c 3. *Educ:* Brooklyn Col, BS, 63; Brandeis Univ, PhD(biol), 67. *Prof Exp:* Fel biol, Univ Wis-Madison, 68. *Concurrent Pos:* Res assoc, Univ Calif, Berkeley, 70; USPHS res career develop award, 72; vis lectr biol chem, Harvard Med Sch, 73-74; vis scientist, Free Univ Berlin, 84, 86, Argonne Nat Lab, 84-87. *Mem:* Genetics Soc Am; Am Soc Photobiol; Am Soc Microbiol. *Res:* Biochemical genetics of yeast; photodynamic action and photosensitivity in microorganisms. *Mailing Add:* Dept Biol Ill Inst Technol 3300 S Federal St Chicago IL 60616-3732. *Fax:* 312-567-3493

ROTH, ROBERT S, GEOLOGY. *Current Pos:* CONSULT, 91- *Personal Data:* b Chicago, Ill, Aug 21, 26; m 54; c 3. *Educ:* Coe Col, BA, 47; Univ Ill, MS, 50, PhD(geol), 51. *Prof Exp:* Res assoc, Eng Exp Sta, Univ Ill, 51; Geologist, Nat Bur Stand, 51-56, solid state physicist, 57-61, res chemist, 62-68, supvr chemist, 69-81, res chemist, 81-91. *Mem:* Geol Soc Am; Mineral Soc Am; Am Crystallog Asn; Mineral Soc Gt Brit & Ireland; Am Ceramic Soc. *Res:* X-ray crystallography and phase equilibria of ceramic materials. *Mailing Add:* 804 Amber Tree Ct Apt 201 Gaithersburg MD 20878-5206

ROTH, ROBERT S, CERAMICS ENGINEERING. *Current Pos:* CHIEF EXEC OFFICER, WORLD OIL MKT CO. *Honors & Awards:* John Jeppson Medal, Am Ceramics Soc, 95. *Mailing Add:* World Oil Mkt Co PO Box 1966 South Gate CA 90280

ROTH, ROBERT STEELE, APPLIED MECHANICS. *Current Pos:* RETIRED. *Personal Data:* b Philadelphia, Pa, July 3, 30; m 66; c 1. *Educ:* Kenyon Col, AB, 53; Carnegie-Mellon Univ, MS, 54; Harvard Univ, PhD(appl math), 62. *Prof Exp:* Engr math, Aberdeen Proving Ground, 54-56; scientist & group leader mech, Systs Div Avco Corp, 62-74; tech staff appl math, Charles Stark Draper Lab, Inc, Cambridge, 74-93. *Concurrent Pos:* Assoc ed, Math Biosci, 72-76. *Mem:* Sigma Xi; Am Acad Mech. *Res:* Structural mechanics; dynamic buckling of thin shells; plastic buckling of thin shells; numerical analysis; nonlinear differential equations; system identification; segmental differential approximation; bioengineering analysis; author of 4 books. *Mailing Add:* 192 Commonwealth Ave Boston MA 02116-2752

ROTH, RODNEY J, MATHEMATICS. *Current Pos:* assoc prof, 71-77, PROF MATH, RAMAPO COL, NJ, 77- *Personal Data:* b Brockway, Pa, Mar 13, 27; m 54; c 2. *Educ:* Pa State Univ, BA, 51; Univ Iowa, MFA, 53; Duke Univ, PhD(math), 62. *Prof Exp:* Asst prof math, Univ Ky, 61-63 & Univ SFla, 63-66; assoc prof & chmn dept, Upsala Col, 66-70. *Mem:* Am Math Soc; Math Asn Am; Sigma Xi. *Res:* Algebra; applications of mathematics in behavioral and social science. *Mailing Add:* 32 Clinton Ave Montclair NJ 07042-2120

ROTH, ROLAND RAY, ECOLOGY, VERTEBRATE BIOLOGY. *Current Pos:* asst prof, 71-77, ASSOC PROF, 77-94, PROF, DEPT ENTOM & APPL ECOL, UNIV DEL, 94- *Personal Data:* b Stuttgart, Ark, Jan 9, 43; m 64; c 3. *Educ:* Univ Ark, Fayetteville, BS, 66; Univ Ill, Urbana, MS, 67, PhD(zool), 71. *Prof Exp:* Res assoc zool, Univ Ill, Urbana, 71. *Mem:* Am Inst Biol Sci; Ecol Soc Am; Am Ornith Union; Cooper Ornith Soc; Soc Conserv Biol; Sigma Xi. *Res:* Habitat quality, selection and use, especially of birds; breeding ecology and population ecology of wood thrush; urban wildlife; effects of forest fragmentation; ornithology; conservation biology. *Mailing Add:* Dept Entom & Appl Ecol Univ Del Newark DE 19717-1303. *Fax:* 302-831-3651

ROTH, RONALD JOHN, ORGANIC CHEMISTRY. *Current Pos:* asst prof, 75-80, ASSOC PROF CHEM, GEORGE MASON UNIV, 81- *Personal Data:* b New York, NY, Feb 1, 47. *Educ:* City Col NY, BS, 67; Columbia Univ, PhD(chem), 72. *Prof Exp:* Res assoc chem, Univ Chicago, 72-73; instr chem, Brown Univ, 74-75. *Mem:* Am Chem Soc; Sigma Xi. *Res:* Synthesis of small strained hydrocarbons and their metal catalyzed transformations. *Mailing Add:* George Mason Univ Dept Chem Fairfax VA 22030

ROTH, ROY WILLIAM, POLYMER CHEMISTRY. *Current Pos:* HQ STAFF, US ARMY RES OFF, 86- *Personal Data:* b Collingswood, NJ, May 27, 29; m 55, 91, Kathie W Young; c Allen D, Douglas M & Margot E (Bennett). *Educ:* Mass Inst Technol, BS, 50; Univ Mich, MS, 51; Mass Inst Technol, PhD(chem), 55. *Prof Exp:* Res chemist, Stamford Labs, Am Cyanamid Co, Conn, 55-60, group leader, 60-64, mgr prod res sect, 64-67, mgr prod develop, Davis & Geck Dept, Lederle Labs, 68-75; dir prod develop, Kendall Co, Colgate-Palmolive, 76-78; res assoc, Pall Corp, 78-79; chief fiber & fabric tech, Natick Labs, US Army, 79-85. *Mem:* Am Chem Soc; Soc Plastics Eng; Am Defense Preparedness Asn. *Res:* Polymer chemistry; medical specialties; product development; non-woven fabrics; specialty filters; sterile-disposable products; chemical protective garments, ballistic protection. *Mailing Add:* US Army Res Off Research Triangle Park NC 27709. *Fax:* 919-549-4248; *E-Mail:* roth@aro.ncren.net

ROTH, SANFORD IRWIN, PATHOLOGY, ELECTRON MICROSCOPY. *Current Pos:* ATTEND PATHOLOGIST, NORTHWESTERN MEM HOSP, CHICAGO, ILL, 80-; PROF, DEPT PATH, MED SCH, NORTHWESTERN UNIV, 80- *Personal Data:* b McAlester, Okla, Oct 14, 32; m 61; c Jeffrey F, Elizabeth F, Gregory J & Suzannah J. *Educ:* Harvard Univ, MD, 56. *Prof Exp:* From intern to asst resident, Mass Gen Hosp, 56-58, actg asst resident, 58-60, asst, 62-64, asst pathologist, 64-70, assoc pathologist, 70-75; prof path & chmn dept, Col Med, Univ Ark, 75-80. *Concurrent Pos:* USPHS res trainee, Mass Gen Hosp, 58-60, teaching fel, Harvard Med Sch, 58-60; instr, Sch Med, Tufts Univ, 58-60; asst, Harvard Med Sch, 62-63, instr, 63-64, assoc, 64-67, from asst prof to assoc prof path, 67-75; fac res assoc, Am Cancer Soc, 67-72; attend pathologist, Northwestern Univ Med Ctr, 80-; fac, res assoc, Am Cancer Soc, US & Can, 67-72; chief lab serv, Vet Admin Lakeside Med Ctr, 80-85. *Mem:* Electron Micros Soc Am; Int Acad Pathologists; Am Soc Cell Biol; Soc Invest Dermat; Am Asn Pathologists; AAAS; Am Soc Bone & Mineral Res. *Res:* Experimental pathology; pathology of the parathyroid glands; dermatopathology; surgical pathology. *Mailing Add:* Dept Path Northwestern Univ Col Med 303 E Chicago Ave Chicago IL 60611. *Fax:* 312-908-3127; *E-Mail:* siroth@nwu.edu

ROTH, SHELDON H, NEUROPHARMACOLOGY, DEVELOPMENTAL NEUROTOXICOLOGY. *Current Pos:* asst prof, Univ Calgary, 73-77, actg head, 77-78 & 89-90, assoc prof, 77-82, assoc prof anesthesia, 81-82, PROF PHARMACOL & THERAPEUT, UNIV CALGARY, 82-, PROF, DEPT ANESTHESIA, 82-, DEP HEAD, DEPT PHARMACOL & THERAPEUTS, 92- *Personal Data:* b Toronto, Ont, June 19, 43; m 68, Karen Ghitter; c Daniel E & Leah H. *Educ:* Univ Toronto, BSc, 66, MSc, 69 & PhD(med & pharmacol), 71. *Prof Exp:* Grad fel, Prov of Ont, 68-71; res fel, Can Med Res Coun, 71-73; lectr pharmacol, Oxford Univ, Eng, 72-73. *Concurrent Pos:* Med Staff, Foothills Hosp, 76-; hon res fel, Univ London, 81; vis lectr, Harvard Med Sch, Boston, 82, vis prof, 86; vis prof, Can Med Res Coun, 83; head toxicol, Univ Calgary, 87-; vis prof, Dept Anesthesia, Univ Saskatoon, Sask; sci officer, P&T Grants Comt, Med Res Coun Can, 91- *Mem:* Pharmacol Soc Can; AAAS; Soc Neurosci; Int Brain Res Orgn; Anaesthesia Res Soc; Soc Toxicol Can. *Res:* Mechanisms of action of anaesthetic agents; toxicology of environmental chemicals; effects of drugs on developing nervous systems; neurotoxicology of volatile organic compounds. *Mailing Add:* Dept Pharmacol-Therapeut Univ Calgary 3330 Hospital Dr NW Calgary AB T2N 4N1 Can. *Fax:* 403-283-2700; *E-Mail:* shroth@acs.ucalgary.ca

ROTH, STEPHEN, MEMBRANE BIOCHEMISTRY, CARBOHYDRATE BIOCHEMISTRY. *Current Pos:* chmn, Dept Biol, 82-88, PROF DEVELOP BIOL, UNIV PA, 80-; CHMN & CHIEF EXEC OFFICER, NEOSE TECHNOL INC. *Personal Data:* b New York, NY, Sept 3, 42; m 81; c 3. *Educ:* Johns Hopkins Univ, AB, 64; Case Western Res Univ, PhD(embryol), 68. *Hon Degrees:* MA, Univ Pa, 80. *Prof Exp:* Fel biochem, Johns Hopkins Univ, 68-70, from asst prof to assoc prof develop biol, 70-80. *Concurrent Pos:* Mem, Cell Biol Study Sect, NIH, 74-78; chmn sci adv bd, Neose Pharmaceut Co, Inc; Res Career Develop Award, NIH, 77-81; res award, Tokyo Med Soc, 87. *Mem:* Am Soc Develop Biol; AAAS; Int Soc Develop Biol; Am Soc Cell Biologists. *Res:* Membrane biochemistry as it controls morphogenesis in vertebrate embryos; glycosyltcans fecases. *Mailing Add:* Neose Technol Inc 102 Witmer Rd Horsham PA 19044

ROTH, THOMAS, PSYCHIATRY. *Current Pos:* DIV HEAD, DEPT PSYCHIAT, HENRY FORD HOSP SLEEP DISORDER RES CTR, 78-; CLIN PROF DEPT PSYCHIAT, SCH MED, UNIV MICH, 79- *Personal Data:* b Czech, July 17, 42; US citizen. *Educ:* City Univ New York, BA, 65; Univ Cincinnati, MA, 69, PhD, 70. *Honors & Awards:* Rush Bronze Award, Am Psychiat Asn, 77; Nathaniel Kleitman Award, Am Sleep Disorders Asn, 90. *Prof Exp:* Res asst, Sleep & Dream Lab, Dept Psychiat, Vet Admin Hosp, Cincinnati, 69-70; res assoc, Dept Psychiat, Col Med, Univ Cincinnati, 70-72, asst prof psychol, 72-76, assoc prof, 76-78. *Concurrent Pos:* Co-dir, Sleep & Dream Lab, Vet Admin Hosp, Cincinnati, 72-78, Sleep Disorder Ctr, Cincinnati Gen Hosp, 77-78; mem res comt, Dept Psychiat, Col Med, Univ Cincinnati, 72-77, fac comt human res, 75-77, adj prof psychol, 76-78; chmn res comt, Xavier Univ, 72-77, assoc prof psychol, 76-78; mem res comt, Dept Psychiat, Henry Ford Hosp, 78-88. *Mem:* AAAS; Am Sleep Disorders Asn (secy-treas, 76-78, pres, 87-88); Am Psychol Asn; Can Sleep Soc; NY Acad Sci; Clin Sleep Soc; Psychonomic Soc; Sleep Res Soc (pres, 78-81). *Res:* Psychiatry; psychology; psychonomics; sleep disorders. *Mailing Add:* Henry Ford Hosp Sleep Disorder Ctr 2799 W Grand Blvd Detroit MI 48202

ROTH, THOMAS ALLAN, metallurgical engineering, materials science; deceased, see previous edition for last biography

ROTH, THOMAS FREDERIC, CELL BIOLOGY, DEVELOPMENTAL BIOLOGY. *Current Pos:* assoc prof, 72-77, PROF BIOL, UNIV MD BALTIMORE CO, 77- *Personal Data:* b Detroit, Mich, Feb 28, 32; m 63, Lorraine M; c Kurt W & Peter H. *Educ:* Tufts Univ, BS, 54; Harvard Univ, MA, 59, PhD(biol), 64. *Prof Exp:* USPHS fel biol, Harvard Univ, 64; fel, Univ Calif, San Diego, 64-66, asst res biologist, 66-67, asst prof biol, 67-72. *Mem:* Soc Develop Biol; Am Soc Cell Biol. *Res:* Molecular biology; biochemistry and ultra structure of receptor mediated protein transport; regulation of coated vesicles; membrane trafficking in cells; discoverer of coated pits and their function. *Mailing Add:* Dept Biol Sci Univ Md Baltimore MD 21228-5398. *Fax:* 301-455-3875; *E-Mail:* roth@umbc.edu

ROTH, WALTER, PHYSICAL CHEMISTRY. *Current Pos:* INDEPENDENT CONSULT, 73- *Personal Data:* b New York, NY, Dec 4, 22; m 47; c 2. *Educ:* City Col New York, BS, 44; NY Univ, MS, 47; Rensselaer Polytech Inst, PhD(chem), 54. *Prof Exp:* Chemist, Kellex Corp, NJ, 44-45; chemist, Carbide & Carbon Chem Co, Tenn, 45-46; phys chemist, US Bur Mines, Pa, 48-53; phys chemist, Res Lab, Gen Elec Co, NY, 54-59; sr physicist, Armour Res Found, Ill Inst Technol, 59-63; mgr gaseous electronics res, Xerox Corp, 63-68; mgr, San Diego Opers, KMS Technol Ctr, 68-70; vpres & tech dir, Diag Instruments, Inc, 70-73. *Concurrent Pos:* Mem, Sci Adv Coun, Rensselaer Polytech Inst, 64-66; arbitrator, Am Arbitration Asn, 71- *Mem:* Am Chem Soc; Am Phys Soc; Sigma Xi. *Res:* Chemical kinetics and mechanisms of light emission; relaxation processes behind shock waves in gases; combustion kinetics and spectroscopy; processes in gas discharges; photochemistry. *Mailing Add:* 8241 El Paseo Grande La Jolla CA 92037

ROTH, WALTER JOHN, operations research, for more information see previous edition

ROTH, WILFRED, ELECTRONICS. *Current Pos:* chmn dept, 64-80, PROF ELEC ENG, UNIV VT, 64- *Personal Data:* b New York, NY, June 24, 22; m 44; c 4. *Educ:* Columbia Univ, BS, 43; Mass Inst Technol, PhD(physics), 48. *Prof Exp:* Mem staff, Radiation Lab, Mass Inst Technol, 43-45, assoc, Res Lab Electronics, 46-47; chief physicist, Rieber Res Lab, NY, 48; develop group leader, Harvey Radio Labs, Mass, 48-49; sect head, Res Div, Raytheon Mfg Co, 49-50; co-dir, Rich-Roth Labs, 50-55; dir, Roth Lab Phys Res, 55-64. *Concurrent Pos:* Partner, Rich Roth Labs, 50-55; treas & dir res, Ultra Viscoson Corp, 52-53; chmn bd dirs, Roth Lab Phys Res, 55-68. *Mem:* AAAS; fel Acoust Soc Am; fel Inst Elec & Electronics Engrs; Sigma Xi. *Res:* Transducers; biomedical engineering; ultrasonic engineering; system dynamics. *Mailing Add:* Univ Vt Burlington VT 05401

ROTHAUS, OSCAR SEYMOUR, MATHEMATICS. *Current Pos:* chmn dept, 73-76, PROF MATH, CORNELL UNIV, 66- *Personal Data:* b Baltimore, Md, Oct 21, 27; m 53; c 1. *Educ:* Princeton Univ, AB, 48, PhD(math), 58. *Prof Exp:* Mathematician, Dept Defense, 53-60; mathematician, Inst Defense Anal, 60-65, dep dir, 63-65; vis prof math, Yale Univ, 65-66. *Mem:* Am Math Soc. *Res:* Lie groups; geometry; several complex variables. *Mailing Add:* Dept Math Cornell Univ White Hall Ithaca NY 14853-7901. *E-Mail:* rothaus@cornell.math.edu

ROTHBART, HERBERT LAWRENCE, PHYSICAL & ANALYTICAL CHEMISTRY, RESEARCH ADMINISTRATION. *Current Pos:* head separation & compos invests, USDA, 66-76, chief phys chem lab, 76-80, dir eastern regional res lab, 80-83, DIR NATLANTIC AREA, AGR RES SERV, USDA, 84- *Personal Data:* b Feb 5, 37; US citizen; m 61, Marian Block; c Bradley. *Educ:* Brooklyn Col, BS, 58; Rutgers Univ, PhD(chem), 63. *Honors & Awards:* Presidential Rank Award, 89. *Prof Exp:* From instr to asst prof chem, Rutgers Univ, 62-66. *Concurrent Pos:* Consult. *Mem:* Am Chem Soc; Inst Food Technol; AAAS. *Res:* Study of the fundamentals of separation processes including equilibrium and transport phenomena; spectroscopy; electron microscopy; computer applications; development of mathematical representations to describe systems and predict efficient separations; physical properties of food components; rapid methods for detection of food pathogens. *Mailing Add:* 411 Norfolk Rd Flourtown PA 19031

ROTHBERG, GERALD MORRIS, SOLID STATE PHYSICS. *Current Pos:* assoc prof, 66-70, head Metallurgy Dept & dir, Cryogenics Ctr, 74-77, prof physics, 70-80, PROF MAT & METALL ENG, STEVENS INST TECHNOL, 80- *Personal Data:* b NJ, May 14, 31; m 54; c 2. *Educ:* Mass Inst Technol, BS, 52; Columbia Univ, PhD(physics), 59. *Honors & Awards:* Jess H Davis Mem Res Award, Stevens Inst Technol, 75. *Prof Exp:* Adams res fel, Univ Leiden, 58-59; asst prof physics, Rutgers Univ, 59-66. *Concurrent Pos:* Fulbright lectr & res, Univ Barcelona, 64-65, Fulbright sr lectr, 72-73. *Mem:* AAAS; Am Phys Soc; Sigma Xi; Am Soc Metals. *Res:* Mossbauer effect; high pressures; cryogenics. *Mailing Add:* Dept Mat Sci & Eng Stevens Inst Technol Hoboken NJ 07030. Fax: 201-216-8306

ROTHBERG, JOSEPH ELI, PHYSICS. *Current Pos:* assoc prof, 69-74, PROF PHYSICS, UNIV WASH, 74- *Personal Data:* b Philadelphia, Pa, May 15, 35; m 58. *Educ:* Univ Pa, BA, 56; Columbia Univ, MA, 58, PhD(physics), 63. *Prof Exp:* Res assoc physics, Yale Univ, 63-64, from instr to asst prof, 64-69. *Mem:* Fel Am Phys Soc. *Res:* Elementary particle physics; experimental physics. *Mailing Add:* Dept Physics Univ Wash Box 351560 Seattle WA 98195

ROTHBERG, LEWIS JOSIAH, QUANTUM CONFINED SEMICONDUCTORS, CONJUGATED POLYMER PHYSICS. *Current Pos:* PROF CHEM, UNIV ROCHESTER, 96- *Personal Data:* b New York, NY, Sept 22, 56. *Educ:* Univ Rochester, BS, 77; Harvard Univ, PhD(physics), 84. *Prof Exp:* Mem tech staff, AT&T Bell Labs, 83-96. *Mem:* Fel Am Phys Soc; Optical Soc Am; Electrochem Soc. *Res:* Transient optical spectroscopy of processes in condensed matter including carrier dynamics in reduced dimensionality semiconductors, protein dynamics and surface adsorbate relaxation. *Mailing Add:* Dept Chem Univ Rochester Rochester NY 14627. Fax: 716-242-9485; E-Mail: ljr@chem.chem.rochester.edu

ROTHBERG, SIMON, BIOCHEMISTRY OF THE SKIN. *Current Pos:* res prof, 70-81, EMER PROF, MED COL VA, VA COMMONWEALTH UNIV, 81- *Personal Data:* b New York, NY, Mar 7, 21; m 46; c 3. *Educ:* Columbia Univ, BS, 48; Georgetown Univ, MS, 52, PhD(biochem), 56. *Prof Exp:* Phys chemist, Nat Bur Stand, 48-53; biochemist, Nat Heart Inst, 53-56; biochemist, Nat Cancer Inst, 57-70. *Concurrent Pos:* NIH res grants, 71-74, 74-78; vis scientist, Cambridge, 64-65; Med Col Va support grants, 78-80. *Mem:* AAAS; Am Chem Soc; Am Soc Biol Chem; Brit Biochem Soc; Sigma Xi; Am Soc Cell Biol. *Res:* Mechanisms of enzymatic reactions; decarboxylation; oxygenases; structure of normal and abnormal keratin; enzymes of epidermis; biochemical regulation of epidermal proliferation and keratinization in normal and pathological skin; role of chalone; DNA catabolism; cyto skeletal proteins of the epidermis. *Mailing Add:* 2717 Kenmore Rd Richmond VA 23225-1427

ROTHBLAT, GEORGE H, BIOCHEMISTRY. *Current Pos:* PROF BIOCHEM, MED COL PA, 76- *Personal Data:* b Willimantic, Conn, Oct 6, 35; m 57; c 2. *Educ:* Univ Conn, BA, 57; Univ Pa, PhD(microbiol), 61. *Prof Exp:* Assoc prof, Wistar Inst, 61-66, assoc mem, 66-71, mem, 71-76. *Concurrent Pos:* Asst prof, Sch Med, Univ Pa, 66-71, assoc prof, 71-76; estab investr, Am Heart Asn, 70-75, fel coun arteriosclerosis. *Mem:* AAAS; Tissue Cult Asn; Am Soc Biol Chemists; Sigma Xi. *Res:* Cellular lipid metabolism; cholesterol metabolism in tissue culture cells. *Mailing Add:* Dept Biochem Allegheny Univ Health Sci 2900 Queen Lane Philadelphia PA 19129-1121. Fax: 215-843-8849

ROTHCHILD, IRVING, REPRODUCTIVE ENDOCRINOLOGY. *Current Pos:* assoc prof obstet & gynec, 55-66, prof, 66-82, EMER PROF REPRODUCTIVE BIOL, SCH MED, CASE WESTERN RESERVE UNIV, 82- *Personal Data:* b New York, NY, Dec 2, 13; m 35, 58; c 1. *Educ:* Univ Wis, BA, 35, MA, 36, PhD, 39; Ohio State Univ, MD, 54. *Prof Exp:* Asst dir chem, Michael Reese Hosp, Chicago, Ill, 41-43; physiologist, USDA, Md, 43-48; asst prof physiol, Sch Med, Univ Md, 48-49; asst prof physiol & obstet & gynec, Ohio State Univ, 49-53. *Concurrent Pos:* Boerhaave prof, Univ Leiden, 77-78. *Mem:* Fel AAAS; Am Soc Zool; Am Physiol Soc; Endocrine Soc; Soc Study Reproduction; Soc Study Fertility. *Res:* Physiology of reproduction. *Mailing Add:* 2441 Kenilworth Rd Cleveland Heights OH 44106-2713

ROTHCHILD, ROBERT, ORGANIC CHEMISTRY, INSTRUMENTATION. *Current Pos:* ASST PROF ORG CHEM, JOHN JAY COL CRIMINAL JUSTICE, CITY UNIV NEW YORK, 78- *Personal Data:* b New York, NY, May 12, 46. *Educ:* City Col New York, BS, 67; Columbia Univ, MA, 68, MPhil, 74, PhD(org chem), 75. *Prof Exp:* Instr org chem, Schwartz Col Pharm & Health Sci, Long Island Univ, 68-72; res asst org chem & instrumentation, Columbia Univ, 72-73; adj asst prof adv pharmaceut synthesis, Schwartz Col Pharm & Health Sci, Long Island Univ, 75-76; lectr org chem, Tex A&M Univ, 76-77; adj asst prof, org chem, Brandeis Univ, 77-78. *Res:* Organic mass spectrometry; organic mechanism and synthesis; nuclear magnetic resonance; chromatographic techniques. *Mailing Add:* Dept Sci John Jay Col Criminal Just 445 W 59th St Rm 4405N New York NY 10019

ROTHE, CARL FREDERICK, PHYSIOLOGY, BIOMEDICAL ENGINEERING. *Current Pos:* from instr to assoc prof, 58-70, PROF PHYSIOL, IND UNIV SCH MED, IND UNIV-PURDUE UNIV, INDIANAPOLIS, 70- *Personal Data:* b Lima, Ohio, Feb 6, 29; m 52, Mary L Hawk; c Sarah K & Thomas H. *Educ:* Ohio State Univ, BSc, 51, MSc, 52, PhD(physiol), 55. *Prof Exp:* Sr asst scientist, USPHS, 55-58. *Concurrent Pos:* Estab investr, Am Heart Asn, 63-69; indust consult biomed instrumentation, 67-; consult, NIH, 71-75, mem cardiovasc renal study sect, Nat Heart & Lung Inst; fel, Circ Sect, Am Physiol Soc. *Mem:* Am Physiol Soc; Microcirculatory Soc; Biomed Eng Soc; fel AAAS; Am Asn Univ Prof; fel Am Heart Asn. *Res:* Cardiovascular physiology; instrumentation for physiological research; computer simulation of physiological systems; bioengineering; control of venous pressure and capacitance vessels. *Mailing Add:* Dept Physiol & Biophys Ind Univ Sch Med 635 Barnhill Dr Indianapolis IN 46202-5120

ROTHE, ERHARD WILLIAM, CHEMICAL PHYSICS, CHEMICAL IMAGING DIAGNOSTICS. *Current Pos:* PROF ENG, CHEM ENG, WAYNE STATE UNIV, 69- *Personal Data:* b Breslau, Ger, Apr 15, 31; US citizen; m 59, Daria Reshetylo; c Lisa & Margaret. *Educ:* Univ Mich, BS, 52, MS, 54, PhD(chem), 59. *Honors & Awards:* Max Planch Res Prize. *Prof Exp:* Staff scientist physics, Gen Dynamics Convair, 59-69. *Concurrent Pos:* Lectr, San Diego State Col, 65-66; consult, Phys Dynamics, Inc, 75-90; adj prof chem, Wayne State Univ, 75-; summer guest researcher, Max Plank Inst, 79-97; Gershenson Distinguished Prof, Wayne State Univ, 86-88. *Mem:* AAAS; Am Chem Soc; fel Am Phys Soc; Sigma Xi. *Res:* Physics and chemistry of atomic and molecular collisions; laser-driven chemistry; laser interaction with surfaces; laser combustion-diagnostics. *Mailing Add:* 1244 Westport Rd Ann Arbor MI 48103. Fax: 313-577-3810; E-Mail: erothe@chem1.eng.wayne.edu

ROTHE, KAROLYN REGINA, limnology, ecology, for more information see previous edition

ROTHEIM, MINNA B, microbial genetics; deceased, see previous edition for last biography

ROTHENBACHER, HANSJAKOB, VETERINARY PATHOLOGY, VETERINARY MICROBIOLOGY. *Current Pos:* from assoc prof to prof, 63-88, EMER PROF VET SCI, PA STATE UNIV, UNIVERSITY PARK, 88-, PATH CONSULT, 88- *Personal Data:* b Blaubeuren, WGer, Jan 21, 28, US citizen; c 3. *Educ:* Univ Munich, dipl vet med, 52, DMV, 53; Mich State Univ, MS, 55, PhD(path), 62; Am Col Vet Pathologists, dipl, 62. *Prof Exp:* Asst prof vet sci, Univ Ark, 55-58; res vet path, Mich State Univ, 58-61, pathologist in chg necropsy, 61-63. *Mem:* Am Asn Avian Path; Wildlife Dis Asn; Int Acad Path; Am Vet Med Asn; Poultry Sci Asn; Animal Sci Asn. *Res:* Ecologic pathology; diseases of fish; pathology of viral, bacterial and nutritional diseases of animals; endocrine pathology. *Mailing Add:* 200 W Prospect Ave State College PA 16801

ROTHENBERG, ALAN S, ORGANIC CHEMISTRY. *Current Pos:* Res chemist monomer synthesis, 77-80, RES GROUP LEADER PROD & PROCESS DEVELOP, STAMFORD RES LABS, AM CYANAMID CO, 81- *Personal Data:* b Harvey, Ill, Jan 30, 51. *Educ:* Univ Utah, BS, 72; Pa State Univ, PhD(org chem), 77. *Mem:* Am Chem Soc. *Res:* Organic synthesis; natural products chemistry; iso- quinoline alkaloids; monomer synthesis; cationic monomers; water treating chemicals. *Mailing Add:* 185 Range Rd Wilton CT 06897-3920

ROTHENBERG, ALBERT, PSYCHIATRY. *Current Pos:* CLIN PROF PSYCHIAT, HARVARD MED SCH, 86- *Personal Data:* b New York, NY, June 2, 30; m 70, Julia Johnson; c Michael, Mora & Rina. *Educ:* Harvard Univ, AB, 52; Tufts Univ, MD, 56; Am Bd Psychiat & Neurol, Dipl Psychiat, 65. *Prof Exp:* Intern, Pa Hosp, 56-57; resident, Dept Psychiat, Sch Med, Yale Univ, 57-60, instr psychiat, 60-61 & 63-64, from asst prof to assoc prof, 64-74; prof psychiat, Sch Med, Univ Conn & chief psychiat clin serv, Univ Health Ctr, 75-79; dir res, Austen Riggs Ctr Inc, 79-94. *Concurrent Pos:* Chief resident, Yale Psychiat Inst, 60-61, asst med dir, 63-64; attend psychiatrist, PR Inst Psychiat, 61-63, chief neuropsychiat, Rodriguez US Army Hosp, 61-63; asst attend psychiatrist, Yale New Haven Hosp, 63-68, attend psychiatrist, 68-84; USPHS res career develop awards, Dept Psychiat, Yale Univ, 64-69 & 69-74; assoc med dir, Yale Psychiat Inst, 63-64, attend Psychiaconist, 64-75; attend psychiatrist, West Haven Vet Admin Hosp, 68-84; vis prof, Pa State Univ, 71, adj prof, 71-79; clin prof psychiat, Yale Univ, 74-84; Guggenheim Found fel, 74-75; attend physician, Dempsey Hosp, Farmington, Conn, 75-79; lectr, Sch Med, Harvard Univ, 82-86; fel, Ctr Advan Study Behav Sci, 86-87 & Neth Inst Advan Study Soc Scis, 92-93; Golestan Found award, 91 & 92. *Mem:* Fel Am Psychiat Asn; Am Soc Aesthetics; fel Am Col Psychoanalysts; AAAS; Sigma Xi. *Res:* Psychological and psychiatric basis of the creative process in pure and applied science, literature, visual and graphic arts, and music; psychotherapy; schizophrenia; anorexia nervosa. *Mailing Add:* 52 Pine Ridge Rd Canaan NY 12029. E-Mail: arothenb@warren.med.harvard.edu

ROTHENBERG, HERBERT CARL, RESEARCH ADMINISTRATION. *Current Pos:* CONSULT, 85- *Personal Data:* b Brooklyn, NY, Mar 9, 19; m 45, Marjorie Smith; c 3. *Educ:* Univ Minn, AB, 38; Pa State Col, PhD(physics), 49. *Prof Exp:* Geophysicist & mathematician, Stand Oil Co, Venezuela, 40-42; res engr, Div Phys War Res, Duke Univ, 42-45; res assoc, Acoust Lab, Pa State Univ, 45-49; fel, Mellon Inst, 49-51; physicist & mgr, Electronic Devices Lab, Gen Elec Co, 51-66; phys scientist, Cent Intel Agency, 66-85. *Concurrent Pos:* Mem res proj, Off Sci Res & Develop. *Mem:* Am Phys Soc; Sigma Xi; AAAS. *Res:* Geophysics; acoustics; electronics; microwaves; solid state. *Mailing Add:* 918 Leigh Mill Rd Great Falls VA 22066-2302

ROTHENBERG, JOSEPH HOWARD, AERONAUTICS & ASTRONAUTICS. *Current Pos:* space telescope opers mgr, NASA Goddard Space Flight Ctr, 83-87, chief, Missions Opers Br, 87-89, dept dir, Mission Opers & Data Systs Directorate, 89-90, assoc dir flight projs, Hubble Space Telescope, 90-94, DIR, NASA GODDARD SPACE FLIGHT CTR, 95- *Personal Data:* b New York, NY, Dec 23, 40; m 64, Frances B Albano; c Edward, Joyce & Annette. *Educ:* State Univ NY, BS, 64; C W Post Col, MS, 73, MS, 77. *Honors & Awards:* Laurel Award, Aviation Week & Space Tech, 93; Collier Trophy, 94; Robert H Goddard Astronaut Award, Am Inst Aeronaut & Astronaut, 94. *Prof Exp:* Proj engr, Grumman Aerospace, 64-78, mgr, Solar Max Mission, 78-81; mgr opers & test projs, Comp Tech Assocs, 81-83; exec vpres, Space Systs Div, CTA Inc, 94-95. *Mem:* Am Inst Aeronaut & Astronaut; Instrument Soc Am. *Mailing Add:* NASA Goddard Space Code 100 Greenbelt MD 20771

ROTHENBERG, LAWRENCE NEIL, MEDICAL PHYSICS. *Current Pos:* ASSOC ATTEND PHYSICIST MED PHYSICS, MEM HOSP, MEM SLOAN-KETTERING CANCER CTR, 78-, ASSOC CLIN MEM, 85- *Personal Data:* b Philadelphia, Pa, July 30, 40; m 71; c 2. *Educ:* Univ Pa, BA, 62; Univ Wis-Madison, MS, 64, PhD(nuclear physics), 70; Am Bd Radiol, cert radiol physics, 76. *Prof Exp:* Teaching asst physics, Univ Wis-Madison, 62-63, from res asst to res assoc nuclear physics, 66-70; from instr to asst prof, Med Col, Cornell Univ, 71-79, assoc prof physics in radiol, 79- *Concurrent Pos:* Am Cancer Soc fel med physics, Mem Hosp, 70; asst physicist, Mem Hosp, Sloan-Kettering Cancer Ctr, 70-73, asst attend physicist, 73-78; asst attend physicist, NY Hosp, 71-; assoc ed, Med Physics; chmn bd dirs, Am Col Med Physics, 87; mem, Nat Coun on Radiation Protection & Measurements, 87- *Mem:* NY Acad Sci; Am Col Radiol; Health Physics Soc; Am Phys Soc; Am Asn Physicists in Med; Am Col Med Physics; Radiol Soc N Am. *Res:* Diagnostic x-ray physics; development of x-ray test methods for United States Public Health Service; computed tomography, mammography, phantoms for abdominal radiography, and magnetic resonance imaging. *Mailing Add:* 1161 York Ave New York NY 10021. *Fax:* 212-717-3010

ROTHENBERG, MORTIMER ABRAHAM, NEUROCHEMISTRY, ENVIRONMENTAL SCIENCES. *Current Pos:* CONSULT, NAT DEFENSE & ENVIRON SCI, 81- *Personal Data:* b New York, NY, June 3, 20; m 44, Adele; c 4. *Educ:* Univ Louisville, BA, 41; NY Univ, MS, 42; Columbia Univ, PhD(biochem), 49. *Prof Exp:* Res assoc neurol & biochem, Columbia Univ, 47-49; res assoc & asst prof, Inst Radiobiol & Biophys, Univ Chicago, 49-51; chief biochemist, Chem Corps Proving Ground, US Dept Army, 51-53, chief chem div, 55-57, sci dir, 57-63, sci dir, Dugway Proving Ground, 63-68, sci dir, Deseret Test Ctr, Ft Douglas, 68-73, sci dir, Dugway Proving Ground, 73-81. *Concurrent Pos:* Mem corp, Woods Hole Marine Biol Lab, Mass. *Mem:* Emer mem AAAS; emer mem Am Chem Soc; fel Am Inst Chemists; NY Acad Sci. *Res:* Physiology and biochemistry of nerve conduction and transmission using inhibitors, drugs pesticides; enzymology and protein isolation and purification; transport and dilution of gases and aerosols in the atmosphere; atmospheric dynamics. *Mailing Add:* 2233 East 3980 S Salt Lake City UT 84124-1857

ROTHENBERG, RONALD ISAAC, MATHEMATICS, OPERATIONS RESEARCH. *Current Pos:* Lectr, 60-62 & 64-66, asst prof, 66-80, ASSOC PROF MATH, QUEEN'S COL, NY, 80- *Personal Data:* b New York, NY; div. *Educ:* City Col New York, BSChE, 58; Northwestern Univ, Evanston, MS, 60; Univ Calif, Davis, PhD(eng), 64. *Concurrent Pos:* Vchair Metrol, NY Chap, Math Asn Am, 87-89. *Mem:* Math Asn Am; Sigma Xi. *Res:* Ordinary and partial differential equations; probability and statistics; engineering mathematics; mathematics for optimization; applied mathematics; author of five books; computing relating to mathematics. *Mailing Add:* Dept Math Queens Col Flushing NY 11367. *E-Mail:* rnrqc@qcvaxa.acc.qc.edu

ROTHENBERG, SHELDON PHILIP, HEMATOLOGY, INTERNAL MEDICINE. *Current Pos:* PROF MED, STATE UNIV NY DOWNSTATE, 80- *Personal Data:* b New York, NY, May 28, 29; m 56; c 2. *Educ:* NY Univ, AB, 50; Chicago Med Sch, MD, 55. *Prof Exp:* From instr to prof med, New York Med Col, 61-80, chief hemat/oncol sect, 69-80. *Mem:* Am Soc Clin Oncol; Am Soc Hemat; Am Soc Clin Invest; Am Fedn Clin Res; Asn Cancer Res; Asn Am Prof. *Res:* Study of metabolism and adsorption of vitamin B-12 and folic acid and the interrelationship of these cofactors in enzymatic reactions in health and disease. *Mailing Add:* Div Hemat & Oncol Dept Med 450 NY Clarkson Ave Brooklyn NY 11203. *Fax:* 718-630-2822

ROTHENBERG, STEPHEN, COMPUTER SYSTEMS. *Current Pos:* PRES, ROTHENBERG COMPUT SYST, INC, 76- *Personal Data:* b New York, NY, Feb 3, 41; div; c 1. *Educ:* Carnegie Inst Technol, BS, 62; Univ Wash, PhD(phys chem), 66. *Prof Exp:* Res assoc, Princeton Univ, 66-68; mgr chem applns, Univ Comput Co, 68-71; mgr tech serv, Info Systs Design, 71-73, vpres comput servs, 73-76. *Concurrent Pos:* Nat Ctr Atmospheric Res fel, 68. *Mem:* Int Word Processing Asn. *Res:* Computer calculation of molecular electronic structure; chemical information systems; programming languages; computer-based office systems; computer systems and applications. *Mailing Add:* 4154 Interdale Way Palo Alto CA 94306

ROTHENBUHLER, WALTER CHRISTOPHER, ZOOLOGY. *Current Pos:* prof, 62-85, EMER PROF APICULT, ETHOLOGY & BEHAV GENETICS, OHIO STATE UNIV, 85- *Personal Data:* b Monroe Co, Ohio, May 4, 20; m 44; c 4. *Educ:* Iowa State Col, BS, 50, MS, 52, PhD(genetics, zool), 54. *Prof Exp:* Res assoc genetics, Iowa State Univ, 50-54, from asst prof to prof apicult, 54-62. *Concurrent Pos:* Mem comt on African honey bee, Nat Res Coun. *Mem:* Entom Soc Am; Int Bee Res Asn; Sigma Xi. *Res:* Biology of honey bees, particularly genetics, gynandromorphism, behavior and disease resistance; animal behavior; behavior genetics of honey bees and other animals. *Mailing Add:* 6226 Alrojo St Worthington OH 43085-3459

ROTHENBURY, RAYMAND ALBERT, ACADEMIC ADMINISTRATION. *Current Pos:* lectr chem, 66-68, chmn technol, 68-75, dir technol & appl arts, 75-81, DEAN TECHNOL & APPL SCI, LAMBTON COL APPL ARTS & TECHNOL, 81- *Personal Data:* b London, Eng, May 14, 37; m 63, Marlene E Sullivan; c David A & Daniel E. *Educ:* Univ Exeter, BSc, 58; Univ London, PhD(chem), 61. *Prof Exp:* Fel inorg chem, McMaster Univ, 61-63; res chemist, Dow Chem Can Ltd, 63-66. *Mem:* Fel Chem Inst Can. *Mailing Add:* Lambton Col Appl Arts & Technol 1457 London Rd Sarnia ON N7S 6K4 Can. *Fax:* 519-542-6901; *E-Mail:* ray@lambton.on.ca

ROTHER, ANA, PHARMACOGNOSY. *Current Pos:* fel, 59-61, res asst, 61-64, from instr to asst prof, 64-70, RES ASSOC PHARMACOG, SCH PHARM, UNIV CONN, 70- *Personal Data:* b Brandenburg/Havel, Ger, July 14, 31. *Educ:* Nat Univ Colombia, BS, 51; Univ Munich, Dr rer nat(pharm), 58. *Prof Exp:* Teaching asst pharm chem, Nat Univ Colombia, 51-53; chemist-analyst, Beneficencia, Bogota, 53-54 & Squibb & Sons, Calif, 58-59. *Mem:* Am Chem Soc; Am Soc Pharmacog; Am Soc Plant Physiol; AAAS; Tissue Cult Asn. *Res:* Isolation, structure and biosynthesis of secondary plant constituents; alkaloids; plant tissue culture. *Mailing Add:* Sch Pharm Univ Conn U-92 Storrs CT 06268

ROTHERHAM, JEAN, BIOCHEMISTRY, HISTONE CHEMISTRY. *Current Pos:* CONSULT, 81- *Personal Data:* b Pompton Lakes, NJ, Jan 4, 22. *Educ:* Montclair State Teachers Col, BA, 42; Univ NC, MS, 52, PhD, 54. *Prof Exp:* Fel, Nat Cancer Inst, 54 & Nat Heart & Lung Inst, 55, biochemist, Nat Cancer Inst, 56-81. *Mem:* Sigma Xi. *Res:* Nucleic acids; intermediary metabolism of normal and tumor tissue; proteins. *Mailing Add:* 1307 Noyes Dr Silver Spring MD 20910-2720

ROTHERMEL, JOSEPH JACKSON, CHEMISTRY, GLASS TECHNOLOGY. *Current Pos:* RETIRED. *Personal Data:* b Reading, Pa, Nov 4, 18; m 43; c 5. *Educ:* Franklin & Marshall Col, BS, 40; Univ Pittsburgh, PhD(chem), 48. *Honors & Awards:* Eugene C Sullivan Award, Corning Sect, Am Chem Soc, 73. *Prof Exp:* Asst chem, Univ Pittsburgh, 40-44; res chemist, Manhattan proj, Sch Med & Dent, Univ Rochester, 44-46; asst chem, Univ Pittsburgh, 46-48; res chemist, Res Labs, Corning Glass Works, 48-58, mgr chem serv, 58-66, mgr tech anal, 66-68, sr eng assoc, Mfg & Eng Div, 68-83. *Mem:* Am Chem Soc; Am Ceramic Soc; Soc Glass Technol. *Res:* Non-silicate glass compositions; glass melting; borate and phosphate glasses; x-ray absorbing transparent barriers. *Mailing Add:* 2834 Powderhouse Rd Corning NY 14830

ROTHFELD, LEONARD B(ENJAMIN), COST ESTIMATING, MINING WASTE DISPOSAL. *Current Pos:* RETIRED. *Personal Data:* b New York, NY, Feb 20, 33; m 67, Mary E Young; c Rebecca R. *Educ:* Cornell Univ, BChE, 55; Univ Wis, MS, 56, PhD(chem eng), 61. *Prof Exp:* Res engr, Emeryville Res Ctr, Shell Develop Co, 61-62, group leader eng res, Houston Res Lab, Shell Oil Co, 62-67, sr engr, NY, 67-70, spec assignment, Shell Int Petrol Maatschapij, The Hague, Holland, 70-71, group leader, Martinez Refinery, Shell Oil Co, Calif, 71-72, spec assignment, Bellaire Res Ctr, Shell Develop Co, 72-73; dir process eng, Synthetic Crude & Minerals Div, Atlantic Richfield Co, Los Angeles, 73-74, mgr process eng, Synthetic Crude & Minerals Div, ARCO Coal Co, 74-81, mgr gen eng, 81-82, assoc res dir, 82, mgr coal res & develop, 82-84, sr consult res engr, 84-85; consult, ARCO Coal Co & Pac Coal, 86-88; environ engr, US Bur Mines, Denver, 88- *Mem:* Soc Mining, Metall & Explor; Air & Waste Mgt Asn; Nat Asn Environ Prof. *Res:* Cost of compliance with environmental regulations at hard-rock mines and minerals processing facilities. *Mailing Add:* 7215 W Eighth Pl Lakewood CO 80215

ROTHFIELD, LAWRENCE I, MICROBIOLOGY, BIOCHEMISTRY. *Current Pos:* chmn dept, 68-80, PROF MICROBIOL, SCH MED, UNIV CONN, 68- *Personal Data:* b New York, NY, Dec 30, 27; m 53, Naomi Fox; c 4. *Educ:* Cornell Univ, AB, 47; NY Univ, MD, 51. *Prof Exp:* From intern to asst resident internal med, Bellevue Hosp, New York, 51-53; asst resident, Presby Hosp, New York, 55-56; asst prof med, NY Univ, 62-64; from asst prof to assoc prof molecular biol, Albert Einstein Col Med, 64-68. *Concurrent Pos:* Assoc ed, J Membrane Biol, 68-83; consult molecular biol sect, NIH, 70-74; mem microbiol & immunol adv comt, President's Biomed Res Panel, 75; chmn, Microbial Physiol Div, Am Soc Microbiol, 75; consult biochem, Biophys Rev Comt, NSF, 79-83; mem microbial physiol & genetics study sect, NIH, 90-94. *Mem:* Am Soc Biol Chem; Am Soc Microbiol. *Res:* Membrane molecular biology; bacterial cell division. *Mailing Add:* Dept Microbiol Univ Conn Sch Med Farmington CT 06030-3205. *Fax:* 860-679-1239; *E-Mail:* lroth@panda.uchc.edu

ROTHFIELD, NAOMI FOX, MEDICINE, RHEUMATOLOGY. *Current Pos:* assoc prof, 68-73, PROF MED, SCH MED, UNIV CONN, 73-, HEAD, ARTHRITIS SECT, 71-, DIR, ARTHRITIS CTR, 78- *Personal Data:* b New York, NY, Apr 5, 29; m 53, Lawrence I; c Susan, Lawrence Jr, John & Jane.

Educ: Bard Col, BA, 50; NY Univ, MD, 55. *Prof Exp:* Clin asst med, Sch Med, Univ Frankfurt, 54-55; intern, Lenox Hill Hosp, New York, 55-56; asst, Sch Med, NY Univ, 59-61, from instr to asst prof med, 61-68. *Concurrent Pos:* Fel, Sch Med, NY Univ, 56-59, Arthritis Found clin scholar, 64-68; consult, Hartford Hosp, 71-, St Francis Hosp, 71- & Newington, Va, 71-; attend, Dempsey Hosp, 75- *Mem:* Am Soc Clin Invest; Am Rheumatism Asn; Am Asn Immunol; Am Fedn Clin Res; Asn Am Physicians. *Res:* Connective tissue diseases and their pathogenesis; antinuclear and anti-DNA antibodies; Lupus; scleroderma. *Mailing Add:* 540 Deercliff Rd Avon CT 06001-2859. *Fax:* 860-679-1287; *E-Mail:* rothfield@wso.uchc.edu

ROTHFUS, JOHN ARDEN, RESEARCH ADMINISTRATION, BIOCHEMISTRY. *Current Pos:* prin res chemist, USDA, 65-70, invest head, 70-73, res leader, 73-90, LEAD SCIENTIST, NAT CTR AGR UTIL RES, AGR RES SERV, USDA, 90- *Personal Data:* b Des Moines, Iowa, Dec 25, 32; m 59, Betty B; c Lee & David. *Educ:* Drake Univ, BA, 55; Univ Ill, PhD(chem), 60. *Prof Exp:* Asst biochem, Univ Ill, 55-59; USPHS fel, Col Med, Univ Utah, 59-61, instr, 61-63; asst prof, Sch Med, Univ Calif, Los Angeles, 63-65. *Mem:* AAAS; Am Chem Soc; NY Acad Sci; Am Soc Plant Physiologists; Am Oil Chemists Soc. *Res:* Protein chemistry; structure and function of conjugated macromolecules; lipid chemistry; computational chemistry; plant biochemistry. *Mailing Add:* 5615 N Sherwood Ave Peoria IL 61614

ROTHFUS, ROBERT R(ANDLE), CHEMICAL ENGINEERING. *Current Pos:* from instr to assoc prof chem eng, 47-59, head dept, 71-78, PROF CHEM ENG, CARNEGIE-MELLON UNIV, 59- *Personal Data:* b Rochester, NY, May 13, 19; m 42; c 3. *Educ:* Univ Pittsburgh, BS, 41; Carnegie Inst Technol, MS, 42, DSc(chem eng), 48. *Prof Exp:* Chem engr, Eastman Kodak Co, NY, 42-46. *Mem:* Am Chem Soc; Am Soc Mech Engrs; Am Inst Chem Engrs. *Res:* Flow of fluids in conduits; heat transfer by convection; fine particle technology; process dynamics and control. *Mailing Add:* 81 Seneca St Pittsburgh PA 15219

ROTHKOPF, MICHAEL H, OPERATIONS RESEARCH. *Current Pos:* RUTGERS CTR OPER RES, 88- *Personal Data:* b New York, NY, May 20, 39; m 60; c Anne & Alan. *Educ:* Pomona Col, BA, 60; Mass Inst Technol, MS, 62, PhD(opers res), 64. *Prof Exp:* Mathematician, Shell Develop Co, Shell Oil Co, 64-67, res supvr, 67-71, head, Planning Methods & Models Div, Shell Int Petrol Co, 71-73; scientist, Xerox Palo Alto Res Ctr, 73-82; prog leader & energy anal, Lawrence Berkeley Lab, 82-88. *Concurrent Pos:* Instr, Univ Calif Exten, 66-78; asst prof math, Calif State Univ, Hayward, 67-69, lectr, Sch Bus & Econ, 74, 76-78; lectr, Dept Med Info Sci, Univ Calif, San Francisco, 74-75; consult, assoc prof, Dept Eng, Econ Syst, Stanford Univ, 80-81; lectr, Grad Sch Bus, Univ Santa Clara, 80; ed, Interfaces, 94-; vis prof, Wharton Sch, Univ Penn, 97. *Mem:* Inst Oper Res & Mgt Sci; Inst Mgt Sci; Am Econ Asn; Int Asn Energy Econ. *Res:* Mathematical modeling useful for improving decisions; management science generally; energy economics; microeconimics; competitive bidding models. *Mailing Add:* Rutgers Ctr Oper Res Rutgers Univ PO Box 5062 New Brunswick NJ 08903. *Fax:* 732-445-5472; *E-Mail:* rothkopf@rutcor.rutgers.edu

ROTHLEDER, STEPHEN DAVID, SYSTEM DESIGN & SYSTEM SCIENCE, UNDERWATER ACOUSTICS. *Current Pos:* Distinguished mem tech staff, Ocean Systs Res Dept, 66-93, DISTINGUISHED MEM TECH STAFF, NETWORK WIRELESS SYSTEMS, BELL LABS, 93- *Personal Data:* b New York, NY, Mar 7, 37; m 60; c 2. *Educ:* NY Univ, BS, 57; Mass Inst Technol, SM, 59, PhD(plasma physics), 62. *Prof Exp:* Res assoc plasma physics lab, Princeton Univ, 62-66. *Mem:* Am Phys Soc. *Res:* Plasma physics; reentry physics; ocean physics; nuclear engineering; wireless communication systems; engineering physics. *Mailing Add:* 3 Trouville Dr Parsippany NJ 07054

ROTHLISBERGER, HAZEL MARIE, MATHEMATICS. *Current Pos:* prof & head dept, 43-76, EMER PROF MATH, UNIV DUBUQUE, 76- *Personal Data:* b Elgin, Iowa, May 10, 11. *Educ:* Iowa State Teachers Col, BA, 38; Univ Wis, MA, 50. *Prof Exp:* Actg prin & teacher high sch, Owasa, Iowa, 40-43. *Mem:* Math Asn Am; Nat Coun Teachers Math. *Mailing Add:* 3598 Filmore Rd Elgin IA 52141

ROTHMAN, ALAN BERNARD, CHEMICAL THERMODYNAMICS, NUCLEAR ENGINEERING. *Current Pos:* chemist, 68-91, CONSULT, ARGONNE NAT LAB, 93- *Personal Data:* b Pittsburgh, Pa, July 5, 27; m 63, Leora R Lubovsky; c Robert S. *Educ:* Univ Pittsburgh, BS, 49; Carnegie Inst Technol, MS, 52, PhD(chem), 54. *Prof Exp:* Sr scientist, Bettis Atomic Power Lab, Westinghouse Elec Co, 53-54; res chemist, Glass Div Res Lab, Pittsburgh Plate Glass Corp, 54-57; assoc chemist, Argonne Nat Lab, 57-60; sr scientist, Astronuclear Lab, Westinghouse Elec Corp, 60-61; mgr flight safety sect, 61-62, adv engr, 62-64, adv scientist, Bettis Atomic Power Lab, 64-65; assoc scientist, Space Div, Chrysler Corp, 65-68; consult, Mac Tech Serv, 91-93. *Mem:* Emer mem Am Nuclear Soc. *Res:* Fields of reactor safety experiments; materials research and development; reactor safety and safeguards analyses; nuclear waste management; electrochemistry. *Mailing Add:* 301 Lake Hinsdale Dr Apt 403 Willowbrook IL 60514

ROTHMAN, ALAN MICHAEL, ANALYTICAL CHROMATOGRAPHY, RADIOTRACER CHEMISTRY. *Current Pos:* SR CHEMIST, ROHM AND HAAS RES LABS, 73- *Personal Data:* b Philadelphia, Pa, July 7, 43; m 72; c 2. *Educ:* Purdue Univ, BS, 65; Pa State Univ, PhD(org chem), 69. *Prof Exp:* Instr radiation safety, Defense Atomic Support Agency Nuclear Weapons Sch, 69-71. *Mem:* Am Chem Soc; Health Physics Soc; Asn Off Analytical Chemists. *Res:* Utilization of radiotracers and chromatography to further research goals of all company research groups, including major fields of plastics, agricultural products, health products, and analysis. *Mailing Add:* 519 Pine Tree Rd Jenkintown PA 19046

ROTHMAN, ALBERT J(OEL), HIGH TEMPERATURE CERAMICS & INSULATION, CHEMISTRY GENERAL. *Current Pos:* CONSULT, 87- *Personal Data:* b Brooklyn, NY, Jan 16, 24; m 47; c 3. *Educ:* Columbia Univ, BS, 44; Polytech Univ NY, MChE, 50; Univ Calif, Berkeley, PhD(chem eng), 54. *Prof Exp:* Chem engr, Stamford Res Labs, Am Cyanamid Co, 44-48; process design engr, Colgate-Palmolive Co, 48-50; res chem engr, Shell Oil Co, 53-56; proj mgr & res assoc corrosion of metals, Eng Res Labs, Columbia Univ, 56-58; chemist ceramic res & develop, Lawrence Livermore Lab, Univ Calif, 58-59, group leader, 59-61, assoc div leader, Inorg Mat, 61-72, dep proj leader, Oil Shale, 72-81, proj leader, nuclear waste isolation, 81-84, sr res chem engr, 84-86, consult, 87-91. *Mem:* Am Chem Soc; Sigma Xi. *Res:* High temperature material for lasers; nuclear waste isolation; research and development shale oil pyrolysis and recovery from oil shale; heat transfer and thermal conductivity of gases; refrigerant substitutions for freon. *Mailing Add:* 503 Yorkshire Dr Livermore CA 94550

ROTHMAN, ALVIN HARVEY, biology; deceased, see previous edition for last biography

ROTHMAN, ARTHUR I, MEDICAL EDUCATION. *Current Pos:* res assoc med educ, Educ Res Unit, 68-69, DIR & PROF MED EDUC, DIV STUDIES MED EDUC, FAC MED, UNIV TORONTO, 69-, PROF HIGHER EDUC GROUP, ONT INST STUDIES EDUC, 76- *Personal Data:* b Montreal, Que, Apr 8, 38; m 60; c 3. *Educ:* McGill Univ, BSc, 59; Univ Maine, MS, 65; State Univ NY Buffalo, EdD(sci educ), 68. *Prof Exp:* Res assoc sci educ, Grad Sch Educ, Harvard Univ, 67-68. *Concurrent Pos:* Hon lectr med educ, Dept Internal Med, Univ Toronto, 69- consult, Can Asn Can Coun fel, 75-76; vis scholar, Univ Teaching Methods Univ, Inst Educ, Univ London, 75-76. *Mem:* Am Educ Res Asn; Can Soc Study Higher Educ; Asn Study Med Educ. *Res:* Examination of programs directed at the development of faculty as teachers; relationships between student characteristics, learning and career selection in medicine; methods of curriculum evaluation in medicine; programs of patient education. *Mailing Add:* Dept Educ Univ Toronto Toronto ON M5S 1A1 Can

ROTHMAN, DAVID J, MEDICINE. *Current Pos:* from asst prof to assoc prof, 67-71, PROF, COLUMBIA UNIV, 71-, BERNARD SCHOENBERG PROF SOCIAL MED & DIR, CTR STUDY SOC & MED. *Personal Data:* b New York, NY, Apr 30, 37; m 60, Sheila Miller; c Matthew & Micol. *Educ:* Columbia Univ, BA, 58; Harvard Univ, MA, 59, PhD, 64. *Honors & Awards:* Albert J Beveridge Prize, Am Hist Asn, 71; Samuel Paley lectr, Hebrew Univ, 77. *Prof Exp:* Fulbright-Hayes prof, Hebrew Univ, Jerusalem, 68-69, India, 82. *Concurrent Pos:* Vis Pinkerton prof, Sch Criminal Justice, State Univ NY, Albany, 73-74; bd dirs, Ment Health Law Proj, 73-80 & 82-; NIMH fel, 74-75 & 78-81; Law Enforcement Assistance Admin fel, 75-76; dir, Proj Community Alternatives, 78-82. *Mem:* Am Hist Asn; Orgn Am Historians; NY State Acad Med. *Res:* Medicine. *Mailing Add:* Ctr Study Soc & Med Columbia Univ Col Physicians & Surgeons 630 W 168th St New York NY 10032

ROTHMAN, FRANCOISE, MEDICINE. *Current Pos:* RETIRED. *Personal Data:* b Paris, France, 23; US citizen. *Educ:* Paris Med Sch, MD, 51. *Prof Exp:* Asst med dir, Med Tribune, 65-73; asst dir clin res, Sandoz Labs, 74-75; area med dir, Abbott Int, 76-77; assoc dir clin res, Merrell Int, 78; assoc med dir, Ayerst Labs, 79-89. *Mem:* Am Asn Study Headache; Drug Info Asn; AMA; NY Acad Sci. *Mailing Add:* 1441 Third Ave New York NY 10028-1977

ROTHMAN, FRANK GEORGE, EDUCATIONAL ADMINISTRATION, BIOCHEMISTRY & GENETICS. *Current Pos:* from asst prof to assoc prof, Brown Univ, 61-70, dean biol, 84-90, provost, 90-95, PROF BIOL, BROWN UNIV, 70- *Personal Data:* b Budapest, Hungary, Feb 2, 30; US citizen; m 53, Joan T Kiernan; c Michael, Jean, Stephen & Maria. *Educ:* Univ Chicago, AB, 48, MS, 51; Harvard Univ, PhD(chem), 55. *Prof Exp:* Res assoc chem, Univ Wis, 57; res assoc biol, Mass Inst Technol, 57-61. *Concurrent Pos:* NSF fel, 56-58; Am Cancer Soc fel, 67-68. *Mem:* Genetics Soc Am; fel AAAS. *Res:* Biochemical genetics; biology of aging. *Mailing Add:* Div Biol & Med Brown Univ Box G-J119 Providence RI 02912-9100. *Fax:* 401-863-2421; *E-Mail:* frank_rothman@brown.edu

ROTHMAN, HERBERT B, TRANSPORTATION ENGINEERING. *Current Pos:* PRIN & DIR TRANSP & BRIDGES, WEIDLINGER ASSOCS, 78- *Personal Data:* b New York, NY, May 27, 24. *Educ:* Rensselaer Polytech Inst, BSCE, 44. *Honors & Awards:* Roebling Award, Am Soc Civil Engrs, Rowland Medal; Arthur J Boase 25th Annual Lectr, Univ Colo, Boulder, 90. *Prof Exp:* Engr railroad design, Gibbs & Hill, 45; struct & hwy engr, Parsons, Brinckenhoff, Quade & Douglas, 45-46; designer to partner bridge, tunnel, transp & spec struct eng, Ammann & Whitney, 46-78. *Concurrent Pos:* Mem, Res Comt, Inst Bridge Tunnel & Turnpike Asn; dep mayor & hwy comnr, Village Laurel Hollow, NY. *Mem:* Nat Acad Eng; Sigma Xi; Am Soc Civil Engrs; Am Concrete Inst; Am Road & Transp Builders Asn; Am Inst Steel Construct; Inst Bridge Integrity & Safety; Struct Stability Res Coun; Int Bridge & Tunnel Turnpike Asn. *Res:* Author of various publications. *Mailing Add:* 375 Hudson St New York NY 10014. *Fax:* 212-564-2279

ROTHMAN, HOWARD BARRY, SPEECH & HEARING SCIENCE. *Current Pos:* res instr, Commun Sci Lab, 69-70, from asst prof to assoc prof 71-88, PROF, DEPT COMMUN PROCESSES & DIS, INST ADVAN STUDY COMMUN PROCESSES, UNIV FLA, 88- *Personal Data:* b New York, NY, July 17, 38; m 79, GloryAnn M Coomer; c Rachel, Gabrielle & Aviva. *Educ:* City Col New York, BA, 61; NY Univ, MA, 64; Stanford Univ, PhD(speech & hearing sci), 71. *Prof Exp:* Clinician aphasia, Inst Phys Med & Rehab, 63-64. *Concurrent Pos:* Consult, Speech Transmission Lab, Royal Inst Technol, Sweden, 72, Defense Res Bd, Defense & Civil Inst Environ Med, Ont, 72, Swed Develop Corp & Swed Nat Defense Works on Underwater Commun, 73, Harbor Br Found/Smithsonian Inst, 73, US Dist Court, Western Dist Tenn, 75 & Alachua County Sheriff's Dept, 75. *Mem:* Acoust Soc Am; Am Asn Phonetic Sci; Am Speech & Hearing Asn; NY Acad Sci; Sigma Xi. *Res:* Acoustic and perceptual aspects of speaker identification; underwater speech communication; acoustic and electromyographic aspects of atypical speech behavior; tape decoding and authentication; perceptual and acoustic analysis of the singing voice. *Mailing Add:* Inst Advan Study Commun & Dept Commun Processes & Dis ASB 63 Univ Fla Gainesville FL 32611. *Fax:* 352-846-0243; *E-Mail:* hrothman@cpd.ufl.edu

ROTHMAN, JAMES EDWARD, BIOCHEMISTRY. *Current Pos:* PAUL A MARKS CHAIR & CHMN, PROG CELLULAR BIOCHEM & BIOPHYS, SLOAN-KETTERING INST, NY, 91- *Personal Data:* b Haverhill, Mass, Nov 3, 50; m 71; c 1. *Educ:* Yale Univ, BA, 71; Harvard Univ, PhD(biochem), 76. *Prof Exp:* Fel, Dept Biol, Mass Inst Technol, 76-78; from asst prof to assoc prof, Dept Biochem, Stanford Univ, 78-88; prof, Dept Molecular Biol, Princeton Univ, NJ, 88-91. *Mem:* Nat Acad Sci; Inst Med-Nat Acad Sci; Am Soc Biol Chemists. *Mailing Add:* Mem Sloan Kettering Cancer Ctr Rockefeller Res Lab 1275 York Ave PO Box 251 New York NY 10021-6007. *Fax:* 212-717-3604

ROTHMAN, KENNETH J, EPIDEMIOLOGY. *Current Pos:* PROF PUB HEALTH, BOSTON UNIV, 89- *Personal Data:* b New York, NY, Nov 2, 45. *Educ:* Colgate Univ, AB, 66; Harvard Univ, DMD, 69, MPH, 70, DrPH, 72. *Honors & Awards:* Adolph G Kammer Award, Am Occup Med Asn, 83; James H Sterner lectr, Univ Calif, Irvine, 87. *Prof Exp:* From asst prof to assoc prof epidemiol, Harvard Univ, 72-84; prof fam & community med, Univ Mass Med Sch, 84-89. *Concurrent Pos:* Res assoc cardiol, Children's Hosp, 73-85; consult epidemiol, Mass Gen Hosp, 75-85; vis epidemiologist, Nat Cancer Inst, 76-77; consult numerous health orgns, 76-88; assoc ed, Am J Epidemiol, 79-82, ed, 82-87; sr epidemiologist, Epidemiol Res Inc, 80-; fac assoc, Univ Mass, 81-85; mem, Adv Comt to Surgeon Gen on Health Consequences of Smokeless Tobacco, 84-85; ed, Epidemiol, 88-; adj prof epidemiol, Harvard Univ, 92- *Mem:* Soc Epidemiol Res (pres, 84-85); Biomet Soc; Int Soc Environ Epidemiol; Am Pub Health Asn; Int Epidemiol Asn; Coun Biol Ed. *Res:* Epidemiologic methods; epidemiology of cancer; birth defects; neurological disease; cardiovascular disease; environmental epidemiology; ethics. *Mailing Add:* Epidemiol Resources Inc One Newton Executive Park Newton Lower Falls MA 02162-1450

ROTHMAN, LAURENCE SIDNEY, ATOMIC PHYSICS, ATMOSPHERIC CHEMISTRY. *Current Pos:* ATOMIC & MOLECULAR PHYSICIST ATMOSPHERIC TRANSMISSION, OPTICAL PHYSICS DIV, AIR FORCE GEOPHYSICS LAB, 68-; STAFF SCIENTIST, HARVARD-SMITHSONIAN CTR ASTROPHYSICS, 94- *Personal Data:* b New York, NY, Jan 20, 40; m 96, Marina Zivkovic. *Educ:* Mass Inst Technol, BS, 61; Boston Univ, MA, 64, PhD(physics), 71. *Honors & Awards:* Fed Lab Consortium Award of Merit; Gunter Loeser Award. *Prof Exp:* Res physicist infrared physics, Block Assoc Inc, Cambridge, Mass, 61-63. *Concurrent Pos:* Invited prof, Univ Paris, 85, 87, 90, 93 & 95; assoc ed, J Quant Spectros & Radiative Transfer; officer, Int Radiation Comn. *Mem:* Sigma Xi; fel Optical Soc Am; Soc Photo Optical Instrument Eng. *Res:* Development of theoretical and analytical methods for the study of molecular physics and infrared absorption; study of mechanisms of attenuation and emission of infrared radiation in model atmospheres. *Mailing Add:* AF Geophysics Directorat PL/GPOS Hanscom AFB MA 01731-3010

ROTHMAN, MILTON A, PLASMA PHYSICS. *Current Pos:* RETIRED. *Personal Data:* b Philadelphia, Pa, Nov 30, 19; m 50; c 2. *Educ:* Ore State Col, BS, 44; Univ Pa, MS, 48, PhD(physics), 52. *Prof Exp:* Physicist, Bartol Res Found, Franklin Inst, Pa, 52-59 & Plasma Physics Lab, Princeton Univ, 59-68; prof physics, Trenton State Col, 68-79; sr res scientist, Franklin Res Ctr, 79-85. *Mem:* Am Phys Soc; AAAS. *Res:* Nuclear physics; plasma physics; heating of magnetically confined plasma by ion cyclotron waves; experimental basis of the fundamental laws of physics. *Mailing Add:* 2020 Chancellor St Philadelphia PA 19103

ROTHMAN, NEAL JULES, MATHEMATICAL ANALYSIS. *Current Pos:* chmn dept, 82-86, PROF, MATH DEPT, IND UNIV-PURDUE UNIV, INDIANAPOLIS, 82- *Personal Data:* b Philadelphia, Pa, Nov 20, 28; m 55, Rozann Cole; c Hal, Elaine & Anne. *Educ:* Univ Del, BS, 51; Tulane Univ, MS, 54; La State Univ, PhD, 58. *Prof Exp:* Sr comput analyst, Burroughs Corp, 54-56; instr & asst math, La State Univ, 56-58; from instr to asst prof, Univ Rochester, 58-62; from asst prof to prof math, Univ Ill, Urbana, 62-82; prog dir modern anal, NSF, Washington, 79-82. *Concurrent Pos:* Vis prof, Hebrew Univ, 68-69, Israel Inst Technol, Haifa, Israel, 71-72, 76-77 & Tel-Aviv Univ, Israel, 89. *Res:* Computer-aided geometric design. *Mailing Add:* Ind Univ-Purdue Univ 402 N Blackford St Indianapolis IN 46202-3272. *Fax:* 317-274-3460; *E-Mail:* nrothman@iupui.math.edu

ROTHMAN, RICHARD HARRISON, ORTHOPEDIC SURGERY, ANATOMY. *Current Pos:* asst prof, 71-73, ASSOC PROF ORTHOP SURG, SCH MED, UNIV PA, 73-; JAMES EDWARDS PROF & CHAIR ORTHOP SURG, THOMAS JEFFERSON UNIV. *Personal Data:* b Philadelphia, Pa, Dec 2, 36; m 60; c 2. *Educ:* Univ Pa, BA, 58, MD, 62; Jefferson Med Col, PhD(anat), 65. *Prof Exp:* NIH fel, Jefferson Med Col, 63-65, dir, Orthop Res Lab, 65-71. *Mem:* Am Asn Anat. *Res:* Blood flow in tendon and bone. *Mailing Add:* 800 Spruce St Philadelphia PA 19107-6130

ROTHMAN, SAM, PHYSICAL CHEMISTRY, RESEARCH ADMINISTRATION. *Current Pos:* res prof, George Washington Univ, 74-75, chmn dept, 75-84, prof, 75-79, EMER PROF ENG ADMIN, GEORGE WASHINGTON UNIV, 90- *Personal Data:* b Brooklyn, NY, Feb 1, 20; m 43; c 2. *Educ:* Long Island Univ, BS, 43; Am Univ, MA, 54, PhD, 59. *Prof Exp:* Chemist, Nat Inst Standards & Technol, 46-55; dep res coordr, Off Naval Res, 55-61, asst res & eng off, Bur Naval Weapons, 61-63, dep dir explor develop, Hq, Naval Mat Command, 63-70, dep dir prog mgt off, 70-74. *Concurrent Pos:* Prof lectr, Am Univ, 59-67, adj prof, 68-74. *Mem:* AAAS; Am Chem Soc; Sigma Xi. *Res:* Polymers in solution; adsorption of macromolecules; research and development management. *Mailing Add:* 613 Hyde Rd Silver Spring MD 20902-3043

ROTHMAN, SARA WEINSTEIN, BACTERIAL TOXINS, PATHOGENESIS. *Current Pos:* res chemist, Dept Biol Chem, 78-89, res chemist, Dept Molecular Path, 89-93, DIR RES MGT, WALTER REED ARMY INST RES, 93- *Personal Data:* b Winthrop, Mass, July 29, 29; div; c Stephen G & Richard M. *Educ:* Simmons Col, BS, 65; Boston Univ, AM, 67, PhD(microbiol), 70. *Prof Exp:* Am Cancer Soc fel, Dept Biochem & Pharmacol, Sch Med, Tufts Univ, 70-73; res assoc, Dept Path, Boston Univ, 73-74, res asst prof, 74-75, res asst prof, Dept Microbiol, Sch Med, Boston Univ, 75-78. *Concurrent Pos:* Res assoc, Mallory Inst Path, 76-78; mem spec sci staff, Boston City Hosp, 76-78; vis prof, Ore Health Sci Univ, 86-87; Secy Army Sci & Eng fel, 86-87; Found microbiol lectr, Am Soc Microbiol, 87-88, Am Acad Microbiol, 90- *Mem:* Am Soc Microbiol; Sigma Xi; Asn Women in Sci; Int Soc Toxicol; The Protein Soc. *Res:* Purification of bacterial toxins and isolation of receptors; biological, physical and genetic characterization of bacterial toxins; molecular pathogenesis of enteric disease; development of cell culture and immunoassays; anaerobic bacteriology; animal models of enteric disease; diagnosis of antibiotic-associated colitis. *Mailing Add:* Off Res Mgt Walter Reed Army Inst Res Washington DC 20307-5100. *Fax:* 202-782-0602; *E-Mail:* rothman@wrair__emh1.army.mil

ROTHMAN, STEPHEN SUTTON, CELL PHYSIOLOGY, CELLULAR BIOPHYSICS. *Current Pos:* founding chair, Prog Biophys, 81-83, PROF PHYSIOL, UNIV CALIF, SAN FRANCISCO, 71-; SR FAC SCIENTIST, LAWRENCE BERKELEY LAB, 87- *Personal Data:* b New York, NY, July 10, 35; m 57, Doreen Zinn; c Jennifer & Peter. *Educ:* Univ Pa, AB, 56, DDS, 61, PhD(physiol), 64. *Prof Exp:* Instr physiol, Univ Pa, 64-65; assoc, Harvard Med Sch, 65-66, asst prof, 66-67, assoc prof, 67-71. *Concurrent Pos:* NIH career develop award, 67-72; mem, prog biophys & med physics, Univ Calif, San Francisco & Univ Calif, Berkeley, 72-, joint prog bioeng, 87; fac mem, Sch Eng, Univ Calif, Berkeley, 88- *Mem:* AAAS; Am Physiol Soc; NY Acad Sci; Biophys Soc; Sigma Xi; Soc Gen Physiologists; Am Soc Zool. *Res:* Soft x-ray microscopy; properties of protein transport. *Mailing Add:* Dept Physiol Univ Calif San Francisco CA 94143. *Fax:* 510-527-8505; *E-Mail:* rothman@itsa.ucsf.edu

ROTHMAN, STEVEN J, PHYSICAL METALLURGY. *Current Pos:* ED, J APPL PHYSICS, 90- *Personal Data:* b Giessen, Ger, Dec 18, 27; US citizen; m 51, Barbara A Kirkpatrick; c Ann (Fritcher) & Nicholas. *Educ:* Univ Chicago, PhB, 47; Stanford Univ, BS, 51, MS, 53, PhD(metall eng), 55. *Honors & Awards:* Fulbright lectr, 73. *Prof Exp:* Asst metallurgist, Argonne Nat Lab, 54-60, assoc metallurgist, 60-77, metallurgist, 77-93. *Concurrent Pos:* NSF fel, 62-63. *Mem:* Am Inst Mining, Metall & Petrol Engrs; Am Phys Soc; Mat Res Soc. *Res:* Diffusion in solids. *Mailing Add:* Argonne Nat Lab Bldg 203 R127 PO Box 8296 Argonne IL 60439-8296. *Fax:* 630-252-4973; *E-Mail:* sj__rothman@anl.gov

ROTHMAN-DENES, LUCIA B, BIOCHEMISTRY, MOLECULAR BIOLOGY. *Current Pos:* fel molecular biol, Dept Biophys, Univ Chicago, 70-72, res assoc, 72-74, from asst prof to prof molecular biol, Dept Biophys & Theoret Biol, 74-84, PROF, DEPT MOLECULAR GENETICS & CELL BIOL, UNIV CHICAGO, 84- *Personal Data:* b Buenos Aires, Arg, Feb 17, 43; US citizen; m 68, Pablo; c Christian Andrew & Anne Elizabeth. *Educ:* Univ Buenos Aires, Lic, 64, PhD(biochem), 67. *Prof Exp:* Fel biochem, Res Inst Biochem, Buenos Aires, 67; fel, Nat Inst Arthritis, Metab & Digestive Dis, 67-69, vis fel genetics, 69-70. *Concurrent Pos:* Nat Res Coun fel, Buenos Aires, 67; NIH spec res fel, 70-72 & res career develop award, 75-80; mem, microbiol genetics & physiol study sect, NIH, 80-84, genertic basis dis study sect, 85-89; chmn, Bacteriophage Div, Am Soc Microbiol, 85, div group 1 rep, 90-92; counr, Am Soc Virol, 88-90; mem, Damon Runyon, Walter Winchell cancer fund sci adv bd, 89-93; biochem panel, NSF, 90-92; mem, Microbiol Genetics & Physiol Study Sect, NIH, 92-96, chair, 94-96. *Mem:* Am Soc Biol Chemists; Am Soc Microbiol; AAAS; Am Soc Virol; fel Am Acad Microbiol. *Res:* Biochemistry and regulation of transcription and DNA replication in bacteriophage infected bacteria; structure function of DNA dependent RNA polymers; DNA structures. *Mailing Add:* Dept Molecular Genetics & Cell Biol Cummings Life Sci Ctr Univ Chicago 920 E 58th St Chicago IL 60637. *Fax:* 773-702-3172; *E-Mail:* lbrd@midway.uchicago.edu

ROTHROCK, GEORGE MOORE, POLYMER CHEMISTRY, PATENT LIAISON. *Current Pos:* RETIRED. *Personal Data:* b Columbus, Ohio, May 5, 19; m 46, 80, Betty E Clay; c Thomas A, Mary C & John L. *Educ:* De Pauw Univ, AB, 41; Purdue Univ, PhD(org chem), 45. *Prof Exp:* Polymer chemist, E I Du Pont De Nemours & Co, Inc, 45-60, sr patent chemist, 60-82. *Mem:* Am Chem Soc. *Res:* Chlorination and fluorination of hydrocarbons; polymer chemistry; polymer solvents; synthetic fibers; non-woven textiles. *Mailing Add:* 29 Commodore Point Rd Lake Wylie SC 29710

ROTHROCK, JOHN WILLIAM, BIOCHEMISTRY. *Current Pos:* RETIRED. *Personal Data:* b Bangor, Pa, Jan 6, 20; m 46, Goldie E Swango; c Janet K & Susan E (Mitchell). *Educ:* Pa State Col, BS, 41; Univ Ill, PhD(biochem), 49. *Prof Exp:* Res chemist, Merck Sharp & Dohme Res Labs, Merck & Co, 49-86. *Mem:* Am Chem Soc; Sigma Xi. *Res:* Antibiotics; growth factors; steroids; enzymes; drugs to lower blood pressure (Enalapril) and cholesterol (Lovastatin). *Mailing Add:* 51 Cardinal Dr Watchung NJ 07060-6108

ROTHROCK, LARRY R, LASER PHYSICS, CRYSTAL GROWTH. *Current Pos:* Res physicist, Union Carbide Corp, 66-68, res assoc, 68-72, mgr, 72-75, mgr res, 75-80, mgr new technol, 80-85, TECHNOL MGR, UNION CARBIDE CORP, 85- *Personal Data:* b Feb 6, 40; m 60; c 2. *Educ:* Oakland City Col, BS, 63. *Mem:* Optical Soc Am; Am Asn Crystal Growth. *Res:* Single crystal mat; laser crystals and sapphire; electro-optics. *Mailing Add:* 13808 Belvedere Dr Poway CA 92064

ROTHROCK, PAUL E, BOTANY, PHYTOPATHOLOGY. *Current Pos:* from asst prof to assoc prof, 81-88, PROF BIOL, TAYLOR UNIV, 88- *Personal Data:* b Newark, NJ, Oct 17, 48; m 73, Mary E Bidwell; c Suzanne. *Educ:* Rutgers Univ, BA, 70; Pa State Univ, MS, 73, PhD(bot), 76. *Prof Exp:* Prof biol, Montreat-Anderson Col, 76-81. *Mem:* Nat Asn Biol Teachers; Torrey Bot Club; Am Soc Plant Taxonomists. *Res:* Systematics of the genus Carex (Cyperaceae). *Mailing Add:* Dept Biol Taylor Univ Upland IN 46989. *E-Mail:* plrothroc@taylor.edu

ROTHROCK, THOMAS STEPHENSON, ORGANIC CHEMISTRY. *Current Pos:* RETIRED. *Personal Data:* b Springdale, Ark, Sept 7, 28; m 54; c 2. *Educ:* Univ Ark, BA, 50, MS, 56, PhD(org chem), 58. *Prof Exp:* Res chemist, Tenn Eastman Corp, 53-54; sr res chemist, Celanese Corp Am, Tex, 57-63; res chemist, Monsanto Co, St Louis, 63-86. *Mem:* Am Chem Soc. *Res:* Carbon-14 tracer studies. *Mailing Add:* 2214 Dehart Farm Rd Glencoe MO 63038-1135

ROTHSCHILD, BRIAN JAMES, FISH BIOLOGY, AQUATIC ECOLOGY. *Current Pos:* DIR, CTR MARINE SCI, ENVIRON & TECHNOL, UNIV MASS, PROF BIOL, 95- *Personal Data:* b Newark, NJ, Aug 14, 34; m 62; c 2. *Educ:* Rutgers Univ, BS, 57; Univ Maine, MS, 59; Cornell Univ, PhD(vert zool), 62. *Prof Exp:* Asst fishery biol, NJ Div Fish & Game, 54-57, zool, Univ Maine, 57-59 & vert zool, Cornell Univ, 59-62; chief skipjack tuna ecol prog, Honolulu Biol Lab, Bur Com Fisheries, 62-68; from assoc prof to prof, Fishery Res Inst & Ctr Quant Sci, Univ Wash, 68-71; dep dir, Northwest Fisheries Ctr, Nat Marine Fisheries Serv, 71-72, dir Atmospheric Admin, 72-75, dir, Extended Jurisdiction Prog Staff, 75-76, dir, Off Policy & Long-Range Planning, 76-77; sr policy adv, Off Admin, Nat Oceanic & Atmospheric Admin, 77-80; prof, Ctr Environ & Estaurine Studies, Chesapeake Biol Lab, Univ Md, 80-95. *Concurrent Pos:* Asst, Inst Fishery Res, Univ NC, 59; affil grad fac, Univ Hawaii, 64-; lectr, 66-67; vis fel biomet, Cornell Univ, 65-66. *Mem:* Fel AAAS; Am Fisheries Soc. *Res:* Ecology of fishes; marine ecology; biology and population dynamics; resource policy. *Mailing Add:* CMAST Univ Mass North Dartmouth MA 02747-2300. *Fax:* 508-999-8197; *E-Mail:* brothschild@umassd.edu

ROTHSCHILD, BRUCE LEE, MATHEMATICS. *Current Pos:* asst prof, 69-73, assoc prof, 73-77, PROF MATH, UNIV CALIF, LOS ANGELES, 77- *Personal Data:* b Los Angeles, Calif, Aug 26, 41. *Educ:* Calif Inst Technol, BS, 63; Yale Univ, PhD(math), 67. *Prof Exp:* Instr math, Mass Inst Technol, 67-69. *Concurrent Pos:* US Air Force grant, Mass Inst Technol, 67-69; consult, Bell Tel Labs, 68-71 & Network Anal Corp, 69; NSF grant, Univ Calif, Los Angeles, 69-; ed, J Combinatorial Theory, 70-; Sloan Found fel, 73-75. *Mem:* AAAS; Am Math Soc; Math Asn Am; Soc Indust & Appl Math; Sigma Xi. *Res:* Combinatorial theory; finite geometries; asymptotic enumeration; Ramsey theory; graph theory; network flows. *Mailing Add:* Dept Math Univ Calif Los Angeles CA 90024

ROTHSCHILD, DAVID (SEYMOUR), ELECTRICAL ENGINEERING, SYSTEMS SCIENCE. *Current Pos:* DERIVATIVES TRADER, BEAR STEARNS, 92- *Personal Data:* b New York, NY, Nov 28, 41; m 74. *Educ:* City Col New York, BEE, 62; NY Univ, MSEE, 66; PhD(elec eng), 71. *Prof Exp:* Asst engr, Sperry Gyroscope Corp, 63; electronics engr, Grumman Aerospace Corp, 63-66; res scientist control syst res, 66-75; cash mgt systs consult, Chase Manhattan Bank, 75-81; decision support systs analyst, Lehman Bros, Kuhn Loeb, 81-85; trader, Bear Stearns, 85-89; options trader, Mabon Nugent, 89-91. *Mem:* Inst Elec & Electronics Engrs. *Res:* Linear optimal control theory; sensitivity analysis; nonlinear stability; estimation theory; research on the design of flight control systems which meet specified goals despite existing disturbances. *Mailing Add:* Am Stock Exchange 86 Trinity Pl New York NY 10006

ROTHSCHILD, GILBERT ROBERT, electrical engineering; deceased, see previous edition for last biography

ROTHSCHILD, HENRY, MOLECULAR BIOLOGY, MEDICINE. *Current Pos:* assoc prof med, 71-75, assoc prof anat, 72-75, ASSOC GRAD FAC, MED CTR, LA STATE UNIV, NEW ORLEANS, 73-, PROF MED & ANAT, 75- *Personal Data:* b Horstein, Germany, June 5, 32; US citizen. *Educ:* Cornell Univ, BA, 54; Univ Chicago, MD, 58; Johns Hopkins Univ, PhD(biol), 68. *Prof Exp:* Intern, Univ Chicago, 58-59; asst resident, Univ Hosp, Baltimore, 59-61; asst physician, Johns Hopkins Univ, 63-66, fel, 67-68; instr med, Mass Gen Hosp, 70-71. *Concurrent Pos:* USPHS spec fel, Mass Gen Hosp, 68-70; King Trust Award, 70-71; vis physician, Charity Hosp, New Orleans, 72-; dir, La Ethnogenetic Dis Screening Prog; consult, La Sickle Cell Educ & Screening Prog; Wellcome res travel grant, 79; vis prof, Fac Med, Univ Autonoma Nuevo Leon, Mex, 81; med dir, New Orleans Home & Rehab Ctr & St Margaret's Daughters Home. *Mem:* Am Fedn Clin Res; Am Col Physicians; Am Asn Cancer Res; Am Soc Human Genetics; Am Soc Path. *Res:* Molecular medicine; oncogenic virology; genetics; gerontology. *Mailing Add:* Dept Med La State Univ Med Ctr 1542 Tulane Ave New Orleans LA 70112-2865. *Fax:* 504-568-5842

ROTHSCHILD, KENNETH J, BIOPHYSICS. *Current Pos:* asst prof physiol, Sch Med & asst prof physics, Boston Univ, 76-81, assoc prof physiol & assoc prof physics, 82-85, prof physics & dir cellular biophys, 86-89, DIR, MOLECULAR BIOPHYS PROG, BOSTON UNIV, 93- *Personal Data:* b New York, NY, Feb 9, 48; m 74, Loan; c David & Brian. *Educ:* Rensselaer Polytech Inst, BS, 69; Mass Inst Technol, PhD(physics), 73. *Honors & Awards:* Whitaker Found Award. *Prof Exp:* Res assoc biophys, Harvard-Mass Inst Technol Prog Health Sci & Technol, 73-75. *Concurrent Pos:* NIH fel, Green Prize, 72-75; NIH fel, Nat Eye Inst, 74, coprin investr, 75; estab investr, Am Heart Asn; vis scientist, Neth Found Basic Sci. *Mem:* Biophys Soc; Sigma Xi; AAAS; fel Am Phys Soc. *Res:* Molecular mechanisms of membrane transport; conformational analysis of photoreceptor membranes using raman spectroscopy, fourier transform IR spectroscopy; purple membrane; nonequilibrium thermodynamics; biotechnology. *Mailing Add:* Dept Physics Boston Univ 590 Commonwealth Ave Boston MA 02215

ROTHSCHILD, MARCUS ADOLPHUS, INTERNAL MEDICINE, NUCLEAR MEDICINE. *Current Pos:* adj prof, 77-90, ADJ PROF, ROCKEFELLER UNIV, 90- *Personal Data:* b New York, NY, June 2, 24; m 65; c 2. *Educ:* Yale Univ, BS, 45; NY Univ, MD, 49; Am Bd Nuclear Med, dipl, 75. *Honors & Awards:* Distinguished Researcher Award, Res Soc Alcoholism, 86. *Prof Exp:* Intern, Beth Israel Hosp, New York, 49-50; resident med, Mt Sinai Hosp, New York, 50-51; resident, Beth Israel Hosp, Boston, Mass, 51-52; chief med resident, Beth Israel Hosp, New York, 52-53; from clin instr to prof med, Sch Med, NY Univ, 55-90. *Concurrent Pos:* Dazian Found fel, Radioisotope Serv, Vet Admin Hosp, NY, 53-55, sect chief gen med & chief radioisotope serv, 55-; lectr physiol, Hunter Col, 54-55; USPHS grants, 56-78; adj prof, Rockefeller Univ, 77-90; spec asst dir med res, Vet Admin Alcohol Res, 78-; ed, Alcoholism Clin Exp Res; clin prof radiol, Univ Miami. *Mem:* Fel Am Col Physicians; Am Soc Clin Invest; Am Asn Study Liver Diseases (secy-treas, 76-81, pres, 85-); Soc Nuclear Med; Asn Am Physicians. *Res:* Protein metabolism. *Mailing Add:* Dept Nuclear Med Vet Admin Med Ctr 1201 NW 16th St Miami FL 33125. *Fax:* 561-852-8430

ROTHSCHILD, RICHARD EISEMAN, X-RAY & GAMMA RAY ASTRONOMY. *Current Pos:* RES PHYSICIST, UNIV CALIF, SAN DIEGO, 77- *Personal Data:* b St Louis, Mo, Nov 27, 43; m 68; c 1. *Educ:* Washington Univ, AB, 65; Univ Ariz, MS, 68, PhD(physics), 71. *Honors & Awards:* NASA Group Achievement Award, Goddard Space Flight Ctr, 78 & 79. *Prof Exp:* Res assoc physics, Univ Ariz, 71-73; Nat Acad Sci/Nat Res Coun fel astrophys, Goddard Space Flight Ctr, NASA, 73-75, astrophysicist, 75-77. *Concurrent Pos:* Co-investr, Cosmic X-ray Exp High Energy Astron Observ, 76-86; prin investr, High Energy X-Ray Timing Exp on X-Ray Timing Explorer, 83- *Mem:* Am Phys Soc; Am Astron Soc. *Res:* Astronomical objects emitting x-rays and gamma rays; data analysis from detector systems. *Mailing Add:* CASS-0111 Univ Calif San Diego 9500 Gilman Dr La Jolla CA 92093

ROTHSCHILD, WALTER GUSTAV, RELAXATION PHENOMENA, FRACTAL PHENOMENA. *Current Pos:* RETIRED. *Personal Data:* b Berlin, Ger, Aug 18, 24; nat US. *Educ:* Tech Univ Berlin, BS, 49; Max Planck Inst, 50; Columbia Univ, MA, 58, PhD, 61. *Honors & Awards:* Donald Julius Groen Prize, Inst Mech Engrs, London, Eng, 86. *Prof Exp:* Res scientist, Electronized Chem Corp, NY, 50-52, Tracerlab, Inc, Mass, 52-54, Brookhaven Nat Lab, 54-57 & Columbia Univ, 57-61; staff scientist, Ford Motor Co, 61-95. *Concurrent Pos:* Guest prof, Dept Physics, Univ Buenos Aires, 69; Fulbright fel, 76-77, NATO res fel, 79-84, 88-90; guest prof, Univ Bordeaux I, France, 76-77, 86 & Univ Vienna, Austria, 77; vis prof, Univ Paris VI, France, 79, 80, 82 & 84; fac, Wayne State Univ, 90-, adj prof, 91- *Mem:* Am Phys Soc. *Res:* Molecular interactions, dynamics and structure; liquid and amorphous-state phenomena; infrared and Raman relaxation phenomena and spectroscopy fractals. *Mailing Add:* 555 E William Apt 10-D Ann Arbor MI 48104-2426

ROTHSTEIN, ASER, BIOPHYSICS, CELL PHYSIOLOGY. *Current Pos:* prof med biophys, Univ Toronto, 73-86, univ prof, 80-86, prof, 80-86, EMER PROF, UNIV TORONTO, 86- *Personal Data:* b Vancouver, BC, Apr 29, 18; nat US; m 40; c 3. *Educ:* Univ BC, BA, 38; Univ Rochester, PhD(biol), 43. *Hon Degrees:* DSc, Univ Rochester, 83. *Honors & Awards:* Gardner Award, 86. *Prof Exp:* Asst biol, Univ Rochester, 40-42, asst physiol, Off Sci Res & Develop Contract, 43, asst, Manhattan Proj, 44-45, assoc, 46-47, from instr to assoc prof pharmacol, 46-72, prof radiation biol, 59-72, co-chmn dept, 65-72, chief physiol sect, 48-60, assoc dir Atomic Energy Proj, 60-65, co-dir, 65-72; dir res inst, Hosp Sick Children, 72-86. *Concurrent Pos:* NSF sr fel, 59-60; vis prof, Dept Radiation Biol & Biophys, Med Sch, Univ Rochester &

Swiss Fed Univ, Weizman Inst. *Mem:* Am Physiol Soc; Biophys Soc; Int Union Physiol Sci; Soc Gen Physiologists; Royal Soc Can. *Res:* Structure and function of cell membranes, especially role of membrane proteins; role of membrane in cell growth and differentiation. *Mailing Add:* Res Inst Hosp Sick Children Toronto 555 University Ave Toronto ON M5G 1X8 Can

ROTHSTEIN, EDWIN C(ARL), TOXICOLOGY, ENVIRONMENTAL SCIENCE. *Current Pos:* PRES, LEBERCO TESTING INC, 82- *Personal Data:* b Brooklyn, NY, Nov 17, 33; m 58, Brenda Rothschild; c Helen L & Debra M. *Educ:* Brooklyn Col, BA, 54; Mass Inst Technol, MS, 56; Polytech Inst Brooklyn, PhD(chem eng), 64. *Honors & Awards:* Roon Award, Fedn Paint Socs, 64. *Prof Exp:* Res technologist, Cent Res Labs, Socony Mobil Oil Co, 56-59; res engr, Res Labs, Keuffel & Esser Co, 59-65; asst tech develop mgr, Indust Chem Div, Geigy Chem Corp, 65-67; chief chemist, Sinclair & Valentine Div, Martin-Marietta Corp, 67-69; dir res & develop, 69-70; tech dir, Equitable Bag Co, Inc, Long Island City, 70-78; tech develop mgr, Sun Chem Corp, 78-82. *Mem:* AAAS; Am Chem Soc; Soc Plastics Engrs; NY Acad Sci; Am Soc Testing & Mat; Asn Off Anal Chemists; Soc Cosmetic Chemists. *Res:* Printing inks and coatings; pigment dispersion rheology; photographic processes; plastics stabilization and testing; toxicology; analytical chemistry. *Mailing Add:* Leberco Testing Inc 123 Hawthorne St Roselle Park NJ 07204-0206. *Fax:* 908-245-6253; *E-Mail:* leberco@celsis.com

ROTHSTEIN, HOWARD, CELL PHYSIOLOGY. *Current Pos:* prof & chmn Dept Biol Sci, 81-86, PROF, FORDHAM UNIV, BRONX, NY, 86- *Personal Data:* b Brooklyn, NY, Aug 25, 35; m 56; c 3. *Educ:* Johns Hopkins Univ, BA, 56; Univ Pa, PhD(gen physiol), 60. *Prof Exp:* Asst instr zool, Univ Pa, 57-60; fel ophthal, Col Physicians & Surgeons, Columbia Univ, 60-62; from asst prof to prof zool, Univ Vt, 62-77; assoc prof ophthal, Kresge Eye Inst, Wayne State Univ Sch Med, Detroit, 77-81. *Mem:* Am Soc Zool; AAAS; Soc Gen Physiol. *Res:* Cell division; hormonal control of growth; vitro culture and wound healing of ocular tissues. *Mailing Add:* 1008 High Point Dr Hartsdale NY 10530

ROTHSTEIN, JEROME, plasma physics, solid state physics; deceased, see previous edition for last biography

ROTHSTEIN, LEWIS ROBERT, CHEMISTRY. *Current Pos:* RETIRED. *Personal Data:* b New York, NY, Oct 4, 20; m 47, Eva; c Susan & Judy. *Educ:* Queens Col NY, BS, 42; Ill Inst Technol, MS, 44, PhD(chem), 49. *Honors & Awards:* Technol Innovation Award, Am Defense Preparedness Asn. *Prof Exp:* Tech dir, Mason & Hanger-Silas Mason Co, 48-60; dir spec projs, Amcel Propulsion, Inc, 60-65; dir chem & munitions dept, Northrop-Carolina Inc, 65-71; spec asst, Naval Weapons Sta, Yorktown, Va, 71-74, asst tech dir, 74-82, tech dir, 82-88. *Concurrent Pos:* Consult, Dept Defense & Dept Defense Private Contractors. *Mem:* Am Chem Soc. *Res:* Physical organic chemistry; predicting detonation and safety characteristics of explosives from their composition and chemical structure alone. *Mailing Add:* 124 Selden Rd Newport News VA 23606

ROTHSTEIN, MORTON, BIOCHEMISTRY. *Current Pos:* chmn dept, 69-70, prof, 65-89, EMER PROF BIOL SCI, STATE UNIV NY, BUFFALO, 89- *Personal Data:* b Vancouver, BC, Sept 8, 22; nat US; m 47; c 3. *Educ:* Univ BC, BA, 46; Univ Ill, MS, 47, PhD(org chem), 49. *Honors & Awards:* Gold Medal for Res, Am Aging Asn, 88. *Prof Exp:* Res assoc tracer chem, Sch Med, Univ Rochester, 49-54; from asst res biochemist to assoc res biochemist, Sch Med, Univ Calif, San Francisco, 54-60; assoc res scientist, Res Inst, Kaiser Found, 60-65. *Concurrent Pos:* Lectr, Sch Med, Univ Calif, San Francisco, 58-65; Nat Inst Child Health & Human Develop res grant, 72-77; Nat Inst Aging res grant, 77-88. *Mem:* AAAS; Am Soc Biol Chem; fel Geront Soc. *Res:* Biochemistry of aging. *Mailing Add:* Div Cell & Molecular Biol State Univ NY Buffalo Buffalo NY 14260-0001

ROTHSTEIN, ROBERT, medical administration, agriculture, for more information see previous edition

ROTHSTEIN, RODNEY JOEL, molecular genetics, for more information see previous edition

ROTHWARF, ALLEN, THEORETICAL SOLID STATE PHYSICS, THEORETICAL WORK IN SUPERCONDUCTIVITY. *Current Pos:* assoc prof, 79-83, PROF ELEC ENG, DREXEL UNIV, PHILADELPHIA, PA, 83-, CONSULT, 79- *Personal Data:* b Philadelphia, Pa, Oct 1, 35; m 57, Bernice Golansky; c Richard, Jeanne & David. *Educ:* Temple Univ, AB, 57; Univ Pa, MS, 60, PhD(physics), 64. *Prof Exp:* Instr physics, Rutgers Univ, 60-62; mem tech staff, RCA Labs, 64-72; fel Sch Metall & Mat Sci, Univ Pa, 72-73; sr scientist, Mgr, Inst Energy Conversion, Univ Del, 73-79. *Mem:* Am Phys Soc; fel Inst Elec & Electronics Engrs. *Res:* Theory of superconductivity; photovoltaics; modeling of new solar cell structures and materials; modeling of power devices, modeling of quantum mechanics and cosmology. *Mailing Add:* Dept Elec & Comput Eng Drexel Univ 32nd & Chesnut Sts Philadelphia PA 19104. *Fax:* 215-895-1695; *E-Mail:* rothwarf@ece.drexel.edu

ROTHWARF, FREDERICK, SOLID STATE PHYSICS, MATERIALS SCIENCE. *Current Pos:* PHYSICIST SOLID STATE PHYSICS, ELECTRONICS TECHNOL & DEVICES LAB, US ARMY, FT MONMOUTH, 71- *Personal Data:* b Philadelphia, Pa, Apr 23, 30; m 51; c 4. *Educ:* Temple Univ, AB, 51, AM, 53, PhD(physics), 60. *Honors & Awards:* Sci Achievement Award, Secy of Army, 74. *Prof Exp:* Physicist antisubmarine warfare, US Naval Air Develop Ctr, Pa, 51-52; asst, Temple Univ, 52-56; physicist, Frankford Arsenal, 56-71. *Concurrent Pos:* Physicist thin film res, Burroughs Corp, Philadelphia, 52-53; health physicist, Radiobiol & X-ray Design, Temple Univ Hosp, 54-55; instr physics, Ogontz Ctr, Pa State Univ, 55-56; consult, Dept Otolaryngol, Presby Hosp, Philadelphia, 62-70; Secy of Army fel, Univ Paris-Orsay, France, 65-66; consult superconductivity, Naval Ships Res & Develop Ctr, Annapolis, Md, 68-72; pres, Terra Systs, Inc, Toms River, 70-; consult magnetics, Harry Diamond Labs, Washington, DC, 72-74. *Mem:* Am Phys Soc; Inst Elec & Electronics Engrs; Electrochem Soc; Am Asn Hydrogen Energy. *Res:* Semiconductor technology of silicon and gallium arsenide; rare earth-cobalt and amorphous magnetic materials; magnetic circuit designs; superconductivity; metal physics; metal hydrides; cryogenics; electronics; health physics. *Mailing Add:* 11722 Indian Ridge Rd Reston VA 22091

ROTHWELL, FREDERICK MIRVAN, MYCOLOGY, PHYSIOLOGICAL ECOLOGY. *Current Pos:* RETIRED. *Personal Data:* b Arena, Wis, May 7, 23; m 45, Claudia Quisenberry; c Lisa, Laura & Lezlie. *Educ:* Eastern Ky Univ, BS, 49; Univ Ky, MS, 51; Purdue Univ, PhD(mycol), 55. *Prof Exp:* USPHS fel, Purdue Univ, 55-56; res microbiologist, Buckman Labs, Inc, Tenn, 56-57, tech rep, 59-61; assoc prof animal dis, Agr Exp Sta, Miss State Univ, 57-59; prof life sci, Ind State Univ, Terre Haute, 61-74; consult, 74-75; microbiologist, US Forest Serv, 75-87. *Concurrent Pos:* Res grants, Com Solvents Corp, 64-66, Tenn Valley Auth, 65-68 & USDA, 67-68; adj prof, Ind Univ Sch Med, Terre Haute Ctr Med Educ & Ind State Univ, 72-75. *Res:* Microbiology associated with revegetation of surface-mined lands; mycorrhizal associates and asymbiotic and symbiotic nitrogen-fixing bacterial species. *Mailing Add:* 504 Center St Berea KY 40403-1739

ROTHWELL, NORMAN VINCENT, CYTOGENETICS. *Current Pos:* RETIRED. *Personal Data:* b Passaic, NJ, Sept 30, 24. *Educ:* Rutgers Univ, BS, 49; Univ Ind, PhD(bot), 54. *Prof Exp:* From lectr to instr bot, Univ Ind, 53-54; assoc prof biol, Southeastern Mo State Col, 54-55; lab instr, Cancer Inst, Univ Miami, Fla, 55-56; prof biol, Long Island Univ, 56- *Concurrent Pos:* Fulbright lectr, Univ Ceylon, 65-66 & 68-69. *Res:* Cytogenetic studies on Claytonia virginica; cellular differentiation in the grass root tip of epidermis. *Mailing Add:* 161 Henry St Brooklyn NY 11201

ROTHWELL, PAUL L, SPACE SCIENCE. *Current Pos:* Res fel elementary particles, Northeastern Univ, 62-67, RES PHYSICIST, AIR FORCE PHILLIPS LAB, 67- *Personal Data:* b Norwood, Mass, Apr 2, 38; m 65, Natalie Chermesino; c Anne & Christina. *Educ:* Harvard Univ, BA, 60; Northeastern Univ, MS, 62, PhD(physics), 67, MBA, 78. *Mem:* Am Geophys Union; Am Phys Soc; Sigma Xi. *Res:* Validity of quantum electrodynamics and the decay modes of the boson resonances; trapped radiation in the Van Allen belts; solar particles; substorm dynamics; magnetosphere-ionosphere coupling. *Mailing Add:* 15 George St Littleton MA 01460

ROTHWELL, WILLIAM STANLEY, OPTICAL OBSERVABLES, X-RAY DIFFRACTION ANALYSIS. *Current Pos:* INDEPENDENT CONSULT & AUTHOR, 86- *Personal Data:* b Wabasha, Minn, May 3, 24; m 46; c 4. *Educ:* US Naval Acad, BS, 45; Univ Wis, MS, 48, PhD(physics), 54. *Prof Exp:* Instr influence mines, US Navy Explosive Ord Disposal Sch, 46-47; instr physics, Racine Exten Ctr, Univ Wis, 49-52; res physicist, Corning Glass Works, 54-57; res group leader, Res Labs, Allis-Chalmers Mfg Co, 57-62; staff scientist, Lockheed Palo Alto Res Lab, 62-81, sr staff scientist, 81-86. *Res:* Solid state physics; small angle x-ray scattering; materials science; aerospace sciences; educational books and software. *Mailing Add:* 343 S Gordon Way Los Altos CA 94022

ROTI ROTI, JOSEPH LEE, RADIATION BIOPHYSICS, THEORETICAL BIOLOGY. *Current Pos:* assoc prof, 85-87, PROF RADIOL, RADIOL ONE CTR, SECT CANCER BIOL, WASHINGTON UNIV SCH MED, 87- *Personal Data:* b Newport, RI, Oct 12, 43; div. *Educ:* Mich Technol Univ, BS, 65; Univ Rochester, PhD(biophys), 72. *Honors & Awards:* Career Develop Award, NIH, 76. *Prof Exp:* Res instr, Univ Utah, 73-76, from asst prof to assoc prof radiol, 79-85. *Concurrent Pos:* Fel, AEC health physics, 65-68; res collabr, Brookhaven Nat Lab, 73-75. *Mem:* Cell Kinetics Soc; Radiation Res Soc; AAAS; Sigma Xi; NY Acad Sci. *Res:* Simulation of cell kinetics in vitro and in vivo using matrix algebra; studies of the effects of x-irradiation and hyperthermia on DNA, chromosomal proteins and cell progression through the cell cycle. *Mailing Add:* 14 Middlesex Dr St Louis MO 63144-1031. *Fax:* 314-362-9790

ROTKIN, ISADORE DAVID, EPIDEMIOLOGY, CANCER. *Current Pos:* from assoc prof to prof, 73-86, EMER PROF PREV MED, UNIV ILL COL MED, 86- *Personal Data:* b Chicago, Ill, June 26, 16; m 42, Patricia A Hughes; c Russ, Leigh & Nora. *Educ:* Univ Chicago, BS, 46; Univ Calif, Berkeley, MS, 49, PhD(genetics), 54. *Prof Exp:* Researcher, Cancer Res Lab, Univ Calif, Berkeley, 50-54; consult sci & indust, 55-59; dir cancer res, Res Inst, Kaiser Found, 59-68; dep chief oper studies, Nat Cancer Control Prog, USPHS, 68; staff consult, Calif Regional Med Progs, 68-70. *Concurrent Pos:* Consult bd med, Nat Acad Sci, Vet Admin Hosp, WSide, Chicago, Zellerbach-Saroni Tumor Inst, Mt Zion Hosp, San Francisco, unit epidemiol & biostatist, WHO, France, inst behav res, Tex Christian Univ, med dept, Pac Tel Co, San Francisco, Dept Chronic Dis, State of Conn & Stanford Res Inst; lectr epidemiol & community health, Sch Med, Univ Calif, San Diego, 70-72; consult, Am Cancer Soc, Alameda & San Francisco Counties, Calif, Oak Forest Hosp, Oak Forest, Ill, Ill Cancer Coun, Comprehensive Cancer Ctr, Chicago, Head & Neck Cancer Network, Rush Med Cancer Ctr, Chicago &

Northwestern Univ Med Sch, Chicago, Ill Inst Technol, Chicago & Pan Am Health Orgn, WHO, Washington, DC; chmn, Task Force Epidemiol & Statist, Ill Comprehensive Cancer Coun, Chicago, 73-; chmn, Panel Anal Epidemiol, XI Int Cancer Congress, Italy, 74; chmn, Legis & Tumor Registry Panels, Ill Cancer Coun, Chicago, 74-; mem, Comt Comprehensive Cancer Ctr Patient Data Syst, Nat Cancer Inst, NIH, 74-; vis prof, Univ Calif, Los Angeles, 80-81. *Mem:* Am Asn Cancer Res; Soc Epidemiol Res; Am Soc Human Genetics; Am Inst Biol Sci; Soc Study Social Biol. *Res:* Cancer and chronic disease epidemiology; sexual data; benign prostatic hypertrophy; case control studies; multidimensional risk studies; disease prevention and control; medical systems; community health; sexual data and counselling. *Mailing Add:* 3317 Cabo Ct Carlsbad CA 92009

ROTMAN, BORIS, MOLECULAR BIOLOGY, IMMUNOLOGY. *Current Pos:* PROF MED SCI, BROWN UNIV, 66- *Personal Data:* b Buenos Aires, Arg, Dec 4, 24; nat US; wid; c 1. *Educ:* Valparaiso Tech Univ, Chile, MS, 48; Univ Ill, PhD(bact), 52. *Honors & Awards:* RI Gov Award for Sci Achievement, 90. *Prof Exp:* Res assoc, Univ Ill, 52-53; Enzyme Inst, Madison, Wis, 53-56; vis prof, Sch Med, Univ Chile, 56-59; res dir, Radioisotope Serv, Vet Admin Hosp, Albany, NY, 59-61; res assoc genetics, Sch Med, Stanford Univ, 61; head biochem sect, Syntex Inst Molecular Biol, Calif, 61-66. *Concurrent Pos:* Am Soc Microbiol pres fel, 58; fel, Harvard Univ, 58. *Mem:* Am Soc Biol Chem; Am Soc Microbiol; Am Asn Cancer Res; Fed Am Scientists; AAAS. *Res:* Chemosensitivity testing; chemotherapy cancer research; short term micro-organ culture to assess chemosensitivity of tumors from individual cancer patients. *Mailing Add:* Div Biol & Med Sci Brown Univ Providence RI 02912

ROTMAN, HAROLD H, EXPERIMENTAL BIOLOGY. *Current Pos:* PROF MED & CHIEF MED SERV, DUKE UNIV, 85- *Mailing Add:* Med Pulmonary Dis Duke Univ Sch Med 1 Duke Med Ctr Durham NC 27710. *Fax:* 704-299-2502

ROTMAN, JOSEPH JONAH, ALGEBRA. *Current Pos:* Res assoc, 59-61, from asst prof to assoc prof, 61-68, PROF MATH, UNIV ILL, URBANA, 68- *Personal Data:* b Chicago, Ill, May 26, 34; m 78, Marganit Weinberger; c Ella R & Daniel A. *Educ:* Univ Chicago, AB, 54, MS, 56, PhD(math), 59. *Concurrent Pos:* Vis prof, Queen Mary Col, Univ London, 65-66 & Hebrew Univ, Jerusalem, 70, 78; ed, Proc, Am Math Soc, 70-73; Lady Davis prof, Israel Inst Technol, Haifa, 77-78, Tel Aviv Univ, 82; vis prof, Bar-ilan Univ Ramat Gan, Israel, 84 & Queen Mary Col, Univ London, 85-86; ann vis, SAfrican Math Soc, 85, Univ Oxford, 90. *Mem:* Math Asn Am; Am Math Soc. *Res:* Algebra. *Mailing Add:* 2203 Edgewater Champaign IL 61821. *E-Mail:* rotman@math.uiuc.edu

ROTMAN, MARVIN Z, MEDICINE. *Current Pos:* PROF & CHMN RADIATION ONCOL, STATE UNIV NY, BROOKLYN, 79- *Personal Data:* b Philadelphia, Pa, Sept 3, 33; c 3. *Educ:* Ursinus Col, BS, 54; Jefferson Med Col, MD, 58. *Prof Exp:* Assoc prof clin radiol, NY Med Col, 71-75, dir radiation oncol, 75-79. *Concurrent Pos:* Dir radiation oncol, Univ Hosp, Long Island Col Hosp & Kings Co Hosp, 79-; consult, Clin Cancer Prog Proj Grant, NIH, 76-85; ed, Int J Radiation Oncol, Biol & Physics, 79-; examnr, Oral Specialty Bds, Am Bd Radiol, 80-85 & 87; pres, SCAROP, 84-86; vpres, Radiol Soc NAm, 87-88. *Mem:* Fel Am Col Radiol; Soc Chmn Acad Radiother Prog (pres, 77-78). *Mailing Add:* Dept Radiation Oncol State Univ NY Health Sci Ctr Brooklyn NY 11203

ROTMAN, WALTER, ELECTRICAL ENGINEERING. *Current Pos:* RETIRED. *Personal Data:* b St Louis, Mo, Aug 24, 22; m 54, Molly Shapiro; c Stanley & Ruth R. *Educ:* Mass Inst Technol, BS, 47, MS, 48. *Prof Exp:* Asst elec eng, Res Lab Electronics, Mass Inst Technol, 47-48; electronic scientist, Air Force Cambridge Res Labs, 48-76 & Rome Air Develop Ctr, 76-80; electronic staff engr, Lincoln Lab, Mass Inst Technol, 80-95. *Concurrent Pos:* Mem comn VI, Int Sci Radio Union. *Mem:* Sigma Xi; fel Inst Elec & Electronics Engrs. *Res:* Development of microwave antennas for radar and communications; millimeter wave satellite communication antennas. *Mailing Add:* 30 Fuller St Apt No 202 Brookline MA 02146. *E-Mail:* wrotman@aol.com

ROTT, NICHOLAS, AERODYNAMICS, ACOUSTICS. *Current Pos:* AFFIL, AERO/ASTRO DEPT, STANFORD UNIV, 83- *Personal Data:* b Budapest, Hungary, Oct 6, 17; nat US; m 44, Rosanna Savedi; c 2. *Educ:* Swiss Fed Inst Technol, Zurich, MME, 40, Dr Sc Tech, 43. *Hon Degrees:* Dr, Fed Inst Technol, Lausanne, 85. *Prof Exp:* Res assoc, Swiss Fed Inst Technol, 43-47, pvt-docent, 47-51; from assoc prof to prof aeronaut eng, Cornell Univ, 51-59; prof eng, Univ Calif, Los Angeles, 59-67; prof, Swiss Fed Inst Technol, 67-83. *Mem:* Nat Acad Eng; Am Inst Aeronaut & Astronaut; Acoust Soc Am; Am Phys Soc. *Res:* High speed aerodynamics; boundary layers; rotating flow and vortices; acoustics, particularly thermal effects and non-linear effects; non-linear dynamics. *Mailing Add:* Stanford Univ Aero-Astro Dept Stanford CA 94305. *E-Mail:* rott@joshua.stanford.edu

ROTTENBERG, HAGAI, BIOENERGETICS, BIOMEMBRANES. *Current Pos:* PROF BIOCHEM, HAHNEMANN UNIV, 78- *Personal Data:* b Haifa, Israel, Aug 21, 36; US citizen. *Educ:* Hebrew Univ, MSc, 63; Harvard Univ, PhD(biophys), 68. *Prof Exp:* Asst prof biochem, Brooklyn Col, 67-69; res assoc biochem, Weizmann Inst, 69-72; assoc prof biochem, Tel Aviv Univ, 72-77 & Univ Pa, 75-76; staff scientist biochem, Bell Labs, 77-78. *Mem:* Biophys Soc; Am Soc Biol Chemists; NY Acad Sci; AAAS. *Res:* Biological membrane transport in cell metabolism and function in animal cells; effect of alcohol and other drugs on biological membrane transport. *Mailing Add:* Allegheny Univ Health Sci Sch Med Dept Path Broad & Vine St Philadelphia PA 19102. *Fax:* 215-448-3274

ROTTER, JEROME ISRAEL, MEDICAL GENETICS, INTERNAL MEDICINE. *Current Pos:* fel med genetics, Los Angeles County Harbor Med Ctr, Univ Calif, Los Angeles, 75-77, sr res fel, 77-78, asst res pediatrician med genetics, 78-79, from asst prof to assoc prof, 79-87, PROF MED & PEDIAT, UNIV CALIF, SCH MED, LOS ANGELES, 87-, DIR, DIV MED GENETICS, CEDARS-SINAI MED CTR, 86- *Personal Data:* b Los Angeles, Calif, Feb 24, 49; m 70; c 3. *Educ:* Univ Calif, Los Angeles, BS, 70, MD, 73. *Honors & Awards:* Richard Weitzman Mem Res Award for Outstanding Young Investr, 83; Ross Joseph A Gene Award, Outstanding Investr, Western Soc Pediat Res. *Prof Exp:* Intern, Harbor Gen Hosp, Torrance, Calif, 73-74; med resident, Wadsworth Vet Admin Hosp, 74-75. *Concurrent Pos:* Res fel, Ctr Ulcer Res & Educ, 76-77, investr, 77-80, key investr, 80-89; res fel, Nat Inst Arthritis, Metab & Digestive Dis, USPHS, 77-79, clin investr, 79-82; dir, Genetic Epidemiol Core, UCLA Ctr Study Inflammatory Bowel Dis, Harbor-UCLA, 85-; chmn, Med Genetics Sect, Med Knowledge Self-Assessment Prog VIII, Am Col Physicians, 86-89; dir Genetic Epidemiol Core, UCLA prog proj Molecular Biol Arteriosclerosis, 88-; Cedars-Sinai Bd Govs Endowed Chair med genetics, 90-, assoc dir, Cedars-Sinai Inflammatory Bowel Dis Ctr, 92- *Mem:* Am Soc Human Genetics; fel Am Col Physicians; Am Heart Asn; Am Gastroenterol Asn; Am Diabetes Asn; Am Soc Clin Invest. *Res:* Genetics of the gastrointestinal disorders and of common diseases, with special interest in diabetes; inflammatory bowel disease; coronary artery disease. *Mailing Add:* Div Med Genetics Cedars-Sinai Med Ctr 8700 W Beverly Blvd Los Angeles CA 90048-1865. *Fax:* 310-659-0491

ROTTINK, BRUCE ALLAN, TREE PHYSIOLOGY, PLANT ECOLOGY. *Current Pos:* CONSULT, BREEDER PROBLEM SOLVING, 90- *Personal Data:* b Minneapolis, Minn, Feb 15, 47; m 71. *Educ:* Univ Minn, St Paul, BS, 69; Mich State Univ, PhD (forestry), 74. *Prof Exp:* Res biologist, Dow Corning Corp, 73-75; res forester, Crown Zellerbach Corp, 75-85. *Mem:* Am Soc Plant Physiologists; Soc Am Foresters; Sigma Xi. *Res:* Plant water relations; reproductive biology of conifers; physiological differences between genotypes of trees; biological nitrogen fixation. *Mailing Add:* 14 Touchstone Lake Oswego OR 97034

ROTTMAN, FRITZ M, BIOCHEMISTRY. *Current Pos:* PROF & CHMN, DEPT MOLECULAR & MICROBIOL, SCH MED, CASE WESTERN RES UNIV, 81- *Personal Data:* b Muskegon, Mich, Mar 29, 37; m 59, Carol J Vanden Bosch; c Barbara, Douglas & Susan. *Educ:* Calvin Col, BA, 59; Univ Mich, PhD(biochem), 63. *Prof Exp:* From asst prof to assoc prof, 66-74, Mich State Univ, prof biochem, 74-81. *Concurrent Pos:* NIH fel, 63-64; Am Cancer Soc fel, NIH, 64-66; vis prof biochem, Univ BC, 74-75. *Mem:* AAAS; Am Soc Biol Chem; Am Chem Soc; Am Soc Microbiol; Endocrine Soc; RNA Soc. *Res:* RNA chemistry; protein biosynthesis; RNA processing and the presence and role of trace nucleotides in RNA molecules. *Mailing Add:* Dept Molecular Biol & Microbiol Case Western Res Univ Sch Med Cleveland OH 44106-4960

ROTTMAN, GARY JAMES, ASTROPHYSICS, ATMOSPHERIC SCIENCE. *Current Pos:* RES ASSOC PHYSICS, LAB ATMOSPHERIC & SPACE PHYSICS, UNIV COLO, 72-, LECTR, DEPT PHYSICS & ASTROPHYS, 74- *Personal Data:* b Denver, Colo, Sept 21, 44; m 78; c 2. *Educ:* Rockhurst Col, BA, 66; Johns Hopkins Univ, MS, 69, PhD (physics), 72. *Honors & Awards:* Group Achievement Award, Nat Aeronaut & Space Admin, 77. *Prof Exp:* Res asst physics, Johns Hopkins Univ, 69-72, teaching asst, 72. *Concurrent Pos:* Scientist, NASA Sounding Rocket Exp, Johns Hopkins Univ & Colo Univ, 69-; co-investr, NASA Orbiting Solar Observ-8, 75-; proj scientist, Solar Mesosphere Explorer Satellite Prog, Lab Atmospheric & Space Physics, NASA, 75-, prin investr, Solar Extreme Ultraviolet Rocket Prog, 77-; consult, Univ Space Res Asn, 77. *Mem:* Am Astronaut Soc; Am Geophys Union. *Res:* Study of the solar atmosphere, in particular the measurement of persistent flows and oscillatory motions in the chromosphere and corona, these observations are made using ultraviolet spectrophotometry from sounding rockets and satellite platforms. *Mailing Add:* Lab Atmospheric & Space Physics 1234 Inovation Dr Boulder CO 80303

ROTTMANN, WARREN LEONARD, CELL BIOLOGY. *Current Pos:* AT DEPT BIOSCI, 3M CO. *Personal Data:* b New York, NY, Dec 23, 43; m 65; c 1. *Educ:* State Univ NY Binghamton, BA, 65; Col William & Mary, MA, 67; Univ Ore, PhD(biol), 71. *Prof Exp:* NIH fel cell biol, Johns Hopkins Univ, 71-73, assoc res fel, 73-74; asst prof zool, Univ Minn, Minneapolis, 74-76; asst prof genetics & cell biol, Univ Minn, St Paul, 76- *Res:* Role of cell surface and plasma membrane in growth control and differentiation; biochemical and cellular mechanisms of intercellular adhesion and cellular invasiveness. *Mailing Add:* Biol Sci Sect Lab 3M Ctr Bldg 270-3N-03 St Paul MN 55144-1000. *Fax:* 612-736-1519

ROTUNNO, RICHARD, METEOROLOGY. *Current Pos:* Fel advan study prog, 76-77, from scientist II to scientist III, 80-89, SR SCIENTIST, NAT CTR ATMOSPHERIC RES, BOULDER, COLO, 89- *Educ:* State Univ NY, Stony Brook, BE, 71, MS, 72; Princeton Univ, MA, 74, PhD(geophys fluid dynamics), 76. *Honors & Awards:* Ted Fujita Award, 83; Banner I Miller Award, Am Meteorol Soc, 92. *Concurrent Pos:* Vis fel, Coop Inst Res Environ Scis, Univ Colo, 77-78, res assoc, 78-79; guest lectr, Dept Math, Monash Univ, Australia, 81 & 84; vis assoc prof, Mass Inst Technol, 85. *Mem:* Fel Am Meteorol Soc. *Res:* Meteorology; atmosphere; ocean waves stability; environmental science; geophysical fluid dynamics. *Mailing Add:* 555 Euclid Ave Boulder CO 80302

ROTZ, CHRISTOPHER ALAN, POLYMER ENGINEERING, MANUFACTURING PROCESSING. *Current Pos:* ASSOC PROF MECH ENG, BRIGHAM YOUNG UNIV, PROVO, UTAH, 85- *Personal Data:* b Van Nuys, Calif, Feb 29, 48; m 73; c 3. *Educ:* Mass Inst Technol, BS, 73, SM, 76, PhD(mech eng), 78. *Prof Exp:* Asst prof mech eng, Univ Tex, Austin, 78-85. *Mem:* Assoc mem Am Soc Mech Engrs; Soc Plastics Engrs. *Res:* Characterization and prediction of viscoelastic properties; injection molding of polymer blends; engineering design with polymers and composites; modeling and control of manufacturing processes; finite element analysis. *Mailing Add:* 1648 S 270 W Orem UT 84058

ROUBAL, RONALD KEITH, INORGANIC CHEMISTRY. *Current Pos:* Assoc prof, 64-76, chmn, Div Sci & Math, 81-90, PROF CHEM, UNIV WIS-SUPERIOR, 76- *Personal Data:* b Omaha, Nebr, Mar 22, 35; m 89, Barbara Rich; c Diana, Laurie & Susan. *Educ:* Creighton Univ, BS, 57, MS, 59; Univ Iowa, PhD(chem), 65. *Mem:* Am Chem Soc; Sigma Xi. *Res:* Synthesis and studies of new borazine compounds; preparation of coordination compounds; natural waters chemistry. *Mailing Add:* 2414 Hughitt Ave Superior WI 54880-2898

ROUBAL, WILLIAM THEODORE, BIOORGANIC CHEMISTRY. *Current Pos:* RES CHEMIST, ENVIRON CONSERV DIV, NAT MARINE FISHERIES SERV, 60- *Personal Data:* b Eugene, Ore, Dec 20, 30; m 53, Carol J Giesy; c Diane J (Daniel), Linda A (Myrick), Sandra M & Cathy L (Hoover). *Educ:* Ore State Univ, BA, 54, MS, 59; Univ Calif, Davis, PhD(biochem), 64. *Honors & Awards:* A E McGee Award, Am Oil Chemist Soc, 64. *Concurrent Pos:* Affil prof, Col Fisheries, Univ Wash, 74-; instr chem technol, Seattle Cent Community Col, 78- *Mem:* Sigma Xi; Am Chem Soc. *Res:* Expression of vitellogenin in immature female fish and in all life cycles of male fish as a means of monitoring the presence of endocrine disruptors in the marine environment; studies on uptake, depuration and metabolism of xenobiotics in aquatic organisms; characterization of glutathione s-transferases in fish exposed to pollutants. *Mailing Add:* Environ Conserv Div Nat Marine Fisheries Serv 2725 Montlake Blvd E Seattle WA 98112

ROUBENOFF, RONENN, RHEUMATOLOGY, NUTRITION. *Current Pos:* SCIENTIST I, USDA HUMAN NUTRIT RES CTR AGING, 96- *Personal Data:* US citizen; m 93, Abby Shevitz; c Ethan. *Educ:* Northwestern Univ, BS, 81, MD, 83; Johns Hopkins Univ, MHS, 90. *Honors & Awards:* Sr Rheumatology Scholar Award, Am Col Rheumatology, 90. *Prof Exp:* Intern-resident, Osler Med Serv, Johns Hopkins Hosp, 83-86, asst chief serv, 86-87; fel epidemiol, Johns Hopkins Sch Pub Health Hyg, 88-90; res assoc nutrit, Tufts Univ Sch Med, 90-92, asst prof med, 92-96. *Concurrent Pos:* Instr med, Johns Hopkins Univ Sch Med, 87-88, fel rheumatology, 87-90; Pew nat nutrit clin investr award, Nat Inst Diabetes, Digestive & Kidney Dis, 92. *Mem:* Fel Am Col Physicians; Am Soc Nutrit Sci; Am Col Rheumatology; AAAS; Am Soc Parenteral & Enteral Nutrit; Am Physiol Soc. *Res:* Effect of chronic inflammation and aging on body composition and nutritional metabolism. *Mailing Add:* USDA Human Nutrit Res Ctr Tufts Univ 711 Washington St Boston MA 02111. *Fax:* 617-556-3224; *E-Mail:* roubenoff@hnrc.tufts.edu

ROUBICEK, RUDOLF V, DESIGN OF BIOREACTORS, PHOTOSYNTHESIS. *Current Pos:* RETIRED. *Personal Data:* b Prosnitz, Austria, Feb 11, 18; Can citizen. *Educ:* Tech Univ, Prague, dipl ing, 46; Tech Univ Czech, Dr Technol(chem eng), 48. *Prof Exp:* Dir res & develop, Spofa-United Pharmaceut Industs, Prague, Czech, 52-68; head fermentation group, Res Ctr, Can Packers Inc, 68-82; dir biochem eng, Ctr Biochem Eng Res, NMex, 82-90; emer prof biochem eng, Indust Waste Treatment & Transp Opers, Dept Chem Eng, NMex State Univ, 81-94, Luke Shires Prof, 85-94. *Concurrent Pos:* Pres, Bio/Film Technol Inc. *Mem:* Soc Indust Microbiol; Am Inst Chem Engrs; Am Chem Soc. *Res:* Biosynthesis and recovery processes of primary and secondary metabolites; photosynthesis; fermented food and single cell proteins; design of bioreactors and photobioreactors; transport operations in biological systems; biochemical engineering fermentation processes. *Mailing Add:* 1304 Delano Las Cruces NM 88011. *Fax:* 505-646-4149

ROUF, MOHAMMED ABDUR, BACTERIOLOGY. *Current Pos:* from asst prof to assoc prof, 64-68, PROF BACT, UNIV WIS-OSHKOSH, 68-, CHMN, DEPT BIOL, 70- *Personal Data:* b Dacca, Bangladesh, May 2, 33; m 65. *Educ:* Univ Dacca, BS, 54, MS, 55; Univ Calif, Davis, MA, 59; Wash State Univ, PhD(bact, biochem), 63. *Honors & Awards:* Duncan Res Award, Univ Wis-Oshkosh, 85. *Prof Exp:* Lectr bot, Govt Col Sylhet, Bangladesh, 55-57; asst bacteriologist, Pullman Div Indust Res, Wash State Univ, 63-64. *Concurrent Pos:* Received grants from various state and fed agencies; NSF fac fel, 76-78. *Mem:* AAAS; Am Soc Microbiol; Sigma Xi; fel Am Acad Microbiol; fel Am Inst Chem. *Res:* Microbial physiology; degradation of uric acid by bacteria; iron and manganese oxidizing bacteria; methanogens; industrial microbiology; quality control; food borne infections. *Mailing Add:* Dept Biol Univ Wis 800 Algoma Blvd Oshkosh WI 54901-3551

ROUFA, DONALD JAY, BIOCHEMISTRY, GENETICS & MOLECULAR BIOLOGY. *Current Pos:* assoc prof biol, 75-81, PROF BIOL, KANS STATE UNIV, 81- *Personal Data:* b St Louis, Mo, Apr 8, 43; m 67, Eileen Weiner; c Karen & Andrew. *Educ:* Amherst Col, AB, 65; Johns Hopkins Univ, PhD(biol), 70. *Prof Exp:* Chemist, Nat Inst Child Health & Human Develop, 69-70; res scientist biochem, NY State Dept Health, Albany, 70-71; from instr to asst prof biochem & med, Baylor Col Med, 71-75. *Mem:* NY Acad Sci; Am Soc Microbiol; Am Soc Biol Chemists. *Res:* Biochemical mechanisms involved in protein synthesis; molecular mechanisms participating in genetic processes; animal cell somatic genetics. *Mailing Add:* Div Biol Kans State Univ Manhattan KS 66506. *Fax:* 785-532-6653; *E-Mail:* droufa@ksu.edu

ROUFFA, ALBERT STANLEY, BOTANY, ECOLOGICAL CONSERVATION & RESTORATION. *Current Pos:* from asst prof to prof, 49-83, chmn dept, 61-63, exec secy dept, 64-68, EMER PROF BIOL SCI, UNIV ILL, CHICAGO, 83- *Personal Data:* b Boston, Mass, Mar 30, 19; wid; c Dorothy (Keagy), Michael & Paul. *Educ:* Mass State Col, BS, 41; Rutgers Univ, MS, 47, PhD(bot), 49. *Prof Exp:* Asst bot, Rutgers Univ, 41-42 & gen biol, 46-49. *Concurrent Pos:* Dir James Woodworth Prairie Preserve, 69- *Mem:* Soc Ecol Restoration; Natural Areas Asn; Am Asn Biol Sci. *Res:* Prairie preserve monitoring and management. *Mailing Add:* 4426 Florence Ave Downers Grove IL 60515

ROUGH, GAYLORD EARL, ENVIRONMENTAL SCIENCES. *Current Pos:* RETIRED. *Personal Data:* b Cochranton, Pa, Nov 17, 24; m 49, Elzada Deeter; c Allan C, Linda S & Shirley A. *Educ:* Univ Pittsburgh, BS, 50, MS, 52, PhD(animal ecol), 61. *Prof Exp:* Instr biol, Alfred Univ, 52-56; asst, Univ Pittsburgh, 56-57, spec lectr, 57-58; from asst prof to chmn dept, Alfred Univ, 69-74, dir environ studies prog, 78-81, from prof to emer prof biol, 66-87. *Mem:* AAAS; Ecol Soc Am; Am Soc Ichthyologists & Herpetologists; Sigma Xi; Am Fisheries Soc; Int Asn Great Lakes Res. *Res:* Radioecology; physiological ecology; respiratory metabolism and thyroid activity in small mammals; animal ecology, especially behavior; limnology, aquatic productivity; population dynamics and meristic characters of freshwater fishes. *Mailing Add:* Dept Biol Alfred Univ Alfred NY 14802. *E-Mail:* frough@bigvax.alfred.edu

ROUGHGARDEN, JONATHAN DAVID, BIOMATHEMATICS. *Current Pos:* from asst prof to assoc prof, 72-81, PROF BIOL, STANFORD UNIV, 81- *Personal Data:* b Paterson, NJ, Mar 13, 46; m 69; c 1. *Educ:* Univ Rochester, AB & BS, 68; Harvard Univ, PhD(biol), 71. *Honors & Awards:* Guggenheim Fel. *Prof Exp:* Asst prof biol, Univ Mass, Boston, 70-72. *Res:* Theoretical population biology; population ecology and genetics; mathematical theory of density-dependent natural selection; niche width, community structure, faunal buildup, population spatial structure and species borders; field work on anolis lizards; intertidal marine community ecology. *Mailing Add:* Dept Biol Sci Stanford Univ Gilbert Hall Stanford CA 94305-9991

ROUGHLEY, PETER JAMES, CARTILAGE PROTEOGLYCAN BIOCHEMISTRY. *Current Pos:* from asst prof to assoc prof, 77-91, PROF, MCGILL UNIV, 91-; RES SCIENTIST, SHRINERS HOSP, CAN, 77- *Personal Data:* b Doncaster, Eng, July 22, 47; m 77, Sheila Stormont; c Fiona & Simon. *Educ:* Nottingham Univ, BSc, 69, PhD(chem), 72. *Prof Exp:* Fel, Charing Cross Hosp, Eng, 72-74, Strangeways Res Lab, Eng, 74-77. *Mem:* Biochem Soc Eng; Orthopaedic Res Soc; Royal Soc Chem Eng. *Res:* Structure and function of the proteoglycans isolated from human articular cartilage; proteinases and proteinase inhibitors present in cartilage; synthesis and degradation of human articular cartilage; genetic disorders of cartilage proteoglycans. *Mailing Add:* Genetics Unit Shriners Hosp 1529 Cedar Ave Montreal PQ H3G 1A6 Can. *Fax:* 514-842-5581; *E-Mail:* proughley@shriners.mcgill.ca

ROUGVIE, MALCOLM ARNOLD, BIOPHYSICS. *Current Pos:* RETIRED. *Personal Data:* b Newton, Mass, Feb 4, 28; m 59. *Educ:* Mass Inst Technol, SB & SM, 51, PhD(biophys), 54. *Prof Exp:* Instr biophys, Mass Inst Technol, 54-55; res assoc, Iowa State Univ, 55-56, asst prof physics, 57-60, from asst prof to assoc prof biophys, 60-91. *Mem:* Biophys Soc; AAAS. *Res:* Structure of proteins by optical and physicochemical methods. *Mailing Add:* 2233 McKinley Ct Ames IA 50010-4508

ROUHANI, SHAHROKH, WATER RESOURCES, ENVIRONMENTAL GEOSTATISTICS. *Current Pos:* PRES, NEWFIELDS, INC, 95- *Personal Data:* b Tehran, Iran, Mar 28, 56; US citizen; m 83, Firouzeh Yekta; c Nina & Shiva. *Educ:* Univ Calif, Berkeley, BS & BA, 78; Harvard Univ, SM, 80, PhD(environ sci), 83. *Prof Exp:* Asst prof, Sch Civil Eng, Ga Inst Technol, 83-90, assoc prof, 90-96. *Concurrent Pos:* Vis scientist, Centre de Geostatistique Ecole Nationale Superieure des Mines de Paris, France, NSF, 87-88; chmn, Task Comt Geostatist Tech Geohydrol, Am Soc Civil Engrs, 87-89, Nat Ground Water Hydrol Comt, 91-92; assoc ed, Water Resources Res, Am Geophys Union, 89-94; sr consult, Dames & Moore, Atlanta, Ga, 90-95; expert mem, Geostatist Stand Comt, Am Soc Testing Mat, US Geol Survey, Environ Protection Agency & Dept Defense, 91-96; adj prof, Sch Civil Eng, Ga Inst Technol, 96- *Mem:* Am Geophy Union; Am Soc Civil Eng; Int Water Resources Asn; Am Water Resources Asn; NAm Coun Geostatist; Int Geostatist Asn; Sigma Xi. *Res:* Environmental system analyses and modeling; development and application of geostatistics in environmental investigations; strategic planning. *Mailing Add:* 1358 W Wesley Rd Atlanta GA 30327-1812. *Fax:* 404-894-2278; *E-Mail:* srouhani@ce.gatech.edu

ROUKES, MICHAEL L, QUANTUM TRANSPORT IN NANOSTRUCTURES, ULTRA-LOW-TEMPERATURE PHYSICS. *Current Pos:* PROF PHYS, CALTECH, 92- *Personal Data:* b Redwood City, Calif, Oct 9, 53. *Educ:* Univ Calif, Santa Cruz, BA(chem) & BA(physics), 78; Cornell Univ, PhD(physics), 85. *Prof Exp:* Collab researcher, T J Watson Res Ctr, IBM, 83-85; mem tech staff & prin investr low temperature physics & quantum struct res, Bell Commun Res, 85-92. *Mem:* Am Phys Soc. *Res:* Electronic and thermal transport physics of nonstructures: theory, low temperature experimentation, techniques for microfabrication; ultra low noise instrumentation design. *Mailing Add:* 1420 San Pasqual Pasadena CA 91106. *Fax:* 626-683-9060; *E-Mail:* roukes@styx.caltech.edu

ROULEAU, WILFRED T(HOMAS), FLUID MECHANICS, ENERGY CONVERSION. *Current Pos:* From asst prof to assoc prof mech eng, 54-65, PROF MECH ENG, CARNEGIE-MELLON UNIV, 65- *Personal Data:* b Quincy, Mass, May 3, 29; m 54, Ruth Osborne; c Richard & Keith. *Educ:* Carnegie Inst Technol, BS, 51, MS, 52, PhD(mech eng), 54. *Concurrent Pos:* Consult, Gulf Res & Develop Labs, Bituminous Coal Res, Inc, Westinghouse Res Labs, Whirlpool Corp, PPG Industs, Mine Safety Appliances Co, Pittsburgh Corning Corp, Colt Industs, Inc, Celanese Fibers Corp, Mat Eng & Testing Co, Air Technologies, Inc. *Mem:* Fel Am Soc Mech Engrs; Sigma Xi. *Res:* Hydrodynamic stability; wave propagation in viscous fluids; viscous flows; biological flows; hydrodynamic lubrication; porous bearings; numerical analysis of fluid flow; jet mixing; magnetohydrodynamics; flow and erosion in turbomachinery; energetics; power. *Mailing Add:* Dept Mech Eng Carnegie Mellon Univ 5000 Forbes Ave Pittsburgh PA 15213-3890

ROULIER, JOHN ARTHUR, MATHEMATICS. *Current Pos:* prof math, Univ Conn, 80-84, prof math & comput sci, 84-86, interim head, 89-90, PROF COMPUT SCI & ENG, DEPT COMPUT SCI & ENG, UNIV CONN, 86- *Personal Data:* b Cohoes, NY, May 3, 41; m 62, Marie DiGesare; c Danelle, Kenneth, Lori & Lanette. *Educ:* Siena Col, NY, BS, 63; Syracuse Univ, MS, 66, PhD(math), 68. *Prof Exp:* Technician, Gen Elec Co, 63-64; asst prof math, Mich State Univ, 68; NSF res assoc math, Rensselaer Polytech Inst, 69; asst prof, Union Col, NY, 69-73; from asst prof math to assoc prof math, NC State Univ, 73-79, prof, 79-80. *Concurrent Pos:* Vis scholar, Rensselaer Polytech Inst, 93. *Mem:* Math Asn Am; Am Math Soc; Soc Indust & Appl Math; Sigma Xi. *Res:* Approximation theory; approximation by polynomials satisfying linear restrictions; weighted approximation; Chebyshev rational approximation on infinite line segments; shape preserving spline interpolation; geometric modeling; computational geometry; computer graphics. *Mailing Add:* Dept Comput Sci & Eng Univ Conn Box U155 Storrs CT 06269-0001

ROULSTON, DAVID J, SEMICONDUCTORS. *Current Pos:* assoc prof, 67-72, PROF ELEC ENG, UNIV WATERLOO, 72- *Personal Data:* b London, Eng, Nov 3, 36; div; c 3. *Educ:* Queen's Univ, Belfast, BSc, 57; Univ London, PhD(elec eng) & DIC, 62. *Prof Exp:* Sci officer, Civil Serv, Portland, Eng, 57-58; engr, CSF Dept, RPC, France, 62-67. *Concurrent Pos:* Vis assoc prof, Univ Waterloo, 66-67; consult engr, Thomson-CSF, France, 73- & Res & Develop Labs in US, Can, Japan, UK & India, UN Indust Develop Orgn, 77-; mem elec eng grants comt, Nat Res Coun Can, 75-78; vis fel, Wolfson Col, Oxford, UK, 88-89. *Mem:* Fel Inst Elec Engrs UK; sr mem Inst Elec & Electronics Engrs. *Res:* Semiconductor devices and circuits; device characterization and modeling using computer aided techniques; microwave bipolar and field effect transistors; integrated circuit modelling; photo diodes and solar cells. *Mailing Add:* Dept Elec Eng Univ Waterloo Waterloo ON N2L 3G1 Can

ROULSTON, THOMAS MERVYN, obstetrics & gynecology, for more information see previous edition

ROUND, FRANK E, BOTANY. *Current Pos:* PROF, DEPT BOT, UNIV BRISTOL, UK. *Honors & Awards:* Gerald W Prescott Award, Psychol Soc Am, 91. *Mailing Add:* Dept Bot Univ Bristol Bristol 8 England

ROUND, G(EORGE) F(REDERICK), CHEMICAL ENGINEERING. *Current Pos:* assoc prof, 68-71, PROF MECH ENG, MCMASTER UNIV, 71- *Personal Data:* b Worcestershire, Eng, Jan 31, 32; m 56, Jean Codling; c 5. *Educ:* Univ Birmingham, BSc, 54, PhD(chem eng), 57, DSc(chem eng), 74. *Honors & Awards:* Henry R Worthington Award, 77; Distinguished Lectr Award, IFPS, 89. *Prof Exp:* Asst res officer, Res Coun Alta, 57-61, assoc res officer, 61-67, sr res officer, 67-68. *Concurrent Pos:* Sr vis, Dept Appl Math & Theoret Physics, Univ Cambridge, 73-74; sr consult, Kuwait Inst Sci Res 78-80; prof chem eng, Kuwait Univ, 78-80; assoc ed, J Pipelines, 85- *Mem:* Chem Inst Can; Royal Soc Arts. *Res:* Fluid dynamics; thermodynamics; author of 75 papers and 3 books on fluid mechanics. *Mailing Add:* Fac Eng McMaster Univ Hamilton ON L8S 4L7 Can. *Fax:* 905-572-7944

ROUNDS, BURTON WARD, FISH & WILDLIFE MANAGEMENT, NATURAL RESOURCE CONSERVATION. *Current Pos:* FISH & WILDLIFE CONSERV CONSULT, 79-; VOL TRAINING OFFICER, WILDLAND FIRE FIGHTERS, 90- *Personal Data:* b Milan, NH, May 6, 24; m 46, Etta R McSpadden-Rounds; c Carol A, George W & Charles B. *Educ:* Colo A&M Col, BS, 48. *Prof Exp:* Wildlife res biologist effects fed projs wildlife, US Fish & Wildlife Serv, 48-58; supvry wildlife res biologist determination causes wetland losses, Bur Sport Fisheries & Wildlife, US Dept Interior, 58-61, supvry wildlife biologist wetlands protection, 61-68, wetlands prog coordr, 68-72, regional supvr, Wildlife Serv, 72; area mgr fish & wildlife admin, US Fish & Wildlife Serv, 72-79. *Concurrent Pos:* Vchmn fish & wildlife resources div, Soil Conserv Soc Am, 72, chmn, 73; fac mem gyroscope, US Fish & Wildlife Serv, 75 & 76, mem pathfinder, 75; mem adv coun to dean sch forestry, Univ Mont, 77-79. *Mem:* Wildlife Soc; Am Soc Mammalogists; Trumpeter Swan Soc; Nat Wildlife Refuge Asn; Nat Animal Damage Control Asn. *Res:* Ecology of prairie wetlands; ecology of wild canids. *Mailing Add:* HC53 Box 541 Columbus MT 59019-9802

ROUNDS, DONALD EDWIN, IMMUNOLOGY. *Current Pos:* CHIEF SCIENTIST, ADVAN MED DIAG, LTD, 90- *Personal Data:* b Maywood, Ill, Jan 17, 26; m 51; c 2. *Educ:* Occidental Col, BA, 51; Univ Calif, Los Angeles, PhD(zool), 58. *Prof Exp:* Lab technician, AEC Proj, 51-54; res assoc exp embryol, Univ Calif, Los Angeles, 54-56; investr tissue cult, Med Br, Univ Tex, 58-59; investr, Tissue Cult Lab, Pasadena Found Med Res, 59-60, assoc dir, Div Cell Biol, 60-64, res dir, 64-90. *Concurrent Pos:* Adj asst prof anat, Univ Southern Calif, 62-70, adj assoc prof, 70-83; consult, Air & Indust Hyg Lab, Dept Pub Health, Calif, 64-66; investr, Huntington Med Res Inst, 64-90; biomed consult, Electro-Optical Systs, Inc, 65-68; asst clin prof path, Sch Med, Loma Linda Univ, 65-74, clin prof, 74-; mem bd dirs, Laser Inst Am, 73- *Mem:* Fel AAAS; Tissue Cult Asn; Am Soc Cell Biol; Soc Gen Physiol; Am Sci Film Asn. *Res:* Development of immunological test systems for tumor markers; tissue culture; cell physiology. *Mailing Add:* 1261 Sonoma Dr Altadena CA 91001

ROUNDS, FRED G, CHEMICAL ENGINEERING. *Personal Data:* b Colfax, Wash, June 4, 25; m 59; c 2. *Educ:* State Col Wash, BS, 49. *Honors & Awards:* Alfred E Hunt Award, Am Soc Lubrication Engrs, 64, Wilbur Deutch Award, 92. *Prof Exp:* From jr res engr to sr res engr, Res Labs, Gen Motors Corp, 49-75, sr staff res engr, 75-90. *Mem:* Am Chem Soc; fel Am Soc Lubrication Engrs. *Res:* Automotive engine exhaust gas emissions; diesel odor; engine combustion; additive mechanisms; lubricant coking; lubricant composition effects on rolling contact fatigue, friction and wear; diesel soot effects on wear; lubricants for alternative refrigerants. *Mailing Add:* 6291 Ledwin Troy MI 48098-1804

ROUNDS, RICHARD CLIFFORD, BIOGEOGRAPHY, RESOURCE GEOGRAPHY. *Current Pos:* from asst prof to prof geog, 70-89, DIR, RURAL DEVELOP, BRANDON UNIV, 89- *Personal Data:* b Rockford Ill, Feb 16, 43; m 65; c 2. *Educ:* Ill State Univ, BSc, 65, MSc, 67; Univ Colo, Boulder, PhD(geog), 71. *Honors & Awards:* Res Award, N Am Bluebird Soc, 85; Conserv Award, Ducks Unlimited, 87. *Prof Exp:* Teaching assoc phys geog, Ill State Univ, 66-67. *Mem:* Can Wildlife Soc; Asn Am Geographers. *Res:* Wildlife resources; tourism and recreation. *Mailing Add:* Rural Develop Inst Brandon Univ 270 18th St Brandon MB R7A 6A9 Can

ROUNSAVILLE, BRUCE J, DRUG ABUSE, PSYCHIATRIC EPIDEMIOLOGY. *Current Pos:* Asst prof psychiat, 78-84, dir res, Drug Dependence Unit, 78-84, ASSOC PROF PSYCHIAT & DIR RES, SUBSTANCE TREATMENT UNIT, SCH MED, YALE UNIV, 84-; PROF PSYCHIAT, SCH MED, UNIV CONN, 84- *Personal Data:* b Ancon, CZ, May 21, 49; US citizen. *Educ:* Yale Univ, BA, 70; Univ Md, MD, 74; Am Bd Psychiat & Neurol, dipl, 79. *Honors & Awards:* Anna Monika Award, Anna Monika Found, 86; Res Scientist Award, Nat Inst Drug Abuse, 88. *Mem:* Asn Clin Psychosocial Res; Am Psychiat Asn; Soc Psychother Res; Am Psychopathol Asn. *Res:* Clinical and epidemiological research on the diagnosis and treatment of substance use disorders and effective disorders. *Mailing Add:* 904 Howard Ave Suite 2A New Haven CT 06519-1108

ROUNSLEY, ROBERT R(ICHARD), DRYING, SIMULATION. *Current Pos:* sr res engr, 57-79, RES FEL, MEAD CORP, 79- *Personal Data:* b Detroit, Mich, Jan 11, 31; m 53, Beatrice A Fulton; c Richard, Suzanne, Pamela, Deborah & David. *Educ:* Mich Technol Univ, BS, 52, MS, 54; Iowa State Univ, PhD(chem eng), 57. *Prof Exp:* Res asst, Argonne Nat Lab, 53-54; instr, Iowa State Univ, 54-57. *Concurrent Pos:* Prof math & eng, Chillicothe Br, Ohio Univ, 63-68. *Mem:* Soc Comput Simulation; Am Inst Chem Engrs; Am Chem Soc; Tech Asn Pulp & Paper Indust. *Res:* Application of computer control in process industries; process simulation; statistics; finishing of paper; drying of paper and coatings. *Mailing Add:* 267 N Woodbridge Ave Chillicothe OH 45601. *Fax:* 740-772-3595

ROUNTREE, JANET, SPECTROSCOPY, ELECTRO-OPTICAL INSTRUMENTS. *Current Pos:* SR SCIENTIST, SCI APPLNS INT CORP, 93-; RES PROF ELEC & COMPUT ENG, UNIV ARIZ, 94- *Personal Data:* b Chicago, Ill, Aug 14, 37. *Educ:* Cornell Univ, AB, 58; Univ Chicago, PhD(astron, astrophys), 67. *Prof Exp:* Res assoc astron, Yerkes Observ, Univ Chicago, 67-68; sci officer, Leiden Observ, Univ Leiden, Neth, 68-70; astronr adjoint, Meudon Observ, Observ Paris, France, 70-71; vis fel astrophys, Joint Inst Lab Astrophys, Univ Colo, 71-72; lectr astron & res astronr, Univ Denver, 72-77, dir, Observ Opers, 74-77; sr res assoc, Goddard Space Flight Ctr, NASA, 77-79; phys scientist, US Dept Air Force, 79-93. *Concurrent Pos:* Eng lang ed & translr, Astron & Astrophys, 69-72; translr, D Reidel Co, Dordrecht, Neth, 69-72 & Joint Publ Res Serv, 73-79; consult, Aerospatiale, 93- *Mem:* Int Astron Union; Am Astron Soc; Royal Astron Soc; Neth Astron Soc; Optical Soc Am. *Res:* Spectral classification of early type stars; short-period variable stars; local galactic structure; advanced optical systems; remote sensing systems; image processing; image data compression. *Mailing Add:* PO Box 65285 Tucson AZ 85728. *Fax:* 520-790-9765; *E-Mail:* rountree@nssdca.gsfc.nasa.gov

ROUQUETTE, FRANCIS MARION, JR, ANIMAL HUSBANDRY, RANGE SCIENCE & MANAGEMENT. *Current Pos:* From asst prof to assoc prof, 70-83, PROF FORAGE PHYSIOL, AGR RES & EXTEN CTR, TEX A&M UNIV, 83- *Personal Data:* b Aransas Pass, Tex, Dec 25, 42; m 64; c 4. *Educ:* Tex A&I Univ, BS, 65; Tex Tech Univ, MS, 67; Tex A&M Univ, PhD(soil & plant sci), 70. *Honors & Awards:* Cert Merit, Am Forage & Grassland Coun. *Mem:* Am Soc Agron; Sigma Xi; Am Soc Range Sci; Am Soc Animal Sci; Am Forage & Grassland Coun. *Res:* Investigation of forage animal systems under various levels of grazing intensity; animal science and nutrition. *Mailing Add:* 504 Cactus St Rockport TX 78382

ROURKE, ARTHUR W, CELL PHYSIOLOGY. *Current Pos:* asst prof biol, 72-77, ASSOC PROF ZOOL & BIOCHEM, UNIV IDAHO, 77- *Personal Data:* b Boston, Mass, Oct 8, 42; m 65; c 2. *Educ:* Lafayette Col, AB, 64; Univ Conn, PhD(cell biol), 70. *Prof Exp:* Fel cell physiol, Univ Conn, 70-72. *Concurrent Pos:* Muscular Dystrophy Asn Am grant, 73; Heart Asn grant, 75. *Mem:* Biophys Soc; Sigma Xi; AAAS; Am Soc Cell Biologists. *Res:* Cellular turnover in eukaryotes. *Mailing Add:* Life Sci Bldg Univ Idaho 375 S Line St Moscow ID 83843-4140

ROUS, STEPHEN N, UROLOGY. *Current Pos:* adj prof, 88-91, PROF SURG, MED SCH, DARTMOUTH COL, 91-; STAFF UROLOGIST, DARTMOUTH-HITCHCOCK MED CTR, 91- *Personal Data:* b New York, NY, Nov 1, 31; m 66, Margot Woolfolk; c Benjamin C S & David G H. *Educ:* Amherst Col, AB, 52; New York Med Col, MD, 56; Univ Minn, MS, 63. *Prof Exp:* Fel, Mayo Grad Sch Med, Univ Minn, 60-63; assoc prof urol, New York Med Col, 68-72, asst dean, 68-70, assoc dean, 70-72; prof surg & chief div urol, Col Human Med, Mich State Univ, 72-75; prof & chmn dept urol, Med Univ SC, 75-88; urologist-in-chief, Med Univ & Charleston County Hosps, SC, 75-88. *Concurrent Pos:* Chief urol, Metrop Hosp Ctr, New York, 68-72; consult, Vet Admins, Roper & St Francis Hosps, Charleston, 75-88; adj prof urol, Med Univ SC, 88-; ed dir, Med Books Div, W W Norton & Co, Pub, 88-; chief urol, Vet Admin Med Ctr, White River Junction, Vt. *Mem:* Am Urol Asn; Am Col Surg; Soc Univ Urol; Pan-Pac Surg Asn; Int Soc Urol; hon Ger Urol Asn; Sigma Xi. *Mailing Add:* Urol Sect Dartmouth-Hitchcock Med Ctr Hanover NH 03756

ROUSE, BARRY TYRRELL, IMMUNOLOGY, VIROLOGY. *Current Pos:* assoc prof, 77-78, PROF IMMUNOL, UNIV TENN, KNOXVILLE, 78- *Personal Data:* b Jan 9, 42; Brit & Can citizen; m 65; c 2. *Educ:* Bristol Univ, BVSc, 65; Univ Guelph, MSc, 67, PhD(immunol), 70. *Prof Exp:* Houseman vet med, Bristol Univ, 65-66; fel immunol, Walter & Eliza Hall, Inst Med Sci, Melbourne, Australia, 70-72; asst prof, Univ Sask, 72-73, assoc prof, 73-77. *Concurrent Pos:* Med Res Coun Can fel, 70-72; mem study sect immunol & transplantation, Med Res Coun Can, 74- 77; ad hoc mem, Study Sect Exp Virol, NIH, 78; mem grant rev panel, Morris Animal Found, 78-80; grants, NIH, Morris Animal Found, Nat Hog Producers. *Mem:* Royal Col Vet Surgeons; Am Asn Immunologists; Infectious Dis Soc Am; Reticuloendothelial Soc; Can Soc Immunol. *Res:* Mechanisms of recovery from herpesvirus infections; treatment methods for canine allergy; immunological diseases of domestic animals. *Mailing Add:* Dept Microbiol Univ Tenn Knoxville TN 37996-0845

ROUSE, CARL ALBERT, THEORETICAL ASTROPHYSICS, THEORETICAL NUCLEAR PHYSICS. *Current Pos:* CONSULT, 89-; PRES & DIR, ROUSE RES INC, 92- *Personal Data:* b Youngstown, Ohio, July 14, 26; m 55, Lorraine Moxley; c Forest, Cecelia & Carolyn. *Educ:* Case Western Reserve Univ, BS, 51; Calif Inst Technol, MS, 53, PhD(physics), 56. *Prof Exp:* Sr res engr, NAm Aviation Inc, 56-57; theoret physicist, Lawrence Radiation Lab, Univ Calif, Berkeley, 57-65, res assoc theoret physics, Space Sci Lab, 65-68; staff physicist, Gulf Radiation Technol, 68-74, Mission Res, 87-89; staff scientist, Ga Technol Inst, 74-87. *Concurrent Pos:* Instr, Exten Div, Univ Calif, Los Angeles, 57; NSF res assoc, E O Hulburt Ctr Space Res, US Naval Res Lab, 65-68; prin investtr, NSF grant, 81-83, San Diego Super-Comput Ctr, 86- *Mem:* Fel Am Phys Soc; Am Astron Soc; Int Astron Union. *Res:* Ionization equilibrium equations of state for monatomic matter; exploding wire phenomena; numerical solutions to the Schrodinger equations; solar and stellar interiors; radiation transport; solar oscillations; original theoretical studies of new shielding materials for fission and fusion nuclear reactors; equation of state for matter at stellar temperatures and densities. *Mailing Add:* 627 15th St Del Mar CA 92014-2524

ROUSE, DAVID B, AQUACULTURE, MARICULTURE. *Current Pos:* adj instr biol & aquatic biol, 77-78, ASST PROF CRUSTACEAN AQUACULT, AUBURN UNIV, 81- *Personal Data:* b Lafayette, Ind, July 15, 49; m 71; c 4. *Educ:* Auburn Univ, BS, 71, MS, 73; Tex A&M Univ, PhD(fisheries), 81. *Prof Exp:* Aquatic biologist, Water Imp Comt, State of Ala, 73-78; res assoc, Tex A&M Univ, 79-81. *Concurrent Pos:* Coop scientist, Univ Agr Sci, India, 84-89; aquacult consult, Traverse Group Inc, Mich, 84-; shrimp specialist, USAID, Honduras, Panama, Ecuador, Madagascar, 81- *Mem:* Am Fisheries Soc; World Aquacult Soc. *Res:* Aquaculture development; fish and shrimp culture; culture of freshwater and saltwater fish and shrimp with applications to the United States and overseas. *Mailing Add:* Dept Fisheries Auburn Univ Auburn AL 36849-3501

ROUSE, GEORGE ELVERTON, MINERALS EXPLORATION PRECIOUS METALS, DIMENSION STONE EXPLORATION. *Current Pos:* mem, GEORGE E ROUSE & ASSOCS, LLC. *Personal Data:* b Chugwater, Wyo, May 4, 34; m 61, Sue Ellen Werber; c Dorthea Lyn (Hoyt), Valerie Sue (Cunningham) & Wendelynn Ann (Nash). *Educ:* Colo Sch Mines, Geol Engr, 61, DSc, 68. *Prof Exp:* Mining geologist, Anglo Am Corp SAfrica, Ltd, 61-64; proj mgr, Mineral Explor Earth Sci Inc, 68-71, vpres & sr proj mgr, 71-81; spec proj mgr, Minerals, Inc, 83-86; vpres, Benton Resources Ltd, 87-89; pres, Bighorn Explor, 81-91; pres, Rouse, Baurer & Assoc Inc, 89-93. *Mem:* Soc Econ Geologists; Am Inst Mining Engrs. *Res:* Global tectonics; gas geochemistry for mineral exploration; geochemistry of metalliferous shales; hydrometallurgy, groundwater hydrology, hazardous materials management, exploration for dimension stone. *Mailing Add:* 9254 Fern Way Golden CO 80403

ROUSE, GLENN EVERETT, palynology, paleobotany, for more information see previous edition

ROUSE, HUNTER, FLUID MECHANICS, HYDRAULICS. *Current Pos:* prof, 39-72, Univ Iowa, assoc dir, Inst Hydraul Res, 42-44, 44-66, dean, Col Eng, 66-72, Carver Prof, 72-74, EMER DEAN ENG, UNIV IOWA, 72-, EMER CARVER PROF HYDRAUL, 74- *Personal Data:* b Toledo, Ohio, Mar 29, 06; m 32; c 3. *Educ:* Mass Inst Technol, SB, 29, SM, 32; Karlsruhe, Dr Ing, 32; Univ Paris, Dr Sci, 59. *Hon Degrees:* Dr Ing, Karlsruhe, 75. *Honors & Awards:* Norman Medal, Am Soc Civil Engrs, 38, Von Karman Medal, 63, Hist & Heritage Award, 80; Westinghouse Award, Am Soc Eng Educ, 48, Bendix Award, 58; John Fritz Award, 91. *Prof Exp:* Asst hydraul, Mass Inst Technol, 31-33; instr civil eng, Columbia Univ, 33-35; asst prof fluid mech, Calif Inst Technol, 35-39. *Concurrent Pos:* Assoc hydraul engr, Soil Conserv Serv, USDA, 36-39; consult, US Off Naval Res, 48-66 & Waterways Exp Sta, US Corps Engrs, 49-68; Fulbright exchange prof, Univ Grenoble, 52-53; NSF sr fel, Univs Goettingen, Rome, Cambridge & Paris, 58-59; sr scholar, Australian-Am Educ Found, 73; vis prof, Col State Univ, 75-86. *Mem:* Nat Acad Eng; hon mem Am Soc Civil Engrs; Am Soc Eng Educ; fel Am Acad Arts & Sci; hon mem Am Soc Mech Engrs; hon mem Venezuela Soc Hydraul Engrs; hon mem Int Asn Hydraul Res. *Res:* Engineering hydraulics; history of hydraulics; engineering education; human ecology. *Mailing Add:* 10814 Mimosa Dr Sun City AZ 85373

ROUSE, IRVING, ANTHROPOLOGY, ARCHEOLOGY. *Current Pos:* asst, Yale Peabody Mus, 34-38, asst cur, 38-47, assoc cur, 47-54, res assoc, 54-62, cur, 77-85, EMER CURATOR ANTRHOP, YALE PEABODY MUS, 85-; EMER PROF ANTHROP, YALE UNIV, 84-, SR RES SCIENTIST ANTHROP, 95- *Personal Data:* b Rochester, NY, Aug 29, 13; m 39, Mary U Mikami; c Peter & David. *Educ:* Yale Univ, BS, 34, PhD, 38. *Hon Degrees:* DPhil & Lett, Ctr Advan Study PR, 90. *Honors & Awards:* A Cressy Morrison Prize in Natural Sci, NY Acad Sci, 51. *Prof Exp:* Instr anthrop, Yale Univ, 39-43, from asst prof to prof, 43-69, Charles J MacCurdy prof, 69-84. *Concurrent Pos:* Guggenheim fel, 63-64. *Mem:* Nat Acad Sci; Am Anthrop Asn (pres, 67-68); Asn Field Archaeol (pres, 77-78); Soc Am Archaeol (pres, 52-53); Am Acad Arts & Sci. *Res:* Anthropology; archaeology; natural science; reconstruct the sequence of human occupations, their origins, and their development on Antigua, the southernmost Leeward Island in the West Indies. *Mailing Add:* Dept Anthrop Yale Univ PO Box 208277 New Haven CT 06520-8277

ROUSE, JOHN WILSON, JR, ELECTRICAL ENGINEERING. *Current Pos:* DEAN ENG, UNIV TEX, ARLINGTON, 81- *Personal Data:* b Kansas City, Mo, Dec 7, 37; m 56; c 1. *Educ:* Purdue Univ, BS, 59; Univ Kans, MS, 65, PhD(elec eng), 68. *Prof Exp:* Engr, Bendix Corp, 59-64; res coordr, Ctr Res, Inc, Univ Kans, 64-68; from asst prof & actg dir to prof elec eng & dir, Remote Sensing Ctr, Tex A&M Univ, 68-78; distinguished prof elec eng, chmn dept & dir, Bioeng Prog, Univ Mo-Columbia, 78-81. *Concurrent Pos:* Mem comn F, Int Union Radio Sci, 69- *Mem:* Inst Elec & Electronics Engrs. *Res:* Electromagnetic and acoustic scattering; radar systems; remote sensor systems; geoscience applications. *Mailing Add:* Southern Res Inst 2000 Ninth Ave S PO Box 55305 Birmingham AL 35255

ROUSE, LAWRENCE JAMES, JR, COASTAL OCEANOGRAPHY, REMOTE SENSING. *Current Pos:* Asst prof physics, Dept Physics, LA State Univ, 72-73, asst prof, Coastal Studies Inst, 73-79, from asst prof to assoc prof phys oceanog, Dept Marine Sci, Coastal Studies Inst, 78-85, chmn, Dept Marine Sci, 83-84, assoc prof phys oceanog, Dept Geol & Geophys, 85-91, ASSOC PROF PHYS OCEANOG, DEPT OCEANOG & COASTAL SCI, COASTAL STUDIES INST, LA STATE UNIV, 91- *Personal Data:* b New Orleans, La, Oct 26, 42; m 74, Kittye L Kiper; c Elliott L & Julia L. *Educ:* Loyola Univ, New Orleans, BS, 64; La State Univ, Baton Rouge, PhD(physics), 72. *Mem:* Sigma Xi; Am Geophys Union; Am Meteorol Soc; Inst Elec & Electronics Engrs; Oceanog Soc; Estuarine Res Fedn. *Res:* Coastal circulation processes and air-sea interactions on continental shelves; remote sensing of these processes; sediment transport processes. *Mailing Add:* Coastal Studies Inst La State Univ Baton Rouge LA 70803. *Fax:* 504-388-2520; *E-Mail:* larry@arcturus.csi.lsu.edu

ROUSE, ROBERT ARTHUR, THEORETICAL CHEMISTRY. *Current Pos:* ASSOC PROF COMPUT SCI, WASH UNIV, 77- *Personal Data:* b St Louis, Mo, Sept 4, 43; m 66; c 3. *Educ:* Wash Univ, AB, 65; Northwestern Univ, PhD(chem), 68. *Prof Exp:* Res assoc chem, Harvard Univ, 68-69; asst prof chem, Univ Mo-St Louis, 69-76. *Mem:* Am Chem Soc; Am Phys Soc; Soc Comput Mach; Sigma Xi. *Res:* Molecular quantum mechanics; interacting molecular systems; reactions in theoretical organic chemistry. *Mailing Add:* Wash Univ CSDP Box 1045 St Louis MO 63130

ROUSE, ROBERT S, ORGANIC CHEMISTRY. *Current Pos:* assoc dean fac, Monmouth Col, 68-73, chmn dept, 67-73, dean fac, 73-80, vpres acad affairs, 73-81, provost, 80-81, PROF CHEM, MONMOUTH COL, 67- *Personal Data:* b Northampton, Mass, Sept 2, 30; m 92, Mary E Morgan; c R Daniel, Roland, James, Katherine, Morgan M & Laura Elizabeth. *Educ:* Yale Univ, BS, 51, MS, 53, PhD(chem), 57. *Prof Exp:* Lab asst, Yale Univ, 51-53 & 55, asst instruction, 56; asst prof chem, Lehigh Univ, 56-62; group leader, Plastics Div, Allied Chem Corp, NJ, 62-66, tech supvr, 66-67. *Concurrent Pos:* Consult, Allied Chem Corp, 68-70; Sabbatical leave, 81-82. *Mem:* Am Chem Soc; fel NY Acad Sci; Sigma Xi. *Res:* Organic reactions and synthesis; environment; energy; science education. *Mailing Add:* 482 Cedar Ave West Long Branch NJ 07764

ROUSE, ROY DENNIS, SOILS AND SOIL SCIENCE. *Current Pos:* Assoc soil chemist, Sch Agr, Auburn Univ, 49-56, prof soils, 56-66, assoc dir, Agr Exp Sta & asst dean, Sch Agr, 66-72, dir & dean, 72-81, EMER DIR, AGR EXP STA & EMER DEAN, SCH AGR, AUBURN UNIV, 82- *Personal Data:* b Andersonville, Ga, Sept 20, 20; m 46, Mary M Mathis; c David B & Sharon R (Breon). *Educ:* Univ Ga, BSA, 42, MSA, 47; Purdue Univ, PhD(soil chem), 49. *Mem:* Fel Soil Sci Soc Am; fel Am Soc Agron; Sigma Xi. *Res:* Soil chemistry of potassium; potassium nutrition of agronomic plants; resource allocation and research administration. *Mailing Add:* 827 Salmon St Auburn AL 36830

ROUSE, THOMAS C, PARASITOLOGY, PHYSIOLOGY. *Current Pos:* from asst prof to assoc prof, 67-85, PROF BIOL, UNIV WIS-EAU CLAIRE, 85- *Personal Data:* b Milwaukee, Wis, Sept 24, 34; m 71; c 2. *Educ:* Univ Wis-Milwaukee, BS, 59; Univ Wis-Madison, MS, 63, PhD(zool), 67. *Prof Exp:* Asst prof, Wis State Univ, Platteville, 65-67. *Mem:* Sigma Xi. *Res:* Effect of exercise on the normal and diseased cardiovascular system. *Mailing Add:* Dept Biol Univ Wis Eau Claire WI 54701

ROUSE, WILLIAM BRADFORD, HUMAN-SYSTEM INTERACTION, ORGANIZATIONAL & INFORMATION SYSTEMS. *Current Pos:* CHIEF EXEC OFFICER, ENTERPRISE SUPPORT SYSTS, 95- *Personal Data:* b Fall River, Mass, Jan 20, 47; m 68, Sandra H Kane; c Rebecca. *Educ:* Univ RI, BS, 69; Mass Inst Technol, MS, 70, PhD(eng), 72. *Honors & Awards:* Schuck Award, Am Automatic Control Coun, 79; Norbert Wiener Award, Syst Soc, 86; Centennial Medal, Inst Elec & Electronics Engrs, 84. *Prof Exp:* Asst prof syst eng, Tufts Univ, 73; prof syst eng, Univ Ill, 74-81, Ga Inst Tech, 81-88; chief exec officer, Search Technol, Inc, 80-95. *Concurrent Pos:* Vis prof, Delft Univ Technol, 79-80; adj prof, Ga Inst Technol, 88- *Mem:* Nat Acad Eng; fel Inst Elec & Electronics Engrs; Systs, Man & Cybernet Soc; Human Factors Soc; sr mem Inst Indust Engrs. *Res:* Human decision making; human-computer interactions; design of information systems; author of many books and articles; organizational systems. *Mailing Add:* 4898 S Old Peachtree Rd Norcross GA 30071. *Fax:* 770-441-9405; *E-Mail:* rouse@searchtech.com

ROUSEK, EDWIN J, AGRICULTURE, ANIMAL SCIENCE. *Current Pos:* RETIRED. *Personal Data:* b Burwell, Nebr, Sept 8, 17; m 45, Anita L Underwood; c Kathryn A & Sarah J. *Educ:* Univ Nebr, BSc, 40; Cornell Univ, MSc, 43. *Honors & Awards:* Noren-Salgo Award, 72. *Prof Exp:* Instr, Cornell Univ, 41-43; chmn dept animal sci, Calif State Univ, Fresno, 48-63 & 70-84, prof animal sci, 48-84. *Concurrent Pos:* Chmn univ senate, Calif State Univ, Fresno, 69-71. *Mem:* Am Meat Sci Asn. *Res:* Animal nutrition and meats. *Mailing Add:* 1175 W San Madele Fresno CA 93711

ROUSELL, DON HERBERT, STRUCTURAL GEOLOGY. *Current Pos:* from asst prof to assoc prof, 63-83, chmn dept 77-78 & 87-90, PROF GEOL, LAURENTIAN UNIV, 83- *Personal Data:* b Winnipeg, Man, Sept 4, 31; m 57; c 2. *Educ:* Univ Man, BSc, 52, Univ BC, MSc, 56; Univ Man, PhD(geol), 65. *Prof Exp:* Geologist, Tidewater Oil Co, 52-53 & Chevron Oil Co Venezuela, 56-59. *Concurrent Pos:* Nat Res Coun Can grants, 68-69, 71-73 & 83-84; grants, Ont Dept Univ Affairs, 68-69, indust, 74-75 & 79-80, Ont Geol Surv, 80-81, Energy Mines & Resources, 86 & 89, Can Geol Found, 87 & Ministry Northern Develop & Mines, 89 & 90; fel, Ctr Tectonophys, Tex A&M Univ, 69-70. *Mem:* Fel Geol Soc Am; fel Geol Asn Can. *Res:* Geology of Northwestern Venezuela; Precambrian geology of Northern Manitoba; geology of the Sudbury Basin; structure of the Greville Front. *Mailing Add:* Geol Laurentian Univ 935 Ramsey Lake Rd Sudbury ON P3E 2C6 Can

ROUSELL, RALPH HENRY, immunology, pharmacology, for more information see previous edition

ROUSH, ALLAN HERBERT, BIOCHEMISTRY. *Current Pos:* From asst prof to assoc prof, 51-62, prof, 62-82, EMER PROF BIOCHEM, ILL INST TECHNOL, 82- *Personal Data:* b Hardin Mont, Feb 24, 18; m 44; c 2. *Educ:* Mont State Col, BS, 40; Univ Wash, PhD(biochem), 51. *Mem:* Am Chem Soc; Am Soc Biol Chemists; Mycol Soc Am. *Res:* Enzymology; nucleic acid metabolism; active transport. *Mailing Add:* 1615 S Black Apt No 72 Bozeman MT 59715-5781

ROUSH, FRED WILLIAM, MATHEMATICS. *Current Pos:* ASST PROF MATH, ALA STATE UNIV, 76- *Personal Data:* b Brooklyn, NY, May 7, 47. *Educ:* Univ NC, AB, 66; Princeton Univ, PhD(math), 72. *Prof Exp:* Asst prof math, Univ Ga, 70-74. *Mem:* Am Math Soc. *Res:* Boolean matrix theory; combinatorics. *Mailing Add:* 3627 Norman Bridge Rd Montgomery AL 36105-2314

ROUSH, MARVIN LEROY, RISK ASSESSMENT, RELIABILITY ANALYSIS. *Current Pos:* from asst prof to assoc prof, 66-80, PROF NUCLEAR ENG, UNIV MD, COLLEGE PARK, 80- *Personal Data:* b Topeka, Kans, Dec 26, 34; m 55, Joanne Witham; c Paul, Brenda & Mark. *Educ:* Ottawa Univ, BSc, 58; Univ Md, PhD(nuclear physics), 64. *Prof Exp:* Asst prof physics, Baker Univ, 59-61 & Tex A&M Univ, 65-66. *Mem:* Am Phys Soc; Am Asn Physics Teachers; Am Nuclear Soc; Inst Elec & Electronics Engrs Reliability Soc; Am Soc Qual Control. *Res:* Risk assessment of nuclear power plants; neutron, gamma-ray and charged particle spectroscopy; system reliability; reliability engineering. *Mailing Add:* Dept Mat & Nuclear Eng Univ Md College Park MD 20742-2115. *Fax:* 301-314-9601; *E-Mail:* roush@eng.umd.edu

ROUSH, WILLIAM BURDETTE, ANIMAL MANAGEMENT DECISIONS. *Current Pos:* Asst prof, 79-88, ASSOC PROF POULTRY SCI, PA STATE UNIV, 88- *Personal Data:* b Sheridan, Wyo, Apr 26, 45; m 73, Noreen Hiatt; c Sarah & Michael. *Educ:* Brigham Young Univ, BS, 72, MS, 75; Ore State Univ, PhD(poultry sci), 79- *Concurrent Pos:* Sect ed, Prod & Educ, Poultry Sci, 94-97. *Mem:* Poultry Sci Asn; Opers Res Soc Am; Am Soc Agr Engrs. *Res:* Management systems analysis for the biological and economical optimization of poultry production. *Mailing Add:* 204 Animal Indust Bldg Dept Poultry Sci Pa State Univ University Park PA 16802. *Fax:* 814-865-5691; *E-Mail:* wbr@psu.edu

ROUSH, WILLIAM R, CHEMISTRY. *Current Pos:* DISTINGUISHED PROF, CHEM DEPT, IND UNIV, BLOOMINGTON. *Educ:* Univ Calif, Los Angeles, BS, 74; Harvard Univ, PhD(chem), 77. *Honors & Awards:* Arthur C Cope Scholar Award, Am Chem Soc, 94. *Mailing Add:* Dept Chem Ind Univ Bloomington IN 47405-4000

ROUSLIN, WILLIAM, BIOCHEMISTRY, BIOENERGETICS. *Current Pos:* asst prof, 77-85, ASSOC PROF PHARMACOL & CELL BIOPHYS, COL MED, UNIV CINCINNATI, 85- *Personal Data:* b Providence, RI, Nov 10, 38; m 70. *Educ:* Brown Univ, AB, 60; Univ Conn, PhD(biochem), 68. *Prof Exp:* NIH res fel, Cornell Univ, 68-70; asst prof biol, Douglass Col, Rutgers Univ, New Brunswick, 70-77. *Concurrent Pos:* Res grants, NIH, 84-87, 87-91 & 91-96. *Mem:* AAAS; Am Asn Pathologists; Am Soc Cell & Develop Biol; Am Physiol Soc; Am Soc Biochem & Molecular Biol; Biophys Soc; Cardiac Muscle Soc; Int Soc Heart Res. *Res:* Mitochondrial ATPase in cardiac muscle. *Mailing Add:* Dept Pharmacol & Cell Biophys Univ Cincinnati Col Med 231 Bethesda Ave ML 575 Cincinnati OH 45267-0575. *Fax:* 513-558-1169

ROUSOU, J A, SURGERY. *Current Pos:* BAY STATE MED CTR. *Res:* Surgery. *Mailing Add:* Cardiac Surg Assoc W Mass 759 Chestnut St Springfield MA 01107

ROUSSEAU, CECIL CLYDE, MATHEMATICS, PHYSICS. *Current Pos:* from asst prof to assoc prof, 76-81, PROF MATH, MEMPHIS STATE UNIV, 81- *Personal Data:* b Philadelphia, Pa, Jan 13, 38; m 65; c 2. *Educ:* Lamar Univ, BS, 60; Tex A&M Univ, MS, 62, PhD (physics), 68. *Prof Exp:* Asst prof physics, Baylor Univ, 68-70; asst prof math, Memphis State Univ, 70-75; Carnegie fel, Univ Aberdeen, 75-76. *Concurrent Pos:* Collab ed, Probs & Solutions, Soc Indust & Appl Math, 71-; vis prof, Univ Waterloo, 87-88. *Mem:* Math Asn Am; Soc Indust & Appl Math; Am Math Soc. *Res:* Graph theory; analysis; mathematical physics; mathematical statistics. *Mailing Add:* Univ Memphis Memphis TN 38152-0001

ROUSSEAU, DENIS LAWRENCE, BIOLOGICAL PHYSICS, PHYSICAL CHEMISTRY. *Current Pos:* AT DEPT PHYSIOL & BIOPHYS, ALBERT EINSTEIN COL MED. *Personal Data:* b Franklin, NH, Nov 18, 40; m 63. *Educ:* Bowdoin Col, BA, 62; Princeton Univ, PhD(phys chem), 67. *Prof Exp:* Res fel, Univ Southern Calif, 67-69; distinguished mem staff, Biophys Res, Bell Labs, Incc, 69- *Mem:* Biophys Soc; fel Am Phys Soc; AAAS; fel Optical Soc Am; Sigma Xi. *Res:* Raman scattering from biological materials; heme proteins; molecular physics. *Mailing Add:* Dept Physiol & Biophys Albert Einstein Col Med ULL-303 Bronx NY 10461. *Fax:* 908-582-2451

ROUSSEAU, RONALD WILLIAM, SEPARATION PROCESSES, PHASE EQUILIBRIA. *Current Pos:* DIR, CHEM ENG, GA INST TECHNOL, 87- *Personal Data:* b Sept 28, 43; US citizen; m 63; c 3. *Educ:* La State Univ, BS, 66, MS, 68, PhD(chem eng), 69. *Honors & Awards:* Outstanding Chem Eng, Am Inst Eng, 86. *Prof Exp:* Instr chem eng, La State Univ, 67; res engr, Westvaco Corp, 69; from asst prof to prof chem eng, NC State Univ, 69-86. *Concurrent Pos:* Vis prof, Princeton Univ, 82-83. *Mem:* Am Inst Chem Engrs; Am Chem Soc. *Res:* Nucleation, growth and crystal size distributions; separation process technology; conditioning gases produced from coal by absorption and stripping; phase equilibria, crystallization and precipitation. *Mailing Add:* Sch Chem Eng Ga Inst Technol Atlanta GA 30332-0100

ROUSSEAU, VIATEUR, ORGANIC CHEMISTRY. *Current Pos:* from assoc prof to prof, 56-82, chmn sci div, 66-68, EMER PROF CHEM, IONA COL, 82- *Personal Data:* b Baie des Sables, Que, July 5, 14; nat US; m 58, Noreen Longo; c Michele, Peter & Jeannine. *Educ:* Am Int Col, BS, 39; NY Univ, PhD(org chem), 48. *Prof Exp:* Anal chemist, Chapman Valve Mfg Co, Mass, 40-42; asst chem, NY Univ, 42-47; instr, Col Mt St Vincent, 47-50, asst prof, 50-56. *Concurrent Pos:* Adj prof, Fordham Univ, 58-73. *Mem:* Am Chem Soc. *Res:* Chemistry of indazoles; synthesis; structural relationships; absorption spectra. *Mailing Add:* 107 Pryer Terr Iona Col New Rochelle NY 10804-4425

ROUSSEL, JOHN S, ENTOMOLOGY, AGRONOMY. *Current Pos:* RETIRED. *Personal Data:* b Hester, La, Nov 23, 21; m 46; c 5. *Educ:* La State Univ, BS, 42, MS, 48; Tex A&M Univ, PhD(entom), 50. *Prof Exp:* From asst prof to entom, La State Univ, Baton Rouge, 49-83, coordr cotton res & asst to dir, Agr Exp Sta, 61-83. *Concurrent Pos:* NSF grant, 57-60. *Mem:* AAAS; Entom Soc Am; Am Inst Biol Sci. *Res:* Cotton production practices and insects. *Mailing Add:* 5032 Perkins Rd Baton Rouge LA 70808

ROUSSEL, JOSEPH DONALD, REPRODUCTIVE PHYSIOLOGY. *Current Pos:* PROF REPROD PHYSIOL, LA STATE UNIV, BATON ROUGE, 72- *Personal Data:* b Paulina, La, Apr 28, 29; m 58; c 2. *Educ:* La State Univ, BS, 58, MS, 60, PhD(reprod physiol), 63. *Prof Exp:* Res asst, La State Univ, 59-63; res assoc, Univ Ark, 63-65 & Delta Regional Primate Res Ctr, 66-72. *Concurrent Pos:* Res grant, 63-66. *Mem:* Am Fertil Asn; Am Dairy Sci Asn; Int Fertil Asn; Brit Soc Study Fertil; Am Soc Animal Sci. *Res:* Environmental reproductive physiology; semen metabolism; enzyme activity in spermatogenesis and physiology factors influencing reproduction; reproduction in primates; nutritional influence in reproduction; ovulation; semen preservation and artificial insemination; embryo transfer. *Mailing Add:* Dept Dairy Sci La State Univ Baton Rouge LA 70803-0001

ROUSSIN, ROBERT WARREN, NUCLEAR ENGINEERING, INFORMATION SCIENCE. *Current Pos:* LEADER, RADIATION INFO ANAL SECT, OAK RIDGE NAT LAB, MARTIN MARIETTA ENERGY SYSTS, 68- *Personal Data:* b Columbia, Mo, Jan 27, 39; m 62. *Educ:* Univ Mo, Rolla, BS, 62; Univ Ill, MS, 64, PhD(nuclear eng), 69, MBA, 86. *Prof Exp:* Co-op student mech eng, McDonnell Aircraft Corp, 57-62; engr mech & nuclear eng, Allis Chalmers, 62. *Concurrent Pos:* Chmn, Cross Sect Eval Working Group, 93. *Mem:* Am Nuclear Soc. *Res:* Promote the exchange of information and computing technology in the field of radiation transport. *Mailing Add:* Oakridge Nat Lab Radiation Inf Anal Sect PO Box 2008 Oak Ridge TN 37831-6362. *Fax:* 423-574-6182; *E-Mail:* rwr@ornl.gov

ROUSSOS, CONSTANTINE, COMPUTER SCIENCE EDUCATION. *Current Pos:* dir comput serv, 81-85, & 94-96, chmn comput sci, 82-88, PROF COMP SCI, LYNCHBURGH COL, 90- *Personal Data:* b Kingston, NY, Sept 22, 47; m 69, Gail Phillips; c Miriam & Damon. *Educ:* Old Dominion Univ, BA, 69; Col William & Mary, MS, 74; Univ Va, PhD(comput sci), 79. *Prof Exp:* Instr math, Tidewater Community Col, 74-75; instr comput sci & math, Wash & Lee Univ, 77-78; vpres software systs, Three Ridges Corp, 79-81. *Concurrent Pos:* Vis researcher, Naval Surface Warfare Ctr, 88; vis prof comput sci, Univ Limerick, Ireland, 89. *Mem:* Asn Comput Mach; Digital Equip User's Soc. *Res:* Data structures and network theory; development of database software; database user interfaces; algorithms for AI applications. *Mailing Add:* 245 Cabell Mt Lane Arlington VA 22922. *E-Mail:* roussos@acavax.lynchburg.edu

ROUTBORT, JULES LAZAR, MATERIALS SCIENCE. *Current Pos:* physicist, mat sci div, 68-92, CERAMIST, ENERGY TECHNOL DIV, ARGONNE NAT LABS, 92- *Personal Data:* b San Francisco, Calif, May 15, 37; m 66, Agnes Eickhorst; c 2. *Educ:* Univ Calif, Berkeley, BS, 60; Cornell Univ, PhD(eng physics), 65. *Prof Exp:* Sci Res Coun fel physics, Cavendish Lab, Cambridge Univ, 64-66; AEC fel, Rensselaer Polytech Inst, 66-68. *Concurrent Pos:* Humboldt fel, Res Inst Transurane, Karlsruhe, 73-74 & Univ Hamburg, Ger, 82; Euratom fel, Res Inst Transurane, 81-82; adj prof mat sci, NC State Univ, Raleigh & mat eng, IIT, Chicago; proj mgr, Off Basic Energy Sci, Dept Energy, Washington, DC, 87-88; assoc ed, Appl Physics Lett. *Mem:* Fel Am Ceramic Soc; Am Phys Soc; Mat Res Soc. *Res:* Mechanical properties of ceramics; diffusion and elastic properties of ceramics. *Mailing Add:* 7220 Wirth Dr Darien IL 60561. *Fax:* 630-252-4798; *E-Mail:* routbort@anl.gov

ROUTH, DONALD KENT, PEDIATRIC PSYCHOLOGY, CLINICAL CHILD PSYCHOLOGY. *Current Pos:* PROF PSYCHOL, UNIV MIAMI, FLA, 85- *Personal Data:* b Oklahoma City, Okla, Mar 30, 37; m 60; c 2. *Educ:* Univ Okla, BA, 62; Univ Pittsburgh, MS, 65, PhD(psychol), 67. *Honors & Awards:* Distinguished Contrib Award, Soc of Pediat Psychol, 81; Nicholas Hobbs Award, Div Child, Youth & Family Serv, Am Psychol Asn, 96. *Prof Exp:* Asst prof psychol, Univ Iowa, 67-70; assoc prof psychol, Bowling Green State Univ, Ohio, 70-71 & Univ NC, Chapel Hill, 71-77; prof, Univ Iowa, 77-85. *Concurrent Pos:* Ed, J Pediat Psychol, 76-82, J Clin Child Psychol, 87-91, J Abnormal Child Psychol, 92-; chmn, Behav Med Study Sect, NIH, 83-85; pres, Div Child, Youth & Family Serv, Am Psychol Asn, 84, Div Ment Retardation, 87-88, Div Clin Psychol, 98. *Mem:* Soc Pediat Psychol (pres, 73-74); Am Psychol Asn. *Res:* Conditioning of infant vocalizations; development of activity level in children; effects of mother presence on children's response to medical stress; phonemic awareness, reading and spelling in children; history of clinical psychology. *Mailing Add:* Dept Psychol Univ Miami PO Box 249229 Coral Gables FL 33124-0721. *Fax:* 305-284-4795; *E-Mail:* drouth@umiami.ir.miami.edu

ROUTH, JOSEPH ISAAC, CLINICAL BIOCHEMISTRY, PATHOLOGY. *Current Pos:* From instr to prof, Univ Iowa, 37-78, dir, clin biochem lab, 52-64, dir spec clin chem lab, 70-78, EMER PROF BIOCHEM, UNIV IOWA, 78- *Personal Data:* b Logansport, Ind, May 8, 10; m 37, 78, Elizabeth M Hayes; c Joseph Hays & John Michael. *Educ:* Purdue Univ, BSChE, 33, MS, 34; Univ Mich, PhD(biochem), 37. *Honors & Awards:* Award Outstanding Efforts Educ & Training Clin Chemists, Am Asn Clin Chem, 73. *Concurrent Pos:* Consult clin chem, Vet Admin Hosp, Iowa City, Iowa, 52- *Mem:* Am Chem Soc; Am Soc Biol Chemists; Am Asn Clin Chem (pres, 57-58); Am Bd Clin Chem (pres, 59-73); fel Am Inst Chem. *Res:* Purification and properties of trypsin inhibitor, levodopa metabolites in Parkinson's disease, enzyme inhibitors; methodology, metabolism and protein binding of analgesic drugs; effects of drugs on clinical chemistry parameters. *Mailing Add:* Box 712 Cherokee Village AR 72525

ROUTIEN, JOHN BRODERICK, MICROBIOLOGY. *Current Pos:* RETIRED. *Personal Data:* b Mt Vernon, Ind, Jan 23, 13; m 44, 67; c Helen H (Boyd) & Constance H (Cook). *Educ:* DePauw Univ, AB, 34; Northwestern Univ, AM, 36; Mich State Col, PhD(mycol), 40. *Honors & Awards:* Com Solvents Award, 50. *Prof Exp:* Instr bot, Univ Mo, 39-42; mycologist, Chemotherapeut Res Labs, Pfizer Inc, 46-73, res adv, Cent Res, 73-77. *Mem:* Bot Soc Am; Mycol Soc Am; Am Soc Microbiol; Soc Indust Microbiol. *Res:* Isolation of microorganisms; culture collection; taxonomy of microorganisms. *Mailing Add:* 318 Grassy Hill Rd Lyme CT 06371

ROUTLEDGE, RICHARD DONOVAN, STATISTICAL METHODOLOGY. *Current Pos:* asst prof math, 80-83, ASSOC PROF MATH & STATIST, SIMON FRASER UNIV, 83- *Personal Data:* b Toronto, Ont, Aug 15, 48; m 70, Louise Weir; c Karen & Laura. *Educ:* Queen's Univ, Kingston, Ont, BSc, 70; Univ Alta, Edmonton, MSc, 72; Dalhousie Univ, Halifax, PhD(biol), 75. *Prof Exp:* Killam fel math, Univ Alta, 75-77, asst prof, 75-80. *Mem:* Biomet Soc; Statist Soc Can; Int Statist Inst. *Res:* Development of statistical methodology and use of mathematical optimization to study problems in population ecology and resource management. *Mailing Add:* Dept Math & Stat Simon Fraser Univ Burnaby BC V5A 1S6 Can

ROUTLY, PAUL MCRAE, ASTROPHYSICS. *Current Pos:* RETIRED. *Personal Data:* b Chester, Pa, Jan 4, 26; m 51; c 2. *Educ:* McGill Univ, BSc, 47, MSc, 48; Princeton Univ, AM, 50, PhD(astrophys), 51. *Prof Exp:* Nat Res Coun Can fel, 51-53; res fel, Calif Inst Technol, 53-54; chmn dept & dir observ, 54-63, from asst prof to prof astron, Pomona Col, 54-63; exec off, Am Astron Soc, 62-68; dir, Div Astrometry & Astrophys, US Naval Observ, 68-77, head explor develop staff, 77-85. *Concurrent Pos:* Vpres, Comn 38, Int Astron Union; 38; vis prof, Rutgers In-Serv Inst, 66; pres, Comn 38, Int Astron Union, 73- *Mem:* Am Astron Soc; Int Astron Union. *Res:* Astrometry; molecular spectroscopy; absolute and relative atomic transition probabilities; stellar parallaxes. *Mailing Add:* 9401 Kentsdale Dr Potomac MD 20854

ROUTSON, RONALD C, SOIL PHYSICAL CHEMISTRY & MINERALOGY. *Current Pos:* CONSULT, 91- *Personal Data:* b Chewelah, Wash, Dec 12, 33; m 58; c 1. *Educ:* Wash State Univ, BS, 58, PhD(soil chem), 70. *Prof Exp:* Sr res scientist & prog mgr, Battelle Pac Northwest Labs, 65-77; staff scientist soil chem, Rockwell Hanford Co, 77-90. *Mem:* Am Soc Agron; Soil Sci Soc Am; Clay Minerals Soc. *Res:* Modeling the movement of radionuclides through soil systems; disposal and fate of wastes in soil; moisture movement in soil systems; plant uptake of pollutants. *Mailing Add:* Knox Rd Benton City WA 99320

ROUTTENBERG, ARYEH, NEUROSCIENCE. *Current Pos:* PROF PSYCHOL & NEUROBIOL & DIR UNDERGRAD NEUROSCI PROG, COL ARTS & SCI & GRAD NEUROSCI PROG, PSYCHOL DEPT, NORTHWESTERN UNIV, 73- *Personal Data:* b Reading, Pa, Dec 1, 39; c 2. *Educ:* McGill Univ, BA, 61; Northwestern Univ, MA, 63; Univ Mich, PhD(neurosci & behav), 65. *Concurrent Pos:* Mem res adv bd, NIMH, 76-80. *Mem:* Neurosci Soc; Am Physiol Soc; Am Soc Neurochem; Am Asn Anatomists; Int Soc Neurochem. *Res:* Brain chemistry; memory and learning. *Mailing Add:* Dept Psychol & Physiol Northwestern Univ 102 Swift Hall Evanston IL 60208-5517

ROUTTI, JORMA TAPIO, agency administration, for more information see previous edition

ROUVRAY, DENNIS HENRY, FUZZY LOGIC IN CHEMISTRY, NATURE OF CHEMICAL CONCEPTS. *Current Pos:* res scientist chem, 84-89, RES PROF, UNIV GA, ATHENS, 89- *Personal Data:* c 3. *Educ:* Imp Col, BSc, 61, ARCS, 61, DIC, 64, PhD(chem), 64. *Prof Exp:* Fel chem, Dalhousie Univ, Halifax, NS, 64-66; fel chem, Univ Liverpool, 65-67; lectr, Univ Witwatersrand, SAfrica, 67-75; res fel, Max Planck Inst, Muelheim, Ger, 75-78; vis prof, Yarmouk Univ, Jordan, 78-79; dir res publ, Diebold Europe Comput Consult, London, 79-84. *Concurrent Pos:* Vis prof, Univ Oxford, UK, 70-71 & 78; ed, J Math Chem, 87-; consult, Du Pont Chem Co, Waynesboro, Va, 88-, Cornell Univ, NY Hosp, 83-87, Glaxo, Research Triangle Park, NC, 90-; co-prin investr, US Off Naval Res, Univ Ga, 84-88; consult, Upjohn Pharm Co, Kalamazoo, Mich, 90- *Mem:* Int Soc Math Chem (secy, 86-). *Res:* Applications of fuzzy logic to chemistry; nature of chemical concepts; role of analogical reasoning in chemistry; theoretical investigation of the foundations of chemistry. *Mailing Add:* Dept Chem Univ Ga Athens GA 30602. *Fax:* 706-542-9454

ROUX, KENNETH H, IMMUNOGENETICS, IMMUNOREGULATION. *Current Pos:* from asst prof to assoc prof, 78-88, PROF IMMUNOL, DEPT BIOL SCI, FLA STATE UNIV, 89- *Personal Data:* b Philadelphia, Pa, May 12, 48; m 70; c 1. *Educ:* Del Valley Col, BS, 70; Tulane Univ, MS, 72, PhD(immunol), 74. *Prof Exp:* Fel immunol, Univ Ill Med Ctr, 75-78. *Concurrent Pos:* Prin investr & prof, Dept Biol Sci, Fla State Univ, 79- *Mem:* Fedn Am Soc Exp Biol; Am Asn Immunologists; AAAS. *Res:* Genetics and regulation of immunoglobulin molecules; electronmicroscopy of immunoglobulin molecules and immune complexes, molecular genetics of antibody diversity; monoclonal antibody (hybridoma) production; electron microscopy; immunochemistry; polymerase chain reaction optimization. *Mailing Add:* Dept Biol Sci Fla State Univ Tallahassee FL 32306-3050

ROUX, STANLEY JOSEPH, PHOTOBIOLOGY, MEMBRANE BIOLOGY. *Current Pos:* from asst prof to assoc prof, 78-86, chmn, Bot Dept, 86-90, PROF BOT, UNIV TEX, AUSTIN, 86- *Personal Data:* b Houston, Tex, Feb 9, 42; m 75; c 2. *Educ:* Spring Hill Col, BS, 66; Loyola Univ, New Orleans, 68; Yale Univ, PhD(biol), 71. *Prof Exp:* Fel, Yale Univ, 71-73; asst prof biol, Univ Pittsburgh, 73-78. *Concurrent Pos:* Consult, Riken Inst, Wako-shi, Japan, 92- *Mem:* AAAS; Am Soc Plant Physiologists; Am Soc Gravitational & Space Biol. *Res:* Identifying cellular mechanisms for the control of plant growth and development by light and for the control of plant tropisms by light and gravity. *Mailing Add:* Dept Bot Univ Tex Austin TX 78712. *Fax:* 512-471-3878

ROVAINEN, CARL (MARX), NEUROPHYSIOLOGY, ENDOTHELIAL CELL BIOLOGY. *Current Pos:* NIH training fel biochem, Wash Univ, 67-68, from instr to asst prof physiol & biophys, 68-73, assoc prof, 73-79, PROF CELL BIOL & PHYSIOL, SCH MED, WASH UNIV, 79- *Personal Data:* b Virginia, Minn, Mar 13, 39; m 66, Leslie Pearson; c Toivo, Ahti & Torsti. *Educ:* Calif Inst Technol, BS, 62; Harvard Univ, PhD(physiol), 67. *Concurrent Pos:* Nat Inst Neurol Dis & Stroke res grant, 70-89; Nat Inst Heart Lung & Blood res grant, 88-96. *Mem:* Soc Neurosci; Am Physiol Soc. *Res:* Lamprey brain and spinal cord; brain blood vessels. *Mailing Add:* Dept Cell Biol & Physiol 660 S Euclid Ave Wash Univ Sch Med St Louis MO 63110. *E-Mail:* rovainen@cellbio.wustl.edu

ROVELLI, CARLO, QUANTUM GRAVITY, GRAVITATION. *Current Pos:* PROF PHYSICS, UNIV PITTSBURGH, PA, 90-; RESEARCHER, UNIV TRENTO, ITALY, 90- *Personal Data:* b Verona, Italy, May 3, 56; m 93, Paola Cesari. *Educ:* Univ Bologna, Italy, Laurea, 81; Univ Padova, Italy, PhD(physics), 84. *Honors & Awards:* Xanthopoulos Award, 95. *Prof Exp:* Fel, Yale Univ, 87; INFN postdoctoral, Univ Roma, Italy, 87-88; contractual prof mech, Univ Dell'aquila, Italy, 89. *Concurrent Pos:* Vis scientist, SISSA, Triestre, Italy, 89-90; prin investr, Res Proj Non Perturbative Quantum Gravity, NSF, 93- *Mem:* Sigma Xi; Int Soc Gen Relativity; Am Phys Soc. *Res:* Construction of a quantistic theory of the gravitational field; general relativity; definition of the concept of time. *Mailing Add:* Physics Dept 100 Allen Hall Univ Pittsburgh Pittsburgh PA 15260. *E-Mail:* rovelli@vms.cis.pitt.edu

ROVELSTAD, GORDON HENRY, DENTISTRY. *Current Pos:* RETIRED. *Personal Data:* b Elgin, Ill, May 19, 21; m 45; c 3. *Educ:* Northwestern Univ, DDS, 44, MSD, 48, PhD(dent), 60; Am Bd Pedodont, dipl. *Hon Degrees:* DSc, Georgetown Univ, 69. *Prof Exp:* Instr dent, Northwestern Univ, 46-49, asst prof pedodont & consult, Cleft Palate Inst, 49-53; res officer, Dent Res Lab, Dent Corps, USN, 54-58, head res & sci div, Dent Sch, 60-65, dir dent res, Dent Res Facil, Training Ctr, 65-67, officer-in-charge & sci dir, Naval Dent Res Inst, Ill, 67-69, prog mgr dent res, Dent Div, Bur Med & Surg, Washington, DC, 69-74; prof pediat dent & assoc prof physiol & biophysics, Sch Dent, Univ Miss Med Ctr, Jackson, 74-81, actg chmn, Dept Pediat Dent & assoc dean educ prog, 77-81; exec dir, Am Col Dentists, 81-93. *Concurrent Pos:* Chief dent staff, Children's Mem Hosp, Chicago, 49-53; consult, Herrick House Rheumatic Fever Inst, 51-53. *Mem:* AAAS; Am Soc Dent Children; Am Dent Asn; Am Acad Pedodontics; NY Acad Sci; Sigma Xi. *Mailing Add:* 11301 Tooks Way Columbia MD 21044

ROVELSTAD, RANDOLPH ANDREW, MEDICINE. *Current Pos:* RETIRED. *Personal Data:* b Elgin, Ill, Mar 11, 20; m 45; c 5. *Educ:* St Olaf Col, BA, 40; Northwestern Univ, MD, 44; Univ Minn, PhD(med), 54. *Prof Exp:* From instr to assoc prof med, Mayo Med Sch, 53-85. *Concurrent Pos:* Consult, Mayo Clin, 52-85. *Mem:* Am Gastroenterol Asn. *Res:* Gastroenterology; gastric secretion; gastric and duodenal pH; enterocutaneous potentials; composition of ascitic fluid. *Mailing Add:* RR 2 Box 2421 Hayward WI 54843-9453

ROVERA, GIOVANNI, HEMATOLOGY. *Current Pos:* from assoc prof to prof cancer res, 75-78, PROF & DIR, WISTAR INST, 91- *Personal Data:* b Cocconato, Italy, Sept, 23, 40; m 79; c 1. *Educ:* Univ Torino, Italy, MD, 64. *Prof Exp:* Fel biochem, Fels Inst, 68-70; resident path, Temple Univ, 70-73, asst prof, 73-75. *Concurrent Pos:* Scholar, Leukemia Soc Am, 74-79; mem, Molecular Biol Grad Group, Univ Pa, 77-91; assoc ed, J Cellular Physiol, 78-91. *Res:* Proliferation and differentiation of leukemia cells; expression of globin genes; mechanisms of tumor promotion. *Mailing Add:* Wistar Inst 3601 Spruce St Philadelphia PA 19104

ROVETTO, MICHAEL JULIEN, PHYSIOLOGY, BIOCHEMISTRY. *Current Pos:* assoc prof, 80-87, PROF PHYSIOL, SCH MED, UNIV MO, 87- *Personal Data:* b Challis, Idaho, Mar 20, 43; m 66, 87; c 2. *Educ:* Utah State Univ, BS, 65; Univ Idaho, MS, 68; Univ Va, PhD(physiol), 70. *Prof Exp:* NIH fel, Hershey Med Ctr, Pa State Univ, 70-71, res assoc physiol, 71-73, asst prof, 73-74; from asst prof to assoc prof physiol, Jefferson Med Col, 74-80. *Concurrent Pos:* Mem, Couns Circulation & Basic Sci, Am Heart Asn. *Mem:* Am Physiol Soc; Biophys Soc; Cardiac Muscle Soc; Am Heart Asn. *Res:* Myocardial energy metabolism; regulation of cardiovascular function; adenine nucleotide metabolism; membrane transport. *Mailing Add:* Physiol Dept Univ Mo Sch Med Columbia MO 65212

ROVICK, ALLEN ASHER, PHYSIOLOGY, SCIENCE EDUCATION. *Current Pos:* assoc prof biomed eng, 75-80, PROF PHYSIOL, RUSH MED SCH, RUSH UNIV, 80- *Personal Data:* b Chicago, Ill, Feb 11, 28; m 49, Renah Reinstein; c Sharon (Keating), Lynn (Cross), Joshua S & Jonathan E. *Educ:* Roosevelt Univ, BS, 51; Univ Ill, MS, 54, PhD(physiol), 58. *Prof Exp:* Instr physiol, Stritch Sch Med, Loyola Univ Chicago, 58-59, assoc, 59, from asst prof to assoc prof, 66-67; Univ Ill Proj, Thailand, 67-68; assoc prof physiol, Univ Ill Med Sch, 69-70; exec secy cardiovasc study sect, Div Res Grants, NIH, 70-71; chief cardiac dis br, Nat Heart & Lung Inst, 71-72. *Mem:* AAAS; Am Physiol Soc; Am Heart Asn; Sigma Xi. *Res:* Metabolic control of local blood circulation; influence of hemodynamics on tissue water partition; local control of blood flow; effect of arterial pulse on blood flow; computer based instruction. *Mailing Add:* Dept Physiol Rush Med Col 1750 W Harrison Chicago IL 60612-3833. *Fax:* 312-942-8711

ROVIT, RICHARD LEE, NEUROSURGERY. *Current Pos:* assoc prof neurosurg, 66-71, PROF CLIN NEUROSURG, SCH MED, NY UNIV, 71-; DIR, DEPT NEUROSURG, ST VINCENT'S HOSP, 66- *Personal Data:* b Boston, Mass, Apr 3, 24; m 53; c 3. *Educ:* Jefferson Med Col, MD, 50; McGill Univ, MSc, 61; Am Bd Neurol Surg, dipl, 62. *Prof Exp:* Asst neurosurgeon, Montreal Neurol Inst, 60-61; assoc prof & surgeon, Jefferson Med Col & Hosp, 61-66, head div neurosurg, 61-65. *Concurrent Pos:* Consult, US Vet Admin Hosps, Philadelphia, 62-64 & Coatesville, 62-66; chief sect neurosurg, Philadelphia Gen Hosp, New York, Columbus Hosp & St Vincent's Hosp; attend neurosurgeon, NY Univ Hosp, 66- *Mem:* AAAS; Am Acad Neurol; Am Epilepsy Soc; Asn Res Nerv & Ment Dis; Am Asn Neurol Surg; Am Col Surgeons; Soc Neurol Surgeons. *Res:* Surgery of epilepsy and neuroendocrinology. *Mailing Add:* St Vincents Med Ctr Dept NS 153 W 11th St New York NY 10011-8305

ROVNER, DAVID RICHARD, ENDOCRINOLOGY, METABOLISM. *Current Pos:* vchmn, Dept Med, Mich State Univ, 71-80, prof endocrinol & metab, Col Human Med, 71-96, chief, Div Endocrinol & Metab, 80-96, ASST-TO-THE-DEAN TECHNOL, MICH STATE UNIV, 96- *Personal Data:* b Philadelphia, Pa, Sept 20, 30. *Educ:* Temple Univ, B, 51, MD, 55. *Prof Exp:* Intern, San Francisco Hosp, Univ Calif Serv, 55-56; resident med, Med Ctr, Univ Mich, 56-57; internist radiobiol, USAF Sch Avaition Med, 57-59; resident med, Med Ctr, Univ Mich, 59-60, from fel to prof endocrinol & metab, 60-71. *Concurrent Pos:* Distinguished Fac Award, Mich State Univ, 84. *Mem:* Endocrine Soc; Am Fedn Clin Res; fel Am Col Physicians; Inst Elec & Electronics Engrs; Cent Soc Clin Res. *Res:* Decision analysis as applied to clinical medicine; endocrine hypertension; data base usage. *Mailing Add:* A108 B E Fee Mich State Univ East Lansing MI 48824. *E-Mail:* rovner@pilot.msu.edu

ROVNER, JEROME SYLVAN, ARACHNOLOGY, ANIMAL BEHAVIOR. *Current Pos:* asst prof, 67-71, assoc prof, 71-77, PROF ZOOL, OHIO UNIV, 77- *Personal Data:* b Baltimore, Md, July 15, 40; m 62; c 2. *Educ:* Univ Md, BS, 62, PhD(zool), 66. *Prof Exp:* NSF fel zool, Gutenberg Univ, Mainz, 66-67. *Concurrent Pos:* Res grant, NSF, 72 & 74; guest researcher, Goethe Univ, Frankfurt, 80. *Mem:* AAAS; Animal Behav Soc; Am Arachnological Soc (pres, 85-87); Brit Arachnological Soc. *Res:* Predatory behavior in spiders; acoustic and chemical communication in spiders; flooding survival in spiders. *Mailing Add:* 18 Franklin Ave Athens OH 45701

ROVNYAK, GEORGE CHARLES, MEDICINAL CHEMISTRY, ORGANIC CHEMISTRY. *Current Pos:* res investr, 70-80, sr res investr med chem, 80-88, RES FEL, E R SQUIBB & SONS, INC, 80- *Personal Data:* b Ford City, Pa, Jan 31, 41; m 63; c 3. *Educ:* St Vincent Col, AB, 62; Univ Pittsburgh, BS, 65, PhD(chem), 70. *Prof Exp:* Chemist, Neville Chem Co, 63-66. *Mem:* Am Chem Soc; NY Acad Sci; Sigma Xi. *Res:* Synthesis and structure-activity relationship of biologically active organic compounds; reaction mechanisms; application of small ring compounds to chemical synthesis; heterocyclic chemistry. *Mailing Add:* 10 W Broad St Hopewell NJ 08525

ROVNYAK, JAMES L, MATHEMATICS. *Current Pos:* assoc prof, 67-73, PROF MATH, UNIV VA, 73- *Personal Data:* b Ford City, Pa, Jan 9, 39; m 63; c 2. *Educ:* Lafayette Col, AB, 60; Yale Univ, MA, 62, PhD(math), 63. *Prof Exp:* Asst prof math, Purdue Univ, 63-67. *Concurrent Pos:* NSF fel, Inst Advan Study, 66-67; Alexander von Humboldt Award, US Sr Scientist, Fed Repub Ger, 79. *Mem:* Am Math Soc. *Res:* Hilbert space; complex analysis. *Mailing Add:* Kerchof Hall Univ Va Charlottesville VA 22903-3199

ROW, CLARK, FOREST ECONOMICS. *Current Pos:* CONSULT RESOURCE ECONOMIST, 84-, SPECIALIST GLOBAL WARMING, 89- *Personal Data:* b Washington, DC, July 24, 34; m 72, Constance Foshay; c Seth & Jess. *Educ:* Yale Univ, BS, 56; Duke Univ, MF, 58; Tulane Univ La, PhD(econ), 73. *Prof Exp:* Res forester, Southern Forest Exp Sta, US Forest Serv, 58-62, proj leader forest prod & mkt res, 62-65; chief, Forest Prods Demand & Price Anal Br, US Forest Serv, 65-67, chief, Forest Econ Br, 68-75, leader, Eval Methods Res Group, 75-84. *Mem:* Am Econ Asn; Soc Am Foresters. *Res:* Economics of forest, range, watershed and outdoor recreation wilderness management; pest control economics; demand for forest products; economics of forest products industries; global climate change mitigation; environmental policies concerning forests. *Mailing Add:* 612 Rivershore Ct Edgewood MD 21040-3603

ROW, THOMAS HENRY, NUCLEAR ENGINEERING. *Current Pos:* res staff, Oak Ridge Nat Lab, 59-67, nat prog coordr, Reactor Containment Spray Syst Prog, Atomic Energy Comn, 67-71, dir, Environ Statements Proj, 71-75, head, Environ Impact Sect, Energy Div, 75-81, dir, Nuclear & Chem Waste Prog, 81-88, dir environ Safety & Health, 88-92, SR STAFF ASST LAB DIR, OAK RIDGE NAT LAB, 92- *Personal Data:* b Blacksburg, Va, May 15; m 91, Patricia Dozier; c Deborah, Stuart, Chris, Robert, Jill, Joel & April. *Educ:* Roanoke Col, BS, 57; Va Polytech Inst & State Univ, MS, 59. *Prof Exp:* Instr math, Roanoke Col, 57. *Concurrent Pos:* Consult, Adv Comt Reactor Safeguards, USAEC, 68-71; mem Stand Comt, Am Nat Stand Inst, 71-72; consult, envir prog, Roane State Community Col, Chattanooga State Tech & Community Col, Midwest Consortium, Hazardous Worker Training, Nat Inst Environ Renewal. *Mem:* Am Nuclear Soc; Sigma Xi. *Res:* Nuclear waste research and operations; environmental effects of energy and industrial facility operation. *Mailing Add:* 114 Nebraska Ave Oak Ridge TN 37830. *Fax:* 423-576-6183; *E-Mail:* rowth@ornl.gov

ROWAN, DIGHTON FRANCIS, MEDICAL VIROLOGY. *Current Pos:* RETIRED. *Personal Data:* b Amsterdam, NY, Dec 31, 14. *Educ:* San Jose State Col, BA, 48; Stanford Univ, MA, 53, PhD(bact & exp path), 54. *Honors & Awards:* Sect Award, Am Pub Health Asn, 61; Outstanding Serv in Educ Recognition Award, Am Soc Clin Pathologists, 68. *Prof Exp:* Instr microbiol virol, Stanford Univ Sch Med, 53-56; instr epidemiol, Sch Trop Med & Pub Health, Tulane Univ, 56-57; asst prof microbiol & virol, Sch Med, Univ Vt, 57-59; prin virologist develop & res, NJ State Dept Health, 59-61; dir, virol lab, Mont State Bd Health, 61-63; prof dir virol dept, Col Dent, Baylor Univ & Med Ctr, 63-73; prof, dir microbiol virol, Adv Microbiol Infectious Dis Div, Sch Med, Southern Ill Univ, 73-84. *Mem:* Fel Am Acad Microbiol; fel Am Pub Health Asn; Am Soc Microbiol; AAAS; Sigma Xi. *Res:* The role of herpes viruses in vulvitis; birth defects and sudden infant death; role of coxsackieviruses in adult myocarditis and pericarditis; respiratory disease and encephalitis surveillance. *Mailing Add:* 300 Davis Circle Midwest City OK 73110

ROWAN, WILLIAM HAMILTON, JR, DATABASE DESIGN, RELATIONAL DATABASE SYSTEMS. *Current Pos:* instr mech, Vanderbilt Univ, 59-60, asst prof math & comput eng, 64-66, chair, Info Eng Dept, 66-69, chair systs & info sci, 69-73, prof systs & info sci, 73-77, prof, 77-95, EMER PROF COMPUT SCI, VANDERBILT UNIV, 95- *Personal Data:* m 73, Sarah Conley; c William H III & Elizabeth (Taylor). *Educ:* Vanderbilt Univ, BE, 55; NC State Univ, PhD(civil eng), 65. *Prof Exp:* Struct engr, Boeing Co, 55-57; electronic engr, State of Tenn, 60-61. *Concurrent Pos:* Staff consult, Aerostruct Div, Avco, 65-70; pres & chief consult, On-Line Comput Inc, 69-84; actg chair Comput Sci Dept, Vanderbilt Univ, 84-85. *Mem:* Inst Elec & Electronics Engrs; Asn Comput Mach; Am Soc Eng Educ. *Res:* Matrix methods of structural analysis and design; finite element methods; man-machine interface in structural design; relational database design; integration of statistical and commercial databases. *Mailing Add:* 604 Summerwind Circle Nashville TN 37215

ROWAND, WILL H, ENGINEERING. *Current Pos:* RETIRED. *Personal Data:* b Mar 20, 08. *Educ:* Cornell Univ, ME, 29. *Honors & Awards:* Newcomen Medal, 54. *Prof Exp:* Mem staff, Babcock & Wilcox, 29-48, chem engr, 48-53, vpres eng, 53-61, vpres mkt, 61-66, vpres nuclear power, 66-72. *Mem:* Nat Acad Eng; fel Am Soc Mech Engrs. *Mailing Add:* 10 Red River Rd Sedona AZ 86351

ROWE, ALLEN MCGHEE, JR, THERMODYNAMICS. *Current Pos:* CONSULT, ENERGY RESOURCE DEVELOP, 90- *Personal Data:* b Columbus, Ohio, May 15, 32. *Educ:* Ohio State Univ, BPetrolEng & MS, 56; Univ Tex, PhD(petrol eng), 64. *Honors & Awards:* Outstanding Achievement Award Eng, Agr Res Ctr Opers, USDA, 84. *Prof Exp:* Jr engr, Texaco, Inc, 56-57, res engr, 57-58; res engr, Esso Prod Res Co, 58-61 & Tex Petrol Res Comt, 61-64; asst prof petrol eng, Okla State Univ, 64-71, assoc prof mech eng, 71-76; sr res engr, Atlantic Richfield Co, 76-85; consult, Microsim Int Inc, 87-90. *Concurrent Pos:* Consult, Continental Oil Co, Okla, 64, Intercomp, Tex, 71 & Marathon Oil Co, 74; NASA fel, 67 & 68; lectr, Stanford Univ, 74. *Mem:* Inst Mining, Metall & Petrol Engrs. *Res:* Calculation of equilibrium compositions of hydrocarbon mixtures; desalination research. *Mailing Add:* 2510 Parkhaven Plano TX 75075. *E-Mail:* amrowe@prodigy.net

ROWE, ANNE PRINE, physical chemistry, for more information see previous edition

ROWE, ARTHUR W(ILSON), BIOCHEMISTRY, CRYOBIOLOGY. *Current Pos:* ADJ PROF, STATE UNIV NY, BINGHAMTON, 88- *Personal Data:* b Newark, NJ, Sept 14, 31; m 57; c 2. *Educ:* Duke Univ, AB, 53; Rutgers Univ, PhD, 60. *Prof Exp:* Res chemist, Linde Div, Union Carbide Corp, 60-64; investr & dir crybiol, NY Blood Ctr, 64-88; assoc prof, 69-83, PROF SCH MED, NY UNIV, 83- *Concurrent Pos:* Consult, Nat Cancer Inst, NIH, 62-66; consult, Lab Exp Med & Surg in Primates, Sch Med, NY Univ, 67-; ed-in-chief, J Cryobiol, 73-; deleg, Am Blood Comn, 76-82; vis prof, Univ Damascus, 77, Helmholtz Inst Aachen, Fed Repub Ger, 84, Jadaupur Univ, 90. *Mem:* Fel AAAS; Am Chem Soc; Soc Cryobiol (treas, 69-72, vpres, 73-76); fel Am Inst Chemists; Transplantation Soc; NY Acad Sci; Sigma Xi. *Res:* Low temperature preservation of bone marrow, stem cells, blood, leukocytes, platelets and tissues and embryos; cryobiology; cellular metabolism and isotopic techniques; immunohematology; cryogenic freezing of tissues. *Mailing Add:* 162 Four Brooks Rd Stamford CT 06903

ROWE, BRIAN H, AIRCRAFT ENGINE DEVELOPMENT. *Current Pos:* var eng pos, Gen Elec Co, 57-68, gen mgr, CF6 Proj Dept, 68-72, vpres & gen mgr, Com Engine Proj Div, 72-74, Airline Prog Div, 74-76 & Aircraft Eng Div, 76-79, sr vpres, 79-95, chmn aircraft engines, 93-95, EMER CHMN AIRCRAFT ENGINES, GEN ELEC CO, CINCINNATI, OHIO, 95- *Personal Data:* b London, Eng, May 6, 31; c 3. *Educ:* Durham Univ, BS, 55. *Mem:* Nat Acad Eng; fel Royal Aeronaut Soc. *Mailing Add:* Mail Drop N178 1 Neumann Way Cincinnati OH 45215-6301

ROWE, BRIAN PETER, CARDIOVASCULAR PHYSIOLOGY & PHARMACOLOGY, NEUROPEPTIDES. *Current Pos:* asst prof, PROF PHYSIOL, EAST TENN STATE UNIV, 81- *Personal Data:* b Shoreham-by-Sea, Eng, May 13, 53; m 87, Rebecca Bowser. *Educ:* Univ Southampton, BSc, 74, PhD(physiol & pharmacol), 77. *Prof Exp:* Res assoc, Univ Mo, Columbia, 77-79, Univ Tenn, 79-81. *Concurrent Pos:* Vis prof vet physiol & pharmacol, Wash State Univ, 95. *Mem:* Am Physiol Soc; Soc Neurosci; Int Brain Res Soc. *Res:* Involvement of angiotensin in cardivascular regulation; pathogenesis of hypertension; role of angiotensin as a neuropeptide. *Mailing Add:* Dept Physiol Col Med E Tenn State Univ Johnson City TN 37614-0576

ROWE, CARLETON NORWOOD, TRIBOLOGY, LUBRICANTS & LUBRICATION. *Current Pos:* sr res chemist, 60-65, res assoc, 65-86, SR RES ASSOC, MOBIL RES & DEVELOP CORP, PRINCETON, NJ, 86- *Personal Data:* b Halifax, Pa, Apr 1, 28; m 56; c 3. *Educ:* Juniata Col, BS, 51; Pa State Univ, MS, 53, PhD(phys chem), 55. *Prof Exp:* Res chemist, Tex Co, 55-60. *Mem:* Am Chem Soc; fel Am Soc Lubrication Engrs (pres, 85-86); Soc Automotive Engrs. *Res:* Lubrication; friction and wear; additive chemistry; contact fatigue; base stock properties; synthetic lubricants. *Mailing Add:* 206 Lenape Trail Wenonah NJ 08090-2007

ROWE, CHARLES DAVID, polymer chemistry, for more information see previous edition

ROWE, DAVID JOHN, MATHEMATICAL PHYSICS. *Current Pos:* assoc prof, 68-74, assoc chmn, Dept Physics, 78-83, assoc dean, Sch Grad Studies, 85-88. *Personal Data:* b Totnes, Eng, Feb 4, 36; m 58; c 2. *Educ:* Cambridge Univ, BA, 59; Oxford Univ, BA, 59, MA & DPhil(nuclear physics), 62. *Honors & Awards:* Rutherford Mem Medal & Prize, Royal Soc Can, 84. *Prof Exp:* Ford Found fel, Niels Bohr Inst, Copenhagen, Denmark, 62-63; UK Atomic Energy Authority res fel, Atomic Energy Res Estab, Harwell, Eng, 63-66; res assoc, Univ Rochester, 66-68. *Concurrent Pos:* Alfred P Sloan fel, 70; chmn, Theoret Physics Div, Can Asn Physists, 70, 71; vis prof, Univ Sao Paulo, 71-72; Isaac Walton Killman fel, 90-92. *Mem:* Can Asn Physicists; fel Royal Soc Can. *Res:* Theory of nuclear structure and reactions; collective motion; group theory. *Mailing Add:* 5 Scarth Rd Toronto ON M4W 2S5 Can. *Fax:* 416-978-2537; *E-Mail:* rowe@physics.utoronto.ca

ROWE, EDWARD C, NEUROPHYSIOLOGY. *Current Pos:* Assoc prof, 61-73, PROF BIOL, EMPORIA STATE UNIV, 73- *Personal Data:* b Oakland, Calif, Dec 23, 33; m 55; c 3. *Educ:* Wesleyan Univ, BA, 55; Univ Mich, MS, 57, PhD(zool), 64. *Concurrent Pos:* NIH res grant physiol ganglia, 66-71. *Mem:* AAAS; Am Soc Zool. *Res:* Comparative neurophysiology. *Mailing Add:* 828 Market St Emporia KS 66801

ROWE, EDWARD JOHN, pharmacy, for more information see previous edition

ROWE, ELIZABETH SNOW, PHYSICAL BIOCHEMISTRY. *Current Pos:* asst prof, Med Sch, Univ Kans, 77-78, adj asst prof, 80-81, from res asst prof to res assoc prof, 81-96, RES PROF, BIOCHEM, MED SCH, UNIV KANS, 96-; ASSOC RES CAREER SCIENTIST, VET ADM ADMIN, 88- *Personal Data:* b Seattle, Wash, Dec 28, 43; m 66; c 2. *Educ:* Duke Univ, BA, 66, PhD(biochem), 71. *Prof Exp:* Fel calorimetry, Med Sch, Johns Hopkins Univ, 71-72; res assoc elec birefringence, Georgetown Univ, 72-75; fel membrane phys chem, Chem Dept, Johns Hopkins Univ, 76-77. *Concurrent Pos:* Dir, Molecular Mech Alcoholism Lab, Vet Admin Med Ctr, Kansas City, 78- *Mem:* Sigma Xi; Am Soc Biol Chemists; Biophys Soc; Res Soc Alcoholism. *Res:* Physical properties of membrane components; effect of anesthetics and alcohol on membranes; thermodynamics of protein structure and function. *Mailing Add:* Phys Biochem Res Lab Vet Admin Med Ctr 4801 Linwood Blvd Kansas City MO 64128. *Fax:* 816-861-1110; *E-Mail:* erowe@kubub.cc.ukaws.edu

ROWE, ENGLEBERT L, physical pharmacy; deceased, see previous edition for last biography

ROWE, GEORGE G, INTERNAL MEDICINE, CARDIOLOGY. *Current Pos:* resident, Med Sch, Univ Wis-Madison, res assoc, 54-55, from asst prof to prof, 57-89, EMER PROF MED, MED SCH, UNIV WIS-MADISON, 89- *Personal Data:* b Vulcan, Alta, May 17, 21; nat US; m 47, Patsy R Barnett; c George L, James A & Jane E. *Educ:* Univ Wis, BA, 43, MD, 45; Am Bd Internal Med, dipl, 55; Am Bd Cardiovasc Dis, dipl, 69. *Prof Exp:* Instr anat, Sch Med, Wash Univ, 48-50; vol res assoc, Hammersmith Hosp, London, 56-57. *Concurrent Pos:* Markle scholar, 55-60. *Mem:* Am Physiol Soc; Am Soc Pharmacol & Exp Therapeut; fel Am Col Physicians; Am Fedn Clin Res; Am Soc Clin Invest; Sigma Xi; Univ Cardiologists Asn (pres, 74-75); fel Am Heart Asn. *Res:* Hemodynamics of the systemic and coronary circulations; congenital and acquired heart disease. *Mailing Add:* Dept Med Med Sch Univ Wis 600 N Highland Ave Madison WI 53792

ROWE, GILBERT THOMAS, OCEANOGRAPHY. *Current Pos:* head, Dept Oceanog, 87-93, PROF, DEPT OCEANOG, TEX A&M UNIV, COL STA, 87- *Personal Data:* b Ames, Iowa, Feb 7, 42; m 62, Judith L Ingram; c Atticus I. *Educ:* Tex A&M Univ, BS, 64, MS, 66; Duke Univ, PhD(zool), 68. *Prof Exp:* From asst to assoc scientist, Woods Hole Oceanog Inst, 68-79; oceanographer, Brookhaven Nat Lab, NY, 79-87. *Mem:* Fel AAAS; Oceanog Soc; Hon Deep Sea Biol Soc; Limnol & Oceanog Soc. *Res:* Benthic ecology; carbon and nitrogen cycles; environmental quality; models of food chains and elemental cycles in marine ecosystems. *Mailing Add:* Dept Oceanog Tex A&M Univ College Station TX 77843. *Fax:* 409-845-6331; *E-Mail:* growe@ocean.tama.edu

ROWE, H(ARRISON) E(DWARD), ELECTRICAL ENGINEERING. *Current Pos:* Anson Wood Burchard Prof, 84-93, EMER PROF ELEC ENG, STEVENS INST TECHNOL, HOBOKEN, NJ, 93- *Personal Data:* b Chicago, Ill, Jan 29, 27; m 51; c 4. *Educ:* Mass Inst Technol, BS, 48, MS, 50, ScD(elec eng), 52. *Hon Degrees:* ME, Stevens Inst Technol, 88. *Honors & Awards:* Microwave Prize, Inst Elec & Electronics Engrs, 72 & David Sarnoff Award, 77. *Prof Exp:* Mem tech staff, Radio Res Lab, Bell Labs, Holmdel, NJ, 52-84. *Concurrent Pos:* Mem comn 6, Int Union Radio Sci; vis lectr, Univ Calif, Berkeley, 63 & Imp Col, Univ London, 68 & 81; res asst, Mass Inst Technol, 48-52; mem, Defense Sci Bd Task Force, 72-74. *Mem:* Fel Inst Elec & Electronics Engrs; Sigma Xi. *Res:* Communications systems; wave guides; optical communication systems; noise and antenna theory; optimizing radio-astronomical observations of incoherent fields with an antenna; terrain mapping by a radiometer; author of 44 publications; random media. *Mailing Add:* 9 Buttonwood Lane Rumson NJ 07760. *Fax:* 732-747-8402; *E-Mail:* hrowe@stevens-tech.edu

ROWE, HENRY A, CHEMISTRY. *Current Pos:* PROF CHEM, NORFOLK STATE UNIV. *Educ:* Univ NC, BS, 76; NC State Univ, PhD(biochem), 81. *Prof Exp:* Arteriosclerosis res fel, Wake Forest Univ, NC, 81-84; biochem/environ consult, US Environ Protection Agency, 86; Fulbright sr scholar biochem, Univ Kelaniya, Sri Lanka, 94-95. *Mem:* AAAS; Am Chem Soc; Am Soc Investigative Path; Sigma Xi. *Res:* Contributed several professional publications. *Mailing Add:* Dept Chem Norfolk State Univ Norfolk VA 23504

ROWE, JACK FIELD, ELECTRICAL ENGINEERING. *Current Pos:* Staff mem, Minn Power & Light Co, 50-66, asst to pres, 66-67, vpres, 67-68, exec vpres, 69-74, chmn, 69-93, pres, 74-84, chief exec officer, 78-89, BD DIRS, MINN POWER & LIGHT CO, 93- *Personal Data:* b Minn, May 10, 27; m 55, Mary E Moen; c Lizette Ann. *Educ:* Univ Minn, BEE, 50. *Honors & Awards:* Outstanding Leadership Award in Energy Conversion Sci, Am Soc Mech Engrs, 80. *Concurrent Pos:* Vchmn, Mid Continent Area Reliability Coun, 70-71, chmn, 72-73. *Mem:* Inst Elec & Electronics Engrs. *Mailing Add:* 4735 Villas Mare Lane Naples FL 33940-3473

ROWE, JAMES LINCOLN, ORGANIC CHEMISTRY. *Current Pos:* RETIRED. *Personal Data:* b Chicago, Ill, Nov 14, 17; m 48, Pauline P Stone; c James L Jr, Robert S & Richard A. *Educ:* Princeton Univ, BA, 39; Univ Chicago, PhD(org chem), 46; Ind Univ, DJ, 68. *Prof Exp:* Chemist, Nat Defense Res Comt, Univ Chicago, 42 & Off Sci Res & Develop, 44-46; res chemist, 46-54, patent agent, 54-68; patent attorney, Eli Lilly & Co, 68-85. *Concurrent Pos:* Mem coun, Woodard, Emhardt, Naughton, Moriarty & McNett, 90- *Mem:* AAAS; Am Chem Soc. *Res:* Mechanisms of organic reactions; free radical reactions; synthesis of synthetic drugs; war gases; nitrogen mustards; decomposition of di-acetyl peroxide in alcohols. *Mailing Add:* 7775 Spring Mill Rd Indianapolis IN 46260-3637

ROWE, JAY ELWOOD, INDUSTRIAL ORGANIC CHEMISTRY. *Current Pos:* res assoc, 74-80, group leader, Res & Develop, 80-92, DIR RES & DEVELOP, CROMPTON & KNOWLES CORP, 92- *Personal Data:* b Tacoma, Wash, Jan 10, 47; m 65; c 3. *Educ:* Bucknell Univ, BS, 68; Lehigh Univ, PhD(org chem), 73. *Prof Exp:* Instr chem, Muhlenberg Col, 72-73, asst prof, 73-74. *Mem:* Am Chem Soc; Am Asn Textile Chemists & Colorists; Sigma Xi. *Res:* Chemistry and theory of acid dyes. *Mailing Add:* RD 1 Box 1163 Hartz Store Rd Mohnton PA 19540

ROWE, JOHN EDWARD, EXPERIMENTAL SOLID STATE PHYSICS. *Current Pos:* Mem tech staff, 69-80, RES HEAD SURFACE PHYSICS, BELL LABS, 80- *Personal Data:* b Jacksonville, Fla, Sept 25, 41; m 65; c 3. *Educ:* Emory Univ, BS, 63; Brown Univ, PhD(physics), 71. *Concurrent Pos:* Mem, Synchrotron Users Exec Comt, Brookhaven Nat Lab; affil prof physics, Univ Fla. *Mem:* Fel Am Phys Soc; Am Vacuum Soc. *Res:* Electron spectroscopy on surfaces and bulk solids using photoemission, electron energy loss and Auger spectroscopies; low energy electron diffraction; studies of chemisorption and of film growth; synchrotron radiation; surface states on semiconductors; chemisorption electronic and structural properties; surface vibrational modes using surface enhanced Raman spectroscopy and high resolution electron energy loss spectroscopy. *Mailing Add:* Rm 3L-401 AT&T Bell Labs 600 Mountain Ave Murray Hill NJ 07974

ROWE, JOHN JAMES, MICROBIAL BIOCHEMISTRY, NITRATE REDUCTION. *Current Pos:* asst prof, 77-83, ASSOC PROF MICROBIOL, DEPT BIOL, UNIV DAYTON, 83- *Personal Data:* b Washington, DC, Aug 2, 44; m 68; c 1. *Educ:* Colo State Univ, BS, 67; Ariz State Univ, MS, 71; Univ Kans, PhD(microbiol), 75. *Prof Exp:* Fel microbiol, Dept Biol, Univ Ga, 75-77. *Mem:* Sigma Xi; Am Soc Microbiol. *Res:* Physiological and genetic studies of bacteria in the genus Pseudomonas; denitrification; inorganic nitrogen metabolism; Pseudomonas aeruginosa vaccine. *Mailing Add:* Dept Biol Univ Dayton 300 College Park Dayton OH 45469-0001

ROWE, JOHN MICHAEL, SOLID STATE PHYSICS. *Current Pos:* RES PHYSICIST, NAT BUR STAND, 73- *Personal Data:* b Oakville, Ont, Apr 9, 39. *Educ:* Queen's Univ, Ont, BSc, 62; McMaster Univ, PhD(solid state physics), 66. *Prof Exp:* Fel physics, Argonne Nat Lab, 66-67, asst staff physicist, 67-72, assoc physicist, 72-73. *Mem:* AAAS; Am Phys Soc. *Res:* Study of lattice and liquid dynamics by slow neutron scattering. *Mailing Add:* Nat Inst Stand & Technol A106 Reactor Bldg Gaithersburg MD 20899

ROWE, JOHN STANLEY, PLANT ECOLOGY. *Current Pos:* prof, 67-85, EMER PROF PLANT ECOL, UNIV SASK, 85- *Personal Data:* b Hardisty, Alta, June 11, 18; m 54; c 2. *Educ:* Univ Alta, BSc, 41; Univ Nebr, MSc, 48; Univ Man, PhD(ecol), 56. *Prof Exp:* Forest ecologist, Can Dept Forestry, 48-67. *Mem:* Can Inst Forestry; Can Bot Asn; Ecol Soc Am. *Res:* Ecology of northern Canada; boreal forest, tundra and peatlands. *Mailing Add:* PO Box 11 New Denver BC V0G 1S0 Can

ROWE, JOHN W, MEDICINE. *Current Pos:* PRES, MT SINAI MED CTR, MT SINAI HOSP & SCH MED, 88-, PROF MED, GERIAT & ADULT DEVELOP, 88- *Personal Data:* Jersey City, NJ, June 20, 44. *Educ:* Canisius Col, BS, 66; Univ Rochester, MD, 70; Am Bd Internal Med, dipl, 73 & 76. *Honors & Awards:* Milo Leavitt Award, Am Geriat Soc, 85; Joseph Freeman Award, Geront Soc Am, 87; Donald P Kent Award, 88; Avery Weissman Award, Am Inst Life-Threatening Illness & Loss, 92; Irving S Wright Award of Distinction, Am Fedn Aging Res, Inc; Allied Signal Achievement Award in Aging. *Prof Exp:* Asst med, Med Sch, Johns Hopkins Univ, 72-74; from instr to prof med, Harvard Med Sch, 75-88. *Concurrent Pos:* Mem bd gov, Am Bd Internal Med; clin fel med, Med Sch, Harvard Univ, 71-72, res fel, 74-75; clin assoc, NIH, 72-74; res & clin fel, Mass Gen Hosp, 74-75; sr physician, Brigham & Women's Hosp & Beth Israel Hosp; dir, Geriat Res Educ Clin Ctr, Vet Admin, Boston; ed, J Gerontol, 80-83; dir, Div Aging, Harvard Med Sch, 80-88; dep dir, Div Health Policy Res & Educ, Harvard Univ, 84-88; vis scientist, Human Nutrit Res Ctr Aging, Tufts Univ, 85-88; actg chmn, Dept Med, Mt Sinai Sch Med, 92-93. *Mem:* Inst Med-Nat Acad Sci; fel NY Acad Med; fel Am Col Physicians; Am Fedn Aging Res (vpres, 84, pres, 87-91); fel Gerontol Soc Am (pres, 89); Am Fedn Clin Res; Am Geriatrics Soc Am. *Res:* Geriatrics; internal medicine. *Mailing Add:* Mt Sinai Med Ctr 1 Gustave L Levy Pl New York NY 10029. *Fax:* 212-996-9763

ROWE, JOHN WESTEL, WOOD CHEMISTRY, BIOCHEMISTRY & ORGANIC CHEMISTRY. *Current Pos:* RETIRED. *Personal Data:* b New York, NY, Sept 3, 24; m 49, Marieli D Lowens; c Peter W, William W & Michael P. *Educ:* Mass Inst Technol, BS, 48; Univ Colo, MS, 52; Swiss Fed Inst Technol, Zurich, ScD(org chem), 56. *Honors & Awards:* Wood Salutes Award, 75. *Prof Exp:* Proj leader & supvry res chemist, Forest Prod Lab, USDA, 57-84. *Concurrent Pos:* Mem, Nat Acad Sci Corrim Comt, 74-75; chmn, Wis Sect, Am Chem Soc, 68-69 & alt counr, 76-78; lectr, Univ Wis. *Mem:* Fel AAAS; Soc Econ Bot; Phytochem Soc NAm; fel Am Inst Chemists; fel Int Acad Wood Sci; Sigma Xi; Am Chem Soc; Tech Asn Pulp & Paper Indust. *Res:* Natural products, especially extractives of wood and bark; higher terpenoids and steroids; improved chemical utilization of wood. *Mailing Add:* 1001 Tumalo Trail Madison WI 53711-3024

ROWE, JOSEPH E(VERETT), ELECTRICAL & COMPUTER ENGINEERING. *Current Pos:* ASSOC VPRES RES & DIR, UNIV DAYTON RES INST, 92- *Personal Data:* b Highland Park, Mich, June 4, 27; m 50, Anne P Prine; c Jonathan D & Carol K (Chorey). *Educ:* Univ Mich, BSE(elec eng) & BSE(math), 51, MSE, 52, PhD(elec eng), 55. *Honors & Awards:* Curtis W McGraw Res Award, Am Soc Eng Educ, 64. *Prof Exp:* Asst, Electron Tube Lab, Eng Res Inst, Univ Mich, Ann Arbor, 51-53, lectr, 52-55, res assoc, 53-55, from asst prof to prof elec eng, 55-74, dir, Electron Physics Lab, 58-68, chmn, Dept Elec & Comput Eng, 68-74; vprovost & dean eng, Case Inst Technol, 74-76, provost, 76-78; vpres & gen mgr technol, Harris Controls Div, Harris Corp, 78-82; exec vpres res & defense systs, Gould Inc, 82-83, vchmn & chief tech officer, 83-86; vpres & chief scientist, PPG Indust Inc, 87-92. *Concurrent Pos:* Chmn, Coalition Adv Indust Technol, 85-86; mem, Army Sci Bd, 85-91, 93-; adv, Group Electron Devices, 93- *Mem:* Nat Acad Eng; fel Inst Elec & Electronics Engrs; Am Phys Soc; Am Soc Eng Educ; fel AAAS. *Res:* Microwave circuits; traveling-wave tubes; crossed-field devices; electromagnetic field theory; noise; computers; lasers; solid state devices; plasmas; integrated circuits; materials science. *Mailing Add:* 856 Timberlake Ct Kettering OH 45429

ROWE, KENNETH EUGENE, EXPERIMENTAL STATISTICS, BIOMETRY. *Current Pos:* from asst prof to assoc prof exp statist, 64-70, assoc prof, 70-80, PROF STATIST, ORE STATE UNIV, 80- *Personal Data:* b Canon City, Colo, Feb 8, 34; m 70; c 4. *Educ:* Colo State Univ, BS, 57; NC State Univ, MS, 60; Iowa State Univ, PhD(animal breeding), 66. *Prof Exp:* Geneticist, Regional Swine Breeding Lab, USDA, Ames, Iowa, 61-64. *Concurrent Pos:* NSF fac develop fel, NC State Univ, 69-70; sr statist adv, Special Studies Staff, IERL, US Environ Protection Agency, NC, 78-79. *Mem:* Biomet Soc; Am Statist Asn; Sigma Xi. *Res:* Applications of statistics, particularly biological problems and quantitative genetics; statistical computation. *Mailing Add:* Dept Statist Ore State Univ Corvallis OR 97331

ROWE, LAWRENCE A, HUMAN-COMPUTER INTERFACES, COMPUTER-INTEGRATED MANUFACTURING. *Current Pos:* PROF COMPUT SCI, UNIV CALIF, BERKELEY, 76- *Personal Data:* b Boston, Mass, Apr 11, 48. *Educ:* Univ Calif, Irvine, BS, 70, PhD(info & computer sci), 76. *Concurrent Pos:* Prin investr, NSF, 78-; founder & dir, Ingres Corp, 80-90; consult, Siemens Corp Res, 87- & Harris Corp, 88-; chmn, Software Systs Awards Comt, Asn Comput Mach, 90. *Mem:* Asn Comput Mach; Inst Elec & Electronics Engrs. *Res:* Design and implementation of computer systems (software and hardware) to solve challenging problems; worked on application development systems, programming languages, databases and computer-integrated manufacturing. *Mailing Add:* Dept Elec Eng & Computer Sci Univ Calif Berkeley CA 94720

ROWE, MARK J, BIOCHEMISTRY. *Current Pos:* PROF BIOCHEM, BRIGHAM YOUNG UNIV, 86- *Personal Data:* b Oakland, Calif, July 16, 43; m 66; c 5. *Educ:* Brigham Young Univ, BS, 68, PhD(biochem), 72. *Prof Exp:* Fel molecular biol, Stanford Univ, 72-73; asst prof Eastern Va Med Sch, 73-78, assoc prof, 78-86; from asst prof to assoc prof biochem, Eastern Va Med Sch, 73-86. *Concurrent Pos:* NIH fel, Dept Biol, Stanford Univ, 72-73. *Mem:* Am Chem Soc; AAAS; Sigma Xi. *Res:* Nucleic acids, protein biosynthesis; mitochondrial membrane biogenesis, protein synthesis and genetics and biochemical genetics; ovarian molecular endocrinology. *Mailing Add:* 305 W 1700 S Orem UT 84058-7541. *Fax:* 801-376-7499

ROWE, MARVIN W, NUCLEAR GEOCHEMISTRY, ARCHAEOLOGICAL CHEMISTRY. *Current Pos:* from asst prof to assoc prof, 75-87, PROF CHEM, TEX A&M UNIV, 87- *Personal Data:* b Amarillo, Tex, July 6, 37; c 4. *Educ:* NMex Inst Mining & Technol, BS, 59; Univ Ark, PhD(chem), 66. *Prof Exp:* Res asst radioactiv, Los Alamos Sci Lab, 60-63; Miller res fel physics, Univ Calif, Berkeley, 66-68; asst prof chem, Univ Wash, 68-69. *Concurrent Pos:* Vis prof, Univ Antwerp, Belgium, 85 & 90, Max Planck Inst, Mainz, WGer, 86-88, Los Alamos Nat Lab, 86-88. *Mem:* Am Chem Soc; Am Soc Archaeology; fel Meteoritical Soc; Int Asn Geochem & Cosmochem. *Res:* Radioactivity, magnetism and noble gas mass spectrometry in meteorites; chronology of early solar system; dating pictographs. *Mailing Add:* Dept Chem Tex A&M Univ College Station TX 77843-3255

ROWE, MARY BUDD, science education; deceased, see previous edition for last biography

ROWE, NATHANIEL H, ORAL PATHOLOGY, ANTIVIRAL CHEMOTHERAPY. *Current Pos:* Prof dent & oral path, Sch Dent, Univ Mich, Ann Arbor, 68-94, assoc prof path, Sch Med, 69-76, assoc dir, Dent Res Inst, 70-89, sr res scientist, 77-89, PROF PATH, SCH MED, UNIV MICH, ANN ARBOR, 76-, WILLIAM R MANN, PROF DENT, 94- *Personal Data:* b Hibbing, Minn, May 26, 31; div; c Bradford Scott, Nathanial E, Lorna M (Twinning) & Jonathan A. *Educ:* Univ Minn, BS, DDS, 55, MSD, 58; Am Bd Oral Path, dipl. *Honors & Awards:* Tiffany Div Nat Award, Am Cancer Soc, 79. *Prof Exp:* Instr, Univ Minn, 58-59; from asst prof to assoc prof gen & oral path & chmn dept, Sch Dent, Wash Univ, 59-69. *Concurrent Pos:* Res fel oral path, Univ Minn, 55-58; consult, Vet Admin, 64- & Ellis Fischel State Cancer Hosp, 66-; assoc res scientist, Cancer Res Ctr, Columbia, Mo, 67-71; mem sci adv bd, Cancer Res Ctr, Columbia Mo, 75-79; civilian prof consult, Off Surgeon, Fifth US Army, 67-83; mem prof adv coun cancer, Mich Asn Regional Med Progs, 69-73, comt cancer control, Mich Dent Asn, 71- & coun dent educ, Am Dent Asn, 71-77, coun on hosp & inst dent, 77-81, coun dental therapeut, 84-90. *Mem:* AAAS; Am Cancer Soc; Am Dent Asn; fel Am Acad Oral Path (pres, 77-78); Am Asn Cancer Res; fel Int Col Dent. *Res:* Effect of environmental variables upon oral cancer induction; etiology and pathogenesis of dental caries; Herpes Simplex virus, antiviral chemotherapy. *Mailing Add:* Univ Mich N University Ave G018K Dent Res Bldg Ann Arbor MI 48109. *Fax:* 313-764-2469

ROWE, PAUL E, PHYSICAL ORGANIC CHEMISTRY. *Current Pos:* CONSULT, 81- *Personal Data:* b Marlboro, Mass, Nov 16, 27; m 53; c David, Cynthia & Ellen. *Educ:* Mass Inst Technol, SB, 48; Boston Univ, PhD(chem), 59. *Prof Exp:* Proj chemist, Nat Northern Div, Am Potash & Chem Co, 53-59; head, Org Develop Dept, Emerson & Cuming, Inc, 69-74, chief chemist, 74-78, dir res & develop, 78-80, partner, Cuming Corp, 80-81. *Mem:* Am Chem Soc. *Res:* Research and development in the explosive and propellant fields and in the plastics and ceramic fields with emphasis on electronic and microwave materials. *Mailing Add:* 71 West Way Mashpee MA 02649-3536

ROWE, RANDALL CHARLES, VEGETABLE PATHOLOGY, POTATO PATHOLOGY. *Current Pos:* asst prof, 74-79, ASSOC PROF VEG PATH, OHIO AGR RES & DEVELOP CTR & OHIO STATE UNIV, 79- *Personal Data:* b Baltimore, Md, Sept 26, 45; m 67; c 2. *Educ:* Mich State Univ, BS, 67; Ore State Univ, PhD(plant path), 72. *Prof Exp:* Res assoc peanut path, NC State Univ, 72-74. *Mem:* Am Phytopath Soc; Potato Asn Am. *Res:* Biology, ecology and control of potato and vegetable diseases with emphasis on soil-borne fungi, verticillium, fusarium, rhizoetonia, fungal-nematode interactions, and fungicide evaluation. *Mailing Add:* Plant Path Ohio State Univ 2021 Coffey Rd Columbus OH 43210-1087

ROWE, RAYMOND GRANT, METALLURGY. *Current Pos:* staff metallurgist, 76-78, METALLURGIST, RES & DEVELOP CTR, GEN ELEC CORP, 78- *Personal Data:* b Seattle, Wash, Oct 24, 41; m 71; c 3. *Educ:* Wash State Univ, BS, 65; Univ Ill, MS, 68, PhD(metall eng), 75. *Prof Exp:* Scientist metall, Battelle-Northwest Labs, 65-67; fels, Jones & Laughlin Steel Co, 67-68 & Am Vacuum Soc, 70-72; adv eng metall, Westinghouse-Hanford Co, 74-76. *Mem:* Am Soc Metals; Metall Soc-Am Inst Mining & Mat. *Res:* Titanium alloys; intermetallic composites; mechanical properties; orthorhombic titanium aluminides. *Mailing Add:* Res & Develop Ctr Gen Elec Corp Schenectady NY 12301. *Fax:* 518-387-5576; *E-Mail:* roweg@ge.crd.com

ROWE, RICHARD J(AY), AGRICULTURAL ENGINEERING. *Current Pos:* PROF AGR ENG, UNIV MAINE, ORONO, 59- *Personal Data:* b Lackawanna, NY, June 12, 30; m 53; c 4. *Educ:* Cornell Univ, BS, 52, PhD, 69; Iowa State Univ, BS, 57, MS, 59. *Prof Exp:* Agr engr, Agr Res Serv, USDA, 57-59. *Mem:* Am Soc Agr Engrs; Am Soc Eng Educ; Sigma Xi. *Res:* Power and mechanization of agricultural operations; systems modeling and simulation. *Mailing Add:* Dept Bio-Resource Eng Univ Maine Orono ME 04469

ROWE, ROBERT S(EAMAN), civil engineering, for more information see previous edition

ROWE, RONALD KERRY, SOIL MECHANICS, ROCK MECHANICS. *Current Pos:* from asst prof to assoc prof, 78-86, PROF CIVIL ENG, UNIV WESTERN ONT, 86-, CHAIR CIVIL ENG, 92- *Personal Data:* b 1951; m 73; c 3. *Educ:* Univ Sydney, BSc, 73, BE, 75, PhD(geotech eng), 79. *Hon Degrees:* DEng, Univ Sydney, 93. *Honors & Awards:* Collingwood Prize, Am Soc Civil Engrs, 85; Can Geotech Soc Prize, 84 & 87, honorable mention, 90; Award of Excellence Grand Prize, NAm Geosynthetics Soc, 91; Shamsher Prakash Res Award, 92. *Prof Exp:* Cadet engr, Australian Dept Construct, 71-74, engr, 75-78. *Concurrent Pos:* Steacie fel, Nat Sci & Eng Res Coun Can, Univ Western Ont, 89-91. *Mem:* Inst Engrs Australia; Asn Prof Engrs Ont; Int Soc Soil Mech & Found Eng; Can Geotech Soc; fel Eng Inst Can; Int Soc Rock Mech; Int Geosynthetics Soc; Can Tunnelling Asn; NAm Geosynthetics Soc. *Res:* Geotechnical and hydrogeologic engineering, with particular emphasis on design and analysis of landfills and contaminant migration through soil and rock; soil and rock-structure interaction problems including tunnelling, shallow foundations, embankments and geosynthesis. *Mailing Add:* Dept Civil & Environ Eng Univ Western Ont London ON N6A 5B9 Can. *Fax:* 519-661-3942

ROWE, THOMAS DUDLEY, pharmacy, for more information see previous edition

ROWE, VERALD KEITH, INDUSTRIAL HYGIENE, INDUSTRIAL TOXICOLOGY. *Current Pos:* Biochemist, Dow Chem Co, 37-44, proj leader, Dow Chem USA, 44-49, toxicologist, 49-52, tech expert, 52-54, lab div leader, 54-64, asst dir, 64-70, dir toxicol & indust hyg, Chem Biol Res, 70-74, res scientist, 73-78, dir toxicol affairs & health & environ sci, 74-79, RES FEL, DOW CHEM CO, 78- *Personal Data:* b Warren, Ill, Oct 5, 14; m 37, Mary; c James & Karen. *Educ:* Cornell Col, AB, 36; Univ Iowa, MS, 38. *Hon Degrees:* ScD, Cornell Col, 71. *Honors & Awards:* Cummings Award, Am Indust Hyg Agency, 79; Borden Award, Am Indust Hyg Asn, 84; Merit Award, Soc Toxicol, 76. *Concurrent Pos:* Mem comt toxicol, Nat Acad Sci-Nat Res Coun, 64-72; mem hazardous mat adv comt, Environ Protection Agency, 75-76. *Mem:* Am Soc Pharmacol & Exp Therapeut; Soc Toxicol (pres, 66-67); Am Chem Soc; Am Indust Hyg Asn; Am Acad Indust Hyg (pres, 72-73). *Res:* Determination of physiological effects of chemicals on animals and man; metabolism of chemicals as they relate to hazards of various types of exposure, both qualitative and quanitative. *Mailing Add:* 9605 Sandstone Dr Dow Chem USA 1803 Bldg Sun City AZ 85351

ROWE, VERNON DODDS, DEVELOPMENTAL NEUROBIOLOGY. *Current Pos:* PRIVATE PRACTICE. *Personal Data:* b Washington, DC, July 11, 44; m 66; c 2. *Educ:* Duke Univ, BS, 65, MD, 69. *Prof Exp:* Resident neurol, Johns Hopkins Hosp, 71-72 & 75-77; res assoc develop neurobiol, Nat Inst Child Health & Human Develop, 72-75; asst prof neurol, Univ Kans Med Ctr, 77-94. *Concurrent Pos:* Staff neurologist, Kansas City Vet Admin Hosp, 77-; Basil O'Connor Starter Grant, Nat Found, 78-80. *Mem:* Sigma Xi. *Res:* Tissue culture of sympathetic and pineal tissue; developmental neurotoxicology. *Mailing Add:* Cons Neuro 2900 Baltimore Suite 630 Kansas City MO 64108-3407

ROWE, WILLIAM BRUCE, BIOCHEMISTRY. *Current Pos:* PRIN, TALIESIN CONSULT, 92- *Personal Data:* b Canon City, Colo, Nov 12, 35; m 78, Frances Martin; c Gavin, Wayne & Gwynne. *Educ:* Colo State Univ, BS, 57; Univ Rochester, MS, 59, PhD(biochem), 67. *Prof Exp:* Instr, Med Col, Cornell Univ, 69-72, asst prof biochem, 72-78; assoc dir, Baxter-Travenol Labs, 78-84, dir, 84-87; dir basic res, Clintec Nutrit Co, 87-92. *Concurrent Pos:* Fel, Sch Med, Tufts Univ, 67 & Med Col, Cornell Univ, 67-69. *Mem:* AAAS; Am Chem Soc; Sigma Xi; NY Acad Sci. *Res:* Amino acid and protein metabolism; enzymology and control mechanisms of intermediary metabolism; clinical nutrition; biotechnology. *Mailing Add:* Taliesin Consult 229 Main St Evanston IL 60202. *Fax:* 847-328-2092

ROWE, WILLIAM DAVID, RISK ANALYSIS, MANAGEMENT SCIENCE & MEASUREMENT THEORY. *Current Pos:* RETIRED. *Personal Data:* b Orange, NJ, Jan 7, 30; m 87, Karen S Terninko; c William D Jr, Andrea L, Deirdre A (Woodcock), Ryan W, Alexandra S Terninko, Miriam S Terninko & John S Terninko. *Educ:* Wesleyan Univ, BS, 52; Univ Pittsburgh, MS, 52; Univ Buffalo, MBA, 61; Am Univ, PhD(bus admin/opers res), 73. *Honors & Awards:* Elizur Wright Award, Risk & Ins Asn. *Prof Exp:* Jr engr, Westinghouse Elec Corp, 52-53, asst engr, Anal Dept, 53-55, assoc engr, 55-56, engr, 56-57, supv engr, Systs Control Dept, 57-61; eng specialist, Advan Systs Lab, Sylvania Electronic Systs, Mass, 61-62, mgr, Digital Systs Dept & Minuteman Syst Task, 62-63, tech dir, Minuteman WS-133B Prog, 63, mem info processing staff, 63-64, sr eng specialist, 63-66, dir advan technol, 66-68; head, Spec Studies Subdept, Mitre Corp, Wash Oper, 68-69, dept head & assoc, 69-72, dep asst adminr radiation progs, US Environ Protection Agency, 72-80; prof decisions & risk anal, Ctr Technol Admin, Am Univ, Washington, DC, & dir, Inst Risk Anal, 80-87; pres, Rowe Res Eng Assocs, Inc, 84-96. *Concurrent Pos:* Head, Environ Systs Dept, Mitre Corp, 69-72; adj prof, Am Univ, 72-80. *Mem:* AAAS; Systs, Man & Cybernet Soc; Soc Risk Anal; sr mem Inst Elec & Electronics Engrs; Sigma Xi; Soc Sci Explor. *Res:* Risk analysis and management; environmental science and radiation protection; risk analysis philosophy and application; uncertainty and measurement theory and application. *Mailing Add:* 309 N Alfred St Alexandria VA 22314. *Fax:* 703-836-0619; *E-Mail:* rowew@erols.com

ROWELL, ALBERT JOHN, INVERTEBRATE PALEONTOLOGY, PALEOZOIC OF ANTARCTICA. *Current Pos:* prof, 67-95, EMER PROF GEOL, UNIV KANS, 95- *Personal Data:* b Ely, Eng, July 19, 29; m 54; c 4. *Educ:* Univ Leeds, BSc, 50, PhD(geol), 53. *Prof Exp:* From asst lectr to lectr geol, Univ Nottingham, 55-64, reader, 64-67. *Concurrent Pos:* Vis prof, Univ Kans, 64-65; Bye fel, Robinson Col, Cambridge, 90- *Mem:* Geol Soc Am; Am Paleont Soc; Geol Soc London; Brit Paleont Asn. *Res:* Application of numerical methods in paleontology; Cambrian stratigraphy and biogeography; Paleozoic inarticulate brachiopods. *Mailing Add:* Univ Kans Univ Kans Rm 120 Lindley Hall Lawrence KS 66045-0501. *E-Mail:* arowell@kuhub.cc.ukans.edu

ROWELL, CHARLES FREDERICK, PHYSICAL ORGANIC CHEMISTRY. *Current Pos:* From asst prof to assoc prof, US Naval Postgrad Sch, 62-79, assoc chmn dept, 81-84, dept chair, 82-86, chmn dept, 84-88, PROF CHEM & CONSULT FORENSIC, US NAVAL ACAD, 79- *Personal Data:* b Lowville, NY, May 29, 35; m 55, Jo A Cowling; c Mark E & Jan E. *Educ:* Syracuse Univ, BS, 56; Iowa State Univ, MS, 59; Ore State Univ, PhD(org chem), 64. *Concurrent Pos:* Vis scientist, Chicago Br, Off Naval Res, 74-75; vis prof, US Naval Acad, 75-76. *Mem:* AAAS; Am Chem Soc; Royal Soc Chem. *Res:* Photochemistry; cyclopropane reactions; water pollution; nitramine chemistry; liquid propellants; azulene derivatives. *Mailing Add:* Dept Chem US Naval Acad Annapolis MD 21402. *Fax:* 410-293-2218; *E-Mail:* rowell@nadn.navy.mil

ROWELL, CHESTER MORRISON, JR, TAXONOMY, BOTANY. *Current Pos:* RETIRED. *Personal Data:* b Burnet, Tex, Dec 2, 25. *Educ:* Univ Tex, BS, 47; Agr & Mech Col, Tex, MS, 49; Okla State Univ, PhD, 67. *Prof Exp:* Asst herbarium, Univ Mich, 53-54; asst prof biol, Agr & Mech Col, Tex, 49-57, assoc prof, Tex Tech Univ, 57-70; prof biol & head dept, Angelo State Univ, 70-79. *Concurrent Pos:* Lectr & consult, rare & endangered species of Tex. *Res:* Seedplants of Texas and Mexico. *Mailing Add:* PO Box 817 Marfa TX 79843. *Fax:* 915-729-3421

ROWELL, JOHN BARTLETT, CEREAL RUST PATHOLOGY. *Current Pos:* RETIRED. *Personal Data:* b Pawtucket, RI, Nov 26, 18; m 44; c 3. *Educ:* RI State Col, BS, 41; Univ Minn, PhD(plant path), 49. *Prof Exp:* Jr res asst plant path, Exp Sta, RI State Col, 40; asst, Univ Minn, St Paul, 41-42 & 46-47; asst, Exp Sta, RI State Col, 47-48, asst res prof, 48-49; res assoc, Univ Minn, St Paul, 49-55, assoc prof, 55-67; plant physiologist, Crops Res Div, USDA, 55-69, res plant pathologist & leader cereal rust lab, Sci & Educ Admin-Agr Res, 69-80; prof plant path, Univ Minn, St Paul, 67-81. *Concurrent Pos:* Consult, Ford Found, 71. *Mem:* Fel AAAS; fel Am Phytopath Soc; Bot Soc Am; Indian Phytopath Soc. *Res:* Control of cereal rusts. *Mailing Add:* 1963 Eustis St St Paul MN 55113-5108

ROWELL, JOHN MARTIN, SUPERCONDUCTIVITY, SUPERCONDUCTING ELECTRONICS. *Current Pos:* chief tech officer, 89-91, pres, 91-96, CHMN, SCI ADV BD, CONDUCTUS INC, 91- *Personal Data:* b Linslade, Eng, June 27, 35; m 59; c 3. *Educ:* Oxford Univ, Eng, BSc, 57, MA & DPhil(physics), 61. *Honors & Awards:* Fritz London Mem Low Temperature Physics Prize, 78. *Prof Exp:* Mem staff, Bell Labs, 61-69, dept head, 69-81, dir, 81-83; asst vpres, Bellcore, 83-89. *Concurrent Pos:* Vis prof, Stanford Univ, 75. *Mem:* Nat Acad Sci; Nat Acad Eng; fel Am Phys Soc; fel Royal Soc London. *Res:* Superconductivity and tunneling; tunneling spectroscopy. *Mailing Add:* Conductus Inc 969 W Maude Ave Sunnyvale CA 94086

ROWELL, LORING B, PHYSIOLOGY. *Current Pos:* from res instr to res asst prof med, 63-68, assoc prof physiol, biophys & med, 70-72, PROF PHYSIOL & BIOPHYS, SCH MED, UNIV WASH, 72- *Personal Data:* b Lynn, Mass, Jan 27, 30; m 56; c 2. *Educ:* Springfield Col, BS, 53; Univ Minn, PhD(physiol), 62. *Honors & Awards:* Joseph B Wolfe Mem Lectr, Am Col Sports Med, 80; Citation Award, Am Col Sports Med, 83; James M Schwinghammer Mem Lectr, Mich State Univ, 84. *Prof Exp:* NIH fel cardiovasc physiol & cardiol, 62-63. *Concurrent Pos:* Estab investr, Am Heart Asn, 66-71; vis prof, Univ Copenhagen, 78-79; vis prof, Ege Univ, 79; vis prof, Univ Antwerp, 79; Ida Bean vis prof, Univ Iowa, 80; assoc ed, J Appl Physiol; adj prof med, Univ Wash, 72- *Mem:* Am Physiol Soc; Sigma Xi; Am Heart Asn. *Res:* Human cardiovascular function; total and regional blood flow; temperature regulation; skeletal muscle and hepatic metabolism; hemodynamics-pressure regulation. *Mailing Add:* Dept Physiol & Biophys Univ Wash Sch Med Box 357290 Seattle WA 98195-7290. *Fax:* 206-685-0619

ROWELL, NEAL POPE, PHYSICS. *Current Pos:* dir Div Eng, 68-72, prof eng, 72-74, PROF PHYSICS, UNIV SALA, 74- *Personal Data:* b Mobile, Ala, Jan 11, 26; m 47; c 5. *Educ:* Univ Ala, BS, 49, MS, 50; Univ Fla, PhD(physics), 54. *Prof Exp:* Instr physics, Univ Ala, 50-51; physicist, Mine Countermeasures Sta, USN, 51-52; instr physics, Univ Fla, 53-54; physicist, Courtaulds, Inc, 54-68. *Mem:* Am Phys Soc; Am Asn Physics Teachers. *Res:* Physical properties of viscose rayon; electron diffraction study of alloys produced by simultaneous vacuum evaporation of aluminum and copper. *Mailing Add:* 354 McDonald Ave Mobile AL 36604

ROWELL, PETER PUTNAM, NEUROCHEMISTRY, TOXICOLOGY. *Current Pos:* from asst prof to assoc prof, 77-92, PROF PHARMACOL, UNIV LOUISVILLE, 92- *Personal Data:* b St Petersburg, Fla, July 24, 46; m 72, Kathryn Johnson; c Julie & David. *Educ:* Stetson Univ, BS, 68; Univ Fla, PhD(pharmacol), 75. *Prof Exp:* Res assoc pharmacol, Vanderbilt Univ, 75-77. *Mem:* Am Soc Pharmacol & Exp Therapeut; Soc Neurosci; Soc Exp Biol & Med; Int Asn Biomed Geront; Am Inst Biol Sci; AAAS. *Res:* Neuropharmacology of nicotine; modulation of neurotransmitter release in the brain; autonomic pharmacology. *Mailing Add:* Dept Pharmacol & Toxicol Univ Louisville Sch Med Louisville KY 40292-0001. *Fax:* 502-852-7868; *E-Mail:* pprowell@ulkyvm.louisville.edu

ROWELL, ROBERT LEE, PHYSICAL CHEMISTRY, COLLOID SCIENCE. *Current Pos:* From instr to assoc prof, 60-78, dir, Res Comput Ctr, 61-64, actg head, 83-86, PROF CHEM, UNIV MASS, AMHERST, 78- *Personal Data:* b Quincy, Mass, July 29, 32; m 56; c 4. *Educ:* Mass State Col Bridgewater, BS, 54; Boston Col, MS, 56; Ind Univ, PhD(phys chem), 60. *Concurrent Pos:* Int Bus Mach Corp fel, Comput Ctr, Mass Inst Technol, 63-64; res assoc, Clarkson Col, 66-70; vis prof, Univ Bristol, Eng, 73-74; Unilever vis prof, 80; assoc ed, Langmuir, 86- *Mem:* Am Chem Soc; Sigma Xi; AAAS; Golden Key Nat Hon Soc. *Res:* Laser light scattering by molecules, macromolecules and colloidal particles; characterization of particle shape and particle size distribution; stability, structure and rheology of coal slurry fuels. *Mailing Add:* Dept Chem GRC-TWR-102 Univ Mass Amherst MA 01003-4510

ROWEN, BURT, AEROSPACE MEDICINE. *Current Pos:* With Med Corps, USAF, 46, instr, USAF Sch Aviation Med, 49-51, asst air attache, Stockholm, Sweden, 52-55, med dir, X-15 Proj, USAF Flight Test Ctr, 56-62, med dir, Dynasoar Proj, Aeronaut Syst Div, 62-64, dep comdr, Aerospace Med Res Labs, 64-65, flight surgeon, Vietnam, 65-66, Hq, 12th Air Force, Waco, Tex, 66-68 & Hq, 17th Air Force, Ramstein, Ger, 68-69, dep surgeon, Hq, USAF Europ, Wiesbaden, Ger, 69-72, comdr, USAF Sch Health Care Sci, Sheppard AFB, 72-74, mem Phys Eval Bd, Air Force Military Manpower Personnel Ctr, Randolph AFB, 74-81, CHIEF MED STAND DIV, MANPOWER & PERSONNEL CTR, USAF, RANDOLPH AFB, 81- *Personal Data:* b New York, NY, Mar 30, 21; m 42; c 3. *Educ:* Lafayette Col, BA, 42; NY Univ, MD, 45; Am Bd Prev Med, dipl, 65. *Mem:* Fel Aerospace Med Asn; Am Col Prev Med; Int Acad Aerospace Med. *Res:* Development of life support systems, including air to ground telemetry of life support parameters and real time ground readout; health care training and management of health care resources; medical manpower and support of tactical air operations; adjudication of medical conditions in relation to the United States Air Force Disability System; medical standards management of United States Air Force active and reserve forces. *Mailing Add:* Med Stand Div USAF MPC/SGM Randolph AFB TX 78148

ROWLAND, ALEX THOMAS, STEROID CHEMISTRY. *Current Pos:* From asst prof to prof, 58-82, chmn dept, 68-82, OCKERSHAUSEN PROF CHEM, GETTYSBURG COL, 82- *Personal Data:* b Kingston, NY, Feb 25, 31; m 53; c 2. *Educ:* Gettysburg Col, AB, 53; Brown Univ, PhD(chem), 58. *Mem:* Am Chem Soc; AAAS. *Res:* Chemistry of highly substituted cyclohexanones. *Mailing Add:* Dept Chem Gettysburg Col Gettysburg PA 17325-1411

ROWLAND, DAVID LAWRENCE, PSYCHOENDOCRINOLOGY, ETHOLOGY. *Current Pos:* assoc prof, 81-89, chmn dept, 83-88, PROF PSYCHOL, VALPARAISO UNIV, 90- *Personal Data:* b Philadelphia, Pa, Sept 30, 50; m 91, Els Houtsmuller; c Clare. *Educ:* Southern Ill Univ, BA, 72; Univ Chicago, MA, 75, PhD(biopsychol), 77. *Prof Exp:* Asst prof psychol & dir, Psychol Animal Lab, Millikin Univ, 76-80; res fel, State Univ NY, Stony Brook, 80-81. *Concurrent Pos:* Proj dir, NSF grants, 79-81; res fel, Stanford Univ, 84-85; vis scientist, Erasmus Univ, Rotterdam. *Mem:* Soc Comp Psychol; Am Asn Univ Prof; Int Acad Sex Researchers. *Res:* Neural and hormonal basis of reproductive behavior; human sexual dysfunction. *Mailing Add:* Dept Psychol Valparaiso Univ Valparaiso IN 46383-6493. *E-Mail:* drowland@exodus.valpo.edu

ROWLAND, FRANK SHERWOOD, ATMOSPHERIC KINETICS. *Current Pos:* prof chem & dept chmn, Univ Calif, 64-70, Daniel G Aldrich Jr, chair prof, 85-89, Donald Bren prof, 89-94, PROF CHEM, UNIV CALIF, IRVINE, 64-, DONALD BREN RES PROF, 94- *Personal Data:* b Delaware, Ohio, June 28, 27; m 52, Joan Lundberg; c Ingrid D & Jeffrey S. *Educ:* Ohio Wesleyan Univ, BA, 48; Univ Chicago, MS, 51, PhD, 52. *Hon Degrees:* Var from US & Can univs, 89-96. *Honors & Awards:* Nobel Prize in Chem, 95; McGregor Lectr, Colgate Univ, 75; Philips Lectr, Haverford Col, 75; Tolman Medal, Am Chem Soc, 76, Environ Sci & Technol Award, 83; Peter Debye Award Phys Chem, 93; Gordon Billard Award Environ Sci, NY Acad Sci, 77; Snider Lectr, Univ Toronto, 80; Humboldt Sr Scientist Award, WGer, 81; Cert Commendation, US Fed Aviation Admin, 82; Tyler World Prize Environ, 83; Whitehead Lectr Chem, Univ Ga, 86; Charles A Dana Award Pioneering Achievement Health, 87; Gustavson Lectr Chem, Univ Chicago, 88; Rachel Carson Award, Soc Environ Toxicol & Chem, 88; King Lectr, Kans State Univ, 91; Robertson Mem lectr, Nat Acad Sci, 93; Roger Revelle Medal, Am Geophys Union, 94. *Prof Exp:* Instr chem, Princeton Univ, 52-56; from asst prof to assoc prof, Univ Kans, 56-63, prof chem, 63-64. *Concurrent Pos:* Mem, Comn Atmospheric Chem & Global Pollution, 79-91; mem, Ozone Comm, Int Asn Meteorol & Atmospheric Physics, 80-88; mem, Fachbeirat, Max Planck Inst Nuclear Phys & Chem, 82-; mem, Bd Environ Studies & Toxicol, US Acad Sci, 86-91; mem, US Nat Comt, Sci Comt Probs Environ, 86-89; mem, Ozone Trends Panel, NASA, 86-88; mem, Comt Atmospheric Chem, US Nat Acad Sci, 87-89, Film Comt, 88-92, Comt Opportunities Appl Environ Res & Develop, 88-91, chmn, Comt Int Orgns & Progs, 93-; Zucker fel, Yale Univ, 91; foreign secy, US Nat Acad Scis, 94- *Mem:* Nat Acad Sci; Inst Med-Nat Acad Sci; fel AAAS (pres-elect, 91, pres, 92); Nat Acad Sci; Am Chem Soc; fel Am Phys Soc; Am Philos Soc; foreign mem Korean Acad Sci & Technol; hon mem Am Meteorol Soc; fel Am Geophys Union; Am Acad Arts & Sci. *Res:* Co-discovered the theory that chlorofluorocarbon gases deplete the ozone layer of the stratosphere with Dr Mario J Molina; research in chemical kinetics; latitudinal variation of trace tropospheric gases; global studies of trace gas concentrations; oxidative capacity of the earth's atmosphere; author of more than 330 scientific publications. *Mailing Add:* Dept Chem Univ Calif Irvine CA 92697-2025

ROWLAND, IVAN W, pharmacy, microbiology; deceased, see previous edition for last biography

ROWLAND, JAMES RICHARD, ELECTRICAL ENGINEERING. *Current Pos:* chmn elec & comput eng, 85-89, PROF ELEC & COMPUT ENG, UNIV KANS, 85- *Personal Data:* b Muldrow, Okla, Jan 24, 40; m 95, Mary Van Dyke Anderson; c Jennifer (Maxwell) & Angela (McComas). *Educ:* Okla State Univ, BS, 62; Purdue Univ, Lafayette, MS, 64, PhD(elec eng), 66. *Honors & Awards:* Centennial Medal, Inst Elec & Electronics Engrs, 84, Educ Soc Achievement Award, 86, Frontiers Educ Conf Award, 88. *Prof Exp:* From asst prof to assoc prof, Ga Inst Technol, 66-71; from assoc prof to prof elec eng, Okla State Univ, 71-85. *Concurrent Pos:* Consult, Lockheed-Ga Co, 66-71, US Army Missile Command, Sandia Nat Lab, 79 & Puritan-Bennett, 92. *Mem:* Fel Inst Elec & Electronics Engrs; Am Soc Eng Educ; Nat Soc Prof Engrs. *Res:* Stochastic modeling; optimal estimation and control. *Mailing Add:* Elec Eng & Comput Sci Univ Kans 1013 Learned Hall Lawrence KS 66045. *Fax:* 785-864-4971; *E-Mail:* jrowland@eecs.ukans.edu

ROWLAND, JOHN H, MATHEMATICS, COMPUTER SCIENCE. *Current Pos:* assoc prof math & comput sci, 66-77, head dept comput sci, 73-79, PROF MATH & COMPUT SCI, UNIV WYO, 77- *Personal Data:* b Bellefonte, Pa, Feb 20, 34; m 56; c 4. *Educ:* Pa State Univ, BS, 56, PhD(math), 66; Univ Wash, MS, 58. *Prof Exp:* Instr math, Univ Nev, 58-61; staff mathematician, HRB Singer, Inc, 61-66. *Concurrent Pos:* NSF fac residency in comput sci, Santa Monica, Calif, 70-71; vis prof appl math, Brown Univ, 78-79; contractor, IBM Tech Educ, Austin, Tex, 85-86; vis prof info & comput sci, Ga Inst Technol, 86-87. *Mem:* Inst Elec & Electronics Engrs Comput Soc; Soc Indust & Appl Math; Asn Comput Mach. *Res:* Theory of program testing; numerical analysis; approximation theory. *Mailing Add:* Dept Comput Sci Univ Wyo Box 3682 Laramie WY 82071-3682

ROWLAND, LENTON O, JR, POULTRY NUTRITION. *Current Pos:* ASST PROF POULTRY NUTRIT, TEX A&M UNIV, 75- *Personal Data:* b Mobile, Ala, Sept 29, 43. *Educ:* Univ Fla, BSA, 65, MS, 67, PhD(animal nutrit), 72. *Prof Exp:* Poultry serviceman layers & pullets, Cent Soya Inc, 65-66; staff mem res & develop animal nutrit, Dow Chem Co, USA, 72-73; mem tech serv, Dow Chem Co, Latin Am, 73-74. *Mem:* Poultry Sci Asn; Am Soc Animal Sci; World Poultry Sci Asn. *Res:* Basic hen and broiler nutrition with particular emphasis on new feed ingredients, energy and amino acid requirements of poultry. *Mailing Add:* 15137 Post Oak Bend Dr College Station TX 77845

ROWLAND, LEWIS PHILLIP, NEUROLOGY. *Current Pos:* PROF NEUROL & CHMN DEPT, COL PHYSICIANS & SURGEONS, COLUMBIA UNIV, 73-, DIR NEUROL SERV, PRESBY HOSP, 73- *Personal Data:* b Brooklyn, NY, Aug 3, 25; m 52; c 3. *Educ:* Yale Univ, BS, 45, MD, 48. *Hon Degrees:* Dr, Univ Aix-marseilles, 86. *Honors & Awards:* Numerous Lect Awards, US & Can Insts. *Prof Exp:* Res asst neuroanat, Columbia Univ, 48; asst med, Yale Univ, 49-50; asst resident, Columbia Univ, 50-52, asst neurol, Col Physicians & Surgeons, 53; clin instr, Georgetown Univ, 53-54; instr, Col Physicians & Surgeons, Columbia Univ, 54-56, assoc, 56-57, from asst prof to prof, 56-67; prof neurol & chmn dept, Univ Pa, 67-73. *Concurrent Pos:* Clin investr, Nat Inst Neurol Dis & Blindness, 53-54; asst neurologist, Montefiore Hosp, New York, 54-57; neurologist, Presby Hosp, 54-67; vis fel, Med Res Coun Labs, London, Eng, 56; co-dir, Neurol Clin Res Ctr, Columbia Univ, 61-67; mem med adv bd, Myasthenia Gravis Found, 63-, pres, 71-73; sci adv bd, Muscular Dystrophy Asns Am, 69-86 & med adv bd, 86-; med adv bd, Multiple Sclerosis Soc, 69-89, hon bd, 89-, Res Progs Adv Comt, 80-82 & 84-88; mem neurol res training comt B, Nat Inst Neurol Dis & Stroke, 71-73, Nat Adv Coun, 85-89, bd sci counc, Nat Inst Neurol Commun Dis Stroke, 78-82, chmn, 81-82; ed-in-chief, Neurol, 77-87; attend/consult, Harlem Hosp, 73-; co-dir, H Houston Merritt Clin Res Ctr Muscular Dystrophy & Related Dis, Columbia-Presby Med Ctr, 74-; secy-treas, Asn Univ Profs Neurol, 69-73, trustee, 73-77 & pres, 77-78; med adv bd, Comt Combat Huntington's Dis, 74-84; consult, Josiah Macy, Jr Found, 80-82 & Klingenstein Found, 81; Steven W Swank vis prof, Univ Oregon, 77, Robert B Aird vis prof neurol, Univ Calif, San Francisco, 79. *Mem:* AAAS; Asn Res Nerv & Ment Dis (pres, 69-70, vpres, 79-80); hon mem Am Neurol Asn (pres elect, 79, pres, 80-81); fel Am Acad Neurol (pres elect, 87-89, pres, 89-90); Soc Neurosci; Am Soc Human Genetics; Sigma Xi; Muscular Dystrophy Asn; Nat Multiple Sclerosis Soc; AMA. *Res:* Neuromuscular disease. *Mailing Add:* Neurol Inst 710 W 168th St New York NY 10032-2603

ROWLAND, NEIL EDWARD, FEEDING BEHAVIOR, THIRST & SODIUM APPETITE. *Current Pos:* assoc prof, 81-86, PROF PSYCHOL, UNIV FLA, 86- *Personal Data:* b London, UK, Feb 20, 47; m 79; c 3. *Educ:* Univ Col London, BSc, 68, MSc, 72; Sussex Univ, MSc, 71; London Univ, PhD(exp psychol), 74. *Prof Exp:* Res assoc, psychobiol, Univ Pittsburgh, 74-81. *Mem:* Am Physiol Soc; Am Inst Nutrit; Am Psychol Asn; Am Diabetes Asn; Soc Neurosci; Soc Study Ingestive Behav. *Res:* Physiological and neural basis of food and fluid intake and selection in rodents. *Mailing Add:* Dept Psychol Univ Fla Gainesville FL 32611-2065. *Fax:* 904-392-7985

ROWLAND, NEIL WILSON, PLANT PHYSIOLOGY, ECOLOGY. *Current Pos:* head dept, Union Col, Nebr, 52-67, acad dean, 67-76, prof biol, 52-77, EMER PROF BIOL, UNION COL, NEBR, 83- *Personal Data:* b Singapore, July 5, 19; US citizen; m 43, Marie Sanders; c Janice, Dale & Bonnie. *Educ:* Union Col, Nebr, BA, 47; Univ Nebr, MA, 52, PhD, 61. *Concurrent Pos:* Dean, Sch Sci & Technol, Mountainview Col, Philippines, 77-83. *Mem:* Sigma Xi. *Res:* Plant physiology; plant transpiration as affected by certain growth substances; ecology: prairie succession as unfluenced depth of natural mulch thickness. *Mailing Add:* 5300 Locust St Lincoln NE 68516

ROWLAND, RICHARD LLOYD, PHYSICAL CHEMISTRY. *Current Pos:* mem fac chem, 72-93, EMER PROF CHEM, COSUMNES RIVER COL, 93- *Personal Data:* b Delaware, Ohio, May 31, 29; m 64. *Educ:* Ohio Wesleyan Univ, BA, 51; Univ Chicago, PhD(chem), 60. *Prof Exp:* Res chemist, Stand Oil Co, Ohio, 61-62, sr res chemist, 62-64; asst prof, Robert Col, Istanbul, 64-67, assoc prof, 67-71; assoc prof, Univ Calif, Irvine, 71-72. *Mem:* Am Chem Soc. *Res:* Solid state diffusion; electrochemistry. *Mailing Add:* 8756 Leo Virgo Ct Elk Grove CA 95624-1796

ROWLAND, ROBERT EDMUND, RADIATION BIOPHYSICS. *Current Pos:* RETIRED. *Personal Data:* b St Charles, Ill, Jan 10, 23; m 44; c 3. *Educ:* Cornell Col, BS, 47; Univ Ill, MS, 49; Univ Rochester, PhD, 64; Univ Chicago, MBA, 75. *Prof Exp:* Assoc physicist, Argonne Nat Lab, 50-62; sr tech assoc, Univ Rochester, 62-64; assoc dir, Radiol Physics Div, Argonne Nat Lab, 64-67, sr biophysicist, 66-83, dir, Radiol & Environ Res Div, 67-81, interim assoc lab dir, biomed & environ res, 81-83. *Concurrent Pos:* Mem, Nat Coun Radiation Protection & Measurements, 71-83. *Mem:* Radiation Res Soc; Health Physics Soc. *Res:* Radiation biology; epidemiology and toxicology of internally deposited radium; significance and biological effects of naturally occurring radioactive elements. *Mailing Add:* 700 W Fabyan-8C Batavia IL 60510. *E-Mail:* rowland@inil.com

ROWLAND, SATTLEY CLARK, MATERIALS SCIENCE, PHYSICS. *Current Pos:* Assoc prof, 66-74, PROF PHYSICS, ANDREWS UNIV, 74- *Personal Data:* b San Jose, Calif, May 15, 38; m 61; c 2. *Educ:* Pac Union Col, BA, 60; Univ Utah, PhD(mat sci), 66. *Concurrent Pos:* NSF grant, Andrews Univ, 69-72; vis prof mat sci, Stanford Univ, 80 & 82; vis scientist, Argonne Nat Lab, 89- *Mem:* AAAS; Am Asn Physics Teachers; Am Phys Soc. *Res:* X-ray diffraction studies of the structure of amorphous and crystalline semiconductors; lattice parameter measurements; high pressure studies of fatigue in metals. *Mailing Add:* 8486 S Hillcrest Dr Berrien Springs MI 49103-9586

ROWLAND, STANLEY PAUL, CELLULOSE STRUCTURE & CHEMISTRY, POLYMER. *Current Pos:* RETIRED. *Personal Data:* b LaCrosse, Wis, Feb 25, 16; m 43; c 4. *Educ:* Univ Minn, BChem, 38; Univ Ill, PhD(org chem), 43. *Honors & Awards:* Anselme Payen Award, Cellulose Div, Am Chem Soc, 81; Olney Medal, Am Asn Textile Chemists & Colorists, 85. *Prof Exp:* Res chemist, Rohm and Haas Co, 43-56; res supvr, US Indust Chem Co, 56-59, asst mgr org chem, 59-61, mgr explor polymer res, 61-63; res leader crosslink struct, Southern Regional Res Ctr, 63-74, res leader nat polymer struct res, 74-84. *Concurrent Pos:* Instr, Tulane Univ, 65-68. *Mem:* Am Chem Soc; Fiber Soc. *Res:* Chemical modification of cellulose; structural characterization of chemically modified and crosslinked celluloses; chemical reactivity of cellulose and synthetic polymers; synthesis of intermediates, resins and polymers; plasticizers; plastics; fabrication; characterization and testing of polymers and plastics; dehydration of hydrobenzoins. *Mailing Add:* 16343 Old Hwy 99 SE Tenino WA 98589-9718

ROWLAND, THEODORE JUSTIN, ELECTRONIC STRUCTURE. *Current Pos:* RETIRED. *Personal Data:* b Cleveland, Ohio, May 15, 27; m 52, 68, Patsy Beard; c Theodore J Jr, Dawson A & Claire M. *Educ:* Western Reserve Univ, BS, 48; Harvard Univ, MA, 49, PhD(appl physics), 54. *Prof Exp:* Res physicist, Res Labs, Union Carbide Metals Co Div, Union Carbide Corp, 54-61; prof phys metall, Univ Ill, Urbana, 61-92. *Concurrent Pos:* Fac res participant, Bell Labs, Murray Hill, NJ, 73, Argonne Nat Lab, 78-84, Ames Lab, Iowa State Univ, 81-82. *Mem:* Fel Am Phys Soc; Sigma Xi; Minerals, Metals & Mat Sci; AAAS; Am Asn Univ Prof. *Res:* Radiospectroscopy; nuclear magnetic resonance in metals; physics of metals, especially solid solutions; nuclear relaxation in polymers. *Mailing Add:* Dept Mat Sci & Eng Univ Ill 1304 W Green St Urbana IL 61801. *Fax:* 217-333-2736

ROWLAND, VERNON, PSYCHIATRY. *Current Pos:* assoc prof, 60-71, PROF PSYCHIAT, MED SCH, CASE WESTERN UNIV, 71- *Personal Data:* b Clevelend Heights, Ohio, Aug 11, 22; m 49; c 2. *Educ:* Harvard Med Sch, MD, 46; Am Bd Psychiat & Neurol, dipl. *Prof Exp:* From intern to asst resident med, Univ Hosps, Cleveland, Ohio, 46-48, resident neuropsychiat, 52-53; resident, Cleveland Vet Admin Hosp, 50-52. *Concurrent Pos:* NIMH & univ res fels psychiat, Western Reserve Univ, 53-55; NIMH career develop award, 55-60; assoc physician, Univ Hosps, 54- *Mem:* AAAS; Pavlovian Soc NAm; Am Psychiat Asn; Sigma Xi. *Res:* Conditioned electrographic response in the brain. *Mailing Add:* 2432 Kenilworth Rd No 5 Cleveland OH 44106

ROWLAND, WALTER FRANCIS, civil engineering, water resources, for more information see previous edition

ROWLAND, WILLIAM JOSEPH, ETHOLOGY, BEHAVIORAL ECOLOGY. *Current Pos:* asst prof, 71-77, ASSOC PROF ZOOL, IND UNIV, BLOOMINGTON, 77- *Personal Data:* b Brooklyn, NY, Dec 15, 43; m 71; c 2. *Educ:* Adelphi Univ, BA, 65; State Univ NY Stony Brook, PhD(biol), 70. *Prof Exp:* Sci co-worker ethol, Zool Lab, Rijksuniversiteit te Groningen, Haren, Neth, 70-71. *Concurrent Pos:* Guest co-worker ethol, Zool Lab, Univ Leiden, Neth, 84. *Mem:* Sigma Xi; Animal Behav Soc; AAAS; Int Asn Fish Ethologists. *Res:* Causation, evolution and function of behavior in fishes and other lower vertebrates; social behavior and behavioral ecology of fishes. *Mailing Add:* Dept Biol Ind Univ Bloomington IN 47405

ROWLANDS, DAVID T, JR, PATHOLOGY, IMMUNOLOGY. *Current Pos:* STAFF MEM, DEPT PATH, COL MED, UNIV SFLA, 79- *Personal Data:* b Wilkes-Barre, Pa, Mar 22, 30; m 58; c 2. *Educ:* Univ Pa, MD, 55. *Prof Exp:* Asst prof path, Univ Colo, 62-64; asst prof biochem, Rockefeller Univ, 64-66; assoc prof path, Duke Univ, 66-70; prof path, Sch Med, Univ Pa, 70-78, chmn dept, 73-78. *Mem:* Am Asn Path & Bact; Fedn Am Socs Exp Biol; Int Acad Path; Am Soc Clin Path. *Res:* Developmental immunology; transplantation immunity. *Mailing Add:* 13804 Cypress Village Circle Tampa FL 33624-4406. *Fax:* 813-888-9419

ROWLANDS, JOHN ALAN, SOLID STATE PHYSICS, MEDICAL PHYSICS. *Current Pos:* ASSOC PROF, DEPT RADIOL & MED BIOPHYS, UNIV TORONTO, 79- *Personal Data:* b Altrincham, Eng, May 4, 45; m 72, Cheryl A Goodfellow; c Brock & Allison. *Educ:* Leeds Univ, BSc, 66, PhD(physics), 71. *Prof Exp:* Killam fel physics, Univ Alta, 71-73, res assoc physics, 71-77; vis asst prof, Dept Physics, Mich State Univ, 77-79. *Mem:* Can Asn Physicists; Am Asn Physicists Med; Soc Electro Optical Eng. *Res:* Physics of diagnostic radiology. *Mailing Add:* Med Physics Reichmann Res Bldg Sunnybrook Health Sci Ctr 2075 Bayview Ave Toronto ON M4N 3M5 Can. *Fax:* 416-480-5714

ROWLANDS, R(ICHARD) O(WEN), MATHEMATICS, ELECTRICAL ENGINEERING. *Current Pos:* assoc prof elec eng, 57-58, assoc prof eng res, 58-64, chmn dept eng acoust, 67-70, prof eng res, 64-79, EMER PROF ENG RES, PA STATE UNIV, 79- *Personal Data:* b Llangefni, Wales, Apr 26, 14; nat US; m 39; c 2. *Educ:* Univ Wales, BS, 36, MS, 50. *Prof Exp:* Head filter design group, Gen Elec Co, Eng, 37-48; sr lectr studio sect, Eng Training Dept, Brit Broadcasting Co, 48-57. *Concurrent Pos:* Liaison scientist, US Off Naval Res, Eng, 70-71. *Mem:* Acoust Soc Am; Inst Elec & Electronics Engrs; Brit Inst Elec Engrs; Sigma Xi. *Res:* Circuit theory; communications; information theory as applied to signal detection; electroacoustics; acoustic telemetry. *Mailing Add:* Appl Res Lab Pa State Univ PO Box 30 State College PA 16804

ROWLANDS, ROBERT EDWARD, STRESS ANALYSIS, FAILURE-STRENGTH. *Current Pos:* from asst prof to assoc prof, 74-80, PROF MECH, UNIV WIS-MADISON, 74- *Personal Data:* b Trail, BC, July 7, 36; m 59; c 2. *Educ:* Univ BC, BASc, 59; Univ Ill, Urbana, MS, 64, PhD(mech), 67. *Honors & Awards:* Hetenyi Award, Soc Exp Stress Anal, 70 & 76, Frocht Award, 88. *Prof Exp:* From res engr to sr res engr, IIT Res Inst, 67-74. *Concurrent Pos:* Consult various orgns, 67- *Mem:* Am Soc Testing & Mat; Am Acad Mech; Am Soc Mech Engrs; fel Soc Exp Stress Anal. *Res:* Experimental stress analysis; photomechanics; fatigue; fracture; composite and advanced materials; numerical processing of experimental data; energy storage; materials at cryogenic environments; wood and paper engineering. *Mailing Add:* Dept Eng Mech Univ Wis-Madison Madison WI 53706

ROWLANDS, STANLEY, MEDICAL BIOPHYSICS, NUCLEAR MEDICINE. *Current Pos:* RETIRED. *Personal Data:* b Liverpool, Eng, July 30, 18; m 42; c 2. *Educ:* Univ Liverpool, BSc, 39, PhD(physics), 42; Univ London, LRCP & MRCS, 56. *Prof Exp:* Lectr physics, Univ Liverpool, 42-44; sr lectr, Univ London, 45-48; lectr med physics, Univ Edinburgh, 48-52; reader physics, Univ London, 52-67; prof med biophys & head dept, Univ Calgary, 67-84, hon prof physics, 77-84. *Concurrent Pos:* Consult physician, St Mary's Hosp, 60-67. *Mem:* Biophys Soc; Soc Nuclear Med; Brit Physiol Soc; Microcirc Soc. *Res:* Cardiovascular biophysics; microcirculation, particularly the mechanical and rheological properties of human erythrocytes. *Mailing Add:* 326 Niagara St Victoria BC V8V 1G6 Can

ROWLETT, ROGER SCOTT, ENZYME KINETICS, PROTEIN CHEMISTRY. *Current Pos:* asst prof, 82-88, ASSOC PROF CHEM, COLGATE UNIV, 88-, CHAIR CHEM, 91- *Personal Data:* b Chickasha, Okla, Jan 1, 55; m 88, Mary J Walsh. *Educ:* Univ Ala, BS, 76, PhD(chem), 81. *Prof Exp:* Fel biochem, Col Med, Univ Fla, 81-82. *Mem:* Am Chem Soc; NY Acad Sci. *Res:* Mechanistic studies of carbonic anhydrase; molecular modeling. *Mailing Add:* Dept Chem Colgate Univ 13 Oak Dr Hamilton NY 13346-1399. *Fax:* 315-824-7831; *E-Mail:* rrowlett@center.colgate.edu

ROWLETT, RUSSELL JOHNSTON, JR, SYNTHETIC ORGANIC CHEMISTRY & ANTI MALARIAL DRUGS, ORGANIC PHOSPHATES & PESICIDES. *Current Pos:* RETIRED. *Personal Data:* b Richmond, Va, Sept 19, 20; m 43, Lillian F German; c Russell J III & William H. *Educ:* Univ Va, BS, 41, MS, 43, PhD(org chem), 45. *Honors & Awards:* Presidential Res Citation, 45; Miles Conrad Award, Nat Fedn Abstracting & Indexing Serv, 80; Herman Skolnik Award, Am Chem Soc, 83 & Distinguished Serv Award, 90. *Prof Exp:* Asst chem, Univ Va, 40-42, assoc, 42-46; chemist, E I du Pont de Nemours & Co, Del, 46; asst ed, Chem Abstr, Ohio State Univ, 47-48, assoc ed, 49-52; patent coordr, Va-Carolina Chem Corp, 52-55, asst dir res, 55-57, asst dir res & develop, 57-60, dir, 60; asst dir, Va Inst Sci Res, 60-67; ed & dir, Chem Absr Serv, 67-79, dir publ & serv, 79-82. *Concurrent Pos:* Mem comt chem info, Nat Res Coun, 68-73; chmn, Gordon Conf Sci Info Prob Res, 74. *Mem:* Fel AAAS; Am Chem Soc; Sigma Xi; hon fel Nat Fedn Abstr & Indexing Serv (secy, 74-76, pres 77-78). *Res:* Synthetic organic chemistry; antimalarial drugs; organic chemical nomenclature; patents; chemistry of phosphorus compounds; scientific information storage and retrieval. *Mailing Add:* Covenant Towers 5001 Little River Rd 502W Myrtle Beach SC 29577-2499

ROWLETT, RUSSELL JOHNSTON, III, TOPOLOGY. *Current Pos:* asst prof, 74-78, ASSOC PROF MATH, UNIV TENN, 78-, DIR, LIBERAL ARTS COOP PROG, 79- *Personal Data:* b Charlottesville, Va, June 26, 45; m 67; c 1. *Educ:* Univ Va, BA, 67, PhD(math), 70. *Prof Exp:* Instr math, Princeton Univ, 70-74. *Mem:* Am Math Soc; Math Asn Am; Am Soc Eng Educ. *Res:* Classification of smooth actions of compact lie groups on compact manifolds; related questions in the theory of compact transformation groups. *Mailing Add:* Ctr Math & Sci Educ Univ NC CB No 3500 Peabody Hall Chapel Hill NC 27599-3500

ROWLEY, DAVID ALTON, PHYSICAL INORGANIC CHEMISTRY. *Current Pos:* From asst prof to assoc prof, 68-81, PROF CHEM, GEORGE WASHINGTON UNIV, 81-, ASST DEAN, GRAD SCH ARTS & SCI, 74- *Personal Data:* b Rochester, NY, July 21, 40; m 62; c 2. *Educ:* State Univ NY Albany, BS, 63, MS, 64; Univ Ill, Urbana, PhD(inorg chem), 68. *Mem:* Am Chem Soc. *Res:* Inorganic electronic absorption spectroscopy; reaction mechanism and reactions of coordinated ligands. *Mailing Add:* Dept Chem George Washington Univ Washington DC 20006

ROWLEY, DONALD ADAMS, EXPERIMENTAL PATHOLOGY, IMMUNOLOGY. *Current Pos:* from instr to asst prof, 54-69, PROF PATH & PEDIAT, UNIV CHICAGO, 69-, DIR, LA RABIDA CHILDREN'S HOSP & RES CTR, LA RABIDA-UNIV CHICAGO INST, 77- *Personal Data:* b Owatonna, Minn, Feb 4, 23; m 48; c 4. *Educ:* Univ Chicago, BS, 45, MS, MD, 50. *Prof Exp:* Sr asst surgeon, Nat Inst Allergy & Infectious Dis, 51-54. *Concurrent Pos:* USPHS sr res fel, 59-69; vis scientist, Sir William Dunn Sch Path, Oxford Univ, 61-62 & 70-71; dir res, La Rabida Children's Hosp & Res Ctr, La Rabida-Univ Chicago Inst, 74-77. *Mem:* Am Soc Exp Path; Am Asn Path & Bact; Am Asn Immunol. *Res:* Immunologic networks and regulation of the immune responses, specific enhancement and suppression by antigen and antibody. *Mailing Add:* Dept Path MC 1089 Univ Chicago 5841 S Maryland Ave Chicago IL 60637

ROWLEY, DURWOOD B, FOOD MICROBIOLOGY. *Current Pos:* RETIRED. *Personal Data:* b Walton, NY, Aug 11, 29; m 50, Shirley Murray; c Stephen, Carol & Gary. *Educ:* Hartwick Col, BS, 51; Syracuse Univ, MS, 53, PhD(microbiol), 62. *Prof Exp:* Asst prof biol, Hartwick Col, 56-59; asst microbiol, Syracuse Univ, 59-62; asst prof, Univ Mass, 62-63; res microbiologist, US Army Natick Labs, 63-70, chief microbiol div, Food Lab, 70-74, head food microbiol group, 74-82, chief biol sci div, Sci & Advan Technol Lab, US Army Natick Res & Develop Ctr, 82-90, chief biotechnology div, 90-92. *Concurrent Pos:* Mem comt nitrate & alternative curing agents in food, Nat Acad Sci; mem, Comn Microbiol Criteria for Foods, Food & Drug Admin, USDA, Nat Marine Fisheries Serv & US Army Natlick Res & Develop Ctr. *Mem:* Sigma Xi; fel Am Soc Microbiol; Inst Food Technol. *Res:* Bacterial spores; radiation microbiology; microbiological safety of mass feeding systems; rapid recovery and estimation of injured and uninjured food-borne bacteria; thermal resistance of food-borne pathogenic and spoilage microorganisms. *Mailing Add:* 144 Spring St Millis MA 02054

ROWLEY, GEORGE RICHARD, BIOCHEMISTRY, PHYSIOLOGY. *Current Pos:* asst prof, 64-68, ASSOC PROF BIOCHEM & ACTG CHMN DEPT, SCH DENT, FAIRLEIGH DICKINSON UNIV, 68- *Personal Data:* b Rahway, NJ, Aug 21, 23. *Educ:* Upsala Col, AB, 49; Rutgers Univ, PhD(biochem), 55. *Prof Exp:* Chem qual control chemist, E R Squibb & Sons, 49-51; USPHS grant psychiat, Coatesville Vet Admin Hosp & Med Sch, Univ Pa, 55-56; assoc res specialist agr chem, Rutgers Univ, 56-57; instr physiol, Col Physicians & Surgeons, Columbia Univ, 57-60; sr res chemist, Colgate-Palmolive Res Lab, 60-64. *Mem:* AAAS; Int Asn Dent Res; Am Chem Soc; NY Acad Sci. *Res:* Blood coagulation and platelet aggregation during hyperlipemia and effects of lipolytic activity; metabolism of vitamin E and vitamin C. *Mailing Add:* 14 Thrumont Rd West Caldwell NJ 07006-7720

ROWLEY, JANET D, CYTOGENETICS. *Current Pos:* res assoc, Argonne Cancer Res Hosp, Univ Chicago, 62-69, assoc prof, 69-77, prof med, Sch Med, Franklin McLean Mem Res Inst, 77-84, BLUM-RIESE DISTINGUISHED SERV PROF, DEPT MED & DEPT MOLECULAR GENETICS & CELL BIOL, UNIV CHICAGO, 84- *Personal Data:* b New York, NY, Apr 5, 25; m 48, Donald A; c Donald (deceased), David, Robert & Roger. *Educ:* Univ Chicago, BS, 46, MD, 48; Am Bd Med Genetics, cert. *Hon Degrees:* DSc, Univ Ariz, 89, Univ Pa, 89, Knox Col, 91, Univ Southern Calif, 92, St Louis Univ, 97. *Honors & Awards:* Kuwait Cancer Prize, 84; A Cressy Morrison Award, NY Acad Sci, 85; Woodward Award, Mem Sloan-Kettering Cancer Ctr, 86; Antoinne Lacassagne Prize, Nat League Against Cancer, 87; Karnofsky Prize, Am Soc Clin Oncol, 87; Co-recipient King Fasial Int Prize in Med, 88; GHA Clowes Award, Am Asn Cancer Res, 89; Wm Proctor Prize, Sigma Xi, 89; Mary Harris Thompson Prize, 90; de Villiers Award, Leukemia Soc Am, 93; Bernard Cohen Mem Lectr, Univ Pa, 93; Katherine D McCormick distinguished lectr, Stanford Univ, 94; Donald D Van Slyke lectr, Brookhaven Nat Lab, 94; Henry Kaprowski lectr, Thomas Jefferson Univ, 94; W Jack Stuckey Jr lectr, Twane Cancer Ctr, 96; Medal of Honor in Basic Sci, Am Cancer Soc, 96. *Prof Exp:* Intern, Marine Hosp, USPHS, 50-51; attend physician, Infant Welfare & Prenatal Clin Dept Pub Health, Montogomery Co, Md, 53-54; res fel, Cook Co Hosp, 55-61; clin instr neurol, Med Sch, Univ Ill, 57-61; spec trainee, Radiobiol Lab, Churchill Hosp, Oxford, Eng, 61-62. *Concurrent Pos:* Julian D Levinson Res Found fel, 55-58; USPHS spec trainee, 61-62; vis scientist, Genetics Lab, Oxford Univ, 70-71; mem, Bd Dirs, Am Soc Human Genetics, 79-84; mem MIT Corp vis comt, Dept Appl Biol Sci, Frederick Cancer Res Fac, 83-86; mem bd, Med Genetics, Am Soc Human Genetics; coun mem, Inst Med, 88. *Mem:* Nat Acad Sci; Inst Med Nat Acad Sci; Am Soc Hemat; Am Soc Human Genetics (pres-elect, 92, pres, 93); Am Asn Cancer Res; Am Acad Arts & Sci; Am Philos Soc; Sigma Xi. *Res:* Human chromosomes; chromosome abnormalities in pre-leukemia as well as in leukemia and lymphoma; quinacrine and Giemsa stains to identify chromosomes in malignant cells; molecular genetic analysis of chromosome translocations and deletions; author of numerous publications. *Mailing Add:* Sect Hemat-Oncol Dept Med Univ Chicago 5841 S Maryland MC2115 Chicago IL 60637

ROWLEY, PETER DEWITT, VOLCANOLOGY, FIELD GEOLOGY. *Current Pos:* GEOLOGIST, US GEOL SURV, 70- *Personal Data:* b Providence, RI, Dec 6, 42; c Scott E & Jill E. *Educ:* Carleton Col, BA, 64; Univ Tex, Austin, PhD(geol), 68. *Honors & Awards:* Antarctic Serv Medal, US Govt, 72; Geog feature named in honor, Rowley Massif, 75; Meritorious Serv Award, Dept Interior, 86; Dibblee Medal, 95. *Prof Exp:* Temp instr geol, Kent State Univ, 68-69; asst prof, Carleton Col, 69-70. *Concurrent Pos:* Leader, NSF-USGS geol expeds, Antarctica, 70-87; spokesman, Mt St Helens Eruptions, US Geol Surv, 80-81; co-chief, Las Vegas Urban Corridor/Nev Test Site Proj. *Mem:* Soc Econ Geologists; fel Geol Soc Am; Am Geophys Union; Am Geol Inst; Rocky Mountain Asn Geologists. *Res:* Geology of Antarctic Peninsula, Antarctica; Antarctic mineral deposits; geology of Iron Springs mining district, Utah; author or co-author of more than 150 published reports and 30 abstracts; geology of eastern Uinta Mountains, Utah-Colorado; geology of Marysvale volcanic field, Utah; geology of Mount St Helen's volcano; geology of Caliente caldera complex, Nevada; environmental and general geology of Las Vegas urban corridor and Nevada test site; tectonics, mineral resources, ground water of Nevada. *Mailing Add:* US Geol Surv Mail Stop 913 Box 25046 Fed Ctr Denver CO 80225-0046. *Fax:* 303-236-0214; *E-Mail:* prowley@ardneh.cr.usgs.gov

ROWLEY, PETER TEMPLETON, HUMAN GENETICS, INTERNAL MEDICINE. *Current Pos:* from asst prof to assoc prof, 63-75, PROF MED, PEDIAT, GENETICS & MICROBIOL, CHMN, DIV GENETICS, SCH MED, UNIV ROCHESTER, 75-, PROF, ONCOL, 91- *Personal Data:* b Greenville, Pa, Apr 29, 29; m 67, Carol Stone; c 2. *Educ:* Harvard Col, AB, 51; Columbia Univ, MD, 55. *Prof Exp:* Intern med, NY Hosp-Cornell Med Ctr, 55-56; resident, Boston City Hosp, 58-60; asst prof med, Stanford Univ, 63-70. *Concurrent Pos:* Hon res asst, Univ Col, Univ London, 60-61; physician & pediatrician, Strong Mem Hosp, 70- *Mem:* Am Soc Human Genetics; Am Fedn Clin Res; Am Col Physicians; Am Soc Hemat. *Res:* Genetics of human cancer; hemoglobinopathies; hematopoietic differentiation; evaluation of genetic screening counseling. *Mailing Add:* Div Genetics Univ Rochester Sch Med Box 641-601 Elmwood Ave Rochester NY 14642

ROWLEY, RICHARD L, THERMODYNAMICS, TRANSPORT PHENOMENA. *Current Pos:* ASST PROF CHEM ENG, RICE UNIV, 78- *Personal Data:* b Salt Lake City, UT, Sept 1, 51; m 72; c 6. *Educ:* Brigham Young Univ, BS, 74; Mich State Univ, PhD(phys chem), 78. *Prof Exp:* Res asst thermodynamics, Ctr Thermochem Studies, 74. *Concurrent Pos:* Consult, Eng Dept, Texaco, Inc, 81. *Mem:* Am Chem Soc; Am Inst Chem Engrs; AAAS; Sigma Xi. *Res:* Measurement and prediction of thermophysical properties, particularly transport coefficients, in liquid mixtures; formulation of liquid mixture models and theories as related to thermodynamic properties. *Mailing Add:* 350 CB Brigham Young Univ Provo UT 84602-1021

ROWLEY, RODNEY RAY, AUDIOLOGY, PSYCHOACOUSTICS. *Current Pos:* DIR AUDIOL, MED CTR, LOMA LINDA UNIV, 73- *Personal Data:* b Cedar City, Utah, Mar 25, 34; m 61; c 4. *Educ:* Brigham Young Univ, BS, 59; Univ Md, MA, 61; Univ Okla, PhD, 66. *Prof Exp:* Assoc prof speech, Univ Utah, 63-73. *Concurrent Pos:* Res audiologist, Vet Admin Hosp, Oklahoma City, 65-66; consult, Utah State Training Sch, 68-73, Mt Fuel Supply, 71-73 & Patton State Hosp, 74- *Mem:* Am Speech & Hearing Asn. *Res:* Loudness; noise and man; behavior modification and hearing loss. *Mailing Add:* 409 Arrowview Dr Redlands CA 92373

ROWLEY, WAYNE A, ENTOMOLOGY. *Current Pos:* asst prof, 67-71, assoc prof, 71-75, PROF ENTOM, IOWA STATE UNIV, 75- *Personal Data:* b Spring Glen, Utah, Aug 27, 33; m 57; c 3. *Educ:* Utah State Univ, BS, 60, MS, 62; Wash State Univ, PhD(med entom), 65. *Prof Exp:* Res entomologist, US Army Biol Labs, Ft Detrick, Md, 65-67. *Mem:* Sigma Xi; Entom Soc Am; Am Mosquito Control Asn; Am Soc Trop Med Hyg; Soc Vector Ecol. *Res:* Insect transmission of vertebrate pathogens; mosquito biology and flight; biology and taxonomy of bloodsucking midges. *Mailing Add:* Dept Entom Iowa State Univ Ames IA 50011. *Fax:* 515-294-5957; *E-Mail:* rowley@iastate.edu

ROWND, ROBERT HARVEY, BIOCHEMISTRY, MOLECULAR BIOLOGY. *Current Pos:* JOHN G SEARLE PROF & CHMN, DEPT MOLECULAR BIOL, MED & DENT SCH, NORTHWESTERN UNIV, 81- *Personal Data:* b Chicago, Ill, July 4, 37; m 59; c 3. *Educ:* St Louis Univ, BS, 59; Harvard Univ, MA, 61, PhD(biophys), 63. *Prof Exp:* USPHS fel molecular biol, Med Res Coun Unit, Cambridge Univ, Eng, 63-65; Nat Acad Sci-Nat Res Coun res fel biochem, Pasteur Inst, Paris, France, 65-66; from asst prof to prof biochem & molecular biol, Univ Wis-Madison, 66-81, chmn, Molecular Biol Lab, 70-81. *Concurrent Pos:* Mem, NSF adv panel for develop biol, 68-71; USPHS res career develop award, NIH, 68-73; mem adv panel grad fel, NSF, 74-77, chmn, 76-77; NATO fel, 79; assoc ed, Plasmid, 77-87; mem, NIH Microbiol Biochem Study Sect, 78-; mem comt human health effects subtherapeut antibiotic use in animal feed, Nat Res Coun, 79-81; ed, J Bacteriol, 81-; mem People to People Prog del microbiologist to China, 83; vis prof, Saint Louis Univ, 84; vchmn Gordon Conf, Extrachromasomal Elements, 84, chmn, 86; assoc ed, J Biotechnol & Med Eng, 86-; sr tech adv recruitment consult, UN Develop Prog, China, 87; hon res prof, biotechnol res ctr, Chines Acad Agr Sci, Beijing, 87- *Mem:* Am Soc Microbiol; Am Acad Microbiol; NY Acad Sci. *Res:* Structure, function and replication of nucleic acids; cellular regulatory mechanisms; genetics and mechanism of drug resistance in bacteria; macromolecular chemistry and biology. *Mailing Add:* Wayne State Univ Sch Med 540 E Canfield St Detroit MI 48201-1928

ROWNTREE, ROBERT FREDRIC, TECHNOLOGY BASE MANAGEMENT, LABORATORY PLANNING. *Current Pos:* RETIRED. *Personal Data:* b Columbus, Ohio, Feb 8, 30; m 56, Esther H Raymand; c Raymond A & Walter R. *Educ:* Miami Univ, BA, 52; Syracuse Univ, MPA, 53; Ohio State Univ, PhD(physics), 63. *Honors & Awards:* Michelson Lab Award, Naval Weapons Ctr, 78; Meritorious Civilian Serv Medal, US Dept Navy, 89. *Prof Exp:* Physicist, Wright Air Develop Ctr, Wright-Paterson AFB, Ohio, 53; asst physics, Ohio State Univ, 56-58, Univ Res Found, 58-59, res assoc, 61-63; physicist, Naval Weapons Ctr, China Lake, Calif, 63-64, assoc missions anal, 64-68, prog dir air strike warfare, 68-72, res & develop planning, Weapons Planning Group, 72-75, head regt group, Off Resource & Technol, 75-76, head, Off Plans & Progs, 76-78, technol base coordr, Lab Directorate, 78-89. *Mem:* Emer mem Optical Soc Am; Am Phys Soc; Sigma Xi. *Res:* Optical properties of solids; instrumentation for infrared spectroscopy; arms control research; military operations research; laboratory management; science policy; understanding complex, technology-influenced organizations and environments, elucidating the critical features in their futures, and communicating findings and suggestions to diverse constituencies. *Mailing Add:* 808 Murray Ave San Luis Obispo CA 93405. *E-Mail:* browntre@slonet.org

ROWOTH, OLIN ARTHUR, POULTRY NUTRITION, POULTRY HUSBANDRY. *Current Pos:* Vitamin chemist, Beacon Milling Co, Spencer Kellogg & Sons, Inc, 47-50, poultry nutritionist, 50-59, asst dir poultry & small animal res, 59-64, dir poultry res, Beacon Feeds, Textron Inc, 64-66, DIR RES & TECH SERV, BEACON MILLING CO, INC, 66-, VPRES SERV, 68- *Personal Data:* b Trenton, Mo, May 6, 21; m 46; c 3. *Educ:* Univ Mo, BA, 43, MA, 48. *Mem:* Poultry Sci Asn; Animal Nutrit Res Coun; World Poultry Sci Asn; Am Soc Animal Sci; Am Poultry Hist Soc. *Res:* Nutrition of chickens, ducks, turkeys, game birds and dogs; feeding systems; nutrient requirements of poultry. *Mailing Add:* 36 Charles St Auburn NY 13021

ROWTON, RICHARD LEE, ORGANIC CHEMISTRY. *Current Pos:* RETIRED. *Personal Data:* b Springfield, Mo, May 29, 28; m 51, Barbara Toalson; c Phillip & Karen. *Educ:* Univ Mo-Rolla, BS, 50, MS, 52; Okla State Univ, PhD(org chem), 59. *Prof Exp:* Sr res chemist, Jefferson Chem Co, 59-77; sr tech serv rep, Texaco Chem Co, 77-87. *Mem:* Am Chem Soc. *Res:* Petrochemicals epoxide reaction mechanisms and isotope effects in chemical reactions; urethane chemistry, foams and elastomers; urethane foam seating; polyoxyalkylene polyamine chemistry. *Mailing Add:* 7607 Delafield Ln Austin TX 78752-1312

ROWZEE, E(DWIN) R(ALPH), CHEMICAL ENGINEERING. *Current Pos:* RETIRED. *Personal Data:* b Washington, DC, May 17, 08; m 35; c 3. *Educ:* Mass Inst Technol, MS, 31. *Hon Degrees:* DSc, Laval Univ, 55. *Honors & Awards:* Purvis Mem Lectr, Soc Chem Indust, 47; R S Jane Mem Lectr, Chem Inst Can, 60; Found Lectr, Brit Inst Rubber Indust, 63. *Prof Exp:* Chem engr, Goodyear Tire & Rubber Co, 31-35, in-charge synthetic rubber develop, 35-42; mgr, Co-Polymer Plant, Can Synthetic Rubber, Ltd, 42-44; dir res, Polymer Corp Ltd, 44-47, mgr prod eng & res, 47-51, mem bd dirs, 50, vpres & mgr, 51-57, pres & managing dir, 57-71, chmn bd dirs, Polymer Corp, 71-78; chmn bd dirs, Urban Transp Develop Corp, 73-83. *Concurrent Pos:* Mem bd gov, Univ Windsor & Ont Res Found; mem, Sci Coun Can, 66-69. *Mem:* Am Chem Soc; Chem Inst Can (pres, 54-55). *Mailing Add:* 580 Woodrowe Ave Sarnia ON N7V 2W2 Can

ROXBY, ROBERT, BIOCHEMISTRY, MOLECULAR BIOLOGY. *Current Pos:* asst prof biochem, 75-81, chmn dept, 84-89, ASSOC PROF BIOCHEM, UNIV MAINE, ORONO, 81- *Personal Data:* b Abington, Pa, June 4, 40; m 65; c 2. *Educ:* Gettysburg Col, BA, 62; Univ NC, Chapel Hill, MA, 65; Duke Univ, PhD(biochem), 70. *Prof Exp:* Fel biochem & biophys, Ore State Univ, 70-72; asst prof biochem, Temple Univ Sch Med, 72-75. *Concurrent Pos:* Vis prof, State Univ, Gruningen, Neth, 81-82; vis scientist, Max Planck Inst Plant Breeding, 89-90. *Mem:* Sigma Xi; AAAS. *Res:* Developmental biology of plants. *Mailing Add:* Dept Biochem Univ Maine Hitchner Hall Rm 177 Orono ME 04469-5735. *Fax:* 207-581-2801

ROXIN, EMILIO O, CONTROL THEORY. *Current Pos:* RETIRED. *Personal Data:* b Buenos Aires, Arg, Apr 6, 22; div; c Ursula & Walter. *Educ:* Univ Buenos Aires, Engr, 47, Dr(math), 58. *Prof Exp:* Asst math & physics, Univ Buenos Aires, 48-56, prof math, 56-67; prof math, Univ RI, 67-92. *Concurrent Pos:* Researcher, AEC, Arg, 53-60 & Res Inst Advan Study, Md, 60-64; res assoc, Brown Univ, 64-65; vis prof, Univ Mich, 67. *Mem:* Am Math Soc; Arg Math Union; Math Asn Am; Soc Indust & Appl Math. *Res:* Ordinary differential equations, especially applied to control theory. *Mailing Add:* 31 Nichols Rd Kingston RI 02881-1803

ROY, AJOY KUMAR, NUCLEAR MAGNETIC RESONANCE SPECTROSCOPY, CHEMOMETRICS & ARTIFICIAL INTELLIGENCE. *Current Pos:* SR STAFF SCIENTIST, AUBURN INT INC, 88- *Personal Data:* b Sylheth, Bangladesh, Dec 12, 51. *Educ:* Dhaka Univ, Bangladesh, BSc, 70, MSc, 74; Clark Univ, MA, 87, PhD(chem), 88. *Concurrent Pos:* Res affil, Mass Inst Technol, 92- *Mem:* Am Chem Soc. *Res:* Application of nuclear magnetic resonance and advanced chemometrics to study chemicals/polymers and develop on-line/lab quality control methodologies for chemical/polymer industries. *Mailing Add:* Auburn Int Inc PO Box 2008 Danvers MA 01923

ROY, ARUN K, MOLECULAR BIOLOGY, ENDOCRINOLOGY. *Current Pos:* PROF OBSTET/GYNEC & CELLULAR & STRUCT BIOL, HEALTH SCI CTR, UNIV TEX, 88- *Personal Data:* b Ganraganis, India, Dec 29, 38; US citizen; m 68; c 1. *Educ:* Univ Calcutta, BS, 58, MS, 60; Wayne State Univ, PhD(biochem), 65. *Prof Exp:* From asst prof to prof biol sci, Oakland Univ, 69-87. *Concurrent Pos:* Res career award, NIH, 76, develop award, 89; mem, Cancer Prog Proj Rev Comt, NIH, 83-87 & Endocrinol Study Sect, 89-93. *Mem:* Fel AAAS. *Mailing Add:* Dept Cellular & Struct Biol Univ Tex Health Sci Ctr 7703 Floyd Curl Dr San Antonio TX 78284-7762. *Fax:* 210-567-3803

ROY, CLARENCE, WATER CHEMISTRY, WATER POLLUTION CONTROL. *Current Pos:* CHEM RESEARCHER, VORTEX WATER SYSTS INC, 90- *Personal Data:* b Cleveland, Ohio, 1928. *Educ:* Ala Polytech Inst, BS, 51; Auburn Univ, MS, 56, PhD(chem), 60. *Honors & Awards:* Indust Achievement Award, Am Electroplaters & Surface Refinishers Soc, 94. *Prof Exp:* Researcher water res & develop, Aqualogic Inc, 66-82; chem researcher, Rainbow Res Inc, 82-90. *Mem:* Fel Am Inst Chemists; Am Chem Soc; Am Electroplaters & Surface Refinishers Soc. *Mailing Add:* Vortex Water Systs Inc PO Box 2313 Stuart FL 34995-2313

ROY, CLAUDE CHARLES, PEDIATRICS, GASTROENTEROLOGY. *Current Pos:* PROF PEDIAT, UNIV MONTREAL, 70- *Personal Data:* b Quebec City, Que, Oct 21, 28; m 62; c 3. *Educ:* Laval Univ, BA, 49, MD, 54, FRCPS(C), 59. *Honors & Awards:* Harry Shuachman Award, NAm Soc Pediat Gastroenterol, 87. *Prof Exp:* NIH res fel, Med Ctr, Univ Colo, Denver, 64-66, from asst prof to assoc prof pediat, 66-70; asst to dir, Dept Pediat, 77-80, dir pediat res ctr, 80-84, CHMN, STE JUSTINE HOSP, 84- *Concurrent Pos:* Chmn med adv bd, Can Cystic Fibrosis Found; mem, med adv bd, Can Found Ileitis & Colitis & Can Liver Found; assoc ed, J Pediat Gastroenterol & Nutrit; chmn, clin investr study sect, Med Res Counc Can. *Mem:* Am Col Nutrit; Can Soc Clin Invest; Soc Pediat Res; Am Gastroenterol Asn; Am Pediat Soc; Soc Exp Biol & Med; Can Asn Gastroenterol. *Res:* Bile salt metabolism and function; bile salt in clinical and experimental disorders of the liver, pancreas and gastrointestinal tract; role of taurine in clinical nutrition, lipoprotein metabolism in malabsorptive disorders; free radicals in chronic liver disease and in disorders of nutrition. *Mailing Add:* Dept Pediat Univ Montreal Fac Med PO Box 6128 Sta A Montreal PQ H3C 3J7 Can

ROY, DAVID C, STRATIGRAPHY, SEDIMENTATION. *Current Pos:* Assoc prof, 70-97, DEPT CHAIR, BOSTON COL, 89-, PROF GEOL, 97- *Personal Data:* b Baton Rouge, La, Nov 14, 37; c 3. *Educ:* Iowa State Univ, BS, 61; Mass Inst Technol, PhD(geol), 70. *Concurrent Pos:* Geologist consult, 70- *Mem:* Fel Geol Soc Am; Sigma Xi; Nat Asn Geol Teachers. *Res:* Stratigraphy in New England geology and experimental sedimentology. *Mailing Add:* 99 LaSalle Ave Framingham MA 01701

ROY, DELLA M(ARTIN), GEOCHEMISTRY, MATERIALS SCIENCE. *Current Pos:* Asst mineral, Pa State Univ, 49-52, res assoc geochem, 52-59, sr res assoc, 59-69, sr res assoc, Mat Res Lab, 63-69, assoc prof mat sci, 69-75, PROF MAT SCI, MAT RES LAB, PA STATE UNIV, UNIVERSITY PARK, 75- *Personal Data:* b Merrill, Ore, Nov 3, 26; m 48, Rustum; c Neill, Ronnen & Jeremy. *Educ:* Univ Ore, BS, 47; Pa State Univ, MS, 49, PhD(mineral), 52. *Honors & Awards:* Jeppson Medal, Am Ceramic Soc, 82, Copeland Award, 87; Slag Award, Am Concrete Inst, 89. *Concurrent Pos:* Mem, Comn A2EO6, Hwy Res Bd, Nat Acad Sci; ed, Cement & Concrete Res; ed-in-chief, Univ Cement & Concrete Res, 71-; chair, NMAB Nat Acad Sci Res Comt on Concrete, 80-83; adv, NMAB Comt Concrete Durability, 86-87; hon fel, Indian Concrete Technol, 87; coun, Mat Res Soc, 88; bd trustees, Am Ceramic Soc, 90. *Mem:* Nat Acad Eng; Mat Res Soc; fel Mineral Soc Am; fel Am Concrete Soc; fel Am Ceramics Soc; Clay Minerals Soc; Concrete Soc; Am Nuclear Soc; Am Soc Testing & Mat; Soc Women Engrs; fel AAAS; Int Acad Ceramics. *Res:* Phase equilibria; materials synthesis; crystal chemistry and phase transitions; crystal growth; cement chemistry, hydration and microstructure; concrete durability; biomaterials; special glasses; radioactive waste management; geologic isolation; chemically bonded ceramics; waste management science. *Mailing Add:* 217 Mat Res Lab Pa State Univ University Park PA 16802

ROY, DEV KUMAR, RECURSIVE FUNCTION THEORY. *Current Pos:* asst prof, 81-86, chmn, Dept Math, 97-94, ASSOC PROF MATH, FLA INT UNIV, 86- *Personal Data:* b Patna, India, July 15, 51; m 85, Maneck Paruwala. *Educ:* Indian Inst Technol, Kharagpur, BS, 71; Indian Inst Technol, Delhi, MS, 73; Univ Rochester, PhD(math), 80. *Prof Exp:* Lectr math, Univ Wis-Milwaukee, 79-81. *Mem:* Asn Symbolic Logic. *Res:* Investigations in recursive algebra and model theory; constructions in recursive ordered structures, hierarchies, and presentations; coding and priority arguments in the context of ordered structures. *Mailing Add:* Dept Math Fla Int Univ Tamiami Trail Miami FL 33199

ROY, DIPAK, HAZARDOUS WASTE MANAGEMENT. *Current Pos:* PROF, POLY TECH UNIV, 95- *Personal Data:* b WBengal, India, Aug 4, 46; m 75; c 2. *Educ:* Jadavpur Univ, India, BCE, 68; Indian Inst Technol, MTech, 71; Univ Ill, Urbana, PhD(civil & environ eng), 79. *Honors & Awards:* Fulbright fel. *Prof Exp:* Scientist res environ eng, Nat Environ Eng Res Inst, 71-73; design engr civil eng, Catalytic, Inc, 73-74; Air Pollution Control, Johns & March, 74-75; asst prof, La State Univ, 79-85, assoc prof environ eng, 85-95. *Concurrent Pos:* Consult, NY Assoc, New Orleans, 80; Woodward-Clyde Consults, 88. *Mem:* Water Pollution Control Fedn; Am Water Works Asn; Am Soc Civil Engrs; Asn Environ Eng Prof; AAAS; Am Chem Soc. *Res:* Destruction of hazardous wastes by photolytic ozonation; removal and inactivation of viruses from water and wastewater; methane generation from waste and organic biomass; mathematical modelling of environmental engineering processes; biodegradation of hazardous waste. *Mailing Add:* 4 Lavender Dr Princeton NJ 08540

ROY, DONALD H, NUCLEAR PHYSICS, REACTOR PHYSICS. *Current Pos:* Reactor physicist, 59-60, sr reactor physicist, 62-63, GROUP SUPVR THEORET PHYSICS & EXP PHYSICS ANAL, BABCOCK & WILCOX CO, 63- *Personal Data:* b Raleigh, NC, July 13, 36; m 65. *Educ:* NC State Univ, BS, 58, PhD(nuclear eng), 62; Mass Inst Technol, MS, 59. *Res:* Advanced computational methods for resonance absorption calculations and prediction of high energy nuclear reaction cross sections and distribution matrices. *Mailing Add:* 1045 Greenway Ct Lynchburg VA 24503

ROY, GABRIEL D, COMBUSTION & PROPULSION SCIENCE, PULSE POWER PHYSICS. *Current Pos:* PROG MGR PROPULSION & PULSE POWER, OFF NAVAL RES, 87- *Personal Data:* b India, July 7, 39; US citizen; m 61; c 4. *Educ:* Univ Kerala, BS, 60, MS, 65; Indian Inst Technol, cert heat transfer, 71; Univ Tenn, PhD(eng sci), 77. *Prof Exp:* Lectr mech eng, Col Eng, Trivandrum, 60-65, asst prof, 65-71; res asst aerospace eng, Univ Tenn, 71-76, sr res engr energy eng, Univ Tenn Space Inst, 76-78, group leader heat transfer, 78-81; prog mgr energy conversion, TRW Inc, 81-87; *Concurrent Pos:* Staff adv, Col Eng, Univ Kerala, 65-71; secy, Trivandrum Arts Group, 69-71; asst prof, Tenn State Univ, 77-78, Univ Tenn, Nashville, 78-79 & Motlow State Col, 79-81; vis prof, Calif State Univ, 83-87; prog reviewer, Dept Energy, Strategic Defense Initiative Orgn, 87-; assoc ed, J Propulsion & Power, Am Inst Aeronaut & Astronaut, 89-, vchmn, Propellants & Combustion. *Mem:* Assoc fel Am Inst Aeronaut & Astronaut; Am Soc Mech Engrs; Sigma Xi. *Res:* Propulsion; pulse power; magnetohydrodynamics; underwater propulsion; fluid dynamics; recipient of 2 patents; author of numerous publications. *Mailing Add:* 9944 Great Oaks Way Fairfax VA 22030

ROY, GABRIEL L, animal breeding, genetics, for more information see previous edition

ROY, GUY, BIOPHYSICS, PHYSIOLOGY GENERAL. *Current Pos:* From asst prof to assoc prof, 68-80, PROF BIOPHYS, UNIV MONTREAL, 80- *Personal Data:* b Que, Apr 10, 39; m 63; c 3. *Educ:* Univ Laval, BSc, 64; Univ Calif, PhD(biophys), 69. *Concurrent Pos:* Vis prof, Dept Physiol, Kyoto Univ, Kyoto, Japan, 75-76, Univ Otago, New Zealand, 83-84. *Mem:* Biophys Soc. *Res:* Ionic currents across artificial and biological membranes; theory and experiments. *Mailing Add:* Univ Montreal CP 6128 Montreal Succursale A PQ H3C 3J7 Can

ROY, HARRY, PLANT MOLECULAR BIOLOGY & BIOCHEMISTRY. *Current Pos:* from asst prof to assoc prof, 76-88, PROF BIOL, RENSSELAER POLYTECH INST, 89- *Personal Data:* b Cincinnati, Ohio, Aug 29, 43; c 1. *Educ:* Brown Univ, AB, 65, ScM, 66; Johns Hopkins Univ, PhD(cell biol), 70. *Prof Exp:* Fel plant biochem, Johns Hopkins Univ, 70-71; NIH fel plant physiol, Cornell Univ, 71-74; asst prof life sci, Polytech Inst NY, 74-76. *Concurrent Pos:* Mem, Capital Dist Plant Res Group; Nat Res Serv Awards fel, Harvard Univ, 83-84. *Mem:* Am Soc Plant Physiologists. *Res:* Synthesis and assembly of chloroplast proteins; molecular chaperones; educational software in genetics. *Mailing Add:* Dept Biol Rensselaer Polytech Inst Troy NY 12180-3590

ROY, HERBERT C, DATABASE MANAGEMENT, STATISTICAL ANALYSIS. *Current Pos:* RES SCIENTIST, NJ DEPT ENVIRON PROTECTION & ENERGY, 89- *Personal Data:* b Lakewood, NJ, Nov 5, 47. *Educ:* Monmouth Col, W Long Br, BS, 69; Drexel Univ, MS, 72, MS, 77; Rutgers Univ, PhD(environ sci), 89. *Prof Exp:* Teaching asst calculus, Drexel Univ, 69-70, res asst atmospheric physics, 70-71; teaching asst gen physics, 71-73, comput programmer biophys, 74-76; comput programmer, Univ Pa, 77-81; res fel, Rutgers Univ, 83-85. *Concurrent Pos:* Adj instr math, Drexel Univ, 78-80; Consult instr math, Satinsky Inst Human Resource Develop, 79-80; comput consult, Rutgers Univ, 84-86, Ctr Alcohol Studies, 87-88. *Mem:* Sigma Xi. *Res:* Perform statistical analysis of radon test data; evaluate Cerenkov light as a dosimeter for electron accelerators. *Mailing Add:* PO Box 501 Cranbury NJ 08512-0501

ROY, JEAN-CLAUDE, RADIOCHEMISTRY, ANALYTICAL CHEMISTRY. *Current Pos:* RETIRED. *Personal Data:* b Quebec, Que, Jan 6, 27; m 56; c 2. *Educ:* Univ Laval, BA, 47, BSc, 51; Univ Notre Dame, PhD(chem), 54. *Prof Exp:* Vis chemist, Carnegie Inst Technol, 54-55; res officer radiochem, Atomic Energy Can, 55-62 & Int Bur Weights & Measures, France, 62-64; prof radiochem, Univ Laval, 64-74, prof chem, 74. *Mem:* Chem Inst Can. *Res:* Methodology and measurement of radioactivity in waters and sediments; x-ray fluorescence analysis. *Mailing Add:* 995 Gerard Morrisset Apt 112 Quebec PQ G1S 4S9 Can

ROY, M S, OPHTHALMOLOGY. *Current Pos:* ASSOC PROF OPHTHAL, UNIV MED & DENT NJ, 89- *Personal Data:* b Libourne, France, May 3, 46; Can citizen; m 74, Alec; c Candice. *Educ:* Univ Bordeaux, MD, 73; Univ London, DO, 76; FRCS(C); 80; FRCophthal, 89; Am Bd Ophthal, cert, 83. *Prof Exp:* Vis scientist retinal dis sect, Nat Eye Inst, 82-89. *Concurrent Pos:* Int Res Group Color Vision Deficiency, 88. *Mem:* Asn Res Vision; Int Soc Ocular Fluorophotom. *Res:* Pathogenesis and treatment of age related maculor degeneration; sickle cell retinopathy and diabetic retinopathy; risk factors for dialetic retinopathy in African-Americans. *Mailing Add:* Dept Ophthal NJ Med Sch Univ Med & Dent 90 Bergen St Newark NJ 07103. *Fax:* 973-982-2068; *E-Mail:* roymo@umdnj.edu

ROY, MARIE LESSARD, OCCUPATIONAL MEDICINE, GENERAL PRACTICE. *Current Pos:* internship, Ont Ministry Labor, 79-80, resident internal med, 80-81, sr med toxicologist, 81-87, prov med toxicologist, 87-93, MED COORDR, WORKERS COMPENSATION BD, ONT MINISTRY LABOR, 94- *Personal Data:* b Fall River, Mass, Mar 1, 44; m 69, Dibyendu; c Ravi & Dia. *Educ:* Albertus Magnus Col, BA, 65; Univ Conn, PhD(org chem), 69, MD, 79; FRCPS(C), 89. *Prof Exp:* Lectr org chem & chem eng, Univ Toronto, 69-73, lectr pharmacol, 73-77. *Concurrent Pos:* Asst prof, Univ Toronto, 84- *Mem:* Am Chem Soc; Sigma Xi; Soc Toxicol Can; Royal Soc Chem; Am Conf Govt Indust Hygienists; Ont Med Asn; NY Acad Sci; Occup Med Asn Can; Am Col Occup Med. *Res:* Evaluation of health effects of hazardous substances in the workplace; health effects of toxic substances; supervised a long-range epidemiology study of health effects on hospital staff due to exposure to waste anaesthetic gases; toxicology of lead. *Mailing Add:* c/o Dr D N Roy 89 Poyntz Ave Willowdale ON M2N 1J3 Can

ROY, PAUL-H(ENRI), CHEMICAL ENGINEERING. *Current Pos:* RETIRED. *Personal Data:* b Quebec City, Que, Apr 19, 24; m 56. *Educ:* Laval Univ, BASc, 48; Univ Mich, MSE, 49; Ill Inst Technol, PhD(chem eng), 55. *Prof Exp:* Proj engr, Res Inst, Univ Mich, 49-51; res engr, E I du Pont de Nemours & Co Inc, 55-60; from asst prof to prof chem eng, Laval Univ, 60-94, vdean fac sci, 61-69. *Concurrent Pos:* Consult, E I du Pont de Nemours & Co Inc, 64-69; mem, Hydro-Que Res Comt, 65-66 & Laval Admin Comn, 65-69; Laval rep, Can Res Mgt Asn, 67-72; rep, Sci Adv Planning Br, Ministry of State Sci & Technol, Govt Can, 72-. *Mem:* Am Inst Chem Engrs; Can Chem Eng Soc; Can Coun Prof Engrs; Sigma Xi. *Res:* Mixing of liquids as related to dynamics of chemical reactors; mechanism of liquid; liquid dispersion; waste water treatment; chemical process economics. *Mailing Add:* 380 Chemin St Louis No 503 Quebec PQ G1S 4M1 Can

ROY, PRADIP KUMAR, thin dielectric process, microelectronics technology development & characterization, for more information see previous edition

ROY, PRODYOT, MATERIALS SCIENCE, PHYSICAL CHEMISTRY. *Current Pos:* engr chem, 68-80, mgr plant mat, 80-83, PRIN SCIENTIST, GEN ELEC CO, SAN JOSE, CA. *Personal Data:* b Calcutta, India, 35; US citizen; m 63; c 2. *Educ:* Univ Calcutta, BS; Univ Calif, Berkeley, MS, PhD(mat sci). *Prof Exp:* Res engr surface chem, Univ Calif, Berkeley, 63-65, res engr chem, 67-68; res fel, Max Planck Inst Phys Chem, 65-67. *Mem:* Am Inst Mining, Metall & Petrol Engrs; fel Am Soc Metals. *Res:* Thermodynamics of metals and alloys; surface chemistry and adsorption phenomenon; solid state electrochemistry; fast breeder coolant chemistry; mechanical properties of materials; corrosion and stress corrosion; terrestial and space power conversion; power storage technology e.g. fuel cells; primary and secondary batteries. *Mailing Add:* GE Nuclear Energy 175 Curtner Ave San Jose CA 95125

ROY, RABINDRA (NATH), PHYSICAL CHEMISTRY, ANALYTICAL CHEMISTRY. *Current Pos:* PROF CHEM & CHMN DEPT, DRURY COL, 73- *Personal Data:* b July 31, 39; m 68. *Educ:* Jadavpur Univ, India, BSc, 59, MSc, 61; La State Univ, Baton Rouge, PhD(chem), 66. *Prof Exp:* Indian Dept Health res scholar phys chem, Jadavpur Univ, India, 61-63; teaching asst chem, La State Univ, Baton Rouge, 65-66; from asst prof to assoc prof phys & analytical chem, Drury Col, 66-71; petrol res fund res assoc phys chem, Univ Fla, 71-73. *Mem:* Am Chem Soc; Royal Soc Chem; Am Soc Test & Mat. *Res:* Thermodynamics and analytical processes of electrolytes and nonelectrolytes in aqueous mixed and nonaqueous solvents from physicochemical measurements; buffer solutions; ion-selective electrode and mixed strong electrolytes. *Mailing Add:* Dept Chem Drury Col Springfield MO 65802

ROY, RAJARSHI, LASER PHYSICS, QUANTUM OPTICS. *Current Pos:* from asst prof to assoc prof, 82-93, PROF PHYSICS, SCH PHYSICS, GA INST TECHNOL, 93- *Personal Data:* b Calcutta, India, June 4, 54; m 82, Katherine Bassein. *Educ:* Delhi Univ, Bsc, 73, MSc, 75; Univ Rochester, MA, 77, PhD(physics), 81. *Prof Exp:* Teaching fel physics, Joint Inst Lab Astrophys, 81-82. *Concurrent Pos:* Vis scientist, Bell Labs, 87. *Mem:* Am Phys Soc; Optical Soc Am. *Res:* Laser physics; quantum optics; experimental tests of statistical theories and non-linear phenomena; quantum fluctuations and their effects on optical devices; control of chaotic systems; nonlinear dynamics. *Mailing Add:* Sch Physics Ga Inst Technol Atlanta GA 30332-0430

ROY, RAM BABU, SYNTHETIC ORGANIC & NATURAL PRODUCTS CHEMISTRY, RANGE SCIENCE & MANAGEMENT. *Current Pos:* PRES, METHODS SUPPORT LAB INC, 95- *Personal Data:* b Shahwaj Pur, India, Jan 15, 33; US citizen; m 52, Sanyukta Devi; c Ranjan S, Sashi B & Samuel J. *Educ:* Bihar Univ, BSc, 56; Patna Univ, MSc, 58; Univ Newcastle, PhD(org chem), 67. *Prof Exp:* Head, Chem Dept, BS Col, India, 59-68; vis prof chem, Univ Mich, Ann Arbor, 68-69, Univ Wash, 69-71; sr res assoc, Princeton Univ, 71-72, Mass Inst Technol, 72-73; sr staff scientist, Technicon Instruments Inc, 73-87; sr process consult, Alfa-Laval Inc, 87-92; dir & prin scientist, Alpkem Corp, 92-95. *Mem:* Am Chem Soc; fel Am Inst Chemists; fel Inst Food Technol; Royal Inst Chem. *Res:* Automation of analytical methods; chemical process development and on-line monitoring of chemical/biochemical reactors in operation; technical consulting for food, pharmaceutical and environmental industries; recovery of materials from waste; extraction, purification and characterization of natural products. *Mailing Add:* Landmark Bldg No 2 Unit 713 Cherry Hill NJ 08034. *Fax:* 609-702-1458

ROY, RAMAN K, BIOCHEMISTRY. *Current Pos:* SR SCIENTIST, ASTRA RES CTR INDIA, 84- *Personal Data:* b Digboi, India, Jan 14, 47; m 72; c 2. *Educ:* Calcutta Univ, BSc, 66, MSc, 68, PhD(biochem), 73. *Prof Exp:* Lectr biochem, Burdwan Univ Med Col, India, 72-73; staff fel, Boston Biomed Res Inst, 74-76, res assoc, 77-79, staff scientist, 80-83. *Concurrent Pos:* Vis scientist, Indian Inst Sci, Bangalore, 84-86. *Mem:* NY Acad Sci; Am Soc Biochem & Molecular Biol. *Res:* Virulence mechanisms of enteropathogens; bacterial cell wall biosynthesis. *Mailing Add:* Astra Res Ctr India 18th Cross Malleswaram PO Box 359 Bangalore 560003 India. *Fax:* 91-812-340449

ROY, RAMENDRA PRASAD, THERMAL SCIENCES, ENERGY SYSTEMS. *Current Pos:* assoc prof mech eng, 81-86, PROF MECH ENG, ARIZ STATE UNIV, 86- *Personal Data:* b Dhanbad, India, Nov 26, 42; US citizen; m 78, Suchitra Mitra; c Rupali & Shilpi. *Educ:* Calcutta Univ, India, BSc, 60; Jadauper Univ, India, BS, 64; Univ Wash, Seattle, MS, 66; Univ Calif, Berkeley, MS, 71, PhD(nuclear eng), 75. *Honors & Awards:* Gold Medal, Indian Zool Soc, 58. *Prof Exp:* Engr, Bechtel Corp, San Francisco, 67-71; asst prof nuclear eng, Univ Ill, Urbana-Champaign, 75-81. *Concurrent Pos:* Consult, Argonne Nat Lab, 78-83, Ariz Pub Serv Co, 88-93; vis prof, Indiana Inst Sci, Bangalore, 87. *Mem:* Sigma XI; Am Soc Mech Engrs. *Res:* Thermal sciences; energy systems. *Mailing Add:* Mech & Aerospace Eng Ariz State Univ Tempe AZ 85287-6106

ROY, ROB, BIOENGINEERING & BIOMEDICAL ENGINEERING, ANESTHESIOLOGY. *Current Pos:* PROF ANESTHESIOL, ALBANY MED COL, 93- *Personal Data:* b Brooklyn, NY, Jan 2, 33; m 59, 96, Judith Webb; c Robert, David & Bruce. *Educ:* Cooper Union, BSEE, 54; Columbia Univ, MSEE, 56; Rensselaer Polytech Inst, DEng Sc(elec eng), 62, Albany Med Col, MD, 76, Am Bd Anesthesiologists, dipl, 85. *Prof Exp:* Sr engr character recognition, Control Instrument Div, Burroughs Corp, 56-60; from instr to assoc prof elec eng, Rensselaer Polytech Inst, 60-68, prof syst eng, 68-79, prof & chmn biomed eng, 79-94. *Concurrent Pos:* Consult, Raytheon Corp, 66-, USAF, 67- & Cornell Aeronaut Lab, 67-; NIH spec fel, 72-74; consult, Searle Corp, 79-, Kendall Corp, 81-, Am Edwards, 85; from asst prof to assoc prof, Albany Med Col, 79-86. *Mem:* Inst Elec & Electronics Engrs; Am Soc Anesthesiologists; Sigma Xi; Biomed Eng Soc; fel Am Col Anesthesiologists. *Res:* Pattern recognition; digital signal processing; process identification; adaptive control systems; biomedical research; biomedical signal processing. *Mailing Add:* 565 Highwood Circle Albany NY 12203. *Fax:* 518-276-3035; *E-Mail:* royr@rpi.edu

ROY, ROBERT FRANCIS, geophysics, for more information see previous edition

ROY, ROBERT MICHAEL MCGREGOR, RADIATION BIOLOGY, CELL BIOLOGY. *Current Pos:* Chmn Dept Biol, Concordia Univ, 77-82, dean sci, 82-85, actg vrector acad, 84-85, PROF BIOL, CONCORDIA UNIV, 70-, CHMN, DEPT BIOL, 93- *Personal Data:* b Nanaimo, BC, Can, June 10, 42; m 67; c 1. *Educ:* Univ Toronto, BSc, 63, MA, 65, PhD(zool), 68. *Res:* Radiation biology; physiological and biochemical effects of ionizing radiation on plants and animals; post radiation modification of damage and repair. *Mailing Add:* Dept Biol Rm 1260 Concordia Univ 1455 de Maisonneuve Blvd W Montreal PQ H3G 1M8 Can. *Fax:* 514-848-2881

ROY, ROBERT RUSSELL, METABOLISM-BIOACTIVATION OF OCCUPATIONAL & ENVIRONMENTAL CHEMICALS, RISK ASSESSMENT & SAFETY EVALUATION OF ENVIRONMENTAL INDUSTRIAL & CONSUMER CHEMICALS. *Current Pos:* staff toxicologist, 90-93, SR TOXICOLOGIST, MINN REGIONAL POISON CTR, ST PAUL-RAMSEY MED CTR, 93- *Personal Data:* b Minneapolis, Minn, Sept 14, 57; m 87, Barbara Richie; c Andrew & Katherine. *Educ:* Augsburg Col, BA, 80; Univ Minn, MS, 86, PhD(toxicol), 89. *Prof Exp:* Res assoc toxicol, Univ Minn, 89; toxicologist, Pace Labs, 89-90; res scientist II toxicol, Minn Dept Health, 90-93. *Concurrent Pos:* Consult toxicologist, J B Stevens & Assocs, 87-89; instr & course dir toxicol, Midwest Ctr Occup Safety & Health, 89-; co-prin investr, St Paul-Ramsey Med Ctr, 93-; mem grad fac, Univ Minn, 93-, adj asst prof pharm, Sch Pub Health, 96- *Mem:* Soc Toxicol; Am Indust Hyg Asn. *Res:* Metabolism and bioactivation of occupational and environmental chemicals; mechanisms of chemical toxicity to the blood and bone marrow; human health risk assessment; safety assessment of consumer products; safety assessment of occupational and agricultural chemicals. *Mailing Add:* 6201 Near Mountain Blvd Chanhassen MN 55317-9117

ROY, RONALD R, CONSUMER FOOD SAFETY. *Current Pos:* Bench chemist, NY Lab, Food & Drug Admin, 72-78, supvry chemist, 78-88, chemist pesticide monitoring foods, 88-91, CHIEF, DOMESTIC PROG BR, DIV FIELD PROG PLANNING & EVAL, CTR FOOD SAFETY & APPL NUTRIT, FOOD & DRUG ADMIN, 91- *Personal Data:* b Brooklyn, NY, May 23, 50. *Educ:* City Univ NY, BS, 71. *Mailing Add:* Off Field Prog Ctr Food Safety & Appl Nutrit FDA 200 C St SW Washington DC 20204. *Fax:* 202-205-9670

ROY, RUSTUM, NEW MATERIALS SYNTHESIS, CRYSTAL CHEMISTRY. *Current Pos:* Fel, Pa State Univ, 48-49, res assoc, 50-51, from asst prof to assoc prof geochem, 51-57, dir, Mat Res Lab, 62-85, prof solid state, 67-81, dir, Sci Technol & Soc Prog, 84-90, PROF GEOCHEM, PA STATE UNIV, 57-, PROF SOLID STATE, 67-, EVAN PUGH PROF SOLID STATE, 81- *Personal Data:* b Ranchi, India, July 3, 24; nat US; m 48, Della; c Neill, Ronnen & Jeremy. *Educ:* Patna Univ, India, BSc, 42, MSc, 44; Pa State Univ, PhD(ceramics), 48. *Hon Degrees:* DSc, Toyko Inst Technol, 87, Alfred Univ, 93. *Honors & Awards:* Mineral Soc Am Award, 57; Welch Lectr, Tex Univ, 74; Sosman Lectr, Am Ceramic Soc, 75, Orton Lectr, 83; Fairchild Lectr, Lehigh Univ, 76; Hibbert Lectr, London Univ, 79; McConnell Lectr, Ore, 88; Harnish Lectr, Fresno State, 89; Gross Lectr, Ind, 91; Nat Advan Award, Fedn Mat Soc, 91; Int Prize, Japan Fine Ceramics Asn, 91; Dupont Award, Am Chem Soc, 93; Centennial Medal, Am Soc Eng Educ, 93. *Concurrent Pos:* Sr sci officer, Cent Glass & Ceramic Res Inst, Calcutta, India, 50; chmn, Solid State Technol Prog, Pa State Univ, 60-67, dir, Mat Res Lab, 62-85, chmn, Sci, Technol & Soc Prog, 69-; consult, Carborundum Co, 62-, Bausch & Laumb, 62-, Xerox Corp, 63-83, Lanxide Corp, 84-; ed, J Mat Educ, 79- *Mem:* Nat Acad Eng; foreign mem Royal Swed Acad Eng Sci; foreign fel Indian Nat Sci Acad; fel Am Ceramic Soc; Eng Acad Japan; hon mem Ceramic Soc Japan; life fel Mineral Soc Am; fel AAAS; fel Am Phys Soc; Mat Res Soc (vpres, 75-76, pres, 76); fel Indian Acad Sci; foreign mem Acad Natural Sci. *Res:* New materials preparation and characterization; crystal chemistry, synthesis, stability, phase equilibria and crystal growth in non-metallic systems; ultrahigh pressure reactions in solids;

radioactive waste forms; nanocomposites, zero-expansion ceramics, diamond films; technology literacy for all citizens; author of 5 books, over 700 scientific and 200 technology and society papers and chapters in books and magazines; granted several patents. *Mailing Add:* 528 S Pugh St State College PA 16801-5312. *Fax:* 814-863-7040

ROY, SAYON, DIABETES, DIABETIC RETINOPATHY. *Current Pos:* res assoc, 90-92, sci assoc, 92-94, ASST SCIENTIST, SCHEPENS EYE RES INST, HARVARD MED SCH, 94- *Personal Data:* b Calcutta, West Bengal, Dec 26, 59; m 84, Sumita Chakravarty; c Sumon. *Educ:* Univ Kalyani, BS, 79, MS, 83; Boston Univ-Harvard Med Sch, PhD(molecular biol), 89. *Honors & Awards:* Nat US Serv Award, NIH, 90. *Prof Exp:* Consult, Biochem & Cell Biol Univ, Schepens Eye Res Inst, 92- *Concurrent Pos:* Fel, Harvard Univ, Harvard Med Sch, 90-94; career develop award, Am Diabetes Asn, 94. *Mem:* Fel Am Diabetes Asn; AAAS. *Res:* Lasting effect of high glucose on human endothelial cells; effects of high glucose in diabetic retinopathy at the level of gene expression. *Mailing Add:* 20 Staniford St Boston MA 02114

ROY, WILLIAM ARTHUR, TERATOLOGY, BONE BIOLOGY. *Current Pos:* STAFF MEM, DEPT ANAT, UNIV MISS MED CTR, 87- *Personal Data:* b Elkins, WVa, July 24, 48. *Educ:* Fairmont State Col, BS, 70; WVa Univ, PhD(anat), 76. *Prof Exp:* Nat res serv award anat, Univ Va, 76-78; asst prof anat & embryol, Sch Dent, Marquette Univ, 78-86; Sch Pediatric Med, Barry Univ, Miami Shores, Fla, 86-87. *Mem:* Teratology Soc; AAAS; Am Asn Anatomists. *Res:* Normal and abnormal craniofacial development during the prenatal and early postnatal periods; pathogenesis and treatment of craniofacial anomalies such as premature craniosynostosis. *Mailing Add:* Phys Ther UMMC/SHRP 2500 N State St Jackson MS 39216-4505

ROY, WILLIAM R, OBSTETRICS & GYNECOLOGY. *Current Pos:* RETIRED. *Personal Data:* b 1926. *Educ:* Ill Wesleyan Univ, BS, 46; NWestern Univ, MD, 49; Washburn Univ, JD, 70. *Prof Exp:* Mem staff, Stormont-Vail Hosp & St Francis Hosp, Topeka, Kans, 55-89. *Mem:* Inst Med-Nat Acad Sci. *Mailing Add:* 6137 SW 38th Terr Topeka KS 66610

ROYAL, GEORGE CALVIN, JR, MEDICAL MICROBIOLOGY. *Current Pos:* from asst prof to assoc prof, 66-82, PROF MICROBIOL, COL MED, HOWARD UNIV, 82- *Personal Data:* b Williamston, SC, Aug 5, 21; m 69; c 6. *Educ:* Tuskegee Inst, BS, 43; Univ Wis, MS, 47; Univ Pa, PhD, 57. *Prof Exp:* Instr bact, Tuskegee Inst, 47-48; asst immunol, Ohio Agr Exp Sta, 50-52; asst prof bact, Agr & Tech Col NC, 52-53, prof, 57-65. *Concurrent Pos:* Fel, Jefferson Med Col, 65-66; dir, Sr Res Proj, US AEC, 58-65; dir, Undergrad Res Partic Prog, NSF, 59-61; mem, Nat Adv Food Comt, Food & Drug Admin, 72- *Mem:* NY Acad Sci; Am Soc Microbiol; fel Am Acad Microbiol; Sigma Xi. *Res:* Virulence factors of candida albicans. *Mailing Add:* 1509 Girard St NE Washington DC 20018-1831

ROYAL, HENRY DUVAL, MEDICINE. *Current Pos:* assoc prof, 87-93, PROF RADIOL, WASH UNIV, 93- *Personal Data:* b Norwich, Conn, May 14, 48; m 72, Christine Gervais; c David, Michael & Catherine. *Educ:* Providence Col, BS, 70; St Louis Univ, MD, 74. *Prof Exp:* From instr to assoc prof radiol, Harvard Univ, 79-86. *Concurrent Pos:* Radiologist, Beth Israel Hosp, 76-86 & Mallinckrodt Inst Radiol, 87- *Mem:* Soc Nuclear Med; Radiol Soc NAm; Health Physics Soc. *Res:* Effects of radiation; health care policy. *Mailing Add:* Mallinckrodt Inst Rad St Louis MO 63110. *Fax:* 314-362-2806; *E-Mail:* royal@mirlink.wustl.edu

ROYALL, RICHARD MILES, MATHEMATICAL STATISTICS. *Current Pos:* From asst prof to assoc prof biostatist, 66-74, assoc prof math sci, 74-76, PROF BIOSTATIST, JOHNS HOPKINS UNIV, 76- *Personal Data:* b Elkin, NC, Aug 13, 39; m 59; c 2. *Educ:* NC State Univ, BS, 62; Stanford Univ, MS, 64, PhD(statist), 66. *Mem:* Int Statist Inst; Biomet Soc; fel Am Statist Asn; Inst Math Statist; Am Public Health Asn. *Res:* Finite population sampling theory; foundations of statistical inference. *Mailing Add:* 2308 South Rd Baltimore MD 21209

ROYALS, EDWIN EARL, organic chemistry; deceased, see previous edition for last biography

ROY-BURMAN, PRADIP, MOLECULAR BIOLOGY, MOLECULAR GENETICS. *Current Pos:* res assoc biochem, Sch Med, Univ Southern Calif, 63-66, asst prof, 67-70, from asst prof to assoc prof biochem & path, 70-78, chmn, grad comt exp path, 78-84, chmn, Biomed Res Support Grant Comt, 84-94, vchmn, Dept Path, 87-95, PROF PATH & BIOCHEM, MED SCH, UNIV SOUTHERN CALIF, 78-, MEM, SCIENTIFIC COUN, HEALTH SCIS CAMPUS, 94-, INTERIM CHMN, DEPT MOLECULAR MICROBIOL & IMMUNOL, 95- *Personal Data:* b Comillah, India, Nov 12, 38; m 63, Sumitra (Ghosh); c Arup & Paula. *Educ:* Univ Calcutta, BSc, 56, MSc, 58, PhD(biochem), 63. *Prof Exp:* Sr res chemist, Dept Bot, Univ Calcutta, 62-63. *Concurrent Pos:* Dernham sr fel oncol, Am Cancer Soc, 66-71, mem, spec grants comt, 74-78, prin investr, res grants & contracts, 68-70; prin investr, res grants & contracts, NIH, 70-, ad hoc mem NIH Path B study sect, 88; prin investr, res grants & contracts, priv founds, 83-; travel grants, Int Mgt, 76-79, 88 & 94; vis scientist, Govt India, 86; mem, NIH Path B Study Sect, 90-94, & Spec Review & Site Visit Comt, Nat Inst Neurolog Dis & Stroke, Extra Mural Res Prog, 92-93, sci coun, Health Sci Campus, Univ Southern Calif, 94- *Mem:* Am Soc Biol Chem & Molecular Biologists; Am Soc Microbiol; Int Asn Comp Res Leukemia & Related Dis; Am Soc Virol; Am Asn Cancer Res; Am Soc Invest Path. *Res:* Molecular biology of retroviruses and endogenous retrovirus genes; viral and cellular oncogenes;

pathogenetic mechanisms in leukemia; recombinant DNA technology in molecular pathology; molecular genetics of prostate cancer. *Mailing Add:* Dept Path Univ Southern Calif Med Sch Los Angeles CA 90033. *Fax:* 213-342-3049; *E-Mail:* royburma@zygote.hsc.usc.edu

ROYCE, BARRIE SAUNDERS HART, SOLID STATE PHYSICS. *Current Pos:* res assoc, 60-61, from asst prof to assoc prof, 61-78, master, Mathey Col, 86-94, PROF SOLID STATE SCI, PRINCETON UNIV, 78-,. *Personal Data:* b Bishop's Stortford, Eng, Jan 10, 33; US citizen; m 64; c Vincent Rene & Marc Edward. *Educ:* Univ London, BSc, 54, PhD(physics), 57. *Prof Exp:* Res assoc physics, Carnegie Inst Technol, 57-60. *Concurrent Pos:* Vis prof, Univ Sao Paulo, 62 & 69 & Nat Polytech Inst, Mex, 67 & 78; Sci Res Coun sr fel, Clarendon Labs, Oxford Univ, Eng, 70; vis prof, Solid State Physics Lab, Orsay, France, 73 & 78, Univ Paris Sud, 73 & 77 & Inst Advan Studies IPN, Mex, 78 & 89. *Mem:* Am Phys Soc; Sigma Xi. *Res:* Relationship between atomic defects in materials and their macroscopic performance; mechanical properties of polymeric fibers and techniques developed to measure their elastic modulus in compression and confined buckling behavior; scanning force microscope employed to measure local elastic modulus across the section of 36 micron fibers and these measurements are being extended to provide elastic constant maps of multi-component fibers of these dimensions. *Mailing Add:* Dept Mech & Aerospace Eng Princeton Univ Princeton NJ 08544. *Fax:* 609-258-1139; *E-Mail:* bshroyce@princeton.edu

ROYCE, GEORGE JAMES, ANATOMY. *Current Pos:* ASSOC PROF ANAT, UNIV WIS-MADISON, 74- *Personal Data:* b Petoskey, Mich, Sept 30, 38. *Educ:* Mich State Univ, BA; Ohio State Univ, MA, 63, PhD(anat), 67. *Prof Exp:* NIH fel, Case Western Reserve Univ, 68-69; instr, Albany Med Col, 69-70, asst prof anat, 70-74. *Mem:* Soc Neurosci. *Res:* Neuroanatomy. *Mailing Add:* Dept Anat Univ Wis 1300 University Ave Madison WI 53706

ROYCE, PAUL C, HEALTH CARE DELIVERY. *Current Pos:* MED DIR, SEGAL CO, NY, 95- *Personal Data:* b Minneapolis, Minn, July 2, 28; m 56, Jacqueline Marofsky; c Sarah (Theis), Rachel & Ethan. *Educ:* Univ Minn, BA, 48, MD, 52; Case Western Res Univ, PhD(physiol), 59. *Prof Exp:* Asst prof med, Albert Einstein Col Med, 61-69; assoc prof, Hahnemann Med Univ, 73-81; dean & prof clin sci, Duluth Sch Med, Univ Minn, 81-87; sr vpres, Monmouth Med Ctr, Long Branch, NJ, 87-95. *Concurrent Pos:* Dir med educ, Guthrie Med Ctr, Sayre, Pa, 70-81; clin prof med, Upstate Med Ctr, State Univ NY, 79-81; emer prof, MCP Hahnemann Sch Med, Philadelphia, Pa. *Mem:* Am Physiol Soc; AAAS; AMA; Fedn Am Scientists; Physicians Social Responsibility. *Res:* Health care delivery. *Mailing Add:* 9 Prospect Rd Atlantic Highlands NJ 07716. *Fax:* 732-872-7049; *E-Mail:* royceassoc@exit.og.com

ROYCE, WILLIAM FRANCIS, FISHERIES, RESOURCE MANAGEMENT. *Current Pos:* CONSULT, FISHERIES SCI & DEVELOP, AQUATIC ENVIRON, 76- *Personal Data:* b DeBruce, NY, Jan 5, 16; m 40, Mary Savage; c James S, William F III & Andrew H. *Educ:* Cornell Univ, BS, 37, PhD(vert zool), 43. *Prof Exp:* From aquatic biologist to fishery res biologist, US Fish & Wildlife Serv, 42-58; prof fisheries, Univ Wash, 58-72, dir, Fisheries Res Inst, 58-67, assoc dean col fisheries, 67-72; assoc dir, Nat Marine Fisheries Serv, 72-76. *Mem:* Fel AAAS; hon mem Am Fisheries Soc. *Res:* Population studies of fish; biological oceanography; life history of fishes; measurement and sampling techniques of fisheries; fishery policy; history of fishery management. *Mailing Add:* 12509 Greenwood Ave N No D-B211 Seattle WA 98133-8073

ROYCHOUDHURI, CHANDRASEKHAR, PHYSICS, OPTICS & PHOTONICS. *Current Pos:* DIR, PHOTONICS RES CTR, UNIV CONN, 92- *Personal Data:* b Barisal, India, Apr 7, 42; m 96, Minati Biswal; c Asim & Onnesha. *Educ:* Jadavpur Univ, BSc, 63, MSc, 65; Univ Rochester, PhD(optics), 73. *Prof Exp:* Sr lectr physics, Univ Kalyani, WBengal, India, 65-68; scientist optics, Nat Inst Astrophys & Optics, Puebla, Mex, 74-78; sr scientist, Space & Technol Group, TRW Systs, 78-86; mgr, Laser Systs, Electro-Optics Technol Div, Perkin Elmer, 86-89; chief scientist, Optics & Appl Technol Lab, United Technol Optical Systs, 89-91. *Concurrent Pos:* Fulbright Scholar, 68; Bd mem, Optical Soc Am; chair, Acad Comt Commun & Info Systs, Conn Acad Sci & Engr. *Mem:* Optical Soc Am; Soc Photo-Optical Instrumentation Engrs; Inst Elec & Electronics Engrs; Am Phys Soc. *Res:* Interferometry; holography; Fourier optics; spectroscopy; interference, diffraction and spectroscopy with ultra-short pulses; conceptual foundations of quantum mechanics; laser communication; applications of semiconductor lasers. *Mailing Add:* 7 Fieldstone Dr Storrs Mansfield CT 06268. *Fax:* 860-486-1033; *E-Mail:* chandra@eng2.conn.edu

ROYER, DENNIS JACK, CHEMICAL ENGINEERING. *Current Pos:* RES FEL & STAFF MEM, DUPONT CO, 85- *Personal Data:* b Lock Haven, Pa, May 24, 41; c 2. *Educ:* Pa State Univ, BS, 62, PhD(chem eng), 67; Carnegie Inst Technol, MS, 64. *Prof Exp:* Dir, Continental Oil Co, 68-80; dir eng res, Chem Res Div, Conoco Inc, 80-85. *Mem:* Am Inst Chem Engrs. *Res:* Petrochemical processes; production scale gas chromatography. *Mailing Add:* Du Pont Co 1007 Market St Wilmington DE 19898

ROYER, DONALD JACK, INORGANIC CHEMISTRY. *Current Pos:* RETIRED. *Personal Data:* b Newton, Kans, May 7, 28. *Educ:* Univ Kans, PhD(chem), 56. *Prof Exp:* From asst prof to prof chem, Ga Inst Technol, 56-93. *Mem:* AAAS; Am Chem Soc. *Res:* Complex inorganic compounds and inorganic stereochemistry. *Mailing Add:* 741 Dudley Lane Longmont CO 80503

ROYER, GARFIELD PAUL, BIOCHEMISTRY, CONTROLLED RELEASE OF MEDICINALS. *Current Pos:* PRES, BUFORD BIOMED, INC, 94- *Personal Data:* b Waynesboro, Pa, Dec 2, 42; m 66; c 3. *Educ:* Juniata Col, BS, 64; WVa Univ, PhD(biochem), 68. *Prof Exp:* NIH postdoctoral fel, Northwestern Univ, 68-70; from asst prof to prof biochem, Ohio State Univ, 70-83; prof biochem, Ohio State Univ, 70-82; mgr, Biotechnol Div, Naperville, Ill, 83-91, consult, 91-94. *Mem:* Am Soc Biol Chemists; Am Chem Soc. *Res:* Enzymology; immobilized enzymes and synthetic enzyme models; advanced drug-delivery systems. *Mailing Add:* PO Box 366 Cashtown PA 17310-0366. *E-Mail:* garroyer@aol.com

ROYER, THOMAS CLARK, PHYSICAL OCEANOGRAPHY. *Current Pos:* SLOVER PROF OCEANOG, OLD DOMINION UNIV, 96- *Personal Data:* b Battle Creek, Mich, Jan 2, 41; m 68, Susan E Burns; c Samantha B & Heather H. *Educ:* Albion Col, AB, 63; Tex A&M Univ, MS, 66, PhD(phys oceanog), 69. *Prof Exp:* From asst prof to prof phys oceanog, Univ Alaska, Fairbanks, 69-96. *Concurrent Pos:* Consult, Sci Applns Inc, Int, Dobrocky-Seatech, NSF, Greenhoun & O'Mora, Exxon; chmn, Bd J Ed, Am Geophys Union, 90-92. *Mem:* Am Geophys Union; Am Meteorol Soc; Sigma Xi; AAAS; Oceanog Soc. *Res:* Ocean circulation, especially the Alaskan Gyre; measurement of currents, water masses and air-sea interactions; long period ocean waves including tsunamis and storm surges. *Mailing Add:* Ctr Coastal Phys Oceanog Old Dominion Univ Norfolk VA 23529. *Fax:* 757-683-5550; *E-Mail:* royer@ccpo.odu.edu

ROYS, CHESTER CROSBY, invertebrate physiology, for more information see previous edition

ROYS, PAUL ALLEN, PHYSICS. *Current Pos:* RETIRED. *Personal Data:* b Evanston, Ill, Apr 3, 26; m 52; c 4. *Educ:* Ill Inst Technol, BS, 48, MS, 50, PhD(physics), 58. *Prof Exp:* Instr physics, Ill Inst Technol, 51-52; sr scientist, Atomic Power Div, Westinghouse Elec Corp, 52-57; from asst prof to assoc prof physics, Univ Wichita, 57-61; prof physics & chmn dept, Carroll Col, Wis, 61-92. *Concurrent Pos:* Consult, Beech Aircraft Corp, 58-61 & Dynex Co, 62-65. *Mem:* Am Phys Soc; Am Asn Physics Teachers; Sigma Xi. *Res:* Low energy nuclear physics; mechanics; instrumentation. *Mailing Add:* 2230 Woodfield Circle Waukesha WI 53188

ROYSE, DANIEL JOSEPH, PLANT PATHOLOGY, MYCOLOGY. *Current Pos:* from instr to assoc prof 78-92, PROF PLANT PATH, PA STATE UNIV, 92- *Personal Data:* b Olney, Ill, Aug 31, 50; m 72; c 2. *Educ:* Eastern Ill Univ, BS, 72, MS, 74; Univ Ill, Urbana, PhD(plant path), 78. *Prof Exp:* Res asst plant path, Univ Ill, 74-78, teaching asst, 75; teaching asst air pollution, Nat Univ Bogota, Colombia, 75. *Concurrent Pos:* Int consult to mushroom indust. *Mem:* Am Phytopath Soc; Mycol Soc Am; Am Mushroom Inst; World Soc Mushroom Biol Mushroom Prod. *Res:* Specialty mushrooms; molecular systematics and selective breeding of Agaricus bisporus and Lentinua edodes; cultivation of Shiitake, Pleurotus and morels on synthetic substrate; edible mushroom cultivation. *Mailing Add:* 316 Buckhout Lab Pa State Univ University Park PA 16802

ROYSTER, JULIA DOSWELL, AUDIOLOGY & OCCUPATIONAL HEARING CONSERVATION. *Current Pos:* vis instr, 86-88, ADJ ASST PROF, DIV SPEECH & HEARING SCI, UNIV NC, CHAPEL HILL, 89-; PRES, ENVIRON NOISE CONSULTS, INC, RALEIGH, NC, 77- *Personal Data:* b Chicago, Ill, Apr 9, 51; m 78, Larry H. *Educ:* Univ NC, Chapel Hill, BA, 72, MS, 75; NC State Univ, PhD, 81. *Prof Exp:* Speech pathologist & audiologist, Savannah Speech & Hearing Ctr, 75-76, Whitaker Rehab Ctr, Forsyth Mem Hosp, Winston-Salem, NC, 76-77 & Hearing & Speech Ctr, NC Mem Hosp, Chapel Hill, 77-78; instr, Dept Psychol, Meredith Col, Raleigh, NC, 79; intern, Gov Advocacy Coun for Persons with Disabilities, Raleigh, NC, 80; vis instr, Dept Psychol & Dept Speech Commun, NC State Univ, Raleigh, 81-82. *Concurrent Pos:* Mem, Tech Comt Noise, Acoust Soc Am, 87-, prog comt, Nat Hearing Conserv Asn, 90-; chair, Comt Regional Chap, Acoust Soc Am, 88-, Accredited Stand Comt Bioacoust, Am Nat Stand Inst, S3, 91-94; consult numerous co. *Mem:* Fel Acoust Soc Am; Am Speech-Lang-Hearing Asn; Nat Hearing Conserv Asn. *Res:* Applied research in occupational hearing conservation (including audiometric data analysis, motivating the correct use of hearing protection, and effective educational strategies); author of books, chapters and papers. *Mailing Add:* 4706 Connell Dr Raleigh NC 27612

ROYSTER, L(ARRY) H(ERBERT), ENGINEERING. *Current Pos:* res engr, 64-67, from instr to prof eng, 67-76, PROF MECH ENG & AEROSPACE ENG, NC STATE UNIV, 76- *Personal Data:* b Durham Co, NC, Sept 22, 36; m 77, Julie Doswell; c Larry Jr & Kirk. *Educ:* NC State Univ, BS, 59, PhD(eng), 68. *Prof Exp:* Res engr, NC State Univ, 59-61; sr dynamics engr, NAm Aviation, Inc, 61-64. *Concurrent Pos:* Consult to numerous industs. *Mem:* Fel Acoust Soc Am; Am Indust Hyg Asn. *Res:* Vibrations, noise control, hearing conservation; effects of noise and vibrations; machine design. *Mailing Add:* Dept Mech & Aerospace Eng NC State Univ Raleigh NC 27695-7910. *Fax:* 919-515-7968; *E-Mail:* 76570.3014@compuserve.com

ROYSTER, ROGER LEE, ANESTHESIOLOGY, CRITICAL CARE MEDICINE. *Current Pos:* from asst prof to assoc prof, 82-92, PROF & VCHMN DEPT ANESTHESIA, BOWMAN GRAY SCH MED, WAKE FOREST UNIV, 92- *Personal Data:* b Shelby, NC, Feb 10, 49; m 80, Mitzi; c Garrett. *Educ:* Univ NC, Chapel Hill, AB, 71; Bowman Gray Sch Med, MD, 76. *Prof Exp:* Resident internal med, NC Baptist Hosp, 76-78, fel cardiol, 78-80, resident anesthesiol, 80-82. *Concurrent Pos:* Oral bd examr, Am Bd Soc Anesthesiol, 88-, sr examiner, 92- *Mem:* Am Heart Asn; fel Am Col Cardiol; Int Anesthesia Res Soc; Am Soc Anesthesiol; Soc Crit Care Med. *Res:* Study of inotropic agents in the cardiac surgery paticut; measurements of myocardial blood flow during cardiac surgery; the cardiac electrophysiologic effects of anesthetic agents; health care reform. *Mailing Add:* Dept Anesthesia Bowman Gray Sch Wake Forest Univ Med Ctr Blvd Winston Salem NC 27157-1009

ROYSTER, WIMBERLY CALVIN, MATHEMATICS, SCIENCE ADMINISTRATION. *Current Pos:* VPRES, KY SCI & TECHNOL COUN, INC, LEXINGTON, 93- *Personal Data:* b Robards, Ky, Jan 12, 25; m 50, Betty Barnett; c David C & Paul B. *Educ:* Murray State Univ, BS, 46; Univ Ky, MA, 48, PhD(math), 52. *Prof Exp:* Asst math, Univ Ky, 46-48, instr, 48-52; asst prof, Auburn Univ, 52-56; from asst prof to assoc prof, Univ Ky, 56-62, chmn, Dept Math, 63-69, dean col arts & sci, 69-72, dean grad sch, 72-88, vchancellor res, 83-88, vpres res, 88-90, prof math, 62-92. *Concurrent Pos:* Mem, Inst Advan Study, 62 & Nat Res Coun, 72-75; mem bd dirs, Oak Ridge Assoc Univs, 78-84; mem bd dirs, Coun Grad Schs, 80-85; mem, Grad Rec Exam Bd, 80-85; chair, bd trustees, South-East Consortium Int Develop, 82-83 & Southeastern Univs Res Asn, 90-92. *Mem:* AAAS; Am Math Soc; Math Asn Am; Sigma Xi. *Res:* Geometric function theory; univalent function theory; expansion in orthonormal functions; approximate methods in difference equations; summability. *Mailing Add:* 773 Malabu Dr Lexington KY 40502. *Fax:* 606-259-0986; *E-Mail:* royster@pop.uky.edu

ROYSTON, RICHARD JOHN, COMPUTER SCIENCE. *Current Pos:* VPRES RES, AOI SYSTS INC, 85- *Personal Data:* b Windlesham, Eng, June 18, 31; US citizen; div; c 2. *Educ:* Oxford Univ, BA, 52, MA, 58; Univ London, BSc, 66. *Prof Exp:* Sci officer appl math, Atomic Energy Res Estab, 52-61; asst mathematician comput sci, Argonne Nat Lab, 62-65; vis scientist, Europ Orgn Nuclear Res, 65-66; assoc mathematician, Argonne Nat Lab, 66-69; sr consult, Scicon Ltd, 69-71; div dir appl math, Argonne Nat Lab, 71-85. *Mem:* Asn Comput Mach; fel Brit Comput Soc; sr mem Inst Elec & Electronics Engrs. *Res:* Networking; pattern recognition; operating systems; vision systems. *Mailing Add:* Aoi Int One Lowell Res Ctr 847 Rogers St Lowell MA 01852

ROYT, PAULETTE ANNE, MICROBIOLOGY. *Current Pos:* asst prof, 77-83, ASSOC PROF, DEPT BIOL, GEORGE MASON UNIV, 83- *Personal Data:* b Brooklyn, NY, June 14, 45; m 71. *Educ:* Am Univ, BS, 67, MS, 71; Univ Md, PhD(microbiol), 74. *Prof Exp:* Fel metab, Nat Heart, Lung & Blood Inst, 75-77. *Mem:* Am Soc Microbiol. *Res:* Protein degradation in microorganisms; glucose transport in yeast; iron transport in pseudomonas aeruginose. *Mailing Add:* 3614 Woodhill Pl Fairfax VA 22031

ROYTBURD, VICTOR, PARTIAL DIFFERENTIAL EQUATIONS. *Current Pos:* asst prof, 81-87, ASSOC PROF MATH, RENSSELAER POLYTECH INST, 87- *Personal Data:* b Moscow, USSR, Nov 28, 45; US citizen; c 2. *Educ:* Moscow State Univ, USSR, MS, 67; Univ Calif, Berkeley, PhD(appl math), 81. *Prof Exp:* Sr researcher, Krzhizhanovsky Energy Inst, Moscow, USSR, 70-79. *Concurrent Pos:* Vis mem, Courant Inst Math Sci, 85-86; sr res mathematician, Princeton Univ, 88-89. *Mem:* Soc Indust & Appl Math. *Res:* Partial differential equations of combustion theory and continuum mechanics; numerical methods for these equations. *Mailing Add:* 73 Fairlawn Dr Latham NY 12110

ROZAS, LAWRENCE PAUL, ESTUARINE ECOLOGY, FISHERY ECOLOGY. *Current Pos:* RES ECOLOGIST, NAT MARINE FISHERIES SERV, NAT OCEANIC & ATMOSPHERIC ADMIN, 92- *Personal Data:* b Cottonport La, Aug 8, 49; m 81, Donna M Gauthier; c Ryan P, Charles M, David J & Mary C. *Educ:* Univ Southwestern La, BS, 75; Univ NC, Wilmington, MS, 82; Univ Va, PhD(environ sci), 87. *Prof Exp:* Res assoc, US Army Chief Engrs, Waterways Exp Sta, Univ Va, 87-89; res assoc, La Univs Marine Consortium, 89-90, asst prof, 90-92. *Concurrent Pos:* Adj asst prof, Univ Southwestern La, 91- *Mem:* Ecol Soc Am; Estuarine Res Fedn; Am Fisheries Soc; Am Inst Biol Sci; Asn Southeastern Biologists; Soc Wetland Scientists. *Res:* Relationships between physical and biological factors in tidal marshes, compares ecological functions among different estuarine habitats, and addresses problems related to marsh habitat creation and restoration in coastal environments. *Mailing Add:* Nat Marine Fisheries Serv 4700 Avenue U Galveston TX 77551. *Fax:* 409-766-3508

ROZDILSKY, BOHDAN, NEUROPATHOLOGY. *Current Pos:* From assoc prof to prof, 64-88, res assoc prof, 56-88, EMER PROF NEUROPATH, UNIV SASK, 88- *Personal Data:* b Wola Ceklynska, Ukraine, Nov 22, 16; m 59; c 3. *Educ:* Univ Lvov, MD, 41; McGill Univ, MSc, 56; Univ Sask, PhD(neuropath), 58; FRCP(C). *Concurrent Pos:* Mem staff, Univ Sask Hosp, 57-, neuropathologist, 62-; lectr, Univ Sask, 59-64; consult, Ment Hosps, Sask. *Mem:* Am Asn Neuropath; Am Acad Neurol; fel Am Soc Clin Path; Can Asn Neuropath; Int Acad Path. *Res:* Cerebrovascular permeability; kernicterus; pathology of neurodegenerative diseases. *Mailing Add:* 515 Lake Crescent Saskatoon SK S7H 3A3 Can

ROZE, ULDIS, ECOLOGY. *Current Pos:* From instr to assoc prof, 64-90, PROF BIOL, QUEENS COL, NY, 91- *Personal Data:* b Riga, Latvia, Jan 3, 38; US citizen; m 66. *Educ:* Univ Chicago, BS, 59; Washington Univ, PhD(pharm), 64. *Concurrent Pos:* Chair, Queens Col, 96- *Mem:* AAAS; Ecol Soc Am; Am Soc Mammalogists. *Res:* Natural history of the porcupine. *Mailing Add:* 240-37 Depew Ave Douglaston NY 11363

ROZEE, KENNETH ROY, MICROBIOLOGY, VIROLOGY. *Current Pos:* RETIRED. *Personal Data:* b Halifax, NS, Feb 7, 31. *Educ:* Dalhousie Univ, BSc, 53, MSc, 55, PhD(microbiol), 58; Univ Toronto, dipl bact, 58. *Prof Exp:* Res asst biol, Dalhousie Univ, 55-59, asst prof, 59-62; assoc prof microbiol, Univ Toronto, 62-67; head dept, Dalhousie Univ, 74-84, prof microbiol, 68-97; staff mem, Dept Microbiol, LCDC, Tuney's Pasture. *Mailing Add:* Dept Microbiol Dalhousie Univ Halifax NS B3H 4H7 Can

ROZEK, CHARLES EDWARD, MOLECULAR GENETICS, RECOMBINANT DNA METHODS. *Current Pos:* asst prof, 83-89, ASSOC PROF, DEPT BIOL, CASE WESTERN RES UNIV, 89- *Personal Data:* b Detroit, Mich, Apr 6, 49. *Educ:* Mich State Univ, BS, 71; Wayne State Univ, PhD(molecular biol), 79. *Prof Exp:* Res assoc, Dept Chem, Calif Inst Technol, 79-83. *Mem:* AAAS; Genetics Soc Am; Am Soc Microbiol. *Res:* Regulation and expression of muscle genes during development of Drosophila. *Mailing Add:* Dept Biol Case Western Res Univ Cleveland OH 44106-1749. *Fax:* 216-368-4672; *E-Mail:* cer2@po.cwru.edu

ROZELLE, LEE T, PHYSICAL CHEMISTRY. *Current Pos:* CONSULT, 92- *Personal Data:* b Rheinlander, Wisc, Mar 9, 33. *Educ:* Univ Wis-Madison, BS, PhD(phys chem). *Honors & Awards:* Spes Hominum Award, Nat Sanit Found, 88; Robert Gans Award, Pac Water Qual Asn, 88; Award Merit, Water Qual Asn, 89. *Prof Exp:* Res chemist, E I du Pont de Nemours & Co, 60-63; prin res scientist & tech coord, Honeywell Inc, 63-67; dir chem div, NStar Res & Develop Inst, 67-74; vpres res & develop, USCI, 74-77; dir res & develop, Permutit Co, 77-80; vpres res & develop, Gelman Sci Inc, 80-82; vpres sci & technol, Culligan Int Co, 82-87; assoc dir res, Olin Corp, 87-92. *Mem:* Am Chem Soc; fel Am Inst Chemists; Water Qual Asn; Pac Water Qual Asn; Am Water Works Asn; Nat Spa & Pool Inst; Int Water Supply Asn; Water Pollution Control Fedn; Filtration Soc; AM Soc Artificial Int Organs; AAAS. *Res:* Thin film composite membranes for water desalination; multitech filtration system for giardia removal from drinking water; ion exhange, membrane and filtration products; residential dry chemical pool feeders. *Mailing Add:* 626 N 23rd St La Crosse WI 54601

ROZELLE, RALPH B, PHYSICAL CHEMISTRY. *Current Pos:* from asst prof to assoc prof, 62-66, chmn dept chem, 65-70, dir grad studies, 67-72, chmn div natural sci & math, 67-77, PROF CHEM, WILKES COL, 66-, DEAN HEALTH SCI, 74-, PROJ DIR, WILKES-HAHNAMANN COOP MED EVAL PROG FAMILY MED, 77- *Personal Data:* b West Wyoming, Pa, July 9, 32; m 57; c 3. *Educ:* Wilkes Col, BS, 54; Alfred Univ, PhD(chem), 61. *Prof Exp:* Instr chem, Alfred Univ, 60-62. *Mem:* Am Chem Soc. *Res:* Fuel cells; heterogeneous catalysis; inorganic chemistry of water pollution. *Mailing Add:* 21 Dana St Forty Fort Wilkes-Barre PA 18704-4104

ROZEMA, EDWARD RALPH, APPROXIMATION THEORY, NUMERICAL ANALYSIS. *Current Pos:* actg head, Dept Math, 93-94, PROF MATH, UNIV TENN, CHATTANOOGA, 73- *Personal Data:* b Chicago, Ill, Nov 16, 45; m 74; c 2. *Educ:* Calvin Col, AB, 67; Purdue Univ, MS, 69, PhD(math), 72. *Honors & Awards:* George Polya Award. *Prof Exp:* Vis asst prof math, Purdue Univ, Calumet Campus, 72-73. *Mem:* Math Asn Am; Soc Indust & Appl Math. *Res:* Numerical analysis; methods of teaching. *Mailing Add:* Univ Tenn Chattanooga TN 37401. *E-Mail:* erozema@utcvm.utc.edu

ROZEN, JEROME GEORGE, JR, SYSTEMATIC ENTOMOLOGY. *Current Pos:* assoc cur hymenoptera, 60-65, chmn dept entom, 60-71, dep dir res, 72-87, CUR, AM MUS NATURAL HIST, 65- *Personal Data:* b Evanston, Ill, Mar 19, 28; m 48, Barbara L Lindner; c Steven G, Kenneth C & James R. *Educ:* Univ Kans, BA, 50; Univ Calif, Berkeley, PhD, 55. *Prof Exp:* Asst instr biol, Univ Kans, 50, instr, 51; asst, Univ Calif, Berkeley, 51-55; entomologist, USDA, US Nat Mus, 56-58; asst prof entom, Ohio State Univ, 58-60. *Concurrent Pos:* Ed pub, Entom Soc Am, 59-60; pres, NY Entom Soc, 64-65. *Mem:* Fel AAAS; Entom Soc Am; Soc Syst Zool; Soc Study Evolution; Orgn Biol Field Stas (pres, 90). *Res:* Ethology, taxonomy and phylogeny of bees; taxonomy, ethology, phylogeny and morphology of Coleoptera larvae; evolution; insect morphology; zoogeography. *Mailing Add:* Am Mus Natural Hist Cent Park W at 79th St New York NY 10024. *Fax:* 212-769-5277

ROZENBERG, J(UDA) E(BER), STRUCTURAL ENGINEERING, CIVIL ENGINEERING. *Current Pos:* assoc prof, 70-79, PROF CIVIL ENG, TENN STATE UNIV, 80- *Personal Data:* b Bocicoul-Mare, Romania, Oct 12, 22; US citizen; m 55; c 4. *Educ:* Berchem Tech Sch Com & Admin, Antwerp, dipl, 39; Univ Notre Dame, BSCE, 63, MSCE, 65, PhD(civil eng), 67. *Prof Exp:* Traffic mgr int freight, Reliable Shipping Co, New York, 55-61; asst prof civil eng, Univ Notre Dame, 67-68 & Christian Bros Col, 68-70. *Concurrent Pos:* Consult, Wright-Patterson AFB Mat Lab, 78-79, Stone & Webster Engr Corp, Boston, Mass, 81-83. *Mem:* Biblical Archeol Soc. *Res:* Systems analysis of structures. *Mailing Add:* 400 N Wilson Blvd Nashville TN 37205-2416

ROZENDAL, DAVID BERNARD, CIVIL ENGINEERING. *Current Pos:* Asst prof, 60-65, ASSOC PROF CIVIL ENG, UNIV TEX, EL PASO, 69- *Personal Data:* b Chamberlain, SDak, Feb 4, 37; m 57, Maribel Smith; c 2. *Educ:* SDak Sch Mines & Technol, BS, 58; Univ Minn, MS, 60; Purdue Univ, PhD(struct eng), 74. *Mem:* Am Soc Civil Engrs. *Res:* Stress analysis; structural engineering. *Mailing Add:* 6368 Monarch Dr El Paso TX 79912

ROZGONYI, GEORGE A, MATERIALS SCIENCE. *Current Pos:* PROF, NC STATE UNIV, 82- *Personal Data:* b Brooklyn, NY, Apr 24, 37; m 63, Norrish Munson; c Amy, Suzanne & Jennifer. *Educ:* Univ Notre Dame, BS, 58, MS, 60; Univ Ariz, PhD(field emission micros), 64. *Honors & Awards:* Recipient Electronics Div Award, Electrochem Soc, 81. *Prof Exp:* Teaching fel eng sci, Univ Notre Dame, 58-60; instr mech eng, Univ Ariz, 60-61, res assoc, Field Emission Lab, 61-63; mem tech staff struct anal & thin film mat, Bell tel Labs, 63-82. *Concurrent Pos:* Electronics ed, J Electrochem Soc, 77-; vis scientist, Max Plank Inst, Stuttgart, WGer, 79-80, Ctr Nat d'Etudes Sci, Microelectronics Lab, Grenoble, France, 81. *Mem:* Am Phys Soc; Electrochem Soc; Am Asn Crystal Growth; Mat Res Soc. *Res:* Application of x-ray, electron diffraction and optical microscopy to the study of native and process-induced defects in films and substrates of metals and semiconductors; thin film growth; vacuum physics; crystal defects. *Mailing Add:* Dept Mat Sci & Eng NC State Univ Raleigh NC 27695-7916. *E-Mail:* rozgonyi@mte.ncsu.edu

ROZHIN, JURIJ, BIOCHEMISTRY. *Current Pos:* CONSULT, 88- *Personal Data:* b Kharkiv, Ukraine, USSR, Mar 19, 31; US citizen; m 60; c 1. *Educ:* Wayne State Univ, BS, 55, PhD(biochem), 67. *Prof Exp:* Res assoc biochem, Child Res Ctr Mich, Detroit, 61-63; fel biochem, Med Sch, Wayne State Univ, 67-69, instr, 71-77, asst prof, Dept Biochem, 77-88. *Concurrent Pos:* Res scientist, Mich Cancer Found, 69-81. *Mem:* Am Chem Soc; Sigma Xi; Am Asn Cancer Res. *Res:* Sulfation of steroids in normal and tumor tissue; promotion of carcinogens in the colon; hydrolases in the plasma membrane of tumor cells. *Mailing Add:* 34510 Richardo Dr Sterling Heights MI 48310-6127

ROZIER, CAROLYN K, ANATOMY. *Current Pos:* DEAN, SCH PHYS THER, TEX WOMAN'S UNIV, 73-, PROVOST, INST HEALTH SCI, 80- *Personal Data:* b Fulton, Mo, Aug 17, 44; div; c 1. *Educ:* Univ Mo, BS, 66; Univ Okla, MS, 71, PhD(anat sci), 72. *Prof Exp:* Staff phys therapist, Gen Leonard Wood Army Hosp, Mo, 66-67; educ coordr & phys therapist, St Anthony Hosp, Oklahoma City, 67-69; asst anat sci, Med Ctr, Univ Okla, 70-72; asst prof anat, Sch Med, Tex Tech Univ, 72-73. *Concurrent Pos:* Res asst, Civil Aeromed Inst, Fed Aviation Admin, Dept Transp, Oklahoma City, 72; instr, Oscar Rose Jr Col, 72. *Mem:* Am Phys Ther Asn. *Res:* Functional and neuroanatomical problems and problems in the field of rehabilitation. *Mailing Add:* 3882 Regent Dr Dallas TX 75229-5244

ROZIN, PAUL, FOOD SELECTION & ATTITUDES. *Current Pos:* from asst prof to assoc prof, 63-70, chmn dept, 78-81, PROF PSYCHOL, UNIV PA, 70- *Personal Data:* b Brooklyn, NY, Aug 3, 36; m 93, Monica Schindlinger; c 4. *Educ:* Univ Chicago, BA, 56; Harvard Univ, MA, 59, PhD(biol & psychol), 61. *Honors & Awards:* Curt Richter lectr psychol, Johns Hopkins Univ, 80; James Ford lectr psychol, Princeton Univ, 83; Edna Park lectr psychol, Univ Toronto, 84; Sigma Xi lectr psychol, Brooklyn Col, 84; F Starling Reid lectr psychol, Univ Va, 85; Robert I Watson lectr, Univ NH, 88. *Prof Exp:* Fel, NIH, 61-63. *Concurrent Pos:* John Simon Guggenheim Fel, 77; Hooker distinguished vis prof, McMaster Univ, 88. *Mem:* Am Psychol Soc; fel Inst Advan Study Behav Sci; Soc Exp Psychologists. *Res:* Biological, psychological and cultural approaches to human food selection; cross-cultural approach to food attitudes; cultural evolution, especially of the emotion of disgust. *Mailing Add:* Dept Psychol Univ Pa 3815 Walnut St Philadelphia PA 19104-6196. *Fax:* 215-898-1982; *E-Mail:* rozin@cattell.psych.upenn.edu

ROZMAN, KARL K, MECHANISM OF TOXICITY OF HALOGENATED AROMATIC HYDROCARBONS, TOXICOKINETICS & METABOLISM OF HALOGENATED AROMATIC HYDROCARBONS. *Current Pos:* from asst prof to assoc prof, 81-85, PROF, DEPT PHARMACOL TOXICOL & THERAPEUT, UNIV KANS MED CTR, 86-; HEAD SECT ENVIRON TOXICOL, INST TOXICOL, NEUHERBURG, GER, 89- *Personal Data:* b Nagycenk, Hungary, July 20, 45; m 77, Maria Tellez; c Marissa, Gabriella, Catarina & Alexandra. *Educ:* Realgymnasium, Austria, Matura, 63; Leopold Franzens Univ, Innsbruck, Cand phil, 70, Dr phil (org & pharm chem), 73. *Honors & Awards:* Carrie-Schneider Award, Ger Dermat Soc, 88. *Prof Exp:* Instr, Inst Org & Pharm Chem, Leopold Franzen's Univ, Austria, 70-73; adj asst prof, Dept Biol, NMex State Univ, Las Cruces, 78-80. *Concurrent Pos:* Res assoc chem, Inst Ecol Chem, Nat Res Ctr Environ & Health, Neuherberg, Ger, 74-77, group leader toxicol, 78-88; vis scientist math, Dept Exp Path, Am Cyanmid Co, 85; distinguished vis prof, NMex State Univ, Las Cruces, 90. *Mem:* Soc Ecotoxicol & Environ Safety; NY Acad Sci; AAAS; Soc Toxicol; Soc Toxicol Pathologists. *Res:* Mechanism of toxicity and toxicokinetics of halogenated hydrocarbons. *Mailing Add:* Bridenthal 1018 3901 Rainbow Blvd Kansas City KS 66160-7417

ROZMIAREK, HARRY, LABORATORY ANIMAL MEDICINE, GNOTOBIOLOGY. *Current Pos:* UNIV VET, PROF & DIR, LAB ANIMAL MED, UNIV PA, 87- *Personal Data:* b Pulaski, Wis, Mar 27, 39; m 62, Jane C Melrose; c Edward, Daniel, Carol & Andrew. *Educ:* Univ Minn, BS, 60, DVM, 62; Ohio State Univ, MS, 69, PhD(microbiol-immunol), 76. *Hon Degrees:* MS, Univ Pa, 87. *Honors & Awards:* Res Award, Am Asn Lab Animal Sci, 80, Griffin Award, 95; Charles River Prize, Am Vet Med Asn, 96. *Prof Exp:* Attend vet, Ft Meyer, Va, 62-64; post vet, Ft Wadsworth, NY, 65 & Ft Hamilton, NY, 65-67; chief vet med & surg, Med Res Lab, Edgewood Arsenal, Md, 69-72; chief lab animal med, Seato Med Res Lab, Bangkok, Thailand, 72-74; dir, Animal Resources Div, US Army Med Res Inst Infectious Dis, Fredrick, Md, 76-83; prof, Ohio State Univ, 83-87. *Concurrent Pos:* Consult, Am Asn Accreditation Lab Animal Care, 71-, Anemia & Malnutrit Res Ctr, Chiang Mai Univ, 72-74, US Army Surgeon Gen, 79-83 & US AID, 81-; prog site visitor & consult, Div Res Resources, NIH, 72-; bd dirs, Am Col Lab Animal Med, 76-79 & 92-94, Pub Responsible

Med & Res, 87-; assoc prof, Col Med, Pa State Univ, 76-83; mem, Comt Care & Use Animals, Nat Res Coun, 82-; vchmn, Am Ans Accreditation Lab Animal Care; bd trustees, Am Asn Accredited Lab Animal Med, 90- Mem: Am Asn Lab Animal Sci (pres, 83-84); Am Vet Med Asn; Am Soc Lab Animal Practr (secy-treas, 79-81, pres, 91-92); Am Col Lab Animal Med (pres, 97-98); Am Asn Accreditation Lab Animal Care. Res: Laboratory animal medicine; spontaneous, zoonotic and latent diseases in laboratory animals; comparative medicine studies using animals as models for human disease and illness; containment of hazardous agents and disease organisms; malaria; animal welfare. Mailing Add: 6491 Drexel Rd Philadelphia PA 19151. Fax: 215-898-0309

ROZNER, ALEXANDER, MATERIAL SCIENCE, MECHANICAL ENGINEERING. Current Pos: PRIN METALLURGIST, NAVAL SURFACE WARFARE CTR, DEPT NAVY, 64- Personal Data: b Krakow, Poland, 1929. Educ: Tech Univ Krakow, BS, 50, MS, 52; Notre Dame Univ, PhD(metal eng), 61. Prof Exp: Res metallurgist, E I Du Pont de Nemours, 61-64. Mem: Am Soc Metals. Mailing Add: 9441 Holbrook Lane Potomac MD 20854-3931

ROZSNYAI, BALAZS, PHYSICS, MATHEMATICS. Current Pos: SR PHYSICIST, LAWRENCE LIVERMORE LAB, UNIV CALIF, 64- Personal Data: b Szekesfehervar, Hungary, Nov 24, 29; US citizen. Educ: Eotvos Lorand Univ, Budapest, MS, 52; Univ Calif, Berkeley, PhD(physics), 60. Prof Exp: Physicist, Cent Res Inst Physics, Budapest, Hunagry, 52-56 & Int Bus Mach Corp, Calif, 60-64. Concurrent Pos: Asst prof, San Jose State Col, 61-63. Mem: Am Phys Soc. Res: Quantum chemistry; electron-molecular scattering; scattering theory; nuclear physics, especially nuclear shell model; optics; thermodynamics; mathematical physics. Mailing Add: Lawrence Livemore Nat Lab L023 PO Box 808 Livermore CA 94550

ROZZELL, THOMAS CLIFTON, ENVIRONMENTAL BIOLOGY, RADIATION BIOLOGY. Current Pos: assoc dir, 86-92, dep dir, 92-94, DIR FEL PROGS, NAT RES COUN, 94- Personal Data: b Gastonia, NC, Apr 5, 37; m 59, Maryann Gay; c Liane, Eric & Jon. Educ: Fisk Univ, BS, 59; Univ Cincinnati, MS, 60; Univ Pittsburgh, ScD(environ radiation), 68. Prof Exp: Radiochemist, USPHS, 60-65; res assoc environ radiation, Univ Pittsburgh, 66-68, asst prof, 68-71; sci officer, Off Naval Res, 71-86. Concurrent Pos: Consult, Bur Health, Manpower & Educ, USPHS, 69-71; Sci Appln Int Corp, 89-91, Europ Bioelectromagnetics Res Ctr, 91-, NIH, 93-; spec asst to vchancellor health professions, Univ Pittsburgh, 70-71. Mem: Health Physics Soc; Int Microwave Power Inst; Bioelectromagnetics Soc; AAAS; Europ Bioelectromagnetics Asn. Res: Radioecology; effect of environmental radiation on man; biological effects of electromagnetic energy, including microwaves, lasers, radio frequency and extremely low frequency fields; bioelectromagnetics. Mailing Add: 3422 Barkley Dr Fairfax VA 22031. Fax: 202-334-3419; E-Mail: trozzell@nas.edu

ROZZI, TULLIO, WAVEGUIDE FIELDS & DISCONTINUITIES, MILLIMETRIC CIRCUITS & ANTENNAS. Current Pos: PROF ELEC ENG, UNIV ANCONA, ITALY, 86-, HEAD, DEPT ELEC ENG, 95- Personal Data: b Civitanova, Italy, Sept 13, 41; Brit & Ital citizen; m 67; c 2. Educ: Pisa Univ, Italy, dottore, 65; Leeds Univ, UK, PhD(elec eng), 68; Bath Univ, DSc, 87. Honors & Awards: Microwave Prize, Inst Elec & Electronics Engrs, 75. Prof Exp: Res scientist, Philips Res Labs, Eindhoven, Holland, 68-78; prof elec eng, Univ Liverpool, UK, 78-81; prof & head electronics, Univ Bath, UK, 81-91. Concurrent Pos: Vis prof, Dept Elec Eng, Univ Ill, Urbana, 75 & Sch Elec Eng, Bath Univ, UK, 92- Mem: Fel Inst Elec & Electronics Engrs; fel Inst Elec & Electronics Engrs UK. Res: Microwave theory and techniques, in particular waveguide fields and discontinuities; integrated optics, planar waveguides; millimetric circuits and antennas; filters; multiplexers. Mailing Add: Dept Electronics & Control Fac Eng Univ Ancona Via Brecce Bianche Ancona 60131 Italy. Fax: 71-2204-8834; E-Mail: t.rozzi@sirio.em.ee.uniam.it

RUBANYI, GABOR MICHAEL, ANIMAL PHYSIOLOGY, MEDICINE. Current Pos: DIR VASCULAR & ENDOTHELIAL RES, BERLEX BIOSCI, 92- Personal Data: b Budapest, Hungary, Jan 7, 47; m 73; c 2. Educ: Semmelweis Med Univ, Hungary, MD, 71; Hungarian Nat Acad Sci, PhD, 80. Prof Exp: Vis prof physiol, Dept Obstet Gynec, Wash Univ, 75-76; assoc prof physiol, Dept Physiol, Semmelweis Med Univ, 71-82; vis prof physiol, Univ Cincinnati Col Med, 82-83; asst prof, Dept Physiol & Biophys, Mayo Clin & Found, 83-86; head cardiovasc pharmacol, Schering-Plough Co, 86-87; dir pharmacol, Belex Labs Inc, 87-90; dir, Inst Pharmacol, Schering Ag, 90-92. Concurrent Pos: Ed, Int J Cardiol & Am J Physiol, Heart & Circulation, 86-, Hypertension, 89-, J Vascular Med Biol, 90- Mem: Am Physiol Soc; fel Am Heart Asn; Int Union Pure & Appl Chem; Europ Soc Clin Invest; Int Soc Oxygen Transp & Tissue. Res: Role of trace metals in ischemic coronary heart diseases; role of endothelium and endothelium-derived vasoactive factors in the normal control and pathophysiology of the cardiovascular system; molecular mechanism of antiatherosclerotic effect of estrogen. Mailing Add: Berlex Biosci Berlex Labs Inc 15049 San Pablo Ave Richmond CA 94804. Fax: 510-669-4246

RUBAS, WERNER, DRUG DELIVERY. Current Pos: SCIENTIST, GENENTECH, INC, 91- Personal Data: b Vienna, Austria, Jan 1, 55; Swiss citizen; m 92, Claudia Kunzler. Educ: ETH-Zurich, Switz, PhD(pharmaceut), 86. Prof Exp: Teaching pharmaceut, Inst Pharm, ETH-Zurich, 86-89; fel, Syntex Res, 89-91. Mem: Am Asn Pharmaceut Scientists; Controlled Release Soc; Mat Res Soc. Res: Mechanistic studies of drug transport across biological membranes, such as skin, intestine and cell monolagers. Mailing Add: Genetech Inc 460 Point San Bruno Ave South San Francisco CA 94080. Fax: 650-225-1418; E-Mail: wr@genie.gene.com

RUBATZKY, VINCENT E, PLANT PHYSIOLOGY, HORTICULTURE. Current Pos: EXTEN VEG CROPS SPECIALIST, UNIV CALIF, DAVIS, 64-, AGRICULTURALIST, COOP EXTEN SERV, 73-, VPRES AGR SCI, VEG CROPS EXTEN, 73- Personal Data: b New York, NY, Oct 24, 32; m 56; c 2. Educ: Cornell Univ, BS, 56; Va Polytech Inst, MS, 60; Rutgers Univ, PhD(plant physiol, biochem, hort), 64. Mem: AAAS; Am Soc Hort Sci. Res: Herbicidal selectivity; biochemistry of tomato internal browning related to tobacco mosaic virus; spacing relating to mechanization and use of growth regulating chemicals. Mailing Add: 3233 Chesapeake Bay Ave Davis CA 95616

RUBBERT, PAUL EDWARD, AERODYNAMICS, MANAGEMENT OF RESEARCH. Current Pos: Res scientist aerodyn, 60-62 & 65-72, supvr aerodyn res, 72-84, UNIT CHIEF, AERODYNAMICS RES, BOEING CO, 84-, TECH FEL, 90- Personal Data: b Minneapolis, Minn, Feb 18, 37; m 89, Rita Dachs; c Mark, David & Stephen. Educ: Univ Minn, BS, 58, MS, 60; Mass Inst Technol, PhD(aerodyn), 65. Honors & Awards: Arch T Colwell Merit Award, Soc Automotive Engrs, 68; Cert Recognition, NASA; Outstanding Tech Mat Award, Am Inst Aeronaut & Astronaut, Wright Brothers Medal; James R & Shirley A Kliegel Lectr, Calif Inst Technol, 96. Concurrent Pos: Assoc ed, J Am Inst Aeronaut & Astronaut, 75-78; mem subcomt, Aerospace Res & Technol, NASA; vis comt, Dept Aeronaut & Astronaut, Mass Inst Technol. Mem: Nat Acad Eng; Sigma Xi; fel Am Inst Aeronaut & Astronaut. Res: Computational fluid dynamics including hydrodynamics; subsonic, transonic and supersonic flows; viscous and inviscid phenomena; steady and unsteady flows; management of research; granted 3 patents; author of over 60 publications. Mailing Add: 20131 SE 23rd Pl Issaquah WA 98029. Fax: 425 865-2776

RUBBIA, CARLO, PHYSICS. Current Pos: mem staff, Lab Particle Physics, Europ Org Nuclear Res, 87-89, gen dir, 89-93, SR PHYSICIST, CERN EUROP LAB PARTICLE PHYSICS, 61- Personal Data: b Gorizia, Italy, Mar 31, 34. Educ: Rome Univ, PhD(physics). Hon Degrees: Numerous from US & foreign univs, 83-94. Honors & Awards: Nobel Prize Physics, 84; Enrico Fermi Lectr; Philip-Burton-Moon Lectr, 84; Bakerian Lectr, 85; Weizmann Lectr, 86; Primakoff Lectr, 86; Sanremo Primavera Prize, 88; Dirac Lectr, 89; Kroton Prize Sci, 91; Prize La Rana d'Oro, 91; Prize Corradi, 92; Heisenberg Lectr, 92; Gold Medal, Ital Phys Soc; Prize Michelangelo, 95. Prof Exp: Prof physics, Harvard Univ, 72-87. Concurrent Pos: Higgins prof physics, Harvard Univ, 70-88. Mem: Foreign mem Nat Acad Sci; Am Acad Arts & Sci; foreign mem Royal Soc; foreign mem Polish Acad Sci; foreign mem USSR Acad Sci; Europ Acad Sci; Ital Acad Advan Studies Am. Mailing Add: CERN Europ Lab Particle Physics CH 1211 Geneva 23 Switzerland

RUBEGA, ROBERT A, ACOUSTICS. Current Pos: RETIRED. Personal Data: b Blackstone, Mass, Aug 2, 27; m 54; c 8. Educ: Univ RI, BS, 51; Univ Rochester, MS, 61, PhD(elec eng), 66. Honors & Awards: Stromberg Carlson Award, 59. Prof Exp: Physicist, US Navy Underwater Sound Lab, 51-56; staff mem res acoust, Gen Dynamics/Electronics, 56-63 mem acoust labs, 63-65, mgr info sci lab, 65-68; dir marine tech serv, Marine Resources Inc, 68-71; supvr physicist, US Naval Underwater Systs Ctr, 71-87. Concurrent Pos: Asst, Univ Rochester, 63-65. Mem: Acoust Soc Am. Res: Acoustics and techniques of signal processing. Mailing Add: 19 Woodland Dr Groton CT 06340

RUBEL, EDWIN W, NEUROBIOLOGY. Current Pos: ASSOC PROF OTOLARYNGOL & PHYSIOL, UNIV VA MED CTR, 77- Personal Data: b Chicago, Ill, May 8, 42; m 63; c 1. Educ: Mich State Univ, BS, 64, MA, 67, PhD(psychol), 69. Prof Exp: Asst physiol psychol, Mich State Univ, 64-66, res asst neurobiol, 66-68; NIMH fel, Univ Calif, Irvine, 69-71; asst prof psychobiol, Yale Univ, 71-77. Mem: AAAS; Am Asn Anatomists; Psychonomic Soc; Sigma Xi. Res: Neuroembryology; behavior development; ethology. Mailing Add: Hearing Develop Lab RL 30 Univ Wash Seattle WA 98195

RUBEL, LEE ALBERT, mathematics; deceased, see previous edition for last biography

RUBEN, HARVEY L, GENERAL ADULT PSYCHIATRY, COMMUNITY MENTAL HEALTH. Current Pos: from asst clin prof to assoc clin prof, 76-93, DIR CONTINUING EDUC, DEPT PSYCHIAT, YALE UNIV SCH MED, 87-, CLIN PROF, 93-; PVT PRACT, 79- Personal Data: b St Louis, Mo, July 25, 41, m; c Adam, Justin & Marc. Educ: Univ Pittsburgh, BS, 63; Northwestern Univ Med Sch, MD, 66; Harvard Sch Pub Health, MPH, 68. Prof Exp: Exec dir, Home Health Care Conn, Inc, 76-78; assoc clin prof, Dept Psychiat, Univ Conn Sch Med, 78-92. Concurrent Pos: Actg dir, Psychiat Emergency Serv, Yale-New Haven Hosp, 82-83; supv psychiatrist, Emergency Serv, Hosp St Raphael, 83-87; Mem, Laughlin Fel Comt, Am col Psychiatrists, 86-89; bd dir, Group Advan Psychiat, 89-91; vpres, Acad Radio & Television Health Communicators, 91-93, pres, 93- Mem: Am Asn Geriatric Psychiat; fel Am Psychiat Asn; Group Advan Psychiat; Am Med Asn; Am Pub Health Asn; fel Am Col Psychiatrists. Res: Presenting psychiatric and mental health topics to non-psychiatric medical and lay audiences via the electronic and print media. Mailing Add: 77 Knollwood Dr New Haven CT 06515

RUBEN, JOHN ALEX, MORPHOLOGY. Current Pos: ASST PROF ZOOL, ORE STATE UNIV, 75- Personal Data: b Los Angeles, Calif, Jan 5, 47; m 73. Educ: Humboldt State Col, BS, 68; Univ Calif, Berkeley, MA, 70. Mem: Soc Vert Paleontologists; AAAS. Res: Functional morphology and physiology of reptiles. Mailing Add: Dept Zool Ore State Univ 3029 Cordley Hall Corvallis OR 97331-2914

RUBEN, LAURENS NORMAN, IMMUNOLOGY. *Current Pos:* RETIRED. *Personal Data:* b New York, NY, May 14, 27; m 50, Judith M Starr; c Bruce, Ellen & Barbara. *Educ:* Univ Mich, AB, 49, MS, 50; Columbia Univ, PhD(zool), 54. *Prof Exp:* Asst, Columbia Univ, 50-53; Nat Cancer Inst fel, Princeton Univ, 54-55; from instr to prof, Reed Col, 55-92, chmn dept, 73-87. *Concurrent Pos:* Vis NATO prof, Dept Human Morphol, Queens Med Ctr, Univ Nottingham, UK. *Mem:* AAAS; Am Soc Zool; Soc Develop Biol; Int Soc Develop & Comp Immunol (pres elect, 86, pres, 88-91); Am Asn Immunologists. *Res:* The evolution and development of humoral immune responses; hapten-carrier immunization of amphibian model systems which represent evolutionary, developmental, anatomical and physiological immunologic progressions. *Mailing Add:* Dept Biol Reed Col 3203 SE Woodstock Blvd Portland OR 97202-8199. *Fax:* 503-777-7773; *E-Mail:* ruben@reed.edu

RUBEN, MORRIS P, PERIODONTOLOGY, ORAL BIOLOGY. *Current Pos:* From asst prof to prof stomatol, 60-73, asst dean, Sch Grad Dent, 61-64, assoc dean grad studies, 69-77, PROF ORAL BIOL, CHMN DEPT & PROF PERIODONT, SCH GRAD DENT, BOSTON UNIV, 73- *Personal Data:* b East Liverpool, Ohio, Aug 27, 19; m 43; c 1. *Educ:* Ohio State Univ, BSc, 40; Loyola Univ, La, DDS, 43; Univ Pa, cert periodont & Boston Univ, cert periodont oral med, 61; Am Bd Periodont, dipl, 66. *Concurrent Pos:* Nat Inst Dent Res fel periodont, Grad Sch Med, Univ Pa, 59-60 & fel stomatol, Sch Med, Boston Univ, 60-61; consult pediat periodont, Kennedy Mem Hosp, Boston; attend dent surgeon, Beth Israel Hosp, Boston. *Mem:* Fel Am Col Dent; Am Acad Periodont; Am Dent Asn; fel Am Acad Dent Sci; fel Int Col Dent. *Mailing Add:* 80 Elinor Rd Newton MA 02161

RUBEN, REGINA LANSING, EXPERIMENTAL ONCOLOGY, DRUG SAFETY SURVEILLANCE & PHARMACOVIGILANCE. *Current Pos:* prin res scientist, DuPont Co, 82-88, prod info scientist, 89-90, sr drug scientist prod safety, 91-94, PROD SAFETY MGR, DUPONT MERCK PHARMACEUT CO, 95- *Personal Data:* b Newark, NJ, Jan 2, 50; m 75, Jeffrey M; c Adam J & Rachel A. *Educ:* Univ Rochester, BA, 72; Ohio State Univ, MS, 74, PhD(anat), 75. *Prof Exp:* Fel anat, Col Med, Univ Ill, 75-78; sr instr, Hahnemann Univ, 78-79, asst prof anat, 79-82, prin investr, 86-88. *Mem:* Soc InVitro Biol; Am Asn Anatomists; Sigma Xi; Am Asn Cancer Res; Drug Info Asn. *Res:* In vitro characterization of human tumor cells; in vitro assessment of novel cancer chemotherapeutic agents; in vitro and ex vitro assessment of novel immunostimulants, cell senescence; in vitro chemical carcinogenesis. *Mailing Add:* DuPont Merck Pharmaceut Co DuPont Merck Plaza-Hickory Run 1128 Wilmington DE 19805

RUBEN, ROBERT JOEL, PEDIATRIC OTOLARYNGOLOGY, DEVELOPMENTAL BIOLOGY. *Current Pos:* PROF OTOLARYNGOL & CHMN DEPT, ALBERT EINSTEIN COL MED, 70-, PROF PEDIAT. *Personal Data:* b New York, NY, Aug 2, 33; m 56; c 4. *Educ:* Princeton Univ, AB, 55; Johns Hopkins Univ, MD, 59. *Prof Exp:* Dir neurophysiol, Sch Med Johns Hopkins Univ, 58-64; res assoc exp embryol, NIH, 65-68; asst prof otolaryngol, Med Ctr, NY Univ, 66-70. *Concurrent Pos:* Attend otolaryngol surg, Montefiore & Morrisania Hosps, 70-; attend & chmn, Dept Otolaryngol, Lincoln Hosp, 71-77; chmn dept, Bronx Munic Hosp Ctr, 71-; attend physician, Albert Einstein Col Med, 71- *Mem:* Acoust Soc Am; Am Asn Anat; Am Acad Ophthal & Otolaryngol; Am Otological Soc; Am Asn Hist Med; Sigma Xi; Asn Res Otolaryngol (pres); Am Soc Pediat Otolaryngol (pres). *Res:* Normal and diseased states of the inner ear, particularly physiological, genetic, cellular pathological, embryological and behavior aspects of genetic deafness. *Mailing Add:* 1025 Fifth Ave Apt 12-C New York NY 10028

RUBENFELD, LESTER A, MATHEMATICAL PHYSICS. *Current Pos:* asst prof, 67-72, ASSOC PROF MATH, RENSSELAER POLYTECH INST, 72- *Personal Data:* b New York, NY, Dec 30, 40; m 64. *Educ:* Polytech Inst Brooklyn, BS, 62; NY Univ, MS, 64, PhD(math), 66. *Prof Exp:* Fel, Courant Inst Math Sci, NY Univ, 66-67. *Mem:* Am Math Soc; Soc Indust & Appl Math. *Res:* Wave propagation in elasticity and electromagnetic theory and asymptotic expansions arising from these fields. *Mailing Add:* Dept Math Rensselaer Polytech Inst Troy NY 12181

RUBENS, SIDNEY MICHEL, PHYSICS. *Current Pos:* CONSULT, 75- *Personal Data:* b Spokane, Wash, Mar 21, 10; m 44; c 1. *Educ:* Univ Wash, BS, 34, PhD(physics), 39. *Honors & Awards:* Meritorious Civilian Serv Award, USN, 45; Info Storage Award, Inst Elec & Electronics Engrs Magnetics Soc, 87. *Prof Exp:* Instr physics, Univ Southern Calif, 39-40; res assoc, Univ Calif, Los Angeles, 40-41; from assoc physicist to physicist, US Naval Ord Lab, 41-46; sr physicist, Eng Res Assocs, Inc, 46-51, staff physicist, 51-52; dir physics, Univac Div, Sperry Rand Corp, 52-55, mgr physics dept, 55-60, mgr phys res, 60-61, dir res, 61-66, staff scientist, Defense Systs Div, 66-69, dir spec projs, Univac Fed Systs Div, 69-71, dir spec tech activities, Defense Systs Div, 71-75. *Concurrent Pos:* Mem res & technol adv subcomt instrumentation & data processing, NASA, 67-69; hon fel, Univ Minn, 77- *Mem:* AAAS; Am Phys Soc; Optical Soc Am; Am Geophys Union; fel Inst Elec & Electronics Engrs. *Res:* Plasma physics; solid state; ferromagnetism; thin films; optics; magnetic measurements; digital computer components; information processing. *Mailing Add:* 1077 Sibley Hwy Apt 506 St Paul MN 55118

RUBENSON, J(OSEPH) G(EORGE), ELECTRONIC & SYSTEMS ENGINEERING. *Current Pos:* RETIRED. *Personal Data:* b Newburgh, NY, Aug 7, 20; m 43; c 3. *Educ:* City Col New York, BS, 40; Polytech Inst Brooklyn, MEE, 46. *Prof Exp:* Proj engr, Nat Union Radio Corp, 41-46 & Polytech Res & Develop Corp, 46-51; sect head, Airborne Instruments Lab, Inc, 51-58; eng specialist, Sylvania Elec Prod, Inc, Gen Tel & Electronics Corp, 58-60; mgr systs div, Watkins-Johnson Co, 60-64; sr res engr, Stanford Res Inst, SRI Int, Calif, 64-70, dir syst eval dept, 70-71, dir, Washington, 71-78; prog mgr, Syst Planning Corp, San Diego, 78-84, dir, 84-89. *Concurrent Pos:* Instr, Polytech Inst Brooklyn, 46-50. *Mem:* Sigma Xi; Inst Elec & Electronics Engrs. *Res:* Electron tubes; industrial electronics; electronic countermeasures; microwave components; electronic reconnaissance; electronic systems; radar systems. *Mailing Add:* 3826 Liggett Dr San Diego CA 92106-2024

RUBENSTEIN, ABRAHAM DANIEL, PUBLIC HEALTH. *Current Pos:* HOSP CONSULT, 69- *Personal Data:* b Lynn, Mass, Nov 19, 07; m 37; c 3. *Educ:* Harvard Univ, AB, 28, MPH, 40; Boston Univ, MD, 33; Am Bd Prev Med, dipl. *Prof Exp:* Intern & res med, Brockton Hosp, 33-35; house officer internal med, Boston City Hosp, 35-36; epidemiologist, Mass Dept Pub Health, 37-42, dist health officer, 42-47, dir, Div Hosp Surv & Construct, 47-50, dir, Div Hosps, 50-54, dir, Bur Hosp Facils & dep comnr, 54-69. *Concurrent Pos:* From asst prof to assoc clin prof, Sch Pub Health, Harvard Univ, 48-60, Simmons Col, 50-59, Boston Col, 50-71 & Sch Med, Tufts Univ, 71-73; sr lectr food sci & nutrit, Mass Inst Technol, 71-74, vis prof, 68-70; pres & trustee, New Eng Sinai Hosp; consult, Jewish Mem Hosp & Beth Israel Hosp, Boston. *Mem:* AMA; Am Pub Health Asn; Am Hosp Asn; Asn Teachers Prev Med; fel Am Col Prev Med. *Res:* Epidemiology of Salmonellosis; medical care programs. *Mailing Add:* 164 Ward St Newton MA 02159-1327

RUBENSTEIN, ALBERT HAROLD, INDUSTRIAL ENGINEERING, TECHNOLOGY MANAGEMENT. *Current Pos:* dir, Eng Mgt Prog, 77-92, PROF INDUST ENG & MGT SCI, NORTHWESTERN UNIV, 59-, WALTER P MURPHY PROF, 86-, DIR, CTR INFO & TELECOMMUN TECHNOL, 86- *Personal Data:* b Philadelphia, Pa, Nov 11, 23; m 49, Hildotte Grossman; c Michael & Lisa. *Educ:* Lehigh Univ, BS, 49; Columbia Univ, MS, 50, PhD(indust eng & mgt), 54. *Hon Degrees:* DSc, Lehigh Univ, 93. *Prof Exp:* Asst to pres, Perry Equip Corp, 40-43; res assoc indust eng, Columbia Univ, 50-53; asst prof indust mgt, Mass Inst Technol, 54-59. *Concurrent Pos:* Ed, Transactions, Inst Elec & Electronics Engrs, 59-85; dir studies col res & develop, Inst Mgt Sci, 60; dir, Narragansett Capital Corp, 60-83; vis prof, Sch Bus, Univ Calif, Berkeley, 64; pres, Int Appl Sci & Technol Assocs, Inc, 77-, Sr Strategy Group, 94-; adj prof, Univ Calif, San Diego, 96- *Mem:* Fel Soc Appl Anthrop; fel Inst Elec & Electronics Engrs; Inst Mgt Sci; fel AAAS. *Res:* Organization, economics and management of research and development and innovation; field research on organizational behavior; empirical, experimental and policy research or technology management. *Mailing Add:* Dept Indust Eng & Mgt Sci Northwestern Univ Evanston IL 60208

RUBENSTEIN, ALBERT MARVIN, PHYSICS, ADVANCED WEAPON SYSTEMS. *Personal Data:* b New York, NY, May 9, 18; m 44; c 2. *Educ:* Brooklyn Col, BA, 39; Univ Md, MS, 49. *Honors & Awards:* Civilian Meritorious Awards, US Navy Bur Ships, 54 & Off Naval Res, 59. *Prof Exp:* Lab asst & specif engr, Micamold Radio Corp, NY, 41-42; unit head submarine radar design, Bur Ships, US Dept Navy, 45-51, mem planning staff in charge of air defense & atomic warfare, Electronics Div, 51-54; head planning staff, 54-56, surveillance warfare syst coordr, Off Naval Res, 56-59; asst chief, Ballistic Missile Defense Br, Adv Res Projs Agency, US Dept Defense, 59-60, actg & asst dir, Ballistic Missile Defense Off, 60-61, asst dir, Ballistic Missile Defense Eng Off, 61-64; tech staff mem, Inst Defense Anal, 64-68; asst dir, Advan Sensor Off, Advan Res Proj Agency, 68-71, dep dir, 71-73; res staff mem, Sci & Technol Div, Inst Defense Anal, 73-94. *Concurrent Pos:* Lectr exten div, Univ Md, 53 & Dept Agr grad sch, 54-60; lectr exten div, Univ Va, 58-59. *Mem:* Am Phys Soc; NY Acad Sci. *Res:* Electronics; radar; air defense; ballistic missile defense systems and space technology; advanced sensors; optics; electro-optics solid state detectors; space systems; reconnaissance and systems analyses; seismic studies and detection of nuclear detonations. *Mailing Add:* 2709 Navarre Dr Chevy Chase MD 20815

RUBENSTEIN, ARTHUR HAROLD, MEDICINE, ENDOCRINOLOGY. *Current Pos:* From asst prof to assoc prof, 68-74, assoc chmn dept, 74-81, PROF MED, UNIV CHICAGO, 74-, CHMN DEPT, 81- *Personal Data:* b Germiston, SAfrica, Dec 28, 37; m 62, Denise Hack; c Jeffrey L & Errol C. *Educ:* Univ Witwatersrand, MBBCh(med), 60. *Honors & Awards:* Lilly Award, Am Diabetes Asn, 73, Banting Medal, 83, S Berson Prize, 85; Sci Award, Juv Diabetes Found, 77; John Phillips Mem Award, Am Col Physicians, 95. *Concurrent Pos:* Smith & Nephew fel, Postgrad Sch Med, Univ London, 65-66; Schweppe Award, Schweppe Found, 70-73; estab investr, Am Diabetes Asn, 75; mem adv coun, Nat Inst Health, Arthritis, Metab Diabetes & Digestive Dis, 77-80 & chmn, Nat Diabetes Adv Bd, 81-; Robert Williams distinguished chair med, Am Prof Med, 97. *Mem:* Inst Med-Nat Acad Sci; master Am Col Physicians; Asn Am Physicians; Endocrine Soc; Am Soc Clin Invest; Am Diabetes Asn; Am Acad Arts & Sci. *Res:* Diabetes mellitus; insulin biosynthesis and secretion; proinsulin; C-peptide; obesity; insulin resistance; immunoassay of hormones and lipoprotein peptides; lipoprotein metabolism. *Mailing Add:* Dept Med MC 6092 Univ Chicago/5841 S Maryland Ave Chicago IL 60637-1470. *Fax:* 773-702-4427; *E-Mail:* arthur@medicine.bsd.uchicago.edu

RUBENSTEIN, DANIEL IAN, BEHAVIORAL ECOLOGY. *Current Pos:* from asst prof to assoc prof, 80-90, PROF, DEPT ECOL & EVOLUTIONARY BIOL, PRINCETON UNIV, 90- *Personal Data:* m 72, Nancy; c Dustin & Alison. *Educ:* Univ Mich, BS, 72; Duke Univ, PhD(zool), 77. *Hon Degrees:* MA, Univ Cambridge, 78. *Prof Exp:* Jr res fel, Kings Col, Cambridge Univ, 77-80. *Concurrent Pos:* NSF-NATO postdoctoral fel,

78-79; presidential young investr award, NSF, 84-90; vis prof, Duke Univ, 85; Japan Soc Prom Sci fel, 93. *Mem:* Sigma Xi; Animal Behav Soc; Ecol Soc Am; Brit Ecol Soc; Soc Conserv Biol; Soc Study Evolution; Int Soc Behav Ecol. *Res:* Adaptive value of animal behavior; focus on understanding how an individual's foraging, mating and social behavior is shaped by its phenotype, ecological circumstances and the actions of other members of the population; applying behavioral ecological principles to understanding population dynamics of flourishing and endangered species. *Mailing Add:* Dept Ecol & Evolutionary Biol Princeton Univ Princeton NJ 08544-1003. *Fax:* 609-258-6818; *E-Mail:* dir@princeton.edu

RUBENSTEIN, EDWARD, INTERNAL MEDICINE. *Current Pos:* ASSOC DEAN POSTGRAD MED EDUC, SCH MED, STANFORD UNIV, 72-, PROF MED, 77- *Personal Data:* b Cincinnati, Ohio, Dec 5, 24; m 54; c 3. *Educ:* Univ Cincinnati, MD, 47. *Honors & Awards:* Kaiser Award, 89; Albion Walter Hewlett Award, 93. *Prof Exp:* Asst, Univ Cincinnati, 46-47; intern internal med, Cincinnati Gen Hosp, Ohio, 47-48, asst resident, 48-50; asst resident, Ward Serv, Barnes Hosp, 52-53; clin instr, Univ Cincinnati, 53-54. *Concurrent Pos:* Ed-in-chief, Sci Am Med. *Mem:* Inst Med-Nat Acad Sci; fel AAAS; fel Royal Soc Med; master Am Col Physicians; Am Clin & Climat Asn. *Res:* Synchrotron radiation; thromboembolism. *Mailing Add:* Dept Med Stanford Univ Sch Med Stanford CA 94305

RUBENSTEIN, HOWARD S, MEDICAL SCIENCES, GENERAL MEDICINE. *Current Pos:* MED CONSULT, DEPT SOCIAL SERV, STATE CALIF, 89- *Personal Data:* b Chicago, Ill, June 14, 31; m 68, Judith Selig; c Emily J, Adam S, Jennifer E & John S. *Educ:* Carleton Col, BA, 53; Harvard Univ, MD, 57. *Prof Exp:* Intern & resident med, Los Angeles Co Gen Hosp, Calif, 57-60; res fel exp surg & bact, Harvard Med Sch, 60-62, Harold C Ernst fel bact, 62-64; res assoc bact, Harvard Med Sch, 64-65, res assoc path, 65-67, clin instr med, 67-89 & chief allergy physician, Harvard Univ Health Serv, 67-89. *Mem:* Fel Am Acad Allergy; Am Col Allergists. *Res:* Mechanism of lethal action of endotoxin; differentiating reticulum cell in antibody formation; influence of environmental temperature on resistance to endotoxin; protection antisera afford against endotoxic death; controlling behavior of patients with bronchial asthma and their overcontrolling mothers; ethical problems posed by bee stings; clinical allergy in China versus United States. *Mailing Add:* 2175 Euclid Ave El Cajon CA 92019-2664

RUBENSTEIN, IRWIN, MOLECULAR BIOLOGY. *Current Pos:* prof genetics & cell biol, 70-88, head, 88-95, PROF PLANT BIOL, COL BIOL SCI, UNIV MINN, ST PAUL, 95- *Personal Data:* b Kansas City, Mo, Sept 6, 31; m 56, Ina Rosen; c Ione C, Ira S & Ilana B. *Educ:* Calif Inst Technol, BS, 53; Univ Calif, Los Angeles, PhD(biophys), 60. *Prof Exp:* Fel, Johns Hopkins Univ, 60-63; from asst prof to assoc prof molecular biophys, Yale Univ, 63-70. *Concurrent Pos:* NIH fel, Carnegie Inst Wash, 69-70; mem biol sci comt, World Book Encycl, 70-96. *Mem:* AAAS; Genetics Soc Am; Am Soc Plant Physiologists; Int Soc Plant Molecular Biol; Sigma Xi. *Res:* Molecular biology of plants. *Mailing Add:* Dept Plant Biol Univ Minn St Paul MN 55108-1095

RUBENSTEIN, JACK HERBERT, PEDIATRICS, HEALTH ADMINISTRATION. *Current Pos:* sr asst res, 55-56, asst med dir & fel pediat outpatient dept, 56-57, ATTENDING PEDIATRICIAN, CHILDREN'S HOSP MED CTR, CINCINNATI, 57- *Personal Data:* b New York, NY, Aug 4, 25; m 52, 90, Marlene F Tibbs. *Educ:* Columbia Univ, AB, 47; Harvard Univ, MD, 52; Am Bd Pediatrics, dipl. *Prof Exp:* Intern pediat, Beth Israel Hosp, Boston, 52-53; intern pediat, Mass Gen Hosp, Boston, 53-54, sr asst res, 54-55. *Concurrent Pos:* dir, Hamilton County Diag Clin Ment Retarded, 57-74, Children's Neuromuscular Diag Clin, 62-74, Univ Affil Clin Prog Ment Retarded, 67-74, Univ Affil Cincinnati Ctr Develop Dis, 74- *Mem:* Fel Am Acad Pediat; Am Pediat Soc; Teratol Soc; Am Asn Ment Retardation; Am Asn Univ Affil Prog Persons Develop Dis (pres, 78-79). *Res:* Reporting Rubinstein-Taybi syndrome, 1963. *Mailing Add:* Univ Affil Cincinnati Ctr Develop Dis Pavillion Bldg 3333 Burnet Ave Cincinnati OH 45229

RUBENSTEIN, NORTON MICHAEL, CLINICAL LABORATORY MEDICINE. *Current Pos:* PRES, RUBENSTEIN & ASSOCS, 81- *Personal Data:* b New York, NY, Aug 25, 36; m 60, 89, Loretta Erb; c Seth & Bryan. *Educ:* Univ Ala, BS, 64, MS, 66; Ohio State Univ, PhD(biol), 69. *Prof Exp:* Teaching asst biol, Univ Ala, 64-66; instr, Ohio State Univ, 66-69; asst prof, Wellesley Col, 69-75; sr scientist, Franklin Inst Res Labs, 77-78 & Sci Data Survs, 79-81. *Concurrent Pos:* Vis prof, Nat Ctr Sci Res, 73-74. *Mem:* Fel NY Acad Sci; Sigma Xi. *Res:* clinical laboratory medicine in managed care environments. *Mailing Add:* 8711 Old Spring Rd Richmond VA 23235. *Fax:* 804-272-4980

RUBENTHALER, GORDON LAWRENCE, CEREAL CHEMISTRY, SOFT WHITE WHEAT. *Current Pos:* CONSULT, 89- *Personal Data:* b Gothenburg, Nebr, Sept 30, 32; m 53, Delores R Ingram; c Rudy L, Randy D, Laura R & Ross D. *Educ:* Kans State Univ, BS, 60, MS, 62. *Prof Exp:* Phys sci aid, Agr Res Serv, USDA, 58-62, cereal technologist, 62-66, res cereal technician, 66-68, res cereal technician in chg wheat res, Wheat Qual Lab, 68-89. *Mem:* Sigma Xi; fel Am Asn Cereal Chemists; Crop Sci Soc Am. *Res:* Improvement of milling, baking, protein and amino acid balance of experimental wheat varieties; efforts to improve nutritional value and utilization of wheat for human consumption in domestic and foreign market. *Mailing Add:* 1951 Golfview Dr Clarkston WA 99403

RUBER, ERNEST, ECOLOGY. *Current Pos:* assoc prof, 68-80, PROF BIOL, NORTHEASTERN UNIV, 80- *Personal Data:* b Berlin, Ger, Aug 21, 34; US citizen; m 55; c 2. *Educ:* Brooklyn Col, BA, 59; Rutgers Univ, PhD(zool), 65. *Prof Exp:* Instr biol, Franklin & Marshall Col, 64-65; asst prof zool, Howard Univ, 65-68. *Mem:* AAAS; Am Soc Limnol & Oceanog; Ecol Soc Am; Sigma Xi; Am Mosquito Control Asn. *Res:* Coastal ecology; ecology and taxonomy of salt marsh Microcrustacea; effects of pesticides. *Mailing Add:* Dept Biol Northeastern Univ Boston MA 02115

RUBIN, ALAN, MEDICINE. *Current Pos:* CLIN PROF OBSTET & GYNEC, TEMPLE UNIV SCH MED, 79- *Personal Data:* b Philadelphia, Pa, Nov 10, 23; m 47, Helen Metz; c Alan M, Stephen & Blake. *Educ:* Univ Pa, MD, 47; Am Bd Obstet & Gynec, dipl, 56. *Prof Exp:* Intern, Univ Hosp, Univ Pa, 47-48, res fel pharmacol, 48-49, res obstet & gynec, 49-51, instr, 51-52, res assoc, 52-72, assoc, 72-79, clin assoc prof obstet & gynec, Sch Med, 80-92. *Concurrent Pos:* Nat Cancer Inst trainee, 51-52; res fel & chief resident, Gynecean Hosp Inst Gynec Res, Univ Pa, 51-52, res assoc, 53-; assoc, Albert Einstein Med Ctr, 55, asst dir, Div Gynec, 68-, actg chmn, Div Obstet & Gynec, 78-80; gynecologist, Grad Hosp Univ Pa, 73-, actg chmn, Dept Gynec, Grad Hosp, 77-78, chmn, 79-; mem, Am Comn Maternal & Infant Health; dir gynec div, Wills Eye Hosp, 77-80; clin prof obstet & gynec, Med Sch, Temple Univ, 81-83. *Mem:* Am Geriat Soc; Am Soc Human Genetics; Am Col Surgeons; Am Col Obstet & Gynec; Sigma Xi. *Res:* Obstetrics and gynecology; infertility; cancer. *Mailing Add:* 1905 Spruce St Philadelphia PA 19103

RUBIN, ALAN A, PHARMACOLOGY, MEDICAL DEVICES & DIAGNOSTICS. *Current Pos:* PRES, ARA ASSOC 91-; BD DIR, LEXINGTON SCI INC, 96- *Personal Data:* b New York, NY, July 10, 26; m 53, Helen Feinstein; c Jeffrey, Ronald & Howard. *Educ:* NY Univ, BA, 50, MS, 53, PhD(biol), 59. *Prof Exp:* Pharmacologist, Schering Corp, 54-64; dir pharmacol, Endo Labs, 64-71, vpres res, 71-74; dir res, DuPont Pharmaceut & DuPont-Merck Pharmaceut, 74-82, dir sci info & technol, 82-87, dir licensing technol, 87-91. *Concurrent Pos:* Ed, Search New Drugs, 72, New Drugs: Discovery & Develop, 78; consult, DuPont-Merck, 91-94, Alanex Ltd, 92-95. *Mem:* AAAS; Am Soc Pharmacol & Exp Therapeut; Am Heart Asn; NY Acad Sci; Soc Exp Biol Med. *Res:* Characterization and evaluation of drugs with special emphasis on the cardiovascular system and central and autonomic nervous systems; assessment of biomedical technology; development of biotechnology products. *Mailing Add:* 207 Hitching Post Dr Wilmington DE 19803. *Fax:* 302-479-5047; *E-Mail:* alanar@juno.com

RUBIN, ALAN BARRY, ORGANIC CHEMISTRY. *Current Pos:* CHIEF RES CHEMIST, ADAMS LABS, INC, 69- *Personal Data:* b Brooklyn, NY, Mar 24, 41; m 63; c 3. *Educ:* Cornell Univ, BA, 62; Univ Rochester, PhD(org chem), 67. *Prof Exp:* Teaching asst org chem, Univ Rochester, 62-66; res chemist, Walter Reed Army Inst Res, Walter Reed Army Med Ctr, 67-69; sect chief, 77-84, br chief, US Environ Protection Agency, 84-; HEAD SPEC CHEM, BRADLEE MED LABS, 69- *Mem:* Am Chem Soc. *Res:* Free radical chemistry; synthesis of antimalarials; medicinal chemistry. *Mailing Add:* 3304 Mill Cross Ct Oakton VA 22124

RUBIN, ALAN EDWARD, METEORITE RESEARCH, COSMOCHEMISTRY. *Current Pos:* staff res assoc, 83-89, asst res geochemist, 89-91, ASSOC RES GEOCHEMIST, UNIV CALIF, LOS ANGELES, 91-, ADJ ASSOC PROF, 94- *Personal Data:* b Chicago, Ill, Feb 3, 53; m 80, Dorene Janet Hamerman; c David, Joshua & Jeremiah. *Educ:* Univ Ill, Urbana, BS, 74; Univ Ill, Chicago, MS, 79; Univ NMex, PhD(geol), 82. *Prof Exp:* Res fel, Smithsonian Inst, 82-83. *Concurrent Pos:* Mem, Comt Meteoritics, Meteoritical Soc, 84 & Antarctic Meteorite Working Group, Lunar & Planet Inst, 91-94. *Mem:* Fel Meteoritical Soc. *Res:* Published more than 90 peer-reviewed scientific papers on the mineralogy and petrology of meteorites and implications for the nature of the solar nebula and the early history of asteroids. *Mailing Add:* Inst Geophys & Planetary Physics Univ Calif Los Angeles CA 90095. *Fax:* 310-206-3051; *E-Mail:* rubin@igpp.ucla.edu

RUBIN, ALAN J, ENVIRONMENTAL CHEMISTRY, SANITARY ENGINEERING. *Current Pos:* RETIRED. *Personal Data:* b Yonkers, NY, Mar 20, 34; m 62; c 1. *Educ:* Univ Miami, BSCE, 59; Univ NC, Chapel Hill, MSSE, 62, PhD(environ chem), 66. *Prof Exp:* Civil engr, Fed Aviation Agency, Tex, 59-60; asst prof environ chem, Univ Cincinnati, 65-68; assoc prof civil eng, Water Resources Ctr, Ohio State Univ, 68-74, prof, 74-92. *Concurrent Pos:* Harry D Pierce vis prof civil eng, Technion-Israel Inst Technol, Haifa, 84. *Mem:* Am Chem Soc; Am Water Works Asn; Water Pollution Control Fedn; Int Asn Water Pollution Res & Control. *Res:* Water chemistry, coagulation and colloid stability; foam separations and flotation; adsorption; aluminum(III) speciation and metal ion hydrolysis, disinfection and inactivation of Naeglaria and Giardia cysts by chloramines, chlorine, ozone, chlorinated isocyanurates, iodine and chlorine dioxide, dewatering of inorganic sludges; physical-chemical water and waste treatment. *Mailing Add:* 1438 Sherbrooke Pl Columbus OH 43209

RUBIN, ALBERT LOUIS, INTERNAL MEDICINE. *Current Pos:* DIR, ROGOSIN LABS, NY HOSP CORNELL MED CTR, 63-, DIR ROGOSIN KIDNEY CTR, 71- *Personal Data:* b Memphis, Tenn, May 9, 27; m 53; c 1. *Educ:* Cornell Univ, MD, 50; Am Bd Internal Med, dipl, 57. *Prof Exp:* Assoc prof med, 59-68, prof biochem & surg, Med Col, Cornell Univ, 69-, prof med, 76- *Concurrent Pos:* Estab investr, Am Heart Asn, 58-63; attend surgeon, NY Hosp, 69- *Res:* Heart and kidney diseases. *Mailing Add:* Cornell Univ Med Col 1300 York Ave New York NY 10021-4805

RUBIN, ALLEN GERSHON, SPACE PHYSICS. *Current Pos:* PHYSICIST, AIR FORCE CAMBRIDGE RES LABS, 63- *Personal Data:* b Lewiston, Maine, July 4, 30. *Educ:* Boston Univ, PhD(physics), 57. *Prof Exp:* Physicist, Oak Ridge Nat Lab, 57-58 & Williamson Develop Co, 58-63. *Mem:* Am Phys Soc; Am Geophys Union; Sigma Xi; Am Inst Aeronaut & Astronaut. *Res:* Nuclear spectroscopy and reactions; plasma acceleration; laboratory astrophysics; lasers; spacecraft changing; computer simulation codes; computer code validation; space environment. *Mailing Add:* 10 Fox Hill Rd Newton Centre MA 02159-3027

RUBIN, ARTHUR I(SRAEL), COMPUTER SCIENCES. *Current Pos:* ACCT EXEC, DEAN WITTER, 84- *Personal Data:* b New York, NY, Dec 3, 27; m 50; c 2. *Educ:* City Col New York, BS, 49; Stevens Inst Technol, MS, 53. *Prof Exp:* Physicist, Picatinny Arsenal, Ord Corps, 50-55; appln engr, Electronic Assocs, Inc, NJ, 55-56, supvr, 57-59, dir comput ctr, 59-62; chief automatic comput, Martin Co, 62-67; mgr hybrid comput sci dept, Orlando Div, Martin Marietta Corp, 67-69; sr tech staff consult, Electronic Assocs, Inc, 69, dir comput ctr, 69-70; mgr anal eng dept, 71-77; dir planning, Autodynamics, Inc, 78-80, dir proj control, 80-84. *Concurrent Pos:* Chmn libr comt, Simulation Coun, 64-77; mem surv comt, Am Fedn Info Processing Socs, 66-69, secy, 68-69. *Mem:* Inst Elec & Electronics Engrs; sr mem Soc Comput Simulation; assoc fel Am Inst Aeronaut & Astronaut. *Res:* Analog and hybrid computer programming and design; thermal physics. *Mailing Add:* 917 Stuart Rd Princeton NJ 08540. Fax: 609-844-7950

RUBIN, BARNEY, CHEMICAL ENGINEERING, TECHNICAL MANAGEMENT. *Current Pos:* RETIRED. *Personal Data:* b Kansas City, Mo, Jan 1, 24; m 48, 84, Evelyn Morris; c 2. *Educ:* Univ Calif, BS, 46, MS, 48, PhD(chem eng), 50. *Prof Exp:* Res chem engr, Radiation Lab, Univ Calif, 50-51 & Calif Res & Develop Co, 51-53; leader, Process & Mat Develop Div, 53-71, sr staff scientist, 71-81, asst assoc dir, 81, communs scientist, 82-83, sr staff scientist, Lawrence Livermore Nat Lab, Univ Calif, 86. *Concurrent Pos:* Consult, Arms Control & Disarmament, The Pentagon, 84-85. *Mem:* Am Chem Soc; Sigma Xi. *Res:* Computer networking assessment; energy technology research and development assessment. *Mailing Add:* 477 Woodbine Lane Danville CA 94526-2653

RUBIN, BENJAMIN ARNOLD, MICROBIOLOGY, EPIDEMIOLOGY. *Current Pos:* RETIRED. *Personal Data:* b New York, NY, Sept 27, 17; m 51, Mae Koenig. *Educ:* City Col, BS, 37; Va Polytech Inst, MS, 38; Yale Univ, PhD(microbiol), 47. *Honors & Awards:* John Scott Award & Medal, 81. *Prof Exp:* Asst bacteriologist, US War Dept, 40-44; res microbiologist, Schenley Res Inst, Ind, 44-45; microbiol chemist, Off Sci Res & Develop, Yale Univ, 45-47; assoc microbiologist, Brookhaven Nat Lab, 47-52; chief microbiologist, Syntex SAm, Mex, 52-54; asst prof pub health, Col Med, Baylor Univ, 54-60; mgr, Biol Prod Develop Dept, Wyeth Labs, Inc, Am Home Prod, 60-84; prof microbiol, Philadelphia Col Osteop Med, 84-96. *Concurrent Pos:* Consult, Space Biol Prog, Gen Elec Corp, 67-75. *Mem:* Am Soc Microbiol; Am Asn Immunol; Harvey Soc; Genetics Soc Am; Radiation Res Soc. *Res:* Immunogenetics; virology; chemical and viral carcinogenesis; bioengineering; immunosuppressants; vaccine development; epidemiology and public health; radiobiology; chemotherapy; injection devices; biomed devices; medical virology (related to dermatology). *Mailing Add:* 50 Belmont Ave No 601 Bala Cynwyd PA 19004. Fax: 215-871-2781

RUBIN, BERNARD, PHARMACOLOGY. *Current Pos:* CONSULT LICENSING, BRISTOL-MYERS SQUIBB PHARMACEUT CO, 84- *Personal Data:* b New York, NY, Feb 15, 19; m 45, Betty Schindler; c Stefi & Robert. *Educ:* Brooklyn Col, BA, 39; Yale Univ, PhD(pharmacol), 50. *Honors & Awards:* Discovery Award, Am Heart Asn. *Prof Exp:* Bact asst respiratory dis, Bur Labs, New York City Health Dept, 40-42, food & drug inspector, Bur Food & Drugs, 44-45; chem lab technician, US Army, 42-43; med lab technician path, Marine Hosp, USPHS, 43-44; res asst pharmacol & chemother, Nepera Chem Co, 45-48; sr res group leader pharmacol, Squibb Inst Med Res, 50-84. *Mem:* AAAS; Am Soc Pharmacol; Soc Exp Biol & Med; NY Acad Sci; Sigma Xi; Am Heart Asn. *Res:* Bioassay of natural products, as veratrum viride and Rauwolfia; chemotherapeutic agents (isoniazid, etc) and their pharmacological characteristics; anesthetics; analgesics; antihistaminics; biometrics; phenothiazine tranquilizers; central nervous system stimulants; antiserotonins; polypeptides; autonomic, vascular and gastrointestinal pharmacology; (teprotide and captopril) inhibitors of angiotensin-converting enzyme; worldwide surveys of drug candidates available for licensing; preparation of licensing candidate summary profile; special reports on drug candidates in a special category, e.g. antidepressants, hypoglycemics, etc. *Mailing Add:* 2 Pine Oak Dr Lawrenceville NJ 08648

RUBIN, BRUCE JOEL, ELECTROPHOTOGRAPHY, FILTRATION. *Current Pos:* Chemist, Eastman Kodak Co, 65-73, sr chemist, 73-78, res assoc, 79-92, prof engr, 93-95, RES ASSOC, EASTMAN KODAK CO, 96- *Personal Data:* b Brooklyn, NY, Nov 24, 42; m 64, Roslyn; c Holly & Michael. *Educ:* City Univ New York, BEchE, 64; Polytech Univ Brooklyn, MchE, 65; Univ Rochester, MBA, 73; Rochester Inst Technol, MEE, 88. *Res:* Filtration and centrifugation of organic chemicals. *Mailing Add:* Eastman Kodak B205 3rd Fl KO ML03084 Rochester NY 14650-3084

RUBIN, BRUCE KALMAN, PEDIATRIC PULMONARY MEDICINE, MUCOLOGY. *Current Pos:* PROF PEDIAT, ST LOUIS UNIV SCH MED, 91- *Personal Data:* b Miami Beach, Fla, May 8, 54; US & Can citizen; m 90, Tomomi Tainaka; c Noah David. *Educ:* Tulane Univ, BS, 75, MEng, 77, MD, 79. *Honors & Awards:* DuPont Young Investr Award, Am Col Chest Physicians, 88, Alfred Soffer Res Award, 90. *Prof Exp:* Rhodes scholar, Oxford Univ, 78-80; pediat resident, Tulane Univ, 80-81; pulmonary fel, Univ Toronto, 81-83; asst prof pediat, Queen's Univ, 83-87 & Univ Alta, 87-91. *Concurrent Pos:* Dir pediat pulmonary med, Cardinal Glennon Children's Hosp, 91- & Asthma Ctr Children, St Louis Univ Sch Med, 92- *Mem:* Fel Am Col Chest Physicians; Soc Pediat Res; fel Am Acad Pediat; Am Physiol Soc; Am Thoracic Soc. *Res:* Regulation of mucous clearance in lung disease; study of cystic fibrosis, asthma, and the effects of tobacco smoke; clinical studies of new therapies for asthma, bronchitis, and cystic fibrosis. *Mailing Add:* Cardinal Glennon Children's Hosp 1465 S Grand Blvd St Louis MO 63104-1003. Fax: 314-268-2798; E-Mail: rubinbk@sluvca.slu.edu

RUBIN, BYRON HERBERT, BIOPHYSICAL CHEMISTRY. *Current Pos:* SR RES SCIENTIST, EASTMAN KODAK, 85- *Personal Data:* b Chicago, Ill, July 25, 43. *Educ:* Reed Col, BA, 65; Duke Univ, PhD(chem), 71. *Prof Exp:* Fel, Dept Biochem, Duke Univ Med Ctr, 70-73; assoc, Inst Cancer Res, 73-77; asst prof chem, Emory Univ, 77-85. *Concurrent Pos:* Assoc prof, Dept Chem, Univ Rochester. *Mem:* Am Chem Soc; Am Crystallog Asn. *Res:* X-ray defraction. *Mailing Add:* 1180 Mendon Ctr Rd Honeoye Falls NY 14472-1294

RUBIN, CAROL MARIE, STRUCTURE & FUNCTION OF REPEATED DNA IN HUMANS, CYTOSINE METHYLATION & ITS EFFECTS ON GENE ACTIVATION. *Current Pos:* indust hygienist, Dept Environ Health & Safety, 83-90, ASST RES GENETICIST, DEPT GENETICS, UNIV CALIF, DAVIS, 91- *Personal Data:* b Chicago, Ill, Sept 19, 48; m 71, Sander; c Miranda & Ethan. *Educ:* Univ Ill, Urbana, BA, 70; Calif State Univ, Dominguez Hills, BA, 76; Univ Calif, Davis, PhD(chem), 81. *Prof Exp:* Assoc res scientist, Connaught Res Inst, Toronto, 81-82. *Mem:* Am Chem Soc; Am Soc Human Genetics. *Res:* Human genome; function and modification of the human genome. *Mailing Add:* Molecular & Cell Biol Univ Calif Davis CA 95616-5224. Fax: 530-752-3085

RUBIN, CHARLES STUART, BIOCHEMISTRY. *Current Pos:* Asst prof neurosci & molecular biol, 72-77, ASSOC PROF MOLECULAR PHARMACOL, ALBERT EINSTEIN COL MED, 78- *Personal Data:* b Scranton, Pa, Nov 24, 43; m 67. *Educ:* Univ Scranton, BS, 65; Cornell Univ, PhD(biochem), 71. *Concurrent Pos:* Damon Runyon fel, Albert Einstein Col Med, 70-72; City of New York Health Res Coun career scientist award, 73; NIH res career develop award, 76. *Mem:* AAAS; Am Chem Soc; Am Soc Biol Chemists. *Res:* Enzymology; enzymes involved in the metabolism and action of cyclic AMP; structure and function of membrane-associated enzymes, especially in the central nervous system; biochemical genetics. *Mailing Add:* Dept Molecular Pharmacol Albert Einstein Col Med 1300 Morris Park Ave Bronx NY 10461-1975. Fax: 718-829-8705

RUBIN, CYRUS E, MEDICINE, GASTROENTEROLOGY. *Current Pos:* from instr to assoc prof, 54-62, PROF MED, UNIV WASH, 62- *Personal Data:* b Philadelphia, Pa, July 20, 21; m 47; c 2. *Educ:* Brooklyn Col, AB, 43; Harvard Med Sch, MD, 45. *Prof Exp:* Intern, Beth Israel Hosp, Boston, Mass, 45-46, resident radiol, 50-51; resident med, Cushing Vet Admin Hosp, Framingham, Mass, 48-50. *Concurrent Pos:* Dazian fel, Univ Chicago, 51-52, Runyon res fel, 52-53; Nat Cancer Inst career res award, 62-; consult, Univ, Children's Orthop, Vet Admin, King County & USPHS Hosps, Seattle, Wash. *Mem:* Am Soc Clin Invest; Am Soc Cell Biol; Am Fedn Clin Res; Am Gastroenterol Asn; Asn Am Physicians; Sigma Xi. *Res:* Structure and function of the human gastrointestinal tract. *Mailing Add:* Dept Med Div Gastroenterol RG-24 Univ Wash Seattle WA 98195-0001

RUBIN, DAVID CHARLES, HERPETOLOGY, ECOLOGY. *Current Pos:* from asst prof to assoc prof, 70-84, PROF BIOL, CENT STATE UNIV, 84- *Personal Data:* b Brooklyn, NY, Feb 9, 43; m 68, Rebecca Allen; c Robert & Beth. *Educ:* Cornell Univ, BS, 63; Ind State Univ, Terre Haute, MA, 65, PhD(systs & ecol), 69. *Prof Exp:* Actg instr biol, Ind State Univ, 66-67; proj writer, interrelated math-sci proj, Broward County, Fla, 69-70. *Concurrent Pos:* Consult interrelated math-sci proj, Broward County, Fla 71 & interdisciplinary environ educ proj, 72; mem Interuniv Comt Environ Qual, Ohio Bd Regents, 72-75; mem adv bd, Ohio Biol Surv, 75-; pres, Cent State Univ chap, Am Asn Univ Profs, 75-77 & 84-86; consult, MacMillian Publ Co, 79-80; consult, State NJ, Dept Educ, 84; chief negotiator, Cent State Univ chap, Am Asn Univ Professors, 88-93, mem, nat coun, 88-91; pres, Ohio Conf, Am Asn Univ Professors, 92-93, chapters serv dir, 93- *Mem:* Soc Study Amphibians & Reptiles; Natural Areas Asn. *Res:* Systematics of Plethodontid salamanders; amphibian and reptile distribution; amphibian and reptile food habits. *Mailing Add:* Dept Biol Cent State Univ Wilberforce OH 45384-9999. Fax: 937-376-6530

RUBIN, DONALD BRUCE, APPLIED STATISTICS. *Current Pos:* PROF DEPT STATIST, HARVARD UNIV, 84-, CHMN DEPT, 85- *Personal Data:* b Washington, DC, Dec 22, 43; m 75; c 2. *Educ:* Princeton Univ, AB, 65; Harvard Univ, MS, 66, PhD(statist), 70. *Honors & Awards:* Wilks Medal, Am Statist Asn, 95; Parzen Prize for Statist Innovation, 96. *Prof Exp:* Lectr statist, Harvard Univ, 70-71; res statistician, Educ Testing Serv, 71-80, chmn statist group, 75-80; mem staff, Math Res Ctr, Univ Wis, 80-81; prof dept statist & educ, Univ Chicago, 81-84. *Concurrent Pos:* Vis lectr statist, Princeton Univ, 71-74; assoc ed, J Am Statist Asn, 75-79, coord & applns ed, 79-82, assoc ed, J Educ Statist, 76-; vis scholar, Univ Calif, Berkeley, 75; vis assoc prof, Univ Minn, 76 & Harvard Univ, 78; Guggenheim fel, 77-78. *Mem:* Fel Am Statist Asn; Biomet Soc; fel Inst Math Statist; Psychometric Soc; fel Int Statist Inst; fel AAAS; Am Acad Arts & Sci. *Res:* Inference for causal effects in randomized and non-randomized studies; analysis of incomplete data; non response in sample surveys; multiple imutation; bayesian statistics; computational statistics EM algorithm and extensions; propersity scope methods. *Mailing Add:* Dept Statist Harvard Univ Cambridge MA 02138. Fax: 617-496-8057

RUBIN, DONALD HOWARD, VIRAL PATHOGENESIS, MUCOSAL IMMUNE RESPONSE. *Current Pos:* asst prof, 80-88, ASSOC PROF, MED & MICROBIOL, UNIV PA, 88-; PHYSICIAN, INFECTIOUS DIS, VET AFFAIRS MED CTR, 85- *Personal Data:* b New York, NY, Feb 3, 48; m 72; c 3. *Educ:* State Univ NY, BA, 69; Cornell Univ Med Col, MD, 74. *Prof Exp:* Employee health physician, Boston Lying-In, 78-80; instr med, Harvard Med Sch, 79-80. *Concurrent Pos:* Res assoc, Vet Affairs Med Ctr, 86-90. *Mem:* Am Soc Clin Invest; fel Infectious Dis Soc; fel Am Col Physicians; Am Soc Microbiol; Am Soc Virol; Am Asn Appl Psychol. *Res:* Viral pathogenesis; infection of gastrointestinal mucosa and hepatocytes with Reovirus; cellular and molecular analysis of viral pathogenesis; mucosal immune response to viral infection. *Mailing Add:* Nashville Va Med Ctr Acss/Res 151 1310 24th Ave S Nashville TN 37212-2637

RUBIN, EDWARD S, MECHANICAL ENGINEERING, ENERGY. *Current Pos:* asst prof mech eng, 69-72, Carnegie-Mellon Univ, asst prof mech eng & pub affairs, 72-74, assoc prof mech eng & eng & pub policy, 74-79, DIR, CTR ENERGY & ENVIRON STUDIES, 78, PROF MECH ENG & ENG & PUB POLICY, CARNEGIE-MELLON UNIV, 79- *Personal Data:* b New York, NY, Sept 19, 41; c 2. *Educ:* City Col New York, BE, 64; Stanford Univ, MS, 65, PhD(mech eng), 69. *Prof Exp:* NSF trainee & res assoc, High Temp Gas Dynamics Lab, Dept Mech Eng, Stanford Univ, 64-68. *Concurrent Pos:* Consult, 70-; mem energy systs task group, Gov Energy Coun, Harrisburg, Pa, 74-76; vis mech engr, Ctr Energy Policy Anal, Brookhaven Nat Lab, 75 & 77; mem air & water qual tech adv comt, Pa Dept Environ Resources, 77-; mem US steering comt-coal task force, Int Inst Appl Syst Anal, Laxenburg, Austria, 77-78; vis prof, Dept Physics (Energy Res Group), Cambridge Univ, Eng, 79-80; vis fel, Churchill Col, 79-80. *Mem:* Am Soc Mech Engrs; Air Pollution Control Asn; AAAS. *Res:* Environmental impacts of coal conversion and utilization; modelling of energy and environmental systems; air quality management; technology assessment and public policy. *Mailing Add:* Dept Eng & Pub Policy Carnegie-Mellon Univ Baker Hall 128-A Pittsburgh PA 15213-3816

RUBIN, EMANUEL, PATHOLOGY. *Current Pos:* GONZALO E APONTE PROF PATH & CHMN DEPT PATH & CELL BIOL, JEFFERSON MED COL, 86- *Personal Data:* b New York, NY, Dec 5, 28; m 55; c 4. *Educ:* Villanova Univ, BS, 50; Harvard Univ, MD, 54. *Honors & Awards:* Maude L Menten Centennial Lect, Univ Pittsburg Sch Med, 87; Whipple Lect, Univ Rochester Med Ctr, 87; Chippy Friedman Mem Lect, Haifa Univ, 88; Maude Abbott Lect, US-Can Acad Path, 90; Reginald G Mason Mem Lect, Univ Utah Sch Med, 92; Marcus Wallenberg Symp, Lund, Swed, 92. *Prof Exp:* Asst attend pathologist, Mt Sinai Hosp, 62-64; assoc attending pathologist, 64-68, prof path, Mt Sinai Sch Med, City Univ New York, 66-72, attend pathologist & dir Hosp Path Serv, 68-72, pathologist-in-chief, 71-76, Irene Heinz & John LaPorte Given prof path & chmn dept, 72-76; prof & chmn, Dept Path & Lab Med, Sch Med, Hahnemann Univ & dir labs, Hahnemann Univ Hosp, 77-86. *Concurrent Pos:* Consult, Nat Task Force Alcohol & Health, Dept Health, Educ & Welfare, 71, 77 & 85; adj prof biochem & biophysics, Sch Med, Univ Pa, 77-88; ed-in-chief, Lab Invest, 82; attend physician-in-chief path, Thomas Jefferson Univ Hosp, Philadelphia, Pa, 86- *Mem:* US-Can Acad Path; Col Am Pathologists; Am Asn Path; Am Col Physicians; Am Asn Study Liver Dis; Am Soc Biochem & Molecular Biol; Am Gastroenterol Asn; Int Asn Study Liver; Am Col Toxicol; Res Soc Alcoholism; Int Soc Biomed Res Alcoholism. *Res:* Function and structure in human and experimental liver disease; effects of ethanol on the liver, heart and other organs. *Mailing Add:* Dept Pathol Anat & Cell Biol Jefferson Med Col Thomas Jefferson Univ 1020 Locust St Suite 279 JAH Philadelphia PA 19107-6799

RUBIN, FRAN AUERBACH, INFECTIOUS DISEASES, VACCINE DEVELOPMENT. *Current Pos:* PROG OFFICER, NAT INST ALLERGY & INFECTIOUS DIS, 97- *Personal Data:* b Baltimore, Md, Mar 9, 43; m 70, Robert J; c Elyse & David. *Educ:* Cornell Univ, BS, 65, PhD(microbiol genetics), 70- *Prof Exp:* Postdoctoral fel, Childrens Hosp Med Ctr, Boston, Mass, 70-72; res assoc, Emory Univ, Atlanta, Ga, 72-73; res microbiologist, Walter Reed Army Inst Res, 81-94; sci reviewer, Ctr Devices & Radiol Health, Food & Drug Admin, 94-97. *Concurrent Pos:* Res fel, Childrens Hosp Med Ctr, Boston, Mass, 80-81; consult, Johns Hopkins Univ, 87-89, Merck, Sharp & Dohme, 89; found lectr, Am Soc Microbiol, 90, mem, Comt Status Women Microbiol, 92-; lectr med, Res Fel Prog, Walter Reed Army Inst Res, 90-94, lab prog rep to Nat Res Coun, 93-94. *Mem:* Am Soc Microbiol. *Res:* Epidemiology and pathogenesis of streptococcal disease; vaccine development; diagnosis of infectious diseases; identification of virulence factors; gene cloning and expression; nucleic acid amplification; development of assays using nucleic acid probes for detection of pathogens; genome sequencing; numerous publications in medial literature; granted one US patent. *Mailing Add:* 6003 Executive Blvd Solar Bldg Bethesda MD 20892-7630. *Fax:* 301-496-8030; *E-Mail:* fr28f@nih.gov

RUBIN, G A, PHYSICS. *Current Pos:* prof, 67-92, EMER PROF PHYSICS, LAURENTIAN UNIV, 92-, DEPT CHMN. *Personal Data:* b Leipzig, Ger, Dec 30, 26; m 55; c 3. *Educ:* Univ Heidelberg, BA, 46; Univ Saarbrucken, dipl, 53, PhD(physics), 55. *Prof Exp:* Instr physics, Univ Saarlandes, 53-56; res scientist, Roechling Steelworks, 56-57; proj group leader mat res, Union Carbide Corp, 57-60; assoc prof physics, Clarkson Tech, 60-65; sr physicist, IIT Res Inst, 65-67. *Concurrent Pos:* Consult, Steinzeug A G, Ger, 62-64; NASA & Nat Res Coun Can grants, 65-; consult, IIT Res Inst, 67-72. *Mem:* Am Phys Soc; Am Ceramic Soc; NY Acad Sci; Can Phys Soc; Ger Phys Soc. *Res:* Acoustic emissions from particulate matter; surface and fine particle physics; charge transportion in solids; ultrasonic fragmentation of rock. *Mailing Add:* Dept Physics & Astron Laurentian Univ Ramsey Lake Rd Sudbury ON P3E 2C6 Can

RUBIN, GERALD M, GENETICS. *Current Pos:* head, Div Genetics, 87-95, JOHN D MACARTHUR PROF GENETICS, DEPT MOLECULAR & CELL BIOL, UNIV CALIF, BERKELEY, 83-, INVESTR, HOWARD HUGHES MED INST, 87-, DIR, DROSPHILA GENOME CTR, 92- *Personal Data:* b Mar 31, 50. *Educ:* Mass Inst Technol, BS, 71; Univ Cambridge, Eng, PhD(molecular biol), 74. *Honors & Awards:* Passano Found Young Scientist Award, 83; Newcomb Cleveland Prize, AAAS, 84; Eli Lilly Award in Biol Chem, Am Chem Soc, 85; US Steel Found Award in Molecular Biol, Nat Acad Sci, 85; Genetics Soc Am Medal, 86. *Prof Exp:* Helen Hay Whitney Found fel, Dept Biochem, Sch Med, Stanford Univ, 74-76; asst prof biol chem, Sidney Farber Cancer Inst, Harvard Med Sch, 77-80; staff mem, Dept Embryol, Carnegie Inst Washington, Baltimore, Md, 80-83. *Concurrent Pos:* Tutor, Bd Tutors in Biomed Sci, Harvard Col, 77-80; assoc ed, Develop Biol, 82-85, Cell, 85-, J Neurosci, 86-, Neuron, 88-; mem bd sci counrs, Nat Inst Environ Health Sci, 84-87; adj prof, Dept Biochem & Biophys, Sch Med, Univ Calif, San Francisco, 87-; mem, Vis Comt, Dept Biochem & Molecular Biol, Harvard Univ, 88-91, Dept Biol, Mass Inst Technol, 88-94, Univ Calif, Davis, 89; ed, Develop, 91-94. *Mem:* Nat Acad Sci; Am Acad Arts & Sci. *Res:* Molecular and cell biology; molecular genetics of development; genome research. *Mailing Add:* Dept Molecular & Cell Biol Univ Calif 539 Life Sci Addn Bldg Berkeley CA 94720-3200

RUBIN, GUSTAV, PROSTHETICS, ORTHOTICS. *Current Pos:* PVT PRACT, 87- *Personal Data:* b New York, NY, May 19, 13; m 46, 65, Esther R Partnow. *Educ:* NY Univ, BS, 34; State Univ NY-Downstate Med Ctr, MD, 39; Am Bd Orthopaedic Surg, dipl. *Honors & Awards:* Olin E Teague Award, Vet Admin, 84; Physician of the Yr Award, Pres Comn Employ of People with Disabilities, 84. *Prof Exp:* Intern, Maimonides Hosp, 39-41; res orthop, Hosp Joint Dis, 41-42, 46; pract med, Brooklyn, 47-56; from orthop surgeon to dir clin, Vet Admin Clin, Brooklyn, 56-70; chief, Spec Prosthetic Clin, Vet Admin Prosthetics Ctr, NY, 70-85, dir spec team, 85-87, mem chief med dir adv group prosthetics svcs, rehab res & develop, 85-87, orthop consult, 70-87. *Concurrent Pos:* Med adv prosthetic res comt, NY State DAV, 70-; lectr prosthetics, Postgrad Med Sch, NY Univ, 72-89; clin prof orthop, NY Col Podiatric Med, 80- *Mem:* Fel Am Acad Orthop Surgeons; fel Am Col Surgeons; fel Am Acad Neurol & Orthop Surgeons; Sigma Xi. *Res:* Talar-tilt, subtalar joint instability, development and testing of new prosthetic and orthotic devices for amputees and other physically challenged individuals. *Mailing Add:* 305 E 24th St Apt 17H New York NY 10010-4028

RUBIN, HARRY, CELL BIOLOGY, CELL AGING & TRANSFORMATION. *Current Pos:* assoc prof, 58-60, PROF VIROL, UNIV CALIF, BERKELEY, 60-, RES VIROLOGIST MOLECULAR BIOL, 73-, PROF MOLECULAR & CELL BIOL, 88- *Personal Data:* b New York, NY, June 23, 26; m 52, Dorothy Shuster; c Andrew L, Janet E, Clinton T & Nell A. *Educ:* Cornell Univ, DVM, 47. *Hon Degrees:* DSc, Guelph, 87. *Honors & Awards:* Rosenthal Award, AAAS, 59; Eli Lilly Award, 61; Lasker Award, 64; Dyer lectr, NIH, 64; Harvey lectr, NY Acad Med, 66. *Prof Exp:* Veterinarian, Foot & Mouth Dis Proj, Mex, 47-48; sr asst veterinarian, Virus Lab, USPHS, Ala, 48-52; res fel virol, Nat Found Infantile Paralysis, Biochem & Virus Lab, Calif, 52-53; res fel, Biol Div, Calif Inst Technol, 53-55, sr res fel, 55-58. *Mem:* Nat Acad Sci; Am Acad Arts & Sci; Int Soc Differentiation. *Res:* Cell growth regulation and malignancy; heritable damage to cells; cellular epigenetics. *Mailing Add:* Dept Molecular & Cell Biol Stanley Donner ASU Univ Calif Berkeley CA 94720. *Fax:* 510-643-9290; *E-Mail:* harry_rubin@maillink.berkeley.edu

RUBIN, HARVEY LOUIS, VETERINARY MICROBIOLOGY, PATHOLOGY. *Current Pos:* RETIRED. *Personal Data:* b San Diego, Calif, Apr 28, 14; m 41, Emily S Scherago; c 1. *Educ:* Auburn Univ, DVM, 39; Univ Ky, MS, 40; Johns Hopkins Univ, MPH, 52; Am Col Vet Prev Med, dipl. *Honors & Awards:* EP Pope Award, Am Asn Vet Lab Diag, 88. *Prof Exp:* Sr technician, Univ Ky, 40; instr vet anat & histol, Agr & Mech Col, Tex, 40-42; instr, Vet Corps, US Army, 42-68; dir, Animal Dis Diag Lab, Live Oak, Fla, 68-77; dir, Bureau Diag Lab, Fla Dept Agri, Kissimmee, Fla, 77-96. *Concurrent Pos:* Adj prof, Col Vet Med, Univ Fla, 77-96. *Mem:* Am Vet Med Asn; Am Asn Vet Lab Diagnosticians; Am Col Vet Toxicol; Sigma Xi; Am Leptospirosis Res Conf. *Res:* Salmonella in hogs; immunology; leptospirosis; zoonoses. *Mailing Add:* PO Box 421836-1836 Kissimmee FL 32742-1836

RUBIN, HERBERT, PHYSICAL CHEMISTRY. *Current Pos:* RETIRED. *Personal Data:* b New York, NY, Oct 9, 23; wid, Sylvia Federbush; c Ann & Charles. *Educ:* NY Univ, BA, 44; Polytech Inst Brooklyn, MS, 49, PhD(phys chem), 53. *Prof Exp:* Res assoc radiation chem, Syracuse Univ, 53-54; sr chemist, Ozalid Div, Gen Aniline & Film Corp, 54-56; sr res engr, Schlumberger Well Surv Corp, 56-63; specialist phys chem, Repub Aviation Corp, 63-64; sr res chemist, Reaction Motors Div, Thiokol Chem Corp, 64-66; prin scientist, Inmont Corp, 66-75, res assoc, 75-85; res assoc, BASF, 85-87. *Mem:* AAAS; Am Chem Soc; Sigma Xi. *Res:* Wide-line nuclear magnetic resonance; electrochemistry; photoreproductive processes; photopolymerization and ultraviolet absorption of inks and coatings; ultraviolet lamp photometry; solvent-polymer solution behavior. *Mailing Add:* 35 Byron Pl Livingston NJ 07039

RUBIN, HERBERT, communications, speech pathology, for more information see previous edition

RUBIN, HERMAN, STATISTICS, MATHEMATICS. *Current Pos:* PROF STATIST, PURDUE UNIV, LAFAYETTE, 67- *Personal Data:* b Chicago, Ill, Oct 27, 26; m 52, Jean E Hirsh; c Arthur L & Leonore A (Findsen). *Educ:* Univ Chicago, BS, 44, MS, 45, PhD(math), 48. *Prof Exp:* Res asst, Cowles Comn Res Econ, Chicago, 44-46, res assoc, 46-47 & 48-49; asst prof statist,

Stanford Univ, 49-55; assoc prof math, Univ Ore, 55-59; prof statist, Mich State Univ, 59-67. *Mem:* Fel AAAS; Am Math Soc; Math Asn Am; fel Inst Math Statist. *Res:* Mathematical statistics; statistical decision theory; mathematical logic and set theory; stochastic processes. *Mailing Add:* Dept Statist Purdue Univ West Lafayette IN 47907-1968. *Fax:* 765-494-0558; *E-Mail:* hrubin@stat.purdue.edu

RUBIN, HOWARD ARNOLD, PHYSICS. *Current Pos:* from asst prof to assoc prof, 66-88, PROF PHYSICS, ILL INST TECHNOL, 88- *Personal Data:* b Baltimore, Md, Jan 4, 40; m 65; c 2. *Educ:* Mass Inst Technol, SB, 61; Univ Md, College Park, PhD(physics), 67. *Mem:* Am Phys Soc. *Res:* High energy physics experiment. *Mailing Add:* Dept Physics Ill Inst Technol Chicago IL 60616. *Fax:* 312-567-3396

RUBIN, ISAAC D, POLYMER CHEMISTRY, ORGANIC CHEMISTRY. *Current Pos:* sr chemist, Texaco Inc, 62-64, res chemist, 64-67, group leader, 67-78, technologist, 78-82, res mgr, 82-85, coordr, 85-87, sr res assoc, 87-88, fel, 88-89, RES FEL, TEXACO INC, 90- *Personal Data:* b Krakow, Poland, Nov 8, 31; US citizen; m 57; c 1. *Educ:* Brooklyn Col, BS, 54; Brooklyn Polytech Inst, MS, 57, PhD(polymer chem), 61. *Prof Exp:* Chemist, Acralite Co, Inc, 54-56, plant mgr, 56-57; develop chemist, Gen Elec Co, 60-62. *Mem:* NY Acad Sci; Am Chem Soc. *Res:* Polymerization mechanisms; structure-property relationships in polymers; lubricants, fuels, energy and petrochemicals; technical writing; science and technology. *Mailing Add:* 14 Michael Dr Wappingers Falls NY 12590

RUBIN, IZHAK, ELECTRICAL ENGINEERING. *Current Pos:* PROF ENG & APPL SCI, UNIV CALIF, LOS ANGELES, 70-; PRES, IRI CORP, 80- *Personal Data:* b Haifa, Israel, May 22, 42; m 65; c 3. *Educ:* Israel Inst Technol, BS, 64, MS, 68; Princeton Univ, PhD(elec eng), 70. *Prof Exp:* Electronics engr, Israel Aircraft Industs, 67-68; res asst elec eng, Princeton Univ, 69-70. *Concurrent Pos:* Off Naval Res grant, Univ Calif, Los Angeles, 72-, NSF res grant, 75-, Naval Res Lab grant, 78-; actg chief scientist, Xerox Telecoms Network, 79-80; consult, Comput Commun Networks, 70-, C3 Systs and Networks, 80- *Mem:* Fel Inst Elec & Electronics Engrs. *Res:* Data and computer communication networks; satellite communication networks; queueing systems; network flows; communication and information theory; stochastic processes; C3 systems and networks; planning and analysis software tools for telecommunications and computer communications networks. *Mailing Add:* Elec Eng Dept Univ Calif Eng IV 56-125B Los Angeles CA 90095

RUBIN, JACOB, SOIL PHYSICS, HYDROLOGY. *Current Pos:* adv solute transport, 74-76, SOIL PHYSICIST, WATER RESOURCES DIV, US GEOL SURV, 62- *Personal Data:* b Wloclawek, Poland, Feb 1, 19; US citizen; m 43; c 3. *Educ:* Univ Calif, Berkeley, BS, 42, PhD(soil sci), 49. *Honors & Awards:* O E Meinzer Award, Geol Soc Am, 77. *Prof Exp:* Soil physicist, Agr Res Sta, Rehovoth, Israel, 50-61, chmn div irrig & soil physics, 56-58, dir inst soils & water, 59-61. *Concurrent Pos:* Adj lectr, Israel Inst Technol, 52-55, adj sr lectr, 56-58, adj assoc prof, 59-61; external lectr, Fac Agr, Hebrew Univ, Israel, 52-61; leader, UN Proj Tech Assistance to Cyprus Govt, 57; consult, Govt Israel, 57-61 & Italian Ministry Agr, 60; consult prof, Stanford Univ, Calif, 75- *Mem:* AAAS; Soil Sci Soc Am; Am Geophys Union; Sigma Xi. *Res:* Movement of water and solutes in the unsaturated zone; flow of fluids and transport of reacting solutes in porous media; evapotranspiration; irrigation practices; soil physical properties in relation to plant growth. *Mailing Add:* 3247 Murray Way Palo Alto CA 94303

RUBIN, JEAN E, MATHEMATICS. *Current Pos:* assoc prof, 68-75, PROF MATH, PURDUE UNIV, 75- *Personal Data:* b New York, NY, Oct 29, 26; m 52, Herman; c Arthur L & Leonore A (Findsen). *Educ:* Queens Col, NY, BS, 48; Columbia Univ, MA, 49; Stanford Univ, PhD(math), 55. *Prof Exp:* Instr math, Queens Col, NY, 49-51; instr, Stanford Univ, 53-55; lectr, Univ Ore, 55-59; asst prof, Mich State Univ, 61-68. *Concurrent Pos:* Reviewer math reviews, 65-79; vis lectr, Math Asn Am, 76-86. *Mem:* Am Math Soc; Asn Symbolic Logic; Math Asn Am. *Res:* Set theory; axiom of choice; cardinal and ordinal numbers; models of set theory; textbook on undergraduate logic; two advanced monographs on set theory. *Mailing Add:* Dept Math Purdue Univ West Lafayette IN 47907-1395. *Fax:* 765-494-0548; *E-Mail:* jer@math.purdue.edu

RUBIN, JOEL E(DWARD), ELECTRICAL ENGINEERING. *Current Pos:* MGR DIR, ARTEC CONSULTS INC, 85- *Personal Data:* b Cleveland, Ohio, Sept 5, 28; m 53; c 3. *Educ:* Case Inst Technol, BS, 49; Yale Univ, MFA, 51; Stanford Univ, PhD(theatre eng), 60. *Honors & Awards:* Founder's Award, US Inst Theatre Technol, 72. *Prof Exp:* vpres illuminating eng, Kliegl Bros Lighting, Long Island City, 54-85. *Concurrent Pos:* Mem, Comt Theatre Eng, US Inst Theatre Technol, 60- *Mem:* US Inst Theatre Technol; Illum Eng Soc; Int Orgn Scenographers & Theatre Technicians (pres, 71-79); fel Am Theatre Asn. *Res:* Theatre technology and illuminating engineering. *Mailing Add:* 24 Edgewood Ave Hastings-on-Hudson NY 10706

RUBIN, KARL C, ALGEBRAIC NUMBER THEORY, ARITHMETIC OF ELLIPTIC CURVES. *Current Pos:* asst prof, 84-87, PROF MATH, OHIO STATE UNIV, 87- *Personal Data:* b Urbana, Ill, Jan 27, 56. *Educ:* Princeton Univ, AB, 76; Harvard Univ, MA, 77, PhD(math), 81. *Honors & Awards:* Cole Prize in Number Theory, Am Math Soc, 92. *Prof Exp:* Vis res fel, Princeton Univ, 81-82; instr math, 82-83; prof, Columbia Univ, 88-89. *Concurrent Pos:* Alfred P Sloan fel, 85; NSF presidential young investr, 88; vis scholar, Harvard Univ, 90-91. *Mem:* Am Math Soc. *Res:* Arithmetic of elliptic curves; Iwasawa theory; special values of L-functions, especially questions related to the Birch and Swinnerton-Dyer conjecture. *Mailing Add:* Ohio State Univ 231 W 18th Ave Columbus OH 43210-1174. *E-Mail:* rubin@math.ohio__state.edu

RUBIN, KENNETH, PHYSICS. *Current Pos:* assoc prof, 64-72, PROF PHYSICS, CITY COL NEW YORK, 72- *Personal Data:* b New York, NY, Feb 28, 28; m 51; c 3. *Educ:* NY Univ, BS, 50, MS, 52, PhD(physics), 59. *Prof Exp:* Asst panel electron tubes, Res Div, NY Univ, 52-53 & Radiation Lab, Columbia Univ, 53-54; instr physics, City Col New York, 54-55; from instr to asst prof, NY Univ, 55-64. *Mem:* Am Phys Soc. *Res:* Atomic beam resonance and atomic scattering experiments utilizing atomic beam techniques. *Mailing Add:* Dept Physics City Col NY Convent Ave & 138th St New York NY 10031

RUBIN, LAWRENCE G, PHYSICS & LOW TEMPERATURE THERMOMETRY, MAGNETIC FIELD MEASUREMENT. *Current Pos:* div head, 77-92, group leader, Adv High Field Facil, 93-95, GROUP LEADER INSTRUMENTATION & OPERS, NAT MAGNET LAB, MASS INST TECHNOL, 64-, VIS SCIENTIST, 96- *Personal Data:* b Brooklyn, NY, Sept 17, 25; m 51, Florence R Kagan; c Michael, Richard & Jeffrey. *Educ:* Univ Chicago, BS, 49; Columbia Univ, MA, 50. *Prof Exp:* Staff mem solid state physics, Res Div, Raytheon Co, Mass, 50-58, mgr instrumentation group, 58-64. *Concurrent Pos:* Mem adv panel, Nat Acad Sci, Nat Bur Stand, 77-82, 85-90; chmn & organizer, Instrument & Measurement Sci Group, Am Phys Soc, 85; chmn Physics Today, Buyers Giude Adv Comt, 87- *Mem:* Fel Am Phys Soc; fel Inst Elec & Electronics Engrs; Instrument Soc Am; Am Vacuum Soc. *Res:* Instrumentation in electronics, vacuum, cryogenics and visible and infrared spectrometry; temperature measurement and control; bulk properties of semiconductors; low level signal processing; high field magnetometry. *Mailing Add:* Bldg NW14-1209 Mass Inst Technol 170 Albany St Cambridge MA 02139. *Fax:* 617-253-5405; *E-Mail:* lrubin@slipknot.mit.edu

RUBIN, LEON E, ANALYTICAL CHEMISTRY. *Current Pos:* scientist, 52-65, res group leader, 65-67, MGR ANALYTICAL CHEM, POLAROID CORP, 67- *Personal Data:* b Winthrop, Mass, Apr 24, 21; m 47; c 3. *Educ:* Mass Inst Technol, BS, 42; Boston Univ, MS, 47; Columbia Univ, PhD(chem), 51. *Prof Exp:* Res assoc phys org chem, Columbia Univ, 51-52. *Mem:* Am Chem Soc. *Res:* Spectrophotometry; titrimetry; chromatography; absorption spectroscopy; kinetics of reactions; photographic chemistry; polymer analysis. *Mailing Add:* 33 E End Ave Apt 12C New York NY 10025

RUBIN, LEONARD ROY, TOPOLOGY. *Current Pos:* From asst prof to assoc prof, 67-78, interim dept chmn, 83-85, PROF MATH, UNIV OKLA, 78-, ASSOC DEPT CHMN, 94- *Personal Data:* b Brooklyn, NY, Nov 16, 39; m 60, Diane Lassen; c Sharon & Jeffrey. *Educ:* Tulane Univ, BS, 61; Univ Miami, MS, 63; Fla State Univ, PhD(math), 65. *Honors & Awards:* Fulbright lectr, Univ Zagreb, Yugoslavia, 85-86. *Concurrent Pos:* Staff mem, Okla Univ Res Inst, 68; vis assoc prof, Univ Utah, 73-74; vis prof, Univ Mex, 92. *Mem:* Am Math Soc. *Res:* Geometric topology and dimension theory. *Mailing Add:* Dept Math Univ Okla 601 Elm Ave Rm 423 Norman OK 73019-0315. *E-Mail:* lrubin@ou.edu

RUBIN, LEONARD SIDNEY, PSYCHOPHYSIOLOGY, PSYCHOPHARMACOLOGY. *Current Pos:* RETIRED. *Personal Data:* b New York, NY, Aug 27, 22; m 50; c 3. *Educ:* NY Univ, PhD(neurosci), 51. *Honors & Awards:* Soc Sci Res Coun Award, Inst Math, Stanford Univ, 55; Hon Award, Soc Biol Psychiat, 59. *Prof Exp:* Asst instr biochem, NY Med Col, 44-45; tutor psychol, City Col NY, 45; instr, Wash Sq Col, NY Univ, 47-50, res assoc col eng, 50-53; chief psychol & Human Eng Br, Med Labs, US Chem Corps, 53-57; head psychobiol, Eastern Pa Psychiat Inst, 57-80; prof physiol & pharm, Philadelphia Col Osteop, 80-92. *Concurrent Pos:* Assoc prof psychiat, Sch Med, Univ Pa, 65-81; adj prof, Sch Med, Temple Univ, 70-74; foreign exchange scholar, Nat Acad Sci, Yugoslavia, 74. *Mem:* Fel Acad Psychosomat Med; Soc Biol Psychiat; fel Am Psychol Asn; Am Psychopath Asn; Soc Psychophysiol Res; Am Physiol Soc. *Res:* Autonomic neurohumoral concomitants of schizophrenia; other behavior disorders; chronic alcoholism; drug abuse; migraine. *Mailing Add:* 706 Powder Mill Lane Wynnewood PA 19016

RUBIN, LOUIS, CHEMISTRY. *Current Pos:* PRIN SCIENTIST, RES OPPORTUNITIES, INC, 90- *Personal Data:* b New York, NY, Aug 19, 22; m 46, Trudy Berman; c David & Harriet. *Educ:* NY Univ, AB, 43; Univ Mo, AM, 47, PhD(chem), 50. *Prof Exp:* Asst chem, Univ Mo, 47-50; chemist, Winthrop Labs, 51-52, dir, Process Develop Lab, 52-59; sr chemist, Rohr Aircraft Corp, 59-61, chief tech staff, 61-64; mem tech staff, Aerospace Corp, 64-75, staff scientist, 75- 90. *Concurrent Pos:* Lectr, Univ Calif, Los Angeles & Exten Div, 63-64; pres, Southern Calif Sect, Soc Plastics Engrs, 76-77. *Mem:* Am Chem Soc; Am Inst Aeronaut & Astronaut; Soc Plastics Engrs; Soc Advan Mat & Process Eng. *Res:* Organic chemistry; reinforced plastics; adhesives; polymer chemistry; ablative materials; hypervelocity erosion; metal-matrix composites; carbon-carbon composites. *Mailing Add:* 2502 E Willow St Signal Hill CA 90806

RUBIN, MARTIN ISRAEL, BIOCHEMISTRY, PHARMACOLOGY. *Current Pos:* prof bioclin chem, Med Sch, Georgetown Univ, 48-52, Sch Med Dent, 58-81, prof, 52-81, EMER PROF, GEORGETOWN UNIV, 81- *Personal Data:* b New York, NY, Nov 2, 15; m 42, Edith Felbau; c Joanne, Richard, Naomi & Deborah. *Educ:* City Col New York, BS, 36; Columbia Univ, PhD(org chem), 42. *Hon Degrees:* DSci, Univ Louis Pasteur, France, 76. *Honors & Awards:* Smith Kline & French Award, Fisher Award, Roe Award & Gemlot Award, Am Asn Clin Chemists. *Prof Exp:* Hernscheim fel, Mt Sinai Hosp, 39-40; res chemist, Wallace & Tiernan Prod, Inc, NJ, 41-46 & Schering Corp, 46-48; res fel, Johns Hopkins Med Sch, 41-42. *Concurrent Pos:* US Chem; consult, WHO, Pan Am Health Orgn, Food & Drug Admin & NIH Comn Clin Chem, Int Union Pure & Appl Chem; pres, Int Fedn Clin

Chem & Int Fedn Chelation Chem. *Mem:* AAAS; Am Chem Soc; Soc Exp Biol & Med; Am Asn Clin Chem; Am Rheumatism Asn; AMA. *Res:* Synthetic drugs; use of radioisotopes in biochemistry and medicine; steroid chemistry; clinical chemistry; synthesis of unsaturated lactones related to the cardiac aglycones; chelate compounds; mineral metabolism. *Mailing Add:* 3218 Pauline Dr Chevy Chase MD 20815

RUBIN, MARYILN BERNICE, GENERAL PHYSIOLOGY, NURSING. *Current Pos:* chairperson, Sect Med-Surg Nursing, St Louis Univ, 71-77, assoc prof, Med-Surg Nursing, Grad Prog, 71-75, actg chairperson, 75, coordr, Grad Med-Surg Nursing, 71-85, PROF, SCH NURSING, ST LOUIS UNIV, ST LOUIS, MO, 75-, DIR RES, 85- *Personal Data:* b St Peter, Ill. *Educ:* Wash Univ, BSN, 59, MSN, 60; Southern Ill Univ, Carbondale, PhD(physiol), 71; Lutheran Hosp Sch Nursing, dipl nursing, 54. *Prof Exp:* Staff nurse, instr & supvr, Operating Rm nursing, Lutheran Hosp, St Louis, Mo, 54-57, instr, Med-Surg Nursing, Team Nursing, 60-61, curric head, Med-Surg Nursing, 65-67; instr, med-surg nursing, grad & undergrad, Wash Univ, St Louis, Mo, 61-65, asst dean, Undergrad Nursing Prog, 62-65, asst prof, Med-Surg Nursing Grad Prog, 68-69; teaching asst physiol, Southern Ill Univ, Carbondale, Ill, 67-68, res asst, 69-70; lectr, Med-Surg Nursing Undergrad Prog, Southern Ill Univ, Edwardsville, Ill, 69-70, asst prof, 70-71. *Concurrent Pos:* Consult, Ind State Univ, 84-87; appointee, Bd Sci Counselor, Nat Inst Occup Safety & Health, 84-87; prin investr, Bedrest Res, 90-91. *Mem:* Am Physiol Soc; AAAS. *Res:* Physiologic effects of bedrest; cutaneous blood perfusion at critical sites on the skin are examined for vasomotor change as well as changes in blood volume, flood flow and blood velocity. *Mailing Add:* Dept Nursing St Louis Univ 3525 Caroline St St Louis MO 63104

RUBIN, MAX, ANIMAL NUTRITION, BIOCHEMISTRY. *Current Pos:* fel, 69-72, FAC RES ASSOC ANIMAL NUTRIT, UNIV MD, COLLEGE PARK, 72- *Personal Data:* b New York, NY, Jan 6, 16; m 42; c 2. *Educ:* Rutgers Univ, BS, 38; Univ Md, MS, 40, PhD(poultry nutrit), 42. *Prof Exp:* Chemist, Chem Warfare Serv, 42-43, physiologist, 43-44; biologist, US Bur Animal Indust, 44-46; nutritionist, Schenley Distillers Corp, 46-47. *Concurrent Pos:* Fel animal nutrit, Univ Md, 42-43. *Mem:* AAAS; Poultry Sci Asn; World Poultry Sci Asn; Am Chem Soc. *Res:* Amino acid metabolism; buphthalmos as it is related to glycine in the diet; lysine and tryptophane from grains which have genetically improved amino acid composition. *Mailing Add:* 15107 Interlachen Dr No 914 Silver Spring MD 20906-5625

RUBIN, MELVIN LYNNE, MEDICINE & OPHTHALMOLOGY, OPTICS & RETINAL DISEASES. *Current Pos:* from asst prof to assoc prof, 63-67, chmn dept, 79-94, PROF OPHTHAL, COL MED, UNIV FLA, 67- *Personal Data:* b San Francisco, Calif, May 10, 32; m 53, Lorna Isen; c Gabrielle, Daniel & Michael. *Educ:* Univ Calif, Berkeley, BS, 53; Univ San Francisco, MD, 57; Univ Iowa, MS, 61. *Honors & Awards:* Statesman Award, Joint Common Allied Health Personnel Opthal, 87; Sr Hon Award, Am Acad Opthal, 86; Shalor Richardson Award for Serv to Med, 95. *Prof Exp:* Exec secy vision res training comn, Nat Inst Neurol Dis & Blindness, 61-63. *Mem:* Asn Res Vision & Ophthal (pres); Am Acad Ophthal (secy, pres, 88); Am Ophthal Soc; Sigma Xi. *Res:* Visual physiology and visual optics; retinal anatomy; microscopic histology and photochemistry; effects of therapy for retinal detachment surgery on the microstructrue of the eye. *Mailing Add:* Dept Ophthal Univ Fla Med Ctr PO Box 100284 Gainesville FL 32610

RUBIN, MEYER, GEOLOGY, GEOMORPHOLOGY & GLACIOLOGY. *Current Pos:* geologist, Mil Geol Br, 50-53, geologist, C-14 Lab, Isotope Geol Br, 53-95, EMER SCIENTIST, US GEOL SURV, 95- *Personal Data:* b Chicago, Ill, Feb 17, 24; m 44; c 3. *Educ:* Univ Chicago, BS, 47, MS, 49, PhD, 56. *Prof Exp:* Asst geol, Univ Chicago, 49-50. *Concurrent Pos:* Instr, Ill Inst Technol, 49 & USDA Grad Sch, 51-52. *Mem:* Geol Soc Am; Am Geophys Union; Am Quaternary Asn; Fedn Am Sci. *Res:* Radiocarbon age determinations of Wisconsin glaciations; sea-level changes; dating volcanic eruptions; tandem accelerator mass spectrometry. *Mailing Add:* US Geol Surv Nat Ctr 971 Reston VA 20192

RUBIN, MILTON D(AVID), SYSTEMS ENGINEERING, COMPUTER GRAPHICS. *Current Pos:* PRIN, MILTON RUBIN ASSOCS, 92- *Personal Data:* b Boston, Mass, July 4, 14; m 44, Tillie E Feingold; c Mark J & Lise D. *Educ:* Harvard Univ, BS, 35. *Prof Exp:* Proj engr, Raytheon Corp, Mass, 44-48; res dir comput, Philbrick Res, Inc, 48-49; proj leader radar & comput, Lab Electronics, Inc, Mass, 49-51; group leader radar, Lincoln Lab, Mass Inst Technol, 51-55; dept mgr anal, Sylvania Elec Prod, Inc, 55-57; systs engr, Lincoln Lab, Mass Inst Technol, 57-59 & Mitre Corp, Mass, 59-69; consult scientist, Raytheon Co, 69-75; pres, Energy Conserv Res Inst, 75-77; staff mem, Lincoln Lab, Mass Inst Technol, 77-85; sr systs engr, Teledyne Brown Eng, Lexington, Mass, 85-87; staff mem, Mitre Corp, 87-92. *Mem:* Fel AAAS; Inst Elec & Electronics Engrs; Int Soc Syst Sci. *Res:* Radar systems engineering; printed circuit techniques; computer and radar circuits; analysis of networks of radars for detection of aircraft, missiles and satellites; general systems research; air traffic control; organization theory and technology; communication systems; energy utilization efficiency; computer graphics. *Mailing Add:* 19 Dorr Rd Newton MA 02158. *E-Mail:* 70410.107@compuserve.com

RUBIN, MORTON HAROLD, THEORETICAL PHYSICS. *Current Pos:* ASSOC PROF PHYSICS, UNIV MD, BALTIMORE COUNTY, 73- *Personal Data:* b Albany, NY, Mar 10, 38; div; c 2. *Educ:* Mass Inst Technol, SB, 59; Princeton Univ, PhD(physics), 64. *Prof Exp:* Jr scientist physics, Avco-Everett Res Corp, 60-61; fel physics, Univ Wis, 64-66, instr, 66-67; asst prof physics, Univ Pa, 67-73. *Concurrent Pos:* Vis asst prof physics, Pahlavi Univ, Shiraz, Iran, 70-71. *Mem:* Am Phys Soc; Am Asn Physics Teachers. *Res:* Critical phenomena; nucleation and condensation; statistical mechanics; non-equilibrium thermodynamics; quantum theory of scattering; quantum measurement theory. *Mailing Add:* Dept Physics Univ Md 5401 Wilkens Ave Baltimore MD 21228

RUBIN, MORTON JOSEPH, METEOROLOGY. *Current Pos:* RETIRED. *Personal Data:* b Philadelphia, Pa, May 15, 17; m 40, 75, Rosa Dockett; c Richard, John & Mary Sue. *Educ:* Pa State Univ, BA, 42; Mass Inst Technol, MS, 52. *Honors & Awards:* Antarctic Serv Medal, 65; Am Meteorol Soc Spec Award, 65; Silver Medal, Dept Com, 69. *Prof Exp:* Meteorologist, Pan-Am Grace Airways, 42-49; res assoc meteorol, Mass Inst Technol, 49-52; res meteorologist, US Weather Bur, Environ Sci Serv Admin, 52-65, sr staff scientist meteorol, 65-67, dep chief plans & requirements div, 67-69, chief off spec studies, 67-69, chief res group, Nat Oceanic & Atmospheric Admin, 69-74; sci officer, World Meteorol Orgn, 74-81; vis scholar, Scott Polar Res Inst, 81-82. *Concurrent Pos:* Mem heat & water panel, Comn Polar Res, Nat Acad Sci, 63-65; chmn, Working Group Antarctic Meteorol, Sci Comt Antarctic Res, 64-82; pres, Int Comn Polar Meteorol, 64-72. *Mem:* Am Meteorol Soc; Am Geophys Union. *Res:* Polar meteorology; heat and water budget; southern hemisphere atmospheric circulation and climate. *Mailing Add:* 8013 Westover Rd Bethesda MD 20814-1146

RUBIN, RICHARD LEE, HARMONIC ANALYSIS, SPECIAL FUNCTIONS. *Current Pos:* asst prof, 76-79, ASSOC PROF MATH, FLA INT UNIV, 79- *Personal Data:* b Cleveland, Ohio, Sept 29, 46. *Educ:* Wash Univ, AB, 68, MA, 70, PhD(math), 74. *Prof Exp:* Asst prof math, Oakland Univ, 74-76. *Concurrent Pos:* Vis prof, Nat Res Coun, Turin, Italy, 82-83; lectr, Fla State Univ Study Ctr, Florence, Italy, 85. *Mem:* Am Math Soc. *Res:* Harmonic analysis on Lie groups; behavior of multiplier operators and singular integrals; analysis of anatogue special functions. *Mailing Add:* Dept Math Fla Int Univ Miami FL 33199

RUBIN, RICHARD MARK, NUCLEAR ENGINEERING, PHYSICS. *Current Pos:* VIS ASST PROF MATH, CHRISTIAN BROS UNIV, 96- *Personal Data:* b Pensacola, Fla, July 26, 37; m 63; c 2. *Educ:* Univ Mich, BSE, 59; Univ Okla, MNE, 61; Kans State Univ, PhD(nuclear eng), 70. *Prof Exp:* Exp supvr, Off Civil Defense Contract, Nuclear Eng Shielding Facil, Kans State Univ, 67-69, instr nuclear eng, 69; asst prof, Miss State Univ, 70-77; proj physicist, Radiation Res Assocs, Inc, 77-85; engr, T U Elec, 85- *Concurrent Pos:* Adj mem grad fac, Tex Christian Univ, 77- *Mem:* Am Nuclear Soc; Am Soc Eng Educ; Sigma Xi. *Res:* Radiation shielding; radiation transport; neutron activation analysis; dosimetry. *Mailing Add:* Christian Bros Univ 650 East Pkwy Mail Box No 36 Memphis TN 38104

RUBIN, ROBERT HOWARD, THEORETICAL ASTROPHYSICS, INFRARED ASTRONOMY. *Current Pos:* sr nat res coun assoc, 81-83, assoc, Kuiper Airborne Observ, 92-96, ASSOC AMES RES CTR, NASA, 83-, HUBBLE SPACE TELESCOPE, 93-, INFRARED SPACE OBSERV, 96- *Personal Data:* b Philadelphia, Pa, Mar 26, 41. *Educ:* Case Inst Technol, BS, 63; Case Western Res Univ, PhD(astrophys), 67. *Prof Exp:* Res assoc, Nat Radio Astron Observ, 67-69; res assoc, Univ Ill, Urbana, 69-71, asst prof astron, 71-72; assoc prof physics, Calif State Univ, Fullerton, 72-81. *Concurrent Pos:* Prin investr, NSF grant, 70-72, NASA IRAS grant, 85-89 & NASA IUE grant, 89-90; fac fel, NASA Ames, Santa Clara Univ, 79 & Stanford Univ, 80 & 81; vis prof & res astromr, Univ Calif, Los Angeles, 83-89, 91-92; vis prof, Stanford Univ, 90-91; pres, Orion Enterprises, Mountain View, Calif, 90- *Mem:* Am Astron Soc; Int Astron Union; Int Sci Radio Union; Sigma Xi. *Res:* Interstellar medium; theoretical computer modeling of gaseous nebulae with emphasis on predicting line intensities; extracting physical information such as elemental abundances and properties of exciting stars. *Mailing Add:* NASA Ames Res Ctr Mail Stop 245-6 Moffett Field CA 94035-1000. *Fax:* 650-604-6779; *E-Mail:* rubin@cygnus.arc.nasa.gov

RUBIN, ROBERT JAY, ENVIRONMENTAL TOXICOLOGY, BIOCHEMISTRY. *Current Pos:* from asst prof to assoc, 64-73, Johns Hopkins Univ, 64-73, dir, div toxicol, 77-79, dir, biochem toxicol prog, 83-87, dep dir, Ctr Environ Health Sci, 87-89, PROF ENVIRON HEALTH SCI, SCH HYG & PUB HEALTH, JOHNS HOPKINS UNIV, 73- *Personal Data:* b Boston, Mass, Mar 25, 32; m 83, Idalea Kofsky; c Ellen J, Howard S & Steven G. *Educ:* Univ Mass, BS, 53; Boston Univ, AM, 55, PhD(pharmacol), 60. *Prof Exp:* Asst prof, Univ Kans, 63-64. *Concurrent Pos:* USPHS fel pharmacol, Sch Med, Yale Univ, 60-63; Res Career Develop Award, Nat Inst Environ Health Sci, 69-74; vis prof, Hebrew Univ, Jerusalem, Israel, 76, Univ Milan Italy, 84, Bethune Univ, Changchun PRC, 86. *Mem:* AAAS; Soc Occup & Environ Health; Soc Toxicol; Am Soc Pharmacol & Exp Therapeut. *Res:* Biochemical toxicology; biochemical mechanisms of action of pharmacologic and toxic agents; drug metabolism and disposition; carcinogenesis. *Mailing Add:* Dept Environ Health Sci Johns Hopkins Sch Hyg & Pub Health Baltimore MD 21205. *Fax:* 410-955-0811

RUBIN, ROBERT JOSHUA, APPLICATION OF RANDOM WALKS IN PHYSICS, CHEMISTRY & BIOLOGY, THEORY OF BROWNIAN MOTION. *Current Pos:* spec expert, 87-89, SPEC VOL, NIH, 89- *Personal Data:* b New York, NY, Aug 17, 26; m 48, Vera Cooper; c David M, Karl C, Judith S (Young) & Allan M. *Educ:* Cornell Univ, AB, 48, PhD(phys chem), 51. *Prof Exp:* Sr mem staff, Appl Physics Lab, Johns Hopkins Univ, 51-55; vis asst prof phys chem, Univ Ill, 55-57; physicist, Nat Bur Stand, 57-87. *Concurrent Pos:* NSF sr fel, 63-64; vis prof, Kyoto Univ, Japan, 68; res physicist, NIH, 76-77; vis prof chem eng, Univ Calif, Berkeley, 81. *Mem:* Fel Am Phys Soc; Am Chem Soc; Biophys Soc; Am Math Soc; fel AAAS; Soc Indust & Appl Math. *Res:* Chemical physics; statistical and quantum mechanics; mathematical physics; biophysics. *Mailing Add:* 3308 McKinley St NW Washington DC 20015. *Fax:* 301-496-0825; *E-Mail:* r1r@cu.nih.gov

RUBIN, ROBERT TERRY, PSYCHIATRY. *Current Pos:* resident psychiat, Sch Med, Univ Calif, 62-65, asst prof, 65-71, vis prof, 72-74, adj prof, 74-77, PROF PSYCHIAT, SCH MED, UNIV CALIF, LOS ANGELES, 77-, MEM, BRAIN RES INST, 69-; PROF NEUROSCI & PSYCHIAT, MCP HAHNEMANN SCH MED, 92- *Personal Data:* b Los Angeles, Calif, Aug 26, 36; m 85, Ada Joan Bailey; c 3. *Educ:* Univ Calif, Los Angeles, AB, 58; Univ Calif, San Francisco, MD, 61; Univ Southern Calif, PhD, 77; Am Bd Psychiat & Neurol, dipl & cert psychiat, 68. *Honors & Awards:* Res Scientist Develop, NIMH, 72, 77, 82, 87 & 93; Fulbright-Hays Res Scholar Award, 83; UK Med Res Coun Sr Vis Scientist Award, 83. *Prof Exp:* Intern, Philadelphia Gen Hosp, 61-62. *Concurrent Pos:* Prof psychiat, Col Med, Pa State Univ, 71-74. *Mem:* Fel Am Psychiat Asn; World Psychiat Asn; fel Am Col Psychiat; Int Soc Psychoneuroendocrinol; fel AAAS; Soc Biol Psychiat. *Res:* Biochemical and neuroendocrine correlates of stress and mental illness. *Mailing Add:* Allegheny Gen Hosp Neurosci Res Ctr 320 E North Ave Pittsburgh PA 15212

RUBIN, RONALD PHILIP, CELLULAR PHARMACOLOGY, SECRETORY MECHANISMS. *Current Pos:* PROF PHARMACOL & HEAD DIV CELLULAR PHARMACOL, MED COL VA, 74- *Personal Data:* b Newark, NJ, Jan 4, 33; m 56; c 3. *Educ:* Harvard Univ, AB, 54, AMT, 58; Yeshiva Univ, PhD(pharmacol), 63. *Prof Exp:* From instr to assoc prof pharmacol, Downstate Med Ctr, State Univ NY, 64-74. *Mem:* AAAS; Am Soc Pharmacol & Exp Therapeut; Endocrine Soc; Harvey Soc; NY Acad Sci. *Res:* Cellular and biochemical events that regulate the secretory process. *Mailing Add:* Dept Pharmacol & Therapeut State Univ NY Farber Hall Rm 102 Buffalo NY 14214-3000. *Fax:* 716-829-2801

RUBIN, SAMUEL H, INTERNAL MEDICINE. *Current Pos:* Assoc prof, NY Med Col, 60-65, prof internal med, 65-84, dir, Cardiovasc Training Prog, 66-71, assoc dean, 71-72, vpres acad affairs, 75-77, dean col, 75-83, provost, 77-83, dir, Inst Med Ethics, 84-86, PROVOST & EMER DEAN, NY MED COL, 84- *Personal Data:* b New York, NY, July 24, 16; m 43; c 2. *Educ:* Brown Univ, AB, 38; Univ Chicago, MS, 55; St Louis Univ, MD, 43; Am Bd Internal Med, dipl. *Concurrent Pos:* Exec dean, NY Med Col, 62-84. *Mem:* Fel Am Col Physicians; NY Acad Sci. *Res:* Clinical and internal medicine; medical education. *Mailing Add:* 425E Heritage Hills Somers NY 10589

RUBIN, SAUL H, ENGINEERING. *Current Pos:* RETIRED. *Personal Data:* b Cleveland, Ohio, Nov 24, 23; m 47; c 4. *Educ:* Case Inst Technol, BS, 44, MS, 47. *Prof Exp:* Res engr, Nat Adv Comt Aeronaut, Ohio, 44-45; asst, Case Inst Technol, 45-46; sci engr, Joy Mfg Co, 47-50; sci engr, Tyroler Metals, Inc, 50-64, pres, 64-88. *Mem:* Am Soc Mech Engrs; Sigma Xi; Nat Soc Prof Engrs; Org Spare Parts & Equipment. *Res:* Test and analysis of aircraft compressors and navy refrigeration coils; analytical design and analysis of axial-flow fans and compressors; design of equipment for salvage and reclamation. *Mailing Add:* 2445 Queenston Rd Cleveland Heights OH 44118

RUBIN, SAUL HOWARD, biochemistry; deceased, see previous edition for last biography

RUBIN, SHELDON, STRUCTURAL DYNAMICS & LIQUID ROCKET DYNAMICS, SHOCK & VIBRATION. *Current Pos:* PRIN ENGR, RUBIN ENG CO, SHERMAN OAKS, CALIF, 96- *Personal Data:* b Chicago, Ill, July 19, 32; m 55, Ann Lustgarten; c Geoffrey, Kenneth & Beth. *Educ:* Calif Inst Technol, BS, 53, MS, 54, PhD(mech eng, physics), 56. *Honors & Awards:* Shuttle Flight Cert Award, NASA, 81. *Prof Exp:* Res engr sound & vibration, Lockheed Aircraft Co, 56-58; head, Tech Eng Sect, Hughes Aircraft Co, 58-62; distinguished engr, Aerospace Corp, Los Angeles, 62-96. *Concurrent Pos:* Consult, 56-; chmn, Aerospace Shock & Vibration Comt, Soc Automotive Engrs, 62- *Mem:* Assoc fel Am Inst Aeronaut & Astronaut; fel Soc Automotive Engrs; Soc Exp Mech. *Res:* Test and analysis of structural vibration; influence of propulsion system on vibration stability of liquid rocket vehicles; test requirements for launch and space vehicles; dynamic characterization of civil structures. *Mailing Add:* Rubin Eng Co 3531 Alana Dr Sherman Oaks CA 91403. *Fax:* 818-986-4069; *E-Mail:* s_arubin@earthlink.net

RUBIN, STANLEY G(ERALD), COMPUTATIONAL FLUID MECHANICS, VISCOUS FLOWS. *Current Pos:* head dept, 79-89, PROF AEROSPACE & ENG MECH, UNIV CINCINNATI, 79- *Personal Data:* b Brooklyn, NY, May 11, 38; m 63, Carol R Kalvin; c Stephany, Elizabeth & Barbara. *Educ:* Polytech Inst Brooklyn, BAE, 59; Cornell Univ, PhD(aerospace eng), 63. *Prof Exp:* Res scientist, Boeing Airplane Co, 63; NSF fel, Henri Poincare Inst, Univ Paris, 63-64; from asst prof to assoc prof eng & appl mech, Polytech Inst New York, 64-73, prof mech & aerospace eng, 73-79, assoc dir, Aerodyn Labs, 77-79; dir, NASA Space Eng Res Ctr, 88-91. *Concurrent Pos:* Vis prof mech eng, Old Dominion Univ, 73-74; consult, Fluid Dynamics Tech Comt, Am Inst Aeronaut & Astronaut, 75-78, Aerospace Corp, 77-82, Allison Gas Turbine, 84-86, NASA aeronaut res technol sub comt, 86-89; vis scientist, Air Force Wright Aeronaut Labs, 87; contractor, USAF Off Sci Res, 67- & NASA, 73-; chief ed, Int J Comput & Fluids, 78; vis prof, Univ Bari, Ital, 96. *Mem:* Fel Am Soc Mech Engrs; Am Soc Eng Educ; assoc fel Am Inst Aeronaut & Astronaut; Sigma Xi. *Res:* High-speed gasdynamics; three-dimensional viscous interactions; asymptotic expansions in viscous flow; numerical analysis of flow problems; particulate flow. *Mailing Add:* 10695 Deershadow Lane Cincinnati OH 45242. *Fax:* 513-556-5308; *E-Mail:* srubin@uceng.uc.edu

RUBIN, VERA COOPER, ASTRONOMY, OBSERVATIONAL COSMOLOGY. *Current Pos:* STAFF MEM, DEPT TERRESTRIAL MAGNETISM, CARNEGIE INST, 65- *Personal Data:* b Philadelphia, Pa, July 23, 28; m 48, Robert J; c David, Judith (Young), Karl & Allan. *Educ:* Vassar Col, BA, 48; Cornell Univ, MA, 51; Georgetown Univ, PhD(astron), 54. *Hon Degrees:* DSc, Creighton Univ, 78, Harvard Univ, 88, Yale Univ, 90, Williams Col, 93 & Univ Mich, 96. *Honors & Awards:* Nat Medal Sci, 93; Grubb Parsons Lectr, Univ Durham, Eng, 93; Jeffrey Bishop Lectr, Columbia Univ, 93; Gold Medal, Royal Astron Soc, 96; Women & Sci Award, Weizmann Ins, 96. *Prof Exp:* Instr math & physics, Montgomery County Jr Col, 54-55; res assoc astron, Georgetown Univ, 55-65, lectr, 59-62, asst prof, 62-65. *Concurrent Pos:* Assoc ed, Astron J, 72- & Astrophys J Letters, 77-; mem, space astron comt, Nat Acad Sci, 72-, US Nat Comt, Int Astron Union, 72-76, Bd of Dirs, Asn Univs Res Astron, Inc, 73-76 & Space Sci Bd, Nat Acad Sci, 74-76; distinguished vis astron, Cerro Tololo, 78; mem, Smithsonian Coun, 79-84; Chancellor's distinguished prof astron, Univ Calif, Berkeley, 81; mem coun, Am Women in Sci, 84-; president's distinguished visitor, Vassar Col, 87; Tinsley vis prof, Univ Tex, 88; mem bd physics & astron, Nat Acad Sci. *Mem:* Nat Acad Sci; Int Astron Union; Am Astron Soc; Astron Soc Pac; Pontif Acad Sci; NY Acad Sci. *Res:* External galaxies; galactic dynamics; spectroscopy; motions of stars in galaxies and motions of galaxies in the universe. *Mailing Add:* Dept Terr Magnet Carnegie Inst 5241 Broad Branch Rd Washington DC 20015

RUBIN, WALTER, GASTROENTEROLOGY, CELL BIOLOGY. *Current Pos:* assoc prof med, 69-70, assoc prof anat, 69-75, CHIEF GASTROENTEROL & VCHMN DEPT MED, MED COL PA, 69-, PROF MED, 70-, PROF ANAT, 75- *Personal Data:* b Worcester, Mass, Aug 15, 33; m 58, Naomi Belle Mel Tzer; c Stuart J, Elizabeth L, Deborah M, Michael B & Adam D. *Educ:* Mass Inst Technol, BS, 55; Cornell Univ, MD, 59. *Prof Exp:* From instr to asst prof med, Med Col, Cornell Univ, 64-69, asst prof anat, 68-69. *Concurrent Pos:* Res fel med, Med Col, Cornell Univ, 62-64; Nat Inst Arthritis & Metab Dis res grant & Am Cancer Soc res grant, Med Col, Cornell Univ, 66-69 & Med Col Pa, 69-88; consult gastroenterol, Mem Hosp, New York, 69-70 & Vet Admin Hosp, Philadelphia, 69-; mem gastrointestinal syst res eval comt, US Vet Admin, 69-71; mem merit rev bd gastroenterol, 72-74; mem ed coun, Ital J Gastroenterol, 70-84; mem gastroenterol adv panel, Subcomt Scope of US Pharmacopeia Comt of Revision, 75-85; chmn, Gen Med A Study Sect, NIH, 82-85. *Mem:* Am Soc Cell Biol; Histochem Soc; fel Am Col Physicians; Am Gastroenterol Asn; Am Soc Clin Invest; Am Asn Study Liver Dis. *Res:* Gastrointestinal epithelia, particularly their fine structure, ontogenesis, differentiation and function in health and disease. *Mailing Add:* Dept Med & Anat Med Col Pa 3300 Henry Ave Philadelphia PA 19129-1121. *Fax:* 215-849-1525

RUBINK, WILLIAM LOUIS, AFRICANIZED HONEY BEE ECOLOGY, TRACHEAL MITE ECOLOGY. *Current Pos:* RES ENTOMOLOGIST, AGR RES SERV, USDA, 83- *Personal Data:* b Sterling, Colo, Apr 5, 47; m 75, Amy H Juan; c Bryan, William & Alan. *Educ:* Utah State Univ, BS, 69, MS, 73; Colo State Univ, PhD(entom), 78. *Prof Exp:* Res asst, Utah State Univ, 71-73; teaching asst, Colo State Univ, 75-78, res assoc, 78-79; res assoc, Ohio State Univ, 79-82. *Mem:* AAAS; Entom Soc Am; Sigma Xi; Am Entom Soc. *Res:* Basic ecology of solitary wasps, including nest site selection; ecology of maize pests and parasitoids, including a tachinid fly, Bonnetia comta; population studies of the honey bee during the process of Africanization. *Mailing Add:* 2116 Nightingale Ave McAllen TX 78504-3803

RUBINO, ANDREW M, INORGANIC CHEMISTRY, PHYSICAL CHEMISTRY. *Current Pos:* dir res & develop, 66-73, vpres-tech dir, 73-78, CONSULT, REHEIS CHEM CO DIV, ARMOUR PHARMACEUT CO, 78- *Personal Data:* b Brooklyn, NY, Apr 30, 22; m 44; c 3. *Educ:* St Johns's Col, NY, BS, 49. *Prof Exp:* Res chemist, Reheis Co Inc, NJ, 51-56, mgr tech serv, 56-60 & res & develop, 60-65; vpres & tech dir, Dragoco Inc, 65-66. *Mem:* AAAS; Am Chem Soc; Soc Cosmetic Chem; NY Acad Sci. *Res:* Aluminum chemistry; chelates; cosmetics; pharmaceuticals and other fine chemicals. *Mailing Add:* 39B Westview Ave New Providence NJ 07974-1522

RUBINOFF, IRA, ZOOLOGY. *Current Pos:* asst dir sci, 65-73, DIR, SMITHSONIAN TROP RES INST, 73- *Personal Data:* b New York, NY, Dec 21, 38; m 78, Anabella Guardia; c Jason, Andres & Ana. *Educ:* Queens Col, BS, 59; Harvard Univ, AM, 61, PhD(biol), 63. *Honors & Awards:* Order of Vasco Nunez De Balboa. *Prof Exp:* Fel evolutionary biol, Harvard Univ, 64; asst cur ichthyol, Mus Comp Zool, 65. *Concurrent Pos:* Assoc ichthyol, Mus Comp Zool, Harvard Univ, 65-79; mem adv sci bd, Gorgas Mem Inst, 74-90; mem bd dirs, Charles Darwin Res Found, 76-, Int Sch Panama, 84-86 & 90-94, Nat Asn Conserv of Nature, Panama, 85-, Fundacion Natura, 90-; trustee, Rare Animal Relief Effort, 76-86; vis fel, Wolfson Col, Oxford Univ, 80-81; hon dir, Latin Am Inst Advan Studies; vis scholar, Mus Comp Zool, Harvard Univ, 87-88. *Mem:* Fel AAAS; Am Soc Nat; Am Soc Ichthyol & Herpet; Soc Study Evolution; fel Linnean Soc London; NY Acad Sci. *Res:* Biological implications of the construction of a sea level canal; zoogeography of the eastern tropical Pacific; strategies for preservation of world's tropical forests; diving physiology of sea snakes. *Mailing Add:* Smithsonian Trop Res Inst Unit 948 APO AA 34002-0948 Panama. *Fax:* 507-32-6197; *E-Mail:* strem002.sivm.si.edu

RUBINOFF, MORRIS, ELECTRICAL ENGINEERING. *Current Pos:* from asst prof to assoc prof, 50-63, PROF ELEC ENG, MOORE SCH ELEC ENG, UNIV PA, 63- *Personal Data:* b Toronto, Ont, Aug 20, 17; nat US; m 41; c 3. *Educ:* Univ Toronto, BA, 41, MA, 42, PhD(external ballistics), 46. *Honors & Awards:* Inst Elec & Electronics Engrs Award, 55. *Prof Exp:* Teach tech sch, Ont, 41; asst, Univ Toronto, 42-44; res fel & instr physics, Harvard Univ, 46-48; res engr, Inst Advan Study, 48-50; pres, Pa Res Assocs, 60-78.

Concurrent Pos: Asst dir, Naval Ord Eng, 43-44; chief engr, Philco Corp, 57-59; trustee, Eng Index, 67-; mem res adv comt commun, instrumentation & data processing, NASA. *Mem:* Asn Comput Mach; Inst Elec & Electronics Engrs. *Res:* Computer logical design; electronic circuit design; mathematical analysis; information retrieval. *Mailing Add:* Univ Pa Philadelphia PA 19174

RUBINOFF, ROBERTA WOLFF, MARINE BIOLOGY. *Current Pos:* asst dir, 80-84, actg dir, 84-85, DIR OFF FEL & GRANTS ADMIN, SMITHSONIAN INST, 85- *Personal Data:* b New York, NY, Aug 26, 39. *Educ:* Queen's Col, BS, 59; Duke Univ, MEM, 81. *Prof Exp:* Biologist res, Smithsonian Trop Res Inst, 66-75, marine sci coordr admin & res, 75-80. *Mem:* AAAS; Am Inst Biol Sci; Am Soc Zoologists. *Res:* Behavior and evolution of transisthmian species of intertidal organisms; taxonomic group speciality is tropical marine inshore fishes. *Mailing Add:* Smithsonian Inst 7000 L'Enfant Plaza Washington DC 20560

RUBINOW, DAVID R, PSYCHIATRY. *Current Pos:* staff psychiatrist, Sect Psychobiol, Biol Psychiat Br, NIMH, 79-82, chief psychiat, Consult-LIaison Serv, 82-92, Unit Peptide Studies, 82-89, Sect Behav Endocrinol, 89-96, dir residency training, 90-96, CLIN DIR, NIMH, 87-, CHIEF BEHAV ENDOCRINOL BR, 96-; CLIN PROF PSYCHIAT, GEORGETOWN UNIV MED SCH, 91- *Personal Data:* b Hartford, Conn, Sept 20, 49; m 71, Carly M; c Tasha, Katya & Dara. *Educ:* Univ Mich, BA, 70; Univ Conn, MD, 75; Am Bd Psychiat & Neurol, dipl, 80. *Honors & Awards:* A E Bennett Neuropsychiat Res Found Award, Soc Biol Psychiat, 85; Res Award, Acad Psychosom Med, 96. *Prof Exp:* Intern & resident psychiat, Yale Univ, 75-79. *Concurrent Pos:* Consult, Nat Cancer Inst Med Br, 80-87; sr staff attending, Psychiat Consult Serv, NIH, 81-87. *Mem:* Endocrine Soc; Soc Biol Psychiat; Am Col Neuropsychopharmacol; fel Acad Behav Med Res; Int Soc Psychoneuroendocrinol. *Mailing Add:* Off Clin Dir NIMH Bldg 10 Rm 3N 238 10 Center Dr MSC 1276 Bethesda MD 20892-1276. *Fax:* 301-402-2588; *E-Mail:* rubinowd@irp.nimh.nih.gov

RUBINS, PHILIP M, SUPERSONIC COMBUSTION & HYPERSONIC APPLICATIONS, COMBUSTION COMPUTER MODELLING FOR EFFICIENCY & POLLUTION CONTROL. *Current Pos:* OWNER & PRES, ENG MGT CONSULTS, 81- *Personal Data:* b Oklahoma City, Okla, Nov 9, 17; m 46. *Educ:* Univ Okla, BS, 41, BS, 48. *Honors & Awards:* Ignitor Award, Am Inst Aeronaut & Astronaut, 61; Wright Brothers Medal, Soc Automotive Engrs, 62. *Prof Exp:* Test engr, Aerophys Lab, Gen Dynamics, 48-54; design engr, Gleason Derrick & Equip Co, 54-55; proj engr, Aircraft Gas Turbine Div, Gen Elec Co, 55-58; res proj engr, Arnold Eng Develop Ctr, USAF, 58-67; sr combustion res engr, United Technol Res Ctr, 67-70; supvr, Combustor Res & Develop, Avco Lycoming Div, 70-79; sr develop engr, Mech Technol Inc, 79-81. *Concurrent Pos:* Chmn educ comt, Tenn Sect, Am Inst Aeronaut & Astronaut, 62-65, Conn Sect, 68-70; mem, Advan Propulsion Comt, Soc Automotive Engrs, 66-71. *Mem:* Assoc fel Am Soc Aeronaut & Astronaut; Am Soc Mech Engrs; Combustion Inst. *Res:* Supersonic combustion; developed concept and experimental verification for shock-induced combustion; hypersonic propulsion flight; co-developer of simplified computer combustion model to improve combustion efficiency and reduce pollutants; author of 13 papers published in field. *Mailing Add:* Eng Mgt Consults 889 Inman Rd Niskayuna NY 12309. *Fax:* 518-346-2528; *E-Mail:* philrub@concentric.net

RUBINS, ROY SELWYN, MAGNETIC RESONANCE. *Current Pos:* from asst prof to assoc prof, 69-82, PROF PHYSICS, UNIV TEX, ARLINGTON, 82- *Personal Data:* b Manchester, Eng, Nov 11, 35; m 63, Patricia M; c Daniel & Jonathan. *Educ:* Oxford Univ, BA, 57, MA & DPhil(physics), 64. *Prof Exp:* Res physicist, Hebrew Univ Jerusalem, 61-63; vis physicist, Battelle Mem Inst, Geneva, 63; res assoc physics, Syracuse Univ, 64-66; asst res physicist & asst prof in residence physics, Univ Calif, Los Angeles, 66-68; lectr, Calif State Col, Los Angeles, 69. *Concurrent Pos:* Michael & Anna Wix fel, Hebrew Univ Jerusalem, 61-62; adj prof, Mont State Univ, 84- *Mem:* Am Phys Soc; Am Asn Physics Teachers. *Res:* Experimental and theoretical studies in electron paramagnetic resonance; nuclear relaxation in hydrogen deuteride; modulated microwave absorption in superconductors; EPR studies of magnetic clusters and low dimensional magnetism in organometallic compounds. *Mailing Add:* Dept Physics Box 19059 Univ Tex 107 F Sci Bldg Arlington TX 76019. *Fax:* 817-273-3637

RUBINSON, JUDITH FAYE, ELECTROCHEMISTRY. *Current Pos:* VIS SCHOLAR, UNIV CINCINNATI, 96- *Personal Data:* b Rose Hill, NC, Nov 14, 52; m 80; c 2. *Educ:* Univ NC, Chapel Hill, BS, 74; Univ Cincinnati, PhD(anal chem), 81. *Prof Exp:* Chemist, Velsicol Chem Corp, 74-75 & Merrell-Nat Labs, 76-77; postdoctoral assoc, Charles F Kettering Res Lab, 81-84; asst prof, Wright State Univ, 85-89 & Univ Dayton, 89-90; asst prof, Col Mt St Joseph, 90-96. *Mem:* Am Chem Soc; Coun Undergrad Res. *Res:* Electrochemistry of biological molecules; electrode modification. *Mailing Add:* Dept Chem ML172 Univ Cincinnati Cincinnati OH 45221-0172. *Fax:* 513-244-4222; *E-Mail:* rubinson@ucbeh.san.uc.edu

RUBINSON, KALMAN, NEUROANATOMY, RETINAL DEVELOPMENT. *Current Pos:* asst prof, 69-74, assoc prof cell biol, 74-78, ASSOC PROF PHYSIOL & BIOPHYS, SCH MED, NY UNIV, 78- *Personal Data:* b New York, NY, Dec 24, 41; wid; c 2. *Educ:* Columbia Univ, AB, 62; State Univ NY Downstate Med Ctr, PhD(anat), 68. *Prof Exp:* Vis asst prof anat, Sch Med, Univ PR, San Juan, 67-68; vis prof, Sch Med, Univ PR, San Juan, 69. *Concurrent Pos:* Nat Inst Neurol Dis & Stroke fel, Lab Perinatal Physiol, PR, 68-69; Nat Inst Neurol Dis & Stroke res grants, Sch Med, NY Univ, 70-72 & Pub Health Res Inst NY, 74-76; assoc, Dept Neurobiol & Behav, Pub Health Res Inst, NY, 69-76. *Mem:* Soc Neurosci; Asn Res Vision & Ophthal. *Res:* Comparative neuroanatomy; development of sensory pathways and retina. *Mailing Add:* Dept Physiol & Biophys Sch Med NY Univ 550 First Ave New York NY 10016-6481

RUBINSON, KENNETH A, PHYSICAL BIOCHEMISTRY, MAGNETIC RESONANCE IMAGING PROBES. *Current Pos:* FIVE OAKS RES INST, 82-; ADJ ASSOC PROF, WRIGHT STATE UNIV, 85-; ADJ ASSOC PROF, SCH MED, UNIV CINCINNATI, 91- *Personal Data:* b June 20, 44; m 81, Judith F; c 2. *Educ:* Oberlin Col, BA, 66; Univ Mich, PhD(phys-inorg chem), 72. *Prof Exp:* Res asst, Univ Chem Lab, Cambridge, UK, 73-78; vis assoc prof & adj prof, Dept Chem, Univ Cincinnati, 79-82, adj asst prof, Sch Med, 85-91. *Concurrent Pos:* Fel, NIH, 73-75 & NATO, 77-78; eng SRC fel, 75-76; hon Ramsey mem fel, 76-78; res serv award, NIH, 76-77. *Mem:* Royal Soc Chem; Am Phys Soc; Int Electronic Paramagnetic Resonance Soc; Am Chem Soc. *Res:* Magnetic resonance; chromatographies; biological macromolecular kinetics. *Mailing Add:* Five Oaks Res Inst 354 Oakwood Park Dr Cincinnati OH 45238

RUBINSTEIN, ASHER A, FRACTURE MECHANICS, FAILURE ANALYSIS. *Current Pos:* ASSOC PROF DEPT MECH ENG, TULANE UNIV, 87- *Personal Data:* b Kishinev, USSR, Sept 16, 47; m 80; c 2. *Educ:* Leningrad Polytech Inst, Dipl, 72; Israel Inst Technol, MSc, 77; Brown Univ, PhD(eng), 81. *Prof Exp:* Design engr equip design, Lenigrad Turbine Blades Plant, 72-74; res engr mat testing, Israel Inst Metals, 74-75; asst prof mech eng, State Univ NY, Stony Brook, 81-87. *Concurrent Pos:* Prin investr, NSF grant, 83-85 & NASA, 86- *Mem:* Soc Eng Sci; Am Soc Mech Engrs; Am Acad Mech. *Res:* Application of theoretical mechanics of materials to problems at interface of continuum mechanics and material science, especially the analysis of problems in the deformation and fracture of solids at both macro and micro scales. *Mailing Add:* Dept Mech Eng Tulane Univ New Orleans LA 70118-5674

RUBINSTEIN, CHARLES B(ENJAMIN), HUMAN FACTORS, SYSTEMS ENGINEERING. *Current Pos:* RETIRED. *Personal Data:* b New York, NY, Dec 25, 33; m 57, Phyllis Strominger; c Barrie, Mindy & Steven. *Educ:* City Col NY, BEE, 59; NY Univ, MEE, 61. *Prof Exp:* Mem tech staff, Res Area, Bell Tel Labs, 59-77, head, Human Factors Dept, 77-82, Int Planning Dept, 82-90, head, Networking & Human Factors Dept, 90-93, head, Cross Platform Customer Solutions Dept, AT&T Bell Labs, 94-97. *Mem:* Fel Optical Soc Am; Asn Res Vision & Ophthal. *Res:* Magneto, electro, geometrical and physical optics; optical properties of materials; crystallographic properties of rare earth crystals; holography; color perception and rendition in complex scenes; digital coding of color pictures; visual threshold; human factors; systems engineering. *Mailing Add:* 210 Richdale Rd Colts Neck NJ 07722. *Fax:* 732-957-5499

RUBINSTEIN, EDUARDO HECTOR, PHYSIOLOGY. *Current Pos:* from asst prof physiol to assoc prof, 67-77, PROF-IN-RESIDENCE ANESTHESIOL & PHYSIOL, UNIV CALIF, LOS ANGELES, 77- *Personal Data:* b Buenos Aires, Arg, July 10, 31; c 2. *Educ:* Univ Buenos Aires, BS, 48, MD, 58, PhD(med), 61. *Prof Exp:* Asst physiol, Sch Med, Univ Buenos Aires, 56-58, asst med, Med Res Inst, 58-61, head neurophysiol sect, 64-67, assoc researcher, 66-67. *Concurrent Pos:* Res fel physiol, Sch Med, Yale Univ, 61-62; res fel physiol, Sch Med, Gotenburg Univ, 62-64; WHO med res grant, Med Res Inst, Univ Buenos Aires, 65-67; estab investr, Nat Res Coun, Arg, 64; asst researcher & lectr, Cardiovasc Res Inst, Univ Calif, San Francisco, 66; sr res investr, Los Angeles County Heart Asn, 67; prin investr, Am Heart Asn grant, Univ Calif, Los Angeles, 69-72. *Mem:* Am Physiol Soc; Soc Neurosci. *Res:* Central nervous control of autonomic functions, especially cardiovascular and gastrointestinal. *Mailing Add:* Dept Anesthesiol & Physiol Univ Calif Los Angeles Sch Med 10833 LeConte Ave Los Angeles CA 90024-1300

RUBINSTEIN, HARRY, ORGANIC CHEMISTRY. *Current Pos:* dean grad sch, 77-87, PROF CHEM, UNIV LOWELL, 65- *Personal Data:* b Cologne, Ger, Dec 19, 30; nat US; m 54, Jean Rauch; c Moira, Felicia & Simone. *Educ:* Brooklyn Col, BS, 53; Purdue Univ, MS, 56, PhD(org chem), 58. *Prof Exp:* Res chemist, Wyandotte Chem Corp, 58-59, Keystone Chemurgic Corp, 59-60 & Merck & Co, 60-63; asst prof chem, Springfield Col, 64-65. *Concurrent Pos:* Vis prof, Harvard Sch Pub Health, 87, Weizman Inst, 71-72. *Mem:* Am Chem Soc; Sigma Xi. *Res:* Heterocyclic compounds; natural products; general organic syntheses; mass spectroscopy; capillary electrophoresis. *Mailing Add:* 15 Fairbanks Rd Chelmsford MA 01824. *Fax:* 978-934-3013; *E-Mail:* rubinsteh@woods.uml.edu

RUBINSTEIN, JACK HERBERT, PEDIATRICS. *Current Pos:* from inst to assoc prof, 56-70, Clin Prog Ment Retarded, 67-74, PROF, UNIV CINCINNATI, 74-; DIR, CTR FOR DEVELOP DISORDERS, 74- *Personal Data:* b New York, NY, Aug 4, 25; m 52, 90, Marlene Florence Tibbs. *Educ:* Columbia Univ, AB, 47; Harvard Univ, MD, 52. *Prof Exp:* Intern pediat, Beth Israel Hosp, 52-53; intern, Mass Gen Hosp, 53-54, sr asst resident, 54-55; sr assdt resident, Children's Hosp Med Ctr, Cincinnati, 55-56, asst med dir & fel, Pediat Outpatient Dept, 56-57. *Concurrent Pos:* Dir, Hamilton County Diag Clin Ment Retarded, Cincinnati, 57-74, Children's Neuromuscular Diag Clin, Cincinnati, 62-74; attending pediatrician, Children's Hosp Med Ctr, 57- *Mem:* Fel Am Acad Pediat; Am Pediat Soc; Teratology Soc; Am Asn Ment Retardation; Am Asn Univ Affil Progs Persons Develop Disabilities. *Res:* Rubinstein-Taybi syndrome. *Mailing Add:* 541 Ludlow Ave Cincinnati OH 45220-1581

RUBINSTEIN, LAWRENCE VICTOR, MEDICAL STATISTICIAN. *Current Pos:* statist fel, 78-83, MATH STATISTICIAN, NAT CANCER INST, 85- *Personal Data:* b Washington, DC, Oct 10, 46; m 80, Yaffa Reuveni; c Tamar, Yael & Daniel. *Educ:* Cornell Univ, BA, 69; Univ Md, MA, 74, PhD(math statist), 78. *Prof Exp:* Programmer, Univac, Apollo Proj, 69-73; teaching asst math, Univ Md, College Park, 73-78; math statistician, Nat Inst

Neurologic Dis & Stroke, 83-85. *Mem:* Am Statist Asn; Biometric Soc. *Res:* Statistical design and analysis of clinical studies in particular; sample size determination and trial monitoring strategies; statistical analysis of in vitro cell-line screens for anti-cancer agents. *Mailing Add:* 5504 Manorfield Rd Rockville MD 20853

RUBINSTEIN, LYDIA, ENDOCRINOLOGY, NEUROENDOCRINOLOGY. *Current Pos:* asst prof, 76-81, ASSOC PROF, DEPT OBSTET & GYNEC, SCH MED, UNIV CALIF, 81- *Personal Data:* b Buenos Aires, Arg, Jan 30, 36; m 59; c 2. *Educ:* Univ Buenos Aires, MD, 59, PhD(physiol), 61. *Prof Exp:* Estab investr, Inst Biol & Exp Med, 61-76. *Concurrent Pos:* Nat Coun Sci Res fel anat, Med Sch, Yale Univ, 61-62 & fel physiol, Gotenburg Univ, 62-64; Ford Found fel anat, Med Sch, Univ Calif, Los Angeles, 68-69. *Mem:* Endocrine Soc; Arg Biol Soc; NY Acad Sci. *Res:* Regulatory mechanisms of reproduction and growth processes. *Mailing Add:* 1100 Glendon Ave Suite 950 Los Angeles CA 90024-3513

RUBINSTEIN, MARK, SOLID STATE PHYSICS. *Current Pos:* RES PHYSICIST, US NAVAL RES LAB, 64- *Personal Data:* b Brooklyn, NY, Dec 26, 35; m 57; c 3. *Educ:* Univ Colo, BA, 57; Univ Calif, PhD(physics), 63. *Prof Exp:* Res assoc solid state physics, Atomic Energy Res Estab, Eng, 63. *Mem:* Am Phys Soc. *Res:* Nuclear magnetic resonance in magnetically ordered systems. *Mailing Add:* 3302 Wessynton Way Alexandria VA 22309

RUBINSTEIN, MOSHE FAJWEL, STRUCTURAL DYNAMICS. *Current Pos:* from asst prof to assoc prof eng, 61-69, coord prof & prog dir continuing educ, Mod Eng for Execs Prog, 65-70, chmn, Eng Systs Dept, 70-75, PROF ENG, SCH ENG & APPL SCI, UNIV CALIF, LOS ANGELES, 69- *Personal Data:* b Miechow, Poland, Aug 13, 30; nat US; m 53; c 2. *Educ:* Univ Calif, Los Angeles, BS, 54, MS, 57, PhD, 61. *Honors & Awards:* Award for Excellence, Am Soc Eng Educ, 65. *Prof Exp:* Designer, Murray Erick Assocs, 54-56; struct designer, Victor Gruen Assocs, 56-61. *Concurrent Pos:* Consult, Pac Power & Light Co, Ore, Northrop Corp, US Army, NASA Res Ctr, Langley, Tex Instruments Co, Hughes Space Syst Div, US Army Sci Adv Comn, Kaiser Aluminum & Chem Corp & IBM; Sussmann chair distinguished vis, Technion Israel Inst Technol, 67-68; Fulbright-Hays fel, Yugoslavia & Eng, 75-76; mem acad rev bd, IBM. *Mem:* Am Soc Chem Engrs; Am Soc Eng Educ; Seismol Soc Am; Sigma Xi; NY Acad Sci. *Res:* Use of computers in structural systems, analysis and synthesis; problem solving and decision theory; author of 70 publications and 6 books which have been translated to foreign languages. *Mailing Add:* 10488 Charing Cross Rd West Los Angeles CA 90024-2646

RUBINSTEIN, ROY, EXPERIMENTAL HIGH ENERGY PHYSICS. *Current Pos:* PHYSICIST, FERMI NAT ACCELERATOR LAB, 73- & ASST DIR. *Personal Data:* b Darlington, Eng, Sept 12, 36; m 68, Nora Dodokin; c 2. *Educ:* Cambridge Univ, BA, 58; Birmingham Univ, PhD(physics), 61. *Prof Exp:* Res assoc, Birmingham Univ, 61-62; res assoc & actg asst prof physics, Cornell Univ, 62-66; from assoc physicist to physicist, Brookhaven Nat Lab, 66-73. *Mem:* Am Phys Soc. *Res:* Elastic scattering and total cross sections of nucleons and mesons on nucleons in the 100 GeV and greater region. *Mailing Add:* Fermi Nat Accelerator Lab PO Box 500 Batavia IL 60510. *Fax:* 630-840-2939; *E-Mail:* royr@fnal.gov

RUBIO, RAFAEL, CARDIOVASCULAR PHYSIOLOGY. *Current Pos:* from asst prof to assoc prof, 69-76, PROF PHYSIOL, UNIV VA, 76- *Personal Data:* b Queretaro, Mex, Feb 15, 28; m 55, 79; c 5. *Educ:* Univ Mex, BS, 63; Univ Va, PhD(physiol), 68. *Honors & Awards:* Fogarty Fel, 83. *Prof Exp:* Res assoc physiol, Syntex, Mex, 52-55; res assoc, Inst Nac Cardiol, Mex, 55-63; res assoc, Case Western Reserve Univ, 64-66. *Concurrent Pos:* NIH fel, Univ Va, 68-69, Am Heart Asn fel, 74; peer rev comt, NIH, 79-82. *Mem:* Mex Physiol Sci Soc; Am Physiol Soc; Biophys Soc; Soc Gen Physiol. *Res:* Blood flow regulation; muscle contraction and metabolism. *Mailing Add:* Dept Physiol Univ Va Sch Med Jordan Hall Charlottesville VA 22908-0001

RUBIS, DAVID DANIEL, PLANT BREEDING, GENETICS. *Current Pos:* RETIRED. *Personal Data:* b Jackson, Minn, May 30, 24; m 59; c 3. *Educ:* Univ Minn, BS, 48; Iowa State Univ, MS, 50, PhD(crop breeding), 54. *Prof Exp:* Res asst, Corn Breeding Proj, Iowa State Univ, 48-52; agent-agronomist, Spec Crops Sect, Agr Res Serv, USDA, 52-56; from asst prof agron & asst agronomist to assoc prof & assoc agron, Univ Ariz, 56-64, prof plant sci & agronomist, 64-86. *Concurrent Pos:* Consult agron. *Mem:* Am Soc Agron; Crop Sci Soc Am; Am Genetic Asn; Genetics Soc Am. *Res:* Genetics and breeding of safflower, soybeans, guayule and plantago; development of new crops; pollination of entomphilous plants; genetics of water use in plants; development of new crops. *Mailing Add:* 11512 N Lone Mountain Pl Tucson AZ 85737

RUBLEE, PARKE ALSTAN, MARINE BIOLOGY, LIMNOLOGY. *Current Pos:* ASST PROF BIOL, UNIV NC, GREENSBORO, 90- *Personal Data:* b Buffalo, NY, June 25, 49; m 77; c 4. *Educ:* Dartmouth Col, BA, 71; NC State Univ, MSc, 74, PhD(zool), 78. *Prof Exp:* Res assoc, Rosenstiel Sch Marine & Atmospheric Sci, 79-80, Chesapeake Bay Ctr Environ Studies, Smithsonian Inst, 80-82; assoc prof biol, Whitman Col, 82-89. *Mem:* Am Soc Limnol & Oceanog; Am Soc Microbiol; AAAS. *Res:* The role of heterotrophic microorganisms in aquatic systems. *Mailing Add:* Biol Dept Univ NC Greensboro 1000 Spring Garden Greensboro NC 27412-0001

RUBLOFF, GARY W, MANUFACTURING INTERREFACES, PROCESS DIAGNOSTICS, SIMULATION & CONTROL. *Current Pos:* ASSOC DIR, NSF ENG RES CTR, ADVAN ELECTRONICS MAT'S PROCESSING, NC STATE UNIV, 93- *Personal Data:* b Peoria, Ill, June 13, 44; m 66; c 2. *Educ:* Dartmouth Col, AB, 66; Univ Chicago, SM, 67, PhD(physics), 71. *Prof Exp:* Res assoc, Physics Dept, Brown Univ, 71-73; res staff mem, IBM Res Div, T J Watson Res Ctr, Yorktown Heights, NY, 73-84, tech asst to vpres, 84-85, mgr, Growth, Interfaces & Offline Processing, 85-87, mgr, Thin Film Mat & Characterization, mgr, Growth, Etching & Integrated Processing, mgr, Thin Film Process Modeling Mfg Res, 89-93. *Concurrent Pos:* Prin investr, Off Naval Res, 75-; ed, Deposition & Growth: Limits for Microelectronics, AIP Conf, Repub of China, 87; chmn, Electronics Mat & Processing, Div Am Vacuum Soc, 87, secy, 90- *Mem:* Fel Am Phys Soc; fel Am Vacuum Soc; Mat Res Soc; sr mem Inst Elec & Electronics Engrs; Electron Device Soc. *Res:* Fundamental chemistry and physics of electronic materials growth, processing and interfaces; ultraclean and integrated processing; CUD & MOS structures; interfacial reactions; surface science; optical properties of solids and surfaces; process diagnostics, simulation and control for manufacturing. *Mailing Add:* NC State Univ Ctr AEMP PO Box 7920 Raleigh NC 27695. *Fax:* 919-515-5055; *E-Mail:* gary_rubloff@ncsu.edu

RUBNITZ, MYRON ETHAN, PATHOLOGY. *Current Pos:* assoc prof, 63-69, PROF PATH, STRITCH SCH MED, LOYOLA UNIV, CHICAGO, 69-; CONSULT, HINES ILL VET ADMIN HOSP, 93- *Personal Data:* b Omaha, Nebr, Mar 2, 24; m 52, Susan Block; c Mary L (Roffe), Peter, Thomas (deceased) & Robert. *Educ:* Univ Nebr, BSc, 45, MD, 47. *Prof Exp:* Fel path, Med Sch, Northwestern Univ, 53-55, assoc path, 55-59, asst prof, 59-63. *Concurrent Pos:* Pathologist, Hines Ill Vet Admin Hosp, 53-56, chief lab serv, 56-91, asst chief, 91-93; clin prof, Dent Sch, 70-; adj prof, Ill State Univ, 79-, Col St Francis, 88-; prof, Northern Ill Univ, 79- *Mem:* Am Soc Clin Path; Col Am Path; Int Acad Path. *Res:* Surgical pathology. *Mailing Add:* 979 Sheridan Rd Winnetka IL 60093. *Fax:* 847-441-0920

RUBOTTOM, GEORGE M, ORGANIC CHEMISTRY. *Current Pos:* PROG DIR CHEM, NSF, 85- *Personal Data:* b London, Eng, Mar 19, 40; US citizen; m 67, 89; c 2. *Educ:* Middlebury Col, AB, 62; Mass Inst Technol, PhD(org chem), 67. *Prof Exp:* Fel org chem, Calif Inst Technol, 66-68; instr, Bucknell Univ, 68-70; from asst prof to assoc prof, Univ PR, 70-74; assoc prof, 75-78, prof org chem, Univ Idaho, 78-85. *Concurrent Pos:* NIH fel, 67-68. *Mem:* Am Chem Soc. *Res:* Chemistry of organo-silicon compounds; chemistry of small ring compounds; chemistry of natural products. *Mailing Add:* NSF 4201 Wilson Blvd Rm 1055 Arlington VA 22230

RUBY, EDWARD GEORGE, MICROBIAL SYMBIOSES, MICROBIAL PHYSIOLOGY. *Current Pos:* ASSOC PROF BIOL SCI, UNIV SOUTHERN CALIF, 82- *Personal Data:* b Rochester, NY, Aug 31, 49. *Educ:* Stetson Univ, BS, 71; Scripps Inst Oceanog, PhD(marine biol), 77. *Prof Exp:* Res fel, Harvard Univ, 77-79, Woods Hole Oceanog Inst, 79-81; res assoc, Univ Calif, Los Angeles, 81-82. *Concurrent Pos:* Adj asst prof microbial physiol, Boston Univ, 78-79. *Mem:* Am Soc Microbiol; Am Soc Limnol & Oceanog; Am Chem Soc; NY Acad Sci. *Res:* Procaryotic cellular differentiation including in the dimorphic growth cycle of the bacterial genus Bdellovibrio; physiological and biochemical studies of their transformation from one cell form to another to understand the processes of development in bacteria. *Mailing Add:* Dept Biol Sci Univ Southern Calif 3616 Trousdale Pkwy Los Angeles CA 90089-0015

RUBY, JOHN L, forest genetics; deceased, see previous edition for last biography

RUBY, JOHN ROBERT, ANATOMY, MEDICAL SCHOOL ADMINISTRATION. *Current Pos:* from asst prof to assoc prof, 67-77, actg head, Dept Pharmacol, 86-88, PROF ANAT, LA STATE UNIV MED CTR, NEW ORLEANS, 77-, VCHANCELLOR INST SERV, 96- *Personal Data:* b Elida, Ohio, May 26, 35; m 57, Sondra Mahon; c Diana, Douglas & Matthew. *Educ:* Baldwin-Wallace Col, BS, 57; St Louis Univ, MS, 59; Univ Pittsburgh, PhD(anat), 63. *Prof Exp:* From instr to asst prof anat, Univ Cincinnati, 63-67; assoc dean fac affairs/admissions, LA State Univ Sch Med, 88-96. *Mem:* Am Asn Anat; Electron Micros Soc Am. *Res:* Development of female reproductive system; ultrastructure of salivary glands; pancreatic cancer. *Mailing Add:* Chancellor's Off La State Univ Sch Med 433 Bolivar St New Orleans LA 70112. *Fax:* 504-565-5575

RUBY, LAWRENCE, NUCLEAR PHYSICS. *Current Pos:* ADJ PROF ELEC ENG, ORE GRAD INST SCI & TECHNOL, 91- *Personal Data:* b Detroit, Mich, July 25, 25; m 51; c 3. *Educ:* Univ Calif, Los Angeles, BA, 45, MA, 47, PhD(physics), 51. *Prof Exp:* Physicist, Lawrence Berkeley Lab, Univ Calif, Berkeley, 50-87, lectr, 60-61, from assoc prof to prof nuclear eng, 61-87; prof nuclear sci & reactor dir, Reed Col, Portland, Ore, 87-91. *Mem:* Am Phys Soc; Am Asn Physics Teachers; Am Nuclear Soc. *Res:* Nuclear spectroscopy; accelerators; reactor dynamics; nuclear fusion. *Mailing Add:* 663 Carrera Lane Lake Oswego OR 97034. *E-Mail:* 105167.1423@compuserve.com

RUBY, MICHAEL GORDON, AIR POLLUTION CONTROL, ENVIRONMENTAL ECONOMICS. *Current Pos:* PRES, ENVIROMETRICS, INC, 84- *Personal Data:* b Muskogee, Okla, May 27, 40; m 68, Edith Henderson. *Educ:* Univ Okla, BS, 62; Univ Wash, MS, 65, MSE, 78, PhD(civil eng), 81. *Prof Exp:* Environ specialist, City Seattle, 72-76; prin, Environ Res Group, 76-81; asst prof civil eng, Univ Cincinnati, 81-84. *Concurrent Pos:* Consult, WHO, AID, World Bank, 79-; dir, Int Environ Eng Inst, 88- *Mem:* Air & Waste Mgt Asn; Am Acad Environ Engrs; Am

Meteorol Asn; Sigma Xi. *Res:* Air pollution measurement and control technology, particularly with reference to combustion and odors; indoor air pollution measurement; benefit-cost analysis of environmental policies and projects. *Mailing Add:* 4128 Burke Ave N Seattle WA 98103-8320. *Fax:* 206-633-4835

RUBY, PHILIP RANDOLPH, ORGANIC CHEMISTRY. *Current Pos:* Res chemist, 53-60, GROUP LEADER, PIGMENTS DIV, AM CYANAMID CO, BOUND BROOK, 60- *Personal Data:* b Aurora, Ill, May 23, 25; m 53; c 1. *Educ:* Univ Ill, BA, 49; Univ Iowa, MS, 51, PhD(org chem), 53. *Mem:* Am Chem Soc. *Res:* Aromatic organic chemistry; organic pigments. *Mailing Add:* 22 Circle Dr Millington NJ 07946

RUBY, RONALD HENRY, BIOPHYSICS. *Current Pos:* from asst prof to assoc prof, 65-79, PROF PHYSICS, UNIV CALIF, SANTA CRUZ, 79- *Personal Data:* b San Francisco, Calif, Dec 1, 32; m 57; c 4. *Educ:* Univ Calif, Berkeley, AB, 54, PhD(physics), 62. *Prof Exp:* Actg asst prof physics, Univ Calif, Berkeley, 62-64; NSF fel biol, Mass Inst Technol, 64-65. *Concurrent Pos:* Sloan Found fel, 66-68. *Mem:* Am Phys Soc. *Res:* Solid state physics; problems of physics in biological systems; energy conversion process in photosynthesis. *Mailing Add:* 214 Highview Dr Santa Cruz CA 95060-2304

RUBY, STANLEY, PHYSICAL CHEMISTRY, MATERIALS SCIENCE. *Current Pos:* RETIRED. *Personal Data:* b Brooklyn, NY, Nov 26, 20; m 46, Gloria Gross; c Jonathan P, Joseph L & Allen M. *Educ:* City Col New York, BS, 41; Columbia Univ, PhD(mining, metall), 54. *Prof Exp:* Res assoc, Manhattan Proj Sam Labs, 43-46; res assoc, Brookhaven Nat Lab, 50-52; group leader ore concentration, Minerals Beneficiation Lab, Columbia Univ, 52-54; sr engr, Sylvania Elec Prod Inc, 54-56; sect chief reentry mat, Res & Adv Develop Div, Avco Corp, 56-62; sr scientist, Allied Res Assocs, 62-64; prog mgr, Advan Res Proj Agency, Arlington, 64-77; prog mgr, Dept Energy, Washington, DC, 78-87. *Concurrent Pos:* Res Assoc, Columbia Univ, 50-51. *Mem:* Am Chem Soc; Am Inst Mining, Metall & Petrol Eng; Sigma Xi; NY Acad Sci. *Res:* Surface chemistry; high temperature chemistry; electrochemistry; ore concentration; winning of metals; radiochemistry. *Mailing Add:* 10913 Kenilworth Ave Garrett Park MD 20896-0025

RUCH, RICHARD JULIUS, PHYSICAL CHEMISTRY, SURFACE & COLLOID CHEMISTRY. *Current Pos:* asst chmn dept, 72-86, assoc prof, 66-90, PROF CHEM, KENT STATE UNIV, 91- *Personal Data:* b Perryville, Mo, June 9, 32; m 54, Leola Sander; c Stephen, David, Susan & Daniel. *Educ:* Southeast Mo State Col, BS, 54; Iowa State Univ, MS, 56, PhD(chem), 59. *Prof Exp:* Asst prof chem, Univ SDak, 59-62; asst prof, Southern Ill Univ, 62-66. *Mem:* Fedn Soc Coatings Technol. *Res:* Surface and colloid chemistry; the stability of colloidal dispersions is studied with the aid of dielectric measurements and with various interfacial techniques. *Mailing Add:* Chem Kent State Univ Main Campus PO Box 5190 Kent OH 44242-0001. *Fax:* 330-672-3816

RUCH, RODNEY R, ANALYTICAL CHEMISTRY, COAL CHARACTERIZATION. *Current Pos:* assoc chemist, Ill State Geol Surv, 66-71, chemist, 71-73, head anal chem sect, 73-84, head minerals eng sect, 84-89, asst br chief, 89-93, SR CHEMIST, ILL STATE GEOL SURV, 93- *Personal Data:* b Springfield, Ill, Aug 18, 33; m 56, Carol; c Stuart, Jefferson & Mary. *Educ:* Univ Ill, BS, 55; Southern Ill Univ, MA, 59; Cornell Univ, PhD(chem), 65. *Honors & Awards:* Gov Award, 71. *Prof Exp:* Res asst chem, Gen Atomic Div, Gen Dynamics Corp, 61-63; res chemist, Nat Bur Stand, 65-66. *Concurrent Pos:* Prin res officer, Broken Hill Proprietary Co, Australia, 80-81. *Mem:* Am Chem Soc; Am Soc Testing & Mat. *Res:* Coal analysis; radiochemical separations; activation analysis; radiochemistry; trace element analysis. *Mailing Add:* 1821 Maynard Dr Champaign IL 61821

RUCHELMAN, MARYON W, SOFTWARE SYSTEMS ENGINEERING & ARTIFICIAL INTELLIGENCE RESEARCH, RESOURCE MANAGEMENT. *Current Pos:* SOFTWARE SYSTS ENGR, LAB ARTIFICIAL INTEL, VET ADMIN HOSP, DALLAS, 87- *Personal Data:* b Mar 19, 21; m 93, Roger Spotswood; c Jack, Susie, David & Phila. *Educ:* Tex A&I Univ, BA, 54, BS, 56, MS, 58; Univ Houston, PhD(chem), 63. *Prof Exp:* Res chemist, Texaco Inc, 58-60; asst prof endocrinol, M D Anderson Hosp & Univ Tex Tumor Inst, 63-70; chem abstr serv, Ohio State Univ, 70-72; sr syst analyst, Stand Oil Co, 73-77; staff mem, Amtrak, Washington, DC, 77-78; coordr & mgr exp develop, Summit Co Welfare, Akron, 79-80; financial exp develop, Ameritrust Bank, 80-81; staff mem, McDonnell Douglas Corp, 81-83; exp develop, Apex Oil, 83-84; software systs engr, Tex Inst Inc, 84-87; vis prof, Comput Sci & Eng Dept, Southern Methodist Univ, 87. *Mem:* Am Asn Artificial Intel; Soc Comput Simulation; Data Processing Mgrs Asn. *Res:* Software systems; published 29 articles and granted 1 patent. *Mailing Add:* 11106-B Valleydale Dr Dallas TX 75230-3332

RUCHKIN, DANIEL S, BIOMEDICAL ENGINEERING, COGNITIVE NEUROSCIENCE. *Current Pos:* assoc prof physiol & comput sci, 71-77, PROF PHYSIOL, SCH MED, UNIV MD, BALTIMORE CITY, 77- *Personal Data:* b New Haven, Conn, June 29, 35; m 58, 85, Elisabeth Mirsky; c Peter. *Educ:* Yale Univ, BE, 56, MEng, 57, DEng, 60. *Honors & Awards:* J Javits neurosci investr, Nat Inst Neurol Dis & Stroke, 86. *Prof Exp:* Instr elec eng, Yale Univ, 59-61; asst prof, Univ Rochester, 61-64; res assoc prof psychiat, NY Med Col, 64-70. *Mem:* AAAS; Inst Elec & Electronics Engrs; Soc Neurosci; fel Am EEG Soc; Soc Psychophysiol Res. *Res:* Cognitive neuroscience; study of human working memory via event-related potentials. *Mailing Add:* Dept Physiol Univ Md Sch Med Baltimore MD 21201. *Fax:* 410-706-8341; *E-Mail:* Bitnet: druchkin@umabnet.ab.umd.edu

RUCHMAN, ISAAC, MICROBIOLOGY, IMMUNOLOGY. *Current Pos:* prof, 63-74, EMER PROF MICROBIOL, UNIV KY, 74- *Personal Data:* b New York, NY, July 2, 09; m 40; c 1. *Educ:* City Col New York, BSc, 37; Univ Cincinnati, MSc, 41, PhD(bact), 44; Am Bd Microbiol, dipl. *Prof Exp:* Tech asst, Rockefeller Inst, 30-39; asst, Children's Hosp Res Found, Cincinnati, Ohio, 39-44, res assoc, 46-52; from instr to asst prof bact, Univ Cincinnati, 44-55; head microbiol, Wm S Merrell Co, 55-63. *Concurrent Pos:* USPHS grant in aid; attend bacteriologist, Cincinnati Gen Hosp, 46-55; adj prof, Col Eng, Off Continuing Educ, Univ Ky, 75-; adj prof, Transylvania Univ, 76- *Mem:* Fel Am Acad Microbiol; Soc Exp Biol & Med; Am Asn Immunol; Am Soc Microbiol; NY Acad Sci. *Res:* Toxoplasmosis; tularemia; virology; immunity in virus infections; herpes simplex; neurotropic viruses; antimicrobial screening; upper respiratory infections; chemotherapy. *Mailing Add:* 365 Garden Rd Lexington KY 40502-2417

RUCHTI, RANDAL CHARLES, HIGH ENERGY PHYSICS, ELEMENTARY PARTICLE PHYSICS. *Current Pos:* from asst prof to assoc prof, 77-86, PROF PHYSICS, UNIV NOTRE DAME, 86- *Personal Data:* b Janesville, Wis, Oct 27, 46; m 70, Peggy Sachse; c 2. *Educ:* Univ Wis-Madison, BS, 68; Univ Ill, Urbana, MS, 70; Mich State Univ, PhD(physics), 73. *Prof Exp:* Res assoc physics, Northwestern Univ, 73-76, asst prof, 76-77. *Mem:* Am Inst Physics; Sigma Xi; Am Phys Soc. *Res:* Strong interactions; collider physics; detector development; scintillating fiber tracking. *Mailing Add:* PO Box 338 Notre Dame IN 46556-0338. *Fax:* 219-631-5952

RUCINSKA, EWA J, RESEARCH ADMINISTRATION, PHARMACOLOGY. *Current Pos:* dir int, 78-84, dir cardiovasc, 84-85, DIR CARDIO-RENAL, MERCK SHARP & DOHME RES LABS, 85- *Personal Data:* b Poland; US citizen; c 1. *Educ:* Med Sch, Gdansk, Poland, MD, 60, PhD(pharmacol), 66. *Prof Exp:* Assoc prof, Dept Pharm, Med Sch, Gdansk, Poland, 67-73; assoc dir, Squibb Inst Med Res, 75-78. *Concurrent Pos:* Dir med teaching prog for students, Gdansk, 63-73; coordr clin res POLFA-Pharm & Dept Pharm, Poland, 67-73; sr lectr, continuing educ prog for physicians & pharmacists, Poland, 70-73. *Mem:* AMA; Am Fedn Clin Res; Am Soc Pharmacol & Exp Therapeut; NY Acad Sci. *Res:* Evaluation of new drugs regarding efficacy and safety in a variety of cardiovascular syndromes; evaluation of the effects of various agents in the renin-angiotension-aldosterone system and the relationships with other humeral systems. *Mailing Add:* Merck Res Labs BLJ 6 PO Box 4 West Point PA 19446

RUCKENSTEIN, ELI, CHEMICAL ENGINEERING. *Current Pos:* fac prof eng, appl sci & chem eng, 73-81, DISTINGUISHED PROF, STATE UNIV NY, BUFFALO, 81- *Personal Data:* b Botosani, Romania, Aug 13, 25; US citizen; m 48, Velina; c Andrel & Lelia. *Educ:* Bucharest Polytech Inst, MS, 49, Dr Eng(chem eng), 66. *Hon Degrees:* Dr, Tech Univ Bucharest, 93. *Honors & Awards:* George Spacu Award, Romanian Acad Sci, 63; Alpha Chi Sigma Award, Am Inst Chem Engrs, 77; Sr Humboldt Award, Alexander Humboldt Found, 85; Kendall Award, Am Chem Soc, 86 & Jacob F Schoellkopf Medal, 91; Walker Award, Am Inst Chem Engrs, 88; EV Murphree Award Indust & Eng Chem, Am Chem Soc, 96. *Prof Exp:* Prof chem eng, Bucharest Polytech Inst, 49-69; NSF sr scientist, Clarkson Col Technol, 69-70; prof, Univ Del, 70-73. *Mem:* Nat Acad Eng; Am Inst Chem Engrs; Am Chem Soc. *Res:* Transport phenomena in fluids and solids; supported metal catalysts; oxide catalysis; zeolite catalysis, enzymatic catalysis, heterogeneous kinetics; thermodynamics and kinetics of interfacial phenomena; micellization; microemulsions and colloids; transport phenomena in colloidal systems; deposition of cells on surfaces; separation processes; polymer composites; membranes for separation processes; reactive polymers. *Mailing Add:* Dept Chem Eng 504 Furnas Hall State Univ NY N Campus Amherst NY 14260. *Fax:* 716-645-3822; *E-Mail:* feaeliru@acsu.buffalo.edu

RUCKER, JAMES BIVIN, GEOLOGY, OCEANOGRAPHY. *Current Pos:* PROJ MGR, TGS, 90- *Personal Data:* b Emporia, Kans, Mar 15, 35; m 57; c 2. *Educ:* Univ Mo, BA, 60, MA, 61; La State Univ, PhD(geol), 66. *Prof Exp:* Oceanographer, US Naval Oceanog Off, 63-72; dir, Miss Marine Resources Coun, 72-74; ecologist, Nat Oceanic & Atmospheric Admin, 75-90. *Concurrent Pos:* Prof lectr, George Washington Univ, 66-84, Johns Hopkins Univ, 84- *Mem:* AAAS; Geol Soc Am; Sigma Xi; Am Soc Limnol & Oceanog. *Res:* Recent marine sediments and benthic biota; environmental impact of deep ocean dumping, remote sensing of environment. *Mailing Add:* 43 Lakeside Carriere MS 39426

RUCKER, ROBERT BLAIN, NUTRITIONAL BIOCHEMISTRY. *Current Pos:* from asst prof to assoc prof nutrit & biol chem, 70-78, chmn dept nutrit, 81-88, PROF NUTRIT & BIOL CHEM, UNIV CALIF, DAVIS, 78- *Personal Data:* b Oklahoma City, Okla, Mar 29, 41; m 67; c 2. *Educ:* Oklahoma City Univ, BA, 63; Purdue Univ, MS, 66, PhD(biochem), 68. *Honors & Awards:* Border Res Award, Am Soc Nutrit Sci. *Prof Exp:* Fel biochem, Univ Mo-Columbia, 68-70. *Concurrent Pos:* Assoc ed, Am J Clin Nutrit. *Mem:* AAAS; Am Soc Nutrit Sci; Am Chem Soc; Am Soc Biochem & Molecular Biol; Soc Exp Biol Med. *Res:* Connective tissue metabolism; selected functions of nutritionally essential trace elements and vitamins; biochemistry of elastin. *Mailing Add:* Dept Nutrit Univ Calif Davis 3135 Meyer Hall Davis CA 95616. *Fax:* 530-752-8966

RUCKERBAUER, GERDA MARGARETA, VETERINARY IMMUNOLOGY. *Current Pos:* RETIRED. *Personal Data:* b Steyr, Austria, Dec 7, 26; Can citizen. *Educ:* Univ Toronto, BA, 51, MA, 55; Ont Vet Col, DVM, 61. *Honors & Awards:* Queen Elizabeth Silver Jubilee Medal. *Prof*

Exp: Tech asst bot, Univ Toronto, 51-52, tech off genetics, 52-53; res fel, Hosp Sick Children, Toronto, 53-55; res off carcinogens, Ont Vet Col, 55-57; vet, Animal Dis Res Inst, Can Dept Agr, 61-78, res scientist serol, Food Prod & Inspection Div, 68-89. *Mem:* NY Acad Sci; Can Vet Med Asn; Can Soc Immunol; Can Micros Soc. *Res:* Methods for diagnosis of animal diseases using serological, elisa and fluorescence microscopical techniques. *Mailing Add:* 19 Barran St Nepean ON K2J 1G3 Can

RUCKLE, WILLIAM HENRY, MATHEMATICS. *Current Pos:* assoc prof, 69-74, PROF MATH SCI, CLEMSON UNIV, 74- *Personal Data:* b Neptune, NJ, Oct 29, 36; m 60; c 1. *Educ:* Lincoln Univ, Pa, AB, 60; Fla State Univ, MS, 62, PhD(math), 63. *Prof Exp:* Assoc prof math, Lehigh Univ, 63-69. *Concurrent Pos:* Vis prof math, Western Wash Univ, 78-79; Fulbright vis scholar, Trinity Col, Dublin; Fulbright fel, 83-84; William C Foster vis fel, US Arms Control & Disarmament Agency, 89-90. *Mem:* Am Math Soc; Soc Indust Appl Math; Irish Math Soc. *Res:* Functional analysis, summability theory, game theory and risk analysis. *Mailing Add:* Dept Math Sci Clemson Univ Clemson SC 29634-1907. *E-Mail:* whrckl@clemson.edu

RUCKLIDGE, JOHN CHRISTOPHER, MINERALOGY, CRYSTALLOGRAPHY. *Current Pos:* from lectr to assoc prof, 65-77, PROF MINERAL, UNIV TORONTO, 77-, ASSOC DIR, ISOTRACE LAB, 81- *Personal Data:* b Halifax, Eng, Jan 15, 38; m 62; c 4. *Educ:* Cambridge Univ, BS, 59; Univ Manchester, PhD(mineral), 62. *Prof Exp:* Res assoc, Univ Chicago, 62-64; res asst, Oxford Univ, 64-65. *Mem:* Mineral Soc Am; Geol Asn Can; Mineral Asn Can; Microbeam Anal Soc; Sigma Xi. *Res:* Electron probe and x-ray crystallographic studies on minerals; ultrasensitive mass spectrometry with tandem accelerators. *Mailing Add:* Dept Geol Univ Toronto Toronto ON M5S 3B1 Can

RUCKMAN, MARK WARREN, SURFACE SCIENCE, THIN FILM GROWTH & SURFACE MODIFICATION. *Current Pos:* asst physicist, Brookhaven Nat Lab, 85-87, assoc physicist, 87-90, physicist, 90-92, PHYSICS ASSOC I, BROOKHAVEN LAB, 92- *Personal Data:* b Rolla, Mo, Dec, 54. *Educ:* Pa State Univ, BS, 77; Rensselaer Polytech Inst, MS, 80, PhD(physics), 84. *Prof Exp:* Res assoc, Univ Minn, 84-85. *Mem:* Am Phys Soc; Am Vacuum Soc; Am Chem Soc; Mat Res Soc; AAAS. *Res:* Use of electron and x-ray spectroscopic probes to study the physical and chemical properties of surfaces films and clusters; elucidation of the relationship between chemisorption and surface electronic structure. *Mailing Add:* Brookhaven Nat Lab Bldg 510B Upton NY 11973. *Fax:* 516-282-2739; *E-Mail:* ruckman@bnl.gov

RUCKNAGEL, DONALD LOUIS, HUMAN GENETICS. *Current Pos:* from asst prof to assoc prof, 64-70, PROF HUMAN GENETICS, UNIV MICH, MED SCH, ANN ARBOR, 70-; PROF INTERNAL MED, SIMPSON MEM INST, 77- *Personal Data:* b St Louis, Mo, May 30, 28; m 55; c 2. *Educ:* Wash Univ, AB, 50, MD, 54; Univ Mich, PhD(human genetics), 64. *Prof Exp:* From intern to jr resident med, Duke Univ Hosp, NC, 54-56; investr human genetics, Nat Inst Dent Res, 57-59. *Concurrent Pos:* Fel, Univ Pittsburgh, 56-57; USPHS sr res fel human genetics, Univ Mich, Med Sch, Ann Arbor, 59-62, res career develop award, 62-69; res assoc internal med, Simpson Mem Inst, 68-77. *Mem:* Am Soc Human Genetics; Am Soc Hemat; Eugenics Soc; Physicians Social Responsibility; Am Fedn Clin Res. *Res:* Internal medicine; hematology; human genetics, especially hemoglobinopathies. *Mailing Add:* Comprehensive Sickle Cell Ctr Childrens Hosp Med Ctr 333 Burnet Ave Cincinnati OH 45229

RUDA, HARRY EUGEN, GROWTH & CHARACTERIZATION OF SEMICONDUCTORS, THEORETICAL STUDIES OF BAND STRUCTURE TRANSPORT & OPTICAL PROPERTIES. *Current Pos:* ASSOC PROF, DEPT METALL & MAT SCI, UNIV TORONTO, 94- *Personal Data:* b London, Eng, Sept 19, 58; Can citizen; m 92, Guela A Solow. *Educ:* London Univ, BSc, 79; Mass Inst Technol, PhD(mat physics), 82. *Prof Exp:* Fel, IBM-Mass Inst Technol, Yorktown Heights, 82-83; sr res physicist, 3M, 84-87, corp res specialist, 87-89. *Res:* Molecular beam epitaxy and liquid phase epitaxy growth of II-VI and III-V compound semiconductors and heterostructures; studies of deep levels, surface and interface states in these heterostructures; modelling of transport and optical properties of semiconductors; studies of optoelectronic devices including lasers, low energy detectors, photodiodes and solar cells. *Mailing Add:* Univ Toronto 184 College St Toronto ON M5S 1A4 Can. *Fax:* 416-978-4155

RUDAT, MARTIN AUGUST, MASS SPECTROMETRY. *Current Pos:* Res chemist, E I du Pont de Nemours & Co, Inc, Wilmington, Del, 78-85, group mgr, 85-94, SR RES SCI, DU PONT ADVAN FIBERS SYSTS, 94- *Personal Data:* b Burbank, Calif, June, 11, 52; m 75; c 3. *Educ:* Harvey Mudd Col, BS, 74; Cornell Univ, MS, 76, PhD(anal chem), 78. *Mem:* Am Chem Soc; Am Soc Mass Spectrometry; Sigma Xi. *Res:* Ionization techniques; mass spectral methods; mass spectral reactions and mechanisms; two dimensional mass spectrometry; linking of mass spectrometry with other techniques; secondary ion mass spectrometry. *Mailing Add:* Dupont Fibersspruance Plant PO Box 27001 Richmond VA 23261-7001

RUDAVSKY, ALEXANDER BOHDAN, CIVIL ENGINEERING. *Current Pos:* DIR & OWNER, HYDRO RES SCI, 64- *Personal Data:* b Poland, Jan 17, 25; US citizen; m 55; c 1. *Educ:* Univ Minn, BS, 53, MS, 55; Hanover Tech Univ, Dr Ing(civil eng), 66. *Prof Exp:* Civil engr, Justin & Courtney, Philadelphia, 56-57 & Iran, 57-58; prof eng, San Jose State Univ, 60-85. *Concurrent Pos:* Vis assoc prof, Stanford Univ, 70. *Mem:* Am Soc Civil Engrs; Am Soc Mech Engrs. *Res:* Hydraulic research, through model studies of engineering problems related to hydraulic structures, rivers, ports and harbors, coastal protection, and sedimentation; development of instrumentation; library documentation system and service; consultative services. *Mailing Add:* PO Box 1321 Pebble Beach CA 93953

RUDAZ, SERGE, ELEMENTARY PARTICLE PHYSICS. *Current Pos:* asst prof, 81-85, assoc prof, 85-87, PROF PHYSICS, UNIV MINN, 87- *Personal Data:* b Verdun, Que, Aug 19, 54; m 83, Risa Cohen; c Jean-Lucien & Francois. *Educ:* Cornell Univ, MS, 79, PhD(physics), 79. *Honors & Awards:* Pres Young Investr Award, 84; Herzberg Medal, Can Asn Physicists, 85. *Prof Exp:* Res fel, European Orgn Nuclear Res, Geneva, 79-81. *Concurrent Pos:* Vis prof, Univ Paris Xl-Orsay, 94-95. *Mem:* Inst Particle Physics Can; fel Am Phys Soc. *Res:* Unified field theories of elementary particle interactions; astroparticle physics and cosmology; models of high energy processes; relativistic many-body theory. *Mailing Add:* Sch Physics & Astron Univ Minn 116 Church St SE Minneapolis MN 55455

RUDBACH, JON ANTHONY, MICROBIOLOGY, IMMUNOLOGY. *Current Pos:* lectr, Univ Mont, 67-70, assoc prof, 70-75, dir, Steela Dincen Mem Res Inst, 79-85, PROF MICROBIOL, UNIV MONT, 75-; VPRES RES & DEVELOP, RIBI IMMUNOCHEM RES LABS, 85- *Personal Data:* b Long Beach, Calif, Sept 23, 37; m 59, Inge Stemcke; c Lucy & Karl. *Educ:* Univ Calif, Berkeley, BA, 59; Univ Mich, MS, 61, PhD(microbiol), 64; Lake Forest Grad Sch Mgt, MBA, 86. *Prof Exp:* Nat Inst Allergy & Infectious Dis fel biophys, Rocky Mountain Lab, USPHS, 64-66, res scientist, 66-67. *Concurrent Pos:* Head, Microbiol Lab, Abbott Labs, 77-79, Infectious Dis & Immunol Res Dept. *Mem:* AAAS; Soc Exp Biol & Med; Am Asn Immunol; Am Soc Microbiol. *Res:* Molecular biology of endotoxins from Gram-negative bacteria; relation of structure of endotoxins to biological activity; detoxification of endotoxins by human plasma; immunology of lipopolysaccharides. *Mailing Add:* 243 Hilltop Dr Hamilton MT 59840. *Fax:* 406-363-6129

RUDD, D(ALE) F(REDERICK), CHEMICAL ENGINEERING. *Current Pos:* fel, Univ Wis-Madison, 61-62, from asst prof to prof, 62-68, Slichter prof, 80-94, SLICHTER EMER PROF CHEM ENG, UNIV WIS-MADISON, 94- *Personal Data:* b Minneapolis, Minn, Mar 2, 35; m 64; c 2. *Educ:* Univ Minn, BS, 56, PhD(chem eng), 60. *Honors & Awards:* Allan P Colburn Award, 71. *Prof Exp:* Asst prof chem eng, Univ Mich, 60-61. *Concurrent Pos:* J S Guggenheim fel, 70. *Mem:* Nat Acad Eng. *Res:* Process engineering. *Mailing Add:* Dept Chem Eng Univ Wis 1415 Johnson Dr Madison WI 53706

RUDD, DEFOREST PORTER, INORGANIC CHEMISTRY. *Current Pos:* RETIRED. *Personal Data:* b Boston, Mass, Aug 17, 23; m 50; c 3. *Educ:* Harvard Univ, BA, 47; Univ Calif, PhD(phys chem), 51. *Prof Exp:* Res assoc, Northwestern Univ, 50-52; prof chem, Lincoln Univ, Pa, 52-88. *Concurrent Pos:* NSF sci fac fel, Cornell Univ, 59-60 & Stanford Univ, 66-67. *Mem:* AAAS; Am Chem Soc. *Res:* Solutions and critical phenomena; reactions of transition metal complexes. *Mailing Add:* 1432 Flamingo Dr Englewood FL 34224

RUDD, MILLARD EUGENE, ATOMIC PHYSICS. *Current Pos:* from assoc prof to prof physics, 65-93, actg chmn dept, 70-72, EMER PROF PHYSICS, UNIV NEBR, LINCOLN, 93- *Personal Data:* b Fargo, NDak, Sept 29, 27; m 53, Eileen L Hovland; c Eric P, Nancy E & Leif E. *Educ:* Concordia Col, BA, 50; Univ Buffalo, MA, 55; Univ Nebr, PhD(physics), 62. *Hon Degrees:* DSc, Concordia Col, 92. *Prof Exp:* From asst prof to prof physics, Concordia Col, 54-65. *Concurrent Pos:* NSF fel, 60-61; mem comm atomic & molecular sci, Nat Acad Sci, 80; vchmn, Div Electron & Atomic Physics, Am Phys Soc, 79, chmn, 80. *Mem:* Am Asn Physics Teachers; fel Am Phys Soc; Hist Sci Soc; Sci Instrument Soc; Antique Telescope Soc. *Res:* Atomic collisions; ion-atom collisions; electron spectroscopy; history of science and scientific instruments. *Mailing Add:* Behlen Lab Physics Univ Nebr Lincoln NE 68588-0111. *Fax:* 402-472-2879; *E-Mail:* erudd@unlinfo.unl.edu

RUDD, NOREEN L, AREUPLOIDY. *Current Pos:* RETIRED. *Personal Data:* b Vancouver, BC, Sept 3, 40; m 74. *Educ:* Univ BC, MD, 65; Am Bd Pediat, dipl, 77; FRCP(C), 73. *Prof Exp:* From asst prof to assoc prof, pediat, Univ Toronto, 73-80; assoc prof, pediat, Univ Calgary, 80-84; assoc staff pediat, Alta Children's Hosp, 80-91; prof, pediat/obstet, Univ Calgary, 84-91. *Concurrent Pos:* Dir, Genetics Clin, Hosp for Sick Children, Toronto, 75-80; assoc staff, Obstet, Toronto Gen Hosp, 78-80; nat comts, Med Res Coun, 86-, Sci Coun Can, 87-; consult, Foothills Hosp, 83-91. *Mem:* Fel Can Col Med Geneticists; Genetics Soc Can; Am Soc Human Genetics; Royal Col Physicians & Surgeons Can. *Res:* Research into the cellular basis of aneuploidy, a common chromosome error recognizable for recurrent abortions, Down Syndrome and some types of cancer. *Mailing Add:* Med Genetics 1820 Richmond Rd SW Alta Childrens Hosp Calgary AB T2T 5C7 Can

RUDD, ROBERT L, ZOOLOGY. *Current Pos:* Asst, Univ Calif, 47-50, assoc zool, 51-52, asst specialist, 52-56, from asst prof to assoc prof, 56-86, EMER PROF ZOOL, UNIV CALIF, 86- *Personal Data:* b Los Angeles, Calif, Sept 18, 21; m 47; c 2. *Educ:* Univ Calif, PhD(zool), 53. *Mem:* Fel AAAS; Soc Study Evolution; Am Soc Mammal; Am Ornith Union; Ecol Soc Am; Cooper Ornith Soc; Asn Trop Biol. *Res:* Pesticides; pollution ecology; vertebrate evolution; population phenomena, chiefly mammals; comparative endocrine structures; tropical ecology; conservation. *Mailing Add:* 2891 Quail St Davis CA 95616-8755

RUDD, VELVA ELAINE, BOTANY. *Current Pos:* SR RES FEL, DEPT BIOL, CALIF STATE UNIV, NORTHRIDGE, 73- *Personal Data:* b Fargo, NDak, Sept 6, 10. *Educ:* NDak Agr Col, BS, 31, MS, 32; George Washington Univ, PhD(bot), 53. *Prof Exp:* Asst bot, NDak Agr Col, 31-32 & Univ Cincinnati, 32-33; instr, Sch Hort, Ambler, Pa, 33-34; supvr sci courses, State Dept Supervised Studies, NDak, 35-37; asst bot, Univ Cincinnati, 37-38; asst sci aide, Bur Plant Indust, USDA, 38-42, personnel classification investr, 42-43; agr prog officer, Food Supply Mission, Inst Inter-Am Affairs, Venezuela, 43-45; agr prog analyst, UNRRA, 45-48; from asst cur to cur, Div Phanerograms, Dept Bot, US Nat Mus, Smithsonian Inst, 48-73. *Concurrent Pos:* Res assoc, Div Phanerograms, Dept Bot, Smithsonian Inst, 73- *Mem:* Fel AAAS; Am Soc Plant Taxonomists; Int Bur Plant Taxon; Soc Bot Mexico; Bot Soc Am; Sigma Xi. *Res:* Systematic botany; plant geography; neotropical legaminasae. *Mailing Add:* PO Box 11 Reseda CA 91337

RUDD, WALTER GREYSON, COMPUTER SCIENCE. *Current Pos:* DEPT COMPUT SCI, ORE STATE UNIV. *Personal Data:* b Teaneck, NJ, Dec 24, 43; m 71; c 1. *Educ:* Rice Univ, BA, 66, PhD(phys chem), 69. *Prof Exp:* Res assoc phys chem, State Univ NY Albany, 69-70, biophys, 70-71; from asst prof to assoc prof, La State Univ, Baton Rouge, 71-81, prof & chem comput sci, 81- *Mem:* AAAS; Asn Comput Mach. *Res:* Statistical mechanics and thermodynamics; theoretical biophysics; analog and hybrid computational techniques; computer simulation of biological systems; small computer system development. *Mailing Add:* 33690 SE Terra Lane Corvallis OR 97333

RUDDAT, MANFRED, HOST-PATHOGEN INTERACTIONS, PLANT MOLECULAR BIOLOGY. *Current Pos:* asst prof bot, Univ Chicago, 64-68, from asst prof to assoc prof biol, 68-84, assoc prof molecular genetics, cell biol, ecol & evolution, 84-90, ASSOC PROF COMT DEVELOP BIOL, ASSOC DEAN STUDENTS, UNIV CHICAGO, 88-, ASSOC PROF ECOL, EVOLUTION & DEVELOP BIOL, 90- *Personal Data:* b Insterburg, Ger, Aug 21, 32; m 62, Helga Kuntzel; c Michael & Monica. *Educ:* Univ Tubingen, Dr rer nat(bot), 60. *Prof Exp:* Sci asst bot, Univ Tubingen, 60-61; NSF res fel plant physiol, Calif Inst Technol, 61-64. *Concurrent Pos:* Ed, Bot Gazette, 74-91 & Int J Plant Scis, 92- *Mem:* Am Bot Soc; AAAS; Am Soc Plant Physiol; Int Soc Molecular Plant-Microbe Interactions; Int Plant Growth Substances Asn. *Res:* Developmental biology of plants; physiology and biochemistry of plant growth regulators; gene expression, host/pathogen interactions. *Mailing Add:* Dept Ecol & Evolution Barnes Lab Univ Chicago 1101 E 57th St Chicago IL 60637. *Fax:* 773-702-9740; *E-Mail:* mdn4@midway.uchicago

RUDDELL, ALANNA, MOLECULAR BIOLOGY. *Current Pos:* ASST PROF, DEPT MICROBIOL & IMMUNOL, UNIV ROCHESTER, 90- *Personal Data:* b Ottawa, Ont, Feb 16, 56. *Educ:* Queen's Univ, BSc, 77; Case Western Reserve Univ, PhD(develop genetics, anat), 83. *Prof Exp:* Postdoctoral, Dept Zool, Univ BC, 83-85, Dept Genetics, Fred Hutchinson Cancer Res Ctr, 85-90. *Mem:* AAAS; Am Soc Microbiol. *Res:* Analysis of role of transcription factors in retroviral oncogenesis, using avian leukosis virus induction of lymphoma as a model system. *Mailing Add:* 180 Labornam Cres Rochester NY 14620

RUDDICK, KEITH, PHYSICS. *Current Pos:* from asst prof to assoc prof, 66-76, PROF PHYSICS, UNIV MINN, MINNEAPOLIS, 76- *Personal Data:* b Haltwhistle, Eng, Dec 2, 39; m 88. *Educ:* Univ Birmingham, BSc, 61, PhD(physics), 64. *Prof Exp:* Res assoc physics, Univ Mich, 64-66. *Mem:* Inst Physics; Am Phys Soc. *Res:* Experimental high energy physics. *Mailing Add:* Sch Physics & Astron Univ Minn 116 Church St SE Minneapolis MN 55455

RUDDLE, FRANCIS HUGH, GENETICS, CELL BIOLOGY. *Current Pos:* from asst prof to assoc prof, Yale Univ, 61-72, chmn, Dept Biol, 77-83, Ross Granville Harrison prof biol, 83-88, chmn, Dept Biol, 88-92, PROF BIOL & HUMAN GENETICS, YALE UNIV, 72-, STERLING PROF BIOL, 88- *Personal Data:* b West New York, NJ, Aug 19, 29; m 64; c 2. *Educ:* Wayne State Univ, BA, 53, MS, 55; Univ Calif, Berkeley, PhD, 60. *Hon Degrees:* MA, Yale Univ, Lawrence Univ, 82; Weizmann Inst, Israel, 83. *Honors & Awards:* Dyer Lectr, NIH, 78; Merck Lectr, Montreal Cancer Inst, 79; Conden Lectr, Univ Ore, 81; Dickson Prize, Univ Pittsburgh, 81; Herman Beerman Award, Soc Invest Dermat, 82; Allan Award, Am Soc Human Genetics, 83; NY Acad Sci Award in Biol & Med Sci, 87; Katherine Berkan Judd Award, 88. *Prof Exp:* NIH fel biochem, Univ Glasgow, 60-61. *Concurrent Pos:* Mem, Cell Biol Study Sect, NIH, 65-70, chmn, Adv Comt, Human Mutant Cell Bank, Nat Inst Gen Med Sci, 72-77, Bd Sci Counselors, Nat Heart, Lung & Blood Inst, 80-84, chmn, Genome Study Sect, NIH, 91-; mem, Bd Dirs, Am Soc Human Genetics, 71-75; mem, Adv Comt, Biol Div, Oak Ridge Nat Lab, 77-80; mem, Panel Cell Biol, Nat Res coun, 85-86; ed-in-chief, J Exp Zool, 85-; co-ed, Genomics, 86-; mem coun, Human Genome Orgn, 88-; mem, Bd Sci Overseers, Jackson Lab, 89-91. *Mem:* Nat Acad Sci; Inst Med-Nat Acad Sci; Soc Develop Biol (pres, 71-72); Am Soc Cell Biol (pres-elect, 86, pres, 87); Am Soc Human Genetics (pres-elect, 84, pres, 85); fel AAAS; Am Soc Zoologists; Am Asn Cancer Res; Am Genetic Asn; fel Am Soc Microbiol; Am Soc Biol Chemists; Genetics Soc Am; Harvey Soc; Pattern Recognition Soc; Sigma Xi. *Res:* Somatic cell genetics and differentiation. *Mailing Add:* Yale Univ Dept Biol PO Box 208103 New Haven CT 06520-8103

RUDDLE, NANCY HARTMAN, IMMUNOLOGY. *Current Pos:* Res assoc & lectr tissue typing, Surgery Dept, Yale Univ, 68-71, fel & lectr microbiol, 71-74, asst prof, 75-80, assoc prof epidemiol, 80-90, PROF BIOL & IMMUNOL, YALE UNIV, 91- *Personal Data:* b St Louis, Mo, Apr 3, 40; m 64; c 2. *Educ:* Mt Holyoke Col, AB, 62; Yale Univ, PhD(microbiol), 68. *Concurrent Pos:* Fel, Damon Runyon Mem Found, Yale Univ, 72; Am Cancer Soc, 73-74 & fac res award, 79-84; vis investr, Basel Inst Immunol, 83; mem review bd, NSF, ACS, 87-90, NIH, 90- *Mem:* Am Soc Microbiol; Sigma Xi; Am Asn Immunol. *Res:* Delayed hypersensitivity; tumor immunology; leukemia virus-lymphocyte interactions; lymphokines; lymphotoxin; tumor necrosis factor. *Mailing Add:* Dept Epidemiol Pub Health & Immunol Yale Univ Sch Med PO Box 208034 815 CEPH New Haven CT 06520-8034. *Fax:* 203-785-7296

RUDDON, RAYMOND WALTER, JR, CANCER BIOLOGY, PHARMACOLOGY. *Current Pos:* DIR, EPPLEY INST RES CANCER, UNIV NEBR MED CTR, 91- *Personal Data:* b Detroit, Mich, Dec 23, 36; m 61; c 3. *Educ:* Univ Detroit, BS, 58; Univ Mich, PhD(pharmacol), 64, MD, 67. *Prof Exp:* From instr to prof pharmacol, Univ Mich, Ann Arbor, 64-76; dir biol marker prog, Nat Cancer Inst, Frederick, Md, 76-81; prof & chmn, Dept Pharmacol, Univ Mich Med Sch, 81-91. *Concurrent Pos:* Teaching fel chem, Univ Detroit, 58-59, NIH predoctoral fel, 59-64; Am Cancer Soc scholar, 64-67. *Mem:* AAAS; Am Soc Pharmacol & Exp Therapeut; Am Asn Cancer Res; Am Soc Biol Chemists; Endocrine Soc. *Res:* Biological markers of neoplasia; protein folding; glycoprotein hormones. *Mailing Add:* Eppley Inst Univ Nebr 600 S 42nd St Omaha NE 68198-6805

RUDDY, ARLO WAYNE, MEDICINAL CHEMISTRY. *Current Pos:* RETIRED. *Personal Data:* b Humboldt, Nebr, Aug 28, 15; m 43, 86; c 4. *Educ:* Univ Nebr, BSc, 36, MSc, 38; Univ Md, PhD(med chem), 40. *Prof Exp:* Sharp & Dohme res assoc, Northwestern Univ, 40-41; res chemist, Sharples Chem, Inc, Pa Salt Mfg Co, Mich, 41-42; sr res chemist, Sterling-Winthrop Res Inst, 42-51; dir org chem res, Chilcott Labs, 51-52, dir chem develop, Warner-Chilcott Res Labs, 52-57, dir org chem, 57-61, dir chem develop, Warner-Lambert Res Inst, 61-78. *Mem:* Am Chem Soc; Am Pharmaceut Asn; Acad Pharmaceut Sci; fel NY Acad Sci. *Res:* Medicinal chemistry, including mercurials, arsenicals, pressor amines, radiopaques, local anesthetics and antispasmodics. *Mailing Add:* 11 Juniper Dr Morris Plains NJ 07950-2193

RUDE, PAUL A, ELECTRONICS ENGINEERING, COMPUTER SCIENCE. *Current Pos:* asst prof elec eng, 63-64, ASSOC PROF ELEC ENG & CHMN DEPT, LOYOLA UNIV, LOS ANGELES, 64- *Personal Data:* b Los Angeles, Calif, Nov 4, 30; m 51; c 6. *Educ:* Univ Calif, Los Angeles, BS, 55; Univ Pittsburgh, MS, 57, PhD(elec eng), 62. *Prof Exp:* Sr engr, Westinghouse Elec Corp, 55-63. *Concurrent Pos:* Lectr, Univ Pittsburgh, 60-61; consult, Space-Gen Corp, 63-64; Pac Tel Co, 64-65 & Hughes Aircraft Co, 66. *Mem:* Am Soc Eng Educ; Inst Elec & Electronics Engrs. *Res:* Medical-optical systems; computer design. *Mailing Add:* Dept Elec Eng & Comput Sci Loyola Marymount Univ 7900 Loyola Blvd Los Angeles CA 90045

RUDE, THEODORE ALFRED, PATHOLOGY, MICROBIOLOGY. *Current Pos:* VET CONSULT, VET CONSULT SERVS, 86- *Personal Data:* b Chuquicamata, Chile, Mar 10, 25; US citizen; m 46; c 5. *Educ:* Univ Pa, VMD, 52; Am Col Vet Path, dipl. *Prof Exp:* Pvt pract, Wis, 52-59; diagnostician, Cent Animal Health Lab, Wis, 59-61, lab supvr, 61-63; staff vet, Norwich Pharmacal Co, NY, 63-64; staff vet, Salsbury Labs, 64-69, mgr path & toxicol, 69-71, biol develop mgr, 71-72, gen mgr, Fromm Labs, 72-80, vpres & gen mgr, 80-82; asst to pres, Salsbury Labs, 83-86. *Concurrent Pos:* Mem, Wis Vet Med Asn & NW Wis Vet Med Asn. *Mem:* Am Vet Med Asn; Am Asn Avian Path; Am Col Vet Pathologist; Am Asn Indust Veterinarians. *Res:* Pathology associated with avian, canine and feline diseases; development of diagnostic reagents, vaccines and bacterins for use with canines and felines; toxicology of chemical compounds. *Mailing Add:* 1716 Laurel Ave PO Box 561 Hudson WI 54016-0561

RUDEE, MERVYN LEA, MATERIALS SCIENCE. *Current Pos:* dean eng, 82-93, PROF MAT SCI & PROVOST, WARREN COL, UNIV CALIF, SAN DIEGO, 74- *Personal Data:* b Palo Alto, Calif, Oct 4, 35; m 58, Elizabeth Eager; c Elizabeth D, & David B. *Educ:* Stanford Univ, BS, 58, MS, 62, PhD(mat sci), 65. *Prof Exp:* From asst prof to prof mat sci, Rice Univ, 64-74, master, Wiess Col, 69-74. *Concurrent Pos:* Guggenheim fel, Cavendish Lab, Cambridge Univ, 71-72; vis scientist, IBM Watson Res Ctr, Yorktown Heights, NY. *Mem:* Am Phys Soc; Micros Soc Am; Mat Res Soc; Sigma Xi. *Res:* Defects in crystals, studies primarily by x-ray diffraction and electron microscopy. *Mailing Add:* 1745 Kearsarge Rd La Jolla CA 92037-3829. *Fax:* 619-534-2486; *E-Mail:* rudee@ucsd.edu

RUDEL, LAWRENCE L, PLASMA LIPOPROTEIN METABOLISM, HEPATIC CHOLESTEROL METABOLISM. *Current Pos:* from asst prof to assoc prof, Wake Forest Univ, 73-82, assoc biochem, 78-87, PROF COMP MED, BOWMAN GRAY SCH MED, WAKE FOREST UNIV, 82-, PROF BIOCHEM, 88- *Personal Data:* b Salt Lake City, Utah, Sept 19, 41; m 68, Katherine Bouwman; c Brian, John & David. *Educ:* Colo State Univ, BS, 63; Univ Ark Med Ctr, MS, 65, PhD(biochem), 69. *Prof Exp:* NIH fel, dept biochem, Univ Ark Med Ctr, 67-69; res fel, Banting & Best Dept Med Res, Can Heart Found, Univ Toronto, 70-71 & Cardiovasc Res Inst, Univ Calif, San Francisco, 72-73. *Concurrent Pos:* Assoc ed, J Lipid Res, 80-90, Atherosclerosis, 89-, Arterio & Thromb, 90-; mem & chmn, Metab Study Sect, NIH, 86-90; mem, Res Rev Comt B, Nat Heart, Lung & Blood Inst, NIH, 91- 95; fel, Arteriosclerosis Coun, Am Heart Asn. *Mem:* AAAS; Am Asn Pathologists; Am Heart Asn; Am Soc Biochem & Molecular Biol; Sigma Xi. *Res:* Evaluation of the role of gene expression in the liver and intestine in cholesterol absorption and transport by lipoproteins of the circulation, including the blood and the lymph; experiments are done in nonhuman primate models of atherosclerosis with emphasis on nutritional effects. *Mailing Add:* Dept Comp Med Bowman Gray Sch Med Wake Forest Univ Winston-Salem NC 27157. *Fax:* 910-716-6279; *E-Mail:* lrudel@bgsm.edu

RUDENBERG, FRANK HERMANN, neurophysiology; deceased, see previous edition for last biography

RUDENBERG, H(ERMANN) GUNTHER, PHYSICS, ELECTRONICS. *Current Pos:* PRIN, RUDENBERG ASSOCS, 83- *Personal Data:* b Berlin, Ger, Aug 9, 20; nat US; m 52; c 3. *Educ:* Harvard Univ, SB, 41, AM, 42, PhD, 52. *Honors & Awards:* Centennial Medal, Inst Elec & Electronics Engrs. *Prof Exp:* Asst electronics, Harvard Univ, 41-42; asst scientist, Los Alamos Sci Lab, 46; physicist res div, Raytheon Mfg Co, 48-52; dir res, Transitron Electronic Corp, 52-62; sr staff mem, Arthur D Little, Inc, 62-83. *Concurrent Pos:* Consult, Spencer-Kennedy Labs, 45-48 & 60-62. *Mem:* Inst Elec & Electronics Engrs. *Res:* Semiconductors; electron ballistics; microwaves; microelectronics; management consulting; technological forecasting; integrated circuits. *Mailing Add:* Rudenberg Assocs Three Lanthorn Lane Beverly MA 01915-4721

RUDERMAN, IRVING WARREN, ELECTROOPTICS. *Current Pos:* FOUNDER & PRES, INRAD, INC, 73- *Personal Data:* b New York, NY, Jan 7, 20; m 45, Carol C Schmied; c Barbara Lee, Clifford Eric, William Brandon & Genevieve Kathryn. *Educ:* Columbia Univ, PhD(chem), 49. *Prof Exp:* Res chemist, St Regis Paper Co, NJ, 40-46; teaching fel, Columbia Univ, 46-47, lectr, 47-48, res scientist, 48-54; consult, 54-56; founder & pres, Isomet Corp, 56-73. *Mem:* Am Chem Soc; Am Phys Soc; Inst Elec & Electronics Engrs; fel NY Acad Sci. *Res:* Solid state physics; crystal growth; lasers; active optics. *Mailing Add:* 45 Duane Lane Demarest NJ 07627. *Fax:* 201-767-9644; *E-Mail:* inrad@aol.com

RUDERMAN, JOAN V, CELL BIOLOGY, CELL DIVISION CYCLE. *Current Pos:* assoc prof biol, 76-86, PROF, HARVARD MED SCH, 89- *Personal Data:* b Mt Vernon, NY; m, Gerald; c Zoe. *Educ:* Barnard Col, Columbia Univ, BA, 69; Mass Inst Technol, PhD(biol), 74. *Prof Exp:* Jane Coffin Childs fel, Mass Inst Technol, 74-76; prof, Duke Univ, 86-89. *Concurrent Pos:* Instr, Marine Biol Lab, 76-, corp mem, 79-, trustee, 86-; Marion V Nelson chair cell biol, Harvard Med Sch; res career develop award, NIH, 80. *Mem:* Am Soc Cell Biol. *Res:* Regulation of the cell cycle. *Mailing Add:* Dept Cell Biol Harvard Med Sch Boston MA 02115. *Fax:* 617-432-1144, 277-2735; *E-Mail:* jruderma@warren.med.harvard.edu

RUDERMAN, MALVIN AVRAM, ASTROPHYSICS. *Current Pos:* PROF PHYSICS, COLUMBIA UNIV, 69-, CENTENNIAL PROF, 80- *Personal Data:* b New York, NY, Mar 25, 27; m 53; c 3. *Educ:* Columbia Univ, AB, 45; Calif Inst Technol, MS, 47, PhD, 51. *Honors & Awards:* Goodspeed-Richards Mem Lectr, Univ Pa, 70; Goldhaber Mem Lectr, Univ Tel Aviv, 72; Boris Pregel Award, NY Acad Sci, 74; Stanley H Kosk Vis Lectr, NY Univ, 77; Boris Jacobson Lectr, Univ Wash, 81. *Prof Exp:* Physicist, Radiation Lab, Univ Calif, 51-52; NSF fel, Columbia Univ, 52-53; from asst prof to prof physics, Univ Calif, Berkeley, 53-64; prof, NY Univ, 64-69. *Concurrent Pos:* Guggenheim fel, Inst Theoret Physics, Copenhagen, 57; Univ, Rome, 58 & Cambridge Univ, Int Astron, 79-80; vis prof, NY Univ, 60 & 64, Stanford Univ, 84-85, Oxford Univ, 90, Univ Calif, San Diego, 91; vis sr res fel, Imp Col, London, 67-68; coun-at-large, Am Phys Soc, 81-, Cong Fel Comt, 81; mem, Pres Peer Rev Comt Acid Rain, 82; mem, Acid Rain Rev Panel, Environ Protection Agency, 83; trustee, Aspen Ctr Physics, 86- *Mem:* Nat Acad Sci; Am Phys Soc; Am Acad Arts & Sci; am Astron Soc; NY Acad Sci. *Res:* Elementary particles; astrophysics. *Mailing Add:* Dept Physics Columbia Univ New York NY 10027. *Fax:* 212-932-3169; *E-Mail:* arb@cuphyf.thys.columbia.edu

RUDERSHAUSEN, CHARLES GERALD, CHEMICAL ENGINEERING. *Current Pos:* RETIRED. *Personal Data:* b Jersey City, NJ, May 26, 28; m 54, Muriel Engel; c 4. *Educ:* Univ Va, BChE, 49; Univ Wis, MS, 50, PhD(chem eng), 52. *Prof Exp:* Sr engr, Eastern Lab, DuPont Chemicals, E I du Pont de Nemours & Co Inc, 52, res chem engr, 53, group leader, 54, sect head, 55-59, tech asst, 59-60, task coordr, 60-61, res sect head, 61-64, res mgr, Newburgh Res Lab, NY & Poromerics Res Lab, Tenn, 64-69, mgr tech progs, Eastern Lab, NJ, 69-72, licensing specialist, 72-76, res assoc, 76-85, sr patents & contracts assoc, 85-93. *Mem:* Sigma Xi. *Res:* Chemical processing; explosives; metallurgy; leather replacement materials; patents; licensing; metal winning; synfuels; catalysis. *Mailing Add:* Taylor Lane Kennett Square PA 19348

RUDESILL, JAMES TURNER, ORGANIC CHEMISTRY. *Current Pos:* from asst prof to assoc prof, 57-67, PROF ORG CHEM, NDAK STATE UNIV, 67- *Personal Data:* b Rapid City, SDak, Nov 26, 23; m 48; c 3. *Educ:* SDak Sch Mines & Tech, BS, 48; Iowa State Col, MS, 50; Purdue Univ, PhD(org chem), 57. *Prof Exp:* Res chemist, Cudahy Packing Co, 50-53; asst, Purdue Univ, 53-57. *Mem:* Am Chem Soc; Royal Soc Chem. *Res:* Determination of configuration in geometrical isomers; additions and substitutions of free radicals; stereochemistry of ring opening processes. *Mailing Add:* Chem Dept NDak State Univ Fargo ND 58105

RUDGE, WILLIAM EDWIN, COMPUTATIONAL PHYSICS. *Current Pos:* SELF EMPLOYED, 96- *Personal Data:* b New Haven, Conn, June 14, 39; m 62, Georgiana Kopal; c Julia, Marian & William. *Educ:* Yale Univ, BS, 60; Mass Inst Technol, PhD(physics), 68. *Prof Exp:* Physicist, Prod Develop Lab, Components Div, IBM Corp, 60-63, staff mem, Res Lab, 68-95. *Res:* Molecular dynamics calculations using special purpose parallel computer. *Mailing Add:* 1187 Washoe Dr San Jose CA 95120-5542. *E-Mail:* werudge@almaden.ibm.com

RUDGERS, ANTHONY JOSEPH, PHYSICS. *Current Pos:* Res physicist, Acoust Div, Washington, DC, 61-76, Naval Res Lab, 76-95, RES PHYSICIST ACOUST, UNDERWATER SOUND REF DETACHMENT, NAVAL UNDERSEA WARFARE CTR, 95- *Personal Data:* b Washington, DC, May 23, 38; m 61, Karen G Jamison; c Nathan S, Benjamin A & Erika M. *Educ:* Univ Md, BS, 61; Cath Univ Am, MSE, 69, PhD(acoust), 77. *Concurrent Pos:* Chmn, Tech Comt Phys Acoust, Acoust Soc Am, 84-87, mem comt, 92-95. *Mem:* Fel Acoust Soc Am; Am Asn Physics Teachers; Sigma Xi; assoc US Naval Inst. *Res:* Acoustics; materials research; radiation, diffraction and scattering theory; random signal theory; elasticity and structural mechanics; linear systems; continuum mechanics. *Mailing Add:* Underwater Sound Ref Detachment Naval Undersea Warfare Ctr PO Box 568337 Orlando FL 32856-8337. *Fax:* 407-857-5103; *E-Mail:* rudgers@newton.nrl.navy.mil

RUDIN, ALFRED, POLYMER SCIENCE. *Current Pos:* assoc prof, Univ Waterloo, 67-69, prof chem, 69-91, prof chem eng, 73-91, adj prof chem, chem eng & physics, 89-91, dir, Inst Polymer Res, 90, EMER PROF CHEM ENG & PHYSICS, UNIV WATERLOO, 91- *Personal Data:* b Edmonton, Alta, Feb 5, 24; m 49, Pearl Gold; c Jonathan, Jeremy & Joel. *Educ:* Univ Alta, BSc, 49; Northwestern Univ, Evanston, PhD(org chem), 52. *Honors & Awards:* Protective Coatings Award, 83; Roon Found Award, 88; Polysar Award, 89. *Prof Exp:* Res chemist, Can Industs, Ltd, 52-60, group leader plastics, 60-64, mgr, Plastics Lab, 64-67. *Mem:* Am Chem Soc; fel Chem Inst Can; Rheology Soc; fel Royal Soc Can. *Res:* Polymer chemistry and engineering. *Mailing Add:* Dept Chem Univ Waterloo Waterloo ON N2L 3G1 Can. *E-Mail:* arudin@chemistry.watstar.uwaterloo.ca

RUDIN, BERNARD D, TECHNICAL MANAGEMENT, COMPUTER SCIENCE. *Current Pos:* MGR, APPLN TECHNOL CTR, IBM, 86- *Personal Data:* b Los Angeles, CA, Nov 18, 27. *Educ:* Calif Inst Technol, BS, 49; Univ Southern Calif, MS, 51; Stanford Univ, PhD(math), 65. *Prof Exp:* Mgr, Lockheed Missile & Space Corp, 56-65. *Mem:* Am Math Soc; Math Asn Am. *Res:* Computational methods in various engineering and scientific disciplines; approximation theory. *Mailing Add:* Austin Lab 9230 IBM 11400 Burnet Rd Austin TX 78758-3406

RUDIN, MARY ELLEN, MATHEMATICS, SET THEORETIC TOPOLOGY. *Current Pos:* lectr & prof math, 58-91, EMER PROF, UNIV WIS-MADISON, 91- *Personal Data:* b Hillsboro, Tex, Dec 7, 24; m 53, Walter; c 4. *Educ:* Univ Tex, PhD(topology), 49. *Hon Degrees:* DSc, Cedar Crest Col, 91, Kenyan Col, 93, Univ of South, 94, Univ NC, Greensboro, 95. *Honors & Awards:* Hedrick lectr, Math Asn Am, 79. *Prof Exp:* Instr math, Duke Univ, 50-53; asst prof, Univ Rochester, 53-57. *Mem:* Am Math Soc; Math Asn Am; Am Math Soc (vpres, 80-83); Asn Symbolic Logic; fel Am Acad Arts & Sci; hon mem Hungarian Acad Sci. *Res:* Set theoretic topology, particularly the construction of counter examples. *Mailing Add:* Dept Math Univ Wis 480 Lincoln Dr Madison WI 53706-1308

RUDIN, WALTER, MATHEMATICS. *Current Pos:* prof, 59-91, EMER PROF MATH, UNIV WIS-MADISON, 91- *Personal Data:* b Vienna, Austria, May 2, 21; m 53; c 4. *Educ:* Duke Univ, BA & MA, 47, PhD(math), 49. *Honors & Awards:* Steele Prize, Am Math Soc, 93. *Prof Exp:* Instr math, Duke Univ, 49-50; Moore instr, Mass Inst Technol, 50-52; from asst prof to prof, Univ Rochester, 52-59. *Mem:* Am Math Soc; Math Asn Am. *Res:* Mathematical analysis, especially abstract harmonic analysis, Fourier series and holomorphic functions of one and several variables. *Mailing Add:* 110 Marinette Trail Madison WI 53705-4717

RUDINGER, GEORGE, FLUID MECHANICS, ENGINEERING PHYSICS. *Current Pos:* CONSULT, 76- *Personal Data:* b Vienna, Austria, May 30, 11; US citizen; m 47, Frances K; c David, Ann, Terri & Mark. *Educ:* Vienna Tech Univ, Ingenieur, 35. *Honors & Awards:* Aerospace Pioneer Award, Am Inst Aeroaut & Astronaut, 74; Centennial Medallion, Am Soc Mech Engrs, 80; Fluids Eng Award, Am Soc Mech Engrs, 83. *Prof Exp:* Res assoc med radiol, Vienna Gen Hosp, Austria, 35-38; physicist, Sydney Hosp, Australia, 39-46; prin physicist fluid mech, Cornell Aeronaut Lab, Buffalo, 46-70; prin scientist, Textron Bell Aerospace Co, Buffalo, 71-76. *Concurrent Pos:* Proj engr, Royal Australian Air Force & Australian Ministry Munitions, 44-46; teacher physics, Sydney Tech Col, 45-46; physicist, Australian Glass Mgrs Pty, Ltd, Sydney, 45-46; adj prof, Dept Mech & Aero Eng, State Univ NY Buffalo, 75- *Mem:* Fel Am Soc Mech Engrs; fel Am Phys Soc; fel Am Inst Aeronaut & Astronaut; Int Soc Biorheology; fel Brit Inst Physics; fel AAAS. *Res:* Gas particle flow, nonsteady duct flow and blood flow; x-ray photography. *Mailing Add:* 47 Presidents Walk Buffalo NY 14221-2426

RUDISILL, CARL SIDNEY, MECHANICAL ENGINEERING. *Current Pos:* assoc prof, 65-75, NASA res grants, 70-73, 75-76, 77-79, PROF MECH ENG, CLEMSON UNIV, 75- *Personal Data:* b Lincolnton, NC, Mar 21, 29; m 60; c 2. *Educ:* NC State Univ, BME, 54, MS, 61, PhD(mech eng), 66. *Prof Exp:* Instr mech eng, NC State Univ, 60-65. *Mem:* Am Inst Aeronaut & Astronaut; Am Soc Mech Engrs. *Res:* Optimization of aircraft structures. *Mailing Add:* 206 Wren St Clemson SC 29631

RUDKO, ROBERT I, ELECTRICAL ENGINEERING. *Current Pos:* chmn, 81-89, CHIEF SCI OFFICER, LASER ENG INC, 89- *Personal Data:* b New York, NY, Apr 24, 42; m 64; c 2. *Educ:* Cornell Univ, BEE, 63, MS, 65, PhD, 67. *Prof Exp:* Sr res scientist, Raytheon Co, 67-77, prin res scientist, Res Div, 77-81. *Mem:* Inst Elec & Electronics Engrs; Am Soc Lasers Med & Surg. *Res:* Laser radars; infrared optics; infrared gas lasers; surgical lasers. *Mailing Add:* PIC Med Systs Forge Park Franklin MA 02038-3137

RUDMAN, ALBERT J, GEOPHYSICS. *Current Pos:* assoc prof geophysics, 65-77, PROF GEOL, IND UNIV, BLOOMINGTON, 77- *Personal Data:* b New York, NY, Nov 14, 28; m 51; c 3. *Educ:* Ind Univ, BS, 52, MA, 54, PhD(geophys), 63. *Prof Exp:* Geophysicist, Carter Oil Co, 54-57 & Ind Geol Surv, 57-65. *Mem:* Soc Explor Geophys; Am Geophys Union. *Res:* Solid earth geophysics, especially exploration. *Mailing Add:* Geol Sci Ind Univ Bloomington IN 47405

RUDMAN, REUBEN, X-RAY CRYSTALLOGRAPHY, STRUCTURAL CHEMISTRY. *Current Pos:* from asst prof to assoc prof, 67-75, PROF CHEM, ADELPHI UNIV, 75- *Personal Data:* b New York, NY, Jan 18, 37; m 58; c 5. *Educ:* Yeshiva Univ, BA, 57; Polytech Inst Brooklyn, PhD(chem), 66. *Prof Exp:* Res assoc chem, Brookhaven Nat Lab, 66-67. *Concurrent Pos:* Vis prof, Hebrew Univ, 73-74; chmn, Comn Crystallog Apparatus, Int Union Crystallog, 75-78; pres, Asn Orthodox Jewish Scientists, 79-80; chmn orientational disorder crystals, Gordon Res Conf, 80; ed, Semi-annual J Assoc Orthodox Jewish Scientists, 85-93. *Mem:* Sigma Xi; AAAS; Am Crystallog Asn; Am Chem Soc. *Res:* X-ray structure analysis; x-ray instrumentation and low-temperature apparatus; study of phase transitions and molecular complexes. *Mailing Add:* Dept Chem Adelphi Univ Garden City NY 11530

RUDMIN, JOSEPH WEBSTER, SCIENCE EDUCATION, CELESTIAL MECHANICS. *Current Pos:* ASSOC PROF, JAMES MADISON UNIV, 78- *Personal Data:* b Lowville, NY, July 27, 42; m 66; c 4. *Educ:* Union Col, NY, BS, 64; Univ Ill, MS, 66; Univ Wis, PhD(physics), 74. *Prof Exp:* Develop engr, Eastman Kodak, 66-68; res assoc, Univ Md, 74-76; temp asst prof, Fla Atlantic Univ, 76-78. *Mem:* Sigma Xi; Am Phys Soc. *Res:* Astronomy; celestial mechanics; CCD applications; asteroid hunting; electronics. *Mailing Add:* Physics Dept James Madison Univ Harrisonburg VA 22807. *E-Mail:* fac__rudmin@jmuvax

RUDMOSE, H WAYNE, PHYSICS, ACOUSTICS. *Current Pos:* RETIRED. *Personal Data:* b Cisco, Tex, Mar 16, 15; wid, Christelle Simmons; c 2. *Educ:* Univ Tex, BA, 35, MA, 36; Harvard Univ, PhD(physics), 46. *Prof Exp:* Asst physics, Univ Tex, 32-35, tutor & chg electronic labs, 35-37; instr, Harvard Univ, 38-39, asst, 39-41, res assoc & group leader, Electro-Acoustic Lab, 41-43; assoc dir, 43-45; from asst prof to prof physics, Southern Methodist Univ, 46-63; group vpres, Sci & Systs Group, Tracor, Inc, 63-80. *Concurrent Pos:* Acoust consult, 46-80; mem comt on hearing & bio-acoustics, Nat Acad Sci, 53, chmn, 75-76. *Mem:* Acoust Soc Am; Am Acad Indust Hyg; Am Indust Hyg Asn; Sigma Xi. *Res:* Audio communication; hearing; architectural acoustics; noise measurement control. *Mailing Add:* 2802 Scenic Dr Austin TX 78703-1041

RUDNER, RIVKA, GENETICS. *Current Pos:* assoc prof, 68-74, PROF BIOL SCI, HUNTER COL, 74- *Personal Data:* b Ramat-Gan, Israel, Apr 9, 35; m 56; c 3. *Educ:* NY Univ, BA, 57; Columbia Univ, MS, 58, PhD(zool), 61. *Prof Exp:* Res worker biochem, Col Physicians & Surgeons, Columbia Univ, 61-62, res assoc, 62-63, asst prof, 63-68. *Mem:* Fedn Am Biochemists. *Res:* Molecular doning in B subtiles of L and H specific operons; sequence analyis and transcriptioner mapping of promotion regions; variation of nucleotide sequences among related Bacillus genomes in conserved and non conserved regions. *Mailing Add:* Dept Biol Sci Hunter Col Columbia Univ NY 695 Park Ave New York NY 10021-5085. *Fax:* 212-772-5227

RUDNEY, HARRY, BIOCHEMISTRY. *Current Pos:* prof biol chem & dir dept, 67-88, interim chmn, Dept Pharmacol, 94-97, EMER PROF, MOLECULAR GENETICS, BIOCHEM & MICROBIOL, COL MED, UNIV CINCINNATI, 88- *Personal Data:* b Toronto, Ont, Apr 14, 18; nat US; m 46, Bernice D Snider; c Joel D & P Robert. *Educ:* Univ Toronto, BA, 47, MA, 48; Western Reserve Univ, PhD(biochem), 52. *Honors & Awards:* G Rieveschel Jr Award, 77. *Prof Exp:* Res asst biochem, Univ Toronto, 46-48; sr instr, Sch Med, Western Reserve Univ, 51-53, from asst prof to prof, 53-67. *Concurrent Pos:* Am Cancer Soc scholar, 55-57; NSF sr res fel, 57-58; USPHS res career develop award, 58-63 & res career award, 63-; vis prof, Case Inst Technol, 65-66; ed, Archiv Biochem & Biophys, 65- & J Biochem, 75-80; mem panel metab biol, NSF, 68-71; mem res career award comt, NIH, 69-71; mem biochem test comt, Nat Bd Med Examr, 74; pres, Dept Biochem, Assoc Med Sch, 81-82. *Mem:* Am Chem Soc; Am Soc Biol Chemists; Am Soc Microbiol; Brit Biochem Soc; AAAS. *Res:* Biosynthesis of isoprenoid precursors of sterols. *Mailing Add:* Dept Molecular Genetics Biochem & Microbiol Univ Cincinnati Col Med Cincinnati OH 45267-0524. *Fax:* 513-558-8474; *E-Mail:* harry.rudney@uc.edu

RUDNICK, ALBERT, VIROLOGY. *Current Pos:* RETIRED. *Personal Data:* b Manchester, NH, Apr 26, 22. *Educ:* Univ NH, BS, 42, MS, 44; Univ Calif, PhD(parasitol), 59. *Prof Exp:* Res asst, Hooper Found, Univ Calif, San Francisco, 47-50; entomologist, State Bur Vector Control, Calif, 52; med entomologist, US Chem Corps, Ft Detrick, Md, 54; res asst, Sch Pub Health, Univ Calif, 55; res assoc, Grad Sch Pub Health, Univ Pittsburgh, 56-60; asst res virologist, Hooper Found, Univ Calif, San Francisco, 60-65, assoc res virologist, 65-71; assoc prog dir, Univ Calif Int Ctr Med Res & Training, 72-74, prog dir, 74-80; prof virol, Dept Epidemiol & Internal Health, Hooper Found, Univ Calif, San Francisco, 74-82. *Concurrent Pos:* Rep, Comn Viral Infections, US Armed Forces Epidemiol Bd, Guam, 48, Tokyo, 49, Manila, 56, assoc mem, 66-72; consult, US Opers Mission, Bangkok, 58; consult to chief surgeon, 13th Air Force, Philippines, 58; actg sr virologist, Inst Med Res, Kuala Lumpur, 62-63; temporary adv, Western Pac Regional Off, WHO, Bangkok, 64; consult, 80- *Mem:* Am Soc Trop Med & Hyg; Wildlife Dis Asn; Am Mosquito Control Asn; Malaysian Soc Parasitol & Trop Med; Pac Sci Asn; Sigma Xi. *Res:* Ecology of dengue and other arboviruses of southeastern Asia. *Mailing Add:* 101 Lombard St Suite 503 W San Francisco CA 94111-1143

RUDNICK, DANIEL LARS, PHYSICAL OCEANOGRAPHY. *Current Pos:* asst prof, 93-97, ASSOC PROF OCEANOG, UNIV CALIF, SAN DIEGO, 97- *Personal Data:* b Los Angeles, Calif, Apr 13, 59. *Educ:* Univ Calif, San Diego, BA, 81, PhD(oceanog), 87. *Prof Exp:* Fel, Woods Hole Oceanog Inst, 87-88, investr, 88-89; asst prof, Univ Wash, 89-93. *Concurrent Pos:* Assoc ed, J Atmospheric & Oceanic Technol, 92- *Mem:* Am Meteorol Soc; Am Geophy Union. *Res:* Observational physical oceanography; physical processes of the upper ocean such as fronts and air-sea interaction and abyssal circulation. *Mailing Add:* Scripps Inst Oceanog 0230 Univ Calif San Diego La Jolla CA 92093-0230. *E-Mail:* drudnick@ucsd.edu

RUDNICK, GARY, BIOCHEMISTRY, PHARMACOLOGY. *Current Pos:* from asst prof to assoc prof, 75-91, PROF PHARMACOL, SCH MED, YALE UNIV, 91- *Personal Data:* b Philadelphia, Pa, Sept 14, 46; m 81; c 2. *Educ:* Antioch Col, BS, 68; Brandeis Univ, PhD(biochem), 74. *Prof Exp:* Fel biochem, Roche Inst Molecular Biol, 73-75. *Concurrent Pos:* Estab investr, Am Heart Asn, 79-84. *Mem:* Am Soc Biochem & Molecular Biol; Soc Neurosci; AAAS. *Res:* Membrane function; mechanisms of solute transport across biological membranes; uptake and storage of neurotransmitters. *Mailing Add:* Dept Pharmacol Yale Univ Sch Med 333 Cedar St PO Box 3333 New Haven CT 06510-8066. *Fax:* 203-785-7670; *E-Mail:* rudnick@biomed.med.yale.edu

RUDNICK, ISADORE, ACOUSTICS, LOW TEMPERATURE PHYSICS. *Current Pos:* RETIRED. *Personal Data:* b New York, NY, May 8, 17; m 39; c 5. *Educ:* Univ Calif, Los Angeles, BA, 38, MA, 40, PhD(physics), 44. *Honors & Awards:* Biennial Award, Acoust Soc Am, 48, Silver Medal, 75, Gold Medal, 82; Fritz London Award, Int Union Pure & Appl Physics, 81. *Prof Exp:* Res physicist, Brown Univ, 42; res physicist, Duke Univ, 42-45; from instr to asst prof physics, Pa State Univ, 45-48; from asst prof to assoc prof, Univ Calif, Los Angeles, 48-58, prof physics, 59-87. *Concurrent Pos:* Fulbright fel, Royal Inst Technol, Copenhagen, 57-58 & Israel Inst Technol, 65; vis prof, Univ Paris, 72, Israel Inst Technol, 73, Univ Tokyo, 77 & Univ Nanjing, China, 79; fac res lectr, Univ Calif, Los Angeles, 75-76; distinguished lectr, Acoust Soc Am, 80- *Mem:* Nat Acad Sci; fel Am Phys Soc; fel Acoust Soc Am (vpres, 62, pres, 69). *Res:* Ultrasonics; high intensity acoustics; cavitation; elastic wave damping in metals; low temperature physics; quantum liquids; non-linear physics. *Mailing Add:* 334 Skyewiay Rd Los Angeles CA 90049

RUDNICK, JOSEPH ALAN, CONDENSED MATTER PHYSICS. *Current Pos:* chmn, Dept Physics, 86-89, PROF PHYSICS, UNIV CALIF, LOS ANGELES, 84- *Personal Data:* b Durham, NC, Feb 1, 44; m 68, Alice A Cook; c 3. *Educ:* Univ Calif, Berkeley, BA, 65; Univ Calif, San Diego, PhD(physics), 70. *Prof Exp:* Res assoc, Univ Wash, 69-72, Technion, Isreal Inst Technol, 72-74 & Case Western Res Univ, 74-78; asst prof physics, Tufts Univ, 78; prof, Univ Calif, Santa Cruz, 78-84. *Concurrent Pos:* Consult, Jet Propulsion Lab, Calif Inst Technol, 85- *Mem:* Am Phys Soc. *Res:* Phase transitions and critical phenomena; physics of disordered systems; structure and dynamics of deposited films; polymer physics; nonlinear dynamics and chaos. *Mailing Add:* 3830 Mandeville Canyon Rd Los Angeles CA 90049. *E-Mail:* jrudnick@uclaph

RUDNICK, LAWRENCE, RADIO ASTRONOMY, ASTROPHYSICS. *Current Pos:* from asst prof to assoc prof, 79-86, PROF ASTRON, UNIV MINN, 86- *Personal Data:* b Philadelphia, Pa, Mar 17, 49; m 70; c 2. *Educ:* Cornell Univ, BA, 70; Princeton Univ, MA, 72, PhD(physics), 74. *Prof Exp:* Res fel radio astron, Nat Radio Astron Observ, 74-76, asst scientist, 76-78, assoc scientist, 78. *Mem:* Am Astron Soc; Int Astron Union. *Res:* Extragalactic radio astronomy; radio galaxies; supernova remnants; relativistic particle acceleration. *Mailing Add:* 5137 Upton Ave S Minneapolis MN 55416

RUDNICK, MICHAEL DENNIS, ANATOMICAL SCIENCES, OTOLOGY. *Current Pos:* DIR & STAFF PHYSICIAN, WESTSIDE NEIGHBORHOOD HEALTH CTR, DENVER, 91- *Personal Data:* b Huntington, NY, Aug 5, 45; c 2. *Educ:* State Univ NY Buffalo, BA, 71, PhD(anat), 78. *Prof Exp:* Resident, Dept Pediat, Univ SFla, Tampa, 87-89; fel pediat med, Univ Colo, 89-91. *Concurrent Pos:* Clin instr, State Univ NY, Buffalo, 78- *Res:* Anatomy, physiology and pathology of the inner ear; aminoglycoside antibiotic ototoxicity; cochlear implant and the function of kinocilia in the vestibular system. *Mailing Add:* Westside Neighborhood Health Ctr Teen Clin 1100 Federal Blvd Denver CO 80204

RUDNICK, STANLEY J, INSTRUMENTATION ENGINEERING. *Current Pos:* engr instrumentation, 61-74, dir electronics div, 74-85, RES PROG MGR, ARGONNE NAT LAB, 85- *Personal Data:* b Chicago, Ill, Oct 10, 37; m 58, Virginia C Richardson; c Katherine, Elizabeth, Jennifer, Thomas & Laura. *Educ:* Northwestern Univ, BS, 59; Univ Ill, MS, 61; Univ Chicago, MBA, 78. *Prof Exp:* Engr electronics, Motorola, Inc, 59-60. *Concurrent Pos:* Mem, Nat Instrumentation Methods Comt, 64- *Mem:* Inst Elec & Electronics Engrs. *Res:* Nuclear instrumentation and systems. *Mailing Add:* Argonne Nat Lab Bldg 207 9700 S Cass Ave Argonne IL 60439. *Fax:* 202-586-0485; *E-Mail:* stan.rudnick@hq.doe.gov

RUDNITSKI, DONALD MICHAEL, GAS TURBINE PERFORMANCE. *Current Pos:* Group leader, Gas Turbine Group, Engine Lab, Div Mech Eng, Nat Res Coun Can, 76-86, head, 85-92, sr policy analyst, Corp Planning & Eval, 92-93, CHIEF AEROPROPULSION, NAT RES COUN CAN, 93- *Educ:* Carleton Univ, BE, 75, ME, 83. *Mem:* Can Aeronaut & Space Inst. *Res:* Mechanical and electrical apparatus. *Mailing Add:* 2043 Palmer Pl Ottawa ON K1H 5Z5 Can

RUDNYK, MARIAN E, PLANETARY GEOLOGY, HISTORICAL ASTRONOMY. *Current Pos:* Planetary photogeol consult, Path Sect, 83-85 & 86-88, astronr, Comet & Asteroid Res Prog, 85-86, MGR, PLANETARY IMAGE FACIL, JET PROPULSION LAB, NASA, 88- *Personal Data:* b Long Island, NY, June 14, 60. *Educ:* Calif State Polytech Univ, BS, 83. *Concurrent Pos:* Lectr astron; mem, Planetary Sci & Imaging Teams, NASA. *Mem:* Am Inst Aeronaut & Astronaut; Soc Ukrainian Engrs Am. *Res:* Astronomical asteroids; historical information and data interpretation of historical NASA and international planetary missions. *Mailing Add:* 732 W Hillcrest Blvd Monrovia CA 91016. *Fax:* 626-359-7149; *E-Mail:* zodanga@aol.com

RUDO, FRIEDA GALINDO, PHARMACOLOGY. *Current Pos:* From instr exp surg to asst prof pharmacol, Univ Md, Sch Med, 60-68, from asst prof to assoc prof, Sch Dent, 68-75, prof, 70-90, EMER PROF PHARMACOL, SCH DENT, UNIV MD, BALTIMORE, 90- *Personal Data:* b New York, NY, Nov 13, 23; m 45; c 2. *Educ:* Goucher Col, AB, 44; Univ Md, MS, 60, PhD(pharmacol), 63. *Hon Degrees:* DSc, Goucher Col, 76. *Concurrent Pos:* Consult, Ohio Chem Co, 60, res grant, 64 - *Mem:* Fel Am Col Dentists; fel Explorer's Club. *Res:* Cardiovascular research using artificial heart; cardiac output studies on new nitrate compounds; pharmacology and toxicity of new anesthetic agents and analgesics. *Mailing Add:* 6008 Ivydene Terr Baltimore MD 21209

RUDOLF, PAUL OTTO, VARIATION IN PINUS & PICEA. *Current Pos:* RETIRED. *Personal Data:* b La Crosse, Wis, Nov 4, 06; m 32; c 2. *Educ:* Univ Minn, BS, 28; Cornell Univ, MF, 29. *Honors & Awards:* Super Serv Award, USDA, 65; Barrington Moore Mem Award, Soc Am Foresters, 88. *Prof Exp:* Res asst forestry, Cornell Univ, 28-29; jr forester, US Forest Serv, Southern Forest Exp Sta, 29-30 & Lake States Forest Exp Sta, 30-35; asst silviculturist, Lake States Forest Exp Sta, 35-37, assoc silviculturist, 37-42, silviculturist, 42-49, forester, 49-59, res forester, 59-65, prin silviculturist, 65; prin silviculturist, N Cent Forest Exp Sta, 66-67, expert, 67-71; lectr appl silvicult & forest ecol, Univ Minn, 67-75, res assoc, 75-82. *Concurrent Pos:* Exec secy, Lake States Forest Tree Improv Comt, 55-66; US rep & chmn, Tree Seed Experts Meeting, Orgn Econ Coop & Develop, 63 & 65; mem, World Forestry Cong, Seattle, 60, Soc of Am Foresters; chmn, Div Silviculture, 61, actg chmn, 65, chmn Tree Seed Comt, 63-64. *Mem:* Fel Soc Am Foresters; fel AAAS; Sigma Xi. *Res:* Reforestation; racial variation in forest trees; forest seeds; silviculture of northern trees; distribution of tree species; forest research history; forest tree improvement. *Mailing Add:* 7244 York Ave S Apt 423 Edina MN 55435-4417

RUDOLPH, ABRAHAM MORRIS, PHYSIOLOGY. *Current Pos:* prof physiol, 74-88, PROF PEDIAT, UNIV CALIF, SAN FRANCISCO, 66-, PROF OBSTET & GYNEC, 74- *Personal Data:* b Johannesburg, SAfrica, Feb 3, 24; nat US; m 49; c 3. *Educ:* Univ Witwatersrand, MB, BCh, 46, MD, 51; Am Bd Pediat, dipl, 53; FRCP(E), 66, FRCP(L), 85. *Honors & Awards:* Mead Johnson Award; Borden Award; Arvo Yippo Award, Helsinki; Merit Award, Nat Heart, Lung & Blood Inst, 86; Res Achievement Award, Am Heart Asn, 91; Joseph W St Geme Leadership Award, Fed Pediat Soc, 93. *Prof Exp:* Fel pediat, Harvard Med Sch, 51-53, res fel physiol, 53-54, Am Heart Asn res fel, 54-55, instr pediat, 55-57, assoc, 57-60; assoc prof, Albert Einstein Col Med, 60-63, prof pediat & assoc prof physiol, 63-66. *Concurrent Pos:* Fel, Children's Med Ctr, Boston, 51-53, from asst cardiologist in chg to assoc cardiologist in chg, Cardiopulmonary Lab, 55-66; Am Heart Asn estab investr, 56-; mem, Nat Adv Heart & Lung Coun. *Mem:* Inst Med-Nat Acad Sci; Am Pediat Soc; Am Physiol Soc; Soc Pediat Res; Am Acad Pediat; Soc Clin Invest; Am Fedn Clin Res. *Res:* Cardiovascular physiology, particularly physiology of the fetus and newborn; physiology of congenital heart disease; pediatric cardiology. *Mailing Add:* Dept Pediat-Obstet-Gynec Univ Calif Med Ctr San Francisco CA 94143-0544. *Fax:* 415-476-0676; *E-Mail:* abraham_rudolph@pedcardgateway.ucsf.edu

RUDOLPH, ARNOLD JACK, pediatrics, neonatal-perinatal medicine; deceased, see previous edition for last biography

RUDOLPH, FREDERICK BYRON, ENZYMOLOGY, METABOLIC REGULATION. *Current Pos:* from asst prof to assoc prof, 72-85, PROF BIOCHEM, RICE UNIV, 85-, DIR, MABEE LAB BIOTECH & GENETIC ENG, 86-, EXEC DIR, INST BIOSCI & BIOENG, 93-, CHAIR BIOCHEM, 95- *Personal Data:* b St Joseph, Mo, Oct 17, 44; m 71, Glenda Myers; c 2. *Educ:* Univ Mo, Rolla, BS, 66; Iowa State Univ, PhD(biochem), 71. *Prof Exp:* NSF fel biochem, Univ Wis, 71-72. *Concurrent Pos:* Consult, World Book Encycl, 72-; assoc ed, Yearbk Cancer, 76-84; adj prof, Univ Tex Med Sch, Houston, 81-; mem, Biochem Study Sect, NIH, 83-87. *Mem:* Am Soc Biochem & Molecular Biol; Am Chem Soc; Am Soc Biotechnol; Coun Undergrad Res; Asn Biol Lab Educ. *Res:* Enzyme studies on nucleotide metabolism; structure and function of enzymes; role of dietary nucleotides in immune function; anaerobic fermentation; protein purification; antimetabolite action. *Mailing Add:* Dept Biochem Rice Univ PO Box 1892 Houston TX 77251-1892. *Fax:* 713-285-5154; *E-Mail:* fbr@rice.edu

RUDOLPH, GUILFORD GEORGE, BIOCHEMISTRY. *Current Pos:* asst dean basic sci, 67-73, head dept, 67-85, PROF BIOCHEM, LA STATE UNIV MED CTR, SHREVEPORT, 67- *Personal Data:* b Kiowa, Kans, Jan 2, 18; m 44; c 3. *Educ:* Univ Colo, BA, 40; Wayne State Univ, MS, 42; Univ Utah, PhD(biochem), 48. *Prof Exp:* Teaching fel biochem, Wayne State Univ, 40-42; instr, Univ Utah, 46-48; asst prof, Vanderbilt Univ, 49-57; assoc prof, Univ Md, 57-60; assoc prof, Vanderbilt Univ, 60-67. *Concurrent Pos:* Am Cancer Soc res assoc, Univ Chicago, 48-49; prin scientist, Vet Admin Hosp, Nashville, Tenn, 49-57; mem grad fac, Med Ctr, La State Univ, 58-; consult, Vet Admin Hosp, 68- *Mem:* AAAS; Am Physiol Soc; Am Asn Clin Chem; Am Chem Soc. *Res:* Clinical chemistry. *Mailing Add:* 550 Dunmoreland Dr Shreveport LA 71106-6125

RUDOLPH, HARVEY, NUCLEAR PHYSICS. *Current Pos:* regulations officer, Bur Radiol Health, Food & Drug Admin, 75-78, chief med pract sect, 78-82, dep dir, planning staff, Ctr Devices & Radiol Health, 82-87, Div Electronics & Comput Sci, 87-88, dir, 88-94, actg dir, Off Sci & Tecchnol, 94-95, ACTG DEP DIR, OFF SCI & TECHNOL, CTR DEVICES & RADIOL HEALTH, FOOD & DRUG ADMIN, 95- *Personal Data:* b Nov 17, 42. *Educ:* Washington Univ, BA, 64; State Univ NY, MA, 66, PhD(nuclear physics), 71. *Prof Exp:* Res assoc, Nuclear Physics Lab, Univ Colo, 70-74; res asst prof physics, Univ Pittsburgh, 74-75. *Concurrent Pos:* Lectr, Physics Dept, Univ Colo, 73-74. *Mem:* Am Phys Soc; Soc Med Decision Making; Am Asn Physicists Med; Sigma Xi. *Res:* Published numerous articles and reports. *Mailing Add:* Ctr Devices & Radiol Health Food & Drug Admin HFZ-100 9200 Corporate Blvd Rockville MD 20850. *E-Mail:* hxr@fdadr.cdrh.fda.gov

RUDOLPH, JEFFREY STEWART, PHARMACY, CHEMISTRY. *Current Pos:* VPRES PHARMACEUT RES & DEVELOP, ICI PHARMACEUT, 88- *Personal Data:* b Chicago, Ill, Oct 30, 42; m 67; c 2. *Educ:* Univ Ill, Chicago, BS, 66; Purdue Univ, Lafayette, MS, 69, PhD(pharm), 70. *Prof Exp:* Sr res pharmacist, Ciba-Geigy Pharmaceut Corp, 70-72; sr scientist, McNeil Labs Div, Johnson & Johnson, 72-75, group leader pharm, Pilot Plant, 75-76; asst dir, 77-80, dir pharmaceut develop, Stuart Pharmaceut Div, ICI Am, Inc, 80-87. *Mem:* Acad Pharmaceut Sci; Am Pharmaceut Asn; Am Asn Pharmaceut Scientist. *Res:* Optimization of drug delivery systems; development of new dosage forms with emphasis on optimum bioavailability; evaluation of pharmaceutical processing equipment. *Mailing Add:* 2201 Patwynn Ct Wynnwood Wilmington DE 19810

RUDOLPH, LEE, KNOT THEORY, COMPLEX PLANE CURVES. *Current Pos:* vis asst prof, 86-87, from asst prof to assoc prof, 87-95, DEPT CHAIR MATH & COMPUT SCI, CLARK UNIV, 91 & 93-, PROF, 95- *Personal Data:* b Cleveland, Ohio, Mar 28, 48; c 2. *Educ:* Princeton Univ, AB, 69, Mass Inst Technol, PhD(math), 74. *Prof Exp:* Researcher, Proj Logo, Artificial Intel Lab, Mass Inst Technol, 74; instr math, Brown Univ, 74-77; asst prof math, Columbia Univ, 77-82; vis asst prof, Brandeis Univ, 83. *Concurrent Pos:* Vis researcher, Univ Geneva, Switz, 82, vis prof math, 83-84; mem, Math Sci Res Inst, Calif, 84-85; vis lectr, Univ Md, 85; vis prof math, Univ Zaragoza, Spain, 86, Univ Nacional Autonoma de Mex, 86, Univ Paul Sabatier, Toulouse, France, 91, Univ Paul Sabatier, 92-93 & Univ Bourgogne, Dijon, 93. *Mem:* Am Math Soc. *Res:* Relationships between low-dimensional topology and several complex variables; knot theory of complex plane curves; theories of braided surfaces, fibered links, enhanced Milnor number, generalized Jones polynomials; homology of arithmetic groups. *Mailing Add:* PO Box 251 Adamsville RI 02801-0251. *E-Mail:* lrudolph@black.clarleu.edu

RUDOLPH, LUTHER DAY, INFORMATION SCIENCE. *Current Pos:* res engr, Res Corp, 64-68, from asst prof to assoc prof syst & info sci, 68-75, PROF SYSTS & INFO SCI, SCH COMPUT & INFO SCI, SYRACUSE UNIV, 75- *Personal Data:* b Cleveland, Ohio, Aug 10, 30; m 54; c 3. *Educ:* Ohio State Univ, BS, 58; Univ Okla, MEE, 64; Syracuse Univ, PhD(systs & info sci), 68. *Prof Exp:* Engr, Gen Elec Co, 58-64. *Mem:* Inst Elec & Electronics Engrs; Am Soc Psychical Res; Parapsychol Asn; Am Math Soc. *Res:* Theory and implementation of error-correcting codes; application of combinatorial mathematics to problems in communication and system science; application of information theory to extrasensory communication. *Mailing Add:* 5191 N Calle Oreo Tucson AZ 85718

RUDOLPH, RAY RONALD, mathematics, for more information see previous edition

RUDOLPH, RAYMOND NEIL, PHYSICAL CHEMISTRY. *Current Pos:* asst prof, 77-83, ASSOC PROF CHEM, ADAMS STATE COL, 83- *Personal Data:* b Lansing, Mich, May 19, 46; m 71; c 2. *Educ:* Univ NMex, BS, 68; Univ Colo, MS, 71, PhD(chem), 77. *Prof Exp:* Lab asst chem, Univ Colo, 68-71; sec teacher physics & math, Koidu Sec Sch, Sierra Leona, Africa, 71-74. *Concurrent Pos:* Am Soc Eng Educ/NASA res fel, 79 & 80. *Mem:* Sigma Xi; Am Chem Soc. *Res:* Ultraviolet/visible spectroscopy; photophysics and photochemistry of small molecules. *Mailing Add:* 511 Brown Ave Alamosa CA 81101

RUDOLPH, WILLIAM BROWN, MATHEMATICS. *Current Pos:* from asst prof to assoc prof, 69-81, PROF MATH & EDUC, IOWA STATE UNIV, 81- *Personal Data:* b St Paul, Minn, Dec 14, 38; m 61, Rosellyn Paige; c Joyce, Bill & Heather. *Educ:* Bethany Col, WVa, BA, 60; Purdue Univ, Lafayette, MS, 65, PhD(math educ), 69. *Prof Exp:* Teacher, Shaker Heights Bd Educ, 61-63; instr math, Menlo Col, 63-66; instr, Univ Santa Clara, 64-66; instr & res asst math educ, Purdue Univ, Lafayette, 66-69. *Concurrent Pos:* Consult, Iowa Dept Pub Instr, 71-; consult & res grant evaluator, North Cent Asn, ESEA Title III & State of Iowa, 71- *Mem:* Sch Sci & Math Asn; Nat Coun Teachers Math; Soc Info Technol. *Res:* Information theory concepts as applied to language analysis; mathematics learning theory; computer assisted instruction; textbook author; distance education. *Mailing Add:* Dept Math Iowa State Univ Ames IA 50011. *Fax:* 515-294-5454; *E-Mail:* rudolph@pollux.math.iastate.edu

RUDOLPHI, THOMAS JOSEPH, COMPUTATIONAL METHODS IN APPLIED MECHANICS, SINGULAR INTEGRAL EQUATIONS. *Current Pos:* PROF ENG MECH, IOWA STATE UNIV, 79- *Personal Data:* b Wendelin, Ill, July 1, 46; m 72, Marlene Ross; c Jacob & Leah. *Educ:* Univ Ill, Urbana, BS, 69, MS, 74, PhD(theoret & appl mech), 77. *Prof Exp:* Engr, Rockwell Int Corp, 69-72; fel, Nat Res Coun, 77-78; engr, Oak Ridge Nat

Lab, 78-79. *Concurrent Pos:* Fulbright fel, Fulbright Found, 92-93. *Res:* Computational techniques in solid mechanics, especially boundary element methods, where singular integral equations are solved numerically; applications of fracture mechanics, non-destructive evaluation, ultrasonics, wave scattering in fluids and solids. *Mailing Add:* 1411 Burnett Ave Ames IA 50010-5545. *Fax:* 515-294-8584; *E-Mail:* rudolphi@iastate.edu

RUDVALIS, ARUNAS, ALGEBRA. *Current Pos:* asst prof, 72-74, ASSOC PROF MATH, UNIV MASS, 75- *Personal Data:* b Bavaria, Ger, June 8, 45; US citizen. *Educ:* Harvey Mudd Col, BS, 65; Dartmouth Col, MA, 67, PhD(math), 69. *Prof Exp:* Eng assoc, Gen Atomic Div, Gen Dynamics, 65; vis asst prof math, Dartmouth Col, 69; res assoc, Mich State Univ, 69-70, asst prof, 70-72. *Concurrent Pos:* NSF res grants, 73, 74 & 75. *Mem:* Am Math Soc. *Res:* Finite simple groups; representations of finite groups; finite geometries; coding theory. *Mailing Add:* 66 Pine Grove Amherst MA 01002

RUDY, BERNARDO, NEUROBIOLOGY, MEMBRANE PHYSIOLOGY. *Current Pos:* asst prof, 79-88, ASSOC PROF PHYSIOL & NEUROSCI, MED CTR, NY UNIV, 88- *Personal Data:* b Mexico City, Mex, March 21, 48; m 89, Olga Rotriquez. *Educ:* Nat Univ, Mex, MD, 71; Centro Invest Estud Avanzados, Mex, PhD(biochem), 72; Cambridge Univ, UK, PhD(physiol), 76. *Prof Exp:* Res assoc, Univ Pa, 76-78. *Mem:* NY Acad Sci; Soc Neurosci. *Res:* Molecular understanding of brain function including studies of the structure of the molecules involved in excitation, as well as their metabolism and genetic control; genetic models of thalamo critical function. *Mailing Add:* Dept Physiol & Neurosci NY Univ Med Ctr 550 First Ave New York NY 10016. *Fax:* 212-689-9060; *E-Mail:* rudyb01@ncrcr0.mert.nyu.edu

RUDY, CLIFFORD R, NUCLEAR MEASUREMENTS. *Current Pos:* sr chemist, Monsanto-Mound, 77-83, prof mgr, 83-85, 85-88, SR RES SPECIALIST, EG&G MOUND, 88- *Personal Data:* b Cleveland, Ohio, Jan 27, 43; m 64. *Educ:* Univ Ariz, BS, 64; Univ Wash, PhD(chem), 70. *Prof Exp:* Postdoctoral res assoc, Kans State Univ, 70-72, Purdue Univ, 76-77. *Mem:* Am Phys Soc; Am Chem Soc; Am Nuclear Soc; Inst Nuclear Mat Mgt. *Res:* Perform applied research in nuclear material safeguards measurements; establish measurement control systems for nuclear accountability. *Mailing Add:* 448 E Linden Ave Miamisburg OH 45342

RUDY, LESTER HOWARD, PSYCHIATRY. *Current Pos:* SR PSYCHIAT CONSULT, HEALTH CARE COMPARE, 88- & BLUE CROSS/BLUE SHIELD, ILL, 96- *Personal Data:* b Chicago, Ill, Mar 6, 18; m 50, Ruth Jean Schmidt; c Sharon Ruth. *Educ:* Univ Ill, BS, 39; Univ Ill Col Med, MD, 41; Northwestern Univ, MSHA, 57. *Honors & Awards:* Bowls Award, Am Col Psychiatrists, 81. *Prof Exp:* Resident psychiat, Downey Vet Admin Hosp, Ill, 46-48, chief serv, 48-54; supt, Galesburg State Res Hosp, Ill, 54-58; dir, Ill State Psychiat Inst, 58-75, Ill Ment Health Insts, 72-75, Univ Ill Hosp, 81-82; prof & head, Dept Psychiat, Col Med, Univ Ill, 75-88; psychiat consult, Circuit Court, Winnebago County, ILL. *Concurrent Pos:* Prof, Dept Psychiat, Univ Ill, 59-; comnr, Joint Comn Accreditation Hosps, 67-76; chmn, NIMH Res Serv Comt, 72-73; sr consult, Vet Admin; exec dir, Am Bd Psychiat & Neurol, 72-86. *Mem:* Fel Am Col Psychiat; fel Am Psychiat Asn; Am Asn Social Psychiat. *Res:* Educational standards and evaluation. *Mailing Add:* 6343 Collingswood Ct Rockford IL 61103

RUDY, PAUL PASSMORE, JR, COMPARATIVE PHYSIOLOGY. *Current Pos:* RETIRED. *Personal Data:* b Santa Rosa, Calif, Aug 29, 33; m 54; c 3. *Educ:* Univ Calif, Davis, AB, 55, MA, 59, PhD(zool), 66. *Prof Exp:* Res asst pesticides, Univ Calif, Davis, 53-54; isopods, 60, lab technician, Marine Aquaria, 62-65; fel salt & water balance in aquatic animals, Univ Birmingham, 66-67; fel Univ Lancaster 67-68; asst prof biol, Univ Ore, 68-71, assoc prof, 71-, dir, Ore Inst Marine Biol, 69-92. *Concurrent Pos:* Teacher pub sch, Calif, 56-62; partic, Int Indian Ocean Exped, Stanford Univ, 64; asst dir, Ore Inst Marine Biol, 69-92; NSF grant, 69-71. *Mem:* AAAS; Am Inst Biol Sci; Am Soc Zool; Sigma Xi. *Res:* Marine biology. *Mailing Add:* 22750 Coast Hwy Jenner CA 95450

RUDY, RICHARD L, veterinary surgery, limited specialty practice primarily orthopedic surgery, for more information see previous edition

RUDY, THOMAS PHILIP, ORGANIC CHEMISTRY, SOLID ROCKET PROPELLANTS. *Current Pos:* CONSULT, 90- *Personal Data:* b Chicago, Ill, Mar 14, 24; m 51. *Educ:* Univ Chicago, MS, 50, PhD(chem), 52. *Prof Exp:* Chemist, Shell Develop Co, 52-56 & 58-62; asst prof chem, Univ Chicago, 56-58; head org chem, United Technol Chem Systs, 62-67, prin scientist, 67-85, chief scientist, 85-90. *Mem:* Am Chem Soc. *Res:* Organic chemistry; lubricants; fuels; antioxidants; polymers; rocket propellant ingredients and combustion. *Mailing Add:* 21142 Sarahills Dr Saratoga CA 95070

RUDY, YORAM, CARDIAC ELECTROPHYSIOLOGY, ELECTROCARDIOGRAPHY. *Current Pos:* Res assoc, Case Western Res Univ, 78-79, vis asst prof, 79-81, from asst prof to assoc prof, 81-89, PROF BIOMED ENG, CASE WESTERN RESERVE UNIV, 89-, PROF BIOPHYS, 91-, PROF MED CARDIOL, 92- *Personal Data:* b Tel-Aviv, Israel, Feb 12, 46. *Educ:* Israel Inst Technol, BSc, 71, MSc, 73; Case Western Res Univ, PhD(biomed eng), 78. *Concurrent Pos:* Vis prof, biomed eng dept, Technion, Israel, 82-83; mem, Cardiovascular & Pulmonary Study Sect, NIH, 84-88; mem, NIH reviewers res, 88-92; vis prof, Dept Physics & Astrono, Tel-Aviv Univ, Isarel, 91; dir, Cardiac Bioelec Res & Training Ctr, Case Western Res Univ. *Mem:* AAAS; fel Inst Elec & Electronics Engrs; sr mem Biomed Eng Soc; Cardiac Electrophysiology Soc; Biophys Soc; fel Am Physiol Soc; Am Heart Asn; Sigma Xi; fel Am Inst Med Biol Eng. *Res:* Model studies of the electrical activity of the heart on the cellular and tissue level; multi-electrode mapping of heart and body surface potentials; forward and inverse problems in electrocardiography; electrocardiographic imaging models of arrhythmias and neural control of the heart. *Mailing Add:* Dept Biomed Eng Case Western Res Univ Cleveland OH 44106-7207

RUDZIK, ALLAN D, PHARMACOLOGY. *Current Pos:* res scientist cent nerv syst, UpJohn Co, 66-72, sr scientist, 72-74, res head, 74-79, mgr cent nerv syst res, 79-81, GROUP MGR THERAPEUT, UPJOHN CO, 81- *Personal Data:* b Mundare, Alta, Nov 30, 34; m 60; c 2. *Educ:* Univ Alta, BSc, 56, MSc, 58; Univ Wis, PhD(pharmacol), 62. *Prof Exp:* Pharmacologist, Ayerst Labs, Que, 62-63; pharmacologist, Pitman-Moore Div, Dow Chem Co, 63-65, sr pharmacologist, 65-66. *Mem:* AAAS; Am Soc Pharmacol & Exp Therapeut; NY Acad Sci; Sigma Xi. *Res:* Autonomic pharmacology as applied to smooth muscle, cardiovascular system and the central nervous system. *Mailing Add:* Berlex Bio Sci 15049 San Pablo Ave PO Box 4099 Richmond CA 94804-0099

RUDZINSKA, MARIA ANNA, zoology, protozoology, for more information see previous edition

RUE, EDWARD EVANS, EXPLORATION GEOLOGY, RESOURCE MANAGEMENT. *Current Pos:* CONSULT GEOLOGIST, 53- *Personal Data:* b Harrisburg, Pa, Oct 3, 24; m 44, Fay Bright; c Fayette, Jonathan R & Georganne. *Educ:* Berea Col, AB, 48; Colo Sch Mines, MS, 49. *Honors & Awards:* Martin Van Couvering Mem Award, Am Inst Prof Geologists, 86. *Prof Exp:* Geologist, Magnolia Petrol Co, Mobil Oil Corp, 49-53. *Mem:* Fel Geol Soc Am; Am Asn Petrol Geol; Soc Petrol Eng; Am Inst Mining, Metall & Petrol Eng; hon mem Am Inst Prof Geologists (secy-treas, 66-67, pres, 79). *Res:* Petroleum geology and engineering; evaluations for industry and governmental agencies; industrial minerals exploration and programming for major producers; geological research coordinated with field work. *Mailing Add:* POD 647 Mt Vernon IL 62864

RUE, JAMES SANDVIK, MATHEMATICS. *Current Pos:* ASSOC PROF MATH, UNIV NDAK, 70- *Personal Data:* b Sheyenne, NDak, Nov 19, 29; m 57; c 2. *Educ:* Mayville State Col, BS, 51; Univ NDak, MS, 55; Iowa State Univ, PhD(math), 65. *Prof Exp:* From instr to asst prof math, Univ NDak, 55-60; mathematician, Boeing Airplane Co, 57-58; instr math, Iowa State Univ, 60-65; asst prof, Univ Wyo, 65-66 & Wash State Univ, 66-70. *Mem:* Am Math Soc; Math Asn Am. *Res:* Functional analysis. *Mailing Add:* Univ NDak Box 8162 Grand Forks ND 58202

RUE, ROLLAND R, PHYSICAL CHEMISTRY. *Current Pos:* Asst prof, 62-70, ASSOC PROF CHEM, SDAK STATE UNIV, 70- *Personal Data:* b Marshfield, Wis, Apr 25, 35; m 58; c 2. *Educ:* Macalester Col, BA, 57; Iowa State Univ, PhD(phys chem), 62. *Mem:* AAAS; Am Chem Soc. *Res:* Interpretation of molecular wave functions; theoretical chemistry; thermodynamic properties of solutions; electrochemistry. *Mailing Add:* 2043 Elmwood Dr Brookings SD 57006-2736

RUEBNER, BORIS HENRY, ANATOMIC PATHOLOGY, GASTROINTESTINAL PATHOLOGY. *Current Pos:* prof path, 68-94, EMER PROF PATH, SCH MED, UNIV CALIF, DAVIS, 94- *Personal Data:* b Dusseldorf, Ger, Aug 30, 23; US citizen; m 57, Susan; c 2. *Educ:* Univ Edinburgh, MB, ChB, 46, MD, 56. *Prof Exp:* Asst prof path, Dalhousie Univ, 57-59; from asst prof to assoc prof, Johns Hopkins Univ, 59-68. *Mem:* Col Am Path; Int Acad Path; Am Asn Pathologists; Am Asn Study Liver Dis; AMA. *Res:* Liver pathology; hepatic carcinogenesis; colonic carcinogenesis. *Mailing Add:* Dept Med Path Univ Calif Davis Sch Med Davis CA 95616-5224

RUECKERT, ROLAND R, VIROLOGY. *Current Pos:* from asst prof to assoc prof, 65-72, PROF BIOCHEM, UNIV WIS-MADISON, 72-, CHMN, INST MOLECULAR BIOL, 88- *Personal Data:* b Rhinelander, Wis, Nov 24, 31; m 59; c 1. *Educ:* Univ Wis, BS, 53, MS, 57, PhD(oncol), 60. *Prof Exp:* Mem res staff, McArdle Mem Lab Cancer Res, Univ Wis, 59-60; asst res virologist, Univ Calif, Berkeley, 62-64, lectr molecular biol, 64-65. *Concurrent Pos:* Fel, Max Planck Res Inst Biochem, Munich, 60-61; Max Planck Res Inst Virol, Tubingen, 61-62. *Mem:* AAAS; Am Soc Microbiol; Am Soc Biol Chemists; Am Soc Virol. *Res:* Structure of animal viruses; mechanism of virus neutralization; structure of biological antivirals. *Mailing Add:* Inst Molecular Virol Univ Wis Madison WI 53706-1596. *Fax:* 608-267-7414

RUEDENBERG, KLAUS, THEORETICAL CHEMISTRY PHYSICS, CHEMICAL BONDING. *Current Pos:* from asst prof to assoc prof, Iowa State Univ, 55-62, prof chem & physics, 64-91, distinguished prof, 78-91, EMER DISTINGUISHED PROF SCI & HUMANITIES, IOWA STATE UNIV, 91-; ASSOC SR CHEMIST, AMES LAB, US DEPT ENERGY, 91- *Personal Data:* b Bielefeld, Ger, Aug 25, 20; m 48, Veronica Kutter; c 4. *Educ:* Univ Fribourg, Lic rer nat, 44; Univ Zurich, PhD(theoret physics), 50. *Hon Degrees:* PhD, Univ Basel, Switz, 75, Univ Bielefeld, Ger, 91 & Univ Siegen, Ger, 94. *Prof Exp:* Asst, Univ Zurich, 46-47; res assoc physics, Univ Chicago, 51-55; from asst prof to assoc prof chem & physics, Iowa State Univ, 55-62; prof chem, Johns Hopkins Univ, 62-64. *Concurrent Pos:* Guggenheim fel, 66-67; vis prof, Swiss Fed Inst Technol, 66-67, Wash State Univ, 70, Univ Calif, Santa Cruz, 73 & Univ Bonn, Ger, 74; adv ed, Int J Quantum Chem & Chem Phys Letts, 67-84; assoc ed, Theoretica Chimica Acta, 67-84, ed-in-chief, 84-; Fulbright sr scholar, Monash Univ & CSIRO Chem Physics Lab, Melbourne, Australia, 82; vis prof, Univ Kaiserslautern, Ger, 87;

ed-in-chief, Theoretica Chimica Acta, 85-96. *Mem:* Fel AAAS; Am Chem Soc; Sigma Xi; fel Am Phys Soc; fel Am Inst Chem; Am Asn Univ Profs; Int Acad Quantum Molecular Sci. *Res:* Atomic and molecular quantum mechanics; chemical binding and reactions; molecular structure and spectra; quantum chemistry; many-electron quantum theory; potential energy surfaces of reactions; about 170 theoretical chemistry publications. *Mailing Add:* Dept Chem Iowa State Univ Ames IA 50011-0061

RUEDISILI, LON CHESTER, HYDROGEOLOGY, ENERGY RESOURCES. *Current Pos:* RETIRED. *Personal Data:* b Madison, Wis, Feb 7, 39; m 65; c 2. *Educ:* Univ Wis, Madison, BS, 61, MS, 65 & 71 PhD(geol), 68. *Prof Exp:* Geologist & geophysicist, Standard Oil Co Calif, 67; asst prof environ geol, Univ Wis, Parkside, 72-74; from assoc prof to prof hydrogeol, Univ Toledo, 74-93. *Concurrent Pos:* Fel water resources specialist, Environ Protection Agency, 71-72; consult hydrogeol, 71-; consult, US Aid Pres, Pakistan, 90-91. *Mem:* Fel Geol Soc Am; Am Water Resources Asn; AAAS; Am Inst Hydrol; Asn Groundwater Scientists & Engrs. *Res:* Applied water, land, and energy resources management; investigating geologic controls to water quality and quantity problems and geologic factors in engineering studies; solid and liquid waste management; environmental impact analysis; petroleum recovery; water law; environmental geology. *Mailing Add:* Ruedisili Inc PO Box 8218 Sylvania OH 43560

RUEGAMER, WILLIAM RAYMOND, BIOCHEMISTRY. *Current Pos:* RETIRED. *Personal Data:* b Huntington, Ind, Dec 15, 22; m 46, Arlene Frankenberg. *Educ:* Ind Univ, BS, 43; Univ Wis, MS, 44, PhD(biochem), 48. *Prof Exp:* Biochemist, Swift & Co, Ill, 48-49; instr biophys, Univ Colo, 49-51; asst chief radioisotope labs, Vet Admin Hosp, Denver, Colo, 51-54; from assoc prof to prof biochem, State Univ NY Upstate Med Ctr, 54-68, actg chmn dept, 67-68; prof biochem & chmn dept, Univ Nebr Med Ctr, Omaha, 68-85, assoc dean, sch allied health prof, 74-85. *Mem:* Am Soc Biol Chem; Am Inst Nutrit; Endocrine Soc; Soc Exp Biol & Med; Am Chem Soc. *Res:* Thyroid metabolism and atherosclerosis. *Mailing Add:* 24 Pine St Sugarmill Woods Homosassa FL 32646

RUEGER, LAUREN J(OHN), SPACECRAFT SYSTEM ENGINEERING. *Current Pos:* CONSULT, 89- *Personal Data:* b Archbold, Ohio, Dec 30, 21; m 44, Florence Scott; c Lauren A, Carol, Beth & Mary. *Educ:* Ohio State Univ, BSc, 43, MSc, 47. *Prof Exp:* Mem staff, Radiation Lab, Mass Inst Technol, 43-45; asst physics, Ohio State Univ, 46-47; res engr, Battelle Mem Inst, 47-49; proj leader, Nat Bur Stand, 49-53; prin prof staff mem, Appl Physics Lab, Johns Hopkins Univ, 53-88. *Concurrent Pos:* Mem, US Study Group 7, Int Radio Consultive Comt; proceedings ed, Dept Defense Precise Time & Time Interval Appl & Planning Conf. *Mem:* Eng Physics Soc (secy, 41, pres, 42); Am Phys Soc; fel Inst Elec & Electronics Engrs; AAAS. *Res:* Satellite system engineering and ground station instrumentation; microwave radar system and component design; shipboard satellite navigation equipment design; electronic system reliability engineering; analysis of nuclear radiation effects in electronic systems; hydrogen maser frequency standard design and applications; precision time frequency technology. *Mailing Add:* 1415 Glenallan Ave Silver Spring MD 20902

RUEGSEGGER, DONALD RAY, JR, RADIOLOGICAL PHYSICS, MEDICAL IMAGING. *Current Pos:* RADIOL PHYSICIST, MIAMI VALLEY HOSP, DAYTON, OHIO, 69-, CHIEF, MED PHYSICS SECT, 82- *Personal Data:* b Detroit, Mich, May 29, 42; m 65, Judith Merrill; c Steven, Susan, Mark & Ann. *Educ:* Wheaton Col, BS, 64; Ariz State Univ, MS, 66, PhD(nuclear physics), 69. *Concurrent Pos:* Consult, Vet Admin Hosp, Dayton, 70-77 & Wright Patterson AFB Med Ctr, 82-84; lectr, Sch X-ray Technol, Miami Valley Hosp, 70-76 & 79-85; from clin asst prof to clin assoc prof radiol, Sch Med, Wright State Univ, Dayton, 76- & dir group radiol physics, 77-; pres, Ohio River Valley Chpt, Am Asn Physicists Med, 82-83 & co-chmn, 84-85. *Mem:* Am Asn Physicists Med; Am Col Med Physics; Am Col Radiol; Health Physics Soc; Am Phys Soc; AAAS. *Res:* Development of new techniques to treat tumors with both ionizing and non-ionizing radiation; clinical program of combining x-rays and microwaves (hyperthemia) for cancer therapy. *Mailing Add:* Med Physics Sect Miami Valley Hosp One Wyoming St Dayton OH 45409

RUEHLE, JOHN LEONARD, PLANT PATHOLOGY. *Current Pos:* RETIRED. *Personal Data:* b Winter Haven, Fla, Feb 4, 31; m 54; c 4. *Educ:* Univ Fla, BSA, 53, MS, 57; NC State Col, PhD(plant path), 61. *Prof Exp:* Plant pathologist, Forestry Sci Lab, Southeastern Forestry Exp Sta, US Forestry Serv, 61-91. *Mem:* Am Phytopath Soc; Soc Nematol. *Res:* Forest nematology, especially host-parasite relationships; Mycorrhiza. *Mailing Add:* Pinetree Terr Lavonia GA 30553

RUEHLI, ALBERT EMIL, CIRCUITS & ELECTROMAGNETICS. *Current Pos:* Res staff mem semiconductor circuits & devices, IBM T J Watson Res Ctr, 63-66, eng & math analyst, Develop Lab, 66-71, res staff mem design automation, 71-78, mgr & res staff mem comput aided design, 78-94, RES STAFF MEM ELECTROMAGNETIC & THERMAL ANALYSIS, IBM T J WATSON RES CTR, 94- *Personal Data:* b Zurich, Switz, June 22, 37; US citizen; m, Robin Waldman. *Educ:* Zurich Tech Sch, Telecom Engr, 63; Univ Vt, PhD(elec eng), 72. *Honors & Awards:* Guillemin-Cauer Award, Inst Elec & Electronics Engrs, 82- *Mem:* Fel Inst Elec & Electronics Engrs; Soc Indust & Appl Math. *Res:* Electrical circuit theory; microwave theory; computer aided design. *Mailing Add:* IBM T J Watson Res Ctr PO Box 218 Yorktown Heights NY 10598. *E-Mail:* ruehli@watson.ibm.com

RUEL, JEAN-CLAUDE, natural regeneration, windthrow, for more information see previous edition

RUEL, MAURICE M J, environmental sciences, for more information see previous edition

RUELIUS, HANS WINFRIED, DRUG METABOLISM. *Current Pos:* vis prof pharmacol, 85-87, CONSULT PHARMACOL, MED SCH JOHNS HOPKINS UNIV, 88- *Personal Data:* b Worms, Ger, Feb 18, 15; nat US; m 46; c 2. *Educ:* Univ Geneva, DSc(chem), 42. *Prof Exp:* Res chemist synthesis pharmaceuts, Kast & Ehinger, Ger, 44-45; res assoc, Med Res Chem Dept, Max-Planck Inst, 46-51; sr res scientist, Wyeth Inst Med Res, Wyeth Labs, 51-66, mgr drug metab dept, res div, 66-78, assoc dir biol res, drug metab, 78-85. *Concurrent Pos:* Res assoc, Univ Pa, 51-53. *Mem:* AAAS; Am Chem Soc; Am Soc Pharmacol & Exp Therapeut; Int Soc Study Xenobiotics. *Res:* Isolation, characterization and structure proof of natural substances; drug metabolism; chemical carcinogens; biochemical mechanisms of drug toxicity. *Mailing Add:* 73 Spruce Hill Rd Weston MA 02193-1058

RUELKE, OTTO CHARLES, AGRONOMY, PLANT PHYSIOLOGY. *Current Pos:* from asst prof to assoc prof, 55-69, PROF AGRON, UNIV FLA, 69- *Personal Data:* b Oshkosh, Wis, Feb 18, 23; m 59; c 3. *Educ:* Univ Wis, BS, 50, MS, 52, PhD(agron), 55. *Prof Exp:* Instr high sch, 50-51; res asst agron, Univ Wis, 52-55. *Concurrent Pos:* Mem staff crop ecol, Forage & Pasture Sci, 55-; mem exec comt, Southern Pasture & Forage Crop Improv Conf, 63-65, chmn, 64; mem, Am Forage & Grassland Coun. *Mem:* Am Soc Agron; Crop Sci Soc Am; Sigma Xi. *Res:* Cold injury; plant growth regulation; microclimatology; forage management and quality evaluations. *Mailing Add:* 1125 SW Ninth Rd Gainesville FL 32601-7828

RUENITZ, PETER CARMICHAEL, MEDICINAL CHEMISTRY, ORGANIC CHEMISTRY. *Current Pos:* from asst prof to assoc prof, 74-88, PROF MED CHEM, SCH PHARM, UNIV GA, 88- *Personal Data:* b Los Angeles, Calif, Nov 10, 43. *Educ:* Univ Minn, BS, 66; Univ Kans, PhD(med chem), 74. *Prof Exp:* Res assoc med chem, Upjohn Co, 66-68. *Concurrent Pos:* Consult, SE Regional Off, Food & Drug Admin, 92- *Mem:* Am Chem Soc; Fedn Am Soc Exp Biol. *Res:* Chemistry of bicyclic amines; nonsteroidal estrogen-antiestrogen metabolism and mechanism of action. *Mailing Add:* Sch Pharm Univ Ga Athens GA 30602-2352. *Fax:* 706-542-5358; *E-Mail:* pruenitz@merc.rx.uga.edu

RUEPPEL, MELVIN LESLIE, AGRICHEMICAL DISCOVERY & DEVELOPMENT, HUMAN RESOURCE MANAGEMENT. *Current Pos:* DIR, CTR ENVIRON SCI & TECHNOL & LAB ENVIRON TRACE SUBSTANCES, UNIV MO, ROLLA, 93- *Personal Data:* b Rolla, Mo, Sept 18, 45; m 69; c 3. *Educ:* Univ Mo, BS, 66; Univ Calif, Berkeley, PhD(chem), 70. *Honors & Awards:* Thomas & Hochwalt Award, 85; MAC Award, 88. *Prof Exp:* NIH fel biochem, Cornell Univ, 70-71; sr res chemist metab, Monsanto Co, 71-75, group leader, 75- 77, res mgr environ process, 77-80, res dir synthesis, 80-82, res dir process technol, 82-85, tech adv patent litigation, 82-86, dir plant protection, 85-86, dir herbicide technol, 86-89, dir global prod develop, 89-90, dir technol, Roundup Div, 91-93. *Concurrent Pos:* Chmn, United Way & Leadership Training Prog; prin, High Output Technol Consult. *Mem:* Am Chem Soc; AAAS; Sigma Xi; Weed Sci Soc; Int Union Pure & Appl Chem. *Res:* Environmental fate and safety of pesticides; agricultural and pesticide chemistry; agrichemical synthesis bioevaluation and development; management, administration and strategy of research; breakthrough project technology; coaching performance. *Mailing Add:* 1904 Grassy Ridge Rd St Louis MO 63122. *Fax:* 573-882-3031

RUESCH, JURGEN, psychiatry, neurosciences; deceased, see previous edition for last biography

RUESINK, ALBERT WILLIAM, PLANT PHYSIOLOGY. *Current Pos:* asst prof, 67-72, assoc prof bot, prof, 72-80, PROF PLANT SCI, IND UNIV, BLOOMINGTON, 80- *Personal Data:* b Adrian, Mich, Apr 16, 40; m 63, Kathleen Cramer; c Jennifer L & Adriana E. *Educ:* Univ Mich, BA, 62; Harvard Univ, MA, 65, PhD(biol), 66. *Prof Exp:* NSF fel bot, Inst Gen Bot, Swiss Fed Inst Technol, 66-67. *Concurrent Pos:* Dir undergrad educ biol sci, Ind Univ, 72-74, 79-81, actg chmn dept biol, 81. *Mem:* AAAS; Am Soc Plant Physiol; Am Inst Biol Sci; Bot Soc Am. *Res:* Relationships between the plant cell plasma membrane and cell wall, especially as related to wall elongation. *Mailing Add:* Dept Biol Ind Univ Bloomington IN 47405. *Fax:* 812-855-6705; *E-Mail:* ruesink@ucs.indiana.edu

RUETMAN, SVEN HELMUTH, ORGANIC CHEMISTRY. *Current Pos:* RETIRED. *Personal Data:* b Rakvere, Estonia, June 14, 27; nat US; m 57, Inge Teel; c Toomas & Andres. *Educ:* Millikin Univ, BS, 53; Univ Utah, PhD(chem), 57. *Prof Exp:* Res chemist, Shell Develop Co, 57-61, Narmco Res & Develop Telecomput Corp, 61-63; res chemist, Dow Chem USA, 63-70, res specialist, 70-77, res leader, central res, 77-92. *Res:* Heterocyclic chemistry; polymer chemistry; process development; pesticides. *Mailing Add:* El Camino Corto Walnut Creek CA 94596

RUEVE, CHARLES RICHARD, MATHEMATICS. *Current Pos:* Chmn dept math & physics, 46-74, PROF MATH, ST JOSEPH'S COL, IND, 46-, CHMN DEPT, 77- *Personal Data:* b Springfield, Ohio, May 25, 18. *Educ:* St Joseph's Col, Ind, AB, 47; Univ Notre Dame, MS, 49, PhD(math), 63. *Mem:* AAAS; Math Asn Am; Am Math Soc. *Res:* Modern abstract algebra; number theory; real analysis; algebraic topology. *Mailing Add:* St Joseph's Col Box 844 Rensselaer IN 47978-0844

RUF, ROBERT HENRY, JR, HORTICULTURE. *Current Pos:* RETIRED. *Personal Data:* b Malden, Mass, Aug 30, 32; m 56. *Educ:* Univ Mass, BS, 55; Cornell Univ, MS, 57, PhD(veg crops), 59. *Prof Exp:* From asst prof to assoc prof hort & from asst horticulturist to assoc horticulturist exp sta, Univ Nev,

Reno, 59-75; pres, Greenhouse Garden Ctr, 74-95. *Concurrent Pos:* Vpres, Geothermal Develop Asn, 78-95. *Res:* Greenhouse management; propagation; geothermal-agricultural research. *Mailing Add:* 4201 Palomino Circle Reno NV 89509

RUFENACH, CLIFFORD L, IONOSPHERIC PHYSICS, PHYSICAL OCEANOGRAPHY. *Current Pos:* CONSULT, 88- *Personal Data:* b Ronan, Mont, Nov 16, 36. *Educ:* Mont State Univ, BS, 62, MS, 63; Univ Colo, PhD(elec eng), 71. *Prof Exp:* Res engr, Electronics Res Lab, Mont State Univ, 62-67; res physicist, Space Environ Lab, Boulder, Colo, 67-75; res physicist, Ocean Remote Sensing Lab, Miami, 75-76, staff mem, Wave Propagation Lab, Nat Oceanic & Atmospheric Admin, Boulder, 76-88. *Mem:* Sr mem Inst Elec & Electronics Engrs; Int Sci Radio Union; Am Geophys Union. *Res:* Remote sensing of the atmosphere and ocean; space science. *Mailing Add:* 1102 Third Ave Longmont CO 80501

RUFF, ARTHUR WILLIAM, METAL PHYSICS. *Current Pos:* RETIRED. *Personal Data:* b Newark, NJ, Aug 18, 30; m 86, Joan Edwards; c Christy, James & Mark. *Educ:* Rice Univ, BS, 52; Univ Ariz, MS, 53; Univ Md, PhD(physics), 63. *Honors & Awards:* Award Merit, Am Soc Testing & Mat; Burgess Award, Am Soc Metals. *Prof Exp:* Physicist, Shell Develop Co, 53-54, Aberdeen Proving Ground, 55-56; sect chief microstruct characterization, Nat Bur Stand, 63-76, chief Metal Sci & Stand Div, 76-79, group leader, Wear & Mech Properties, Nat Inst Stand & Technol, 80-87, Physicist, 57-94. *Concurrent Pos:* Fac, Mats & Nuclear Eng Dept, Univ Md. *Mem:* Fel Am Soc Metals; fel Am Soc Testing & Mat. *Res:* Dislocation; defects in crystals; plastic deformation; electron microscopy; metal physics; wear; tribology; mechanical properties. *Mailing Add:* A256 MATLS Nat Inst Stand & Technol Gaithersburg MD 20899

RUFF, GEORGE ANTONY, PHYSICS. *Current Pos:* from asst prof to assoc prof, Bates Col, 68-79, chmn physics dept, 76-85, chmn, Div Nat Sci & Math, 77-82, PROF PHYSICS, BATES COL, 79-, CHMN, DIV NAT SCI & MATH, 85-, CHARLES A DANA PROF PHYSICS, 85- *Personal Data:* b Bay Shore, NY, May 10, 41; m 66; c 4. *Educ:* Le Moyne Col, NY, BS, 62; Princeton Univ, MA, 64, PhD(physics), 66. *Prof Exp:* Res assoc physics, Cornell Univ, 66-68. *Concurrent Pos:* Vis assoc prof, Univ Ariz, 75-76; vis prof, Univ Freiburg, Ger, 82-83; vis res prof, Univ Va, 89-90. *Mem:* Am Phys Soc; Am Asn Physics Teachers. *Res:* Optical and atomic physics; quantum electronics. *Mailing Add:* Dept Physics Bates Col Lewiston ME 04240

RUFF, GEORGE ELSON, PSYCHIATRY. *Current Pos:* vchmn, Sch Med, Univ Pa, 74-82, actg chmn, 82-84, assoc dean, Med Student Progs, 76-80, PROF PSYCHIAT, SCH MED, UNIV PA, 56- *Personal Data:* b Wilkes-Barre, Pa, Jan 12, 28; m 51, Jean Heron; c Lynne, John, Susan, Carol & Nancy. *Educ:* Haverford Col, AB, 48; Univ Pa, MD, 52. *Honors & Awards:* Longacre Award, Aerospace Med Asn, 59. *Prof Exp:* Intern, Univ Mich, 52-53, resident psychiat, 53-56. *Concurrent Pos:* USPHS fel, Inst Neurol Sci, Sch Med, Univ Pa, 56-57; USPHS career investr, 59-64; consult, USAF, 60-63, NASA, 62-63 & 88- & Vet Admin, 64-82. *Mem:* Am Col Psychoanalysts; Am Psychiat Asn; Am Col Psychiat. *Res:* Psychiatric and psychophysiologic studies of human stress; medical education; rehabilitation; geriatric psychiatry. *Mailing Add:* Univ Pa 3615 Chestnut St Philadelphia PA 19104. *Fax:* 215-898-9114

RUFF, IRWIN S, METEOROLOGY. *Current Pos:* res meteorologist, US Weather Bur, 59-65 & Nat Earth Satellite Serv, 65-85, RES METEOROLOGIST, SATELLITE RES LAB, DEPT RES, NAT OCEANOG & ATMOSPHERIC ADMIN, 85- *Personal Data:* b New York, NY, Oct 11, 32; m 59; c 2. *Educ:* City Col New York, BS, 53; NY Univ, MS, 57. *Prof Exp:* Asst res scientist, Dept Meteorol, NY Univ, 55-59. *Mem:* Am Meteorol Soc; Am Geophys Union; Asn Orthodox Jewish Scientists. *Res:* Reflection properties of the earth and atmosphere in solar wavelengths; satellite determinations of terrestrial radiative properties and influence on climate; climatic change; scene identification from satellites. *Mailing Add:* 14421 Barkwood Dr Rockville MD 20853

RUFF, JOHN K, INORGANIC CHEMISTRY. *Current Pos:* assoc prof chem, 68-95, LAB COORDR, DEPT CHEM, UNIV GA, 95- *Personal Data:* b New York, NY, Feb 19, 32; m 54; c 3. *Educ:* Haverford Col, BS, 54; Univ NC, PhD(chem), 59. *Prof Exp:* Asst phys chem, Univ NC, 54-56; chemist, Rohm & Haas Co, 57-68. *Mem:* Am Chem Soc; Royal Soc Chem. *Res:* Organometallic chemistry of boron, aluminum and gallium; fluorine chemistry; nitrogen fluorides; hypofluorites; sulfur oxyfluoride derivatives. *Mailing Add:* Dept Chem Univ Ga Athens GA 30602

RUFF, MICHAEL DAVID, PARASITOLOGY. *Current Pos:* res leader, Protozoan Dis Lab, Animal Parasitol Inst, 77-93, technol transfer coordr, 93-96, DEP ASST ADMINR, OFF TECHNOL TRANSFER, USDA, 97- *Personal Data:* b Newton, Kans, July 22, 41; m 63; c Brian & Eric. *Educ:* Kans State Univ, BS, 64, MS, 66, PhD(parasitol), 68; Bowie State Univ, MBA, 93. *Prof Exp:* Instr biol, Marymount Univ, 67-68; parasitologist, 406th Med Lab, Japan, 68-71; NIH res fel, Rice Univ, 71-72; from asst prof to assoc prof poultry sci, Univ Ga, 72-77. *Mem:* Poultry Sci Asn; Am Soc Parasitol; Am Asn Vet Parasitol; Am Asn Avian Pathologists; World Poultry Sci Asn. *Res:* Physiology and biochemistry of parasites; metabolism of larval trematodes; schistosomiasis; avian coccidia, host parasite interactions. *Mailing Add:* Agr Res Ctr LPSI Bldg 1040 Beltsville MD 20705

RUFF, ROBERT LAVERNE, BEAR ECOLOGY, WILDLIFE MANAGEMENT. *Current Pos:* from asst prof to assoc prof, 70-81, EXTENT WILDLIFE SPECIALIST, UNIV WIS-MADISON, 70-, WATER RESOURCES MGR FAC, 71-, PROF WILDLIFE ECOL, 81-, CHNM DEPT, 87- *Personal Data:* b Laurel, Mont, Mar 4, 39; c 2. *Educ:* Univ Mont, BS, 61, MS, 63; Utah State Univ, PhD(ecol), 71. *Prof Exp:* Furbearer biologist, Mont Fish & Game Dept, 61; NIH res asst parasitol bighorn sheep, Univ Mont, 61-62; res asst magpie predation on pheasant nests, Mont Coop Wildlife Res Unit, 62-63, res assoc ecol grizzly bears & elk, 64-66; NIH res asst behav ground squirrels, Utah State Univ, 66-70. *Concurrent Pos:* Chmn, wildlife mgt on pvt lands comt, The Wildlife Soc, 84-87, pres, Wis Chap, 85; chair, exten comt, Nat Asn Univ Fish & Wildlife Progs, 95- *Mem:* Audubon Soc; Animal Behav Soc; Wildlife Soc; Bear Biol Asn; Nat Wildlife Fedn; Nature Conservancy. *Res:* Human dimensions of wildlife management on private lands; environmental impact assessment; ecology of black bear populations; ecology of European brown bears in National Parks of Yugoslavia; ecology of coyotes in Yellowstone National Park. *Mailing Add:* Dept Wildlife Ecol Univ Wis 226 Russell Labs Madison WI 53706

RUFFA, ANTHONY RICHARD, CHEMICAL PHYSICS, SOLID STATE PHYSICS. *Current Pos:* THEORET SOLID STATE PHYSICIST, ALGORISYMS RES INST, 83- *Personal Data:* b Pittsburgh, Pa, Dec 12, 33; m 59; c 5. *Educ:* Carnegie Inst Technol, BS, 55, MS, 57; Catholic Univ, PhD(physics), 60. *Prof Exp:* Theoret solid state physicist, Nat Bur Stand, 60-66 & Naval Res Lab, 66-83. *Concurrent Pos:* Lectr, Am Univ, 59-60 & Georgetown Univ, 63-64. *Mem:* Phys Soc; NY Acad Sci; Sigma Xi. *Res:* Thermal, optical and magnetic properties of crystals; theory of chemical bonding in crystals; quantum theory of atomic and molecular structure. *Mailing Add:* PO Box 4587 Silver Spring MD 20914

RUFFER, DAVID G, VERTEBRATE ZOOLOGY. *Current Pos:* STAFF, DAYTON SOC NATURAL HIST, 95- *Personal Data:* b Archbold, Ohio, Aug 25, 37; m 58; c 3. *Educ:* Defiance Col, BS, 59; Bowling Green State Univ, MA, 60; Univ Okla, PhD(zool), 64. *Prof Exp:* From instr to assoc prof biol, Defiance Col, 64-73, dean, 69-73; provost, Elmira Col, 73-78; pres, Albright Col, 78-91; pres, Univ Tampa, 91-95. *Mem:* AAAS; Am Soc Mammal; Ecol Soc Am; Animal Behav Soc. *Res:* Ecology and behavior of Cricetid rodents; evolution of behavior in the grasshopper mice. *Mailing Add:* Dayton Soc Natural Hist 2600 De Weese Pkwy Dayton OH 45414

RUFFIN, SPAULDING MERRICK, BIOLOGICAL CHEMISTRY. *Current Pos:* RETIRED. *Personal Data:* b Emporia, Va, Apr 8, 23; m 58; c 3. *Educ:* Hampton Inst, BS, 43; Mich State Univ, MA, 53, PhD(animal nutrit), 56. *Prof Exp:* Teacher pub schs, NC, 46-52; prof chem, Southern Univ, Baton Rouge, 56- *Mem:* Am Chem Soc. *Res:* Vitamins; amino acids; intermediary metabolism; biochemistry; organic chemistry. *Mailing Add:* Dept Chem Southern Univ A&M Col Baton Rouge LA 70813-0401

RUFFINE, RICHARD S, PHYSICS. *Current Pos:* SPECIALIST TECHNOL & ANALYSIS OFF DIR, DEFENSE RES ENG, 75- *Personal Data:* b New York, NY, July 28, 28; m 60; c 3. *Educ:* Queens Col, NY, BS, 50; Syracuse Univ, MS, 53; NY Univ, PhD(physics), 60. *Honors & Awards:* Meritorious Civilian Serv, US Army, 75. *Prof Exp:* Instr physics, Hunter Col, 54-55; instr, NY Univ, 58-59, res assoc, 59-60; staff scientist, GC Dewey Corp, 60-62; mem tech staff, RCA Labs, 62-67; prog mgr, Advan Res Proj Agency, US Dept Defense, 67-68; asst dir & chief reentry physics div, US Army Advan Ballistic Missile Defense Agency, 68-75. *Concurrent Pos:* Adj asst prof, NY Univ, 60-61; consult, Inst Defense Anal, 60-61. *Mem:* AAAS; Am Phys Soc; Am Geophys Union; Am Inst Aeronaut & Astronaut. *Res:* Atomic physics; electromagnetic scattering, re-entry physics. *Mailing Add:* 4050 N 27th Rd Arlington VA 22207. *Fax:* 202-693-7093

RUFFNER, JAMES ALAN, HISTORY OF SCIENCE, SCIENCE INFORMATION. *Current Pos:* from asst prof to assoc prof natural sci, Monteith Col, 64-78, ACAD SERV OFFICER, SCI LIBR, WAYNE STATE UNIV, 78- *Personal Data:* b Akron, Ohio, Sept 6, 30; m 59, Trenna Edmonson; c 2. *Educ:* Ohio State Univ, BSc, 51; Univ Mich, MS, 58; Ind Univ, MA, 63, PhD(hist sci), 66. *Prof Exp:* Physicist, Battelle Mem Inst, 51-52; instr earth sci, ETex State Col, 58-60. *Mem:* Am Libr Asn; Am Meteorol Soc; Soc Social Study Sci. *Res:* Bibliometrics; communication networks in science. *Mailing Add:* 1347 Bedford Rd Grosse Pointe Park MI 48230

RUFFOLO, JOHN JOSEPH, JR, cell biology, protozoology, for more information see previous edition

RUFFOLO, ROBERT RICHARD, JR, PHARMACOLOGY, NEUROBIOLOGY. *Current Pos:* DIR, CARDIOVASC & RENAL PHARMACOL, SMITH KLINE & FRENCH LABS, 84- *Personal Data:* b Yonkers, NY, Apr 14, 50. *Educ:* Ohio State Univ, BS, 73, PhD(pharmacol), 76. *Prof Exp:* Res assoc, Am Found Pharmaceut Educ, 73-76; res assoc pharmacol, NIH, 77-78; sr pharmacologist, Lilly Res Labs, 78-82, res scientist, 82-84. *Concurrent Pos:* Res assoc & fel pharmacol, Nat Inst Gen Med Sci, 77-78. *Mem:* Fedn Am Scientists; Am Soc Pharmacol & Exp Therapeut. *Res:* Pharmacology of vascular smooth muscle; adrenergic receptors; hypertension; congestive heart failure. *Mailing Add:* Pharmacol Sci PO Box 1539 UW 2523 Smith Kline Beecham Pharmaceut King of Prussia PA 19406-0939. *Fax:* 215-270-4114

RUGGE, HENRY F, medical technology, plasma physics, for more information see previous edition

RUGGE, HUGO R, PHYSICS, SPACE SCIENCE & TECHNOLOGY. *Current Pos:* Mem tech staff, Aerospace Corp, 62-68, dept head, 68-79, prin dir, Lab Opers, 79-81, dir, Space Sci Lab, 81-89, vpres, Lab Opers, 89-90, VPRES TECH OPERS, AEROSPACE CORP, 90- *Personal Data:* b San Francisco, Calif, Nov 7, 35; m 69; c 2. *Educ:* Univ Calif, Berkeley, AB, 57, PhD(physics), 63. *Concurrent Pos:* Mem, Adv Group Aerospace Res & Develop. *Mem:* Int Astron Union; fel Am Phys Soc; Am Geophys Union; Am Astron Soc. *Res:* Space science; solar x-rays; upper atmosphere, infrared astronomy, high energy physics; satellite instrumentation. *Mailing Add:* 216 Monte Grigio Dr Pacific Palisades CA 90272-3108

RUGGERI, ZAVERIO MARCELLO, MEDICINE, MEDICINAL SCIENCES. *Current Pos:* asst mem, dept immunol & basic & clin res, Scripps Clin & Res Found, 82-85, ASSOC MEM, DEPT BASIC & CLIN RES, DIV EXP HEMOSTASIS, SCRIPPS CLIN & RES FOUNDM 85- *Personal Data:* b Bergamo, Italy, Jan 7, 45; m 71. *Educ:* Univ Milan, Italy, MD, 70. *Prof Exp:* Res fel, hemophilia, Hemophilia Ctr, Univ Milan, 70-72; asst prof, 72-80; assoc dir FVIII/vWF, hemophilia & thrombosis ctr, Policlinico Hosp Milan, 80-82. *Concurrent Pos:* Postdoctoral hemat, Univ Pavia, Italy, 73; vis investr, St Thomas Hosp, London, 74-75, St Bantholomeuis Hosp, London, 76, Res Inst Scripps Clin, 79-80. *Mem:* NY Acad Sci; Int Soc Thrombosis & Hemostasis; Am Heart Asn; World Fed Hemophilia; AAAS; Am Soc Hemat. *Res:* Platelet adhesive functions; platelet receptors for adhesive molecules; mechanisms of cell adhesion. *Mailing Add:* Scripps Res Inst 5BR8 10666 N Torrey Pines Rd La Jolla CA 92037

RUGGERO, MARIO ALFREDO, NEUROPHYSIOLOGY, AUDITORY PHYSIOLOGY. *Current Pos:* HUGH KNOWLES PROF HEARING SCI, DEPT COMMUN SCI & DIS, NORTHWESTERN UNIV, HEAD AUDIOL & HEARING SCI PROG, 96- *Personal Data:* b Resistencia, Argentina, Nov 7, 43; m 73, Elsa L Statzner. *Educ:* Cath Univ Am, BA, 65; Univ Chicago, PhD(physiol), 72. *Prof Exp:* From asst prof to prof, Otolaryngol & Neurosci, Univ Minn, 75-93. *Concurrent Pos:* NIH fel, neurophysiol, Univ Wis, 72-75; assoc ed, J Neurosci, 89-95; mem, Commun Dis Rev Comt, Nat Inst Deafness & other Commun Dis, NIH, 90-94. *Mem:* AAAS; Soc Neurosci; Acoust Soc Am; Asn Res Otolaryngol; Am Asn Univ Prof. *Res:* Physiology and biophysics of the ear and of the auditory nerve. *Mailing Add:* Commun Sci & Dis Northwestern Univ 2299 N Campus Dr Evanston IL 60208-3550. *Fax:* 847-491-2523; *E-Mail:* mruggero@nwu.edu

RUGGIERI, MICHAEL RAYMOND, NEUROPHARMACOLOGY, RECEPTOR PHARMACOLOGY. *Current Pos:* Res assoc, 85-86, dir urol basic res, 87-90, RES ASST PROF SURG, UNIV PENN, 86-;ASSOC PROF & DIR UROL RES, TEMPLE UNIV MED CTR, 90- *Personal Data:* b Quantico, Va, Mar 2, 54; m 81, Nicole R DeMicco; c Michael R. *Educ:* Temple Univ, BS, 76; Univ Pa, PhD(pharmacol), 84. *Prof Exp:* Prin investr, NIH, 85- *Mem:* AAAS; Am Soc Microbiol; Am Urol Assoc; Am Soc Pharmacol & Exp Therapeut; Soc Neurosci. *Res:* Basic and applied investigations of mechanisms of smooth muscle and epithelial function using bladder and prostate as model systems; neurotransmitter receptor mechanisms and excitation contraction coupling; etiology of interstitial cystitis. *Mailing Add:* Urol Res Labs 3400 N Broad St Philadelphia PA 19140. *Fax:* 215-707-4565; *E-Mail:* rugg@vm.temple.edu

RUGGIERO, ALESSANDRO GABRIELE, PARTICLE PHYSICS, ACCELERATOR PHYSICS. *Current Pos:* sr physicist & head accelerator, Physics Div, 87-92, SR PHYSICIST WITH TENURE, AGS & DAT, BROOKHAVEN, UPTON, LONG ISLAND, NY, 93- *Personal Data:* b Rome, Italy, Apr 10, 40; m 65; c Sara & Filippo. *Educ:* Univ Rome, Italy, PhD(physics), 64. *Prof Exp:* Physicist, Nat Lab Frascati, Italy, 62-65, & 69-70, Europ Orgn Nuclear Res, Geneva, Switz, 66-69, Fermi Nat Accelerator Lab, Batavia, Ill, 70-84; sr physicist, Argonne Nat Lab, Argonne, Ill, 85-86. *Mem:* Am Physics Soc; NY Acad Sci. *Res:* Accelerator physics; design construction and operation of large accelerators, proton-proton and electron-positron storage and colliding devices for high energy physics experiment; design of proton-antiproton colliders; study of methods to collect anti-matter conceptual design of Tevatron I; new methods of acceleration; invention of the wakeatron; design of the relativistic heavy ion collidor (RHIC) at Brookhaven National Laboratory; feasibility studies of advanced hadron facilities; cooling techniques for heavy ions; feasibility study of crystalline beams, muson collider, nuclear fusion with accelerator technology; spallation neutron sources. *Mailing Add:* 33 Inlet View Path W East Moriches NY 11940. *Fax:* 516-344-5954; *E-Mail:* agr@bnl.gov

RUGGIERO, DAVID A, CENTRAL NEUROTRANSMISSION, CENTRAL CARDIOVASCULAR REGULATION. *Current Pos:* fel neurol, Med Col, Cornell Univ, 77-79, instr, 80-81, asst prof, 81-88, ASSOC PROF NEUROL MED COL, CORNELL UNIV, 88-; DIR NEUROL RES INST LUBEC, 93- *Personal Data:* b New York, NY, May 2, 49; m 77, Anke Nolting. *Educ:* Queens Col, NY, BA, 72; Col Physicians & Surgeons, Columbia Univ, MA, 76, MPhil & PhD(anat), 77. *Honors & Awards:* Harriet Ames Award, NY Heart Asn, 79. *Prof Exp:* Instr neuroanat & gross anat, Col Physicians & Surgeons, Columbia Univ, 74-76; course dir neurosci, NY Col Podiatric Med, 76-77. *Concurrent Pos:* Reviewer, study sect, Drug Abuse, Biomed Res Rev Comt, 87; reviewer, Study Sect Drug Abuse, Biomed Res Rev Comt, 87; consult, Vet Health Serv & Res Admin, 90-, NSF, 90-, Neurosci Rapid Response Network & Instnl Animal Care & Use Comt, Cornell Univ Med Col, 91- *Mem:* Soc Neurosci; Sigma Xi; Am Asn Anatomists; Int Brain Res Orgn; Am Soc Hypertension. *Res:* Central regulation of arterial blood pressure and cerebrovascular mechanisms; immunochemical identification of structures in brain which play a role in the tonic and reflex control of the circulation; central regulation of arterial blood pressure and cerebral blood flow; neural networks involved in behavioral expression; expression of immediate-early genes as a monitor of functional activity in the brain; cocaine related cardiac death (central mechanisms); restoration of function. *Mailing Add:* Dept Neurol Col Med Cornell Univ New York NY 10021. *Fax:* 212-988-3672

RUGGLES, IVAN DALE, MATHEMATICS. *Current Pos:* SCI PROF SPECIALIST APPL MATH, LOCKHEED MISSILES & SPACE CO, 66- *Personal Data:* b Omaha, Nebr, Dec 7, 27; m 60; c 2. *Educ:* Nebr Wesleyan Univ, AB, 49; Univ Wyo, MA, 51; Iowa State Col, PhD(math), 58. *Prof Exp:* Instr math, Iowa State Col, 57-58; from asst prof to assoc prof, San Jose State Col, 58-65; opers analyst, Stanford Res Inst, 65-66. *Mem:* AAAS; Am Math Soc; Soc Indust & Appl Math; Math Asn Am; Asn Comput Mach. *Res:* Real variables; elementary number theory; numerical analysis. *Mailing Add:* 127 Belvue Dr Los Gatos CA 95032-5114

RUGH, WILSON J(OHN), II, ELECTRICAL ENGINEERING. *Current Pos:* From asst prof to assoc prof, 69-79, PROF ELEC ENG, JOHNS HOPKINS UNIV, 79- *Personal Data:* b Tarentum, Pa, Jan 16, 44; m 76, Theresa M Winter; c David & Karen. *Educ:* Pa State Univ, BS, 65; Northwestern Univ, MS, 67, PhD(elec eng), 69. *Concurrent Pos:* Vis prof, Princeton Univ, 84, Beijing Inst Tech, 82. *Mem:* Fel Inst Elec & Electronics Engrs; Soc Indust & Appl Math; Inst Elec & Electronics Engrs Control Systs Soc. *Res:* Systems and control theory; particularly nonlinear control & gain scheduling. *Mailing Add:* Dept Elec & Comput Eng Johns Hopkins Univ 34th & Charles Sts Baltimore MD 21218-2689

RUGHEIMER, NORMAN MACGREGOR, PHYSICS. *Current Pos:* from asst prof to assoc prof, Mont State Univ, 64-80, asst dean, Col Letters & Sci, 69-, prof physics, 80-, EMER PROF PHYSICS, MONT STATE UNIV, 93- *Personal Data:* b Charleston, SC, Feb 10, 30; m 58, 82; c 4. *Educ:* Col Charleston, BS, 50; Univ NC, PhD(physics), 65. *Prof Exp:* Instr physics, The Citadel, 57-59. *Concurrent Pos:* Adv on energy to comnr higher educ, State Mont, 75- *Mem:* Am Asn Physics Teachers. *Res:* Transmission and reflection coefficients and properties of thin superconducting films; holography. *Mailing Add:* 6500 Leverich Lane Bozeman MT 59915

RUH, EDWIN, CERAMICS, CHEMISTRY. *Current Pos:* PRES, RUH INT INC, 76- *Personal Data:* b Westfield, NJ, Apr 22, 24; m 52, Elizabeth J Mundy; c Elizabeth J & Edwin Jr. *Educ:* Rutgers Univ, BSc, 49, MSc, 53, PhD(ceramics, chem), 54. *Honors & Awards:* Pace Award, Nat Inst Ceramic Engrs, 63; Greaves-Walker Roll of Hon, Keramos, 76; Bleinger Award, Am Ceramics Soc, 90. *Prof Exp:* Res engr, Harbison-Walker Refractories Co, 54-57, asst dir res, Garber Res Ctr, 57-70, dir res, 70-73, dir advan technol, 73-74; vpres res, Vesuvius Crucible Co, 74-76; sr lectr & assoc head dept metall & mat sci, Carnegie-Mellon Univ, 76-84; res prof, Dept Cermaics, Rutgers Univ, 84-95. *Concurrent Pos:* Ed, Metall Trans, 78-83. *Mem:* AAAS; fel Am Ceramic Soc (pres, 85-86); Nat Inst Ceramic Engrs; Am Inst Mining, Metall & Petrol Engrs; fel Inst Mat Ceramics UK; Sigma Xi; Am Soc Testing Mat; Keramos-Prof Ceramic Eng Fraternity (pres, 76-72); Metall Soc; Am Soc Metals Int; Acad Ceramics. *Res:* Refractories and refractory technology, manufacture, applications, failure analysis; ceramics and refractories. *Mailing Add:* 892 Old Hickory Rd Pittsburgh PA 15243. *Fax:* 412-561-1993

RUH, MARY FRANCES, PHYSIOLOGY, ENDOCRINOLOGY. *Current Pos:* from asst prof to assoc prof, 71-84, PROF PHYSIOL, SCH MED, ST LOUIS UNIV, 84- *Personal Data:* b Chicago, Ill, July 18, 41; m 68; c 2. *Educ:* Marquette Univ, BS, 63, MS, 66, PhD(physiol), 69. *Prof Exp:* Instr pub health, Univ Mass, Amherst, 66-67; instr physiol, Univ Ill, Urbana, 69-71. *Mem:* Am Soc Cell Biol; Am Physiol Soc; Endocrine Soc; Sigma Xi. *Res:* Steroid hormone action; mammalian reproductive physiology; environmental estrogens; toxicology. *Mailing Add:* Dept Pharmacol & Physiol Sci St Louis Univ Sch Med 1402 S Grand Blvd St Louis MO 63104. *Fax:* 314-577-8233; *E-Mail:* ruhmf@sluvca.slu.edu

RUH, ROBERT, CERAMICS, MATERIALS SCIENCE. *Current Pos:* res ceramist, Aerospace Res Labs, Wright Patterson AFB, 66-67, res ceramist, Processing & High Temperature Mat Br, Air Force Mat Lab, 67-70, sr proj engr, Processing & High Temperature Mat Br, 70-86, SIGNATURE TECHNOL OFF, WRIGHT LAB, WRIGHT-PATTERSON AFB, 86- *Personal Data:* b Plainfield, NJ, Aug 2, 30; m 52; c Robert Jr, Susan P & William N. *Educ:* Rutgers Univ, BS, 52, MS, 53, PhD(ceramics), 60. *Prof Exp:* Res ceramist, Aerospace Res Labs, Wright-Patterson AFB, Ohio, 58-65 & Chem Res Labs, Commonwealth Sci & Indust Res Orgn, Australia, 65-66. *Concurrent Pos:* Ian Potter Found fel, 65-66. *Mem:* Fel Am Ceramic Soc; Nat Inst Ceramic Engrs; Ceramic Educ Coun; fel Am Inst Chem. *Res:* Development of improved ceramic materials through fabrication, characterization and property studies. *Mailing Add:* 4225 Murrel Dr Dayton OH 45429

RUHE, CARL HENRY WILLIAM, MEDICAL ADMINISTRATION. *Current Pos:* RETIRED. *Personal Data:* b Wilkinsburg, Pa, Dec 1, 15; m 43, 74, Dorothy Duncan; c Barbara R (Grumet), Nancy C & David R. *Educ:* Univ Pittsburgh, BS, 37, MD, 40. *Prof Exp:* From instr to assoc prof physiol & pharmacol, Sch Med, Univ Pittsburgh, 37-60, from asst dean to assoc dean, 55-60; from asst secy to secy, Coun Med Educ, AMA, 60-67, group vpres, 76, sr vpres, 76-82. *Mem:* AAAS; Am Physiol Soc; Sigma Xi. *Res:* Human blood values; blood volume; hypothermia. *Mailing Add:* 19027 E Tonto Trail Rio Verde AZ 85263

RUHL, ROLAND LUTHER, MECHANICAL DESIGN, DYNAMICS OF PHYSICAL SYSTEMS. *Current Pos:* PRES, RUHL & ASSOC CONSULT ENGRS, 73- *Personal Data:* b Chicago, Ill, Dec 13, 42; m 65; c 3. *Educ:* Cornell Univ, BME, 65, MBA, 66, PhD(eng), 70. *Concurrent Pos:* Adj prof, Univ Ill, Urbana-Champaign, 70- *Mem:* Am Soc Mech Engrs; Am Soc Safety Engrs; Soc Automotive Engrs; Soc Mfg Engrs. *Res:* Design automation and in particular simulation and dynamics of mechanical systems. *Mailing Add:* 1906 Fox Dr Suite G Champaign IL 61820

RUHLING, ROBERT OTTO, EXERCISE PHYSIOLOGY. *Current Pos:* chmn, Dept Health, Sport & Leisure Studies, 87-91, Dept Human Serv, 91-93, PROF & GRAD COORD, GEORGE MASON UNIV, 87-, COL NURSING & HEALTH SCI, ASSOC DEAN, HEALTH SCI, 93- *Personal Data:* b Takoma Park, Md, Dec 3, 42; m 64, Holly L Gilbert; c Alice, Grant, Lara, Erin, Minna, Blair, Jeanne, Roy & Heidi. *Educ:* Univ Md, BS, 64, MA, 66; Mich State Univ, PhD(phys educ), 70. *Prof Exp:* NIH trainee cardiovasc physiol, Inst Environ Stress, Univ Calif, Santa Barbara, 70-71, res physiologist, 71-72; dir, Human Performance Res Lab, Col Health, Univ Utah, 72-84, from asst prof to prof exercise physiol, 72-87, chmn dept phys educ, 84-86, assoc dean, 86-87. *Concurrent Pos:* Mem Utah Gov's Adv Coun on Phys Fitness; mem, sports med deleg Peoples' Repub China, 85, Repub SAfrica, 88; distinguished vis scholar, James Cook Univ, Townsville, Australia, 86, Liverpool John Moore Univ, UK, 93. *Mem:* Fel Am Alliance Health, Phys Educ & Recreation; fel Am Col Sports Med; Sigma Xi. *Res:* Investigate the effects of exercise and the environment on the cardiovascular, respiratory, muscular, and nervous systems of the mammalian body. *Mailing Add:* Dept Health Fitness Recreation Resources 1F6 George Mason Univ 4400 University Dr Fairfax VA 22030-4444. *E-Mail:* rruhling@gmu.edu

RUHMANN WENNHOLD, ANN GERTRUDE, SUBSTANCE ABUSE, POST TRAUMATIC STRESS DISORDER. *Current Pos:* Res asst radiobiol, Univ Utah, 60-61, USPHS res fel, 61-63, from instr to assoc res prof anat, 65-78, res scientist med, 67-81, assoc res prof med, 78-80, asst prof 85-89, asst dean student affairs, Sch Med, 90-95, ASSOC PROF PSYCHIAT, UNIV UTAH, 89-, ASSOC DEAN STUDENT AFFAIRS & EDUC, 95-; CHIEF PSYCHIAT, SALT LAKE VET ADMIN MED CTR, 90- *Personal Data:* b Brooklyn, NY, June 12, 32; m 67, Phil; c Kim & BJ. *Educ:* Seton Hill Col, BA, 54; State Univ NY Downstate Med Ctr, MD, 58; Am Bd Psychiat & Neurol, Dipl. *Concurrent Pos:* Staff psychiatrist, Salt Lake Vet Admin Med Ctr, 84-90, 94- *Mem:* Am Fedn Clin Res. *Res:* Clinical in nature, involving malondial-dehyde in the urine of alcohol and drug abusers; use of B-blockers in post-traumatic stress disorder and bromocriptine treatment of cocaine cravings. *Mailing Add:* 2180 Belaire Dr Salt Lake City UT 84109. *Fax:* 801-584-2507

RUHNKE, LOTHAR HASSO, ATMOSPHERIC ELECTRICITY. *Current Pos:* RETIRED. *Personal Data:* b Ger, Mar 2, 31; US citizen; m 59; c 2. *Educ:* Tech Univ, Munich, MS, 55; Univ Hawaii, PhD(geosci), 69. *Honors & Awards:* Outstanding Achievement Award, Nat Oceanic & Atmospheric Admin & NASA, 72. *Prof Exp:* Res asst, Electrophys Inst, Munich, 54-57; res physicist, Meteorol Div, US Army Res & Develop Lab, Ft Monmouth, 57-61; res scientist, Appl Sci Div, Litton Indust Inc, 61-65; sci dir, Mauna Loa Observ, Nat Oceanic & Atmospheric Admin, Hawaii, 65-68, res physicist, Atmospheric Physics & Chem Lab, Environ Res Lab, 68-72; br head atmospheric physics, Naval Res Lab, 72-90. *Concurrent Pos:* Mem, Int Comn Atmospheric Elec, 63-, secy, 75-84, pres, 88-92. *Mem:* Am Geophys Union. *Res:* Basic and applied research in atmospheric electricity, electrostatics, lightning. *Mailing Add:* 11208 Wedge Dr Reston VA 20190. *E-Mail:* lrunke@aol.com

RUI, HALLGEIR, SIGNAL TRANSDUCTION, CANCER RESEARCH. *Current Pos:* ASST PROF PATH, UNIFORMED SERV UNIV HEALTH SCI, 95- *Personal Data:* b Rissa, Norway, Dec 13, 61. *Educ:* Univ Oslo MD, 87, PhD(path), 88. *Honors & Awards:* Fulbright Award, 89; Lillemor Grobstock Award, Norweg Cancer Soc, 89, 92, 93, 94 & 95; Alexander Malthe Award, Norweg Med Asn, 89, 90 & 91; Henrichsen Award Ministry Sci & Cult, 90, 91 & 92; Norweg Coun Sci Award, 90. *Prof Exp:* Clin fel, Notodden County Hosp, 87-89; post doctoral fel, Norweg Cancer Soc, 89, Univ SFla, 89-91; vis scientist, Nat Cancer Inst, 91-95. *Concurrent Pos:* Fogarty Award, Johne E Fogarty Int Ctr, Md, 91-95. *Mem:* AAAS; NY Acad Sci; Int Soc Interferon & Cytokine Res; Cytokine Soc. *Res:* Signal transduction and gene regulation by growth factors and differentation agents; breast and prostate cancer; author of over seventy articles in international medical journals. *Mailing Add:* Uniformed Serv Univ Health Sci-Path 4301 Jones Bridge Rd Bethesda MD 20814. *Fax:* 301-295-1640; *E-Mail:* hrui@usuhs.mil

RUIBAL, RODOLFO, VERTEBRATE ZOOLOGY. *Current Pos:* from instr to assoc prof, 54-70, PROF ZOOL, UNIV CALIF, RIVERSIDE, 70- *Personal Data:* b Cuba, Oct 27, 27; nat US; c 1. *Educ:* Harvard Univ, AB, 50; Columbia Univ, MA, 52, PhD(zool), 55. *Prof Exp:* Instr biol, City Col NY, 52-54. *Concurrent Pos:* Guggenheim fel, 70; res assoc, Smithsonian Inst; vis prof, Univ Chile, 68; ed, J Herpet, 80-; chmn, Nongame Adv Comt, Calif Dept Fish & Game. *Mem:* Soc Study Evolution; Am Soc Zool; Am Soc Ichthyol & Herpet. *Res:* Evolution and ecology. *Mailing Add:* Dept Biol Univ Calif Riverside CA 92521

RUINA, J(ACK) P(HILIP), ELECTRICAL ENGINEERING. *Current Pos:* vpres spec labs, 66-70, PROF ELEC ENG, MASS INST TECHNOL, 63- *Personal Data:* b Rypin, Poland, Aug 19, 23; nat US; m 47; c 3. *Educ:* City Col, BS, 44; Polytech Inst Brooklyn, MEE, 49, DEE, 51. *Honors & Awards:* Fleming Award, 62. *Prof Exp:* From instr to assoc prof elec eng, Brown Univ, 50-54; res assoc prof, Control Systs Lab, Univ Ill, 54-59, res prof, Coord Sci Lab & prof elec eng, 59-63. *Concurrent Pos:* Dep for res to Asst Secy Res & Eng, USAF, 59-60; asst dir defense res & eng, Off Secy Defense, 60-61, dir adv res projs agency, US Dept Defense, 61-63; pres, Inst Defense Anal, 64-66; mem gen adv comt, Arms Control & Disarmament Agency, 69-73; mem, Int Sci Radio Union; consult, var govt agencies; mem panel on telecommun, Nat Acad Eng; sr consult, Off Sci & Technol Policy, 77- *Mem:* Fel AAAS; fel Am Acad Arts & Sci; fel Inst Elec & Electronics Engrs; Inst Strategic Studies. *Res:* Statistical theory of noise; radar systems. *Mailing Add:* Dept Elec Eng Mass Inst Technol Cambridge MA 02139

RUIZ, CARL P, reactor chemistry, radiochemistry, for more information see previous edition

RUIZ, JOAQUIN, GEOSCIENCE. *Current Pos:* from asst prof to assoc prof, 83-93, PROF GEOSCI, UNIV ARIZ, 93-, HEAD, DEPT GEOSCI, 95- *Educ:* Univ Miami, BSc & BS, 77; Univ Mich, MS, 80, PhD(geol), 83. *Prof Exp:* Asst prof geosci, Univ Miami, 82-83. *Concurrent Pos:* Grantee, NSF, 83-, panel mem, 88, 90 & 91-93; mem, Student Affairs Comt, Soc Econ Geologists, 88-89; vis researcher, Lawrence Livermore Nat Lab, 91; vis assoc prof geosci, Univ Calif, Berkeley, 91; secy, Volcanol Sect, Am Geophys Union, 96-98. *Mem:* Fel Geol Soc Am; Am Geophys Union; Am Chem Soc; Geochem Soc. *Mailing Add:* Dept Geosci Univ Ariz Tucson AZ 85721

RUIZ-PETRICH, ELENA, CARDIAC ELECTROPHYSIOLOGY. *Current Pos:* from asst prof to assoc prof, 68-77, chmn, dept biophys, 78-84, PROF BIOPHYS, FAC MED, UNIV SHERBROOKE, 77-, CHMN, DEPT PHYSIOL BIOPHYS, 87- *Personal Data:* b Mendoza, Arg, Nov 19, 33; wid. *Educ:* Univ Cuyo, MD, 59. *Hon Degrees:* DSc, Univ Cuyo, 76. *Prof Exp:* Sr instr physiol, Fac Med, Univ Cuyo, 65-68. *Concurrent Pos:* Res fel heart physiol, Fac Med, Univ Cuyo, 59-63; Arg Nat Coun Sci & Technol Invest fel, 60-62, grant, 66-67; fel heart electrophysiol, Univ Southern Calif, 63-65; Med Res Coun Ottawa grants, 67-71; Que Heart Found grant, 69-73; fel, Can Heart Found, 69-70, res scholar, 71-75. *Mem:* Int Soc Heart Res; Can Physiol Soc; Am Physiol Soc. *Res:* Electrical activity of the heart and ionic distribution; anoxia and ischemia; atrioventricular conduction; membrane impedance and cytoplasmic resistivity in skeletal and cardiac muscle. *Mailing Add:* Dept Physiol & Biophys Fac Med Univ Sherbrooke 3001 12th Ave Sherbrooke PQ J1H 5N4 Can. *Fax:* 819-819-5399

RUKAVINA, NORMAN ANDREW, SEDIMENTOLOGY, LIMNOLOGY. *Current Pos:* RES SCIENTIST, CAN CTR INLAND WATERS, ENVIRON DEPT CAN, 66- *Personal Data:* b Ft William, Ont, June 20, 37; m 60; c 4. *Educ:* Univ Toronto, BA, 59; Univ Western Ont, MSc, 61; Univ Rochester, PhD(geol), 65. *Prof Exp:* NSF grant fel & lectr basic mineral, Univ Rochester, 65-66. *Concurrent Pos:* Ed, Proc Conf Great Lakes Res, 72-75; assoc ed, Geosci Can, 73-76 & J Great Lakes Res, 76-79. *Mem:* Sigma Xi; fel Geol Soc Am; Soc Econ Paleont & Mineral; Int Asn Gt Lakes Res; Am Geol Union. *Res:* Nearshore sedimentology of the Great Lakes; lakeshore erosion; coastal geomorphology; acoustics of sediments; sedimentology of contaminated sediments. *Mailing Add:* Can Ctr Inland Waters PO Box 5050 Burlington ON L7R 4A6 Can

RUKHIN, ANDREW LEO, STATISTICAL DECISION THEORY. *Current Pos:* PROF MATH STATIST, UNIV MD BALTIMORE CO, 89- *Personal Data:* b Leningrad, USSR, Oct 1, 46; US citizen; m 73; c 2. *Educ:* Leningrad State Univ, MS, 67; Steklov Math Inst, PhD(math & statist), 70. *Honors & Awards:* Sr Distinguished Scientist Award, Alexander von Humboldt Found, 90. *Prof Exp:* Res assoc, Steklov Math Inst, Acad Sci USSR, 70-74; assoc prof statist, Purdue Univ, 77-80, prof, 82-86. *Concurrent Pos:* Lectr, Leningrad Technol Inst, 68; vis asst prof, Leningrad State Univ, 72; vis prof, Rome Univ, Italy, 77, Univ Mass, Amherst, 82. *Mem:* fel Inst Math Statist; Am Statist Asn. *Res:* Description of universal statistical estimators; adaptive procedures for a finite parameter; characterizations of probability distributions. *Mailing Add:* 628 S Lakewood Ave Baltimore MD 21224

RUKNUDIN, ABDUL MAJEED, PHYSIOLOGY OF FERTILIZATION, ION CHANNELS IN MEMBRANES. *Current Pos:* postdoctoral res assoc electron micros, 88-91, RES ASST PROF BIOPHYS, STATE UNIV NY, 91- *Personal Data:* b India, Feb 16, 52; m 92; c 2. *Educ:* Univ Madras, India, BS, 72, MS, 74, PhD(physiol), 82. *Prof Exp:* Asst prof, Univ Madras, India, 75-84; res assoc electron micros, Univ Paris VI, 85-86; vis researcher path, Univ Bristol, UK, 86-87. *Mem:* Electron Micros Soc Am; Am Cell Biol; Soc Study Reproduction; Soc Study Fertil. *Res:* Physiology of reproduction in insects; ultrastructural aspects of mammalian fertilization; biophysical aspects of mechanotransducing ion channels in heart cells. *Mailing Add:* Dept Microbiol & Immunol Univ Md 655 W Baltimore St Baltimore MD 21201

RULE, ALLYN H, IMMUNOCHEMISTRY, BIOCHEMISTRY. *Current Pos:* asst prof immunochem & biochem, 66-74, ASSOC PROF GRAD DEPT BIOL, BOSTON COL, 77-; res fel dermat & res assoc, 74-77, ASST PROF OBSTET-GYN, SCH MED, TUFTS UNIV, 80- *Personal Data:* b New York, NY, June 18, 34; m 70; c 4. *Educ:* Cent Conn State Col, BSA, 56; Boston Univ, PhD(biol), 65. *Prof Exp:* NIH fel biochem, Brandeis Univ, 65-66; asst prof immunochem & biochem, Boston Col, 66-74; res fel dermat & res assoc med, Sch Med, Tufts Univ, 74-77. *Concurrent Pos:* Aid to Cancer res grant, 67-71; NASA res grant, 70-73; asst res prof, Mt Sinai Med Sch, 70-74. *Mem:* Am Asn Immunologists; AAAS; Path Soc. *Res:* Antigenic purification, characterization and haptenic inhibitions of glycoproteins from blood group substances, lymphocytes, muscle, skin, tumors, carcinoembryonic antigens as well as studies in immune response, suppression and autoimmunity. *Mailing Add:* Dept Biol Boston Col 140 Commonwealth Ave Chestnut Hill MA 02167-3800

RULE, DONALD, PHYSICS. *Current Pos:* RES SCIENTIST, NAVAL SURFACE WARFARE CTR. *Mailing Add:* Naval Surface Warfare Ctr 10901 New Hampshire Ave Silver Spring MD 20903-1048

RULE, JOSEPH HOUSTON, GEOCHEMISTRY & PHYTOCHEMISTRY OF TRACE ELEMENTS, PLANTS AS PHYTOMONITORS. *Current Pos:* ASSOC PROF GEOL SCI, OLD DOMINION UNIV, 76-, ASSOC PROF BIOL, 80- *Personal Data:* b Knoxville, Tenn, Feb 22, 43; m 73, Anna M. *Educ:* Univ Tenn, Knoxville, BS, 67, MS, 70; Univ Mo, Columbia, PhD(agron), 72. *Honors & Awards:* Fulbright Lecture Award, Comp & Int Educ Soc, 91. *Prof Exp:* Res fel, Trace Substances Res Ctr, Univ Mo, 73-74; vis asst prof geol sci, Univ Tenn, Knoxville, 74-76. *Mem:* Soil Sci Soc Am; Am Soc Agron; Water Environ Fedn; Geol Soc Am. *Res:* Geochemical specialization of trace elements in soils and sediments; trace element uptake by plants and aquatic organisms; biological effects of trace elements; the use of vegetative plants as phytomonitors of trace elements in the environment. *Mailing Add:* Geol Sci Old Dominion Univ Norfolk VA 23529-1000. *Fax:* 757-683-5194; *E-Mail:* jhr100f@oduum.cc.odu.edu

RULF, BENJAMIN, PHYSICAL MATHEMATICS, MATH & SCIENCE EDUCATION. *Current Pos:* TEACHER PHYSICS, ESSEX CO VOC SCH, BLOOMFIELD, NJ. *Personal Data:* b Jerusalem, Israel, Nov 6, 34; US citizen; m 68; c 4. *Educ:* Technion Israel Inst Technol, BSc, 58, MSc, 61; Polytech Univ, PhD(electroph), 65. *Prof Exp:* Res scientist, Courant Inst Math Sci, 65-67; sr lectr appl math, Tel Aviv Univ, 67-71, assoc prof, 73-79; assoc prof, Rensselaer Polytech Inst, 71-73; res officer, Nat Res Coun Can, 76-77; mem tech staff, MITRE Corp, 79-83; dir res, Radant Technols, 83- 85; mgr advan technol, Lockheed Electronics Co, 85-90; sr staff scientist, Grumman Co, 90-92. *Concurrent Pos:* Adj prof, Princeton Univ, 87, NJ Inst Technol, 86, Tufts Univ, 83-85; adj assoc prof, Univ Mass, Amherst, 81-83; lectr, Tufts Univ, 78-81; mem, Bd Educ, Westfield, NJ, 88-93. *Mem:* Sr mem Inst Elec & Electronics Engrs. *Res:* Electromagnetic and acoustic wave propagation and diffraction theory; antenna theory and design; science and math education. *Mailing Add:* 955 S Springfield Ave No C-105 Springfield NJ 07081

RULFS, CHARLES LESLIE, ANALYTICAL CHEMISTRY, INORGANIC CHEMISTRY. *Current Pos:* from asst prof to assoc prof, 49-61, PROF CHEM, UNIV MICH, ANN ARBOR, 61- *Personal Data:* b St Louis, Mo, Oct 21, 20; m 42; c 5. *Educ:* Univ Ill, BS, 42; Purdue Univ, PhD(chem), 49. *Prof Exp:* Res chemist, Res Labs, Linde Air Prods Co Div, Union Carbide Corp, 42-45. *Concurrent Pos:* Consult, Los Alamos Sci Lab, 60- *Mem:* Am Chem Soc. *Res:* Chemistry of technetium and rhenium; polarographic theory and applications; unusual oxidation levels; microanalytical techniques. *Mailing Add:* Brookhaven Manor No 142 401 Oakbrook Ann Arbor MI 48103

RULIFFSON, WILLARD SLOAN, biochemistry, for more information see previous edition

RULIFSON, JOHNS FREDERICK, INFORMATION SCIENCE. *Current Pos:* ENG DIR, SOFTWARE PROD, SUN MICROSYSTS, 87- *Personal Data:* b Bellefontaine, Ohio, Aug 20, 41; m 64; c 2. *Educ:* Univ Wash, BS, 66; Stanford Univ, PhD(comput sci), 73. *Prof Exp:* Res mathematician comput sci, Stanford Res Inst, 66-73; mem res staff comput sci, Xerox Palo Alto Res Ctr, 73-80; eng mgr, Rohm Corp, 80-85; eng mgr artificial intel, Syntelligence, 85-87. *Mem:* Asn Comput Mach; Inst Elec & Electronics Engrs. *Res:* Office automation, especially written communications in managerial and office environments and the design and evaluation of computer systems; human interface technologies; expert systems; window systems. *Mailing Add:* Sun Microsysts Inc 2550 Garcia Ave Mountain View CA 94043

RULIFSON, ROGER ALLEN, ANADROMOUS FISHES, FISHERIES. *Current Pos:* sci inst coastal marine res, 83-92, assoc prof, 87-92, PROF, BIOL DEPT & SR SCIENTIST, ECAROLINA UNIV, 92-, DIR, FIELD STA COASTAL STUDIES MATTAMUSKEET, 95- *Personal Data:* b Manchester, Iowa, Nov 13, 51; m 81, Gayle Gwennap; c Heather & Eric. *Educ:* Univ Dubuque, BS, 73; NC State Univ, MS, 75, PhD(marine sci eng), 80. *Prof Exp:* Res asst, NC Coop Fishery Res Unit, Dept Zool, NC State Univ, 73-75; leader, Fish Distrib & Vulnerability Assessment Task, Ecol Serv Group, Tex Instruments Inc, 75-77; res asst, Dept Zool, NC State Univ, 77-80; res assoc, NC Coop Fishery Res Unit, Dept Zool, 80-81; asst prof fisheries, marine sci, Ctr Environ Sci, Unity Col, 81-83. *Concurrent Pos:* Consult, US Fish & Wildlife Serv, Fishery Resources, Region 4, Atlanta, Ga, 80-82; vis scientist, Acadia Univ, Nova Scotia, 87- *Mem:* Am Fisheries Soc; Estuarine Res Fedn; Sigma Xi; Am Inst Fisheries Res Biologists; Atlantic Extuarine Res Soc. *Res:* Life history aspects of striped bass, alewife, blueback herring, and American shad; evolutionary ecology of man-created wetlands for mitigation purposes; tidal power effects on fish and fisheries; hydroelectric generation effects on fisheries. *Mailing Add:* Inst Coastal Marine Res ECarolina Univ Greenville NC 27858-4353. *Fax:* 919-328-4265; *E-Mail:* cmrulifs@ecuvm.cis.ecu.edu

RULON, RICHARD M, PHYSICAL CHEMISTRY, CERAMICS. *Current Pos:* CONSULT, D G O'BRIEN NH, CORNING GLASS, NY, 84- *Personal Data:* b Babylon, NY, Oct 29, 22; m 43; c 4. *Educ:* Alfred Univ, BS, 43; Univ Pittsburgh, PhD(phys chem), 51. *Prof Exp:* Engr, Radio Corp Am, Pa, 43-45; teacher high sch, NY, 45-46; instr physics, Alfred Univ, 46-47; AEC fel binary metal alloys, Univ Pittsburgh, 50-51; from sr engr to engr-in-charge, Sylvania Elec Prod Inc, Gen Tel & Electronics Corp, Mass, 51-60; res dir glass to metal seals, Hermetite Corp, 60-62; from assoc prof to prof chem, Alfred Univ, 62-84. *Concurrent Pos:* Lectr & coordr, Northeastern Univ, 55-61; consult, Mass & Tetron, Inc, NY, 62-76 and others; mem comt nomenclature for electron-optical devices, Joint Comt Inst Elec Eng & Inst Radio Eng, 57-60. *Mem:* Am Ceramic Soc; Electrochem Soc; Nat Inst Ceramic Eng; Sigma Xi. *Res:* Electroluminescent and electron optical devices; dielectric ceramic materials; glass to metal seals for electronic and hermetic devices. *Mailing Add:* 3811 Ebury St Houston TX 77066

RULON, RUSSELL ROSS, MUSCLE & ANIMAL PHYSIOLOGY. *Current Pos:* asst prof, 63-72, PROF BIOL, LUTHER COL, IOWA, 72- *Personal Data:* b Apr 26, 36; m 63, Joan Scholtes; c Brita R (Loynachan), Amber S (Myers) & Ryan R. *Educ:* Luther Col (Iowa), BA, 58; Univ Iowa, MS, 60, PhD(physiol), 61. *Prof Exp:* Instr physiol, Col Med, Univ Iowa, 61-63. *Concurrent Pos:* USPHS trainee, Med Sch, Univ Va, 69-70; vis scientist cardiol res, Mayo Clin, 75-76; vis scientist, Inst Arctic Biol, Fairbanks, Alaska, 89. *Mem:* Am Physiol Soc. *Res:* Muscle physiology; physiological ecology; electrophysiology; comparative physiology of neurogenic and myogenic hearts; environmental physiology; effect of toxic materials on heart metabolism. *Mailing Add:* Dept Biol Luther Col 700 College Dr Decorah IA 52101-1045. *Fax:* 319-387-1080; *E-Mail:* rulonrus@luther.edu

RUMACK, BARRY H, TOXICOLOGY, PEDIATRICS. *Current Pos:* PRES, CEO MICROMEDEX INC, 74- *Personal Data:* b Chicago, Ill, Nov 1, 42; m 64, Carol Masters; c Becky & Marc. *Educ:* Univ Chicago, BS, 64; Univ Wis, MD, 68; Am Bd Pediatrics, dipl. *Prof Exp:* Intern, Univ Colo, 68-69, pediat res, 71-72, fel, Med Ctr, 72-73, from assoc prof pediat to prof, 78-92; clin assoc, Regional Treat Ctr, Royal Infirmary, Edinburgh, 73. *Concurrent Pos:* Dir, Rocky Mountain Poison Ctr, Univ Colo, 74-92, drug assay lab, 75-77; chmn pharm & therapeut comn, 76-80; consult, Nat Clearinghouse Poison Control Ctrs, 75-91; chmn, Int Cong Clin Toxicol Colo, 82; comn to advise Red Cross, 84-91. *Mem:* Fel Am Acad Clin Toxicol; fel Am Acad Pediat; Am Asn Poison Control Ctrs (vpres, 80-82, pres, 82-84); Soc Pediat Res; Soc Toxicol; Am Col Emergency Med; NAm Mycological Asn. *Mailing Add:* 33 Silver Fox Circle Littleton CO 80121

RUMBACH, WILLIAM ERVIN, SCIENCE ADMINISTRATION. *Current Pos:* dir Div Natural Sci, 67-78, chmn & prof, Dept Sci, 78-87, PROF BIOL & BOTANY, CENT FLA COMMUNITY COL, 88- *Personal Data:* b Weston, WVa, Mar 15, 34; m 55, Janice C Seckman; c William G, Nancy O (Coogler) & Jeffery D. *Educ:* Glenville State Col, BS, 55; WVa Univ, MS, 58. *Prof Exp:* Instr genetics, WVa Univ, 57-60; instr biol, Cent Fla Jr Col, 60-67. *Concurrent Pos:* Consult, Crystal River Marine Sci Res Sta, 66-68. *Mailing Add:* Cent Fla Community Col PO Box 1388 Ocala FL 34478-1388

RUMBARGER, JOHN H, BALL & ROLLER BEARING TECHNOLOGY. *Current Pos:* CONSULT ENGR, JOHN H RUMBARGER, PE, INC, 91- *Personal Data:* b Norfolk, Va, Dec 27, 25; m 51, 82; c 9. *Educ:* Lehigh Univ, BSME, 49; Univ Pa, MSME, 63. *Honors & Awards:* Silver Snoopy Astronauts Personal Achievement Award, NASA, 90. *Prof Exp:* Prin engr, Franklin Inst Res Labs, 65-75, dir eng, 76-85, program mgr, Calspan, 86-88, exec engr, 89-90. *Mem:* Am Soc Mech Engrs. *Res:* Ball and roller bearing design, application, test and evaluation; tribology. *Mailing Add:* 123 Poplar Ave Wayne PA 19087

RUMBAUGH, MELVIN DALE, CROP BREEDING. *Current Pos:* RETIRED. *Personal Data:* b Pella, Iowa, Sept 13, 29; m 53, Annabelle Eis; c Alan L, Rosemary A, David J & Steven T. *Educ:* Cent Col (Iowa), BS, 51; Univ Nebr, MS, 53, PhD(agron), 58. *Prof Exp:* Asst prof agron, Colo State Univ, 58-59; from asst prof to prof, SDak State Univ, 59-76; res geneticist, USDA-Agr Res Serv, Logan, Utah. *Concurrent Pos:* Vis scientist, People's Repub China, 87 & 90 & Russia, 95. *Mem:* Fel Crop Sci Soc Am; fel Am Soc Agron; Soc Range Mgt. *Res:* Biometrical genetics and breeding of plants, especially of Medicago sativa; utilization of legume species for improvement of range. *Mailing Add:* RR 3 Box 125 Humboldt NE 68376

RUMBLE, DOUGLAS, III, METAMORPHIC PETROLOGY, STABLE ISOTOPE GEOCHEMISTRY. *Current Pos:* PETROLOGIST, GEOPHYS LAB, CARNEGIE INST WASH, 73- *Personal Data:* b Atlanta, Ga, June, 15, 42; m 67; c 2. *Educ:* Columbia Col, NY, BA, 64; Harvard Univ, PhD(geol), 69. *Prof Exp:* Asst prof geol, Univ Calif, Los Angeles, 71-73. *Concurrent Pos:* Prog dir, NSF, 85-87; coun, Mineral Soc Am, 86-89; pres, Geol Soc Washington, 88; ed, J Petrol, 89-93. *Mem:* Mineral Soc Am; Am Geophys Union. *Res:* Nature of fluid-rock interaction during metamorphism through chemical thermodynamics and stable isotope geochemistry. *Mailing Add:* Geophys Lab 5251 Broad Branch Rd NW Washington DC 20015-1305. *Fax:* 202-686-2419; *E-Mail:* rumble@gl.ciw.edu

RUMBLE, EDMUND TAYLOR, III, NUCLEAR ENGINEERING. *Current Pos:* PRIN, POLESTAR APPL TECHNOL, INC, 92- *Personal Data:* b Philadelphia, Pa, Oct 26, 42; m 76. *Educ:* US Naval Acad, BS, 65; Univ Calif, Los Angeles, MS, 71, PhD(nuclear eng), 74. *Prof Exp:* Mem staff reactor safety, Sci Applns Inc, 74-77, div mgr nuclear mat, 77-92. *Mem:* Am Nuclear Soc. *Res:* Reactor safety and performance. *Mailing Add:* 580 Madison Palo Alto CA 94303

RUMBURG, CHARLES BUDDY, AGRONOMY. *Current Pos:* AGRONOMIST, SOC RANGE MGT, 92- *Personal Data:* b Welch, WVa, Dec 12, 31; m 54; c 3. *Educ:* Colo State Univ, BS, 54; Rutgers Univ, MS, 56, PhD(farm crops), 58. *Prof Exp:* Res asst farm crops, Rutgers Univ, 54-58; res agronomist, Agr Res Serv, USDA, 58-70, supt, Colo Mountain Meadow Res

Ctr, 70-77, agronomist, Coop State Res Serv, 77-92, dep admin, 85-92. *Concurrent Pos:* Fel, Ore State Univ, 65-66; assoc prof agron, Colo State Univ, 70-77. *Mem:* Am Soc Agron. *Res:* Quantity and quality of forage from native meadows; increasing the efficiency of nitrogen fertilizer. *Mailing Add:* Soc Range Mgt 1839 York St Denver CO 80206

RUMELY, JOHN HAMILTON, PLANT TAXONOMY, PLANT ECOLOGY. *Current Pos:* from asst prof to prof, 56-85, cur herbartium, 73-88, EMER PROF BOT, MONT STATE UNIV, 85- *Personal Data:* b New York, NY, Jan 14, 26; m 48, Constance M Dudley; c Robert S, Katherine L (Griffing) & Elizabeth A (Plumbo). *Educ:* Oberlin Col, AB, 48; Wash State Univ, PhD(bot), 56. *Prof Exp:* Instr biol, Wash State Univ, 55-56. *Concurrent Pos:* Ed, Mont Acad Sci, 84-88. *Res:* Flora of Montana; vegetation constitution and succession; plant life histories; grasses especially trisetum. *Mailing Add:* Dept Biol Mont State Univ Bozeman MT 59717-0346

RUMER, RALPH R, CIVIL ENGINEERING, HYDRAULIC ENGINEERING. *Current Pos:* assoc prof eng, State Univ NY, Buffalo, 63-69, actg head, Dept Civil Eng, 66-67, chmn dept, 67-74, prof, 69-76, chmn dept, 84-87, PROF CIVIL ENG, STATE UNIV NY, BUFFALO, 78- *Personal Data:* b Ocean City, NJ, June 22, 31; wid; c Sherri R (Cooper), Sue R (O'Donnell), Sandra & Sarah R (Brodeur). *Educ:* Duke Univ, BS, 53; Rutgers Univ, MS, 59; Mass Inst Technol, ScD(civil eng), 62. *Prof Exp:* Engr, Luken Steel Co, Pa, 53-54; instr civil eng, Rutgers Univ, 56-59; engr, Soil Conserv Serv, USDA, NJ, 57-59, res asst hydraul, Mass Inst Technol, 61-62, asst prof civil eng, 62-63; exec dir, NY Ctr Hazardous Waste Mgt, 87-95. *Concurrent Pos:* Ford Found fel, 62-63; NIH res grant, 65-69; sr res fel, Calif Inst Technol, 70-71; prin tech consult, Lake Erie Wastewater Mgt Study, Buffalo Dist, US Army Corps Engrs, 73-; prof civil eng & chmn dept, Univ Del, 76-78; dir, Great Lake Prog, 86-91; interim dir, Inst Environ, 95-; vis prof, Duke Univ, 96-97. *Mem:* Fel Am Soc Civil Engrs; Am Geophys Union; Int Asn Hydraulic Res; Int Asn Gt Lakes Res; Sigma Xi. *Res:* Water resources, flow through porous media; lake dynamics; hydraulic modelling; hydraulic processes related to water quality control; ice engineering. *Mailing Add:* 821 Eggert Rd Buffalo NY 14226

RUMFELDT, ROBERT CLARK, PHOTOCHEMISTRY, INORGANIC CHEMISTRY. *Current Pos:* asst prof, 65-68, ASSOC PROF CHEM, UNIV WINDSOR, 68- *Personal Data:* b Shawinigan Falls, Que, Nov 28, 36; m 59; c 5. *Educ:* Loyola Univ, Can, BSc, 59; Univ Alta, PhD(radiation chem), 63. *Prof Exp:* Gen Elec Res Found fel, Univ Leeds, 63-65. *Mem:* Chem Inst Can. *Res:* Spectroscopy and photochemistry of inorganic systems. *Mailing Add:* Dept Chem Univ Windsor Windsor ON N9B 3P4 Can

RUMMEL, DON, AGRONOMY. *Current Pos:* AGRONOMIST, AGR RES & EXTEN CTR, TEX A&M UNIV. *Honors & Awards:* Ciba-Geigy Agron Award, Am Soc Agron, 90. *Mailing Add:* Agr Res Exten Ctr Tex A&M Univ Rte 3 PO Box 219 Lubbock TX 79401

RUMMEL, ROBERT WILAND, AERONAUTICAL ENGINEERING. *Current Pos:* PRES, ROBERT W RUMMEL ASSOCS, INC, 77- *Personal Data:* b Dakota, Ill, Aug 4, 15; m 39, Majorie B Cox; c Linda, Sharon, Susan, Robert & Diana. *Educ:* Curtiss Wright Tech Inst, Dipl aero eng, 34. *Honors & Awards:* Distinguished Pub Serv Medal, NASA, 79. *Prof Exp:* Stress analyst, Hughes Aircraft Co, Calif, 35 & Lockheed Aircraft Corp, 36; detail designer, Aero Eng Corp, 36 & Nat Aircraft Co, 37; chief engr, Rearwin Aircraft Co, Mo, Ken Royce Eng Co & Rearwin Aircraft & Engines, 37-43; chief engr, Trans World Airlines, 43-46, vpres eng, 56-59, vpres planning & res, 59-69 & tech develop, 69-77. *Concurrent Pos:* Mem comn on aircraft operating probs, NASA, 63-69, mem res comn on aeronaut, 69-70; mem panel on Supersonic Transport environ effects, Commerce Tech adv bd, 71-72; consult, NASA, 72-78; mem, Presidental Comn Space Shuttle Challenger Accident. *Mem:* Nat Acad Eng; fel Am Inst Aeronaut & Astronaut (treas, 71-72); fel Soc Automotive Engrs (vpres, 56). *Res:* Aeronautical research relating to aircraft transport design and operations. *Mailing Add:* Robert W Rummel Assocs Inc PO Box 7330 Mesa AZ 85206

RUMMENS, F H A, MOLECULAR SPECTROSCOPY, PHYSICAL CHEMISTRY. *Current Pos:* RETIRED. *Personal Data:* b Eindhoven, Neth, May 20, 33; m 60; c 3. *Educ:* Univ Leiden, Drs, 58; Oxford Univ, Brit Coun bursary, 58; Eindhoven Technol Univ, DSc, 63; Univ Sask, PhD, 72. *Prof Exp:* Sci co-worker, Eindhoven Technol Univ, 59-67; from assoc prof to prof chem, Univ Regina, 67-96. *Concurrent Pos:* Niels Stensen fel, 63-64; Nat Res Coun Can fel, 64-65; vis prof chem, Univ Colo, 67; France-Can exchange fel, 74. *Mem:* Fel Chem Inst Can; Spectros Soc Can; Int Soc Magnetic Resonance. *Res:* Nuclear magnetic resonance, infrared and ultraviolet spectroscopy; structure of simple molecules; effects of medium on spectra; analytical spectroscopy. *Mailing Add:* Birkenshaw 605 13th Ave SW Suite 1014 Calgary AB T2R 0K6 Can

RUMMERY, TERRANCE EDWARD, SOLID STATE CHEMISTRY. *Current Pos:* RETIRED. *Personal Data:* b Brockville, Ont, Nov 16, 37; m 67; c 2. *Educ:* Queen's Univ, Ont, BSc, 61, PhD(chem), 66. *Prof Exp:* Nat Res Coun Can overseas fel, Univ Col, Univ London, 66-67; assoc res scientist mat chem, Ont Res Found, 68-69; scientist phys chem, Airco Speer Res Labs, 69-71; assoc res officer phys chem, Atomic Energy Can, Ltd, 71-76, sr res officer & head, Res Chem Br, 76-79, dir, Waste Mgt Div, 79-84, gen mgr, Mkt & Sales, 86-87, gen mgr, Marine Propulsion Unit, 87-90, pres, 90-95. *Mem:* Fel Chem Inst Can; Can Nuclear Soc. *Res:* Physical chemistry of power reactor coolant systems; basic science underlying nuclear waste management. *Mailing Add:* 5611 Watterson St Manotick ON K4M 1C6 Can

RUMPEL, MAX LEONARD, INORGANIC CHEMISTRY, CHEMICAL EDUCATION. *Current Pos:* From instr to assoc prof, 61-68, Chmn dept, 72-88 PROF CHEM, FT HAYS STATE UNIV, 68- *Personal Data:* b WaKeeney, Kans, Mar 17, 36; m 61; c 2. *Educ:* Ft Hays Kans State Col, AB, 57; Univ Kans, PhD(chem), 62. *Concurrent Pos:* Mem, NSF Res Partic Prog Col Teachers, Univ Colo, 65-66 & Wash State Univ, 71. *Mem:* Am Chem Soc; Sigma Xi. *Res:* Unusually low oxidation states of metals; electrochemistry; computer programming for chemistry; instrumentation. *Mailing Add:* Dept Chem Ft Hays State Univ 600 Park St Hays KS 67601-4099

RUMPF, JOHN L, CIVIL ENGINEERING. *Current Pos:* dean, Col Eng Technol, Temple Univ, 69-76, vpres acad affairs, 76-82, vpres, 82-84, EMER PROF CIVIL ENG, TEMPLE UNIV, 86- *Personal Data:* b Philadelphia, Pa, Feb 21, 21; m 44; c 2. *Educ:* Drexel Inst Technol, BS, 43; Univ Pa, MS, 54; Lehigh Univ, PhD, 60. *Prof Exp:* From instr to assoc prof civil eng, Drexel Inst Technol, 47-56; res instr, Lehigh Univ, 56-60; prof, Drexel Univ, 60-64, head dept, 64-69. *Concurrent Pos:* Chmn, Res Coun Riveted & Bolted Struct Joints, 65-71; consult struct eng, 50- *Mem:* Am Soc Civil Engrs; Am Soc Eng Educ; Nat Soc Prof Engrs; Am Concrete Inst; Sigma Xi. *Res:* Behavior of steel structures and their component parts and connections. *Mailing Add:* Dept Civil-Construct Eng Temple Univ Col Eng 12th & Norris St Philadelphia PA 19122

RUMPF, R(OBERT) J(OHN), AERONAUTICAL ENGINEERING. *Current Pos:* ENG CONSULT, TRW VEHICLE SAFETY SYSTS INC, 86- *Personal Data:* b Auburn, NY, July 31, 16; m 40. *Educ:* Univ Notre Dame, BS, 39. *Prof Exp:* Design engr, Stinson Aircraft Co, 39-45 & Bendix Aviation Corp, 45-46; res engr, Univ Mich, 46-55; prin res engr, Ford Motor Co, 55-70; dir res & develop, Hamill Mfg Co Div, Firestone Tire & Rubber Co, 70-86. *Mem:* Soc Automotive Engrs. *Res:* Aircraft development; guided missile, air defense and highway control systems; automotive safety; automotive restraint systems. *Mailing Add:* 37 Fisher Rd Grosse Pointe MI 48230

RUMSEY, THERON S, RUMINANT NUTRITION. *Current Pos:* Res animal scientist, 65-86, res leader, Ruminant Nutrit Lab, 86-94, RES ANIMAL SCIENTIST, LIVESTOCK & POULTRY SCI INST, AGR RES SERV, USDA, 94- *Personal Data:* b Whitley Co, Ind, Mar 11, 39. *Educ:* Purdue Univ, BS, 61, MS, 63, PhD(animal sci), 65. *Concurrent Pos:* Ed-in-chief, J Animal Sci, 93-96. *Mem:* Am Soc Animal Sci; Am Inst Nutrit; Am Dairy Sci Asn; Am Registry Prof Animal Scientists; Coun Biol Ed. *Mailing Add:* Animal Sci Inst Beltsville MD 20705. *Fax:* 301-504-8162

RUMSEY, VICTOR HENRY, APPLIED PHYSICS. *Current Pos:* RETIRED. *Personal Data:* b Devizes, Eng, Nov 22, 19; m 42, Doris Herring; c John D, Peter A & Catherine A. *Educ:* Cambridge Univ, BA, 41, DSc, 73; Tohoku Univ, Japan, PhD, 62. *Honors & Awards:* Liebmann Prize, Inst Elec & Electronics Engrs, 62; George Sinclair Award, Ohio State Univ, 83. *Prof Exp:* From asst to sr sci officer, Sci Civil Serv, Gt Brit, 41-45; mem staff theoret physics, Atomic Energy Estab, 45-48; from asst prof to assoc prof elec eng, Ohio State Univ, 48-54; prof, Univ Ill, 54-57 & Univ Calif, Berkeley, 57-69; prof appl physics, Univ Calif, San Diego, 69-87. *Concurrent Pos:* Head, Antenna Lab, Ohio State Univ, 48-54; Guggenheim fel, 65. *Mem:* Nat Acad Eng; Inst Elec & Electronics Engrs; Am Astron Soc; Int Sci Radio Union. *Res:* Theory of electromagnetic waves; antennas; physics of atomic piles; wave propagation in a turbulent medium. *Mailing Add:* 2199 Bohemian Hwy PO Box 400 Occidental CA 95465

RUMSEY, WILLIAM LEROY, NUCLEAR MEDICINE, CELLULAR PHYSIOLOGY. *Current Pos:* postdoctoral, 85-89, RES ASSOC BIOCHEM, SCH MED, UNIV PA, 89-; SR RES INVESTR RADIOPHARMACEUT, BRISTOL-MYERS SQUIBB PHARMACEUT RES INST, 89- *Personal Data:* b Philadelphia, Pa, Nov 5, 51; m 72; c 2. *Educ:* Pa State Univ, BS, 73; Temple Univ, MEd, 80, PhD(physiol & biochem), 85. *Prof Exp:* Therapeut actg supvr psychol, Norristown State Hosp, 73-80. *Concurrent Pos:* Co-prin investr, Dept Biochem & Biophys, Sch Med, Univ Pa, 89-; reviewer, Am J Physiol, 89- *Mem:* Am Physiol Soc; AAAS; Int Soc Oxygen Transport to Tissue. *Res:* Mechanisms responsible for oxygen sensing; cellular events that bring about a change in oxygen delivery to tissue. *Mailing Add:* Zeneca Pharmaceut 1800 Concord Pke Box 5437 Wilmington DE 19850-5437. *Fax:* 732-519-3175

RUNCO, PAUL D, PHYSICS, ELECTRICAL ENGINEERING. *Current Pos:* DEVELOP ENGR & QUAL CONTROL ENGR, FORE SYST, INC, 91- *Personal Data:* b Pittsburgh, Pa, Feb 22, 57. *Educ:* Carnegie Mellon, BS, 81, MS, 82. *Prof Exp:* Scientist, Carnegie Mellon, 84-91. *Res:* Design of apparatus and procedures for sensor technology, materials science and communications technology; development and manufacturing of asynchronous transmission mode computer network switching products. *Mailing Add:* 256 Emerson St Pittsburgh PA 15209. *Fax:* 412-772-6500; *E-Mail:* runco@fore.com

RUND, JOHN VALENTINE, INORGANIC CHEMISTRY. *Current Pos:* Asst prof, 63-69, ASSOC PROF CHEM, UNIV ARIZ, 69- *Personal Data:* b Champaign, Ill, Mar 9, 38; m 61. *Educ:* Univ Ill, BS, 59; Cornell Univ, PhD(chem), 62. *Mem:* Am Chem Soc; Royal Soc Chem; Sigma Xi. *Res:* Reaction mechanisms of coordination complexes; photochemistry; metalloenzyme models. *Mailing Add:* Dept Chem Univ Ariz Tucson AZ 85721

RUNDEL, PHILIP WILSON, PLANT ECOLOGY, ECOSYSTEM STUDIES. *Current Pos:* assoc dir, 83-89, PROF BIOL, LAB BIOMED ENVIRON SCI, UNIV CALIF, LOS ANGELES, 83- *Personal Data:* b Palo Alto, Calif, Aug 7, 43; c Alexandra, Colin & Tyler. *Educ:* Pomona Col, BA, 65; Duke Univ, AM, 67, PhD(bot), 69. *Prof Exp:* Instr bot, Duke Univ, 68-69; asst prof pop & environ biol, Univ Calif, Irvine, 69-74, from assoc prof to prof ecol & evolutionary biol, 74-83. *Concurrent Pos:* Vis prof, Univ Chile, Santiago, 72, Lehrstuhl Botanik II Univ, WGer, 76 & Univ Hawaii, 83, Univ Catolica, Valparaib, Chile, 94; Alexander Humboldt fel, 76. *Mem:* Ecol Soc Am; Am Bryol & Lichenological Soc; Brit Ecol Soc; Asn Trop Biol. *Res:* Physiological plant ecology; arid ecosystems; tropical ecosystems. *Mailing Add:* Dept Biol Univ Calif Los Angeles CA 90095. *Fax:* 310-825-9433; *E-Mail:* rundel@lbiology.ucla.edu

RUNDEL, ROBERT DEAN, PHYSICS. *Current Pos:* PHYSICIST, JANDEL SCI, 91- *Personal Data:* b Palo Alto, Calif, Jan 9, 40. *Educ:* Dartmouth Col, BA, 61; Univ Wash, PhD(physics), 65. *Prof Exp:* Res assoc physics, Culham Lab, Eng, 65-68; sr res assoc space sci, Rice Univ, 68-69, instr physics, 69-70, asst prof, 70-77, adj prof space physics & astron, 77-80; from assoc prof to prof physics, Miss State Univ, 80-91. *Concurrent Pos:* Staff scientist, Johnson Space Ctr, NASA, 74-80. *Mem:* Am Asn Physics Teachers; Am Soc Photobiol; Sigma Xi. *Res:* Atomic collision physics. *Mailing Add:* 141 Nantucket Curve San Rafael CA 94901

RUNDELL, CLARK ACE, CLINICAL CHEMISTRY. *Current Pos:* CLIN CHEMIST, MAINE MED CTR, 75-, DIR CHEM, 80- *Personal Data:* b Verndale, Minn, Sept 1, 38; m 61; c 2. *Educ:* St Cloud State Col, BS, 61; Univ NDak, MS, 63, PhD(phys chem), 66; Am Bd Clin Chem, dipl, 76. *Prof Exp:* Dept Defense res fel, Purdue Univ, Lafayette, 65-66; res chemist, W R Grace & Co, Clarksville, 66-73; res assoc, Univ Md Hosp, 73-75. *Mem:* Am Chem Soc; Am Asn Clin Chemists; Clinical Legend Assay Soc. *Res:* Enzymology catalysis; kinetics; data processing. *Mailing Add:* Hearthside N Standish ME 04062

RUNDELL, HAROLD LEE, ZOOLOGY, PARASITOLOGY. *Current Pos:* assoc prof, 59-71, head dept, 59-81, PROF BIOL, MORNINGSIDE COL, 71- *Personal Data:* b Hurley, SDak, Dec 1, 22; m 47, Fern Swansan; c Phyllis A. *Educ:* SDak State Col, BS, 52; Univ Iowa, PhD(zool), 57. *Prof Exp:* Assoc prof biol, Parsons Col, 57-59. *Mem:* AAAS. *Res:* Fine structure of animal parasites, chiefly tapeworms. *Mailing Add:* 14 Eastview Dr Morningside Col Sioux City IA 51106

RUNDELL, MARY KATHLEEN, MICROBIOLOGY, VIROLOGY. *Current Pos:* asst prof, 76-82, ASSOC PROF MICROBIOL, MED CTR, NORTHWESTERN UNIV, 82- *Personal Data:* b Cleveland, Ohio, Nov 19, 46; m 76. *Educ:* Univ Rochester, BA, 68; Case Western Reserve Univ, PhD(microbiol), 73. *Prof Exp:* Fel biochem, Univ Calif, Berkeley, 74; fel pharmacol, Case Western Reserve Univ, 74-75; fel microbiol, State Univ NY Stony Brook, 75-76. *Concurrent Pos:* Nat Cancer Inst fel, 75-76 & res grant, 77-; Am Cancer Soc res grant, 76-77; NSF res grant, 80-82. *Mem:* Am Soc Microbiol; AAAS. *Res:* Molecular virology and viral genetics; viral transformation. *Mailing Add:* Dept Microbiol-Immunol Northwestern Univ Med Sch 303 E Chicago Ave Chicago IL 60611-3072

RUNDENSTEINER, ELKE ANGELIKA, OBJECT-ORIENTED DATABASE TECHNOLOGY, ENGINEERING & SCIENTIFIC APPLICATION DATABASES. *Current Pos:* ASST PROF, ELEC ENG & COMPUT SCI DEPT, UNIV MICH, 92- *Personal Data:* b Hanau, Ger, Feb 21, 62; m 92, Frank E Lovering. *Educ:* J W Goeth Univ, Frankfurt, Ger, BS, 83, MS, 84; Fla State Univ, MS, 87; Univ Calif, Irvine, PhD(comput sci), 92. *Honors & Awards:* Res Initiation Award, NSF, 93; Fac Fel Award, Univ Mich, 93. *Prof Exp:* Programmer, Honeywell, Doernigheim, Ger, 82-83; teaching asst, Comput Sci Dept, J W Goeth Univ, Frankfurt, Ger, 83-84, Fla State Univ, 84-86; res asst, Comput Sci Dept, Fla State Univ, 86-87. *Concurrent Pos:* Res asst, Mech Eng Dept, Fla State Univ, 85-86; res asst, Info & Comput Sci Dept, Univ Calif, Irvine, 87-92; mem rev panel, NSF, 92; exec comn, Human Genome Ctr, Univ Mich, 92-; co-chmn, Eng Conf, Object-Oriented Prog, Univ Mich, 93, 94; prin investr, Genomic Database Tools, Univ Mich, Partnership Res, 93-94, Educ Training Grant, 93-94, Object-Oriented Comput Asst Drafting, Fac Grant, 93-95, I V H S Ctr Excellence Proj, 94-, NSF Database Res Proj, NSF, 93-; NSF young investr award, 94; eng res initiation award, Eng Found/Intel, 94. *Mem:* Asn Comput Mach; Inst Elec. *Res:* Database technology for support of newly emerging application domains-such as space sciences, the Human Genome Project and manufacturing; developing advanced object-oriented database technology, in particular, view integration mechanisms, transparent schema change tools and data discovery systems. *Mailing Add:* Elec Eng & Comput Sci Dept Univ Mich 1301 Beal Ave Ann Arbor MI 48109. *E-Mail:* rundenst@eecs.umich.edu

RUNDO, JOHN, RADIOLOGICAL PHYSICS, HUMAN RADIOBIOLOGY. *Current Pos:* RETIRED. *Personal Data:* b London, Eng, Dec 27, 25; US citizen; m 53, M Katrine Have; c Elizabeth, Marie & David. *Educ:* Univ London, BSc, 49, PhD(radiation biophys), 58, DSc, 80. *Prof Exp:* Sci officer, Atomic Energy Res Estab, Harwell, UK, 49-51; sr sci officer, Finsen Lab, Copenhagen, Denmark, 52-54; prin sci officer, Atomic Energy Res Estab, Harwell, UK, 55-69; assoc scientist, Argonne Nat Lab, 69-74, sr biophysicist, 74-91, head, Ctr Human Radiobiol, 80-83, interim assoc lab dir, 83, dep head, 83-84, actg head, Human Radiobiol Sect, 84-85, prog mgr, Int Prog, 85-90, head, Environ Health Sect, 90-91; consult, Int Atomic Energy Agency, 93-95. *Concurrent Pos:* Task group mem, Int Comn Radiol Units & Measurements, 65-70; consult, 81-85. *Mem:* Health Physics Soc. *Res:* Metabolism, dosimetry, and late biological effects of natural and artificial radioactivity in the human body. *Mailing Add:* 142 56th St Downers Grove IL 60516. *Fax:* 630-964-1217; *E-Mail:* gbcoils@msn.com

RUNECKLES, VICTOR CHARLES, PLANT PHYSIOLOGY. *Current Pos:* RETIRED. *Personal Data:* b London, Eng, Sept 2, 30; m 53; c 2. *Educ:* Univ London, BSc, 52, PhD(plant physiol), 55, Imp Col, dipl, 55. *Prof Exp:* fel plant physiol, Nat Res Coun Can, Queen's Univ, Ont, 55-57; head dept, Univ BC, 69-88, prof plant sci, 69-96. *Concurrent Pos:* Lectr, Sir George Williams Univ. *Mem:* Am Soc Plant Physiol; Phytochem Soc NAm (secy, Plant Phenolics Group NAm, 61-66, vpres, 66, pres, 67; Am Phytopath Soc; Air Pollution Control Asn; AAAS. *Res:* Chemistry and metabolism of secondary plant products; pyrolysis of natural products; effects of air pollution on vegetation, cold hardiness; free radicals in plants. *Mailing Add:* Dept Plant Sci Univ BC 2357 Main Mall Rm 344 Vancouver BC V6T 1Z4 Can

RUNEY, GERALD LUTHER, PHYSIOLOGY. *Current Pos:* Assoc prof biol, 67-80, PROF BIOL, THE CITADEL, 80- *Personal Data:* b Charleston, SC, Feb 16, 38; m 69. *Educ:* Col Charleston, BS, 60; Univ SC, MS, 63, PhD(physiol), 67. *Mem:* Sigma Xi. *Res:* Endocrine control of lipid metabolism. *Mailing Add:* Dept Biol The Citadel Charleston SC 29409

RUNG, DONALD CHARLES, JR, MATHEMATICAL ANALYSIS. *Current Pos:* From asst prof to assoc prof, 61-72, PROF MATH, PA STATE UNIV, UNIVERSITY PARK, 72-, HEAD DEPT, 75- *Personal Data:* b Rome, NY, Sept 12, 32; m 56; c 6. *Educ:* Niagara Univ, BA, 54; Univ Notre Dame, MS, 57, PhD(math), 61. *Concurrent Pos:* Sr Fulbright lectr, Nat Tsing Hua Univ, Taiwan, 67-68; vis sr res scientist, Carleton Univ, Ottawa, 74-75. *Mem:* Math Asn Am; Am Math Soc. *Res:* Complex function theory, especially cluster set theory. *Mailing Add:* Pa State Univ 203 McAllister Bldg University Park PA 16802-6401

RUNGE, EDWARD C A, AGRONOMY, SOILS & SOIL SCIENCE. *Current Pos:* PROF SOIL & CROP SCI & HEAD DEPT, TEX A&M UNIV, 80- *Personal Data:* b St Peter, Ill, Aug 4, 35; m 56; c Kim (Overton) & Jeffrey. *Educ:* Univ Ill, BS, 55, MS, 57; Iowa State Univ, PhD(agron-soil), 63. *Hon Degrees:* Dr, Univ Agr, Nitra Slovakia, 96. *Honors & Awards:* Agron Serv Award, Am Soc Agron, 95. *Prof Exp:* Instr & res assoc, Iowa State Univ, 59-63, asst prof, 63; from asst prof to prof, Univ Ill, 63-73; prof & chmn dept agron, Univ Mo, 73-80. *Concurrent Pos:* Mem bd dirs, Coun Agr, Sci & Technol, 82-85, Tropsoils, Soil Mgt Entity, 83-, Found Agr Res, 85-94 & Miss Chem Corp, 86-95; mem adv coun, Potash & Phosphate Inst, 83-88; chmn, Tex State Seed & Plant Bd, 83-95, Agron Sci Found, 89-; secy, Sect & Renewable Resources, AAAS, 89- *Mem:* Fel Soil Sci Soc Am (pres, 85); fel AAAS; fel Am Soc Agron (pres, 89); Soil Conserv Soc Am. *Res:* Soil genesis and classification; soil chemical relationships; soil water-climate-crop yield modeling; dynamic nature of soil development processes; interdependence of soil moisture-rainfall-temperature on corn and soybean yields. *Mailing Add:* Dept Soil & Crop Sci Tex A&M Univ College Station TX 77843-2474. *Fax:* 409-845-0456; *E-Mail:* e_tune@tamu.edu

RUNGE, RICHARD JOHN, WELL LOGGING THEORY & PHYSICAL BASIS, DOWNHOLE EXPLORATION. *Current Pos:* RES CONSULT, PETROSOFT CO, 86- *Personal Data:* b Buffalo, NY, Sept 20, 21; m 57; c 3. *Educ:* Univ Chicago, BS, 44; Univ NMex, MS, 49, PhD(physics), 52. *Prof Exp:* Asst prof physics, Univ NMex, 49-52 & Tulsa Univ, 53-55; res asst, Stanolind Amoco Tulsa Labs, 55-56; res assoc, Chevron Oil Field Res Co, 56-86. *Mem:* Soc Prof Well Log Analysts. *Res:* Exploration geophysics and well logging with emphasis on computer applications; nmr and epr logging theory; long range electric logging. *Mailing Add:* 2106 E Sycamore Anaheim CA 92806

RUNGE, THOMAS MARSCHALL, CARDIOVASCULAR DISEASES. *Current Pos:* PROF BIOMED ENG, UNIV TEX, AUSTIN, 68-; PROF SURG, HEALTH SCI CTR, UNIV TEX, SAN ANTONIO, 88- *Personal Data:* b Mason, Tex, Jan 24, 24; m 47, Gretchen Herrmann; c 3. *Educ:* Univ Tex Med Br Galveston, MD, 47; Am Bd Internal Med, dipl, 55; Am Bd Cardiovasc Dis, dipl, 67. *Prof Exp:* Intern med, Milwaukee Co Gen Hosp, Wis, 47-48; resident, Hosp Univ Pa, 48-51; pvt pract, 53-68. *Concurrent Pos:* Fel, Hosp Univ Pa, 48-51; fel cardiol, St Luke's Hosp, Tex Med Ctr, 65-66; med dir, Noninvasive Cardiol, Brackenridge Hosp. *Mem:* AMA; Am Heart Asn; fel Am Col Physicians; fel Am Col Cardiol; fel Am Col Chest Physicians. *Res:* Cardiac devices; pulsatile flow cardiopulmonary bypass pumps; contrasting pharmacodynamic action of polar and nonpolar cardiac glycosides as delineated by noninvasive techniques; pulsatile flow hemodialysis; granted three US patents. *Mailing Add:* 610 Engineering Sci Bldg Univ Tex Austin TX 78712

RUNGTA, RAVI, CORROSION ENGINEERING, JOINING TECHNOLOGY. *Current Pos:* sr engr, 88-90, staff engr, 91-93, MGR CORROSION & COATINGS DEPT, DELHI HARRRISON THERMAL SYST, GEN MOTORS, 93- *Personal Data:* b Calcutta, India, Feb 10, 54; US citizen; m 75, Renu Agarwal; c Ankur & Vishal. *Educ:* Birla Inst Technol & Sci, India, BE, 75; Ohio State Univ, MS, 78. *Prof Exp:* Res asst, Ohio State Univ, 78-79; res scientist, Batelle Mem Inst, 79-85, prin res scientist, 85-88. *Concurrent Pos:* Mem, Fatigue Crack Growth Rate Comt, Metal Properties Coun, 81-86; assoc mem, Int Group, Int Cyclic Crack Growth Rate Group, 81-88. *Mem:* AAAS; Metal Soc; Am Soc Metals Int; Nat Asn Corrosion Engrs; Soc Automotive Engrs. *Res:* Author of 30 publications; granted three patents; edited three proceedings of conferences. *Mailing Add:* 256 Quail Hollow Lane East Amherst NY 14051. *Fax:* 716-439-2891

RUNION, HOWELL IRWIN, ELECTROPHYSIOLOGY. *Current Pos:* assoc prof, 69-80, PROF ELECTROPHYSIOL, SCH PHARM, UNIV PAC, 80- *Personal Data:* b Ann Arbor, Mich, Oct 26, 33; m 59; c 2. *Educ:* Col of the Pac, BA, 56; Univ Ore, MS, 63; Univ Glasgow, PhD(electrophysiol), 68; Stanford Univ Med Sch, PA, 80. *Prof Exp:* Chmn, Lincoln Unified Sch Dist, Calif, 58-65; res asst electrophysiol, Univ Glasgow, 65-68; res specialist, Univ Calif, Berkeley, 68-69. *Concurrent Pos:* Sci adv, Esten Corp, 60-65, Aquatic Res Inst, Port Stockton, 63-65, & Etec Corp, 72-75 & Elec Hazards, Underwriters Med-Dent Inst Bd, 75-; mem bd dirs, Alcoholism Coun Calif, 77-87 & San Joaquin County Alcoholism Adv Bd, 78-80. *Mem:* Am Inst Biol Sci; Brit Soc Exp Biol; Int Asn Elec Inspectors; Am Acad Physician Assts; Sigma Xi. *Res:* Pathological mechanisms involved in atrophy and neuropathy secondary to electrical injury and electrical burns. *Mailing Add:* 6324 Plymouth Rd Stockton CA 95207-3259

RUNK, BENJAMIN FRANKLIN DEWEES, botany; deceased, see previous edition for last biography

RUNKA, GARY G, AGRICULTURE. *Current Pos:* PRES, GG RUNKA LAND SENSE, INC. *Concurrent Pos:* Fel, Agr Inst Can, 90. *Mailing Add:* GG Runka Land Sense Ltd Box 80356 Burnaby BC V5H 3X6 Can

RUNKE, SIDNEY MORRIS, METALLURGY. *Current Pos:* RETIRED. *Personal Data:* b Greenwood, SDak, Dec 23, 11; m 42; c 2. *Educ:* Univ Ariz, BS, 35, MS, 36, EMet, 56. *Prof Exp:* Mill foreman, Cia Huanchaca de Bolivia, 36-39 & Coconino Copper Co, Ariz, 40; educ analyst, US Dept Educ, Washington, DC, 42; metall engr, US Bur Mines, Mo, 42-45 & Ark, 45-47, metallurgist, SDak, 47-56; mill supt, Rare Metals Corp Am, Ariz, 57-60, chief metallurgist, Utah, 60-62 & El Paso Natural Gas Co, 62-77. *Mem:* Am Inst Mining, Metall & Petrol Engrs. *Res:* Ore benefication, geology and chemistry. *Mailing Add:* 632 Londonderry Rd El Paso TX 79907

RUNKEL, RICHARD A, INDUSTRIAL PHARMACY. *Current Pos:* RETIRED. *Personal Data:* b La Crosse, Wis, Aug 21, 32; m 57; c 6. *Educ:* Univ Wis, BS, 58, PhD(pharm), 67. *Prof Exp:* Lectr, Univ Wis, 66; staff researcher, Syntex Res, 67-75, head dept drug metab, 75-89. *Mem:* Am Pharmaceut Asn; Pharmaceut Soc Japan. *Res:* Drug availability, disposition, metabolism, absorption and excretion. *Mailing Add:* 741 Garland Dr Palo Alto CA 94303

RUNKLE, JAMES READE, FOREST TREE DYNAMICS, LANDSCAPE ECOLOGY. *Current Pos:* from asst prof to assoc prof, 79-93, PROF BIOL, WRIGHT STATE UNIV, 93- *Personal Data:* b Grove City, Pa, July 3, 51; m 73, Janet Kreps; c Benjamin, Matthew, William & Jennifer. *Educ:* Ohio Wesleyan Univ, BA, 73; Cornell Univ, PhD(ecol), 79. *Prof Exp:* Vis asst prof biol & ecol, Univ Ill, Chicago, 78-79. *Concurrent Pos:* Vis sci, Res Inst, Christchurch, NZ, 88-89. *Mem:* AAAS; Am Inst Biol Sci; Am Soc Naturalists; Brit Ecol Soc; Ecol Soc Am; Int Asn Vegetation Sci; Natural Areas Asn. *Res:* Distribution and role of small scale disturbances (gaps) in forest regeneration; effect of human landscape patterning on forest composition. *Mailing Add:* Dept Biol Sci Wright State Univ Dayton OH 45435. *E-Mail:* jrunkle@desire.wright.edu

RUNKLES, JACK RALPH, SOIL PHYSICS. *Current Pos:* prof soil sci, 64-83, dir Tex Water Resources Inst, 74-83, EMER PROF SOIL SCI, TEX A&M UNIV, 83- *Personal Data:* b San Angelo, Tex, Sept 4, 22; m 45; c 4. *Educ:* Agr & Mech Col Tex, BS, 50, MS, 52; Iowa State Col, PhD(soil physics), 56. *Prof Exp:* Res assoc, Iowa State Col, 53-55; from asst prof to assoc prof soil physics, SDak State Col, 55-64. *Mem:* Soil Sci Soc Am; Am Soc Agron; Am Geophys Union. *Res:* Agronomy; soils; mathematics; physics; physical chemistry; hydrology. *Mailing Add:* PO Box 1133 Eldorado TX 76936-1133

RUNNALLS, O(LIVER) JOHN C(LYVE), metallurgy, ceramics, for more information see previous edition

RUNNELLS, DONALD DEMAR, GEOCHEMISTRY, HYDROGEOLOGY. *Current Pos:* VPRES ENG CONSULT, FT COLLINS, 93- *Personal Data:* b Eureka, Utah, Dec 30, 36; m 58; c 2. *Educ:* Univ Utah, BS, 58; Harvard Univ, MA, 60, PhD(geol), 64. *Prof Exp:* Geochemist, Shell Develop Co, 63-67; asst prof geol, Univ Calif, Santa Barbara, 67-69; assoc prof, Univ Colo, Boulder, 69-75, prof, 75-, chair geol sci, 90-93. *Concurrent Pos:* NSF grad fel, 58-62; regional ed, J Explor Geochem, 71-75; consult, numerous pvt co & govt agencies, Los Alamos Sci Lab, 75-76 & Argonne Nat Lab, 80-84; assoc ed, J Chem Geol, 80-88. *Mem:* Fel Geol Soc Am; Asn Explor Geochem; Soc Econ Paleont & Mineral; Geochem Soc; Asn Ground Water Scientists & Engrs; Asn Explor Geochemists (pres, 90-91). *Res:* Geochemistry of natural waters; low-temperature geochemistry; water pollution; geochemical exploration; geochemistry of trace substances. *Mailing Add:* 8032 Al Lott Ave Ft Collins CO 80525

RUNNELS, JOHN HUGH, ANALYTICAL CHEMISTRY. *Current Pos:* sect supvr, Anal Br, 68-91, tech environ specialist, 91-92, TECH MGR, PHILLIPS PETROL CO, 92- *Personal Data:* b Mize, Miss, Mar 30, 35; m 60, Carol J Cole; c 3. *Educ:* Univ Denver, BS, 63; Colo State Univ, PhD(chem), 68. *Prof Exp:* Chemist, W P Fuller & Co, 58-60 & Marathon Oil Co, 60-64. *Mem:* Am Chem Soc. *Res:* Developing, testing, and applying new technologies for the clean-up of contaminated air, soils, and groundwaters. *Mailing Add:* 3625 Silver Lake Pl Bartlesville OK 74006. *Fax:* 918-662-1097

RUNNELS, KELLI, CHEMICAL PHYSICS, MATHEMATICAL PHYSICS. *Current Pos:* HEAD MASTER, RUNNELS SCH, 95- *Personal Data:* b Perry, Okla, June 9, 38. *Educ:* Rice Univ, BA, 60; Yale Univ, MS, 61, PhD(chem), 63. *Prof Exp:* From asst prof to prof chem, La State Univ, Baton Rouge, 63-95. *Concurrent Pos:* Sloan Found fel, 66-70. *Res:* Statistical mechanics of liquids, dense gases and surface-adsorbed phases; theory of phase transitions; theory of liquid crystals; properties of ice. *Mailing Add:* Runnels Sch 17255 S Harrell's Ferry Rd Baton Rouge LA 70816

RUNNELS, ROBERT CLAYTON, meteorology; deceased, see previous edition for last biography

RUNNER, MEREDITH NOFTZGER, LIMB MORPHOGENESIS. *Current Pos:* chmn dept, Univ Colo, Boulder, 62-63, dir inst develop biol, 66-71, prof, 62-84, EMER PROF BIOL, 84- *Personal Data:* b Schenectady, NY, Jan 7, 14; m 41, Helen Falacy; c Carol, Charles, Marilyn, Peter & Suzanne. *Educ:* Ind Univ, AB, 37, PhD(zool), 42. *Prof Exp:* Instr zool, Univ Conn, 42-46; Finney-Howell fel, Jackson Mem Lab, 46-48, res assoc, 48-57, staff scientist, 57-62. *Concurrent Pos:* Res biologist, Roswell Park Mem Inst, 55-56; prog dir develop biol, NSF, 59-62; mem panel develop biol, 62-64; mem study sect cell biol, NIH, 64-68, human embryol & develop, 69-73; mem, Study Sect Cell Biol, NIH, 64-68, Study Sect Human Embryol & Develop, 69-73, Breast Cancer Task Force, NIH, 75-78. *Mem:* AAAS; Genetics Soc Am; Am Soc Zool; Am Asn Anat; Teratol Soc (pres, 67); Soc Develop Biol (pres, 68-69). *Res:* Transplantation of embryonic primordia in mammals; transplantation and explantation of the mouse ovum; physiology of reproduction and hormonal balance in the mouse; mechanism of action of teratogenic agents; genetics of development; limb morphogenesis; staging system for mouse embryo morphogenesis; retinoic acid interaction with gene morpho-regulatory networks. *Mailing Add:* Dept Molecular Cellular & Develop Biol Univ Colo Box 347 Boulder CO 80309

RUNQUIST, ALFONSE WILLIAM, SUPPLYING RESEARCHERS IN ALL FIELDS OF CHEMISTRY WITH PRODUCTS THEY NEED FOR RESEARCH. *Current Pos:* develop chemist, Aldrich Chem Co, 76-79, mgr tech servs, 79-90, mgr chem prods, 90-96, MGR, PROD TECH SERV ALDRICH CHEM CO, INC, 96- *Personal Data:* b Hibbing, Minn, Apr 4, 45; m 74, Jennifer A Jackson. *Educ:* Hamline Univ, BS, 67; Northwestern Univ, PhD(synthetic org chem), 74. *Prof Exp:* Instr org chem, Northwestern Univ, 73-74; fel, Johns Hopkins Univ, 74-76. *Mem:* Am Chem Soc. *Res:* Supplying researchers with the products that they need to do their research. *Mailing Add:* Aldrich Chem Co Inc PO Box 355 Milwaukee WI 53201

RUNQUIST, OLAF A, ORGANIC CHEMISTRY, CHEMICAL EDUCATION. *Current Pos:* asst prof, 57-73, prof org chem, 73-77, PROF CHEM, HAMLINE UNIV, 77- *Personal Data:* b Lohrville, Iowa, Apr 11, 31; m 51; c 4. *Educ:* Iowa State Univ, BS, 52; Univ Minn, PhD(chem), 56. *Prof Exp:* From instr to asst prof org chem, Col St Thomas, 55-57. *Concurrent Pos:* Consult, Minn Mining-Rayette, Inc, 56-57; instr, Exten Div, Univ Minn, 58-59. *Mem:* Am Chem Soc. *Res:* Chemistry of glycosylamines; base strengths of amines. *Mailing Add:* 1536 Hewitt Ave St Paul MN 55104-1205

RUNSTADLER, PETER WILLIAM, JR, FLUID DYNAMICS. *Current Pos:* vpres res & develop, 68-75, VPRES & TECH DIR, CREARE PROD INC, 75- *Personal Data:* b San Francisco, Calif, Jan 19, 34. *Educ:* Stanford Univ, BA, 55, MS, 56, PhD, 61. *Prof Exp:* Teaching asst mech eng, Stanford Univ, 58, res assoc, 60-61. *Concurrent Pos:* Adj prof, Thayer Sch Eng, Dartmouth Col, 68- *Mem:* Am Soc Mech Engrs; Sigma Xi. *Mailing Add:* Four Freeman Rd Hanover NH 03755

RUNYAN, JOHN WILLIAM, JR, INTERNAL MEDICINE. *Current Pos:* from instr to prof, 53-87, UNIV DISTINGUISHED PROF, ALBANY MED COL, 87- *Personal Data:* b Memphis, Tenn, Jan 23, 24; m 49, Barbara Zerbe; c John W III, Scott Baylor & Keith Roberts. *Educ:* Washington & Lee Univ, AB, 44; Johns Hopkins Univ, MD, 47; Am Bd Internal Med, dipl, 55. *Honors & Awards:* John D Rockefeller III Award Pub Serv Health, 77; Rosenthal Award, Am Col Physicians, 80; Upjohn Award, Am Diabetes Asn, 81. *Prof Exp:* Intern, Johns Hopkins Hosp, 47-48; resident internal med, Albany Hosp, 48-49, chief resident, 49-50; res assoc & fel metab dis, Thorndike Mem Lab, Harvard Med Sch, 50-53; from instr to asst prof, Albany Med Col, 53-60; from assoc prof to prof med, Univ Tenn, Memphis, 60-73, chief sect endocrinol, 64-73, dir, Div Health Care Sci, 72-80, prof community med & chmn dept, Col Med, 73-94, prog dir geront, 80-86. *Concurrent Pos:* Clin dir, Albany Med Ctr Group Clin, 59-60; consult, Memphis Vet Admin Hosp, 62-; prof & chmn, Dept Prev Med, Family Health Plan, 72-94, assoc med dir, 94- *Mem:* Am Diabetes Asn; fel Am Col Physicians; Am Fedn Clin Res. *Res:* Endocrinology and metabolism. *Mailing Add:* 66 N Pauline Suite 633 Memphis TN 38103-2813

RUNYAN, THORA J, medical sciences, for more information see previous edition

RUNYAN, WILLIAM SCOTTIE, NUTRITION, CELL BIOLOGY. *Current Pos:* RETIRED. *Personal Data:* b Merrill, Wis, June 24, 31; m 54; c 2. *Educ:* Univ Idaho, BS, 60, MS, 62; Harvard Univ, DSc(nutrit), 68. *Prof Exp:* Res asst tissue cult, Harvard Univ, 61-63; from asst prof to assoc prof food & nutrit, Iowa State Univ, 68-93, Nutrit Found Future Leader Grant, 70-71. *Mem:* Am Heart Asn; Tissue Cult Asn; NY Acad Sci. *Res:* Relationships between nutritional status and physical activity; diet and coronary disease. *Mailing Add:* 2117 Kellogg Ave Ames IA 50010

RUOF, CLARENCE HERMAN, CHEMISTRY. *Current Pos:* RETIRED. *Personal Data:* b Hummelstown, Pa, Sept 6, 19; m 45, Catherine Carns; c Mary Ellen (Van Pelt) & Susan Melinda (Haas). *Educ:* Gettysburg Col, BA, 41; Haverford Col, MS, 42; Pa State Univ, PhD(org chem), 48. *Prof Exp:* Asst chem, Haverford Col, 41-42 & Pa State Univ, 42-48; mem staff, Coal Res Lab, Carnegie Inst Technol, 48-54; sr fel, Mellon Inst, 54-60; staff scientist, Ford Motor Co, 60-69, prin staff engr & supvr fuels & lubricants, 69-86. *Mem:* Soc Automotive Engrs; Am Soc Testing & Mat; Am Chem Soc; Sigma Xi. *Res:* Steroids; high octane gasoline components; aromatic acids from coal; structure of coals; plastics; automotive lubricants. *Mailing Add:* 13080 West Shore Dr Unit 3 Houghton Lake MI 48629-9732

RUOFF, ARTHUR LOUIS, PHYSICAL CHEMISTRY. *Current Pos:* From asst prof to assoc prof eng mat, 55-65, PROF MAT SCI & APPL PHYSICS, CORNELL UNIV, 65-, DIR & CHAIRED PROF, 77- *Personal Data:* b Ft Wayne, Ind, Sept 17, 30; m 54, Enid Seaton; c William L, Stephen A, Rodney S, Jeffrey K & Kenneth J. *Educ:* Purdue Univ, BS, 52; Univ Utah, PhD(phys chem), 55. *Honors & Awards:* PW Bridgman Award. *Concurrent Pos:* NSF sci fac fel & vis assoc prof, Univ Ill, 61-62. *Mem:* Fel Am Phys Soc; Mat Res Soc; Am Ceramics Soc; fel Bohnische Phys Soc. *Res:* Multimegabar pressures; electronic and structural transitions at high pressures; optical reflectivity, absorption and raman spectroscopy; metallization of ionic and molecular solids. *Mailing Add:* Dept Mat Sci & Eng Cornell Univ Ithaca NY 14853

RUOFF, WILLIAM (DAVID), ORGANIC CHEMISTRY. *Current Pos:* From asst prof to assoc prof, 66-74, PROF CHEM, FAIRMONT STATE COL, 74-, CHMN DIV SCI, 68- *Personal Data:* b Reading, Pa, Apr 4, 40; m 60; c 3. *Educ:* Albright Col, BS, 62; Univ Del, MS, 65, PhD(chem), 67. *Mem:* Am Chem Soc. *Res:* Physical organic and synthetic organic chemistry. *Mailing Add:* Fairmont State Col Fairmont WV 26554-2489

RUOTSALA, ALBERT P, MINERALOGY. *Current Pos:* from asst prof to assoc prof, 64-74, prof, 74-88, EMER PROF MINERAL, MICH TECHNOL UNIV, 88- *Personal Data:* b Morse Twp, Minn, Sept 16, 26; m 50; c 3. *Educ:* Univ Minn, BA, 52, MS, 55; Univ Ill, PhD, 62. *Prof Exp:* Jr geologist, Bear Creek Mining Co, 52-54; geologist, C&NW Rwy, 55-56; instr geol, Tex Tech Col, 56-57; asst prof, Tex Western Col, 57-60 & Northern Ill Univ, 62-64. *Mem:* AAAS; Geochem Soc; Am Geophys Union; Mineral Soc Am; Geol Soc Am. *Res:* Clay mineralogy; igneous and metamorphic petrology; economic geology; mineralogy and chemistry of soils. *Mailing Add:* 310 S Tenth Apt 5 Escanaba MI 49629-3444

RUPAAL, AJIT S, NUCLEAR PHYSICS. *Current Pos:* from asst prof to assoc prof, 64-73, chmn, 80-89, PROF PHYSICS, WESTERN WASH UNIV, 74- *Personal Data:* b Sangrur, Panjab, India, June 25, 33; m 63; c 2. *Educ:* Panjab Univ, India, BSc, 54, MSc, 55; Univ BC, PhD(nuclear physics), 63. *Prof Exp:* Lectr, Ramgarhia Col, Panjab, 55-56; sr res scholar physics, Panjab Univ, 56-57. *Concurrent Pos:* Nat Res Coun Can fel, Chalk River Nuclear Labs, 63-64. *Mem:* Am Asn Physics Teachers; Can Asn Physicists. *Res:* Neutron gamma angular correlations and gamma branching ratios in C; interpretations of Fresnel's equations; neutron time-of-flight spectrometer; positron transmission in thin foils; negative work function of positrons in metals; electrical breakdown of ceramic insulators; low energy positive muon beam development; solid oxide fuel cell. *Mailing Add:* 805 Queen St Bellingham WA 98226

RUPERT, CLAUD STANLEY, BIOPHYSICS. *Current Pos:* prof biol, Univ Tex, Dallas, 69-92, dean natural sci & math, 75-80, Lloyd Viel Berkner prof, 81-89, assoc to vpres acad affairs, 88-92, actg vpres, 91-92, EMER PROF BIOL, UNIV TEX, DALLAS, 92- *Personal Data:* b Porterville, Calif, Feb 24, 19; m 54; c 2. *Educ:* Calif Inst Technol, BS, 41; Johns Hopkins Univ, PhD(physics), 51. *Honors & Awards:* Finsen Medal, Int Comn Photobiol, 64. *Prof Exp:* Eng trainee & sr detail draftsman, Lockheed Aircraft Corp, 41-42; jr instr physics, Johns Hopkins Univ, 46-50, res asst to Prof Strong, 50-52, Am Cancer Soc fel biophys, 52-54, asst prof, 54-57, res assoc, Sch Hyg & Pub Health, 57-58, from asst prof to assoc prof, 58-65; prof biol, SW Ctr Advan Studies, 65-69. *Concurrent Pos:* USPHS sr res fel, 58-65; lab guest, Inst Microbiol, Copenhagen, Denmark, 61-62; mem impact stratospheric change comt, Nat Res Coun, 75-79. *Mem:* AAAS; Biophys Soc; Am Soc Photobiol. *Res:* Infection and transformation of cells by nucleic acids; cell biology; photobiology; photoenzymology; radiation biology. *Mailing Add:* Prog Biol PO Box 830688 Richardson TX 75083-0688

RUPERT, EARLENE ATCHISON, plant genetics, taxonomy, for more information see previous edition

RUPERT, GERALD BRUCE, GEOPHYSICS. *Current Pos:* assoc prof rock mech res & mining eng, 69-74, SR INVESTR ROCK MECH & EXPLOR RES CTR, 74-, PROF GEOPHYS & CHMN DEPT GEOL & GEOPHYS, UNIV MO-ROLLA, 76- *Personal Data:* b Akron, Ohio, Aug 23, 30; m 54; c 2. *Educ:* Ind Univ, BS, 56, MA, 58; Univ Mo-Rolla, PhD(geophys), 64. *Prof Exp:* Sr seismic comput, Texaco, Inc, 57-60; from asst instr to instr mining engr, Univ Mo-Rolla, 60-64, asst prof geophys, 64-66; res geophysicist, Western Geophys Co, 66-67, mgr, Milano Digital Ctr, Italy, 67-69; sr seismic analyst, Mobil Oil, 69. *Mem:* Soc Explor Geophys; Am Geophys Union; Seismol Soc Am; Earthquake Eng Res Inst. *Res:* Exploration geophysics; digital filtering; rock mechanics, particularly wave propagation; earthquake mechanisms; viscoelasticity. *Mailing Add:* 11611 County Rd 8070 Rolla MO 65401

RUPERT, JOHN PAUL, POLYMER SCIENCE. *Current Pos:* MONSANTO INDUST CHEM CO, BROKER, EDWARD JONES, 90- *Personal Data:* b Delphos, Ohio, Oct 14, 46; m 68; c 2. *Educ:* Heidelberg Col, BS, 68; Akron Univ, PhD(polymer sci), 75. *Prof Exp:* Tech supvr eng, Goodyear Tire & Rubber Co, 68-72; fel chem, Inst Polymer Sci, Akron Univ, 75; chemist polymer physics, Union Carbide Corp, 75-76; sr chemist polyurethane raw mat facia develop, 76-78; sr res chemist new appln urethane technol, BASF Wyandotte, 78- *Mem:* Am Chem Soc. *Res:* Effect of polymerization variables on anionic polymerizations, polymer characterization and structure-property and rheology-property relationships of engineering thermoplastics; nuclear magnetic resonance of polymers. *Mailing Add:* 5541 Liberty Ave Vermilion OH 44089

RUPF, JOHN ALBERT, JR, ELECTRICAL ENGINEERING. *Current Pos:* ASSOC PROF, SOUTHERN COL TECHNOL, 93- *Personal Data:* b Wichita, Kans, Apr 8, 39; m 60; c 3. *Educ:* Univ Kans, BSEE, 61; Mass Inst Technol, MSEE & EE, 64; Purdue Univ, Lafayette, PhD(elec eng), 69. *Prof Exp:* Instr elec eng, Purdue Univ, Lafayette, 64-69; asst prof elec eng, Bur Child Res, Univ Kans, 69-72, assoc prof & res assoc, 72-82; sr engr, Chevron Geosci Co, 82-86; sr eng specialist, Gen Dynamics, Tex, 87-91; assoc prof elec eng, Tex A&M Univ, 91; staff engr, Lockheed Aeronaut Syst Co, 92-93. *Mem:* Acoust Soc Am; Inst Elec & Electronics Engrs; Inst Noise Control Eng. *Res:* Speech perception, analysis and synthesis; human factors engineering; digital signal processing; noise control. *Mailing Add:* 2160 Southbrook Ridge Kennesaw GA 30144

RUPICH, MARTIN WALTER, ELECTRONIC MATERIAL SYNTHESIS, OPTICAL & ELECTROCHEMICAL SENSORS. *Current Pos:* SR SCIENTIST, EIC LABS INC, 80- *Personal Data:* b Youngstown, Ohio, Feb 3, 52; m; c 2. *Educ:* John Carroll Univ, Cleveland, Ohio, BS, 74; Northeastern Univ, PhD(inorg chem), 80. *Prof Exp:* Chemist, New Eng Nuclear Corp, 75-76. *Mem:* Am Chem Soc; AAAS; Mat Res Soc; Electrochem Soc. *Res:* Synthesis and characterization of advanced materials for optical, electronic and catalytic applications, specifically high temperature oxide superconductors, non-linear optical materials, supported catalyst, battery cathodes; development of sensors for atmospheric gases. *Mailing Add:* Am Super Conductor Corp 2 Technol Dr Westborough MA 01581

RUPLEY, JOHN ALLEN, PROTEIN CHEMISTRY, ENZYME CHEMISTRY. *Current Pos:* from asst prof to prof chem, 61-78, PROF BIOCHEM, UNIV ARIZ, 78- *Personal Data:* b Brooklyn, NY, July 15, 33; m 60; c 1. *Educ:* Princeton Univ, AB, 54; Univ Wash, PhD(biochem), 59. *Prof Exp:* NIH fel, Cornell Univ, 59-61. *Concurrent Pos:* Consult, Fel Panel, NIH, 68-70 & Biochem Study Sect, 71-75; consult, W R Grace & Co, 68-; NIH spec fel, Oxford Univ, 70; mem biochem carcinogen panel, Am Cancer Soc, 72-76; mem pub affairs comt, Fedn Am Soc Exp Biol, 74-77; hon assoc mem, Inst Josef Stefan, Yugoslavia, 74-; co-chmn proteins, Gordon Conf, 83. *Mem:* Am Chem Soc; Am Soc Biol Chemists; AAAS; Am Inst Chemists; NY Acad Sci; Sigma Xi. *Res:* Correlation of protein structure and properties; mechanism of action of enzymes; thermochemistry. *Mailing Add:* Dept Biochem 30 Calle Belleza Tucson AZ 85716

RUPP, JOHN JAY, INORGANIC CHEMISTRY, CHEMICAL EDUCATION COMPUTER ASSISTED INSTRUCTION. *Current Pos:* From asst prof to assoc prof, 66-87, PROF CHEM, ST LAWRENCE UNIV, 87- *Personal Data:* b Archbold, Ohio, Sept 28, 40; m 63, Elinore Boehm; c Jeffrey & Richard. *Educ:* Ohio Univ, BS, 62; Northwestern Univ, PhD(chem), 67. *Concurrent Pos:* NSF instrnl equip prog grant, 69-71; vis prof, Univ Hawaii, Manoa, 84-85, 91-92. *Mem:* Am Chem Soc; Sigma Xi. *Res:* Preparative and physical inorganic chemistry, especially unusual Lewis acid-base addition compounds, organometallics and x-ray crystallography and molecular modeling. *Mailing Add:* 52 Spears St Canton NY 13617. *Fax:* 315-379-7421; *E-Mail:* jrupp@vm.stlawu.edu

RUPP, RALPH RUSSELL, AUDIOLOGY, SPEECH PATHOLOGY. *Current Pos:* PROF SPEC EDUC & AUDIOL, SPEECH & HEARING SCI, SCH EDUC, UNIV MICH, ANN ARBOR, 65-; COORDR AUDIOL, EASTERN MICH UNIV, 85- *Personal Data:* b Saginaw, Mich, Apr 12, 29; m 55; c 2. *Educ:* Univ Mich, BA, 51, MA, 52; Wayne State Univ, PhD(audiol, speech path), 64. *Honors & Awards:* Distinguished Serv Award and Honors Asn, Michigan Speech-Lang-Hearing Asn. *Prof Exp:* Speech & hearing consult, Detroit Pub Schs, Mich, 52-59; exec dir, Detroit Hearing Ctr, 59-62; assoc audiol, Henry Ford Hosp, 62-65. *Concurrent Pos:* Consult audiol, C S Mott Children's Health Ctr, Mich, 66-, Ann Arbor Vet Admin Hosp, 67-, St Joseph Mercy Hosp, Ann Arbor, 67 & Dept Hearing Speech & Lang, Kenny-Mich Rehab Found, Pontiac Gen Hosp. *Mem:* Fel Am Speech & Hearing Asn. *Res:* Effect of excessively loud rock 'n roll music on the human hearing mechanisms; improvement of hearing efficiency of the elderly; audiological assessment techniques; language ability of hearing-impaired children; speech audiometry; auditory processing and listening skills in children. *Mailing Add:* 4099 Green Meadows Blvd Ypsilanti MI 48197-2207

RUPP, W DEAN, MOLECULAR GENETICS, GENETIC ENGINEERING. *Current Pos:* Res assoc radiobiol, 65-69, asst prof, 69-74, assoc prof, 74-81, PROF THERAPEUT RADIOL, MOLECULAR BIOPHYS & BIOCHEM, SCH MED, YALE UNIV, 81- *Personal Data:* b Archbold, Ohio, Aug 24, 38; m 62; c 1. *Educ:* Oberlin Col, AB, 60; Yale Univ, PhD(pharmacol), 65. *Concurrent Pos:* Res assoc biol chem, Harvard Univ, 67-68. *Mem:* Biophys Soc; Radiation Res Soc; Am Soc Microbiol. *Res:* Cloning of genes and characterization of enzymes involved in DNA repair; expression of proteins from cloned genes. *Mailing Add:* Dept Therapeut Radiol Yale Univ Sch Med 333 Cedar St New Haven CT 06510-3219. *Fax:* 203-785-6309

RUPP, WALTER H(OWARD), CHEMICAL ENGINEERING. *Current Pos:* PRES, HYLO CO, 68- *Personal Data:* b Pittsburgh, Pa, Dec 22, 09; m 37, Sidney Stanton; c Margaret Sidney, John Stanton & Leila Jane. *Educ:* Univ Pittsburgh, BS, 30. *Prof Exp:* Jr engr, Standard Oil Co, NJ, 30-36, group head, Esso Res & Eng Co, 36-44, asst div head, 44-49, supv engr, 49-54, tech adv, 54-56, staff engr, 56-62, head tech info ctr, 62-68. *Concurrent Pos:* Independent consult, 68- *Mem:* Am Inst Chem Engrs. *Res:* Petroleum refining; design engineering; air pollution; advanced information systems for engineers; granted numerous patents. *Mailing Add:* 359 Dogwood Way Mountainside NJ 07092

RUPPEL, EARL GEORGE, PLANT PATHOLOGY, VIROLOGY. *Current Pos:* plant pathologist, Tropic & Subarctic Res Br, Crops Res Div, Sci & Educ Admin-Agr Res, 63-65, PLANT PATHOLOGIST, AGR RES SERV, USDA, 65-, RES LEADER SUGARBEET RES, 92-; MEM AFFIL FAC, BIOAGRIC SCI & PEST MGT DEPT, COLO STATE UNIV, 70- *Personal Data:* b Milwaukee, Wis, Nov 10, 32; m 58, Joyce Port; c Susan (Erickson), Julia (Crawmer) & Michael. *Educ:* Univ Wis-Milwaukee, BS, 58; Univ Wis-Madison, PhD(plant path), 62. *Honors & Awards:* Meritorious Serv Award, Am Soc Sugar Beet Technologists, 87. *Prof Exp:* Wis Alumni Res Found-Am Cancer Soc res grant, 62-63. *Concurrent Pos:* Mem grad fac, Colo State Univ, 71- *Mem:* Fel Am Phytopath Soc; Mycol Soc Am; Am Soc Sugar Beet Technol; Int Soc Plant Path. *Res:* Epidemiology of sugarbeet diseases; physiological and biochemical nature of disease resistance; physiology and properties of pathogens; breeding for disease resistance in sugarbeet; genetics. *Mailing Add:* USDA-Agr Res Serv Crops Res Lab 1701 Center Ave Ft Collins CO 80526-2083. *E-Mail:* eruppel@lamar.colostate.edu

RUPPEL, EDWARD THOMPSON, STRUCTURAL GEOLOGY. *Current Pos:* Geologist, US Geol Surv, 48-86, DIR & STATE GEOLOGIST, MONT BUR MINES & GEOL, 86- *Personal Data:* b Ft Morgan, Colo, Oct 26, 25; m 56, Phyllis B Tanner; c Lisa, David, Douglas & Kristin. *Educ:* Univ Mont, BA, 48; Univ Wyo, MA, 50; Yale Univ, PhD(geol), 58. *Mem:* Fel Geol Soc Am; fel Soc Econ Geologists; Am Inst Prof Geologists. *Res:* Structural geology; economic geology; geomorphology; geologic mapping and related structural, stratigraphic and resource studies in Montana and adjacent states. *Mailing Add:* Box K Twin Bridges MT 59754-0402

RUPPEL, ROBERT FRANK, ENTOMOLOGY. *Current Pos:* assoc prof, 63-68, liaison agr proj, 66-67, PROF ENTOM, MICH STATE UNIV, 68- *Personal Data:* b Detroit, Mich, June 2, 25; m 48; c 2. *Educ:* Mich State Col, BS, 48; Ohio State Univ, MS, 50, PhD(entom), 52. *Prof Exp:* Res asst, Mich State Col, 48; from asst entomologist to entomologist, Rockefeller Found, Columbia Univ, 52-62; res biologist, Niagara Chem Div, FMC Corp, 62. *Concurrent Pos:* Tech dir, Entom Prog, Dept Agr Res, Govt Colombia, 58-62; res assoc, Univ Calif, 60. *Mem:* AAAS; Entom Soc Am; Am Inst Biol Sci. *Res:* Economic entomology; insect ecology; chemical control; taxonomy. *Mailing Add:* Dept Entomol Mich State Univ East Lansing MI 48824

RUPPEL, THOMAS CONRAD, PHYSICAL CHEMISTRY. *Current Pos:* res chemist, 65-76, chem engr, 76-87, ENVIRON ENGR, DEPT ENERGY, 87- *Personal Data:* b Pittsburgh, Pa, June 30, 30; m 57; c 4. *Educ:* Duquesne Univ, BS, 52; Univ Pittsburgh, BS, 59, MS, 68. *Prof Exp:* Res asst, Heat Insulation fel, Mellon Inst, 52-53 & Phys Chem Dept, 53-57, res assoc, Food Packaging fel, 57-58 & Protective Coatings fel, 58-60; chemist, Res Ctr, Koppers Co, Inc, 60-63; sr res asst water pollution, Grad Sch Pub Health, Univ Pittsburgh, 63-65. *Concurrent Pos:* Chmn, Pittsburgh Sect, Am Chem Soc, 88, dir, 89-91. *Mem:* Air & Waste Mgt Asn; Am Chem Soc. *Res:* Thermal diffusion; physical adsorption at elevated pressure; chemistry of gaseous non-disruptive electrical discharges; chemical reaction engineering; thermodynamic coal conversion process calculations; on-line engineering database development; environmental engineering; federal environmental laws and regulations. *Mailing Add:* PO Box 195 Bethel Park PA 15102. *Fax:* 412-892-4775

RUPPERT, DAVID, STOCHASTIC APPROXIMATION, REGRESSION MODELING. *Current Pos:* PROF, OPERS RES, CORNELL UNIV, 87- *Educ:* Cornell Univ, BA, 70; Univ Vet, MA, 73; Mich State Univ, PhD(statist), 77. *Honors & Awards:* Wilcoxon Prize, Am Soc Quality Control, 86. *Prof Exp:* From asst prof to assoc prof statist, Univ NC, 83-87. *Mem:* Inst Math Statist; Am Statist Asn; Math Asn Am; Opers Res Soc Am; Sigma Xi. *Res:* Recursive estimation and stochastic approximation, robustness and regression; biological modeling and natural research management. *Mailing Add:* 154 Ellis Hollow Creek Rd Ithaca NY 14850

RUPPRECHT, KEVIN ROBERT, MOLECULAR GENETICS, GENETIC ENGINEERING. *Current Pos:* RES ASSOC, UNIV CHICAGO, 81- *Personal Data:* b Trenton, NJ, Apr 14, 55; m 79; c 1. *Educ:* Cornell Univ, BS, 76; Univ Notre Dame, MS, 80, PhD(microbiol), 81. *Mem:* Am Soc Microbiol; AAAS. *Res:* Discerning the role of the E coli K12 gene ion in capsule production and cell division using recombinant DNA techniques. *Mailing Add:* Dept 09A1 Dept 9TV Bldg AP20 100 Abbott Park Rd Abbott Park IL 60064-3500

RUPRECHT, RUTH MARGRIT, RETROVIROLOGY, ONCOLOGY. *Current Pos:* asst prof, 84-91, ASSOC PROF MED, HARVARD MED SCH, 91-; CHIEF, LAB VIRAL PATHOGENESIS, DANA-FARBER CANCER INST, 91- *Personal Data:* b Baden, Switz, Apr 10, 47; US citizen; div; c David E & Adam E. *Educ:* Univ Zurich, Switz, predipl, 70; Columbia Univ, NY, PhD (human genetics), 73; Univ Miami Sch Med, MD, 77. *Prof Exp:* Asst prof med, Mt Sinai, Sch Med, 83-84. *Concurrent Pos:* Consult, maj pharmaceut co, 88-91, WHO, 89; chief, Lab Viral Pathogenesis, Dana Farber Cancer Inst, 91-; mem, Sci Adv Comt, Pediat AIDS Found, 91- *Mem:* AAAS; NY Acad Sci; Am Col Physicians; Am Asn Cancer Res. *Res:* Retroviral pathogenesis and acquired immune deficiency syndrome research; study antiviral chemotherapy and the nature of host immunity against retroviruses in animals, including primates. *Mailing Add:* Dana-Farber Cancer Inst 44 Binney St Boston MA 02115-6084. *Fax:* 617-632-3719; *E-Mail:* ruth_ruprecht@dfci.harvard.edu

RUSAY, RONALD JOSEPH, ORGANIC CHEMISTRY, BIOLOGICAL CHEMISTRY. *Current Pos:* chair, Dept Chem, 93-96, VIS SCHOLAR, UNIV CALIF, BERKELEY, 96-; SR PROD MGR, DIABLO VALLEY COL, 90- *Personal Data:* b New Brunswick, NJ, Dec 21, 45; m 67, Suzanne Hendrickson; c Christopher & Sylvia. *Educ:* Univ NH, BA, 67, MS, 69; Ore State Univ, PhD(org chem, oceanog), 76. *Prof Exp:* Teacher chem, Bridgton Acad, 71-73; Am Chem Soc-Petrol Res Fund res fel, Ore State Univ, 74-76; res chemist synthesis, Pac Basin, Stauffer Chem Co, 76-80, res analyst, 81-83, mgr prod develop, 84-88; sr prod mgr, ICI/Zeneca, UK, 88-90. *Concurrent Pos:* Fac affil, Peregrine Publ. *Mem:* AAAS; Am Chem Soc; Sigma Xi; NY Acad Sci. *Res:* Developed organic compounds of agricultural and pharmaceutical importance; interested in meltacognition, learning in higher education and applications of web based instruction. *Mailing Add:* 1030 Leland Dr LaFayette CA 94549-4130. *Fax:* 510-685-1551; *E-Mail:* rrusay@viking.dvc.edu

RUSCELLO, DENNIS MICHAEL, SPEECH PATHOLOGY. *Current Pos:* from asst prof to assoc prof, 77-85, PROF SPEECH PATH, WVA UNIV, 85- *Personal Data:* b Washington, Pa, Sept 2, 47; m 68, Edith W Watt; c Scott, Craig & Mark. *Educ:* Calif State Col, BS, 69; WVa State Univ, MS, 72; Univ Ariz, PhD(speech path), 77. *Prof Exp:* Speech clinician speech path, Allegheny Intermediate 3, Pittsburgh, Pa, 69-74; res assoc, Univ Ariz, 74-77. *Concurrent Pos:* Ed consult, Lang, Speech, Hearing in Schs & J Commun Dis. *Mem:* Fel Am Speech & Hearing Asn; Am Cleft Palate Asn. *Res:* Investigation of speech problems exhibited by young children and persons with cranio-facial anomalies. *Mailing Add:* Dept Speech Path & Audiol WVa Univ PO Box 6122 Morgantown WV 26506-0001. *Fax:* 304-293-7565

RUSCH, DONALD HAROLD, WILDLIFE ECOLOGY, VERTEBRATE BIOLOGY. *Current Pos:* asst leader, 73-74, LEADER, WIS COOP WILDLIFE RES UNIT, US FISH & WILDLIFE SERV, 74- *Personal Data:* b Appleton, Wis, Dec 22, 38; m 65, Doris Peterson; c Jennifer. *Educ:* Univ Wis-Madison, BS, 62, PhD(wildlife ecol, zool), 70; Utah State Univ, MS, 65. *Honors & Awards:* Meritorious Serv Award, US Dept Interior, 92. *Prof Exp:* Res specialist birds, Man Dept Natural Resources, 71-72, actg chief wildlife res, 72-73. *Concurrent Pos:* Asst prof, Dept Wildlife Ecol, Univ Wis, 73-79, assoc prof, 79-83, prof, 83- *Mem:* Wildlife Soc; Ecol Soc; Sigma Xi. *Res:* Population ecology; vertebrate predation; waterfowl migration; grouse ecology; population indices; analysis of wildlife habitat. *Mailing Add:* Wis Coop Wildlife Res Unit Univ Wis Madison WI 53706

RUSCH, PETER FREDERICK, TECHNICAL MANAGEMENT. *Current Pos:* dir, 75-90, VPRES, DIALOG INFO SERV, INC, 90- *Personal Data:* b Dallas, Tex, May 26, 43; m 66; c 2. *Educ:* Southern Methodist Univ, BS, 65, MS, 66; Univ Tex, Austin, PhD(chem), 71. *Prof Exp:* Fel, Ctr Nat Res Sci, 71-72; info scientist, Chem Abstr Serv, 73-75. *Concurrent Pos:* Res fel, NSF/Nat Ctr Sci Res, 71. *Mem:* Am Chem Soc; Am Inst Chemists; Sigma Xi; Chem Struct Asn. *Res:* Accessing databases composed of textual numeric and image information including chemical and other scientific or technical content. *Mailing Add:* 355 Verano Dr Los Altos CA 94022-2345

RUSCH, WILBERT H, SR, BIOLOGY, GEOLOGY. *Current Pos:* div chmn, 63-73 & 74-75, actg pres, 73-74, acad dean, 75-77, prof biol & geol, 63-80, EMER PROF BIOL & GEOL, CONCORDIA LUTHERAN COL, MICH, 80- *Personal Data:* b Chicago, Ill, Feb 19, 13; m 37; c 5. *Educ:* Ill Inst Technol, BS, 34; Univ Mich, MS, 52; Eastern Mich Univ, SpS, 69. *Hon Degrees:* LLD, Concordia Sem, Mo, 75. *Prof Exp:* Instr music & math, Concordia Teachers Col, Nebr, 32-33; instr physics & math, Concordia Col, Ind, 37-46, assoc prof biol, 46-57; assoc prof, Concordia Teachers Col, Nebr, 57-60, prof biol & geol, 60-63. *Concurrent Pos:* Kellogg Found fel, 73. *Mem:* Nat Asn Biol Teachers; Nat Asn Geol Teachers; Nat Sci Teachers Asn; fel Creation Res Soc (pres). *Res:* Trees of Great Lake States. *Mailing Add:* 2717 Cranbrook Rd Ann Arbor MI 48104

RUSCHAK, KENNETH JOHN, CHEMICAL ENGINEERING. *Current Pos:* RES SCIENTIST, EASTMAN KODAK CO, 74- *Personal Data:* b Homestead, Pa, March 3, 49; m 78; c 2. *Educ:* Carnegie-Mellon Univ, BS, 71; Univ Minn, PhD(chem eng), 74. *Honors & Awards:* C E K Mees Award for Sci, Eastman Kodak Co, 83. *Mem:* Am Inst Chem Engrs. *Res:* Capillary hydrodynamics, perturbation methods, and numerical simulation of fluid flow with applications to coating technology. *Mailing Add:* 236 Wimbledon Rd Rochester NY 14617

RUSCHER, PAUL H, SYNOPTIC & MESOSCALE METEOROLOGY, BOUNDARY LAYER STUDIES. *Current Pos:* asst prof, 88-94, ASSOC PROF METEOROL, FLA STATE UNIV, 94- *Personal Data:* b Mt Vernon, NY, June 8, 55; m 75. *Educ:* State Univ NY, Oneonta, BS, 76; Ore State Univ, MS, 81, PhD(atmospheric sci), 88. *Prof Exp:* Vis asst prof meteorol, Tex A&M Univ, 83-84, Fla State Univ, 84; instr atmospheric sci, Creighton Univ, 85-86; res assoc & instr atmospheric sci, Ore State Univ, 86-88. *Concurrent Pos:* Prin investr res grants, Fla State Univ, 88-; mem, Comt Boundary Layers & Turbulence, Am Meteorol Soc, 90-, Comt Undergrad Scholarships &

Awards, 91-; proj dir, Tallahassee Area Rain Gauge Proj, 91- *Mem:* Am Meteorol Soc; Am Geophys Union; Can Meteorol & Oceanog Soc; Nat Weather Asn. *Res:* Synoptic studies; mesoscale meteorology especially of coastal winds; boundary layer studies, observational and modelling aspects; weather education; physical and applied climatology; severe storms; turbulence; diffusion and air pollution problems. *Mailing Add:* Meteorol Fla State Univ 600 W College Ave Tallahassee FL 32306-1096

RUSCHMEYER, ORLANDO R, PUBLIC HEALTH BIOLOGY, AQUATIC MICROBIOLOGY. *Current Pos:* Asst microbiol, 52-56, instr pub health biol, 59-65, ASST PROF PUB HEALTH BIOL, UNIV MINN, MINNEAPOLIS, 66- *Personal Data:* b Stewart, Minn, Feb 27, 25; m 51; c 2. *Educ:* Univ Minn, Minneapolis, BA, 51, MS, 56, PhD(environ health), 65. *Concurrent Pos:* Consult biologist, Int Joint Comn Boundary Waters of US & Can, 61-62. *Mem:* AAAS; Am Soc Limnol & Oceanog; Am Soc Microbiol; Int Asn Theoret & Appl Limnol; Sigma Xi. *Res:* Transformations of organic compounds by soil microflora; limnology of western Lake Superior; water pollution biology; environmental microbiology. *Mailing Add:* 1798 Carl St St Paul MN 55113-5202

RUSH, BENJAMIN FRANKLIN, JR, SURGERY. *Current Pos:* RETIRED. *Personal Data:* b Honolulu, Hawaii, Jan 14, 24; m 48, Norah Grant; c 2. *Educ:* Univ Calif, AB, 44; Yale Univ, MD, 48. *Honors & Awards:* Sheen Award, Am Col Surgeons, 94. *Prof Exp:* Res asst, Sloan-Kettering Div, Med Col, Cornell Univ, 54-57; instr surg, Sch Med, Johns Hopkins Univ, 57-59, asst prof, 59-62; from assoc prof to prof, Col Med, Univ Ky, 62-69; prof, Univ Med & Dent, NJ, Newark, 69-71, chmn dept, 69-94, distinguished prof surg, 71-90. *Concurrent Pos:* Resident, Mem Ctr Cancer & Allied Dis, 53-57; asst chief surg, Baltimore City Hosps, 59-62; consult, Nat Cancer Plan, Nat Cancer Inst. *Mem:* Am Fedn Clin Res; fel Am Col Surgeons; Am Asn Cancer Educ (pres); Am Surg Asn; Sigma Xi; Soc Surg Oncol (pres). *Res:* Fluid balance and renal physiology in relation to surgery; surgical oncology. *Mailing Add:* 90 Bergen St, Suite 7200 Newark NJ 07103-2499. *Fax:* 973-982-6803

RUSH, CECIL ARCHER, MICROCHEMISTRY. *Current Pos:* CONSULT MICROCHEM, ANAL CHEM, CHEM & PHYS MICROS, 81- *Personal Data:* b Dillwyn, Va, Apr 14, 17; m 57, Betty A Morgan; c Gordon D. *Educ:* Col William & Mary, BS, 38. *Prof Exp:* Anal chemist, Edgewood Arsenal, Chem Res Labs, 40-44, microchemist, 44-50, supvr microanal lab, 50-60, chief microchem lab, Chem Res Labs, 60-80. *Concurrent Pos:* Chem consult. *Mem:* Am Microchem Soc; Am Chem Soc; Sigma Xi; Am Crystallog Asn. *Res:* Analytical chemistry; crystallography; chemical microscopy; chemical warfare agents. *Mailing Add:* 1410 Northgate Rd Baltimore MD 21218-1549

RUSH, CHARLES KENNETH, MECHANICAL ENGINEERING. *Current Pos:* from assoc prof to prof, 63-86, EMER PROF MECH ENG, QUEEN'S UNIV, ONT, 86- *Personal Data:* b Toronto, Ont, Jan 15, 21; m 46; c 4. *Educ:* Queen's Univ, Ont, BSc, 44; McGill Univ, Dipl, 62; Carleton Univ, Can, MEng, 63. *Prof Exp:* Res engr, Nat Res Coun Can, 44-63. *Mem:* Am Soc Eng Educ; Am Soc Heating Refrigerating Air-Conditioning Engrs; Int Solar Energy Soc; Can Soc Mech Eng. *Res:* Aircraft icing; energy utilization; solar energy. *Mailing Add:* 801-185 Ontario St Kingston ON K7L 2Y7 Can

RUSH, CHARLES MERLE, IONOSPHERIC PHYSICS. *Current Pos:* MEM STAFF, NAT OCEANIC & ATMOSPHERIC ADMIN, 77- *Personal Data:* b Philadelphia, Pa, Oct 10, 42; m 64; c 2. *Educ:* Temple Univ, BA, 64; Univ Calif, Los Angeles, PhD(meteorol), 67. *Prof Exp:* Staff scientist, Space Systs Div, Avco Corp, Mass, 67-69; res physicist, Air Force Cambridge Res Labs, 69-77. *Mem:* Am Meteorol Soc; Am Geophys Union; Sigma Xi. *Res:* Dynamics and structure of the earth's ionized atmosphere. *Mailing Add:* 6541 Bay Tree Ct Falls Church VA 22041

RUSH, DAVID EUGENE, MATHEMATICS. *Current Pos:* from asst prof to assoc prof, 71-82, PROF MATH, UNIV CALIF, RIVERSIDE, 82- *Personal Data:* b Carthage, Mo, Mar 5, 43; m 66; c 2. *Educ:* Southwest Mo State Col, BSEd, 65; Western Wash State Col, MS, 68; La State Univ, Baton Rouge, PhD(math), 71. *Prof Exp:* High sch teacher, Mo, 65-67. *Concurrent Pos:* Dept Chair, Univ Calif, Riverside, 85-88. *Mem:* Am Math Soc; Math Asn Am. *Res:* Commutative algebra. *Mailing Add:* Univ Calif Riverside CA 92521-0001

RUSH, JAMES E, LIBRARY & INFORMATION SCIENCE, SYSTEM DESIGN. *Current Pos:* EXEC DIR, PALINET, 88- *Personal Data:* b Warrensburg, Mo, July 18, 35; m 58, Delores A Lee; c Susan, Pamela, Adam & Jennifer. *Educ:* Cent Mo State Univ, BS, 57; Univ Mo, PhD(org chem), 62. *Prof Exp:* Asst ed, Org Index Ed Dept, Chem Abstr Serv, Am Chem Soc, 62-65, asst head, Chem Info Procedures Dept, 65-68; from asst prof to assoc prof comput & info sci, Ohio State Univ, 68-73; dir res & develop, OCLC, Inc, 73-80; pres, James E Rush Assoc, Inc, 80-88. *Concurrent Pos:* Ed, Chem Lit, 70-73; adj prof comput & info sci, Ohio State Univ, 73-80; adj prof libr & info sci, Univ Ill, 80-83. *Mem:* Sigma Xi; Am Chem Soc; Am Soc Info Sci. *Res:* Organoboron compounds; organometallic and coordination chemistry; stereochemistry; information storage and retrieval; library automation; telecommunication and networks. *Mailing Add:* 673 Old Eagle Sch Rd Stafford PA 19087. *Fax:* 215-382-0022; *E-Mail:* rush@palinet.org

RUSH, JOHN EDWIN, JR, THEORETICAL PHYSICS. *Current Pos:* RES SCIENTIST, KAMAN SCI CORP, HUNTSVILLE, ALA, 83- *Personal Data:* b Birmingham, Ala, Aug 11, 37; m 63, 82; c 5. *Educ:* Birmingham-Southern Col, BS, 59; Vanderbilt Univ, PhD(physics), 65. *Prof Exp:* From instr to asst prof physics, Univ of the South, 64-67; from asst prof to assoc prof physics, Univ Ala, Huntsville, 67-83, chmn dept, 69-72, dean sch grad studies & res, 72-76. *Mem:* Am Phys Soc; Sigma Xi. *Res:* Nuclear weapons effects. *Mailing Add:* 100 Kathy Circle Madison AL 35758

RUSH, JOHN JOSEPH, SOLID STATE PHYSICS, PHYSICAL CHEMISTRY. *Current Pos:* phys chemist, 62-71, chief neutron-solid state physics sect, Nat Measurements Lab, 71-81, LEADER, NEUTRON-CONDENSED MATTER SCI GROUP, NAT BUR STAND, 81- *Personal Data:* b Brooklyn, NY, Apr 20, 36; m 61. *Educ:* St Francis Col, NY, BS, 57; Columbia Univ, MA, 58, PhD(phys chem), 62. *Honors & Awards:* Gold & Silver Medals, Com Dept. *Prof Exp:* Asst, Columbia Univ, 57-62. *Concurrent Pos:* Guest scientist, Solid State Sci Div, Argonne Nat Lab, 62-65. *Mem:* AAAS; Am Phys Soc; fel Nat Inst Stand & Technol. *Res:* Study of molecular solids, catalysts and hydrogen in metals by thermal neutron scattering and other spectroscopic techniques; vibrations and rotations in condensed systems; structure; phase transitions. *Mailing Add:* Bldg G235 Nat Inst Stand & Technol Mat Sci & Eng Lab Gaithersburg MD 20879

RUSH, KENT RODNEY, ORGANIC CHEMISTRY. *Current Pos:* RETIRED. *Personal Data:* b Quakertown, Pa, Sept 5, 38; m 59, Paticia Hunsworth; c Susan, Michael & Melissa. *Educ:* Franklin & Marshall Col, BS, 60; Univ Minn, PhD(org chem), 63. *Prof Exp:* Res chemist, Distillation Prod Indust Div, Eastman Kodak Co, 63-65, res assoc res labs, 65-78, prod develop mgr, 78-92, consult, 92-97. *Mem:* Am Chem Soc. *Res:* Chemistry of nitrogen heterocycles, polyenes; carotenoids; photographic chemistry; imaging science. *Mailing Add:* 74 Brush Creek Dr Rochester NY 14612

RUSH, RICHARD MARION, PHYSICAL CHEMISTRY. *Current Pos:* CHEMIST, OAK RIDGE NAT LAB, 56- *Personal Data:* b Bristol, Va, Dec 5, 28; m 55; c 2. *Educ:* Princeton Univ, AB, 49; Univ Va, MS, 52, PhD(chem), 54. *Prof Exp:* Asst chem, Mass Inst Technol, 53-54; asst prof, Haverford Col, 54-56. *Mem:* Fel AAAS; Am Chem Soc; Am Nuclear Soc; fel Am Inst Chemists; Sigma Xi. *Res:* Physical chemistry; inorganic solution chemistry; thermodynamics of electrolyte solutions; environmental impact assessment. *Mailing Add:* 102 Dana Dr Oak Ridge TN 37830

RUSH, RICHARD WILLIAM, GEOLOGY. *Current Pos:* RETIRED. *Personal Data:* b Austin, Minn, July 14, 21; div; c 4. *Educ:* Univ Iowa, BA, 45; Columbia Univ, MA, 48, PhD (geol), 54. *Prof Exp:* Consult, River Prod Corp, 61-64; assoc prof, Northern Ariz Univ, 63-69; consult geol, 69-86. *Mem:* Am Inst Prof Geol; AAAS; Sigma Xi; Geol Soc Am; Am Geophys Union; Am Asn Petrol Geologists. *Res:* Siluvian stratigraphy; geomorphology; conceptual design of new surface mining techniques; regional tectonics; suspect or exotic terranes; computer techniques to aid fundamental geologic research in regional tectonics; expert systems. *Mailing Add:* 337 W Pasadena No 16 Phoenix AZ 85013

RUSH, STANLEY, ELECTRICAL ENGINEERING. *Current Pos:* assoc prof, 62-67, PROF ELEC ENG, UNIV VT, 67- *Personal Data:* b New York, NY, June 17, 20; m 52; c 1. *Educ:* Brooklyn Col, BA, 42; Syracuse Univ, MEE, 58, PhD(elec eng), 62. *Prof Exp:* Design engr, RCA Victor Div, Radio Corp Am, 46-47; supvry electronic scientist, Rome Air Develop Ctr, US Air Force, 47-57; instr elec eng, Syracuse Univ, 57-62. *Mem:* Inst Elec & Electronics Engrs; NY Acad Sci. *Res:* Current flow in body from heart and brain generators; interpretation of electrocardiogram on physical basis; electrophysiology of the heart; tissue impedance at gross and cellular level; electromagnetic field theory. *Mailing Add:* Dept Elec Eng Univ Vt Burlington VT 05401

RUSHFORTH, CRAIG KNEWEL, ELECTRICAL ENGINEERING. *Current Pos:* PROF ELEC ENG, UNIV UTAH, 73- *Personal Data:* b Ogden, Utah, Sept 4, 37; m 58; c 5. *Educ:* Stanford Univ, BS, 58, MS, 60, PhD(elec eng), 62. *Prof Exp:* Res asst radio propagation, Stanford Univ, 58-59; res engr, Stanford Res Inst, 63; asst prof elec eng, Utah State Univ, 62-66; assoc prof, Mont State Univ, 66-72, prof, 72-73. *Concurrent Pos:* Lectr, Stanford Univ, 63; consult panel synthetic aperture optics, Nat Acad Sci, 67; mem staff, Inst Defense Analyses, 67-68. *Mem:* Inst Elec & Electronics Engrs. *Res:* Communication theory; digital signal processing. *Mailing Add:* Dept Elec Eng Univ Utah Merrill Eng Bldg Salt Lake City UT 84112

RUSHFORTH, NORMAN B, ANIMAL BEHAVIOR, EPIDEMIOLOGY. *Current Pos:* From instr to assoc prof biol, 61-72, asst prof biostatist, 63-72, ASSOC PROF BIOSTATIST & PROF BIOL, CASE WESTERN RESERVE UNIV, 72-, CHMN DEPT, 71- *Personal Data:* b Blackpool, Eng, Dec 27, 32; m 56; c 2. *Educ:* Univ Birmingham, BSc, 54; Cornell Univ, MS, 58, PhD(statist), 61. *Honors & Awards:* Brit Johnson Found Fel, 56; Woodrow Wilson Fel, 59. *Res:* Application of quantitative methods in biological research; animal behavior; epidemiological studies of violent behavior. *Mailing Add:* Dept Epidemiol Pub Health Case Western Res Sch Med 2119 Abington Cleveland OH 44106-2333

RUSHFORTH, SAMUEL ROBERTS, ENVIRONMENTAL SCIENCES, ENVIRONMENTAL POLICY. *Current Pos:* From asst prof to assoc prof, 70-80, PROF BOT, BRIGHAM YOUNG UNIV, 80- *Personal Data:* b Salt Lake City, Utah, Nov 24, 45; m 64; c 4. *Educ:* Weber State Col, BS, 66; Brigham Young Univ, MS, 68, PhD(bot), 70. *Mem:* Int Phycol Soc; Sigma Xi; Phycol Soc Am; Soc Conserv Biol. *Res:* Taxonomic and ecological investigation of the algae of western America; effects of pollutants on aquatic communities. *Mailing Add:* Dept Bot Brigham Young Univ 401 Widb Provo UT 84602-1049

RUSHING, ALLEN JOSEPH, CONTROL SYSTEMS. *Current Pos:* RES ASSOC, EASTMAN KODAK CO, 73- *Personal Data:* b Charlottesville, Va, Oct 23, 44; m 73; c 3. *Educ:* Univ Denver, BSEE, 66; Univ Mo-Rolla, MSEE, 70, PhD(elec eng), 73. *Prof Exp:* Elec engr instruments, Monsanto Co, 67-70. *Concurrent Pos:* Mem adj fac, Rochester Inst Technol, 75-87. *Mem:* Sr mem Inst Elec & Electronics Engrs. *Res:* Applications of control theory to electrophotography. *Mailing Add:* Eastman Kodak Co Off Imaging Res & Technol Develop 2nd Floor Bldg 6 Elmgrove Plant Rochester NY 14653-6402

RUSHING, FRANK C, ELECTRICAL ENGINEERING. *Current Pos:* RETIRED. *Personal Data:* b Nordheim, Tex, July 11, 06; m 34, Viola Clarke; c James C, Vernon C & Mary J. *Educ:* Univ Tex, BS, 28; Univ Pittsburgh, MS, 30. *Honors & Awards:* George Westinghouse Career Innovation Award, 94. *Prof Exp:* Eng consult, Westinghouse Corp, 28-90. *Mem:* Fel Am Soc Mech Engrs; fel Inst Elec & Electronics Engrs; Sigma Xi. *Mailing Add:* 6436 Belleview Dr Columbia MD 21046-1015

RUSHING, THOMAS BENNY, GEOMETRIC TOPOLOGY. *Current Pos:* from asst prof to assoc prof, 69-77, chmn dept, 85-93, PROF MATH, UNIV UTAH, 77-, DEAN, COL SCI, 93- *Personal Data:* b Marshville, NC, Oct 30, 41; m 62; c 2. *Educ:* Wake Forest Univ, BS, 64, MA, 65; Univ Ga, PhD(math), 68. *Prof Exp:* Asst prof math, Univ Ga, 68-69. *Concurrent Pos:* Vis prof, Univ Fla, 74 & 81; Nat Acad Sci exchange scientist, Univ Zagreb, Yugoslavia, 75-76 & 83; vis fel, Warwick Math Inst, Eng, 76; David P Gardner fac fel, Univ Utah, 77; visitor, Inst Math, Nat Univ, Mex, 82, Banach Math Ctr, Warsaw, Poland, 84 & Math Inst, Univ Heidelberg, Ger, 85; mem, Inst Advan Study, Princeton, 82-83 & 88-89. *Mem:* Am Math Soc; Math Asn Am. *Res:* Topology of manifolds; embedding problems; piecewise linear topology; fibrations and bundle theories, dynamical systems. *Mailing Add:* Col Sci 220 JTB Univ Utah Salt Lake City UT 84112-1107

RUSHMER, ROBERT FRAZER, BIOENGINEERING. *Current Pos:* from asst prof to prof physiol, Sch Med, Univ Wash, 47-68, prof bioeng, 68-86, dir, Ctr Advan Studies Biomed Sci, 78-84, EMER PROF BIOENG, UNIV WASH, 86- *Personal Data:* b Ogden, Utah, Nov 30, 14; m 42, Estella Dix; c Donald S, Anne & Betsy (Harris). *Educ:* Univ Chicago, BS, 35; Rush Med Col, MD, 39. *Hon Degrees:* PhD, Univ Linkoping, Sweden, 77, Inst Med, 81. *Honors & Awards:* Ida B Gould Award, AAAS, 62; Modern Med Award, 62; Pioneer Award Hist Med Ultrasound, 88. *Prof Exp:* Intern, St Luke's Hosp, San Francisco, 39-40; fel pediat, Mayo Found, Univ Minn, 40-42; assoc prof aviation med, Sch Med, Univ Southern Calif, 46-47. *Concurrent Pos:* Asst, Sch Aviation Med, Randolph Field, Tex, 41-42. *Mem:* Inst Med-Nat Acad Sci; Am Physiol Soc; Am Heart Asn; AAAS; hon fel Am Col Cardiol; Biomed Eng Soc; fel Int Asn Med & Biol Environ. *Res:* Comprehensive engineering analysis of cardiovascular function and control in intact, unanesthetized animals; non-invasive analysis of cardiovascular function in man. *Mailing Add:* 10901 176th Circle NE No 3526 Redmond WA 98052

RUSHTON, ALAN R, GENETICS, PEDIATRICS. *Current Pos:* ASSOC CLIN PROF PEDIAT, ROBERT W JOHNSON MED SCH, 80- *Personal Data:* b Oak Park, Ill, Mar 10, 49; m 73, Nancy Spencer; c Andrew & Daniel. *Educ:* Earlham Col, BA, 71; Univ Chicago, PhD(genetics), 75, MD, 77. *Prof Exp:* Resident pediat, Yale-New Haven Hosp, 77-80. *Concurrent Pos:* Pediatrician, Hunterdon Med Ctr, 80-; lectr human genetics, Princeton Univ, 80-84. *Mem:* Fel Am Acad Pediat; fel Am Col Med Genetics; Am Asn Hist Sci; fel NY Acad Med; Hist Sci Soc; fel Royal Soc Med. *Res:* Historical research; history of genetics in US and British medicine 1800 to 1939. *Mailing Add:* Dept Pediat Hunterdon Med Ctr Flemington NJ 08822

RUSHTON, BRIAN MANDEL, CHEMISTRY. *Current Pos:* VPRES RES & DEVELOP, AIR PROD & CHEM, INC, 81- *Personal Data:* b Sale, Eng, Nov 16, 33; m 58; c 3. *Educ:* Univ Salford, ARIC, 57; Univ Minn, MS, 59; Univ Leicester, PhD(chem), 63. *Prof Exp:* Sr res chemist, Petrolite Corp, 63-65, group leader, 65-66; sect mgr, Asland Chem Co, 66-69; corp res mgr, Hooker Chem Corp, 69-72, dir polymer & plastics res & develop, 72-74, vpres res & develop, 74-75; pres, Celanese Res Corp, 75-80, corp vpres-technol, 80-81. *Concurrent Pos:* Mem, Nat Mats Adv Bd, Nat Res Coun, Nat Acad Sci/Nat Acad Eng, 80-84; mem gov bd, Coun Chem Res, 81-87; mem, Life Sci Vis Comt, Lehigh Univ, 83-86; chairperson, Vis Comt, Ctr Surface & Coatings, 86-89; mem, Adv Comt Pa, Ben Franklin Prog, Northeast Tier, 86-88; mem bd trustees, Textile Res Inst, 86-89; mem bd dir, Indust Res Inst, 90- & Mich Molecular Inst, 91- *Mem:* Coun Chem Res (treas, 81-87); Textile Res Inst; Am Chem Soc; Soc Chem Indust; Indust Res Inst (pres-elect, 90-). *Res:* Polymer chemistry; general chemistry. *Mailing Add:* 3366 Bingen Rd Bethlehem PA 18015

RUSINKO, FRANK, JR, FUEL TECHNOLOGY & MATERIALS RESEARCH, MANAGEMENT. *Current Pos:* SR SCIENTIST & DIR, CARBON RES CTR, ENERGY & FUELS RES CTR, PA STATE UNIV, 91-; UTI Inc, 76-89, PRES & CHMN, EDIMAX TRANSOR, 82-, PRES, INTECH EDM ELECTROTOOLS, 89- *Personal Data:* b Nanticoke, Pa, Oct 12, 30; m 57, Lucy Geryak; c Nancy & Lawrence. *Educ:* Pa State Univ, BS, 52, MS, 54, PhD(fuel technol, phys chem), 58. *Prof Exp:* Res assoc, Pa State Univ, 58-59; scientist, Speer Carbon Co, Air Reduction Co, 59-61, mgr develop, Carbon Prod Div, 61-62; mgr develop, IGE Div, Airco, Inc, 62-67, dir develop & technol serv, 67-70, vpres & tech dir, Airco Speer Carbon-Graphite Div, 70-76; vchmn, Powder Tech, 85-86; pres, Electrotools, Inc, UTI, 76-89; pres & chmn Edimax Transor, 82-91; pres, Intech EDM Electrotoools, 89-91. *Concurrent Pos:* Bd mem, C-Cor Electronics, State Col, Pa, 90-; bd chmn, Transor Filter USA, Elk Grove Vill, Ill, 91. *Mem:* Am Chem Soc; Am Carbon Soc. *Res:* Carbon and graphite; gas-solid reactions; gas adsorption; coal carbonization; irradiation of coal and graphite; nuclear graphite; catalysis of heterogeneous carbon reactions; fuel cells; surface chemistry; research and development management; high temperature materials technology; electrical discharge machine technology, including electrode materials, accessories, dielectrics and dielectric oil filtration. *Mailing Add:* C204 Coal Utilization Lab Energy Fuels Res Ctr Pa State Univ University Park IL 16802-2323. *Fax:* 814-863-7432

RUSKAI, MARY BETH, MATHEMATICAL PHYSICS, OPERATOR THEORY. *Current Pos:* from asst prof to assoc prof, 77-86, PROF MATH, UNIV LOWELL, 86- *Personal Data:* b Cleveland, Ohio, Feb 26, 44. *Educ:* Notre Dame Col, Ohio, BS, 65; Univ Wis-Madison, MA, 69, PhD(chem), 69. *Prof Exp:* Battelle fel math physics, Theoret Physics Inst, Univ Geneva, 69-71; res assoc math, Mass Inst Technol, 71-72; res assoc theoret physics, Univ Alta, 72-73; asst prof math, Univ Ore, 73-76. *Concurrent Pos:* Consult, Bell Labs, NJ, 72, 83 & 88-89; vis asst prof, Rockefeller Univ, 80-81; guest prof, Univ Vienna, Austria, 81; sci scholar, Mary Ingraham Bunting Inst, 83-85; vis assoc math, Calif Inst Technol, 84; vis mem, Courant Inst Math Sci, NY Univ, 88-89; vis scientist, Inst Theoret Atomic & Molecular Physics, Harvard-Smithsonian Ctr Astrophys, 90; pres, Fac Senate, Univ Lowell, 90-91; vis prof, Univ Mich, 91-92. *Mem:* Am Math Soc; Math Asn Am; Am Phys Soc; Int Asn Math Physics; Asn Women in Math; Sigma Xi; fel AAAS. *Res:* Operator theory; statistical mechanic; multi-particle Coulomb system. *Mailing Add:* Univ Mass Lowell MA 01854. *E-Mail:* bruska@cs.uml.edu

RUSKIN, ARNOLD M(ILTON), PROJECT MANAGEMENT, SYSTEM ENGINEERING. *Current Pos:* network syst engr, Jet Propulsion Lab, Calif Inst Technol, 78-80, mgr network strategy develop, 80-86, dep mgr, Syst Eng Resource Ctr, 86-90, training mgr, Systs, Software & Opers Resource Ctr, 87-90, planning mgr, Cassini Proj, 91-94, mgr planning, assesment & integration, Pluto Express Preproj, 95-96, PROF MGR, ADMIN PROCESS ENG, CALIF INST TECHNOL, 96- *Personal Data:* b Bay City, Mich, Jan 4, 37. *Educ:* Univ Mich, BSE(chem eng) & BSE(mat eng), 58, MSE, 59, PhD(eng mat), 62; Claremont Grad Sch, MBE, 70. *Prof Exp:* Instr mat eng, Univ Mich, 61-62; lectr appl physics, Rugby Col Eng Technol, Eng, 62-63; from asst prof to prof eng, Harvey Mudd Col, 63-73; eng mgr, Everett/Charles, Inc, 73-74; vpres & prog mgr, Claremont Eng Co, 74-78. *Concurrent Pos:* Res engr, E I du Pont de Nemours & Co, Inc, 58; dir joint col & indust libr study, Harvey Mudd Col, 63-65; Union Oil Co fel eng, 66-73, asst dir, Freshman Div Fac, 71-72, dir, 72-73; assoc instnl res, Claremont Univ Ctr, 65-67, from assoc prof to prof econ & bus, Grad Sch, 70-73; fac fel, Pac Coast Banking Sch, Univ Wash, Seattle, 67; visitor, Prog Indust Metall & Mgt Techniques, Univ Aston, Birmingham, Eng, 69; continuing educ specialist, Univ Calif, Los Angeles, 74-84, lectr, 75-77, adj prof eng, 77-84, dir eng exec prog, 78-84; Zambelli fel, syst eng & proj mgt, Royal Melbourne Inst Technol, Australia, 90. *Mem:* Proj Mgt Inst; Am Soc Engr Mgt; assoc fel Am Inst Aeronaut & Astronaut; Am Inst Chem Engrs; Metall Soc; Am Soc Metals Int. *Res:* Engineering management; project management; system engineering methodology; risk management; strategic and tactical planning. *Mailing Add:* 4525 Castle Lane La Canada CA 91011-1436. *Fax:* 818-249-5811; *E-Mail:* 103673.3400@compuserve.com

RUSKIN, RICHARD A, OBSTETRICS & GYNECOLOGY. *Current Pos:* from instr to assoc prof, 52-72, PROF OBSTET & GYNEC, MED COL, CORNELL UNIV, 72- *Personal Data:* b New Rochelle, NY, Oct 1, 24; m 46, Clara L Johnson; c 1. *Educ:* Duke Univ, BA, 40, MD, 44; Am Bd Obstet & Gynec, dipl, 54. *Prof Exp:* Resident obstet & gynec, New York Lying-In-Hosp, 47-52. *Concurrent Pos:* Resident, Kings Co Hosp, New York, 46-47; resident, New York Polyclin Med Sch & Hosp, 47-52, clin prof, 65-; attend obstetrician & gynecologist, New York Lying-In-Hosp, 65-, attend, 72-, clin prof, 72, prof, 72; consult, Workmans Compensation Bd; attend obstet & gynec, Roosevelt Hosp, 76-; prof & attend, New York Polyclin Med Sch & Hosp, 65-76. *Mem:* Fel Am Col Obstet & Gynec; fel Am Col Surg; Geriat Soc Am. *Res:* Oxytocin and vasopressin in clinical obstetrics. *Mailing Add:* 415 E 52nd St New York NY 10022

RUSKIN, ROBERT EDWARD, ATMOSPHERIC PHYSICS. *Current Pos:* Physicist, Uranium Isotope Separation Proj, Naval Res Lab, 42-47, head instrument sect, Atmospheric Physics Br, 47-71, actg head, 71-72, asst head, 72-79. *Personal Data:* b Sioux Falls, SDak, Oct 30, 16; m 42; c 2. *Educ:* Kans State Col, AB, 40. *Honors & Awards:* Meritorious Civilian Serv Award, US Navy, 45, Superior Accomplishment Award, 65. *Concurrent Pos:* Vis prof, Colo State Univ, 70; consult atmospheric physicist, 82- *Mem:* Fel AAAS; Am Phys Soc; Sigma Xi; Am Meteorol Soc; fel Instrument Soc Am. *Res:* Cloud physics; physics of interactions of the atmosphere; aircraft instrumentation; air pollution; marine fog and haze interactions with electrooptical systems; marine salt aerosol in relation to gas turbine ship engines. *Mailing Add:* 1406 Ruffner Rd Alexandria VA 22302

RUSLING, JAMES FRANCIS, BIOELECTROCHEMISTRY & ELECTROCATALYSIS. *Current Pos:* asst prof, 79-85, assoc prof, 85-89, PROF ANALYTICAL CHEM, UNIV CONN, 90- *Personal Data:* b Philadelphia, Pa, Nov 4, 46; m, Penelope Williams; c Matthew. *Educ:* Drexel Univ, BSc, 69; Clarkson Univ, PhD(anal chem), 79. *Prof Exp:* Spectroscopist anal chem, Sadtler Res Co, 72-73; anal chemist, Wyeth Labs, 73-76. *Concurrent Pos:* Mem, Inst Mat Sci & Environ Res Inst, Univ Conn, 81- *Mem:* Am Chem Soc; Am Asn Univ Profs; Electrochem Soc; Soc Electroanal Chem. *Res:* Development of electrocatalytic systems in organized media for redox transformations of organic compounds; applications of such systems to destroying pollutants and modeling of biological redox events; development of biosensors; development of computerized methods for data interpretation. *Mailing Add:* Chem Dept Univ Conn Box U 60 Storrs CT 06269-3060. *Fax:* 860-486-2981; *E-Mail:* jrusling@nucleus.chem.uconn.edu

RUSOFF, IRVING ISADORE, NUTRITION. *Current Pos:* CONSULT, 85- *Personal Data:* b Newark, NJ, Jan 29, 15; m 41, 87, Lillian Skora; c Susan & Arnold. *Educ:* Univ Fla, BS, 37, MS, 39; Univ Minn, PhD(physiol chem), 43. *Honors & Awards:* Charles N Frey Award, Am Asn Cereal Chemists, 84. *Prof Exp:* Asst, Nutrit Lab, Exp Sta, Univ Fla, 37-39, asst dairy res, 39-40; fels, Nat Found Infantile Paralysis, Univ Minn, 43-44, Off Sci Res & Develop, 44-45 & US Naval Ord, 45-46; head nutrit lab, Stand Brands, Inc, 46-47; head biochem sect, Res Ctr, Gen Foods Corp, 47-57, head nutrit sect, 57-61, group leader fats & oils, 61-62; mgr res & res serv, DCA Food Industs, 62-63; mgr nutrit & biochem & coordr spec proj res, Beech-Nut Life Savers, Inc, 63-66; head biol sci & asst to res dir, Nat Biscuit Co, 66-67, mgr develop res, 67-68; dir basic studies, Nabisco Brands Inc, 68-70, dir sci, 71-76, sr scientist, 76-85, dir nutrit sci, 78-85. *Concurrent Pos:* Assoc ed, Am Oil Chemists Soc J, 60-62; mem, ad hoc comt food sci abstracts, Food & Nutrit Bd, Nat Res Coun, 79-80, mem chmn indust, Laison Panel, 79-83; chmn & liason, Nat Inventors Hall of Fame, Inst Food Technologists, 80-; chmn, Food & Nutrit Conf, Gordon Res Conf, 81. *Mem:* Am Chem Soc; Am Inst Nutrit; fel Inst Food Technologists; NY Acad Sci; Am Pub Health Asn; Am Asn Cereal Chemists. *Res:* Human and animal nutrition; vitamin and mineral metabolism; trace elements and nutrients; biomedicine. *Mailing Add:* 65 Central Blvd Brick NJ 08724-2451

RUSOFF, LOUIS LEON, ANIMAL NUTRITION, NUTRITION. *Current Pos:* RETIRED. *Personal Data:* b Newark, NJ, Dec 23, 10; m 45, Sylvia Levin; c Gail & Marsha. *Educ:* Rutgers Univ, BS, 31; Pa State Col, MS, 32; Univ Minn, PhD(agr biochem, nutrit), 40. *Honors & Awards:* Charles E Coates Award, Am Chem Soc, 59; Borden Award, Am Dairy Sci Asn, 65; Hon Scroll, Am Inst Chem, 82. *Prof Exp:* Asst, Nutrit Lab, Exp Sta, Univ Fla, 32-35, lab asst & instr animal nutrit, 35-37, asst & asst prof, 37-42; assoc dairy nutritionist, Exp Sta, La State Univ, Baton Rouge, 42-50, assoc prof dairy nutrit, 48-50, prof dairy nutrit & dairy nutritionist, 50-81. *Mem:* AAAS; Am Chem Soc; Am Soc Animal Sci; Am Dairy Sci Asn; Am Inst Nutrit. *Res:* Vitamin assays; minerals and alkaloids; biochemistry of blood; trace elements in animal nutrition; milk analysis; feeding and digestion trials; molasses; urea feeding; antibiotics in food and silage preservation; fluoridation of milk; nutritive value of aquatic plants as foodstuffs for animals and man. *Mailing Add:* 1704 Myrtledale Ave Baton Rouge LA 70808-2868

RUSS, CHARLES ROGER, INORGANIC CHEMISTRY. *Current Pos:* asst prof, 65-71, ASSOC PROF CHEM, UNIV MAINE, ORONO, 71- *Personal Data:* b New London, Wis, July 2, 37; m 61; c 3. *Educ:* Marquette Univ, BS, 59, MS, 61; Univ Pa, PhD(chem), 65. *Prof Exp:* Asst chem, Marquette Univ, 59-61 & Univ Pa, 61-65. *Mem:* Am Chem Soc. *Res:* Synthesis and properties of silicon or germanium compounds. *Mailing Add:* Dept Chem Univ Maine 333 Aubery Hall Orono ME 04473

RUSS, DAVID PERRY, TECTONIC GEOMORPHOLOGY, QUATERNARY GEOLOGY. *Current Pos:* GEOLOGIST, US GEOL SURV, 75- *Personal Data:* b Wilmington, Del, May 7, 45. *Educ:* Pa State Univ, BS, 67, PhD(geol), 75; WVa Univ, MS, 69. *Prof Exp:* Geologist, Waterways Exp Sta, US Army Corps Engrs, 70-72. *Mem:* Geol Soc Am. *Res:* Geological and geophysical investigations of earthquake hazards; seismotectonics of the New Madrid seismic zone. *Mailing Add:* 2363 Venetion Ct Reston VA 20191

RUSS, GERALD A, NUCLEAR MEDICINE. *Current Pos:* ASST PROF RADIOL, UNIV ROCHESTER MED CTR, 82-; HEAD RADIOPHARM, DIV NUCLEAR MED, STRONG MEM HOSP, 82- *Personal Data:* b Washington, DC, Oct 17, 36; m 65, Lana Cohen; c David, Daniel & Joseph. *Educ:* Univ Md, BS, 64; Georgetown Univ, PhD(biochem), 74. *Prof Exp:* Res asst physiol, Georgetown Univ, 62-64; res technician cytogenetics, Radiol Health, USPHS, 64; res assoc biochem, Georgetown Univ, 64-72; res assoc biophys, mem Sloan-Kettering Cancer Ctr, 73-76, assoc biophys, 76-82. *Concurrent Pos:* Instr biophys, Sloan-Kettering Div, Grad Sch Med Sci, Cornell Univ, 74-77, asst prof biophys, 77-82, asst prof pharmacol exp ther, 80-82. *Mem:* Am Chem Soc; Soc Nuclear Med; NY Acad Sci. *Res:* Distribution and kinetics of radiolabeled compounds and the physiological interpretations of these; emphasis on short-lived, gamma-emitting compounds. *Mailing Add:* Dept Nuclear Med Univ Rochester Med Ctr PO Box 620 Rochester NY 14642. *Fax:* 716-273-1022; *E-Mail:* russ@rad.rochester.edu

RUSS, GUSTON PRICE, III, MASS SPECTROMETRY, ISOTOPE GEOCHEMISTRY. *Current Pos:* CHEMIST, LAWRENCE LIVERMORE NAT LAB, 81- *Personal Data:* b Mobile, Ala, Apr 5, 46; m 71; c 2. *Educ:* Univ of the South, BA, 68; Calif Inst Technol, PhD(chem), 74. *Prof Exp:* Fel, Univ Calif, San Diego, 74-77; asst prof chem, Univ Hawaii, 77-81. *Mem:* Am Geophys Union. *Res:* Nuclear geochemistry; lunar regolith studies; inductively coupled plasma mass spectrometry; chronology; isotope ratio mass spectrometry; environmental analytical chemistry. *Mailing Add:* Lawrence Livermore Nat Lab MS L-231 PO Box 808 Livermore CA 94550

RUSS, JAMES STEWART, HIGH ENERGY PHYSICS. *Current Pos:* from asst prof to assoc prof, 67-80, PROF PHYSICS, CARNEGIE-MELLON UNIV, 80- *Personal Data:* b Canton, Ohio, Aug 22, 40; m 63, 81; c 3. *Educ:* Ind Univ, BS, 62; Princeton Univ, MA, 64, PhD(physics), 66. *Prof Exp:* Instr physics, Princeton Univ, 66-67. *Concurrent Pos:* Vis scientist, Cern, 85-86. *Mem:* Am Phys Soc; Sigma Xi; Am Asn Physics Teachers. *Res:* Elementary particle physics; experiments using electronic detectors; computer-oriented data-handling systems; computer simulation of experimental data. *Mailing Add:* Dept Physics Carnegie-Mellon Univ Schenley Park Pittsburgh PA 15213

RUSSEK, ARNOLD, PHYSICS. *Current Pos:* from asst prof to assoc prof, 55-65, PROF PHYSICS, UNIV CONN, 65- *Personal Data:* b New York, NY, July 13, 26; m 56; c 2. *Educ:* City Col New York, BS, 47; NY Univ, MS, 48, PhD(physics), 53. *Prof Exp:* Instr physics, Univ Buffalo, 53-55. *Mem:* Fel Am Phys Soc. *Res:* Nuclear structure; atomic structure and atomic collisions; electromagnetic diffraction theory. *Mailing Add:* Rte 175 Campton NH 03223

RUSSEK-COHEN, ESTELLE, MULTIVARIATE METHODS, BIOASSAY METHODS. *Current Pos:* asst prof, 78-83, ASSOC PROF BIOSTATIST, UNIV MD, 83- *Personal Data:* b Brooklyn, NY, July 23, 51; m; c 1. *Educ:* State Univ NY, Stony Brook, BS, 72; Univ Wash, Seattle, PhD(biomath), 79. *Prof Exp:* Programmer, NY Life Ins, 72-73; res asst biostat, Univ Wash, 73-75, teaching asst, 75-76, instr, 77-78. *Concurrent Pos:* Consult, Univ Md Sea Grant Prog & Joint Consult Lab, USDA, Univ Md, 81- *Mem:* Am Statist Asn; Biomet Soc; Classification Soc. *Res:* Biostatistics. *Mailing Add:* Dept Animal Sci Univ Md College Park MD 20742-0001

RUSSEL, DARRELL ARDEN, AGRONOMY. *Current Pos:* RETIRED. *Personal Data:* b McPherson, Kans, May 26, 21; m 49; c 9. *Educ:* Kans State Univ, BS, 43; Univ Ill, MS, 47, PhD(soil fertil, anal chem), 55. *Prof Exp:* Spec asst soil fertil, Univ Ill, 46-47, asst soils, 51-55; instr soils, Iowa State Univ, 47-49, dist exten dir, Agr Exten Serv, 49-51; asst prof soil chem, N La Hill Farm Exp Sta, La State Univ, 55-60; agriculturist, Div Agr Develop, Tenn Valley Authority, 60-78, asst adminr, Int Fertilizer Prog, 78-81, head, Educ & Commun Serv Staff, Div Agr Develop, Nat Fertilizer Develop Ctr, 81-82. *Concurrent Pos:* AID consult, Morocco, 66, Bolivia, 69, Paraguay, 70, Indonesia, 71, Ghana, 72 & 74, Cent Treaty Orgn, 74, UN India Develop Orgn, 76 & Int Fertilizer Develop Ctr, 81. *Mem:* Fel Soil Sci Soc Am; fel Am Soc Agron; Crop Sci Soc Am; Am Chem Soc; Coun Agr Sci & Technol. *Res:* Analytical procedures for soil testing; effect of fertilizers on soil fertility, crop growth and crop quality; fertilizer education. *Mailing Add:* 501 W Cleveland Ave Florence AL 35630

RUSSEL, MARJORIE ELLEN, MOLECULAR GENETICS. *Current Pos:* fel genetics, 77-87, asst prof, 87-92, ASSOC PROF, ROCKEFELLER UNIV, 92- *Personal Data:* b New York, NY, July 16, 44; m 81; c 1. *Educ:* Oberlin Col, BA, 66; Univ Wis, MS, 68; Univ Colo, PhD(molecular biol), 77. *Prof Exp:* Res asst molecular biol, Dept Genetics, Univ Wash, 68-70 & Dept Molecular Biol, Univ Geneva, 71-73. *Concurrent Pos:* Damon Runyon-Walter Winchell Cancer Fund fel, 77-78. *Mem:* Am Soc Microbiol; Am Soc Virol. *Res:* Control of gene expression in prokaryotes; mechanisms of protein transport into and across bacterial membranes. *Mailing Add:* Rockefeller Univ Dept Genetics 1230 York Ave New York NY 10021

RUSSEL, WILLIAM BAILEY, COLLOID SCIENCE. *Current Pos:* from asst prof to assoc prof, 74-83, chmn chem eng, 87-96, PROF CHEM ENG, PRINCETON UNIV, 83-, DIR, PRINCETON MAT INST, 96- *Personal Data:* b Corpus Christi, Tex, Nov 17, 45; m 72; c 2. *Educ:* Rice Univ, BA & MChE, 69; Stanford Univ, PhD(chem eng), 73. *Honors & Awards:* William H Walker Award, Am Inst Chem Engrs, 92. *Prof Exp:* NATO fel appl math, Dept Appl Math & Theoret Physics, Cambridge Univ, 73-74. *Concurrent Pos:* Olaf A Hougen prof, Univ Wis, 84. *Mem:* Nat Acad Eng; Soc Rheology; Am Inst Chem Engrs; Am Chem Soc; Mat Res Soc. *Res:* Fluid mechanics; colloidal suspensions; polymer solutions. *Mailing Add:* Dept Chem Eng Princeton Univ Princeton NJ 08544

RUSSELL, ALAN JAMES, APPLIED ENZYMOLOGY, PROTEIN ENGINEERING. *Current Pos:* PROF CHEM ENG, UNIV PITTSBURGH, 89-, ASSOC DIR, CTR BIOTECHNOL, PROF BIOCHEM & MOLECULAR BIOL, UNIV PITTSBURGH MED CTR, CHMN, DEPT CHEM ENG. *Personal Data:* b Salford, Eng, Aug 8, 62; m 87, Janice Quoresimo; c Hannah & Vincent. *Educ:* Univ March Inst Technol Brit, BS, 84, Imp Col, PhD, 87, DIC, 87. *Prof Exp:* NATO fel chem, Mass Inst Technol, 87-89. *Concurrent Pos:* NSF presidential young investr, 90; assoc dir, Pittsburgh Tissue Eng Initiative Inc. *Mem:* Am Chem Soc; Am Inst Chem Engrs; Biochem Soc; Tissue Eng Soc. *Res:* Study of enzymes in extreme environments; using protein engineering to design enzymes in organic solvents and at high temperatures and pressures; design of biomaterials for tissue engineering. *Mailing Add:* 113 Foxwood Dr Wexford PA 15090-7100. *Fax:* 412-624-9639; *E-Mail:* ajrchet@pitt.edu

RUSSELL, ALLAN MELVIN, PHYSICS. *Current Pos:* assoc prof, Hobart & William Smith Cols, 67-70, assoc provost, 67-68, provost & dean fac, 68-72, PROF PHYSICS, HOBART & WILLIAM SMITH COLS, 70- *Personal Data:* b Newark, NJ, Feb 2, 30; m 51; c 5. *Educ:* Brown Univ, ScB, 51, ScM, 53; Syracuse Univ, PhD(physics), 57. *Prof Exp:* Res assoc physics, Syracuse Univ, 57-58; asst prof, Univ Calif, 58-64; assoc prof, Wesleyan Univ, 64-67. *Mem:* Am Phys Soc; Am Asn Physics Teachers; Sigma Xi. *Res:* Low energy electron diffraction; field emission; measurement; molecular beams; paleomagnetism; epistemology; philosophy of science. *Mailing Add:* Hobart & Wm Smith Cols Physics Dept Geneva NY 14456

RUSSELL, ALLEN STEVENSON, CHEMISTRY, ENGINEERING. *Current Pos:* RETIRED. *Personal Data:* b Bedford, Pa, May 27, 15; m 41. *Educ:* Pa State Univ, BS, 36, MS, 37, PhD(phys chem), 41. *Honors & Awards:* Karl J Bayer Medallist, 81; Gold Medal, Am Soc Metals, 82; Chem Pioneer Award, 83; James Douglas Gold Medal, 87. *Prof Exp:* Chemist, Bell Tel Labs, 37; asst, Pa State Univ, 37-40; chemist, Aluminum Co Am, 40-44, asst chief, Phys Chem Div, 44-53, chief, 53-55 & Process Metall Div, 55-69, asst dir res, 69-74, assoc dir, 74, vpres, 74-78, vpres sci & technol, 78-81, vpres & chief scientist, Alcoa Labs, 81-82. *Concurrent Pos:* Adj prof, Univ Pittsburgh. *Mem:* Nat Acad Eng; Am Chem Soc; fel Am Soc Metals; Sigma Xi; fel Am Inst Mining, Metall & Petrol Engrs. *Res:* Process metallurgy of aluminum. *Mailing Add:* Nine N Caliboque Cay Rd Hilton Head Island SC 29928

RUSSELL, ANTHONY PATRICK, HERPETOLOGY, MAMMALOGY. *Current Pos:* asst prof, Univ Calgary, 73-80, assoc prof biol, 80-87, asst dean, 85-89, ASSOC DEAN FAC SCI, UNIV CALGARY, 89-, PROF BIOL, 87- *Personal Data:* b London, Eng, Sept 10, 47; m 70; c 3. *Educ:* Univ Exeter, BSc, 69; Univ London, PhD(zool), 72. *Prof Exp:* Lectr zool, Univ Botswana, Lesotho & Swaziland, 73. *Concurrent Pos:* Res assoc, Dept Herpetol, Royal Ont Mus, 80-, Royal Tyrrell Mus Paleont, Drumheller, Alta, 87- *Mem:* Am Soc Zoologists; Soc Syst Biol; Linnean Soc London; Zool Soc London; Can Soc Zoologists; Soc Study Evolution; Am Soc Ichthyol & Herpetol; Herpetol League; Paleontol Soc; Soc Preserv Nat Hist Collections. *Res:* Investigation of the functional biology and evolutionary morphology of reptiles and mammals, particularly locomotor and feeding mechanisms. *Mailing Add:* Dept Biol Sci Univ Calgary 2500 University Dr NW Calgary AB T2N 1N4 Can

RUSSELL, B DON, ELECTRIC POWER SYSTEMS, REAL-TIME COMPUTER CONTROL. *Current Pos:* RES ENGR, TEX ENG EXP STA, 76-, PROF ELEC ENG, 88-, ASSOC DEAN ENG, 94- *Personal Data:* b Denison, Tex, May 25, 48; m 73; c 4. *Educ:* Tex A&M Univ, BS, 70, ME, 71; Univ Okla, PhD(elec eng), 75. *Honors & Awards:* Outstanding Achievement Award, Nat Soc Prof Engrs. *Prof Exp:* Instr elec eng, Tex A&M Univ, 70-71; instr physics, Abilene Christian Univ, 71-73; instr elec eng, Univ Okla, 73-75; res engr power systs, Okla Gas & Elec, & Elec Power Res Inst, 75; from asst prof to prof, Tex A&M Univ, 76-88. *Concurrent Pos:* Consult numerous indust orgns, 73-90; prin investr, Tex A&M Univ Res Found, 76-90; pres, Micon Eng, Inc, 77-90; assoc dir, Inst for Ventures & New Technol, 83-85; assoc ed, Elec Power Systs Res, 85-90. *Mem:* Fel Inst Elec & Electronics Engrs; sr mem Power Eng Soc; Instrument Soc Am. *Res:* Applications of advanced computer technology to solution of power systems problems; automation, control and protection of power systems; development of fault detection systems for power lines to improve efficiency and safety of power system operation. *Mailing Add:* Dept Elec Eng Tex A&M Univ College Station TX 77846

RUSSELL, BRENDA, ANATOMY, PHYSIOLOGY. *Current Pos:* PROF, UNIV ILL, 88-, ASSOC DEAN GRAD EDUC, 94- *Personal Data:* b Eng, Oct 11, 42; m 64; 93; c 4. *Educ:* Univ London, BSc, 65, PhD(physiol), 71. *Prof Exp:* Teaching fel, Univ Calif, Los Angeles, 71-72, asst res biochemist, 72-74, adj asst prof med, 74-76; from asst prof & prof physiol, Rush Med Col, 76-83, dir, Cell Biol Dept, 78-88. *Concurrent Pos:* Vis prof, Univ Chicago, 85-86; assoc ed, Am J Anat, 85-92; ed, Am J Physiol Cell, 93-97. *Mem:* Am Soc Cell Biol; Biophys Soc; Am Asn Antomists; Am Heart Asn; Am Physiol Soc; Am Col Sports Med. *Res:* Adaption of muscle structure to function; cell and molecular biology. *Mailing Add:* Dept Physiol Univ Ill 835 S Wolcott Ave M/C 901 Chicago IL 60612-7342. *Fax:* 312-996-6312; *E-Mail:* russell@uic.edu

RUSSELL, CATHERINE MARIE, MEDICAL MICROBIOLOGY, MEDICAL PARASITOLOGY. *Current Pos:* from instr to assoc prof microbiol, 48-77, from assoc prof to prof clin path, 63-77, EMER PROF PATH, MED SCH, UNIV VA, 77- *Personal Data:* b Tuckahoe, NY, Nov 20, 10. *Educ:* Col of Mt St Vincent, BS, 32; Columbia Univ, MA, 48; Univ Va, PhD(biol), 51; Am Bd Med Microbiol, dipl. *Prof Exp:* Technician, Res & Diag Labs, State Dept Health, NY, 39-41; technician, New York Med Col, 41-42, instr bact & parasitol, 42-48. *Mem:* Am Soc Trop Med & Hyg; Am Soc Parasitol; Am Soc Microbiol; Sigma Xi. *Res:* Trematode infections; development of the egg of Plagitura salamandra; leptospirosis; pathogenesis and identification of the organism; virus-cell relationship. *Mailing Add:* 511 N First St No 505 Charlottesville VA 22901

RUSSELL, CHARLES ADDISON, POLYMER CHEMISTRY, ANALYTICAL CHEMISTRY. *Current Pos:* mem tech staff, 59-66, supvr atmospheric effects, microchem & contact group, 66-83, DIST RES MGR, BELL COMMUN RES, 84- *Personal Data:* b Danielson, Conn, Jan 12, 21; m 47; c 3. *Educ:* Yale Univ, BSc, 42, MSc, 44, PhD(org chem), 49. *Prof Exp:* Assoc prof phys chem, Bucknell Univ, 48-52; chemist, Nat Lead Co, 52-59. *Mem:* AAAS; Am Chem Soc. *Res:* Effects of contamination on telephone equipment; interaction of various materials with environment and each other; behavior of telephone contacts. *Mailing Add:* 106 Kenley Way Sun City Center FL 33573

RUSSELL, CHARLES BRADLEY, MATHEMATICS, STATISTICS. *Current Pos:* Asst prof, 67-72, ASSOC PROF MATH SCI, CLEMSON UNIV, 72- *Personal Data:* b Evanston, Ill, Apr 8, 40; m 68. *Educ:* Univ of the South, BA, 62; Fla State Univ, MS, 63, PhD(statist), 68. *Mem:* Inst Math Statist; Am Statist Asn; Opers Res Soc Am; Inst Mgt Sci. *Res:* Probability theory; stochastic processes; management science. *Mailing Add:* Dept Math Sci Clemson Univ Clemson SC 29634-1907

RUSSELL, CHARLES CLAYTON, NEMATOLOGY, ENTOMOLOGY. *Current Pos:* RETIRED. *Personal Data:* b Key West, Fla, Oct 9, 37; m 58; c 2. *Educ:* Univ Fla, BSA, 60, MSA, 62, PhD(nematol), 67. *Prof Exp:* Nematologist, Okla State Univ, 67-, prof, Dept Plant Path, 80- *Mem:* Am Phytopath Soc; Soc Nematol; Sigma Xi. *Res:* Plant parasitic; free-living nematodes. *Mailing Add:* RR2 PO Box 70 Glencoe OK 74032

RUSSELL, CHARLES ROBERTS, ENERGY SOURCES. *Current Pos:* CONSULT, 80- *Personal Data:* b Spokane, Wash, July 13, 14; m 43, Dolores Kopriva; c Ann E, John C, David F & Thomas R. *Educ:* Wash State Univ, BS, 36; Univ Wis, PhD(chem eng), 41. *Prof Exp:* Engr, div reactor develop, Atomic Energy Comn, Washington, 50-56, Gen Motors Tech Ctr, Warren, Mich & Santa Barbara, Calif, 56-68; assoc dean eng, Calif Polytech State Univ, 68-73, prof mech eng, 73-80. *Concurrent Pos:* secy adv comn reactor safeguards, AEC, 50-55; mem nuclear stand bd, Am Nat Stand Inst, 56-78. *Mem:* Am Chem Soc. *Res:* Author of four books. *Mailing Add:* 3071 Marilyn Way Santa Barbara CA 93105-2040

RUSSELL, CHARLOTTE SANANES, BIOCHEMISTRY, ORGANIC CHEMISTRY. *Current Pos:* from instr to assoc prof, 54-72, PROF CHEM, CITY COL NEW YORK, 72- *Personal Data:* b Brooklyn, NY, Jan 4, 27; m 47, Joseph B; c James R & Joshua S. *Educ:* Brooklyn Col, AB, 46; Columbia Univ, AM, 47, PhD(org chem), 51. *Prof Exp:* Lectr org chem, Brooklyn Col, 49; res assoc biochem, Col Physicians & Surgeons, Columbia Univ, 51-54. *Concurrent Pos:* Vis asst prof, Col Physicians & Surgeons, Columbia Univ, 63-64; prin investr, res grants; reviewer, prof journals & granting agencies. *Mem:* Sigma Xi; AAAS; Am Chem Soc; Am Soc Biochem & Molecular Biol. *Res:* Biochemistry of heme compounds; enzymology of heme biosynthesis; invertebrate lectins; lipid hemagglutinins; solid state reactions in organic chemistry. *Mailing Add:* Dept Chem City Col New York New York NY 10031. *E-Mail:* chrcc@cunyvm.cuny.edu

RUSSELL, CHRISTOPHER THOMAS, PLANETARY MAGNETISM, MAGNETOPHERIC PHYSICS. *Current Pos:* Res geophysicist, 68-81, PROF GEOPHYS, INST GEOPHYS & PLANETARY PHYSICS, UNIV CALIF, LOS ANGELES, 82- *Personal Data:* b London, Eng, May 9, 43; m 66, Arlene Ann Thompson; c Jennifer A & Danielle S. *Educ:* Univ Toronto, BSc, 64; Univ Calif, Los Angeles, PhD(space physics), 68. *Honors & Awards:* Macelwane Award; Harold Jeffreys lectr, Royal Astron Soc, 87. *Concurrent Pos:* Prin investr, Int Sun Earth Explorer, 72-87; mem, USNC Int Union Radio Sci, 75-81; prin investr, Pioneer Venus Orbiter, 75-94; assoc ed, J Geophys Res, 76-78, Geophys Res Letter, 79-81, ed, Solar Wind Three, 74, Auroral Processes, 79, IMS Source Book, 82, Space Sci Revs, 83-, Planetary & Space Sci, 84-, Solar Wind Interactions, 86, Multipoint Magnetoshperic Measurements, 88, Physics of magnetic fluxropes, 90, Venus Aeronomy, 91, Galileo Mission, 92, Global Geospace Mission, 95, Introduction to Space Physics & Physics of Collisionless Shocks, 95-; chair, NAS/Space Sci Bd Comt on Data Mgmt & Comput, 85-88; chair, Int Sci Comn D Cospar, 82-86 & NASA, Planetary Sci Data Steering Group, 84-85 & 92-95; pres, Solar Terrestrial Relationships Sect, Am Geophys Union, 88-90; interdisciplinary scientist, Galileo mission, 77-, prin invest, Polar Mission, 83- *Mem:* Fel Am Geophys Union; Int Astron Union; fel AAAS; Am Astron Soc; Europ Geophys Soc; assoc Royal Astronomical Soc. *Res:* Magnetospheric physics; solar-terrestrial relationships; planetary and terrestrial lightning; planetary magnetospheres; heliospheric physics; sun-earth connections; space weather; planetary magnetic fields. *Mailing Add:* Inst Geophys & Planetary Physics Univ Calif Los Angeles CA 90095-1567. *Fax:* 310-206-3051; *E-Mail:* ctrussell@igpp.ucla.edu

RUSSELL, DALE A, VERTEBRATE PALEONTOLOGY. *Current Pos:* SR CUR PALEONT, NC STATE UNIV MUS NATURAL SCI, 95- *Personal Data:* b San Francisco, Calif, Dec 27, 37; m 64; c 3. *Educ:* Univ Ore, BA, 58; Univ Calif, Berkeley, MA, 60; Columbia Univ, PhD(geol), 64. *Honors & Awards:* Bancroft Award, Royal Soc Can, 96- *Prof Exp:* NSF fel, Yale Univ, 64-65; cur fossil vert, Mus Nature, Nat Mus Can, 65-77, chief, Paleobiol Div, 77-95. *Concurrent Pos:* Vis prof, Dept Marine, Earth & Atmospheric Sci, NC State Univ, 95- *Mem:* Soc Vert Paleont. *Res:* Mesozoic, particularly Cretaceous, reptiles; Cretaceous-Tertiary boundary problems. *Mailing Add:* NC State Univ Mus Natural Sci PO Box 29555 Raleigh NC 07695-8208

RUSSELL, DAVID A, AERONAUTICAL & ASTRONAUTICAL ENGINEERING, ENGINEERING PHYSICS. *Current Pos:* res assoc prof, Univ Wash, 67-70, assoc prof, 70-74, chair dept, 77-92, PROF AERONAUT & ASTRONAUT, UNIV WASH, 74- *Personal Data:* b St John, NB, April 25, 35; US citizen; m 57, Hazel Garnett; c Karen, Kristen & Kathryn. *Educ:* Univ Southern Calif, BEng, 56; Calif Inst Technol, MSc, 57, PhD(aeronauts & physics), 61. *Prof Exp:* Sr scientist, Jet Propulsion Lab, Calif Inst Technol, 61-67. *Concurrent Pos:* Consult, pvt firms & govt labs, 67-; prin investr, NASA, 69-72, 84-86 & 95-96, Dept Defense, 69-71 & 73-81, indust, 85-86 & 91-95; mem, Plasma Dynamics Tech Comt, Am Inst Aeronaut & Astronaut, 70-72 & 86-92; mem Kirkland Planning Comn, Wash, 71-79, chair, 77-79, chair, Kirkland Land Use Policy Plan Comn, 77-79, mem City Coun, 84-, mayor of Kirkland, 92-96; exec coun, Fluid Dynamics Div, Am Phys Soc, 77. *Mem:* Fel Am Phys Soc; fel Am Inst Aeronaut & Astronaut. *Res:* Fluid mechanics and gas physics with applications to aerodynamics, shock processes and gas lasers. *Mailing Add:* 4507 105th Ave NE Kirkland WA 98033

RUSSELL, DAVID L, MATHEMATICS. *Current Pos:* FAC, VA POLYTECH INST. *Personal Data:* b Orlando, Fla, May 1, 39; m 60; c 2. *Educ:* Andrews Univ, BA, 60; Univ Minn, PhD(math), 64. *Prof Exp:* From asst prof to assoc prof math & comput sci, Univ Wis-Madison, 64-77, prof L&S math, 77- *Concurrent Pos:* Res consult, Honeywell, Inc, 63-6. *Mem:* Am Math Soc; Soc Indust & Appl Math. *Res:* Control theory of ordinary and partial differential equations; asymptotic theory of ordinary differential equations. *Mailing Add:* Math Dept Va Polytech Inst & State Univ 418 McBryde Hall Blacksburg VA 24061-4002

RUSSELL, DENNIS C, MATHEMATICAL ANALYSIS & APPROXIMATION THEORY. *Current Pos:* chmn dept, 62-69, prof, 62-89, EMER PROF MATH, YORK UNIV, 89- *Personal Data:* b Southampton, Eng, Sept 4, 27; m 51, Joyce Brown; c Julian & Jeremy. *Educ:* Univ Sheffield, BSc, 48; Univ London, MSc, 52, PhD(math anal), 58, DSc, 72. *Prof Exp:* Asst lectr math, Northampton Col Advan Technol, 48-52; demonstr, Univ Col London, 53-55; asst lectr, Keele Univ, 55-57, lectr, 57-60; assoc prof, Mt Allison Univ, 60-62. *Concurrent Pos:* Nat Res Coun Can sr res fel, 68; Can Coun leave fel, 69 & 76-77; hon res fel, Birkbeck Col, London, 68-69; Ger Acad Exchange Serv res fel, 71; Nuffield Found res travel award, 73 & Nat Sci Eng Res Coun Can travel grants, 76, 80 & 83, collaborative res grant, 82, res operating grants, 69-91; consult grad prog, Univ Calgary, 78; vis prof, Tel-Aviv Univ, 81. *Mem:* Am Math Soc; Math Asn Am; Can Math Soc; London Math Soc; fel Inst Math & Applns. *Res:* Mathematical analysis; matrix transformations on sequence spaces, and summability of sequences, series and integrals; approximation theory; inequalities. *Mailing Add:* Dept Math York Univ Toronto ON M3J 1P3 Can

RUSSELL, DONALD GLENN, PETROLEUM ENGINEERING. *Current Pos:* CHMN & CHIEF EXEC OFFICER, SONAT EXPLOR CO, 88-, EXEC VPRES, SONAT INC, 91- *Personal Data:* b Kansas City, Mo, Nov 24, 31; m 53; c 2. *Educ:* Sam Houston State Univ, BS, 53; Univ Okla, MA, 55. *Honors & Awards:* John Franklin Carll Award, Soc Petrol Engrs, Am Inst Mining Metall & Petrol Engrs, 80, Cedric K Ferguson Medal & DeGolyer Medal. *Prof Exp:* Var eng assignments, Tex, La & NY, Shell Oil, 56-72, gen mgr, info & comput serv, Houston, 72-76, vpres corp planning, 77-78, vpres, Int Explor & Prod, 78-80, vpres prod, Houston, 80-87. *Concurrent Pos:* Mem bd dirs, Am Petrol Inst. *Mem:* Nat Acad Eng; Nat Gas Supply Asn; Am Petrol Asn; Soc Petrol Engrs; Am Inst Mining Metall & Petrol Engrs (vpres, 73, pres, 74). *Mailing Add:* Sonat Exploration Co PO Box 1513 Houston TX 77251-1513

RUSSELL, DOUGLAS STEWART, ANALYTICAL CHEMISTRY, TRACE INORGANIC ANALYSIS. *Current Pos:* RETIRED. *Personal Data:* b Georgetown, Ont, June 16, 16; m 45, Loreen Myers; c Margaret, Robert & Donald. *Educ:* Univ Toronto, BA, 40, MA, 41. *Honors & Awards:* Fisher Sci Lectr Award, Chem Inst Can, 79. *Prof Exp:* Asst chem, Univ Toronto, 40-42; supvr anal chem, Welland Chem Works, Ltd, 42-44; asst res officer radiochem, Can Atomic Energy Proj, 44-46; asst res officer, Nat Res Coun Can, 46-51, sr res officer, 52-70, head anal sect, Div Chem, 52-81, prin res officer, 70-81. *Mem:* Am Chem Soc; Chem Inst Can; hon mem Spectros Soc Can (vpres, 68-69, pres, 69-70); Int Colloquial Spectros (secy, 67). *Res:* Development of methods for the determination of trace impurities in highly purified metals, ultrapure acids, reagents and semiconductor materials; using optical emission spectrometry, spark source mass spectrometry and stable isotope dilution. *Mailing Add:* 44 Tower Rd Nepean ON L2G 2E7 Can

RUSSELL, ELIZABETH SHULL, MAMMALIAN GENETICS. *Current Pos:* RETIRED. *Personal Data:* b Ann Arbor, Mich, May 1, 13; m 36; c 4. *Educ:* Univ Mich, AB, 33; Columbia Univ, MA, 34; Univ Chicago, PhD(zool), 37. *Hon Degrees:* DSc, Univ Maine, Farmington, 75, Colby Col, 84, Med Col Ohio & Bowdoin Col. *Prof Exp:* Asst zool, Univ Chicago, 35-37; independent investr, Jackson Lab, 39-40, res assoc, 46-57, sr staff scientist, 57-82, emer sr scientist, 82-88. *Concurrent Pos:* Nourse fel, Am Asn Univ Women, 39-40; Finney-Howell fel, 47; Guggenheim fel, 58-59. *Mem:* Nat Acad Sci; Am Acad Arts & Sci; Genetics Soc Am; Am Soc Naturalists; Soc Develop Biol; Am Physiol Soc. *Res:* Mammalian physiological genetics; action of deleterious genes; mouse anemias and hemoglobins; coat color; muscular dystrophy; genetic effects on aging. *Mailing Add:* HCR 62-223 Mt Desert ME 04660

RUSSELL, EMILY W B, HISTORICAL ECOLOGY, CONSERVATION. *Current Pos:* RES ASSOC PROF, DEPT GEOL SCI, RUTGERS UNIV, 81- *Personal Data:* b Birminham, Ala, Feb 10, 45; m 68, Frederick H. *Educ:* Denison Univ, BS, 66; Duke Univ, MA, 70; Rutgers Univ, MA, 74, PhD(bot), 79. *Concurrent Pos:* Vis prof, Bot Dept, Duke Univ, 89-90; vis scholar, Harvard Univ, 95- *Mem:* AAAS; Ecol Soc Am; Int Asn Landscape Ecologists; Sigma Xi; Am Quatarnary Asn. *Res:* Using historical documents and pollen analysis to detect the residual effects on ecosystems of past human activities especially in northeastern North America. *Mailing Add:* Dept Geol Sci Rutgers Univ Newark NJ 07102. *E-Mail:* russell@crssa.rutgers.edu

RUSSELL, ERNEST EVERETT, GEOLOGY. *Current Pos:* from asst prof to assoc prof, 55-68, prof, 68-, EMER PROF GEOL, MISS STATE UNIV, 85- *Personal Data:* b Jackson, Miss, Apr 16, 23; m 49; c 3. *Educ:* Miss State Univ, BS, 49, MS, 55; Univ Tenn, PhD(geol), 65. *Prof Exp:* Instr geol, Univ Tenn, 54-55. *Concurrent Pos:* Consult geologist, Tenn Div Geol, 58-70, WAE, US Geol Surv, 61-68, Tenn Valley Authority, 75-83. *Mem:* Fel Geol Soc Am; Paleont Soc; Am Inst Prof Geologists. *Res:* Upper Cretaceous Litho and Biostratigraphy of the eastern Gulf Coastal Plain; Lithofacies relations in Mesozoic and Cenozoic sediments. *Mailing Add:* 970 Sandhurst St Starkville MS 39759

RUSSELL, FINDLAY EWING, PHYSIOLOGY, TOXINOLOGY. *Current Pos:* RES PROF HEALTH SCI, UNIV ARIZ, 80- *Personal Data:* b San Francisco, Calif, Sept 1, 19; m 50, Marilyn R Strickland; c Christa, Sharon, Robin, Connie & Mark. *Educ:* Walla Walla Col, BA, 41; Loma Linda Univ, MD, 50; Univ Santa Barbara, PhD, 74. *Hon Degrees:* LLD, Univ Santa Barbara, 88. *Honors & Awards:* F Redi Medal, 66; J Stefan Award, 78; C H Thienes Award, 85. *Prof Exp:* Intern, White Mem Hosp, Los Angeles, 50-51; res fel biol, Calif Inst Technol, 51-53; physiologist, Inst Med Res, Huntington Mem Hosp, Pasadena, 53-55; res prof neurosurg, Loma Linda Univ, 55-66; prof neurol, physiol & biol, Univ Southern Calif, 66-80. *Concurrent Pos:* Dir lab neurol res, Los Angeles Co Hosp, 55-66; vis physiologist, Lab Marine Biol Asn, Eng, 58; vis prof, Cambridge Univ, 62-63 & 70-71, Ain Shams Univ Cairo, 63 & Univ Ljubljana, 75-76; ed, Toxicon, 62-68; G Griffith Scholar, Am Col Physicians, 86. *Mem:* Fel Am Col Physicians; fel NY Acad Sci; Int Soc Toxinology (pres, 62-66); fel Royal Soc Trop Med & Hyg; Am Physiol Soc. *Res:* Venoms. *Mailing Add:* Dept Pharmacol & Toxicol Col Pharm Univ Ariz Tucson AZ 85721. *Fax:* 520-626-2466

RUSSELL, FREDERICK A(RTHUR), ELECTRICAL ENGINEERING. *Current Pos:* RETIRED. *Personal Data:* b New York, NY, Apr 18, 15; m 47, Virginia McCullough; c David A & Jane S (Lysebo). *Educ:* Newark Col Eng, BS, 35, EE, 39; Stevens Inst Technol, MS, 41; Columbia Univ, ScD(eng), 53. *Honors & Awards:* Sr Sci Simulation Award, Electronic Assocs, 66. *Prof Exp:* From instr to asst prof elec eng, Newark Col Eng, 37-44; sr proj engr, Div War Res, Columbia Univ, 44-45; exec assoc, NJ Inst Technol, 45-56, from asst prof to assoc prof elec eng, 45-53, chmn dept, 56-75, prof, 53-67, distinguished prof, 67-80, asst to pres & dir planning, 75-80, adj prof, 80-85. *Concurrent Pos:* Consult, Franklin Inst, 45-46 & Bell Tel Labs, Inc, 57-70. *Mem:* Am Soc Eng Educ; fel Inst Elec & Electronics Engrs; Sigma Xi. *Res:* Digital and analog computer simulation; control systems. *Mailing Add:* 101 Elkwood Ave New Providence NJ 07974

RUSSELL, GEORGE A, PHYSICS. *Current Pos:* RETIRED. *Personal Data:* b Bertrand, Mo, July 12, 21; m 44; c 4. *Educ:* Mass Inst Technol, BS, 47; Univ Ill, MS, 52, PhD(physics), 55. *Prof Exp:* Physicist, Bur Aeronaut, US Navy, 55-59 & Antisubmarine Warfare Develop Squadron, 59-60; assoc prof physics, Southern Ill Univ, 60-62; assoc prof, Univ Ill, Urbana, 62-65, prof physics & assoc dir, Mat Res Lab, 65-74, head, Dept Physics, 68-74, assoc dean, Grad Col, 70-72, assoc vchancellor res & develop, 72-74, dean, Grad Col, 71-78, vchancellor res, 74-78; pres, Univ Mo Syst, 78-96. *Concurrent Pos:* Consult, Off Naval Res, 60; chancellor, Univ Mo-Kansas City, 77- *Mem:* Am Phys Soc; Am Asn Physics Teachers; Sigma Xi. *Res:* Color centers in ionic crystals; infrared radiation; antisubmarine warfare; utilization of educated manpower; university administration. *Mailing Add:* 3601 Augusta Columbia MO 65203

RUSSELL, GEORGE ALBERT, AUTOMATIC CONTROL SYSTEMS. *Current Pos:* asst prof, 67-70, ASSOC PROF MECH ENG, UNIV MASS, AMHERST, 70- *Personal Data:* b Chicago Heights, Ill, Aug 29, 36; m 57; c 3. *Educ:* Mass Inst Technol, BS, 58; Ariz State Univ, MS, 61; Univ Conn, PhD(elec eng), 67. *Prof Exp:* Develop engr, AiRes Mfg Co Div, Garrett Corp, 58-61, eng specialist, 64-67. *Concurrent Pos:* Consult, AiRes Mfg Co Div, Garrett Corp, Springfield Wire Inc. *Mem:* Acoust Soc Am; Am Soc Mech Engrs. *Res:* Gas turbine hydromechanical controls. *Mailing Add:* Dept Mech Eng Univ Mass 17 Gunness Bldg Amherst MA 01003

RUSSELL, GEORGE K(EITH), PLANT PHYSIOLOGY, BIOCHEMISTRY. *Current Pos:* from asst prof to assoc prof, 67-77, PROF BIOL, ADELPHI UNIV, 77- *Personal Data:* b Bronxville, NY, Dec 13, 37; m 70, Lenore De Sylva. *Educ:* Princeton Univ, AB, 59; Harvard Univ, PhD(biol), 63. *Prof Exp:* NSF fel biochem, Cornell Univ, 63-64; NSF fel biol, Brandeis Univ, 64-65; asst prof, Princeton Univ, 65-67. *Mem:* Am Soc Plant Physiologists; AAAS; Sigma Xi; Am Inst Biol Sci. *Res:* Genetic and biochemical control of photosynthesis and chloroplast development; genetics. *Mailing Add:* Dept Biol Adelphi Univ One South Ave Garden City NY 11530-4213. *Fax:* 516-877-4191

RUSSELL, GERALD FREDERICK, FOOD SAFETY, COMPUTERS IN FOOD SCIENCE & NUTRITION. *Current Pos:* ASSOC PROF FOOD SCI, UNIV CALIF, DAVIS, 68- *Personal Data:* b Edmonton, Alta, Feb 29, 44. *Educ:* Univ Alta, BSc, 64; Univ Calif, PhD(agr chem), 68. *Concurrent Pos:* Vis assoc prof, Eppley Inst Res in Cancer, Med Col, Univ Nebr, 75-76. *Mem:* Am Chem Soc; Inst Food Technologists; Am Soc Mass Spectrometry; AAAS; Sigma Xi. *Res:* Chemistry of food volatiles; chemistry of Maillard reaction in foods; structure and mechanisms of flavor compounds; agents and mechanisms of toxic and carcinogenic substances in foods; computers in food science and nutrition. *Mailing Add:* Dept Food Sci & Technol Univ Calif Davis CA 95616-5200

RUSSELL, GLEN ALLAN, ORGANIC CHEMISTRY. *Current Pos:* assoc prof, 58-62, prof chem, 62-72, DISTINGUISHED PROF, IOWA STATE UNIV, 72- *Personal Data:* b Rensselaer Co, NY, Aug 23, 25; m 53, Martha E Havill; c Susan Ann & June Ellen. *Educ:* Rensselaer Polytech Inst, BChE, 47, MS, 48; Purdue Univ, PhD(chem), 51. *Honors & Awards:* Am Chem Soc Award, 65 & 72, James Flack Norris Award, 83; Fulbright-Hays Lectr, Univ Wurzburg, 66; Reilly Lectr, Univ Notre Dame, 66. *Prof Exp:* Res assoc, Res Lab, Gen Elec Co, 51-58. *Concurrent Pos:* Sloan Found fel, 59-62; vis prof, Univ Wyo, 67, Univ Grenoble, France, 85, Guggenheim fel, Nuclear Res Ctr, Grenoble, France, 72; fel Japan Soc Prom Sci, 83. *Mem:* AAAS; Am Chem Soc; The Chem Soc. *Res:* Physical organic chemistry; reactions of free radicals and atoms; chlorination; oxidation; application of electron spin resonance spectroscopy to organic molecules. *Mailing Add:* Dept Chem Iowa State Univ Ames IA 50011-0061. *Fax:* 515-294-0105; *E-Mail:* grussell@iastate.edu

RUSSELL, GLENN C, SOIL CHEMISTRY. *Current Pos:* RETIRED. *Personal Data:* b Taber, Alta, June 6, 21; m 47; c 5. *Educ:* Brigham Young Univ, BS, 43; Univ Mass, MS, 49; Purdue Univ, PhD(soil chem), 52. *Prof Exp:* Instr, Univ Mass, 47-49; fel, Purdue Univ, 49-51; res officer, Agr Res Sta, Can Dept Agr, Lethbridge, 51-54, head soils sect, 54-66, dir exp farm, PEI, 66-70, dir res sta, Ont, 70-75, dir res sta, Summerland, BC, 75-85. *Mem:* Soil Sci Soc

Am; Am Soc Agron; Can Soc Soil Sci; Agr Inst Can; Can Soc Agron. *Res:* Effect of fertilizers and soil amendments on chemical changes in the soil and on crop production. *Mailing Add:* 1448 Dartmouth St Penticton BC V2A 4B6 Can

RUSSELL, GRANT E(DWIN), CHEMICAL ENGINEERING. *Current Pos:* RETIRED. *Personal Data:* b Asheville, NC, June 5, 16; m 42; c 6. *Educ:* Wash Univ, BSChE, 38, MSChE, 50. *Prof Exp:* Chemist, Reardon Co, 38-40; anal chemist, Monsanto Co, 40-41, tech asst, 42-45, chem engr, 45-48, supv engr, 48-52, asst eng supt, 52-57, eng mgr, 57-65, sr eng specialist, 65-68, sr res specialist, 68-74; sr chem eng, SRI Int, 75-80, consult process econ, 80-86. *Mem:* Am Inst Chem Engrs. *Res:* Economic evaluation of research projects; preliminary process design; design and economic evaluation of chemical process. *Mailing Add:* 1033 Havre Ct Sunnyvale CA 94087

RUSSELL, HENRY FRANKLIN, ORGANIC CHEMISTRY, HETEROCYCLIC CHEMISTRY. *Current Pos:* PROF CHEM, JOHNSON C SMITH UNIV, 79- *Personal Data:* b Glenolden, Pa, July 18, 40; m 68, Beverly Maulden; c 2. *Educ:* Univ Del, BS, 63, MS, 65; Univ Va, PhD(org chem), 73. *Prof Exp:* Instr chem, US Naval Acad, 66-68; process & develop chemist, Am Cyanamid Co, 73-79. *Concurrent Pos:* Minority Access to Res Careers Progs prin investr, NIH, 80-, Minority Biomed Res Support Prog, 82- *Mem:* Am Chem Soc. *Res:* Synthesis of melatonin analogs, substituted indoles and precursors; anti-mitotic activity. *Mailing Add:* 3739 Severn Ave Charlotte NC 28210-6213. *Fax:* 704-378-4050; *E-Mail:* hrussell@jcsu.edu

RUSSELL, HENRY GEORGE, STRUCTURAL ENGINEERING. *Current Pos:* exec dir, 87-88, pres, 89-91, VPRES, CONSTRUCT TECHNOL LABS, 91- *Personal Data:* b Eng, June 12, 41. *Educ:* Univ Sheffield, BEng, 62, PhD(struct eng), 65, Lake Forest Grad Sch Mgt, MBA, 91. *Honors & Awards:* Martin P Korn Award, Prestressed Concrete Inst, 80; Delmar L Bloem Award, Am Concrete Inst, 86, Wason Medal, 92. *Prof Exp:* Jr res fel struct eng, Bldg Res Sta Eng, 65-68; struct engr, Portland Cement Asn, 68-74, mgr, 74-79, dir, 79-86. *Mem:* Fel Am Concrete Inst; Prestressed Concrete Inst; Transp Res Bd. *Res:* Shrinkage compensating concretes; time dependent behavior of reinforced concrete columns and posttensioned concrete bridges; high strength concrete; construction failures. *Mailing Add:* 720 Cornet Rd Glenview IL 60025. *Fax:* 847-998-0292

RUSSELL, JAMES, POLYMER CHEMISTRY, PHYSICAL CHEMISTRY. *Current Pos:* CONSULT, 86- *Personal Data:* b Leeds, Eng, Feb 14, 28; m 51, Dorothy Russell; c Linda M (Margraf) & J Michael. *Educ:* Univ London, BSc, 50, PhD(polymer chem), 53. *Prof Exp:* Fel, Cornell Univ, 53-55; res chemist, Am Viscose Corp, 55-61; res assoc, St Regis Paper Co, NY, 61-67, mgr res & develop, 67-71, dir corp prod develop, 71-75; vpres res & develop, Sylvachem Corp, 75-86. *Mem:* Am Chem Soc; Tech Asn Pulp & Paper Indust. *Res:* Wood chemistry and its application to pulping and byproducts; polymer chemistry and its application to packaging. *Mailing Add:* 2938 Jenks Ave Panama City FL 32405-4315

RUSSELL, JAMES A(LVIN), JR, ELECTRICAL ENGINEERING. *Current Pos:* RETIRED. *Personal Data:* b Lawrenceville, Va, Dec 25, 17; m 43; c 2. *Educ:* Oberlin Col, AB, 40; Bradley Univ, BS, 41, MS, 50; Univ Md, EdD(indust ed), 67. *Hon Degrees:* LLD, St Paul's Col, Va, 84. *Prof Exp:* Instr elec technol, US Naval Training Sch, 42-45 & St Paul's Col, 45-50; assoc prof electronics eng, Hampton Inst, 50-58, div dir technol, 63-68, prof electronics, 67-71; pres, St Paul's Col, Va, 71-81; prof indust technol & chmn div professional studies, WVA State Col, 82-86, acting pres, 86-87, exec asst pres, 87-88. *Concurrent Pos:* Res engr, Thomas J Watson Res Ctr, IBM Corp, 68-69; chmn dept electronics technol, Hampton Inst, 58-68, chmn dept eng & dir eng & technol div, 68-71. *Mem:* Am Soc Eng Educ; Inst Elec & Electronics Engrs; Tech Educ Asn. *Res:* Industrial education; investigation into changes in critical thinking and achievement in electronics as the result of exposure of subjects to specific techniques of critical thinking. *Mailing Add:* 811 Grandview Dr Dunbar WV 25064

RUSSELL, JAMES CHRISTOPHER, ATHEROSCLEROSIS, CLINICAL CHEMISTRY. *Current Pos:* univ fel chem, Univ Alta, 64-67, asst prof biochem in surg & dir, Biochem Lab, Surg-Med Res Inst, 67-72, assoc prof, 72-81, PROF SURG, DIV EXP SURG, UNIV ALTA, 81- *Personal Data:* b Montreal, Que, Oct 24, 38; m 61, Wendy Spencer; c Katrina. *Educ:* Dalhousie Univ, BSc, 58; Univ Sask, MSc, 59, PhD(radiation chem), 62. *Prof Exp:* Gen Elec Co fel phys chem, Univ Leeds, 62-64. *Concurrent Pos:* Consult med staff sci & res, Univ Alta Hosp, 69- *Mem:* Can Soc Clin Chemists; Can Pysiol Soc; Can Soc Clin Invest; Can Athero Soc; Can Acad Clin Biochem; Nat Acad Clin Biochem. *Res:* Clinical chemistry in both humans and animals; animal models of cardiovascular disease; biochemistry of exercise; diabetes and obesity in rodents; maintain colony of JRC: LA-corpulent. *Mailing Add:* Dept Surg Univ Alta 275 Heritage Med Res Ctr Edmonton AB T6G 2S2 Can. *Fax:* 403-492-4923; *E-mail:* jrussell@pop.stu.ualberta.ca

RUSSELL, JAMES E(DWARD), ROCK MECHANICS, MINING ENGINEERING. *Current Pos:* PROF PETROL ENG & GEOPHYS, TEX A&M UNIV, 78- *Personal Data:* b Rapid City, SDak, May 20, 40; m 63; c 2. *Educ:* SDak Sch Mines & Technol, BS, 63, MS, 64; Northwestern Univ, Evanston, PhD(theoret & appl mech), 66. *Prof Exp:* Sr res engr, Southwest Res Inst, 66-67; from asst prof to assoc prof civil eng, SDak Sch Mines & Technol, 67-71, from assoc prof to prof civil & mining eng, 71-76; proj mgr rock mech, Off Waste Isolation, Union Carbide Corp, 77-78. *Concurrent Pos:* Vpres struct & mech systs, RE/SPEC, Inc, 69-76; Brokett prof, 82-83, Halliburton prof, 85-86. *Mem:* Am Soc Civil Engrs; Am Inst Mining, Metall & Petrol Engrs; Am Acad Mech; Am Geophys Union. *Res:* Rock mechanics; nuclear waste disposal and underground storage; in situ gasification of coal-subsidence. *Mailing Add:* Dept Petrol Eng Tex A&M Univ College Station TX 77843-3116

RUSSELL, JAMES EDWARD, ATOMIC PHYSICS. *Current Pos:* assoc prof, 65-74, PROF PHYSICS, UNIV CINCINNATI, 74- *Personal Data:* b Ft Wayne, Ind, Sept 27, 31; m 77. *Educ:* Yale Univ, BS, 53, MS, 54, PhD(physics), 58. *Prof Exp:* Fel, Univ Va, 57-58; res assoc physics, Ind Univ, 58-60; res physicist, Carnegie-Mellon Univ, 60-62; vis asst prof, Univ Padua, 62-63; sr res officer, Univ Oxford, 63-65. *Concurrent Pos:* Vis scientist, CERN, 74; consult, Lawrence Berkeley Labs, 75; vis, Int Ctr Theoret Physics, 70, 74 & 85. *Res:* Exotic atoms; chemical physics. *Mailing Add:* Dept Physics Univ Cincinnati Cincinnati OH 45221. *Fax:* 513-556-3425; *E-Mail:* james.russell@uc.edu

RUSSELL, JAMES MADISON, III, atmospheric science, electrical engineering, for more information see previous edition

RUSSELL, JAMES N(ELSON), JR, chemical engineering, for more information see previous edition

RUSSELL, JAMES T, MEMBRANE TRANSPORT PROCESS, SIGNAL TRANSDUCTION. *Current Pos:* sr staff fel neurobiol, 78-83, RES CHEMIST, NIH, 84- *Personal Data:* b Nagercoil, India, Sept 26, 44; US citizen; m 90, Andra E Miller; c Ivan G & Kamala R. *Educ:* Univ Madras, BVSc, 66; Post Grad Inst Med Educ & Res, MSc, 71; Copenhagen Univ, Lic Med, 74. *Prof Exp:* Adj lectr physiol, Copenhagen Univ, Denmark, 74-76; fel biochem, St Louis Univ, 76-77. *Concurrent Pos:* Vet asst surgeon, Madras Animal Husb Serv, India, 66-67; vet officer, Amul Dairy, India, 67-68; vis scientist, Med Physiol Inst, Copenhagen Univ, Denmark, 80. *Mem:* Soc Neurosci; Scand Soc Physiologists. *Res:* Presynaptic mechanisms of neurotransmitter secretion & its modulation; molecular description of neuronal excitability and presynaptic plasticity; functional organization of the nerve terminal; neuronal-glial signalling; glial cell development; muscle biochemisty. *Mailing Add:* NIH Bldg 49 Rm 5A32 9000 Rockville Pike Bethesda MD 20892

RUSSELL, JAMES TORRANCE, APPLIED PHYSICS, ELECTRONICS. *Current Pos:* CONSULT PHYSICS, RUSSELL ASSOC INC, 85- *Personal Data:* b Bremerton, Wash, Feb 23, 31; m 53, Barbara Giblett; c Janet, James & Kristen. *Educ:* Reed Col, BA, 53. *Prof Exp:* Physicist, Hanford Atomic Prod Oper, Gen Elec Co, 53-60, sr physicist, 60-65; res assoc exp physics, Pac Northwest Labs, Battelle Mem Inst, 65-66, sr res assoc appl physics, 66-80; vpres & tech dir, Digital Rec Corp, 80-85. *Concurrent Pos:* Vpres res, Info Optics Corp. *Mem:* AAAS; Am Phys Soc; Inst Elec & Electronics Engrs; Soc Photo-Optical Instrumentation Engrs; Optical Soc Am. *Res:* Optical data storage; sensor development; physics of instrumentation; high resolution optical systems; laser devices; development of techniques for experimental physics; granted 46 US patents. *Mailing Add:* Russell Assocs 14589 SE 51st St Bellevue WA 98006-3509

RUSSELL, JESSE E, SR, ELECTRONICS ENGINEERING, COMMUNICATIONS. *Current Pos:* Mem tech staff, AT&T Labs, 72-78, supvr, Special Serv Circuit Design Group, 78-81, head, Network Performance Objectives Dept, 81-82, Intergrated Loop Systs Design Dept, 82-84, Cellular Base Sta Software Design Dept, 84-86, dir, Cellular Commun Lab, 86-88 & Cellular Transmission Lab, 88-91, chief tech officer, Network Wireless Business Univ, vpres, Advan Wireless Techn ol Lab, 91-92, chief wireless architect & managing dir, Wireless Commun Ctr Excellence, 92-95, VPRES AT&T ADVAN COMMUN LAB, 96- *Personal Data:* b Nashville, Tenn, Apr 26, 48; c 4. *Educ:* Tenn State Univ, BSEE, 72; Stanford Univ, MSEE, 73. *Honors & Awards:* Scientist of the Year Award, Nat Tech Assocs Inc, 80; Outstanding Scientist Award, Nat Soc Black Engrs, 82. *Concurrent Pos:* Vchmn, Int Regulatory & Stand Comt on Third Generation Wirless Commun Systs; mem, Info Technol Coun, Am Mgt Asn. *Mem:* Nat Acad Eng; sr fel Inst Elec & Electronics Engrs. *Res:* Personnel communication services, cellular systems and architectures as well as digital cellular technologies and systems; published 12 articles; granted 15 US patents. *Mailing Add:* AT & T Labs 67 Whippamy Rd Whippany NJ 07981. *Fax:* 973-386-3302; *E-Mail:* jerussell@att.com

RUSSELL, JOEL W, PHYSICAL CHEMISTRY. *Current Pos:* from asst prof to assoc prof, 66-82, interim dean grad study, 84-85, PROF CHEM, OAKLAND UNIV, 82-, INTERIM DEAN SCH HEALTH SCI, 83- *Personal Data:* b Elkhart, Ind, May 18, 39; m 61; c 5. *Educ:* Northwestern Univ, BA, 61; Univ Calif, Berkeley, PhD(chem), 65. *Prof Exp:* Res fel, Univ Minn, 65-66. *Concurrent Pos:* Vis mem staff, Australian Nat Univ, 72-73; res fel, Southampton Univ, 80-81; vis scholar, Univ Mich, 88-89. *Mem:* Am Chem Soc; Sigma Xi; Am Asn Univ Prof. *Res:* Molecular structure and dynamics; infrared and raman spectroscopy; studies of means to enhance teaching and learning for chemistry. *Mailing Add:* 1564 Charter Oak Dr Rochester MI 48309

RUSSELL, JOHN ALBERT, ASTRONOMY, METEORS. *Current Pos:* head dept astron, Univ Southern Calif, 46-69, from asst prof to prof, 46-78, chmn div phys sci & math, 59-62, assoc dean natural sci & math, Col Lett, Arts & Sci, 63-68, emer prof, 78-83, DISTINGUISHED EMER PROF ASTRON, UNIV SOUTHERN CALIF, 83- *Personal Data:* b Ludington, Mich, Mar 23, 13; m 36, Phyllis Rock; c Stanton J & Carolyn R (Gold). *Educ:*

Univ Calif, AB, 35, AM, 37, PhD(astron), 43. *Honors & Awards:* Univ Assocs Award, 60. *Prof Exp:* Guide, Griffith Observ, 35; asst, Univ Calif, 36-39; instr astron, Pasadena City Col, 39-41, Exten Div, Univ Calif, Los Angeles, 41, Santa Ana Army Air Base, 42 & Pasadena City Col, 46. *Concurrent Pos:* Fac res lectr, Univ Southern Calif, 57-; mem comn interplanetary dust, Int Astron Union; mem bd dirs, Astron Soc Pac, 60-63. *Mem:* Fel AAAS; Am Astron Soc; fel Meteoritical Soc (secy, 49-58, pres, 58-62); fel Astron Soc Pac. *Res:* Meteor spectroscopy and statistics. *Mailing Add:* 5654 Coliseum St Los Angeles CA 90016-5006

RUSSELL, JOHN ALVIN, TRIBOLOGY. *Current Pos:* RETIRED. *Personal Data:* b San Antonio, Tex, Aug 15, 34; m 58; c 2. *Educ:* Univ Tex, BS, 57; St Mary's Univ, MS, 64. *Prof Exp:* Assoc engr, Convair Astronaut, San Diego, 57; proj officer nuclear weapons, US Air Force, 57-60; mgr special proj fuels & lubricants, Alcor Inc, 60-71; mgr synthetic fuels develop, Southwest Res Inst, 71-90; dir, Alternative Fuels, US Dept Energy, 90-96. *Concurrent Pos:* Sr res engr tribology, Southwest Res Inst, 60-66; mem, Fuels & Lubricants Comt, Coord Res Coun, 67-; mem tech adv panel, Alternative Fuels, US Dept Energy, 76- *Mem:* Soc Automotive Engrs (pres, 72-73); Am Soc Mech Engrs (vpres, 65-66); Am Soc Lubrication Engrs; Sigma Xi. *Res:* Synthetic fuels and lubricants performance in aviation and automotive power plants; cryogenic tribology; hydrocarbon fuels utilization projection analysis. *Mailing Add:* 7215 Brookside San Antonio TX 78209

RUSSELL, JOHN BLAIR, INORGANIC CHEMISTRY. *Current Pos:* from asst prof to prof, 56-93, EMER PROF CHEM, HUMBOLDT STATE UNIV, 93- *Personal Data:* b Rochester, NY, Dec 13, 29; m 55, Barbara Woods; c Deborah. *Educ:* Oberlin Col, AB, 51; Cornell Univ, PhD(chem), 56. *Prof Exp:* Instr & res assoc chem, Cornell Univ, 55-56. *Mem:* Am Chem Soc; Sigma Xi. *Res:* Solutions of metals in liquid ammonia; electrochemistry in aqueous and non-aqueous solvents; complex ions; author, general chemistry texts. *Mailing Add:* Dept Chem Humboldt State Univ Arcata CA 95521

RUSSELL, JOHN GEORGE, ORGANIC CHEMISTRY. *Current Pos:* asst prof, 69-74, ASSOC PROF CHEM, CALIF STATE UNIV, SACRAMENTO, 74- *Personal Data:* b Manila, Philippines, Dec 19, 41; US citizen; m 66. *Educ:* Purdue Univ, BS, 63; Univ Minn, PhD(org chem), 68. *Prof Exp:* Res assoc chem, Ohio State Univ, 68. *Mem:* Am Chem Soc. *Res:* Nuclear magnetic resonance spectroscopy; conformational analysis; synthesis, rate and equilibria studies of organometallic compounds. *Mailing Add:* Dept Chem Calif State Univ Sacramento CA 95819-4698

RUSSELL, JOHN LYNN, JR, NUCLEAR PHYSICS. *Current Pos:* CHIEF EXEC OFFICER & CHMN BD, MATSI INC, 93- *Personal Data:* b Woodsborough, Tex, Aug 5, 30; m 51; c 3. *Educ:* Univ Tex, BS, 51; Rice Univ, MA, 54, PhD(physics), 56. *Prof Exp:* Theoret physicist, Vallecitos Atomic Lab, Gen Elec Co, 56-60, mgr exp reactor physics, 60-62; mgr spec projs, Gen Atomic Co, San Diego, Calif, 62-78; prof, Dept Nuclear Eng, Ga Inst Technol, 78-83, dir, Frank H Neely Nuclear Res Ctr, 79-83; pres & chmn bd, Theragenics Corp, 83-89; consult, 89-94. *Concurrent Pos:* Vpres res & develop, Int Brachyther, SA, 95- *Mem:* Am Nuclear Soc; Am Phys Soc. *Res:* Pulsed neutron measurements; fast neutron spectra in bulk media; fast reactors; control of nuclear reactors; solar energy; hydrogen production; charged particle scattering; radiopharmaceuticals; solar neutrinos. *Mailing Add:* 110 Westchester Way Alpharetta GA 30202. *E-Mail:* russellji@aol.com

RUSSELL, JOHN MCCANDLESS, PHYSIOLOGY OF MEMBRANE TRANSPORT OF IONS, REGULATION OF INTRACELLULAR PH AND OF CELL VOLUME. *Current Pos:* CONSULT, 86-; PROF & CHAIR, MED COL PA, 92- *Personal Data:* b Drumright, Okla; m 91, Janice R Hall; c Joshua C & Gregory M G. *Educ:* Univ NMex, BS, 66; Univ Utah, PhD(pharmacol), 71. *Honors & Awards:* Jacob K Javits Neurosci Award. *Prof Exp:* NIH fel, Dept Physiol & Biophys, Sch Med, Wash Univ, 72-73; from asst prof to assoc prof, Univ Tex Med Br, 74-85, prof & actg chmn, 85-86. *Concurrent Pos:* Mem, Physiol Study Sect, NIH, 83-87; Cellular Cardiovasc Physiol & Pharmacol Study Sect, Am Heart Asn, 88-89. *Mem:* Biophys Soc; Soc Gen Physiologists; AAAS; Red Cell Club; Am Physiol Soc. *Res:* Mechanisms involved in the membrane translocation of ions, especially the chloride anion and its role in intracellular pH and volume regulation in biological tissue. *Mailing Add:* Dept Physiol Allegheny Univ Health Sci Philadelphia PA 19129. *Fax:* 215-843-8493; *E-Mail:* russell@allegheny.edu

RUSSELL, JOHN MASTERS, FLUID DYNAMICS. *Current Pos:* ASSOC PROF, DEPT MECH & AERO ENG, FLA INST TECHNOL, 87- *Personal Data:* b Paterson, NJ, Sept 4, 51; m 84, Marilyn Lazenby; c Grace & Stuart. *Educ:* Mass Inst Technol, BS(math) & BS(aeronaut & astronaut eng), 76, MS, 78, ScD, 81. *Prof Exp:* Asst prof, Sch Aerospace Mech & Nuclear Eng, Univ Okla, 81-87. *Concurrent Pos:* Fel, USAF, 82 & 90; NASA summer res fel, 88, 89, 93, 94, 95 & 96; fel, USN, 91. *Mem:* Assoc fel Am Inst Aeronautics; Sigma Xi; Am Phys Soc. *Res:* Exact analytical solution of the Rayleigh, Orr-Sommerfeld and related equations for some simple mean velocity distributions. *Mailing Add:* Aerospace Eng Prog Florida Inst Technol 150 W University Blvd Melbourne FL 32901. *Fax:* 407-768-8000 Ext 8813; *E-Mail:* russell@zach.fit.edu

RUSSELL, JOSEPH LOUIS, FLUORINE CHEMISTRY. *Current Pos:* from asst prof to assoc prof, 74-93, PROF CHEM, ALCORN STATE UNIV, 93- *Personal Data:* b Vicksburg, Miss, June 18, 36; m 62; c 1. *Educ:* Alcorn State Univ, BS, 60; Marquette Univ, MS, 71, PhD(inorg chem), 74. *Prof Exp:* Teacher math, Natchez Pub Schs, 60-64; control chemist, Liquid Glaze Chem Co, 65; scientist chem, Battelle-Northwest Lab, 66-69; teaching asst chem, Marquette Univ, 69-74. *Concurrent Pos:* Lab instr chem, Ala State Col, 65. *Mem:* Am Chem Soc. *Res:* Reactions in anhydrons liquid hydrogen fluoride; transition metal bonding to plant harmones; photochemical catalyzed decomposition of volatile Freons. *Mailing Add:* Dept Chem & Physics Alcorn State Univ 1000 ASU Drive No 780 Lorman MS 39096-9402

RUSSELL, KENNETH CALVIN, METALLURGY, MATERIALS SCIENCE. *Current Pos:* from asst prof to assoc prof metall, 64-78, PROF METALL & NUCLEAR ENG, MASS INST TECHNOL, 78- *Personal Data:* b Greeley, Colo, Feb 4, 36; m 63; c 2. *Educ:* Colo Sch Mines, MetE, 59; Carnegie Inst Technol, PhD(metall eng), 64. *Honors & Awards:* Sauveur Memorial Award, Am Soc Metals Int, Boston, 77. *Prof Exp:* Asst engr, Westinghouse Elec Corp, 59-61; NSF fel, Oslo, 63-64. *Concurrent Pos:* Ford Found fel eng, 64-66. *Mem:* Am Inst Mining, Metall & Petrol Engrs; Am Phys Soc; fel Am Soc Metals. *Res:* Phase transformations; lattice defects in solids; radiation damage. *Mailing Add:* 21 Taft Ave Lexington MA 02173

RUSSELL, KENNETH EDWIN, POLYMER CHEMISTRY. *Current Pos:* lectr, 54-56, from asst prof to prof, 56-90, EMER PROF CHEM, QUEEN'S UNIV, ONT, 90- *Personal Data:* b Barnwell, Eng, Dec 9, 24; m 55; c 3. *Educ:* Cambridge Univ, BA, 45, PhD(chem), 48. *Prof Exp:* Vis asst prof chem, Pa State Col, 48-50; asst lectr, Manchester Univ, 50-52; fel, Princeton Univ, 52-54. *Mem:* Am Chem Soc; fel Chem Inst Can; Royal Soc Chem. *Res:* hydrogen abstraction reactions in solution; studies of ethylene copolymers; phase structure of polyethylene; polymer grafting. *Mailing Add:* Dept Chem Queen's Univ Kingston ON K7L 3N6 Can. *Fax:* 613-545-6669

RUSSELL, KENNETH HOMER, PHYSICAL CHEMISTRY. *Current Pos:* from asst prof to assoc prof, 63-72, PROF CHEM, CALIF STATE UNIV, FRESNO, 72- *Personal Data:* b Portland, Ore, June 7, 33; m 54; c 3. *Educ:* Portland State Col, BS, 58; Washington State Univ, PhD(phys chem), 64. *Prof Exp:* Instr chem, Portland State Col, 58-59. *Concurrent Pos:* Lectr solar energy; partner, Solar Design & Mfg Co. *Mem:* AAAS; Am Chem Soc; Royal Soc Chem; Int Solar Energy Soc. *Res:* Molecular structure and infrared spectroscopy of inorganic compounds in the solid state. *Mailing Add:* Chem Calif State Univ 2555 E San Ramon Fresno CA 93740-8034

RUSSELL, LEONARD NELSON, NUCLEAR PHYSICS. *Current Pos:* RETIRED. *Personal Data:* b Coldwater, Mich, Jan 15, 22; m 47, Lavon M; c Linda C (Mach) & Janet A (Messaras). *Educ:* Kalamazoo Col, AB, 47; Ohio State Univ, PhD(physics), 52. *Prof Exp:* Res physicist, Mound Lab, 47-54, from asst prof to prof physics & math, Ohio Wesleyan Univ, 54-85. *Mem:* Sigma Xi. *Res:* Proton capture studies with van de Graaff generator; beta ray spectroscopy. *Mailing Add:* 45 Westgate Dr Delaware OH 43015

RUSSELL, LIANE BRAUCH, MUTAGENESIS. *Current Pos:* biologist, Oak Ridge Nat Lab, 48-75, corp res fel, 73-88, head, Mamalian Genetics & Develop Sect, 75-95, SR RES FEL, OAK RIDGE NAT LAB, 88- *Personal Data:* b Vienna, Austria, Aug 27, 23; nat US; m 47; c 2. *Educ:* Hunter Col, AB, 45; Univ Chicago, PhD(zool), 49. *Honors & Awards:* Int Roentgen Medal, 73; Fermi Award, 95. *Prof Exp:* Asst, Jackson Mem Lab, 45, 46, Dept Zool, Univ Chicago, 46-47. *Concurrent Pos:* Sci adv to US deleg, First Atoms-for-Peace Conf, 55; mem comt energy & the environ, Nat Acad Sci, 75-77, biol effects of ionizing radiations, 77-80; mem sci comt 1 task group, Nat Coun for Radiation Protection & measurements, 75-77; assoc ed, Mutation Res, 76-, Environ Mutagenesis, 80-83; mem comt, Int Comn for Protection against Mutagens & Carcinogens, 77-83; mem, Int Comt Standardized Genetic Nomenclature for Mice, 77-90; mem, Gene-Toxicol Prog Coord Comt, Environ Protection Agency, 79-, mem sci adv bd, Rev Panel on Mutagenicity Guidelines, 85-86; chmn, Mammalian Mutagenesis Group, Int Agency Res Cancer, 79; mem, Tech Support Group, Environ Protection Agency Risk Assessment, Reproductive & Teratogenic Effects, 80-81; mem, Bd Toxicol & Environ Health Hazards, Nat Acad Sci, 81-; mem sci adv panel, Off Technol Assessment, 85; mem bd, Environ Studies & Toxicol, Nat Acad Sci, 86-90; fel, Environ Health Inst, 87- *Mem:* Nat Acad Sci; fel AAAS; Genetics Soc Am Soc; Environ Mutagen Soc (pres, 84). *Res:* Induced and spontaneous genetic changes in mammalian germ cells; genetic analysis of the mouse genome; functional mapping with deletion complexes; genetic activity of the mammalian X chromosome; developmental genetics; teratogenesis. *Mailing Add:* Biol Div Oak Ridge Nat Lab PO Box 2009 Oak Ridge TN 37831-8077. *Fax:* 423-574-1283; *E-Mail:* russellb@bioax1.bio.ornl.gov

RUSSELL, LORIS SHANO, PALEONTOLOGY. *Current Pos:* chief biologist, 63-71, EMER CUR, ROYAL ONT MUS, 71- *Personal Data:* b Brooklyn, NY, Apr 21, 04; m 38. *Educ:* Univ Alta, BSc, 27, LLD, 58; Princeton Univ, AM, 29, PhD(paleont), 30. *Hon Degrees:* LLD, Univ Alta, 58. *Honors & Awards:* Willet G Miller Medal, Royal Soc Can, 59; Can Jubilee Medal, 78; Elkanah Billings Medal, Geol Soc Can, 84; Romer-Simpson Medal, Vert Paleont Soc, 93. *Prof Exp:* Field officer, Geol Div, Res Coun, Alta, 28-29; asst paleontologist, Geol Surv Can, 30-37; from asst dir to dir, Royal Ont Mus, 37-50; chief zoologist, Nat Mus Can, 50-56, dir, 56-63. *Concurrent Pos:* From asst prof to prof paleont, Univ Toronto, 37-70, emer prof, 70- *Mem:* Geol Soc Am; Paleont Soc; Soc Vert Paleont; Can Mus Asn; Royal Soc Can. *Res:* Vertebrate paleontology; fossil vertebrates and mollusks of western North America; Cretaceous and Tertiary stratigraphy of western North America. *Mailing Add:* Royal Ont Mus 100 Queens Pike Toronto ON M5S 2C6 Can

RUSSELL, LYNN DARNELL, THERMODYNAMICS, HEAT TRANSFER. *Current Pos:* DEAN ENG, UNIV ALA, HUNTSVILLE, 87- *Personal Data:* m 63, Elaine Lowery; c Kathy (Mucher), Brent, Mark & Jeffrey. *Educ:* Miss State Univ, BS, 60, MS, 61; Rice Univ, PhD(mech eng), 66. *Prof Exp:* Proj engr, Marshall Space Flight Ctr, NASA, 61-63, Johnson Space Ctr, 63-64; assoc res scientist, Lockheed, 66-67; mem tech staff, TRW Systs, 67-69; dir/dean eng, Univ Tenn, Chattanooga, 69-79; prof mech eng, Miss State Univ, 79-87. *Concurrent Pos:* Chair, Grad Studies Div, Am Soc Eng Educ, 94-95. *Mem:* Fel Am Soc Mech Engrs; Am Soc Eng Educ; Sigma Xi; Nat Soc Prof Engrs; Int Solar Energy Soc. *Res:* Heat transfer; thermodynamics and solar energy; co-author of one textbook on thermodynamics. *Mailing Add:* 218 Nale Dr Madison AL 35758

RUSSELL, MARVIN W, PHYSICS, APPLIED MATHEMATICS. *Current Pos:* head, Dept Physics, Western Ky Univ, 62-65, prof, 64-94, dean, 65-80, EMER PROF PHYSICS, OGDEN COL SCI & TECHNOL, WESTERN KY UNIV, 94- *Personal Data:* b Poole, Ky, Aug 26, 27; m 48; c 4. *Educ:* Western Ky Univ, BS, 50; Univ Fla, MS, 52, PhD(physics), 54. *Prof Exp:* Physicist, Gen Elec Co, 54-61; sr res scientist physics, Kaman Nuclear, 61-62. *Concurrent Pos:* Vis lectr, Ky Wesleyan Col, 56-60. *Mem:* Am Phys Soc; Inst Elec & Electronics Engrs; Am Asn Physics Teachers. *Res:* Electron and heat transfer physics; mass spectrometry; applied mathematics; ion mobility and recombination phenomena; mathematical models; atmospheric physics; science education. *Mailing Add:* 531 Claremoor Dr Bowling Green KY 42101

RUSSELL, MICHAEL W(ILLIAM), MUCOSAL IMMUNOLOGY, ORAL MICROBIOLOGY. *Current Pos:* vis investr, Inst Dent Res, Univ Ala, Birmingham, 79-81, res asst prof, 82-86, res assoc prof, 86-92, RES PROF, DEPT MICROBIOL, UNIV ALA AT BIRMINGHAM, 92- *Personal Data:* b Epsom, Eng, July 12, 44. *Educ:* Univ Cambridge, Eng, BA, 66, MA, 70; Univ Reading, Eng, PhD(microbiol), 73. *Prof Exp:* Researcher, Nat Inst Res Dairying, Univ Reading, UK, 68-72; res fel, Dept Oral Immunol, Med & Dent Schs, Guy's Hosp, UK, 72-79. *Concurrent Pos:* Investr, Inst Dent Res, Univ Ala at Birmingham, 82-86, Res Ctr Oral Biol, 87-92; vis assoc prof, Dept Oral Biol, Royal Dent Col, Aarhus, Denmark, 87-88; assoc scientist, Ctr AIDS Res, Univ Ala, Birmingham, 88-92; sr scientist, Ctr AIDS Res & Res Ctr Oral Biol, 92-, Comprehensive Cancer Ctr & Arthritis Ctr, 93-; chair, Immunol Sect, Am Soc Microbiol, 96-97. *Mem:* Brit Soc Immunol; Int Asn Dent Res; Am Soc Microbiol; Am Asn Immunologists; Soc Mucosal Immunol. *Res:* Induction and biological functions of immunoglobulin A antibodies; immunity to dental caries; protein antigens of Streptococcus mutans; mucosal vaccine development; immunopathology of periodontal disease; mucosal immunity in gonorrhea. *Mailing Add:* Dept Microbiol Univ Ala Birmingham 845 19th St S Birmingham AL 35294-2170. *Fax:* 205-934-3894; *E-Mail:* medmo12@uabdpo.dpo.uab.edu

RUSSELL, MORLEY EGERTON, PHYSICAL CHEMISTRY. *Current Pos:* assoc prof, 65-93, PROF PHYS CHEM, NORTHERN ILL UNIV, 93- *Personal Data:* b Los Angeles, Calif, June , 29; m 63, Marueen McLaughlin; c Vance & Trevor. *Educ:* Col Wooster, AB, 51; Mass Inst Technol, SM, 53; Univ Mich, PhD(chem), 58. *Prof Exp:* Fel phys chem, Nobel Inst Chem, Sweden, 58-59; asst prof, Mich State Univ, 59-64. *Mem:* Am Soc Mass Spectrometry; Am Chem Soc. *Res:* Kinetics of homogeneous reactions; mass spectrometry. *Mailing Add:* Dept Chem Northern Ill Univ DeKalb IL 60115. *Fax:* 815-753-4802

RUSSELL, NANCY JEANNE, biology, pharmacology, for more information see previous edition

RUSSELL, PAUL E(DGAR), ELECTRICAL & ENERGY SYSTEMS ENGINEERING, CONTROLS ENGINEERING. *Current Pos:* CONSULT ENGR, 90- *Personal Data:* b Roswell, NMex, Oct 10, 24; m 43, Lorna Clayshulte; c Carol (Potter), Janice (Gregory), & Gregory. *Educ:* NMex State Univ, BS, 46 & 47; Univ Wis, MS, 50, PhD(elec eng), 51. *Prof Exp:* From instr to asst prof elec eng, Univ Wis, 47-52; sr dynamics engr, Gen Dynamics/Convair, 52-54; prof elec eng, Univ Ariz, 54-63, head dept, 58-63, dir, Appl Res Lab, 56-58, 60-63; prof elec eng & dean col eng, Kans State Univ, 63-67; prof eng, Ariz State Univ, 67-90, dir, Sch Construct & Tech, 88-90. *Concurrent Pos:* Consult, NSF, Dynamic Sci, Westinghouse, Motorola, AiResearch, US Army Electronic Proving Grounds & numerous univs, UN. *Mem:* Am Soc Eng Educ; fel Inst Elec & Electronics Engrs; Nat Soc Prof Engrs; Sigma Xi. *Res:* Control systems analysis and design; computers; photovoltaic power systems; Energy systems; power quality. *Mailing Add:* 5902 E Caballo Lane Scottsdale AZ 85253

RUSSELL, PAUL SNOWDEN, SURGERY, IMMUNOLOGY. *Current Pos:* JOHN HOMANS PROF SURG, HARVARD MED SCH, 62- *Personal Data:* b Chicago, Ill, Jan 22, 25; m 52; c Katherine, Paul, Allene & Laura. *Educ:* Univ Chicago, PhB, 44, BS, 45, MD, 47; Am Bd Surg, dipl, 57; Am Bd Thoracic Surg, dipl, 60. *Hon Degrees:* MA, Harvard Univ, 62. *Prof Exp:* Surg intern, Mass Gen Hosp, 48-49, asst surg resident, 49-51 & 53-55; teaching fel surg, Harvard Univ, Sch Med, 56, instr, 57-59; clin assoc surg & tutor med sci, 59-60; assoc prof surg, Col Physicians & Surgeons, Columbia Univ, 60-62. *Concurrent Pos:* USPHS res fel, 54-55; resident, Mass Gen Hosp, 56, asst surg, 57-60; assoc attend surgeon, Presby Hosp & assoc vis surgeon, Francis Delafield Hosp, 60-62; USPHS career develop award, 60-62; chief gen surg serv, Mass Gen Hosp, 62-69, vis surgeon, 69-; mem comts trauma & tissue transplantation, Div Med Sci, Nat Acad Sci-Nat Res Coun, 63; mem allergy & immunol study sect, Div Res Grants, NIH, 63-65, chmn, 65; secy, Dept Surg, Harvard Med Sch, 65-70. *Mem:* Fel Am Col Surg; Am Asn Thoracic Surg; Soc Clin Surg; fel Royal Soc Med; Transplantation Soc (pres, 70-72); Sigma Xi. *Res:* Production of stable immunological tolerance in adult individuals; successful transplantation of animal organs to patients; better understanding of transplant arteriopathy. *Mailing Add:* Dept Surg Mass Gen Hosp Boston MA 02114. *Fax:* 617-726-3713; *E-Mail:* russell@helix.mgh.harvard.edu

RUSSELL, PAUL TELFORD, BIOCHEMISTRY. *Current Pos:* HEAD, ANIMAL CONSERVATION DIV, CINCINNATI ZOO & BOTANICAL GARDENS, 92- *Personal Data:* b San Francisco, Calif, June 5, 35; m 59; c 3. *Educ:* Univ Calif, Berkeley, BA, 59; Univ Ore, MS, 61, PhD(biochem), 63. *Prof Exp:* Trainee, Steroid Training Prog, Clark Univ & Worcester Found Exp Biol, 63-64; fel chem, Univ Miss, 64-66; asst prof obstet & gynec, Ohio State Univ, 66-68; asst prof obstet, gynec & biol chem, Med Sch, Univ Cincinnati, 68-76, assoc prof res obstet & gynec, 76-92, assoc prof pediat, 78-92. *Res:* Pathways and mechanisms of biosynthesis and metabolism of steroidal compounds; metabolic pathways of prostaglandins. *Mailing Add:* Dept Reproduction & Infertil The Christ Hosp 2139 Auburn Ave Cincinnati OH 45219

RUSSELL, PERCY J, BIOCHEMISTRY. *Current Pos:* ASSOC PROF BIOCHEM, UNIV CALIF, SAN DIEGO, 70- *Personal Data:* b New York, NY, May 29, 26; m 55; c 3. *Educ:* City Col New York, BS, 50; Brooklyn Col, MA, 55; Western Reserve Univ, PhD(biochem), 59. *Prof Exp:* Res fel bact, Harvard Univ, 59-61; from asst prof to assoc prof biochem, Univ Kans, 61-70. *Res:* Immunochemistry; enzyme mechanisms; phospholipid metabolism. *Mailing Add:* Dept Biol 0601 2130 Bonner Hall Univ Calif San Diego M-001 La Jolla CA 92093-5003. *Fax:* 619-534-0128

RUSSELL, PETER BYROM, ORGANIC CHEMISTRY. *Current Pos:* mgr org develop lab, 57-59, DIR RES, WYETH LABS DIV, AM HOME PROD CORP, 59- *Personal Data:* b Manchester, Eng, Oct 24, 18; nat US; m 45; c 2. *Educ:* Univ Manchester, BSc, 40, MSc, 41, PhD, 45, DSc, 54. *Prof Exp:* Sr res chemist, Burroughs Wellcome & Co, Inc, 47-56; dir res, John Wyeth & Brother Ltd, Eng, 56-57. *Concurrent Pos:* Chmn ad hoc study group med chem, Walter Reed Army Inst Res, 73-75. *Mem:* Am Chem Soc. *Res:* Isolation and synthesis of natural products; synthesis of chemotherapeutically active compounds; medicinal chemistry; pharmaceutical chemistry. *Mailing Add:* 1708 Sherwood Circle Villanova PA 19085-1910

RUSSELL, PETER JAMES, MOLECULAR BIOLOGY, MICROBIOLOGY. *Current Pos:* From asst prof to assoc prof, 72-84, PROF BIOL & GENETICS, REED COL, 84- *Personal Data:* b Kent, Eng, Oct 30, 47; div; c 2. *Educ:* Univ Sussex, BSc, 68; Cornell Univ, PhD(genetics), 72. *Concurrent Pos:* Vis assoc prof, Dept Physiol Chem, Univ Wis, 80-81; ed-in-chief, Fungal Genetics Newslett, 80-; mem bd, Ore Res & Technol Develop Corp, 86-89; vis prof, Dept Molecular, Cellular & Develop Biol, Univ Colo, Boulder, 89-91. *Mem:* Am Soc Microbiol; Genetics Soc Am. *Res:* Genetics of yeast virus double-stranded RNA replication. *Mailing Add:* Dept Biol Reed Col Portland OR 97202-8199. *Fax:* 503-777-7773; *E-Mail:* yeast@reed.edu

RUSSELL, PHILIP BOYD, REMOTE SENSING. *Current Pos:* chief, Atmosphere Exp Br, 82-89, actg chief & actg dep chief, Earth Syst Sci Div, 88-89, CHIEF, ATMOSPHERIC CHEM & DYNAMICS BR, NASA AMES RES CTR, 89- *Personal Data:* b Buffalo, NY, Mar 15, 44; div. *Educ:* Wesleyan Univ, BA, 65; Stanford Univ, MS, 67, 90, PhD(physics), 71. *Prof Exp:* Fel, Nat Ctr Atmospheric Res, 71-72; physicist, SRI Int, 72-76, sr physicist, 76-82. *Concurrent Pos:* Prin investr grants, NSF, NASA & Army Res Off, 74-82; mem, Army Basic Res Adv Comn, Nat Res Coun, 79-81, Solar Terrestrial Observ Sci Study Group, NASA, 79-80 & Atmospheric Lidar Working Group, 77-79; chmn, Comn Laser Atmosphere Studies, Am Meteorol Soc, 79-82, mem, Comn Radiation Energy, 79-81 & Comn Atmospheric Environ, Am Inst Aeronaut & Astronaut, 84-; mem, Interagency Task Group Airborne Geosci; guest ed, 3 J Geophys Res issues on satellite validation & stratosphere-troposphere exchange. *Mem:* Am Meteorol Soc; Optical Soc Am; Am Geophys Union; AAAS; Sigma Xi; Am Inst Aeronaut & Astronaut. *Res:* Atmospheric science; remote sensing and radiative transfer; radiative and climatic effects of aerosols and gases; aircraft and stellite measurements; laser and acoustic radar; data validation and error analysis; atmospheric multi-sensor experiment design. *Mailing Add:* 1464 Wessex Ave Los Altos CA 94024. *Fax:* 650-604-3625; *E-Mail:* philip_russell@qmgate.arc.nasa.gov

RUSSELL, PHILIP KING, INFECTIOUS DISEASES, VIROLOGY. *Current Pos:* RETIRED. *Personal Data:* b Syracuse, NY, Jan 26, 32; m 55; c 3. *Educ:* Johns Hopkins Univ, AB, 54; Univ Rochester, MD, 58; Am Bd Internal Med, dipl. *Honors & Awards:* Gorgas Medal; Smadel Mem Medal; Paul Siple Medal. *Prof Exp:* Med Corps, US Army, 58-, intern med, NC Mem Hosp, 58-59, lab officer, Walter Reed Army Inst Res, 59-61, resident med, Univ Hosp, Baltimore, 61-63, clin investr infectious dis, Pakistan Med Res Ctr, 63-64, res officer, Walter Reed Army Inst Res, 64-65, mem, Seato Med Res Lab, 65-68, chief dept virus dis, 68-71, dep dir, 76-79, dir & commandant, 79-83, dir, Div Commun Dis & Immunol, Walter Reed Army Inst Res, 71-90, comdr, Fitzsimmons Army Med Ctr, 83-90. *Concurrent Pos:* Mem bd dir, Gorgas Mem Inst; sci adv comt denque & yellow fever, Pan Am Health Orgn; tech adv comt, Denque haemorrhnqic Fever, WHO, Infectious Dis Comt & Task Force Virology, Nat Inst Allergy & Infectious Dis, NIH; chmn steering comt, Sci Working Group Immunol Malaria, WHO, 80-; sci adv group experts, WHO, 85- *Mem:* Am Soc Trop Med & Hyg; Am Soc Microbiol; Am Asn Immunol; Am Epidemiol Soc; Infectious Dis Soc Am. *Res:* Virus diseases; immunology; pathogenesis of virus diseases; epidemiology of arboviruses. *Mailing Add:* 11909 Coldstream Dr Potomac MD 20854

RUSSELL, RAYMOND ALVIN, PHYSIOLOGY. *Current Pos:* RETIRED. *Personal Data:* b Buffalo, NY, Jan 16, 17; m 43, Ruth L MacClaren; c Raymond A Jr & Daniel M. *Educ:* Hamilton Col, AB, 38; Univ Rochester, MS, 41, PhD(physiol), 51. *Prof Exp:* Asst agr biochem, Univ Minn, 41-42; asst invest chem, NY Agr Exp Sta, 42-44; from instr to assoc prof, La State Univ Med Ctr, New Orleans, 51-80. *Concurrent Pos:* Consult, Southern Baptist Hosp, New Orleans, La, 59-76. *Mem:* Am Physiol Soc; AAAS. *Res:* Secretion of the small intestine; myocardial metabolism; circulatory shock. *Mailing Add:* 5619 Old Wake Forest Rd Raleigh NC 27609-5056

RUSSELL, RICHARD DONCASTER, GEOPHYSICS, INSTRUMENTATION. *Current Pos:* head dept, 68-79, assoc vpres acad, 83-86, PROF GEOPHYS, UNIV BC, 63- *Personal Data:* b Toronto, Ont, Feb 27, 29; m 51; c 3. *Educ:* Univ Toronto, BA, 51, MA, 52, PhD(physics/geophys), 54. *Prof Exp:* Lectr physics, Univ Toronto, 54-56, asst prof, 56-58, prof, 62-63; assoc prof, Univ BC, 58-62. *Mem:* Am Geophys Union; fel Royal Soc Can; Geol Asn Can; Can Soc Explor Geophysicists. *Res:* Mass spectrometry; seismology; electronics; histroy of the earth; geochronology; physics of geophysical instruments and geochemistry. *Mailing Add:* Dept Geophysics & Astronomy Univ BC 1292219 Main Mall, Vancouver BC V6T 1Z4 Can

RUSSELL, RICHARD LAWSON, DEVELOPMENTAL NEUROGENETICS. *Current Pos:* assoc prof, 76-84, PROF BIOL SCI, UNIV PITTSBURGH, 84- *Personal Data:* b Bar Harbor, Maine, Nov 24, 40; m 62, 77, Barbara J Attardi; c Kerstin, Daniel & David. *Educ:* Harvard Col, BA, 62; Calif Inst Technol, PhD(genetics), 67. *Prof Exp:* Asst prof genetics, Cornell Univ, 66-67; mem staff, Lab Molecular Biol, Med Res Coun, Cambridge Univ, 67-70; asst prof biol, Calif Inst Technol, 70-76. *Concurrent Pos:* NSF fel, 67-68; NATO fel, 68-69; Am Heart Asn fel, 69-70; mem, NIH Molecular Cytol Study Sect, 80-84. *Mem:* AAAS; Fedn Am Scientists; Genetics Soc Am. *Res:* Genetic analysis of structure and function in simple nervous systems. *Mailing Add:* Dept Biol Sci univ Pittsburgh A-234 Langley Hall Pittsburgh PA 15260-0001. *Fax:* 412-624-4759

RUSSELL, RICHARD OLNEY, JR, CARDIOLOGY. *Current Pos:* from instr to prof med, 64-81, CLIN PROF, UNIV ALA, BIRMINGHAM, 81-; CARDIOLOGIST, CARDIOVASC ASSOCS, 81- *Personal Data:* b Birmingham, Ala, July 9, 32; m 63, Phyllis Hutchinson; c Scott R, Katherine H, Meredith C & Stephen W. *Educ:* Vanderbilt Univ, BA, 53, MD, 56. *Concurrent Pos:* Co-dir, Myocardial Infarction Res Unit, Univ Ala, Birmingham, 70-75. *Mem:* Am Fedn Clin Res; Am Col Cardiol. *Res:* Ischemic heart disease; acute myocardial infarction; hemodynamics of acute and chronic ischemic heart disease. *Mailing Add:* Cardiovasc Assocs 880 Montclair Rd Suite 170 Birmingham AL 35213

RUSSELL, ROBERT JOHN, LABORATORY ANIMAL MEDICINE. *Current Pos:* DIR, ANIMAL MED LAB, HARLAN SPRAGUE DAWLEY, INC, INDIANAPOLIS, 96- *Personal Data:* b Ballymena, Northern Ireland, Jan 21, 38; US citizen; m 71; c 2. *Educ:* Univ Ill, BS, 60, DVM, 62; Tex A&M Univ, MS, 69. *Prof Exp:* Clin pract vet med, Roseland Animal Hosp, Chicago, 62; base vet, USAF, Norton AFB, Calif, 62-64 & Royal Air Force, Wethersfield, Eng, 64-67; resident lab animal med, Tex A&M Univ & Brooks AFB, 67-69; dir, Vet Serv, Cam Rahn Bay 20th Hosp, USAF, Vietnam, 69-70, dir, Lab Animal Med, Armed Forces Inst Path, Washington, 70-76, Naval Med Res Inst, Bethesda, Md, 76-82 & Prog Resources, Inc, Frederick, Md, 82-85. *Concurrent Pos:* Consult, NIH, Bethesda, 72-82, Bioqual, Inc, Rockville, Md, 78-; adj fac, NVa Community Col, Herndon, Va, 76- *Mem:* Am Vet Med Asn; Am Asn Lab Animal Sci. *Res:* Laboratory animal management; infectious disease; animal reproduction; hypobaric medicine; author of various publications. *Mailing Add:* Harlan Sprague Dawley Inc 298 S County Line Rd Indianapolis IN 46250

RUSSELL, ROBERT LEE, PHYSIOLOGY, PHARMACOLOGY. *Current Pos:* Asst physiol & pharmacol, 50-53, from asst instr to prof pharmacol, 53-89, EMER PROF PHARMACOL, UNIV MO-COLUMBIA, 89- *Personal Data:* b Independence, Mo, June 27, 27; m 50; c 2. *Educ:* Univ Mo, PhD(physiol, pharmacol), 54. *Mem:* Fel AAAS; Soc Exp Biol & Med; Am Soc Pharmacol & Exp Therapeut. *Res:* Drugs affecting lipid metabolism. *Mailing Add:* 12301 Rte N Columbia MO 65203-9343

RUSSELL, ROBERT M, GASTROENTEROLOGY. *Current Pos:* DIR HUMAN STUDIES, HUMAN NUTRIT RES CTR-TUFTS UNIV, USDA, 81-, PROF MED & NUTRIT, 88- *Personal Data:* b Boston, Mass, Apr 9, 41; m 68, Sharon Stanton; c Kimberley & Brooke. *Educ:* Harvard Univ, BA, 63; Columbia Univ, MD, 67. *Honors & Awards:* Res Award, Chicago Soc Gastroenterol, 74; Grace A Goldsmith Award, Am Col Nutrit, 94; Ethyl Austin Martin Distinguished Lectr Human Nutrit, 95. *Prof Exp:* Vis asst prof med, Shiraz Univ, Shiraz, Iran, 74-75; from asst prof to assoc prof, Sch Med, Univ Md, 75-81; res & develop assoc, Vet Admin Med Ctr, Baltimore, 75-79; staff physician gastroenterol, Univ Md Hosp & Vet Admin Hosp, 75-81; assoc prof med, Sch Med, Tufts Univ, 81-86, adj assoc prof nutrit, 82-86. *Concurrent Pos:* Consult, Food & Drug Admin, 74-79 & Nat Iranian Cancer Found, 78; clin investr, Vet Admin Career Develop Prog, Baltimore, 79-81; mem, Comt Nutrit Res, Am Soc Clin Nutrit, 80-84; staff physician, New Eng Med Ctr, Boston, 81; mem bd dirs, Am Col Nutrit, 81-; actg dir, Human Nutrit Res Ctr-Tufts Univ, USDA, 83-85 & 85-86, assoc dir, 87-; mem, Nat Dairy Coun Sci Adv Bd, 87-91, chmn, 90-91; nutrit consult, Am Bd Internal Med, 90-93; coun, Am Soc Clin Nutrit, 92-95; mem, Expert Adv Comm Older Americans, Am Dietetic Asn, 96; panel mem, folate & B vitamins, Food & Nutrit Bd, Nat Acad Sci, 96. *Mem:* Am Gastroenterol Asn; fel Am Col Physicians; Am Inst Nutrit; Am Fedn Clin Res; Am Soc Clin Nutrit; Gastroenterol Res Group. *Res:* Gastrointestinal absorptive function of micronutrients; effect of aging on gastrointestinal function; folic acid and retnoid metabolism. *Mailing Add:* USDA Human Nutrit Res Ctr Aging Tufts Univ 711 Washington St Boston MA 02111-1525. *Fax:* 617-556-3295

RUSSELL, ROBERT RAYMOND, CHEMISTRY. *Current Pos:* RETIRED. *Personal Data:* b Beach, Wash, July 3, 20; m 43; c 3. *Educ:* Graceland Col, AB, 43, MA, 46; Univ Kans, PhD(chem), 49. *Prof Exp:* prof chem, Univ Mo-Rolla, 48- *Mem:* Am Chem Soc. *Res:* Organic chemical reaction mechanisms. *Mailing Add:* Box 766 Rolla MO 65402

RUSSELL, ROSS F, CHEMICAL ENGINEERING, POLYMER CHEMISTRY. *Current Pos:* VPRES, MESERAN CO, 83- *Personal Data:* b Auburn, Nebr, May 7, 19; m 44; c 4. *Educ:* Peru State Col, BA, 41; Iowa State Univ, PhD(chem eng), 50. *Prof Exp:* Engr, E I du Pont de Nemours & Co, Inc, 50-57, process supvr, 57-67, sr res engr, 67-82. *Mem:* Am Chem Soc; Am Inst Chem Engrs. *Res:* Plant installations of solvent extraction, distillation and polymerization equipment; computerized analytical instruments. *Mailing Add:* 701 Highview Dr Chattanooga TN 37415-2915

RUSSELL, RUTH LOIS, MICROBIOLOGY. *Current Pos:* from asst prof to assoc prof microbiol, 63-72, prof, 72-73, actg dean, Grad Studies, 74-77, DIR ENVIRON STUDIES, CALIF STATE UNIV, LONG BEACH, 77- *Personal Data:* b San Diego, Calif, July 22, 28; m 54; c 1. *Educ:* Univ Calif, Los Angeles, BA, 52, PhD(microbiol), 63. *Prof Exp:* Asst bact, Univ Calif, Los Angeles, 52-55; instr biol, Occidental Col, 56-57; med bacteriologist, San Fernando Vet Admin Hosp, Calif, 59-61; res microbiologist, Olive View Hosp, 61-62; med bacteriologist, San Fernando Vet Admin Hosp, Calif, 62-63. *Concurrent Pos:* Consult microbiologist, var clin & biomed labs. *Mem:* AAAS; Am Soc Microbiol; Am Pub Health Asn; NY Acad Sci; Am Soc Qual Control. *Res:* Pub health microbiology; medical bacteriology; environmental microbiology. *Mailing Add:* Dept Microbiol Calif State Univ 3702 Csulb Long Beach CA 90840-0004

RUSSELL, SCOTT D, CYTOLOGY. *Current Pos:* From asst prof to assoc prof, 81-92, DIR S R NOBLE ELEC MICROS LAB, UNIV OKLA, 84-, PROF STRUCTURAL BOT, 92- *Personal Data:* b Milwaukee, Wis, Dec 8, 52; m 93, Vivian Linke; c 1. *Educ:* Univ Wis-Madison, BA, 75; Northern Ariz Univ, MS, 77; Univ Alta, PhD, 81. *Honors & Awards:* Jeanette Siron Pelton Award, Bot Soc Am, 88. *Concurrent Pos:* prin investr, 2 NSF grants, 3 USDA grants, 1 Dept Educ grant, 82-; vis scientist, Univ Melbourne, Australia, 84; vis prof, Ecole Normal Superieure, Lyon, France, 89. *Mem:* Bot Soc Am; AAAS; Int Soc Plant Morpholog; Elec Micros Soc Am; Microbeam Anal Soc; Am Soc Plant Physiologists. *Res:* Structural basis of double fertilization and male cytoplasmic transmission in angiosperms; reproductive plant cytology and ultrastructure. *Mailing Add:* Dept Bot & Microbiol Univ Okla Norman OK 73019. *Fax:* 405-325-7619; *E-Mail:* srussell@ou.edu

RUSSELL, SHARON MAY, growth hormones, for more information see previous edition

RUSSELL, STEPHEN MIMS, ORNITHOLOGY. *Current Pos:* asst prof, 64-70, ASSOC PROF ZOOL, UNIV ARIZ, 70-, CUR BIRDS, 64- *Personal Data:* b Hot Springs, Ark, Sept 16, 31. *Educ:* Va Polytech Inst, BS, 53; La State Univ, PhD(zool), 62. *Prof Exp:* From instr to asst prof biol, La State Univ, 58-64. *Mem:* Fel Am Ornith Union; Cooper Ornith Soc; Wilson Ornith Soc; Sigma Xi. *Res:* Biology of desert and neotropical birds, especially behavior, ecology, distribution. *Mailing Add:* 2850 Camino de Oeste Tucson AZ 85745

RUSSELL, STUART JONATHAN, MACHINE LEARNING, LIMITED RATIONALITY. *Current Pos:* ASST PROF COMPUTER SCI, UNIV CALIF, BERKELEY, 86- *Personal Data:* b Portsmouth, UK, Feb 25, 62. *Educ:* Oxford Univ, BA Hons, 82; Stanford Univ, PhD(comput sci), 86. *Concurrent Pos:* Consult, MCC, 86-89; vis prof, Oxford Univ, 90; mem rev panel, Nat Res Coun, 90; NSF presidential young investr, 90. *Mem:* Am Asn Artificial Intel; Asn Comput Mach. *Res:* Artificial intelligence; machine learning, knowledge-based induction; limited rationality-decision-theoretic-metareasoning; analogical reasoning; real time decision making. *Mailing Add:* 1567 Mallorca Dr Vista CA 92083

RUSSELL, T W FRASER, CHEMICAL ENGINEERING. *Current Pos:* prof chem eng, 64-81, chmn dept, 86-91, ALLAN P COLBURN PROF CHEM ENG, UNIV DEL, 81-, CHIEF ENGR, INST ENERGY CONVERSION, 96- *Personal Data:* b Moose Jaw, Sask, Aug 5, 34; m 56; c 3. *Educ:* Univ Alta, BSc, 56, MSc, 58; Univ Del, PhD(chem eng), 64. *Honors & Awards:* Leo Friend Award, Am Chem Soc, 82; 3M Chem Eng Div Award, Am Soc Eng Educ, 84; Award in Chem Eng Pract, Am Inst Chem Engrs, 87, Thomas H Chilton Award, 88. *Prof Exp:* Res chem engr, Res Coun Alta, 56-58; design engr, Union Carbide Can, 58-61. *Concurrent Pos:* Consult, E I du Pont de Nemours & other chem & electronics firms, 61-94; dir, Inst Energy Conversion, 79-96. *Mem:* Nat Acad Eng; Am Chem Soc; Am Soc Eng Educ; fel Am Inst Chem Engrs. *Res:* Semi-conductor reaction and reactor engineering with application to commercial scale manufacture of photovoltaic modules/multi-phase fluid mechanics with application to the design of process equipment; economics of the chemical process industries. *Mailing Add:* Inst Energy Conversion Univ Del Newark DE 19716-0001. *Fax:* 302-831-6226; *E-Mail:* russell@che.udel.edu

RUSSELL, TERRENCE R, HIGHER EDUCATION ADMINISTRATION. *Current Pos:* EXEC DIR, ASN INSTNL RES, 91- *Personal Data:* b Chicago, Ill, Dec 22, 40; m 65, Linda Martin; c Joshua. *Educ:* Southern Ill Univ, BA, 67, MS, 69, PhD(soc sci), 79. *Prof Exp:* Res assoc, Nat Surv Community Corrections Progs Ctr Study Crime, Delinquency & Corrections, 71-72; instr social & co-founder, co-dir Urban Studies Prog, Ill Wesleyan Univ, 72-77; asst prof social & dir res internship prog, Ill State Univ, 77-80; asst prof soc, Northern Ky Univ, 80-84; sr res assoc, Work Force Analysis, 84-85, prof relations prog mgr, 85-88, mgr, Am Chem Soc, 88-91. *Concurrent Pos:* Mem, Comt Measuring Nat Needs for Scientists to Yr 2000, chair, Social Sci Sect, 87; adv comt, Div Sci Resources Studies, NSF, 87-89; comn prof sci & technol, Prof Soc Ethis Goup, AAAS; vis assoc prof, Georgetown Univ, 87-, chmn, Engrs & Scientists' Joint Comt on Pensions, Am Asn Eng Soc, 91; grant, Occup Mobility Studies, NSF, 88-89. *Mem:* Acad Mgt; Am Chem Soc; Am Soc Asn Exec; Am Sociol Asn; Asn Inst Res; Soc Social Study Sci. *Res:* Development, implementation and marketing of programs serving the professional and information needs of Association for Institutional Research members; studies of issues concerning the scientific and technical labor force.. *Mailing Add:* Assn Inst Res 114 Stone Bldg Fla State Univ Tallahassee FL 32306-3038. *Fax:* 850-644-8824; *E-Mail:* air@mailer.fsu.edu

RUSSELL, THOMAS EDWARD, PLANT PATHOLOGY. *Current Pos:* asst plant pathologist, 71-76, ASSOC RES SCIENTIST PLANT PATH, UNIV ARIZ, 76- *Personal Data:* b Tucson, Ariz, May 8, 42; m 65; c 1. *Educ:* Univ Ariz, BS, 65, MS, 67; Tex A&M Univ, PhD(plant path), 70. *Prof Exp:* Agr specialist pesticide res, Buckman Labs, Tenn, 70-71. *Mem:* Am Phytopath Soc. *Res:* Diseases of vegetable crops, turf and cotton. *Mailing Add:* PO Box 420 Waddell AZ 85355

RUSSELL, THOMAS J, JR, biochemistry, for more information see previous edition

RUSSELL, THOMAS PAUL, POLYMER PHYSICS. *Current Pos:* RES STAFF MEM POLYMER PHYSICS, IBM RES LABS, 81- *Personal Data:* b Boston, Mass, Nov 18, 52; m 78, Catherine Gulla; c Justin, Katie & Sebastian. *Educ:* Boston State Col, BS, 74; Univ Mass, Amherst, MA, 77, PhD(polymer sci), 79. *Honors & Awards:* A Doolittle Award, Am Chem Soc, 85. *Prof Exp:* Res fel polymer physics, Univ Mainz, W Germany, 79-81. *Concurrent Pos:* Mem, Nat Steering Comt for Advan Neutron Source, Prog Adv Comt, Los Alamos Nat Lab; chmn, Div Polymer Physics Prog Comt, Am Phys Soc. *Mem:* Fel Am Phys Soc; Am Chem Soc; Am Crystallog Asn; Sigma Xi; Mat Res Soc. *Res:* The physics of high polymers in the solid state; characteristics of high temperature polymers for use in the microelectronics industry; compatibility, phase separation kinetics and crystallization of polymer mixtures and their interdiffusion by use of small angle x-ray, light and neutron scattering; time resolved scattering techniques using synchrohon radiation; x-ray and neutron reflectivity on thin polymer films. *Mailing Add:* Dept Polymer Sci & Eng Univ Mass Amherst MA 01003. *Fax:* 408-927-3310; *E-Mail:* trussell@almaden.ibm.com

RUSSELL, THOMAS SOLON, STATISTICS. *Current Pos:* from asst statistician to assoc statistician, 56-63, prof agr & statistician, Agr Exp Sta, 63-85, EMER PROF AGR, WASH STATE UNIV, 85- *Personal Data:* b Bracey, Va, June 27, 22; m 49; c 4. *Educ:* Wake Forest Col, BS, 44; Va Polytech Inst, MS, 53, PhD(statist), 56. *Prof Exp:* Instr math, Capitol Radio Engrs Inst, 46-47; instr, Va Polytech Inst, 47-51, asst statistician, Agr Exp Sta, 53-56. *Mem:* Biomet Soc; Am Statist Asn; Inst Math Statist; Sigma Xi. *Res:* Mathematical statistics. *Mailing Add:* SW 910 Fountain St Pullman WA 99163

RUSSELL, THOMAS WEBB, HETEROGENEOUS CATALYSIS, ORGANIC REDUCTIONS. *Current Pos:* PRES, LONE STAR VINEYARD CO, 84- *Personal Data:* b Greenville, Tex, Dec 17, 40; m 64. *Educ:* Tex Col Arts & Indust, BSc, 62; Univ Colo, MSc, 64, PhD(chem), 66. *Prof Exp:* Vis asst prof chem, La State Univ, 66-67; asst prof chem, Eastern NMex Univ, 67-72, assoc prof, 72-79, prof, 79-81; sr res chemist, El Paso Petrochem Co, 81-83. *Concurrent Pos:* Am Chem Soc Petrol Res Fund fel, NSF fel. *Mem:* AAAS; Am Chem Soc. *Res:* Heterogeneous hydrogenation and methanation catalysts; organic synthesis; groundwater quality and control. *Mailing Add:* 14017 W Co Rd No 124 Odessa TX 79765-9801

RUSSELL, WILBERT AMBRICK, plant breeding, genetics, for more information see previous edition

RUSSELL, WILLIAM CHARLES, THIN FILM SCIENCE, CHEMICAL VAPOR DEPOSITION PROCESS MODELING. *Current Pos:* ADV ENGR, VALENITE, INC, 88- *Personal Data:* b New Brunswick, NJ, Nov 11, 55; m 86; c 2. *Educ:* Rutgers Univ, BS, 77; Univ Ky, MS, 86, PhD(mat sci), 88. *Prof Exp:* Ceramic engr, Corhart Refractories Co, 77-78. *Mem:* Mat Res Soc. *Res:* Thin refractory ceramic coatings deposition by chemical vapor deposition and related methods on cemented carbides for the metal cutting industry; thin film analytical techniques; thermodynamics. *Mailing Add:* Valenite Inc 1711 Thunderbird Troy MI 48084

RUSSELL, WILLIAM LAWSON, GENETIC RISK FROM RADIATION & CHEMICALS. *Current Pos:* prin geneticist, 47-77, CONSULT GENETICS, OAK RIDGE NAT LAB, 77- *Personal Data:* b Newhaven, Eng, Aug 19, 10; nat US; m 36, 47; c 6. *Educ:* Oxford Univ, BA, 32; Univ Chicago, PhD, 37. *Honors & Awards:* Roentgen Medal, 73; Distinguished Achievement Award of Health, Physics Soc, 76; Enrico Fermi Award, 77; Environ Mutagen Soc Award, 89. *Prof Exp:* Asst zool, Univ Chicago, 34-36; res assoc, Jackson Mem Lab, 37-47. *Concurrent Pos:* Adv, US deleg to UN Sci Comt Effects Atomic Radiation, 62-86; mem, various other int and nat comts on genetic risks of radiation and chemicals. *Mem:* Nat Acad Sci; Genetics Soc Am (pres, 65); Environ Mutagen Soc. *Res:* Genetics of the mouse; genetic effects of radiation and chemicals. *Mailing Add:* Life Sci Oak Ridge Nat Lab PO Box 2009 Oak Ridge TN 37831-8077. *Fax:* 423-574-1283

RUSSELL, WILLIAM T(RELOAR), mechanical & electrical engineering; deceased, see previous edition for last biography

RUSSEY, WILLIAM EDWARD, ORGANIC CHEMISTRY. *Current Pos:* From asst prof to assoc prof, 66-75, chmn dept, 68-75, PROF CHEM, JUNIATA COL, 75- *Personal Data:* b Kalamazoo, Mich, Apr 5, 39; div; c 2. *Educ:* Kalamazoo Col, AB, 61; Harvard Univ, AM, 64, PhD(chem), 67. *Concurrent Pos:* NSF fac sci fel, Max Planck Inst Coal Res, Muelheim/Ruhr, WGer, 75-76, 80 & 81; Fulbright vis prof, Fachhochschule Muenster & Univ Marburg, W Germany, 82-83. *Mem:* Am Chem Soc; Royal Soc Chem. *Res:* Steroid biogenesis; olefin cyclization reactions; molecular rearrangements; fossil fuel chemistry. *Mailing Add:* Dept Chem Juniata Col Huntingdon PA 16652-2196

RUSSFIELD, AGNES BURT, PATHOLOGY. *Current Pos:* SCIENTIST, MASON RES INST, 75- *Personal Data:* b Portland, Ore, Jan 9, 17; m 54. *Educ:* Reed Col, BA, 35; Univ Calif, MA, 37; Univ Chicago, PhD(zool), 43; Cornell Univ, MD, 49. *Prof Exp:* Asst zool, Univ Calif, Los Angeles, 35-36; asst, Univ Chicago, 37-39 & 40-41, asst, Off Sci Res & Develop Proj, 42-43; intern, Mass Gen Hosp, 49-50, asst resident, 50-51, fel path, 51-54, asst, 54-57, asst pathologist, 57-58; assoc, Bio-Res Inst Inc, 59-61; res assoc, Children's Cancer Res Found, 61-67; resident, Mallory Inst Path, 67-68, asst pathologist, 68-71; res assoc, Bio-Res Inst, Inc, 72-73; staff pathologist, St Vincent Hosp, 74-75. *Concurrent Pos:* From instr to assoc clin prof, Harvard Med Sch, 52-68; coop scientist, Worcester Found Exp Biol, 65-67 & 68-; assoc prof, Med Sch, Tufts Univ, 68-71 & Med Sch, Univ Mass, 75-78. *Mem:* Am Asn Cancer Res; Endocrine Soc; Am Asn Path; Am Soc Cytol; Soc Toxicol Path. *Res:* Endocrine changes in cancer; carcinogenesis. *Mailing Add:* Egg/Mason Res Inst 57 Union St Worcester MA 01608-1114

RUSSIN, NICHOLAS CHARLES, PHYSICAL CHEMISTRY. *Current Pos:* RETIRED. *Personal Data:* b Butler, Pa, Feb 6, 22; m 47; c 3. *Educ:* Washington & Jefferson Col, AB, 43; Carnegie Inst Technol, MS, 49, DSc, 50. *Prof Exp:* develop assoc, Tenn Eastman Co, 50-85. *Mem:* Am Chem Soc; fel Am Inst Chemists; Am Asn Textile Technol. *Res:* Thermodynamic properties of solutions; man-made fibers. *Mailing Add:* 312 McTeer Dr Kingsport TN 37663

RUSSO, ANTHONY R, REEF ECOLOGIST. *Current Pos:* asst prof oceanog, 70-82, PROF OCEANOG, LEEWARD COL, UNIV HAWAII, 82- *Personal Data:* b Trenton, NJ, May 14, 37; m 61; c 3. *Educ:* US Naval Acad, BS, 58; Univ Wis, MS, 66; Univ Hawaii, MS, 78; Fla Inst Technol, PhD(oceanog), 86. *Prof Exp:* Nuclear engr, Gulf Gen Atomic Lab, 66-69; researcher, Univ Calif, San Diego, 68-70. *Concurrent Pos:* Consult, Univ Hawaii, 72-; vis prof, Oxford Univ, Eng, 76-77, Univ Naples, 80 & Univ Thessaloniki, Greece, 89-90. *Mem:* Am Soc Naturalists; Nature Conservancy. *Res:* Structure and dynamics of coral reef invertebrate fauna; factors which regulate epifaunal invertebrate populations; effects of pollution stress on coral reef communities. *Mailing Add:* 1088 Bishop St Apt 1225 Honolulu HI 96813

RUSSO, DENNIS CHARLES, BEHAVIORAL MEDICINE, PEDIATRIC PSYCHOLOGY. *Current Pos:* ASSOC CLIN PROF PSYCHIAT, HARVARD MED SCH, 86-; SR VPRES CLIN SERV, MAY INST, 91- *Personal Data:* b Cleveland, Ohio, Feb 11, 50; m 85; c 1. *Educ:* Univ Calif, Santa Barbara, BA, 72, PhD(educ psychol), 75. *Prof Exp:* Asst prof psychiat & pediat, Sch Med, Johns Hopkins Univ, 77-79; asst prof psychiat, Harvard Med Sch, 79-86. *Concurrent Pos:* Dir training & clin serv, behav pscyhol, John F Kennedy Inst, Baltimore, 75-79; dir behav med, Childrens Hosp, Boston, 79-89, sr assoc psychol, 82-89; distinguished vis prof, USAF Wilword Hall Med Ctr, 81-88. *Mem:* Fel Am Psychol Asn; fel Soc Behav Med; Asn Advan Behav Ther (secy-treas, 83-86, pres, 87-88); Am Bd Behav Psychol. *Res:* Psychological sequelae of chronic illness in children with particular reference to the relationship between physiology and behavior; development of psychological treatment for chronic illness management. *Mailing Add:* May Inst 220 Norwood Park S Norwood MA 02062. *Fax:* 781-440-0401

RUSSO, EDWIN PRICE, MECHANICAL & ELECTRICAL ENGINEERING. *Current Pos:* PROF MECH ENG, UNIV NEW ORLEANS, 77- *Personal Data:* b New Orleans, La, June 4, 38; m 83, Barbara Chartier; c Christopher, Darren, David & Anne-Marie. *Educ:* Tulane Univ, BS, 60, MS, 62; La State Univ, PhD(mech eng), 68. *Prof Exp:* Elec engr, Chevron Oil Co, 62-63; res engr, Boeing Co, 63-66; instr eng mech, La State Univ, Baton Rouge, 66-68; assoc prof eng sci, La State Univ, New Orleans, 68-77. *Concurrent Pos:* Act chmn mech eng, Univ New Orleans. *Mem:* Fel Am Soc Mech Engrs. *Res:* Stress analysis; fluid mechanics; heat transfer; oceanography. *Mailing Add:* Dept Mech Eng Univ New Orleans New Orleans LA 70148-0001. *Fax:* 504-288-5539; *E-Mail:* eprme@uno.edu

RUSSO, EMANUEL JOSEPH, PHARMACEUTICS. *Current Pos:* group leader pharmaceut develop, 63-78, mgr oral & topical prod, 78-90, DIR, PHARMACEUT SCI, WYETH LABS, 90- *Personal Data:* b Philadelphia, Pa, Jan 23, 34; m 65. *Educ:* Philadelphia Col Pharm, BSc, 55; Temple Univ,

MSc, 57; Univ Wis, PhD(pharm), 60. *Prof Exp:* Chemist, Phys Chem Dept, Schering Corp, NJ, 60-63. *Mem:* Am Pharmaceut Asn; Acad Pharmaceut Sci. *Res:* Study of physical and chemical properties of drugs, before and after their inclusion into a finished dosage form in order to formulate the most stable and efficacious product. *Mailing Add:* 8 Morris Philadelphia PA 19148

RUSSO, JOHN A, JR, METEOROLOGY. *Current Pos:* PRES, JUST RESTAURANTS BUS BROKERS, 86- *Personal Data:* b New York, NY, June 24, 33; m 59; c 7. *Educ:* City Col New York, BS, 55; Univ Conn, MBA, 68. *Prof Exp:* Weather forecaster, US Weather Bur, 55-56; res asst statist & meteorol, Univ Ariz, 57-60; res assoc radar meteorol, Travelers Res Corp, Conn, 60-63, assoc scientist, 63-66, res scientist, 66-68, dir opers res, 68-71; vpres, Group Dept, Hartford Ins Group, 71-86. *Mem:* Am Meteorol Soc. *Res:* Meteorological statistics; design and development of information systems; weather sensitivity analysis; business administration. *Mailing Add:* 311 Cedarwood Lane Newington CT 06111

RUSSO, JOSE, EXPERIMENTAL PATHOLOGY, PATHOLOGY. *Current Pos:* CHMN, DEPT PATH, FOX CHASE CANCER CTR, 91- *Personal Data:* b Mendoza, Argentina, Mar 24, 42; m 69; c 1. *Educ:* A Alvarez Col, Argentina, BA & BS, 59; Sch Med, Univ Cuyo, Argentina, Physician, 67, Med Dr, 68; Bd Cert Path, 82. *Prof Exp:* Instr path, Inst Gen Exp Path, Sch Med, Mendoza, Argentina, 61-66, instr histol & embryol, Inst Histol & Embryol, 66-69, chief instr embryol, 69-71; res fel, Inst Molecular Cell Evolution, Univ Miami, Fla, 71-73; sr res scientist, Mich Cancer Found, 73-74, chief, Exp Path Lab, 74-79, chmn, dept path, 79-91. *Concurrent Pos:* Fel, Nat Coun Res, Argentina, 67-69 & 69-71; assoc mem, Mich Cancer Found, 70-; assoc clin prof path, Wayne State Univ, 79-; grants, Am Cancer Soc & Nat Cancer Inst. *Mem:* Foreign mem Soc Study Reproduction; Am Soc Cell Biol; Soc Exp Biol & Med; Electron Micros Soc Am; Am Asn Cancer Res; Am Col Path; Am Soc Clin Pathologists; Am Cancer Soc, Nat Cancer Inst; Am Col Pathologists, Int Acad Pathologists. *Res:* Study of the etiology and pathogenesis of human breast cancer, and pathogenesis of the same disease in experimental models; chemical carcinogenesis; oncogenes; cell transformation. *Mailing Add:* Fox Chase Cancer Ctr 7701 Burholme Ave Philadelphia PA 19111. *Fax:* 215-728-2899

RUSSO, JOSEPH MARTIN, AGRICULTURAL METEOROLOGY, SYSTEMS SCIENCE. *Current Pos:* RES SCIENTIST, ZEDX INC, 87- *Personal Data:* b Middletown, Conn, Feb 6, 49. *Educ:* St Louis Univ, BS, 71; McGill Univ, MSc, 74; Cornell Univ, PhD(agrometeorol), 78. *Prof Exp:* Res assoc, Agron Dept, Cornell Univ, 78-79, Dept Entom, NY State Agr Exp Sta, 79-81; asst prof, Dept Hort, Pa State Univ, 81-87. *Concurrent Pos:* Res consult, 78-79; vis fel, Agron Dept, Cornell Univ, 79. *Mem:* Am Meteorol Soc; Am Soc Agron; Soil Sci Soc Am; Am Soc Hort Sci; Int Soc Biometeorol. *Res:* Theory and experimental designs for agricultural production systems. *Mailing Add:* 228 W Pine St Boalsburg PA 16827. *Fax:* 814-466-6691

RUSSO, MICHAEL EUGENE, CHEMISTRY. *Current Pos:* Investr chem res & develop, Mallinckrodt Chem Works, 67-74, RES MGR, MALLINCKRODT, INC, 74- *Personal Data:* b St Louis, Mo, Aug 5, 39. *Educ:* Wash Univ, AB, 61, PhD(chem), 70. *Concurrent Pos:* Vpres & dir, Parkside Develop Corp; dir, Montecello Corp. *Res:* Physical and inorganic chemistry; molecular spectroscopy. *Mailing Add:* Ten Kingsbury Pl St Louis MO 63112

RUSSO, RALPH P, MATHEMATICAL STATISTICS. *Current Pos:* AT DEPT STATIST & MATH, UNIV IOWA. *Personal Data:* b New York, NY, Dec, 29, 52; m 76; c 1. *Educ:* State Univ NY, Binghamton, MA & PhD(math), 80. *Prof Exp:* Asst prof Statist, State Univ NY, Buffalo, 80- *Mem:* Am Statist Asn; Inst Math Statist. *Mailing Add:* Dept Statist Univ Iowa 101 Maclean Hall Iowa City IA 52242

RUSSO, RAYMOND JOSEPH, ENTOMOLOGY, ECOLOGY. *Current Pos:* ASSOC PROF ECOL, IND UNIV-PURDUE UNIV, INDIANAPOLIS, 76- *Personal Data:* b St Louis, Mo, May 30, 44; m 70; c 2. *Educ:* Southeast Mo State Univ, BS, 66; Northeast Mo State Univ, MA, 71; Univ Notre Dame, PhD(entom), 76. *Concurrent Pos:* Consult, Ind State Bd Health, 78. *Mem:* Entom Soc Am; Soc Neurosci; Sigma Xi. *Res:* Insect neurobiology; computer applications to biology; medical entomology. *Mailing Add:* Dept Biol Ind Univ-Purdue Univ 1100 W Michigan St Indianapolis IN 46202-2880

RUSSO, RICHARD F, OPERATIONS RESEARCH, SYSTEMS ANALYSIS & PROJECT MANAGEMENT. *Current Pos:* RETIRED. *Personal Data:* b Somerville, Mass, Apr 22, 27; wid; c Richard, Albert, Sara, John, Elizabeth, Carolyn & Andrea. *Educ:* Mass Maritime Acad, BS, 47; Boston Col, AB, 51, AM, 53. *Prof Exp:* Develop physicist, Am Optical Co, 52-55; staff mem, Lincoln Lab, Mass Inst Technol, 55-57; sr engr, Shipbldg Div, Bethlehem Steel Co, 57-64; mathematician, Dewey & Almy Chem Div, W R Grace & Co, 64-66; mgr corp mgt sci, Itek Corp, 66-69, sr analyst innovative software, 70-71; res systs analyst, New Eng Life Inst Co, Mass, 71-73; systs planning specialist, United Illum Co, 73-75; pvt pract, 75-77; sr bus analyst, Honeywell Info Systs, 77-79, tech support adminr, 79-83; systs proj mgr, Blue Cross, 83-91. *Mem:* Opers Res Soc Am. *Res:* Application of advanced mathematical techniques and computer technology to the solution of business and industrial problems. *Mailing Add:* 170 Crosby St Arlington MA 02174

RUSSO, ROY LAWRENCE, ELECTRICAL ENGINEERING, DESIGN AUTOMATION ENGINEER. *Current Pos:* RETIRED. *Personal Data:* b Kelayres, Pa, Nov 6, 35; m 59; Elizabeth J Tautkus; c Mark, Keith, Aileen & Linda. *Educ:* Pa State Univ, BS, 57, MS, 59, PhD(elec eng), 64. *Honors & Awards:* Leonard A Doggett Award, 66; Int Bus Mach Corp Outstanding Contrib Award, 68, 89, Invention Achievement Award, 78; Centennial Medal, Inst Elec & Electronic Engrs, 84; Distinguished Serv Award, Computer Soc, 85, 90, Merwin Award, 93. *Prof Exp:* From instr to asst prof elec eng, Pa State Univ, 59-65; res staff mem, IBM Corp, 65-68, 83-85, mgr design automation, 68-78, sr engr, 78-81, mgr design automation strategy, 81-82, mgr design automation lab, 85-94. *Concurrent Pos:* Consult prof elec eng, Stanford Univ, 82-83. *Mem:* Fel Inst Elec & Electronics Engrs Computer Soc (pres, 86-87). *Res:* Logic design of computers; computer reliability; design automation. *Mailing Add:* 1793 Blossom Ct Yorktown Heights NY 10598

RUSSO, SALVATORE FRANKLIN, PHYSICAL BIOCHEMISTRY. *Current Pos:* from asst prof to assoc prof, 68-83, PROF CHEM, WESTERN WASH UNIV, 83- *Personal Data:* b Hartford, Conn, Feb 6, 38; m 67, Judy Watke; c Amy & Alan. *Educ:* Wesleyan Univ, BA, 60; Northwestern Univ, PhD(phys chem), 64. *Prof Exp:* Instr, Northwestern Univ, 63-64; res assoc phys biochem, Univ Wash, 64-65; asst prof, Sacramento State Col, 67-68. *Concurrent Pos:* NIH fel, 65-67; adjoint prof, Univ Colo, 77-78, vis prof, 84-85, vis fel, 93-94; vis fac, Wash State Univ, 80; vis scientist, COBE Labs, Inc, 81. *Mem:* Am Chem Soc; Sigma Xi; Am Asn Univ Professors; Protein Soc. *Res:* Conformational changes in proteins; fluorescent probes of protein structure; hydrogen bonds between model peptide groups; blood plasma exchange; biochemistry of blood pressure regulation; site specific mutagenesis; oligonucleotides for antisense therapy; thermophilic enzymes. *Mailing Add:* Dept Chem Western Wash Univ Bellingham WA 98225-9150. *Fax:* 360-650-2826; *E-Mail:* russo@chem.wwu.edu

RUSSO, THOMAS JOSEPH, ORGANIC CHEMISTRY. *Current Pos:* from instr to asst prof, 64-71, ASSOC PROF CHEM, PA STATE UNIV, ALTOONA, 71- *Personal Data:* b Brooklyn, NY, Feb 10, 36; m 88; c 4. *Educ:* Polytech Inst Brooklyn, BSc, 57; Pa State Univ, PhD(org chem), 65. *Prof Exp:* Instr chem, Bucknell Univ, 62 & Juniata Col, 62-64. *Mem:* Am Chem Soc. *Res:* Physical organic chemistry. *Mailing Add:* Dept Chem Pa State Univ Ivyside Park Altoona PA 16603. *E-Mail:* tjr4@psu.edu

RUSSOCK, HOWARD ISRAEL, ETHOLOGY. *Current Pos:* from asst prof to assoc prof, 76-87, PROF BIOL, WESTERN CONN STATE UNIV, 88- *Personal Data:* b Philadelphia, Pa, Dec 22, 47; m 91, Christine Niewenhous; c Victor. *Educ:* Western Md Col, BA, 69; Pa State Univ, MS, 71; WVa Univ, PhD(biol), 75. *Prof Exp:* Eli Lilly Endowment Inc internship, Purdue Univ, 75-76. *Concurrent Pos:* Investr, NSF fac fel awards, Rockefeller Univ, 79-81; vis fac fel, Yale Univ, 84-85; Conn St Univ-Am Asn Univ Professors res grants, 86, 87-88, 88-89, 90-91, 92-93, 93-94, 95-96, 96-97, fac ombudsman, 88-90, Univ senate pres, 92 & 94. *Mem:* AAAS; Am Soc Zoologists; Animal Behav Soc; Sigma Xi. *Res:* Developmental and social behavior; effects and importance of early experience in birds and cichlid fish. *Mailing Add:* Dept Biol Sci Western Conn State Univ Danbury CT 06810. *E-Mail:* russock@wcsub.ctstateu.edu

RUSSU, IRINA MARIA, BIOPHYSICS. *Current Pos:* asst prof, 86-93, ASSOC PROF, WESLEYAN UNIV, 93- *Personal Data:* b Bucharest, Romania, Aug 15, 48. *Educ:* Univ Bucharest, MS, 70; Univ Pittsburgh, PhD(biophys), 79. *Prof Exp:* Res assoc, Univ Pittsburgh, 79-80; res asst prof, Carnegie-Mellon Univ, 80-86. *Mem:* Am Biophys Soc. *Res:* Structure-function relationships in proteins and nucleic acids by means of nuclear magnetic resonance spectroscopy. *Mailing Add:* Dept Molecular Biol & Biochem Hall-Atwater & Shanklin Labs 203 Wesleyan Univ Middletown CT 06459-0175

RUST, CHARLES CHAPIN, ZOOLOGY. *Current Pos:* RETIRED. *Personal Data:* b Medford, Wis, June 13, 35; m 56; c 3. *Educ:* Wis State Univ, BS, 60; Univ Wis-Madison, MS, 61, PhD(zool), 64. *Honors & Awards:* Am Soc Mammalogists Annual Award, 64. *Prof Exp:* From asst prof to prof zool, Univ Wis Ctr Syst, 64-90. *Concurrent Pos:* Vis scientist, Regional Primate Ctr, 68-69. *Mem:* AAAS; Am Soc Zoologists; Am Soc Mammalogists. *Res:* Endocrinology of mammalian reproductive and pelage cycles. *Mailing Add:* 3501 Hackdarth Rd Janesville WI 53545

RUST, DAVID MAURICE, ASTROPHYSICS. *Current Pos:* PHYSICIST, PRIN PROF STAFF, APPL PHYS LAB, JOHNS HOPKINS UNIV, 83- *Personal Data:* b Denver, Colo, Dec 9, 39; m 63, Gail Gochenour; c Amy & Harlan. *Educ:* Brown Univ, ScB, 62; Univ Colo, PhD(astrophys), 66. *Prof Exp:* Res fel solar physics, Nat Ctr Atmospheric Res, 63-66; Carnegie fel astrophys, Mt Wilson & Palomar Observ, 66-68; astrophysicist, Sacramento Peak Observ, Air Force Cambridge Res Labs, 68-74; sr staff scientist, Am Sci & Eng, Inc, 74-83. *Concurrent Pos:* Consult, Lockheed Calif, 66-70; vis assoc prof, Univ Md, 71; chmn, Working Group Solar Maximum Year, Int Astron Union, 73; vis astronr, Observ of Paris, 78; consult, NASA, 78-; assoc ed, Geophys Res Lett, 90-94; chmn, Users Comt, Natl Solar Observ. *Mem:* Am Geophys Union; Am Astron Soc; Int Astron Union. *Res:* Solar physics and magnetic fields; astronomical instrumentation; solar flares and x-ray emission; satellite-borne and balloon-borne telescopes. *Mailing Add:* Applied Phys Lab Johns Hopkins Univ Johns Hopkins Rd Laurel MD 20723-6099

RUST, JAMES HAROLD, NUCLEAR ENGINEERING. *Current Pos:* RETIRED. *Personal Data:* b Peoria, Ill, Sept 19, 36. *Educ:* Purdue Univ, BS, 58, PhD(nuclear eng), 65; Mass Inst Technol, SM, 60. *Prof Exp:* Asst prof nuclear eng, Univ Va, 64-67; from assoc prof to prof nuclear eng, Ga Inst Technol, 67-81. *Mem:* Am Soc Eng Educ; Am Nuclear Soc; Am Soc Mech Engrs; Nat Soc Prof Engrs. *Res:* Heat transfer and fluid mechanics pertinent to nuclear reactors, especially liquid metals and two phase systems. *Mailing Add:* 340 Garden Lane NW Atlanta GA 30309

RUST, JOSEPH WILLIAM, ANIMAL HUSBANDRY, ANIMAL NUTRITION. *Current Pos:* asst proj dairy husb, NCent Exp Sta, Univ Minn, 63-64, from asst prof to assoc prof animal husb, 64-80, prof animal husb & supt, 80-92, EMER PROF ANIMAL HUSB, NCENT EXP STA, UNIV MINN, 92- *Personal Data:* b Butler, Ky, Oct 1, 25. *Educ:* Univ Ky, BS, 53, MS, 57; Iowa State Univ, PhD(animal nutrit), 63. *Prof Exp:* Instr dairying, Univ Ky, 53-59; res assoc dairy sci, Iowa State Univ, 59-63. *Mem:* Am Dairy Sci Asn; Am Soc Animal Sci. *Mailing Add:* 807 Third Ave SW Grand Rapids MN 55744

RUST, LAWRENCE WAYNE, JR, MATHEMATICS, STATISTICS. *Current Pos:* PRES, APPL ANALYSIS SERV, 93- *Personal Data:* b St Paul, Minn, Mar 25, 37; m 64; c 3. *Educ:* Univ Minn, BS, 59, MS, 61, PhD(aeronaut eng), 64. *Prof Exp:* Sr engr, Ventura Div, Northrop Corp, 64-65 & Appl Sci Div, Litton Industs, 65-66; res engr, NStar Res & Develop Inst, 66-76; dp mgr, Filmtec Corp, 84-93. *Res:* Mathematical modeling; computer simulation; statistical data analysis; heat and mass transfer; fluid mechanics. *Mailing Add:* 1826 N Alameda St St Paul MN 55113

RUST, MICHAEL KEITH, ENTOMOLOGY. *Current Pos:* PROF ENTOM, UNIV CALIF, RIVERSIDE, 75- *Personal Data:* b Akron, Ohio, Aug 26, 48; m 70; c 2. *Educ:* Hiram Col, BA, 70; Univ Kans, MA, 73, PhD(entom), 75. *Concurrent Pos:* Pres, Pac Br, Entom Soc Am, 85-86. *Mem:* Entom Soc Am; Animal Behav Soc; Sigma Xi. *Res:* Urban entomology, especially biology and control of cockroaches, fleas and termites; chemical factors influencing termite feeding. *Mailing Add:* Dept Entom Univ Calif Riverside CA 92521

RUST, PHILIP FREDERICK, BIOSTATISTICS, STATISTICS. *Current Pos:* asst prof, 79-83, ASSOC PROF BIOMETRY, MED UNIV SC, 83- *Personal Data:* b Oakland, Calif, 1947; m. *Educ:* Calif Inst Technol, BS, 69; Univ Calif, Berkeley, MA, 71, PhD(biostatist), 76. *Prof Exp:* Lt biostatist, Ctr Dis Control, USPHS, 71-73; asst prof statist, Univ Mo-Columbia, 76-79. *Concurrent Pos:* Consult, Med Ctr, Univ Mo, 76-78, Med Univ SC, 79-; Environ Protection Agency; Rippel Found grant, 82-84. *Mem:* Am Statist Asn; Biomet Soc; Sigma Xi; Soc Epidemiol Res. *Res:* Applied stochastic processes; biometry; epidemiology; statistical distributions. *Mailing Add:* Dept Biometry & Epidemiol Med Univ SC 171 Ashley Ave Charleston SC 29425-2503

RUST, RICHARD HENRY, SOIL SCIENCE. *Current Pos:* asst prof, 56-71, PROF SOILS, UNIV MINN, ST PAUL, 71- *Personal Data:* b Bunker Hill, Ill, Oct 12, 21; m 42; c 5. *Educ:* Univ Ill, BS, 47, MS, 50, PhD(agron), 55. *Prof Exp:* Asst prof soil physics, Univ Ill, 55-56. *Concurrent Pos:* Consult to indust & govt. *Mem:* Fel Am Soc Agron; Soil Conserv Soc Am. *Res:* Soil genesis, classification and physical chemistry; properties related to clay mineralogy of soils; soil productivity evaluation. *Mailing Add:* 1922 Autumn St St Paul MN 55113

RUST, RICHARD W, INSECT ECOLOGY. *Current Pos:* FAC MEM BIOL, UNIV NEV, 78- *Personal Data:* b Logan, Utah, Oct 11, 42. *Educ:* Utah State Univ, BS, 65, MS, 67; Univ Calif, PhD(entom), 72. *Prof Exp:* Res asst pollination, Wild Bee Pollination Lab, USDA, 65-67; field biologist parasites, Field Mus Nat Hist, Chicago, 69; teaching asst zool, Univ Calif, 72; fac mem entom, Univ Del, 73-78. *Mem:* Am Entom Soc (rec secy, 74-); Soc Study Evolution; Soc Syst Zoologists; Ecol Soc Am. *Res:* Pollination ecology. *Mailing Add:* Dept Biol Univ Nev Reno NV 89557-0001

RUST, STEVEN RONALD, EXTENSION, FEEDLOT MANAGEMENT. *Current Pos:* ASSOC PROF ANIMAL NUTRIT, MICH STATE UNIV, 85- *Educ:* Univ Wis-River Falls, BS, 77; Okla State Univ, MS, 78, PhD(animal nutrit), 83. *Prof Exp:* Asst prof animal nutrit, Mont State Univ, 82-84. *Mem:* Am Soc Animal Sci; Animal Nutrit Res Coun; Am Registry Prof Animal Scientists. *Res:* Ruminant nutrition; efficient utilization of high grain diets in beef cattle; forage utilization. *Mailing Add:* 600 N Aurelius Rd Mason MI 48854

RUST, VELMA IRENE, MATHEMATICAL STATISTICS, ECONOMETRICS. *Current Pos:* RETIRED. *Personal Data:* b Edmonton, Alta, May 22, 14; wid. *Educ:* Univ Alta, BSc, 34, MEd, 44, BEd, 47; Univ Ill, PhD(math, math educ), 59. *Prof Exp:* Teacher math & sci, Alta, 36-42 & 43-44; admin secy fac educ, Univ Alta, 44-52, from lectr to asst prof math educ & dir, Student Teaching Prog, 52-56; researcher personnel planning, RCAF Hq, Can Dept Nat Defence, Ont, 60-62; chief staff training, Inspection Serv, 62-65; statistician, Origin & Destination Statist, Govt Can, 65-67; sr policy analyst, Can Dept Health & Welfare, 67-79. *Concurrent Pos:* Asst, Univ Ill, 56-59; sessional lectr, Carleton Univ, 59-62. *Res:* Social security; aviation; education. *Mailing Add:* 811 Adams Ave Ottawa ON K1G 2Y1 Can

RUST, WALTER DAVID, ATMOSPHERIC PHYSICS. *Current Pos:* US Nat Res Coun res assoc, 73-75, ATMOSPHERIC PHYSICIST, US DEPT COM, NAT OCEANIC & ATMOSPHERIC ADMIN, 75- *Personal Data:* b Randolph AFB, Tex, Oct 8, 44; m 66; c 2. *Educ:* Southwestern Univ, BS, 66; NMex Inst Mining & Technol, MS, 69, PhD(physics), 73. *Mem:* Am Geophys Union; Am Meteorol Soc; Royal Meteorol Soc Eng; Sigma Xi. *Res:* Cloud electrification; lightning suppression by chaff dispersal within thunderstorms; distribution of electric fields; use of atmospheric electric measurements to assess possibility of triggered lightning by rockets launched near thunderstorms; remote detection of corona; severe storm electricity. *Mailing Add:* Nat Severe Storms Lab 1313 Halley Dr Norman OK 73069

RUSTAD, DOUGLAS SCOTT, INORGANIC CHEMISTRY, PHYSICAL CHEMISTRY. *Current Pos:* from asst prof to assoc prof, 69-79, PROF INORG CHEM, SONOMA STATE UNIV, 79- *Personal Data:* b Juneau, Alaska, Sept 25, 40; m 67. *Educ:* Univ Wash, BS, 62, MS, 64; Univ Calif, Berkeley, PhD(chem), 67. *Prof Exp:* Lectr inorg chem, Univ West Indies, 67-69. *Mem:* Am Chem Soc. *Res:* High temperature spectroscopic and thermodynamic studies of transition metal halides. *Mailing Add:* Dept Chem Sonoma State Univ Rohnert Park CA 94928

RUSTAGI, JAGDISH S, BIOSTATISTICS. *Current Pos:* from assoc prof to prof math, Ohio State Univ, 63-70, prof statist, 70-88, chmn dept, 79-88, EMER PROF & CHMN STATIST, OHIO STATE UNIV, 88- *Personal Data:* b Sikri, India, Aug 13, 23; m 49; c 3. *Educ:* Univ Delhi, BA, 44, MA, 46; Stanford Univ, PhD(statist), 56. *Prof Exp:* Lectr math, Hindu Col, Univ Delhi, 46-52; asst prof, Carnegie Inst Technol, 55-57; asst prof statist, Mich State Univ, 57-58; reader, Aligarh Muslim Univ, 58-60; assoc prof math, Univ Cincinnati, 60-63. *Concurrent Pos:* NIH res grants, 62-68; consult, Toxic Hazards Unit, Wright-Patterson AFB, Ohio, 64-65; Air Force Off Sci Res grants, 67-; vis scholar, Stanford Univ, 71-72 & 83 & Off Naval Res, 78-; adj prof prev med, Col Med, Ohio State Univ, 67-75; vis prof, Univ Philippines, 88-89; vis scientist, IBM Corp, San Jose, Calif, 90-91. *Mem:* Fel Inst Math Statist; Biomet Soc; fel Am Statist Asn; fel Indian Soc Med Statist; Indian Soc Agr Statist; Int Statist Inst. *Res:* Mathematical statistics; medical statistics; operations research; optimization techniques in statistics. *Mailing Add:* 18531 Oak Dr Los Gatos CA 95030

RUSTAGI, KRISHNA PRASAD, FOREST BIOMETRICS, LAND USE PLANNING. *Current Pos:* asst prof, 73-79, ASSOC PROF FORESTRY, UNIV WASH, 79- *Personal Data:* b Khurja, India, Jan 1, 32; m 56; c 2. *Educ:* Agra Univ, India, BSc, 51, MSc, 53; Yale Univ, PhD(forestry), 73. *Prof Exp:* Asst conservator, Forest Dept, India, 55-61, dep conservator, 61-64; lectr, Forest Res Inst & Col, 64-69. *Mem:* Soc Am Foresters. *Res:* Biometric investigations in growth and yield of forest stands and trees; operations research application in land use; forest management planning. *Mailing Add:* Dept Forest Resources AR-10 Univ Wash Seattle WA 98195-0001

RUSTED, IAN EDWIN L H, ENDOCRINOLOGY, HEALTH SCIENCES EDUCATION. *Current Pos:* actg dir postgrad & continuing med educ, Mem Univ Nfld, 66-67; coodr, Med Sch Planning, 66-67, dean med, 67-74, vpres health sci, 74-79, pro vchancellor & vpres health sci & prof, 81-88, PROF MED, MEM UNIV NFLD, 67-, EMER DEAN, 89- *Personal Data:* b Nfld, July 12, 21; m 49; c 2. *Educ:* Univ Toronto, BA, 43; Dalhousie Univ, MD, CM, 48; McGill Univ, MSc, 49; FRCP(C), 53. *Hon Degrees:* LLD, Dalhousie Univ & Mt Allison Univ; DSL, Univ Toronto. *Honors & Awards:* Officer Order of Can, 85. *Prof Exp:* Med consult, Dept Health, Nfld, 52-67. *Concurrent Pos:* Physician & dir med educ, St John's Gen Hosp, 53-67, chmn, Dept Med, 67-68; mem coun, Royal Col Physicians & Surgeons Can, 61-70, vpres, 68-70; vis prof, Univ Toronto & Laval Univ, 74-75; vchmn, Bd Regents, Am Col Physicians, 85-86; chmn, Int Med Activ Subcomt, 85-88; mem, Nat Coun Bioethics Human Res, 88-93. *Mem:* Col Family Physicians Can; Asn Can Med Col (vpres, 73-74); fel Am Col Physicians. *Res:* Thyroid disorders; hypertension, especially epidemiology. *Mailing Add:* Health Sci Ctr Mem Univ St John's NF A1B 3V6 Can

RUSTGI, MOTI LAL, nuclear & medical physics, atomic & solid state physics; deceased, see previous edition for last biography

RUSTGI, OM PRAKASH, SPECTROSCOPY, SOLID STATE PHYSICS. *Current Pos:* from asst prof to assoc prof, 73-85, PROF PHYSICS, STATE UNIV NY COL BUFFALO, 85- *Personal Data:* b Delhi, India, Aug 1, 31; US citizen; m 63, Meena Rohatgi; c Arju & Arun. *Educ:* Univ Delhi, BS, 52, MS, 54; Univ Southern Calif, PhD(physics), 60. *Prof Exp:* Head optics div, Proj Celescope, Smithsonian Astrophys Observ, 60-62; physicist ultraviolet radiation, Northrop Corp, 63-67; mem prof staff space res, TRW Systs Inc, 67-71; vis assoc prof physics, Univ Ill, 71-73. *Concurrent Pos:* Consult, Smithsonian Astrophys Observ, 63-64 & Lawrence Livermore Lab, 74-76; prog mgr, Northrop Corp, 65-67; vis assoc prof physics, Univ Nebr, 81-82. *Mem:* Am Phys Soc; Optical Soc Am; Sigma Xi; Am Asn Physics Teachers. *Res:* Optical properties of thin films; photoionization in gases and light elements; lasers and holography; x-rays and crystal structure; laser plasma interaction studies. *Mailing Add:* 362 Sunrise Blvd Williamsville NY 14221. *Fax:* 716-878-4524; *E-Mail:* rustgiop@snybufaa.cs.snybuf.edu

RUSTIGIAN, ROBERT, MEDICAL MICROBIOLOGY. *Current Pos:* RETIRED. *Personal Data:* b Boston, Mass, July 26, 15; m 56; c 2. *Educ:* Univ Mass, BS, 38; Brown Univ, MS, 40, PhD, 43. *Prof Exp:* Nat Res Coun fel bact & immunol, Harvard Med Sch, 46-48, instr, 48-49, assoc instr, 49; asst prof microbiol, Univ Chicago, 49-55; asst prof, Sch Med, Tufts Univ, 55-61, assoc prof, 61-67; chief virologist, Vet Admin Hosp, 67-86; assoc prof microbiol &

moelcular genetics, Harvard Med Sch, 75-86. *Mem:* Am Soc Microbiol; Am Asn Immunol. *Res:* Biological and biochemical studies of virus-host interactions in chronic viral infections of neural and non-neural cells; virology and immunology. *Mailing Add:* Gilmore Rd North Easton MA 02356

RUSTIONI, ALDO, NEUROBIOLOGY, ANATOMY. *Current Pos:* ASSOC PROF ANAT & PHYSIOL, UNIV NC, CHAPEL HILL, 73- *Personal Data:* b Porto Ceresio, Italy, July 22, 41; m 69; c 2. *Educ:* Univ Parma, MD, 65. *Prof Exp:* Asst prof neuroanat, Erasmus Univ, Rotterdam, Holland, 68-72; sr asst prof, 72-73. *Concurrent Pos:* Vis investr, Nat Inst Health & Med Res, Paris, 72-73; Europ Training Prog Brain & Behav fel, 72-73; grants, Dutch Orgn Fundamental Res Med, 72-73, USPHS, 75-81 & 80-85 & Nat Found March Dimes, 78-80. *Mem:* Europ Neurosci Asn; Am Asn Anatomists; Soc Neurosci; AAAS; Am Acad Neurobiol. *Res:* Neuroanatomy; neurocytology; neurohistochemistry; electron microscopy; neurophysiology; somatosensory system. *Mailing Add:* Dept Cell Biol & Anat Univ NC CB 7090 108 Taylor Hall Chapel Hill NC 27599

RUSTON, HENRY, SOFTWARE ENGINEERING & PROGRAMMING LANGUAGES. *Current Pos:* assoc prof, 64-86, PROF, POLYTECH UNIV, 86- *Personal Data:* b Lodz, Poland, July 23, 29; US citizen; m 59, Janet R Margulies; c Anne, Lillian & Eileen. *Educ:* Univ Mich, BSE(math) & BSE(elec eng), 52, PhD(elec eng), 60; Columbia Univ, MS, 55. *Prof Exp:* Intermediate test engr, Wright Aeronaut Div, Curtiss-Wright Corp, NJ, 55; elec engr, Reeves Instrument Co, NY, 55-56; res asst, Eng Res Inst, Univ Mich, 56-58, res assoc, 58-60, assoc res engr, 60; asst prof elec eng, Moore Sch Elec Eng, Univ Pa, 60-64. *Concurrent Pos:* Lectr, Univ Mich, 60; indust consult, 61- *Mem:* Sr mem Inst Elec & Electronics Engrs; Asn Comput Mach. *Res:* Circuit theory; computer simulation; software engineering; programming languages. *Mailing Add:* 222 Exeter St Brooklyn NY 11235. *Fax:* 718-260-3136; *E-Mail:* hruston@pzism.poly.edu

RUSY, BEN F, PHARMACOLOGY, ANESTHESIOLOGY. *Current Pos:* PROF, DEPT ANESTHESIOL, UNIV HOSP, UNIV WIS-MADISON, 77- *Personal Data:* b Sturgeon Bay, Wis, July 12, 27; m 57; c 4. *Educ:* Univ Wis, BS, 52, MD, 56; Temple Univ, MS, 59; Am Bd Anesthesiol, dipl, 62. *Prof Exp:* Asst instr anesthesiol, Med Sch, Temple Univ, 59-60, instr anesthesiol & pharmacol, 60-62, from asst prof to prof anesthesiol & pharmacol, 62-77. *Concurrent Pos:* NIH fel, 59-61; NIH res grant, 62-, 75-78, 82-85; mem coun basic sci & coun circulation, Am Heart Asn, 65-; USPHS spec res fel, Heart & Lung Inst, 71-72; hon res fel, Dept Physiol, Univ Col, Univ London, 71-72. *Mem:* AAAS; Am Soc Anesthesiol; Am Soc Pharmacol & Exp Therapeut. *Res:* Effect of anesthetics and antihypertensive drugs on cardiac function. *Mailing Add:* Dept Anesthesiol Univ Wis Clin Sci Ctr Madison WI 53792-3216. *Fax:* 608-263-0575

RUTAN, ELBERT L, RESEARCH ADMINISTRATION. *Current Pos:* PRES, RUTAN AIRCRAFT FACTORY, INC, 74-; PRES & CHIEF EXEC OFFICER, SCALED COMPOSITES, INC, 82- *Personal Data:* b June, 1943. *Educ:* Calif Polytech Univ, BS, 65, DSc, 87; Daniel Webster Col, Dr, 87; Lewis Univ, Dr, 88; Delft Univ Technol, Dr, 90. *Honors & Awards:* Outstanding New Design, Exp Aircraft Asn, 75, 76 & 78; Aircraft Design Cert of Merit, Am Inst Aeronaut & Astronaut, 86, Struct Dynamics & Mat Award, 92; Presidential Citizen's Medal, 86; Award for Unique & Useful Plastic Prod, Soc Plastics Engrs, 87; W Randolph Lovelace Award, Soc NASA Flight Surgeons, 87; Distinguished Serv Award, Acad Model Aeronaut, 87; J H Doolittle Award, Soc Exp Test Pilots, 87; Collier Trophy, Nat Aeronaut Asn & Nat Aviation Club, 87; Meritorious Serv Award, Nat Bus Aircraft Asn, 87; Spirit St Louis Medal, Am Soc Mech Engrs, 87; Brit Gold Medal Aeronauts, Royal Aeronaut Soc, 87; Franklin Medal, Franklin Inst, 88; Leroy Randle Krumman Medal, 89; George Lubin Award, Soc Advan Mat & Process Eng, 95; Freedom of Flight Award, 96. *Prof Exp:* Flight test proj engr, Air Force Flight Test Ctr, Edwards AFB, 65-72; dir, Bede Test Ctr, Bede Aircraft, Newton, Kans, 72-74. *Mem:* Nat Acad Eng; Exp Aircraft Asn; Soc Flight Test Engrs; Acad Model Aeronaut; Soc Exp Test Pilots; Aircraft Owners & Pilots Asn. *Res:* Granted 3 patents. *Mailing Add:* Scaled Composites Inc 1624 Flight Line Hangar 78 Airport Mojave CA 93501. *Fax:* 805-824-4174

RUTENBERG, AARON CHARLES, PHYSICAL CHEMISTRY. *Current Pos:* DEVELOP CHEMIST, MARTIN MARIETTA ENERGY SYSTS, Y-12 PLANT, 72- *Personal Data:* b Chicago, Ill, July 28, 23; m 64, Elizabeth; c Amy & Alan. *Educ:* Univ Chicago, PhD(chem), 50. *Prof Exp:* Jr inspector, US War Dept, 42; res assoc, Univ Chicago, 50-51; chemist, Oak Ridge Nat Lab, 51-71. *Mem:* Am Chem Soc. *Res:* Nuclear magnetic resonance spectroscopy. *Mailing Add:* 101 Monticello Rd Oak Ridge TN 37830-8227

RUTENBERG, MORTON WOLF, STARCH CHEMISTRY, CARBOHYDRATE CHEMISTRY. *Current Pos:* CONSULT STARCH CHEM & TECHNOL, EMMAR CONSULT, 90- *Personal Data:* b Philadelphia, Pa, Jan 10, 21; m 42, Ruth Joffe; c Joel M. *Educ:* Univ Pa, BS, 42, MS, 47, PhD(org chem), 49. *Honors & Awards:* Melville L Wolfrom Award, Div Carbohydrate Chem, Am Chem Soc, 87. *Prof Exp:* Jr chemist, Eastern Regional Res Lab, USDA, 42-43; res group supvr, Nat Starch Prod, Inc, 49-58, res sect leader, 58-75, assoc dir, 75-80, dir starch res, 80-84, vpres natural polymer res, 84-86, div vpres res & develop, Food Prod & Indust Starch Divisions, Nat Starch & Chem Corp, 87-90. *Mem:* AAAS; Am Chem Soc; fel Am Inst Chem; Royal Soc Chem; Am Asn Cereal Chemists; Sigma Xi. *Res:* Synthetic organic, carbohydrate and polysaccharide chemistry; starch chemistry and technology; polysaccharides. *Mailing Add:* 587 Rockview Ave North Plainfield NJ 07063-1850

RUTFORD, ROBERT HOXIE, GEOLOGY. *Current Pos:* PRES, UNIV TEX, DALLAS, 82- *Personal Data:* b Duluth, Minn, Jan 26, 33; m 54; c 3. *Educ:* Univ Minn, BA, 54, MA, 63, PhD(geol), 69. *Honors & Awards:* Antarctic Serv Medal, US Secy Defense, 68; Distinguished Serv Award, NSF, 77. *Prof Exp:* Res assoc geol, Univ Minn, 62-67; from asst prof to assoc prof, Univ SDak, 67-72, actg chmn dept geol, 68-69, chmn, 69-71, chmn,dept geol & physics, 71-72; co-dir, Ross Ice Shelf Proj, Univ Nebr-Lincoln, 72-73, dir, 73-75; head, Off Polar Progs, NSF, 75-77; interim chancellor, Univ Nebr-Lincoln, 80-81, vchancellor res & grad studies, 77-82. *Concurrent Pos:* NSF res grant, 68-69; mem,panel geol & geophys, comt polar res, Nat Acad Sci, 68-73, mem, Ross Ice Shelf Proj steering group, 72-73, antarctic adv panel, Deep Earth Sampling Proj, Joint Oceanog Inst; chmn, Interagency Arctic Res Coord Comt, 75-77; mem, comt int rels, Nat Res Coun, Nat Acad Sci, 77-81 & Polar Res Bd, 80-; mem, Antartic Sect, Ocean Affairs Adv Comt, Dept State, 78-; US deleg, Sci Comt Antarctic Res, 88-; chmn, Nat Res Coun Polar Res Bd, 90- *Mem:* Fel Geol Soc Am; Arctic Inst NAm; Sigma Xi; Nat Coun Univ Res Admin; Nat Asn Geol Teachers. *Res:* Antarctic geology; geomorphology; glacial geology in eastern South Dakota. *Mailing Add:* 1882 Quail Lane Richardson TX 75080

RUTGER, JOHN NEIL, GENETICS, PLANT BREEDING. *Current Pos:* DIR, NAT RICE GERMPLASM CTR, STUTTGART, AR, 93- *Personal Data:* b Noble, Ill, Mar 3, 34; m 58, P J Kuyoth; c Ann & Robyn. *Educ:* Univ Ill, BS, 60; Univ Calif, Davis, MS, 62, PhD(genetics), 64. *Prof Exp:* Asst prof plant breeding, Cornell Univ, 64-70, assoc prof, 70; res geneticist, Agr Res Serv, USDA, Davis, Calif, 70-88, assoc area dir, Midsouth Area, 89-93. *Mem:* Fel AAAS; fel Am Soc Agron; fel Crop Sci Soc Am. *Res:* Rice genetics and breeding; inheritance of semi-dwarfism, male sterility and other hybrid rice mechanisms; cold tolerance. *Mailing Add:* USDA Agr Res Serv PO Box 287 Stuttgart AR 72160-0287

RUTGERS, JAY G, ANALYTICAL CHEMISTRY. *Current Pos:* RES SCIENTIST, WYETH LABS, INC, 61- *Personal Data:* b Holland, Mich, Feb 16, 24; m 55; c 1. *Educ:* Hope Col, BA, 49; Northwestern Univ, PhD(anal chem), 55. *Prof Exp:* Res assoc, Merck Sharp & Dohme Res Labs, 54-61. *Mem:* Am Chem Soc. *Res:* Analytical method development for pharmaceuticals; purity testing of new drugs. *Mailing Add:* 232 Upper Valley Rd North Wales PA 19454-2445

RUTH, BYRON E, CIVIL ENGINEERING, TRANSPORTATION. *Current Pos:* assoc prof, 70-77, PROF CIVIL ENG, UNIV FLA, 77- *Personal Data:* b Chicago, Ill, Mar 25, 31; m 60, Margarete R Rohweder; c Boyd & Toni. *Educ:* Mont State Univ, BSCE, 55; Purdue Univ, MSCE, 59; WVa Univ, PhD(civil eng), 67. *Prof Exp:* Asst dir res & develop, Symons Mfg Co, 60-61; from instr to asst prof civil eng, WVa Univ, 61-70. *Concurrent Pos:* Mem, Transp Res Bd, Nat Acad Sci-Nat Res Coun, chmn, Comt Gen Asphalt Problems; chmn, Comt D4 Rd & Paving Mat, Am Soc Testing & Mat, 91-93. *Mem:* Am Soc Civil Engrs; Am Soc Testing & Mat; Am Soc Photogram & Remote Sensing; Asn Asphalt Paving Technol (pres, 86); Sigma Xi. *Res:* Bituminous materials; concrete and aggregate materials; soil exploration and testing; remote sensing applications to terrain analysis and site selection; flexible and rigid pavement response; nondestructive testing and evaluation of pavements; low temperature behavior of asphalt and mixtures for pavement analysis; asphalt age hardening prediction and effects. *Mailing Add:* Dept Civil Eng Univ Fla Gainesville FL 32611. *Fax:* 352-392-3394

RUTH, DOUGLAS WARREN, CORE ANALYSIS, TRANSPORT PHENOMENA IN POROUS MEDIA. *Current Pos:* res assoc, 74-75, PROF & HEAD, DEPT MECH & INDUST ENG, UNIV MAN, 90- *Personal Data:* b Winnipeg, Man, Oct 16, 48. *Educ:* Univ Man, BSc, 70, MSc, 72; Univ Waterloo, PhD, 77. *Prof Exp:* Res engr, Temro, 72-74; asst prof mech eng, Univ Calgary, 77-80; sr res engr, Petro-Canada Resources, 80-84; mgr prod res, Geotech Resources Ltd, 84-87. *Mem:* Soc Petrol Engrs; Petrol Soc-Can Inst Mining; Soc Core Analysts. *Res:* Developing predictive models for transport processes in porous media; developing precise and accurate methods for performing core analysis. *Mailing Add:* Dept Mech & Indust Eng Univ Man Winnipeg MB R3T 2N2 Can. *Fax:* 204-275-7507; *E-Mail:* druth@bldgeng.lanl.umanitoba.ca

RUTH, JAMES ALLAN, PHARMACOLOGY, MEDICINAL CHEMISTRY. *Current Pos:* ASST PROF MED CHEM & PHARMACOL, SCH PHARM, UNIV COLO, 78- *Personal Data:* b Wichita, Kans, Dec 24, 46. *Educ:* Univ Kans, BS, 68; Northwestern Univ, Evanston, PhD(org chem), 74. *Prof Exp:* Res assoc med chem, Univ Kans, 74-76, res assoc pharmacol, 76-78. *Concurrent Pos:* NIH fels med chem, 74-76; Am Heart Asn fels pharmacol, 76-78. *Mem:* Am Chem Soc; Royal Soc Chem. *Res:* Neurochemistry; neuropharmacology. *Mailing Add:* Univ Co Health Sci Ctr 4200 E Ninth Ave PO Box C-238 Denver CO 80262-0238

RUTH, JOHN MOORE, PHYSICAL CHEMISTRY. *Current Pos:* RES CHEMIST, AGR ENVIRON QUAL INST, AGR RES SERV, USDA, 66- *Personal Data:* b Pittsboro, NC, May 26, 24. *Educ:* Univ NC, BS, 44, PhD(phys chem), 59. *Prof Exp:* Chemist, Dockery Labs, 45-46; jr chemist, Oak Ridge Nat Lab, 47-48, assoc chemists, 48-50, 52; staff mem, Los Alamos Sci Lab, 54-55; staff mem dacron res lab, E I du Pont de Nemours & Co, Inc, 57-59; sr chemist, Res Dept, Liggett & Myers Tobacco Co, 59-66. *Concurrent Pos:* Staff mem, Los Alamos Sci Lab, 53, 55 & E I du Pont de Nemours & Co, 56. *Mem:* Fel AAAS; Am Chem Soc; fel Am Inst Chem; Am Soc Mass Spectrometry. *Res:* Mass spectrometry; molecular spectroscopy; identification of organic compounds; determination of molecular structures. *Mailing Add:* PO Box 450 College Park MD 20740-0450

RUTH, ROYAL FRANCIS, EMBRYOLOGY, IMMUNOLOGY. *Current Pos:* RETIRED. *Personal Data:* b Des Moines, Iowa, Oct 3, 25; m 50; c 1. *Educ:* Grinnell Col, AB, 49; Univ Wis, MS, 53, PhD(zool), 54. *Prof Exp:* Fel embryol, Ind Univ, 54-56; from asst prof to prof zool, Univ Alta, 61-91. *Concurrent Pos:* Vis prof zool, Univ Wis, 61 & 62; mem, Animal Welfare Comt, Alta, 61-72; mem, Grants Comt Cell Biol & Genetics, Nat Res Coun Can, 69-72, chmn, 71-72; prof biol & chmn dept, Washington & Lee Univ, 75-76; mem, Comt Post-Doctoral Fel, Natural Sci & Eng Res Coun Can, 79-82, chmn, 81-82; mem, Sci Comt, Alta Heritage Found Med Res, 80-81, chmn, Capital Grants Comt, 81-82. *Mem:* Radiation Soc. *Res:* Immediate lethal effects of ionizing radiation; clinical radiation-hypotension and early reactor-accident deaths. *Mailing Add:* 1814 Oakland Ave Des Moines IA 50314-3329

RUTHERFORD, CHARLES, CELL BIOLOGY, BIOCHEMISTRY. *Current Pos:* from asst prof to assoc prof, 72-83, PROF BIOL, VA POLYTECH INST & STATE UNIV, 83- *Personal Data:* b Trenton, Mo, May 17, 39; m 63; c 1. *Educ:* William Jewell Col, BA, 61; Col William & Mary, MA, 63; Univ Miami, PhD(cell & molecular biol), 68. *Prof Exp:* Fel biochem, Med Sch, Washington Univ, 68-69; fel biochem develop, Retina Found, 69-71. *Concurrent Pos:* Fel, Boston Biomed Res Inst, 69-72. *Mem:* Am Soc Biochem & Molecular Biol. *Res:* Molecular biology of development. *Mailing Add:* Dept Biol Va Polytech Inst & State Univ Derring Hall Rm 2031 Blacksburg VA 24061

RUTHERFORD, JAMES CHARLES, INVERTEBRATE ECOLOGY. *Current Pos:* HEAD TELECOMMUN, FLA CTR FOR BLIND, 97- *Personal Data:* b Oakland, Calif, Aug 27, 46. *Educ:* Calif State Col, Hayward, BS, 68; Univ Calif, Berkeley, MA, 71, PhD(zool), 75. *Prof Exp:* Asst prof zool, Ore State Univ, 75-76; asst prof biol, Hilo Col, Univ Hawaii, 76-80, Hawaii Prep Acad, 85-86; math-sci teacher, Honokaa High Sch, 87-88; sci dept head, Parker Sch, Kamuela, 88-95. *Concurrent Pos:* Comput coordr, Parker Sch, Kamuela, Hawaii, 92- *Mem:* Ecol Soc Am; Sigma Xi; AAAS. *Res:* Quantitative invertebrate natural history with emphasis on ecological and evolutionary theory especially as it relates to marine intertidal and benthic invertebrates, echinoderms in particular. *Mailing Add:* 7895 NW 110th St Reddick FL 32686. *Fax:* 808-885-9341; *E-Mail:* james_c_rutherford@portal.com.cup

RUTHERFORD, JOHN GARVEY, NEUROANATOMY. *Current Pos:* From asst prof to assoc prof, 70-91, assoc dean, Fac Grad Studies, 91-96, PROF ANAT & NEUROBIOL, FAC MED, DALHOUSIE UNIV, 91- *Personal Data:* b Baltimore, Md, Sept 25, 42; m 65; c 2. *Educ:* Cornell Univ, AB, 64; Syracuse Univ, MS, 68; State Univ NY Upstate Med Ctr, PhD(anat), 72. *Mem:* Can Asn Anatomists; Am Asn Anatomists; Soc Neurosci. *Res:* Ultrastructure and connections of mammalian brain stem nuclei. *Mailing Add:* Dept Anat & Neurobiol Dalhousie Univ Halifax NS B3H 4H7 Can. *E-Mail:* john.rutherford@dal.ca

RUTHERFORD, JOHN L(OFTUS), METALLURGY, MATERIALS SCIENCE. *Current Pos:* res mgr, 69-80, dir, Mat & Processes Lab, Kearfott Div, Singer Co, 80-85, DIR MFG, KEARFOTT CORP, 85- *Personal Data:* b Philadelphia, Pa, Mar 6, 24; m 47, Sara Richards; c David & Peter. *Educ:* Univ Pa, BA, 52, MS, 61, PhD(metall), 63; Rutgers Univ, MA, 81. *Prof Exp:* Proj engr, Sharples Corp, Pa, 45-52; res physicist, Franklin Inst, 52-60; sr staff scientist, Aerospace Group, Gen Precision, Inc, 63-69. *Mem:* Am Soc Metals; Am Inst Mining, Metall & Petrol Engrs; Am Inst Aeronaut & Astronaut; Sigma Xi. *Res:* Micro-mechanical properties of metals, polymers, and fiber-reinforced composites; relationships between atomic structure and properties; deformation and mechanisms in materials; surface topology in friction and wear. *Mailing Add:* 161 Pershing Ave Ridgewood NJ 07450

RUTHERFORD, MALCOLM JOHN, PETROLOGY. *Current Pos:* asst prof, 70-75, ASSOC PROF GEOL, BROWN UNIV, 75- *Personal Data:* b Durham, Ont, July 6, 39; m 62; c 2. *Educ:* Univ Sask, BScEng, 61, MSc, 63; Johns Hopkins Univ, PhD(geol), 68. *Prof Exp:* Fel, Univ Calif, Los Angeles, 68-69, asst prof geol, 69-70. *Mem:* AAAS; Geol Soc Am; Mineral Soc Am; Am Geophys Union; Mineral Soc Can. *Res:* Chemistry variations and origin of igneous and metamorphic rocks in the earth's crust and the lunar crust through a combination of analytical studies and laboratory synthesis; origin and processes involved in formation of economic metal; sulfide deposits in association with igneous rocks. *Mailing Add:* Geol Brown Univ Providence RI 02912-9127

RUTHERFORD, PAUL HARDING, PLASMA PHYSICS. *Current Pos:* mem res staff, Princeton Univ, 65-68, res physicist, 68-72, head, Theoret Div, 72-79, assoc dir, 80-95, LECTR PLASMA PHYSICS, PRINCETON UNIV, 68-, SR RES PHYSICIST, PLASMA PHYSICS LAB, 72-, ASSOC DIR, 80- *Personal Data:* b Shipley, Eng, Jan 22, 38; m 59, Audrey Irvine; c Andrea & Julia. *Educ:* Cambridge Univ, BA, 59, PhD(plasma physics), 63. *Honors & Awards:* E O Lawrence Mem Award, US Dept Energy, 83. *Prof Exp:* Res assoc plasma physics, Princeton Univ, 62-63; res assoc, Culham Lab, UK Atomic Energy Auth, 63-65. *Mem:* Fel Am Phys Soc. *Res:* Theoretical plasma physics. *Mailing Add:* Plasma Physics Lab Princeton Univ PO Box 451 Princeton NJ 08543. *E-Mail:* rutherfo@pppl.gov

RUTHVEN, DOUGLAS M, chemical engineering, physical chemistry, for more information see previous edition

RUTISHAUSER, URS STEPHEN, BIOCHEMISTRY, EMBRYOLOGY. *Current Pos:* PROF, DEPT GENETICS, CASE WESTERN RES UNIV. *Personal Data:* b Altadena, Calif, Feb 27, 46; m 89. *Educ:* Brown Univ, ScB, 67; Rockefeller Univ, PhD(biochem), 73. *Honors & Awards:* McKnight Scholar. *Prof Exp:* Jane Coffin Childs fel, Weizmann Inst Sci, Israel, 73-74; asst prof biochem, Rockefeller Univ, 74-79, assoc prof, 79- *Mem:* Soc Neurosci; Am Asn Cell Biol; Soc Develop Biol; AAAS. *Res:* Developmental and cell biology; cell-cell interactions; neurobiology. *Mailing Add:* Dept Genetics Sch Med Case Western Res Univ Cleveland OH 44106-2333. *Fax:* 216-368-3182; *E-Mail:* uxr@po.cwru.edu

RUTKIN, PHILIP, COSMETIC CHEMISTRY. *Current Pos:* SR DIR, GRYPHON DEVELOP, 96- *Personal Data:* b New York, NY, Sept 17, 33; m 57; c 4. *Educ:* City Col New York, BS, 55; NY Univ, PhD(org chem), 60. *Prof Exp:* Res chemist, Faberge, 58-60, dir res, 60-66, vpres res, 66-70; sr vpres, Estee Lauder, 75-90. *Concurrent Pos:* Eve sessions instr, Farleigh Dickinson Univ, 59-, NY Univ, 61 & City Col New York, 62-; gen mgr, Chemspray Div, ATI; vpres, Revlon-Int. *Mem:* Am Chem Soc; Soc Cosmetic Chemists; AAAS; Acad Sci. *Res:* Cosmetic chemistry. *Mailing Add:* 6 Henhawk Rd Great Neck NY 11024-2107

RUTLAND, LEON W, MATHEMATICS. *Current Pos:* chmn dept, 64-70, PROF MATH, VA POLYTECH INST & STATE UNIV, 64- *Personal Data:* b Commerce, Tex, Aug 24, 19; m 44; c 2. *Educ:* Univ Colo, PhD, 54. *Prof Exp:* From asst prof to assoc prof appl math, Univ Colo, 54-64. *Mem:* Am Math Soc; Am Soc Eng Educ; Soc Indust & Appl Math; Math Asn Am. *Res:* Applied mathematics. *Mailing Add:* 1391 Locust Ave Blacksburg VA 24060-5626

RUTLEDGE, CARL THOMAS, MICROCOMPUTER INTERFACING. *Current Pos:* assoc prof, 81-87, PROF PHYSICS, E CENT UNIV, 87- *Personal Data:* b Fayetteville, Ark, Sept 17, 44; m 67; c 2. *Educ:* Univ Ark, BS, 66, MS, 69, PhD(physics), 71. *Prof Exp:* prof physics, Southern Ark Univ, 70-81. *Mem:* Sigma Xi; Am Asn Physics Teachers. *Res:* X-ray diffraction studies of liquids; interferometry and physical optics; improvements in teaching basic astronomy and physics; microcomputer software and interfacing. *Mailing Add:* Dept Physics E Cent Univ Ada OK 74820-6899

RUTLEDGE, CHARLES O, PHARMACOLOGY. *Current Pos:* PROF PHARMACOL, SCH PHARM, PURDUE UNIV, 87-, DEAN SCH PHARM, NURSING & HEALTH SCI, 87- *Personal Data:* b Topeka, Kans, Oct 1, 37; m 61, Jane E Crow; c David O, Susan H, Elizabeth J & Karen A. *Educ:* Univ Kans, BS, 59, MS, 61; Harvard Univ, PhD(pharmacol), 66. *Prof Exp:* NATO fel pharmacol, Gothenburg Univ, 66-67; from asst prof to assoc prof, Med Ctr, Univ Colo, Denver, 67-75; prof pharmacol & toxicol & chmn dept, Sch Pharm, Univ Kans, 75-87. *Mem:* Am Pharmaceut Asn; Am Soc Pharmacol & Exp Therapeut (pres, 96-97); Am Soc Health Syst Pharmacists; Soc Neurosci; Am Asn Cols Pharm (pres, 96-97); Am Asn Pharmaceut Scientists. *Res:* Autonomic, behavioral and biochemical pharmacology; interactions of drugs with the synthesis, storage, uptake, release and metabolism of neurotransmitters in the central nervous system to produce alterations in behavior. *Mailing Add:* Sch Pharm Purdue Univ Robert E Heine Bldg West Lafayette IN 47907-1330. *Fax:* 765-494-7880; *E-Mail:* chipr@pharmacy.purdue.edu

RUTLEDGE, DAVID B, PHYSICS. *Current Pos:* PROF ELEC ENG, CALIF INST TECHNOL, 80- *Educ:* Williams Col, BA, 73; Cambridge Univ, MA, 75; Berkeley, PhD(elec eng), 80. *Honors & Awards:* Microwave Prize, Microwave Theory & Tech Soc, 93. *Prof Exp:* Aerosyst engr, Gen Dynamics Corp, 75-76. *Concurrent Pos:* Consult, Aerospace Corp, Litton, Army Night Vision Lab, United Technol, TRW; pres young investr award, NSF, 84-86; distinguished lectr, Antennas & Propagation Soc, 91-93. *Mem:* Fel Inst Elec & Electronics Engrs. *Res:* Integrated-circuit antennas, including lens coupled antennas for focal plane arrays; anisotropic etching for fabricating horns and membrane technology for suspending metal antennas; active grid components, including phase shifters, oscillators, mixers and amplifiers; author of 3 publications; granted one US patent. *Mailing Add:* Dept Elec Eng Calif Inst Tech M/S 13693 Pasadena CA 91125

RUTLEDGE, DELBERT LEROY, THERMAL PHYSICS. *Current Pos:* from asst prof to prof, 57-88, EMER PROF PHYSICS, OKLA STATE UNIV, 88- *Personal Data:* b Mooreland, Okla, July 20, 25; m 47; c 2. *Educ:* Univ NMex, BS, 46; Okla State Univ, MS, 48, EdD, 58. *Prof Exp:* Asst prof physics, Cent State Col, Okla, 47-57. *Concurrent Pos:* Assoc prog dir, NSF Div Undergrad Educ, 65-66. *Mem:* Am Asn Physics Teachers; Am Phys Soc; Am Soc Eng Educ. *Mailing Add:* 1924 McElroy Stillwater OK 74075

RUTLEDGE, DOROTHY STALLWORTH, MATHEMATICS, COMPUTER SCIENCE. *Current Pos:* asst prof, 69-72, ASSOC PROF MATH, GA STATE UNIV, 72- *Personal Data:* b Tuscaloosa, Ala, May 3, 30; m 49; c 2. *Educ:* Birmingham-Southern Col, BA, 51; Emory Univ, MS, 60, PhD(math), 66. *Prof Exp:* Asst prof math, Agnes Scott Col, 66-69. *Mem:* Am Math Soc; Math Asn Am. *Res:* Analysis; functional analysis. *Mailing Add:* 7120 Beaver Trail Apex NC 27502-9549

RUTLEDGE, FELIX N, GYNECOLOGIC ONCOLOGY. *Current Pos:* PROF GYNEC, UNIV TEX, M D ANDERSON HOSP & TUMOR INST, 54- *Personal Data:* b Anniston, Ala, Nov 20, 17; m 50; c 1. *Educ:* Univ Ala, BS, 39; Johns Hopkins Univ, MD, 43; Am Bd Obstet & Gynec, dipl, 51. *Mem:* Am Asn Obstet & Gynec; Am Gynec Soc; Am Radium Soc; Soc Pelvic Surg; Soc Gynec Oncol. *Res:* Diagnosis and treatment of female pelvic malignancies. *Mailing Add:* Dept Gynec Oncol 67 Univ Tex M D Anderson Cancer Ctr Houston TX 77030-4095. *Fax:* 713-792-7586

RUTLEDGE, GENE PRESTON, PHYSICAL CHEMISTRY, RESEARCH ADMINISTRATION. *Current Pos:* RES DIR & OWNER, PAC POLAR RIMS, 78- *Personal Data:* b Spartanburg, SC, Dec 3, 25; m 50; c 4. *Educ:* Wofford Col, BS, 46; Univ Tenn, MS, 48. *Hon Degrees:* DSc, Wofford Col, 71. *Honors & Awards:* Creative Res Award, Div Fluorine Chem, Am Chem Soc, 93. *Prof Exp:* Res chemist & proj engr, Lab & Eng Div, Union Carbide Nuclear Co, Tenn, 48-54; supvry engr, Develop Eng Div, Goodyear Atomic Corp, Ohio, 54-56, sr scientist, S5W & Pressurized Water Reactor Projs, Westinghouse Elec Corp, 56-59, supvry scientist, Naval Reactors Facil, Bettis Atomic Power Lab, 60-67; exec dir, Idaho Nuclear Energy Comn, 67-76; energy scientist, Off Gov, State of Alaska, 76-78. *Concurrent Pos:* Mem bd dirs, Western Interstate Nuclear Compact, 69; mem, Gov Task Force Radioactive Waste Mgt, 71; consult, high technol firms throughout USA. *Mem:* Am Nuclear Soc; Am Chem Soc; Am Inst Chem Eng. *Res:* Energy development including nuclear, geothermal, solar, geosolar, hydrogen and wind and environmental; forestry, agriculture, mining and research using nuclear methods; author and co-author four books. *Mailing Add:* 6930 Oakwood Dr Anchorage AK 99507-2442

RUTLEDGE, HARLEY DEAN, SOLID STATE PHYSICS. *Current Pos:* RETIRED. *Personal Data:* b Omaha, Nebr, Jan 10, 26; m 54; c 5. *Educ:* Tarkio Col, AB, 50; Univ Mo, MS, 56, PhD(photoelec emission), 66. *Prof Exp:* Assoc prof physics, Cent Methodist Col, 57-60; instr, Univ Mo, 60-61; from assoc prof to prof physics, Southeast Mo State Univ, 63-86, head dept, 64-86. *Mem:* Am Asn Physics Teachers. *Res:* Experimental study of photoelectric emission from strontium oxide sprayed cathodes; theoretical analysis of photoelectric emission from semiconductors. *Mailing Add:* 1817 Westridge Cape Girardeau MO 63701-2939

RUTLEDGE, JACKIE JOE, ANIMAL BREEDING. *Current Pos:* asst prof, 75-77, assoc prof, 77-80, prof animal breeding, 80-87, PROF & CHMN, UNIV WIS, 88- *Personal Data:* b Woodward, Okla, Dec 20, 41; m 66; c 2. *Educ:* Okla State Univ, BS, 68; NC State Univ, MS, 71, PhD(animal breeding), 73. *Prof Exp:* Res asst animal breeding, NC State Univ, 68-72; res assoc animal breeding, Univ Wis, 72-74; asst prof animal breeding, Univ Vt, 74-75. *Mem:* Am Soc Animal Sci; Genetics Soc Am; Sigma Xi; Am Dairy Sci Asn; Am Genetic Asn; Biomet Soc. *Res:* Dynamics of genetic variances and covariances among and within populations; multivariate statistical theory applications to genetic problems; realized heritability of and correlated predictors of fecundity in economic and laboratory animals. *Mailing Add:* Animal Sci 256 Univ Wis 1675 Observatory Dr Madison WI 53706-1205

RUTLEDGE, JAMES LUTHER, SOLID STATE PHYSICS, ELECTRONICS. *Current Pos:* mgr, Gov Res & Develop Progs, Motorola Semiconductor Prod, 93-95, MGR PACKING RES & DEVELOP, MOTOROLA INC, 95- *Personal Data:* b Woodward, Okla, Oct 1, 37; m 63, Barbara Johns; c Matthew B & Kathleen M. *Educ:* Okla State Univ, BS, 63, MS, 66, PhD(physics), 68. *Prof Exp:* Sr physicist, Motorola Semiconductor Prod, Inc, 67-74, proj leader res & develop, Fairchild Semiconductor, 74, mgr, Adv Prod Res & Develop Labs, 74-84, vpres tech staff, 84-91; dir univ & nat labs progs, Sematech, 91-93. *Mem:* Inst Elec & Electronics Engrs; Am Phys Soc. *Res:* Solid state surface physics; electrical properties of semiconductors; physics of semiconductor devices. *Mailing Add:* 8518 Dunsmere Dr Austin TX 78749-3435

RUTLEDGE, JOSEPH DELA, MATHEMATICS, COMPUTER SCIENCES. *Current Pos:* STAFF MEM, RES DIV, T J WATSON RES CTR, IBM CORP, 58- *Personal Data:* b Selma, Ala, Aug 9, 28; m 54, Barbara Bruce; c 4. *Educ:* Swarthmore Col, BA, 50; Cornell Univ, PhD(math), 59. *Prof Exp:* Sr systs engr, Remington Rand Univac Div, Sperry Rand Corp, 50-53; asst bact, Univ Hosp, Univ Pa, 53-55; asst math, Cornell Univ, 55-58. *Concurrent Pos:* Vis lectr, Wesleyan Univ, 65-67; lectr, Univ Grenoble, 67-68; adj prof, NY Univ, 69-70; IBM vis prof, Spelman Col, 71-72. *Mem:* Asn Symbolic Logic; Asn Comput Mach; Math Asn Am; Sigma Xi. *Res:* Theory of automatation and computation; computer design and applications, especially man-machine communication and problem specification; programming and programming language. *Mailing Add:* 11 Sycamore Terr RD 2 Mahopac NY 10541-3140

RUTLEDGE, LESTER T, PHYSIOLOGY. *Current Pos:* from res assoc to assoc prof, 56-67, chmn, Neurosci Prog, 72-84, PROF PHYSIOL, MED SCH, UNIV MICH, ANN ARBOR, 67- *Personal Data:* b Big Sandy, Mont, June 12, 24; m 49. *Educ:* Univ Utah, MA, 52, PhD(physiol, psychol), 53. *Prof Exp:* Res assoc & res instr physiol, Univ Utah, 53-56. *Concurrent Pos:* NIH sr res fel, 58-62, career develop award, 63-68. *Mem:* AAAS; Soc Neurosci; Am Physiol Soc. *Res:* Integrative processes of central nervous systems; electrophysiology of cortical and subcortical relationships; neural basis of learning; spinal and supraspinal reflexes; association cortex; epilepsy; neurological teaching; alcohol effects on cortex. *Mailing Add:* Dept Physiol Univ Mich 3718 Salish Tr Stevensville MT 59870-6544

RUTLEDGE, ROBERT B, MATHEMATICS, ELECTRICAL ENGINEERING. *Current Pos:* From asst prof to assoc prof math & appl sci, 62-69, assoc prof eng, 69-73, PROF MATH, SOUTHERN ILL UNIV, 73- *Personal Data:* b St Louis, Mo, Dec 9, 35; m 60; c 4. *Educ:* St Louis Univ, BS, 58, MS, 59, PhD(math), 62. *Concurrent Pos:* Consult electromagnetic sensor lab, Emerson Elec Co, 62- *Mem:* Math Asn Am; Soc Indust & Appl Math. *Res:* Analysis of advanced radar processing techniques using stochastic models; digital simulation techniques. *Mailing Add:* Div Eng Southern Ill Univ Edwardsville IL 62026-1002

RUTLEDGE, ROBERT L, PHYSICAL CHEMISTRY. *Current Pos:* res chemist, 60-70, res specialist, 70-78, SR RES SPECIALIST, MINN MINING & MFG CO, 78- *Personal Data:* b Pocahontas, Miss, June 23, 30; m 58; c 5. *Educ:* Miss State Univ, BS, 52; Univ Ill, MS, 53, PhD(phys chem), 58. *Prof Exp:* Sr res chemist, Socony Mobil Oil Co, Tex, 58-60. *Mem:* Soc Photog Sci & Eng. *Res:* Image evaluation of photographic media; novel imaging systems. *Mailing Add:* 2220 Powers Ave St Paul MN 55119

RUTLEDGE, THOMAS FRANKLIN, ORGANIC CHEMISTRY, CATALYSIS. *Current Pos:* RETIRED. *Personal Data:* b Cordova, Tenn, June 1, 21; m 43; c 3. *Educ:* Univ Ark, BS, 43; Univ Del, PhD(org chem), 50. *Prof Exp:* Chemist, Res Labs, Socony-Vacuum Oil Co, 43-44, 47-48; sr res chemist, Monsanto Chem Co, 50-51; sect head org div, Res Labs, Air Reduction, Inc, 51-57; mgr org & catalysis res, Corp Res Dept, ICI-Am, 57-81. *Concurrent Pos:* Vpres, Develop Solar Elec Corp, 84. *Mem:* Am Chem Soc. *Res:* Mechanisms of chemical oxidations via chromic acid; preparation of synthetic lubricants of hydrocarbon type; catalyst preparation; acetylene and hydrocarbon chemistry; urea chemistry; polyurethanes; polymers; catalytic oxidation; polymerization; electrochemistry. *Mailing Add:* 124 Uxbridge Cherry Hill NJ 08034-1519

RUTLEDGE, WYMAN COE, APPLIED PHYSICS, INSTRUMENTS. *Current Pos:* sr res physicist, Mead Corp, 56, sr res fel, Cent Res Labs, 56-68, inst syst consult, 68-86, PRIN SCIENTIST, MEAD CORP, 86- *Personal Data:* b Abrahamsville, Pa, Dec 15, 24; m 45, Mary Louise Jones; c Paul, Nancy & Mark. *Educ:* Hiram Col, AB, 44; Univ Mich, MS, 48, PhD(physics), 52. *Hon Degrees:* PhD, Miami Univ, 91. *Honors & Awards:* Phoenix Post Doct Fel. *Prof Exp:* Lab instr, Hiram Col, 43-44; res asst, Oceanog Inst, Woods Hole, 46-47; res assoc, Univ Mich, 47-48, res asst, 48-50; jr physicist, Argonne Nat Lab, 50-52; res physicist, Philip Labs, Inc, 52-56. *Concurrent Pos:* Part-time instr, Ohio Univ, 58-68; mem, Simulation Coun, Inc; mem measurement technol comt, Am Inst Paper Res, process systs & controls comt, Tech Asn Pulp & Paper Indust; mem particulate subcomt, Inter Socs Air Sampling Comt, 72-84; mem, Environ Res Tech Comt, Instrument Soc Am; Adv Bd Trustees, Ohio Univ, Chillicothe, vpres, 80-82, pres, 82-84, emer, 85-; mem, Bd Trustees, Hiram Col, 80-86; mem, Advan Sensor Comt, Dept Energy, 82-; distinguished vpres, Instrument Soc Am, 74-76, vpres technol, 76-78. *Mem:* Am Phys Soc; Optical Soc Am; fel Instrument Soc Am; Measurements & Data Soc; Sigma Xi; fel Tech Asn Pulp Paper Indust. *Res:* Underwater research; upper atmosphere; nuclear spectroscopy; thermionic emission; instrumentation and automation; computer systems application; basic phenomena; air and water quality instrumentation; sensors. *Mailing Add:* 704 Ashley Dr Chillicothe OH 45601

RUTMAN, ROBERT JESSE, BIOCHEMISTRY, MOLECULAR BIOLOGY. *Current Pos:* res assoc biol, Univ Pa, 54-56, chem, 57-64, assoc prof, 64-69, prof, 69-87, chmn, Lab Biochem, Dept Animal Biol, 71-73, & 78-79, EMER PROF MOLECULAR BIOL, SCH VET MED, UNIV PA, 87- *Personal Data:* b Kingston, NY, June 23, 19; wid, Geraldine Burwell; c Rose, Randi, Stephen, Brian, David & Ellen. *Educ:* Pa State Univ, BS, 40; Univ Calif, PhD(biochem), 50. *Hon Degrees:* MS, Univ Pa, 72. *Prof Exp:* Asst prof biochem, Jefferson Med Col, 50-53. *Concurrent Pos:* Prof biochem & chmn dept, Philadelphia Col Osteopath, 59-62; consult, Hartford Found, Presby Hosp, Philadelphia, 63-65; vis prof, Univ Ibadan, Nigeria, 73-74; external examnr, 81; legal consult, Environ Carcinogenesis. *Mem:* AAAS; Am Chem Soc; Am Soc Biol Chem; Am Asn Cancer Res; Am Asn Vet Educr; Vet Oncol Soc. *Res:* Cancer chemotherapy; mechanism of action of chemotherapeutic drugs; nucleic acid metabolism; biochemical thermodynamics; nucleic acid metabolism in nucleus and mitochondria with particular reference to effect of clinically important anti-cancer drugs; biological response modifiers, liposomes/transport; carcinogenesis; environmental contamination, environmental science; oncology. *Mailing Add:* Dept Animal Biol Sch Vet Med Univ Pa Philadelphia PA 19104-6046

RUTNER, EMILE, CHEMICAL PHYSICS. *Current Pos:* RETIRED. *Personal Data:* b Budapest, Hungary, Apr 28, 21; nat US. *Educ:* Carnegie Inst Technol, BS, 43; Cornell Univ, PhD(chem), 51. *Prof Exp:* Chemist, Control Lab, Koppers Co, 43; anal develop, Publicker Industs, 43-45; asst, Cornell Univ, 47-50; phys chemist, Wright Air Develop Ctr, US Dept Air Force, 51-56; physicist, Lewis Res Ctr, NASA, 56-60; chemist, 60-75, physicist, US Air Force Mat Lab, Wright Patterson AFB, 75-83. *Concurrent Pos:* Res assoc, Forrestal Res Ctr, Princeton Univ, 51-52. *Mem:* Am Chem Soc; Am Phys Soc. *Res:* Spectra; thermophysics; solid state; radiation effects; kinetics; high energy laser effects. *Mailing Add:* 34 Columbia Ave Takoma Park MD 20912. *Fax:* 301-270-6973

RUTOWSKI, RONALD LEE, ANIMAL BEHAVIOR. *Current Pos:* Asst prof, 76-80, assoc prof, 80-88, PROF ZOOL, ARIZ STATE UNIV, 88- *Personal Data:* b Van Nuys, Calif, May 16, 49; m 74; c 2. *Educ:* Univ Calif, Santa Cruz, BA, 71; Cornell Univ, PhD(behav), 76. *Concurrent Pos:* Prin investr, NSF grants, 78-80, 80-82, 83-85 & 86-88; vis scientist, Archbold Biol Sta, Lake Placid, Fla, 81, Long Marine Lab, Univ Calif, Santa Cruz, 82, Dept Zool, James Cook Univ, Townsville, Queensland, Australia, 89; lectr, Univ Stockholm, 84, vis scientist, 94. *Mem:* Animal Behav Soc; AAAS; Am Soc Naturalists; Lepidopterists Soc; Int Soc Behav Ecol; Sigma Xi. *Res:* Animal communication, especially in invertebrates; reproductive behavior. *Mailing Add:* Dept Zool Ariz State Univ Tempe AZ 85287. *Fax:* 602-965-2519; *E-Mail:* r.rutowski@asu.edu

RUTSCHKY, CHARLES WILLIAM, ENTOMOLOGY. *Current Pos:* prof, 65-86, EMER PROF ENTOM, PA STATE UNIV, 86- *Personal Data:* b Pottstown, Pa, May 2, 23; m 45; c 4. *Educ:* Pa State Univ, BS, 43; Cornell Univ, PhD(entom), 49. *Prof Exp:* Investr fruit insects, NY Agr Exp Sta, 47-49; from asst prof to assoc prof entom, Pa State Univ, 49-62; prof, Univ Hawaii, 62-64. *Mem:* Entom Soc Am. *Mailing Add:* 1016 Taylor St State College PA 16803

RUTSTEIN, MARTIN S, MINERALOGY, GEOCHEMISTRY. *Current Pos:* asst prof, 70-72, chmn dept, 72-74, actg assoc vpres acad affairs, 74-75, ASSOC PROF GEOL SCI, STATE UNIV NY COL NEW PALTZ, 72-, CHMN DEPT, 76- *Personal Data:* b Boston, Mass, Apr 1, 40; m 62; c 2. *Educ:* Boston Univ, BA, 61, MA, 62; Brown Univ, PhD(mineral), 69. *Prof Exp:* Teaching asst geol, Boston Univ, 60-62; chief geol & soils sect, US Army Eng Sch, 62-64; res asst geol-mineral, Brown Univ, 64-68; asst prof mineral, Juniata Col, 68-70. *Concurrent Pos:* Pa Res Found fel, Juniata Col, 69-70; NY Res Found & Geol Soc Am Penrose Fund fels, State Univ NY Col New Paltz, 71-72, NSF fel, 72-73. *Mem:* Mineral Soc Am. *Res:* High temperature-pressure chain silicate phase relations; crystal chemistry of sulphides; environmental geology and human health; petrology. *Mailing Add:* Geol State Univ NY Col 75 S Manheim Blvd New Paltz NY 12561-2400

RUTTAN, VERNON W, AGRICULTURAL ECONOMICS. *Current Pos:* prof & head, Dept Agr Econ, Univ Minn, 65-70, prof & dir, Econ Develop Ctr, 70-73, prof, Dept Agr & Appl Econ & Dept Econ, 78-86, REGENTS PROF, DEPT APPL ECON, UNIV MINN, 86- *Personal Data:* b Alden, Mich, Aug 16, 24. *Educ:* Yale Univ, BA, 48; Univ Chicago, MA, 50, PhD, 52. *Hon Degrees:* LLD, Rutgers Univ, 78; Doktor der Agrarwissenschaften ehrenhalber, Christian Albrechts Universitat, Kiel, Ger, 86; DAgr, Purdue Univ, 91. *Honors & Awards:* B Y Morrison Mem Lectr, USDA, 83, Distinguished Serv Award, 86; Nat Award Agr Excellence, Nat Agri-Mkt Asn, 89. *Prof Exp:* Economist, Div Regional Studies, Tenn Valley Authority, 51-53, Off Gen Mgr, 54-55; from asst prof to prof, Dept Agr Econ, Purdue Univ, 55-63; agr economist, Rockefeller Found, Int Rice Res Inst, Philippines, 63-65; pres, Agr Develop Coun, Inc, 73-77. *Concurrent Pos:* Assoc agr economist, Giannini Found Agr Econ, Univ Calif, Berkeley, 58-59; mem, Comt New Orientations Agr Econ Res, Am Agr Econ Asn, 59-63, Comt Prof Problems Int Res, 67-69, chmn, 68-69; US coun mem, Int Asn Agr Economists, 69-72; mem, Tech Adv Comt, Consult Group Int Agr Res, 73-77, bd dirs, Int Serv Nat Agr Res, 79-86, Res Adv Comt, USAID, 67-75 & 83-86 & var agr comts, Nat Res Coun, Social Sci Res Coun, 71-; Alexander von Humboldt award, 84. *Mem:* Nat Acad Sci; fel Am Acad Arts & Sci; fel Am Agr Econ Asn (vpres, 67-68, pres, 71-72); Am Econ Asn; fel AAAS; Int Asn Agr Economists. *Res:* Agricultural economics; author and co-author of nine books and numerous technical publications. *Mailing Add:* Dept Agr & Appl Econ Univ Minn 1994 Buford Ave St Paul MN 55108. *Fax:* 612-625-2729; *E-Mail:* vruttan@maroon.pc.umn.edu

RUTTEN, MICHAEL JOHN, GASTROENTEROLOGY, GROWTH FACTOR RESEARCH. *Current Pos:* res physiologist, Kansas City, Mo, 87-91, RES PHYSIOLOGIST, VET ADMIN MED CTR, PORTLAND, ORE, 92-; ASST PROF SURG, ORE HEALTH SCI UNIV, 91- *Personal Data:* b San Bernardino, Calif, May 8, 49; m 78, Layne Lindquist; c Heather Linquist, Jonathan & Matthew. *Educ:* Calif State Univ, BA, 71, MA, 75; Univ Calif, Berkeley, PhD(endocrinol-physiol), 80. *Prof Exp:* Fel, Ctr Ulcer Res & Educ, Univ Calif Los Angeles Sch Med, 80-81; physiol instr, Dept Physiol, Harvard Med Sch, 81-86, res assoc, Dept Anat-Cell Biol, 81-87; res asst prof physiol, Kans Univ Med Sch, 87-91. *Concurrent Pos:* Prin investr, NIH, 82-87, Monsanto Corp, 89-92, Vet Admin, 89- *Mem:* AAAS; Am Gastroenterol Asn; Am Physiol Soc. *Res:* Investigating the role of growth factors in gastric epithelial repair and cancer; indentifying the cellular signals for epidermal growth factor, transforming growth factor alpha, and amphiregulin in normal cultures of gastric surface epithelial cells and in cultures of gastric cancer cells; specific effects these growth factors have on membrane ion channels, cell Ca2+, cyclic-AMP, inositol phosphates, protooncogene expression, and receptor mRNA levels; develop methods of in vivo retroviral growth factor transfection in animal stomachs as a model to help us better understand the gastric repair and cancer processes in the hope of designing better therapeutic treatments. *Mailing Add:* Vet Admin Med Ctr 3710 Veterans Hosp Rd Portland OR 97201. *Fax:* 503-220-3420

RUTTENBERG, HERBERT DAVID, PEDIATRICS, CARDIOLOGY. *Current Pos:* assoc prof pediat cardiol & chmn div, 69-78, prof pediat & chmn, Div Pediat Cardiol, 78-84, PROF PEDIAT & PATH, SCH MED, UNIV UTAH, 84- *Personal Data:* b Philadelphia, Pa, June 14, 30; m 55; c 4. *Educ:* Univ Calif, Los Angeles, BA, 52, MD, 56. *Prof Exp:* Fel pediat, Med Sch, Univ Minn, 57-58 & 60-61, USPHS fel pediat cardiol, 61-63; NIH trainee cardiovasc res technol, Wash Univ, 63-64; asst prof pediat cardiol, Sch Med, Univ Calif, Los Angeles, 64-69. *Concurrent Pos:* Res assoc cardiovasc path, Charles T Miller Hosp, St Paul, Minn, 62-63; regional vpres, Am Heart Asn, 87-88. *Mem:* Fel Am Acad Pediat; fel Am Col Cardiol; fel NY Acad Sci; Am Fedn Clin Res; fel Am Pediat Soc. *Res:* Neurohumoral control of cardiac function; adreneric receptors; cardiovascular function in clinical and experimental complete heart block; exercise physiology and preventive cardiology. *Mailing Add:* PC Med Ctr 100 N Medical Dr Salt Lake City UT 84113-1103. *Fax:* 801-588-2612

RUTTENBERG, STANLEY, ATMOSPHERIC PHYSICS, INTERNATIONAL DATA EXCHANGE. *Current Pos:* asst to dir, Nat Ctr Atmospheric Res, 64-73, mem sr mgt, 73-79, dir, Off Sci Prog Develop, UN Corp for Atmospheric Res, 79-84, dir, 84-86, SR MGT, UN CORP FOR ATMOSPHERIC RES PROJ, 86- *Personal Data:* b St Paul, Minn, Mar 12, 26; m 55; c 2. *Educ:* Mass Inst Technol, BS, 46; Univ Calif, Los Angeles, MA, 51. *Prof Exp:* Res asst geophys, Inst Geophys, Univ Calif, Los Angeles, 49-55; prog officer, US Nat Comt, Int Geophys Yr, Nat Acad Sci, 55-56, head prog officer, 57-60; secy, Panel World Magnetic Surv, Spec Comt Int Yrs Quiet Sun, Geophys Res Bd, 61-62, exec secy, US Nat Comt, 62-64. *Concurrent Pos:* Chmn, ICSU Panel World Data Ctrs, 88-; mem, US Nat Comt for Codata. *Mem:* Am Geophys Union. *Res:* Atmospheric physics; space-based observational techniques; geophysical data storage and access. *Mailing Add:* UN Corp Atmospheric Res PO Box 3000 Boulder CO 80307

RUTTER, EDGAR A, JR, MATHEMATICS. *Current Pos:* prof, 77-92, CHMN DEPT, WRIGHT STATE UNIV, 78-, FREDRICK A WHITE DISTINGUISHED PROF MATH, 92- *Personal Data:* b Newark, NJ, Feb 3, 37; wid; c David & Katherine. *Educ:* Marietta Col, BA, 59; Iowa State Univ, PhD(math), 65. *Prof Exp:* Asst prof math, NMex State Univ, 65-66; asst prof math, Univ Kans, 66-69, assoc prof, 69-76, prof, 76-77. *Mem:* Am Math Soc; Math Asn Am. *Res:* Ring theory; commutative algebra. *Mailing Add:* Dept Math Wright State Univ Colonel Glenn Hwy Dayton OH 45435. *Fax:* 937-775-2081; *E-Mail:* erutter@math.wright.edu

RUTTER, EDWARD WALTER, JR, PHOTOIMAGEABLE POLYMER SYSTEMS. *Current Pos:* PROJ LEADER, MAT SCI & DEVELOP LAB, CENT RES & DEVELOP, DOW CHEM CO, 89- *Personal Data:* b Wilmington, Del, Aug 4, 60. *Educ:* Univ Del, BS, 82, BA, 83; Univ Wis-Madison, PhD(inorg chem), 89. *Mem:* Am Chem Soc; Int Electronics Packaging Soc. *Res:* Development of photodefinable benzocyclobutene films as interlayer dielectric insulators for MCM-D technology; mechanistic organometallic chemistry of heterobimetallic Re- Pf complexes. *Mailing Add:* Shipley Co 455 Forest St Marlborough MA 01752. *Fax:* 517-636-6558

RUTTER, HENRY ALOUIS, JR, TOXICOLOGY, BIOCHEMISTRY. *Current Pos:* res coordr chem pharmacol, Hazelton Labs, Inc, 60-61, sr chemist, 61-63, sci dir chem dept, 63-64, res coordr pharmacol dept, 64-66, PROJ MGR TOXICOL DEPT, HAZLETON LABS, INC, 66- *Personal Data:* b Richmond, Va, Mar 28, 22; m 55; c 1. *Educ:* Va Polytech Inst, BS, 43; Univ Richmond, MS, 47; Georgetown Univ, PhD(biochem), 52. *Prof Exp:* Chemist, Stand Oil Co, La, 43; chemist, US Naval Ord Lab, 43-45; asst, Univ Tenn, 48-49; instr chem, Am Univ, 49-50; assoc prof org chem, Carson-Newman Col, 50-51; instr phys chem, Georgetown Univ, 51-52; biochemist & mem staff, Biochem Res Found, Franklin Inst, 52-55; chemist, Walter Reed Army Inst Res, 56-59; chief res chemist, Dept Surg, Baltimore City Hosps, 59-60. *Mem:* Am Chem Soc; Soc Cryobiol; Soc Toxicol; Am Inst Chemists. *Res:* Drugs and industrial chemicals; medical application of plastics; environmental sciences. *Mailing Add:* 2110 Mc Kay St Falls Church VA 22043-1522

RUTTER, MICHAEL L, PSYCHIATRY. *Current Pos:* PROF & HEAD, DEPT CHILD & ADOLESCENT PSYCHIAT, INST PSYCHIAT, UNIV LONDON, 73- *Hon Degrees:* Dr, Univ Leiden, 85, Cath Univ, 90; DSc, Univ Birmingham, 90, Univ Chicago, 91, Univ Minn, 93, Univ Ghent, 94; MD, Univ Edinburgh, 90; DPsychol, Univ Syvaskyla, 96. *Prof Exp:* Res fel, Dept Pediat, Albert Einstein Col Med, NY, 61-62; social psychiat unit, Med Res Coun, 62-65. *Mem:* Foreign assoc mem Inst Med-Nat Acad Sci; hon fel Brit Psychol Soc; hon fel Am Acad Pediat; hon mem Am Acad Child Psychiat; fel Royal Soc; foreign hon mem Am Acad Arts & Sci; foreign assoc mem Nat Acad Educ; Soc Res Child Develop (pres-elect, 97). *Res:* Stress resistance in children; developmental links between childhood and adult life; schools as social institutions; interviewing skills; neuropsychiatry; infantile autism and psychiatric epidemiology; author of 28 books and over 220 papers. *Mailing Add:* Inst Psychiat Univ London 16 De Crespigny Park Denmark Hill London SE5 8AF England

RUTTER, NATHANIEL WESTLUND, QUATERNARY GEOLOGY. *Current Pos:* from assoc prof to prof, 75-97, chmn dept, 80-89, UNIV PROF, UNIV ALTA, 97- *Personal Data:* b Omaha, Nebr, Nov 22, 32; Can citizen; m 61, Mary Munson; c Todd & Christopher. *Educ:* Tufts Univ, BS, 55; Univ Alaska, MS, 62; Univ Alta, PhD(geol), 66. *Prof Exp:* Explor geologist, Venezuelan Atlantic Ref Co, 55-58; res scientist, Geol Surv, Can, 65-74, head urban projs, 73-74; environ adv, Nat Energy Bd, 74-75. *Concurrent Pos:* Instr, Dept Archaeol, Univ Calgary, 67-73; pres, Westlund Consults Ltd; ed bd, Quaternary Rev; mem subcomt, NAm Stratig; pres, Int Quaternary Asn Cong, Ottawa, 87; assoc ed, Geosci Can, & Arctic; mem, Can Nat Comt, Int Geol Correlation Prog, 87-91; mem adv bd, Alta Geol Surv; mem, ICSU-IGBP Sci Steering Comt Global Changes of the Past; mem, Task Force Global Change, Int Union Geol Sci; hon vis prof, Acad Sci, China; mem, Can Nat Comt, Int Union Quaternary Res, Global Change Prog; ed-in-chief, Quaternary Int; sr res fel, Wissen Shaftskolleazu Berlin, 89; Annual Killam prof, Univ Alta, 93; hon prof, Chinese Acad Sci, 94; mem, Sci Bd-VNESCO-IGCP; nat lectr, Sigma Xi, 95-97. *Mem:* Fel Geol Soc Am; fel Geol Asn Can; fel Arctic Inst NAm; Sigma Xi; Int Union Quaternary Res (vpres, 82-87, pres, 89-91); Can Quaternary Asn. *Res:* Quaternary sedimentary and stratigraphy of the Rocky Mountains, Canada; paleosol investigations of glaciated and unglaciated surfaces; terrain analysis and land classification; northern Canada; amino acid dating methods; sea level changes, Argentina; Loess statigraphy, China; quaternary sedimentation, Southwest Africa; high Andes, Columbia. *Mailing Add:* Dept Earth & Atmospheric Sci Univ Alta Edmonton AB T6G 2E3 Can. *Fax:* 403-492-2030

RUTTER, WILLIAM J, MOLECULAR BIOLOGY. *Current Pos:* CHMN BD, CHIRON CORP, 81- *Personal Data:* b Malad City, Idaho, Aug 28, 28; m 71; c 2. *Educ:* Harvard Univ, BA, 49; Univ Utah, MS, 50; Univ Ill, PhD(biochem), 52. *Honors & Awards:* Pfizer Award, Am Chem Soc, 67; J J Berzelius Award, Karolinska Inst, 83; Brown-Haxen Lectr, Dept Pub Health,

State NY, 86. *Prof Exp:* USPHS fel, Inst Enzyme Res, Univ Wis, 52-54; USPHS fel biochem, Nobel Inst, Sweden, 54-55; from asst prof to prof, Univ Ill, Urbana, 55-65; prof biochem & genetics, Univ Wash, 65-69; chmn, Dept Biochem & Biophys, Univ Calif, San Francisco, 69-82, Hertz Stein prof biochem, 69-91, dir, Hormone Res Inst, 83-89. *Concurrent Pos:* Consult, Abbott Labs, 60-75, Eli Lilly Co, 77-80 & Merck & Co, 77-81; vis scientist, Guggenheim Mem fel, Stanford Univ, 62-63; mem & chmn basic sci adv comn, Nat Cystic Fibrosis Res, 69-74, mem, Pres Adv Coun, 74-75; mem, Develop Biol Panel, NSF, 71-73; pres, Pac Slope Biochem Conf, 71-73; mem, Bd Sci Counrs, Nat Inst Environ Health Sci, NIH, 76-81; mem bd dirs, Hana Biologics, Berkeley, Calif, 80-83, Keystone Life Sci Study Ctr, 83-; chmn bd dirs & founder, Chiron Corp, Emeryville, Calif, 81- & Meridian Instruments, Ann Arbor, Mich, 82-88; Kroc vis prof, Joslin Diabetes Ctr, Harvard Univ, Cambridge, Mass & Health Sci Ctr, Univ Tex, Dallas, 86. *Mem:* Nat Acad Sci; Am Soc Cell Biol; Am Soc Biol Chemists (treas, 70-76); Am Soc Develop Biol (pres-elect, 74-75, pres, 75-76); Am Chem Soc; Am Acad Arts & Sci; fel Am Acad Microbiol. *Res:* Control of gene expression; mechanisms of cytodifferentiation; regulation of cell proliferation; mechanism of enzyme action; macromolecular variation and evolution. *Mailing Add:* Chivon Corp 4560 Horton St Emeryville CA 94608. *Fax:* 510-655-3282

RUTTIMANN, URS E, MEDICAL IMAGE PROCESSING. *Current Pos:* sr scientist, Diag Syts Br, Nat Inst Dent Res, 86-91, SR SCIENTIST, LAB CLIN STUDIES, NAT INST ALCOHOL ABUSE & ALCOHOLISM, NIH, 91-; RES PROF CHILD HEALTH & DEVELOP, GEORGE WASHINGTON UNIV, 93- *Personal Data:* b Switz, July 28, 38; US citizen. *Educ:* HTL, Burgdorf, Switz, BS, 61; Swiss Fed Inst Technol, MS, 66; Univ Pa, PhD(biomed eng), 72. *Prof Exp:* Asst prof, Dept Clin Eng, George Wash Univ, 73-79, assoc prof child health & develop, 80-93. *Mem:* Biomed Eng Soc; Inst Elec & Electronics Engrs Eng Med & Biol Soc; Inst Elec & Electronics Engrs Comput Soc; Inst Elec & Electronics Engrs Acoust Speech & Signal Processing Soc; Soc Photo-Optical Instrumentation. *Mailing Add:* Lab Clin Studies NIAAA NIH Bldg 10-3C102 9000 Rockville Pike Bethesda MD 20892. *Fax:* 301-402-0445; *E-Mail:* ursr@nih.gov

RUTZ, LENARD O(TTO), CHEMICAL ENGINEERING. *Current Pos:* CONSULT CHEM ENGR, SAN MARINO, 84- *Personal Data:* b Franklin, Wis, Jan 27, 24; m 53; c 2. *Educ:* Marquette Univ, BChE, 45; Univ Wis, BS, 52, MS, 53; Univ Iowa, PhD(chem eng), 58. *Prof Exp:* Engr, Allis-Chalmers Mfg Co, 45-47, asst engr mining & mineral dressing div, 47-50; res chem engr, E I du Pont de Nemours & Co, 53-54; instr chem eng, Univ Iowa, 56-58, asst prof, 58-61; res engr, Missile & Space Systs Div, Douglas Aircraft Co, Inc, 61, supvr adv space tech, 62-63, chief eng res sect adv biotech, 63-65, sr staff specialist, Astropower Lab, Newport Beach, 65-77; chem engr, Procon Int Inc, 77-83. *Concurrent Pos:* Res fel, Eudora Hull Spalding Lab, Calif Inst Technol, 61-62; consult, Douglas Aircraft Co, Inc, 61-62; adj prof chem eng, Calif Polymer Univ, 78-84 & Univ Southern Calif, 84-92. *Mem:* Am Inst Aeronaut & Astronaut; Am Chem Soc; Am Inst Chem Eng; Am Soc Eng; Nat Soc Prof Engrs. *Res:* Applied thermodynamics; batteries; bioscience and biotechnology; desalination; fuel cells; heat transfer; membrane separation processes; nuclear engineering; physical and flow properties of porous media; sorption processes; transport phenomena; ultra-high vacua; petroleum refining processing; synfuels; alternate energy systems. *Mailing Add:* 2075 Del Mar Ave San Marino CA 91108-2809

RUTZ, RICHARD FREDERICK, SEMICONDUCTOR DEVICES & MATERIALS. *Current Pos:* RETIRED. *Personal Data:* b Alton, Ill, Feb 9, 19; m 45; c 3. *Educ:* Shurtleff Col, BA, 41; State Univ Iowa, MS, 46. *Prof Exp:* Staff mem electronics, Sandia Corp, 48-51; mgr semiconductor devices, T J Watson Res Ctr, IBM Corp, 51-80, mem staff, 80-87. *Mem:* Am Inst Physics; fel Inst Elec & Electronics Engrs. *Res:* Experimental semiconductor device technology; method of fabrication of crystalline shapes; high speed switching transistors; 20 publications and 50 US patents on transistors, lasers and tunnel diode devices in germanium, gallium arsenide, silicon carbon and aluminum nitrate. *Mailing Add:* Nine Burgundy Ct Grand Junction CO 81503

RUUD, CLAYTON OLAF, RESIDUAL STRESS, MANUFACTURING PROCESSES. *Current Pos:* PROF INDUST ENG, CO-DIR, QUAL MFG MNG PROG, DIR NDT&E PROG, ASST DIR, MAT RES LAB & ASSOC PROF ENG SCI, PA STATE UNIV, 79- *Personal Data:* b Glasgow, Mont, July 31, 34; m 90, Paula Mannino; c Kelley & Kirsten. *Educ:* Wash State Univ, BS, 57; San Jose State Univ, MS, 67; Denver Univ, PhD(mat sci), 70. *Honors & Awards:* IR 100 Award, Int Crystallog Data Pattern Contribution; Gov New Prod Award, Prof Eng Soc. *Prof Exp:* Asst remelt met, Kaiser Aluminum & Chem Corp, 57-58; develop engr, Boeing Aircraft Co, 58-61; res engr, Lockheed Missiles & Space Corp, 62-64, FMC Corp, 64-67; sr res scientist, Denver Univ, 70-79. *Concurrent Pos:* Ed, Advances X-Ray Anal, 70-80, X-Ray Spectros, 77-85; dir, Denver X-ray conf, 70-79; chmn, Particulates Subcomt, Safe Drinking Water Comt, Nat Acad Sci, dir, 75-77; chmn, Educ Subcomt, Joint Comt Powder Diffraction Stand, 80-85; pres, Denver X-ray Instruments, Inc. *Mem:* Am Soc Metals; Am Soc Metall Engrs; Soc Exp Stress Anal; Am Soc Testing Mat; Soc Mfg Engrs. *Res:* Manufacturing processing of materials; material properties and quality; cause and effect of residual stresses in metallic components, especially measurement methods and instrumentation; nondestructive materials characterization; published over 100 publications and granted seven patents. *Mailing Add:* Pa State Univ 207 HB State College PA 16801-6239

RUUS, E(UGEN), HYDRAULICS. *Current Pos:* lectr civil eng, 57-58, from asst prof to prof, 58-84, EMER & HON PROF CIVIL ENG, UNIV BC, 84- *Personal Data:* b Parnu, Estonia, Aug 19, 17; Can citizen; m 45; c 3. *Educ:* Univ Technol, Tallinn, Estonia, Dipl civil eng, 41; Karlsruhe Tech Univ, DrEng(civil eng), 57. *Prof Exp:* Sr asst & lectr civil eng, Univ Technol, Tallinn, Estonia, 42-43; designer, Dept War, Finland, 44; A B Skanska Cementgjuteriet, Sweden, 45-50 & Wagner & Oliver Consult Engrs, Ont, 50-51; hydraul & sr design engr, B C Eng Co, 51-56. *Res:* Water power development; hydraulic transients and turbine governing; pumping and pumped discharge lines. *Mailing Add:* 1819 Knox Rd Vancouver BC V6T 1S4 Can

RUVALCABA, ROGELIO H A, PEDIATRIC ENDOCRINOLOGY. *Current Pos:* trainee pediat endocrinol & metab dis, Univ Wash, 62-64, chief trainee, 64-66, from instr to assoc prof pediat endocrinol, 65-77, actg head, Div Pediat Endocrinol, 77-92, PROF PEDIAT ENDOCRINOL, UNIV WASH, 77- *Personal Data:* b Tepic, Mex, Apr 16, 34; US citizen; m 61; c 3. *Educ:* Univ Guadalajara, MD, 57. *Prof Exp:* Rotating intern med & surg, Hotel Dieu Hosp, New Orleans, 59, resident pediat, 60; resident, Children's Mem Hosp, Omaha, Nebr, 61; resident, Creighton Mem Hosp, 62. *Concurrent Pos:* Dir, Endocrinol Clin, Rainier Sch, 66-; mem human res rev bd, Dept Social & Health Serv, 75-78; dir, Pediat Endocrine Clin, Mary Bridge Children's Hosp, Tacoma, 75- *Mem:* Endocrine Soc; Lawson Wilkins Pediat Endocrine Soc; Western Soc Pediat Res; Am Acad Pediat. *Res:* Metabolic and endocrine disorder in children. *Mailing Add:* 1280 SW 301st St Federal Way WA 98023-3413

RUVALDS, JOHN, PHYSICS. *Current Pos:* from asst prof to assoc prof, 69-76, PROF PHYSICS, UNIV VA, 76- *Personal Data:* b Jelgava, Latvia, Mar 26, 40; US citizen; div. *Educ:* Grinnell Col, BA, 62; Univ Ore, MA, 65, PhD(physics), 67. *Prof Exp:* Res assoc physics, James Franck Inst, Univ Chicago, 67-69. *Mem:* Am Phys Soc; NY Acad Sci. *Res:* Theoretical solid state physics; superconductors. *Mailing Add:* Dept Physics Univ Va Charlottesville VA 22901

RUWART, MARY JEAN, gastroenterology, drug delivery, for more information see previous edition

RUWE, WILLIAM DAVID, THERMOREGULATION, FEVER & ANTIPYRESIS. *Current Pos:* ASST PROF PHYSIOL, UNIV ARK MED SCH, 86- *Personal Data:* b Lafayette, Ind, Feb 18, 53; m 90. *Educ:* Wabash Col, AB, 75; Purdue Univ, MS, 77, PhD(neurobiol), 80. *Prof Exp:* Res asst physiol psychol, Purdue Univ, W Lafayette, Ind, 75-78; res asst, Univ NC, 78-80, fel, 80-81; fel, Univ Calgary, Alta, Can, 80-85; res assoc, Ft Detrick, Frederick, Md, 85-86. *Concurrent Pos:* Prin investr, Nat Inst Neurol & Commun Disorders & Stroke, NIH, 88- & Univ Ark Med Sch, 88- *Mem:* Am Physiol Soc; Soc Neurosci; AAAS; Soc Exp Biol & Med; Sigma Xi; Int Brain Res Orgn. *Res:* Thermoregulatory processes and their possible mediation by neuroactive substances of the hypothalamus; the febrile state and associated acute response; mechanisms of antipyresis, both endogenous and exogenous; addictive processes, especially withdrawal; the alterations occurring in some of these processes that are altered during aging. *Mailing Add:* Dept Clin Psychol George Fox Col 420 N Meridian St SUB #5968 Newburg OR 97132-2699

RUYLE, WILLIAM VANCE, organic chemistry, pharmaceutical chemistry; deceased, see previous edition for last biography

RUZE, JOHN, ELECTRONICS ENGINEERING. *Current Pos:* RETIRED. *Personal Data:* b New York, NY, May 24, 16; m 56; c 4. *Educ:* City Col New York, BS, 38; Columbia Univ, MS, 40; Mass Inst Technol, ScD(electronic eng), 52. *Prof Exp:* Sect head antenna design, Signal Corps Radar Labs, 40-46; asst lab head, Air Force Cambridge Res Labs, 46-52; dir, Gabriel Lab, 52-54; pres, Radiation Eng Lab, 54-62; Sr Staff Mem, Lincoln Labs, Mass Inst Technol, 62- *Concurrent Pos:* Ed, Inst Elec & Electronics Engrs Trans Antennas & Propagation, 67-69. *Mem:* Fel Inst Elec & Electronics Engrs; Int Union Radio Sci. *Res:* Microwave optics; large antenna systems; electromagnetic theory. *Mailing Add:* 4 Concord Green Apt 6 Concord MA 01742

RUZICKA, FRANCIS FREDERICK, JR, RADIOLOGY. *Current Pos:* RETIRED. *Personal Data:* b Baltimore, Md, June 30, 17; m 41; c 6. *Educ:* Col Holy Cross, AB, 39; Johns Hopkins Univ, MD, 43. *Prof Exp:* Roentgenologist, Cancer Detection Ctr, Univ Minn, 48-49, instr radiol, Univ Hosps, 49-50; chmn dept radiol, St Vincent's Hosp & Med Ctr, New York, 50-73; from assoc chmn dept to chmn dept, Med Ctr, Univ Wis-Madison, 73-81, prof, 73-84, emer prof radiol, 84-88. *Concurrent Pos:* Consult radiol, St Elizabeth's Hosp, Elizabeth, NJ, Overlook Hosp, Summit, NJ & Columbus Hosp, New York; assoc clin prof radiol, Sch Med, NY Univ, 50-53, clin prof, 54-73; consult comt Vet Admin health resources, Nat Acad Sci, 75-76; chief, Diag Imaging Res Br, Radiation Res Prog, Nat Cancer Inst, NIH, Md, 84-88. *Mem:* Radiol Soc NAm; AMA; emer fel Am Col Radiol; Am Roentgen Ray Soc; emer fel Soc Cardiovasc & Interventional Radiol. *Res:* Roentgen vascular aspects of the liver and the portal venous system; Xeromammography; double contrast techniques in gastrointestinal radiology including the use of drugs. *Mailing Add:* PO Box 763 St Michaels MD 21663

RYALL, A(LBERT) LLOYD, HORTICULTURE. *Current Pos:* RETIRED. *Personal Data:* b Phoenix, Ariz, June 25, 04; m 28, Mary E Newton; c Patricia J, Philip L, Pamela K & Peter N. *Educ:* NDak Agr Col, BS, 26; Ore Agr Col, MS, 28. *Prof Exp:* Jr pomologist, USDA, Yakima, Wash, 28-41, assoc horticulturist, Harlingen, Tex, 42-49, horticulturist, Fresno, 49-57, sr horticulturist, Beltsville, Md, 57-62, prin horticulturist, Washington, 62-69; asst prof, NMex State Univ, Las Cruces, 71-75. *Concurrent Pos:* hort consult various produce & transp co, 70- *Mem:* Fel AAAS; fel Am Soc Hort Sci; Am

Inst Biol Sci. *Res:* Development of advanced applications in precooling, special storage requirements, packaging and transportation services for fresh fruits and vegetables. *Mailing Add:* 6101 Camelot Dr Harlingen TX 78550-8420

RYALL, ALAN S, JR, seismology, for more information see previous edition

RYALS, GEORGE LYNWOOD, JR, GENETIC IDENTITY TESTING. *Current Pos:* DIR, PATERNITY DIV, ROCHE BIOMED, 92- *Personal Data:* b Erwin, NC, Nov 14, 41; m 93, Mary Anne Elder; c Jennifer & Mackenzie. *Educ:* Elon Col, AB, 66; Appalachian State Univ, MA, 67; Clemson Univ, PhD(zool), 75. *Prof Exp:* Asst prof biol, Lees-McRae Col, 67-69 & Southeastern Col, 69-70; assoc prof & chmn dept, Elon Col, 73; dir, Genetic Design, 85-92. *Concurrent Pos:* dir & vpres, Micro Diag, Inc. *Mem:* Am Inst Biol Sci; AAAS; Am Soc Zoologists; NAm Benthological Soc; Am Asn Blood Banks; Am Soc Histocompatibility & Immunogenetics. *Res:* Structure and function of benthic communities; seasonal regulation in Chironomidae and Odonata. *Mailing Add:* 806 Tarleton Ave Burlington NC 27215

RYAN, ALLAN JAMES, MEDICAL EDITING. *Current Pos:* RETIRED. *Personal Data:* b Brooklyn, NY, Dec 9, 15; m 42; c 3. *Educ:* Yale Univ, BA, 36; Columbia Univ, MD, 40; Am Bd Surg, dipl, 47. *Hon Degrees:* Doctor Sports Sci, US Sports Acad, 83. *Prof Exp:* From assoc prof to prof rehab med & phys educ, Univ Wis-Madison, 65-76; athletic teams physician, 65-76; ed-in-chief, Postgrad Med, 76-79, The Physician & Sports Med, 73-86, Fitness in Bus, 87-89. *Concurrent Pos:* Pvt pract, gen surg, Meriden, Conn, 46-65. *Mem:* Hon fel Brit Asn Sport & Med; fel Am Col Sports Med. *Res:* Sports medicine; physical education; causation, prevention and treatment in head, back and ankle injuries in sports and dance. *Mailing Add:* 5800 Jeff Pl Edina MN 55436-1938

RYAN, ANNE WEBSTER, ORGANIC CHEMISTRY, INFORMATION SCIENCE. *Current Pos:* Asst ed, 49-51 & 52-64, group leader, 64-65, asst dept head, 65-67, MGR, CHEM ABSTRACTS SERV, 67- *Personal Data:* b Lowell, Mass, Apr 17, 27; wid; c 2. *Educ:* Simmons Col, BS, 49. *Concurrent Pos:* Tech librn res & develop, Lever Bros Co, 51-52. *Mem:* Am Chem Soc. *Res:* Chemical information, storage and retrieval. *Mailing Add:* 1785 Northwest Ct Apt F Columbus OH 43212-1527

RYAN, BILL CHATTEN, METEOROLOGY. *Current Pos:* RES METEOROLOGIST, USDA FOREST SERV, 67- *Personal Data:* b Long Beach, Calif, Oct 2, 28; m 50; c 4. *Educ:* Univ Nev, Reno, BS, 50; Tex A&M Univ, MS, 64; Univ Calif, Riverside, PhD(geog), 74. *Honors & Awards:* Outstanding Meteorologist Award, Riverside-San Bernardino Chap, Am Meteorol Soc, 75. *Prof Exp:* Officer electronics, US Air Force, 51-58, officer meteorol, 58-65; res meteorologist, Meteorol Res Inc, 65-67. *Concurrent Pos:* Mem, Sci Comt Riverside Air Pollution Control Dist, 69- *Mem:* Am Meteorol Soc. *Res:* Development of a mathematical model to diagnose and predict wind in remote areas of mountainous terrain. *Mailing Add:* 2291 Quartz Pl Riverside CA 92507

RYAN, CARL RAY, SATELLITE COMMUNICATION SYSTEMS FOR MILITARY APPLICATIONS. *Current Pos:* mem tech staff, 63-77 & 79-89, vpres, 89-90, DIR, STRATEGIC ELECTRONICS DIV, MOTOROLA INC, 90- *Personal Data:* b Gateway, Ark, Mar 3, 38; m 64; c 2. *Educ:* Univ Ark, BSEE, 62; Iowa State Univ, MS, 63; Univ Mo, Rolla, PhD, 69. *Prof Exp:* Prof elec, Mich Technol Univ, 77-79. *Concurrent Pos:* Dan Nobel fel, Motorola Inc, 75; adj prof, Ariz State Univ, 81-89; gen chmn, Phoenix Conf Comput & Commun, 88; mem, Eng Acceleration Comn, 88- *Mem:* Fel Inst Elec & Electronics Engrs; Am Defense Preparedness Asn. *Res:* Very high data rate communication equipment; channel models, computer simulation, coders, modems and circuits; computer aided design of communication system hardware. *Mailing Add:* RR 2 Box 2386 Cassville MO 65625-9640

RYAN, CECIL BENJAMIN, POULTRY SCIENCE. *Current Pos:* from asst prof to prof, 47-81, EMER PROF POULTRY SCI, TEX A&M UNIV, 81- *Personal Data:* b Runge, Tex, Aug 4, 16; m 41; c 2. *Educ:* Tex Col Arts & Indust, BS, 38; Tex A&M Univ, MS, 47, PhD, 62. *Prof Exp:* Teacher pub sch, 38-42. *Concurrent Pos:* Piper Prof, 66. *Mem:* Fel AAAS; Poultry Sci Asn (secy-treas, 54-77, first vpres, 78-79, pres, 79-80); Genetics Soc Am; World Poultry Sci Asn. *Res:* Environmental physiology and management. *Mailing Add:* Dept Poultry Sci Tex A&M Univ College Station TX 77843-2472

RYAN, CHARLES EDWARD, JR, ELECTRICAL ENGINEERING. *Current Pos:* CONSULT, 91- *Personal Data:* b Crestline, Ohio, Mar 30, 38; m 62; c Patricia, Deirdre, Charles, Michael & Sean. *Educ:* Case Inst Technol, BSc, 60; Ohio State Univ, MSc, 61, PhD(elec eng), 68. *Prof Exp:* Eng asst, North Elec Co, 56-60; res asst, Electrosci Lab, Ohio State Univ, 60-62, res assoc, 62-68, asst supvr, 68-71; chief, Electromagnetic Effectiveness Div, Ga Inst Technol, 80-88, sr res engr, Eng Exp Sta, 71-76, prin res engr, 76-91. *Mem:* Fel Inst Elec & Electronics Engrs; Sigma Xi. *Res:* Electromagnetic theory applied to antennas and scattering; radar cross section studies; computer analysis. *Mailing Add:* 2499 Kingsland Dr Doraville GA 30360

RYAN, CHARLES F, CLINICAL PHARMACOLOGY, DRUG DEVELOPMENT. *Current Pos:* dir clin develop, 89-92, DIR PROJ MGT, PHARMACO, 93- *Personal Data:* b Terre Haute, Ind, Dec 30, 41; m 62; c 1. *Educ:* Purdue Univ, BS, 63, MS, 66, PhD(pharmacol), 69. *Prof Exp:* Asst prof pharmacol, Univ Wisc, 68-72; assoc prof & chmn pharmacol, Univ Nebr, 72-79; prof & dep dean pharm, Wayne State Univ, 79-82; dir clin res, Harris Labs, 82-89. *Concurrent Pos:* Adj prof, Univ Nebr, 82-89. *Mem:* Acad Pharmaceut Sci; Am Asn Pharmaceut Scientists; Am Soc Clin Pharmacol & Therapeut; Am Soc Pharmacol & Exp Therapeut; Am Pharmaceut Asn; Drug Info Asn. *Res:* Clinical research and drug development. *Mailing Add:* Pharmaco 706A Ben White Blvd W Austin TX 78704

RYAN, CLARENCE AUGUSTINE, JR, PLANT PHYSIOLOGY, PLANT BIOCHEMISTRY. *Current Pos:* asst agr chemist, Wash State Univ, 64-68, assoc prof biochem & assoc agr chemist, 68-72, chmn, Dept Agr Chem, 78-80, PROF BIOCHEM & FEL, INST BIOL CHEM, WASH STATE UNIV, 72- *Personal Data:* b Butte, Mont, Sept 29, 31; m 54; c 4. *Educ:* Carroll Col, Mont, BA, 53; Mont State Univ, MS, 56, PhD(chem), 59. *Honors & Awards:* Merck Award, 59; Steven Holes Prize, Am Soc Plant Phys, 92; Kenneth Spencer Award, Am Chem Soc, 93; Silverstein-Simeone Award, Int Soc Chem Ecol. *Prof Exp:* Fel, Ore State Univ, 59-61; fel, Western Regional Lab, USDA, 61-63, chemist, 63-64. *Concurrent Pos:* USPHS Career Develop Award, 64-74; prog mgr competitive grants, Biol Stress, USDA, 83-84; mem bd dirs, Int Soc Plant Molecular Biol, 88-91; consult, Kemin Ind, Des Moines, Iowa; non-resident fel plant biol, Noble Found, Ardmore, OK, 96- *Mem:* Nat Acad Sci; Am Soc Biol Chemists; Am Chem Soc; Am Soc Plant Phys; Int Soc Plant Molecular Biol; Int Soc Chem Ecol; AAAS. *Res:* Protein chemistry; plant proteolytic enzymes, naturally occurring proteinase inhibitors; plant molecular biology; signal transduction in plants. *Mailing Add:* Inst Biol Chem Wash State Univ Pullman WA 99164-6340

RYAN, CLARENCE E, JR, organic coatings for metal, for more information see previous edition

RYAN, DAVID GEORGE, PARTICLE PHYSICS. *Current Pos:* from asst prof to assoc prof, 67-81, PROF PHYSICS, MCGILL UNIV, 81- *Personal Data:* b Quebec, Que, Dec 31, 37. *Educ:* Queen's Univ, Ont, BSc, 59, MSc, 61; Univ Birmingham, PhD(physics), 65. *Prof Exp:* Res fel physics, Univ Birmingham, 65-66; res assoc, Cornell Univ, 66-67. *Mem:* Am Phys Soc. *Res:* Interactions and decays of elementary particles. *Mailing Add:* Dept Physics McGill Univ 3600 University Montreal PQ H3A 2T8 Can

RYAN, DONALD EDWIN, MATHEMATICS, ASTRONOMY. *Current Pos:* assoc prof, 68-74, PROF MATH, NORTHWESTERN STATE UNIV, 74- *Personal Data:* b San Diego, Calif, July 1, 35. *Educ:* Univ Tex, BA, 57, MA, 61, PhD(math), 64. *Prof Exp:* Aero-engr, Pensacola Naval Air Sta, 55; test engr, Convair Astronaut Div, Gen Dynamics Corp, 57-59; instr math, Univ Tex, 59-63, 63-64; asst prof math, Eastern Mich Univ, 64-65; asst prof, Bowling Green State Univ, 65-68. *Concurrent Pos:* NSF consult, India, 67; chmn gifted & talented adv comt, Northwestern State Univ. *Mem:* Am Math Soc; Math Asn Am. *Res:* Functions of a complex variable which are ecart fini and their topological structures. *Mailing Add:* Dept Math & Sci Northwestern State Univ Natchitoches LA 71497-0003

RYAN, DONALD F, PHYSICS. *Current Pos:* from asst prof to assoc prof, 66-72, chmn dept physics & earth sci, 70-72, PROF PHYSICS, STATE UNIV NY, COL PLATTSBURGH, 72- *Personal Data:* b Syracuse, NY, July 24, 30; m 59; c 4. *Educ:* LeMoyne Col, NY, BS, 57; Cath Univ Am, MS, 60, PhD(physics), 63. *Prof Exp:* Res fel physics, Cath Univ Am, 63-64, from res asst prof to res assoc prof, 64-66. *Mem:* Am Phys Soc. *Res:* Cosmic ray and elementary particle research. *Mailing Add:* 4 Valcour Blvd Plattsburgh NY 12901

RYAN, DOUGLAS EARL, INORGANIC CHEMISTRY, ANALYTICAL CHEMISTRY. *Current Pos:* from asst prof to assoc prof, 51-63, chmn, Dept Chem, 69-73, MCLEOD PROF, DALHOUSIE UNIV, 63-, DIR, TRACE ANAL RES CTR, 71-, DIR, SLOWPOKE FACIL, 76-, EMER PROF CHEM, 87- *Personal Data:* b Can, Jan 21, 22; m 45, Nanette Pritchard; c Lorne, Michelle & Kelly. *Educ:* Univ NB, BSc, 44; Univ Toronto, MA, 46; Imp Col, London, dipl & PhD(chem), 51; Univ London, DSc, 65. *Honors & Awards:* Fisher Sci Lect Award, Chem Inst Can, 72. *Prof Exp:* Asst prof chem, Univ NB, 46-48. *Concurrent Pos:* Nat Res Coun Can traveling fel, 59-60; exec dir, Ctr Anal Res & Develop, Univ Colombo, Sri Lanka, 80-85; Erskine fel, Univ Canterbury, NZ, 86. *Mem:* Fel Chem Inst Can. *Res:* Metal chelates; molecular spectroscopy; neutron activation and trace analysis in general. *Mailing Add:* Dept Chem Dalhousie Univ Halifax NS B3H 4J1 Can. *Fax:* 902-494-1310

RYAN, EDWARD MCNEILL, GEOLOGY. *Current Pos:* prof, 46-84, EMER PROF GEOL, STEPHENS COL, 84- *Personal Data:* b St Louis, Mo, May 24, 20; m 76; c 3. *Educ:* Miami Univ, BA, 41; Univ Mo, Columbia, MA, 43. *Prof Exp:* Aerial phototopographer, US Army Corp Engrs, 43-46. *Mem:* Nat Asn Geol Teachers. *Res:* Geologic travel and color photography in fifty states, most provinces of Canada, Virgin Islands and East Africa. *Mailing Add:* 505 S Garth Columbia MO 65203

RYAN, FREDERICK MERK, PHYSICS. *Current Pos:* RETIRED. *Personal Data:* b Pittsburgh, Pa, Jan 20, 32; m 52; c 2. *Educ:* Carnegie-Mellon Univ, BS, 54, MS, 56, PhD(physics), 59. *Prof Exp:* Res physicist, Westinghouse Elec Corp, 59-61, sr physicist, 61-66, fel scientist, 66-72, adv scientist, 72-85, consult scientist, 85-90, leader Instrument Develop Group, 90-93. *Concurrent Pos:* Rosemount anal instr, 90- *Mem:* Am Phys Soc; Electrochem Soc. *Res:* Experimental solid state physics; luminescence; optical physics; optical analytical instrumentation. *Mailing Add:* PO Box 406 New Alexandria PA 15670

RYAN, GEORGE FRISBIE, HORTICULTURE. *Current Pos:* assoc horticulturist, 67-79, HORTICULTURIST, WESTERN WASH RES & EXTEN CTR, WASH STATE UNIV, 79- *Personal Data:* b Yakima, Wash, July 28, 21; m 47; c 1. *Educ:* State Col Wash, BS, 47; Univ Calif, Los Angeles, PhD(hort sci), 53. *Prof Exp:* Res asst hort, Univ Calif, Los Angeles, 48-52, instr & jr horticulturist, 52-54, asst horticulturist, 54-60, assoc specialist, 60-61; asst prof & asst horticulturist, Citrus Exp Sta, Univ Fla, 61-67. *Mem:* Am Soc Hort Sci; Weed Sci Soc Am; Int Plant Propagation Soc; Sigma Xi. *Res:* Chemical regulation of plant growth and flowering; nutrition of ornamental plants; chemical weed control. *Mailing Add:* 1877 Skyline Dr Tacoma WA 98406-1930

RYAN, JACK A, geophysics, for more information see previous edition

RYAN, JACK LEWIS, INORGANIC CHEMISTRY, ACTINIDE & LANTHANIDE CHEMISTRY. *Current Pos:* sr res scientist, 65-69, res assoc, 69-93, SR RES SCIENTIST, PAC NORTHWEST LABS, BATTELLE MEM INST, 93- *Personal Data:* b Dallas, Ore, May 14, 33; m 82, JoAnne M Liesy; c Rex C. *Educ:* Ore State Univ, BS, 53, MS, 56. *Prof Exp:* Chemist, Hanford Lab, Gen Elec Co, 55-60, sr scientist, 60-65. *Concurrent Pos:* Consult, Lawrence Berkeley Lab, Univ Calif, 74; lectr, Joint Ctr Grad Study, Richland, Wash, 74-92; consult, PDI Technol, Palos Verde, Calif, 94, Geosate Corp, Richland, WA, 94- *Mem:* AAAS; Am Chem Soc. *Res:* Inorganic and physical chemistry of actinide and lanthanide elements; coordination chemistry; absorption spectroscopy; ion exchange; solvent extraction; non-aqueous solutions; electrochemistry, chemical processing of actinide elements. *Mailing Add:* 1326 Broadview Dr West Richland WA 99352. *Fax:* 509-376-3566

RYAN, JAMES ANTHONY, SOIL CHEMISTRY, SOIL BIOCHEMISTRY. *Current Pos:* soil scientist, Munic Environ Res Lab, 74-77, mem staff, Ultimate Disposal Res Prog, 77-90, SOIL SCIENTIST, LAND REMEDIATIION POLLUTION CONTROL, ENVIRON PROTECTION AGENCY, 90- *Personal Data:* b Cairo, Ill, Mar 16, 43; m 63; c 3. *Educ:* Murray State Univ, BS, 66; Univ Ky, MS, 68, PhD(soils), 71. *Prof Exp:* Fel soil sci, Univ Wis-Madison, 71-74. *Mem:* Am Soc Agron; Soil Sci Soc Am; Water Pollution Control Fedn; AAAS; Sigma Xi. *Res:* Nitrogen transformations in soils; sewage sludge disposal on agricultural lands; transformation of heavy metals in soils in relation to their phytotoxic effects. *Mailing Add:* US Environ Protection Agency 5995 Center Hill Ave Cincinnati OH 45224

RYAN, JAMES M, CHEMICAL ENGINEERING. *Current Pos:* mgr res & develop, 81-88, dir process design & evaluation, 88-91, ENG FEL, KOCH PROCESS SYSTS, INC, 91- *Personal Data:* b Milwaukee, Wis, Feb 20, 32; m 55, 89; c 8. *Educ:* Univ Mich, BS & MS, 55; Mass Inst Technol, ScD(chem eng), 58. *Prof Exp:* Technologist, Shell Chem Co, 58-63, res engr, 63-65; proj leader gas chromatography, Abcor, Inc, 65-66, prog mgr, 66-70, mgr eng, 70-71, mgr commercial plants eng, 71-73, vpres, Abcor Japan, 73-75, dir technol, Abcor, Inc, 75-78; mgr process & prod develop, Helix Process Systs Inc, 78-81. *Mem:* Am Chem Soc; Am Inst Chem Engrs; Soc Petrol Engrs. *Res:* Chemical process development; membrane process and equipment design, engineering, plants; separation processes; gas chromatography; large scale liquid chromatography; reaction kinetics; chemical manufacturing economics; process simulation; mass transfer; cryogenic gas field separations; large scale simulation. *Mailing Add:* Seven Swallow Lane Wichita KS 67230-6619

RYAN, JAMES MICHAEL, GAMMA RAY ASTRONOMY, SOLAR PHYSICS. *Current Pos:* Res scientist, 78-84, RES PROF PHYSICS, UNIV NH, 84- *Personal Data:* b Chicago, Ill, Oct 9, 47; m 79, Nancy Glick. *Educ:* Univ Calif Riverside, BA, 70, PhD(physics), 78; Univ Calif San Diego, MS, 73. *Concurrent Pos:* Prin investr, Univ NH, 88- *Mem:* Am Geophys Union; Am Astron Soc; Sigma Xi; Am Phys Soc. *Res:* Comptel instrument on gamma ray observatory; gamma ray astronomy; solar flare physics (gamma and x-ray measurements); cosmic ray production and acceleration theory; atmospheric gamma ray and neutron measurements. *Mailing Add:* 18 Belle Lane Lee NH 03824-6438

RYAN, JAMES PATRICK, GASTROINTESTINAL PHYSIOLOGY. *Current Pos:* asst prof, 75-80, ASSOC PROF, SCH MED, TEMPLE UNIV, 80- *Personal Data:* b Philadelphia, Pa, Jan 10, 47; m 68; c 2. *Educ:* Villanova Univ, BS, 68, MS, 70; Hahnemann Med Col, PhD(physiol), 74. *Prof Exp:* Fel, Sch Med, Univ Pa, 74-75. *Concurrent Pos:* Lectr, Gwynedd Mercy Col, 76- *Mem:* NY Acad Sci; Sigma Xi. *Res:* Neural and hormonal control of gastrointestinal smooth muscle motility, including how motor patterns are affected during pregnancy. *Mailing Add:* Dept Physiol Med Sch Temple Univ Philadelphia PA 19140

RYAN, JAMES WALTER, MEDICINE, BIOCHEMISTRY. *Current Pos:* PROF ANESTHESIOL & PHARM & TOXICOL, MED COL GA, 95- *Personal Data:* b Amarillo, Tex, June 8, 33; div; c James P, Alexandra L & Amy J. *Educ:* Dartmouth Col, AB, 57; Cornell Univ, MD, 61; Oxford Univ, DPhil(biochem), 67. *Honors & Awards:* Louis & Artur Luciano Award, McGill Univ, 85-85. *Prof Exp:* Intern med, Montreal Gen Hosp, Can, 61-62, resident, 62-63; res assoc, NIH, 63-65; hon med officer to Regius prof med, Oxford Univ, 65-67; asst prof biochem, Rockefeller Univ, 67-68; from assoc prof to prof med, Sch Med, Univ Miami, 68-95. *Concurrent Pos:* USPHS fel, Oxford Univ, 65-67; USPHS spec fel, Rockefeller Univ, 67-68, career develop award, 68; sr scientist, Papanicolaou Cancer Res Inst, 72-77; vis prof, Clin Res Inst Montreal, 74; mem, Coun Cardiopulmonary Dis & Med Adv Bd, Coun High Blood Pressure, Am Heart Asn; investr, Howard Hughes Med Inst, 68-71; Pfizer travelling fel, Univ Montreal, 74; vis fac, Mayo Clin, 74. *Mem:* Am Heart Asn; Am Chem Soc; Am Soc Biol Chemists; Brit Biochem Soc; AAAS; Biochem Soc; NY Acad Sci; Sigma Xi; Europ Microcirulation Soc. *Res:* Action and metabolism of the vasoactive polypeptides; bradykinin and angiotensin, and their relation to diseases of high blood pressure. *Mailing Add:* Vascular Biol Ctr Med Col Ga Augusta GA 30912-5000. *Fax:* 706-721-9799; *E-Mail:* jryan@mail.mcg.edu

RYAN, JOHN DONALD, geology; deceased, see previous edition for last biography

RYAN, JOHN F, ANESTHESIOLOGY. *Current Pos:* ASST PROF ANESTHESIOL, HARVARD MED SCH & MASS GEN HOSP, 69- *Personal Data:* b Boston, Mass, May 16, 35; m 59; c 3. *Educ:* Boston Col, AB, 57; Columbia Univ, MD, 61. *Prof Exp:* Asst prof anesthesiol, Col Physicians & Surgeons, Columbia Univ & Columbia-Presby Med Ctr, 68-69. *Res:* Pediatric anesthesia; biochemistry of the myoneural junction; hypotensive anesthesia and malignant hyperpyrexia. *Mailing Add:* Dept Anesthesiol Mass Gen Hosp Fruit St Boston MA 02114-2620

RYAN, JOHN PETER, PHYSICAL CHEMISTRY. *Current Pos:* res chemist radiochem, 51-61, mgr nuclear prod dept, 61-73, MGR STATIC CONTROL SYSTS DEPT, 3M CO, 73- *Personal Data:* b St Paul, Minn, July 28, 21; m 44; c 5. *Educ:* Col St Thomas, BS, 43; Univ Minn, PhD(phys chem), 52. *Prof Exp:* Instr chem, Col St Thomas, 46-51. *Mem:* Am Nuclear Soc; Am Chem Soc. *Res:* Development of commercial and medical products containing radioactive isotopes. *Mailing Add:* 360 Edith Dr West St Paul MN 55118-3008

RYAN, JOHN WILLIAM, ORGANIC CHEMISTRY. *Current Pos:* Proj leader org chem res, 57-65, supvr, 65-68, personnel coordr res, develop & eng, 68-69, mgr tech serv & develop, resins & chem bus, 69-73, MGR RES & DEVELOP SILICONE FLUIDS, DOW CORNING CORP, 73- *Personal Data:* b La Crosse, Wis, Sept 8, 26; m 52; c 3. *Educ:* Loras Col, BS, 48; Univ Iowa, MS, 51; Univ Ky, PhD(org chem), 57. *Mem:* Sigma Xi. *Res:* Organosilicone and organometallic compounds. *Mailing Add:* 514 Linwood Midland MI 48640-3447

RYAN, JON MICHAEL, CELL BIOLOGY, LARGE SCALE CELL CULTURE. *Current Pos:* cell biologist, Abbott Labs, 81-83, cell biol group leader, 84-89, assoc res fel, 89-96, SECT MGR, ABBOTT LABS, 89-, RES FEL, 96- *Personal Data:* b Ottumwa, Iowa, Nov 14, 43; m 65, Penny Millen; c 1. *Educ:* William Penn Col, BA, 65; Univ Nebr, Lincoln, MS, 67; Iowa State Univ, PhD(cell biol), 70. *Prof Exp:* NIH fel, 70-71, res asst, 72-76, res assoc cell biol, Wistar Inst Anat & Biol, 76; res scientist, Res Inst, Ill Inst Technol, 76-78, sr scientist, 78-81. *Mem:* AAAS; Tissue Cult Asn. *Res:* Control of cellular proliferation in tissue culture; aging; large scale cell culture; virus production; plasminogen activators; recombinant cell culture. *Mailing Add:* 266 Woodstock Clarendon Hills IL 60514

RYAN, JULIAN GILBERT, PETROLEUM CHEMISTRY. *Current Pos:* RETIRED. *Personal Data:* b Metamora, Ill, Oct 6, 13; m 36, Helen F Roberts; c Mary J Villani. *Educ:* Univ Ill, BS, 35. *Prof Exp:* Res chemist, Shell Oil Co, 35-42, supvr fuels & lubricants develop, 46-63, tech adv to res dir, 63-70, staff res engr, 70-78. *Concurrent Pos:* Group leader, Coord Res Coun, 53-66, mem diesel div, 66-76; chmn, St Louis Sect, Soc Auto Engrs, 64-65. *Mem:* AAAS; Am Chem Soc; Soc Automotive Eng. *Res:* Corrosive and abrasive wear of engines; gasoline oxidation stability; tetraethyl lead antagonism by sulfur compounds; antiknock performance and abnormal combustion phenomena; aviation and automotive fuels and lubricants; automotive engines exhaust emission; patents and publications in fuels and lubricants. *Mailing Add:* 664 Halloran Ave Wood River IL 62095

RYAN, KENNETH JOHN, ENDOCRINOLOGY, BIOCHEMISTRY. *Current Pos:* dir, Lab Human Reproduction & Reproductive Biol, Harvard Med Sch, 74-93, Kate Macy Ladd prof & chmn dept, 73-93, Kate Macy Ladd distinguished prof, 93-96, EMER PROF, OBSTET & GYNEC, HARVARD MED SCH, 96- *Personal Data:* b New York, NY, Aug 26, 26; m 48; c 3. *Educ:* Harvard Med Sch, MD, 52; Am Bd Obstet & Gynec, dipl, 64. *Honors & Awards:* Ernst Oppenheimer Award, Endocrine Soc, 64; Weinstein Award United Cerebral Palsy, 71. *Prof Exp:* Intern med, Mass Gen Hosp, Boston, 52-53, resident, 53-54, fel biochem, 54-55, Am Cancer Soc fel, 54-56; asst resident, Columbia-Presby Med Ctr, 56-57; resident, Boston Lying-In-Hosp & Free Hosp Women, 57-60; dir, Fearing Lab, Free Hosp Women, 60-61; Arthur H Bill prof obstet & gynec & chmn dept, Sch Med, Case Western Res Univ, 61-70, chmn, Dept Reprod Biol, 68-70, coordr biol sci, 69-70; prof reprod biol & chmn, Dept Obstet & Gynec, Univ Calif, San Diego, 70-72, chief-of-staff, Boston Hosp Women, 73-80; chmn, Dept Obstet & Gynec, Brigham & Women's Hosp, 80-93. *Concurrent Pos:* Fel med, Harvard Med Sch, 53-54 & 55-56, teaching fel obstet & gynec, 57-60, instr, 60-61; dir, Fearing Res Lab, 60-70; dir, Dept Obstet & Gynec, Univ Hosps Cleveland, 61-70; mem, Pres Comt Ment Retardation, 68-72; chmn, Nat Comn Protection Human Subjects, 74-78; Henry J Kaiser Sr fel, 82; chmn, Ethics Comt, Am Col Obstet & Gynec, 84-88 & Brigham & Women's Hosp. *Mem:* Inst Med-Nat Acad Sci; Am Soc Biol Chemists; Endocrine Soc; fel Am Col Obstet & Gynec; Soc Gynec Invest; Henry J Kaiser Sr fel, 82. *Mailing Add:* Brigham & Women's Hosp 75 Francis St Boston MA 02115

RYAN, KEVIN WILLIAM, ANIMAL VIRUS ASSEMBLY & REPLICATION, PATHOLOGY OF VIRUS INFECTIONS. *Current Pos:* res asst, 86-89, ASST MEM, DEPT VIROL & MOLECULAR BIOL, ST JUDE CHILDREN'S RES HOSP, 89-; ASST PROF, DEPT PATH, COL MED, UNIV TENN, 94- *Personal Data:* b Ft Dodge, Iowa, Dec 8, 52; m 74, Mary Lyman; c Matthew L & Mark J. *Educ:* Univ Iowa, BS, 78; Univ Mich, PhD(cellular & molecular biol), 84. *Prof Exp:* Teaching asst med microbiol, Dept Microbiol & Immunol, Univ Mich, 81-82; fel, Mich Cancer Res Inst, 82-84; staff fel, Lab Infectious Dis, Nat Inst Allergy & Infectious Dis, 84-86. *Concurrent Pos:* Fel, Mich Cardiol Res Inst, 82-84; prin investr, Nat Inst Allergy & Infectious Dis, 92- *Mem:* AAAS; Am Soc Microbiol; Am Soc Virol; Sigma Xi; Soc Gen Microbiol. *Res:* Molecular biology of virus assembly, gene expression and replication; RNA viruses causing respiratory infections; virus biochemistry; development of effective antiviral drugs and vaccines. *Mailing Add:* PO Box 318 Memphis TN 38101. *E-Mail:* kevin.ryan@stjude.org

RYAN, MARK R, ENDANGERED SPECIES CONSERVATION, UNIVERSITY EDUCATION. *Current Pos:* ASSOC PROF WILDLIFE CONSERV, UNIV MO, 84- *Personal Data:* b Rochester, Minn, Oct 26, 51; m 92, Carol A Mertensmeyer; c Gena-Marie & Samantha Jo. *Educ:* Univ Minn, BS, 73; Iowa State Univ, MS, 78, PhD(animal ecol), 82. *Prof Exp:* Asst prof zool, NDak State Univ, 82-84. *Concurrent Pos:* Assoc ed, J Wildlife Mgt, 93-95; chmn, Univ Ed Working Group, Wildlife Soc, 95-97. *Mem:* Wildlife Soc; Am Ornithologists Union; Soc Conserv Biol; Wilson Ornith Soc; Cooper Ornith Soc; Soc Field Ornithologists. *Res:* Population ecology; habitat modeling of rare and endangered birds in wetland and grassland ecosystems. *Mailing Add:* Univ Mo Stephens Hall Columbia MO 65211. *Fax:* 573-884-5070; *E-Mail:* remmr@muccmail.missouri.edu

RYAN, MICHAEL G, ECOSYSTEMS ECOLOGY, PLANT PHYSIOLOGICAL ECOLOGY. *Current Pos:* RES FOREST ECOLOGIST, USDA FOREST SERV, ROCKY MOUNTAIN EXP STA, 90- *Personal Data:* m 85, Linda J. *Educ:* Univ Pittsburgh, BS, 76; Northern Ariz Univ, MS, 78; Ore State Univ, PhD(forest serv), 88. *Prof Exp:* Fel, Ecosysts Ctr, Marine Biol Lab, 88-90. *Concurrent Pos:* Affil fac, Dept Forest Sci, Colo State Univ, 91- *Mem:* Ecol Soc Am; Am Inst Biol Sci; AAAS. *Res:* Effect of climate, species, and nutrition on the carbon balance and allocation of carbon in terrestrial forest ecosystems; autotrophic respiration costs and carbon use efficiency of forests in response to climate and species. *Mailing Add:* Rocky Mountain Exp Sta 240 W Prospect Rd Ft Collins CO 80526. *Fax:* 970-498-1010; *E-Mail:* mryan@lamar.colostate.edu

RYAN, MICHAEL T, BIOCHEMISTRY, CHEMISTRY. *Current Pos:* RETIRED. *Personal Data:* b Tipperary, Ireland, Sept 29, 25; Irish & Can citizen; m 55; c 3. *Educ:* Univ Col, Dublin, BSc, 46, MSc, 47; McGill Univ, PhD(biochem), 55. *Prof Exp:* Asst chem, Univ Col, Galway, 47-49; from lectr to assoc prof, Fac Med, Univ Ottawa, 49-71; prof biochem, Fac Med & Sci, 71-86. *Mem:* Can Biochem Soc. *Res:* Interaction of steroids and proteins. *Mailing Add:* 2380 Georgina Dr Ottawa ON K2B 7M7 Can

RYAN, NORMAN DANIEL, HOT DEFORMATION, CONSTITUTIVE ANALYSIS OF STAINLESS & COMPOSITE MATERIALS. *Current Pos:* ADJ ASSOC PROF MAT ENG AEROSPACE, CONCORDIA UNIV, 89- *Personal Data:* b Ayr Queensland, Australia, Dec 10, 33; wid; c Daniel & Patrick. *Educ:* Loyola Col, BSc, 72; Concordia Univ, BA, 76, MEng, 82, PhD(mech eng), 89; McGill Univ, MEd, 76. *Honors & Awards:* Prime Minister's Award for Teaching Excellence in Sci, Technol & Math, 93. *Concurrent Pos:* Vis prof, Univ Ancona, Italy, 86; teacher coordr astronaut & space technol, Comn Scolaire, 91-; consult, Can Space Agency, 93- *Mem:* Am Soc Metals; Can Aeronaut & Space Inst; Can Inst Mining & Metall; Sigma Xi; Can Soc Mech Engrs; Welding Inst Can. *Res:* Hot deformation behavior of austenitic, ferritic and martensitic stainless steels is imperative to improving product quality and lowering cost. *Mailing Add:* 2941 Blais St Longueuil PQ J4M 1K5 Can. *Fax:* 514-848-3175

RYAN, NORMAN W(ALLACE), COMBUSTION & FLUID DYNAMICS. *Current Pos:* from assoc prof to prof, 48-84, EMER PROF CHEM ENG, UNIV UTAH, 84- *Personal Data:* b Casper, Wyo, Feb 9, 19; m 42, Elsie Schwemmer; c Philip W, Nancy A, Gwen J & Timothy A. *Educ:* Cornell Univ, BChem, 41, ChemE, 42; Mass Inst Technol, ScD, 49. *Prof Exp:* Chem engr, Stand Oil Co, Ind, 42-46. *Concurrent Pos:* Consult. *Mem:* Am Chem Soc; Am Inst Chem Engrs; Sigma Xi. *Res:* Combustion; fluid dynamics in product synthesis, in chemical propulsion systems - both rockets and air-breathing engines and as related to air quality. *Mailing Add:* Dept Chem Eng Univ Utah Salt Lake City UT 84112-1102

RYAN, PATRICK WALTER, ORGANIC POLYMER CHEMISTRY. *Current Pos:* TECH CONSULT, 86- *Personal Data:* b Chicago, Ill, Nov 14, 33; m 56; c 4. *Educ:* Loyola Univ Chicago, BS, 55; Purdue Univ, PhD(chem), 59. *Prof Exp:* From res chemist to sr res chemist, Sinclair Res Inc, 59-65, group leader, 65-68, div dir, 68-69; res mgr, Arco Chem Co, 69-84; mgr, Technol Transfer, Atlantic Richfield Co, 84-86. *Mem:* Am Chem Soc; Sigma Xi. *Res:* Syntheses of low molecular weight organic polymers and their applied chemistry; chemicals for tertiary oil recovery and basic petrochemicals. *Mailing Add:* 3567 Via La Primavera Thousand Oaks CA 91360-1873

RYAN, PETER MICHAEL, MATHEMATICS. *Current Pos:* ASSOC PROF MATH & COMPUT SCI, JACKSONVILLE UNIV, 78- *Personal Data:* b Quincy, Mass, Aug 6, 43; m 68; c 2. *Educ:* Calif Inst Technol, BS, 65; Dartmouth Col, AM, 67, PhD(math), 70. *Prof Exp:* Asst prof math, Gustavus Adolphus Col, 69-76; asst prof math, Moorhead State Univ, 76-78. *Mem:* AAAS; Am Math Soc; Math Asn Am; Soc Indust Appl Math. *Res:* Frames; complete Brouwerian lattices. *Mailing Add:* Jacksonville Univ Jacksonville FL 32211-6369

RYAN, RICHARD ALEXANDER, VERTEBRATE ZOOLOGY. *Current Pos:* RETIRED. *Personal Data:* b Detroit, Mich, Feb 27, 25; m 47; c 3. *Educ:* Cornell Univ, AB, 48, MS, 49, PhD(zool), 51. *Prof Exp:* From instr to prof biol, Hobart & William Smith Cols, 52-87, chmn dept, 66-69, 74-75. *Mem:* AAAS; Am Soc Ichthyol & Herpet; Am Soc Mammal; Wildlife Soc. *Res:* Life history of vertebrates. *Mailing Add:* 4532 Lakeview Rd Dundee NY 14837

RYAN, RICHARD PATRICK, PATENT AGENT. *Current Pos:* sr scientist, 67-71, group leader, 71-75, sr clin res assoc, Mead Johnson Res Ctr, 75-80, patent coord, 80-82, patent agent, 82-86, SR PATENT AGENT, BRISTOL MYERS CO, 86- *Personal Data:* b Decatur, Ill, May 4, 38; m 60; c 3. *Educ:* Millikin, BA, 60; Univ Ky, PhD(org chem), 68. *Prof Exp:* Chemist, Neisler Labs, Inc, Union Carbide Corp, 60-63. *Concurrent Pos:* Lectr, Univ Evansville, 69-73. *Mem:* Fel Am Geriat Soc; Am Chem Soc; Sigma Xi; Am Heart Asn; AAAS. *Res:* Preparation and prosecution of patent applications covering pharmaceutical and nutritional inventions; synthesis of biologically active heterocyclic compounds; correlation of chemical structure with biological activity; drug therapy of cardiovascular, central nervous system, respiratory, neoplastic and nutritional diseases. *Mailing Add:* Patent Dept 851 5 Res Pkwy PO Box 5100 Wallingford CT 06492-7660

RYAN, ROBERT DEAN, MATHEMATICS. *Current Pos:* RETIRED. *Personal Data:* b Upland, Calif, Mar 3, 33; m 61; c Michael J & Celene E. *Educ:* Calif Inst Technol, BS, 54, PhD(math), 60; Harvard Univ, MPA, 71. *Prof Exp:* Res assoc math, Calif Inst Technol, 60-61; asst prof, US Army Math Res Ctr, Wis, 61-63, asst prof, Univ, 63-65; mathematician, Math Br, Off Naval Res, Washington, DC, 65-69, prog dir oper res, 69-71, spec asst res, 71-86, dir, Spec Prog Off, 86-89, liaison scientist, London, 89-93. *Mem:* Am Math Soc; Math Asn Am; Soc Indust & Appl Math. *Res:* Harmonic analysis and measure theory. *Mailing Add:* 12 Blvd Edgar Quinet 75014 Paris France

RYAN, ROBERT F, SURGERY, PLASTIC SURGERY. *Current Pos:* from instr to assoc prof plastic surg, 56-67, prof surg, 67-87, CHIEF SECT PLASTIC SURG, TULANE UNIV, 69-, EMER PROF, 87- *Personal Data:* b Hoquiam, Wash, June 23, 22; div. *Educ:* Stanford Univ, MD, 47; Univ Minn, MS, 56. *Honors & Awards:* Hoekton Gold Medal, AMA, 59. *Prof Exp:* Resident surg, Emergency Hosp, Washington, DC, 50-51. *Mem:* AMA; Am Surg Asn; Am Asn Plastic Surgeons; Am Soc Plastic & Reconstruct Surg. *Res:* Plastic surgery; tissue transplantation; wound healing; cancer. *Mailing Add:* Perdido Bay Country Club 5068 Shoshone Dr Pensacola FL 32507

RYAN, ROBERT J, BIOCHEMISTRY, ENDOCRINOLOGY. *Current Pos:* prof, 85-90, EMER PROF BIOCHEM, MAYO MED SCH, 90- *Personal Data:* b Cincinnati, Ohio, July 18, 27; m 54; c 6. *Educ:* Univ Cincinnati, MD, 52. *Honors & Awards:* Robert H Williams Award, Endocrine Soc, 84; Daniel Drake Medal, Univ Cincinnati, 90; Carl G Hartman Award, Soc Study Reproduction, 91. *Prof Exp:* Intern, Henry Ford Hosp, Detroit, 52-53; res fel, Univ Ill Col Med, 53-54, resident med, Res & Educ Hosp, 54-57; Am Col Physicians res fel endocrinol, New Eng Ctr Hosp, 57-58; from instr to assoc prof, Univ Ill Col Med, 58-67; from assoc prof to prof med, 67-79, chmn dept molecular med, Mayo Clin, 73-79, prof cell biol, Mayo Grad Sch Med, Univ Minn, 79-85. *Concurrent Pos:* Mem staff, Mayo Clin, 67-90, chmn dept endocrine res, 70-79; mem reproductive biol study sect, NIH; mem pop res comn, Nat Inst Child Health & Human Develop; mem med adv bd, Nat Pituitary Agency. *Mem:* Endocrine Soc (vpres, 77-78); Am Soc Biol Chemists; Soc Study Reprod (pres, 87-88); Soc Exp Biol & Med; Am Soc Clin Invest. *Res:* Structure and function of human gonadotropic hormones. *Mailing Add:* 5810 Sumac Lane NE Rochester MN 55906-8555

RYAN, ROBERT PAT, ULTRASOUND. *Current Pos:* SOFTWARE DEVELOPER, 87- *Personal Data:* b Pensacola, Fla, May 1, 25; m 50, Mary C Skipper; c Kenneth & Janet. *Educ:* Rice Univ, BS, 45; Brown Univ, ScM, 59, PhD(physics), 63. *Prof Exp:* Physicist, USN Mine Defense Lab, Fla, 47-58; asst prof physics, Univ Ky, 63-65; Nat Acad Sci-Nat Res Coun res assoc solid state physics, Res Dept, Naval Ord Lab, Md, 65-66; physicist, NASA Electronics Res Ctr, 66-70; physicist, Mech Eng Div, Dept Transp, 70-82, staff engr, Transp Systs Ctr, 82-87. *Mem:* Acoust Soc Am; Inst Elec & Electronics Engrs; Am Soc Nondestructive Test; Sigma Xi. *Res:* Underwater sound noise measurement; analysis; guided mode and finite-amplitude propagation; ultrasonic relaxations in glasses; second-order optical effects; piezo and ferroelectricity; ultrasonic techniques for nondestructive testing; ultrasonic imaging; signal processing; pattern recognition; software development. *Mailing Add:* My Word Micro Enterprises 110 Quincy Ave Braintree MA 02184-4429. *E-Mail:* rpr@world.std.com

RYAN, ROBERT REYNOLDS, ACTINIDE CHEMISTRY, ORGANIC EXPLOSIVES. *Personal Data:* b Klamath Falls, Ore, July 29, 36. *Educ:* Portland State Univ, BS, 61; Ore State Univ, PhD(chem), 65. *Prof Exp:* Fel x-ray diffraction, Swiss Fed Inst Technol, Zurich, 65-66; fel vibrational spec, Los Alamos Nat Lab, 66-67, staff mem, 67-80, dep group leader, 80-93. *Mem:* Am Chem Soc; Am Crystallog Asn. *Res:* Transition metal chemistry; actinide chemistry; continuous phase changes; small molecule activation; organic explosives; vibrational spectroscopy; x-ray diffraction; gas phase electron diffraction. *Mailing Add:* 291 Acorn Dr Roseburg OR 97470-0346

RYAN, ROGER BAKER, INSECT ECOLOGY & BIOLOGICAL CONTROL. *Current Pos:* PROF, DEPT FOREST SCI, ORE STATE UNIV, 89- *Personal Data:* b Port Chester, NY, May 5, 32; m 55, Joan Bennett; c James, Ann, Joseph & Patrick. *Educ:* State Univ NY Col Forestry, Syracuse, BS, 53; Ore State Univ, MS, 59, PhD(entom, plant path), 61. *Honors & Awards:* Superior Serv Honor Award, USDA, 86. *Prof Exp:* Entomologist, Forestry & Range Sci Lab, US Forest Serv, 61-65, res entomologist, 65-89. *Mem:* Entom Soc Am; Entom Soc Can; Int Orgn Biol Control. *Res:* Biological control, physiology and behavior of insects; biological control of forest insect pests using introduced parasitoids and predators (acquisition, propagation, release, evalation and population dynamics). *Mailing Add:* Dept Forest Sci Ore State Univ Corvallis OR 97331-5705

RYAN, SIMEON P, BIOLOGY. *Current Pos:* RETIRED. *Personal Data:* b New York, NY, May 30, 22. *Educ:* St Francis Col, BS, 51; St Louis Univ, MS, 53, PhD(biol), 57. *Prof Exp:* From instr to assoc prof biol, St Francis Col, NY, 57-70, dir pre-med & pre-dent training, 58-66, actg head, Dept Biol, 66-70; from asst prof to assoc prof biol, Nassau Community Col, 70-92. *Mem:* AAAS; NY Acad Sci. *Res:* Cytological nutritional effects; cytopathology. *Mailing Add:* 53 Morris Pkwy Valley Stream NY 11580

RYAN, STEPHEN JOSEPH, RETINA & VITREOUS DISEASE & SURGERY, SUBRETINAL NEOVASCULARIZATION MACULAR DEGENERATION & OCULAR TRAUMA. *Current Pos:* med dir, 77-86, GRACE & EMERY BEARDSLEY PROF & CHMN, DEPT OPHTHAL, SCH MED, LOS ANGELES, 74-, DEAN, 91-, SR VPRES MED AFFAIRS, 94-; PRES, DOHENY EYE INST, LOS ANGELES, 87- *Personal Data:* b Honolulu, Hawaii, Mar 20, 40; m 65, Ann Mullady; c Patricia Anne. *Educ:* Providence Col, AB, 61; Johns Hopkins Univ, MD, 65. *Hon Degrees:* DSc, Providence Col, 77. *Honors & Awards:* Cert of Merit, Am Med Asn, 71; Award of Merit, Am Acad Ophthal, 75, Sr Hon Award, 88, Guest of Hon Award, 94. *Prof Exp:* Instr ophthal, Sch Med, Johns Hopkins Univ, 70-71, from asst prof to assoc prof, 71-74. *Concurrent Pos:* Ophthalmologist, Johns Hopkins Hosp, 71-94; assoc ed, Ophthal Surg, 74-85; pres, Estelle Doheny Eye Med Clin, Inc, 75-92, Doheny Eye Med Group, 92-93, Alliance Eye & Vision Res, 93-; bd dirs, Doheny Eye Med Group, Inc, Los Angeles, 75-96, Doheny Eye Inst, 77-87, Charles R Drew Univ Med Sci, Inglewood, Calif, 91-94, Norris Cancer Ctr, 91-, Huntington Mem Hosp, Pasadena, 93-, W M Keck Found, 96-; consult, Children's Hosp Los Angeles, 77-85 & Dept Vet Affairs, 92- *Mem:* Inst Med-Nat Acad Med; Am Acad Ophthal; Macula Soc (pres, 86-88); Am Bd Ophthal; Asn Univ Profs Ophthal; Am Med Asn; Retina Soc; Pan Am Asn Ophthal (secy, 81-83, pres, 83-85); NIH; Am Acad Ophthal. *Res:* Developed experimental model of proliferative vitreoretinopathy which provided insight into the role of macrophages in the pathogenesis of this condition; developed experimental model of subretinal neovascularization and perfected drug delivey via intraocular cannula system to study pathogenesis of this disease. *Mailing Add:* Doheny Eye Inst 1450 San Pablo St Los Angeles CA 90033-4681. *Fax:* 213-342-6447, 224-7090

RYAN, STEWART RICHARD, APPLIED PHYSICS. *Current Pos:* asst prof, 77-82, ASSOC PROF PHYSICS, UNIV OKLA, 82- *Personal Data:* b Schenectady, NY, Jan 26, 42; m 66, Rita Sandman; c Kathleen, Colleen & Ellen. *Educ:* Univ Notre Dame, BS, 64; Univ Mich, MS, 65, PhD(physics), 71. *Prof Exp:* Res staff physicist, Yale Univ, 71-73, instr, 73-74; res assoc, Univ Ariz, 74-76, staff physicist, 76-77. *Mem:* Am Phys Soc; Am Asn Physics Teachers; Am Asn Eng Educ; Sigma Xi. *Res:* Molecular dissociation processes; atom-molecule collisions; electron-molecule collisions; low temperature properties of helium 3 & helium 4 mixtures; applied physics; instrumentation; energy conservation. *Mailing Add:* Dept Physics & Astron Univ Okla Norman OK 73019

RYAN, THOMAS ARTHUR, JR, STATISTICS. *Current Pos:* asst prof, 69-75, ASSOC PROF STATIST, PA STATE UNIV, UNIVERSITY PARK, 75- *Personal Data:* b Ithaca, NY, June 12, 40; m 66. *Educ:* Wesleyan Univ, BA, 62; Cornell Univ, PhD(math), 68. *Prof Exp:* Instr math statist, Columbia Univ, 67-68, asst prof, 68-69. *Mem:* Inst Math Statist; fel Am Statist Asn; Asn Comput Mach; Inst Elec & Electronics Engrs. *Res:* Statistical computing. *Mailing Add:* Dept Statist Pa State Univ 219 Pond Lab University Park PA 16802-6106

RYAN, THOMAS JOHN, BIOCHEMISTRY, ORGANIC CHEMISTRY. *Current Pos:* fel biochem, 72-74, RES SCIENTIST BIOCHEM, DIV LABS & RES, DEPT HEALTH, ALBANY, NY, 74-; CHIEF LAB MOLECULAR DIAG, WADSWORTH CTR. *Personal Data:* b New York, NY, June 12, 43; m 70; c 3. *Educ:* Manhattan Col, BS, 65; State Univ NY, Stony Brook, PhD(org chem), 70. *Prof Exp:* Res assoc org chem, Johns Hopkins Univ, 69-71; assoc, Rensselaer Polytech Inst, 71-72. *Mem:* Am Chem Soc; AAAS. *Res:* Fibrinolysis; coagulation; enzyme mechanism and structure. *Mailing Add:* Dept Health Empire State Plaza Albany NY 12201

RYAN, THOMAS WILTON, SYSTEMS DESIGN, SYSTEMS SCIENCE. *Current Pos:* STAFF SCIENTIST, SCI APPLN, INC, 79- *Personal Data:* b San Mateo, Calif, March 20, 46; m 69; c 2. *Educ:* Univ Santa Clara, BS, 68; Univ Ariz, MS, 71, PhD(elec eng), 81. *Prof Exp:* Teacher math & physics, Green Fields Sch, 71-76; res asst, Univ Ariz, 76-79. *Mem:* Inst Elec & Electronics Engrs; Soc Photo-Optical Instrumentation Engrs. *Res:* Applications of signal processing in radar signal analysis; image processing. *Mailing Add:* Sci Appln Int Corp 5151 Broadway Suite 900 Tucson AZ 85711

RYAN, UNA SCULLY, VASCULAR BIOLOGY, COMPLEMENT, ENDOTHELIUM. *Current Pos:* VPRES RES & CHIEF SCI OFFICER, T CELL SCI, INC, 93- *Personal Data:* b Kuala Lumpur, Malaysia, Dec 18, 41; Brit citizen; m 73; c 2. *Educ:* Bristol Univ, BSc, 63; Cambridge Univ, PhD(cell biol), 68. *Honors & Awards:* Louis & Artur Lucian Award, 85; Lamport lectr, 85; Lillie Award, 89. *Prof Exp:* From instr to assoc prof, Sch Med, Univ Miami, 67-80, prof med, 80-89; dir, Health Sci, Monsanto Co, 90-93. *Concurrent Pos:* Vis investr, Lab Cardiovasc Res, Howard Hughes Med Inst, Miami, 67-71, dir, Lab Ultrastruct Studies, 70-71; adj asst prof biol, Univ Miami, 68-; sr scientist, Papanicolaou Cancer Res Inst, 72-77; estab investr, Am Heart Asn, 72-77, mem basic sci coun, 77-, mem, Microcirculation Coun, 78-; mem pulmonary dis adv comt, Nat Heart, Lung & Blood Inst, 73-76, mem res rev comt A, 77-81, chmn, 80-81; Wellcome vis prof, 89-90. *Mem:* Royal Entom Soc London; Am Soc Cell Biol; Europ Soc Endocrinol; Tissue Cult Asn; NY Acad Sci; Am Thoracic Soc; Am Microcirculatory Soc; Sigma Xi (pres, 88-89). *Res:* Application of advanced techniques of electron microscopy and cell culture to studies of the endocrine or non-ventilatory functions of the lung, with particular emphasis on correlations of fine structure of endothelial cells with specific metabolic activities; application of cellular and molecular biology to understanding of vascular biology in health and disease; specific focus on endothelial injury and responses, role of complement, T cells and other immuno-inflammatory mechanisms. *Mailing Add:* Pres & CEO T Cell Sci Inc 119 4th Ave Needham MA 02194-2725

RYAN, VICTOR ALBERT, NUCLEAR CHEMISTRY, ACADEMIC & INDUSTRIAL SAFETY. *Current Pos:* RETIRED. *Personal Data:* b Laramie, Wyo, Aug 11, 20; m 50; c 4. *Educ:* Univ Wyo, BS, 42; Univ Minn, PhD(phys chem), 51. *Prof Exp:* Chemist, E I du Pont de Nemours & Co, Tenn, 51-53; chemist, Dow Chem Co, Colo, 53-58; from asst prof to prof chem, 58-84, prof chem eng, Univ Wyo, 80-, safety dir, 74- *Mem:* Am Chem Soc; Am Nuclear Soc; Am Asn Univ Profs; Sigma Xi. *Res:* Photochemistry; flash photolysis; industrial chemistry; lanthanide and actinide chemistry; prompt and ordinary activation analysis. *Mailing Add:* 1202 Grand Ave Laramie WY 82070-7752

RYAN, WAYNE L, BIOCHEMISTRY, IMMUNOLOGY. *Current Pos:* pres, 87-91, CHMN BD & CHIEF EXEC OFFICER, STRECK LABS, 91-; RES PROF OBSTET GYNEC, UNIV NEBR CTR, 67- *Personal Data:* b Corning, Iowa, June 14, 27; m 48, Eileen; c Tim, Carol, Connie, Stacy & Steve. *Educ:* Creighton Univ, BS, 49, MS, 51; Univ Mo, PhD(biochem), 53. *Prof Exp:* Instr microbiol & asst prof biochem, Sch Med, Creighton Univ, 53-61, assoc prof biochem, 61-64; from assoc prof to prof biochem, Univ Nebr Ctr, 64-87, res assoc prof obstet & gynec, 64-67, asst dean res, 73-79. *Mem:* Am Chem Soc; Am Asn Cancer Res; Soc Exp Biol & Med. *Res:* Cell fusion; diagnostic control methods. *Mailing Add:* Streck Labs Inc 14306 Industria Rd PO Box 37625 Omaha NE 68137-0625

RYAN, WEN, MICROBIAL FERMENTATION PROCESS DEVELOPMENT, RECOMBINANT PROTEIN PRODUCTION. *Current Pos:* RES SCIENTIST, AMGEN INC, 93- *Personal Data:* b Taipei, Taiwan, Nov 3, 59; m 85, Lee Rei-min; c Kai-cheng. *Educ:* Tunghai Univ, Taiwan, BS, 82; Ill Inst Technol, PhD(chem eng), 90. *Prof Exp:* Bioengr, Schering-Plough Corp, 90-93, fermentation pilot plant supvr, 93. *Mem:* Am Inst Chem Engrs; Am Chem Soc; AAAS; Soc Indust Microbiol; Sigma Xi. *Res:* Develop fermentation and recovery processes for the production of recombinant human proteins as well as non-recombinant microbial metabolites. *Mailing Add:* Amgen Ctr 185-A-373 Thousand Oaks CA 91320-1789

RYAN, WILLIAM B F, OCEANOGRAPHY, GEOLOGY. *Current Pos:* res asst geol, 62-74, SR RES ASSOC GEOL, LAMONT-DOHERTY GEOL OBSERV, COLUMBIA UNIV, 74- *Personal Data:* b Troy, NY, Sept 1, 39; m 62, Judith Lingle; c Sarah L, Ashley R (Gaddis) & Sean H. *Educ:* Williams Col, BA, 61; Columbia Univ, PhD(geol), 71. *Honors & Awards:* Shepard Medal, Soc Sedimentologists. *Prof Exp:* Res asst oceanog, Woods Hole Oceanog Inst, 61-62. *Mem:* Am Geophys Union; Sigma Xi. *Res:* Marine geology and geophysics. *Mailing Add:* 12 Clinton Ave South Nyack NY 10960-4716. *E-Mail:* billr@lamont.ldeo.columbia.edu

RYAN, WILLIAM GEORGE, PSYCHOPHARMACOLOGY, TREATMENT OF PSYCHOTIC DISORDERS. *Current Pos:* Asst prof, 82-87, ASSOC PROF PSYCHIAT, SCH MED, UNIV ALA, 87- *Personal Data:* b Berkeley, Calif, Jan 7, 51; m 91, Lynn Bledsoe; c Ethan, Emily, Marilyn & Daniel. *Educ:* Ind Univ, AB, 74, Ind Univ Sch Med, MD, 78. *Mem:* Fel Am Psychiat Asn; Soc Biol Psychiat; Am Acad Clin Psychiatrists. *Res:* Psychopharmacology and the neuroendorine (particularly thyroid) aspects of schizophrenia and the major mood disorders. *Mailing Add:* Dept Psychiat Univ Ala Birmingham AL 35294. *Fax:* 205-975-8950; *E-Mail:* bryan@smopsy1.his.uab.edu

RYANT, CHARLES J(OSEPH), JR, ENGINEERING, ENVIRONMENTAL ENGINEERING. *Current Pos:* CONSULT, C J RYANT, JR & ASSOC, 80- *Personal Data:* b Chicago, Ill, Apr 1, 20; m 77, Rosalind Bailey. *Educ:* Armour Inst Technol, BS, 40; Ill Inst Technol, MS, 41, PhD(chem eng), 47. *Prof Exp:* Instr chem eng, Ill Inst Technol, 40-41, instr chem, 46-47; chem engr, Sinclair Refining Corp, Ind, 41 & Wurster & Sanger, Inc, 41-43; sr proj engr, Standard Oil Co, Ind, 43-59; consult, 59-68; tech consult, Joint Ill House & Senate Air Pollution Study Comt, 68-69; vpres & dir eng, Sparkleen Systs, Inc, 69-70; exec dir, Midwest Legis Coun Environ, Univ Ill, Chicago Circle, 70-80. *Concurrent Pos:* Civilian with AEC, 44; instr, Ill Inst Technol, 53-; chmn, Calumet City Environ Control Comn, 74-81; secy, Cleveland Twp Planning Comn, 81-87, chmn, 94- *Mem:* Am Inst Chem Engrs. *Res:* Filtration and sedimentation; heat transfer; conditioning of air; heat transfer in a double exchanger; petroleum refinery furnaces. *Mailing Add:* 504 W Ryant Rd PO Box 250 Maple City MI 49664-0250

RYASON, PORTER RAYMOND, PHYSICAL CHEMISTRY. *Current Pos:* FEL, CHEVRON RES & TECH CO, CHEVRON CORP, 78- *Personal Data:* b Bridgeport, Nebr, Jan 18, 29; div; c Rhian, Arne, Heather & Sten. *Educ:* Reed Col, BA, 50; Harvard Univ, MA, 52, PhD(chem), 54. *Prof Exp:* Sr res assoc, Chevron Res Co, Stand Oil Co Calif, 53-73; mem tech staff, Jet Propulsion Lab, Calif Inst Technol, 73-78. *Concurrent Pos:* Mem, Coop Air Pollution Eng Proj Group, 58-68, 68-; mem, Nat Air Pollution Control Admin Adv Comt Chem & Physics, Dept Health, Educ & Welfare, 68-70; mem, Task Force Hydrocarbon Reactivities, Am Petrol Inst, 69-70, Task Force Aerometric Data Anal, 70- *Mem:* AAAS; Am Chem Soc; Am Phys Soc. *Res:* Molecular spectroscopy; gas phase chemical kinetics; fast reactions; combustion and flame; infrared spectra of adsorbed species; air pollution; aerochemistry; solar photochemical conversion; tribology. *Mailing Add:* 60 Madrone Rd Fairfax CA 94930-2120

RYBA, EARLE RICHARD, X-RAY CRYSTALLOGRAPHY. *Current Pos:* Asst prof, 60-65, ASSOC PROF METALL, PA STATE UNIV, UNIVERSITY PARK, 65- *Personal Data:* b Elyria, Ohio, June 27, 34; m 54, 83, Kathy A Lansberry; c Elizabeth A (Maza), David M, Beth A (Sparkman), Anya K & Janos K. *Educ:* Mass Inst Technol, BS, 56; Iowa State Univ, PhD(phys metall), 60. *Mem:* Am Crystallog Asn; Am Inst Metall Engrs; Int Ctr Diffraction Data. *Res:* Crystal structures, properties and theory of bonding in intermetallic compounds; quasicrystals; characterization of materials by x-ray diffraction techniques; structure of polymer films and metal/polymer interfaces. *Mailing Add:* Rm 304 Steidle Bldg Pa State Univ University Park PA 16802. *Fax:* 814-865-3760; *E-Mail:* ryba@ems.psu.edu

RYBACK, RALPH SIMON, NEUROPSYCHIATRY. *Current Pos:* ASSOC CLIN PROF, UNIFORM SERV UNIV HEALTH SCI, 81- *Personal Data:* b Detroit, Mich, Oct 17, 40; m 76, Susan King; c Dylan, Luke & Jesse. *Educ:* Wayne State Univ, BA, 63, MD, 66. *Prof Exp:* Res fel, Harvard Med Sch, 67-68; teaching fel psychiat, 70-72, instr, 72-73, asst prof, 73-77; vis scientist, Nat Inst Alcohol Abuse & Alcoholism, 76-77, med officer, lab clin studies, 77-84. *Concurrent Pos:* Dir, Alcohol & Drug Abuse Serv, McLean Hosp, Div Mass Gen Hosp, 72-76; assoc clin prof, George Washington Univ, Med Sch, 79-80; dir, Adolescent Servs, Potomac Ridge Treatment Ctr. *Mem:* Am Psychiat Asn. *Res:* Interrelationships of commonly order clinical chemistries for the diagnosis of alcoholism and related illness including nonalcoholic liver diseases; use of the EEG and anticonvulsant medication in psychiatric illness. *Mailing Add:* 18572 Office Park Dr Gaithersburg MD 20879

RYBICKI, EDMUND FRANK, RESIDUAL STRESSES, THERMAL SPRAY COATINGS. *Current Pos:* PROF & CHAIR, DEPT MECH ENG, UNIV TULSA, 79- *Personal Data:* b Cleveland, Ohio, Oct 7, 41; m 64; c 3. *Educ:* Case Inst Technol, BS, 63, MS, 65; Case Western Res Univ, PhD(eng), 68. *Prof Exp:* Res engr, Battelle Columbus Labs, 68-79. *Mem:* Fel Am Soc Mech Engrs; Am Welding Soc; Nat Asn Corrosion Engrs; Am Soc Eng Educ; Nat Soc Prof Engrs. *Res:* Residual stresses due to welding; weld induced deflections; debonding of laminated composites and thermal spray coatings; erosion; finite element analysis; composite materials. *Mailing Add:* 10524 S 68th E Pl Tulsa OK 74133

RYCHECK, MARK RULE, INORGANIC CHEMISTRY, TECHNICAL INFORMATION SCIENCE. *Current Pos:* SR INFO SCIENTIST, UPJOHN CO, 89- *Personal Data:* b Racine, Wis, Dec 30, 37; m 62; c 3. *Educ:* St Francis Col, Pa, BS, 59; Univ Cincinnati, PhD(chem), 67. *Prof Exp:* Res asst spectros, Mellon Inst Sci, 61-62; Ohio State Univ Res Found fel, Ohio State Univ, 66-68; from res chemist to sr res chemist, Phillips Petrol Co, 68-77, sr patent develop chemist, 78-84, sr info scientist, Petrol Res Ctr, 85-89. *Mem:* Am Chem Soc; Am Soc Info Sci. *Res:* Coordination compounds; catalysis. *Mailing Add:* 3806 Edinburgh Dr Kalamazoo MI 49006-5445

RYCHECK, RUSSELL RULE, MEDICINE, EPIDEMIOLOGY. *Current Pos:* res fel epidemiol, 62-64, asst prof, 64-67, ASSOC PROF EPIDEMIOL, GRAD SCH PUB HEALTH, UNIV PITTSBURGH, 67-, ASST PROF PEDIAT & MED, 72- *Personal Data:* b Racine, Wis, June 11, 32; m 62; c 2. *Educ:* Univ Pittsburgh, MD, 57, MPH, 59, DrPH, 64; Am Bd Prev Med, dipl, 68. *Prof Exp:* Teaching fel, Children's Hosp, Pittsburgh, 59-61, res fel pediat, 61-62. *Concurrent Pos:* Consult, Allegheny Co Health Dept, Pa, 64- *Mem:* Am Col Prev Med; Am Pub Health Asn; Soc Epidemiol Res. *Res:* Epidemiology of infectious diseases in hospitals and civilian communities. *Mailing Add:* Dept Epidemiol Univ Pittsburgh Grad Sch Pub Health Pittsburgh PA 15261. *Fax:* 412-624-1736; *E-Mail:* rrrteach@ums.cis.pitt.edu

RYCHLIK, WOJCIECH, POLYMERASE CHAIN REACTION, MOLECULAR BIOLOGY SOFTWARE DEVELOPMENT. *Current Pos:* DIR MOLECULAR BIOL SERVS, NAT BIOSCI INC, 91- *Personal Data:* b June 2, 53; m 76, Barbara Piotrowska; c Adam & Maia. *Educ:* Polish Acad Sci, PhD(biochem), 80. *Prof Exp:* Res asst, Polish Acad Sci, 76-80; res assoc, Univ Tex, Austin, 80-83; res assoc, Univ Ky, Lexington, 83-88, res asst prof, 88-91. *Mem:* Am Soc Biochem & Molecular Biol. *Res:* Cloned and studied human translational initiation factor elf-4E; developed primer design software OLIGO. *Mailing Add:* Dept Molec Biol Nat Biosci Inc 15200 25th Ave N Suite 110 Plymouth MN 55447-1968. *Fax:* 612-550-9625; *E-Mail:* nbi@epx.cis.umn.edu, nbi@biotechnet.com

RYCKMAN, DEVERE WELLINGTON, ENVIRONMENTAL ENGINEERING, SANITARY ENGINEERING. *Current Pos:* consult, Ryckman, Edgerley, Tomlinson & Assocs, 72-75, PRES, RYCKMAN'S EMERGENCY ACTION & CONSULT TEAM, 75-; FOUNDER & PRES, D W RYCKMAN & ASSOCS, INC. *Personal Data:* b South Boardman, Mich, May 27, 24; m; c 3. *Educ:* Rensselaer Polytech Inst, BS, 44; Mich State Univ, MS, 49; Mass Inst Technol, ScD, 56; Environ Eng Intersoc, dipl, 78. *Honors & Awards:* Resources Div Award, Am Water Works Asn, 62 & George Warren Fuller Award, 65; Grand Conceptor Award, Am Consult Engrs Coun, 69, Nat Design Award. *Prof Exp:* From instr to asst prof environ & civil eng, Mich State Univ, 46-53; res asst environ & sanit eng, Mass Inst Technol, 53-55; from assoc prof environ & sanit eng to prof & dir dept, Wash Univ, 56-72. *Concurrent Pos:* USPHS res & prog grants & consult, 56-; mem eng coun prof develop, Sanit Eng Accreditation Comt, 62; Mo Gov's Sci Adv Comt, 62-; vis lectr, Univ Hawaii, 63 & Vanderbilt Univ, 64; USAF Sch Aerospace Med, 64; Mfg Chem Asn res grant, 65-68; mem Nat Sci Traineeship Rev Comt, 65; consult Nat Energy Res & Develop Admin, 77-; environ engr, Frank R Theroux & Assocs, East Lansing, Mich; ensign-proj engr, 121st Naval Res, Outer Pac Area; founding fel, Ctr Biol Natural Complex Systs, Wash Univ; mem, Nat Hazardous Substance Comt, Am Water Works Asn; past pres & dir, Mo Consult Engrs Coun; chmn awards coun, Am Consult Engrs Coun. *Mem:* Am Water Works Asn; Am Pub Health Asn; Am Soc Civil Engrs; Am Soc Eng Educ; Dipl Am Acad Environ Engrs; Air & Waste Mgt Asn; Am Consult Engrs Coun; Am Pub Works Asn; Nat Soc Prof Engrs; Sigma Xi; Water Environ Fedn. *Res:* Industrial water; wastewater; solid waste problems; significance of chemical structure in biodegradation of pesticides, synthetic detergents and other organic chemicals; environmental and energy engineering, hazardous substances and environmental crises engineering research. *Mailing Add:* 339 Alverston Ct Ballwin MO 63021

RYCKMAN, RAYMOND EDWARD, MEDICAL ENTOMOLOGY, PARASITOLOGY. *Current Pos:* Asst prof entom & head dept, Sch Trop & Prev Med, 50-59, from asst prof to assoc prof, 59-72, chmn dept, 80-87, PROF MICROBIOL, LOMA LINDA UNIV, 72- *Personal Data:* b Shullsburg, Wis, June 19, 17; m 43; c 3. *Educ:* Univ Calif, BS, 50, MS, 57, PhD, 60. *Mem:* Entom Soc Am; Nature Conservancy; Soc Vector Ecologists; Audubon Soc; Nat Wildlife Fedn; Sierra Club. *Res:* Biosystematics; ecology of blood feeding insects and their vertebrate hosts; taxonomy, ecology and vector potential of insects of medical and veterinary importance; world bibliography and literature to the parasitic Hemiptera. *Mailing Add:* 25877 Chula Vista St Redlands CA 92373

RYDER, D(AVID) F(RANK), CHEMICAL ENGINEERING. *Current Pos:* RETIRED. *Personal Data:* b Seekonk, Mass, Aug 22, 19; m 57; c 1. *Educ:* Tufts Univ, BS, 41. *Prof Exp:* Res engr, E I DuPont de Nemours & Co, Inc, 41-55, sr res engr, 55-75, develop assoc, 75-80. *Mem:* Am Chem Soc. *Res:* Synthetic and textile fibers; industrial fibers. *Mailing Add:* 101 Watford Rd Westgate Farms Wilmington DE 19808-1423

RYDER, EDWARD JONAS, LETTUCE BREEDING, GENETICS. *Current Pos:* Res leader veg prod res, 72-94, location leader, 82-89, GENETICIST, PAC WEST AREA, AGR RES SERV, USDA, 57- *Personal Data:* b New York, NY, Oct 6, 29; m 62; Elouise Jones; c Robert G, Lawrence D & Deborah (Ryder). *Educ:* Cornell Univ, BS, 51; Univ Calif, PhD(genetics), 54. *Honors & Awards:* Scientist of the Yr, Pac W Area, Agr Res Serv, USDA; Outstanding Researcher Award, Am Soc Hort Sci, 95. *Concurrent Pos:* Instr, Monterey Peninsula Col, 58-64; mem hort adv bd, AVI Publ Co, 76-85. *Mem:* AAAS; Am Genetic Asn; fel Am Soc Hort Sci. *Res:* Quantitative genetics; evolution; breeding new cultivars of lettuce with improvements in disease, insect and stress resistance, horticultural quality and uniformity; gene identification and linkage studies in lettuce; genetic-physiological basis for resistance. *Mailing Add:* USDA Agr Res Serv 1636 E Alisal St Salinas CA 93905. *Fax:* 408-753-2866

RYDER, KENNETH WILLIAM, JR, CLINICAL CHEMISTRY, LABORATORY MANAGEMENT. *Current Pos:* From asst prof to assoc prof, 78-88, PROF PATH, SCH MED, IND UNIV, 88-, ASSOC CHMN DEPT, 87- *Personal Data:* b Mobile, Ala, May 1, 45; m 71; c 3. *Educ:* Knox Col, BA, 67; Ind Univ, PhD(biochem), 72; Univ Ill, MD, 75. *Honors & Awards:* Joseph Kleiner Award, Am Soc Med Technol, 87. *Concurrent Pos:* Dir labs, Wishard Hosp, Indianapolis, 86- *Mem:* AMA; Am Soc Clin Pathologists; Am Asn Clin Chem; Col Am Pathologists; Clin Lab Mgt Asn. *Res:* Improvement of clinical laboratory tests by reducing interferences and enhancing specificity. *Mailing Add:* Dept Path Wishard Mem Hosp 1001 W Tenth St Indianapolis IN 46202-2859

RYDER, OLIVER A, CONSERVATION BIOLOGY, ENDANGERED SPECIES. *Current Pos:* geneticist, 78-86, KLEBERG GENETICS CHAIR, SAN DIEGO ZOO, 86- *Personal Data:* b Alexandria, Va, Dec 27, 46; m 70, Cynthia Ryan; c Kerry & Ryan. *Educ:* Univ Calif, Riverside, BA, 68, San Diego, PhD(biol), 75. *Prof Exp:* Fel geneticist, Sch Med, Univ Calif, 75-77. *Concurrent Pos:* Species coordr, Asian Wild Horse Species Survival Plan, 82-; mem, Wildlife Conserv Comn, Am Asn Zool Parks & Aquaria, 84-90, Conserv Comn, Am Soc Mammalogists, 85-92; adj assoc prof biol, Univ Calif, San Diego, 87-; coun mem, Am Genetics Asn, 90-; secretariat, Przewalski's Horse Global Mgt Plan Working Group, 90- *Mem:* Am Genetics Asn; Am Soc Mammalogists; Am Asn Zool Parks & Aquaria; Soc Study Evolution; Soc Conserv Biol. *Res:* Genetics in support of conservation programs for endangered species in captivity and in the wild; species conservation; molecular and chromosomal evolution; conservation education in primary and secondary schools, colleges and for general public. *Mailing Add:* San Diego Zoo PO Box 551 San Diego CA 92112-0551

RYDER, RICHARD ARMITAGE, FISHERIES ECOLOGY, LIMNOLOGY. *Current Pos:* RETIRED. *Personal Data:* b Windsor, Ont, Feb 25, 31; m 56, Sonja Thomson; c Vikki & Jeffrey. *Educ:* Univ Mich, BSc, 53, MSc, 54. *Honors & Awards:* Award of Excellence, Am Fisheries Soc. *Prof Exp:* Res asst, US Fish & Wildlife Serv, 53-54; dist biologist fisheries, Ont Ministry Natural Resources, 54-58, biologist-in-chg inventory, 58-61, res scientist, 62-96. *Concurrent Pos:* Consult to var int pub & pvt orgn, 71-88; comt mem, Man & Biosphere, 73-76 & Int Joint Comn, 73-90; bd tech experts, Great Lakes Fishery Comn, 82-87. *Mem:* Am Soc Fishery Res Biologists; Am Fisheries Soc (pres, 80); Int Asn Theoret & Appl Limnol; Am Soc Limnol & Oceanog; Int Asn Great Lakes Res; Can Conf Fish Res (pres, 88). *Res:* Methods of determining levels of fish production from global waters; defining concepts necessary for a basic understanding of fish communities in fresh water. *Mailing Add:* 1265 Lakeshore Dr Thunder Bay ON P7B 5E4 Can

RYDER, RICHARD DANIEL, PHYSICS. *Current Pos:* Staff mem physics, 77-86, dep group leader, Accelerator & Beam Line Develop, 86-93, lampf facil eng coordr, 93-94, TECH AREA 53 FACIL MGR, LOS ALAMOS NAT LAB, UNIV CALIF, 94- *Personal Data:* b Providence, RI, Oct 1, 44; m 81; c 1. *Educ:* Univ RI, BS, 66; Brown Univ, ScM, 73, PhD(physics), 74. *Res:* Accelerator physics; particle beam optics. *Mailing Add:* 390 Richard Ct Los Alamos NM 87544. *E-Mail:* ryder@lanl.gov.

RYDER, ROBERT J, CERAMICS. *Personal Data:* b Olean, NY, Apr 19, 31; m 54; c 5. *Educ:* Alfred Univ, BS, 53; Pa State Univ, MS, 55, PhD(ceramics), 59. *Prof Exp:* Res scientist, Brockway Glass Co Inc, 59-62, asst dir res develop, 62-69, dir res & develop, 69-78, vpres, 78-88; staff, Owens Ill Co, Toledo, 88-94. *Concurrent Pos:* Chmn, Air & Water Qual Comt, Glass Container Mfrs Inst, 68-75. *Mem:* Fel Am Ceramic Soc; Soc Glass Technol; Am Chem Soc. *Res:* Physical chemistry of glass melting process; colored glasses; physical properties of glasses; reactivity of glass surfaces. *Mailing Add:* 1253 Treasure Lake DuBois PA 15801

RYDER, ROBERT M, BIOMEDICAL ENGINEERING, MEDICAL INFORMATICS. *Current Pos:* ASST PROF, UNIV SOUTHERN ALA, 95- *Personal Data:* b Niagara Falls, NY, Nov 9, 39. *Educ:* State Univ NY, Buffalo, BS, 66, MS, 69; Clemson Univ, PhD(biomed eng), 92. *Prof Exp:* Consult, Med Informatics, 84-87; pres, Intelligent Med Systs, 92-95. *Mem:* Am Informatics Asn; Am Asn Cardiovasc & Pulmonary Rehab. *Mailing Add:* 8690 Byrnes Lake Rd Bay Minette AL 36507

RYDER, ROBERT THOMAS, STRATIGRAPHY, PETROLEUM GEOLOGY. *Current Pos:* eastern region coordr, Nat Oil & Gas Assessment, 93, GEOLOGIST, US GEOL SURV, 74- *Personal Data:* b Bowling Green, Ohio, Sept 23, 41; m 68, Marlene Myers; c Robert M & Renee M. *Educ:* Mich State Univ, BS, 63; Pa State Univ, PhD(geol), 68. *Prof Exp:* Geologist, Shell Develop Co, Tex, 69-72, Shell Oil Co, 72-74. *Concurrent Pos:* Mem, Am Sedimentary Basins Deleg, Peoples Repub China, 85; mem, US Geol Surv, CMGMR Deleg, Peoples Repub China, 91. *Mem:* Geol Soc Am; Am Asn Petrol Geologists. *Res:* Seismic detection of stratigraphic traps; sedimentation and tectonics; regional stratigraphy; nonmarine depositional environments; petroleum geology of the Appalachian basin. *Mailing Add:* US Geol Surv MS 956 Nat Ctr Reston VA 20192. *E-Mail:* rryder@usgs.gov

RYDER, RONALD ARCH, WILDLIFE MANAGEMENT. *Current Pos:* from asst prof wildlife mgt to prof wildlife biol, 58-85, chmn dept biol majors, 69-72, EMER PROF WILDLIFE BIOL, COL FORESTRY & NATURAL RESOURCES, COLO STATE UNIV, 85- *Personal Data:* b Kansas City, Kans, Feb 3, 28; m 55, Audrey Teele; c Raymond T & Helen A. *Educ:* Colo Agr & Mech Col, BS, 49, MS, 51; Utah State Univ, PhD(wildlife mgt), 58. *Prof Exp:* Wildlife technician, Dept Game & Fish, Colo, 48-49, 54-55; instr, Wartburg Col, 57-58. *Concurrent Pos:* NSF fel, Univ BC, 65-66; vis prof, Mem Univ Nfld, 72-73; vis prof, Univ Otago, New Zealand, 81. *Mem:* Wildlife Soc; Cooper Ornith Soc; Wilson Ornith Soc; Am Ornith Union. *Res:* Waterfowl ecology and management; bird banding; distribution of Colorado birds; nongame wildlife management. *Mailing Add:* 748 Eastdale Dr Ft Collins CO 80524

RYDZ, JOHN S, PHYSICS, ELECTRONICS. *Current Pos:* VPRES TECHNOL, EMHART CORP. *Personal Data:* b Milwaukee, Wis, May 7, 25; m 46; c 2. *Educ:* Mass Inst Technol, BS, 52; Univ Pa, MS, 56. *Prof Exp:* Proj engr, Radio Corp Am, 52-56, eng group leader, Appl Physics Group, 56-59, mgr new bus develop, 59-61; mgr new prod develop & dir, Nuclear Corp Am, 61-63; mgr new prod develop, 63-66; vpres res & develop, Diebold, Inc, Ohio, 66-71; vpres & tech dir, N Atlantic Consumer Prod Group, NY, 71-74, vpres eng, Sewing Prod Group, Singer Co, 74- *Mem:* Inst Elec & Electronics Engrs; Optical Soc Am. *Res:* Spectrophotometry and colorimetry; masers; color electrofax; molecular resonance; zener diodes; nuclear instrumentation; electrostatic printing; closed circuit television techniques; information search and retrieval; consumer products. *Mailing Add:* Univ Conn 29 Ariel Way Avon CT 06001

RYE, DANNY MICHAEL, GEOCHEMISTRY. *Current Pos:* res staff geologist, Yale Univ, 72-74, instr, 74-75, asst prof, 75-80, assoc prof, 80-90, PROF GEOL, YALE UNIV, 90- *Personal Data:* b Glendale, Calif, Feb 21, 46; m 67; c 4. *Educ:* Occidental Col, AB, 67; Univ Minn, PhD(geol), 72. *Honors & Awards:* Lindgren Award, Soc Econ Geologists, 76. *Prof Exp:* Fel geol, Purdue Univ, 72. *Concurrent Pos:* Ed, Am J Sci, 86- *Mem:* Soc Econ Geologists; Geochem Soc; Geol Soc Am. *Res:* Isotopic composition of carbon, hydrogen, oxygen and sulfur to obtain information about the volatile phases present during hydrothermal ore formation, or during the formation of metamorphic rocks. *Mailing Add:* Geol & Geophys Yale Univ Box 208109 New Haven CT 06511-8109

RYE, ROBERT O, ECONOMIC GEOLOGY. *Current Pos:* GEOLOGIST, US GEOL SURV, 64- *Personal Data:* b Los Angeles, Calif, Nov 29, 38; m 64, Frances Rini; c David, Mark & Jonathan. *Educ:* Occidental Col, AB, 60; Princeton Univ, PhD(geol), 65. *Honors & Awards:* Lindgren Award, Soc Econ Geologists, 73, Silver Medal, 92. *Mem:* Fel Geol Soc Am; Geochem Soc; Soc Econ Geologists. *Res:* Stable isotope studies of ore deposits; stable isotope geochemistry as applied to mineral resources, global change, hazards and the environment; geochemistry of ore deposits and related phenomona. *Mailing Add:* 11863 W 27th Dr Lakewood CO 80215. *Fax:* 303-236-4930

RYEBURN, DAVID, GENERAL TOPOLOGY. *Current Pos:* ASST PROF MATH, SIMON FRASER UNIV, 66- *Personal Data:* b Cincinnati, Ohio, June 19, 35; m 57; c 3. *Educ:* Kenyon Col, AB, 54; Ohio State Univ, PhD(math), 62. *Prof Exp:* Instr math, Kenyon Col, 56-57; asst, Ohio State Univ, 58-61, instr, 61-62; asst prof, Kenyon Col, 62-66. *Mem:* AAAS; Am Math Soc; Math Asn Am; Can Math Soc. *Mailing Add:* PO Box 387 Lynden WA 98264-0387

RYEL, LAWRENCE ATWELL, BIOSTATISTICS, WILDLIFE RESEARCH. *Current Pos:* Game biologist, Mich Dept Conserv, 53-61, biometrician, 61-64, biomet supvr, Res & Develop Div, 64-72, chief div, 72-73, chief, Off Surv & Statis Serv, 73-78, chief, Surv & Statist Serv, Environ Serv Div, 78-80, HEAD, SURV & STATIST SERV WILDLIFE DIV, MICH DEPT NATURAL RESOURCES, 80- *Personal Data:* b Farmington, Mich, Feb 22, 30; m 52; c 2. *Educ:* Mich State Univ, BS, 51, MS, 53, PhD(zool), 71. *Concurrent Pos:* Vis prof wildlife sci, Utah State Univ, 77. *Mem:* Biomet Soc; Wildlife Soc; Am Soc Mammal; Wilson Ornith Soc; Sigma Xi. *Res:* Wildlife population dynamics; sample survey design; consultation in design and analysis of fisheries and wildlife research studies. *Mailing Add:* 882 N 300 E Logan UT 84321

RYERSON, GEORGE DOUGLAS, ORGANIC CHEMISTRY. *Current Pos:* sr assoc ed, 67-75, SR ED, CHEM ABSTR SERV, 75- *Personal Data:* b East Orange, NJ, Apr 29, 34. *Educ:* Lehigh Univ, BS, 55; Mass Inst Technol, PhD(org chem), 60. *Prof Exp:* Chemist, Esso Res & Eng Co, 60-67. *Mem:* AAAS; Am Chem Soc; Am Soc Info Sci; Sigma Xi. *Res:* Macromolecular chemistry. *Mailing Add:* 2407 Ravenel Dr Columbus OH 43209-3308. *E-Mail:* gdr59@cas.org

RYERSON, JOSEPH L, electrical engineering; deceased, see previous edition for last biography

RYFF, JOHN V, MATHEMATICAL ANALYSIS. *Current Pos:* PROG DIR, DIV MATH SCI, NSF, 79- *Personal Data:* b Jersey City, NJ, Oct 18, 32; m 58. *Educ:* Syracuse Univ, AB, 57; Stanford Univ, PhD(math), 62. *Prof Exp:* Benjamin Peirce instr math, Harvard Univ, 62-64; Off Naval Res assoc, Univ Wash, 64-65, asst prof, 65-67; Inst Advan Study, 67-68 & Inst Defense Anal, 68; prog dir math sci sect, NSF, 69-72; prof math & head dept, Univ Conn, 72-79. *Mem:* Soc Indust & Appl Math. *Res:* Real and complex function theory; harmonic analysis. *Mailing Add:* PO Box 12 South Harwich MA 02661. *Fax:* 703-306-0550; *E-Mail:* jryff@nsf.gov

RYKBOST, KENNETH ALBERT, POTATO VARIETY DEVELOPMENT. *Current Pos:* SUPT, KLAMATH EXP STA, ORE STATE UNIV, 87- *Personal Data:* b Marion, NY, June 5, 41; m 68, Shirley Merrill; c James E & Ronny A. *Educ:* Cornell Univ, BS, 63, MS, 66; Ore State Univ, PhD(soil sci), 73. *Prof Exp:* Res assoc, Long Island Res Sta, Cornell Univ, 73-76; crop scientist, McCain Foods Ltd, NB, Can, 76-87. *Concurrent Pos:* Mem, Western Regional Potato Variety Develop Comn, 87-94, chmn, 90; mem, Tri-State Potato Variety Develop Comm, 87-94, chmn, 89. *Mem:* Potato Asn Am; Am Soc Agron. *Res:* Cultural management of potatoes with emphasis on fertility, population density, control of diseases and pests, and seed handling; new cultivars. *Mailing Add:* Klamath Exp Sta Ore State Univ 6941 Washburn Way Klamath Falls OR 97603. *Fax:* 541-883-4596; *E-Mail:* rykbostk@ccmail.orst.edu

RYKER, LEE CHESTER, BIOACOUSTICS, FOREST ENTOMOLOGY. *Current Pos:* ADJ PROF BIOL, SOUTHERN ORE STATE COL, 84- *Personal Data:* b Indianapolis, Ind, July 1, 40; m 86, Cassie L Giorgi; c Jason & Treva. *Educ:* Franklin Col, Ind, BA, 63; Univ Mich, MS, 65; Univ Ore, MS, 71; Ore State Univ, PhD(entom), 75. *Prof Exp:* Res assoc bioacoust, Entom Dept, Ore State Univ, 75-82; res assoc forest entom, Simon Fraser Univ, 83-84. *Mem:* Coleopterists Soc. *Res:* Chemoacoustic communication research on species of bark beetles destructive to economically important western coniferous trees; ecology of birds-insects; song behavior of birds; communication and behavior of hydrophilid beetles. *Mailing Add:* PO Box 267 Jacksonville OR 97530-0267

RYLANDER, HENRY GRADY, JR, MECHANICAL ENGINEERING. *Current Pos:* from asst prof to assoc prof, 47-68, res scientist, 50, JOE J KING PROF MECH ENG, UNIV TEX, AUSTIN, 68- *Personal Data:* b Pearsall, Tex, Aug 23, 21; m 43; c 4. *Educ:* Univ Tex, BS, 43, MS, 52; Ga Inst Technol, PhD(mech eng), 65. *Prof Exp:* Design engr, Steam Div, Aviation Gas Turbine Div, Westinghouse Elec Corp, 43-47. *Concurrent Pos:* Design engr, Fargo Eng Co, 49-50; eng consult, Mobil Oil Corp, 56-70, Tracor, Inc, 60-72 & CMI Corp, 70- *Mem:* Fel Am Soc Mech Engrs; Am Soc Lubrication Engrs. *Res:* Machine design lubrication and bearing performance including the effects of solids in bearing lubrication. *Mailing Add:* 2500 Spanish Oak Trail Round Rock TX 78681

RYLANDER, MICHAEL KENT, VERTEBRATE BEHAVIOR, VERTEBRATE NEUROANATOMY. *Current Pos:* From asst prof to assoc prof, 65-75, PROF BIOL, TEX TECH UNIV, 75- *Personal Data:* b Hillsboro, Tex, Dec 25, 35; m, Laura Ronstadt; c Michael K & Sharon A. *Educ:* NTex State Univ, BA, 56, MS, 62; Tulane Univ, PhD(biol), 65. *Res:* Comparative neuroanatomy; behavior of vertebrates, chiefly birds and mammals in North and South America. *Mailing Add:* Dept Biol Sci Tex Tech Univ Lubbock TX 79409. *E-Mail:* icrmk@ttacs.ttu.edu

RYMAL, KENNETH STUART, FOOD SCIENCE. *Current Pos:* RETIRED. *Personal Data:* b Winnepeg, Man, Sept 13, 22; m 49; c 5. *Educ:* Mass Inst Technol, BS, 49; Univ Fla, MS, 66; Univ Ga, PhD(food sci), 73. *Prof Exp:* Chemist fish prods, Assoc Fish By-Prods Inc, 49-51; res & develop food mfg, John E Cain Co, 51-52; owner-mgr, Rymal's Restaurant, 52-64; res assoc, Univ Fla, 64-66; from asst prof to prof hort, Auburn Univ, 66-90. *Mem:* Inst Food Technologists; Am Soc Hort Sci; Asn Anal Chem; Asn Off Anal Chemists. *Res:* Chemistry of horticultural crops; composition, flavor and nutritive content; chemical nature of insect resistance in horticultural crops. *Mailing Add:* 363 Lee Rd No 23 Auburn AL 36830

RYMER, WILLIAM ZEV, NEUROPHYSIOLOGY, NEUROLOGY. *Current Pos:* asst prof physiol & neurol, 78-81, assoc prof rehab med & assoc prof biomed eng, 83-87, ASSOC PROF PHYSIOL & NEUROL, MED SCH, NORTHWESTERN UNIV, 81-, PROF PHYSIOL REHAB MED, 87-; JOHN G SEARLE PROF REHAB & DIR RES, REHAB INST CHICAGO, 89- *Personal Data:* b Melbourne, Australia, June 3, 39; m 77; c 3. *Educ:* Melbourne Univ, Australia, MBBS, 62; Monash Univ, Australia, PhD(neurophysiol), 73. *Prof Exp:* Resident internal med, Dept Med, Monash Univ, Australia, 63-67 & grad scholar neurophysiol, 67-72; Fogarty fel, Lab Neural Control, Nat Inst Neurol & Commun Dis & Stroke, NIH, 72-74; res assoc, Med Sch, Johns Hopkins Univ, 75-76; asst prof neurosurg & physiol, Med Sch, State Univ NY, 77-78. *Concurrent Pos:* Instr, Cold Spring Harbor Lab, 80-81; mem, Muscle Skeletal & Orthop Study Sect, NIH, 83-87; consult spasticity res, Warner-Lambert Drug, Co. *Mem:* Soc Neurosci; AAAS. *Res:* Neural control of movement using animal models, normal and neurologically impaired human subjects; interneuronal circuitry of the spinal cord; neurophysiological basis of spasticity. *Mailing Add:* 2029 Bennett Ave Evanston IL 60201-2115

RYMON, LARRY MARING, ANIMAL ECOLOGY, RAPTOR CONSERVATION. *Current Pos:* assoc prof, 68-71, PROF BIOL, E STROUDSBURG UNIV, 71-, CUR, NATURAL HIST MUS, 71- *Personal Data:* b Portland, Pa, Nov 16, 34; m 62, Barbara Persons; c Tyler & Holly. *Educ:* East Stroudsburg Univ, BS, 58, MEd, 64; Ore State Univ, PhD(biol), 69. *Prof Exp:* Test dept expediter, Electronics, Electro-Mech Res, Fla, 58. *Concurrent Pos:* Danforth Assoc, 70; coordr, Environ Studies Inst, 74- *Mem:* Wildlife Soc; Am Inst Biol Sci; Sigma Xi. *Res:* Osprey reintroduction; river otter reintroduction and management. *Mailing Add:* 214 Timberline Dr Sequim WA 98382

RYNARD, HUGH C, CIVIL ENGINEERING. *Current Pos:* Design engr, Acres Int Ltd, 51-53, liaison engr, Bersimis 1 Proj, 53-56, asst resident engr, 57-59, actg resident engr, 60, head construct dept, 60-64, vpres & dir, 62, mgr, 64-67, pres, 71-78, CHMN, ACRES INT LTD, 87- *Educ:* Univ Toronto, BASc, 51. *Honors & Awards:* Julian C Smith Medal, Eng Inst Can, 91. *Mem:* Asn Consult Engrs Can; Eng Inst Can. *Mailing Add:* 49A Castlefield Ave Toronto ON M4R 1G5 Can

RYNASIEWICZ, JOSEPH, ANALYTICAL CHEMISTRY, METALLURGY. *Current Pos:* RETIRED. *Personal Data:* b Pawtucket, RI, May 22, 17; m 47, Erma J Schultz; c John J & Robert A. *Educ:* Univ RI, BS, 41, MS, 44. *Prof Exp:* Asst agr chem, Exp Sta, Univ RI, 41-45; asst org & anal chem, Northwestern Univ, 45-46; asst anal chem, Knolls Atomic Power Lab, Gen Elec Co, 46-52, res assoc, 52-57, mgr, 57-62, consult anal chem, 62, corrosion engr, 62-64, supvr chem anal, Lamp Metals & Components Dept, 64-71, mgr anal chem, refratory metals prod dept, 71-83. *Mem:* Am Chem Soc; Am Soc Testing & Mat. *Res:* Soil chemistry; analytical chemistry of nuclear reactor materials; micro separations of uranium and transuranium elements; high temperature thermal analysis; analytical chemistry of tungsten, molybdenum; corrosion of zircaloy and reactor fuels. *Mailing Add:* 5245 E Farnhurst Rd Lyndhurst OH 44124

RYNASIEWICZ, ROBERT ALAN, QUANTUM MECHANICS. *Current Pos:* from asst prof to assoc prof, 92-96, PROF PHILOS, JOHNS HOPKINS UNIV, 96- *Personal Data:* b Schenectady, NY, Apr 23, 52; m 78, Barbara Shellhorn; c Samuel & John. *Educ:* Brown Univ, ScB, 74; Univ Minn, PhD(philos), 81. *Prof Exp:* Instr, Sch Physics & Astron, Univ Minn, 77-78; fel, Hist & Philos of Sci, Univ Pittsburgh, 81-82, Sage Sch Philos, Cornell Univ, 82-83; asst prof philos, Case Western Res Univ, 83-86. *Mem:* Philos Sci Asn; Hist Sci Soc; AAAS. *Res:* Foundational problems in theories of space, time and motion from 17th Century to present; foundations of quantum mechanics; methodological problems of mathematics and the physical sciences. *Mailing Add:* Dept Philos Johns Hopkins Univ Baltimore MD 21218. *Fax:* 410-516-6848; *E-Mail:* ryno@ryno.phl.jhu.edu

RYNBRANDT, DONALD JAY, TOXICOLOGY, PATHOLOGY. *Current Pos:* SUPVR CHEM, VET ADMIN MED CTR. *Personal Data:* b Jamestown, Mich, Apr 8, 40; m 67; c 1. *Educ:* Hope Col, BA, 62; Mich State Univ, PhD(biochem), 67. *Prof Exp:* Assoc dir chem, Drug Anal Sects, St Lukes Hosp, 68-90; sci dir, Forensic Toxicol Assocs, 87-92. *Concurrent Pos:* Instr, Case Western Res Univ, 68-70, adj sr instr, 70-75, adj asst prof, 75-; Ohio Thoracic grant, 72-73. *Mem:* Am Asn Clin Chemists; Clin Ligand Assay Soc; Clin Lab Mgt Asn. *Res:* Development of biochemical mechanisms for pulmonary diseases; isolation of lung proteolytic enzymes and proteolytic enzyme inhibitors; development of clinical chemistry tests; development of forensic toxicol tests. *Mailing Add:* Vet Admin Med Ctr 10000 Brecksville Rd Brecksville OH 44141

RYND, JAMES ARTHUR, BIOORGANIC CHEMISTRY, PROTEIN STRUCTURE. *Current Pos:* PROF CHEM, BIOLA UNIV, 70- *Personal Data:* b Chicago, Ill, Nov 8, 42; m 68; c 2. *Educ:* Univ Ill, BS, 66; Univ Calif, Riverside, PhD(chem), 71. *Concurrent Pos:* Fel, Univ Calif, Riverside, 72 & 73; res assoc, Col Med, Univ Calif, Irvine, 77-78, Calif State Univ, Fullerton, 80. *Mem:* Am Chem Soc; AAAS; Am Sci Affil. *Res:* X-ray crystal structure of organic compound; enzyme model systems involving flavins and prostaglandins. *Mailing Add:* Dept Chem Biola Col 13800 Biola Ave La Mirada CA 90639-0002

RYNN, NATHAN, FUNDAMENTAL PLASMA PHYSICS EXPERIMENTS, CONTROLLED FUSION. *Current Pos:* prof elec eng & physics, 66-69, prof physics, 69-93, EMER PROF PHYSICS & ASTRON & RES PROF, UNIV CALIF, IRVINE, 93- *Personal Data:* b New York, NY, Dec 2, 23; m 89, Glenda Brown; c Jonathan M, Margaret E & David A. *Educ:* City Col New York, BEE, 44; Univ Ill, MS, 47; Stanford Univ, PhD(elec eng), 56. *Prof Exp:* Res asst, Univ Ill, 46-47 & Stanford Univ, 52-56, res assoc, 58; res engr, RCA Labs, Princeton, NJ, 47-52; mem tech staff, Ramo Wooldridge Corp, 56-57; supvr, Huggins Labs, 57-58; res staff physicist, Plasma Physics Lab, Princeton Univ, 58-65. *Concurrent Pos:* Consult, Curtiss-Wright Corp, 64-65, Maxwell Labs, 72-73, Lawrence Livermore Labs, 75-80, Hughes Aircraft, Malibu, Calif, 77-78; vis lectr, Univ Calif, Berkeley, 65-66; prin investr, NSF grants, 67-96; vis scientist, Fontenay aux Roses Nuclear Res Ctr, France & Ecole Polytech, Paris, 75; Fulbright sr res fel, Ecole Polytech, Paliseau, France, 78; consult, TRW, Inc, 80-82; vis prof, Ecole Polytech, Lausanne, Switz, 86-91. *Mem:* Fel Am Phys Soc; fel Inst Elec & Electronics Engrs; Am Geophys Union; Sigma Xi; fel AAAS. *Res:* Experimental plasma physics in the Q-machine; transport phenomena in plasmas; plasma turbulence; controlled fusion; plasma diagnostics; LIF physics of the magnetosphere; plasma applications; stochasticity and chaos in plasma; microwave electronics; plasma science and engineering microwave tubes. *Mailing Add:* Dept Physics & Aston Univ Calif Irvine CA 92697-4575. *Fax:* 714-824-5903; *E-Mail:* nrynn@uci.edu

RYNTZ, ROSE A, PAINTS, COATINGS. *Current Pos:* TECH SPECIALIST, FORD MOTOR CO, 92- *Personal Data:* b Detroit, Mich, July 23, 57. *Educ:* Wayne State Univ, BS, 79; Univ Detroit, PhD(chem), 83. *Prof Exp:* Res chemist, Dow Chem Co, 83-85 & Ford Motor Co, 85-86; sr res chemist, E I du Pont de Nemours, 86-88; sr proj chemist, Dow Corning Corp, 88-89; tech dir, Akzo Coatings, Inc, 89-92. *Concurrent Pos:* Adj prof, Univ Detroit, 86-; tech chair, Fedn Socs Coatings Technol-Detroit Soc, 87-, prof develop comt chair, 91-; chair, Younger Chemists Comt, Am Chem Soc, 88-90; prof Develop Comt, Fedn Soc Coatings Technol, 91-; lectr, Univ Wis, 91- *Mem:* Am Chem Soc; Soc Automotive Engrs. *Res:* Innovative coating development in areas of waterborne primers and basecoats; new crosslinking technology clearcoats; adhesion to plastics; high solids dispersion technology. *Mailing Add:* 36056 Farmbrook Dr Mt Clemens MI 48043-1505. *Fax:* 313-592-2467

RYON, ALLEN DALE, CHEMICAL ENGINEERING, INORGANIC CHEMISTRY. *Current Pos:* RETIRED. *Personal Data:* b Republic, Ohio, Mar 18, 20; m 42; c 3. *Educ:* Heidelberg Col, BS, 41. *Prof Exp:* Chemist, Basic Refractories Inc, Ohio, 41-42, Basic Magnesium Inc, Nev, 42-44 & Tenn Eastman Corp, Tenn, 44-48; chem engr, Oak Ridge Nat Lab, 48-62, asst sect chief nuclear fuel processing, 62-83. *Concurrent Pos:* Consult, 83- *Mem:* Am Chem Soc. *Res:* Separation and purification by solvent extraction and chromatography. *Mailing Add:* 125 Goucher Circle Oak Ridge TN 37830-7011

RYPKA, EUGENE WESTON, MICROBIOLOGY. *Current Pos:* ADJ PROF BIOL, UNIV NMEX, 95- *Personal Data:* b Owatonna, Minn, May 6, 25; m 67; c 2. *Educ:* Stanford Univ, BA, 50, PhD(med microbiol), 58. *Prof Exp:* Asst prof biol, Univ NMex, 57-62; assoc bacteriologist, Leonard Wood Mem Leprosy Res Lab, Johns Hopkins Univ, 62-63; sr scientist, Lovelace Med Ctr, 63-70, head, Sect Microbiol, 70-93. *Concurrent Pos:* Vis lectr, Univ NMex, 67-68 & 70-71; adj prof biol, Univ NMex, 72- *Mem:* AAAS; Am Soc Microbiol; Am Soc Cybernet; Inst Elec & Electronics Engrs; Am Statist Asn; Int Soc Systs Sci; Am Med Informatics Asn. *Res:* Bacterial physiology; immunology; medical microbiology; systems and cybernetics; genetics definition and comprehension; NP-complete problems. *Mailing Add:* PO Box 706 Cedar Crest NM 87008

RYSCHKEWITSCH, GEORGE EUGENE, INORGANIC CHEMISTRY. *Current Pos:* from asst prof to assoc prof, 56-65, PROF CHEM, UNIV FLA, 65- *Personal Data:* b Frankfurt, Ger, July 8, 29; nat US; m 50; c 3. *Educ:* Univ Dayton, BS, 52; Ohio State Univ, PhD(chem), 55. *Prof Exp:* Fel, Ohio State Univ, 56. *Mem:* Am Chem Soc. *Res:* Chemistry of Group III elements; boron hydrides; molecular addition compounds; inorganic reaction mechanisms. *Mailing Add:* 10 SW 41st St Gainesville FL 32607-2760

RYSER, FRED A, JR, ZOOLOGY. *Current Pos:* from asst prof to assoc prof biol, 53-70, PROF BIOL, UNIV NEV, RENO, 70- *Personal Data:* b Albion, Mich, Feb 29, 20; m 45; c 4. *Educ:* Univ Wis, PhD(zool), 52. *Prof Exp:* Res assoc, Univ Wis, 52-53. *Mem:* Am Soc Mammal; Cooper Ornith Soc; Am Ornith Union; Sigma Xi. *Res:* Temperature regulation and metabolism of mammals; avian and mammalian ecology. *Mailing Add:* Box 8156 University Sta Reno NV 89507

RYSER, HUGUES JEAN-PAUL, CELL BIOLOGY, PHARMACOLOGY. *Current Pos:* PROF PATH & PHARMACOL, BOSTON UNIV, 72-, PROF PUB ENVIRON HEALTH, SCH PUB HEALTH, 80-, PROF BIOCHEM, SCH MED, 81- *Personal Data:* b La Chaux-de-Fonds, Switz, June 11, 26; m 61; c 3. *Educ:* Univ Berne, MD, 53, DrMed(pharmacol), 55. *Prof Exp:* Asst biochem, Med Sch, Univ Berne, 52-55; Swiss Nat Found Sci Res fel med, Univ Med Hosp, Univ Lausanne, 55-56, asst, 56-58; res fel, Harvard Med Sch, 58-60, from instr to asst prof pharmacol, 60-69; assoc prof cell biol & pharmacol, Med Sch, Univ Md, Baltimore, 69-70, prof, 70-72. *Concurrent Pos:* Clin & res fel med, Mass Gen Hosp, Boston, 58-64; prin investr, Nat Inst Gen Med Sci grant, 61-67; Lederle med fac award, 64-67; consult, George Washington Univ, 67-69; career develop award, Nat Cancer Inst, 68-69, grant, 65-; mem adv group biol & immunol segment carcinogenesis prog, 72-75; mem adv comt inst grants, Am Cancer Soc, 76-81; mem med res comt, Mass Div, Am Cancer Soc, 79-, mem bd dirs, 83- *Mem:* Histochem Soc; Am Asn Cancer Res; Am Soc Cell Biol; Soc Gen Physiol; Am Soc Pharmacol & Exp Therapeut; Am Asn Path. *Res:* Enzymatic studies on milligram amounts of diseased human liver; penetration and fate of macromolecules into mammalian cells in culture; interaction of basic polymers with cell membranes; molecular mechanisms in chemical carcinogenesis; macromolecular carriers for cancer chemotherapy and drug targeting. *Mailing Add:* Dept Path L804 Boston Univ Sch Med 80 E Concord St Boston MA 02118-2307. *Fax:* 617-638-4085

RYSKIN, GREGORY, POLYMER PHYSICS, FLUID MECHANICS. *Current Pos:* ASSOC PROF, DEPT CHEM ENG, NORTHWESTERN UNIV, 83- *Personal Data:* b Russia. *Educ:* Polytech Inst, Russia, BS, 70; Calif Inst Technol, PhD(chem eng), 83. *Mem:* Am Phys Soc. *Res:* Polymer physics; fluid mechanics. *Mailing Add:* Dept Chem Eng Northwestern Univ 2145 Sheridan Rd Evanston IL 60208

RYSTEPHANICK, RAYMOND GARY, THEORETICAL PHYSICS. *Current Pos:* asst prof, 67-71, assoc prof, 71-81, PROF PHYSICS, UNIV REGINA, 81- *Personal Data:* b Erickson, Man, Aug 24, 40; m 63. *Educ:* Univ Man, BSc, 62, MSc, 63; Univ BC, PhD(physics), 65. *Prof Exp:* Fel, McMaster Univ, 65-67. *Mem:* Am Phys Soc; Can Asn Physicists; AAAS. *Res:* Calculation of soft x-ray emission spectra in metals; gravitational effects in metals. *Mailing Add:* Dept Physics Univ Regina Regina SK S4S 0A2 Can. *Fax:* 306-585-4894

RYTI, RANDALL TODD, ECOLOGICAL MODELING & RISK ASSESSMENT, STATISTICAL PLANNING & ANALYSIS OF ENVIRONMENTAL SURVEYS. *Current Pos:* ENVIRON SCIENTIST, NEPTUNE & CO, INC, 92- *Personal Data:* b Chicago, Ill, Mar 12, 58. *Educ:* Univ Calif, Los Angeles, BA, 79; Univ Calif, San Diego, PhD(biol), 86. *Prof Exp:* Res scientist, Mont State Univ, 87-92. *Concurrent Pos:* Adj asst prof biol, Mont State Univ, 88-92. *Mem:* Am Soc Naturalists; Ecol Soc Am; Soc Environ Toxicol & Chem; Am Statist Asn. *Res:* Application of community ecological models to ecological risk assessment, including sensitivity analysis and statistical assessment of uncertainty in risk estimation. *Mailing Add:* 1874 Camino Manzana Los Alamos NM 87544. *E-Mail:* tnneptuneco@technet.nm.org

RYTTING, JOSEPH HOWARD, PHYSICAL CHEMISTRY, PHARMACEUTICS. *Current Pos:* From asst prof to assoc prof, 69-80, PROF PHARM, UNIV KANS, 80- *Personal Data:* b Rexburg, Idaho, June 12, 42; m 65, Barbara K Smith; c Barbara, Michael, Kiersten, Rebecca, Melinda, Heather, Erik, Cheryl, Nathan, Megan, Janae & Matthew. *Educ:* Brigham Young Univ, BA, 66, PhD(phys chem), 69. *Honors & Awards:* Tensiochimica Int Prize Surfactant Chem, Italian Oil Chemist's Soc, 74. *Concurrent Pos:* Prof, Upjohn Co, 78; assoc ed, Int J Pharmaceut, 84-93, ed-in-chief, 94- *Mem:* Am Chem Soc; Sigma Xi; Calorimetry Conf; fel Am Asn Pharm Scientists; Controlled Release Soc; Am Asn Cols Pharm. *Res:* Application of solution thermodynamics to drug design and delivery; physical chemistry of biologically active agents; effects of pressure and temperature on biologicals and pharmaceutical products; stability; rectal, transdermal, intraoral and intestinal drug absorption; insulin absorption. *Mailing Add:* Pharmaceut Chem Dept Univ Kans 2095 Constant Ave Lawrence KS 66047. *Fax:* 785-749-7393; *E-Mail:* rytting@smissman.hbc.ukans.edu

RYUGO, KAY, POMOLOGY, PLANT PHYSIOLOGY. *Current Pos:* From asst pomologist to assoc pomologist, 55-69, POMOLOGIST, UNIV CALIF, DAVIS, 69-, LECTR, 76- *Personal Data:* b Sacramento, Calif, Apr 10, 20; m 55; c 5. *Educ:* Univ Calif, BS, 49, MS, 50, PhD, 54. *Concurrent Pos:* NATO fel, Univ Bologna, 72. *Mem:* Int Soc Hort Sci; Am Soc Hort Sci; Bot Soc Am; Scand Soc Plant Physiol; Am Soc Plant Physiol. *Res:* Physiology and biochemistry; native growth regulators in fruits and trees. *Mailing Add:* 523 A St Davis CA 95616

RYZLAK, MARIA TERESA, ENZYMOLOGY, RECEPTOR PROTEINS. *Current Pos:* ADJ ASST PROF, UNIV MED & DENT NJ, 92- *Personal Data:* b Augustow, Poland, Feb 27, 38; US citizen; m 59; c 2. *Educ:* Univ Manchester, Eng, BSc, 66; NJ Inst Technol, Newark, MS, 70; Univ Med & Dent NJ, PhD(biochem), 86; Rutgers Univ, New Brunswick, PhD(biochem), 86. *Prof Exp:* Res chemist org synthesis, Troy Chem Co, Newark, NJ, 64-68; teaching fel, Chem Lab, NJ Inst Technol, Newark, 68-69; res asst, Endocrinol Lab, Worcester Found Exp Biol, 69-71, sr res asst molecular biol, 71-74; res assoc biochem, Temple Univ, Med Sch, 74-77; chemist, US Naval Air Develop Ctr, 77-78; res assoc biochem, McNeil Pharmaceut, 78-81; grad res asst, Rutgers Univ, 82-86, res assoc biochem, 89-92. *Concurrent Pos:* Busch fel, Waksman Inst, Rutgers Univ, 86-89; postdoctoral fel, Charles & Johanna Busch Mem Found, 86-89. *Mem:* Sigma Xi; Soc Exp Biol & Med; Res Soc Alcoholism. *Res:* Purification and characterization of aldehyde dehydrogenases from the human liver and prostate; study of the metabolism of acetaldehyde and biogenic aldehydes arising from the oxidation of biogenic anines, putrescine, spermine and spermidine; study of oxysterols, specific receptor proteins, regulation of HMG-CoA-reductase and carcinogenesis by oxysterols of the human and rat prostates; mechanism of carcinogenesis of the human liver and prostate due to ethanol metabolism. *Mailing Add:* 303 Woodstock Dr Cherry Hill NJ 08034

RYZNAR, JOHN W, ANALYTICAL & PHYSICAL CHEMISTRY. *Current Pos:* RETIRED. *Personal Data:* b Sharpsburg, Pa, May 27, 12; m. *Educ:* Kent State Univ, BS, 34; Ohio State Univ, MS, 35, PhD(anal & phy sci), 37. *Prof Exp:* Dir res & tech dir, Nalco Chem Co, Ill, 37-73. *Res:* Ryznar stability index used in water treatment. *Mailing Add:* 278 Stonegate Rd Clarendon Hills IL 60514

RZAD, STEFAN JACEK, PHYSICAL CHEMISTRY. *Current Pos:* PHYS CHEMIST, CORP RES & DEVELOP CTR, GEN ELEC CO, 74- *Personal Data:* b Warsaw, Poland, Mar 15, 38; m 63; c 2. *Educ:* Univ Louvain, MS, 60, PhD(phys chem), 64. *Prof Exp:* Fel radiation lab, Univ Notre Dame, 64-66 & radiation labs, Mellon Inst, Carnegie-Mellon Univ, 67-74. *Mem:* Am Chem Soc; Inst Elec & Electronics Engrs; Sigma Xi. *Res:* Reactions of radicals in electron irradiated liquids; gas-phase vacuum ultraviolet photochemistry; ionic processes; conduction and mechanisms of electrical breakdown in liquids, solids and gases; high voltage phenomena; plasma enhanced chemical vapor deposition of organic and inorganic materials. *Mailing Add:* 140 Appleton Rd Rexford NY 12148

RZESZOTARSKI, WACLAW JANUSZ, RADIOPHARMACEUTICALS. *Current Pos:* DIR MED CHEM, NOVA PHARMACEUT CORP, 85- *Personal Data:* b Warsaw, Poland, Apr 14, 36; US citizen. *Educ:* Gdansk Inst Technol. MS, 59; Polish Acad Sci, PhD(chem), 64. *Prof Exp:* Res assoc med chem, Univ Calif, Santa Barbara, 66-68 & Wash Hosp Ctr, 68-75; from asst prof to prof med chem, George Washington Univ, 75-85. *Mem:* Am Chem Soc; AAAS; Nuclear Med Soc; Polish Inst Arts & Sci; Pilsudski Inst Am. *Res:* Medicinal chemistry; drug design, synthesis and development; pharmaceutical effect on central nervous system. *Mailing Add:* 407 Buckspur Ct Millersville MD 21108-1764

S

SAACKE, RICHARD GEORGE, REPRODUCTIVE PHYSIOLOGY, CYTOLOGY. *Current Pos:* asst prof, 65-68, PROF DAIRY SCI, VA POLYTECH INST & STATE UNIV, 68- *Personal Data:* b Newark, NJ, Oct 31, 31; m 54; c 5. *Educ:* Rutgers Univ, BS, 53; Pa State Univ, MS, 55, PhD(dairy sci), 62. *Honors & Awards:* Res Award, Nat Asn Animal Breeders, 85. *Prof Exp:* Dairy exten specialist, Univ Md, 57-58; from instr to asst prof dairy physiol, Pa State Univ, 58-65. *Concurrent Pos:* Nat Inst Child Health & Human Develop res grant, 65-69. *Mem:* AAAS; Am Dairy Sci Asn; Am Soc Animal Sci; Soc Study Reprod; Sigma Xi. *Res:* Cytology and physiology of bovine spermatozoa; ultrastructural study of the bovine mammary gland with emphasis on milk synthesis and secretion; sperm transport in the female and male-related embryonic death. *Mailing Add:* Dept Dairy Sci Va Polytech Inst & State Univ Blacksburg VA 24061-0315

SAADA, ADEL SELIM, SOIL MECHANICS & MECHANICS OF GEO-MATERIALS. *Current Pos:* From asst prof to assoc prof, 62-88, CHMN DEPT, CASE WESTERN RES UNIV, 78-, FRANK H NEFF PROF CIVIL ENG, 88- *Personal Data:* b Heliopolis, Egypt, Oct 24, 34; US citizen; m 60, Nancy Hernan; c Christiane & Richard. *Educ:* Ecole Centrale de Paris, France, Engr, 58; Univ Grenoble, MS, 59; Princeton Univ, PhD(soil mech), 61. *Honors & Awards:* Richard J Carrol Lectr, Johns Hopkins Univ, 90; Telford Prize, Inst Civil Eng, UK, 95. *Prof Exp:* Res assoc civil eng, Princeton Univ, 61-62. *Concurrent Pos:* NSF res grant soil mech, 65-; US-France res grant civil eng & Army Res Off grant fracture mech, 83-; soils & foundations consult; Air Force Off Sci Res grant, 88. *Mem:* Am Soc Testing & Mat; fel Am Soc Civil Engrs; Int Soc Soil Mech; Brit Geotech Soc. *Res:* Mechanical behavior of soils under different stress systems; fracture mechanics applied to soils, shear banding and liquefaction of soils. *Mailing Add:* Dept Civil Eng Case Western Res Univ University Circle Cleveland OH 44106. *Fax:* 216-368-5229; *E-Mail:* arcs31@po.cwru.edu

SAALFELD, FRED ERICH, PHYSICAL CHEMISTRY, INORGANIC CHEMISTRY. *Current Pos:* dir, 87-93, DEPUTY CHIEF NAVAL RES & TECHNICAL DIR, OFF NAVAL RES. 93- *Personal Data:* b Joplin, Mo, Apr 9, 35; m 58, Elizabeth Renner; c Fred E Jr. *Educ:* Southeast Mo State Col, BS, 57; Iowa State Univ, MS, 59, PhD(chem), 61. *Honors & Awards:* Presidential Distinguished & Meritorious Ranks Award, President of US, 86 & 89; Robert Dexter Conrad Award, Secy of the Navy, 89. *Prof Exp:* Fel, Iowa State Univ, 61-62; sect head mass spectronomy, Naval Res Lab, 62-74, head, phys chem br, 74-76, supt, Chem Div, 76-82, assoc dir res, 82. *Concurrent Pos:* Chief scientist, Off Naval Res, London Br Off, 79-80. *Mem:* Fel AAAS; Am Chem Soc; Am Soc Mass Spectrometry (secy, 70-74); fel Chem Soc London; Mass Spectros Soc Japan; Combustion Inst. *Res:* Application of mass spectrometry to chemical problems; investigation of ion-molecule reaction and the kinetics of chemical reactions occuring in flames and chemical laser; analysis of exceedingly complex mixtures. *Mailing Add:* 5510 Ventnor Lane Springfield VA 22151-1420. *Fax:* 703-696-4065; *E-Mail:* saalfeld@tomcat.onr.navy.mil

SAARI, DONALD GENE, MATHEMATICAL ECONOMICS, CELESTIAL MECHANICS. *Current Pos:* from asst prof to assoc prof, 68-74, PROF MATH, NORTHWESTERN UNIV, 74-, PROF ECON, 88- *Personal Data:* b Ironwood, Mich, Mar 9, 40; m 66, Lillian Kalinen; c Katri & Anneli. *Educ:* Mich Technol Univ, BS, 62; Purdue Univ, MS, 64, PhD(math), 67. *Hon Degrees:* PhD(appl math & econ), Purdue Univ, 88. *Honors & Awards:* Lester Ford Award, Math Asn Am, 85; Duncan Black Award, Pub Choice Soc, 91. *Prof Exp:* Res staff astronr, Yale Univ, 67-68. *Concurrent Pos:* Consult, Nat Bur Stand, 79-86; ed, Soc Indust & Appl Math, 81-86; Guggenheim fel, 88. *Mem:* Am Math Soc; Math Asn Am; Soc Indust & Appl Math; Am Astron Soc; Economet Soc. *Res:* Qualitative behavior of the N-body problem of celestial mechanics; behavior of expanding gravitational systems; dynamical systems; mathematical economics; decision analysis; voting theory. *Mailing Add:* Dept Math Northwestern Univ Evanston IL 60208-2730. *Fax:* 847-491-8906

SAARI, EUGENE E, phytopathology, for more information see previous edition

SAARI, JACK THEODORE, CARDIOVASCULAR PHYSIOLOGY. *Current Pos:* RES PHYSIOLOGIST, USDA AGR RES SERV HUMAN NUTRIT RES CTR, GRAND FORKS, NDAK, 87- *Personal Data:* b Virginia, Minn, Jan 1, 43; m 74; c 2. *Educ:* Univ Minn, Minneapolis, BChE, 65, PhD(physiol), 70. *Prof Exp:* Instr physiol, Univ Minn, Minneapolis, 70-71; res assoc biophys, Univ Calgary, 71-75; asst prof physiol, Sch Dent, Marquette Univ, 75-78; from asst prof to assoc prof physiol, Sch Med, Univ NDak, 78-87. *Concurrent Pos:* William H Davies Mem Res fel, Div Med Biophys, Univ Calgary, 72-74, Med Res Coun Can prof asst, 74-75. *Mem:* Sigma Xi; Am Physiol Soc; Am Heart Asn. *Res:* Microvascular permeability and vasoactivity; calcium kinetics in cardiac muscle; trace mineral metabolism and cardiovascular function. *Mailing Add:* USDA Agr Res Serv Human Nutrit Res Ctr PO Box 9034 Univ Sta Grand Forks ND 58202-9034

SAARI, WALFRED SPENCER, ORGANIC CHEMISTRY. *Current Pos:* sr res chemist, 59-75, SR INVESTR, MERCK SHARP & DOHME RES LABS, 75- *Personal Data:* b Lonsdale, RI, Feb 6, 32; m 53; c 4. *Educ:* Brown Univ, ScB, 53; Mass Inst Technol, PhD(org chem), 57. *Prof Exp:* Res chemist, Shell Develop Co, Calif, 57-59. *Mem:* Am Chem Soc. *Res:* Medicinal chemistry. *Mailing Add:* 3435 N Druid Hills Rd Apt S Decatur GA 30033

SAARLAS, MAIDO, AERONAUTICAL & MECHANICAL ENGINEERING. *Current Pos:* PROF AERONAUT ENG, US NAVAL ACAD, 80- *Personal Data:* b Tartu, Estonia, Feb 5, 30; US citizen; m 56; c 2. *Educ:* Univ Ill, Urbana, BS, 53, MS, 54 & 57; Univ Cincinnati, PhD(mech eng), 66. *Prof Exp:* Res engr, Univ Chicago, 54-56 & Douglas Aircraft Co, 56; sr engr, Autonetics Div, NAm Rockwell Corp, 58-59 & Aeronutronic Div, Ford Motor Co, 59-61; res assoc, Univ Cincinnati, 61-65 & Kinetics Corp, 65-67; sr engr, Gen Elec Co, 67-69. *Concurrent Pos:* Lectr, Univ Calif, Los Angeles, 58-61; consult, Douglas Aircraft Co, 65, Gen Elec Co, 65-67, Trident Eng, 69- & Cadcom, Inc, 70- *Mem:* Am Inst Aeronaut & Astronaut; Am Soc Mech Engrs. *Res:* Fluid mechanics and heat transfer, flight mechanics and dynamics; turbo-machinery. *Mailing Add:* 225 Mill Harbor Dr Arnold MD 21012

SAATY, THOMAS L, MATHEMATICS. *Current Pos:* prof statist & oper res, 69-79, UNIV PROF, UNIV PITTSBURGH, 79- *Personal Data:* b Mosul, Iraq, July 18, 26; US citizen; m 48; c 5. *Educ:* Cath Univ, MS, 49; Yale Univ, MA, 50, PhD, 53. *Honors & Awards:* Lester R Ford Award, Math Asn Am, 73; Inst Mgt Sci Award, 77. *Prof Exp:* Mathematician, Melpar, Inc, 53-54; mathematician & sci analyst, Mass Inst Technol, 54-57; mathematician, US Dept Navy, 57-58, sci liaison officer, Off Naval Res, Eng, 58-59, dir adv planning, 59-61, head math br, 61-63, mathematician, US Arms Control & Disarmament Agency, Dept State, 63-69. *Concurrent Pos:* Lectr, Am Univ & USDA Grad Sch, 54-; prof lectr, Catholic Univ, George Washington Univ & Exten Div, Univ Calif, Los Angeles; Ford Found lectr, Nat Planning Inst, Cairo, 59 & 64; mathematician, US Dept Air Force & Nat Bur Stand, 51-52; consult var corps, US govt agencies & depts & foreign govts; exec dir, Conf Bd Math Sci, AAAS, 65-67. *Mem:* Fel AAAS; Am Math Soc; Math Soc Am; Opers Res Soc Am; Royal Span Acad. *Res:* Optimization; nonlinear processes; graph theory; queueing theory and stochastic processes; operations research, especially in underdeveloped countries; mathematical methods and military uses; models of arms reduction; systems; planning; decision making; conflict resolution. *Mailing Add:* 4922 Ellsworth Ave Pittsburgh PA 15213-2807. *Fax:* 412-648-1693; *E-Mail:* saaty@vms.sys.pitt.edu

SAAVEDRA, JUAN M, PHARMACOLOGY, PSYCHIATRY. *Current Pos:* Vis fel, NIH, 71-73, vis scientist pharmacol, 73-79, med officer, 79-89, CHIEF, SECT PHARMACOL, NIH, 89- *Personal Data:* b Buenos Aires, Arg, Oct 5, 41. *Educ:* Univ Buenos Aires, MD, 65. *Honors & Awards:* Adminr Award Meritorious Achievement, Dept Health Human Serv, Alcohol Drug Abuse & Ment Health Admin, 87. *Concurrent Pos:* Res prof psychiat, Uniformed Serv Univ Health Sci. *Mem:* Int Soc Hypertension; Int Soc Neurochem; Soc Neurosci; Int Brain Res Orgn. *Res:* Psychopharmacology; biological psychiatry; neural regulation of blood pressure; central control of automatic functions; stress and central nervous system. *Mailing Add:* 9510 Kingsley Ave Bethesda MD 20814. *Fax:* 301-402-0337

SABA, GEORGE PETER, II, RADIOLOGY, BIOPHYSICS. *Current Pos:* ASST PROF RADIOL, JOHNS HOPKINS HOSP, 74- *Personal Data:* b Wilkes-Barre, Pa, Sept 30, 40; m 67; c 4. *Educ:* Pa State Univ, BS, 62, MS, 64; State Univ NY, Buffalo, MD, 68. *Prof Exp:* Asst physics, Pa State Univ, 62-64; intern med, Buffalo Gen Hosp, 68-69; clin assoc, Nat Heart Inst, 69-71. *Concurrent Pos:* Consult physician radiol, Union Mem Hosp, 73-, Havre de Grace Hosp, 74- & Md Gen Hosp, 74- *Res:* Clinical medicine; pancreatic studies and gastrointestinal radiology. *Mailing Add:* Dept Radiol Johns Hopkins Hosp Baltimore MD 21205

SABA, SHOICHI, ELECTRICAL ENGINEERING, SCIENCE POLICY. *Current Pos:* Mem, Toshiba Corp, 42-68, chief engr, Heavy Apparatus Div, 68-70, dir & gen mgr, 70-80, pres & chief exec officer, 80-86, chmn bd & exec officer, 86-87, ADV TO BD, TOSHIBA CORP, 87- *Personal Data:* b Tokyo, Japan, Feb 28, 19; wid; c 3. *Educ:* Univ Tokyo, BSc, 41. *Honors & Awards:* Develop Award, Inst Elec Engrs Japan, 58. *Concurrent Pos:* Dir, Japan Atomic Power Co, 81, Tokyo Bay Hilton Co Ltd, 85; chmn, bd trustees, Int Christian Univ, 92; pres, Global Infrastruct Fund Res Found, 89; chmn, Japanese Panel, Japan-US Conf Cult & Educ Interchange, 91; pres, Japanese Indust Stand Comt, 94-; adv, Japan Fed Econ Orgn, 94- *Mem:* Foreign assoc Nat Acad Eng; fel Inst Elec & Electronics Engrs. *Res:* Author or co-author of 4 books and 10 technical papers; holder of 2 patents. *Mailing Add:* Toshiba Corp 1-1 Shibaura 1-Chome Minato-Ku Tokyo 105 Japan

SABA, THOMAS MARON, MEDICAL PHYSIOLOGY, BIOPHYSICS. *Current Pos:* PROF PHYSIOL & CHMN DEPT, ALBANY MED COL, 73- *Personal Data:* b Wilkes Barre, Pa, Mar 8, 41; m 63; c 3. *Educ:* Wilkes Col, BA, 63; Univ Tenn, PhD(physiol, biophys), 67. *Prof Exp:* Lab asst biol, Wilkes Col, 61-62; instr physiol & biophys, Med Units, Univ Tenn, 67-68; from asst prof to assoc prof physiol, Univ Ill Col Med, 68-73. *Concurrent Pos:* Consult physiologist, Vet Admin Hosp, Hines, Ill, 70-73; clinical physiologist, Albany Med Ctr, 73-; adj prof biomed eng, Rensselaer Polytech Inst. *Mem:* AAAS; Reticuloendothelial Soc; Soc Exp Biol & Med; Am Asn Study Liver Dis; Am Physiol Soc; Shock Soc; Surg Infection Soc. *Res:* Cardiovascular and metabolic aspects of the liver; physiology and physiopathology of the reticuloendothelial system; physiological mechanisms of host-defense; plasma fibronection and phagocytores; lung vascular injury; pathophysiology of traumatic shock; lung and peripheral vascular permeability. *Mailing Add:* Dept Physiol & Cell Biol A-134 Albany Med Col 47 New Scotland S Albany NY 12208-3479. *Fax:* 518-262-5669

SABA, WILLIAM GEORGE, PHYSICAL CHEMISTRY. *Current Pos:* phys chemist, Heat Div, Nat Bur Stand, 61-69, PATENT EXAM, PATENT OFF, DEPT COM, 69- *Personal Data:* b Wilkes-Barre, Pa, Aug 15, 32; m 60; c 4. *Educ:* Wilkes Col, BS, 54; Univ Pittsburgh, PhD(phys chem), 61. *Prof Exp:* Asst chem, Univ Pittsburgh, 54-55, phys chem, 55-61. *Mem:* Am Chem Soc; Am Phys Soc; AAAS. *Res:* Thermodynamic properties of solid solutions; low-temperature calorimetry; solid state electronics; semiconductor design and processing. *Mailing Add:* 2623 Kinderbrook Lane Bowie MD 20715

SABACKY, M JEROME, ORGANIC CHEMISTRY, PROCESS CHEMISTRY. *Current Pos:* Sr res chemist, Org Chem Div, Monsanto Co, 66-75, from res specialist to sr res specialist, Nutrit Chem Div, 75-85, fel, Animal Sci Div, 85-91, New Prod Div, Monsanto Agr Group, 91-94, FEL, MONSANTO AGR CO, 95- *Personal Data:* b Cedar Rapids, Iowa, June 22, 39; m 67, Jane; c Kevin & Alisa. *Educ:* Coe Col, BA, 61; Univ Ill, MS, 63, PhD(chem), 66. *Honors & Awards:* Thomas & Hochwalt Award, 81. *Mem:* Am Chem Soc. *Res:* Magnetic resonance studies of ortho-substituted derivatives of triphenylmethane; homogeneous catalysis; catalytic asymmetric synthesis employing transition metal complexes; enzyme inhibitors; plant scale-ups and start-ups; protein formulations; agricultural chemicals process development. *Mailing Add:* 324 Holloway Ballwin MO 63011

SABADELL, ALBERTO JOSE, CHEMICAL ENGINEERING. *Current Pos:* phys scientist, bur sci & technol, 83-87, DEP DIR OFF ENERGY, BUR SCI & TECHNOL, USAID, 88- *Personal Data:* b Barcelona, Spain, Oct 31, 29; m 56, Nora Filangeri; c Silvia, Gabriel & Laura. *Educ:* Univ Buenos Aires, Lic chem, 54; Princeton Univ, MSE, 63. *Prof Exp:* Chemist, Invests Inst Sci & Tech Armed Forces, 55-56, chief env explosives and propellants, 57-60; prof theory explosives, Eng Sch Army, Argentinian Army, 60-61; res asst rocket propulsion, Forrestal Res Ctr, Princeton Univ, 62-63; assoc prof combustion, Sch Eng, Univ Buenos Aires, 64-65; res engr, Princeton Chem Res, 66 & Aerochem Res Labs Inc, Sybron Corp, 67-75; tech staff, Metrek Div, Mitre Corp, 76-82. *Concurrent Pos:* NASA fel, Princeton Univ, 61-63; hon mem space tech comt, Arg Space Nat Comn, 64-65; panel mem, Nat Res Coun, 82- *Mem:* Am Chem Soc. *Res:* Energy. *Mailing Add:* 20265 Island View Ct Sterling VA 20165

SABATH, LEON DAVID, MEDICINE, MICROBIOLOGY & INFECTIOUS DISEASES. *Current Pos:* STAFF PHYSICIAN, UNIV MINN HOSPS, 74- *Personal Data:* b Savannah, Ga, July 24, 30; div; c Natasha R, Joanna T & Rachel T. *Educ:* Harvard Univ, AB, 52; Harvard Med Sch, MD, 56. *Prof Exp:* Intern med, Peter Bent Brigham Hosp, Boston, 56-57; jr resident, Bellevue Hosp, New York, 59-60; res fel, Harvard Med Sch, 60-62; sr resident, Peter Bent Brigham Hosp, 62-63; spec fel, Oxford Univ, 63-65; assoc med, Harvard Med Sch, 65-68, from asst prof to assoc prof, 68-74; head sect infectious dis, 74-83, PROF MED, UNIV MINN, MINNEAPOLIS, 74- *Concurrent Pos:* Spec fel, Nat Inst Allergy & Infectious Dis, 63-67, Res Career Develop Award, 69-74; attend physician, Vet Admin Hosp, West Roxbury, 68-74; assoc physician, Boston City Hosp, 69-74. *Mem:* Am Fedn Clin Res; Soc Gen Microbiol; Am Soc Microbiol; Soc Clin Pharmacol & Therapeut; fel Am Col Physicians; Am Soc Clin & Infectious Dis; fel Infectious Dis Soc Am. *Res:* Antibiotics; infectious diseases; bacterial resistance to antibiotics; antibiotic assays; clinical pharmacology; penicillins, penicillinases; bacterial cell walls. *Mailing Add:* Univ Minn Div Infectious Dis Dept Med Box 489 UMHC Rm 14-168A 516 Delaware Sr SE Minneapolis MN 55455-0356. *Fax:* 612-625-4410

SABATINI, DAVID DOMINGO, CELL BIOLOGY, BIOCHEMISTRY. *Current Pos:* prof, 72-74, FREDERICK L EHRMAN PROF & CHMN, DEPT CELL BIOL, SCH MED, NY UNIV, 75-, DIR, MD-PHD PROG, 87- *Personal Data:* b Bolivar, Arg, May 10, 31; US citizen; m 60, Zulema Lena; c Bernardo L & David M. *Educ:* Nat Univ Litoral, MD, 54; Rockefeller Univ, PhD(biochem), 66. *Honors & Awards:* Wendell Griffith Mem Lect, St Louis Univ, Mo, 77; Mary Peterman Mem Lectr, Mem-Sloan Kettering Inst, New York, NY, 77; 25th Robert J Terry Lectr, Washington Univ, 78; Samuel Roberts Noble Res Recognition Award, 80; E B Wilson Award, Am Soc Cell Biol, 86; Seventh Annual Kenneth F Naidorf Mem Lectr, Columbia Univ, 89. *Prof Exp:* Instr, lectr & assoc prof histol, Inst Gen Anat & Embryol & dir admis, Med Sch, Univ Buenos Aires, Arg, 57-60; Rockefeller Found fel, Med Sch, Yale Univ, 61 & Rockefeller Inst, 61-62; res assoc, Cell Biol Lab, Rockefeller Univ, New York, NY, 61-63; from asst prof to assoc prof cell biol, 60-72. *Concurrent Pos:* Fel, Nat Acad Med, Arg, 56; UNESCO fel, Biophys Inst, Rio de Janeiro, 57; Pfizer travelling fel, 72; mem, Molecular Biol Study Sect, NIH, 73-77, chmn, 76-77; coun mem, Am Soc Cell Biol, 74-77; ed, J Cellular Biochem, 80-84, Molecular & Cellular Biol, 80-82, Biol Cell, 86- & Current Opinions Cell Biol, 90-; bd dirs, Pub Health Res Inst, 80-88; mem, Bd Basic Biol, Nat Res Coun, 86- *Mem:* Nat Acad Sci; Am Soc Cell Biol (pres, 78-79); fel NY Acad Sci; Harvey Soc (vpres, 85-86, pres, 86-87); fel Am Acad Arts & Sci. *Res:* Mechanisms by which newly synthesized proteins are targeted to their sites of function in the different membranes and organelles that characterize the eukaryotic cell. *Mailing Add:* 77 Wellington Ave New Rochelle NY 10804-3705. *Fax:* 212-263-5813; *E-Mail:* sabatini@nyumed.med.nyu.edu

SABBADINI, EDRIS RINALDO, IMMUNOBIOLOGY. *Current Pos:* asst prof, 69-72, assoc prof, 72-80, PROF IMMUNOL, UNIV MAN, 80- *Personal Data:* b Anzio, Italy, Apr 1, 30; Can citizen; m 60; c 2. *Educ:* Univ Pavia, MD, 54; McGill Univ, PhD(exp surg), 67. *Prof Exp:* Asst surg, Univ Pavia, 58-63; lectr exp surg, McGill Univ, 68-69. *Mem:* Can Soc Immunol; Am Asn Immunologists; Transplantation Soc; NY Acad Sci. *Res:* Transplantation and tumor immunology; regulation of cell-mediated immunity. *Mailing Add:* Dept Immunol Univ Man 795 McDermot St Winnipeg MB R3E 0W3 Can

SABBAGH, HAROLD A(BRAHAM), ELECTRICAL ENGINEERING, PHYSICS. *Current Pos:* PRES, SABBAGH ASSOC, INC, 80- *Personal Data:* b W Lafayette, Ind, Jan 9, 37; m 66, Sandra C Abookive; c Elias H, Kahlil G & Amira A. *Educ:* Purdue Univ, BSEE & MSEE, 58, PhD(elec eng), 64. *Prof Exp:* Instr elec sci, US Naval Acad, 59-61; asst prof elec eng, Rose-Hulman Inst Technol, 64-67, assoc prof, 67-70, prof elec eng & physics, 70-72; electronics engr, Naval Weapons Support Ctr, 72-80. *Mem:* Inst Elec & Electronics Engrs; Sigma Xi; Appl Computational Electromagnetic Soc. *Res:* Electromagnetic waves; electroacoustic waves; nondestructive evaluation, computational electromagnetics. *Mailing Add:* Sabbagh Assoc Inc 4635 Morningside Dr PO Box 7706 Bloomington IN 47407

SABBAGHIAN, MEHDY, ENGINEERING SCIENCE. *Current Pos:* from asst prof to assoc prof, 64-74, PROF ENG SCI, LA STATE UNIV, BATON ROUGE, 74- *Personal Data:* b Tehran, Iran, Nov 22, 35; m 63; c 1. *Educ:* Abadan Inst Technol, Iran, BSc, 58; Case Inst Technol, MSc, 63; Univ Okla, PhD(eng sci), 64. *Prof Exp:* Proj engr, Iranian Oil Ref Co, 58-60 & Viking Air Prod, 61-62. *Concurrent Pos:* Consult, Hydro Vac Inc, 70-71, Gamma Indust, 72- & Nuclear Systs Inc, 73. *Mem:* Am Soc Mech Engrs; Am Soc Eng Educ. *Res:* Viscoelastic materials and their physical behaviors; thermoviscoelasticity with time dependent properties. *Mailing Add:* 6821 Perkins Rd Baton Rouge LA 70808

SABBAN, ESTHER LOUISE, NEUROCHEMISTRY. *Current Pos:* from asst prof to assoc prof, 83-90, PROF BIOCHEM & MOLECULAR BIOL, NY MED COL, 91- *Personal Data:* b Detroit, Mich, July 21, 48. *Educ:* Hebrew Univ, BSc, 70, MSc, 72; NY Univ, PhD (biochem), 77. *Honors & Awards:* NIH Career Develop Award. *Prof Exp:* Asst res scientist cell biol, Med Ctr, NY Univ, 77-80, res asst prof cell biol & psychol, 80-83. *Mem:* NY Acad Sci; Am Soc Biol Chemists; Am Soc Cell Biol; Soc Neurosci; AAAS. *Res:* Regulation of biosynthesis of dopamine beta-hydroxylase and tyrosine hydroxylase; stress induced changes of gene expression; molecular regulation of neurotransmitter biosynthesis. *Mailing Add:* Dept Biochem & Molecular Biol NY Med Col Valhalla NY 10595. *Fax:* 914-993-4058; *E-Mail:* Sabban@nymc.edu

SABELLI, HECTOR C, PSYCHIATRY, NEUROPHARMACOLOGY. *Current Pos:* asst prof psychiat, 79-84, ASSOC PROF PSYCHIAT & PROF PHARMACOL, RUSH UNIV, 84- *Personal Data:* b Buenos Aires, Arg, July 25, 37; nat US; m 60; c 2. *Educ:* Univ Buenos Aires, MD, 59, DrMed, 61. *Honors & Awards:* Soc Biol Psychiat Award, 63; Sci Res Award, Interstate Postgrad Med Sch Asn NAm, 70; Clin Res Award, Am Acad Clin Psychiatrists, 84. *Prof Exp:* Res fels, Arg Soc Advan Sci, 59-60 & Arg Coun Res, 60-61; asst prof pharmacol, Chicago Med Sch, 62-64; career investr, Arg Coun Res, 64-66; vis prof pharmacol, Chicago Med Sch, 66-67, actg chmn dept, 70, chmn dept, 71-75. *Concurrent Pos:* Prof & chmn, Inst Pharmacol, Nat Univ Litoral, 65-66; psychiatrist, Rush-Presby, St Lukes Hosp, dir, Psychobiol Lab, 79- *Mem:* Soc Biol Psychiat; Am Soc Pharmacol & Exp Therapeut; Soc Neurosci. *Res:* Biogenic amines psychiatric disorders and drug therapy; psychodynamics and pharmacotherapy of depression. *Mailing Add:* 2400 N Lakeview 2802 Chicago IL 60614

SABELLI, NORA HOJVAT, THEORETICAL CHEMISTRY, COMPUTER SCIENCE. *Current Pos:* prog dir, 92-, SR DIR, NSF. *Personal Data:* b Buenos Aires, Argentina, Dec 22, 36; m 60; c 2. *Educ:* Univ Buenos Aires, MS, 58, PhD(chem), 64. *Prof Exp:* Res assoc chem, Univ Chicago, 61-63; instr phys chem, Univ Buenos Aires, 64-65; asst prof, Nat Univ Litoral, 65-66; chemist, Univ Chicago, 67-69; instr comput sci, Univ Ill Chicago Circle, 69-75, assoc prof comput sci & chem, 75-92; sr res scientist, NCSA, 89-92. *Concurrent Pos:* Career investr, Argentine Nat Res Coun, 64-66; vis resident assoc, Argonne Nat Labs, 74-84. *Mem:* Am Chem Soc; AAAS. *Res:* Theoretical organic chemistry; molecular orbital and semiempirical methods; computational chemistry; ab initio methods; potential curves. *Mailing Add:* NSF 4201 Wilson Blvd Arlington VA 22230

SABERSKY, ROLF H(EINRICH), HEAT TRANSFER, FLUID MECHANICS. *Current Pos:* from instr to prof, 49-88, PROF EMER MECH ENG, CALIF INST TECHNOL, 88- *Personal Data:* b Berlin, Ger, Oct 20, 20; nat US; m 46, Bettina S Schuster; c Carol M & Sandra S. *Educ:* Calif Inst Technol, BS, 42, MS, 43, PhD, 49. *Honors & Awards:* Heat Transfer Mem Award, Am Soc Mech Engrs, 77. *Prof Exp:* Develop engr, Aerojet-Gen Corp, Gen Tire & Rubber Co, 43-46. *Concurrent Pos:* Consult, Aerojet-Gen Corp, 49-71, var aerospace & high tech co, 71- *Mem:* Fel Am Soc Mech Engrs. *Res:* Heat transfer to granular materials and complex fluids. *Mailing Add:* 1060 Fallen Leaf Rd Arcadia CA 91006-1903

SABES, WILLIAM RUBEN, ORAL PATHOLOGY. *Current Pos:* RETIRED. *Personal Data:* b St Paul, Minn, Jan 18, 31; m 51, Evelyn Bellman; c 3. *Educ:* Univ Minn, BS & DDS, 59, MSD, 61; Am Bd Oral Path, dipl, 69. *Honors & Awards:* Award, Am Acad Dent Med, 59. *Prof Exp:* Fel, Univ Minn, 59-61; asst prof oral histopath, Sch Dent, Temple Univ, 61-63; asst prof histol & path & chmn sect, Sch Dent, Univ Detroit, 63-65, from asst prof to assoc prof histopath & diag, 65-68, chmn dept, 66-68; assoc prof, Col Dent, Univ Ky, 68-71; prof oral path & chmn dept, 71-78; prof path dept, Sch Dent, Univ Detroit, 78-91. *Concurrent Pos:* Consult, Vet Admin Hosps, Philadelphia, 61-63, Dearborn, Mich, 65-68, Lexington, Ky, 73-78, Allen Park, Mich, 78- & Mich Dent Asn Comn Cancer Control, Hosp & Inst Dent Servs, 85-86; vis prof, Sch Dent, Univ Calif, Los Angeles, 76; clin assoc prof, Dept Path Sch Med, Wayne State Univ, 79-84; coun mem, Am Acad Oral Path, 80-83; consult, Am Cancer Soc, Mich Div, Prof Educ Comm, 85-86; dent chmn, Am Asn Cancer Educ, 77-78, exec coun mem, 90-91; sec path sect, Am Asn Dent Schs, 72-73, chmn elect path sect, 73-74, chmn path sect, 74-75. *Mem:* Am Dent Asn; Am Acad Oral Path; Am Asn Cancer Educ; AAAS; Am Asn Univ Professors; Am Asn Dent Schs; fel Am Col Dentists. *Res:* Experimental carcinogenesis. *Mailing Add:* 2803 Murray Hill Pike Louisville KY 40242

SABESIN, SEYMOUR MARSHALL, INTERNAL MEDICINE, GASTROENTEROLOGY. *Current Pos:* DYRENFORTH PROF MED & CHMN DIV GASTROENTEROL, RUSH-PRESBY-ST LUKE'S MED CTR, CHICAGO, 85- *Personal Data:* b Riga, Latvia, Nov 27, 32; US citizen; m 57; c 3. *Educ:* City Col New York, BS, 54; NY Univ, MD, 58. *Honors & Awards:* Rorer Award, Am Col Gastroenterol, 70 & 71. *Prof Exp:* Clin fel exp path, Lab Path, Nat Cancer Inst, 59-61; resident internal med, New York Hosp-Cornell Med Ctr, 62-63; instr med, Harvard Med Sch, 63-65, assoc, 65-69; assoc prof med & path & dir electron micros lab, Jefferson Med Col, 69-73; prof med & dir div gastroenterol, Col Med, Univ Tenn, Memphis, 73-85. *Concurrent Pos:* Nat Inst Arthritis & Metab Dis fel, Mass Gen Hosp & Harvard Med Sch, 62-64, clin & res fel gastroenterol, 63-65; assoc investr, Metab Res Ctr, Mass Gen Hosp, 65-69; consult, Vet Admin Hosp, 69-; NIH & Am Heart Asn grants, Jefferson Med Col, 72-; mem, Gen Med A Study Sect, NIH, 78-; fel Coun Arteriosclerosis, Am Heart Asn; assoc ed, Lipids; counr, cent soc clin res, 84. *Mem:* Am Soc Cell Biol; Am Gastroenterol Asn; fel Am Col Physicians; Am Fed Clin Res; Am Heart Asn; Am Asn Study Liver Dis; fel Am Col Gastroenterol; fel Am Heart Asn Coun Arteriosclerosis. *Res:* Biochemical pathology of the liver; mechanisms of lipid transport in intestine and liver; lipoprotein metabolism; experimental liver injury. *Mailing Add:* Dept Digest Dis Rush Med Col 1725 W Harrison Suite 204 Chicago IL 60612-3864. *Fax:* 312-666-5114

SABET, TAWFIK YOUNIS, IMMUNOBIOLOGY. *Current Pos:* assoc prof, 67-72, PROF HISTOL, COL DENT, UNIV ILL MED CTR, 72- *Personal Data:* b Egypt, Nov 24, 26; nat US; m 53; c 1. *Educ:* Cairo Univ, BSc, 48, MS, 52, PhD(microbiol), 55. *Prof Exp:* Asst bacteriologist, Cairo Univ, 48-51, instr microbiol, 55-56; res assoc, Univ Ill, 57-64; NIH spec fel, 65 & 66. *Concurrent Pos:* Guest investr, US Naval Res Unit 3, 55-56; res assoc, Presby-St Luke's Hosp, Chicago, 57-64. *Mem:* AAAS; Am Soc Microbiol; Am Asn Immunol; Reticuloendothelial Soc; Sigma Xi. *Res:* Macrophage activation; macrophage phagocytosis; neutrophil function. *Mailing Add:* Dept Oral Biol M/C690 Univ Ill at Chicago 801 S Paulina St Chicago IL 60612-7213. *Fax:* 202-364-4507

SABEY, BURNS ROY, SOILS. *Current Pos:* PROF SOIL SCI, COLO STATE UNIV, 69- *Personal Data:* b Magrath, Alta, May 17, 28; m 48; c 6. *Educ:* Brigham Young Univ, BSc, 53; Iowa State Col, MS, 54, PhD, 58. *Prof Exp:* Instr soils, Iowa State Col, 54-58; from asst prof to prof soil microbiol, Univ Ill, Urbana, 58-69. *Concurrent Pos:* NSF fac fel, 67-68. *Mem:* Fel Am Soc Agron; fel Soil Sci Soc Am. *Res:* Soil microbes and their influence on plant nutrient transformations in the soil; nitrification; denitrification; ammonification; organic waste recycling on land; mine land reclamation; revegetation of oil shale retorted. *Mailing Add:* 3505 Canadian Pkwy Ft Collins CO 80524

SABHARWAL, CHAMAN LAL, MATHEMATICS, COMPUTER SCIENCE. *Current Pos:* PROF, UNIV MO, ROLLA, 85- *Personal Data:* b Ludhiana, India, Aug 15, 37; m 68, Chander; c Anup & Aman. *Educ:* Panjab Univ, India, BA, 59, MA, 61; Univ Ill, Urbana, MS, 66, PhD(math), 67. *Prof Exp:* Lectr math, D A V Col, Hoshiarpur, 61-63; teaching asst, Univ Ill, Urbana, 63-67; from asst prof to prof math, St Louis Univ, 67-83; software engr, McDonnell Douglas McAir, 83-85. *Concurrent Pos:* NSF res grant, McDonnell Douglas Lab, 79; A I grants, McDonnell Douglas Res Lab. *Mem:* Am Math Soc; Math Asn Am; Asn Comput Mach; Am Asn Artificial Intel; Inst Elec & Electronic Engrs; NY Acad Sci. *Res:* Mathematical physics; functional analysis; software engineering; algorithm development; robotics; graphics; artificial intelligence. *Mailing Add:* 5892 Chrisbrook Dr St Louis MO 63128. *Fax:* 314-516-5434; *E-Mail:* chaman@umr.edu

SABHARWAL, KULBIR, FOOD SCIENCE, TECHNOLOGY. *Current Pos:* VPRES TECH SERVS, GALAXY FOODS, ORLANDO, 91- *Personal Data:* b Punjab, India, Jan 5, 43; m 76, Karuna Puri; c Sabina & Aunish. *Educ:* Punjab Agr Univ, India, BSc, 64, MSc, 66; Ohio State Univ, MS, 69, PhD(food sci nutrit), 72. *Prof Exp:* Res asst, Ohio State Univ, 67-69, res assoc, 69-72; dir res & develop prod develop, An Amfac Co, Wapakoneta, Ohio, 72-86; food consult, 86-87, dir, Tech Serv, Gilardis Frozen Foods & Bakery, 87-90; dir, Tech Serv, Nu-Tek Foods, 90-91. *Mem:* Inst Food Technologists; Am Dairy Sci Asn; Am Cult Dairy Prod Inst; Am Chem Soc; Am Oil Chemists Soc. *Res:* Development of various cheese substitutes in addition to process cheese and cheese products; functional food ingredients of dairy and non-dairy source; improvement of pizza crust, sauce and other toppings; setting up of new cheese operation; development of low-fat, no fat, no lactose, no cholesterol dairy product alternatives. *Mailing Add:* 2441 Viscount Row Orlando FL 32809. *Fax:* 407-855-7485

SABHARWAL, PRITAM SINGH, DEVELOPMENTAL BIOLOGY. *Current Pos:* asst prof, 66-71, ASSOC PROF BOT, UNIV KY, 71- *Personal Data:* b Jehlum, Punjab, India, Apr 22, 37; US citizen; m 65; c 2. *Educ:* Univ Delhi, BSc, 57, MSc, 59, PhD(bot), 63. *Prof Exp:* Res asst bot, Univ Delhi, 59-63, asst prof, 63-64; NSF fel & res assoc, Univ Pittsburgh, 64-65 & Ind Univ, Bloomington, 65-66. *Concurrent Pos:* USDA contract, 69-72. *Mem:* AAAS; Tissue Cult Asn; Int Soc Plant Morphol; Bot Soc Am. *Res:* Control of differentiation in plants. *Mailing Add:* 604 Lakeshore Dr Lexington KY 40502

SABHARWAL, RANJIT SINGH, PURE MATHEMATICS. *Current Pos:* assoc prof, 68-74, PROF MATH, CALIF STATE UNIV, HAYWARD, 74- *Personal Data:* b Dhudial, Pakistan, Dec 11, 25; nat US; m 48; c 3. *Educ:* Sikh Nat Col, Lahore, BA, 44; Punjab Univ, India, MA, 48; Univ Calif, Berkeley, MA, 62; Wash State Univ, PhD(math), 66. *Prof Exp:* Lectr math, Khalsa Col, Bombay, 51-58; teaching asst, Univ Calif, 58-62; instr, Portland State Col, 62-63; instr, Wash State Univ, 63-66; asst prof, Kans State Univ, 66-68. *Concurrent Pos:* Trustee-secy, Sikh Found, USA. *Mem:* Am Math Soc; Math Asn Am; Sigma Xi; AAAS. *Res:* Non-Desarguesian planes. *Mailing Add:* Digital Comput Exchange Inc 2487 Indust Pkwy W Hayward CA 94540

SABIA, RAFFAELE, materials science; deceased, see previous edition for last biography

SABIDUSSI, GERT OTTO, MATHEMATICS, ALGEBRA. *Current Pos:* dir math res ctr, 71-72, PROF MATH, UNIV MONTREAL, 69- *Personal Data:* b Graz, Austria, Oct 28, 29; m 72; c 1. *Educ:* Univ Vienna, PhD, 52. *Prof Exp:* Mem, Inst Adv Study, NJ, 53-55; instr, Univ Minn, 55-56; res instr math, Tulane Univ, 56-57, asst prof, 57-60; from assoc prof to prof, McMaster Univ, 60-69. *Concurrent Pos:* Fulbright grant, 53-54. *Mem:* Can Math Soc; Sigma Xi. *Res:* Graph theory; combinatorics; automata. *Mailing Add:* Dept Math CP6128 Succ A Univ Montreal Montreal PQ H3C 3J7 Can

SABIN, JOHN ROGERS, ENERGY DEPOSITION, OSCILLATOR STRENGTH DISTRIBUTION. *Current Pos:* from assoc prof to prof physics, 77-80, PROF PHYSICS & CHEM, UNIV FLA, 80- *Personal Data:* b Springfield, Mass, Apr 29, 40; m 88, Birgit Horn; c Peter B, Amanda B, Lene E & Neils K. *Educ:* Williams Col, BA, 62; Univ NH, PhD(radiation chem), 66. *Prof Exp:* NIH fel, Quantum Chem Group, Univ Uppsala, 66-67; fel chem, Northwestern Univ, 67-68; asst prof, Univ Mo-Columbia, 68-71. *Concurrent Pos:* Assoc ed, Int J Quantum Chem, 73-; consult, Phys Sci Dir, Micom-Redstone Arsenal, 72-77; vis prof, Odense Univ, Denmark, 80-91, adj prof, 92-; ed, Adv Quantum Chem, 85-; Fulbright res scholar, Denmark, 86, 91. *Mem:* Am Chem Soc; fel Am Phys Soc; Danish Phys Soc; Danish Spectros Soc. *Res:* Energy deposition characteristics of swift, massive charged particles in materials; determination of microscopic and macroscopic properties of materials; calculational quantum mechanics of thin metal films, polymers and small molecules. *Mailing Add:* Dept Physics Univ Fla PO Box 118435 Gainesville FL 32611-8435. *Fax:* 352-392-8722; *E-Mail:* sabin@qtp.ufl.edu, jrs@dou.dk

SABIN, THOMAS DANIEL, NEUROLOGY. *Current Pos:* assoc dir, 70-75, DIR NEUROL UNIT, BOSTON CITY HOSP, 75-; PROF NEUROL & PSHTCHIAT, BOSTON UNIV, 81- *Personal Data:* b Webster, Mass, Apr 28, 36; m 58; c 3. *Educ:* Tufts Univ, BS, 58, MD, 62. *Prof Exp:* Resident neurol, Boston City Hosp, 64-66; assoc chief rehab, USPHS Hosp, Carville, La, 67-70. *Concurrent Pos:* Asst prof neurol, Tufts Univ, 70-; assoc prof, Sch Med, Boston Univ, 75-; lectr neurol, Harvard Med Sch, 75-80; consult ed, J Phys Ther, 75-80. *Mem:* AAAS; Am Acad Neurol; Soc Clin Neurologists; Int Leprosy Asn. *Res:* Clinical problems in peripheral nerve disorders; application of computerized tomography of the brain to behavioral disorders and dementia; treatment of end stage parkinsonism; pathogenesis of peripheral neuropathies. *Mailing Add:* Neurol Unit Boston City Hosp 818 Harrison Ave Boston MA 02118-2999. *Fax:* 617-534-4550; *E-Mail:* tsabin@bu.edu

SABINA, LESLIE ROBERT, VIROLOGY, MICROBIOLOGY. *Current Pos:* RETIRED. *Personal Data:* b Ft Erie, Ont, Nov 28, 28; m 55; c 2. *Educ:* Cornell Univ, AB, 52; Univ Nebr, MS, 56, PhD(microbiol), 60. *Prof Exp:* Bacteriologist, Ont Dept Health, 52-53; bacteriologist, Mt Sinai Hosp, Toronto, 53-54; asst animal path, Univ Nebr, 56-59, instr vet sci, 59-60; sr res asst virol, Connaught Med Res Labs, Toronto, 60-62, res assoc, 62-63; Upjohn Co, 64-65; from asst prof to prof virol, Univ Windsor, 65-95. *Concurrent Pos:* Registered, Nat Registry Microbiol. *Mem:* Am Soc Microbiol; Can Soc Microbiol; Can Col Microbiol. *Res:* Host-virus interactions; viral chemotherapeutics; tissue culture cell nutrition. *Mailing Add:* 2717 Longfellow Windsor ON N9E 2L1 Can

SABINS, FLOYD F, REMOTE SENSING. *Current Pos:* PRES, REMOTE SENSING ENTERPRISES INC, 82- *Personal Data:* b Houston, Tex, Jan 5, 31; m 54; c 2. *Educ:* Univ Tex, BS, 52; Yale Univ, PhD(geol), 55. *Honors & Awards:* Pecora Award, 83; Alan Gordon Award, 81. *Prof Exp:* Sr res geologist, Chevron Res Co, 55-67, sr res assoc, 67-88, sr res scientist, Chevron Oil Field Res Co, 88-92. *Concurrent Pos:* Asst prof, Calif State Col Fullerton, 65-66; adj prof, Univ Southern Calif, 66-76; regents prof, Univ Calif, Los Angeles, 75- *Mem:* Fel Geol Soc Am; Am Soc Photogram; Am Asn Petrol Geologists. *Res:* Remote sensing; sedimentary petrology; stratigraphy; structural geology. *Mailing Add:* Remote Sensing Enterprises Inc 1724 Celeste Lane Fullerton CA 92833

SABISKY, EDWARD STEPHEN, SOLID STATE PHYSICS. *Current Pos:* VPRES, IDM, 89- *Personal Data:* b Middleport, Pa, Sept 11, 32; m 55; c 2. *Educ:* Pa State Univ, BS, 56; Univ Southern Calif, MS, 59; Univ Pa, PhD(physics), 65. *Prof Exp:* Mem tech staff, Hughes Aircraft Co, 56-59; mem tech staff, RCA Res Labs, 59-80; mem staff, Solar Energy Res Inst, 80-88, sr scientist & prog mgr, 88. *Mem:* Am Phys Soc; Inst Elec & Electronics Engrs. *Res:* Spin-phonon interaction; liquid helium films; tunable phonon spectrometer; dispersion in sound velocity in liquid helium; masers; double resonance employing optical-microwave techniques; spin memory; circular dichroism in solids; paramagnetic resonance of ions in solids; atomic hydrogen maser. *Mailing Add:* 11 Carnation Pl Trenton NJ 08648

SABISTON, CHARLES BARKER, JR, MICROBIOLOGY, DENTISTRY. *Current Pos:* from assoc prof to prof periodont, 72-87, PROF FAMILY DENT, COL DENT, UNIV IOWA, 87- *Personal Data:* b Wake Forest, NC, July 22, 33; m 59; c 2. *Educ:* Wake Forest Univ, BS, 53; Univ NC, DDS, 57; Va Commonwealth Univ, PhD(microbiol), 68; Univ Iowa, cert periodont, 75. *Prof Exp:* Pvt pract dent, NC, 60-64; Nat Inst Dent Res fel & Dent Res Training Prog fel, Va Commonwealth Univ, 64-67, assoc prof periodont, Med Col Va, 67-72. *Concurrent Pos:* Nat Inst Dent res grants, Va Commonwealth Univ, 71-72 & Col Dent, Univ Iowa, 72-78, consult, coun therapeut, Am Dent Asn, 71-89; consult, J Am Dent Asn, 78-89. *Mem:* Am Soc Microbiol; Am Dent Asn; Int Asn Dent Res; Am Asn Dent Res; Am Acad Periodont. *Res:* Microbial factors in periodontal disease etiology; non-sporing anaerobic bacteria; clinical dental microbiology; dentinal hypersensitivity. *Mailing Add:* 107 Potomac Dr Iowa City IA 52245

SABISTON, DAVID COSTON, JR, GENERAL SURGERY, CARDIOTHORACIC SURGERY. *Current Pos:* prof & chmn dept, 64-96, JAMES B DUKE PROF SURG, MED CTR, DUKE UNIV, 96- *Personal Data:* b Jacksonville, NC, Oct 4, 24; m 55; c 3. *Educ:* Univ NC, BS, 43; Johns Hopkins Univ, MD, 47. *Honors & Awards:* Sci Councils' Distinguished Achievement Award, Am Heart Asn, 83; Michael E DeBakey Award for Outstanding Achievement, 84; Col Medalist, Am Col Chest Physicians, 87. *Prof Exp:* Intern surg, Johns Hopkins Hosp, 47-48, asst surg, Johns Hopkins Univ, 48-49, Cushing fel, 49-50, from asst to assoc prof surg, 55-59, prof, 64. *Concurrent Pos:* Investr, Howard Hughes Med Inst, 55-61; NIH res career award, 62-64; consult, NIH & Womack Army Hosp; chmn, Surg Study sect, NIH, 70-72; ed, Annals Surg, co-ed, Surg Chest; chmn, Am Bd Surg, 71-72; chmn, Accreditation Coun Grad Med Educ, 85-86. *Mem:* Inst Med-Nat Acad Sci; Am Asn Thoracic Surgeons (pres, 84-85); Am Col Surg (pres, 85-86); Soc Univ Surg (pres, 68-69); Am Surg Asn (pres, 77-78); Soc Surg Chmn (pres, 74-76). *Res:* General and cardiovascular surgery; basic physiology of coronary blood flow and myocardial metabolism; clinical revascularization of myocardium; congenital heart surgery. *Mailing Add:* Dept Surg Duke Univ Med Ctr MSRB-475 Research Dr Durham NC 27710

SABLATASH, MIKE, COMMUNICATIONS & INFORMATION THEORY & APPLICATIONS. *Current Pos:* SR RES SCIENTIST, COMPUT COMMUN IMAGE PROCESSING DIGITAL COMMUN & INFO TECHNOL, DEPT COMMUN & COMMUN RES CENT, 76- *Personal Data:* b Bienfait, Sask, Sept 30, 35; m 61; c Tania D, Lisa G (Dillon). *Educ:* Univ Man, BScEng, 57, MSc, 64; Univ Wis-Madison, PhD(elec eng), 68. *Prof Exp:* Commun engr, Sask Power Corp, 57; mem common sci staff, Res & Develop Labs, Northern Elec Co, 61-65; asst prof elec eng, Univ Toronto, 68-72; statistician V, Energy Bd Can, 72-76. *Concurrent Pos:* Lab demonstr, Univ Man, 57-60, res asst, 58-59; lectr, Univ Ottawa, 64-65; teaching asst, Univ Wis, 65-68; consult, Consociates Ltd, 68-72; Nat Res Coun grant, Univ Toronto, 68-72; adj prof, Carleton Univ, 79; sci info technol adv, Commun res Ctr, Dept Commun, Govt Can, 80-; guest prof, Univ Man, 81, Tokyo Inst Technol. *Mem:* Sigma Xi; Inst Elec & Electronics Engrs; sr mem Can Soc Elec Comput Eng; Asn Prof Engrs Ont. *Res:* Communication signals, networks and systems and their optimal design; statistical communication and information theory; mathematical programming, functional analysis; computer communications in information systems and technology; high definition television; wavelet tehory and applications; error-correcting; modulation and adaptive equalization for transmission of high-definition television and digital radio broadcasts. *Mailing Add:* 23 A Bertona St Nepean ON K2G 4G6 Can. *Fax:* 613-998-2433; *E-Mail:* mike@dgbt.doc.ca

SABLE, EDWARD GEORGE, STRUCTURAL GEOLOGY, STRATIGRAPHY-SEDIMENTATION. *Current Pos:* Geologist petrol explor, 48-56, geologist mineral explor, 57-81, GEOLOGIST FRAMEWORK MAPPING, US GEOL SURV, 81-, EMER GEOLOGIST. *Personal Data:* b Rockford, Ill, Dec 12, 24; m 54; c 2. *Educ:* Univ Minn, BA, 48; Univ Mich, MS, 59, PhD, 65. *Honors & Awards:* Case Mem Award, Univ Mich, 59; Meritorious Serv Award, Dept Interior, 87. *Concurrent Pos:* Instr, Univ Ky, Elizabethtown, 65-66. *Mem:* AAAS; Geol Soc Am; Arctic Inst NAm. *Res:* Mesozoic and Paleozoic stratigraphy and structural and economic geology of Arctic Alaska; tectonics of arctic regions; petroleum exploration of Alaska; granite emplacement; regional Mississippian stratigraphy of Eastern Interior Basin, United States; coordination of Devonian stratigraphic data; petroleum source rock studies; oil and gas appraisal; precambrian of southern Arabian shield; stratigraphy and structure of southern Utah; coal, north slope of Alaska. *Mailing Add:* US Geol Surv Box 25046 Denver Fed Ctr Lakewood CO 80225

SABLIK, MARTIN J, MAGNETIC PROPERTIES OF MATERIALS, COMPUTER MODELING IN APPLIED PHYSICS. *Current Pos:* sr res scientist, 80-87, STAFF SCIENTIST, SW RES INST, SAN ANTONIO, TEX, 87- *Personal Data:* b Brooklyn, NY, Oct 21, 39; m 65, Beverly; c Jeanne, Karen, Marjorie & Larry. *Educ:* Cornell Univ, BA, 60; Univ Ky, MS, 65; Fordham Univ, PhD(theoret solid state physics), 72. *Honors & Awards:* Imagineer Award, Mind Sci Found, 89. *Prof Exp:* Jr engr, Martin Co, Orlando, Fla, 62-63; instr physics, Univ Ky, Lexington, 63-65; from assoc, Fairleigh Dickinson Univ, Teaneck, NJ, 65-67; from instr to assoc prof, 67-80. *Concurrent Pos:* Mem adv comt, Conf Properties & Applications of Magnetic Mat, 90-; local chmn, 1995 Intermag Conf, 93-; interim exec bd mem topical group on magnetism & appln, Am Phys Soc, 96- *Mem:* Am Phys Soc; Am Soc Nondestructive Testing; Inst Elec & Electronics Engrs; Am Asn Physics Teachers; Am Geophys Union. *Res:* Magnetism-modeling effects of stress and microstructure on hysteresis of magnetic properties for use in nondestructive evaluation; space science-computer simulation of electrostatic analyzers; geophysics-electrical resistance tomographic imaging; superconductivity-melt processing of ceramic superconductors; nondestructive evaluation-modeling for electromagnetic characterization of defects; acoustics-statistical energy analysis of structure-borne sound; condensed matter theory-rare earth physics; quadrupolar excitations and aspherical coulomb scattering; Monte Carlo simulations of phase transitions. *Mailing Add:* SW Res Inst PO Drawer 28510 San Antonio TX 78228-0510. *E-Mail:* msablik@swri.edu

SABLOFF, JEREMY ARAC, ARCHAEOLOGY. *Current Pos:* CHARLES K WILLIAMS II DIR, UNIV PA MUS ARCHAEOL & ANTHROP, 94- *Personal Data:* b New York, NY, Apr 16, 44; m 68, Paula L Weinberg; c Joshua & Saralinda. *Educ:* Univ Pa, BA, 64; Harvard Univ, MA, PhD, 69. *Hon Degrees:* MA, Univ Pa, 94. *Prof Exp:* From asst prof to assoc prof, Harvard Univ, 69-76; assoc prof anthrop, Univ Utah, 76-77; prof anthrop, Univ NMex, 78-86, chmn dept, 80-83; chmn, Dept Anthrop, Univ Pittsburgh, 90-92, prof anthrop, hist & philos sci, 86-94. *Concurrent Pos:* Nat Geog Soc grant, 72-74, NSF grant, 83-88, NEH grant, 90-91; curator anthrop, Utah Mus Nat Hist, Salt Lake City, 76-77; sr fel, Pre-Columbian Studies, Dumbarton Oaks, 86-92, chmn, 89-92; res asn, Carnegie Mus Nat Hist, 87-; fel, Ctr Philos Sci, Univ Pittsburgh, 87-, chancellor's distinguished res award, 93. *Mem:* Nat Acad Sci; fel AAAS; fel Royal Anthrop Inst; fel Soc Antiq London; Soc Am Archaeol (pres, 89-91); Am Philol Soc; Sigma Xi; Am Anthrop Asn. *Res:* Ancient Maya civilization; development of pre-industrial civilizations; rise of early cities; history of archaeological theory and method. *Mailing Add:* Univ Pa Mus Archaeol & Anthrop 33rd & Spruce Sts Philadelphia PA 19104-6324

SABNIS, ANANT GOVIND, ELECTRONICS, SOLID STATE PHYSICS. *Current Pos:* MEM STAFF, BELL LABS, 80- *Personal Data:* b Chandgad, India, Feb 22, 44; m 73; c 1. *Educ:* Univ Bombay, BE, 65; SDak Sch Mines & Technol, MS, 71, PhD(elec eng), 74. *Prof Exp:* Elec engr elec mach, Cropton-Greaves Ltd, Bombay, 65-66; lectr elec eng, Shri Bhagubhai Mafatlal Polytech, Bombay, 66-69; vis asst prof elec eng, Univ Pittsburgh, 74-75, asst prof, 75-80. *Mem:* Inst Elec & Electronics Engrs; Sigma Xi. *Res:* Solid state device physics; thin-films; integrated circuits design and modeling; material characterization. *Mailing Add:* AT&T Bell Labs 555 Union Blvd Allentown PA 18103

SABNIS, GAJANAN MAHADEO, STRUCTURAL ENGINEERING, REHABILITATION ENGINEERING. *Current Pos:* assoc prof, 74-80, PROF CIVIL ENG, HOWARD UNIV, 80- *Personal Data:* b Belgaum, India, June 11, 41; nat US; m 69, Sharda; c Rahul & Madhavi. *Educ:* Univ Bombay, BE, 61; Indian Inst Technol, Bombay, MTech, 63; Cornell Univ, PhD(struct eng), 67. *Prof Exp:* Res assoc struct eng, Cornell Univ, 67, fel, Univ Pa, 68; res engr, Am Cement Corp, Calif, 68-69; eng supvr, Bechtel Power Corp, 70-74. *Concurrent Pos:* Consult engr, Bombay, 63-64; consult, Technol Transfer Consults, Inc; pres, KC Eng, PC, 83- *Mem:* Fel Am Concrete Inst; Am Soc Civil Engrs; Am Soc Eng Educ; Soc Exp Stress Anal; Inst Engrs India. *Res:* Structural models, shear strength of concrete slabs; deflection of structures; properties of concretes; nuclear power plants; structural failure investigations; ferrocement; rehabilitation of bridges and buildings. *Mailing Add:* 13721 Townline Rd Silver Spring MD 20906. *Fax:* 301-460-7756

SABNIS, SUMAN T, CHEMICAL ENGINEERING, STATISTICS. *Current Pos:* OWNER, KSS ASSOCS, 88- *Personal Data:* b Rajkot, India, Nov 27, 35; US citizen; m 60, Vasumati Kulkarni; c Samir, Sushil & Kalpana. *Educ:* Christ Church Col, India, BSc, 54; Harcourt Butler Tech Inst, BS, 57; Lehigh Univ, MS, 60, PhD(chem eng), 67; Rutgers Univ, MS, 64. *Prof Exp:* Chem engr, Union Carbide Plastics Co, NJ, 60-63; sr chem engr, Monsanto Co, 66-68, group leader, Kinetics Polymer Systs, 68-74; mgr mat res & develop, Kerite Co, Harvey Hubbell Inc, 74-76, mgr process eng, 76-81; vpres eng, Laribee Wire Mfg Co, Inc, 81-84, vpres, Eng Sales, 84-88. *Mem:* Am Inst Chem Engrs; Am Chem Soc; Inst Elec & Electronics Engrs; Soc Plastics Engrs; Sigma Xi. *Res:* Mixing studies in polymeric systems, kinetics of polymer systems, statistics and process development in area of polymers; compounding of rubber and plastic compounds; vulcanization techniques for insulated wire and cable. *Mailing Add:* 843 Garden Rd Orange CT 06477-1513

SABO, JULIUS JAY, ENVIRONMENTAL ENGINEERING, POLLUTION CONTROL. *Current Pos:* CONSULT ENGR HAZARDOUS WASTE CONTROL, 80- *Personal Data:* b Cleveland, Ohio, May 27, 21; m 48; c 2. *Educ:* Fenn Col, BME, 48; Univ Colo, MPA, 81. *Prof Exp:* Chem engr, Repub Steel Corp, 48-52; consult engr, Reserve Mining Co, 52-55; develop engr, Gen Elec Co, 55-58; chief monitoring, Reactor Testing Sta, US Pub Health Serv, Idaho, 58-60, chief nuclear anal, 60-64, asst chief res grants, Div Radiol Health, 65-67, chief res grants prog & exec secy radiol health study sect, 67-69; dir off grants admin, Environ Control Admin, 69-71; grants info off, Environ Protection Agency, 71-75; mem fac, Colo Tech Col, 78-79. *Concurrent Pos:* Tech chmn, Non Conventional Energy Resources Comt & Conf, 75-77; mgr dir, Analysis Non Conventional Energy Resources. *Mem:* Am Acad Environ Engrs; fel Royal Soc Health. *Res:* Environmental aspects of developing non-conventional energy resources. *Mailing Add:* 6935 Blackhawk Pl Colorado Springs CO 80919

SABOL, GEORGE PAUL, NUCLEAR MATERIALS. *Current Pos:* sr engr phys metall, Westinghouse Res & Develop Ctr, 67-72, fel engr, 72-76, adv engr, 76, mgr mat applications, 87-91, MGR CORE MAT DEVELOP NUCLEAR MAT, WESTINGHOUSE RES & DEVELOP CTR, 76-94, MGR DEVELOP PROG, 94-, CONSULT ENGR, WESTINGHOUSE, 91- *Personal Data:* b Clairton, Pa, Oct 17, 39; m 63; c 4. *Educ:* Pa State Univ, BS, 61; Carnegie Inst Technol, MS, 64, PhD(mat sci), 67. *Prof Exp:* Engr superalloy res & develop, Colwell Res Ctr, TRW Inc, 65-67. *Mem:* Am Soc Metals; Am Inst Mining & Metall Engrs; Am Nuclear Soc. *Res:* Processing, corrosion response and mechanical behavior of zirconium-based alloys; performance of nuclear fuel in light water reactors; physical metallurgy of nickel-based superalloys. *Mailing Add:* Westinghouse PO Box 355 Pittsburgh PA 15230

SABOL, STEVEN LAYNE, BIOCHEMISTRY. *Current Pos:* sr staff fel, 77-79, SR INVESTR, LAB BIOCHEM GENETICS, NAT HEART LUNG & BLOOD INST, NIH, 79- *Personal Data:* b Phoenix, Ariz, Sept 21, 44; m 95; c 1. *Educ:* Yale Col, BS, 66; NY Univ, MD & PhD(biochem), 73. *Prof Exp:* Intern med, Duke Univ Med Ctr, 73-74, res assoc, 74-77. *Mem:* Am Soc Biochem & Molecular Biol; Soc Neurosci; Am Soc Neurochem. *Res:* Protein and peptide biosynthesis; regulation of gene expression in the nervous system; apoptosis. *Mailing Add:* NIH Bldg 36 Rm 1C-06 Bethesda MD 20892. *Fax:* 301-402-0270; *E-Mail:* sabol@codon.nih.gov

SABOUNGI, MARIE-LOUISE JEAN, PHYSICAL CHEMISTRY, PHYSICS. *Current Pos:* CHEMIST, CHEM TECH DIV, ARGONNE NAT LAB, 73- *Personal Data:* b Tripoli, Lebanon, Jan 1, 48; m 76, 89; c 2. *Educ:* Univ Aix, Marseilles, France, PhD(thermodyn), 73. *Mem:* Electrochem Soc; AAAS. *Res:* Molten salt chemistry; alloy thermodynamics; statistical mechanics; electrochemistry. *Mailing Add:* 5492 S Everett Ave Chicago IL 60615. *Fax:* 630-252-7777

SABOUR, MOHAMMAD PARVIZ, BIOTECHNOLOGY, ANIMAL BREEDING & GENETICS. *Current Pos:* RES SCIENTIST CELL & MOLECULAR BIOL, CTR FOOD & ANIMAL RES, AGR & AGRI-FOOD, CAN, 84- *Personal Data:* b Bakharz, Iran, Apr 24, 36; c 3. *Educ:* Utah State Univ, BSc, 63; Univ Calif, Berkeley, PhD(genetics), 69. *Prof Exp:* Res geneticist, Univ Calif, Berkeley, 69-70; prof genetics, Nat Univ Iran, 70-72, Univ Tehran, 72-80; prof genetics & cell biol, Bishop Univ, 81-82; res scientist cell biol, Carleton Univ, 82-83, Atomic Energy Can Lab, 83-84. *Concurrent Pos:* Adj grad adv, Univ Guelph, 90-94, McGill Univ, 94-96; secy & chairperson, Expert Comt Animal Breeding & Reproduction, Can Agr Res Coun, 92-96. *Mem:* Genetics Soc Am; Genetics Soc Can; Am Soc Cell Biol; AAAS; Int Mammalian Genome Soc; Int Soc Animal Genetics. *Res:* Molecular cytogenetics of mealybugs; DNA repair in human cells; molecular genetics of endogenous viral genes in chicken; molecular genetics of quantitative traits; genetics and molecular genetics of reproductive longevity in mice. *Mailing Add:* Ctr Food & Animal Res Bldg 20 Agr & Agri Food Can Ottawa ON K1A 0C6 Can. *E-Mail:* sabourp@em.agr.ca

SABOURIN, THOMAS DONALD, PRODUCT REGISTRATION. *Current Pos:* VPRES, PRO-2-SERVE. *Personal Data:* b Bay City, Mich, May 31, 51; m 74. *Educ:* Univ Mich, BA, 73; Calif State Univ, MA, 77; La State Univ, PhD(physiol), 81. *Prof Exp:* Anal chemist, Sel Rex Div Occidental Petrol, 73-75; teaching asst physiol, Calif State Univ, Hayward, 75-76; teaching asst biol, physiol & marine, La State Univ, 78-80; Nat Inst Environ Health Sci fel, Environ Health Sci Ctr, Ore State Univ, 81-82; res scientist, Battelle Columbus Opers, 82-85, prin res scientist, 85-88, mgr, Agr Chem Projs, 88-89, vpres, chem regist, 89- *Concurrent Pos:* Prin investr, Sigma Xi grant, 80-81, Lerner Fund Marine Res grant, 80-82 & alternatives toxicity testing, 82-88; consult, Browning & Ferris Industs, 80-81; adj asst prof zool, Ohio State Univ, 86- *Mem:* Sigma Xi; AAAS; Am Soc Testing & Mat; Soc Toxicol; Soc Environ Toxicol & Chem. *Res:* Development, validation and implementation of test systems with nonmammalian organisms for use in screening and monitoring potential adverse effects of environmental agents to humans; environmental physiology. *Mailing Add:* Pro-2-Serve 14255 US Hwy I Juno Beach FL 33408

SABOURN, ROBERT JOSEPH EDMOND, GEOLOGY. *Current Pos:* CONSULT, 88- *Personal Data:* b Sturgeon Falls, Ont, July 6, 26; m 53; c 2. *Educ:* Univ Ottawa, BSc, 47; Laval Univ, BAppSc, 51, MSc, 52, DSc(geol), 55. *Prof Exp:* From asst prof to prof, Laval Univ, 55-77, chmn dept geol & mineral, 65-71. *Concurrent Pos:* Mem, AID Proj, Senegal, WAfrica, 63. *Mem:* Geol Soc Am; fel Geol Asn Can; Can Inst Mining & Metall. *Res:* Engineering, field and areal geology; geomorphology. *Mailing Add:* 1914 Bourbonniere Sillery PQ G1S 1N4 Can

SABROSKY, CURTIS WILLIAMS, ENTOMOLOGY, TAXONOMY. *Current Pos:* entomologist, Entom & Plant Quarantine, USDA, 46-53 & Entom Res Br, 53-67, Dir syst entom lab, 67-73, res entomologist, 73-80, COOP SCIENTIST, USDA, 80- *Personal Data:* b Sturgis, Mich, Apr 3, 10; wid; c Alan N. *Educ:* Kalamazoo Col, AB, 31; Kans State Univ, MS, 33. *Hon Degrees:* ScD, Kalamazoo Col, 66. *Honors & Awards:* Distinguished Serv Award, Kans State Univ, 65; Superior Serv Award, USDA, 62, Distinguished Serv Award, 80. *Prof Exp:* From instr to asst prof entom, Mich State Univ, 36-45. *Concurrent Pos:* Mem, Int Comn Zool Nomenclature, 63-85, pres, 77-83; mem permanent comt, Int Cong Entom, 60-80; pres & chmn orgn comt, XV Int Cong Entom, 73-76. *Mem:* AAAS; hon mem Entom Soc Am (pres, 69); Soc Syst Zool (pres, 62); hon fel Entom Soc Can; hon foreign mem Entom Soc USSR; hon mem Int Cong Entom; hon pres Entom Soc Washington. *Res:* Taxonomy of higher flies; problems of zoological nomenclature. *Mailing Add:* 205 Medford Leas Medford NJ 08055-2236

SABRY, ZAKARIA I, NUTRITION, BIOCHEMISTRY. *Current Pos:* PROF PUB HEALTH, UNIV CALIF, BERKELEY, 84- *Personal Data:* b Tanta, Egypt, Aug 16, 32; Can citizen; m 56; c 2. *Educ:* Univ Ain Shams, Cairo, BSc, 52; Univ Mass, MSc, 54; Pa State Univ, PhD(biochem), 57. *Prof Exp:* From asst prof to assoc prof food technol & nutrit, Am Univ Beirut, 57-64; head dept, 61-64; from assoc prof to prof nutrit, Univ Toronto, 64-72; pres, Nutrit Res Consults, Inc, 74-79; dir food policy & nutrit div, Food & Agr Orgn, UN, 79-84. *Concurrent Pos:* Nat Res Coun Can fel, 61-62; nat coordr, Nutrit Can, Health Protect Br, Can Dept Health & Welfare, 69-74; prof appl human nutrit, Univ Guelph, 76-79. *Mem:* Am Inst Nutrit; AAAS; Soc Nutrit Educ; Sigma Xi. *Res:* Relationships of diet and disease; development of risk factors of coronary heart disease and cancer; nutrition survey; assessment of nutritional status in man. *Mailing Add:* 421 Warren Hall Univ Calif Berkeley CA 94720-0001. *Fax:* 510-643-6981

SABSHIN, MELVIN, PSYCHIATRY. *Current Pos:* MED DIR, AM PSYCHIAT ASN, 74- *Personal Data:* b New York, NY, Oct 28, 25; m 55; c 1. *Educ:* Univ Fla, BS, 44; Tulane Univ, MD, 48. *Honors & Awards:* Distinguished Serv Award, Am Psychiat Asn, 86, Admin Psychiat Award, 88; Salmon Award, NY Acad Sci, 96. *Prof Exp:* Resident psychiat, Tulane Univ, 49-52; res psychiatrist, Psychosom & Psychiat Inst, Michael Reese Hosp, 53-55, asst dir, 55-57, assoc dir, 57-61; prof psychiat & head dept, Col Med, Univ Ill, 61-74. *Concurrent Pos:* Fel, Ctr Advan Study Behav Sci, 67-68; assoc ed, Am J Psychiat, 71-74; actg dean, Abraham Lincoln Sch Med, Univ Ill, 73-74. *Mem:* AAAS; Am Col Psychiat (pres, 73-74); Am Psychiat Asn; AMA; Am Psychosom Soc; Group Advan Psychiat; World Psychiat Asn (treas, 93-96). *Res:* Social psychiatry; empirical studies of adaptive behavior. *Mailing Add:* 1400 K St NW Washington DC 20005

SABY, JOHN SANFORD, PHYSICS, TECHNICAL MANAGEMENT. *Current Pos:* res physicist, Electronics Lab, Gen Elec Co, 51-52, supvr semiconductor components develop, 52-55, mgr, Semiconductor & Solid State, 55-56, Lamp Res Lab, 56-71, Lamp Phenomena Res Lab, 71-82, CONSULT, GEN ELEC CO, 82- *Personal Data:* b Ithaca, NY, Mar 21, 21; m 45, Mary E Long; c Arthur, Thomas, Jean & Joe. *Educ:* Gettysburg Col, AB, 42; Pa State Univ, MS, 44, PhD(physics), 47. *Hon Degrees:* ScD, Gettysburg Col, 69. *Honors & Awards:* Centennial Award, Inst Elec & Electronics Engrs, 87. *Prof Exp:* Lab instr physics, Gettysburg Col, 40-42; asst, Pa State Univ, 42-47; instr, Cornell Univ, 47-50. *Mem:* Am Phys Soc; fel Inst Elec & Electronics Engrs; Sigma Xi. *Res:* X-ray liquid diffraction; atmospheric ultrasonics; wave mechanics of interacting particles; x-ray solid state; p-n-p transistor; p-n junction studies; power transistors; luminescence; electroluminescence; gas discharge physics; electron emission; antiquarian horology. *Mailing Add:* 8 Tamarac Terr Hendersonville NC 28791

SACCO, ANTHONY G, IMMUNO-REPRODUCTION. *Current Pos:* from asst prof to assoc prof, 74-85, PROF, DEPTS OBSTET, GYNEC, IMMUNOL & MICROBIOL, SCH MED, WAYNE STATE UNIV, 85- *Personal Data:* b Utica, NY, Nov 2, 44; m 67; c 2. *Educ:* Univ Rochester, BA, 66; Univ Tenn, MS, 68, PhD(zool), 71. *Prof Exp:* Res assoc, Inst Cancer Res, 72-74. *Concurrent Pos:* Non-clin assoc, Dept Path, Hutzel Hosp, Wayne State Univ, 75- & co-dir, in vitro fertil prog, 83- *Mem:* Soc Study Reprod; Sigma Xi; Am Fertil Soc. *Res:* Immuno-reproduction: antigenic properties and possible reproductive roles of antigens present in female and male reproductive tissues, tract secretions, and ova and sperm; fertility control: immunocontraception; mammalian reproductive biology: sperm-egg/ova interaction and recognition during the fertilization process. *Mailing Add:* 1682 Hallmark Dr Troy MI 48098-4349

SACCO, LOUIS JOSEPH, JR, ORGANIC CHEMISTRY. *Current Pos:* process res chemist & sr res asst, 58-70, tech counr, 70-72, process res chemist & sr res asst, 73-75, supvr, Process Improv Lab, 75-80, SUPVR SAFETY, TRAINING & WASTE MGT, G D SEARLE & CO, 81- *Personal Data:* b Chicago, Ill, Mar 24, 24; m 51; c 5. *Educ:* DePaul Univ, ScB, 48, ScM, 50. *Prof Exp:* Res chemist, Baxter Lab, Inc, 50-56 & Nalco Chem Co, 56-57; res & develop chemist, Alkydol Lab, Inc, 57-58. *Concurrent Pos:* Lectr, Chicago City Jr Col, 65-70 & DePaul Univ, 69-71 & 78-81. *Mem:* Am Chem Soc. *Res:* Amino acids; carbohydrate chemistry; fatty acids; steroids; prostaglandins. *Mailing Add:* 3348 N Panama Ave Chicago IL 60634

SACCOMAN, FRANK (MICHAEL), ANATOMY, ZOOLOGY. *Current Pos:* RETIRED. *Personal Data:* b Hibbing, Minn, July 31, 31; c 4. *Educ:* Bemidji State Col, BS, 58; Univ Minn, PhD(anat), 64. *Prof Exp:* Instr anat, Univ Mich, 64-66; from asst prof to prof biol, Div Sci & Math, Bemidji State Univ, 66-80, chmn dept, 66-80, dean, 80-90. *Concurrent Pos:* NSF fel, Univ Minn, 70. *Res:* Radioautographic studies of developing extraembryonic membranes in the mouse; cellular migration in developing extraembryonic membranes with the use of radioautography; DNA synthesis in freshwater algae. *Mailing Add:* 4227 Waville Rd E Bemidji MN 56601

SACCOMAN, JOHN JOSEPH, MATHEMATICAL ANALYSIS, HISTORY OF MATHEMATICS. *Current Pos:* From instr to asst prof, 61-81, ASSOC PROF MATH, SETON HALL UNIV, 81- *Personal Data:* b Paterson, NJ, Sept 10, 39; m 63; c 2. *Educ:* Seton Hall Univ, BS, 60; NY Univ, MS, 62, PhD(math educ), 74. *Mem:* Am Math Soc; Math Asn Am. *Res:* Development of a set of normability conditions for topological vector spaces using a generalized Hahn-Banach theorem; applications of non-standard analysis to functional analysis; historical aspects of the Hahn Banach theorem; historical aspects of Krein-Milman theorem; historical aspects of functional analysis and topological vector spaces, eg, origin of weak convergence and the Banach-Alaogu theorem; precursors of the Krein-Rutman theorem; origin and ramifications of the Banach-Saks property; rearrangements of series in banach spaces; basic sequences. *Mailing Add:* Dept Math & Comput Sci Seton Hall Univ South Orange NJ 07079-2687. *E-Mail:* saccomjj@lawmail.shu.edu

SACHAN, DILEEP SINGH, NUTRITIONAL BIOCHEMISTRY, MICROBIOLOGY. *Current Pos:* assoc prof, 79-87, PROF NUTRIT & BIOCHEM, DEPT NUTRIT, UNIV TENN, KNOXVILLE, 87-, DIR, NUTRIT INST, 93- *Personal Data:* b Makhauli, India, Dec 18, 38; US citizen; m 68, Cheryl L Hill; c Rashmi, Ravi & Vinay. *Educ:* M P Vet Col, India, BVSc, 61, MVSc, 63; Univ Ill, Urbana, MS, 66, PhD(nutrit), 68. *Prof Exp:* Lectr obstet & gynec, M P Vet Col, India, 63-64; res asst nutrit, Univ Ill, Urbana, 64-69; res assoc pharmacol & microbiol, Case Western Reserve Univ, 69-71; asst prof pharmacol, Meharry Med Col, 71-76; res chemist, Vet Admin Hosp, 76-78; fel nutrit & gastroenterol, Vanderbilt Univ Med Ctr, Nashville, 78-79. *Concurrent Pos:* NIH fel, Case Western Res Univ, 69-71; consult clin path, Vet Admin Hosp, 78-80; prin investr res grants, NSF, NIH, USDA & AID. *Mem:* Am Inst Nutrit; NY Acad Sci; Am Col Nutrit; AAAS; Biochem Pharmacol; Am Soc Clin Nutrit. *Res:* Nutrient-nutrient and nutrient-drug interactions; lipid metabolism; carnitine nutriture; bioavailability of vitamins; nutritional supplements. *Mailing Add:* Dept Nutrit Col Human Ecol Univ Tenn Knoxville TN 37996-1900. *Fax:* 423-974-3491; *E-Mail:* dsachan@utkux.utcc.utk.edu

SACHDEV, GOVERDHAN PAL, BIOCHEMISTRY, BIO-ORGANIC CHEMISTRY. *Current Pos:* ASSOC RES PROF, COL PHARM, UNIV OKLA HSC, 84- *Personal Data:* b Lahore, India, July 17, 41; m 68; c 2. *Educ:* Univ Delhi, BSc, 61, MSc, 63, PhD(chem), 67. *Honors & Awards:* Eason Award, Eason Oil Co-Okla Geol Soc, 78. *Prof Exp:* Lectr chem, Ramjas Col, Univ Delhi, 63-64; res fel, Univ Delhi, 64-67, sr res fel, 67-68; res assoc biochem, Yale Univ, 68-75; asst mem, Okla Med Res Found, 76-84. *Mem:* Am Chem Soc; AAAS; Sigma Xi; Soc Complex Carbohydrates; Am Asn Col Pharm. *Res:* Structure and function of biological membrane-bound enzymes; role of glycoproteins and proteins in obstructive pulmonary diseases. *Mailing Add:* Col Pharm Univ Okla Health Sci Ctr PO Box 26901 Oklahoma City OK 73126-0901

SACHDEV, OM PRAKASH, CLINICAL RESEARCH, ONCOLOGY. *Current Pos:* DIR, NON-DERMAT RES & DEVELOP, CHEMEX PHARMACEUT, 92- *Personal Data:* b Allahabad, India, May 15, 49; US citizen; m 74, Chander P Lulla; c Bindu & Nina. *Educ:* Allahabad Univ, BSc, 69, MSc, 71; Howard Univ, PhD(biochem), 80. *Prof Exp:* Sr anal biochemist, Lederele Labs, Am Cyanamid Co, 84-88, clin res scientist, Med Res Div, 89-92. *Concurrent Pos:* Lectr biochem, Govt Med Col, Jabalpur, India, 71-74. *Mem:* Am Asn Pharmaceut Scientists; fel Am Inst Chemists; NY Acad Sci. *Res:* Cardiovascular, oncology and virology; numerous publication in peer reviewed journals; preclinical and clinical aspects of drug development (pharmaceuticals, biologicals and biopharmaceuticals). *Mailing Add:* 4 Candlewood Ct New City NY 10956-2712. *Fax:* 201-944-9474

SACHDEV, SHAM L, CHEMISTRY. *Current Pos:* MEM STAFF, ENV HEALTH SERV, 78- *Personal Data:* b Hoshiarpur, India, Dec 21, 37; m 67; c 2. *Educ:* Panjab Univ, India, BS, 59, MS, 60; La State Univ, PhD(chem), 66; Am Bd Indust Hyg, cert; Int Hazard Control Cert Bd, Hazard Control Mgr. *Prof Exp:* Vis res assoc chem, La State Univ, 65-66, vis asst prof, 66-70; anal specialist, Kem-Tech Labs, Inc, 70-74, mgr methods & develop, 74-78. *Concurrent Pos:* USPHS fel, La State Univ, 65-67, Air Pollution Control Admin fel, 68-69, NSF fel, 69-70. *Mem:* AAAS; Am Chem Soc; Air Pollution Control Asn. *Res:* Determination and significance of trace elements in environmental samples such as air, water, food and others; study of trace elements in the environment. *Mailing Add:* Entek Labs Inc 14285 Airline Hwy Baton Rouge LA 70817-6232

SACHDEV, SUBIR, PHYSICS. *Current Pos:* asst prof, 87-89, ASSOC PROF PHYSICS, YALE UNIV, 89- *Personal Data:* b New Delhi, India, Dec 2, 61; m 85; c 1. *Educ:* Mass Inst Technol, Cambridge, SB, 82; Harvard Univ, MS, 84, PhD(physics), 85. *Prof Exp:* Postdoctoral fel, AT&T Bell Labs, Murray Hill, 85-87. *Mem:* Am Phys Soc. *Res:* Theory of strongly correlated electronic systems with applications to superconductors, semiconductors and magnetism. *Mailing Add:* Dept Physics Yale Univ PO Box 208120 New Haven CT 06520

SACHDEV, SURESH, SEMICONDUCTOR PROCESS DEVELOPMENT, CHEMICAL VAPOR DEPOSITION & THIN FILMS. *Current Pos:* prog mgr/sr engr thin films & engr, CVD technol develop, Intel Corp, Livermore, Calif, 80-84, prog mgr technol develop, Santa Clara, Calif, 85-90, mfg mgr programmable logic oper, Folsom, Calif, 90-91, MFG INTEGRATION MGR, TECHNOL & DEVELOP, INTEL CORP, SANTA CLARA, CALIF, 91- *Personal Data:* b New Delhi, India, Sept 17, 54; m 80; c 2. *Educ:* Inst Technol, Banaras Hindu Univ, Varanasi, India, BTech Hon, 76; Univ Ill, MS, 80; Univ Calif, Berkeley, cert, 89. *Prof Exp:* Prod develop engr super refractories, Carborundum Universal, Madras, India, 76-77; res & teaching asst elec ceramics & glass, Univ Ill, Urbana, 78-80; dir applications & develop, Genus Inc, Mountain View, Calif, 84-85. *Mem:* Inst Elec & Electronics Engrs; Am Ceramic Soc. *Mailing Add:* Intel Corp FMS-73 1900 Prairie City Rd Folsom CA 95630

SACHDEVA, BALDEV KRISHAN, APPLIED MATHEMATICS. *Current Pos:* dir acad affairs, 82-83, chmn dept, 84-89, PROF MATH, UNIV NEW HAVEN, CONN, 79- *Personal Data:* b India, Oct 15, 39; m 78. *Educ:* Univ Delhi, India, BSc Hons, 59, MA, 61; Pa State Univ, PhD(math), 73. *Prof Exp:* Lectr math, Univ Delhi, 64-69; res assoc math & elec eng, Carleton Univ, Ottawa & Nat Res Coun, 73-74; lectr math, Univ Wis-Milwaukee, 75-77; vis prof math, Panjab Univ, Chandigarh, India, 77-79. *Mem:* Am Math Soc; Soc Indust & Appl Math; Math Asn Am. *Res:* Scattering of acoustic and electromagnetic waves; general applied mathematics; numerical analysis. *Mailing Add:* Dept Math Univ New Haven West Haven CT 06516-1999

SACHER, ALEX, BIOENGINEERING & BIOMEDICAL ENGINEERING. *Current Pos:* PRES, UNIVERSAL PETROCHEM, INC, MAPLEWOOD, NJ, 63- *Personal Data:* b Brooklyn, NY, July 24, 22; m 43; May Goldstein; c Joel, Stephen, Felice & Lisa. *Educ:* City Col NY, BS, 43; Polytech Univ, MS, 46, PhD(polymer chem), 48. *Honors & Awards:* Spec Award, Soc Plastics Engrs, 59; Award Recognition, Am Soc Testing & Mat, 96; Distinguished Serv Award, Chem Specialties Mfrs Asn, 96. *Prof Exp:* Asst, Polytech Inst Brooklyn, 45-46 & 47-48; assoc tech dir, Maybunn Chem Co, NY, 48-49; fel synthetic rubber, Mellon Inst, 49-51; asst res mgr, Irvington Varnish & Insulator Div, Minn Mining & Mfg Co, 51-55; tech dir, Stand Insulation Co, 55-58; vpres commercial develop, Hudson Pulp & Paper Corp, NY, 58-59; pres, Dimensional Pigments, Inc, 60-62. *Concurrent Pos:* Adj prof, NY Inst Technol, 59. *Mem:* Fel AAAS; fel Am Inst Chemists; Am Soc Testing & Mat; fel NY Acad Sci; Soc Plastics Engrs; Am Chem Soc; Am Soc Biomech; Am Acad. *Res:* specialty floor maintenance chemicals; Application of forensic biomechanics to the analysis and reconstruction of slip-trip-stumble and fall accidents. *Mailing Add:* 92 Van Ness Ct Maplewood NJ 07040

SACHER, EDWARD, PHYSICAL CHEMISTRY OF SURFACES. *Current Pos:* RES PROF, DEPT ENG & PHYS, ECOLE POLYTECH, 82- *Personal Data:* b New York, NY, June 3, 34; m 62; c 3. *Educ:* City Col New York, BS, 56; Pa State Univ, PhD(phys chem), 60. *Prof Exp:* Fel, Ohio State Univ, 60-61 & Ottawa Univ, Ont, 61-63; res chemist, E I du Pont de Nemours & Co, Inc, 63-68; staff chemist, IBM Corp, 68-70, adv chemist, Mat Lab, Systs Prod Div, 70-80, Gen Technol Div, 80-82. *Concurrent Pos:* Adj prof, McGill Univ. *Mem:* Fel Royal Soc Chem; Sigma Xi; fel Inst Elec & Electronics Engrs. *Res:* Chemical kinetics; AC and DC dielectric properties of polymeric solids; structure and motions of polymeric solid surfaces; polymer-metal adhesion. *Mailing Add:* Eng Physics Ecole Polytech Montreal PQ H3C 3A7 Can. *Fax:* 514-340-3218; *E-Mail:* sacher@phys.polymtl.ca

SACHER, ROBERT FRANCIS, GENETIC IMPROVEMENT OF PROCESSING PERFORMANCE IN CROP PLANTS. *Current Pos:* PRIN SCIENTIST & BIOTECHNOL COORDR, HUNTWESSON, FULLERTON, CALIF, 89- *Personal Data:* b Chicago, Ill, July 23, 47; m 73. *Educ:* Univ Ill, BS, 75, MS, 77; Wash State Univ, PhD(hort), 80. *Prof Exp:* Assoc, Boyce Thompson Inst Plant Res, Cornell Univ, 80-81, res assoc, 81-84; res assoc, Univ Wis, 84-89. *Concurrent Pos:* Mem, Aflatoxic Multi-Crop Working Group, Agr Res Serv, USDA. *Mem:* Am Soc Plant Physiol; Am Soc Hort Sci; AAAS. *Mailing Add:* Huntwesson 1645 W Valencia Dr Fullerton CA 92633-3899

SACHLEBEN, RICHARD ALAN, CHEMICAL SEPARATIONS, SOLVENT EXTRACTION. *Current Pos:* fel, 86-87, RES STAFF, OAK RIDGE NAT LAB, US DEPT ENERGY, 87- *Personal Data:* b Madison, Ind, Feb 9, 56. *Educ:* Ga Inst Technol, BSci, 79; W M Rice Univ, PhD(org chem), 85. *Prof Exp:* Student res assoc, US Environ Protection Agency, 76-79; vis asst prof, Colo Sch Mines, 84-86, Univ Colo, Boulder, 85. *Mem:* Am Chem Soc; AAAS. *Res:* Design and synthesis of metal specific ligands; chemical and structural principles of separations by solvent extraction; incorporation of metals into nucleic acids and DNA. *Mailing Add:* MS-6119/ Bldg 4500 PO Box 2008 Oak Ridge TN 37831-6119. *Fax:* 423-574-4939; *E-Mail:* sachlebenra@ornl.gov

SACHS, BENJAMIN DAVID, BEHAVIORAL NEURO-ENDOCRINOLOGY, BEHAVIOR-ETHOLOGY. *Current Pos:* From asst prof to prof, 68-92, EMER PROF PSYCHOL, UNIV CONN, 92- *Personal Data:* b Madrid, Spain, Mar 4, 36; US citizen; m 65; c 1. *Educ:* City Col New York, BA, 57, MSEd, 61; Univ Calif, Berkeley, PhD(comp psychol), 66. *Concurrent Pos:* Nat Inst Child Health & Human Develop fel, Rutgers Univ, Newark, 66-68; mem adv bd, Current Contents/Life Sci, 70-96; consult ed, J Comp & Physiol Psychol, 79-81, J Comp Psychol, 88-92, Physiol Behav, 89- & Horm Behav, 97-; prin investr, NICHD res grants, 69-94; NSF res grant, 97- *Mem:* Fel Am Psychol Soc; Animal Behav Soc; Soc Behav Neuroendocrinol; Soc Neurosci; Int Acad Sex Res. *Res:* Neuroendocrine aspects of reproductive behavior; sexually dimorphic behavior patterns. *Mailing Add:* Dept Psychol U-20 Univ Conn 406 Babbidge Rd Storrs CT 06269-1020. *Fax:* 860-486-2760; *E-Mail:* bsachs@uconnvm.uconn.edu

SACHS, DAVID, MATHEMATICS. *Current Pos:* assoc prof, 66-71, PROF MATH, WRIGHT STATE UNIV, 71- *Personal Data:* b Chicago, Ill, Aug 18, 33. *Educ:* Ill Inst Technol, BS, 55, MS, 57, PhD(math), 60. *Prof Exp:* Instr math, Ill Inst Technol, 59-60; from instr to asst prof, Univ Ill, Urbana, 60-66. *Mem:* Am Math Soc; Math Asn Am; Sigma Xi. *Res:* Lattice theory; exchange geometries; foundations of geometry. *Mailing Add:* Dept Math & Statist Wright State Univ Dayton OH 45435-0001

SACHS, DAVID HOWARD, TRANSPLANTATION, IMMUNOGENETICS. *Current Pos:* DIR, TRANSPLANTATION BIOL RES CTR, MASS GEN HOSP, 91-; P S RUSSELL/WARNER-LAMBERT PROF SURG & IMMUNOL, HARVARD MED SCH, 91- *Personal Data:* b New York, NY, Jan 10, 42; m 69, Kristina; c Michelle, Karin, Jessica & Teviah. *Educ:* Harvard Col, AB, 63, MD, 68; Univ Paris, DES, 64. *Honors & Awards:* Medal, Swedish Soc Med, 95. *Prof Exp:* Intern surg, Mass Gen Hosp, 68-69, res fel, 69-70; res assoc biochem, Lab Chem Biol, Nat Inst Arthritis & Metab Dis, NIH, 70-72, sr investr, Immunol Br, Nat Cancer Inst, 72-74, sect chief, Transplanation Biol Sect, 74-82, br chief, Immunol Br, 82-90. *Concurrent Pos:* Teaching asst org chem, Harvard Univ, 62-65; vis prof, Dept Cell Res, Wallenberg Lab, Univ Uppsala, Sweden, 84-85; ed-in-chief, Xenotransplantation, 94-97, founding ed, 94- *Mem:* Inst Med-Nat Acad Sci; Am Asn Immunologists; Am Soc Biochem & Molecular Biol; Transplantation Soc; Am Soc Hemat; Am Soc Histocompatibility & Immunogenetics; Am Soc Blood & Bone Marrow Transplantation; Belgian Xenotransplantation Soc; Am Soc Transplant Surgeons; Am Soc Transplant Physicians. *Res:* Investigations in basic immunology with particular emphasis on studies of the major histocompatibility complex and its role in transplantation in animal models and in man. *Mailing Add:* Mass Gen Hosp Transplantation Biol Res Ctr MGH E Bldg 149-9019 13th St Boston MA 02129. *Fax:* 617-726-4067, 301-496-0832

SACHS, FREDERICK, BIOPHYSICS. *Current Pos:* asst prof pharmacol, 75-80, asst prof biophys, 80-81, assoc prof biolphys, 81-88, PROF BIOPHYS, STATE UNIV NY BUFFALO, 88- *Personal Data:* b New York, NY, Jan 8, 41; m 83, Susan Lankenan; c Shosashana, Christopher, Janna, Benjamin & Robert. *Educ:* Univ Rochester, BA, 62; State Univ NY Upstate Med Ctr, PhD(physiol), 72. *Prof Exp:* Assoc engr electromagnetic compatibility, Douglas Aircraft Co, 62-64; jr researcher biophys, dept biochem & biophys, Univ Hawaii, 69-71; staff fel, Biophys Lab, Nat Inst Neurol Dis & Stroke, 71-75. *Concurrent Pos:* Fogarty fel, 91. *Mem:* Biophys Soc; AAAS; Soc Gen Physiol. *Res:* Mechanisms of ion transport in cells, excitability; mechanical transduction; instrumentation design. *Mailing Add:* Dept Biophys Sci State Univ NY 120 Cary Hall Buffalo NY 14214-3005. *Fax:* 716-829-2028; *E-Mail:* sachs@sun1.med.buffalo.edu

SACHS, FREDERICK LEE, INTERNAL MEDICINE. *Current Pos:* instr, 69-70, asst prof med, 70-77, ASSOC CLIN PROF MED, SCH MED, YALE UNIV, 77- *Personal Data:* b Brooklyn, NY, Feb 28, 38; m 60; c 3. *Educ:* Princeton Univ, AB, 59; Columbia Univ, MD, 63. *Honors & Awards:* Upjohn Award, 69. *Prof Exp:* From intern to chief resident med, Yale-New Haven Hosp, 63-69. *Concurrent Pos:* Winchester fel chest dis, Sch Med, Yale Univ, 69-70; consult, Vet Admin Hosp, West Haven, 69- *Mem:* AAAS; Am Thoracic Soc; Sigma Xi. *Res:* Alveolar macrophages. *Mailing Add:* 42 Indian Trail Woodbridge CT 06525-1441

SACHS, GEORGE, BIOCHEMISTRY. *Current Pos:* from asst prof to assoc prof med & physiol, 63-70, assoc prof physiol & biophys, 77-80, PROF MED, SCH MED, UNIV ALA, BIRMINGHAM, 70-, PROF PHYSIOL & BIOPHYS & DIR, MEMBRANE BIOL UNIT, 80- *Personal Data:* b Vienna, Austria, Aug 26, 36; US citizen; m 63; c 4. *Educ:* Univ Edinburgh, BSc, 57, MB, ChB, 60,. *Hon Degrees:* DSc, Univ Edinburgh, 80. *Prof Exp:* Instr biochem, Albert Einstein Col Med, 61-62. *Concurrent Pos:* Fel biochem, Albert Einstein Col Med, 61; res fel, Columbia Univ, 62-63. *Mem:* Biophys Soc; Brit Biochem Soc; NY Acad Sci; Soc Exp Biol & Med; Am Physiol Soc. *Res:* Physiology and biochemistry of transport. *Mailing Add:* Membrane Biol Lab Ctr Ulcer Res Bldg 113 Rm 324 West Los Angeles Vet Admin Med Ctr 11301 Wilshire Blvd Los Angeles CA 90073. *Fax:* 310-206-1699

SACHS, HARVEY MAURICE, GEOLOGY, ENERGY. *Current Pos:* CONSULT, 90-; DIR POLICY RES, UNIV MD, COLLEGE PARK, 91- *Personal Data:* b Atlanta, Ga, Dec 10, 44; m 67; c 1. *Educ:* Rice Univ, AB, 67; Brown Univ, PhD(geol), 73. *Prof Exp:* Fel oceanog, Ore State Univ, 72-74; asst prof, Case Western Res Univ, 74-76; asst prof geol, Princeton Univ, 77-82, consult, 82-84; mem tech staff, AT&T Bell Labs, 84-87; asst comnr energy, State NJ, 87-89. *Concurrent Pos:* Prin investr var grants, NSF & Pa Power & Light Co, 81-82. *Mem:* AAAS; Am Geophys Union; Geol Soc Am; Sigma Xi. *Res:* Engineering and evaluation of energy efficiency modifications for dwellings; side effects of conservation; geology of radon distribution; energy efficiency and policy; geology, applied, economic and engineering; oceanography; stratigraphy-sedimentation. *Mailing Add:* 1442 Oakview Dr McLean VA 22101

SACHS, HOWARD GEORGE, DEVELOPMENTAL BIOLOGY, ANATOMY. *Current Pos:* ASSOC DEAN & PROF BIOL, PA STATE UNIV, HARRISBURG, 88- *Personal Data:* b New York, NY, Dec 12, 43; m 68, Martha Sandrof; c Emily & Mark. *Educ:* Worcester Polytech Inst, BS, 65; Clark Univ, PhD(biol), 71. *Prof Exp:* Fel develop biol, Carnegie Inst, 70-72; from asst prof to assoc prof & asst dean, Grad Col, Univ Ill, 72-80; assoc provost & assoc prof anat, Ohio State Univ, 80-83; provost & vpres acad affairs, Univ Maine, Farmington, 83-86. *Mem:* Am Asn Anatomists; NY Acad Sci; AAAS; Sigma Xi; Am Heart Asn. *Res:* Cardiac biology and pathology. *Mailing Add:* Res & Grad Studies Pa State Univ at Harrisburg Middletown PA 17057. *Fax:* 717-948-6008; *E-Mail:* hgsi@oas.psu.edu

SACHS, JOHN RICHARD, HEMATOLOGY, PHYSIOLOGY. *Current Pos:* assoc prof, 75-77, PROF MED, SCH MED, STATE UNIV NY, STONY BROOK, 77- *Personal Data:* b Brooklyn, NY, July 29, 34; m 59, Marilyn F Mahn; c Caroly, John & Jennifer. *Educ:* Manhattan Col, BS, 56; Columbia Univ, MD, 60. *Prof Exp:* Res hematologist, Walter Reed Army Inst Res, 66-69; from asst prof to assoc prof physiol, Sch Med, Yale Univ, 69-75. *Mem:* Am Physiol Soc; Biophys Soc; Soc Gen Physiologists. *Res:* Cation transport, membrane physiology; sodium potassium pump kinetics and structure; cell volume regulation; biophysics. *Mailing Add:* Dept Med State Univ NY Stony Brook NY 11794

SACHS, LEO, MOLECULAR GENETICS, CANCER. *Current Pos:* prof & head, Dept Genetics, Weizmann Inst Sci, Rehovot, Israel, 62-89, dean, Fac Biol, 74-79, RES SCIENTIST, WEIZMANN INST SCI, REHOVOT, ISRAEL, 52-, OTTO MEYERHOF PROF BIOL, 68- *Personal Data:* b Leipzig, Ger, Oct 14, 24; m 70, Pnina Salkind; c 4. *Educ:* Univ Col N Wales, BSc, 48; Univ Cambridge, PhD, 51. *Hon Degrees:* Doctor, Univ Bordeaux, 85; MD, Univ Lund, 97. *Honors & Awards:* Israel Prize for Natural Sci, 72; Harvey Lectr, Rockefeller Univ, 72; Rothschild Prize in Biol Sci, Israel, 77; Wolf Prize in Med, 80; Bristol-Myers Award for Distinguished Achievement in Cancer Res, 83; Royal Soc Wellcome Found Prize, 86; Jan Waldenstrom Lectr, Swedish Soc Med, 87; Alfred Sloan Prize, Gen Motors Cancer Res Found, 89; Warren Alpert Found Prize, Harvard Med Sch, 97. *Prof Exp:* Res scientist genetics, John Innes Inst, Eng, 51-52. *Concurrent Pos:* Fogarty scholar, NIH, 72; Samuel Rudin vis prof, Col Physicians & Surgeons, Columbia Univ, 79; Charles B Smith vis res prof, Mem Sloan-Kettering Cancer Ctr, NY, 81. *Mem:* Foreign assoc Nat Acad Sci; fel Royal Soc; corresp mem Am Asn Cancer Res; Israel Acad Sci & Humanities; Europ Molecular Biol Orgn; fel Royal Soc. *Mailing Add:* Dept Molecular Genetics Weizmann Inst Sci Rehovot 76100 Israel. *Fax:* 972-8-9344108

SACHS, LESTER MARVIN, THEORETICAL PHYSICS, INFORMATION SCIENCE. *Current Pos:* syst develop specialist, 75-80, TECH ADV, SOCIAL SECURITY ADMIN, 80- *Personal Data:* b Chicago, Ill, May 16, 27; m 57, Blanche Cohen; c Deborah. *Educ:* Ill Inst Technol, BS, 50, MS, 54, PhD(physics), 61. *Prof Exp:* Instr physics, Univ Ill, 55-58; student resident assoc, Argonne Nat Lab, 59-60; asst prof physics, Wayne State Univ, 60-64; scientist, Res Inst Advan Studies, 65-69; pres, Comput Prog Assocs, Inc, Md, 69-71; independent consult, 71-72; comput systs analyst, Bur Labor Statist, 72-75. *Mem:* Am Phys Soc; Sigma Xi. *Res:* Atomic and molecular structure; solid state theory; microcomputers; telecommunications theory; televideo compression algorithms. *Mailing Add:* 8823 Stonehaven Rd Randallstown MD 21133-4223

SACHS, MARTIN M, ANAEROBIC STRESS IN MAIZE, MAIZE BIOCHEMICAL & MOLECULAR GENETICS. *Current Pos:* RES GENETICIST PLANTS, USDA-AGR RES SERV, 92- *Educ:* City Univ NY, BS, 75; Univ Calif, Berkeley, PhD(genetics), 81. *Prof Exp:* Res scientist, Commonwealth Sci & Indust Res Orgn, Australia, 81-84; asst prof, Wash Univ, 84-91; res asst prof, Univ Mo, Columbia, 91-92. *Concurrent Pos:* Dir, Maize Genetics Coop-Stock Ctr, 92-; asst prof, Dept Agron, Univ Ill, 92- *Mem:* Genetics Soc Am; Int Soc Plant Molecular Biol; Am Soc Plant Physiologists; Am Soc Agron. *Res:* Analysis of anaerobic (flooding) stress responses in maize; molecular-genetic analysis of mutant alleles in maize; analysis of DNA polymorphism and gene evolution in maize. *Mailing Add:* 602 W Main St Urbana IL 61801. *E-Mail:* msachs@uiuc.edu

SACHS, MARTIN WILLIAM, INPUT-OUTPUT ARCHITECTURE, DATA COMMUNICATION. *Current Pos:* RES STAFF MEM, DEPT COMPUT SCI, IBM T J WATSON RES CTR, 76- *Personal Data:* b New Haven, Conn, Sept 30, 37; m 68, June Sugarman. *Educ:* Harvard Univ, AB, 59; Yale Univ, MS, 60, PhD(physics), 64. *Prof Exp:* Dept guest nuclear physics, Weizmann Inst, 64, inst fel, 64, NATO fel, 65, res asst, 66; res assoc, Nuclear Struct Lab, Yale Univ, 67-72; sr res assoc & lectr, 72-76. *Concurrent Pos:* Mem panel on-line comput nuclear res, Nat Res Coun, 68-70. *Mem:* Asn Comput Mach; Am Phys Soc; Sigma Xi; fel Inst Elec & Electronics Engrs. *Res:* Computer systems and communications. *Mailing Add:* IBM PO Box 704 Yorktown Heights NY 10598. *E-Mail:* sachs@watson.ibm.com

SACHS, MARVIN LEONARD, INTERNAL MEDICINE, VASCULAR DISEASES. *Current Pos:* instr, 55-61, physician-in-chg, Univ Pa Div Med Clin, Philadelphia Gen Hosp, 60-78, assoc, 61-69, ASST PROF MED, SCH MED, UNIV PA, 69-, CHIEF, MED VASCULAR SERV & DIR, MED VASCULAR LAB, HOSP UNIV PA. *Personal Data:* b Allentown, Pa, Aug 31, 26; m 74; c 1. *Educ:* Yale Univ, BA, 46; Harvard Univ, MD, 50; Am Bd Internal Med, dipl, 58. *Hon Degrees:* MA, Univ Pa, 71. *Prof Exp:* Intern surg, obstet & pediat, Allentown Gen Hosp, Pa, 50; intern med, Univ Hosps Cleveland, 51-52, resident, 52-53. *Concurrent Pos:* Nat Heart Inst fel cardiovasc dis, Hosp Univ Pa, 55-57; mem cardiovasc sect, Dept Med, Univ Pa, 57-; consult, Food & Drug Admin, Dept Health, Educ & Welfare, 64; consult, Archit Res Unit, Univ City Sci Ctr, Philadelphia, 65-; lectr, Wharton Sch, 66-; mem res in nursing in patient care rev comt, USPHS, 67-70; attend physician, Vet Admin Hosp, 67-; mem coun arteriosclerosis, coun circulation & mem adv bd, Am Heart Asn. *Mem:* Fel Am Col Physicians; AMA; Am Fedn Clin Res; Am Thyroid Asn; Sigma Xi; Soc Vascular Med & Biol. *Res:* Peripheral vascular diseases; patient care research and education; organization and design of health care facilities. *Mailing Add:* Hosp Univ Pa 3400 Spruce St Philadelphia PA 19104-4274

SACHS, MENDEL, THEORETICAL PHYSICS. *Current Pos:* PROF PHYSICS, STATE UNIV NY, BUFFALO, 66- *Personal Data:* b Portland, Ore, Apr 13, 27; m 52, Yetty Herman; c Robert R, Daniel E, Carolyn T & Michael G. *Educ:* Univ Calif, Los Angeles, AB, 49, MA, 50, PhD(physics), 54. *Prof Exp:* Theoret physicist, Radiation Lab, Univ Calif, 54-56; res scientist, Lockheed Missiles & Space Co, 56-61; res prof, McGill Univ, 61-62; assoc prof physics, Boston Univ, 62-66. *Concurrent Pos:* Asst prof, San Jose State Col, 57-61. *Res:* Relativity; field theory; quantum electrodynamics; elementary particles; philosophy of science; physical applications of group theory; astrophysics and cosmology. *Mailing Add:* Dept Physics State Univ NY Buffalo Buffalo NY 14260. *Fax:* 716-645-2507; *E-Mail:* msachs@ubvms.cc.buffalo.edu

SACHS, MURRAY B, HEARING SCIENCES. *Current Pos:* from asst prof to assoc prof biomed eng, 70-80, dir, Ctr Hearing Sci, 86-91, MASSEY PROF & DIR, DEPT BIOMED ENG, JOHNS HOPKINS UNIV, 91- *Educ:* Mass Inst Technol, BS, 62, MS, 64, PhD(elec eng & auditory physiol), 66. *Prof Exp:* Fel, Univ Cambridge, Eng, 68-69. *Concurrent Pos:* Mem, Comn Commun & Control, Int Union Pure & Appl Biophys, 75-80; mem, Commun Dis Panel & Basic Sci Task Force, Nat Inst Neurol & Commun Dis & Stroke, NIH, 77-78, chmn, Commun Dis Rev Comt, 77-79, ad hoc adv comt, Commun Dis Prog, 79-86, sci prog adv comt, 84-86; prof biomed eng, Johns Hopkins Univ, 80-, prof neurosci, 81-, prof otolaryngol-head & neck surg, 83-; mem, Sensory Physiol & Perception Panel, NSF, 82-85; Jacob Javitz neurosci investr, 85; mem, Comt Hearing & Bioacoust, Nat Acad Sci, 85-88. *Mem:* Inst Med-Nat Acad Sci; Sigma Xi; fel Am Inst Med & Biol Eng. *Res:* Neural mechanisms of auditory perception; mathematical models for signal processing in the nervous system. *Mailing Add:* Sch Med Johns Hopkins Univ 720 Rutland Ave Baltimore MD 21205. *Fax:* 410-955-0549

SACHS, RAINER KURT, THEORETICAL PHYSICS. *Current Pos:* PROF PHYSICS & MATH, UNIV CALIF, BERKELEY, 69- *Personal Data:* b Frankfurt, Ger, June 13, 32; US citizen; div; c 4. *Educ:* Mass Inst Technol, BSc, 53; Syracuse Univ, PhD(physics), 58. *Prof Exp:* Fel physics, Univ Hamburg, 59-60; fel, Univ London, 60-61; asst prof, Stevens Inst Technol, 62-63; from assoc prof to prof, Univ Tex, 63-69. *Mem:* Am Phys Soc; Am Astron Soc. *Res:* General relativity; cosmology. *Mailing Add:* 5300 Shafter Ave Oakland CA 94618

SACHS, ROBERT GREEN, ELEMENTARY PARTICLE PHYSICS, FIELD THEORY. *Current Pos:* prof, 64-86, EMER PROF PHYSICS, UNIV CHICAGO, 86- *Personal Data:* b Hagerstown, Md, May 4, 16; m 41, 50, 68, Carolyn Levin; c Rebecca, Jennifer, Jeffrey, Judith, Joel, Thomas (Wolf), Jacqueline & Katherine (Wolf). *Educ:* Johns Hopkins Univ, PhD(physics), 39. *Hon Degrees:* DSc, Purdue Univ, 67, Univ Ill, 77, Elmhurst Col, 87. *Honors & Awards:* Distinguished Serv Citation, Col Eng Univ Wis, 77. *Prof Exp:* Res fel theoret physics, George Washington Univ, 39-41 & Univ Calif, 41; instr physics, Purdue Univ, 41-43; chief air blast sect, Ballistic Res Lab, Aberdeen Proving Ground, 43-46; dir, Theoret Physics Div, Argonne Nat Lab, 46-47, assoc lab dir high energy physics, 64-68, dir, 73-79; from assoc prof to prof physics, Univ Wis, 47-64; dir, Enrico Fermi Inst, 68-73 & 83-86. *Concurrent Pos:* Consult, Argonne Nat Lab, 46-52, 60-63 & Ballistic Res Lab, Aberdeen Proving Ground, 46-59; Higgins vis prof, Princeton Univ, 55-56; consult, Lawrence Radiation Lab, Univ Calif, 55-59; mem adv panel physics, NSF, 58-61; Guggenheim fel & vis prof, Ecole Normale Superieure, Univ Paris, 59-60; vis scientist, Europ Orgn Nuclear Res, 59 73-79; mem, Sci Policy Comt, Stanford Linear Accelerator Ctr, 66-70; high energy physics adv panel, US AEC, 67-69; vis prof, Tohoku Univ, Japan, 74; mem, Physics Surv Comt & chmn, Elem Particle Physics Panel, Physics Surv Comt, Nat Acad Sci; mem, Task Force Energy Res Priorities, Dept Energy, 91-93. *Mem:* Nat Acad Sci; AAAS; fel Am Phys Soc; fel AAAS (vpres, 79-83); Am Inst Physics. *Res:* High energy physics; fundamental particles; nuclear theory; solid state; terminal ballistics; nuclear power reactors; physics of time reversal; author or co-author of over 100 publications and 2 books. *Mailing Add:* 5490 S Shore Dr Apt 9N Chicago IL 60615. *Fax:* 773-702-1914

SACHS, ROY M, PLANT PHYSIOLOGY. *Current Pos:* from asst plant physiologist to assoc plant physiologist, 58-70, prof, 70-, PLANT PHYSIOLOGIST & EMER PROF ENVIRON HORT, UNIV CALIF, DAVIS. *Personal Data:* b New York, NY, Apr 1, 30; m 53; c 5. *Educ:* Mass Inst Technol, BS, 51; Calif Inst Technol, PhD(plant physiol), 55. *Prof Exp:* Fulbright fel, Univ Parma, 55-56; jr res botanist, Univ Calif, Los Angeles, 56-58, asst plant physiologist, 58-61. *Mem:* Am Soc Plant Physiol; Am Soc Hort Sci; Agron Soc Am. *Res:* Vegetative growth; flowering; growth substances. *Mailing Add:* Environ Hort Univ Calif Davis CA 95616-5224

SACHS, THOMAS DUDLEY, PHYSICAL ACOUSTICS, BIOPHYSICS. *Current Pos:* asst prof, 62-77, ASSOC PROF PHYSICS, UNIV VT, 77- *Personal Data:* b St Louis, Mo, Jan 29, 25; m 61, 88; c 4. *Educ:* Univ Calif, Berkeley, BA, 51; Innsbruck Univ, PhD(physics, math), 60. *Prof Exp:* Pub sch teacher, Calif, 52-53 & high sch & jr col teacher, 53-55; res investr chem, Western Reserve Univ, 60-62. *Concurrent Pos:* Consult, Jr High Sch Sci Exp Prog, 62-65, Ladd Res, IBM Corp & Varian Corp; pres, Electronic Educator, Inc, 69-79; mem, Vt Regional Cancer Ctr, 80-; mem, Cell Biol Group, Univ Vt, 84-; res dir, Wellen Assocs, Inc, 88- *Mem:* AAAS; Am Phys Soc; Acoust Soc Am; Inst Elec & Electronics Engrs. *Res:* Perturbed acoustic propagation parameter measurements in liquids, plasmas and biological tissues with applications to liquid structure, cavitation, solar dynamics and mechanics; thermo-acoustic tissue characterization, non-invasive biopsy, perfusion and non-invasive temperature measurement by thermo-acoustic sensing technique (TAST). *Mailing Add:* 21 Grandview Ave Essex Junction VT 05452. *Fax:* 802-878-5084

SACHSE, WOLFGANG H, PHYSICAL ACOUSTICS. *Current Pos:* from asst prof to assoc prof, 70-83, PROF APPL MECH, CORNELL UNIV, 83- *Personal Data:* b Berlin-Charlottenburg, Ger, Mar 22, 42; US citizen; m 70; c 3. *Educ:* Pa State Univ, University Park, BS, 63; Johns Hopkins Univ, MSE, 66, PhD(mech), 70. *Prof Exp:* Ger acad exchange fel, Inst Metall, Aachen, 69-70. *Concurrent Pos:* Consult; Ger acad exchange fel, Nat Bur Standards, 77-78. *Mem:* Acoust Soc Am; Inst Acoust; Inst Elec & Electronics Engrs; Sigma Xi; Exp Mech Soc. *Res:* Mechanics of materials; wave propagation in solids; ultrasonics; acoustic emission; non-destructive testing of materials; transducers. *Mailing Add:* Dept Theoret & Appl Mech Thurston Kimball Halls Cornell Univ Ithaca NY 14853

SACHTLEBEN, CLYDE CLINTON, PHYSICS, SCIENCE EDUCATION. *Current Pos:* From instr to assoc prof, 60-68, PROF PHYSICS, HASTINGS COL, 68-, CHMN DEPT, 62- *Personal Data:* b Lincoln, Nebr, May 4, 36; m 58; c 2. *Educ:* Nebr Wesleyan Univ, BA, 57; Univ Nebr, MA, 60; Univ Iowa, PhD(sci educ), 67. *Concurrent Pos:* US AEC lectr, Oak Ridge Radioisotope-Mobile Lab, 65-, res assoc, Oak Ridge Assoc Univs, 72; vis prof physics, Univ Nebr, 65-81 & Univ Colo, 90-91; NSF fel, Univ Iowa, 66-67. *Mem:* Am Asn Physics Teachers. *Res:* Atomic and nuclear physics. *Mailing Add:* 623 N Shore Dr Hastings NE 68901

SACHTLER, WOLFGANG MAX HUGO, CATALYSIS. *Current Pos:* PROF CHEM, NORTHWESTERN UNIV, 83- *Personal Data:* b Delitzsch, Ger, Nov 8, 24; m 53; c 3. *Educ:* Univ Technol Braunschweig, MS, 49, PhD(chem), 52. *Honors & Awards:* Numerous invited lects throughout the world; R L Burwell Award, NAm Catalysis Soc, 85; E V Murphree Award, Am Chem Soc, 87. *Prof Exp:* Res chemist, Kon-Shell Lab, Amsterdam, 52-60, Shell Res Ctr, Emeryville, LA, 60-61, sect leader, Kon-Shell Lab, Amsterdam, 61- 72, dir, 73-83. *Concurrent Pos:* Prof chem, Univ Leiden, 63-84. *Mem:* Royal Acad Sci Neth; Am Chem Soc; Neth Chem Soc; Sigma Xi. *Res:* Heterogeneous catalysis; surface science; thermodynamics; electron emission. *Mailing Add:* Chem Dept Northwestern Univ Evanston IL 60208

SACK, E(DGAR) A(LBERT), JR, ELECTRICAL ENGINEERING, SOLID STATE ELECTRONICS. *Current Pos:* CHMN & CHIEF EXEC OFFICER, ZILOG CORP, 84- *Personal Data:* b Pittsburgh, Pa, Jan 31, 30; m 52, Eugenia Ferris; c Elaine K & Richard W. *Educ:* Carnegie Inst Technol, BS, 51, MS, 52, PhD(elec eng), 54. *Honors & Awards:* Hammerschlag Lectr, 95. *Prof Exp:* Res engr, Carnegie Inst Technol, 51-54; res engr, Res Labs, Westinghouse Elec Corp, 54-56, proj leader, TV Sect, 56-57, sect mgr, Dielec Devices, 57-60, dept mgr, Electronics, 60-61, dept mgr, Solid State Devices, 61-62, mgr eng, Molecular Electronics Div, 62-65, mgr tech opers, 65-66, asst gen mgr, 66-67, gen mgr, Integrated Circuits Div, 67-69; vpres & gen mgr, Integrated Circuits Div, Gen Instrument Corp, 69-70, vpres opers, Microelectronics, 70-71, vpres comput prod, 71-73, vpres & gen mgr, Microelectronics, 73-76, sr vpres, 76-84. *Concurrent Pos:* Dir, Regional Indust Tech Educ Coun, 80-82; fel, Polytechnic Inst, 81; dir, Semiconductor Indust Asn, 80-82; dir, Catalyst Semiconductor Inc, 93-95. *Mem:* Fel Inst Elec & Electronics Engrs; Sigma Xi. *Res:* Ferroelectrics; electroluminescence; nonlinear circuits; integrated circuit design and processing; technical and general management; MOS memory device; solid state devices; consumer electronics products. *Mailing Add:* 21412 Sarahills Ct Saratoga CA 95070

SACK, FRED DAVID, PLANT CELL BIOLOGY & DEVELOPMENT. *Current Pos:* ASSOC PROF PLANT ANAT, DEPT BOT, OHIO STATE UNIV, 84- *Personal Data:* b New York, NY, May 22, 47; m 92, Dian Clare. *Educ:* Antioch Univ, BA, 69; Cornell Univ, PhD(plant biol), 82. *Prof Exp:* Res fel, Boyce Thompson Inst Plant Sci, Cornell, 81-84. *Mem:* Am Soc Plant Physiologists; Am Soc Gravitational & Space Biol; Am Soc Cell Biol; AAAS; Bot Soc Am. *Res:* Stomatal development; plant graviperception. *Mailing Add:* Dept Plant Biol Ohio State Univ 1735 Neil Ave Columbus OH 43210-1220. *Fax:* 614-292-6345; *E-Mail:* sack1@osu.edu

SACK, GEORGE H(ENRY), JR, MEDICAL GENETICS, GENE ORGANIZATION. *Current Pos:* fel med genetics, Johns Hopkins Univ, 75-76, asst prof med pediat, 76-84, asst prof physiol chem, 80-84, ASSOC PROF MED, PEDIAT & BIOL CHEM, JOHNS HOPKINS UNIV, 84- *Personal Data:* b Baltimore, Md, Apr 17, 43. *Educ:* Johns Hopkins Univ, BA, 65, MD, 68, PhD(molecular biol & microbiol), 75. *Prof Exp:* Intern med, Johns Hopkins Hosp, 68-69, asst resident, 69-70, fel microbiol, 70-73; major med, US Army Med Corps, 73-75. *Concurrent Pos:* Biochemist, Kennedy Inst, 81-93. *Mem:* Am Soc Human Genetics; AAAS; AMA; fel Am Col Med Genetics. *Res:* Molecular biology: human gene structure, organization, expression, polymorphisms; clinical applications of genetic principles and technology; medical genetics; amyloidosis. *Mailing Add:* Div Med Genetics Blalock 1008 Johns Hopkins Hosp Baltimore MD 21287. *E-Mail:* gsack@welchlink.welch.jhu.edu

SACK, RICHARD BRADLEY, MEDICINE, MICROBIOLOGY. *Current Pos:* fel path, Sch Pub Health, Johns Hopkins Univ, 65-68, from instr to assoc prof, Sch Med, 66-79, head, Div Geog Med, 77-90, PROF MED, JOHNS HOPKINS UNIV, 79-, PROF INT HEALTH, 85- *Personal Data:* b Le Sueur, Minn, Oct 25, 35; m 55, Josephine Nystrom; c Collette E, Daniel B, James G & Jonathan A. *Educ:* Lewis & Clark Col, BS, 56; Univ Ore, MS & MD, 60; Johns Hopkins Univ, ScD(pathobiol), 68. *Prof Exp:* Internship, Univ Wash, Seattle, 60-61, int med residency, 61-62 & 64-65; John Hopkins Hosp fel med, Calcutta, 62-64; assoc prof, Sch Med, Univ Ore, 70-72. *Concurrent Pos:* Assoc dir & head, Div Community Health & Lab Scis, Int Ctr Diarrheal Dis Res, Bangladesh, 91- *Mem:* Infectious Dis Soc Am; Am Soc Microbiol; Am Fedn Clin Res; Am Soc Clin Invest. *Res:* Cholera; diarrheal diseases; bacterial enterotoxins. *Mailing Add:* Dept Int Health Johns Hopkins Univ 615 N Wolfe St Baltimore MD 21205

SACK, ROBERT A, BIOCHEMISTRY, VISUAL SCIENCES. *Current Pos:* ASSOC PROF BASIC SCI, STATE UNIV NY, 72- *Personal Data:* b Mar 14, 44; US citizen; m 78; c 1. *Educ:* NY Med Col, PhD(biochem), 72. *Concurrent Pos:* Guest res assoc, Brookhaven Nat Lab, 71- *Res:* Regeneration of visual pigments; cryobiochemistry; ocular microbiology and immunology. *Mailing Add:* 235 Beaver Dam Rd Brookhaven NY 11719

SACK, RONALD LESLIE, SOLID MECHANICS, STRUCTURAL ENGINEERING. *Current Pos:* assoc prof, 70-74, PROF CIVIL ENG, UNIV IDAHO, 74- *Personal Data:* b Minneapolis, Minn, Mar 29, 35; m 58; c 2. *Educ:* Univ Minn, BS, 57, MSCE, 58, PhD(civil eng), 64. *Prof Exp:* Asst prof civil eng, Clemson Univ, 64-65; res engr, Boeing Co, 65-70. *Concurrent Pos:* Vis lectr, Dept Mech Eng, Seattle Univ, 67-68 & Dept Civil Eng, Univ Wash, 68-70; NASA-Am Soc Eng Educ summer fel, Stanford Univ & Moffet Field, 71; Royal Norwegian Coun Sci & Indust Res fel, Trondheim, Norway, 76-77. *Mem:* Am Soc Civil Engrs; Am Soc Eng Educ; Sigma Xi. *Res:* Application of approximate numerical methods to structural engineering problems; investigation of structural stability problems; seismic design; wind and snow loading on structures. *Mailing Add:* Nat Sci Found 4201 Wilson Blvd Rm 545 Arlington VA 22230

SACK, WOLFGANG OTTO, ANATOMY, VETERINARY MEDICINE. *Current Pos:* assoc prof, Cornell Univ, 64-73, mem fac vet anat, 64-91, prof, 73-91, EMER PROF, CORNELL UNIV, 91- *Personal Data:* b Leipzig, Ger, Mar 17, 28; US citizen; m 55; c 2. *Educ:* Univ Toronto, DVM, 57; Univ Edinburgh, PhD(vet anat), 62; Univ Munich, Dr med vet, 72. *Prof Exp:* Asst prof vet anat, Ont Vet Col, Toronto, 58-60, assoc prof, 62-64. *Concurrent Pos:* Mem, Int & Am Comts Vet Anat Nomenclature, 64-; guest prof, Univ Munich, 71-72; chair, Int Comt Vet Embryol Nomenclature, 87- *Mem:* Am Asn Vet Anat (pres, 81-82); Am Asn Anat; Am Vet Med Asn; World Asn Vet Anat (gen secy, 83-91, pres, 91-); Royal Col Vet Surg. *Res:* Developmental anatomy of domesticated animals; gross anatomy of the horse. *Mailing Add:* 36 Woodcrest Ave Ithaca NY 14850

SACKEIM, HAROLD A, CLINICAL PSYCHOLOGY, NEUROPSYCHOLOGY. *Current Pos:* CHIEF, BIOL PSYCHIAT, NY STATE PSYCHIAT INST, 91-; PROF DEPT, PSYCHIAT & RADIOL, COLUMBIA UNIV, 91- *Personal Data:* b Hackensack, NJ, July 13, 51; m 77, Donna M Zucchi; c Alexander. *Educ:* Columbia Col, BA, 72; Oxford Univ, BA & MA, 74; Univ Pa, PhD(psychol), 77. *Honors & Awards:* Estab Investr Award, Nat Alliance Res Schizophrenia & Depressions, 89; Merit Award, NIMH, 90; Joel Elkes Int Award, Am Col Neuropsychopharmacol, 94. *Prof Exp:* Asst prof psychol, Columbia Univ, 77-79; asst prof, NY Univ, 79-81; dep chief biol psychiat, NY State Psychiat Inst, 81-91; assoc prof psychol, NY Univ, 81-87. *Concurrent Pos:* Lectr psychiat, Col Physicians & Surgeons, Columbia, 80-; consult ed, Imagination, Cognition & Personality, 80-; assoc ed, J Social & Clin Psychol, 81, Convulsive Ther; estab investr award, NARSAD, 96. *Mem:* Hon fel Am Psychiat Asn; AAAS; Int Neuropsychol Soc; Soc Biol Psychiat; Am Psychopathological Asn; Asn Res Nerv & Ment Dis; Am Col Neuropsychopharmacol. *Res:* The role of functional brain asymmetry in the regulation of emotion; psychobiology and treatment of affective disorders; dissociation and consciousness. *Mailing Add:* Dept Biol Psychiat NY State Psychiat Inst 722 W 168th St New York NY 10032. *Fax:* 212-960-5854; *E-Mail:* has1@columbia.edu

SACKETT, DAVID LAWRENCE, CLINICAL TRIALS, CLINICAL EPIDEMIOLOGY. *Current Pos:* assoc prof, 67-70, PROF MED, DEPT CE&B, MCMASTER UNIV, 69-; HEAD, DIV GEN INTERNAL MED, 88- *Personal Data:* m, Barbara Bennett; c David, Charles, Andrew & Robert. *Educ:* Lawrence Col, BA, 56; Univ Ill, BSc, 58, MD, 60. *Honors & Awards:* J Allyn Taylor Int Prize in Med, 87. *Concurrent Pos:* Founding chair, Dept CE&B, McMaster Univ, 67-73; chair, Health Pub Policy Comt, Royal Col Physicians & Sug, 88-92; physician-in-chief med, Chedoke-McMaster Hosp, 86-88. *Mem:* Asn Am Physicians; Am Soc Clin Invest; Am Fedn Clin Res; Sydenham Soc; Royal Soc Can; Can Soc Clin Invest. *Res:* Randomized controlled trials and other studies of medical therapeutics and diagnosis; teach evidence-based medicine. *Mailing Add:* Nuffield Dept Clin Med Univ Oxford John Radcliffe Hosp Level 5 Headington Oxford OX39DU Ireland. *Fax:* 905-575-7320

SACKETT, JOHN I, FAST REACTORS SAFETY. *Current Pos:* Engr, Argonne Nat Lab, 70-75, mgr aparatus anal, 75-80, assoc div dir, 80-86, div dir, EBR II Div, 86-92, DEP ASSOC LAB DIR, ARGONNE NAT LAB, 90- *Personal Data:* m 65, Karen King; c Brent & Erik. *Educ:* Univ Idaho, BS, 65; Univ Ariz, PhD(nuclear eng), 70. *Honors & Awards:* Award for Pioneering Work Post Fracture Safety, Am Nuclear Soc, 91, Walker Cissles Award, 96. *Concurrent Pos:* Bd dirs, Am Nuclear Soc. *Mem:* Am Nuclear Soc. *Res:* Fast reactor safety, including emphasis on passively safe response to upsets. *Mailing Add:* 3490 S Handly Ave Idaho Falls ID 83404

SACKETT, W(ILLIAM) T(ECUMSEH), JR, ELECTRICAL ENGINEERING. *Current Pos:* CHMN BD, ALTEC SOLUTIONS INC & INFRARED SOLUTIONS INC, 94- *Personal Data:* b Xenia, Ohio, Jan 28, 21; m 46, M Louise Kelly; c William T III, Brian E, John T & R Henry. *Educ:* Johns Hopkins Univ, BEE, 41, DrEng(elec eng), 50. *Prof Exp:* Engr, Duquesne Light Co, 41-42; elec engr, US Naval Ord Lab, 42-50; asst chief, Elec Eng Div, Battelle Inst, 50-55; mgr res, Kuhlman Elec Co, 55-59; dir res, Honeywell Inc, 60-77, dir, Syst & Res Ctr, 77-80, vpres, Corp Technol Ctr, 80-84, vpres corp res, 84-86; assoc dean, Inst Technol, Univ Minn, 86-89; pres, XOX Corp, 89-92. *Concurrent Pos:* Instr, Johns Hopkins Univ, 47-48. *Mem:* AAAS; Inst Elec & Electronics Engrs; Sigma Xi. *Res:* Contact resistance; instrumentation; insulation; research administration; aerospace sciences. *Mailing Add:* 1349 Pike Lake Dr New Brighton MN 55112

SACKETT, WILLIAM MALCOLM, GEOCHEMISTRY, CHEMISTRY. *Current Pos:* prof marine sci & chmn dept, 79-83, GRAD RES PROF, UNIV SFLA, 83- *Personal Data:* b St Louis, Mo, Nov 14, 30; m 56, Mary A Huchey; c Susan A & Karen L. *Educ:* Wash Univ, BA, 53, PhD(chem), 58. *Prof Exp:* Chemist, Carbide & Carbon Chem Corp, Ky, 53-54 & Mallinckrodt Chem Co, Mo, 54; vis asst res chemist, Scripps Inst Oceanog, Univ Calif, San Diego, 58-59; sr res engr, Pan Am Petrol Corp, 59-61, tech group supvr, 61-62; asst prof geol, Columbia Univ, 62-64; assoc prof chem, Univ Tulsa, 65-68; from assoc prof to prof oceanog, Tex A&M Univ, 68-79. *Concurrent Pos:* Von Humboldt fel, 76-77; fel, Richard Moht Gowery Field, Am Geophys Union, 86-87. *Mem:* Am Geophys Union; Geochem Soc; Sigma Xi. *Res:* Isotope geochemistry of carbon, uranium-thorium series of radioactive elements; organic geochem marine pollutions. *Mailing Add:* 2500 Driftwood Rd SE St Petersburg FL 33705. *Fax:* 813-893-9189

SACKHEIM, ROBERT LEWIS, AEROSPACE ENGINEERING. *Current Pos:* proj mgr, TRW, 64-69, sect head, 72-76, dept mgr, 76-81, mgr new bus, 81-86, lab mgr, 86-90, dep ctr dir, 90-93, CTR DIR, TRW, 93- *Personal Data:* b New York, NY, May 16, 37; m 64, Babette Freund; c Karen Holly & Andrew Frederick. *Educ:* Univ Va, BS, 59; Columbia Univ, MS, 61. *Honors & Awards:* Group Achievement Award, NASA, 70, 78 & 86; Shuttle Flag Award, Am Inst Astronaut & Aeronaut, 84, J H Wyld Propulsion Award, 92. *Prof Exp:* Chief, Titan II Propulsion Sect, USAF, 61-63; proj engr, Comsat Corp, 69-72. *Concurrent Pos:* Instr, Univ Calif Los Angeles Eng Exten, 86; mem, Aeronaut & Space Eng Bd, Nat Res Coun, 94- *Mem:* Fel Am Inst Astronaut & Aeronaut; Int Acad Astronaut. *Res:* Granted seven patents for spacecraft propulsion systems, devices and components; author of two books; contributed over 90 articles to professional journals. *Mailing Add:* TRW Space & Elec Group Bldg 01/Rm 2010 1 Space Park Blvd Rm 2010 Redondo Beach CA 90278-1001. *Fax:* 310-812-59799; *E-Mail:* robert.sackheim@trw.com

SACKMAN, GEORGE LAWRENCE, ELECTRICAL ENGINEERING. *Current Pos:* PROF ELEC ENG, WATSON SCH, 84- *Personal Data:* b Baxley, Ga, Mar 15, 33; m 63; c 2. *Educ:* Univ Fla, BME, 54, BEE, 57, MSE, 59; Stanford Univ, PhD(elec eng), 64. *Prof Exp:* Res engr, Electron Tube Div, Litton Industs, Inc, 64-65; from assoc prof to prof elec eng, Naval Postgrad Sch, 65-84. *Concurrent Pos:* Consult, Lansmont Corp, 74- *Mem:* Inst Elec & Electronics Engrs; Acoust Soc Am; Sigma Xi; Res Soc Am. *Res:* Underwater acoustics; ultrasonic image systems; acoustic signal processing. *Mailing Add:* Elec Eng TJ Watson Sch Eng State Univ NY Binghamton NY 13902

SACKMAN, JEROME L(EO), ENGINEERING. *Current Pos:* from asst prof to assoc prof, 60-66, PROF CIVIL ENG, UNIV CALIF, BERKELEY, 66-, VCHMN DIV STRUCT ENG & STRUCT MECH, 67- *Personal Data:* b Rockaway Beach, NY, June 16, 29; m 51; c 2. *Educ:* Cooper Union, BCE, 51; Columbia Univ, MS, 55, ScD, 59. *Prof Exp:* Civil engr, Eng Res & Develop Labs, US Dept Army, Ft Belvoir, Va, 51-52; asst thermal inelasticity, Inst Flight Struct, Columbia Univ, 56-57; from instr to asst prof appl mech, 57-60. *Concurrent Pos:* Sci consult, Paul Weidlinger, Consult Eng, NY, 59-, Math Sci, Wash, 67-, Lockheed Propulsion Co, Calif, 67- & Physics Int Co, 70-; mem at large, US Nat Comt Theoret & Appl Mech, 75-78. *Mem:* AAAS; Am Soc Civil Engrs; Am Soc Mech Engrs; Soc Eng Sci; Soc Exp Stress Anal; Sigma Xi. *Res:* Mechanics of solids; stress and stability analysis of deformable solids; wave propagation in deformable solids. *Mailing Add:* 576 The Alameda Berkeley CA 94707-1653

SACKMANN, I JULIANA, ASTROPHYSICS. *Current Pos:* res fel, Calif Inst Technol, 71-74, res assoc, Jet Propulsion Lab & vis assoc, 74-76, sr res fel astrophys, 76-81, FAC ASSOC, CALIF INST TECHNOL, 81- *Personal Data:* b Schoenau, EGer, Feb 8, 42; US citizen; m 73; c 2. *Educ:* Univ Toronto, BA, 63, MA, 65, & PhD(astrophys), 68. *Prof Exp:* Nat Res Coun Can fel astrophys, Univ Observ, Gottingen, WGer, 68-71; Alexander von Humboldt fel, Max Planck Inst Physics & Astrophys, Munich, WGer, 69-71. *Mem:* Am Astron Soc; Can Astron Soc. *Res:* Violent helium shell flashes in stars and their consequences on new element nucleosynthesis explaining carbon stars; new convective breakthroughs in the interior; observable surface variabilities on short timescales; FG Sagittae; mass loss and the sun. *Mailing Add:* Kellogg Radiation Lab 106-38 Calif Inst Technol Pasadena CA 91125

SACKNER, MARVIN ARTHUR, PULMONARY PHYSIOLOGY. *Current Pos:* DIR, MED CTR, MT SINAI HOSP. *Personal Data:* b Philadelphia, Pa, Feb 16, 32; m 56; c 3. *Educ:* Temple Univ, BS, 63; Jefferson Med Col, MD, 57; Am Bd Internal Med, dipl, 65; Am Bd Pulmonary Dis, dipl, 69. *Prof Exp:* Intern med, Philadelphia Gen Hosp, 57-58, resident, 58-61; Am Col Physicians res fel physiol, Grad Sch Med, Univ Pa, 61-64, instr, 63-64; chief div pulmonary dis, Mt Sinai Med Ctr, 64-78, dir med serv, 74-; prof med, Univ Miami, 73- *Concurrent Pos:* Pa Heart Asn fel cardiol, 58-59; Am Col Physicians Brower traveling fel, 66; mem pulmonary dis adv comt, Nat Heart & Lung Inst; mem, Am Bd Pulmonary Dis, 74; mem, Am Bd Internal Med, chmn, Subspecialty Bd Pulmonary Dis, 78-79. *Mem:* Am Fedn Clin Res; fel Am Col Physicians; Am Thoracic Soc (pres, 80-81); Am Physiol Soc. *Res:* Pulmonary circulation; mucociliary clearance; mechanics of breathing, non-invasive cardiopulmonary monitoring. *Mailing Add:* Dept Med Serv Mt Sinai Hosp 4300 Alton Rd Miami Beach FL 33140-2849

SACKOFF, MARTIN M, TECHNICAL MANAGEMENT IN CHEMISTRY, LEGAL CHEMICAL INVESTIGATIONS. *Current Pos:* dir special proj, 79-85, EXEC DIR LABS, INT TESTING LABS, 85- *Personal Data:* b Philadelphia, Pa, Mar 3, 18; m 46, Evelyn E Silver; c Ellen J. *Educ:* Philadelphia Col Pharm & Sci, BSc, 41; Univ Del, MSc, 51, PhD(org polymer), 53. *Prof Exp:* Sr chemist res & develop, Scott Paper Co, 53-55; group leader, Borden Chem Co, 56-58; mat staff consult, Philco-Ford Corp, 58-63; dir res & develop, Girder Process Co, 63-66, United Merchants & Mfrs, 67-77. *Mem:* Am Chem Soc; Tire Soc; Soc Plastics Engrs. *Res:* Polymeric coatings; different types of adhesives; synthetic polymeric activities; synthetic fethers; melamine and formaldehyde laminates. *Mailing Add:* Int Testing Labs 580 Market St Newark NJ 07105

SACKS, CLIFFORD EUGENE, ORGANIC CHEMISTRY & MANAGEMENT. *Current Pos:* res chemist, Upjohn Co, 79-85, assoc dir process res & develop, 85-90, assoc dir chem res prep, 91-92, ASSOC DIR PROCESS RES & DEVELOP, UPJOHN CO, 92- *Personal Data:* b Carlisle, Pa, Oct 18, 53; m 77, Cheryl; c Ryan, Rachel & Justin. *Educ:* Purdue Univ, BS, 75; Calif Inst Technol, PhD(chem), 80. *Mem:* Am Chem Soc; AAAS. *Res:* Process research and development including steroids, heterocycles and insecticidal agents. *Mailing Add:* Upjohn Co 1500-91-2 Portage MI 49002. *Fax:* 616-329-9158

SACKS, DAVID B, PATHOLOGY. *Current Pos:* ASST PROF PATH, HARVARD MED SCH, 89- *Personal Data:* b Cape Town, SAfrica, Mar 20, 50; US citizen. *Educ:* Univ Cape Town, MBChB, 76. *Prof Exp:* Instr path & med, Sch Med, Wash Univ, 88-89. *Concurrent Pos:* Young investr award with distinction, Acad Clin Lab Physicians & Scientists, 87; asst pathologist, Barnes Hosp, 88-89; med dir clin chem, Brigham Womens Hosp, 89- *Mem:* Am Soc Biochem & Molecular biol; fel Am Col Physicians; fel Am Col Pathologists; Am Diabetes Asn; Am Fedn Clin Res; Am Asn Clin Chem. *Res:* Mechanism of insulin action, including intracellular signal transduction; calmodulin function. *Mailing Add:* Dept Path Harvard Med Sch Brigham & Women's Hosp 75 Francis St Boston MA 02115-6195. *Fax:* 617-731-4872

SACKS, GERALD ENOCH, COMPUTER PROGRAMMING. *Current Pos:* PROF MATH, MASS INST TECHNOL, 67-; PROF MATH, HARVARD UNIV, 72- *Personal Data:* b Brooklyn, NY, Mar 22, 33; m 55, 83, Lulsa Raposo; c Matthew, Natalie, Paul & Ella. *Educ:* Cornell Univ, BEE & MEE, 58, PhD(math), 61. *Hon Degrees:* MA, Harvard Univ, 73. *Prof Exp:* NSF fel math, Inst Advan Study, 61-62; from asst prof to assoc prof, Cornell Univ, 62-67. *Concurrent Pos:* Guggenheim fel, 66-67; Inst Advan Study fel, 73-74. *Mem:* Am Math Soc; Asn Symbolic Logic. *Res:* Mathematical logic; recursive function theory; set theory. *Mailing Add:* Dept Math Harvard Univ One Oxford St Cambridge MA 02138. *E-Mail:* sacks@zariski.harvard.edu

SACKS, IVOR SELWYN, GEOPHYSICS. *Current Pos:* fel seismol, 62-63, STAFF MEM, CARNEGIE INST WASH DEPT TERRESTRIAL MAGNETISM, 64- *Personal Data:* b Johannesburg, SAfrica, Mar 20, 34; m 62, Pamela; c 1. *Educ:* Univ Witwatersrand, BSc, 54, PhD(geophys), 62. *Prof Exp:* Staff mem seismol & geophys, Bernard Price Inst Geophys Res, Univ Witwatersrand, 55-62. *Concurrent Pos:* Mem bd dirs, Geophys Inst Peru, 65-73, Inc Res Inst Seismol, 84-88; mem, Seismol Comt, Nat Res Coun, Nat Acad Sci, 72-75, 86-89, Geodynamics Comt, 84-88, chmn, Panel Real Time Earthquake Warning, 88-; mem, Nat Earthquake Prediction Eval Comt, 84-88, Standing Comt, Prog Array Seismic Studies Continental Lithosphere, 84-86; co-chair, Instrumentation Design Team, 84-87, Lithosphere-Asthenosphere Sounding, 86- *Mem:* Fel Am Geophys Union. *Res:* Seismology; attenuation of seismic waves in various regions of the earth; deep structure of continents and oceans; heterogeneity of the lower mantle; strain and earthquakes; author of numerous publications. *Mailing Add:* Dept Terrestrial Magnetism Carnegie Inst Wash 5241 Broad Branch Rd NW Washington DC 20015

SACKS, JEROME, MATHEMATICS. *Current Pos:* assoc prof, 61-66, PROF MATH, NORTHWESTERN UNIV, 66- *Personal Data:* b New York, NY, May 8, 31. *Educ:* Cornell Univ, BA, 52, PhD, 56. *Prof Exp:* Instr math, Calif Inst Technol, 56-57; asst prof math statist, Columbia Univ, 57-60; asst prof math, Cornell Univ, 60-61; prof statist, Rutgers Univ, 79-81. *Mem:* Am Statist Asn; Inst Math Statist. *Res:* Statistics; calibration; regression analysis; time series; robustness. *Mailing Add:* PO Box 14162 Research Triangle NC 27709

SACKS, JONATHAN, GEOMETRY, TOPOLOGY. *Current Pos:* SOFTWARE ENGR, INTERACTIVE DATA CORP, 97- *Personal Data:* b Worcester, S Africa, Oct 26, 43; m 69; c 1. *Educ:* Univ Cape Town, BSc, 68, MSc, 70; Univ Calif, Berkeley, PhD(math), 75. *Prof Exp:* Vis lectr math, Univ Ill, Urbana-Champaign, 75-77; lectr math, Univ Chicago, 77-82; software engr, Applicon Inc, Billerica, Mass, 91-94. *Mem:* Am Math Soc. *Res:* Eigenvalues of the Laplacian on Riemannian manifolds; application of the study of the topology of function spaces to variational problems in Riemannian geometry. *Mailing Add:* 375 Broadway Apt 2-R Cambridge MA 02139

SACKS, LAWRENCE EDGAR, MICROBIOLOGY. *Current Pos:* RETIRED. *Personal Data:* b Los Angeles, Calif, Mar 9, 20; m 63; c 2. *Educ:* Univ Calif, Los Angeles, AB, 41; Univ Wash, MS, 43; Univ Calif, PhD(microbiol), 48. *Prof Exp:* Asst bacteriologist, Comt Lignin & Cellulose Res, 43-44; bacteriologist, USDA, 48-62, prin chemist, 62-72, microbiologist, Western Regional Res Ctr, Sci & Educ Admin-Agr Res, 72-89. *Mem:* AAAS; Am Soc Microbiol; Am Chem Soc. *Res:* Action of antibiotics and surface active agents on bacteria; bacterial denitrification; Arthrobacter; spores; Clostridium perfringens; mutagen screening. *Mailing Add:* 681 Woodmont Ave Berkeley CA 94708-1235

SACKS, LAWRENCE J, INORGANIC CHEMISTRY. *Current Pos:* PROF CHEM, CHRISTOPHER NEWPORT COL, 70- *Personal Data:* b Newark, NJ, June 12, 28; m 55; c 3. *Educ:* Drew Univ, AB, 52; Pa State Univ, MS, 58; Univ Ill, PhD(inorg chem), 64. *Prof Exp:* Instr chem, Pa State, 53-55; res chemist, Monsanto Chem Co, 55-56; asst prof chem, Reed Col, 60-63 & Rose Polytech, 64-65; assoc prof, State Univ NY Col Buffalo, 65-68; prof, Hampton Inst, 68-70. *Concurrent Pos:* Assoc dir, Lab Chem Evolution, Dept Chem, Univ Md, College Park, 85-86. *Mem:* AAAS; Am Chem Soc. *Res:* Thermodynamics; theoretical calculations of bond energies, dipole movements and steric effects. *Mailing Add:* 542 Burcher Rd Newport News VA 23606-1502

SACKS, MARTIN, invertebrate zoology; deceased, see previous edition for last biography

SACKS, MARTIN EDWARD, CHEMICAL ENGINEERING, COAL SCIENCE. *Current Pos:* ENG CONSULT, 89- *Personal Data:* b Bronx, NY, Nov 22, 43; m 67; c 1. *Educ:* Cooper Union, BChE, 65; Univ Mich, MSE, 66; Stevens Inst Technol, PhD(chem eng), 72. *Prof Exp:* Res engr coal conversion, FMC Corp, 66-70; sr res engr, Cogas Develop Co, 72-78, process design supvr coal gasification, 78-80, eng mgr, 80-81; prin process engr & sect mgr, FMC Corp, 81-89. *Mem:* Am Inst Chem Engrs; Am Chem Soc. *Res:* Coal conversion, especially pyrolysis and gasification. *Mailing Add:* 11 Wickham Lane East Windsor NJ 08520-1209

SACKS, WILLIAM, POLYMER CHEMISTRY, POLYMER ENGINEERING. *Current Pos:* EXEC DIR, PLASTICS INST AM, 88- *Personal Data:* b Toronto, Ont, Jan 30, 26; m 52, Irene Ziebell; c David, Judi, Elaine & Patricia. *Educ:* Univ Toronto, BASc, 48, MASc, 49; McGill Univ, PhD(chem), 54. *Prof Exp:* Res officer, Nat Res Coun Can, Ottawa, 49-52, fel, McGill Univ, 52-54; res engr & res sect mgr, Visking Div, Union Carbide Corp, 54-61, group leader, Plastics Div, 61-65; res assoc & res mgr, Gen Chem & Fabricated Prod Div, Allied Corp, 66-73, tech dir, Films Dept, 73-79, dir, New Bus Develop, 79-87. *Mem:* Am Chem Soc; Chem Inst Can; Soc Plastics Engrs; Sigma Xi; NY Acad Sci. *Res:* Physical chemistry of polymers; properties and applications of polymer films; processing behavior of synthetic polymers; plastics recycling. *Mailing Add:* 686 Long Hill Rd Gillette NJ 07933-1346. *Fax:* 201-808-5953

SACKSTEDER, RICHARD CARL, MATHEMATICS. *Current Pos:* assoc prof, 65-67, PROF MATH, CITY UNIV NEW YORK, 67- *Personal Data:* b Muncie, Ind, Feb 11, 28; m 52; c 2. *Educ:* Univ Chicago, BS, 48, PhB, 46; Johns Hopkins Univ, PhD, 60. *Prof Exp:* Res mathematician, Ballistics Res Lab, US Dept Army, Aberdeen Proving Ground, Md, 54-59; vis mem, Inst Math Sci, NY Univ, 60-62; asst prof math, Barnard Col & Columbia Univ, 62-65. *Concurrent Pos:* Jr instr, Johns Hopkins Univ, 57-59; lectr, Goucher Col, 58. *Mem:* Am Math Soc; Catgut Acoust Soc. *Res:* Differential geometry; fluid dynamics. *Mailing Add:* City Univ New York Grad Sch & Univ Ctr 33 W 42nd St New York NY 10036-8003

SACKSTON, WALDEMAR E, PLANT PATHOLOGY. *Current Pos:* from asst plant pathologist to plant pathologist, 46-58, sr plant pathologist & head plant path sect, 58-60, chmn dept, 60-69, prof, 60-83, EMER PROF PLANT PATH, MACDONALD CAMPUS MCGILL UNIV, 83- *Personal Data:* b Manitoba, Jan 4, 18; m 41; c 2. *Educ:* Univ Manitoba, BSA, 38; McGill Univ, MSc, 40; Univ Minn, PhD(plant path), 49. *Honors & Awards:* Pustovoit Award, Int Sunflower Asn, 82; D L Bailey Award, Can Phytopath Soc, 83. *Prof Exp:* Asst, Macdonald Col, McGill Univ, 38-40; agr asst, Dom Lab Plant Path, Can Dept Agr, 41-46. *Concurrent Pos:* Specialist & consult, Point IV Prog, Chile, 54 & Uruguay, 56-57; at Res Ctr on Oilseed Crops, Cordoba, Spain, 72-77. *Mem:* fel Am Phytopath Soc; Indian Phytopath Soc; Int Sunflower Asn (pres, 78-80); fel Can Phytopath Soc (vpres, 58-60, pres, 60-61); Sigma Xi. *Res:* Diseases of oilseed crops; soilborne and seedborne diseases; epidemiology. *Mailing Add:* Dept Plant Sci Macdonald Campus McGill Univ Ste Anne de Bellevue PQ H9X 3V9 Can

SACLARIDES, THEODORE JOHN, SPHINCTER-SAVING ALTERNATIVES FOR RECTAL CANCER, FECAL INCONTINENCE & INFLAMMATORY BOWEL DISEASE. *Current Pos:* Asst prof surg, 88-93, ASSOC PROF SURG, RUSH MED COL, 93-, ASST PROF OBSTET & GYNEC & ASST PROF THERAPEUT RADIOL, 93-; HEAD, SECT COLON & RECTAL SURG, DEPT GEN SURG, RUSH-PRESBY-ST LUKE'S MED CTR, 91- *Personal Data:* b Clearwater, Fla, Oct 12, 56; m 80, Elena Economou; c Kathryn T, Evthokia S, Constantine P, Alexandra E & Theodora K. *Educ:* Vanderbilt Univ, BA, 78; Univ Miami, MD, 82. *Honors & Awards:* Young Investigators Award, Am Soc Colon & Rectal Surgeons, 93. *Concurrent Pos:* Residency surg, Rush-Presby-St Luke's Med Ctr, Chicago, 82-87, attend surgeon, 88-; fel colon & rectal surg, Mayo Clin, Rochester, 87-88; attend surgeon, Rush North Shore Med Ctr, Skokie, 91-. *Mem:* Fel Am Col Surgeons; fel Am Soc Colon & Rectal Surgeons; Soc Am Gastrointestinal Endoscopic Surgeons; Soc Surg Alimentary Tract; Am Soc Gastrointestinal Endoscopy. *Res:* Sphincter-saving approaches to rectal cancer, histopathological and survival studies of colon cancer; studies of inflammatory bowel disease and functional results following surgery. *Mailing Add:* 1653 W Congress Pkwy Chicago IL 60612. *Fax:* 312-942-2867

SADAGOPAN, VARADACHARI, MATERIALS SCIENCE. *Current Pos:* res staff mem phys sci, T J Watson Res Ctr, 68-72, mgr univ rel, 72-76, mgr tech rel, Off Res & Develop Coord, IBM Europe, 76-79, mgr tech rel, 79-88, DIV MGR UNIV REL, IBM RES DIV, IBM CORP, 88- *Personal Data:* b Uppiliappan Koil, Madras, India; US citizen; m 62. *Educ:* Univ Madras, BSc, 53; Annamalai Univ, Madras, MA, 55; Indian Inst Sci, DIISc, 58; Mass Inst Technol, SM, 60, MetE, 61. *Hon Degrees:* ScD, Mass Inst Technol, 64. *Prof Exp:* Asst econ affairs off, Hq, UN, 62, spec asst to secy-gen & chief liaison off for dels from Asia & Far East, UN Europ Off, Geneva, 63; res assoc mat sci, Mass Inst Technol, 64-67; prin res scientist, Avco Corp, Mass, 67-68. *Concurrent Pos:* Consult, Asian Bank, Manila, 71- *Mem:* Am Phys Soc; Inst Elec & Electronics Engrs. *Res:* Electronic materials. *Mailing Add:* IBM Res Div PO Box 218 Yorktown Heights NY 10598

SADANA, AJIT, BIOSENSORS, BIOSEPARATIONS-PROTEIN ADSORPTION. *Current Pos:* assoc prof, 81-90, PROF CHEM ENG, UNIV MISS, 90- *Personal Data:* b Rawalpindi, Pakistan, Feb 14, 47; US citizen; m 73, Lopa Tandon; c Neeti & Richa. *Educ:* Indian Inst Technol, BTech, 69; Univ Del, MCE, 72, PhD(chem eng), 75. *Prof Exp:* Sr sci officer, Nat Chem Lab, Coun Sci & Indust Res, India, 75-80; vis assoc prof chem eng, Auburn Univ, 80-81. *Concurrent Pos:* Consult, First Chem Corp, 88, DuPont de Nemours & Co, 88, Naval Res Lab, Wash, 90-91, NIH, 93; vis res scientist, E I DuPont de Nemours & Co, 88; sr fel, Naval Res Lab, Wash, DC, 90; vis scientist, Oak Ridge Nat Lab, 94, 95 & 96. *Mem:* Am Inst Chem Engrs. *Res:* Applications of fractals to antigen-antibody binding kinetics for biosensor applications; quality of product in bioseparations; protein adsorption on biomaterials; author of 2 books. *Mailing Add:* Chem Eng Dept Univ Miss University MS 38677-9740. *Fax:* 601-236-5282; *E-Mail:* cmsadana@olemiss.edu

SADANA, YOGINDER NATH, INORGANIC CHEMISTRY. *Current Pos:* assoc prof, 66-77, PROF CHEM, LAURENTIAN UNIV *Personal Data:* b Peshawar, India, May 15, 31; m 62; c 2. *Educ:* Univ Agra, BSc, 51, MSc, 53; Univ BC, PhD(chem), 63. *Prof Exp:* Sr res fel electrodeposition of metals & alloys, Nat Metall Lab, India, 54-58; res asst, Res Inst Precious Metals & Metall Chem, Ger, 58-59; instr chem, Wash State Univ, 62-63; res engr, Cominco Ltd, Can, 64-66 *Concurrent Pos:* Nat Res Coun Can res grants, 66-; fels, Chem Inst Can & Inst Metal Finishing; hon prof, Nanchang Inst Aero-Technol, China, 89. *Mem:* Am Chem Soc; Chem Inst Can. *Res:* Electrodeposition of metals and alloys; surface finishing techniques; electrodeposition of gold and gold alloys and their x-ray structures. *Mailing Add:* Chem Laurentian Univ 935 Ramsey Lake Rd Sudbury ON P3E 2C6 Can

SADANAGA, KIYOSHI, GENETICS. *Current Pos:* RETIRED. *Personal Data:* b Onomea, Hawaii, Feb 6, 20; m 66; c 2. *Educ:* Univ Hawaii, BS, 42; Iowa State Univ, MS, 51, PhD(genetics), 55. *Prof Exp:* Asst genetics, Sugar Cane Exp Sta, Hawaii Sugar Planters Asn, 52-53; geneticist, Oat Proj, USDA, 56-76, geneticist soybean res, 76-; prof genetics, Iowa State Univ, 59-83. *Concurrent Pos:* Fulbright scholar, Kyoto Univ, 60-61. *Res:* Genetics and cytogenetics of soybeans. *Mailing Add:* 1307 Sequoia Pl Davis CA 95616

SADAVA, DAVID ERIC, CELL BIOLOGY. *Current Pos:* from asst prof to assoc prof, 72-83, PROF BIOL, CLAREMONT COLS, 83-, CHMN JOINT SCI DEPT, 80- *Personal Data:* b Ottawa, Ont, Mar 14, 46; m 72, Angeline Douvas; c Dana. *Educ:* Carleton Univ, BSc, 67; Univ Calif, San Diego, PhD(cell biol), 71. *Prof Exp:* Researcher entomol, Can Dept Agr, 65-66; adv sci policy, Sci Secretariat, Can, 67; teaching asst biol, Univ Calif, San Diego, 67-71; researcher marine biol, Scripps Inst Oceanog, 72. *Concurrent Pos:* Woodrow Wilson Found fel, 67; vis prof, Univ Colo, 77-, Univ Calif, 86; vis scientist med oncol, City Hope. *Mem:* AAAS; Soc Pediat Res; Asn Politics Life Sci; Am Asn Cancer Res. *Res:* Cancer chemotherapy; biochemistry of development; pharmacology. *Mailing Add:* Joint Sci Dept Claremont Cols Claremont CA 91711. *E-Mail:* dsadava@jsd.claremont.edu

SADEE, WOLFGANG, MOLECULAR PHARMACOLOGY, NEUROSCIENCES. *Current Pos:* from asst prof to assoc prof, 74-81, PROF PHARM & PHARMACEUT CHEM, UNIV CALIF, SAN FRANCISCO, 81- *Personal Data:* b Bad Harzburg, WGer, Mar 25, 42; m 74. *Educ:* Free Univ Berlin, Dr rer nat, 68. *Honors & Awards:* First Res Achievement Award in Biotechnol, Am Asn Pharmaceut Scientists. *Prof Exp:* NATO fel, Univ Calif, San Francisco, 69; res assoc fel clin pharmacol, Free Univ Berlin, 70-71; asst prof pharm & med, Univ Southern Calif, 71-74. *Concurrent Pos:* Ed-in-chief, Pharmaceut Res. *Mem:* AAAS; Am Asn Pharmaceut Scientists. *Res:* Study of the structure, function, activation, and regulation of opioid and muscarinic receptors addresses the mechanism of narcotic addition and of memory. *Mailing Add:* Sch Pharm Univ Calif San Francisco Med Sch 513 Parnassus Ave San Francisco CA 94122-2722

SADEGH, ALI M, ORTHOPOATIC ENGINEERING, DESIGN & ANALYSIS OF DEVICE IMPLANTS. *Current Pos:* from asst prof to assoc prof, 82-92, PROF MECH ENG, DEPT MECH ENG, CITY UNIV NY, 92- *Personal Data:* b Tehran, Iran, Sept 1, 50; m 80, Guita Miremadi; c Mietra, Cameron, Mona, Jasmin & David. *Educ:* Sharif Univ Technol, BS, 72; Mich State Univ, MS, 75, PhD(mech), 78. *Honors & Awards:* Melville Medal, Am Soc Mech Engrs, 93. *Prof Exp:* Mech engr, Mfg Dept, Danube Corp, Tehran, 72-73; design engr, Eng Div, Nat Radio & TV, Tehran, 72-74; postdoctoral scholar, Dept Appl Mech Eng Sci, Univ Mich, 78-79; asst prof, Dept Mech Eng, Sharif Univ Technol, 79-81; vis asst prof, Dept Metall Mech & Mat Sci, Mich State Univ, 81-82. *Concurrent Pos:* Consult various private cos & govt agencies, 79-96; chmn, Dept Mech Eng, Sch Eng, City Univ NY City Col, 93-96. *Mem:* Fel Soc Mfg Engrs; fel Am Soc Mech Engrs; Sigma Xi; Am Acad Mech; Biomed Eng Soc; Soc Automotive Engrs; Am Soc Eng Educ; Nat Soc Inventors. *Res:* Biomechanics particularly bone remodeling, bone and implants interactions, implant design, biodynamics, modeling of cervical spine, head and neck injuries; computational mechanics, boundary element method, fracture-damage of materials, mathematical modeling and mechanical systems analysis, design and manufacturing; published over 80 research papers and 41 technical reports; granted 4 patents. *Mailing Add:* Dept Mech Eng City Col NY New York NY 10031. *E-Mail:* sadegh@me-mail.engr.ccny.cuny.edu

SADEGHI, FARSHID, ENGINEERING. *Current Pos:* asst prof, 86-91, ASSOC PROF, PURDUE UNIV, 91- *Personal Data:* b Masjed Solaiman, Iran, Dec 23, 56; m 84, Brenda Stevens; c Nina M & Sara A. *Educ:* Univ Tenn, MS, 81; NC State Univ, PhD, 85. *Honors & Awards:* Burt L Newkirk Award, Am Soc Metall Engrs, 91. *Prof Exp:* Res asst, Univ Tenn, Chattanooga, 79-81; teaching asst, NC State Univ, 81-83, res asst, 83-85. *Mem:* Am Soc Metall Engrs; Soc Automotive Engrs. *Res:* Discovery that temperature effects in lubricated contacts are significant and cannot be neglected. *Mailing Add:* 3716 Chancellor Way West Lafayette IN 47906

SADEH, WILLY ZEEV, ENGINEERING. *Current Pos:* from asst prof to assoc prof, 68-76, PROF CIVIL ENG, COLO STATE UNIV, 76- *Personal Data:* b Galatz, Romania, Oct 13, 32; nat US; m 56; c 2. *Educ:* Israel Inst Technol, BSc, 58, MSc, 64; Brown Univ, PhD(eng), 68. *Honors & Awards:* Cert appreciation, Technol Utilization Prog, NASA, 71. *Prof Exp:* Res engr, Gen Aero M Dassault, Paris, 58-59, Nat Sci Res Ctr, 59-60 Desalination Plants, Israel, 60-62 & Negev Inst Arid Zone Res, 62; instr mech eng, Israel Inst Technol, 62-64; fel eng, Brown Univ, 64-65, res asst, 65-68. *Mem:* AAAS; Am Soc Mech Engrs; Am Asn Univ Professors; assoc fel Am Inst Aeronaut & Astronaut; Am Soc Eng Educ; Sigma Xi. *Res:* Fluid mechanics; turbulent flow; instrumentation; structural aerodynamics; atmospheric turbulence; air pollution; turbomachinery; boundary-layer flow. *Mailing Add:* Dept Civil Eng Colo State Univ Ft Collins CA 80523

SADIK, FARID, PHARMACEUTICS. *Current Pos:* assoc prof, 73-76, PROF PHARMACEUT, ASSOC DEAN & DIR GRAD STUDIES, COL PHARM, UNIV SC, 76- *Personal Data:* b Taibeh, Palestine, July 3, 34; US citizen; m 59; c 4. *Educ:* Univ Ga, BSPharm, 58; Univ Miss, PhD(pharmaceut), 68. *Prof Exp:* Pharmacist, 58-65; instr pharmaceut, Univ Miss, 65-68, asst prof, 68; asst prof, Northeast La Univ, 68-71; assoc prof, Univ Miss, 71-73. *Concurrent Pos:* Fulbright scholar, 87-88. *Mem:* Am Pharmaceut Asn. *Res:* Clinical pharmacy; effect of particle size of drugs on absorption. *Mailing Add:* Col Pharm Univ SC Columbia SC 29208-0001

SADJADI, FIROOZ AHMADI, SIGNAL & IMAGE PROCESSING, AUTOMATIC OBJECT RECOGNITION. *Current Pos:* STAFF SCIENTIST, LOCKHEED MARTIN CORP, 93- *Personal Data:* b Tehran; US citizen. *Educ:* Purdue Univ, BS, 72, MS, 74; Univ Southern Calif, EEE, 76; Univ Tenn, PhD(elec eng). *Prof Exp:* Res asst image processing, Image Processing Inst, Univ Southern Calif, 74-77; res asst image & signal processing, Image & Pattern Anal Lab, Univ Tenn, 77-83; prin res scientist signal & image processing, Honeywell Systs & Res Ctr, 83-93. *Concurrent Pos:* Consult image processing, Oak Ridge Nat Lab; prin investr, Defense Advan Res Projs Agency, Army & Air Force, 84-; lectr, George Washington Univ, Univ London, Univ Md, Calif, Los Angeles, Int Soc Optical Eng, Gov Res Ctrs, 88-; guest ed, Optical Eng J, 91 & 92, Int Soc Elec & Electronics Engrs Comput, 97. *Mem:* Sigma Xi; sr mem Inst Elec & Electronics Engrs; Int Soc Optical Eng. *Res:* Modeling, algorithm design, sensor fusion, performance evaluation for the development of adaptive millimeter wave radar, infrared, radar and sonar signal processing systems for a variety of applications: automatic object recognition, enhanced vision for autonomous landing, remote sensing, seafloor mapping; environmental monitoring; agriculture automation; granted 6 patents with several pending and published more than 100 articles, one book and editor of 12 books. *Mailing Add:* 3400 Highcrest Rd NE Minneapolis MN 55418

SADLER, ARTHUR GRAHAM, CHEMISTRY, CERAMICS. *Current Pos:* RETIRED. *Personal Data:* b Pontefract, Eng, Oct 20, 25; Can citizen; m 57; c 4. *Educ:* Univ Leeds, BSc, 51, PhD(ceramics), 56. *Prof Exp:* Mem, Electronic Ceramics, Dept Mines & Tech Surv, Govt Can, 57-59, sr sci staff, 59-62; mem sci staff ferrites, Northern Elec Co Ltd, Ont, 62-63, dept chief magnetic mat, 63-67, mgr phys sci, 67-69; mgr electronic mat & processes, Bell-Northern Res Ltd, 69-72, mgr, Sta Apparatus Br Lab, 72- *Mem:* Can Ceramic Soc (pres, 69-70); fel Brit Inst Ceramics; fel Chem Inst Can. *Res:* Chemistry of high temperature reactions in inorganic materials; chemistry and physics of electronic ceramics; research management. *Mailing Add:* 480 Cloverdale Rd Rockcliffe ON K1M 0Y6 Can

SADLER, CHARLES ROBINSON, JR, LOW BACK PAIN, COMPUTERS-IN-MEDICINE. *Current Pos:* ASST CLIN PROF ORTHOP SURG, UNIV SOUTHERN CALIF, 90- *Personal Data:* b Richmond, Va, June 17, 50; m; c 1. *Educ:* Rice Univ, Houston, Tex, BSEE, 72, MEE, 73; Baylor Col Med, MD, 76. *Concurrent Pos:* Consult orthop surg, Rancho Los Amigos Hosp, 84-; pres, Charles Sadler MD PC, 86-; vpres, US Sect Int Col Surgeons, 90- *Res:* Orthopedic surgery. *Mailing Add:* 8447 Wilshire Blvd No 424 Beverly Hills CA 90211-3209

SADLER, G(ERALD) W(ESLEY), mechanical engineering, for more information see previous edition

SADLER, GEORGE D, FOOD PACKAGING SAFETY ISSUES, MIGRATION OF ORGANIC COMPOUNDS IN PLASTICS. *Current Pos:* STAFF MEM, NAT CTR FOOD SAFETY & TECHNOL, 92- *Personal Data:* b Long Beach, Miss, Mar 17, 52; m 75, Cynthia A Tompkins; c Michael, Emily, Philip & Elizabeth. *Educ:* Fla State Univ, BS, 74; Brigham Young Univ, MS, 80; Purdue Univ, PhD(food chem), 84. *Prof Exp:* Res & develop technician, Energy Systs Div, Olin Industs, 74-76, opers control technician, 76-77; res fel, Purdue Univ, 84-86; from asst prof to assoc prof food chem, Univ Fla, 86-92. *Mem:* Inst Food Technologists; Am Chem Soc. *Res:* Impact of organic compound migration on quality and safety of organic compounds in plastics and paper food packaging materials. *Mailing Add:* 9317 Waterford Lane Orland Park IL 60462. *Fax:* 708-563-1873; *E-Mail:* mtcsadler@minna.cns.iit.edu

SADLER, J(ASPER) EVAN, HEMATOLOGY. *Current Pos:* ASSOC INVESTR, HOWARD HUGHES MED INST, 84- *Personal Data:* b Huntington, WVa, Nov 9, 51; m 81; c 2. *Educ:* Princeton Univ, AB, 73; Duke Univ, PhD(biochem), 78, MD, 79. *Prof Exp:* Intern internal med, Duke Univ Med Ctr, 79-80, resident, 80-81; fel hemat, Univ Wash, Seattle, 81-84; from asst prof to assoc prof, Sch Med, Wash Univ, 84-89, asst prof biochem & molecular biophys, 85- *Concurrent Pos:* Mem Coun Thrombosis, Am Heart Asn. *Mem:* Am Soc Clin Invest; Am Heart Asn; Int Soc Thrombosis & Hemostasis; Am Fedn Clin Res; Am Soc Hemat; Am Soc Biochem & Molecular Biol. *Res:* Regulation and structure-function relationships of hemostatic proteins. *Mailing Add:* Dept Med HHMI Wash Univ Sch Med 660 S Euclid Box 8022 St Louis MO 63110. *Fax:* 314-454-3012; *E-Mail:* sadlerj@ustg.edu

SADLER, JAMES C, METEOROLOGY. *Current Pos:* from assoc prof to prof meteorol, 65-87, EMER PROF, UNIV HAWAII, 87- *Personal Data:* b Silver Point, Tenn, Feb 9, 20; m 41; c 2. *Educ:* Tenn Polytech Inst, BS, 41; Univ Calif, Los Angeles, MA, 47. *Honors & Awards:* Banner Miller Award, Am Meteorol Soc. *Prof Exp:* Mil dir, Sacramento Peak Observ, US Air Force, 51-53, res meteorologist, Air Force Sch Aviation Med, 53-55; dir trop meteorol course, Air Weather Serv, Univ Hawaii, 55-59; chief satellite meteorol br, Air Force Cambridge Res Labs, 59-62, chief satellite utilization, Int Indian Ocean Exped, 62-65. *Concurrent Pos:* Consult, US Air Force, 67- & US Navy, 68- *Mem:* AAAS; fel Am Meteorol Soc; Am Geophys Union. *Res:* Kinematic description of the general circulation of the tropics and its relation to satellite determined cloud climatology and life history of tropical cyclones. *Mailing Add:* 1489 Kalaepohaku St Honolulu HI 96816

SADLER, MICHAEL ERVIN, PHYSICS, ELEMENTARY PARTICLE PHYSICS. *Current Pos:* PROF PHYSICS, ABILENE CHRISTIAN UNIV, 80-; ASST PROF PHYSICS, ABILENE UNIV, 88- *Personal Data:* b Tex, May 18, 48; m 73, Virginia Gustafson; c Lela J & Laura J. *Educ:* Tex Tech Univ, BA, 71; Ind Univ, MS, 74, PhD(physics), 77. *Prof Exp:* Res physicist, Univ Calif Los Angeles, 77-80. *Mem:* Am Phys Soc; Am Asn Phys Teachers. *Res:* Pion-nucleon scattering; structure of the nucleon and its excited states. *Mailing Add:* 1233 Piedmont Dr Abilene TX 79601. *Fax:* 915-674-2202; *E-Mail:* sadler@acuvax.ace.edu

SADLER, MONROE SCHARFF, PHYSICAL CHEMISTRY. *Current Pos:* RETIRED. *Personal Data:* b Natchez, Miss, Oct 2, 20; m 43, Barbara Livingston; c Nora. *Educ:* Mass Inst Technol, SB, 42; Carnegie Inst Technol, MS, 48, DSc(chem), 49. *Prof Exp:* Res chemist, E I du Pont de Nemours & Co, Inc, 49-53, res supvr, 53-59, lab dir, 59-63, dir mat res, 63-66, asst dir res & develop, 66-68, asst dir, Develop Dept, 68-70, dir develop dept, 70-75, asst dir, Cent Res & Develop Dept, 75-80. *Mem:* Am Chem Soc; Am Phys Soc. *Res:* Physics of high pressure; ultrasonics; nuclear magnetic resonance; ferromagnetic materials. *Mailing Add:* 8510 Sandy Oak Lane Sarasota FL 34238

SADLER, STANLEY GENE, MECHANICAL & AEROSPACE SCIENCES. *Current Pos:* dynamic staff specialist, Bell Helicopter Textron, 78-80, chief rotor dynamics, 81-83, group engr aeromech, 83-89, staff engr aeromech, 89-93, PRIN ENGR, BELL HELICOPTER TEXTRON, 93- *Personal Data:* b Spring Lake, Utah, Mar 6, 38; m 63, Suzanne Rich; c Nathan, Rebecca, Jennifer, Jared & Rachelle. *Educ:* Univ Utah, BS, 62; Univ Rochester, MS, 64, PhD(mech & aerospace sci), 68. *Prof Exp:* Lab asst, High Velocity Impact Lab, Univ Utah, 62-63; res engr, Rochester Appl Sci Assocs, 67-71, group head aerodyn & hydrodyn res, 71-72; sr proj engr, Homelite Textron, 72-78. *Mem:* Am Soc Mech Engrs; Am Helicopter Soc. *Res:* Statics and dynamics of elastic systems; fluid dynamics and stability; helicopter rotor dynamics and noise; shell analysis; rotating system vibration and stability. *Mailing Add:* 1002 Curtis Ct Arlington TX 76012-5327

SADLER, THOMAS WILLIAM, TERATOLOGY, DEVELOPMENTAL BIOLOGY. *Current Pos:* assoc prof anat, 82-88, PROF CELL BIOL & ANAT, SCH MED, UNIV NC, 85- *Personal Data:* b Portsmouth, Ohio, Feb 25, 49; m 76; c 2. *Educ:* Wake Forest Univ, BS, 71; Univ Va, PhD(anat), 76. *Prof Exp:* Asst prof anat, Univ Va, 76-79; assoc prof anat, Col Med, Univ Cincinnati, 79-82. *Concurrent Pos:* Vis prof, Downing Col, Cambridge Univ, Eng, 76. *Mem:* Teratol Soc; Am Asn Anatomists; AAAS. *Res:* Investigation of normal and abnormal events during embryogenesis; development of techniques for maintaining mammalian embryos in culture during organogenesis. *Mailing Add:* Dept Cell Biol & Anat Univ NC CB No 7090 312 Taylor Hall Mason Farm Rd Chapel Hill NC 27599-7090

SADLER, WILLIAM OTHO, limnology; deceased, see previous edition for last biography

SADOCK, BENJAMIN, MEDICINE, PSYCHIATRY. *Current Pos:* PROF PSYCHIAT & DIR STUDENT HEALTH PSYCHIAT, NY UNIV, 80-, DIR, UNDERGRAD EDUC, 86- *Personal Data:* b New York, NY, Dec 22, 33; m 63, Virginia Alcott; c James & Victoria. *Educ:* Union Col, NY, AB, 55; New York Med Col, MD, 59; Am Bd Psychiat, dipl, 66. *Prof Exp:* Instr psychiat, Univ Tex Southwestern Med Sch Dallas, 64-65; from instr to assoc prof psychiat, NY Med Col, 65-75, prof, 75-80, co-dir, Sexual Ther Ctr, 72-80, dir continuing educ psychiat, 75-80. *Concurrent Pos:* Consult, Wichita Falls State Hosp, Tex, 64-65; chief psychiat consult, Student Health Serv, New York Med Col, 66-, dir div group process, 68-; assoc examr, Am Bd Psychiat, 67-; clin asst prof, Sch Med, NY Univ, 69-73; vchmn, Dept Psychiat, NY Univ, 84-, co-dir, grad med educ, 86- *Mem:* Am Psychiat Asn; NY Acad Med; fel Am Col Physicians. *Mailing Add:* Four E 89th St New York NY 10128-0636

SADOCK, VIRGINIA A, PSYCHIATRY. *Current Pos:* Asst clin prof psychiat, Med Col, 74-80, CLIN PROF PSYCHIAT, NY UNIV MED CTR, 80- *Personal Data:* b Bulgaria, Nov 25, 38; US citizen; m 63; c James & Victoria. *Educ:* Bennington Col, AB, 60; New York Med Col, MD, 70. *Concurrent Pos:* Dir prog human sexuality & sex therapy, Dept Psychiat, New York Univ Med Ctr, 80. *Mem:* AMA; fel Am Psychiat Asn; Am Med Womens Asn; Am Asn Sex Educrs & Counrs; fel Acad Med. *Mailing Add:* Four E 89th St New York NY 10128-0636

SADOFF, AHREN J, ELEMENTARY PARTICLE PHYSICS, PHYSICS. *Current Pos:* PROF PHYSICS, ITHACA COL, 88- *Personal Data:* b Ithaca, NY, May 26, 36. *Educ:* Mass Inst Technol, BS, 58; Cornell Univ, PhD(physics), 64. *Prof Exp:* Res assoc Lab Nuclear Studies, Cornell Univ, 64-65. *Concurrent Pos:* Vis scientist, Lawrence Livermore Radiation Lab, Berkeley, Calif, 80; vis prof, Cornell Univ, 86-88. *Mem:* Am Phys Soc; Sigma Xi. *Mailing Add:* Dept Physics Ithaca Col Ithaca NY 14850

SADOFF, HAROLD LLOYD, MICROBIOLOGY, BIOCHEMISTRY. *Current Pos:* from asst prof to assoc prof, 55-65, PROF MICROBIOL, MICH STATE UNIV, 65-, PROF PUB HEALTH, 77- *Personal Data:* b Minneapolis, Minn, Sept 17, 24; m 46, Gertrude H Lax; c David Z, Barbara R, Daniel A & Mark J. *Educ:* Univ Minn, BChEng, 47; Univ Ill, MS, 52, PhD(microbiol, biochem), 55. *Prof Exp:* Res assoc chem eng, Univ Ill, 54-55. *Concurrent Pos:* USPHS fel, Univ Wash, 61-62 & Stanford Univ, 70-71; mem microbiol chem study sect, NIH, 71-73. *Mem:* AAAS; Am Soc Microbiol; Am Soc Biol Chemists; NY Acad Sci; Soc Appl Bact; Sigma Xi. *Res:* The biochemistry and molecular biology of cell differentiation of microorganisms. *Mailing Add:* Dept Microbiol & Pub Health Col Human Med Michi State Univ East Lansing MI 48824

SADOSKY, ALESIA BETH, molecular pathogenesis, microbiology, for more information see previous edition

SADOULET, BERNARD, ASTROPHYSICS. *Current Pos:* sabbatical, 84-85, PROF PHYSICS, UNIV CALIF, BERKELEY, 85-, DIR, CTR PARTICLE ASTROPHYS, NSF SCI & TECHNOL CTR, 88- *Personal Data:* b Nice, France, Apr 23, 44; m 67, Elisabeth Chaine; c Loic, Helene & Samuel. *Educ:* Serie A & Math Elementaries, Lyon, Baccalaureat, 60-61; Univ Paris, License, 65; Ancien Eleve l'Ecole Polytech, Paris, dipl, 63-65; Univ Orsay, France, dipl, 65-66, PhD(phys sci), 71. *Prof Exp:* Fel, Lawrence Berkeley Lab, Univ Calif, Berkeley, 73-76, physicist, 76-81, sr physicist, 81-84; fel & staff, Europ Orgn Nuclear Res, 66-73. *Mem:* Am Phys Soc; AAAS; Am Astron Soc; Am Asn Physics Teachers. *Res:* Search for dark matter particles with ionization and cryogenic detectors and development of gas scintillation drift chambers for x-ray astrophysics. *Mailing Add:* Dept Physics Univ Calif Berkeley Berkeley CA 94720. *Fax:* 510-642-5719; *E-Mail:* sadoulet@lbl.gov

SADOVNIK, ISAAC, MAGNETOHYDRODYNAMICS, ENERGY CONVERSION & PROPULSION. *Current Pos:* PRIN RES ENGR, TEXTRON SYSTS CO, 81- *Personal Data:* b Lima, Peru, Sept 15, 53; US citizen; m 94, Joan Cooper; c Eli. *Educ:* Mass Inst Technol, SB, 74, SB, 75, SM, 76, PhD(physics of fluids), 81. *Honors & Awards:* Jimmy Hamilton Award, Am Soc Naval Engrs, 92. *Res:* Magnetohydrodynamic propulsion for submarines; magnetohydrodynamic energy conversion and electric discharge phenomena in plasmas. *Mailing Add:* 201 Lowell St Wilmington MA 01887. *E-Mail:* isadovni@systems.textron.com

SADOWAY, DONALD ROBERT, MOLTEN SALT CHEMISTRY. *Current Pos:* NATO fel, 77-78, asst prof, 78-82, ASSOC PROF MAT ENG, MASS INST TECHNOL, 82- *Personal Data:* b Toronto, Can, Mar 7, 50; m 73; c 3. *Educ:* Univ Toronto, BASc, 72, MASc, 73, PhD(chem metall), 77. *Mem:* Minerals, Metals, & Mat Soc; Electrochem Soc; Can Inst Mining & Metall; Int Soc Electrochem; AAAS. *Res:* Electrochemical processing of materials in molten salts and in cryogenic media. *Mailing Add:* 100 Memorial Dr Cambridge MA 02142

SADOWSKI, CHESTER M, LASER PHOTOCHEMISTRY. *Current Pos:* asst prof natural sci, York Univ, 67-70, chair natural sci, 77-80 & sci studies, 86-89, ASSOC PROF CHEM, YORK UNIV, 70-, CHAIR, DEPT CHEM, 96- *Personal Data:* b Toronto, Ont, Aug 10, 36; m 79, Philippa Harper; c Emma & Alexandra. *Educ:* Univ Toronto, BA, 57, PhD(chem kinetics), 61. *Prof Exp:* Res asst high temperature chem kinetics, Cornell Univ, 61-62; defence serv sci officer, Can Armament Res & Develop Estab, 62-67. *Concurrent Pos:* Guest worker, Nat Oceanic & Atmospheric Admin, 73-74; sabbaticant, Univ Cambridge, UK, 81-82, Univ Oxford, 94-95; assoc dean, Atkinson Col, 91-92; vis fel, Trinity Col, Oxford Univ, 94-95. *Mem:* Fel Chem Inst Can; Inter-Am Photochem Soc. *Res:* Laser assisted kinetic studies of free radical reactions; laser photochemistry of small molecules; rotational energy transfer. *Mailing Add:* Dept Chem York Univ 4700 Keele St North York ON M3J 1P3 Can. *Fax:* 416-736-5936; *E-Mail:* chesters@turing.sci.yorku.ca

SADOWSKI, IVAN J, TRANSCRIPTION, SIGNAL TRANSDUCTION. *Current Pos:* asst prof biochem, 90-95, ASSOC PROF, DEPT BIOCHEM, UNIV BC, 95- *Personal Data:* b Sask, Can, Oct 31, 60; m 83, Shelley Iona; c Eric, Ethan & Andrea. *Educ:* Univ Sask, BSc, 82; Univ Man, MSc, 84; Univ Toronto, PhD(med biophys), 87. *Prof Exp:* Fel molecular biol, Harvard Univ, 87-90. *Concurrent Pos:* Dir res & develop, Tatalus Molecular Inc, Vancouver, BC. *Mem:* Am Soc Microbiol; Am Soc Genetics; AAAS; Am Soc Biol. *Res:* Regulation to transcription by signal transduction pathways. *Mailing Add:* Dept Biochem Univ BC Vancouver BC V6T 1W5 Can

SADOWSKY, JOHN, SIGNAL & IMAGE PROCESSING, DESIGN & ANALYSIS OF ALGORITHMS. *Current Pos:* SR MATHEMATICIAN & ASST GROUP SUPVR, M S EISENHOWER RES CTR, APPL PHYSICS LAB, JOHNS HOPKINS UNIV, 89- *Personal Data:* b Worcester, Mass, Aug 27, 49; m 72, Emilie Hoffman; c Rebecca, Joshua & David. *Educ:* Johns Hopkins Univ, AB, 71; Univ Md, College Park, MA, 73, PhD(math), 80. *Prof Exp:* Mathematician, Soc Sec Admin, 73-77 & US Bur Census, 77-79; software engr, Hadron, Inc, 79-81; prin scientist & sect mgr, Syst Eng & Develop Corp, 81-89. *Concurrent Pos:* Adj grad fac computer sci, Whiting Sch Eng, Johns Hopkins Univ, 81-; secy & treas, Johns Hopkins Chapter, Sigma Xi. *Mem:* Am Math Soc; Math Asn Am; Sigma Xi. *Res:* Signal and image processing; diophantine approximation; applied number theory; computational complexity and algorithm analysis; signal analysis, representations, and decomposition; computational architectures; wavelet analysis; sensory engineering and synthetic environments. *Mailing Add:* 9006 Scotch Pine Ct Columbia MD 21045-2355. *Fax:* 410-953-6904; *E-Mail:* js@aplcomm.jhuapl.edu

SADOWSKY, MICHAEL JAY, SOIL MICROBIOLOGY, MICROBIAL ECOLOGY. *Current Pos:* ASSOC PROF SOIL SCI & MICROBIOL, UNIV MINN, 89- *Personal Data:* b Milwaukee, Wis, Jan 12, 55; m, Suzanne Caroll; c Alexander & Katherine. *Educ:* Univ Wis, BS, 77, MS, 79; Univ Hawaii, PhD(microbiol), 83. *Honors & Awards:* Young investr award, Am Soc Microbiol, 90. *Prof Exp:* Fel, Dept Biol, McGill Univ, 83-85; molecular biologist, Allied Chem Corp, 85; microbiologist, Agr Res Serv, USDA, 86-89. *Concurrent Pos:* Assoc ed, Appl Environ Microbiol, 89- *Mem:* Am Soc Microbiol; Soil Sci Soc Am; Int Soc Molecular, Plant & Microbe Interactions. *Res:* Ecological and genetic interaction of root-nodule bacteria with leguminous plants; role of environmental factors in transmission of DNA from genetically engineered organisms to native microbial populations; biodegradation of halogenated solvents and pesticides. *Mailing Add:* 710 Lovell Ave Roseville MN 55113. *E-Mail:* sadowsky@soil.umn.edu

SADRI, F, COMPUTER SCIENCE. *Current Pos:* ASSOC PROF MATH SCI, UNIV NC, GREENSBORO. *Educ:* Tehran Univ, Iran, BS, 72; Univ Wash, MS, 76; Princeton Univ, PhD, 80. *Res:* Modeling uncertainty; object-oriented databases; multi database systems. *Mailing Add:* Dept Math Univ NC Greensboro NC 27412-5001. *E-Mail:* sadri@uncg.edu

SADTLER, PHILIP, ANALYTICAL CHEMISTRY. *Current Pos:* PRES, SANDA CORP, 70- *Personal Data:* b Flourtown, Pa, July 19, 09; m 40, 64; c 3. *Educ:* Lehigh Univ, BS, 34. *Prof Exp:* Pres, Sadtler Res Labs Inc, 34-69; Sandia, Inc, 70-90. *Concurrent Pos:* Consult fluorine damage, infra-red & thermometric titration. *Mem:* Franklin Inst; Am Chem Soc; Am Soc Testing & Mat; Soc Appl Spectros; Am Mgt Asn. *Res:* Molecular studies with infrared spectrophotometry, ultraviolet, nuclear magnetic resonance; analyses, diesel engines; polymers; air pollution; explosion; synthesis of new materials; computerization of analytical instruments; digitization of spectral data. *Mailing Add:* 3555 W School House Lane Philadelphia PA 19144-5427

SADUN, ALBERTO CARLO, EXTRAGALACTIC JETS, FLUX VARIABILITY FROM ACTIVE GALACTIC NUCLEI. *Current Pos:* ASSOC PROF ASTRON, AGNES SCOTT COL, 84-; DIR ASTROPHYS, BRADLEY OBSERV, 84- *Personal Data:* b Atlanta, Ga, Apr 28, 55. *Educ:* Mass Inst Technol, BS, 77, PhD(physics), 84. *Prof Exp:* ASSOC PROF ASTRON, AGNES SCOTT COL, 84- *Concurrent Pos:* Adj prof, Ga State Univ, 86-; res affil, ANSA-Caltech Jet Propulsion Lab. *Mem:* Am Astron Soc; Astron Soc Pac; fel Royal Astron Soc; Int Astron Union; Sigma Xi; NY Acad Sci. *Res:* High-energy extragalactic astrophysics, particularly observations and some theoretical modeling; dynamics and morphology of optical and radio jets; flux variations of active galactic nuclei. *Mailing Add:* 4739 Springfield Dr Atlanta GA 30338

SADURSKI, EDWARD ALAN, INORGANIC CHEMISTRY, ORGANOMETALLIC CHEMISTRY. *Current Pos:* ASSOC PROF CHEM, OHIO NORTHERN UNIV, 80- *Personal Data:* b Detroit, Mich, June 12, 49; m 71; c 2. *Educ:* Oakland Univ, BS, 71; Wayne State Univ, PhD(inorg chem), 78. *Prof Exp:* Instr chem, Mich Christian Col, 70-72; vis asst prof inorg chem, Miami Univ, 78-80. *Mem:* Am Chem Soc; Sigma Xi. *Res:* Main group organometallics; nuclear magnetic resonance spectroscopy and single crystal x-ray crystallography. *Mailing Add:* Dept Chem Ohio Northern Univ Ada OH 45810

SAE, ANDY S W, BIOCHEMISTRY. *Current Pos:* Assoc prof, 69-80, chmn dept sci, 77-87, PROF CHEM, EASTERN NMEX UNIV, 80-, ACTG GRAD ASST DEAN, 88- *Personal Data:* b Hong Kong, Jan 5, 41; c 1. *Educ:* Kans State Univ, BS, 64, MS, 66, PhD(biochem), 69. *Concurrent Pos:* Tour speaker, Am Chem Soc. *Mem:* Am Chem Soc; Nat Sci Teacher Asn. *Res:* Chemical education; immobilized enzymes; enzyme isolation purification; peroxidases. *Mailing Add:* Dept Phys Sci Eastern NMex Univ Portales NM 88130

SAEGEBARTH, KLAUS ARTHUR, ORGANIC CHEMISTRY, AGRICULTURAL CHEMISTRY. *Current Pos:* RETIRED. *Personal Data:* b Berlin, Ger, Jan 5, 29; nat US; m 53, Mary A Douglas; c Eric, Katherine & Margaret. *Educ:* Univ Calif, BS, 53, Univ Wash, PhD(chem), 57. *Prof Exp:* Chemist, Radiation Lab, Univ Calif, 50; res chemist, Elastomer Chem Dept, E I du Pont de Nemours & Co Inc, 57-65, res & develop suprv, 65-67, res div head, 67-69, lab dir, Fabrics & Finishes Dept, Exp Sta, 69-70, res & develop mgr, Marshall Lab, 71-72, asst nat mgr indust finishes, 72-73, nat mgr trade finishes, 73-74, asst dir, Finishes Div, 74-78, dir res & develop, Fabrics & Finishes Dept, 78-80, dir, Agrichem Res & Develop Div, 80-88, dir, 88-90, vpres fibers res & develop, 90-92. *Concurrent Pos:* Trustee, Textile Res Inst, Princeton. *Mem:* Am Chem Soc; Sigma Xi; Soc Chem Indust. *Res:* Oxidation mechanisms; organometallics; catalysis; elastomers; finishes; agricultural chemicals. *Mailing Add:* 604 Haverhill Rd Sharpley Wilmington DE 19803

SAEGER, VICTOR WILLIAM, ENVIRONMENTAL CHEMISTRY, ANALYTICAL CHEMISTRY. *Current Pos:* RES SPECIALIST, MONSANTO CO, ST LOUIS, 60- *Personal Data:* b Kansas City, Mo, May 17, 33; m 62; c 2. *Educ:* Univ Mo-Kansas City, BA, 53; Iowa State Univ, PhD(phys chem), 60. *Mem:* Am Chem Soc; Am Soc Microbiol; Sigma Xi. *Res:* Environmental fate testing and assessment. *Mailing Add:* 870 N Dickson Kirkwood MO 63122-3075

SAEGUSA, TAKEO, POLYMER SCIENCE. *Current Pos:* From asst prof to prof, 57-91, EMER PROF, KYOTO UNIV, 91-; EXEC VPRES, KANSAI RES INST, 91- *Personal Data:* b Mukden, China, Oct 18, 27; m 56, Ayako; c Yumiko & Mamiko. *Educ:* Kyoto Univ, B, 50, D, 56. *Honors & Awards:* Award, Chem Soc Japan, 78; H F Mark Medal, Austrian Inst Sci & Res; Purple Ribbon Medal, Japanese Gout, 92; Award Polymer Chem, Am Chem Soc, 93. *Concurrent Pos:* Pres, Macromolecular Div, Int Pure & Appl Sci, Oxford, Eng, 85-89, Pac Polymer Fedn, Tokyo, 91-92. *Mem:* Hon mem Soc Polymer Sci. *Res:* Organic and inorganic polymer hybrids; no catalyst copolymerization via zwitterion intermediate; new catalysts for the ring-opening polymerization reactions; creation of novel non-ionic hydrogels; invention of new types of non-ionic surfactants; contributed over 500 papers on polymer science to journals. *Mailing Add:* Kyoto Univ 8-22 Toji-in Kitamachi Kyoto Kita-Ku 603 Japan

SAEKS, RICHARD E, ELECTRICAL ENGINEERING, APPLIED MATHEMATICS. *Current Pos:* AT DEPT ELEC ENG & COMPUT SCI, ARIZ STATE UNIV. *Personal Data:* b Chicago, Ill, Nov 30, 41. *Educ:* Northwestern Univ, Evanston, BS, 64; Colo State Univ, MS, 65; Cornell Univ, PhD(elec eng), 67. *Prof Exp:* From asst prof to assoc prof elec eng, Univ Notre Dame, 67-73; from assoc prof to prof elec eng & math, Tex Tech Univ, 73-79, Paul Whitfield prof eng, math & comput sci, 79- *Concurrent Pos:* NASA fel, Marshall Space Flight Ctr, 69-70; consult, Res Triangle Inst, 78-; ed-at-large, Marcell Dekker Inc, 78-; distinguished fac res award, Tex Tech Univ, 78- *Mem:* Am Soc Eng Educ; fel Inst Elec & Electronics Engrs; Soc Indust & Appl Math; Am Math Soc. *Res:* Fault analysis; large-scale systems; mathematical system theory. *Mailing Add:* Accurate Automation Corp 7001 Shallow Pond Rd Chattanooga TN 37421

SAEMAN, W(ALTER) C(ARL), CHEMICAL ENGINEERING, GLASS MAKING. *Current Pos:* RETIRED. *Personal Data:* b Norlina, NC, Apr 15, 14; m 40, 67, Cynthia Williams; c Betty A. *Educ:* Ga Inst Technol, BS, 40. *Prof Exp:* From jr to assoc chem engr, Chem Eng Div, Wilson Dam, Tenn Valley Authority, 40-46, proj leader, 47-52; sr chem engr, Oak Ridge Nat Lab, 46-47; engr, Olin Indust, Inc, 52-58, res proj mgr, Olin Corp, New Haven, 58-70, asst res dir, 70-77, prin engr, 77-81. *Concurrent Pos:* Mem bd dirs, Carolina Meadows, 85-92. *Mem:* Am Chem Soc; Am Inst Chem Eng; NY Acad Sci. *Res:* Drying; crystallization; ammonium nitrate; process control; nuclear energy development design of experiments; mathematics; natural philosophy; awarded more than 40 US patents. *Mailing Add:* Carolina Meadows Villa 123 Chapel Hill NC 27514

SAEMANN, JESSE C(HARLES), JR, ENGINEERING MECHANICS. *Current Pos:* From instr to prof, 46-83, EMER PROF ENG MECH, UNIV WIS-MADISON, 83- *Personal Data:* b Adell, Wis, Sept 16, 21; m 58; c 2. *Educ:* Univ Wis, BS, 43, MS, 50, PhD(eng mech), 55. *Mem:* Sigma Xi. *Res:* Shrinkage cracking of concrete block; variation of concrete masonry; soil mechanics. *Mailing Add:* 4421 Waite Lane Madison WI 53711

SAENGER, EUGENE L, RADIOLOGY, NUCLEAR MEDICINE. *Current Pos:* From asst to assoc prof, Univ Cincinnati, 43-62, prof radiol, 62-87, dir radioisotope lab, 50-87, EMER PROF RADIOL & EMER DIR, RADIOISOTOPE LAB, COL MED, UNIV CINCINNATI, 87- *Personal Data:* b Cincinnati, Ohio, Mar 5, 17; m 41, Sue Rieis; c Katherine. *Educ:* Harvard Univ, AB, 38; Univ Cincinnati, MD, 42; Am Bd Radiol, dipl, 46, cert nuclear med, 72. *Honors & Awards:* Aubrey Hampton lectr, Mass Gen Hosp, 71; Twenty Eighth George Charles de Hevesy Nuclear Pioneer Award, 87; Gold Medal, Radiol Soc NAm, 93. *Concurrent Pos:* Radiation therapist, Children's Hosp, Cincinnati, 46-47; pvt pract, 46-62; mem subcomt sealed gamma sources, Nat Comt Radiation Protection; Am Roentgen Ray Soc rep, Nat Coun Radiation Protection & Measurements, mem bd dirs, chmn sci comt brachyther, 68-; prog dir radiol sci, Nat Inst Gen Med Sci; consult to dir, Bur Radiol Health & to Surgeon Gen, USAF. *Mem:* Am Roentgen Ray Soc; fel Am Col Radiol; Health Physics Soc; Soc Nuclear Med; Am Radium Soc; Sigma Xi. *Res:* Radiobiology; cancer; radiological sciences; public health. *Mailing Add:* 9160 Given Rd Cincinnati OH 45243

SÁENZ, ALBERT WILLIAM, THEORETICAL PHYSICS. *Current Pos:* physicist, Naval Res Lab, 52-64, head, Anal & Theory Br, Radiation Div, 64-66, head, Theory Br, Nuclear Sci Div, 66-74, head, Theory Br, Nuclear Tech Div, 74-76, HEAD THEORY CONSULT STAFF, CONDENSED MATTER & RADIATION SCI DIV, NAVAL RES LAB, 76-; RES PROF PHYSICS DEPT, CATH UNIV, WASHINGTON, DC, 81- *Personal Data:* b Medellín, Colombia, Aug 27, 23; nat US; m 57. *Educ:* Univ Mich, BS, 44, MA, 45, PhD(physics), 49. *Prof Exp:* Physicist, Naval Res Lab, 50-51; physicist, Inst Appl Math, Ind Univ, 51-52. *Concurrent Pos:* Vis scientist, Mass Inst Technol, 57 & Oak Ridge Nat Lab, 58; vis fel, Johns Hopkins Univ, 64 & Princeton Univ, 76-77; lectr, Univ Md grad prog, Nat Res Lab, 50-51, 54-55 & 63-64. *Mem:* Fel Am Phys Soc; NY Acad Sci; Sigma Xi. *Res:* Special and general relativity; symmetry and degeneracy in quantum mechanics; equilibrium and nonequilibrium statistical mechanics; spin-wave theory and inelastic magnetic scattering of neutrons; quantum scattering theory. *Mailing Add:* Naval Res Lab Code 6693 Washington DC 20375-0001

SAENZ, REYNALDO V, PHARMACEUTICAL CHEMISTRY. *Current Pos:* ASST DEAN, UNIV NMEX, 89- *Personal Data:* b San Juan, Tex, Sept 29, 40; m 66. *Educ:* Univ Tex, BS, 62, MS, 65, PhD(pharmaceut chem), 67. *Prof Exp:* Assoc prof pharmaceut chem, Sch Pharm, Northeast La Univ, 66-89. *Mem:* Am Pharmaceut Asn; Am Chem Soc; Am Asn Col Pharm. *Res:* Synthesis of agents acting on the central nervous system or peripheral nervous system based on known compounds already established as active. *Mailing Add:* Col Pharm Univ NMex Main Campus 1 University Campus Albuquerque NM 87131-0001

SAETHER, OLE ANTON, LIMNOLOGY, ENTOMOLOGY. *Current Pos:* PROF SYST ZOOL & HEAD DEPT, UNIV BERGEN, 77- *Personal Data:* b Kristiansand, Norway, Dec 9, 36; m 66, Unni Soemhovd; c Trine, Beate & Tore K. *Educ:* Univ Oslo, Cand Mag, 60, Cand Real, 63. *Honors & Awards:* August Thienemann lectr, 88. *Prof Exp:* Sci asst limnol, Univ Oslo, 61-63, Nansen Fund fel, 62-69, lectr hydrobiol, 63-69; res scientist, Freshwater Inst, Fisheries Res Bd Can, 69-77. *Concurrent Pos:* Vis scientist, Fisheries Res Bd Can, 67-68; consult, Indust Bio-Test Lab, Inc, 71-80; adj prof entom, Univ Man, 73-77; adj res scientist, Freshwater Inst, Dept Environ, Man, Can, 78-; consult, Duke Power Co, 78-; ed, Fauna Norveg Ser B, 79-85; vis scientist, Kans Biol Surv, Univ Kans, Lawrence, 92-93, Univ Ghana, Accra, Ghana, 93, 94, 95 & 96. *Mem:* Int Asn Theoret & Appl Limnol; Am Soc Limnol & Oceanog; Entom Soc Can; Norweg Entom Soc; NAm Benthol Soc. *Res:* Taxonomy, morphology and ecology of Chironomidae, Chaoboridae and Hydracarina; benthic fauna; zooplankton; phytoplankton; systematic zoology. *Mailing Add:* Dept Syst Zool Univ Bergen Norway 5007 Norway. *Fax:* 47-55-58-9675; *E-Mail:* ole.sather@zmb.uib.no

SAEVA, FRANKLIN DONALD, CHEMISTRY. *Current Pos:* SR SCIENTIST, EASTMAN KODAK CO, 79- *Personal Data:* b Rochester, NY, Nov 28, 38; m 63; c 3. *Educ:* Bucknell Univ, BS, 60; State Univ NY Buffalo, PhD(org chem), 68. *Prof Exp:* Sr scientist, Xerox Corp, 68-79. *Mem:* Am Chem Soc. *Res:* Organic reaction mechanisms and photochemistry. circular dichroism studies; liquid crystals; organic synthesis; electrochemical behavior of organics. *Mailing Add:* 1219 Gerrads Crossing Webster NY 14580-9151

SAEZ, JUAN CARLOS, cell biology, phosphorylation, for more information see previous edition

SAFADI, M OUSSAMA, STRESS ANALYSIS, STRUCTURAL ANALYSIS & DYNAMICS. *Current Pos:* LECTR MECH & AERONAUT ENG, UNIV SOUTHERN CALIF, 91-; LECTR CIVIL ENG, UNIV CALIF, LOS ANGELES, 91-; PRES, ENG RES & CONSULT, 92- *Personal Data:* b Damascus, Syria, Feb 21, 56; US citizen. *Educ:* Calif State Univ, Northridge, BS, 82; Univ Calif, Los Angeles, MS, 85, PhD(civil eng). 91. *Prof Exp:* Asst prof civil & mech eng, Calif State Univ, 85-91. *Mem:* Am Soc Eng Educ; Math Asn Am. *Res:* Structural dynamics and finite element analysis. *Mailing Add:* PO Box 24344 Los Angeles CA 90024. *E-Mail:* safadi@usc.edu

SAFAI, BIJAN, DERMATOLOGY. *Current Pos:* PROF & CHMN, DEPT DERMAT, NY MED COL, 93-; DIR DERMAT, WESTCHESTER MED CTR, 93- *Personal Data:* b Mar 26, 40; US citizen; m 78, Vera P; c Matthew. *Educ:* Tehran Univ Med Sch, Iran, MD, 65; Univ Goteborg, Swed, DSc, 81. *Prof Exp:* Teaching clin asst, Dept Dermat, NY Univ Med Col, 73-74; from asst prof to prof med & dermat, Cornell Univ, Med Col, 74-93, assoc prof clin med dermat, 79-80. *Concurrent Pos:* Asst attend physician, Dermat Serv, Mem Hosp, NY, 74-79, actg chief, 78-79, chief, 79-93, assoc attend physician, 79-81, attend physician, 81-93; res assoc, Sloan-Kettering Inst Cancer & Allied Dis, NY, 77-79, asst mem, 79-83, assoc mem, 83-88, mem, 88-93; assoc attend physician, Div Dermat, Dept Med, NY Hosp, Cornell Univ Med Col, 80-85, attend physician, 85-93; assoc mem, Mem Sloan-Kettering Cancer Ctr, 83-88, mem, 88-93; comt AIDS, Am Acad Dermat, 89-91; chmn, Dermat Sect, NY Acad Med, 89-90; pres, NY Dermat Soc, 90-91, Z & E Fisher Med Found, 93- *Mem:* AMA; Soc Invest Dermat; Am Acad Dermat; Int Soc Trop Dermat; Am Fedn Clin Res; Am Dermat Soc Allergy & Immunol; NY Acad Sci. *Mailing Add:* Dept Dermat NY Med Col Valhalla NY 10595. *Fax:* 914-993-4019; *E-Mail:* safai@aol.com

SAFAI, MORTEZA, SPECKLE SHEARING INTERFEROMETRY NONDESTRUCTIVE TESTING, INFRARED IMAGING NONDESTRUCTIVE TESTING. *Current Pos:* SR RES ENGR, QUEST INT, INC, 94- *Personal Data:* b Iran, Feb 14, 64; US citizen; m 87, Rebecca. *Educ:* Univ Utah, BS, 87, MS, 89. *Prof Exp:* Res engr, Becton Dickenson Med Co, 87-88; res asst, Univ Utah, 88-89; specialist engr, Boeing Defense & Space Group, 89-94. *Mem:* Am Soc Nondestructive Testing; Int Soc Optical Eng. *Res:* Development of a laser-based speckle shearing interferometry and thermal imaging techniques for nondestructive testing of advanced materials and aerospace structures; designing and implementation of the technology in conjunction with proper excitation techniques. *Mailing Add:* 3005 26th Ave W Seattle WA 98119. *Fax:* 253-872-8967

SAFANIE, ALVIN H, ANATOMY, HISTOLOGY. *Current Pos:* RETIRED. *Personal Data:* b Washington, DC, Dec 27, 24; m 50; c 4. *Educ:* Cornell Univ, DVM, 47; Mich State Univ, MS, 50; Univ Ill, PhD(anat), 62. *Prof Exp:* Instr anat, Col Vet Med, Mich State Univ, 47-51, asst prof, 51-52; from instr to prof anat, Col Vet Med, Univ Ill, Urbana, 52-77, prof vet anat & histol, 77-85. *Mem:* Am Vet Med Asn; Am Asn Vet Anatomists; Am Soc Zoologists. *Res:* Vagus nerve of pig; embryology of domestic animals. *Mailing Add:* 4103 Amherst Dr Champaign IL 61821-9794

SAFAR, MICHAEL, INFORMATION SCIENCE. *Current Pos:* info spec, Mfg Tech Info Analysis Ctr, 85-87, tech coordr, 87-90, MGR, RES MFG DEPT, ILL INST TECHNOL RES CTR, 85-, DIR, 90- *Educ:* Butler Univ, BA, 72; Rosary Col, MLS, 82. *Prof Exp:* Credit reporter, Dun & Bradstreet, 72-73, supvr serv, 74-75, supvr, Tel Order Dept, 76, sales rep 77, admin asst, 78; supvr, Chicago Blue Cross & Blue Shield, 79-81; asst librn, East-West Univ, Chicago, 83-85. *Mem:* Am Libr Asn; Am Soc Info Sci; Am Defense Preparedness Asn. *Mailing Add:* ITT Res Inst Mfg Productivity Ctr 3350 S Federal St Chicago IL 60616-3703

SAFAR, PETER, ANESTHESIOLOGY, CRITICAL CARE MEDICINE. *Current Pos:* prof anethesiol/critical care med & chmn dept, Sch Med, 61-78, DISTINGUISHED PROF RESUSCITATION MED & FOUND DIR, RESUSCITATION RES CTR, UNIV PITTSBURGH, 78- *Personal Data:* b Vienna, Austria, Apr 12, 24; nat US; m 50; c 2. *Educ:* Univ Vienna, MD, 48; Am Bd Anesthesiol, dipl. *Hon Degrees:* Dr, Univ Mainz, 72. *Prof Exp:* Resident path & surg, Univ Vienna, 48-49; fel surg, Yale Univ, 49-50; resident anesthesiol, Univ Pa, 50-52; chief dept, Nat Cancer Inst, Lima, Peru, 52-53; asst prof, Sch Med, Johns Hopkins Univ, 54-61. *Concurrent Pos:* Clin assoc prof, Sch Med, Univ Md, 55-61; chief, Baltimore City Hosps, Md, 55-61; res contractor, US Army Res & Develop Div, Off Surgeon Gen, 57-69; vis scientist, Cardiovasc Res Inst, Univ Calif, San Francisco, 69-70; mem comts resuscitation, emergency & critical care, Nat Res Coun, Am Heart Asn & other nat orgns; mem, Interagency White House Comt Emergency Med Serv; Wattie prof, NZ, 81; F S Cheeves prof, Pittsburgh. *Mem:* Am Physiol Soc; Am Soc Anesthesiol; Soc Critical Care Med (pres, 73); Sigma Xi. *Res:* Resuscitation; neurosciences; author or coauthor of over 500 publications. *Mailing Add:* Dept Anesthesiol/CCM Safar Ctr Resuscitation Res Univ Pittsburgh 3434 Fifth Ave Pittsburgh PA 15260-0001

SAFDARI, YAHYA BHAI, ENGINEERING. *Current Pos:* PRES, SAF ENERGY CONSULTS, INC, 79- *Personal Data:* b Amravati, India, July 25, 30; US citizen; m 62; c 4. *Educ:* Aligarh Muslim Univ, India, BSME, 52, BSEE, 53; Univ Wash, MSME, 59; NMex State Univ, DSc(mech eng), 64. *Prof Exp:* Asst engr, Delhi Cloth Mills, India, 54-56; res asst mech engr, Univ Wash, Seattle, 57-58; design engr, Refrig Co, Wash, 58-61; instr mech eng, NMex State Univ, 61-64; assoc prof, 64-69, PROF, DEPT MECH ENG, BRADLEY UNIV, 69- *Concurrent Pos:* Pres, Sun Systs Inc, 76-79; vis prof & planner, dept mech eng, Makkah Univ, Saudi Arabia, 83-85. *Mem:* Am Soc Heating, Refrig & Air-Conditioning Engrs; Am Soc Mech Engrs; Int Solar Energy Soc; Int Solar Energy Soc; Solar Energy Indust Asn; Am Solar Energy Soc; Sigma Xi. *Res:* Heat transfer in transparent media; convection heat transfer in nuclear reactors; solar energy; energy management; photovollair remote application; solar grain drying. *Mailing Add:* Dept Mech Eng Bradley Univ Peoria IL 61606

SAFDY, MAX ERROL, ORGANIC CHEMISTRY, MEDICINAL CHEMISTRY. *Current Pos:* Res scientist, Corp Res Div, Miles Labs, Inc, 70-76, sr res scientist, Ames Div, 77-83, supvr diag res & develop, 84-87, mfg develop diag, 87-88, MGR, PILOT PLANT OPERS, DIAG DIV, BAYER CORP, 88- *Personal Data:* b Brooklyn, NY, Nov 9, 41; m 68; c 1. *Educ:* Polytech Inst Brooklyn, BS, 63; Univ NC, PhD(org chem), 69. *Mem:* Am Chem Soc. *Res:* Medical diagnostics, cardiovascular agents, biogenic amines, amino acids and peptides; microencapsulation; medical instrumentation. *Mailing Add:* Bayer Corp 1884 Miles Ave Elkhart IN 46514

SAFER, BRIAN, MOLECULAR BIOLOGY, PHARMACOLOGY. *Current Pos:* sr staff fel, Nat Heart & Lung Inst, 73-79, CHIEF SECT PROTEIN BIOSYNTHESIS, NAT HEART, LUNG, & BLOOD INST, NIH, 79- *Personal Data:* b Brooklyn, NY, Dec 3, 42; m 69. *Educ:* Columbia Univ, BA, 64; Baylor Col Med, MS, 67, MD, 69; Univ Pa, PhD(molecular biol), 72. *Honors & Awards:* Louis N Katz Prize, Am Heart Asn, 73. *Prof Exp:* USPHS fel, Univ Pa, 69-71, Pa Plan fel, 71-73. *Mem:* Am Chem Soc; Sigma Xi; Am Heart Asn; Am Soc Biol Chemists. *Res:* Regulation of protein synthesis; initiation factor characterization; eucaryotic transcription factors. *Mailing Add:* Nat Heart Lung & Blood Inst NIH Bldg 10 Rm 7N316 Bethesda MD 20892-1654. *Fax:* 301-496-9985

SAFERSTEIN, LOWELL G, POLYMER CHEMISTRY, ORGANIC CHEMISTRY. *Current Pos:* RETIRED. *Personal Data:* b Newark, NJ, July 25, 40; m 76; c 1. *Educ:* Rutgers Univ, BS, 62, MS, 65, PhD(org chem), 67. *Prof Exp:* Res chemist, Celanese Res Co, 67-76; sr res chemist, Ethicon Inc, 76-77. *Mem:* Am Chem Soc; Am Inst Chemists; Sigma Xi. *Res:* Synthesis of high performance polymers; synthesis of biopolymers. *Mailing Add:* 14 Currey Lane West Orange NJ 07052-2164

SAFERSTEIN, RICHARD, FORENSIC SCIENCE. *Current Pos:* CHIEF CHEMIST, FORENSIC SCI BUR, NJ STATE POLICE, 70- *Personal Data:* b Brooklyn, NY, July 17, 41; m 75; c 2. *Educ:* City Col New York, BS, 63, MA, 66, PhD(org chem), 70. *Prof Exp:* Chemist, US Treasury Dept, NY, 64-69; chemist, Shell Chem Co, 69-70. *Concurrent Pos:* Instr, Trenton State Col & Ocean County Col, 72- *Mem:* Am Chem Soc; Am Acad Forensic Sci; Forensic Sci Soc; Int Asn Forensic Sci; Can Soc Forensic Scientists. *Res:* Application of chemical ionization mass spectroscopy to forensic science; forensic characterization of polymers by pyrolysis-gas chromatography. *Mailing Add:* 20 Forrest Ct Mt Laurel NJ 08054

SAFF, EDWARD BARRY, MATHEMATICAL ANALYSIS. *Current Pos:* dir, Ctr Math Serv, 78-83, from assoc prof to prof, 69-86, UNIV DISTINGUISHED PROF MATH, UNIV SFLA, 86-, GRAD RES PROF, 86- *Personal Data:* b New York, NY, Jan 2, 44; m 66; c 3. *Educ:* Ga Inst Technol, BS, 64; Univ Md, College Park, PhD(math), 68. *Honors & Awards:* Sigma Xi Outstanding Researcher Award, Univ South Fla, 84. *Prof Exp:* Fulbright grant, Imp Col, Univ London, 68-69. *Concurrent Pos:* NSF grant, Univ South Fla, 69-72 & 80-; Air Force res grant, 73-79; Guggenheim fel, Oxford Univ, 78; assoc dir, Ctr for Excellence in Math, Sci Comput & Technol, 83-; ed-in-chief, Construct Approximation J, 83-; dir, Inst Constructive Math, 85-; Fulbright fel, 82; hon prof math, Zhejiang Normal Univ, China. *Mem:* Am Math Soc; Math Asn Am; Sigma Xi. *Res:* Approximation in complex domain; approximate solutions of differential equations; Pade approximants; geometry of polynomials. *Mailing Add:* 11738 Lipsey Rd Tampa FL 33618-3620

SAFFER, ALFRED, PHYSICAL CHEMISTRY. *Current Pos:* RETIRED. *Personal Data:* b New York, NY, Dec 3, 18; m 42, 85, Doris Graubard; c Anita C (Horowitz) & Martin K. *Educ:* NY Univ, AB, 39, MS, 41, PhD(phys chem), 43. *Honors & Awards:* Chem Pioneer Award, Am Inst Chemists, 82. *Prof Exp:* Asst chem, NY Univ, 40-43; res assoc, Princeton Univ, 43-45; sr res chemist, Firestone Tire & Rubber Co, 45-48; sr vpres mfg, Halcon Int Inc, NY, 48-70; pres, Oxirane Int, NJ, 71-78; vchmn, Halcon Int Inc, 78-81. *Concurrent Pos:* Pres, Catalyst Develop Corp, NJ, 57-70. *Mem:* Nat Acad Eng; Am Chem Soc; Soc Chem Indust; Am Inst Chem; Sigma Xi. *Res:* Oxidation of hydrocarbons in gas and liquid phases; processes for manufacture of petrochemicals; manufacture of catalysis; mechanisms of organic reactions. *Mailing Add:* 16629 Ironwood Dr Delray Beach FL 33445

SAFFER, CHARLES MARTIN, JR, INDUSTRIAL CHEMISTRY. *Current Pos:* RETIRED. *Personal Data:* b Salem, Mass, Dec 15, 14; m 42; c 1. *Educ:* Mass Inst Technol, SB, 36, SM, 37, PhD(chem), 38. *Hon Degrees:* MA, Christ Church, Oxford Univ, 73. *Prof Exp:* Moore traveling fel, Oxford Univ, 39-40; res asst, Harvard Univ, 40-41; res chemist, Aerojet Eng Corp, Calif, 46-48; scientist, Bur Aeronaut, US Dept Navy, 48-51; vpres, Microcard Corp, 51-54; dir res, Nat Fireworks Ord Corp, 53-57; asst mgr nat northern div, Am Potash & Chem Corp, 57-58, head propellant chem res, 58-60; asst dir res planning, Thiokol Chem Corp, 60-65, tech consult, 65-66; tech dir, Sonneborn Div, Witco Chem Corp, 66-70, Activated Carbon Div, 70-75, Inorganic Specialties Div, 75-82. *Concurrent Pos:* Officer, US Navy, 41-46. *Mem:* Am Chem Soc. *Res:* Organo-silicon synthesis; synthetic estrogens; sodium triphenylmethyl; smokeless propellants; explosives. *Mailing Add:* Two Rockwood Rd Levittown PA 19056-2308

SAFFER, HENRY WALKER, PHYSICAL CHEMISTRY, TEXTILE CHEMISTRY. *Current Pos:* Res chemist, E I DuPont de Nemours & Co, Inc, 62-66, sr res chemist, 66-72, res supvr, 72-75, mkt develop supvr, 75-76, strategist, Textile Fibers Dept, 76-77, prog mgr, 78-79, bus serv mgr, 80-82, site mgr, 83-84, admin mgr, 85-91, PLANNING MGR, DUPONT RES & DEVELOP, E I DUPONT DE NEMOURS & CO INC, 92- *Personal Data:* b New York, NY, Apr 4, 35; c 3. *Educ:* NC State Col, BS, 56, MS, 58; Princeton Univ, MA, 60, PhD(phys chem), 63. *Res:* Protein chemistry; nuclear magnetic resonance spectroscopy of fibers; textile warp sizing; engineering fibers for special end uses; nonwoven products and processes; business diversification and development; laboratory administration. *Mailing Add:* DuPont CR & D Experimental Sta E I DuPont de Nemours & Co Inc Rte 141 & Henry Clay St PO Box 80328 Wilmington DE 19880-0328

SAFFERMAN, ROBERT S, MICROBIOLOGY. *Current Pos:* microbiologist, US Environ Protection Agency, 70-74, chief virol sect, 74-88, chief virol br, 88-94, chief, Virol & Parasitol Br, Environ Monitoring Systs Lab, 94-95, CHIEF, BIOHAZARD ASSESSMENT RES BR, US ENVIRON PROTECTION AGENCY, 95- *Personal Data:* b Bronx, NY, Dec 19, 32; m 58, Jewel S Reisman; c Karen, Sharon & Steven. *Educ:* Brooklyn Col, BS, 55; Rutgers Univ, PhD(microbiol), 60. *Honors & Awards:* Gans Medal, Soc Water Treatment & Examination, UK, 70. *Prof Exp:* Res fel microbiol, Inst Microbiol, Rutgers Univ, 55-59; microbiologist, USPHS, 59-64 & US Dept Interior, 64-70. *Mem:* Am Soc Microbiologists; Phycol Soc Am; Sigma Xi; fel Am Acad Microbiol; Int Comt Taxon Viruses. *Res:* Survival and persistence of viruses in water sources; phycoviruses; virus monitoring methodology; medical aspects of phycology. *Mailing Add:* US Environ Protection Agency 26 W Martin Luther King Dr Cincinnati OH 45268

SAFFIOTTI, UMBERTO, ONCOLOGY, CYTOLOGY. *Current Pos:* assoc sci dir carcinogenesis, Etiology Area, Nat Cancer Inst, 68-72, assoc dir carcinogenesis, Div Cancer Cause & Prev, 72-76, chief, Exp Path Br, 74-78, CHIEF LAB EXP PATH, DIV CANCER ETIOLOGY, NAT CANCER INST, 78-, ACTG HEAD, REGISTRY EXP CANCERS, 88- *Personal Data:* b Milan, Italy, Jan 22, 28; US citizen; m 58; c Luisa M & Maria F. *Educ:* Univ Milan, MD, 51, dipl occup med, 57. *Honors & Awards:* Superior Serv Honor Award, HEW, 71; Pub Interest Sci Award, Environ Defense Fund, 77; Pub Health Serv Spec Recognition Award, HEW, 80. *Prof Exp:* Fel, Inst Path Anat, Univ Milan, 51-52; res asst oncol, Chicago Med Sch, 52-54, res assoc, 54-55; chief pathologist, Inst Occup Med & asst occup med, Univ Milan, 56-60; fel, Inst Gen Path, 57-60; from asst prof to prof oncol, Chicago Med Sch, 60-68. *Concurrent Pos:* Mem comt young scientists in cancer res, Int Union Against Cancer, 56-58, mem comt cancer prev, 59-66 & mem panel on carcinogenicity, 63-66; NIH career develop award, 64-68; mem path B study sect, NIH, 64-68; partic panel carcinogenesis, Secy's Comn Pesticides & Environ Health, Dept Health, Educ & Welfare, 69, chmn ad hoc comt eval low levels environ carcinogenesis, Surg Gen, 69-70 & mem comt coord toxicol & related prog, 73-76; mem working groups, Eval Carcinogenic Risk of Chem to Man, Int Agency Res Cancer, 70-88; mem adv comt to scholars-in-residence prog, Fogarty Int Ctr, NIH, 73-77; mem bd dirs, Rachel Carson Trust for Living Environ, Inc, 76-79; chmn carcinogenesis contract prog mgt group, Div Cancer Cause & Prev, Nat Cancer Inst, 68-76, mem occup cancer task force & chmn comt carcinogenesis, 78-80; mem, Cancer Prev Task Force, 79-; partic, Work Group on Assessment, Interagency Regulatory Liaison Group, 79-80 & Work Group on Regulation of Carcinogens, US Regulatory Coun, 79-80. *Mem:* AAAS; Am Asn Cancer Res; Am Soc Investigative Path; fel NY Acad Sci; Sigma Xi; Soc Toxicol. *Res:* Experimental pathology of chemical carcinogenesis, especially respiratory; cell culture carcinogenesis models; combined effects of carcinogens; identification and evaluation criteria for carcinogens; occupational and environmental carcinogenesis; pneumoconioses. *Mailing Add:* NCI NIH Bldg 41 Rm C105 Bethesda MD 20892-0041. *Fax:* 301-402-1829

SAFFIR, ARTHUR JOEL, DENTAL SCIENCE, NUTRITION. *Current Pos:* dir oral health res, 73-81, PRES BIOSYST RES, 81- *Personal Data:* b Chicago, Ill, May 11, 41; m 63; c 2. *Educ:* Mass Inst Technol, PhD(nutrit), 70; Tufts Univ, DMD, 64. *Prof Exp:* Res assoc, Mass Inst Technol, 64-70; dir res & develop, Mat Analysis, 70; pvt consult, 70-73. *Mem:* Int Asn Dent Res. *Res:* Dental research; statistical analysis; electron optics; nutrition clinical research. *Mailing Add:* 2057 Summit Dr SW Lake Oswego OR 97034

SAFFMAN, PHILIP GEOFFREY, APPLIED MATHEMATICS, FLUID MECHANICS. *Current Pos:* prof fluid mech, 64-69, PROF APPL MATH, CALIF INST TECHNOL, 69- *Personal Data:* b Leeds, Eng, Mar 19, 31; m 54; c 3. *Educ:* Cambridge Univ, BA, 53, PhD(appl math), 56. *Prof Exp:* Lectr appl math, Cambridge Univ, 58-60; reader, King's Col, Univ London, 60-64. *Concurrent Pos:* Res fel, Trinity Col, Cambridge Univ, 55-59; vis prof, Mass Inst Technol, 70-71. *Mem:* Fel Am Acad Arts & Sci; fel Royal Soc London. *Res:* Turbulence; viscous flow; wave interactions; vortex motion. *Mailing Add:* 399 Ninita Pkwy Pasadena CA 91106

SAFFO, MARY BETH, SYMBIOSIS, MARINE BIOLOGY. *Current Pos:* ASSOC RES MARINE BIOLOGIST, INST MARINE SCI, UNIV CALIF, SANTA CRUZ, 85-, LECTR, 88- *Personal Data:* b Inglewood, Calif, Apr 8, 48; m 78; c 1. *Educ:* Univ Calif, Santa Cruz, BA, 69; Stanford Univ, PhD(biol), 77. *Prof Exp:* Miller res fel, Dept Bot, Univ Calif, Berkeley, 76-78; asst prof biol, Swarthmore Col, 78-85. *Concurrent Pos:* Independent investr, Marine Biol Lab, 79-80; fel, Am Assoc Univ Women, Univ Calif, Berkeley, 81-82; prog officer, Div Invertebrate Zool, Am Soc Zoologists, 85-87, Comt Ensure Equal Opportunity, 88-92; chair, AAAS, 91-92. *Mem:* Sigma Xi; Am Soc Zoologists; Soc Study Evolution; Mycol Soc Am; Soc Evolutionary Protistology; fel AAAS. *Res:* Biology symbiosis especially microbial-invertebrate symbioses; nitrogen excretion; physiological ecology; tunicate biology; protist biology. *Mailing Add:* Arts & Sci Ariz State Univ W 4701 W Thunderbird Glendale AZ 85306-4900

SAFFORD, LAWRENCE OLIVER, FORESTRY, ECOLOGY. *Current Pos:* Res forester, Maine, 62-68, 69-70, RES FORESTER, NORTHEASTERN FOREST EXP STA, US FOREST SERV, USDA, NH, 70- *Personal Data:* b Bremen, Maine, Dec 27, 38; div; c 3. *Educ:* Univ Maine, BS, 61, PhD(plant sci), 68; Yale Univ, MFor, 62. *Concurrent Pos:* WVa Pulp & Paper Co fel, Yale Univ, 68-69. *Mem:* Soc Am Foresters; AAAS; Am Soc Agron; Sigma Xi. *Res:* Soil-tree relationships; soil moisture and nutrient requirements of forest trees. *Mailing Add:* Rte 202A Stratford NH 03884

SAFFRAN, JUDITH, BIOCHEMISTRY, TOXICOLOGY. *Current Pos:* asst prof, Med Col Ohio, 74-76, assoc prof obstet, gynec & biochem, 76-79, clin chemist, 79-85, TOXICOLOGIST, MED COL OHIO, 85- *Personal Data:* b Montreal, Que, Nov 5, 23; m 47, Murray; c David, Wilma, Arthur & Richard. *Educ:* McGill Univ, BSc, 44, PhD(biochem), 48. *Prof Exp:* Melville Trust fel biochem, Univ Edinburgh, 58-59; biochemist, Jewish Gen Hosp, Montreal, 55-58 & 61-69; sr res fel, Med Res Inst, Toledo Hosp, 69-74. *Concurrent Pos:* Adj asst prof, Med Col Ohio, 70-74; asst prof path, Med Col Ohio, 70- *Mem:* Can Biochem Soc; Am Soc Biol Chemists; Am Asn Clin Chem. *Res:* Steroid hormones; mechanism of action; reproductive physiology. *Mailing Add:* 2331 Hempstead Rd Toledo OH 43606

SAFFRAN, MURRAY, DRUG DELIVERY. *Current Pos:* chmn dept, 69-80, PROF BIOCHEM, MED COL OHIO, 69-, ASST DEAN, MED EDUC, 90- *Personal Data:* b Montreal, Que, Oct 30, 24; US citizen; m 47, Judith Cohen; c Michael D, Wilma A, Arthur M & Richard E. *Educ:* McGill Univ, BSc, 45, MSc, 46, PhD(biochem), 49. *Honors & Awards:* Ayerst Award, Endocrine Soc, 67. *Prof Exp:* Lectr psychiat, McGill Univ, 48-52, from asst prof to assoc prof psychiat, 53-65, from assoc prof to prof biochem, 59-69, bldg dir, McIntyre Med Sci Bldg, 63-65; Life Ins Med Res Fund fel, Copenhagen Univ, 52-53; Founds Fund Res Psychiat fel, Univ Edinburgh, 58-59. *Concurrent Pos:* Mem endocrinol study sect, NIH, 64-68, mem neurol A study sect, 77-81; mem biochem test comt, Nat Bd Med Examrs, 65-69, fel, 79; vis lectr, Ctr Pop Studies, Sch Pub Health, Harvard Univ, 67-68; chmn biochem test comt, Nat Bd Podiatry, 78-; consult, Pharmaceut Indust; vis prof, Ben Gurion Univ, 81, Armenian Acad Sci, 88. *Mem:* AAAS; Endocrine Soc; Am Soc Biol Chemists; Am Diabetes Asn; Int Brain Res Orgn. *Res:* Neuroendocrinology; peptide hormones; intestinal absorption of peptides; oral adimistration of peptide drugs. *Mailing Add:* Dept Biochem & Molecular Biol Med Col Ohio PO Box 10008 Toledo OH 43699-0008. *Fax:* 419-381-6141; *E-Mail:* msaffran@vortex.mco.edu

SAFFREN, MELVIN MICHAEL, MATHEMATICAL PHYSICS, FLUID DYNAMICS. *Current Pos:* RETIRED. *Personal Data:* b Brooklyn, NY, Sept 13, 29; div, Ballen; c Paul, David & Joshua. *Educ:* City Col NY, Bs, 51; Mass Inst Technol, PhD(physics), 59. *Prof Exp:* Asst physics, Brookhaven Nat Lab, 52; asst physics, Mass Inst Technol, 52-59; physicist, Res Lab, Gen Elec Co, 59-62; mem tech staff, Jet Propulsion Lab, Calif Inst Technol, 62-67, supvr theoret physics group, 67-71, space sci div rep to off res & advan develop, 71-76, staff scientist, 76-94. *Concurrent Pos:* Consult & mem vis fac, Univ Southern Calif, 66-68; mem physics subcomt, Bluebook Update Task, NASA, 70-71, mem physics & chem in space working group, 72-, proj scientist, Drop Dynamics Module Proj, 75-; chmn steering comt, Int Colloquium on Drops & Bubbles, 74-, co-ed proceedings, 76; exec secy, Int Symp Relativity Exp Space, 77. *Mem:* Am Phys Soc; Inst Elec & Electronics Engrs; Math Asn Am; Am Math Soc; Asn Comput Mach. *Res:* Theory and computation of energy bands in solids; superconductivity; many body problem; interaction of radiation with matter; low temperature physics; superfluidity; physics and chemistry experiments in earth-orbiting laboratories; programming; dynamics of liquid drops and bubbles; theory of theta functions; theory of Hilbert transforms. *Mailing Add:* 226 Edelen Ave Los Gatos CA 95030

SAFIR, SIDNEY ROBERT, MEDICINAL CHEMISTRY. *Current Pos:* RETIRED. *Personal Data:* b Trenton, NJ, June 17, 16; m 42; c 2. *Educ:* Univ Mich, BS, 37, MS, 38, PhD(org chem), 40. *Prof Exp:* Fuller fel, Univ Mich, 40-41; org chemist, Am Cyanamid Co, 41-46 & Schenley Distillers Co, 46-47; org chemist, Lederle Labs, Am Cyanamid Co, 47-82. *Mem:* Am Chem Soc; Sigma Xi. *Res:* Synthesis of novel antipsychotic, anxiolytic and analgetic agents. *Mailing Add:* 7775 Beltane Dr San Jose CA 95135-2138

SAFKO, JOHN LOREN, PHYSICS. *Current Pos:* From asst prof to assoc prof, 64-78, PROF PHYSICS & ASTRON, UNIV SC, 79- *Personal Data:* b San Diego, Calif, Oct 29, 38; m 64, Peggy J Ferrell; c Tanya D & John L Jr. *Educ:* Case Inst Technol, BS, 60; Univ NC, PhD(physics), 65. *Concurrent Pos:* Rep, Southern Atlantic Coast Sect, Am Asn Physics Teachers; treas, SC Acad Sci. *Mem:* Am Phys Soc; Am Asn Physics Teachers; Am Astron Soc; Int Astron Union; Int Soc Gen Relativity & Gravitation; fel AAAS. *Res:* General relativity and gravitation theory; teaching methods; astrophysical investigations related to relativity; astronomy education. *Mailing Add:* Dept Physics & Astron Univ SC Columbia SC 29208. *Fax:* 803-777-3065; *E-Mail:* d530001@univscvm.csd.scarolina.edu

SAFLEY, LAWSON MCKINNEY, JR, SANITARY & ENVIRONMENTAL ENGINEERING. *Current Pos:* PRES, AGRO WASTE TECH. *Personal Data:* b Fayetteville, Tenn, Jan 13, 50; m 73; c 3. *Educ:* Univ Tenn, BS, 72; Cornell Univ, MS, 74, PhD(agr eng), 77. *Prof Exp:* Res support specialist, Cornell Univ, 76-77; asst prof agr eng, Univ Tenn, 77-81; assoc prof, NC State Univ, 81-87, prof bio & agr eng, 87- *Mem:* Am Soc Agr Engrs; Sigma Xi; Am Soc Agr Consults. *Res:* Manurial nutrient loss during storage; land application of manure; systems analysis of animal manure systems; anaerobic digestion systems. *Mailing Add:* Agro Waste Tech 700-108 Blue Ridge Rd Raleigh NC 27606

SAFONOV, MICHAEL G, CONTROL THEORY, SIGNAL PROCESSING. *Current Pos:* from asst prof to assoc prof, 77-88, assoc dept chair, 89-93, PROF ELEC ENG, UNIV SOUTHERN CALIF, 88- *Personal Data:* b Pasadena, Calif, Nov 1, 48; m 68, 85, Janet Sunderlad; c Alexander M & Peter G. *Educ:* Mass Inst Technol, BS & MS, 71, PhD(elec eng), 77. *Prof Exp:* Res & teaching asst, Mass Inst Technol, 75-77. *Concurrent Pos:* Consult, Anal Sci Corp, Systs Control, Honeywell, Northrup, TRW, Lear-Siegler, Lear Astronics & United Technologies; vis prof, Cambridge Univ, 83-84, Imperial Col, 87, Caltech, 90-91. *Mem:* Fel Inst Elec & Electronics Engrs; Sigma Xi. *Res:* Control and feedback theory; aircraft flight control; hierarchical decomposition methods; multivariable control synthesis; stability theory. *Mailing Add:* Dept Elec Eng Systs Univ Southern Calif Los Angeles CA 90089-2563. *Fax:* 213-740-4449; *E-Mail:* safonov@bode.usc.edu

SAFRAN, SAMUEL A, COLLOID PHYSICS. *Current Pos:* actg dept head, Polymer Dept, 90, PROF, WEIZMANN INST SCI, 90- *Personal Data:* b Brooklyn, NY, Nov 22, 51; m 75; c 3. *Educ:* Yeshiva Univ, BA, 73; Mass Inst Technol, PhD(physics), 78. *Prof Exp:* Postdoctoral fel, mem tech staff, Bell Labs, 78-80; sr staff physics, Exxon Res & Eng, 80-90. *Concurrent Pos:* Coordr, Inst Theoret Physics prog self-assembling syst, 89. *Mem:* Fel Am Phys Soc; Am Chem Soc. *Res:* Theoretical condensed matter physics; complex fluid physics; structure and phase behavior of microemulsion surfactants, polymers, colloids; structure of interfaces in both fluids and solids. *Mailing Add:* Dept Mat & Interfaces Weizmann Inst Sci Perlman Bldg Rehovot 76100 Israel

SAFRANYIK, LASZLO, FOREST ENTOMOLOGY. *Current Pos:* Res officer forest entom, Can Dept Forestry, 64-69, sect head, 69-72, RES SCIENTIST FOREST ENTOM, CAN FORESTRY SERV, 69- *Personal Data:* b Besenyszog, Hungary, Feb 13, 38; Can citizen; m 66, Elizabeth Jozsa; c 2. *Educ:* Univ BC, BSF, 61, MF, 63, PhD(pop dynamics), 69. *Mem:* fel Entom Soc Can (pres, 94-95); Can Inst Forestry. *Res:* Population dynamics and management of bark and wood boring insects. *Mailing Add:* 141 Durrance Rd Victoria BC V8X 4M6 Can

SAFRON, SANFORD ALAN, PHYSICAL CHEMISTRY, SURFACE CHEMISTRY & PHYSICS. *Current Pos:* from asst prof to assoc prof, 70-91, PROF CHEM, FLA STATE UNIV, 91- *Personal Data:* b Chicago, Ill, July 24, 41; m 80, Penny J Gilmer; c Helena M & Nathaniel S. *Educ:* Univ Calif, Berkeley, BS, 63; Harvard Univ, MA, 65, PhD(chem), 69. *Prof Exp:* Guest researcher, Physics Inst, Univ Bonn, 69-70. *Concurrent Pos:* Res Corp-Cottrell grant, Fla State Univ, 71, Petrol Res Fund-Am Chem Soc grant, 71-74; Res Corp-Cottrell grant, 76, NSF-URP grant, 79 & DOE grant, 85, 88, 91 & 94; vis prof, Max Planck Inst, Gottingen, 80; chair, Fla Sect, Am Chem Soc, 96. *Mem:* AAAS; Am Phys Soc; Am Chem Soc; Am Vacuum Soc; Sigma Xi. *Res:* Dynamics of chemical reactions; dynamics of crystal surfaces; helium atom-surface scattering. *Mailing Add:* Dept Chem Fla State Univ Tallahassee FL 32306-3006. *Fax:* 850-644-8281; *E-Mail:* safron@chem.fsu.edu

SAGAL, MATTHEW WARREN, PHYSICAL CHEMISTRY. *Current Pos:* dir, Int Strategic Planning & Bus Develop, AT&T Tech Systs, 83-88, VPRES BUS DEVELOP AT&T MICROELECTRONICS, 88- *Personal Data:* b Brooklyn, NY, Nov 23, 36; m 59; c 3. *Educ:* Cornell Univ, BChE, 58; Mass Inst Technol, PhD(phys chem), 61. *Prof Exp:* Mem tech staff chem, Bell Tel Labs, 61-66; res leader, Western Elec Co, 66-67, asst dir mat & chem processes, 67-69, dir mat & chem process, 69-76, mgr prod planning, 76-79, dir eng, Allentown Works, 79-83. *Mem:* Electrochem Soc; sr mem Inst Elec & Electronics Engrs. *Res:* Electronic materials; manufacturing processes; environmental analysis; plastics; ceramics. *Mailing Add:* 29 Cinnamon Tree Lane Berkeley Heights NJ 07922

SAGALYN, PAUL LEON, solid state physics, materials science, for more information see previous edition

SAGALYN, RITA C, SPACE PHYSICS, IONOSPHERIC PHYSICS. *Current Pos:* res physicist, Air Force Cambridge Res Labs, 48-58 & Aeronomy & Ionospheric Physics Labs, 58-69, br chief space physics, Ionospheric Physics Lab, 69-75, br chief, Elec Processes Bd, 75-81, dir, Space Physics Div, Geophys Directorate, 81-96, SR SCIENTIST, USAF CAMBRIDGE RES LABS, 96- *Personal Data:* b Lowell, Mass, Nov 24, 24; m 52, 90, Sidney Bowhill; c Michael & Roger. *Educ:* Univ Mich, Ann Arbor, BS, 48; Radcliffe Col, MS, 50. *Honors & Awards:* Guenther Loeser Award, Air Force Cambridge Res Labs, 58; Patricia Kayes Glass Award, USAF, 66. *Concurrent Pos:* Mem, Space Sci Comt, Nat Acad Sci. *Mem:* Sigma Xi; Am Geophys Union; AAAS. *Res:* Upper atmospheric and space research; study experimentally and theoretically the influence of soft particle fluxes, solar ultraviolet, terrestrial electric and magnetic fields, plasma motions and instabilities on spatial distribution and temporal behavior of environmental plasma; develop solar-terrestrial physics bond models. *Mailing Add:* 555 Annursnac Hill Rd Concord MA 01742

SAGAN, CARL, planetary sciences; deceased, see previous edition for last biography

SAGAN, HANS, SPACE-FILLING CURVES. *Current Pos:* prof, 63-93, EMER PROF MATH, NC STATE UNIV, 94- *Personal Data:* b Vienna, Austria, Feb 15, 28; nat US; m 54, Ingeborg Ulbrich; c Ingrid. *Educ:* Univ Vienna, PhD, 50. *Honors & Awards:* Poteat Award, NC Acad Sci, 66. *Prof Exp:* Asst prof math, Vienna Tech Univ, 50-54 & Mont State Univ, 54-57; assoc prof, Univ Idaho, 57-61, prof & head dept, 61-63. *Concurrent Pos:* Assoc ed, Math Mag, 63-73; Math Asn Am lectr, 63-73, 77-; vis prof, Munich Tech Univ, 64; vis prof, Univ Vienna, 72. *Mem:* Math Asn Am. *Res:* Probability; calculus of variations and optimal control theory; operations research; space-filling curves. *Mailing Add:* 5004 Glen Forest Dr Raleigh NC 27612-3132

SAGAN, LEON FRANCIS, MATHEMATICS. *Current Pos:* PROF MATH, ANNE ARUNDEL COMMUNITY COL, 64- *Personal Data:* b Chicopee Falls, Mass, May 23, 41. *Educ:* Towson State Col, BS, 62; Col William & Mary, MA, 64; Univ Md, College Park, PhD(math educ), 71. *Mem:* Math Asn Am; Nat Coun Teachers Math; Am Math Asn. *Res:* Remedial math; college algebra and trigonometry; calculus. *Mailing Add:* Dept Math Anne Arundel Community Col 101 College Pkwy Arnold MD 21012-1857

SAGAN, LEONARD A, INTERNAL MEDICINE, ENVIRONMENTAL MEDICINE. *Current Pos:* RETIRED. *Personal Data:* b San Francisco, Calif, Feb 18, 28; m 54; c 3. *Educ:* Stanford Univ, AB, 50; Univ Chicago, MD, 55; Harvard Univ, MPH, 65; Am Bd Internal Med, dipl, 64. *Prof Exp:* Intern, Univ Calif Hosp, 55-56, resident internal med, 56-61; physician, Atomic Bomb Casualty Comn, Japan, 61-64; physician, US AEC, Washington, DC, 65-68; physician, Palo Alto Med Clin, 68-78, assoc dir, Dept Environ Med, 71-78; sr scientist, Elec Power Res Inst, 78- *Mem:* Fel Am Col Physicians; Nat Coun Radiation Protection. *Res:* Late effects of radiation; non-ionizing radiation. *Mailing Add:* 177 Toyon Rd Atherton CA 94027

SAGAR, WILLIAM CLAYTON, SYNTHETIC ORGANIC CHEMISTRY. *Current Pos:* from asst prof to assoc prof chem, 61-70, PROF CHEM, CENTRE COL KY, 70-, CHMN, DIV SCI & MATH, 72- *Personal Data:* b Columbus, Ohio, Oct 17, 29; m 53; c 3. *Educ:* Capital Univ, BS, 51; Ohio State Univ, MSc, 54, PhD(chem), 58. *Prof Exp:* Res chemist, Ethyl Corp, 58-61. *Mem:* Am Chem Soc. *Res:* Synthesis of insecticides; aldol condensations. *Mailing Add:* 698 East Dr Danville KY 40422-1912

SAGARAL, ERASMO G (RAS), PLANT GROWTH REGULATORS PGRS, MANAGEMENT OF SOYBEANS & SMALL GRAINS BREEDING. *Current Pos:* PROF LECTR, BIOL SCI DEPT, RUTGERS STATE UNIV, 97- *Personal Data:* b Camiguin, Philippines, June 2, 36; m 60, Betty Catindig; c Emmanuel, Elenn, Ervi, Emelou & Erasmo Jr. *Educ:* Cent Mindanao Univ, BSA, 59; Univ Philippines, MS, 68; Va Polytech Inst & State Univ, PhD(plant physiol), 78. *Prof Exp:* Farm mach teacher agr, Bohol Agr Col, 59-62; voc agr teacher farm mech, Cent Mindanao Univ, 62-65; asst prof agron, Xavier Univ, 69-73, head dept, 69-75 & 78-79, assoc prof agron, 73-75 & 78-79; sr scientist, Dole Philippines, Inc, 79-85; res specialist physiol, Va Polytech Inst & State Univ, 85-87, supt res & admin, Eastern Va Agr Res & Exten Ctr, 87-96. *Concurrent Pos:* Prof lectr, Southeast Asia Rural Social Leadership Inst, 78-79; consult, Coconut Fedn Philippines, 78-79. *Mem:* Am Soc Agron; Plant Growth Regulator Soc Am. *Res:* Weed control in rice (rainfed and flooded conditions); developed research programs on nutrition, weed control and cultural management practices for pineapples and bananas; evaluated the performance of plant growth regulators in soybeans, wheat and barley; coordinating research on soybeans and small grains breeding program at Eastern Virginia Agricultural Research and Extension Center. *Mailing Add:* 5 Bay St Glen Ridge NJ 07028. *Fax:* 973-743-8942

SAGAWA, YONEO, CYTOGENETICS. *Current Pos:* dir, Harold L Lyon Arboretum, 67-91, PROF HORT, UNIV HAWAII, 64- *Personal Data:* b Keeau, Hawaii, Oct 11, 26; wid; c Penelope (Toshiko) & Irene (Teruko). *Educ:* Washington Univ, AB, 50, MS, 52; Univ Conn, PhD(cytogenetics), 56. *Prof Exp:* Res assoc biol, Brookhaven Nat Lab, 55-57, guest biol, 58; from asst prof to assoc prof bot, Univ Fla, 57-64. *Concurrent Pos:* Dir undergrad sci educ prog & undergrad res participation & independent study, NSF, Univ Fla, 64; consult, Biosatellite Proj, NASA, 66-67, USAID-ASAP, 93, VOCA, 93-96 & UNDP-UNISTAR, 93; res assoc, Univ Calif, Berkeley, 70; ed, Hawaii Orchid J, 72-; fel, Agr Univ, Neth, 79-80; res assoc, Bishop Mus, Honolulu, 92-; Bot Res Inst Tex, 93-; external assessor, Univ Pertanian, Malaysia, 94-; res assoc, Hawaii Trop Bot Garden, 95- *Mem:* Bot Soc Am; Int Soc Hort Sci; AAAS; Am Soc Hort Sci; Int Asn Plant Tissue Culture; Sigma Xi; Am Anthurium Soc; Am Inst Biol Sci; Am Orchid Soc. *Res:* Cytogenetics of cultivated plants, especially subtropical plants; morphogenesis; tissue culture; tissue culture for micropropagation, germplasm storage and disease elimination; propagation and preservation of native Hawaiian plants. *Mailing Add:* Univ Hawaii Dept Hort 3190 Maile Way Honolulu HI 96822-2279. *Fax:* 808-956-3894; *E-Mail:* yoneo@hawaii.edu

SAGDEEV, ROALD ZINNUROVI, PHYSICS. *Current Pos:* DISTINGUISHED PROF PHYSICS, UNIV MD, COLLEGE PARK, 90-; DIR, EAST-WEST SPACE SCI CTR, 90- *Educ:* Moscow State Univ, BSc, 55; Moscow Inst Phys Problems, PhD(theoret physics), 60. *Honors & Awards:* John T Tate Int Award, Am Inst Physics, 92. *Prof Exp:* Head plasma theory lab, Inst Nuclear Physics, Novosibirsk, Russia; mem, Inst High-Temp Physics, Moscow, 71-73; dir, Inst Space Res, Moscow, 73-90. *Mailing Add:* Dept Physics Univ Md Bldg 82 Rm 4310 College Park MD 20742

SAGE, ANDREW PATRICK, DECISION SUPPORT SYSTEMS. *Current Pos:* assoc vpres acad affairs, 84-85, dean, Sch Info Technol & Eng, 85-86, FIRST AM BANK PROF INFO TECHNOL, GEORGE MASON UNIV, 84-, FOUNDING EMER DEAN, 96-, UNIV PROF, 96- *Personal Data:* b Charleston, SC, Aug 27, 33; m 62, LaVerne Galhouse; c Theresa, Karen & Philip. *Educ:* The Citadel, BS, 55; Mass Inst Technol, MS, 56; Purdue Univ, PhD(elec eng), 60. *Hon Degrees:* DEngr, Univ Waterloo, Can, 87. *Honors & Awards:* Barry Carlton Award, Inst Elec & Electronics Engrs, 70, Norbert Wiener Award, 81 & Centennial Medal, 84, Joseph G Wohl Outstanding Career Award, 91, Donald G Fink Prize, 94; Frederick Emmonds Terman Award, Am Soc Eng Educ, 70; Outstanding Serv Award, Int Fedn Automotive Control, 90. *Prof Exp:* Instr elec eng, Purdue Univ, 56-60; assoc prof, Univ Ariz, 60-63; tech staff mem, Aerospace Corp, Calif, 63-64; prof elec eng, Univ Fla, 64-67, prof nuclear eng, 66-67; prof & dir info & control sci ctr, Inst Technol, Southern Methodist Univ, 67-74, head dept elec eng, 72-74; chmn, Dept Chem Eng, Univ Va, 74-75, assoc dean, 74-80, Lawrence R Quarles Prof Eng & Appl Sci & Chmn, Dept Eng Sci & Systs, 77-84. *Concurrent Pos:* Consult var corp & insts, 57-; ed, Trans on Systs, Man & Cybernet, Inst Elec & Electronics Engrs; ed, Automatica, 80-96; co-ed-in-chief, Chief Info & Systs Eng, 82-; mem bd trustees, CNA Corp, 90-95. *Mem:* Fel AAAS; Inst Mgt Sci; fel Inst Elec & Electronics Engrs; Am Soc Eng Educ; Inst Mgt Sci. *Res:* Systems engineering and management; software systems engineering, expert systems; decision support systems; systems engineering; education; optimization and estimation theory; information technology and management. *Mailing Add:* 8011 Woodland Hills Lane Fairfax VA 22039-2433. *Fax:* 703-978-9716; *E-Mail:* asage@gmu.edu

SAGE, GLORIA W, PHYSICAL CHEMISTRY, ANALYTICAL CHEMISTRY. *Current Pos:* SR SCIENTIST, SYRACUSE RES CORP, 80- *Personal Data:* b Brooklyn, NY, Mar 7, 36; m 58, Martin L; c Daniel S. *Educ:* Cornell Univ, AB, 57; Radcliffe Col, AM, 58; Harvard Univ, PhD(phys chem), 63. *Prof Exp:* Jr chemist, Res & Adv Develop Div, Avco Corp, 57-58; res assoc chem, Univ Ore, 61-63; instr, 63-66, res assoc, 66-67; res assoc, Syracuse Univ, 67-70; res assoc biochem, State Univ NY Upstate Med Ctr,

70-72, asst prof med technol, 72-76, res assoc pediat, 76-77; res assoc chem, Tel Aviv Univ, 77-78. *Concurrent Pos:* Consult, 78-80. *Mem:* AAAS; Am Chem Soc. *Res:* Design and development of data bases containing chemical properties, environmental, health and safety and regulatory information on tracking systems; writing environmental fate and exposure assessments of chemicals; use of mosses to monitor pollution. *Mailing Add:* Syracuse Res Corp Merrill Lane Syracuse NY 13210. *E-Mail:* sage@syrres.com

SAGE, HARVEY J, IMMUNOCHEMISTRY, BIOCHEMISTRY. *Current Pos:* asst prof biochem, 64-71, ASST PROF PATH, DUKE UNIV, 64-, ASSOC PROF BIOCHEM, 71-, ASSOC PROF IMMUNOL, 74- *Personal Data:* b New York, NY, Jan 5, 33; m 68; c 1. *Educ:* Polytech Inst Brooklyn, BS, 54; Yale Univ, PhD(chem), 58. *Prof Exp:* Res assoc hemat, Sch Med, Yale Univ, 58-60; res assoc biochem, St Luke's Hosp, Cleveland, 60-62; res assoc, Brandeis Univ, 62-64. *Mem:* AAAS; Am Soc Biochem; Am Asn Immunologists. *Res:* Specificity of antigen-antibody reactions; in vitro lymphocyte culture and isolation of lymphocyte surface membrane proteins; protein structure; use of synthetic polypeptides as models for protein structure and as immunogens. *Mailing Add:* Dept Biochem Duke Univ Sch Med Duke Med Ctr Durham NC 27710-7599

SAGE, HELENE E, VASCULAR BIOLOGY, CONNECTIVE TISSUE PROTEINS. *Current Pos:* Res asst prof, dept biochem, 80-82, asst prof, dept biol struct, 82-85, ASSOC PROF, DEPT BIOL STRUCT, UNIV WASH, 85- *Personal Data:* b Philadelphia, Pa, Oct 6, 46; m 85. *Educ:* Mt Holyoke Col, AB, 69; Univ Utah, PhD(biol sci), 77. *Concurrent Pos:* Investr, Am Heart Asn, 81-86; vis assoc prof, Univ Med & Dent NJ, 85 & Nat Ctr Sci Res-LGME, Strasbourg, France, 85-86. *Mem:* Am Soc Cell Biol; Am Chem Soc; Am Soc Biochem & Molecular Biol. *Res:* Protein synthesis by cells in vitro; protein structure, especially elastin and collagen; relationship of cell behavior to extracellular matrix; control of gene expression and cellular phenotypic modulation. *Mailing Add:* Dept Biol Struct Univ Wash SM-20 PO Box 357420 Seattle WA 98195-7420. *Fax:* 206-543-1524

SAGE, JAY PETER, SUPERCONDUCTING ELECTRONICS, RESONANT-TUNNELING DIODES. *Current Pos:* MEM TECH STAFF, LINCOLN LAB, MASS INST TECHNOL, 81- *Personal Data:* b Pittsburgh, Pa, Nov 8, 43; m 71; c 2. *Educ:* Harvard Univ, BA, 64, MA, 65, PhD(physics), 69. *Prof Exp:* Sr res scientist, Res Div, Raytheon Co, Waltham, Mass, 68-81. *Concurrent Pos:* Raytheon exchange scientist, Toshiba Res & Develop Ctr, Japan, 73-74. *Mem:* Inst Elec & Electronics Engrs. *Res:* Superconducting circuits, resonant-tunneling-diode circuits, charge-coupled devices and metal oxide semiconductor integrated circuitry for signal processing. *Mailing Add:* Lincoln Lab Mass Inst Technol 244 Wood St Lexington MA 02173-9108. *E-Mail:* sage@ll.mit.edu

SAGE, JOSEPH D, SOIL MECHANICS, ENGINEERING GEOLOGY. *Current Pos:* from instr to prof, 57-96, EMER PROF CIVIL ENG, WORCESTER POLYTECH INST, 96- *Personal Data:* b Leonardo, NJ, July 14, 31; m 51; c 7. *Educ:* Rutgers Univ, BS, 53, MS, 58; Clark Univ, PhD(geog), 74. *Prof Exp:* Pres & mem bd, Geotechnics Inc, 59-65. *Concurrent Pos:* Prin investr, Dept Transp & NSF; partner, Sage & D'andrea, 77- *Mem:* Sigma Xi; Am Soc Civil Engrs; Portuguese Soc Geotechnol. *Res:* Rock mechanics; frost action in particulate systems; mathematical synthesis of climatological time series. *Mailing Add:* 2 Riches Ave Paxton MA 01612

SAGE, MARTIN, ZOOLOGY, PHYSIOLOGY. *Current Pos:* assoc prof, 74-77, chmn dept, 75-81, PROF BIOL, UNIV MO, ST LOUIS, 77-, ASSOC DEAN, COL ARTS & SCI, 83-85 & 86- *Personal Data:* b Torquay, Eng, Dec 6, 35; m 65, Linda C Harrop; c Mark & Hannah. *Educ:* Univ Nottingham, BSc, 57, PhD(zool), 60. *Prof Exp:* Demonstr zool, Univ Nottingham, 59-60; from asst lectr to lectr zool, Univ Leicester, 60-66, lectr physiol, 66-69; assoc prof zool, Univ Tex, Austin, 69-74, assoc prof marine studies, 73-74. *Concurrent Pos:* Tutor, Univ Nottingham, 60; resident tutor, Univ Leicester, 60-65; Wellcome fund travel grant & asst zoologist, Cancer Res Genetics Lab & Bodega Marine Lab, Dept Zool, Univ Calif, Berkeley, 68-69; res scientist, Marine Sci Inst, Port Aransas, 69-74; reader, Marine Biol Lab, Woods Hole, 81-82. *Mem:* Res Defense Soc; Am Soc Zool. *Res:* Comparative endocrinology and physiology; evolution of vertebrate endocrine and neuroendocrine control systems; evolution of biological activity of hormones; endocrine control of osmoregulation; hormones and behavior; biological rhythms; human population biology. *Mailing Add:* Dept Biol Univ Mo St Louis MO 63121-4499. *Fax:* 314-553-5415; *E-Mail:* smsage@umslvma.umsl.edu

SAGE, MARTIN LEE, CHEMICAL PHYSICS. *Current Pos:* assoc prof, 67-85, PROF CHEM, SYRACUSE UNIV, 85-, DIR TECHNOL & PUB AFFAIRS PROG, 88- *Personal Data:* b New York, NY, Mar 4, 35; m 58, Gloria A Welt; c Daniel. *Educ:* Cornell Univ, AB, 55; Harvard Univ, MA, 48, PhD(chem physics), 59. *Prof Exp:* Fel physics, Brandeis Univ, 59-61; asst prof chem & theoret sci, Univ Ore, 61-67. *Concurrent Pos:* Vis assoc prof chem, Tel Aviv Univ, Israel, 77-78; vis, Dept Theoret Chem, Univ Oxford, Eng, 85-86. *Mem:* AAAS; Am Phys Soc; Am Chem Soc; Am Asn Univ Professors; Nat Asn Sci Teachl & Soc. *Res:* Quantum chemistry; intramolecular dynamics; multiphoton photochemistry; computer algebra. *Mailing Add:* Dept Chem Syracuse Univ Syracuse NY 13244. *Fax:* 315-443-4070; *E-Mail:* mlsage@mailbox.syr.edu

SAGE, NATHANIEL MCLEAN, JR, RESEARCH ADMINISTRATION. *Current Pos:* RETIRED. *Personal Data:* b Boston, Mass, Feb 4, 18; m 55, 72; c 5. *Educ:* Mass Inst Technol, SB, 41, SM, 51, PhD, 53. *Prof Exp:* Teacher high sch, Conn, 46-49; asst to dir admis, Mass Inst Technol, 49-50; from instr to asst prof geol, Amherst Col, 51-55; from asst prof to assoc prof, Univ NH, 55-60, chmn dept, 57-60; assoc dir sponsored res, Mass Inst Technol, 60-68; coordr res, Univ RI, 68-83, emer coordr res, 83. *Mem:* Fel Geol Soc Am; Am Asn Petrol Geologists. *Res:* Invertebrate paleontology; carboniferous of Nova Scotia and Pennsylvania anthracite region. *Mailing Add:* 957 Saugatucket Rd Peacedale RI 02879

SAGE, ORRIN GRANT, ENVIRONMENTAL GEOLOGY. *Current Pos:* PRIN, SAGE ASSOCS, 75-; EXTEN LECTR WILDERNESS SURVIVAL, UNIV CALIF, 75- *Personal Data:* b Los Angeles, Calif, May 31, 46; m 70. *Educ:* Univ Calif, BA, 69, MA, 71, PhD(geol), 73. *Prof Exp:* Environ scientist environ mgt, Multran Am Corp & Henningson, Durham & Richardson, 72-75; lectr environ studies, Univ Calif, Santa Barbara, 73-88. *Concurrent Pos:* NSF fel, 70-73. *Mem:* Geol Soc Am; Soc Range; Soil & Water Conserv Soc. *Res:* Tectonic evolution of western California; environmental assessment and land use planning; environmental effects of California agriculture; agricultural economics. *Mailing Add:* 1396 Danielson Rd Santa Barbara CA 93108

SAGER, CLIFFORD J, PSYCHIATRY, MARITAL & FAMILY THERAPY. *Current Pos:* CLIN PROF PSYCHIAT, NEW YORK HOSP/CORNELL MED CTR, 80-, ATTEND PSYCHIAT, 80- *Personal Data:* b New York, NY, Sept 28, 16; m, Anne Scheinmann; c Rebecca (Riviere), Philip T, Barbara & Anthony E. *Educ:* Pa State Col, BS, 37; NY Univ, MD, 41; Am Bd Psychiat & Neurol, dipl, 48; NY Med Col, cert psychoanal, 49. *Honors & Awards:* Ann Award for Distinguished Prof Contrib to Family Ther, 83, Am Asn Marriage & Family Therapists, 83. *Prof Exp:* Consult psychiat, Family Welfare Orgn, Allentown, Pa, 46-47; assoc dean & dir therapeut serv, Postgrad Ctr Ment Health, 48-60; dir clin serv, NY Med Col, 60-63, chief family treatment & study unit, 64-70, prof psychiat & dir partial hosp prog, 66-70; clin prof psychiat, Mt Sinai Sch Med, City Univ New York, 70-80, attend psychiat, Mt Sinai Hosp, 74-80. *Concurrent Pos:* Asst adj psychiatrist, Beth Israel Hosp, 48-50; vis psychiatrist, Metrop Hosp, 60-70; attend psychiatrist, Flower & Fifth Ave Hosp, 60-70; chief family treatment & study unit, Beth Israel Med Ctr, 70-74, assoc dir family & group ther, 71-73, chief behav sci serv prog, Ctr & Hosp, 71-73; dir psychiat, Gouverneur Hosp, 70-73; psychiat dir, Jewish Family Serv, New York, 73-; ed, J Sex & Marital Ther, 74-; dir family psychiat, Jewish Bd Family & Children's Serv, New York, 78-, dir, Sex Therapy Clin & Remarried Consult Serv; psychiatric counr, Corp Health Prog, Jewish Bd for Family Childrens Serv; dir marital & family clin, NY Hosp, 91- & Payne-Whitney Clin, 85-; ed, J Sex & Marital Ther. *Mem:* Fel Am Psychiat Asn; fel Am Med Asn; fel Am Acad Psychoanal; fel Am Orthopsychiat Asn; fel Am Group Psychother Asn (pres, 68-70); charter fel Am Family Therapy Asn; fel Am Asn Marriage & Family Therapists; Soc Med Psychiat (pres, 60-61); Soc Sex Therapy & Res; Am Soc Advan Psychother. *Res:* The marital couple and the development of suitable methods of bringing psychiatric treatment to those segments of the population previously not reached by effective psychological and social forms of treatment; new methods of treating the sexual dysfunctions; family process; marital interaction; typography of marriages; problems of remarriage. *Mailing Add:* 65 E 76th St New York NY 10021

SAGER, EARL VINCENT, ENGINEERING PHYSICS. *Current Pos:* RES ANALYST, SYST PLANNING CORP, 78- *Personal Data:* b Buffalo, NY, Sept 24, 45; m 79. *Educ:* State Univ NY, Buffalo, BA, 67, MA, 69; Univ Md, PhD(physics), 79. *Mem:* Am Phys Soc. *Res:* Radar digital signal processing. *Mailing Add:* 6730 White Post Rd Centreville VA 20121

SAGER, JOHN CLUTTON, ENVIRONMENTAL CONTROL. *Current Pos:* SR ENG & RES MGR, BIOL RES & LIFE SUPPORT, NASA, 86- *Personal Data:* b New Castle, Pa, Mar 15, 42; m 64, Barbara Fleeger; c Scott A & Kathryn A. *Educ:* Pa State Univ, BS, 64, MS, 70, PhD(agr eng), 73. *Honors & Awards:* Arch T Colwell Merit Award, Soc Agr Eng. *Prof Exp:* Agr res eng, Radiation Biol Lab, Smithsonian Inst, 73-86. *Concurrent Pos:* Instr pilot, Ag Rotors Inc, 69; res asst, Agr Eng Dept, Pa State Univ, 68-69 & 70-73, instr, 70; adj asst prof, Agr Eng Dept, Univ Md, 84-86. *Mem:* Am Soc Agr Eng; Am Soc Hort Sci. *Res:* Direct development of advanced life support systems based on a research program on environmental effects on plants with emphasis on life support elements and resource recovery; design new or modify equipment to provide control of environmental factors critical to the research program with emphasis on electromagnetic radiation (light) and biological recycling of waste. *Mailing Add:* NASA JJ-G Kennedy Space Center FL 32899. *Fax:* 407-853-4165; *E-Mail:* john.sager-1@ksc.nasa.gov

SAGER, RAY STUART, INORGANIC CHEMISTRY, PHYSICAL CHEMISTRY. *Current Pos:* ASSOC PROF CHEM, PAN AM UNIV, 75- *Personal Data:* b Cuero, Tex, Feb 24, 42; m 62; c 2. *Educ:* Tex Lutheran Col, BS, 64; Tex Christian Univ, PhD(chem), 68. *Prof Exp:* Asst prof chem, Concordia Col, Moorhead, Minn, 68-69; from asst prof to assoc prof, Capital Univ, 69-74. *Mem:* Am Chem Soc. *Res:* Structure and properties of copper II complexes of schiff bases containing amino acids. *Mailing Add:* Dept Chem Victoria Col Victoria TX 77901-4494

SAGER, RONALD E, CRYOGENICS, MAGNETIC MEASUREMENTS. *Current Pos:* VPRES, QUANTUM MAGNETICS, INC, CALIF, 87- *Personal Data:* b Adrian, Mich, Aug 8, 47; m 69; c 2. *Educ:* Mich State Univ, BS, 69; Univ Calif, San Diego, MS, 74, PhD(physics), 77. *Prof Exp:* Res physicist, Physical Dynamics, Calif, 77-79 & S H E Corp, Calif, 79-82; sr res physicist, Quantum Design, Inc, Calif, 82-87. *Concurrent Pos:* Prin investr, Dept Energy, 79-82, Dept Defense, 85-91 & Dept Transp, 87-91; guest instr, Mgt Technol Sem, Univ Minn, 91. *Mem:* Am Phys Soc. *Res:* Cryogenic instrumentation development for commercial applications; superconducting quantum interference devices to make extremely sensitive magnetic measurements in field from 1 millioersted to 70,000 oersted and over temperatures from 1.7 kelvin to 800 kelvin. *Mailing Add:* Quantum Magnetics 11578 Sorrento Valley Rd San Diego CA 92121. *Fax:* 619-481-7410

SAGER, RUTH, genetics; deceased, see previous edition for last biography

SAGER, THOMAS WILLIAM, STATISTICS. *Current Pos:* vis asst prof math & bus, Univ Tex, Austin, 78-79, asst prof, 79-82, assoc prof, 82-93, PROF STATIST, UNIV TEX, AUSTIN, 93- *Personal Data:* US citizen. *Educ:* Univ Iowa, BA, 68, MS, 71, PhD(statist), 73. *Prof Exp:* Asst prof statist, Stanford Univ, 73-78. *Concurrent Pos:* Co-dir, Ctr Statist Sci, Univ Tex, Austin. *Mem:* Inst Math Statist; Am Statist Asn; Sigma Xi. *Res:* Spatial patterns; density estimation; isotonic regression; environmental statistics; computational statistics; sampling. *Mailing Add:* Dept Man Sci/Info Syst-CBA 5202 Univ Tex Austin TX 78712. *E-Mail:* tomsager@mail.utexas.edu

SAGER, WILLIAM FREDERICK, PHYSICAL ORGANIC CHEMISTRY. *Current Pos:* prof chem, 65-86, head dept, 65-80, EMER PROF CHEM, UNIV ILL, CHICAGO, 86- *Personal Data:* b Ill, Jan 22, 18; m 41, Marilyn Williams; c Karen (Dickinson), Judith (Peyton) & Kathryn (Potts). *Educ:* George Washington Univ, BS, 39, MA, 41; Harvard Univ, PhD(chem), 48. *Prof Exp:* Chemist, Tex Co, 41-45; from asst prof to prof chem, George Washington Univ, 48-64. *Concurrent Pos:* Guggenheim fel, Oxford Univ, 54-55; consult, Bur Weapons, US Dept Navy, Army Chem Ctr, NIH, W Grace Co & Houdry Process Co. *Mem:* Am Chem Soc; Sigma Xi. *Res:* Mechanisms of organic reactions; chemistry of high explosives. *Mailing Add:* 1552 John Anderson Dr Ormond Beach FL 32176

SAGERMAN, ROBERT H, RADIATION ONCOLOGY, RADIOLOGY. *Current Pos:* PROF RADIOL, RADIOTHER DIV, STATE UNIV NY, HEALTH SCI CTR, 68- *Personal Data:* b Brooklyn, NY, Jan 23, 30; m 54; c 4. *Educ:* NY Univ, BA, 51, MD, 55; Am Bd Radiol, dipl, 61. *Prof Exp:* Clin instr radiol, Med Sch, Tulane Univ, 56-57; instr, Sch Med, Stanford Univ, 61-64; asst prof, Columbia-Presby Med Ctr, 64-68. *Mem:* AAAS; Am Soc Therapeut Radiol; Radiol Soc NAm; Am Radium Soc; Radiation Res Soc. *Res:* Therapeutic radiology; radiation biology. *Mailing Add:* Radiation Oncol Div State Univ NY Health Sci Ctr 750 E Adams St Syracuse NY 13210. *Fax:* 315-464-5934

SAGERS, CYNTHIA LOUISE, EVOLUTIONARY ECOLOGY OF PLANT-ANIMAL INTERACTIONS. *Current Pos:* ASST PROF, DEPT BIOL, UNIV ARK, 94- *Personal Data:* b Maquaketa, Iowa, Sept 4, 59; m 93, R David Evans. *Educ:* Univ Iowa, BA, 82; Univ Utah, PhD(ecol & evolutionary biol), 93. *Mem:* Ecol Soc Am; Bot Soc Am; Asn Trop Biologists; Am Soc Naturalists; Soc Study Evolution. *Res:* Quantitative genetics approach to study the evolution of plant-animal interactions. *Mailing Add:* Dept Biol Sci Univ Ark Fayetteville AR 72701. *Fax:* 501-575-4010

SAGERS, RICHARD DOUGLAS, BIOCHEMISTRY. *Current Pos:* From asst prof to assoc prof, 58-64, assoc dean, Col Biol & Agr, 80-86, PROF MICROBIOL, BRIGHAM YOUNG UNIV, 64- *Personal Data:* b Tooele, Utah, Dec 19, 28; m 50, Pauline Shields; c Richard C, Michael, John, David, James & Paul. *Educ:* Brigham Young Univ, BS, 54, MS, 55; Univ Ill, PhD(bact), 58. *Honors & Awards:* NIH career development award, 63-68. *Mem:* Am Soc Microbiologists; Am Soc Biol Chemists; Sigma Xi. *Res:* Metabolic pathways, energy relationships and biosynthetic mechanisms in anaerobic microorganisms; metabolism of natural products; antimicrobial enhancement. *Mailing Add:* Dept Microbiol Brigham Young Univ 775 Widb Provo UT 84602-1049

SAGERT, NORMAN HENRY, PHYSICAL & RADIATION CHEMISTRY, SURFACE SCIENCE. *Current Pos:* RETIRED. *Personal Data:* b Midland, Ont, Mar 31, 36; m 59, Marilyn I McArton; c 3. *Educ:* Queen's Univ, BSc, 59, MSc, 60; Ottawa Univ, PhD(phys chem), 63. *Prof Exp:* Fel phys chem, Cambridge Univ, 63-64; asst res officer, Atomic Energy Can Ltd, 64-68, assoc res officer, 68-76, sr res officer, 76-90, mgr res chem, 90-93, sr sci adv, 93-94. *Concurrent Pos:* Ed, Electrochem, Solution Chem & Thermochem, Can J Chem, 84-89; counr, Chem Inst Can, 87-90. *Mem:* Fel Chem Inst Can. *Res:* Surface and colloid science; radiation chemistry of hydrocarbons and iodine containing solutions; high temperature mass spectrometry. *Mailing Add:* 56 Glencoe Ave Winnipeg MB R2K 0G7 Can. *Fax:* 204-753-2635; *E-Mail:* sagertn@wl.aecl.ca

SAGGIOMO, ANDREW JOSEPH, MEDICINAL CHEMISTRY, QUALITY ASSURANCE. *Current Pos:* RETIRED. *Personal Data:* b Philadelphia, Pa, Mar 20, 31; m 53, Dolores Durelli; c Andrew Jr, Michael & David. *Educ:* La Salle Col, BA, 52; Temple Univ, MA, 54. *Prof Exp:* Chemist, Philadelphia Qm Depot, 52; asst, Duquesne Univ, 52-53; res fel, Res Inst, Temple Univ, 53-56; res assoc, Germantown Labs, Inc, 56-61, proj dir, 61-69, financial mgr, 69-72, vpres & treas, 72-80; admin mgr, Franklin Res Ctr, Defense Personnel Support Ctr, 80-85, mgr qual assurance, 82-85, qual assurance specialist, 86-93. *Mem:* Am Chem Soc. *Res:* Organic fluorine chemistry; dyes; polymers; organometallics; medicinals; anticancer and anti-inflammatory agents; psychotropic drugs; antimalarials; polychlorinated biphenyl disposal methods. *Mailing Add:* 1817 Schley St Philadelphia PA 19145

SAGI, CHARLES J(OSEPH), MECHANICAL ENGINEERING. *Current Pos:* sr res engr, Spec Progs Dept, Gen Motors Res Labs, 68-77, res engr, 77-80, staff res engr, Fluid Dynamics Res Dept, 80-85, STAFF RES ENGR, FLUID MECH DEPT, GEN MOTORS RES LABS, 85- *Personal Data:* b Phillipsburg, NJ, Mar 10, 35; m 59; c 2. *Educ:* Lehigh Univ, BS, 56; Stanford Univ, MS, 61, PhD(mech eng), 65. *Prof Exp:* Develop engr, Ingersoll-Rand Co, 56-59; asst prof mech eng, Stanford Univ, 64-65; assoc sr res engr, Gen Motors Corp, 65-67; sr res engr, Creare, Inc, 67-68. *Mem:* Am Soc Mech Engrs. *Res:* Fluid mechanics of internal flow; aerodynamics of ground vehicles. *Mailing Add:* 5607 Thorny Ash Rochester MI 48306-2861

SAGIK, BERNARD PHILLIP, VIROLOGY. *Current Pos:* prof biol sci & vpres acad affairs, 80-88, PROF BIOSCI & BIOTECH, DREXEL UNIV, 88-, OBOLD PROF, 91- *Personal Data:* b New York, NY, May 8, 25. *Educ:* City Col New York, BS, 47; Univ Ill, MS, 48, PhD, 52; Am Bd Med Microbiol, dipl pub health & virol. *Prof Exp:* Asst bact, Univ Ill, 48-52; Nat Found Infantile Paralysis fel & instr biophys, Sch Med, Univ Colo, 52-54; sect head virol, Upjohn Co, 54-62; dir viral chemother, Ciba Pharmaceut Co, 62-66; from assoc prof to prof microbiol, Univ Tex, Austin, 66-73; prof microbiol, Univ Tex Health Sci Ctr, San Antonio, 73-80, prof life sci, 73-80, dean, Col Sci & Math, 73-80. *Concurrent Pos:* Vis scholar, Univ Ill, 60-61; lectr, City Univ New York, 63-66 & Drew Univ, 66; adj prof environ health eng, Univ Tex, Austin, 73-80. *Mem:* Am Soc Microbiologists; Am Acad Microbiol. *Res:* Virus-host cell interactions; pathogenesis of virus infections; arbovirus genetics; viruses, sewage and terrestrial waste disposal. *Mailing Add:* Drexel Univ 3141 Chestnut St Philadelphia PA 19104-2816. *Fax:* 215-895-1273; *E-Mail:* sagikbp@duvm.ocs.drexel.edu

SAGLE, ARTHUR A, DIFFERENTIAL GEOMETRY, SYSTEMS THEORY. *Current Pos:* PROF MATH, UNIV HAWAII, 72- *Personal Data:* b Honolulu, Hawaii; m 60; c 1. *Educ:* Univ Wash, BS, 56, MS, 57; Univ Calif, Los Angeles, PhD(math), 60. *Honors & Awards:* Oberwolfach lectr, Ger Govt, 68. *Prof Exp:* Instr math, Univ Chicago, 60-62; asst prof, Syracuse Univ, 62-64; ONR fel & res instr, Univ Calif, Los Angeles, 64-65; res fel, Yale Univ, 65-66; prof, Univ Minn, 66-72. *Concurrent Pos:* NSF grants, 60-72; invit lectr, Am Math Soc, 64; vis prof, Univ Tex, 71; mem, Hadronic Mech Conf, Como, Italy, 84; ed, J Algebras Groups Geometries, 85; mem, Int Cong Math, 86; lectr, Math Theory Networks Systs, 87, Soc Indust & Appl Math, 92 & lectr algebra & applns, Oviedo, Spain, 93; vis scholar, Univ Utah, 88. *Mem:* Sigma Xi; Am Math Soc; London Math Soc; Soc Indust & Appl Math. *Res:* Investigation of the interdependency of differential geometry; systems; lie groups and non-associative algebras; stability and bifurcations of quadratic systems. *Mailing Add:* Univ Hawaii Hilo HI 96720-4091

SAGRIPANTI, JOSE-LUIS, DEVELOPMENT OF DNA PROBE & POLYMERASE CHAIN REACTION TECHNOLOGY, DEVELOPMENT & EVALUATION OF LIQUID DISINFECTANTS & VIRUCIDAL AGENTS. *Current Pos:* RES CHEMIST, FOOD & DRUG ADMIN, 84- *Personal Data:* b Rosario, Arg, Jan 14, 54. *Educ:* Univ Rosario, Arg, Bachelor, 71, Biochemist, 77; Univ Buenos Aires, Doctor Sci, 83. *Honors & Awards:* Cert Recognition, Sigma Xi, 88 & 92. *Prof Exp:* Teaching asst physics, Rosario Univ, 75-78, asst prof immunol, 79-80, chief lab teaching, 82-84; Fogarty vis fel, NIH, 80-82. *Mem:* Europ Soc Radiation Biol; Soc Gen Microbiol; Int Soc Electrochem; Bioelectromagnetic Soc. *Res:* Biotechnology; evaluate current methods and develop new formulations for disinfection and sterilization of medical devices; develop DNA technology for in vitro diagnosis of infectious and genetic diseases; assess the health risk of metallic compounds present in implantable medical devices such as copper in intrauterine devices and iron-alloy prostheses. *Mailing Add:* 5600 Fishers Lane HFZ-113 Rockville MD 20857. *Fax:* 301-594-6775

SAH, CHIH-HAN, MATHEMATICS. *Current Pos:* PROF MATH, STATE UNIV NY, STONY BROOK, 70- *Personal Data:* b Peiping, China, Aug 16, 34; US citizen; m 66, Analee Feldsher; c Adam, Jason & Deborah. *Educ:* Univ Ill, BS, 54, MS, 56; Princeton Univ, PhD(math), 59. *Prof Exp:* Instr math, Princeton Univ, 59-60; Benjamin Peirce instr, Harvard Univ, 60-63; from asst prof to prof, Univ Pa, 63-70. *Concurrent Pos:* Vis lectr, Harvard Univ, 67-68; vis prof, Univ Calif, Berkeley, 69-70 & 76-77, Yale Univ, 84, Columbia Univ, 85. *Mem:* Am Math Soc; AAAS. *Res:* Finite groups; algebraic number theory; rings; cohomology of groups; classical geometry; applications to physics and chemistry. *Mailing Add:* Dept Math State Univ NY Stony Brook NY 11794-3651

SAH, CHIH-TANG, ENGINEERING PHYSICS, ELECTRICAL ENGINEERING. *Current Pos:* PITTMAN EMINENT SCHOLAR CHAIR, UNIV FLA, GAINESVILLE, 88-, GRAD RES PROF CHAIR, 88- *Personal Data:* b Beijing, China, Nov 10, 32; nat US; m 59; c 2. *Educ:* Univ Ill, BS(eng physics) & BS(elec eng), 53; Stanford Univ, MS, 54, PhD(elec eng), 56. *Hon Degrees:* Dr, Univ Leuven, Belg, 75. *Honors & Awards:* Browder J Thompson Prize, Inst Radio Eng, Inst Elec & Electronics Engrs, 62, Jack Morton Award, 88; Franklin Inst Award Develop Stable MOS Transistors, 75; J J Ebers Award, Electron Device Soc, 81; Achievement Award, High Technol, Asian Am Mfg Asn, 84. *Prof Exp:* Res asst, Electronics Lab, Stanford Univ, 54-56, res assoc, 56-57; mem sr staff, Semiconductor Lab, Shockley Transistor Corp, 56-59; sr mem tech staff, Fairchild Semiconductor Corp, 59-61; prof elec eng & physics, Univ Ill, Urbana, 63-88. *Concurrent Pos:* Mgr & head physics dept, Fairchild Semiconductor Res Lab, 61-65; US Nat Acad Sci Committeeman, 75-78; life fel, Franklin Inst, Philadelphia. *Mem:* Nat Acad Eng; fel Am Phys Soc; fel Inst Elec & Electronics Engrs. *Res:* Solid state and semiconductor electronics and physics. *Mailing Add:* Dept Elec Eng Univ Fla Gainesville FL 32611

SAHA, ANIL, immunology; deceased, see previous edition for last biography

SAHA, BIJAY S, magnetic ceramics, xerography, for more information see previous edition

SAHA, GOPAL BANDHU, NUCLEAR CHEMISTRY, RADIOPHARMACY. *Current Pos:* staff nuclear chemist, 84-88, DIR, NUCLEAR CHEM & PHARM, DEPT NUCLEAR MED, CLEVELAND CLIN FOUND, 88- *Personal Data:* b Chittagong, Bangladesh, Apr 30, 38; US citizen; m 65, Sipra Saha; c Prantik & Trina. *Educ:* Dacca Univ, Bangladesh, BSc, 59, MSc, 60; McGill Univ, PhD(chem), 65; Am Bd Radiol, cert med nuclear physics, 79, Am Bd Nuclear Med Sci, 79. *Prof Exp:* Teaching fel biochem, Dacca Univ, 60-61; asst prof chem, Purdue Univ, 65-66; teaching asst, McGill Univ, 61-64, res assoc, 66-69, asst prof diag radiol, 70-75; from assoc prof to prof radiol & nuclear med, Univ Ark Med Sci, 76-82, dir radiopharmaceut prog & assoc prof, Col Health Related Profs, 76-82, prof pharm, Col Pharm, Univ NMex, 82-84. *Concurrent Pos:* Radiopharmacist nuclear med, Royal Victoria Hosp, Montreal, 70-75. *Mem:* Soc Nuclear Med; Am Chem Soc; AAAS; Am Asn Physicists Med; Radiol Soc NAm. *Res:* Radiochemistry; reactor and cyclotron production of radionuclides and their chemical processing; surface chemistry; separation chemistry of different elements and compounds; activation analysis; preparation of radiopharmceuticals and study of their in vivo distribution; dosimetry of various radionuclides; quality control of radiopharmaceuticals; high performance liquid chromatography. *Mailing Add:* Dept Nuclear Med Cleveland Clin Found 9500 Euclid Ave Cleveland OH 44195. *Fax:* 216-444-3943; *E-Mail:* saha@maria.nvemed.ccf.org

SAHA, JADU GOPAL, PESTICIDE CHEMISTRY. *Current Pos:* RETIRED. *Personal Data:* b Bengal, India, Dec 1, 31; Can citizen; m 57; c 1. *Educ:* Univ Calcutta, BSc, 53, MSc, 56; Univ Sask, PhD(org chem), 62. *Prof Exp:* Sr sci asst, Cent Fuel Res Inst, Dhanbad, India, 56-59; res fel org chem, Radiation Lab, Univ Notre Dame, 62-63; res fel, Univ Sask, 63-64; res officer, Chem & Biol Res Inst, Can Dept Agr, 65-66, res scientist, 67-75, dir, 75-; dir gen, Health & Welfare Can. *Mem:* AAAS; Am Chem Soc; Chem Inst Can; Royal Soc Chem. *Res:* Utilization of coal tar and mechanism of aromatic substitution reactions; persistence, translocation, photodecomposition and metabolism of pesticides. *Mailing Add:* 11 Weatherwood Crescent Nepean ON K2E 7C5 Can

SAHA, PAMELA S, MEDICINE. *Current Pos:* ASST RES GEOL, YALE UNIV, 74-, RES ASST BIOCHEM, 78- *Personal Data:* b Washington, DC, July 10, 51; m 72; c 2. *Educ:* Stanford Univ, BS, 72; La State Univ, MD, 89. *Concurrent Pos:* Resident pgy I&II, Vet Hosp, Shreveport, 89-91; resident physician, La State Univ, Med Ctr, Shreveport, 89-91; resident doctor, Martin Luther King/Drew Med Ctr, 91- *Mem:* Am Med Asn; Am Psychiat Asn. *Res:* Published papers in national and international journals on bioethics, ethical issues in bioengineering, ethical issues related to animal research, ethical issues related to aids treatment. *Mailing Add:* 1373 S Center St Redlands CA 92373

SAHA, SUBRATA, BIOMECHANICS, BIOMATERIALS. *Current Pos:* ASSOC PROF BIOMED ENG, LA TECH, 79-; PROF & COORDR BIOENG, LA STATE UNIV MED CTR, SHREVEPORT, 79-, ASSOC PROF PHYSIOL & BIOPHYS, 80-; DIR, BIOENG ALLIANCE SC & PROF BIOENG, CLEMSON UNIV, 96- *Personal Data:* b Kushita, India, Nov 2, 42; US citizen; m 72; c 2. *Educ:* Calcutta Univ, BE, 63; Tenn Tech, MS, 69; Stanford Univ, PhD(appl mech), 73. *Honors & Awards:* Fulbright Award, 82; W C Hall Res Award, 87; Eng Achievement Award, Econ, Statist & Coop Serv, 91. *Prof Exp:* Teaching & res asst, Stanford Univ, 71-73; prof, Dept Anat, prof & vchmn res, Univ Med Ctr, Loma Linda Univ. *Concurrent Pos:* Mem, Sch Grad Studies, Med Ctr, La State Univ, 80-, Biomech Comt, Am Soc Civil Engrs, 81-, Long-Range Planning Comt, Shreveport Sigma Xi, 87-88; grad fac, Med Ctr, La State Univ, 87-; chmn, Steering Comt, Southern Biomed Eng Conf, 81-83 & 84; mem-at-large, Health Care Tech Policy Comt, Inst Elec & Electronics Engrs. *Mem:* Am Soc Mech Engrs; Alliance Eng Med Biol; Soc Biomat; Am Soc Civil Engrs; Am Acad Mech; Soc Biomech; Orthop Res Soc; Inst Elec & Electronics Engrs Eng in Med & Biol Soc; Biomed Eng Soc; Am Soc Eng Educ; fel Am Inst Med & Biol Eng. *Res:* Author of over 400 publications in national and international journals and conference proceedings in bioengineering, biomechanics and biomaterials. *Mailing Add:* Dir Bioeng Alliance SC Clemson Univ 501 Rhodes Res Ctr Clemson SC 29634-0905

SAHAI, HARDEO, STATISTICS, BIOSTATISTICS. *Current Pos:* PROF, DEPT BIOSTATS & EPIDEMIOL, UNIV PR MED SCIS, SAN JUAN, 86-, SR RESEARCHER, CTR EVAL & SOCIOMED RES, SCH PUB HEALTH, 86- *Personal Data:* b Bahraich, India, Jan 10, 42; m 73, Lillian; c Amogh, Mrisa & Pankaj. *Educ:* Lucknow Univ, India, BSc, 62; Banaras Hindu Univ, MSc, 64; Univ Chicago, MS, 68; Univ Ky, PhD(statist), 71. *Honors & Awards:* Gold Medal, Banaras Hindu Univ; Medal of Honor, Univ Granada, 94. *Prof Exp:* Lectr math, Banaras Hindu Univ, 64-65; statist officer, Durgapur Steel Plant, India, 65; statistician, Blue Cross Asn, Chicago, 66; statist programmer, Cleft Palate Ctr, Univ Ill, Chicago, 67 & Chicago Health Res Found, 68; asst statist, Univ Ky, 68-71; mgt scientist, Burroughs Corp, Mich, 72; asst prof, Univ PR, Mayaguez, 72-75, assoc prof, 76-80, prof statist, 81-82; sr res statistician, Travenol Labs, Inc, Round Lake, Ill, 82-83; chief statist, US Army Hq, Ft Sheridan, Ill, 83-84; sr math statist, US Bur of Census, Dept Com, Washington, 84-85; sr ops res analyst Defense Logistics Agency Dept Defense, Chicago, 85-86. *Concurrent Pos:* Statist consult, PR Driving Safety Eval, San Juan, 73 & PR Univ Consult Corp, 77-78; res investr, Water Resources Inst, Mayaguez, 75-76; vis res prof, Dept Statist & Appl Math, Fed Univ Ceara, Brazil, 78-79; hon res fel statists, Harvard Univ; fel, Univ Chicago; mem, Int Statist Inst, Bernalli Soc Math Statists & Probability; contrib ed, Indian J Statists; sr researcher, Res Inst, PR Dept Anti Addiction Servs, 87-; vis prof, Dept Health Care Sci, George Washington Univ, 93, Dept Biostatist, Univ Granada, Spain; consult, Dept Consumer Affairs Servs, Commonwealth, San Juan, PR, 93, Dept Anti-Addiction Servs, Commonwealth, San Juan, PR, Inst Acquired Immune Deficiency Syndrome, Municipality San Juan, Vet Admin Med Ctr, San Juan; hon prof, Nat Univ Peru, 94- *Mem:* Am Statist Asn; Inst Math Statist; Int Biomet Soc; Am Pub Health Asn; fel AAAS; NY Acad Sci; fel Royal Statist Soc; Sigma Xi; fel Inst Math & Applns UK; Int Stat Inst; Fulbright Found; Int Asn Teaching Statist. *Res:* Design and analysis for variance components, biostatistics, epidemiology, statistical consultation, statistical training and education, statistical computer packages, medical decision making, computer-assisted clinical diagnosis and environmetrics. *Mailing Add:* Terrace Calle Dr Gautier Texidoz K-5-B Mayaguez PR 00680. *Fax:* 787-834-0422; *E-Mail:* h__sahai@rumac.upr.clu.edu

SAHAI, YOGESHWAR, MATERIALS PROCESSING, MATHEMATICAL MODELLING. *Current Pos:* from asst prof to assoc prof, 83-92, PROF MAT SCI & ENG, OHIO STATE UNIV, 92- *Personal Data:* m 71, Usha Saxena; c Smita & Vivek. *Educ:* Univ Roorkee, BE, ME, 73; Imp Col Sci & Technol, Eng, DIC, 79; Univ London, PhD(process metall), 79. *Prof Exp:* Lectr metall eng, Univ Roorkee, 68-75; res assoc, McGill Univ, 79-82. *Concurrent Pos:* Dir, Ohio Mining & Minerals Resources Res Inst, 92- *Mem:* Metals Mat Minerals Soc; Iron Steel Soc; Electrochem Soc; Japan Iron & Steel Inst. *Res:* Processing of metals and materials through physical and mathematical modelling; design optimization of process reactors. *Mailing Add:* 2041 College Rd Ohio State Univ Columbus OH 43210

SAHAKIAN, ALAN VARTERES, CARDIAC ELECTROPHYSIOLOGY, NON-DESTRUCTIVE TESTING IN AEROSPACE & MEDICAL APPLICATIONS. *Current Pos:* asst prof, 84-90, ASSOC PROF ELEC ENG, COMPUT SCI & BIOMED ENG, NORTHWESTERN UNIV, 90- *Personal Data:* b Long Island, NY, Oct 21, 54; m 83, Jill Morrison. *Educ:* Univ Wis-Parkside, BS, 76, Univ Wis-Madison, MS, 79, PhD(elec eng), 84. *Prof Exp:* Sr elec engr, Medtronic, Inc, 79-80; elec engr, Bahr Technols, 82-84. *Concurrent Pos:* Assoc prof staff, Evanston Hosp, 85-; resident vis scholar, Air Force Inst Technol, 87. *Mem:* Inst Elec & Electronics Engrs; Sigma Xi. *Res:* Electrophysiology of cardiac arrhythmias and their automatic diagnosis and treatment by implanted devices; instrumentation for non-destructive testing in aerospace and medical applications. *Mailing Add:* 1872 Kiest Ave Northbrook IL 60062-3639. *E-Mail:* sahakian@eecs.nwu.edu

SAHASRABUDHE, MADHU R, FOOD SCIENCE & TECHNOLOGY, NUTRITION. *Current Pos:* RETIRED. *Personal Data:* b Apr 1, 25; Can citizen; m 50; c 2. *Educ:* Agra Univ, BSC, 44; Banaras Hindu Univ, MSc, 46; Univ Bombay, PhD(biochem & nutrit), 52. *Prof Exp:* Res assoc food sci, Univ Ill, 54-57; tech officer, Kraft Foods Ltd, 57-58; head food additives, Nat Health & Welfare, Can, 58-68; mgr res & develop, Salada Foods Ltd, Salada Kelloggs, 69-72; actg dir, Agr Can, 73-74 & 84-85, sr res scientist food sci, Food Res Inst, 74-83, res coordr food, 83-84, asst dir food res, 85-92. *Mem:* Am Oil Chemists' Soc; Can Inst Food Sci & Technol; Chem Inst Can; Inst Food Technol; Asn Food Scientist & Technologists India. *Res:* Plant lipids; chemistry; nutrition/processing; analytical methods; toxic compounds; safety food additives. *Mailing Add:* 15 Cramer Dr Nepean ON K2H 5X2 Can

SAHATJIAN, RONALD ALEXANDER, ORGANOMETALLIC CHEMISTRY, POLYMER SCIENCE. *Current Pos:* VPRES RES, MEDI-TECH, 87-; VPRES CORP TECHNOL, BOSTON SCI, 90- *Personal Data:* b Cambridge, Mass, Oct 1, 42; m 66. *Educ:* Tufts Univ, BS; Univ Mass, MS, 68, PhD(chem), 69. *Prof Exp:* Res chemist, Film Dept, E I du Pont de Nemours & Co, Inc, 69-71; scientist & supvr positive evaluation group, Polaroid Corp, Cambridge, 71-75, res group leader, 75-80, res lab mgr, 80-84, Chem Fabrics, 84-86. *Mem:* AAAS; Soc Photog Scientist & Engr; Am Chem Soc. *Res:* Organometallic carbonium ions; polymeric Schiff bases; dye diffusion processes in photography; non-silver imaging systems; organometallic polymers; medical polymers. *Mailing Add:* 29 Saddle Club Rd Lexington MA 02173

SAHBARI, JAVAD JABBARI, MICRO-ELECTRONICS CHEMICALS RESEARCH & DEVELOPMENT, PHOTOLITHOGRAPHY & OPTICAL SPECTROSCOPY. *Current Pos:* CHIEF EXEC OFFICER & PRES, SILICON VALLEY CHEM LABS, INC, 89- *Personal Data:* b Marand, Iran, Nov 13, 44; m 66; c 3. *Educ:* Univ Tehran, Iran, BS, 71; Univ Shiraz, Iran, MS, 75; Univ Calif, Davis, PhD(chem), 83. *Prof Exp:* Lectr gen/phys chem, Tabriz Univ, Iran, 75-77; sr appln consult, Molecular Design Ltd, 85-86; sr chemist anal, Carter Anal Labs Inc, 86-87; res & develop mgr, EMT, Inc (Brent Chem Int), 87-89. *Mem:* Am Chem Soc; Semiconductor Equip & Mat Int. *Res:* Author of several publications; x-ray crystallographic structures of acetylacetonate complexes and optical detection on magnetic resonance spectroscopy; granted several patents; polymeric coating materials; micro-electronics process; chemical development. *Mailing Add:* Silicon Valley Chem Labs Inc 245 Santa Ana Ct Sunnyvale CA 94086. *Fax:* 408-732-0733

SAHINEN, WINSTON MARTIN, MINING ENGINEERING, GEOLOGICAL ENGINEERING. *Current Pos:* PRES, SAHINEN MINING & GEOL SERV CO, 80- *Personal Data:* b Butte, Mont, Aug 4, 31; m 57, Catherine H Perrick; c Rose M (Wheeler), Christina D (Portillo), Steven J & Mark U. *Educ:* Mont Col Mineral Sci & Technol, BS, 53. *Prof Exp:* Res engr, Zonolite Co, 57-60; mine supt, Werdenhoff Mining Co, 60-61; sr mining engr, Pac Power & Light Co, 61-73; mining & geol engr, John T Boyd Co, 73-76, vpres, 76-80. *Mem:* Am Inst Mining, Metall & Petrol Engrs. *Res:* Mineral and fossil fuel exploration tools and techniques; mineral benefication and material handling; surface and underground excavation and stability. *Mailing Add:* 510 Bayou Knoll Dr Houston TX 77079

SAHLI, BRENDA PAYNE, OCCUPATIONAL HEALTH. *Current Pos:* CONSULT OCCUP HEALTH & ENVIRON TOXICOL, 84- *Personal Data:* b Richmond, Va, Sept 28, 42; m 67, Muhammad Saleh; c Andrea L, Kevin J & Heather F. *Educ:* Richmond Prof Inst, BS, 64; Med Col Va, MS, 67; Va Commonwealth Univ, PhD(pharmaceut chem), 74. *Prof Exp:* Res asst anal res, Am Tobacco Co, 64-65; chemist, Firestone Synthetic Fibers & Textiles Co, 67-69; teaching asst, Health Sci Ctr, Va Commonwealth Univ, 70-73; res chemist polymer res, Textile Fibers Dept, E I du Pont de Nemours & Co, 74-77; toxicologist, Va Dept Health, 77-82, vol compliance dir occup health, 82-83, dir toxic substance info, 83-84. *Concurrent Pos:* Adj prof, Acad Ctr, Va Commonwealth Univ, 75-77 & Falls Church Regional Ctr, Univ Va, 84-87; mem comt D-22, Am Soc Testing & Mat, & chmn E-34 task force, Acrylonitrile & MSDS, 79-83; Gubernatorial appointee, Va Pesticide Control Bd, 89-91, 91-95; mem, Va Pesticide & Groundwater Task Force, 92-93; mem, MAL(Iota Sigma Pi) Scholar Comt, 92-93, chmn, 93-96. *Mem:* Am Col Toxicol; Sigma Xi; Am Conf Govt Indust Hygienists; Soc Occup & Environ Health; Am Pub Health Asn. *Res:* Development of analytical test procedures for raw materials and fibers; bovine albumin tryptic hydrolyzate; isothermal compressibility of organic liquids; analytical ultracentrifugation; flame retardants; coatings for spun-bonded products; health hazard evaluation of substances with respect to conditions and circumstances of use. *Mailing Add:* 2900 Wicklow Lane Richmond VA 23236-1338. *Fax:* 804-276-0675; *E-Mail:* bps1@uno.com

SAHLI, MUHAMMAD S, ORGANIC CHEMISTRY, POLYMER CHEMISTRY. *Current Pos:* PRES, HEALTH CARE CONCEPT, 92- *Personal Data:* b Haifa, Palestine, June 8, 35; m 67, Brenda Payne; c Andrea, Kevin & Heather. *Educ:* Am Univ Beirut, BSc, 60; Univ SC, PhD(org chem), 66. *Prof Exp:* Instr chem, Am Univ Beirut, 60-61; res chemist, Film Res & Develop Lab, E I du Pont de Nemours & Co, Inc, 66-75; sr res scientist monomer technol, Fibers & Plastics Co, Allied Corp, 75-83; pres, Copy Van, Inc, 83-90 & Harmon/Commonwealth Corp, 90-92. *Concurrent Pos:* Adj prof, Va Commonwealth Univ, 66-; mem, Sharp Electronics Corp Adv Coun, 84-89. *Mem:* Sigma Xi. *Res:* Organic synthesis; elucidation of structure of alkaloids; mechanism of pyrolysis of sulfoxides; emulsion polymerization and properties of dispersion coatings; formulation of coatings and characterization of polymers; industrial toxicology; Bechman rearrangement byproducts and mechanisms. *Mailing Add:* 2900 Wicklow Lane Richmond VA 23236-1338. *Fax:* 804-276-0675

SAHNEY, VINOD K, OPERATIONS MANAGEMENT & PLANNING. *Current Pos:* PROF INDUST ENG, WAYNE STATE UNIV, 79-; VPRES, CORP PLANNING & MARKETING, HENRY FORD HEALTH CARE CORP, 84-, SR VPRES PLANNING & DEVELOP, 92- *Personal Data:* b Amritsar, India, Nov 16, 42; US citizen; m 70, J Gail Meyst; c Mira S & Vikram S. *Educ:* Ranchi Univ, BSc, 63; Purdue Univ, MSME, 65; Univ Wis-Madison, PhD(indust eng), 70. *Honors & Awards:* Dean Connelly Award, Am Col Healthcare Execs; Qual Award, Healthcare Info Mgt Systs Soc. *Prof Exp:* From asst prof to assoc prof indust eng, Wayne State Univ, 70-77; assoc prof health policy & mgt, Harvard Univ, 77-79. *Concurrent Pos:* Vis lectr, Exec Prog Health Policy & Mgt, Harvard Univ, 79-81; mem, Health Care Technol Study Sect, Dept Health & Human Serv, 80-; consult, Nat Ctr Health Serv Res, 80-; adminr, Henry Ford Hosp, Detroit, 81-; pres, Fairlane Health Serv Corp; bd dirs, Fairlane Health Serv Corp & Health Alliance Plan, Fla, Inst Healthcare Improv. *Mem:* Inst Med-Nat Acad Sci; fel Inst Indust Engrs; fel Hosp Info Mgt Systs Soc; Opers Res Soc. *Res:* Strategic planning and operations management in health services delivery organizations; developing better methods of planning and management control, including operations planning, staffing, and scheduling and managing the introduction of technology; total quality management. *Mailing Add:* 4727 Burnley Dr Bloomfield Hills MI 48304-3725. *Fax:* 313-876-9243

SAHNI, SARTAJ KUMAR, ALGORITHMS, DESIGN AUTOMATION. *Current Pos:* PROF COMPUT SCI, CIS DEPT, UNIV FLA, 90- *Personal Data:* b Poona, India, July 22, 49; m 75, Neeta; c Agam, Neha & Param. *Educ:* Indian Inst Technol, BTech, 70; Cornell Univ, MS, 72, PhD(comput sci), 73. *Prof Exp:* Prof comput sci, Univ Minn, Minneapolis, 81-90. *Concurrent Pos:* Chmn, Comput Sci, Nat Tech Univ, Colo; co-ed, J Parallel & Distrib Comput. *Mem:* Asn Comput Mach; fel Inst Elec & Electronics Engrs; Soc Indust & Appl Math. *Res:* Design and analysis of computer algorithms; parallel computing; design automation of electronic circuits. *Mailing Add:* CSE 301 Univ Fla Gainesville FL 32611. *E-Mail:* sahni@cis.ufl.edu

SAHNI, VIRAHT, MANY-BODY DENSITY-FUNCTIONAL THEORY. *Current Pos:* from instr to assoc prof, 72-81, PROF PHYSICS, BROOKLYN COL, 82- *Personal Data:* b Lahore, India, Dec 31, 44; m 91, Catherine Quinn; c Vishal R & Vikram D. *Educ:* Indian Inst Technol, India, BTech, 65; Polytech Inst Brooklyn, MS, 68, PhD(physics), 72. *Prof Exp:* Polytech fel elec engr, Polytech Inst Brooklyn, 65-68; instr, Pratt Inst, 68-70; sr res asst physics, Polytech Inst Brooklyn, 70-72. *Concurrent Pos:* Instr & fel, Brooklyn Col, 72-74; City Univ New York Res Found fac res grants, 73-74, 75-87, 89-90 & 94-98; vis res physicist, Inst Theoret Physics, Univ Calif, 83; grantee, NSF & Am Chem Soc, 91-93. *Mem:* Am Phys Soc; Sigma Xi. *Res:* Many-body theory of the inhomogeneous electron gas in atoms, molecules and metallic surfaces. *Mailing Add:* Dept Physics Brooklyn Col Brooklyn NY 11210. *Fax:* 718-951-4407; *E-Mail:* vvvbc@cunyvm.cuny.edu

SAHOO, MAHI, PHYSICAL METALLURGY, CASTING SOLIDIFICATION. *Current Pos:* res scientist, Metals Technol Lab, Can Ctr Mineral & Energy Technol, 77-84 & 87-88, asst dir, Res Prog Off, 85-86, Head, Foundry Sect, Metals Technol Lab, 89-93, PROG MGR CASTING TECHNOL, CAN CTR MINERAL & ENERGY TECHNOL, 93- *Personal Data:* b India, Apr 7, 43; Can citizen; m 71, Saudamini Mahapatra; c Daisy & Debashish. *Educ:* Utkal Univ, India, BSc (Hons), 64; Indian Ist Sci, Bangalore, BE, 67; Univ BC, Vancouver, PhD(phys metall), 71. *Honors & Awards:* Merit Award, Dept Energy, Mines & Resources, 87; Award of Excellence, Treasury Bd, Govt Can, 88; Sci Merit Award, Am Foundrymen's Soc, 89, Gold Medal, 94. *Prof Exp:* Nat Res Coun fel, Dept Metall Eng, Queens Univ, Kingston, 71-73, res assoc, 73-77. *Mem:* Fel Am Soc Metals Int; Am Foundrymen's Soc; Am Soc Testing & Mat; Can Inst Mining Metall & Petrol. *Res:* Solidification; gating and risering design; alloy development; vacuum pouring; evaporative pattern casting; gravity permanent mold casting; low pressure die casting; metal matrix composite casting; strip casting of ferrous and non-ferrous alloys; author of numerous publications and granted 2 patents. *Mailing Add:* CANMET Metals Technol Lab 568 Booth St Ottawa ON K1A 0G1 Can. *Fax:* 613-992-8735

SAHOO, PRASANNA, FUNCTIONAL EQUATIONS & INEQUALITIES, COMPUTER VISION & IMAGE PROCESSING. *Current Pos:* from asst prof to assoc prof, 88-97, PROF MATH, UNIV LOUISVILLE, 97- *Personal Data:* b Rampella, India, Mar 10, 51. *Educ:* Univ Regina, Can, MSc, 79; Univ Waterloo, Can, PhD(appl math), 86. *Prof Exp:* Res asst, Univ Regina, 79-80; postdoctoral fel, Univ Waterloo, 86-87. *Mem:* Am Math Soc; Math Asn Am; Can Appl Math Soc; Inst Elec & Electronics Engrs; Sigma Xi. *Res:* Characterized probabilistic information measures using functional equations; theory of price discrimination and computer vision. *Mailing Add:* Dept Math Univ Louisville Louisville KY 40292-0001. *Fax:* 502-852-7132; *E-Mail:* pksaho01@homer.louisville.edu

SAHOTA, AJIT SINGH, VERIFICATION OF GENETIC PURITY OF PEDIGREE SEEDS OF FIELD CROPS, METHOD DEVELOPMENT FOR GENETIC PURITY TESTING OF FIELD CROPS. *Current Pos:* CHIEF BIOLOGIST VARIETY VERIFICATION, AGR & PLANT BREEDING, LAB SERV DIV, CAN AGR & AGR FOOD, 80- *Personal Data:* m 69, Surinder K Rai; c Deep K, Tegh S & Harminder S. *Educ:* Punjab Agr Univ, BSc, 64, MSc, 69. *Prof Exp:* Seed analyst, Can Dept Agr, 71-75, agr officer, 75-80. *Mem:* Agr Inst Can; Inst Seed Testing Asn; Asn Seed Analysts Am; assoc mem Can Seed Growers Asn; Indian Soc Seed Technol. *Res:* Monitoring of Canada's pedigree seed multiplication for genetic purity to ensure that it meets the standards laid out in Canadian seeds act and regulation and international seed pedigree standards of various countries under the Econ Coop Develop seed pedigreeing schemes; method development in testing seeds for genetic purity and identity. *Mailing Add:* Agr Can & Agr Food Cent Exp Farm Bldg 18 Ottawa ON K1A 0C6 Can. *Fax:* 613-759-1260

SAHU, SAURA CHANDRA, CANCER RESEARCH, OXYGEN RADICALS. *Current Pos:* RES CHEMIST, US FOOD & DRUG ADMIN, 88- *Personal Data:* b Cuttack, India, June 29, 44; US citizen; m 66; c 3. *Educ:* Uktal Univ, India, BS, 64; Columbia Univ, MS, 67; Univ Pittsburgh, PhD(chem), 71. *Honors & Awards:* Fel, Indian Atomic Energy Comn, 64-66. *Prof Exp:* Res assoc biophys, Mich State Univ, 71-72 & C F Kettering Res Lab, 72-74; asst res prof biochem, Duke Univ, 74-79; res biochemist, US Consumer Prod Safety Comn, 79-88. *Concurrent Pos:* Fel, Indian Atomic Energy Comn, 64-66. *Mem:* Am Soc Biol Chemists; Am Soc Pharmacol & Exp Therapeut; Soc Toxicol; Soc Complex Carbohydrates; NY Acad Sci; Oxygen Soc; Am Soc Cancer Res. *Res:* Molecular mechanisms of carcinogenesis; cancer biochemistry and free radical biochemistry. *Mailing Add:* Div Toxicol Res US Food & Drug Admin 8301 Muirkirk Rd Laurel MD 20708

SAHYUN, MELVILLE RICHARD VALDE, PHOTOGRAPHIC CHEMISTRY. *Current Pos:* res specialist, Imaging Res Lab, 3M Co, 66-74, sr res specialist, Systs Res Lab, 74-81, staff scientist, Corp Res Lab, 81-89, STAFF SCIENTIST, GRAPHIC RES LAB, 3M CD, 90- *Personal Data:* b Santa Barbara, Calif, Feb 11, 40; m 66, Irene M Nordquist; c Steven & Michael. *Educ:* Univ Calif, Santa Barbara, AB, 59; Univ Calif, Los Angeles, PhD(chem), 63. *Prof Exp:* Sr asst scientist, Nat Cancer Inst, 62-65; NIH res fel chem, Calif Inst Technol, 65-66. *Concurrent Pos:* Assoc ed, J Imaging Sci. *Mem:* Am Chem Soc; fel Soc Photog Sci & Eng. *Res:* Photographic science; photography; reaction kinetics; organic photochemistry; solid state science; computer modelling. *Mailing Add:* 2458 Hillwood Dr Maplewood MN 55119

SAID, MOSTAFA MOHAMED, biochemical evaluation of drugs & newly synthetic compounds, quality control in biological purposes, for more information see previous edition

SAID, RUSHDI, GENERAL EARTH SCIENCE, GEOLOGY. *Current Pos:* CONSULT, 78- *Personal Data:* b Cairo, Egypt, May 12, 20; US citizen; m 53, Wadad; c Kareem & Sawsan. *Educ:* Cairo Univ, BSc, 41 & MSc, 44; Harvard Univ, PhD(geol), 50. *Hon Degrees:* Dr, Tech Univ, Berlin, 86. *Honors & Awards:* Medal Sci & Arts, Egyptian Govt, 62; Nachtigal Medal, Geog Soc Berlin, 86. *Prof Exp:* Lectr geol, Cairo Univ, 51-57, asst prof, 57-64; prof geol, Alexandria Univ, 64-68; pres, Mining Orgn, Egypt, 68-70; Geol Surv Egypt, 70-78. *Concurrent Pos:* Mem bd, Int Geol Correlation Prog, 73-75; vpres, Arab Mining Co, Amman, Jordan, 75-78; sr res scientist, Inst Earth & Man, Southern Methodist Univ, Dallas, 78-; assoc ed, J African Earth Sci, 83-95; fel, Inst Advan Studies, Berlin, 89- *Mem:* Egyptian Acad Sci; hon fel Geol Am Soc; Third World Acad Sci; hon mem Geol Soc Africa; emer mem Am Asn Petrol Geol; Inst Egypt. *Res:* Author of a large number of publications dealing primarily with different aspects of geology of Egypt and evaluation of River Nile. *Mailing Add:* 3801 Mill Creek Dr Annandale VA 22003. *Fax:* 703-207-0341

SAID, SAMI I, PULMONARY DISEASE, PEPTIDES. *Current Pos:* PROF & ASSOC HEAD RES, DEPT MED, UNIV ILL COL MED & VET ADMIN WESTSIDE MED CTR, 87-, MED INVESTR, VET ADMIN, 88- *Personal Data:* b Cairo, Egypt, Mar 25, 28. *Educ:* Univ Cairo, MB, BCh, 51. *Honors & Awards:* William S Middleton Award, Vet Admin, 81; Smith-Kline Award, Can Cong Clin Chem, 83. *Prof Exp:* Intern, Univ Hosp, Univ Cairo, 51-52, resident internal med, 53; asst resident, Bellevue & Univ Hosps, Postgrad Med Sch, NY Univ, 53-55, instr med, Sch Med, 55, NY Heart Asn res fel, Bellevue Hosp, 55-57; asst physician & fel, Sch Med, Johns Hopkins Univ & Johns Hopkins Hosp, 57-58; from asst prof to prof, Med Col Va, 58-71; prof internal med & pharmacol, Univ Tex Health Sci Ctr, 71-81; chief, Pulmonary Dis Sect, Dallas Vet Admin Med Ctr, 71-81; prof med, chief, pulmonary dis & critical care sect, Univ Okla Health Sci Ctr, 81-87. *Concurrent Pos:* Fulbright res fel, Naval Med Res Unit 3, 52-53; Fulbright traveling fel, 53; Nat Heart Inst res career develop award, 62-71; vis scientist, Karolinska Inst, Sweden, 68-70; dir, Pulmonary Specialized Ctr Res, Dallas, 71-81; mem merit rev bd respiration, Vet Admin, 72-75; mem pulmonary-allergy clin immunol adv comt, Bur Drugs, Food & Drug Admin,772-76 & pulmonary dis adv comt, Vet Admin, 79-81; exchange scientist, Vet Admin-INSERM, France, 73; mem, rev panel nat res & demonstration ctrs, Nat Heart & Lung Inst, NIH, 74; assoc ed, Peptides, 80- *Mem:* Am Soc Clin Invest; Asn Am Physicians; Soc Neurosci; Am Gastroenterol Asn; Endocrine Soc; hon mem Royal Belgian Soc Gastroenterol; Sigma Xi; Am Psysiol Soc; Am Soc Pharmacol Exp Ther. *Res:* Mediators of pulmonary responses in health and disease; biology and biochemistry of vasoactive intestinal peptide and related peptides. *Mailing Add:* Dept Med State Univ NY Stony Brook Health Sci Ctr T17040 Stony Brook NY 11794-8172. *Fax:* 516-444-1754

SAIDAK, WALTER JOHN, WEED SCIENCE. *Current Pos:* RETIRED. *Personal Data:* b Ottawa, Ont, May 10, 30; m 56; c 2. *Educ:* Ont Agr Col, BSA, 53; Cornell Univ, MS, 55, PhD(veg crops), 58. *Prof Exp:* Res officer, Plant Res Inst, Can Dept Agr, 58-62, res scientist, Res Sta, 62-73, res coordr weeds, Res Br, Cent Exp Farm, 73-89. *Mem:* Weed Sci Soc Am; Agr Inst Can. *Res:* Weed control in field and horticultural crops; translocation of herbicides. *Mailing Add:* 50 Kilmory Crescent Nepean ON K2E 6N1 Can

SAIDE, JUDITH DANA, MUSCLE STRUCTURE & CHEMISTRY. *Current Pos:* asst biochem, 75-77, asst prof, 77-82, ASSOC PROF, DEPT PHYSIOL, SCH MED, BOSTON UNIV, 82- *Personal Data:* b Worcester, Mass, Feb 21, 44. *Educ:* Vassar Col, AB, 65; Boston Univ, PhD(physiol), 72. *Prof Exp:* Res fel, Dept Med, Mass Gen Hosp, 72-75. *Concurrent Pos:* Res fel biol chem, Harvard Med Sch, 72-75, instr, Dept Physiol, 75-77; establ investr, Am Heart Asn, 77. *Mem:* AAAS; Am Heart Asn. *Res:* Identification, characterization and assembly of proteins of the z-band of striated muscle. *Mailing Add:* 457 Beacon St Boston MA 02115

SAIDEL, GERALD MAXWELL, BIOMEDICAL ENGINEERING. *Current Pos:* From asst prof to assoc prof, 67-81, PROF BIOMED ENG, CASE WESTERN RES UNIV, 81-, CHMN, 87- *Personal Data:* b New Haven, Conn, May 27, 38; m 69; c 2. *Educ:* Rensselaer Polytech Inst, BChE, 60; Johns Hopkins Univ, PhD(chem eng), 65. *Concurrent Pos:* Res engr, Vet Admin Med Ctr, Cleveland, 70-85; sect ed, Annals of Biomed Eng, 79-85; fel, City Col NY, 85-86; vis prof, Techion-Israel Inst Tech, 85-86. *Mem:* Am Inst Chem Eng; Biomed Eng Soc (pres, 87-88); Am Asn Univ Professors; Inst Elec & Electronics Engrs Engrs Biol Med Soc; fel Am Inst Med & Biol Eng. *Res:* Heat and mass transport; modeling and computer simulation; parameter estimation of dynamic systems; optimal experiment design; metabolic systems analysis. *Mailing Add:* Dept Biomed Eng Case Western Res Univ Wickenden Bldg Cleveland OH 44106. *Fax:* 216-368-4969; *E-Mail:* gms3@po.cwru.edu

SAIDEL, LEO JAMES, BIOCHEMISTRY. *Current Pos:* RETIRED. *Personal Data:* b Lanark, Ill, Aug 22, 16; m 43, Helen A Fabricant; c Lou E, Matthew L & Tobi J. *Educ:* Univ Chicago, BS, 38; Georgetown Univ, MS, 41, PhD(biochem), 46. *Prof Exp:* Lab aide, Food & Drug Admin, USDA, 38 & Bur Dairy Indust, 38-40, jr chemist, 40-42; res assoc, Col Physicians & Surgeons, Columbia Univ, 42-46; chemist, G Barr & Co, Ill, 46-47; assoc, Univ Chicago, 47; from instr to prof biochem, Chicago Med Sch, 47-82, chmn dept, 75-76. *Mem:* Am Chem Soc; Am Soc Biochem & Molecular Biol; AAAS; Sigma Xi. *Res:* Composition, structure and properties of peptides and proteins; ultraviolet absorption spectra of proteins and related materials. *Mailing Add:* PO Box 1205 Lyons CO 80540

SAIDHA, TEKCHAND, ENZYMES OF SULFATE METABOLIC PATHWAYS-SULFOLIPID BIOSYNTHESIS IN CHLOROPLASTS & MITOCHONDRIA, PURIFICATIONS & CHARACTERIZATION OF ENZYMES & LIPIDS. *Current Pos:* res fel, 84-87, res assoc, 87-91, SR RES ASSOC, BRANDEIS UNIV, 92- *Personal Data:* b Hyderabad, India, June 1, 52; US citizen; m 84, Laxmi N A Maher; c Sheela & Ashwin. *Educ:* Andhra Pradesh Agr Univ, BS, 74; Univ Agr Sci, MS, 76; Tamil Nadu Agr Univ, PhD(hort), 82. *Prof Exp:* Vis scientist, Hebrew Univ, Jerusalem, 82-84. *Mem:* Am Soc Plant Physiol; Am Soc Hort Sci. *Res:* Involved in research in the areas of cell biology, biochemistry and enzymology; specific activities include purification, characterization and cellular localization of enzymes of sulfate, carbohydrate and glycolipid metabolic pathways; isolation, analysis and identification of intermediates; chemical and enzymatic synthesis and purification of radio labeled and non-radio labeled esters, sugars, sulfonic acids, amino acids and adenine nucleotides. *Mailing Add:* 14111 Bramble Apt 103 Laurel MD 20708. *Fax:* 781-736-2689

SAIDUDDIN, SYED, ENDOCRINOLOGY, REPRODUCTIVE PHYSIOLOGY. *Current Pos:* from asst prof, 71-76 to assoc prof, 76-79, PROF VET PHYSIOL, COL VET MED, OHIO STATE UNIV, 79- *Personal Data:* b Kakinada, India, Dec 7, 38; m 67, Jamu Ramdas; c Shafi. *Educ:* Sri Venkateswara Univ, India, BVSc, 59; Indian Vet Res Inst, NDAG, 62; Univ Nev, Reno, MS, 64; Univ Wis-Madison, PhD(endocrinol), 68. *Prof Exp:* Proj assoc, Univ Wis, 67-69; NIH res fel, Med Sch, Tufts Univ, 69-71. *Mem:* Soc Study Reproduction; Endocrine Soc; Am Physiol Soc. *Res:* Endocrine control of ovarian follicular growth; mechanism of action of estrogen and progesterone. *Mailing Add:* Dept Vet Physiol Ohio State Univ Col Vet Med Columbus OH 43210. *Fax:* 614-292-2077

SAIED, FAISAL, NUMERICAL ANALYSIS, PARALLEL COMPUTATION. *Current Pos:* ASST PROF COMPUT SCI, UNIV ILL, URBANA-CHAMPAIGN, 89- *Personal Data:* b Karachi, Pakistan, July 14, 51; US citizen; m 82; c 2. *Educ:* Trinity Col, Cambridge, Eng, BA Hons, 73; Gottingen Univ, Ger, dipl math, 77; Yale Univ, PhD(comput sci), 90. *Mem:* Soc Indust & Appl Math. *Res:* Numerical analysis; scientific computation; partial differential equations; parallel algorithm; ocean acoustics. *Mailing Add:* Dept Comput Sci Univ Ill 1304 W Springfield Ave Urbana IL 61801-2910

SAIER, MILTON H, JR, MOLECULAR TRANSPORT, CELL REGULATION. *Current Pos:* From asst prof to assoc prof, 72-82, PROF BIOL, UNIV CALIF, SAN DIEGO, 82- *Personal Data:* b Palo Alto, Calif, July 30, 41; m 61, Jeanne Woodhams; c Hans H, Anila J & Amanda L. *Educ:* Univ Calif, Berkeley, BS, 63, PhD(biochem), 68. *Concurrent Pos:* Fel, Alexander von Humboldt Soc Ger. *Mem:* Am Soc Microbiol; Soc Gen Microbiol, Gt Brit; Fedn Am Soc Exp Biol. *Res:* Mechanism and regulation of sugar transport in bacteria; transcriptional regulation and catabolite repression in bacteria; multidrug resistance in bacteria; genome sequence analyses. *Mailing Add:* Dept Biol 0116 Univ Calif San Diego La Jolla CA 92093-0116. *Fax:* 619-534-7108; *E-Mail:* msaier@ucsd.edu

SAIF, LINDA JEAN, MICROBIOLOGY, IMMUNOLOGY & VIROLOGY. *Current Pos:* instr microbiol, Ohio Agr Res & Dev Ctr, 72-74, res assoc, 75-76, res assoc fel, 77-78, asst prof, Dept Vet Sci, 79-85, assoc prof, Food Animal Health Res Prog, 85-90, PROF, OHIO AGR RES & DEVELOP CTR, 90- *Personal Data:* b Columbus, Ohio, June 29, 47; m 70, Y M; c Justin. *Educ:* Col Wooster, BA, 69; Ohio State Univ, MS, 71, PhD(microbiol), 76; Am Col Vet Microbiologists, dipl, 90. *Honors & Awards:* Distinguished Vet Immunologist Award, Am Asn Vet Immunologists, 95. *Prof Exp:* Res asst, Dept Microbiol, Case Western Res Univ, 69-70. *Concurrent Pos:* Vis prof, Col Vet Med, Univ Guelph, Ont, Can, 87; consult, FAO & Interam Develop Bank; Fulbright res scholar, Inst Virol, CICV-INTA, Arg, 92. *Mem:* Am Soc Microbiol; Conf Res Workers Animal Dis; Am Soc Virol; Am Asn Vet Immunol; fel AAAS. *Res:* Basic mechanisms of the immune response of swine and cattle; mechanisms of protection against enteric viral infections; identification and purification of bovine and porcine enteric viruses and immunoglobulins; preparation of enteric vaccines. *Mailing Add:* Food Animal Health Res Prog Ohio Agr Res & Develop Ctr Ohio State Univ Wooster OH 44691. *Fax:* 330-263-3677; *E-Mail:* saif.2@osu.edu

SAIF, YEHIA M(OHAMED), VETERINARY IMMUNOLOGY, INFECTIOUS DISEASES. *Current Pos:* res asst vet sci, Ohio State Univ, 65-67, fel, 67-68, from asst prof to assoc prof, 68-77, PROF VET PREV MED & HEAD, FOOD ANIMAL HEALTH RES PROG, OHIO AGR RES & DEVELOP CTR, OHIO STATE UNIV, 77- *Personal Data:* b Minia, Egypt, Dec 23, 34; US citizen; m 70, Linda J Marsch; c Justin N. *Educ:* Cairo Univ, DVM, 59; Ohio State Univ, MSc, 64, PhD(vet prev med), 67; Am Col Vet Microbiol, dipl. *Honors & Awards:* Upjohn Res Achievement Award, Am Asn Avian Pathologists, 87; Res Award, Nat Turkey Fedn, 88; Beecham Award for Res Excellence, 90. *Prof Exp:* Teaching asst vet med, Cairo Univ, 59-62. *Mem:* Am Col Vet Microbiol; Am Col Poultry Vet. *Res:* Immune response of poultry; poultry diseases. *Mailing Add:* Food Animal Health Res Prog Ohio Agr Res & Develop Ctr Ohio State Univ Wooster OH 44691

SAIFER, MARK GARY PIERCE, SUPEROXIDE DISMUTASE, ORGOTEIN. *Current Pos:* VPRES & SCI DIR, MOUNTAIN VIEW PHARMACEUT INC, 95- *Personal Data:* b Philadelphia, Pa, Sept 16, 38; m 94, Merry R Sherman; c Scott & Alandria. *Educ:* Univ Pa, AB, 60; Univ Calif, Berkeley, PhD(biophys), 67. *Prof Exp:* Actg asst prof zool, Univ Calif, Berkeley, 66; sr cancer res scientist, Roswell Park Mem Inst, 68-70; lab dir enzym, Diag Data, Inc, 70-78; vpres, DDI Pharmaceut Inc, 78-95. *Concurrent Pos:* Am Cancer Soc fel, Dept Bacteriol & Immunol, Univ Calif, Berkeley, 67-68; Damon Runyon Mem Fund grant, 68-70; res develop award, Health Res Inc, Buffalo, 68-70. *Mem:* AAAS; NY Acad Sci; Parenteral Drug Asn. *Res:* Regulation of synthesis, compartmentalization and secretion of proteins; biological and medical effects of superoxide dismutase; immunology and pharmacology of proteins; suppression of immunogenicity by chemical modification of proteins; long-acting derivatives of proteins. *Mailing Add:* 1114 Royal Lane San Carlos CA 94070. *Fax:* 650-632-1616; *E-Mail:* msaifer@mvpharm.com

SAIFF, EDWARD IRA, ZOOLOGY, ANATOMY. *Current Pos:* asst prof, 72-75, assoc prof, 75-80, PROF BIOL, RAMAPO COL, NJ, 80- *Personal Data:* b New Brunswick, NJ, Oct 11, 42; m 67, Roberta Lichter; c Beth & Joshua. *Educ:* Rutgers Univ, BA, 64, PhD(zool), 73; State Univ NY, Buffalo, MA, 68. *Prof Exp:* Instr zool, Rutgers Univ, 70-71, lectr, 71-72. *Concurrent Pos:* Dir, Sch Theoret & Anal Sci, Ramapo Col, 84-93. *Mem:* Am Ornith Union; Am Soc Zoologists; Soc Syst Zoology; Linnean Soc London; Sigma

Xi; AAAS; NY Acad Sci; Soc Neurosci. *Res:* Avian anatomy, particularly of the middle ear region; anatomical correlates of hearing in birds; evolutionary theory; CNS receptor sites; neurohistology. *Mailing Add:* Theoret & Appl Sci Ramapo Col 505 Ramapo Valley Rd Mahwah NJ 07430. *Fax:* 201-529-7637; *E-Mail:* esaiff@.ramapo.edu

SAIGAL, SUNIL, COMPUTATIONAL MECHANICS, NUMERICAL METHODS. *Current Pos:* asst prof, 89-91, ASSOC PROF CIVIL ENG, CARNEGIE MELLON UNIV, 91- *Personal Data:* b Karnal, India, July 13, 57; m 89, VanDana; c Rohan & Vandana. *Educ:* Punjab Eng Col, Chandigarh, India, BS, 78; Indian Inst Sci, Bangalore, India, MS, 80; Purdue Univ, PhD(aerospace eng), 85. *Prof Exp:* Postdoctoral fel aerospace eng, Purdue Univ, 85-86; asst prof mech eng, Worcester Polytech Inst, 86-89. *Concurrent Pos:* NASA-CASE res fel, Lewis Res Ctr, Ohio, 89; NSF presidential young investr, 90; prog dir mech & mat, NSF. *Mem:* Am Soc Civil Engrs; Am Soc Mech Engrs; Am Inst Aeronaut & Astronaut. *Res:* Finite element, boundary element, and meshless analyisis methodologies, mechanics of materials, biomechanics of orthopaedic implants; inverse problems in engineering and shape optimization with boundary elements; computational bounds for equivalent material properties of woven composites. *Mailing Add:* Dept Civil Eng Carnegie Mellon Univ Pittsburgh PA 15213. *Fax:* 412-268-7813; *E-Mail:* ssaigal@andrew.cmu.edu

SAIGO, ROY HIROFUMI, PLANT ANATOMY, PLANT PATHOLOGY. *Current Pos:* CHANCELLOR, AUBURN UNIV, MONTGOMERY, 94- *Personal Data:* b Sacramento, Calif, Aug 6, 40; m 67. *Educ:* Univ Calif, Davis, BA, 62; Ore State Univ, PhD(plant anat), 69. *Honors & Awards:* Charles E Bessey Award, Bot Soc Am. *Prof Exp:* Asst dean, Univ Wis-Eau Claire, 81-84; sci & agr dean, Southeastern La Univ, 84-90, prof biol, provost & vpres acad & student affairs, 90-94. *Concurrent Pos:* Fac res grants, Univ Wis-Eau Claire, 68-69 & 71-72, teacher improv assignment, 70, asst to dean arts & sci, 80-; acad affairs intern, Univ Wis Syst, 75-76; sci & agr dean, Univ Northern Iowa, 84-90, dean nat sci, 84-90. *Mem:* Fel AAAS; Bot Soc Am; Am Inst Biol Sci. *Res:* Effect of insects on the bark of coniferous trees; ultrastructural investigation of the phloem of lower vascular plants and protein body development in oats. *Mailing Add:* Auburn Univ Montgomery PO Box 244023 Montgomery AL 36124

SAI-HALASZ, GEORGE ANTHONY, MICROELECTRONICS, COMPUTER DESIGN. *Current Pos:* res staff mem, 74-84, RES MGR, IBM WATSON RES LAB, 84- *Personal Data:* b Budapest, Hungary, Dec 7, 43; m 70, 90, Ildiko Medve; c Christine, Adria & Kathleen. *Educ:* Eotvos Roland Sci Univ, Budapest, dipl physics, 66; Case Western Reserve Univ, PhD(physics), 72. *Honors & Awards:* Cledo Brunetti Award, Int Elec & Electronics Engrs, 97. *Prof Exp:* Fel, Univ Pa, 72-74. *Mem:* Am Phys Soc; fel Int Elec & Electronics Engrs. *Res:* Computer systems and design; silicon technology; past activity in solid state physics. *Mailing Add:* IBM T J Watson Res Ctr PO Box 218 Yorktown Heights NY 10598. *Fax:* 914-945-3613; *E-Mail:* sai@watson.ibm.com

SAILA, SAUL BERNHARD, FISH BIOLOGY. *Current Pos:* from asst prof marine biol to assoc prof oceanog, Univ RI, 56-67, coordr comput lab, 59-76, dir, Marine Exp Sta, 66-76, prof, 67-, EMER PROF OCEANOG, UNIV RI. *Personal Data:* b Providence, RI, May 23, 24; m 49; c 3. *Educ:* Univ RI, BS, 49; Cornell Univ, MS, 50, PhD(fishery biol), 52. *Honors & Awards:* Am Fisheries Soc Award, 59. *Prof Exp:* Res assoc zool, Ind Univ, 52-54; fishery biologist, Div Fish & Game, RI Dept Agr & Conserv, 54-56. *Mem:* AAAS; Am Fisheries Soc; Am Soc Limnol & Oceanog; Inst Fishery Res Biologists; Int Asn Theoret & Appl Limnol. *Res:* Fish population dynamics. *Mailing Add:* 317 Switch Rd Hope Valley RI 02832

SAILOR, MICHAEL JOSEPH, MATERIALS CHEMISTRY. *Current Pos:* asst prof chem, 90-91, MEM, MAT SCI DIV, UNIV CALIF, SAN DIEGO, 91- *Personal Data:* b Redwood City, Calif, May 18, 61. *Educ:* Harvey Mudd Col, BS, 83; Northwestern Univ, PhD(chem), 88. *Honors & Awards:* NSF Young Investr, 93; Beckman Young Investr, Arnold & Mabel Beckman Found, 93. *Prof Exp:* Fel, Stanford Univ & Calif Inst Technol, 87-90. *Concurrent Pos:* Consult, 3-M Co, 89, Hughes Aircraft Corp, 91- *Mem:* Am Chem Soc; AAAS; Mat Res Soc; Electrochem Soc. *Res:* Synthesis and study of materials with interesting electronic properties; quantum-size semiconductor particles, luminescent porous silicon and electronically conductive polymers. *Mailing Add:* Dept Chem Univ Calif San Diego La Jolla CA 92093-0358

SAILOR, VANCE LEWIS, NUCLEAR SCIENCE. *Current Pos:* CONSULT, NUCLEAR POWER PLANT SAFETY, 85- *Personal Data:* b Springfield, Mo, June 28, 20; m 43, Marguerite Erdman; c Richard V, Nancy A & John K. *Educ:* DePauw Univ, AB, 43; Yale Univ, MS, 47, PhD(physics), 49. *Prof Exp:* From assoc physicist to physicist, Brookhaven Nat Lab, Upton, 49-67, sr physicist, 67-85. *Concurrent Pos:* Dir systs anal proj, Int Energy Agency. *Mem:* Am Phys Soc; Am Nuclear Soc; Sigma Xi. *Res:* Neutron and reactor physics; charged particle reactions; low temperature physics; nuclear energy; environmental effects of energy production and usage. *Mailing Add:* 100 Durkee Lane East Patchogue NY 11772

SAIN, MICHAEL K(ENT), CONTROL SYSTEMS. *Current Pos:* From asst prof to prof, 65-82, FRANK M FREIMANN PROF ELEC ENG, UNIV NOTRE DAME, 82- *Personal Data:* b St Louis, Mo, Mar 22, 37; m 63; c 3. *Educ:* St Louis Univ, BS, 59, MS, 62; Univ Ill, PhD(elec eng), 65. *Honors & Awards:* Centennial Medal, Inst Elec & Electronics Engrs, 84. *Concurrent Pos:* Vis scientist, Univ Toronto, 72-73; res grants, NASA, 75-85, Airforce Off Sci Res, 76-78, NSF, 66-71, 73-77, 81-85 & 91-94, Off Naval Res, 79-81, Army Res Off, 88-89, Clark Components Int, 90-; mem rev panel, NSF, 76, 79 & 84; ed, Transactions on Automatic Control, Inst Elec & Electronics Engrs, 79-83, vpres admin, Circuits & Systs Soc, 92-93, vpres tech activ, 94; distinguished vis prof, Ohio State Univ, 87. *Mem:* Fel Inst Elec & Electronics Engrs; Soc Indust & Appl Math; Am Soc Eng Educ; distinguished mem Inst Elec & Electronics Engrs Control Syst Soc. *Res:* Nonlinear multivariable control systems; hysteretic circuits, systems and control; structural control for earthquake hazard mitigation; gas turbine engine control; pressure modelling in internal combustion engines; global zeros and feedback properties; hybrid models and autonomous control; algebraic system theory and applications. *Mailing Add:* Dept Elec Eng Univ Notre Dame Notre Dame IN 46556-0398

SAINI, GIRDHARI LAL, MATHEMATICS. *Current Pos:* assoc prof, 67-76, PROF MATH, UNIV SASK, 76- *Personal Data:* b Hariana, India, Aug 2, 31; m 49; c 3. *Educ:* Panjab Univ, India, BS, 55, MA, 57; Indian Inst Technol, Kharagpur, PhD(math), 61. *Prof Exp:* Assoc lectr math, Indian Inst Technol, Kharagpur, 60, lectr, 60-62; vis asst prof, Math Res Ctr, Univ Wis-Madison, 62-64; asst prof, Indian Inst Technol, New Delhi, 64-67. *Concurrent Pos:* Res mem, US Army Res Ctr, Univ Wis-Madison, 62-64. *Mem:* Am Math Soc; Can Math Soc. *Res:* Relativistic fluid mechanics. *Mailing Add:* Dept Math & Statist Univ Sask 106 Wiggins Rd Saskatoon SK S7N 5E6 Can

SAINI, RAVINDER KUMAR, CLINICAL CARDIOVASCULAR PHARMACOLOGY, CLINICAL CARDIOLOGY. *Current Pos:* ASSOC DIR CARDIOVASC CLIN, BRISTOL-MYERS SQUIBB CO. *Personal Data:* b Hoshiarpur, India, Jan 28, 46; US citizen; m 71; c 2. *Educ:* Col Vet Med, Hissar, India, DVM, 68; Postgrad Med Res Inst, Chandigarh, India, MS, 71; Univ Naples, Italy, PhD(pharmacol), 73. *Prof Exp:* Res assoc pharmacol, Sch Med, Univ Pa, 73-74; res fel pharmacol, Univ Wis, Madison, 74-76; res assoc pharmacol, Sch Med, Univ Miami, Fla, 76-78; res pharmacologist, Merrell Res Ctr, Cincinnati, Ohio, 78-79; SR RES INVESTR PHARMACOL, SQUIBB INST MED RES, 79- *Concurrent Pos:* Res grant investr, Tobacco Inst, 73-74, Am Lung Asn, 74-76 & NIH Cardiovasc Training, 76-78. *Mem:* Am Soc Pharmacol & Exp Therapeut; fel Am Col Angiol; Int Soc Heart Res; fel Am Col Cardiol. *Res:* Planning, development and management of cardiovascular clinical programs for arrhythmias, hypertension and lipid-lowering agents. *Mailing Add:* Dept Cardiovasc Clin Res Bristol Myers Squibb Co Rte J4008 Princeton NJ 08543-4000. *Fax:* 609-252-6003

SAINSBURY, ROBERT STEPHEN, NEUROPSYCHOLOGY. *Current Pos:* From asst prof to assoc prof, 69-80, PROF PSYCHOL, UNIV CALGARY, 80- *Personal Data:* b Halifax, NS, Apr 16, 43; m, Anne Mahoney; c Pamela. *Educ:* Mt Allison Univ, BA, 63; Dalhousie Univ, MA, 65; McMaster Univ, PhD(psychol), 69. *Mem:* Soc Neuroscience; Int Neuropsychol Soc. *Res:* Effects of brain lesions on species typical behavior in small mammals; affective discrimination in brain damaged populations. *Mailing Add:* Dept Psychol Univ Calgary 2500 Univ Dr Calgary AB T2N 1N4 Can. *Fax:* 403-282-8249; *E-Mail:* sainsbur@acs.ucalgary.ca

ST AMAND, PIERRE, GEOPHYSICS. *Current Pos:* OWNER, ST-AMAND SCI SERV, 80-; VPRES TECHNOL, MUETAL INC, 94- *Personal Data:* b Tacoma, Wash, Feb 4, 20; m 48, Marie Poss; c Gene, Barbara, Denal & David. *Educ:* Univ Alaska, BS, 48; Calif Inst Technol, MS, 51, PhD(geophys, geol), 53. *Hon Degrees:* DSc, Univ Los Altos, Tepotitlan, Jalisco, Mex, 92. *Honors & Awards:* Distinguished Civilian Serv Medal, US Navy, 67 & Meritorious Serv Medal; Spec Award, Philippine Air Force; L T E Thompson Award, Naval Weapon Ctr, 74; Distinguished Pub Serv Award, 76; Thunderbird Award, Weather Modification Asn; Dipl de Honor, Soc Geol de Chile, 65. *Prof Exp:* Magnetic observer, Carnegie Inst, Alaska, 41-42, mem geophys inst, 46-48; physicist, Earth & Planetary Sci Div & Spec Projs Off, 50-61, head, 61-81, sr exec serv, Off Tech Dir, 81-88. *Concurrent Pos:* Asst, Seismol Lab, Calif Inst Technol, 52-54; Fulbright scholar, France, 54-55; Int Coop Admin prof sch geol, Univ Chile, 58-61; consult, UN Chilean & Arg Govts, 60, Mex, Can & States of Calif, SDak, NDak, Ore & Wash; dir, Ridgecrest Community Hosp, 63-83, Indian Wells Valley Water Dist; consult, Orgn Am States, 65-72; adj prof atmospheric sci, Univ Ndak, geol, McKay Sch Mines, Univ Nev, Reno; dir & chmn, Indian Wells Valley Airport Dist. *Mem:* Fel AAAS; Seismol Soc Am; fel Geol Soc Am; Am Geophys Union; Weather Modification Asn; Earthquake Eng Res Inst. *Res:* Auroral height measurement; atmospheric refraction; terrestrial magnetism; ionosphere; light of night sky; seismology; earthquakes; structural geology; electronics and instrumentation; circum pacific tectonics; weather modification; oceanography; deep sea research; Arctic research; geomorphology; desert processes. *Mailing Add:* 1748 Las Flores Ridgecrest CA 93555. *Fax:* 760-375-0481

ST AMAND, WILBROD, CYTOGENETICS. *Current Pos:* from assoc prof to prof, 58-88, EMER PROF BIOL, UNIV MISS, 88- *Personal Data:* b Old Town, Maine, May 5, 27; m 50. *Educ:* Univ Maine, BA, 48; Univ Tenn, MS, 49, PhD(zool, entom), 54. *Prof Exp:* Asst zool, Univ Tenn, 48-49; instr, Exten Serv, 50; res assoc radiation biol, Oak Ridge Nat Lab, 54-55, biologist, 55-58. *Mem:* AAAS; Am Micros Soc; Am Soc Zoologists; Genetics Soc Am; Am Inst Biol Sci. *Res:* Radiation cytology; radiosensitivity of the stages of mitosis; mouse genetics. *Mailing Add:* 134 County Rd 401 Oxford MS 38655

ST ANGELO, ALLEN JOSEPH, LIPIDOXIDATION, ENZYMOLOGY. *Current Pos:* Res chemist, 58-79, actg res leader, 79-82, RES CHEMIST, SOUTHERN REGIONAL RES CTR, USDA, 82- *Personal Data:* b New Orleans, La, April 11, 32; m 58, Althea T Finnin; c William J, Laura M, Terri F & Michael J. *Educ:* Southeastern La Univ, BS, 57; Tulane Univ, MS, 65,

PhD(biochem), 68. *Honors & Awards:* Invention Award, USDA, 89. *Concurrent Pos:* Vis adj prof, Food Sci Dept, Va Polytech Inst & State Univ, Blacksburg, Va. *Mem:* Am Chem Soc; Am Oil Chemists Soc; Inst Food Technol; Sigma Xi. *Res:* Develop methodology for assessing overall quality of meat, poultry and fish; determine mechanism for formation of warmed-over flavor in meat and design procedure for its prevention; author of 150 publications including 28 book chapters and editor of 3 books. *Mailing Add:* Southern Regional Res Ctr USDA PO Box 19687 New Orleans LA 70179. *Fax:* 504-286-4419

SAINT-ARNAUD, RAYMOND, ELECTRICAL ENGINEERING. *Current Pos:* asst prof elec eng, 65-70, ASSOC PROF ELEC ENG, LAVAL UNIV, 70- *Personal Data:* b Shawinigan, Que, Sept 23, 35; m 62; c 2. *Educ:* Laval Univ, BA, 55, BScAppl, 61, Dipl Adm, 72; Univ Strathclyde, PhD(elec eng), 66. *Prof Exp:* Engr, Hydro-Quebec, Montreal, 61-62; res asst eng, Univ Strathclyde, 62-65. *Concurrent Pos:* Res assoc, Dept Exp Med, Laval Univ, 71- *Mem:* Inst Elec & Electronics Engrs. *Res:* High voltage engineering; ionization phenomena; gas lasers; electrostatics; bioelectricity; biometeorology. *Mailing Add:* Head Genie Elec Gen Delivery Ste Foy PQ G1K 7P4 Can

ST ARNAUD, ROLAND JOSEPH, SOILS. *Current Pos:* from asst prof to prof, 56-89, EMER PROF SOIL SCI, UNIV SASK, 89- *Personal Data:* Can citizen; m 57, Therese M Blondeau; c Lise, Rene & Marc. *Educ:* Univ Sask, BSA, 48, MSc, 50; Mich State Univ, PhD(soils), 61. *Prof Exp:* Res officer, Sask Soil Surv, Can Dept Agr, 50-56. *Concurrent Pos:* Sci ed, Can Soc Soil Sci, 63-66. *Mem:* Clay Minerals Soc; Fel Can Soc Soil Sci (pres, 74-75); Am Soc Agron; Agr Inst Can. *Res:* Soil classification; mineralogical studies and micropedology. *Mailing Add:* 1302 Preston Ave Saskatoon SK S7H 2V4 Can

ST CLAIR, ANNE KING, BIOCHEMISTRY. *Current Pos:* polymer res chemist, NASA, 77-81, sr scientist, 81-86, mgr, Advan Aircraft Prog, Mat Div, 86-93, CHIEF SCI, MAT DIV, LANGLEY RES CTR, NASA, 93- *Personal Data:* b Bluefield, WVa, May 31, 47; m 71; c 1. *Educ:* Queens Col, BA, 69; Va Polytech & State Univ, MS, 72. *Honors & Awards:* IR-100 Award, 81. *Prof Exp:* Res assoc, Nat Aeronaut & Space Admin, 72-77. *Concurrent Pos:* Mem, Speakers Bur, Soc Advan Mat Process Engrs, 80-; lectr, State Univ NY, 81 & 82, sci prog chmn & lectr, course on high temperature polymers, 84-, Ehime Univ, Tokyo, Japan, 87; chmn, tech sessions, Am Chem Soc, Soc Advan Mat Process Engrs & Gordon Res Conf; chmn, Potentially Hazardous Mat Comt, NASA-Langley, 83-87; elected vchmn, Gordon Res Conf Films & Coatings, 89. *Mem:* Am Chem Soc; Soc Advan Mat Process Engrs; Asn Women Sci. *Res:* Synthesis, characterization and development of high-performance aerospace materials for applications as structural adhesives, advanced composites, films and fibers; author or coauthor of 35 publications; granted 16 patents. *Mailing Add:* Langley Res Ctr NASA Mail Stop 227 Hampton VA 23681-0001

ST CLAIR, RICHARD WILLIAM, BIOCHEMISTRY, PATHOBIOLOGY. *Current Pos:* PROF PATH & PHYSIOL, BOWMAN GRAY SCH MED, WAKE FOREST UNIV, 65- *Personal Data:* b Sioux Falls, SDak, Oct 10, 40; m 62; c 2. *Educ:* Colo State Univ, BS, 62, PhD(physiol), 65. *Concurrent Pos:* NIH fel aging, Bowman Gray Sch Med, 65-67; fel coun arteriosclerosis, Am Heart Asn, estab investr, 70-75, chmn, 90-92; Fogerty int fel, 85-86. *Mem:* Am Soc Exp Path; Tissue Culture Asn; Soc Exp Biol Med; Sigma Xi; AAAS. *Res:* Atherosclerosis research; arterial metabolism; lipoprotein metabolism in nonhuman primates; cellular lipoprotein metabolism. *Mailing Add:* Dept Path (Pysiol) Bowman Gray Sch Med Med Ctr Blvd Winston-Salem NC 27517-1072. *Fax:* 919-748-6279

ST CLAIR, TERRY LEE, POLYMER CHEMISTRY. *Current Pos:* chemist adhesives, Langley Res Ctr, NASA, 72-75, aerospace technologist polymers, 75-80, res chemist polymers, 80-84, HEAD-POLYMERIC MAT BR, LANGLEY RES CTR, NASA, 84- *Personal Data:* b Roanoke, Va, June 18, 43; m 71; c 1. *Educ:* Roanoke Col, BS, 65; Va Polytech Inst & State Univ, PhD(org chem), 73. *Honors & Awards:* Sci Achievement Medal, NASA; IR-100, 79 & 81. *Prof Exp:* Chemist quality control, E I du Pont de Nemours & Co, Inc Orlon, 65-67;; solid propellants engr, Hercules Inc-Radford Army Ammo Plant, 67-68. *Concurrent Pos:* Chmn, Gordon Conf-Adhesion, 86. *Mem:* Am Chem Soc; Sigma Xi; Soc Aerospace Mat & Process Engrs; Adhesion Soc (pres, 90-92). *Res:* Preparation and development of adhesives and composite matrix resins for aerospace applications. *Mailing Add:* 17 Roberts Landing Dr Poquoson VA 23662

SAINTE-MARIE, BERNARD, BENTHOS, POPULATION DYNAMICS. *Current Pos:* RES SCIENTIST INVERTEBRATES, INST MAURICE LA MONTAGNE, 87-, HEAD, CRUSTACEAN SECT, 91- *Personal Data:* b Montreal, Que, Can, Nov 15, 56; c 1. *Educ:* Univ Montreal, BSc, 78, MSc, 81; Dalhousie Univ, PhD(biol), 86. *Concurrent Pos:* Assoc prof, A Rimouski Oceanog Dept, Univ Que, 88-, Univ Laval, 92- *Mem:* Crustacean Soc; Can-Fr Asn Advan Sci. *Res:* Reproductive biology and population dynamics of benthic marine crustaceans, mainly amphipods and brachyurans; behavior of benthic marine scavengers. *Mailing Add:* Dept Fisheries & Oceans Inst Maurice LaMontagne 850 Rte de la Mer CP1000 Mont-Joli PQ G5H 3Z4 Can. *Fax:* 418-775-0542

SAINTE-MARIE, GUY, LYMPHOLOGY, HEMATOLOGY. *Current Pos:* assoc prof, 66-69, chmn dept, 77-85, PROF ANAT, UNIV MONTREAL, 69- *Personal Data:* b Montreal, Que, May 22, 28; m 55; c 3. *Educ:* Col Ste-Marie, BA, 50; Univ Montreal, MD, 55; McGill Univ, PhD(histol), 62. *Prof Exp:* From asst prof to assoc prof anat, Univ Western Ont, 61-66. *Concurrent Pos:* Nat Cancer Inst Can fel, 58-60; res fel bact & immunol, Harvard Univ, 60-61; Med Res Coun Can res assoc, 66. *Mem:* Am Soc Anat. *Res:* Histology and physiology of lymph nodes. *Mailing Add:* Dept Anat Univ Montreal Fac Med CP 6128 Montreal PQ H3C 3J7 Can

ST JEAN, JOSEPH, JR, INVERTEBRATE PALEONTOLOGY. *Current Pos:* RETIRED. *Personal Data:* b Tacoma, Wash, July 24, 23; m 71, Elena Melnikove. *Educ:* Col Puget Sound, BS, 49; Ind Univ, AM, 53, PhD(geol), 56. *Prof Exp:* Instr geol, Kans State Col, 51-52; from instr to asst prof, Trinity Col, Conn, 55-57; from asst prof to assoc prof, Univ NC, Chapel Hill, 57-66, prof geol, 66-90. *Concurrent Pos:* Partic, Nat Acad Sci-USSR Acad Sci Exchange Prog, 65. *Mem:* Paleont Res Inst; Paleont Soc; Soc Econ Paleont & Mineral; Int Paleont Union; Paleont Asn London. *Res:* Stromatoporoidea; systematics, evolution and paleobiology of Paleozoic Stromatoporoidea (Porifera). *Mailing Add:* Dept Geol CB 3315 Univ NC Chapel Hill NC 27599-3315. *Fax:* 919-966-4519

ST JOHN, BILL, PETROLEUM EXPLORATION. *Current Pos:* INT CONSULT, PETROL EXPLOR & MGT, 94- *Personal Data:* b Wink, Tex, Jul 27, 32. *Educ:* Univ Tex, Austin, BS, 53, MA, 60, PhD(geol), 65. *Prof Exp:* Sr geologist, Esso Explor/Esso Prod Res, 65-73; chief frontier geologist, LVO Int, 73-74, vpres, 74-78; exec vpres, Agri Petro, 78-80, pres, 80-81; pres, Primary Fuses Inc, 81-89; consult, Ethiopia, 90; vpres, Hunt Oil Co, Ethiopia & Niger, 91-94. *Mem:* Am Asn Petrol Geologists; Am Geophys Union; Geol Soc Am. *Res:* Sedimentary basins of the world, giant oil & gas fields, petroleum potential of antarctica. *Mailing Add:* PO Box 185 Vanderpool TX 78885

ST JOHN, DANIEL SHELTON, PHYSICAL CHEMISTRY. *Current Pos:* RETIRED. *Personal Data:* b San Diego, Calif, June 25, 23; m 43, Rosemary Rowlands; c Penelope, Priscilla, Pamela & Peter H. *Educ:* Univ Calif, BS, 43; Univ Wis, PhD(chem), 49. *Prof Exp:* Jr technologists, Shell Oil Co, 43-44; engr, Los Alamos Sci Lab, Univ Calif, 44-47; chemist, E I Du Pont de Nemours & Co, 49-58, res mgr, 58-64, mem, Develop Dept, 64-66; pres, Holotron Corp, 66-69; res mgr, E I Du Pont de Nemours & Co, Inc, 70-74, res fel, Polymer Intermediates Dept, 74-80, res fel, Petrochem Dept, 80-83, dept res fel, 84-85. *Mem:* Fel Am Nuclear Soc; Am Chem Soc; AAAS; Am Geophys Union; Sigma Xi. *Res:* Theoretical reactor physics; chemical engineering; physical optics; heterogeneous catalysis; chemical reaction kinetics; computer programming. *Mailing Add:* 532 Ashland Ridge Rd Hockessin DE 19707-9662

ST JOHN, FRAZE LEE, ZOOLOGY. *Current Pos:* res specialist, 69-70, asst prof, 70-79, ASSOC PROF ZOOL, OHIO STATE UNIV, 79- *Personal Data:* b Lebanon, Ohio, May 23, 39; m 62, Mary Kindell; c James & David. *Educ:* Miami Univ, BS, 61; Ind Univ, Bloomington, MA, 63; Ohio State Univ, PhD(zool), 70. *Prof Exp:* Instr zool, Miami Univ, 63-65; naturalist biol, Wahkeena State Mem, Ohio, 68. *Mem:* Sigma Xi. *Res:* Invertebrate ecology. *Mailing Add:* Dept Zool Ohio State Univ Newark OH 43055

ST JOHN, JUDITH BROOK, BIOCHEMISTRY, PLANT PHYSIOLOGY. *Current Pos:* PLANT PHYSIOLOGIST, RES LEADER WEED SCI LAB, AGR RES, USDA, 67-, DIR, PLANT SCI INST. *Personal Data:* b Memphis, Tenn, Aug 15, 40; m 67, Peter A; c Alan & Katherine. *Educ:* Millsaps Col, BS, 62; Univ Fla, PhD(bot), 66. *Prof Exp:* Res fel plant physiol, Univ Fla, 66-67. *Mem:* Am Soc Plant Physiologists; Am Inst Biol Sci; Weed Sci Soc Am; Am Chem Soc. *Res:* Mechanisms of herbicide action; plant lipid biochemistry. *Mailing Add:* Agr Res Ctr Bldg 005 10400 Baltimore Ave Riverdale MD 20705

ST JOHN, PETER ALAN, ANALYTICAL CHEMISTRY. *Current Pos:* PRES, ST JOHN ASSOCS, INC, 84- *Personal Data:* b Ashtabula, Ohio, May 11, 41; m 67; c 2. *Educ:* Univ Fla, BS, 63, PhD(anal chem), 67. *Prof Exp:* Sr res chemist, instrument develop, AMINCO, 67-70, proj mgr, New Prod Develop, 71-79, prog mgr, 79-81, asst vpres eng, Instrument Div, Baxter Travenol Labs, Inc, 81-82; vpres eng, Am Res Prod Inc, 82-83. *Mem:* Am Chem Soc; Sigma Xi. *Res:* Atomic and molecular spectroscopy; chromatography; biochemistry; microbiology. *Mailing Add:* 3306 Sellman Rd Hyattsville MD 20783

ST JOHN, PHILIP ALAN, CELL PHYSIOLOGY, VERTEBRATE REGENERATION. *Current Pos:* RETIRED. *Personal Data:* b Lexington, Mass, Feb 13, 24; m 51; c 2. *Educ:* Univ NH, BS, 49, MS, 51; Harvard Univ, PhD, 56. *Prof Exp:* From instr to asst prof biol, Brandeis Univ, 56-67; prof biol, Butler Univ, 67- *Mem:* AAAS. *Res:* Invertebrate cell culture; physiology of regeneration of Turbellaria and vertebrates parasite chemotherapy. *Mailing Add:* 1557 Brewster Rd Indianapolis IN 46260

ST JOHN, RALPH C, STATISTICS. *Current Pos:* from asst prof to assoc prof, 73-83, dir, Statist Consult Ctr, 77-84, PROF STATIST, BOWLING GREEN STATE UNIV, 83- *Personal Data:* b Ft Kent, Maine, Aug 29, 42; m 69; c 2. *Educ:* Univ Maine, Orono, BS, 64; Univ Mass, MS, 68; Univ Wis, PhD(statist), 73. *Prof Exp:* Mathematician statist, IBM, 64-66. *Mem:* Am Statist Asn; Am Soc Qual Control. *Res:* Regression; design for regression; experiments with mixtures. *Mailing Add:* 610 Rosewood Dr Bowling Green OH 43402

ST JOHN, ROBERT MAHARD, EXPERIMENTAL ATOMIC PHYSICS. *Current Pos:* From asst prof to prof, 54-90, EMER PROF PHYSICS, UNIV OKLA, 90- *Personal Data:* b Westmoreland, Kans, Mar 20, 27; m 49, Phyllis Frank; c Glenn & Carol. *Educ:* Kans State Univ, BS, 50, MS, 51; Univ Wis, PhD(physics), 54. *Mem:* Fel Am Phys Soc; Am Asn Physics Teachers. *Res:* Gaseous electronics; atomic and electronic collisions. *Mailing Add:* 1523 Rosemont Norman OK 73072

ST JOHN, WALTER MCCOY, NEUROPHYSIOLOGY. *Current Pos:* Parker B Francis Found fel & res assoc physiol, 76-77, from asst prof to assoc prof, 77-83, PROF PHYSIOL, DARTMOUTH MED SCH, 83- *Personal Data:* b Providence, RI, Apr 23, 44; m 70; c 2. *Educ:* Brown Univ, AB, 66; Univ NC, Chapel Hill, PhD(physiol), 70. *Prof Exp:* From instr to asst prof physiol, Med Ctr, Univ Ark, Little Rock, 70-74; sr fel & staff assoc, Col Physicians & Surgeons, Columbia Univ, 74-75, res assoc pharmacol, 75-76. *Concurrent Pos:* Vis scientist, Fac St Jerome, Marseilles, France, 80-81. *Mem:* Am Physiol Soc. *Res:* Neural control of respiration. *Mailing Add:* Dept Physiol Dartmouth Med Sch Dartmouth-Hitchcock Med Ctr Lebanon NH 03756

ST LAWRENCE, PATRICIA, genetics; deceased, see previous edition for last biography

ST LEGER, RAYMOND JOHN, MOLECULAR BIOLOGY & BIOCHEMISTRY OF FUNGI, ENTOMOPATHOGENIC FUNGI. *Current Pos:* fel, Boyce Thompson Inst Plant Res, Inc, 87-89, res assoc, 89-92, sr res assoc, 92, INSECT PATHOLOGIST, BOYCE THOMPSON INST PLANT RES, INC, 92- *Personal Data:* b London, Eng, Apr 1, 57. *Educ:* Exeter Univ, BSc Hons, 78; London Univ, MSc, 80; Bath Univ, PhD(insect control with microbes), 85. *Prof Exp:* Fel, Bath Univ, 85-87. *Concurrent Pos:* Res grants, USDA, 87-; consult, Eco Sci Labs, 92-; assoc ed, J Invert Path, 93- *Mem:* Soc Invert Path; Soc Gen Microbiol. *Res:* Insect mycoses including molecular biology of mechanisms used by fungi to overcome insects; enzymes and toxins produced by entomopathogenic fungi; insect cuticle and its degradation; insect immune responses. *Mailing Add:* 12 Gaslight Village Apt Ithaca NY 14853. *Fax:* 607-254-1242; *E-Mail:* rs50@cornell.edu

ST LOUIS, ROBERT VINCENT, PHYSICAL CHEMISTRY. *Current Pos:* PROF CHEM, UNIV WIS-EAU CLAIRE, 68- *Personal Data:* b Los Angeles, Calif, Dec 15, 32; m 60, Nadine Small; c Paula. *Educ:* Univ Calif, Los Angeles, BS, 54; Univ Minn, PhD(phys chem), 62. *Prof Exp:* Res assoc far-infrared spectros, Johns Hopkins Univ, 62-63; res chemist, US Borax Res Corp, 63-66; res assoc far-infrared spectros, Univ Southern Calif, 66-68. *Concurrent Pos:* Res fel, Ctr Interdisciplinary Res, Univ Bielefeld, WGer, 85-86. *Mem:* Am Chem Soc. *Res:* Chemical infrared spectroscopy; colloid chemistry; solvent effects. *Mailing Add:* Dept Chem Univ Wis Eau Claire WI 54701. *Fax:* 715-836-2380; *E-Mail:* stlouis@cnsvax.uwec.edu

ST MARY, DONALD FRANK, NUMERICAL SOLUTIONS OF PARTIAL DIFFERENTIAL EQUATIONS, SCIENTIFIC COMPUTATION. *Current Pos:* from asst prof to assoc prof, 68-83, PROF MATH, UNIV MASS, AMHERST, 83-, DEPT HEAD, 94- *Personal Data:* b Lake Charles, La, July 22, 40; m 63, LaVerne G Frilot; c Colette, Germaine & Michele. *Educ:* McNeese State Col, BS, 62; Univ Kans, MA, 64; Univ Nebr, Lincoln, PhD(math), 68. *Prof Exp:* Instr math, Univ Nebr, Lincoln, 66-67 & Iowa State Univ, 67-68. *Concurrent Pos:* Vis fac, Univ Okla, 75-76; prin investr, NSF, 81-87, Off Naval Res, 85-87 & 88-94, Nat Cancer Inst, 88-94; vis res fel, Yale Univ, 83, 90; summer fac res assoc, Navy/ASEE, 83, 84 & 87; consult, Naval Underwater Systs Ctr, 83-87; mem, Comt Equal Opportunity Sci & Eng, NSF, 86-91. *Mem:* Am Math Soc; Math Asn Am; Soc Indust & Appl Math; Am Acoust Soc; Nat Asn Math; Asn Women Math. *Res:* Numerical solutions of partial differential equations; current applications being parabolic and elliptic problems in underwater acoustics. *Mailing Add:* Dept Math Statist Univ Mass Amherst MA 01003-4515. *Fax:* 413-545-1801; *E-Mail:* stmary@math.umass.edu

ST OMER, LUCY, BIOLOGICAL SCIENCES, ECOLOGY. *Current Pos:* ASSOC PROF BIOL SCI, SAN JOSE STATE UNIV, CALIF. *Concurrent Pos:* Fulbright grantee ecol, Univ WIndies, St Augustine, Trinidad, 95. *Res:* Coastal ecology; global environmental issues. *Mailing Add:* Dept Biol Sci San Jose State Univ San Jose CA 95192-0135

ST OMER, VINCENT VICTOR, NEUROSCIENCE, VETERINARY PHARMACOLOGY. *Current Pos:* assoc prof vet anat-physiol, Col Vet Med & asst prof pharmacol, 74-84, PROF VET BIOMED SCI & ASSOC PROF PHARMACOL, SCH MED, UNIV MO, COLUMBIA, 84- *Personal Data:* b Castries, BWI, Nov 16, 34; m 62; c 4. *Educ:* Univ Guelph, DVM, 62, PhD(pharmacol), 69; Univ Man, MSc, 65. *Prof Exp:* Res assoc bur child res, Univ Kans, 68-71; asst prof vet pharmacol, Col Vet Med, Kans State Univ, 72-74. *Concurrent Pos:* Adj prof, Univ Kans, 70-73. *Mem:* Sigma Xi; Am Soc Vet Physiologists & Pharmacologists; Soc Neurosci; fel Am Acad Vet Pharmacol & Therapeut; NY Acad Sci; Behav Teratology Soc. *Res:* Adverse drug interaction; behavioral and development toxicology and neurotoxicology. *Mailing Add:* 2504 Mallard Ct Columbia MO 65201

ST ONGE, G H, ENGINEERING. *Current Pos:* PRIN, ST ONGE ASSOC INC. *Mailing Add:* 60 Olcott Ave Bernardsville NJ 07924

ST PIERRE, GEORGE R(OLAND), METALLURGY, MATERIALS SCIENCE & ENGINEERING. *Current Pos:* from asst prof to prof metall eng, Ohio State Univ, 57-88, assoc dean, 64-66, chmn dept, 84-88, PRESIDENTIAL PROF MAT SCI & ENG, OHIO STATE UNIV, 88-, DEPT CHMN, 88- *Personal Data:* b Cambridge, Mass, June 2, 30; m 57, 76, Elizabeth Adams; c 4. *Educ:* Mass Inst Technol, SB, 51, ScD(metall), 54. *Honors & Awards:* Bradley Stoughton Award, Am Soc Metals, 61, Gold Medal, 87, Albert Easton Award, 97; Mining Indust Educ Award, Am Inst Mining Engrs, 87; Elliott Lectr, Iron & Steel Soc, 94; Educr Award, Minerals Metals & Mat Soc, 96. *Prof Exp:* Sr res metallurgist, Inland Steel Co, 54-56; proj off, USAF, 56-57. *Concurrent Pos:* Consult, Gen Elec, USAF, Battelle & others; chief scientist, Mat Dir, Wright-Patterson AFB, 95-96. *Mem:* Fel Am Soc Metals; fel Am Inst Mining, Metall & Petrol Engrs; Sigma Xi; Iron & Steel Soc; Mat Res Soc. *Res:* Chemical and process metallurgy; high-temperature materials. *Mailing Add:* 4495 Carriage Hill Lane Columbus OH 43220. *Fax:* 614-292-1537; *E-Mail:* stpierre.2@osu.edu

SAINT-PIERRE, GUY, CIVIL ENGINEERING. *Current Pos:* pres, chief exec officer & bd dirs, 89-96, CHMN BD, SNC-LAVALIN GROUP INC, 96- *Personal Data:* b Windsor Mills, Que, Aug 3, 34; m 57, Francine Garneau; c Marc, Guylaine & Nathalie. *Educ:* Laval Univ, BCE, 57; Univ London, DIC, 58, MSc, 59. *Hon Degrees:* LLD, Concordia Univ, 92; DSc, Laval Univ, 92, Sherbrooke, 94; DSe, Montreal Univ. *Honors & Awards:* Sir John Medal, 93. *Prof Exp:* Dir, Irnes Inc, 66-67; vpres, Acres Que, 67-70; minister educ, Govt Que, 70-72, minister indust com, 72-76; pres & chief oper officer, Ogilvie Mills Ltd, 77-80. *Concurrent Pos:* Asst to pres, John Labatt Ltd, 77-80; chmn, Bus Coun Nat Issues, 95-; dir, Gen Motors Can, Royal Bank, BCE Inc, Purolator Can & Alcan Aluminum. *Mem:* Eng Inst Can; Brit NAm Com; Can Mfr Asn(pres, 87); Coun Can Unity (vpres). *Mailing Add:* 1227 Sherbrooke St W Montreal PQ H3G 1G1 Can

ST PIERRE, JEAN CLAUDE, AGRONOMY, PLANT PHYSIOLOGY. *Current Pos:* Res scientist forage crops, 70-81, prog anal res mgt, 81-, DIR GEN EXP FARM RES CTR, AGR CAN, OTTAWA. *Personal Data:* b St Jean, Que, Aug 21, 42; m 63; c 2. *Educ:* Laval Univ, BScA, 64, MSc, 67; Cornell Univ, PhD(agron), 70. *Mem:* Am Soc Agron; Can Soc Agron; Crop Sci Soc Am. *Res:* Forage crop production and quality; management and fertilization of grasses; plant physiology applied to breeding. *Mailing Add:* Nat Resources Can 555 Booth St Ottawa ON K1A 1G0 Can

ST PIERRE, LEON EDWARD, POLYMER CHEMISTRY. *Current Pos:* chmn, 72-76, prof, 65-90, EMER PROF POLYMER CHEM, McGILL UNIV, 90- *Personal Data:* b Edmonton, Alta, Sept 1, 24; m 49; c 7. *Educ:* Univ Alta, BSc, 51; Notre Dame Univ, PhD, 55. *Honors & Awards:* Notre Dame Univ Centennial of Sci Award, 65. *Prof Exp:* Res chemist, Res Lab, Gen Elec Co, 54-65. *Mem:* Chem Inst Can; Soc Plastics Eng; Am Chem Soc. *Res:* Polymers from epoxides; chemo-rheology and radiation of polymers; surface chemistry on films generated in ultra high vacuum; polymers for medical applications. *Mailing Add:* Dept Chem McGill Univ Sherbrooke St W PO Box 6070 Sta A Montreal PQ H3A 2M5 Can

ST PIERRE, P(HILIPPE) D(OUGLAS) S, POWDER TECHNOLOGY, ABRASIVES & BIOMATERIALS. *Current Pos:* ADJ PROF BIOMAT, UNIV ILL, CHICAGO, 96- *Personal Data:* b Liverpool, Eng, Sept 10, 25; nat US; m 48, Sylvia Hill; c Anthony & Adrienne. *Educ:* Royal Sch Mines, BS, 45; Univ London, PhD, 52. *Prof Exp:* Metallurgist, Mines Br, Govt Can, 48-55; metallurgist, Gen Elec Res Lab, Gen Elec Co, 55-67, mgr diamond eng, Mich off, 67-68, mgr eng, Specialty Mat Dept, 68-88, consult superabrasives, 88-90. *Concurrent Pos:* Nuffield traveling fel, 47; mem, Comt Export Technol, Dept Com, 84-88. *Mem:* Fel Am Ceramic Soc. *Res:* Special ceramics; materials processing; education; biomaterials. *Mailing Add:* 235 Medick Way Worthington OH 43085

ST PIERRE, RONALD LESLIE, HISTOLOGY, IMMUNOLOGY. *Current Pos:* ASSOC VPRES HEALTH SERV & ACAD AFFAIRS, 81- *Personal Data:* b Dayton, Ohio, Feb 2, 38; m 61; c 2. *Educ:* Ohio Univ, BS, 61; Ohio State Univ, MSc, 62, PhD(anat), 65. *Prof Exp:* From instr to assoc prof, 65-72, assoc dir, Cancer Ctr, 74-78, prof anat & chmn dept, Ohio State Univ, 72-81. *Concurrent Pos:* Lederle med fac award, 68-71; vis res assoc, Med Ctr, Duke Univ, 66-67. *Mem:* AAAS; Transplantation Soc; Am Asn Anat; Am Asn Immunologists; Reticuloendothelial Soc. *Res:* Role of lymphoid organs, especially bursa of Fabricius and thymus, in immunity; histocompatibility testing for organ transplantation; clinical and developmental immunology; cancer immunology. *Mailing Add:* 218 Meiling Hall Ohio State Univ 370 W Ninth Ave Columbus OH 43210

SAIRAM, M RAM, PROTEIN HORMONES & RECEPTORS, GONADAL FUNCTION. *Current Pos:* from asst prof to assoc prof, 75-85, RES PROF, DEPT MED, UNIV MONTREAL, 85-; DIR, REPRODUCTION RES LAB, CLIN RES INST, 74- ; RES DIR, DIV EXP MED & ADJ PROF, DEPT PHYSIOL, McGILL UNIV, MONTREAL, 79- *Personal Data:* b Mysore, India, Jan 10, 43; Can citizen; m 69, Jayashree N Murthy; c Ashwin M & Charith M. *Educ:* Mysore Univ, BSc, 61, MSc, 63; Indian Inst Sci, PhD(biochem), 69. *Honors & Awards:* Marcel Piche Prize. *Prof Exp:* Res biochemist, Hormone Res Lab, Univ Calif, San Francisco, 69-73. *Concurrent Pos:* Res Coun mem, Int Soc Biomed Endocrine, 78-87; vis scientist, Indian Inst Sci, 86; fel TOKTEN, UN Develop Prog, 93; fel, NIH & Med Res, France, 94-95. *Mem:* Endocrine Soc Am; AAAS; Am Soc Biochem & Molecular Biol; Soc Study Reproduction; Can Soc Biochem & Molecular Biol; Can Fertility & Andrology Soc. *Res:* Establish structure and function of protein hormones and their receptors in animals and man; develop new methods of contraception, fertility improvement and targeted drug delivery for gonadal cancer; vaccine development. *Mailing Add:* Clin Res Inst Montreal 110 Ave des Pins Ouest Montreal PQ H2W 1R7 Can. *Fax:* 514-987-5688; *E-Mail:* sairamm@ircm.umontreal.ca

SAITO, TAKUMA, CYTOLOGY. *Current Pos:* PROF ANAT, JICHI MED SCH, 76- *Personal Data:* b Fukui, Japan, July 14, 32; m 62; c 2. *Educ:* Kyoto Univ, BA, 52, MS, 54, PhD(biol), 66; Kansai Med Sch, MD, 69. *Honors & Awards:* Seto Prize, Japanese Soc Electron Micros, 90. *Prof Exp:* Res assoc anat, Kansai Med Sch, 57-64, from instr to asst prof, 64-67 & 69-71; res fel path, M D Anderson Hosp, 67-69; sect chief morphol, Inst Develop Res, 71-76. *Mem:* Am Soc Cell Biol; Histochem Soc; Japanese Asn Anatomists; Japan Soc Histochem & Cytochem; Japanese Soc Develop Biol; Soc Develop Biol; Japan Soc Cell Biol. *Res:* Enzyme histochemistry of retina. *Mailing Add:* Dept Anat 3311 Yakushiji Jichi Med Sch Minamikawachi-Machi Tochigi-ken Japan 32904

SAITO, THEODORE T, OPTICS. *Current Pos:* dep prog leader, Precision Eng Prog, Lawrence Livermore Nat Lab, 84-87, dep dept head, Defense Sci, 88-89, group leader optical sci & eng, 89-93, actg leader, Precision Eng Prog, 93-94, Dept Energy sci adv, 94-96, PHYSICIST, LAWRENCE LIVERMORE NAT LAB, 96- *Personal Data:* b Poston, Ariz, Sept 9, 42; m 68, Diane G Signorino; c Jennifer A & Paul H. *Educ:* USAF Acad, Colo, BS, 64; Mass Inst Technol, MS, 66; Pa State Univ, PhD(physics), 70. *Honors & Awards:* Tech Achievement Award, Photo Optical Instrumentation Engrs; Indust Res 100 Award, 92; Lowell King Award, 92. *Prof Exp:* Proj officer optical tech, Air Force Weapons Lab, USAF, 70-71, group leader optical eval facil, 71-73, optical coating, 73-74, leader, Energy Res & Develop Admin, Dept Defense, Lawrence Livermore Nat Lab, 74-77; dir, Mfg Tech Transfer Prog, Air Force Mat Lab, 79-80, dir aerospace mech, 80-83, comdr, 83-84. *Mem:* Fel Photo Optical Instrumentation Engrs (Pres, vpres, secy); fel Optical Soc Am; Am Soc Precision Eng; Am Asn Eng Soc. *Res:* Developing and commercializing diamond turning of optics; laser damage of optical materials; manufacturing technology and technology transfer; optical metrology; lasers; optical fabrication; spectroscopy. *Mailing Add:* Lawrence Livermore Nat Lab 644 PO Box 808 Livermore CA 94551. *E-Mail:* saito1@llnl.gov

SAJBEN, MIKLOS, TRANSONIC & SUPERSONIC INTERNAL FLOWS. *Current Pos:* PROF AEROSPACE ENG, UNIV CINCINNATI, 93-, DIR FLUID MECH LAB, 93- *Personal Data:* b Bekescsaba, Hungary, July 31, 31; US citizen; m 63, Mary T McCauley; c F Paul, Stephen L & Jeanne M. *Educ:* Budapest Tech Univ, Mech Engr, 53; Univ Pa, MS, 61; Mass Inst Technol, ScD(magnetohydrodyn), 64. *Prof Exp:* Develop engr, Westinghouse Elec Co, Pa, 57-61; res asst magnetohydrodyn, Mass Inst Technol, 61-64; asst prof aeronaut, Calif Inst Technol, 64-70; prin scientist, McDonnell Douglas Res Labs, 70-83, McDonnell Douglas fel, 83-90, prog dir, 90-93. *Concurrent Pos:* Consult, Shock Hydrodyn, Inc, 66 & McDonnell Douglas Astronaut Co, 66-70, fel, 83; assoc ed, Am Inst Aeronaut & Astronaut J, 86-88; affil prof mech eng, Washington Univ, St Louis, 87-92; mem adv comt, Bur Eng Res, Univ Tex, Austin, 88-89. *Mem:* Fel Am Inst Aeronaut & Astronaut; Sigma Xi; Am Soc Mech Engrs. *Res:* Internal and unsteady flows; supersonic inlets; aerodynamic experimentation. *Mailing Add:* 4 Coventry Ct Cincinnati OH 45140-8207. *Fax:* 513-556-5038; *E-Mail:* m.sajben@uc.edu

SAK, JOSEPH, STATISTICAL MECHANICS. *Current Pos:* from asst prof to assoc prof, 73-85, PROF PHYSICS, RUTGERS UNIV, 85- *Personal Data:* b Zlin, Czech, Nov 20, 39; m 61; c 1. *Educ:* Charles Univ, Prague, MS, 61; Inst Solid State Physics, Prague, PhD(physics), 68. *Prof Exp:* Res assoc physics, Univ Chicago, 69-71; instr, Cornell Univ, 71-73. *Mem:* Am Phys Soc. *Res:* Critical phenomena; renormalization group; kinetic theory; many body theory. *Mailing Add:* Dept Physics Rutgers Univ Busch Campus Piscataway NJ 08854

SAKAGAWA, GARY TOSHIO, FISHERIES. *Current Pos:* fishery biologist, 72-79, chief, Oceanic Fisheries Resources Div, 79-86, CHIEF, PELOGIC FISHERIES RESOURCES DIV, SOUTHWEST FISHERIES CTR, NAT MARINE FISHERIES SERV, 86- *Personal Data:* b Honolulu, Hawaii; c 2. *Educ:* Univ Hawaii, BA, 63; Univ Mich, MSc, 67; Univ Wash, PhD(fisheries), 72. *Prof Exp:* Res assoc, Fisheries Res Inst, Univ Wash, 67-72. *Concurrent Pos:* Sci adv US deleg, Int Comn for Conserv Atlantic Tunas, 72 & 75-85 & Inter-Am Trop Tuna Comn, 73 & 79-86; mem, Billfish Mgt Plan Develop Team, Pac Fishery Mgt Coun, 78-79, convener, subcomt skipjack tuna, Int Comn for Conserv Atlantic Tunas, 78-84; dir, Am Inst Fishery Res Biologists, 79-81; res assoc, Scripps Int Oceanog, 80-; consult stock assessment of tuna, Indian Ocean, Pac Tuna Prog, food & Agr Orgn, 86- *Mem:* Am Fisheries Soc (pres, 81-82); Am Inst Fishery Res Biologists; Sigma Xi. *Res:* Stock assessment and fishery evaluation of tunas and billfishes; stock assessment and management of marine mammals. *Mailing Add:* 5871 Soledad Rd La Jolla CA 92037-7055

SAKAGUCHI, DIANNE KOSTER, SYSTEM ENGINEERING. *Current Pos:* Mem tech staff, 72-80, proj engr, 80-86, MGR SYST REQUIREMENTS, AEROSPACE CORP, 86- *Personal Data:* b Rockville Ctr, NY, Feb 27, 46; m 74. *Educ:* Hofstra Univ, BA, 66; Adelphi Univ, MS, 68, PhD(numerical anal), 72. *Res:* Intelligent systems; space flight requirements; system design. *Mailing Add:* Aerospace Corp PO Box 92957 Los Angeles CA 90009-2957

SAKAI, ANN K, EVOLUTIONARY ECOLOGY, PLANT ECOLOGY. *Current Pos:* ASSOC PROF, DEPT ECOL & EVOL BIOL, UNIV CALIF, IRVINE, 96- *Personal Data:* b Boston, Mass, Jan 15, 51. *Educ:* Oberlin Col, AB, 72; Univ Mich, MS, 73, PhD(bot), 78. *Prof Exp:* from asst prof to assoc biol, Oakland Univ, 78-84; res assoc & lectr, Dept Biol, Univ Chicago, 84-87; res scientist, Biol Sta, Univ Mich, 87-96. *Concurrent Pos:* Prog dir, Div Environ Biol, NSF. *Mem:* Soc Study Evolution; Ecol Soc Am; Bot Soc Am; Soc Conserv Biol. *Res:* Ecology and evolution of plant breeding systems; Hawaiian conservation biology; dynamics of forest succession. *Mailing Add:* Dept Ecol & Evol Biol Univ Calif Irvine Irvine CA 92697. *Fax:* 714-824-2181; *E-Mail:* aksakai@uci.edu

SAKAI, HIROSHI, ELECTRICAL ENGINEERING. *Current Pos:* prof, 63-87, EMER PROF, ELEC ENG, SOPHIA UNIV, JAPAN, 87- *Personal Data:* b Tokyo, Japan, Nov 9, 21; m 54, Shigeko; c Izumi & Masumi. *Educ:* Lu-Shun Inst Eng, BS, 44; Kyo-to Univ, Dr, 53. *Prof Exp:* Asst engr, Ministry Transp, 45-49; chief researcher, Toho Construct Co, 49-58; asst prof, Tokyo Metrop Univ, 58-63. *Concurrent Pos:* Consult, Sakai's Consult Off, 72- *Mem:* Fel Inst Elec & Electronics Engrs. *Res:* Gas filled communication cablesystem; analysis on electric-magnetic interference. *Mailing Add:* 5-38-3 Narita Higashi Suginami Tokyo 166 Japan

SAKAI, SHOICHIRO, MATHEMATICS. *Current Pos:* assoc prof, 64-69, PROF MATH, UNIV PA, 69- *Personal Data:* b Japan, Jan 2, 28; m 58; c 2. *Educ:* Univ Tohuku, Japan, BS, 53, PhD(math), 61. *Prof Exp:* Asst math, Univ Tohuku, Japan, 53-60; asst prof, Wasedu Univ, Japan, 60-64; vis lectr, Yale Univ, 62-64. *Concurrent Pos:* Guggenheim fel, 70 & 71; invited speaker, Int Cong Math, Helsinki, 78. *Mem:* Am Math Soc; NY Acad Sci; AAAS; Japan Math Soc. *Res:* Functional analysis. *Mailing Add:* 205 Green Hts 5-1-6 Odawara Sendai Japan

SAKAI, TED TETSUO, STRUCTURAL CHEMISTRY. *Current Pos:* asst prof biochem, 79-85, ASSOC SCIENTIST, COMPREHENSIVE CANCER CTR, UNIV ALA, 76-, RES ASSOC PROF BIOCHEM, 85- *Personal Data:* b Newell, Calif, April 12, 45. *Educ:* Univ Calif, Berkeley, BS, 67; Univ Calif, Santa Barbara, PhD(bioorg chem), 71. *Prof Exp:* Fel biochem & microbiol, Univ Colo Med Ctr, 71-76. *Mem:* Am Chem Soc; AAAS. *Res:* Mechanism of action of chemotherapeutic agents; drug-nucleic acid interactions; polyamines; protein structures. *Mailing Add:* Comprehensive Cancer Ctr Univ Ala-Birmingham Rm CHSB B-31 Birmingham AL 35294. *E-Mail:* ted@mozart.nmrcore.uab.edu

SAKAI, WILLIAM SHIGERU, BOTANY, ELECTRON MICROSCOPY. *Current Pos:* from asst prof to assoc prof, 76-83, actg dean Col Agr, 82-83, PROF HORT, UNIV HAWAII, HILO, 83- *Personal Data:* b Cody, Wyo, Sept 9, 42; m 69. *Educ:* Univ Mich, Ann Arbor, BS, 66; Univ Hawaii, PhD(bot), 70. *Prof Exp:* Teaching asst bot, Univ Hawaii, Manoa, 69-70, asst prof, 70-71, asst soil scientist agron & soil sci, 71-74; vpres prod & res, The Flower Cart, Inc, 74-76. *Mem:* AAAS; Bot Soc Am; Am Soc Plant Physiol; Sigma Xi; Am Soc Hort Sci; Int Plant Growth Regulator Soc. *Res:* Cell biology; plant anatomy and physiology; horticulture. *Mailing Add:* Col Agr Univ Hawaii 200 W Kawili St Hilo HI 96720-4075

SAKAKIBARA, SHUMPEI, CHEMISTRY. *Current Pos:* DIR, PROTEIN RES FOUND, JAPAN, 71-; PRES, PEPTIDE INST INC, 77- *Personal Data:* b Kobe, Japan, Oct 26, 26; m 55, Keiko Kado; c Toshiro & Tomoko. *Educ:* Osaka Univ, PhD, 60. *Honors & Awards:* Ralph F Hirschmann Peptide Chem Award, Am Chem Soc, 95. *Prof Exp:* Assoc prof, Osaka Univ, 63-71. *Mem:* Am Chem Soc; Japan Chem Soc. *Mailing Add:* 23-3 Fujishirodai 2 Suita-shi Osaka 565 Japan

SAKAKINI, JOSEPH, JR, MATERNAL-FETAL MEDICINE, CLINICAL RESEARCH. *Current Pos:* CHMN OBSTET & GYNEC MATERNAL-FETAL MED, TEX TECH MED SCH, EL PASO, 83- *Personal Data:* b Norfolk, Va, Oct 18, 32; m 58; c 5. *Educ:* Va Mil Inst, BA, 55; Med Col Va, MD, 59. *Prof Exp:* Dir residency obstet & gynec, Madigan Army Hosp, 71-74; fel maternal-fetal med, William Beaumont Army Hosp, 74-76; chief obstst & gynec, Madigan Army Hosp, 77-81; dir, Tacoma Gen Hosp, 81-83. *Concurrent Pos:* Consult, Surgeon Gen US Army, 80-83; mem, Nurse Pract Exam Bd, Nurse Asn, Am Col Obstet & Gynec, 82-86, vchmn, AFD, 82-85; vis prof, Med Sch, Tex A&M Univ, 83; mem, Am Bd Obstet & Gynec, 84- *Mem:* Am Col Obstetricians & Gynecologists; Soc Perinatal Obstetricians; Nurse Asn-Am Col Obstet & Gynec; Am Bd Obstet & Gynec. *Res:* Pain medication to ease post partum and post operative discomfort; viral infections in pregnancy. *Mailing Add:* Dept Obstet & Gynec Tex Tech Univ Sch Med 4800 Alberta Ave El Paso TX 79905-2700. *Fax:* 915-545-6946

SAKAKURA, ARTHUR YOSHIKAZU, THEORETICAL PHYSICS. *Current Pos:* physicist, 66-68, ASSOC PROF PHYSICS, COLO SCH MINES, 68- *Personal Data:* b San Francisco, Calif, May 24, 28; m 56. *Educ:* Mass Inst Technol, BS, 49, MS, 50; Univ Colo, PhD(physics), 60. *Prof Exp:* Physicist, US Geol Surv, Colo, 50-58; physicist, Res Ctr, IBM Corp, 60-63; physicist, Joint Inst Lab Astrophys, Univ Colo, 63-65, physicist, Dept Physics, 65-66. *Mem:* Am Phys Soc. *Res:* Statistical mechanics; quantum mechanical many-body problems. *Mailing Add:* 3420 Longwood Ave Boulder CO 80303. *Fax:* 303-273-3919

SAKALOWSKY, PETER PAUL, JR, PHYSICAL GEOGRAPHY. *Current Pos:* assoc prof, 70-80, PROF GEOG, SOUTHERN CONN STATE COL, 80- *Personal Data:* b Worcester, Mass, July 29, 42; m 69; c 3. *Educ:* Worcester State Col, BSEd, 64; Clark Univ, MA, 66; Ind State Univ, PhD(geog), 72. *Prof Exp:* Instr geog, Bloomsburg State Col, 66; instr, Briarcliff Col, 66-68. *Res:* Geomorphology, climatology, coastal processes and beach morphology; historical coastline changes; interrelationship of coastal processes and man, microclimates; regional geography of Anglo-America; meandering streams; general physical geography. *Mailing Add:* Dept Geog Southern Conn State Col 501 Crescent St New Haven CT 06515-1330

SAKANO, THEODORE K, PHYSICAL CHEMISTRY. *Current Pos:* PROF SCI DEPT, ROCKLAND COMMUNITY COL. *Personal Data:* b Portland, Ore, Sept 24, 38; m 87. *Educ:* Ore State Col, BS, 60; Univ Wis, PhD(phys chem), 66. *Prof Exp:* From instr to assoc prof, 65-75, prof Chem, 75-87, dept chmn Rose-Hulman Inst Technol 80-83. *Mem:* Am Chem Soc. *Mailing Add:* Sci Dept Rockland Community Col Suffern NY 10901

SAKHARE, VISHWA M, MATHEMATICS. *Current Pos:* assoc prof, 65-76, PROF MATH, ETENN STATE UNIV, 76- *Personal Data:* b Belgaum, India, Aug 28, 32; m 56, Sheela Batli; c Raj, Ravi & Anil. *Educ:* Karnatak Univ, India, BS, 51; Cambridge Univ, BA & MA, 54; Univ Tenn, Knoxville, PhD(math), 73. *Prof Exp:* Teaching asst math, Univ Idaho, 59-62, instr, 62-65. *Mem:* Math Asn Am; Am Math Soc. *Res:* Applied mathematics. *Mailing Add:* ETenn State Univ PO Box 23086 Johnson City TN 37614

SAKHNOVSKY, ALEXANDER ALEXANDROVITCH, PHYSICAL CHEMISTRY. *Current Pos:* PRES, CONSTRUCT RES LAB, 68- *Personal Data:* b Asheville, NC, July 14, 26; m; c 2. *Educ:* Univ NC, AB, 49, MA, 50. *Honors & Awards:* Charles Martin Hall Award, Architectural Aluminum Mfr Asn, 74. *Prof Exp:* Jr chemist, Erwin Chem Lab, 51-52; res instr, Univ Miami, 52-56, res asst prof, Indust Chem Res Lab & Housing Res Lab, 56-68. *Concurrent Pos:* Asst mgr paint proving grounds, Sun Tests, 50-55. *Mem:* Am Chem Soc; Am Soc Testing & Mat; fel Am Inst Chem. *Res:* Refrigeration chemistry; dehydration of refrigeration systems; desiccants; oil-refrigerant reactions; physical testing of building components; building water leakage. *Mailing Add:* 7600 NW 79th Ave Miami FL 33166-2308

SAKITA, BUNJI, THEORETICAL HIGH ENERGY PHYSICS. *Current Pos:* DISTINGUISHED PROF PHYSICS, CITY COL NEW YORK, 70- *Personal Data:* b Toyama-ken, Japan, June 6, 30; c 2. *Educ:* Kanazawa Univ, Japan, BS, 53; Nagoya Univ, MS, 56; Univ Rochester, PhD(physics), 59. *Honors & Awards:* Nishina Prize, 74. *Prof Exp:* Res assoc physics, Univ Wis, 59-62, asst prof, 62-64; assoc physicist, High Energy Physics Div, Argonne Nat Lab, 64-66; prof physics, Univ Wis-Madison, 66-70. *Concurrent Pos:* Guggenheim fel, 70; fel, Japan Soc Prom Sci, 75, 80, 87 & 95. *Mem:* Fel Am Phys Soc. *Res:* Elementary particles; symmetries of hadrons; weak interactions; field theories. *Mailing Add:* Dept Physics City Col New York Convent Ave & 138th St New York NY 10031

SAKITT, BARBARA, vision, for more information see previous edition

SAKITT, MARK, ELEMENTARY PARTICLE PHYSICS. *Current Pos:* Res assoc physics, 64-66, from asst physicist to physicist, 66-80, SR PHYSICIST, BROOKHAVEN NAT LAB, 80-, ASST DIR PLANNING & POLICY, 90- *Personal Data:* b Brooklyn, NY, Apr 7, 38; m 63. *Educ:* Polytech Inst Brooklyn, BEE, 58; Univ Md, PhD(physics), 65. *Concurrent Pos:* Mem Adv Bd Arms Control, Disarmamant & Peace Studies, Res Ctr, State Univ NY, Stony Brook & adj lectr defense policy; adj lectr defense policy, State Univ NY, Stony Brook; sci fel, Ctr Int Security & Arms Control, Stamford Univ, 86-87; Carnegie sci fel, 86-87. *Mem:* Fel Am Phys Soc; NY Acad Sci; Sigma Xi. *Res:* High energy experimental physics; defense policy. *Mailing Add:* Dirs Off Bldg 460 Box 5000 Brookhaven Nat Lab Upton NY 11973

SAKMANN, BERT, cell physiology, membrane biology; deceased, see previous edition for last biography

SAKMAR, ISMAIL AYDIN, ELEMENTARY PARTICLE PHYSICS & THEORETICAL PHYSICS, NUMBER THEORY. *Current Pos:* GRANTEE, UNIV S FLA, 92- *Personal Data:* b Istanbul, Turkey, Sept 29, 25; div. *Educ:* Istanbul Univ, 51; Univ Calif, Berkeley, PhD(physics), 63. *Prof Exp:* Lectr physics, Univ Calif, Santa Barbara, 63-64; asst prof, Univ Miami, 64-67; from assoc prof to prof appl math, Univ Western Ont, 67-86, Nat Res Coun Can Grant, 68-86; grantee, Univ Md, 86-91. *Concurrent Pos:* Vis scientist, Int Ctr Theoret Physics, Italy, 65, 69, 70, 78 & 83, Europ Orgn Nuclear Res, Switz, 72 & Lab de Phys Theorique, Univ de Nice, France, 79; Near Eastern Col fel, Rockefeller Found; Alexander von Humboldt Stiftung. *Mem:* Am Phys Soc; Ital Phys Soc; Math Asn Am. *Res:* Elementary particles; S-matrix theory; Regge pole hypothesis; model independent calculations in particle physics; application of variational techniques with infinite variables and inequality constraints; number theoretical problems. *Mailing Add:* 518 Chickadee Ct Plant City FL 33565. *Fax:* 813-974-5813; *E-Mail:* dkhamaa@cfrvm.cfr.usf.edu

SAKO, KUMAO, MEDICINE, SURGERY. *Current Pos:* RETIRED. *Personal Data:* b Sebastopol, Calif, Oct 31, 24; m 66. *Educ:* Univ Ill, BS, 50, MD, 52; Am Bd Surg, dipl, 59. *Prof Exp:* Intern, Cook Co Hosp, Chicago, 52-53; resident surg, Augustana Hosp, 53-55; resident, Roswell Park Mem Inst, 55-57, sr cancer res surgeon, 57-58, assoc cancer res surgeon, 58-61, assoc chief head & neck surgeon, 61-90. *Concurrent Pos:* Asst, Sch Med, Univ Buffalo, 59-60, clin instr, 60-62, clin assoc, 62-65, res assoc, 65-75, res asst clin prof, 75-79. *Mem:* Fel Am Col Surg; Soc Head & Neck Surgeons; Am Soc Clin Oncol; Soc Surg Oncol; Am Asn Cancer Res. *Res:* Cancer research; head, neck and general surgery. *Mailing Add:* 226 Brantwood Rd Snyder NY 14226

SAKO, YOSHIO, SURGERY. *Current Pos:* From instr to assoc prof, 52-66, PROF SURG, UNIV MINN, MED SCH, MINNEAPOLIS, 66- *Personal Data:* b Forestville, Calif, Jan 25, 18; m 54; c 3. *Educ:* Univ Minn, MD, 47, PhD(surg), 51. *Concurrent Pos:* Nat Heart Inst trainee, 51-52; assoc chief surg & chief cardiovasc surg sect, Vet Admin Hosp, Minneapolis, 55- *Mem:* AMA; fel Am Col Surg. *Res:* Cardiovascular surgery. *Mailing Add:* Vet Admin Hosp 1 Veterans Dr Minneapolis MN 55417

SAKODA, WILLIAM JOHN, THEORETICAL COMPUTER SCIENCE. *Current Pos:* PRIN ENG, SYMBOL TECHNOL, 96- *Personal Data:* b Brooklyn, NY, Feb 25, 51; m 77. *Educ:* Harvard Col, AB, 72; Univ Calif, PhD(comput sci), 78. *Prof Exp:* Res asst, Univ Calif, 74-78, instr, 78; asst prof comput sci, Columbia Univ, 78-80 & Pa State Univ, 80-86; asst prof comput sci, Pa State Univ, 80-86; res asst prof, Comput Sci Dept, NY State Univ, 86-96. *Mem:* Asn Comput Mach; AAAS; Sigma Xi. *Res:* Parallel algorithms for picture analysis; artificial intelligence. *Mailing Add:* Symbol Technol 1 Symbol Plaza MS B-15 Holtsville NY 11742-1300

SAKSENA, VISHNU P, ZOOLOGY, AQUATIC BIOLOGY. *Current Pos:* assoc prof, 68-76, chmn dept, 80-85 & 90-93, PROF BIOL, MUSKINGUM COL, 76- *Personal Data:* b Shahjahanpur, India, July 15, 34; m 62, Sudha. *Educ:* Banaras Hindu Univ, BSc, 52, MSc, 54; Univ Okla, PhD(zool), 63. *Prof Exp:* Asst prof biol, Janta Vidyalaya Col, 54-55; res asst animal genetics, Indian Vet Res Inst, 55-57; from asst prof to assoc prof biol, Youngstown State Univ, 63-68. *Mem:* Fel Am Inst Fishery Res Biologists; Am Fisheries Soc; Am Inst Biol Sci; World Maricult Soc; Indian Acad Life Sci. *Res:* Physiology of air breathing fishes; ecology of marine fish larvae; effect of pollution on fishes; fish reproduction and development. *Mailing Add:* Biol Muskingum Col New Concord OH 43762-1199

SAKSHAUG, EUGENE C, LIGHTING PROTECTION. *Current Pos:* RETIRED. *Personal Data:* b Mandan, NDak, Oct 18, 23. *Educ:* NC State Univ, BEE, 52. *Honors & Awards:* WRG Baker Prize Award, Inst Elec & Electronics Engrs, 78; Lamme Medal, 89. *Prof Exp:* Power tech, Ray Chem, 85-86, consult, 86-92. *Concurrent Pos:* Mem, Surge Protective Devices Comt, Inst Elec & Electronics Engrs, 81, 82 & 92, comt award, 83. *Mem:* Nat Acad Eng; fel Inst Elec & Electronics Engrs; Sigma Xi. *Mailing Add:* PO Box 1531 Lanesboro MA 01237

SAKURA, JOHN DAVID, BIOCHEMISTRY. *Current Pos:* RES ASSOC BIOCHEM, DEPT BIOL CHEM, HARVARD MED SCH, 71- *Personal Data:* b Seattle, Wash, Mar 28, 36. *Educ:* Wheaton Col, BS, 58; Univ Ariz, PhD(biochem), 70. *Prof Exp:* Res asst, Dept Chem, Univ Ore, 61-64. *Concurrent Pos:* Nat Res Coun fel, Dept Biochem, Brandeis Univ, 70-71; asst biochemist, Ralph Lowell Labs, Harvard Med Sch, 71-80. *Mem:* Am Chem Soc; Am Soc Neurochem; Sigma Xi. *Res:* Structure and function of proteins; lipid-protein interactions; isolation and characterization of proteolipids; proteolipids in membrane transport. *Mailing Add:* 72 Chester St Arlington MA 02174

SAKURAI, TOSHIO, SURFACE SCIENCE. *Current Pos:* PROF, INST MAT RES, TOHOKU UNIV, 89- *Personal Data:* b Osaka, Japan, Jan 17, 45; m 70; c 2. *Educ:* Univ Tokyo, BS, 67, MS, 69; Pa State Univ, PhD(physics), 74. *Prof Exp:* Mem tech staff, Bell Tel Labs, Murray Hill, 74-76; asst prof physics, Pa State Univ, 77-80; assoc prof, Inst Solid State Physics, Univ Tokyo, 81-89. *Concurrent Pos:* Mem bd dirs, Rev Sci Instrumentation, 86-89. *Mem:* Am Phys Soc; Am Vacuum Soc; Phys Soc Japan. *Res:* Development of an atom-probe field ion microscope and its applications to surface physics; experimental study of surface electronic structures of semiconductors by ultraviolet photoemission and ion neutralization spectroscopies and scanning tunneling microscopy. *Mailing Add:* 2384 Shagbark Ct State College PA 16803. *Fax:* 814-865-2917

SAKURAI, YOSHIFUMI, MAGNETIC MEMORY, CONTROL DEVICE. *Current Pos:* PROF ELEC ENG, FAC ENG, SETSUNAN UNIV, 84- *Personal Data:* b Tokyo, Japan, Mar 30, 21; m 49; c 2. *Educ:* Osaka Univ, BS, 43, MS, 45, Dr Eng, 58. *Prof Exp:* Lectr elec eng, Fac Eng, Osaka Univ, 46-48, asst prof, 48-59, prof nuclear eng, 59-65, prof control eng, Fac Eng Sci, 65-84. *Mem:* Fel Inst Elec & Electronics Engrs. *Res:* Magnetic materials, especially rare-earth transition metal alloy thin films used in large capacity magneto-optical memory. *Mailing Add:* Minoo 2-Chome 9-18 Minoo Osaka 562 Japan

SALA, LUIS FRANCISCO, SURGERY. *Personal Data:* b New York, NY, Dec 13, 19; m 43, Judith Colon; c Luis E, Francisco A, Jorge P & Jose M. *Educ:* Georgetown Univ, BS, 39, MD, 43; Univ Pa, MSc, 51; Am Bd Surg, dipl. *Honors & Awards:* Dr Luis F Sasa Medal, Acad Med, 95. *Prof Exp:* Intern resident, Presby Hosp, San Juan, PR, 43-45; chief resident, Grad Hosp, Univ Pa, 47-51, instr surg, 50-51; chmn, Dept Surg, Damas Hosp, Ponce, PR, 55-88; prof surg, Univ PR Sch Med, 68-88; pres, dean & prof surg, Ponce Sch Med, PR, 88-94. *Concurrent Pos:* Deleg, PR Med Asn, 60-93. *Mem:* Int Soc Surg; fel Am Col Surgeons. *Res:* Contributed articles to professional journals. *Mailing Add:* 43 Calle Concordia Ponce PR 00731-4984

SALADIN, JURG X, NUCLEAR PHYSICS. *Current Pos:* from asst prof to assoc prof, 61-69, PROF PHYSICS, UNIV PITTSBURGH, 69-, DIR NUCLEAR PHYSICS LAB, 80- *Personal Data:* b Solothurn, Switz, July 25, 29; m 63; c 2. *Educ:* Swiss Fed Inst Technol, dipl, 54, PhD(nuclear physics), 59. *Prof Exp:* Res asst physics, Swiss Fed Inst Technol, 54-59; res assoc, Univ Wis, 59-61. *Concurrent Pos:* Vis prof, Univ Basel, Switz, 69-70, & Inst Atomic Physics, Univ Bucharest, Romania, 73; fel, Oak Ridge Assoc Univs, 86; chmn, Exec Comt User Group, 80-81, & Mem Exec Comt, NSCL, 86- *Mem:* Fel Am Phys Soc; Swiss Phys Soc; Sigma Xi; Europ Phys Soc. *Res:* Experimental nuclear physics; nuclear reactions and structure; electromagnetic properties of nuclei; nuclear shapes; collective properties of nuclei; coulomb excitation; physics of high spin states. *Mailing Add:* Dept Physics Univ Pittsburgh Pittsburgh PA 15213

SALADIN, KENNETH S, ETHOLOGY PARASITISM, INVERTEBRATE SENSORY PHYSIOLOGY. *Current Pos:* From asst prof to assoc prof, 77-89, PROF BIOL, GA COL, 89- *Personal Data:* b Kalamazoo, Mich, May 6, 49; m 79, C Diane Campbell; c Emory M & Lisa N. *Educ:* Mich State Univ, BS, 71; Fla State Univ, PhD(parasitol), 79. *Honors & Awards:* Elon E Byrd Award, Southeast Soc Parasitologists, 78. *Concurrent Pos:* Ed assoc, Humanist Mag, Amherst, NY, 79-82, sci columnist, 80-83; mem, bd dirs, Nat Ctr Sci Educ, 82-87. *Mem:* Am Soc Zoologists; Animal Behav Soc; AAAS; Nat Ctr Sci Educ (treas, 82-87); Human Anat Physiol Soc. *Res:* Sensory capacities and host-finding behavior of parasitic invertebrates, with emphasis on chemical and photosensory ecology of Digenea, Acari, Siphonaptera and Hymenoptera. *Mailing Add:* 114 Nature Creek Trail SW Milledgeville GA 31061

SALAFIA, W(ILLIAM) RONALD, PSYCHOBIOLOGY, HUMAN FACTORS ENGINEERING. *Current Pos:* from instr to assoc prof, 65-74, chmn, Psychol Dept, 75-77, Decamp prof health sci, 84-87, PROF PSYCHOBIOL, FAIRFIELD UNIV, 74- *Personal Data:* b Baltimore, Md, Dec 28, 38; div; c 2. *Educ:* Loyola Col, BS, 60; Fordham Univ, MA, 63, PhD(exp psychol), 67. *Prof Exp:* Lectr psychol, Hunter Col City Univ New York, 63-65. *Concurrent Pos:* Consult, Naval Underwater Syst Ctr, New London, Conn, 87- *Mem:* Psychonomic Soc; Soc Neurosci; AAAS; NY Acad Sci; Am Psychol Soc; Human Factors Soc. *Res:* Neural mechanisms of learning and memory; classical (Pavlovian) conditioning; human factors of sonar displays. *Mailing Add:* Dept Psychol Fairfield Univ Fairfield CT 06430-7524

SALAFSKY, BERNARD P, PHARMACOLOGY, PARASITOLOGY. *Current Pos:* prof, Dept Biomed Sci, 77-82, DIR, COL MED, UNIV ILL, ROCKFORD, 82- *Personal Data:* b Chicago, Ill, Dec 27, 35; m 61, Marilyn Ritchie; c 3. *Educ:* Philadelphia Col Pharm & Sci, BS, 58; Univ Wash, MS, 61, PhD(pharmacol-toxicol), 62. *Honors & Awards:* Fulbright Lectr, Malaysia, 68. *Prof Exp:* Instr pharmacol, Univ Wash, 62-64; from asst prof to assoc prof, Univ Ill Col Med, 64-70; adj assoc prof, Med Sch, Univ Pa, 70-72; WHO consult, SEARO-Indo 00l, 73-75. *Concurrent Pos:* Nat Inst Neurol Dis & Stroke res grant, 65-71; Muscular Dystrophy Asn Am spec fel, 72; spec fel, Med Sch, Univ Bristol, 72-74; vis prof, Med Sch, Pahlavi Univ, Iran, 70-72; lectr toxicol, Univ Calif, Berkeley, 78-80; consult indust, 79-81; consult, WHO. *Mem:* AAAS; Soc Trop Dis Hyg; Am Soc Pharmacol & Exp Therapeut; Royal Soc Trop Med & Hyg. *Res:* Biology of skin penetrating parasites; tropical disease pharmacology/parasitology. *Mailing Add:* Dean Off Col Med Univ Ill 1601 Parkview Rockford IL 61101. *Fax:* 815-395-5887

SALAH, JOSEPH E, INCOHERENT SCATTER RADAR SYSTEMS, RADIO ASTRONOMY TECHNIQUES. *Current Pos:* Group leader, Lincoln Lab, 66-83, DIR, HAYSTACK OBSERV, MASS INST TECHNOL, 83- *Personal Data:* b Jerusalem, Feb 27, 44; US citizen; m 65; c 1. *Educ:* Univ Ill, Urbana, BSc, 65 & MSc, 66; Mass Inst Technol, PhD(meteorol), 72. *Concurrent Pos:* Mem, comt solar terrestrial res, Nat Astron Soc & Nat Res Coun, 85-88, adv comt astron sci, 85-88, Cedar Sci Steering Coun, Nat Sci Found, 87-; prin res scientist & sr lectr, Earth, Atmospheric & Planetary Sci Dept, Mass Inst Technol, 83- *Mem:* Am Geophys Union; Am Astron Soc; Am Meterol Soc; Union Radio Sci Int. *Res:* Structure and dynamics of the earth's inosphere and thermosphere; development of techniques and applications for high-power radar studies of the atmosphere; development of observational techniques for radio astronomy. *Mailing Add:* Haystack Observ Mass Inst Technol Route 40 Westford MA 01886

SALAHUB, DENNIS RUSSELL, THEORETICAL CHEMISTRY, THEORETICAL SOLID STATE PHYSICS & BIOMOLECULAR MODELING. *Current Pos:* from asst prof to prof, 76-90, MCCONNELL PROF CHEM, UNIV MONTREAL, 90- *Personal Data:* b Castor, Alta, 1946; m 70. *Educ:* Univ Alta, BSc, 67; Univ Montreal, PhD(chem), 70. *Honors & Awards:* Noranda Award, Can Chem Soc, 87; Int Union Pure & Appl Chem Award, 84; Killam fel, 90. *Prof Exp:* Fel chem, Univ Sussex, 70-72; res assoc, Univ Waterloo, 72-74 & Johns Hopkins Univ, 74; chemist, Res & Develop, Gen Elec Co, 75-76. *Mem:* Am Chem Soc; fel Chem Inst Can; Can Asn Physicists. *Res:* Quantum theoretical studies of the electronic structure and properties of molecules, clusters and solids; development and application of quantum chemical and molecular dynamics wetlands for biomolecular modeling. *Mailing Add:* Dept Chem CP 6128 Univ Montreal Montreal PQ H3C 3J7 Can

SALAITA, GEORGE N, NUCLEAR GEOPHYSICS, NUCLEAR WELL-LOGGING. *Current Pos:* SR RES ASSOC, CHEVRON PETROL TECH CO. *Personal Data:* m 59, Linda G; c Nicholas G, John G & Nadya. *Educ:* Millikin Univ, BS, 57; Tex A&M, MS, 59; Va Polytech Inst & State Univ, PhD(physics), 66. *Prof Exp:* Res technologist, Humble Oil Res & Develop Lab, 59-62; asst prof, Southern Methodist Univ, 66-70, assoc prof, 70-74, prof, 74-81. *Concurrent Pos:* Consult, Gearhart Indust, 71-80. *Mem:* Am Nuclear Soc; Soc Petrol Eng; Soc Prof Well Log Anal. *Res:* Apply nuclear methods to formation evaluation in both open and closed holes; evaluate new technology and interpret well logging data. *Mailing Add:* 7125 E Columbus Dr Anaheim CA 92807

SALAM, FATHI M A, NEURAL COMPUTATIONAL SYSTEMS, ADAPTIVE CONTROL SYSTEMS. *Current Pos:* asst prof systs & circuit, 85-87, ASSOC PROF NONLINEAR SYSTS, MICH STATE UNIV, 87-, PROF ENG, 91- *Educ:* Univ Calif, Berkeley, BS, 76, MS, 79, MA, 83, PhD(elec eng), 83. *Prof Exp:* Vis asst prof control systs, Univ Calif, Berkeley, 83; asst prof dynamical systs, Drexel Univ, 83-85; vis prof, Calif Inst Technol, 92; vis lect scientist, Univ Minn, Math Inst, 93. *Concurrent Pos:* Prin investr, NSF, 84-90; assoc ed, Inst Elec & Electronics Engrs, Inc, 85-87, guest ed, 87-88; finance chmn, Inst Elec & Electronics Engrs & Systs, 88-90. *Mem:* Fel Inst Elec & Electronics Engrs; Int Soc Optical Eng. *Res:* Nonlinear phenomena in circuits and systems; analysis and design of neural networks, adaptive systems, control and compliance of robot manipulators; stability of power systems. *Mailing Add:* Dept Elec Eng Mich State Univ East Lansing MI 48824

SALAMA, CLEMENT ANDRE TEWFIK, ELECTRICAL ENGINEERING. *Current Pos:* from asst prof to assoc prof, 67-77, J M Ham chair microelectronics, 87-97, PROF SOLID STATE ELECTRONICS, UNIV TORONTO, 77-, UNIV PROF, 92- *Personal Data:* b Heliopolis, Egypt, Sept 27, 38; Can citizen; m 74, Rhoda; c Nicole. *Educ:* Univ BC, BAS, 61, MAS, 63, PhD(elec eng), 66. *Honors & Awards:* Izaak Walton Killam Prize. *Prof Exp:* Mem sci staff, Bell-Northern Res Labs, Ottawa, 66-67. *Concurrent Pos:* Natural Sci & Eng Res Coun grant, 67-, Defence Res Bd Can grant, 67-75; consult, Elec Eng Consociates, Ltd, 69-, dir, 69-76; vis prof, Cath Univ Leuven, Belg, 75-76; chmn, Natural Sci & Eng Coun, Nat Microelectronics Fac Comt, 83-84, Toronto Sect, Inst Elec & Electronics Engrs, 85-87; mem bd dirs & chmn bd, Can Microelectronics Corp, 84-87; mem, Tech Prog Comt, Int Electron Devices Meeting, 87-88, Int Symp Circuits & Systs, 88-, Can Conf VLSI, 84-87, chmn, 85; assoc ed, Inst Elec & Electronics Engrs Trans Circuits & Systs, 87-89; prin investr, Info Technol Res Ctr, 87-92; prog leader & mem bd dirs, Micronet. *Mem:* Fel Inst Elec & Electronics Engrs; Electrochem Soc; Can Res Mgt Asn. *Res:* Solid state electronics; integrated circuits; electronic circuits. *Mailing Add:* Dept Elec & Comput Eng Univ Toronto Toronto ON M5S 1A4 Can. *Fax:* 416-978-4516; *E-Mail:* salama@vrg.utoronto.ca

SALAMA, GUY, VOLTAGE-SENSITIVE DYES. *Current Pos:* asst prof, 80-87, ASSOC PROF PHYSIOL, SCH MED, UNIV PITTSBURGH, 87- *Personal Data:* b Cairo, Egypt, Apr 23, 47; US citizen. *Educ:* City Col New York, BS, 68; Univ Pa, MS, 71, PhD(biophysics), 77. *Honors & Awards:* Res Car Div Award, NIH. *Prof Exp:* Teaching asst physics, Univ Pa, 70-71, res fel physiol, 73-77, res fel biochem & biophysics, 77-80. *Concurrent Pos:* Lectr physics, Spring Garden Col, Philadelphia, Pa, 69-70; investr, Marine Biol Lab, Woods Hole, Mass, 80-81. *Mem:* Biophys Soc; Soc Gen Physiologists; Am Heart Asn. *Res:* Development and application of voltage-sensitive dyes to measure transmembrane electrical potential in heart muscle and in the sarcoplasmic reticulum; optical recordings of cardiac action potentials, optical maps of action potential activation and repolarization in perfused hearts, cardiac arrhythmics; excitation-contraction coupling in mammalian skeletal muscle. *Mailing Add:* Dept Physiol Sch Med Univ Pittsburgh 3500 Terrace St Pittsburgh PA 15261. *Fax:* 412-648-8330; *E-Mail:* ggs@pittmed.edu

SALAMA, KAMEL, MATERIALS ENGINEERING, PHYSICAL METALLURGY. *Current Pos:* PROF, UNIV HOUSTON, 73- *Personal Data:* b Bahgoura, Egypt, Apr 1, 32; m 71; c 2. *Educ:* Cairo Univ, BSc, 51, MSc, 55, PhD(physics), 59. *Honors & Awards:* Jacob Wallenberg Found Award, Swed Acad Eng, Stockholm, 82. *Prof Exp:* Res asst physics, Cairo Univ, 51-60, lectr, 60-65; res consult, Ford Sci Lab, 66-68; fel mat sci, Rice Univ, 68-71, sr res scientist, Mat Sci Dept, 71-73. *Concurrent Pos:* Partic, Int Seminar Res & Educ Physics, Uppsala Univ, Sweden, 62-63, fel, 62-64; distinguished vis scientist, NASA Langley Res Ctr, Hampton, Va, 83- *Mem:* Am Soc Metals; Am Inst Mining, Metall & Petrol Engrs; Am Phys Soc; Soc Metallurgical Engrs; Am Soc Nondestructive Testing. *Res:* Elastic and mechanical properties of solids; work hardening in environmental effects; mechanical behavior of metals and alloys; ultrasonic nondestructive characterization of materials properties and residual stresses. *Mailing Add:* 13818 Kimberley Lane Houston TX 77079

SALAMO, GREGORY JOSEPH, QUANTUM OPTICS. *Current Pos:* from asst prof to assoc prof, 75-85, PROF PHYSICS, UNIV ARK, 85- *Personal Data:* b Brooklyn, NY, Sept 19, 44; m 87. *Educ:* Brooklyn Col, BS, 66; Purdue Univ, MS, 68; City Univ New York, PhD(physics), 74. *Prof Exp:* Resident visitor physics, Bell Labs-Murray Hill, 71-73; res assoc, Rochester Univ, 73-75. *Mem:* Sigma Xi; Am Phys Soc. *Res:* Design and use of lasers and related optical systems for coherent optical experiments and spectroscopic experiments with some useful application in mind. *Mailing Add:* Dept Physics Phys 226 Univ Ark Fayetteville AR 72701-1202

SALAMON, IVAN ISTVAN, BIOCHEMISTRY, ORGANIC CHEMISTRY. *Current Pos:* RETIRED. *Personal Data:* b Budapest, Hungary, Sept 10, 18; nat US; m 50, 68, Karlene Williams; c Peter. *Educ:* Swiss Fed Inst Technol, ChemEng, 41; Univ Basel, PhD(chem), 49. *Prof Exp:* Lab instr & asst, Univ Basel, 42-50; USPHS res fel, Med Col, Cornell Univ, 50-52; res fel biochem, Sloan-Kettering Inst, 52-54, from asst biochem to assoc biochem, 54-63; asst mem div endocrinol, Res Labs, Albert Einstein Med Ctr, Philadelphia, 63-68; biochemist, Hektoen Inst Med Res, Cook Co Hosp, 68-93. *Mem:* emer mem Am Chem Soc; emer mem Swiss Chem Soc; fel Nat Acad Clin Biochem; emer mem Am Asn Clin Chemists. *Res:* Steroid chemistry and biochemistry; phospholipids. *Mailing Add:* 6007 N Sheridan Rd No 24C Chicago IL 60660-3008

SALAMON, KENNETH J, TOXICOLOGY, ECOLOGY. *Current Pos:* PROJ TOXICOLOGIST & ECOLOGIST, RAY J WESTON, INC, 80- *Personal Data:* US citizen. *Educ:* Fordham Col, BS, 67, MS, 75, PhD(physiol ecol), 79. *Prof Exp:* Mem staff, Consolidated Edison Co, NY, 76-77, Inst Environ Med, NY Univ, 79-80. *Concurrent Pos:* Mem, Advan Study Inst, NATO. *Mem:* Am Fisheries soc; Am Soc Limnol & Oceanog; AAAS; Sigma Xi. *Res:* Aquatic toxicology; fish physiology; bioassay and ecological investigations; estuarine biology; power plant impact studies; marine and freshwater phytoplankton and zooplankton physiology and ecology. *Mailing Add:* Roy F Weston Inc 619 Westbourne Rd West Chester PA 19382

SALAMON, MYRON B, SUPERCONDUCTIVITY, MAGNETISM. Current Pos: from asst prof to assoc prof, 66-74, dir, NSF-Mat Res Lab, 83-90, PROF PHYSICS, UNIV ILL, URBANA, 74- Personal Data: b Pittsburgh, Pa, June 4, 39; m 60, Sonya Blank; c David & Aaron. Educ: Carnegie Inst Technol, BS, 61; Univ Calif, Berkeley, PhD(physics), 66. Prof Exp: NSF fel, 65-66. Concurrent Pos: Vis scientist, Inst Solid State Physics, Univ Tokyo, 71 & Tech Univ Munich, 74-75; Alfred P Sloan Found res fel, 71-72; Humboldt Found fel, 74; Inst Laue Langevin & Nat Ctr Sci Res, Grenoble, 81-82; distinguished vis prof, Univ Tsukuba, Japan, 95; Berndt Matthias fel, Los Alamos Nat Lab, 95-96. Mem: Am Phys Soc. Res: Experimental studies of phase transitions in magnets, superconductors and modulated structures. Mailing Add: Dept Physics Univ Ill 1110 W Green St Urbana IL 61801. Fax: 217-244-2278; E-Mail: salmon@uiuc.edu

SALAMON, RICHARD JOSEPH, SCIENCE EDUCATION. Current Pos: PROF SCI & SCI EDUC, CENT CONN STATE UNIV, 66- Personal Data: b Palmer, Mass, Apr 27, 32; m 60; c 1. Educ: Col Holy Cross, BS, 53; Am Int Col, MA, 60; Univ Conn, Prof Dipl Educ, 64, PhD(sci educ), 68. Prof Exp: Instr high sch, Mass, 59-65. Mem: Asn Educ Teachers Sci; Nat Sci Teachers Asn; Nat Asn Res Sci Teaching; Sch Sci & Math Asn. Res: Elementary, middle school, high school and college science instruction. Mailing Add: Dept Physics & Earth Sci Cent Conn State Univ 1615 Stanley St New Britain CT 06050

SALAMONE, JOSEPH C, ORGANIC POLYMER CHEMISTRY. Current Pos: from asst prof to prof, Univ Mass, Lowell, 70-89, chmn dept, 75-78, actg dean, Col Pure & Appl Sci, 78-81, dean, Col Pure & Appl Sci, 81-84, chmn, Coun Deans, 81-83, EMER PROF CHEM, UNIV MASS, LOWELL, 89- Personal Data: b Brooklyn, NY, Dec 27, 39; m 78; c 3. Educ: Hofstra Univ, BSc, 61; Polytech Inst Brooklyn, PhD(org chem), 67. Prof Exp: Res Liverpool, 66-67; res assoc, Univ Mich, Ann Arbor, 67-70, secy, Macromolecular Res Ctr, 68-70. Concurrent Pos: Secy-treas, Pac Polymer Fedn, 87-90, counr, 90-92 & pres 94-; treas, Polymer Chem Div, Am Chem Soc, 74-78, chmn, 82; distinguished res fel, Univ Mass, Lowell, 84-90; ed-in-chief, Polymer Sci & Technol Series, 93- Mem: Am Chem Soc; Am Acad Ophthal; Soc Plastics Engrs. Res: Syntheses of new monomers and polymers; copolymerization of ionic monomers; polyampholytes and ampholytic ionomers; solution properties of polymers. Mailing Add: Dept Chem Univ Mass Lowell MA 01854. Fax: 561-997-7249; E-Mail: jsalamone@crcpress.com

SALAMUN, PETER JOSEPH, BOTANY. Current Pos: from instr to prof, 48-84, chmn dept, 60-64, EMER PROF BOT, UNIV WIS-MILWAUKEE, 84- Personal Data: b La Crosse, Wis, June 12, 19; m 46; c 8. Educ: Wis State Teacher's Col, BS, 41; Univ Wis-Madison, MS, 47, PhD(bot), 50. Prof Exp: Asst, Univ Wis, 45-48. Concurrent Pos: Dir, Herbarium. Mem: AAAS; Am Inst Biol Sci; Bot Soc Am; Am Soc Plant Taxonomists; Am Meteorol Soc; Ecological Soc Am; AAAS. Res: Floristic and monographic work in plant taxonomy. Mailing Add: Dept Biol Sci Univ Wis Milwaukee WI 53201

SALAND, LINDA C, ANATOMY, CYTOLOGY. Current Pos: sr res assoc, 71-78, from asst prof to assoc prof, 78-89, PROF ANAT, SCH MED, UNIV NMEX, 89- Personal Data: b New York, NY, Oct 24, 42; m 64; c 2. Educ: City Col New York, BS, 63, PhD(biol), 68; Columbia Univ, MA, 65. Prof Exp: Res assoc anat, Col Physicians & Surgeons, Columbia Univ, 68-69. Concurrent Pos: Assoc ed, Anat Record; ad hoc reviewer endocrinol & neuroendocrinol; chair, Women in Neurosci Steering Comt, 91-93. Mem: Am Asn Anat; Am Soc Cell Biol; Soc Neurosci. Res: Pituitary cytology; electron microscopic autoradiography; hypothalamic cytology; receptor autoradiography; opiate peptides; neuroendocrine function; neural-immune interactions. Mailing Add: Dept Anat Univ NMex Sch Med Albuquerque NM 87131-5211. E-Mail: lsaland@salud.unm.edu

SALANECK, WILLIAM R, SOLID STATE PHYSICS. Current Pos: Scientist, Xerox Corp, Rochester, 68-72, mgr mat sci areas, 72-73, mgr photo & insulator physics area, 74, SR SCIENTIST MOLECULAR & ORG MAT AREA, XEROX WEBSTER RES CTR, 74-, PROF, SURFACE PHYSICS & CHEM, UNIV LINKPING, SWEDEN, 83- Personal Data: b Pottstown, Pa, Aug 19, 41; m 67; c 2. Educ: Albright Col, BS, 63; Univ Pa, MS, 64, PhD(physics), 68. Concurrent Pos: NSF grants, NATO Advan Study Inst, 66 & Army res grant, 67; adj assoc prof physics, Univ Pa, 80- Mem: Am Phys Soc; European Phys Soc; Swedish Phys Soc; Europ Mat Res Soc. Res: Electron physics; photoelectron spectroscopy; electronic structure of molecular solids; electronic structure of conducting polymers; focused upon insulating or electrically conducting organic polymers, their surfaces, as well as polymer-metal interfaces, and model molecular systems for polymer-metal interfaces. Mailing Add: Inst Physics & Measurement Technol Univ Linkoping S-58183 Linkoping Sweden

SALANITRE, ERNEST, MEDICINE, ANESTHESIOLOGY. Current Pos: Instr, Columbia Univ, 53-54, assoc, 55-58, from asst prof to prof, 59-86, EMER PROF ANESTHESIOL, COL PHYSICIANS & SURGEONS, COLUMBIA UNIV, 86- Personal Data: b New York, NY, Feb 3, 15; m 45, Gabriella Vichi; c Susan & Laurie. Educ: City Col New York, BS, 36; Univ Rome, MD, 42. Honors & Awards: Robert M Smith Award in Pediat Anesthesiol, Am Acad Pediat, 90. Prof Exp: From asst attend to assoc attend, Columbia-Presby Med Ctr, 53-71, attend, 71-86, emer consult, 90- Mem: Am Soc Anesthesiol; AMA; Am Acad Pediat. Res: Pediatric anesthesiology; uptake and elimination of inhalational anesthetic agents in man. Mailing Add: 5933 Fieldston Rd New York NY 10471

SALANS, LESTER BARRY, MEDICINE, METABOLISM. Current Pos: VPRES, SANDOZ RES INST. Personal Data: b Chicago Heights, Ill, Jan 25, 36; m 58, Lois Kapp; c Laurence E & Andrea S Kramer. Educ: Univ Mich, Ann Arbor, BA, 57; Univ Ill, Chicago, MD, 61. Prof Exp: Intern med, Stanford Med Sch, 61-62, resident, 62-64; asst prof, Rockefeller Univ, 67-68; from asst prof to assoc prof med, Dartmouth Med Sch, 71-78; chief, Lab Cellular Metab & Obesity & assoc dir diabetes, endocrinol & metab dis, Nat Inst Arthritis, Diabetes, Digestive & Kidney Dis, NIH, 78-81, dir, 81-84. Concurrent Pos: Fel, Stanford Med Sch, 63-64, USPHS fel, 64-65; USPHS spec fel, Rockefeller Univ, 65-67, Nat Inst Arthritis & Metab Dis grant, 68-77 & res career develop award, 72-77; adj prof med, Med Sch, Dartmouth Col, 78-; adj fac, Rockefeller Univ, 84-; adj prof, Mt Sinai Med Sch & Hosp, 87- Mem: Fel Am Col Physicians; Asn Am Physicians; Endocrine Soc; Am Soc Clin Invest; Am Diabetes Asn. Res: Intermediary carbohydrate/lipid metabolism related to diabetes mellitus, obesity and atherosclerosis. Mailing Add: Sandoz Res Inst Rte 10 East Hanover NJ 07936. Fax: 973-503-6976

SALANT, ABNER SAMUEL, FOOD TECHNOLOGY. Current Pos: dir, food eng dir, 76-88, DIR, SCI & ADV TECH DIR, US ARMY NATICK RES DEVELOP ENG CTR, 88- Personal Data: b Cincinnati, Ohio, Mar 18, 30; m 52; c 3. Educ: NY Univ, BA, 50; Rutgers Univ, PhD(food technol), 53. Prof Exp: Res asst, Rutgers Univ, 51-53; assoc technologist, Gen Foods Corp, 53-56; proj leader, Tenco Div, Coca-Cola Co, 56-62; proj mgr org chem div, Monsanto Co, Inc, 62-68, vpres, Monsanto Flavor Essence Inc, 68-75. Mem: AAAS; Am Chem Soc; Inst Food Technologists; Am Inst Chemists; fel NY Acad Sci; Soc Flavor Chemists. Res: Food chemistry; beverage and dessert products; dehydration; evaporation; extraction; classification; blending; commercial development; flavor and fragrance products; low-calorie foods and beverages; nutrition. Mailing Add: US Army Natick Rd & E Ctr Kansas St Natick MA 01760-5020

SALANT, RICHARD FRANK, FLUID SEALING TECHNOLOGY, TRIBOLOGY. Current Pos: PROF MECH ENG, GA INST TECHNOL, 87- Personal Data: b New York, NY, Sept 4, 41; m 62, Barbel Lang; c Scott & Stephanie. Educ: Mass Inst Technol, BS & MS, 63, DSc(mech eng), 67. Honors & Awards: Henry R Worthington Medal, Am Soc Mech Engrs, 96. Prof Exp: Asst prof mech eng, Univ Calif, Berkeley, 66-68; from asst prof to assoc prof mech eng, Mass Inst Technol, 68-72; mgr fluid mech res, Borg Warner Corp, 72-79, mgr fluid mech & heat transfer, 79-80, mgr fluid mech, heat transfer & appl physics, 80-83, head dept fluid mech & heat transfer, 83-87. Concurrent Pos: Consult, Veriflo Corp, 67-68, United Aircraft Res Labs, 69-71, BW/IP Int, 87-96 & CR Industs, 89-; mem educ coun, Mass Inst Technol, 81-87; assoc ed, J Fluids Eng, 85-88 & J Tribology, 93- Mem: Fel Am Soc Mech Engrs; Soc Tribologists & Lubrication Engrs. Res: Fluid sealing technology; tribology; fluid mechanics; two-phase flow. Mailing Add: Sch Mech Eng Ga Inst Technol Atlanta GA 30332. Fax: 404-894-8336; E-Mail: richard.salant@me.gatech.edu

SALARI, HASSAN, ENZYME BIOCHEMISTRY, INFLAMMATORY DISEASES. Current Pos: res assoc, 85-87, ASST PROF MED & ASSOC PROF PHARMACOL, UNIV BC, 87- Personal Data: b Iran, Aug 27, 53; Can citizen; m 82; c 2. Educ: Tehran Univ, BSc, 76; Southampton Univ, Eng, PhD, 80. Prof Exp: Post doc immunol, McGill Univ, 82, biochem, Laval Univ, 85. Mem: Can Soc Biochem; Can Soc Pharmacol. Res: Cellular biochemistry related to lung and heart diseases. Mailing Add: Med Pulmonary Dis Univ Brit Col Faculty Med 2194 Health Sci Mall Vancouver BC V6T 1Z3 Can. Fax: 604-875-4497

SALAS, PEDRO JOSE I, CELL BIOLOGY OF EPITHELIA, IMMUNOCYTOCHEMISTRY. Current Pos: STAFF RES MEM, INST INVEST BIOCHEM FUNDACION CAMPOMAR, BUENOS AIRES, 88-; ASST PROF CELL BIOL, UNIV BUENOS AIRES, 90- Personal Data: b Buenos Aires, Arg, Nov 29, 54; m 82; c 2. Educ: Univ Buenos Aires, MD, 76, Master, 80, PhD(biophys), 81. Prof Exp: From instr to head instr cell biol, Univ Buenos Aires, 72-82; postdoctoral, State Univ NY Downstate, 82-84; res assoc, Cornell Univ Med Col, 84-88. Concurrent Pos: Res fel, Nat Res Coun, 78-82. Mem: Am Soc Cell Biol. Res: Plasma membrane polarization in epithelial cells; role of the cytoskeleton; early polarization; vacuolar apical compartment; selective anchoring of plasma membrane proteins to critical cytoskeleton. Mailing Add: Dept Cell Biol Univ Miami Sch Med R-124 PO Box 16960 Miami FL 33101. Fax: 305-545-7166

SALAS-PRATO, MILAGROS, CELL BIOLOGY, OPHTHALMOLOGY. Current Pos: fel, Cancer Inst, Notre Dame Hosp & Univ Montreal, 76-78, asst res prof, 82-85, Ste Justine Hosp, 85-86, vis researcher, Maissonoeuve/ Rosemont Hosp & Univ Montreal, 89-92, VIS RESEARCHER, NOTRE-DAME HOSP & UNIV MONTREAL, 92- Personal Data: b Caracas, Venezuela, May 17, 51; Venezuelan & Can citizen; m 73, Pedro J Araujo; c Mila, Lisa-Marie, Peter-Emmanuel & Sara. Educ: Loyola Col, Montreal, BSc, 70; Univ Montreal, MSc, 74, PhD(exp med & surg), 77. Prof Exp: Prof asst, Lady Davis Inst, Jewish Gen Hosp, McGill Univ, 78-79; vis scholar, Dept Biol & Cancer Ctr, Univ Calif, San Diego, 79-82; vis assoc prof, Vet Admin/West Los Angeles Med Ctr, Univ Calif, Los Angeles, 86-89. Concurrent Pos: Centennial fel, Med Res Coun Can, 79; Smith Kline Beckman career develop award, Univ Calif, Los Angeles, 86; vis researcher, Que Med Res Coun, 89. Mem: Asn Res Vision & Ophthal; Am Asn Cell Biol; Invitro Soc Develop & Cell Biol; NY Acad Sci. Res: Invitro growth of human tenons capsule fibroblasts by hormones, growth factors and drugs; development of in vivo models of eye fibroblast proliferation and its inhibition by drugs and other agents. Mailing Add: 4548 Coolbrook Ave Montreal PQ H3X 2K6 Can. Fax: 514-876-6630, 876-5111

SALAS-QUINTANA, SALVADOR, biotechnology, for more information see previous edition

SALATI, OCTAVIO M(ARIO), ELECTRICAL ENGINEERING. *Current Pos:* from asst prof to assoc prof, 63-75, PROF ELEC ENG, UNIV PA, 75-, PROJ DIR, INST COOP RES, 48-, DIR, TV SYST, 70- *Personal Data:* b Philadelphia, Pa, Dec 12, 14; m 51; c 3. *Educ:* Univ Pa, BS, 36, MS, 39, PhD(elec eng), 63. *Prof Exp:* Trainee, Radio Corp Am, 37-38, develop engr, 39; develop engr, C G Com Ltd, 39-42; sr engr, Hazeltine Electronics Corp, 42-48. *Concurrent Pos:* Vis prof, Pahlavi Univ, Iran, 69 & People's Repub China, 81; consult, USAF & Naval Med Res Inst, 77-; in charge design, construct & oper, Eng Schs Instrnl TV Syst, Univ Pa, dir eng schs, grad TV syst & dir continuing eng educ. *Mem:* AAAS; fel Inst Elec & Electronics Engrs; Sigma Xi. *Res:* Radio interference in communications and radar systems; microwave tubes; biological effects of microwave radiation; studies of out of band performance of antennas and radio propagation studies; BNC electrical connector and microwave absorber; shielding systems. *Mailing Add:* Univ Pa Col Eng & Appl Physics 103 Moore Sch D2 Philadelphia PA 19104

SALAZAR, HERNANDO, pathology, public health, for more information see previous edition

SALCE, LUDWIG, ORGANIC CHEMISTRY. *Current Pos:* VPRES, CHEM PROD DEVELOP, CONAIR CORP, 92- *Personal Data:* b New York, NY, Feb 3, 34; m 67, Gloria Ferro; c Peter. *Educ:* Fordham Univ, BS, 55, PhD(chem), 67; NY Univ, MS, 61. *Prof Exp:* Chemist, Petrotex Div, Food Mach Chem Corp, 55-56, Burroughs Wellcome & Co, 56-59 & Col Physicians & Surgeons, Columbia Univ, 59-62; sr chemist, Merck & Co, Inc, 66-70; res chemist, Cybertek & Co, 71-72; res chemist, Evans Chemetics Inc, Conn, 72-82; res dir, Zotos Int Inc, Darien, Conn, 82-92. *Mem:* Am Chem Soc; Soc Cosmetic Chemists. *Res:* Purines; pyrimidines; glycosides; amino acids; peptides; aromatic hydrocarbons; steroids; heterocyclics; synthesis of biologically active compounds; synthesis of sulfur compounds; cosmetics and hair research. *Mailing Add:* 32 Brynwood Lane Greenwich CT 06831-3312

SALCH, RICHARD K, PLANT PATHOLOGY. *Current Pos:* from asst prof to assoc prof, 69-73, PROF BIOL, EAST STROUDSBURG STATE COL, 73- *Personal Data:* b Union City, NJ, Sept 10, 40; m 69; c 1. *Educ:* Cent Col, Iowa, BA, 61; Rutgers Univ, MS, 62, PhD(plant biol), 69. *Prof Exp:* Lab technician, Boyce Thompson Inst Plant Res, NY, 63-66. *Mem:* Sigma Xi; Am Inst Biol Sci. *Res:* Biological methods of plant disease control pollution problems and how they effect agriculture; control of fungus diseases of plants; physiology of fungus. *Mailing Add:* RR 3 Box 3578 Saylorsburg PA 18353-9601

SALCMAN, MICHAEL, NEUROLOGICAL SURGERY, NEURO-ONCOLOGY. *Current Pos:* from asst prof to prof neurosurg, 76-91, head neurosurg, 84-91, CHIEF NEURO-ONCOL, SCH MED, UNIV MD, 78-, CLIN PROF NEUROSURG, GEORGE WASHINGTON UNIV, 91-; CHIEF NEUROSURG, SINAI HOSP, BALTIMORE, 96- *Personal Data:* b Pilsen, Czech, Nov 4, 46; US citizen; m 69, Ilene Rebarber; c Joshua & Dara. *Educ:* Boston Univ, BA & MD, 69. *Prof Exp:* Intern surg, Univ Hosp, Boston Univ Med Ctr, 69-70; res assoc neurophysiol, Lab Neural Control, Nat Inst Neurol Dis & Stroke, 70-72; resident neurosurg, Neurol Inst NY, Columbia Univ, 72-76. *Concurrent Pos:* Co-prin investr cats' visual cortex, Nat Eye Inst, NIH, 72-78 & hyperthermal radiotherapy, Am Cancer Soc, 78-80; assoc ed, Neurosurg, 82- *Mem:* Cong Neurol Surgeons; Am Asn Neurol Surgeons; Asn Advan Med Instrumentation; fel Am Col Surgeons; NY Acad Sci; Soc Neurol Surg. *Res:* Biology and treatment of brain tumors using microsurgery, laser, microwave hyperthermia, reversal of blood-brain barrier and chemotherapy; chronic microelectrode technology for single unit neurophysiology and neural prosthesis development. *Mailing Add:* 120 Sister Pierre Dr Suite 107 Towson MD 21204. *E-Mail:* msalch@erols.com

SALCUDEAN, MARTHA EVA, HEAT TRANSFER, FLUID FLOW. *Current Pos:* prof & head, Univ BC, 85-93, Killiam Res Prize, 93, assoc vpres res, 93-96, vpres res, 95, WEYERHAEUSER INDUST RES CHAIR COMPUTATIONAL FLUID DYNAMICS, UNIV BC, 96- *Personal Data:* b Cluj, Romania, Feb 26, 34; m 55; c Tim. *Educ:* Univ Cluj, BEng, 56, MEng, 62; Inst Polytech, Brasov, Romania, PhD(mech), 69. *Hon Degrees:* Dr, Univ Ottawa, 92. *Honors & Awards:* Gold Medal Appl Sci & Eng, Sci Coun BC, 91; Julian C Smith Medal, Eng Inst Can, 95. *Prof Exp:* Engr, Armatura, Cluj, Romania, 56-60; design engr, Nat Ctr Indust Automatics, Bucharest, 60-63; sr res officer, Nat Res Ctr Metall, Bucharest, 63-75; lectr, Univ Ottawa, 76-77, from assoc prof to prof, 77-85. *Concurrent Pos:* Consult pulp & paper indust. *Mem:* Am Soc Mech Engrs; fel Can Soc Mech Eng; Tech Asn Pulp & Paper Indust; fel Can Acad Eng; fel Royal Soc Can. *Res:* Computational heat transfer and fluid dynamics; convective heat transfer in laminar and turbulent flows; two phase flow and heat transfer in vertical and horizontal channels; void formation in two phase flow at low pressures; film cooling of turbine blades; mathematical modelling of recovery boilers; mathematical modelling of flow in hydrocyclones and headboxes. *Mailing Add:* Dept Mech Eng Univ BC 2324 Main Mall Vancouver BC V6T 1Z4 Can. *Fax:* 604-822-6295

SALDANHA, LEILA GENEVIEVE, DIETETICS, NUTRITION. *Current Pos:* MGR NUTRIT PROGS, KELLOGG CO. *Personal Data:* b Bangalore, India, Jan 11, 55. *Educ:* Univ Bombay, India, BSc, 74; Kans State Univ, Manhattan, MS, 83, PhD(food & nutrit), 85. *Prof Exp:* Prod supvr, Mafco Ltd, Bombay, India, 76-80; asst prof nutrit, Dept Animal Sci, Food & Nutrit, Southern Ill Univ, 85- *Concurrent Pos:* Clin dietician, Holy Family Hosp, New Delhi, 75; Fel, Gen Foods Fund, 83-85; Mae Baird Mem Scholar, 83-85; exten asst, Exten Serv, Kans State Univ, 84, asst instr dietetics, Dept Housing, 84. *Mem:* Am Dietetic Asn; Sigma Xi; Inst Food Technologists; Am Inst Nutrit; Am Soc Clin Nutrit. *Res:* Food labelling and fortification regulations; breakfast and fortification-related research. *Mailing Add:* Kellogg Co PO Box 1145 Battle Creek MI 49016

SALDARINI, RONALD JOHN, PHYSIOLOGY, BIOCHEMISTRY. *Current Pos:* RETIRED. *Personal Data:* b Paterson, NJ, Nov 6, 39; m 62; c 3. *Educ:* Drew Univ, BA, 61; Univ Kans, PhD(biochem, physiol), 67. *Prof Exp:* Sr res scientist, Metab Dis Ther Res Sect, Lederle Labs, 69-74, group leader respiratory & skin dis, 74, head, Dept Biol, Metal Dis Sect, 74-, pres, Lederle-Praxis Biol. *Concurrent Pos:* NIMH training fel biochem & physiol, Brain Res Inst, Sch Med, Univ Calif, Los Angeles, 67-68, NIH fel, 68-69. *Mem:* AAAS; Soc Study Reproduction; Brit Soc Study Fertil; Int Soc Fertil. *Res:* Estrogen and progestin receptors in uterus and corpus luteum; immunological regulation of immediate hypersensitivity disease states; cyclic nucleotide involvement in proliferative skin disease; sperm metabolism in monkeys. *Mailing Add:* 6 Surrey Lane Mahwah NJ 07430

SALDICH, ROBERT JOSEPH, ELECTRONICS. *Current Pos:* from mgr finance & personnel to divs gen mgr, Raychem Corp, Menlo Park, Calif, 64-83, off pres, 83-87, subsid pres, Raynet Corp, 87-88, sr vpres telecommun & technol, 88-90, PRES & CHIEF EXEC OFFICER, RAYCHEM CORP, MENLO PARK, CALIF, 90- *Personal Data:* b New York, NY, June 7, 33; m 63, 68, Virginia Vaughan; c Alan, Tad Thomas, Stan Thomas, Melinda Thomas & Margaret Thomas. *Educ:* Rice Univ, BSChe, 56; Harvard Univ, MBA, 61. *Prof Exp:* Mfg mgr, Proctor & Gamble Mfg Co, Dallas & Kansas City, 56-59; res asst, Harvard Bus Sch, Boston, 61-62; asst to pres, Kaiser Aluminum & Chem Corp, Calif, 62-64. *Mailing Add:* Raychem Corp-Mailstop 120/7815 300 Constitution Dr Menlo Park CA 94025-1140

SALDICK, JEROME, PHYSICAL CHEMISTRY. *Current Pos:* RETIRED. *Personal Data:* b Brooklyn, NY, Mar 24, 21; m 51; c 2. *Educ:* Brooklyn Col, BA, 40; Columbia Univ, MA, 41, PhD(phys chem, kinetics), 48. *Prof Exp:* Chemist, Kellex Corp, 48-51; assoc chemist, Brookhaven Nat Lab, 51-54; tech engr, Aircraft Nuclear Propulsion Dept, Gen Elec Co, 54-56; assoc, Astra, Inc, 56-58; pres, Gen Radionuclear Co, 58-59; resident scientist, Indust Reactor Labs, Am Mach & Foundry Co, 59-63; group leader, Princeton Chem Res Inc, 64-66; sr res chemist, FMC Corp, 66-73, res assoc, 73-83. *Mem:* Am Chem Soc. *Res:* Radiation chemistry; heterogeneous catalysis; applied microbiology. *Mailing Add:* 24 Randall Rd Princeton NJ 08540-3610

SALE, PETER FRANCIS, BEHAVIORAL ECOLOGY, TROPICAL ECOLOGY. *Current Pos:* PROF & HEAD BIOL SCIS, UNIV WINDSOR, 94- *Personal Data:* b Jan 12, 41; Can citizen; m 71; c 1. *Educ:* Univ Toronto, BSc, 63, MA, 64; Univ Hawaii, PhD(zool), 68. *Honors & Awards:* Stoye Award, Am Soc Ichthyologists & Herpetologists, 68. *Prof Exp:* Lectr, Univ Sydney,68-74, sr lectr, 75-81, assoc prof biol sci 82-87; asst dir, Inst Marine Ecol, 84-87; prof & chmn, Dept Zool, Univ NH, 88-92, dir, Ctr Marine Biol, 90-93. *Concurrent Pos:* Adv Comt Crown-of-Thorns res grant, Australia, 72-73; Australian Res Grants Comt grant, 74-87; mem bd, Heron Island Res Sta, 74-85; mem consult bd, Lizard Island Res Sta, Australia, 75-87; Australian Marine Sci & Technol grant, 80-88, mem adv comt, 84-86; dir, Sydney Univ One Tree Island Field Sta, 74-87; mem, Crown-of-Thorns Starfish adv res comt, 86-88, Australasia Region Comt, CIES; life mem, Australian Coral Reef Soc, 87; Fulbright Awards Prog, 90-93; prin investr, NSF, 91-, Nat Oceanic & Atmospheric Admin, 91-94; Glaser vis fel, Fla Int Univ, 93. *Mem:* Am Soc Naturalists; Soc Animal Behav; Sigma Xi; Ecol Soc Am; Am Soc Ichthyologists & Herpetologists; AAAS. *Res:* Ecology of coral reef communities, especially fish and their high diversity; role of recruitment in mediating structure of communities; demography of coral reef fish; larval and juvenile ecology of temperate coastal fishes. *Mailing Add:* Dept Biol Scis Univ Windsor Windsor ON N9B 3P4 Can

SALEEB, FOUAD ZAKI, SURFACE CHEMISTRY, PHYSICAL CHEMISTRY. *Current Pos:* sr chemist, 72-80, prin scientist, 80-87, RES FEL, TECH CTR, GEN FOODS CORP, 87- *Personal Data:* b Toukh, Egypt, Sept 7, 34; m 66; c 3. *Educ:* Univ Alexandria, BS, 56; Univ London, PhD(phys chem) & DIC, 63. *Prof Exp:* Egyptian Govt fel, Imp Col, Univ London, 63-64; res scientist surface chem, Nat Res Ctr, Cairo, Egypt, 64-69; res assoc, Mass Inst Technol, 69-72. *Mem:* Am Chem Soc; NY Acad Sci; Inst Food Technol; Control Rel Soc. *Res:* Surface chemistry of emulsions, foams and suspensions; electrokinetic properties of carbons, minerals and hydroxyapatites; monomolecular films and mass transfer. *Mailing Add:* Tech Ctr Kraft Foods Tarrytown NY 10591

SALEEBY, JASON BRIAN, GEOLOGY. *Current Pos:* ASSOC PROF GEOL, CALIF INST TECHNOL, 78- *Personal Data:* b Los Angeles, Calif, Oct 24, 48; m 78; c 1. *Educ:* Univ Calif, Santa Barbara, PhD(geol), 75. *Prof Exp:* Asst prof geol, Univ Calif, Berkeley, 75-78. *Concurrent Pos:* Mem, US Geol Surv, 75- *Mem:* Geol Soc Am; Am Geophys Union. *Res:* Tectonic and paleogeographic development of western North America; processes of accretion of ocean floor and island areas to continental edges by use of geochronology; field structure and petrology. *Mailing Add:* Div Geol & Planetary Sci 170-25 Calif Inst Technol 1201 E California Pasadena CA 91125-0001

SALEH, ADEL ABDEL MONEIM, ELECTRICAL ENGINEERING. *Current Pos:* MEM TECH STAFF ELEC ENG, BELL TEL LABS, 70- *Personal Data:* b Alexandria, Egypt, July 8, 42; m 70. *Educ:* Univ Alexandria, BSc, 63; Mass Inst Technol, SM, 67, PhD(elec eng), 70. *Prof Exp:* Instr elec eng, Univ Alexandria, 63-65. *Concurrent Pos:* Consult engr, Sylvania Elec Prod, Inc, Mass, 68-70. *Mem:* Sr mem Inst Elec & Electronics Engrs. *Res:* Microwave and millimeter-wave circuits and communication systems research, including power amplifiers nonlinearities and efficiency, power combining networks, mixers and frequency converters, automated microwave measurements, and quasi-optical components. *Mailing Add:* AT&T Bell Labs 791 Holmdel-Keyport Rd PO Box 400 Holmdel NJ 07733

SALEH, BAHAA E A, OPTICAL PROCESSING, IMAGE PROCESSING. *Current Pos:* PROF & CHMN, DEPT ELEC & COMPUT ENG, BOSTON UNIV, 94- *Personal Data:* b Egypt, Sept 30, 44; US citizen. *Educ:* Cairo Univ, BS, 66; Johns Hopkins Univ, PhD(elec eng), 71. *Prof Exp:* Asst prof elec eng, Univ Santa Catarina, Brazil, 71-74; res assoc, Max Planck Inst, Gottingen, Ger, 74-77; from asst prof to prof, Univ Wis-madison, 81-94, chmn, 90-94. *Concurrent Pos:* Ed, J Optical Soc Am; Guggenheim fel, 84-85. *Mem:* Fel Optical Soc Am; fel Inst Elec & Electronics Engrs. *Res:* Image processing, optical information processing, optical communication, quantum optics, statistical optics and vision. *Mailing Add:* Dept Elec & Comput Eng Boston Univ 44 Cummington St Boston MA 02215-2407. *Fax:* 617-353-6440; *E-Mail:* besaleh@bu.edu

SALEH, FARIDA YOUSRY, ENVIRONMENTAL CHEMISTRY, ANALYTICAL CHEMISTRY. *Current Pos:* from asst prof to assoc prof, Dept Chem, 82-89, assoc prof, Div Environ Sci, PROF, UNIV NTEX, 94- *Personal Data:* b Cairo, Egypt, June 17, 39; m 59, Hasny G; c Maggie (Fox) & Nagwa (Pfingston). *Educ:* Ain-Shams Univ, Cairo, Egypt, BS, 59; Alexandria Univ, Egypt, MS 67; Univ Tex, Dallas, PhD(environ chem), 76. *Honors & Awards:* Outstanding Serv Award, US Environ Protection Agency Off Explor Res, 93. *Prof Exp:* Anal chemist, Alexandria Labs, Alexandria, Egypt, 62-68; res chemist, Res Ctr, Dallas Water Reclamation, 68-75; res scientist, Ctr Environ Studies, Univ Tex, Dallas, 75-77; res fel, Dept Chem, Tex A&M Univ, College Station, Tex, 77-78; res scientist, II-Res, NTex State Univ, Denton, 78-83, res scientist III-Res, Inst Appl Sci, 83-85. *Concurrent Pos:* Res scientist, II-Res, NTex State Univ, Denton, 78-83, Inst Appli Sci, 83-85. *Mem:* Am Chem Soc; Int Union Pure & Appl Chem; Int Humic Substances Soc; Asn Women Sci. *Res:* Environmental chemistry; transport and fate of chemicals in the environment; analytical chemistry of pollutants with emphasis on utilization of advanced spectroscopic techniques to identify and measure pollutants. *Mailing Add:* Grad Environ Sci Prof Univ NTex Box 13078 Denton TX 76203-3078. *Fax:* 817-565-4297; *E-Mail:* saleh@cas.unt.edu

SALEH, WASFY SELEMAN, SURGERY, UROLOGY. *Current Pos:* UROLOGIST, QUEENS WAY CARLTON HOSP, 77- *Personal Data:* b Egypt, Jan 23, 32; Can citizen; m 64; c 3. *Educ:* Cairo Univ, MB, Bch, 57; McGill Univ, PhD(exp surg), 70. *Prof Exp:* Asst prof surg, Ottawa Univ, 70-73; asst prof urol, Univ Sherbrooke, 73-77. *Mem:* Am Col Surgeons; Int Transplantation Soc; Royal Col Surgeons & Physicians Can; Am Urol Asn. *Res:* Studies in graft versus host reactions. *Mailing Add:* 3029 Carling Ave Suite 203 Ottawa ON K2B 8E8 Can

SALEHI, HABIB, MATHEMATICAL ANALYSIS. *Current Pos:* from asst prof to assoc prof, 65-74, PROF MATH & STATIST, MICH STATE UNIV, 74- *Personal Data:* b Iran, Jan 29, 35; m 62; c 2. *Educ:* Univ Tehran, BA, 58; Ind Univ, MA, 62, PhD(math), 65. *Prof Exp:* Instr math, Univ Tehran, 58-60. *Concurrent Pos:* Nat Inst Gen Med Sci grant, 66-; NSF grants, Mich State Univ, 67-71. *Mem:* Am Math Soc; Inst Math Statist. *Res:* Prediction theory of stochastic processes as initiated by N Wiener and A N Kolmogorov; powerful tools and techniques used in mathematical analysis to solve various problems in prediction and communication theory. *Mailing Add:* Dept Statist & Prob Mich State Univ A-415 Wells Hall East Lansing MI 48824-0001. *Fax:* 517-336-1405

SALEL, ANTONE FRANCIS, CARDIOLOGY. *Current Pos:* CARDIOLOGIST, NORTH CO CARDIOVASC MED GROUP, INC, 76-; SR STAFF MEM, SCRIPPS MEM HOSP, LA JOLLA & ENCINITAS, 76-; ASSOC CLIN PROF MED CARDIOL, DEPT MED, UNIV CALIF, SAN DIEGO SCH MED, 91- *Personal Data:* b Oakland, Calif, Aug 9, 38; c 3. *Educ:* St Marys Col, BS, 60; Georgetown Univ, MD, 64; Am Bd Internal Med, cert, 72, recert, 80. *Prof Exp:* Intern Med, Boston City Hosp, Boston Univ Sch Med, 64-65, resident med, 65-66; officer internal med, Med Corps, US Army, 66-67, chief outpatient & mil dispensary, 66-67, chief clin labs, Beach Army Hosp, 66-67, battalion surgeon, 8th Infantry, 4th Infantry Div, Rep, Viet Nam, 67-68; cardiovasc training prog, Univ Wash Sch Med, 68, sr res fel, Dept Physiol, Div Bioeng, 68-70; fel cardiol, Sch Med, Univ Calif, Davis, 70-72, asst prof med, chief lipid lab & chief cardiovasc bioeng, Dept Internal Med, Sect Cardiovasc Med, 72-76, asst prof eng, 73-76; attending, Univ Hosp, Univ Calif, San Diego, 76-85; asst clin prof med cardiol, Dept Med, Univ Calif, San Diego Sch Med, La Jolla, 85-90. *Concurrent Pos:* Consult aerojet gen implantable artificial heart power syst, Nat Heart & Lung Inst, 72-76; consult cardiol, Martinez Vet Admin Hosp, 74-76; chmn, Cardiopulmonary Comt, Scripps Mem Hosp, La Jolla, 78-80, vchmn, 79-80, chmn, Dept Med, 78-80, dir, Intensive Care Unit, 78-, co-dir, Cardiac Catheterization Lab, 78-, chief of staff, 91-; fel, Coun Clin Cardiol, Am Heart Asn, fel, Coun Atherosclerosis & assoc fel, Coun Epidemiol. *Mem:* Am Fedn Clin Res; Am Heart Asn; fel Am Col Physicians; fel Am Col Chest Physicians; fel Biomed Eng Soc; fel Am Col Cardiol. *Res:* Lipid-lipoprotein metabolism and nutrition; cardiovascular bioengineering, cardiac assist devices, cardiac pacemakers; clinical cardiovascular pharmacology; author of numerous publications. *Mailing Add:* 320 Santa Fe Dr Suite 211 Encinitas CA 92024

SALEM, HARRY, PHARMACOLOGY, TOXICOLOGY. *Current Pos:* CHIEF SCIENTIST, EDGEWOOD RES DEVELOP & ENG CTR, APG, MD, 94- *Personal Data:* b Windsor, Ont, Mar 21, 29; US citizen; m 57, Florence Rosenbaum; c Jerry Sheldon. *Educ:* Univ Western Ont, BA, 50; Univ Mich, BSc, 53; Univ Toronto, MA, 55, PhD(pharmacol), 58. *Honors & Awards:* Cert Appreciation, Soc Toxicol, 90. *Prof Exp:* Res asst, Univ Toronto, 58-59; pharmacologist, Air-Shields Inc, 59-62; sr pharmacologist, Smith Kline & French Labs, 62-65; pres, Whittaker Toxigenics, Inc, Decatur, Ill, 80-84; dir phamacol & toxicol, Cooper Labs, Cedar Knolls, NJ, 72-77; pres & chief toxicologist, Cannon Labs, Inc, 77-80; pres, Whittaker Toxigenics, INC, Decatur, Ill, 80-84; chief, Toxicol Div, Res Develop & Eng Ctr, Md, 84-94. *Concurrent Pos:* From instr to asst prof, Sch Med, Univ Pa, 60-75, assoc prof, 75-; adj prof environ health, Sch Pharm, Temple Univ, 76; chmn, tech comt, Inhalation Specialty Sect, Soc Toxicol; ed-in-chief, J Appl Technol; councilor & chmn, Tech Comt, Specialty Sect on Inhalation, Soc Toxicol; prof chemtoxicol, Drexel Univ, 92- *Mem:* AAAS; Am Chem Soc; fel Am Col Clin Pharmacol; charter mem Am Col Toxicol; Am Conf Govt Indust Hyg Inc; Am Soc Clin Pharmacol & Therapeut; Am Soc Pharmacol & Exp Therapeut; chem Corps Asn Inc; fel NY Acad Sci; Soc Comp Ophthal (vpres); Sigma Xi; Soc Toxicol; Fel Acad Toxicol Soc. *Res:* Respiratory, cardiovascular, ocular and general pharmacology, physiology and toxicology. *Mailing Add:* 200F Foxhall Dr Bel Air MD 21015. *Fax:* 440-671-2447; *E-Mail:* hxsalem@cbdcom.apgea.army.mil

SALEM, MOHAMMED A, PHARMACEUTICAL SCIENCES, PRECLINICAL DEVELOPMENT & REGULATORY AFFAIRS. *Current Pos:* DIR PRECLIN DEVELOP & REGULATORY AFFAIRS, BOSTON LIFE SCI INC, 97- *Personal Data:* b Kenya, May 2, 55; US citizen. *Educ:* Kuwait Univ, BSc, 77; Univ Mich, MS, 81; Univ Nebr, PhD(biochem), 86. *Prof Exp:* Assoc sr scientist, Marion Merrell Dow Inc, 92-93; head preclin pharmacol & toxicol, Autoimmune Inc, 94-97. *Concurrent Pos:* Res assoc, Whittier Inst, Scripps Mem Hosp, 87-89; sr pharmacologist, Marion Labs Inc, 89-92. *Mem:* Am Soc Biochem & Molecular Biol; Endocrine Soc; Soc Exp Biol & Med; Fedn Am Soc Exp Biol; Regulatory Affairs Prof; Soc Tooxicol. *Res:* Inflammatory diseases and metabolic diseases; autoimmune diseases and genetically derived in born errors of metabolism such as diabetes, multiple sclerosis, arthritis and atherosclerosis; areas of biotechnology and cancer therapeutics. *Mailing Add:* 31 Newbury St Suite 300 Boston MA 02116

SALEM, NORMAN, JR, LIPID CHEMISTRY, POLYUNSATURATED FATTY ACID METABOLISM. *Current Pos:* CHIEF SECT ANAL CHEM, NAT INST ALCOHOL ABUSE & ALCOHOLISM, 83- *Personal Data:* b Cleveland, Ohio, Feb 14, 50; m. *Educ:* Miami Univ, BS, 72; Univ Rochester, PhD(neurobiol), 78. *Concurrent Pos:* Adj prof, Dept Physiol & Biophys, Georgetown Univ; NIH staff fel, 77-81, sr fel, Develop Metabolic Neurol Br, 81-83. *Mem:* Am Soc Neurochem; Am Soc Molecular Biol & Biochem; Soc Exp Biol & Med; Int Soc Study Fatty Acids & Lipids; Res Soc Alcoholism. *Res:* Over 70 publications on lipid biochemistry; specialist in omega-3 fatty acid area; mechanisms of action of alcohol; molecular structure of biomembranes. *Mailing Add:* 12501 Washington Ave Lab Membrane Biochem & Biophys Rockville MD 20852. *Fax:* 301-594-0035

SALEM, SEMAAN IBRAHIM, PHYSICS. *Current Pos:* chmn dept physics, 79-88, from asst prof to assoc prof, 61-68, PROF PHYSICS, CALIF STATE UNIV, LONG BEACH, 68- *Personal Data:* b Bterram, Lebanon, Apr 4, 27; US citizen; c 3. *Educ:* Am Univ, Cairo, BSc, 55; Univ Tex, PhD(physics), 59. *Honors & Awards:* Lebanon Govt Nat Award for the Best Article of the Year, 63. *Prof Exp:* Teacher physics & math, Tripoly Col & Tripoly Boys Sch, 55-56; consult radiation, NAm Aviation, Inc, 58-59; asst prof physics, Univ Tex, Arlington, 59-61. *Concurrent Pos:* Gen Elec Co educ grant, 64; Res Corp res grants, 64-66; res physicist, Lawrence Livermore Nat Lab, 67-68; vis scientist, Calif Inst Technol, 76. *Mem:* Am Phys Soc; Nat Asn Physics Teachers; Arab Phys Soc. *Res:* Measurement of x-ray line width; interaction of charged particles with metals; x-ray spectra; channeling; transition probabilities; sets of energy levels in the rare earth and transition elements. *Mailing Add:* 3443 Fanwood Ave Long Beach CA 90808

SALEMME, ROBERT MICHAEL, CHEMICAL & SYSTEMS ENGINEERING. *Current Pos:* Staff engr, 69-75, tech adminr, 75-77, MGR ENERGY CONVERSION SYSTS, GEN ELEC CORP RES & DEVELOP, 77- *Personal Data:* b Boston, Mass, June 17, 43; c 1. *Educ:* Tufts Univ, BS, 64, MS, 67, Case Western Reserve Univ, 70. *Mem:* Am Inst Chem Engrs. *Res:* Energy conversion systems analysis and development of advanced energy conversion technologies; development and analysis of synthetic fuel processes. *Mailing Add:* 1156 Stratford Schenectady NY 12308

SALERNI, ORESTE LEROY, ORGANIC CHEMISTRY, MEDICINAL CHEMISTRY. *Current Pos:* assoc prof, 69-77, PROF MED CHEM, COL PHARM, BUTLER UNIV, 77- *Personal Data:* b Bolivar, Pa, June 11, 34. *Educ:* Duquesne Univ, BS, 57, MS, 59; Univ Ill, PhD(pharmaceut chem), 63. *Prof Exp:* Assoc chemist, Midwest Res Inst, 62-65, sr chemist, 65-69. *Concurrent Pos:* Res grant, 66-67. *Mem:* Am Chem Soc; Royal Soc Chem. *Res:* Synthesis of organic compounds with potential biological activity. *Mailing Add:* Col Pharm Butler Univ Indianapolis IN 46208-3485

SALERNO, ALPHONSE, SURGERY, BIOLOGY. *Current Pos:* PVT PRACT. *Personal Data:* b Newark, NJ, Apr 3, 23; m 66; c 2. *Educ:* Seton Hall, BS, 44; Philadelphia Col Osteopath Med, DO, 48; Guadalajara Mex, cert(gen surg), 67 & abdominal surg, 86. *Prof Exp:* Chmn bd cert surg & pres acad surg, 76; chief surg, Livingston Community Hosp, 76-, chief staff, 86-88. *Mem:* NY Acad Sci. *Mailing Add:* 613 Park Ave East Orange NJ 07017

SALERNO, JOHN CHARLES, BIOENERGETICS, SPECTROSCOPY. *Current Pos:* asst prof, 80-86, ASSOC PROF BIOL, RENSSELAER POLYTECH INST, 86- *Personal Data:* b Troy, NY, May 23, 49; m 74; c 1. *Educ:* Mass Inst Technol, BSc, 72; Univ Pa, PhD(biophys), 77. *Prof Exp:* Res assoc biophys, Univ Pa, 77-78; NIH fel biochem, Duke Univ, 78-80. *Concurrent Pos:* NIH fel, 78-80; adj asst prof, dept biol, State Univ NY, Albany, 83- *Mem:* Biophys Soc. *Res:* Structure and function of electron transfer complexes using spectroscopic methods and computer modeling; thermodynamics of electron and proton transfer in energy conserving systems; membrane bound and multicomponent enzymes-electron paramagnetic resonance. *Mailing Add:* Biol Dept Rensselaer Polytech Inst Troy NY 12180

SALERNO, JUDITH A, OCCUPATIONAL MEDICINE. *Current Pos:* chief, Geriatric Sect & dir, Geriat Eval & Mgmt Unit, 93-96, assoc chief staff, Geriats & Extended Care, 95-96, ASST CHIEF MED DIR & CHIEF CONSULT, GERIATS & EXTENDED CARE, VETERANS HEALTH ADMIN, DEPT VET AFFAIRS, 96- *Educ:* Stonehill Col, BA, 73; Harvard Univ, MS, 76, MD, 85; Am Bd Internal Med, dipl, 88. *Mem:* Am Col Physicians; Am Geriats Soc; Gerontol Soc Am; AMA; Am Pub Health Asn. *Res:* Cognitive function and brain imaging in patients with geriatric hypertension and Alzheimer's disease; experience in positron emission tomography and structural brain imaging methods and analysis; author of numerous publications in field. *Mailing Add:* Vet Health Admin Geriat & Extended Care Serv 810 Vermont Ave Washington DC 20420

SALERNO, LOUIS JOSEPH, CRYOGENICS. *Current Pos:* Res scientist, Space Proj Div, Ames Res Ctr, NASA, 79-89, sci instrument engr, 89-90, atmospheric entry proj engr, 90-94, RES SCIENTIST, SPACE TECHNOL DIV, AMES RES CTR, NASA, 96- *Personal Data:* b San Mateo, Calif, Mar 5, 49; m 94. *Educ:* Univ Calif, Santa Barbara, BA, 74; San Jose State Univ, BS, 79; Stanford Univ, MS, 82. *Concurrent Pos:* Lectr, Dept Mech Eng, San Jose State Univ, 80- *Res:* Thermal conductance of pressed metallic contacts at liquid helium temperatures; instruments for atmospheric entry vehicles; liquid helium transfer in space, especially fluid management, metering; advanced space transportation; thermal protection systems. *Mailing Add:* NASA Ames Res Ctr Mail Stop 234-1 Moffett Field CA 94035-1000

SALERNO, RONALD ANTHONY, BIOLOGICAL QUALITY CONTROL, VIROLOGY. *Current Pos:* SR PROJ DEVELOP BIOLOGIST, BIOL QUAL CONTROL TECH SERV, MERCK SHARP & DOHME, 81- *Personal Data:* b Philadelphia, Pa, Dec 13, 42; m 64; c 4. *Educ:* St Vincent Col, BA, 64; Villanova Univ, MS, 67; Univ Md, College Park, MS, 70, PhD(zool), 71. *Prof Exp:* Teaching asst biol, Villanova Univ, 64-66; teaching asst zool, Univ Md, College Park, 66-69; sr technologist, Microbiol Assocs, Inc, 69-70, asst scientist, 70-71, asst investr, 71-73; sr virologist, Merck Sharp & Dohme Res Labs, 73-81. *Concurrent Pos:* Mem fac, Dept Biol, Grad Sch, Villanova Univ, 81- *Mem:* AAAS; NY Acad Sci. *Res:* Biology of the type C RNA tumor and herpes simplex viruses; viral vaccine development; biological assay development. *Mailing Add:* 619 Brookwood Lane North Wales PA 19454

SALES, BRIAN CRAIG, HIGH-TEMPERATURE SUPERCONDUCTIVITY, PHOSPHATE GLASSES. *Current Pos:* staff scientist, 81-87, CO-GROUP LEADER, SOLID STATE DIV, OAK RIDGE NAT LAB, TENN, 87- *Personal Data:* b Durham NC, Dec 19, 47; m 74; c 2. *Educ:* Carnegie-Mellon Univ, BS, 69; Univ Calif San Diego, PhD(physics), 74. *Honors & Awards:* Mat Sci Award, US Dept Energy, 84. *Prof Exp:* Fel, Univ Cologne, WGer 74-76; res physicist, Univ Calif, San Diego, 76-81. *Mem:* Am Phys Soc; Mat Res Soc; Am Ceramic Soc; Am Asn Crystal Growth. *Res:* Fundamental structure properties of phosphate glasses and crystals; synthesis of cuprate-based high temperature superconductors. *Mailing Add:* Oak Ridge Nat Lab Solid State Div Bldg 2000 MS 6056 Box 2008 Oak Ridge TN 37830

SALESSE, CHRISTIAN, VISION RESEARCH, MODEL MEMBRANES. *Current Pos:* PROF, UNIV QUE, TROIS-RIVIERES, 90- *Personal Data:* b Jonquiere, Que, Oct 14, 55; m 80, Lise Lebel; c Frederick, Charles & Helene. *Educ:* Univ Que, Trois-Rivieres, BSc, 79, MSc, 81, PhD(biophys), 86. *Concurrent Pos:* Adj prof, Dept Ophthal, Laval Univ, 90-, Jilin Univ, China, 95-; vpres, Int Coord Expert Coun, Russian State Comt Higher Educ, 93-96; mem, Int Comt, Int Conf Organized Molecular Films, 93- *Mem:* AAAS; Asn Res Vision & Ophthal; Biophys Soc; Int Soc Eye Res; Can-Fr Asn Advan Sci. *Res:* Visual transduction; mechanism of activation of phosphodiesterase by transducin and crystallization of rhodopsin; interaction between photoreceptors and the pigment epithelium; expression of integrins and phospholipases; involvement of integrins in corneal wound healing. *Mailing Add:* Ctr Rech Photobiophys Univ Quebec a Trois-Rivieres CP 500 Trois-Rivieres PQ G9A 5H7 Can. *Fax:* 819-376-5057; *E-Mail:* christian_salesse@uqtr.uquebec.ca

SALEUDDIN, ABU S, INVERTEBRATE NEUROENDOCRINOLOGY. *Current Pos:* from asst prof to assoc prof, York Univ, 67-78, chair biol, 84-86, assoc dean fac grad studies, 83-88, chair senate, 93, PROF BIOL, YORK UNIV, 78- *Personal Data:* b Faridpur, Bangladesh, Jan 14, 37; m 66, Robertson; c 1. *Educ:* Univ Dacca, BSc, 55, MSc, 57; Univ Reading, PhD(marine ecol), 63. *Prof Exp:* Lectr invert zool, Univ Dacca, 58-60 & 63-64; Nat Res Coun Can fel invert physiol, Univ Alta, 64-66; instr cell physiol, Duke Univ, 66-67. *Mem:* Am Soc Zoologists. *Res:* Physiology of biological calcification with special interest in shell regeneration in molluscs; neurosecretion in invertebrates; hormonal physiology in mollures. *Mailing Add:* Dept Biol York Univ 4700 Keele St North York ON M3J 1P3 Can

SALGADO, ERNESTO D, PATHOLOGY. *Current Pos:* assoc prof, 61-68, PROF PATH, COL MED & DENT NJ, 68- *Personal Data:* b Spain, Nov 16, 23; m 52; c 4. *Educ:* Univ Zaragosa, AB, 40; Univ Madrid, MD, 47; Univ Montreal, PhD, 55. *Prof Exp:* Resident, Univ Madrid Hosp, 47-50; asst, Univ Montreal, 50-52, res assoc, 52-54; sr biologist, Nepera Chem Co, NY, 54-55, dir biol res, 55-57; endocrinologist, Pfizer Therapeut Inst, NY, 57-58. *Concurrent Pos:* Fel path, Col Med & Dent NJ, 58-61; consult, Pfizer Therapeut Inst, 58-59. *Mem:* AAAS; Am Soc Exp Path; Am Physiol Soc; fel NY Acad Sci. *Res:* Experimental and clinical pathology. *Mailing Add:* Dept Path Univ Med Dent NJ Med Sch Newark NJ 07103-2714

SALGANICOFF, LEON, PHARMACOLOGY, BIOCHEMISTRY. *Current Pos:* assoc prof, 68-76, PROF PHARMACOL, DEPT PHARMACOL, MED SCH, TEMPLE UNIV, 76- *Personal Data:* b Buenos Aires, Arg, Sept 11, 24; US citizen; m 54; c 2. *Educ:* Univ Buenos Aires, MS, 47, DSc, 55. *Prof Exp:* Chief clin path, Military Hosp, Buenos Aires, 55-59; chief neurochem, Med Sch, Univ Buenos Aires, 59-64; res fel biochem, Dept Biophys Chem, Univ Pa, 65-68. *Concurrent Pos:* Mem, Nat Res Coun, 60-64; sect head pharmacol, Thrombosis Res Ctr, Med Sch, Temple Univ, 72-84; vis prof, Dept Gen Path, State Univ Rome, Italy, 80-; mem Coun Thrombosis, Am Heart Asn. *Mem:* Am Heart Asn; Sigma Xi. *Res:* Second messenger control of platelet function. *Mailing Add:* Dept Pharmacol Med Sch Temple Univ 3400 N Broad St Philadelphia PA 19140-5104. *Fax:* 215-221-7068

SALHANICK, HILTON AARON, OBSTETRICS & GYNECOLOGY. *Current Pos:* head, dept pop sci, 71-73, PROF OBSTET & GYNEC, SCH MED, HARVARD UNIV, 62-, FREDERICK LEE HISAW PROF REPRODUCTIVE PHYSIOL, 70- *Personal Data:* b Fall River, Mass, Sept 17, 24; m 55; c 2. *Educ:* Harvard Univ, AB, 47, MA, 49, PhD(biol), 50; Univ Utah, MD, 56. *Honors & Awards:* Distinguished Serv Award, Endocrine Soc, 89. *Prof Exp:* Asst endocrinol, Harvard Univ, 47-50; res assoc obstet & gynec, Col Med, Univ Utah, 52-56; intern, St Louis Maternity Hosp, 56-57; from resident to chief resident, Col Med, Univ Nebr, 57-59, from asst prof to assoc prof, 57-62, asst prof biochem, 57-62; obstetrician-gynecologist-in-chief, Beth Israel Hosp, Boston, 62-65. *Concurrent Pos:* Mem, Endocrinol Study Sect, NIH, 61-65, chmn, 65-66; mem, Ctr Pop Studies, Sch Pub Health, Harvard Univ, 65- *Mem:* AAAS; Am Chem Soc; fel Am Col Obstet & Gynec; Endocrine Soc; Soc Gynec Invest. *Res:* Endocrinology of reproductive system; conception control. *Mailing Add:* 87 Colchester St Brookline MA 02146

SALHANY, JAMES MITCHELL, BIOPHYSICS. *Current Pos:* res asst prof biochem, 75-79, assoc prof, dept internal med, 79-89, PROF DEPTS INTERNAL MED & BIOCHEM, UNIV NEBR MED CTR, 89- *Personal Data:* b Detroit, Mich, Mar 27, 47; m 84. *Educ:* Univ Fla, BS, 72; Univ Chicago, PhD(biophys), 74. *Prof Exp:* Fel biophys, Bell Tel Labs, 74-75. *Concurrent Pos:* Established investr, Am Heart Asn, 80-85. *Mem:* Am Chem Soc; Biophys Soc. *Res:* Membrane biophysics, ion transport and protein associations; Band 3 protein. *Mailing Add:* Swanson Hamm Med Ctr Rm 4060 600 S 42nd St Omaha NE 68189-5290

SALIBA, TONY ELIAS, PROCESS MODELING OF COMPOSITE MATERIALS MANUFACTURING, PROCESS CONTROL. *Current Pos:* From asst prof to assoc prof, 86-95, PROF & CHMN CHEM ENG, UNIV DAYTON, 95- *Personal Data:* m, Susan Shappert; c Lawrence J & Justin A. *Educ:* Univ Dayton, BS, 81, MS, 82, PhD(mat eng). 86. *Concurrent Pos:* Consult curric develop, Winona State Univ, 90. *Mem:* Soc Advan Mat & Process Eng; Am Inst Chem Engrs. *Res:* Develop mathematical models, sensors and process control strategies to develop and manufacture intelligently high performance composite materials. *Mailing Add:* 4045 N Emerald Ct Dayton OH 45430

SALIHI, JALAL T(AWFIQ), ELECTRICAL ENGINEERING. *Current Pos:* DIR RES, OTIS ELEVATOR CO, FARMINGTON, CONN; VPRES RES & DEV, US ELEVATOR CO. *Personal Data:* b Sulaymania, Iraq, Dec 6, 25; m 57; c 2. *Educ:* Univ Leeds, BSc, 48; Univ Calif, Berkeley, MS, 54, PhD(elec eng), 58. *Prof Exp:* Staff engr, Lenkurt Elec Co, Calif, 57-59; asst prof elec eng, Univ Baghdad, 59-61, head dept, 61-63; supvry res engr, Gen Motors Defense Res Labs, Calif, 63-71, supvry res engr elec propulsion dept, Res Labs, Gen Motors Tech Ctr, Mich, 71; chief hybrid & elec systs br, Environ Protection Agency, 71-72, asst dir, Div Advan Automotive Power Systs Develop, 72- *Mem:* Inst Elec & Electronics Engrs; Soc Automotive Engrs. *Res:* Magnetic amplifiers and other types of nonlinear magnetic circuits; servomechanisms and control; power conversion; electric propulsion. *Mailing Add:* 1586 Kimberly Woods Dr El Cajon CA 92020

SALIK, JULIAN OSWALD, RADIOLOGY. *Current Pos:* from asst prof to assoc prof, 56-82, EMER ASSOC PROF RADIOL, SCH MED, JOHNS HOPKINS UNIV, 82-; EMER RADIOLOGIST-IN-CHIEF, SINAI HOSP, 82- *Personal Data:* b Czech, Sept 17, 09; nat US; m 39. *Educ:* Jagiellonian Univ, MD, 36; Cambridge Univ, DMRE, 41. *Prof Exp:* Clin clerk radiol, Holzknecht Inst, Vienna, Austria, 37; Paean Hosp, Cracow, Poland, 38 & Middlesex, London, Eng, 39; resident, Columbia-Presby Med Ctr, NY, 42-44; dir dept radiol, Halloran Vet Admin Hosp, Staten Island, NY, 47-49. *Concurrent Pos:* Asst resident, Col Physicians & Surgeons, Columbia Univ, 42-44; radiologist, Levindale Home for Aged & Chronic Dis Hosp, Baltimore, Md, 51-82 & Hopkins Hosp, 56-82, emer radiologist, 82-; radiologist-in-chief, Sinai Hosp, 49-82. *Mem:* Emer mem Radiol Soc NAm; emer mem AMA; emer fel Am Col Radiol; emer fel NY Acad Med; emer mem Brit Inst Radiol. *Res:* Diagnostic radiology of gastrointestinal tract, pancreas and lungs; vascular anatomy and pathology; genito-urinary tract. *Mailing Add:* 4000 N Charles St Baltimore MD 21218

SALIN, MARVIN LEONARD, BIOCHEMISTRY. *Current Pos:* asst prof, 78-80, ASSOC PROF, MISS STATE UNIV, 80-. PROF, 87- *Personal Data:* b Brooklyn, NY, July 14, 46; m 90, Delmy Calderon; c Tod, Andy & Gilda. *Educ:* Brooklyn Col, City Univ New York, BS, 67; Fla State Univ, MS, 69, PhD(biol sci), 72. *Honors & Awards:* Fel, Juan March Found, Madrid, Spain. *Prof Exp:* Assoc biochem, Univ Ga, 73-74; NIH fel, Duke Univ, 74-76, assoc biochem, 76-78. *Concurrent Pos:* Humboldt Found fel, Max Planck Inst Biochem, Munich, WGer, 86; Fulbright fel, Univ Malta, 90; vis prof, US Mil Acad, West Point, NY. *Mem:* Am Soc Photobiol; Sigma Xi; Am Soc Biol Chemists; Am Soc Microbiol. *Res:* Free radicals of oxygen, bioenergetics metabolism, oxidases, oxygenases and peroxidases; halophilie protein, photooxidations. *Mailing Add:* Dept Biochem & Molecular Biol Miss State Univ Mississippi State MS 39762. *Fax:* 601-325-8664; *E-Mail:* mlsl@ra.msstate.edu

SALINAS, DAVID, ENGINEERING, APPLIED MATHEMATICS. *Current Pos:* ASSOC PROF MECH ENG, US NAVAL POSTGRAD SCH, 70- *Personal Data:* b New York, NY, Feb 25, 32. *Educ:* Univ Calif, Los Angeles, BS, 59, MS, 62, PhD(eng), 68. *Prof Exp:* Sr res engr, Space & Info Div, NAm Aviation, Inc, 62-65; scholar eng mech, Univ Calif, Los Angeles, 68-70. *Mem:* Am Soc Civil Engrs; Am Soc Mech Engrs; Am Acad Mech; Sigma Xi. *Res:* Optimization of structures; micromechanics of composite materials; finite element methods; inelastic behavior of structures; mechanics of composite materials; optimization of structures; finite element analysis of nonlinear field problems. *Mailing Add:* Mech Engr Code ME/SA US Naval Postgrad Sch Monterey CA 93940

SALINAS, FERNANDO A, ONCOLOGY, IMMUNOPATHOLOGY. *Current Pos:* SR ONCOLOGIST, DEPT ADVAN THERAPEUT, CANCER CONTROL AGENCY BC, VANCOUVER, CAN, 76- *Personal Data:* b Santiago, Chile, Oct 30, 39; Can citizen; m 64; c 2. *Educ:* Univ Chile, BSc, 57, DVM, 63. *Prof Exp:* Instr biol, Sch Vet Med, Univ Chile, Santiago, 50-63, asst prof morphol, Sch Med, 63-67, asst prof exp med, 67-70; asst prof med, Sch Med, Univ Southern Calif, Los Angeles, 73-76; assoc prof, 76-83, prof path, Fac Med, Univ BC, 84- *Concurrent Pos:* Mem, biohazards comt, Cancer Control Agency of BC, 85- *Mem:* Int Soc Exp Hemat; Am Asn Cancer Res; Am Asn Immunologists; Am Soc Clin Oncol; Chilean Soc Biol; Int Soc Interferon Res; AAAS. *Res:* Pathogenic and prognostic role of circulating immune complexes in cancer patients; immunoregulatory implications of oncofetal antigens in human cancer; new approaches to cancer treatment by use of biological response modifiers, emphasis in monoclonal antibodies and interferon. *Mailing Add:* 9520 Snowdon Ave Richmond BC V7A 2M1 Can

SALINGAROS, NIKOS ANGELOS, NUCLEAR FUSION, MAGNETOHYDRODYNAMICS. *Current Pos:* from asst prof to assoc prof, 83-95, PROF MATH, UNIV TEX, SAN ANTONIO, 95- *Personal Data:* b Perth, Australia, Jan 1, 52; m 86, Marielle Blum. *Educ:* Univ Miami, BSc, 71; State Univ Stony Brook, MA, 74, PhD(physics), 78. *Prof Exp:* Asst prof physics, Univ Mass, Boston, 79-80, Univ Crete, Greece, 80-81 & math, Univ Iowa, Iowa City, 81-83. *Concurrent Pos:* Vis assoc prof physics, Univ Rochester, 88-89; vis prof, Univ Tex, Arlington, 91-93; vis scientist, Superconducting Super Collider, 91-93. *Mem:* Sr mem Inst Elec & Electronics Engrs; Am Phys Soc; Int Asn Math Physics. *Res:* Developed the Clifford Algebras into a practical tool for field theory; thermonuclear fusion reactors; magnetohydrodynamic dynamos; author of 57 publications; developing a mathematical theory of architecture. *Mailing Add:* Div Math Univ Tex San Antonio TX 78249-0664. *Fax:* 210-458-4439; *E-Mail:* salingar@ringer.utsa.edu

SALINGER, GERHARD LUDWIG, LOW TEMPERATURE PHYSICS. *Current Pos:* PROG DIR, NSF, ARLINGTON, VA, 91- *Personal Data:* b Berlin, Ger, Aug 25, 34; US citizen; m 58; c 3. *Educ:* Yale Univ, BS, 56; Univ Ill, MS, 58, PhD(physics), 62. *Prof Exp:* Asst physics, Univ Ill, 56-61; vis res prof, Univ Sao Paulo, 61-64; instr asst prof to prof physics, Rensselaer Polytech Inst, 64-91, chmn dept, 78-88. *Concurrent Pos:* Vis assoc prof, Iowa State Univ, 74-75. *Mem:* Am Phys Soc; Am Asn Physics Teachers. *Res:* Low temperature thermal properties of amorphous materials. *Mailing Add:* 3174 Cantrell Lane Fairfax VA 22031

SALINGER, RUDOLF MICHAEL, QUALITY ASSURANCE. *Current Pos:* res chemist, Dow Corning Corp, 64-68, group leader, Res Eng Sect, 68-75, sr res group leader, 75-77, sect mgr anal serv, 77-80, corp qual assurance mgr, 80-82, sect mgr metall silicon, 82-85, process res mgr, adv ceramics prog, 85-90, global analytical technol coordr, 90-94, QUAL SYSTS & ISO/QS PROG MGR, DOW CORNING CORP, 94- *Personal Data:* b Berlin, Ger, July 24, 36; US citizen; m 61, Sharon; c 2. *Educ:* Cooper Union, BChE, 58; Univ Wis, MS, 60; Univ Cincinnati, PhD(org chem), 63. *Prof Exp:* Fel, Stanford Univ, 63-64. *Mem:* Am Inst Chem Engr; Am Chem Soc; Sigma Xi; Am Soc Qual Control. *Res:* Organosilicon chemistry. *Mailing Add:* Dow Corning Corp PO Box 0995 Midland MI 48686-0994

SALIS, ANDREW E, ELECTRICAL ENGINEERING. *Current Pos:* chmn Dept Elec Eng, 59-70, PROF ELEC ENG, UNIV TEX, ARLINGTON, 5-, DEAN ENG, 70- *Personal Data:* b Boston, Mass, Oct 10, 15; m 41; c 3. *Educ:* Auburn Univ, BSc, 39, MSc, 40, Prof degree, 48; Tex A&M Univ, PhD(elec eng), 51. *Prof Exp:* From instr to assoc prof elec eng, Tex A&M Univ, 40-51; sr group engr, Gen Dynamics Corp, 51-59. *Concurrent Pos:* Consult, LTV Corp & Gen Dynamics-San Diego Dallas Power & Light Co, 59-71. *Mem:* Inst Elec & Electronics Engrs; Am Soc Eng Educ. *Res:* High frequencies and natural electrical phenomena. *Mailing Add:* 4105 Shady Valley Ct Arlington TX 76013

SALISBURY, DONALD CHARLES, RELATIVITY THEORY, NUMERICAL RELATIVITY. *Current Pos:* asst prof, 87-90, ASSOC PROF PHYSICS, AUSTIN COL, 90- *Personal Data:* b Pulaski, NY, May 6, 46; m 87, Maria Cecilia Sandoval de Arteaga. *Educ:* Oberlin Col, BA, 68; Syracuse Univ, PhD(physics), 77. *Prof Exp:* Postdoctoral researcher, Free Univ Berlin, 80-82; vis asst prof, Reed Col, 83-85; asst prof physics, Hobart & William Smith Col, 85-87. *Concurrent Pos:* Prin investr, NSF, 92-96; assoc ed, Coun Undergrad Res, 95-96, Physics & Astron Coun, 95- *Mem:* Am Phys Soc; Coun Undergrad Res; Int Soc Gen Relativity & Gravitation. *Res:* Development and implementation of connection-based procedures in numerical relativity for fixing and monitoring gravitational waves; coordinate and gauge symmetries in Lagrangian and Hamiltonian dynamical theories. *Mailing Add:* Austin Col Sherman TX 75090. *Fax:* 903-813-2420; *E-Mail:* dsalis@austinc.edu

SALISBURY, FRANK BOYER, PLANT PHYSIOLOGY. *Current Pos:* head, Dept Plant Sci, 66-70, PROF PLANT PHYSIOL, UTAH STATE UNIV, 66-, PROF BOT, 68- *Personal Data:* b Provo, Utah, Aug 3, 26; m 49, 91, Mary B Thorpe; c Frank C, Steven S, Michael J, Cynthia K, Phillip B (deceased), Rebecca L & Blake C. *Educ:* Univ Utah, BS, 51, MA, 52; Calif Inst Technol, PhD(plant physiol, geochem), 55. *Honors & Awards:* Cert Merit, Bot Soc Am, 82. *Prof Exp:* Asst prof bot, Pomona Col, 54-55; asst prof, Colo State Univ, 55-61, prof, 61-66. *Concurrent Pos:* AEC fel, 51-53, McCallum fel, 53-54 & Lady Davis fel, Hebrew Univ, Jerusalem, 83; NSF sr fel, Univ Tubingen, Ger & Univ Innsbruck, Austria, 62-63; plant physiologist, US AEC, 73-74; vis prof, Univ Innsbruck, Austria & Hebrew Univ, Jerusalem, 83; mem aerospace med adv comt, NASA; chmn, Controlled Ecol Life Support Syst Working Group, NASA; ed, Am & Pac Rim Countries, J Plant Physiol, 89- *Mem:* AAAS; Am Soc Plant Physiologists; Ecol Soc Am; Am Inst Biol Sci; Bot Soc Am; Sigma Xi; Am Soc Gravitational & Space Biol. *Res:* Physiology of flowering; space biology; physiological ecology; plant responses to gravity; maximum yield of wheat in controlled environments; growth of wheat plants in microgravity. *Mailing Add:* Dept Plants Soils & Biometeorol Utah State Univ Logan UT 84322-4820. *Fax:* 435-797-3376

SALISBURY, JEFFREY L, CELL BIOLOGY. *Current Pos:* ASSOC PROF BIOCHEM & MOLECULAR BIOL, MAYO CLIN/FOUND, 89- *Personal Data:* b Sept 21, 50; US citizen. *Educ:* Ind State Univ, BS, 73; Rutgers Univ, MS, 75; Ohio State Univ, PhD(bot), 78. *Prof Exp:* Postdoctoral fel, Albert Einstein Col Med, 78-82, asst prof anat, 82-84; asst prof molecular genetics & anat, Case Western Reserve Univ, 84-88, assoc prof, Neurosci Ctr, 88-89. *Mem:* AAAS; Phycol Soc Am; Soc Protozoologists; Am Soc Cell Biol. *Res:* Research of centrin, a calcium-binding phosphoprotein associated with centrosomes and mitotic spindle poles; centrin is involved with processes that affect the dynamic behavior of the cell's major microtubule organizing centers during the cell cycle. *Mailing Add:* Dept Biochem & Molecular Biol Mayo Clin-Found 200 First St SW Rochester MN 55905-0001. *Fax:* 507-284-1767

SALISBURY, JOHN WILLIAM, JR, REMOTE SENSING. *Current Pos:* RES PROF, DEPT EARTH & PLANETARY SCI, JOHNS HOPKINS UNIV, 89- *Personal Data:* b Palm Beach, Fla, Feb 6, 33; m 57, Lynne Trowbridge; c John & Matthew. *Educ:* Amherst Col, BA, 55; Yale Univ, MS, 57, PhD(geol), 59. *Honors & Awards:* Outstanding Contribution to Mil Sci Award, US Air Force, 61; Gunter Loeser Award, Air Force Cambridge Res Labs, 69 & Sci Achievement Award, 74; Meritorious Serv Award, Dept Interior, 90. *Prof Exp:* Res scientist, Air Force Cambridge Res Labs, 59-61, chief, Lunar Planetary Res Br, 61-70 & Spectros Studies Br, 70-76; chief, Geothermal Energy Br, 76-81, div dir, Dept Energy, 80-81; chief, Earth Resources Observation Syst Off, US Geol Surv, 81-83, res geologist, Geophys Br, 83-89. *Concurrent Pos:* Vis prof, Purdue Univ, 61-64; guest lectr, Hayden Planetarium, Am Mus, 64-75. *Mem:* AAAS; Am Geophys Union; fel Geol Soc Am. *Res:* Terrestrial and extraterrestrial geological remote sensing; geology of moon and planets; nature and extent of geothermal resources. *Mailing Add:* Dept Earth & Planetary Sci Johns Hopkins Univ Baltimore MD 21218. *Fax:* 410-516-7933; *E-Mail:* salisburys@worldnet.att.net

SALISBURY, MATTHEW HAROLD, GEOPHYSICS. *Current Pos:* head, Regional Reconnaissance, 88-90, SR RES SCIENTIST, GEOL SURV CAN, 90- *Personal Data:* b Far Rockaway, NY, Mar 17, 43; m 67, Jean McQuarrie; c Cameron & Meredith. *Educ:* Mass Inst Technol, BS, 68; Univ Wash, MS, 71, PhD(geol sci), 74. *Prof Exp:* Technician geophys, Woods Hole Oceanog Inst, 64, res asst, 65; res asst seismol, Dept Geol & Geophys, Mass Inst Technol, 66-67; sr observer satellite geodesy, Smithsonian Astrophys Observ, 68-70; asst prof geophys, State Univ NY, Binghamton, 74-76; asst res geol, Scripps Inst Oceanog, 76-79, assoc chief scientist, Deep Sea Drilling Proj, 79-85; prof geophys, Dalhousie Univ, Halifax, 85-88. *Concurrent Pos:* Asst proj officer, Deep Sea Drilling Proj, NSF, 74-75; vis prof, Ore State Univ, Corvallis, 78; adj prof, Dalhousie Univ, Halifax, 88-; co-chief scientist, Deep Sea Drilling/Ocean Drilling Proj Legs 53,78B,102; assoc ed, J Geophys Res, 92-93. *Mem:* Am Geophys Union. *Res:* Determination of the petrology of the crust through comparison of seismic and logging data with laboratory-determined physical properties of geologic materials at high confining pressures; acoustic properties of ores. *Mailing Add:* 55 Peregrine Crescent Bedford NS B4A 3B9 Can

SALISBURY, NEIL ELLIOT, FLUVIAL GEOMORPHOLOGY, NATURAL RESOURCES. *Current Pos:* PROF GEOG, UNIV OKLA, 79- *Personal Data:* b New Orleans, La, Oct 27, 28; m 80; c 4. *Educ:* Univ Minn, BA, 52, PhD(geog), 57. *Prof Exp:* Prof geog, Univ Iowa, 55-79. *Mem:* Asn Am Geographers; Geol Soc Am; Am Geophys Union; Am Water Resources Asn; Nat Coun Geog Educ. *Res:* Fluvial geomorphology, slope development and mass-wasting processes; natural resources, agricultural land quality and water resources. *Mailing Add:* Geog Univ Okla Main Campus 900 Asp Ave Norman OK 73019-4050

SALISBURY, STANLEY R, NUCLEAR & ATOMIC PHYSICS, ARTIFICIAL INTELLIGENCE. *Current Pos:* res scientist, Lockheed Palo Alto Res Lab, 62-68, from staff scientist to sr staff scientist, 69-81, consult scientist, 81-86, SR SCIENTIST, LOCKHEED PALO ALTO RES LAB, 86- *Personal Data:* b Milwaukee, Wis, Oct 2, 32; m 56; c 6. *Educ:* Marquette Univ, BS, 55; Univ Wis, MS, 56, PhD(nuclear physics), 61. *Prof Exp:* Res fel nuclear physics, Univ Wis, 61-62. *Mem:* Am Phys Soc. *Res:* X-ray phenomenology; Van de Graaff accelerators; neutron induced reactions; neutron cross sections; level parameters; aurora phenomenon; charged particle x-ray and neutron flux measurements from satellites; measurement of x-rays for environmental effects experiments; program management; systems design and fabrication; artificial intelligence; expert systems. *Mailing Add:* Dept 52-10 3251 Hanover St Bldg 203 Palo Alto CA 94304

SALITA, MARK, ROCKET SCIENCE. *Current Pos:* SR SCIENTIST, BALLISTIC MISSILE DIV, TRW, 93- *Personal Data:* m 66, Alice Kanthor; c Karen & Joshua. *Educ:* Rensselaer Polytech Inst, BAe, 65; Pa State Univ, MS, 67; NY Univ, PhD(aerospace eng), 71. *Prof Exp:* Res asst, Pa State Water Tunnel, 65-67; asst proj engr, Pratt & Whitney Aircraft, 72-76; sr scientist, Thiokol Corp, 77-92. *Mem:* Am Inst Aeronaut & Astronaut. *Res:* Analytical models to analyze flow problems in and around solid rocket motors; combustion thermochemistry, propellant ignition and two-phase flow; seal leakage, slag generation, and plume characteristics; droplet dynamics material heating and ablation. *Mailing Add:* 332 W 3275 N Ogden UT 84414. *E-Mail:* mark.salita@trw.com

SALIVAR, CHARLES JOSEPH, ORGANIC CHEMISTRY. *Current Pos:* RETIRED. *Personal Data:* b New York, NY, Feb 15, 23; m 45, 75; c 4. *Educ:* Queens Col, NY, BS, 43. *Prof Exp:* Res chemist, Chas Pfitzer & Co, Inc, 45-55, pharmaceut res supvr, 55-62; dir pharm res & develop, Mallinckrodt Chem Works, St Louis, 62-69, dir opers, 69-73; vpres & tech dir, KV Pharmaceut Co, 73-75; dir develop & qual assurance, Emko Co, 75-76, vpres tech, 76-77, mem bd dirs, 76-78, vpres mfg & tech opers, 78-84. *Concurrent Pos:* Dir opers, Schering-Plough Corp, St Louis, 78-86. *Mem:* Am Pharmaceut Asn; Am Chem Soc. *Res:* Antibiotics; vitamins; medicinals; pharmaceutical dosage forms. *Mailing Add:* 15 Webster Oak Dr St Louis MO 63119-4663

SALK, DARRELL JOHN, MEDICAL GENETICS, MEDICAL CYTOGENETICS. *Current Pos:* CONSULT, BIOTECH MED REG, SEATTLE WA. *Personal Data:* b Ann Arbor, Mich, Mar 30, 47; m 76; c 2. *Educ:* Stanford Univ, BA, 69; Johns Hopkins Univ, MD, 74. *Prof Exp:* Intern pediat, Children's Orthop Hosp Med Ctr, Seattle, Wash, 74-75; resident, Univ Wash, 75-78, fel med genetics, 78-80; asst prof, Univ Wuerzburg, WGer, 80-81; from asst prof to assoc prof path & pediat, Univ Wash, 81-87; dir cytogenetics lab, Children's Orthop Hosp Med Ctr, 83-87; assoc med dir, Neorx Corp, 87-90, vpres med & regulatory affairs, 90-93. *Concurrent Pos:* Co-dir Cytogenetics Lab, Univ Hosp, Seattle, 81-83. *Mem:* Am Soc Human Genetics; AAAS. *Res:* monoclonal antibodies for cancer detection and therapy. *Mailing Add:* Biotech Med/Reg 3011 Webster Pt Rd NE Seattle WA 98105-5339. *Fax:* 206-524-9759

SALK, JONAS EDWARD, medicine, immunology; deceased, see previous edition for last biography

SALK, MARTHA SCHEER, TERRESTRIAL PLANT ECOLOGY. *Current Pos:* RES STAFF, OAK RIDGE NAT LAB, 75- *Personal Data:* b Detroit, Mich, Apr 16, 45; m 67; c 2. *Educ:* Albion Col, BA, 67; Univ Iowa, MS, 69; Univ Louisville, PhD(bot & ecol), 75. *Prof Exp:* Terrestrial ecologist, Gilbert/Commonwealth, Reading, Pa, 74-75. *Mem:* Ecol Soc Am. *Res:* Environmental laws and regulations. *Mailing Add:* Environ Sci Div Bldg 1505 MS 6036 Oak Ridge Nat Lab PO Box 2008 Oak Ridge TN 37831-6036

SALK, SUNG-HO SUCK, PHYSICS, CHEMISTRY. *Current Pos:* PROF PHYSICS, POHANG INST SCI & TECHNOL, S KOREA, 88- *Personal Data:* b Seoul, Korea, Apr 14, 39; m 68; c 2. *Educ:* Midwestern Univ, BS, 66; Univ Houston, MS, 68; Univ Tex, Austin, PhD(physics), 72. *Prof Exp:* Res fel, Univ Tex, 72-74, res assoc chem, 74-77; from asst prof to assoc prof, Univ Mo, 77-87. *Mem:* Am Phys Soc. *Res:* Condensed matter physics related superconductivity, surface physics and semi-conductivity; nucleation; collision theory; atomic and molecular physics. *Mailing Add:* Dept Physics Pohang Inst Sci & Technol PO Box 125 Pohang Kyungbuk 790600 South Korea

SALKIN, DAVID, MEDICINE. *Current Pos:* dir res & educ, 71-75, med dir, 75-77, dir med res, 77-83, MED RES, LA VINA HOSP, 83- *Personal Data:* b Ukraine, Russia, Aug 8, 06; nat US; m 34, Bess Adelman; c Barbara. *Educ:* Univ Toronto, MD, 29. *Prof Exp:* Intern, St Mary's Hosp, Detroit, Mich, 29-30; pathologist, Mich State Sanitarium, 33-34; demonstr med, Sch Med, WVa Univ, 35-38, from instr to asst prof, 38-48; chief med serv, San Fernando Vet Admin Hosp, 48-61, chief of staff, 61-71, hosp dir, 67-71. *Concurrent Pos:* Fel path, H Kiefer Hosp, 33; med dir, Hopemont Sanitarium, 34-41, supt, 41-48; assoc clin prof med, Univ Calif, Los Angeles, 51-61; clin prof, Loma Linda Univ, 60- & Univ Southern Calif, 64-71 (emer). *Mem:* Fel Am Soc Clin Pharmacol & Therapeut; fel Am Thoracic Soc; fel AMA; fel Am Col Chest Physicians; fel Am Col Physicians. *Res:* Pneumoperitoneum; intestinal tuberculosis; pulmonary cavities; physiology of pneumothorax; chemotherapy of tuberculosis; bronchiectasis and bronchitis; coccidiodomycosis; BCG treatment of cancer; various mycobacteria (atypical tuberculosis). *Mailing Add:* 1820 Linda Vista Ave Pasadena CA 91103

SALKIN, IRA FRED, MEDICAL MYCOLOGY. *Current Pos:* res scientist III, NY State Dept Health, 70-77, res scientist IV, 77-84, res scientist V, 84-93, HEALTH PROG DIR II, NY STATE DEPT HEALTH, 93- *Personal Data:* b Chicago, Ill, Dec 21, 41; m 91; c 4. *Educ:* Northwestern Univ, Evanston, BA, 63, MS, 64; Univ Calif, Berkeley, PhD(bot), 69. *Honors & Awards:* Meridian Award Clin Microbiol. *Prof Exp:* Lectr, biol, Univ Calif, Santa Barbara, 69-70. *Concurrent Pos:* Mem adj fac, Dept Biol, Russell Sage Col, 77-88 & Union Col, NY, 78-84, Dept Biomed Sci, Sch Pub Health, State Univ NY, 87- *Mem:* Med Mycol Soc Am; Int Soc Human & Animal Mycol; Mycol Soc Am; Brit Mycol Soc; Sigma Xi; Am Soc Microbiol. *Res:* Development and improvement of diagnostic procedures; taxonomy of zoopathogenic fungi and studies of the physiologic factors associated with pathogenicity in the fungi. *Mailing Add:* Div Labs & Res Empire State Plaza Albany NY 12201

SALKIND, ALVIN J, ELECTROCHEMICAL ENGINEERING, BIOENGINEERING. *Current Pos:* PROF & CHIEF, BIOENG SECT, DEPT SURG, ROBERT WOOD JOHNSON MED SCH, UNIV MED & DENT, 70- *Personal Data:* b New York, NY, June 12, 27; m 65; c 2. *Educ:* Polytech Inst New York, BChE, 49, MChE, 52, DChE, 58. *Honors & Awards:* Spec Award & Plaque, Int Technol Exchange Soc, 92. *Prof Exp:* Engr energy res, US Elec Mfg Co, 52-54; sr scientist energy res, Sonotone Corp, 54-56; res assoc, Polytech Inst NY, 56-58; sr scientist energy conversion, ESB Inc, 58-63, head, Lab Electrochem, 63-68, mgr electromed prod, 68-71, vpres technol, 71-79, pres, 77-79. *Concurrent Pos:* Adj prof chem eng, Polytech Inst New York, 60-70; consult, Dept Space Sci, Univ Mo, 68-70; consult, Hahnemann Med Sch, 69-71, Nat Res Coun & Dept Energy, 79-; vis prof, Case Western Res Univ, 81-82; vis scientist, Yugoslavian Acad Sci, 82; prof chem & biochem eng, Rutgers Univ, 85-; assoc dean & dir, Bur Eng Res, 89- *Mem:* Fel AAAS; fel Am Col Cardiol; Asn Advan Med Instrumentation; Am Inst Chem Engrs; Electrochem Soc. *Res:* Energy storage devices; batteries; electromedical devices. *Mailing Add:* 51 Adams Dr Princeton NJ 08540. *Fax:* 732-445-5313; *E-Mail:* salkind@rci.rutgers.edu

SALKIND, MICHAEL JAY, RESEARCH MANAGEMENT, STRUCTURES & MATERIALS. *Current Pos:* PRES, OHIO AEROSPACE INST, 90- *Personal Data:* b New York, NY, Oct 1, 38; m 59, 90, Carol Gill; c Michael Jr, Elizabeth, Jonathan & Joshua. *Educ:* Rensselaer Polytech Inst, BMetE, 59, PhD(mat eng), 62. *Honors & Awards:* Von Karman Award, TRE Corp, 74. *Prof Exp:* Asst to chief res, US Army Watervliet Arsenal, 62-64; chief, advan metall, United Technol Res Ctr, United Technol Corp, 64-68, chief, structures & mat, Sikorsky Aircraft, 68-75; dir prod develop, syst div, Avco, 75-76; mgr structures, NASA HQ, 76-80; dir aerospace sci, Air Force Off Sci Res, 80-89. *Concurrent Pos:* Lectr eng mat, Trinity Col Conn, 67-68, Univ Md, 81-84 & Johns Hopkins Univ, 85-89; chmn Conn Dept Environ Protection Tech Adv Group, 72-75. *Mem:* Am Soc Mech Engrs; Am Inst Aeronaut & Astronaut; Am Inst Mining, Metall & Petrol Engrs; Am Soc Metals; Am Soc Testing & Mat; Sigma Xi. *Res:* Fatigue in composites; fatigue and fracture behavior of titanium. *Mailing Add:* Ohio Aerospace Inst 22800 Cedar Point Rd Cleveland OH 44142

SALKOFF, LAWRENCE BENJAMIN, NEUROGENETICS, NEUROBIOLOGY. *Current Pos:* ASSOC PROF ANAT-NEUROBIOL & GENETICS, WASH UNIV, ST LOUIS, 84- *Personal Data:* b Brooklyn, NY, Mar 3, 44; m 68, Susan Baumer; c Leah, David & Elizabeth. *Educ:* Univ Calif, Los Angeles, BA, 67; Univ Calif, Berkeley, PhD(genetics), 79. *Honors & Awards:* John Belling Prize, 80. *Prof Exp:* Teaching assoc genetics, Univ Calif, Berkeley, 76-79; fel, Dept Biol, Yale Univ, 79-83. *Concurrent Pos:* Kliengenstein fel, 86-89. *Mem:* Genetics Soc Am; Soc Neurosci; AAAS; Biophys Soc. *Res:* Neurogenetics; identification and characterization of genes that affect the function and development of the nervous system. *Mailing Add:* Dept Anat-Neurobiol Sch Med Wash Univ 660 S Euclid Ave St Louis MO 63110. *Fax:* 314-362-3446; *E-Mail:* salkoffL@thalamus.wustl.edu

SALL, THEODORE, MICROBIOLOGY. *Current Pos:* CONSULT, 92- *Personal Data:* b Paterson, NJ, Feb 22, 27; m 53; c 3. *Educ:* Univ Louisville, AB, 49, MS, 50; Univ Pa, PhD(microbiol), 55. *Prof Exp:* Biochemist, Vet Admin Hosp, Philadelphia, 55-56; microbiologist & res assoc, Sch Med, Univ Pa, 56-61; staff scientist, RCA Space Ctr, 61-64; chief bact, Pepper Lab, Univ Pa Hosp, 64-68; from asst prof to assoc prof microbiol, NY Med Col, 68-72; prof life sci, Ramapo Col, NJ, 72-92. *Concurrent Pos:* Consult, Vet Admin Hosp, Philadelphia; chief microbiol serv, Metrop Hosp, New York, 68-71, dir, 71-72; Ethicon Corp, 76-78; res adv, Biorecovery Technol, Inc, 82-85; Biometallics Inc, 87- *Mem:* AAAS; Am Chem Soc; Am Soc Microbiol; fel NY Acad Sci; dipl Am Acad Microbiol. *Res:* Diagnostic bacteriology; microchemical analysis of bacteria; bacterial morphology; electron microscopy; fermentation chemistry; sterilization techniques. *Mailing Add:* 47 Lakeview Dr Old Tappan NJ 07675

SALLAVANTI, ROBERT ARMANDO, PHYSICAL CHEMISTRY. *Current Pos:* ASSOC PROF CHEM, UNIV SCRANTON, 69- *Personal Data:* b Scranton, Pa, July 24, 42; m 64; c 3. *Educ:* Wilkes Col, BS, 63; Univ Pa, PhD(chem), 66. *Prof Exp:* Advan Res Projs Agency fel, Univ Pa, 66-67; USPHS fel, Yale Univ, 67-69. *Concurrent Pos:* Asst prof, Quinnipiac Col, 68-69. *Mem:* Am Chem Soc; fel Am Inst Chemists; Sigma Xi. *Res:* Molecular orbital theory of organic and biological molecules; intermolecular potentials of the rare gases; transport properties of systems involving critical phenomena. *Mailing Add:* 104 Miles St Dalton PA 18414-9118

SALLEE, G THOMAS, MATHEMATICS. *Current Pos:* From asst prof to assoc prof, 66-75, PROF MATH, UNIV CALIF, DAVIS, 75- *Personal Data:* b Ontario, Ore, Feb 21, 40; m 66; c 4. *Educ:* Calif Inst Technol, BS, 62; Univ Calif, Berkeley, MA, 64; Univ Wash, PhD(math), 66. *Mem:* Math Asn Am; Am Math Soc. *Res:* Geometry, especially geometry of convex sets, sets of constant width and polytopes. *Mailing Add:* Univ Calif Davis CA 95616-8633

SALLEE, VERNEY LEE, RECEPTORS, GLAUCOMA. *Current Pos:* SR SCIENTIST, DEPT PHARMCOL, ALCON LABS, FT WORTH, 84- *Personal Data:* b Amarillo, Tex, June 26, 42; m 64; c 2. *Educ:* Hardin-Simmons Univ, BA, 64; Univ NMex, PhD(med sci, physiol), 70. *Prof Exp:* Fel physiol, Southwestern Med Sch, Univ Tex Health Sci Ctr, 70-72, asst prof, 72-78; asst prof, Tex Col Osteop Med, 78-81, assoc prof physiol, 81-84. *Mem:* Am Physiol Soc; Asn Res Vision & Ophthal; Int Soc Eye Res. *Res:* Glaucoma pharmacology; ocular physiology; aqueous humor dynamics. *Mailing Add:* Dept Glaucoma Res Alcon Labs Inc 6201 South Freeway Ft Worth TX 76134-2099. *Fax:* 817-551-4584

SALLEE, WESLEY WILLIAM, NEUTRON SPECTROSCOPY, GAMMA RAY SPECTROSCOPY. *Current Pos:* NUCLEAR PHYSICIST, DIRECTORATE APPL TECHNOL, TEST & SIMULATION, 83- *Personal Data:* b Perry, Okla, June 5, 51. *Educ:* Okla State Univ, BS, 74; Univ Ark, PhD(nuclear chem), 83. *Mem:* Am Soc Testing & Mat. *Res:* Testing of material to neutron and gamma ray radiation; field strength and spectrum measurements. *Mailing Add:* 1515 Dorothy Circle Las Cruces NM 88001-1625

SALLER, CHARLES FREDERICK, NEUROPHARMACOLOGY, NEUROCHEMISTRY. *Current Pos:* PRES, ANALTICAL BIOL SERV INC, 90- *Personal Data:* b Wheeling, WVa, Jan 8, 50. *Educ:* Georgetown Univ, BS, 71; Univ Pittsburgh, MS, 78, PhD(biol sci & psychobiol), 79. *Prof Exp:* Pharmacol res assoc, Nat Inst Mental Health, 79-81; res pharmacologist, Stuart Pharmaceuts, 82-85, sr res pharmacologist, ICI Pharma, ICI Am Inc, 86-91. *Concurrent Pos:* Pres, Del area chap Neurosci, 89. *Mem:* NY Acad Sci; Sigma Xi; Soc Neurosci; Am Soc Pharmacol & Exp Therapeut; Int Brain Res Orgn. *Res:* Explored the biochemical, physiological and behavioral responses to manipulations of brain monoamine neurotransmitter systems; particular emphasis on the effects of antipsychotic drugs. *Mailing Add:* Analytical Biol Serv Inc 104 Warwick Dr Wilmington DE 19803-2626. *Fax:* 302-654-8046

SALLET, DIRSE WILKIS, mechanical engineering, fluid dynamics; deceased, see previous edition for last biography

SALLEY, JOHN JONES, ORAL PATHOLOGY. *Current Pos:* EMER PROF ORAL PATH, MED COL VA, 91- *Personal Data:* b Richmond, Va, Oct 29, 26; m 50, Jean; c Katharine, John Jr & Martha. *Educ:* Med Col Va, DDS, 51; Univ Rochester, PhD(path), 54. *Hon Degrees:* DSc, Boston Univ, 75. *Honors & Awards:* Award, Int Asn Dent Res, 53; Presidential Award, Am Asn Hosp Dentists, 84. *Prof Exp:* Instr histol, Eastman Dent Hyg, 52-54; instr path diag & therapeut, Med Col Va, 54-55, from asst prof to chmn & prof path, 55-63; assoc vpres, 74-80, vpres res & grad affairs, Va Commonwealth Univ, 80-85; actg pres & vpres, Va Ctr Innovative Technol, 85-87; prof path & dean, Sch Dent, 63-74, emer dean, Univ MD, Baltimore, 87-, consult, 90- *Concurrent Pos:* Consult, Off Chief Med Examr, Commonwealth of Va, 56-90, Vet Admin Hosp, 59, NIH, 62-66 & USPHS, 63-74; mem adv comt regional med prog in Md, 66-74; consult, WHO, 68-; hon prof, Univ Peru Cayetano Heredia, 70; pres, Am Asn Dent Sch, 71-72; dent educ rev comt, Bur Health Manpower Educ, 72-76; sr prog consult, Robert Wood Johnson Found, 79-85; pres, Conf Southern Grad Schs, 83-84; prof oral path, Med Col Va, 87-90. *Mem:* Fel AAAS; Am Dent Asn; Am Acad Oral Path; Int Asn Dent Res; Nat Coun Univ Res Admir; Sigma Xi; hon mem Am Acad Oral Med. *Res:* Dental school administration; experimental carcinogenesis in oral tissues, including predisposing factors to oral cancer; etiological factors in periodontal diseases; hospital dentistry. *Mailing Add:* PO Box 838 Urbanna VA 23175. *E-Mail:* salleyj@aol.com

SALLEY, JOHN JONES, JR, PHARMACEUTICAL CHEMISTRY. *Personal Data:* b Rochester, NY, June 2, 54; m 78; c 2. *Educ:* Randolph-Macon Col, BS, 76; Med Col Va, PhD(med chem), 80. *Prof Exp:* Fel org chem, Univ Ala, 80-81; res scientist, Norwich-Eaton Pharmaceut, Div Procter & Gamble, 81-84; group leader, 84-85, sect head, 85-92. *Mem:* Am Chem Soc. *Res:* New ethical pharmaceutical products, specifically in the area of cardiovascular and anti-inflammatory agents; development of novel organic chemical methodology and techniques. *Mailing Add:* 110 New St Ashland VA 23005

SALLOS, JOSEPH, electronics, for more information see previous edition

SALMASSY, OMAR K, MECHANICAL ENGINEERING. *Current Pos:* RETIRED. *Personal Data:* b McConnelsville, Ohio, Sept 22, 25; m 54; c 3. *Educ:* Purdue Univ, BSME, 49, MSE, 51. *Prof Exp:* Asst dynamic strain anal, Purdue Univ, 49-50; mech engr, Repub Steel Corp, 50-51; prin mech engr, Mat Res, Battelle Mem Inst, 51-56; sr scientist, Avco Corp, 56-58, group leader, 58-59, from chief mat res, Res & Develop Div to sr consult scientist, Res & Advan Develop Div, 59-61 & 64-67; proj officer, Apollo Spacecraft Struct, Off Manned Space Flight, NASA Hq, Washington, DC, 61-64; br chief, Composites Mat Res & Develop, McDonnell Douglas Astronaut Co, 67-73, mat specialist, 73-81, sr scientist composites, 81-94. *Concurrent Pos:* Staff asst vol, mech & aerospace eng, Univ Calif, Los Angeles. *Mem:* Am Soc Mec Engrs. *Res:* High-modulus fiber reinforced composites; carbon/carbon, graphite and ceramic composites; cryogenic insulations; thermal protection systems; re-entry, antiballistic missile interceptor and space vehicle materials technology; ablation, vulnerability and hardening, inelasticity, dust erosion and fracture phenomenology; liquified natural gas insulation system development. *Mailing Add:* 850 Toyopa Ave Pacific Palisades CA 90272. *Fax:* 310-206-4830

SALMINEN, SEPPO OSSIAN, PLANT PHYSIOLOGY. *Current Pos:* RES ASSOC, OHIO AGR RES & DEVELOP CTR, OHIO STATE UNIV, 84- *Personal Data:* b Helsinki, Finland, Feb 5, 39; Can citizen. *Educ:* Univ Calif, Los Angeles, BA, 64; Calif State Univ, Los Angeles, MA, 68; Univ Calif, Riverside, PhD(plant physiol), 73. *Prof Exp:* Fel, Univ Man, 73-77; res assoc, Nat Res Coun, Can, 77-82; lectr, Univ Alta, 82-83. *Mem:* Am Soc Plant Physiologists; Sigma Xi. *Res:* Symbiotic nitrogen fixation; bacteroid metabolism. *Mailing Add:* Hort & Crop Sci Agr Res & Develop Ctr Ohio State Univ Wooster OH 44691

SALMOIRAGHI, GIAN CARLO, physiology, for more information see previous edition

SALMON, CHARLES G(ERALD), STRUCTURAL & ENGINEERING. *Current Pos:* From instr to assoc prof, 56-67, prof, 67-89, EMER PROF CIVIL ENG, UNIV WIS-MADISON, 67- *Personal Data:* b Detroit, Mich, Oct 28, 30; m 53, Elizabeth E Corbett; c Margaret E, David C & Martha A. *Educ:* Univ Mich, BS, 52, MS, 54; Univ Wis, PhD(struct eng), 61. *Honors & Awards:* Delmar L Bloehm Award & Joe W Kelly Award, Am Concrete Inst; Western Elec Award, Am Soc Eng Educ. *Mem:* Fel Am Soc Civil Engrs; Int Asn Bridge & Structural Eng; fel Am Concrete Inst; Am Soc Eng Educ; Nat Soc Prof Engrs; Am Soc Testing & Mat; Am Welding Soc. *Res:* Stability and stresses in edge loaded triangular plates; design methods and behavior of reinforced and prestressed concrete; design methods and behavior of steel structures. *Mailing Add:* 1720 Griffith Ave Las Vegas NV 89104-3639

SALMON, EDWARD DICKINSON, CELL BIOLOGY. *Current Pos:* asst prof zool, 77-89, PROF BIOL, UNIV NC, 89- *Personal Data:* b Montclair, NJ, Mar 1, 44; m 67; c 1. *Educ:* Brown Univ, BS, 67; Univ Pa, PhD(biomed eng), 73. *Prof Exp:* Staff scientist cell motility, Marine Biol Lab, Woods Hole, 73-77. *Concurrent Pos:* Corp mem, Bermuda Biol Sta Res & Marine Biol Lab, Woods Hole. *Mem:* Am Soc Cell Biol; Sigma Xi. *Res:* Molecular mechanisms of cell motility especially the mitotic mechanisms of motility and the physiological effects of deep-sea cold temperatures and high hydrostatic pressures on cellular processes. *Mailing Add:* Dept Biol CB 3280 Univ NC 607 Fordham Chapel Hill NC 27599-3280

SALMON, JAMES HENRY, NEUROSURGERY. *Current Pos:* PVT PRACT NEUROSURG, 77- *Personal Data:* b Centerville, Pa, Feb 25, 32; m 67; c 2. *Educ:* Pa State Univ, BS, 53; Hahnemann Med Col, MD, 57; Am Bd Neurol Surg, dipl, 68. *Prof Exp:* Resident neurosurg, Yale Univ, 61-65, instr neurol surg, Sch Med, 64-65; from instr to assoc prof neurosurg, Sch Med, Univ Cincinnati, 66-72; prof neurosurg & chmn div, Sch Med, Southern Ill Univ, 72-77. *Concurrent Pos:* Knight fel neuropath, Sch Med, Yale Univ, 62-63; NIH fel, Univ London, 65; chief neurosurg, Cincinnati Vet Admin Hosp, 66-72; asst dir neurosurg, Children's Hosp, Cincinnati; attend neurosurgeon, Cincinnati Gen Hosp & Christian R Holmes Hosp, Cincinnati; consult neurosurg, Bur Serv Crippled Children, Hamilton County Neuromuscular Diag Clin & Shriners Burns Inst. *Mem:* Cong Neurol Surg; Asn Acad Surg; Int Soc Pediat Neurosurg; fel Am Col Surg; Am Asn Neurol Surg. *Res:* Hydrocephalus, adult and childhood; cerebral blood flow, cortical function; electron microscopy, cerebral capillaries in traumatic encephalopathy; neonatal meningitis, treatment, ultrastructure of brain. *Mailing Add:* 220 Anderson Dr Erie PA 16509-3205

SALMON, MARLA ELIZABETH, PUBLIC HEALTH SERVICE. *Current Pos:* assoc prof, 86-91, PROF PUB HEALTH NURSING, SCH PUB HEALTH, UNIV NC, CHAPEL HILL, 91-; DIR, DIV NURSING, US DEPT HEALTH & HUMAN SERV, PUB HEALTH SERV, HEALTH RESOURCES & SERVS ADMIN, BUR HEALTH PROF, ROCKVILLE, MD, 91- *Educ:* Univ Portland, BA, 71, BS, 72; Johns Hopkins Univ, DS, 77. *Hon Degrees:* DPS, Univ Portland, 93. *Honors & Awards:* Catherine Dempsey Spec Recognition Award, Am Asn Occup Health Nurses, 92; Achievement Award, Nat Black Nurses Found, 94; Presidential Rank Award, White House, 95. *Prof Exp:* Adj fac & mgt preceptor, Div Health Servs Orgn, Sch Hyg & Pub Health, Johns Hopkins Univ, 77-78; from asst prof to assoc prof, Sch Pub Health, Univ Minn, 78-82, asst dir, Proj Nursing Admin, Sch Pub Health, 78-79, actg dir, 79-80, dir, Pub Health Nursing Prog, 80-85, actg div head, Div Community Pub Health Progs, 83-84, dir, Pub Health Nursing Policy Ctr, Pub Health Nursing Prog, 84-86. *Concurrent Pos:* Dir nursing & assoc dir, Dept Emergency Med, Johns Hopkins Hosp, Md, 75-78; fel, W K Kellogg Found, 84-87, Hubert H Humphrey Inst Pub Affairs, Univ Minn, 85-86; chairperson, Curric Pub Health Nursing, Sch Pub Health, Univ NC, Chapel Hill, fac mem, Exec Inst Community Health Nurses, Sch Nursing & Sch Pub Health, 88-89; chief nurse, Bur Health Prof, 91-, Health Resources & Servs Admin, 92-; fac mem, Primary Care fel prog, USPHS, 91-. *Mem:* Inst Med-Nat Acad Sci; Sigma Xi; fel Am Acad Nursing; hon mem Am Acad Nurse Practr. *Res:* Health services and policy research with a focus on health workforce, including demand, requirements and supply; outcomes of nursing care and educational financing. *Mailing Add:* 1090 Pipestem Pl Rockville MD 20854

SALMON, MICHAEL, ANIMAL BEHAVIOR. *Current Pos:* PROF, BIOL SCI, FLA ATLANTIC UNIV, 90- *Personal Data:* b New York, NY, Apr 8, 38. *Educ:* Earlham Col, BS, 59; Univ Md, MS, 62, PhD(zool), 64. *Prof Exp:* Asst animal behav, Univ Md, 59-64; NIH fel, Univ Hawaii, 64-65; asst prof biol, DePaul Univ, 65-67; from asst prof to assoc prof zool, Univ Ill, Urbana-Champaign, 67-77, prof ecol, Ethology & Evolution, 77-90. *Mem:* AAAS; Animal Behav Soc; Crustacean Soc; Am Soc Zoologists. *Res:* Marine bioacoustics of crustaceans and fishes; sensory mechanisms; orientation and navigation by sea turtle; mating systems and sexual selection within the crustacea. *Mailing Add:* Dept Biol Sci Fla Atlantic Univ 500 NW 20th St Boca Raton FL 33431

SALMON, OLIVER NORTON, PHYSICAL CHEMISTRY. *Current Pos:* RETIRED. *Personal Data:* b Syracuse, NY, Mar 24, 17; m 45; c 4. *Educ:* Cornell Univ, AB, 40, PhD(phys chem), 46. *Prof Exp:* Lab asst animal nutrit, Cornell Univ, 40-41; chemist, Corning Glass Works, NY, 41-43; res asst, Off Sci Res & Develop, Cornell Univ, 43-45, res assoc, Off Res & Inventions, US Dept Navy, 46-47; phys chemist, Knolls Atomic Power Lab, Gen Elec Co, 47-56 & Electronics Lab, 56-60; res specialist, 3M Co, 60-62, supvr, 62-64, mgr mat physics res, 64-72, mgr basic & pioneering res, 72-73, sr res specialist, 73-81, sr res specialist, 3M Indust & Consumer Sector Res Lab, 81-82. *Mem:* Am Chem Soc; Am Ceramic Soc; Int Solar Energy Soc. *Res:* Solar energy; solid state physics and chemistry; chemical thermodynamics; liquid metals; hydrogen isotopes. *Mailing Add:* Rte 7 Bemidji MN 56601

SALMON, PETER ALEXANDER, SURGERY. *Current Pos:* assoc prof, 66-72, PROF SURG, UNIV ALTA, 72- *Personal Data:* b Victoria, BC, Aug 5, 29; US citizen; m 53, Janet N Zeeb; c Steven, David & Peter. *Educ:* Univ Wash, BS, 51, MD, 55; Univ Minn, Minneapolis, MS & PhD(surg), 61; Am Bd Surg, dipl, 64; FACS, 68; FRCS(C), 71. *Prof Exp:* Asst prof surg, Med Sch, Univ Minn, Minneapolis, 62-66. *Concurrent Pos:* Hartford Found grant, Mt Sinai Hosp, Minneapolis, 63-67, dir surg educ & res, 63-66; USPHS res grant, 64-65; Med Res Coun Can grant, Univ Alta, 67-90; dir surg educ & res, Mt Sinai Hosp, Minneapolis, 63-66. *Mem:* AAAS; Soc Res Biol & Med; fel Am Col Surg; fel Royal Col Surg; Soc Univ Surgeons; Assoc Acad Surg. *Res:* Gastrointestinal physiology, secretion, motility; gastrointestinal transplantation, especially intestine, pancreas, liver; surgical treatment of obesity. *Mailing Add:* 606 Montana Way Eugene OR 97405

SALMON, RAYMOND EDWARD, POULTRY NUTRITION. *Current Pos:* RETIRED. *Personal Data:* b Vancouver, BC, Apr 14, 31; m; c 3. *Educ:* Univ BC, BSA, 54, MSA, 57; Univ Sask, PhD, 72. *Prof Exp:* Nutritionist, Buckerfield's Ltd, 58-67; res scientist, Can Agr Res Br, 67-91. *Mem:* Poultry Sci Asn; Worlds Poultry Sci Asn. *Res:* Turkey nutrition research; utilization of fats and oils; rapeseed meal research; author of over 50 science publications. *Mailing Add:* 1458 Ashley Dr Swift Current SK S9H 1N5 Can

SALMON, VINCENT, ACOUSTICS. *Current Pos:* CONSULT PROF, STANFORD UNIV, 77- *Personal Data:* b Kingston, BWI, Jan 21, 12; nat US; wid, Madeline Giuffra; c Margaret S (Goodman) & Jean L (Salmon). *Educ:* Temple Univ, AB, 34, AM, 36; Mass Inst Technol, PhD(physics), 38. *Honors & Awards:* Biennial Award, Acoust Soc Am, 46 & Silver Medal, 84. *Prof Exp:* Physicist, Jensen Radio Mfg Co, 37, physicist in charge res & develop, Jensen Mfg Co, 38-49; mgr, sonics sect, SRI Int, 49-65, mgr, sonic prog, 65-70, staff scientist physics, Sensory Sci Res CTr, 70-76. *Concurrent Pos:* Ed, Audio Eng Soc J, 54-55; consult, acoust, 46-, Nat Acad Sci, 65- & Nat Acad Eng, 73-74; pres, Nat Coun Acoust Consults, 69-71; mem, Inst Noise Control Eng & pres, 74; vpres, Indust Health Inc, 72-77. *Mem:* Fel Acoust Soc Am (pres, 70-71); fel Audio Eng Soc; Inst Noise Control Eng. *Res:* Theory of acoustic radiators; electroacoustics; underwater sound; industrial acoustics; audio engineering; sound recording; noise control; architectural acoustics; nondestructive sonic testing. *Mailing Add:* 765 Hobart St Menlo Park CA 94025

SALMON, WILLIAM COOPER, MECHANICAL ENGINEERING. *Current Pos:* EXEC OFFICER, NAT ACAD ENG, WASHINGTON, 86- *Personal Data:* b New York, NY, Sept 3, 35; m 67, Josephine Stone; c William C, Mary B & Pauline A. *Educ:* Mass Inst Technol, SB, 57, MS, 58, ME, 59 & SM, 69. *Honors & Awards:* Superior Honor Award, US Dept State, 64; Meritorious Serv Award, Pres US, 84; Karl Taylor Compton Award, Mass Inst Technol, 57; Kenneth Rowe Award, Am Asn Eng Soc, 96. *Prof Exp:* Res & teaching asst, Mass Inst Technol, 57-59, Sloan fel, 68; asst sci adv, US Dept State, Washington, 61-74, sr adv sci & technol, 78-86; counr sci & technol, Am Embassy, Paris, 74-78. *Concurrent Pos:* dir, Jr Eng Tech Soc; dir, US Found World Commun Develop. *Mem:* Fel Am Soc Mech Engrs; Nat Soc Prof Engrs; Am Soc Eng Educ. *Res:* Performance of a reciprocating expansion engine. *Mailing Add:* Nat Acad Eng 2101 Constitution Ave NW Washington DC 20418. *E-Mail:* wsalmon@nae.edu

SALMOND, WILLIAM GLOVER, SYNTHETIC ORGANIC CHEMISTRY, STEROID CHEMISTRY. *Current Pos:* sr res scientist chem, 72-77, res mgr, 77-82, dir, chem res & develop, 82-84, vpres, 84-90, VPRES CHEM OPERS, UPJOHN CO, 90- *Personal Data:* b West Wemyss, Scotland, May 29, 41; US citizen; m 68. *Educ:* St Andrews Univ, BSc, 63, PhD(chem), 66. *Prof Exp:* Scientist chem, Sandoz-Wander Inc, 70-72. *Mem:* Am Chem Soc. *Res:* Commercially viable synthesis of complex natural products; application of organometallic chemistry to organic synthesis. *Mailing Add:* 9990 W PQ Ave Mattawan MI 49071

SALMONS, JOHN ROBERT, CIVIL ENGINEERING. *Current Pos:* assoc prof, 65-80, PROF CIVIL ENG, UNIV MO-COLUMBIA, 80- *Personal Data:* b Climax Springs, Mo, Sept 12, 32; m 57; c 2. *Educ:* Univ Mo, BSCE, 60; Univ Ariz, MSCE, 65, PhD(civil eng), 66. *Prof Exp:* Detailer, Bridge Div, Mo State Hwy Dept, 57-59; asst civil eng, Univ Ariz, 61-64. *Concurrent Pos:* Res engr, Prestressed Div, United Mat Inc, Ariz; instr, Off Civil Defense, 63-; Am Soc Eng Educ-Ford Found engr in residency with Wilson Concrete Co, Nebr, 69-70; mem bd dirs & vpres, Wilson Concrete Co, Nebr, 73- *Mem:* Am Soc Civil Engrs; Am Concrete Inst; Prestressed Concrete Inst. *Res:* Evaluation of precast-prestressed composite u-beam bridge slabs; continuity of precast-prestressed bridge members; large panel prefabricated concrete building construction; design of precast-prestressed concrete structures. *Mailing Add:* 3234 S Oak Ave Springfield MO 65804-4750

SALO, WILMAR LAWRENCE, BIOCHEMISTRY. *Current Pos:* asst prof, Univ, 69-74, ASSOC PROF BIOCHEM, SCH MED, UNIV MINN, DULUTH, 74- *Personal Data:* b Nichols Twp, Minn, Aug 22, 37; m 60; c 3. *Educ:* Univ Minn, BS, 59, PhD(biochem), 67; Univ Wis, MS, 62. *Prof Exp:* Staff fel, NIH, 67-69. *Mem:* Am Soc Biol Chemists; AAAS. *Res:* Biochemistry of complex carbohydrates; enzymology. *Mailing Add:* Biochem Univ Minn Duluth Sch Med Ten University Dr Duluth MN 55812-2487

SALOM, SCOTT MICHAEL, FOREST ENTOMOLOGY. *Current Pos:* res assoc, 89-92, res scientist, 92-93, ASST PROF FOREST ENTOM, VA POLYTECH INST & STATE UNIV, 93- *Personal Data:* b Sept 14, 59; m 87, Siti M Hasim. *Educ:* Iowa State Univ, BS, 81; Univ Ark, MS, 85; Univ BC, PhD(forestry), 89. *Prof Exp:* Res assoc, Univ Wis, 89. *Concurrent Pos:* Prin investr, US Forestry Serv, 91-, Va Agr Coun, 92-94 & USDA, 92-95. *Mem:* Soc Am Foresters; Entom Soc Am; AAAS; Sigma Xi. *Res:* Behavior and ecology of forest pests with special emphasis on Saturn pine beetle, pales weevil, and hemlock woolly adelgid. *Mailing Add:* Dept Entom Va Polytech Inst & State Univ 216 Price Hall Entom Div Blacksburg VA 24061-0319. *Fax:* 540-231-9131

SALOMAN, EDWARD BARRY, LASER SPECTROSCOPY, ELECTRONIC COMMERCE IN SCIENTIFIC AND ENGINEERING DATA. *Current Pos:* physicist far ultraviolet physics & photon physics, electron & optical physics div, 72-94, MGR, OFF ELECTRONIC COM IN SCI & ENG DATA, PHYSICS LAB, NAT INST STAND & TECHNOL, 94- *Personal Data:* b New York, NY, May 30, 40; m 68, Ora Frishberg. *Educ:* Columbia Univ, AB, 61, MA, 62, PhD(atomic physics), 65. *Prof Exp:* Res physicist, Columbia Univ, 65-66; asst prof physics, Brown Univ, 66-72. *Concurrent Pos:* Sr tech staff, Nat Initiative for Prod Data Exchange, 93-95; mem, Libr Liaison Comt, Optical Soc Am, 94- *Mem:* AAAS; Am Phys Soc; Optical Soc Am. *Res:* Atomic spectroscopy; radiometry; resonance physics; optical resonance studies of stable and radioactive atoms; relaxation of optically oriented atoms; far ultraviolet physics; effect of external fields on autoionizing states of atoms and molecules, soft x-ray cross section data; atomic physics with synchrotron radiation; relativistic calculations of atomic energy levels and transition probabilities; resonance ionization spectroscopy. *Mailing Add:* B-161 Bldg 225 Nat Inst Stand & Technol Gaithersburg MD 20899. *E-Mail:* ebs@nist.gov

SALOMON, LOTHAR L, BIOCHEMISTRY. *Current Pos:* RETIRED. *Personal Data:* b Buedingen, Ger, Nov 8, 21; nat US; c 3. *Educ:* Columbia Univ, BS, 49, MA, 50, PhD(chem), 52. *Prof Exp:* Asst chem, Columbia Univ, 49-52; instr biochem & nutrit, Univ Tex Med Br, 52-53, from asst prof to assoc prof, 53-64; chief biol div, Dugway Proving Ground, 64-72; dep dir test opers, Deseret Test Ctr, 72-78; dep dir mat test directorate, Dugway Proving Ground, 78-81, sci dir, 81-89. *Concurrent Pos:* Consult isotopically labelled carbohydrates, 58-62. *Mem:* Fel AAAS; assoc AMA; Am Chem Soc; Soc Exp Biol & Med; fel Am Inst Chem; Sigma Xi. *Res:* Biosynthesis and metabolism of ascorbic acid and carbohydrates; membrane transport of carbohydrates; aerobiology; research and development administration. *Mailing Add:* 9710 Grand Oak Dr Austin TX 78750-3803

SALOMON, MARK, PHYSICAL CHEMISTRY. *Current Pos:* CONSULT, 97- *Personal Data:* b Brooklyn, NY, June 2, 35; m 59, Carol L Linden; c 3. *Educ:* Hunter Col, BA, 57; Brooklyn Col, MA, 61; Univ Ottawa, PhD(chem), 64. *Prof Exp:* Chemist, Leesona-Moos Labs, 58-61; NSF res assoc chem, Princeton Univ, 64-65; asst prof, Rutgers Univ, 65-67; chemist, NASA, 67-72; chemist, US Army Aeromed Res Lab, Ft Monmouth, 72-97. *Concurrent Pos:* Res scientist physics, Boston Col, 72-; titular mem comn V8, Int Union Pure & Applied Chem. *Mem:* Electrochem Soc; Int Union Pure & Appl Chem. *Res:* Chemical kinetics; biochemical kinetics; electrochemistry; thermodynamics. *Mailing Add:* 65 Island View Way Sea Bright NJ 07760. *Fax:* 732-544-3665; *E-Mail:* msalomon@monmouth-etdl1.army.mil

SALOMON, ROBERT EPHRIAM, PHYSICAL CHEMISTRY. *Current Pos:* from asst prof to assoc prof phys chem, 61-67, chmn dept chem, 68-74, PROF PHYS CHEM, TEMPLE UNIV, 67- *Personal Data:* b Brooklyn, NY, June 8, 33; m 61, Rosalyn Greenstein; c Alexander & Lawrence. *Educ:* Brooklyn Col, BA, 54; Univ Ore, PhD(phys chem), 60. *Prof Exp:* Lectr chem, Brooklyn Col, 57; Sloan res fel, 60. *Concurrent Pos:* Consult, Frankford Arsenal, Pa, 61, Gen Elec Co, 66 & Nuclear Regulatory Comn, 79- *Mem:* Am Chem Soc; Am Asn Univ Prof; Sigma Xi; Electrochem Soc. *Res:* Spectroscopic and electrical properties of solids; conversion of ocean wave energy and solar heat into electricity using electrochemical hydrogen concentration cells; inorganic superconductors. *Mailing Add:* Dept Phys Chem Temple Univ Philadelphia PA 19122. *Fax:* 215-205-1532

SALOMONSON, VINCENT VICTOR, METEOROLOGY, HYDROLOGY. *Current Pos:* Res hydrologist, Lab Meteorol & Earth Sci, NASA, 68-74; head, Hydrospheric Sci Br, Lab Atmospheric Sci, 74-80, chief, Lab Terrestial Physics, 80-88, dep dir, Space & Earth Sci Directorate, 88-90, DIR, EARTH SCI DIRECTORATE, GODDARD SPACE FLIGHT CTR, NASA, 90- *Personal Data:* b Longmont, Colo, July 19, 37; m 63; c 5. *Educ:* Colo State Univ, BS, 59, PhD(atmospheric sci), 68; Univ Utah, BS, 60; Cornell Univ, MS, 64. *Honors & Awards:* Cert for Outstanding Performance, Goddard Space Flight Ctr, NASA, 74, 75, 76 & 77, NASA, Except Sci Achievement Medals, 76, 83; Distinguished Achievement Award, Inst Elec & Electronics Engrs GeoSci & Remote Sensing Soc, 86; William T Pecora Award, 87. *Concurrent Pos:* Mem, Working Group Remote Sensing Hydrol, US Int Hydrol Decade-Nat Acad Sci, 71-74; US co-chmn, Remote Sensing Subcomt, Int Field Year Great Lakes, 72-74; proj scientist, Landsat 4 & 5, 77-88; sci team leader, Earth Observing Syst (EOS) Modis, 88- *Mem:* Am

Meterol Soc; Am Geophys Union; fel Am Soc Photogrammetry & Remote Sensing (vpres, 89-90, pres elect, 90-91, pres, 91-92); Inst Elec & Electronics Engrs Geosci & Remote Sensing Soc (vpres, 95-96). *Res:* Author of over 110 publications on remote sensing applications and studies in hydrology, atmospheric science and earth resource management. *Mailing Add:* 2812 Spindle Lane Bowie MD 20715. Fax: 301-286-1733; E-Mail: vsalomon@pop900.gsfe.nasa.gov

SALOT, STUART EDWIN, INORGANIC CHEMISTRY. *Current Pos:* PRES, CTL ENVIRON SERV, 75- *Personal Data:* b Los Angeles, Calif, Oct 23, 37; m 68; c 2. *Educ:* Univ Calif, Berkeley, BA, 60; Univ Southern Calif, PhD(chem), 69; Am Bd Indust Hyg, cert, 78. *Prof Exp:* Asst prof chem, San Fernando Valley State Col, 68-69; asst prof, Calif State Polytech Col, 69-72; dir tech serv, Daylin Corp, Los Angeles, 72-75. *Mem:* AAAS; Am Chem Soc; Am Crystallog Asn; Am Bd Indust Hyg; Am Indust Hyg Asn. *Res:* Industrial environment pollution abatement studies; synthetic inorganic chemistry; reactions in non-aqueous solvent systems; non-stoichiometric compounds. *Mailing Add:* 24404 S Vermont Ave No 307 Harbor City CA 90710

SALOTTO, ANTHONY W, CHROMATOGRAPHY. *Current Pos:* assoc prof, 69-77, asst chmn dept, 75-77, PROF CHEM, PACE UNIV, WESTCHESTER CAMPUS, 77-, CHMN, DEPT CHEM, 77- *Personal Data:* b Yonkers, NY, Aug 28, 36; c 3. *Educ:* Mass Inst Technol, BS, 58, MS, 59; NY Univ, PhD(chem), 69. *Prof Exp:* Res engr, Calif Res Corp, 59-61; instr chem, Sacramento City Col, 62-63; asst prof, Dutchess Community Col, 63-66. *Mem:* AAAS; Am Chem Soc. *Res:* Analytical chemistry; environmental chemistry; liquid chromatography. *Mailing Add:* Dept Chem Pace Univ Pleasantville NY 10570-2799. Fax: 914-773-3418; E-Mail: salotto@pace.edu

SALOVEY, PETER, SOCIAL-PERSONALITY PSYCHOLOGY, HEALTH PSYCHOLOGY. *Current Pos:* Asst prof, Yale Univ, 86-90, assoc prof psychol, 90-95, assoc prof epidemiol & pub health, 94-95, DIR GRAD STUDIES, YALE UNIV, 92-, PROF PSYCHOL & EPIDEMIOL & PUB HEALTH, 95- *Personal Data:* b Cambridge, Mass, Feb 21, 58; m 86, Marta E Moret. *Educ:* Stanford Univ, BA & MA, 80; Yale Univ, MS, 83, PhD(psychol), 86. *Honors & Awards:* Presidential Young Investr Award, Nat Sci Found, 90. *Concurrent Pos:* Consult psychologist health psychol, West Haven Vet Admin Med Ctr, 86-92; prin investr, Nat Ctr Health Statist, 88-91, Nat Cancer Inst, 89-, NSF, 90- & AM Cancer Soc, 93-; assoc ed, Psychol Bull, 91-; ed, Rev Gen Psychol, 96- *Mem:* Sigma Xi; Int Soc Res Emotion (treas, 92-96); Soc Exp Social Psychol; Soc Personality & Social Psychol; Am Psychol Soc; fel Am Psychol Asn; Soc Psychol Study Social Issues. *Res:* Psychological significance of human moods and emotions, especially the impact of emotion on cognition, social behavior and health; application of principles derived from social psychology to the promotion of health protective behaviors, especially the role of message framing in cancer and AIDS prevention. *Mailing Add:* Dept Psychol Yale Univ PO Box 208205 New Haven CT 06520. Fax: 203-432-8430; E-Mail: psalove@yalevm.ycc.yale.edu

SALOVEY, RONALD, PHYSICAL CHEMISTRY, POLYMER CHEMISTRY. *Current Pos:* actg chmn chem eng, 87-89, PROF CHEM ENG & MAT SCI, UNIV SOUTHERN CALIF, 75-, CHMN CHEM ENG, 89- *Personal Data:* b New York, July 11, 32; m 54; c 3. *Educ:* Brooklyn Col, BS, 54; Harvard Univ, AM, 58, PhD(phys chem), 59. *Prof Exp:* Res chemist, Interchem Corp, 54-55; mem tech staff, Bell Tel Labs, Inc, 58-70; res supvr, Hooker Res Ctr, Occidental Petrol Corp, Niagara Falls, 70-73, mgr res, 73-75. *Concurrent Pos:* Dir, Los Angeles Rubber Group Inc Found, 75-; adv bd, Polymer Eng & Sci & J Appl Polymer Sci. *Mem:* Am Chem Soc; Am Phys Soc; Soc Plastics Eng; Am Inst Chem Eng. *Res:* Physical chemistry of polymers. *Mailing Add:* Dept Chem Eng HED 311 Univ S Calif Los Angeles CA 90089-1211. Fax: 213-740-8053

SALOWE, SCOTT P, ENZYMOLOGY. *Current Pos:* SR RES BIOCHEMIST, MERCK RES LABS, 90- *Personal Data:* b Glen Ridge, NJ, Mar 3, 60. *Educ:* Haverford Col, BA, 82; Univ Wis-Madison, PhD(biochem), 87. *Prof Exp:* Fel, Chem Dept, Johns Hopkins Univ, 87-90. *Mem:* Am Chem Soc. *Res:* Characterization and mechanistic studies on enzymes of pharmaceutical interest. *Mailing Add:* Merck & Co PO Box 2000 Rahway NJ 07065. Fax: 732-594-6100; E-Mail: scott_salowe@merck.com

SALPETER, EDWIN ERNEST, ASTROPHYSICS. *Current Pos:* res assoc, 49-53, from assoc prof to prof physics & astrophys, 53-72, J G WHITE DISTINGUISHED PROF PHYS SCI, CORNELL UNIV, 72- *Personal Data:* b Vienna, Austria, Dec 3, 24; nat US; m 50, Miriam Mark; c 2. *Educ:* Univ Sydney, MSc, 45; Univ Birmingham, PhD, 48. *Hon Degrees:* DSc, Univ Chicago, 69, Case Western Res Univ, 70, Sydney Univ, 94 & Univ NSW, 96. *Honors & Awards:* Award, Carnegie Inst, 59; Gold Medal, Royal Astronomical Soc, 63; J R Oppenheimer Mem Prize, 74; H N Russell lectr, 74; Bruce Medal, 87; DeVaucouleur Medal, 92; Dirac Medal, 96; Crafoord Prize, Royal Swed Acad Sci, 97. *Prof Exp:* Res fel sci & indust res, Univ Birmingham, 48-49. *Concurrent Pos:* Vis prof, Australian Nat Univ, 53-54; mem, Int Sci Radio Union; mem, US Nat Sci Bd, 78-84. *Mem:* Nat Acad Sci; Akad Leopoldina; Am Philos Soc; Am Astron Soc (vpres, 71-73); Int Astron Union; foreign mem Royal Soc. *Res:* Quantum theory of atoms; quantum electrodynamics; nuclear theory; energy production stars; theoretical astrophysics. *Mailing Add:* 612 Space Sci Bldg Cornell Univ Ithaca NY 14853

SALPETER, MIRIAM MIRL, NEUROBIOLOGY, CYTOLOGY. *Current Pos:* NIH fel biol, Cornell Univ, 57-60, res assoc, 60-64, sr res assoc, 64-66, assoc prof neurobiol, 66-73, chair, 82-88, PROF NEUROBIOL & BEHAV, CORNELL UNIV, 73- *Personal Data:* b Riga, Latvia, Apr 8, 29; US citizen; m 50, Edwin; c Judy & Shelley. *Educ:* Hunter Col, AB, 50; Cornell Univ, AM, 51, PhD(psychobiol), 53. *Concurrent Pos:* NIH career develop award, 62-72. *Mem:* Fel AAAS; Electron Micros Soc Am; Am Soc Cell Biol; Soc Neurosci. *Res:* Cell biology; electron microscopy; regeneration; neurocytology; molecular organization of neuromuscular junctions; neurotropic phenomena. *Mailing Add:* Neurobiol Cornell Univ W 363 Seeley Mudd Ithaca NY 14853-0001

SALSBURY, JASON MELVIN, INDUSTRIAL ORGANIC CHEMISTRY. *Current Pos:* DIR, INDEPENDENT OPPORTUNITIES CTR, GA INST TECH, 82- *Personal Data:* b Richmond, Va, June 12, 20; m 46; c 2. *Educ:* Univ Richmond, BS, 40; Univ Va, MS, 43, PhD(org chem), 45. *Prof Exp:* Asst, Nat Defense Res Comt, Univ Va, 41-44 & Off Sci Res & Develop, 44-45; chemist, Am Cyanamid Co, 46-53, group leader, 54, mgr textile resin res, 54-57, mgr tech dept, Santa Rosa Plant, 57-61, dir fibers res, Fibers Div, Stamford Labs, 61-63, dir res, 63-64, dir res & commercial develop, 64-65, dir res, 65-66, tech dir, 66-67, vpres res & develop, Formica Corp, 67-72, dir, Chem Res Div, 72-81; pres, Saljas Mgt & Consult, Inc, 81- *Concurrent Pos:* Mem, Indust Res Inst. *Mem:* Am Chem Soc. *Res:* Polymer chemistry; synthetic organic chemistry; analysis of organic compounds; B-alkyl aminoalkyl esters of alkozybenzoic acids for local anesthetics; synthetic fibers; textile chemicals; laminates; panels; paper chemistry; polymers; resins; catalysts. *Mailing Add:* 20110 Boca W Dr Suite 258 Boca Raton FL 33434-5246

SALSBURY, ROBERT LAWRENCE, RUMINANT NUTRITION, POULTRY NUTRITION. *Current Pos:* RETIRED. *Personal Data:* b Vancouver, BC, July 4, 16; nat US; m 45. *Educ:* Univ BC, BA & BSA, 42; Mich State Univ, PhD(animal nutrit), 55. *Prof Exp:* Jr chemist, Can Dept Pub Works, 42-45; control chemist, E R Squibb & Sons, 45-46; res assoc, NJ Agr Exp Sta, 46-47; bacteriologist, State Dept Health, Mich, 47-49; biochemist, 49-50; agent bur dairy indust, USDA, 52-54; asst prof agr chem, Mich State Univ, 55-61; from assoc prof to prof animal sci & agr biochem, Univ Del, 61-86. *Mem:* Am Chem Soc; Am Dairy Sci Asn; Am Soc Animal Sci; Am Soc Microbiol; Poultry Sci Asn; Sigma Xi. *Res:* Mineral balance of poultry diets; interactions amoung dietary ingredients; physiological effects of ionophores in poultry. *Mailing Add:* 726 Loveville Rd No 36 Hockessin DE 19707-1521

SALSER, WINSTON ALBERT, MOLECULAR BIOLOGY. *Current Pos:* from asst prof to assoc prof, 68-75, PROF MOLECULAR BIOL, UNIV CALIF, LOS ANGELES, 75- *Personal Data:* b Wichita, Kans, May 5, 39; m 63; c 3. *Educ:* Univ Chicago, BS, 63; Mass Inst Technol, PhD(molecular biol), 66. *Prof Exp:* Helen Hay Whitney fel, Inst Molecular Biol, Geneva, Switz, 65-67 & Inst Biophys & Biochem, Paris, France, 67-68. *Mem:* AAAS. *Res:* Chromosome structure and gene expression in mammalian genomes; insertion of selected mammalian genes into bacterial plasmids; nucleotide sequence analysis of hemoglobin mRNAs and mammalian satellite DNAs. *Mailing Add:* Dept Biol Univ Calif 405 Hilgard Ave Los Angeles CA 90024-1301

SALSIG, WILLIAM WINTER, JR, mechanical engineering; deceased, see previous edition for last biography

SALSTEIN, DAVID A, ATMOSPHERIC DYNAMICS. *Current Pos:* SR STAFF SCIENTIST METEOROL, ATMOSPHERIC & ENVIRON RES, INC, 82-, MGR, GEN CIRCULATION DIAG, 90- *Personal Data:* b New York, NY. *Educ:* Mass Inst Technol, SB, 72, SM, 73, PhD(meteorol), 76. *Prof Exp:* Fel, Nat Ctr Atmospheric Res, 76-77; sr staff scientist meteorol, Environ Res & Technol, Inc, 78-82. *Mem:* Am Meteorol Soc; Am Geophys Union. *Res:* General circulation of the atmosphere. *Mailing Add:* Atmospheric & Environ Res Inc 840 Memorial Dr Cambridge MA 02139

SALSTROM, JOHN STUART, MOLECULAR BIOLOGY, BIOCHEMISTRY. *Current Pos:* MOLECULAR GENETICS, INC. *Personal Data:* b Greensboro, NC, Jan 25, 45; m 67; c 2. *Educ:* Miami Univ, BA, 67; Univ Wis, MS, 70, PhD(molecular biol), 77. *Prof Exp:* Res scientist, Harvard Univ, 77- *Concurrent Pos:* NIH fel, 77- *Res:* Molecular biology of transcriptional controls over gene expression in E-coli and its phages. *Mailing Add:* 1250 W Minnehaha Pkwy Minneapolis MN 55419

SALT, DALE L(AMBOURNE), CHEMICAL ENGINEERING. *Current Pos:* from asst prof to assoc prof, 54-70, PROF CHEM ENG, UNIV UTAH, 70- *Personal Data:* b Salt Lake City, Utah, July 1, 24; m 50; c 3. *Educ:* Univ Utah, BS, 48, MS, 49; Univ Del, PhD(chem eng), 59. *Honors & Awards:* A E Marshall Award, Am Inst Chem Engrs, 48. *Prof Exp:* Chem engr, Utah Oil Refining Co, 49-51; res fel chem eng, Univ Del, 51-54. *Mem:* Am Soc Eng Educ; Am Inst Chem Engrs; Combustion Inst. *Res:* Gaseous combustion; rheology; accelerated particle dynamics; interphase transfer processes. *Mailing Add:* 1571 Logan Ave Salt Lake City UT 84105

SALT, GEORGE WILLIAM, ANIMAL ECOLOGY. *Current Pos:* assoc, Univ Calif, Davis, 49-50, lectr, 50-51, instr, 51-53, from asst prof to prof, 53-90, EMER PROF ZOOL, UNIV CALIF, DAVIS, 90- *Personal Data:* b Spokane, Wash, Oct 9, 19; m 42; c 3. *Educ:* Univ Calif, Los Angeles, BA, 42; Univ Calif, MA, 48, PhD(zool), 51. *Prof Exp:* Asst zool, Univ Calif, Berkeley, 46-49. *Concurrent Pos:* NSF sr fel, 59-60; Rockefeller Found affiliate & vis prof, Univ Valle, Colombia, 71-72; ed, Am Naturalist, 79-84. *Mem:* Brit Ecol Soc; Am Soc Limnol Oceanog; Cooper Ornith Soc; Am Ornith Union; Am Naturalist Soc; Ecol Soc Am. *Res:* Faunal analysis and community structure; feeding in Protozoa; predator-prey interactions. *Mailing Add:* 310 East 12th St Davis CA 95616

SALT, WALTER RAYMOND, histology; deceased, see previous edition for last biography

SALTER, ROBERT BRUCE, ORTHOPEDIC SURGERY. *Current Pos:* emer surgeon-in-chief, 66-76, SR EMER SCIENTIST, RES INST, HOSP SICK CHILDREN, 76-; EMER PROF SURG, UNIV TORONTO, 95- *Personal Data:* b Stratford, Ont, Dec 15, 24; m 48; c 5. *Educ:* Univ Toronto, MD, 47, MS, 60; FRCPS(C), 55; FRACS, 77; FRCS(I), 78. *Honors & Awards:* Medal Surg, Royal Col Physicians & Surg Can, 60; Centennial Medal, Govt Can, 67; Gairdner Int Award Med Sci, 69; hon fel, Royal Col Physicians & Surg Glasgow, 70, Royal Col Surgeons Edinburgh, 73, Col Surgeons SAfrica, 73 & Royal Col Surgeons Eng; Sir Arthur Sims Commonwealth Traveling Prof, 73; Nicolas Andry Award, Asn Bone & Joint Surgeons, 74; Charles Mickle Award, Univ Toronto; Officer of Order of Can, 77. *Prof Exp:* Clin teacher orthop, Univ Toronto, 55-57, from asst prof to prof surg, 62-95; orthop surgeon, Hosp Sick Children, 55-57, chief orthop surg, 57-66; asst prof to prof surg, Univ Toronto, 62-95. *Concurrent Pos:* R S McLaughlin traveling fel, London Hosp, Eng, 54-55; consult, Ont Soc Crippled Children, 55-; mem, Med Res Coun Can, 67-69. *Mem:* Fel Am Col Surg; Am Orthop Asn; Int Soc Orthop Surg & Traumatol; Can Orthop Res Soc; Royal Col Physicians & Surgeons Can (vpres, 70-, pres, 78-80). *Res:* Articular cartilage degeneration; avascular necrosis of epiphyses; epiphyseal injuries, congenital dysplasia and dislocation of the hip; Legg Perthes disease; experimental arthritis. *Mailing Add:* RR3 Schomberg ON L0G 1T0 Can. *Fax:* 416-813-6414

SALTER, ROBERT MUNKHENK, JR, ELEMENTARY PARTICLE PHYSICS, APPLIED PHYSICS. *Current Pos:* phys scientist appl physics, 68-81, CONSULT, RAND CORP, 68-81. *Personal Data:* b Morgantown, WVa, Apr 24, 20; m 77, Darlene Oliva; c Robert M, Wendy L (Reynolds) & Gary (Coddington). *Educ:* Ohio State Univ, BME, 41; Univ Calif, Los Angeles, MA, 58, PhD(nuclear physics), 65. *Honors & Awards:* Space Pioneer Medal, DOD, 85. *Prof Exp:* Res engr metall & adv eng, Gen Motors Res Lab, 41-42; Lt propulsion, US Navy Aeronaut Exp Sta, Philadelphia & Exp Engines Sect, Bur Aeronaut, Washington, DC, 42-46; res engr, Aerophysics Lab, NAm Aviation, Inc, 46-48; dir proj feedback space systs res, Rand Corp, 48-54; dept mgr satellite br, USAF Satellite Prog Develop, Lockheed Missiles & Space Co, 54-58; corp consult, Litton Indust, 65-85. *Concurrent Pos:* Pres & gen mgr, Sigma Corp, 59-60 & Quantatron, 60-62; consult, Lockheed Missiles & Space Co, 59-65 & RCA Labs, 62-65; chmn bd, Telic Corp, 68-71; mem, Nuclear Propulsion Comt, Am Inst Aeronaut & Astronaut, 70-72 & Ad Hoc Comt Early Warning Physics, Adv Res Proj Agency, 72-76; pres, Xerad Inc, 57- & Spectravision Inc, 71- *Mem:* Sigma Xi. *Res:* Experimental and theoretical determination of neutron-neutron forces in nucleus through decay of di-neutron formed from pion absorption in deuteron; application of advanced physics in conceptualization of new devices in optics, electronics and aero-space systems. *Mailing Add:* 3277 Peacock Lane Machipongo VA 23405. *Fax:* 310-394-0936

SALTHE, STANLEY NORMAN, EVOLUTIONARY SYSTEMS. *Current Pos:* RETIRED. *Personal Data:* b Oct 16, 30; US citizen; m 59, Barbara May; c Rebecca & Eric. *Educ:* Columbia Univ, BS, 59, MA, 60, PhD(zool), 63. *Prof Exp:* Am Cancer Soc fel, Brandeis Univ, 63-65; from asst prof to prof biol, Brooklyn Col, 65-91. *Concurrent Pos:* NSF res grants, 66-71; City Univ New York res grants, 71-72 & 72-73. *Mem:* Am Soc Naturalists; Int Soc Systs Sci; Wash Evolutionary Systs Soc; Int Soc Hist, Philos & Social Studies Biol; Gen Evolutionary Group. *Res:* Application of hierarchy theory to evolutionary process; infodynamics and development theory; macroevolution. *Mailing Add:* 228 Laurel Bank Ave Deposit NY 13754

SALTIEL, ALAN ROBERT, BIOCHEMISTRY. *Current Pos:* DIR SIGNAL TRANSDUCTION, PARKE-DAVIS/WARNER-LAMBERT CO, 90- *Personal Data:* b New Brunswick, NJ, Nov 29, 53; m 81; c 3. *Educ:* Duke Univ, AB, 75; Univ NC, PhD(biochem), 80. *Honors & Awards:* John Jacob Abel Award, Am Soc Pharmacol & Exp Therapeut, 90. *Prof Exp:* Res scientist, Burroughs-Wellcome Co, 80-84; asst prof, Rockefeller Univ, 84-90; assoc prof, Univ Mich, 90- *Concurrent Pos:* Irma T Hirschl Scholar, Hirschl/ Caulier Trust, 86. *Mem:* Am Soc Biochem & Molecular Biol; Am Soc Pharmacol & Exp Therapeut; Endocrine Soc; Harvey Soc. *Res:* Investigated the molecular events involved in the initial phase of receptor activation by the hormones insulin, epidermal growth factor and nerve growth factor, to understand the key mechanisms responsible for the regulation of cellular metabolism and growth; molecular characterization of receptors that are coupled to guanyl nucleotide binding G protein; growth factor receptors and protein phosphorylation; hormonal control of carbohydrate and lipid metabolism. *Mailing Add:* Warner-Lambert Parke-Davis Co 2800 Plymouth Rd Ann Arbor MI 48105-2430. *Fax:* 313-996-5668

SALTIEL, JACK, PHOTOCHEMISTRY. *Current Pos:* from asst prof to assoc prof, 65-69, PROF CHEM, FLA STATE UNIV, 75- *Personal Data:* b Salonica, Greece, Feb 14, 38; US citizen; m 65, Terri. *Educ:* Rice Univ, BA, 60; Calif Inst Technol, PhD(chem), 64. *Honors & Awards:* R A Welch Found Lectr, 90. *Prof Exp:* NSF fel, Univ Calif, Berkeley, 63-64. *Concurrent Pos:* Consult, Eli Lilly & Co, 65-67; Alfred P Sloan fel, 71-73. *Mem:* Am Chem Soc; Sigma Xi; Inter-Am Photochem Soc; Am Soc Photobiol; Europ Photochem Asn. *Res:* Photochemistry and photophysics of organic molecules. *Mailing Add:* Dept Chem Fla State Univ Tallahassee FL 32306-3006. *Fax:* 850-644-8281; *E-Mail:* saltiel@chem.fsu.edu

SALTMAN, DAVID J, FIELDS, DIVISION ALGEBRAS. *Current Pos:* assoc prof, 82-87, Joe B & Louis Cook prof math, 87-89, KERR PROF MATH, UNIV TEX, AUSTIN, 89- *Personal Data:* b New York, NY, Mar 23, 51; m 72; c 3. *Educ:* Univ Chicago, BA & MS, 72; Yale Univ, PhD(math), 76. *Prof Exp:* Dickson instr math, Univ Chicago, 76-78; asst prof, Yale Univ, 78-82. *Mem:* Am Math Soc; Asn Women Math. *Res:* Division algebras, fields, Braver group and related areas of algebra and algebraic geometry. *Mailing Add:* Univ Tex Austin TX 78712-1082

SALTMAN, PAUL DAVID, BIOCHEMISTRY, NUTRITION. *Current Pos:* provost, Revelle Col, 67-72, vchancellor acad affairs, 72-80, PROF BIOL, UNIV CALIF, SAN DIEGO, 67- *Personal Data:* b Los Angeles, Calif, Apr 11, 28; m 49, Barbara J Golden; c David R & Joshua F. *Educ:* Calif Inst Technol, BS, 49, PhD(biochem), 53. *Prof Exp:* From instr to prof biochem, Univ Southern Calif, 53-67. *Concurrent Pos:* NIH sr fel, 60-; sr Fulbright scholar, Perth, Australia, 81; Lady Davis prof, Jerusalem, Israel, 87. *Mem:* Am Chem Soc; Am Soc Plant Physiol; Am Soc Biol Chemists; Am Inst Nutrit. *Res:* Biological transport mechanisms; trace metal metabolism; photosynthesis; metabolism of higher plants; plant growth hormones; communication of science through films, television and radio. *Mailing Add:* Dept Biol Univ Calif San Diego La Jolla CA 92093-0322. *Fax:* 619-534-0936; *E-Mail:* psaltman@ucsd.edu

SALTMAN, ROY G, INTEGRITY & SECURITY OF COMPUTERIZED VOTING, USE OF ELECTRONIC DATA INTERCHANGE. *Current Pos:* COMPUT SCIENTIST, COMPUT SYSTS LAB, NAT INST, STAND & TECHNOL, 69- *Personal Data:* b New York, NY, July 15, 32; m 59, 92, Joan Ettinger; c David, Eve & Steven. *Educ:* Rensselaer Polytech Inst, Troy, NY, BEE, 53; Mass Inst Technol, MSEE, 55; Columbia Univ, EE, 62; Am Univ, MPA, 76. *Honors & Awards:* E U Condon Award, Nat Bureau Standards, 78; Bronze Medal, US Dept Com, 81. *Prof Exp:* Res engr, Sperry Gyroscope Co, 55-64; adv syst analyst, IBM Corp, 64-69. *Concurrent Pos:* Intergovt Affairs fel, State Minn/US Civil Serv Comn, 75; exec secy, Comt Automation Opportunities Serv Sector, Fed Coun Sci & Technol, 72-75; com sci fel, US Dept Com/US House Reps, 77-78; dep mem, US Bd on Geog Names, 79-87; John & Mary R Markle Found grant, 86; rep, US Dept Com, 89- *Mem:* Inst Elec & Electronics Engrs; Asn Comput Mach; Archaeol Conservancy; Nature Conservancy. *Res:* Productivity in federal computer use; policy implications of information systems; computer security in election administration; use of electronic data interchange. *Mailing Add:* 5025 Broken Oak Lane Columbia MD 21044. *Fax:* 301-948-1784; *E-Mail:* saltman@enh.nist.gov

SALTMAN, WILLIAM MOSE, RUBBER CHEMISTRY, KINETICS. *Current Pos:* CONSULT, RUBBER & PLASTICS, 82- *Personal Data:* b Perth Amboy, NJ, Nov 19, 17; m 43, Juliet Zion; c 3. *Educ:* Univ Mich, BS(chem eng) & BS(eng math), 38, MS, 39; Univ Chicago, PhD(phys chem), 49. *Prof Exp:* Testing chemist, State Hwy Dept, NJ, 40-42; res assoc, Calif Inst Technol, 45; sr chemist, Shell Chem Co, Colo, 49-54; sr chemist, 55-64, sect head budene & ethylene-propylene rubbers, 64-75, mgr stereo rubbers dept, 75-77, mgr specialty polymers dept, Res Div, 77-80, mgr, Polymer Serv, Goodyear Tire & Rubber Co, 80-82. *Concurrent Pos:* Vis prof, Ohio State Univ, 67. *Mem:* Am Chem Soc. *Res:* Stereospecific catalysts; rubber technology; polymerization; kinetics; polymer physical properties. *Mailing Add:* 12973 Candela Pl San Diego CA 92130-1857

SALTON, GERARD, information retrieval language processing; deceased, see previous edition for last biography

SALTON, MILTON ROBERT JAMES, MICROBIOLOGY. *Current Pos:* PROF MICROBIOL & CHMN DEPT, SCH MED, NY UNIV, 64- *Personal Data:* b NSW, Australia, Apr 29, 21; m 51; c 2. *Educ:* Univ Sydney, BSc, 45; Cambridge Univ, PhD(biochem), 51; ScD, Cambridge Univ, 67. *Hon Degrees:* Dr Med, Univ Liege, 67. *Honors & Awards:* Ciba Lectr, Rutgers Univ, 60. *Prof Exp:* Res officer microbiol, Commonwealth Sci & Indust Res Orgn, Australia, 45-48; res fel biochem, Cambridge Univ, 48-54, Beit Mem res fel, 50-52, demonstr, 57-61; prof, Univ New South Wales, 62-64. *Concurrent Pos:* Merck Int fel, Univ Calif, 52-53; reader, Manchester Univ, 57-61; lectr, Off Naval Res, 60. *Mem:* Am Soc Microbiol; Am Soc Biol Chem; Harvey Soc; Royal Soc Med; Brit Biochem Soc; fel Royal Soc London; hon mem Brit Soc Antimicrobial Chemother. *Res:* Chemistry and biochemistry of microbial cell surfaces. *Mailing Add:* Dept Microbiol NY Univ Sch Med 550 First Ave New York NY 10016-6402. *Fax:* 212-263-8276

SALTONSTALL, CLARENCE WILLIAM, JR, SYNTHETIC MEMBRANE TECHNOLOGY, POLYMER CHEMISTRY. *Current Pos:* CONSULT MEMBRANE TECHNOL, 78- *Personal Data:* b El Centro, Calif, Jan 26, 25; m 46; c 3. *Educ:* Pomona Col, BA, 48; Columbia Univ, PhD(org chem), 57. *Prof Exp:* Res chemist, Photo Prod Dept, E I du Pont de Nemours & Co, Inc, 53-58; res chemist, Chem Div, Aerojet-Gen Corp, 58-62, asst sr chemist, Solid Rocket Res Div, 62-63, sr chemist, 63-64, sr chemist, Chem & Struct Prod Div, 64-67, mgr res & develop, Phys Processes Dept, Environ Systs Div, 67-70, mgr desalination res, Water Purification Systs Oper, Envirogenics Co, 70-75; dir res & develop, Envirogenics Systs Co, 75-78. *Mem:* Am Chem Soc; Sigma Xi; AAAS. *Res:* Synthesis of monomers, polyelectrolytes, cellulose derivatives, elastomers and novel heterocyclic polymers; solid propellants; membranes for water desalination and the mechanism of reverse osmosis; manufacture of membranes and membrane systems. *Mailing Add:* 30031 Running Deer Lane Laguna Niguel CA 92677-2024. *Fax:* 714-495-2857

SALTSBURG, HOWARD MORTIMER, PHYSICAL CHEMISTRY. *Current Pos:* PROF MAT SCI, CHEM ENG & CHEM, UNIV ROCHESTER, 69- *Personal Data:* b New York, NY, Sept 12, 28; m 51; c 2. *Educ:* City Col New York, 50; Boston Univ, MA, 51, PhD(phys chem), 55. *Prof Exp:* Chemist, Geophys Res Directorate Air Force Cambridge Res Labs, 51-54; Henry & Camille Dreyfus Found fel chem, Univ Rochester, 54-55; chemist, Knolls Atomic Power Lab, Gen Elec Co, 55-57, missiles & space vehicles dept, 57-59; res & develop staff mem, Gen Atomic Div, Gen Dynamics Corp, 59-69. *Mem:* Am Phys Soc; Am Chem Soc; Sigma Xi. *Res:* Nucleation; surface thermodynamics; evaporation; adsorption on oxides; electrical conductivity of oxides; molecular beam scattering from surfaces. *Mailing Add:* Dept Chem Eng Gavett Hall Univ Rochester Rochester NY 14627-0166

SALTVEIT, MIKAL ENDRE, STRESS PHYSIOLOGY, POSTHARVEST PHYSIOLOGY. *Current Pos:* asst, 83-89, ASSOC, VEG CROPS DEPT, UNIV CALIF, DAVIS, 89- *Personal Data:* b Minneapolis, Minn, Nov 11, 44; m 78, Pamela A Lehnert; c Mikai & Kyle. *Educ:* Univ Minn, BA, 67, MS, 72; Mich State Univ, PhD(hort & bot), 77. *Honors & Awards:* Outstanding Publ Award, Am Soc Hort Sci, 88, 89. *Prof Exp:* Mgr, Biol Labs Antartica, Antartic Res Prog, Nat Sci Found, 68-69 & 70-71; res botanist, NASA Space Prog, Agr Res Serv, US Dept Agr, 72-73; res asst plant physiol, Dept Hort, Mich State Univ, 73-77, res assoc ethylene physiol, Plant Res Lab, 77-78; asst prof postharvest physiol, Hort Dept, NC State Univ, 78-83. *Concurrent Pos:* Assoc ed, Am J Hort Sci; dir, Louis K Mann Lab, Post Harvest Biol & Technol Prog, Univ Calif. *Mem:* Am Soc Hort Sci; Am Soc Plant Physiol; AAAS; Sigma Xi; Scand Soc Plant Physiol. *Res:* Physiological response of plants to abiotic stresses: chilling injury, physical wounding, altered gaseous atmospheres; postharvest physiology of fruit and vegetable crops (apples, carrots, lettuce, tomatoes). *Mailing Add:* Mann Lab/Veg Crops Dept Univ Calif Davis CA 95616-8631

SALTZ, DANIEL, MATHEMATICS. *Current Pos:* assoc prof, 59-70, PROF MATH, SAN DIEGO STATE UNIV, 70- *Personal Data:* b Chicago, Ill, July 25, 32; div; c 4. *Educ:* Univ Chicago, BA, 52, BS, 53; Northwestern Univ, MS, 55, PhD(math), 58. *Prof Exp:* Instr math, Northwestern Univ, 58-59. *Mem:* Am Math Soc; Am Math Asn. *Res:* Fourier analysis; differential equations; generalized function theory. *Mailing Add:* 5720 Eldergardens St San Diego CA 92120

SALTZ, JOEL HASKIN, COMPILERS, HIGH PERFORMANCE COMPUTING. *Current Pos:* staff scientist, 85-86, LEAD COMPUTER SCIENTIST, INST COMPUTER APPLNS SCI & ENG, LANGLEY RES CTR, NASA, 89- *Personal Data:* b Champaign, Ill, June 4, 56; m 79; c 2. *Educ:* Univ Mich, Ann Arbor, BS & MA, 78; Duke Univ, MD, 86, PhD(computer sci), 86. *Prof Exp:* Scientist ocean acoust modeling, Sci Applns Inc, 78-79; asst prof computer sci, Yale Univ, 86-89. *Concurrent Pos:* Res scientist, Yale Univ, 89-; adj asst prof, William & Mary Col, 90-; ed, Appl Numerical Math, 90- *Mem:* Inst Elec & Electronics Engrs; Asn Comput Mach; AMA. *Res:* Development of tools and compilers capable of mapping sparse, irregular, adaptive and geometrically complex problems onto a variety of multiprocessor architectures; multiprocessor solution methods for sparse matrix problems; adaptive and unstructured mesh page-directory entry problems; molecular dynamics simulations. *Mailing Add:* Dept Comput Sci Yale Univ Box 2158 Yale Sta New Haven CT 06520

SALTZBERG, BURTON R, COMMUNICATION THEORY. *Current Pos:* MEM TECH STAFF, AT&T BELL LABS, 57- *Personal Data:* b New York, New York, June 20, 33; m 59; c 3. *Educ:* NY Univ, BS, 54, ScD(elec eng), 64; Univ Wisconsin, MS, 55. *Mem:* Fel Inst Elec & Electronics Engrs; Sigma Xi. *Res:* Data communications. *Mailing Add:* 91 Southview Terr Middletown NJ 07748-2412

SALTZBERG, THEODORE, electrical engineering, for more information see previous edition

SALTZER, CHARLES, MATHEMATICS. *Current Pos:* PROF MATH, OHIO STATE UNIV, 62- *Personal Data:* b Cleveland, Ohio, Feb 3, 18; m 40; c 1. *Educ:* Western Reserve Univ, BA, 41; Univ Nebr, MA, 42; Brown Univ, MSc, 45, PhD(math), 49. *Prof Exp:* Instr math, Brown Univ, 44-48; from instr to assoc prof, Case Western Reserve Univ, 48-60; prof appl math, Univ Cincinnati, 60-62. *Concurrent Pos:* Fulbright award, 50-51; consult, Electronics Lab, Gen Elec Co, 56-58; Thompson-Ramo-Wooldridge, Inc, 58-61 & Bell Tel, 61-63. *Mem:* Am Math Soc; Math Asn Am; Sigma Xi; Inst Elec & Electronics Engrs. *Res:* Numerical analysis; partial difference equations; conformal mapping; computer theory; network theory; theory of distributions; control and communication theory; automata theory. *Mailing Add:* Dept Math Ohio State Univ 231 W 18th Ave Columbus OH 43210

SALTZER, JEROME H(OWARD), COMPUTER SYSTEMS. *Current Pos:* From instr to assoc prof elec eng, 63-76, PROF COMPUT SCI, MASS INST TECHNOL, 76- *Personal Data:* b Nampa, Idaho, Oct 9, 39; m 61; c 3. *Educ:* Mass Inst Technol, SB, 61, SM, 63, ScD, 66. *Concurrent Pos:* Tech dir, Mass Inst Technol, Proj Athena, 84-89; mem, Comt Comput & Pub Policy, Asn Comput Mach, 85-; mem, Comput Sci & Telecommun Bd, Nat Res Coun, 90-93. *Mem:* Fel AAAS; Asn Comput Mach; fel Inst Elec & Electronics Engrs. *Res:* Design of computer systems; data communication networks; information protection and privacy; impact of computer systems on society; digital library systems. *Mailing Add:* 54 Gammons Rd Waban MA 02168-1216. *E-Mail:* saltzer@mit.edu

SALTZMAN, BARRY, METEOROLOGY, CLIMATE DYNAMICS. *Current Pos:* chmn dept, 88-91, PROF GEOPHYS, YALE UNIV, 68- *Personal Data:* b New York, NY, Feb 26, 31; m 62, Sheila Eisenberg; c Matthew & Jennifer. *Educ:* City Col New York, BS, 52; Mass Inst Technol, SM, 54, PhD(meteorol), 57. *Hon Degrees:* MA, Yale Univ, 68. *Prof Exp:* Res asst meteorol, Mass Inst Technol, 52-57, res staff, 57-61; sr res scientist, Travelers Res Ctr, Inc, 61-66, res fel, 66-68. *Concurrent Pos:* Assoc ed, J Geophys Res, 71-74; chmn, Comt Atmospheric Sci & Biometeorol, Yale Univ, 74-; ed, Advances Geophys, 77- *Mem:* Fel AAAS; fel Am Meteorol Soc; Am Geophys Union; Sigma Xi; hon foreign mem Acad Sci Lisbon; Europ Geophys Soc. *Res:* Geophysical fluid dynamics; theory of climate and the atmospheric general circulation. *Mailing Add:* Dept Geol & Geophys Yale Univ New Haven CT 06511

SALTZMAN, BERNARD EDWIN, INDUSTRIAL HYGIENE, AIR POLLUTION. *Current Pos:* res prof environ health, 67-71, prof, 71-86, EMER PROF ENVIRON HEALTH, KETTERING LAB, COL MED, UNIV CINCINNATI, 86- *Personal Data:* b New York, NY, June 24, 18; m 49, Martha H Schneider; c Phyllis, Gregory & Barbara. *Educ:* City Col New York, BChE, 39; Univ Mich, MS, 40; Univ Cincinnati, PhD(chem eng), 58; Am Bd Indust Hyg, cert. *Honors & Awards:* Wiley Award, Asn Off Anal Chemists, 78; Borden Award, Am Indust Hyg Asn, 89. *Prof Exp:* Chem engr, Joseph E Seagram & Sons, Inc, 40-41; jr pub health engr, USPHS, 41-43, from asst engr to sr asst engr, 43-49, from sanit engr to sr sanit engr, 49-61, sanit engr dir & dep chief, Chem Res & Develop Sect, 61-67. *Concurrent Pos:* Consult, Occup Safety & Health Admin, Nat Inst Occup Safety & Health, Nat Res Coun & WHO. *Mem:* Am Chem Soc; hon mem Am Indust Hyg Asn; Am Conf Govt Indust Hygienists; Air Pollution Control Asn; Asn Off Anal Chem; Am Soc Testing & Mat. *Res:* Air pollution chemistry; administration of research; industrial hygiene. *Mailing Add:* 504 Williamsburg Rd Cincinnati OH 45215-5238. *E-Mail:* saltzmbe@ucbeh.san.uc.edu

SALTZMAN, HERBERT A, MEDICINE. *Current Pos:* asst dir, Hyperbaric Unit & asst prof med, Duke Univ, 63-64, dir, F G Hall Lab Environ Res, 64-77, assoc prof, 65-69, co-dir, EG Hall Lab Environ Res, 77-81, PROF MED, MED CTR, DUKE UNIV, 69- *Personal Data:* b Philadelphia, Pa, Nov 27, 28; m 54, Charlotte Wolf; c 3. *Educ:* Jefferson Med Col, MD, 52; Am Bd Internal Med, dipl, 60; Am Bd Pulmonary Dis, dipl, 71. *Honors & Awards:* Boerema Award. *Prof Exp:* Chief pulmonary dis, Vet Admin Hosp, Durham, NC, 58-63. *Concurrent Pos:* Mem, Comt Underwater Physiol & Med, Nat Res Coun, 72-75. *Mem:* Am Heart Asn; Am Physiol Soc; Am Soc Clin Invest; Undersea Med Soc; Am Thoracic Soc. *Res:* Environmental research; respiratory physiology; pulmanary embolism; hyperbaric and high altitude medicine; physiology. *Mailing Add:* Duke Univ Med Ctr Box 3838 Durham NC 27710

SALTZMAN, MARTIN D, ORGANIC CHEMISTRY. *Current Pos:* asst prof chem, 69-74, assoc prof found sci & spec lectr chem, 74-81, PROF NATURAL SCI & SPEC LECTR CHEM, PROVIDENCE COL, 81- *Personal Data:* b Brooklyn, NY, Mar 20, 41; m 73; c 1. *Educ:* Brooklyn Col, BS, 61, MA, 64; Univ NH, PhD, 68. *Prof Exp:* Res assoc, Brandeis Univ, 68-69. *Res:* History of chemistry. *Mailing Add:* Nat Sci Prog Providence Col Providence RI 02918

SALTZMAN, MAX, COLOR TECHNOLOGY. *Current Pos:* CONSULT COLOR TECHNOL, 93- *Personal Data:* b Brooklyn, NY, Apr 17, 17; m 41, 52, Barbara Fish; c 2. *Educ:* City Col New York, BS, 36. *Honors & Awards:* Bruning Award, Fedn Soc Coatings Technol; Hon Mem, Int Soc Color Coun, 85, MacBeth Award, 86. *Prof Exp:* Inspector, NY Inspection Div, Chem Warfare Serv, 41-46; res chemist, B F Goodrich Chem Co, 46-52; vpres, Phipps Prod Corp, 52-55; develop supvr, Harmon Colors, 55-61, tech asst to vpres, Nat Aniline Div, 61-66, sr scientist, Indust Chem Div, 66-69, mgr color technol specialty, Chem Div, Allied Chem Corp, 69-73; res specialist, Inst Physics & Planetary Physics, Univ Calif, Los Angeles, 73-93. *Concurrent Pos:* Chmn tech comt, Dry Color Mfrs Asn, 66-84; adj prof, Rensselaer Polytech, 66-84. *Mem:* Am Chem Soc; Optical Soc Am; Brit Soc Dyers & Colourists; Fedn Socs Paint Technol; Am Asn Textile Chem & Colorists. *Res:* Color measurement; spectrophotometry; color technology; archaeological chemistry; analytical dyes in ancient textiles. *Mailing Add:* 16428 Sloan Dr Los Angeles CA 90049. *Fax:* 310-442-1172; *E-Mail:* bfish@ucla.edu

SALTZMAN, W MARK, CHEMICAL ENGINEERING. *Current Pos:* Asst prof, 87-92, ASSOC PROF CHEM ENG, JOHNS HOPKINS UNIV, 92- *Personal Data:* b Des Moines, Iowa, Sept 8, 59. *Educ:* Iowa State Univ, BS, 81; Mass Inst Technol, MS, 84, PhD(med eng), 87. *Concurrent Pos:* Camille & Henry Dreyfus teacher scholar award, Dreyfus Found, 90. *Mem:* Am Inst Chem Engrs; Biomed Eng Soc; Controlled Release Soc; Am Chem Soc; Soc Study Reproduction. *Mailing Add:* Sch Chem Eng Cornell Univ 120 Olin Hall Ithaca NY 14853

SALU, YEHUDA, MEDICAL PHYSICS. *Current Pos:* asst prof, 80-82, ASSOC PROF PHYSICS, HOWARD UNIV, 82- *Personal Data:* b Tel-Aviv, Israel, Feb 17, 41; m 64; c 2. *Educ:* Hebrew Univ, MSc, 64; Tel-Aviv Univ, PhD(physics), 73. *Prof Exp:* Asst scientist, Univ Iowa, 73-78, assoc scientist, 78-80. *Concurrent Pos:* Prin investr, NIH, 78- *Res:* Bioelectricity of the human heart, its modeling, measurements and interpretation; models and simulations of nerve networks. *Mailing Add:* 14326 Stilton Circle Silver Spring MD 20905

SALUJA, JAGDISH KUMAR, ROBOTICS, NEW COAL TECHNOLOGIES. *Current Pos:* PRES, VIKING SYSTS INT, PITTSBURGH, PA, 78- *Personal Data:* b Jhelum, Pakistan, Jan 14, 34; US citizen; m 67; c 2. *Educ:* Univ Bombay, India, BSc, 55, Univ Mich, Ann Arbor, BSE, 57, BSE, 58, MSE, 59; Univ Fla, Gainesville, PhD(nuclear eng), 66. *Honors & Awards:* Small Bus Innovation Res Award, Off Energy Res, US Dept Energy, 83, 84-92 & 93. *Prof Exp:* Jr engr, Cornell Dublier, Los Angeles, Calif, 57-58; control engr, Argonne Nat Lab, 59-61; sr nuclear engr, Westinghouse Elec, Pittsburgh, Pa, 67-77. *Mem:* Am Nuclear Soc; AAAS; Soc Mfg Engrs; Am Chem Soc. *Res:* Robot systems for work in hazardous environments; coal conversion and biomass conversion technologies; aging of nuclear plant components; manufacture of electronics calibration equipment; manufacture of helicopter restrainer sets; environmental restoration and waste management; utilization of combustion ash for useful products. *Mailing Add:* 105 Wynnwood Dr Pittsburgh PA 15215. *Fax:* 412-826-3353

SALUJA, PREET PAL SINGH, HAZARDOUS & RADIOACTIVE WASTE, MANAGEMENT & INSTRUMENTATION. *Current Pos:* ADJ PROF CHEM, ROOSEVELT UNIV, 92- *Personal Data:* b Kanpur, India; Can citizen; m 74; c 2. *Educ:* Banaras Hindu Univ, India, BSc Hons, 64, MSc, Hons, 66; Univ Pa, PhD(electrochem), 71. *Prof Exp:* NIH fel, Cornell Univ, 71-73; Robert A Welch fel, Univ Houston, 75-76; sr res assoc, Univ Alta, Can, 76-80; assoc res officer, Nat Res Coun, Can, 80-81; assoc res officer, Whiteshell Nuclear Res Estab, Atomic Energy Can Ltd, 81-82, res officer hazardous & radioactive waste mgt, 83-91; sci educ, Western Mich Univ, 91-92. *Concurrent Pos:* Lectr chem, Banaras Hindu Univ, India, 66, vis fac, 73-75; exec, Chem Inst Can & Can Nat Comn Steam, 87-89. *Mem:* Am Chem Soc; Chem Inst Can. *Res:* Gas phase ion chemistry and important mass-spectrometry applications; in situ chemical kinetic at high pressures; instrumentation and innovation; waste management both hazardous and nuclear; development of a particle mass-spectrometer. *Mailing Add:* 3935 Gregory Dr Northbrook IL 60062-7107

SALUNKHE, DATTAJEERAO K, FOOD TECHNOLOGY. *Current Pos:* prof, 76-80, PROF EMER, NUTRIT & FOOD SCI, UTAH STATE UNIV, 86- *Personal Data:* b Kolhapur, India, Nov 7, 25; m 55; c 2. *Educ:* Univ Poona, BSc, 49; Mich State Univ, MS, 51, PhD(food technol), 53. *Prof Exp:* From asst prof to prof hort 54-67, prof nutrit & food sci, Utah State Univ, 67-75; vchancellor & pres, Marathwada Agr Univ, India, 75-76, Mahatma Phule Agr Univ, India, 80-86. *Mem:* Fel Inst Food Technologists. *Res:* Post-harvest physiology, pathology and microscopy of fruits and vegetables; horticultural processing; radiation effects on horticultural plants and plant products; food toxicology; mycotoxins and naturally occurring toxicants in plant foods; food and nutrition. *Mailing Add:* 384 Lauralin Dr Logan UT 84321

SALUTSKY, MURRELL LEON, water chemistry; deceased, see previous edition for last biography

SALVADOR, RICHARD ANTHONY, PHARMACOLOGY. *Current Pos:* group chief, Hoffmann-La Roche Inc, 70-75, asst dir, Dept Pharmacol, 75-79, dir exp therapeut, 79-83, asst vpres & dir exp therapeut, 83-85, VPRES & DIR PRECLIN DEVELOP, HOFFMANN-LA ROCHE INC, 85- *Personal Data:* b Albany, NY, May 19, 27; m 66; c 2. *Educ:* St Bernadine of Siena Col, BS, 51; Boston Univ, AM, 53; George Washington Univ, PhD(pharmacol), 56. *Prof Exp:* Res instr pharmacol, Sch Med, Wash Univ, 58-60; sr pharmacologist, Wellcome Res Labs, 60-69. *Concurrent Pos:* Nat Inst Neurol Dis & Blindness fel, 57. *Mem:* AAAS; Am Soc Pharmacol & Exp Therapeut; Am Chem Soc; NY Acad Sci; Fedn Am Socs Exp Biol; Sigma Xi. *Res:* Lipid metabolism; autonomic drugs; hypolipemic drugs; feasability of altering collagen metabolism with drugs. *Mailing Add:* Hoffmann-La Roche Inc 340 Kingsland St Nutley NJ 07110-1150. *Fax:* 973-235-6617

SALVADOR, ROMANO LEONARD, MEDICINAL CHEMISTRY. *Current Pos:* RETIRED. *Personal Data:* b Montreal, Que, Dec 12, 28; m 54; c 3. *Educ:* St Mary's Col, AB, 50; Univ Montreal, BSc, 54, MSc, 56; Purdue Univ, PhD(pharmaceut chem), 60. *Prof Exp:* From asst prof to assoc prof, Univ Montreal, 59-70, prof Pharmaceut chem & vdean fac pharm, 70-92. *Mem:* Am Chem Soc; Can Soc Chemother; Chem Inst Can. *Res:* Cholinergic-anticholinergic drugs; cholinesterase regenerators; analgesics; central nervous system drugs; acetylenic drugs. *Mailing Add:* 417 Des Prairies Blvd Laval PQ H7N 2W7 Can

SALVADORI, ANTONIO, computer science, solid state physics, for more information see previous edition

SALVADORI, M(ARIO) G(IORGIO), ENGINEERING, MATHEMATICAL PHYSICS. *Current Pos:* lectr civil eng, Columbia Univ, 40-41, from instr to prof, 41-59, prof, Sch Archit, 59-75, James Renwick prof, 60-68, chmn, Archit Tech Div, 65-73, EMER PROF ARCHIT & JAMES RENWICK EMER PROF CIVIL ENG, COLUMBIA UNIV, 68- *Personal Data:* b Rome, Italy, Mar 19, 07; nat US; m 75, Carol B Bookmen; c Vieri. *Educ:* Univ Rome, DCE, 30, DrMath, 33, Libero Docente, 37. *Hon Degrees:* DrSc, Columbia Univ, 77. *Honors & Awards:* Topaz Medalion, Am Inst Architects, 92. *Prof Exp:* Secy, Civil Eng Div, Nat Ital Res Coun, 34-38; chmn bd, Weidlinger Assocs, 83-90. *Concurrent Pos:* Consult, Calculus Applns Inst, Italy, 34-38; asst prof, Univ Rome, 37-38; fel, Int Inst Cult Rels, 38; lectr, Princeton Univ, 55-60; partner, Paul Weidlinger, Consult Eng, 56-83; hon prof, Univ Minas Gerais; hon chmn bd, Salvador Educ Ctr Built Environ, 65-90; spec lectr, Columbia Univ, 68-90. *Mem:* Nat Acad Eng; hon mem Am Soc Civil Engrs; fel Am Soc Mech Engrs; fel NY Acad Sci; hon mem Am Inst Architects. *Res:* Theory of structures; applied mathematics and mechanics. *Mailing Add:* 2 Beekman Pl New York NY 10022-8058. *Fax:* 212-564-2279

SALVAGGIO, JOHN EDMOND, INTERNAL MEDICINE, IMMUNOLOGY. *Current Pos:* DIR IMMUNOL & CLIN ALLERGY UNIT, CHARITY HOSP, 64-, VCHANCELLOR RES, 88. *Personal Data:* b New Orleans, La, May 19, 33; m 58; c 5. *Educ:* Loyola Univ, BS, 54; La State Univ, MD, 57; Am Bd Internal Med & Am Bd Allergy, dipl. *Prof Exp:* From instr to assoc prof med, La State Univ, 63-72; chmn Dept Med, 83-88, Henderson prof med, Tulane Med Sch, New Orleans, 75-; prof med, Sch Med, LA State Univ, 72- *Concurrent Pos:* NIH res fel immunol & allergy, Dept Med, Mass Gen Hosp & Harvard Med Sch, 61-63; NIH res spec fel, Sch Med, Univ Colo, 72; dir USPHS Training Prog Clin Immunol & Allergy, Tulane Med Sch, 64- *Mem:* AAAS; Am Fedn Clin Res; Am Soc Clin Invest; Am Thoracic Soc; Am Asn Immunol; Asn Am Physicians. *Res:* Immediate and delayed hypersensitivity. *Mailing Add:* Tulane Univ Sch Med 1430 Tulane Box SL-76 New Orleans LA 70112-2699. *Fax:* 504-584-3686

SALVENDY, GAVRIEL, HUMAN-COMPUTER INTERACTION, COMPUTERIZED MANUFACTURING. *Current Pos:* from assoc prof to prof, 71-84, NEC PROF INDUST ENG, PURDUE UNIV, 84-; PRES & CHIEF SCIENTIST, ERGOTECH INC, 85- *Personal Data:* b Budapest, Hungary, Sept 30, 38; m 66, Catherine V Dees; c Laura D & Kevin D. *Educ:* Brunel Univ, UK, dipl, 64; Univ Birmingham, UK, dipl, 65, MSc, 66 & PhD(human factors), 68. *Hon Degrees:* Dr, Chinese Acad Sci, 95. *Honors & Awards:* Mikhail Vasilievich Lomonosov Medal, USSR Acad Sci, 91. *Prof Exp:* Asst prof, State Univ NY, Buffalo, 68-71. *Concurrent Pos:* Fulbright distinguished prof, Tel Aviv Univ, Israel, 79-81; mem, Nat Res Coun, 85-86; founding ed, Int J Human-Comput Interaction, 88- & Int J Human Factors Mfg, 89-; founding chmn, Int Comn Human Aspect Comput, 86-91 & chmn, Int Conf Human-Comput Interaction, 84- *Mem:* Nat Acad Eng; Am Psychol Asn; fel Human Factors Soc; fel Ergonomics Soc; Asn Comput Mach; Am Inst Indust Eng. *Res:* Human aspects in computing; human-computer interactive tasks and cognitive engineering in the design and use of expert systems. *Mailing Add:* Purdue Univ Sch Indust Eng 1287 Grissom Hall West Lafayette IN 47907-1287. *Fax:* 765-494-0874; *E-Mail:* salvendy@ecn.purdue.edu

SALVESEN, ROBERT H, ORGANIC CHEMISTRY, POLYMER CHEMISTRY. *Current Pos:* CONSULT, MGT OILS, SOLVENTS & HAZARDOUS WASTES, 83- *Personal Data:* b Staten Island, NY, Jan 31, 24; m 48, Alice Knutson; c Diane (Bell), Susan & Robert A. *Educ:* Wagner Col, BS, 48; Univ Buffalo, MA, 51; Polytech Inst Brooklyn, PhD(org chem), 58. *Prof Exp:* Proj leader petrol specialties, Tech Serv Labs, Socony Mobil Oil Co, NY, 52-59; res assoc, Esso Agr Chem Lab, Exxon Res & Eng Co, 59-71, Govt Res Lab, 71-79, Prod Res Div, 79-82. *Mem:* Am Chem Soc. *Res:* Research and development of agricultural products; wax emulsions and coatings; specialty petroleum products and refinery by-products; new product development activities in polymers; design of oily waste treatment and disposal equipment; hazardous waste mgt; petroleum technologies. *Mailing Add:* 119 Driftwood Dr Bayville NJ 08721-1954. *Fax:* 732-237-0818

SALVETER, SHARON CAROLINE, INTELLIGENT SYSTEMS, DATABASE SYSTEMS. *Current Pos:* asst prof, 82-85, ASSOC PROF COMPUT SCI, BOSTON UNIV, 85- *Personal Data:* b Pasadena, Calif, June 9, 49; m 84; c 1. *Educ:* Univ Calif, San Diego, BS, 69; Univ Ore, MS, 71; Univ Wis, PhD(comput sci), 78. *Prof Exp:* Instr comput sci, Univ Ore, 71-73; asst prof comput sci, State Univ NY, Stony Brook, 78-82. *Concurrent Pos:* Prin investr, NSF, 79-81 & 83-, co prin investr, 81-83; consult, Bell Labs, 80, co-prin investr, 87-; sabattical fel comput sci, Int Bus Mach, 81. *Mem:* Sigma Xi; Asn Comput Mach; Asn Comput Linguistics; Inst Elec & Electronics Engrs; Cognitive Sci Soc. *Res:* Investigation of computer learning mechanisms; applying artificial intelligence techniques in support of natural language front ends to databases. *Mailing Add:* Boston Univ 5247 S University Ave Chicago IL 60615-4405

SALVI, RICHARD J, PHYSIOLOGICAL PSYCHOLOGY. *Current Pos:* MEM FAC, UNIV TEX, DALLAS, 80- *Personal Data:* b Chisholm, Minn, June 30, 46. *Educ:* NDak State Univ, BS, 68; Syracuse Univ, PhD(psychol), 75. *Prof Exp:* Asst prof otolaryngol, Upstate Med Ctr, State Univ NY, 75-80. *Mem:* AAAS; Acoust Soc Am; Neurosci Asn Res Otolaryngol. *Res:* Auditory physiology; auditory psychophysics. *Mailing Add:* 2 Goldfinch Ct Buffalo NY 14228

SALVIN, SAMUEL BERNARD, IMMUNOLOGY, MYCOLOGY. *Current Pos:* PROF MICROBIOL & IMMUNOL, SCH MED, UNIV PITTSBURGH, 67- *Personal Data:* b Boston, Mass, July 10, 15; c 3. *Educ:* Harvard Univ, AB, 35, EdM, 37, AM, 38, PhD(biol), 41. *Prof Exp:* Asst, Radcliffe Col & Harvard Univ, 37-41; instr, Harvard Univ, 41-43; immunologist & mycologist, Rocky Mountain Lab, Nat Inst Allergy & Infectious Dis, 46-64; head immunol, Res Div, Ciba Pharmaceut Co, 65-67. *Mem:* Bot Soc Am; Am Soc Microbiol; Am Asn Immunol; NY Acad Sci; Am Acad Microbiol. *Res:* Hypersensitivity and cellular immunity; antibody formation; immunological tolerance; autoimmune disease; immunology of pathogenic fungi; immunoregulation; lymphokines. *Mailing Add:* Dept Microbiol Scaife Hall Rm E1240 Univ Pittsburgh Sch Med Pittsburgh PA 15261-0001

SALVINI, GIORGIO, PHYSICS. *Current Pos:* INSTR & RESEARCHER, PHYSICS DEPT, UNIV ROME, 90- *Personal Data:* b Milan, Italy, Apr 24, 20; m 51, Costanza Catenacci; c Paola, Francesco, Stefano, Giovanna & Pietro. *Educ:* Univ Milan, dipl, 42. *Hon Degrees:* Dipl, Univ L'Aquila, 91. *Prof Exp:* Assoc prof, Superior Physics, Milan, 45-48; vis researcher, Univ Princeton, 49; instr, Univ Cagliari, 51-52; proj dir, Univ Pisa, 53-55; fac gen physics, Physics Inst, Rome, 55-65; researcher, Nat Labs, Italy, 66-74, Cent

Europ Nuclear Res, Rome, 75-89. *Concurrent Pos:* Instr physics, Univ La Sapienze, 59-89; pres, Comt Exact & Natural Sci, UNESCO, Rome, 89-; pres, Com Int Security & Arms Control, Rome, 90-; minister, Univ & Sch Res, 95- *Mem:* Europ Comt Future Accelerators (pres, 71-73). *Res:* Contributed articles to professional journals. *Mailing Add:* Via Senafe 19 Rome 00199 Italy

SALVINO, JOSEPH MICHAEL, PHARMACEUTICAL CHEMISTRY, ORGANIC CHEMISTRY. *Current Pos:* SR RES CHEMIST, RHONE POULENC-ROHRER, 95- *Personal Data:* b Philadelphia, Pa, Dec 6, 58; m 88, Susan J Beaty; c John V & Sarah J. *Educ:* Kutztown State Col, BS, 80; Bucknell Univ, MS, 83; Brown Univ, PhD(org chem), 88. *Prof Exp:* Res, Univ Pa, 88-89; from res investr to sr res investr, Sterling Winthrop, 89-94, sr res chemist, 89-95. *Mem:* Am Chem Soc. *Res:* Design of Brady Kinin B2 receptor antagonists; design of enzyme inhibitors, specifically interleuken 1 beta protease and collogenase; inflammation and arthritis. *Mailing Add:* Rhone Poulenc-Rohrer 500 Arcola Rd MS No 8W8 PO Box 1200 Collegeville PA 19426

SALVO, JOSEPH J, MOLECULAR BIOLOGY. *Current Pos:* MOLECULAR BIOLOGIST, BIOL SCI LAB, GEN ELEC CORP RES & DEVELOP CTR, SCHENECTADY, NY, 88- *Personal Data:* b Lawrence, Mass, May 4, 58; m 87. *Educ:* Harvard Univ, BA, 80; Yale Univ, MPhil, 82, PhD(molecular biophys & biochem), 87. *Concurrent Pos:* Adj asst prof, Dept Microbiol & Immunol, Albany Med Col, 89-, State Univ NY, Albany, 90- *Mem:* Am Chem Soc. *Res:* Genetic regulation of secondary metabolism and sporulation in the filamentous fungus Aspergillus parasiticus; elucidating the enzymatic pathways which produce specific para-hydroxylated aromatic compounds; kinship of early human ancestors from pre-Columbian South America and the prevalence of endemic infectious diseases and environmental pollutants; author of several publications. *Mailing Add:* GE Corp Res & Develop PO Box 8 K-1 3C21 Schenectady NY 12301-0008. *E-Mail:* salvo@erdge.com

SALWEN, HAROLD, THEORETICAL PHYSICS, FLUID DYNAMICS. *Current Pos:* asst prof, 59-65, assoc prof, 65-81, PROF PHYSICS, STEVENS INST TECHNOL, 81- *Personal Data:* b New York, NY, Jan 30, 28; m 50; c 6. *Educ:* Mass Inst Technol, SB, 49; Columbia Univ, PhD(physics), 56. *Prof Exp:* Asst physics, Columbia Univ, 50-53; asst, Watson Lab, Int Bus Mach Corp, 53-55; res assoc statist mech, Syracuse Univ, 55-57; res fel solid state physics, Div Eng & Appl Physics, Harvard Univ, 57-59. *Concurrent Pos:* Vis scientist math dept, Imp Col Sci & Technol, London, 80 & Nat Maritime Inst, Teddington, Eng, 82; adj prof oceanog, Old Dominion Univ, 81-; vis prof math, Rensselaer Polytechnic Inst, 82. *Mem:* AAAS; Am Phys Soc; Sigma Xi. *Res:* Magnetic resonance; molecular structure; statistical mechanics of irreversible processes; kinetic theory; solid state theory; hydrodynamics; quantum-mechanical many-body problem. *Mailing Add:* 703 Riverview Ave Teaneck NJ 07666

SALWEN, MARTIN J, CLINICAL PATHOLOGY, LABORATORY ADMINISTRATION. *Current Pos:* DIR PATH, KINGS CO HOSP CTR, 79-; DIR LABS, UNIV HOSP BROOKLYN, 86- *Personal Data:* b Brooklyn, NY, Sept 21, 31; m 79, Jane Stafford; c John P, Julie D, Jonathan M, Jennifer A & Zachary D. *Educ:* City Col NY, BS, 53; State Univ NY, MD, 57. *Prof Exp:* Chief lab, USAF Hosp, Tachikawa, Japan, 64-66; dir path, Monmouth Med Ctr, 67-78. *Concurrent Pos:* Attend path, Yale-New Haven Hosp, 61-67; instr, Yale Univ Sch Med, 61-64, asst prof, 66-67, asst clin prof, 67-71; prof path, Hahnemann Med Col, 71-79; clin prof, State Univ NY Sci Ctr Brooklyn, 79-; counr, Am Soc Clin Pathologists, 88-; distinguished serv prof, State Univ NY, Health Sci Ctr, Brooklyn, 93- *Mem:* Fel Am Soc Clin Pathologists; fel Col Am Pathologists; Am Asn Clin Chem; Am Asn Blood Bank; fel Am Clin Scientists; fel NY Acad Med. *Res:* Laboratory computers; medical informatics. *Mailing Add:* 934 Albemarle Rd Brooklyn NY 11218-2708. *Fax:* 718-270-1683; *E-Mail:* salwen@hscbklyn.edu

SALWIN, ARTHUR ELLIOTT, SOFTWARE ENGINEERING. *Current Pos:* mem tech staff, 81-83, group leader, 83-95, PRIN ENG, MITRE CORP, 96- *Personal Data:* b Chicago, Ill, Feb 18, 48; m 77; c 2. *Educ:* Univ Md, BS, 70; Princeton Univ, PhD(phys chem), 75. *Prof Exp:* Sr analyst comput sci, Xonics Inc, 75-76; sr staff scientist, Appl Physics Lab, Johns Hopkins Univ, 76-78; mem res staff, Riverside Res Inst, 78-80. *Concurrent Pos:* Inst Elec & Electronics Engrs comt on software eng; canvassee Ada 9x, comput rev, Asn Comput Mach; lectr phys chem, Georgetown Univ Grad Sch, 80-82; computer prog instr, Fairfax Co Adult Educ, 82-92, internet instr, 93- *Res:* Systems engineering intelligent vehicle-highway systems; studies in state-of-the-art software engineering and Ada practices; applications of computer technology to scientific problems. *Mailing Add:* 10 Sunnymeade Ct Potomac MD 20854

SALWIN, HAROLD, FOOD TECHNOLOGY, AGRICULTURAL & FOOD CHEMISTRY. *Current Pos:* RETIRED. *Personal Data:* b Kansas City, Mo, Nov 24, 15; m 43, Shirley Minsk; c Arthur E, Barbara C (Finkelstein). *Educ:* Univ Chicago, BS, 41. *Honors & Awards:* Outstanding Employee Award, Dept Army, 60; Rohland A Isker Award, 62. *Prof Exp:* Chemist, Tenn Valley Authority, 42-43, Explosives Res Lab, US Bur Mines, 43-45 & US Customs Lab, 45-48; res chemist, Armed Forces, Qm Food & Container Inst, 48-58, head food biochem lab, 58-61, actg chief chem br, 61; res chemist, Div Food Chem, Food & Drug Admin, 61-64, head decomposition & preservation sect, 64-71, chief protein & cereal prod br, 71-79. *Mem:* Am Chem Soc; Inst Food Technol; fel Asn Official Anal Chemists. *Res:* Food science and technology; chemistry of food deterioration; food dehydration; analytical methods. *Mailing Add:* 14809 Pennfield Circle No 309 Silver Spring MD 20906-1593

SALYERS, ABIGAIL ANN, MOLECULAR BIOLOGY OF ANAEROBES. *Current Pos:* ASSOC PROF MICROBIOL, UNIV ILL, 78- *Educ:* George Washington Univ, PhD(physics), 69. *Res:* Polysaccharide catabolism. *Mailing Add:* Dept Microbiol Univ Ill 407 S Goodwin 131 Burrill Hall Urbana IL 61801

SALZANO, FRANCIS J(OHN), CHEMICAL ENGINEERING, MATERIAL SCIENCE. *Current Pos:* SR CHEM ENGR, BROOKHAVEN NAT LAB, 56- *Personal Data:* b Brooklyn, NY, Mar 23, 33; m 58; c 3. *Educ:* City Univ New York, BChE, 55. *Prof Exp:* Aeronaut res scientist, Lewis Flight Propulsion Lab, Cleveland, 55-57. *Mem:* AAAS. *Res:* Fused salt chemistry; surface adsorption; inorganic carbon chemistry; solid state electrolytes; chemistry of the alkali-metals, especially sodium; atmospheric chemistry; synthetic clean fuels; industrial energy conservation; batteries, fuel cells and advanced materials; strategies for long range research; research/ technology transfer to industry; environment materials management. *Mailing Add:* 144 Avery Ave Patchogue NY 11772

SALZARULO, LEONARD MICHAEL, physics, chemical engineering, for more information see previous edition

SALZBERG, BERNARD, ELECTRONICS. *Current Pos:* CONSULT, 72- *Personal Data:* b New York, NY, July 22, 07; m 41; c Margaret C Jones. *Educ:* Polytech Univ, EE, 29, MEE, 33, DEE, 41. *Honors & Awards:* Mod Pioneer Award, Nat Asn Mfrs, 40; Diamond Award, Inst Radio Engrs, 55; Meritorious Civilian Award, US Navy, 56. *Prof Exp:* Engr res & develop, RCA Commun, Inc, 29-31 & RCA Mfg Co, 31-41; assoc supt, Radio Div, Naval Res Lab, 41-52, assoc supt & consult, Electronics Div, 52-56; chief scientist, AIL Div, Cutler-Hammer, Inc, 56-72. *Mem:* Am Phys Soc; fel Inst Elec & Electronics Engrs. *Res:* Semiconductors; microwaves; electrophysics; electron tubes. *Mailing Add:* 15 Ridge Rock Lane East Norwich NY 11732

SALZBERG, BETTY, DATA BASE. *Current Pos:* From asst prof to assoc prof math, 71-82, assoc prof comput sci, 82-, PROF, NORTHWESTERN UNIV, 90- *Personal Data:* b Denver, Colo, Jan 19, 44; m 78; c 1. *Educ:* Univ Calif, Los Angeles, BA, 64; Univ Mich, MA, 66, PhD(math), 71. *Mem:* Am Math Soc; Asn Comput Mach. *Res:* Finite groups of Lie type; search structures for data bases. *Mailing Add:* Col Comput Sci Northeastern Univ Boston MA 02115

SALZBERG, BRIAN MATTHEW, NEUROBIOLOGY, BIOPHYSICS. *Current Pos:* from asst prof to prof physiol, 75-93, PROF NEUROSCI & PHYSIOL, SCH MED, UNIV PA, 93- *Personal Data:* b New York, NY, Sept 4, 42. *Educ:* Yale Univ, BS, 63; Harvard Univ, AM, 65, PhD(physics), 71, Univ Pa, AM, 80. *Honors & Awards:* Marine Biol Lab Prize, 81; Arturo Rosenblueth Prof, Mex City, 87. *Prof Exp:* Res asst high energy physics, Harvard Univ, 65-71; fel neurobiol, Sch Med, Yale Univ, 71-74, res assoc physiol, 74-75. *Concurrent Pos:* Investr neurobiol, Marine Biol Lab, Woods Hole, 72-, mem coun, 74-, trustee, 80-84, 88-94; mem, Inst Neurol Sci, Univ Pa, 76-; guest fel, Royal Soc, 91; mem coun, Soc Gen Physiologists. *Mem:* Soc Neurosci; fel Am Phys Soc; Soc Gen Physiologists; fel AAAS; fel Japan Soc Prom Sci. *Res:* Development of molecular probes of membrane potential and their application to neurophysiology; optical recording of neuronal activity; excitation-secretion coupling; light scattering. *Mailing Add:* Dept Neurosci Univ Pa 234 Stemmler Hall Philadelphia PA 19104-6074. *Fax:* 215-573-2015; *E-Mail:* bmsalzbe@mail.med.upenn.edu

SALZBERG, DAVID AARON, BIOCHEMISTRY. *Current Pos:* FEL NEUROBIOL, MED SCH, STANFORD UNIV, 69-, PVT CONSULT, 73- *Personal Data:* b Kansas City, Mo, May 5, 20; m 44; c Philip, Judith, Joel & Daniel. *Educ:* Univ Chicago, BS, 40; Univ Calif, MS, 48; Stanford Univ, PhD(biochem), 50. *Prof Exp:* Chemist, Ala Ord Works, 42-43 & US Engr Dist, Hawaii, 43-45; USPHS res asst, Stanford Univ, 49-50; biochemist, Palo Alto Med Res Found, 52-62, head, Basic Cancer Res Div, 58-62; asst res prof biochem, Univ San Francisco, 62-64; dir res, Arequipa Found, 63-67; pres, Tahoe Col, 67-68. *Concurrent Pos:* Am Cancer Soc fel, 50-52 & scholar cancer res, 53-58; mem adv bd, Miramonte Found Ment Health & Great Books Found. *Mem:* Am Asn Cancer Res; Am Chem Soc. *Res:* Diabetes and hormone relationships in cancer; mutagenesis; genetic changes in cancer induction; azo-dye hepatocarcinogenesis; maternal and foster nursing in carcinogenesis; nutritional evaluation of biochemical intermediates; physiology of stress and emotion; brain hormones; nervous system regulation of growth. *Mailing Add:* 815 N Humboldt Ave No 303 San Mateo CA 94401

SALZBERG, HUGH WILLIAM, PHYSICAL CHEMISTRY. *Current Pos:* from instr to assoc prof, 54-70, PROF CHEM, CITY COL NEW YORK, 70- *Personal Data:* b New York, NY, June 27, 21; m 52. *Educ:* City Col New York, BS, 42; NY Univ, MS, 47, PhD(phys chem), 50. *Prof Exp:* Res chemist, US Naval Res Lab, 50-53; res chemist, Columbia Univ, 53-54. *Mem:* AAAS; Am Chem Soc; Electrochem Soc; Sigma Xi. *Res:* Electrodeposition and preparative electrochemistry; kinetics. *Mailing Add:* Dept Chem City Col New York NY 10031

SALZBRENNER, RICHARD JOHN, MECHANICAL PROPERTIES, ALLOY DEVELOPMENT. *Current Pos:* MEM TECH STAFF, WESTERN ELEC, SANDIA NAT LAB, 78- *Personal Data:* b Douglas, Ariz, July 25, 48; m 76. *Educ:* Univ Notre Dame, BS, 70; Univ Denver, PhD(mat sci), 73. *Prof Exp:* Res assoc, Mass Inst Technol, 73-78. *Mem:* Am Soc Metals; Am Inst Metall Engrs. *Res:* Mechanical property measurement; structure-property relationships in ferrous and non-ferrous alloys; low alloy steel development; martensitic transformations; corrosion fatigue; formability; fracture toughness; internal friction. *Mailing Add:* 1400 Caballero Dr SE Albuquerque NM 87123

SALZENSTEIN, MARVIN A(BRAHAM), SAFETY ENGINEERING, MACHINE DESIGN. *Current Pos:* PRES, POLYTECH, INC, 61- *Personal Data:* b Chicago, Ill, May 12, 29; m 58; c 2. *Educ:* Ill Inst Technol, BS, 51. *Prof Exp:* Asst res mech engr, Armour Res Found, Ill Inst Technol, 49-51; sales engr, Sci Instruments, W H Kessel & Co, 53-57; assoc engr, Walter C McCrone Assocs, Inc, 57-61. *Concurrent Pos:* Res engr, White Sands Proving Grounds. *Mem:* Am Soc Mech Engrs; Am Soc Safety Engrs; Am Gas Asn; Nat Fire Protection Asn; Am Nat Standards Inst. *Res:* Industrial zoning; combustion; safety. *Mailing Add:* 3740 W Morse Ave Chicago IL 60645

SALZER, JOHN M(ICHAEL), ELECTRICAL ENGINEERING, SEMICONDUCTOR EQUIPMENT & PROCESSES. *Current Pos:* PRES, SALZER TECHNOL ENTERPRISES, INC, 77- *Personal Data:* b Vienna, Austria, Sept 12, 17; nat US; m 44, Eva R Arvay; c Arleen J, Ronald E, Myra L & Gary P. *Educ:* Case Inst Technol, BS, 47, MS, 48; Mass Inst Technol, ScD(elec eng), 51. *Prof Exp:* Instr elec eng, Case Inst Technol, 47-48; res assoc, Digital Comput Lab, Mass Inst Technol, 48-51; mem tech staff, Res & Develop Labs, Hughes Aircraft Co, 51-54; dir systs, Res Labs, Magnavox Co, 54-59; dir intellectronics labs, Thompson Ramo Wooldridge, Inc, 59-63; vpres tech & planning, Librascope Group, Gen Precision, Inc, 63-68; pres, Salzer Technol Enterprises, 68-72; prin, Darling & Alsobrook, 72-75; sr vpres, Darling, Paterson & Saltzer, 75-77. *Concurrent Pos:* Lectr, Univ Calif, Los Angeles, 52-62. *Mem:* Int Soc Hybrid Microelectronics; Semiconductor Equip & Mat Inst; Sigma Xi; fel Inst Elec & Electronics Engrs; fel Inst Advan Eng. *Res:* Digital computers and control systems; sampled data systems; information systems; electronic components. *Mailing Add:* Salzer Technol Enterprises 909 Berkeley St Santa Monica CA 90403-2307

SALZMAN, EDWIN WILLIAM, SURGERY. *Current Pos:* SURGEON & ASSOC DIR SURG SERV, BETH ISRAEL HOSP, BOSTON, 66-; SR RES ASSOC, MASS INST TECHNOL, 67- *Personal Data:* b St Louis, Mo, Dec 11, 28; m 54; c 3. *Educ:* Wash Univ, AB, 50, MD, 53; Harvard Univ, MA, 69. *Prof Exp:* Asst in surg, Mass Gen Hosp, 61-65, asst surgeon, 65-66; instr, Harvard Med Sch, 61-65, assoc prof, 69-71, prof surg, 72- *Concurrent Pos:* NIH fel, Radcliffe Infirmary, Oxford Univ, 59; Am Cancer Soc clin fel, Mass Gen Hosp, Boston, 60-61, Med Found, Inc fel, 62-65; Markle scholar acad med, 68; assoc, Univ Seminar Biomat, Columbia Univ, 67-, chmn, 68; consult, Am Nat Res Cross, 68- & thrombosis adv comt, NIH, 70-; mem steering comt, Harvard Univ-Mass Inst Technol Prog Health Sci & Technol, 70-; dep ed, New Eng J Med. *Mem:* Am Physiol Soc; Soc Univ Surg; Soc Vascular Surg; Am Surg Asn; Am Soc Clin Invest. *Res:* Hemostasis and thrombosis; biochemistry of blood platelets; surgical physiology. *Mailing Add:* Dept Surg Harvard Med Sch Beth Israel Hosp 330 Brookline Ave Boston MA 02215-5491

SALZMAN, GARY CLYDE, CLINICAL LABORATORY DATA ANALYSIS. *Current Pos:* mem staff & presidential intern fel physics, Los Alamos Nat Lab, 72-73, staff mem, Biophys & Instrumentation Group, 73-86, biophys sect leader, Biochem Biophys Group, 87-91, STAFF MEM, LIFE SCI DIV, LOS ALAMOS NAT LAB, 91- *Personal Data:* b Palo Alto, Calif, May 25, 42; m 65, Joan C Hoyer; c Sonja & Eric. *Educ:* Univ Calif, Berkeley, AB, 63, Univ Ore, MS, 68, PhD(nuclear physics), 72. *Prof Exp:* Peace Corps teacher physics & math, Ghana, 65-67. *Concurrent Pos:* Adj assoc prof path, Univ NMex Med Sch, 86- *Mem:* AAAS; Int Soc Anal Cytol; Inst Elec & Electronics Engrs; Comput Soc. *Res:* Light scattering from biological cells, automated cytology, instrumentation and techniques for cell identification and cancer diagnosis; cluster analysis for immunophenotyping in the clinical laboratory. *Mailing Add:* 108 Sierra Vista Dr Los Alamos NM 87544. *Fax:* 505-665-3024; *E-Mail:* gary_salzman@lanl.gov

SALZMAN, GEORGE, THEORETICAL PHYSICS. *Current Pos:* PROF PHYSICS, UNIV MASS, BOSTON, 65- *Personal Data:* b Newark, NJ, Sept 8, 25; m 48; c 2. *Educ:* Brooklyn Col, BS, 49; Univ Ill, PhD(physics), 53. *Prof Exp:* Instr physics, Univ Ill, 53-55; res assoc, Univ Rochester, 55-56, asst prof, 55-58; from asst prof to assoc prof, Univ Colo, 58-65. *Concurrent Pos:* Ford Found fel, Theory Group, Europ Orgn Nuclear Res, Switz, 58-59; Fulbright res scholar, Frascati Nat Lab, Italy, 61-62; NSF res grant, 62-; vis assoc prof, Northeastern Univ, 64-65, vis fac mem, Oglala Lakota Col, SDak, 94-95. *Res:* Development of a science for humane survival; theory of elementary particles; high energy scattering theory; electromagnetic structure of nucleons; theory of relativity. *Mailing Add:* Dept Physics Univ Mass Boston MA 02125. *Fax:* 617-287-6053; *E-Mail:* salzman@umbsky.cc.umb.edu

SALZMAN, LEON, PSYCHIATRY. *Current Pos:* PROF CLIN PSYCHIAT, MED SCH, GEORGETOWN UNIV, 75- *Personal Data:* b New York, NY, July 10, 15; m 50; c 4. *Educ:* City Col New York, BS, 35; Royal Col Physicians & Surgeons, MD, 40. *Prof Exp:* Prof clin psychiat, Med Sch, Georgetown Univ, 45-67; prof psychiat, Med Sch, Tulane Univ, La, 67-69; clin prof psychiat, Albert Einstein Col Med, 69-75. *Concurrent Pos:* Dep dir, Bronx State Hosp, 70-75; pvt pract psychiat & psychoanal, 75-. *Mem:* Am Acad Psychoanal (pres); Am Psychiat Asn; Am Psychoanal Asn. *Res:* Sex behavior; obsessive and compulsive states. *Mailing Add:* 1800 R St NW Washington DC 20009-1625

SALZMAN, LOIS ANN, VIROLOGY, MOLECULAR BIOLOGY. *Current Pos:* Res chemist, 68-84, spec asst to sci dir, Nat Inst Allergy & Infectious Dis, 84-85, DEP DIR INTRAMURAL RES, NAT INST DENT RES, NIH, 85- *Personal Data:* b Philadelphia, Pa, Oct 19, 39; m 59, Richard S; c John & Andrew. *Educ:* Univ Pa, BA, 58; Columbia Univ, MA, 59; Georgetown Univ, PhD(microbiol), 66. *Concurrent Pos:* Reviewer sci jour. *Mem:* AAAS; Am Soc Microbiol; NY Acad Sci; Fedn Am Soc Exp Biol; Am Soc Virol. *Res:* Replication of viruses in infected cells; primarily replication of nucleic acids and proteins; study of viral enzymes required for virus replication. *Mailing Add:* NIDR NIH Bldg 31 Rm 2C34 Bethesda MD 20892-0001

SALZMAN, NORMAN POST, VIROLOGY. *Current Pos:* mem, Virol Study Sect, 71-73, BIOCHEMIST, NAT INST ALLERGY & INFECTIOUS DIS, 55-, CHIEF LAB BIOL VIRUSES, 68- *Personal Data:* b New York, NY, Aug 14, 26; m 54; c 3. *Educ:* City Col New York, BS, 48; Univ Mich, MS, 49; Univ Ill, PhD(biochem), 53. *Prof Exp:* Res asst, Squibb Inst Med Res, 49-50; biochemist, Nat Heart Inst, 53-55. *Concurrent Pos:* Ed, J Virol, 67-75; vis prof, Univ Geneva, 73-74; prof lectr, Georgetown Univ. *Mem:* Am Soc Cell Biol; Am Soc Biol Chem; Am Asn Immunol; Am Soc Microbiol. *Res:* Virus replication; viral oncology. *Mailing Add:* Lab Retrovirol SAIC NCI Frederick Cancer R&D Ctr Bldg 550 Frederick MD 21702-1201. *Fax:* 202-687-1319

SALZMAN, STEVEN KERRY, PHARMACOLOGY, NEUROPHYSIOLOGY. *Current Pos:* RES ANALYST, ECRI, 95- *Personal Data:* b New York, NY, Feb 19, 52; m 74; c 2. *Educ:* Univ Fla, BS, 74; Univ Conn, PhD(neuropharmacol), 79. *Prof Exp:* Assoc prof, Thomas Jefferson Univ; assoc scientist & dir med sci, Alfred I Du Pont Inst. *Mem:* Soc Neurosci; Neurotrauma Soc; Am Soc Pharmacol Exp Therapeut. *Res:* Characterization, detection and prevention of acute responses to spinal trauma and ischemia; control of surgical stress. *Mailing Add:* 15 Ridgeway Sq Wilmington DE 19810

SALZMAN, WILLIAM RONALD, THEORETICAL PHYSICAL CHEMISTRY. *Current Pos:* from asst prof to assoc prof, 67-79, from actg head dept to head dept, 77-83, PROF CHEM, UNIV ARIZ, 79- *Personal Data:* b Cutbank, Mont, Feb 27, 36; m, Virginia A Harbin; c Suzanne R (Barnes) & Sandra R (Kavanangh). *Educ:* Univ Calif, Los Angeles, BS, 59, MS, 64, PhD(chem), 67. *Prof Exp:* Res metallurgist, Southern Res Inst, Ala, 61-62. *Concurrent Pos:* Am Chem Soc-Petrol Res Fund grant, Univ Ariz, 68-70. *Mem:* AAAS; Am Phys Soc; Sigma Xi; Am Asn Univ Professors; Am Chem Soc. *Res:* Application of quantum theory to problems of chemical interest; semiclassical and quantum radiation theory; theory of circular dichroism; circular dichroism in molecular rotational spectroscopy. *Mailing Add:* Dept Chem Univ Ariz Tucson AZ 85721. *Fax:* 520-621-8407; *E-Mail:* salzman@ccit.arizona.edu

SAM, JOSEPH, PHARMACEUTICAL CHEMISTRY. *Current Pos:* from assoc prof to prof, 59-86, chmn dept, 63-69, DEAN GRAD SCH & DIR UNIV RES, UNIV MISS, 68-, ASSOC VCHANCELLOR RES, 81-, EMER PROF PHARMACEUT CHEM, 86- *Personal Data:* b Gary, Ind, Aug 15, 23; m 45; c 3. *Educ:* Univ SC, BS, 48; Univ Kans, PhD(pharmaceut chem), 51. *Honors & Awards:* Found Res Award Pharmaceut & Med Chem, Am Pharmaceut Asn, 68. *Prof Exp:* Instr org chem, Univ SC, 47-48; asst pharmaceut chem, Univ Kans, 48-49; sr res chemist, McNeil Labs, Inc, 51-54; Bristol Labs, 55-57 & E I du Pont de Nemours & Co, 57-59. *Concurrent Pos:* Fulbright lectr, Cairo Univ, 65-66; mem, Pharm Rev Comt, Bur Health Manpower Educ, Dept Health, Educ & Welfare, 67-71; mem exec comt, Coun Res Policy & Grad Educ, Nat Asn State Univs & Land Grant Cols, 69-71 & 74-76. *Mem:* Am Chem Soc; Am Pharmaceut Asn; fel Acad Pharmaceut Sci; Am Asn Cols Pharm. *Res:* Medicinal chemistry. *Mailing Add:* PO Box 351 University MS 38677

SAMAAN, NAGUIB A, endocrinology; deceased, see previous edition for last biography

SAMAGH, BAKHSHISH SINGH, VETERINARY MEDICINE, SEROLOGY & IMMUNOLOGY. *Current Pos:* vet scientist, 75-78, HEAD DIAG SEROL, ANIMAL DIS RES INST, AGR CAN, 78- *Personal Data:* b Abohar, India, Oct 1, 38; Can citizen; m 66; c 2. *Educ:* Panjab Univ, BVSc & AH, 60, MSc, 63; Univ Guelph, MSc, 68, PhD(serol), 72, DVM, 75. *Prof Exp:* Dist vet, Panjab Govt, India, 60-61; lectr microbiol, various univs, India, 63-66; fel, Univ Guelph, 66-75. *Mem:* Can Soc Immunol; Can Vet Med Asn; Am Asn Vet Lab Diagnosticians; Am Asn Vet Immunologists. *Res:* Research and development on immune response and sero-diagnosis of bacterial, viral and protozoan diseases of animals. *Mailing Add:* 3 Arbuckle Crescent Nepean ON K2G 5G9 Can

SAMANEN, JAMES MARTIN, PEPTIDE CHEMISTRY, SYNTHETIC ORGANIC CHEMISTRY. *Current Pos:* RES CHEMIST, BIOPRODS DEPT, BECKMAN INSTRUMENTS INC, 77- *Personal Data:* b Detroit, Mich, June 17, 47. *Educ:* Kalamazoo Col, BA, 69; Univ Mich, PhD(org chem), 75. *Prof Exp:* Res assoc, Mass Inst Technol, 75-77. *Mem:* Am Chem Soc. *Res:* Synthesis and chemistry of peptides, alkaloids, heterocycles, natural products. *Mailing Add:* Smith Kline & French L412 PO Box 1539 King of Prussia PA 19406-0939

SAMARA, GEORGE ALBERT, PHYSICS, CHEMICAL ENGINEERING. *Current Pos:* staff mem phys res, Sandia Labs, 62-63, div supvr, High Pressure Physics Div, 67-71, dept mgr physics solids res, 71-89, dept mgr, Condensed Matter & Device Physics, 79-83, dept mgr condensed matter & surface sci res, 83-89, dept mgr condensed matter res, 89-93, DEPT MGR, NANO STRUCT & ADVAN MAT CHAM, SANDIA NAT LABS, 93- *Personal Data:* b Lebanon, Dec 5, 36; US citizen. *Educ:* Univ Okla, BS, 58; Univ Ill, Urbana, MS, 60, PhD(chem eng, physics), 62. *Honors & Awards:* Ipatieff Prize, Nat Acad Eng, 74. *Concurrent Pos:* US Army Signal Corps, 63-65. *Mem:* Nat Acad Eng; Am Phys Soc; Mat Res Soc; Am Inst Chem Engrs; AAAS. *Res:* Effects of high pressure and temperature on the physical properties of solids especially ferroelectric, ferromagnetic and semiconductor properties. *Mailing Add:* Dept 1103-MS-1421 Sandia Nat Labs Box 5800 Albuquerque NM 87185

SAMBORSKI, JAN, MICROWAVE AMPLITUDE MODULATED LINK, CATV DISTRIBUTION NETWORK. *Current Pos:* MICROWAVE TRANSMISSION SYSTS ENGR, AML WIRELESS SYSTS, 92- *Personal Data:* m, Malgorzata Samborska Witoslawska; c Michael & Aleksandra. *Educ:* Univ Wroclaw, Poland, MSEE, 75, PhD(elec eng), 80. *Prof Exp:* TV engr, Ministry Info, 91-92. *Mem:* Inst Elec & Electronics Engrs. *Res:* Microwave amplitude modulated link; equipment design and test engineering. *Mailing Add:* AML Wireless Systs Inc 260 Saulteaux Crescent Winnipeg MB R3J 3T2 Can

SAMBROTTO, RAYMOND NICHOLAS, PLANKTON PRODUCTION, MARINE CARBON & NITROGEN CYCLING. *Current Pos:* assoc res scientist, Lamont-Doherty Earth Observ, 85-96, RES SCIENTIST, COLUMBIA UNIV, 96- *Personal Data:* b Buffalo, NY, May 19, 51; m 71, Beverly Walker; c Colby & Lia. *Educ:* State Univ NY, Buffalo, BA, 73, MS, 75; Univ Alaska, Fairbanks, PhD(oceanog), 83. *Prof Exp:* Assoc, Univ Alaska, Fairbanks, 83-84. *Concurrent Pos:* Asst prog mgr, NSF, 86-88; adj fac, Fairleigh-Dickinson Univ, 90-93, Univ Conn, 92-, Barnard Col, 96. *Mem:* Am Soc Limnol & Oceanog; Sigma Xi; Am Geophys Union. *Res:* Measure plankton growth in the ocean for an analysis of its role in the cycling of substances through the biosphere, particularly for climaticly significant substances such as carbon dioxide. *Mailing Add:* Lamont-Doherty Earth Observ Palisades NY 10964. *Fax:* 914-365-8150; *E-Mail:* sambrott@ldeo. columbia.edu

SAMEJIMA, FUMIKO, MATHEMATICAL PSYCHOLOGY & STATISTICS, PSYCHOMETRICS. *Current Pos:* PROF PSYCHOL, UNIV TENN, KNOXVILLE, 73- *Personal Data:* b Tokyo, Japan, Dec 25, 30. *Educ:* Keio Univ, Tokyo, BA, 53, MA, 56, PhD(psychol), 65. *Prof Exp:* Res psychologist, Educ Testing Serv, 66-67; res fel, Psychometric Labs, Univ NC, 67-68; asst prof psychol, Univ NB, Can, 68-70; assoc prof, Bowling Green State Univ, 70-73. *Concurrent Pos:* Nat Res Coun Can grant, 69-70; Off Naval Res grant, 77-; consult ed, Appl Psychol Measurement, 75-; assoc ed, Educ Statist, 78-81; bd trustees, Psychometric Soc, 90. *Mem:* Sigma Xi; Psychometric Soc; Am Statist Soc; Am Educ Res Asn; Am Asn Univ Professors. *Res:* Mathematical statistics and psychometrics; mathematical model buildings in many applied areas. *Mailing Add:* 7910 High Health Knoxville TN 37919

SAMELSON, HANS, MATHEMATICS. *Current Pos:* PROF MATH, STANFORD UNIV, 60- *Personal Data:* b Strassburg, Ger, Mar 3, 16; nat US; m 40, 56; c 3. *Educ:* Swiss Fed Inst Technol, DSc(math), 40. *Prof Exp:* Mem, Inst Advan Study, 41-42, 52-54 & 60-61; instr math, Univ Wyo, 42-43; asst prof, Syracuse Univ, 43-46; from asst prof to prof, Univ Mich, 46-60. *Mem:* Am Math Soc; Math Asn Am. *Res:* Topology of group manifolds; differential geometry. *Mailing Add:* 841 Esplanada Way Stanford CA 94305

SAMELSON, LAWRENCE ELLIOT, BIOCHEMISTRY, MOLECULAR IMMUNOLOGY. *Current Pos:* fel, Lab Immunol, Nat Inst Allergy & Infectious Dis, NIH, 80-83, expert, 83-85, sr staff fel immunol, Cell Biol & Metab Br, Nat Inst Child Health & Develop, 85-88, sr investr, 88-94, DEPT CHIEF, CELL BIOL & METAB BR, NAT INST CHILD HEALTH & HUMAN DEVELOP, NIH, 94-, CHIEF, SECT LYMPHOCYTE SIGNALING, 94- *Personal Data:* b Chicago, Ill, Apr 18, 51; m 80; c 2. *Educ:* Univ Rochester, BA, 72; Yale Univ, MD, 77. *Prof Exp:* Resident med, Univ Chicago Hosp & Clins, 77-80. *Mem:* Am Soc Clin Invest; Am Asn Immunologists. *Res:* How the t-cell receptor is coupled to intracellular signaling and identification of the components of these biochemical pathways. *Mailing Add:* Cell Biol & Metab Br Nat Inst Child Health & Human Develop Bldg 18T Rm 101 Bethesda MD 20892. *E-Mail:* samelson@helix.nih.gov

SAMES, RICHARD WILLIAM, BACTERIOLOGY. *Current Pos:* dean natural sci, 72-75, asst vpres acad affairs, 75-78, actg vpres acad affairs, 78-79, PROF BIOL, SANGAMON STATE UNIV, 79- *Personal Data:* b Louisville, Ky, Apr 13, 28; m 55; c 5. *Educ:* Ind Univ, AB, 51, MA, 54, PhD, 56. *Prof Exp:* Assoc prof biol & chmn dept, Bellarmine Col, Ky, 56-66, prof biol & dir sci develop, 66-68; dean col, Benedictine Col, 68-72. *Concurrent Pos:* Dir, Instructional Sci Equip Prog, NSF, 65-66, consult, 66-, consult, Col Sci Improv Prog, 71-74; consult, Developing Insts Prog, US Off Educ, 68-74; gov task force on sci & technol, 79-80. *Mem:* Am Soc Microbiol; AAAS. *Res:* Bacterial viruses for anaerobic bacteria; science and public policy. *Mailing Add:* 2001 Schoolhouse Lane Springfield IL 62704

SAMET, JONATHAN MICHAEL, EPIDEMIOLOGY. *Current Pos:* from asst prof to prof med, Univ NMex, Albuquerque, 78-94, assoc prof family, community & emergency med, 85-88, prof, 86-94, CLIN PROF MED, UNIV NMEX, ALBUQUERQUE, 94-; PROF & CHMN, DEPT EPIDEMIOL, JOHNS HOPKINS UNIV, 94- *Personal Data:* b Va, Mar 26, 48. *Educ:* Harvard Univ, AB, 66, MS, 77; Univ Rochester, MD, 70; Am Bd Internal Med, dipl. *Honors & Awards:* Surgeon Gen Medallion, 90; Award for Excellence in Environ Health Res, Lovelace Inst, 96. *Prof Exp:* Intern med, Univ Ky Med Ctr, Lexington, 70-71; asst resident mem, Univ NMex Affil Hosps, Albuquerque, 73-74; sr resident, 74-75; res fel clin epidemiol, Channing Lab, Harvard Med Sch, 75-78, res assoc med, 78-83. *Concurrent Pos:* Epidemiologist, Cancer Res & Treatment Ctr, Univ NMex, Albuquerque, 80-; chief, Pulmonary Div, Univ NMex Hosp, Albuquerque, 85-94, Pulmonary & Crit Care Div, Dept Med, 86-94; mem, Indoor Air Qual & Total Human Exposure Comt, US Environ Protection Agency, 87-; ed pro tem, Am J Epidemiol, 91-92, ed, 97-; consult ed, Tobacco Control: An Int J, 91-; chmn, Biol Effects Ionizing Radiation VI Comt, Nat Res Coun, 94-; ed, Epidemiol Rev, 94-; co-dir, Ctr Risk Sci & Pub Policy Inst, Johns Hopkins Univ, 95- *Mem:* Inst Med-Nat Acad Sci; fel AAAS; fel Am Col Epidemion; Soc Epidemiol Res (pres-elect, 88-89, pres, 89-90); Am Thoracic Soc; Int Epidemiol Asn; Int Soc Indoor Air Qual & Climate. *Mailing Add:* Dept Epidemiol Johns Hopkins Univ 615 N Wolfe St Suite 6030 Baltimore MD 21205-2103

SAMET, PHILIP, INTERNAL MEDICINE, CARDIOLOGY. *Current Pos:* from instr to assoc prof, 55-70, PROF MED, SCH MED, UNIV MIAMI, 70-; CHIEF, DEPT CARDIOL, PHILIP SAMET CARDIOL ASSOC. *Personal Data:* b New York, NY, Jan 30, 22; m 47; c 3. *Educ:* NY Univ, BA, 42, MD, 47. *Prof Exp:* Intern, Mt Sinai Hosp, New York, 47-48; resident internal med, Bronx Vet Hosp, 48-51; from instr to assoc prof, Univ Miami, 55-70, prof med, Sch Med, 70- *Concurrent Pos:* Res fel, Cardiopulmonary Lab, Bellevue Hosp, 51-53; chief, Div Cardiol, Mt Sinai Hosp, Miami Beach, Fla, 55- *Mem:* Am Thoracic Soc; Am Physiol Soc; Am Heart Asn; AMA; Am Col Cardiol. *Res:* Cardiac and pulmonary physiology. *Mailing Add:* Dept Cardiol Mt Sinai Med Ctr 4300 Alton Rd Miami Beach FL 33140

SAMI, SEDAT, FLUID MECHANICS, HYDRAULICS. *Current Pos:* from asst prof to assoc prof, 66-72, actg chmn, Dept Eng Mech & Mat, 78-79, PROF FLUID MECH & HYDRAUL, SOUTHERN ILL UNIV, 72-, CHMN, DEPT CIVIL ENG, 92- *Personal Data:* b Istanbul, Turkey, Oct 23, 28; m 58, Dagmar E Ellwanger; c Iskender & Elisabeth. *Educ:* Tech Univ Istanbul, MSCE, 51; Univ Iowa, MS, 57, PhD(fluid mech), 66. *Prof Exp:* Design engr, Chase T Main, Inc, Turkey, 51-53, asst chief engr, 54-56; chief design engr, Eti Yapi Ltd, Turkey, 58-60, tech dir, 60-62; asst prof civil eng, Middle East Tech Univ, Ankara, 62-63. *Mem:* Fel Am Soc Civil Engrs; Int Asn Hydraul Res; Sigma Xi. *Res:* Turbulence, fluctuating velocities and pressures; turbulent flows; electro-osmotic dewatering of ultrafine coal; aircraft refueling systems. *Mailing Add:* Dept Civil Eng Southern Ill Univ Carbondale IL 62901-6603. *Fax:* 618-453-3044; *E-Mail:* sami@ce.siu.edu

SAMIOS, NICHOLAS PETER, PHYSICS. *Current Pos:* from asst physicist to physicist, Brookhaven Nat Lab, 59-68, chmn, Dept Physics, 75-81, dep dir high energy & nuclear physics, 81-82, SR PHYSICIST, BROOKHAVEN NAT LAB, 62-, DIR, 82- *Personal Data:* b New York, NY, Mar 15, 32; m 58, Mary Linakis; c Peter, Gregory & Alexandra. *Educ:* Columbia Univ, AB, 53, PhD(physics), 57. *Hon Degrees:* DSc, Dowling Col, 92. *Honors & Awards:* E O Lawrence Mem Award, 80; Phys & Math Sci Award, NY Acad Sci, 80; WKH Panofsky Prize, 93. *Prof Exp:* Instr physics, Columbia Univ, 56-59. *Concurrent Pos:* Prof, Dept Particles & Fields, 75-76; chmn, PEP Exp Prog Ctr, 76-78; chmn, Physics Planning Ctr Am Phys Soc, 95. *Mem:* Nat Acad Sci; fel Am Phys Soc; fel Am Acad Arts & Sci; AAAS; corresp mem Akademia Athenon. *Res:* High energy particle and nuclear physics. *Mailing Add:* Dir Off 460 Brookhaven Nat Lab Upton NY 11973-5000

SAMIR, URI, SPACE PHYSICS. *Current Pos:* PROF SPACE PHYSICS, TEL-AVIV UNIV, ISRAEL, 84- *Personal Data:* b Tel-Aviv, Israel, Sept 14, 30; m 67, Violet H Witherow; c Tamar & Aurit. *Educ:* Hebrew Univ, Israel, MSc, 60; Univ London, PhD(physics), 67. *Prof Exp:* Teaching asst physics, Israel Inst Technol, 58-60, researcher, Israeli Defence Syst, 60-62; res assoc ionospheric physics, Univ Col, Univ London, 62-67; sci consult Gemini 10 & 11 spacecraft, Electro-Optical Systs, Inc, Calif, 67-68; from assoc res physicist, to res physicist Space Physics, Res Lab, Univ Mich, Ann Arbor, 69-84. *Concurrent Pos:* Prof, Dept Geophys & Planetary Sci, Tel-Aviv Univ, Israel, 74-85; mem, Sci Adv Bd Plasma Physics Exp on Future Space-Shuttles & Space Sta, 72-; mem steering & working group, Atmospheric-Magnetospheric & Plasmas in Space, 73-; chmn, Plasma Interaction Sect, NASA-Aircraft Multispectral Photog Syst Sci Definition Working Group, 75-76 & Israeli Nat Comt Res & Technol, 85-; mem, Subsatellite Sci Definition Team, 77-78 & Tetler Shuttle Working Group, 84- *Mem:* Am Phys Soc; Am Geophys Union; fel Brit Interplanetary Soc; Israel Phys Soc. *Res:* Flows of space-plasmas over bodies; ionospheres of the earth and planets; physics of cosmic rays; laboratory simulation of space physics and rarefied plasma physics phenomena and processes; space plasma expansion into a vacuum; laboratory simulation and measurements from space platforms; application of plasma expansion properties to the wake structure behind artificial satellites and behind non-magnetized planets and moons; interactions between large spacecraft and the terrestrial ionosphere. *Mailing Add:* 18 Hakneset Hagdola Str Tel-Aviv 62917 Israel

SAMIS, HARVEY VOORHEES, JR, BIOCHEMISTRY, PHYSIOLOGY. *Current Pos:* CONSULT, 87- *Personal Data:* b Easton, Md, July 14, 31; m 56; c 4. *Educ:* Wash Col, BS, 56; Brown Univ, PhD(biochem physiol), 63. *Prof Exp:* Instr biol, Washington Col, 55-56; res scientist, Masonic Med Res Lab, 63-75, dir exp geront prog, Utica, NY, 63-75; sr scientist, Med Res Serv, Vet Admin Med Ctr, Bay Pines, Fla, 75-87, coordr res & develop, 77-87. *Concurrent Pos:* Vis lectr biol, Syracuse Univ, 73-75; vis assoc prof & adj prof chem, Univ SFla, Tampa, 77- *Mem:* AAAS; Soc Gen Physiol; fel Geront Soc; Soc Develop Biol; fel Am Inst Chemists; Inter-Am Soc Chemother. *Res:* Chelation chemistry of biomolecules; alcoholism effect of aging on properties of biological macromolecules and their functions; effects of age on the temporal organization of biological systems; molecular genetics and neoplasia; nucleic acid metabolism. *Mailing Add:* 5301 14th Ave S St Petersburg FL 33707

SAMITZ, M H, DERMATOLOGY. *Current Pos:* From instr to asst prof, Grad Sch Med, 40-53, from asst prof to assoc prof, Sch Med, 49-67, prof & dir grad dermat, 67-75, EMER PROF DERMAT, SCH MED, UNIV PA, 75- *Personal Data:* b Philadelphia, Pa, Dec 18, 09; m 45; c 2. *Educ:* Temple Univ, MD, 33; Univ Pa, MSc, 45. *Concurrent Pos:* Med dir, Skin & Cancer Hosp, Philadelphia, 53-54; prin investr, USPHS res grants, 58-75; consult, US Naval Hosp, 65-; consult & vis prof, Pa Col Podiat Med, 65-75, emer prof dermat,

75-; vis prof, Hahnemann Med Col, 67-, Univ Dar es Salaam, 75-; chief dept dermat, Grad Hosp, Univ Pa, 67-; mem comt, Div Educ, Nat Prog Dermat, 71-; mem comt on nickel, Nat Res Coun; consult, Food & Drug Admin, Dermat Adv Comt, 77-78; US-Poland health scientist exchange fel, 80; mem bd dirs, Found Int Dermatol Educ, 75-, pres, 79- *Mem:* AAAS; Am Acad Dermat; Am Col Physicians; Am Col Allergists; Soc Invest Dermat. *Res:* Industrial dermatology, particularly effects of chromium salts and nickel on the skin; clinical investigations in various aspects of clinical dermatology. *Mailing Add:* 226 W Rittenhouse Sq Apt 805 Philadelphia PA 19103-5742

SAMLOFF, I MICHAEL, MEDICINE, GASTROENTEROLOGY. *Current Pos:* ASSOC CHIEF STAFF RES, VET ADMIN MED CTR, 80- *Personal Data:* b Rochester, NY, Jan 24, 32; m 54; c 2. *Educ:* State Univ NY, MD, 56. *Prof Exp:* Instr med, Sch Med & Dent, Univ Rochester, 62-64, sr instr med & psychiat, 64-65, asst prof, 65-68; assoc prof, 68-72; prof med, Sch Med, Univ Calif, Los Angeles, 72- *Concurrent Pos:* USPHS fel med, Strong Mem Hosp, 58-59, fel psychiat, 61-62 & trainee med, 61-63; Am Cancer Soc advan clin fel, 63-66; chief, Gastroenterol Div, Harbor Hosp, Univ Calif, Los Angeles Med Ctr, 68-80. *Mem:* Am Fedn Clin Res; Am Psychosom Soc; Am Gastroenterol Asn; Am Soc Clin Invest; fel Am Col Physicians. *Res:* Gastritis; ulcer. *Mailing Add:* Vet Admin Med Ctr 16111 Plummer St Sepulveda CA 91343-2036. *Fax:* 818-895-9554

SAMMAK, EMIL GEORGE, EMULSION POLYMERIZATION, RHEOLOGY. *Current Pos:* RETIRED. *Personal Data:* b Brooklyn, NY, Apr 3, 27; div; c Paul, Karen & Mark. *Educ:* Polytech Inst Brooklyn, BS, 49, PhD(polymer sci), 58. *Prof Exp:* Sr res chemist, Chem Div, Int Latex & Chem Corp, 55-60, mgr basic polymer res, 60-68; mgr basic res, Standard Brands Chem Industs, Inc, 68-76; mgr polymer & anal res, Emulsion Polymers Div, Reichhold Chem Inc, 76-92. *Concurrent Pos:* Adj prof, Wesley Col, 82, Del State Univ, 88-97. *Mem:* AAAS; Am Chem Soc. *Res:* Synthesis, characterization and mechanical properties of butadiene latex, polyelectrolytes, polyacrylates, polyurethanes, allyl and formaldehyde resins; ionic polymerization; grafting olefin copolymers; starch utilization; rheology, computer applications, pollution control, analytical research. *Mailing Add:* English Village No G 3 Dover DE 19904

SAMMAK, PAUL J, SIGNAL TRANSDUCTION ANGIOGENESIS. *Current Pos:* ASST PROF, DEPT PHARMACOL, UNIV MINN, 92- *Personal Data:* b Dover, Del, Feb 8, 56; c 2. *Educ:* Hampshire Col, BA, 78; Univ Wis-Madison, MS, 80, PhD(biophys), 88. *Honors & Awards:* Edward Livingston Trudeau Award, Am Lung Asn, 95. *Prof Exp:* Res asst, Physics Dept, Amherst Col, 78, Chem Dept, Univ Wis, 79-80; Lab Molecular Biol, Univ Wis, 81-88; res pharmacologist, Dept Pharmacol, Univ Calif, San Diego, 89-90; res physiologist, Dept Molecular & Cellular Biol, Univ Calif, Berkeley, 91-92. *Concurrent Pos:* Teaching & lab asst, Physics Dept, Univ Wis, 78-80; lectr & reader, Physiol Dept, Univ Calif, Berkeley, 89, res physiologist, NIH Cancer Res Lab, 89; NIH fel, 90-92. *Mem:* Am Soc Cell Biol; AAAS; Am Soc Pharmacol & Exp Therapeut. *Res:* Mechanisms and regulation of cell movement and growth during wound healing and during angiogenesis; wound healing. *Mailing Add:* Pharmacol 3-249 Millard Univ 435 Delaware St SE Minneapolis MN 55455

SAMMARCO, PAUL WILLIAM, CORAL REEF ECOLOGY, CHEMICAL ECOLOGY. *Current Pos:* exec dir, 91-95, PROF, LA UNIVS MARINE CONSORTIUM, 95- *Personal Data:* b Hackensack, NJ, Oct 18, 48; m 71, Jean Sogioka; c Mimi C, Dustin P & Jack I. *Educ:* Syracuse Univ, BA, 70; State Univ NY, Stony Brook, PhD(ecol & evolution), 77. *Prof Exp:* Asst prof, Dept Biol, Clarkson Univ, 77-79; from res scientist to sr res scientist, Australian Inst Marine Sci, 79-89; dir environ res, Resource Assessment Comn, 89-90, prin assessment officer, Coastal Zone Inquiry, Dept Prime Minister & Cabinet, 90-91. *Concurrent Pos:* Researcher, Clarkson Col, 77-; vis asst prof trop ecol, State Univ NY, Potsdam, Dept Biol, St Croix, US Virgin Islands, 79; vis eminant scientist, Univ SFla, St Petersburg, 87; adj prof biol, Univ Southwestern La, oceanog & coastal sci, La State Univ A&M & zool & physiol; vis prof, Dept Geol, McMaster Univ, 88-89; adj prof biol, Univ New Orleans, 92-, Nicholls State Univ, 93-; counr, Int Soc Reef Studies. *Mem:* AAAS; Int Soc Reef Studies; Australian Marine Sci Asn; Int Soc Chem Ecol. *Res:* Coral reef research; chemical ecology of soft corals, larval dispersal and recruitment processes in corals, bioerosion in corals, stable isotope geochemistry of corals, grazing in coral reef ecosystems. *Mailing Add:* Lumcon 8124 Hwy 56 Chauvin LA 70344. *Fax:* 504-851-2874; *E-Mail:* psammarco@lumcon.edu

SAMMELWITZ, PAUL H, REPRODUCTIVE PHYSIOLOGY, ENVIRONMENTAL PHYSIOLOGY. *Current Pos:* Asst prof, 59-68, ASSOC PROF AVIAN & MAMMALIAN PHYSIOL & GENETICS, UNIV DEL, 68- *Personal Data:* b Buffalo, NY, Mar 13, 33; m 62, Diane Lease; c Michael, Christopher & Ellen F (Casey). *Educ:* Cornell Univ, BS, 55; Univ Ill, MS, 57, PhD(reproductive physiol), 59. *Mem:* Fel AAAS; fel Coun Agr Sci & Technol; Am Soc Animal Sci; Poultry Sci Asn; World Poultry Sci Asn; Asn Develop Comput Based Instruct Systs; Nat Asn Cols & Teachers Agr. *Res:* Mammalian and avian reproductive physiology; avian heat stress physiology; endocrine factors influenced by moderate dietary vitamin A deficiency; genetic resistance to Marek's disease; computer assisted instruction; multimedia lecture tools. *Mailing Add:* Dept Animal Sci Univ Del Newark DE 19717-0001. *Fax:* 302-831-3654

SAMMET, JEAN E, SOFTWARE HISTORY, PROGRAMMING LANGUAGES. *Current Pos:* CONSULT, PROG LANG, 89- *Personal Data:* b New York, NY, Mar 23, 28. *Educ:* Mt Holyoke Col, BA, 48; Univ Ill, MA, 49. *Hon Degrees:* DSc, Mt Holyoke Col, 78. *Prof Exp:* Teaching asst math, Univ Ill, 48-51; dividend technician, Metrop Life Ins Co, 51-52; teaching asst, Barnard Col, Columbia Univ, 52-53; engr, Sperry Gyroscope Co, 53-58; sect head, Mobidic Prog, Sylvanaia Elec Prod, 58-59, staff consult prog res, 59-61; mgr, Boston Adv Prog, IBM Corp, 61-65, Prog Lang Tech, 65-68, Prog Technol Planning, 68-74, Prog Lang Technol, 74-79, Div Software Technol, 79-83 & Prog Lang Technol, 83-88. *Concurrent Pos:* Lectr, Adelphi Col, 56-58, Northeastern Univ, 67, Univ Calif, Los Angeles, 67-72 & Mt Holyoke Col, 74; ed-in-chief, Comput Rev & Am Comput Mach Guide Comput Lit, 79-87. *Mem:* Nat Acad Eng; Asn Comput Mach (vpres, 72-74, pres, 74-76); Math Asn Am. *Res:* High level programming languages; use of computers for non-numerical mathematics; formula manipulation systems; programming systems; language measurement; practical uses of artificial intelligence; use of natural language on a computer; history of software; history of programming languages. *Mailing Add:* PO Box 30038 Bethesda MD 20824-0038

SAMMONS, DAVID JAMES, AGRONOMY, PLANT BREEDING. *Current Pos:* ASSOC DEAN AGR & DIR INT PROGS AGR, PURDUE UNIV, 93- *Personal Data:* b Columbus, Ohio, Sept 2, 46; m 70, Rebecca Bell; c Amy E & Rachel A. *Educ:* Tufts Univ, BS, 68; Harvard Univ, AM, 72; Univ Ill, PhD(agron), 78. *Prof Exp:* Vol, Peace Corps, Philippines, 68-70; asst biol, Harvard Univ, 70-72; assoc dir natural hist, Norwalk Mus & Zoo, Conn, 72; teacher-naturalist, Nat Audubon Soc, 72-75; res asst, Univ Ill, 75-78; from asst prof to prof agron, Univ Md, 78-93, assoc dean undergrad studies, 89-91, assoc dean agr, 92-93. *Concurrent Pos:* Mem fac adv comt, Univ Ill, 75-76; curric consult, Sinclair Community Col, Dayton, Ohio, 73-74; mem environ qual bd, Dept Urban Develop, New Towns Prog, 73-74; mem curric develop, Govt Philippines, 68-70; fac adv & partic, Study Abroad Prog, Univ Md, Asia, 79, Caribbean, 81 & PR, 83; fac mem, Grad Sch, USDA, Washington, DC, 80-83; vis prof, Berkeley Col, Yale Univ, 81; consult, Off Int Coop & Develop, The Gambia, USDA, 84, Proj Sci Technol Coop, AID, 84-85; vis lectr, Egerton Univ, Njoro, Kenya, 86-87; mem bd dirs, Consortium Int Crop Protection, 86-89, chmn, Eastern Wheat Region, 87-90; Fulbright award, Kenya, 86-87; Rotary Int teaching fel, Kenya, 86-87; mem, Nat Wheat Improv Comt, 87-93; coordr, Grad Studies Agron, Univ Md, 87-; mem, Nat Barley Improv Comt, 88-91; distinguished scholar/teacher, Univ Md, 88-89; mem bd dirs, Int Sorghum-Millet Collab Res Support Proj & Bean-Cowpea Collab Res Support Proj. *Mem:* Crop Sci Soc Am; Am Soc Agron; Asn Asian Studies-Middle Atlantic Region. *Res:* Applied breeding research designed to improve barley and wheat cultivars for producers in Maryland and the Mid-Atlantic region; small grain production, breeding and physiology; factors affecting quality in wheat. *Mailing Add:* Agr Admin Bldg Int Progs Agr Purdue Univ West Lafayette IN 47906. *Fax:* 765-494-9613; *E-Mail:* djs@admin.agad.purdue.edu

SAMMONS, JAMES HARRIS, FAMILY PRACTICE, MEDICINE. *Current Pos:* CONSULT, 91- *Personal Data:* b Montgomery, Ala, March 13, 27; c 4. *Educ:* Washington & Lee Univ, BS; St Louis Univ, MD. *Hon Degrees:* LHD, Tex Univ Sci Ctr. *Prof Exp:* Dep med examr, Harris Co, Tex, 62-74; clin asst prof family med, Dept Community Med, Baylor Col Med, 72-75, clin assoc prof family pract, Family Pract Ctr, 73-74, vis assoc prof family pract, 74-91. *Mem:* Inst Med-Nat Acad Sci; Am Pub Health Asn; AMA; Am Acad Gen Pract; Am Asn Med Soc Execs. *Mailing Add:* 161 E Chicago Ave Apt 49E Chicago IL 60611. *Fax:* 312-464-5969

SAMN, SHERWOOD, MATHEMATICS. *Current Pos:* MATHEMATICIAN, BROOKS AFB, USAF, SAN ANTONIO, TEX, 74- *Personal Data:* b Los Angeles, Calif, Apr 20, 41; m 68; c 2. *Educ:* Univ Calif, Berkeley, BA, 63, PhD(math), 68. *Prof Exp:* Asst prof math, Ind Univ-Purdue Univ, Indianapolis, 68-74. *Mem:* Am Math Soc; Soc Indust & Appl Math. *Res:* Differential equations; cardiovascular system modeling; operations research. *Mailing Add:* 8807 Cattail Creek San Antonio TX 78239-2717

SAMOILOV, SERGEY MICHAEL, POLYMER CHEMISTRY, CATALYSIS. *Current Pos:* RETIRED. *Personal Data:* b Baku, USSR, Dec 17, 25; US citizen; m 61, Elena Krasnostchekova; c Michael. *Educ:* Moscow Inst Fine Chem Technol, MS, 49; USSR Acad Sci, PhD(chem), 58. *Prof Exp:* Engr catalysis, USSR Nat Res Inst Artificial Fuel, 49-51, USSR Petrochem Plant No 16, 51-55; res assoc, USSR Acad Sci, 58-61; sr res assoc polymers, USSR Nat Res Inst Petrochem, 62-76; res assoc, Columbia Univ, 77-78; res assoc polymers, Celanese Res Co, 78-81; sr res chemist polymers, Allied-Signal Corp, 81-90. *Concurrent Pos:* Abstractor, Chem Abstracts J, Inst Sci Info, USSR Acad Sci, 56-76. *Mem:* Am Chem Soc. *Res:* Synthesis and investigation of polyolefins; radical pressure copolymerization of lower olefins; polymer emulsions; metalorganic polymers; structural and relaxational properties of polymers; Ziegler catalysis. *Mailing Add:* 225 Hampton Park Dr Athens GA 30606. *Fax:* 706-613-9203; *E-Mail:* sergeysa@aol.com

SAMOLLOW, PAUL B, ECOLOGICAL GENETICS. *Current Pos:* post doctoral scientist, Dept Genetics, SW Found Biomed Res, Tex, 81-84, asst scientist, 84-87 & 91-96, adj asst scientist biochem & genetics, 87-91, ASSOC SCIENTIST, DEPT GENETICS, SW FOUND BIOMED RES, TEX, 96- *Personal Data:* b San Francisco, Calif, Mar 20, 48; m 68; c 2. *Educ:* Univ Calif, BA, 71; Ore State Univ, PhD(zool), 78. *Prof Exp:* Lectr genetics & evolution, Humboldt State Univ, 78; asst prof, Univ Mont, 79; fel, Hawaii Inst Marine Biol, 79-81; asst prof evolution & genetics, Lehigh Univ, 87-91. *Concurrent Pos:* Teaching & res asst, Dept Zool, Ore State Univ, 71-77, instr, 78; lectr, Dept Biol, Humboldt State Univ, 78; asst prof, Dept Zool, Univ Mont, 79; res assoc, Univ Hawaii, Hawaii Inst Marine Biol, 79-81; Nat Serv Res Award, NIH, 83-89; asst prof, Dept Biol, Lehigh Univ, Pa, 87-91. *Mem:* Genetics Soc Am; Soc Study Evolution; AAAS. *Res:* Physical and linkage mapping of marsupial genomes; evolution of mammalian sex chromosomes; marsupial X-chromosome inactivation; genetic regulation of normal quantitative variation in human thyroid and thyroid-related hormone levels. *Mailing Add:* Southwest Found Biomed Res PO Box 760549 San Antonio TX 78245-0549. *Fax:* 210-670-3317; *E-Mail:* pbs@darwin.sfbr.org

SAMOLS, DAVID R, RECOMBINANT DNA. *Current Pos:* asst prof, 80-88, ASSOC PROF BIOCHEM, MED SCH, CASE WESTERN RESERVE UNIV, 88- *Personal Data:* b Washington, DC, Aug 31, 45; m 76; c 2. *Educ:* Earlham Col, BS, 67; Univ Chicago, PhD(biol), 76. *Prof Exp:* Fel, Roche Inst Molecular Biol, 76-79; res assoc, Inst Molecular Biol, Univ Ore, 79. *Mem:* Am Soc Cell Biol; Am Soc Biochem & Molecular Biol. *Res:* Signal and mechanism by which tissue injury and infection induce the liver to secrete c-reactive protein; types of genetic rearrangements and alterations caused by chemical carcinogenesis. *Mailing Add:* Dept Biochem Case Western Reserve Univ 10900 Euclid Ave Cleveland OH 44106-4935. *Fax:* 216-368-4544; *E-Mail:* samols@biochemistry.cwru.edu

SAMORAJSKI, THADDEUS, ANATOMY. *Current Pos:* mem staff, 74-89, EMER PROF, TEX RES INST MENT SCI, 89- *Personal Data:* b Shelburne, Mass, Oct 29, 23; m 52; c 2. *Educ:* Univ Mich, BS, 48; Univ Chicago, PhD(anat), 56. *Honors & Awards:* Cralow Medal, Polish Acad Sci. *Prof Exp:* Asst & instr, Univ Chicago, 55-56; instr anat, Ohio State Univ, 56-60; dir lab neurochem, Cleveland Psychiat Inst, 60-74. *Concurrent Pos:* Adj prof, Dept Biol, Tex Women's Univ, 78- & Dept Neurobiol & Anat, Sch Med, Univ Tex, 80- *Mem:* Soc Neurosci; Geront Soc. *Res:* Neurochemistry, particularly in relation to neurobiology of aging; environmental modification of life span; radiation neuropathology; myelin formation and degeneration; catecholamine metabolism. *Mailing Add:* 1208 Howard Lane Bellaire TX 77401

SAMOUR, CARLOS M, CHEMISTRY. *Current Pos:* CHMN & SCI DIR, MACROCHEM CORP, 82- *Educ:* Am Univ Beirut, BA, 42, MA, 44; Mass Inst Technol, MS, 47; Boston Univ, PhD, 50. *Prof Exp:* Res fel, Boston Univ, 50-52; res chemist, Kendall Co, 52-57, dir, Theodore Clark Lab, 57-73, Lexington Res Lab, 73-81,; pres, Samour Assocs, 81-84. *Concurrent Pos:* Sect chmn, Int Union Pure & Appl Chem, Univ Mass, 82; session chmn, Biomat, Sardinia, 88, int conf, Mass Inst Technol, 82, technol adv; pres & chmn, Augusta Epilepsy Res Found, Washington, 89-; Adv univs & med ctrs. *Mem:* Am Chem Soc; Am Asn Pharmaceut Sci; Controlled Release Soc. *Res:* Polymer chemistry, biomaterials, pharmaceuticals and dental materials; over 50 US patents and over 200 foreign patents. *Mailing Add:* Macrochem Corp 110 Hartwell Ave Lexington MA 02173-3123

SAMPLE, HOWARD H, solid state physics, for more information see previous edition

SAMPLE, JAMES HALVERSON, ORGANIC POLYMER CHEMISTRY. *Current Pos:* CONSULT, 80- *Personal Data:* b Cicero, Ill, Feb 27, 14; m 40; c 3. *Educ:* Elmhurst Col, BS, 35; Univ Ill, MS, 36, PhD(org chem), 39. *Prof Exp:* Asst chem, Univ Ill, 36-39; prof, Ind Cent Col, 39-42; prof, Franklin Col, 42-44; res chemist, Sherwin Williams Co, 44-47, chem res supvr, 47-58, asst dir resin dept, 58-65, dir, 66-73, dir polymer & mat res-coating, 74-79. *Mem:* Am Chem Soc. *Res:* Resins for surface coatings; alkyds. *Mailing Add:* 1206 E 165th Pl South Holland IL 60473

SAMPLE, JOHN THOMAS, NUCLEAR REACTIONS. *Current Pos:* from asst prof to prof, 58-90, chmn dept physics, 67-76, EMER PROF PHYSICS, UNIV ALTA, 90- *Personal Data:* b Kerrobert, Sask, May 4, 27; m 53, Dorothy Lambe; c Catherine, Rick, Irene, Michael & Patricia. *Educ:* Univ BC, BA, 48, MA, 50 & PhD, 55. *Prof Exp:* Sci officer, Defence Res Bd, Can, 55-58; dir res, Secretariat BC, 81-88. *Concurrent Pos:* Vis scientist, Brookhaven Nat Lab, 65-66; bd mem, Pac Isotopes & Pharmaceut Ltd, 83-89; dir, TRIUMF, Univ BC, 76-81; gen mgr, Ebco Technologies, 88-91. *Mem:* Am Inst Physics; Am Phys Soc; Can Asn Physicists. *Res:* Reactions of low and intermediate energy nuclear physics; design of nuclear medicine equipment. *Mailing Add:* TRIUMF 4004 Wesbrook Mall Vancouver BC V6T 1W5 Can. *Fax:* 604-222-1074; *E-Mail:* sample@triumf.ca

SAMPLE, PAUL E(DWARD), CHEMICAL ENGINEERING, POLYMER MORPHOLOGY. *Current Pos:* CONSULT, SAMPLES INC, 90- *Personal Data:* b Chicago, Ill, Nov 24, 28; m 53, Jacqulyn Smith; c Gary L, Ronald L, Kimberly A, Bradley E & Whitney S. *Educ:* Ill Inst Technol, BS, 51; Univ WVa, MS, 55, PhD(chem eng), 57. *Prof Exp:* Asst, Exp Sta, Univ WVa, 54, 54-57; res engr, Film Dept, E I Du Pont de Nemours & Co, Inc, 57-59, group leader, Chem Develop, 59-60, supvr, Mfg Div, 60-62, tech rep, Mkt Div, 62-66, res supvr, Res & Develop Div, 66-69, group mgr, 69-72, tech consult, Res & Develop Div, 72-90. *Mem:* Am Chem Soc; Am Soc Metals; Am Inst Chem Engrs; Sigma Xi; Am Soc Testing & Mat; Am Soc Plastics Eng. *Res:* Process automation and instrumentation; packaging systems and packaging materials; morphology of engineering polymers in failure analysis and prevention. *Mailing Add:* 308 Walden Rd Wilmington DE 19803. *Fax:* 302-656-3212; *E-Mail:* sample@bellatlantic.net

SAMPLE, STEVEN BROWNING, ELECTROHYDRODYNAMICS. *Current Pos:* PRES & PROF ELEC ENG, UNIV SOUTHERN CALIF, 91- *Personal Data:* b St Louis, Mo, Nov 29, 40; m 61, Kathryn Brunkow; c Michelle & Melissa. *Educ:* Univ Ill, Urbana, BS, 62, MS, 63, PhD(elec eng), 65. *Prof Exp:* Scientist, Melpar, Inc, 65-66; from asst prof to assoc prof elec eng, Purdue Univ, 66-73; prof elec eng & exec vpres, Univ Nebr, 74-82, dean, Grad Col, 77-82; pres & prof elec eng, State Univ NY, Buffalo, 82-91. *Concurrent Pos:* Dep dir, Ill Bd Higher Educ, 71-74; mem bd dirs, Design & Mfr Corp, Connersville, Ill, 77- & Moog Inc, 82-; mem ednl activ bd, Inst Elec & Electronics Engrs, 82-84; mem exec comt, Nat Asn State Univs & Land-Grant Cols, 85-, chmn coun pres's, 85-86, chmn ednl & telecommun comt, 85-86. *Mem:* Sigma Xi; Inst Elec & Electronics Engrs. *Res:* Electrohydrodynamic instability of liquid drops in electric fields; harmonic electrical spraying of liquids from capillaries; solid-state digital control systems for appliances. *Mailing Add:* Off Pres Univ Southern Calif University Park Los Angeles CA 90089-0012

SAMPLES, RONALD EUGENE, COAL ENGINEERING. *Current Pos:* staff mem, 66-73, vpres eng & explor, 73, pres & chief oper officer, 75-77, CHMN & CHIEF EXEC OFFICER, CONSOL COAL CO, 77-; PRES COAL & MINERALS OPERS, CONOCO INC, 80- *Personal Data:* b Boonville, Ind, Apr 23, 26; m 50, Virginia A Derr; c Ronald E II, Rebecca L, Thomas H & Susan A. *Educ:* NMex Sch Mines, BSEM, 49. *Honors & Awards:* Erskine Ramsay Gold Medal, Soc Mining Metall & Explor, 94. *Prof Exp:* Staff mem, Peabody Coal Co, St Louis, 49-66, regional chief engr, 60-66; sr vpres opers, Amax Coal Co, Indianapolis, 73-75, exec vpres engr opers, exploration, purchasing, 75. *Concurrent Pos:* Bd dir, United Way, Pittsburgh, 77-90. *Mem:* Am Inst Mining, Metall & Petrol Engrs; Nat Coal Asn. *Mailing Add:* Arch Mineral Corp One Cityplace Dr Suite 3 St Louis MO 63141-7065

SAMPLES, WILLIAM R(EAD), SANITARY ENGINEERING, ENVIRONMENTAL ENGINEERING. *Current Pos:* coordr, Wheeling-Pittsburgh Steel Corp, 71-78, mgr environ control, 78-85, eng & environ control, 85-90, DIR ENVIRON CONTROL, WHEELING-PITTSBURGH STEEL CORP, 90- *Personal Data:* b Whipple, WVa, Oct 17, 31; m 53; c 4. *Educ:* Univ WVa, BS, 53; Harvard Univ, MS, 55, PhD(eng), 59. *Prof Exp:* Asst prof civil eng, Calif Inst Technol, 59-65; fel water resources, Mellon Inst, 65-68, sr fel & head water resources, 68-71. *Concurrent Pos:* Nat Air Pollution Control Techniques Adv Comt, Environ Protection Agency. *Mem:* Am Soc Civil Engrs; Water Pollution Control Fedn; Am Inst Chem Engrs; Air Pollution Control Asn; Am Iron & Steel Inst. *Res:* Industrial waste water control; air pollution; industrial hygiene; water quality; water and sewage treatment. *Mailing Add:* 2293 Weston Dr Pittsburgh PA 15241

SAMPLEY, MARILYN YVONNE, NUTRITION. *Current Pos:* CHMN, DEPT HUMAN SCI, MOREHEAD STATE UNIV, KY. *Personal Data:* b Ala. *Educ:* Auburn Univ, BS, 57; Univ Ala, MS, 61; Tex Woman's Univ, PhD(nutrit, biochem & foods), 69. *Prof Exp:* Instr nutrit & chief dietician, Sacred Heart Dominican Col, St Joseph Hosp, Houston, 57-58; teacher, K J Clark Jr High Sch, Mobile Ala, 59-60; res asst, Univ Ala, 60-61; instr nutrit & chief dietician, Sacred Heart Dominican Col, St Joseph Hosp, Houston, 62; dir food serv, Dickinson Sch Dist, Dickenson, Tex, 63-67; res asst, Tex Woman's Univ, 67-69; assoc prof & chmn, Dept Home Econ, Tex A&I Univ, 72- *Mem:* Am Pub Health Asn; AAAS; Soc Nutrit Educ; Nat Coun Admin Home Econ; Nat Educ Asn. *Res:* Eating and food buying habits. *Mailing Add:* Dept Human Sci Morehead State Univ 150 University Blvd Morehead KY 40351-1684

SAMPSON, CALVIN COOLIDGE, MEDICINE, PATHOLOGY. *Current Pos:* From asst prof to assoc prof, 58-69, PROF PATH, COL MED, HOWARD UNIV, 69- *Personal Data:* b Cambridge, Md, Feb 1, 28; m 53; c 2. *Educ:* Hampton Inst, BS, 47; Meharry Med Col, MD, 51. *Concurrent Pos:* Asst ed, J Nat Med Asn, 65-77, ed, 78- *Mem:* Nat Med Asn; Int Acad Path; fel Col Am Path. *Res:* Importance of estrogen and progesterone receptors in African American women with breast cancer, investigated over a 10 year period. *Mailing Add:* 1614 Varnum Pl NE Washington DC 20017-3141

SAMPSON, CHARLES BERLIN, STATISTICS, INFORMATION SCIENCE. *Current Pos:* RETIRED. *Personal Data:* b Iowa Falls, Iowa, Dec 15, 39; m 65, Vicki; c Eric, Brenda & Carl. *Educ:* Univ Iowa, BS, 61, MS, 63; Iowa State Univ, PhD(statist), 68. *Prof Exp:* Qual Engr, Int Bus Mach, 63-64; sr statistician, Eli Lilly & Co, 68-73, res scientist 73-74, head, Statist & Math Serv, 74-81, head, Sci Info Serv, 81-87, mgr, med info serv & statist, 87-88, dir statist & math sci, 89-93, dir decision sci, 93-94. *Concurrent Pos:* Mem bd dir, Am Statist Asn, 82-83, 88-89, coun, Biometrics Soc, 84-86; vis lectr, Comt Pres of Statist Soc, 84-; chmn nominations comt, Am Statist Asn, 89, mem comt nat & int statist stand, 91- *Mem:* Fel Am Statist Asn; Biometric Soc. *Res:* Application of statistical and mathematical models to biological, medical, and chemical research; design of experiments; pharmaceutical quality control. *Mailing Add:* 11716 Eden Estates Dr Carmel IN 46033-3249

SAMPSON, DAVID ASHMORE, METABOLISM, METHODOLOGY. *Current Pos:* RES NUTRIT SCIENTIST, WESTERN HUMAN NUTRIT RES CTR, AGR RES SERV, USDA, SAN FRANCISCO, 84- *Educ:* Colo State Univ, PhD(nutrit biochem), 82. *Mailing Add:* Dept Food Sci & Human Nutr Colo State Univ Gifford Bldg Rm 227 Ft Collins CO 80523-0001. *Fax:* 970-491-7252

SAMPSON, DEXTER REID, GENETICS, PLANT BREEDING. *Current Pos:* Res officer hort crops, 55-66, RES SCIENTIST CEREAL CROPS, CAN DEPT AGR, 66- *Personal Data:* b New Glasgow, NS, Can, Sept 9, 30; m 58; c 2. *Educ:* Acadia Univ, BSc, 51; Harvard Univ, AM, 54, PhD, 56. *Mem:* Genetics Soc Can; Can Bot Asn; Sigma Xi; Can Soc Agron; Agr Inst Can. *Res:* Genetics of self-incompatability in angiosperms; genetics of Brassica and oats; breeding soft white pastry winter wheat and hard red winter wheat for milling and baking quality, high yield, winter survival and disease resistance. *Mailing Add:* 1189 Cline Cresent Ottawa ON K2C 2P3 Can

SAMPSON, DOUGLAS HOWARD, ATOMIC PHYSICS. *Current Pos:* assoc prof, 65-70, PROF ASTROPHYS, PA STATE UNIV, 70- *Personal Data:* b Devils Lake, NDak, May 19, 25; m 56, Carlyn Grutzner; c 4. *Educ:* Concordia Col, Moorhead, Minn, BA, 51; Yale Univ, MA, 53, PhD(theoret physics), 56. *Prof Exp:* Staff mem, Theoret Div, Los Alamos Sci Lab, NMcx, 56-61; theoret physicist, Space Sci Lab, Gen Elec Co, Pa, 61-64; group leader atomic & radiation physics, 64-65. *Concurrent Pos:* Consult, Lawrence Livermore Nat Lab. *Mem:* Fel Am Phys Soc; Am Astron Soc; Int Astron Union. *Res:* Atomic physics of very highly charged ions; theoretical astrophysics; statistical mechanics and kinetic theory; radiative transport. *Mailing Add:* Dept Astron & Astrophys Pa State Univ 525 Davey Lab University Park PA 16802-6305. *Fax:* 814-863-3399; *E-Mail:* sampson@astro.psu.edu

SAMPSON, HENRY T, NUCLEAR ENGINEERING. *Current Pos:* mem tech staff, 67-81, DIR PLANNING & OPERS, SPACE TEST PROG, AEROSPACE CORP, 81- *Personal Data:* b Jackson, Miss, Apr 22, 34; m 61; c 2. *Educ:* Purdue Univ, BS, 56; Univ Calif, Los Angeles, MS, 61; Univ Ill, PhD(nuclear eng), 67. *Prof Exp:* Res engr, US Naval Weapons Ctr, 56-62. *Mem:* AAAS; Am Nuclear Soc; Am Inst Aeronaut & Astronaut. *Res:* Research and development of rocket propellants and plastic bonded explosives; direct conversion of nuclear energy to electrical energy; analysis of space electrical power systems; granted 1 US patent. *Mailing Add:* Aerospace Corp PO Box 92957 Mail Stop M-5-656 Los Angeles CA 90009-2957

SAMPSON, HERSCHEL WAYNE, CELL CALCIUM, MINERALIZATION. *Current Pos:* assoc prof, 79-93, PROF ANAT, MED SCH, TEX A&M UNIV, 93- *Personal Data:* b Greenville, Tex, June 28, 44; m 65, Patricia J Hudson; c Nathan P & Susan D. *Educ:* Arlington State Col, BS, 67; Baylor Univ, PhD(anat), 70. *Prof Exp:* Asst prof anat, Sch Med, Creighton Univ, 70-72; assoc prof, Baylor Col Dent, 72-77 & Col Med & Dent, Oral Roberts Univ, 77-78. *Mem:* Am Asn Anat; Am Soc Bone & Mineral Res; Am Physiol Soc; Electron Microscope Soc Am; Res Soc Alcoholism. *Res:* Calcium transfer and homeostasis at the cell level; bone and joint disease mechanisms; mineralization; alcohol and bone. *Mailing Add:* Dept Human Anat Tex A&M Univ Med Sch College Station TX 77843-1114. *Fax:* 409-845-0790; *E-Mail:* sampson@tamu.edu

SAMPSON, JOHN LAURENCE, PHYSICS. *Current Pos:* PHYSICIST, NORTHEAST PHOTOSCI, 90- *Personal Data:* b Lynn, Mass, Dec 14, 29; m 52, Georgette McMurray; c Thomas, Gail & Elizabeth. *Educ:* Mass Inst Technol, BS, 51; Tufts Univ, MS, 54, PhD, 62. *Prof Exp:* Physicist, Air Force Cambridge Res Labs, 51 & 55-59; instr physics, Tufts Univ, 54-55, asst, 59-61; physicist, Arthur D Little, Inc, 61-62; physicist, Air Force Rome Air Develop Ctr, Bedford, 62-90. *Mem:* Sigma Xi. *Res:* Holography and fiber optics. *Mailing Add:* 8 Bedford St Lexington MA 02173

SAMPSON, JOSEPH HAROLD, MATHEMATICS. *Current Pos:* chmn dept, 70-80, PROF MATH, JOHNS HOPKINS UNIV, 65- *Personal Data:* b Spokane, Wash, Sept 14, 25. *Educ:* Princeton Univ, MA, 49, PhD(math), 51. *Prof Exp:* Res grant, Off Naval Res, 51-52; C L E Moore instr math, Mass Inst Technol, 52; asst prof, Johns Hopkins Univ, 52-64; prof assoc, Univ Strasbourg, 64-65 & 68-69, Univ Grenoble, 74-75. *Concurrent Pos:* Prof assoc, Univ Strasbourg, 68-69; ed, Am J Math, 78- *Mem:* Am Math Soc; Math Soc France; Italian Math Union; Sigma Xi. *Res:* Algebraic geometry; geometry of manifolds; geometric applications of partial differential equations, especially as connected with the Laplace operator; gave the first general description of harmonic mappings; number-theoretic applications of algebraic geometry; global analysis. *Mailing Add:* Dept Math Johns Hopkins Univ Baltimore MD 21218-2689

SAMPSON, PAUL, SYNTHETIC ORGANIC CHEMISTRY, SYNTHETIC ORGANOFLUORINE CHEMISTRY. *Current Pos:* asst prof, 85-92, ASSOC PROF ORG CHEM, KENT STATE UNIV, 92- *Personal Data:* b Keighley, Eng, Jan 4, 59; UK citizen; m 90, Janice M Sawer; c Hannah & Emma. *Educ:* Univ Birmingham, Eng, BSc, 80, PhD(org chem), 83. *Prof Exp:* Res assoc org chem, Univ Iowa, 83-85. *Mem:* Am Chem Soc; Royal Soc Chem. *Res:* Development of synthetic methods aimed at syntheses of paslitaxel analogs; synthesis of macrocyclic and medium-sized rings; synthetic organofluorine chemistry; synthesis of fluorinated liquid crystals florinated carbasugars. *Mailing Add:* 508 Bowman Dr Kent OH 44240-4512. *Fax:* 330-672-3816; *E-Mail:* psampson@kentvm.kent.edu

SAMPSON, ROBERT NEIL, AGRONOMY. *Current Pos:* PRES, SAMPSON GROUP INC, 96- *Personal Data:* b Spokane, Wash, Nov 29, 38; m 60, Jeanne L Stokes; c Robert W, Eric S, Christopher B & Heidi L. *Educ:* Univ Idaho, BS, 60; Harvard Univ, MPA, 74. *Honors & Awards:* Hugh Hammond Bennett Award, Soil & Water Conserv Soc, 92. *Prof Exp:* Soil conservationist, Soil Conserv Serv, Burley, Idaho, 60-61, work unit conservationist, Orofino, 62-65, agronomist, Idaho Falls, 67-68, info specialist, Boise, 68-70, area conservationist, 70-72, land use specialist, Washington, 74-77, dir, Environ Servs Div, 77-78; land use prog mgr, Idaho Planning & Community Affairs Agency, Boise, 72-73; exec vpres, Nat Asn Conserv Dist, Washington, 78-84; exec vpres, Am Forestry Asn Washington, 84-95. *Concurrent Pos:* Instr soils & land use, Boise State Univ, 72; dir, Am Land Forum, Washington, 78-88; chmn, Nat Comn Wildfire Disasters, 92-94; sr fel, Am Forests, Washington, 95- *Mem:* Fel Soil & Water Conserv Soc; Soc Am Foresters. *Res:* Contributes articles to professional publications on forests, forestry, land management, biomass and climate change. *Mailing Add:* 5209 York Rd Alexandria VA 22310-1126

SAMPSON, RONALD N, CHEMICAL ENGINEERING. *Current Pos:* RETIRED. *Personal Data:* b Pittsburgh, Pa, Sept 16, 30; m 53; c 4. *Educ:* Carnegie-Mellon Univ, BS, 52 & 57. *Prof Exp:* Engr, Mat Eng Dept, Westinghouse Elec Corp, 52-57, supvry engr, Chem Appln Sect, 57-62, mgr insulation, 62-80, mgr, Chem Sci Div, Res Labs, 80-88, tech dir, 88-89. *Mem:* Am Chem Soc; Soc Plastics Engrs; AAAS; Inst Elec & Electronics Engrs. *Res:* Research and development of polymers and plastics in areas of electrical insulation, laminates, molding materials, adhesives and films. *Mailing Add:* 4250 Bulltown Rd Murrysville PA 15668-9503

SAMPSON, SANFORD ROBERT, PHYSIOLOGY, PHARMACOLOGY. *Current Pos:* DEPT LIFE SCI, BAR-ILAN UNIV, ISRAEL. *Personal Data:* b Los Angeles, Calif, Feb 27, 37; m 59; c 2. *Educ:* Univ Calif, Berkeley, BA, 59; Univ Utah, PhD(pharmacol), 64. *Prof Exp:* Lectr, 68-69, asst prof pharmacol, 69-71, from asst prof to assoc prof psysiol, Med Ctr, Univ Calif, San Francisco, 71- *Concurrent Pos:* Fel pharmacol, Albert Einstein Col Med, 64-66; res fel, Cardiovasc Res Inst, Med Ctr, Univ Calif, San Francisco, 66-69, Nat Heart Inst spec fel, 69-71; Macy fac scholar, 78-79; vis scientist, Weizmann Inst Sci, 78-79. *Mem:* Am Physiol Soc; Soc Neurosci; Am Soc Pharmacol & Exp Therapeut; Int Soc Develop Neurosci. *Res:* Membrane channels and electro-genic pumps in excitable membranes. *Mailing Add:* Dept Life Sci Bar-Ilan Univ Ramat-Gan Israel. *Fax:* 972-3-535-1824

SAMPSON, WILLIAM B, PHYSICS. *Current Pos:* PHYSICIST, ACCELERATION DEPT, BROOKHAVEN NAT LAB, 62- *Personal Data:* b Toronto, Ont, Aug 31, 34; m 55; c 2. *Educ:* Univ Toronto, BA, 58, MA, 59, PhD(physics), 62. *Mem:* Am Phys Soc. *Res:* Superconductivity and applications to high energy physics. *Mailing Add:* Accelerator Dept Brookhaven Nat Lab Upton NY 11973

SAMPSON-HEIMER, PHYLLIS MARIE, BIOCHEMISTRY. *Current Pos:* RETIRED. *Personal Data:* b New York, NY, Sept 13, 28; m 74, Ralph; c Robert & Paul. *Educ:* Hunter Col, BA, 50; Columbia Univ, PhD(biochem), 72. *Prof Exp:* Res assoc chem, Yeshiva Univ, 72-73; res assoc biochem, Columbia Univ, 73-76; res assoc med, Univ Pa, 76-84, res assist prof, 84-90. *Mem:* Sigma Xi; Soc Complex Carbohydrates; AAAS; NY Acad Sci. *Res:* Proteoglycan and glycosaminoglycan distribution in normal and pathological lung tissue and production by lung cells in tissue and organ culture; biochemistry and chemistry of carbohydrates. *Mailing Add:* 235 S Third St Philadelphia PA 19106

SAMPUGNA, JOSEPH, BIOCHEMISTRY, NUTRITION. *Current Pos:* asst prof, 68-72, ASSOC PROF BIOCHEM, UNIV MD, COLLEGE PARK, 72-, DIR, CHEM & BIOCHEM UNDERGRAD PROGS, 95- *Personal Data:* b Sept 27, 31; US citizen; m 57, Dorothy J Leduc; c Joseph A & Theresa A (Otley). *Educ:* Univ Conn, BA, 59, MA, 62, PhD(biochem), 68. *Prof Exp:* Res asst biochem, Univ Conn, 62-68. *Concurrent Pos:* Vpres, Chem Asn Md, 73-80, treas, 80- *Mem:* Am Chem Soc; Am Oil Chem Soc; Am Inst Nutrit. *Res:* Lipid biochemistry; membrane structure and function; metabolism of dietary lipids; trans fatty acids. *Mailing Add:* Dept Chem & Biochem Univ Md College Park MD 20742. *Fax:* 301-314-9121; *E-Mail:* js8@umail.umd.edu

SAMS, BRUCE JONES, JR, HEALTH ECONOMICS. *Current Pos:* RETIRED. *Personal Data:* b Savannah, Ga, Jan 24, 28; m; c 3. *Educ:* Ga Inst Technol, BS, 51; Harvard Univ, MD, 55. *Prof Exp:* Intern, NC Mem Hosp, Chapel Hill, 55-56; asst resident, Univ Calif, San Fransisco, 56-57; res fel hemat, Mass Gen Hosp, Boston, 57-59; dir, Med Residency Prog, Kaiser Permanente Med Ctr, San Francisco, 64-71, chief med, 65-71, chief staff educ, 66-69, physician-in-chief, 71-75; exec dir-elect, Permanente Med Group, Oakland, Calif, 75-76, exec dir, 76-91. *Concurrent Pos:* Clin instr med, Univ Calif, San Francisco, 61-62, assoc clin prof, 63-; physician, Kaiser Permanente Med Ctr, 62-; mem, Clin Pract Subcomt, Am Col Physicians; mem bd, Group Health Asn Am. *Mem:* Inst Med-Nat Acad Sci; fel Am Col Physicians; AMA; Am Col Physician Execs. *Mailing Add:* 88 Lagoon Rd Belvedere Tiburon CA 94920

SAMS, BURNETT HENRY, III, DATABASES, MULTIPROCESSING. *Current Pos:* MGR INTEGRATED SYSTS, NAT BROADCASTING CO, 81- *Personal Data:* b Seattle, Wash, Apr 30, 31; m 56; c 2. *Educ:* Univ Wash, BS, 51; Univ Ill, MS, 53, PhD(math), 58. *Honors & Awards:* David Sarnof Achievement Award Sci. *Prof Exp:* Res assoc, Control Systs Lab, Univ Ill, 57-58 & Comput Ctr, Mass Inst Technol, 58-59; proj leader, Astro-Electronics Prods Div, Radio Corp Am, 59-61, mgr, Prog Sci Sect, Data Systs Ctr, 62-64; systs res lab, RCA Labs, 64-76, head comput aided mfg, Solid State Technol Ctr, 76-81. *Concurrent Pos:* Instr, Dartmouth Col, 58-59; prof, Dept Elec Eng & Comput Sci, Stevens Inst Technol, 72-82. *Mem:* AAAS; Asn Comput Mach; Math Asn Am; Am Math Soc; Inst Elec & Electronics Engrs; Soc Motion Picture TV Engrs. *Res:* Computer system architecture; distributed systems, multiprocessing; information storage and retrieval; data communications; process control; software engineering; television control systems; high definition TV; spectrum utilization. *Mailing Add:* 513 Prospect Ave Princeton NJ 08540-4032

SAMS, CARL EARNEST, STRESS PHYSIOLOGY HORTICULTURAL CROPS. *Current Pos:* asst prof, 83-85, ASSOC PROF, UNIV TENN, 85- *Personal Data:* b Knoxville, Tenn, Dec 8, 51; m 71; c 3. *Educ:* Univ Tenn, BS, 74, MS, 76; Mich State Univ, PhD(hort), 80. *Prof Exp:* Res plant physiologist, USDA, 80-83. *Mem:* Am Soc Hort Sci; Int Soc Hort Sci; Am Soc Plant Physiologists. *Res:* Stress physiology of horticultural crops: mineral nutrition, water stress, temperature stress and the relationship between stress related disorders and crop productivity and senescence; postharvest physiology. *Mailing Add:* Dept Plant & Soil Sci Univ Tenn PO Box 1071 Knoxville TN 37901-1071

SAMS, EMMETT SPRINKLE, MATHEMATICS EDUCATION. *Current Pos:* RETIRED. *Personal Data:* b Burnsville, NC, July 17, 20; m 46; c 2. *Educ:* Western Carolina Univ, BS, 41; George Peabody Col, MA, 49, NC State Univ, 58; Cornell Univ, 60; Univ Kans, 64. *Honors & Awards:* Robert S Gibbs Distinguished Teacher Award, Mars Hill Col, 80, W W Rankin Award Excellence in Math Educ, 83. *Prof Exp:* Teacher math, Yancey Co Bd Educ,

41-45; teacher, Madison Co Bd Educ, 45-47; from instr to assoc prof math, Mars Hill Col, 47-57, prof, 57-92. *Mem:* Math Asn Am; Nat Coun Teachers Math; NC Council of Teachers of Math. *Res:* Serial correlation. *Mailing Add:* PO Box 501 Mars Hill NC 28754

SAMS, JOHN ROBERT, JR, CHEMICAL PHYSICS, ORGANOMETALLIC CHEMISTRY. *Current Pos:* from asst prof to assoc prof, 63-72, PROF CHEM, UNIV BC, 72- *Personal Data:* b Kinston, NC, Feb 16, 36; m 63; c 2. *Educ:* Amherst Col, BA, 58; Univ Wash, PhD(phys chem), 62. *Prof Exp:* NATO fel, Imp Col, Univ London, 62-63. *Mem:* NY Acad Sci. *Res:* Moessbauer spectroscopy; theoretical chemistry; magnetochemistry. *Mailing Add:* Dept Chem Univ BC 2075 Westbrook Pl Vancouver BC V6T 1W5 Can

SAMS, LEWIS CALHOUN, JR, INORGANIC CHEMISTRY. *Current Pos:* from asst prof to assoc prof inorg chem, 63-81, PROF CHEM, TEX WOMAN'S UNIV, 81- *Personal Data:* b Dallas, Tex, Sept 13, 28; m 52; c 2. *Educ:* Midwestern Univ, BS, 50; Tex A&M Univ, MS, 54, PhD(inorg chem), 61. *Prof Exp:* Microanalyst, Ft Worth Gen Depot, US Army, 54-56; chemist, Celanese Chem Corp, 56-57; instr chem, ETex State Univ, 57-59; asst prof chem, Trinity Col, Tex, 61-63. *Mem:* Am Chem Soc. *Res:* Microwave spectroscopy; inorganic fluorine synthesis. *Mailing Add:* 2611 Crestwood Pl Denton TX 76201

SAMS, RICHARD ALVIN, ANALYTICAL CHEMISTRY. *Current Pos:* ASST PROF PHARMACOL & VET CLIN SCI, COL VET MED, OHIO STATE UNIV, 76- *Personal Data:* b Lebanon, Ohio, Aug 28, 46. *Educ:* Ohio State Univ, BS, 69, PhD(pharm), 75. *Prof Exp:* Sr scientist anal res, Pharmaceut Div, Ciba-Geigy Corp, 74-75. *Mem:* Am Chem Soc. *Res:* Investigation of high-pressure liquid chromatography and gas liquid chromatography separation mechanisms; investigation of comparative pharmacokinetics in various animal species. *Mailing Add:* 3416 Polley Rd Columbus OH 43221-4704

SAMS, WILEY MITCHELL, JR, DERMATOLOGY. *Current Pos:* PROF DERMAT & CHMN DEPT, UNIV ALA, 81- *Personal Data:* b Ann Arbor, Mich, Apr 15, 33; m 59, Marion Yount; c Robert, Hunter & Margery. *Educ:* Univ Mich, BS, 55; Emory Univ, MD, 59; Am Bd Dermat, dipl. *Prof Exp:* Intern, Emory Univ Hosp, 59-60; asst resident & resident dermat, Duke Univ Hosp, 60-62, assoc, Med Ctr, 63-64; asst clin prof, Med Ctr, Univ Calif, San Francisco, 65-66; from asst prof to assoc prof, Mayo Grad Sch Med, Univ Minn, 66-72; prof dermat & head div, Univ Colo Med Ctr, Denver, 72-76; prof, Univ NC, Chapel Hill, 76-80. *Concurrent Pos:* Nat Cancer Inst fel, 62-64. *Mem:* Am Acad Dermat; Soc Invest Dermat; Am Fedn Clin Res. *Res:* Immunology of skin diseases. *Mailing Add:* Dept Dermat Univ Ala University Sta KB101 Birmingham AL 35294

SAMSON, CHARLES HAROLD, STRUCTURAL ENGINEERING, QUALITY MANAGEMENT & SYSTEMS ENGINEERING. *Current Pos:* head, Civil Eng Dept, Tex A&M Univ, 64-79, actg pres, 80-81, vpres planning, 81-82, prof aerospace & civil eng, 60-80, prof, 80-94, EMER PROF CIVIL ENG, TEX A&M UNIV, 94- *Personal Data:* b Portsmouth, Ohio, July 12, 24; m 47, Ruth A Baumbach; c Peggy A & Charles H III. *Educ:* Univ Notre Dame, BSCE, 47, MSCE, 48; Univ Mo, PhD(struct eng), 53. *Honors & Awards:* Eng Honor Award, Univ Notre Dame, 82. *Prof Exp:* Asst to field rep, Loebl, Schlossman & Bennett, Ill, 48-49; struct engr, Gen Dynamics-Convair, Tex, 51-52, sr struct engr, 52-53; asst prof civil eng, Univ Notre Dame, 53-56; proj aerodyn engr, Gen Dynamics-Ft Worth, 56-58, proj struct engr, 58-60. *Concurrent Pos:* Lectr, Southern Methodist Univ, 52-53 & 56-60. *Mem:* Am Soc Civil Engrs; Am Soc Eng Educ; Nat Soc Prof Engrs (pres, 87-88); Am Soc Qual Control; Am Soc Eng Mgt; Int Coun Syst Eng. *Res:* Systems engineering; quality management; engineering education. *Mailing Add:* 810 Dogwood Lane Bryan TX 77802-1144. *Fax:* 409-779-0486

SAMSON, FREDERICK EUGENE, JR, PHARMACOLOGY. *Current Pos:* From asst prof to prof physiol, Med Ctr, Univ Kans, 52-73, actg chmn, Dept Biochem & Physiol, 61-62, chmn, Dept Physiol & Cell Biol, 62-73, dir, R L Smith Res Ctr, 73-89, EMER PROF, MED CTR, UNIV KANS, 89- *Personal Data:* b Medford, Mass, Aug 16, 18; m 45, Camila Albert; c Cecile, Julie & Renee. *Educ:* Univ Chicago, BS, 48, PhD(physiol), 52; Mass Col Osteop, DO, 40. *Concurrent Pos:* Staff scientist, Neurosci Res Prog, Mass Inst Technol, 65-82. *Mem:* Am Physiol Soc; Soc Neurosci; Am Soc Neurochem; Am Soc Cell Biol; fel AAAS; Oxygen Soc. *Res:* Neurochemistry; brain metabolism; brain regional functional mapping; experimental studies on neurological systems involved in seizures, toxicity and anesthesia; role of the brain extracellular compartment and brain cell microenvironment in central nervous system functions, seizures and toxins; role of free radicals in brain damage and in normal functions. *Mailing Add:* 171 Lake Shore S Lake Quivira KS 66106-9516. *Fax:* 913-588-5677; *E-Mail:* fsamson1@kumc.edu

SAMSON, JAMES ALEXANDER ROSS, ATOMIC PHYSICS. *Current Pos:* prof, 70-81, CHARLES MACH DISTINGUISHED PROF PHYSICS, UNIV NEBR-LINCOLN, 81- *Personal Data:* b Scotland, Sept 9, 28; nat US; m 54; c 2. *Educ:* Univ Glasgow, BSc, 52, DSc, 70; Univ Southern Calif, MS, 55, PhD(physics), 58. *Prof Exp:* Asst physics, Univ Southern Calif, 53-58, res assoc, 58-60; res physicist, Univ Mich & Harvard Univ, 60-61, GCA Corp, Mass, 61-70. *Concurrent Pos:* Assoc ed, J of the Optical Soc Am, 70-81; mem adv screening comt physics, Coun for Int Exchange of Scholars, 78-81; vis prof, Univ Southampton, Eng, 72, Bonn Univ, W Ger, 76, Daresbury Synchrotron Lab, Eng, 76-77, Phys Res Lab, Ahmedabad, India, 77, Univ Hawaii, Honolulu, 80 & Australian Nat Univ, Canberra, 82; mem, Comt Line Spectra Elements-Atomic Spectros, Nat Res Coun, 81-84; chmn, Int Prog Comt, 6th Int Conf Vacuum Ultraviolet Radiation Physics, 80, mem, 83; mem, Comt Appln Physics, Am Phys Soc, 81-85; mem, X-ray & Ultraviolet Tech Comt, Optical Soc Am & Mees Medal Comt, 83, chmn, 85. *Mem:* fel Am Phys Soc; fel Optical Soc Am; Sigma Xi. *Res:* Vacuum ultraviolet spectroscopy; atomic and molecular physics; photoelectron spectroscopy. *Mailing Add:* Dept Physics Univ Nebr Lincoln NE 68588-0111

SAMSON, LINDA FORREST, HEALTH CARE FINANCE, PERINATAL NURSING. *Current Pos:* asst prof nursing, 89-93, head, Dept Bacc Nursing, 90-92, DEAN, SCH HEALTH SCI, CLAYTON COL & STATE UNIV, 92-, ASSOC PROF NURSING, 93- *Personal Data:* b Miami, Fla, Dec 7, 49; m 72, Mark; c Amy & Josh. *Educ:* Emory Univ, BSN, 72, MN, 73; Univ Pa, PhD(nursing admin/health policy), 89. *Prof Exp:* Perinatal clin specialist, Our Lady Lourdes Med Ctr, 78-82; lectr-perinatal nursing, Univ Pa, 81-88; asst prof nursing, Kennesaw Col, 88-89. *Concurrent Pos:* Bd dirs, Nat Perinatal Asn, 86-89, Am AACN Cert Corp & Am Asn Critical Care Nursing, 87-90; consult, 85- *Mem:* Am Asn Crit Care Nursing; Soc Critical Care Med; Am Nurses Asn; Nat League Nursing. *Res:* Cost of health care, liability issues and perinatal infection; pulmonary problems of newborns. *Mailing Add:* 2915 Four Oaks Dr Atlanta GA 30360. *Fax:* 770-961-3639; *E-Mail:* samson@cc.clayton.edu

SAMSON, STEN, CHEMISTRY. *Current Pos:* res fel, Calif Inst Technol, sr res fel, 61-73, res assoc, 73-80, sr res assoc, 80-86, EMER SR RES ASSOC CHEM, CALIF INST TECHNOL, 86- *Personal Data:* b Stockholm, Sweden, Mar 25, 16; m 48, Lalli Sandstrom; c Karin & Karl, O. *Educ:* Univ Stockholm, Fil Kand, 53, Fil Lic, 56, Fil Dr, 68. *Prof Exp:* Res fel chem, Univ Stockholm, 48-53. *Concurrent Pos:* Consult, Comn Crystal Data, Int Union Crystal, 67-73, Syst Anal Instruments, 69-71 & Advan Res & Applications Corp, 80-; mem, US Panel Joint US Brazil Study Group Grad Training & Res Brazil, 75-76. *Mem:* Am Crystallog Asn. *Res:* Crystal structures of very complex intermetallic compounds; crystallographic tranformations associated with changes in physical properties, paralelectric and ferroelectric, conductors and insulator transitions especially in one-dimensional conductors; structures of quasi-crystalline substances. *Mailing Add:* Beckman Inst Calif Inst Technol MC 139-74 Pasadena CA 91125

SAMSON, WILLIS KENDRICK, NEUROENDOCRINOLOGY, PEPTIDE NEUROCHEMISTRY. *Current Pos:* CHMN, DEPT PHYSIOL, UNIV NDAK, 92- *Personal Data:* b Syracuse, NY, May 15, 47. *Educ:* Duke Univ, AB, 68; Univ Tex Health Sci Ctr Dallas, PhD(physiol), 79. *Prof Exp:* Asst prof physiol, Univ Tex Health Sci Ctr, 81-88; assoc prof aton, Univ Miss, Sch Med, 88-92. *Mem:* Endocrine Soc. *Res:* Neuroendocrinology; brain and gut peptides; control of anterior pituitary function. *Mailing Add:* Physiol Dept Univ NDak Sch Med 501 N Columbia Rd Rm 3700 Grand Forks ND 58202-9037

SAMTER, MAX, CLINICAL MEDICINE, ALLERGY & CLINICAL IMMUNOLOGY. *Current Pos:* SR CONSULT, MAX SAMTER INST ALLERGY & CLIN IMMUNOL, GRANT HOSP, CHICAGO, 84- *Personal Data:* b Berlin, Ger, Mar 3, 08; nat US; m 47; c 1. *Educ:* Univ Berlin, MD, 33; Univ Ill, MS, 47; Am Bd Internal Med & Am Bd Allergy & Immunol, dipl, 49 & 74. *Honors & Awards:* Outstanding Clinician Award, Am Acad Allergy & Immunol, 90. *Prof Exp:* Asst dispensary physician, Sch Med, Johns Hopkins Univ, 37-38; asst biochem, 46, from instr to prof med, 46-80, head sect allergy & clin immunol, 47-75, assoc dean clin affairs, 74-75, chief of staff, Univ Hosp, 74-75, emer prof med, Abraham Lincoln Sch Med, Univ Ill Med Ctr, 80- *Concurrent Pos:* Consult, Chicago West Side, Hines Vet Admin & West Suburban Hosps; dir, Max Samter Inst Allergy & Clin Immunol, Grant Hosp, Chicago, 75-84. *Mem:* Am Med Asn; fel Am Col Physicians; Am Acad Allergy & Immunol (treas, 54, pres, 58); Int Asn Allergol & Clin Immunol; Interasma; Sigma Xi. *Res:* Function of eosinophils; mechanism of drug reactions; pathogenesis of bronchial asthma. *Mailing Add:* 645 Sheridan Rd Evanston IL 60202-2533

SAMUEL, ALBERT, MOLECULAR BIOLOGY. *Current Pos:* PROF BIOL, DEPT SCI, FREDERICK COMMUNITY COL, MD, 86-, CHMN, DEPT SCI. *Personal Data:* b Tanjore, India, Feb 27, 37; US citizen; m 69, Jean L Wuori; c Paul, Joseph & Mark. *Educ:* Univ Madras, India, BA, 59, MSc, 61; Oberlin Col, Ohio, MA, 65; Mich State Univ, PhD(entomol), 71. *Prof Exp:* Demonstr zool, Am Col, Madurai, India, 61-63; fel entom, Mich State Univ, 71-73; prof biol & chmn, Dept Sci & Math, St Paul's Col, Va, 73-83; dir biomed res activ, 73-83. *Concurrent Pos:* NIH fac fel, 77-79; res biologist, Lawrence Livermore Lab & Naval Med Res Inst, Bethesda, 81-83. *Mem:* AAAS; Cell Kinetic Soc; Am Inst Biol Sci. *Res:* Aging in cells in vitro; kinetics of tumor cells and its application in chemotherapy; expression of cell surface antigens and correlated cell cycle phases in t-cell lines; pluripotent stem cell identification by monoclonal antibodies. *Mailing Add:* Dept Sci Frederick Community Col 7932 Opposumtown Pike Frederick MD 21702. *Fax:* 301-846-2498

SAMUEL, ARYEH HERMANN, OPERATIONS RESEARCH. *Current Pos:* RETIRED. *Personal Data:* b Hildesheim, Ger, Feb 19, 24; US citizen; wid; c Joshua R. *Educ:* Univ Ill, BS, 43; Northwestern Univ, MS, 46; Univ Notre Dame, PhD(chem), 53. *Honors & Awards:* Lanchester Prize, Oper Res Soc Am, 62. *Prof Exp:* Scientist, Broadview Res, 56-60, Stanford Res Inst, 60-65; res leader phys chem, Gen Precision, 65-67; sr scientist, Stanford Res Inst, 67-72; criminalist, County Santa Clara, Calif, 72-74; sr scientist, Vector Res Inc, 74-77; prin res scientist, Battelle Mem Inst, 77-87; Consult, 88-92. *Mem:* Inst Opers Res & Mgt Sci. *Res:* Operations research-public systems, especially military and postal; remote sensing; chemical effects of radiations. *Mailing Add:* 10861 Bucknell Dr Wheaton MD 20902

SAMUEL, CHARLES EDWARD, VIROLOGY, INTERFERON. *Current Pos:* from asst prof to assoc prof biol, 74-83, chmn, Prog Molecular Biol & Biochem, 88-95, PROF BIOCHEM & MOLECULAR BIOL, UNIV CALIF, SANTA BARBARA, 83-, MEM, MATS RES LAB, 92-, CHMN, DEPT MOLECULAR, CELLULAR & DEVELOP BIOL. *Personal Data:* b Portland, Ore, Nov 28, 45; m 68; c 2. *Educ:* Mont State Univ, BS, 68; Univ Calif, Berkeley, PhD(biochem), 72. *Honors & Awards:* Merit Award, NIH; Wellcome Vis Prof Award, Fedn Am Soc Exp Biol. *Prof Exp:* Damon Runyon Scholar, Duke Univ Med Ctr, 72-74. *Concurrent Pos:* Fel, Damon Runyon-Walter Winchell Cancer Fund, 72-74 & Duke Med Sch, 74; prin investr, Nat Inst Allergy & Infectious Dis 75-, Am Cancer Soc, 75-85; Res Career Develop Award, NIH, 79-84; assoc ed, Virol, 80-, J Interferon Res, 80-, J Virol, 83-95 & J Biol Chem, 89-93, 96-; consult, NIH, 80-; vis prof, Univ Zurich, 86-87. *Mem:* Am Soc Biol Chemists; Am Soc Microbiol; Am Soc Virol; Int Soc Interferon Cytokine Res. *Res:* Biochemistry of animal virus-cell interactions; mechanism of interferon action; molecular biology of reoviruses; translational control mechanisms. *Mailing Add:* Dept Molecular Cellular & Develop Biol Univ Calif Santa Barbara CA 93106. *Fax:* 805-893-4724; *E-Mail:* samuel@lifesci.lscf.ucsb.edu

SAMUEL, DAVID EVAN, WILDLIFE BIOLOGY, ORNITHOLOGY. *Current Pos:* instr zool, 68-69, assoc prof, 69-97, ASSOC WILDLIFE BIOLOGIST, WVA UNIV, 76-, PROF WILDLIFE BIOL, 97- *Personal Data:* b Johnstown, Pa, July 28, 40; m 66. *Educ:* Juniata Col, BS, 62; Pa State Univ, MS, 64; Univ WVa, PhD(zool), 69. *Prof Exp:* Instr biol, Bethany Col, 64-66. *Concurrent Pos:* USDA grant. *Mem:* Am Ornith Union; Wildlife Soc; Wilson Ornith Soc; Nat Audubon Soc. *Res:* Behavior. *Mailing Add:* Div Forestry WVa Univ Box 6125 Morgantown WV 26506-6125

SAMUEL, EDMUND WILLIAM, DEVELOPMENTAL BIOLOGY. *Current Pos:* from asst prof to assoc prof biol, 60-71, PROF BIOL, ANTIOCH COL, 72- *Personal Data:* b Canton, Ohio, Sept 17, 24; m 63. *Educ:* Case Western Reserve Univ, BSEE, 45, MS, 49; Princeton Univ, MS, 59, PhD(biol), 60. *Prof Exp:* Res investr theoret physics, Sperry Gyroscope Corp, 49-50; res asst med physics, Mass Gen Hosp, Boston, 52-53. *Concurrent Pos:* NSF instrumentation grant, 62-64, undergrad res partic grant, 65-66. *Res:* Biophysics; theoretical and molecular biology; history and philosophy of science; East Asian science such as Japanese medicine; bioethics. *Mailing Add:* Dept Biol Southern Conn St Col 501 Crescent St New Haven CT 06515-1330

SAMUEL, JAY MORRIS, WELDING METALLURGY, WELDING PROCESSES. *Current Pos:* ASST PROF MECH ENG, UNIV WIS, MADISON, 79- *Personal Data:* b Stuttgart, WGer, Jan 24, 46. *Educ:* Rensselaer Polytech Inst, BS, 67, PhD(mat eng), 79. *Honors & Awards:* Clyde Sanders Award, Foundry Educ Found & Am Colloid Co, 82. *Prof Exp:* Adj prof mech tech, Hudson Valley Community Col, 77-79. *Mem:* Am Welding Soc; Am Soc Metals. *Res:* Solidification mechanics; physical metallurgy of weldments; control of welding processes; structure; properties of engineering materials. *Mailing Add:* 766 S Gammon Rd Madison WI 53719

SAMUEL, MARK AARON, THEORETICAL HIGH ENERGY PHYSICS. *Current Pos:* Asst prof, 69-75, assoc prof, 75-81, PROF PHYSICS, OKLA STATE UNIV, 81- *Personal Data:* b Montreal, Que, Jan 26, 44; div; c 2. *Educ:* McGill Univ, BSc, 64, MSc, 66; Univ Rochester, PhD(physics), 69. *Honors & Awards:* Masua Lectr. *Concurrent Pos:* Consult, NSF Educ Res Grant, Okla State Univ, 72-75; vis scientist, Stanford Linear Accelerator Ctr, 73, 75, 94, 95 & 96, Niels Bohr Inst, Copenhagen, Denmark, 77, Aspen Ctr Physics, 81, 85, 86, 87, 91, 95 & 96, Argonne Nat Lab, 95. *Mem:* Am Phys Soc; Am Asn Physics Teachers; Can Asn Physicists. *Res:* Field theory; particle physics; atomic physics; tests of quantum electrodynamics and quantum chromodynamics; applied mathematical techniques. *Mailing Add:* Dept Physics Okla State Univ Stillwater OK 74078. *Fax:* 405-744-6811; *E-Mail:* physmas@mus.ucc.okstate.edu

SAMUEL, WILLIAM MORRIS, PARASITOLOGY. *Current Pos:* Fel parasitol, Univ Alta, 69-71, from asst prof to assoc prof, 71-78, assoc dean res, 91-92, PROF ZOOL, UNIV ALTA, 81-, ASSOC CHMN GRAD STUDIES, 94- *Personal Data:* b Windber, Pa, July 28, 40; m 96, Donette M Williams. *Educ:* Juniata Col, BSc, 62; Pa State Univ, MSc, 65; Univ Wis, PhD(vet sci, zool), 69. *Mem:* Am Soc Parasitol; Wildlife Dis Asn; Wildlife Soc; Can Soc Zoologists; Entom Soc Am. *Res:* Ecology of wildlife parasites; importance for host populations; emphasis on big game. *Mailing Add:* Dept Biol Sci Univ Alta Edmonton AB T6G 2E9 Can. *Fax:* 403-492-9234

SAMUEL-CAHN, ESTER, DECISION THEORY, SEQUENTIAL ANALYSIS. *Current Pos:* PROF STATIST, HEBREW UNIV, 62- *Personal Data:* b Oslo, Norway, May 16, 33; Israeli citizen; m 70, Aron Cahn; c Amotz, Oded, Michal & Eitan. *Educ:* Hebrew Univ, BA, 58; Columbia Univ, NY, MA, 59, PhD(statist), 61. *Concurrent Pos:* Vis prof, Columbia Univ, 80 & Rutgers Univ, 81; chmn, Israel Statist Asn. *Mem:* Fel Inst Math Statist; fel Am Statist Asn; Int Statist Inst; Israel Statist Asn; Israel Soc Oper Res; Norweg Acad Sci & Letters. *Res:* Empirical Bayes decision problems; Bomber Problem; univariate and multivariate optimal stopping problems; prophet inequalities; secretary problems and other problems in statistics and applied probability. *Mailing Add:* Dept Statist Hebrew Univ Jerusalem 91905 Israel. *Fax:* 972-2-5322545; *E-Mail:* msdoronz@pluto.mscc.huji.ac.il

SAMUELS, ARTHUR SEYMOUR, PSYCHOANALYTIC MEDICINE, PSYCHOSOMATIC MEDICINE. *Current Pos:* DIR, STRESS TREATMENT CTR, NEW ORLEANS, 87- *Personal Data:* b New York, NY, July 24, 25; c 4. *Educ:* Cornell Univ, BA, 44, MA, 49; Tulane Univ, MD, 53. *Prof Exp:* Dir, New Orleans Mental Health Clinic, 56-58; teacher group psychotherap, New Orleans Ctr Psychotherap, 76-77; assoc prof clin psychiat, LA State Univ Med Sch, 79- *Concurrent Pos:* Pvt pract pyschiat, 58-; dir, Biofeedback Ctr New Orleans, 76- *Mem:* Fel Am Acad Psychoanal; Fel Am Psychiat Asn. *Res:* The production of essential hypertension through automatic conditioning techniques; evaluation of various phenothiazine drugs in psychosis; the role of the composition of group in the efficacy of group therapy; using a group approach for reducing inter-racial prejudice; the combined use of hypnosis and biofeedback in the treatment of stress related illnesses; geriatric medicine. *Mailing Add:* 4829 Prytania St Suite 200 New Orleans LA 70155-4046

SAMUELS, BRIAN LOUIS, MEDICAL ONCOLOGY. *Current Pos:* fel, Univ Ill, Chicago, 84-88, instr med, 88-89, asst prof med, 89-95, ASSOC PROF MED, UNIV ILL, CHICAGO, 96- *Personal Data:* b Harare, Zimbabwe, May 5, 54; US citizen; m 79, Lesley Margaret Blake; c David, Mark & Emma. *Educ:* Univ Rhodesia, MBChB, 76. *Prof Exp:* Intern, Univ Rhodesia; flight surgeon, Rhodesian Air Force, 78; med resident, Albert Einstein Med Ctr, 79-81 & 83-84, Univ Witwatersrand, 81-83. *Mem:* Fel Am Col Physicians; Am Soc Clin Oncol; Am Asn Cancer Res; Am Fed Clin Res; Cent Soc Clin Res; Connective Tissue Oncol Soc. *Res:* Conduct of clinical trials in cancer therapy with specific emphasis on adult soft tissue and bone sarcomas. *Mailing Add:* 1700 Luther Lane Park Ridge IL 60062. *Fax:* 847-723-8250; *E-Mail:* brian.samuels_md@advocatehealth.com

SAMUELS, JOHN M, JR, MECHANICAL ENGINEERING, SYSTEMS DESIGN. *Current Pos:* Dir indust eng, Conrail Corp 79-80, asst vpres eng, 80-90, vpres continuous qual improv, 90-92, vpres eng, 92-94, vpres mech eng, 94-96, VPRES OPER ASSETS, CONRAIL CORP, 96- *Personal Data:* b Trenton, NJ, July 8, 43. *Educ:* Gen Motors Inst, BS, 66; Pa State Univ, MS, 68, PhD, 72. *Mem:* Nat Acad Eng; Am Railway Eng Asn; Nat Coun Indust Eng; Inst Indust Eng. *Mailing Add:* Consolidated Rail Corp 2001 Market St 15B PO Box 41415 Philadelphia PA 19101-1415. *Fax:* 215-209-1310; *E-Mail:* john.samuels@conrail.com

SAMUELS, MARTIN E(LMER), CHEMICAL ENGINEERING. *Current Pos:* RETIRED. *Personal Data:* b Dayton, Ohio, Apr 24, 18; m 43, Jeannette Rubin; c Joel & Paula. *Educ:* Univ Dayton, BChE, 39. *Prof Exp:* Chemist, Dayton Tire & Rubber Co, 39-43; chemist, Copolymer Rubber & Chem Corp, 43-45, develop supvr, 45-47, develop mgr, 57-61, prod qual mgr, 61-67, mgr tech serv, 67-81, asst to vpres mkt, 81-82. *Concurrent Pos:* Lectr. *Mem:* Am Chem Soc. *Res:* Development, evaluation, quality control, end uses and utilization of synthetic latexes and elastomers. *Mailing Add:* 8021 Owen St Baton Rouge LA 70809-1633

SAMUELS, REUBEN, ENGINEERING. *Current Pos:* PRIN ENG CONSULT, PARSONS BRINCKERHOFF, INC, 90- *Mem:* Nat Acad Eng. *Mailing Add:* Parsons Brinckerhoff Inc One Penn Plaza 3rd Floor New York NY 10119

SAMUELS, ROBERT, PROTOZOOLOGY. *Current Pos:* prof biol & chmn dept, 79-83, prof, 83-88, EMER PROF, ETENN STATE UNIV, 88- *Personal Data:* b Philadelphia, Pa, June 12, 18; m 48, Gloria Siegel; c Deborah, Noel & Leslie. *Educ:* Univ Pa, AB, 38, MA, 40; Univ Calif, PhD(zool), 52. *Prof Exp:* Jr entomologist, USPHS, 41-43; teaching asst zool, Univ Calif, 46-49, assoc, 49-52; instr biol, Calif State Polytech Col, 53; from instr to asst prof microbiol, Sch Med, Univ Colo, 53-63, vis prof, 63; prof, Merharry Med Col, 63-67; prof biol, Purdue Univ, Indianapolis, 67-70; prof biol, Ind Univ-Purdue Univ, Indianapolis, 70-78, chmn dept, 72-76. *Concurrent Pos:* Sect rep, Purdue Univ, 69-70; lectr, Sch Med, Univ Colo; consult, Indian Health Surv, Wyo State Bd Health, USPHS, Wetherill Mesa Archaeol Proj, Nat Park Serv & Nat Geog Surv. *Mem:* Soc Protozool (asst treas, 58-60, treas, 60-66, pres, 72-73); Am Soc Microbiol; AAAS; Soc Exp Biol & Med; Am Soc Parasitol; Sigma Xi. *Res:* Cytology; physiology; molecular biology of parabasalid flagellate protozoa. *Mailing Add:* Dept Biochem Box 70581 ETenn State Univ Johnson City TN 37614. *E-Mail:* gsamu26968@aol.com

SAMUELS, ROBERT BIRELEY, FOOD CHEMISTRY. *Current Pos:* PRES, ALLERGAN HUMPHREY, 87- *Personal Data:* b Palo Alto, Calif, Feb 27, 40; m 60; c 3. *Educ:* Calif State Polytech Col, BS, 62; Univ Ill, PhD(food sci), 65. *Prof Exp:* USPHS trainee fel, 65-66; res chemist, Beckmam Instruments, Inc, Palo Alto, 66-67, sr res chemist, 67, group supvr chromatography res, 67-68, group supvr chromatography res & appln, 68-71, prog coordr bioprod, 71-72, chemotherapy prog mgr, 72-73, mgr bioprod, Spino Div, 73-; mem staff, Smith Kline Beckman, Philadelphia, 73-87. *Mem:* AAAS; Am Chem Soc; Inst Food Technologists; Sigma Xi. *Res:* Lipid chemistry; lipoprotein structure; peptide synthesis and purification; instrumentation. *Mailing Add:* One Bayberry St Portola Valley CA 94028

SAMUELS, ROBERT JOEL, PHYSICAL CHEMISTRY, POLYMER PHYSICS. *Current Pos:* PROF, GA INST TECHNOL, 79- *Personal Data:* b Brooklyn, NY, Jan 8, 31; m 86; c 2. *Educ:* Brooklyn Col, BS, 52; Stevens Inst Technol, MS, 55; Univ Akron, PhD(polymer chem), 61. *Honors & Awards:* Am Chem Soc Award, 71; Soc Plastics Engrs Award, 83. *Prof Exp:* Res chemist, Picatinny Arsenal, 52-55, Res Ctr, Goodyear Tire & Rubber Co, 57-59 & Inst Rubber Res, Akron, 59-60; res chemist, Res Ctr, Hercules Inc, 60-67, sr res chemist, 67-70, res scientist, 70-79. *Concurrent Pos:* Adj prof,

Dept Chem Eng, Univ Del, 72-79; affil prof, Dept Chem Eng, Univ Wash, 78-80. *Mem:* Am Chem Soc; Am Phys Soc; Soc Plastics Engrs; Polymer Processing Soc. *Res:* Polymer morphology and mechanics; small and wide angle x-ray diffraction; infrared spectroscopy; birefringence and refractometry; small-angle light scattering, sonic and mechanical properties of polymers; chemical stress relaxation of polymers; polymer chromatography; physical chemistry of stress relaxation of polymers; polymer chromatography; physical chemistry of dilute solutions; polyolefins, polymides, polyesters and others. *Mailing Add:* Sch Chem Eng Ga Inst Technol Atlanta GA 30332

SAMUELS, STANLEY, NEUROCHEMISTRY. *Current Pos:* asst prof, 64-69, ASSOC PROF EXP NEUROL, SCH MED, NY UNIV, 69- *Personal Data:* b New York, NY, Oct 13, 29; m 51; c 3. *Educ:* Syracuse Univ, AB, 51, MS, 54, PhD(biochem), 58. *Prof Exp:* Asst instr zool, Syracuse Univ, 52-54 & 55-57; asst biochem, Col Med, Univ Ill, 54-55; instr ophthalmic res, Col Med, Western Reserve Univ, 57-59; instr, Albert Einstein Col Med, 61-63. *Concurrent Pos:* Nat Inst Neurol Dis & Blindness fel neurol, Albert Einstein Col Med, 59-61; Nat Multiple Sclerosis Soc fel, 61-63; consult, NY Eye & Ear Infirmary, 61-63. *Mem:* AAAS; Harvey Soc; Asn Res Nerv & Ment Dis; Int Soc Neurochem; Am Soc Neurochem; Am Chem Soc. *Res:* Amino acid transport; thin-layer and high performance liquid chromatography; inborn metabolic errors; brain biochemistry. *Mailing Add:* Ten Crest Dr White Plains NY 10607. *E-Mail:* samues01@mcneu.med.nyu.edu

SAMUELSON, CHARLES R, BOTANY, ZOOLOGY. *Current Pos:* RETIRED. *Personal Data:* b Crookston, Minn, Feb 10, 27; m 56; c 3. *Educ:* Moorhead State Univ, BS, 52; Univ Northern Colo, Greeley, MA, 56; NDak State Univ, Fargo, PhD(entom), 76. *Prof Exp:* Teacher biol & chem, Dawson, Minn pub sch, 52-54 & Thief River Falls, 55-65; prof biol, Northland Community Col, Thief River Falls, Minn, 65-92. *Concurrent Pos:* Survey entomologist, Dept Agr, Minn, 58-81; consult entomologist, 81- *Mem:* Entom Soc Am; Nat Asn Biol Teachers; Am Registry Prof Entomologists; Nat Educ Asn; Am Fedn Teachers. *Res:* Life cycle and associated environmental factors of the sunflower midge, Contarinia Schulzi Gagne in northwest Minnesota and northeast North Dakota; diptera: chironomidae in municipal sewage lagoons, (chironomid midges) biology and control. *Mailing Add:* 206 S Maple Thief River Falls MN 56701

SAMUELSON, DON ARTHUR, ZINC, GLAUCOMA. *Current Pos:* Asst prof, 82-88, ASSOC PROF VET OPHTHAL, COL VET MED, UNIV FLA, 88-, ASSOC CHAIR RES & GRAD STUDIES, 96- *Personal Data:* b Boston, Mass, Aug 30, 48; m 77, Leslie Gilbert; c Peter & Eric. *Educ:* Boston Univ, BA, 71; Univ Fla, PhD(mycol), 77, MS, 82. *Mem:* Asn Res Vision & Ophthal; Int Soc Eye Res; Am Asn Anatomists. *Res:* Aqueous humor dynamics in vertebrate eyes; spontaneous glaucoma in the dog and monkey; zinc nutrition and age related macular degeneration; mercury neurotoxicosis in wildlife species; melanin. *Mailing Add:* Univ Fla Box 100-126 Gainesville FL 32610. *Fax:* 352-392-6125; *E-Mail:* das@vetmed3.vetmed.ufl.edu

SAMUELSON, DONALD JAMES, MATHEMATICS. *Current Pos:* asst prof, 75-77, ASSOC PROF MATH, PA STATE UNIV, UNIVERSITY PARK, 77- *Personal Data:* b Warren, Pa, May 15, 40; m 65; c 2. *Educ:* Cornell Col, BA, 62; Univ Calif Berkeley, MA, 65; Univ Calif, Santa Barbara, PhD(math), 69. *Prof Exp:* Asst prof math, Cornell Col, 65-67, Univ Hawaii, 69-71 & Pa State Univ, McKeesport, 71-75. *Mem:* Am Math Soc. *Res:* Universal algebra. *Mailing Add:* San Jose City Col 2100 Moorpark Ave San Jose CA 95128-2799

SAMUELSON, H VAUGHN, FIBER ENGINEERING, STATIC CHARGE CONTROL. *Current Pos:* Res chemist, 65-67, sr res chemist, 67-79, RES ASSOC, PIONEERING RES LAB, DUPONT CO, 79- *Personal Data:* b Uniontown, Pa, Dec 1, 38; m 67; c 3. *Educ:* Pa State Univ, BS, 60; Western Reserve Univ, MS, 63, PhD(chem), 65. *Mem:* NY Acad Sci; Sigma Xi. *Res:* Research and development on fibers and fiber systems: regulate static charging, aesthetics, membranes and bioreactors, spinneret technology, fiber engineering and spinning dynamics, conductive polymers, polymer blends and multicomponent fibers; recipient of 10 patents. *Mailing Add:* 69 Old Orchard Lane Chadds Ford PA 19317-9165

SAMUELSON, PAUL ANTHONY, ECONOMICS. *Current Pos:* from prof to inst prof, 40-66, EMER PROF ECON & GORDON BILLARD FEL, MASS INST TECHNOL, 86- *Personal Data:* b Gary, Ind, May 15, 15; m 57, 81, Risha Eckaus; c Jane (Kendall), Margaret (Wray), William F, Robert J, John, Paul R & Susan (Miller). *Educ:* Univ Chicago, BA, 35; Harvard Univ, MA, 36, PhD, 41. *Hon Degrees:* Various from US & foreign univs, 61-91. *Honors & Awards:* Nat Medal Sci, 96; John Bates Clark Medal, Am Econ Asn, 47; Alfred Nobel Mem Prize, 70; Albert Einstein Commemorative Award, 71; Brittanica Award, 89; Gold Scanno Prize, Italy, 90; Medal Honor, Club Econ & Mgt, Spain, 90. *Concurrent Pos:* Consult, Nat Res Planning Bd, 41-43; mem, Radiation Lab, 44-45; prof int econ rels, Fletcher Sch Law & Diplomacy, 45; consult, WPB, 45, US Treas, 45-52 & 61-74, Bur Budget, 52 & Rand Corp, 48-75; econ adv, Pres Kennedy, 59-63; comnr res adv bd, Com Econ Develop, 59-60; coun, Econ Adv, 60-68; consult, Fed Res Bd, 65-, Cong Budget Off, 65-; sr adv, Brookings Panel Econ Activ; mem comn soc scis, NSF, 67-68; vis prof polit econs, Ctr Japan-US Bus & Econ Studies, NY Univ, 87- *Mem:* Nat Acad Sci; Corresp fel Brit Acad; AAAS; fel Am Philos Soc; fel Econometric Soc (vpres, 50, pres, 51); fel Am Econ Asn (pres, 61); Int Econ Asn; Comn Econ Develop. *Res:* Author of numerous books and articles. *Mailing Add:* Dept Econ Mass Inst Technol E52-383B Cambridge MA 02139. *Fax:* 617-253-0560

SAMUELSSON, BENGT INGEMAR, MEDICAL CHEMISTRY. *Current Pos:* Asst prof, Karolinska Inst, Stockholm, 61-66, chmn, Physiol Chem Dept, & dean med fac, 78-83, pres, 83-95, PROF MED & PHYSIOL CHEM, KAROLINSKA INST, STOCKHOLM, 72- *Personal Data:* b Halmstad, Sweden, May 21, 34; m 58, Karin Bergstein; c Bo, Elisabet & Astrid. *Educ:* Karolinska Inst, Stockholm, DMS, 60, MD, 61. *Hon Degrees:* DSc, Univ Chicago, 78, Univ Ill, 83. *Honors & Awards:* Nobel Prize in Physiol/Med, 82; Albert Lasker Basic Med Res Award, 77; Gairdner Found Award, 81; Heinrich Wieland Prize, 81; Nobel Prize in Physiol or Med, 82; Waterford Bio-Med Sci Award, 82; Int Asn Alergol & Clin Immunol Award, 82; Gregory Pincus Mem Award, 84; Abraham White Sci Achievement Award, 84 & 91; Charles E Culpepper Award, 85; Supelco Award, Am Oil Chemists Soc, 85; City of Med Award, 92. *Concurrent Pos:* Res fel, Harvard Univ, 61-62; prof med chem, Royal Vet Col, Stockholm, 67-72; Harvey lectr, NY, 79; mem, Nobel Comn Physiol & Med, 84-, chmn comn, 87-89; mem res adv bd, Swedish Govt, 85-88; mem, Nat Comn Health Policy, 87-90; chmn, Nobel Found, Stockholm, 93-; mem, Europ Sci & Tech Assembly, 94- *Mem:* Foreign assoc Nat Acad Sci; foreign assoc Inst Med-Nat Acad Sci; Mediterranean Acad Sci; Acad Europaea; French Acad Sci; Asn Am Physicians; Swedish Med Asn; Am Soc Biol Chemists; Int Soc Hemat; Royal Swed Acad; Span Soc Allergol & Clin Immunol; hon mem Royal Nat Acad Med Spain; hon mem Int Acad Sci; hon mem AAAS. *Res:* Thromboxanes which are involved in thrombosis and diseases such as strokes and coronary infarcts; discovered leukotrienes, substances that play a role in inflammation and asthma and other allergic diseases. *Mailing Add:* Frannsvagen 6 S-18263 Djursholm Sweden

SAMULON, HENRY A, ELECTRONICS. *Current Pos:* RETIRED. *Personal Data:* b Graudenz, Ger, Dec 26, 15; nat US; m 43, Fanny Sogolow; c 2. *Educ:* Swiss Fed Inst Technol, MS, 39. *Prof Exp:* Res engr & instr, Acoust Lab, Swiss Fed Inst Technol, 43-44, assoc, Inst Commun Technol, 44-47; mem staff, Electronics Lab, Gen Elec Co, 47-51, mgr, Eng Anal Subsect, 51-55; gen mgr, Electronic Systs Div, TRW Systs, 55-71, vpres, 64-71, vpres electronics equip, TRW Electronics, 71-74; vpres & mgr, Electronics Div, Xerox Corp, 74-81; pres, H A Samulon Consult, 81-89. *Mem:* Fel Inst Elec & Electronics Engrs. *Res:* Circuitry; color television; space and missile guidance and communication systems; microelectronics; general management. *Mailing Add:* 575 Muskingum Pacific Palisades CA 90272

SAMULSKI, EDWARD THADDEUS, PHYSICAL CHEMISTRY, POLYMER CHEMISTRY. *Current Pos:* PROF CHEM, UNIV NC, 88- *Personal Data:* b Augusta, Ga, May 23, 43; m 76; c 1. *Educ:* Clemson Univ, BS, 65; Princeton Univ, PhD(chem), 69. *Prof Exp:* NIH fel, State Univ Groningen, 69-70; univ fel, Univ Tex, Austin, 71-72; from asst prof to prof chem, Univ Conn, 72-88. *Mem:* AAAS; Am Chem Soc; Sigma Xi. *Res:* Liquid crystals; biological macromolecules and synthetic polymers; application of magnetic resonance techniques to study molecular dynamics of polymer solutions and liquid crystal phases. *Mailing Add:* Dept Chem Univ NC Chapel Hill NC 27599-0001

SAMWORTH, ELEANOR A, PHYSICAL CHEMISTRY. *Current Pos:* from asst prof to assoc prof, 64-81, PROF CHEM, SKIDMORE COL, 81-, DEPT CHAIR, 85- *Personal Data:* b Wilmington, Del, May 10, 36. *Educ:* Wilson Col, AB, 58; Johns Hopkins Univ, MA, 60, PhD(phys chem), 63. *Prof Exp:* Nat Cancer Inst fel phys chem, Harvard Univ, 63-64. *Mem:* Am Phys Soc; Sigma Xi; Am Chem Soc. *Res:* Molecular structure; vibrational spectroscopy; inorganic synthesis; computer applications to chemical education. *Mailing Add:* 75 Ludlow St Saratoga Springs NY 12866-3509

SANABOR, LOUIS JOHN, CHEMICAL ENGINEERING. *Current Pos:* Asst shift foreman, Butadiene Div, 43-45, from pilot plant group leader to sr chem engr, Res Dept, 45-58, staff asst to mgr explor res sect, 58-65, pilot plant group leader, Cost Anal & Design Group, 65-81, SR CHEM ENGR, ENG EVAL GROUP, RES DEPT, KOPPERS CO, INC, 70- *Personal Data:* b Cleveland, Ohio, Dec 2, 20; m 45; c 1. *Educ:* Case Inst Technol, BS, 42; Carnegie Inst Technol, MS, 54. *Mem:* Am Inst Chem Engrs; Am Chem Soc. *Mailing Add:* 311 Parkridge Dr Pittsburgh PA 15235-3430

SANADI, D RAO, BIOCHEMISTRY. *Current Pos:* dir, Dept Cell Physiol, 66-92, exec dir, 69-71 & 75-77, SR, SCIENTIST, BOSTON BIOMED RES INST, 92- *Personal Data:* b India, July 8, 20; nat US; m 50; c 2. *Educ:* Univ Calif, PhD(biochem), 49. *Prof Exp:* Fel, Nat Cancer Inst, 49-52, res assoc, 52-53; asst prof biochem, Univ Wis, 53-55; asst prof, Univ Calif, 55-58; chief sect comp biochem, NIH, 58-66. *Concurrent Pos:* Estab investr, Am Heart Asn, 54-58; chmn, Gordon Res Conf Energy Coupling Mechanisms, 69, 72 & 74; chmn, Gordon Res Conf Biol of Aging, 74; mem adult develop & aging res & training comt, Nat Inst Child Health & Human Develop, 70-73; mem adv panel metab biol, NSF, 71-74; assoc prof, Dept Biol Chem, Harvard Med Sch, 75-; ed, J Bioenergetics Biomembrane, 75-90. *Mem:* AAAS; Am Chem Soc; Am Soc Biol Chem; fel Geront Soc; Biophys Soc. *Res:* Intermediary metabolism; bioenergetics; enzymology; isotopes; aging. *Mailing Add:* Dept Cell Physiol Boston Biomed Res Inst 20 Staniford St Boston MA 02114-2500

SAN ANTONIO, JAMES PATRICK, HORTICULTURE, PHYSIOLOGY. *Current Pos:* RETIRED. *Personal Data:* b New York, NY, June 4, 25; m 51; c 3. *Educ:* Univ Chicago, SB, 48, PhD(physiol), 51. *Prof Exp:* Res assoc mycol physiol, Univ Chicago, 51-53; plant physiologist, Sect Cotton & Other Fiber Crops & Dis, Agr Res Serv, 53-55, Veg & Ornamentals Res Br, Crops Res Div, 55-72, horticulturist, Plant Genetics & Germplasm Inst, Sci & Educ Admin-Agr Res, USDA, 72-88. *Mem:* Am Soc Plant Physiol; Bot Soc Am; Am Soc Hort Sci; Mycological Soc Am. *Res:* Cultivation of edible fungi. *Mailing Add:* 12411 Salem Lane Bowie MD 20715

SANATHANAN, C(HATHILINGATH) K, COMPUTER CONTROL, CONTROL SYSTEM DESIGN. *Current Pos:* assoc prof info eng, 68-71, PROF ELEC ENG, UNIV ILL, CHICAGO, 71- *Personal Data:* b Kerala, India, Feb 17, 36; m 63, 88. *Educ:* Univ Madras, BS, 59; Case Western Reserve Univ, MS, 62, PhD(eng), 64. *Prof Exp:* Asst nuclear engr, Argonne Nat Lab, Ill, 63-68. *Mem:* Am Nuclear Soc; Inst Elec & Electronics Engrs. *Res:* Automation control theory; control of aircrafts chemical processes and power plants; simulation of large scale systems; control and simulation; urban mass transportation. *Mailing Add:* Dept Elec Eng & Comput Sci, Univ Ill Mc 154 851 S Morgan St Chicago IL 60607

SANATHANAN, LALITHA P, applied statistics, mathematical statistics, for more information see previous edition

SANAZARO, PAUL JOSEPH, MEDICINE. *Current Pos:* RETIRED. *Personal Data:* b Sanger, Calif, Sept 27, 22; m 74. *Educ:* Univ Calif, AB, 44, MD, 46; Am Bd Internal Med, dipl, recert, 77. *Prof Exp:* From asst prof to assoc prof med, Sch Med, Univ Calif, San Francisco, 53-62; dir, Div Educ, Asn Am Med Cols, Ill, 62-68; dir, Nat Ctr Health Serv, Res & Develop, 68-72; assoc dep adminr develop, Health Serv & Ment Health Admin, US Dept Health, Educ & Welfare, 72-73; dir pvt initiative, Prof Stand Rev Orgn, 73-77, dir, pvt initiative qual assurance, 78-82; clin prof med, Sch Med, Univ Calif, San Francisco, 75-90. *Concurrent Pos:* Clin assoc prof, Univ Ill Col Med, 62-67, clin prof, 67-68; consult, NIH & Dept Health & Human Serv; pvt consult, health serv res & develop. *Mem:* Fel Am Col Physicians. *Res:* Health services research and development, especially quality of medical care. *Mailing Add:* PO Box 1715 Harwich MA 02645-5062

SANBERG, PAUL RONALD, ANIMAL MODELS OF NEURODEGENERATIVE DISORDERS, BRAIN-BEHAVIOR RELATIONS. *Current Pos:* DIR, RES & PROF SURG NEUROL, PSYCHIAT, PSYCHOL, PHARMACOL & THERAPEUT, UNIV S FLA, 92-; CHAIR NEUROSCI PROG, 97- *Personal Data:* b Coral Gables, Fla, Jan 4, 55; m 96, Deanna Maureen Koss; c Nicole D. *Educ:* York Univ, BSc, 76; Univ BC, MSc, 79; Australian Nat Univ, PhD (behav biol), 81; GDipl, Curtin Univ, 85. *Honors & Awards:* Young Investr Award, Am Col Neuropsychopharmacol; Ove Ferno Prize, Int Col Neuropsychopharmacol. *Prof Exp:* Res neurosci, Johns Hopkins Med Sch, 81-83; asst prof psychol, Ohio Univ, Athens, 83-86; assoc prof psychiat, Univ Cincinnati Med Sch, 86-89, prof, 89-; sci dir, Cellular Transplants, Inc, 90-92; prof psychiat, Brown Univ, 90-92. *Concurrent Pos:* Vis scholar, dept neurosci, Univ Calif, San Diego, 80; prin investr grants, NIH, Huntington's Dis Found, Hereditary Dis Found, Tourette Syndrome Asn, Pratt Found, 82- *Mem:* Soc Neurosci; fel Am Psychol Asn; fel AAAS; fel Int Behav Neurosci Soc (pres, 94); Sigma Xi; fel Am Soc Neural Transplantation (pres, 95); Am Col Neuropsychopharmacol; Cell Transplant Soc (pres, 96); fel NY Acad Sci. *Res:* Understanding how the brain controls movement and behavior; develop animal models of various neuropsychiatric disorders, in order to test various experimental treatments; studying the ability of brain tissue transplants into animal models of Parkinson's, Huntington's and Alzheimer's diseases. *Mailing Add:* Dept Surg MDC Univ SFla 12901 Bruce B Downes Blvd PO Box 16 Tampa FL 33612-4799. *Fax:* 813-974-3078; *E-Mail:* psanberg@com1.med.usf.edu

SANBORN, ALBERT FRANCIS, GEOLOGY. *Current Pos:* GEOL CONSULT, 78- *Personal Data:* b Calif, June 21, 13; m 36, 71, Marie Clayton; c 2. *Educ:* Fresno State Col, AB, 48; Stanford Univ, MS, 50, PhD(geol), 52. *Prof Exp:* Div stratigrapher, Western Opers, Standard Oil Co, Calif, 55-63, sr geologist, Western Div, Calif Oil Co, 63-66, sr explor geologist, Western Div, Chevron Oil Co, Denver, 66-78. *Mem:* Soc Independent Prof Earth Scientists; Am Asn Petrol Geologists. *Res:* Petroleum geology; stratigraphy; mineralogy-petrology. *Mailing Add:* 460 S Marion Pkwy No 1552B Denver CO 80209

SANBORN, CHARLES E(VAN), CHEMICAL ENGINEERING, MATHEMATICS. *Current Pos:* RETIRED. *Personal Data:* b Mankato, Minn, July 11, 19; m 41, 80, Norma Gary; c Charles E Jr, James M, Jane A & Rachel E. *Educ:* Univ Minn, BChE, 41, PhD(chem eng), 49. *Prof Exp:* Engr, Shell Develop Co, Calif, 49-72, Shell Oil Co, 72-73, staff res engr, 73-82. *Mem:* Am Inst Chem Engrs. *Res:* Process development; industrial chemicals. *Mailing Add:* 925 Risdon Ct Concord CA 94518

SANBORN, I B, AUTOMATIC CONTROL SYSTEMS. *Current Pos:* Proj engr, Consol Papers, Inc, 61-65, process engr, 65-67, mgr process control, 67-68, mgr process develop & control, 68-76, ASSOC DIR RES DEVELOP, CONSOL PAPERS, INC, 76- *Personal Data:* b Pepperell, Mass, Apr 29, 32; m 53; c 6. *Educ:* Rensselaer Polytech Inst, BChE, 54; Inst Paper Chem, MCh, 56, PhD, 61. *Mem:* Tech Asn Pulp & Paper Indust; Instrument Soc Am. *Res:* Application of automatic control principles to the control of the paper making process. *Mailing Add:* Consol Papers Inc PO Box 8050 Wisconsin Rapids WI 54494

SANBORN, MARK ROBERT, VIROLOGY, IMMUNOLOGY. *Current Pos:* ASST PROF VIROL & IMMUNOL, OKLA STATE UNIV, 76- *Personal Data:* b Mason City, Iowa, Mar 17, 46; m 68; c 2. *Educ:* Univ Northern Iowa, BA, 68, MA, 71; Iowa State Univ, PhD(bacteriol), 76. *Mem:* Am Soc Microbiol; Sigma Xi; NY Acad Sci; AAAS. *Res:* Early events in paramyxovirus infection; induction of neurological autoimmune disease; immunological assay for gene expression. *Mailing Add:* 1845 Saddle Rd Libertyville IL 60048

SANBORNE, PAUL MICHAEL, SYSTEMATICS, EVOLUTION. *Current Pos:* INSECT IDENTIFICATION SERV & CONSULT, AGR CAN, 93- *Personal Data:* b London, Ont, Can, Jan 18, 50. *Educ:* Carleton Univ, Ottawa, Ont, BSc, 77; Lakehead Univ, Thunder Bay, Ont, MSc, 79; McMaster Univ, Hamilton, Ont, PhD(entom), 82. *Prof Exp:* Nat Sci & Eng Res Coun fel syst entom, Carleton Univ, 83-85, E B Eastburn fel syst entom, 85-86; asst prof entom, MacDonald Col, McGill Univ & cur, Lyman Mus, 86-93. *Concurrent Pos:* Vis cur, Biosyst Res Inst, Agr Can, Ottawa, Ont, 85 & 94; vis lectr, Univ Zimbabwe, SAfrica, 91 & 93; vis researcher, Agr Can, St Jean sur Richelieu Que, 93-94. *Mem:* Entom Soc Can; Coleopterists Soc; Willi Henig Soc. *Res:* Systematics, evolution and biogeography of Ichneumonidae (hymenoptera); behavior and ecology of Diptera, Coleoptera and Mecoptera; larval forms of curculionoidea; mecoptera. *Mailing Add:* 4 Rue Pacifique No 3 Ste Anne de Bellevue PQ H9X 1C6 Can

SANCAKTAR, EROL, ADHESION & ADHESIVES, COMPOSITE MATERIALS. *Current Pos:* PROF POLYMER ENG, UNIV AKRON, 95- *Personal Data:* b Ankara, Turkey, July 13, 52; US citizen; m 79, Teresa S Davis; c Orhan A & Errol A. *Educ:* Robert Col, Turkey, BS(Hons), 74; Va Polytech Inst & State Univ, MS, 75, PhD(eng mech), 79. *Prof Exp:* Instr mat testing, Va Polytech Inst & State Univ, 77-78; from instr to asst prof mech eng, Clarkson Univ, 78-84, dept lab dir, 84-85, assoc prof mech & aeronaut eng, 84-95. *Concurrent Pos:* Prin investr, NSF, 80-83 & 84-87, NASA, 82-83 & 83-84, Kendall Co, 86, IBM Co, 92-93 & US Army, 93-94; eng consult, UN, Alcoa, Kendall Co, US Army, Zinc Corp & Champion Int, 84-; vis scholar, Lexington Res Labs, Kendall Co, 85-86; co-prin investr, Grumman Corp, 86-89 & NY State Sci & Technol Found, 92- *Mem:* Am Soc Mech Engrs. *Res:* Constitutive modelling and fracture behavior of adhesives in the bulk and bonded states; stress analysis and failure prediction for adhesive joints; effects of processing conditions on the mechanical behavior of adhesives and bonded joints; substrate/adhesive interphase modelling; composite materials design. *Mailing Add:* Dept Polymer Univ Akron Akron OH 44325-0301. *Fax:* 330-258-2339; *E-Mail:* erol@uakron.edu

SANCAR, AZIZ, DNA REPAIR, CHEMICAL CARCINOGENESIS. *Current Pos:* assoc prof, 82-88, PROF BIOCHEM & BIOPHYS, SCH MED, UNIV NC, CHAPEL HILL, 88- *Personal Data:* b Sept 8, 46; m, Gwendolyn Boles. *Educ:* Istanbul Med Sch, MD, 69; Univ Tex, Dallas, PhD(molecular biol), 77. *Honors & Awards:* Res Award, Am Soc Photobiol, 90; Basic Sci Award, Turkish Sci Res Coun, 95. *Concurrent Pos:* Presidential Young Investr Award, NSF, 84-89; assoc fel, Third World Acad Sci, 95. *Mem:* Am Soc Microbiol; Am Soc Biol Chemists; Am Chem Soc. *Res:* Enzyme mechanisms; molecular mechanisms of DNA repair mechanisms including DNA photolyase, excision repair and transcription-coupled repair. *Mailing Add:* Dept Biochem & Biophys Sch Med Univ NC CB No 7260 Chapel Hill NC 27599-7260. *Fax:* 919-966-2852

SANCAR, GWENDOLYN BOLES, DNA REPAIR, GENE REGULATION. *Current Pos:* ASST PROF BIOCHEM, UNIV NC, CHAPEL HILL, 87- *Personal Data:* b Waco, Tex, Sept 10, 49; m 78. *Educ:* Baylor Univ, BS, 72; Univ Tex-Dallas, MS, 74, PhD(molecular biol), 77. *Prof Exp:* Fel hemat, State Univ NY Downstate, Brooklyn, 77-80; fel radiobiol, Yale Univ Sch Med, 80-82, res asst prof biochem, 82-86. *Mem:* Am Soc Microbiol; Am Soc Photobiol; Am Soc Biochem & Molecular Biol. *Res:* Molecular mechanism of repair of ultraviolet induced DNA damage and the regulation of genes whose products are involved in repair. *Mailing Add:* Dept Biochem Univ NC CB No 7260 Chapel Hill NC 27599-7260. *Fax:* 919-966-2852; *E-Mail:* gsancar@uncmed.bitnet

SANCES, ANTHONY, JR, BIOMEDICAL ENGINEERING. *Current Pos:* PROF BIOMED ENG & CHMN PROG, MED COL WIS, 64- *Personal Data:* b Chicago, Ill, July 13, 32; m 65; c 3. *Educ:* Am Inst Technol, BSEE, 53; DePaul Univ, MS, 59; Northwestern Univ, PhD(biomed eng), 63. *Prof Exp:* Res engr, Mech Res Dept, Am Mach & Foundry Co, 53-59; mgr, Advan Res Dept, Sunbeam Corp, 59-60; asst prof, Am Inst Technol, 60-61; consult numerous firms, 61-64; prof elec eng & neurosurg & dir biomed eng, Marquette Univ, 64- *Concurrent Pos:* Walter Murphy fel, 62-63; NIH fel, 63-64; staff, Wood Vet Admin Hosp, 64-, Milwaukee County Gen Hosp, 64- & Deaconness Hosp, Milwaukee, 72- *Mem:* Biophys Soc; sr mem Inst Elec & Electronics Engrs; Instrument Soc Am; Neuroelec Soc (pres); Alliance Eng Med & Biol (past pres); Sigma Xi. *Res:* Nervous system research related to biomedical engineering and biomechanics. *Mailing Add:* Neurosurg 9200 W Wisconsin Milwaukee WI 53226-3522

SANCETTA, CONSTANCE ANTONINA, MARINE GEOLOGY, MICROPALEONTOLOGY. *Current Pos:* ASSOC PROG DIR, MARINE GEOL & GEOPHYSICS NSF, 94- *Personal Data:* b Richmond, Va, Apr 17, 49; div. *Educ:* Brown Univ, BA, 71, MS, 73; Ore State Univ, PhD(oceanog), 76. *Prof Exp:* Res assoc geol, Stanford Univ, 76-78; assoc res scientist, Lamont-Doherty Geol Observ, Columbia Univ, 79-83, res scientist, 84-87, sr res scientist, 88-94. *Concurrent Pos:* NSF Ocean Sci Exec Adv Comt, 81-86; mem, Educ & Human Resource Comt, Am Geophys Union, 81-88, Planning Comt, 84-88; assoc ed, Marine Micropaleont, 83-; co-chmn, Geol Sect, NY Acad Sci, 83-85; mem, Artic Marine Sci Comt, Nat Res Coun, 84-86n, 81-88, Planning Comt, 84-88; mem comt, Geol Soc Am, 85-87; mem, Cent & E Pac Regional Ocean Drilling Prog, 86-89; secy, Ocean Sci Sect, Am Geophys Union, 88-90; counr, Am Quaternary Asn, 88-& Oceanograph Soc, 89-; NSF Ocean Sci Adv Panel, 89. *Mem:* Fel Geol Soc Am; Am Geophys Union; fel AAAS; Oceanog Soc. *Res:* Cenozoic paleoceanography; marine diatoms, biostratigraphy and paleoecology; depositional processes and generation of fossil assemblages. *Mailing Add:* NSF-Ocean Sci Div Rm 725 4201 Wilson Blvd Arlington VA 22230

SANCHEZ, ALBERT, NUTRITION, BIOCHEMISTRY. *Current Pos:* DIR SPAN DEPT & PROG COORDR, PAC HEALTH EDU CTR, 91- *Personal Data:* b Solomonsville, Ariz, Feb 10, 36; m 62, Aneva Lonise Allred; c Ruth, Joan, Alina & Albert. *Educ:* Loma Linda Univ, BA, 59, MS, 62; Univ Calif, Los Angeles, DrPH, 68. *Prof Exp:* Biochemist, Int Nutrit Res Found, 61-65; from asst prof to prof nutrit, Loma Linda Univ, 68-91; prof biochem & nutrit, Sch Med, Montemorelos Univ, Mex, 74-80. *Concurrent Pos:* Pres, Int Nutrit Res Found, Inc. *Mem:* Am Dietetic Asn; Latin Am Nutrit Soc; Am Inst Nutrit; Am Soc Clin Res; Soc Int Nutrit Res; Nat Coalition Hosp Health Human Serv Orgn. *Res:* Protein and amino acid nutrition; role of nutritional factors as they relate to public health problems. *Mailing Add:* Pac Health Edu Ctr 5300 California Ave Bakersfield CA 93309

SANCHEZ, ANTHONY DE JESUS, SYNTHESIS OF PHARMACEUTICAL ANALOG, CONJUGATIONS OF HAPTENS TO PROTEINS ENZYMES & DNA. *Current Pos:* SR SCIENTIST, BOEHRINGER MANHEIMS CORP, 95- *Personal Data:* b Pasco, Wash, July 14, 65. *Educ:* Reed Col, BA, 87; Univ Calif, Santa Cruz, PhD(org chem), 94. *Prof Exp:* Postdoctoral fel, Univ Calif, Santa Cruz, 94-95, Microgenics Corp, 94-95. *Mem:* Am Chem Soc. *Res:* Synthesis of pharmaceutical analogs and their linkage to proteins, enzymes and DNA for use in the manufacture of immunoassays. *Mailing Add:* 3173 Claudia Dr Concord CA 94519

SANCHEZ, DAVID A, MATHEMATICS. *Current Pos:* PROF MATH, TEX A&M UNIV, 96- *Personal Data:* b San Francisco, Calif, Jan 13, 33; m 58, Joan Thomas; c Bruce & Christina. *Educ:* Univ NMex, BS, 55; Univ Mich, MA, 60, PhD(math), 64. *Prof Exp:* Res asst, Radar Lab, Inst Sci & Technol, Univ Mich, 59-63; instr math, Univ Chicago, 63-65; from asst prof to prof, Univ Calif, Los Angeles, 65-77; prof, Univ NMex, 77-86; provost, Lehigh Univ, 86-90; asst dir, NSF, 90-92, Los Alamos Nat Lab, 92-93; vchancellor acad affairs, Tex A&M Univ Syst, 93-96. *Concurrent Pos:* Vis lectr, Univ Manchester, 65-66. *Mem:* Am Math Soc; Math Asn Am; Soc Indust & Appl Math. *Res:* Direct methods in the calculus of variations; nonlinear ordinary differential equations. *Mailing Add:* Math Dept Tex A&M Univ College Station TX 77843-3368

SANCHEZ, IGNACIO, PHARMACEUTICAL COMPOUNDS. *Current Pos:* RES MGR, GREAT LAKES CHEM CORP, 93- *Personal Data:* b Mexico City, Mex, Aug 14, 47. *Educ:* Nat Univ Mex, BS, 69; Univ BC, PhD(org synthesis), 75; Rejis Univ, MS, 93. *Prof Exp:* Res fel, Nat Prod Res Ctr, Univ NB, 75-77; prof chem, Inst Chem, Nat Univ Mex, 77-84; mgr neotechnol, Syntex Technology Ctr, 87-93. *Mem:* Am Chem Soc; fel Am Inst Chemists; Chem Soc Mex. *Mailing Add:* 44 Jester Ct Lafayette IN 47905

SANCHEZ, ISAAC CORNELIUS, POLYMER PHYSICS. *Current Pos:* PROF CHEM ENG, UNIV TEX, 88- *Personal Data:* b San Antonio, Tex, Aug 11, 41; m 76, Karen P Horton; c Matthew & Timothy. *Educ:* St Mary's Univ, Tex, BS, 63; Univ Del, PhD(phys chem), 69. *Honors & Awards:* Bronze & Silver Medal, US Dept Com. *Prof Exp:* Nat Res Coun-Nat Acad Sci assoc, Nat Bur Stand, Washington, DC, 69-71; assoc scientist polymer sci, Xerox Corp, 71-72; asst prof polymer sci & eng, Univ Mass, Amherst, 72-77; res chemist, Inst Mat Sci & Eng, Nat Bur Stand, 77-86; res fel, Alcoa Res Labs, 86-88. *Mem:* Nat Acad Eng; fel Am Phys Soc; Am Inst Chem Eng; AAAS; Mat Res Soc; Am Chem Soc. *Res:* Application of statistical mechanics to problems in polymer science. *Mailing Add:* Chem Eng Dept Univ Tex Austin TX 78712-1062. *Fax:* 512-471-7060; *E-Mail:* sanchez@che.utexas.edu

SANCHEZ, JOSE, ORGANIC CHEMISTRY. *Current Pos:* GROUP LEADER, PEROXIDES, LUCIDOL DIV PENNWALT CORP, 67- *Personal Data:* b Suffern, NY, June 30, 36; m 62; c 2. *Educ:* Univ Rochester, BS, 58; Brown Univ, PhD(org chem), 66. *Prof Exp:* Res chemist, F & F Dept, E I du Pont de Nemours, 65-67. *Mem:* Am Chem Soc. *Res:* Synthesis, evaluation, process development and production troubleshooting in the areas of organic peroxides and organic specialty compounds. *Mailing Add:* 1624 Huth Rd Grand Island NY 14072-1799

SANCHEZ, PEDRO ANTONIO, TROPICAL SOILS, AGROFORESTRY. *Current Pos:* prof soil sci & leader, Trop Soils Prog, 79-91, EMER PROF SOIL SCI & FORESTRY, NC STATE UNIV, 91-; DIR GEN, INT CTR RES AGR FORESTRY, UN, 91- *Personal Data:* b Havana, Cuba, Oct 7, 40; US citizen; m 65, 90, Cheryl Palm; c Jennifer, Evan & Juliana. *Educ:* Cornell Univ, BS, 62, MS, 64, PhD(soil sci), 68. *Honors & Awards:* Int Soil Sci Award, 93; Serv Agron Award, 93. *Prof Exp:* Asst soil sci, Philippine Prog, Cornell Univ, 65-68; asst prof soil sci & co-leader, Nat Rice Res Prog Mission Peru, NC State Univ, 68-71; assoc prof, 71-77; coordr, Trop Pastures Prog, Cent Int Agr Trop, 77-79. *Concurrent Pos:* Chief, NC State Univ Mission Peru, Lima, 82-83; adj prof trop conserv, Duke Univ, 90; dir, Ctr World Environ & Sustainable Develop, Duke Univ, NC State Univ & Univ NC-Chapel Hill, Raleigh, 91. *Mem:* Fel Am Soc Agron; fel Soil Sci Soc Am; Int Soc Soil Sci; Brazilian Soc Soil Sci; Colombian Soc Soil Sci. *Res:* Fertility and management of tropical soils; fertility and management of rice soils and tropical pastures; low input systems; agro forestry; tropical soil and climate change; tropical conservation and sustainable development. *Mailing Add:* Int Ctr Res Agr Forestry PO Box 30677 UN Nairobi Gigiri Kenya. *Fax:* 254-2-520023; *E-Mail:* p.sanchez@cqnet.com

SANCHEZ, ROBERT A, BIO-ORGANIC CHEMISTRY, ORGANIC CHEMISTRY. *Current Pos:* VPRES CHEM, VYREX CORP, 91- *Personal Data:* b Colombia, SAm, Feb 4, 38; US citizen; m 60, Beverly Joan Woods; c 4. *Educ:* Pomona Col, BA, 58; Kans State Univ, PhD(org chem), 62. *Prof Exp:* Fel org chem, Univ Colo, 62-64, asst prof, 63-64; asst prof, Haverford Col, 64-65; sr res assoc, Salk Inst Biol Studies, 65-72; dir res, Terra-Marine Biores, Inc, 72-74; dir bio-org res & develop, Calbiochem-Behring Corp, 74-80, sr res scientist, 80-89, vpres prod & res & develop, Calbiochem Corp, 89-91. *Concurrent Pos:* Consult biochem, pharmaceut & nutrit industs. *Mem:* AAAS; NY Acad Sci; Am Chem Soc; Sigma Xi. *Res:* Fundamental and developmental research; pharmaceuticals and biochemicals; pre-biological chemistry and origins of life; bio-organic chemistry and natural products; small molecule therapeutics. *Mailing Add:* 5531 West 13680 S Riverton UT 84065. *Fax:* 801-253-9959; *E-Mail:* rsanchez@inconnect.com

SANCHEZ ALVARADO, ALEJANDRO, EPIMORPHIC REGENERATION IN METAZOANS, MORPHOGENESIS. *Current Pos:* postdoctoral fel, 94-96, STAFF ASSOC, CARNEGIE INST WASHINGTON, 96- *Personal Data:* b Caracas, Venezuela, Feb 24, 64; US citizen. *Educ:* Vanderbilt Univ, BS, 86; Univ Cincinnati, PhD(pharmacol & cell biophysics), 92. *Prof Exp:* Res asst, Col Med, Univ Cincinnati, 87-88, grad assoc, 88-92, res assoc, 92-94. *Mem:* AAAS; Am Soc Cell Biol; Soc Develop Biol; Singer Soc Regeneration. *Res:* Embryology; molecular biology; cell biology. *Mailing Add:* Dept Embryol Carnegie Inst Wash 115 W University Pkwy Baltimore MD 21210. *Fax:* 410-243-6311; *E-Mail:* sanchez@mail1.cuwemb.edu

SANCIER, KENNETH MARTIN, PHYSICAL CHEMISTRY. *Current Pos:* PHYS CHEMIST, SRI INT, 54- *Personal Data:* b New York, NY, June 21, 20. *Educ:* Polytech Inst Brooklyn, BS, 42; Johns Hopkins Univ, MA, 47, PhD(chem), 49. *Prof Exp:* Phys chemist gas chem, Linde Air Prod Co, Union Carbide & Carbon Corp, 42-46; lab instr, Johns Hopkins Univ, 46-49; phys chemist low temperature chem, Brookhaven Nat Lab, 49-53. *Concurrent Pos:* Vis instr chem, Conn Col, 48; fel, Standard Oil Ind, 48-49; NSF vis scientist, Univ Tokyo, 66-67. *Mem:* Am Chem Soc; Sigma Xi; AAAS. *Res:* Photochemistry related to solar energy conversion; energy transfer processes in solution and between gases and solids; hydrogen bonding; absorption spectroscopy, particularly at low temperature; heterogenous catalysis; electron spin resonance of gaseous atoms, gas-solid interactions, and biochemical systems. *Mailing Add:* 561 Berkeley Ave Menlo Park CA 94025

SANCILIO, LAWRENCE F, PHARMACOLOGY. *Current Pos:* PHARMACOLOGIST, DRUG DEPT, FOOD & DRUG ADMIN, 90- *Personal Data:* b Brooklyn, NY, Dec 13, 32; m 60; c 5. *Educ:* St John's Univ, NY, BS, 54; Georgetown Univ, PhD(pharmacol), 60. *Prof Exp:* Teaching asst pharmacol, Georgetown Univ, 58-59; res pharmacologist, Miles Labs, Inc, Ind, 60-68; assoc res pharmacologist, A H Robbins, Inc, 68-71, group mgr pharmacol res sect, 71-81, dir pharmacol, 81-90. *Mem:* Soc Exp Biol & Med; Am Soc Pharmacol & Exp Therapeut (chmn, 85); Inflammation Res Asn (pres, 78-80). *Res:* Analgesia; mechanism of inflammation and the evaluation of systemic nonsteroidal and topical steroidal anti-inflammatory agents; immediate hypersensitivity. *Mailing Add:* Dept Oncol & Pulmonary Drug Prod HFD 150 17B-20 Food & Drug Admin 5600 Fishers Ln Rockville MD 20857-0001

SANCTUARY, BRYAN CLIFFORD, NUCLEAR MAGNETIC RESONANCE-THEORY, PROTEIN STRUCTURE & QUANTUM MECHANICS. *Current Pos:* from asst prof to assoc prof, 76-86, dir chem grad studies, 91-96, PROF CHEM, MCGILL UNIV, MONTREAL, 86- *Personal Data:* b Yorkshire, Eng, Jan 25, 45; Can citizen; m 67, Mingy Woo; c Mark C, Colin S & Hillary A. *Educ:* Univ BC, BSc, 67, PhD(chem theory), 71. *Prof Exp:* Resident theorecian molecular physics, Kamerlingh Onnes Lab, Holland, 72-76; asst prof chem, Univ Wis-Madison, 76. *Concurrent Pos:* Vis prof chem, Univ York, UK, 81-82; vis prof chem, Res Sch Chem, ANU, Australia, 89-90; hon prof, E China Inst Technol; pres, Can Asn Theoret Chemists, 91-93. *Mem:* Am Inst Physics; Can Inst Chem. *Res:* Theoretical investigation on systems containing angular momentum; development of the multipole theory of nuclear magnetic resonance; structure of biomolecules from 2-D nuclear magnetic resonance quantum dynamics and statistical mechanics applied to non-spherical molecules in all phases. *Mailing Add:* Dept Chem McGill Univ 801 Sherbrooke St W Montreal PQ H3A 2K6 Can. *Fax:* 514-398-3797; *E-Mail:* bryans@omc.lan.mcgill.ca

SAND, RALPH E, PHYSICAL ORGANIC CHEMISTRY. *Current Pos:* RETIRED. *Personal Data:* b Stamford, Conn, May 16, 21; c 2. *Educ:* Univ Conn, BS, 42; Polytech Inst Brooklyn, MS, 48, PhD(org chem), 50. *Prof Exp:* Proj leader, Lab Advan Res, Remington Rand, Inc, 50-53; group leader, Res Ctr, Gen Foods, Inc, 53-61; sr chemist, Pratt & Whitney Div, United Aircraft Corp, 61-66; mgr pioneering res, Nat Biscuit Co, 66-70; dir tech develop, CPC Int, 70-71; sr chemist anal methods develop, Anderson Clayton Res Ctr, 71-88. *Mem:* Am Chem Soc; Sigma Xi; Inst Food Technologists; Am Asn Cereal Chemists. *Res:* Enzyme models; organic, photographic, lithographic, food, natural polymers, carbohydrates and proteins. *Mailing Add:* 182 Moonlight Dr Plano TX 75094

SANDAGE, ALLAN REX, ASTRONOMY. *Current Pos:* asst astronr, 52-56, ASTRONR, CARNEGIE OBSERV, 56-; SR RES SCIENTIST, SPACE TELESCOPE SCI INST, 87- *Personal Data:* b Iowa City, Iowa, June 18, 26; m 59; c 2. *Educ:* Univ Ill, AB, 48, DSc, 67; Calif Inst Technol, PhD(astron), 53. *Hon Degrees:* DSc, Yale Univ, 69, Univ Chicago & Univ Ill, 67; LLD, Univ Southern Calif, 71; ScD, Miami Univ, 74 & Graceland Col, 85. *Honors & Awards:* Warner Prize, Am Astron Soc, 58; Eddington Medal, Royal Astron Soc, 63; Gold Medal, 70; Pope Pius XI Gold Medal, Pontifical Acad Sci, 66; Nat Medal Sci, 71; Cresson Medal, Franklin Inst, 73; Russell Prize, Am Astron Soc, 73; Bruce Gold Medal, Astron Soc Pac, 75; Crafoord Prize, Swed Acad Sci, 91; Adion Medal, 91; Tomalla Prize, Swiss Phys Soc, 91. *Prof Exp:* Homewood prof physics, Johns Hopkins Univ, 87-89. *Concurrent Pos:*

Rouse Ball lectr, Cambridge Univ, 57; lectr, Harvard Univ, 57 & Haverford Col, 58 & 66; consult, NSF, 62-63; mem vis comt, Nat Radio Astron Observ, 63-64, chmn, 65; mem, Comt Astron Facil, Nat Acad Sci, 65-65 & Comt Sci & Pub Policy, 65; fel, Australian Nat Univ, 68-69 & 72; Fulbright-Hays scholar, Australia, 72-73; res scholar, Univ Basel, 85 & Univ Calif, San Diego, 85-86; adj astronr, Univ Hawaii, 86. Mem: AAAS; Am Astron Soc; Royal Astron Soc; Int Astron Union. Res: Stellar evolution; photoelectric photometry; observational cosmology; galaxies; stellar kinematics; quasi-stellar radio sources; extragalactic distance scale; age and evolution of the universe; galactic structure; curvature of space. Mailing Add: Carnegie Observ 813 Santa Barbara Dr Pasadena CA 91101. Fax: 626-795-8136

SANDALL, ORVILLE CECIL, CHEMICAL ENGINEERING. Current Pos: PROF CHEM ENG, UNIV CALIF, SANTA BARBARA, 66- Personal Data: b Cupar, Sask, July 4, 39; m 61, Patricia J Sullivan; c Erin K, Shannon E, Brendan P & Colleen C. Educ: Univ Alta, BS, 61, MS, 63; Univ Calif, Berkeley, PhD(chem eng), 66. Concurrent Pos: Consult. Mem: Am Inst Chem Engrs; Am Chem Soc; Sigma Xi; Am Soc Eng Educ. Res: Gas absorption, heat and mass transfer in turbulent flow; separation processes. Mailing Add: Dept Chem Eng Univ Calif Santa Barbara CA 93106

SANDBERG, ANN LINNEA, MICROBIOLOGY. Current Pos: res biologist, 72-76, CHIEF, MICROBIAL RECEPTORS & PATHOGENESIS SECT, LAB MICROBIAL ECOL, NAT INST DENT RES, 76- Personal Data: b Denver, Colo. Educ: Mont State Univ, BS, 60; Univ Chicago, PhD(pharmacol), 64. Prof Exp: USPHS training grant, Med Sch, Tufts Univ, 65-67; assoc immunol, Pub Health Res Inst, New York, 68-72. Concurrent Pos: Res assoc prof, Med Sch, NY Univ, 71-72. Mem: AAAS; Am Asn Immunol; Am Soc Microbiol. Res: Alternate pathway of complement activation; definition of system and its biological consequences; host defense systems; molecular mechanisms of bacterial attachment. Mailing Add: DER NIDR NIH Bldg 45 Rm 4AN-24A Bethesda MD 20892-0001

SANDBERG, AVERY ABA, INTERNAL MEDICINE. Current Pos: DIR CANCER CTR, SOUTHWEST BIOMED RES INST, SCOTTSDALE, ARIZ, 88- Personal Data: b Poland, Jan 29, 21; nat US; m 43; c 4. Educ: Wayne Univ, BS, 44, MD, 46; Am Bd Internal Med, dipl, 48. Prof Exp: Intern, Receiving Hosp, Detroit, Mich, 46-47; resident cardiol, Mt Sinai Hosp, New York, 49-50; resident med, Vet Admin Hosp, Salt Lake City, Utah, 50-51; resident instr med, Col Med, Univ Utah, 52-53, instr med, 53-54; assoc chief med, Roswell Park Mem Inst, 54-57, chief med, 57-88. Concurrent Pos: Dazian Found Med Res fel, 50; univ fel med & NIH res fel, Col Med, Univ Utah, 51-52, Dazian Found Med Res fel, 52-53, Am Cancer Soc scholar, 53-56; asst prof, Med Sch, Univ Buffalo, 54-, asst res prof, Grad Sch, 56-57, res prof, 57-; res prof, Canisius Col, 69- & Niagara Univ, 69-; consult, Med Found Buffalo, NY. Mem: Am Soc Clin Invest; Endocrine Soc; Am Soc Hemat; Am Asn Cancer Res; Am Fedn Clin Res. Res: Metabolism of steroids; metabolic changes in leukemia; cytogenetics of human leukemia and cancer. Mailing Add: Cancer Ctr Southwest Biomed Res Inst 6401 E Thomas Rd Scottsdale AZ 85251. Fax: 602-947-8220

SANDBERG, CARL LORENS, POLYMER CHEMISTRY. Current Pos: RETIRED. Personal Data: b Aniwa, Wis, July 24, 22; m 51; c 4. Educ: Univ Wis, BS, 48, MS, 49. Prof Exp: Chemist, Minn Mining & Mfg Co, 50-54, res chemist, 54-67, res specialist, 67-76, sr res specialist, 3M Co, 76-86. Mem: Am Chem Soc. Res: Synthesis and characterization of organic and fluoro-organic polymers. Mailing Add: 1736 Rowe Pl St Paul MN 55106-6831

SANDBERG, EUGENE CARL, OBSTETRICS & GYNECOLOGY. Current Pos: RETIRED. Personal Data: b Ashtabula, Ohio, Jan 4, 24; div; c Kristin E & Kerk A. Educ: Univ Calif, AB, 45, MD, 48; Am Bd Obstet & Gynec, dipl, 59 & 79. Prof Exp: Intern, San Francisco City & County Hosp, 48-49; intern, Vanderbilt Univ Hosp, 49-50, asst resident, 50-51 & 53-54, resident, 54-55; from instr to assoc prof obstet & gynec, Sch Med, Stanford Univ, 55-87. Concurrent Pos: Trainee steroid biochem, Worcester Found Exp Biol, 61-62; Macy Found fel, Col Physicians & Surgeons, Columbia Univ, 62-63. Mem: Am Col Obstet & Gynec; Soc Gynec Invest; Endocrine Soc. Mailing Add: 1788 Oak Creek Dr Apt 407 Palo Alto CA 94304-2131

SANDBERG, I(RWIN) W(ALTER), NON-LINEAR SYSTEMS. Current Pos: HOLDER COCKRELL FAMILY REGENTS CHAIR, NO 1 ELEC & COMPUT ENG, UNIV TEX, AUSTIN, 86- Personal Data: b New York, NY, Jan 23, 34; m 58, Barbara Ann Zimmerman; c 1. Educ: Polytech Inst Brooklyn, BEE, 55, MEE, 56, DEE, 58. Honors & Awards: Centennial Medal, Inst Elec & Electronics Engrs; Tech Achievement Award, Circuits & Systs Soc. Prof Exp: Mem tech staff, Bell Labs, 56 & 58-67, head, Systs Theory Res Dept, 67-72, mem staff, Math Sci Res Ctr, 72-86. Concurrent Pos: Vchmn, Inst Elec & Electronics Engrs Group on Circuit Theory; guest ed, Inst Elec & Electronics Engrs Trans on Circuit Theory, Spec Issue on Active & Digital Networks; Distinguished lectr, Inst Elec & Electronics Engrs; adv, Inst Elec & Commun Engrs of Japan & Am Men & Women Sci. Mem: Nat Acad Eng; fel Inst Elec & Electronics Engrs; fel AAAS; Sigma Xi; Soc Indust & Appl Math. Res: Non-linear analysis; network theory; theory of feedback systems; communication systems; differential equations; integral equations; functional analysis; numerical analysis; neural networks; published more than 165 papers and holds 9 United States patents. Mailing Add: Eng Sci Bldg Univ Tex Austin TX 78712-1084

SANDBERG, PHILIP A, geology, paleontology, for more information see previous edition

SANDBERG, ROBERT GUSTAVE, CLINICAL BIOCHEMISTRY, ABIOSENSORS & IMMUNOASSAY. Current Pos: mkt planning mgr automatic clin anal, E I Du Pont De Nemours & Co, Inc, 75-80, mkt tech mgr, 80-92, specialty diag mgr, 82-85, bus develop mgr, 85-89, vpres mkt, Ohmicron Corp, 89-96, PROD SUPVR CLIN CHEM, E I DU PONT DE NEMOURS & CO, INC, 71-, TECH MGR MKT, 80-, PRES, PISCES GROUP, 96- Personal Data: b Minneapolis, Minn, Mar 20, 39; m 59; c 3. Educ: Hamline Univ, BS, 61; Ohio State Univ, MS, 63. Prof Exp: Group leader polymers, Cargill Inc, 63-66; sr chemist, Hoerner-Waldorf Inc, 66-69; clin chemist, St John's Hosp, 69-71. Concurrent Pos: Bd dirs, asn Off Anal Chemists Res Inst, 93-94. Mem: Am Asn Clin Chem; Biomed Mkt Asn (pres, 79); Am Chem Soc. Res: Standards and control materials for clinical chemistry; development and marketing; automated clinical chemistry analyzers; preparation of stable enzyme solutions for verification of standard methods; evaluation of automated clinical chemistry and immunoassay methods; biosensor development; immunoassay calibrations. Mailing Add: 110 Hobson Dr Hockessin DE 19707-2105

SANDBORN, VIRGIL A, AERONAUTICAL ENGINEERING. Current Pos: prof aerodyn & fluid mech, 62-77, prof civil eng, 77-88, EMER PROF, COLO STATE UNIV, 88- Personal Data: b Conway Springs, Kans, Apr 30, 28; m 55, Virginia R Cerny; c Peter & Patricia. Educ: Univ Kans, BS, 50; Univ Mich, MS, 54. Prof Exp: Aeronaut res scientist, Nat Adv Comt Aeronaut, 51-58; aerospace res scientist, NASA, 58-62; consult scientist, Avco Corp, 62-63. Concurrent Pos: Vis prof, Purdue Univ, 66-75. Mem: Am Inst Aeronaut & Astronaut. Res: Turbulent air flow; turbulent boundary layer flow; separation of boundary layers from surfaces. Mailing Add: Dept Civil Eng Colo State Univ Ft Collins CO 80523-0001

SANDE, RONALD DEAN, VETERINARY RADIOLOGY. Current Pos: resident vet med & surg, 68-69, instr, 69-70, from asst prof vet radiol to assoc prof, 71-77, assoc prof, 77-79, PROF VET CLIN MED & SURG, WASH STATE UNIV, 77- Personal Data: b Twin Falls, Idaho, July 3, 42; m 64; c 3. Educ: Wash State Univ, DVM, 66, MS, 71, PhD(vet sci), 76. Prof Exp: Res vet radionuclides, Univ Utah, 66-67. Concurrent Pos: Vis prof, Norweg Col Vet Med, 92-93. Mem: Am Col Vet Radiologists; Am Vet Radiol Soc; Am Vet Med Asn; Vet Ultrasound Soc. Res: Inherited metabolic bone disorders in animals; animal models; aguaculture. Mailing Add: RR 2 Pullman WA 99163

SANDEFUR, KERMIT LORAIN, OPTICS. Current Pos: CONSULT, 87- Personal Data: b Arkansas City, Kans, Sept 1, 25; m 46, Elsie C Osborn; c John T & Mark M. Educ: Univ Kans, BS, 50 & 51. Prof Exp: Assoc physicist, Midwest Res Inst, 51-56; sr res scientist, Hycon Mfg Co, Calif, 56-69; res & develop eng, Lockheed-Calif Co, 69-87. Res: Photographic reconnaissance and infrared systems; supersonic flow; ballistics; optical systems analysis. Mailing Add: 3635 Landfair Rd Pasadena CA 91107

SANDEFUR, WILLIAM MARION, NUCLEAR PHYSICS. Current Pos: STAFF SCIENTIST, SEAR-BROWN GRP, 68- Personal Data: b Cincinnati, Ohio, May 13, 47. Educ: Univ Ky, BS, 69; Univ Ill, MS, 71, PhD(physics), 77. Mem: Am Phys Soc. Mailing Add: 660 E Charles St Batesville AR 72501-3711

SANDEL, BILL ROY, SPACE PHYSICS. Current Pos: assoc res scientist, 84-91, SR RES SCIENTIST, LUNAR & PLANETARY LAB, UNIV ARIZ, 91- Personal Data: b Brady, Tex, Nov 19, 45; m 80; c 2. Educ: Rice Univ, BA, 68, MS, 71, PhD(space sci), 72. Honors & Awards: Excep Sci Achievement Award, NASA, 81. Prof Exp: Sr assoc-in-res, Kitt Peak Nat Observ, 73-78; res assoc planetary atmospheres, Lunar & Planetary Lab, Univ Ariz, 78-79; res scientist, Earth & Space Sci Inst, Univ Southern Calif, 79-83. Concurrent Pos: Co-investr Voyager ultraviolet spectrometer exp, Galileo Ultraviolet Spectrometer Exp. Mem: Am Geophys Union; Am Astron Soc. Res: Atmospheric and space physics of the outer planets; ultraviolet spectroscopy; development of ultraviolet imaging detectors. Mailing Add: Lunar & Planetary Lab Gould Simpson Bldg Rm 901 Univ Ariz Tucson AZ 85721

SANDEL, VERNON RALPH, PHYSICAL ORGANIC CHEMISTRY. Current Pos: RETIRED. Personal Data: b Marquette, Mich, June 4, 33; m 59; c 2. Educ: Mich Tech Univ, BS, 55; Northwestern Univ, PhD(org photochem), 62. Prof Exp: Chemist, Ethyl Corp, 55-57; spec proj chemist, Dow Chem Co, Mich, 61-62; res chemist, Eastern Res Lab, Mass, 63-67; assoc prof chem, Mich Technol Univ, 67-84. Mem: Am Chem Soc; Sigma Xi. Res: Nuclear magnetic resonance of carbanions; carbanion chemistry; organic reaction mechanisms. Mailing Add: Chippewa Trail Dollar Bay MI 49922

SANDELL, LIONEL SAMUEL, AGRICULTURAL FORMULATIONS CHEMISTRY, WATER GEL EXPLOSIVES CHEMISTRY. Current Pos: res chemist colloid chem, Pigments Dept Du Pont Co, 73-78, sr chemist water gel explosives, Petrochem Dept, 78-82, res assoc, Agr Prod Dept, 82-90, SR RES ASSOC, AGR PROD DEPT, DU PONT CO, 90- Personal Data: b Montreal, Que, May 29, 45; US citizen; m 71, Nancy Stuzin; c Lisa & Sharon. Educ: McGill Univ, BSc, 66, PhD(phys chem), 70. Prof Exp: From assoc to res assoc, Col Environ Sci & Forestry, State Univ NY, 70-73. Mem: Am Chem Soc. Res: Product and process development for agricultural formulations; chemistry of water gel explosives; agricultural formulations for sulfonylureas. Mailing Add: 2900 Bodine Dr Wilmington DE 19810-2247. Fax: 302-695-7804; E-Mail: sandell@esvax.dnet.dupont.com

SANDELL, RICHARD ARNOLD, APPLICATIONS OF SYSTEMS IN ECONOMIC RESEARCH, INTERNATIONAL TRADE & TECHNOLOGY TRANSFER. *Current Pos:* exec vpres & chief operating officer, 74-80, PRES & CHIEF EXEC OFFICER, AURA TECHNOL CORP, 80- *Personal Data:* b Buenos Aires, Arg, Oct 22, 37; US citizen; m 68, Phyllis Levinson; c Laurie Alyssa, Karyn Joy & Sylvie Jennine. *Educ:* Univ Buenos Aires, BA, 57, JD, 59; Univ San Marcos, MS, 60; NY Univ, LLM, 62; Columbia Univ, PhD(sociol & econs), 72, MBA, 77. *Hon Degrees:* DSc, Univ Auckland, NZ, 72, Sofia Univ Japan, 83; LLD, Cath Univ Santiago, Chile, 76; LHD, Univ San Carlos, Guatemala, 78. *Honors & Awards:* San Martin Medal Honor, Nat Acad Lett, 93. *Prof Exp:* Int trade mgr, Guerrero Mercantile Int Ltd, 57-59, dir bus planning, 59-62; spec forces, US Army, Vietnam, 62-65; gen mgr, Acquatronic Universal, Matsushita Corp, 65-68; vpres indust econ, Mgt Analyst Group Inc, 68-70; exec vpres, AIM Int Corp, 70-71; pres & chief exec officer, 71-74. *Concurrent Pos:* From asst prof to assoc prof econ, Food Res Inst, Stanford Univ, 70-75, assoc prof int trade, Sch Bus Admin, 75-77; prof int law, McGeorge Sch Law, Univ Pac, 72-77; dir & vpres Latin Am, Int Inst Cert Mgt Consults, 75-80; prof int bus, Univ Am States, Miami, 77-79; prof int mgt, Univ Francisco Marroquin, Guatemala, 77-79; dir grad enterprise studies & prof int bus & govt, Mercy Col, Long Island Univ, 79-83; prof int finance & bus & chair bus enterprise, Ramapo Col, State Univ NJ, 83-88; prof int trade, sr res fel & dir, World Free Enterprise Studies Prog, Am Res Inst Soc & Econ, 89- *Mem:* Fel AAAS; fel NY Acad Sci; fel Royal Soc Arts, Mfrs & Com; fel Am Econ Asn; fel Inst Mgt Sci. *Res:* International trade policies for agricultural commodities in common markets; economic trade areas; customs unions; free enterprise zones; mapping their coherent study by means of electronic systems; communication methodology applications. *Mailing Add:* PO Box 1367 Scarsdale NY 10583-9367. *Fax:* 914-833-0930; *E-Mail:* rsandell@aura.com

SANDER, C MAUREEN, MEDICINE, PATHOLOGY. *Current Pos:* From instr to assoc prof, 65-76, PROF, DEPT PATH, COLS MED, COL HUMAN MED, MICH STATE UNIV, 76- *Personal Data:* b Lansing, Mich, Mar 2, 33. *Educ:* Mich State Univ, BS, 55; Univ Mich, MD, 58; Univ London, dipl clin path, 64; Am Bd Path, dipl, 66. *Concurrent Pos:* Fulbright fel, 63-64; dir, Mich Placental Tissue Registry, 76- *Res:* Pathology of the placenta; perinatal pathology. *Mailing Add:* Dept Path Mich State Univ A630 E FEE Hall East Lansing MI 48824

SANDER, DONALD HENRY, AGRONOMY. *Current Pos:* assoc prof, 67-73, PROF AGRON, EXTEN, UNIV NEBR, LINCOLN, 73- *Personal Data:* b Creston, Nebr, Apr 21, 33; m 53; c 2. *Educ:* Univ Nebr, BS, 54, MS, 58, PhD(agron, soils), 67. *Honors & Awards:* Agron Achievement Award-Soils, Am Soc Agron, 85; Soil Sci Appl Res Award, Soil Sci Soc Am, 89. *Prof Exp:* Soil scientist, US Forest Serv, 58-64; asst prof agron, Exten, Kans State Univ, 64-67. *Mem:* Fel Am Soc Agron; fel Soil Sci Soc Am. *Res:* Influence soil properties, especially nutrients and nutrient interactions on plant growth and composition. *Mailing Add:* Dept Agron Univ Nebr Rm 253 Keim Hall Lincoln NE 68583-0915

SANDER, DUANE E, ELECTRICAL ENGINEERING. *Current Pos:* assoc prof elec eng, 67-75, PROF ELEC ENG, SDAK STATE UNIV, 75-, HEAD DEPT GEN ENG, 85- *Personal Data:* b Sioux Falls, SDak, Feb 14, 38; m 60; c 4. *Educ:* SDak Sch Mines & Technol, BS, 60; Iowa State Univ, MS, 62, PhD(elec eng), 64. *Prof Exp:* Instr elec eng, Iowa State Univ, 60-63, res asst, 63-64; intel analyst, US Army Foreign Sci & Technol Ctr, Washington, DC, 65-67. *Concurrent Pos:* Consult, Med Eng Serv Asn, 77- *Mem:* Inst Elec & Electronics Engrs; Int Soc Hybrid Microelectronics; Am Soc Hosp Eng; Nat Soc Prof Eng. *Res:* Bioengineering and data acquisition; clinical engineering. *Mailing Add:* Dean Eng SDak State Univ Ceh 201 Box 2219 Brookings SD 57007

SANDER, EUGENE GEORGE, ENZYMOLOGY. *Current Pos:* PROF, DEPT BIOCHEM, UNIV ARIZ, 87-, VPROVOST & DEAN, COL AGR, 87- *Personal Data:* b Fargo, NDak, Sept 17, 35; m 79, Louise Canfield; c 2. *Educ:* Univ Minn, BS, 57; Cornell Univ, MS, 59, PhD(biochem), 65. *Prof Exp:* NIH fel biochem, Brandeis Univ, 65-67; from asst prof to prof, Dept Biochem, Univ Fla, 67-76; prof & chmn dept, WVa Univ, 76-80; prof & head, Dept Biochem & Biophys, Tex A&M Univ, 80-86, dep chancellor biotech develop, Tex A & M Univ Syst, 86-87. *Mem:* Am Chem Soc; Am Soc Biol Chemists; Sigma Xi; Biophys Soc. *Res:* Mechanism of action of enzymes involved in dihydropyrimidine synthesis and degradation along with related organic model systems. *Mailing Add:* Forbes Bldg Rm 306 Univ Ariz Tucson AZ 85721. *Fax:* 520-621-7196; *E-Mail:* egsander@az.arizona.edu

SANDER, GARY EDWARD, CARDIOVASCULAR DISEASE, CLINICAL PHARMACOLOGY. *Current Pos:* PROF MED & CARDIOL, LA STATE UNIV, 92-, DIR, CARDIOL TRAINING PROG, 94- *Personal Data:* b New Orleans, LA, Feb 14, 47; m 73, Patricia Pruett; c Edward, Andrew & Philip. *Educ:* Tulane Univ, PhD(biochem), 71, MD, 74. *Prof Exp:* Prof med cardiol, Sch Med, Tulane Univ, 80-92. *Mem:* Fel Am Col Physicians; Am Soc Hypertension; fel Am Col Cardiol; Am Soc Pharmacol & Exp Therapeut; Am Heart Asn. *Res:* Clinical pharmacology of hypertension, heart failure and platelet inhibitors in acute ischemic syndromees; various aspects of cardiomyopathy; basic research including cardiovascular regulation by peptides and the effects of diabetes on the heart. *Mailing Add:* Sch Med La State Univ 1542 Tulane Ave New Orleans LA 70112. *Fax:* 504-568-4655; *E-Mail:* gsroses@aol.com

SANDER, IVAN LEE, SILVICULTURE, FOREST MANAGEMENT. *Current Pos:* RETIRED. *Personal Data:* b Cape Girardeau, Mo, Mar 13, 28; m 49; c 3. *Educ:* Univ Mo, BSF, 52, MS, 53. *Prof Exp:* Res forester, Cent States Forest Exp Sta, USDA Forest Serv, 53-65, Northeastern Forest Exp Sta, 66-70 & NCent Forest Exp Sta, 71-74, proj leader, 75-; res assoc, Sch Forestry, Fisheries & Wildlife, Univ Mo, 71- *Mem:* Soc Am Foresters; Sigma Xi. *Res:* Determination of the critical biological, environmental and ecological factors that control hardwood reproduction establishment and growth with emphasis on oaks; development of systems to ensure harvested stands will be regenerated to oaks and other important hardwoods. *Mailing Add:* 5500 N Rte E Columbia MO 65202

SANDER, LEONARD MICHAEL, STATISTICAL PHYSICS. *Current Pos:* from asst prof to assoc prof, 69-80, PROF PHYSICS, UNIV MICH, ANN ARBOR, 80- *Personal Data:* b St Louis, Mo, Aug 17, 41; m 64; c 1. *Educ:* Washington Univ, BS, 63; Univ Calif, Berkeley, MA, 66, PhD, 68. *Prof Exp:* NSF fel physics, Univ Calif, San Diego, 68-69. *Concurrent Pos:* Vis prof, Univ Paris, 89-90. *Mem:* Fel Am Phys Soc; Mat Res Soc. *Res:* Theory of physical processes far from equilibrium; theoretical solid state physics. *Mailing Add:* Physics Dept Univ Mich Ann Arbor MI 48109-1120. *E-Mail:* lsander@umich.edu

SANDER, LINDA DIAN, MEDICAL PHYSIOLOGY, GASTROINTESTINAL ENDOCRINOLOGY. *Current Pos:* ASSOC PROF, DEPT PHYSIOL, MEHARRY MED COL, 82- *Personal Data:* b Harrisburg, Pa, Sept 2, 47; m 70; c 2. *Educ:* Ariz State Univ, BS, 69; Univ Okla, PhD(physiol), 73. *Prof Exp:* Fel, dept physiol, Med Sch, Univ Tex, Houston, 73-76; asst prof, dept physiol, Med Ctr, La State Univ, New Orleans, 76-82. *Concurrent Pos:* Prin investr, NIH grant. *Mem:* Am Physiol Soc; Soc Exp Biol & Med. *Res:* Role of gastrointestinal hormones and brain-gut polypeptides on pituitary adrenal hormonal secretion and circadian rhythms; influence of stress on gastrointestinal function; gastrointestinal endocrinology. *Mailing Add:* Meharry Med Col 1005 D B Todd Jr Blvd Nashville TN 37208. *Fax:* 615-327-6655

SANDER, LOUIS W, PSYCHIATRY. *Current Pos:* EMER PROF PSYCHIAT, SCH MED, UNIV COLO, 78- *Personal Data:* b San Francisco, Calif, July 31, 18; m 53, Betty Thorpe; c Mark, Rebecca & David. *Educ:* Univ Calif, AB, 39, MD, 42; Boston Psychoanal Inst, grad, 61; Am Bd Psychiat & Neurol, dipl, 51. *Honors & Awards:* Grete Simpson Award, Univ Calif Med Sch. *Prof Exp:* Asst psychiat, Sch Med, Boston Univ, 47-51, instr, 51-57, asst prof, 54-58, res psychiatrist, Univ Med Ctr, 54-78, from asst res prof to assoc res prof, 58-68, prof psychiat, 68-78. *Concurrent Pos:* Asst, Mass Mem Hosps, 48-55, asst vis physician, 55-59, assoc vis physician, 59-78; mem staff, James Jackson Putnam Children's Ctr, 50-53; jr vis physician, Boston City Hosp, 53-57, assoc vis physician, Pediat Serv, 57-78; USPHS grants, 54-78, career develop award, 63-68; consult, Bd Missions, Methodist Church, 54-60; res scientist award, NIMH, 68-73 & 73-78; vis prof, Univ Calif Med Sch, 84. *Mem:* Am Psychiat Asn; Am Acad Child Psychiat; Soc Res Child Develop; Am Col Psychoanalysts; AAAS. *Res:* Early personality development, especially in relation to the influence of maternal personality on mother-child interactions; investigation of neonatal state regulation in the caretaking systems by non-intrusive bassinet monitoring; twenty-five year longitudinal study of personality development. *Mailing Add:* 2525 Madrona Ave St Helena CA 96574

SANDER, MICHAEL JAMES, CORPORATE REENGINEERING, AEROSPACE SYSTEMS PROCESS ENGINEERING. *Current Pos:* Dir, Ground Syst Develop Voyager Proj, Jet Propulsion Lab, NASA, 76-79, dep div dir, Life Sci Div, Hq, 79-82, div dir, Shuttle Payloads Eng Div, 82-85, mgr, Flight Proj Support Off, Jet Propulsion Lab, 85-90, proj mgr, SIR-C Proj, 90-95, DEP DIR, EARTH & SPACE SCI PROG DIRECTORATE, JET PROPULSION LAB, NASA, 95- *Personal Data:* b Jerusalem, Palestine, Aug 3, 42; US citizen; m 68, Jane Sinko; c Viathleen & Danielle. *Educ:* Occidental Col, BS, 63. *Mem:* AAAS; assoc fel Am Inst Aeronaut & Astronaut. *Mailing Add:* 324 Queensbury Ave Thousand Oaks CA 91360

SANDER, WILLIAM AUGUST, III, COMMUNICATIONS, SIGNAL PROCESSING. *Current Pos:* staff scientist, Res Mgt, 75-89, command, control & commun mgr, Res & Technol Integration Off, 89-91, ASSOC DIR, ELECTRONICS DIV, US ARMY RES OFF, 91- *Personal Data:* b Charleston, SC, May 11, 42; m 67, Helen R Childress; c Todd R & Kathryn E. *Educ:* Clemson Univ, BS, 64; Duke Univ, MS, 67, PhD(elec eng), 73. *Prof Exp:* Res asst, Duke Univ, 67-70; engr, Commun & Electronics Bd, US Army Airborne, 70-75. *Concurrent Pos:* Instr, Fayetteville State Univ, 74-75. *Mem:* Inst Elec & Electronics Engrs; Sigma Xi. *Res:* Signal processing; communications; computer-aided design of integrated circuits. *Mailing Add:* US Army Res Off PO Box 12211 Research Triangle Park NC 27709-2211

SANDERFER, PAUL OTIS, ORGANIC CHEMISTRY. *Current Pos:* Asst prof chem, 65-71, ASSOC PROF CHEM & PHYSICS, WINTHROP COL, 71-, ACTG CHMN, DEPT CHEM & PHYSICS, 81- *Personal Data:* b Union City, Tenn, Mar 1, 37; m 59; c 1. *Educ:* Union Univ, BS, 59; Univ Fla, PhD(org chem), 65. *Mem:* Am Chem Soc. *Res:* Kinetic studies of reaction mechanisms; organic synthesis. *Mailing Add:* Dept Chem & Physics Winthrop Univ 701 W Oakland Ave Rock Hill SC 29733-0001

SANDERS, BARBARA, PHYSICAL THERAPY. *Current Pos:* PROF PHYS THER, SW TEX STATE UNIV, 84- *Personal Data:* b Covington Ky, Mar 31, 50; m 78, Michael T; c Whitney M. *Educ:* Univ Ky, BSPT, 72, MS, 76; Univ Tex, Austin, PhD(educ admin), 91. *Prof Exp:* Phys therapist, Good Samaritan

Hosp, 72-74; instr, Univ Ky, 76-77; sr phys therapist, St Cloud Hosp, 77-78; instr phys ther, Univ Wis-LaCrosse, 78-83; sr phys therapist, Ft Sanders Regional Med Ctr, 83-86. *Concurrent Pos:* Consult, 85-; prin investr, US Dept Educ, 91-; adj fac phys ther, Inst Phys Ther, 93-; chair, Adv Panel Educ, Am Phys Ther Asn, 93-; pres, Tex Phys Ther Asn, 96- *Mem:* Am Phys Ther Asn; Am Asn Univ Women. *Res:* Sports physical therapy; education and selective admissions. *Mailing Add:* 8206 Cache Dr Austin TX 78749-3814. *Fax:* 512-245-8736; *E-Mail:* bs5331@samson.health.swt.edu

SANDERS, BARBARA A, TECHNICAL MANAGEMENT. *Current Pos:* Dept head, Composites Mat Characterization, Gen Motors, 79-80, mgr composites processing, 80-82, CAD/CAM Tooling Group, 82-84, dir artificial intel, 84-85, prog mgr, Truck & Bus Group, 89-90, dir, Advan Mfg Eng, 91-, DIR, ENG-ADVAN DEVELOP, INLAND FISHER GUIDE DIV, GEN MOTORS. *Personal Data:* b New Orleans, La, Oct 20, 47; m 73; c 1. *Educ:* Southern Univ, BS, 69; Rutgers Univ, MS, 72. *Concurrent Pos:* Mem & ed, Marine Composites, Nat Res Coun, 89-91. *Mem:* Soc Automotive Engrs; Soc Mfg Engrs. *Res:* Research and development management; assembly systems-automotive advanced manufacturing engineering. *Mailing Add:* 5865 Clearview Dr Troy MI 48098

SANDERS, BOBBY GENE, IMMUNOGENETICS. *Current Pos:* assoc prof, 68-74, PROF ZOOL, UNIV TEX, AUSTIN, 74-, ASSOC DEAN, COL NATURAL SCI, 85- *Personal Data:* b Rhodell, WVa, Apr 16, 32; m 51; c 4. *Educ:* Concord Col, BS, 54; Pa State Univ, MEd, 58, PhD(genetics), 61. *Prof Exp:* Asst prof biol, Lafayette Col, 61-64; fel immunogenetics, Calif Inst Technol, 64-66, asst prof biol, 66-68. *Mem:* Am Asn Immunologists; Am Genetic Asn. *Res:* Cell surface antigens in normal erythroid differentiation and retrovirus-induced erythro leukemia; immunochemical characterization of chicken major histocompatibility complex products. *Mailing Add:* Dept Zool Univ Tex Austin TX 78712-1026

SANDERS, BOBBY LEE, APPLIED MATHEMATICS. *Current Pos:* PARTNER, SANDERS & SANDERS, 77- *Personal Data:* b Ben Wheeler, Tex, Jan 12, 35; m 54; c 2. *Educ:* ETex State Univ, BS, 56; Fla State Univ, MS, 58, PhD(math), 62; Southern Methodist Univ, JD, 77. *Prof Exp:* Instr math, Fla State Univ, 57-58; from asst prof to prof math, Tex Christian Univ, 62-77. *Mem:* Am Math Soc; Math Asn Am. *Res:* Structure theory of Banach spaces; functional analysis; categorical applications; applications of finite mathematical structures; quantitative and qualitative applications of mathematics to judicial problems and processes. *Mailing Add:* Sanders & Sanders PO Box 416 Canton TX 75103

SANDERS, BRENDA MARIE, TOXICOLOGY, MOLECULAR BIOLOGY. *Current Pos:* assoc prof physiol, 86-91, ASSOC DIR, MOLECULAR ECOL INST, CALIF STATE UNIV, LONG BEACH, 86-, PROF PHYSIOL, 91- *Personal Data:* b Island Falls, Maine, Mar 31, 51; m 83; c 1. *Educ:* Wesleyan Univ, BA, 75; Univ Del, PhD(marine biol), 81. *Prof Exp:* Res assoc, Duke Univ Marine Lab, 80-83, res asst prof, 83-86. *Concurrent Pos:* NAm ed, Ecotoxicol Sci, 91-; ed, Rev Aquatic Sci, 91-93; consult, JSA Inc, 91- *Mem:* AAAS; Am Soc Zoologists; Sigma Xi; Soc Environ Toxicol & Chem; Am Physiol Soc. *Res:* Molecular mechanisms by which organisms adapt to their environment; stress proteins as biological markers; aquatic toxicology; ecological assessments. *Mailing Add:* 1250 Bellflower Blvd Cal State Univ Long Beach CA 90840. *Fax:* 562-985-5244

SANDERS, CHARLES ADDISON, CARDIOLOGY. *Current Pos:* RETIRED. *Personal Data:* b Dallas, Tex, Feb 10, 32; m 56, Ann; c 4. *Educ:* Univ Tex Southwestern Med Sch Dallas, MD, 55. *Hon Degrees:* DSc, Suffolk Univ, 77, Mass Col Pharm, 82. *Prof Exp:* Intern & asst resident med serv, Boston City Hosp, Mass, 55-57, chief resident, 57-58; clin & res fel cardiol, Mass Gen Hosp, 58-60, prog dir, Myocardial Infarction Res Unit, 67-72, prog dir medlab systs, 69-73, assoc physician, 70-73, chief, Cardiac Catheter Unit, 62-72, gen dir, 72-81, physician, 73-81; exec vpres, Squibb Corp, 81-88, vchmn, 88-89; chief exec officer, Glaxo, Inc, 89-94, chmn 92-95. *Concurrent Pos:* Instr, Harvard Med Sch, 64-66, assoc, 66-68, from asst prof to prof, 69-84; dir, Merrill Lynch & Co, Morton Int Inc & Reynolds Metals Co. *Mem:* Inst Med-Nat Acad Sci; Am Col Physicians; Asn Univ Cardiol. *Mailing Add:* Europa Ctr 100 Europa Dr Suite 170 Chapel Hill NC 27514

SANDERS, CHARLES F(RANKLIN), JR, HEAT TRANSFER, COMBUSTION. *Current Pos:* from asst prof to prof eng, Calif State Univ, Northridge, 62-83, chmn dept thermal-fluid systs, 69-72, dean, Sch Eng & Comput Sci, 72-81, EMER PROF ENG, CALIF STATE UNIV, NORTHRIDGE, 83-; EXEC VPRES & DIR, ENERGEO, 89- *Personal Data:* b Louisville, Ky, Dec 22, 31; m 56, Marie A Galuppo; c Karen (Parks), Craig & Keith. *Educ:* Univ Louisville, BChE, 54, MChE, 58; Univ Southern Calif, PhD(chem eng), 70. *Prof Exp:* Engr, Esso Res & Eng Co, 55-62. *Concurrent Pos:* Consult, KVB Eng Co, 70-80; dir, Rusco Industs Corp, 80-83, pres & chief exec officer, 81-82; exec vpres, Energy Systs Assocs, 82-89; dir, Datametrics Corp, 82-86; dir, Uniforms Unlimited, 85-; dir, Advan Combustion Technol, 91- *Mem:* Am Inst Chem Engrs; Am Soc Eng Educ; Combustion Inst; Nat Soc Prof Engrs. *Res:* Combustion; pollution from combustion; radiative transfer through particulate clouds; combustion modelling; fluid-bed combustion; biomass combustion. *Mailing Add:* 28531 La Maravilla Aliso Viejo CA 92677. *Fax:* 714-733-1364

SANDERS, CHARLES LEONARD, JR, RADIOBIOLOGY. *Current Pos:* VPRES, GAIL'S BOOKS, 95- *Personal Data:* b Chicago, Ill, Dec 27, 38; m 63; c 3. *Educ:* Col William & Mary, BS, 60; Tex A&M Univ, MS, 63; Univ Rochester, PhD(radiobiol), 66. *Prof Exp:* AEC fel, Life Sci Dept, Pac Northwest Labs Battelle Mem Inst, 66-68, res assoc, 68-78, staff scientist inhalation toxicol, 78-92; prof, Sch Pharm, Wash State Univ, Spokane, 92-93; sr res scientist, Inhalation Toxicol Res Inst, Albuquerque, NMex, 94- *Concurrent Pos:* Affil asst prof, Univ Wash, 75-80, affil prof, 80-; mem, Nat Coun Radiation Protection & Measurements. *Res:* Inhalation toxicology and carcinogenesis of plutonium and other transuranic elements, and of beryllium, lead, mercury, cadmium, asbestos, silica and volcanic ash; general radiobiology and toxicology of energy effluents. *Mailing Add:* 1943 Davison Richland WA 99352

SANDERS, CHRISTINE CULP, MEDICAL MICROBIOLOGY, INFECTIOUS DISEASES. *Current Pos:* from asst prof to assoc prof, 73-85, PROF MICROBIOL, SCH MED, CREIGHTON UNIV, 85-; DIR, CTR FOR RES ANTI-INFECTIVES & BIOTECHNOLO, 93- *Personal Data:* b Tampa, Fla, Sept 3, 48; m 74, W Eugene Jr. *Educ:* Univ Fla, BS, 70, PhD(med microbiol), 73. *Honors & Awards:* Burlington Northern Award for Res, 86. *Prof Exp:* Technician microbiol, Shands Teaching Hosp & Clin, 69-70; chief technologist, Alachua Gen Hosp, 70. *Concurrent Pos:* Res award, Sigma Xi, 74; ed, Antimicrobial Agents & Chemother, 84-94. *Mem:* Am Soc Microbiol; Am Fedn Clin Res; Infectious Dis Soc Am; NY Acad Sci; fel Am Acad Microbiol. *Res:* Bacterial drug resistance; evaluation of new antimicrobial agents; genetics of drug resistance; antimicrobial antagonisms; pharmacodynamics. *Mailing Add:* Dept Med Microbiol Sch Med Creighton Univ Omaha NE 68178

SANDERS, DARRYL PAUL, URBAN ENTOMOLOGY, MEDICAL & VETERINARY ENTOMOLOGY. *Current Pos:* assoc dean agr, 82-86, PROF, ENTOM DEPT, UNIV MO, 86- *Personal Data:* b Arch, NMex, Feb 11, 36; m 62, Mary Acker; c Cori Lynn & Kim Andra. *Educ:* Tex Tech Col, BS, 59; Purdue Univ, MS, 64, PhD(entom), 67. *Honors & Awards:* Distinguished Serv Award, Entom Soc Am; John Veach Award, Mo Pest Control Asn. *Prof Exp:* Exten entomologist, Purdue Univ, 65-67; teaching & res entomologist, Tex A&M Univ, 67-70; teaching & exten entomologist, Purdue Univ, West Lafayette, 70-75; prof entom & chmn dept, Tex Tech Univ, 76-82. *Mem:* Entom Soc Am; Am Mosquito Control Asn; Sigma Xi. *Res:* Insects affecting man and livestock; household invading insects, particularly ants; household pesticide application. *Mailing Add:* Dept Entom Univ Mo Rm 1-87 Agr Bldg Columbia MO 65211. *Fax:* 573-882-1469; *E-Mail:* agosande@muccmail.missouri.edu

SANDERS, DOUGLAS CHARLES, HORTICULTURE, PLANT PHYSIOLOGY. *Current Pos:* from exten asst prof to exten assoc prof, 70-82, PROF HORT, NC STATE UNIV, 82- *Personal Data:* b Lansing, Mich, May 21, 42; m 65. *Educ:* Mich State Univ, BS, 65; Univ Minn, MS, 69, PhD(hort), 70. *Honors & Awards:* Outstanding Exten Educr, Am Soc Hort Sci. *Prof Exp:* Res fel hort, Univ Minn, 69-70. *Concurrent Pos:* Consult, Latin Am. *Mem:* Fel Am Soc Hort Sci; Am Soc Agron; Crop Sci Soc Am; Sigma Xi; Coun Agr Sci Technol; Potato Asn Am. *Res:* Vegetable crop cultural practices; crop microclimate modification; influence of climate on plant physiology; plasticulture drip irrigation plant nutrition. *Mailing Add:* NC State Univ Box 7609 Raleigh NC 27695-7609. *Fax:* 919-515-7747; *E-Mail:* doug_sanders@ncsa.edu

SANDERS, F KINGSLEY, BIOLOGICAL SCIENCES, CELL BIOLOGY & VIROLOGY. *Current Pos:* RETIRED. *Personal Data:* b Oct 1, 17; wid; c Francis & Virginia. *Educ:* Oxford Univ, Eng, DPhil, 42. *Prof Exp:* Dir, Virus Res Unit, Med Res Coun, UK, 55-67; prof cell biol, Grad Sch Med Sci, Cornell Univ, 67-80. *Concurrent Pos:* Mem, Sloan-Kettering Inst Cancer Res, 67-80. *Mailing Add:* 358 Kelly Rd East Chatham NY 12060

SANDERS, FRANK CLARENCE, JR, ATOMIC PHYSICS, MOLECULAR PHYSICS. *Current Pos:* asst prof, 69-77, ASSOC PROF PHYSICS, UNIV SOUTHERN ILL, CARBONDALE, 77- *Personal Data:* b Tiquisate, Guatemala, Dec 26, 40; US citizen; m 63; c 2. *Educ:* Univ Tex, Austin, BS, 63, PhD(physics), 68. *Prof Exp:* Asst prof physics, Univ Tex, Austin, 68-69. *Mem:* Am Phys Soc; Am Asn Physics Teachers. *Res:* Theoretical atomic and molecular physics; perturbation theory and its application to simple atomic and molecular systems. *Mailing Add:* Dept Physics Southern Ill Univ Carbondale IL 62901. *Fax:* 618-453-1056

SANDERS, FREDERICK, METEOROLOGY, SYNOPTIC. *Current Pos:* asst, 49-52, from instr to prof , 52-84, EMER PROF METEOROL, MASS INST TECHNOL, 84- *Personal Data:* b Detroit, Mich, May 17, 23; m 46; c 3. *Educ:* Amherst Col, BA, 44; Mass Inst Technol, ScD, 54. *Honors & Awards:* Special Award, Am Meteorol Soc, 91. *Prof Exp:* Aviation forecaster, US Weather Bur, 47-49. *Mem:* Fel Am Meteorol Soc; Royal Meteorol Soc. *Res:* Synoptic meteorology; maritime cyclogenesis; mesoscale meterology; fronts and frontogenetical processes; cumulus convective systems; symmetric instability; trends in forecast kill. *Mailing Add:* 9 Flint St Marblehead MA 01945

SANDERS, GARY HILTON, PARTICLE PHYSICS. *Current Pos:* DEP DIR, LIGO LAB, CALIF INST TECHNOL, 95- *Personal Data:* b New York, NY, Aug 27, 46; m 73; c 2. *Educ:* Columbia Univ, AB, 67; Mass Inst Technol, PhD(physics), 71. *Prof Exp:* Res asst high energy physics, Mass Inst Technol, 67-71; res assoc physics, Princeton Univ, 71-73, asst prof, 73-78; staff mem, Los Alamos Nat Lab, 78-94. *Concurrent Pos:* Vis scientist, Deutsches Elektronen Synchrotron, Hamburg, 68-71; NSF fel, 71-72; vis scientist, Brookhaven Nat Lab, 71-74, 84- & Fermi Nat Accelerator Lab, 75-79. *Mem:* Am Phys Soc; Sigma Xi. *Res:* Experimental studies of elementary particles including quantum electrodynamics, hadronic production of dimuons, new particles, rare decays of muons and kaons; particle beam physics; neutrino physics. *Mailing Add:* Calif Inst Technol Ms 18-34 Pasadena CA 91125. *Fax:* 505-665-3858

SANDERS, HARVEY DAVID, PHARMACOLOGY, PHYSIOLOGY. *Current Pos:* RETIRED. *Personal Data:* b Winnipeg, Man, June 22, 25; m 59; c 4. *Educ:* Univ BC, BSP, 59, MSP, 61, MD, 72; Univ Man, PhD(pharmacol), 63; FRCP(C), 77. *Prof Exp:* Lectr pharmacog, Univ BC, 59-60, lectr chem, 60-61, from instr to assoc prof pharmacol, 64-95. *Concurrent Pos:* Ford fel, 63-64; McEachern fel, 64-66. *Mem:* Am Soc Pharmacol & Exp Therapeut; Am Fedn Clin Res; NY Acad Sci; Can Med Asn; Am Col Physicians. *Res:* Effects of centrally active drugs on responses of the cerebral cortex to electrical stimulation; intracellular and extracellular recordings; cardiovascular effects of local anesthetics; pharmacology of the human urinary bladder. *Mailing Add:* Dept Med Univ BC Vancouver Gen Hosp Vancouver BC V5Z 1M9 Can

SANDERS, HOWARD L(AWRENCE), ECOLOGY, DEEP SEA BIOLOGY. *Current Pos:* RETIRED. *Personal Data:* b Newark, NJ, Mar 17, 21; m 49; c 2. *Educ:* Univ BC, BA, 49; Univ RI, MS, 51; Yale Univ, PhD(zool), 55. *Prof Exp:* Res assoc, Woods Hole Oceanog Inst, 55-63, assoc scientist, 63-65, sr scientist, 65-86,. *Concurrent Pos:* Instr, Marine Biol Lab, Woods Hole, 60-68; mem, Environ Biol Panel, NSF, 66-68; adj prof biol sci, State Univ NY, Stony Brook, 69-75, res affil, Marine Sci Res Ctr, 69-80; assoc invert zool, Harvard Univ, 69-80; mem adv panel, Cent Am Sea Level Canal, Nat Acad Sci, 69-70; res assoc, Smithsonian Trop Res Inst, 70; corresp, Nat Mus Natural Hist, 75-; coun deleg sect G, biol sci, AAAS, 80-82; mem, Int Asn Biol Oceanog Working Group, High Diversity Marine Ecosyts, UNESCO, 86. *Mem:* Nat Acad Sci; fel AAAS; Soc Am Naturalists. *Res:* Ecology as applied to marine benthic communities; crustacean phylogeny; protobranch bivalves; deep-sea biology; oil pollution biology; author or co-author of about 64 scientific publications. *Mailing Add:* 7 Oyster Pond Rd Falmouth MA 02540

SANDERS, J(OHN) LYELL, JR, STRUCTURAL MECHANICS. *Current Pos:* vis lectr struct mech, Harvard Univ, 57-58, lectr, 58-60, assoc prof, 60-64, Gordon McKay prof, 64-95, EMER PROF STRUCT MECH, HARVARD UNIV, 95- *Personal Data:* b Highland, Wis, Sept 11, 24; m 60, Mary Jane Wade; c Alice E, William L & Jeanne F. *Educ:* Purdue Univ, BSc, 45; Mass Inst Technol, ScM, 50; Brown Univ, PhD(appl math), 54. *Hon Degrees:* MA, Harvard Univ, 60. *Prof Exp:* Res engr, Nat Adv Comt Aeronaut, 47-57. *Concurrent Pos:* NSF sr fel, Delft Technol Univ, 67-68. *Mem:* Fel Am Soc Mech Engrs; fel Am Acad Arts & Sci; fel Am Acad Mech. *Res:* Theory of thin shells; theory of plasticity and fracture mechanics. *Mailing Add:* Pierce Hall Harvard Univ Cambridge MA 02138

SANDERS, JAMES GRADY, TRACE METAL BIOGEOCHEMISTRY, PHYTOPLANKTON ECOLOGY. *Current Pos:* from asst curator to assoc cur, 81-90, LAB DIR, BENEDICT ESTUARINE RES LAB, DIV ENVIRON RES, ACAD NAT SCI, 83-, CUR, 90- *Personal Data:* b Norfolk, Va, June 10, 51; m 72. *Educ:* Duke Univ, BS, 73; Univ NC, Chapel Hill, MS, 75, PhD(marine sci), 78. *Prof Exp:* Fel, Woods Hole Oceanog Inst, 78-80; vis asst prof, Chesapeake Biol Lab, Ctr Environ & Estuarine studies, Univ Md, 80-81. *Concurrent Pos:* Vis lectr, Dept Earth Sci, Bridgewater State Col, 80; adj assoc prof, Chesapeake Biol Lab, Ctr Environ & Estuarine studies, Univ Md, 82-89. *Mem:* AAAS; Am Soc Limnol & Oceanog; Estuarine & Coastal Sci Asn; Estuarine Res Fedn; Phycol Soc Am; Am Geophys Union; Oceanog Soc. *Res:* Impact of marine phytoplankton on trace metal transfer in food webs; biogeochemical cycling of metals and metalloids; effects of sublethal concentrations of toxic substances on the morphology growth, and community structure of marine phytoplankton and zooplankton. *Mailing Add:* 1726 Sollers Wharf Rd Lusby Rd MD 20657

SANDERS, JAMES VINCENT, UNDERWATER ACOUSTICS, FLUID DYNAMICS. *Current Pos:* Asst prof, 61-68, ASSOC PROF PHYSICS, NAVAL POSTGRAD SCH, 68- *Personal Data:* b Twinsburg, Ohio, July 24, 32; m 55; c 4. *Educ:* Kent State Univ, BS, 54; Cornell Univ, PhD(physics), 61. *Res:* Fluid mechanics of non-Newtonian fluids; large amplitude standing acoustic waves; interaction of acoustic waves with fluid flow; acoustic properties of the ocean. *Mailing Add:* Dept Physics Naval Postgrad Sch 1 Univ Circle Monterey CA 93943-5000

SANDERS, JAY W, AUDIOLOGY. *Current Pos:* RETIRED. *Personal Data:* b Baltimore, Md, July 26, 24; m 50; c 3. *Educ:* Univ NC, AB, 50; Columbia Univ, MA, 51; Univ Mo, PhD(speech path), 57. *Prof Exp:* Instr speech, Univ Mo, 52-57; from asst prof to assoc prof, Trenton State Col, 57-62; from asst prof to assoc prof, 64-70, Prof Audiol, Vanderbilt Univ, 70- *Concurrent Pos:* Nat Inst Neurol Dis & Blindness fel audiol, Northwestern Univ, 62-64; consult, St Francis Hosp, Hearing & Speech Ctr, Trenton, NJ, 61-62; asst prof, Vanderbilt Univ, 64-65, assoc prof, 65-70; mem staff, Bill Wilkerson Hearing & Speech Ctr, 64- *Mem:* Am Speech & Hearing Asn. *Res:* Audition; disorders of audition and diagnostic audiology. *Mailing Add:* 5518 Vanderbilt Rd Old Hickory TN 37138

SANDERS, JOAN ELIZABETH, BIOMECHANICS, TISSUE ENGINEERING. *Current Pos:* teaching asst, Ctr Bioeng & Elec Eng Dept, Univ Washington, 86-87, res asst, Rheumatology Dept, 87, Mech Eng Dept, 87-88, Ctr Bioeng, 86, 88, 90, res fel, Dept Rehab Med, 88-89, ASST PROF, CTR BIOENG, UNIV WASHINGTON, 92- *Personal Data:* b Santa Monica, Calif, May 11, 61. *Educ:* Stanford Univ, BS, 83; Northwestern Univ, MS, 85; Univ Washington, PhD(bioeng), 91. *Honors & Awards:* Soc Women Engrs Award, 87. *Prof Exp:* Mech engr, Gekee Fiberoptics, 83; teaching & res asst, Mech Eng Dept, Northwestern Univ, 84; res engr, Artificial Organs Div, Baxter Travenol Labs, Inc, 84; engr, Tyler Builders, 85; grader, Math Dept, Stanford Univ, 85; res scientist, Prosthetics Res Study, 90-91, dir tissue mech res, 91-92. *Concurrent Pos:* Adj asst prof, Univ Wash, 93- *Mem:* Int Soc Prosthetics Orthotics; Soc Exp Mech; Rehab Eng Soc NAm; Inst Elec & Electronics Engrs; Biomed Eng Soc; Am Soc Mech Engrs. *Res:* Soft tissue biomechanics; adaptive biomaterials; soft tissue mechanical characterization; prosthetic evaluation; non-invasive assessment of skin structures; soft tissues for load-bearing functions; immediate post surgical techniques; prosthetic interfaces. *Mailing Add:* Ctr Bioeng WD-12 Univ Wash Seattle WA 98195. *Fax:* 206-543-6124; *E-Mail:* jsanders@uwashington.edu

SANDERS, JOHN CLAYTOR, MECHANICAL ENGINEERING, AERONAUTICS. *Current Pos:* RETIRED. *Personal Data:* b Roanoke, Va, Oct 29, 14; m 54; c 2. *Educ:* Va Polytech Inst, BS, 36, MS, 37. *Prof Exp:* Indust engr, Aluminum Co Am, 37-39; aeronaut res scientist, NASA, 39-58, asst chief, Wind Tunnel & Flight Div, Lewis Res Ctr, 58-77. *Concurrent Pos:* Mem subcomt internal flow, Nat Adv Comt Aeronaut, 47-48, subcomt power plant controls, NASA, 53-58 & subcomt struct dynamics, 63-64; consult indust automation & control; pres city coun, Strongsville, Ohio, 66-67. *Mem:* Fel Am Soc Mech Engrs. *Res:* Dynamics and control of aircraft and missile propulsion systems, including propeller engines, jet engines, chemical rockets and nuclear rockets. *Mailing Add:* 15305 Forest Park Dr Strongsville OH 44136

SANDERS, JOHN D, ELECTRICAL ENGINEERING. *Current Pos:* CHIEF EXEC OFFICER, TECH NEWS INC, 89- *Personal Data:* b Louisville, Ky, Aug 2, 38; m 67; c 1. *Educ:* Univ Louisville, BEE, 61; Carnegie-Mellon Univ, MS, 62, PhD(elec eng), 65. *Prof Exp:* Develop engr, Receiving Tube Dept, Gen Elec Co, Ky, 61; mem tech staff, Radio Corp Am Labs, NJ, 62; instr elec eng, Carnegie-Mellon Univ, 62-64; Proj officer, US Cent Intel Agency, 64-68; vpres, Wachtel & Co, Inc, 68-89. *Concurrent Pos:* Asst prof lectr, George Washington Univ, 67-68; financial adv, Indust Training Corp, Radiation Systs, Inc, Tork, Inc, Fla Glass Indust, Temporaries, Inc & Data Measurement Corp. *Mem:* Inst Elec & Electronics Engrs; Financial Analysts Fedn; Nat Security Traders Asn. *Res:* Aiding management of small technical companies, primarily in communications and electronics. *Mailing Add:* Washington Tech Newspaper 8500 Leesburg Pike Suite 7500 Vienna VA 22182

SANDERS, JOHN ESSINGTON, GEOLOGY. *Current Pos:* ADJ STAR PROF, HOFSTRA UNIV, 90- *Personal Data:* b Des Moines, Iowa, May 5, 26; m 52; c 3. *Educ:* Ohio Wesleyan Univ, BA, 48; Yale Univ, PhD(geol), 53. *Hon Degrees:* DSc, Ohio Wesleyan, 68. *Prof Exp:* Nat Res Coun fel, geol surv, Smithsonian Inst, 52-53 & Brit Mus Natural Hist, Neth, 53-54; instr geol, Yale Univ, 54-56, asst prof, 56-64; sr res assoc, Hudson Labs, Barnard Col, Columbia Univ, 64-69, vis prof, 68-69, prof geol, 69-89. *Concurrent Pos:* NSF fac fel sci, Yale Univ & Mass Inst Technol, 62-63; assoc ed, J Sedimentary Petrol, 62-76; mem, bd dirs, Mutual Oil Am, Inc, 69-75; mem NY State Dept Environ Conserv Hudson River PCB Settlement Adv Comt, 76-, chmn, 77; mem Nat Res Coun Comt Assess PCB's in Environ, 78. *Mem:* Fel AAAS; fel Geol Soc Am; Soc Econ Paleontologists & Mineralogists; Am Asn Petrol Geologists; NY Acad Sci. *Res:* Sedimentology; stratigraphy; paleogeography; primary structures in sedimentary deposits; Mississippian of southern Appalachians; Mississippian Brachiopoda; Triassic-Jurassic of Connecticut, New York and New Jersey; nearshore marine sediments; geological applications of side-looking sonar; origin and occurrence of petroleum; geology of New York metropolitan area. *Mailing Add:* Dept Geol Hofstra Univ 114 Gittleson Hall Rm 156 Hempstead NY 11550-1090

SANDERS, JOHN P(AUL), SR, CHEMICAL & NUCLEAR ENGINEERING. *Current Pos:* res staff mem, 65-80, SR RES STAFF MEM, OAK RIDGE NAT LAB, 80- *Personal Data:* b Hope, Ark, July 4, 26; m 57; c 2. *Educ:* Univ Ark, BSChE, 50, MS, 52; Ga Inst Technol, PhD(chem eng), 63. *Prof Exp:* Instr chem eng, Univ Ark, 50-52; engr, Oak Ridge Nat Lab, 52-55; assoc prof chem eng, Univ Ark, 57-65. *Concurrent Pos:* Lectr, Oak Ridge Assoc Univ. *Mem:* Am Inst Chem Engrs; Sigma Xi. *Res:* Heat removal from nuclear reactor cores; transfer of heat through outer wall of annulis as a function of the system parameters; evaluation of the performance of the cores of nuclear reactors; computational procedures for systems analysis. *Mailing Add:* 116 Nebraska Ave Oak Ridge TN 37830

SANDERS, KENTON M, SMOOTH MUSCLE ELECTROPHYSIOLOGY. *Current Pos:* Assoc prof, 82-86, PROF PHYSIOL, SCH MED, UNIV NEV, 86- *Personal Data:* b Oakland, Calif, June 16, 50. *Educ:* Univ Calif, Los Angeles, PhD(physiol), 76. *Mem:* Biophys Soc; Am Physiol Soc; Am Gastroenterol Asn; Am Motility Soc. *Mailing Add:* Dept Physiol & Cell Biol Univ Nev Sch Med Anderson Med Sci Bldg Reno NV 89557. *Fax:* 702-784-6903

SANDERS, LOUIS LEE, INTERNAL MEDICINE, BIOCHEMISTRY. *Current Pos:* from instr to asst prof, 62-69, assoc prof, 69-80, PROF INTERNAL MED, SCH MED, UNIV ARK, LITTLE ROCK, 80-; CHIEF METAB SECT, LITTLE ROCK VET ADMIN HOSP, 69- *Personal Data:* b Little Rock, Ark, May 18, 29; m 58; c 4. *Educ:* Univ Ark, BS, 51, MD, 55, MS, 61. *Prof Exp:* Asst chief med serv, Little Rock Vet Admin Hosp, 75-94. *Concurrent Pos:* Asst dir clin res ctr, Univ Ark, Little Rock, 62-65; attend physician, Little Rock Vet Admin Hosp, 62-65, staff physician, 66-69 & 94- *Mem:* Fel Am Col Physicians. *Res:* Diabetes mellitus; insulin metabolism in adult-onset diabetes; effect of oral hypoglycemic agents on insulin metabolism. *Mailing Add:* Little Rock Vet Admin Hosp 4300 W Seventh Little Rock AR 72205-5411

SANDERS, MARILYN MAGDANZ, BIOCHEMISTRY, MOLECULAR BIOLOGY. *Current Pos:* from instr to assoc prof, 73-87, PROF PHARMACOL, ROBERT WOOD JOHNSON MED SCH, UNIV MED & DENT NJ, 87- *Personal Data:* b Norfolk, Nebr, Aug 12, 42; div. *Educ:* Stanford Univ, BSc, 64; Univ Wash, PhD(biochem), 69. *Prof Exp:* From instr to res assoc biochem sci, Princeton Univ, 71-73. *Concurrent Pos:* Med Res Coun Can grant, Univ BC, 69-71. *Mem:* Am Chem Soc; Am Soc Cell Biol; Genetics Soc Am; Am Soc Biol Chemists. *Res:* Mechanism of induction of the heat shock response; gene regulation in heat shock in Drosophilia melanogaster; regulation of development and gene expression in eukaryotic organisms. *Mailing Add:* Pharmacol Dept Robert Wood Johnson Med Sch Univ Med & Dent NJ 675 Hoes Lane Piscataway NJ 08854-5635. *Fax:* 732-235-4073

SANDERS, MARTIN E, IMMUNOLOGY. *Current Pos:* DIR RHEUMATOLOGY-IMMUNOL RES, CENTOCOR, INC, 90- *Personal Data:* b Appleton City, Mo, Feb 1, 54. *Educ:* Univ Mo, AB, 75; Univ Chicago, MD, 79. *Prof Exp:* Med staff fel immunol, Nat Inst Allergy & Infectious Dis, NIH, 82-85, Nat Cancer Inst, 85-88; physician-scientist, Upjohn Co, 88-90. *Concurrent Pos:* Fel rheumatology, Johns Hopkins Univ, 84-85. *Mem:* Am Fedn Clin Res; Am Col Rheumatology; Am Asn Immunologists; AAAS; Am Col Physicians; Clin Immunol Soc. *Res:* Pharmaceutical research; development with particular emphasis on therapies for autoimmune and inflammatory disease. *Mailing Add:* Centocor Inc 200 Great Valley Pkwy Malvern PA 19355-1307. *Fax:* 215-640-1385

SANDERS, MARY ELIZABETH, GENETICS. *Current Pos:* RETIRED. *Personal Data:* b Kobe, Japan, Mar 1, 17; US citizen. *Educ:* Mt Holyoke Col, AB, 38; Cornell Univ, MS, 40; Smith Col, PhD(genetics), 47. *Prof Exp:* Asst, Dept Genetics, Carnegie Inst, 40-41; teacher sch, SDak, 41-42; asst bot, Conn Col, 42-43; asst Genetics Exp Sta, Smith Col, 43-46; instr bot, Mt Holyoke Col, 46-47; asst bot, Yale Univ, 47-48; instr & res assoc integrated lib studies & bot, Univ Wis, 48-54; instr biol sci, Northwestern Univ, 54-55; res assoc agron, SDak State Col, 55-62; res assoc, Arnold Arboretum, Harvard Univ, 62-65, Am Asn Univ Women fel, 64-65; from asst prof to prof bot, Mont Alto Campus, Pa State Univ, 65-77. *Res:* Genetics and embryo culture of Datura; origin of colchicine-induced diploid sorghum mutants with multiple changed characters, many mutants immediately true-breeding; investigations of tomato for responses to colchicine similar to those found in sorghum. *Mailing Add:* 500 E Marylyn Ave State College PA 16801

SANDERS, OLIVER PAUL, MATHEMATICS. *Current Pos:* prof & head dept, 62-65, acad dean, 65-68, provost, 68-70, vpres acad affairs, 70-74, prof, 74-87, EMER PROF MATH, APPALACHIAN STATE UNIV, 87- *Personal Data:* b Caney, Okla, Dec 26, 24; m 45; c 2. *Educ:* Southeastern State Col, BA, 47; Okla State Univ, MS, 49, PhD, 56. *Prof Exp:* Asst prof math, Arlington State Col, 49-51 & Southeastern State Col, 51-54; instr, Okla State Univ, 54-56; asst prof, Univ Ark, 56-57; assoc prof, La Polytech Univ, 57-59; prof & head dept, Hardin-Simmons Univ, 59-62. *Mem:* Math Asn Am. *Res:* Partial differential equations. *Mailing Add:* 1004 St Johns Ave Green Cove Springs FL 32043

SANDERS, PATRICIA A, TEST SYSTEM EVALUATION & ENGINEERING. *Current Pos:* DIR TEST SYST EVAL & ENG, DEPT DEFENSE, 97- *Educ:* Wayne State Univ, PhD(math), 72. *Concurrent Pos:* Fel, NSF, 72. *Mailing Add:* Dept Defense-Test & Eval 3110 Defense Pentagon Washington DC 20301

SANDERS, RAYMOND THOMAS, PHYSIOLOGY. *Current Pos:* from asst prof to prof physiol, Utah State Univ, 58-70, prof zool, 70-77, prof biol, 77-88, EMER PROF BIOL, UTAH STATE UNIV, 88- *Personal Data:* b Ogden, Utah, June 23, 23; m 47; c 1. *Educ:* Univ Utah, BS, 49, MS, 50; Stanford Univ, PhD(biol), 56. *Prof Exp:* Nat Found Infantile Paralysis fel, Physiol Inst, Univ Uppsala, 56-58. *Concurrent Pos:* Dir, Hons Prog, Utah State Univ, 74-89. *Mem:* Am Soc Zoologists; Am Gen Physiol. *Res:* Permeability phenomena in cells and model systems; role of salts in metabolism; sensory physiology of invertebrates. *Mailing Add:* PO Box 242 Richmond UT 84333

SANDERS, RICHARD PAT, GEOLOGY. *Current Pos:* ASST PROF GEOL, WGA COL, 74- *Personal Data:* b Chicago, Ill, Mar 18, 43; m 67. *Educ:* Northern Ill Univ, BS, 65, MS, 68; Univ Ill, PhD(geol), 71. *Prof Exp:* Asst prof geol, Univ Wis-Stevens Point, 71-74. *Mem:* Am Geophys Union; Geol Soc Am; Sigma Xi. *Res:* Igneous and metamorphic petrology; mode of implacement of igneous plutons and volcanics. *Mailing Add:* Dept Geol WGa Col 1601 Maple St Carrollton GA 30118-0001

SANDERS, ROBERT B, BIOLOGICAL CHEMISTRY. *Current Pos:* from asst prof to assoc prof, Univ Kans, 66-86, assoc dean, Grad Sch, 87-96, assoc vchancellor, Res Grad Studies Pub Serv, 89-96, PROF BIOCHEM, UNIV KANS, 86- *Personal Data:* b Augusta, Ga, Dec 9, 38; m 61, Gladys Nealous; c Sylvia L & William N. *Educ:* Paine Col, BS, 59; Univ Mich, MS, 61, PhD(biochem), 64. *Prof Exp:* Am Cancer Soc fel biochem, Univ Wis, 64-66. *Concurrent Pos:* Battelle Mem Inst fel, 70 & 71; consult, Interex Res Corp, 72-80, NIH & NSF; vis assoc prof, Dept Pharmacol, Sch Med, Univ Tex, Houston, 74-75; NIH fel, 74-75; prog dir, Regulatory Biol Prog, NSF, Washington, DC, 78-79, assoc dir, Jr Sci Humanities Symp, Kan-Neb-Okla Region, 83-93, dir, 93- *Mem:* Sigma Xi; Am Soc Biol Chemists; Am Soc Pharmacol & Exp Therapeut. *Res:* Biochemistry of hormone action; cyclic nucleotides; biochemistry of reproduction. *Mailing Add:* 1220 W 29th Ct Lawrence KS 66046. *Fax:* 785-864-5321; *E-Mail:* bsanders@research.rgsps.ukans.edu

SANDERS, ROBERT CHARLES, NUCLEAR ENGINEERING, THERMAL HYDRAULICS. *Current Pos:* ENGR CONSULT, MPR ASSOCS, 79- *Personal Data:* b Anaconda, Mont, Dec 17, 42; m 70; c 1. *Educ:* Ore State Univ, BS, 66. *Hon Degrees:* ScD, Mass Inst Techol, 70. *Honors & Awards:* Gold Medal, Soc Am Military Engr. *Prof Exp:* Nuclear engr, Div Naval Reactors, US Dept Energy, 70-75; asst prof, Univ Mo, 75-79. *Concurrent Pos:* Consult, Consumers Power Co, 77. *Mem:* Am Nuclear Soc; Nat Soc Prof Engrs; Sigma Xi; NY Acad Sci. *Res:* Nuclear power plant thermal-hydraulics, safety, and reliability; waste heat utilization; neutron activation analysis; fluid systems design and analysis; design and analysis of heat transfer equipment. *Mailing Add:* 9405 Kilimanjaro Columbia MD 21045-3952

SANDERS, ROBERT W, FOOD WEB DYNAMICS. *Current Pos:* ASST PROF BIOL, TEMPLE UNIV, 96- *Personal Data:* b Washington, DC, Feb 25, 52; m 76, Elizabeth Davies; c Nicholas E & Katherine H. *Educ:* Univ Va, BA, 79; Univ Maine, MS, 82; Univ Ga, PhD(zool), 88. *Prof Exp:* Res assoc, Univ Ga, 88-89; asst cur, Acad Natural Sci, Philadelphia, 89-95. *Concurrent Pos:* Prin investr, NSF, 90-92, NJ Sea Grant Prog, 91-93 & 93-; adj asst prof, Univ Pa, 93- *Mem:* Sigma Xi; Am Soc Limnol & Oceanog; Am Soc Microbiol; Soc Protozoologists; Ecol Soc Am. *Res:* Ecology of aquatic organisms, with emphasis on protists and their trophic interactions; food web transfer of toxic materials; dissolved organic compounds and eutrophication. *Mailing Add:* Dept Biol Temple Univ Philadelphia PA 19122. *Fax:* 215-299-1028; *E-Mail:* rsanders@say.acnatsci.org

SANDERS, RONALD L, BIOCHEMISTRY. *Current Pos:* ADJ ASSOC PROF RADIOL, DUKE UNIV, 87- *Personal Data:* b Greenway, Ark, June 19, 47; m 88, Donna Tucceru; c Elizabeth. *Educ:* Wash Univ, AB, 70; St Louis Univ, PhD(biochem), 75. *Prof Exp:* Res assoc, Dept Biochem, Univ Colo Med Ctr, 75-76; fel, W Alton Jones Cell Sci Ctr, 76-78; res asst prof anat & cell biol & biochem, Sch Med, Tufts Univ, 79-86, res asst prof biochem, 85-86. *Concurrent Pos:* Sr clin res scientist, Burroughs Wellcome Co, 86-96,. *Mem:* Am Chem Soc; Am Phys Soc; Am Soc Biol Chem; Am Thoracic Soc; Am Col Chest Physicians. *Res:* Pulmonary biochemistry, phospholipid and surfactant metabolism, type II culture. *Mailing Add:* Dept Radiol Erwin Rd Duke Univ Durham NC 27710

SANDERS, SAMUEL MARSHALL, JR, HEALTH PHYSICS, RADIOBIOLOGY. *Current Pos:* RETIRED. *Personal Data:* b Charleston, SC, July 26, 28; div; c Melissa S (Walker) & S Marshall III. *Educ:* The Citadel, BS, 49; La State Univ, Baton Rouge, MS, 52; Am Bd Health Physics, dipl, 61; Med Col Ga, PhD(radiobiol), 74. *Honors & Awards:* Elda E Anderson Mem Award, Health Physics Soc, 68. *Prof Exp:* Sr supvr, Bio-Assay Lab, Savannah River Plant, E I Du Pont de Nemours & Co, Inc, 52-55, chemist, Health Physics Sect, 55-60 & 62-64, sr res chemist, Environ Sci Sect, Savannah River Lab, 64-89; sr scientist, Westinghouse Savannah River Co, 89-93. *Concurrent Pos:* Partic, Traveling Lect Prog, Oak Ridge Asn Univs, 63-67; consult, Dept Radiol, Med Col Ga, 68-74. *Mem:* Health Physics Soc. *Res:* Metabolism of water with the fixing of hydrogen in non-labile positions in macromolecules of plants and animals; microbeam analysis of plutonium-bearing microaerosols from fuel reprocessing facilities. *Mailing Add:* 1220 Fernwood Ct Aiken SC 29803-5206

SANDERS, T H, JR, PHYSICAL METALLURGY. *Current Pos:* PROF MAT ENG, SCH MAT ENG, GA INST TECH, 87- *Personal Data:* b Philadelphia, Pa, July 23, 43. *Educ:* Ga Inst Technol, BS, 66, MS, 69, PhD(metall), 74. *Prof Exp:* Res scientist, Aluminum Co Am, Alcoa Ctr, Pa, 74-79, Fracture & Fatigue Res Lab, Metall Prog, Ga Inst Technol, 79-81; assoc prof phys metall, Purdue Univ, 81-87, prof metall, 85-87. *Mem:* Am Inst Mining, Metall & Petrol Engrs; Am Soc Metals; Am Soc Eng Educ. *Res:* Aluminum alloy development for aerospace applications; microstructural mechanisms of fracture and fatigue, solidification and microstructure, and primary processing to improve properties. *Mailing Add:* Dept Mat Engr Ga Inst Tech Atlanta GA 30332-0001

SANDERS, THEODORE MICHAEL, JR, PHYSICS. *Current Pos:* vis prof, 63-64, PROF PHYSICS, UNIV MICH, ANN ARBOR, 64- *Personal Data:* b New York, NY, Sept 14, 27; wid; c 2. *Educ:* Harvard Univ, AB, 48; Columbia Univ, MS, 51, PhD(physics), 54. *Prof Exp:* Asst physics, Columbia Univ, 49-51; res assoc, Stanford Univ, 53-55; from asst prof to prof, Univ Minn, 55-63. *Concurrent Pos:* Sloan fel, 58-62. *Mem:* Fel Am Phys Soc. *Res:* Physics of atoms, molecules and solids; radio frequency spectroscopy; low temperature physics. *Mailing Add:* H M Randall Physics Lab Univ Mich Ann Arbor MI 48109

SANDERS, TIMOTHY D, PHYSICS. *Current Pos:* asst prof physics & math, Occidental Col, 64-69, asst dean fac, 68-70, assoc prof, 69-77, PROF PHYSICS, OCCIDENTAL COL, 77- *Personal Data:* b Laramie, Wyo, Apr 1, 35; m 57; c 2. *Educ:* Stanford Univ, BS, 57, MSc, 59, PhD(physics), 62. *Prof Exp:* Res assoc theoret physics, Washington Univ, 62-64. *Concurrent Pos:* NSF sci fac fel, Stanford Linear Accelerator Ctr, 71-72. *Mem:* AAAS; Am Phys Soc; Am Math Soc; Sigma Xi. *Res:* Elementary particles; hyper-nuclei and light nuclei; group theory and its applications to quantum theory. *Mailing Add:* 1912 Campus Rd Los Angeles CA 90041-3009

SANDERS, W EUGENE, JR, MEDICINE, MICROBIOLOGY. *Current Pos:* PROF MED & MED MICROBIOL & CHMN DEPT MED MICROBIOL, SCH MED, CREIGHTON UNIV, 72- *Personal Data:* b Frederick, Md, June 25, 34; m 72, Christine Culp; c Eugene III, Sherri L, John W, & Lisa-Marie (Barbour). *Educ:* Cornell Univ, AB, 56, MD, 60; Am Bd Internal Med, dipl,

68. *Prof Exp:* Intern med, Johns Hopkins Hosp, 60-61, resident, 61-62; epidemic intel serv officer, Commun Dis Ctr, USPHS, 62-64; chief resident med, Teaching Hosps, Col Med, Univ Fla, 64-65, from asst prof to assoc prof med & microbiol, 65-72. *Concurrent Pos:* Am Soc Pharmacol & Exp Therapeut travel award, 67; NIH res career develop award, 68-; Markle scholar acad med, 68-; instr, Sch Med, Emory Univ, 62-64; bd trustees, Inter-Am Soc Chemotherapy, 80-90; Arminit T Wilson Mem Orator, 83; ed, Am J Epidemiol, 84-; distinguished prof, 87; lectr Pasteur Inst, Paris, France, Jules Bordet Inst, Brussels, Belgium. *Mem:* AAAS; Am Pub Health Asn; Am Fedn Clin Res; Am Soc Microbiol; Infectious Dis Soc am; Am ColEpidemiol. *Res:* Internal medicine; infectious diseases and epidemiology; bacterial interference; antimicrobial agents and chemotherapy; bacterial carrier states; resistance to antimicrobial agents; inventor/co-inventor 9 US and foreign patents. *Mailing Add:* Creighton Univ Sch Med 2500 California St Omaha NE 68178-0001. *Fax:* 402-280-1225

SANDERS, W(ILLIAM) THOMAS, SOLID MECHANICS, MECHANICAL ENGINEERING. *Current Pos:* asst prof mech eng, 62-66, ASSOC PROF MECH ENG, COLUMBIA UNIV, 66- *Personal Data:* b Owensboro, Ky, June 13, 33; m 54; c 2. *Educ:* Purdue Univ, BS, 54; NY Univ, MS, 57; Columbia Univ, ScD(mech eng), 62. *Prof Exp:* Engr, Dow Chem Co, 54; engr-trainee, Oak Ridge Nat Lab, 54-55; engr, Combustion Eng, Inc, 55-57 & Am Mach & Foundry Co, 57-60. *Concurrent Pos:* Consult, Am Mach & Foundry Co, Avion Corp & Columbia Broadcasting Syst Labs. *Mem:* Am Phys Soc; Am Soc Mech Engrs; Sigma Xi. *Res:* Solid state engineering; dislocations in crystals; solar energy applications. *Mailing Add:* PO Box 9353 Bardonia NY 10954

SANDERS, W(ALLACE) W(OLFRED), JR, CIVIL ENGINEERING, STRUCTURAL ENGINEERING. *Current Pos:* assoc prof, Iowa State Univ, 64-70, asst dir, Eng Res Inst, 80-84, assoc dir, 84-91, assoc dean, Col Eng, 88-91, interim vprovost res, 91-92, PROF CIVIL ENG, IOWA STATE UNIV, 70- *Personal Data:* b Louisville, Ky, June 24, 33; m 56, Julia Howard; c Linda & David. *Educ:* Univ Louisville, BCE, 55, MEng, 73; Univ Ill, MS, 57, PhD(civil eng), 60. *Honors & Awards:* Adams Mem Award, Am Welding Soc, 70; R C Reese Res Prize, Am Soc Civil Engrs, 78. *Prof Exp:* Asst civil eng, Univ Ill, 55-59, res assoc, 59-60, asst prof, 60-64. *Mem:* Am Soc Civil Engrs; Am Welding Soc; Am Rwy Eng Asn; Am Soc Eng Educ. *Res:* Fatigue of welded joints in structural metals; behavior of timber, steel and concrete bridges. *Mailing Add:* Iowa State Univ 374 Town Eng Bldg Ames IA 50011. *Fax:* 515-294-8216; *E-Mail:* wsanders@iastate.edu

SANDERS, WALTER L, science teaching, computer programming, for more information see previous edition

SANDERS, WALTER MACDONALD, III, CIVIL & SANITARY ENGINEERING. *Current Pos:* SR CONSULT, MR CHASMAN & ASSOCS PC, 87- *Personal Data:* b Bluefield, WVa, Dec 5, 30; m 56, Emily Joyce; c Walter M IV, Albert B & Stephen C. *Educ:* Va Mil Inst, BS, 53; Johns Hopkins Univ, MS, 56, PhD(sanit eng), 64. *Honors & Awards:* Gold Medal, US Environ Protection Agency, 85. *Prof Exp:* Eng asst, WVa Water Serv Co, 47-52; sanit engr, Greeley & Hansen Engrs, 53; res sanit engr, USAF MSc, Ft Detrich, Md, 53-55; asst, dept sanit eng, Johns Hopkins Univ, 55-56; sanit eng consult, USPHS, Div Int Health, 56-58, asst chief, Water Supply Sect, Dept Water Supply & Pollution Control, 58-60, res sanit engr, Southeast Region USPHS, Clemson Univ, 62-64, chief, Freshwater Ecosyts Br, US Environ Protection Agency/USPHS, 64-76, assoc dir water qual res, Athens Environ Res Lab USPHS, 76-85. *Concurrent Pos:* Adj prof, Div Interdisciplinary Studies, Clemson Univ, 62-75; res assoc & prof, Ecol Inst, Univ Ga, 67- & adj res assoc, Dept Microbiol, 72-85, adj prof, Sch Pharm, 85-; consult environ, 85- *Mem:* Am Soc Civil Engrs; AAAS. *Res:* Aquatic ecosystem studies and use of controlled environmental chamber-stream ecosystem complex to develop predictive models for future water quality and stream conditions; environmental pollution; ecological engineering; sanitary engineering; water quality management; control of toxic chemicals; environmental exposure and risk assessments; environmental assessments; wetlands assessments; groundwater protection and assessment. *Mailing Add:* 195 Xavier Dr Athens GA 30606. *Fax:* 706-548-4697

SANDERS, WILLIAM ALBERT, THEORETICAL CHEMISTRY, CHEMICAL DYNAMICS. *Current Pos:* asst prof, 65-69, ASSOC PROF CHEM, CATH UNIV AM, 69-, CHMN DEPT, 81- *Personal Data:* b Lafayette, Ind, Apr 28, 33; m 56; c 4. *Educ:* Purdue Univ, BSChE, 55, PhD(phys chem), 63; Georgetown Univ, MS, 61. *Prof Exp:* Instr chem, US Naval Acad, 57-60; NSF fel theoret chem, Univ Wis, 63-65, res assoc, 65. *Concurrent Pos:* Consult, Phys Res Labs, Edgewood Arsenal, 68-70 & Naval Res Lab, 78- *Mem:* Sigma Xi; Am Chem Soc. *Res:* Gas phase kinetics; theory of molecular beam scattering; applications of perturbation theory; theory of inter- and intramolecular forces; chemical dynamics. *Mailing Add:* 16 Stone Cliff Dr Niantic CT 06357-1514

SANDERS, WILLIAM MACK, MATHEMATICS. *Current Pos:* PROF MATH & HEAD DEPT, JAMES MADISON UNIV, 69- *Personal Data:* b West Point, Ark, June 12, 26; m 49; c 3. *Educ:* Ark State Teachers Col, BS, 49; Univ Ark, MA, 52; Univ Ill, Urbana, PhD(math), 65. *Prof Exp:* Instr math, SMiss Univ, 52-55, assoc prof, 58-64; assoc prof, Lawrence Univ, 64-69. *Mem:* Math Asn Am; Am Math Soc. *Res:* Foundations of geometry, especially abstract models of geometries. *Mailing Add:* Dept Math James Madison Univ Harrisonburg VA 22807-0002

SANDERS-BUSH, ELAINE, SEROTONIN. *Current Pos:* NIMH fel, 67-69, from instr to assoc prof, 68-80, PROF PHARMACOL, SCH MED, VANDERBILT UNIV, 80-, PROF PSYCHIAT, 86- *Personal Data:* b Russellville, Ky, Apr 27, 40; m 67, 87; c Katherine. *Educ:* Western Ky Univ, BS, 62; Vanderbilt Univ, PhD(pharmacol), 67. *Concurrent Pos:* NIMH res scientist develop award, 74; counr, Serotonin Club, 86-93; ed bd, Neurochemistry Int, 88; field ed, J Pharmacol Exp Therapeut, 92- *Mem:* Am Soc Pharmacol & Exp Therapeut; Am Col Neuropsychopharmacol; Neurosci Soc; Serotonin Club (vpres, 90-92, pres, 92-94). *Res:* Psychopharmacology; serotonin receptor subtypes; biogenic amines; second messengers. *Mailing Add:* Dept Pharmacol Vanderbilt Univ Sch Med Nashville TN 37232-6600

SANDERS-LOEHR, JOANN, BIOCHEMISTRY. *Current Pos:* PROF CHEM & BIOL SCI, ORE GRAD INST, 84- *Personal Data:* b New York, NY, Sept 2, 42; m 65. *Educ:* Cornell Univ, BS, 64, PhD(biochem), 69. *Prof Exp:* Fel biochem, Ore Health Sci Univ, 69-71; from asst prof to prof chem, Portland State Univ 71-84. *Concurrent Pos:* NIH fel, 70-71; Cottrell res grant, 72-74; NIH grant, 75-; vis assoc chem, Calif Inst Technol, Pasadena, 78-79. *Mem:* Am Soc Microbiol; Am Chem Soc; Am Soc Biochem & Molecular Biol. *Res:* Role of metal ions in biological systems; metalloprotein structure and function. *Mailing Add:* Dept chem Biochem & Molecular Biol Ore Grad Inst Sci & Technol PO Box 91000 Portland OR 97291-1000

SANDERSON, ARTHUR CLARK, ROBOTICS, INTELLIGENT SYSTEMS. *Current Pos:* PROF & DEPT HEAD, ELEC, COMPUT & SYSTS ENG DEPT, RENSSELAER POLYTECH INST, 87- *Personal Data:* b Providence, RI, Oct 23, 46; m 71, Susan; c Angeline & Andrew. *Educ:* Brown Univ, BS, 68; Carnegie-Mellon Univ, MS, 70, PhD(elec eng), 72. *Prof Exp:* Res engr, Res & Develop Lab, Westinghouse, 68-71; fel, Delft Univ Technol, 72-73; asst prof elec eng, Carnegie-Mellon Univ, 73-75; vis prof biomed eng, Univ Iberoamericana, Mex, 76-77; assoc prof, 77-81, prof elec eng & dir, Robotics Inst, Carnegie-Mellon Univ, 81-87. *Concurrent Pos:* Vis scientist, Inst Politech Nat, Mex, 76-77; adj prof, Med Sch, Univ Pittsburgh, 80-; res dir, Philips Res Lab, NY, 85-87. *Mem:* Fel Inst Elec & Electronics Engrs; AAAS; Sigma Xi. *Res:* Signal processing and pattern recognition applied to robotics and biomedicine; sensor based control of robots; intelligent systems. *Mailing Add:* Rensselaer Polytech Inst Elec Eng Dept Troy NY 12180-3590. *Fax:* 518-276-4897; *E-Mail:* acs@cat.rpi.edu

SANDERSON, BENJAMIN S, PHYSICAL CHEMISTRY. *Current Pos:* RETIRED. *Personal Data:* b Buffalo, NY, Mar 18, 22; m 52; c 4. *Educ:* Hobart Col, BS, 42; Ohio State Univ, PhD(phys chem), 55. *Prof Exp:* Tech supvr, Holston Ord Works, Tenn Eastman Corp, 43-44; res chemist, NL Industs, Inc, 55-58, group leader, 58-68, sect mgr, Anal Sect, 68-72, process supt, Res Lab, 72-82. *Concurrent Pos:* Lectr, Rutgers Univ, 62-71. *Mem:* Am Chem Soc; Am Statist Asn; fel Am Inst Chemists. *Res:* X-ray diffraction and spectroscopy; statistics; use of computers in research; infrared spectroscopy; quality control. *Mailing Add:* 80 Lyme Rd Apt 211 Hanover NH 03755-1230

SANDERSON, DONALD EUGENE, GEOMETRIC, SET-THEORETIC. *Current Pos:* from instr to prof, 53-91, EMER PROF MATH, IOWA STATE UNIV, 91- *Personal Data:* b Oskaloosa, Iowa, Feb 4, 26; wid; c Robert, Mark & Karen. *Educ:* Cornell Col, BA, 49; Calif Inst Technol, MS, 51; Univ Wis, PhD(math), 53. *Honors & Awards:* Allendoerfer Award, Math Asn Am, 80. *Prof Exp:* Asst instr math, Calif Inst Technol, 49-51. *Concurrent Pos:* Vis assoc prof, Mich State Univ, 62-63. *Mem:* Am Math Soc; Math Asn Am. *Res:* Topology of manifolds; general topology, infinite dimensional topology; set-theoretic topology. *Mailing Add:* Dept Math Iowa State Univ Ames IA 50011-0001

SANDERSON, EDWIN S, ORGANIC CHEMISTRY, POLYMER CHEMISTRY. *Current Pos:* RETIRED. *Personal Data:* b Mannville, Alta, Aug 19, 20; m 42, Louise Sweet; c Judith, Dianne, Jacqueline & Robert. *Educ:* Univ Alta, BSc, 50; McGill Univ, PhD(cellulose & wood chem), 53. *Prof Exp:* Res chemist, Visking Corp, 53-54; mgr cellulose & casing res, 54-57; plant mgr, Visking Div, Union Carbide Can, Ltd, 57-60, admin mgr, 60-62, dir res & develop plastic prod, 62-66; dir technol br, Dept Indust, Trade & Com, 66-81. *Mem:* Chem Inst Can; Am Chem Soc; Can Inst Food Technol; Sigma Xi. *Res:* Cellulose and high polymer chemistry; food packaging and preservation. *Mailing Add:* 1538 Stableview Way Greeley ON K4P 1P2 Can

SANDERSON, GARY WARNER, FOOD CHEMISTRY. *Current Pos:* vpres res, 78-88, VPRES TECHNOL, UNIVERSAL FOODS CORP, 89- *Personal Data:* b Thermal, Calif, Dec 17, 34; m 53; c 4. *Educ:* Univ Calif, Davis, BS, 56; Univ Nottingham, PhD(bot), 61. *Prof Exp:* Biochemist & head biochem div, Tea Res Inst, Ceylon, 62-66; mgr tea res, Thomas J Lipton, Inc, 66-71, asst dir tea res & develop, 71-75, dir beverage prod res, 76-78. *Concurrent Pos:* Adj prof, Col New Rochelle, 75; mem sci adv comt, Am Inst Baking, indust adv comt, Food Sci Dept, Univ Wis-Madison; chmn indust adv bd biol, Marguette Univ, Milwaukee, Wis. *Mem:* NY Acad Sci; fel Inst Food Technologists; Am Asn Cereal Chemists; Am Chem Soc; Brit Biochem Soc; World Aquacult Soc. *Res:* Plant biochemistry and physiology; food chemistry; tea chemistry and biochemistry; fermentation science and microbiology; biotechnology. *Mailing Add:* Universal Foods Corp 433 E Michigan Milwaukee WI 53202-5104

SANDERSON, GEORGE ALBERT, GEOLOGY, PALEONTOLOGY. *Current Pos:* CONSULT, 90- *Personal Data:* b New Haven, Conn, Aug 22, 26; m 61, Helen Greenlee; c Robert, George & Charles. *Educ:* Trinity Col, Conn, BS, 49; Univ Wis, PhD(geol), 54. *Prof Exp:* Asst geol, Univ Wis, 50-54; geologist, Shell Develop Co, Tex, 54-55, jr stratigr, Shell Oil Co, 55, paleontologist, 55-64; sr res scientist, Pan Am Petrol Corp, 64-65, staff res scientist, 65-69, res group supvr, 69-77, spec res assoc, 77-83, sr res assoc, Amoco Prod Co, 83-89. *Mem:* Paleont Soc; Soc Econ Paleontologists & Mineralogists. *Res:* Paleozoic micropaleontology; paleoecology and biostratigraphy, especially Fusulinidae and small Foraminifera; biometrics; detailed biostratigraphy, especially Pennsylvanian and Permian. *Mailing Add:* 2643 E 26th St Tulsa OK 74114. *Fax:* 918-743-6103

SANDERSON, GLEN CHARLES, ZOOLOGY, PHYSIOLOGY. *Current Pos:* game biologist, Ill Dept Conserv & Ill Natural Hist Surv, 55-60, assoc wildlife specialist, Ill Natural Hist Surv, 60-63, wildlife specialist, 63-64, actg head, Sect Wildlife Res, 63-64, head Sect Wildlife Res, 64-90, EMER PRIN SCIENTIST, ILL NATURAL HIST SURV, 90- *Personal Data:* b Wayne Co, Mo, Jan 21, 23; m 47, Beverley Carrick; c James W & Laurie J. *Educ:* Univ Mo, BS, 47, MA, 49; Univ Ill, PhD, 61. *Honors & Awards:* Oak Leaf Award, Nature Conservancy, 75. *Prof Exp:* Game biologist, Iowa State Conserv Comn, 49-55. *Concurrent Pos:* Prof, Univ Ill, 65-; adj res prof, Southern Ill Univ, 64, adj prof, 64-84; ed, J Wildlife Mgt, 71-72. *Mem:* Am Soc Mammal; Wildlife Soc; AAAS; Am Inst Biol Sci. *Res:* Population dynamics of wild animals, especially furbearers; physiological factors of reproductive and survival rates; lead poisoning in waterfowl. *Mailing Add:* 711 S State St Champaign IL 61820-5114. *Fax:* 217-333-4949

SANDERSON, H PRESTON, CHEMISTRY, ENVIRONMENTAL HEALTH. *Current Pos:* RETIRED. *Personal Data:* b Midgell, PEI, Aug 28, 25; m 51, Thelma June MacDougall; c Susan Marie & John Dougall. *Educ:* Dalhousie Univ, BSc, 49; Univ Minn, Minneapolis, MPH, 62, PhD(environ health), 69. *Prof Exp:* Plant chemist, Can Packers Ltd, 49; chemist sci serv, Can Dept Agr, NS, 49-51, chemist plant prod serv, Ont, 51-54; chemist, Int Joint Comn, 54-56; res scientist, Occup Health Div, Dept Nat Health & Welfare, 56-70; res officer, Nat Res Coun Can, Environ Secys, Div Biol, 70-77; chief, Atmospheric Chem Criteria & Stand, Atmospheric Eval Serv, 77-86. *Concurrent Pos:* Resource staff, Endownment Fund, Morris Katz Lectr, Ctr Atmospheric Chem, 86- *Mem:* Can Stand Asn; Am Indust Hyg Asn; Air Pollution Control Asn. *Res:* Compilation of scientific data related to cause and effects of pollutants on receptors; air pollution; atmospheric chemistry; acidification of precipitation; toxic chemicals; oxidants and photochemical reaction; effects of pollutants on vegetation; industrial hygiene. *Mailing Add:* 42 Millgate Crescent Willowdale-North York ON M2K 1L6 Can. *Fax:* 416-221-6133

SANDERSON, JAMES GEORGE, NUMERICAL ANALYSIS. *Current Pos:* STAFF MEM, THEORET DESIGN DIV, LOS ALAMOS SCI LAB, 76- *Personal Data:* b Somerset, NJ, Oct 10, 49. *Educ:* Lafayette Col, BS, 71; Univ NMex, MA, 73, PhD(math), 76. *Mem:* Soc Indust & Appl Math; Ecol Soc Am; Soc Conservation Biologists. *Res:* Mathematical ecology, population models, community structure, ecological models. *Mailing Add:* RR 1 Box 92 Santa Fe NM 87501

SANDERSON, JUDSON, MATHEMATICS. *Current Pos:* assoc prof, 56-75, PROF MATH, UNIV REDLANDS, 75- *Personal Data:* b Orrick, Mo, July 15, 21; m 54; c 3. *Educ:* Univ Ill, BS, 47, MS, 48, PhD(math), 50. *Prof Exp:* Asst math, Univ Ill, 47-48; asst prof, Tulane Univ, 50-51; assoc prof, USAF Inst Technol, 51-56. *Concurrent Pos:* Lectr, Ohio State Grad Ctr, Wright-Patterson AFB, 53-56; consult, San Bernardino County Sch Syst, 63-66. *Mem:* Am Math Soc; Math Asn Am. *Res:* Real variable measure theory and foundations of mathematics. *Mailing Add:* 1408 Garden Redlands CA 92373

SANDERSON, KENNETH CHAPMAN, FLORICULTURE, WASTE UTILIZATION. *Current Pos:* WRITER & CONSULT, 94- *Personal Data:* b Woodbury, NJ, Jan 9, 33; m 61, Barbara J; c Lesley M & Kenneth H. *Educ:* Cornell Univ, BS, 55; Univ Md, MS, 58, PhD(hort), 65. *Prof Exp:* Teaching asst hort, Univ Md, 55-56; retail florist, C J Sanderson Florist, 58-60; greenhouse mgr, Univ Md, 60-65; asst prof floricult, La State Univ, 65-66; from asst prof to prof floricult, Auburn Univ, 66-94. *Concurrent Pos:* Vis prof, Calif Polytech State Univ, 76-77 & 84-85; assoc ed, Hortsci & J Am Soc Hort Sci, 77-81; chmn, Environ Pollution Comt, Am Soc Hort Sci, 73-75, Munic Agr & Indust Waste Comt, 80-84, Floricult Work Group, 90- *Mem:* Sigma Xi; Plant Growth Regulator Soc Am; fel Am Soc Hort Sci; Prof Plant Growers Asn. *Res:* Greenhouse construction and management, florist crop production, pest control; floral design, retail flower shop management; plant propagation; environmental control, pollution; waste utilization; plant growth regulators; tropical foliage plants; interiorscaping. *Mailing Add:* 222 Green St Auburn AL 36830

SANDERSON, KENNETH EDWIN, MICROBIAL GENETICS. *Current Pos:* from asst prof to assoc prof, 66-73, PROF BIOL SCI, UNIV CALGARY, 73- *Personal Data:* b Holland, Man, Sept 14, 34; m 62; c 4. *Educ:* Univ Man, BSA, 56, MSc, 57; Cornell Univ, PhD(genetics), 62. *Prof Exp:* Res assoc genetics, Cornell Univ, 61-62; AEC res assoc, Brookhaven Nat Lab, 62-64, vis biologist, 64-65; Wellcome Trust fel genetics, Lister Inst Prev Med, London, 65; microbial genetics res unit, Hammersmith Hosp, London, 65-66. *Concurrent Pos:* Nat Res Coun Can grants, 66-80; NSF grant, 68-76; Humboldt fel, Max Planck Inst, Freiburg, Ger, 72-73; vis scientist, Stanford Univ, 79-80, Univ Victoria, 87. *Mem:* Genetics Soc Am; Am Soc Microbiol; Genetics Soc Can; Can Soc Microbiol; Sigma Xi. *Res:* Mechanisms of parasexual recombination in fungi; genetic structure of the chromosome of Salmonella typhimurium; genetic basis of cell wall synthesis in Salmonella typhimurium; recombinant DNA methods. *Mailing Add:* Dept Biol Sci Univ Calgary 2500 University Dr Calgary AB T2N 1N4 Can. *Fax:* 403-289-9311; *E-Mail:* kesander@acs.vcalgary.ca

SANDERSON, MARIE ELIZABETH, PHYSICAL GEOGRAPHY. *Current Pos:* ADJ PROF, UNIV WATERLOO, 88- *Personal Data:* b Chesley, Ont, Nov 16, 21; m 46; c 3. *Educ:* Univ Toronto, BA, 44; Univ Md, MA, 46; Univ Mich, PhD(geog), 65. *Honors & Awards:* Award of Merit, Can Asn Geographers & Asn Am Geographers. *Prof Exp:* Res scientist, Ont Res Found, 46-50; res assoc climat, C W Thornwaite Asn Lab Climat, NJ, 50-51; from asst prof to prof geol, Univ Windsor, 74-88, dir, Great Lakes Inst, 81-87. *Concurrent Pos:* Vis prof, Univ Hawaii, 79-86; dir, Water Network, 88-; Ryerson fel, Ryerson Tech Univ, Toronto, 93. *Mem:* Can Asn Geogrs (pres, 80-81); Asn Am Geogrs; Am Water Resources Asn; Can Meteorol Soc; Can Water Resources Asn. *Res:* Climatology; water balance of the Great Lakes; hydrology; climate change. *Mailing Add:* Dept Geog Univ Waterloo 200 University Ave W Waterloo ON N2L 3G1 Can. *Fax:* 519-746-2031

SANDERSON, RICHARD BLODGETT, PHYSICS. *Current Pos:* PHYSICIST, USAF WRIGHT-AERONAUT LAB, 72- *Personal Data:* b Waltham, Mass, July 20, 35. *Educ:* Mass Inst Technol, BS, 57; Syracuse Univ, PhD(physics), 63. *Prof Exp:* Res assoc physics, Ohio State Univ, 62-64, vis asst prof, 65, asst prof, 65-71. *Mem:* Optical Soc Am. *Res:* Infrared spectroscopy; optical properties of materials; infrared sensors. *Mailing Add:* 2317 Pine Knott Dr Dayton OH 45431

SANDERSON, RICHARD JAMES, BIOPHYSICS, CELL BIOLOGY. *Current Pos:* STAFF INVESTR MICROBIOL, WEBB-WARING LUNG INST, SCH MED, UNIV COLO, 72- *Personal Data:* b Sydney, Australia, Aug 4, 33; m 58; c 1. *Educ:* Univ Sydney, BE, 54; Univ Denver, MS, 71, PhD(appl physics), 74. *Prof Exp:* Aerodynamicist, English Elec Aviation, Eng, 55-61; sect chief, Stanley Aviation, Denver, 61-63; sr res scientist, Martin Marietta Corp, Denver, 63-72. *Res:* Function of human peripheral cells in the immune response and their isolation into pure populations; red cell aging; biophysics of lung surfactant. *Mailing Add:* Dept Microbiol Univ Colo Health Sci 4200 E Ninth Ave Denver CO 80220-3706

SANDFORD, MAXWELL TENBROOK, II, ASTROPHYSICS, MATHEMATICAL PHYSICS. *Current Pos:* STAFF MEM, LOS ALAMOS SCI LAB, 71- *Personal Data:* b Kansas City, Mo, Nov 7, 44; m 71; c 1. *Educ:* Univ Kans, AB(math), AB(physics) & AB(astron), 66, MA, 68; Univ Ind, Bloomington, PhD(astrophys), 71. *Mem:* Sigma Xi; Royal Astron Soc; Am Astron Soc. *Res:* Radiative transfer; hydrodynamics of dusty objects; digital vidicon observations. *Mailing Add:* 160 Monte Rey S Los Alamos NM 87544

SANDHAM, HERBERT JAMES, ORAL BIOLOGY, MICROBIOLOGY. *Current Pos:* assoc prof prev dent, 71-77, prof microbiol, Fac Dent, 77-97, EMER PROF UNIV TORONTO, 97- *Personal Data:* b Lethbridge, Alta, Sept 30, 32; m 55, Isabel J Bowman; c 4. *Educ:* Univ Alta, DDS, 57; Univ Man, MSc, 63, PhD(oral biol), 67. *Prof Exp:* Asst prof med microbiol, Univ Man, 66-68; asst prof microbiol & dent, Univ Ala, Birmingham & investr microbiol, Inst Dent Res, 68-71. *Concurrent Pos:* Hon prof, Hubei Med Col, Wuhan, People's Repub China, 87. *Mem:* Int Asn Dent Res; Can Asn Dent Res (pres, 88-90). *Res:* Dental caries etiology and prevention; oral microbiology; chemotherapeutic prevention of dental caries. *Mailing Add:* Fac Dent Univ Toronto Toronto ON M5G 1G6 Can. *E-Mail:* sandham@dental.utoronto.ca

SANDHU, HARBHAJAN SINGH, PHYSICS. *Current Pos:* PROF PHYSICS, UNIV VICTORIA. *Personal Data:* b Sarih, India, May 1, 32; m 62; c 2. *Educ:* Punjab Univ, India, BSc, 54, MSc, 55; Pa State Univ, PhD(physics), 61. *Prof Exp:* Res assoc physics, Col William & Mary, 61-62 & Univ Southern Calif, 62-64; asst prof physics, Calif State Univ, Northridge, 64-68, prof, 68- *Mem:* Am Phys Soc. *Res:* Pair and multiplet production by 5-90 million electron volt x-rays; charged particle nuclear reaction cross sections. *Mailing Add:* Dept Physics & Astron Univ Victoria PO Box 3055 Victoria BC V8W 2Y2 Can. *E-Mail:* sandhu@uvvm.uvic.ca

SANDHU, JATINDER SINGH, GEOGRAPHIC INFORMATION SYSTEMS, TRANSPORTATION LOGISTICS & SITE SELECTION. *Current Pos:* Software engr, 90-92, SR SOFTWARE ENGR, ENVIRON SYSTS RES INST, 92- *Personal Data:* b Punjab, India, Apr 28, 61; m 88, Balwinder Hundal; c Jasdeep & Jasmine. *Educ:* State Univ NY, BA, 86, MA, 88; Ohio State Univ, PhD(geog info systs), 90. *Concurrent Pos:* Adj prof geog, Calif State Univ, San Bernardino, 93- *Mem:* Asn Comput Mach; Asn Am Geogr. *Res:* Development of geographic information systems that primarily deal with transportation applications such as pavement data management, logistic applications such as vehicle routing and site selection; temporal geographic information and its visualization aspects. *Mailing Add:* Environ Systs Res Inst 380 New York St Redlands CA 92373. *E-Mail:* jsandhu@esri.com

SANDHU, M AKRAM, ORGANIC POLYMER CHEMISTRY. *Current Pos:* sr res chemist, Eastman Kodak Co, 70-77, sr staff, 77-79, lab head, Eastman Chem Co, 79-84, dir sci affairs, Pharmaceut Kodak, 84-86, dir, New Bus Develop, Eastman Pharmaceut, 86-89, dir, New Prod Develop, Winthrop Pharmaceut, 89-91, dir, Special Proj-MREO Gen, Kodak, 91-95, VPRES, PARTICULATE PROSPECTS CORP, KODAK, 95- *Personal Data:* b Baddomahli, Pakistan, Mar 26, 36; m 62; Bushra; c 3. *Educ:* Univ Punjab, Pakistan, BSc, 58, MSc, 61; Univ Strathclyde, PhD(chem), 67. *Honors & Awards:* Hamilton Barrett Res Prize, Univ Strathclyde, 65. *Prof Exp:* Res chemist, Pakistan Coun Sci & Indust Res, 61-64; res specialist, Univ Minn, Minneapolis, 67-70. *Concurrent Pos:* Assoc, Royal Inst Chem, 66; Walter Reed Army Inst Res fel, Univ Minn, Minneapolis, 67-69, NIH fel, 69-70. *Mem:* Royal Soc Chem; Am Chem Soc; Sigma Xi. *Res:* Organic syntheses, polymer for photographic, electrographic and electronic imaging systems; aromatic, heterocyclic and natural products; organic chemistry of Ferrocene. *Mailing Add:* Eastman Kodak Co 1669 Lake Ave Rochester NY 14652-4707. *E-Mail:* akram@kodak.com

SANDHU, RANBIR SINGH, CIVIL ENGINEERING, STRUCTURAL MECHANICS. *Current Pos:* assoc prof, 69-73, PROF CIVIL ENG, OHIO STATE UNIV, 73- *Personal Data:* b Lyallpur, Pakistan, Jan 19, 28; US citizen; m 57, Surinder K Sarkaria; c Manjot, Anahat & Gurdal. *Educ:* Univ Punjab, Pakistan, BA, 46; E Panjab Univ, India, BSc, 49; Univ Sheffield, MEng, 62; Univ Calif, Berkeley, PhD(civil eng), 68. *Prof Exp:* Asst engr to dep dir designs, Irrig Dept, Govt of Punjab, India, 50-63; assoc prof civil eng, Punjab Eng Col, India, 63-65; sr engr, Harza Eng Co, Ill, 68-69. *Concurrent Pos:* Consult applications finite element method, var agencies, 66-; vis scientist, Norweg Geotech Inst, 77 & Univ Dayton, 79; guest prof, Univ Stuttgart, WGer, 80; Ohio State Univ Col Eng res award, 89. *Mem:* Am Soc Civil Engrs. *Res:* Soil and structural mechanics; mathematical, numerical and variational methods; approximate solution of boundary value problems; theoretical and applied mechanics; mechanics of continua; finite element methods; composite laminates. *Mailing Add:* 5743 Rushwood Dr Dublin OH 43017. *E-Mail:* sandhu.2@osu.edu

SANDHU, SHINGARA SINGH, SOIL CHEMISTRY. *Current Pos:* PROF CHEM, CLAFLIN COL, 70- *Personal Data:* b Pauhowind, India, Oct 10, 32; m 60; c 4. *Educ:* Panjab Univ, BS, 52, MS, 54; Utah State Univ, PhD(soil chem), 70. *Prof Exp:* Asst prof chem, Punjab Agr Univ, India, 55-65; assoc prof, Alcorn Agr & Mech Col, 68-69. *Concurrent Pos:* Res affil, Punjab Agr Univ, India, 72. *Mem:* AAAS; Am Chem Soc; Soil Sci Soc Am. *Res:* Pollutants in rural drinking water supplies. *Mailing Add:* Dept Chem Claflin Univ Orangeburg SC 29115

SANDIFER, JAMES ROY, ELECTROCHEMISTRY. *Current Pos:* RES CHEMIST, EASTMAN KODAK CO, 73- *Personal Data:* b Blakely, Ga, May 21, 45; m 68. *Educ:* Miss Col, BS, 67; Univ NC, Chapel Hill, PhD(anal chem), 73. *Mem:* Am Chem Soc. *Res:* Mass transport properties of membranes, their electrical characteristics and their use in the fabrication of ion selective electrodes. *Mailing Add:* 231 Pearson Lane Rochester NY 14612-3521

SANDIFER, MYRON GUY, JR, PSYCHIATRY. *Current Pos:* assoc dean acad affairs, 69-75, PROF PSYCHIAT, UNIV KY, 66-, PROF FAMILY PRACT, 74- *Personal Data:* b Lowrys, SC, Sept 4, 22; m; c 2. *Educ:* Davidson Col, BS, 43; Harvard Med Sch, MD, 47; Am Bd Psychiatry, dipl, 54; Am Bd Internal Med, dipl, 74. *Prof Exp:* Instr psychiat, Sch Med, Univ NC, 55-58, asst prof, 58-59, from clin asst prof to clin assoc prof, 59-65; clin prof, Columbia Univ, 65-66. *Concurrent Pos:* Dir res, NC Dept Ment Health, 59-65. *Mem:* AMA; Am Psychiat Asn. *Res:* Psychiatric diagnosis. *Mailing Add:* 4008 Mayflower Lane Med Ctr Univ Ky Lexington KY 40504

SANDIFER, PAUL ALAN, MARINE ZOOLOGY. *Current Pos:* DIR MARINE RES, DEPT NATURAL RESOURCES SC, 84- *Personal Data:* b Cincinnati, Ohio, Jan 3, 47; m 66; c 4. *Educ:* Col Charleston, BS, 68; Univ Va, PhD(marine sci), 72. *Prof Exp:* Asst marine scientist, Dept Wildlife & Marine Resources, Marine Resources Res Inst, SC, 72-74, assoc marine scientist, 74-76, asst dir, 76-84. *Mem:* Am Soc Zoologists; SE Estuarine Res Soc; World Maricult Soc (secy-treas, 75, pres, 79). *Res:* Culture, ecology and taxonomy of decapod crustacean larvae; mariculture of crustaceans; biology of commercially important crustaceans; ecosystem analysis; research management. *Mailing Add:* 921 Parrot Creek Way Charleston SC 29412

SANDIFER, RONDA MARGARET, ORGANIC CHEMISTRY. *Personal Data:* b Barnwell, SC, May 31, 54. *Educ:* Newberry Col, BS, 76; Vanderbilt Univ, PhD(chem), 80. *Prof Exp:* NIH fel, Univ Utah, 80-82; asst prof, Dept Chem, Memphis State Univ, 82-84; asst prof, Chem Dept, Reed Col, 84-88. *Mem:* Am Chem Soc. *Res:* Mechanisms of the enzymatic synthesis of terpenes, in particular inhibition of squalene synthetase. *Mailing Add:* 1625 N Highland St Portland OR 97217

SANDIFER, SAMUEL HOPE, MEDICINE. *Current Pos:* prof, 68-81, EMER PROF PREV MED, MED UNIV SC, 81- *Personal Data:* b Walterboro, SC, May 27, 16; c 3. *Educ:* The Citadel, BS, 37; Med Univ SC, MD, 41. *Prof Exp:* Prof mil sci, Med Col Va, 47-49; asst clin prof med, Univ Ga, 55-56; assoc clin prof pediat cardiol, Sch Med, Univ Louisville, 64-65. *Mem:* AAAS; fel Am Col Cardiol; fel Am Col Prev Med; fel Am Col Physicians. *Res:* Preventive medicine; pesticide study. *Mailing Add:* Prev Med Aero Med Harborview Towers Med Univ SC Charleston SC 29425-0001

SANDIN, THOMAS ROBERT, SOLID STATE PHYSICS. *Current Pos:* assoc prof, 68-77, PROF PHYSICS, NC A&T STATE UNIV, 77- *Personal Data:* b Beloit, Wis, July 19, 39; m 60, Emilie Hall; c Kathleen, Michael, John, Margaret & Elizabeth. *Educ:* Univ Santa Clara, BS, 60; Purdue Univ, Lafayette, MS, 62, PhD(physics), 68. *Prof Exp:* Instr physics, Purdue Univ, Indianapolis, 62-65. *Concurrent Pos:* Lectr, Ind Univ, Kokomo Campus, 62-64. *Mem:* Am Asn Physics Teachers; Fedn Am Scientists. *Res:* Low temperature solid state; Mossbauer effect; author of textbooks on classical and modern physics. *Mailing Add:* Dept Physics NC A&T State Univ Greensboro NC 27411. *Fax:* 910-334-7283; *E-Mail:* sandint@athena.ncat.edu

SANDINE, WILLIAM EWALD, BACTERIOLOGY, MICROBIOLOGY. *Current Pos:* from asst prof to assoc prof, 60-66, PROF MICROBIOL, ORE STATE UNIV, 66- *Personal Data:* b Des Moines, Iowa, June 6, 28; m 55; c 1. *Educ:* Iowa State Univ, BS, 50; NC State Univ, MS, 55; Ore State Univ, PhD(bact), 58. *Honors & Awards:* Pfizer Paul Lewis Award, 64. *Prof Exp:* Instr bact, Ore State Col, 58-59; res assoc dairy biochem, Univ Ill, 59-60. *Mem:* Am Soc Microbiol; Am Dairy Sci Asn. *Res:* Lactic acid bacteria, especially bacteriophage, growth, taxonomy, metabolism and genetics; Staphylococci in food; microbiology of cheese; ecology of lactic acid bacteria including their role in human and animal nutrition. *Mailing Add:* Microbiol Dept Ore State Univ 220 Nash Hall Corvallis OR 97331-3804

SANDLER, HAROLD, MEDICINE, PHYSIOLOGY. *Current Pos:* RETIRED. *Personal Data:* b Cincinnati, Ohio, Nov 24, 29; m 61; c 2. *Educ:* Univ Cincinnati, BS, 51, MD, 55. *Prof Exp:* Intern med, Univ Chicago, 55-56; asst med, Univ Wash, 56-58, res fel cardiol, 58-61, from instr to asst prof med, 63-65; clin investr cardiol, Vet Admin Hosp, Seattle, Wash, 63-65; res med officer cardiovasc physiol, Biomed Res Div, NASA-Ames Res Ctr, Moffett Field, 65-69, actg chief div, 69- 72, chief biomed res div, 72-84, Moffett Field, 72- *Concurrent Pos:* Wash State Heart Asn fel, 58-59; NIH fel, 59-61; asst clin prof, Sch Med, Stanford Univ, 66-71, assoc clin prof, 71-78, clin prof med, 78- *Mem:* AMA; Am Fedn Clin Res; Aerospace Med Asn; Am Col Cardiol. *Res:* Internal medicine; cardiology; angiocardiography and cineangiocardiography; cardiovascular physiology; aerospace medicine; space bioscience; biophysics; bioengineering. *Mailing Add:* 241 Lovell Ave SW Bainbridge Island WA 98110-0176

SANDLER, MELVIN, ELECTRICAL ENGINEERING, ENERGY CONVERSION. *Current Pos:* assoc prof, Cooper Union, 69-77, chmn admis comt, 71-77, chmn, Dept Elec Eng, 75-77, PROF ELEC ENG, COOPER UNION, 77-, CHMN, DEPT ELEC ENG, 86- *Personal Data:* b Brooklyn, NY, July 1, 37; m 61; c 3. *Educ:* Polytech Inst Brooklyn, BEE, 58, MEE, 60, PhD(electrophys), 65. *Prof Exp:* Instr elec eng, Polytech Inst Brooklyn, 59-60; res assoc comput sci, Microwave Res Inst, 60-62, sr res assoc, Farmingdale Grad Ctr, 62-64; group leader, Airborne Instruments Lab, Div, Cutler-Hammer, 64-68; sr venture specialist, W R Grace & Co, 68-69. *Concurrent Pos:* Dir Russian Prog, 92- *Mem:* Inst Elec & Electronics Engrs; Sigma Xi. *Res:* Communication theory; application of phase and injection lock techniques to signal processing and communication systems; power electronics. *Mailing Add:* Dept Elec Eng Cooper Union 51 Astor Pl New York NY 10003

SANDLER, RIVKA BLACK, GERONTOLOGY. *Current Pos:* from asst prof to assoc prof, Univ Pittsburgh, 64-78, prof sci, Sch Health Related Professions, Interdisciplinary Progs, 78-89, prof, 83-89, EMER PROF GERONTOL & EPIDEMIOL, UNIV PITTSBURGH, 89- *Personal Data:* b Warsaw, Poland, Feb 20, 18; US citizen; m 47; c 2. *Educ:* Hebrew Univ, MSc, 42, PhD(endocrinol), 50. *Prof Exp:* Instr, Hebrew Univ, 47-50; lectr pharmacol, Sch Med, Univ Ottawa, 50-52. *Mem:* Fel Geront Soc Am. *Res:* Gerontolog; osteoporosis. *Mailing Add:* 5743 Fifth Ave Pittsburgh PA 15232

SANDLER, SAMUEL, COMBUSTION ENGINEERING, ANALYTICAL CHEMISTRY. *Current Pos:* RETIRED. *Personal Data:* b Lipivitz, USSR, Jan 1, 21; Can citizen; m 48; c 3. *Educ:* Univ Toronto, BASc, 44, MASc, 48. *Prof Exp:* Lab supvr, Defence Indusrs Ltd, 44-45; instr chem eng, Univ Toronto, 46-48, from asst prof to prof, 58-90; prin sci res officer, Defence Res Bd Can, 48-58; from asst prof to prof chem eng, Univ Toronto, 58-90. *Concurrent Pos:* Instr, Can Voc Training Inst, 46-48; consult, Chem Eng Res Consult, Ltd, 62- *Mem:* Fel Chem Inst Can. *Res:* Kinetics and mechanisms of oxidation, decomposition, ignition and detonation of fuel vapors and gases; associated instrumental methods of chemical analysis; flame arrestor design. *Mailing Add:* 5 Evanston Dr North York ON M3H 5N9 Can

SANDLER, SHELDON SAMUEL, BIOPHYSICS, APPLIED PHYSICS. *Current Pos:* from asst prof to assoc prof, 62-81, PROF ELEC & COMPUT ENG, NORTHEASTERN UNIV, 81- *Personal Data:* b Cleveland, Ohio, Dec 17, 32; m 58; c 1. *Educ:* Case Western Reserve Univ, BSEE, 54; Yale Univ, MEng, 55; Harvard Univ, MS, 58, PhD(appl physics), 62. *Prof Exp:* Res assoc, Horizons, Inc, 56-57; mem staff, Lincoln Lab, Mass Inst Technol, 58-59; sr engr, Electronic Commun, Inc, 59-60. *Concurrent Pos:* Consult, Harvard Col Observ, 62-63; res fel appl physics, Harvard Univ, 63-; consult, Raytheon Corp, 63-64; guest prof, Swiss Fed Inst Technol, 64-65; consult, US Naval Res Lab, 65-69; vis scholar, Med Res Coun Lab Molecular Biol, Eng, 69-70; consult, Geosci Surv, 70-72, Block Eng, 73-74 & Am Sci & Eng, 74-75 & Geo-Ctr Inc; mem, Comt VI, Int Union Radio Sci; vis prof, Univ Zurich, 76-77, Robotics Res Ctr, Univ RI, 83-84; vis scholar, Harvard Univ, 90-91. *Mem:* Sigma Xi. *Res:* Pattern recognition; picture processing and reconstruction; electromagnetics; geophysical exploration; bioengineering; biomedical engineering. *Mailing Add:* Dept Elec Eng Northeastern Univ 360 Huntington Ave Boston MA 02115-5096

SANDLER, STANLEY I, THERMODYNAMICS, CHEMICAL ENGINEERING. *Current Pos:* from asst prof to prof & chmn dept, 82-86, interim dean eng, 92, H B DUPONT PROF CHEM ENG DEPT, UNIV DEL, 82-, DIR, CTR MOLECULAR & ENG THERMODYNAMICS, 92-, PROF CHEM & BIOCHEM, 93- *Personal Data:* b New York, NY, June 10, 40; m 62; c 3. *Educ:* City Col New York, BChE, 62; Univ Minn, PhD(chem eng), 66. *Honors & Awards:* Prof Prog Award, Am Inst Chem Eng, 84; 3M Lectureship Award, Chem Eng Div, Am Soc Eng Educ, 88; Phillips lectr, Okla State Univ, 93; Warren K Lewis Award, Am Inst Chem Engrs, 96. *Prof Exp:* NSF fel, Inst Molecular Physics, Univ Md, 66-67. *Concurrent Pos:* Camille & Henry Dreyfus fac scholar, 71; consult, Mobil Res & Develop

Corp, 77-, Chevron, 78-, Union Carbide Corp, 82- & Du Pont, 85-; vis prof, Imp Col, London, 73-74, Tech Univ Berlin, 81 & 88-89, Univ Del Sur Argentina, 85, Univ Queensland, Australia, 89 & 96 & Univ Calif, Berkeley, 95; Alexander von Humboldt US sr scientist prize, 88. *Mem:* Nat Acad Eng; Fel Am Inst Chem Engrs; Am Chem Soc; Am Soc Eng Educ; Sigma Xi. *Res:* Thermodynamic properties modelling and measurement; predict properties of fluids under extreme conditions; phase equilibrium prediction and measurement; computer-aided design; author or co-author of 225 referenced scientific papers. *Mailing Add:* Dept Chem Eng Univ Del Newark DE 19716. *Fax:* 302-831-4466; *E-Mail:* sandler@sche.udel.edu

SANDLIN, ALLISON C, AEROSPACE TECHNOLOGY & POLICY. *Current Pos:* PRIN MEM TECH STAFF, ANALYTIC SCI CORP, 97- *Personal Data:* b Birmingham, Ala, May 2, 63; m 83, Thomas; c Grant & Alexandra. *Educ:* Univ Ala, Birmingham, BS, 85, MS, 87, PhD(mat eng), 87. *Prof Exp:* Nat Res Coun fel, Nat Inst Stand & Technol, 89-91; sr prog officer, Aeronaut & Space Eng Bd, Nat Acad Sci, 91-97. *Concurrent Pos:* Tech analyst & mem, Synthesis Group, White House Panel Space Exp Initiative, 90-91. *Mem:* Am Inst Aeronaut & Astronaut; Nat Space Soc; Am Asn Space. *Res:* Conduct high-level, technical and policy assessments on aerospace issues of national interest; areas of interest include GPS, small spacecraft technology, cost reduction and launch vehicles. *Mailing Add:* 1619 Lozano Dr Vienna VA 22182. *E-Mail:* sandlin@erols.com

SANDLIN, BILLY JOE, PHYSICS. *Current Pos:* ASSOC PROF PHYSICS, TEX TECH UNIV, 59- *Personal Data:* b Hunt Co, Tex, Jan 10, 27; m 49; c 2. *Educ:* ETex State Univ, BS, 48, MS, 49; Univ Tex, PhD, 60. *Prof Exp:* Instr physics, ETex State Teachers Col, 46-49; instr, LeTourneau Tech Inst, 49; instr physics, geol & math, Odessa Col, 49-53; asst prof physics, Tex Tech Col, 55-57; instr math, Univ Tex, 57-58. *Mem:* Am Phys Soc; Am Asn Physics Teachers. *Res:* Measurements of high accuracy and precision involving electrical and electronic techniques; temperature and temperature-difference measurements; properties of solids at low temperatures; electronic circuit development. *Mailing Add:* Dept Physics Tex Tech Univ Lubbock TX 79409

SANDMANN, WILLIAM HENRY, ASTRONOMY, EXPERIMENTAL PHYSICS. *Current Pos:* assoc prof, 63-72, prof 73-, EMER PROF PHYSICS, HARVEY MUDD COL. *Personal Data:* b Yakima, Wash, Jan 15, 28; m 53; c 3. *Educ:* Reed Col, BA, 53; Univ Utah, PhD, 60. *Prof Exp:* Asst prof physics, Grinnell Col, 59-63. *Concurrent Pos:* Vis scholar, Univ Tex, Austin, 72-73 & 76-77; vis prof, Univ Capetown & Sutherland Observ, 76-77. *Mem:* Am Astron Soc. *Res:* Observational astronomy; astronomical instrumentation. *Mailing Add:* 6453 Cape George Rd Port Townsend WA 98368

SANDMEIER, HENRY ARMIN, NUCLEAR PHYSICS. *Current Pos:* PHYSICIST, NAT SECURITY PROG, LOS ALAMOS NAT LAB, 63- *Personal Data:* b Antwerp, Belg, Mar 17, 20; nat US; m 61, Antoinette; c Robert & Monica. *Educ:* Swiss Fed Inst Technol, dipl, 49, DSc(elec eng), 54, PhD(physics), 59; Mass Inst Technol, SM, 52, EE, 54. *Prof Exp:* Mem res staff, Mass Inst Technol, 51-54; assoc physicist, Argonne Nat Lab, 56-61; liaison scientist, London Br, US Off Naval Res, London Embassy, UK, 61-63. *Concurrent Pos:* Vis prof nuclear eng, Purdue Univ, 66; consult, US Naval Weapons Eval Facility, 66-, Army Res Off, 70-; vis prof, Univ Stuttgart, 68-69; consult, Defense Depts, Switz, Norway, Sweden & Ger, 68- *Mem:* Am Phys Soc; Am Nuclear Soc; Sigma Xi. *Res:* Reactor physics and engineering; engineering education; assay techniques of fissionable materials; vulnerability of nuclear weapons and nuclear weapons effects; international scientific liaison and consulting. *Mailing Add:* 809 Camino del Este Santa Fe NM 87501

SANDMEIER, RUEDI BEAT, CHEMISTRY. *Current Pos:* VPRES RES, SANDOZ CROP PROTECTION, 87- *Personal Data:* b Basel, Switz, Apr 25, 45; m 70, Susan Guggenbuhl; c Corinna D & Franziska C. *Educ:* Univ Basel, Switz, BS, 68, PhD(chem), 73. *Prof Exp:* Fel, Syntex Corp, Palo Alto, Calif, 73-74; sr res chemist, Sandoz Ltd, Basel, 74-85; dir biosci, Northrup King Seeds, Stanton, Minn, 85-87. *Mem:* Soc Chem Indust; Int Soc Plant Molecular Biol; Am Chem Soc. *Res:* Granted 1 US patent; chemistry; plant molecular biology; crop protection. *Mailing Add:* 1709 Joel Way Los Altos CA 94024

SANDMEYER, ESTHER E, PETROLEUM, INDUSTRIAL HEALTH. *Current Pos:* CONSULT, TRANSCONTEC, 76- *Personal Data:* b Winterthur, Switz, Aug 9, 29; US citizen. *Educ:* Winterthur Tech Univ, Switz, BSc, 51; Ohio State Univ, MSc, 60, PhD(biochem), 65. *Prof Exp:* Chemist, Nuffield Lab, Univ Birmingham, 52-53, Feldm hle, Rorschach, Switz, 53-55, Bell Tel Labs, Inc, NJ, 55-57 & Chem Abstr, Ohio, 58-60; asst prof chem, Friends Univ, 65 & biochem, Univ Nev, Reno, 65-70; trainee physiol & biophys, Hahnemann Med Col, 70-71 & toxicol, Sch Med, Univ Calif, San Francisco, 71-72; biochemist-toxicologist, Gulf Oil Corp, 72-75, toxicologist & dir Biochem Lab, 75. *Concurrent Pos:* Desert Res Inst grant, 66-67; prog chmn, Int Cong Technol & Technol Transfer, 84. *Mem:* AAAS; Am Chem Soc; Soc Environ Health. *Res:* Biochemistry, chemical engineering; feasibility studies; literature surveys; training of toxicologists and toxicology managers; establishing organic analytical division for commercial laboratory. *Mailing Add:* 7305 Live Oak Dr Kelseyville CA 95451-9677

SANDO, JULIANNE J, CARCINOGENESIS & TUMOR PROMOTION, CELLULAR SIGNAL TRANSDUCTION. *Current Pos:* asst prof, 82-88, ASSOC PROF PHARMACOL, UNIV VA, CHARLOTTESVILLE, 88- *Personal Data:* b Santa Maria, Calif, July 16, 52. *Educ:* Ind Univ Pa, BS, 74; Univ Mich, Ann Arbor, PhD(pharmacol), 79. *Prof Exp:* Res fel immunol & carcinogenesis, NIH, Bethesda, Md, 79-81, staff fel, Nat Cancer Inst, 81. *Concurrent Pos:* Prin investr, NIH grant, 82- *Mem:* Am Asn Cancer Res; Am Soc Pharmacol & Exp Therapeut; AAAS; Am Soc Biochem & Molecular Biol. *Res:* Understanding, at the cellular and biochemical level, the role of hormones, immunological mediators and tumor promoters in controlling cell proliferation and the expression of specific cell products; mechanisms by which phorbol ester tumor promoters activate protein kinase C and lead to transcriptional effects; molecular endocrinology. *Mailing Add:* Dept Pharmacol Jordan 5227 Univ Va Sch Med Box 448 1300 Jefferson Pk Charlottesville VA 22908-0001. *E-Mail:* jjs@virginia.edu

SANDO, KENNETH MARTIN, THEORETICAL CHEMISTRY. *Current Pos:* asst prof chem, 69-73, ASSOC PROF CHEM, UNIV IOWA, 73- *Personal Data:* b Oglivie, Minn, May 15, 41; m 66. *Educ:* Univ Minn, BCh, 61; Univ Wis, PhD(chem), 68. *Prof Exp:* Physicist, Smithsonian Astrophys Observ, 68-69. *Concurrent Pos:* Guest worker, Nat Bur Standards, 75-76. *Mem:* Am Phys Soc; Am Chem Soc. *Res:* Quantum chemistry; atomic and molecular processes. *Mailing Add:* Univ Iowa Dept Chem Iowa Advan Tech Lab Iowa City IA 52242-1000

SANDO, RODNEY W, FORESTRY. *Current Pos:* dir, Div Forestry, Minn Dept Nat Resources, 78-79, adminr real estate mgt bur, 81-90, adminr mgmt info syst bur, 90-91, COMMISSIONER, MINN DEPT NAT RESOURCES, 91- *Honors & Awards:* Pres Conserv Achievement Award, Nature Conservancy, 95. *Prof Exp:* Reg dir, Ruffed Grouse Soc, 79-80. *Mailing Add:* Minn Dept Nat Resources 500 Lafayette Rd St Paul MN 55155-4037

SANDO, WILLIAM JASPER, stratigraphy, paleontology; deceased, see previous edition for last biography

SANDOK, PAUL LOUIS, ZOOLOGY, IMMUNOLOGY. *Current Pos:* SR ENGR, BECHTEL SAVANNA RIVER, 92- *Personal Data:* b Rice Lake, Wis, Aug 18, 43; m 69; c 5. *Educ:* Univ Wis, Madison, BS, 68, MS, 71, PhD(bact), 74, Univ NC, Charlotte, BSEE, 87. *Prof Exp:* Proj asst, Med Sch, Univ Wis-Madison, 68-69, res asst, Dept Bact, 69-74; Hormel fel, Hormel Inst, Univ Minn, 74-77, res assoc, 77-78; asst prof microbiol, Univ NC, Charlotte, 78-85; process instrument engr, C T Main, Inc, 87-91. *Mem:* Sigma Xi; Am Soc Microbiol; Inst Elec & Electronics Engrs; AAAS. *Res:* Host-parasite interaction, at the cellular and molecular levels; portable cardiac monitoring devices; biochemistry; granted 1 US patent. *Mailing Add:* 10315 Starwood Dr Charlotte NC 28215-9664

SANDOR, GEORGE N(ASON), MECHANICAL ENGINEERING, DESIGN ENGINEERING. *Current Pos:* res prof mech eng & dir, Mech Eng Design & Rotordynamics Labs, 76-89, EMER RES PROF, UNIV FLA, GAINESVILLE, 89- *Personal Data:* b Budapest, Hungary, Feb 24, 12; US citizen; m 64; c 2. *Educ:* Univ Polytech, Budapest, Dipl Ing, 34; Columbia Univ, New York, DEngSc, 59. *Hon Degrees:* Dr, Technol Univ Budapest, 86. *Honors & Awards:* Machine Design & Applied Mechanisms Awards, Am Soc Mech Engrs, 75. *Prof Exp:* Asst chief engr, Hungarian Rubber Co, Dunlop Ltd, 35-37, head mfg dept, 37-38; design engr, Babcock Printing Press Corp, Conn, 39-44; vpres & chief engr, Harry W Faeber Corp, NY, 44-50; chief engr, Graphic Arts Res Lab, Time Inc, Conn, 50-61 & Huck Design Co, NY, 61; assoc prof mech eng, Yale Univ, 61-66; Alcoa Found prof mech design, Rensselaer Polytech Inst, 66-75, chmn, Div Machines & Struct, Sch Eng, 67-74, dir, Ctr Eng Design, 74-75. *Concurrent Pos:* Instr, Univ Conn, 41-44; lectr, Columbia Univ, 61-62; consult, Graphic Arts Res Lab, Time Inc, 61-63, McCall's Corp, 61-62 & Huck Design Co, 61-67; mem bd dirs, Huck Co, Inc, 67-71; consult, Xerox Corp, 71- & Instituto Politecnico Olivetti, Ivrea, Italy; consult engr, 71-; NSF, NASA & Army Res Off grants; mem, Graphic Arts Tech Found. *Mem:* Fel Am Soc Mech Engrs; Am Soc Eng Educ; Nat Soc Prof Engrs; NY Acad Sci; Am Acad Mech; hon mem Int Fedn Theory Mach & Mechanisms. *Res:* Methodology and philosophy of engineering design; design and development of automatic machinery; printing, paper processing and allied machine design; kinematic and kineto-elastodynamic synthesis of planar and spatial mechanisms; hard automation for high productivity in manufacturing; computer-aided experimental design; design optimization; robotics. *Mailing Add:* Broadview Acres Highlands NC 28741

SANDOR, THOMAS, BIOCHEMISTRY, ENDOCRINOLOGY. *Current Pos:* SR RES SCIENTIST, LAB ENDOCRINOL, HOSP NOTRE DAME, 59- *Personal Data:* b Budapest, Hungary, Nov 3, 24; Can citizen; m 49, Vera Varkonyi; c Catherine S (Heuser). *Educ:* Pazmany Peter Univ, Budapest, dipl chem, 48; Univ Toronto, PhD(path chem), 60. *Prof Exp:* Res biochemist, Clin Res Dept, Hotel-Dieu Hosp, 56-59; from res asst prof med to res assoc prof, Univ Montreal, 61-70, res prof, 70-93. *Concurrent Pos:* Career investr, Med Res Coun Can, 62-91; Nuffield Found traveling fel, 64; Sci Res Coun sr vis res fel, 66 & 79-80; Schering traveling fel, 66; Endocrine Soc traveling fel, 68; assoc mem exp med, McGill Univ, 69-; vis prof zool, Univ Sheffield, 70-71 & 79-80; corres[ed, J Steroid Biochem, 70-79; hon vis prof,Dept Biol Chem, Fac Exact & Natural Sci, Univ Buenos Aires, 74. *Mem:* Endocrine Soc; Can Biochem Soc; Can Soc Clin Invest; Royal Soc Med; Brit Soc Endocrinol; Biochem Soc, Gt Brit; fel Royal Soc Can; Am Soc Zoologists; Europ Soc Camp Endocrinologists; Endocrine Soc. *Res:* Steroid biochemistry; comparative steroid endocrinology; mechanism of steroid hormone action; steroid hormone receptors. *Mailing Add:* 5194 W Broadway Montreal PQ H4V 2A2 Can

SANDORFI, ANDREW M J, NUCLEAR & ELEMENTARY PARTICLE PHYSICS. *Current Pos:* Staff scientist, 79-92, SR SCIENTIST, BROOKHAVEN NAT LAB, 92- *Personal Data:* b Toronto, Ont, Aug 27, 50; m 75, Juliet A Fischette; c 2. *Educ:* Univ Toronto, BS, 73, MS, 74, PhD(physics), 76. *Honors & Awards:* Gov Gen Can Medal, 73. *Prof Exp:* Nat Res Coun (Can) Fel, High Energy Physics Lab, Stanford Univ, 77-79. *Concurrent Pos:* Rutherford Mem Fel, Royal Soc Canada, 77; group leader, Laser-Electron-Gamma-Source, Brookhaven Nat Lab. *Mem:* Fel Am Phys Soc. *Res:* Experimental studies of the structure of nucleons and light nuclei using elctromagnetic probes, particularly utilizing polarization degrees of freedom. *Mailing Add:* Brookhaven Nat Lab Bldg 510 Upton NY 11973. *Fax:* 516-344-2049; *E-Mail:* sandorfi@bnl.gov

SANDORFY, CAMILLE, FAR ULTRAVIOLET PHOTOELECTRON INFARED SPECTROSCOPY, HIGHER EXCITED STATES OF POLYATOMIC MOLECULES. *Current Pos:* Nat Res Coun Can fel, Univ Montreal, 54, from asst prof to prof, 54-88, EMER PROF CHEM, UNIV MONTREAL, 88- *Personal Data:* b Budapest, Hungary, Dec 9, 20; Can citizen; m 71, Rolande Cayla. *Educ:* Univ Szeged, BS, 43, PhD(chem), 46, Sorbonne, DSc, 49. *Hon Degrees:* PhD, Univ Moncton, 86, Univ Szeged, 88. *Honors & Awards:* Herzberg Medal, Spectros Soc Can, 80; Medal, Chem Inst Can, 83; Medal, World Orgn Theoret Organic Chemists, 90; Heyrovsky Gold Medal, Czech Acad Sci, 93. *Prof Exp:* Res assoc, Tech Univ Budapest, 46; researcher, Nat Ctr, Sci Res, 47-51, 53; fel, Nat Res Coun, Can, 51-53. *Concurrent Pos:* Vis prof, Univ Pierre & Marie Curie, Paris, 68, Italian Nat Res Coun, 69, Univ Rio de Janeiro & San Paulo, 70, Fed Univ Rio de Janeiro, 82, Univ Paris, 74-75, Infared Spectros Lab, 87, Nat Ctr Res, France; lectr, China Tour, 87. *Mem:* Int Acad Quantum Molecular Sci; Europ Acad Arts Sci & Humanities; hon mem Can Asn Advan Sci; Hungarian Acad Sci; fel Royal Soc Can. *Res:* Initiated quantum chemistry of polyatomic sigma electron systems; far ultraviolet spectroscopy of typical organic molecules, transitions to Rydberg and intravalency transitions; application to the chromophore of visual pigments; the nature of hydrogen bonding and vibrational anharmonicity; application to the mechanisms of general anesthesia; author of about 250 publications. *Mailing Add:* PO Box 6128 Sta Ctr-Ville Montreal PQ H3C 3J7 Can. *Fax:* 514-343-7586; *E-Mail:* majorc@ere.umontreal.ca

SANDOVAL, HOWARD KENNETH, MICROBIOLOGY. *Current Pos:* asst prof, 69-72, ASSOC PROF BIOL, MIAMI-DADE COMMUNITY COL N, 72- *Personal Data:* b New York, NY, Aug 15, 31; m 51. *Educ:* City Col New York, BS, 53; Columbia Univ, AM, 56; Cornell Univ, PhD(microbiol), 64. *Prof Exp:* Teacher high sch, NY, 56-58; res asst, Sloan-Kettering Inst Cancer Res, NY, 58-59; Sloan fel, 64-65; instr biol, Brooklyn Col, 65-67; microbiologist, Lederle Labs, NY, 67-69. *Mem:* Am Soc Microbiol. *Res:* Colicins; lysogeny; microbial genetics; electron microscopy of bacterial viruses. *Mailing Add:* Dept Biol Miami-Dade Comm Col N 11380 NW 27th Ave Miami FL 33167-3418

SANDOW, BRUCE ARNOLD, REPRODUCTIVE BIOLOGY, HISTOLOGY. *Current Pos:* ASST PROF ANAT & ASST PROF OBSTET GYNEC, EASTERN VA MED SCH, 81- *Personal Data:* b Los Angeles, Calif, Jan 26, 45; m 71. *Educ:* Univ Calif, Berkeley, BA, 67, MA, 70, PhD(endocrinol), 78. *Prof Exp:* Res fel, Ore Regional Primate Res Ctr, 76-81. *Mem:* Sigma Xi; Am Fertil Soc; Am Asn Anatomists. *Res:* In vitro fertilization; oocyte maturation; hormonal regulation of follicular function. *Mailing Add:* Dept Anat E Va Med Sch PO Box 1980 Norfolk VA 23501-1980

SANDOZ, GEORGE, METALLURGICAL ENGINEERING. *Current Pos:* RETIRED. *Personal Data:* b Toledo, Ohio, Jan 24, 21; m 61; c 3. *Educ:* Wayne State Univ, BS, 43; Univ Mich, MS, 45; Univ Md, PhD(metall), 59. *Prof Exp:* Metallurgist, Chevrolet Motor Co, 43-44 & US Naval Res Lab, 46-72; mertallurgist, Chicago Br Off, Off Naval Res, 72-77, dir sci, 77-85. *Concurrent Pos:* Mem malleable iron comt, Welding Res Coun, 56-57. *Mem:* Am Soc Metals. *Res:* Reaction kinetics; mechanical properties; fracture and corrosion of steel and cast iron; protective coatings for refractory metals; mechanical properties of intermediate phases; electric and magnetic alloys; stress corrosion and hydrogen embrittlement. *Mailing Add:* 2030 Glencoe Wheaton IL 60187

SANDQUIST, GARY MARLIN, NUCLEAR & MECHANICAL ENGINEERING. *Current Pos:* Teaching asst mech eng, Univ Utah, 59 & 61-62, instr, 62-63 & 64-65, from asst prof to assoc prof, 65-75, res assoc prof surg, 78-86, actg chair mech eng, 84-85, DIR NUCLEAR ENG, UNIV UTAH, 66-, PROF MECH ENG, 75- *Personal Data:* b Salt Lake City, Utah, Apr 19, 36; m 92, Kristine Brock; c Titia, Julia, Taunia, Cynthia & Carl. *Educ:* Univ Utah, BSME, 60, PhD(mech eng), 64; MBA, 95; Univ Calif, Berkeley, MS, 61. *Honors & Awards:* Glen Murphy Award, Am Soc Eng Educ, 84. *Concurrent Pos:* Vis scientist, NSF fac fel, Mass Inst Technol, 69-70, sabbatical, Technion, Haifa, Israel & Ben Gurion Univ, Beer Shiva, Israel, 69-70; chief scientist, Rogers & Assocs Eng Corp, 80-; adj prof civil eng, Univ Utah, 93-; expert nuclear sci, Int Atomic Energy Agency, UN, 80-; affiliate fac prof, Idaho State Univ, 96- *Mem:* Fel Am Nuclear Soc; Am Soc Eng Educ; fel Am Soc Mech Engrs; Nat Soc Prof Engrs; Health Physics Soc; sr mem Am Soc Qual Control. *Res:* Safety and environment aspects of nuclear energy; nuclear fusion; biomedical engineering; applied mathematics; system analysis; risk analysis; waste management. *Mailing Add:* 2564 Neffs Circle Salt Lake City UT 84109-4055. *Fax:* 801-581-8692; *E-Mail:* sandquist@me.mech.utah.edu

SANDRA, ALEXANDER, CELL BIOLOGY, HORMONAL CONTROL OF DEVELOPMENT. *Current Pos:* ASSOC PROF ANAT, UNIV IOWA, 83- *Educ:* Case Western Reserve Univ, PhD(anat), 76. *Res:* Hormonal cellular action. *Mailing Add:* Dept Anat Univ Iowa 1-530 Bowen Sci Bldg Iowa City IA 52242-1109

SANDRAPATY, RAMACHANDRA RAO, ENERGY & ENVIRONMENTAL ENGINEERING. *Current Pos:* PROF MECH & INDUST ENG & CHMN DEPT, SC STATE UNIV, ORANGEBURG, 73- *Personal Data:* b Eluru, India, Feb 15, 42; nat US; m 66, Kalyani K Kappuravuri; c Ravichandra & Kiran. *Educ:* Andhra Univ, Waltair, India, BE Hons, 63; Univ Roorkee, India, ME, 65; Univ SC, Columbia, MS, 71, PhD(mech eng), 74. *Prof Exp:* Proj engr, Cent Mech Eng Res Inst, Durgapur, India, 66-67; prod eng & bus partner, SGKR Mill-B, Elura, AP, India, 67-69. *Concurrent Pos:* Sr res fel, Govt India, 66-67; vis prof, IBM Corp, Res Triangle Park, NC, 74; adj staff mem, SC Energy Res Inst, 77-; engr consult, Appl Eng Co, Orangeburg, SC, 78; fac fel, Western Elec, Chicago, Ill, 79, US Dept Transp, Cambridge, Mass, 80 & NASA Lewis Res Ctr, Cleveland, Ohio, 82; vis fac scientist, Lawrence Berkeley Lab, Calif, 81; distinguished fac chair, SC State Univ, 87, 90 & 91. *Mem:* Am Soc Mech Engrs; Am Soc Eng Educ; Am Asn Univ Prof; Air & Waste Mgt Asn; Inst Indust Engrs. *Res:* Energy and thermal sciences; air pollution control; combustion research; environmental engineer. *Mailing Add:* Dept Indust Elec Eng Technol SC State Univ Orangeburg SC 29117-0001. *Fax:* 803-533-3623

SANDRI, JOSEPH MARIO, ORGANIC CHEMISTRY. *Current Pos:* AT CALLOWAY CHEM CO. *Personal Data:* b Chicago, Ill, Mar 9, 29; m 59; c 4. *Educ:* Ill Inst Technol, BS, 52; Mich State Univ, PhD(chem), 56. *Prof Exp:* Res proj chemist, Am Oil Co, 56-61, sr proj chemist, 61-62; sr group leader, Nalco Chem Co, Ill, 62-70; dir res & develop, Ott Chem Co, 71-72, Story Chem Co, 72-80. *Mem:* AAAS; Am Chem Soc; Royal Soc Chem; Am Asn Textile Chemists & Colorists. *Res:* Isocyanates; phosgene and medicinal chemistry; amino acids; agricultural and paper chemicals; chemicals, latices and resins for textiles; surfactants; macrocyclic chemistry; fragrance chemicals; polymers; reaction mechanisms. *Mailing Add:* Calloway Chem Co PO Box 2335 Columbus GA 31993-3599

SANDRIDGE, ROBERT LEE, ANALYTICAL CHEMISTRY, ORGANIC POLYMER CHEMISTRY. *Current Pos:* AT MILES INC, 88-, CONSULT, 92- *Personal Data:* b Junior, WVa, June 12, 32; m 53, Ilene; c Michael, Jennifer, Becky, Brian & Susan. *Educ:* WLiberty State Col, BS, 54; WVa Univ, MS, 58, PhD(org chem), 69. *Prof Exp:* Chemist, NC State Univ, 54; group leader anal chem, Mobay Chem Corp, 58-73, mgr, Anal Group, Process Res Dept, 73-78, mgr anal & environ res, 78-88; pres, Proctor Consult, 88-92. *Concurrent Pos:* Chmn, NAm Anal Comt, Int Isocyanate Inst. *Mem:* Am Chem Soc; Am Soc Testing & Mat; Soc Plastics Indust; AAAS. *Res:* Isocyanates; urethanes; polycarbonates; amines; spectroscopy and spectrometry; long path fourier transform infared development; environmental analysis. *Mailing Add:* RD 1 Box 65 Proctor WV 26055

SANDRIK, JAMES LESLIE, DENTAL MATERIALS. *Current Pos:* From asst prof to prof, 72-93, chmn dept, 82-93, EMER PROF DENT MAT, SCH DENT, LOYOLA UNIV CHICAGO, 93- *Personal Data:* b Chicago, Ill, July 7, 38; m 71, Joan Kaye; c Timothy & Kathleen. *Educ:* Northwestern Univ, PhB, 67, MS, 68, PhD(biol mat), 72. *Concurrent Pos:* NIH fel, Northwestern Univ, 72; dir, Tech Serv, Teledyne Water Pic, Chicago, 93 & Tech Affairs, Bisco, Inc, Itasca, IL, 94- *Mem:* Am Dent Asn; Am Soc Metals; Int Asn Dent Res; Sigma Xi. *Res:* Polymeric restorative and reconstructive materials; adhesive dental materials; composite dental materials. *Mailing Add:* 409 S Clifton Park Ridge IL 60068-3950

SANDS, DAVID CHANDLER, PLANT PATHOLOGY, BACTERIOLOGY. *Current Pos:* from asst prof to assoc prof, 77-89, PROF PLANT PATH, MONT STATE UNIV, 89- *Personal Data:* b Los Angeles, Calif, Aug 30, 41; m 69; c 3. *Educ:* Pomona Col, AB, 63; Univ Calif, Berkeley, PhD(plant path), 69. *Prof Exp:* NSF fel soil microbiol, Div Soils, Commonwealth Sci & Indust Res Orgn, Australia, 69-70; asst plant pathologist, Conn Agr Exp Sta, 70-77. *Concurrent Pos:* Adj assoc prof microbiol, Mont State Univ, 81-; Environ Protection Agency Rev Panels, 86-88; proj leader, US Agency Int Develop-Int Ctr Agr Res Dry Areas, Middle East, N & W Africa & SAm. *Mem:* AAAS; Am Phytopath Soc; Am Soc Microbiol; Brit Soc Gen Microbiol; Am Inst Biol Sci; Arab Soc Plant Protection. *Res:* Physiology, taxonomy and ecology of bacterial plant pathogens, especially Pseudomonas; ecology and general physiological differences between plant pathogenic pseudomonads and saprophytes; bacterial diseases of cereal crops; selection of high lysine lines of bacteria for food fermentation and high lysine lines of cereal crops; ice nucleating bacteria; biocontrol of weeds; expert systems in prediction of plant disease epidemics. *Mailing Add:* Dept Plant Path Mont State Univ Bozeman MT 59717-0001. *Fax:* 406-994-1906; *E-Mail:* uplds@msu.oscs.montana.edu

SANDS, DONALD EDGAR, PHYSICAL CHEMISTRY. *Current Pos:* from asst prof to prof, Univ Ky, 62-68, dir gen chem, 74-75, assoc dean advan studies, Col Arts & Sci, 75-80, actg dean, 80- 81, assoc vpres acad affairs, 81-84, vchancellor acad affairs, 84-89, PROF CHEM, UNIV KY, 68-, CHMN, DEPT CHEM, 93- *Personal Data:* b Leominster, Mass, Feb 25, 29; m 56, Elizabeth Stoll; c Carolyn (Looff) & Stephen R. *Educ:* Worcester Polytech Inst, BS, 51; Cornell Univ, PhD, 55. *Prof Exp:* Res assoc, Cornell Univ, 55-56; crystallographer, Lawrence Radiation Lab, 56-62; sect head, Networking & Teacher Prep, NSF, 89-91. *Mem:* Sigma Xi; AAAS; Am Chem Soc; Am Crystallog Asn; NY Acad Sci. *Res:* Crystallography; thermodynamics. *Mailing Add:* Dept Chem Univ Ky Lexington KY 40506-0055. *Fax:* 606-323-1069; *E-Mail:* sands@pop.uky.edu

SANDS, ELAINE S, SPEECH-LANGUAGE PATHOLOGY. *Current Pos:* asst prof, 70-80, ASSOC PROF SPEECH PATH & AUDIOL, ADELPHI UNIV, 80-, DEPT CHAIR, 89- *Personal Data:* b Brooklyn, NY, Jan 25, 40; m 64; c 2. *Educ:* Brooklyn Col, AB, 60; Univ Mich, MS, 61; NY Univ, PhD(speech path, audiol), 77. *Prof Exp:* Speech pathologist, Med Ctr, NY Univ, 61-70. *Concurrent Pos:* Consult, New York Vet Admin Hosp, 76- *Mem:* Acad Aphasia; fel Am Speech, Hearing & Language Asn. *Res:* Neurological aspects of language; aphasia in adults; recovery from aphasia. *Mailing Add:* Dept Speech Adelphi Univ Garden City NY 11530-4299

SANDS, GEORGE DEWEY, physical chemistry; deceased, see previous edition for last biography

SANDS, HOWARD, PHARMACOLOGY, BIOCHEMISTRY. *Current Pos:* SR FEL, BIOL SPARTA PHARMACEUT, 96- *Personal Data:* b New York, NY, Aug 20, 42; m 68, Michele Berkowitz; c Andrea, Michael & Deborah. *Educ:* Rutgers Univ, New Brunswick, BA, 64; Case Western Res Univ, PhD(pharmacol), 69. *Prof Exp:* NIH training grant renal dis, Northwestern Univ, 69-71; pharmacologist, Nat Jewish Hosp & Res Ctr, 71-81; group leader, pharmacol/toxicol, New Eng Nuclear, 81-83; group leader, Immunopharmaceut, 83-88; prin res scientist, DuPont Merck Pharmaceut, 89-94; prin investr, Lexin Pharmaceut, 94-96. *Concurrent Pos:* Pharmacologist, Vet Admin Res Hosp, 70-71; asst prof, Dept Oral Biol, Sch Dent, Univ Colo, 75-77. *Mem:* Am Asn Cancer Res. *Res:* Physiology of drug delivery; radio pharmaceutical research and related immunology; cancer therapeutics; pharmacokinetics and biodistribution of macromolecules. *Mailing Add:* 2417 Landon Dr Wilmington DE 19810

SANDS, JEFFREY ALAN, BIOPHYSICS. *Current Pos:* From asst prof to assoc prof, 73-82, PROF BIOPHYSICS, LEHIGH UNIV, 82- *Personal Data:* b Kingston, Pa, Jan 16, 48; m 73. *Educ:* Univ Del, BS, 69; Pa State Univ, MS, 71, PhD(biophys), 73. *Mem:* Biophys Soc; Am Soc Microbiol. *Res:* Molecular virology, antiviral agents, virus-cell interactions, glycoprotein transport. *Mailing Add:* Dept Biol Lehigh Univ 27 Memorial Dr W Bethlehem PA 18015-3044

SANDS, MATTHEW, PHYSICS, ACCELERATOR PHYSICS. *Current Pos:* vchancellor sci, 69-72, prof physics, 69-86, EMER PROF PHYSICS, UNIV CALIF, SANTA CRUZ, 86- *Personal Data:* b Oxford, Mass, Oct 20, 19; m, Freya E Kidner; c Walter, Michael, Richard & Michelle. *Educ:* Clark Univ, BA, 40; Rice Inst, MA, 41; Mass Inst Technol, PhD(physics), 48. *Prof Exp:* Physicist, US Naval Ord Lab, 41-43 & Los Alamos Sci Lab, 43-46; res assoc, Mass Inst Technol, 46-48, asst prof physics, 48-50; sr res fel, Calif Inst Technol, 50-52, from assoc prof to prof, 52-63; prof & dep dir, Linear Accelerator Ctr, Stanford Univ, 63-69. *Concurrent Pos:* Fulbright scholar, Italy, 52-53; consult, Inst Defense Anal, 60-68, Off Sci & Technol, 61-66 & Arms Control & Disarmament Agency, 62-66; mem, Comn Col Physics, 60-66, chmn, 64-66; mem, Pugwash Conf Sci & World Affairs, 61-62; pres, Sands-Kidner Assoc, Inc, 86-91; consult, Linear Accelerator Ctr, Stanford Univ, 86-92. *Mem:* Fel Am Phys Soc; Am Asn Physics Teachers; Fedn Am Sci; AAAS. *Res:* Electronic instrumentation; cosmic rays; accelerators; high-energy physics; education; science and public affairs. *Mailing Add:* 160 Michael Lane Santa Cruz CA 95060. *E-Mail:* sanos@scipp.ucsc.edu

SANDS, RICHARD DAYTON, ORGANIC CHEMISTRY. *Current Pos:* from asst prof to prof, Alfred Univ, 56-70, Ferro prof, 70-80, prof chem, 70-92, chmn div math & sci, 74-76, chmn div phys sci, 76-80, chmn dept chem, 80-85, COLE PROF, ALFRED UNIV, 92- *Personal Data:* b Skaneateles, NY, Nov 18, 29; m 53, Margery M Wilson; c Marguerite, Virginia & Elizabeth. *Educ:* Oberlin Col, AB, 51; Syracuse Univ, MS, 54, PhD(org chem), 59. *Honors & Awards:* Scholes Lectureship, Alfred Sigma Xi Club; Sullivan Award, Corning Sect, Am Chem Soc, 96. *Prof Exp:* Asst instr chem, Syracuse Univ, 52-56. *Concurrent Pos:* Chmn, Corning Sect, Am Chem Soc, 72-73. *Mem:* Am Chem Soc. *Res:* Ring size in the pinacol rearrangement of alicyclic glycols; synthesis and cleavage of aliphatic bicyclic compounds. *Mailing Add:* Dept Chem Alfred Univ Alfred NY 14802

SANDS, RICHARD HAMILTON, BIOPHYSICS, ATOMIC PHYSICS. *Current Pos:* from asst prof to prof, 57-94, chmn, Dept Physics, 77-82, RES BIOPHYSICIST, UNIV MICH, ANN ARBOR, 65-, EMER PROF PHYSICS, 94- *Personal Data:* b San Diego, Calif, Sept 28, 29; m 51; c 4. *Educ:* Univ Redlands, BS, 50; Washington Univ, PhD(physics), 54. *Honors & Awards:* Cert of Literature Award, Philalethes Soc, 81. *Prof Exp:* Res assoc & instr physics, Stanford Univ, 54-57. *Mem:* AAAS; Am Asn Physics Teachers; Am Phys Soc; Biophys Soc. *Res:* Magnetic and optical resonance fluorescence in atomic and solid state physics; biophysical applications of electron paramagnetic resonance spectrometry; Mossbauer spectroscopy and electron-nuclear double resonance spectrometry. *Mailing Add:* Chem Bldg Rm 3204 Univ Mich Ann Arbor MI 48109

SANDS, SEYMOUR, TEXTILE CHEMISTRY. *Current Pos:* RETIRED. *Personal Data:* b New York, NY, Mar 16, 18. *Educ:* City Col, BS, 39; NY Univ, MS, 48; Polytech Inst Brooklyn, PhD(chem), 53. *Prof Exp:* Org chemist, Fleischmann Distilling Co, 46-49; res chemist, 53-82, develop assoc, Textile Fibers Dept, E I du Pont de Nemours & Co, Inc, 68-82. *Mem:* Am Chem Soc; Sigma Xi. *Res:* Polymer chemistry pertaining to fiber technology. *Mailing Add:* 23 Riddle Ave Wilmington DE 19806

SANDSON, JOHN IVAN, MEDICINE, RHEUMATOLOGY. *Current Pos:* prof, 74-96, dean, 74-88, EMER DEAN, SCH MED, BOSTON UNIV, 88-, EMER PROF MED, 96- *Personal Data:* b Jeannette, Pa, Sept 20, 27; m 57, Hannah E Ney; c Jennifer M & Thomas A. *Educ:* Wash Univ, MD, 53; Am Bd Internal Med, dipl, 60. *Honors & Awards:* Maimonides Award, Anti Defamation League, 86. *Prof Exp:* From intern to asst resident med serv, Presby Hosp, New York, 53-56; fel rheumatol, Albert Einstein Col Med, Bronx, NY, 57-60, from assoc med to prof med, 60-74, from asst dean to assoc dean health servs, 59-66, hosp med dir, 69-74. *Concurrent Pos:* Nat Inst Arthritis & Metab Dis trainee, Albert Einstein Col Med, 57-59, Arthritis & Rheumatism Found fel, 57-60, chief resident, 57, asst vis physician, Bronx Munic Hosp Ctr, 57-66, vis physician, 66-, head, Arthritis Group, 68-72; attend physician, Bronx Vet Admin Hosp, 57-66; investr health res coun, City New York, 61-71; consult, study sect, NIH, 71-74; mem gen med A study sect & gen res support study sect, 85-89. *Mem:* AAAS; Am Soc Clin Invest; Harvey Soc; Am Rheumatism Asn; Am Asn Physicians; AMA. *Res:* Chemical and immunological studies of the proteoglycans of synovial fluid and cartilage. *Mailing Add:* Sch Med Boston Univ 80 E Concord St Boston MA 02118

SANDSTEAD, HAROLD HILTON, INTERNAL MEDICINE, HUMAN NUTRITION. *Current Pos:* chmn, 85-90, PROF, DEPT PREV MED & COMMUNITY HEALTH, MED BR, UNIV TEX, GALVESTON, 85-, PROF INTERNAL MED, 86-, PROF HUMAN BIOL CHEM & GENETICS, 86-, PROF PREV MED & COMMUNITY HEALTH, 90- *Personal Data:* b Omaha, Nebr, May 25, 32. *Educ:* Ohio Wesleyan Univ, BA, 54; Vanderbilt Univ, MD, 58; Am Bd Internal Med, dipl, 67. *Honors & Awards:* Hull Gold Medal Award, AMA, 70; Meade Johnson Award, Am Inst Nutrit, 72; W O Atwater Mem Lectr, USDA, 84; Ellen Swallow Richards Mem Lectr, Univ NC, 85; Sam & Mary E Roberts Nutrit Medal, 85. *Prof Exp:* From intern to asst resident med, Barnes Hosp, St Louis, Mo, 58-60; asst resident path, Vanderbilt Hosp, Nashville, Tenn, 60-61; res asst resident med, Vet Admin Hosp, 63-64; Hugh J Morgan resident int med, Vanderbilt Hosp, 64-65; from instr to asst prof med, Sch Med, Vanderbilt Univ, 65-71, asst prof biochem, 65-77, asst prof med & nutrit, 67-70, assoc prof nutrit, 70-71; adj prof biochem & clin internal med, Sch Med, Univ NDak, 71-84; dir, Grand Forks Human Nutrit Res Ctr, Agr Res Serv, USDA, 71-84; dir, Human Nutrit Res Ctr Aging & prof nutrit, Sch Nutrit, Tufts Univ, 84-85. *Concurrent Pos:* Nutrit Found Future leader, 68-71; Welcome vis prof basic sci, Fedn Am Soc Exp Biol, Pa State Univ, 88. *Mem:* Fel Am Col Physicians; Am Soc Nutrit Sci; Am Soc Clin Nutrit (secy-treas, 72-73, secy, 73-75, pres elect, 81-82, pres, 82-83); Southern Soc Clin Invest; Cent Soc Clin Res. *Res:* Clinical nutrition; zinc metabolism; essential and toxic trace elements; nutrition, brain development and function; nutrition pregnancy; nutrition and growth. *Mailing Add:* Dept Prev Med & Community Health 1109 Univ Tex Med Br Galveston TX 77555-1109. *Fax:* 409-772-6287; *E-Mail:* harold.sandstead@utmb.edu

SANDSTED, ROGER FRANCE, VEGETABLE CROPS. *Current Pos:* from asst prof to assoc prof, 57-77, prof veg crops, Exten, 77-83, EMER PROF, DEPT FRUIT & VEG SCI, CORNELL UNIV, 83- *Personal Data:* b Holdrege, Nebr, Aug 5, 18; m 49; c 3. *Educ:* Univ Nebr, BS, 48; Univ Minn, PhD, 54. *Prof Exp:* Asst hort, Univ Nebr, 48-50 & Univ Minn, 52-54; asst horticulturist, Parma Br Exp Sta, Idaho, 54-57. *Mem:* Am Soc Hort Sci. *Res:* Legume vegetables; dry beans; cultural problems. *Mailing Add:* 22 Dutcher Rd Freeville NY 13068

SANDSTROM, DONALD JAMES, METALLURGY OF URANIUM ALLOYS, DEFORMATION PROCESSING OF REFRACTORY MATERIALS. *Current Pos:* Group leader, Mat Technol Group, Los Alamos Nat Lab, 75-81, assoc div leader, Mat Sci & Technol Di,, 81-85, dep div leader, 85-89, div leader, Mat Sci & Technol Div, 89-94, MGR, SPECIAL PROGS, LOS ALAMOS NAT LAB, 94- *Personal Data:* b Chicago, Ill, July 26, 37; m 59; c 3. *Educ:* Univ Ill, BS, 58; Univ NMex, MS, 68. *Mem:* Fel Am Soc Mat; Am Inst Mining Metall & Petrol Engrs. *Res:* Material science and technology; Dept Defense and Dept Energy activities associated with uranium. *Mailing Add:* Los Alamos Nat Lab PO Box 1663 MS M713 Los Alamos NM 87545

SANDSTROM, DONALD RICHARD, PHYSICS. *Current Pos:* eng staff & mgt, Boeing Defense & Space Group, 84-94, SR PRIN ENG, BOEING INFO & SUPPORT SERV, 95- *Personal Data:* b Spokane, Wash, May 9, 40; m 63, Monika nee Nichaus; c Ian. *Educ:* Wash State Univ, BS, 63, PhD(physics), 67. *Prof Exp:* NSF fel, Univ Bonn, 67; NSF & UK Atomic Energy Authority fel, Univ Liverpool, 67-69; from asst prof to assoc prof, Wash State Univ, 69-81, prof physics & chem phyuics, 81-84. *Concurrent Pos:* Guest worker, Nat Bur Standards, 74-75. *Mem:* Am Phys Soc; AAAS. *Res:* Development of advanced processes for aerospace manufacture. *Mailing Add:* 6130 E Mercer Way Mercer Island WA 98040. *Fax:* 425-865-2966; *E-Mail:* donald.r.sandstrom@boeing.com

SANDSTROM, WAYNE MARK, UNDERWATER ACOUSTICS, ORDNANCE. *Current Pos:* RETIRED. *Personal Data:* b Seattle, Wash, Feb 17, 27; m 53, Ann Lomen; c Mark, Robert & Carol. *Educ:* Univ Wash, BS, 48, PhD(physics), 53. *Honors & Awards:* David Bushnell Award, Am Defense Preparedness Asn, 90. *Prof Exp:* From assoc physicist to sr physicist, Appl Physics Lab, Univ Wash, 52-59, asst dir, 59-64, dep dir, 64-70; pres, Henderson Tech Corp, 70-93. *Concurrent Pos:* Consult, US Naval Undersea Warfare Ctr, Wash, 70-93. *Mem:* Am Phys Soc. *Res:* Electromagnetics. *Mailing Add:* 6215 54th NE Seattle WA 98115

SANDUS, OSCAR, PHYSICAL CHEMISTRY. *Current Pos:* RETIRED. *Personal Data:* b New York, NY, July 29, 24; m 46; c 3. *Educ:* Univ Ky, BS, 49; Univ Chicago, MS, 50; Ill Inst Technol, PhD(chem), 55. *Prof Exp:* Asst chemist, Argonne Nat Lab, 55-58; res assoc phys chem, Radiation Lab, Univ Mich, 58-60, assoc res phys chemist, 60-61; res phys chemist, Conductron Corp, 62-63; sr chemist, Chemotronics, Inc 63-64; assoc res chemist, Infrared Physics Lab, Univ Mich, Ann Arbor, 64-67; res chemist, Energetics & Warheads Div, Army Armament Res Eng & Develop Ctr, US Army, 68-89. *Mem:* AAAS; Am Chem Soc; Sigma Xi. *Res:* Thermodynamics and properties of nonelectrolytic solutions; uranium fuel and feed materials process development; dielectric relaxation; electromagnetic materials; electroplating process and plastic foam process development; fundamental aspects of physics and chemistry relating to missile reentry; photochemistry; spectroscopy; explosives. *Mailing Add:* 9 Farmstead Dr Parsippany NJ 07054-1533

SANDUSKY, HAROLD WILLIAM, COMBUSTION, DETONATION PHYSICS. *Current Pos:* MECH ENGR, NAVAL SURFACE WARFARE CTR, 76- *Personal Data:* b Baltimore, Md, Sept 12, 49; m 78. *Educ:* Georgia Tech, BAE, 71; Princeton Univ, MSE, 73, MA, 74, PhD(aerospace & mech sci), 76. *Res:* Nitric oxide emissions from turbojet combustors and cigarette burning; deflagration and shock to detonation transition for explosives and propellants. *Mailing Add:* 9307 Old Scaggsville Rd Laurel MD 20723. *Fax:* 301-394-4634; *E-Mail:* hsandus@nswc.navy.mil

SANDVIG, ROBERT L(EROY), CHEMICAL ENGINEERING. *Current Pos:* instr chem, SDak Sch Mines & Technol, 49-50, asst prof chem & chem eng, 51-55, from assoc prof to prof, 56-87, head dept, 73-87, EMER PROF CHEM ENG, SDAK SCH MINES & TECHNOL, 87- *Personal Data:* b Lead, SDak, Sept 11, 23; m 57; c 3. *Educ:* SDak Sch Mines & Technol, BS, 44; Univ Cincinnati, MS, 48; Univ Colo, PhD(chem eng), 53. *Prof Exp:* Mech engr, Nat Adv Comt Aeronaut, Va, 44; instr chem, SDak Sch Mines & Technol, 46-47; chem engr, Darling & Co, Ohio, 48-49. *Concurrent Pos:* Instr, Univ Colo, 52-53; consult, Rocky Flats Plant, Dow Chem Co, 69-75, Rocky Flats Plant, Rockwell Int, 75-87 & SD Forest Products, Inc. 86-66. *Mem:* Am Chem Soc; Am Soc Eng Educ; Am Inst Chem Engrs; Sigma Xi. *Res:* Development of substitute for chloride road deicer and development of process for enhancing the color of softwoods throughout the entire cross section of the wood. *Mailing Add:* 442 James Ave Apt 4 Mankato MN 56001

SANDWEISS, JACK, PHYSICS. *Current Pos:* from instr to prof, 57-80, chmn dept, 77-80, DONNER PROF PHYSICS, YALE UNIV, 80- *Personal Data:* b Chicago, Ill, Aug 19, 30; m 56; c 3. *Educ:* Univ Calif, BS, 52, PhD(physics), 56. *Prof Exp:* Physicist, Radiation Lab, Univ Calif, 56-57. *Concurrent Pos:* Consult, Lab Marine Physics, Yale Univ, 57-60, Brookhaven Nat Lab, 61-, Argonne Nat Lab & Nat Accelerator Lab; chmn, High Energy Physics Adv Panel, US Dept Energy, 83- *Mem:* Nat Acad Sci; Am Phys Soc. *Res:* High energy physics; streamer chamber technique; physics of strange particles and charmed and beauty particles; counter and spark chamber techniques; high energy heavy ion reactions. *Mailing Add:* Physics Dept Yale Univ PO Box 208101 New Haven CT 06520-8121

SANDWITH, COLIN JOHN, MECHANICAL ENGINEERING. *Current Pos:* asst prof, 66-74, RES ASSOC PROF MECH ENG, UNIV WASH, 74-, SR ENGR, MECH ENG, APPL PHYSICS LAB, 85- *Personal Data:* b Friday Harbor, Wash, Nov 9, 36; m 57; c 4. *Educ:* Univ Wash, BSME, 61; Ore State Univ, PhD(mat sci), 67. *Honors & Awards:* Gold Medal Valor Award, US Dept Interior, 66; Ralf Teetor Award, Soc Automotive Engrs, 72. *Prof Exp:* Draftsman, Com Airplane Div, Boeing Airplane Co, 57-58 & Duffy, Lawyer & Kumpf Eng Consult Co, 59; mech engr, Hanford Atomic Prod Opers, Gen Elec Co, 61-62; mech engr, Albany Res Ctr, US Bur Mines, 63-66. *Concurrent Pos:* NIH grant, Univ Wash, 67-69, NASA grant, 68-70; contracts, USN. *Mem:* Am Soc Metals; Am Soc Mech Engrs; Nat Asn Corrosion Engrs; Am Soc Eng Educ; Soc Mfg Engrs. *Res:* Corrosion, failure analysis, design, materials, ceramic coatings; structural failures; biomedical instrumentation; fiberoptic cardiovascular catheters; marine and industrial corrosion; mechanical behavior of materials; manufacturing processes; video tape documentation and post-mortem analysis of Navy instruments to determine design wisdom; accident reconstruction and analysis. *Mailing Add:* 4030 NE 95th St Seattle WA 98115

SANDZA, JOSEPH GERARD, biochemistry, for more information see previous edition

SANES, JOSHUA RICHARD, DEVELOPMENTAL NEUROBIOLOGY. *Current Pos:* Asst prof physiol, 80-85, assoc prof, 85-88, PROF ANAT, WASHINGTON UNIV, 89- *Personal Data:* b Buffalo, NY, Sept 5, 49; m 82, Susan Corcoran; c Jesse & Amelia. *Educ:* Yale Univ, BA, 70; Harvard Univ, MA & PhD(neurobiol), 76. *Concurrent Pos:* Counr, Soc Neurosci, 90-; mem bd sci counrs, NIH. *Mem:* Fel AAAS; Soc Neurosci. *Res:* Roles of cell surface molecules, extracellular matrix molecules, and cell lineage in synaptic specificity. *Mailing Add:* Dept Anat Med Ctr Washington Univ St Louis MO 63110

SAN FILIPPO, JOSEPH, JR, organic chemistry, organometallic chemistry, for more information see previous edition

SANFORD, ALLAN ROBERT, GEOPHYSICS. *Current Pos:* PROF GEOPHYS, NMEX INST MINING & TECHNOL, 57-, COORDR GEOPHYS, 78- *Personal Data:* b Pasadena, Calif, Apr 25, 27; m 56, Alice Carlson; c Robert & Colleen. *Educ:* Pomona Col, BA, 49; Calif Inst Technol, MS, 54, PhD(geophys), 58. *Mem:* Fel AAAS; Soc Explor Geophysicists; Seismic Soc Am; Am Geophys Union; Sigma Xi. *Res:* Seismology and seismicity; crustal exploration; tectonophysics; gravity. *Mailing Add:* Dept Geosci NMex Inst Mining & Technol Socorro NM 87801

SANFORD, BARBARA ANN, MICROBIOLOGY, IMMUNOLOGY. *Current Pos:* from instr to asst prof, 68-77, ASSOC PROF MICROBIOL, UNIV TEX MED SCH SAN ANTONIO, 77- *Personal Data:* b Beaumont, Tex, Aug 5, 41. *Educ:* Hardin-Simmons Univ, BA, 62; Baylor Univ, MS, 65, PhD(microbiol), 68. *Prof Exp:* From res asst to res assoc immunol, Med Ctr, Baylor Univ, 63-68. *Mem:* Am Soc Microbiol; Sigma Xi. *Res:* Development of in vitro models of delayed hypersensitivity to chemical carcinogens in humans and experimental animal models. *Mailing Add:* Dept Microbiol Univ Tex Med Sch San Antonio 7703 Floyd Curl Dr San Antonio TX 78284-6200

SANFORD, EDWARD RICHARD, PHYSICS. *Current Pos:* assoc prof, 61-66, chmn dept, 78-90, PROF PHYSICS, OHIO UNIV, 66- *Personal Data:* b Clifton, NJ, Feb 15, 28; m 57, Elise Mitchell; c Michael. *Educ:* Iowa State Univ, BS, 49, MS, 50, PhD(physics), 59. *Prof Exp:* Sr scientist, Bettis Atomic Power Lab, Westinghouse Elec Corp, 53-61. *Mem:* Am Phys Soc; Am Nuclear Soc; Inst Elec & Electronics Engrs; Am Asn Physics Teachers. *Res:* Solid state physics; nuclear reactor physics and engineering. *Mailing Add:* Dept Physics & Astron Ohio Univ Athens OH 45701. *Fax:* 740-593-0433; *E-Mail:* sanford@ouvaxa.cats.ohiou.edu

SANFORD, GARY L, LUNG DEVELOPMENT, LUNG & VASCULAR CELL BIOLOGY. *Current Pos:* Asst prof, 82-90, ASSOC PROF BIOCHEM, MOREHOUSE SCH MED, 90- *Personal Data:* b Birmingham, Ala, June 16, 50; m 73, Birdie Mattison; c Gary M. *Educ:* Miles Col, BA, 72; Brown Univ, PhD(biochem), 78. *Prof Exp:* Fel, Albert Einstein Col Med, 78-80, Univ Miami Sch Med, 80-82. *Concurrent Pos:* Prin investr res grant, Am Lung Asn, 79-81, Ga Lung Asn, 83-84, NIH, 83-87, NIH Nat Heart, Lung Blood Inst, 87-92, Am Lung Asn, 89-94; adj fac, Biol Dept, Clark Atlanta Univ, 83- & Chem Dept, Ga State Univ, 88-; prog dir, NASA, 92-94. *Mem:* AAAS; Am Chem Soc; Am Asn Cell Biol; Am Thoracic Soc. *Res:* Role of non-hormonal factors in post-lung development and in the pathogenesis of clinical disorders involving vascular remodeling; role of galaptin in vascular cell growth. *Mailing Add:* Dept Biochem Morehouse Sch Med 720 Westview Dr SW Atlanta GA 30310-1495

SANFORD, JAMES R, PHYSICS. *Current Pos:* SR PHYSICIST & ASST DIR, SUPERCONDUCTING SUPER COLLIDER LAB, 89- *Personal Data:* b Zanesville, Ohio, Jan 29, 33; m 56; c 2. *Educ:* Oberlin Col, AB, 55; Yale Univ, MS, 57, PhD(physics), 61. *Prof Exp:* Fel, Yale Univ, 61-62; physicist, Brookhaven Nat Lab, 62-69; head exp facil sect, Nat Accelerator Lab, 69-72, assoc dir, Fermi Nat Accelerator Lab, 72-76; assoc dir, Brookhaven Nat Lab, 76-81, sr physicist, 76-90. *Concurrent Pos:* Mem high energy physics adv panel, Dept Energy; design team mem, Superconducting Super Collider, 83-89. *Mem:* Am Phys Soc. *Res:* High energy particle physics and the use of accelerators. *Mailing Add:* 17 Otis Ln Bellport NY 11713. *Fax:* 972-708-4021

SANFORD, JAY PHILIP, infectious diseases; deceased, see previous edition for last biography

SANFORD, KARL JOHN, clinical biochemistry, biotechnology, for more information see previous edition

SANFORD, KATHERINE KOONTZ, GENERAL BIOLOGY. *Current Pos:* RETIRED. *Personal Data:* b Chicago, Ill, July 19, 15; m 71. *Educ:* Wellesley Col, BA, 37; Brown Univ, MA, 39, PhD(zool), 42. *Hon Degrees:* DSc, Med Col Pa, Philadelphia, 74, Catholic Univ Am, Washington, DC, 88. *Prof Exp:* Asst biol, Brown Univ, 37-41; instr, Western Col, 41-42 & Allegheny Col, 42-43; asst dir sch nursing, Johns Hopkins Univ Hosp, 43-47; res biologist, Nat Cancer Inst, 47-73, chief cell physiol & oncogenesis, Lab Biochem, 73-77, chief, In Vitro Carcinogenesis Sect, Cancer Etiology Div, Lab Cellular & Molecular Biol, 77-94. *Concurrent Pos:* USPHS, 47; Ross Harrison fel, 54; mem, Cell Cult Collection Adv Comt, Am Type Cult Collection, 60- *Mem:* Tissue Cult Asn; Am Soc Cell Biol; Am Asn Cancer Res; Int Soc Cell Biol; Sigma Xi. *Res:* Physiological genetics of Cladocera; nutrition of tissue cells grown in culture; characteristics of malignant cells in vitro; carcinogenesis studies in vitro; DNA damage and repair. *Mailing Add:* 101 Steuart Dr Dover DE 19901

SANFORD, L G, ENTOMOLOGY, VERTEBRATE ZOOLOGY. *Current Pos:* from assoc prof to prof, 69-93, EMER PROF BIOL, JACKSONVILLE STATE UNIV, 93- *Personal Data:* b Parrish, Ala, Sept 16, 30; m 55; c 2. *Educ:* Florence State Col, BS, 57; Auburn Univ, MS, 63, PhD(entom), 65. *Prof Exp:* Biol aide, Fisheries Dept, Tenn Valley Authority, 56-58; teacher high sch, Ala, 58-60; instr zool, Auburn Univ, 60-63, res asst entom, 63-65. *Mem:* Am Inst Biol Sci. *Res:* Mammalogy and Siphonaptera. *Mailing Add:* 1003 Tenth Ave NE Jacksonville AL 36265

SANFORD, LINDA S, HARDWARE SYSTEMS. *Current Pos:* Engr, IBM, 75-94, mgr hardware & software prod, 79, asst to chmn, 85-87, prod mgr, Distributed Prog Exec, 87-89, dir, Networking Systs, 89-92, lab dir, Enterprise Systs, 92-83, gen mgr, Syst/390 Systs, 93-95, GEN MGR, SYST/390 DIV, IBM, 95- *Personal Data:* b Jan 21, 53; c William J & Catherine A. *Educ:* St John's Univ, BA; Rensselaer Poly Tech Inst, MS. *Mem:* Nat Acad Eng; Nat Asn Engrs. *Mailing Add:* IBM Systs 390 Div Bldg 504 Rte 9 Fishkill NY 12533. *Fax:* 914-892-7530

SANFORD, MALCOLM THOMAS, APICULTURE. *Current Pos:* PROF & EXTEN APICULTURIST, UNIV FLA, 81- *Personal Data:* b Miami Beach, Fla, Oct 23, 42; m 70. *Educ:* Univ Tex, BA, 64; Thunderbird Grad Sch Int Mgt, Ariz, BFT, 67; Univ Ga, MA, 73, PhD, 77. *Prof Exp:* Res assoc geog, Univ Ga, 70-73, res asst apicult, 74-77, lectr, 77; asst prof apicult, Ohio State Univ, 78-81. *Mem:* Am Beekeeping Fedn; Int Bee Res Asn; Am Asn Prof Apiculturists; Entom Soc Am. *Res:* Transmission and scanning electron microscopy to study abdominal glands of queen honey bee; honey bee management in tropical and temperate lands; beekeeping industry of Yucatan; modeling populations by computer simulation; financial analysis of apicultural operations by personal computer. *Mailing Add:* Entomol & Nematol Dept Bldg 970 Univ Fla Gainesville FL 32611-0620

SANFORD, RICHARD FREDERICK, kinetics, ore deposits, for more information see previous edition

SANFORD, RICHARD SELDEN, electrical engineering, control systems, for more information see previous edition

SANFORD, ROBERT ALOIS, ORGANIC CHEMISTRY. *Current Pos:* RETIRED. *Personal Data:* b East St Louis, Ill, Mar 1, 22; m 46; c 4. *Educ:* St Louis Univ, BS, 43; Purdue Univ, PhD(chem eng & chem), 49. *Prof Exp:* Asst org chem, Univ Pittsburgh, 43-44; res chemist, Manhattan Proj, Univ Rochester, 44-46; res chemist, Catalysis Res Div, Sinclair Res Labs, Inc, Ill, 49-52, res chemist, Petrochem Div, 52-53, group leader, 53-57, asst dir, Res Div, 57-60, dir, Explor Div, 60-66; dir, Brown & Williamson Tobacco Co, 66-79, vpres res & develop, 79-83, vpres sci & technol, 83- *Res:* Chemical engineering; heterogeneous catalysis; petrochemicals; organic chemistry. *Mailing Add:* 7404 Shadwell Lane Prospect KY 40059

SANFORD, ROBERT LAURIE, JR, BIOGEOCHEMISTRY, ENVIRONMENTAL HISTORY. *Current Pos:* asst prof, 92-95, ASSOC PROF PLANT & SOIL BIOL, DEPT BIOL SCI, UNIV DENVER, 95- *Personal Data:* b Glen Ridge, NJ, Jan 6, 54; m 86, Sara E Molden; c Luke & Katherine. *Educ:* Univ Mich, BS, 77; Univ Calif, Berkeley, MS, 80, PhD(wildland resource sci), 85. *Prof Exp:* Teaching asst trop biol, Orgn Trop Studies, Costa Rica, 78; res asst, Dept Plant & Soil Biol, Univ Calif, Berkeley, 81-84, teaching asst, Dept Forestry & Resource Mgt, 79-85; fel biol, Dept Biol Sci, Stanford Univ, 85-86; asst res prof forest ecol, Dept Forestry, NC State Univ, 86-88, Dept Forest Sci, Colo State Univ, 88-91. *Concurrent Pos:* Res sta mgr, Cent Am, La Selva Biol Sta, Costa Rica, 78, Ivic San Carlos de Rio Negro, Venezuela, 82; res asst tree genetics, US Forest Serv, Ariz, 79; res intern forest soils, Potlach Corp, Idaho, 81; consult forest inventory, Southern Pac Land Co, Calif, 83; dir site productivity proj, Dept Forestry, NC State Univ, 86-88; sr res scientist ecosyst ecol, Nat Resource Ecol Lab, Colo State Univ, 88-, acad coordr, Prog Ecol Studies, Grad Sch, 90-91; Fulbright scholar trop resource mgt, Ctr Appl Soc Sci, Univ Zimbabwe, 96; distinguished scholar, Univ Denver, 97. *Mem:* Sigma Xi; AAAS; Am Inst Biol Sci; Asn Trop Biol; Ecol Soc Am; Int Soc Soil Sci; Int Asn Trop Foresters; Soc Conserv Biol; Soil Sci Soc Am. *Res:* Land use history, fire ecology and biogeochemistry of terrestrial ecosystems, especially following disturbances and perturbations. *Mailing Add:* Dept Biol Sci Univ Denver Denver CO 80208. *Fax:* 303-871-3471; *E-Mail:* rsanford@du.edu

SANFORD, THOMAS BAYES, PHYSICAL OCEANOGRAPHY, MARINE GEOPHYSICS. *Current Pos:* PRIN OCEANOGR, APPL PHYSICS LAB, PROF, SCH OCEANOG, UNIV WASH, SEATTLE, 79- *Personal Data:* b Toledo, Ohio, Apr 22, 40; m 62, Marilyn Wilmore; c James, Cynthia & Craig. *Educ:* Oberlin Col, AB, 62; Mass Inst Technol, PhD(oceanog), 67. *Honors & Awards:* A F Bulgin Premium, Inst Electronic & Radio Engrs, UK, 72. *Prof Exp:* Physicist, NASA, 62-63; instr oceanog, Mass Inst Technol, 66-67; from asst scientist to assoc scientist, Woods Hole Oceanog Inst, 67-79. *Concurrent Pos:* Vis scientist, Inst fur Meereskunde Kiel FRG, 76; consult, Sippican Ocean Systs Inc, 79-85, Endeco, 85; dir res, Horizon Marine Inc, 82-90 & Transtrack Inc, 86-89. *Mem:* AAAS; fel Am Geophys Union; Sigma Xi; Am Meteorol Soc; Oceanog Soc. *Res:* Motionally induced electromagnetic fields in the sea; marine magneto-tellurics; ocean circulation; internal waves; eddy motion; marine acoustics. *Mailing Add:* Appl Physics Lab Univ Wash 1013 NE 40th St Seattle WA 98105. *Fax:* 206-543-6785; *E-Mail:* sanford@apl.washington.edu

SANG, QING-XIANG, BIOCHEMISTRY & CELL BIOLOGY OF MATRIX METALLOPROTEINASES, BREAST CANCER & PROSTATE CANCER. *Current Pos:* res assoc, 90-92, NIH fel, 92-93, ASST RES SCHOLAR/SCIENTIST & INSTR BIOCHEM, FLA STATE UNIV, 92- *Personal Data:* m. *Educ:* Hunan Normal Univ, China, BS, 84; Georgetown Univ, PhD(cell biol & anat), 90. *Concurrent Pos:* Prin investr, Fla State Univ, 92- *Mem:* Am Soc Cell Biol; Sigma Xi. *Res:* Biochemistry and cell biology of matrix metalloproteinases; extracellular matrix; breast and prostate cancer cell invasion and metastasis. *Mailing Add:* Dept Chem Inst Molec Biophys Fla State Univ Tallahassee FL 32306-3006. *Fax:* 850-644-8281

SANGER, ALAN RODNEY, CATALYSIS, ORGANOMETALLIC CHEMISTRY & APPLIED CHEMISTRY. *Current Pos:* ADJ PROF, CHEM ENG DEPT, UNIV ALTA, 93-; PROPRIETOR, ALAN R SANGER CONSULT, 93- *Personal Data:* b Southampton, Eng, Apr 23, 43; Can citizen; m 80; c 2. *Educ:* Univ Sussex, BSc, 65, MSc, 66, DPhil(inorg chem), 69. *Prof Exp:* Teaching fel chem, Univ Alta, 69-72 & Simon Fraser Univ, 73; res officer chem, Alta Res Coun, 73-93. *Mem:* Fel Chem Inst Can. *Res:* Preparation, characterization and evaluation of inorganic and organometallic materials of use as homogeneous or heterogeneous catalysts; c-1 chemistry. *Mailing Add:* Alan R Sanger Consult 2833 123rd St Edmonton AB T6J 6A6 Can. *Fax:* 403-492-2881; *E-Mail:* alan.sanger@ualberta.ca

SANGER, FREDERICK, MOLECULAR BIOLOGY. *Current Pos:* RETIRED. *Personal Data:* b Rendcomb, Eng, Aug 13, 18; m 40, Joan Howe; c Robin, Peter F & Sally J. *Educ:* St John's Col, BA; Cambridge Univ, PhD, 43. *Hon Degrees:* DSc, Leicester Univ, 68, Oxford Univ, 70, Strasbourg Univ, 70. *Honors & Awards:* Nobel Prize in Chem, 56, 80; Royal Medal, Royal Soc, 69; William Bait Hardy Prize, Cambridge Philos Soc, 76; Copley Medal, Royal Soc, 77; Wheland Award, 78; Gold Medal, Royal Soc Med, 83. *Prof Exp:* Res worker biochem, Cambridge Univ, 40-60; div head, Lab Molecular Biol, Med Res Coun, 62-83. *Mem:* Nat Acad Sci; Am Acad Arts Sci; Am Soc Biol Chemist. *Res:* Development of methods for sequencing amino acids in proteins and nucleotides in RNA & DNA; determination of structures of insulin, bacteriophage phi chi, human mitochondria, bacteriophage lambda. *Mailing Add:* Far Leys Fen Lane Swaffham Bulbeck Cambridge CB5 0NJ England

SANGER, GREGORY MARSHALL, OPTICAL ENGINEERING, MATERIALS SCIENCE. *Current Pos:* VPRES OPERATIONS, ITHACO, 93- *Personal Data:* b Spokane, Wash, Feb 2, 46; m 72; c 1. *Educ:* Calif State Univ, BS, 68; Univ Ariz, MS, 71, PhD(optics), 76. *Prof Exp:* Res assoc, Optical Sci Ctr, Univ Ariz, 71-72, proj engr, 72-76; group leader, Lawrence Livermore Lab, 76-86; opers mgr, Perkin-Elmer, 87-89; dir opers, Contraues USA, 89-93. *Mem:* Optical Soc Am; fel Soc Photo-Optical Instrumentation Engrs; Sigma Xi. *Res:* Physics, engineering, manufacturing and metrology of high precision optical surfaces as applied to advanced aerospace, astronomical and energy related applications. *Mailing Add:* 8 Estates Dr Ithaca NY 14850-9792

SANGER, JEAN M, CELL BIOLOGY. *Current Pos:* res assoc cell biol, Univ Pa, 74-80, sr res investr, 80-82, res asst prof, 82-92, RES ASSOC PROF, CELL & DEVELOP BIOL, SCH MED, UNIV PA, 88- *Personal Data:* b New York, NY, June 13, 41; m 64, Joseph W; c John & Matthew. *Educ:* Marymount Col, BS, 63; Dartmouth Col, PhD(molecular biol), 68. *Prof Exp:* Res fel biol, Dartmouth Col, 68. *Concurrent Pos:* Corp mem, Bermuda Biol Sta Res, 75-; vis scientist cell biol, Europ Molecular Biol Lab, 79-80; corp mem, Marine Biol Lab, 81- *Mem:* Am Soc Cell Biol. *Res:* Cell biology; cell motility; cell differentiation. *Mailing Add:* Dept Cell & Develop Biol Univ Pa Sch Med Philadelphia PA 19104-6058

SANGER, JON EDWARD, AQUATIC ECOLOGY. *Current Pos:* from asst prof to assoc prof, 69-78, PROF BOT & MICROBIOL & CHMN DEPT, OHIO WESLEYAN UNIV, 78- *Personal Data:* b Minneapolis, Minn, May 31, 39. *Educ:* Univ Minn, Minneapolis, BS, 61, MS, 64, PhD(plant ecol), 68. *Prof Exp:* Asst prof bot, Univ Minn, 68-69. *Concurrent Pos:* Prin co-investr, NSF Grant, Ohio Wesleyan Univ & Univ Minn, 70-72, Off Water Resources Res Grant, 73-77, 87-, US Geol Surv, 79-83 & Howard Hughes Med Inst. *Mem:* AAAS; Sigma Xi; Int Asn Pure & Appl Limnol; Am Quaternary Asn; Am Soc Limnol & Oceanog. *Res:* Geochemical studies on lakes, with special emphasis on productivity indices; historical aspects of lake eutrophication; landscape erosion, soil weathering and climate change; paleoecology. *Mailing Add:* Dept Bot & Microbiol Ohio Wesleyan Univ 70 S Henry St Delaware OH 43015

SANGER, JOSEPH WILLIAM, CELL & MOLECULAR BIOLOGY, DEVELOPMENTAL BIOLOGY. *Current Pos:* trainee cell differentiation, Univ Pa, 68-71, assoc anat, 71-72, from asst prof to prof, 72-92, PROF CELL & DEVELOP BIOL, SCH MED, UNIV PA, 92- *Personal Data:* b New York, NY, Feb 25, 41; m 64, Jean McGilvray; c John M & Matthew K. *Educ:* Manhattan Col, BS, 62; Dartmouth Col, PhD(molecular biol), 68. *Hon Degrees:* MA, Univ Pa, 76. *Honors & Awards:* Latsis Pub Lectr, ETH, Zurich, Switz, 89; Christiana Smith Lectr, Mt Holyoke Col, MA, 93. *Prof Exp:* Trainee physiol, Dartmouth Med Sch, 67-68. *Concurrent Pos:* Pa Plan scholar, Sch Med, Univ Pa, 71-74; corp mem, Bermuda Biol Sta for Res trustee, 77-82, Marine Biol Lab trustee, 90-; Pa Muscle Inst, 73-; vis scientist, Europ Molecular Biol Lab, 79-80; Alexander von Humboldt fel, 79-80; ed staff, J Cell Motility and the Cytoskeleton, 86-; chair, Univ Pa Cell Biol Grad Prog, 90-95; mem study sect, Biol Sci, NIH, 91-95; ed staff, J Struct Biol, 93- *Mem:* Am Soc Cell Biol; fel AAAS; Soc Develop Biol. *Res:* Cell biology and differentiation; cytology; muscle structure and function; motility; embryology. *Mailing Add:* Dept Cell & Develop Biol Univ Pa Philadelphia PA 19104-6058

SANGER, WARREN GLENN, MEDICAL GENETICS. *Current Pos:* Res assoc cytogenetics, 73-74, ASST PROF HUMAN GENETICS, UNIV NEBR MED CTR, OMAHA, 75-, PROF PEDIAT & PATH, 79- *Personal Data:* b Minden, Nebr, Oct 6, 45; m 69; c 1. *Educ:* Kearney State Col, BS, 67; Univ Nebr, Lincoln, MS, 69, PhD(genetics), 74. *Concurrent Pos:* Coordr, Nebr Tay-Sachs Screening Prog, Univ Nebr Med Ctr, Omaha, 73-, dir, Ctr Human Genetics, 75-79, lab dir, Genetic Semen Bank, 75-79, dir, Ctr Human Genetics & Cytogenetics & Semen Bank, 79-88. *Mem:* Sigma Xi; Am Soc Human Genetics; Am Genetics Asn; Tissue Cult Asn; Am Asn Tissue Banks. *Res:* Prenatal diagnosis of genetic defects and the cytogenetics of infertility; cancer cytogenetics. *Mailing Add:* Dept Pediatrics Univ Nebr Col Med 6005 42nd St Omaha NE 68198-0001

SANGIOVANNI-VINCENTELLI, ALBERTO LUIGI, COMPUTER-AIDED DESIGN, INTEGRATED CIRCUITS. *Current Pos:* from asst prof to assoc prof, 76-83, PROF ELEC ENG & COMPUT SCI, UNIV CALIF, BERKELEY, 83- *Personal Data:* b Milan, Italy, June 23, 47; c 1. *Educ:* Milan Polytech, Dr Eng, 71. *Honors & Awards:* Guillemin-Cauer Award, Inst Elec & Electronics Engrs, 83, Darlington Award, 88. *Prof Exp:* From asst prof to assoc prof elec eng & comput sci, Milan Polytech, 71-76. *Concurrent Pos:* Vchmn dept elec eng & comput sci, Univ Calif, Berkeley, 82-85; vis scientist, IBM, 80-81; consult, Honeywell, SGS-Thomson, 81-, IBM, JJ Watson Res Ctr, 80-86, Cadence Syst, 83-, Nynex, 87-; vis prof, Mass Inst Tech, 87; corp fel, Harris Co, 80-, Thinking Mach, 86-, Synopsys, 86-, Actel, 89-, Crosscheck, 89-, Greylock, 90-, Biocad, 90-; bd dir, Cadence. *Mem:* Fel Inst Elec & Electronics Engrs; Asn Comput Mach. *Res:* Algorithms for computer-aided design of electronic systems including simulation, synthesis, layout, testing and formal verification; software systems for computer aided design and hardware platforms. *Mailing Add:* Dept Elec Eng & Comput Sci Univ Calif Berkeley CA 94720. *Fax:* 510-643-5052; *E-Mail:* alberto@ic.berkeley.edu

SANGREN, WARD CONRAD, APPLIED MATHEMATICS. *Current Pos:* DIR INFO SYST & ANALYSIS, SAN FRANCISCO STATE UNIV, 76- *Personal Data:* b Kalamazoo, Mich, Apr 20, 23; m 44; c 3. *Educ:* Princeton Univ, AB, 43; Univ Mich, MA, 47, PhD(math), 50. *Prof Exp:* Asst prof math, Miami Univ, 49-51; sr mathematician, Oak Ridge Nat Lab, 51-55; chief math & comput res div, Curtiss-Wright Corp, 55-56, chief gen atomic div, Gen Dynamics Corp, 56-62; vpres, Comput Applns Inc, Calif, 62-70; coordr comput activities, Univ Calif, Berkeley, 70-76. *Mem:* Am Math Soc; Soc Indust & Appl Math; Math Asn Am; Asn Comput Mach. *Res:* Boundary value and eigenvalue problems; high speed calculation of reactors; nonlinear differential equations. *Mailing Add:* 121 Bates Ct Orinda CA 94563-2901

SANGREY, DWIGHT A, CIVIL & GEOTECHNICAL ENGINEERING. *Current Pos:* assoc prof, 70-77, PROF CIVIL & ENVIRON ENG, CORNELL UNIV, 77- *Personal Data:* b Lancaster, Pa, May 24, 40; m 64; c 3. *Educ:* Lafayette Col, BS, 62; Univ Mass, MS, 64; Cornell Univ, PhD(civil eng), 68. *Honors & Awards:* Res Award, Am Soc Testing & Mat, 69. *Prof Exp:* Engr, H L Griswold, Consult Engrs, 60-64; proj engr, Shell Oil Co, Tex, 64-65; asst prof civil eng, Queen's Univ, Ont, 67-70; dept head, Dept Civil Eng, Carnegie-Mellon Univ, 87-88. *Concurrent Pos:* Mem hwy res bd, Nat Res Coun; pres, Ore Grad Inst, Portland, 88-95. *Mem:* Am Soc Civil Engrs; Am Soc Testing & Mat; Am Soc Eng Educ; Int Soc Soil Mech & Found Engrs. *Res:* Shear strength and stress-strain behavior of soils; repeated and dynamic loading of soils; organic soils; slope stability; offshore, marine and coastal engineering; engineering geology; solid waste management and disposal. *Mailing Add:* 2383 Palisades Crest Dr Lake Oswego OR 97034

SANGSTER, RAYMOND CHARLES, INORGANIC CHEMISTRY, METROLOGY & STANDARDS. *Current Pos:* CONSULT & TECH WRITER, 89- *Personal Data:* b Lyons, Kans, Mar 15, 28; m 55, 80, 93, Kathie Bryant; c Lynne, Rebecca, David & Lisa. *Educ:* Univ Chicago, PhB, 46, BS, 47; Mass Inst Technol, PhD(chem), 51. *Prof Exp:* Asst chem, Mass Inst Technol, 48-49, res assoc, 51-52; mem tech staff, Semiconductor Res & Develop Dept, Hughes Aircraft Co, 52-54; mem tech staff, Cent Res Lab, Tex Instruments, Inc, 54-57, dir, Mat Res Dept, 57-58, res assoc, 58-62, dir, Semiconductor Exp Lab, 62-65; dir res, Bayside Lab, Gen Tel & Electronics Labs, Inc, NY, 65-68; chief, Electromagnetics Div, Inst Basic Stand, Nat Bur Stand, 69-74, prog mgr strategic planning, 74-78, sr scientist, 78-79; sr scientist, GE-Tempo, Santa Barbara, Calif, 79-80; guest scientist & staff mem, Gmelin Inst, Frankfurt, WGer, 80-85; sr scientist, Raytheon Serv Co, Hsinchu, Taiwan, 86-87; consult, Nat Acad Sci, Bangkok, Thailand, 88-89; contract writer, Omelen Inst, 89-; Unido consult, Addis Ababa, Ethiopia, 92. *Concurrent Pos:* Chmn, Gordon Conf Chem & Metall Semiconductors, 67; chmn, NASA Working Group Electronic Mat, 68-70; US chmn, Marine Commun & Electronics Panel, US-Japan Natural Resources Comn, 69-71. *Mem:* Am Chem Soc; Am Phys Soc; Inst Elec & Electronics Engrs; fel Am Inst Chemists; Sigma Xi. *Res:* Research management; semiconductor materials and devices; organic scintillators; science and technology for development; preparation and reactions of silicon nitride. *Mailing Add:* 4232 Shadow Cym Rd Templeton CA 93465

SANGSTER, WILLIAM M(CCOY), HYDRAULIC ENGINEERING, ENGINEERING MECHANICS. *Current Pos:* prof civil eng & dir Sch Civil Eng, 67-74, DEAN, COL ENG, GA INST TECHNOL, 74- *Personal Data:* b Austin, Minn, Dec 9, 25; m 46; c 3. *Educ:* Univ Iowa, BS, 47, MS, 48, PhD, 64. *Prof Exp:* Asst instr, Univ Iowa, 48; from asst prof to prof civil eng, Univ Mo, Columbia, 48-67, assoc dean col eng & assoc dir eng exp sta, 64-67. *Mem:* Am Soc Civil Engrs (pres, 74-75); Am Soc Eng Educ; Eng Joint Coun; Engrs Coun Prof Develop; Sigma Xi. *Res:* Hydrodynamic stability of stratified flows; orbital mechanics; general hydraulics. *Mailing Add:* 3050 Vinings Ferry Dr SE Atlanta GA 30339

SANI, BRAHMA PORINCHU, BIOCHEMISTRY, CANCER. *Current Pos:* sr biochemist, 74-78, HEAD, PROTEIN BIOCHEM SECT, SOUTHERN RES INST, 79-, SR STAFF SCIENTIST, 88- *Personal Data:* b Trichur, India, Sept 13, 37; m 67, Alice C Matthai; c Anita & Renoju. *Educ:* Univ Kerala, BS, 60; Holkar Sci Col, MS, 62; Indian Inst Sci, Bangalore, PhD(biochem), 67. *Prof Exp:* Res scholar biochem, Indian Inst Sci, Bangalore, 62-65, Univ Grants Comn India jr res fel, 65-67, Coun Sci & Indust Res India sr res fel, 67-68; staff fel, Boston Biomed Res Inst, Retina Found, 68-71; res assoc, Inst Cancer Res, Philadelphia, 71-74. *Concurrent Pos:* Res consult, Cornea Res Dept, Retina Found, Boston, 68-70; res grants, NIH, Coun Tobacco Res, WHO, Am Inst Cancer Res & Nat Cancer Inst. *Mem:* AAAS; Am Asn Cancer Res; Am Soc Biol Chemists; Sigma Xi. *Res:* Molecular mechanism of chemical carcinogenesis and anticarcinogenesis; anti-carcinogen-protein interactions; modern molecular biology and hybridoma techniques; characterization of a retinoic acid-binding protein, a retinol-binding protein and a selenium-binding protein which may be involved in the control of epithelial differentiation and anticarcinogenesis; discovered specific retinoid-binding proteins in several filarial parasites. *Mailing Add:* Southern Res Inst 2000 Ninth Ave S Birmingham AL 35255-5305. *Fax:* 205-581-2877

SANI, ROBERT L(E ROY), CHEMICAL ENGINEERING. *Current Pos:* PROF CHEM ENG, UNIV COLO, BOULDER, 76- *Personal Data:* b Antioch, Calif, Apr 20, 35; m 66, Martha J Marr; c Cynthia, Jeffrey & Elizabeth. *Educ:* Univ Calif, Berkeley, BS, 58, MS, 60; Univ Minn, PhD(chem eng), 63. *Prof Exp:* Instr math, Rensselaer Polytech Inst, 63-64; from asst prof to assoc prof chem eng, Univ Ill, Urbana, 64-76. *Concurrent Pos:* Guggenheim fel, 70-71; consult, Atmospheric Sci Div, Lawrence Livermore Labs, 71-84. *Mem:* Am Inst Chem Engrs; Soc Appl & Indust Math. *Res:* Nonlinear aspects of the dynamics of physical systems exhibiting transport and transformation processes that are coupled at the macroscopic level; computational fluid dynamics. *Mailing Add:* Dept Chem Eng Campus Box 424 CHI-72 Univ Colo Boulder CO 80309. *Fax:* 303-492-4341; *E-Mail:* sani@pastis.colorado.edu

SANIEE, IRAJ, COMBINATORIAL OPTIMIZATION, CONTROL OF EPIDEMIC PROCESSES. *Current Pos:* mem tech staff systs, 85-92, distinguished mem tech staff, 92-94, SR RES SCIENTIST, BELL COMMUN RES, 94- *Personal Data:* b Jan 21, 56; m 87, Marjan Nirou. *Educ:* Cambridge Univ, Eng, BA, 79, MPhil, 81, MA, 83, PhD(opers res), 84. *Honors & Awards:* Franz Edelman Finalist Award. *Prof Exp:* Lectr applicable math, Churchill Co, Cambridge Univ, 83-84. *Concurrent Pos:* Adj prof, Fairleigh Dickinson Univ, 88-90. *Mem:* Soc Indust & Appl Math; Opers Res Soc Am. *Res:* Deterministic and stochastic optimization as applied to control or contain performance of static and dynamic systems; EG telecommunications networks, performance control, their associated economics and implications on regulatory issues; patentee in field. *Mailing Add:* MCC 1A 328B 445 South St Morristown NJ 07960-6454

SANK, DIANE, BIOLOGICAL ANTHROPOLOGY, GENETICS. *Current Pos:* PROF ANTHROP, CITY COL NY, CITY UNIV NY, 68- *Personal Data:* b New York, NY, Dec 22, 27; div; c Brian, Dean & Gayle. *Educ:* Long Island Univ, BS, 49; Univ Ill, MS, 51; Columbia Univ, PhD(human variations), 63. *Prof Exp:* Sr res scientist, NY State Psychiat Inst, 52-67; prof anthrop, Hunter Col, 67-68, chmn dept, 69-71 & 87-88. *Concurrent Pos:* Res assoc psychiat, Col Physicians & Surgeons, Columbia Univ, 53-67, lectr, 67-71, assoc, Univ Sem Genetics & Evol Man, 67-; prof doctoral prog, Grad Ctr, City Univ New York, 67-71; consult human genetics, NS Kline Psychiat Res Inst, 67-84. *Mem:* Fel Int Soc Twin Studies; Am Soc Human Genetics; Am Soc Primatologists; Soc Anthrop Visual Commun; fel AAAS; fel Am Anthrop Asn. *Res:* Hereditary and bio-social studies of mental illness, mental retardation, deafness, learning disability and normal human behavior; primate behavior. *Mailing Add:* 173 Chalotte Pl Englewood Cliffs NJ 07632

SANK, VICTOR J, ENGINEERING PHYSICS. *Current Pos:* CONSULT, VJ SYSTS, 72-; CONSULT NASA, FH&A, 85- *Personal Data:* b Washington, DC, Sept 17, 44; m 65, Catherine Shaer; c Michael, Jeffrey & Daniel. *Educ:* Polytech Inst Brooklyn, BS, 66, PhD(physics), 71. *Prof Exp:* Instr physics, Polytech Inst Brooklyn, 68-71; res asst, 70-71; asst prof, Quinnipiac Col, 71-75; asst prof, San Antonio Col, 75-79; res physicist neuroradiol & comput tomography, NIH, 79-82, res physicist, biomed eng & instrumentation br, 82-85. *Concurrent Pos:* Electronic engr, Schulz Controls, 74-75; res assoc, Dept Radiol, Univ Tex Health Sci Ctr, San Antonio, 75-78; assoc prof imaging physics, Georgetown Univ, 86-87; adj prof telecommun mgt, Univ Md, 90- *Mem:* Am Phys Soc; Inst Elec & Electronics Engrs; Soc Magnetic Resonance in Med. *Res:* Mathematics and computer interfacing for diagnostic medical imaging; computerized tomography; positron-emission tomography; nuclear magnetic resonance. *Mailing Add:* FH&A Code 534 12/N120 Goddard Space Flight Ctr Greenbelt MD 20771

SANKAR, D V SIVA, BIOCHEMISTRY, CHEMICAL PATHOLOGY. *Current Pos:* PRES, AM HEALTH SCI SYSTS CORP, 81- *Personal Data:* b Vizianagram, India, Apr 7, 27; nat US; m 59; c 3. *Educ:* Univ Madras, MSc, 49, PhD(biochem), 51; Am Bd Clin Chemists, dipl. *Honors & Awards:* Indian Chem Soc Gold Medal, 53; Dr Quinn Medal. *Prof Exp:* Fulbright fel, Mass Inst Technol, 53-55; NSF fel, Johns Hopkins Univ, 56; asst prof biochem, Adelphi Col, 56-58; sr res scientist & head biochem res lab, Children's Unit, Creedmoor State Hosp, 58-63, assoc res scientist, 63-69; chief lab res, Queen's Children's Hosp, 69-81. *Concurrent Pos:* Adj prof, Long Island Univ, 64-, Fordham Univ, 70-78 & St Johns Univ, 71-74, NY Col Osteop Med, 86, Schwartz Col Pharm; adj assoc prof psychiat, NY Univ Med Ctr, 76-; ed, J Med. *Mem:* Am Psychol Asn; Am Chem Soc; Am Soc Microbiol; Am Soc Pharmacol & Exp Therapeut; Am Asn Clin Chem. *Res:* Molecular mechanisms of metabolism; drug actions and pathogenesis; biosynthetic mechanisms, vitamins, enzymes, structure-activity relations; neurochemical and psychobiological research on drug actions and on mental health; hypothesis that sleep is a detoxification mechanism for the metabolic oxidative burdens of the wakeful state; rapid eye movement state results from a hypoxic condition in the brain areas; quantitative and mathematical psychology; pharmacology. *Mailing Add:* PO Box 966 Westbury NY 11590-0966. *Fax:* 516-626-5546

SANKAR, SESHADRI, computer aided design, vibration control, for more information see previous edition

SANKAR, SURYANARAYAN G, SOLID STATE CHEMISTRY. *Current Pos:* SR SCIENTIST & ADJ PROF, CARNEGIE MELLON UNIV, 86- *Personal Data:* b Madras, India, July 1, 42; m 74; c 2. *Educ:* Andhra Univ, BSc, 62, MSc, 63; Poona Univ, PhD(solid state chem), 68. *Prof Exp:* Fel chem, Tex Tech Univ, 70; fel, Univ Pittsburgh, 70-73, from res asst prof to res assoc prof, 73-78; sr res chemist, Mat Res Ctr, Allied Corp, 78-82; sr res assoc, Mat Res Lab, Pa State Univ, 82-85. *Mem:* Mat Res Soc; Am Chem Soc; fel Am Inst Chemists. *Res:* Study of structural and magnetic properties of permanent magnets; study of the influence of paramagnetic impurities in superconductors; heterogeneous catalysis; metal hydrides. *Mailing Add:* 1224 Ridgewood Rd Pittsburgh PA 15241

SANKAR, THIAGAS SRIRAM, mechanical engineering, for more information see previous edition

SANKOFF, DAVID, MATHEMATICS. *Current Pos:* RES, CTR RECH MATH, UNIV MONT, 69- *Personal Data:* b Montreal, Quebec, Can, Dec 31, 42. *Educ:* McGill Univ, PhD(math), 69. *Honors & Awards:* Vincent Prize, Can Fr Asn Adv Sci,77; Can Inst Advan Res, Fel, 87- *Mem:* Soc Indust & Appl Math; Linguistics Soc Am. *Res:* Statistical procedures for the analysis of sociolinguistic data; algorithms for the study of macromolecular structure and evolution; mathematics applied to natural and social science and the humanities. *Mailing Add:* Ctr Rech Math Univ Montreal cp 6128 Montreal PQ H3C 3J7 Can. *Fax:* 514-343-2254; *E-Mail:* sankoff@ere.umontreal.ca

SANMANN, EVERETT EUGENE, optical physics, for more information see previous edition

SANN, KLAUS HEINRICH, ELECTRONICS, RADAR SYSTEMS. *Current Pos:* RETIRED. *Personal Data:* b Driesen, Ger, Aug 6, 19; m 44; c 2. *Educ:* Technische Universitat Berlin, Diplom-Ingenieur, 51. *Honors & Awards:* Hinman Award, Harry Diamond Labs, 76. *Prof Exp:* Electronics engr, Telefunken GmbH, Berlin, 51-53, asst lab mgr, 53-56, lab mgr, 56-58; electronics engr, 59-69, chief, advan res br, Harry Diamond Labs, 69- *Concurrent Pos:* Mem working group on Radar Minimum Performance, Radio Adv Comt, 67. *Mem:* Sr mem Inst Elec & Electronics Engrs; affil Nat Soc Prof Engrs. *Res:* Advanced development of fuzzing systems and solid state microwave sources; conceives and coordinates research programs of substantial importance to installation. *Mailing Add:* 4910 Bangor Dr Kensington MD 20895

SANNELLA, JOSEPH L, MATERIALS SCIENCE ENGINEERING. *Current Pos:* supvr chem res, Ball Corp, 67-74, dir res, res develop & eng, 74-85, dir corp lab serv, 85-88, DIR LAB SERV, METAL CONTAINER OPERS, BALL CORP, 88- *Personal Data:* b Boston, Mass, July 27, 33; m 59, Nancy Marshall; c Joseph, Sue A & Stephen. *Educ:* Harvard Univ, AB, 55; Univ Mass, MS, 58; Purdue Univ, PhD(biochem), 63; Univ Del, MBA, 69. *Prof Exp:* Res chemist, Am Viscose Div, FMC Corp, Pa, 62-67. *Concurrent Pos:* Chmn packaging adv panel, Nat Food Processors Asn, mem lab mgt comt. *Mem:* Am Chem Soc; Soc Plastics Engrs; Nat Metal Decorators Asn. *Res:* Process chemistry; analytical chemistry; plastics; packaging; glass; coatings; materials. *Mailing Add:* 2803 W Woodbridge Muncie IN 47304

SANNER, JOHN HARPER, PROSTAGLANDINS. *Current Pos:* RETIRED. *Personal Data:* b Anamosa, Iowa, Apr 29, 31; m 58, Marilyn J Eichorst; c Linda L (Costanzo) & Steven B. *Educ:* Univ Iowa, BS, 54, MS, 61, PhD(pharmacol), 64. *Prof Exp:* From res investr to res fel pharmacol, G D Searle & Co, 63-86. *Mem:* Soc Pharmacol & Exp Therapeut. *Res:* Pharmacological antagonists; pharmacology of vasoactive peptides and prostaglandins; pharmacological mechanisms of smooth muscle; anti-inflammatory mechanisms. *Mailing Add:* 959 Appletree Lane Deerfield IL 60015

SANNES, FELIX RUDOLPH, elementary particle physics; deceased, see previous edition for last biography

SANNES, PHILIP LOREN, ENVIRONMENTAL HEALTH, CELL BIOLOGY. *Current Pos:* ASST PROF ENVIRON HEALTH SCI, JOHNS HOPKINS UNIV, 78-, ASST PROF CELL BIOL & ANAT, 79-; ASSOC PROF, DEPT ANAT, PHYSIOL SCI & RADIOL, NC STATE UNIV COL VET MED, 88- *Personal Data:* b Canton, Ohio, Mar 10, 48; m 73; c 1. *Educ:* Ohio State Univ, BA, 70, MSc, 73, PhD(anat), 75. *Prof Exp:* Instr path, Med Univ SC, 75-77, asst prof, 77-78. *Concurrent Pos:* NIH fel, Inst Gen Health Sci, 77-78; assoc sr investr, path, Smith Kline & French Lab, 88. *Mem:* Am Asn Anatomists; Histochem Soc; Soc Cell Biol; Electrophoresis Soc. *Res:* Cell biology: ultrastructure and cytochemistry; alteration of lung structure and function relationships by environmental agents. *Mailing Add:* Dept Anat Physiol Sci & Radiol NC State Univ Col Vet Med 4700 Hillsborough St Raleigh NC 27606-1428. *Fax:* 919-829-4465

SANNINO, ANTHONY PASCAL, ANALYTICAL & NUMERICAL MODELING. *Current Pos:* SR ADV DEVELOP ENGR, SEAGATE TECHNOL, 96- *Personal Data:* b Marseille, France, Aug 22, 68. *Educ:* Clemson Univ, BS, 91, MS, 93, PhD(mat sci & eng), 96. *Mem:* Am Soc Mech Engrs; Am Soc Metals; Minerals, Metals & Mat Soc. *Res:* Analytical and numerical modeling, including finite element modeling of surface tension influence of polyethylene-based adhesive in stress condition of wafer bar for manufacturing computer hard drive transducers. *Mailing Add:* 1100 Legion St Shakopee MN 55379

SANNUTI, PEDDAPULLAIAH, CONTROL SYSTEMS, INFORMATION SCIENCE. *Current Pos:* PROF ELEC ENG, RUTGERS UNIV, NEW BRUNSWICK, 68- *Personal Data:* b Rajupalem, India, Apr 2, 41; m 65; c 1. *Educ:* Eng Col, Anantapur, India, BE, 63; Indian Inst Technol, Kharagpur, MTech, 65; Univ Ill, Urbana, PhD(elec eng), 68. *Mem:* Fel Inst Elec & Electronics Engrs. *Res:* Communication systems; filtering; H2 optimal control; control of linear systems with saturating actuators. *Mailing Add:* 64 Valley Forge Dr East Brunswick NJ 08816

SANNY, CHARLES GORDON, ALDEHYDE DEHYDROGENASES. *Current Pos:* assoc prof, 85-89, PROF BIOCHEM, COL OSTEOP MED, OKLA STATE UNIV, 89- *Personal Data:* b Aug 25, 47; m 72; c 1. *Educ:* Okla Baptist Univ, BS, 70; Univ Okla, PhD(biochem), 75. *Prof Exp:* Assoc prof biochem, Univ Osteop Med & Health Sci, Des Moines, Iowa, 81-85. *Mem:* Am Soc Biochem & Molecular Biol; Sigma Xi. *Mailing Add:* Biochem-Col Osteop Med Okla State Univ 1111 W 17th St Tulsa OK 74107. *Fax:* 918-561-8412

SANOFF, HENRY, BEHAVIORAL DESIGN, PROGRAMMING & POST OCCUPANCY EVALUATION. *Current Pos:* PROF ARCHIT, NC STATE UNIV, 67- *Personal Data:* b New York, Jan 16, 34; m 57, Joan D; c Ari & Zoe. *Educ:* Pratt Inst, BArchit, 57, MArchit, 62. *Honors & Awards:* Award of Honor, Environ Design Res Asn, 77; Statute Victory, World Cult Prize for Lett, Arts & Sci, 85. *Prof Exp:* Asst prof archit, Univ Calif, Berkeley, 63-67. *Concurrent Pos:* Founder & chmn, Environ Design Res Assoc, 68-72, bd mem, 72-75; distinguished univ prof, Univ Col, London, 81-82, Univ Melbourne, Australia, 87; vis prof, Oxford Univ, 82, Inst SAfrican Archit, 85 & 86; Chettle scholar, Univ Sydney, Australia, 90; distinguished Fulbright scholar, Seoul Nat Univ, Korea, 90-91; US ed, J Design Studies. *Mem:* Am Inst Archit; Environ Degree Res Asn; Int Asn People-Environ Studies. *Res:* Research and writing focus on citizen participation in design and planning decisions; developed techniques and strategies to effectively involve non-designers in the process of designing buildings and planning urban development. *Mailing Add:* Sch Design NC State Univ Raleigh NC 27695. *Fax:* 919-515-7330; *E-Mail:* henry_sanoff@ncsu.edu

SAN PIETRO, ANTHONY, PLANT BIOCHEMISTRY. *Current Pos:* RETIRED. *Personal Data:* b Apr 22, 22. *Educ:* NY Univ, BA, 42; Columbia Univ, PhD(biochem), 51. *Honors & Awards:* US Sr Scientist Award, Humboldt Found, 77. *Prof Exp:* Res assoc, Biochem Dept, Columbia Univ, 51-52; Nat Polio Found fel, Johns Hopkins Univ, 52-54; from asst prof to assoc prof biol & McCollum-Pratt Inst, 54-62; sr investr, Kettering Res Lab, 62-64, asst dir, 64-68; chmn & prof, Dept Plant Sci, Ind Univ, 68-77, distinguished prof plant biochem, 75-88, prof, Dept Biol, 77-88. *Concurrent Pos:* Prof chem, Antioch Col, 62-68; US-China lectr exchange prog, Nat Acad Sci, 80; sci adv, Off Pres, Ind Univ, 80-, spec consult, Off Vchancellor Undergrad Educ, 90-; vis scientist, Inst Phys & Chem Res, Japan, 85; mem bd gov, Ben Gurion Univ, Israel, 85; mem, Bd Sci & Technol Int Develop, Nat Res Coun, Nat Acad Sci, 86-89; vchmn, Biotechnol Comt, Corp Sci & Technol, 87-88. *Mem:* Nat Acad Sci; Am Soc Biochem. *Mailing Add:* Dept Biol Jordan Hall Ind Univ Bloomington IN 47405

SANS, JOHN RUDOLFS, GEOCHEMISTRY, ENVIRONMENTAL CHEMISTRY. *Current Pos:* LAB SUPVR, SD MYERS INC, 88- *Personal Data:* b Celle, Ger, Apr 19, 50; US citizen; m 78, Barbara Ann Urban; c Peter, Amanda, John Jr, Victoria & Matthew. *Educ:* Univ Chicago, BA, 72, PhD(geochem), 83; Yale Univ, MS, 74. *Prof Exp:* Res specialist, Va Polytech & State Univ, 78-80; asst prof, Ball State Univ, 81-86; prin scientist, Lockheed, Johnson Space Ctr, NASA, 86-88. *Mem:* Am Chem Soc; Am Soc Testing & Mat; Inst Elec & Electronics Engrs. *Res:* Product configuration baseline abatement in electrical power equipment; development of diagnostic methods for trouble-shooting of power transformers; develop methods to extend life of power transformers. *Mailing Add:* 180 South Ave Tallmadge OH 44278-2813. *Fax:* 330-633-8168

SANSING, NORMAN GLENN, BIOCHEMISTRY, PLANT PHYSIOLOGY. *Current Pos:* asst prof biochem & bot, 64-72, ASSOC PROF BIOCHEM, UNIV GA, 72- *Personal Data:* b Woodstock, Ala, Aug 17, 32; m 55; c 3. *Educ:* Auburn Univ, BS, 54, MS, 59; Iowa State Univ, PhD(plant physiol), 62. *Prof Exp:* Res assoc nucleic acid enzym, Biol Div, Oak Ridge Nat Lab, 62-64. *Mem:* AAAS; Am Soc Plant Physiologists. *Res:* Nucleic acid enzymology; isolation and characterization of plant nucleases. *Mailing Add:* Dept Biochem Univ Ga 1180 E Broad St Athens GA 30601-3040

SANSLONE, WILLIAM ROBERT, NUTRITIONAL BIOCHEMISTRY. *Current Pos:* RETIRED. *Personal Data:* b Vineland, NJ, Feb 16, 31; m 60, Alice Koury; c Catherine S (Downs). *Educ:* Rutgers Univ, BS, 53, PhD(biochem), 61; Univ NH, MS, 55. *Honors & Awards:* Cavaliere della Republica, Ital Govt, 96- *Prof Exp:* Asst, Univ NH, 53-55 & Rutgers Univ, 58-61; inst biochem, State Univ NY Downstate Med Ctr, 61-64, from asst prof to assoc prof, 64-71; sr proj scientist, NIH, 71-73, exec secy biochem study sect, Div Res Grants, 73-75, prog dir review, Div Extramural Activ, Nat Cancer Inst, 75-83, assoc dir sci prog opers, Div Lung Dis, Nat Heart, Lung & Blood Inst, 83-87, dir, Off Prog Planning & Eval, Nat Inst Arthritis & Musculoskeletal & Skin Dis, NIH, 87-96. *Concurrent Pos:* Vis assoc prof, Med Col Pa, 70-71. *Mem:* AAAS; Am Inst Nutrit; Soc Exp Biol & Med; Sigma Xi. *Res:* Muscle and nutritional biochemistry; health-science administration; analyses of cost savings attributable to health research. *Mailing Add:* 6835 Old Stage Rd Rockville MD 20852-4359. *E-Mail:* txpf32a@prodigy.com

SANSONE, ERIC BRANDFON, INDUSTRIAL HYGIENE, SAFETY. *Current Pos:* MEM STAFF, FREDERICK CANCER RES DEVELOP CTR, NAT CANCER INST, 74-, DIR ENVIRON CONTROL & RES PROG, 79- *Personal Data:* b New York, NY, Mar 26, 39; c 2. *Educ:* City Col New York, BChE, 60; Univ Mich, MPH, 62, PhD(indust health), 67. *Prof Exp:* From asst prof to assoc prof, Indust Hyg & Air Eng, Univ Pittsburgh, 67-74. *Mem:* AAAS; Am Indust Hyg Asn; NY Acad Sci; Brit Occup Hyg Soc; Soc Occup Environ Health; Am Chem Soc; Health Physics Soc. *Res:* Risk assessment and environmental monitoring. *Mailing Add:* 1104 Wilshire Ct Champaign IL 61821

SANSONE, FRANCES MARIE, HUMAN ANATOMY. *Current Pos:* instr, 64-68, asst prof histol & neuroanat, 68-76, clin asst prof, 76-81, ASSOC PROF ANAT SCI, SCH MED, STATE UNIV NY BUFFALO, 81- *Personal Data:* b Birmingham, Ala, June 30, 31. *Educ:* Cath Univ Am, AB, 52; Marquette Univ, MS, 56; Univ Tex, PhD(anat), 65. *Prof Exp:* Teaching asst histol & neuroanat, Dent Br, Univ Tex, 57-60. *Mem:* Am Asn Anatomists; Soc Neurosci; Am Soc Cell Biol; Sigma Xi; Electron Mic Soc Am. *Res:* environmental neurotoxins and the epidemiology of neural tumors. *Mailing Add:* Dept Anat Sci State Univ NY 317 Farber Hall Buffalo NY 14214

SANSONE, FRANCIS JOSEPH, ORGANIC BIOGEOCHEMISTRY, CHEMICAL OCEANOGRAPHY. *Current Pos:* Asst prof, 80-87, ASSOC PROF OCEANOG, UNIV HAWAII, MANOA, 87- *Personal Data:* b Dayton, Ohio, July 25, 51. *Educ:* Rensselaer Polytech Inst, BS, 73; Univ NC, Chapel Hill, MS, 76, PhD(marine sci), 80. *Mem:* Am Soc Limnol & Oceanog; Am Soc Microbiol; Am Geophys Union; Am Chem Soc. *Res:* Marine organic geochemistry; microbially-mediated anaerobic decomposition in sediments; tropical seawater chemistry; anaerobic diagenesis of marine carbonates. *Mailing Add:* 3032 Alencastre Pl Honolulu HI 96816

SANSONE, FRED J, mathematics, for more information see previous edition

SANSONETTI, S JOHN, METALLURGY. *Current Pos:* RETIRED. *Personal Data:* b Blairsville, Pa, Aug 18, 14; m 48; c 2. *Educ:* Ind Univ, BS, 36; Carnegie Mellon Inst, BS, 41. *Prof Exp:* Dir metall res, Reynolds Metals Co, 45-80. *Concurrent Pos:* Instr, Am Inst Mgt, 58-78. *Mem:* Fel Am Soc Metals Int; Am Chem Soc; Am Phys Soc; Optical Soc Am; Am Inst Mech Engrs; Nat Corrosion Eng Soc. *Res:* Methods of applications of aluminum development of alloys. *Mailing Add:* 503 Ridge Top Rd Richmond VA 23229-6935

SAN SOUCIE, ROBERT LOUIS, MATHEMATICS, RESEARCH ADMINISTRATION. *Current Pos:* MANAGING DIR, MILL RIVER VENTURES LTD, 75- *Personal Data:* b Adams, Mass, Apr 30, 27; m 53; c 3. *Educ:* Univ Mass, BA, 49; Univ Wis, MA, 50, PhD(math), 53. *Prof Exp:* Wis Alumni Res Found asst math, Univ Wis, 49-51, univ asst, 51-52; instr, Univ Ore, 53-55, asst prof, 55-57; head math sect, Sylvania Electronic Systs Div, Gen Tel & Electronics Corp, 57-59, mgr adv commun, 59-61, mgr systs projs, 61-62; vpres eng electronics & space div, Emerson Elec Co, 62-64, pres & gen mgr, 64-67, exec vpres, 67-71; pres, DLJ Capital Corp, Subsidiary of Donaldson, Lufkin & Jenrette, Inc, 71-75. *Concurrent Pos:* Trustee, St Louis Univ, 71-82. *Mem:* Am Math Soc; Am Mgt Asn; Sigma Xi; Phi Beta Kappa. *Res:* Right alternative rings; additive and multiplicative systems; error correcting codes and management information systems. *Mailing Add:* 68 Dortmunder Dr Manalapan NJ 07726

SANTACANA, GUIDO E, IONIC TRANSPORT IN THE LIVER CELL & EFFECTS OF TOXINS, AIRWAY SMOOTH MUSCLE PHYSIOLOGY. *Current Pos:* from asst prof to assoc prof, 84-87, PROF & CHMN, DEPT PHYSIOL, UNIV CENT DEL CARIBE, 2000- *Personal Data:* b Placetas, Cuba, Dec 25, 52; US citizen; m 78, Maria E Laffitte; c Guido E. *Educ:* Univ PR, BS, 75, PhD(physiol), 82. *Prof Exp:* Instr, Univ Sacred Heart, 76, asst prof, 83-84; instr, Sch Pharm, Univ PR, 79; San Juan Bautista Sch Med, 82-83. *Concurrent Pos:* Prin investr, NIH, 79-82, coordr, Res Info Ctr, 91-; prin investr, Res Ctrs Minority Inst Progs, 85-91. *Mem:* Am Phys Soc; Am Asn Chmn Depts Physiol. *Res:* Effects of cocaine on several aspects of airway smooth muscle physiology, including tension development and changes in intracellular calcium level. *Mailing Add:* Dept Physiol Univ Central Caribe Sch Med Hosp U Ramon Ruiz Arnau Bayamon PR 00621-6032. *Fax:* 787-740-4390

SANTACANA-NUET, FRANCISCO, ANALYTICAL CHEMISTRY. *Current Pos:* RETIRED. *Personal Data:* b Barcelona, Spain, Jan 16, 31; US citizen; div; c 4. *Educ:* Barcelona Indust Col, BSc, 51; Purdue Univ, MS, 59. *Prof Exp:* Chemist, S A Rovira, Bachs & Macia, 50-53, chief anal sect, 53-56, consult dye chem, 59-60; res chemist, Org Chem Div, Am Cyanamid Co, Stamford, Conn, 60-70, group leader anal res & develop, 70-71, group head, Chem Res Div, Bound Brook, NJ, 71-80, mgr anal serv, 80-88, dir sci serv, Chem Res Div, 88-93. *Concurrent Pos:* Consult. *Mem:* Am Chem Soc. *Res:* Chromatography; automation and instrumentation; spectrophotometry; identification of organic structures; nuclear magnetic resonance; mass spectrometry; management; microscopy. *Mailing Add:* 34 Spinning Wheel Rd Fairfield CT 06430-6362

SANTAMARIA, VITO WILLIAM, TECHNICAL MANAGEMENT. *Current Pos:* TECH DIR, JAMESTOWN PAINT & VARNISH CO, 90- *Personal Data:* b Cleveland, Ohio, Aug 19, 48; m 89, Diane Groff; c 6. *Educ:* Cleveland State Univ, BS, 70. *Prof Exp:* Sr technician, Lamp Glass Div, Gen Elec, 69-70; sect head, Indust Coatings-Appliance, Glidden, 70-77; tech mgr, Indust Coatings, Stand T Chem, 77-80, Coatings Div, Whittaker Corp, Batavia, 80-81; Extrusion Coatings, Valspar Corp, 81-86; tech dir, Indust Coatings Div, Pratt & Lambert, 86-89. *Concurrent Pos:* Mem, corrosion comt, Fedn Soc Coatings Technol, 87- *Mem:* Asn Finishing Processes; Fedn Soc Coatings Technol; Nat Paint & Coatings Asn; Chem Coaters Asn; Steel Structure Painting Coun. *Res:* OEM finishes technology advancement of protective and ornamental products which are ecologically sound forming films through evaporation, oxidation, thermal reactivity, and chemical reaction. *Mailing Add:* 10903 Fawnview Dr Houston TX 77070

SANT'AMBROGIO, GIUSEPPE, RESPIRATORY PHYSIOLOGY, NEUROPHYSIOLOGY. *Current Pos:* assoc prof, 75-77, PROF, DEPT PHYSIOL, UNIV TEX MED BR, GALVESTON, 77- *Personal Data:* b Milano, Italy, Nov 28, 31; m 58; c 3. *Educ:* Univ Milan, MD, 56. *Prof Exp:* From asst prof physiol to prof, Med Sch, Univ Milan, 57-76. *Concurrent Pos:* Res fel, Dept Physiol, Univ Ky, 58-59 & 60-61, Univ Oxford, 63-64; vis prof, Dept Physiol, McGill Univ, 73. *Mem:* Italian Soc Physiol; Brit Physiol Soc; Europ Soc Respiratory Pathophysiol; Am Physiol Soc; Soc Exp Biol & Med. *Res:* Neural control of breathing in mammals. *Mailing Add:* Dept Physiol Univ Tex Med Br 301 University Blvd Galveston TX 77555-0641. *Fax:* 409-772-3381

SANTAMOUR, FRANK SHALVEY, JR, PLANT GENETICS, BIOCHEMISTRY. *Current Pos:* RES GENETICIST, AGR RES SERV, USDA, 67- *Personal Data:* b Lowell, Mass, Mar 7, 32; m 52; c 1. *Educ:* Univ Mass, BS, 53; Yale Univ, MF, 54; Harvard Univ, AM, 57; Univ Minn, PhD(forestry, plant genetics), 60. *Honors & Awards:* Jackson Dawson Medal, Univ Ma, 84. *Prof Exp:* Geneticist northeast forest exp sta, US Forest Serv, 57-64; geneticist, Morris Arboretum, Univ Pa, 64-67. *Concurrent Pos:* Am Philos Soc grants, 66, 71, 80; Holly Soc Am grants, 71, 85; Hort Res Inst grants, 76, 79; Int Soc Arboriculture grant, 82. *Mem:* Soc Am Foresters; Bot Soc Am; Am Hort Soc; Int Soc Arboriculture (pres, 84). *Res:* Genetics and breeding of shade trees and wood ornamentals for urban areas; biochemistry of incompatabilities and pest resistance; biochemical systematics; cytology. *Mailing Add:* US Nat Arboretum 3501 New York Ave NE Washington DC 20002

SANTANGELO, GEORGE MICHAEL, MOLECULAR GENETICS. *Current Pos:* asst prof, 89-94, ASSOC PROF, UNIV SOUTHERN MISS, 95- *Personal Data:* b Bronx, NY, Nov 14, 56. *Educ:* Univ Pa, BA, 78; Yale Univ, PhD(genetics), 84. *Prof Exp:* Researcher, Univ Calif, Irvine, 83-85; asst res biologist, Univ Calif, Santa Cruz, 85-87; asst prof biochem, Ore Health Sci Univ, 87; adj asst prof biol, Portland State Univ, 87-89. *Mem:* Genetics Soc Am; Am Soc Microbiol; AAAS. *Res:* Transcriptional regulation of gene expression in eukaryotes, particularly with respect to control of cellular metabolism and growth rate. *Mailing Add:* Dept Biol Sci Univ Southern Miss Hattiesburg MS 39406-5018. *E-Mail:* santnglo@whale.st.usm.edu

SANTARE, MICHAEL HAROLD, ENGINEERING MECHANICS, MECHANICAL ENGINEERING. *Current Pos:* Asst prof, 86-91, ASSOC PROF MECH ENG, UNIV DEL, 91-, ASSOC PROF BIOMECH & MOVEMENT SCI, 94- *Personal Data:* b Brooklyn, NY, Nov 25, 59; m 81; c 3. *Educ:* Rensselaer Polytech Inst, BS, 81; Northwestern Univ, MS, 84, PhD(T&AM), 87. *Concurrent Pos:* Dir, Orthop & Biomech Eng Ctr, 93. *Mem:* Am Acad Mech; Am Soc Mech Engrs; Sigma Xi. *Res:* Mechanical behavior of inhomogeneous materials; orthopaedic biomechanics; crack-inclusion interaction. *Mailing Add:* Dept Mech Eng Univ Del Newark DE 19716. *Fax:* 302-831-3619; *E-Mail:* santare@me.udel.edu

SANTE, DANIEL P(AUL), ELECTRONICS. *Current Pos:* asst prof elec eng, 64-72, ASSOC PROF ELEC ENG, ERIE COMMUNITY COL, 72- *Personal Data:* b Lackawanna, NY, Nov 16, 19; m 58. *Educ:* Tri-State Col, BS, 41. *Prof Exp:* Jr engr, Colonial Radio Corp, 41-42; sr design engr, Sylvania Electric Prod Co, 43-48; assoc electronics engr, Cornell Aeronaut Lab, Inc, 48-52, res engr, 52-59; sect head, Sylvania Elec Prod Inc Div, Gen Tel & Electronics Corp, 59-63. *Res:* Radio telemetry; communications systems; missile systems; establishment of reliability techniques in a circuit sense for electronics equipment. *Mailing Add:* 4530 Greenbriar Rd Buffalo NY 14221

SANTELMANN, PAUL WILLIAM, AGRONOMY, WEED SCIENCE. *Current Pos:* from assoc prof to prof, 62-74, regents prof, 74-78, PROF AGRON & HEAD DEPT, OKLA STATE UNIV, 78- *Personal Data:* b Ann Arbor, Mich, Oct 18, 26; m 50; c 4. *Educ:* Univ Md, BS, 50; Mich State Col, MS, 52; Ohio State Univ, PhD(agron), 54. *Prof Exp:* Asst prof agron, Univ Md, 54-61, assoc prof, 61-62. *Concurrent Pos:* Mem adv group pest mgt & res, President's Coun Environ Qual; mem herbicide study group, Environ Protection Agency; mem study probs pest control team, Nat Acad Sci; mem bd dirs, Coun Agr Sci & Technol, 75-78; ed, newslett, Weed Sci Soc Am; res award, Sigma Xi. *Mem:* Am Inst Biol Sci; AAAS; fel Weed Sci Soc Am (pres, 78); fel Am Soc Agron; Weed Sci Soc; Sigma Xi. *Res:* Crop and weed management and ecology; herbicide persistence and activity. *Mailing Add:* 4920 Woodlawn Dr Stillwater OK 74074

SANTEN, RICHARD J, ENDOCRINOLOGY. *Current Pos:* from asst prof to prof, 71-86, EVAN PUGH PROF MED, M S HERSHEY MED CTR, PA STATE UNIV, 86-; CHIEF DIV ENDOCRINOL, 79- *Personal Data:* b Cincinnati, Ohio, Apr 2, 39; c 3. *Educ:* Holy Cross Col, AB, 61; Univ Mich, Ann Arbor, MD, 65; Am Bd Int Med, dipl, 70 & 76. *Prof Exp:* Instr med, Univ Wash Sch Med, 70-71. *Concurrent Pos:* Vis prof, Univ Liege, Belgium, 78-79, Hosp Necker, Paris, 85-86; consult physician, Lebanon Vet Admin Hosp, Pa, 80- *Mem:* Endocrine Soc; fel Am Col Physicians; Am Soc Androl; Am Soc Clin Invest; Am Soc Clin Oncol. *Res:* Hormonal control of breast and prostate cancer; experimental therapy of breast and prostate cancer; control gonudotropin secretion. *Mailing Add:* 39 Beverly Rd Detroit MI 48236

SANTER, JAMES OWEN, ORGANIC CHEMISTRY. *Current Pos:* SR RES SPECIALIST, MONSANTO POLYMERS & RESINS CO, 65- *Personal Data:* b Benenden, Eng, May 3, 31; m 57; c 4. *Educ:* Univ London, BSc, 55; Ill Inst Technol, PhD(chem), 61. *Prof Exp:* Res chemist, Shawinigan Resins Corp, 61-65. *Mem:* Am Chem Soc. *Res:* Chemistry and technology of aminoplast resins in surface coatings. *Mailing Add:* 15 Pleasant Pl East Longmeadow MA 01028-2421

SANTER, MELVIN, MICROBIOLOGY. *Current Pos:* from asst prof to assoc prof biol, 56-68, PROF BIOL, HAVERFORD COL, 68- *Personal Data:* b Boston, Mass, Aug 23, 26; m 55; c 3. *Educ:* St John's Univ, NY, BS, 49; Univ Mass, MS, 51; George Wash Univ, PhD(bact), 54. *Prof Exp:* Nat Found Infantile Paralysis fel, Yale Univ, 54-55, NIH fel, 55-56. *Concurrent Pos:* Lalor fac award, 58; NSF sr fel, 62-63; Weizmann Inst Sci fel, 69-70. *Mem:* AAAS; Am Soc Microbiol; Am Soc Biol Chemists. *Res:* Biochemistry of autotrophic bacteria; ribosome structure and RNA sequence work. *Mailing Add:* Dept Biol Haverford Col Haverford PA 19041-1392. *Fax:* 215-896-1224; *E-Mail:* unixmsanter@haverford.edu

SANTERRE, ROBERT FRANK, CELL CULTURE, MICROBIOLOGY. *Current Pos:* RES SCIENTIST MOLECULAR BIOL, LILLY RES LABS, 75- *Personal Data:* b Hanover, NH, June 28, 40; m 58, Virginia J Blaisdell; c 4. *Educ:* Southern Conn State Col, BS, 65; Univ NH, MS, 67, PhD(zool), 70. *Honors & Awards:* Muscular Dystrophy Res Fel, 72-73. *Prof Exp:* Fel biol, Mass Inst Technol, 70-73 & Univ Calif, San Diego, 73-75. *Concurrent Pos:* Pub Health fel, NIH, 70-72; Am Heart Asn fel, San Diego, 74-75. *Mem:* Sigma Xi; AAAS; Am Soc Microbiol; Am Soc Bone & Mineral Soc. *Res:* Oxidative phosphorylation and lipid metabolism; in vitro studies of insulin biosynthesis; development of cloning vectors for gene analysis and expression in higher eukaryotic cells; cytokine gene regulation in transgenic animals; transgenics; myogenesis; alzheimers disease; osteoporosis; biotechnology; neurosciences. *Mailing Add:* Endocrinol Res Lilly Res Labs Lilly Corp Ctr Indianapolis IN 46285. *Fax:* 317-276-1414; *E-Mail:* santerre_robert@lilly.com

SANTI, DANIEL V, ORGANIC CHEMISTRY, BIOCHEMISTRY. *Current Pos:* assoc prof pharmaceut chem & biochem, 70-76, PROF PHARMACEUT CHEM & BIOCHEM, UNIV CALIF, SAN FRANCISCO, 76- *Personal Data:* b Buffalo, NY, Feb 6, 42. *Educ:* State Univ NY, Buffalo, BS, 63, PhD(med chem), 67. *Prof Exp:* Asst prof chem, Univ Calif, Santa Barbara, 66-70. *Mem:* Am Chem Soc. *Res:* Enzyme mechanisms; protein biosynthesis; design of enzyme inhibitors; model enzyme reactions; nucleic acids; heterocyclic chemistry. *Mailing Add:* Dept Biochem Univ Calif San Francisco Third & Parnassus San Francisco CA 94143-0448. *Fax:* 415-476-0473

SANTIAGO, JULIO VICTOR, DIABETES, PEDIATRIC ENDOCRINOLOGY. *Current Pos:* DIR RES, DIABETES RES & TRAINING CTR, 77-, PROF PEDIAT, WASH UNIV MED SCH, 83- *Personal Data:* b San German, PR, Jan 13, 42; m 63; c 4. *Educ:* Manhattan Col, New York, BS, 63 & Univ PR, MD, 67; Univ Montevideo, Uraguay, PhD, 84. *Concurrent Pos:* Prin investr, Diabetes Cent & Complications Trial, 83- *Mem:* Am Soc Clin Invest; Soc Ped Res; Am Diabetes Asn. *Res:* Treatment of diabetes mellitus, longterm complications of diabetes, insulin induced hypoglycemia, pediatric endocrinology. *Mailing Add:* Washington Sch Med 400 S Kings Hwy St Louis MO 63110-1014

SANTIAGO-ACEVEDO, NOEMI, DRUG DELIVERY, ORAL VACCINATION. *Current Pos:* DIR, EMISPHERE TECH, INC, 89- *Personal Data:* b San Juan, PR, Dec 28, 53; m, Michael Kmetz; c Phillip & David. *Educ:* Univ PR, BS, 74, MS, 78, PhD(immunol & microbiol), 85. *Prof Exp:* Instr biol, Sacred Heart Univ, 78-80 & Univ PR, 80-82; asst prof immunol & parasitol, Cayey Sch Med, 86-88. *Concurrent Pos:* Consult, Marc Prog, NIH, 83-84; vis prof, Univ PR, Cayey Campus, 87-88. *Mem:* Am Asn Immunologists; NY Acad Scis; Am Mgt Asn; Controlled Release Soc. *Res:* Oral delivery system based on microencapsulation with a protein-like polymer for delivery of proteins and other drugs as well as for oral vaccination. *Mailing Add:* Emisphere Tech, Inc 15 Skyline Dr Hawthorne NY 10532-1361. *Fax:* 914-347-2498

SANTIAGO-MELENDEZ, MIGUEL, STRUCTURAL ENGINEERING. *Current Pos:* CONSULT. *Personal Data:* b Corozal, PR, Sept 28, 30; m 54, 80; c 6. *Educ:* Univ PR, Mayaguez, BSCE, 54; Tex A&M Univ, MCE, 60, PhD(struct eng), 62. *Prof Exp:* Instr mech, Univ PR, Mayaguez, 54-59, prof struct eng, 62-69; exec dir, Commonwealth of PR, 69-73; chmn, Dept Civil Eng, 77-80, assoc dean eng, Univ PR, 83-86; prof eng, Carribean Univ, Bayamon. *Concurrent Pos:* Consult, PR Planning Bd, 63-69; vis scholar, Univ Calif, Berkeley, 76-77. *Mem:* Am Concrete Inst; Am Soc Civil Engrs; Am Soc Eng Educ; Earthquake Eng Res Inst. *Res:* Shear and diagonal tension in reinforced concrete members, especially beams. *Mailing Add:* Post No 63N Mayaguez PR 00680

SANTIDRIAN, SANTIAGO, NUTRITION, PROTEIN & CHOLESTEROL METABOLISM. *Current Pos:* asst prof biochem, Sch Med, 76-77, assoc prof physiol, 81-83, PROF PHYSIOL, UNIV NAVARRA, SPAIN, 87-, HEAD, DEPT PHYSIOL, 87- *Personal Data:* b Burgos, Spain, Nov 16, 50; m 79. *Educ:* Univ Navarra, Spain, BSc, 73, MB, 74, PhD(pharmaceut physiol), 76. *Prof Exp:* Postdoctoral fel nutrit biochem, Mass Inst Technol, 77-78, res assoc nutrit biochem physiol, 78-81; prof physiol, Univ Granada, Spain, 83-84; prof, Univ La Laguna, Spain, 84-87. *Concurrent Pos:* Res award, Royal Acad Pharm, 88. *Mem:* Am Inst Nutrit; Am Soc Animal Sci; NY Acad Sci. *Res:* Effect of hormones and diets on protein metabolism; effects of legumes on protein metabolism, immune response and cholesterol metabolism; effect of antibiotics on intestinal absorption of sugars and amino acids. *Mailing Add:* Dept Physiol Univ Navarra Sch Med Pamplona 31008 Spain

SANTILLI, ARTHUR A, ORGANIC CHEMISTRY. *Current Pos:* sr res scientist, 60-65, group leader, 65-86, res supvr & prin scientist, 86-88, RES FEL, WYETH-AYERST RES, 88- *Personal Data:* b Everett, Mass, July 25, 29; m 64; c 1. *Educ:* Boston Univ, AB, 51; Tufts Col, MS, 52; Univ Mass, PhD(chem), 58. *Prof Exp:* Asst chem, Univ Mass, 54-57; fel, Tufts Univ, 58-60. *Concurrent Pos:* Manuscript Reviewer, J Med Chem & Med Chem Res. *Mem:* Am Chem Soc; Int Union Pure & Appl Chem. *Res:* Synthesis of heterocyclic compounds of possible medicinal interest. *Mailing Add:* 1737 Sue Ellen Dr Havertown PA 19083-1227

SANTISTEBAN, GEORGE ANTHONY, NEUROENDOCRINOLOGY, CARDIOVASCULAR DISEASES. *Current Pos:* head, Dept Biol, Seattle Univ, 64-65, assoc prof, 68-75, prof, 75-84, EMER PROF BIOL, SEATTLE UNIV, 88- *Personal Data:* b Mex, Apr 12, 18; nat US; m 42; c 3. *Educ:* Univ Mont, BA, 45; Univ Utah, MA, 49, PhD(human anat), 51. *Prof Exp:* Asst zool, Univ Mont, 47-48; lectr anat, Univ Utah, 49-51, res instr anat & radiobiol, 51-53; asst prof anat, Med Col Va, 53-54; asst prof sch med, Univ Southern Calif, 54-59, asst prof physiol, 59-64. *Concurrent Pos:* Sr biologist, Pac Northwest Res Found, 68-; USPHS spec fel, Gothenburg Univ, 66-67; affil investr, Fred Hutchinson Cancer Ctr, 73- *Mem:* AAAS; Am Asn Cancer Res; NY Acad Sci; Am Asn Anat. *Res:* Effects of early experience as a modifying influence upon the function of the hypothalamus; psychosocial stress and development of hypertension, cardiovascular disease and malignancy; interrelationship between stress imprinting and intraneuronal RNA; psychosocial stress; hyperglycemia and tumor growth. *Mailing Add:* 9116 227th SW Edmonds WA 98029

SANTNER, JOSEPH FRANK, MATHEMATICAL STATISTICS, OPERATIONS RESEARCH. *Current Pos:* RETIRED. *Personal Data:* b Chicago, Ill, Aug 19, 19; m 46; c 5. *Educ:* St Louis Univ, BS, 50, MS, 52. *Prof Exp:* Mathematician, McDonnell Aircraft Corp, 52-54; opers res analyst, NAm Aviation, Inc, 54-55; lectr, Xavier Univ, Ohio, 55-58, asst prof, 58-62; math statistician, Robert A Taft Sanit Eng Ctr, US Dept Health, Educ & Welfare, 62-65, head math sci, 65-70; head math sci, Environ Protection Agency, 70-82. *Mem:* Am Statist Asn. *Res:* Mathematical logic; non-parametric statistical methods; design and analysis of experiments; applied mathematics. *Mailing Add:* 2124 Glenside Ave Cincinnati OH 45212

SANTNER, THOMAS JOSEPH, MATHEMATICAL STATISTICS, ANALYSIS OF DISCRETE DATA. *Current Pos:* PROF STATIST, DEPT STATIST, OHIO STATE UNIV, 89-, CHMN, DEPT STATIST, 92- *Personal Data:* b St Louis, Mo, Aug 29, 47; m 70, Gail DeFord; c Emily, Matthew, Abigail & Dominick. *Educ:* Univ Dayton, BS, 69; Purdue Univ, MS, 71, PhD(math statist), 73. *Prof Exp:* Fel, Nat Sci Found, 69-72; from asst prof to prof statist, Sch Opers Res & Indust Eng, Cornell Univ, 73-89. *Concurrent Pos:* Vis scientist & prin investr, NSF grant, 75-77, vis scientist & co-prin investr, 77-79; vis assoc prof biostatist, Univ Wash, 81-82; vis scientist, biometry br, Nat Cancer Inst, 78-79. *Mem:* Inst Math Statist; fel Am Statist Asn; Biometric Soc. *Res:* Analysis of discrete data; selection and ranking theory applied statistics. *Mailing Add:* Dept Statist Ohio State Univ 1958 Neil Ave 141 Cockins Hall Columbus OH 43210. *Fax:* 614-292-2096; *E-Mail:* tjs@osustat.mps.ohio_state.edu

SANTO, GERALD S(UNAO), PLANT NEMATOLOGY. *Current Pos:* PROF/NEMATOLOGIST, WASH STATE UNIV, 74- *Personal Data:* b Olaa, Hawaii, Dec 22, 44; m 68, Leatrice Y Miura; c Daron, Derek & Jeremy. *Educ:* Univ Hawaii, BS, 67, MS, 69; Univ Calif, Davis, PhD(plant path), 74. *Honors & Awards:* Ciba-Geigy Recognition Award, Soc Nematologists. *Mem:* Soc Nematologists (pres); Am Phytopath Soc; Coun Agr & Sci Technol; Orgn Trop Am Nematologists; Potato Asn Am; Europ Soc Nematologists. *Res:* Study of biology, pathogenicity and control of plant-parasitic nematodes on potato, mint, apple and grape. *Mailing Add:* Dept Plant Path Wash State Univ 24106 Bunn Rd Prosser WA 99350-9687. *Fax:* 509-786-9370; *E-Mail:* gsanto@tricity.wsu.edu

SANTORA, NORMAN JULIAN, CHEMICAL INFORMATION, QUANTITATIVE DRUG DESIGN. *Current Pos:* chem info specialist, 81-83, SR INFO CHEMIST, SMITH KLINE & FRENCH CORP, 84- *Personal Data:* b Camden, NJ, Sept 17, 35; m 62; c 3. *Educ:* Temple Univ, AB, 57, AM, 60, PhD(org chem), 65. *Prof Exp:* Asst chem, Temple Univ, 57-60 & 61-65; fel, Univ Pa, 65-68; res assoc med chem, Wm H Rorer, Inc, 68-81. *Concurrent Pos:* Adj prof comput sci, Spring Garden Col, 84- *Mem:* Am Chem Soc; Am Pharmaceut Asn. *Res:* Pyrimidine chemistry; synthesis and characterization of analogs of sulfonamides and nucleosides; quantitative structure-activity relationship studies. *Mailing Add:* 1323 Partridge Rd Roslyn PA 19001-2807

SANTORO, THOMAS, microbiology; deceased, see previous edition for last biography

SANTOS, EUGENE (SY), COMPUTER SCIENCE, MATHEMATICS. *Current Pos:* assoc prof, 68-74, PROF MATH, YOUNGSTOWN STATE UNIV, 74- *Personal Data:* b Manila, Philippines, Feb 15, 41; m 67; c 2. *Educ:* Mapua Inst Technol, BSME, 61; Univ Philippines, MSc, 63; Ohio State Univ, PhD(math), 65. *Prof Exp:* Instr math, Mapua Inst Technol, 62-63; teaching asst, Ohio State Univ, 63-65, asst prof, 65-68. *Mem:* Asn Comput Mach. *Res:* Theory of automata, computability and formal languages; software systems, artificial intelligence. *Mailing Add:* 3460 Almerinda Dr Canfield OH 44406

SANTOS, GEORGE WESLEY, ONCOLOGY, IMMUNOLOGY. *Current Pos:* from instr to assoc prof med, 62-68, PROF ONCOL & MED, 73-, PHYSICIAN, SCH MED, JOHNS HOPKINS UNIV, 62- *Personal Data:* b Oak Park, Ill, Feb 3, 28; m 52, Joanne A Corrigan; c Susan (Carey), George W II, Kelly A & Amy C (Cauley). *Educ:* Mass Inst Technol, BS & MS, 51; Johns Hopkins Univ, MD, 55; Am Bd Internal Med, dipl, 62. *Hon Degrees:* Doctoris Med Grad Honoris Causa, Ludwig-Maximillians-Univ Munich, 89. *Honors & Awards:* Bristol-Meyers Award, 88. *Prof Exp:* Intern med, Johns Hopkins Hosp, 55-56, asst resident, 58-60, fel, 60-62. *Concurrent Pos:* Leukemia Soc scholar, 61-66; asst dir med oncol unit, Baltimore City Hosps, 62-, asst physician-in-chief, 63-65; mem, Cancer Clin Investigative Rev Comt & Immunol-Epidemiol Spec Virus-Cancer Prog, NIH, 69-73 & Cell Biol-Immunol-Genetics Res Evaluations Comt, Vet Admin, 69-71; chmn, Bone Marrow Transplant Registry & mem, Int Comt Organ Transplant Registry, Am Col Surgeons-NIH, 69-73; mem bd dir, Leukemia Soc Am, 73-76 & Am Nat Bd, Trustees, 87. *Mem:* Am Soc Hemat; Transplantation Soc; Am Asn Immunologists; Am Asn Cancer Res; Int Soc Exp Hemat. *Res:* Transplantation immunology. *Mailing Add:* Oncol 3-127 Johns Hopkins Hosp 600 N Wolfe Baltimore MD 21287. *Fax:* 410-955-1969

SANTOS-BUCH, CHARLES A, EXPERIMENTAL PATHOLOGY. *Current Pos:* assoc prof, 68-76, assoc dean, 70-74, PROF MATH, MED COL, CORNELL UNIV, 76-; DIR, PAPANICOLAOU CYTOL LAB, NEW YORK HOSP, 79- *Personal Data:* b Santiago, Cuba, Mar 20, 32; US citizen; m 56; c 3. *Educ:* Harvard Univ, BA, 53; Cornell Univ, MD, 57. *Prof Exp:* Asst path, Med Col, Cornell Univ, 58-61, instr neuropath, 61-62; from asst prof to prof path, Sch Med, Emory Univ, 62-68. *Concurrent Pos:* USPHS res training fel, 59-62; Markle scholar acad med, 64. *Mem:* Am Soc Exp Path; Am Asn Path & Bact; NY Acad Sci; Pan-Am Med Asn; Am Soc Cytol. *Res:* Diseases of small arteries; high resolution enzyme histochemistry; immunology of hypersensitivity diseases; molecular and biochemical parasitology. *Mailing Add:* Dept Path Cornell Univ Med Col 525 & 68th St New York NY 10021-4896

SANTOS-MARTINEZ, JESUS, PHYSIOLOGY, PHARMACOLOGY. *Current Pos:* mem fac, Dept Physiol & Pharmacol, 79-86, PROF & CHMN, DEPT PHARMACOL, SCH MED, UNIV CENT DEL CARIBE, 86-, DIR PROG GRAD STUDIES, 89- *Personal Data:* b Vieques, PR, Mar 5, 24; m 55, Maria F de Jesus; c Jose A, Miguel A, Jose R & Magali P. *Educ:* Univ PR, BS, 46; Univ Ill, MS, 48; Purdue Univ, PhD(pharmacol), 54. *Prof Exp:* Asst instr pharm, Col Pharm, Univ PR, San Juan, 46-47, instr, 47-51, asst prof pharmacol, 51-55, from asst prof to prof physiol, Sch Med, 55-72, lectr pharmacol, Sch Pharm, 58, prof basic sci & chmn dept, Sch Dent, 72-76, prof pharmacol, Sch Med, 76-80. *Concurrent Pos:* Nat Inst Arthritis & Metab Dis fel, Med Ctr, Ind Univ, 66-67; vis prof, Univ Col WI, 60 & Sch Med, Univ Nicaragua, 62. *Mem:* AAAS; Am Physiol Soc; Am Soc Nephrology; Int Soc Nephrology; Soc Exp Biol Med. *Res:* Renal physiology; electrolyte distribution. *Mailing Add:* Dept Pharmacol Univ Central Caribe Sch Med Call Box 60-327 Bayamon PR 00960-6032

SANTULLI, THOMAS V, SURGERY. *Current Pos:* Assoc prof, 55-67, CHIEF PEDIAT SURG, COL PHYSICIANS & SURGEONS, COLUMBIA UNIV, 55-, PROF SURG, 67- *Personal Data:* b New York, NY, Mar 16, 15; m 43; c 2. *Educ:* Columbia Univ, BS, 35; Georgetown Univ, MD, 39; Am Bd Surg, dipl, 47, cert spec competence pediat surg, 75. *Concurrent Pos:* Consult, Monmouth Mem & Fitkin Mem Hosps, NJ, 50-, St Joseph's Hosp, Yonkers, NY, 53- & St Joseph's Hosp, Stamford, Conn, 59-; attend surgeon, Presby Hosp, NY, 60- *Mem:* Fel Am Col Surg; fel Am Acad Pediat; Am Surg Asn; Am Pediat Surg Asn (pres, 80-81); Brit Asn Pediat Surg. *Res:* Pediatric surgery. *Mailing Add:* 3959 Broadway Babies Hosp NYC New York NY 10032-1537

SANUI, HISASHI, BIOPHYSICS & CELL PHYSIOLOGY, ION TRANSPORT & MEMBRANES. *Current Pos:* RETIRED. *Personal Data:* b Orosi, Calif, Jan 7, 24; m 54, Peggy T Furuhashi; c Lester M & Sharon K (Sakanashi). *Educ:* Univ Calif, AB, 51, PhD(biophys), 58. *Prof Exp:* Jr res physiologist, Univ Calif, Berkeley, 57-59, lectr physiol, 60-61, from asst res physiologist to res physiologist, 61-86. *Mem:* AAAS; Am Physiol Soc; Biophys Soc; NY Acad Sci; Sigma Xi; Am Soc Cell Biol. *Res:* Active ion transport by living cells; subcellular morphology and biochemistry; ion binding by biological materials; atomic absorption spectrophotometry; role of cell membrane and ions in cell transformation; role of inorganic cations in cell growth regulation; mechanisms of heavy metal action on cells. *Mailing Add:* 506 Albemarle St El Cerrito CA 94530

SANWAL, BISHNU DAT, TISSUE CULTURE, MOLECULAR BIOLOGY. *Current Pos:* PROF BIOCHEM, UNIV WESTERN ONT, 73- *Educ:* Fed Inst Technol, Zurich, DSc(bot), 53. *Mailing Add:* Dept Biochem Univ Western Ont London ON N6A 5C1 Can. *Fax:* 519-661-3175

SANYER, NECMI, WOOD CHEMISTRY. *Current Pos:* supvry chemist, 59-73, SUPVR RES CHEM, FOREST PRODS LAB, US FOREST SERV, 73- *Personal Data:* b Konya, Turkey, Oct 5, 19; nat US; m 53; c 2. *Educ:* Inst Agr, Ankara, Turkey, BS, 41; State Univ NY, MS, 50, PhD, 53. *Prof Exp:* Hibbert Mem fel, McGill Univ, 53-54; res chemist, Mead Corp, 54-59. *Mem:* Fel Am Inst Chemists; Am Chem Soc. *Res:* Lignin, cellulose and pulping chemistry. *Mailing Add:* 1442 W Skyline Dr Madison WI 53705-1135

SANZONE, GEORGE, CHEMICAL PHYSICS, CHEMICAL KINETICS. *Current Pos:* asst prof, 69-81, ASSOC PROF CHEM, VA POLYTECH INST & STATE UNIV, 81- *Personal Data:* b Brooklyn, NY, Jan 13, 34; m 56; c 3. *Educ:* Univ Ill, Urbana, BS, 65, MS, 67, PhD(chem), 69. *Prof Exp:* Designer, Burton Rodgers, Inc, Ohio, 59-60; proj engr, Bendix Corp, 60-63; engr dept chem, Univ Ill, Urbana, 63-65. *Mem:* Am Chem Soc; Am Phys Soc; Am Soc Mass Spectros. *Res:* High temperature, fast chemical reaction studies employing shock tubes with mass spectrometric and optical detection techniques; molecular beam fluorescence; reactions in high-velocity flows. *Mailing Add:* Chem Va Polytech Inst PO Box 0212 Blacksburg VA 24063-0001

SAPAKIE, SIDNEY FREIDIN, CHEMICAL ENGINEERING, FOOD ENGINEERING. *Current Pos:* Res engr, Gen Mills Inc, 67-70, group leader, Betty Crocker Div, 70-73, asst prod mgr mkt, Protein Div, 73-74, develop leader, Spec Technol Activ, 74-77, dir res, Gorton Group, 77-78, dir, Subsid Res & Develop, 78-80, appl eng & new process develop, 80-84, res & develop, Big G Div, 84-90, vpres cereaL res & technol, 90-94, VPRES INT RES & DEVELOP, GEN MILLS INC, 94- *Personal Data:* b Port Chester, NY, May 10, 45; m 72, Linda Fuller; c Rebecca & Johanna. *Educ:* Univ Mich, BSChEng, 67; Univ Minn, MBA, 72. *Concurrent Pos:* Adj fac, Dept Food Sci, Univ Minn; dir, Am Inst Chem Engrs. *Mem:* Am Inst Chem Engrs; Inst Food Technologists; Am Asn Cereal Chemists. *Res:* Food sterilization, especially thermal processing, aseptic processing and microwave processing; food extrusion, especially math modeling and development; engineering economics; cereal processing. *Mailing Add:* Gen Mills Inc 9000 Plymouth Ave N Minneapolis MN 55427

SAPATNEKAR, SACHIN SURESH, COMPUTER AIDED DESIGN OF VERY LARGE SCALE INTEGRATED SYSTEMS, DIGITAL HARDWARE DESIGN. *Current Pos:* ASSOC PROF ELEC ENG, UNIV MINN, 97- *Educ:* Indian Inst Technol, Bombay, BTech, 87; Syracuse Univ, MS, 89; Univ Ill, PhD(elec eng), 92. *Honors & Awards:* Fac Early Career Develop Award, NSF, 95. *Prof Exp:* Mem tech staff, Tex Instruments Inc, 90; asst prof elec & comput eng, Iowa State Univ, 92-97. *Concurrent Pos:* Prin investr, NSF, 95; consult, Cadence Design Systs Inc, 95-96. *Mem:* Inst Elec & Electronics Engrs; Asn Comput Mach. *Res:* Computer aided design strategies and algorithms for very large scale integrated systems; estimating and optimizing the timing and power of circuits and on the automated layout design of very large scale integrated circuits. *Mailing Add:* 201 Coover Hall Dept Elec Eng Iowa State Univ Ames IA 50011. *E-Mail:* sachin@iastate.edu

SAPEGA, A(UGUST) E(DWARD), ELECTRICAL ENGINEERING. *Current Pos:* From instr to assoc prof, 51-67, chmn dept, 71-81, PROF ENG, TRINITY COL, CONN, 67- *Personal Data:* b Bridgeport, Conn, Dec 10, 25; m 55; c 2. *Educ:* Columbia Univ, BS, 46, MS, 51; Worcester Polytech Inst, PhD, 72. *Mem:* Am Soc Mech Engrs; Inst Elec & Electronics Engrs. *Res:* Electrical engineering circuits and devices; semiconductor physics and circuits; computer applications. *Mailing Add:* 27 Pelham Rd West Hartford CT 06107-2717

SAPEGA, ALEXANDER ANDREW, SPORTS MEDICINE, KNEE ARTHROSCOPY. *Current Pos:* fel orthop surg res, 81-82, asst instr, 82-85, ASSOC PROF ORTHOP SURG, UNIV PA SCH MED, PHILADELPHIA, 86-, ASST PROF ORTHOP SURG HOSP UNIV PA, 92- *Personal Data:* b Chicago, Ill, Oct 23, 52; m 77, Sally; c Marissa & Danielle. *Educ:* Cornell Univ, BS, 75; Temple Univ Sch Med, MD, 80; Am Bd Orthop Surg, dipl, 89. *Honors & Awards:* Elizabeth Winston Lanier Award, Am Acad Orthop Surgeons, Orthop Res Soc, 86. *Prof Exp:* Clin res assoc, Inst Sports Med & Athletic Trauma, Dept Orthop Surg, Lenox Hill Hosp, New York, NY, 75-76; asst lab instr clin anat, Temple Univ Sch Allied Health Sci, Philadelphia, 78-80, clin instr orthop surg, Dept Orthop Surg, Sch Med, 85-86; surg internship, Hosp Univ Pa, Philadelphia, 80-81. *Concurrent Pos:* Clin residency orthop surg, Hosp Univ Pa, Philadelphia, 82-85, attend staff, 86-; fel arthroscopic & athletic trauma surg, Temple Univ Ctr Sports Med & Sci, Philadelphia, 85-86; attend surg staff, Dept Orthop Surg, Temple Univ Hosp, Philadelphia, 85-86; assoc investr, NIH Grant, 82-85; Richards Mfg Corp med res grant, 82, Vet Admin Merit Rev grant renewal, 82, 85-86 & 88-90; prin investr, Advan Technol Ctr Southeastern Pa Partnership Challenge Grant, 86 & NIH, 89; attend staff, Dept Orthop Surg, Grad Hosp, Philadelphia, 86-, Mt Sinai Hosp, Philadelphia 89-; chief, Sports Med Serv, Philadelphia Vet Admin Hosp, 86-92; lectr var univs & hosps. *Mem:* Orthop Res Soc; Can Asn Appl Sports Sci; Arthroscopy Asn NAm; Am Orthop Soc Sports Med; fel Am Acad Orthop Surgeons. *Res:* Knee ligament biomechanics and applied anatomy; muscle metabolism and physiology; knee injuries and surgery; author of numerous publications and granted 2 patents. *Mailing Add:* Penn Sports Med Ctr Univ Pa 235 S 33rd St Philadelphia PA 19104. *Fax:* 215-349-5847

SAPER, CLIFFORD B, NEUROBIOLOGY, NEUROLOGY. *Current Pos:* CHIEF NEUROL, BETH ISRAEL HOSP, 92-; CHMN, DEPT NEUROL, HARVARD MED SCH, 92-, JAMES JACKSON PUTNAM PROF NEUROL & NEUROSCI, 92- *Personal Data:* b Chicago, Ill, Feb 20, 52; m 73; c 3. *Educ:* Univ Ill, BS & MS, 72; Wash Univ, PhD(neurobiol) & MD, 77. *Hon Degrees:* MA, Harvard Univ, 92. *Honors & Awards:* Jacob Javits Neurosci Award, Nat Inst Neurol & Commun Dis & Stroke. *Prof Exp:* Intern med, Jewish Hosp St Louis, 77-78; resident neurol, NY Hosp-Cornell Med Ctr, 78-81; asst prof neurol & anat, Sch Med, Wash Univ, 81-85; from assoc prof to prof pharm, physiol & neurol, Univ Chicago, 85-92, chmn neurol biol, 87-92. *Concurrent Pos:* Teacher-investr Develop Award, Nat Inst Neurol & Commun Dis & Stroke, 81; McKnight Found scholar, 83; ed chief, J Comp Neurol, 94- *Mem:* Soc Neurosci; Am Acad Neurol; Am Physiol Soc; Am Asn Anatomists; AAAS; Am Neurol Asn. *Res:* Neuroanatomy and neurophysiology of central nervous system control of the cardiovascular system and its integration with ongoing behaviour and arousal. *Mailing Add:* Beth Israel Hosp Dept Neurol 330 Brookline Ave Boston MA 02215. *Fax:* 617-667-2987; *E-Mail:* csaper@idmc.harvard.edu

SAPER, MARK A, MACROMOLECULAR CRYSTALLOGRAPHY, PROTEIN STRUCTURE. *Current Pos:* ASST PROF, UNIV MICH, 90- *Personal Data:* b New York, NY, Sept 29, 54; m 85; c 3. *Educ:* Univ Conn, BS, 76; Rice Univ, PhD(biochem), 83. *Prof Exp:* Res assoc, Rice Univ, 83-84 & Weizmann Inst Sci, 84-86; res assoc, Howard Hughes Med Inst, Harvard Univ, 86-90. *Mem:* Am Crystallographic Asn; Protein Soc. *Res:* Answering immunological questions using the techniques of structural biology; protein phosphatases and plant lectins with x-ray crystallography. *Mailing Add:* Biophys Res Div Univ Mich 3040 Chem Bldg 930 N University Ave Ann Arbor MI 48109-1055. *Fax:* 313-764-3323; *E-Mail:* saper@umich.edu

SAPERS, GERALD M, FOOD SCIENCE. *Current Pos:* res chemist, 68-80, res leader, 80-85, RES FOOD TECHNOLOGIST, EASTERN REGIONAL RES CTR, AGR RES SERV, USDA, 85- *Personal Data:* b Brookline, Mass, Jan 17, 35; m 60, Eleanor Clark; c Steven P & Tamara B. *Educ:* Mass Inst Technol, SB & SM, 59, PhD(food technol), 61. *Prof Exp:* Food scientist, Pioneering Res Div, US Army Natick Labs, 61-63; sr res assoc, Lever Bros Co, NJ, 63-64; unit leader food res, Corn Prod Food Technol Inst, Mass, 64-68. *Mem:* AAAS; Inst Food Technologists; Am Chem Soc. *Res:* Flavor chemistry and stability of dehydrated potato products and other dehydrated foods; quality of fruit and vegetable products; fruit and vegetable processing; natural pigments; home canning safety. *Mailing Add:* 812 Triumphe Way Warrington PA 18976. *Fax:* 215-233-6406

SAPERSTEIN, ALVIN MARTIN, THEORETICAL PHYSICS, PEACE & CONFLICT STUDIES. *Current Pos:* assoc prof, Wayne State Univ, 63-68, dir, Prog Environ Studies, 78-80, chmn exec bd & dir res, Ctr Peace & Conflict Studies, 85-87, secy, Fac Coun, Col Sci, 92-93, PROF PHYSICS, WAYNE STATE UNIV, 68- *Personal Data:* b Bronx, NY, June 3, 30; m 56, Harriet; c Shira & Rina. *Educ:* NY Univ, BA, 51; Yale Univ, MS, 52, PhD(physics), 56. *Prof Exp:* Asst physics, Yale Univ, 52, res asst, 52-56; res physicist, Eng Res Inst, Univ Mich, 56-57; res assoc, Brown Univ, 57-59, Argonne Nat Lab, 62-63; asst prof physics, Univ Buffalo, 59-62. *Concurrent Pos:* NSF res grant, 65-67 & 67-71; hon res assoc, Univ Col, Univ London, 69-70 & 76-77; prof sci & technol, Weekend Col, Wayne State Univ, 74-75; vis prof, Open Univ, Eng, 76-77, 84; vis res fel, Stockholm Int Peace Res Inst, 83, Int Inst Strategic Studies, London, 84; mem exec bd, Ctr Peace & Conflict Studies, Wayne State Univ; Fulbright res scholar, Peace Res Inst Oslo, Norway, 87; vis prof, dept physics, Univ Md, 94; William Foster fel, US Arms Contol & Disarmament Agency, 94-95; chair, Forum on Physics & Soc Am Phys Soc, 94-95; ed, Physics & Soc, 96- *Mem:* Fel AAAS; fel Am Phys Soc; Fedn Am Sci; Am Asn Physics Teachers; Union Concerned Scientists. *Res:* Scattering of nucleons from nucleons and nuclei; general theory of nuclear reactions; elementary particle reactions; general scattering theory; interaction between science and society; chaos and models of war initiation and war fighting; mathematical models of military strategy and international relations; use of computers in teaching elementary physics. *Mailing Add:* Dept Physics Wayne State Univ Detroit MI 48202. *Fax:* 313-577-3932; *E-Mail:* ams@hal.physics.wayne.edu

SAPERSTEIN, DAVID DORN, PHYSICAL CHEMISTRY. *Current Pos:* adv scientist, Instruments Div, IBM, 81-84, tech support mgr, 84-85, adv chemist, Storage Systs Div, 85-90, ADVAN DISK DEVELOP MGR, IBM, 91- *Personal Data:* b New York, NY, June 30, 46; m 76; c Robert E. *Educ:* Johns Hopkins Univ, BA, 67; NY Univ, PhD(chem), 73. *Prof Exp:* Sr res chemist, Merck Sharp & Dohme Res Labs, 73-77, res fel, 77-81. *Concurrent Pos:* Chmn, Western Spectros Asn, 87. *Mem:* Am Chem Soc; AAAS; Soc Appl Spectros; Western Spectros Asn (secy, 83-86). *Res:* Molecular investigations using physical, spectroscopic and analytic chemical methods; vibrational spectroscopy of adsorbates on surfaces; structure and properties of amorphous carbon. *Mailing Add:* Stor Media 385 Reed St Santa Clara CA 95050. *E-Mail:* dsaperstein@ibm.com

SAPERSTEIN, LEE W(ALDO), MINING ENGINEERING, ENVIRONMENTAL ENGINEERING. *Current Pos:* DEAN & PROF MINING ENG, SCH MINES & METALL, UNIV MO, ROLLA, 93- *Personal Data:* b New York, NY, July 14, 43; m 67, Priscilla F Hickson; c Adam G & Clare F. *Educ:* Mont Sch Mines, BS, 64; Oxford Univ, DPhil(eng sci), 67. *Prof Exp:* From asst prof to assoc prof mining eng, Pa State Univ, 67-78, prof & sect chmn, 78-87; prof & chmn mining eng, Univ Ky, 87-93. *Concurrent Pos:* Mem comt mineral technol, Nat Res Coun, 76-78, comt surface mining & reclamation, 78-79 & comt abandoned mine lands, 85-86; chmn, Eng Accreditation Comn, Accreditation Bd Eng & Technol, 89-90; dir, Accreditation Bd Eng & Technol, 92-, secy, 95-97. *Mem:* Distinguished mem Soc Mining, Metall & Explor; Nat Soc Prof Engrs; Soc Eng Educ; fel Accreditation Bd Eng & Technol. *Res:* Materials handling in mines and tunnels; rapid excavation; noise in underground mines; rock fragmentation; mined-land reclamation; surface mining for coal; quarries; pre-mining planning; mining training, subsidence, advances in mining sciences. *Mailing Add:* Univ Mo-Rolla 305 V H McNutt Hall Rolla MO 65409-0810. *Fax:* 573-341-4192; *E-Mail:* saperste@umr.edu

SAPERSTEIN, SIDNEY, NUTRITION. *Current Pos:* asst dir nutrit sci, Syntex Labs, Inc, 71-73, prin scientist, Inst Agr Sci Nutrit, 73-78, clin trials mgr, 78-81, ASSOC DIR, SCI AFFAIRS, SYNTEX LABS, INC, 81- *Personal Data:* b Brooklyn, NY, Apr 2, 23; m 47; c 3. *Educ:* Brooklyn Col, AB, 47; Univ Calif, Los Angeles, MA, 48; Univ Calif, PhD(microbiol), 53. *Prof Exp:* Asst bact, Univ Calif, 49-53; res assoc antileukemics, Col Dent, NY Univ, 53-54; bacteriologist, Borden Co, 54-56, supvr microbiol res & develop, Borden Spec Prod Co, 56-65, res assoc, 65-66, dir res pharmaceut div, Borden Foods Co, 67-71. *Concurrent Pos:* Mem tech adv group, Comn Nutrit, Am Acad Pediat, 75-81. *Mem:* Am Chem Soc; Am Inst Nutrit; Am Soc Clin Nutrit; AAAS; Sigma Xi; Am Dietetic Asn. *Res:* Bacteriology; biochemistry; allergy; nutrition; pharmacology. *Mailing Add:* 281 S Balsamina Way Portola Valley CA 94028

SAPHIER, DAVID, NEUROENDOCRINOLOGY, CENTRAL NERVOUS SYSTEM-IMMUNE SYSTEM INTERACTIONS. *Current Pos:* ASSOC PROF PHARMACOL, LA STATE UNIV MED CTR, SHREVEPORT, 90- *Personal Data:* b Bristol, UK, July 7, 57. *Educ:* Univ Col N Wales, Bangor, BSc, 75; Inst Biol, UK, CBiol & MIBiol, 75; Univ Cambridge, UK, PhD(neuroendocrinol), 86. *Honors & Awards:* Curt P Richter Prize, Int Soc Psychoneuroendocrinol, 88. *Prof Exp:* Sr scientist neurol, Hadassah Univ Hosp, Jerusalem, Israel, 83-90. *Concurrent Pos:* External lectr endocrinol, Hebrew Univ Med Sch, Jerusalem, Israel, 85-90; ed referee, numerous journals, 86-; consult, Teva Pharmaceut, Rehovot, Israel, 89-90. *Mem:* Int Soc Psychoneuroendocrinol; Europ Neurosci Asn; Soc Neurosci. *Res:* Neural regulation of adrenocortical secretion; effects of immunoactivation upon neural and neuroendocrine function; physiology of cotransmitter substances in relation to classical neurotransmission and neuroendocrine events. *Mailing Add:* Dept Pharmacol La State Univ Med Ctr Box 33932 Shreveport LA 71130-3932. *Fax:* 318-675-7857; *E-Mail:* dsaphi@lsumc.edu

SAPICO, FRANCISCO L, INFECTIOUS DISEASES, CLINICAL MICROBIOLOGY. *Current Pos:* from asst prof to assoc prof, 77-90, PROF MED, DEPT MED, UNIV SOUTHERN CALIF, 90-; PHYSICIAN SPECIALIST, RANCHO LOS AMIGOS MED CTR, 77-, CHIEF, INFECTIOUS DIS DIV, 95- *Personal Data:* b Manila, Philippines, July 18, 40; US citizen; m 69, Margaret; c Erica & Derek. *Educ:* Univ Philippines, MD, 65. *Prof Exp:* Rotating intern, Philippine Gen Hosp, 64-65 resident internal med, 65-67; resident internal med, State Univ NY Upstate Med Ctr, Syracuse, NY, 67-69; teaching fel infectious dis, Ctr Health Sci, Univ Calif, Los Angeles, 69-71, adj asst prof med, Dept Med, 72-77; res fel infectious dis, Wadsworth Vet Admin Ctr, 71-72, staff physician, Dept Med, 72-77. *Concurrent Pos:* Prof med, Dept Med, Univ Calif, Los Angeles, 72-77; assoc chief infectious dis, Rancho Los Amigos Med Ctr, 77-95, chmn, Hosp Inspection Comt, 85-91. *Mem:* Fel Am Col Physicians; fel Infectious Dis Soc Am; Am Soc Microbiol. *Res:* Anaerobic infections; soft tissue and bone infections; new antibiotics; methicillin-resistant staphylococci; infections in diabetics. *Mailing Add:* Rancho Los Amigos Med Ctr 7601 E Imperial Hwy Downey CA 90242

SAPIR, DANIEL GUSTAVE, MEDICINE. *Current Pos:* instr, 66-68, asst prof, 68-73, ASSOC PROF, SCH MED, JOHNS HOPKINS UNIV, 73- *Personal Data:* b Brussels, Belgium, May 21, 35; US citizen; m 62; c 2. *Educ:* Brown Univ, AB, 56; Johns Hopkins Univ, MD, 60. *Prof Exp:* Fel nephrol, Tufts New Eng Med Ctr, 64-66. *Concurrent Pos:* Consult var pvt & pub orgn, 67-; Irvine-Blum scholar, Sch Med, Johns Hopkins Univ, 77. *Mem:* Am Fedn Clin Res; Am Soc Nephrol; Sigma Xi. *Res:* Renal metabolism; nutrition. *Mailing Add:* 10755 Falls Rd No 320 Lutherville MD 21093

SAPIRSTEIN, JONATHAN ROBERT, ATOMIC & MOLECULAR PHYSICS. *Current Pos:* from asst prof to assoc prof, 84-92, PROF PHYSICS, UNIV NOTRE DAME, 92- *Personal Data:* b Los Angeles, Calif, Mar 1, 51; m 72, Patricia Northern; c Philip & David. *Educ:* Stanford Univ, Calif, BS, 73, PhD(physics), 79. *Prof Exp:* Researcher physics, Univ Calif, Los Angeles, 79-80, adj asst prof, 80-82; res assoc, Cornell Univ, 82-84. *Mem:* Fel Am Phys Soc. *Res:* Higher order quantum electrodynamics calculations in one electron atoms; many body perturbation theory calculations in heavy atomic systems. *Mailing Add:* Dept Physics Univ Notre Dame Notre Dame IN 46556. *Fax:* 219-631-5952; *E-Mail:* jonathan@atomic4.phys.nd.edu

SAPOLSKY, ASHER ISADORE, BIOCHEMISTRY. *Current Pos:* VIS SCIENTIST VOL RES, MIRIAM HOSP, 80- *Personal Data:* b Naroditch, Ukraine, USSR, Oct 2, 09; US citizen; m 40, Eva Rosenthal; c Walter T, Steven W & Wanda L (Needleman). *Educ:* Univ Pa, BS, 33; Philadelphia Col Pharm & Sci, BS, 35; Univ Miami Med Sch, PhD(biochem), 69. *Prof Exp:* Res asst prof, Univ Miami Sch Med, 69-79. *Mem:* Am Soc Biochem & Molecular Biol; Am Col Rheumatology; Orthop Res Soc. *Res:* Cartilage proteases which may be involved in the pathogenesis of osteoarthritis; discovered and isolated from human cartilage the neutral, metal-dependent proteoglycanase and now investigating possible inhibitors. *Mailing Add:* Miriam Hosp 205 Sessions St Providence RI 02906-3442

SAPONARA, ARTHUR G, BIOCHEMISTRY, MOLECULAR BIOLOGY. *Current Pos:* BIOCHEMIST, LOS ALAMOS NAT LAB, UNIV CALIF, 64- *Personal Data:* b Newark, NJ, Nov 27, 36; m 59; c 2. *Educ:* Rutgers Univ, AB, 58; Univ Wis, MS, 61, PhD(biochem), 64. *Mem:* AAAS; Am Chem Soc. *Res:* Amino acid activation in protein biosynthesis; ribonucleic acid biosynthesis and modification in mammalian cells. *Mailing Add:* 328 Venado Los Alamos NM 87544-2435. *E-Mail:* 7667.1323@compuserve.com

SAPONARO, JOSEPH A, MATHEMATICS. *Current Pos:* mgr, 69-79, vpres & gen mgr, 79-86, CHIEF EXEC OFFICER & PRES, INTERMETRICS INC, CAMBRIDGE, 86- *Personal Data:* b Boston, Mass, Sept 24, 39; m 60, Susan L. *Educ:* Mass Maritime Acad, BS, 59; Northeastern Univ, MS, 68. *Honors & Awards:* Appreciation Award for Apollo Work, Mass Inst Technol, 69; Appreciation Award for Space Shuttle Work, NASA, 73. *Prof Exp:* Third officer, Grace Lines, MMP, NY, 59-60; analyst, Harvard Univ, 60-62;

programmer, Sylvania, Needham, Mass, 62-64; proj mgr, Syst Develop Corp, Lexington, Mass, 64-69. *Concurrent Pos:* Bd dirs, Nat Security Indust Asn, 88-, Am Elec Asn, 89- & Mass High Tech Coun. *Mem:* Am Elec Asn; Nat Security Indust Asn (pres, 88-). *Mailing Add:* Intermetrics Inc 733 Concord Ave Cambridge MA 02138-1002

SAPORITO, MICHAEL S, REGULATION OF NEUROTROPHIC FACTOR EXPRESSION, MECHANISMS & MODELS OF NEURODEGENERATION. *Current Pos:* res scientist I, 91-92, res scientist II, 91-94, RES SCIENTIST III, CEPHALON, INC, 94- *Personal Data:* b Haddonfield, NJ, Apr 11, 61; m 90, Mary A Bryant. *Educ:* Juniata Col, BS, 83; Phila Col Pharm & Sci, PhD(pharmacol), 89. *Prof Exp:* Fel, Dept Neurol & Pharmacol, Robert Wood Johnson Med Sch, Univ Med & Dent NJ, 89-90, Gov Comt Ment Retardation & Develop Dis, 90-91. *Mem:* Soc Neurosci; NY Acad Sci. *Res:* Pharmacological regulation of neurotrophic factor expression as a potential strategy for treating non-degenerative disorders; mechanisms and models of neurodeneration, specifically Parkinson's disease; identification of novel targets for therapeutic intervention in neurodegenerative disorders. *Mailing Add:* Cephalon Inc 145 Brandywine Pkwy West Chester PA 19380. *Fax:* 215-344-0065; *E-Mail:* msaporit. cephalon@notes.ccmail.comuserve.com

SAPOROSCHENKO, MYKOLA, PHYSICS. *Current Pos:* from asst prof to assoc prof, 65-82, PROF PHYSICS & ASTRON, SOUTHERN ILL UNIV, CARBONDALE, 82- *Personal Data:* b Ukraine, May 19, 24; nat US; m 60; c 2. *Educ:* Ursinus Col, BS, 52; Wash Univ, AM, 54, PhD(physics), 58. *Prof Exp:* Asst prof physics, Univ Ark, 58-59 & Ill Inst Technol, 59-60; res assoc, Wash Univ, 60-62, asst prof, 62-65. *Mem:* Am Phys Soc. *Res:* Gaseous electronics; ion-molecule reactions; mass spectrometry; mrossbaner spectroscopy. *Mailing Add:* 1520 W Taylor Dr Carbondale IL 62901-4399

SAPORTA, SAMUEL, NEUROANATOMY, NEUROBIOLOGY. *Current Pos:* asst prof, 77-83, ASSOC PROF ANAT, UNIV SFLA, 83- *Personal Data:* b Athens, Greece, Mar 30, 46; m 70; c 2. *Educ:* Univ Calif, Davis, BA, 67; Univ Southern Calif, PhD(physiol psychol), 73. *Prof Exp:* Instr anat, Univ Calif, Los Angeles, 76, res asst, 76-77. *Concurrent Pos:* NIMH fel, 70-73, NIH fel, 74-76. *Mem:* Am Asn Anatomists; Soc Neurosci; Sigma Xi; AAAS; Int Asn Study Pain. *Res:* Neuroanatomical and physiological organization of the somatosensory system; response of the nervous system to damage. *Mailing Add:* Dept Anat Col Med Univ SFla 12901 N 30th St Tampa FL 33612. *E-Mail:* ssaporta@com1.med.usf.edu

SAPP, RICHARD CASSELL, LOW TEMPERATURE PHYSICS, MAGNETISM. *Current Pos:* from asst prof to assoc prof, 57-67, PROF PHYSICS, UNIV KANS, 67- *Personal Data:* b Kokomo, Ind, Sept 8, 28; m 57; c 2. *Educ:* Wilmington Col, BSc, 49; Ohio State Univ, PhD(physics), 55. *Prof Exp:* Res assoc physics, Ohio State Univ, 55; Welch Found fel, Rice Univ, 55-57. *Concurrent Pos:* Sloan Found fel, 62-64. *Mem:* Fel Am Phys Soc; Am Asn Physics Teachers. *Res:* Low temperature physics; magnetic relaxation; spin glasses; superconductivity. *Mailing Add:* 1021 Avalon Rd Lawrence KS 66044

SAPP, WALTER J, cell biology, for more information see previous edition

SAPPENFIELD, ROBERT W, MEDICINE. *Current Pos:* RETIRED. *Personal Data:* b Bedford, Ind, Oct 2, 24; m 48; c 3. *Educ:* Ind Univ, MD, 47. *Prof Exp:* Intern, Med Ctr, Ind Univ, 47-48 & 49, resident pediat, 49-51; resident, Chicago Contagious Dis Hosp, 48; resident, La Rabida Sanitarium Rheumatic Fever, 48-49; epidemiologist, State Bd Health, La, 51-52; from instr to assoc prof pub health & pediat, Sch Med, La State Univ Med Ctr, New Orleans, 53-63, prof prev med, pub health & pediat & head dept pub health & prev med, 63-72, assoc dean, 72-79, prof prev med & pub health, 79-88. *Concurrent Pos:* Res fel, Children's Hosp, 52-53; proj dir, Collab Child Develop Prog, Charity Hosp New Orleans, 60-62. *Mem:* Am Col Prev Med; Asn Teachers Prev Med; Am Acad Pediat. *Res:* Preventive medicine; pediatrics; epidemiology, especially communicable disease and perinatal problems. *Mailing Add:* 4809 Henican Pl Metairie LA 70003-1113

SAPPENFIELD, WILLIAM PAUL, AGRONOMY, PLANT BREEDING. *Current Pos:* from assoc prof to prof, 56-88, EMER PROF AGRON, UNIV MD, COLUMBIA, 89- *Personal Data:* b Lee's Summit, Mo, Apr 10, 23; m 51, Ruth E Yates; c Charles R, Mary Anne (Williams), William Jr & Eric. *Educ:* Univ Mo, BS, 48, PhD(plant breeding), 52. *Prof Exp:* Instr agron, Univ Mo, 48-51; agronomist, NMex State, 51-54 & Univ Calif, Davis, USDA, 54-56. *Concurrent Pos:* Mem, Nat Cotton Testing Comt, Crop Variety Regist Comt & Nat Comt Res Task Force Comt; chmn, Miss Delta Cotton Variety Testing Comt; rep comt cotton quality, State Agr Exp Sta, USDA; res grants, Cotton Inc; consult, 88- *Mem:* Am Soc Agron; Crop Sci Soc Am. *Res:* Cotton breeding, host plant resistance, and fiber technology; production systems; commercial cotton breeding and varietal development. *Mailing Add:* 115 Mango Cove Leesburg FL 34748-8608. *Fax:* 352-787-2911

SAPRA, VAL T, PLANT BREEDING, PLANT CYTOGENETICS. *Current Pos:* fel, 72-73, assoc prof plant breeding & plant cytogenetics, 73-80, PROF AGRON, ALA A&M UNIV, 80- *Personal Data:* b Beawar, India, Nov 15, 42; m 73. *Educ:* Kans State Univ, PhD(plant breeding, genetics), 72. *Prof Exp:* Res asst plant breeding, Govt of Rajastham, India, 65-68; res asst, Kans State Univ, 68-72. *Concurrent Pos:* Consult, Somdiaa, Paris, France; agronomist, WCent Africa. *Mem:* Crop Sci Soc Am; Am Soc Agron; Can Soc Genetics; Can Soc Agron. *Res:* Triticale breeding and cytogenetics; development of new triticale strains through conventional and mutation breeding procedures. *Mailing Add:* Dept Plant Sci Ala A&M Univ PO Box 285 Normal AL 35762-0285

SAPRU, HREDAY N, CIRCULATION, RESPIRATION. *Current Pos:* PROF PHARMACOL, UNIV MED & DENT, NJ MED SCH, NEWARK, 74- *Educ:* Columbia Univ, PhD(neuro-pharmacol), 74. *Mailing Add:* Dept Neurosurg & Dept Pharmacol MSB H586 NJ Med Sch 185 S Orange Ave Newark NJ 07103. *Fax:* 973-982-2333

SAR, MADHABANANDA, VETERINARY MEDICINE, PHYSIOLOGY. *Current Pos:* res assoc neuroendocrinol, Labs Reprod Biol, 69-77, res asst prof, 77-78, RES ASSOC PROF ANAT, SCH MED, UNIV NC, CHAPEL HILL, 78- *Personal Data:* b Palchakada, India, Dec 31, 33; m 56; c 3. *Educ:* Bihar Univ, BVSc & AH, 56; Mich State Univ, MS, 64, PhD(physiol), 68. *Prof Exp:* Vet asst surg, Dept Vet Serv & Animal Husb, India, 56-59; instr parasitol, Orissa Col Vet Sci & Animal Husb, 59-61; res assoc neuroendocrinol, Univ Chicago, 68-69, res assoc, 69-70, instr & res assoc pharmacol, 69. *Mem:* AAAS; Endocrine Soc; Soc Study Reprod; Int Brain Res Orgn; Am Physiol Soc. *Res:* Neuroendocrinology; endocrinology; reproductive physiology; hormone localization in brain and peripheral target tissues by autoradiography and immunohistochemistry. *Mailing Add:* Dept Cell Biol & Anat Div Health Affairs CB 7090 108 Taylor Hall Univ NC Chapel Hill NC 27599-0001. *Fax:* 919-966-1856

SARA, RAYMOND VINCENT, MATERIALS SCIENCE. *Personal Data:* b Carbondale, Pa, Jan 24, 27; m 52, Anne M Geschke; c Carl M, Robert J, Mary J & Stephen S. *Educ:* Pa State Univ, BS, 50, MS, 52. *Prof Exp:* Corp fel, UCAR Carbon Co, 52-92. *Concurrent Pos:* Consult. *Mem:* Am Ceramic Soc. *Res:* Phase equilibria and thermal behavior of refractory materials, mechanical and thermal properties of metal/non-metal fiber and ceramic composite systems, oxidation and diffusion phenomenon, oxidation protective coatings, graphitization and intercalation; abradable seals; high performance ceramics. *Mailing Add:* 22146 Meadow N Ct Cleveland OH 44145

SARABANDI, KAMAL, RADAR REMOTE SENSING, ELECTROMAGNETIC SCATTERING. *Current Pos:* asst res scientist, 89-92, asst prof, 92-96, ASSOC PROF, UNIV MICH, 96- *Personal Data:* b Tehran, Iran, Nov 4, 56; m 85, Shiva Goltalab-Rad; c Arya Joseph. *Educ:* Sharif Univ Technol, BS, 80; Univ Mich, MSE, 86, MS, 89, PhD(elec eng), 89. *Honors & Awards:* Second Prize, Inst Elec & Electronics Engrs Antenna & Propagation Soc, 95. *Prof Exp:* Microwave engr, Iran's Telecommun Res Ctr, 80-84. *Concurrent Pos:* Consult, TRW Co, 93, Phoenix Int 95-, Raytheon Co, 97; co-founder, EMG Technologies, Inc, 96-; prin investr, NASA, Gen Motors Corp, Army Res Off Naval Res, Army Res Lab & Jet Propulsion Lab. *Mem:* Sr mem Inst Elec & Electronics Engrs; Int Union Radio Sci; Electromagnetic Acad. *Res:* Microwave and millimeter-wave radar remote sensing; authored 60 papers. *Mailing Add:* 3118 EECS Bldg 1301 Beal Ave Ann Arbor MI 48109. *Fax:* 313-647-2106; *E-Mail:* saraband@eecs.umich.edu

SARACENO, ANTHONY JOSEPH, VENT STACK SAMPLING TECHNOLOGY, PROCESS CHEMISTRY. *Current Pos:* supvr, Chem & Mat Tech Dept, Martin Marietta Energy Systs, Inc, 84-89, supvr, Chem Technol Dept, 89-90, head, Chem Technol Dept, 90-93, HEAD, CHEM TECHNOL DEPT, MARTIN MARIETTA UTILITY SERVS, INC, 93- *Personal Data:* b Reggio, Italy, June 20, 33; nat US; m 70, Edith Landpraf; c Rochelle. *Educ:* St Vincent Col, BS, 55; Univ Notre Dame, PhD(chem), 58. *Prof Exp:* Res assoc, Univ Notre Dame, 56-58; res chemist, Gulf Res & Develop Co, 58-61; sr chemist, Pennwalt Corp, 61-64, proj leader, 65-67; group leader, Goodyear Atomic Corp, 67-73, sect head, 73-82, supvr, Chem Dept, 82-84. *Mem:* AAAS; Am Chem Soc. *Res:* Coordination compounds; solid state inorganic chemistry; inorganic polymers; infrared spectroscopy; organometallic compounds; lubricants; coatings; process development; air-water pollution control; halogen chemistry; metal corrosion. *Mailing Add:* 276 Crestwood Dr Forest Hills Waverly OH 45690-9658. *Fax:* 740-897-5734

SARACHEK, ALVIN, MICROBIOLOGY. *Current Pos:* DISTINGUISHED EMER PROF, 92- *Personal Data:* b Pittsburgh, Pa, July 29, 27; m 56, 76. *Educ:* Univ Mo, Kansas City, BA, 48, MA, 50; Kans State Univ, PhD(microbiol genetics), 58. *Prof Exp:* Instr biol, Univ Mo, Kansas City, 50-51; res assoc biol res lab, Univ Southern Ill, 51-54; fel microbial biochem, Inst Microbiol, Rutgers Univ, 57-58; from asst prof to prof, Wichita State Univ, 58-72, chmn dept biol, 61-74, distinguished prof natural sci, 72- *Concurrent Pos:* Microbial geneticist, US AEC, 65-66, mem adv comt prog in food irradiation, 67-72; chmn panel student oriented prog, NSF, 71-75; chmn grants & awards comt, Am Cancer Soc, Kans Div, 70-76, mem exec comt, 70-78; prof assoc, Sci Educ Directorate, NSF, 77-78; mem, Dept Energy adv coun life sci prog, Argonne Nat Lab, 78-80 & NSF adv panel, 81-; NATO sci fel, 81-; consult, Div Biol Energy Res, US Dept Energy, 80-; chair, External Peer Oversight Comt; NATO postdoctoral fel prog, NSF, 87-90; vis scientist to minority insts, Am Soc Microbiol. *Mem:* Am Cancer Soc; Am Soc Microbiol; Genetics Soc Am; Int Soc Human & Animal Mycol; fel Am Acad Microbiol. *Res:* Genetics and physiology of microorganisms; radiobiology; radiation genetics and chemical mutagenesis in fungi. *Mailing Add:* 1828 W 18th St No 1208 Wichita KS 67203

SARACHIK, EDWARD S, DYNAMIC METEOROLOGY, OCEANOGRAPHY. *Current Pos:* res prof, 88-93, PROF, DEPT ATMOSPHERIC SCI & ADJ PROF, SCH OCEANOG, UNIV WASH, 93- *Personal Data:* b New York, NY, Apr 22, 41; div. *Educ:* Queens Col, NY, BS, 60; Brandeis Univ, MS, 63, PhD(physics), 66. *Prof Exp:* Res assoc, Linear Acceleration Ctr, Stanford Univ, 65-67; staff physicist, Electronics Res Ctr, NASA, 67-70; staff mathematician, Dept Transport, Transport Systs Ctr, 70-71; NSF fel & res assoc meteorol, Mass Inst Technol, 71-73; res fel & lectr atmospheric physics, Harvard Univ, 73-78, res assoc & proj mgr, Ctr Earth & Planetary Physics, 78-83, sr res fel, Dynamical Meteorol & Oceanog, 83-85; oceanogr, Nat Oceanic & Atmospheric Admin/PAC Marine Environ Lab, Seattle, 84-87. *Concurrent Pos:* Mem, Climate Res Comt, Nat Acad Sci/Nat Res Coun, 85-88, Panel Model Assimilated Data Sets, 89-90, chair, Toga Panel, 92-96, mem, Deccen Panel, 95-, mem, Comt Global Change Res, 95-; assoc ed, J Atmospheric Sci, 81-90 & J Phys Oceanog, 84- *Mem:* Am Phys Soc; fel Am Meteorol Soc; Am Geophys Union; Oceanog Soc; Soc Indust & Appl Math. *Res:* The role of the ocean in climate variability and in climate prediction. *Mailing Add:* Dept Atmospheric Sci AK-40 Univ Wash Box 351640 Seattle WA 98195-1640. *Fax:* 206-685-3397; *E-Mail:* sarachik@utmas.washington.edu

SARACHIK, MYRIAM PAULA, SOLID STATE PHYSICS. *Current Pos:* from asst prof to prof, 65-94, DISTINGUISHED PROF PHYSICS, CITY COL NEW YORK, 95-. *Personal Data:* b Antwerp, Belgium, Aug 8, 33; US citizen; m 54, Philip; c Karen. *Educ:* Barnard Col, BA, 54; Columbia Univ, MS, 57, PhD(physics), 60. *Prof Exp:* From res asst to res assoc exp solid state physics, IBM Watson Lab, Columbia Univ, 55-61; mem tech staff, Bell Tel Labs, NJ, 62-64. *Concurrent Pos:* Exec officer, PhD prog Physics, City Univ New York, 75-78. *Mem:* Nat Acad Sci; fel NY Acad Sci; fel Am Phys Soc. *Res:* Magnetic and transport properties of semiconductors; disordered systems; semiconductors; the metal insulator transition; macroscopic quantum tunneling. *Mailing Add:* Dept Physics City Col New York Convent Ave at 138th St New York NY 10031. *E-Mail:* sarachik@sci.ccny.cuny.edu

SARACHIK, PHILIP E(UGENE), CONTROL SYSTEMS, COMMUNICATION NETWORKS. *Current Pos:* PROF ELEC ENG, POLYTECH UNIV, 73-. *Personal Data:* b New York, NY, Dec 3, 31; m 64; c 1. *Educ:* Columbia Univ, AB, 53, BS, 54, MS, 55, PhD(elec eng), 58. *Prof Exp:* Staff engr, Int Bus Mach Res Lab, NY, 58-60; from asst prof to assoc prof elec eng, Columbia Univ, 60-64; assoc prof, NY Univ, 64-67, prof elec eng, 67-73. *Concurrent Pos:* Consult, Aerospace Group, Gen Precision, Inc, 63-68; vis prof, control, commun & comput systs dept, Tel Aviv Univ, 79-80. *Mem:* fel Inst Elec & Electronics Engrs; Soc Indust & Appl Math. *Res:* Applications of computers to real time control systems; problems in optimal and adaptive control systems; management and control of communication networks. *Mailing Add:* Dept Elec Eng Polytech Univ 333 Jay St Brooklyn NY 11201

SARACINO, DANIEL HARRISON, EXISTENTIAL COMPLETENESS, HOMOGENEOUS STRUCTURES. *Current Pos:* from asst prof to assoc prof, 74-84, chmn, 86-95, PROF MATH, COLGATE UNIV, 84-, CHARLES A DANA PROF MATH, 92-. *Personal Data:* b Ellenville, NY, Mar 25, 47. *Educ:* Cornell Univ, AB, 68; Princeton Univ, MA, 70, PhD(math), 72. *Prof Exp:* Gibbs instr math, Yale Univ, 72-74. *Concurrent Pos:* Guest researcher, Math Inst, Heidelberg, Ger, 75; prin investr, NSF Res Grant, 76-78; vis asst prof, Wesleyan Univ, 77-78, vis assoc prof, 80-81, van Vleck vis assoc prof, 82-83, van Vleck vis prof, Wesleyan Univ, 90-96; vis Inst Advan Study, Princeton, 86. *Mem:* Asn Symbolic Logic. *Res:* Model-theoretic algebra; existential completeness and homogeneity in various algebraic contexts. *Mailing Add:* Dept Math Colgate Univ Hamilton NY 13346-1398

SARADA, THYAGARAJA, SPECTROSCOPY, POLYMERS. *Current Pos:* sr chemist, 82-84, mgr chem res, 85-, MGR PRINTING TECHNOL, PITNEY BOWES. *Personal Data:* b Madras, India, Apr 19, 29; US citizen. *Educ:* Annamalai Univ, Madras, BSc, 51; Am Univ, MS, 70, PhD(phys chem), 72. *Prof Exp:* Lectr & head, Dept Chem, St Mary's Col, Madras, 51-52, SPW Col, Tirupati, India, 52-63; prof, Am Univ, Wash, 63-67, head, Dept Chem, 52-67, fel phys chem, 73-74, res asst, 75-78, asst prof, 78-79; sr chemist, Celanese Res Co, 79-82. *Concurrent Pos:* Dreyfus & Camille Found fel, Am Univ, 73-74; sci pool officer, CLRI, Madras, 74-75; res asst, ERDA, 75-76 & US Defense, 76-78. *Mem:* Am Chem Soc; Tech Asn Paper Pulp Indust; Am Soc Test & Mat. *Res:* Optical properties of liquid crystals; physico-chemical, electrical properties and characterization of fuel cell electrolytes and electrodes; electrochemical corrosion, complex ion theory; membranes; fuel cells, batteries, lithium batteries; ink-paper interactions; adhesives; ink jet technology; piezoceramic materials; inks; flourescence; dyes. *Mailing Add:* 120 Homestead Lane Brookfield CT 06804

SARAKWASH, MICHAEL, STATISTICS, RELIABILITY & QUALITY CONTROL. *Current Pos:* RETIRED. *Personal Data:* b South River, NJ, Feb 20, 25; m 72, Elizabeth M Weaver. *Educ:* Columbia Univ, BS, 50; Stevens Inst Technol, MS, 58, PE, 78. *Prof Exp:* Mathematician, Evans Signal Lab, 50-53; sr qual control engr propeller div, Curtiss-Wright Corp, 53-58; sr mathematician reaction motors div, Thiokol Chem Corp, Denville, 58-63, reliability statistician reaction, Motors Div, Hiokol Chem Corp, Denville, NJ, 63-67; consult statist & exp design, MS Assocs, 67-74; sr reliability engr, Res-Cottrell, NJ, 74-77; consult statist, reliability, qual control & exp design, MS Assocs, 77-80; dir, statist & anal div, Mil Sealift Command, Motby, Bayonne, NJ, 80-87; consult probability theory, statist & assoc fields, MS Assocs, 87. *Mem:* Am Statist Asn; Am Soc Qual Control; NY Acad Sci. *Res:* Industrial quality control; marketing and market research; specialist in graphic statistics; reliability; industrial application of probability theory and statistics. *Mailing Add:* 377 Colfax Ave Clifton NJ 07013-1703

SARAN, CHITARANJAN, SAFETY, HEALTH & ENVIRONMENTAL PROTECTION. *Current Pos:* coordr, St Louis Degree Prog, 75-78 & 88-90, assoc prof, 75-80, PROF INDUST SAFETY & HYG, CENT MO STATE UNIV, WARRENSBURG, 80-. *Personal Data:* b Lucknow, India, Sept 22, 39; US citizen; m 69; c 1. *Educ:* Indian Inst Technol, BTech, 62, MTech, 63; NC State Univ, PhD(bioeng, agr eng), 67. *Prof Exp:* Asst, NC State Univ, 63-67; asst agr engr, Univ PR, 67-68, from instr to asst prof math, 68-71; USPHS Trainee, Med Ctr & Ctr Safety, NY Univ, 71-73, asst prof safety, Ctr Safety, 73-75. *Concurrent Pos:* Vis prof/scholar, Sweden, 86 & 90, India, 86-87 & Raleigh, 89. *Mem:* Am Soc Agr Engrs; Inst Eng, India; Am Soc Safety Engrs; Human Factors Soc; Sigma Xi; Safety, Health & Environ Protection Int. *Res:* Ergonomics, Safety, Health and Environmental Protection International and Holistic; loss control; applied to occupations, industries, and agriculture. *Mailing Add:* 191 SE 411 Warrensburg MO 64093-9307. *Fax:* 660-747-8065; *E-Mail:* csaran@cmsuvmb.cmsu.edu

SARANTAKIS, DIMITRIOS, MEDICINAL CHEMISTRY. *Current Pos:* GROUP LEADER ORG CHEM, WYETH LABS INC, PHILADELPHIA, PA, 71-. *Personal Data:* b Nafplion, Greece, May 20, 36; m 65; c 2. *Educ:* Nat Univ Athens, BSc, 59; Imp Col, dipl, 65, Univ London, PhD(org chem), 65. *Prof Exp:* Res fel org chem, Univ Leicester, 65-66; res assoc, Royal Res Estab, Greece, 66-67; res assoc, Univ Wash, 67-71; chief chemist, Fox Chem Co, 71. *Mem:* Am Chem Soc. *Res:* Synthesis of biologically active polypeptides; synthesis of biologically active organic compounds. *Mailing Add:* 262 Sentinel Ave Newtown PA 18940-1166

SARANTITES, DEMETRIOS GEORGE, NUCLEAR CHEMISTRY, NUCLEAR PHYSICS. *Current Pos:* assoc prof, 75-76, PROF NUCLEAR CHEM, WASHINGTON UNIV, 76-. *Personal Data:* b Athens, Greece, May 5, 33; m 65; c 1. *Educ:* Mass Inst Technol, PhD (nuclear and inorganic chem), 63. *Prof Exp:* Radiochemist, Cyclotron Lab, Mass Inst Technol, 60-63; res assoc nuclear chem, Washington Univ, 63-65, from asst prof to assoc prof, 65-74; vis prof, Res Inst Physics, Stockholm, 74-75. *Mem:* Am Phys Soc; Sigma Xi. *Res:* Investigations of nuclear reaction mechanisms and of nuclear structure with emphasis on the electromagnetic and nuclear properties of the high spin states. *Mailing Add:* 7132 Waterman Ave St Louis MO 63130

SARASON, DONALD ERIK, MATHEMATICS. *Current Pos:* from asst prof to assoc prof, 64-70, PROF MATH, UNIV CALIF, BERKELEY, 70-. *Personal Data:* b Detroit, Mich, Jan 26, 33. *Educ:* Univ Mich, BS, 55, AM, 57, PhD(math), 63. *Prof Exp:* Mem math, Inst Adv Study, 63-64. *Concurrent Pos:* NSF fel, 63-64; Sloan fel, 69-71. *Mem:* Am Math Soc; Math Asn Am. *Res:* Functional analysis. *Mailing Add:* Univ Calif Berkeley CA 94720-3840

SARASON, LEONARD, mathematics; deceased, see previous edition for last biography

SARAVANAMUTTOO, HERBERT IAN H, MECHANICAL ENGINEERING. *Personal Data:* b Monkton, Scotland, June 20, 33; Can citizen; m 60, Helen Buckner; c Colin, Malcolm & Neil. *Educ:* Glasgow Univ, BSc, 55; Bristol Univ, PhD(mech), 68. *Prof Exp:* Engr, Orenda Engines, 55-59; analyst, KCS Ltd, Toronto, 59; engr, Orenda Engines, 59-64; lectr mech eng, Bristol Univ, 64-70; assoc prof aerothermodyn, 70-75, prof mech & aeronaut eng & chmn dept, Carleton Univ, 75-80, 82-88; dir, Gas Tops Ltd, Ottawa, 80-94. *Concurrent Pos:* Consult, Rolls Royce Ltd, 66-70, Brit Aircraft Corp, 75 & Avionics Div, Smith's Indust, 75-76; vis res fel, Royal Naval Eng Col, 80-81. *Mem:* Fel Can Aeronaut & Space Inst (vpres, 78-79, pres 79-80); fel Brit Inst Mech Engrs; fel Am Soc Mech Engrs. *Res:* Dynamic response of gas turbines; improvement of part load performance; engine health monitoring. *Mailing Add:* Dept Mech & Aerospace Eng Carleton Univ Ottawa ON K1S 5B6 Can. *Fax:* 613-520-5715; *E-Mail:* hsaravan@alfred.ccs.carleton.ca

SARAVIA, NANCY G, IMMUNOPARASITOLOGY. *Current Pos:* SCIENTIST & GEN COORDR, ICIDR, TULANE UNIV, 85- *Educ:* Vanderbilt Univ, PhD(microbiol & immunol), 78. *Mailing Add:* CIDEIM Apdo Aereo 5390 Cali Colombia

SARAVIS, CALVIN, IMMUNOLOGY. *Current Pos:* ASSOC PROF SURG-BIOCHEM, HARVARD MED SCH, 84- *Personal Data:* b Englewood, NJ, Feb 27, 30; m 54; c 4. *Educ:* Syracuse Univ, AB, 51; WVa Univ, MS, 55; Rutgers Univ, PhD(zool), 58. *Prof Exp:* Asst physiol, serol & immunol, Rutgers Univ, 55-58; head antiserum prod & develop, Blood Grouping Lab, Mass, 58-59; dir immunochem lab, Blood Res Inst, Inc, 59-72; prin assoc surg & mem fac med, Harvard Med Sch, 71-84; res assoc, 74-83, ASSOC RES PROF PATH, SCH MED, BOSTON UNIV, 83- *Concurrent Pos:* Assoc med, Peter Bent Brigham Hosp, 61-69; res assoc, Harvard Med Sch, 62-71; chief, Immunol Div, Harvard Surg Unit, Boston City Hosp, 66-68; sr res assoc & asst dir, Gastrointestinal Res Lab, Mallory Inst Path Found, 74-; mem spec sci staff, Boston City Hosp & Mallory Inst Path, 78-; sr res assoc, Cancer Res Inst, New Eng Deaconess Hosp, Boston, 79- *Mem:* Transplantation Soc; Am Asn Immunologists. *Res:* Transplantation immunology; cancer immunology; isolation and identification of antibodies and antigens; hepatitis; detection, isolation and characterization of human cancer markers. *Mailing Add:* Dept Surg Harvard Med Sch 110 Evelyn Rd Newton MA 02168-1021. *Fax:* 617-732-9897

SARAZIN, CRAIG L, THEORETICAL ASTROPHYSICS. *Current Pos:* from asst prof to prof, 77-96, chmn, 92-95, W H VANDERBILT PROF ASTRON, UNIV VA, 96-. *Personal Data:* b Milwaukee, Wis, Aug 11, 50; m 71, Jane Curry; c Stephen & Andrew. *Educ:* Calif Inst Technol, BS, 72; Princeton Univ, MA, 74, PhD(physics), 75. *Honors & Awards:* Haren Fisher Physics Prize, 71. *Prof Exp:* Millikan fel physics, Calif Inst Technol, 75; mem, Inst Advan Study, 75-77. *Concurrent Pos:* Vis fel, Inst Astron, Cambridge Univ, 76 & 87; vis scientist, Nat Radio Astron Observ, 77-81; vis asst prof, astron dept, Univ Calif, Berkeley, 79; vis mem, Inst Advan Study, 81-82; Joint Inst Lab Astrophys vis fel, Univ Colo & Nat Bur Stand, 85-86; vis prof, Scuola Normale, Pisa, 92; vis scientist, Inter-Univ, Ctr Astron & Astrophys, Dune, India, 95. *Mem:* Am Astron Soc; Int Astron Union. *Res:* Interstellar medium; clusters of galaxies; x-ray emission; extragalactic astronomy. *Mailing Add:* Dept Astron Univ Va PO Box 3818 Charlottesville VA 22903-0818. *Fax:* 804-924-3104; *E-Mail:* cls7i@virginia.edu

SARBACH, DONALD VICTOR, product engineering, elastomers marketing; deceased, see previous edition for last biography

SARBER, RAYMOND WILLIAM, MEDICAL BACTERIOLOGY. *Current Pos:* RETIRED. *Personal Data:* b Hammond, Ind, Apr 15, 16; m 37, Nilo P Miller; c Nancy S (Simmons) & Judith L (Petrie). *Educ:* Western Mich Univ, AB, 38; Univ Cincinnati, MS, 41. *Prof Exp:* Asst bact, Univ Mich, 40; asst prof col pharm, Univ Cincinnati, 40-42; sr res bacteriologist, Parke, Davis & Co, 42-59; exec secy, Am Acad Microbiol, 68-78; exec secy, Am Soc Microbiol, 59-82, emer exec secy, 82-85; exec secy, Nat Pediat Infectious Dis Sem, 81-90. *Concurrent Pos:* Consult, Clopay Corp, 41-43; ed, Am Soc Microbiol News, 59-72; registr, Nat Registry Microbiol, 68-74; secy, Am Bd Med Microbiol, 68-74; secy gen, XIII Int Cong Microbiol, 81. *Mem:* Am Soc Microbiol; Sigma Xi; AAAS. *Res:* Tuberculosis antigens; tuberculins; pertussis, biological and chemical tuberculosis antigens; germicide testing methods; tissue culture. *Mailing Add:* 2212 Great Falls St Falls Church VA 22046

SARCHET, BERNARD REGINALD, ENGINEERING MANAGEMENT. *Current Pos:* chmn, Dept Eng Mgt, Univ Mo, Rolla, 67-81, exec dir, External Affairs, 75-79, prof, 67-87, EMER PROF ENG MGT, UNIV MO, ROLLA, 87- *Personal Data:* b Byesville, Ohio, June 13, 17; m 41, Lena V Fisher; c Renee (Erickson), Dawne & Melanie (Koewing). *Educ:* Ohio State Univ, BChE, 39; Univ Del, MChE, 41. *Prof Exp:* Asst, Univ Del, 39-41; operator, Eng & Construct Div, Koppers Co, Inc, Pa, 41-42, gen foreman, Butadiene Div, 42-45, supv chem engr, Res Div, 45-46, supvr, Eng & Construct Div, 46-47, mgr, Oil City Plant, 47-50, mgr, Kobuta Plant, 50-53, asst mgr sales, Chem Div, 54-56, mgr, Develop Dept, 56-58, mgr prod develop, Plastics Div, 58-61, mgr, Panel Dept, 61-64, dir com develop, 64-67. *Mem:* Am Chem Soc; fel Am Soc Eng Educ; Am Inst Chem Engrs; fel Am Soc Eng Mgt. *Res:* Absorption distillation; robotics and impact on management; housing construction panels; engineering management; co-authored two books and nearly 50 articles. *Mailing Add:* PO Box 68 Rolla MO 65401-0068. *E-Mail:* sarchet@shuttle.cc.umr.edu

SARCIONE, EDWARD JAMES, BIOCHEMISTRY. *Current Pos:* RETIRED. *Personal Data:* b Lawrence, Mass, Dec 3, 25; m 53; c 3. *Educ:* St Michael's Col, BS, 48; Univ Kans, PhD(biochem), 57. *Prof Exp:* Biochemist, Dept Pub Health, Mass, 49-50; asst instr biochem, Sch Med, Univ Kans, 50-55; assoc cancer res scientist, Roswell Park Mem Inst, 55-72, prin cancer res scientist & prof & chmn physiol oneg, 72-91. *Mem:* AAAS; Am Soc Biol Chemists; Am Chem Soc; Am Asn Cancer Res; Soc Exp Biol & Med. *Res:* Biosynthesis of glycoproteins and fetal proteins; molecular diseases. *Mailing Add:* 110 Boxwood Circle Hamburg NY 14075

SARD, RICHARD, SURFACE CHEMISTRY, SCIENCE MANAGEMENT. *Current Pos:* EXEC VPRES INT, ETHONE-OMI INC, 89- *Personal Data:* b Brooklyn, NY, Apr 19, 41; m 63; c 2. *Educ:* Stevens Inst Technol, BE, 62, MS, 63, PhD(phys metall), 68. *Prof Exp:* Electron microscopist, Cent Res Labs, Air Reduction Corp, 63-64; mem tech staff, Bell Tel Labs, 68-73, supvr plated film properties & interface studies, 73-78, supvr mat develop & comput applns, 78-79; dir technol, Plating Systs Div, Occidental Petrol Corp, 79-83; vpres technol, OMI Int Corp, 83-88. *Mem:* AAAS; Electrochem Soc; Am Electroplaters Soc; Sigma Xi. *Res:* Structure and properties of electrodeposits and other coatings in relation to process conditions; electrodeposition; surface characterization; physical properties; device phenomena; process control sensors; microprocessor applications. *Mailing Add:* 1180 Willow Lane Birmingham MI 48009

SARD, ROBERT DANIEL, experimental high energy physics; deceased, see previous edition for last biography

SARDANA, MOHINDER K, PROTEIN CHARACTERIZATION, ENZYMOLOGY. *Current Pos:* res fel, 87-91, ASST DIR, MERCK RES LABS, 91- *Personal Data:* m 80, Vinod Virmani; c Niti. *Educ:* Indian Inst Sci, PhD(biochem), 77. *Prof Exp:* Asst prof, Rockefeller Univ, 83-87. *Mem:* Protein Soc; AAAS. *Res:* Protein structure determination and disulfide connectivities; peptide mapping and amino acid analysis for protein characterization; isolation of proteins-peptides of therapeutic function. *Mailing Add:* Merck Sharp & Dohme Inc West Point PA 19486

SARDELLA, DENNIS JOSEPH, ORGANIC CHEMISTRY, PHYSICAL CHEMISTRY. *Current Pos:* from asst prof to assoc prof, 67-81, PROF CHEM, BOSTON COL, 81-, DIR, PRESIDENTIAL SCHOLARS PROG, 90- *Personal Data:* b Lawrence, Mass, July 3, 41; m 66; c 4. *Educ:* Boston Col, BS, 62; Ill Inst Technol, PhD(phys org chem), 67. *Prof Exp:* Nat Res Coun Can fel, Univ Western Ont, 66-67. *Concurrent Pos:* Vis lectr biol chem, Sch Med, Harvard Univ, 73-75. *Mem:* Am Chem Soc. *Res:* Nuclear magnetic resonance spectroscopy; structural chemistry; theoretical organic chemistry. *Mailing Add:* Dept Chem Boston Col Chestnut Hill MA 02167. *Fax:* 617-552-2705; *E-Mail:* dennis.sardella@bc.edu

SARDESAI, VISHWANATH M, BIOCHEMISTRY, CLINICAL CHEMISTRY. *Current Pos:* asst prof, 63-69, ASSOC PROF BIOCHEM, SCH MED, WAYNE STATE UNIV, 69- *Personal Data:* b Goa, India, Nov 17, 32; m 66. *Educ:* Univ Bombay, BS, 54, MS, 57; Wayne State Univ, PhD(physiol chem), 62. *Prof Exp:* Instr chem, Univ Bombay, 54-57; res chemist, Zandu Pharmaceut Works Ltd, India, 57-59; teaching asst biochem, Wayne State Univ, 59-60; instr, Sch Med, Tulane Univ, 62-63. *Mem:* AAAS; Am Physiol Soc; Am Inst Nutrit; Am Chem Soc; NY Acad Sci; Sigma Xi; Am Asn Clin Chem; Shock Soc. *Res:* Porphyrin biosynthesis and metabolism; oxidative phosphorylation; alcohol metabolism; metabolism in shock; clinical methods; tryptophan metabolism. *Mailing Add:* Dept Surg Sch Med Wayne State Univ 6C UHC 4201 St Antoine Detroit MI 48201

SARDINAS, AUGUST A, MATHEMATICAL ANALYSIS. *Current Pos:* ASSOC PROF MATH, VILLANOVA UNIV, 63- *Personal Data:* b Bronx, NY, June 19, 22; m 44; c 3. *Educ:* Brooklyn Col, BA, 43; Harvard Univ, MA, 47; Univ Pa, PhD(math), 62. *Prof Exp:* Res asst info theory, Univ Pa, 49-50; staff engr, Burroughs Corp, 50-63. *Concurrent Pos:* Logical design consult, Burroughs Corp, 65- *Mem:* Math Asn Am. *Res:* Information theory; logical design; analysis. *Mailing Add:* 55 Eastwood Rd Berwyn PA 19312

SARDISCO, JOHN BAPTIST, PHYSICAL CHEMISTRY. *Current Pos:* Sect supvr phys chem sect, Res Eng & Develop Dept, Pennzoil United, Inc, 61-75, mgr anal sect, Technol Div, 85-92, DIV MGR INORGANIC RES, RES & DEVELOP DEPT, PENNZOIL CO, 75-, DIR ANALYTICAL SERVS DEPT, TECHNOL DIV, 93- *Personal Data:* b Shreveport, La, July 27, 34; m 59; c 1. *Educ:* Spring Hill Col, BS, 56; La State Univ, MS, 58, PhD(phys chem), 60. *Prof Exp:* Consult, Anal Serv, Inc, 79- *Mem:* Am Chem Soc; Sigma Xi; Am Inst Chemists; Smithsonian Inst. *Res:* Corrosion research and control; inorganic process development; hydrometallurgical refining of metals; instrumental inorganic analysis; water pollution control and water purification; environmental analysis; analytical chemistry. *Mailing Add:* 98 E Morning Cloud Circle Spring TX 77381

SAREM, AMIR M SAM, CHEMICAL & PETROLEUM ENGINEERING, RESERVOIR CHARACTERIZATION. *Current Pos:* PRES, IMPROVED PETROL RECOVERY CONSULT, 93- *Personal Data:* b Teheran, Iran, Sept 5, 30; US citizen; m 57, Loretta Richison; c Susan K (Beckwith), Elaine Z (Gilmore), David A & Scott A. *Educ:* Univ Tulsa, BSPE, 54, MSPE, 56; Univ Okla, PhD(eng sci), 64. *Prof Exp:* Jr engr, Sinclair Res Inc, Okla, 54-55, intermediate res engr, 55-59, res engr, 59-61; teaching asst petrol eng, Univ Okla, 61-64; res engr, Unocal Sci & Technol, Union Oil Co Calif, 64-66, sr res engr, 66-77, res assoc, 77-83, sr res assoc, 83-86, comput coordr, 85-92, supvr & mgr, Reservoir, Eng, 86-88, staff consult, 89-93. *Concurrent Pos:* Lectr, Sinclair Res Lab, Inc, 59-61 & 64, Calif State Univ, Fullerton, 73-75, Univ Southern Calif, 80-92; lectr exten sch, Univ Calif, Los Angeles, 65-67; mem, Orange Co Eng Coun; distinguished lectr, Soc Petrol Engrs, 83 & 84. *Mem:* Am Inst Mining, Metall & Petrol Engrs; Am Chem Soc; Am Inst Chem Engrs; Soc Rheol; fel Am Inst Advan Eng; Soc Petrol Engrs. *Res:* Petroleum reservoir engineering; P-V-T properties of hydrocarbon systems; fluid flow mechanics in porous media; viscous and surfactant water flood of oil fields; rheological properties of polymer solutions; pipeline flow drag reduction; mobility controlled caustic flooding; enhanced oil recovery; over 30 US & foreign patents. *Mailing Add:* 18741 La Casita Ave Yorba Linda CA 92886. *Fax:* 714-693-0663; *E-Mail:* sam4iprc@aol.com

SARETT, HERBERT PAUL, NUTRITION, MEDICAL FOODS. *Current Pos:* CONSULT NUTRIT SCI, 81- *Personal Data:* b Brooklyn, NY, Feb 5, 16; m 48, Helen Statsinger; c David C, Mark E & Joshua D. *Educ:* Brooklyn Col, BA, 36; Cornell Univ, MS, 39; Duke Univ, PhD(biochem), 42; Am Bd Nutrit, dipl, 52. *Prof Exp:* Instr biochem, Sch Med, Duke Univ, 42-43; asst prof & res assoc, Ore State Col, 43-45; res assoc med div, Chem Warfare Serv, US Dept Army, Md, 45; asst prof biochem & med, Sch Med, Tulane Univ, 46-51, assoc prof, 51-52; dir nutrit res, Mead Johnson Res Ctr, 52-67, dir nutrit & biochem res, 58-62, vpres nutrit sci, 67-71, vpres nutrit sci resources, 71-81. *Concurrent Pos:* Mem tech adv group comt nutrit, Am Acad Pediat, 61-67, 69-81, chmn, 71-74; mem panel new foods, White House Conf Foods, Nutrit & Health, 69; mem food standards & fortification policy, Food & Nutrit Bd, Nat Acad Sci, 70-72; chmn nutrit sci comt, Infant Formula Coun, 71-81; indust adv to US deleg comt foods for spec dietary uses, Codex Alimentarius Comn, 71-81. *Mem:* Fel Am Inst Nutrit; Soc Exp Biol & Med; Am Soc Clin Nutrit; Am Chem Soc; Am Soc Biochem & Molecular Biol. *Res:* Foods for special dietary uses; protein evaluation; infant nutrition; milk substitute formulas; formulas for infants with metabolic disorders; formula diets; meal replacements; medium chain triglycerides; cholestyramine; nutrition regulations; vitamin, mineral and fluoride supplements. *Mailing Add:* 7325 Links Ct Sarasota FL 34243-4638

SARETT, LEWIS HASTINGS, RESEARCH ORGANIZATION, LIFE SCIENCES. *Current Pos:* RETIRED. *Personal Data:* b Champaign, Ill, Dec 22, 17; m 44, 69; c 4. *Educ:* Northwestern Univ, BS, 39; Princeton Univ, PhD(chem), 42. *Hon Degrees:* DSc, Northwestern Univ, 72, Bucknell Univ, 77. *Honors & Awards:* Sci Award, Bd Dirs, Merck & Co, Inc, 51; Baekeland Award, Am Chem Soc, 51, Award, 64; Julius W Sturmer Mem Lectr, 59; Medal, Synthetic Org Chem Mfrs Asn, 64; William Scheele Lectr, Royal Pharmaceut Inst, Stockholm, Sweden, 64; Chem Pioneer Award, Am Inst Chem, 72; Nat Medal Sci, 75; Perkin Medal Award, Soc Chem Indust, 76; Gold Medal, Am Inst Chemists, 81. *Prof Exp:* Res chemist, Merck & Co, Inc, 42-48, asst dir, Dept Org Chem & Biochem Res, 48-52, dir, Dept Med Chem, 52-56, dir, Dept Synthetic Org Chem, 56-62, exec dir fundamental res, 62-66, vpres basic res, 66-69, pres, Merck Sharp & Dohme Res Labs, 69-76, sr vpres sci & technol, Merck & Co, Inc, 75-82, dir, Start Up Biotechnol Cos, 82-95. *Concurrent Pos:* Consult, Med Chem Sect, USPHS, 64-67; mem, Res & Eval

Comt, Nat Cystic Fibrosis Res Found, 64-69; trustee, Cold Spring Harbor Lab Quant Biol, 68-70; rep, Indust Res Inst, 68-, dir, 74-77; rep, Pharmaceut Mfrs Asn, 69-; mem, Vis Comt Div Biol, Calif Inst Technol, 69-76, chmn, 72-76; mem, Dirs Indust Res, 70-, secy, 71-72, chmn, 72-73; mem bd trustees, Med Ctr, Princeton Univ, 77-79; mem, Sci & Technol Panel, Reagan Transition Team, 80-81, Drugs for Rare Dis, Pharmaceut Mfrs Asn Comn, 81-; mem bd dirs, Immunex Corp, Resonex Corp, Vestar Corp & Hybertech Corp; indust consult life sci, 82- *Mem:* Nat Acad Sci; Inst Med-Nat Acad Sci; Am Inst Chem. *Res:* Biomedical research organization. *Mailing Add:* 1488 Marshall Rd Viola ID 83872

SARFARAZI, MANSOOR, HUMAN DISEASE GENE MAPPING, HUMAN POPULATION GENETICS. *Current Pos:* asst prof human genetics, 89-92, assoc prof, Dept Pediat, 92-93, ASSOC PROF HUMAN GENETICS DEPT SURG, UNIV CONN HEALTH CTR, 93- *Personal Data:* b Mashad, Iran, June 24, 52. *Educ:* Univ Mashad, Iran, BSc, 75; Univ Wales, PhD(human genetics), 81. *Prof Exp:* Res fel human genetics, Col Med, Univ Wales, 81-85, sr res fel, 86-89. *Concurrent Pos:* Teacher human genetics-pedigree linkage anal, Europ Sch Med Genetics, 87 & 91; prin investr, Univ Conn Health Ctr, 90, 92, 93 & 94, NATO Collaborative Res, 93-94, Int Glaucoma Asn, 93-, Am Health Assistance Found, 93-, Nat Eye Inst, 93-, Knights Templar Eye Found, Inc, 94-, Fight for Sight-Nat Soc to Prevent Blindness, 94- *Mem:* Asn Res Vision & Opthal; Am Soc Human Genetics. *Res:* Participated in mapping the genes for at least 14 different human disorders; gene mapping of three different eye diseases, two different limb deformities, two cardiovascular abnormalities and one type of learning disorder; advanced molecular genetics techniques to identify the chromosomal location of the above mentioned genes; scientific publications include 72 papers and 108 abstracts. *Mailing Add:* Univ Conn Sch Med 263 Farmington Ave Farmington CT 06030-0001. *Fax:* 860-679-2451; *E-Mail:* sarfarazi@mbcg.uchc.edu

SARGE, THEODORE WILLIAM, PHYSICAL ORGANIC CHEMISTRY. *Current Pos:* RETIRED. *Personal Data:* b Taunton, Mass, Feb 4, 18; m 44; c 5. *Educ:* Col Holy Cross, BS, 40, MS, 41. *Prof Exp:* Chemist, Dow Chem Co, 41-44, chemist, Saran Develop Lab, 44-56, res admin asst Petrochem & Gen Res, Saginaw Bay Res Dept, 56-67, res admin asst New Prod, 67-69, res admin asst Pilot Plant & Process Develop & Eng Admin, 69-74, mem staff, Patent Dept, 74-83. *Mem:* AAAS; Am Chem Soc; Sigma Xi. *Res:* Vinyl polymerizations; polymer properties; polymeric film applications and properties, especially water vapor and gas transmissions; petrochemicals-hydrocarbons processing and extraction; research administration, especially research and development, patents, safety and training. *Mailing Add:* 3307 Kentwood Dr Midland MI 48642-3732

SARGEANT, PETER BARRY, FIBER PRODUCTION, RESEARCH ADMINISTRATION. *Current Pos:* Res chemist, Cent Res Dept, Dacron Div, E I Dupont De Nemours & Co, Kinston, NC, 62-66, sr res chemist, Textile Fibers Dept, Va, 66-69, res supvr, Dacron Res Lab, NC, 69-71, res suppvr, Textile Res Lab, 71-73, sr supvr process, 73-75, sr supvr, 75-83, tech supvr, 83-86, TECH GROUP MGR, DACRON DIV, EI DUPONT DE NEMOURS & CO, KINSTON, NC, 86- *Personal Data:* b Cedar Rapids, Iowa, Jan 18, 36; m 56, Patricia Pisney; c Jeffrey, James & Jonathan. *Educ:* Iowa State Univ, BS, 58; Ohio State Univ, PhD, 62. *Prof Exp:* Res asst, Ohio State Univ, 58-59, NSF fel, 60-62. *Res:* Polymer chemistry; fiber technology. *Mailing Add:* 1703 St George Pl Kinston NC 28504. *Fax:* 919-522-6597

SARGENT, ANNEILA ISABEL, ASTRONOMY, ASTROPHYSICS. *Current Pos:* Sr res asst, Calif Inst Technol, 67-70 & 72-74, res fel astron, 77-81, mem prof staff, 81-88, sr res fel, 88-90, SR RES ASSOC, CALIF INST TECHNOL, 90-, EXEC DIR, OWENS VALLEY RADIO OBSERV, 96- *Personal Data:* b Kirkcaldy, Scotland; m 64; c 2. *Educ:* Univ Edinburgh, BSc, 63; Calif Inst Technol, MS, 67, PhD(astron), 77. *Mem:* Am Astron Soc; Royal Astron Soc; Int Astron Union. *Res:* Millimeter-wave studies of regions of star formation; star formation in galaxies; proto-planetary disks. *Mailing Add:* Dept Astron Calif Inst Technol 105-24 Pasadena CA 91125

SARGENT, BERNICE WELDON, nuclear physics, for more information see previous edition

SARGENT, CHARLES, CIVIL ENGINEERING. *Current Pos:* from asst prof to prof, 53-61, dean math phys sci & eng, 61-67, EMER DEAN MATH, PHYS SCI & ENG, UNIV ALASKA, COLLEGE, 70- *Personal Data:* b Mitchell, Nebr, May 24, 13; m 38, Betty Ann King; c Charles King. *Educ:* Univ Idaho, BS, 48, CE, 52; Stanford Univ, MS, 58. *Prof Exp:* Asst prof civil eng, Univ Idaho, 48-53. *Concurrent Pos:* Consult engr, 48-; exec dir planning & opers, Univ Alaska, 67-70; prof construct mgt, NDak State Univ, 70-75. *Mem:* Am Soc Civil Engrs; Am Soc Eng Educ. *Res:* Economic problems in engineering construction, particularly concrete aggregates. *Mailing Add:* 2501 E Sherman Ave No 201 Coeur d'Alene ID 83814-5859

SARGENT, DAVID FISHER, X-RAY CRYSTALLOGRAPHY, MEMBRANE ELECTRICAL PROPERTIES. *Current Pos:* fel biophys, 71-74, res asst biophys, 75-94, STAFF SCIENTIST, FED INST TECH, ZURICH, 94- *Personal Data:* b Victoria, BC, June 29, 45; m 67, Hedi Emch; c Mark. *Educ:* Univ BC, BSc, 66; Univ Western Ont, PhD(biophys), 71. *Prof Exp:* Fel biochem, Univ Sydney, 74-75. *Concurrent Pos:* Med Res Coun Can fel, 71-74. *Mem:* Biophys Soc; Union Swiss Soc Exp Biol; Swiss Crystallog Soc. *Res:* Structure/function of DNA/protein complexes (x-ray crystallography); lipid/peptide interactions (lipid bilayer membranes: electrical properties). *Mailing Add:* Inst Molecular Biol & Biophys ETH-Hoenggerberg Zurich 8093 Switzerland. *Fax:* 8011-411-633-1073; *E-Mail:* sargent@mol.biol.ethz.ch

SARGENT, FRANK DORRANCE, QUANTITATIVE GENETICS. *Current Pos:* Res asst animal breeding, NC State Univ, 57-63, instr dairy husb, 63-65, from asst prof exten dairy husb to prof exten dairy husb, 65-81, PROF ANIMAL SCI, NC STATE UNIV, 81- *Personal Data:* b Concord, NH, July 9, 35; m 59; c 2. *Educ:* Univ NH, BS, 57; NC State Univ, MS, 60, PhD(animal sci), 65. *Mem:* Am Dairy Sci Asn; Sigma Xi. *Res:* Dairy cattle breeding; dairy herd management; production record systems; reproductive physiology. *Mailing Add:* PO Box 2135 Cary NC 27512

SARGENT, FREDERICK PETER, NUCLEAR WASTE DISPOSAL. *Current Pos:* res officer chem, 69-77, mem plutonium chem group, 77-78, sect leader exp pathways anal radionuclide migration in geologic formations, 78-81, HEAD, GEOCHEM & APPL CHEM BR, ATOMIC ENERGY CAN LTD, 81- *Personal Data:* b Plymouth, UK, July 26, 40; m 67; c 2. *Educ:* Univ Exeter, BS, 61; Univ Leeds, MS, 63, PhD(chem), 65. *Prof Exp:* Nat Res Coun Can fel, Univ Sask, 65-67; Sci Res Coun UK fel, Univ Leeds, 67-69. *Mem:* Fel Chem Inst Can; Can Nuclear Soc. *Res:* Fundamental processes in radiation chemistry; electron spin resonance; leaching; nuclide sorption; ion exchange; geochemical and geophysical aspects of nuclear waste disposal; product and process development for immobilization of nuclear waste. *Mailing Add:* Atomic Energy Can Ltd Pinawa MB R0E 1L0 Can

SARGENT, GORDON ALFRED, MATERIALS SCIENCE. *Current Pos:* dean eng, 85-91, VPRES GRAD STUDIES & RES DEAN GRAD STUDIES, UNIV DAYTON, 91- *Personal Data:* b Winterton, Eng, Apr 8, 38; m 66, Amy T Skinner; c Andrew, Anne, Mark, Adrian, Maria, Sarah & Susan. *Educ:* Univ London, BSc, 60, DIC, 63, PhD(metall), 64; Royal Sch Mines, ARSM, 60. *Prof Exp:* Res fel, Mellon Inst, 63-67; from asst prof to assoc prof mat sci, Univ Ky, 67-77, prof metall eng & mat sci, 77-82, chmn dept, 82-85. *Mem:* Fel Am Soc Metals; Am Inst Mining, Metall & Petrol Engrs; fel Am Soc Mat; Sigma Xi. *Res:* Deformation and physical properties of materials under high pressures; properties of materials subjected to irradiation damage; erosion damage to materials. *Mailing Add:* 1937 Rich Rd Dayton OH 45432

SARGENT, HOWARD HARROP, III, SOLAR-TERRESTRIAL PHYSICS. *Current Pos:* instrumentation engr solar radio astron, 71-73, gen phys scientist solar physics, 73-77, SPACE SCIENTIST SOLAR PHYSICS, NAT OCEANIC & ATMOSPHERIC ADMIN, 77- *Personal Data:* b Hartford, Conn, June 12, 36; m 68; c 2. *Educ:* Univ Conn, BS, 63; Univ Colo, MS, 72. *Honors & Awards:* Spec Achievement Award, Nat Oceanic & Atmospheric Admin, 75. *Prof Exp:* Engr-in-charge ionospheric physics, Nat Bur Stand, S Pole Sta, Antarctica, 63-64; res asst, Stanford Univ, 65-66; instrumentation engr, Environ Sci Serv Admin, 68-71. *Mem:* Am Geophys Union; Sigma Xi. *Res:* Geophysical, including weather, effects of solar activity; intra-cycle changes in solar behavior; solar and geomagnetic activity prediction techniques; long-term solar variability; time series analysis. *Mailing Add:* Space Environ Lab 325 Broadway Boulder CO 80303

SARGENT, KENNETH ALBERT, geology, for more information see previous edition

SARGENT, MALCOLM LEE, BIOCHEMISTRY, GENETICS. *Current Pos:* asst prof bot, 68-73, ASSOC PROF PLANT BIOL, UNIV ILL, URBANA, 73- *Personal Data:* b Grayling, Mich, Sept 14, 37; c 3. *Educ:* Univ Mich, BS, 60; Stanford Univ, PhD(biol), 66. *Prof Exp:* NIH fel bot, Univ Mich, 66-68. *Mem:* Am Bryolog & Lichenological Soc; Am Soc Plant Physiol; Genetics Soc Am. *Res:* Biochemical-genetics of circadian rhythms and development in Neurospora and other fungi; reproductive and developmental physiology of bryophytes. *Mailing Add:* Dept Plant Biol Univ Ill Urbana 505 S Goodwin Ave Urbana IL 61801-3707

SARGENT, MURRAY, III, QUANTUM OPTICS, COMPUTER SCIENCE. *Current Pos:* asst prof optical sci, 69-72, assoc prof optical sci & comput sci, 72-74, assoc prof, 74-77, PROF OPTICAL SCI, UNIV ARIZ, 77-, PRES, SCROLL SYSTS, 81- *Personal Data:* b New York, NY, Aug 18, 41; m 67; c 2. *Educ:* Yale Univ, BS, 63, MS, 64, PhD(physics), 67. *Prof Exp:* Fel physics, Yale Univ, 67; mem tech staff, Bell Tel Labs, 67-69. *Concurrent Pos:* Humboldt sr scientist award, Fed Repub Ger, 75; guest prof, Univ Stuttgart, 75-76 & Max Planck Inst for Quantum Optics, 75-76 & 80-85. *Mem:* Am Phys Soc; fel Optical Soc Am. *Res:* Laser physics and applications; micro computer systems; technical word processing. *Mailing Add:* 11108 NE 106th Pl Kirkland WA 98033-5084

SARGENT, ROBERT GEORGE, OPERATIONS RESEARCH, DISCRETE EVENT SIMULATION. *Current Pos:* from asst prof to assoc prof, 66-82, PROF INDUST ENG & OPERS RES, SYRACUSE UNIV, 82- *Personal Data:* b Port Huron, Mich, June 14, 37; m 70; c Tiffany. *Educ:* Univ Mich, BSE, 59, MS, 63, PhD(indust eng), 66. *Honors & Awards:* Distinguished Serv Award, Tims Col. *Prof Exp:* Electronics engr, Hughes Aircraft Co, 59-61; grad asst & lectr eng, Univ Mich, 62-66. *Concurrent Pos:* Vis assoc prof, Cornell Univ, 81-82; dept ed, Simulation Modeling & Statist Comput, 80-85; nat lectr, Asn Comput Mach, 85-89. *Mem:* Opers Res Soc Am; Inst Mgt Sci; Am Inst Indust Engrs; Asn Comput Mach; Soc Comput Simulation. *Res:* Discrete event & digital simulation; modelling and performance evaluation of computer systems; production and inventory control; model validation. *Mailing Add:* Dept Indust Eng & Opers Res Syracuse Univ Syracuse NY 13244

SARGENT, ROGER GARY, PARASITOLOGY. *Current Pos:* Off Econ Opportunity fel malnutrit & parasitism, 70-71, dir fac res develop & lectr biol, 71-74, asst dean, Col Health & Phys Educ, 74-81, ASSOC PROF BIOL, UNIV SC, 74-, ASSOC DEAN COL HEALTH, 81- *Personal Data:* b Sandborn, Ind, Mar 7, 39; m 62; c 2. *Educ:* Ind State Univ, BS, 62, MS, 64; Univ SC, PhD(parasitol), 71. *Concurrent Pos:* Jannsen Pharmaceut fel clin drug eval, 71-72, res grant, 75; mem, Nat Coun Univ Res Adminr. *Mem:* Am Soc Parasitol; Am Zool Soc; Am Asn Health, Phys Educ & Recreation; Sigma Xi. *Res:* Intestinal parasites Ascaris lumbricoides and Trichuris trichura with emphasis in drug regimens and ovicidal effects of various compounds; comparative drug studies establishing efficacy of current drugs of choice for Ascaris lumbricoides to investigational drugs. *Mailing Add:* Univ SC Columbia SC 29208-0001

SARGENT, ROGER N, ANALYTICAL CHEMISTRY, PHYSICAL CHEMISTRY. *Current Pos:* MEM FAC, COL HEALTH PHYS EDUC, UNIV SC, 80- *Personal Data:* b Stelton, NJ, June 3, 28; m 52; c 2. *Educ:* Lafayette Col, BS, 51; Rutgers Univ, PhD(anal chem), 56. *Prof Exp:* Shift supvr styrene control lab, Koppers Co, 51-52; asst chem, Rutgers Univ, 52-56, res fel, 56-57; sr res chemist ion exchange div, Dow Chem Co, Mich, 57-68, group leader anal chem, 68-76, sr res specialist, Human Health Res & Develop Lab, 76-80. *Mem:* Am Chem Soc; Sigma Xi. *Res:* Chromotographic separation and purification of organic compounds with ion exchange resins; ion-exchange chromatography and exclusion; salting-out chromatography. *Mailing Add:* Health Educ Univ SC Columbia SC 29208-0001

SARGENT, THEODORE DAVID, ZOOLOGY. *Current Pos:* Instr zool, 63-64, from asst prof to assoc prof, 64-75, PROF ZOOL, UNIV MASS, AMHERST, 75- *Personal Data:* b Peabody, Mass, Oct 25, 36; m 67; c 2. *Educ:* Univ Mass, BS, 58; Univ Wis, MS, 60, PhD(zool), 63. *Concurrent Pos:* Ed, J. Lepidop Soc, 72-74. *Mem:* Animal Behav Soc; Soc Study Evolution; Lepidop Soc (pres, 79). *Res:* Cryptic moths, behavior, ecology, genetics; melanism in North American moths; bird behavior; moths of the genus Catocala. *Mailing Add:* Biol Univ Mass Amherst MA 01003-0002

SARGENT, THORNTON WILLIAM, III, NUCLEAR MEDICINE, BIOCHEMICAL PHARMACOLOGY. *Current Pos:* RETIRED. *Personal Data:* b St Louis, Mo, June 25, 28; m 52; c 2. *Educ:* Reed Col, BA, 51; Univ Calif, Berkeley, PhD(biophys), 59. *Prof Exp:* Physicist, Michelson Lab, US Naval Ord Test Sta, Calif, 51-52; res biophysicist, Lawrence Berkeley Lab, Res Med & Radiation Biophys Div, Univ Calif, Berkeley, 59-77, sr biophysicist, 59-91. *Concurrent Pos:* Prin investr, Dept Energy, 59-90, NIMH, 82-94. *Mem:* Soc Nuclear Med; Soc Biol Psychiat; Sigma Xi. *Res:* In vivo radionuclide research in human disease; chromium metabolism in diabetes; iron absorption in hematologic disorders; bioamine, amino acid and methyl carbon metabolism in schizophrenia and manic depressive illness; positron emission tomography of metabolism and cerebral blood flow in psychosis and Alzheimers disease. *Mailing Add:* Lawrence Berkeley Lab 1 Cylcotron Rd Berkeley CA 94720

SARGENT, WALLACE LESLIE WILLIAM, ASTROPHYSICS. *Current Pos:* from asst prof to prof astron, 66-81, exec officer, 75-81, IRA S BOWEN PROF ASTRON, CALIF INST TECHNOL, 81-, EXEC OFF, 96- *Personal Data:* b Elsham, Eng, Feb 15, 35; m 64, Anneila Cassells; c Lindsay & Alison. *Educ:* Univ Manchester, BSc, 56, MSc, 57, PhD(astron), 59. *Honors & Awards:* Helen B Warner Prize, Am Astron Soc, 69, Heineman Prize, 91; George Darwin Lectr, Royal Astron Soc, 87; Bruce Gold Medal, Astron Soc Pac, 94; Thomas Gold Lectr, Cornell Univ, 94; Sackler Lect, Harvard Univ, 95, Univ Calif, 95. *Prof Exp:* Res fel astron, Calif Inst Technol, 59-62; sr res fel, Royal Greenwich Observ, Eng, 62-64; asst prof physics, Univ Calif, San Diego, 64-66. *Concurrent Pos:* Hon vis fel, Australian Nat Univ, 65 & 67; Alfred P Sloan Found fel, 68-70; vis fel, Cambridge Univ, 68-72, 74-75, 79, 82, 87, Oxford Univ, 73, Univ Groningen, 78, Univ Florence, 81, Europ Southern Observ, 80, 83 & 85, Astrophys Inst, Paris, 84, Max Planck Inst, Astron, Heidelberg, 92-94; mem staff, Owens Valley Radio Observ, 78- *Mem:* Am Astron Soc; fel Am Acad Arts & Sci; fel Royal Astron Soc; Int Astron Union; fel Royal Soc London. *Res:* Stellar and extragalactic spectroscopy; evolution of galaxies; clusters of galaxies; quasars; cosmology. *Mailing Add:* 400 S Berkeley Ave Pasadena CA 91107-5062. *Fax:* 626-568-9352; *E-Mail:* wws@astro.caltech.edu

SARGENT, WILLIAM QUIRK, FLUID METABOLISM, ELECTROLYTE METABOLISM. *Current Pos:* CENT REGION MGR, SCI & TECHNOL AFFAIRS, HOECHST-ROUSSEL PHARMACEUT, MEMPHIS, DIR, DRUG & REGULATORY AFFAIRS, 93- *Personal Data:* b Bell, Calif, Jan 26, 45; m 69; c 3. *Educ:* Johns Hopkins Univ, BA, 67; Univ Tenn, PhD(physiol), 73. *Prof Exp:* USPHS trainee, Col Basic Med Sci, Univ Tenn, 69-71, teaching fel, 71-73; fel, Alcohol & Drug Res Ctr, Tenn Psychol Hosp, 73-75. *Mem:* Am Physiol Soc. *Res:* Renal and gastrointestinal electrolyte metabolism during long term drug administrations (ie, ethanol). *Mailing Add:* Lorex Pharmaceut Box 5110 Chicago IL 60680-5110

SARGENTINI, NEIL JOSEPH, MUTAGENESIS, DNA REPAIR. *Current Pos:* ASST PROF MICROBIOL & IMMUNOL, KIRKSVILLE COL OSTEOP MED, MO, 91- *Personal Data:* b San Francisco, Calif. *Educ:* Calif State Univ, Fresno, BA, 69, MA, 73; Stanford Univ, PhD(med microbiol), 80. *Prof Exp:* Res assoc radiation oncol, Sch Med, Stanford Univ, 80-84, sr res assoc, 84-91. *Mem:* Am Soc Microbiol; Radiation Res Soc; Sigma Xi; Environ Mutagen Soc; AAAS. *Res:* Spontaneous mutagenesis; mutagenesis, DNA repair and survival of gamma or UV-irradiated Escherichia coli cells. *Mailing Add:* RR 1 Box 358A Kirksville MO 63501

SARGES, REINHARD, ORGANIC CHEMISTRY. *Current Pos:* res chemist, Pfizer Inc, 65-75, proj leader, 75-81, prin investr, 81-85, RES ADV, PFIZER INC, 85- *Personal Data:* b Siegen, Ger, July 25, 35; US citizen; m 80, Divina Valder; c Heike, Michael & Philip. *Educ:* Univ Frankfurt, dipl, 60, PhD(peptide chem), 62. *Prof Exp:* Vis fel chem, NIH, 62-64, vis assoc, 64-65. *Mem:* Am Chem Soc. *Res:* Peptide and medicinal chemistry; biochemistry; CNS agents; antidiabetic drugs; aldose reductase inhibitors. *Mailing Add:* 1063 River Rd Mystic CT 06355. *Fax:* 860-441-4111

SARGESON, ALAN MCLEOD, CHEMISTRY. *Current Pos:* res fel, John Curtin Sch Med Res, Australian Nat Univ, 58-67, sr fel, 67-68, prof fel, 68-78, prof, 78-96, EMER PROF INORG CHEM, RES SCH CHEM, AUSTRALIAN NAT UNIV, 96- *Personal Data:* b Armidale, Australia, Oct 13, 30. *Educ:* Univ Sydney, BSc, 52, Dipl Ed, 55, PhD, 56. *Hon Degrees:* DSc, Univ Sydney, 90. *Honors & Awards:* Burrows Award Inorg Chem, 75; Award Inorg Chem, Am Chem Soc, 80; Nyholm Medal, Royal Soc Chem, 83, Centenary Medal, 92. *Prof Exp:* Lectr, Univ Technol, Sydney, 55, Univ Adelaide, 56. *Concurrent Pos:* Res consult, Dept Chem & Biochem, James Cook Univ; Int Rel Comt, Royal Australian Chem Inst & Australian Acad Sci; chmn, Comn Nomenclature Inorg Chem 11-2, Int Union Pure & Appl Chem. *Mem:* Foreign assoc Nat Acad Sci; fel Australian Acad Sci; foreign mem Royal Danish Acad Sci; fel Royal Soc; fel Royal Australian Chem Inst. *Mailing Add:* Res Sch Chem Australian Nat Univ Canberra ACT 0200 Australia. *Fax:* 616-249-0760

SARHAN, FATHEY, PLANT PHYSIOLOGY. *Current Pos:* PROF PLANT PHYSIOL & BIOCHEM, UNIV QUE, MONTREAL, 79- *Personal Data:* b Cairo, Egypt, Mar 28, 45; Can citizen. *Educ:* Cairo Univ, BSc, 65; Univ Montreal, MSc, 73, PhD(plant physiol), 77. *Prof Exp:* Agronomist, Ministry Agr, Cairo, Egypt, 66-70. *Concurrent Pos:* Lab instr, Univ Montreal, 71-76; res asst, McGill Univ, Montreal, 72-73; lectr, Univ Que, Montreal, 76-78; vis prof, Inst Grad Studies & Res, Alexandria Univ, 84-85. *Mem:* Can Soc Plant Physiol; Am Soc Plant Physiol; NY Acad Sci; Egyptian Soc Genetics. *Res:* Protein and nucleic acid synthesis mechanisms relative to cold hardiness in wheat; molecular and genetic manipulations of plant genes. *Mailing Add:* Dept Biol Sci Univ Que CP8888 Succ A Montreal PQ H3C 3P8 Can

SARI, JAMES WILLIAM, SPACE SCIENCE, PLASMA PHYSICS. *Current Pos:* SR PHYSICIST, APPL PHYSICS LAB, JOHNS HOPKINS UNIV, 77- *Personal Data:* b Buffalo, NY, Oct 13, 42; m 71. *Educ:* Oberlin Col, BA, 64; Univ Md, PhD(physics), 72. *Prof Exp:* Physicist plasma physics, Cornell Aeronaut Lab, 72-77. *Mem:* Am Geophys Union. *Res:* Interplanetary magnetic fields; cosmic-ray propagation; geomagnetic micropulsations; ocean magnetic fields. *Mailing Add:* Appl Physics Lab John Hopkins Univ John Hopkins Rd MS 7-362 Laurel MD 20723-6099

SARIASLANI, SIMA, MICROBIOLOGY, BIOCHEMISTRY. *Current Pos:* PRIN INVESTR MICROBIOL & BIOCHEM, E I DU PONT DE NEMOURS, 84- *Educ:* Univ Kent, UK, PhD(microbiol & biochem), 74. *Mem:* Am Chem Soc; Am Soc Microbiol; Soc Indust Microbiol. *Res:* Biochemistr and molecular biology of microbial xenobiotic metabolism and biotransformation. *Mailing Add:* DuPont Exp Sta E173/118 Wilmington DE 19880-0173

SARIC, WILLIAM SAMUEL, HYDRODYNAMIC STABILITY. *Current Pos:* assoc prof, 75-79, prof mech eng, 79-84, PROF MECH & AEROSPACE ENG, VA POLYTECH INST & STATE UNIV, 84- *Personal Data:* b Chicago, Ill, Sept 28, 40; m 62, 90; c 1. *Educ:* Ill Inst Technol, BS, 63, PhD(mech), 68; Univ NMex, MS, 65. *Prof Exp:* Staff mem environ testing, Sandia Labs, 63-66; instr, Ill Inst Technol, 66-68; staff mem, Sandia Labs, 68-75. *Concurrent Pos:* Adj prof, Univ NMex, 72 & Va Polytech Inst & State Univ, 74-75; mem, Nat Tech Comt Fluid Dynamics, Am Inst Aeronaut & Astronaut, 75-78; consult, Sandia Labs, 75-81, Ecodynamics Corp, 76, Ballistic Res Labs, 76 & Lockheed-Ga, 77-; invited guest & researcher, USSR Acad Sci, 76 & 81. *Mem:* Fel Am Inst Aeronaut & Astronaut; fel Am Phys Soc; fel Am Soc Mech Engrs; Am Soc Eng Educ. *Res:* Hydrodynamic stability; boundary-layer transition; nonlinear waves; nonlinear dynamics; transpiration cooling; boundary-layer flows; laminar flow control; electron-beam induced nuclear fusion; stability of stratified flows. *Mailing Add:* Dept Mech & Aerospace Eng Ariz State Univ Box 876106 Tempe AZ 85287-6106

SARICH, VINCENT M, PHYSICAL ANTHROPOLOGY. *Current Pos:* asst prof, 67-70, assoc prof, 70-81, PROF ANTHROP, UNIV CALIF, BERKELEY, 81- *Personal Data:* b Chicago, Ill, Dec 13, 34; m 61; c 2. *Educ:* Ill Inst Technol, BS, 55; Univ Calif, Berkeley, PhD(anthrop), 67. *Prof Exp:* Instr anthrop, Stanford Univ, 65. *Mem:* AAAS; Am Asn Phys Anthrop; Am Soc Mammal; Sigma Xi. *Res:* Construction of quantitative phylogenies by the use of comparative molecular data; evolutionary and selective bases of human variation. *Mailing Add:* Dept Anthrop Univ Calif Berkeley CA 94720-3710

SARID, DROR, SCANNING TUNNELING MICROSCOPY, LIGHT SCATTERING. *Current Pos:* PROF PHYSICS, OPTICAL SCI CTR, UNIV ARIZ, 80- *Personal Data:* b Haifa, Israel, Dec 13, 38; US citizen; m 63; c Uri & Rami. *Educ:* Hebrew Univ, Jerusalem, BSc, 66, MSc, 68, PhD(physics), 72. *Prof Exp:* Fel physics, Univ Calif, Santa Barbara, 72-74; scientist, Xerox Webster Res Ctr, 74-78; sr lectr, Hebrew Univ, Jerusalem, 78-80. *Concurrent Pos:* Consult, EG&G, Santa Barbara, 74; vis scholar, Univ Calif, Santa Barbara, 75; consult, Xerox Webster Res Ctr, 78-81, US Army, 81-93. *Mem:* Optical Soc Am; Am Phys Soc; Electrochem Soc; AAAS; NY Acad Sci. *Res:* Laser light scattering, nonlinear optics scanning tunneling microscopy; atomic force microscopy. *Mailing Add:* 4149 E Sixth St Tucson AZ 85711

SARIDIS, GEORGE N, ELECTRICAL ENGINEERING. *Current Pos:* PROF ELEC, COMPUT & SYSTS ENG & DIR, ROBOTICS & AUTOMATION LAB, RENSSELAER POLYTECH INST, 81- *Personal Data:* b Athens, Greece, Nov 17, 31; m 85, Panayota Dimarogona. *Educ:* Athens Tech Univ, Dipl, 55; Purdue Univ, MSEE, 62, PhD(optimal control), 65. *Honors & Awards:* Centennial Medal, Inst Elec & Electronics Engrs, 84. *Prof Exp:* Instr elec mech, Athens Tech Univ, 55-63; from instr to prof elec eng, Purdue Univ, West Lafayette, 63-81; dir, NASA Ctr Intelligent Robotic Systs Space Explor, 87-92. *Concurrent Pos:* Engr, Telecommun Orgn Greece, 55-56 & Pub Power Corp Greece, 57-63. *Mem:* Fel Inst Elec & Electronics Engrs; NY Acad Sci; Am Soc Mech Engrs; Am Soc Eng Educ; Soc Mfg Engrs; Control Systs Soc. *Res:* Optimal control theory and applications; adaptive and learning systems; self-organizing control systems; bioengineering systems; prosthetics and robotics; intelligent systems. *Mailing Add:* Dept Elec Comput/Systs Eng Rensselaer Polytech Inst Troy NY 12180-3590. *Fax:* 518-276-8715; *E-Mail:* saridis@ral.rpi.edu

SARIN, PREM S, BIOCHEMISTRY, BIOTECHNOLOGY, IMMUNOLOGY. *Current Pos:* ADJ PROF BIOCHEM, GEORGE WASHINGTON UNIV, SCH MED, 87-92 & 96- *Personal Data:* US citizen; m 65; c 2. *Educ:* Univ Delhi, BSc, 54, MSc, 56, PhD(chem), 59; Cambridge Univ, PhD(chem), 62. *Prof Exp:* Lectr chem, Univ Delhi, 57-60; res fel, Harvard Univ, 63-65; biochemist, Univ Toronto, 65-67; head sect nucleic acids, Merck Sharp & Dohme, NJ, 67-70; dir molecular biol, Litton Bionetics, Md, 71-72; vis scientist, Nat Cancer Inst, 72-74, dept chief, Lab Tumor Cell Biol, 74-91. *Concurrent Pos:* Vis prof, Univ del Rosario, Columbia, 84; vpres res infectious dis, Cal-Sci Corp, 93- *Mem:* Am Soc Cell Biol; Am Chem Soc; Am Soc Biol Chem; Am Asn Cancer Res. *Res:* Immunology & pathogenesis of human retroviruses including HIV and AIDS; search for drugs for treatment and preventive and therapeutic vaccines for HIV; elicitation of cellular and humoral immune responses of viral antigens. *Mailing Add:* Wash Univ Med Ctr 2300 Eye St NW Ross Hall 530 Washington DC 20037

SARJEANT, PETER THOMSON, PAPER CHEMISTRY, ENGINEERING. *Current Pos:* RETIRED. *Personal Data:* b Orillia, Ont, June 24, 29; m 56; c 2. *Educ:* Queens Univ, BSc, 53, MSc, 56; Pa State Univ, PhD(mat sci), 67. *Prof Exp:* Prod supvr pharmaceut, Merck Sharpe & Dohme, 54-57; res engr wood prod, Westvco Corp, 57-60, prod develop supr lignin prod, 60-63, res chemist electrocopy, 63-64, res chemist paper coatings, 67-69, group leader, 69-70, assoc res dir, 70-71, res dir, 71-78, res group mgr, 78-89. *Mem:* Tech Asn Pulp & Paper Indust; Am Chem Soc; AAAS. *Res:* Process control of papermaking and chemical recovery processing; wood pulping processes; refining; cleaning; fourdrinier optimization; converting equipment for paper and board; history of papermaking; wood by-product chemicals. *Mailing Add:* Chestnut Lane Highlands NC 28741

SARJEANT, WALTER JAMES, PHYSICS, ELECTRICAL ENGINEERING. *Current Pos:* JAMES CLERK MAXWELL PROF DEPT ELEC ENG, STATE UNIV NY, BUFFALO, 81- *Personal Data:* b Strathroy, Ont, Apr 7, 44; m 67; c 2. *Educ:* Univ Western Ont, BSc, 66, MSc, 67, PhD(physics), 71. *Prof Exp:* Asst dir res & develop, Gen-Tec Inc, 71-73; scientist, Lumonics Res Ltd, 73-75; scientist, Nat Res Coun Can, 75-78; scientist, Los Alamos Sci Labs, 79-81. *Concurrent Pos:* Indust fel, Gen-Tec Inc, 71-73; consult, Dept Nat Defence, 71-73, Atomic Energy Can Ltd, 75-; adj prof elec eng, Tex Tech Univ, 77-; adj prof physics, Univ Ill, 79-; scientific adv, DARDA, 81-; consult, Los Alamos Nat Lab, 81- & Defense Nuclear Agency, 85- *Mem:* Fel Inst Elec & Electronics Engrs; Asn Prof Engrs. *Res:* High repetition rate power conditioning systems; gas discharge laser physics and chemical kinetics; generation and measurement of picosecond electrical impulses; electrical insulation and breakdown processes. *Mailing Add:* Dept Elec Eng Bonner Hall Rm 312 State Univ NY Buffalo Buffalo NY 14260

SARJEANT, WILLIAM ANTONY SWITHIN, PALEONTOLOGY, HISTORY OF GEOLOGY. *Current Pos:* assoc prof, 72-80, PROF GEOL SCI, UNIV SASK, 80- *Personal Data:* b Sheffield, Eng, July 15, 35; m 66, Anne M Crowe; c Nicola R, Rachel P & Juliet K. *Educ:* Univ Sheffield, BSc Hons, 56, PhD(geol), 59; Univ Nottingham, DSc(geol), 72. *Honors & Awards:* Sue Tyler Friedman Medal, Geol Soc London, 90; Founders Medal, Soc Hist Natural Hist, 91; Hist Geol Award, Geol Soc Am, 91. *Prof Exp:* Demonstr temp lectr geol, Univ Col N Staffordshire, Eng, 60-61; res fel, Univ Reading, 61-62; from asst lectr to lectr, Univ Nottingham, 63-72. *Concurrent Pos:* Vis prof geol & geophys, Univ Okla, 68-69; consult numerous petrol industs, Eng, France, US & Brazil. *Mem:* Fel Geol Soc London; fel Linnean Soc London; Geol Soc France; Paleont Asn; Am Asn Stratigraphical Palynologists; fel Geol Soc Am; Explorers Club; hon mem, Sociedad Venezolana Historia Geociencios; fel Royal Soc Can. *Res:* Dinoflagellate cysts and acritarchs of the Triassic to Quaternary, Great Britain, France, Germany, Greenland, Algeria, Iran, and Canada; fossil vertebrate footprints and trace-fossil classification, Canada, United States, British Isles and Brazil; history and bibliography of the geological sciences; history of science. *Mailing Add:* Univ Sask Dept Geol Sci 114 Science Pl Saskatoon SK S7N 5E2 Can. *Fax:* 306-966-8593

SARKAR, BIBUDHENDRA, BIOCHEMISTRY, PHYSICAL CHEMISTRY. *Current Pos:* PROF, UNIV TORONTO , 78-; HEAD, BIOCHEM RES, HOSP SICK CHILDREN, 90- *Personal Data:* b Kushtia, India, Aug 2, 35; wid; c Paul & Uma. *Educ:* Banares Univ, India, BPharm, 56, MPharm, 57; Univ Southern Calif, PhD(biochem), 64. *Honors & Awards:* Nuffield Found Award. *Prof Exp:* Vis prof, Inst Phys Chem Biol, Univ Paris, 76-77 & Cambridge, 77. *Mem:* AAAS; Can Biochem Soc; Am Chem Soc; fel Chem Inst Can; Am Soc Biochem & Molecular Biol; Int Asn Bioinorg Sci; Protein Soc. *Res:* Chemical and physico chemical studies related to coordination compounds of metals with proteins, peptides, amino acids, sugars and nucleic acids conducted for understanding their biochemical role in physiological systems and pathological conditions; molecular design to mimic functional sites of biomolecules. *Mailing Add:* Res Inst Hosp for Sick Children 555 University Ave Toronto ON M5G 1X8 Can. *Fax:* 416-813-5379; *E-Mail:* bsarkar@sickkids.on.ca

SARKAR, FAZLUL HOQUE, GENE EXPRESSION & REGULATION, VIROLOGY-HPV & HUMAN CANCER. *Current Pos:* ASSOC PROF PATH & DIR MOLECULAR BIOL, WAYNE STATE UNIV SCH MED, 90- *Personal Data:* b Naroshingapur, India, Jan 26, 52; US citizen; m 83, Nahar; c Sarah F, Sanila F & Shaan M. *Educ:* Calcutta Univ, BS, 71; Aligarh Muslim Univ, MS, 74; Banaras Hindu Univ, PhD(biochem), 78. *Prof Exp:* Res assoc virol & molecular biol, Mem Sloan Kettering Cancer Ctr, 78-81, asst researcher interferon, 81-84; asst prof res gene expression steroid, Oakland Univ, 84-87; dir res mutagenesis, Oxford Biomed Res, 87-88; dir, tumor & molecular biol, Henry Ford Hosp, 88-90. *Concurrent Pos:* From adj asst prof to adj assoc prof, Oakland Univ, 88-93; sci dir res, Oxford Biomed Res, 88- *Mem:* AAAS; Am Soc Biochem & Molecular Biol; Am Asn Cancer Res. *Res:* Expression and regulation of cellular genes in human solid tumors; studies on the mechanism of the role of human papillomavirus in human cancer; patented breast cancer gene; federal funding to conduct cancer research. *Mailing Add:* Dept Path Wayne State Univ Sch Med Detroit MI 48201. *Fax:* 313-745-9299

SARKAR, GOBINDA, MOLECULAR BASIS OF DRUG RESISTANCE IN CARTILAGE TUMORS, ROLE OF BETA TRANSFORMING GROWTH FACTOR RECEPTORS IN FRACTURE HEALING. *Current Pos:* res assoc, 86-91, ASSOC CONSULT, MAYO CLIN & FOUND, 91- *Personal Data:* b Berhampore, W Bengal, India, Jan 1, 50; m 86, Suhla Biswas; c Ameet J. *Prof Exp:* Fel, McGill Univ, 82-85. *Mem:* AAAS; Am Soc Human Genetics. *Res:* Molecular mechanism of chemoresistance in chondrosarcoma; contribution of tumor growth factor and related proteins and their cognate receptors in fracture repair. *Mailing Add:* 1929 Stonewall Lane SW Rochester MN 55902. *Fax:* 507-284-5075

SARKAR, KAMALAKSHA, COMPUTER-AIDED DESIGN. *Current Pos:* PRIN MATS ENG, PHARMACIA DELTEC, INC, 92- *Personal Data:* b Calcutta, India, Sept 27, 47; m 78; c 2. *Educ:* Bengal Eng Col, Sibpur, India, BE, 68; Indian Inst Technol, Kanpur, MTech, 74; Univ Tenn, Knoxville, PhD(eng sci), 80. *Prof Exp:* Structural engr, Indian Space Res Orgn, Trivandrum, 69-74; develop engr, Allied Signal Inc, Morristown, NJ, 80-84, sr res engr, 84-88, res assoc, 88-92. *Concurrent Pos:* Assoc ed, Appl Mech Rev, 84-86. *Mem:* Am Soc Mech Engrs. *Res:* Computer-aided design to develop materials and components using an interdisciplinary approach (mechanical, structural, metallurgical and materials); composite material; fracture mechanics; fluid dynamics; finite element analysis and computational fluid dynamics. *Mailing Add:* 665 Oakwood Dr St Paul MN 55126

SARKAR, NIKHIL KUMAR, BIOMEDICAL ENGINEERING. *Current Pos:* assoc prof, 80-85, actg head biomat, 80-83, HEAD BIOMAT, LA UNIV SCH DENT, 83-, PROF, 85- *Personal Data:* b Jan 21, 43; nat US; m 67, Joysri Sengupta; c Abheek. *Educ:* Calcutta Univ, BE, 66; Univ Alta, MSc, 69; Northwestern Univ Dent Sch, PhD(biol mat), 73. *Honors & Awards:* Award Winner Res Contest, Am Asn Dent Res, 75. *Prof Exp:* Grad engr metall steel, Durgapur Steel Plant, India, 66-67; lab instr physics, Univ Alta, 68-69; res asst, Northwestern Univ Dent Sch, 69-72, fel, 72-73; res assoc, Kerr Mfg Co, Syborn Corp, 73-74, Am Dent Asn, 74- 77. *Concurrent Pos:* Prin investr, Nat Inst Dent Res, 74-88; adj asst prof eng, Tulane Univ, 78-; adj assoc prof mech eng, Univ New Orleans, 84-85, adj prof, 85-; consult, TOKTEN prog, UN Develop Prog & Coun Sci & Indust Res, India, 86 & 92. *Mem:* Fel Acad Dent Mat; Am Soc Metals; Nat Asn Corrosion Engrs; Inst Mining Metall & Petrol Engrs; Int Asn Dent Res; Am Asn Dent Res. *Res:* Structure and corrosion of dental alloys; degradation of dental cements; wear mechanism of restorative resins; bonding mechanism of porcelain-fused-to-metal restorations; dentin bonding agents; metal-reinforced glass-ionomers; degradation of composite resins. *Mailing Add:* 7211 Westhaven Rd New Orleans LA 70126

SARKAR, NILIMA, MOLECULAR BIOLOGY. *Current Pos:* STAFF SCIENTIST, DEPT METABOLIC REGULATION, BOSTON BIOMED RES INST, 76- *Personal Data:* b India, June 2, 35; US citizen; m 61; c 2. *Educ:* Univ Calcutta, India, BS, 53, MS, 55; Northwestern Univ, PhD(biochem), 61. *Prof Exp:* Fel, Dept Biochem, Univ Chicago, 61-63; fel, Dept Microbiol, Tufts Univ, 63-64; res fel, Harvard Med Sch, 64-67, res assoc, 67-69, assoc, 69-75, lectr, Dept Biol Chem, 75- *Mem:* Am Soc Biol Chemists; Am Soc Cell Biol; Am Chem Soc; AAAS. *Res:* Mechanisms of replication of the chromosome, especially in relation to the involvement of RNA primers; poly(A) RNA in bacteria with respect to structure, function and biosynthesis, using the technique of cloning of DNA. *Mailing Add:* Boston Biomed Res Inst 20 Staniford St Boston MA 02114-2500. *Fax:* 617-956-6536

SARKAR, NITIS, WATER SOLUBLE POLYMERS, MINERAL ENGINEERING. *Current Pos:* ASSOC SCIENTIST, FUNCTIONAL POLYMERS RES, DOW CHEM CO, MIDLAND, MI, 68- *Personal Data:* b Gauhati, India, Dec 1, 38; m 70, Chandana Sen; c Richik & Prateek. *Educ:* Gauhati Univ, India, BS, 57; Univ Calcutta, MS, 60; Mass Inst Technol, ScD(mineral eng), 65. *Honors & Awards:* MASTL (Dow) Scientists' Award, 84. *Prof Exp:* Res trainee, Fuel Res Inst, India, 60-61; lectr, Barasat Govt Col, 61-62; res asst, Mass Inst Technol, 62-65; res chemist chem lab, Dow Chem Co, 65-68 & Betz Labs, Inc, 68. *Mem:* Am Chem Soc. *Res:* Flocculation; water treatment; characterization of water soluble polymers; rheology of polymer solutions; detergency; dispersion; adhesion; paints; latexes;

thickeners; enhanced oil recovery, cellulosic polymers, surface and colloid chemistry flotation; use of polymer in food; suspension polymerization; engineering thermoplastics and blends. *Mailing Add:* 4794 Washtenaw Ave Apt B1 Ann Arbor MI 48108

SARKAR, SATYAPRIYA, MOLECULAR & CELLULAR BIOLOGY OF MUSCLE DEVELOPMENT. *Current Pos:* ASSOC PROF, DEPT ANAT & CELL BIOL, TUFTS UNIV MED SCH, 86- *Personal Data:* b Khanjanagar, India, Mar 1, 34; m 61; c 2. *Educ:* Univ Calcutta, BSc, 53, MSc, 56; Northwestern Univ, PhD(biochem), 61. *Prof Exp:* Sr staff scientist, Boston Biomed Res Inst, 72-86; mem grad prog, Cell & Develop Biol, Sch Med, Harvard Univ, 80-86. *Concurrent Pos:* Consult, NIH Nat Heart, Lung & Blood Inst, 81-, mem, Biomed Sci Study Sect, NIH, 87-, mem, res peer rev comt, Am Heart Asn Mass Affiliate, 87-90, prin investr, NIH grant, 69- *Mem:* Am Chem Soc; Am Soc for Biochem & Molecular Biol; Am Soc for Cell Biol; NY Acad Sci; AAAS. *Res:* Molecular mechanism of gene expression in muscle cell; regulation of human myogenesis in normal and pathological conditions. *Mailing Add:* Dept Anat Cellular Biol & Comp Med Health Sci Ctr M&V 519 Tufts Univ 136 Harrison Ave Boston MA 02111-1800. *Fax:* 617-956-6536

SARKARIA, GURMUKH S, ENGINEERING ADMINISTRATION. *Current Pos:* CONSULT, 87- *Personal Data:* b 1925. *Educ:* Punjab Univ, BS, 45; Polytech Inst, Brooklyn, MS, 47; Harvard Univ, MSE, 48. *Prof Exp:* Vpres, Morrison Knudsen Inc, 70-81, sr vpres, 81-86. *Concurrent Pos:* Gen coordr, Hydroelec Proj Bet, Paraguay-Brazil, 75-81; consult to Chinese Govt for Three Gorges hydroelec power plant. *Mem:* Nat Acad Eng; Am Soc Civil Engrs. *Mailing Add:* 2378 San Clemente Way Vista CA 92084

SARKISOV, PAVEL JEBRAELOVICH, CHEMISTRY & TECHNOLOGY OF HIGH MELTING MATERIALS, SYNTHESIS OF GLASS-CRYSTALLINE MATERIALS. *Current Pos:* res, asst prof, vice-prof, dean, 62-84, PROF CHEM TECHNOL, MENDELEYEV UNIV CHEM TECHNOL RUSSIA, 85- *Personal Data:* b Tbilisi, Ga, Russia, Sept 19, 32; m 60, Svetlana Jabotinskaya; c Corine & Elizabeth. *Educ:* Moscow D I Mendeleyev Inst Chem Technol, MS, 59, PhD(technol glass), 63, DSc, 76. *Honors & Awards:* Laureate of Ukraine State Prize, 82; Order of Red Banner State Prize, 85. *Prof Exp:* Technologist, Crystal Glass Plant, Ministry Indust & Eng, Gus-Khrustalny, 56-59. *Concurrent Pos:* Consult, Plant Avtosteko, Ukraine, 70-80; mem, Sci Coun, State Inst Glass, 70-94; supvr, high schs, Kazakhstan, Russia, 75-80; chmn, Sci Coun Chem, State Comt Higher Educ, 75-; lectr, Claustal Univ, Ger, 80; mem, Sci Coun Heat-Resistant Mat, Russian Acad Sci, 80-94; bd mem, Am Inst Chem, 91. *Mem:* Corresp mem Acad Sci Russia. *Res:* Glass technology. *Mailing Add:* Mendeleyev Univ Chem Technol Russia Miusskaya Sq 9 Moscow 125190 Russia. *Fax:* 7-095-200-4204; *E-Mail:* Sarkisov@mhti.msk.su

SARKISSIAN, NAVER AGOP, MEDICAL VIROLOGY. *Current Pos:* RES SCIENTIST, DEPT PATH, COL PHYSICIANS & SURGEONS, COLUMBIA UNIV, 96- *Personal Data:* b Varna, Bulgaria, Apr 12, 60; m 95, Assen Petrov Bugdanov. *Educ:* Med Col Varna, Bulgaria, BS, 80, MD, 87; Med Acad, Moscow, PhD(med), 93. *Prof Exp:* Lab technologist, Med Sch, Varna, Bulgaria, 80-81; physician & clin virologist, Div Med Microbiol, Inst Epidemiol, Varna, Bulgaria, 87-89; postdoctoral res assoc, Dept Infectious Dis & Virol & Molecular Biol, St Jude Children's Res Hosp, 94-96. *Mem:* Am Soc Virol. *Res:* Molecular mechanisms of human immunodeficiency virus assembly and entry into host cells; evaluation of antiviral compounds to HIV; interaction between HIV and various infectious agents; anti-HIV gene therapy. *Mailing Add:* 515 W 59th St No 10J New York NY 10019. *Fax:* 212-582-5027; *E-Mail:* nas35@columbia.edu

SARKO, ANATOLE, POLYMER CHEMISTRY, POLYMER PHYSICS. *Current Pos:* res assoc chem, 66-67, from asst prof to assoc prof, 67-76, PROF CHEM, STATE UNIV NY COL ENVIRON & FORESTRY, 76-, CHMN DEPT, 84- *Personal Data:* b Tallinn, Estonia, May 27, 30; m 55; c 1. *Educ:* Upsala Col, BS, 52; NY Univ, MS, 60; State Univ NY Col Forestry, Syracuse, PhD(phys chem), 66. *Prof Exp:* Mem biochem staff, Gen Foods Corp, NY, 52-60, sr chemist, 60-63. *Concurrent Pos:* Vis scientist, Univ Frieburg, Ger & Nat Ctr Sci Res-CERMAV, Grenoble, France, 78. *Mem:* AAAS; Am Chem Soc; Am Phys Soc. *Res:* Physical chemistry of polymers; conformation of cellulose and other polysaccharides in solid and solution states and their structure-function relationships; x-ray techniques of polymers; computer techniques in chemistry. *Mailing Add:* 212 Kittell Rd Fayetteville NY 13066-1623

SARLES, F(REDERICK) WILLIAMS, ELECTRICAL ENGINEERING. *Current Pos:* PRES & CONSULT ENGR, FWS ENG, LEXINGTON, MASS, 82- *Personal Data:* b Cincinnati, Ohio, Sept 27, 31; m 60; c 2. *Educ:* Duke Univ, BSEE, 53; Mass Inst Technol, MS, 55, ScD(elec eng), 61. *Prof Exp:* Res asst compound components & systs group, Lincoln Lab, Mass Inst Technol, 53-61, mem staff div sponsored res, 61, mem staff space commun, 61-69, asst group leader, 69-71, group leader spacecraft technol group, 71-78, sr staff mem, 78-80, vpres, Tri Solar Corp, Bedford, Mass, 80-82. *Concurrent Pos:* Lectr, Northeastern Univ, 67-71. *Mem:* Sr mem Inst Elec & Electronics Engrs; AAAS; Sigma Xi. *Res:* Design of control and communication systems; telemetry systems; design of space experiments; photovoltate systems; industrial controls and communication. *Mailing Add:* 54 Ledgelawn Ave Lexington MA 02173-3449

SARLES, LYNN REDMON, INSTRUMENTATION DESIGN. *Current Pos:* CONSULT, SPECTRONICS, INC, 89- *Personal Data:* b Grand Forks, NDak, Jan 22, 30; m 51, Lucretia Zopf; c Laura, Jennifer, Jeffrey & Christopher. *Educ:* Univ Calif, Berkeley, BA, 51; Stanford Univ, PhD(physics), 57. *Prof Exp:* Sloan fel physics, Univ Calif, 57-58; res physicist, Varian Assocs, 58-62; mgr phys optics, Maser Optics-West, 62-63; mgr geophys res, Varian Assocs, 63-67; dir admin, Ore Grad Ctr, 67-68, vpres, 68-72; vpres res, Systs Mgt Assoc, Inc, 71-93. *Mem:* Fel AAAS. *Res:* Magnetic resonance; optical pumping; geomagnetism; lasers; instrumentation; technological forecasting. *Mailing Add:* PO Box 253 Keyport WA 98345. *E-Mail:* lsarles@sprintmail.com

SARMA, ATUL C, CERAMIC & REFRACTORY BINDING SYSTEMS. *Current Pos:* RES ASSOC MAT SCI & DIR, RES & DEVELOP & PROD, WHIP MIX CORP, 73- *Personal Data:* b Mangaldoi, Assam, India, Feb 1, 39; US citizen; m 79; c 2. *Educ:* Cotton Col, India, BSc Hons, 61; Guwahati Univ, MSc, 63; Univ Minn, MS, 67; Univ Louisville, PhD(inorg chem), 71. *Prof Exp:* Lectr chem, Cotton Col, India, 63-65; res assoc environ chem, Univ Louisville, 71-73. *Concurrent Pos:* Instr, Univ Louisville, 71-73, adj assoc prof, 76-83; mem & secy, specif comt waxes, Am Nat Standards Inst, 81-, chmn, specif comt dent stones, plasters & casting refractories, 85- *Mem:* Am Chem Soc; Am Ceramic Soc; Int Asn Dent Res; Sigma Xi. *Res:* Solid state, environmental and ceramic chemistry; precision casting technology; reactions in solids; high-technology ceramics; waxes, gypsum products and dental materials. *Mailing Add:* Whip Mix Corp PO Box 17183 Louisville KY 40217-0183

SARMA, DITTAKAVI S R, BIOCHEMISTRY, EXPERIMENTAL PATHOLOGY. *Current Pos:* assoc prof, 77-86, PROF PATH, UNIV TORONTO, 86- *Personal Data:* b Tenali, India, June 15, 36; m 72. *Educ:* Andhra Univ, India, BSc, 54; Univ Nagpur, MSc, 57; Univ Madras, PhD(biochem), 62. *Prof Exp:* Coun Sci & Indust Res sr res fel, Dept Biochem, Indian Inst Sci, Bangalore, 62-65; res assoc exp path, Sch Med, Univ Pittsburgh, 65-70, asst res prof, 70-71; asst res prof chem carcinogenesis, Fels Res Inst, Med Sch, Temple Univ, 71-77. *Mem:* Am Soc Exp Path; Am Asn Cancer Res; Environ Mutagen Soc; NY Acad Sci. *Res:* Chemical carcinogenesis; DNA repair. *Mailing Add:* Dept Path Med Sci Bldg Univ Toronto Toronto ON M5S 1A8 Can

SARMA, PADMAN S, VIROLOGY, VETERINARY MEDICINE. *Current Pos:* PROG DIR, RNA VIRUS STUDIES I, BIOL CARCINOGENESIS BR, NAT CANCER INST, NIH, 83- *Personal Data:* b India, Dec 3, 31; US citizen; c 2. *Educ:* Madras Vet Col, India, DVM, 53; Univ Minn, MS, 57, PhD(virol), 59. *Prof Exp:* Asst lectr animal husb & microbiol, Madras Vet Col, 53-55; res officer, Pasteur Inst, India, 59-61; asst prof microbiol, Univ Ky, 61-62; vis scientist, NIH, 62-64; proj dir viral carcinogenesis, Microbiol Assoc Inc, 64-68; res microbiologist & chief, Sec Ecol & Epizool, Viral Carcinogensis Br, 68-77, chief, Animal Virol & Field Studies Sect, Lab Cellular & Molecular Biol, 77-83. *Concurrent Pos:* Instr lectr, Med Virol Course, 83- *Mem:* AAAS; Am Vet Med Asn. *Res:* Elucidation of the prevalence, etiological role and control of retroviruses responsible for the causation of naturally-occurring cancers in a variety of avian and mammalian species, including man; more recently, scientific program administration of NIH extramural grants and contracts in this area; author of 93 scientific publications in leading scientific journals. *Mailing Add:* 14124 Rippling Brook Dr Silver Spring MD 20906

SARMA, RAGHUPATHY, MOLECULAR BIOLOGY, BIOCHEMISTRY. *Current Pos:* asst prof, 71-77, assoc prof, 78-80, PROF BIOCHEM, STATE UNIV NY, STONY BROOK, 80- *Personal Data:* b Udipi, India, Feb 18, 37; m 63; c 2. *Educ:* Presidency Col, Madras, BSc, 57; Univ Madras, MSc, 58, PhD(physics), 63. *Prof Exp:* Fel & res assoc, Royal Inst, London, 63-66 & Oxford Univ, 66-68; vis assoc, NIH, 68-71. *Mem:* Am Crystallog Asn. *Res:* Structure and function of biological macromolecules; x-ray crystallography; crystallographic computing. *Mailing Add:* Dept Biochem State Univ NY 100 Nicholls Rd Stony Brook NY 11794-0001

SARMA, RAMASWAMY HARIHARA, BIOCHEMISTRY. *Current Pos:* asst prof, 70-75, assoc prof, 75-77, PROF CHEM, STATE UNIV NY ALBANY, 77-, DIR, INST BIOMOLECULAR STEREODYNAMICS, 77-, DIR, CTR BIOL MACROMOLECULES, 81- *Personal Data:* b Perumbavoor, India, May 10, 39; m 63. *Educ:* Univ Kerala, BSc, 59, MS, 61; Brown Univ, PhD(chem), 67. *Prof Exp:* Fel biochem, Brandeis Univ, 67-69; fel, Univ Calif, San Diego, 69-70. *Mem:* AAAS; Am Inst Chem; NY Acad Sci; Am Soc Biol Chemists. *Res:* Nucleic acid structures and their complexes with anticancer agents. *Mailing Add:* State Univ NY 1400 Washington Ave Albany NY 12222-1000

SARMIENTO, JORGE LOUIS, BIOGEOCHEMISTRY. *Current Pos:* assoc prof, 86-91, PROF GEOL & GEOPHYS SCI DEPT, ATMOSPHERIC & OCEANIC SCI PROG, PRINCETON UNIV, 91- *Personal Data:* b Lima, Peru, Feb 7, 46; m 78, Lucia Acosta; c Jonathan D & Sara A. *Educ:* Swarthmore Col, BS, 48; Columbia Univ, MA, 74, MPh, 76, PhD(geol), 78. *Prof Exp:* Res assoc, 78-80, asst prof, 80-86. *Concurrent Pos:* Dir, Atmospheric & Oceanic Sci Prog, Princeton Univ, 80-91. *Mem:* Am Geophys Union; Am Soc Limnol & Oceanog; Sigma Xi; Am Meterol Soc; Oceanog Soc. *Res:* Published numerous articles in various journals, modeling of global biogeochemical cycles, primarily the cycling of carbon in the oceans. *Mailing Add:* GFD Prog Princeton Univ PO Box 308 Princeton NJ 08540. *Fax:* 609-258-2850; *E-Mail:* jls@splash.princeton.edu

SARMIENTO, RAFAEL APOLINAR, CHROMATOGRAPHIC & SPECTROSCOPIC ANALYSIS. *Current Pos:* RETIRED. *Personal Data:* b Manila, Philippines, Jan 8, 37; m 66, Loreta Moyco; c Andre & John. *Educ:* Wash Col, Md, BS, 61; Am Univ, Wash, DC, MS, 69, PhD(org-analytic chem), 75. *Prof Exp:* Chemist, Entom Res Div, Agr Res Serv, USDA, 61-66, res chemist, Agr Environ Qual Inst, 66-75; adv, Int Atomic Energy Agency, Vienna, 75-79, proj dir, 79-83; sect head, Chem Coord Unit, USDA, 85-86, lab mgr, Fed Grain Inspection Serv, 88-90, asst dir, Field Mgt Div, Fed Grain Inspection Serv, 90-91; anal chemist, Anal Chem Lab, Environ Protection Agency, 86-88; sr chemist, Bur Alcohol, Tobacco & Firearms, Dept Treas, 91-94. *Concurrent Pos:* Lectr, Univ Md, 73-75; gen mgr, Mikael Assoc, 90-. *Mem:* Am Chem Soc; Am Inst Chemists; Am Asn Univ Profs; Entom Soc Am. *Res:* Development of chromatographic and spectrometric analysis of agricultural and environmental contaminants and pest control agents. *Mailing Add:* The Pentagon House Mayayap Sur Cabanatuan 3100 Philippines. *Fax:* 301-413-9463

SARNA, SUSHIL K, PHYSIOLOGY. *Current Pos:* PROF SURG & PHYSIOL, MED COL WIS, 81-, CHIEF, DEPT SURG RES SECT, 84-, DIR, INTERDEPT RES UNIT DIGESTIVE SYST RES, 87- *Personal Data:* b Rawalpindi, India, Mar 2, 42; m; c 1. *Educ:* Univ Alta, PhD(biomed eng), 71. *Honors & Awards:* Career Scientist Award, Vet Admin, 84, Outstanding Performance Award, 86, 88 & 89. *Prof Exp:* Asst prof, depts pharmacol & elec eng, Univ Alta, 71-74; assoc prof, depts surg & elec eng, McMaster Univ, 74-80. *Concurrent Pos:* Mem prog comt, Am Gastrointestinal Soc, 84 & 85, Am Motility Soc, 84; mem, Digestive Dis Core Ctr Site comts, NIH, 84 & 85; ad hoc mem, Physiol Study sect, NIH, 85; ed, J Gastrointestinal Motility. *Res:* Gastrointestinal smooth muscle motor function. *Mailing Add:* Dept Surg Zablocki Vet Admin Med Ctr Surg Res 15 5000 W National Ave Milwaukee WI 53295-8001. *Fax:* 414-384-1906

SARNA-WOJCICKI, ANDREI M, TEPHROCHRONOLOGY, NEOTECTONICS. *Current Pos:* GEOLOGIST, US GEOL SURV, 71- *Personal Data:* b Gdynia, Poland, May 30, 37; US citizen; m 79, Deborah R Harden; c Matthew, Martin, Daniel & Margaret. *Educ:* Columbia Col, NY, BA, 59; Univ Calif, Berkeley, PhD(geol), 71. *Mem:* Friends of the Pleistocene. *Res:* Correlation of volcanic ash layers (tephrochronology) in the western United States; assessment of volcanic and seismic hazards in the western United States; application of volcanic ash chronology to climate studies. *Mailing Add:* 708 Garland Dr Palo Alto CA 94303

SARNER, STANLEY FREDERICK, PHYSICAL CHEMISTRY. *Current Pos:* RES CHEMIST, REACTION INSTRUMENTS, 71- *Personal Data:* b New York, NY, Oct 15, 31; m 67; c 2. *Educ:* City Col New York, BSc, 52; Univ Cincinnati, MSc, 61; Univ Del, PhD, 70. *Honors & Awards:* Bendix Aviation Corp Award, 57; Del Award, Am Chem Soc, 70. *Prof Exp:* Chemist, Picatinny Arsenal, NJ, 52-54; res chemist flight propulsion labs, Gen Elec Co, Ohio, 56-61; sr chemist, Thiokol Chem Corp, Md, 61-66, staff chemist, 66-67; res chemist, F&M Sci Div, Hewlett-Packard Co, Pa, 67-68; res chemist exp sta, E I du Pont de Nemours & Co, Inc, 68-70; res chemist, Chem Data Systs, 70-71. *Concurrent Pos:* Sr res assoc & instr chem, Univ Del, 71-; Archmere Acad, 74- *Mem:* Am Chem Soc; Am Inst Aeronaut & Astronaut; Brit Interplanetary Soc. *Res:* High temperature reactions; thermodynamics and kinetics; rocket propellants; pyrolysis; gas chromatography; instrument research. *Mailing Add:* 2635 Sherwood Dr Wilmington DE 19808

SARNESKI, JOSEPH EDWARD, ANALYTICAL CHEMISTRY, INORGANIC CHEMISTRY. *Current Pos:* asst prof, 78-80, ASSOC PROF CHEM, FAIRFIELD UNIV, 80- *Personal Data:* b East Orange, NJ, Oct 27, 44; m 75. *Educ:* Kings Col, BS, 66; Case Western Reserve Univ, PhD(chem), 71. *Prof Exp:* Res assoc, Univ NC, Chapel Hill, 72-75; vis asst prof anal chem, Duke Univ, 75-78. *Mem:* Am Chem Soc. *Res:* Nuclear magnetic resonance; analytical and structural applications; chelate chemistry; conformation analysis; chromatography. *Mailing Add:* Dept Chem Fairfield Univ Fairfield CT 06430-6018

SARNGADHARAN, MANGALASSERIL G, BIOCHEMISTRY, RETROVIROLOGY. *Current Pos:* DIR DEPT CELL BIOL, ADVAN BIOSCI LABS, 77-, VPRES SCI AFFAIRS, 87- *Personal Data:* b 1937; m 67; c 2. *Educ:* Univ Delhi, PhD(chem), 66. *Mem:* Am Soc Biochem & Molecular Biol; Am Asn Cancer Res; fel Am Acad Microbiol; Int Asn Comp Res Leukemia & Related Dis; Int AIDS Soc. *Res:* Protein chemistry; immunochemistry; study of human retroviruses in relation to cancer and immune deficiency; develop sensitive and specific methods to detect infection; design strategies for control and prevention of retroviral infection. *Mailing Add:* Advan BioSci Labs Inc 5510 Nicholson Lane Kensington MD 20895-1042

SAROFF, HARRY ARTHUR, ORGANIC CHEMISTRY. *Current Pos:* from chemist to chief sect, 50-74, CHIEF SECT MACROMOLECULES, LAB BIOPHYS CHEM, NAT INST ARTHRITIS & METAB DIS, 74- *Personal Data:* b New York, NY, Mar 8, 14; m 50; c 3. *Educ:* Rensselaer Polytech Inst, BS, 36, MS, 37, PhD(org chem), 40. *Prof Exp:* Res exec chem, US Naval Med Res Inst, 47-50. *Mem:* AAAS; Am Soc Biol Chemists; Biophys Soc; Am Chem Soc. *Res:* Physical chemistry of proteins; protein modification reactions; binding of ions and small molecules to proteins; action of hemoglobin. *Mailing Add:* NIH Bldg 8 Bethesda MD 20892. *Fax:* 301-402-0240

SAROFIM, ADEL FARES, CHEMICAL ENGINEERING. *Current Pos:* From asst prof to assoc prof chem eng, 61-72, Joseph R Mares prof, 81-84, PROF CHEM ENG, MASS INST TECHNOL, 72-, LAMMOT DU PONT PROF, 89- *Personal Data:* b Cairo, Egypt, Oct 21, 34; US citizen; m 67; c 1. *Educ:* Oxford Univ, BA, 55; Mass Inst Technol, SM, 57, ScD(chem eng), 62. *Honors & Awards:* Kuwait Petrochem Eng Prize, 83; Sir Alfred Egerton Medal, Combustion Inst, 84; Hottel lectr, Combustion Inst, 86; Lacey lectr, Calif Inst Technol, 87; Walter Ahlstrom Prize, 93. *Concurrent Pos:* Vis prof, Scheffield Univ, Eng, 71, Univ Naples, Italy, 83; mem, Panel Hazardous Trace Substances, Off Sci & Technol, 72 & 74, Comt Health & Ecol Effect Increased Utilization, Dept HEW, 77 & Energy Eng Bd, Nat Acad Sci, 83-88; Chevron vis prof, Calif Inst Technol, 78; comt hazardous waste in lab, Nat Acad Sci, 81-84, Chem Eng Res Frontiers, 85-87. *Mem:* Am Chem Soc; Am Inst Chem Engrs; Combustion Inst. *Res:* Radiative heat transfer, combustion, fluidization, gas-solid reactions, aerosol formation. *Mailing Add:* Bldg 20, 18 Vassar St Mass Inst Technol 66-572 Cambridge MA 02139. *Fax:* 617-253-2072; *E-Mail:* sarofim@athena.mit.edu

SARPHIE, THEODORE G, HISTOCHEMISTRY. *Current Pos:* ASST PROF ANAT, HAHNEMANN MED COL, 79- *Personal Data:* b Hattiesburg, Miss, July 18, 44; m 73; c 2. *Educ:* Univ Southern Miss, BS, 66, MS, 68; Univ Miss, PhD(anat & path), 72. *Prof Exp:* Asst prof anat, Univ S Ala, 72-79. *Mem:* Am Soc Cell Biol; Histochem Soc; Am Asn Anatmists. *Res:* Macromolecular response of endothelial cell surfaces to hemodynamic forces and pathological conditions; using transmission and scanning electron microscopy and histo-cytochemistry. *Mailing Add:* Dept Anat La State Univ Sch Med 1542 Tulane Ave New Orleans LA 70112-2825

SARPKAYA, TURGUT, MECHANICAL ENGINEERING, MATHEMATICS. *Current Pos:* prof, 67-76, chmn dept, 67-71, DISTINGUISHED PROF MECH ENG, NAVAL POSTGRAD SCH, MONTEREY, CALIF, 76- *Personal Data:* b Turkey, May 7, 28; US citizen; m 62. *Educ:* Tech Univ Istanbul, BS & MS, 50; Univ Iowa, PhD(eng mech), 54. *Honors & Awards:* L F Moody Award, Am Soc Mech Engrs, 67; Collingwood Prize, Am Soc Civil Engrs, 57; Fluids Eng Award, 90. *Prof Exp:* Res engr, Hydrodyn Lab, Mass Inst Technol, 54-55; lectr hydrodyn, Univ Paris, 55-56; from asst prof to prof eng mech, Univ Nebr, Lincoln, 57-64, Fawick prof, 64-66, prof mech eng, 66-67. *Concurrent Pos:* Res vis prof, Univ Manchester; aerodyn res inst, Univ Gottingen, 71-72; Sigma Xi res award, 71. *Mem:* Int Asn Hydraul Res; Am Soc Mech Engrs; Am Soc Civil Engrs; Am Inst Aeronaut & Astronaut; Sigma Xi. *Res:* Hydrodynamics; heat transfer; unsteady fluid motions; turbulence; biomedical engineering; vortex motion; stability of flows; fluidics; pulsating flows in rigid and elastic systems. *Mailing Add:* Dept Mech Eng-ME 700 Dyer Rd Bldg 245 Naval Postgrad Sch One University Ctr Monterey CA 93943-5146

SARRAM, MEHDI, NUCLEAR SYSTEMS ENGINEERING. *Current Pos:* MGR NUCLEAR ANALYSIS, UNITED ENGRS & CONSTRUCTORS INC, 82- *Personal Data:* b Kerman, Iran, June 28, 42; m 68; c 2. *Educ:* Univ Mich, BS, 65, MS, 66; Univ Teheran, PhD, 70. *Prof Exp:* Asst prof nuclear eng, Univ Tehran, 67-73; dir nuclear safeguards, Atomic Energy Orgn, Iran, 73-81; consult nuclear safeguards, Int Atomic Energy Agency, Vienna, Austria, 81-82. *Concurrent Pos:* Nuclear reactor supv, Tehran Nuclear Ctr, 67-73; dir nuclear training, Atom Energy Orgn, Iran, 73-81; invited lectr, Sandia Lab, 82; invited prof, Univ Pa, 84. *Mem:* Am Nuclear Soc. *Res:* Nuclear safeguards and physical security. *Mailing Add:* 5225 Pooks Hill Rd Bethesda MD 20814-2052

SARRAS, MICHAEL P, JR, CELL BIOLOGY, ANATOMY. *Current Pos:* ASST PROF ANAT, MED CTR, UNIV KANS, 82- *Educ:* La State Univ, PhD(anat & cell biol), 78. *Res:* Developmental biology; biochemistry. *Mailing Add:* Dept Anat Cell Biol Univ Kans Med Ctr 3901 Rainbow Blvd Kansas City KS 66160-7400. *Fax:* 913-588-1412

SARRIF, AWNI M, pharmacology, toxicology, for more information see previous edition

SARTAIN, JERRY BURTON, SOIL SCIENCE, STATISTICS. *Current Pos:* From asst prof to assoc prof, 74-86, PROF, DEPT SOIL SCI, UNIV FLA, 86- *Personal Data:* b Walnut, Miss, May 29, 45; m 65; c 1. *Educ:* Miss State Univ, BS, 67, MS, 70; NC State Univ, PhD(soil sci), 74. *Mem:* Am Soc Agron; Soil Sci Soc Am; Soil & Crop Sci Soc Fla. *Res:* Turf and ornamental soil fertility. *Mailing Add:* 8001 SW 103rd Ave Gainesville FL 32608

SARTELL, JACK A(LBERT), METALLURGY. *Current Pos:* CONSULT, MATH & PROCESSES, HONEYWELL RES CTR, 87- *Personal Data:* b St Cloud, Minn, June 18, 24; m 51; c 1. *Educ:* Univ Minn, BS, 49, MS, 51; Univ Wis, PhD(metall), 56. *Prof Exp:* Res engr, Res Lab, Aluminum Co Am, 51-52; instr, Univ Wis, 52-56; sr res scientist, 56-63, staff scientist, 63-64, head res sect, 64-67, mgr appl physics dept, 67-86. *Mem:* Fel Am Soc Metals; Am Inst Mining, Metall & Petrol Engrs; Brit Inst Metals. *Res:* Oxidation of metals and alloys; magnetics; computer memories and process control. *Mailing Add:* 167 Spring Valley Dr Minneapolis MN 55420

SARTIN, AUSTIN ALBERT, carbonate petrography; deceased, see previous edition for last biography

SARTIN, JAMES L, JR, GROWTH HORMONE-IGF AXIS, ENDOCRINE SYSTEM & DISEASE. *Current Pos:* from asst prof to assoc prof, 82-92, PROF PHYSIOL, DEPT PHYSIOL & PHARMACOL, COL VET MED, AUBURN UNIV, 92- *Personal Data:* b Jacksonville, NC, Feb 15, 52; m 76, Eva Martin; c Matthew & Scott. *Educ:* Auburn Univ, BA, 73, MS, 76; Okla State Univ, PhD(physiol), 78. *Prof Exp:* Postdoctoral trainee, Temple Univ, 79-82. *Concurrent Pos:* Ed, Domestic Animal Endocrinol, 83-; vis prof, Univ Ala, Birmingham, 89-90, Emory Univ, 97. *Mem:* Endocrine Soc; Am Soc Animal Sci; Int Soc Neuroendocrinol; AAAS; Am Physiol Soc. *Res:* Growth hormone, insulin-like factor synthesis and release; role of hormones in disease processes; growth hormone signal transduction. *Mailing Add:* Dept Physiol Pharmacol Auburn Univ Col Vet Med Auburn AL 36849-5520. *E-Mail:* jsartin@acesag.auburn.edu

SARTOR, ALBIN FRANCIS, JR, PETROLEUM CHEMISTRY. *Current Pos:* RETIRED. *Personal Data:* b Bartlett, Tex, Oct 14, 19; m 50, Leela Cardwell; c Carol L. *Educ:* Rice Inst, BA, 41. *Prof Exp:* Jr res chemist, Shell Oil Co, 41-44, from res chemist to sr res chemist, 44-56, supvr, 56-63, sr res chemist, 63-86. *Mem:* Am Chem Soc. *Res:* Process and catalyst development; hydrogenation; technical information. *Mailing Add:* 3314 Country Meadows Ct Pearland TX 75584-2079

SARTOR, ANTHONY, CHEMICAL ENGINEERING, ENVIRONMENTAL ENGINEERING. *Current Pos:* EXEC VPRES, PAULUS, SOKOLOWSKI & SARTOR INC, 78- *Personal Data:* b Englewood, NJ, Mar 28, 43; m 64, Maria Crisonino; c Colette, Lisanne & John. *Educ:* Manhattan Col, BChE, 64; Univ Mich, Ann Arbor, MSE, 65, PhD(chem eng), 68. *Prof Exp:* Develop engr, Celanese Plastics Co, 68-70; sr water qual engr, Consol Edison of NY, Inc, 70-72; dir environ affairs, NY Power Pool, 72-77; pres, Sartor Assocs, 77-78. *Mem:* Am Inst Chem Eng; Am Chem Soc. *Res:* Effects of power plant discharges on the environment. *Mailing Add:* Paulus Sokolowski & Sartor Inc 67A Mountain Blvd Ext Warren NJ 07059-0039

SARTORELLI, ALAN CLAYTON, BIOCHEMICAL PHARMACOLOGY, CANCER RESEARCH. *Current Pos:* from asst prof to assoc prof pharmacol, Sch Med, Yale Univ, 61-67, head, Develop Therapeut Prog, Cancer Ctr, 74-90, chmn dept, 77-84, dep dir, Yale Comprehensive Cancer Ctr, 82-84 & Cancer Prev Res Unit Conn, 89-91, dir, Yale Comprehensive Cancer Ctr, 84-93, actg dir, Cancer Prev Res Unit Conn, 89-93, PROF PHARMACOL, SCH MED, YALE UNIV, 67-, ALFRED GILMAN PROF PHARMACOL, 87-, PROF EPIDEMIOL, 91- *Personal Data:* b Chelsea, Mass, Dec 18, 31; m 69, Alice Anderson; c Linda, Suzanne & Sandra. *Educ:* Northeastern Univ, BS, 53; Middlebury Col, MS, 55; Univ Wis, PhD(oncol), 58. *Hon Degrees:* MA, Yale Univ, 67. *Honors & Awards:* Paul K Smith lectr, George Washington Univ, 78; Rufus Cole lectr, Rockefeller Univ, 80; Walter Hubert lectr, Brit Asn Cancer Res, 85; Pfizer lectr, Univ Conn Health Ctr, 85; Award in Exp Therapeut, Am Soc Pharmacol & Exp Therapeut, 86; Mike Hogg Award, Univ Tex Anderson Cancer Ctr, 89. *Prof Exp:* Asst chem, Middlebury Col, 53-55; asst oncol, Univ Wis, 55-58; from res chemist to sr res chemist, Biomed Div, Samuel Roberts Noble Found, 58-61. *Concurrent Pos:* Mem, Cancer Clin Invest Rev Count, NIH, 68-72, consult, Psoriasis Topical Chemother Planning comt, 72; regional ed, Am Continent, Biochem Pharmacol, 68-; consult biochem, Univ Tex M D Anderson Hosp & Tumor Inst, Houston, 70-76; mem, Adv Comt, Cancer Res Ctr, Mallinckrodt Inst Radiol, Sch Med, Washington Univ, 71-75, mem, Inst Res Grants Comt, Am Cancer Soc, 71-75; mem, Exp Therapeutic Study Sect, USPHS, 73-77; mem, Bd Dirs, Am Asn Cancer Res, 75-78 & 84-87; mgt consult, Off Dir, Div Cancer Treat, Nat Cancer Inst, 75-76, mem, Bd Sci Counr, 78-82; mem, Bristol-Myers Award, Distinguished Achievement Career Res, 77-85, 88-93, chmn, 79-80, 89-92; Charles B Smith vis res prof, Mem Sloan Kettering Cancer Ctr, 79; mem, Nat Prog Comt, 13th Int Cancer Cong, 79-81, Publ Comt, Am Asn Cancer Res, 79-82, chmn comt, 81-82; consult, Bristol-Myers Squibb, 82-93; mem, External Adv Comt, Duke Comprehensive Cancer Ctr, 83-, Univ Southern Calif, 83-93, Bd Dirs, Metastasis Res Soc, 84-90, bd adv, Grace Cancer Drug Ctr, Roswell Park Mem Inst, 86-89, Award Comt, Am Soc Pharmacol & Therapeut, 88, chmn, Award Comt, 92, Forum Drug Develop & Regulation, Inst Med, 89-93, bd vis, Moffitt Cancer Ctr, Univ SFla, 89-92, consult group, Cancer Ctr Prog, Nat Cancer Inst, 89-91 & Nat Bd, Cosmetic, Toiletry & Fragrance Asn, 89+; William N Creasy vis prof clin pharmacol, Wayne State Univ, 83 & Bowman Gray Sch Med, 86; Mayo Found vis prof oncol, Mayo Clin, 83; chmn, Sci Adv Comt, Columbia Univ Comprehensive Cancer Ctr, 86- & bd dirs, Asn Am Cancer Inst, 88; ed-in-chief, Oncol Res/Cancer Commun, 89-; Wellcome vis prof basic sci, Univ Pittsburgh Sch Med, 90; mem, Adv Comt, SLSB Partners, 92-96; chmn, Spec Rev Comt, outstanding investr research applications, Nat Cancer Inst, 92; chmn ad hoc, Contracts Tech Rev Group, Nat Cancer Inst, mgt & oper, Frederick Cancer Res & Develop Ctr, 93. *Mem:* Inst Med Nat Acad Sci; Am Soc Cell Biol; Am Soc Pharmacol & Exp Therapeut; Biochem & Molecular Biol; fel NY Acad Sci; Am Asn Cancer Res (vpres, 85, pres, 86); Asn Am Cancer Insts (vpres, 86, pres, 87); fel AAAS. *Res:* Molecular pharmacology; action of growth-inhibitory agents; nucleotide metabolism; mechanisms of cell death; cell membranes; oncology; mechanisms of cell differentiation; mechanisms of drug resistance; drug development. *Mailing Add:* 4 Perkins Rd Woodbridge CT 06525-1616. *Fax:* 203-737-2045; *E-Mail:* alan_sartorelli@qm.yale.edu

SARTORI, LEO, THEORETICAL ASTROPHYSICS, RELATIVITY. *Current Pos:* chmn dept, 72-78, PROF PHYSICS, UNIV NEBR, LINCOLN, 72-, PROF POLIT SCI, 83- *Personal Data:* b Milan, Italy, Dec 9, 29; nat US; m 61, Eva Martin; c Anne & Jennifer. *Educ:* Mass Inst Technol, SB, 50, PhD(physics), 56. *Prof Exp:* Physicist, Brookhaven Nat Lab, 55-56; instr physics, Princeton Univ, 56-59; asst prof, Rutgers Univ, 59-63; mem res staff sci teaching ctr, Mass Inst Technol, 63-66, lectr, 66-68, assoc prof, 68-72. *Concurrent Pos:* Consult, Lockheed Aircraft Corp, 58-63, Arms Control & Disarmament Agency, 78-81, Dept of Energy, 81-88 & 89; Fulbright fel, Univ Torino, 53; chmn, Forum Physics & Soc, 84-85; vis scholar, Stanford Ctr Int Security & Arms Control, 85, 86 & 88. *Mem:* Fel Am Phys Soc; Arms Control Asn; Am Asn Physics Teachers; Fedn Am Sci; Int Astron Union. *Res:* High-energy astrophysics; supernovas; radio and x-ray sources; defense policy and arms control; theory of synchroton radiation; relativity. *Mailing Add:* Behlen Lab Physics Univ Nebr Lincoln NE 68588-0111. *Fax:* 402-472-2879; *E-Mail:* lsartori@unlinfo.unl.edu

SARTORIS, DAVID JOHN, DIAGNOSTIC RADIOLOGY, MUSCULOSKELETAL IMAGING. *Current Pos:* asst prof radiol, Univ Calif, San Diego, 85-87, chief, Musculoskeletal Imaging, Med Ctr, 85-91, chief, quant bone densitometry, 85-94, ASSOC PROF RADIOL, UNIV CALIF, SAN DIEGO, 87-, PROF RADIOL, MUSCULOSKELETAL IMAGING SECT, SCH MED. *Personal Data:* b Chicago, Ill, Nov 25, 55. *Educ:* Stanford Univ, BS, 76, MD, 80; Am Board Radiol, cert, 84. *Honors & Awards:* Wallace Graham Lectr, Univ Ottawa, 87. *Prof Exp:* Intern diag radiol, Stanford Univ Med Ctr, 80-81; resident, Stanford Univ Affil Hosps, 81-84; fel musculo skeletal radiol, Univ Calif Affil Hosps, San Diego, 84-85. *Concurrent Pos:* Vis prof, Univ Calif, Davis, 85, Univ Calif, Irvine, 86, Maricopa Med Ctr & St Joseph's Hosp, Phoenix, Ariz, 86, Univ Pittsburgh Sch Med & Doris Palmer Arthritis Ctr, St Margaret Mem Hosp, Pittsburgh, 88 & 90, Vet Admin Med Ctr, Long Beach, Calif, 90, Wyeth-Ayerst Lab, Vis Prof Prog, 91, Nebr Radiol Soc, Creighton Univ Med Ctr, 93 & Western Pa Hosp, 95; mem, ed adv bd, Chem Rubber Co Press Inc, 85-, Diag Imaging Mag, 87 & Thieme Med Publ Inc, 86-; mem, Res Grant Rev Bd, The Arthritis Soc, 86- & bd consult, Bd Trustees Res Initiative Comt, Radiol Soc NAm, 87-; mem, Comt Prof Self-Eval & Continuing Educ, Am Col Radiol, 85-88, Prog Comt Subcomt Gen Diag, Radiol Soc NAm, 87-88, Am Soc Emergency Radiol, 93-, Med Ethics Comt, Univ Calif, San Diego, 94- & steering comt, San Diego Sci Alliance, 95; instr, Diag Imaging Musculoskeletal Syst, Univ Calif, San Diego & San Diego State Univ, 87-88 & 88-89; vis fel, Magnetic Resonance Imaging, Univ Calif, Med Ctr, San Diego & Am Med Inst Magnetic Resonance Inst, 89-; NIH res fel, 93. *Mem:* Am Col Radiol; Am Roentgen Ray Soc; Asn Univ Radiologists; Radiol Soc NAm; Int Skeletal Soc; New Bone Densitometry Soc; Bone Dysplasia Soc; Soc Advan Women's Imaging; Am Soc Bone & Mineral Res. *Res:* Osteoporosis; noninvasive bone densitometry; musculoskeletal magnetic resonance imaging; diagnostic imaging of the musculoskeletal system; imaging-pathologic correlation in musculoskeletal disease; sports medicine; musculoskeletal trauma; temporomandibular joint dysfunction; author of numerous publications. *Mailing Add:* Radiol Dept H-756 Univ Calif Med Ctr 225 Dickinson St San Diego CA 92103

SARTORIS, NELSON EDWARD, ORGANIC CHEMISTRY. *Current Pos:* From asst prof to assoc prof, 68-80, PROF CHEM, WITTENBERG UNIV, 80-, CHMN DEPT, 84- *Personal Data:* b Auburn, Ill, Aug 2, 41; m 64; c 2. *Educ:* MacMurray Col, AB, 63; Northwestern Univ, PhD(org chem), 68. *Concurrent Pos:* Vis prof chem, Rice Univ, 81-82. *Mem:* Am Chem Soc; AAAS. *Res:* Base catalyzed reactions; addition of ketenes to olefins; stereochemistry. *Mailing Add:* Dept Chem Wittenberg Univ Springfield OH 45501

SARTWELL, PHILIP EARL, EPIDEMIOLOGY. *Current Pos:* From asst prof to prof, 47-73, EMER PROF EPIDEMIOL, SCH HYG & PUB HEALTH, JOHNS HOPKINS UNIV, 73- *Personal Data:* b Salem, Mass, Sept 11, 08; m 36; c 2. *Educ:* Boston Univ, MD, 32; Harvard Univ, MPH, 38. *Honors & Awards:* John Snow Award, Am Pub Health Asn. *Concurrent Pos:* Consult, WHO, NIH & USPHS; vis lectr, Harvard Sch Pub Health, 75-89; adj prof epidemiol & biostatist, Pub Health, Boston Univ, 83-89. *Mem:* Am Epidemiol Soc; hon mem Royal Soc Med. *Res:* Epidemiology of acute and chronic conditions, including adverse effects of oral contraceptives; ionizing radiation. *Mailing Add:* 38 Cloutman Lane Marblehead MA 01945-1545

SARUKHAN, JOSE, BIOLOGY. *Current Pos:* INVESTR, INST ECOL, CIUDAD UNIV. *Mem:* Nat Acad Sci. *Mailing Add:* Inst de Exologia Ciudad Univ Amexo & Jardin Botonica 2nd piso Ecologia de Pablaciones Del Coyoacan 04510 Mexico. *Fax:* 52-5-622-9018

SARVER, EMORY WILLIAM, ANALYTICAL CHEMISTRY. *Current Pos:* CHEMIST, PHYS RES DIV, CHEM SYST LAB, ABERDEEN PROVING GROUND, 71- *Personal Data:* b Bluefield, WVa, Oct 1, 42; m 63; c 3. *Educ:* WVa Univ, AB, 64; Marshall Univ, MS, 66; Lehigh Univ, PhD(chem), 69. *Mem:* Am Chem Soc; Sigma Xi. *Res:* Characterization of biological materials by pyrolysis-mass spectrometer; development of methods for analysis of these reactants in dilute aqueous and nonaqueous systems. *Mailing Add:* US Army Res Div SMECR-DDT/Sarver Aberdeen Proving Ground MD 21010

SARVEY, JOHN MICHAEL, NEUROPHARMACOLOGY, ELECTROPHYSIOLOGY. *Current Pos:* asst prof, 79-85, ASSOC PROF PHARMACOL, UNIFORMED SERV UNIV HEALTH SCI, 85- *Personal Data:* b North Tonawanda, NY, Dec 31, 46; m 80. *Educ:* Williams Col, BA, 69; State Univ NY, Buffalo, PhD(pharmacol), 76. *Prof Exp:* Vis scientist, Max Planck Inst Brain Res, Ger, 76-79. *Mem:* Soc Neurosci. *Res:* Electrophysiological investigation of synaptic pharmacology neurotransmitter function, and neuronal plasticity in the rat hippocampus in situ and in thin hippocampal slices in vitro and in rat visual cortical slices; effects of anticholinesterases on hippocampol slices. *Mailing Add:* Dept Pharmacol Uniformed Serv Univ Health Sci Bethesda MD 20814-4799. *Fax:* 202-295-3220; *E-Mail:* Bitnet: sarvey@usuhs

SARWAR, GHULAM, PROTEIN & AMINO ACID NUTRITION, SAFETY OF NUTRITIONAL ASSESSMENT OF NOVEL FOODS. *Current Pos:* sci evaluator regulatory affairs, 77-82, RES SCIENTIST NUTRIT, HEALTH & WELFARE CAN, 82- *Personal Data:* b DI Khan, Pakistan, Jan 8, 43; Can citizen; m 69; c 3. *Educ:* Univ Peshawar, Pakistan, BSc, 64, MSc, 68; Univ Sask, MSc, 71, PhD(nutrit), 74. *Prof Exp:* Res assoc nutrit, Univ Sask, 75-77. *Concurrent Pos:* Postdoctoral fel, Univ Alta, 73-75; mem, Codex Comt Veg Proteins, Can Deleg, 82-89; auxiliary prof, Laval Univ, 85-89, McGill Univ, 85-91; off analyst, Health Protection Br, Govt Can, 85-91; sci adv, Food & Agr Orgn, UN, 89-90; sci consult, UN Develop Prog, Pakistan, 90. *Mem:* Am Inst Nutrit; Can Soc Nutrit Sci. *Res:* Protein nutrition such as analysis of proteins and amino acids in foods and determination of their biological effects and requirements, with emphasis on infant formulas. *Mailing Add:* Nutrit Res Div Bur Nutrit Sci Health Protection Br Banting Bldg Tunney's Pasture Ottawa ON K1A 0L2 Can. *Fax:* 613-957-1907

SARWATE, DILIP VISHWANATH, ELECTRICAL ENGINEERING, COMPUTER SCIENCE. *Current Pos:* Res assoc, 73-74, asst prof, 74-80, assoc prof elec, 80-84, PROF, UNIV ILL, 84- *Personal Data:* b Nagpur, India, Dec 25, 45; c 2. *Educ:* Univ Jabalpur, BSc, 65; Indian Inst Sci, Bangalore, India, BE, 68; Princeton Univ, PhD(elec eng), 73. *Concurrent Pos:* Sr investr, Joint Serv Electronics Prog, 73-90; fac investr, NSF grant, 73-76, co-prin investr, 76-80; co-prin investr, Army Res Off contract, 78-91, Technol Challenge grant, State Ill, 90-; co-chmn, 18th & 19th Ann Allerton Conf Commun, 80-81; consult ITT Corp, Aerospace & Optical Div Systs, 85-; treas, Inst Elec & Electronics Engrs Info Theory Group, 81-83; assoc ed, coding theory, Inst Elec Eng Electronics, info theory, 83-85; co-chmn, army res office, workshop for spread spectrum systs, 85-; Battelle Columbus Labs, short term anal prog, 85-86. *Mem:* Fel Inst Elec & Electronics Engrs. *Res:* Multiple-access communications; spread-spectrum communication; coding theory; analysis of algorithms. *Mailing Add:* Coord Sci Lab 1308 W Main St Urbana IL 61801

SARWER-FONER, GERALD, PSYCHOANALYSIS & NEUROPSYCHOPHARMACOLOGY, PSYCHOTHERAPY & FORENSIC PSYCHIATRY. *Current Pos:* PROF PSYCHIAT, WAYNE STATE UNIV MED SCH, DETROIT, MI, 89- *Personal Data:* b Poland, Dec 6, 24; nat Can; m 50, Ethel Sheinfeld; c Michael, Gladys, Janice, Henry & Brian. *Educ:* Univ Montreal, BA, 45, MD, 51; Royal Col Physicians Can, cert psychiat, 55; Am Bd Psychiat & Neurol, dipl, 57; FRCP(C), 71, FRCPsychiat, 73. *Honors & Awards:* Hassan Azima Mem Lectr, Soc Biol Psychiat, 63; Silver Apple Award, Am Acad Psychiat Law, 77; First Samuel Bellet Mem Lectr, Inst Law & Psychiat, Univ Pa, 78; Karl Stern Mem Lectr, Univ Ottawa Fac Med, 79; Simon Bolivar Lectr, Am Psychiat Asn, New Orleans, 81; Sigmund Freud Award, Am Asn Psychoanal Physicians, 82; Laughlin Award, Am Col Psychoanal; William Silverburg Award, Am Acad Psychoanal, 90; Knight Malta. *Prof Exp:* Intern, Univ Montreal Hosps, 50-51, clin lectr psychiat, Fac Med, 53-55; sr asst resident, Western Res Univ Hosps, Cleveland, Ohio, 52-53; clin demonstr, Fac Med, McGill Univ, 54-55, demonstr, 55-58, lectr, 58-62, asst prof, 62-66, assoc prof psychiat, 66-71; dir, Dept Psychiat & psychiatrist-in-chief, Queen Elizabeth Hosp, 66-71; dir, Dept Psychiat, Ottawa Gen Hosp, 71-88, chmn dept, 74-86, prof psychiat, Fac Med, Univ Ottawa, 71-; dir, Lafayette Clin, Detroit, Mich, 89. *Concurrent Pos:* Fel, Butler Hosp, Providence, RI, 51-52; asst resident, Queen Mary Vet Hosp, 53-54, chief resident, 54-55, dir psychiat res, 55-60; dir psychiat res, Jewish Gen Hosp, 55-65, assoc psychiatrist, 55-71; vis prof, Fac Med, Laval Univ, 64-76; consult, Notre Dame Hosp, Montreal, 64-71; vis prof, Chicago Med Sch, 68-76; consult, Ottawa Civic Hosp, 71-, Royal Ottawa Hosp, 71-, Pierre Janet Ctr Hosp, 72- & Nat Defense Med Ctr, 74- *Mem:* Fel Royal Col Psychiatrists; fel Am Col Psychiat; fel Am Col Psychoanalysts (pres, 84-85); fel Int Col Psychom Med (secy, 79-81); Am Acad Psychiat & Law (pres, 75-77); Soc Biol Psychiat (pres, 83-84); Can Psychoanal Soc (pres, 77-81); Can Asn Prof Psychiat (pres, 76-77 & 82-86); Am Asn Social Psychiat (pres elect, 91, pres, 92). *Res:* Dynamics of psychiatric drug therapy; adaptive difficulties of immigrant groups; psychoanalytic psychotherapy of marital problems; object relationship classification of depressive illnesses; human territoriality and instinct theory; obsessive compulsive states; schizophrenia; depressive illness. *Mailing Add:* 3220 Bloomfield Shores Dr West Bloomfield MI 48323-3300. *Fax:* 248-855-8321

SARWINSKI, RAYMOND EDMUND, SUPERCONDUCTING INSTRUMENTS & MAGNETS. *Current Pos:* CONSULT, CRYOGENIC DESIGNS, 82- *Personal Data:* b La Salle, Ill, Jan 11, 36; div; c 2. *Educ:* Univ Ill, Urbana, BS, 60, MS, 61, PhD(physics), 66. *Prof Exp:* Fel physics, Ohio State Univ, 66-67, asst prof, 67-72; mgr advan develop, SHE Corp, 72-82. *Concurrent Pos:* Consult, Gen Atomic, Appl Superconetics, Quantum Design, Jet Propulsion Lab, Hughes, Ball Aerospace, Aerojet Gen, GWR, Nat Radio Astron Observ. *Mem:* Am Phys Soc. *Res:* Cryogenic instruments and measurements; MRI superconducting magnets; squid instruments; special dewars and cryostats; JT refrigeration systems; thermometers and coil foil material. *Mailing Add:* 2655 Soderbloom Ave San Diego CA 92122

SARYAN, LEON ARAM, BLOOD LEAD TESTING, INDUSTRIAL HYGIENE. *Current Pos:* TECH DIR TOXICOL, WEST ALLIS MEM HOSP, 82- *Personal Data:* b Wilmington, Del, July 18, 48; m 81; c 2. *Educ:* Johns Hopkins Univ, BA, 70, PhD(biol chem), 75. *Honors & Awards:* Ralston Purina Bright Idea Award, 79. *Prof Exp:* Lab tech chem, Allied Kid Co, 64-68; engr air pollution, DuPont Co Petrol Lab, 68-69; NSF fel cancer res, Roswell Park Mem Inst, 70; res fel chem, Univ Wis-Milwaukee, 75-81, adj asst prof chem, 81-82. *Concurrent Pos:* Asst clin prof, Dept Path, Med Col Wis, 91- *Mem:* Am Chem Soc; Am Indust Hyg Asn; Armenian Engrs & Scientists Am. *Res:* Heavy metal toxicology including blood lead testing for industrial and environmental exposures; cancer research and trace element analysis and metabolism, asbestos, and environmental science. *Mailing Add:* Indust Toxicol Lab West Allis Mem Hosp 8901 W Lincoln Ave West Allis WI 53227. *Fax:* 414-328-8560

SAS, DARYL, TISSUE CULTURE, ANTIBODY PRODUCTION. *Current Pos:* RES FEL, MAYO CLIN, 85- *Educ:* Univ Minn, PhD(cell & develop biol), 82. *Mailing Add:* Dept Biol Geneva Col Beaver Falls PA 15010-3557

SASAKI, CLARENCE TAKASHI, OTORHINOLARYNGOLOGY, NEUROPHYSIOLOGY. *Current Pos:* from instr to assoc prof, 73-82, PROF SURG, YALE SCH MED, 82-, CHIEF, SECT OTOLARYNGOL, 81-, VCHAIR, SURG, 96- *Personal Data:* b Honolulu, Hawaii, Jan 24, 41; m 67; c 2. *Educ:* Pomona Col, BA, 62; Yale Univ, MD, 66. *Honors & Awards:* First Prize Clin Res, Am Acad Ophthalmol & Otolaryngol, 72; Edmund Prince Fowler Award, Triol Soc, 79. *Prof Exp:* Intern, Univ Calif, San Francisco, 66-67; resident surg, Dartmouth Med Ctr, 67-68 & Yale-New Haven Med Ctr, 70-73. *Concurrent Pos:* Attend surg, Yale-New Haven Hosp; attend surg, West Haven Vet Admin Hosp, 73-76, consult, 73-, Windham Community Hosp, 80- & Backas Hosp, 81-; mem, Commmun Sci Study Sect, NIH, 80-83; prin investr, NIH grant, Hearing Res Study Sect, 83-84, Sensory Dis & Lang Study Sect, 85-88; atten surgeon, Hosp St Raphael, 96. *Mem:* Sigma Xi; Am Col Surgeons; Am Soc Head & Neck Surg; Psychol Res Soc; Am Laryngol Soc; Am Acad Otolaryngol; Soc Neurosci; Asn Res Otolaryngol; NY Acad Sci; Soc Neurovascular Surg; Soc Head & Neck Surgeons; Am Otol Soc; Am Neurobiol Soc; NAm Skull Base Soc; Am Bronchoesoph Asn. *Res:* Neurophysiology of the larynx; postnatal development as related to the sudden infant death syndrome; tinnitus, development of a neurophysiologic correlate. *Mailing Add:* Dept Surg Yale Sch Med 333 Cedar St PO Box 208041 New Haven CT 06520-8041. *Fax:* 203-785-3970

SASAKI, GORDON HIROSHI, PLASTIC SURGERY, GENERAL SURGERY. *Current Pos:* asst prof, Surg & Plastic Surg, 82-85, CLIN ASSOC PROF, DEPT PLASTIC SURG, UNIV SOUTHERN CALIF, LOS ANGELES, 85- *Personal Data:* b Honolulu, Hawaii, July 27, 42; m 69; c 1. *Educ:* Pomona Col, BA, 64; Yale Univ, MD, 68. *Prof Exp:* Intern, Health Sci Ctr, Univ Ore, 68-69, surg resident, 69-70, surg res fel, 72-74, gen surg, 74-77; chief res plastic surg, Med Sch, Yale Univ, 77-79; asst prof plastic surg, Southwestern Med Sch, Univ Tex, 79-82. *Concurrent Pos:* Instr gen surg & res assoc, Med Sch, Yale Univ, 78-79; fel, Surg Hand, Univ Conn, 78-79; attend staff, Vet Admin Hosp & Children's Hosp, Dallas, Tex, 79-82; attend surg, Huntington Mem Hosp, 85- *Mem:* AMA; fel Am Col Surg; Asn Acad Surg; Am Asn Plastic Surg; Am Asn Hand Surg; Am Bd Surg; Am Bd Plastic Surg. *Res:* Steroid and peptide hormones in breast cancer and other target tissues; microcirculation in skin; prostaglandins and microcirculation; macrophage-myofitonblast and wound contraction. *Mailing Add:* 800 S Fairmount Ave 319 Pasadena CA 91105

SASAKI, HIDETADA, GERIATRIC MEDICINE, RESPIRATORY MEDICINE. *Current Pos:* PROF & CHMN, DEPT GERIAT MED, 87- *Personal Data:* b Akita, Japan, July 28, 41; m 71; c 2. *Educ:* Tohoku Univ, Dr, 66, PhD(med), 71. *Honors & Awards:* Kumagai Award, Japanese Thoracic Soc, 83. *Mem:* Am Thoracic Soc; Am Physiol Soc; Am Col Chest Physicians. *Res:* Aspiration pneumonia; bronchial asthma; Alzheimer's disease; chronic obstructive pulmonary disease; fibrosing lung disease. *Mailing Add:* Dept Geriat Med Sch Med Tohoku Univ 1-1 Seiryo-machi Aobaku Sendai 980 Japan. *Fax:* 81-22-717-7186

SASAKI, SHIN-ICHI, COMPUTER CHEMISTRY. *Current Pos:* VCHMN, SCIENCE-CREATE CORP, 96- *Personal Data:* b Tokyo, Japan, Nov 25, 25; m 51, Kotoji Saito; c Fumiko & Hiroshi. *Educ:* Tohoku Univ, BS, 49, DSc, 59. *Honors & Awards:* Award, Japan Soc Anal Chem, 74; Award, Japan Inf Ctr Sci & Technol, 80. *Prof Exp:* Res assoc, Tohoku Univ, 49-62, assoc prof, 63-70; prof, Miyagi Univ Educ, 70-79; prof, Toyohashi Univ Technol, Japan, 79-84, vpres, 84-90, pres, 90-96. *Concurrent Pos:* Res assoc, Mass Inst Technol, 59-61; pres, Asn Japan-Germany Toyohoshi, 91- *Mem:* Am Chem Soc; Japan Acad Eng; Chem Soc Japan; Japan Soc Anal Chem; Japan Asn Int Chem Info (pres). *Res:* Inventor of chemical structure elucidation system, chemics. *Mailing Add:* Science-Create Corp Nishimiynki Toyohashi Aichi 441 Japan. *Fax:* 81-532-44-1122; *E-Mail:* sasaki@tsc.co.jp

SASAKI, YOSHI KAZU, DYNAMIC METEOROLOGY. *Current Pos:* res scientist, 60-62, adj assoc prof, 61-64, assoc prof, 64-67, PROF METEOROL, UNIV OKLA, 67-, GEORGE LYNN CROSS RES PROF, 74- *Personal Data:* b Akita, Japan, Jan 2, 27; m 54; c 4. *Educ:* Univ Tokyo, BS, 50, PhD, 55. *Honors & Awards:* Prize, Meteorol Soc Japan, 55. *Prof Exp:* Res scientist meteorol res found, Agr & Mech Col, Tex, 56-60, prin investr, 58-60, mem fac, 59-60. *Concurrent Pos:* Res dir, Naval Environ Prediction Res Fac, 74-75; dir, Coop Inst Mesoscale Meteorol Studies, 80- *Mem:* Fel Am Meteorol Soc; Meteorol Soc Japan. *Res:* Mesometeorology; numerical weather prediction; variational methods. *Mailing Add:* 906 W Timberdell Rd Norman OK 73072

SASAMORI, TAKASHI, METEOROLOGY. *Current Pos:* RETIRED. *Personal Data:* b Tokyo, Japan, Feb 1, 30; m 58; c 3. *Educ:* Tohoku Univ, Japan, BSc, 53, MSc, 55, DrSc(meteorol), 58. *Prof Exp:* Res assoc meteorol, Geophys Inst, Tohoku Univ, Japan, 58-60; staff scientist, Tech Inst, Japan Defense Agency, 60-64, 65-66; res assoc dept astron & geophys, Univ Colo, 64-65; staff scientist, Nat Ctr Atmospheric Res, 67-78; prof meteorol, Univ Ill, Urbana-Champaign, 78-93. *Concurrent Pos:* Fel, Univ Colo, 64-65. *Mem:* Am Geophys Union; Am Meteorol Soc; Meteorol Soc Japan. *Res:* Radiation transfer in planetary atmosphere; numerical modelling of planetary boundary layer. *Mailing Add:* 2307 Brookens Circle Urbana IL 61801

SASENICK, JOSEPH ANTHONY, PHARMACEUTICAL CHEMISTRY. *Current Pos:* PRES & CHIEF EXEC OFFICER, ALCIDE CORP, WASHINGTON, 91- *Personal Data:* b Chicago, Ill, May 18, 40; m 62, Barbara Ellen Barr; c Richard Allen, Susan Marie & MIchael Joseph. *Educ:* DePaul Univ, BA, 62; Univ Okla, MA, 66. *Prof Exp:* Staff mem, Miles Labs Inc, 63-70; prod mgr, Alka-Seltzer, 66-88, dir mktg, Grocery Prod Div, 68-70; staff mem, Gillette Corp, Boston, 70-79, dir, New Prod/New Ventures, Personal Care Div, 77; mkt dir, Braun AG, Kronberg, WGer, 70-73, chmn managing dir, Braun UK Ltd, 73-77; vpres diversified cosmetics & pres, Jafra Cosmetics Worldwide, 77-79; staff mem, Abbott Labs, North Chicago, 79-84, corp vpres, Consumer Prod Div, 79-84; pres & chief exec officer, Moxie Indust, 84-87 & Personal Monitoring Technologies, Rochester, NY, 87; pres, Bioline Labs, Ft Lauderdale, 88; managing dir & partner, Vista Resource Group, Newport Beach, Calif, 88-90. *Mailing Add:* 1301 Spring St Seattle WA 98104-1354

SASHIHARA, THOMAS F(UJIO), CHEMICAL ENGINEERING. *Current Pos:* RETIRED. *Personal Data:* b Los Angeles, Calif, May 7, 29; m 57; c 3. *Educ:* Ohio State Univ, BChE & MSc, 53, PhD(chem eng), 57. *Prof Exp:* Instr chem eng, Ohio State Univ, 55-56; chem engr, Polychem Dept, E I Du Pont de Nemours & Co, Inc, 56-63, sr res engr, Plastics Dept, 63-71, supt res lab, Plastics Dept, 71-92. *Mem:* Am Chem Soc; Am Inst Chem Engrs. *Res:* Chemical processes. *Mailing Add:* 3 Roan Ct Wilmington DE 19803

SASHIN, DONALD, PHYSICS IN POSITRON EMISSION TOMOGRAPHY, RADIOLOGICAL PHYSICS. *Current Pos:* from instr to assoc prof radiol & radiation health, 67-74, dir radiol imaging, 75-84, ASSOC PROF RADIOL, SCH MED, UNIV PITTSBURGH, 74- *Personal Data:* b New York, NY, Dec 11, 37; m 67, Kathleen Flaherty; c Deirdre & Courtenay. *Educ:* Mass Inst Technol, BS, 60; Carnegie Inst Technol, MS, 62; Carnegie-Mellon Univ, PhD(medium energy physics), 68. *Prof Exp:* Proj physicist, Carnegie Inst Technol, 62-67. *Concurrent Pos:* Pa Lions Sight Conserv & Eye Res Found grants, 71-86; Nat Cancer Inst contract, 73-75; Am Cancer Inst grant, 77-79; Nat Heart, Lung & Blood Inst contracts, 77-79, 80-83 & 83-88; Western Pa Advan Tech Ctr grant, 86-89; Philips Med Systs, Inc grant, 81-84. *Mem:* Sigma Xi; Am Phys Soc; Health Physics Soc; Am Asn Physicists in Med; Inst Elec & Electronics Engrs; Soc Nuclear Med. *Res:* Quantitative three-dimensional data acquisition techniques in a whole body positron-emission tomography septa retracted to improve imaging of subtle changes in the body. *Mailing Add:* Univ Pittsburgh Med Ctr Pet Facil 200 Lothrop St Rm B938 Pittsburgh PA 15213. *Fax:* 412-647-0700; *E-Mail:* don@pet.upmc.edu

SASHITAL, SANAT RAMANATH, SOLID STATE PHYSICS, MATERIALS SCIENCE. *Current Pos:* mgr, 88-90, SR SECT HEAD, MAT PROCESSING, TRW, 88- *Personal Data:* b Bagalkot, India; US citizen. *Educ:* Univ Bombay, BSc, 59, MSc, 61; Pa State Univ, PhD(solid state sci), 67. *Prof Exp:* Physicist, Res Labs, Zenith Radio Corp, 69-74; vis scholar, Dept Mat Sci, Northwestern Univ, 74-76; mem tech staff, Res Labs, Hughes Aircraft Co, 76-88. *Mem:* Am Asn Crystal Growth; Am Vacuum Soc. *Res:* Crystal growth; epitaxial growth; thin films, structure and properties; electro-optic materials; restricted access memory materials. *Mailing Add:* 13 Mallard Irvine CA 92604

SASIADEK, JERZY Z, ROBOTICS, CONTROL SYSTEMS. *Current Pos:* PROF & DIR AEROSPACE ENG, CARLETON UNIV, 82- *Educ:* Tech Univ Wroclaw, BSc, 71, MSc, 72, PhD(control systs), 75, DSc, 76. *Prof Exp:* Prof, Tech Univ Wroclaw, 75-79, Univ Alta, 79-80, Concordia Univ, 80-82. *Concurrent Pos:* Dir advan technologies, Alta Res Coun, 85-87; vis prof, Can Space Agency, 90-92; control eng react, Int Fedn Automatic Ctr, 92-, ed, 94- *Mem:* Fel Am Inst Aeronaut & Astronaut. *Res:* Various aspects of control systems, guidance and navigation with application to aerospace systems, robotics and power plants. *Mailing Add:* Dept Mech & Aerospace Carleton Univ Ottawa ON K1S 5B6 Can. *Fax:* 613-520-5715

SASIELA, RICHARD, OPTICS. *Current Pos:* MEM STAFF, LINCOLN LAB, MASS INST TECHNOL, 69- *Personal Data:* b Brooklyn, NY, June 1, 40; m 62, Dethlefs; c Amy & Dawn. *Educ:* Polytech Inst Brooklyn, BEE, 61, MS, 62, PhD(electrophys), 67. *Prof Exp:* Res engr, Microwave Assocs, Inc, 67-69. *Mem:* Inst Elec & Electronics Engrs; Sigma Xi. *Res:* Analysis of electromagnetic wave propragation in turbulence and development of adaptive-optics systems. *Mailing Add:* Mass Inst Technol Lincoln Lab 244 Wood St PO Box 73 Lexington MA 02173. *E-Mail:* sasiela@ll.mit.edu

SASIN, RICHARD, ORGANIC CHEMISTRY. *Current Pos:* RETIRED. *Personal Data:* b Warsaw, Poland, Nov 16, 22; nat US; m 57; c 1. *Educ:* Drexel Inst, BS, 47; Temple Univ, MA, 49, PhD(chem), 54. *Prof Exp:* Asst chem, Temple Univ, 47-51; instr, Drexel Inst, 51-53, asst prof, 53-57, assoc prof, 57-60, prof, 60-68; prof chem & dean div sci & math, Millersville State Col, 68- 89. *Concurrent Pos:* Consult, Hardesty Industs, 55-57; Fatty Acid Producers Coun fel, Eastern Regional Res Lab, USDA, 57-58. *Mem:* AAAS; Am Chem Soc; Am Oil Chem Soc; Sigma Xi. *Res:* Nitrogen heterocyclics; organotin compounds; derivatives of long-chain fatty acids; sulfur compounds and phosphorus derivatives of fatty acids. *Mailing Add:* 1142 Olde Hickory Rd Lancaster PA 17601-4938

SASKI, WITOLD, BIOPHARMACEUTICS. *Current Pos:* From asst prof to prof, 52-93, EMER PROF PHARM, MED CTR, UNIV NEBR, OMAHA, 93- *Personal Data:* b Poland, Dec 4, 09; nat US; wid. *Educ:* Batory Univ, Poland, MPharm, 33; Univ Bologna, DPharm, 46; Inst Optical Sci, London, Eng, dipl, 50; Univ Nebr, BSc, 54. *Prof Exp:* Practicing pharmacist, Poland, 33-36; pharmaceut inspector, Polish Ministry Soc Welfare, 37-39; chief pharmacist med clin, Eng, 47-48; sr pharmacist supplies div, Brit Ministry Health, 48-51; asst prof pharm, Mont State Univ, 51-52. *Concurrent Pos:* Vis assoc prof, Sch Pharm, Univ Calif, San Francisco, 59-60; Fulbright scholar, Univ Pisa, 67-68; Nat Acad Sci exchange scientist, Poland, 70. *Mem:* Fel Am Acad Pharmaceut Sci; Am Asn Cols Pharm. *Res:* Surface-active agents and drug absorption mechanisms; medicinal product formulation; experimental pharmaceutical technology; author of nearly 350 publications. *Mailing Add:* 2600 S 46th St Lincoln NE 68506-2520

SASLAW, LEONARD DAVID, BIOCHEMISTRY, TOXICOLOGY. *Current Pos:* RETIRED. *Personal Data:* b Brooklyn, NY, Aug 27, 27. *Educ:* City Col New York, BS, 49; George Washington Univ, MS, 54; Georgetown Univ, PhD(chem), 63. *Prof Exp:* Chemist, Nat Cancer Inst, NIH, 51-57; chemist, Div Biophys, Sloan-Kettering Inst, 57-58; chemist, Biochem Br, Armed Forces Inst Path, 58-64; dir div biochem pharmacol, Cancer Chemother Dept, Microbiol Assocs, Inc, 65-68; sr biochemist, Nat Drug Co, 68-69; chief, Lab Cellular Biochem, Albert Einstein Med Ctr, 69-70; clin lab dir, Med Diag Ctrs, Inc, 70-71; lab dir & res assoc, Renal Lab, New York Med Col, 71-73; mgr biochem invests, Bio Dynamics Inc, NJ, 73-74; prof assoc, Smithsonian Sci Info Exchange, 75-77; physiologist, Div Toxicol, Bur Foods, Food & Drug Admin, 78-83; toxicologist, Ctr Vet Med, 83-92. *Concurrent Pos:* Consult, Burton Parsons, Inc, 77-78. *Mem:* Sigma Xi; Am Soc Pharmacol & Exp Therapeut Assay Soc; Am Asn Cancer Res. *Res:* Drug metabolism; analytical biochemistry; cancer research; oxidation of unsaturated fatty acids; clinical chemistry; toxicology. *Mailing Add:* 2939 Van Ness St NW Apt 120 Washington DC 20088

SASLOW, WAYNE MARK, LOW TEMPERATURE PHYSICS, SOLID STATE SCIENCE. *Current Pos:* asst prof, 71-77, assoc prof, 77-83, PROF PHYSICS, TEX A&M UNIV, 83- *Personal Data:* b Philadelphia, Pa, Aug 11, 42; m 71, Mary Liani; c 2. *Educ:* Univ Pa, BA, 64; Univ Calif, Berkeley, MA, 67; Univ Calif, Irvine, PhD(physics), 68. *Prof Exp:* Res assoc, Univ Pittsburgh, 69-71. *Concurrent Pos:* Joliot-Curie fel & vis prof, Univ Paris, 80-81. *Mem:* Am Phys Soc; Electrochem Soc. *Res:* Theory of liquid helium, solid state theory; surface physics; spin glasses; hydrodynamics of condensed matter systems; disordered magnetic systems, transport in electrolytes, batteries. *Mailing Add:* Dept Physics Tex A&M Univ College Station TX 77843-4242. *E-Mail:* saslow@phys.tamu.edu

SASMAN, ROBERT T, HYDROLOGY & WATER RESOURCES. *Current Pos:* RETIRED. *Personal Data:* b Plattsburgh, NY, July, 23, 23; m 51, Julia Vos; c Gary, Dean & Marcia. *Educ:* Univ Wis-Madison, BS, 47. *Honors & Awards:* Fuller Award, Am Water Works Asn, 76. *Prof Exp:* Soil analyst, Univ Wis, 47; soil scientist, US Soil Conserv Serv, 47-48, geologist, 48-51; asst hydrologist, Ill State Water Surv Div, 51-57, hydrologist, 57-87; consult hydrologist, 87-96. *Concurrent Pos:* Lectr numerous cols, univ & orgn, 57-88; dir, Am Water Works Asn, 75-78, Groundwater Protection Adv Workgroup, 87-93, chair, Groundwater Comt, 89-94. *Mem:* Hon mem Am Water Works Asn. *Res:* Analysis of groundwater resources of northern Illinois including availability, quantity and quality of shallow and deep aquifers, groundwater withdrawals, water-level trends, and feasibility of artificial recharge. *Mailing Add:* 200 Wyndemere Circle E336 Wheaton IL 60187-2430

SASNER, JOHN JOSEPH, COMPARATIVE PHYSIOLOGY, INVERTEBRATE ZOOLOGY & ALGAL TOXINS. *Current Pos:* asst prof zool, Univ NH, 65-69, assoc prof, 69-81, chair, 91-95, PROF ZOOL, UNIV NH, 81- *Personal Data:* b Lawrence, Mass, June 15, 36; m 58; c 3. *Educ:* Univ NH, BA, 57, MS, 59; Univ Calif, Los Angeles, PhD(comp physiol), 65. *Prof Exp:* Res assoc physiol & biophys, Univ Ill, 62-63; res & develop off, USAF Sch Aerospace Med, 63-65. *Res:* Effects of naturally occurring microorganism toxins on excitable membranes. *Mailing Add:* Dept Zool Univ NH Rudman Hall Durham NH 03824

SASS, DANIEL B, PALEONTOLOGY, ENVIRONMENTAL SCIENCES. *Current Pos:* from asst prof to prof geol, Alfred Univ, 52-82, chmn dept, 52-74, coordr environ studies prog, 74-80, EMER PROF GEOL, ALFRED UNIV, 82- *Personal Data:* b Rochester, NY, Mar 28, 19; m 59, Mary J Moler; c Danny A & Elizabeth E. *Educ:* Univ Rochester, BA & MS, 51; Univ Cincinnati, PhD, 59. *Honors & Awards:* Scholes Sigma Xi lectr, 65. *Prof Exp:* Soils geologist, Capitol Eng, 51-52. *Concurrent Pos:* mus cur & consult, 82- *Mem:* Fel Geol Soc Am; Paleont Soc; Electron Micros Soc; Sigma Xi. *Res:* Devonian stratigraphy and paleontology; electron microscopy; ultrastructure of bivalve shells; biomedical research; kirlian photography. *Mailing Add:* 27 High St Alfred NY 14802-1302. *Fax:* 607-871-2746

SASS, JOHN HARVEY, GEOPHYSICS. *Current Pos:* Chief, Earthquake Drilling Proj, 84-85, on-site sci mgr, Salton Sea Sci Drilling Proj, 85-86, GEOPHYSICIST, US GEOL SURV, 67-, CHIEF, GEOTHERMAL STUDIES PROJ, 84- *Personal Data:* b Chatham, Ont, July 20, 37; m 61. *Educ:* Univ Western Ont, BS, 59, MS, 61; Australian Nat Univ, PhD(geophys), 65. *Concurrent Pos:* Nat Res Coun Can fel, Univ Western Ont, 64-66; vis fel, Australian Nat Univ, 71-72 & Stanford Univ, 72. *Mem:* AAAS; Am Geophys Union; Can Geophys Union. *Res:* Earth's heat and internal temperatures; continental scientific drilling. *Mailing Add:* US Geol Surv 2255 N Gemini Dr Flagstaff AZ 86001-1637

SASS, LOUIS CARL, EXPLORATION. *Current Pos:* RETIRED. *Personal Data:* b Chicago, Ill, Dec 18, 10. *Educ:* Univ Chicago, BS, 32. *Prof Exp:* Explor geol, Gulf Oil Corp, 33-65. *Mem:* Geol Soc Am; Sigma Xi; Am Asn Prof Geologists; Soc Econ Paleontologist & Mineralogists. *Mailing Add:* 3083 S Spruce Way Denver CO 80231

SASS, NEIL LESLIE, NUTRITIONAL BIOCHEMISTRY, TOXICOLOGY. *Current Pos:* toxicologist, Bur Foods, Food & Drug Admin, 77-82, SPEC ASST TO DIR, CTR FOOD SAFETY & APPL NUTRIT, FOOD & DRUG ADMIN, 82-, DIR, DIV TOXICOL RES. *Personal Data:* b Baltimore, Md, Oct 24, 44; m 84, Paige Munnikhuysen; c 3. *Educ:* Wake Forest Col, BS, 66; WVa Univ, MS, 69, PhD(biochem), 71; Johns Hopkins, MS, 84. *Prof Exp:* Res toxicologist, Chem-Toxicol, Biomed Lab, US Army Edgewood Arsenal, 71-73, res anal chemist explosives, Chem Lab, 73-74; chief lab serv, Med Res & Develop, William Beaumont Army Med Ctr, 74-77. *Concurrent Pos:* Fel, Appl Behav Sci/Orgn Develop, Johns Hopkins Univ; comdr, Disaster Med Assistance Team, USPHS Prev Med Unit. *Mem:* Sigma Xi; Soc Appl Spectroscopy; Am Chem Soc; Soc Armed Forces Med Lab Scientists; Am Col Toxicol; NY Acad Sci; Am Soc Training & Develop; Appl Res Ethics Nat Asn. *Res:* Biochemical mechanisms of the chemical pain response; mechanisms of idiopathic respiratory distress syndrome; reptilian venoms as presynaptic acetylcholine inhibitors; radioimmunoassay development for thyroid hormone precursors; thyroid hormone actions; biochemical toxicology; motivational aspects of human performance; psychosocial aspects of eating disorders. *Mailing Add:* 12900 Fork Rd Baldwin MD 21013-9345. *Fax:* 202-205-5025; *E-Mail:* nls@vm.cfsaw.fda.gov

SASS, RONALD L, BIOPHYSICAL CHEMISTRY. *Current Pos:* from asst prof to assoc prof, 58-66, PROF CHEM & BIOL, RICE UNIV, 66- *Personal Data:* b Davenport, Iowa, May 26, 32; m 52, 69, Margie Macy; c Denise, Andria, Hartley & Dennis. *Educ:* Augustana Col, BA, 54; Univ Southern Calif, PhD, 57. *Honors & Awards:* Salgo-Noren Distinguished Prof Award, 66. *Prof Exp:* Res fel chem, Brookhaven Nat Lab, 57-58. *Concurrent Pos:* Guggenheim fel, Cambridge Univ, 65; adj prof, Baylor Col Med, 70-; fel, Nat Res Coun, 88. *Mem:* Am Geophys Union. *Res:* Ecology; atmospheric science; biogeochemistry. *Mailing Add:* Dept Ecol Rice Univ Houston TX 77251. *E-Mail:* sass@pop.rice.edu

SASS, STEPHEN L, MATERIALS SCIENCE. *Current Pos:* from asst prof to assoc prof, 67-79, PROF MAT SCI, CORNELL UNIV, 79- *Personal Data:* b New York, NY, Mar 11, 40; m 66, Karen Sande; c 2. *Educ:* City Col New York, BChE, 61; Northwestern Univ, PhD(mat sci), 66. *Prof Exp:* Res asst mat sci, Northwestern Univ, 61-66; Fulbright scholar, Delft Univ, 66. *Concurrent Pos:* Max-Planck fel, 80-81; Krengel vis prof, Technion, 80-81. *Mem:* Am Inst Metall Engrs; Am Ceramic Soc; Electron Micros Soc Am; Am Soc Metals; fel Am Phys Soc; AAAS. *Res:* Electron microscopy; electron diffraction; x-ray diffraction; diffraction from crystalline imperfections; internal interfaces; metal-ceramic microstructures. *Mailing Add:* Dept Mat Sci & Eng Cornell Univ Ithaca NY 14853. *Fax:* 607-255-2365

SASSA, SHIGERU, HEMATOLOGY, BIOCHEMISTRY. *Current Pos:* res assoc, 68-71, asst prof hemat & biochem, 71-75, ASSOC PROF HEMAT & BIOCHEM & PHYSICIAN, ROCKEFELLER UNIV, 75-, HEAD, LAB BIOCHEM HEMAT, 92- *Personal Data:* b Tokyo, Japan, Mar 3, 35; m 63, Reiko Arakawa; c Junko & Osamu. *Educ:* Univ Tokyo, MD, 61, DrMedSci, 66. *Prof Exp:* Res assoc med, Fac Med, Univ Tokyo, 68. *Mem:* Am Soc Biochem & Molecular Biol; Am Soc Hemat; Am Soc Clin Invest. *Res:* Heme biosynthesis; the regulatory mechanism of enzyme induction; genetic defects of heme synthesis. *Mailing Add:* Rockefeller Univ New York NY 10021

SASSAMAN, ANNE PHILLIPS, BLOOD DISEASES, ENVIRONMENTAL HEALTH. *Current Pos:* DIR, DIV EXTRAMURAL RES & TRAINING, NAT INST ENVIRON HEALTH SCI, 86- *Personal Data:* b LaGrange, Ga, Jan 7, 44; m 66, 83, Jan F; c Kristen A (Ball) & John R (Ball). *Educ:* Auburn Univ, BS, 65; Duke Univ, PhD(immunol), 70. *Prof Exp:* Res assoc, Dept Surg, Med Ctr, Duke Univ, 70-71; Dept Biochem, 71-74; chemist, Bur Biol, Food, Drug & Admin, 74-76; scientist-adminr, 76-79, chief, Blood Dis Br, Nat Heart, Lung & Blood Inst, 79-86. *Concurrent Pos:* Fel cardiol, Dept Med, Med Ctr, Duke Univ, 71-74. *Mem:* Soc Toxicol; Am Soc Hemat; Am Heart Asn; AAAS; Sigma Xi; Am Pub Health Asn. *Res:* Biochemistry of blood coagulation and fibrinolysis; blood diseases, including thrombosis and hemostasis and red cell disorders. *Mailing Add:* Nat Inst Environ Health Sci Box 12233 Research Triangle Park NC 27709. *Fax:* 919-541-2843; *E-Mail:* sassaman@niehs.nih.gov

SASSAMAN, CLAY ALAN, INVERTEBRATE ZOOLOGY, EVOLUTIONARY GENETICS. *Current Pos:* from asst prof to assoc prof, 76-88, PROF BIOL, UNIV CALIF, RIVERSIDE, 88-, CHAIR DEPT, 90- *Personal Data:* b Washington, DC, Dec 27, 48; m 92, Trudy Mahoney; c Alex H. *Educ:* Col William & Mary, BS, 70; Stanford Univ, PhD(biol), 76. *Prof Exp:* Scholar, Woods Hole Oceanog Inst, 75-76. *Mem:* Am Inst Biol Sci; AAAS; Crustacean Soc. *Res:* Population genetics and evolutionary genetics of crustaceans; evolution of sex determination. *Mailing Add:* Dept Biol Univ Calif 900 University Ave Riverside CA 92521-0101. *Fax:* 909-787-4286

SASSE, EDWARD ALEXANDER, CLINICAL CHEMISTRY, CLINICAL PATHOLOGY. *Current Pos:* asst prof, 70-74, ASSOC PROF PATH, MED COL WIS, 74- *Personal Data:* b Amarillo, Tex, July 10, 38; m 60; c 2. *Educ:* Arlington State Col, BS, 63; Univ Tenn, Memphis, PhD(biochem), 68; Am Bd Clin Chem, dipl, 73. *Prof Exp:* From instr to asst prof clin path, Sch Med, Univ Ala, Birmingham, 68-70. *Concurrent Pos:* Consult scientist, Univ Ala Hosps & Clins, 68-70; co-dir clin chem sect, Dept Path & Labs, Milwaukee County Gen Hosp, 70- *Mem:* AAAS; Am Chem Soc; Am Asn Clin Chem. *Res:* Clinical chemistry methodology; toxicology; endocrinology; physical and chemical properties of proteins; enzyme immunoassay. *Mailing Add:* 1550 Green Valley Blvd Brookfield WI 53045

SASSELOV, DIMITAR D, STELLAR PHYSICS, RADIATIVE TRANSFER. *Current Pos:* Postdoctoral fel, 90-93, Hubble fel, 93-96, ASTROPHYSICIST, SMITHSONIAN ASTROPHYS OBSERV, HARVARD-SMITHSONIAN CTR ASTROPHYS, 96- *Personal Data:* b Nessebar, Bulgaria, Aug 15, 61; m 96, Sheila A Doran. *Educ:* Univ Sofia, Bulgaria, MSc, 86, PhD(physics), 88; Univ Toronto, Can, PhD(astrophys), 90. *Concurrent Pos:* Lectr astron, Harvard Univ, 93- *Mem:* Am Astron Soc; Can Astron Soc; Royal Astron Soc; Int Astron Union. *Res:* Radiative transfer and hydrodynamics in stellar atmospheres and their environment; stability of stars; measuring distances and the extragalactic distance scale; study of helium content in the universe; gravitational lensing of stars. *Mailing Add:* Harvard Smithsonian Ctr Astrophys 60 Garden St Cambridge MA 02138. *E-Mail:* dsasselov@cfa.harvard.edu

SASSENRATH, ETHELDA NORBERG, BEHAVIORAL PHYSIOLOGY, PSYCHOPHARMACOLOGY. *Current Pos:* res specialist, Nat Ctr Primate Biol, 64-68, lectr behav biol, Sch Med, 68-73, res behav biologist, Calif Primate Res Ctr, 73-76, ASSOC PROF BEHAV BIOL, SCH MED, UNIV CALIF, DAVIS, 76-, PROF PSYCHIAT, 80- *Personal Data:* b Dubuque, Iowa, Feb 21, 21; m 51; c 2. *Educ:* Dubuque Univ, AB, 42; Iowa State Univ, PhD(chem), 49. *Prof Exp:* Asst res biochemist, Sch Med, Univ Calif, 49-59; res assoc psychopharmacol, Ind Univ, 59-64. *Mem:* AAAS; Soc Neurosci; Soc Exp Biol & Med; Sigma Xi. *Res:* Mechanisms of psychoactive drug action; endocrine correlates of behavior; psycho endocrine correlates of stress and aging. *Mailing Add:* 4234 Cowell Blvd Davis CA 95616-4323

SASSER, JOSEPH NEAL, NEMATOLOGY. *Current Pos:* from asst prof to prof, 53-84, EMER PROF PLANT PATH, NC STATE UNIV, 84- *Personal Data:* b Goldsboro, NC, May 19, 21; m 45, Laura E Long; c Anita G (Chappell), Joseph N, Betty L (Wilder) & Laura A (Young). *Educ:* NC State Col, BS, 43, MS, 50; Univ Md, PhD, 53. *Honors & Awards:* OMax Gardner Award, 82; Adventurers in Agr Sci Award of Distinction, 79. *Prof Exp:* Asst nematologist, USDA, 51-53. *Concurrent Pos:* Tech consult, Rockefeller Found, Chile, 63-64; ed, Am Phytopath Soc, 63-65; prin investr, Int Meloidogyne Proj, 75-84 & Crop Nematode Res & Control Proj, 84-89; hon mem, Orgn Trop Am Nematologists. *Mem:* Hon mem Soc Nematol (vpres, 61-63, pres, 63-64); Am Phytopath Soc. *Res:* Nematode diseases of plants. *Mailing Add:* 200 W Cornwall Rd No 121 Cary NC 27511-3802

SASSER, LYLE BLAINE, TOXICOLOGY, NUTRITION. *Current Pos:* sr res scientist, 81-87, STAFF SCIENTIST, BATTELLE PAC NORTHWEST LABS, 87- *Personal Data:* b Tremonton, Utah, Feb 20, 39; m 63, Sonja Nelson; c Bruce, Kyla, Kirt & Jenise. *Educ:* Univ Idaho, BS, 61; Colo State Univ, MS, 65, PhD(nutrit), 68. *Prof Exp:* Asst prof animal sci, Fresno State Col, 67; asst prof, Univ Tenn-AEC Agr Res Lab, 68-72; from asst prof to assoc prof nutrit, Univ Tenn-Oak Ridge, 73-81. *Concurrent Pos:* consult, Sci Appln, Inc, 79-81; lectr, Washington State Univ, 85- *Mem:* Bioelectromagnetics Soc; Am Inst Nutrit; Soc Exp Biol & Med; Soc Toxicol. *Res:* Metabolism of trace elements in animal nutrition; radioisotope tracers; trace element absorption studies; toxicity of heavy metals; interaction of heavy metals and dietary nutrients; body composition; effects of radiation on domestic animals; toxicology and risk evaluation of environmental contaminants, toxic agents and chemicals, and ionizing and non-ionizing and radiation; animal cancer models, bioeffects of electromagnetic fields. *Mailing Add:* Battelle Pac Northwest Labs Battelle Blvd Richland WA 99352. *Fax:* 509-376-0302; *E-Mail:* lbsasser@pnl.gov

SASSERATH, JAY N, SEMICONDUCTOR MANUFACTURING, THIN FILM PROCESSING. *Personal Data:* b Flushing, NY, Feb, 1962; m 90; c 1. *Educ:* Rensselaer Polytech Inst, BS, 84; State Univ NY, Stony Brook, MS, 87, PhD(mat sci), 90. *Honors & Awards:* Commendation Outstanding Res, US Army, 92. *Prof Exp:* Process engr, Stand Microsysts, 85-88; mgr process eng, Hypres, 88-90; mgr, Mat Res Corp, 90, dir, Appl Lab, 91-96. *Mem:* Electrochem Soc; Int Soc Optical Eng. *Res:* Metallurgy and physical metallurgical engineering. *Mailing Add:* 1922 NE Illinois Ave St Petersburg FL 33703. *Fax:* 914-425-7606

SASSONE-CORSI, PAOLO, MOLECULAR BIOLOGY. *Current Pos:* UL Pasteur fel, postdoctoral, Nat Ctr Sci Res, 79-83, assoc res fel, 84-85, charge res first class, 84-85, DIR, RES DRZ, NAT CTR SCI RES, FRANCE, 90- *Personal Data:* b Naples, Italy, June 8, 56; m 80, Emilia Borrelli. *Educ:* Univ Naples, PhD(biol sci), 79. *Honors & Awards:* Gold Medal, Europ Molecular Biol Org, 94; Rosen Med Res Prize, Endocrinol Soc, 95. *Concurrent Pos:* Fel, Found Med Res, France, 84-85; Am-Ital Found Cancer Res, NY, 86-87; vis res scientist, Molecular BBiol & Virol Lab, Salk Inst, 86-89; sr fel, Am Cancer Soc, 87-88; teacher, Int Ctr Genetic Eng & Biotech, UN Indust Develop Orgn, 90; prof biol chem, Univ Naples, 92. *Mem:* Europ Molecular Biol Orgn; Europ Cellular Biol Orgn; Endocrinal Soc. *Res:* Patentee in field for transcription factor crem antibodies. *Mailing Add:* IGBMC Inst Gen et Bio Molec 10 Rue Schimper Strasbourg 67000 France

SASSOON, HUMPHREY FREDERICK, TOXICOLOGY. *Current Pos:* RETIRED. *Personal Data:* b Barnes, Eng, Aug 18, 20; US citizen; m 56, M Patricia Bourd; c Timothy, Mark & Clare. *Educ:* Oxford Univ, BA & MA, 46, BA, 48; Bristol Univ, PhD(animal sci), 64. *Prof Exp:* Res assoc nutrit biochem, Univ Ill, 64-65; sr investr biochem, Okla Med Res Found & Med Sch, Univ Okla, 65-70; res specialist alcoholism, Tex Res Inst Ment Sci, 70-71; res assoc, Life Sci Res Off, Fedn Am Socs Exp Biol, 71-73; sr scientist, Tracor Jitco Inc, 73-76; sr scientist, Envirocontrol Inc, 76-81; proprietor, Jefferson Fruit Farm, 81-90. *Concurrent Pos:* Founder & dir, Washington Grove Singers, 75-80; consult, Merrill Math, Merrill Publ Co, 83-85. *Mem:* AAAS; Brit Nutrit Soc; Am Inst Nutrit. *Res:* Adaptation of enzyme systems to dietary carbohydrates and fats; color vision anomalies in school children and in families of alcoholics; nutritional toxicology; human cultural evolution. *Mailing Add:* 1561 St Luke Rd Woodstock VA 22664

SASTRI, SURI A, PHYSICAL METALLURGY, MATERIALS SCIENCE. *Current Pos:* PRES, SURMET CORP, 83- *Personal Data:* b Tanjore, India, Dec 26, 39; m 69. *Educ:* Banaras Hindu Univ, BSc, 60; Univ London, PhD(eng) & DIC, 64. *Prof Exp:* Australian Inst Nuclear Sci & Eng fel mat physics, Australian Atomic Energy Comn Res Labs, Sydney, 64-66; AEC res assoc metall, Ames Inst Atomic Res, Iowa State Univ, 67-68; res & develop scientist, Microphys Div, Gillette Safety Razor Co, 68-69, chief res & develop scientist, 69-71, group mgr mat res, 71-76, dir, chem & mat res, Boston Res & Develop Labs, 76-83. *Mem:* Electron Micros Soc Am; Am Soc Metals; Am Inst Mining, Metall & Petrol Engrs; Brit Iron & Steel Inst. *Res:* Application of electron microscopy to the understanding of the relationship between microstructure and mechanical properties of materials; phase transformations and strengthening mechanisms in materials. *Mailing Add:* 10 Bicentennial Dr Lexington MA 02173

SASTRI, VINOD RAM, POLYMER BLENDS, POLYMER SYNTHESIS. *Current Pos:* RES CHEMIST, ALLIED SIGNAL, INC, 89- *Personal Data:* b Lucknow, India, Jun 20, 57; US citizen. *Educ:* Madras Univ, BSc, 76; Indian Inst Tech, MSc, 78; Rutgers Univ, PhD(org chem), 84. *Prof Exp:* Fel, Polytech Univ, 84-87; sr res chemist, BASF, Clifton, 87-88. *Concurrent Pos:* Adj prof, Va Commonwealth Univ, 92- *Mem:* Am Chem Soc; Soc Plastics Eng; Am Inst Chem. *Res:* Synthesis of novel polymeric systems for a wide spectrum of end-uses, and polymer blends with value-added properties for fibers, films and engineering plastics. *Mailing Add:* Allied Signal Inc PO Box 31 Petersburg VA 23804-0031. *Fax:* 804-520-3644

SASTRY, BHAMIDIPATY VENKATA RAMA, PHARMACOLOGY, MEDICINAL CHEMISTRY. *Current Pos:* res assoc, 59-60, from instr to assoc prof, 60-71, PROF PHARMACOL, VANDERBILT UNIV, 71- *Personal Data:* b Andhra, India, Oct 21, 27; nat US; m 68; c 1. *Educ:* Andhra Univ, India, BSc, 49, MSc, 50, DSc(med chem), 56; Emory Univ, MS, 59; Vanderbilt Univ, PhD(pharmacol), 62. *Prof Exp:* Demonstr pharmaceut chem, Andhra Univ, India, 51-52, lectr, 52-56; res asst pharmacol, Emory Univ, 56-59. *Mem:* AAAS; Soc Exp Biol & Med; fel Am Inst Chem; Soc Toxicol; Am Soc Pharmacol & Exp Therapeut. *Res:* Physiology, pharmacology and toxicology of radionuclides and insecticides; synthesis and screening of psychotherapeutic agents; pharmacology and structure-activity drugs active on autonomic nervous system. *Mailing Add:* Dept Anesthesiol Vanderbilt Univ Med Ctr Nashville TN 37232-2125

SASTRY, SHANKARA M L, METALLURGY. *Current Pos:* from res scientist to sr scientist phys metall, 77-90, PROG DIR, METALS & COMPOSITES, MCDONNEL DOUGLAS RES LABS, 90- *Personal Data:* b India, June 11, 46; m 74; c 3. *Educ:* Bangalore Univ, BS, 65; Indian Inst Sci, BEng, 68, MEng, 70; Univ Toronto, PhD(metall & mat sci), 74. *Prof Exp:* Vis scientist metall, Air Force Mat Lab, Wright Patterson AFB, 74-76. *Concurrent Pos:* Prin investr, var res contracts, 78- *Mem:* Metall Soc Am. *Res:* Rapid solidification processing of titanium and aluminum alloys; novel consolidation techniques (explosive and dynamic compaction) of rapidly solidified powders; advanced titanium fabrication techniques; laser processing of materials. *Mailing Add:* 1305 Sheperd Hollow Glencoe MO 63038

SASTRY, VANKAMAMIDI VRN, PILE FOUNDATIONS, DYNAMICS OF PARTICLE. *Current Pos:* dir, Div Eng, 87-96, PROF, ST MARY'S UNIV, 96- *Personal Data:* b Guntur, India, Sept 1, 40; m 68; c 2. *Educ:* Osmania Univ, BE Hons, 60; Indian Inst Sci, ME, 62; Tech Univ NS, Can, PhD(civil eng), 77. *Prof Exp:* Asst engr, Heavy Eng Corp, India, 62-65; assoc prof civil eng, Osmania Univ, 65-82; res assoc, Tech Univ NS, 82-87. *Concurrent Pos:* Consult, Nolan Davis & Assocs Ltd, Can, 82- *Mem:* Can Geotech Soc; Asn Prof Engrs. *Res:* Behavior of pile foundations driven in homogeneous and layered soil systems and subjected to inclined and eccentric loads by studying fully instrumented, rigid and flexible piles under such loadings. *Mailing Add:* Dept Eng St Mary's Univ Robie St Halifax NS B3H 3C3 Can

SASYNIUK, BETTY IRENE, CARDIAC PHARMACOLOGY. *Current Pos:* Asst prof pharmacol, 71-78, ASSOC PROF CARDIOVASC PHARMACOL, MCGILL UNIV, 78- *Personal Data:* b Jan 19, 42; c Kenneth & Christopher. *Educ:* Univ Sask, BSP, 64; Univ Man, PhD(pharmacol), 68. *Concurrent Pos:* Med Res Coun fel, 68-71, scholar, 71-76. *Mem:* Pharmacol Soc Can; Am Soc Pharmacol & Exp Ther; Can Soc Clin Invest; Cardiac Electrophysiol Soc; Can Cardiovasc Soc; Int Soc Heart Res. *Res:* Cardiac electro-physiology; antiarrhythmic drugs; mechanisms of torsade de pointe arrhythmias; potassium channel blockers; potassium currents; patch clamping. *Mailing Add:* Dept Pharmacol McGill Univ 3655 Drummond St Montreal PQ H3G 1Y6 Can

SATAS, DONATAS, CHEMICAL ENGINEERING. *Current Pos:* CONSULT, SATAS & ASSOCS, 75- *Personal Data:* b Lithuania, Apr 7, 29; US citizen; m 53; c 3. *Educ:* Ill Inst Technol, BS, 53. *Prof Exp:* Res engr, Armour Res Found, 55-57; group leader, Kendall Co, 57-69; tech dir, Whitman Prod Ltd, 69-75. *Mem:* Am Inst Chem Engrs; Soc Plastics Engrs; Asn Consult Chemists & Chem Engrs; Am Lithuanian Engrs & Architects Asn; fel Am Inst Chemists; Adhesion Soc; Tech Asn Pulp & Paper Indust. *Res:* Adhesives and coating technology; pressure sensitive adhesives; emulsion and solution polymerization; paper coating and saturation; coating and lamination equipment; author/editor of six books. *Mailing Add:* 99 Shenandoah Rd Warwick RI 02886. *Fax:* 401-884-7620; *E-Mail:* 76660.74@compuserve.com

SATCHER, DAVID, MEDICAL GENETICS, MEDICAL EDUCATION. *Current Pos:* DIR, CTR DIS CONTROL & PREV, 93-; ADMINR, AGENCY TOXIC SUBSTANCES & DIS REGISTRY, 93- *Personal Data:* b Anniston, Ala, Mar 2, 41; m; c 4. *Educ:* Morehouse Col, BS, 63; Case Western Res Univ, MD & PhD(cytogenetics), 70; Am Bd Family Pract, cert, 76 & 82. *Hon Degrees:* DSc, Med Col Pa, 86. *Honors & Awards:* Breslow Award in Pub Health, 95; Dr Nathan B Davis Award, AMA, 96. *Prof Exp:* Fac fel community med, Charles R Drew Med Sch, Los Angeles, 72-74, prof & chmn, Dept Family Med, actg dean, 75-79; prof & chmn, Dept Community & Family Med, Sch Med, Morehouse Col, Atlanta, 79-82; pres, Meharry Med Col, Nashville, 82-93. *Concurrent Pos:* Assoc dir, King-Drew Sickle Cell Ctr, Los Angeles, Calif, 73-75, dir, 74-79; asst prof epidemiol, Univ Calif, Los Angeles, 74-76, Robert Wood Johnson Clin scholar & sr family pract resident, 75076; prin investr grants, Dept Health & Human Serv, 85-90 & 88-91, Nat Cancer Inst, 88-91, NSF, 87-; pres, Asn Minority Health Professions Schs; mem bd dirs, Univ Pa Med Ctr, First Am Bank, Nashville. *Mem:* Inst Med-Nat Acad Sci; fel Am Acad Family Physicians; AAAS; Am Cancer Soc; Am Health Asn; AMA; Am Soc Human Genetics; Nat Med Asn. *Res:* Medical genetics, community and family medicine; author or co-author of over 35 publications. *Mailing Add:* Off Dir Ctr Dis Control Bldg 16 Rm 5132 1600 Clifton Rd NE Atlanta GA 30333. *Fax:* 404-639-7111

SATCHLER, GEORGE RAYMOND, THEORETICAL PHYSICS. *Current Pos:* RES PROF, UNIV TENN, KNOXVILLE, 94- *Personal Data:* b London, Eng, June 14, 26; m 48, Pat Gibson; c Ann & Jacqui. *Educ:* Oxford Univ, BA & MA, 51, DPhil(physics), 55. *Hon Degrees:* DSc, Oxford Univ, 89. *Honors & Awards:* Tom W Bonner Prize, Am Phys Soc, 77. *Prof Exp:* Sr studentship, Clarendon Lab, Oxford Univ, 51-56, Imp Chem Industs res fel, 56-59; physicist, Oak Ridge Nat Lab, 59-94, corp res fel, 76-94. *Concurrent Pos:* Res assoc, Univ Mich, 56-57. *Mem:* Fel Am Phys Soc. *Res:* Theory of nuclear structure and nuclear reactions. *Mailing Add:* Physics Div Oak Ridge Nat Lab PO Box 2008 Oak Ridge TN 37831-6373

SATEEV, JOHN, PHYSICS. *Current Pos:* PROF, PHYSICS DEPT, UNIV TORONTO. *Honors & Awards:* Gerhard Herzberg Medal, Can Asn Physicists, 95. *Mailing Add:* Univ Toronto 60 St George St Toronto ON M5S 1A1 Can

SATER, VERNON E(UGENE), CHEMICAL ENGINEERING. *Current Pos:* from asst prof to assoc prof, 62-74, PROF CHEM ENG & ACTG CHMN, ARIZ STATE UNIV, 74- *Personal Data:* b Rock Rapids, Iowa, Apr 10, 35; m 57; c 3. *Educ:* Ill Inst Technol, BS, 57, MS, 59, PhD(chem eng), 63. *Prof Exp:* Instr chem eng, Ill Inst Technol, 62. *Mem:* Am Chem Soc; Am Inst Chem Engrs. *Res:* Process control; process simulation; microcomputer. *Mailing Add:* Dept Chem Biol & Mat Eng Ariz State Univ PO Box 876006 Tempe AZ 85287-6006

SATHE, SHARAD SOMNATH, ORGANIC & MEDICINAL CHEMISTRY. *Current Pos:* res investr, 73-79, tech supvr, 79-81, GROUP LEADER RES & DEVELOP, MALLINCKRODT INC, 81- *Personal Data:* b Bombay, India, Oct 10, 40; m 66; c 2. *Educ:* Bombay Univ, BSc, 60; Banaras Hindu Univ, BPharm, 63; Ind Univ, PhD(org chem), 71. *Prof Exp:* Analytical chemist, Hoffman-La Roche Co, India, 63-65; res asst chem, CIBA Res Ctr, India, 65-67; assoc, Res Triangle Inst, 71-73. *Mem:* Am Chem Soc; Am Inst Chem; NY Acad Sci. *Res:* Research and development in organic chemistry related to drug products, drug intermediates and fine organic chemicals. *Mailing Add:* Mallinckrodt Inc 3600 N Second St St Louis MO 63147-3458

SATHE, SHRIDHAR KRISHNA, AGRICULTURAL & FOOD CHEMISTRY, FOOD SCIENCE & TECHNOLOGY. *Current Pos:* from asst prof to assoc prof, 88-97, PROF FOOD SCI, FLA STATE UNIV, 91- *Personal Data:* b Pune, India, Oct 30, 50; m 84, Sandhya; c Sonal S. *Educ:* Bombay Univ, BSc Hons, 71, BSc Tech Hons, 74, MSc Tech, 77; Utah State Univ, PhD(food sci), 82. *Prof Exp:* Assoc lectr food technol, Bombay Univ, 76-77; fel food sci & biochem, Univ Ariz, 81-85 & food sci, Purdue Univ, 86-88. *Concurrent Pos:* Invited speaker, Cambridge Univ, UK, 83 & Univ Irapuato, Mex, 85; mem, Ann Meeting Prog Comt, Inst Food Technologists, 90-97. *Mem:* Inst Food Technologists; Am Asn Cereal Chemists; Am Oil Chemists Soc; Am Dairy Sci Asn; Sigma Xi. *Res:* Chemical and biochemical aspects of foods and their relation to nutrition and functionality; biochemistry of legumes with special emphasis on proteins, carbohydrates, and antinutritional factors. *Mailing Add:* Dept Nutrit Food & Movement Sci Fla State Univ Tallahassee FL 32306-2033. *Fax:* 850-644-0700; *E-Mail:* ssathe@mailer.fsu.edu

SATHER, BRYANT THOMAS, PHYSIOLOGY, ECOLOGY. *Personal Data:* b Wallace, Idaho, Feb 8, 35; m 63. *Educ:* Univ Idaho, BS, 57; Univ Hawaii, PhD(zool), 65. *Prof Exp:* Asst physiologist, Pac Biomed Res Ctr, Univ Hawaii, 64-66; asst prof zool NC State Univ, 66-67; from asst prof to assoc prof physiol, Rutgers Univ, Newark, 67-85. *Mem:* AAAS; Am Soc Zoologists; Am Physiol Soc. *Res:* Comparative and ecological physiology; osmoregulation and electrolyte balance; mineral metabolism; renal physiology. *Mailing Add:* 944 S 25th St Easton PA 18042

SATHER, DUANE PAUL, MATHEMATICS. *Current Pos:* assoc prof, 70-74, PROF MATH, UNIV COLO, BOULDER, 74- *Personal Data:* b Minneapolis, Minn, Sept 19, 33; m 55; c 3. *Educ:* Univ Minn, BPhys, 59, MS, 60, PhD(math), 63. *Prof Exp:* Instr math, Univ Minn, 63-64; res assoc, Univ Md, 64-65; asst prof, Cornell Univ, 65-68; assoc prof math, Math Res Ctr, US Army, Univ Wis-Madison, 68-70. *Mem:* Am Math Soc; Soc Natural Philos. *Res:* Partial differential equations; applied mathematics. *Mailing Add:* 850 Circle Dr Boulder CO 80302

SATHER, GLENN A(RTHUR), CHEMICAL ENGINEERING, SOLUTION THERMODYNAMICS. *Current Pos:* From asst prof to prof, 59-91, EMER PROF CHEM ENG, UNIV WIS-MADISON, 91- *Personal Data:* b Franklin, Minn, Jan 18, 28; m 52, Eleanor Severeid; c 1. *Educ:* Univ Minn, BCE & BBA, 52, PhD(chem eng), 59. *Concurrent Pos:* NSF sci fac fel, Imp Col, Univ London, 66-67; year-in-indust prof, E I du Pont de Nemours & Co, 73-74. *Mem:* Am Inst Chem Engrs; Am Chem Soc; Am Soc Eng Educ. *Res:* Cryogenics; thermodynamics. *Mailing Add:* 1111 Woodland Way Madison WI 53711-2535

SATHER, J HENRY, ZOOLOGY, ECOLOGY. *Current Pos:* prof biol & dean grad sch, 55-80, EMER DEAN GRAD SCH & PROF BIOL SCI, WESTERN ILL UNIV, 80- *Personal Data:* b Presho, SDak, July 12, 21; m 48, Shirley M Johnson; c Kristi, Signe & Ingrid. *Educ:* Univ Nebr, BSc, 43, PhD(zool), 53; Univ Mo, AM, 48. *Honors & Awards:* Patriotic Civilian Serv Award, US CEngr, 83; Spec Recognition Serv Award, Wildlife Soc, 87. *Prof Exp:* Sr biologist fur invests, Game, Forestation & Parks Comn, Nebr, 48-53, leader game res, 53-55; wetland ecologist, US Fish & Wildlife Serv, 80-88. *Concurrent Pos:* Mem, Nat Wetlands Tech Coun, 76-; adv to proj leader, Nat Wetland Inventory, 76-88; wetland res adv, Bombay Natural Hist Soc, 80- *Mem:* AAAS; Explorers Club; Ecol Soc Am; Sigma Xi; Am Inst Biol Sci. *Res:* Mammals, upland game birds and wetland ecosystems. *Mailing Add:* 103 Oakland Lane Macomb IL 61455-1219

SATHER, NORMAN F(REDRICK), BIOTECHNOLOGY, ENVIRONMENTAL CONTROL TECHNOLOGY. *Current Pos:* chem engr energy & environ systs, 74-79, assoc div dir, 79-83, dep div dir, 83-89, DIV DIR, ARGONNE NAT LAB, 89- *Personal Data:* b Elmhurst, Ill, Sept 17, 36; m 57; c 3. *Educ:* Univ Ill, BS, 58; Univ Minn, PhD(chem eng), 62. *Prof Exp:* From asst prof to prof chem eng, Univ Wash, 62-74. *Concurrent Pos:* Fel, Univ Cambridge, Eng, 71-72; consult, Ocean Thermal Energy Conversion to Ministry, Int Trade & Indust, Japan, 79. *Mem:* Am Inst Chem Eng; AAAS; Am Soc Mech Engr. *Res:* Development of ocean thermal energy converison power systems components and designs; thermochemical and biological processes for conversion of biomass to fuels and chemicals, and environmental control technology for coal combustion and gasification. *Mailing Add:* 9700 S Cass Ave Argonne Nat Lab Lemont IL 60439

SATHOFF, H JOHN, GENERAL PHYSICS. *Current Pos:* asst prof physics & chem, 61-64, assoc prof physics, 64-69, chmn dept, 64-81, PROF PHYSICS, BRADLEY UNIV, 69- *Personal Data:* b Peoria, Ill, Sept 21, 31; m 54; c 2. *Educ:* Bradley Univ, BS, 53; Ohio State Univ, MS, 55, PhD(nuclear physics), 60. *Prof Exp:* Res assoc physics, Ohio State Univ, 61. *Mem:* Am Asn Physics Teachers; Am Chem Soc; Sigma Xi. *Res:* Acoustics; physics; computing. *Mailing Add:* Dept Physics Bradley Univ Peoria IL 61625-0001

SATHYAMOORTHY, MUTHUKRISHNAN, NONLINEAR MECHANICS, COMPOSITE MATERIALS. *Current Pos:* from asst prof to assoc prof mech eng, Clarkson Univ, 79-94, exec officer, 92-97, PROF MECH ENG, CLARKSON UNIV, 94-, CHMN MECH ENG, 97- *Personal Data:* b Sathanur, India, Feb 21, 46; US citizen; m 71, Chitra; c Mohan & Kumaran. *Educ:* Madras Univ, BS, 67; Indian Inst Technol, MS, 69, PhD(aeronaut eng), 73. *Honors & Awards:* Nat Fac Adv Award, Am Soc Mech Engrs, 93. *Prof Exp:* Lectr aeronaut eng, Indian Inst Technol, 69-74 & 76-77; res fel mech eng, Univ Birmingham, Eng, 74-76; vis res fac civil eng, Univ Calgary, Can, 77-79. *Concurrent Pos:* Consult, Gen Motors, 84-85, US Army Ballistic Res Lab, 88-95; co-prin investr, Off Sci Res, USAF, 84-87; prin investr, US Army Ballistic Res Lab, 89-90. *Mem:* Fel Am Soc Mech Engrs; fel Aeronaut Soc India; assoc fel Am Inst Aeronaut & Astronaut. *Res:* Nonlinear mechanics; composite materials, stiffened structures; finite element methods, vulnerability analysis. *Mailing Add:* 177 Regan Rd Potsdam NY 13676. *Fax:* 315-268-6438, 268-6695; *E-Mail:* salty@sun.soe.clarkson.edu

SATIJA, KANWAR (KEN) SAIN, fluid mechanics, hydraulics, for more information see previous edition

SATINOFF, EVELYN, PHYSIOLOGICAL PSYCHOLOGY, BEHAVIORAL NEUROSCIENCE. *Current Pos:* PROF & CHAIR, PSYCHOL DEPT, UNIV DE, 93- *Personal Data:* b Brooklyn, NY; div; c 2. *Educ:* Brooklyn Col, NY, BS, 58; Univ Pa, Philadelphia, PhD(physiol psychol), 63. *Prof Exp:* NIH fel & res assoc psychol, Univ Pa, 63-73; prof, Univ Ill, 73-93. *Concurrent Pos:* Vis investr, Inst Invests Cerebral, Mexico City, 67-68; sr res assoc, Ames Res Ctr, Moffett Field, Calif, 75-76; mem, Thermal Physiol Comn, Int Union Physiol Sci, 77-83, Exec Comn Div Six, 81-84 & Fels Comt Div Three, Six & Twenty-eight, Am Psychol Asn, 84-86 & Neurosci Steering Comn, Am Physiol Soc, 83-86; vis prof, Bar Ilan Univ, Ramat Gan, Israel & sch med, Tel Aviv Univ, 79, NY Hosp, Cornell Med Ctr, White Plains, NY, 87-88; mem biopsychol study sect, NIH, 79-83; J S Guggenheim fel, 87-88. *Mem:* Am Psychol Asn; Am Physiol Soc; Soc Neurosci; Sleep Res Soc; Int Union Physiol Sci; Soc Exp Psychologists. *Res:* Neural and pharmacological substrates of motivated behavior; thermoregulation; sleep-wakefulness; circadian rhythms. *Mailing Add:* Dept Psychol Univ Del Newark DE 19716-2577. *Fax:* 302-831-3645; *E-Mail:* esatinof@spsychuicc.edu

SATIR, BIRGIT H, MEMBRANE BIOLOGY, CELL BIOLOGY. *Current Pos:* prof & dir, Anal Ultrastruct Ctr, 77-84, PROF, ALBERT EINSTEIN COL MED, NY, 77- *Personal Data:* b Copenhagen, Denmark, Mar 22, 34; m 62; c 2. *Educ:* Univ Copenhagen, Cand Phil, 55, Magistra (biochem), 61. *Prof Exp:* Res assoc, Fibiger Lab, Copenhagen, 61-62 & Univ Chicago, 62-66; asst res physiologist, Univ Calif, Berkeley, 67-74, assoc res physiologist, 74-76, adj assoc prof, 76-77. *Concurrent Pos:* Res fel, Univ Geneva, Switz, 65-66; spec fel, Univ Tokyo, Japan, 72-73; ed-in-chief, Mod Cell Biol, 80-; dir biol, Electron Micros Soc, 82-84. *Mem:* Am Soc Cell Biol; Electron Micros Soc; Soc Protozool. *Res:* Regulation of signal transduction in stimulus-exocytosis-coupling using secretory mutants of the ciliated protozoa; ultrastructural and biochemical analyses. *Mailing Add:* Dept Anat & Struct Biol Albert Einstein Col Med 1300 Morris Park Ave Bronx NY 10461-1975. *Fax:* 212-518-7236; *E-Mail:* bastir@aecom.yu.edu

SATIR, PETER, CELL BIOLOGY, CELL MOTILITY. *Current Pos:* PROF ANAT & STRUCT BIOL & CHMN DEPT, ALBERT EINSTEIN COL MED, 77- *Personal Data:* b New York, NY, July 28, 36; m 62; c 2. *Educ:* Columbia Col, AB, 56; Rockefeller Inst, PhD, 61. *Prof Exp:* Instr biol & zool, Univ Chicago, 61-63, asst prof, 63-67; assoc prof anat, Univ Calif, Berkeley, 67-73, dir, Electron Micros Lab, 69-76, prof physiol-anat, 73-77. *Concurrent Pos:* Mem Nat Bd Med Examrs, 85- *Mem:* AAAS; Am Soc Cell Biol; Soc Protozool; Am Asn Anatomists; Biophys Soc. *Res:* Cell biology, ciliary motility; cytoplasmic and membrane organization; signal transduction in control of cell movement. *Mailing Add:* Dept Anat & Struct Biol Albert Einstein Col Med 1300 Morris Park Ave Bronx NY 10461-1975. *Fax:* 718-518-7236

SATKIEWICZ, FRANK GEORGE, PHYSICAL CHEMISTRY. *Current Pos:* SR STAFF, APPL PHYSICS LAB, JOHNS HOPKINS UNIV, 73- *Personal Data:* b Cambridge, Mass, Mar 6, 27; m 51; c 4. *Educ:* Northeastern Univ, BS, 47; Wesleyan Univ, MA, 49; Mass Inst Technol, PhD(phys chem), 58. *Prof Exp:* Radiochemist, Tracerlab, Inc, 49-52; head high sch math dept, 52-54; res assoc, Norton Co, 58-63; staff scientist, GCA Corp, 63-69, prin scientist, 69-73. *Mem:* Am Chem Soc; Am Soc Mass Spectrometry. *Res:* Solid state chemistry and physics; sputter-ion source mass spectrometry of solids; ion-acoustics. *Mailing Add:* 3453 Nanmark Ct Ellicott City MD 21042-3715

SATO, AKIO, PHYSIOLOGY. *Current Pos:* head, Second Dept Physiol, 72-80, dir, Dept Physiol, 80-90, VDIR, TOKYO METROPOLITAN INST GERONT, 90- *Personal Data:* b Hokkaido, Japan, June 21, 34; m 60, Yuko Otsuka; c Ikuko & Reiko. *Educ:* Hokkaido Univ, MD, 59, PhD, 64. *Honors & Awards:* Max Planck Res Award, 91. *Prof Exp:* Instr, Dept Physil, Hokkaido Univ Sch Med, 64-65; study fel, China Med Bd, Downstate Med Ctr, State Univ NY, 66-67; NIH postdoctoral fel, Univ Utah Sch Med, 67-69; Alexander von Humboldt Stiftung fel, Univ Heidelberg, 69-72. *Concurrent Pos:* Assoc ed, Neurosci Lett, 75-, J Autonomic Nervous Syst, 79- *Mem:* Int Union Physiol Sci; Int Brain Res Orgn; Int Asn Study Pain; Soc Neurosci; foreign mem Polish Acad Sci. *Res:* Contributed articles to professional journals. *Mailing Add:* Tokyo Metrop Inst Geront 35-2 Sakaecho Itabashiku Tokyo 173 Japan

SATO, DAIHACHIRO, MATHEMATICS, MATHEMATICAL EDUCATION. *Current Pos:* instr, 62-63, lectr, 63, from asst prof to assoc prof, 63-71, PROF MATH, UNIV REGINA, 71- *Personal Data:* b Fujinomiya-Shi, Japan, June 1, 32; m 56, Yoriko; c Mika Elaine, Kimihiko Ernst & Yusuke Ellis. *Educ:* Tokyo Univ Educ, BS, 55; Univ Calif, Los Angeles, MA, 57, PhD(math), 63. *Honors & Awards:* Lester R Ford Award, Math Asn Am, 77. *Prof Exp:* Reader math, Univ Calif, Los Angeles, 57-58, from asst to assoc, 58-61; asst prof, San Fernando Valley State Col, 61; instr, Tokai Univ, Japan, 61-62. *Concurrent Pos:* Vis asst prof & NSF fel, Univ Calif, Los Angeles, 64; Can Math Cong res fel, Queen's Univ, Ont, 65, Univ Alta, 66 & 71, Univ BC, 67, Univ Man, 68 & 69, Carlton Univ, 73, Univ Calgary, 74 & 75 & Res Inst Math Sci, Kyoto Univ, 76, 83. *Mem:* Am Math Soc; Math Asn Am; Soc Indust & Appl Math; Can Math Cong; Math Soc Japan. *Res:* Integer valued entire functions; generalized interpolations by analytic functions; prime representing functions; function theory; number theory; p-adic analysis; transcendentality problems; mathematics education; computer sciences; operations research; translatable GCD and LCM identities of binomial and multinomial coefficients. *Mailing Add:* Dept Math Univ Regina Regina SK S4S 0A2 Can. *Fax:* 306-586-0679; *E-Mail:* sato@math.uregina.ca

SATO, GENTEI, ANTENNAS, MICROWAVE TRANSMISSION DEVICES. *Current Pos:* prof, 64-92, EMER PROF ELEC ENG, SOPHIA UNIV, 92-; PRES, ANTENNA GIKEN CO, LTD, 92- *Personal Data:* b Sendai, Japan, Mar 15, 26; m 56, Mutsuko Ikeda; c Motoyuki, Mazuko & Tomonavi. *Educ:* Tohoku Univ, BS, 47, PhD(elec eng), 61. *Prof Exp:* Res asst elec eng, Tohoku Univ, 47-56, assoc prof, 56-57; dir, Yagi Antenna Co, Ltd, 57-64. *Concurrent Pos:* Lectr, Shibaura Inst Technol, 65-68, vis prof, 87; vis prof, Tsinghua Univ, 90. *Mem:* Fel Inst Elec & Electronics Engrs; Electromagnetic Acad. *Res:* Phased array antennas; satellite communication antennas; direction finding antennas; broadcasting antennas; microwave devices such as directional couplers, phase shifters, attenuators. *Mailing Add:* Antenna Giken Co Ltd 4-72 Kamikizaki Omiya 330 Japan

SATO, GORDON HISASHI, BIOLOGY. *Current Pos:* RETIRED. *Personal Data:* b Los Angeles, Calif, Dec 17, 27; m 52; c 6. *Educ:* Univ Southern Calif, BA, 51; Calif Inst Technol, PhD(biophys), 55. *Honors & Awards:* Edwin J Cohn Lectr, Harvard Univ; Rosenstiel Award, 82. *Prof Exp:* Teaching asst microbiol, Calif Inst Technol, 53-55; jr res virologist, Univ Calif, 56; instr molecular genetics, Med Sch, Univ Colo, 56-58; from asst prof to prof, Dept Biochem, Brandeis Univ, Waltham, Mass, 58-69; prof, Biol Dept, Univ Calif, San Diego, 69-83; dir, W Alton Jones Cell Sci Ctr, Inc, Lake Placid, NY, 83-92; scientist, Upstate Bio Technol, 92-94. *Concurrent Pos:* Panel mem, Molecular Biol Study Sect, NIH, 68-73, Breast Cancer Task Force, Nat Cancer Inst, 70-74; adj fac, Med Sch, Univ Vt, Burlington, 85; adj prof, Dept

Biochem, Albany Med Col Union Univ, NY, 85; distinguished res prof & dir, Lab Molecular Biol, Clarkson Univ, Potsdam, NY, 87. *Mem:* Nat Acad Sci; AAAS; Am Asn Immunologists; Endocrine Soc; Asn Biol Chem; Sigma Xi; Tissue Cult Asn (pres, 84-86); Int Cell Res Orgn; Am Soc Biol Chemists; fel Am Acad Arts & Sci. *Res:* Animal cell culture; endocrinology; bacteriophage; author of various publications. *Mailing Add:* 190 POB 190 Lake Placid NY 12946

SATO, HIROSHI, SOLID STATE PHYSICS. *Current Pos:* Ross distinguished prof, 84-89, prof, Sch Mat Eng, 74-89, EMER ROSS DISTINGUISHED PROF ENG, PURDUE UNIV, WEST LAFAYETTE, 89- *Personal Data:* b Matsuzaka, Japan, Aug 31, 18; nat US; m 47, Kyoko Amemiya; c Norie, Albert & Erika. *Educ:* Hokkaido Univ, MSc, 41; Univ Tokyo, DSc, 51. *Honors & Awards:* Prize, Japan Inst Metals, 51; Alexandar von Humboldt US sr scientist award, 80. *Prof Exp:* Res assoc physics, Hokkaido Univ, 42, asst prof, Inst Low Temperature Res, 42-43; res physicist, Inst Phys Chem Res, Tokyo, 43-45; prof metal physics, Res Inst Iron, Steel & Other Metals, Tohoku Univ, Japan, 45-57; prin res physicist, Sci Lab, Ford Motor Co, Mich, 56-74. *Concurrent Pos:* Res physicist, Res Lab, Westinghouse Elec Corp, 54-56; Guggenheim Mem fel, 66-67; consult, Solid State Div, Oak Ridge Nat Lab, 78-80; vis prof, Univ Hannover, 80-81; affil prof, Univ Wash, Seattle, 86-89; collabr, Los Alamos Nat Lab, NMex, 89- *Mem:* Fel Am Phys Soc; Phys Soc Japan; Am Ceramic Soc; Metall Soc; NY Acad Sci; hon mem Japan Inst Metals. *Res:* Metal physics; magnetism; diffusion and ion transport phenomena; high temperature ceramic materials; super ionic conductors; composite sic materials; kinetics of phase transitions; crystal growth; transmission electron microscopy; high temperature superconductors. *Mailing Add:* School Mat Eng Purdue Univ West Lafayette IN 47907-1289. *E-Mail:* sato@ecn.purdue.edu

SATO, MAKIKO, PLANETARY ATMOSPHERES. *Current Pos:* sci analyst planetary sci, Sigma Data Serv Corp, 80-94, SR SCIENTIST ANALYST, GODDARD INST SPACE STUDIES, NASA, 94- *Personal Data:* b Nishinomiya, Hyogo, Japan, May 29, 47; m 69; c 1. *Educ:* Osaka Univ, BS, 70; Yeshiva Univ, MA, 72, PhD(physics), 78. *Prof Exp:* Res scientist, Columbia, Univ, 78; res assoc, State Univ NY, Stony Brook, 78-79. *Concurrent Pos:* Co-investr, Voyager Spacecraft Mission, 80- *Mem:* Am Astron Soc; Planetary Soc. *Res:* Determination of the chemical compositions, cloud-haze structure and temperature profiles of the atmospheres of the outer planets by analyzing visible and infrared spectra. *Mailing Add:* Goddard Inst Space Studies 2880 Broadway New York NY 10025

SATO, MASAHIKO, BIOPHYSICS, CELL BIOLOGY. *Current Pos:* SR SCIENTIST, 91- *Personal Data:* b Aug 19, 55; m, Joan Frelond; c Michael & Amy. *Educ:* Dartmouth Col, PhD(cell biol), 83. *Prof Exp:* Res fel anat, Sch Med, Johns Hopkins Univ, 84-86. *Concurrent Pos:* Res fel, Merck Sharp Dohme; adj assoc prof, Dept Anat, Sch Med, Ind Univ. *Mem:* Am Soc Cell Biol; Am Soc Biochem & Molecular Biol; Am Soc Bone & Mineral Res. *Res:* Cell biology of bone resorption; pharmacology; bone biology. *Mailing Add:* Dept Endocrine Res Lilly Corp Ctr MC797 Indianapolis IN 46285. *Fax:* 317-276-9086

SATO, MIKIO, MATHEMATICS. *Current Pos:* prof res ins math sci, 70-72, EMER PROF, KYOTO UNIV, 92- *Personal Data:* b Tokyo, Japan, Apr 18, 28; m 80, Yasuko; c 2. *Educ:* Univ Tokyo, PhD(math), 60. *Honors & Awards:* Culture Contrib, Japanese Govt, 84. *Prof Exp:* Prof, Osaka Univ, 63-66, Univ Tokyo, 68-70. *Concurrent Pos:* Vis prof, Columbia Univ, 64-66 & 92, Nice Univ, France, 72-73. *Mem:* Nat Acad Sci; Math Soc Japan; Nat Acad Sci; Inst Advan Study. *Mailing Add:* Res Inst Math Sci Kyoto Univ Yoshida-Honmachi, Sakyo-ku Higasihiaki Kyoto 606 Japan

SATO, MOTOAKI, GEOCHEMISTRY, EARTH SCIENCES. *Current Pos:* res geologist, 63-65, proj leader, 65-95, EMER SCIENTIST, US GEOL SURV, 95- *Personal Data:* b Tokyo, Japan, Oct 11, 29; div; c 3. *Educ:* Univ Tokyo, BS, 53, MS, 55; Univ Minn, Minneapolis, PhD(geol), 59. *Prof Exp:* Res fel geophys, Harvard Univ, 59-61; assoc prof geol, Inst Thermal Springs Res, Okayama Univ, 61-63. *Concurrent Pos:* Apollo 12-17 prin investr oxygen fugacity studies lunar basalts, NASA. *Mem:* Am Geophys Union; Geochem Soc. *Res:* Electrochemistry of minerals; redox evolution of rocks; origin of sulfide self-potentials; geochemistry of gas-forming elements; electrochemical sensors for volcanic gas monitoring; oxygen fugacities of planetary rocks and meteorites; thermochemistry of fossil fuels; earthquake prediction by gas monitoring. *Mailing Add:* 11173 Lake Chapel Lane Reston VA 22091. *Fax:* 703-648-6419; *E-Mail:* motoaki@aol.com

SATO, PAUL HISASHI, ENZYME DEFICIENCY DISEASE, ENZYME ADMINISTRATION. *Current Pos:* ASSOC PROF PHARMACOL & TOXICOL, MICH STATE UNIV, 83- *Personal Data:* b Mar 22, 49; m, Jean Ellen Courville. *Educ:* New York Univ, PhD(pharmacol), 75. *Res:* Ascorbic acid biosynthesis. *Mailing Add:* Dept Pharmacol & Toxicol/8430 Life Sci Mich State Univ East Lansing MI 48824. *Fax:* 517-353-8915; *E-Mail:* sato@pilot.msu.edu

SATOH, PAUL SHIGEMI, BIOCHEMISTRY. *Current Pos:* sr res scientist III immunol, 72-79, MGR RES & DEVELOP, UPJOHN DIAG, THE UPJOHN CO, 79- *Personal Data:* b Osaka, Japan, Nov 6, 36; US citizen; c 2. *Educ:* St Paul's Univ, Tokyo, BA, 59; Wayne State Univ, PhD(biochem), 64. *Prof Exp:* Res assoc immunochem, Wayne State Univ, 64-66; res staff tumor immunol, Aichi Cancer Ctr, Nagoya, Japan, 66-68; sr res assoc protein chem, Med Sch, Tufts Univ, 68-72. *Mem:* Sigma Xi; NY Acad Sci; Am Chem Soc. *Res:* Immunological diagnosis of human cancer; enzyme-immunoassay; immunology of mediaters; lymphocytemembrane; cell mediated immunology of cancer patients, and immunosuppressive drugs; radioimmunoassay; bioluminescence. *Mailing Add:* PO Box 1987 Portage MI 49081-1987

SATRAN, RICHARD, NEUROLOGY. *Current Pos:* Instr neurol & EEG, Univ Rochester Med Ctr, 62-63, dir, EEG Lab, 62-70, sr instr neurol, 63-64, from asst prof to assoc prof, 64-75, actg chmn div, 66, actg chmn dept, 84-86, vchmn dept, 79-86, PROF NEUROL, UNIV ROCHESTER MED CTR, 75-, ASSOC CHMN DEPT, 86- , ASSOC DEAN MED SCH ADMIS, 90- *Personal Data:* b New York, NY, Oct 3, 28; m 51; c 2. *Educ:* Univ Louisville, BA, 49, MD, 56; NY Univ, MA, 51. *Mem:* Fel Am Col Physicians; fel Am Acad Neurol; Sigma Xi; hon mem Fr Soc Neurol; fel Am Heart Asn. *Res:* Electroencephalography; cerebrovascular disease; medical history. *Mailing Add:* Dept Neurol 601 Elmwood Ave Rochester NY 14642-0001

SATRE, RODRICK IVERSON, PROCESS ENGINEERING OF WASTE TREATMENT-CLEAN UP-WASTE MINIMIZATION, INCINERATOR DESIGN OPERATIONS. *Current Pos:* ASSOC, BLASLAND, BOUCK & LEE, 96; ENG MGR, ATI ENG SERVS INC, 97. *Personal Data:* b Geneseo, NY, July 14, 51; m 78, Bonita M Daley. *Educ:* Clarkson Univ, BS, 73; J F Kennedy Univ, MBA, 89. *Prof Exp:* Design engr, Chevron Chem Co, Ortho Agr, 74-75, plant engr, 75-77, operating asst, 77-78, area supvr, 78-80, sr opers analyst, 80-85, group leader process improv, 85-87, sr res engr, 87-89; proj mgr, IT Corp, 90-92, gen mgr, 92-93; prin engr & group mgr eng, Harding Lawson Assocs, 93-95; proj dir, Vpres Environ Solutions Inc, 95-96. *Concurrent Pos:* Prin SSD, Consult, 89-; assoc, Kertez Int, Inc, 90-; guest lectr environ eng, Univ Calif, 91- *Mem:* Am Inst Chem Engrs. *Res:* Specialization in applied technology/business development; activities are all commercially driven; qualified in process engineering, product development and process/product improvement; technical management; granted two US patents and one European patent. *Mailing Add:* 625 Morgan Ave Point Richmond CA 94801. *Fax:* 415-951-9451

SATTAR, SYED ABDUS, MEDICAL & ENVIRONMENTAL MICROBIOLOGY. *Current Pos:* assoc prof, 70-82, PROF MICROBIOL, UNIV OTTAWA, 82- *Personal Data:* b Hyderabad, India, Mar 23, 38; m 70, Parveen; c Saleem & Sara. *Educ:* Univ Karachi, BSc, 58, MSc, 60; Univ Toronto, dipl bact, 62, MA, 64; Univ Ottawa, PhD(microbiol), 67. *Prof Exp:* Asst lectr microbiol, Univ Karachi, 60-61; res fel, Univ Ottawa, 64-67; lectr, Univ Karachi, 68-70. *Mem:* Can Soc Microbiologists; Int Am Soc Microbiol; Can Asn Microbiol & Infectious Dis; Community & Hosp Infectious Control Asn Can; Asn Off Anal Chemists; Asn Practr Infectious Control; Can Col Microbiologists. *Res:* Study of human pathogenic viruses in air, surface and the water environment; viral gastroenteritis; disinfection of viruses; non-tuberculous mycobacteria in water; survival and inactivation of cryptosporidium and giardia in water. *Mailing Add:* Dept Microbiol Fac Med Univ Ottawa Ottawa ON K1H 8M5 Can. *E-Mail:* ssatter@uottawa.ca

SATTEN, ROBERT A, SOLID STATE SPECTROSCOPY. *Current Pos:* from asst prof to prof, 53-91, EMER PROF PHYSICS, UNIV CALIF, LOS ANGELES, 91- *Personal Data:* b Chicago, Ill, Aug 4, 22; m 46, Erica Semone; c Corey & Glen. *Educ:* Univ Chicago, BS, 44; Univ Calif, Los Angeles, MA, 47, PhD(physics), 51. *Prof Exp:* Instr physics, Univ Calif, Los Angeles, 51-52; asst prof, Mass Inst Technol, 52-53. *Concurrent Pos:* Consult, Argonne Nat Lab, 59-72, Hughes Res Lab, 59-67 & Lockheed Res Lab, 63-65; Fulbright res fel, France, 61-62 & Ger, 69-70; vchmn dept physics, Univ Calif, Los Angelos, 68-73 & 87-; vis Erskine fel, Univ Canterbury, 71. *Mem:* Fel Am Phys Soc; Am Asn Physics Teachers. *Res:* Rare earth and actinide spectra in solids, vibronic spectra in crystals; optical detection of spin-lattice relaxation. *Mailing Add:* Dept Physics Univ Calif Los Angeles Los Angeles CA 90024. *E-Mail:* satten@physics.ucla.edu

SATTER, LARRY DEAN, ANIMAL NUTRITION. *Current Pos:* mem staff, 81-87, DIR, US DAIRY FORAGE RES CTR, UNIV WIS, USDA, 87- *Personal Data:* b Madelia, Minn, July 30, 37; m 66; c 1. *Educ:* SDak State Univ, BS, 60; Univ Wis, MS, 62, PhD(biochem, dairy sci), 64. *Honors & Awards:* Am Feed Mfrs Award, 77. *Prof Exp:* From asst prof to assoc prof dairy sci, Univ Wis-Madison, 64-73, prof, 73-81. *Mem:* Am Dairy Sci Asn; Am Soc Animal Sci; Am Inst Nutrit; Brit Nutrit Soc. *Res:* Digestive phenomena occurring in the rumen and quantitative aspects of the rumen fermentation. *Mailing Add:* 1925 W Linden Dr Univ Wis 1925 W Linden Dr W Madison WI 53706-1108. *Fax:* 608-264-5275

SATTERFIELD, CHARLES N(ELSON), CHEMICAL ENGINEERING, HETEROGENEOUS CATALYSIS. *Current Pos:* Res engr, 43-45, from asst prof to prof, 46-92, EMER PROF CHEM ENG, MASS INST TECHNOL, 92- *Personal Data:* b Dexter, Mo, Sept 5, 21; m 46, Anne Pettingell; c Mark & Joye. *Educ:* Harvard Univ, SB, 42; Mass Inst Technol, SM, 43, ScD(chem eng), 46. *Honors & Awards:* Wilhelm Award, Am Inst Chem Engrs; Kelly lectr, Purdue Univ, 71; Plenary lectr, Int Symposium Chem React Eng, 74; Van Winkle lectr, Univ Tex, 79. *Concurrent Pos:* Vis lectr, Harvard Univ, 48-57; consult, 48-; consult, US Res & Develop Bd, 52-53 & US Dir Defense Res & Eng, 53-60; mem, Comt Chem Kinetics, Nat Acad Sci-Nat Res Coun, 60-66; mem adv bd, Indust & Eng Chem, 66-68, Energy & Fuels, 91-, Appl Catalysis, 94- & Comt Air Qual Mgt & chmn ad hoc panel, Abatement Nitrogen Oxides Emissions Stationary Sources, Nat Acad Eng, 70-72, Nat Res Coun Panel, Direct Combustion Coal, 75-77. *Mem:* Am Chem Soc; Am Inst Chem Engrs; fel Am Acad Arts & Sci. *Res:* Applied chemical kinetics and heterogeneous catalysis; mass transfer in chemical reactors; author and co-author of six books and about 150 research papers; holds three patents. *Mailing Add:* 38 Tabor Hill Rd Lincoln MA 01773. *Fax:* 617-253-9695

SATTERLEE, JAMES DONALD, BIOINORGANIC & PHYSICAL CHEMISTRY. *Current Pos:* asst prof, 81-84, ASSOC PROF, DEPT CHEM, UNIV NMEX, 84- *Personal Data:* b Seattle, Wash, Feb 16, 48; c 1. *Educ:* Cent Wash Univ, BA, 70, MS, 71; Univ Calif, Davis, PhD(chem), 75. *Prof*

Exp: Res fel chem biol, Dept Chem, Calif Inst Technol, 75-78; asst prof, Dept Chem, Northern Ill Univ, 78-81. *Concurrent Pos:* Alfred P Sloan Found fel, 83-86; NIH res career develop award, 86- *Mem:* Am Chem Soc; Biophys Soc; Protein Soc. *Res:* Chemistry; metal ions in biology; nuclear magnetic resonance spectroscopy in chemical and biochemical systems; electron transfer in biology. *Mailing Add:* Dept Chem Wash State Univ Pullman WA 99164-4630. *Fax:* 509-335-8867

SATTERLEE, LOWELL DUGGAN, FOOD CHEMISTRY, BIOCHEMISTRY. *Current Pos:* DEAN, COL AGR, NDAK STATE UNIV, 92- *Personal Data:* b Duluth, Minn, July 30, 43; m 63; c 2. *Educ:* SDak State Univ, BS, 65; Iowa State Univ, MS, 66, PhD(biochem), 68. *Prof Exp:* Asst prof food technol, Iowa State Univ, 68-69; from asst prof to prof food sci, Univ Nebr, Lincoln, 69-, head food sci, 83-; prof food sci & technol, Pa State Univ. *Concurrent Pos:* Viobin Labs indust grant, 69-73; Nebr Agr Asn grants, 72-79; NSF grant, 74-79 & 79-82. *Mem:* AAAS; Inst Food Technologists; Am Chem Soc. *Res:* Isolation, characterization and utilization of human food proteins. *Mailing Add:* Agr NDak State Univ Main Campus Fargo ND 58105

SATTERLIE, RICHARD A, ZOOLOGY. *Current Pos:* from asst prof to assoc prof, 80-91, PROF, DEPT ZOOL, ARIZ STATE UNIV, 91- *Personal Data:* b Feb 3, 50. *Educ:* Sonoma State Univ, BA, 73; Univ Calif, Santa Barbara, PhD, 78. *Prof Exp:* Postdoctoral fel, Univ Alta, 78-80, lectr, 79-80. *Concurrent Pos:* Grass Found fel neurobiol, Marine Biol Lab, Woods Hole, Mass, 78; Fulbright grantee, Univ St Andrews, 94-95. *Mem:* AAAS; Am Soc Zoologists; Sigma Xi; Soc Neurosci. *Res:* Contributed numerous publications in field. *Mailing Add:* Dept Zool Univ Ariz Box 871501 Tempe AZ 85287

SATTERLUND, DONALD ROBERT, FORESTRY. *Current Pos:* from asst prof to assoc prof, 64-71, PROF FORESTRY, WASH STATE UNIV, 71- *Personal Data:* b Polk Co, Wis, Apr 10, 28; m 55; c 3. *Educ:* Univ Mich, BSF, 51, MF, 55, PhD(forestry), 60. *Prof Exp:* Asst forestry, Univ Mich, 53-58; instr forest influences, State Univ NY Col Forestry, Syracuse, 58-60, asst prof, 60-64. *Mem:* Soc Am Foresters; Soil Conserv Soc Am; Am Geophys Union. *Res:* Watershed management; forest influences and ecology. *Mailing Add:* 1400 NW Clifford St Pullman WA 99163

SATTERLY, GILBERT T(HOMPSON), CIVIL ENGINEERING. *Current Pos:* assoc prof, 70-76, PROF CIVIL ENG, PURDUE UNIV, 76- *Personal Data:* b Detroit, Mich, Sept 27, 29; m 52; c 4. *Educ:* Wayne State Univ, BS, 52, MS, 61; Northwestern Univ, PhD(transp eng), 65. *Prof Exp:* Detailer struct design, Giffels & Vallet, Inc, 53-54; asst civil engr, Bur Hwy & Expressways, City of Detroit, 54-56; struct engr, Stran-Steel Corp, 56-57; instr transp & struct eng, Wayne State Univ, 57-59; sr asst engr, Bur Hwy & Expressways, City of Detroit, 59-60; lectr transp & traffic eng, Northwestern Univ, 63-65, asst prof, 65-66; assoc prof, Univ Mich, Ann Arbor, 66-68; assoc prof, Wayne State Univ, 68-70. *Concurrent Pos:* Mem, Hwy Res Bd, Nat Acad Sci-Nat Res Coun. *Mem:* Am Soc Civil Engrs; Am Soc Eng Educ; Inst Traffic Engrs. *Res:* Transportation and traffic engineering. *Mailing Add:* 136 Blackhawk Lane West Lafayette IN 47906

SATTERTHWAITE, CAMERON B, HYDROGEN IN METALS. *Current Pos:* chmn dept, 79-82, prof, 79-85, EMER PROF PHYSICS, VA COMMONWEALTH UNIV, 85-; EMER PROF PHYSICS, DEPT PHYSICS & MAT RES LAB, UNIV ILL, URBANA, 79- *Personal Data:* b Salem, Ohio, July 26, 20; div; c Mark C, Tod F, Tracy L, Keith A & Craig E (deceased). *Educ:* Col Wooster, BA, 42; Univ Pittsburgh, PhD(phys chem), 51. *Prof Exp:* Res assoc cryogenics res found, Ohio State Univ, 44-45, res chemist, Mound Lab, 45-46, group leader, 46-47; res chemist, E I du Pont de Nemours & Co, 50-53; res physicist, Westinghouse Elec Co, 53-61; from assoc prof to prof, Dept Physics & Mat Res Lab, Univ Ill, Urbana, 61-79. *Concurrent Pos:* On leave, Iowa State Univ, 70-71; prog dir, NSF, 75-76; emer prof physics, Dept Physics & Mat Res Lab, Univ Ill, Urbana, 79- *Mem:* AAAS; fel Am Phys Soc; Fedn Am Scientists (pres, 69). *Res:* Low temperature properties of metals, particularly superconductors; properties of metal hydrides; hydrogen in metals. *Mailing Add:* 803 S Coler Ave Urbana IL 61801-4009

SATTERWHITE, RAMON S(TEWART), ELECTRICAL ENGINEERING. *Current Pos:* VPRES, SOUTHERN AVIONICS CO, 76- *Personal Data:* b Little Rock, Ark, Feb 9, 40; m 62; c 2. *Educ:* Univ Ark, BSEE, 62; Univ NMex, MS, 64; Ohio State Univ, PhD(elec eng), 69. *Prof Exp:* Staff mem, Sandia Corp, 62-66; from asst prof to assoc prof elec eng, Lamar Univ, 69-76. *Mem:* Inst Elec & Electronics Engrs; Sigma Xi. *Res:* Electromagnetic field theory. *Mailing Add:* Southern Avionics Co 5000 Belmont Box 5345 Beaumont TX 77707

SATTIN, ALBERT, NEUROPHARMACOLOGY. *Current Pos:* assoc prof psychiat, 77-84, ASSOC PROF PSYCHIAT & NEUROBIOL, SCH MED & GRAD SCH, IND UNIV, 84-; CHIEF, ANTIDEPRESSANT NEUROPHARMACOL LAB, DVA SEPULVEDA MED CTR, 91-, DVA W LOS ANGELES MED CTR, 94- *Personal Data:* b Cleveland, Ohio, Oct 5, 31; m 62; c 2. *Educ:* Western Res Univ, BS, 53, MD, 57; Am Bd Psychiat & Neurol, dipl, 79. *Prof Exp:* Intern med, Barnes Hosp, Wash Univ Med Ctr, 57-58; resident psychiat, Univ Hosp, Western Res Univ, 58-62, teaching fel, 62-64; fel neurochem, Dept Biochem, Inst Psychiat, Univ London, 65-66; instr psychiat, Case Western Res Univ, 66-68, sr instr, 68-69, asst prof pharmacol, 69-70 & asst prof psychiat & pharmacol, 70-77. *Concurrent Pos:* Res assoc, Dept Pharmacol, Case Western Res, 65-68, instr, 68-69, sr instr psychiat, 69-70; prin investr, NIMH, 68-74 & 77-82 & NSF, 75-77 & Vet Admin, 83-; staff physician, R L Roudebush Vet Admin Ctr, 77-91; assoc prof psychiat, Dept Psychiat Behav Sci, Sch Med, Univ Calif, Los Angeles, 91-, mem, Brain Res Inst, 97- *Mem:* AAAS; fel Am Psychiat Asn; Int Soc Neurochem; Soc Biol Psychiat; Soc Neurosci. *Res:* Discovery of the adenosine receptor and the effect of caffeine; discovery of the neuroregulatory role of TRH in the brain and its role in antidepressant treatment. *Mailing Add:* PO Box 84122 Los Angeles CA 90073. *E-Mail:* asattin@ucla.edu

SATTINGER, DAVID H, DIFFERENTIAL EQUATIONS. *Current Pos:* PROF MATH, UNIV MINN, MINNEAPOLIS, 72- *Personal Data:* b Ft Wayne, Ind, Apr 3, 40. *Educ:* Oberlin Col, BA, 62; Mass Inst Technol, PhD(math), 65. *Mem:* Am Math Soc. *Mailing Add:* Sch Math Rm 227 Vincent Hall Univ Minn Minneapolis MN 55455

SATTINGER, IRVIN J(ACK), ELECTRICAL ENGINEERING. *Current Pos:* RES ENGR, ENVIRON RES INST MICH, ANN ARBOR, 73- *Personal Data:* b Indianapolis, Ind, Nov 1, 12; m 37. *Educ:* c David & Michael. *Educ:* Univ Mich, BSE, 33, MS, 35. *Prof Exp:* Jr engr, Cent Ohio Light & Power Co, 36-37; elec draftsman, Commonwealth & Southern Corp, Mich, 37-38 & Loup River Pub Power Dist, Nebr, 38-39; asst engr, Ind Serv Corp, 39-41; elec designer, Basic Magnesium, Inc, Nev, 41-43; design engr, Lear, Inc, Mich, 43-48; res engr, Willow Run Labs, Inst Sci & Technol, Univ Mich, Ann Arbor, 48-73. *Mem:* Sr mem Inst Elec & Electronics Engrs. *Res:* Application of computers to scientific problems; electronic measurement and control systems, particularly for aerospace and ground vehicles; applications of airborne and spacecraft remote sensing systems; energy studies; infrared and electro-optical technology. *Mailing Add:* 410 Keech Ave Ann Arbor MI 48103

SATTIZAHN, JAMES EDWARD, JR, PHYSICAL CHEMISTRY. *Current Pos:* RETIRED. *Personal Data:* b Moline, Ill, June 26, 20; wid; c 2. *Educ:* Lawrence Col, BA, 42; Univ NMex, PhD(chem), 57. *Prof Exp:* Chemist, E I du Pont de Nemours & Co, 42-46; mem staff, Los Alamos Nat Lab, 46-85. *Res:* Fission product behavior in various matrices. *Mailing Add:* 1422 44th St Los Alamos NM 87544

SATTLER, ALLAN R, ATOMIC PHYSICS, NUCLEAR PHYSICS. *Current Pos:* STAFF MEM, SANDIA CORP, 63- *Personal Data:* b Los Angeles, Calif, June 28, 32; m 59; c 1. *Educ:* Univ Calif, Los Angeles, BA, 54; Pa State Univ, MS, 59, PhD(physics), 62. *Prof Exp:* Eng aide, Univ Calif, Los Angeles, 53-54; jr engr, Douglas Aircraft Co, Inc, 54; physicist atomic power equip dept, Gen Elec Co, 56-57. *Concurrent Pos:* Fulbright travel grant, 62-63; mem staff, Asse Nuclear Waste Repository, 77. *Mem:* Am Phys Soc. *Res:* Atomic particle energy; channelling; radiation effect; neutron cross section measurements; nuclear waste technology; earth sciences; fuel technology and petroleum engineering. *Mailing Add:* Sandia Nat Labs MS 0706 PO Box 5800 Albuquerque NM 87185-0706

SATTLER, CAROL ANN, BIOLOGICAL STRUCTURE. *Current Pos:* Res assoc path, Med Sch, 74-75, proj assoc oncol, McArdle Lab Cancer Res, 75-77, asst scientist, 77-82, ASSOC SCIENTIST, MCARDLE LAB CANCER RES, UNIV WIS-MADISON, 82- *Personal Data:* b DuBois, Pa, Sept 23, 46; m 71, Gerald L; c Matthew & Andrew. *Educ:* Thiel Col, BA, 68; Univ Colo, PhD(biol), 74. *Mem:* Am Soc Cell Biol; AAAS. *Res:* Ultrastructure of cilia and the oral cavity of Tetrahymena pyriformis; ultrastructure of cultured epithelial cells in rat hepatocytes and human mammary; Mitosis and gap junctions in cultured rat hepatocytes; ultrastructure of Drosophila ommatidia. *Mailing Add:* McArdle Lab Cancer Res Univ Wis 1400 University Ave Madison WI 53706-1599. *E-Mail:* sattlerc@oncology.wisc.edu

SATTLER, FRANK A(NTON), CHEMICAL ENGINEERING. *Current Pos:* RETIRED. *Personal Data:* b New England, NDak, July 5, 20; m 45; c 9. *Educ:* Univ NDak, BS, 42. *Prof Exp:* Res engr, Res Labs, Westinghouse Elec Corp, 42-54, supv chemist, 54-73, mgr wire, 73-78, adv scientist, Westinghouse Res & Develop Ctr, 78-83. *Mem:* Am Chem Soc. *Res:* Development of electrical insulating materials. *Mailing Add:* RR 1 Monroeville PA 15146

SATTLER, JOSEPH PETER, LASERS, RADAR. *Current Pos:* CHIEF SCIENTIST, SENSORS DIRECTORATE, ARMY RES LABS, ADELPHI, MD, 92- *Personal Data:* b New York, NY, Oct 19, 40; m 68, Jane Schoonover; c Emily, Timothy & Anna. *Educ:* Iona Col, BS, 62; Georgetown Univ, MS, 66, PhD(physics), 69. *Honors & Awards:* Res & Develop Achievement Award, US Army, 75; Hinman Tech Achievement Award, Harry Diamond Labs, 78. *Prof Exp:* Physicist, Harry Diamond Labs, 66-88, chief scientist, 88-92. *Concurrent Pos:* Army Dep (A) Technol & Req, 85-87. *Mem:* Am Phys Soc; Inst Elec & Electronics Engrs; Sigma Xi. *Res:* High resolution infrared and submillimeter wave spectroscopy; solid state physics; quantum electronics; electron paramagnetic resonance. *Mailing Add:* 1320 Woodside Pkwy Silver Spring MD 20910-1551. *Fax:* 301-394-5420; *E-Mail:* jsattler@adelphi_emh1.army.mil

SATTLER, ROBERT E(DWARD), CHEMICAL ENGINEERING, MATHEMATICS. *Current Pos:* RETIRED. *Personal Data:* b St Louis, Mo, Mar 31, 25; m 50, Helen E Roney; c Richard A & Kathryn A (Gatz). *Educ:* Wash Univ, St Louis, BS, 49; Univ Mo, MS, 52. *Prof Exp:* Process engr, Lago Oil & Transport Co, Ltd, 49-51; process design engr, Phillips Petrol Co, 52-57, planning & correlation engr, 57-61, theoret develop engr, 61-63, mgr process fundamentals sect, 63-66, rate processes sect, 66-69, sr engr kinetics & mass transfer sect, 69-73, res & develop engr, Hydrocarbon Processes Br, 73-77, res & develop engr, Coal Processes Sect, Alt Energy Br, Res & Develop Dept, 77-85. *Mem:* AAAS; Am Inst Chem Eng; Am Chem Soc. *Res:* Heat transfer; reaction kinetics; reactor design. *Mailing Add:* 1245 Grandview Bartlesville OK 74006

SATTLER, ROLF, PLANT MORPHOLOGY, BIOPHILOSOPHY. *Current Pos:* from asst prof to assoc prof, 64-77, PROF BOT, MCGILL UNIV, 77- *Personal Data:* b Goppingen, Ger, Mar 8, 36; div. *Educ:* Univ Munich, PhD(taxon), 61. *Hon Degrees:* DSc, Open Int Univ Complementary Med, Colubo, Sri Lanka, 95. *Honors & Awards:* Lawson Medal, Can Bot Asn, 74. *Prof Exp:* NATO fel, 62-64. *Concurrent Pos:* mem, Sci & Med Network, Ctr Process Studies, 96. *Mem:* Can Bot Asn; fel, Linnean Soc London; Sigma Xi; Int Soc Hist, Philos & Social Studies Biol; Int Asn New Sci. *Res:* Philosophy of biology: basic biological concepts (including complementarity) and their relevance to the human condition; process philosophy and process morphology; process language i.e. verb-based language structures. *Mailing Add:* Dept Biol McGill Univ Montreal PQ H3A 1B1 Can. *Fax:* 514-398-5069; *E-Mail:* rolf__sattler@maclean.mcgill.ca

SATTSANGI, PREM DAS, ORGANIC CHEMISTRY. *Current Pos:* pool officer, Pa State Univ, 68-70, asst prof chem, 70-73, res assoc, 73-77, ASST PROF CHEM, PA STATE UNIV, 77- *Personal Data:* b Ghazipur City, India, May 2, 39; m 68; c 2. *Educ:* Univ Allahabad, India, BS, 58, MS, 60, PhD(chem), 64. *Prof Exp:* Res assoc chem, Univ Ill, Urbana, 65-68. *Mem:* Am Chem Soc; Royal Soc Chem; Sigma Xi. *Res:* Synthesis of fluorescent probes; fluorescent modification of polypeptides of physiological interest; synthesis of heterocyclic compounds of biological interest. *Mailing Add:* Pa State Univ Fayette Campus Rte 119 N PO Box 519 Uniontown PA 15401-0519

SATTUR, THEODORE W, ANALYTICAL CHEMISTRY. *Current Pos:* CONSULT CHEM, 82- *Personal Data:* b Passaic, NJ, Oct 20, 20; m 41, Greta Lund; c Theodore W III, Gary S & Russell W. *Educ:* Rutgers Univ, BS, 42. *Prof Exp:* Chemist, Raritan Copper Works, 42-43; res chemist, Metal & Thermit Corp, 43-47; res chemist, Cent Res Labs, Am Smelting & Refining Co, NJ, 47-60, asst chief chemist, 60-73, sr res chemist, 73-76, res assoc, 76-82. *Mem:* Am Chem Soc; Sigma Xi; Soc Appl Spectros; fel Am Inst Chemists. *Res:* Methods for trace determination of halogens, sulfur and arsenic; application of atomic absorption spectroscopy. *Mailing Add:* 21 Hudson Pkwy Whiting NJ 08759

SATURNO, ANTONY FIDELAS, CHEMICAL PHYSICS. *Current Pos:* assoc prof, 66-71, PROF CHEM, STATE UNIV NY ALBANY, 71-, CHMN DEPT, 74- *Personal Data:* b Rochester, NY, Apr 7, 31; m 56; c 4. *Educ:* Univ Rochester, BS, 54; Carnegie Inst Technol, MS, 57, PhD(chem), 59. *Prof Exp:* Instr chem, Carnegie Inst Technol, 58-59; from asst prof to assoc prof, Univ Tenn, 59-66. *Concurrent Pos:* Consult, Metal & Ceramics Div, Oak Ridge Nat Lab, 63-66. *Mem:* AAAS; Am Chem Soc; Am Phys Soc; Sigma Xi. *Res:* Quantum chemistry, especially the application of high speed computers to chemical problems concerning the electronic structure of small molecules and atoms. *Mailing Add:* Chem State Univ NY 1400 Washington Ave Albany NY 12222-1000

SATYA, AKELLA V S, MATERIALS SCIENCE, PHYSICAL METALLURGY. *Current Pos:* adv engr, 69-80, mgr, 80-82, SR ENGR, DIAG DEVELOP, IBM CORP, 82- *Personal Data:* b Madras, India, Nov 21, 39; m 64; c 2. *Educ:* Indian Inst Technol, Kharagpur, BTech, 60, MTech, 62; Mich State Univ, PhD(mat sci), 69. *Honors & Awards:* Outstanding Innovation Award, IBM, 77. *Prof Exp:* Assoc lectr phys metall, Indian Inst Technol, Kharagpur, 60-62; chief metallurgist, Midwest Mach Co Ind, Inc, Mich, 64-66, consult, 66-67. *Concurrent Pos:* Hon lectr, Indian Inst Sci, Bangalore, 62; consult, Nat Aeronaut Labs, Bangalore, 62. *Mem:* Am Phys Soc; Electrochem Soc; Indian Inst Metals (treas-secy, 60-62); Sigma Xi; Inst Elec & Electronics Engrs. *Res:* Microelectronic device design and processing; metal-SC contacts, ion implantation, thin films; low-temperature specific heats, electronic energy bands, metal and semiconductor physics; charge coupled devices; system reliability; semiconductor device diagnostics methodologies, yield modeling/forecasting and test structures, yield and reliability management; solid state physics; electronics engineering. *Mailing Add:* 38 Tor Rd Wappingers Falls NY 12590

SATYANARAYANA, UPADHYAYULA V, POINT SET TOPOLOGY, NUMBER THEORY. *Current Pos:* PROF MATH, CALIF STATE UNIV, NORTHRIDGE, 71- *Personal Data:* b Andrapradesh, India, Dec 24, 35; m, Padria Rambhatla; c Sekhar C, Sridevi V & Saila R. *Educ:* Andhra Univ, India, BA, 54, MA, 55; Univ Calif Santa Barbara, PhD(math), 71. *Prof Exp:* Lectr & asst prof, Andhdra Univ, Waltair, India, 54-66; teaching & res asst, Univ Calif, Santa Barbara, 66-71. *Mem:* Math Asn Am; Am Math Soc; Indian Math Soc. *Res:* Involved in lecture notes for undergraduates in topology, fundamentals of math for computer science majors. *Mailing Add:* Calif State Univ Northridge CA 91330-0001

SATYANARAYANAN, MAHADEV, DISTRIBUTED SYSTEMS & MOBILE COMPUTING, FILE SYSTEMS & DATABASES. *Current Pos:* Syst designer, Info Technol Ctr, 83-86, from asst prof to assoc prof, 86-95, PROF COMPUT SCI, SCH COMPUT SCI, CARNEGIE-MELLON UNIV, 95- *Personal Data:* b 1953; US citizen; m 90, Deborah Kelly. *Educ:* Indian Inst Technol, Madras, BTech, 75, MTech, 77; Carnegie-Mellon Univ, PhD(comput sci), 83. *Concurrent Pos:* NSF presidential young investr, 87. *Mem:* Asn Comput Mach; Inst Elec & Electronics Engrs Comput Soc; Sigma Xi; Usenix Asn. *Res:* Design, development and evaluation of distributed systems that provide shared access to information; distributed file systems and databases, network protocols, security, performance evaluation, mobile computing. *Mailing Add:* Sch Comput Sci Carnegie-Mellon Univ Pittsburgh PA 15213-3890

SATYA-PRAKASH, K L, CANCER CYTOGENETICS. *Current Pos:* ASST PROF PATH & DIR, CANCER CYTOGENETICS LAB, SCH MED, MED COL GA, 86- *Personal Data:* b Mysore City, India, Dec 10, 47; m 72; c 2. *Educ:* Univ Mysore, India, PhD(cell biol), 76. *Mem:* Am Soc Human Genetics; AAAS; NY Acad Sci; Genetic Toxicol Assoc. *Res:* Cancer cytogenetics-management of the cancer patient. *Mailing Add:* Dept Path Med Col Ga Sch Med 1120 15th St Augusta GA 30901-3181

SATZ, HELMUT T G, elementary particle thermodynamics, for more information see previous edition

SATZ, RONALD WAYNE, SOFTWARE PACKAGE DESIGN & PRODUCTION, ENGINE DESIGN. *Current Pos:* chief prod engr, 76-77, PRES, TRANSPOWER CORP, 82- *Personal Data:* b Seattle, Wash, May 24, 51. *Educ:* Rensselaer Polytech Inst, BSc, 74, MEng, 74; Columbia Pac Univ, PhD(systs eng), 91. *Prof Exp:* Design engr, Int Harvester Co, 73; res engr, Caterpillar Tractor Co, 75; advan proj engr, 3M Co, 77-78; prod res engr, Budd Co, 78-80; sr syst engr, Gen Elec Co, 80-82. *Mem:* Am Soc Mech Engrs; Soc Automotive Engrs; Opers Res Soc Am; AAAS; Int Soc Unified Sci (secy, 71-91, pres, 91-95); Asn Automated Reasoning. *Res:* Systems engineering; product engineering; project engineering; theoretical physics; computer simulation and design of complex machines and processes, including engines; linear and nonlinear optimization programs. *Mailing Add:* PO Box 7132 Penndel PA 19047. *Fax:* 215-355-7804; *E-Mail:* transpower@201.com

SAUBERLICH, HOWERDE EDWIN, BIOCHEMISTRY, MICROBIOLOGY. *Current Pos:* PROF & DIR, DIV EXP NUTRIT, UNIV ALA, BIRMINGHAM. *Personal Data:* b Ellington, Wis, Jan 23, 19; m 45, Irene K Cartwright; c Melissa K (Philbin) & Howerde E II. *Educ:* Lawrence Univ, BA, 44; Univ Wis, MS, 46, PhD(biochem), 48. *Honors & Awards:* Johnson Award, 52 & Borden Award, 71, Am Inst Nutrit; Meritorious Civilian Serv Award, US Army, 64; McLester Award, 65; Diag Lab Award, Can Soc Clin Chemists, 83. *Prof Exp:* Assoc animal nutritionist, Exp Sta, Auburn Univ, 48-50, prof & animal nutritionist, 50-58; assoc prof animal husb, Iowa State Univ, 59; chief chem div, Med Res & Nutrit Lab, Fitzsimons Gen Hosp, US Dept Army, Denver, 59-74; chief dept nutrit, Western Human Nutrit Res Ctr, USDA, Letterman Army Inst Res, Presidio of San Francisco, 74-83, 82- *Concurrent Pos:* Res fel, Univ Tenn, 51; prof, Univ Indonesia, 57-59; prof, Colo State Univ, 64-74; vis prof, Vanderbilt Univ, 70-71; Dept Army res & study fel award, 70; adj prof, Univ Calif, Berkeley, 92, Univ Miami. *Mem:* Soc Exp Biol & Med; Am Soc Biochem & Molecular Biol; Am Soc Animal Sci; Am Soc Microbiol; Am Soc Clin Nutrit; fel Am Inst Nutrit. *Res:* Protein, amino acid, vitamin and mineral metabolism in the human, rat, monkey and mouse; nutrition of microorganisms; nutritional assessment and surveillance; vitamin metabolism; human nutrition; mineral and lipid metabolism; nutrition and acquired immunodeficiency syndrome. *Mailing Add:* Dept Nutrit Sci Univ Ala Birmingham AL 35294. *Fax:* 205-934-7049

SAUCEDO, ISMAEL G, STEELMAKING & CASTING OF STEEL, APPLICATION OF MAGNETOHYDRODYNAMICS TO STEEL PROCESSES. *Current Pos:* scientist, sr staff engr, Inland Steel Co, 84-91, sect mgr primary processes, 91-94, sect mgr process res, 94-96, MGR PROCESS RES, INLAND STEEL CO, 96- *Personal Data:* b San Diego, Mich, Mex, June 19, 51; US citizen; m 77, Silvia Uribe; c Rodrigo. *Educ:* Univ Mex, BS, 71, IQM, 76; Pan Am Course, MS, 77; Sheffield Univ, UK, PhD(solidification of steel), 81. *Hon Degrees:* MPhil, Sheffield Univ, 78. *Honors & Awards:* Brunton Medal for Metall Res, Eng, 81. *Prof Exp:* Supvr, Poroflex, Mex, 68-71; res asst, UNAM, Mex, 72-75; res scientist, IMIS-CONACYT, Mex, 75-77, dep dir, IMIS, 81-84; sr res engr, Brit Steel, Eng, 80-81. *Concurrent Pos:* Supvr, Banamex, Mex, 69-71; lectr basic sci, Univ Mex, 74-75, metall, Sheffield Univ, Eng, 78-81, math, North Park Col, Chicago, 86-89; vpres bd, San Diego Chem, Mexico City, Mex, 85-; pres, Sauz Metals, Ind, 88-94. *Mem:* Iron & Steel Soc; Inst Mat. *Res:* Developed understanding of oscillation marks and breakout formation during the continuous casting of steel with corresponding means to reduce or eliminate them; developed electromagnetic techniques for steel containment in twin roll casters which make steel strip casting feasible. *Mailing Add:* Inland Steel Co 3001 E Columbus Dr East Chicago IN 46312. *Fax:* 219-399-6562; *E-Mail:* saucedo@inland.com

SAUCIER, ROGER THOMAS, PHYSICAL GEOGRAPHY, ARCHEOLOGICAL GEOLOGY. *Current Pos:* RETIRED. *Personal Data:* b New Orleans, La, Aug 30, 35; m 57, Anita R Wood; c Brian & Connie (Reeves). *Educ:* La State Univ, BA, 57, MA, 58, PhD, 68. *Honors & Awards:* Roald Fryxell Medal Interdisciplinary Res, Soc Am Archeol, 85. *Prof Exp:* Res asst geol, Coastal Studies Inst, La State Univ, 59-61; geog, Geol Br, Soils Div, US Army Eng Waterways Exp Sta, 59-61, spec asst, 74-81, phys scientist, Environ Lab, 81-94. *Concurrent Pos:* Consult earth scientist, 80- *Mem:* Am Quaternary Asn; Soc Am Archaeol; fel Geol Soc Am; Asn Eng Geologists; Soc Prof Archeologists. *Res:* Applied research in geomorphology; alluvial and coastal morphology; sedimentology and areal geographic and geologic mapping as related to engineering design and construction activities; anthropology; quaternary and environmental geology; earth sciences. *Mailing Add:* 4325 Winchester Rd Vicksburg MS 39180. *Fax:* 601-634-2854

SAUCIER, WALTER JOSEPH, METEOROLOGY. *Current Pos:* prof, 69-86, EMER PROF METEOROL, NC STATE UNIV, 86- *Personal Data:* b Moncla, La, Oct 5, 21; m 43; c 7. *Educ:* Univ Southwestern La, BA, 42; Univ Chicago, SM, 47, PhD(meteorol), 51. *Prof Exp:* Asst meteorol, Univ Chicago, 46-48, instr, 48-52; from asst prof to prof, Tex A&M Univ, 52-60; prof, Univ Okla, 60-69. *Concurrent Pos:* mem bd cert consult meteorologists, Am Meteorol Soc, 70-75, chmn, 71-75; consult, Nat Acad Sci-Nat Res Coun, 71-77; mem bd dirs, Triangle Univs Consortium on Air Pollution, 72-86. *Mem:* Fel AAAS; Sigma Xi; fel Am Meteorol Soc; Am Geophys Union. *Res:* Atmospheric circulations and weather analysis. *Mailing Add:* 2000 Hillock Dr Raleigh NC 27612

SAUDEK, CHRISTOPHER D, DIABETES, LIPID METABOLISM. *Current Pos:* ASSOC PROF MED, SCH MED, JOHNS HOPKINS UNIV, DIR, DIABETES CTR & PROG DIR, CLIN RES CTR, 81- *Personal Data:* b Bronxville, NY, Oct 8, 41; m 66; c 3. *Educ:* Harvard Univ, BA, 63; Cornell Univ, MD, 67. *Prof Exp:* Intern med, Presby-St Luke's Hosp, 67-68, resident, 68-69; resident, Harvard Med Serv, Boston City Hosp, 69-70; fel metab, Thorndike Mem Lab, 70-72; instr med, Harvard Med Sch, 72-73; asst prof, Sch Med, Cornell Univ, 73-79, assoc clin prof, 79-81. *Concurrent Pos:* Dir, Metab Lab, Sch Med, Cornell Univ, 73-, dir, Clin Res Ctr, 74-; adj asst prof, Rockefeller Univ, 74-; mem, Coun Arteriosclerosis, Am Heart Asn; dir, Johns Hopkins, Clin Res Ctr. *Mem:* Am Fedn Clin Res; Am Heart Asn; NY Acad Sci. *Res:* Insulin delivery systems for diabetes. *Mailing Add:* 600 N Wolfe St Bldg 576 Baltimore MD 21205-2104

SAUDER, DANIEL NATHAN, DERMATOLOGY, INTERNAL MEDICINE. *Current Pos:* PROF & CHIEF DERMAT, DEPT MED, UNIV TORONTO, 90-, DIR GEN RES PROG, SUNNYBROOK HEALTH SCI CTR, 93- *Personal Data:* b Hamilton, Ont, Apr 15, 49; c 3. *Educ:* York Univ, Toronto, BA, 71, MA, 72; McMaster Univ, Hamilton, MD, 75; FRCP(C), 80. *Honors & Awards:* Henry W Stelwagon Award, 79; Lila Gruber Cancer Res Award, 84. *Prof Exp:* Intern, Royal Victoria Hosp, PQ, 75-76; resident II internal med, McMaster Univ, 76-77; fel dermat, Cleveland Clin Found, Ohio, 77-79; from asst prof to prof dermat, McMaster Univ, Hamilton, 82-90. *Concurrent Pos:* Vis assoc dermat, Nat Cancer Inst, NIH, Bethesda, Md, 79-82; prof, Dept Med Biophys, Inst Med Sci, 92-; chmn AIDS Acad & Res Subcomt, Hamilton-Wentworth Regional Health Coun, 87-90, mem, Subcomt Provision Clin Servs, 87-90. *Mem:* Fedn Am Soc Exp Biol; Can Soc Immunologists; Can Soc Clin Invest; Am Soc Immunologists; Am Acad Dermat; Soc Invest Dermat; Am Soc Clin Invest; Can Med Asn; Am Col Physicians; Am Fedn Clin Res; Can Dermat Asn; Am Dermat Asn. *Res:* Purification to homogeneity of several other epidermal immunoregulatory cytokines, particularly B-cell growth and differentiation factor epidermal derived interleukin-3 and epidermal derived colony stimulating factors; evaluation of the basic biology of these homogeneous and cloned factors, and their potential significance in inflamatory and immunologic conditions that effect the skin; cytokines secreted by direct stimulation of the skin; regulation of cytokines in the skin utilizing models of inflammation and skin cancer. *Mailing Add:* Dept Med Div Dermat Univ Toronto Sunnybrook Health Sci 2075 Bayview Ave Toronto ON M4N 3M2 Can. *Fax:* 416-480-4707

SAUDER, WILLIAM CONRAD, PHYSICS, X-RAY SPECTROSCOPY. *Current Pos:* From instr to assoc prof, 55-68, chmn dept, 79-84, PROF PHYSICS, VA MIL INST, 68- *Personal Data:* b Wheeling, WVa, Jan 3, 34; m 55; c 2. *Educ:* Va Mil Inst, BS, 55; Johns Hopkins Univ, PhD(physics), 63. *Concurrent Pos:* Consult, Nat Bur Standards, 65-81. *Mem:* Am Phys Soc; Am Asn Physics Teachers. *Res:* Atomic constants; x-ray and gamma ray spectroscopy; ultrasonic interferometry; acoustic interferometry. *Mailing Add:* Dept Physics & Astron Va Mil Inst Lexington VA 24450. *Fax:* 540-464-7214

SAUER, BARRY W, medical research center administration, bioengineering; deceased, see previous edition for last biography

SAUER, BRIAN L, DNA RECOMBINATION. *Current Pos:* EXPERT, NAT INST DIABETES, DIGESTIVE & KIDNEY DIS, 93- *Personal Data:* b Columbus, Wis, Sept 18, 49. *Educ:* Univ Wis, BS, 72; Univ Calif, Berkeley, PhD(molecular biol), 79. *Prof Exp:* Damon Runyon-Walter Winchell fel, Stanford Univ, 79-81, NIH fel, 81-82; staff scientist, Frederick Cancer Res Facil, 82-84; prin investr, DuPont Co, 84-90; sr res scientist, DuPont-Merck Pharm Co, 91-93. *Concurrent Pos:* Vis prof, Hood Col, 83. *Mem:* Genetics Soc Am; Am Soc Microbiol. *Res:* Developing new methods for introducing genes into transgenic mice and controlling their expression, primarily by exploiting site-specific DNA recombination systems. *Mailing Add:* Nat Inst Diabetes Digestive & Kidney Dis NIH Bldg 10 Rm 9B15 Bethesda MD 20892. *Fax:* 301-496-0839; *E-Mail:* sauer@helix.nih.gov

SAUER, DAVID BRUCE, PLANT PATHOLOGY. *Current Pos:* RES PLANT PATHOLOGIST, US GRAIN MKT RES CTR, AGR RES SERV, USDA, 67- *Personal Data:* b Akron, Ohio, Sept 20, 39; m 61, Lois Lauck; c Scott, Susan, Karen, Kathleen & Judith. *Educ:* Kent State Univ, BA, 61; Univ Minn, MS, 64, PhD(plant path), 67. *Mem:* Am Phytopath Soc; Sigma Xi; Am Asn Cereal Chemists. *Res:* Ecology and control of microorganisms in stored grain, including grain quality surveys, grain drying, mycotoxins, moisture relations, odor detection, testing of grain preservatives. *Mailing Add:* US Grain Mkt Res Ctr 1515 College Ave Manhattan KS 66502. *Fax:* 785-776-2792; *E-Mail:* dsauer@ksu.ksu.edu, dave@usgmrl.ksu.edu

SAUER, DENNIS THEODORE, INORGANIC CHEMISTRY. *Current Pos:* staff scientist, 72-82, tech supt, 82-83, tech mgr lasers, 83-84, prog mgr, DS Propellants, 84-87, MGR, ROCKET TECHNOL, HERCULES, INC, 87- *Personal Data:* b Lamont, Wash, Oct 26, 44; m 69. *Educ:* Whitworth Col, BS, 66; Cent Wash State Col, MS, 68; Univ Idaho, PhD(inorg chem), 72. *Prof Exp:* Asst chem, Cent Wash State Col, 66-68; res fel, Univ Idaho, 68-71; fac intern chem, Univ Utah, 71-72. *Mem:* Am Chem Soc. *Res:* Fluorine chemistry; phosphorus and boron chemistry; laser systems. *Mailing Add:* 7854 Deer Creek Rd Salt Lake City UT 84121-5719

SAUER, GORDON CHENOWETH, DERMATOLOGY. *Current Pos:* clin assoc & actg head dermat sect, 55-59, consult dermat, 59-67, CLIN PROF, UNIV MO, 67-; EMER CLIN PROF, UNIV KANS, 92- *Personal Data:* b Rutland, Ill, Aug 14, 21; m 44, 82, Marion Green; c Elisabeth R, Gordon C, Margaret L & Amy K. *Educ:* Univ Ill, BS, 43, MD, 45. *Prof Exp:* Intern, Cook County Hosp, 45-46; resident dermat & syphilol, NY-Univ, Bellevue Med Ctr, 48-51; dermatologist, Thompson-Brumm-Knepper Clin, 51-54; assoc instr, Univ Kans, 51-56, vchmn dermat sect, 56-58, head dermat sect, 58-70, assoc clin prof, 60-64, clin prof, 64-92. *Concurrent Pos:* Pvt pract, 54-; consult, Munson Army Hosp, Ft Leavenworth, 59-68; mem dermat panel & drug efficacy panel, Nat Acad Sci-Food & Drug Admin, 67-69. *Mem:* Fel Am Acad Dermat & Syphilol (vpres, 80); Dermat Found; Am Ornith Union; Royal Australasian Ornithologists Union; Am Dermat Asn; Wilson Ornith Soc. *Res:* Published 12 books on dermatology. *Mailing Add:* 6400 Prospect Ave Kansas City MO 64132-1181

SAUER, HARRY JOHN, JR, MECHANICAL & AEROSPACE ENGINEERING. *Current Pos:* assoc prof, 62-66, dean grad study, 84-92, PROF MECH & AERO ENG, UNIV MO, ROLLA, 66- *Personal Data:* b St Joseph, Mo, Jan 27, 35; m 56, Patricia Zbierski; c Harry III, Elizabeth, Carl, Robert, Katherine, Deborah, Victoria, Valerie & Joseph. *Educ:* Mo Sch Mines, BS, 56, MS, 58; Kans State Univ, PhD(heat transfer), 63. *Honors & Awards:* Hermann F Spoehrer Mem Award, Am Soc Heat, Refrig & Air-Conditioning Engrs, 79, E K Campbell Award, 83. *Prof Exp:* From instr to asst prof mech eng, Mo Sch Mines, 57-60; instr, Kans State Univ, 60-62. *Concurrent Pos:* Sr eng & consult, Midwest Res Inst, 63-70. *Mem:* Fel Am Soc Mech Engrs; fel Am Soc Heat, Refrig & Air-Conditioning Engrs; Soc Automotive Engrs; Am Soc Eng Educ; Nat Soc Prof Engrs. *Res:* Heat transfer; thermophysical properties; environmental control; photographic science. *Mailing Add:* Dept Mech & Aerospace Eng Univ Mo Rolla MO 65401-0249. *Fax:* 573-341-4607

SAUER, HELMUT WILHELM, DEVELOPMENTAL BIOLOGY. *Current Pos:* PROF BIOL, TEX A&M UNIV, 81- *Personal Data:* b Kassel, WGer, Aug 12, 36; m 68; c 2. *Educ:* Univ Marburg, WGer, Dr rer nat, 65. *Prof Exp:* Asst prof, Univ Heidelberg, 65-73; assoc prof, Univ Konstanz, 73-76; prof, Univ Wurzburg, 76-81. *Concurrent Pos:* Fel cell biol, McArdle Lab Cancer Res, Univ Wis, Madison, 67-69; hon prof, Univ Wurzburg, 85- *Mem:* Ger Soc Zool; Ger Soc Biol Chemists; Ger Soc Entwicklungsbiol; Am Soc Zoologists; Soc Develop Biol; Int Soc Develop Biologists; Am Soc Cell Biol; Int Cell Cycle Soc. *Res:* Control of cellular growth and differentiation, employing a simple eukaryotic model Physarum and analyzing the mechanism of genome expression. *Mailing Add:* Dept Biol Tex A&M Univ College Station TX 77843-3258

SAUER, HERBERT H, MAGNETOSPHERIC PHYSICS. *Current Pos:* RETIRED. *Personal Data:* b Newark, NJ, Dec 9, 29; m 57; c 4. *Educ:* Rutgers Univ, BSc, 53; Univ Iowa, PhD(physics), 62. *Prof Exp:* Vacuum tube engr, Fed Telecommun Labs, NJ, 53-54; physicist, Inst Telecommun & Aeronomy, Environ Sci Serv Admin, Nat Oceanic & Atmospheric Admin, 63-70, physicist, Space Environ Lab, 70-94. *Concurrent Pos:* Vis lectr, Univ Colo, 65, 68, 72, 77; vis prof, Univ Calgary, 69. *Mem:* Am Phys Soc; Am Geophys Union; Sigma Xi. *Res:* Magnetospheric and cosmic ray physics. *Mailing Add:* 350 Auburn St Boulder CO 80303

SAUER, JOHN A, SOLID STATE PHYSICS & MATERIAL SCIENCE, POLYMER SCIENCE & CHEMISTRY. *Current Pos:* prof & chmn, 63-83, emer prof, Dept Mech & Mat Sci, 83-95, EMER PROF, DEPT CHEM & BIOCHEM ENG, RUTGERS UNIV, 95- *Personal Data:* b Oct 26, 12; m 44, Marion Short; c Virginia & Pamela. *Educ:* Rutgers Univ, BS, 34, MS, 36; Cambridge Univ, PhD(math physics), 42. *Honors & Awards:* Linbach Award, 75; Rutger Univ Award, 88. *Prof Exp:* Instr math & mech, Union Jr Col, 34-38; instr, Rutgers Univ, 36-38; fel & sr fel, Mellon Inst Indust Res, Pittsburgh, 41-44; asst & dir res eng, Elastic Stop Nut Corp, 44-46; prof & chmn, Dept Eng Mech, Pa State Univ, 46-53, prof & chmn, Dept Physics, 53-63. *Concurrent Pos:* Consult, Amerace-ESNA Corp, 51-84; vis prof, Clarendon Lab, Oxford Univ, 52-53; Guggenheim fel, 59-60; Rutgers res fel, Dept Eng Sci, 69-70; vis prof, Dept Eng Sci, Oxford Univ, 77-78; vis lect, Am Inst Physics, 71-72; vpres, Rutgers Chap, Sigma Xi, 71-72, pres, 72-73; invited prin lect, Ger Phys Soc, Wurtzburg, & conf high pressure, Kyotto, Japan, 74; vis prof, Dept Eng Sci, Oxford Univ, 83-85. *Mem:* fel Am Phys Soc; fel AAAS; Am Chem Soc; Sigma Xi. *Res:* Polymer physics; physical properties of polymers; effects of molecular structure, temperature, pressure, radiation and chemical environment on mechanical and relaxation behavior of polymers and relation of properties to structure; author of many research articles and co-author of one book. *Mailing Add:* 33 Patton Dr East Brunswick NJ 08816-1128

SAUER, JOHN ROBERT, ENTOMOLOGY, PHYSIOLOGY. *Current Pos:* From asst prof to assoc prof, 69-77, PROF INSECT PHYSIOL, OKLA STATE UNIV, 77-, REGENTS PROF, 87-, SARKEYS DISTINGUISHED PROF ENTOM, 89- *Personal Data:* b Aberdeen, SDak, Aug 1, 36; m 62,

Margie Baker; c Marilyn, Ruth A & Teresa. *Educ:* St John's Univ, Minn, BS, 59; NMex Highlands Univ, MS, 64; Tulane Univ, PhD(biol), 69. *Concurrent Pos:* Mem, Trop Med, Parasitol, NIH; NIH res grant. *Mem:* Sigma Xi; Entom Soc Am; Am Soc Zool; Am Soc Parasitol; AAAS; Soc Vector Ecol. *Res:* Insect physiology; tick physiology; role of salivary glands in tick feeding; control of tick salivary glands; factors in tick saliva. *Mailing Add:* 1304 W Osage Stillwater OK 74075-2143. *Fax:* 405-744-6039

SAUER, JON ROBERT, HIGH ENERGY PHYSICS, ACCELERATOR PHYSICS. *Current Pos:* ON LOAN AS CHIEF SCIENTIST TO CTR OPTOELECTRONIC COMPUT SYSTS, COLO UNIV, BELL LABS, 84- *Personal Data:* b Schenectady, NY, Nov 24, 40; m 72; c 2. *Educ:* Stanford Univ, BS, 62; Tufts Univ, PhD(physics), 70. *Prof Exp:* Staff physicist accelerator physics, Stanford Linear Accelerator Ctr, 62-64, Cambridge Electron Accelerator, 69-70 & Fermilab, 70-77; sr res assoc high energy physics, Ind Univ, 77-78; asst physicist high energy physics, Argonne Nat Lab, 78-81; mem tech staff, Bell Labs, 81-83; prod mgr, Adv Systs, Denelcor Supercomput, 83-84. *Mem:* Sigma Xi; Am Phys Soc. *Mailing Add:* 1851 Alma Lane Superior CO 80027

SAUER, JONATHAN DEININGER, BIOGEOGRAPHY. *Current Pos:* prof geol, 67-88, EMER PROF GEOG, UNIV CALIF, LOS ANGELES, 88- *Personal Data:* b Ann Arbor, Mich, July 5, 18; m 46; c 1. *Educ:* Univ Calif, AB, 39; Washington Univ, MA, 48, PhD(genetics), 50. *Prof Exp:* From instr to assoc prof bot, Univ Wis-Madison, 50-59, from assoc prof to prof bot & geog, 59-67; vis prof geog, La State Univ, 67. *Concurrent Pos:* Vis assoc cur, Herbarium, Univ Mich, 55-56; dir bot gardens & herbarium, Univ Calif, Los Angeles, 74-80. *Mem:* Brit Ecol Soc; Ecol Soc Am; Am Soc Plant Taxon; Org Trop Studies; Soc Econ Bot. *Res:* Recent plant migration and evolution; systematics of Amaranthus, Canavalia and Stenotaphrum; dynamics of seacoast and riverbank pioneer vegetation. *Mailing Add:* 659 Erskine Dr Pacific Palisades CA 90272

SAUER, KENNETH, BIOPHYSICAL CHEMISTRY. *Current Pos:* NIH res fel, Univ Calif, Berkeley, 60-63, from asst prof to assoc prof, 63-72, MEM SR STAFF, LAB STRUCT BIOL, UNIV CALIF, BERKELEY, 62-, PROF CHEM, 72- *Personal Data:* b Cleveland, Ohio, June 19, 31; m 58; c 4. *Educ:* Oberlin Col, AB, 53; Harvard Univ, MA, 54, PhD(chem), 58. *Honors & Awards:* Res Award, Am Soc Photobiol, 93. *Prof Exp:* From instr to asst prof chem, Am Univ Beirut, 57-60. *Concurrent Pos:* Guggenheim fel, 76-77; Alexander von Humboldt Award, 85, 86 & 95. *Mem:* Fel AAAS; Am Chem Soc; Biophys Soc; Am Soc Photobiol; Sigma Xi. *Res:* Photosynthetic energy conversion; biological molecular structure; molecular spectroscopy; fluorescence lifetimes; excitation transfer. *Mailing Add:* Dept Chem Univ Calif Berkeley CA 94720

SAUER, LEONARD A, CELL BIOLOGY, BIOCHEMISTRY. *Current Pos:* RES PHYSICIAN, MARY IMOGENE BASSETT HOSP, 73- *Personal Data:* b Schenectady, NY, Aug 20, 29; m 56; c 3. *Educ:* Cornell Univ, BS, 56; Univ Rochester, MD, 60; Rockefeller Univ, PhD(cell biol), 66. *Prof Exp:* From instr to assoc prof med, Sch Med, Yale Univ, 67-73. *Concurrent Pos:* USPHS spec fel, Univ Marburg, 66-67. *Mem:* Am Soc Biol Chemists; Am Soc Cell Biol; Endocrine Soc; Soc Exp Biol & Med; Am Asn Cancer Res. *Res:* Cell regulatory processes; mitochondrial physiology; adrenal steroidogenesis; tumor biology. *Mailing Add:* Bassett Res Inst Mary Imogene Bassett Hosp Cooperstown NY 13326-1301. *Fax:* 607-547-3061; *E-Mail:* isaver@research.bassett.org

SAUER, MYRAN CHARLES, JR, RADIATION CHEMISTRY. *Current Pos:* Resident res assoc, 59-61, asst chemist, 61-63, ASSOC CHEMIST, ARGONNE NAT LAB, 63- *Personal Data:* b Pittsburgh, Pa, Nov 30, 33; m 59, Mary Benedict; c Bryan, Willard & Andrea. *Educ:* Carnegie Inst Technol, BS, 55; Univ Wis, PhD(chem), 58. *Mem:* Am Chem Soc; Radiation Res Soc. *Res:* Kinetics and mechanisms of reactions initiated by ionizing radiation and light. *Mailing Add:* 85060 Creek Dr Naperville IL 60565

SAUER, PETER WILLIAM, ELECTRICAL ENGINEERING. *Current Pos:* from asst prof to assoc prof, 77-85, PROF ELEC ENG, UNIV ILL, URBANA, 85- *Personal Data:* b Winona, Minn, Sept 20, 46; m 69, Sylvia L Stenzel; c Katherine D & Daniel A. *Educ:* Univ Mo, Rolla, BS, 69; Purdue Univ, MS, 74, PhD(elec eng), 77. *Prof Exp:* Design engr, USAF Tactical Air Command, 69-73; res asst, elec eng dept, Purdue Univ, 73-77; prog dir, NSF, 91-92. *Concurrent Pos:* Elec power consult, US Army Corps Eng Res Lab, 75-; prin investr, NSF grant, 78-; res dir, Ill Power Affil Prog, 78-; Grainger assoc, 82- *Mem:* Sigma Xi; fel Inst Elec & Electronics Engrs; Acad Elec Eng. *Res:* Electrical power system simulation and analysis; electric power system operation and planning methods; electric power system dynamics and control. *Mailing Add:* 337 Everitt Lab Univ Ill 1406 W Green St Urbana IL 61801. *Fax:* 217-333-1162; *E-Mail:* sauer@ece.uiuc.edu

SAUER, RICHARD JOHN, ENTOMOLOGY. *Current Pos:* dep vpres, 83-85, DIR, MINN AGR EXP STA, UNIV MINN, ST PAUL, 80-, VPRES, AGR, FORESTRY & HOME ECON, 85-; PRES & CHIEF EXEC OFFICER, NAT 4H COUN, CHEVY CHASE, MD, 89- *Personal Data:* b Walker, Minn, Nov 15, 39; m 62; c 4. *Educ:* St John's Univ, Minn, BS, 62; Univ Mich, Ann Arbor, MS, 64; NDak State Univ, PhD(entom), 67. *Prof Exp:* Teaching asst zool, Univ Mich, Ann Arbor, 62-64; asst prof biol, St Cloud State Col, 67-68; asst prof biol & entom, Mich State Univ, 68-70, exten entom, 70-72, assoc prof exten entom & exten pesticide coordr, 72-76; prof exten & head dept, Kans State Univ, 76-80. *Concurrent Pos:* Entom consult, Coop State Res Serv, USDA, 74-75. *Mem:* Entom Soc Am. *Res:* Taxonomy and biology of spiders; clearance of minor use pesticides; pesticide usage and safety. *Mailing Add:* Nat 4H Coun 7100 Connecticut Ave Chevy Chase MD 20815

SAUER, ROBERT THOMAS, MOLECULAR GENETICS, BIOPHYSICAL CHEMISTRY. *Current Pos:* From asst prof to prof, 78-91, ASSOC HEAD, DEPT BIOL, MASS INST TECHNOL, 89-, WHITEHEAD PROF BIOL, 91- *Personal Data:* b Cornwall, NY, July 13, 48; m 81, Karen Nestler; c Jessica A & Rebecca J. *Educ:* Amherst Col, BA, 72; Harvard Univ, PhD(biochem), 79. *Concurrent Pos:* Consult, Genentech Inc, 88-, Scriptech Inc, 93-; chmn, Bd Sci Counrs, Nat Ctr Biotechnol Info, NIH, 90- *Mem:* Nat Acad Sci; Protein Soc; Am Soc Biochem & Molecular Biol; fel Am Acad Arts & Sci; Am Soc Microbiol. *Res:* Macromolecular folding and function using protein biochemistry, combinatorial mutagenesis and x-ray crystallography; protein DNA interactions in repressor-operator systems. *Mailing Add:* Dept Biol Mass Inst Technol Cambridge MA 02139

SAUERBRUNN, ROBERT DEWEY, ANALYTICAL CHEMISTRY, POLYMER CHEMISTRY. *Current Pos:* Develop assoc res & develop, 53-62, sr res chemist polymer chem, 62-63, SUPVR RES & DEVELOP, E I DU PONT DE NEMOURS & CO, INC, 63- *Personal Data:* b Jonesboro, Ill, Dec 27, 22; m 47; c 2. *Educ:* Southern Ill Univ, BS, 47; Univ Minn, PhD(analytical chem), 53. *Mem:* Am Chem Soc. *Res:* Electrochemical and spectrophotometric analyses; chemical kinetics and polymer chemistry. *Mailing Add:* 904 Robin Dr Seaford DE 19973-1134

SAUERLAND, EBERHARDT KARL, ANATOMY, PSYCHIATRY. *Current Pos:* ASSOC PROF PSYCHIAT & PROF ANAT, UNIV TEX HEALTH SCI CTR, SAN ANTONIO, 88- *Personal Data:* b Ger, Dec 17, 33; US citizen; m 86; c 3. *Educ:* Univ Kiel, MD, 60. *Prof Exp:* From intern to resident, St John Gen Hosp, NB, 60-62; res scientist aerospace med, Lockheed-Calif Co, Burbank, 62-64; asst prof anat, Sch Med, Univ Calif, Los Angeles, 64-70, assoc prof anat & oral med, 70-71; prof anat, Univ Tex Med Br Galveston, 71-80; dir, Clin Invest Fac, Wilford Hall, USAF Med Ctr, Lackland AFB, Tex, 80-83, resident diag radiol, 80-81; resident psychiat, 84-87, chief resident psychiat, 86-87, fel acad psychiat, Loma Linda Univ Med Ctr, 87-88. *Concurrent Pos:* Adj prof anat, Univ Tex Med Br Galveston, 80-85; vis prof anat, USUHS, 80. *Mem:* Am Asn Anat; Am Asn Psychiatrists. *Res:* Interaction of brain and reflex mechanisms; electromyography; psychodynamics. *Mailing Add:* Dept Anat Univ Tex Med Sch San Antonio 7703 Floyd Curl Dr San Antonio TX 78284-6200

SAUERS, RICHARD FRANK, ORGANIC CHEMISTRY. *Current Pos:* sr res chemist, 69-80, RES SUPVR, E I DU PONT DE NEMOURS & CO, INC, 80- *Personal Data:* b Philadelphia, Pa, Apr 4, 39; m 66; c 4. *Educ:* LaSalle Col, BA, 65; Univ Minn, PhD(org chem), 69. *Prof Exp:* Chemist, Smith Kline & French Labs, 63-65. *Mem:* Am Chem Soc. *Res:* Biologically active materials. *Mailing Add:* 11 Polaris Dr Newark DE 19711

SAUERS, RONALD RAYMOND, ORGANIC CHEMISTRY. *Current Pos:* from instr to assoc prof, 57-70, PROF CHEM, RUTGERS UNIV, NEW BRUNSWICK, 70- *Personal Data:* b Pittsburgh, Pa, June 19, 32; div; c 2. *Educ:* Pa State Univ, BS, 53; Univ Ill, PhD(chem), 56. *Prof Exp:* USPHS fel, Univ Ill, 56-57. *Concurrent Pos:* Vis fel, Princeton Univ, 66-67; USPHS spec fel, Brandeis Univ, 72-73. *Mem:* Am Chem Soc. *Res:* Stereochemistry of organic reactions; polycyclic hydrocarbon systems; organic photochemistry. *Mailing Add:* 150 Montgomery St Highland Park NJ 08904-2628

SAUL, FRANK PHILIP, PALEOPATHOLOGY, FORENSIC ANTHROPOLOGY. *Current Pos:* from asst prof to prof anat, Med Col Ohio, 69-93, asst dean res, 84-90, assoc dean, continuing med educ, 89-93, EMER PROF ANAT, MED COL OHIO, 94-, EMER ASSOC DEAN CONTINUING MED EDUC, 94- *Personal Data:* b New York, NY, Oct 31, 30; m 64, Julie Mather; c Joseph M & Jennifer M. *Educ:* Brooklyn Col, AB, 52; Harvard Univ, AM, 59, PhD, 72; Am Bd Forensic Anthrop, dipl, 78. *Prof Exp:* Field asst, archaeol exped to SDak, Univ Mus, Kans, 50; asst phys anthrop, Am Mus Natural Hist, 51-52; phys anthropologist, Aero Med Lab, Wright Air Develop Ctr, US Dept Air Force, 53-58 & Natick Qm Res & Eng Ctr, US Dept Army, 58-59; field study Hutterite morphol, Harvard Univ, 59, teaching fel anthrop, 59-62; instr, Pa State Univ, 62-67, asst prof anthrop & phys anthropologist, Eastern Pa Archaeol Projs, 67-69. *Concurrent Pos:* Consult, forensic anthrop, 54-, human factors, 59- & anthrop, Lab Cent Nervous Syst Studies, NIH, 79-84; res assoc, Boston Mus Sci, 60-62; phys anthropologist Maya area projs, Peabody Mus, Harvard Univ, 62-68; biol anthropologist Maya area projs, Cambridge Univ, 70-80; regional lectr, Sigma Xi, 71-76 & 89; hon cur biomed anthrop, Toledo Mus Health & Natural Hist, 77-80; vis prof phys anthrop, Univ Cambridge, 78; adj cur, hist of health & med in Mex & Cent Am, Nat Mus Health & Med, 87-; guest fac, forensic anthrop course, Am Regist Path & Armed Forces Inst Path, 89-; mem, sci adv bd, Armed Forces Inst Path, 89-95; forensic anthropologist, Nat Disaster Mortuary Assistance Team, USPHS, 95-; consult Fed Bur Invest Evidence Response Team, Cleveland, 95-, Wayne Co Med Examrs Off, 96-; dir, Am Bd Forensic Anthropol, 96-; vis prof archael, Univ Sheffield, 96-; consult, Wayne Co Med Exam Off, 96- *Mem:* Fel Am Anthrop Asn; Am Asn Phys Anthrop; fel Royal Anthrop Inst; fel AAAS; fel Am Acad Forensic Sci; Paleopath Asn. *Res:* Osteology; human factors; origin and evolution of the Maya; biomedical anthropology; paleopathology; forensic anthropology. *Mailing Add:* Sr Consult Lucas Co Coroner 2025 Arlington Ave Toledo OH 43609-1983. *Fax:* 419-382-2049; *E-Mail:* fsaul@opus.mco.edu

SAUL, GEORGE BRANDON, II, GENETICS. *Current Pos:* chmn dept, 68-76 & 91-93, acad vpres, 76-79, PROF BIOL, MIDDLEBURY COL, 67- *Personal Data:* b Hartford, Conn, Aug 8, 28; m 53, Sue Williams. *Educ:* Univ Pa, AB, 49, AM, 50, PhD(zool), 54. *Prof Exp:* Asst instr zool, Univ Pa, 50-52; from instr to assoc prof, Dartmouth Col, 54-67. *Concurrent Pos:* NSF sci fac fel, Univ Zurich, 59-60; res fel biol, Calif Inst Technol, 64-65; vis scientist,

Boyce Thompson Inst Plant Res, 72-73. *Mem:* Fel AAAS; Radiation Res Soc; Genetics Soc Am; Am Genetic Asn; Sigma Xi; NY Acad Sci. *Res:* Cytogenetics; biochemical genetics; embryological genetics of Nasonia vitripennis; extranuclear genetics. *Mailing Add:* Dept Biol Middlebury Col Middlebury VT 05753. *Fax:* 802-443-2072

SAUL, JULIE MATHER, FORENSIC ANTHROPOLOGY, PALEOPATHOLOGY. *Current Pos:* RES ASSOC BIOMED ANTHROP, DEPT ANAT, MED COL OHIO, 69-; DIR, FORENSIC ANTHROP LAB, LUCAS CO CORONER'S OFF, 90- *Personal Data:* b Indianapolis, Ind, May 23, 41; m 64, Frank P; c Joseph M & Jennifer M. *Educ:* Pa State Univ, BA, 63. *Prof Exp:* Res technician agron, Pa State Univ, 60-61, res asst anthrop, 64-69. *Concurrent Pos:* Consult forensic anthrop, Lucas Co, Ohio, Coroner, Monroe Co, Mich Chief Med Examr, 76-; co-leader, Nat Geog Maya Res Proj, 81-82, field investr, Ceren Res Proj, El Salvador, 89, 92, Cuello Res Proj, Belize, 92, 93 & La Milpa Res Proj, Belize, 93-; co-prin invest, NSF Maya Res Proj, 81-82,; co-chmn ann meeting, Paleopath Asn, 82-83; guest fac, Am Registry Path & Armed Forces Inst Path, 88-; adj assoc cur, Hist Health & Med, Nat Mus Health & Med, Mex & Cent Am, 93-; forensic anthropologist, Nat Disaster Mortuary Assistance Team, USPHS, 95-; consult, Fed bur Invest Evidence Response Team, Cleveland, 95-, Wayne Med Examrs Off, 96-; vis res assoc archaeol, Univ Sheffield, 96- *Mem:* Sigma Xi; AAAS; Am Anthrop Asn; Am Asn Phys Anthropologists; Paleopath Asn; Am Acad Forensic Sci. *Res:* Origin and evolution of the Maya; paleopathology; osteology; forensic anthropology. *Mailing Add:* Dir Forensic Anthrop Lab Lucas Co Coroner's Off 2025 Arlington Ave Toledo OH 43609-1983. *Fax:* 419-382-2049; *E-Mail:* fsaul@opus.mco.edu

SAUL, LEON JOSEPH, psychiatry; deceased, see previous edition for last biography

SAUL, LOUELLA RANKIN, EVOLUTION MOLLUSKS, PALEONTOLOGY. *Current Pos:* RETIRED. *Personal Data:* b Lenox, Calif, July 28, 27; US citizen; m 49, Richard B; c R Brant & Robert L. *Educ:* Univ Calif Los Angeles, BA, 49, MA, 59. *Prof Exp:* Mus scientist cur, Geol Dept, Univ Calif, Los Angeles, 51-85; collection mgr invert paleont, Natural Hist Mus, Los Angeles Co, 85-93. *Concurrent Pos:* Lectr earth & space sci, Univ Calif Los Angeles, 82- *Mem:* Paleont Soc; Geol Soc; AAAS; Sigma Xi; Paleont Asn; Soc Study Evolution. *Res:* Study of mollusks, bivalves and gastropods of Cretaceous through early Tertiary age from the Pacific slope of North America. *Mailing Add:* Earth Sci Div Natural Hist Mus Los Angeles Co 900 Exposition Blvd Los Angeles CA 90007. *Fax:* 213-746-7646; *E-Mail:* lulasaul@aol.com

SAUL, WILLIAM EDWARD, STRUCTURAL ENGINEERING, CIVIL ENGINEERING. *Current Pos:* CHAIRPERSON & PROF, DEPT CIVIL & ENVIRON ENG, MICH STATE UNIV, 90- *Personal Data:* b New York, NY, May 15, 34; m, J Muriel Held Eagleburger. *Educ:* Mich Technol Univ, BS, 55, MS, 61; Northwestern Univ, PhD(civil eng), 64. *Prof Exp:* Mech engr, Shell Oil Co, 55-59; teaching asst, Mich Technol Univ, 59-60, instr eng mech, 60-62; from asst prof to prof, Univ Wis, 64-84, chmn dept, 76-80; prof civil eng & dean engr, Univ Idaho, 84-90. *Concurrent Pos:* Indust consult, 64-; vis prof, Inst Aircraft & Space Struct Eng, Univ Stuttgart, 70-71, Fulbright travel grant, Alexander von Humboldt Found & Univ Wis Alumni Res Found grant. *Mem:* Fel Am Soc Civil Engrs; Int Asn Bridge & Struct Engrs; Sigma Xi; Am Soc Eng Educ; Am Concrete Inst; Nat Soc Prof Engr. *Res:* Dynamic response of structures; computer methods in structural analysis; theory of structures; reinforced concrete structures; applications in the response of structures due to high intensity forces such as earthquake, blast or storm; pile foundations. *Mailing Add:* 1971 Cimmarron Dr Okemos MI 48864-3905. *Fax:* 517-336-1827; *E-Mail:* saul@cee.egr.msu.edu

SAUNDERS, B DAVID, COMPUTER ALGEBRA. *Current Pos:* COMPUT & INFO SCI, UNIV DEL, 85- *Personal Data:* b Bryan, Tex, Apr 12, 44; m 68; c 3. *Educ:* Univ Wis, BA, 70, PhD(math), 75. *Prof Exp:* Prof math & comput sci, Rensselaer Polytech Inst, 75-84. *Mem:* Asn Comput Mach; Math Asn Am; AAAS. *Res:* Systems and algorithms for symbolic mathematical computation. *Mailing Add:* Dept Comput & Info Sci Univ Del Newark DE 19716

SAUNDERS, BURT A, ELECTRONIC IMAGING, COLOR REPRODUCTION. *Current Pos:* PRIN IMAGING CONSULT, ROCHESTER INST TECHNOL RES CORP, 86-; PRES GOLDEN COLOR INC, NUNDA, 93- *Personal Data:* b Rochester, NY, July 20, 49. *Educ:* Rochester Inst Technol, BS, 72; State Univ NY-Geneseo, MA, 76. *Concurrent Pos:* Consult, 80- *Mem:* Tech Asn Graphic Arts; Soc Info Display. *Res:* Control and reproduction of color in electronic imaging. *Mailing Add:* 8384 Short Tract Nunda NY 14517

SAUNDERS, DONALD FREDERICK, EXPLORATION GEOLOGY, PETROLEUM. *Current Pos:* MGR INTEGRATED EXPLOR, RECON EXPLORATION INC, 87- *Personal Data:* b Utica, NY, Nov 9, 24; m 50, Winifred W Miller; c Richard P, David A & Paul W. *Educ:* St Lawrence Univ, BS, 46; Univ Wis, PhD(chem), 50. *Prof Exp:* Proj assoc, Univ Wis, 50-53; sr engr, Tex Instruments, Inc, 53-57; chief res geochemist, Geophys Serv, Inc, 57-62; mem tech staff, Tex Instruments Inc, 62-67, mgr radiation sci, 67-70, mgr new prog develop, 70-73, sr geoscientist, 73-83; vpres, Petrominex, 83-84, pres, 84-87. *Mem:* Asn Explor Geologists; Am Asn Petrol Geologists; Asn Petrol Geochem Explorationists; Soc Explor Geophysicists. *Res:* Thermoluminescence of rocks and minerals; geochemistry of the origin of uranium deposits; geochemical prospecting; nuclear arms control studies; remote sensing of natural resources; geological interpretation of satellite imagery; environmental studies. *Mailing Add:* 4057 Northaven Rd Dallas TX 75229

SAUNDERS, DONALD ROY, TOXICOLOGY, ENVIRONMENTAL SCIENCES. *Personal Data:* b Chicago, Ill, June 2, 40; m 79, Nancy S Wendt. *Educ:* Leland Stanford Jr Univ, BA, 63; Purdue Univ, MS, 70, PhD(pharmacol, toxicol), 73; Am Bd Toxicol, dipl, 81. *Prof Exp:* Sr toxicologist, Riker Labs Inc, 73-76; res toxicologist, Stauffer Chem Co, 76-77, sr toxicologist, 77-78, toxicol contract admin, 78-82, mgr toxicol planning & contracts, 82-84, dir, Toxicol Dept, 84-88; dir, Environ Health Ctr, Agr Div, Ciba-Geigy Corp, 88-92, dir toxicol, 92-97. *Concurrent Pos:* Mem, Gov Task Force Water Qual, Conn Dept Health, 84-92. *Mem:* Soc Toxicol; AAAS; Sigma Xi. *Res:* Safety evaluation of agricultural chemicals. *Mailing Add:* 3001 County Clare Rd Greensboro NC 27407. *E-Mail:* don__saunders@alumni.stanford.org

SAUNDERS, EDWARD A, SOLID STATE ELECTRONICS, NUCLEAR SCIENCE. *Current Pos:* Instr electronics, 51-54, prof elec, 61-65, PROF PHYSICS & HEAD DEPT, US MIL ACAD, 65-; DEAN OF ACAD, TRIDENT TECH COL. *Personal Data:* b Manilla, Iowa, Mar 30, 25; m 46; c 4. *Educ:* US Mil Acad, BSMSE, 46; Purdue Univ, MS, 51; Rensselaer Polytech Inst, PhD(nuclear sci), 65. *Mem:* Am Asn Physics Teachers; Am Soc Eng Educ. *Res:* Radiation damage on semiconductor materials. *Mailing Add:* 1417 Patriot Dr Melbourne FL 32940

SAUNDERS, FRANK AUSTIN, REHABILITATION ENGINEERING, PSYCHOLOGY. *Current Pos:* PRAC ADMIN, OBSTET & GYNEC ASN SAN FRANCISCO, 90- *Personal Data:* b Suffolk, Va, Dec 4, 40; m 63, 86, Barbara Day; c 3. *Educ:* Juilliard Sch, BS, 61; Ind Univ, Bloomington, PhD(psychol), 65. *Honors & Awards:* Hektoen Award, Am Med Asn, 72 & 77. *Prof Exp:* Res psychologist, Langley Porter Neuropsychiat Inst, 66-68; res assoc & sr scientist, Smith-Kettlewell Inst Visual Sci, 68-90. *Concurrent Pos:* Fel med psychol, Langley Porter Neuropsychiat Inst, San Francisco, 65-66; clin instr med psychol, Sch Med, Univ Calif, San Francisco, 68-; lectr psychol, San Francisco State Col, 68- *Mem:* Am Psychol Asn; Acoust Soc Am; Inst Elec & Electronics Engrs; Biomed Eng Soc. *Res:* Development of electrotactile displays and sensory aids for deaf and blind persons. *Mailing Add:* 1431 Marlin Ave Foster City CA 94404

SAUNDERS, FRANK LINWOOD, PHYSICAL CHEMISTRY. *Current Pos:* Proj leader, 56-66, group leader, 66-75, sr res specialist, 75-80, res assoc, 80-86, ASSOC SCI, DOW CHEM CO, 86- *Personal Data:* b Moline, Ill, July 26, 26; m 49; c 2. *Educ:* Augustana Col, AB, 50; Case Western Reserve Univ, MS, 52, PhD(chem), 53. *Mem:* Am Chem Soc; Sigma Xi. *Res:* Polymer and colloid chemistry; latexes; stereospecific polymers. *Mailing Add:* 3718 Devonshire Midland MI 48642-4914

SAUNDERS, FRANK WENDELL, MATHEMATICS. *Current Pos:* dir grad studies in math, 70-76, actg chmn dept, 76-78, PROF MATH, ECAROLINA UNIV, 61- *Personal Data:* b Reidsville, NC, Sept 27, 22; m 51; c 3. *Educ:* Univ NC, AB, 45, MA, 47. *Prof Exp:* Instr math, Univ NC, 47-49; prof, Coker Col, 49-61. *Res:* Number theory. *Mailing Add:* 1713 Morningside Pl Greenville NC 27834

SAUNDERS, FRED MICHAEL, WATER & WASTEWATER TREATMENT, HAZARDOUS WASTE TREATMENT. *Current Pos:* from asst prof to assoc prof, 74-89, PROF CIVIL ENG, GA INST TECHNOL, 89-, PROG COORDR ENVIRON ENG, 89- *Personal Data:* b Lawton, Okla; c 3. *Educ:* Va Polytech Inst, BS, 67, MS, 69; Univ Ill, Urbana-Champaign, PhD(civil eng), 75. *Honors & Awards:* Excellence in Presentation Award, Am Electroplaters Soc, 80, Sam Wyman Mem Award, 84. *Prof Exp:* Design engr, Wiley & Wilson Consults, Inc, 74. *Concurrent Pos:* Mem, Standard Methods Comt, Water Pollution Control Fedn, 75-82, Toxic Substances Comt, 77-82 & Prog Comt, chmn, Res Comt, 83-86; mem, Distiguished Lectr Comt, Asn Environ Eng Prof, 77-82, Pub Comt Abstract Rev Comt, Nat Environ Eng, 81-88 & US Mat Comt, Int Asn Water Pollution Res & Control & US Nat Comt, 88-; ed, Am Soc Civil Engrs Nat Conf Environ Eng, 81, US regional ed, Environ Technol Lett, 85-89; mem bd dirs, Asn Environ Eng Prof, 83-86; vchmn, Water Pollution Mgt Comt, Environ Eng Div, Am Soc Civil Engrs, 85, chmn, 86; mem organizing comt, Int Asn Water Pollution Res & Control 1992 Biennial Conf, 86-; mem, Task Force Wastewater Mgt, Atlanta Regional Comn, 88-91; assoc ed, J Environ Eng, Am Soc Civil Engrs, 88-89; ed, J Water Pollution Control Fedn, 89-; mem exec comt, Environ Eng Div, Am Soc Civil Engrs, 88-, secy, 88-91, vchair, 91-; liasion, US Nat Comt to Int Asn Water Pollution Res & Control, Am Soc Civil Engrs, 88-, secy-treas, 90-; mem publ comt, WPCF, 89-; dipl, Am Acad Environ Engrs. *Mem:* Am Soc Civil Engrs; Int Asn Water Pollution Res & Control; Water Pollution Control Fedn; Am Chem Soc; Asn Environ Eng Prof (pres, 85-86); Am Water Works Asn; Am Acad Environ Engrs; Sigma Xi; Nat Water Well Asn. *Res:* Investigation of unit operations and processes used in treatment, reclamation and disposal of industrial and domestic waters, wastewaters and residues; in situ biological treatment of ground water; solid & liquid separations; hazardous waste management; residue treatment. *Mailing Add:* Environ Eng MC0512 Ga Inst Technol Atlanta GA 30332-0001

SAUNDERS, GRADY FRANKLIN, MOLECULAR BIOLOGY. *Current Pos:* from asst prof to assoc prof, 66-78, PROF BIOCHEM, UNIV TEX, M D ANDERSON CANCER CTR, 78- *Personal Data:* b Bakersfield, Calif, July 11, 38; m 59; c 1. *Educ:* Ore State Univ, BS, 60, MS, 62; Univ Ill, Urbana, PhD(microbiol), 65. *Prof Exp:* USPHS fel, Inst Physicochem Biol, Univ Paris, 65-66. *Concurrent Pos:* US-USSR exchange scientist, Inst Molecular Biol, USSR Acad Sci, Moscow, 72. *Mem:* Am Chem Soc; Biophys Soc; Am Soc Biol Chemists; Am Soc Cell Biol; Am Soc Human Genetics. *Res:* Regulation of gene activity; chromosome anatomy. *Mailing Add:* Dept Biochem & Molecular Biol Univ Tex M D Anderson Cancer Ctr 1515 Holcombe Blvd Box 117 Houston TX 77030-4009

SAUNDERS, JACK PALMER, PHARMACOLOGY. *Current Pos:* prof & dean, 74-87, EMER PROF PHARMACOL & TOXICOL & DEAN, GRAD SCH BIOMED SCI, UNIV TEX MED BR, GALVESTON, 87- *Personal Data:* b London, Eng, Sept 11, 15; nat US; m 42, Margaret Siebert; c George P II & Margaret S (Adam). *Educ:* City Col New York, BS, 36; Univ Md, MS, 49, PhD(biochem), 53. *Prof Exp:* Chemist, R H Macy & Co, NY, 39-41; pharmacologist, Pharmacol Br, Chem Corps Med Labs, US Army Chem Ctr, Md, 46-48, 50-56, dep chief, 54-56; biochemist, USPHS Nutrit Unit, State Dept Health, Md, 48-50; exec secy, Pharmacol Exp Therapeut Study Sect, NIH, 56-57, asst chief extramural progs, Nat Inst Allergy & Infectious Dis, 57, exec secy, Cancer Chemotherapy Study Sect, 57-59, exec secy, Metab Study Sect, 59, asst chief biol sci, Res Grants Rev Br, Div Res Grants, 59-60, chief, 61-64, assoc chief, Div Res Grants, 64-65, dep sci dir chemother, Nat Cancer Inst, 65-67, assoc dir extramural activities, 67-72, dir div cancer grants, 72-73, dir div cancer res resources & ctr, 73-74. *Concurrent Pos:* Consult, Nat Cancer Inst, 74-; co-chmn, Int Symp Immunol Cancer, Univ Tex Med Br-Montpellier Univ, France, 80. *Mem:* AAAS; Am Soc Pharmacol & Exp Therapeut; Am Chem Soc; Soc Toxicol; fel Am Acad Forensic Sci. *Res:* Toxicology; pharmacology of pesticides; nutrition; mechanisms of atherosclerotic plaque formation. *Mailing Add:* Dept Pharmacol & Toxicol Univ Texas Med Br Galveston TX 77550-2779

SAUNDERS, JAMES ALLEN, PLANT BIOCHEMISTRY, PLANT PHYSIOLOGY. *Current Pos:* PRES, NATIVE SEEDS, INC, 80-; RES BIOCHEMIST, BARC-WEST, USDA, 77- *Personal Data:* b Cleveland, Ohio, Oct 4, 49; m 87, June M Gillespie; c 2. *Educ:* Univ SFla, BA, 71; Miami Univ Ohio, PhD(bot), 75. *Prof Exp:* Teaching assoc, Miami Univ Ohio, 71-75; res biochemist, Univ Calif, Davis, 75-77. *Concurrent Pos:* Adj assoc prof entom, Univ Md, 83-, adj assoc prof agron, 93- *Mem:* Sigma Xi; Am Soc Plant Physiologists; Phytochem Soc NAm; AAAS. *Res:* Secondary natural products in plants and their biosynthetic enzyme complexes including flavonoids, cyanogenic glucosides, alkaloids and phenolics; health related problems from tobacco use; electrofusion and electroporation in plants, pollen and plant gene transfer; drug crops, genetics and chemistry, including opium, poppy, coca, cannabis. *Mailing Add:* Biotechnol Lab Bldg 9 Rm 5 Natural Prod Inst USDA Beltsville MD 20705. *Fax:* 301-504-6478; *E-Mail:* saund10449@aol.com

SAUNDERS, JAMES CHARLES, PHYSIOLOGICAL PSYCHOLOGY, ANIMAL PHYSIOLOGY. *Current Pos:* from asst to assoc prof, 73-89, PROF OTORHINOLARYNGOL, SCH MED, UNIV PA, 89- *Personal Data:* b Elizabeth, NJ, May 8, 41; m 67, Elaine P Edwards; c Breton M & Drew C. *Educ:* Ohio Wesleyan Univ, BA, 63; Conn Col, MA, 65; Princeton Univ, PhD(psychol), 68. *Hon Degrees:* MA, Univ Pa, 80. *Honors & Awards:* Claude Pepper Award for Res Excellence, Nat Inst Neurol Commun Dis, 88. *Prof Exp:* Asst prof psychol, Monash Univ, Australia, 69-72; res assoc, Cent Inst Deaf, St Louis, 72-73. *Concurrent Pos:* Fel, Auditory Labs, Princeton Univ, 68; res fel, Dept Physiol, Univ Western Australia, 70; med assoc, Philadelphia Gen Hosp, 75-77; res assoc, Philadelphia Vet Hosp, 77-78; actg dir, Inst Neurol Sci, Univ Pa, 80-83, assoc dir, 83-; fel, Am-Scand Found, 84-85 & Swed Med Res Coun, 84-85; guest researcher, Karolinska Inst, Stockholm, Sweden, 84-85; mem, Comt Hearing & Bio-Acoust, Nat Res Coun, 86-; mem, study sect, Nat Inst Neurol & Commun Dis, 87-, mem exec coun, Asn Res Otolaryngol, 88-; dir, Auditory Res Lab & Ctr Hearing Sci, Univ Pa. *Mem:* Acoust Soc Am; Asn Res Otolaryngol; AAAS; Neurosci Soc; NY Acad Sci; Am Acad Otolaryngol; Soc Gen Physiol. *Res:* Communicative science; communicative disorders; audition; auditory neurobiology; animal psychoacoustics; physiological acoustics; developmental neurobiology; auditory psychology; hearing sciences; physiology of normal hearing; effects of intense sound on hearing loss; role of hair cell regeneration; hair cell micro mechanical; hearing development. *Mailing Add:* Dept Otorhinolaryngol Head Neck Surg 5 Silverstein OTO 3400 Spruce St Philadelphia PA 19104. *Fax:* 215-898-7504; *E-Mail:* saunderj@mail.med.upenn.edu

SAUNDERS, JAMES HENRY, POLYMER CHEMISTRY, ORGANIC CHEMISTRY. *Current Pos:* TECH CONSULT, 86- *Personal Data:* b Ames, Iowa, May 3, 23; m 46, Mary P Carter; c James H Jr, Stephen C, Charles W & Thomas D. *Educ:* Univ Ky, BS, 44; Univ Ill, PhD(org chem), 46. *Prof Exp:* Spec asst rubber res, Univ Ill, 44-47, group leader, 46-47; chemist, Monsanto Chem Co, 47-50, group leader, 50-54; group leader, Mobay Chem Co, Pa, 54-55, asst dir res, 55-59, dir res, 59-67; mgr nylon res, Monsanto Textiles Co, 68-69, dir nylon & polyester res, 69-75, dir res, Tech Ctr, 76-78, dir polyester res & develop, 79-80, gen mgr technol, 81-82; gen mgr res & develop, Monsanto Fiber & Intermediates Co, 83-85. *Concurrent Pos:* Affil prof, Dept Eng & Policy, Washington Univ, St Louis, Mo, 87-89; adj prof, Univ WFla, Pensacola, 90-92. *Mem:* AAAS; fel Am Inst Chemists; NY Acad Sci; Am Chem Soc; Fiber Soc; Sigma Xi; Soc Plastics Engrs. *Res:* Emulsion polymerization; synthesis of substituted styrenes and butadienes; biphenyl and phosgene chemistry; preparation, reactions and applications of isocyanates; polyesters; polycarbonates; polyethers; polyurethanes; polyamides; synthetic foams; elastomers; coatings; adhesives; thermoplastics; synthetic fibers; technical management. *Mailing Add:* 691 Tennyson Pl Pensacola FL 32503-3233

SAUNDERS, JAMES ROBERT, VETERINARY PATHOLOGY, VETERINARY MICROBIOLOGY. *Current Pos:* RETIRED. *Personal Data:* b Simcoe, Ont, Oct 6, 31; m 55; c 4. *Educ:* Ont Vet Col, Univ Guelph, DVM, 54; Univ Toronto, dipl vet pub health, 57; Univ Wis, PhD(vet sci, cell physiol), 61. *Prof Exp:* Vet practitioner, Sask, 54-56; res asst microbiol vet sci, Univ Wis, 57-60; vet pathologist, Sask Dept Agr, 60-61; asst prof vet path & microbiol, Purdue Univ, 61-65; from assoc prof to prof vet microbiol, Univ Sask, 65-93, chmn dept, 74-93. *Concurrent Pos:* NIH gen res grant, 63-65; Nat Res Coun Can grant, 66-67. *Mem:* Am Asn Avian Path; Am Col Vet Path; Conf Res Workers Animal Dis; Am Vet Med Asn; Can Vet Med Asn. *Res:* Role of viruses in pneumonias of cattle; pathology of encephalitic diseases; pseudorabies in swine; toxoplasmosis and Marek's disease in chickens; etio-pathogenesis of clostridial infections in birds and animals; ocular diseases of animals; congenital disorders of central nervous system of swine. *Mailing Add:* 20109 36 A Ave Langley BC V3A 2R9 Can

SAUNDERS, JEFFREY JOHN, PALEONTOLOGY. *Current Pos:* Res assoc vert paleont, Ill State Mus Soc, 75-78, CUR VERT PALEONT, ILL STATE MUS, 78- *Personal Data:* b Minneapolis, Minn, Dec 12, 43. *Educ:* Univ Minn, Minneapolis, BA, 66; Univ Ariz, MS, 70, PhD(geosci), 75. *Mem:* Soc Vert Paleont; Am Quaternary Asn; Sigma Xi. *Res:* Taphonomy of spring deposits and the paleoecology of fossil Proboscidea. *Mailing Add:* 730 N Bruns Lane Apt J Springfield IL 62702-3544

SAUNDERS, JOHN WARREN, JR, EMBRYOLOGY, TERATOLOGY. *Current Pos:* prof, 67-85, EMER PROF BIOL SCI, STATE UNIV NY, ALBANY, 85- *Personal Data:* b Muskogee, Okla, Nov 12, 19; m 42; c Mary K (Brown), Sarah E (Reeder), John W, Margaret A (Geist) & William M (deceased). *Educ:* Univ Okla, BS, 40, MS, 41; Johns Hopkins Univ, PhD(embryol), 48. *Honors & Awards:* Conklin Medal, Soc Develop Biol, 96. *Prof Exp:* Instr zool, Univ Chicago, 48-49; from asst prof to prof, Marquette Univ, 49-66, chmn dept, 57-65; prof anat, Univ Pa, 66-67. *Concurrent Pos:* Consult Develop Biol Prog, NSF, 62-66, Div Biol & Med Sci, 69-71, chmn, 71. *Mem:* Am Soc Zoologists (secy, 64-66); Soc Develop Biol (pres, 67-68); Am Asn Anatomists; fel AAAS. *Res:* Experimental morphogenesis; chick limb bud and feather tracts; cellular death in embryogenesis. *Mailing Add:* PO Box 3381 Waquoit MA 02536

SAUNDERS, KIM DAVID, EXPLOSIVE WELDING, CUTTING & FORMING. *Current Pos:* OCEANOGR, NAVAL RES LAB, STENNIS SPACE CTR, MISS, 78- *Personal Data:* b Chicago, Ill, Jan 21, 45; m 93, Joan; c 2. *Educ:* Rose Polytech Inst, BSc, 66; Mass Inst Technol, PhD(oceanog), 71. *Prof Exp:* Res assoc oceanog, Mass Inst Technol, 71-72; NATO fel, Inst Geophys, Univ Bergen, 72-73, Royal Norwegian Coun Sci & Indust Res fel, 73-74; asst environ scientist, Environ & Energy Systs Div, Argonne Nat Lab, 74-78. *Concurrent Pos:* Consult engr underwater explosion damage prev & explosive welding, 80- *Mem:* AAAS; Am Geophys Union; Sigma Xi; Inst Elec & Electronics Engrs; Marine Technol Soc; Am Soc Civil Engrs; Am Soc Mech Engrs; Int Soc Explosive Engrs; Nat Soc Prof Engrs. *Res:* Near shore circulations; high frequency internal waves; oceanographic instrumentation; geophysical fluid dynamics; numerical analysis and data quality control; ocean simulation. *Mailing Add:* 302 Country Club Dr Picayune MS 39466-5004. *Fax:* 228-688-5997; *E-Mail:* kim@nrlssc.navy.mil

SAUNDERS, LEON Z, VETERINARY PATHOLOGY, HISTORY OF VETERINARY. *Current Pos:* RETIRED. *Personal Data:* b Winnipeg, Man, Dec 16, 19; nat US; m 65, Marliese Janz; c Christine. *Educ:* Univ Toronto, VS & DVM, 43; Iowa State Col, MS, 46; Cornell Univ, PhD(vet path), 51. *Hon Degrees:* Dr Med Vet, Vet Col Vienna, 68; DSc, Univ Guelph, 93. *Honors & Awards:* Schofield Mem Medal, 73; Theodor Kitt Medal, Munich, 82; Armed Forces Inst Pathol Medallion, 91. *Prof Exp:* Instr vet path, Iowa State Col, 46-48; asst, Cornell Univ, 48-51; pathologist, Chem Corps Med Labs, US Army Chem Ctr, Md, 51-52; assoc vet, Brookhaven Nat Lab, 52-54, vet, 55-58; head path & toxicol sect, Smith Kline & French Labs, 58-68, dir path & toxicol, Smith Kline Beecham Pharmaceut, 68-80, vpres drug safety eval, 80-83, vpres & sr consult pathologist, 83-90, consult toxicol pathologist, 90-92. *Concurrent Pos:* Vis asst prof, Univ Pa, 58-62, vis assoc prof, 62-63, adj prof, 64-; vpres, World Fedn Vet Path, 59-67, pres, 67-71; ed, Pathologia Veterinaria, 63-67; managing ed, Vet Path, 68-89; mem, sci adv bd, Armed Forces Inst Path, Washington, DC, 85-91. *Mem:* Am Vet Med Asn; distinguished mem Am Col Vet Path (vpres, 67-, pres, 68); Am Asn Hist Med; US-Can Acad Path; Am Asn Pathologists; Am Col Vet Ophthal; Soc Tox Path. *Res:* Animal ophthalmic pathology; history of veterinary pathology; papers and books on the history of veterinary pathology in North America and in Europe. *Mailing Add:* 628 Sussex Rd Wynnewood PA 19096

SAUNDERS, MARTIN, ORGANIC CHEMISTRY. *Current Pos:* From instr to assoc prof chem, 55-70, PROF CHEM, YALE UNIV, 70-, FEL, BRANFORD COL, 70- *Personal Data:* b Brooklyn, NY, Jan 10, 31; m 82; c 2. *Educ:* City Col, BS, 52; Harvard Univ, PhD(org chem), 56. *Concurrent Pos:* Yale Univ jr fac fel sci, 62-63; Sloan fel, 65-69; spec award, von Humboldt Found, 77-78 & 85; Kharasch award, Univ Chicago, 82-83. *Mem:* Am Chem Soc; fel AAAS. *Res:* Applications of nuclear magnetic resonance spectroscopy to organic chemistry; study of stable carbonium ion solutions; molecular modeling. *Mailing Add:* Sterling Chem Lab Yale Univ 225 Prospect St New Haven CT 06520

SAUNDERS, PETER REGINALD, physical chemistry, physics, for more information see previous edition

SAUNDERS, PRISCILLA PRINCE, biochemical pharmacology, purine metabolism, for more information see previous edition

SAUNDERS, RICHARD L DE C H, NEUROANATOMY, RADIOLOGY. *Current Pos:* from asst prof to assoc prof anat, Dalhousie Univ, 38-48, prof path anat & dir med mus, 48-49, prof anat & head dept, 49-73, EMER PROF ANAT, DALHOUSIE UNIV, 74- *Personal Data:* b Grahamstown, SAfrica, May 29, 08; m 36, Sarah C MacIntyre; c Alastair C de C M. *Educ:* Univ Edinburgh, MB, ChB, 32; MD, 40. *Hon Degrees:* Dipl radiol, Univ Lisbon, 65. *Prof Exp:* Vis physician, Settlers Hosp, SAfrica, 32; house surgeon,

Bradford Royal Infirmary, Eng, 33; lectr anat, Univ Edinburgh, 33-37. *Concurrent Pos:* Res prof neuroanat, Radcliffe Infirmary, Oxford, Eng, 74-79; consult microfocal radiography, Cerebrovasc Proj, NIH, Winston-Salem, NC, 84-92. *Mem:* Fel Royal Micros Soc; Am Asn Anatomists; fel Royal Soc Edinburgh. *Res:* Microfocal radiography in experimental and clinical medicine, with special emphasis on cerebral microcirculation and neural structure. *Mailing Add:* W Jeddore by Head Jeddore Halifax NS B0J 1P0 Can

SAUNDERS, RICHARD LEE, PHYSIOLOGY. *Current Pos:* RETIRED. *Personal Data:* b Lynn, Mass, June 24, 28; m 55; c 3. *Educ:* Univ Mass, BS, 51; Univ Toronto, MA, 53, PhD(zool), 60. *Prof Exp:* Res scientist, Can Dept Fisheries & Oceans, 60-96, emer scientist, Biol Sta. *Mem:* Am Fisheries Soc; Can Soc Zoologists; World Aquacult Soc; Aquacult Asn Can. *Res:* Environmental physiology; fish respiration and metabolism; osmotic and ionic changes resulting from stress; endocrinological control of salmon smolting and growth; Atlantic salmon biology; salmonid genetics; salmonid aquaculture. *Mailing Add:* 309 Montague PO Box 156 St Andrews NB E0G 2X0 Can

SAUNDERS, ROBERT M(ALLOUGH), ELECTRICAL ENGINEERING. *Current Pos:* asst to chancellor, 64-65, dean sch eng, 65-73, PROF ELEC ENG, UNIV CALIF, IRVINE, 65- *Personal Data:* b Winnipeg, Man, Sept 12, 15; nat US; m 43, Elizabeth Lenander. *Educ:* Univ Minn, BEE, 38, MS, 42. *Hon Degrees:* DEng, Tokyo Inst Technol, 71. *Honors & Awards:* Centennial Medal, Inst Elec & Electronics Engrs, 84, Hariden Pratt Award, 90. *Prof Exp:* Instr elec eng, Univ Minn, 42-44; US Navy, 44-46; from lectr to prof elec eng, Univ Calif, Berkeley, 46-65, chmn dept, 59-63. *Concurrent Pos:* Vis assoc prof, Mass Inst Technol, 54-55; mem eng educ & accreditation comt, Eng Coun Prof Develop, 65-71, chmn, 69-70, mem bd dirs, 71-75; mem, Eng Adv Comt, NSF, 68-71; mem bd visitors, Army Transp Sch, Ft Eustis, Va, 70-73 & Secy Navy's Bd Educ & Training, 72-78; consult, Defense Res Labs, Gen Motors Corp, 63-69, Apollo Support Dept, Gen Elec Co, 63-68, Aerospace Corp, El Segundo, 71-78, Rohr Corp, Chula Vista, Hughes Aircraft Co, Fullerton, 80-82 & Sundstrand, Rockford, Ill, 85-88; secy, Nat Comn Eng Films, NSF. *Mem:* Am Soc Eng Educ; fel Inst Elec & Electronics Engrs; fel AAAS; fel Accreditation Bd Eng & Technol. *Res:* Electrical machinery theory; feedback control systems; applications of digital computers to electrical machine design; theory of electromechanical energy converters; system simulation and optimization. *Mailing Add:* Univ Calif Elec Eng Irvine CA 92717. *Fax:* 612-722-1878

SAUNDERS, ROBERT NORMAN, ATHEROSCLEROSIS, THROMBOSIS. *Current Pos:* RETIRED. *Personal Data:* b Fairbury, Ill, Sept 25, 38; m 81; c 3. *Educ:* Purdue Univ, BS, 61, MS, 66, PhD(pharmacol), 68. *Prof Exp:* Res scientist, G D Searle Co, 68-77, group leader, 77-80; sect head, Sandoz Inc, 80-84, dept head, 84-85, dir, 85-96. *Concurrent Pos:* Res comt chmn, G D Searle Co, 71-80, proj coordr, 73-79. *Mem:* Am Soc Pharmacol & Exp Therapeut; Int Soc Thrombosis & Haemostasis; Soc Exp Biol & Med; Am Heart Asn. *Res:* Diabetes and intermediary metabolism cholesterol synthesis regulation; smooth muscle cell proliferation; growth factors especially PDGF; platelet function and activity modification; prostaglandin synthesis and pharmacological activity; platelet activating factor activity and inhibition. *Mailing Add:* 1 Powder Horn Dr Convent Station NJ 07961

SAUNDERS, RONALD STEPHEN, GEOLOGY, PLANETOLOGY. *Current Pos:* Sr scientist, 69-74, mem tech staff, 74-86, SR RES SCIENTIST, JET PROPULSION LAB, 86- *Personal Data:* b Parsons, Kans, Oct 8, 40; c 3. *Educ:* Univ Wis-Madison, BS, 63; Brown Univ, MSc, 68, PhD(geol), 70. *Honors & Awards:* Except Serv Medal, NASA, 86, Except Sci Achievement, 91. *Concurrent Pos:* Proj scientist, Magellan, 81- *Mem:* Sigma Xi; Am Geophys Union; Soc Econ Paleontologists & Mineralogists; AAAS; Geol Soc Am. *Res:* Planetary geology of the moon, Mars, and Venus. *Mailing Add:* 1976 E Crary St Pasadena CA 91104

SAUNDERS, SAM CUNDIFF, MATHEMATICAL STATISTICS & PROBABILITY. *Current Pos:* PROF PURE & APPL MATH, WASH STATE UNIV, 72- *Personal Data:* b Richland, Ore, Feb 24, 31; m 54; c 3. *Educ:* Univ Ore, BS, 52; Univ Wash, PhD(math statist), 56. *Prof Exp:* Mathematician, Math Serv Unit, Boeing Airplane Co, 56-58 & Math Res Lab, 58-60; asst prof math, Math Res Ctr, Univ Wis, 60-61; staff mem, Math Res Lab, Boeing Sci Res Labs, Wash, 61-72. *Concurrent Pos:* Consult, Nuclear Regulatory Comn. *Mem:* Am Math Soc; Soc Indust & Appl Math; Math Asn Am; Inst Math Statist; fel Am Statist Asn. *Res:* Non-parametric methods; reliability theory; statistical inference. *Mailing Add:* Dept Math Wash State Univ Pullman WA 99164-0001

SAUNDERS, SHELLEY RAE, EVOLUTIONARY THEORY. *Current Pos:* from asst prof to assoc prof, 81-94, PROF ANTHROP, MCMASTER UNIV, 94- *Personal Data:* b Toronto, Can, Feb 28, 50; m 71; c 2. *Educ:* Univ Toronto, BA, 72, MA, 73, PhD(phys anthrop), 77. *Prof Exp:* Lectr & sr demonstr, McGill Univ, 76-79; asst prof, Univ Toronto, 79-81. *Concurrent Pos:* Ed, J Can Asn Phys Anthropologists, 78-81. *Mem:* Am Asn Phys Anthropologists; AAAS; Human Biol Coun; Can Asn Phys Anthropologists (secy treas, 83-); Am Anthrop Asn; Sigma Xi. *Res:* Investigation of bone growth remodeling of human infracranial bone; morphological variation of human bone; evolutionary changes of past human populations. *Mailing Add:* Dept Anthrop McMaster Univ 1280 Main St W Hamilton ON L8S 4L9 Can. *E-Mail:* saunders@mcmail.mcmaster.ca

SAUNDERS, VIRGINIA FOX, NEUROPSYCHOLOGY, NEUROSCIENCES. *Current Pos:* from asst prof to assoc prof, 67-76, PROF PSYCHOL, SAN FRANCISCO STATE UNIV, 76- *Personal Data:* b Roanoke, Va, May 31, 38; m 63; c 2. *Educ:* Univ Mich, BA, 60; Ind Univ, PhD(psychol & neurophysiol), 66. *Prof Exp:* Fel, Interdisciplinary Training Prog, Univ Calif Med Ctr, 65-67. *Concurrent Pos:* Spec progs coordr, Kentfield Sch Dist, Calif, 74-76; mem, Res & Eval Comt, Redwood High Sch, Calif, 75-77. *Res:* Physiological and pharmacological factors in sensation, perception, learning and memory. *Mailing Add:* Dept Psychol San Francisco State Univ 1600 Holloway Ave San Francisco CA 94132-1722

SAUNDERS, WILLIAM BRUCE, INVERTEBRATE PALEONTOLOGY, GEOLOGY. *Current Pos:* Asst prof, 70-76, chmn geol, 80-81, ASSOC PROF GEOL, BRYN MAWR COL, 76- *Personal Data:* b Tuscaloosa, Ala, Nov 12, 42; m 64; c 1. *Educ:* Univ Ark, BSc, 66, MSc, 68; Univ Iowa, PhD(geol), 71. *Concurrent Pos:* Exchange scientist, Nat Acad Sci-USSR Acad Sci, 74-75; prin investr, NSF grants marine biol, paleobiol, 75-77, 77-79, 80-84 & RV Alpha Helix, Philippines, 79. *Mem:* Int Union Geol Sci; Am Soc Am; Int Paleont Asn; Paleont Soc; fel Explorers Club. *Res:* Evolution and paleobiology of fossil cephalopods, cephalopod biostratigraphy and biology of cephalopods; particularly living nautilus. *Mailing Add:* Dept Geol Bryn Mawr Col 101 N Merian Ave Bryn Mawr PA 19010

SAUNDERS, WILLIAM H, OTOLARYNGOLOGY. *Current Pos:* From asst prof to assoc prof, 54-60, actg chmn dept, 61-63, PROF OTOLARYNGOL, COL MED, OHIO STATE UNIV, 60-, CHMN DEPT, 63- *Personal Data:* b Omaha, Nebr, Jan 7, 20; c 4. *Educ:* Univ Omaha, AB, 39; Univ Iowa, MD, 43. *Concurrent Pos:* Dir, Am Bd Otolaryngol, 74. *Mem:* AMA; Am Acad Ophthal & Otolaryngol; Am Laryngol, Rhinol & Otol Soc; Am Laryngol Asn; Am Otol Soc. *Res:* Otology. *Mailing Add:* Dept Chem Univ Rochester Rochester NY 14627-1001

SAUNDERS, WILLIAM HUNDLEY, JR, PHYSICAL ORGANIC CHEMISTRY, AB INITIO CALCULATIONS. *Current Pos:* from instr to prof chem, Univ Rochester, 53-91, chmn dept, 66-70, fac sr assoc, 91, EMER PROF, UNIV ROCHESTER, 96- *Personal Data:* b Pulaski, Va, Jan 12, 26; wid; c Anne & Claude. *Educ:* Col William & Mary, BS, 48; Northwestern Univ, PhD(chem), 52. *Prof Exp:* Res assoc chem, Mass Inst Technol, 51-53. *Concurrent Pos:* Guggenheim fel & hon res assoc, Univ Col, Univ London, 60-61; Sloan Found fel, 61-64; NSF sr fel & guest researcher, Univ Gothenburg, 70-71; ed, Tech of Chem, 85-94. *Mem:* Am Chem Soc; Royal Soc Chem. *Res:* Isotope effects and isotopic tracers; mechanisms of organic reactions, especially elimination and other proton transfer processes; the role of tunneling in proton transfers; ab initio calculations on proton transfers and eliminations. *Mailing Add:* Dept Chem Univ Rochester Rochester NY 14627. *Fax:* 716-473-6889; *E-Mail:* saunders@chem.chem.rochester.edu

SAUPE, ALFRED (OTTO), physics, physical chemistry, for more information see previous edition

SAURO, JOSEPH PIO, PHYSICS. *Current Pos:* from assoc prof to prof physics, Univ Mass, Dartmouth, 66-93, dean, Col Arts & Sci, 69-80, dean grad sch, 69-71, dir, Col Sci Improv Prog, 69-71, interim dean, Col Eng, 78-80, dir, Steps Towards Abstract & Reasoning Prog, 80-92, EMER PROF, UNIV MASS, DARTMOUTH, 95- *Personal Data:* b New Rochelle, NY, Apr 4, 27; m 48, Elizabeth J Schellman; c Brian, Michael & Joseph. *Educ:* Polytech Univ, BS, 55, MS, 58, PhD(physics), 66. *Prof Exp:* Instr physics, Polytech Inst Brooklyn, 56-65. *Mem:* Am Phys Soc; Sigma Xi; Am Asn Physics Teachers. *Res:* Scattering of x-rays by thin films; dielectric properties of phosphors. *Mailing Add:* 8 Captain Wing Rd PO Box 28 East Sandwich MA 02537-0028

SAURO, MARIE D, HYPERTENSION, VASCULAR SMOOTH MUSCLE FUNCTION. *Current Pos:* ASST PROF & RES SCIENTIST, DEPT PHARMACOL & ANESTHESIOL, STATE UNIV NY, HEALTH SCI CTR, SYRACUSE, 94- *Personal Data:* b Syracuse, NY, Dec 5, 59; m 83, Nicolas J. *Educ:* Union Col, Schenectady, BS, 82; Univ SFla, MS, 87, PhD(med sci), 89. *Honors & Awards:* Acad Award Excellence, Josten Educ Found, 80. *Prof Exp:* Asst, Dept Pharmacol, Univ SFla, Col Med, 85-89, clin asst prof, 90-91; fel, H Lee Moffitt Cancer Inst, Tampa, Fla, 89-91; res scientist, Masonic Med Lab, Utica, NY, 91-94. *Concurrent Pos:* Res award, Sigma Xi, 87 & 88; fel, Am Heart Asn, 89-90, Coun High Blood Pressure, 92-; nat res serv award fel, NIH, 90-93; comt mem, Am Soc Pharmacol & Exp Therapeut, 92-; exec bd dirs, Asn Women Sci, 93- *Mem:* Am Soc Pharmacol & Exp Therapeut; Asn Women Sci; Am Heart Asn. *Res:* Vascular smooth muscle pharmacology; molecular biology; physiology and biochemistry as it relates to hypertension; signal transduction mechanisms in hypertension; cGMP, protein tyrosine kinases and protein kinase C. *Mailing Add:* Dept Pharmacol State Univ NY Health Sci Ctr 750 E Adams St Syracuse NY 13210. *Fax:* 315-464-8000

SAUSE, H WILLIAM, ORGANIC CHEMISTRY. *Current Pos:* RETIRED. *Personal Data:* b Baltimore, Md, Sept 29, 20; m 44, Norah A Brooks; c David, Anne & Barbara. *Educ:* Johns Hopkins Univ, AB, 48, MA, 50, PhD(chem), 53. *Prof Exp:* Jr instr chem, Johns Hopkins Univ, 48-52; res assoc, Northwestern Univ, 52-54; res chemist, 54-77, clin pharm assoc, Searle Labs, Chicago, 77-86. *Mem:* AAAS; Am Chem Soc. *Res:* Natural products; pharmaceutical chemistry; heterocyclic chemistry; clinical pharmacy. *Mailing Add:* 1061 Springfield Ave Deerfield IL 60015-3030

SAUSEN, GEORGE NEIL, ORGANIC CHEMISTRY. *Current Pos:* DIR INTELLECTURE PROPERTY, CEPHALON, INC, WEST CHESTER, PA, 92- *Personal Data:* b St Paul, Minn, Aug 14, 27; m 51; c 5. *Educ:* Col St Thomas, BS, 49; Univ Wis, PhD(chem), 53. *Prof Exp:* Res chemist, E I du Pont de Nemours & Co, Inc, 53-63, supvr, 64-67, sr res chemist, 68-71, patent liaison & suprv patents & tech info, 71-88, mgr corp info sci, Cent Res & Develop Dept, 88-92. *Mem:* Am Chem Soc. *Res:* Angular methylation studies of steroid intermediates; cyanocarbons; fluorine chemistry; polymer intermediates. *Mailing Add:* 322 Brockton Rd Wilmington DE 19803-2412

SAUSVILLE, EDWARD ANTHONY, ONCOLOGY. *Current Pos:* med staff fel, Nat Cancer Inst, 82-85, sr investr, 85-88, sr investr, 90-91, CHIEF, LAB BIOL CHEM, NAT CANCER INST, BETHESDA, 94-, ASSOC DIR, DEVELOP THERAPEUT PROG. *Personal Data:* b Albany, NY, Apr 3, 52; m 75, Carol A Cassidy; c Justin, Brendan, Elizabeth, Rebecca & Paul. *Educ:* Manhattan Col, BS, 73; Albert Einstein Col Med, MD, PhD, 79. *Prof Exp:* Med house staff, Brigham & Womens Hosp, Boston, 79-82; assoc prof med, Georgetown Univ, Sch Med, Wash, 88-90. *Mem:* Am Asn Cancer Res; Am Soc Clin Oncol; Am Soc Biochem & Molecular Biol; Am Fedn Clin Res. *Res:* Mechanisms of bleomycin action; bombesin-related peptic gene expression and response in lung cancer; optimal treatment and staging of cutaneous T-cell lymphoma; author of 1 publication. *Mailing Add:* Develop Therapeut Prog Nat Cancer Inst EPN 843 Bethesda MD 20892-0001. *Fax:* 301-402-0831; *E-Mail:* sausville@dtpaxz.ncifcrf.gov

SAUSVILLE, JOSEPH WINSTON, HIGH TEMPERATURE CHEMISTRY, ENGINEERING MANAGEMENT. *Current Pos:* mgr phosphor advan develop, 67-70, MGR PHOSPHOR DEVELOP, FLUORESCENT & VAPOR LAMP DIV, WESTINGHOUSE ELEC CORP, 70- *Personal Data:* b Brooklyn, NY, Oct 17, 18; m 45; c 3. *Educ:* Polytech Inst Brooklyn, BS, 41; Univ Iowa, PhD(phys chem), 48. *Prof Exp:* Chemist, Tenn Eastman Corp, 44-46 & Nuclear Energy Propulsion Aircraft Div, Fairchild Eng & Airplane Corp, 47-48; from asst prof to assoc prof phys chem, Univ Cincinnati, 48-56, chmn grad studies, 51-56; mgr nuclear mat, Res Div, Curtiss-Wright Corp, Pa, 56-61, eng head advan develop metall, Wright Aero Div, NJ, 62-67. *Mem:* Am Chem Soc; Am Inst Chemists; Illum Eng Soc; Am Soc Photobiol. *Res:* Fundamental properties of matter; high temperature materials fabrication and evaluation; effects of ionizing radiations. *Mailing Add:* PO Box 366 Garfield NJ 07026-0366

SAUTE, ROBERT E, PHARMACY, COSMETIC SCIENCES. *Current Pos:* OWNER, SAUTE CONSULTS, 74- *Personal Data:* b West Warwick, RI, Aug 18, 29; m 57; c 3. *Educ:* RI Col Pharm, BS, 50; Purdue Univ, MS, 52, PhD(pharm), 53. *Honors & Awards:* Fel Soc Cosmetic Chemists. *Prof Exp:* Tech asst to gen mgr, Lafayette Pharmacol Co, 55-56; res chemist, H K Wampole Co, 56-58; plant supt, Strong Cobb Arner Co, 58-60; res chemist, Avon Prod Inc, NY, 60-64; dir prod & process develop & dir res & develop admin, 64-68; res dir, Toiletries Div, Gillette Co, 68-71; group vpres, Dart Industs Inc, 71-74. *Mem:* AAAS; Soc Invest Dermat; Am Pharmaceut Asn; Acad Pharmaceut Sci; NY Acad Sci; Soc Cosmetic Chemists; Sigma Xi. *Res:* Consulting in the cosmetic, drug, toiletries and fragrance industries. *Mailing Add:* 10236 Mossy Rock Circle Los Angeles CA 90077

SAUTER, FREDERICK JOSEPH, ORGANIC CHEMISTRY. *Current Pos:* Sr res chemist, 69-76, RES ASSOC EASTMAN KODAK CO, 76- *Personal Data:* b Pittsburgh, Pa, Dec 12, 43; m 66; c 3. *Educ:* Duquesne Univ, BS, 65; Mass Inst Technol, PhD(org chem), 69. *Mem:* AAAS; Am Chem Soc. *Res:* Organic syntheses and reaction mechanisms as applied to conventional and unconventional imaging systems. *Mailing Add:* 203 Dohrcrest Dr Rochester NY 14612-4139

SAUTHOFF, NED ROBERT, PLASMA PHYSICS. *Current Pos:* Res physicist, Plasma Physics Lab, Princeton Univ, 75-84, head, Tokamak Fusion Test Reactor Exp, Comput Br, 80-84, dep head, Comput Div, 83-86, head, Comput Div, 86-88, head, Princton Beta Exp, 88-94, head, Exp Projs Dept, 90-92, PRIN RES PHYSICIST, PRINCETON UNIV, 84-, HEAD, PHYSICS DEPT, 92-, HEAD, PLASMA SCI & TECHNOL DEPT, 94- *Personal Data:* b Belleville, Ill, Apr 14, 49; m 75, Ana; c Ana Maria. *Educ:* Mass Inst Technol, SB & SM, 72; Princeton Univ, PhD(astrophys), 75. *Mem:* Fel Am Phys Soc; Sigma Xi; sr mem Inst Elec & Electronics Engrs. *Res:* Plasma physics in general; x-ray techniques; magnetohydrodynamics in tokamaks by x-ray imaging and tomography. *Mailing Add:* Plasma Physics Lab Princeton Univ PO Box 451 Princeton NJ 08543

SAUTTER, CHESTER A, EXPERIMENTAL ATOMIC PHYSICS, ENVIRONMENTAL PHYSICS. *Current Pos:* ASSOC PROF PHYSICS, CONCORDIA COL, MOORHEAD, MINN, 65- *Personal Data:* b Scotia, Nebr, Nov 16, 33; m 59; c 4. *Educ:* Nebr Wesleyan Univ, AB, 55; Univ Nebr, MA, 58, PhD(physics), 63. *Prof Exp:* Fulbright travel grant & guest physicist, Inst Physics, Aarhus, Denmark, 63-64. *Concurrent Pos:* Consult & vis prof, Wash State Univ, 74-75; consult, Lutheran Coun, USA & Lutheran World Ministries, 81-82. *Mem:* Am Asn Physics Teachers; Am Phys Soc; Int Solar Energy Soc; Hist Sci Soc; Sigma Xi. *Res:* Charge exchange of slow atoms and ions in gases; stopping power of ions and atoms in carbon and hydrocarbon films; ion channelling in single crystals and neutron activation analysis; residual environmental effects of Church Rock, New Mexico 1979 uranium mill tailings spill; development of response procedures to nuclear criticality accidents at the Idaho National Engineering Laboratory. *Mailing Add:* 1305 Elm St Moorhead MN 56560

SAUTTER, JAY HOWARD, VETERINARY PATHOLOGY. *Current Pos:* Instr vet med, 47-48, assoc prof vet path, 48-52, PROF VET PATH, UNIV MINN, ST PAUL, 52- *Personal Data:* b Waynesburg, Ohio, Nov 11, 12; m 37; c 3. *Educ:* Ohio State Univ, DVM, 44; Univ Minn, PhD(path), 48. *Concurrent Pos:* AID consult, Peru, 65; tech asst, Nebr Proj, Columbia Univ, 70-71; tech asst, Food & Agr Orgn, Dom Repub, 72; prof & head dept path & microbiol, Ahmadu Bella Univ, Nigeria, 74-76; tech asst, Kans AID Proj, Ahmadu Bella Univ, 74- *Mem:* Am Asn Avian Pathologists; Am Vet Med Asn; Am Col Vet Pathologists; Nigerian Vet Med Asn; Am Asn Pathologists. *Mailing Add:* 1550 Fulham Ave St Paul MN 55108

SAUVAGE, LESTER ROSAIRE, CARDIOVASCULAR SURGERY & RESEARCH. *Current Pos:* FOUNDER & DIR, HOPE HEART INST, 59-; PVT PRACT CARDIOVASC PEDIAT SURG, 59- *Personal Data:* b Wapata, Wash Nov 15, 26; m 56; c 8. *Educ:* St Louis Univ Sch Med, MD, 48. *Hon Degrees:* ScD, Gonzaga Univ, 82. *Honors & Awards:* Clemson Award, Soc Biomats, 82; Jefferson Award, Am Inst Pub Serv, 83. *Concurrent Pos:* Chmn dept surg, Providence Med Ctr, 65-74; dir surg educ, 68-73; dir cardiac surg, Childrens Orthop Hosp & Med Ctr, 65-74; clin prof surg, Univ Wash. *Mem:* Am Col Surgeons; Int Cardiovasc Soc; Soc Vascular Surg; Neurovascular Soc NAm. *Res:* Synthetic blood vessel prostheses; vascular surgical techniques; prediction and prevention of thrombotic complications of atherosclerosis; endothelial cell function; vascular autografts; approximately 175 articles. *Mailing Add:* Hope Heart Inst 528 18th St Seattle WA 98122

SAVAGE, ALBERT B, POLYMER CHEMISTRY, SYNTHETIC ORGANIC & NATURAL PRODUCTS CHEMISTRY. *Current Pos:* RETIRED. *Personal Data:* b Minneapolis, Minn, Dec 22, 12; wid, Esther C Anderson; c John G & Marjorie E (Abbott). *Educ:* Univ Minn, BChE & BA, 35, MS, 37. *Prof Exp:* Sr res specialist, Cellulose Res, Designed Polymers Res Lab, Dow Chem Co, 37-76. *Mem:* Sigma Xi. *Res:* Etherification; cellulose; soluble polymers; plastics. *Mailing Add:* 122 Varner Ct Midland MI 48640-3508

SAVAGE, BLAIR DEWILLIS, ASTRONOMY. *Current Pos:* from asst prof to assoc prof, 68-78, PROF ASTRON, UNIV WIS-MADISON, 78- *Personal Data:* b Mt Vernon, NY, June 7, 41; m 66; c 1. *Educ:* Cornell Univ, BEngrPhysics, 64; Princeton Univ, PhD(astron), 67. *Prof Exp:* Res assoc astron, Princeton Univ, 67-68. *Concurrent Pos:* Vis fel, Joint Inst Lab Astrophys, Colo, 74-75. *Mem:* Am Astron Soc; Int Astron Union. *Res:* Ultraviolet space astronomy; interstellar matter, high resolution spectroscopy. *Mailing Add:* Washburn Observ Univ Wis Madison WI 53706

SAVAGE, CARL RICHARD, JR, biochemistry, endocrinology, for more information see previous edition

SAVAGE, CHARLES, PSYCHIATRY. *Current Pos:* PHYSICIAN & INTERPRETER, CHICHICASPENASGO, GUATAMALA MAYA QUICHE EPISCOPAL SEM, 93- *Personal Data:* b Berlin, Conn, Sept 25, 18; wid; m Emmy & Charles W III. *Educ:* Yale Univ, BA, 39; Univ Chicago, MD, 44; Am Bd Psychiat & Neurol, dipl, 51. *Honors & Awards:* David C Wilson Soc Lectr, Univ Va, 67. *Prof Exp:* Intern, Univ Chicago, 45; asst resident psychiat, Yale Univ, 46; resident psychiat, US Naval Hosp, Md, 47-48, chief psychiatrist, SC, 48-49; res psychiatrist, Naval Med Res Inst, Nat Naval Med Ctr, 49-52; actg chief adult psychiatrist, NIMH, 53-58; psychiatrist, Livermore Sanitarium, 58-60 & Stanford Vet Admin Hosp, 61-62; med dir, Int Found Advan Study, 62-64; psychiatrist, Co Santa Clara, 64-65; dir res, Spring Grove State Hosp, 65-68; from clin asst prof to assoc prof, Inst Psychiat & Human Behav, Univ Md, 65-80, prof psychiat, 72-86; psychiatrist, Div Ment Health, Dept Health, VI Govt, 86-92; chief geriat psychiat, Eastern Shore Hosp Ctr, Cambridge, Md, 92-93. *Concurrent Pos:* Prin investr, Nat Inst Ment Health grant, Studies of Selected Narcotic Agonists & Antagonists, 72-75; chief, Psychiat Serv & Drug Treatment Ctr, Vet Admin Hosp, 72-82; fel, Ctr Advan Study Behav Sci, 57-58; emer asst prof psychiat, Johns Hopkins Univ, 82- *Mem:* Fel Am Psychiat Asn; Am Psychoanal Asn; Am Electroencephalogram Soc; AAAS. *Res:* Treatment of drug and alcohol abuse; cross cultural studies of mental illness; psychopharmacology. *Mailing Add:* PO Box 307 Sherwood Forest MD 21405

SAVAGE, CHARLES FRANCIS, AERONAUTICAL & ASTRONAUTICAL ENGINEERING. *Current Pos:* RETIRED. *Personal Data:* b Maywood, Ill, Feb 24, 06; m 30, 74, Ruth Sununu; c Edward S & Ruth (Ashworth). *Educ:* Ore State Univ, BSEE, 28. *Honors & Awards:* Centennial Medal, Inst Elec & Electronics Engrs, 84. *Prof Exp:* Div engr, Gen Elec Co, 28-71; exec dir, Coun Eng Law, 71-77; staff consult eng law, Engrs Joint Coun, 77-80. *Concurrent Pos:* Chmn nuclear cong, Am Soc Mech Engrs, 54-55; conf bd indust, Nat Soc Prof Engrs, 56-59, eng sect, AAAS, 57-58; hon mem, Coun Eng & Sci Soc Exec, 70- *Mem:* Fel Inst Elec & Electronics Engrs; fel Am Soc Mech Engrs; Nat Soc Prof Engrs; Am Soc Eng Educ; fel AAAS; fel Am Inst Elec Engrs; hon mem Coun Eng & Sci Soc Execs; assoc fel Am Inst Aeronaut & Astronaut. *Res:* Electrical measurement, especially in aircraft engine, guidance and control. *Mailing Add:* 3609 Palmer Ct Clovis NM 88101-3142

SAVAGE, DANIEL DEXTER, FETAL ALCOHOL SYNDROME RESEARCH, EPILEPSY RESEARCH. *Current Pos:* From asst prof to assoc prof, 83-94, PROF PHARMACOL, UNIV NMEX, 94- *Personal Data:* b June 27, 51; m 78, Holly Horuff; c Jennifer L & Jessica L. *Educ:* Univ Richmond, BS, 73; Univ Pa, PhD(pharmacol), 80. *Mem:* Soc Neurosci; Res Soc Alcoholism; Int Soc Biomed Res Alcoholism. *Res:* Pharmacological mechanisms and neurobiological consequences of ethanol's teratogenic effects on developing brain, with special emphasis on excitatory amino acid neurotransmitter systems in limbic brain regions. *Mailing Add:* Univ NMex Med Sch 1 University Campus Albuquerque NM 87131-0001. *Fax:* 505-277-2070

SAVAGE, DENNIS JEFFREY, ORGANIC CHEMISTRY. *Current Pos:* SR RES CHEMIST, EASTMAN KODAK CO, 70- *Personal Data:* b Warren, Ohio, Oct 13, 42; m 68, Gabrielle Simard; c Liza & Cary. *Educ:* Univ Colo, Boulder, BA, 65; Univ Ariz, PhD(chem), 71. *Res:* Organometallic chemistry; organic polymer synthesis. *Mailing Add:* Eastman Kodak Co 343 State St Rochester NY 14650

SAVAGE, DONALD ELVIN, paleontology, for more information see previous edition

SAVAGE, DWAYNE CECIL, MOLECULAR & MICROBIAL ECOLOGY. *Current Pos:* dept head, 88-96, PROF MICROBIOL, UNIV TENN, 96- *Personal Data:* b Arco, Idaho, Aug 8, 34; m 57; c Marco & Clark. *Educ:* Univ Idaho, BS, 56; Univ Calif, Berkeley, MA, 61, PhD(bact), 65. *Prof Exp:* Guest investr & fel, Rockefeller Univ, 65-67; from asst prof to assoc prof, Univ Tex, Austin, 67-73; from assoc prof to prof microbiol, Univ Ill & Sch Basic Med Sci, Col Med, 73-88. *Concurrent Pos:* Nat Inst Allergy & Infectious Dis res proj grant, 68-92; vis assoc prof, Sch Med, Univ Colo, Denver, 70, consult, Div Gastroenterol, 70-73; Am Soc Microbiol Found Lectr, 72-73; res grant rev, NIH, 74-78, 77-78 & 79-85, Nat Health Med Res Coun, Australia, 79-, Med Res Coun, N Zealand, 80- & Am Inst Biol Sci, 85-90; consult, Nat Res Coun-Nat Acad Sci, 79, NSF, 86; indust consult, 79-87; vis scientist, Australian Soc Microbiol, 82. *Mem:* Am Acad Microbiol; Am Soc Microbiol; Sigma Xi; fel AAAS; Soc Gen Microbiol UK. *Res:* Molecular properties of anaerobic gastrointestinal microorganisms including adhesion of lactobacilli to tissue surfaces and bile salt hydrolase genetics and function in lactobacilli and bifidobacteria. *Mailing Add:* Dept Microbiol Univ Tenn M409 Walters Life Sci Bldg Knoxville TN 37996-0845. *Fax:* 423-974-4007

SAVAGE, E LYNN, SEDIMENTOLOGY, MEDICAL GEOLOGY. *Current Pos:* Annual lectr, 66-67, from instr to assoc prof, 67-86, PROF GEOL, BROOKLYN COL, CITY UNIV NEW YORK, 87- *Personal Data:* b New York, NY. *Educ:* Brooklyn Col, BS; NY Univ, MS; Rutgers Univ, PhD (sedimentol, stratig) 67. *Honors & Awards:* John Moss Award, Nat Assn Geol Teachers. *Concurrent Pos:* Adj assoc prof, Hunter Col, 78-; conf dir & chmn, Environ Health, Med Geol, Earth Day, 89. *Mem:* Fel Geol Soc Am; Soc Econ Paleontologists & Mineralogists; NY Acad Sci; Sigma Xi; Int Soc Sedimentologists. *Res:* Relevance of aluminum and acid rain to etiology of Alzheimer's disease; sedimentology of sandstones; application of geology to disease patterns; environmental health problems; physicians who practiced geology, (and why). *Mailing Add:* Dept Geol Brooklyn Col City Univ New York Brooklyn NY 11210

SAVAGE, EARL JOHN, plant pathology, mycology, for more information see previous edition

SAVAGE, ELDON P, PUBLIC HEALTH. *Current Pos:* RETIRED. *Personal Data:* b Bedford, Iowa, Apr 4, 26; m 48; c 2. *Educ:* Univ Kans, BA, 50; Tulane Univ, MPH, 57; Univ Okla, PhD(prev med, pub health), 67. *Prof Exp:* Entomologist, Tech Br, Nat Commun Dis Ctr, Kans, 50-51, WVa, 51-52, Ga, 53-54, proj entomologist, Kans, 54-55, demonstration entomologist, Iowa, 56-57, proj dir environ control, 57-58, dir commun dis control demonstration, Pa, 58-64, asst chief state aids sect, 64-66, chief state serv pesticides prog, Ga, 67-70; dep dir, Inst Rural Environ Health, Colo State Univ, 70-84, prof environ health & toxicol, chief chem epidemiol sect, Inst Rural Environ Health, 70-94, dir, 84-94. *Concurrent Pos:* Prof & head, Dept Environ Health, dir, Environ Health Serv, Colo State Univ. *Mem:* Sigma Xi; Res Soc Am; Nat Environ Health Asn; Am Acad Sanitarians; NY Acad Sci. *Res:* Ecology of flies; environmental sanitation; human ecology; environmental toxicology; chemical pesticides; chemical pollutants in mother's milk; epidemiology; chronic effects of pesticide exposure. *Mailing Add:* 5220 Apple Dr Ft Collins CO 80526

SAVAGE, GEORGE ROLAND, MICROBIOLOGY. *Current Pos:* RETIRED. *Personal Data:* b Ft Worth, Tex, Apr 2, 29; m 55; c 4. *Educ:* NTex State Univ, BS, 49; Univ Tex, MA, 50; Nat Registry Microbiol, cert, 66. *Prof Exp:* Res technician, Samuel Roberts Noble Res Found, Okla, 50-51; bacteriologist & serologist, NMex Dept Pub Health, 51-52; chief clin lab, Carlsbad Mem Hosp, NMex, 52-55; asst dir admin, Carnegie Inst, Ohio, 55-58; microbiologist, Directorate Biol Opers, Dept Army, 59-62, chief bact & fungal develop sect, 62-64, chief viral & rickettsial labs, 64-67; sr microbiologist, Biol Sci Div, Midwest Res Inst, Mo, 67-73; environ scientist, Black & Veatch Engrs-Architects, 73-94. *Mem:* Am Soc Microbiol; NY Acad Sci; Sigma Xi. *Res:* Environmental studies related to the establishment and operation of energy production facilities; physiological and genetic problems associated with large-scale growth of pathogenic bacteria, viruses and rickettsia. *Mailing Add:* 9801 Bluejacket Dr Overland Park MO 66214

SAVAGE, GODFREY H, MECHANICAL ENGINEERING, OCEAN ENGINEERING. *Current Pos:* PROF MECH ENG & DIR ENG DESIGN LAB, UNIV NH, 65- *Personal Data:* b Niagara Falls, NY, June 13, 27; m 60, Joanne Goodhue; c 3. *Educ:* Princeton Univ, BSE, 50; Stanford Univ, MS, 51, PhD(earth sci), 70; Harvard Univ, MBA, 54. *Prof Exp:* Petrol engr, Stand Oil Co Calif, 51-52; staff mem, Arthur D Little, Inc, 54-55, assoc & proj leader, 55-58; asst to dean grad sch bus, Harvard Univ, 58-59; asst vpres overseas opers, Leesona Holt Ltd, Eng & Leesona Corp, RI, 59-60; staff engr, Nat Acad Sci, 60-61; res engr, Woods Hole Oceanog Inst, 63-65. *Concurrent Pos:* Vis engr, Mass Inst Technol, 63-66; founding co-chmn, Maine-NH Bi-State Comn Oceanog, 66-68; chmn, NH State Port Authority & Tidelands Conserv Authority, 67-69; pres, Ocean Technol Explor Co, 73-; Fulbright fel & vis prof, Heriot Watt Univ, 75-76; chief eng adv, Ocean Margin Drill Prog, JOI Inc, 79-81; chmn, Ocean Eng Bldg Construct Panel, Univ NH, 93- *Mem:* Marine Technol Soc; Inst Offshore Eng, Scotland; Am Soc Mech Engrs. *Res:* Invention and development of structural and mechanical-electrical systems for ocean exploration and commerce: buoy systems, deep diving systems and vehicles; wave energy measurement and finfish cage aquaculture. *Mailing Add:* Dept Mech Eng Univ NH Durham NH 03824. *Fax:* 603-862-1864; *E-Mail:* ghs@christa.unh.edu

SAVAGE, I RICHARD, STATISTICS. *Current Pos:* prof, 74-91, EMER PROF STATIST, YALE UNIV, 91- *Personal Data:* b Detroit, Mich, Oct 26, 25; m 50; c 2. *Educ:* Univ Chicago, BS, 44; Univ Mich, MS, 45; Columbia Univ, PhD(statist), 54. *Honors & Awards:* Founders Award, Am Statist Asn, 93. *Prof Exp:* Statistician, Nat Bur Stand, 51-54; actg asst prof statist, Stanford Univ, 54-57; from assoc prof to prof, Univ Minn, 57-63; prof, Fla State Univ, 63-74. *Concurrent Pos:* Consult, Ctr Advan Study Behav Sci, 56, NSF sr fel, 70-71; vis assoc prof, Sch Bus, Harvard Univ, 60-61; vis prof, Yale Univ, 67-68; ed, Ann of Statist, 74-77. *Mem:* Fel Am Statist Asn (pres, 84); Am Math Soc; fel Inst Math Statist; Int Statist Inst. *Res:* Government statistics; non-parametric techniques; control theory. *Mailing Add:* 123 York St Apt 21A New Haven CT 06511

SAVAGE, JANE RAMSDELL, NUTRITION, BIOCHEMISTRY. *Current Pos:* from asst prof to prof, 73-86, assoc dean, 84-86, EMER PROF NUTRIT, UNIV TENN, KNOXVILLE, 86- *Personal Data:* b Boston, Mass, Sept 23, 25. *Educ:* Simmons Col, BS, 46, MS, 49; Univ Wis, PhD(nutrit, biochem), 63. *Prof Exp:* Asst chem, Simmons Col, 46-49; asst prof nutrit & chem, Univ Tenn, 49-59; res asst nutrit, Univ Wis, 59-62. *Mem:* Am Chem Soc; Am Home Econ Asn; Sigma Xi. *Res:* Tryptophan metabolism; niacin containing co-enzymes; amino acid imbalance. *Mailing Add:* 9131 Wesley Pl Dr Knoxville TN 37922-5945

SAVAGE, JAY MATHERS, HERPETOLOGY, EVOLUTION. *Current Pos:* chmn dept, 82-87, PROF BIOL, UNIV MIAMI, 82- *Personal Data:* b Santa Monica, Calif, Aug 26, 28; m 81, Rebecca E Papendick; c Nancy D & Charles R. *Educ:* Stanford Univ, AB, 50, MA, 54, PhD(biol sci), 55. *Prof Exp:* Asst gen biol, Stanford Univ, 50-53, asst comp vert anat & embryol, 54; asst prof zool, Pomona Col, 54-56; from instr to assoc prof biol, Univ Southern Calif, 56-64, vchmn, Nat Oceanog Lab Syst, 71-74, prof & assoc dir, Allan Hancock Found, 64-82. *Concurrent Pos:* Mem, Stanford field exped, Mex, 50; herpetologist, Sefton Found-Stanford Exped, Gulf of Calif & Mex, 52; actg asst cur herpet, Philadelphia Acad Natural Sci, 54; Guggenheim Found fel, 63-64; dir advan sci sem trop biol, Univ Costa Rica, 61-63, prof & tech adv to dept biol, 63-66; res assoc, Los Angeles County Mus; mem bd dirs, Orgn Trop Studies, Inc, 63-, exec secy, 63-65, pres, 74-80; chmn, comt select biol problems in the humid tropics, Nat Acad Sci/Nat Res Coun, 80-81, comt formation, Nat Biol Surv, 93; int dir, Sch Int Rel, 79-81; chair, dept biol, Univ Miami, 82-87; mem, Int Comn Zool Nomen, 82- *Mem:* AAAS; Soc Study Evolution; Am Soc Ichthyologists & Herpetologists (treas, 60-63, pres, 82); Soc Study Amphibians & Reptiles; Sigma Xi; Soc Syst Biol (pres, 95-96); Soc Europ Herp; fel Linnear Soc, London; Brit Herpetologists Soc; Asn Trop Biol. *Res:* Ecology and evolution of amphibians and reptiles; ecology of midwater fishes; herpetofauna of tropical America; biosystematics frog genus Eleutherodactylus; ecological dynamics and evolution in the tropics; biogeography; evolution of consciousness; tropical biology. *Mailing Add:* Biol Dept Univ Miami PO Box 249118 Coral Gables FL 33124-0421. *Fax:* 305-284-3039

SAVAGE, JIMMIE EUEL, POULTRY NUTRITION. *Current Pos:* from asst prof to assoc prof, Univ Mo, Columbia, 55-64, prof poultry nutrit, 64-90, chmn dept, 66-90, EMER PROF POULTRY NUTRIT, ANIMAL SCI DEPT, UNIV MO, COLUMBIA, 90- *Personal Data:* b Calico Rock, Ark, Feb 15, 20; m 48; c 2. *Educ:* Univ Ark, BSA, 43; Univ Mo, MA, 48, PhD(agr chem), 55. *Prof Exp:* Nutritionist, Farm Bur Mills, Ark, 50-54. *Mem:* AAAS; Am Inst Nutrit; Poultry Sci Asn (pres, 73-74). *Res:* Amino acid; trace mineral and unrecognized vitamin requirements of poultry. *Mailing Add:* 116 Animal Sci Ctr Univ Mo Columbia MO 65211

SAVAGE, JOHN EDMUND, COMPUTER SCIENCE. *Current Pos:* chmn, Dept Comput Sci, 85-91, PROF COMPUT SCI & ENG, BROWN UNIV, 67- *Personal Data:* b Lynn, Mass, Sept 19, 39; m 66, Patricia Landers; c Elizabeth, Keven, Christopher & Timothy. *Educ:* Mass Inst Technol, ScB & ScM, 62, PhD(elec eng), 65. *Prof Exp:* Res asst elec eng, Mass Inst Technol, 62-65; mem tech staff, Bell Tel Labs, NJ, 65-67. *Concurrent Pos:* Consult, Codex Corp, Mass, 67-68, Fed Systs Div, IBM Corp, Md, 68-69, Jet Propulsion Lab, 69-74, Lincoln Lab, Mass Inst Technol, 72, Battelle Inst, 77 & Davis Hoxie, NY, 82-; Guggenheim fel & Fulbright-Hays fel, 73; assoc ed, Inst Elec & Electronics Engrs Trans Comput, 76-78; vis prof comput sci, Univ Paris, 80-81; NSF fel; mem bd dirs, Comput Res Asn, 90-96; vis comt, Dept Elec Eng & Computer Sci, MIT Corp, 91- *Mem:* Fel Inst Elec & Electronics Engrs Comput Soc; fel Asn Comput Mach; Sigma Xi; fel AAAS. *Res:* Applied theory of computation; algorithms and analysis for very large scale integrated systems; computational complexity; high-performance computing; parallel computation; applied theory of computation with particular application to problems in high-performance computing and very large scale integration system. *Mailing Add:* Dept Comput Sci Brown Univ PO Box 1910 Providence RI 02912. *E-Mail:* jes@cs.brown.edu

SAVAGE, JOHN EDWARD, MEDICINE. *Current Pos:* RETIRED. *Personal Data:* b Philadelphia, Pa, June 11, 07; wid; c 2. *Educ:* Univ Md, BS, 28, MD, 32; Am Bd Obstet & Gynec, dipl, 40. *Prof Exp:* Asst clin prof obstet & gynec, Sch Med, Univ Md, 46-61; chief of staff, Greater Baltimore Med Ctr, 65-68, chief obstet, 65-73. *Concurrent Pos:* Lectr, Johns Hopkins Univ, 58-73, emer lectr, 73- *Mem:* Fel Am Gynec & Obstet Soc; fel Am Col Obstet & Gynec; fel Am Col Surgeons. *Mailing Add:* 3100Club Dr No 232 Lawrenceville GA 30244

SAVAGE, MARTHA KANE, SEISMOLOGY, TECTONICS. *Current Pos:* lectr, 95-96, SR LECTR, VICTORIA UNIV, WELLINGTON, 97- *Personal Data:* b Schenectady, NY, June 28, 57; m 82, Michael L; c Patrick E & Kelly R. *Educ:* Swarthmore Col, BA, 79; Univ Wis, MS, 84, PhD(geophys), 87. *Prof Exp:* From res asst prof to res assoc prof, Univ Nev, Reno, 87-94. *Concurrent Pos:* Vis investr, Dept Terrestrial Magnetism, Carnegie Inst Wash, 88-; mem, Data Mgt Comt, Inc Res Inst Seismol, 93-94. *Mem:* Am Geophys Union; Seismol Soc Am; Sigma Xi. *Res:* Seismology and its relation to tectonics and to earthquake hazards. *Mailing Add:* Inst Geophys Box 600 Victoria Univ Wellington New Zealand

SAVAGE, MICHAEL, MECHANICAL ENGINEERING. *Current Pos:* assoc prof, 79-86, PROF MECH ENGR, UNIV AKRON, 86- *Personal Data:* b Yonkers, NY, Sept 6, 41; m 66, Helen M Long; c Maureen J, Deborah A, Daniel S & Tara E. *Educ:* Manhattan Col, BME, 63; Purdue Univ, Lafayette, MSME, 65, PhD(mech eng), 69. *Honors & Awards:* Tech Achievement Award, Cleveland Tech Soc Coun, 77. *Prof Exp:* Consult engr, Res Div, United Shoe Mach Co, Mass, 65-66; asst prof, Wash State Univ, 69-70; asst prof eng, Case Western Res Univ, 70-76; chief engr, Erickson Tool Co, 76-77; assoc prof mech eng, Purdue Univ, Calumet Campus, 77-79. *Mem:* Fel Am Soc Mech Engrs; Am Gear Manufacturers Asn; Sigma Xi. *Res:* Kinematic analysis and synthesis; applications of analysis to the design of machinery; dynamics of machinery; mechanical design; reliability in design; computer assisted design. *Mailing Add:* 2547 Celia Dr Stow OH 44224-1905. *Fax:* 330-972-6027; *E-Mail:* savage@uakron.edu

SAVAGE, NEVIN WILLIAM, mathematics, for more information see previous edition

SAVAGE, NORMAN MICHAEL, PALEONTOLOGY, STRATIGRAPHY. *Current Pos:* assoc prof, Univ Ore, 71-79, head dept, 79-85, pres, Univ Ore Senate, 90-91, PROF GEOL, UNIV ORE, 79- *Personal Data:* b Dover, Eng, Aug 23, 36; m 64, Conolly; c Jane, Wendy & Michael. *Educ:* Bristol Univ, BS, 59; Univ Sydney, PhD(geol), 68. *Prof Exp:* Teaching fel geol, Univ Sydney, 62-66; res fel, Univ Col Swansea, Wales, 66-68; lectr, Univ Natal, 68-71. *Concurrent Pos:* Consult, US Geol Surv, 74-76; Life Mem, Clare Hall, Cambridge, Eng; res assoc, Nat Mus Wales, UK. *Mem:* Fel Geol Soc London; fel Geol Soc Am; Brit Palaeont Asn; Paleont Soc. *Res:* Lower Paleozoic Brachiopods and conodonts. *Mailing Add:* Dept Geol Univ Ore Eugene OR 97403

SAVAGE, PETER, EPIDEMIOLOGY. *Current Pos:* Chief, Clin & Genetic Epidemiol Br, 86-97, DEP DIR, DIV EPIDEM & CLIN APPLN, NAT HEART, LUNG & BLOOD INST, NIH, 97- *Personal Data:* b Gardner, Mass, May 13, 42. *Educ:* Boston Col, BA, 64; Tufts Univ, MD, 68. *Mem:* Am Heart Asn; Am Diabetes Asn. *Mailing Add:* Div Epidemiol & Clin Appln 2 Rockledge Ctr MS 7934 6701 Rockledge Dr Bethesda MD 20892

SAVAGE, PHILLIP E, CHEMICAL KINETICS, REACTION AT SUPERCRITICAL CONDITION. *Current Pos:* asst prof, 86-92, ASSOC PROF CHEM ENG, UNIV MICH, 92- *Personal Data:* b Rochester, Pa, Jan 28, 61; m 83, Elaine Schiever; c Bethany, Stephen & Michael. *Educ:* Pa State Univ, BS, 82; Univ Del, MChE, 85, PhD(chem eng), 86. *Prof Exp:* Indust intern, E I DuPont de Nemours & Co Inc, 82-83. *Concurrent Pos:* Prin investr, NSF, Dept Energy & Environ Protection Agency, 87- *Mem:* Am Inst Chem Eng; Am Chem Soc; Am Soc Eng Educrs. *Res:* Reaction pathways, kinetics and mechanisms with focus on thermal and oxidative degradation reactions; free-radical reactions; reactions in supercritical fluids. *Mailing Add:* Chem Eng Dept Univ Mich Ann Arbor MI 48109-2136. *E-Mail:* psavage@umich.edu

SAVAGE, ROBERT E, CELL BIOLOGY. *Current Pos:* from asst prof to assoc prof, 71-76, chmn dept, 76-81, PROF BIOL, SWARTHMORE COL, 76-, ISAAC H CLOTHIER JR PROF BIOL, 83- *Personal Data:* b Middlebury, Vt, Dec 8, 32; m 64, Gisela C Bergau; c Anna M (Kruse) & Eric E. *Educ:* Oberlin Col, BA, 54; Univ Wis, MS, 58, PhD(bot), 63. *Prof Exp:* Lectr biol, Queens Col, NY, 62-63, from instr to asst prof, 63-67. *Concurrent Pos:* Vis researcher, Dept Med Cell Genetics, Karolinska Inst, Sweden, 70-71, 74, 86 & Inst Physiol Bot, Univ Uppsala, Sweden, 79, Bot Dept, Univ Mass, 90. *Mem:* AAAS; Am Soc Cell Biol; Tissue Cult Asn; Sigma Xi. *Res:* Chromosomal chemistry and structure; somatic cell hybridization; nucleolar proteins; auxin receptors. *Mailing Add:* 411 Vasar Ave Swarthmore PA 19081. *Fax:* 610-328-8663; *E-Mail:* rsavage1@cc.swarthmore.edu

SAVAGE, STEVEN PAUL, PHYSICAL ANTHROPOLOGY. *Current Pos:* Asst prof, 75-81, ASSOC PROF ANTHROP, EASTERN KY UNIV, 81-, DEPT CHMN, 87- *Personal Data:* b Topeka, Kans, Apr 8, 50; m 71, Ballou Waldron; c Eric, Mark & Scott. *Educ:* Univ Kans, BA, 71; Univ Colo, MA, 73, PhD(anthrop), 78. *Prof Exp:* Proj dir, NSF grant, 78-81. *Mem:* Am Asn Phys Anthropologists; Paleopath Asn. *Res:* Photobiology; growth; osteology. *Mailing Add:* Dept Anthrop Sociol & Social Work Eastern Ky Univ Richmond KY 40475. *E-Mail:* antsavag@acs.eku.edu

SAVAGE, STUART B, APPLIED MECHANICS, FLUID MECHANICS. *Current Pos:* lectr civil eng, 64-67, from asst prof to assoc prof, 67-77, PROF CIVIL ENG, MCGILL UNIV, 77- *Personal Data:* b Far Rockaway, NY, Oct 18, 32; m 68. *Educ:* McGill Univ, BEng, 60, PhD(eng mech), 67; Calif Inst Technol, MSc, 61, AeroE, 62. *Prof Exp:* Prin aerodyn engr, Appl Res & Develop Lab, Repub Aviation Corp, NY, 62-64. *Concurrent Pos:* Acad visitor, Imp Col, Univ London, 71-72 & Cambridge Univ, 77-80. *Mem:* Am Soc Civil Engrs; Am Soc Mech Engrs; Am Acad Mech; Int Asn Hydraul Res; Sigma Xi. *Res:* Storage and flow of bulk solids; pneumatic transport; incompressible fluid mechanics. *Mailing Add:* Dept Civil Eng McGill Univ Sherbrooke St W Montreal PQ H3A 2M5 Can

SAVAGE, WILLIAM F(REDERICK), NUCLEAR ENGINEERING, MECHANICAL ENGINEERING. *Current Pos:* RETIRED. *Personal Data:* b Anchorage, Alaska, May 23, 23; m 49; c 2. *Educ:* Rensselaer Polytech Inst, BAeroE, 43; Purdue Univ, MAeroE, 49. *Prof Exp:* Aerodynamicist, Consol Aircraft Co, Tex, 44-46; instr mech & aeronaut eng, Univ Ky, 46-48, assoc prof, 49-52; chief engr, Kett Corp, 53-55; prin engr, Aircraft Nuclear Propulsion Dept, Gen Elec Co, 55-58, supvr preliminary design, 58, mgr applns tech anal, 59-60; dir nuclear prod area, Adv Progs, Martin Co, 61-64, mgr resources planning, 65-67; asst dir eng & develop, Off Saline Water, US Dept Interior, 67-74, chief advan systs eval, 74-81; dir utility coordr, US Dept Energy, 81-85, dep dir, Nuclear Plant Performance, 85-90. *Mem:* Am Nuclear Soc. *Res:* Advanced nuclear systems technology, power plant technology, desalting technology. *Mailing Add:* Rte 1 Box 546 Jonesville VA 24263

SAVAGE, WILLIAM ZUGER, ROCK MECHANICS, GEOMECHANICS. *Current Pos:* GEOLOGIST, US GEOL SURV, DENVER, COLO, 75- *Personal Data:* b Duluth, Minn, June 20, 42; m 68; c 2. *Educ:* Lawrence Univ, BA, 65; Syracuse Univ, MS, 68; Tex A&M Univ, PhD(geol), 74. *Prof Exp:* Staff scientist, Systs, Sci & Software, La Jolla, Calif, 72-75. *Concurrent Pos:* Prin investr, Landslide Dynamics & Kinematics Proj, US Geol Surv, Denver, Colo, 83-; adj assoc prof, Dept Civil, Archit & Environ Eng, Sec & Third Summer Schs Hydrogeol Hazards Studies, Univ Perugia, Italy, 88-, adj vis prof, 89-90 & 92; supvry geologist, US Geol Surv, Denver, Colo, 88-90. *Mem:* Am Geophys Union; Int Soc Rock Mech; Int Asn Eng Geologists; Am Acad Mech. *Res:* Development and application of continuum mechanics concepts and methods to model deformation and flow of surficial geologic materials and the distribution of near-surface in-situ stresses associated with these processes. *Mailing Add:* US Geol Surv MS 966 Denver Fed Ctr Box 25046 Denver CO 80225

SAVAGEAU, MICHAEL ANTONIO, BIOCHEMICAL NETWORKS, GENE CIRCUITS & NONLINEAR SYSTEMS ANALYSIS. *Current Pos:* from asst prof to assoc prof, Univ Mich, 70-78, actg chmn, 79-80, interim chmn, 82-85, dir, Cellular Biotechnol Lab, 88-91, PROF MICROBIOL, UNIV MICH, ANN ARBOR, 78-, CHAIR, 93- *Personal Data:* b Fargo, NDak, Dec 3, 40; m 67, Ann E Birky; c Mark E, Patrick D & Elisa M. *Educ:* Univ Minn, BS, 62; Univ Iowa, MS, 63; Stanford Univ, PhD(cell physiol, syst sci), 67. *Prof Exp:* Res asst, Stanford Univ, 63-64, lectr, 69-70. *Concurrent Pos:* NIH fel, Stanford Univ, 64-67, 68-70, Univ Calif, Los Angeles, 67-68; prin investr, NSF & NIH grants, Univ Mich, Ann Arbor, 71-; Guggenheim fel & Fulbright sr res fel, Max Planck Inst Biophys Chem, Gottingen, Ger, 76-77; consult, Upjohn, 80-81, Off Technol Assessments, 82-83, & Synergen, 85-87; NIH, Spec Study Sect Biochem Modelling, 81-82; vis scientist & fel, Commonwealth Sci & Indust Res Org, Div Comput Res, John Curtin Sch Med Res, Australian Nat Univ, Canberra, 83-84; bd dirs, Soc Math Biol, 86-90; lectr, Am Soc Microbiol, 93-95; vis prof, Univ Ariz, 94; NIH Consult, 95. *Mem:* AAAS; Am Soc Microbiol; Inst Elec & Electronics Engrs; Soc Math Biol; NY Acad Sci; Soc Gen Physiologists. *Res:* Development of a general-purpose nonlinear system theory, including optimal strategies for nonlinear modeling and computer analysis of organizationally complex systems; application of such methods to understand function, design and evolution of integrated biological networks in terms of their underlying molecular determinants. *Mailing Add:* 900 Lincoln Ann Arbor MI 48104. *Fax:* 313-763-7163; *E-Mail:* savageau@umich.edu

SAVAIANO, DENNIS ALAN, INTESTINAL METABOLISM OF NUTRIENTS. *Current Pos:* Asst prof, 80-86, ASSOC PROF NUTRIT, UNIV MINN, 86- *Personal Data:* b Pomona, Calif, Dec 28, 53; m 75; c 2. *Educ:* Claremont McKenna Col, BA, 75; Univ Calif, Davis, MS, 77, PhD(nutrit), 80. *Mem:* Am Inst Nutrit; Inst Food Technol. *Res:* Intestinal purine metabolism; lactose digestion and tolerance; intestinal carnitine metabolism. *Mailing Add:* Sch Consumer & Family Sci Purdue Univ 1260 Stone Hall Rm 110 West Lafayette IN 47907-1260. *Fax:* 612-625-5767; *E-Mail:* saviano@mailche.umn.edu

SAVARD, GS, EARTH SCIENCES. *Honors & Awards:* Falconbridge Innovation Award, Can Mining & Metall, 92. *Mailing Add:* Xerox Tower Suite 1210 3400 de Maisonneuve Blvd W Montreal PQ H3Z 3B8 Can

SAVARD, JEAN YVES, SOLID STATE PHYSICS. *Current Pos:* Asst prof elec eng, 61-67, ASSOC PROF ELEC ENG, LAVAL UNIV, 67- *Personal Data:* b Quebec, Que, Jan 25, 35; m 58; c 2. *Educ:* Laval Univ, BASc, 57; Univ London, PhD(microwaves), 61. *Mem:* Am Phys Soc. *Res:* Paramagnetic resonance in solids. *Mailing Add:* Dept Elec Eng Laval Univ Quebec PQ G1K 7P4 Can

SAVAS, OMER, FLUID DYNAMICS. *Current Pos:* ASSOC PROF, DEPT MECH ENG, UNIV CALIF, BERKELEY, 91- *Personal Data:* b Turkey, Oct 30, 52. *Educ:* Turkey Univ, BS, 74; Calif Inst Technol, MS, 75, PhD(aeronaut), 79. *Mem:* Am Phys Soc. *Res:* Fluid dynamics. *Mailing Add:* 215 Cambridge Ave Berkeley CA 94708

SAVEDOFF, LYDIA GOODMAN, CHEMISTRY. *Current Pos:* from asst prof to assoc prof, 60-67, PROF CHEM, CALIF STATE UNIV, NORTHRIDGE, 67- *Personal Data:* b New York, NY, Dec 23, 20. *Educ:* Hunter Col, BA, 41; Columbia Univ, MA, 44, PhD(chem), 47. *Prof Exp:* Technician, Manhattan Proj, SAM Labs, Columbia Univ, 42-43, asst univ, 43-47; assoc supvr, Ohio State Univ, 47-49; res assoc, Sch Med, Univ Wash, 49-52; instr chem, Gonzaga Univ, 52-54, asst prof, 54-59; NSF fac fel, Univ Calif, Los Angeles, 59-60. *Mem:* AAAS; Am Chem Soc; Am Phys Soc; Sigma Xi. *Res:* Physical properties and conductance of electrolyte and polyelectrolyte solutions. *Mailing Add:* 3249 A San Amadeo Laguna Hills CA 92653-3035

SAVEDOFF, MALCOLM PAUL, ASTROPHYSICS. *Current Pos:* res assoc & asst prof physics, Univ Rochester, 53-56, asst prof optics, 56-59, Sloan Found res fel, 56-60, from asst prof to assoc prof physics & astron, 57-64, prof astron, 64-91, EMER PROF ASTRON, UNIV ROCHESTER, 91- *Personal Data:* b New York, NY, July 4, 28; m 48, Roberta Lazoff; c Allen M, Barbara E & William D. *Educ:* Harvard Univ, AB, 48; Princeton Univ, MA, 50, PhD(astron), 51. *Prof Exp:* Nat Res Coun fel, Mt Wilson & Palomar Observs, Calif Inst Technol, 51-52; NSF fel, Leiden Observ, 52-53. *Concurrent Pos:* Dir, C E Kenneth Mees Observ, 64; NSF fel, Univ Leiden, 64-65; Nat Res Coun sr assoc, Goddard Space Flight Ctr, NASA, 79-80. *Mem:* Sigma Xi; Am Phys Soc; Am Astron Soc; Int Astron Union. *Res:* Interstellar material; stellar interiors. *Mailing Add:* 10 Cranston Rd Pittsford NY 14534-2944. *E-Mail:* mpsa@pas.rochester.edu

SAVEREIDE, THOMAS J, INDUSTRIAL ORGANIC CHEMISTRY. *Current Pos:* Sr res chemist, St Paul, Minn, 61-64, supvr org res, 64-69, tech mgr chem div, 69-73, tech dir, Chem Resources Div, 73-80, TECH DIR, SUMITOMO DIV 3M CO, TOKYO, JAPAN, 81- *Personal Data:* b Rockford, Ill, Nov 18, 32; m 57; c 3. *Educ:* St Olaf Col, BA, 57; Northwestern Univ, PhD(org chem), 61. *Mem:* Am Chem Soc. *Res:* Organic synthesis; polymer chemistry. *Mailing Add:* 211 Eastbank Ct N Hudson WI 54016-1084

SAVERY, CLYDE WILLIAM, ENERGY CONVERSION, TECHNOLOGY TRANSFER. *Current Pos:* chair mech eng, 80-89, vprovost grad studies & res, 89-92, PROF MECH ENG, PORTLAND STATE UNIV, 92-, TECHNOL TRANSFER OFFICER, 92- *Personal Data:* b White Plains, NY, Jan 3, 35; m 58, Meredith Gore; c Caitlin (Szieff) & Benjamin D. *Educ:* Univ Ill, Urbana, BS, 57; Univ Wash, MS, 60; Univ Wis-Madison, PhD(mech eng), 69. *Honors & Awards:* Ralph Teetor Award, Soc Automotive Engrs, 71. *Prof Exp:* Res & develop assoc, Gen Atomic Div, Gen Dynamics, 60-66; from asst prof to prof mech eng, Drexel Univ, 69-80. *Concurrent Pos:* Consult, Choice Mag, 69- & Gilbert Assoc, Inc, 72-77; res grants, NSF, US Dept Energy, HUD & Elec Power Res Inst, 73-; Fulbright sr res fel, Univ Maribor, Slovenia, 88; vis fel, Battelle Pac Northwest Lab, 92. *Mem:* Soc Automotive Engrs; Am Soc Mech Engrs; Am Soc Heating, Refrig, Air Conditioning Engrs; Asn Univ Technol Mgrs. *Res:* Heat and mass transfer with applications to vaporization, combustion, environmental remediation; control engineering with applications to energy conservation. *Mailing Add:* Mech Eng Portland State Univ PO Box 751 Portland OR 97207-0751. *Fax:* 503-725-4298; *E-Mail:* savery@eas.pdx.edu

SAVERY, HARRY P, PHYSIOLOGY, ENDOCRINOLOGY. *Current Pos:* RETIRED. *Personal Data:* b Coffeyville, Kans, Jan 4, 20; m 50; c 4. *Educ:* Colo Agr & Mech Col, BS, 49; Univ Wyo, MS, 50; Tex A&M Univ, PhD(reproduction physiol), 54. *Prof Exp:* from assoc prof to prof biol, Cent Mo State Univ, 60-87, head dept, 71-87. *Mem:* AAAS; Am Soc Animal Sci; Am Soc Zoologists; Am Inst Biol Sci. *Res:* Cytological studies of normal and superovulated ova. *Mailing Add:* 261 SE 101st Rd Warrensburg MO 64093

SAVIC, MICHAEL I, AUTOMATIC SPEAKER RECOGNITION & SIGNAL RECOGNITION, DIGITAL SIGNAL & SPEECH PROCESSING. *Current Pos:* assoc prof, 82-91, PROF ELEC ENG, RENSSELAER POLYTECH INST, TROY, NY, 91- *Personal Data:* b Belgrade, Yugoslavia, Aug 4, 29; US citizen; m 61; c Alice. *Educ:* Univ Belgrade, dipl ing, 55, Dr Eng Sc, 65. *Honors & Awards:* Cert Appreciation, Inst Elec & Electronics Engrs, 72. *Prof Exp:* Res & develop engr indust electronics, Kretztech Zipf, Austria, 56; res engr vacuum tubes, Tungsram Vienna, Austria, 57-58; asst prof elec eng, Univ Belgrade, 59-67; researcher ultrasound, Yale Univ, New Haven, Conn, 67-78; prof elec eng, Western New Eng Col, Springfield, Mass, 68-82. *Concurrent Pos:* Prin investr, NSF grant, 75-76 & Comput Controlled Cryosurg, Zacarian Res Found, 78-80; chmn, Elec Eng Dept, Western New Eng Col, 77-82; vis prof elec eng, Rensselaer Polytech Inst, Troy, NY, 80, 81 & 82, prin investr, Signal Recognition, 84-, Speaker Verification, 85-, Speech Recognition, 88-, Voice Character Transformation, 89- & Lang Identification, 89-, Pipeline Leak Detection, 90-, speaker separation, 92- & detection of accumulations of cholesterol in bloodvessels, 93- *Mem:* Sr mem Inst Elec & Electronics Engrs; Int Asn Sci & Technol Develop. *Res:* Digital signal processing algorithms; hardware and software; speaker verification; signal identification; speech recognition; language identification; pipeline leak detection; voice character transformation; granted five patents. *Mailing Add:* Elec Comput & Syst Eng Dept Rensselaer Polytech Inst Troy NY 12180-3590. *Fax:* 518-276-6261; *E-Mail:* savic@ecse.rpi.edu

SAVIC, STANLEY D, PRODUCT SAFETY, ACCIDENT INVESTIGATIONS. *Current Pos:* Res scientist, Univ Chicago, 64-72, mgr, 72-78, DIR, ZENITH ELECTRONICS, 78- *Personal Data:* b Belgrade, Yugoslavia, Dec 30, 38; US citizen. *Educ:* Roosevelt Univ, BS, 62; Univ Ill, MS, 69. *Honors & Awards:* Distinguished Contrib Award, Electronics Industs Asn, 87. *Concurrent Pos:* Consult, Univ Chicago, 65-78 & pvt, 78- *Mem:* NY Acad Sci; sr mem Inst Elec & Electronics Engrs; Nat Fire Protection Asn; Am Soc Testing & Mat; Am Asn Physicists Med; Health Physics Soc. *Res:* Medical physics radiation treatment planning research using computer simulations; electronic product safety research and cataode ray tube x-radiation and phospitor research. *Mailing Add:* Zenith Radio Corp 1000 Milwaukee Ave Glenview IL 60025

SAVICKAS, DAVID FRANCIS, THEORETICAL PHYSICS. *Current Pos:* ASSOC PROF PHYSICS, WESTERN NEW ENG COL, 69- *Personal Data:* b Chicago, Ill, Nov 9, 40. *Educ:* St Mary's Col, BA, 62; Mich State Univ, MS, 64, PhD(physics), 66. *Prof Exp:* Asst prof, Bucknell Univ, 66-69. *Mem:* Am Phys Soc. *Res:* Relativity theory; astrophysical kinematics. *Mailing Add:* Dept Physics Western New Eng Col 1215 Wilbraham Rd Springfield MA 01119

SAVIDGE, JEFFREY LEE, THERMODYNAMICS & MATERIAL PROPERTIES. *Current Pos:* res engr, 86-87, PROG MGR THERMODYN, GAS RES INST, 87- *Personal Data:* b Omaha, Neb, Dec 27, 52; m 78; c 1. *Educ:* Okla City Univ, BS, 77; Univ Okla, MS, 83, PhD(chem engr), 86. *Prof Exp:* Lab chemist, Okla Med Res Found, 78-80; res assoc, Univ Okla, 85-86, vis assoc prof chem engr, 86. *Mem:* Am Inst Chem Engrs; Sigma Xi. *Res:* High accuracy thermodynamic properties of natural gas and related fluids. *Mailing Add:* 11 Haverford Ct Algonquin IL 60102

SAVILE, DOUGLAS BARTON OSBORNE, BOTANY. *Current Pos:* Agr asst, Agr Can, 36-39, agr scientist, 39-53, sr mycologist, 53-57, prin mycologist, 57-74, EMER RES ASSOC, BIOSYST RES INST, AGR CAN, OTTAWA, 74- *Personal Data:* b Dublin, Ireland, July 19, 09; m 39; c 2. *Educ:* McGill Univ, BSA, 33, MSc, 34; Univ Mich, PhD(bot), 39. *Hon Degrees:* DSc, McGill Univ, 78. *Honors & Awards:* Lawson Medal, Can Bot Asn, 76. *Mem:* AAAS; Mycol Soc Am; Am Soc Plant Taxon; fel Arctic Inst NAm; fel Royal Soc Can. *Res:* Mycology; taxonomy of parasitic fungi; biology of rusts; co-evolution of rusts and host plants; arctic biology; avian aerodynamics. *Mailing Add:* 357 Hinton S Ottawa ON K1Y 1A6 Can

SAVILLE, D(UDLEY) A(LBERT), CHEMICAL ENGINEERING, FLUID MECHANICS. *Current Pos:* from asst prof to assoc prof, 68-71, PROF CHEM ENG, PRINCETON UNIV, 77- *Personal Data:* b Lincoln, Nebr, Feb 25, 33; m 59; c 2. *Educ:* Univ Nebr, Lincoln, BS, 54, MS, 59; Univ Mich, Ann Arbor, PhD(chem eng), 66. *Prof Exp:* Engr chem eng, Union Carbide Corp, 54-55; res engr, Calif Res Corp, 59-61 & Shell Develop Co, 66-68. *Mem:* Am Inst Chem Engrs; Am Chem Soc; Am Phys Soc. *Res:* Colloid science; electrokinetics and other colloidal phenomena; hydrodynamic stability; electrohydrodynamics; heat and mass transfer in particulate suspensions; crystal growth. *Mailing Add:* 244 Dodds Lane Princeton NJ 08540

SAVILLE, THORNDIKE, JR, CIVIL & COASTAL ENGINEERING. *Current Pos:* hydraul engr, Beach Erosion Bd & Coastal Eng Res Ctr, Corps Engrs, 49-81, asst chief res div, 53-64, chief gen proj br, 54-64, chief res div, 64-71, tech dir, 71-81, CONSULT, COASTAL ENG & COASTAL RES APPLICATIONS, 81- *Personal Data:* b Baltimore, Md, Aug 1, 25; m 50, Janet Foster; c 3. *Educ:* Harvard Univ, AB, 47; Univ Calif, MS, 49. *Honors & Awards:* Huber Res Award, Am Soc Civil Engrs, 63, Moffatt-Nichol, Award, 79, Int Coastal Eng Award, 91. *Prof Exp:* Res asst, Univ Calif, 47-49. *Concurrent Pos:* Mem, Coun Wave Res, Eng Found, 54-64; mem, Permanent Int Asn Navig Cong, 56-, secy, US Deleg, Sect II, London, 57 & Baltimore, Md, 61, liaison officer, Int Comn Force of Waves & chmn, Am Sect Subcomt, 64-72; mem adv bd, Nat Oceanog Data Ctr, 64-72, chmn, 68; mem, Comt Tidal Hydraul, US Army CEngrs, 64-81; gen chmn, Specialty Conf Coastal Eng, Santa Barbara, 65 & Washington, DC, 71; liaison rep, Panel Coastal Eng & Inland Waters, Comt Earthquake Eng Res, Nat Acad Eng, 66-70, Marine Bd, 79-81; mem coun, AAAS, 71-77; US mem, Permanent Int Comn, Pianc, 71-78; adv ed, Coastal Eng, 71-94; dir, Am Shore Beach Preserv Asn, 76-, vpres, 88-96; mem, Tech Coun Res, Am Soc Civil Engrs, 83-88, chmn, 85-87; US rep, PTC II (Ocean Navig) Permanent Int Asn Navig Cong, 91- *Mem:* Nat Acad Eng; fel AAAS; fel Am Soc Civil Engrs; Am Geophys Union; Am Shore & Beach Preserv Asn; hon mem Int Asn Navig Cong. *Res:* Basic laws governing wave and surge action on beaches and shore structures and application of these to engineering design; coastal erosion processes and littoral tranpost; hydraulic model studies; over 75 articles in engineering and scientific publications. *Mailing Add:* 5601 Albia Rd Bethesda MD 20816-3304

SAVIN, SAMUEL MARVIN, GEOCHEMISTRY, GEOLOGY. *Current Pos:* From asst prof to assoc prof, 67-76, chmn dept, 77-82, PROF GEOL SCI, CASE WESTERN RES UNIV, 76-, ASSOC DEAN ARTS & SCI, 93- *Personal Data:* b Boston, Mass, Aug 31, 40; m 78, Norma Gouldes; c 2. *Educ:* Colgate Univ, BA, 61; Calif Inst Technol, PhD(geochem), 67. *Concurrent Pos:* Assoc ed, Geuchimica et Cosmochimica Acta, 76-79; mem, Earth Sci Adv Panel, NSF, 78-81; ed, Marine Micropaleont, 79-87, Paleogeog Paleoclimatol Paleoecol, 87- *Mem:* Fel Geol Soc Am; Geochem Soc; fel AAAS; Am Geophys Union; Clay Minerals Soc; Am Asn Petrol Geologists. *Res:* Stable isotope geochemistry; low temperature geochemistry; shore erosion; stable isotopes in medicine; paleoceanography. *Mailing Add:* 2236 Demington Dr Cleveland Heights OH 44106

SAVINELLI, EMILIO A, CHEMISTRY. *Current Pos:* res dir, 60-62, div mgr, 62-68, dir mkt, 64-68, vpres, 68-71, PRES, DREW CHEM CORP, 71- *Personal Data:* b New York, NY, May 7, 30; c 8. *Educ:* Manhattan Col, BCE, 50; Univ Fla, MSE, 51, PhD(chem), 55. *Prof Exp:* Engr, Du Pont Co, 56-60. *Mem:* Nat Acad Sci; Am Chem Soc; Am Soc Mech Engrs. *Mailing Add:* 34 Molbrook Dr Wilton CT 06897

SAVIT, CARL HERTZ, geophysics, reflection seismology; deceased, see previous edition for last biography

SAVIT, JOSEPH, REPROGRAPHY, INFORMOGRAPHY. *Current Pos:* PRES, SAVIT ENTERPRISES, INC, 73- *Personal Data:* b Chicago, Ill, Oct 23, 21; m 42; c 4. *Educ:* Univ Chicago, BS, 42. *Prof Exp:* Res assoc gas warfare, Univ Chicago, 42-46; pres & mgr, Travelers Hotel Co, Calif, 47-51; plant chemist, Reproduction Prod Co, 52-53; staff chemist, A B Dick & Co, 53-56; chief chemist, Huey Co, 56-57; mgr res & develop, Eugene Dietzgen Co, 58-63 & Colonial Carbon Co, 63-64; mgr, Microstatics Div, SCM Corp, 64-66; dir res & asst vpres, Apeco Corp, 66-73. *Mem:* Tech Asn Pulp & Paper Indust; Am Chem Soc; Soc Photog Sci & Eng; fel Am Inst Chem. *Res:* Reprography, especially electrography and electrophotography; office print out; non-impact computer print-out systems; paper and film coatings; offset printing systems; ink-jet printing systems. *Mailing Add:* 751 Vernon Ave Glencoe IL 60022-1562

SAVIT, ROBERT STEVEN, DYNAMICAL SYSTEMS, ECONOMICS & FINANCE. *Current Pos:* assoc res scientist & lectr, 78-83, assoc prof, 83-89, PROF PHYSICS DEPT, UNIV MICH, 90-, DIR, PROG STUDY COMPLEX SYSTS, 94- *Personal Data:* b Chicago, Ill, Aug 21, 47. *Educ:* Univ Chicago, BA, 69; Stanford Univ, MS, 70, PhD(physics), 73. *Prof Exp:* Res assoc theoret physics, Stanford Linear Accelerator Ctr, 73; vis scientist, Europ Orgn Nuclear Res, 74-75; res assoc theoret physics, Fermi Nat Accelerator Lab, 73-74; physicist, 75-78. *Concurrent Pos:* NATO fel, NSF, 74-75; grant recipient, Am-Swiss Found Sci Exchange, 74-75; assoc ed, Nuclear Phys Field Theory & Statist Systs, 80-; res fel, Sloan Found, 81-83, Columbia Futures Ctr, 88-89; vis scientist, Inst Theoret Physics, Santa Barbara, 81-82; vis prof, Hebrew Univ Jerusalem, Weizmann Inst Sci, 86-87. *Res:* Field theory; critical phenomena; statistical mechanics; equilibrium and non-equilibrium growth; dynamical systems; chaos; finance and economics; time series analysis; applied mathematics and statistics; dynamics of biological systems. *Mailing Add:* Physics Dept Univ Mich Ann Arbor MI 48109. *E-Mail:* savit@umich.edu

SAVITCH, WALTER JOHN, COMPUTER SCIENCE, MATHEMATICS. *Current Pos:* Assoc prof info & comput sci, 69-80, PROF ELEC ENG & COMPUT SCI, UNIV CALIF, SAN DIEGO, 80- *Personal Data:* b Brooklyn, NY, Feb 21, 43. *Educ:* Univ NH, BS, 64; Univ Calif, Berkeley, MA & PhD(math), 69. *Concurrent Pos:* NSF res grant, 70-76. *Mem:* Am Math Soc; Asn Comput Mach; Asn Symbolic Logic; Soc Indust & Appl Math. *Res:* Theoretical computer science; complexity of algorithms; formal languages; automata theory; mathematical logic. *Mailing Add:* Comput Sci Eng 0114 Univ Calif San Diego 9500 Gilman Dr La Jolla CA 92093-0114

SAVITSKY, DANIEL, NAVAL ARCHITECTURE. *Current Pos:* dir, Davidson Lab, 47-89, prof, 67-89, EMER PROF OCEAN ENG, 89- *Personal Data:* b New York, NY, Sept 26, 21; m 62, Mary Wysocki; c Jean, James & Anne. *Educ:* City Col New York, BCE, 42; Stevens Inst Technol, MSc, 52; NY Univ, PhD, 71. *Honors & Awards:* Adm Cochrane Award, Soc Naval Archit & Marine Eng, 67, Davidson Medal, 96. *Prof Exp:* Struct engr, Edo Corp, 42-44; aeronaut res scientist, Nat Adv Comt Aeronaut, 44-47. *Concurrent Pos:* Ottens res award, Stevens Inst Technol, 68; consult, indust & USN; consult, Naval Studies Bd, Nat Res Coun; T&R Comt, Soc Naval Architects & Marine Engr, 85- *Mem:* Soc Naval Archit & Marine Eng; Am Soc Naval Eng; Sigma Xi. *Res:* Hydrodynamics; ocean science and engineering. *Mailing Add:* 597 Delcina Dr River Vale NJ 07675

SAVITSKY, GEORGE BORIS, PHYSICAL CHEMISTRY. *Current Pos:* from assoc prof to prof, 65-90, EMER PROF CHEM, CLEMSON UNIV, 90- *Personal Data:* b Harbin, China, Mar 10, 25; nat US; m 48; c 3. *Educ:* Aurora Univ, China, BS, 47; Univ Fla, PhD(chem), 59. *Prof Exp:* Res assoc chem, Princeton Univ, 59-61; asst prof, Univ Calif, Davis, 61-65. *Mem:* AAAS; fel Am Inst Chem; Am Chem Soc; Sigma Xi. *Res:* Spectroscopy; nuclear magnetic resonance spectroscopy. *Mailing Add:* 204 Brook St Clemson SC 29631

SAVITZ, DAVID ALAN, ENVIRONMENTAL EPIDEMIOLOGY, REPRODUCTIVE EPIDEMIOLOGY. *Current Pos:* asst prof, 85-88, ASSOC PROF EPIDEMIOL, SCH PUB HEALTH, UNIV NC, 88- *Personal Data:* b Hamilton, Ohio, Mar 14, 54; m 83; c 2. *Educ:* Brandeis Univ, BA, 75; Ohio State Univ, MS, 78; Univ Pittsburgh, PhD(epidemiol), 82. *Prof Exp:* Researcher epidemiol, Battelle Mem Inst, 76-79; asst prof prev med, Sch Med, Univ Colo, 81-85. *Mem:* Soc Epidemiol Res (secy & treas, 87-91); Am Pub Health Asn; Int Epidemiol Asn. *Res:* Occupational and environmental exposures in relation to reproductive health outcomes and cancer; epidemiologic methods. *Mailing Add:* Dept Epidemiol Univ NC Chapel Hill NC 27599-7400

SAVITZ, JAN, LIMNOLOGY. *Current Pos:* asst prof, 69-74, ASSOC PROF BIOL, LOYOLA UNIV CHICAGO, 74- *Personal Data:* b Sellersville, Pa, Apr 8, 41; m 68. *Educ:* Pa State Univ, BS, 63; Ind Univ, PhD(limnol), 67. *Honors & Awards:* Mary Ashby Cheek Award, 68. *Prof Exp:* Asst prof biol, Rockford Col, 67-69. *Mem:* AAAS; Am Fisheries Soc; Am Inst Biol Sci; Am Soc Limnol & Oceanog; Ecol Soc Am. *Res:* Protein metabolism of fish; fish predation on benthic organisms. *Mailing Add:* Dept Biol Loyola Univ Lake Shore Campus 6525 N Sheridan Rd Chicago IL 60626-5311

SAVITZ, MAXINE LAZARUS, ORGANIC CHEMISTRY, ELECTROCHEMISTRY. *Current Pos:* asst vpres eng, 85-87, GEN MGR, ALLIED-SIGNAL CERAMIC CORP, 87- *Personal Data:* b Baltimore, Md, Feb 13, 37; m 61, S Alan; c Adam & Alison. *Educ:* Bryn Mawr Col, AB, 58; Mass Inst Technol, PhD(org chem), 61. *Prof Exp:* NSF fel, Univ Calif, Berkeley, 61-62; instr chem, Hunter Col, 62-63; res chemist, Elec Power Div, US Army Eng Res & Develop Lab, Ft Belvoir, 63-68; assoc prof chem, Fed City Col, 68-71, prof, 71-72; prof mgr, Res Appl Nat Needs, NSF, 72-73; chief bldgs conserv policy res, Fed Energy Admin, 73-75; div dir bldgs & indust conserv, Dept Energy, Energy Res & Develop Admin, 75-76; div dir bldgs & community systs, 76-79, dep asst secy conserv, 79-83; pres, Lighting Res Inst, 83-85. *Concurrent Pos:* Mem, Energy & Eng Bd, Nat Acad Eng, 86-92; mem, Off Technol Assessment, Demand Bd, 87-89, Nat Mat Adv Bd Nat Res Coun, 89-94, pres, US Advan Ceramic Asn, 91; secy, Energy Adv Bd, 92-; sci bd, Dept Defense, 93-96; vis comt, Advand Technol, 93- *Mem:* Nat Acad Eng; AAAS; Am Ceramic Soc. *Res:* Free radical mechanisms; fuel cells; more efficient use of energy in buildings; community systems; appliances; agriculture and industrial processes; transportation; batteries and other storage systems; new materials; advanced structural ceramic materials and components. *Mailing Add:* 10350 Wilshire Blvd Los Angeles CA 90024. *Fax:* 310-512-5901; *E-Mail:* maxine.savitz@alliedsignal.com

SAVITZKY, ABRAHAM, ANALYTICAL CHEMISTRY, COMPUTER SCIENCE. *Current Pos:* PRES, SILVERMINE RESOURCES INC, 85- *Personal Data:* b New York, NY, May 29, 19; m 42 Evelyn R; c Stephen R & Alan H. *Educ:* State Univ NY, BA, 41; Columbia Univ, MA, 47, PhD(phys chem), 49. *Honors & Awards:* Williams-Wright Award, Coblentz Soc, 86. *Prof Exp:* Res assoc electron micros, Columbia Univ, 49-50; staff scientist, Perkin-Elmer Corp, 50-71, sr staff scientist, Corp Comput Facil, 71-79, prin scientist, Instrument Group, 80-85. *Concurrent Pos:* Mem, Nat Acad Sci-Nat Res Coun Eval Panel Atomic & Molecular Physics, Nat Bur Stand, 70-72; dir, Time Share Peripherals Corp, 70-77; Sci Apparatus Makers Asn rep, Am Nat Stand Comt X-3 Comput & Data Processing, 72-80. *Mem:* Am Chem Soc; Am Phys Soc; Optical Soc Am; hon mem Soc Appl Spectros; Asn Comput Mach. *Res:* Development of laboratory and process analytical instrumentation; infrared spectroscopy; computer aided experimentation and data reduction; time sharing systems and languages; computer plotting; user interfacing; personal computers. *Mailing Add:* 3 Mail Coach Ct Wilton CT 06897. *Fax:* 203-762-8146; *E-Mail:* savitzkya@acm.org

SAVITZKY, ALAN HOWARD, HERPETOLOGY. *Current Pos:* AT BIOL SCI DEPT, OLD DOMINION UNIV, NORFOLK. *Personal Data:* b Danbury, Conn, June 23, 50; m 72; c 2. *Educ:* Univ Colo, BA, 72; Univ Kans, MA, 74, PhD(biol), 79. *Prof Exp:* Fel, Nat Mus Natural Hist, Smithsonian Inst, 76-78; mem staff, Sect Ecol & Systemetics, Cornell Univ, 78- *Mem:* Am Soc Ichthyologists & Herpetologists; Am Soc Zoologists; Herpetologists League; Soc Study Amphibians & Reptiles; Soc Syst Zool; Sigma Xi. *Res:* Relationship between phylogeny and adaptation, especially among snakes; morphological correlates of specialized feeding habits; parallel evolution of complex adaptations. *Mailing Add:* Biol Sci Dept Old Dominion Univ Norfolk VA 23529-0266

SAVKAR, SUDHIR DATTATRAYA, FLUID MECHANICS, ACOUSTICS. *Current Pos:* Res engr, 66-78, mgr eng mech, 78-83, MGR FLUID SYSTS, GEN ELEC CORP RES & DEVELOP, 83- *Personal Data:* b Poona, India, Sept 27, 39; US citizen; m 64; c 2. *Educ:* Catholic Univ Am, BS, 61; Univ Mich, MS, 63, PhD(mech eng), 66. *Concurrent Pos:* Adj assoc prof, Nuclear Eng Dept, Rensselaer Polytech Inst, 77- *Mem:* Assoc fel Am Inst Aeronaut & Astronaut; Sigma Xi. *Res:* Unsteady flow and structural interaction; acoustics; combustion instability; electro-hydrodynamics; plasma physics. *Mailing Add:* 2344 Jade Lane Schenectady NY 12309

SAVOIE, RODRIGUE, PHYSICAL CHEMISTRY. *Current Pos:* From asst prof to assoc prof, 65-75, PROF CHEM, LAVAL UNIV, 75- *Personal Data:* b Carleton, Que, Oct 1, 36; m 60; c 3. *Educ:* Univ of the Sacred Heart, BA, 56; Laval Univ, BSc, 60, PhD(chem), 63. *Concurrent Pos:* Vis prof, Univ Ore, 76-77. *Mem:* Chem Inst Can; Spectros Soc Can; French Can Asn Advan Sci. *Res:* Infrared and Raman spectroscopy; molecular and crystal structures. *Mailing Add:* Dept Chem Laval Univ Pavillon Vachon Quebec PQ G1K 7P4 Can

SAVOL, ANDREJ MARTIN, MACHINE VISION, IMAGE PROCESSING. *Current Pos:* sr specialist engr, Boeing Aerospace Co, 77-90, ASSOC TECH FEL, BOEING COM AIRPLANE GROUP, 90- *Personal Data:* b Slovakia, Feb 4, 40; US citizen; m 69, Toni Griglak; c Lee, Andrej & Jaro. *Educ:* Carnegie-Mellon Univ, BS, 67; Univ Pittsburgh, MS, 75, PhD(elec eng), 79. *Honors & Awards:* Outstanding Tech Achievement Award, Pac Northwest Sect, Am Inst Aeronaut & Astronaut, 78. *Prof Exp:* Comput programmer, Westinghouse Indust Systs Div, 67-69; head, comput servs, Mellon Inst, 69-72. *Mem:* Soc Mfg Eng. *Res:* Applications of computerized pattern recognition; computer analysis of images in manufacturing and inspection; integration of machine vision subsystems into manufacturing and assembly cells. *Mailing Add:* 4710 Lakeridge Dr E Sumner WA 98390

SAVORY, JOHN, CLINICAL CHEMISTRY, PATHOLOGY. *Current Pos:* MEM FAC, DEPT PATH CLIN LABS, MED CTR, UNIV VA, 77- *Personal Data:* b Lancashire, Eng, Apr 4, 36; US citizen; m 77; c 2. *Educ:* Univ Durham, BSc, 58, PhD(chem), 61. *Prof Exp:* Res chemist, Chemstrand Res Ctr, NC, 63-64; dir clin chem & instr path, Univ Fla, 66-67; asst dir clin labs & asst prof path, 67-72; assoc prof med & dir clin chem, Univ NC, Chapel Hill, 72-77; med & dir clin chem, Univ NC, Chapel Hill, 72-77. *Concurrent Pos:* Res fel chem, Univ Fla, 61-63; sr fel biochem, Univ Wash, 64-66; dir exp & clin path grad prog, Col Med, Univ Fla, 66-72; consult, Vet Admin Hosp, Gainesville, Fla, 67-72. *Mem:* Am Asn Clin Chemists; Am Chem Soc; Asn Clin Sci; Royal Soc Chem; Sigma Xi. *Res:* Organic fluorine chemistry; biochemistry. *Mailing Add:* Dept Path Clin Labs Box 168 Univ Va Med Ctr Charlottesville VA 22908

SAVORY, LEONARD E(RWIN), CHEMICAL ENGINEERING. *Current Pos:* RETIRED. *Personal Data:* b Denver, Colo, Jan 11, 20; m 47; c 3. *Educ:* Univ Denver, BSChE, 42; Ill Inst Technol, MSChE, 44. *Prof Exp:* Asst, Manhattan Proj, SAM Labs, Columbia Univ, 44-45; res technologist, Tenn Eastman Corp, 45-46; asst prof chem eng, Univ Denver, 46-50; mem staff, Los Alamos Sci Lab, NMex, 50-53; res proj supvr, Res Dept, United Gas Corp, 53-60, asst dir res, 60-66, mgr admin div, Res, Eng & Develop Dept, Pennzoil United, Inc, 67-73, sr tech adv, Environ, Safety & Health Affairs Dept, Pennzoil Co, 73-81. *Mem:* AAAS; Am Chem Soc; Am Inst Chem Engrs. *Res:* Nuclear energy; natural gas technology; pollution control. *Mailing Add:* 319 Parkview Lane Estes Park CO 80517

SAVRUN, ENDER, ELECTRON MICROSCOPY & X-RAY MICROANALYSIS, FAILURE ANALYSIS. *Current Pos:* PRES, SIENNA TECHNOL, 94- *Personal Data:* b Adana, Turkey, July 29, 53; m 79; c 1. *Educ:* Istanbul Tech Univ, Turkey, BS, 76, MS, 78; Univ Wash, PhD(ceramic eng), 86. *Prof Exp:* Res scientist ceramics, Flow Industs, 85-87, Photon Sci, 87-88; res mgr, Montedison, 88-89, vpres res ceramics, 89-94. *Concurrent Pos:* Consult, Charlton Industs, 84-85. *Mem:* Am Ceramic Soc; Am Soc Metals; Am Soc Mech Engrs. *Res:* Processing of monolithic ceramics & ceramic matrix composites; mechanical behavior of structural ceramics; ceramic faced composite armor systems; ceramic cutting tools. *Mailing Add:* 9004 Inverness Dr NE Seattle WA 98115

SAWAN, MAHMOUD EDWIN, SYSTEMS DESIGN & SYSTEMS SCIENCE, ELECTRICAL ENGINEERING. *Current Pos:* asst prof, 79-85, assoc prof elec eng, 85-89, PROF, WICHITA STATE UNIV, 89-, GRAD COORD, 93- *Personal Data:* b Damanhor, Egypt, July 28, 50; US citizen; m 76; c 1. *Educ:* Univ Alexandria, Egypt, BS, 73, MS, 76; Univ Ill, Urbana, PhD(elec eng), 79. *Prof Exp:* Lectr automatic control, Univ Alexandria, 73-76; res asst, Univ Ill, Urbana, 76-79. *Concurrent Pos:* Secy, Wichita Sect, Inst Elec & Electronics Engrs, 85-87, vchmn, 87-89. *Mem:* Sr mem Inst Elec & Electronics Engrs. *Res:* Application of control theory: development of robust control design techniques for systems with slow and fast modes. *Mailing Add:* Elec Eng Dept Box 44 Wichita State Univ Wichita KS 67260-0044. *Fax:* 316-978-3853; *E-Mail:* ed@ee.twsu.edu

SAWAN, SAMUEL PAUL, POLYMER CHEMISTRY, BIOPOLYMERS. *Current Pos:* PROF, DEPT CHEM, UNIV MASS, LOWELL. *Personal Data:* b Akron, Ohio, Apr 18, 50. *Educ:* Univ Akron, BS, 72, PhD(polymer sci), 76. *Prof Exp:* Data analyst, Akron Regional Air Pollution Control Agency, 73-74; scholar, Dept Pharmaceut Chem, Univ Calif, San Francisco, 76-78. *Concurrent Pos:* Prin investr, 4 grants. *Mem:* Am Chem Soc; Sigma Xi; AAAS; Soc Plastics Engrs; Asn Res Vision & Ophthal; Int Union Pure & Appl Chem. *Res:* Biocompatible polymeric materials; controlled release drugs delivery; polysilanes; surface modification; plasma chemistry; plasma polymerization. *Mailing Add:* Chem Dept Univ Lowell Lowell MA 01854. *Fax:* 978-934-3028; *E-Mail:* sawans@woods.uml.edu

SAWARDEKER, JAWAHAR SAZRO, PHYSICAL PHARMACY, ANALYTICAL CHEMISTRY. *Current Pos:* DIR QUAL CONTROL & VPRES MFG, GLAXO INC, 81-, VPRES INT QUAL ASSURANCE, GLAXO HOLDINGS, 90- *Personal Data:* b Goa, India, Nov 22, 37; m 66; c 3. *Educ:* Univ Bombay, BS, 57; Univ Iowa, MS, 61, PhD(pharm), 64. *Prof Exp:* Res chemist, USDA, Ill, 64-66; assoc scientist, Ortho Pharmaceut Corp, 67-69, group leader scientist, 69-73; group mgr, Whitehall Labs, 73-77, dir qual control, 77-81. *Mem:* Am Pharmaceut Asn; Am Chem Soc; Am Soc Qual Control. *Res:* Gas chromatography application to pharmaceutical systems and carbohydrate chemistry; exploration of analytical techniques and development of procedures; preformulation research; bioavailability studies. *Mailing Add:* RRI PO Box 271 Ft Lauderdale FL 33326

SAWATARI, TAKEO, OPTICS. *Current Pos:* PRES, SENTEC CORP, 81- *Personal Data:* b Okayama, Japan, Feb 7, 39; US citizen; m 66, Yoshiko Terashima; c Atomu, Ken & Yoh. *Educ:* Waseda Univ, Tokyo Japan, BS, 62, PhD(appl physics), 70. *Prof Exp:* Researcher, Canon Camera, 62-65; res assoc, Univ Tokyo, 65-66; physicist, Optics Technol Inc, 66-70; prin physicist, Bendix Res Lab, 70-77, mem tech staff, Bendix Advan Technol Ctr, 77-81. *Concurrent Pos:* Lectr, Univ Mich, Dearborn, 78, Oakland Univ, 81. *Mem:* Optical Soc Am. *Res:* Development of fiber optics and its applications; optics; signal processing; laser applications; author of over 50 technical papers and contributor to two fiber optic textbooks. *Mailing Add:* 6105 Gilbert Lake Rd Bloomfield Hills MI 48301. *Fax:* 248-960-1814

SAWATZKY, ERICH, PHYSICS. *Current Pos:* RES STAFF SCIENTIST, SAN JOSE RES LAB, IBM CORP, 62- *Personal Data:* b Cholm, Poland, Apr 21, 34; US citizen; m 61; c 3. *Educ:* Univ BC, BSc, 58, MSc, 60, PhD(physics), 62. *Mem:* Am Phys Soc; Inst Elec & Electronics Engrs. *Res:* Magnetism in solid state materials; nuclear magnetic resonance, preparation and characterization of physical properties of thin films; magnetic and magneto-optic properties of thin films. *Mailing Add:* 1077 Trevino Terrace San Jose CA 95120

SAWAYA, RAYMOND, BRAIN TUMORS, CANCER RESEARCH. *Current Pos:* PROF & CHMN, DEPT NEUROSURG, M D ANDERSON CANCER CTR, UNIV TEX, 90- *Personal Data:* b Latakia, Syria, May 5, 49; US citizen; m 95, Kristin E Tveit; c Marc Emile & Corinne. *Educ:* St Joseph Univ, Beirut, Lebanon, MD, 74. *Honors & Awards:* Wilder Penfield Award, Middle E Neurosurg Soc, 92. *Prof Exp:* Internship surg, Beeckman Downtown Hosp, 75; residency surg, State Univ NY, 76; pediat neurosurg, Children's Hosp, Cincinnati, Ohio, 77; residency neurosurg, Univ Cincinnati, 76-80; Fogarty int fel, NIH, 81-82; from asst prof to assoc prof neurosurg, Univ Cincinnati, 82-90; ADJ PROF, BAYLOR COL MED, 91- *Concurrent Pos:* Chief neurosurg serv, Vet Admin Med Ctr, 83-90; dir div neuro-oncol, Univ Cincinnati Col Med, 85-90; mem res comt, Jt Sect Brain Tumors, Am Asn Neurol Surgeons & Cong Neurol Surgeons, 85-, mem, Joint Tumor Comt, 90-; chmn, Qual Control subcomt, Cancer Comt, Univ Cincinnati, 85-86; consult, Johnson & Johnson Inc, 87-88 & Osteotech Inc, 88; assoc ed, J Neuro-Oncol, 91-, guest ed, 93; chmn, Scientific Session VI, Middle East Neurosurg Soc, 92; contrib ed, Cancer Bull, 92, guest ed, 93; consult, Ministry Health, Govt Singapore, 92; ed, Jt Sect Brain Tumors newslett, 92- *Mem:* Am Radium Soc; Soc Surg Oncol; Am Asn Neurol Surgeons; Cong Neurol Surgeons. *Res:* Molecular make-up of brain tumors; specific products of tumor cells, particularly enzymes and their inhibitors, play major roles in allowing tumors to grow and spread within the substance of the brain; ability to understand the mechanisms involved and in turn prevent the process from taking place carry the potential to cure brain tumors. *Mailing Add:* M D Anderson Cancer Ctr 1515 Holcombe Box 064 Houston TX 77030. *Fax:* 713-794-4950

SAWCHUK, ALEXANDER ANDREW, ELECTRICAL ENGINEERING, OPTICS. *Current Pos:* from asst prof to assoc prof elec eng, 71-82, PROF ELEC ENG, UNIV SOUTHERN CALIF, 82-, DIR SIGNAL & IMAGE PROCESSING INST, 78-88 & 90- *Personal Data:* b Washington, DC, Feb 20, 45; m 71; c 2. *Educ:* Mass Inst Technol, SB, 66; Stanford Univ, MS, 68, PhD(elec eng), 72. *Prof Exp:* Elec engr, Goddard Space Flight Ctr, NASA, Md, 66 & Commun Satellite Corp, Washington, DC, 67. *Concurrent Pos:* Consult, TRW Defense & Space Systs Group, 77-; founder dir, Optivision Inc, 83. *Mem:* Inst Elec & Electronics Engrs; Optical Soc Am; Soc Photo-Optical Instrumentation Engrs; Soc Info Display. *Res:* Digital image processing; statistical optics; optical information processing; multidimensional signal processing and system theory. *Mailing Add:* Dept Elec Eng Univ Southern Calif Mc 2564 Eeb 404b Los Angeles CA 90089

SAWCHUK, RONALD JOHN, PHARMACOKINETICS, MEDICAL RESEARCH. *Current Pos:* From asst prof to assoc prof, 72-83, PROF PHARMACEUT, COL PHARM, UNIV MINN, MINNEAPOLIS, 83-, DIR GRAD STUDIES PHARMACEUT, 83- *Personal Data:* b Toronto, Ont, May 29, 40; m 67; c David, Heather & Holly. *Educ:* Univ Toronto, BScPh, 63, MScPhm, 66; Univ Calif, San Francisco, PhD(pharmaceut), 72. *Concurrent Pos:* Actg chmn, Dept Pharmaceut, Univ Minn, 83-86, dir, Clin Pharmacokinetics Lab, 82-; mem comt rev, US Pharmacopeial Con. *Mem:* Fel AAAS; Am Pharmaceut Asn; Am Asn Cols Pharm; Acad Pharmaceut Sci; Controlled Release Soc; fel Am Asn Pharmaceut Sci; NY Acad Sci. *Res:* Pharmacokinetics and kinetic modeling; drug distribution, metabolism and excretion; drug-drug interactions; quantitative analysis of foreign compounds in biological fluids; absorption of drugs using in situ animal models; pharmocokinetics utilizing microdialysis. *Mailing Add:* Dept Pharmaceut 5-130 HS Unit F Univ Minn 308 Harvard St SE Minneapolis MN 55455-0353. *Fax:* 612-624-0951; *E-Mail:* sawch001@maroon.tc.umn.edu

SAWERS, JAMES RICHARD, JR, DOCUMENTATION FOR REGULATORY COMPLIANCE, ENGINEERING PHYSICS. *Current Pos:* PRES, KNOWLEDGE TECHNOL, 85- *Personal Data:* b Memphis, Tenn, Feb 4, 40; m 61; c Pamela L & Laura R (Ault). *Educ:* Duke Univ, BS, 62, PhD(nuclear physics), 66. *Prof Exp:* Res physicist, Du Pont Instruments, Del, 66-71; sr scientist, 71-73; tech supvr, du Pont Biomed, 74-75, mgr microtomy prod, 76-77, mgr clinprod, 77-78, mgr instrument prod, E I du Pont de Nemours & Co Inc, 78-79, mgr instrument mfr, 79-83, mgr du Pont Learning Systs, 83-85; adj prof, Temple Univ, 85, Willmington Col, 86, James Madison Univ, 87. *Concurrent Pos:* Post doctorate, Univ Mich, 68, Univ RI, 69, Univ Pa, 74. *Mem:* Am Inst Chem Engrs; Electron Micros Soc Am; Am Phys Soc; Sigma Xi; Soc Photog Scientists & Engrs; Inst Mgt Consults. *Res:* Regulatory compliance documentation for OSHA, EPA; Neutron polarization; magnetism; photochemistry; electroluminescence; electron imaging; submicron particle size analysis; diamond knives; computer analysis; biomedical instrumentation; process and pollution control instrumentation; industrial and manufacturing engineering; general computer sciences; technical management; electrical engineering; engineering and general physics; electromagnetism. *Mailing Add:* Knowledge Technologies 16 Harleston Pl Charleston SC 29401. *Fax:* 803-723-0411; *E-Mail:* jlmknowledgetech@msn.com

SAWHILL, ROY BOND, transportation, civil engineering, for more information see previous edition

SAWHNEY, VIPEN KUMAR, PLANT DEVELOPMENT & PHYSIOLOGY. *Current Pos:* from asst prof to assoc prof, 75-86, asst head biol dept, 87-90, PROF BIOL, UNIV SASK, 86- *Personal Data:* b India; c 1. *Educ:* Univ Punjab, BSc, 65, MSc, 67; Univ Western Ont, PhD(plant sci), 72. *Prof Exp:* Post doc fel biol, Simon Fraser Univ, 72-74. *Concurrent Pos:* Vis fel, Yale Univ, 82-83. *Mem:* Can Soc Plant Physiologists; Can Bot Asn; Bot Soc Am; Am Soc Plant Physiologists. *Res:* Growth regulation of vegetative and floral apecies of normal and mutant plants; physiological and biochemical studies on male sterility in plants. *Mailing Add:* Dept Biol Sci Univ Sask Saskatoon SK S7N 5E2 Can

SAWICKA, BARBARA DANUTA, PROPERTIES OF MATERIALS, SOLID STATE PHYSICS. *Current Pos:* RES SCIENTIST, CHALK RIVER NUCLEAR LABS, ONT, CAN, 85- *Personal Data:* b Debica, Poland; m 64, Jerzy Sawicki; c Marcin. *Educ:* Jagiellonian Univ, Cracow, Poland, MSc, 64, PhD(scis), 70; Inst Nuclear Physics, Cracow, Habilitation(physics), 80. *Honors & Awards:* Res Award, Atomic Energy Comn, Poland, 76-80. *Prof*

Exp: From res asst to assoc prof, Inst Nuclear Physics, Cracow, Poland, 64-84. *Concurrent Pos:* Vis res scientist, Joint Inst Nuclear Physics, Dubna, USSR, 64-66, Johns Hopkins Univ, Baltimore, 80, Rijksuniversitet Groningen, Neth, 82-83, Max Planck Inst Plasma Physics, 84-85; vis res assoc, Tech Univ, Otaniemi, Finland, 71; vis asst prof, Inst Physics, Zurich Univ, Switz, 74-75; vis assoc prof, Universite Lyon, France, 81. *Mem:* Polish Phys Soc; Am Phys Soc; Europ Phys Soc; Am Ceramic Soc. *Res:* Solid state physics problems and properties of materials studied by nuclear techniques; computed tomography, digital radiography and related techniques; hyperfine interactions; particle-solid interactions; influence of energetic beams on materials properties; advanced ceramics; nondestructive testing. *Mailing Add:* AECL Res Chalk River Labs Chalk River ON K0J 1J0 Can. *Fax:* 613-584-4523; *E-Mail:* sawickab@crl.aecl.ca

SAWICKI, JOHN EDWARD, EXPERIMENTALIST, REACTION KINETICS. *Current Pos:* sr prin res engr, Air Prod & Chem, Inc, 78-81, technol mgr & group leader, 81-87, process technologist, 87-92, eng assoc, 92-94, SR ENG ASSOC, AIR PROD & CHEM, INC, 94- *Personal Data:* b Philadelphia, Pa, March 10, 44; m 71; Geraldine A Rogalski; c Christian J & Mara B. *Educ:* Drexel Univ, BS, 67, MS, 68; Univ Va, PhD(chem eng), 72. *Prof Exp:* Sr res officer, Chem Eng Group, SAfrica Coun Sci & Indust Res, 72-74; res engr & group leader, Joseph Schlitz Brewing Co, 74-78. *Mem:* Am Inst Chem Engrs. *Res:* Applied and basic research in aromatic nitgration processes and chemistry; unit operations and plant optimization; process development; environmental engineering. *Mailing Add:* 1862 Kecks Rd Breinigsville PA 18031

SAWICKI, STANLEY GEORGE, VIROLOGY, TISSUE CULTURE. *Current Pos:* ASST PROF MICROBIOL, MED COL OHIO, 77- *Personal Data:* b Oklahoma City, Okla, Feb 23, 42; m 69. *Educ:* Georgetown Univ, BS, 64; Columbia Univ, MA & PhD(pathobiol), 74. *Prof Exp:* Fel molecular cell biol, Rockefeller Univ, 74-77. *Mem:* AAAS; Am Soc Microbiol; Sigma Xi. *Res:* RNA and protein synthesis in eukaryotic cells; control of the replication cycle in alphaviruses and arenaviruses. *Mailing Add:* 2940 Talmadge Rd Toledo OH 43606-2251

SAWIN, CLARK TIMOTHY, THYROID DISEASE. *Current Pos:* CHIEF, ENDOCRINE-DIABETES SECT, BOSTON VET ADMIN MED CTR, 66-; PROF MED, TUFTS MED SCH, 81- *Personal Data:* b Boston, Mass, May 23, 34; m 82; c 3. *Educ:* Brandeis Univ, BA, 54; Tufts Univ, MD, 58. *Honors & Awards:* Reynolds Award, Am Physiol Soc, 90. *Concurrent Pos:* Prin investr res projs, Dept Vet Affairs, 66- *Mem:* Endocrine Soc; Am Thyroid Asn; Am Asn Hist Med; Am Geront Soc; Am Diabetes Asn. *Res:* Endocrine changes with aging in man; history of endocrinology. *Mailing Add:* Endocrine-Diabetes Sect Vet Admin Med Ctr 150 S Huntington Ave Boston MA 02130

SAWIN, STEVEN P, POLYMER REACTOR DESIGN. *Current Pos:* Sr engr res & develop, Polyolefins Div, Union Carbide Corp, 70-74, group leader, 74-81, assoc dir, 81-85, DIR POLYPROPYLENE RES & DEVELOP, UNION CARBIDE CORP, 85- *Personal Data:* b Mason City, Iowa, Oct 19, 44; m 66; c 4. *Educ:* Iowa State Univ, BS, 66; Univ Ill, MS, 68, PhD(chem eng), 71. *Mem:* Am Inst Chem Engrs; Am Chem Soc. *Res:* The UNIPOL process technology for polyethylene extended to polypropylene; all types of polypropylene homopolymers, random and impact copolymers are produced; new products and advanced catalyst system being developed. *Mailing Add:* 865 Madison Ave Bridgewater NJ 08807

SAWINSKI, VINCENT JOHN, PHYSICAL SCIENCES, ADMINISTRATION. *Current Pos:* RETIRED. *Personal Data:* b Chicago, Ill, Mar 28, 25; m 52, Florence L Whitman; c Christine & Michael. *Educ:* Loyola Univ, Chicago, BS, 48, MA, 50, PhD(biochem), 62. *Prof Exp:* Asst prof biochem, Loyola Univ, 49-67; assoc prof, Wilbur Wright Col, City Cols Chicago, 67-70, prof & chmn phys sci, 71-90. *Concurrent Pos:* Supvry res scientist, Vet Admin, 61-66. *Mem:* Sr mem Am Chem Soc; fel AAAS; Sigma Xi; sr mem Nat Sci Teachers Asn; fel Am Inst Chemist. *Res:* Biochemistry lab research and article abstracts; chemical research and education. *Mailing Add:* 1945 N 77th Ct Elmwood Park IL 60707-3623

SAWITSKY, ARTHUR, HEMATOLOGY, ONCOLOGY. *Current Pos:* chief div hemat, 55-84, EMER DIR CANCER PROGS, LONG ISLAND JEWISH MED CTR, 85-; PROF MED ALBERT EINSTEIN COL MED, STATE UNIV NY, STONY BROOK, 91- *Personal Data:* b Jersey City, NJ, Jan 31, 16; m, Barbara Polak; c Edith & Kitt. *Educ:* NY Univ, BA, 36, MD, 40; Am Bd Internal Med, dipl, 52, cert hemat, 72. *Prof Exp:* Intern, Kings County Hosp, 40-42; fel hemat, Dept Therapeut, Col Med, NY Univ, 46-47; asst resident med, Goldwater Mem Hosp, NY Univ Div, 47-48; assoc med, NY Med Col, 50-54; prof med & clin path, State Univ Ny, Stony Brook, 71-91. *Concurrent Pos:* Asst vis physician, Goldwater Mem Hosp, NY Univ Div, 48-52; assoc vis physician hemat & physician-in-chg blood bank, Queens Hosp Ctr, 48-64; assoc vis physician hemat, Jamaica Hosp, 49-54; asst vis physician hemat, Flushing Hosp, 50-55; attend hematologist, North Shore Hosp, Manhasset, NY, 54-67; attend physician-in-chg, Long Island Jewish Hosp-Queens Hosp Ctr Affil, 64-84; clin assoc prof, State Univ NY Downstate Med Ctr, 69-73; NIH grants, 61-84; fels, Pall Found, 64-72, Nat Leukemia Soc & United Leukemia Soc, 64-, Zelda Grossberg Found, 65-72 & Dennis Klar Mem Fund, 69-; res collabr, Brookhaven Nat Lab; sr immuno hematologist, New York City Dept Health, 74-; consult hematologist, North Shore Hosp, Manhasset, Huntington Hosp, St Francis Hosp, Roslyn, Flushing Hosp & Peninsula Gen Hosp, Edgemere, NY. *Mem:* Am Soc Hemat; Soc Exp Biol & Med; Am Fedn Clin Res; Am Asn Cancer Res; Am Soc Clin Oncol; Sigma Xi; Am Asn Blood Banks. *Res:* Biology and classification of sub-populations of patients in the chronic leukemias; basic understanding of the defect in the syndrome of the sea-blue histiocyte and lipidoses. *Mailing Add:* 52 Acorn Ponds Dr North Hills NY 11576-2818. *Fax:* 718-470-0169

SAWOROTNOW, PARFENY PAVOLICH, HILBERT SPACES, BANACH ALGEBRAS. *Current Pos:* From instr to prof, 54-96, EMER PROF MATH, CATH UNIV AM, 97- *Personal Data:* b Ust-Medvedyskaya, Russia, Feb 20, 24; nat US. *Educ:* Harvard Univ, MA, 51, PhD, 54. *Concurrent Pos:* NSF grants, 67 & 70. *Mem:* Sigma Xi; Am Asn Univ Professor; Am Math Soc; Math Asn Am; NY Acad Sci. *Res:* Functional analysis; Hilbert spaces; Banach algebras; vector measures; probability; generalization of classical result, characterization of systems in functional analysis. *Mailing Add:* 6 Avon Pl Avondale MD 20782

SAWUTZ, DAVID G, RECEPTOR PHARMACOLOGY. *Current Pos:* SR RES INVESTR, DEPT ENZYMOL & RECEPTOR BIOCHEM, STERLING DRUG, INC, 87- *Personal Data:* b Montclair, NJ, July 14, 54. *Educ:* Univ Cincinnati, PhD(pharmacol), 84. *Prof Exp:* Res fel, Mass Gen Hosp, 84-87. *Mem:* Am Soc Pharmacol & Exp Therapeut; AAAS. *Mailing Add:* Berlex Biosci 15049 San Pablo Ave Richmond CA 94804. *Fax:* 215-640-8800

SAWYER, BALDWIN, PHYSICS OF SOLIDS, METALLURGY. *Current Pos:* RETIRED. *Personal Data:* b Naragansett Pier, RI, July 21, 22; m 47, Dorothy Straker; c Dorothy C, Ann S (Williams), Charles B & Elizabeth R. *Educ:* Yale Univ, BE, 43; Carnegie Inst Technol, DSc(physics), 52. *Prof Exp:* Jr metallurgist, Manhattan Proj, Univ Chicago, 43-46; instr & res assoc, Carnegie Inst Technol, 48-51; mem tech staff, Bell Tel Labs, Inc, 51-53, group supvr, 53-57; treas & chief engr, Sawyer Res Prods, Inc, 57-60, vpres eng, 60-64, exec vpres, 64-73, vchmn & dir technol, 84-86. *Concurrent Pos:* Chmn, quartz mats stand comt, Electronic Industs Asn, 85-, Int Electrotech Comn, 86-; mem, Natural Mats Adv Bd, Nat Acad Sci, 85. *Mem:* AAAS; Am Phys Soc; Electrochem Soc; Inst Elec & Electronics Engrs; Sigma Xi. *Res:* Cultured quartz crystals; plasma spray coatings; growth and characterization. *Mailing Add:* 1659 Berkshire Rd PO Box 96 Gates Mills OH 44040-0096. *Fax:* 216-351-4462

SAWYER, C GLENN, CARDIOLOGY. *Current Pos:* RETIRED. *Personal Data:* b New Bern, NC, Feb 27, 22; c 4. *Educ:* Bowman Gray Sch Med, MD, 44; Am Bd Internal Med, dipl, 52. *Prof Exp:* From intern to chief med resident, Peter Bent Brigham Hosp, Boston, Mass, 44-50; instr med, Harvard Med Sch, 50-51; from instr to assoc prof, Bowman Gray Sch Med, 51-63, chief cardiol, 63-81, prof med, 63-88. *Concurrent Pos:* Fel clin coun cardiol, Am Heart Asn. *Mem:* Am Heart Asn; AMA; fel Am Col Physicians; fel Am Col Cardiol; Asn Univ Cardiol. *Mailing Add:* 905 Goodwood Rd Winston-Salem NC 27106

SAWYER, CHARLES HENRY, NEUROENDOCRINOLOGY. *Current Pos:* prof, 51-85, chmn dept, 55-63, EMER PROF ANAT, SCH MED, UNIV CALIF, LOS ANGELES, 85- *Personal Data:* b Ludlow, Vt, Jan 24, 15; m 41, Ruth Schaeffer; c Joan. *Educ:* Middlebury Col, AB, 37; Yale Univ, PhD(zool), 41. *Hon Degrees:* ScD, Middlebury Col, 75. *Honors & Awards:* Koch Res Medal, Endocrine Soc, 73; Hartman Award, Soc Study Reprod, 77; Henry Gray Award, Am Asn Anatomists, 84. *Prof Exp:* Instr anat, Stanford Univ, 41-44; assoc, Duke Univ, 44-45; from asst prof to prof, 45-51, chmn, Dept Anat, Univ Calif, Los Angeles, 55-63, fac res lectr, 66-67; commonwealth Found fel, 58-59; mem anat panel, Nat Bd Med Examr, 60-64, chmn, 64; mem-fel rev bd pharmacol & endocrinol, USPHS, 61-63 & 68-70; mem neuroendocrine panel, Int Brain Res Orgn, 61-, mem cent coun, 64-67; mem neurol study sect, NIH, 63-67. *Mem:* Nat Acad Sci; hon mem Hungarian Soc Endocrinol & Metab; Am Asn Anatomists (vpres, 68-70); Soc Study Reprod; fel Am Acad Arts & Sci; hon mem Japan Endocrine Soc. *Res:* Neuroendocrinology of reproduction; nervous control of pituitary secretion; function, distribution, ontogenesis and properties of cholinesterases; effects of hormones on brain function. *Mailing Add:* Dept Neurobiol Med Sch Univ Calif Los Angeles CA 90095. *Fax:* 310-825-2224

SAWYER, CONSTANCE B, ASTROPHYSICS, OCEANOGRAPHY. *Current Pos:* RETIRED. *Personal Data:* b Lewiston, Maine, June 3, 26; div; c Sarah H (Charlock), David Warwick, Rachel Warwick & Joel McCulloch. *Educ:* Smith Col, AB, 47; Harvard Univ, AM, 48, PhD, 52. *Prof Exp:* Res asst, Sacramento Peak Observ, 53-55; mem staff, High Altitude Observ, Univ Colo, 55-58; astronr, Space Environ Lab, 58-75; phys scientist, Atlantic Oceanog Meteorol Labs, 75-76, phys scientist, Pac Marine Environ Lab, Nat Oceanic & Atmospheric Admin, 76-79; staff scientist, High Altitude Observ, 79-82; scientist, Radiophysics Inc, 83-94. *Concurrent Pos:* Satellite oper, NASA, 80; consult, D-Peek, 83; res assoc, Univ Colo, 84-85. *Mem:* Int Astron Union; Int Union Geod & Geophys; AAAS; Am Geophys Union; Am Astron Soc; Sigma Xi. *Res:* Solar physics and solar-terrestrial relations; ocean remote sensing; internal waves; planetary radio emission; planetary magnetic-field modeling. *Mailing Add:* 850 20th St 705 Boulder CO 80302-7749. *E-Mail:* sawyer@stripe.colorado.edu

SAWYER, DAVID ERICKSON, OPTICS. *Current Pos:* CONSULT, 90- *Personal Data:* b Boston, Mass, Feb 6, 27; m; c 3. *Educ:* Clark Univ, BA, 53; Univ Ill, MS, 55; Worcester Polytech Inst, PhD, 76. *Honors & Awards:* Indust Res 100 Award, 76. *Prof Exp:* Res staff mem, Lincoln Lab, Mass Inst Technol, 55-59; develop staff mem, Int Bus Mach Corp, NY, 59-61; res staff mem, Sperry Rand Res Ctr, Mass, 61-66; sect head & sr scientist semiconductor device res, Electronics Res Ctr, NASA, 66-70; group leader, Electron Device Div, Nat Bur Stand, 70-75, sr staff mem, 75-79; sr res engr, Chevron Res Co, 79-85; optics res group leader & res & develop dept head, Systron Donner Co, 85-90. *Mem:* Soc Photo-Optical Instrumentation Engrs; Inst Elec & Electronics Engrs. *Res:* Solid-state physics and devices; energy conversion; exploratory measurement techniques. *Mailing Add:* 1120 Toedtli Dr Boulder CO 80303

SAWYER, DAVID W(ILLIAM), PETROLEUM, ORGANIC CHEMISTRY. *Current Pos:* CONSULT, 75- *Personal Data:* b Pittsburgh, Pa, Feb 1, 10; m 38; c 1. *Educ:* Univ Pittsburgh, BS, 33. *Prof Exp:* Asst civil engr, City Planning Comn, Pittsburgh, Pa, 33-34; fel petrol, Mellon Inst, 34-35; res chemist, Gulf Res & Develop Co, 34-43; res engr, Alcoa Res Labs, Aluminum Co Am, 43-53, sr res engr, Lubricants Div, Alcoa Tech Ctr Pittsburgh, 53-75. *Concurrent Pos:* Mem interim subcomt turbine-gear oils, US Dept Navy, 53- *Mem:* Am Chem Soc; fel Am Inst Chemists; Soc Tribologists & Lubrication Engrs; Sigma Xi. *Res:* Lubricants; lubrication; petroleum refining; corrosion. *Mailing Add:* 620 12th St Oakmont PA 15139

SAWYER, DONALD C, ANESTHESIOLOGY. *Current Pos:* assoc prof & head anesthesia sect, 70-77, actg assoc dean, 74-75, PROF VET MED & ANESTHESIA, MICH STATE UNIV, 77-, CVM OUTREACH, 86- *Personal Data:* b New York, NY, Aug 23, 36; m 62; c 3. *Educ:* Mich State Univ, BS, 59, DVM, 61, MS, 62; Colo State Univ, PhD(vet anesthesiol), 69; Am Col Vet Anesthesiologists, dipl. *Hon Degrees:* Hon Dipl, Am Bd Vet Practr. *Prof Exp:* Asst instr vet med, Mich State Univ, 61-62; pvt pract, 62-63; NIH spec fel, Colo State Univ & Univ Calif, 65-70. *Concurrent Pos:* Support grant, 70-72, pharmacol res, 72-88; consult, NIH, 85. *Mem:* Am Vet Med Asn; Am Soc Vet Anesthesiol (pres, 72); Am Soc Anesthesiol; Am Col Vet Anesthesia (pres, 78); Am Bd Vet Practitioners (pres, 79-82). *Res:* Cardiovascular effects of anesthetics; metabolism of inhalation anesthetics; effects of analgesics for pain relief. *Mailing Add:* Col Vet Med A-133 E Fee Hall Mich State Univ East Lansing MI 48824-1316

SAWYER, DONALD TURNER, JR, OXYGEN CHEMISTRY, BIOINORGANIC CHEMISTRY. *Current Pos:* staff, 85-96, EMER, TEX A&M UNIV, 96-; FAC, INST BIOSCI & TECHNOL, 96- *Personal Data:* b Pomona, Calif, Jan 10, 31; m 52, Shirley Scott; c Sharon, Robert & Andrew. *Educ:* Univ Calif, Los Angeles, BS, 53, PhD(chem), 56. *Honors & Awards:* Richard C Tolman Medal, Am Chem Soc, 82; Henry Werner lectr, Univ Kans, 91. *Prof Exp:* Guggenheim fel, Cambridge, 62-63 & 75; vis res fel, Merton Col, Oxford Univ, 70; chmn, Gordon Res Conf Anal Chem, 71; mem adv comt, Res Corp, 78-84; fac res lectr, Univ Calif, Riverside, 79; sci adv, US Food & Drug Admin, Calif, 75-82. *Concurrent Pos:* Fac, Univ Calif, Riverside, 56-86, Rice Univ, 96- *Mem:* Fel AAAS. *Res:* Electroanalytical chemistry; physical chemical studies of metal chelates; chemical instrumentation; optical, nuclear magnetic resonance and electron spin resonance spectroscopy; model studies of metalloenzymes; nuclear magnetic resonance studies of coordination complexes; oxygen activation by metalloproteins and transition metal complexes; oxygen chemistry. *Mailing Add:* Inst Biosci & Technol Tex A&M Univ Houston TX 77030-3303. *Fax:* 713-677-7958; *E-Mail:* sawyer@ibt.tamu.edu

SAWYER, FREDERICK GEORGE, COMMUNICATION, WRITING & SPEAKING. *Current Pos:* CONSULT, FREDERICK G SAWYER & ASSOCS, 78- *Personal Data:* b Brooklyn, NY, Mar 14, 18; m 50; c 2. *Educ:* Polytech Inst Brooklyn, BChE, 39, MChE, 41, DChE, 43. *Prof Exp:* Res chem engr, Eastman Kodak Co, 41; instr chem eng, Polytech Inst Brooklyn, 42-43; chem engr, Am Cyanamid Co, Conn, 43-45; tech serv, NY, 45-46; assoc ed, Indust & Eng Chem & Chem & Eng News, Am Chem Soc, 46-50; adminr air pollution res, Stanford Res Inst, 50-51, asst to dir res, 51-53; dir info, Ralph M Parsons Co, 53-57; vpres, Jacobs Eng Co, 57-63; consult corp commun & mkt, 63-72; vpres, Reynolds Environ Group, 72-78. *Concurrent Pos:* Lectr, Stanford Univ, 52-53, Univ Southern Calif, 67-69, Univ Calif, Los Angeles, 68, Saddleback Col, 77-, Calif State Univ, Pomona, 79- & Univ Calif, Irvine, 82-; pres, Vita-Cell Prod, 64; dir, Econ Int, Inc, 65-; mem, Advan Technol Consults Corp; asst dean, Sch Eng & lectr, Univ Calif, Irvine, 79-91. *Mem:* AAAS; Am Inst Chem Engrs; Chem Mkt Res Asn; Asn Mgt Consults; Am Chem Soc. *Res:* Corporate and scientific communications; technical public relations; business development; lexical research; environmental planning and assessment; handmade paper. *Mailing Add:* 12922 Keith Pl Tustin CA 92780-3513

SAWYER, FREDERICK MILES, FOOD TECHNOLOGY, NUTRITION. *Current Pos:* RETIRED. *Personal Data:* b Brockton, Mass, Nov 30, 24; m 48. *Educ:* Mass Inst Technol, SB, 48; Univ Calif, MS, 51, PhD(nutrit), 58. *Prof Exp:* Food technologist seafoods div, Gen Foods Corp, 48-49; sr lab technician, Univ Calif, 50-57; from asst prof to prof res food sci, Univ Mass, Amherst, 57-89. *Mem:* AAAS; Am Chem Soc; Inst Food Technologists. *Res:* Flavor chemistry; biochemistry of food spoilage; frozen foods; sensory analysis of foods. *Mailing Add:* PO Box 547 Amherst MA 01004

SAWYER, GEORGE ALANSON, PLASMA PHYSICS. *Current Pos:* RETIRED. *Personal Data:* b Chicago, Ill, July 20, 22; m 47, Ruth Wilson; c Robert & Mark. *Educ:* Univ Mich, BSE, 44, MS, 48, PhD(physics), 50. *Prof Exp:* Mem staff, Los Alamos Nat Lab, 50-72, group leader, 72-74, alt div leader, 74-79, prog mgr, 80-86, sr adv, 86-91. *Mem:* Sigma Xi; Am Phys Soc. *Res:* Plasma physics; nuclear reactions; radioactivity; x-ray and visible spectroscopy; controlled thermonuclear research; particle accelerators. *Mailing Add:* 2519 35th St Los Alamos NM 87544

SAWYER, JAMES W, MANAGEMENT SCIENCE, SYSTEMS ENGINEERING. *Current Pos:* SR SCIENTIST, ERCO, 81- *Personal Data:* b Malone, NY, June 30, 33; m 66. *Educ:* Clarkson Col Technol, BChE, 54; Univ Pa, MS, 70, PhD(systs eng), 73. *Prof Exp:* Res chem eng, E I du Pont de Nemours & Co Inc, 54-68; res assoc, Resources for the Future, 73-75, sr res assoc, Qual Environ Prog, 75-76, fel & asst dir, 76-78; prin analyst, Congressional Budget Off, 78-81. *Concurrent Pos:* Sr energy specialist, Nat Transp Policy Studies Comn 77-78. *Mem:* Inst Elec & Electronics Engrs; Am Inst Chem Engrs; Inst Mgt Sci; Am Chem Engrs; Am Econ Asn. *Res:* Environmental quality policy; water resources; secondary materials (scrap) studies; mathematical modeling of water, secondary materials, fossil fuel and synfuel studies with emphasis on environmental quality; policy aspects. *Mailing Add:* 430 Rockewell Rd Hampton VA 23669

SAWYER, JANE ORROCK, MATHEMATICS, STATISTICS. *Current Pos:* qual engr, Am Safety Razor Co, 81-84, sr eng specialist, 84-89, mgr data processing, 89-95, MGR CORP SYST DEVELOP, AM SAFETY RAZOR CO, 95- *Personal Data:* b Richmond, Va, June 15, 44; div; c 2. *Educ:* Va Polytech Inst & State Univ, BS, 66, MS, 68, PhD(math), 75. *Prof Exp:* From instr to assoc prof math, Mary Baldwin Col, 69-81. *Concurrent Pos:* Coordr & researcher, NASA, 75-76, prin investr, 76-77. *Mem:* Am Math Soc; Math Asn Am; Asn Women Math; Soc Mfg Engrs. *Res:* Rings of continuous functions, specifically pseudocompact topological spaces and pseudocompactifications. *Mailing Add:* 22 Marlene Pl Verona VA 24482

SAWYER, JOHN ORVEL, JR, PLANT ECOLOGY. *Current Pos:* from asst prof to assoc prof ecol, 66-75, PROF BOT, HUMBOLDT STATE UNIV, 75- *Personal Data:* b Chico, Calif, Nov 22, 39; m 60; c 2. *Educ:* Chico State Col, AB, 61; Purdue Univ, MS, 63, PhD(plant ecol), 66. *Prof Exp:* Ecologist, Wilson Nuttall Raimond Engrs, Inc, 64-66. *Mem:* Ecol Soc Am; Sigma Xi. *Res:* Vegetation of northern California. *Mailing Add:* Dept Biol Humboldt State Univ Arcata CA 95521

SAWYER, JOHN WESLEY, OPERATIONS RESEARCH. *Current Pos:* RETIRED. *Personal Data:* b Raleigh, NC, Nov 2, 17; m 39, Edna Matthews; c John W Jr. *Educ:* Wake Forest Col, AB, 38, AM, 43; Univ Mo, AM, 48, PhD(math), 51. *Prof Exp:* Instr high sch math, NC, 38-46 & Mo, 46-50; from asst prof to assoc prof math, Univ Ga, 50-53; assoc prof, Univ Richmond, 53-56; assoc prof, Wake Forest Univ, 56-61, prof math, 61-88. *Concurrent Pos:* Consult, R J Reynolds Industs, 58-83. *Mem:* Math Asn Am; Opers Res Soc Am; fel AAAS. *Res:* Differential and distance geometry; operations research; computer science. *Mailing Add:* 5401 Indiana Ave Apt N-174 Winston-Salem NC 27106-2884

SAWYER, PAUL THOMPSON, PLANT TAXONOMY. *Current Pos:* Asst prof, 69-76, ASSOC PROF BIOL, MONT COL MINERAL SCI & TECHNOL, 76- *Personal Data:* b Hanover, NH, Aug 7, 40. *Educ:* Univ Vt, BS, 65; Mont State Univ, MS, 67, PhD(bot), 70. *Mem:* Bot Soc Am; Am Soc Plant Taxon; Int Asn Plant Taxon. *Res:* Systematic investigations of the genera Delphinium and Ledum using chromatographic procedures; investigations of environmental changes occurring when grassland-shrub communities influenced by mining activities are reforested. *Mailing Add:* Dept Biol Sci Mont Col Mineral Sci & Technol Butte MT 59701

SAWYER, PHILIP NICHOLAS, THORACIC SURGERY. *Current Pos:* from instr to assoc prof surg, 57-66, PROF SURG, STATE UNIV NY DOWNSTATE MED CTR, 66-, HEAD VASCULAR SURG SERV & BIOPHYS & ELECTROCHEM LABS, 64- *Personal Data:* b Bangor, Maine, Oct 25, 25; m 53; c 4. *Educ:* Univ Pa, MD, 49; Am Bd Surg, dipl, 58; Am Bd Thoracic Surg, dipl, 60. *Honors & Awards:* Clemson Award Basic Res Biomat. *Prof Exp:* Asst, Harrison Dept Surg Res, Univ Pa, 47-49, intern, Hosp Univ Pa, 49-50; staff mem, Naval Med Res Inst, 51-53; chief resident, St Luke's Hosp, New York, 56-57. *Concurrent Pos:* Fel surg, Univ Pa, 53-56, Nat Cancer Inst res fel biophys, Johnson Found Med Physics, 50; fel path, St Luke's Hosp, New York, 57; Markle scholar, 59-64; vis surgeon, Kings County Hosp & univ hosp, State Univ NY; assoc attend surgeon, St John's Episcopal Hosp & Methodist Hosp, Brooklyn; consult vascular surg, USPHS Hosp, Staten Island, NY, 66. *Mem:* AAAS; Am Chem Soc; Am Heart Asn; Am Physiol Soc; Am Soc Artificial Internal Organs. *Res:* Tissue electrical potential differences and metabolism; ionic movement across cellular membranes; etiology of vascular thrombosis; preservation of tissues; homotransplantation techniques; cardiovascular surgery. *Mailing Add:* 7600 Ridge Blvd Brooklyn NY 11209-3008

SAWYER, RALPH STANLEY, PHYSICS, ENGINEERING. *Current Pos:* RETIRED. *Personal Data:* b Gray, Maine, Jan 9, 21; m 51, Margaret Helen Howard; c Nancy Ellen & Michael Howard. *Educ:* Tufts Univ, BS, 44. *Honors & Awards:* Exceptional Serv Medals, Nat Aeronaut & Space Admin, 69; Centennial Medal, Inst Elec & Electronics Engrs, 84; Outstanding Leadership Medal, Nat Aeronaut & Space Admin, 81. *Prof Exp:* Res & lab instr piezo elec, Tufts Univ, 46-47; res engr instrumentation, Nat Adv Comt Aeronaut Labs, Langley Field, Va, 47-48; electronic engr, Indust Instrument Div, Minneapolis-Honeywell Regulator Co, 50; electronics engr commun, Hastings Instrument Co, Hampton, Va, 50-51; supvry electronic control engr, US Naval Weapons Sta, Yorktown, Va, 51-53; head, Range Data & Homing Test Sect, US Naval Underwater Ordnance Sta, Newport, RI, 53-54; head Ballistic Instrumentation Br, & consult, Missile Br, Spec Projs Off, US Naval Bur Weapons Labs, Dahlgren, Va, 54-59; res engr & head, commun sect, Space Task Group, Nat Aeronaut & Space Admin, Langley Field, Va, 59-61; head, Elec Systs Br, Johnson Space Ctr, Houston, 61-62, chief, Instrumentation & Electronic Systs Div, 62-69, chief, Tracking & Commun Develop Div, 69-89. *Mem:* Fel Inst Elec & Electronics Engrs; Am Inst Aeronaut & Astronaut; Nat Telecommunications Conf (chmn, 72); Aerospace & Electronic Systs Soc. *Res:* Responsible for the research, development, and test of all tracking, television, telemetry and communications systems used on all current and past manned space flight programs sponsored by the United States. *Mailing Add:* 510 N Shadow Bend Ave Friendswood TX 77546

SAWYER, RAYMOND FRANCIS, THEORETICAL PHYSICS. *Current Pos:* PROF PHYSICS, UNIV CALIF, SANTA BARBARA, 65- *Personal Data:* b Northfield, Minn, Aug 30, 32; m 56; c 2. *Educ:* Swarthmore Col, AB, 53; Harvard Univ, MA, 55, PhD, 58. *Prof Exp:* NSF fel physics, Europ Orgn Nuclear Res, Geneva, 58-59; Wis Alumni Res Found fel, Univ Wis, 59-60, from asst prof to prof, 60-65. *Mem:* Am Phys Soc. *Res:* High energy physics; fundamental particle theory. *Mailing Add:* Dept Physics Univ Calif Santa Barbara CA 93106

SAWYER, RICHARD TREVOR, mononuclear phagocyte biology, cell kinetics, for more information see previous edition

SAWYER, ROBERT FENNELL, MECHANICAL ENGINEERING, COMBUSTION. *Current Pos:* from asst prof to assoc prof, Univ Calif, Berkeley, 66-75, prof mech eng, 75-91, Class 1935 Prof Energy, 88-91, PROF GRAD SCH, UNIV CALIF, BERKELEY, 93- *Personal Data:* b Santa Barbara, Calif, May 19, 35; m 57, Barbara L White; c Lisa Marie & Allison Jean (Shaffer). *Educ:* Stanford Univ, BS, 57, MS, 58; Princeton Univ, MA, 63, PhD(aerospace & mech sci), 66. *Prof Exp:* Instr physics, Antelope Valley Col, 58-61; mem res staff, Princeton Univ, 65-66. *Concurrent Pos:* Res engr, USAF Rocket Propulsion Lab, 58-61, chief liquid systs anal, 61; consult to various co & govt agencies, 64-; mem, Calif Air Resources Bd, 75-76; chmn, Energy & Resources Group, Univ Calif, Berkeley, 84-88; sr policy adv, US Environ Protection Agency, 95-96; vis prof energy & environ, Univ Col, London. *Mem:* Am Inst Aeronaut & Astronaut; Am Soc Mech Engrs; fel Am Soc Eng Educ; Soc Automotive Engrs; Combustion Inst (pres, 92-96). *Res:* Propulsion; combustion; air pollution; chemical kinetics; fire science; regulatory policy. *Mailing Add:* Dept Mech Eng Univ Calif Berkeley CA 94720-1740. *Fax:* 510-642-1850; *E-Mail:* rsawyer@enter.me.berkeley.edu

SAWYER, ROGER HOLMES, DEVELOPMENTAL BIOLOGY. *Current Pos:* from asst prof to assoc prof, 75-83, PROF BIOL, UNIV SC, 83-, CHMN DEPT, 86- *Personal Data:* b Portland, Maine, Sept 5, 42; m 61, 83; c 5. *Educ:* Univ Maine, BA, 65; Univ Mass, PhD(zool), 70. *Prof Exp:* NIH fel, Univ Calif, Davis, 70-71, NSF res assoc genetics, 71-72, asst res anatomist develop biol, Calif Primate Res Ctr, 73-74. *Concurrent Pos:* Mem, NIH Study Sect Biol. *Mem:* Sigma Xi; Soc Develop Biol; Am Soc Zoologists; NY Acad Sci; Int Soc Develop Biologists; fel AAAS; Am Soc Cell Biol; Linnean Soc. *Res:* Control of biochemical and morphological differentiation by epithelial-mesenchymal interactions during skin organogenesis and the action of mutant genes and teratogens on these interactions. *Mailing Add:* Dept Biol Univ SC Columbia SC 29208-0001

SAWYER, S PRENTISS, physics, for more information see previous edition

SAWYER, STANLEY ARTHUR, MATHEMATICAL STATISTICS. *Current Pos:* PROF MATH, GENETICS & BIOSTATIST, WASHINGTON UNIV, 84- *Personal Data:* b Juneau, Alaska, Mar 19, 40. *Educ:* Calif Inst Technol, BS, 60, PhD(math), 64. *Hon Degrees:* AM, Brown Univ, 69. *Prof Exp:* Courant instr math, Courant Inst, NY Univ, 65-67; from asst prof to assoc prof, Brown Univ, 67-69; from asst prof to prof math, Yeshiva Univ, 69-77; prof math & statist, Purdue Univ, 78-84. *Concurrent Pos:* Assoc ed, Molecular Biol & Evolution, 94-; probability ed, Proceedings Am Math Soc, 96- *Mem:* Am Math Soc; Genetics Soc Am; fel Inst Math Statist. *Res:* Probability; population genetics. *Mailing Add:* Dept Math Washington Univ St Louis MO 63130

SAWYER, WILBUR HENDERSON, ENDOCRINE PHARMACOLOGY, COMPARATIVE ENDOCRINOLOGY. *Current Pos:* from assoc prof to prof, 57-78, Gustavus A pfeiffer prof pharmacol, 78-90, EMER PROF PHARMACOL, COL PHYSICIANS & SURGEONS, COLUMBIA UNIV, 91- *Personal Data:* b Brisbane, Australia, Mar 23, 21; US citizen; m 42, 82; c 4. *Educ:* Harvard Univ, AB, 42, MD, 45, PhD(biol), 50. *Hon Degrees:* DSc, Med Col Ohio, 94. *Prof Exp:* Instr biol, Harvard Univ, 50-53; asst prof physiol, Col Med, NY Univ, 53-57. *Concurrent Pos:* Lederle med fac award, 55-57; mem adv panel regulatory biol, NSF, 59-62; mem gen med B study sect, Div Res Grants, NIH, 70-74; sr res scholar, Australian-Am Educ Found, 74; vis res fel, Howard Florey Inst Exp Biol & Med, Univ Melbourne, Australia, 74. *Mem:* Endocrine Soc; Am Soc Pharmacol & Exp Therapeut; Soc Endocrinol; Am Soc Zool; Soc Gen Physiol; Am Physiol Soc. *Res:* Comparative endocrinology; renal physiology; pharmacology of neurohypophysial hormones. *Mailing Add:* 1490 Kings Lane Palo Alto CA 94303-2836

SAWYER, WILLIAM D, MICROBIOLOGY, INTERNAL MEDICINE. *Current Pos:* PRES, CHINA MED BD NY INC, 88- *Personal Data:* b Roodhouse, Ill, Dec 28, 29; m 51, Jane A Stewart; c Dale S & Carde A (Bolin). *Educ:* Univ Ill, 47-50; Wash Univ, MD, 54. *Hon Degrees:* ScD, Mahidol Univ, Thailand, 88; DPH, Chiang Mai Univ, Thailand, 93. *Prof Exp:* Asst prof microbiol, Sch Med, Johns Hopkins Univ, 64-67; mem staff, Rockefeller Found, 67-73; prof microbiol & immunol & chmn dept, Sch Med, Ind Univ, Indianapolis, 73-80; prof, microbiol & immunol, dept med, Wright State Univ, Ohio & dean, Sch Med, 81-87. *Concurrent Pos:* Fel med, Sch Med, Wash Univ, 58-60; consult, Army Med Res & Develop Command, 65-67, Armed Forces Inst Path, 79- & Lobund Adv Bd, Notre Dame Univ, 79-86; vis prof & chmn, dept microbiol, Mahidol Univ, Thailand, 67-73; consult, WHO Immunol Res & Training Ctr, Singapore, 69-73; chmn, Consortium Affils Int Progs, AAAS; hon prof, Sun Yat Sen Univ Med Sci, Guangzhou, Peoples Rep China. *Mem:* Am Soc Microbiol; Am Col Physicians; Am Acad Microbiol; Soc Exp Biol Med; Am Asn Pathologists; AAAS. *Res:* Bacterial infection, genetics and physiology. *Mailing Add:* China Med Bd 750 Third Ave New York NY 10017-2703. *Fax:* 212-949-8726; *E-Mail:* 75460.452@compuserve.com

SAWYERS, JOHN LAZELLE, SURGERY. *Current Pos:* From asst prof to prof surg, 69-83, JOHN CLINTON FOSHEE DISTINGUISHED PROF SURG & CHMN DEPT, VANDERBILT UNIV, 83- *Personal Data:* b Centerville, Iowa, July 26, 25; m 57; c 3. *Educ:* Univ Rochester, BA, 46; Johns Hopkins Univ, MD, 49. *Concurrent Pos:* Dir, Sect Surg Scis, Vanderbilt Univ, 83- *Mem:* Soc Univ Surg; Am Asn Thoracic Surg; Am Col Surg; Am Surg Asn; Int Cardiovasc Soc. *Res:* Surgery of the alimentary tract. *Mailing Add:* Vanderbilt Univ Med Ctr 1001 Oxford House Nashville TN 37232-4730

SAWYERS, KENNETH NORMAN, APPLIED MATHEMATICS. *Current Pos:* from asst prof to assoc prof, Ctr Appln Math, 69-82, PROF MECH ENGR & MECHS, LEHIGH UNIV, 83-, ASSOC DEAN & APPL SCI, 90- *Personal Data:* b Chicago, Ill, May 19, 36; m 62; c 2. *Educ:* Ill Inst Technol, BS, 62; Brown Univ, PhD(appl math), 67. *Prof Exp:* Math physicist, Stanford Res Inst, 66-69. *Mem:* Am Acad Mech. *Res:* Theoretical seismology; mechanics of fluids and solids; stability theory. *Mailing Add:* 1822 Monocaly St Bethlehem PA 18018-1916. *E-Mail:* kns0@lehigh.edu

SAX, KARL JOLIVETTE, chemistry, for more information see previous edition

SAX, MARTIN, CRYSTALLOGRAPHY, MACROMOLECULAR & BIORELEVANT STRUCTURES. *Current Pos:* RES CHEMIST & DIR, BIOCRYSTALLOG LAB, VET AFFAIRS MED CTR, PITTSBURGH, 66-, ASSOC CHIEF STAFF RES & DEVELOP, 72- *Personal Data:* b Wheeling, WVa. *Educ:* Univ Pittsburgh, BS, 41, PhD(phys chem), 61. *Prof Exp:* Res chemist, Trojan Powder Co, 41-44 & Glyco Prod Co, 51-59; asst biochemist, W Pa Hosp, 46-57; postdoctoral crystallog, Univ Pittsburgh, 61-63, asst res prof, 63-66. *Concurrent Pos:* Adj assoc prof crystallog, Univ Pittsburgh, 66-71, adj prof, 71- *Mem:* AAAS; Am Crystallog Asn; Am Chem Soc. *Res:* Three dimensional structures and the functions of biological macromolecules as ascertained by x-ray diffractions from single crystals. *Mailing Add:* Vet Affairs Med Ctr Univ DsC PO Box 12055 Pittsburgh PA 15240-0055

SAX, ROBERT LOUIS, GEOPHYSICS. *Current Pos:* sr geophysicist, United Earth Sci Div, Teledyne Indust, 62-68, SR SCIENTIST, TELEDYNE INC, GEOTECH CORP, 68- *Personal Data:* b Wheeling, WVa, Apr 7, 28; m 58; c 2. *Educ:* Mass Inst Technol, BS, 52, PhD(geophys), 60. *Prof Exp:* Geologist-geophysicist, Standard Oil Co Calif, 52-56; mem tech staff, Ramo-Wooldridge Labs, 59-60 & Hughes Aircraft Corp, 60-62. *Mem:* AAAS; Am Geophys Union; Soc Explor Geophys; Seismol Soc Am; Inst Elec & Electronics Engrs. *Res:* Interpretation of earth gravity measurements; design of systems for probing and analyzing planetary atmospheres; wave propagation and source mechanisms in a solid earth; theory of seismic noise. *Mailing Add:* 3707 Cameron Mills Rd Alexandria VA 22305

SAX, SYLVAN MAURICE, CLINICAL CHEMISTRY. *Current Pos:* RETIRED. *Personal Data:* b Wheeling, WVa, Feb 8, 23; m 57; c 3. *Educ:* Univ Pittsburgh, BS, 44, PhD(org chem), 53; Am Bd Clin Chem, Dipl, 60. *Honors & Awards:* Fisher Award, Am Asn Clin Chem. *Prof Exp:* Group leader res, Glyco Prods Co, 53-55; clin biochemist, Western Pa Hosp, 55-85, clin chem consult, 85- *Concurrent Pos:* Instr & adj asst prof, Sch Med, Univ Pittsburgh, 57- *Mem:* Am Chem Soc; Am Asn Clin Chem. *Res:* Clinical chemistry methodology and control. *Mailing Add:* 6490 Monitor St Pittsburgh PA 15217-2722

SAXE, HARRY CHARLES, CIVIL & STRUCTURAL ENGINEERING. *Current Pos:* dean, Speed Sci Sch, 69-80, prof, 69-83, DEAN & EMER PROF CIVIL ENG, UNIV LOUISVILLE, 83- *Personal Data:* b Long Island City, NY, Mar 18, 20; m 45; c 2. *Educ:* City Col New York, BCE, 42; Univ Fla, MSE, 49; Mass Inst Technol, ScD, 52. *Prof Exp:* Asst civil eng, Univ Fla, 48-49, instr, 49-50; res asst, Mass Inst Technol, 50-52; assoc prof, Ga Inst Technol, 52-56; engr, Praeger-Kavanagh & Assocs, NY, 56-57; assoc prof civil eng, Polytech Inst Brooklyn, 57 & Univ Cincinnati, 57-59; prof & head dept, Univ Notre Dame, 59-60 & 61-65, actg dean col eng, 60-61 & 66-67, chmn dept civil eng, 67-69. *Concurrent Pos:* NSF sci fac fel & vis prof, Imp Col, Univ London, 65-66; pres, Univ Louisville Inst Indust Res, 69-74; mem, Ky Sci & Technol Adv Coun, 70-75; Ky Bd Registr for Prof Engrs & Land Surveyors, 72-80; mem, energy res bd, Ky Dept Energy, 76-80; Louis S Le Tellier distinguished vis prof, Dept Civil Eng, The Citadel, Mil Col SC, 83-85 & 86-; Fredrik Wachtmeister distinguished prof eng, Va Mil Inst, 83; vis prof civil, Univ Md, Col Park, 85-86. *Mem:* Fel Am Soc Civil Engrs; Am Soc Eng Educ; Nat Soc Prof Engrs; Soc Am Mil Engrs; Am Soc Testing & Mat; Sigma Xi. *Res:* Structural mechanics including computer applications. *Mailing Add:* 612 Harbor Creek Pl Charleston SC 29412

SAXE, LEONARD, PSYCHOLOGY. *Current Pos:* ADJ PROF, BRANDEIS UNIV, 88- *Personal Data:* b New York, NY, June 12, 47; m 70; c 1. *Educ:* Univ Pittsburgh, BS, 69, MS, 72, PhD(social psychol), 76. *Prof Exp:* Assoc prof psychol, Boston Univ, 75. *Concurrent Pos:* Consult, US Cong, Off Technol Assessment, 80-88; Fulbright lectr, Univ Haifa, Israel, 81-82; dir, Ctr Appl Social Sci, Boston Univ, 85-88. *Mem:* Am Psychol Asn; Soc Psychol Study Soc Sci. *Res:* Mental health policy; use of social research in the development of social policy; lie detectors; polygraph tests; substance abuse treatment evaluation. *Mailing Add:* Heller Sch Brandeis Univ Waltham MA 02254

SAXE, STANLEY RICHARD, GERIATRIC DENTISTRY, PERIODONTOLOGY. *Current Pos:* from asst prof to assoc prof, Col Dent, Univ Ky, 62-67, chmn dept, 66-69, prof periodont, 77-97, prof geriatric dent oral health sci, 87-97, EMER PROF, COL DENT, UNIV KY, 97- *Personal Data:* b Chelsea, Mass, Feb 1, 32; m 58, Judith Shapiro; c Harriet, Natalie & Neal. *Educ:* Boston Univ, AB, 53; Harvard Univ, DMD, 58; Univ Wash, MSD, 60. *Honors & Awards:* Geriat Oral Health Award, Am Dent Asn, 89. *Prof Exp:* Instr periodont, Sch Dent, Univ Wash, 60-62. *Concurrent Pos:* Consult, Vet Admin Hosp, Am Lake, Wash, 61-62, Lexington, Ky, 62- & USPHS Hosp, 62-76; vis prof, Hadassah Sch Dent Med, Hebrew Univ Jerusalem, 70 & Sanders-Brown Res Ctr on Aging, Lexington, Ky, 84. *Mem:* Am Soc Aging; Am Acad Periodont; Int Asn Dent Res; Am Soc Geriat Dent. *Res:* Oral health care strategies for the older adult; etiology, assessment and treatment of periodontal disease; relationship of dental amalgam experience brain mercury level and Alzheimer's disease. *Mailing Add:* Geriatric Oral Health 201 Med Ctr Annex 5 Lexington KY 40536-0078

SAXENA, BRIJ B, BIOCHEMISTRY, ENDOCRINOLOGY. *Current Pos:* assoc prof biochem, Dept Med, 66-72, assoc prof endocrinol, Dept Obstet & Gynec, 70-72, PROF BIOCHEM, DEPT MED & PROF ENDOCRINOL, DEPT OBSTET & GYNEC, MED COL, CORNELL UNIV, 72-, DIR, DIV REPRODUCTIVE ENDOCRINOL, DEPT OBSTET & GYNEC, 80- *Personal Data:* b India, July 6, 30. *Educ:* Lucknow Univ, PhD(biochem), 54; Univ Munster, Dr rer nat(physiol), 57; Univ Wis, PhD(biochem, endocrinol), 61. *Prof Exp:* Lectr biol, Lucknow Univ, 54-55; res assoc endocrinol, Univ Wis, 57-62; from asst prof to assoc prof biochem, NJ Col Med, 62-66. *Concurrent Pos:* Career sci award, Health Res Coun, New York, 69. *Mem:* AAAS; Endocrine Soc; NY Acad Sci; fel Royal Soc Med; Harvey Soc; Sigma Xi. *Res:* Physiology, biochemistry and molecular biology of pituitary hormones and gonadal receptors. *Mailing Add:* NY Hosp-Cornell Med Ctr 525 E 68th St New York NY 10021. *Fax:* 212-746-4964; *E-Mail:* msingh@mail.med.cornell.edu

SAXENA, NARENDRA K, MARINE SURVEYS, GEODESY. *Current Pos:* asst prof surv, Univ Hawaii, 78-81, assoc prof, 81-86, PROF CIVIL ENG, UNIV HAWAII, 86-, CHMN, 94- *Personal Data:* b Agra, India, Oct 15, 36; US citizen; m 70, Cecilia HSI; c Sarah V & Lorelle S. *Educ:* Agra Univ, BSc, 55; Hannover Tech Univ, dipl Ing, 65; Graz Tech Univ, Dr tech (satellite geod), 72. *Honors & Awards:* Fel, Marine Technol Soc. *Prof Exp:* Proj-in-charge satellite geod, Space Sci & Technol Ctr, India, 69; res assoc geod, Ohio State Univ, 69-74; asst prof geod eng, Univ Ill, Urbana, 74-78. *Concurrent Pos:* Mem, Spec Study Group, Int Asn Geod, 73-80; ed-in-chief, Marine Geod J Int J Ocean Surv Mapping & Sensing, 77-; co-chmn, Pac Cong Marine Technol, 84, 86 & 88; adj res prof oceanog, Naval Postgrad Sch, Monterey, 84-; pres, Pacon Int, 92- *Mem:* Marine Technol Soc; Am Geophys Union; Tsunami Soc; Am Soc Civil Engrs. *Res:* Ocean survey and navigation; computational methods to solve large systems; engineering survey; space geodesy. *Mailing Add:* Dept Civil Eng Univ Hawaii Honolulu HI 96822. *Fax:* 808-956-5014; *E-Mail:* saxema@wiliki.eng.hawaii.edu

SAXENA, SATISH CHANDRA, POLLUTION CONTROL, WASTE MANAGEMENT. *Current Pos:* PROF CHEM ENG, UNIV ILL, 68- *Personal Data:* b Lucknow, India, June 24, 34; US citizen; m 61, Asha; c Alka, Alok, Anup & Anil. *Educ:* Lucknow Univ, BSc, 51; MSc, 53; Calcutta Univ, PhD(physics), 56. *Prof Exp:* Res assoc, Univ Md, 56-58, Columbia Univ, 58-59; res assoc physics, Yale Univ, 59; engr, Bhabha Atomic Res Ctr, India, 59-61; reader & head, Dept Physics, Rajasthan Univ, India, 61-66; assoc prof, Purdue Univ, 66-68. *Concurrent Pos:* Sr res assoc, Ames Res Ctr, NASA, 69 & 70, Argonne Nat Lab, 77; consult, Purdue Univ, Argonne Nat Lab, E I du Pont de Nemours & Co Inc, Oak Ridge Nat Lab & Gen Elec Co, Morgantown Energy Technol Ctr, WVa, Inst Gas Technol, Chicago, Ortho Inc, Chicago & Maremac Corp, Pittsburgh Energy Technol Ctr; vis prof, Huazhong Univ Sci Tech, Wuhan, China, Banaras Hinda Univ, India, King Fahd Univ Petrol & Minerals, Saudi Arabia. *Mem:* Am Inst Chem Engrs. *Res:* Transport properties of gases and gaseous mixtures; modeling of fluidized bed operations, coal combustion, coal gasification and indirect coal liquefaction; solid waste management. *Mailing Add:* Dept Chem Eng M/C 110 Univ Ill 810 S Clinton Chicago IL 60607-7000. *Fax:* 312-996-0808; *E-Mail:* saxena@uic.edu

SAXENA, SUBHASH CHANDRA, FINITE GEOMETRY, GRAPH THEORY. *Current Pos:* assoc prof, 73-77, chmn, 87-93, PROF MATH, UNIV SC, COASTAL, 77- *Personal Data:* b Etawah, UP, India; US citizen; m 59, Pushpa Rani; c Anita & Anil. *Educ:* Univ Delhi, BA(hons), 52, MA, 54, PhD(math), 58. *Prof Exp:* Instr math, Defense Acad, India, 58; fel, Univ Delhi, 58-59; from asst prof to assoc prof, Atlanta Univ, 59-63; assoc prof, Northern Ill Univ, 63-68 & Univ Akron, 68-73. *Concurrent Pos:* Exchange res prof, Univ SC, Columbia, 80; vis res scientist, Indian Inst Technol, Delhi, India, 81-82. *Mem:* Am Math Soc; Math Asn Am; Nat Coun Teachers Math; Sigma Xi. *Res:* Differential geometry; finite geometry; combinatorial mathematics; real analysis; discrete mathematics; geometry at the college level; author of several publications. *Mailing Add:* 4407 Greenbay Trail Myrtle Beach SC 29577. *Fax:* 803-349-2990; *E-Mail:* saxenas@coastal.edu

SAXENA, UMESH, INDUSTRIAL ENGINEERING. *Current Pos:* PROF INDUST ENG, UNIV WIS-MILWAUKEE, 68- *Personal Data:* b Pilibhit, India; m, Nirmala; c Priya, Ila & Juhi. *Educ:* Univ Roorkee, BS, 60; Univ Wis-Madison, MS, 65, PhD, 68. *Prof Exp:* Lectr mech eng, Indian Inst Technol, Delhi, 62-64. *Concurrent Pos:* Dir, Energy Analysis & Diag Ctr. *Mem:* Oper Res Soc Am; Am Inst Indust Engrs. *Res:* Health care systems and delivery; application of quantitative methods in analysis and control of industrial and service systems; energy and environment management and conservation. *Mailing Add:* Indust & Systs Eng Univ Wis Col Appl Sci & Eng Milwaukee WI 53201. *Fax:* 414-229-6958; *E-Mail:* uksaxena@convex.csd.uwm.edu

SAXENA, VINOD KUMAR, METEOROLOGY, CLOUD PHYSICS. *Current Pos:* assoc prof meteorol, 79-88, PROF METEOROL, NC STATE UNIV, 88- *Personal Data:* b Agra, India, May 23, 44; m 87, Beena Sharma; c Rita & Victor. *Educ:* Agra Univ, BS, 61, MS, 63; Univ Rajasthan, PhD(physics), 69. *Honors & Awards:* Meterol Award, Univ Utah, 79. *Prof Exp:* Lectr physics, Agra Col, 63-64; asst prof, Univ Saugar, 67-68; Off Naval Res fel, Univ Mo, Rolla, 68-71; res assoc cloud physics, Univ Denver, 71-73, cloud physicist & lectr physics, Denver Res Inst, 73-77; res assoc prof meteorol, Univ Utah, 77-79. *Concurrent Pos:* Fac mem invited sem, NC Ctr Advan Teaching, Western Carolina Univ; US grants, NSF, US Environ Protection Agency, NSF Dept Energy, US Bur Mines, NASA. *Mem:* Am Meteorol Soc; Am Geophys Union; fel Royal Meteorol Soc, UK; Am Asn Areasol Res; Air Pollution Control Asn; European Asn Areasol Res. *Res:* Cloud and aerosol physics; air pollution meteorology; condensation and nucleation phenomena; cloud-aerosol interactions; instrumentation for simulating atmospheric environment regional aerosol-cloud-climate interactions; cloud and ice-forming nuclei. *Mailing Add:* Dept Marine Earth & Atmospheric Sci Box 8208 NC State Univ Raleigh NC 27695-8208. *Fax:* 919-515-7802; *E-Mail:* saxena@eos.nesu.edu

SAXER, RICHARD KARL, METALLURGICAL ENGINEERING. *Current Pos:* CHIEF EXEC OFFICER, UNIVERSAL TECH CORP, 91- *Personal Data:* b Toledo, Ohio, Aug 31, 28; m 52, Marilyn D Mersereau; c Jane L, Robert K, Kris R & Ann L. *Educ:* US Naval Acad, BS, 52; Air Force Inst Technol, MS, 57; Ohio State Univ, PhD(metall eng), 62. *Prof Exp:* Comdr 2nd lt, USAF, 52, adv through ranks to lt gen, 76; electronics & mech officer, Tactical Air Command, Sandia Base, NMex, 53-54; SAC 6th Aviation Depot Squadron, French Morocco, 54-55; proj engr, Mech Equip Br, Air Force Spec Weapons Ctr, Kirtland AFB, NMex, 57-59; proj officer, Nuclear Safety Div, 59-60; assoc prof, Dept Eng Mech, Air Force Inst Technol, 62-66; assoc prof & dep dept head, USAF Acad, 66-70; comdr & dir, Air Force Mat Lab, Wright-Patterson AFB, 71-74; dep, Re-entry Syst Space & Missile Systs Orgn, 74-77; dep aero equip, Aero Systs Div, 77-80, dep tactical systs, 80, vcomdr, 81-83; aero systs div dir, Defense Nuclear Agency, 83-85; pres, R K Saxer & Assoc, 85-91. *Concurrent Pos:* Mem Nat Mil Adv Bd, 71-74, NATO Adv Group Res & Develop, 73-74; res & tech comn mat & struct, NASA, 73-74; chmn plan group aerospace mat, Interagency Coun Mat, 73-74. *Mem:* Am Defense Preparedness Asn; Sigma Xi. *Mailing Add:* 215 Dalfaber Lane Springboro OH 45066

SAXINGER, W(ILLIAM) CARL, DIAGNOSTIC IMMUNOLOGY. *Current Pos:* RES PROF, LAB CHEM EVOLUTION, DEPT CHEM, UNIV MD, 72- *Personal Data:* b Chicago, Ill, Oct 4, 41; m 67; c 3. *Educ:* Univ Ill, BS, 63, PhD(microbiol), 69. *Prof Exp:* Nat Acad Sci & Nat Res Coun res assoc exbiol & chem evolution, Ames Res Ctr, NASA, 69-71; res assoc chem evolution, dept chem, Univ Md, 71-72; staff fel tumor virol, 72-74, sr investr human retrovirol, Lab Tumor Cell Biol, Div Cancer Treat, Nat Cancer Inst, 74- *Res:* Processes of infection and immunity to human retroviruses causing human leukemia and immunosuppression. *Mailing Add:* 6814 Renita Lane Bethesda MD 20817

SAXON, DAVID STEPHEN, THEORETICAL NUCLEAR PHYSICS. *Current Pos:* EMER PROF, UNIV CALIF. *Personal Data:* b St Paul, Minn, Feb 8, 20; m 40; c 6. *Educ:* Mass Inst Technol, BS, 41, PhD(physics), 44. *Hon Degrees:* LHD, Hebrew Union Col, 76, Univ Judaism, 77; LLD, Univ SCalif, 78. *Prof Exp:* Mem staff, Radiation Lab, Mass Inst Technol, 42-46; assoc physicist, Philips Lab, Inc, NY, 46-47; physicist, Inst Numerical Anal, Nat Bur Stand, Calif, 50-53; from asst prof to prof physics, Univ Calif, Los Angeles, 47-83, chmn dept, 63-66, dean phys sci, 66-70, vchancellor, 68-74, exec vchancellor, 74-75, pres, 75-83; off chmn corp, Mass Inst Technol, Cambridge, 83-90, hon chmn, 90- *Concurrent Pos:* Guggenheim Mem fel, 56-57 & 61-62; Fulbright lectr, 61-62; consult, Systs Corp Am, 58-63, Convair Div, Gen Dynamics Corp, 60-63 & E H Plessit Assoc, 61-63; emer pres & emer prof physics, Univ Calif, Los Angeles, 83-; mem bd dirs, Mass Ctrs Excellence Corp, Ford Tech Adv panel & Harvard Overseer's comt to visit Med Sch & Sch Dent Med. *Mem:* Fel Am Phys Soc; Am Asn Physics Teachers; Sigma Xi; fel Am Acad Arts & Sci; Am Philos Soc; fel AAAS; Am Inst Physics. *Res:* Electromagnetic theory; quantum theory; nuclear physics; author of 1 book and author or coauthor of 3 physics texts and many scientific articles in professional journals. *Mailing Add:* Dept Physics 2 130J KnudsonHall Univ Calif 405 Hilgard Ave Los Angeles CA 90024. *Fax:* 310-206-5668

SAXON, JAMES GLENN, ANATOMY. *Current Pos:* from asst prof to assoc prof, 74-82, PROF ANAT, SOUTHERN COL OPTOM, 83- *Personal Data:* b Marlin, Tex, July 16, 41; m 68; c 2. *Educ:* Baylor Univ, BS, 63, MS, 66; Tex A&M Univ, PhD(wildlife sci), 70. *Prof Exp:* Asst prof biol, Memphis State Univ, 69-70; asst prof & chmn dept, Erskine Col, 70-74. *Mem:* AAAS. *Res:* Anatomy and reproductive physiology of amphibians and ocular reptiles. *Mailing Add:* 5988 Diplomat Pl Memphis TN 38134

SAXON, ROBERT, POLYMER CHEMISTRY. *Current Pos:* CONSULT, 86- *Personal Data:* b Brooklyn, NY, June 3, 24; m 60; c 2. *Educ:* Northwestern Univ, PhD(chem), 52. *Prof Exp:* Res chemist, US Indust Chem Co, 43-49; asst chem, Northwestern Univ, 50-52; res assoc, Harris Res Labs, 52-56; res chemist, Am Cyanamid Co, 56-72, mgr res & develop, 72-86. *Mem:* AAAS; Am Chem Soc. *Res:* Organic synthesis and mechanisms; urethane chemistry and technology; surface coatings; laminated plastics; elastomer synthesis and technology. *Mailing Add:* 199 Laurel Circle Princeton NJ 08540-2718. *Fax:* 609-683-5799; *E-Mail:* rsaxon@delphi.com

SAXON, ROBERTA POLLACK, CHEMICAL PHYSICS, ATOMIC & MOLECULAR PHYSICS. *Current Pos:* chem physicist, 74-79, sr chem physicist, 79-91, DEPT DIR, PHYS SCI DIV, SRI INT, 91- *Personal Data:* b Chicago, Ill, July 19, 46; m 92, Michael Sasnett. *Educ:* Cornell Univ, BA, 67; Univ Chicago, MA, 69, PhD(chem), 71. *Prof Exp:* Fel, Argonne Nat Lab, 72-73, Univ Wash, 73-74. *Concurrent Pos:* Mem, Comt Atomic Molecular Optical Sci, Nat Res Coun, 89-92, Panel Opportunities Plasma Sci, 92-93. *Mem:* Fel Am Phys Soc; Am Chem Soc; AAAS. *Res:* Ab initio molecular structure calculations predicting structure and energy of small organic species and transition states and excited state potential energy curves including Rydbug states; photodissociation; multiphoton process; theory of reactive, inelastic, and elastic collisions. *Mailing Add:* SRI Int PS277 333 Ravenswood Ave Menlo Park CA 94125-3434

SAXTON, HARRY JAMES, MATERIALS SCIENCE. *Current Pos:* mem tech staff, 71-74, div supvr, 74-76, dept mgr, 76-83, DIR, SANDIA NAT LABS, 83- *Personal Data:* b Bell, Calif, July 2, 39; m 61, 83; c 2. *Educ:* Stanford Univ, MS, 62, PhD(mat sci), 69. *Prof Exp:* Systs analyst, Ctr Naval Anal, 69-71. *Concurrent Pos:* Consult, Lawrence Livermore Lab, 66-71. *Mem:* Am Soc Metals. *Res:* Relation of materials microstructure to macroscopic properties; development and production of integrated circuits; quartz oscillators; electromechanical devices; explosive devices; battery research and development. *Mailing Add:* Sandia Nat Labs Org 1800 MS 1435 Albuquerque NM 87185

SAXTON, KEITH E, AGRICULTURAL ENGINEERING. *Current Pos:* HYDRAUL ENGR, FED RES, SCI & EDUC ADMIN, USDA, 61- *Personal Data:* b Crawford, Nebr, Dec 22, 37; m 57; c 2. *Educ:* Univ Nebr, BS, 61; Univ Wis, MS, 65; Iowa State Univ, PhD, 72. *Mem:* Am Soc Agr Engrs; Am Soc Civil Engrs. *Res:* Hydrologic research on small agricultural watersheds. *Mailing Add:* NW 1830 Deane Pl Pullman WA 99163

SAXTON, LAWRENCE VICTOR, OBJECT-ORIENTED DATABASE THEORY, ORDERED DATA. *Current Pos:* From asst prof to assoc prof, 73-94, PROF & HEAD, COMPUT SCI DEPT, UNIV REGINA, CAN, 94- *Personal Data:* b St Catherines, Ont, May 26, 46. *Educ:* Univ Waterloo, BMath, 69, MMath, 70, PhD(comput sci), 73. *Concurrent Pos:* Vis asst prof, Vanderbilt Univ, 82-83; vis researcher, Ind Univ, 90-91. *Mem:* Asn Comput Mach; Inst Elec & Electronics Engrs Comput Soc; Can Info Processing Soc; Soc Indust & Appl Math. *Res:* Theoretical and implementation issues arising in database programming languages as a result of allowing complex data types. *Mailing Add:* Dept Comput Sci Univ Regina Regina SK S4S 0A2 Can. *E-Mail:* saxton@cs.uregina.ca

SAXTON, WILLIAM REGINALD, PULP CHEMISTRY. *Current Pos:* RETIRED. *Personal Data:* b Montreal, Que, May 3, 28; m 53, Diane Mary Morrison; c 2. *Educ:* McGill Univ, BSc Hons, 49. *Honors & Awards:* Environ Improv Award, Chem Inst Can; Tappi Fel Award, 87. *Prof Exp:* Mgr rayon res, Indust Cellulose Res Ltd, 58-62, mgr res planning, 62-65; mgr new prod develop, Int Cellulose Res Ltd, 65-68; asst to vpres res & develop, Int Paper Co, 68-71; pres, Can-Pac-Forest Prod Res Ltd, 71-89. *Mem:* Can Pulp & Paper Asn; Can Res Mgt Asn; Tech Asn Pulp & Paper Indust. *Res:* Chemical and mechanical wood pulps for printing and industrial papers, paper board packaging, tissue products, conversion to rayon, cellophane and other cellulosic products. *Mailing Add:* 29 Country Club Pl Brockville ON K6V 6T6 Can

SAYALA, CHHAYA, OIL EXPLORATION CHEMICALS, NITRO COMPOUND EXPLOSIVES. *Current Pos:* PATENT EXAMR, US PATENT & TRADEMARK OFF, 89- *Personal Data:* b Bangalore, India, Apr 16, 50; US citizen; m 78; c Seema. *Educ:* Bangalore Univ, India, BSc, 70, MSc, 72; Indian Inst Technol, India, PhD(chem), 76. *Prof Exp:* Res fel, Univ Agr Sci, India, 77-78; res fel, Univ Nijmegen, Neth, 78-79; lectr, Diablo Valley Col, 84, Ohlone Col, 85, George Mason Univ, 86-88. *Concurrent Pos:* Res fel, Coun Sci & Indust Res, India, 76 & 77-78, Univ Nijmegen, Neth, 78-79; lectr, San Jose State Univ, 85, Northern Va Community Col, 88-89. *Res:* Synthetic organometallic chemistry: syntheses and characterization of thiourea, & dithiocarbamate compounds with selenium, tellurium, transition metals. *Mailing Add:* 1887 Cold Creek Ct Vienna VA 22182

SAYALA, DASHARATHAM (DASH), MINERAL EXPLORATION, ENVIRONMENTAL RISK ASSESSMENTS. *Current Pos:* PRIN MGR, ENVIRON DIV, INT BUS & TECH CONSULT. *Personal Data:* b Hyderabad, AP, India, Sept 12, 43; US citizen; m 78; c 1. *Educ:* Osmania Univ, India, BSc, 62, MSc, 64; Univ NMex, MS, 72; George Wash Univ, PhD(geochem), 79. *Honors & Awards:* Cert Appreciation, US Dept Energy, 86. *Prof Exp:* Teaching fel, Univ NMex, 66-68; proj mgr min explor, Uranium King Corp, 68-74; asst prof, Howard Univ, 75-77; lectr, George Washington Univ, 77-78; adv res geoscientist, Bendix Field Eng Corp, 79-83; sr geochemist, Woodward-Clyde Consult, 83-85; tech staff, Mitre Corp, 85-91. *Concurrent Pos:* Mem bd dirs, Am Uranium Asn. *Mem:* Nat Wellwater Asn. *Res:* Trace element geochemistry and isotope geochemistry; application in mineral exploration and environmental studies, including ground water hydrology; fate and transport of hazardous chemicals and radionuclides. *Mailing Add:* 1887 Cold Creek Ct Vienna VA 22182. *Fax:* 703-749-0110; *E-Mail:* dsayala@ibtci.com

SAYEED, MOHAMMED MAHMOOD, MEMBRANE TRANSPORT, CIRCULATORY SHOCK PHYSIOLOGY. *Current Pos:* PROF PHYSIOL, STRITCH SCH MED, LOYOLA UNIV, 76- *Personal Data:* b Dec 8, 37; m 61; c 4. *Educ:* Univ Miami Sch Med, PhD(physiol), 65. *Prof Exp:* from asst prof to assoc prof physiol surg, Wash Univ Sch Med, 68-76. *Concurrent Pos:* Assoc prof physiol surg, Wash Univ Sch Med, 74-76; dir div cellular physiol, Jewish Hosp, St Louis, 70-76; study sect on biomed sci, NIH, 86-90. *Mem:* Am Physiol Soc; Soc Exp Biol Med; Shock Soc. *Res:* Cellular mechanics of pathogenesis of sepsis/septic shock. *Mailing Add:* Dept Physiol & Surg Burn & Shock Trauma Inst Loyola Univ Stritch Sch Med 2160 S First Ave Maywood IL 60153-5589

SAYEG, JOSEPH A, BIOPHYSICS. *Current Pos:* ASSOC PROF RADIATION MED, COL MED, UNIV KY, 67-, CHMN DEPT HEALTH RADIATION SCI, COL ALLIED HEALTH PROF, 68- *Personal Data:* b Fresno, Calif, Sept 22, 25; m 56; c 2. *Educ:* Univ Calif, Berkeley, AB, 47, PhD(biophys), 54; Am Bd Health Physics, dipl, 66; Am Bd Radiol, dipl, 69. *Prof Exp:* Res asst biophys, Donner Lab Med Physics & Biophys, Univ Calif, Berkeley, 49-54; biophysicist, Los Alamos Sci Lab, 54-61; sci specialist, Santa Barbara Labs, Edgerton, Germeshausen & Grier Inc, 61-66; assoc prof health physics, Univ Pittsburgh, 66-67. *Concurrent Pos:* Consult, Nat Comt Radiation Protection, 58-70, Armed Forces Radiobiol Res Inst, 63-64, Walter Reed Army Inst Res, 65-67 & Mercy Hosp, Pittsburgh, Pa, 66-67; lectr, Univ Calif, Santa Barbara, 62-65. *Mem:* Am Asn Physicists in Med; Soc Nuclear Med; Health Physics Soc; Radiation Res Soc. *Res:* Radiation dosimetry, including x-rays, neutrons and heavy charge particles; health physics; neutron dosimetry for personnel dose evaluation; radiobiology; effect of radiation on unicellular organisms. *Mailing Add:* 1948 Blairmore Rd Lexington KY 40502

SAYEGH, FAYEZ S, microscopic anatomy; deceased, see previous edition for last biography

SAYEGH, JOSEPH FRIEH, GAS CHROMATOGRAPHY, MASS-SPECTROMETRY. *Current Pos:* RETIRED. *Personal Data:* b Rmeimeen, Jordan, Mar 5, 28; m 55, Ida Hamway; c Roger, Jumana, Jeffrey & Randy. *Educ:* NY Univ, BA, 54, MS, 65, PhD(biol), 69. *Prof Exp:* Teacher sci & math, Al-Ahlyam Col, Jordan, 54-56, St George Col, 56-60; res scientist, Res Ctr, Rockland State Hosp, 60-69; sr res scientist, Nathan Klini Inst, 70-78; scientist V, 85-97. *Concurrent Pos:* Asst res prof, NY Univ, 85-97. *Mem:* NY Acad Sci; Clin Ligand & Assay Soc; Am Soc Neurochem. *Res:* Development of analytical methodologies for biomolecules; hormones and psychoactive drugs; gas chromatography; interfaced gas chromatography-mass spectrometry; high pressure liquid chromatography; infrared ultra violet; fluorometry; radioimmunoassay and enzyme immunoassays; column liquid chromatography; protein synthesis and amino acids uptake by the brains. *Mailing Add:* 47 Shelbourne Rd Yonkers NY 10710. *Fax:* 914-365-2214

SAYEKI, HIDEMITSU, MATHEMATICS. *Current Pos:* Nat Res Coun Can fel, Univ Montreal, 66-67, asst prof, 67-70, ASSOC PROF MATH, UNIV MONTREAL, 70- *Personal Data:* b Yokohama, Japan, July 2, 33; m 59; c 1. *Educ:* Univ Tokyo, BSc, 56; Univ Warsaw, MA, 61, PhD, 65. *Mem:* Asn Symbolic Logic; Math Soc Japan; Can Math Cong; Am Math Soc. *Res:* Mathematical logic; set theory. *Mailing Add:* Dept Math Univ Montreal Box 6128 Montreal PQ H3C 3J7 Can

SAYER, JANE M, BIO-ORGANIC CHEMISTRY. *Current Pos:* RES CHEMIST, NAT INST DIABETES, DIGESTIVE & KIDNEY DIS, 85- *Personal Data:* b Keene, NH, Mar 7, 42. *Educ:* Middlebury Col, BA, 63; Yale Univ, PhD(biochem), 67. *Prof Exp:* NIH fel biochem, Brandeis Univ, 67-69, sr res assoc, 69-74; asst prof, Univ Vt, 74-79, res asst prof chem, 79-83. *Concurrent Pos:* Sabbatical leave, Nat Inst Diabetes, Digestive & Kidney Dis, NIH, 79-83, spec expert, 83-85. *Mem:* Sigma Xi; Am Chem Soc. *Res:* Mechanisms of catalysis in enzymatic and related non-enzymatic reactions of carbonyl, imino and acyl compounds and epoxides; organic oxidation-reduction reactions of biochemical interest, reaction mechanisms and structure-activity; relationships of ultimate carcinogens; DNA polymerases. *Mailing Add:* Nat Inst Diabetes Digestive & Kidney Dis NIH Bldg 8 Rm 1A11 LBC 8 Center Dr MSC 0820 Bethesda MD 20892-0820. *Fax:* 301-402-0008

SAYER, JOHN SAMUEL, INFORMATION SCIENCE, SYSTEMS ENGINEERING. *Current Pos:* PRES, DAKOTA MGT CORP, 85-; INDEPENDENT CONSULT. *Personal Data:* b St Paul, Minn, July 27, 17; m 40, Elizabeth Hughes; c Stephen, Susan, Kathryn & Nancy. *Educ:* Univ Minn, BSME, 40. *Prof Exp:* Supvr plant develop, E I du Pont de Nemours & Co, 47-52, eng planning, 52-54, sect mgr plant eng, 54-56, mgt sci, 56-60; exec vpres, Documentation Inc, 60-62; vpres mgt sci, Auerbach Corp, 62-65; vpres, Info Dynamics Corp, 65-66; pvt consult info sci, Mass, 66-69; exec vpres, Leasco Systs & Res, Md, 69; pvt consult, 70-71; exec vpres, Leasco Info Prod, 72-75; pres, REMAC Info Corp, 75-84. *Concurrent Pos:* Pres, John Sayer Assocs, Inc. *Mem:* Asn Info & Image Mgt; Am Soc Info Sci; Am Soc Mech Engrs. *Res:* Large scale information systems concepts and designs, users needs, value functions and use patterns, in management and in scientific and engineering fields. *Mailing Add:* 13209 Colton Lane Gaithersburg MD 20878

SAYER, MICHAEL, ENGINEERING PHYSICS, CERAMICS ENGINEERING. *Current Pos:* from assoc prof to prof physics, Queen's Univ, Ont, 62-82, head dept, 75-82, assoc res dean, Fac Appl Sci, 84-87, PROF PHYSICS, QUEEN'S UNIV, ONT, 89-, PROF MAT & METALL ENG, 91- *Personal Data:* b Newport, Eng, Nov 6, 35; m 60; c 2. *Educ:* Univ Birmingham, BSc, 57; Univ Hull, PhD(physics), 61, PEng, 80. *Prof Exp:* Nat Res Coun Can fel, 60-62; dir res, Almax Industs Ltd, 87-88. *Concurrent Pos:* Vis asst prof, Univ Trent, 65-66; vis fel physics, Univ Sheffield, 72-73; mem,

Can Eng Accreditation Bd, 88-; ed, J Can Ceramic Soc, 88- *Mem:* Can Ceramic Soc; Am Ceramic Soc. *Res:* Superionic conductors; amorphous and vitreous semiconductors; dielectric; thin film devices; piezoelectric devices and materials; industrial instrumentation; materials science engineering. *Mailing Add:* Dept Physics Queen's Univ Kingston ON K7L 3N6 Can. *Fax:* 613-545-6463

SAYER, ROYCE ORLANDO, NUCLEAR PHYSICS. *Current Pos:* comput appln specialist, 74-80, COMPUT CONSULT, OAK RIDGE NAT LAB, 80- *Personal Data:* b Toccoa, Ga, Apr 29, 41; m 64; c 2. *Educ:* Furman Univ, BS, 62; Univ Tenn, PhD(physics), 68. *Prof Exp:* Physicist, US Army Nuclear Effects Lab, 68-70; asst prof physics, Furman Univ, 70-73; res assoc, Vanderbilt Univ, 73-74. *Concurrent Pos:* Oak Ridge Assoc Univs fac res partic, Oak Ridge Nat Lab, 71; consult, Union Carbide Corp, 72- *Mem:* Am Phys Soc; Am Chem Soc; Sigma Xi. *Res:* Coulomb excitation of nuclear levels; gamma ray angular correlations; accelerator ion optics; heavy-ion physics; MHD stability; graphical display systems. *Mailing Add:* Fed Bldg Oak Ridge Nat Lab PO Box 2008 Oak Ridge TN 37831. *Fax:* 423-576-5436

SAYERS, DALE EDWARD, SOLID STATE PHYSICS. *Current Pos:* from asst prof to assoc prof, 76-84, PROF PHYSICS, NC STATE UNIV, 84- *Personal Data:* b Seattle, Wash, Nov 29, 43; div; c 2. *Educ:* Univ Calif, Berkeley, BA, 66; Univ Wash, MS, 68, PhD(physics), 71. *Honors & Awards:* Sidhu Award, Pittsburgh X-ray Diffraction Conf, 73; Bertram Eugene Warren Award, Am Crystallog Asn. *Prof Exp:* Res engr physics, Boeing Aerospace Co, 72-73; sr res assoc physics, Univ Wash, 74-76. *Concurrent Pos:* Vis assoc prof, Univ Paris-Sud, 83-84; Case centennial scholar, Case Western Reserve Univ. *Mem:* AAAS; Am Phys Soc; Sigma Xi; Am Chem Soc. *Res:* Development of the extended x-ray absorption fine structure technique and its application to structural studies of amorphous materials, biological systems, catalysts and other systems. *Mailing Add:* PO Box 8202 Raleigh NC 27695. *Fax:* 919-515-3031

SAYERS, EARL ROGER, GENETICS, PLANT BREEDING. *Current Pos:* Asst prof genetics, 63-66, asst acad vpres, 71-76, dean acad develop, 72-76, assoc acad vpres, 76-80, ASSOC PROF GENETICS, UNIV ALA, 66-, ACAD VPRES, 80- *Personal Data:* b Sterling, Ill, July 20, 36; m 58; c 3. *Educ:* Univ Ill, BS, 58; Cornell Univ, MS, 61, PhD(plant breeding), 64. *Concurrent Pos:* Dir arboretum, Univ Ala, 64-66, actg head dept biol, 66-68, asst dean col arts & sci, 68-70, spec asst off acad affairs, 70-71, dean spec progs, 71-72; fel, Am Coun Educ; mem, Acad Admin Internship Prog. *Mem:* Genetics Soc Am. *Res:* Self and cross incompatibility in cultivated alfalfa; genetics of the colonial green alga Volvox aureus. *Mailing Add:* 190 The Highlands Tuscaloosa AL 35404

SAYERS, GEORGE, ENDOCRINOLOGY. *Current Pos:* ADJ PROF, DEPT PHYSIOL & ANAT, ENVIRON PHYSIOL LAB, UNIV CALIF, BERKELEY. *Personal Data:* b Glasgow, Scotland, June 10, 14; nat US; m 66; c 4. *Educ:* Wayne Univ, BS, 34, MS, 41; Univ Mich, MS, 36; Yale Univ, PhD(biochem), 43. *Honors & Awards:* Abel Award, Am Soc Pharmacol & Exp Therapeut, 47; Ciba Award, Endocrine Soc, 49. *Prof Exp:* Asst & instr biochem, Sch Med, Yale Univ, 43-45; from asst prof to assoc prof pharmacol, Sch Med, Univ Utah, 45-52; chmn dept, Sch Med, Case Western Reserve Univ, 52-76, prof physiol, 52- *Mem:* AAAS; Endocrine Soc; Soc Exp Biol & Med; Am Soc Pharmacol & Exp Therapeut; Am Physiol Soc. *Res:* Pituitary and adrenocortical physiology. *Mailing Add:* 1441 Campus Dr Berkeley CA 94708-2005

SAYETTA, THOMAS C, STATISTICAL PHYSICS, GENERAL PHYSICS LAB EXPERIMENTS. *Current Pos:* ASSOC PROF PHYSICS, ECAROLINA UNIV, 64- *Personal Data:* b Williamsport, Pa, Apr 12, 37; m 68, Anne Sherrill; c Susan. *Educ:* Univ SC, BS, 59, PhD(physics), 64. *Prof Exp:* Engr, Radio Corp Am, NJ, 59-60. *Concurrent Pos:* Nat treas, Chi Beta Phi Sci Fraternity, 74-78; asst ed, Int J Math & Math Sci, 79-83. *Mem:* Am Asn Physics Teachers; Sigma Xi. *Res:* Quantum chemistry and electron spin resonance. *Mailing Add:* Dept Physics ECarolina Univ Greenville NC 27858. *Fax:* 919-328-6314

SAYKALLY, RICHARD JAMES, LASER SPECTROSCOPY. *Current Pos:* from asst prof to assoc prof, Univ Calif, Berkeley, 79-86, Miller res prof, 85-86, vchmn, 88-91, PROF, UNIV CALIF, BERKELEY, 86- *Personal Data:* b Rhinelander, Wis, Sept 10, 47. *Educ:* Univ Wis, BS, 70, PhD, 77. *Honors & Awards:* Bergman Lectr, Yale Univ, 87; Merck-Frost Lectr, Univ BC, 88; Michelson Prize, Coblentz Soc, 89; E K Pyler Prize, Am Physics Soc, 89; Bourke-Lectr, Royal Soc Chem, UK, 92; E R Lipincott Medal, Optical Soc, Am Soc Appl Spectros, 92; Harrison Howe Award, Am Chem Soc, 92; L J Bircher Lectr, Vanderbilt Univ, 93. *Prof Exp:* Nat Coun Res fel, 77; fel, Nat Bur Stand, Boulder, Colo, 77-79; Dreyfuss Found fel, 79. *Concurrent Pos:* Bd dirs, Space Sci Lab, Univ Calif, Berkeley, 83-86; prin investr, Lawrence Berkeley Lab, 83-91, NSF; pres young investr, NSF, 84-88; vis prof, Univ Nijmegen, 91, Max-Planck Inst Fluid Dynamics- Gottingen, 91. *Mem:* Fel Royal Soc Chem; fel Am Physics Soc; Am Asn Univ Profs; AAAS; Am Chem Soc; fel Optical Soc Am. *Res:* Laser spectroscopy; molecular ions; clusters; intermolecular forces; molecular dynamics; molecular spectroscopy; astrophysics; astrochemistry. *Mailing Add:* Dept Chem Univ Calif Berkeley CA 94720-1460. *Fax:* 510-642-8369; *E-Mail:* rjs@hydrogen.cchem.berkeley.edu

SAYLAK, DONALD, INDUSTRIAL BY-PRODUCT UTILIZATION & RECYCLING, HIGHWAY MATERIALS RESEARCH. *Current Pos:* prof mat sci, Civil Eng Dept, 72-94, DIR BY-PROD UTILIZATION & RECYCLING RES CTR, CIVIL ENG DEPT, TEX A&M UNIV, 94-; RES ENGR, TEX TRANSP INST, 72- *Personal Data:* m 51, Genevieve Komichak; c Daniel & Thomas. *Educ:* Univ Pittsburgh, BS, 50; Univ Del, MS, 62; Tex A&M Univ, PhD(interdisciplinary eng), 72. *Prof Exp:* Design & res engr, E I du Pont de Nemours & Co, 53-60; head, Mech & Mats Res Lab, Thiokol Chem Corp, 60-66, Solid Rocket Mech Behav Sect, Rocket Propulsion Lab, USAF, 66-72. *Concurrent Pos:* Pres, Joint Army-Navy-NASA-Air Force, 68-71; consult, Lockheed, 71-73, Nat Acad Sci, 73-74, Tex Coal Ash Utilization Group, 75- & Elec Power Res Inst, 82-; mem, Transp Res Bd, 76-; expert witness mats, highways & air fields, 85- *Mem:* Am Asn Asphalt Paving Tech; Sigma Xi; Am Soc Chem Engrs. *Res:* Experimental stress analysis and materials development for the solid propellants, highways and airfield; building construction and municipal and industrial waste utilization and recycling industries. *Mailing Add:* 841 N Rosemary Dr Bryan TX 77802

SAYLE, WILLIAM, II, ELECTRONICS ENGINEERING. *Current Pos:* from asst prof to assoc prof, 70-82, PROF ELEC ENG, GA INST TECHNOL, 82-, ASSOC DIR, 89- *Personal Data:* b Baytown, Tex, Sept 30, 41; m 89, Joyce C Gross; c Amy E. *Educ:* Univ Tex, Austin, BSEE, 63, MSEE, 64; Univ Wash, PhD(elec eng), 70. *Prof Exp:* Res engr, Boeing Co, 65-67, sr engr, 70. *Concurrent Pos:* Consult prof, UNESCO, Venezuela, 73-74; consult, Hughes Aircraft, 78-80 , Hewlett-Packard, 81, Motorolo, 83, Lockheed, 85, 86. *Mem:* Sr mem Inst Elec & Electronics Engrs; Am Asn Univ Prof. *Res:* Solid-state power electronics; computer-aided electronic circuit design. *Mailing Add:* Sch Elec & Comput Eng Ga Inst Technol Atlanta GA 30332-0001. *Fax:* 404-853-9171; *E-Mail:* bill.sayle@ee.gatech.edu

SAYLER, GARY S, MICROBIOLOGY. *Current Pos:* PROF, UNIV TENN, KNOXVILLE. *Honors & Awards:* Proctor & Gamble Award Appl & Environ Microbiol, Am Soc Microbiol, 94. *Mailing Add:* Univ Tenn Ctr Environ Technol 676 Dabney Hall Knoxville TN 37996-1605

SAYLES, DAVID CYRIL, EXPLOSIVES & PROPELLANTS, COMPOSITE MATERIALS. *Current Pos:* chief, Res Plans Br, Ord Missile Command, US Dept Army, Redstone Arsenal, 58-60, actg dep chief, Res Plans Div, 61-63, group leader propellants & mat, Propulsion Lab, US Army Missile Command, 63-66, res phys scientist, Propulsion Technol & Mgt Ctr, 66-70, gen engr, Missile Develop Div, Advan Ballistic Missile Defense Agency, 70-75, gen engr, interceptor directorate, Ballistic Missile Defense Advan Technol Ctr, 75-82, GEN ENGR, US ARMY SPACE & STRATEGIC DEFENSE COMMAND, 82- *Personal Data:* b Scollard, Alta, Mar 23, 17; nat US; m 51, Marion K Zelter; c Lance H & Lynn R. *Educ:* Univ Alta, BSc, 39; Univ Chicago, MS, 41; Purdue Univ, PhD(chem), 46. *Honors & Awards:* Hon Scroll, Am Inst Chemists, 65, 67 & 68; Res Achievement Award, Chem Inst Can, 70. *Prof Exp:* Asst, Univ Alta, 38-39, Univ Chicago, 40-41 & Purdue Univ, 43-44; instr gen eng chem, 45-46; prof org chem & head dept chem, Ferris Inst, 46-47; dep dir res, Lowe Bros Co, 47-52; chief chem prod & equip unit, Wright Air Develop Ctr, Wright-Patterson AFB, Ohio, 52-53, chief high explosives & propellants unit, 53-54, chief ammunition sect, Gun & Rocket Br, 54-56; from asst chief to chief, Gun & Ammunition Br, Munitions Develop Labs, Armament Ctr, Eglin AFB, Fla, 56-57, tech adv, Tech Planning Group, 57-58. *Concurrent Pos:* Consult, C C Letroy & Co, 46-47, Harrow Enterprises, 46-49, Sayles Chem Consults, 46-49 & Glo-Rnz, Inc, 54-58; consult, Hopestone Co Inc, 46-49, Lockheely Distribrs, 50, Holland Chem Co, 56, Res & Develop Corp, 70-75, Saycore Int, 80-, Technol Recognition Corp, 87- *Mem:* Am Chem Soc; Am Inst Chemists; Am Ord Asn; Sigma Xi. *Res:* Reactions of organometallic compounds; diethylstilbesterol analogs; lysine; alkyd resins; silicones; epichlorohydrin-bisphenol A resins; surface coatings; synthetic drying oils; lacquers; linoleum; laminates; high explosives; liquid propellants; solid and hybrid materials and propellants; ammunition development; missile, rocket and interceptor propulsion subsystems, materials and propulsion technology; granted 256 patents. *Mailing Add:* 9616 Dortmund Dr SE Huntsville AL 35803

SAYLES, EVERETT DUANE, ZOOLOGY. *Current Pos:* prof, 54-74, chmn, biol dept & sci div, 61-74, EMER PROF BIOL, EASTERN COL, 74- *Personal Data:* b Hillsdale, Mich, July 27, 03; wid; c 4. *Educ:* Kalamazoo Col, AB, 27; Kans State Col, MS, 28; Univ Chicago, PhD(zool), 42. *Hon Degrees:* LLD, Eastern Col, 75. *Prof Exp:* Instr biol, Va Jr Col, Minn, 30-45; prof, Thiel Col, 45-54. *Concurrent Pos:* Vis prof, Fla Mem Col, 61-62. *Mem:* Fel AAAS; Am Inst Biol Sci; emer mem Sigma Xi; emer mem Sci Res Soc NAm. *Res:* Biology of male in mammals; castration of male guinea pig; male guinea pig post natal sexual differentiation; identification and culturing of Archiannelid worms (Dinophilus) and other microscopic Annelid worms. *Mailing Add:* 2247 Sandrala Dr Sarasota FL 34231-4447

SAYLES, FREDERICK LIVERMORE, GEOCHEMISTRY, MARINE CHEMISTRY. *Current Pos:* Fel, 68-69, asst scientist, 69-73, ASSOC SCIENTIST MARINE CHEM, WOODS HOLE OCEANOG INST, 73- *Personal Data:* b New York, NY, May 1, 40. *Educ:* Amherst Col, BA, 62; Univ Calif, Berkeley, MA, 66; Univ Manchester, PhD(geochem), 68. *Mem:* AAAS; Geochem Soc Am; Am Geophys Union. *Res:* Geochemical mass balances in the oceans; the cycling of elements in the oceans and the geochemistry of sediments. *Mailing Add:* PO Box 655 Woods Hole MA 02543-0655

SAYLOR, LEROY C, FORESTRY, GENETICS. *Current Pos:* RETIRED. *Personal Data:* b Cedar Rapids, Iowa, July 17, 31; m 55; c 3. *Educ:* Iowa State Univ, BS, 58; NC State Univ, MS, 60, PhD(genetics), 62. *Honors & Awards:* NC State Col Chap Res Award, Sigma Xi, 67. *Prof Exp:* Asst geneticist, NC State Univ, 61-62, from asst prof to prof genetics & forestry, 62-89, asst dean, Sch Forest Resources, 69-74, assoc dean, Sch Forest Resources, 74-89, asst dir, Agr Res Serv, 87-89. *Concurrent Pos:* NSF res grants, 61-66; McIntire-Stennis res grants, 64-72. *Mem:* Genetics Soc Am; Soc Am Foresters; AAAS; Am Forestry Asn; Sigma Xi. *Res:* Cytogenetics of forest tree species; speciation and introgression in forest tree species. *Mailing Add:* 809 Merwin Rd Raleigh NC 27606

SAYLOR, PAUL EDWARD, NUMERICAL ANALYSIS. *Current Pos:* From asst prof to assoc prof, 67-91, PROF COMPUT SCI, UNIV ILL, URBANA, 91- *Personal Data:* b Dallas, Tex, Mar 19, 39; m 64, Cynthia V Staay; c Gerrit & Gerard. *Educ:* Stanford Univ, BS, 61; Univ Tex, MA, 63; Rice Univ, PhD(math), 68. *Concurrent Pos:* Vis prof, Inst Fluid Dynamics & Appl Math, Univ Md, College Park, 73-74 & Swiss Fed Inst Technol, 91; hydrologist, US Geol Surv, Reston, Va, 75. *Mem:* Am Math Soc; Soc Indust & Appl Math; Sigma Xi. *Res:* Solution of linear systems arising from partial differential equations with applications to groundwater hydrology, numerical relativity and computational fluid dynamics. *Mailing Add:* Dept Comput Sci Univ Ill 1304 W Springfield Urbana IL 61801

SAYRE, CLIFFORD M(ORRILL), JR, CHEMICAL ENGINEERING. *Current Pos:* RETIRED. *Personal Data:* b Springfield, Mass, Dec 17, 30; m 59; c 2. *Educ:* Mass Inst Technol, SB, 52. *Prof Exp:* Develop engr, Tech Sect Polychem Dept, E I du Pont de Nemours & Co, Inc, 52-56, engr, Plants Tech Mgr Off, 56-57, asst tech supt, 57-58, res supvr, 58-59, res supvr, Indust & Biochem Dept, 59-63, sr res engr, Plastics Dept, 63-66, sr res supvr, 66, div supt process res, Victoria Plant, 66-69, tech supt, Pontchartrain Works, 69-72, mgr financial & bus anal, Polymer Intermediates, 72-73, intermediates studies mgr, 73-74, mat & distrib mgr, 74-76, planning mgr, Nylon Intermediates, 76-77, mgr, Div Transp & Distrib, 77-81, dir, Int Div, 82-83, Logistics, 83-88 & 89-90, Corp Studies, 88-89, vpres, Mat, Logistics & Serv, 90-92. *Concurrent Pos:* Mem, Marine Bd, Nat Res Coun; chmn, Sea Transp Comt, US Coun for Int Bus; dir, Nat Indust Transp League; chmn, Shippers Competitive Ocean Transp & Compressed Gas Asn; vis comt, Mass Inst Technol Ctr Transp Studies. *Mem:* Fel AAAS; fel Am Inst Chemists; Am Chem Soc; Am Inst Chem Engrs; Nat Freight Trans Asn; Coun Logistics Mgt. *Res:* Nylon and polymer intermediates; industrial chemicals; plastics and environmental control; business and financial analysis; petrochemicals; transportation and distribution of chemicals; maritime research; transportation policy, domestic and international. *Mailing Add:* 30 Southridge E Kennett Square PA 19348

SAYRE, DAVID, X-RAY MICROSCOPY, X-RAY CRYSTALLOGRAPHY. *Current Pos:* RETIRED. *Personal Data:* b New York, NY, Mar 2, 24; m 47, Anne Bowns. *Educ:* Yale Univ, BS, 43; Ala Polytech Inst, MS, 49; Oxford Univ, DPhil(chem crystallog), 51. *Honors & Awards:* Fankuchen Award, Am Crystallog Asn, 89. *Prof Exp:* Mem staff radiation lab, Mass Inst Technol, 43-46; consult, US Off Naval Res, 51; assoc biophys, Johnson Res Found, Univ Pa, 51-55; mathematician, IBM Corp, 55-60, dir prog, 60-62, mgr mach reasoning, 62-64, mgr exp prog, 64-69, res staff mem, 69-90. *Concurrent Pos:* Mem nat comt crystallog, Nat Res Coun, 57-59 & 81-86; vis fel, All Souls Col, Oxford Univ, 72-73; fac mem, Int Sch Crystallogr, Erice, 74, 76, 78, Prague, 75, Ottawa, 81; guest scientist physics, State Univ NY, Stony Brook, 78-; guest scientist, Nat Synchrotron Light Source, Brookhaven Nat Lab, 78-; guest scientist chem, Rutgers Univ, New Brunswick, NJ, 96- *Mem:* Am Crystallog Asn (treas, 53-55, pres, 81). *Res:* X-ray diffraction imaging with soft x-rays and non-periodic microspecimens; x-ray holography; x-ray microscopy with focusing optics; mathematical methods in x-ray crystallography. *Mailing Add:* 15 Jefferson Ct Bridgewater NJ 08807. *E-Mail:* sayre@bnl.gov

SAYRE, EDWARD VALE, PHYSICAL CHEMISTRY. *Current Pos:* RES PHYS SCIENTIST, SMITHSONIAN INST, 84- *Personal Data:* b Des Moines, Iowa, Sept 8, 19; m 43. *Educ:* Iowa State Col, BS, 41; Columbia Univ, AM, 43, PhD(chem), 49. *Honors & Awards:* George Hevesy Medal, 84. *Prof Exp:* Chemist, Manhattan Dist Proj, SAM Labs, Columbia Univ, 42-45 & Eastman Kodak Co, 49-52; sr chemist, Brookhaven Nat Lab, 52-84. *Concurrent Pos:* Vis lectr, Stevens Inst, 55-63; consult fel, Conserv Ctr, Inst Fine Arts, NY Univ, 60-67, adj prof, 65-74; Guggenheim fel, 69; distinguished vis prof, Am Univ Cairo, 69-70; regents prof, Univ Calif, Irvine, 72; head res lab, Mus Fine Arts, Boston, 75-78, sr scientist, 78-; Alexander von Humboldt US sr scientist award, Berlin, 80. *Mem:* Fel Int Inst Conserv Hist & Artistic Works; Am Chem Soc; fel Am Inst Conserv. *Res:* Technical study of fine art and archaeological materials; single crystal spectra, cryogenic measurements; catalyst exchange and surface chemistry studies. *Mailing Add:* 2106 Wilkinson Pl Alexandria VA 22306-2540

SAYRE, FRANCIS WARREN, BIOCHEMISTRY. *Current Pos:* PROF BIOCHEM, UNIV OF THE PAC, 68- *Personal Data:* b Larchwood, Iowa, Nov 20, 24; m 54; c 1. *Educ:* Univ Calif, AB, 49, PhD(biochem), 55; Col Pacific, MA, 51. *Prof Exp:* Chemist, Aluminum Co Am, 43-44; asst chem, Modesto Jr Col, 45-46 & Col Pacific, 50-51; chemist, Agr Lab, Shell Develop Co, 51; res scientist, Clayton Found Biochem Inst, Univ Tex, 51-52; asst biochem, Univ Calif, 52-55; res assoc, City of Hope Med Ctr, 55-58; assoc res scientist, 59-62, res scientist, Kaiser Found Res Inst, 62-68. *Concurrent Pos:* Mem biochem subsect, Am Chem Soc Exam Comt, 74- *Mem:* Am Chem Soc; Brit Biochem Soc; AAAS; NY Acad Sci; Sigma Xi. *Res:* Growth and metabolic regulation; specific recognition sites in proteins; cellular aging; carcinogenesis; specific growth factors; enzyme synthesis; nutrition; nutrient interrelationships. *Mailing Add:* 4922 Cozad Way Stockton CA 95212

SAYRE, RICHARD MARTIN, PLANT PATHOLOGY. *Current Pos:* RETIRED. *Personal Data:* b Hillsboro, Ore, Mar 25, 28; m 62, Diane S Pringle; c Janet. *Educ:* Ore State Univ, BS, 51, MS, 54; Univ Nebr, PhD(plant nematol), 58. *Prof Exp:* Nematologist, Harrow Res St, Can Dept Agr, 58-65; nematologist, USDA, 65-95. *Mem:* Am Phytopath Soc; Soc Nematol. *Res:* Biological control of plant parasitic nematodes; isolates, identifies, and evaluates species of soil bacteria that are parasites or antagonists of plant-parasitic nematodes for their potential as biological control agents against plant nematode diseases. *Mailing Add:* 6100 Westchester Dr No 1004 College Park MD 20740-2848

SAYRE, RICHARD THOMAS, PLANT BIOCHEMISTRY, PHOTOSYNTHESIS. *Current Pos:* asst prof, 85-91, ASSOC PROF, PLANT BIOL & BIOCHEM DEPT, OHIO STATE UNIV, 91- *Personal Data:* b Iowa City, Iowa, May 24, 51; m 74, Kathleen M Slattery; c Matthew P & Robert L. *Educ:* Humboldt State Univ, BA, 74; Univ Iowa, MS, 76, PhD(bot), 78. *Prof Exp:* Res assoc, Inst Molecular Biophys, Fla State Univ, 78-79, Dept Agron, Univ Ky, 79-82 & Dept Cellular & Develop Biol, Harvard Univ, 82-85. *Concurrent Pos:* Vis prof, Dept Cellular & Develop Biol, Harvard Univ, 85-86. *Mem:* AAAS; Int Soc Plant Molecular Biologists; Am Soc Plant Physiologists; Genetic Soc Am; Am Soc Biochem & Molecular Biol. *Res:* Structure and function of photosynthetic complexes in the thylakoid membranes of chloroplasts; cyanogenesis in the tropical crop cassava; plant molecular biology. *Mailing Add:* Dept Biochem & Plant Biol Ohio State Univ 202 Kottman Hall 2021 Coffey Rd Columbus OH 43210. *Fax:* 614-292-7162; *E-Mail:* rsayre@magnus.acs.ohio_state.edu

SAYRE, ROBERT NEWTON, AGRICULTURAL CHEMISTRY, HISTOLOGY. *Current Pos:* RETIRED. *Personal Data:* b Cottonwood Falls, Kans, July 25, 32; m 54; c 4. *Educ:* Kans State Univ, BS, 54; Univ Wis, MS, 61, PhD(biochem, meat sci), 62. *Prof Exp:* Asst co agr agent, Kans Agr Exten Serv, USDA, 56-58; res asst muscle biochem, Univ Wis, 58-62; food technologist, Am Meat Inst Found, Ill, 62-64; res chemist poultry meat invests, Western Regional Res Ctr, USDA, 64-70, freeze damage reduction in plant tissue, 70-71, res chemist food technol-potato invests, 72-79, res chemist, Food Qual Res Unit-Grain Compos, 79-96. *Mem:* Inst Food Technol; Am Chem Soc; Am Asn Cereal Chemists. *Res:* Investigation of rice and rice by product processing and product development; processing of other cereal grains and vegetables. *Mailing Add:* 739 Bay Tree Lane El Cerrito CA 94530

SAYRE, WILLIAM OLAF, SURFACE WATER HYDROLOGY, WATER RIGHTS ADMINISTRATION. *Current Pos:* PROF GEOL, DEPT SCI & MATH, COL SANTA FE, 91- *Personal Data:* b Fairfield, Iowa, Apr 7, 54; m 89, Patricia Roberts; c Adam T. *Educ:* Western Wash Univ, BS, 76; Univ Southampton, UK, PhD(geophys oceanog), 81. *Prof Exp:* Asst prof geol & appl geophys, Iowa State Univ, 79-83; geologist, US Geol Surv, 83-84; assoc prof marine geol & coastal geol, Eckerd Col, 84-91. *Concurrent Pos:* Mem & chmn, Fla Bd Prof Geologists, 89-91; adj prof geol, Northern Ariz Univ, 89- *Mem:* Am Geophys Union; Geol Soc Am. *Res:* Water availability and water quality in New Mexico; geology of Capulin Volcano National Monument. *Mailing Add:* Col Santa Fe Dept Math & Sci 1600 St Michaels Dr Santa Fe NM 87505-7634. *Fax:* 505-473-6399; *E-Mail:* sayre@santafe.edu

SAYRES, ALDEN R, NUCLEAR PHYSICS. *Current Pos:* RETIRED. *Personal Data:* b New York, NY, Mar 7, 32; m 72. *Educ:* Dartmouth Col, AB, 53; Columbia Univ, PhD(physics), 60. *Prof Exp:* Res assoc physics, Columbia Univ, 60-65; from asst prof to prof physics, Brooklyn Col, 65-90. *Mem:* NY Acad Sci; Am Phys Soc; Am Asn Physics Teachers; Sigma Xi. *Res:* Nuclear particle detection and nuclear spectroscopy. *Mailing Add:* 113 Crest Dr Summit NJ 07901-4115

SAZ, ARTHUR KENNETH, MICROBIOLOGY. *Current Pos:* prof microbiol & chmn dept, Sch Med & Dent, 64-84, prof, 84-88, EMER PROF MICROBIOL, GEORGETOWN UNIV, 88- *Personal Data:* b New York, NY, Dec 2, 17; m 45; c 1. *Educ:* City Col New York BS, 38; Univ Mo, MA, 39; Duke Univ, PhD(bact), 43; Am Bd Microbiol, dipl. *Prof Exp:* Asst pharmacol, Sch Med, Duke Univ, 40-42, instr bact, 42-43; instr, New York Med Col, 46-47; asst prof, Iowa State Col, 48-49; bacteriologist, Nat Inst Allergy & Infectious Dis, 48-57, chief med & physiol bact sect, 57-64. *Concurrent Pos:* Fel, Rockefeller Inst, 47-49; endowed lectr, Mico-Immunol Ann. *Mem:* AAAS; Am Soc Microbiol; Am Acad Microbiol. *Res:* Microbial biochemistry; bacterial physiology and mode of action of antibiotics; penicillinase induction; resistance to penicillin in staphylococcus and gonococcus; bacteriophages of Bacillus cereus; microbial interactions in periodontitis and disease in general; biochemistry of the gonococcus. *Mailing Add:* 6507 Pyle Rd Bethesda MD 20817

SAZ, HOWARD JAY, BIOCHEMISTRY, PARASITE BIOCHEMISTRY. *Current Pos:* PROF BIOL SCI, UNIV NOTRE DAME, 69- *Personal Data:* b New York, NY, Sept 29, 23; m 46, Rosalyn Pollack; c Daniel, Marjory & Wendy. *Educ:* City Col, BS, 48; Western Reserve Univ, PhD(microbiol), 52. *Honors & Awards:* Bueding & von Brand Mem Award, Am Soc Parasitol, 89. *Prof Exp:* Res assoc microbiol, Western Reserve Univ, 52-53,; Nat Found Infantile Paralysis fel, biochem & microbiol, Univ Sheffield, 53-54; res assoc pharmacol, La State Univ, 54-55, from asst prof to assoc prof, 55-60; assoc prof pathobiol, Sch Hyg & Pub Health, Johns Hopkins Univ, 60-69. *Concurrent Pos:* Mem trop med & parasitol study sect, USPHS, 65-69, chmn, 69-70; mem Army Res & Develop Study Group, Parasitic Dis, 73-77; mem Nat Sci Found, Regulatory Biol Panel, 84-86. *Mem:* Am Soc Microbiol; Sigma Xi; Brit Biochem Soc; Am Soc Parasitol; Am Soc Biochem & Molecular Biol. *Res:* Bacterial and helminth biochemistry; comparative biochemistry employing isotopic tracers and enzyme purification techniques. *Mailing Add:* Dept Biol Sci Col Sci Univ Notre Dame Notre Dame IN 46556. *Fax:* 219-631-7413

SAZAMA, KATHLEEN, BLOOD BANKING, TRANSFUSION MEDICINE. *Current Pos:* PROF PATH & LAB MED & DIR CLIN LABS, MED COL PA, 94-; DIV DIR, ROTH LAB MED, ALLEGANY UNIV, 94- *Personal Data:* b Sutherland, Nebr, May 8, 41; m 62, Franklin J; c 2. *Educ:* Univ Nebr, Lincoln, BS, 62; Am Univ, Washington, DC, MS, 69; Georgetown Univ, MD, 76; Cath Univ, JD, 90. *Prof Exp:* Pathologist, Suburban Hosp, Bethesda, Md, 79-84; chief path, Mem Med Ctr Mich, Ludington, 84-86; chief blood bank pract, Food & Drug Admin, 86-89; consult, Ober, Kales, Grimes & Shriver, Baltimore, Md, 89-90; assoc med dir, Sacramento Med Found, 90-92, dir, Ctr Blood Res, 90-92; assoc prof clin path, Med Ctr, Univ Calif, Davis, 92-94. *Concurrent Pos:* Med dir, Metrop Wash Blood Banks, 82-84; clin asst prof, Uniformed Serv Univ Health Sci, 80-89; liaison, Nat Coun Health Lab Serv, 83-85; consult, Civil Aviation Med Asn, 84-85. *Mem:* AMA; Am Asn Blood Banks; Am Soc Clin Path; Col Am Pathologists; Am Soc Apheresis. *Res:* Laboratory reaction to emergencies, dealing with DRG payment system, fatalities and other errors in blood banks; medicolegal issues. *Mailing Add:* Allegany Univ Hosp Hahnemann Broadevine St MS 435 Philadelphia PA 19102

SBARRA, ANTHONY J, BACTERIOLOGY. *Current Pos:* asst prof bact, 59-65, assoc prof obstet & gynec, 65-73, PROF OBSTET & GYNEC, MED SCH, TUFTS UNIV, 73- *Personal Data:* b Victor, NY, Sept 3, 22; m 56; c 3. *Educ:* Siena Col, BS, 48; Ind Univ, BA, 51; Univ Ky, MS, 51; Univ Tenn, PhD(bact), 54; Am Bd Microbiol, dipl. *Prof Exp:* Assoc biologist, Oak Ridge Nat Lab, 53-56; res assoc, Harvard Med Sch, 56-60, instr, 60. *Concurrent Pos:* Res fel bact & immunol, Harvard Med Sch, 56-58; lectr, Univ Tenn, 54-55; assoc dir dept path & med res, St Margaret's Hosp, 59-74, dir dept, 74-; biochem sect ed, Res, 66-73, mem adv bd, 74-; ed, J Infection & Immunol, 73- & Proc Soc Exp Biol & Med, 74. *Mem:* Am Soc Microbiol; Am Soc Exp Path; Reticuloendothelial Soc; affil AMA; fel Infectious Dis Soc. *Res:* Biological and biochemical approach to the host-parasite relationships; stem cell biology. *Mailing Add:* 54 Cypress Rd Milton MA 02186

SCACCIA, CARL, BIOENGINEERING, POLYMER CHEMISTRY. *Current Pos:* dir res & develop, 81-91, VPRES & GEN MGR, SPECIALITY POLYMERS & ADHESIVES DIV, ASHLAND CHEM, 91- *Personal Data:* B Aug 23, 46; c 1. *Educ:* State Univ NY, Buffalo, BS, 68, PhD (eng), 73; Univ Rochester, MS, 70. *Prof Exp:* Supvr, process & prod develop chem eng, Union Carbide, 73-79; mgr technol, chem eng, Combustion Eng, 79-81. *Concurrent Pos:* Adj prof, State Univ NY, Buffalo, 77-81, Ohio State Univ, 81-; bd mem adv comt, Cent Ohio Tech Col, 81-90. *Mem:* Am Ins Chem Eng; Am Chem Soc; Am Soc Mech Engrs; Soc Plastics Indust; Soc Advan Mat & Process Eng. *Res:* Research and commercial development in various chemicals fields; acquisition evaluations, technology feasibility analysis; operations research, strategic planning; first of a kind product process commercialization. *Mailing Add:* 8422 Tibbermore Ct Dublin OH 43017-9721

SCADDEN, DAVID T, ACQUIRED IMMUNE DEFICIENCY SYNDROME. *Current Pos:* clin fel med, Harvard Med Sch, 80-84, res fel, 84-86, instr, 86-87 & 88-91, ACTIVE STAFF, HARVARD MED SCH, 88-, ASST PROF MED, NE DEACONESS HOSP, 91-; AT MASS GEN HOSP CANCER CTR-CNYM. *Personal Data:* b Passaic, NJ, Jan 28, 53; c 3. *Educ:* Bucknell Univ, BA, 75; Case Western Res Univ, MD, 80; Am Bd Internal Med, dipl, 83. *Prof Exp:* Clin fel hemat & oncol, Dana-Farber Cancer Inst, Brigham & Women's Hosp, 83-84; assoc, Howard Hughes Med Inst, 85-87; instr med, Tufts Univ Sch Med, 87-88; staff physician hemat & oncol, NE Med Ctr Hosps, 88; active staff, NE Deaconess Hosp, 88- *Concurrent Pos:* Intern & med house officer, Brigham & Women's Hosp, 80-81, resident, 81-83, res clin fel, 85-87; res fel, NE Med Ctr, 87-88; mem, Educ Session on Acquired Immune Deficiency, Am Soc Hemat, 91, chair, 93. *Mem:* AAAS; Am Soc Clin Oncol; Am Col Physicians; Am Soc Hemat; Am Soc Microbiol; Int Soc Exp Hemat. *Res:* Hematopoietic stem cell regulation; effects of human immunodeficiency virus-1 on hematopoiesis; biology and treatment of acquired immune deficiency syndrom; biochemistry of tyrosine kinases. *Mailing Add:* Mass Gen Hosp Cancer Ctr CNYM Bldg 149 Boston MA 02129. *Fax:* 617-566-8043

SCADDING, STEVEN RICHARD, LIMB DEVELOPMENT & LIMB REGENERATION ESPECIALLY IN THE AMPHIBIANS, DEVELOPMENTAL BIOLOGY. *Current Pos:* asst prof, 74-84, ASSOC PROF, DEPT ZOOL, UNIV GUELPH, 84- *Personal Data:* b Toronto, Ont, Apr 4, 44; m 67, Susan A Hill; c Andrew, Joel & Matthew. *Educ:* Univ Toronto, BSc, 66, MSc, 68, PhD(develop biol), 73; Cambridge Univ, Eng, cert theol, 69. *Prof Exp:* Med Res Coun fel, Banting-Best Dept Biomed Res, Univ Toronto, 73-74. *Concurrent Pos:* Vis scientist, Nat Inst Med Res, Mill Hill, London, Eng, 84-85 & Develop Biol Res Ctr, King's Col, Univ London, Eng, 92-93. *Mem:* Can Soc Cellular Molecular Biol; Can Asn Anatomists; Can Soc Zoologists; Sigma Xi; Can Sci Christian Affil (secy, 80-92); Soc Teaching Learning Higher Educ. *Res:* Limb development and limb regeneration; why limbs of urodele amphibians can regenerate following amputation while those of other vertebrates do not; control of growth and pattern formation during limb development and limb regeneration; publications include about 45 papers in referred journals. *Mailing Add:* Dept Zool Univ Guelph Guelph ON N1G 2W1 Can. *Fax:* 519-767-1656; *E-Mail:* scadding@uoguelph.ca

SCADRON, MICHAEL DAVID, THEORETICAL PHYSICS, HIGH ENERGY PHYSICS. *Current Pos:* vis prof, 70-71, PROF PHYSICS, UNIV ARIZ, 71- *Personal Data:* b Chicago, Ill, Feb 12, 38; m 60, Arlene Weininger; c 2. *Educ:* Univ Mich, BS, 59; Univ Calif, Berkeley, PhD(physics), 64. *Prof Exp:* Fel physics, Lawrence Radiation Lab, 64-66; NSF fel, Imp Col, Univ London, 66-68; asst prof, Northwestern Univ, 68-70. *Concurrent Pos:* Vis scientist, Int Ctr Theoret Physics, Trieste, 67, 72, 78, 83, 87, 89; sr res fel, Imp Col, Univ London, 72 & 78, Univ Durham, 78; Fulbright scholar, Pakistan, 79 & India, 85 & 93; Australian fel, NSF, Univ Tasmania & Melbourne, 79, 85, 86; Can fel, Univ Western Ont, 91. *Mem:* Am Phys Soc; Fedn Am Sci. *Res:* Elementary particle theory; strong, electromagnetic and weak interactions. *Mailing Add:* 220 N Stewart Ave Tucson AZ 85716

SCAFE, DONALD WILLIAM, GEOLOGY, OCEANOGRAPHY. *Current Pos:* WITH RES OFF, ALTA RES COUN, 67- *Personal Data:* b Highgate, Ont, Nov 30, 37; m 62, Velma Dunn. *Educ:* Univ Western Ont, BSc, 60; Univ Kans, MS, 63; Tex A&M Univ, PhD(oceanog), 68. *Mem:* Clay Minerals Soc; Assn Prof Engrs. *Res:* Bentonite; ceramic clays; volcanic ash; industrial minerals. *Mailing Add:* Alta Res Coun Box 8330 Edmonton AB T6H 5X2 Can. *Fax:* 403-438-7633; *E-Mail:* scafe@terrace.arc.ab.ca

SCAGLIONE, PETER ROBERT, PEDIATRICS & PEDIATRIC NEPHROLOGY. *Current Pos:* PROF CLIN PEDIAT, NY MED COL, 82- *Personal Data:* b Tampa, Fla, Oct 9, 25; m 56; c 4. *Educ:* City Col New York, BS, 48; Columbia Univ, MD, 52. *Prof Exp:* Asst pediat, Columbia Univ, 54-57, instr, 57-61, assoc, 61-65; pediatrician-in-chief, Brooklyn-Cumberland Med Ctr, 65-74; prof clin pediat, Med Ctr, NU Univ, 74-82; dir pediat, St Vincent's Hosp & Med Ctr. *Concurrent Pos:* From clin asst prof to clin assoc prof pediat, State Univ NY Downstate Med Ctr, 65-74; mem coun kidney in cardiovasc dis, Am Heart Asn, 73- *Mem:* Am Soc Nephrology; Int Soc Nephrology; Am Soc Pediat Nephrology. *Res:* Pediatric renal and acid-base disorders. *Mailing Add:* Dept Pediat St Joseph's Hosp & Med Ctr 703 Main St Paterson NJ 07503

SCAIANO, JUAN C, CHEMISTRY. *Current Pos:* RES CHEMIST, DEPT CHEM, UNIV OTTAWA. *Honors & Awards:* Henry Marshall Tory Medal, Roy Soc Can 95. *Mailing Add:* Dept Chem Univ Ottawa Sta A 550 Cumberland St PO Box 450 Ottawa ON K1N 6N5 Can

SCAIFE, CHARLES WALTER JOHN, INORGANIC CHEMISTRY, SCIENCE EDUCATION. *Current Pos:* chmn & assoc prof, 72-78, PROF CHEM, UNION COL, NY, 82- *Personal Data:* b Williamsport, Pa, Jan 27, 38; m 64; c 2. *Educ:* Cornell Univ, BA, 59, PhD(inorg chem), 66. *Prof Exp:* NSF fel, York, Eng, 66-67; asst prof chem, Middlebury Col, 67-72. *Concurrent Pos:* Vis prof, NMex State Univ, 78-79. *Mem:* Am Chem Soc. *Res:* New laboratory experiments in general and inorganic chemistry; crystal growth on NASA space shuttle. *Mailing Add:* Dept Chem Union Col Schenectady NY 12308

SCALA, ALFRED ANTHONY, PHOTOCHEMISTRY. *Current Pos:* from asst prof to assoc prof, 66-75, head dept chem, 77-80, PROF ORG CHEM, WORCESTER POLYTECH INST, 75- *Personal Data:* b Brooklyn, NY, Apr 29, 36; m 57; c 3. *Educ:* Brooklyn Col, BS, 57, MA, 61; Polytech Inst Brooklyn, PhD(org chem), 65. *Prof Exp:* Res chemist, Pfister Chem Works, 57-61; res assoc, Nat Res Coun, Nat Bur Stand, 64-66. *Mem:* Am Chem Soc. *Res:* Radiation chemistry; zeolite catalysis. *Mailing Add:* Dept Chem Worcester Polytech Inst Worcester MA 01609. *E-Mail:* aascala@wpi.edu

SCALA, E(RALDUS) (PETE), METALLURGY, COMPOSITE MATERIALS ENGINEERING. *Current Pos:* RETIRED. *Personal Data:* b Trieste, Italy, June 22, 22; nat US; m 48, Phyllis Pofenz; c Phyllis, Ralda, Elise & Chris. *Educ:* City Col New York, BS, 43; Columbia Univ, MS, 48; Yale Univ, DEng(metall), 53. *Prof Exp:* Metall chemist, Ledoux & Co, 43; res assoc, AEC Proj, Columbia Univ, 47-48; res metallurgist, Chase Brass & Copper Co, 48-52, training dir, 52-53, head, Phys Metall Sect, 53-55; mgr, Mat Dept, Res & Adv Develop Div, Avco Corp, 55-61; prof metall & mat sci, Cornell Univ, 61-68; dir, US Army Mat & Mech Res Ctr, Mass, 68-70; prof mat sci & eng, Cornell Univ, 70-72; dir, Cortland Line Co, 74-81, pres, Cortland Cable Co, 81-88. *Concurrent Pos:* Guggenheim fel, Delft Technol Univ, 67-68; consult, Aerospace Corp, Man Labs & Air Force Ballistic Missile Re-entry Systs, Battelle Mem Inst; mem adv bd mat, NASA, mem res adv comt mat; mem mat adv bd, Nat Acad Sci; consult eng, Scala & Co, 78- *Mem:* Am Inst Aeronaut & Astronaut; Am Soc Metals; Am Inst Mining, Metall & Petrol Engrs; Marine Technol Soc. *Res:* Physical metallurgy; high strength fibers and composites; cables and ropes; marine cable technology. *Mailing Add:* Cortland Cable Co PO Box 330 Cortland NY 13045. *Fax:* 607-753-3183; *E-Mail:* eps@baka.com

SCALA, JAMES, BIOCHEMISTRY & NUTRITION. *Current Pos:* vpres res & develop, 78-87, CONSULT, AUTHOR & LECTR, SHAKLEE CORP, 88- *Personal Data:* b Ramsey, NJ, Sept 16, 34; m 57; c 4. *Educ:* Columbia Col, AB, 60; Cornell Univ, PhD(biochem), 64. *Prof Exp:* Biochemist, Miami Valley Labs, Procter & Gamble Co, 64-66; sr res scientist, Owens-Ill Glass Inc, 66-68; chief life sci, Tech Ctr, 68-69; dir fundamental res, 69-71; dir appl nutrit, Tech Res, Thomas J Lipton, Inc, 71-75; dir nutrit & health sci, Gen Foods Corp, Tarrytown, NY, 75-78. *Concurrent Pos:* Lectr & adj prof, Med Col, Ohio Univ; lect prof, Georgetown Univ Sch Med, 73-85; instr, Univ Calif, Berkeley. *Mem:* Am Chem Soc; Am Soc Cell Biol; Inst Food Technol; Am Inst Nutrit; Am Col Nutrit; Brit Nutrit Soc; Am Dietetic Asn. *Res:* Selenium metabolism in microorganisms and mammalian systems; percutaneous absorption; control mechanisms in protein biosynthesis; intermediary metabolism, especially the interrelationship of carbohydrate and lipid metabolism; relationship between metabolism and exercise physiology with emphasis on stress; interrelationship between nutrition and dental health; nutritional supplementation. *Mailing Add:* 44 Los Arabis Circle Lafayette CA 94549-2746

SCALA, JOHN RICHARD, NUMERICAL MODELING, FIELD METEOROLOGY. *Current Pos:* POSTDOCTORAL FEL, GODDARD SPACE FLIGHT CTR, NASA, 90- *Personal Data:* b Rochester, NY, May 21, 58; m 86; c 1. *Educ:* Univ Rochester, BS, 80; Univ Va, MS, 84, PhD(environ sci), 90. *Mem:* Am Meteorol Soc; Am Geophys Union; Sigma Xi. *Res:* Field observation and study of convective clouds; convective-scale dynamics and transport structure; impact of convection on vertical distribution of trace gases. *Mailing Add:* 12 Indian Hill Dr Rochester NY 14420

SCALA, LUCIANO CARLO, ORGANIC CHEMISTRY. *Current Pos:* RETIRED. *Personal Data:* b Rome, Italy, July 24, 23; nat US; m 51, Rosemary Durnan; c 7. *Educ:* Univ Bologna, DSc(chem), 48. *Prof Exp:* Instr chem, Univ Bologna, 47-49; res assoc, Mass Inst Technol, 50-51; res chemist, Conn Hard Rubber Co, 51-53; mgr res labs, Westinghouse Elec Corp, 53-87, consult scientist res labs, 87-89. *Concurrent Pos:* Fulbright fel, 50. *Mem:* Sr mem Am Chem Soc. *Res:* Organic synthesis; high temperature insulation; thermal degradation mechanisms; organic monolayers; photoresists; electrophoretic processes; liquid crystals; radiation chemistry; reverse osmotic membranes. *Mailing Add:* 3359 Fawnway Dr Murrysville PA 15668-1422

SCALA, ROBERT ANDREW, ENVIRONMENTAL HEALTH. *Current Pos:* RETIRED. *Personal Data:* b Utica, NY, Nov 14, 31; m 57, Janet Eddy; c John, Anne, Peter & Jeanne. *Educ:* Hamilton Col, AB, 53; Univ Rochester, MS, 56, PhD(physiol), 58; Am Bd Toxicol, dipl, 80. *Honors & Awards:* Shaw-Mudga Award, Cosmatic Chemists, 72; Merit Award, Soc Toxicol, 95. *Prof Exp:* Res asst toxicol, Nat Acad Sci-Nat Res Coun, 58-60; sect supvr, Toxicol-Pharmacol Dept, Hazleton Labs, Inc, 60-61, asst chief, 62, dir lab opers, 62-65; toxicologist, Med Res Div, Esso Res & Eng Co, Exxon Biomed Sci, Inc, 65-74, dir toxicol, 74-81, sr sci adv, 81-91. *Concurrent Pos:* Adj prof environ med, NY Univ, 70, environ & community med, Robert Wood Johnson Med Sch, 82-; affil assoc prof pharmacol, Med Col Va, 78-; adj prof toxicol, Rutgers Univ, 82- *Mem:* Soc Toxicol (pres, 76-77); fel Acad Toxicol Sci. *Res:* Relation of chemical structure to biological function or activity; toxicology of chemicals used in foods, drugs, pesticides, cosmetics, industry and military chemicals. *Mailing Add:* 506 Scarborough Ave Rehoboth Beach DE 19971

SCALA, SINCLAIRE M(AXIMILIAN), aeronautical science, space science, for more information see previous edition

SCALAPINO, DOUGLAS J, PHYSICS. *Current Pos:* PROF PHYSICS, UNIV CALIF, SANTA BARBARA, 69- *Personal Data:* b San Francisco, Calif, Dec 10, 33; m 55, Diane Lappe; c 5. *Educ:* Yale Univ, BS, 55; Stanford Univ, PhD(physics), 61. *Prof Exp:* Res assoc physics, Wash Univ, 61-62; res assoc, Univ Pa, 62-64, from asst prof to prof, 64-69. *Concurrent Pos:* Sloan fel, 64-66, Guggenheim fel, 76-77; consult, E I du Pont de Nemours & Co, Inc, 64-87, IBM, 88-92, STI, 92- *Mem:* Nat Acad Sci; fel Am Phys Soc. *Res:* Many-body problems; superconductivity; magnetism; surfaces; statistical mechanics; phase transitions. *Mailing Add:* Dept Physics Univ Calif Santa Barbara CA 93106. *Fax:* 805-893-8838; *E-Mail:* djs@spock.physic.ucsb.edu

SCALES, JOHN ALAN, COMPUTATIONAL PHYSICS, INVERSE THEORY. *Current Pos:* ASST PROF GEOPHYS, COLO SCH MINES, GOLDEN, 92- *Personal Data:* b Louisville, Ky, June 24, 57; m 79; c 1. *Educ:* Univ Del, BS, 79; Univ Colo, PhD(physics), 84. *Prof Exp:* Consult, Tulsa Res Ctr, Amoco Prod Co, 85-86, res scientist, 86-89, sr res scientist, 89-92. *Mem:* Fel Royal Astron Soc; Am Phys Soc; Soc Indust & Appl Math; Am Geophys Union; Sigma Xi. *Res:* Geophysical inverse theory; statistical physics; global optimization methods; large scale linear algebra, especially sparse linear systems and eigenvalue problems; wave propagation in complex media. *Mailing Add:* Dept Geophys Colo Sch Mines Golden CO 80401

SCALES, STANLEY R, HEAT TREATMENT OF METALS. *Current Pos:* RETIRED. *Personal Data:* b Summitville, NY, Apr 24, 23; m, Lois McDowell; c Stephen & Laura. *Educ:* Univ Mo, Rolla, BS, 50. *Prof Exp:* Chief metallurgist, Hughes Tool Co, 50-85. *Concurrent Pos:* Chmn, Houston Sect, Am Welding Soc, 70-71; dir, Houston Mat Conf, 87. *Mem:* Fel Am Soc Metals Int. *Res:* Heat treatment of alloy steels; hard surfacing as pertains to oil well drilling tools; author of numerous technical publications; awarded 11 US patents. *Mailing Add:* 410 Axilda Houston TX 77017

SCALET, CHARLES GEORGE, FISH BIOLOGY, ICHTHYOLOGY. *Current Pos:* from asst prof to assoc prof, 73-82, PROF WILDLIFE & FISHERIES SCI, SDAK STATE UNIV, 82-, DEPT HEAD, 76- *Personal Data:* b Chicago, Ill, Sept 9, 42; m 66; c 3. *Educ:* Southern Ill Univ, Carbondale, BA, 64, MA, 67; Univ Okla, PhD(zool), 71. *Prof Exp:* Asst prof zool, Cent State Univ, 71-72; instr, Iowa State Univ, 72-73. *Mem:* Am Fisheries Soc; Am Soc Ichthyologists & Herpetologists; Wildlife Soc. *Res:* Management of South Dakota waters for fish production; culture of fishes; description of the life histories and ranges of South Dakota fishes. *Mailing Add:* Wildlife SDak State Univ Box 2206 Brookings SD 57007-0001

SCALETTAR, RICHARD, THEORETICAL PHYSICS. *Current Pos:* PROF PHYSICS & CHMN DEPT PHYSICS-ASTRON, CALIF STATE UNIV, LONG BEACH, 68- *Personal Data:* b New York, NY, Dec 9, 21; m 58; c 2. *Educ:* City Col NY, BS, 41; Univ Wis, MA, 43; Cornell Univ, PhD(physics), 59. *Prof Exp:* Physicist, Metall Lab, Univ Chicago, 43-44 & Clinton Labs, Oak Ridge, Tenn, 44-46; asst prof physics, Univ Rochester, 49-51; physicist, Curtiss-Wright Corp, 52-53; asst prof physics, Univ Southern Calif, 53-59; sr theoret physicist, John Jay Hopkins Lab Pure & Appl Sci, Gen Atomic, 60-68. *Concurrent Pos:* Consult, Aerojet Gen Corp, 56; lectr, Edwards AFB, 57; consult, Atomics Int, 58-59. *Mem:* Am Phys Soc. *Res:* Electron and gamma ray transport; interaction of electromagnetic radiation with plasmas; statistical mechanics and transport theory; reactor kinetics; particle and field theory. *Mailing Add:* Lake Forest 24782 Winterwood Dr El Toro CA 92630

SCALETTI, JOSEPH VICTOR, BACTERIOLOGY. *Current Pos:* assoc prof 64-70, PROF MICROBIOL, UNIV NMEX, 70-, CHMN DEPT, 76-, VPRES, 85- *Personal Data:* b New London, Conn, July 22, 26; m 51; c 2. *Educ:* Univ Conn, BA, 50, MS, 53; Cornell Univ, PhD(bact), 57. *Prof Exp:* Instr bact, Univ Conn, 52-53; asst, Cornell Univ, 53-56; bacteriologist, Am Cyanamid Co, 56-57; res assoc pub health, Univ Minn, St Paul, 57-58, asst prof animal husb, 58-64. *Mem:* Am Soc Microbiol; Am Pub Health Asn; Am Acad Microbiol. *Res:* Nucleic acid metabolism as related to bacteriophage-bacterial systems; growth characteristics of psychrophilic microorganism. *Mailing Add:* Dept Microbiol Univ NMex Med Sch Albuquerque NM 87131

SCALFAROTTO, ROBERT EMIL, PIGMENTS CHEMISTRY, PAPER CHEMISTRY. *Current Pos:* CONSULT, 84- *Personal Data:* b Alexandria, Egypt, June 4, 20; US citizen; m 46; c 1. *Educ:* Univ Genoa, DSc(indust chem), 48. *Prof Exp:* Chemist, Lechner & Muratori Co, 46-50, tech dir pigments, 50-57; tech mgr gen chem, Mercantile Develop, Inc, 57-58; appl res chemist, Pigments Div, Am Cyanamid Co, 58-63; asst mgr pigments div, Ciba Chem & Dye Co, NJ, 63-67, promotion coordr, 67-70, mgr tech develop, Pigments Dept, Ciba-Geigy Corp, NY, 70-76; mgr int indust chems res & develop, Am Cyanamid Co, 76-78, mgr new prod testing, 78-80, mgr prod develop, 80-84. *Concurrent Pos:* Consult, Shell Ital Chem Serv, 50-54. *Mem:* Am Chem Soc; NY Soc Coatings-Technol; Tech Asn Pulp & Paper Indust. *Res:* Paper chemicals; pigments chemistry. *Mailing Add:* PO Box 362 Ocean View DE 19970-0362

SCALIA, FRANK, NEUROBIOLOGY. *Current Pos:* From instr to assoc prof, 63-77, PROF ANAT, STATE UNIV NY DOWNSTATE MED CTR, 77- *Personal Data:* b Brooklyn, NY, Mar 18, 39; m 60; c 2. *Educ:* NY Univ, BA, 59; State Univ NY, PhD(anat), 64. *Mem:* AAAS; Am Asn Anat; Soc Neurosci. *Res:* Experimental neuroanatomy; neuroembryology; vision; olfaction. *Mailing Add:* Dept Anat State Univ NY Health Sci Ctr 450 Clarkson Ave Brooklyn NY 11203

SCALLAN, ANTHONY MICHAEL, PAPER CHEMISTRY. *Current Pos:* PRIN SCIENTIST & HEAD, FIBER CHEM SECT, PULP & PAPER RES INST CAN, 63- *Personal Data:* b Blackpool, Eng, Apr 12, 36; m 61, Sandra Reynolds; c Adrian, Michael, Julian, Christopher & Susan. *Educ:* Univ Liverpool, BSc, 57, PhD(polymer chem), 63. *Honors & Awards:* Res & Develop Award, Tech Asn Pulp & Paper Indust, 95. *Prof Exp:* Chemist, Roan Antelope Copper Mines, Zambia, 57-59. *Concurrent Pos:* Assoc sci ed, J Pulp Paper Sci, 90-95. *Mem:* Can Pulp & Paper Asn; fel Tech Asn Pulp & Paper Indust. *Res:* Physical chemistry of pulping and papermaking with emphasis on aspects related to the porous structure of wood and paper; ionic chemistry of paper making fibers. *Mailing Add:* Pulp & Paper Res Inst Can 570 St Johns Rd Pointe Claire PQ H9R 3J9 Can. *Fax:* 514-630-4134; *E-Mail:* scallan@paprican.ca

SCALLEN, TERENCE, BIOCHEMISTRY. *Current Pos:* From asst prof to assoc prof, 65-76, PROF BIOCHEM, SCH MED, UNIV NMEX, 76- *Personal Data:* b Minneapolis, Minn, Jan 16, 35; m 57; c 4. *Educ:* Col St Thomas, BS, 57; Univ Minn, Minneapolis, MD, 61, PhD(biochem, org chem), 65. *Concurrent Pos:* Am Col Cardiol young investr award, 69. *Mem:* Am Chem Soc; Am Soc Biol Chemists; Am Soc Cell Biol. *Res:* Mechanisms of sterol and lipid biosynthesis; application of physical techniques to problems of steroid structure; sterol carrier protein. *Mailing Add:* 15220 Avenida Rorras San Diego CA 92128. *Fax:* 505-277-7621

SCALLET, BARRETT LERNER, FOOD CHEMISTRY, GRAIN PRODUCTS CHEMISTRY. *Current Pos:* PRES, CENT RES, INC, 80- *Personal Data:* b St Louis, Mo, May 13, 16; m 43; c 3. *Educ:* Wash Univ, BS, 37, MS, 43, PhD(org chem), 46. *Prof Exp:* Control chemist, Anheuser-Busch, Inc, 37-38, res chemist, 38-46, res group leader, 46-47, res proj leader, 47-48, sect dir, 48-52, dir corn prod sect, Cent Res Dept, 52-55, assoc dir, 55-75, dir corn prod res, 75-80. *Mem:* Am Chem Soc; Am Asn Cereal Chem; Tech Asn Pulp & Paper Indust. *Res:* Physical study of proteins and starches; electrophoresis; ultracentrifugation; chemistry of zein; beer proteins; corn syrups and starches; industrial utilization of corn products; food products; consumer products; new corn genetic varieties; glass fracture. *Mailing Add:* 244 Christopher Ct Sanibel FL 33957

SCALORA, FRANK SALVATORE, MATHEMATICS, OPERATIONS RESEARCH. *Current Pos:* RETIRED. *Personal Data:* b New York, NY, June 16, 27. *Educ:* Harvard Univ, AB, 49; Univ Ill, AM, 51, PhD(math), 58. *Prof Exp:* Asst math, Univ Ill, 49-54; mathematician, Repub Aviation Corp, 54; mathematician, IBM Corp, 56-63, info planning mgr, World Trade, 63-67, data mgt mgr, 67-71, sr analyst, 71-74, sr analyst, Data Processing div, 74-79, corp staff, 79-82, sr analyst, Acad Info Systs, 82-87; prof, Fordham Univ, 87-89. *Concurrent Pos:* Adj prof, Polytech Inst Brooklyn, 60-61; adj asst prof, Courant Inst Math Sci, NY Univ, 61-63. *Mem:* Am Math Soc; Inst Math Statist. *Res:* Probability theory and stochastic processes; measure theory; statistics; operations research; bank asset and liability management. *Mailing Add:* 225 E 57th St Apt 10-S New York NY 10022

SCALZI, FRANCIS VINCENT, ORGANIC CHEMISTRY. *Current Pos:* PROF CHEM, HIRAM COL, 64- *Personal Data:* b Reading, Pa, Dec 4, 33; m 63; c 2. *Educ:* Gettysburg Col, BA, 55; Univ Del, MS, 60, PhD(chem), 63. *Prof Exp:* Res chemist, Firestone Tire & Rubber Co, Pa, 56-58; lectr chem, Rutgers Univ, 63-64. *Concurrent Pos:* NSF res participation col teachers grant, 64-66; vis assoc prof, Univ Wis-Milwaukee, 70-71; NSF spec proj grant, 70-72; prof, Univ Akron, 76-84, Case Western Reserve Univ, 85, 90 & Kent State Univ, 87. *Mem:* Am Chem Soc. *Res:* N-halamine chemistry; aromatic substitution; thermal degradation of organic compounds. *Mailing Add:* Chem Hiram Col PO Box 1778 Hiram OH 44234-1778

SCALZI, JOHN BAPTIST, STRUCTURAL ENGINEERING, CIVIL ENGINEERING. *Current Pos:* PROG DIR, NSF, 73- *Personal Data:* b Milford, Mass, Nov 13, 15; m 40; c 2. *Educ:* Worcester Polytech Inst, BS, 38; Mass Inst Technol, SM, 40, ScD, 51. *Prof Exp:* Field engr, Metcalf & Eddy, Mass, 39; struct engr, Curtiss-Wright Corp, NY, 40-45; engr, Eng Div, Nat Aniline Div, 45-46; prof struct eng, Case Inst Technol, 46-60; engr, Mkt Develop Div, US Steel Corp, 60-62; dir mkt tech serv, 62-71; engr res & technol, HUD, 71-73. *Concurrent Pos:* Lectr, Exten Eng Sci & Mgt War Training Prog, Cornell Univ, 42-45 & Univ Buffalo, 45; prof lectr, Western Reserve Univ, 46-60; lectr, Carnegie-Mellon Univ, 65-71 & George Washington Univ, 72-83; struct consult, Cleveland eng firms. *Mem:* Am Soc Civil Engrs; Sigma Xi. *Res:* Earthquake engineering; general civil engineering; infrastructure. *Mailing Add:* NSF 4201 Wilson Blvd Rm 545 Arlington VA 22230

SCALZO, FRANK M, PHARMACOLOGY, TOXICOLOGY. *Current Pos:* res asst prof, Dept Pediat, Univ Ark Med Sci, 89-90, asst prof, 90-92, Pediat Res, Ark Children's Hosp Res Inst, 92-95, Dept Pharmacol, 93-95 & Grad Sch, 94-95, INSTR, DEPT PSYCHOL, UNIV ARK, 94- ASSOC PROF, GRAD SCH & DEPT PEDIAT, PHARMACOL & TOXICOL, 95- *Personal Data:* b Albany, NY, May 24, 58. *Educ:* St Bonaventure Univ, BS, 80; State Univ NY, Binghamton, MA, 82, PhD(psychol), 85. *Prof Exp:* Postdoctoral fel, Dept Develop Psychobiol, NY State Psychiat Inst & Dept Psychiat, Col Physicians & Surgeons, Columbia Univ, 85-87; Nat Ctr Toxicol Res fel, Div Reproductive & Develop Toxicol, Oakridge Assoc Univs, 87-90. *Concurrent Pos:* Nat Res Serv award, NIMH, 85-87; instr, Columbia Univ, 86-87; grantee, Nat Inst Drug Abuse, 88, 92-95 & 94-99, Nat Acad Sci, 91, March of Dimes Birth Defects Found, 93, Am Heart Asn, 93-95; first independent res award, Nat Inst Drug Abuse, 90-95; guest worker, Div Reproductive & Develop Toxicol, Nat Ctr Toxicol Res, Ark, 90-; lectr, Dept Pediat, Pharmacol & Toxicol, Univ Ark Med Scis, 90-; E Europe Exchange Prog, Nat Acad Scis, Slovenia, 92; mem, comt Soc Neurosci, 93, coun & chair, Neurobehav Teratology Soc, 95-; Fulbright scholar, Dept Pharm, Univ Ljubljana, 95-96, vis prof, 95-96. *Mem:* Soc Neurosci; Int Soc Develop Psycholbiol; AAAS; Teratology Soc; Neurobehav Teratology Soc; Sigma Xi. *Mailing Add:* Pediat Res S Campus Room R-2052-C Ark Children's Hosp Res Inst 800 Marshall St Little Rock AR 72202

SCAMEHORN, RICHARD GUY, ORGANIC REACTION MECHANISMS, CHEMICAL EDUCATION. *Current Pos:* From asst prof to assoc prof, 68-82, chmn dept, 85-92, PROF CHEM, RIPON COL, 82-, BARBER DISTINGUISHED PROF, 92- *Personal Data:* b Elkhart, Ind, June 20, 42; m 64, Sandra S Nice; c David J & Richard T. *Educ:* Hanover Col, BA, 64; Northwestern Univ, PhD(org chem), 68. *Concurrent Pos:* Res assoc, Univ Calif, Santa Cruz, 75-76; vis prof, Univ Wis, 84 & 92. *Mem:* Am Chem Soc; Sigma Xi. *Res:* Organic reaction mechanisms; carbanion rearrangement reactions; kinetics; radical chain substitution reactions; chemical education. *Mailing Add:* 627 Sunset Circle Ripon WI 54971-1608. *Fax:* 920-748-7243; *E-Mail:* scamehornr@acad.ripon.edu

SCANDALIOS, JOHN GEORGE, GENETICS. *Current Pos:* prof genetics & head dept, 75-85, DISTINGUISHED UNIV PROF, NC STATE UNIV, 85- *Personal Data:* b Nysiros, Greece, Nov 1, 34; US citizen; m 61, Penelope Lawrence; c Artemis, Melissa & Nikki. *Educ:* Univ Va, BA, 57; Adelphi Univ, MS, 60; Univ Hawaii, PhD(genetics), 65. *Hon Degrees:* DSc, Aristotelian Univ Thessaloniki, Greece, 86. *Prof Exp:* Instr biol, Hunter Col, 59-60; res assoc bact genetics, Cold Spring Harbor Lab, 60-63; NIH res fel molecular genetics, Univ Hawaii, 65; from asst prof to assoc prof res genetics, AEC Plant Res Lab, Mich State Univ, 65-72; prof genetics & head, Dept Biol, Univ SC, 72-75. *Concurrent Pos:* Instr radiation biol, biol & genetics, Adelphi Univ, 60-62; vis prof, Univ Calif, Davis, 68 & Orgn Am States, Arg, 72; mem, Recombinant DNA Adv Comt, NIH, 80-85; ed, Develop Genetics & Advances Genetics. *Mem:* Fel AAAS; Genetics Soc Am; Soc Develop Biol (treas, 79-81); Am Genetic Asn (pres, 81-82); Int Soc Differentiation; Am Soc Biochem & Molecular Biol; Am Soc Plant Physiol; Int Soc Plant Nuclear Biol. *Res:* Developmental-molecular genetics of eukaryotes; genetics, structure and function of isozymes; genetic regulation; biotechnology; plant molecular biology; molecular biology of antioxidant defense genes. *Mailing Add:* Dept Genetics NC State Univ Raleigh NC 27695-7614

SCANDRETT, JOHN HARVEY, PHYSICS. *Current Pos:* assoc prof, 66-81, PROF PHYSICS, WASH UNIV, 81- *Personal Data:* b Liberal, Kans, July 7, 33; m 54; c 3. *Educ:* La State Univ, BS, 54; Univ Wis, MS, 56, PhD(physics), 63. *Prof Exp:* Lectr physics, Mich State Univ, 60-62; lectr, Ind Univ, 62-63; asst prof, 63-66. *Mem:* Am Phys Soc. *Res:* Medical physics; image processing. *Mailing Add:* 6829 Waterman St St Louis MO 63130

SCANDURA, JOSEPH M, INTELLIGENT SYSTEMS, CASE. *Current Pos:* PROF & DIR, INTERDISCIPLINARY STUDIES IN STRUCT LEARNING & INSTRNL SCI, UNIV PA, 66- *Personal Data:* b Bay Shore, NY, Apr 29, 32; m 60; c Jeanne (Bodine), Janette, Joseph IV & Julie. *Educ:* Univ Mich, BA, 53, MA, 55; Syracuse Univ, PhD(math educ), 62; Univ Pa, MS, 74. *Hon Degrees:* MS, Univ Pa, 71. *Prof Exp:* Math teacher, NY, 53-55; asst prof math, Col Oswego, State Univ NY, 55-56; instr, Syracuse Univ, 56-63; asst prof math & educ, State Univ NY Buffalo, 63-64; res prof math educ, Fla State Univ, 64-66. *Concurrent Pos:* Consult, Merge Res Inst; pres, Intel Micro Systs. *Mem:* AAAS; fel Am Psychol Asn; Am Educ Res Asn. *Res:* Theory and research in structural learning, cognitive psychology, instructional systems design and intelligent computer-based instruction; computer aided system engineering; cognitive methodology for software engineering and re- engineering. *Mailing Add:* 1249 Greentree Suite 100 Narberth PA 19072. *Fax:* 215-664-7276; *E-Mail:* jms@pobox.upenn.edu

SCANES, COLIN G, HORMONES & GROWTH. *Current Pos:* assoc prof physiol, 78-81, CHMN DEPT ANIMAL SCI, RUTGERS UNIV, 81-, PROF ANIMAL SCI, 82- *Personal Data:* b London, Eng, July 11, 47; m 76, Carla J Turk; c Rosalind A, Jacqueline D & Meredith L. *Educ:* Univ Hull, UK, BS, 69; Univ Wales, PhD(zool), 72. *Hon Degrees:* DSc, Univ Hull, UK, 85. *Honors & Awards:* Merck Award for Excellence-Poultry Sci Res, Rutgers Univ, 86. *Prof Exp:* Lectr animal physiol & nutrit, Univ Leeds, UK, 72-78. *Concurrent Pos:* Prog mgr, Competitive Grants Prog, USDA, 89-90; prof, Cath Univ Leuven, 90-91. *Mem:* Am Physiol Soc; Poultry Sci Asn; Am Soc Zoologists; Endocrine Soc; Am Soc Animal Sci; Soc Exp Biol. *Res:* Hormonal control of growth metabolism and reproduction, particularly in the domestic fowl and other farm animals. *Mailing Add:* Dept 1A Agr & Home Econ Exp Sta Iowa State Univ 123S Curtis Hall Ames IA 50011-1050. *Fax:* 732-932-6996

SCANIO, CHARLES JOHN VINCENT, ORGANIC CHEMISTRY, ORGANIC PROCESS RESEARCH & DEVELOPMENT. *Current Pos:* PRES, SECANT CHEM, INC, 92- *Personal Data:* b Ann Arbor, Mich, June 23, 40; m 65, Kaaren Wellman; c Erik & Kurt. *Educ:* Univ Mich, BS, 62; Northwestern Univ, PhD(org chem), 66. *Prof Exp:* From instr to asst prof chem, Iowa State Univ, 66-72; staff chemist, Pfizer Inc, 72-77; head process res, UpJohn Inc, 77-84; corp dir, res & develop, Chem Design Corp, 84-86; exec vpres, Chem Sultants Int Inc, 86-92. *Mem:* Am Chem Soc; Brit Chem Soc. *Res:* Processes to manufacture fine chemicals and pharmaceutical intermediates. *Mailing Add:* 300 High St Po Box 246 Winchendon MA 01475-0246. *Fax:* 978-297-1518; *E-Mail:* cscanio@juno.com

SCANLAN, J(ACK) A(DDISON), JR, mechanical engineering, for more information see previous edition

SCANLAN, MARY ELLEN, SCIENCE COMMUNICATIONS. *Current Pos:* asst mgr, 82-90, mgr ed off, Jour Dept, 91-96, DIR, J PUBL OPERS, AM CHEM SOC, 96- *Personal Data:* b New York, NY, Sept 20, 42. *Educ:* Chestnut Hill Col, BS, 64; Univ RI, PhD(org chem), 70. *Prof Exp:* Sr assoc ed, Dept Org Chem, Chem Abstr Serv, 70-82. *Mem:* Am Chem Soc. *Mailing Add:* Am Chem Soc 1155 16th St NW Washington DC 20036. *Fax:* 202-872-6060; *E-Mail:* mscanlan@acs.org

SCANLAN, RICHARD ANTHONY, FOOD SCIENCE. *Current Pos:* asst food sci, Ore State Univ, 64-67, from asst prof to assoc prof, 67-78, dept head, 85-89, PROF FOOD SCI, ORE STATE UNIV, 78- , DEAN RES, ADMIN BLDG, 89- *Personal Data:* b Syracuse, NY, Dec 13, 37; m 59, Margaretta Smith; c 5. *Educ:* Cornell Univ, BS, 60, MS, 62; Ore State Univ, PhD, 67. *Honors & Awards:* Sigma Xi Res Award, Ore State Univ, 83; Distinguished Serv Award, Am Chem Soc, 88. *Prof Exp:* Res & develop coordr, US Army Natick Labs, Mass, 62-64. *Concurrent Pos:* Prin investr, res grants. *Mem:* AAAS; Am Chem Soc; Sigma Xi; Inst Food Technologists. *Res:* Food toxicology; chemistry of formation and inhibition of N-nitrosamines; development of analytical methodology for nitrosamines; biological effects of N-nitrosamines; food chemistry; flavor chemistry. *Mailing Add:* Res Off Ore State Univ Corvallis OR 97333. *Fax:* 541-737-3093; *E-Mail:* scanlanr@ccmail.orst.edu

SCANLAN, ROBERT HARRIS, STRUCTURAL DYNAMICS. *Current Pos:* PROF CIVIL ENG, JOHNS HOPKINS UNIV, 85- *Personal Data:* b Chicago, Ill, Aug 15, 14; m 39; c 4. *Educ:* Univ Chicago, SB, 36, SM, 39; Mass Inst Technol, PhD(math), 43; Univ Paris, Dr es Sci(mech), 56. *Honors & Awards:* State-of-the Art in Civil Eng Award, Am Soc Civil Engrs, 69, Wellington Prize, 86, Newmark Medal, 86; T R Higgins Nat Lectr, 76. *Prof Exp:* Assoc prof aeronaut, Rensselaer Polytech Inst, 46-51; Nat Res Coun-Nat Adv Comt Aeronaut fel, France, 51-52; res fel aeronaut, Nat Sci Res Ctr, France, 52-55; res engr, Nat Off Aeronaut Studies & Res, France, 55-57; Schlumberger Corp, Tex, 58-60; prof mech, Case Inst Technol, 60-66; prof civil eng, Princeton Univ, 66-85. *Concurrent Pos:* Sloan vis prof, Princeton Univ, 64-65; vis prof, Rice Univ, Univ Calif, Berkeley, 78; consult, Pvt US, Fr & Japanese firms. *Mem:* Nat Acad Eng; Am Inst Aeronaut & Astronaut; Am Soc Mech Engrs; hon mem Am Soc Civil Engrs; fel Am Acad Mech; Nat Acad Eng. *Res:* Acoustics; aeroelasticity; vibrations; applied mechanics; wind engineering; bridge aerodynamics. *Mailing Add:* Dept Civil Eng Johns Hopkins Univ Baltimore MD 21218

SCANLEY, CLYDE STEPHEN, WATER SOLUBLE POLYMERS. *Current Pos:* PROPRIETOR, CHEM RES & DEVELOP CONSULT, JEITO RES, 83- *Personal Data:* b Milwaukee, Wis, June 16, 21; div; c 3. *Educ:* Univ Wis, BS, 43, PhD(org chem), 49. *Prof Exp:* Chemist, Standard Oil Co, Ind, 49-53; group leader, Am Cyanamid Co, 53-73; mgr res, Drew Chem Corp, 74-83. *Mem:* Am Chem Soc; Tech Asn Pulp & Paper Indust. *Res:* Vinyl polymers, especially polyelectrolyte flocculants, polycrylamides, surfactants, organic synthesis and process development. *Mailing Add:* 330 Speedwell Ave Morristown NJ 07960-2929

SCANLON, ANDREW, STRUCTURAL ENGINEERING. *Current Pos:* PROF, PA STATE UNIV, UNIVERSITY PARK, 87- & DIR, TRANSP STRUCT PROG, PA TRANSP INST, 93- *Personal Data:* b Bridge of Allan, Scotland, Apr 16, 44; m 78, Mary E Kendall; c Mark & Christina. *Educ:* Univ Glasgow, BSc, 66; Univ Alta, PhD, 72. *Honors & Awards:* Le Prix P L Pratley Award, Can Soc Civil Eng, 90. *Prof Exp:* Civil engr, Pub Works Can, St John, NB, 66-67; proj engr, NB Develop Corp, Fredericton, 67-68; assoc prof civil eng, Univ Alta, Edmonton, 82-83, prof, 83-87; struct design engr, Duthie Newby & Assocs, Edmonton, 71-73; struct div head, Reid Crowther & Partners Ltd, Edmonton, 73-78; sr struct engr, Struct Eval Sect, Construct Tech Labs Inc, 78-80, mgr, Anal Design Sect, 80-82. *Concurrent Pos:* Actg head dept, Pa State Univ, 91; mem, Coun Tall Buildings & Urban Habitat. *Mem:* Am Soc Civil Engrs; Am Concrete Inst. *Res:* Bridge engineering; earthquake engineering. *Mailing Add:* Pa State Univ 212 Sackett Bldg University Park PA 16802. *Fax:* 814-863-7304; *E-Mail:* axs21@psu.edu

SCANLON, CHARLES HARRIS, FLIGHT MANAGEMENT RESEARCH. *Current Pos:* SR RESEARCHER, NASA, 90- *Personal Data:* b Austin, Tex, Oct 13, 37; c Judy, Charlotte & Nicholas. *Educ:* Univ Tex, BA, 61, MA, 63, PhD(math), 67. *Prof Exp:* Prof math & comput sci, Ark State Univ, 70-90. *Mem:* Am Inst Aeronaut & Astronaut. *Res:* Aronautical digital communicators; cockpit weather information; airborn information for lateral spacing. *Mailing Add:* NASA Langley Res Ctr MS 156A Hampton VA 23681. *Fax:* 757-864-8858; *E-Mail:* c.h.scanlon@larc.nasa.gov

SCANLON, JACK M, COMPUTER SCIENCE, ELECTRICAL ENGINEERING. *Current Pos:* VPRES, PROCESSOR & SOFTWARE SYSTS, WESTERN ELECTRONIC CO; VPRES & GEN MGR, INT CELLULAR INFRASTRUCT, MOTOROLA, INC, ARLINGTON HEIGHTS, 90- *Personal Data:* b Binghamton, NY, Jan 3, 42; m 63; c 4. *Educ:* Univ Toronto, BASc, 64; Cornell Univ, MS, 65. *Prof Exp:* Mem staff elec eng, 65-68; supvr comput sci, Bell Labs, 68-74, dept head electronic switching syst design, 74-77, dir, Software & Syst Design Lab, 77-79, exec dir, Processor & Common Software Systs Div, 79-; vpres, prod develop, AT&T Info Syst. *Concurrent Pos:* NSF fel, 64-65; comput sci & technol bd, Nat Res Coun-Nat Acad Sci. *Mem:* Inst Elec & Electronics Engrs. *Res:* Computer science; communications science; physics, mathematics. *Mailing Add:* Motorola 1501 W Shore Dr Barrington IL 60010

SCANLON, JOHN EARL, MEDICAL ENTOMOLOGY. *Current Pos:* RETIRED. *Personal Data:* b New York, NY, Nov 29, 25; m 47; c 2. *Educ:* Fordham Univ, BS, 50; Cornell Univ, MS, 55; Univ Md, PhD, 60. *Prof Exp:* Med entomologist, Far East Med Res Unit, US Army, Tokyo, 50-53, Med Field Serv Sch, San Antonio, 55-56, Walter Reed Army Inst, 56-58, SEATO, Bangkok, 60-64 & Walter Reed Army Inst, 64-69; prof med zool, Sch Pub Health, Univ Tex, Houston, 69-75, assoc dean, 75-87. *Mem:* AAAS; Am Soc Trop Med & Hyg (secy-tres, 80-). *Res:* Epidemiology of malaria and arbovirus; taxonomy and ecology of mosquitoes. *Mailing Add:* 17 Trails End Rd Boerne TX 78006

SCANLON, PATRICK FRANCIS, REPRODUCTIVE PHYSIOLOGY, WILDLIFE RESEARCH. *Current Pos:* from asst prof to assoc prof wildlife physiol, 71-78, PROF, DEPT FISHERIES & WILDLIFE SCI, VA POLYTECH INST & STATE UNIV, 78- *Personal Data:* b Athlone, Ireland, Sept 16, 41; m 67; c 4. *Educ:* Nat Univ Ireland, BAgrSci, 65, MAgrSci, 66, PhD(animal physiol), 70. *Prof Exp:* Res demonstr animal physiol, Fac Agr, Univ Col, Dublin, 65-66, res scholar, 66-69; res assoc appl physiol, Univ Guelph, 69-73. *Concurrent Pos:* Vis prof, Telemark, Norway. *Mem:* Am Soc Animal Sci; Wildlife Soc; Am Soc Mammal; Wildlife Dis Asn; Soc Environ Toxicol & Chem. *Res:* Reproductive physiology of wild animals; influences of environmental contaminants on wild animals; vertebrate pest control; control of reproduction in wild and domestic animals. *Mailing Add:* Dept Fisheries & Wildlife Sci Va Polytech Inst & State Univ PO Box 0321 Blacksburg VA 24063-0001

SCANNELL, EDWARD PERRY, PLASMA PHYSICS. *Current Pos:* RESEARCHER, US ARMY, 91- *Personal Data:* b New Orleans, La, Aug 31, 40. *Educ:* Tulane Univ, BS, 65; NC State Univ, PhD(physics), 76. *Prof Exp:* Opers mgr, AI Corp, 84-91. *Mem:* Am Phys Soc. *Mailing Add:* 14 Wetherbee Ct Phoenix MD 21131

SCANNELL, JAMES PARNELL, BIOCHEMISTRY. *Current Pos:* RETIRED. *Personal Data:* b Oak Park, Ill, Jan 16, 31; m 56; c 4. *Educ:* Univ Ill, BA, 51; Univ Calif, Berkeley, PhD(biochem), 60. *Prof Exp:* Fel biochem, Univ Calif, San Francisco, 60; lectr chem, Southern Ill Univ, 60-61; sr chemist, Papst Res Biochem, Pabst Brewing Co, 61-63 & Burroughs Wellcome & Co, 64-65; sr chemist, Hoffman-La Roche & Co, 66-75, res fel, 75-81, sr res fel, 81-85. *Mem:* Am Chem Soc. *Res:* Isolation and characterization of natural products; chemistry and metabolism of nucleosides, amino acids and antibiotics. *Mailing Add:* 376 Guthrie Ashland OR 97520

SCANU, ANGELO M, MEDICINE, BIOCHEMISTRY. *Current Pos:* asst prof, 63-66, res assoc biochem, 65-66, assoc prof internal med & biochem, 66-70, PROF INTERNAL MED BIOCHEM & MOLECULAR BIOL, MED SCH, UNIV CHICAGO, 70-, DIR, LIPOPROTEIN STUDY UNIT, 73-, DIR, CTR MOLECULAR MED, 87- *Personal Data:* b Bonnanaro, Italy, Dec 16, 24; m 58; c 2. *Educ:* Univ Sassari, MD, 49. *Honors & Awards:* Res Career Develop Award, 65-75. *Prof Exp:* From intern to resident, Med Sch, Univ Sassari, 49-52; asst prof internal med, Med Sch, Univ Naples, 53-55; res assoc, Cleveland Clin, 58, staff asst, 59-62; Res fel, Med Sch, Univ Barcelona, 52 & Med Sch, Univ Lund, 53; Fulbright scholar & res fel, Res Div, Cleveland Clin, 55-57; Fulbright scholar, Univ Nice, 80. *Mem:* Am Soc Biol Chemists; Am Chem Soc; Am Physiol Soc; Biophys Soc; Am Soc Clin Invest; Asn Am Physicians. *Res:* Structure and function of serum lipoproteins in normal and disease states; lipoprotein cell interactions; genetics of lipoprotein disorders. *Mailing Add:* Dept Med Biochenm & Molecular Biol Univ Chicago Pritzker Med Sch 5841 S Maryland Ave MC 5041 Chicago IL 60637-1463. *Fax:* 773-702-4534

SCAPINO, ROBERT PETER, ANATOMY, DENTISTRY. *Current Pos:* From instr to assoc prof, 65-75, PROF ORAL ANAT, COL DENT, COL MED, UNIV ILL, 75- *Personal Data:* b Chicago, Ill, July 20, 36; m 58; c 3. *Educ:* Univ Ill, BS, 59, DDS, 62, MS, 63, PhD(anat), 68. *Concurrent Pos:* Nat Inst Dent Res fel anat, 62-65. *Mem:* Fel AAAS; Sigma Xi; Am Dent Assn. *Res:* Biomechanics of feeding in carnivores; comparative and human anatomy; function and pathology of jaw joints. *Mailing Add:* 917 Foxworth Blvd Lombard IL 60148-4815

SCARATT, DAVID J, MARINE BIOLOGY. *Current Pos:* CONSULT, DAVID SCARATT & ASSOCS, HALIFAX, NS, 92- *Personal Data:* b Liverpool, Eng, Dec 21, 35; m 62; Irene S Grant; c Michael G & Alison M. *Educ:* Univ Wales, BS, 58, PhD, 61. *Prof Exp:* Res scientist, Govt Can Fisheries, St Andrews, NB, 61-85, Halifax, NS, 85-92. *Mem:* Nat Shellfisheries Asn; World Aquacult Asn; Can Aquacult Asn. *Res:* Shellfish culture development. *Mailing Add:* David Scaratt & Assocs PO Box 1564 Halifax NS B3J 2Y7 Can. *Fax:* 902-423-2720; *E-Mail:* scarratt@atcon.com

SCARBOROUGH, CHARLES SPURGEON, INVERTEBRATE ZOOLOGY, ACAROLOGY. *Current Pos:* asst zool, Mich State Univ, 59-63, from instr to assoc prof natural sci, 63-77, from asst dir resident instr to dir resident instr, 71-77, from asst dean to actg dean, 77-81, PROF NATURAL SCI, MICH STATE UNIV, 77-, DIR, LYMAN BRIGGS SCH, 81- *Personal Data:* b Goodman, Miss, May 20, 33; m 70. *Educ:* Rust Col, BA, 55; Northwestern Univ, Evanston, MS, 58; Mich State Univ, PhD(zool), 69. *Prof Exp:* Instr bot & zool, Alcorn Agr & Mech Col, 57-59. *Mem:* AAAS. *Res:* Free-living mites associated with bracket fungi, their taxonomy and biology. *Mailing Add:* Ctr Integrated Studies Mich State Univ 100 N Kedzie Lab East Lansing MI 48824-1031

SCARBOROUGH, ERNEST N, AGRICULTURAL ENGINEERING, AUTOMOTIVE ENGINEERING. *Current Pos:* from assoc prof to prof, 55-83, chmn dept, 68-81, EMER PROF AGR ENG, UNIV DEL, 83- *Personal Data:* b Annapolis, Md, May 21, 22; m 44; c 4. *Educ:* Iowa State Col, BS, 43, MS, 47. *Honors & Awards:* Award, Christian R & Mary H Lindbach Found, 64. *Prof Exp:* Asst prof agr eng, NC State Col, 48-52; assoc prof, Tenn Polytech Inst, 52-53; sr test engr, Thompson Prod Co, 53-54, prod analyst, 54-55. *Mem:* Am Soc Agr Engrs. *Res:* Farm machinery and power; crop processing; environmental control; soil and water conservation. *Mailing Add:* 1002 Lakeside Dr Newark DE 19711

SCARBOROUGH, GENE ALLEN, BIOCHEMISTRY. *Current Pos:* assoc prof pharmacol, 77-82, PROF PHARMACOL, UNIV NC, CHAPEL HILL, 82- *Personal Data:* b Hugo, Colo, Oct 8, 40; m 66. *Educ:* Univ Ariz, BS, 63; Univ Calif, Los Angeles, PhD(biochem), 66. *Prof Exp:* From asst to assoc prof biochem, Sch Med, Univ Colo, 76-77. *Concurrent Pos:* Whitney fel, Harvard Med Sch, 67-68. *Mem:* AAAS; Am Soc Biol Chemists; Am Soc Microbiol; Biophys Soc. *Res:* Phospholipid biosynthesis; structure and function of biomembranes. *Mailing Add:* Dept Pharmacol Univ NC Sch Med 1005A FLOB 231H Chapel Hill NC 27599

SCARBOROUGH, VERNON LEE, ARCHAEOLOGICAL METHOD & TECHNIQUE. *Current Pos:* ASSOC PROF ANTHROP, UNIV CINCINNATI, 88- *Personal Data:* M 84, Pat Mora; c 4. *Educ:* Univ Ore, BS, 73; Southern Methodist Univ, PhD(anthrop), 80. *Prof Exp:* Lectr archaeol, Univ Khartoum, Sudan, 81-82, Univ Tex, El Paso, 82-87; Fulbright fel archaeol, Univ Peshawar, Pakistan, 86. *Concurrent Pos:* Weatherhead fel, Sch Am Res, Santa Fe, NM, 94-95. *Mem:* Am Anthrop Asn; Am Assn; Asn Field Archaeol; Sigma Xi; Soc Am Archaeol. *Res:* Ancient water management systems as well as related landscape engineering principally in the Maya lowlands and North American Southwest. *Mailing Add:* Dept Anthrop Univ Cincinnati PO Box 210380 Cincinnati OH 45221. *Fax:* 513-556-2778

SCARBROUGH, FRANK EDWARD, CHEMISTRY. *Current Pos:* DIR, OFF FOOD LABELING, FOOD & DRUG ADMIN, 92- *Personal Data:* b Knoxville, Tenn, Sept 27, 42. *Educ:* Univ Tenn, BS, 64; Harvard Univ, PhD(chem), 71. *Prof Exp:* Res assoc, Univ Bern, Switz, 71-73; instr, Univ Pa, 73-76. *Mem:* Am Soc Clin Nutrit; Inst Food Technologists; Am Chem Soc. *Res:* Public health policy-food labeling; food fortification; dietary supplements, etc. *Mailing Add:* FDA 200 C St SW HFS-150 Washington DC 20204-0001. *Fax:* 202-205-4594

SCARDERA, MICHAEL, INDUSTRIAL ORGANIC CHEMISTRY. *Current Pos:* RETIRED. *Personal Data:* b Providence, RI, May 11, 35; m 62; c 4. *Educ:* Brown Univ, BS, 57; Univ Bridgeport, MBA, 63. *Prof Exp:* Res chemist fuels res, Olin Corp, 57-63, sr res chemist, 64-75, sr res assoc surface active agents, 76-91. *Concurrent Pos:* Instr, Southern Conn State Col, 65-75. *Mem:* Sigma Xi; Am Oil Chem Soc. *Res:* Synthesis and application of surface active agents. *Mailing Add:* 81 Manor St Hamden CT 06517

SCARDINA, JOHN A, ARCHITECTURE & SYSTEMS ENGINEERING. *Current Pos:* staff, 75-96, leader, Air Traffic Mgt Integrated Prod Team, DIR, ARCHIT & SYST ENG DIRECTORATE, FED AVIATION ADMIN, 96-, LEADER, FED AVIATION ADMIN/NASA INTERAGENCY INTEGRATED PROD TEAM, 96- *Educ:* Va Polytech Inst, BSEE, 64; Ga Inst Technol, MS, 66, PhD(elec eng), 68. *Prof Exp:* Group leader, Mitre Corp, Va. *Res:* Advanced automation program, weather program; remote maintenance monitoring; collision avoidance systems; oceanic automation; automation systems and satellite applications. *Mailing Add:* Fed Aviation Admin Systs Archit & Integration Asn-100 800 Independence Ave SW Washington DC 20591. *Fax:* 202-358-5298

SCARDINO, PETER T, OBSTETRICS & GYNECOLOGY. *Current Pos:* from asst prof to assoc prof, 79-86, PROF UROL, BAYLOR COL MED, HOUSTON, 86-, RUSSELL & MARY HUGH SCOTT PROF & CHMN, DEPT UROL, 89- *Personal Data:* b Portsmouth, Va, Sept 28, 45; m 65, Alice Barrow Myrick Barrie; c Allison Kelly, Peter Daniel Robinson & Elizabeth Barrow. *Educ:* Yale Univ, BA, 67; Duke Univ, MD, 71; Am Bd Urol, cert, 81. *Honors & Awards:* George Slotkin Hon Lectr, Am Urol Asn, 85 & 95; Gold Cystoscope Award, 89; Eugene Fuller Triennial Prostate Award, 95; Pres Award, Am Found Urologic Dis, 96. *Prof Exp:* Surg resident, Mass Gen Hosp, Boston, 71-73; clin assoc, Surg Br, Nat Cancer Inst, NIH, 73-76; urol resident, Sch Med, Univ Calif, Los Angeles, 76-79, instr, 78-79. *Concurrent Pos:* Sr attending Urol, Methodist Hosp, 79-, chief urol serv, 89-,; courtesy staff, Vet Admin Med Ctr, 79, Tex Children's Hosp, 79-; active staff urol, St Luke's Episcopal Hosp, 79-, Ben Taub Gen Hosp, 79- & chief urol serv, 89- *Mem:* Inst Med-Nat Acad Sci; Am Asn Cancer Res; AAAS; Int Urol Soc; Clin Soc Genitourinary Surgeons; Soc Univ Surgeons; fel Am Col Surgeons; Am Asn Genitourinary Surgeons; Am Soc Clin Oncol; Am Urol Asn; Am Inst Ultrasound Med; NY Acad Sci; AMA. *Res:* Translational research in prostate cancer; gene therapy for prostate cancer; controlled clinical trials in urologic oncology; techniques for radical surgery for genitourinary cancers. *Mailing Add:* 6560 Fannin Suite 1004 Houston TX 77030-2706

SCARFE, COLIN DAVID, OBSERVATIONAL STELLAR ASTRONOMY. *Current Pos:* From asst prof to assoc prof, 65-81, PROF ASTRON, UNIV VICTORIA, BC, 81- *Personal Data:* b Danbury, Eng, Dec 17, 40; Can citizen; m 67, R Ann M Thompson; c Sarah M & M Jean. *Educ:* Univ BC, BSc, 60, MSc, 61; Cambridge Univ, PhD(astron), 65. *Concurrent Pos:* Mem comns, Int Astron Union, 26, 30, 42; sabbatical, Observs, Cambridge, Eng, 71-72 & Mt John Observ, NZ, 78-79, Dominion Astrophys Observ, Victoria, Can, 85-86; vis fel, Mt Stromlo Observ, Australia, 78-79; mem, Assoc Comt Astron, Nat Res Coun Can, 77-83, chmn, Optical Astron Subcomt, 80-83; chmn, organizing comt, Can Asn Physicists meeting, Can Astron Soc, 83; vpres, Comn 30, Int Astron Union, 91-94; Sabbatical, Copenhagen Univ, Cambridge Univ & Dom Astrophys Observ, 92-93; pres, Comm 30, Inst Astron Union, 94-97, pres, Div IX, 94-97. *Mem:* Am Astron Soc; Royal Astron Soc Can; fel Royal Astron Soc; Can Astron Soc; Astron Soc Pac. *Res:* Spectroscopy and photometry of binary and multiple stars; determination of pendamental stellar properties. *Mailing Add:* Dept Physics & Astron Univ Victoria Victoria BC V8W 3P6 Can

SCARFONE, LEONARD MICHAEL, PHYSICS. *Current Pos:* from asst prof to assoc prof, 63-70, PROF PHYSICS, UNIV VT, 70- *Personal Data:* b North Adams, Mass, Oct 5, 29; m 55; c 3. *Educ:* Williams Col, BA, 53, MA, 55; Rensselaer Polytech Inst, PhD(physics), 60. *Prof Exp:* Instr physics, Rensselaer Polytech Inst, 60-61; fel, Fla State Univ, 61-62, asst prof, 62-63. *Mem:* Am Phys Soc; Am Asn Physics Teachers. *Res:* Quantum field theory; quantum theory of scattering; mathematical physics; elementary particles; theoretical solid state. *Mailing Add:* Cook Phys Sci Bldg Univ Vt Burlington VT 05401

SCARGLE, JEFFREY D, ASTRONOMY. *Current Pos:* RES SCIENTIST, AMES RES CTR, NASA, 75- *Personal Data:* b Evanston, Ill, Nov 24, 41; div; c 2. *Educ:* Pomona Col, BA, 63; Calif Inst Technol, PhD(astron), 68. *Prof Exp:* Fel astron, Univ Calif, Berkeley, 68; instr astron & jr astronr, Univ Calif, Santa Cruz, 68-69, asst prof astron & astrophys, 69-74. *Mem:* Am Astron Soc; Int Astron Union. *Res:* Plasma astrophysics; quasars; The Crab Nebula; radiative transfer; statistical analysis of random processes; infrared astronomy; time series analysis; planetary detection astrometry. *Mailing Add:* Theoret Studies MS-245-3 NASA Ames Res Ctr Moffett Field CA 94035

SCARINGE, RAYMOND PETER, CHEMISTRY, X-RAY DIFFRACTION. *Current Pos:* RES CHEMIST, EASTMAN KODAK CO, 78- *Personal Data:* b Albany, NY, July 31, 50. *Educ:* State Univ NY, Plattsburgh, BA, 72; Univ NC, PhD(inorg chem), 76. *Prof Exp:* Fel chem, Northwestern Univ, 76-78. *Mem:* Am Chem Soc; Am Crystallog Asn. *Res:* Structural, electrical and magnetic properties in the solid state. *Mailing Add:* 26 Moorland Rd Rochester NY 14612-3423

SCARINGE, ROBERT P, SOFTWARE SYSTEMS. *Current Pos:* prof heat transfer, 82-86, RES PROF THERMODYN HEAT TRANSFER, FLA INST TECHNOL, 86-; PRES, MAINSTREAM ENG CORP, 86- *Personal Data:* US citizen. *Educ:* Rensselaer Polytech Inst, BS, 74, MS, 75, PhD(mech eng), 78. *Prof Exp:* Res scientist, Gen Elec Res & Develop, 78-82. *Concurrent Pos:* Fel, Dupont, Fa, Ford, 77; adj proj thermodyn heat transfer, Rensselaer Polytech Inst, 78-82. *Mem:* Am Soc Mech Engrs. *Res:* Thermal control; chemical research; software development; hardware development; working fluid research; computer simulation of thermal management systems. *Mailing Add:* 6191 Anchor Lane Rockledge FL 32955

SCARL, DONALD B, PHYSICS. *Current Pos:* from assoc prof to prof, 74-95, EMER PROF, POLYTECH UNIV, 95- *Personal Data:* b Easton, Pa, Sept 17, 35; m 79; c 1. *Educ:* Lehigh Univ, BA, 57; Princeton Univ, PhD(physics), 62. *Prof Exp:* Res assoc physics, NY Univ, 62-63; instr, Cornell Univ, 63-65, instr elec eng, 65-66; from asst prof to assoc prof physics, Polytech Inst Brooklyn, 66-74. *Concurrent Pos:* Consult, Hazeltine Corp, 82-84, Naval Res Lab, 84-89. *Mem:* Am Phys Soc; Optical Soc Am; AAAS. *Res:* Quantum optics, particularly photon correlations and temporal coherence, lasers. *Mailing Add:* 8 Woodland Rd Glen Cove NY 11542-1727. *E-Mail:* dscarl@pb.net

SCARLATOS, PANAGIOTIS DIMITRIOS, SEDIMENT TRANSPORT, STRATIFIED FLOW. *Current Pos:* ASSOC PROF, DEPT OCEAN ENG, FLA ATLANTIC UNIV, 89- *Personal Data:* b Thessaloniki, Greece, Feb 14, 48; US citizen; m 72, Evagelia Romanos; c 2. *Educ:* Aristotle Univ Thessaloniki, Greece, Dipl Eng, 72, DrEng, 81. *Prof Exp:* Second Lt, CEngr, Greek Army, 72-74; civil engr, Orgn Greek Rwy, 74-75; asst engr, Hydrol Struct Lab, Aristotle Univ, 75-81, lectr, 81-82; res assoc, Ctr Wetland Resources, La State Univ, 82-83, res assoc, La Water Resources Res Inst, 84-85; water res engr, SFla Water Mgt Dist, 85-86, staff water res engr, 86-89. *Concurrent Pos:* Consult, 72-83; NATO res scholar, Univ Fla, Gainesville, 78-80; adj asst prof, Dept Ocean Eng, Fla Atlantic Univ, 86-89, prin investr, 89-93; Fulbright res fel, Univ Thessaloniki, Greece, 92; chair, Tidal Hydraul Comt, Am Soc Civil Engrs, 93-94. *Mem:* Am Water Resources Asn; Am Geophys Union; Int Asn Hydrol Res; Am Soc Civil Engrs. *Res:* Dynamics of river and estuarine sediments; aquatic pollution; mathematical modeling; water resources. *Mailing Add:* 12890 Meadowbend Dr West Palm Beach FL 33414

SCARPA, ANTONIO, BIOENERGETICS, MEMBRANE TRANSPORT. *Current Pos:* PROF & CHMN DEPT PHYSIOL & BIOPHYS, SCH MED, CASE WESTERN RESERVE UNIV, 85- *Personal Data:* b Padua, Italy, July 3, 42; US citizen. *Educ:* Univ Padua, MD, 66, PhD(gen path), 70. *Hon Degrees:* MS, Univ Pa, 76. *Prof Exp:* Asst prof gen path, Univ Padua, 69-71; from asst prof to prof biochem & biophys, Sch Med, Univ Pa, 73-85, dir, Biomed Instrumentation Group, 82-85. *Concurrent Pos:* Nat Res Coun Italy exchange fel biochem, Univ Bristol, 68; Dutch Orgn Advan Pure Res fel biochem, Univ Utrecht, 70; NATO fel, Johnson Found, Univ Pa, 71; estab investr, Am Heart Asn, 73-78; prog chmn, US Bioenergetics Group, Biophys Soc, 74-75 & 84-85; assoc ed, Biophys J; adv bd, Biophys Soc Coun, 79-83; consult, Phys Biochem Study Sect, NIH, 83-87; nat res comt, Am Heart Asn; mem, Review Comt A, Nat Heart, Lung, Blood Inst, NIH, 90- *Mem:* Am Phys Soc; Biophys Soc; Am Soc Biol Chemists; Soc Gen Physiologists; Am Soc Physiologists. *Res:* Structure and function of biological membranes; ion transport; regulation of contraction of heart muscle; mechanisms secretion; structure and function of isolated sarcoplasmic reticulum with x-ray crystallography and neutron diffraction; intracellular Ca2; mechanism by which catecholamines are accumulated in chromaffin granules; secretion coupling in isolated bovine parathyroid cells. *Mailing Add:* Dept Physiol & Biophys Case Western Res Univ Sch Med 10090 Euclid Ave Cleveland OH 44106-4970. *Fax:* 216-368-5586

SCARPACE, PHILIP J, AGING, ADRENERIGIC PHARMACOLOGY. *Current Pos:* assoc prof, 87-93, PROF PHARMACOL, UNIV FLA, 94-; RES DIR, GERIAT RES EDUC & CLIN CTR, VET ADMIN MED CTR, GAINESVILLE, 87- *Personal Data:* b Buffalo, NY, Jan 4, 48; c 2. *Educ:* Calif State Univ, San Jose, BS, 70; Univ Rochester, PhD(biophys), 74. *Prof Exp:* Asst prof geriat & pharmacol, Univ Calif, Los Angeles, 77-87; lab chief, Geriat Res Ctr, Vet Admin Med Ctr, Sepalveda, Calif, 77-87. *Concurrent Pos:* Asst prof math, Calif State Univ, Northridge, 79-81; assoc dir, Ctr Res Oral Health & Aging, Univ Fla, 88-93. *Mem:* Am Soc Pharmacol & Exp Therapeut; AAAS; Geront Soc Am. *Res:* Loss of responsiveness to adrenerigic agents with age; defective receptor signal transduction in the membranes of heart cells. *Mailing Add:* Geriat Res Educ Clin Ctr VA Med Ctr Gainesville FL 32602. *Fax:* 352-374-6142

SCARPELLI, DANTE GIOVANNI, EXPERIMENTAL PATHOLOGY. *Current Pos:* chmn dept, 76-92, PROF PATH, NORTHWESTERN UNIV MED SCH, CHICAGO, 76- *Personal Data:* b Padua, Italy, Feb 5, 27; nat US; m 51, Harriett Shonwiler; c Michael, April & Harriett. *Educ:* Baldwin-Wallace Col, BS, 50; Ohio State Univ, MS, 53, MD, 54, PhD, 60. *Hon Degrees:* DSc, Baldwin-Wallace Col, 66. *Honors & Awards:* Silver Medal, Am Soc Clin Path, 56; K P DuBois Award, Soc Toxicol, 93. *Prof Exp:* From instr to prof path, Ohio State Univ, 58-66; dean fac & acad affairs, Univ Kans Med Ctr, Kansas City, 72-73; prof path & oncol & chmn dept, 66-76. *Mem:* AAAS; Am Asn Cancer Res; Am Soc Invest Path (pres, 72); Histochem Soc; US Can Acad Path; Am Soc Cell Biol. *Res:* Ultrastructural cytochemistry; carcinogenesis; comparative pathology; molecular events in pancreatic carcinogenesis; differentiation; comparative pathology. *Mailing Add:* Dept Path Northwestern Univ Med Sch Ward Bldg 303 E Chicago Ave Chicago IL 60611-3072

SCARPELLI, EMILE MICHAEL, PEDIATRICS, CARDIOPULMONARY PHYSIOLOGY. *Current Pos:* AT PULMONARY & CRITICAL CARE MED DIV, SCHNEIDER CHILDRENSS'S HOSP, LONG ISLAND JEWISH-HILLSIDE MED CTR. *Personal Data:* b New York, NY, July 24, 31; m 52; c 7. *Educ:* Fordham Univ, BS, 51; Duke Univ, MD, 60, PhD(physiol), 62. *Prof Exp:* Instr pediat & physiol, Albert Einstein Col Med, 62-64, res asst prof pediat, 64-66, assoc prof, 68-72, asst prof physiol, 64-71, assoc prof, 71-, prof pediat, 73-, dir pediat pulmonary div, 64- *Concurrent Pos:* Res grants, New York Heart Asn, 63-76, John Polachek Found Med Res, 65-66 & NIH career develop award, 66-76; mem, Int Med Comt, Lourdes; Nat Heart & Lung Inst, NIH Prog-Proj, 73-78 & training grant, 75-80. *Mem:* AAAS; Am Physiol Soc; Soc Pediat Res; NY

Acad Sci; Am Heart Asn. *Res:* Cardiovascular physiology and disease, including dynamics of cardiac arrhythmias and circulatory shunts; pulmonary physiology and disease, including airway dynamics and the physiology, chemistry and morphology of lung surfactant. *Mailing Add:* Perinatol Ctr Cornell Univ Med Ctr 133 Constitution Dr Orangeburg NY 10962

SCARPINO, PASQUALE VALENTINE, ENVIRONMENTAL ENGINEERING. *Current Pos:* from asst prof to assoc prof environ eng, 63-71, PROF ENVIRON ENG, UNIV CINCINNATI, 71-, PROF ENVIRON HEALTH, 86- *Personal Data:* b Utica, NY, Feb 13, 32; m 86; c 2. *Educ:* Syracuse Univ, BA, 55; Rutgers Univ, MS, 58; PhD(microbiol), 61. *Prof Exp:* USPHS res asst microbiol, Rutgers Univ, 58-61; asst prof biol sci, Fairleigh Dickinson Univ, 61-63. *Concurrent Pos:* Water pollution control admin, USPHS res award, 65-68; NASA Space Inst grant, Univ Cincinnati, 67-69; Fed Water Pollution Control Admin res contract, 69-71; US Environ Protection Agency grants, 72-82 & 84-86; chmn, Water Subcomt, Environ Task Force, City of Cincinnati, 72-73; Citizen-Scientist Comt Drinking Water Qual & Water Comt Environ Adv Coun, 75-76, chmn, Environ Adv Coun, 80-82, chmn, "Right to Know" Ordinance Tech Adv Comt, 83-88; Dept Defense res grant, 83-84; chmn, Pub Interest Adv Comt, Ohio River Valley Water Sanit Comn, 84-85, Ohio comnr, 85-, chmn, 89-90; res grant, Nat Inst Environ Health Sci, 88- *Mem:* Am Water Works Asn; Int Asn Water Pollution Res & Control; Am Soc Microbiol; Sigma Xi; fel Am Soc Microbiol. *Res:* Environmental microbiology; halogen inactivation of viruses in water and waste water; microbial food production; microbial survival in water, landfills and landfill leachates; dissemination of microbes in sewage treatment plant aerosols; risk assessment; biodegradation; bioaerosols; outdoor and indoor air pollution. *Mailing Add:* 3843 Middleton Ave Cincinnati OH 45220-1126

SCARR, HARRY ALAN, federal agency administration; deceased, see previous edition for last biography

SCARR, SANDRA WOOD, PSYCHOLOGY. *Current Pos:* Commonwealth prof, 83-96, chmn, Dept Psychol, 84-90, EMER PROF PSYCHOL, UNIV VA, CHARLOTTESVILLE, 96- *Personal Data:* b Washington, DC, Aug 8, 36; m 61, 82, James C Walker; c Phillip, Karen, Rebbecca & Stephanie. *Educ:* Vassar Col, AB, 58; Harvard Univ, AM, 63, PhD, 65. *Honors & Awards:* Distinguished Contrib to Res on Pub Policy, Am Psychol Asn, 88; James McKeen Cattell Award, Am Psychol Soc, 93. *Prof Exp:* Asst prof psychol, Univ Md, College Park, 64-67; assoc prof, Univ Pa, Philadelphia, 67-71; prof, Univ Minn, Minneapolis, 71-77, Yale Univ, 77-83. *Concurrent Pos:* Grant, NIH, NSF & others, 67-; fel, Ctr Advan Studies, Stanford Univ, 76-77; ed, J Develop Psychol, 80-86; chmn & chief exec officer, KinderCare Learning Ctrs, Inc, 95-97. *Mem:* Fel AAAS; fel Am Psychol Asn; fel Am Psychol Soc; Am Acad Arts & Sci; Behav Genetics Asn (pres, 85-86); Soc Res Child Develp (pres, 89-91); Int Soc Study Behav Develop. *Res:* Genetic variability in human behavior, particularly intelligence and personality; effects of variation in quality of home and child care environments on children's development. *Mailing Add:* 2636 Capstone Montgomery AL 36106. *E-Mail:* sandrascar@aol.com

SCARRATT, DAVID JOHNSON, MARINE BIOLOGY. *Current Pos:* AT DAVID SCARRATT & ASSOC, 92- *Personal Data:* b Liverpool, Eng, Dec 21, 35; m 62; c 2. *Educ:* Univ Wales, BSc, 58, PhD(marine zool), 61. *Prof Exp:* Scientist, Sci Br, Dept Fisheries & Oceans, Halifax Fisheries Lab, 61-92. *Mem:* Aquacult Asn Can; World Aquacult Soc. *Res:* The ecology and behavior of larval, juvenile and adult stages of North American lobster; effects of pollutants; industrial developments and fishing practices on commercial fisheries; marine resource inventories and atlases; vertebrate and molluscan aquaculture research; uptake and elimination marine toxins by molluscs. *Mailing Add:* PO Box 1564 Halifax NS B3J 2Y3 Can. *Fax:* 902-426-2760; *E-Mail:* scarratt@coton.com

SCATLIFF, JAMES HOWARD, RADIOLOGY. *Current Pos:* PROF RADIOL & CHMN DEPT, SCH MED, UNIV NC, CHAPEL HILL, 66- *Personal Data:* b Chicago, Ill, July 9, 27; m 61; c 2. *Educ:* Northwestern Univ, BS, 49, MD, 52. *Prof Exp:* Intern, Cook County Hosp, Chicago, 52-53; resident radiol, Michael Reese Hosp, Chicago, 53-56; from instr to assoc prof, Sch Med, Yale Univ, 57-66. *Concurrent Pos:* NIH fel neuroradiol, St George's Hosp, London, Eng, 62-63; consult radiologist, Watts Hosp, Durham, NC, 66- *Mem:* AMA; Asn Univ Radiol (pres, 71-72); fel Am Col Radiol; Radiol Soc NAm; Am Soc Neuroradiol; Sigma Xi. *Res:* Microvasculature, neuroradiology and cardiac radiology. *Mailing Add:* Dept Radiol Univ NC Sch Med Chapel Hill NC 27514

SCATTERDAY, JAMES WARE, GEOLOGY. *Current Pos:* from asst prof to prof geol, 63-91, chmn, Dept Geol Sci, 69-77, EMER PROF GEOL, COL ARTS & SCI, STATE UNIV NY, GENESEO, 91- *Personal Data:* b Westerville, Ohio, Dec 10, 35; m 59, Sandra Hawkey. *Educ:* Denison Univ, BS, 57; Ohio State Univ, PhD(geol), 63. *Mem:* Paleont Soc; Palaeont Asn; Sigma Xi; Paleont Res Inst. *Res:* Ecology and sediments of recent coral reefs; stratigraphic and conodont biostratigraphic study of the Mississippian System of Ohio; stratigraphic and paleontologic studies of the Silurian and Devonian Systems of New York. *Mailing Add:* RD 1 3527 Abel Hill Rd Mt Morris NY 14510

SCATTERGOOD, EDGAR MORRIS, CHEMICAL ENGINEERING, BIOCHEMICAL ENGINEERING. *Current Pos:* RES FEL, MERCK SHARP & DOHME RES LABS, 73- *Personal Data:* b Philadelphia, Pa, Mar 2, 36; m 65; c 2. *Educ:* Mass Inst Technol, BS, 58; Univ Wis-Madison, PhD(chem eng), 66. *Prof Exp:* Design engr, Standard Oil Co of Calif, 59-61; res asst transport properties ion-exchange membranes, Univ Wis, 62-66; res engr, Gen Mills, Inc, 66-69 & North Star Res & Develop Inst, 69-70; res fel, St Olaf Col, 70-72; chem engr, Calgon Havens Systs, 72-73. *Mem:* Am Chem Soc; Am Inst Chem Engrs. *Res:* Transport properties of ion-exchange membranes; food processing; membrane processes; artificial biological membranes; mass tissue culture, virology, bacterial fermentation and vaccines. *Mailing Add:* 1375 Steven Lane Lansdale PA 19446-4745

SCATTERGOOD, LESLIE WAYNE, FISH BIOLOGY. *Current Pos:* RETIRED. *Personal Data:* b Seattle, Wash, May 22, 14; m 40; c Charles E, Leslie Jr, Elizabeth P & Margaret K. *Educ:* Univ Wash, BS, 36. *Prof Exp:* Aquatic biologist, US Fish & Wildlife Serv, 39-49, fisheries res biologist, 49-58, dir, Fisheries Biol Lab, 58-61, chief, Br of Reports, 61-68, chief, Div Publ, 68-70; chief, Bd Br, Nat Oceanic & Atmospheric Admin, 70-71, chief, Sci & Tech Publ Div, 71-80; fishery consult, 80-81. *Concurrent Pos:* Sci asst, Int Pac Salmon Comn, Can, 38; biologist, Wash State Dept Fisheries, 39; local coordr, Off Coord Fisheries, Washington, DC, 43-45; fishery off, Panama, 52-53; Fulbright scholar, Fiskeridirektoratets, Bergen, Norway, 53-54; mem res comt, Int Passamaquoddy Fisheries Bd, 56-59. *Mem:* AAAS; Am Fisheries Soc; Inst Fishery Res Biol. *Res:* Life history of marine animals; science information. *Mailing Add:* 1951 Sagewood Lane Apt 425 Reston VA 20191

SCATTERGOOD, RONALD O, METALLURGY. *Current Pos:* PROF MAT ENG, NC STATE UNIV, 81- *Personal Data:* b Philadelphia, Pa, June 27, 37; m 66; c 1. *Educ:* Lehigh Univ, SB, 60; Mass Inst Technol, SM, 63, ScD(metall), 68. *Prof Exp:* Assoc metallurgist, Argonne Nat Lab, 68-81. *Mem:* Am Inst Mining, Metall & Petrol Engrs; Am Soc Metals. *Res:* Deformation of metals; dislocation theory; radiation effects. *Mailing Add:* Dept Mat Eng NC State Univ Box 7907 Raleigh NC 27695-7907

SCAVEN, GREGORY JOSEPH, AEROSPACE & DEFENSE ENGINEERING, AUTOMOTIVE SAFETY ENGINEERING. *Current Pos:* proj engr, 91-96, SR ENGR, TALLEY DEFENSE SYSTS, 96- *Personal Data:* b Philadelphia, Pa, Apr 9, 63; m 90, Lorraine Gilmore; c Victoria & Joseph. *Educ:* Lehigh Univ, BS, 85; Univ Pa, MS, 87. *Prof Exp:* Proj mgr, US Army, 89-91. *Mem:* Am Inst Chem Engrs; Am Chem Soc; Soc Automotive Engrs; Int Pyrotech Soc. *Res:* Design, development and demonstration of solid propellant based systems used in defense and automotive applications. *Mailing Add:* PO Box 849 Mesa AZ 85211. *Fax:* 602-898-2347; *E-Mail:* gscaven@talleyds.com

SCAVIA, DONALD, LIMNOLOGY, MODELING. *Current Pos:* RETIRED. *Personal Data:* b Schenectady, NY. *Educ:* Rensselaer Polytech Inst, BS, 73, MS, 74; Univ Mich, PhD, 80. *Prof Exp:* Res assoc aquatic modeling, Freshwater Inst, Rensselaer Polytech Inst, 74-75; res scientist nutrients & ecosyst dynamics, Great Lakes Environ Res Lab, Nat Oceanic & Atmospheric Admin, 75-84. *Concurrent Pos:* Adj asst prof, Div Biol Sci, Univ Mich, 81- *Mem:* Am Soc Limnol & Oceanog; Int Asn Great Lakes Res; AAAS; Int Soc Ecol Modelling; Soc Int Limnol. *Res:* Investigation of biological, chemical and physical controls of nutrient cycles and carbon flow in the aquatic environment with particular emphasis on the use of models in the analysis; experimental analysis of ecological aspects of phytoplankton and zooplankton interactions in the control of primary production and nutrient cycling. *Mailing Add:* 2573 Braeburn Ann Arbor MI 48108

SCAVUZZO, RUDOLPH J, JR, MECHANICAL ENGINEERING. *Current Pos:* prof mech eng & head dept, 73-83, PROF MECH ENG, UNIV AKRON, 83- *Personal Data:* b Plainfield, NJ, Jan 21, 34; m 55; c 10. *Educ:* Lehigh Univ, BSME, 55; Univ Pittsburgh, MSME, 59, PhD(mech eng), 62. *Prof Exp:* Sr engr, Bettis Atomic Power Lab, Westinghouse Elec Corp, 55-64; from asst prof to assoc prof mech eng, Univ Toledo, 64-70; assoc prof mech eng, Hartford Grad Ctr, Rensselaer Polytech Inst Conn, Inc, 70-73. *Concurrent Pos:* Adj instr, Univ Pittsburgh, 63-64. *Mem:* Am Soc Mech Engrs; Am Soc Eng Educ; Am Indust Arts Asn; Soc Mech. *Res:* Solid mechanics; mechanical vibrations; dynamic shock analysis. *Mailing Add:* 4366 Shaw Rd Akron OH 44333

SCHAAD, LAWRENCE JOSEPH, PHYSICAL CHEMISTRY. *Current Pos:* from asst prof to assoc prof, 61-72, PROF CHEM, VANDERBILT UNIV, 72- *Personal Data:* b Columbus, Ohio, Sept 23, 30; m 54. *Educ:* Harvard Univ, AB, 52; Mass Inst Technol, PhD, 57. *Prof Exp:* Res assoc & NIH fel, Math Inst, Oxford Univ, 56-58; res assoc chem, Univ Ind, 59-61. *Mem:* Am Chem Soc; Am Phys Soc. *Res:* Quantum chemistry. *Mailing Add:* Dept Chem Vanderbilt Univ Box 1822 Sta B Nashville TN 37235

SCHAAD, NORMAN W, BACTERIOLOGY, ECOLOGY. *Current Pos:* RES LEADER, USDA/AGR RES SERV, FOREIGN DIS WEED SCI, 92- *Personal Data:* b Myrtle Point, Ore, Nov 9, 40; m, Yvette Berthier; c Sandra R & Kristina D. *Educ:* Univ Calif, Davis, BS, 64, MS, 66, PhD(plant path), 69. *Prof Exp:* Fel plant path, Univ Calif, Davis, 69-71; from asst prof to prof phytobacteria, taxon ecol & serol, Univ Ga, 71-82; prof dept plant sci, Univ Idaho, 82-88; dir biotechnol, Harris Moran Seed Co, 88-92. *Concurrent Pos:* NSF vis prof, Univ Brasilia, 77; mem outstanding grant activ, Univ Ga, 79-80; adj prof, Hassen II, Morocco, 85-92. *Mem:* Am Soc Microbiol; Am Phytopath Soc; Int Seed Testing Asn; Int Soc Plant Path. *Res:* Serology of phytobacteria; ecology of phytobacteria; seed pathology; molecular detection and identification of phytobacteria. *Mailing Add:* USDA/ARS Foreign Dis Weed Sci Bldg 1301 Frederick MD 21702. *Fax:* 301-619-2880; *E-Mail:* schaad@ncifcrf.gov

SCHAAF, NORMAN GEORGE, MAXILLOFACIAL PROSTHETICS, PROSTHODONTICS. *Current Pos:* Resident, Sch Dent, State Univ NY, Buffalo, 63-64, instr prosthodontics, 64-65, from asst prof to assoc prof, 65-74, PROF MAXILLOFACIAL PROSTHETICS, STATE UNIV NY, BUFFALO, 74-, DIR, REGIONAL CTR MAXILLOFACIAL PROSTHETICS, 67-; CHIEF, DENT SERV, ROSWELL PARK MEM INST, 68- *Personal Data:* b Buffalo, NY, May 29, 36; m 59; c 3. *Educ:* Univ Buffalo, DDS, 60; Am Bd Prosthodontics, dipl, 71. *Concurrent Pos:* Prosthodontic consult, J Sutton Regan Cleft Palate Found, Children's Hosp, Buffalo, 63-; consult hosp, 65-; consult, Eastman Dent Ctr; univ assoc, Buffalo Gen Hosp, 73-; maxillofacial prosthodontic consult, Buffalo Vet Hosp, 74- *Mem:* Am Cleft Palate Asn; Am Acad Maxillofacial Prosthetics; Soc Head & Neck Surgeons; Am Dent Assoc. *Res:* Anatomic, functional and cosmetic reconstruction, by the use of non-living substitutes, of those regions of the head and neck that are missing or defective whether from congenital anomaly, injury or disease. *Mailing Add:* Dept Dent Maxillofacial Prosthetics Roswell Park Cancer Inst Elm & Carlton St Buffalo NY 14263

SCHAAF, ROBERT LESTER, ORGANIC CHEMISTRY. *Current Pos:* From res chemist to sr res chemist, 55-67, res assoc, 67-77, sr res staff mem, 77-82, QUAL ASSURANCE ENGR, BASF CORP, 82- *Personal Data:* b Baptistown, NJ, June 17, 29. *Educ:* Rutgers Univ, BS, 50; Univ Mich, MS, 52, PhD(pharmaceut chem), 55. *Mem:* Am Chem Soc. *Mailing Add:* 1455 Oak St Wyandotte MI 48192

SCHAAF, THOMAS KEN, MEDICINAL CHEMISTRY. *Current Pos:* res chemist, Pfizer Inc, 70-74, proj leader, 74-76, mgr, 76-81, asst dir med sci chem, 81- 83, dir Animal Health Med Chem, 84-89, DIR, US ANIMAL DISCOVERY RES, PFIZER INC, 90- *Personal Data:* b Louisville, Ky, July 17, 43; m 84; c 3. *Educ:* Kalamazoo Col, BA, 65; Stanford Univ, PhD(chem), 69. *Prof Exp:* Res fel, Harvard Univ, 69-70. *Mem:* Am Chem Soc. *Res:* Antibacterial, antiparasitic and immune modulating agents. *Mailing Add:* Pfizer Cent Res Eastern Point Rd Groton CT 06340-5196

SCHAAF, WILLIAM EDWARD, FISHERIES RESOURCE MODELING. *Current Pos:* RETIRED. *Personal Data:* b Martins Ferry, Ohio, Aug 9, 38; m 61; c 3. *Educ:* Duke Univ, BS, 61; Univ NC, MS, 63; Univ Mich, PhD(fisheries), 72. *Prof Exp:* Biostatistician, NIH, 63-66; biometrician, Inst Fisheries Res, Mich Dept Natural Resources, 66-69; biometrician, Nat Marine Fisheries Serv, Dept Com, 69-88. *Mem:* Am Statist Asn; Am Fisheries Soc. *Res:* Modeling the population dynamics of exploited marine fishes, emphasizing optimal management strategies; developing ecosystem models of multi-species fisheries; investigation impacts of environmental variability, and life history strategies on expected yields. *Mailing Add:* 251 Schaaf Lane Gloucester NC 28528

SCHAAL, BARBARA ANNA, POPULATION BIOLOGY, MOLECULAR EVOLUTION. *Current Pos:* PROF BIOL, WASHINGTON UNIV, ST LOUIS, 80-, CHMN DEPT, 93- *Personal Data:* b Berlin, Ger, Sept 17, 47; US citizen; m 76, Wesley J Leverich; c Leah S & Joseph P. *Educ:* Univ Ill, Chicago, BS, 69; Yale Univ, MPhil, 71, PhD(pop biol), 74. *Prof Exp:* Asst prof, Univ Houston, 74-76; asst prof bot, Ohio State Univ, 76-80. *Concurrent Pos:* Res assoc, Mo Bot Garden. *Mem:* Fel AAAS; Genetics Soc Am; Soc Study Educ; Brit Ecol Soc; Ecol Soc; Bot Soc Am. *Res:* Genetic structure of outbreeding plant population; plant demographic genetics; molecular evolution. *Mailing Add:* Dept Biol Washington Univ St Louis MO 63130. *Fax:* 314-935-4432; *E-Mail:* schaal@biodec.wustl.edu

SCHAAP, A PAUL, ORGANIC CHEMISTRY. *Current Pos:* Asst prof, 70-74, assoc prof, 74-79, PROF CHEM, WAYNE STATE UNIV, 79- *Personal Data:* b Scottsburg, Ind, June 4, 45. *Educ:* Hope Col, AB, 67; Harvard Univ, PhD(org chem), 70. *Concurrent Pos:* Alfred P Sloan Res Fel, 74-76. *Mem:* Am Chem Soc; Royal Soc Chem; Sigma Xi. *Res:* Photo-oxidation; chemistry of singlet oxygen; chemiluminescence; 1,2-dioxetanes. *Mailing Add:* Lumigen Inc 24485 W 10 Mile Rd Southfield MI 48034-2931

SCHAAP, LUKE ANTHONY, ORGANIC CHEMISTRY. *Current Pos:* RETIRED. *Personal Data:* b South Holland, Ill, Nov 11, 31; m 59, Pauline Klompien; c 4. *Educ:* Calvin Col, AB, 53; Northwestern Univ, PhD(org chem), 57. *Prof Exp:* Instr, Northwestern Univ, 53-54; res chemist, Am Oil Co, Whiting, Ind, 57-74, Res Ctr, Amoco Oil Co, 74-92. *Concurrent Pos:* Instr, Trinity Christian Col, 64-65. *Mem:* Am Chem Soc; Am Soc Testing & Mat; Soc Tribologists & Lubrication Engrs; Soc Automotive Engrs. *Res:* Base catalyzed reactions of hydrocarbons; high pressure and petroleum chemistry; olefin hydration; chemistry of nitrogen fluorides; lubricant research and development; fuels research and development. *Mailing Add:* 463 E 163rd St South Holland IL 60473

SCHAAP, WARD BEECHER, INORGANIC CHEMISTRY, ANALYTICAL CHEMISTRY. *Current Pos:* from instr to assoc prof chem, Ind Univ, Bloomington, 50-63, assoc dean, Col Arts & Sci, 66-71, assoc dean, Res & Develop, 71-73, actg vchancellor admin & budgetary planning, 73-76, prof chem, 63-88, dean admin & budgetary planning, 76-88, EMER PROF CHEM, IND UNIV, BLOOMINGTON, 88- *Personal Data:* b Holland, Mich, Sept 15, 23; m 44; c 3. *Educ:* Wheaton Col, Ill, BS, 44; Univ Ill, MS, 48, PhD(inorg chem), 50. *Prof Exp:* Anal chemist, Metall Lab, Univ Chicago, 44; res chemist, Manhattan Proj, Oak Ridge Nat Lab, 44-47. *Concurrent Pos:* Consult, Union Carbide Nuclear Corp, 56- & E I du Pont de Nemours & Co, 58-60; NSF fel, Univ Calif, 60-61. *Mem:* Am Chem Soc. *Res:* Metal chelate compounds; polarography; electrochemistry in nonaqueous solvents; kinetics of inorganic reactions. *Mailing Add:* 819 S Jordan Ave Bloomington IN 47401

SCHABER, GERALD GENE, GEOLOGY, ASTROGEOLOGY & RADAR GEOLOGY. *Current Pos:* Geologist, 65-95, EMER GEOLOGIST LUNAR & PLANETARY EXPLOR RES, FLAGSTAFF FIELD CTR, US GEOL SURV, 95- *Personal Data:* b Covington, Ky, May 29, 38; m 61; c 3. *Educ:* Univ Ky, BS; Univ Cincinnati, MS, 62, PhD(geol), 65. *Honors & Awards:* Spec Commendation for Apollo Astronaut Training, Geol Soc Am, 73; Group Achievement Award for Apollo Traverse Planning, NASA, 71; Group Achievement Award, NASA, 82; Autometric Award, Am Soc Photogrammetry, 82; Meritorious Serv Award, US Dept Interior, 88. *Concurrent Pos:* Private consult, radar remote sensing & radar geol interpretation. *Mem:* Geol Soc Am; Am Geophys Union. *Res:* Lunar and planetary geologic mapping; terrestrial and planetary remote sensing; terrestrial and planetary radar-geology. *Mailing Add:* Flagstaff Field Ctr US Geol Surv 2255 N Gemini Drive Ave Flagstaff AZ 86001

SCHABRON, JOHN F, ENVIRONMENTAL ANALYSIS, MONITORING & FIELD SCREENING, PETROLEUM RESIDUA CHARACTERIZATION. *Current Pos:* sr res chemist, 84, DIV MGR, WESTERN RES INST, 85- *Personal Data:* b Carson City, Nev, Nov 2, 50. *Educ:* Regis Univ, BS, 72; Creighton Univ, MS, 75; Univ Wyo, PhD(anal chem), 78. *Prof Exp:* Res chemist, Phillips Petrol Res Ctr, 79-84. *Mem:* Am Chem Soc; Air & Waste Mgt Asn; Anal Lab Mgrs Asn. *Res:* Developing new analytical methods and devices for field screening and downhole monitoring for environmental analysis; developed separation and analytical schemes for fossil fuel and petroleum residue evaluation; developed methods for extraction and determination of polymer additives. *Mailing Add:* 1805 Arnold St Laramie WY 82070

SCHACH, STEPHEN RONALD, SOFTWARE ENGINEERING. *Current Pos:* ASSOC PROF COMPUT SCI, VANDERBILT UNIV, 83- *Personal Data:* b Cape Town, S Africa, Dec 3, 47; US citizen; m 74, Sharon M Stein; c David & Lauren. *Educ:* Univ Cape Town, BSc, 66, MSc, 69, PhD(appl math), 73; Weizmann Inst Sci, MSc, 72. *Prof Exp:* Lectr appl math, Univ Cape Town, 72-75, from lectr to assoc prof comput sci, 76-83. *Concurrent Pos:* Vis scientist, Weizmann Inst Sci, Israel, 78-79. *Mem:* Asn Comput Mach; Inst Elec & Electronics Engrs Computer Soc. *Res:* Software engineering; software maintenance; software reuse; software testing; software process. *Mailing Add:* Dept Comput Sci Vanderbilt Univ Box 70 Sta B Nashville TN 37235

SCHACHER, GORDON EVERETT, ATMOSPHERIC SCIENCES, SOLID STATE PHYSICS. *Current Pos:* from asst prof to assoc prof, Naval Postgrad Sch, 64-80, chmn, Physics Dept, 81-85, dean sci & eng, 86-88, dean fac, 88-94, PROF PHYSICS, NAVAL POSTGRAD SCH, 80- *Personal Data:* b Portland, Ore, Aug 24, 35; m 79; c 6. *Educ:* Reed Col, AB, 56; Rutgers Univ, PhD(physics), 61. *Prof Exp:* Instr physics, Rutgers Univ, 60-61; fel, Argonne Nat Lab, Ill, 61-64. *Mem:* Am Phys Soc; Am Asn Physics Teachers; Sigma Xi; Soc Photo-optical Instrumentation Engrs; Am Meteor Soc. *Res:* Marine atmospheric boundary layer processes; electromagnetic propagation in the atmosphere; transport and dispension; chemical and biological defense. *Mailing Add:* Dept Physics Naval Postgrad Sch Monterey CA 93943

SCHACHER, JOHN FREDRICK, PARASITOLOGY, INFECTIOUS DISEASES. *Current Pos:* PROF EMERITUS, UNIV CALIF, LOS ANGELES. *Personal Data:* b Jamestown, NDak, July 17, 28; m 52; c 3. *Educ:* NDak State Univ, BS, 53; Tulane Univ, MS, 56, PhD(parasitol), 61. *Prof Exp:* Tulane Univ prof asst parasitol, Univ Malaya, Singapore, 56-58; from asst prof to assoc prof trop dis, Am Univ Beirut, 60-69; assoc prof, Univ Calif, Los Angeles, 69-72, prof infectious trop dis & epidemiol, 72-, asst dean Acad Affairs, 80- *Concurrent Pos:* NIH res grant, Am Univ Beirut & Univ Calif, Los Angeles, 63-76; Interam fel trop med, La State Univ, 66; consult, La Fisheries & Wildlife Comn, 54-55; mem expert comt filariasis, WHO, 73-, mem sci tech comt onchocerciasis control, 74- *Mem:* Int Filariasis Asn; Am Soc Parasitol; Am Soc Trop Med & Hyg; Royal Soc Trop Med & Hyg; Malaysian Soc Parasitol Trop Med. *Res:* Parasitology, especially helminthology, filariasis; host-parasite relations and pathology, taxonomy and identification of parasites in tissue. *Mailing Add:* 3120 Castle Heights Ave Los Angeles CA 90034

SCHACHMAN, HOWARD KAPNEK, MOLECULAR BIOLOGY, BIOCHEMISTRY. *Current Pos:* from instr to assoc prof biochem, Univ Calif, Berkeley, 48-59, prof biochem & molecular biol, 59-91, chmn, Dept Molecular Biol & dir, Virus Lab, 69-76, emer prof, Dept Molecular & Cell Biol, 91-94, PROF, GRAD SCH, UNIV CALIF, BERKELEY, 94- *Personal Data:* b Philadelphia, Pa, Dec 5, 18; m 45; c 2. *Educ:* Mass Inst Technol, BS, 39; Princeton Univ, PhD(phys chem). *Hon Degrees:* DSc, Northwestern Univ, 74; DMed, Univ Naples, 90. *Honors & Awards:* E H Sargent & Co Award, Am Chem Soc, 62; Warren Prize, Mass Gen Hosp, 65; Carter-Wallace Lectr, Princeton Univ, 76; Gardiner Mem Lectr, NMed State Univ, 76; Jesse W Beams Mem Lectr, Univ Va, Charlottesville, 78; Merck Award, Am Soc Biol Chemists, 86; Bernard Axelrod Lectr, Purdue Univ, Lafayette, 86; Behring Diag Lectr, Univ Calif, San Diego, 87; Alta Heritage Found Lectr, Univ Alta, 87; William Lloyd Evans Award lectr, Ohio State Univ, 88; Alexander von Humboldt Award, 90; Carland Gerty Cori Lectr, Wash Univ Sch Med, 93; Herbert A Sober Award Lectr, Am Soc Biochem & Molecular Biol, 94; Pub Serv Award, Fedn Am Soc Exp Biol, 94. *Prof Exp:* Chem engr, Continental Distilling Corp, Pa, 39-40; res asst, 42; tech asst, Rockefeller Inst, 41-44. *Concurrent Pos:* Guggenheim fel, 57-58; Fogarty Int Sch, NIH, 77-78; mem, Bd Sci Counrs, Nat Inst Arthritis, Diabetes & Digestive & Kidney Dis, NIH, 83-87, Bd Sci Consults, Mem Sloan-Kettering Cancer Ctr, 88-; Sci Coun & Sci Adv Bd, Stazione Zoologica, Naples, Italy, 88-; chair, Pub Affairs Comt, Am Soc Biochem & Molecular Biol, 89- & Biochem Sect, Nat Acad Sci, 90-93; mem, Panel Sci Responsibility & Conduct Res, Nat Acad Sci, 90-92; fac res lectr, Univ Calif, 94. *Mem:* Nat Acad Sci; Sigma Xi; Am Chem Soc;

Am Soc Biochem & Molecular Biol (pres, 87-88); Am Acad Arts & Sci; Fed Am Soc Exp Biol (pres, 88-89). *Res:* Physical chemistry of macromolecules of biological interest; structure, function and interactions of proteins, nucleic acids and viruses; development and application of the ultracentrifuge. *Mailing Add:* Dept Molecular & Cell Biol Univ Calif MCB Stanley Hall ASU 229 Stanley Hall No 3206 Berkeley CA 94720-3206

SCHACHT, JOCHEN (HEINRICH), NEUROCHEMISTRY. *Current Pos:* Asst res biochemist, 69-72, from asst prof to assoc prof, 73-84, PROF BIOL CHEM OTORHINOL, KRESGE HEARING RES INST, UNIV MICH, 84-, ASSOC DIR, 89- *Personal Data:* b Konigsberg, Ger, July 2, 39; m 67; c 2. *Educ:* Univ Bonn, BS, 62; Univ Heidelberg, MS, 65, PhD(biochem), 68. *Honors & Awards:* Animal Welfare Award, Erna-Graff-Found, Berlin, Ger, 87. *Concurrent Pos:* Fogarty Int fel, 79-80; vis prof, Dept Otolaryngol, Karolinska Inst, Stockholm, Sweden, 79-80; Sen Jacob Javits Neurosci Investr Award, 84-91; chercheur entranger, INSERM, France, 86-87; mem, Hearing Res Study Sect, NIH/NINCDS, 86-89. *Mem:* Ger Soc Biol Chem; Am Soc Biol Chemists; Soc Neurosci; Asn Res Otolaryngol; Int Soc Neurochem. *Res:* Biochemistry of hearing and deafness; metabolism and function of phosphoinositides. *Mailing Add:* Kresge Hearing Res Inst Univ Mich Ann Arbor MI 48109-0506. *Fax:* 313-764-0014; *E-Mail:* jochenschach@medumichedu

SCHACHT, LEE EASTMAN, HUMAN GENETICS. *Current Pos:* RETIRED. *Personal Data:* b Detroit, Mich, Sept 13, 30. *Educ:* Dartmouth Col, AB, 52; Univ NC, MA, 55, PhD(zool), 57. *Prof Exp:* Instr human genetics, Univ Mich, 57-60; supvr, Human Genetics Unit, State Dept Health, Minn, 60-91. *Concurrent Pos:* Lectr, Sch Pub Health, Univ Minn, 64-74, adj asst prof to adj assoc prof, 74-92, emer prof, 93- *Mem:* Am Soc Human Genetics. *Res:* Genetics in public health; genetic counseling. *Mailing Add:* 100 SE Second St No 802 Minneapolis MN 55414

SCHACHTELE, CHARLES FRANCIS, DENTAL RESEARCH, MICROBIOLOGY. *Current Pos:* Asst prof, Sch Dent, Univ Minn, Minneapolis, 68-72, assoc prof, 72-78, assoc prof microbiol, 74-78, PROF DENT, SCH DENT, UNIV MINN, MINNEAPOLIS, 78-, PROF MICROBIOL, 78- *Personal Data:* b Kearny, NJ, May 3, 42. *Educ:* Macalester Col, BA, 63; Univ Minn, Minneapolis, MS, 65, PhD(microbiol), 68. *Concurrent Pos:* USPHS res career develop award, 71. *Mem:* AAAS; Am Soc Microbiol; Int Asn Dent Res. *Res:* Dental caries and periodontal disease. *Mailing Add:* Dent Res Inst 18-104 Moos Tower Univ Minn Minneapolis MN 55455

SCHACHTER, DAVID, MEDICINE. *Current Pos:* From asst prof to assoc prof med, 57-69, PROF PHYSIOL, COL PHYSICIANS & SURGEONS, COLUMBIA UNIV, 69- *Personal Data:* b New York, NY, Oct 29, 27; m 56. *Educ:* NY Univ, BS, 46, MD, 49; Am Bd Internal Med, dipl, 55. *Mem:* AAAS; Soc Exp Biol & Med; Am Soc Clin Invest; Am Gastroenterol Asn; Am Physiol Soc. *Res:* Calcium transport and metabolism; membrane function and organization; active transport mechanisms. *Mailing Add:* Dept Physiol Col Physicians & Surgeons 11-427 Columbia Univ 630 W 168th St New York NY 10032-3702

SCHACHTER, E NEIL, INTERNAL MEDICINE, PULMONARY MEDICINE. *Current Pos:* PROF MED, MT SINAI SCH MED, 84-, MED DIR RESPIRATORY CARE, 84- *Personal Data:* b New York, NY, May 10, 43; m 69, Deborah; c Lauren & Karen. *Educ:* Columbia Col, AB, 64; NY Univ, MD, 68. *Prof Exp:* From asst prof to assoc prof Med, Yale Sch Med, 74-84. *Concurrent Pos:* E L Trudeau fel, Am Thoracic Soc, 75; Maurice Hexter chair pulmonary med, Mt Sinai Sch Med, 87, assoc dir, Pulmonary Div, 90- *Mem:* Am Physiol Soc; Am Fedn Clin Res; Am Thoracic Soc; fel Am Col Physicians; Nat Asn Med Dirs (pres-elect, 89-91); fel Am Col Chest Physicians. *Res:* Occupational and environmental lung disease using clinical studies as well as in vitro pharmacologic studies; pulmonary medicine; epidemiology. *Mailing Add:* Mt Sinai Med Ctr 1 Gustave L Levy Pl New York NY 10029. *Fax:* 212-831-3560

SCHACHTER, H, BIOCHEMISTRY, GLYCOPROTEINS & GLYCOSYL TRANSFERASES. *Current Pos:* From asst prof to assoc prof, 64-70, PROF BIOCHEM, UNIV TORONTO, 70- *Personal Data:* b Vienna, Austria, Feb 25, 33; Can citizen; m 58, Judith Jakubovic; c Aviva & Asher. *Educ:* Univ Toronto, BA, 55, MD, 59, PhD(biochem), 64. *Honors & Awards:* Boehringer-Mannheim Can Prize, Can Biochem Soc, 85. *Concurrent Pos:* Cystic Fibrosis Res Found fel, 66-68; head, Res Div, Dept Biochem, Hosp Sick Children. *Mem:* Am Soc Biol Chem; Can Biochem Soc; UK Biochem Soc; Gylocobiol Soc. *Res:* Glycoprotein biosynthesis and metabolism; differentiation. *Mailing Add:* 555 University Ave Toronto ON M5G 1X8 Can. *Fax:* 416-813-5022; *E-Mail:* harry@sickkids.on.ca

SCHACHTER, JOSEPH, PSYCHIATRY, PSYCHOANALYSIS. *Current Pos:* RETIRED. *Personal Data:* b New York, NY, Aug 26, 25; m 49, Judith Spector; c Rachel, Beth & Daniel. *Educ:* Dartmouth Col, AB, 46; Harvard Univ, PhD, 55; NY Univ, MD, 52. *Prof Exp:* Res assoc psychiat, Col Physicians & Surgeons, Columbia Univ, 56-60, asst clin prof, Univ & Columbia Psychoanal Clin Training & Res, 60-68, dir postdoctoral res training prog, 65-68; dir res child psychiat, Sch Med, Univ Pittsburgh, 68-74, assoc prof, 68-76, res assoc prof psychiat, 76-86, assoc prof epidemiol, Grad Sch Pub Health, 79-86. *Concurrent Pos:* Found Fund Res Psychiat fel, Columbia Univ & NY State Psychiat Inst, 55-56; pres, Pittsburgh Psychoanal Ctr, 78-80, Pittsburg Psychoanal Soc, 87-89. *Mem:* Am Psychosom Soc; Am Psychiat Asn; Am Col Psychoanalysts. *Res:* Psychoanalystic theory of technique. *Mailing Add:* Schachter & Schahter Psychiat Assocs Inc 401 Shady Ave Pittsburgh PA 15217-4409. *Fax:* 412-661-7006

SCHACHTER, JULIUS, PUBLIC HEALTH & EPIDEMIOLOGY, LABORATORY DIAGNOSIS. *Current Pos:* Grad res microbiol, Univ Calif, San Francisco, 60-65, asst res microbiologist, 65-68, from asst prof to assoc prof epidemiol & med, 68-75, asst dir, G W Hooper Found, 72-76, actg dir, 77-81, PROF EPIDEMIOL, UNIV CALIF, SAN FRANCISCO, 75-, PROF LAB MED, 80- *Personal Data:* b New York, NY, June 1, 36; wid; c Marc & Sara. *Educ:* Columbia Col, BA, 57; Hunter Col, MA, 60; Univ Calif, PhD(bact), 65. *Honors & Awards:* Karl F Meyer Gold Headed Cane Award, Am Vet Epidemiol Soc, 84; Thomas Parran Award, Am Venereal Dis Asn, 91. *Concurrent Pos:* Mem viral & rickettsial registry comt, Am Type Cult Collection; co-dir, Collab Centre Reference & Res on Trachoma & Other Chlamydial Infections, WHO, 72-77, dir, 77-; mem, expert panel trachoma, WHO, 72-, expert panel venereal dis, 80-; bd govs, Am Acad Microbiol, 86-; ed, Sexually Transmitted Dis, 89- *Mem:* Infectious Dis Soc Am; Am Soc Microbiol; Soc Exp Biol & Med; Am Venereal Dis Asn; Am Acad Microbiol; Am Epidemiol Soc. *Res:* Chlamydial infections, including psittacosis, trachoma, inclusion conjunctivitis, lymphogranuloma venereum, venereal diseases and perinatal infection; microbiology; epidemiology; host-parasite relationships. *Mailing Add:* Lab Med Univ Calif San Francisco Med Sch 513 Parnassus Ave San Francisco CA 94122-2722. *Fax:* 415-821-8945

SCHACHTER, MICHAEL B, MEDICAL NUTRITION, CHELATION THERAPY. *Current Pos:* FOUNDER, OWNER & DIR, SCHACHTER CTR COMPLEMENTARY MED, 96- *Personal Data:* b Brooklyn, NY, Jan 15, 41; m 67, 82, 94, Lisa Lackhai; c Brian J, Amy, Stefan J, Adam E, Jason N & Seth A. *Educ:* Columbia Col, BA, 61, MD, 65. *Honors & Awards:* Carlos Lamar Pioneer Mem Award, Am Acad Med Preventics, 79. *Prof Exp:* Intern, Hosp Joint Dis & Med Ctr, 65-66; psychiatric resident, Downstate Med Ctr, King County Hosp, 66-69; co-dir, Psychiat Outpatient Dept, Keesler AFB, Biloxi, Miss, 69-71; dir, Psychiat Emergency & Admis Dept, Rockland County Community Health Ctr, 71-72, psychiat outpatient clin, 72-74; founder, owner & dir, Mountainview Med Assocs, 74-90 & Michael B Schachter MD, PC, 90-96. *Concurrent Pos:* Bd dirs, Am Bd Chelation Ther, 83-88; vpres, Found Advan Innovative Med, 86-93, pres, 93- *Mem:* Am Col Adv Med (vpres, 85-87, pres elec, 87-89, pres, 89-91); Am Bd Chelation Therapy; Acad Orthomolecular Psychiat (vpres, 81-83); Am Psychiat Asn; Am Col Nutrit; Am Acad Environ Med. *Res:* Degenerative diseases are largely caused by environmental factors. Prevention & treatment should focus on eliminating toxic factors and instituting positive life style changes, including improved diet, nutritional supplements, exercise and stress management. *Mailing Add:* 2 Executive Blvd Suite 202 Suffern NY 10901-4164. *Fax:* 914-368-4727; *E-Mail:* mbschachter@mbschachter.com

SCHACHTER, ROZALIE, DEVICE PHYSICS & ENGINEERING, PRODUCT APPLICATIONS & MARKETING. *Current Pos:* DIR BUS DEVELOP, GEN MICROWAVE, 90- *Personal Data:* b Rumania, Oct 14, 46; US citizen; m 67; c 2. *Educ:* Brooklyn Col, BS, 68; Yeshiva Univ, MS, 70; New York Univ, PhD(physics), 79. *Prof Exp:* APS fel, Stauffer Chem Co, 79-80, group leader, 80-86; tech dir, Am Cyanamid, 86-90. *Mem:* Am Phys Soc; Inst Elec & Electronics Engrs. *Res:* Compound semiconductor (III-V) optoelectronic devices (lasers, detectors) for communication and instrumentation; research on MOCVD epitaxial growth, electro-optical characterization and device fabrication and test; application of safe chemical sources to semiconductor processes; application of microwave radar sensors. *Mailing Add:* Gen Microwave Corp 5500 New Horizons Blvd Amityville NY 11701

SCHACH VON WITTENAU, MANFRED, ORGANIC CHEMISTRY, DRUG METABOLISM. *Current Pos:* res chemist, 58-64, group supvr drug metab, 64-67, mgr drug metab, 67-71, from asst dir to dir, Dept Drug Metab, 71-74, exec dir, Safety Eval & Drug Metab, 74-81, VPRES SAFETY EVAL, PFIZER, INC, 81- *Personal Data:* b Pennekow, Ger, June 19, 30; m 55; c 3. *Educ:* Univ Heidelberg, BS, 52, MS, 55, PhD(org chem), 57. *Prof Exp:* Fel, Mass Inst Technol, 57-58. *Mem:* Am Chem Soc; Soc Ger Chem; Am Soc Pharmacol & Exp Therapeut; Soc Toxicol. *Res:* Medicinal chemistry; analytical chemistry; toxicology. *Mailing Add:* 59 Button Rd Cent Res Eastern Point Rd North Stonington CT 06359

SCHACK, CARL J, INORGANIC CHEMISTRY. *Current Pos:* Sr res engr, 64-68, MEM TECH STAFF, ROCKETDYNE DIV, ROCKWELL INT, 68- *Personal Data:* b St Louis, Mo, Dec 26, 36; m 59; c 2. *Educ:* St Louis Univ, BSChem, 58; Polytech Inst Brooklyn, PhD(inorg chem), 64. *Mem:* Am Chem Soc; Royal Soc Chem. *Res:* Fluorine chemistry; synthesis and material characterization of inorganic oxidizers, fluorine compounds including fluorocarbons and boron-nitrogen species. *Mailing Add:* 20744 Tribune St Chatsworth CA 91311-1528

SCHACTER, BERNICE ZELDIN, IMMUNOGENETICS, BIOCHEMISTRY. *Current Pos:* CONSULT, 93- *Personal Data:* b Philadelphia, Pa, June 20, 43; m 68; c 2. *Educ:* Bryn Mawr Col, AB, 65; Brandeis Univ, PhD(biol), 70. *Prof Exp:* Charles F Kettering fel photosynthetic membrane, Lawrence Berkeley Lab, 70-71, res chemist, 71; Fla Heart Asn fel, Sch Med, Univ Miami, 72, instr pharmacol of cell membranes, 72-73; fel tumor cell membrane immunol, Oncol Ctr, Johns Hopkins Univ, 73-74, instr med & oncol, Sch Med, 74-76; mem staff, Dept Immunopath, Cleveland Clin, 76-77; from asst prof to assoc prof exp path, Case Western Res Univ, 77-84; sr res scientist, Bristol-Myers, Squibb, 84-87, assoc dir, Immunol Dept, 88-91; vpres, BioTransplant Inc, 91- 93. *Concurrent Pos:* Adj prof, Univ Conn, Wesleyan Univ. *Mem:* Am Asn Immunologists; Am Soc Human Genetics; Am Asn Clin Histocompatibility Testing. *Res:* Immunobiology and immunogenetics; transplantation; tumor cell biology. *Mailing Add:* 748 Durham Rd Madison CT 06443

SCHACTER, BRENT ALLAN, MEDICAL RESEARCH & ONCOLOGY, HEMATOLOGY. *Current Pos:* From asst prof to assoc prof, 72-87, PROF INTERNAL MED, UNIV MAN, 87-; PRES & CHIEF EXEC OFFICER, MAN CANCER TREATMENT & RES FOUND, 93- *Personal Data:* b Winnipeg, Man, June 1, 42; m 81, Sora Ludwig; c Miriam, Isanne & Jennifer. *Educ:* Univ Man, BSc & MD, 65; FRCP(C), 71. *Concurrent Pos:* Fel, Med Res Coun Can, 70-72, scholar, 75-80. *Mem:* Am Soc Clin Oncol; Am Fedn Clin Res; Can Soc Clin Invest; Am Soc Hemat; Am Asn Study Liver Dis; Can Asn Med Oncologists. *Res:* Investigation of the mechanism of action of heme oxygenase and the nature of the regulation of heme catabolism by this enzyme. *Mailing Add:* Man Cancer Treatment & Res Found 100 Olivia St Winnipeg MB R3E 0V9 Can. *Fax:* 204-787-1184; *E-Mail:* brent.schacter@mctrf.mb.ca

SCHAD, GERHARD ADAM, PARASITOLOGY. *Current Pos:* prin investr parasitol, Univ Pa, 72-79, assoc prof, 73-77, head, Lab Parasitol, 74-83, chmn, Grad Group Parasitol, 78-84, PROF PATHOBIOL, SCH VET MED, UNIV PA, 77- *Personal Data:* b Brooklyn, NY, Apr 2, 28; m 53, Donna J Crawford; c Eric J & Lisa A. *Educ:* Cornell Univ, BS, 50; McGill Univ, MSc, 52, PhD(parasitol), 55. *Hon Degrees:* MSc, Univ Pa, 75. *Prof Exp:* Scripps res fel, Biol Res Inst, San Diego Zool Soc, 53; parasitologist, USDA, 55-58; asst prof parasitol, Inst Parasitol, Macdonald Col, McGill Univ, 58-64; from asst prof to assoc prof pathobiol, Johns Hopkins Univ, 64-73. *Concurrent Pos:* Prin investr parasitol, Johns Hopkins Univ Ctr Med Res & Training, Calcutta, 64-66 & 68-70, NIH, 79-81 & 85-, WHO, 79-81 & 84- & USDA, 81-85; mem, Nat Selection Comt, US Educ Found, India, 68-69. *Mem:* Fel AAAS; Am Asn Vet Parasitol; Am Soc Trop Med & Hyg; Royal Soc Trop Med & Hyg; Am Soc Parasitol (pres, 90). *Res:* Developmental and neurobiology of parasitic heiminths. *Mailing Add:* Parasitol/213 Vet/H1 Sch Vet Med Univ Pa Philadelphia PA 19104

SCHAD, THEODORE M(ACNEEVE), PUBLIC ADMINISTRATION, RESEARCH. *Current Pos:* CONSULT, APOGEE RES, 92- *Personal Data:* b Baltimore, Md, Aug 25, 18; m 44, 95, Margot Cornwell; c MaryJane & Rebecca. *Educ:* Johns Hopkins Univ, BE, 39. *Honors & Awards:* Iben Award, Am Water Resource Asn, 78; Caulfield Award, 90; Julian Hinds Award, Am Soc Civil Engrs, 92. *Prof Exp:* Eng aide, US Army Corps Engrs, Md, 39-40, chief, Specif Sect, Washington, 42-45, engr, 45-46; jr engr, US Bur Reclamation, Colo, 40-42, engr, 46-49, chief, Coord Plans Sect, 50-51, asst chief, Prog Coord Div, 51-54; budget exam, US Bur Budget, 54-58; sr specialist eng & pub works, Legis Ref Serv, Libr Cong, 58-68, actg chief, Sci Policy Res Div, 66-67, dep dir, 67-68; exec dir, US Nat Water Comn, 69-73; exec secy, Environ Studies Bd, 73-77, dep exec dir, Comn Nat Resources, Nat Res Coun, 77-83; sr fel, Off Technol Assessment, 92-93; exec dir, Nat Ground Water Policy Forum, 84-86. *Concurrent Pos:* Staff dir, Select Comt Nat Water Resources, US Senate, 59-61; consult, Comt Interior & Insular Affairs, 63, Comt Water Resources Res, Fed Coun Sci & Tech, 62-64, Comt Sci & Tech & Astron, House of Rep, 63-64, Off Saline Water, 64-67, A T Kearney, Inc, 79-80, Gambia River Basin Develop Orgn, 86- & Apogee Res, 88-90; mem Permanent Int Comn, Permanent Int Asn Navig Cong, 63-70; mem, US Comt Large Dams, Int Comn Large Dams, 64-; vis fel, Woodrow Wilson Nat Fel Found, 73-81; sr fel, Conserv Found, 86-, Ronco Consult Corp, 86-90. *Mem:* Fel Am Soc Civil Engrs; Am Geophys Union; Nat Speleol Soc; hon mem Am Water Works Asn; Am Acad Environ Engrs; Nat Acad Pub Admin. *Res:* Water resources policy; federal policies and programs; water resources research; environmental policy; ground water management. *Mailing Add:* 4540-25th Rd N Arlington VA 22207

SCHADLER, DANIEL LEO, PLANT PATHOLOGY, BIOCHEMISTRY. *Current Pos:* from asst prof to assoc prof, 75-84, PROF BIOL, OGLETHORPE UNIV, 84-, CHMN, 83- *Personal Data:* b Dayton, Ky, Apr 5, 48. *Educ:* Thomas More Col, AB, 70; Cornell Univ, MS, 72, PhD(plant path), 74. *Prof Exp:* Res assoc, Univ Wis, 74-75. *Mem:* Am Phytopath Soc; Int Soc Plant Path; Am Chem Soc; AAAS. *Res:* Physiology and biochemistry of plant disease and of plant pathogens, especially phytotoxins. *Mailing Add:* Dept Biol 4484 Peachtree Rd NE Atlanta GA 30319-2797. *Fax:* 404-364-8500; *E-Mail:* dschadle@oglethorpe.edu

SCHADLER, HARVEY W(ALTER), METALLURGY. *Current Pos:* RETIRED. *Personal Data:* b Cincinnati, Ohio, Jan 4, 31; m 54; c 3. *Educ:* Cornell Univ, BMetE, 54; Purdue Univ, PhD, 57. *Honors & Awards:* Geisler Award, Am Soc Metals. *Prof Exp:* Metallurgist, Res Labs, Gen Elec Res & Develop Ctr, 57-69, mgr, Surfaces & Reactions Br, 69-71, Phys Metall Br, 71-73 & Mat Res Ctr, 73-96. *Mem:* Nat Acad Eng; Am Inst Mining, Metall & Petrol Engrs; Sigma Xi; fel Am Soc Metals. *Res:* Physical metallurgy; brittle fracture; diffusion; crystal perfection; plastic deformation; superconductivity. *Mailing Add:* 1333 Lowell Rd Schenectady NY 12308

SCHADT, FRANK LEONARD, III, PHYSICAL ORGANIC CHEMISTRY, PHOTOGRAPHIC CHEMISTRY. *Current Pos:* Res chemist, Photosysts & Electronic Prod Dept, E I du Pont de Nemours & Co, Inc, 74-80, sr res chemist, 80-86, res assoc, Electronics Dept, 86-92, SR RES ASSOC, ELECTRONIC MAT, E I DU PONT DE NEMOURS & CO, INC, 92- *Personal Data:* b Syracuse, NY, Feb 3, 47; m 88, Margaret A Conley; c 2. *Educ:* Le Moyne Col, BS, 68; Princeton Univ, MA, 71, PhD(chem), 74. *Mem:* Am Chem Soc; Sigma Xi; fel Am Inst Chemists. *Res:* Mechanistic organic chemistry; photochemically induced polymerization and rearrangement; photographic chemistry; photopolymer resists for electronics; synthesis of specialized polymers and reagents; electrically conductive coatings; Agx imaging systems; polymer structure and properties; photoresist technology. *Mailing Add:* 2305 W 17th St Wilmington DE 19806-1330

SCHADT, JAMES C, CARDIOVASCULAR CONTROL, NEUROPHYSIOLOGY. *Current Pos:* ASST PROF & RES INVESTR NEUROPHYSIOL, DALTON RES CTR, 78- *Educ:* Tex Tech Univ, PhD(physiol), 78. *Mailing Add:* Dalton Cardivasc Res Ctr Univ Mo Columbia MO 65211-0001

SCHADT, RANDALL JAMES, SOLID STATE NUCLEAR MAGNETIC RESONANCE, NUCLEAR MAGNETIC RESONANCE SIMULATIONS. *Current Pos:* POLYMER SCIENTIST, POLYMER DIV, NAT INST STAND & TECHNOL, 93- *Personal Data:* b Highland Park, Ill, Apr 14, 60. *Educ:* Univ Neb, BS, 82; Univ Mo, MS, 84; NC State Univ, PhD(physics), 90. *Prof Exp:* Res asst physics, Physics Dept, Univ Mo, 83-85; teaching asst physics, Physics Dept, Univ Ill, 85-87; res asst polymer chem, Physics Dept, NC State Univ, 87-90; vis scientist polymer physics, Max Planck Inst Polymer Sci, 90-91; Dupont Ctr Res & Develop, 91-93. *Mem:* Am Phys Soc; Am Chem Soc. *Res:* Modern solid state nuclear magnetic resonance methods are used as the principal tools to probe molecular dynamics/structural correlations at various length scales in polymers and their relationship to measured macroscopic properties. *Mailing Add:* Hoffman La Roche Inc 340 Kingsland St Bldg 86 Nutley NJ 07110

SCHAECHTER, MOSELIO, MICROBIOLOGY, MOLECULAR BIOLOGY. *Current Pos:* from assoc prof to prof, 62-87, CHMN DEPT, TUFTS UNIV, 70-, DISTINGUISHED PROF MICROBIOL, 87- *Personal Data:* b Milan, Italy, Apr 26, 28; US citizen; wid; c 2. *Educ:* Univ Kans, MA, 51; Univ Pa, PhD(microbiol), 54. *Prof Exp:* From instr to assoc prof microbiol, Univ Fla, 58-62. *Concurrent Pos:* Am Cancer Soc grant, State Serum Inc, Copenhagen, Denmark, 56-58; mem bact & mycol study sect, NIH, 75-79, chmn, 78-79; mem, Microbiol Test Comt, Nat Bd Med Examr, 82-85; chmn, Asn Med Sch Microbiol & Immunol, pres, 84-85. *Mem:* Am Soc Microbiol (pres, 85-86); Soc Gen Microbiol; Sigma Xi. *Res:* The role of the cell membrane in bacterial DNA replication and segregation. *Mailing Add:* 6345 Rockhurst Dr San Diego CA 92120

SCHAEDLE, MICHAIL, PLANT PHYSIOLOGY. *Current Pos:* RETIRED. *Personal Data:* b Tallinn, Estonia, Dec 27, 27; US citizen; m 66; c 1. *Educ:* Univ BC, BSA, 57, MSA, 59; Univ Calif, Berkeley, PhD(plant physiol), 64. *Prof Exp:* Fel, Univ Calif, Berkeley, 64-65; from asst prof to assoc prof, 65-81, prof bot, State Univ NY, Col Environ Sci & Forestry, 81-95. *Mem:* AAAS; Am Inst Biol Sci; Am Soc Plant Physiol; Sigma Xi. *Res:* Plant nutrition; ion transport and cell permeability; photosynthesis in tissues of perennial plants; calcium and aluminum problems. *Mailing Add:* State Univ NY Col Environ Sci & Forestry Syracuse NY 13210

SCHAEDLER, RUSSELL WILLIAM, MEDICINE, MICROBIOLOGY. *Current Pos:* PROF MICROBIOL & CHMN DEPT, JEFFERSON MED COL, 68- *Personal Data:* b Hatfield, Pa, Dec 17, 27. *Educ:* Ursinus Col, BS, 49; Jefferson Med Col, MD, 53. *Prof Exp:* Intern hosp, Jefferson Med Col, 53-54; asst & asst physician med & microbiol, Rockefeller Univ, 54-57, asst prof & resident assoc physician, 57-61, assoc prof & physician, 61-68. *Mem:* Harvey Soc; Am Soc Microbiol; Am Gastroenterol Asn; Infectious Dis Soc Am; Am Asn Immunol; Sigma Xi. *Res:* Influence of environmental factors and nutrition on host resistance; ecology of the flora of the digestive tract and diarrheal diseases. *Mailing Add:* Dept Miocrobiol & Immunol Jefferson Med Col Thomas Jefferson Univ 1020 Locust St Philadelphia PA 19107-6731

SCHAEFER, ALBERT RUSSELL, OPTICAL DETECTORS & CHARGE COUPLED DEVICES, RADIOMETRIC PHYSICS. *Current Pos:* SR SCIENTIST, SCI APPLICATIONS INT CORP, 87- *Personal Data:* b Oklahoma City, Okla, Oct 13, 44; m 68; c 2. *Educ:* Univ Okla, BS, 66, PhD(physics), 70. *Honors & Awards:* Bronze Medal, Dept Com, 81. *Prof Exp:* Physicist, Optical Radiation Sect, Nat Bur Standards, 70-86; chief scientist, Western Res Corp, 86-87. *Concurrent Pos:* Instr, Montgomery Col, 74-77, adj prof, 78- *Mem:* Am Phys Soc; Optical Soc Am; Soc Photo-Optical Instrumentation Engrs. *Res:* Transition probabilities; radiometric physics; electro-optic devices; lifetimes; radiometry; photometry; spectroscopy; silicon detectors; astrophysics; charge coupled devices (CCD's). *Mailing Add:* SAIC Elec Vision Syst Div 4161 Campus Point Dr San Diego CA 92121-1513. *Fax:* 619-646-9252; *E-Mail:* a.russell.schaefer@cpmx.saic.com

SCHAEFER, CARL FRANCIS, CIRCULATORY SHOCK, ANESTHESIOLOGY. *Current Pos:* fel psychosom med, 71-74, asst prof res med, 74-76, asst prof res anesthesiol, 76-80, ASSOC PROF ANESTHESIOL, UNIV OKLA HEALTH SCI CTR, 80-, DIR ANESTHESIA RES LAB, 88- *Personal Data:* b Schenectady, NY, Mar 20, 41; m 75; c 2. *Educ:* Univ Toronto, BA; Univ Rochester, PhD(physiol psychol), 72. *Prof Exp:* Asst prof psychol, Wilkes Col, 70-71. *Concurrent Pos:* NIMH res grant, 77-78, Vet Admin res grant, 87- *Mem:* Am Psychol Asn; Sigma Xi; NY Acad Sci; Am Soc Anesthesiol; Am Physiol Soc; Shock Soc. *Res:* Physiological mechanisms of circulatory shock; cardiovascular effects of anesthetic agents; oxidative metabolism, small intestinal pathology and circulatory shock; development of anesthetic and physiological monitoring methods for small animals such as rats. *Mailing Add:* Dept Anesthesiol Univ Okla Health Sci Ctr PO Box 26901 Oklahoma City OK 73190-0001

SCHAEFER, CARL W, II, ENTOMOLOGY. *Current Pos:* from asst prof to assoc prof, 66-75, PROF BIOL, UNIV CONN, 76- *Personal Data:* b New Haven, Conn, Sept 6, 34; div; c Ann & Madelyn. *Educ:* Oberlin Col, BA, 56; Univ Conn, PhD(entom), 64. *Prof Exp:* From instr to asst prof biol, Brooklyn Col, 63-66. *Concurrent Pos:* Grantee, City Univ NY Grad Div, 64-66, Univ Conn Res Found, 66-67 & NSF, 67-69, 79-81; co-ed, Ann Entom Soc Am,

73- Mem: Hon mem Entom Soc Am; Soc Syst Zool; Soc Study Evolution; Indian Entom Soc. Res: Comparative morphology, biology and phylogeny of the terrestrial Heteroptera. Mailing Add: Dept Ecol Evolutionary Biol Univ Conn U-43 Storrs CT 06269-3043

SCHAEFER, CHARLES HERBERT, ENTOMOLOGY, AGRICULTURAL CHEMISTRY. Current Pos: RETIRED. Personal Data: b Albany, Calif, Sept 24, 35; m 57; c 2. Educ: Univ Calif, Berkeley, BS, 58, PhD(entom), 62. Prof Exp: Insect physiologist, US Forest Serv, Md, 62-64 & Shell Develop Co, Calif, 64-67; dir, Mosquito Control Res Lab, Univ Calif, 67-93. Mem: AAAS; Entom Soc Am; Entom Soc Can; Mosquito Control Asn Am. Res: New approaches to insect control; biochemical relationships between insects and their respective plant hosts; mechanisms of insecticide degradation by target insects and by the environment. Mailing Add: 7740 E Saginaw Way Fresno CA 93727

SCHAEFER, DALE WESLEY, EDUCATION ADMINISTRATION. Current Pos: DEAN, COL ENG, UNIV CINCINNATI, 97- Personal Data: b Willoughby, Ohio, May 17, 41; m 62; c Joel W & Jeanne (Williams). Educ: Wheaton Col, BS, 63; Mass Inst Technol, PhD(phys chem), 68. Honors & Awards: Chemist Award, Am Inst Chemists, 63; Outstanding Sustained Res Award, Dept Energy Basic Energy Sci, 86. Prof Exp: Fel physics, Mass Inst Technol, 68-70 & T J Watson Res Ctr, IBM Corp, 70-72; mem tech staff, Sandia Nat Labs, 72-80, supvr, Corrosion Div, 80-82, supvr, Chem Physics Div, 82-88, mgr, Org & Elec Mat Dept, 89-91, mgr mat res, Energy & Environ Tech Dept, 91-94; sr tech adv, US Dept Energy, 94-97. Concurrent Pos: NSF fel, 64; Int Sci Orgn Comt, Statphys 16, 85-86; chmn, Symposium Fractal Aspects Mat, Mat Res Soc, 86; Los Alamos Neutron Scattering Ctr Adv Comt, 87-91; mem meeting chain, Mat Res Soc spring meeting, 91 & panel, Chaos & Nonlinear Math, Nat Res Ctr, 92-94. Mem: Fel Am Phys Soc; Mat Res Soc; Am Chem Soc; Am Ceramic Soc; Sigma Xi; fel Am Inst Chemists. Res: Polymer physics light scattering; small angle x-ray scattering; colloid physics; structure of fluids; neutron scattering; ceramic and polymer materials science. Mailing Add: Col Eng Univ Cincinnati Cincinnati OH 45221. E-Mail: dwschae@sandia.gov

SCHAEFER, DANIEL M, RUMEN BACTERIOLOGY, RUMINANT NUTRITION. Current Pos: from asst prof to assoc prof, 81-90, PROF ANIMAL SCI, UNIV WIS-MADISON, 90- Personal Data: b Kewaskum, Wis, Sept 12, 51; m 75, Gail Kottke; c Jeremy & Mary. Educ: Univ Wis-Madison, BS, 73, MS, 75; Univ Ill, PhD(nutrit sci), 79. Prof Exp: Asst prof animal sci, Purdue Univ, 79-81. Mem: Am Soc Animal Sci; Am Dairy Sci Asn; Am Soc Microbiol. Res: Understanding and manipulation of ruminal microbes to obtain nutritional advantantages for the host ruminant; stabilization of fresh beef color with dietary vitamin E. Mailing Add: Animal Sci Dept Univ Wis Madison WI 53706-1284. Fax: 608-262-5157

SCHAEFER, ERNST J, LIPOPROTEINS, ATHEROSCLEROSIS. Current Pos: ASSOC PROF MED & CHIEF, LIPID METAB LAB, TUFTS UNIV, 82- Personal Data: b Bad Nauheim, Germany, Nov 18, 45. Educ: Mt Sinai Sch Med, New York City, MD, 72. Mem: Am Heart Asn; Am Inst Nutrit; Am Fedn Clin Res. Mailing Add: Lipid Metab Lab USDA Human Nutrit Res Ctr on Aging Tufts Univ 711 Washington St Boston MA 02111-1524. Fax: 617-556-3103

SCHAEFER, FRANCIS T, CIVIL ENGINEERING, HYDROLOGY. Current Pos: RETIRED. Personal Data: b Hamilton, Mont, Mar 11, 13; m 37; c 2. Educ: Univ Minn, BCE, 34. Prof Exp: Observer, US Coast & Geod Surv, 34-35; surveyman, Corps Engrs, New Orleans, La, 35-36; engr, Gulf Res & Develop Co, 36-37; hydraul engr, Surface Water Br, Ark, Tenn & Okla, US Geol Surv, 37-42, off engr, Nebr, asst dist engr, Ky, 49-54, dist engr, Wis, 54-60, br area chief, 60-64, asst regional hydrologist, Water Resources Div, 64-86. Concurrent Pos: Delaware River Master, US Geol Surv, 75-; consult, Govt Brazil, 73. Mem: Fel Am Soc Civil Engrs. Res: Science administration. Mailing Add: 6801 Lemon Rd McLean VA 22101

SCHAEFER, FRANK WILLIAM, III, ANIMAL PARASITOLOGY, ENVIRONMENTAL PARASITOLOGY. Current Pos: MICROBIOLOGIST, US ENVIRON PROTECTION AGENCY, 78- Personal Data: b Dayton, Ohio, Sept 1, 42. Educ: Miami Univ, BA, 64; Univ Cincinnati, MS, 70, PhD(biol), 73. Honors & Awards: Bronze Medal, US Environ Protection Agency, 84. Prof Exp: Res assoc parasitol, Univ Notre Dame, 73-78. Concurrent Pos: Adj asst prof, Dept Path & Lab Med, Med Sch, Univ Cincinnati, 84- Mem: AAAS; Sigma Xi; Am Soc Parasitol; Am Soc Microbiol; Soc Protozoologists; Am Water Works Asn; Am Soc Testing & Mat. Res: In vitro cultivation of helminth and protozoan parasites; physiological studies relating to the viability and infectivity of these parasites. Mailing Add: Nat Exposure Res Lab 26 West M L King Dr Cincinnati OH 45268. E-Mail: schaefer.frank@eramail.epa.gov

SCHAEFER, FREDERIC CHARLES, ORGANIC CHEMISTRY. Current Pos: res chemist, 43-56, RES ASSOC, AM CYANAMID CO, 56-, PROJ LEADER, 74- Personal Data: b Syracuse, NY, Nov 28, 17; m 45; c 3. Educ: Syracuse Univ, BS, 39; Univ Akron, MS, 40; Mass Inst Technol, PhD(org chem), 43. Prof Exp: Res chemist, Goodyear Tire & Rubber Co, Ohio, 40-41. Concurrent Pos: Am Cyanamid Co fel, Inst Org Chem, Univ Munich, 62-63. Mem: Am Chem Soc. Res: Organic nitrogen chemistry; heterocycles, s-triazines; reactive polymerizable materials; synthetic resin intermediates; keratin chemistry; hair care science. Mailing Add: 506 Jadetree Ct West Columbia SC 29169-4962

SCHAEFER, FREDERICK VAIL, DNA DIAGNOSTIC MEDICINE, DEVELOPMENTAL BIOLOGY. Current Pos: fel res, 79-81, res assoc, 81-84, CLIN ASST PROF PEDIAT, INST CANCER RES, 85-, DIR, MOLECULAR GENETICS, 85- Personal Data: b Fort Dix, NJ, May 25, 49; m 69. Educ: Univ Md, BS, 71; NC State Univ, PhD(biochem), 79. Prof Exp: Res technician, Electronucleonics Lab, 71-73. Concurrent Pos: Res fel, NIH, 80-81. Mem: Sigma Xi; Am Soc Human Genetics; Am Chem Soc; AAAS. Res: Molecular basis of carcinogensis; develop testing protocols for cancer diagnosis; determine molecular changes in the growth hormone related genes. Mailing Add: 5429 S 72nd East Ave Tulsa OK 74145

SCHAEFER, GEORGE, OBSTETRICS & GYNECOLOGY. Current Pos: from asst prof to prof, 51-78, EMER PROF OBSTET & GYNEC, MED COL, CORNELL UNIV, 78- Personal Data: b New York, NY, May 30, 13; m 44, Shirley Plaut; c Jay Lloyd & Michael Lee. Educ: NY Univ, BS, 33; Cornell Univ, MD, 37; Am Bd Obstet & Gynec, dipl, 48. Prof Exp: Attend obstetrician & gynecologist, Sea View Hosp, 40-48. Concurrent Pos: Consult, Booth Mem Hosp, 63-; attend, NY Hosp, 62-78; dir, obstet & gynec residency training prog, Mercy Hosp & Med Ctr, San Diego, 80-86; clin prof reproductive med, San Diego, Calif, 83-86. Mem: Fel Am Col Surg; fel Am Col Obstet & Gynec; hon fel Span Gynec Soc. Res: Tuberculosis in obstetrics and gynecology; study of the expectant father. Mailing Add: 6144 Laport La Mesa CA 91942-4313

SCHAEFER, GERALD J, BEHAVIORAL PHARMACOLOGY, BEHAVIORAL TOXICOL. Current Pos: DIR NEUROSCI, MPI RES, 95- Personal Data: b Sheboygan, Wis, Aug 12, 44; c Kristen. Educ: Univ Wis-Milwaukee, BA, 68; Univ Akron, Ohio, MA, 70; Vanderbilt Univ, PhD(neurosci), 74; Ga State Univ, JD, 94. Prof Exp: Postdoctoral fel pharmacol, 74-76, assoc prof psychiat & asst prof pharmacol, Emory Univ, 82-92; res scientist neuropharmacol, Dept Human Resources, State of Ga, 76-91; dir neurosci, Int Res & Develop Corp, 93-95. Mem: AAAS; Am Soc Pharmacol & Exp Therapeut; Sigma Xi; Soc Neurosci; Int Brain Res Orgn; Soc Toxicol. Res: Behavioral and biochemical effects of psychoactive drugs in animals; behavioral toxicology and safety evaluation, including pathology of drugs used to treat neurological and mental health problems. Mailing Add: MPI Res 54943 N Main St Mattawan MI 49071. Fax: 616-668-4151

SCHAEFER, HENRY FREDERICK, III, THEORETICAL CHEMISTRY. Current Pos: GRAHAM PERDUE PROF CHEM & DIR CTR COMPUTATIONAL QUANTUM CHEM, UNIV GA, 87- Personal Data: b Grand Rapids, Mich, June 8, 44; m 66, Karen R Rasmussen; c Charlotte, Theodore, Pierre, Rebecca & Caleb. Educ: Mass Inst Technol, SB, 66; Stanford Univ, PhD(chem), 69. Honors & Awards: Am Chem Soc Pure Chem Award, 79, Leo Hendrik Baekeland Award, 83; Ann Award, World Asn Theoret Org Chemists, 90; Albert Einstein Centennial Lectr, Nat Univ Mex, 79, Lester P Kuhn Lectr, Johns Hopkins Univ, 82, John Howard Appleton Lectr, Brown Univ, 85, J A Erskine Lectr, Univ Canterbury, Christchurch, New Zealand, 86, Edward Curtis Franklin Lectr, Univ Kans, 86, John Lee Pratt Lectr, Univ Va, 88, Louis Jacob Bircher Lectr, Vanderbilt Univ, 88, Harry Emmett Gunning Lectr, Univ Alta, 90, Guelph-Waterloo distinguished Lectr, Univ Guelph & Univ Waterloo, Ont, 91, John M Templeton Lectr, Case Western Res Univ, 92 & Herbert H King Lectr, Kans State Univ, 93; Centenary Medal, Royal Soc Chem London, 92; Francis A Schaeffer Lectr, Covenant Theol Semi, 94; Mary Kapp Lectr Va Commonwealth Univ, 96; Abbott Lectr, Univ NDak, 97; C S Lewis Lectr, Univ Tenn, 97. Prof Exp: From asst prof to prof chem, Univ Calif, Berkeley, 69-87, staff mem, Nuclear Chem Div, Lawrence Berkeley Lab, 71-75, staff mem, Molecular & Mat Res Div, 75-87; Wilfred T Doherty prof chem & dir Inst Theoret Chem, Univ Tex, Austin, 79-80. Concurrent Pos: Joint study proj, Univ Calif-IBM Res Lab, 72-77; Alfred P Sloan Res Fel, 72-74; Consult, Eastman Kodak, 74, Lawrence Livermore Lab, 68-80 & Energy Conversion Devices, 82-86, Dow Chem Co, 87, IBM Corp, 87; John Simon Guggenheim Fel, 76-77; chmn, Subdiv Theoret Chem, Phys Chem Div, Am Chem Soc, 82, mem exec comt, 84-87, vchair, 90, chair, 92; mem NSF adv comt chem, 89-92; ed-in-chief, Molecular Physics, 95-; pres, World Asn Theoretically Oriented Chemists, 95- Mem: Fel Am Phys Soc; fel Int Acad Quantum Molecular Sci. Res: Rigorous quantum mechanical studies of the electronic structure of atoms and molecules. Mailing Add: Ctr Computational Quantum Chem Univ Ga Chem Bldg Rm 404 Athens GA 30602. Fax: 706-542-0406; E-Mail: hfsiii@uga.cc.uga.edu

SCHAEFER, JACOB FRANKLIN, PHYSICAL CHEMISTRY. Current Pos: PROF CHEM, WASH UNIV, 86- Personal Data: b San Francisco, Calif, Aug 13, 38; m 62; c 3. Educ: Carnegie Inst Technol, BS, 60; Univ Minn, PhD(phys chem), 64. Prof Exp: Res chemist phys chem, Monsanto Co, 64-74, sci fel, 74-86. Mem: Am Chem Soc; Am Phys Soc. Res: Nuclear magnetic resonance spectroscopy of polymers and proteins in the solid state. Mailing Add: Dept Chem Wash Univ St Louis MO 63130-4899. Fax: 314-935-4481; E-Mail: schaefer@wuchem.wustl.edu

SCHAEFER, JACOB W, COMMUNICATIONS, SYSTEMS ENGINEERING. Current Pos: Engr, Bell Tel Labs, 41-42, 46-50, supvr Nike Ajax & Hercules syst design, 50-57, dept head Nike Zeus res, 57-61, asst dir, Nike Zeus Proj, 61-63, dir, Kwajalien Field Sta, 63-65, dir, Data Commun Lab, 65-68, exec dir, Data & PBX Div, 68-70, exec dir customer switching servs, 70-81, exec dir, Mil Systs Div, 81-84, CONSULT, MIL SYSTS DIV, AT&T BELL LABS, 84- Personal Data: b Paullina, Iowa, June 27, 19; m 41, Mary Carter; c Joanna (Fiori), James C & William S. Educ: Ohio State Univ, BME, 41. Hon Degrees: DSc, Ohio State Univ, 76. Prof Exp: Capt, US Army Ordance, 42-46. Concurrent Pos: Mem subcomt, Air Force Sci Adv Bd, 61-63. Mem: Nat Acad Eng; Am Ord Asn; fel Inst Elec & Electronics Engrs; Sigma Xi. Res: Servomechanisms for missile control surfaces; missile guidance and air defense missile systems; design of data communication terminals; initial design of cellular telephone system. Mailing Add: 115 Century Lane Watchung NJ 07060

SCHAEFER, JOSEPH ALBERT, SOLID STATE PHYSICS. *Current Pos:* From instr to assoc prof, 64-80, PROF PHYSICS, LORAS COL, 80- *Personal Data:* b Bellevue, Iowa, Dec 24, 40; m 65, Carol Deppe; c Sarah & Amy. *Educ:* Loras Col, BS, 62; Univ Toledo, MS, 64; Northwestern Univ, Evanston, PhD(physics), 72. *Concurrent Pos:* Res fel, Northwestern Univ, Evanston, 74; consult, John Deere Co, 80; NSF sci fac prof develop fel, Iowa State Univ, 81-82; assoc res scientist, Iowa Inst Hydraul Res, 85-90 & 91. *Mem:* Am Asn Physics Teachers; Am Soc Eng Educ. *Res:* Magnetoresistance of potassium; transport properties of metals; switching varistors; ice engineering. *Mailing Add:* Dept Physics & Eng Sci Loras Col 1450 Alta Vista Dubuque IA 52004-0178. *Fax:* 319-588-7964; *E-Mail:* schaefer@loras.edu

SCHAEFER, JOSEPH THOMAS, FORECASTING, WIND ENGINEERING. *Current Pos:* DIR, STORM PREDICTION CTR, NAT WEATHER SERV, 96- *Personal Data:* b Milwaukee, Wis, Oct 23, 43; m 68, Sharon Gibson; c Christopher, Thomas & John. *Educ:* St Louis Univ, BS, 65, PhD(meteorol), 73. *Honors & Awards:* Bronze Medal, Dept Com. *Prof Exp:* Meteorologist, Nat Weather Serv, St Louis, Mo, 66-69; res meteorologist, US Navy Weather Res Facil, 69-71; res meteorologist, Nat Severe Storms Lab, Nat Oceanic & Atmospheric Admin, 71-76, chief, Tech Develop Unit, Nat Severe Storms Forecast Ctr, 76-83, chief sci serv, Nat Weather Serv Cent Region, 83-91, dir, Nat Weather Serv Training Ctr, 91-96. *Concurrent Pos:* Mem, US/Japan Panel Wind & Seismic Effects, 79-93; instr, Univ Mo, Kansas City, 85-86 & 92-93; adj prof, Univ Okla, 97- *Mem:* Fel Am Meteor Soc; Am Geophys Union; Nat Weather Asn; Can Meteorol & Oceanog Soc. *Res:* Weather forecasting; tornado climatology; severe thunderstorm environment; severe thunderstorm dynamics and structure; atmospheric boundary layer structure; mesoscale numerical atmospheric modelling; cumulus dynamics. *Mailing Add:* 2203 Parkland Way Norman OK 73069. *Fax:* 405-579-0700; *E-Mail:* joseph.schaefer@noaa.gov

SCHAEFER, PAUL THEODORE, MATHEMATICS. *Current Pos:* PROF MATH, STATE UNIV NY COL GENESEO, 67- *Personal Data:* b Rochester, NY, Mar 7, 30; m 51. *Educ:* Univ Rochester, AB, 51, MA, 56; Univ Pittsburgh, PhD(infinite series), 63. *Prof Exp:* Instr math, Rochester Inst Tech, 55-56; from asst prof to prof, State Univ NY Albany, 56-67. *Concurrent Pos:* First vchmn seaway sect, Math Asn Am, 76-77, chmn, 77-78; vis prof, Calif State Univ, Los Angeles, 78-79. *Mem:* Am Math Soc; Math Asn Am. *Res:* Series; summability; real and complex analysis. *Mailing Add:* 5215 Deuel Rd Honeoye NY 14471-9752

SCHAEFER, PHILIP WILLIAM, APPLIED MATHEMATICS, ELLIPTIC PARTIAL DIFFERENTIAL EQUATIONS. *Current Pos:* assoc prof, 67-77, PROF MATH, UNIV TENN, KNOXVILLE, 77- *Personal Data:* b Baltimore, Md, Feb 16, 35; m 58, Patricia E Kirby; c Daniel, Barbara, Michael & Susan. *Educ:* John Carroll Univ, BS, 56, MS, 57; Univ Md, PhD(math), 64. *Prof Exp:* Instr math, Loyola Col, Md, 59-60; asst prof, Univ SFla, 64-67. *Mem:* Am Math Soc; Soc Indust & Appl Math. *Res:* Elliptic partial differential equations; maximum principles and solution bounds; overdetermined boundary value problems; Phragmen-Lindelof and Liouville type theorems. *Mailing Add:* Dept Math Univ Tenn Knoxville TN 37996-1300. *Fax:* 423-974-6576; *E-Mail:* schaefer@novell.math.utk.edu

SCHAEFER, ROBERT J, phase transformations, for more information see previous edition

SCHAEFER, ROBERT WILLIAM, ANALYTICAL CHEMISTRY. *Current Pos:* Asst prof, 49-51, from asst prof to assoc prof, 52-81, chairperson, 79-85, PROF ANALytical CHEM, UNION COL, 81- *Personal Data:* b Schenectady, NY, Dec 5, 27; m 54; c 4. *Educ:* Siena Col, BS, 49; Union Col, NY, MS, 51. *Concurrent Pos:* Develop chemist, Willsboro Mining Co, 50; asst, Univ Ky, 51; sr sanit chemist, State Dept Health, NY, 54-60; lectr, Bard Col, 55; consult, Power Technol Inc, Schenectady, NY, 80-84; Welch Chem Co, Schenectady, NY, 85-86. *Mem:* Am Chem Soc. *Res:* Instrumental analytical chemistry; sanitary chemistry; methods for trace metals. *Mailing Add:* 30 Featherfoil Way Ballston Spa NY 12020

SCHAEFER, THEODORE PETER, PHYSICAL CHEMISTRY. *Current Pos:* from asst prof to prof, 58-82, univ distinguished prof chem, 82-97, SR SCHOLAR, UNIV MAN, 97- *Personal Data:* b Gnadenthal, Man, July 22, 33; m 60, Nicola Sewell; c Catherine, Dominic & Benjamin. *Educ:* Univ Man, BSc, 54, MSc, 55; Oxford Univ, DPhil(chem), 58. *Hon Degrees:* DSc, Univ Winnipeg, 82. *Honors & Awards:* Noranda Award, Chem Inst Can, 73; Herzberg Award, Spectros Soc Can, 75. *Concurrent Pos:* Nat Res Coun Can sr res fel, 64-65; mem, Chem Grants Comt, Nat Res Coun Can, 75-77; mem, Natural Sci & Eng Res Coun Can, 80-84, Publ Grants Comt, 87-89; mem, Publ Grants Comt, Natural Sci & Eng Res Coun, Can 87-89. *Mem:* Fel Royal Soc Can; fel Chem Inst Can. *Res:* Nuclear magnetic resonance spectroscopy in chemistry. *Mailing Add:* Dept Chem Univ Man Winnipeg MB R3T 2N2 Can

SCHAEFER, WILBUR CARLS, AGRICULTURAL CHEMISTRY. *Current Pos:* CONSULT, 87- *Personal Data:* b Beardstown, Ill, Sept 18, 25; m 49, Naomi Carpenter; c Gregory & Kurt. *Educ:* Bradley Univ, BS, 49, MS, 50. *Prof Exp:* Res chemist, Agr Res Serv, USDA, 50-61, asst to dir, Northern Regional Res Ctr, 61-72, prog analyst, 72-87. *Mem:* AAAS; Am Asn Cereal Chem (treas, 72-74); Am Chem Soc. *Res:* Utilization of cereal grains and oilseeds; starch and dextran structure; starch derivatives; wheat gluten properties; histochemistry of wheat endosperm; chemical research administration; carbohydrate and protein chemistry. *Mailing Add:* 2208 W Newman Pkwy Peoria IL 61604

SCHAEFER, WILLIAM PALZER, X-RAY CRYSTALLOGRAPHY. *Current Pos:* sr res fel, Calif Inst Technol, 68-77, registrar, 71-77, dir financial aid, 72-77, res assoc, 77-81, sr res assoc, 81-94, dir, X-Ray Diffraction Facil, 86-94, EMER SR RES ASSOC, CALIF INST TECHNOL, 94- *Personal Data:* b Bisbee, Ariz, Jan 13, 31; m 54, Margaret Durfy; c Peter L & Michael J. *Educ:* Stanford Univ, BS, 52; Univ Calif, Los Angeles, MS, 54, PhD(anal chem), 60. *Prof Exp:* From instr to asst prof chem, Calif Inst Technol, 60-66; asst prof, Univ Calif, Davis, 66-68. *Mem:* Am Crystallog Asn; fel AAAS. *Res:* Structure and stability of complexes of the transition metals; x-ray crystallography; structural chemistry. *Mailing Add:* Beckman Inst 139-74 Calif Inst Technol Pasadena CA 91125. *Fax:* 626-449-4159; *E-Mail:* wps@xray.caltech.edu

SCHAEFERS, GEORGE ALBERT, ENTOMOLOGY. *Current Pos:* RETIRED. *Personal Data:* b Erie, Pa, Mar 19, 29; m 60; c 3. *Educ:* Univ Calif, BS, 55, PhD, 58. *Prof Exp:* From asst prof to prof, NY State Col Agr, 58-, chmn dept, 83-; emer prof entom, NY State Agr Exp Sta, Cornell Univ. *Concurrent Pos:* Vis scientist, Int Inst Trop Agr, 74-75 & Coop State Res Serv, USDA, 81-82. *Mem:* Entom Soc Am. *Res:* Economic entomology; small fruit insects; insect vectors plant diseases; Aphid biology. *Mailing Add:* Dept Entom Cornell Univ NY State Agr Exp Sta PO Box 462 Geneva NY 14456-0462

SCHAEFF, CATHERINE MARGARET, POPULATION GENETICS OF ENDANGERED SPECIES, CONSERVATION WITH EMPHASIS ON SOCIAL BEHAVIOR. *Current Pos:* ASST PROF, AM UNIV, 93- *Personal Data:* b Brampton, Ont, Mar 16, 62; m 89, Patricia Rivera Spencer; c Caitlin Rivera-Schaeff. *Educ:* Univ Toronto, BSc, 83; Univ Ottawa, MSc, 88; Queen's Univ, PhD(conserv biol & pop genetics), 93. *Mem:* Can Soc Zoologists; Soc Study Evolution; Soc Conserv Biologists; AAAS. *Res:* Molecular techniques (DNA fingerprints, sequencing, net DNA restriction fragment length polymorphism) to assess levels of genetic relatedness and then investigate how relatedness influences social behavior (mating, courtship, fostering) habitat use and population recovery rates; conservation biology. *Mailing Add:* Amer Univ 4400 Massachusetts Ave NW Washington DC 20016-8001. *Fax:* 202-885-2182; *E-Mail:* schaeff@american.edu

SCHAEFFER, BOBB, VERTEBRATE PALEONTOLOGY. *Current Pos:* EMER CUR VERT PALEONT, AM MUS NATURAL HIST, 76- *Personal Data:* b New Haven, Conn, Sept 27, 13; m 41; c 2. *Educ:* Cornell Univ, BA, 36; Columbia Univ, MA, 37, PhD(zool), 41. *Prof Exp:* Demonstr histol & embryol, Jefferson Med Col, 41-42; asst cur vert paleont, Am Mus Natural Hist, 46-49, assoc cur fossil fishes, 49-55, chmn dept, 66-76; vis assoc prof zool, Columbia Univ, 55-57, adj prof, 57-59, prof, 59-78. *Concurrent Pos:* Cur vert paleont, Am Mus Natural Hist, 55-76. *Mem:* Soc Vert Paleont (actg secy, 52-53, pres, 53); Soc Syst Zool; Soc Study Evolution; fel Geol Soc Am; Sigma Xi. *Res:* Systematics; morphology and embryology of fishes; systematic theory. *Mailing Add:* 1400 East Ave Apt 505 Rochester NY 14610-1648

SCHAEFFER, CHARLES DAVID, INORGANIC CHEMISTRY. *Current Pos:* asst prof, 76-81, assoc prof chem, 81-91, AC BAUGHER PROF, ELIZABETHTOWN COL, 91- *Personal Data:* b Allentown, Pa, June 14, 48. *Educ:* Franklin & Marshall Col, BA, 70; State Univ NY, Albany, PhD(chem), 74. *Prof Exp:* Fel inorg chem, Yale Univ, 74-76. *Concurrent Pos:* Res grant, Cottrell Col, 77-78 & 82-84, NSF, 91; Petrol Res Fund, Am Chem Soc grant, 78-80, 84-86, 86-88, 88-91, 92-94, 94-96 & 97- *Mem:* Am Chem Soc; Royal Soc Chem, London. *Res:* Main group organometallic chemistry; nuclear magnetic resonance spectroscopy. *Mailing Add:* Chem Dept Elizabethtown Col Elizabethtown PA 17022

SCHAEFFER, DAVID GEORGE, MATHEMATICS. *Current Pos:* asst prof, 70-75, ASSOC PROF MATH, MASS INST TECHNOL, 75- *Personal Data:* b Cincinnati, Ohio, Oct 6, 42; m 70. *Educ:* Univ Ill, Urbana, BS, 63; Mass Inst Technol, PhD(math), 68. *Prof Exp:* Instr math, Brandeis Univ, 68-70. *Mem:* Am Math Soc. *Res:* Partial differential equations; approximations by finite differences; functional analysis. *Mailing Add:* Dept Math Duke Univ Durham NC 27708-0251

SCHAEFFER, DAVID JOSEPH, ENVIRONMENTAL TOXICOLOGY, RISK ASSESSMENT. *Current Pos:* ENVIRON TOXICOLOGIST, CORPS ENGRS, CONSTRUCT ENG RES LAB, 85- *Personal Data:* b Brooklyn, NY, Feb 7, 43; m 70; c 2. *Educ:* Brooklyn Col, BS, 63; Northwestern Univ, MS, 65; City Univ NY, PhD(org chem), 69. *Prof Exp:* Lectr, Brooklyn Col, 65-69; res assoc, State Univ NY Binghamton, 69-70; asst prof, Sangamon State Univ, 70-72; adv environ sci, Ill Environ Protection Agency, 72-85. *Concurrent Pos:* Adj assoc prof toxicol, Southern Ill Univ, 79-; adj asst prof health serv, Sangamon State Univ, 80; Hill scholar in residence, Univ Minn, 85. *Mem:* Am Chem Soc; NY Acad Sci; Int Asn Gt Lakes Res; Am Statist Asn; Nat Speleol Soc. *Res:* Environmental chemistry of water pollutants; statistical properties, chance mechanisms and quality control of environmental data. *Mailing Add:* 3502 Roxford Dr Champaign IL 61821-5228

SCHAEFFER, GENE THOMAS, METALLURGY. *Current Pos:* ADVAN DEVELOP ENGR, CHEM & METALL DIV, GTE SYLVANIA INC, 65- *Personal Data:* b Reading, Pa, Jan 15, 32; m 57; c 3. *Educ:* Albright Col, BS, 56; Syracuse Univ, MS, 61, PhD(solid state sci & technol), 65. *Prof Exp:* Process engr, Western Elec Co, Inc, 56-57. *Mem:* Am Inst Mining, Metall & Petrol Engrs; Am Soc Metals; Sigma Xi. *Res:* Heavy metals; mechanical properties of materials; properties and processing of incandescent lamp metals. *Mailing Add:* 16 Thomas St Towanda PA 18848-1526

SCHAEFFER, HAROLD F(RANKLIN), CHEMICAL MICROSCOPY, PHYSICAL CHEMISTRY. *Current Pos:* prof, 59-68, res prof, 68-76, EMER PROF CHEM, WESTMINSTER COL, 76-; CONSULT, SCHAEFFER RES ASSOC, 76- *Personal Data:* b Philadelphia, Pa, Sept 21, 99; m 32, Katherine A Fisher; c 1. *Educ:* Muhlenberg Col, BSc, 22; Univ NH, MSc, 26. *Prof Exp:* High sch teacher, Pa, 22-24; asst agr chem, Univ NH, 24-26; prof chem, Waynesburg Col, 26-42, head dept, 40-42; instr, Univ Mo, 42-43; prof, Col Our Lady of the Elms, 43-44; res assoc in chg sulfur-org res lab, Univ Ala, 44-48; asst prof chem, Valparaiso, 48-52; res scientist, US Army Ord, Rensselaer Polytech, 52-53; prof chem, Grove City Col, 53-55; prof & head dept, Col Emporia, 55-59. *Concurrent Pos:* Abstractor, Chem Abstracts, 48-76; Res Corp grants, 54, 57 & 60; vist scientist, Mo high schs, 65-67. *Mem:* AAAS; Am Chem Soc; Am Microchem Soc; Sigma Xi. *Res:* Direct sulfuration of organic compounds; microscopic methods in chemistry; chemical microscopy of platinum metals; quantitative microscopy; thermal microscopy; reactions of organic squarates and other heterocyclic amines. *Mailing Add:* 15 E Chestnut St Fulton MO 65251-1501

SCHAEFFER, HOWARD JOHN, MEDICINAL CHEMISTRY. *Current Pos:* mem staff, 77-, VPRES RES, DEVELOP & MED, BURROUGHS WELLCOME CO, 86- *Personal Data:* b Rochester, NY, Mar 14, 27; m 50; c 4. *Educ:* Univ Fla, PhD(pharmaceut chem), 55. *Honors & Awards:* Ebert Prize, Am Pharmaceut Asn; Bristol Award Chemotherapy. *Prof Exp:* Sr scientist, Southern Res Inst, 55-57, head pharmaceut chem sect, 57-59; assoc prof med chem & actg chmn dept, State Univ NY Buffalo, 59-63, prof, 63-70, chmn dept, 65-70; dept head org chem, Wellcome Res Labs, Burroughs Wellcome Co, 70-74; mem fac, Med Col Va, Va Commonwealth Univ, 74-77. *Mem:* Am Chem Soc; Acad Pharmaceut Sci; Sigma Xi. *Res:* Enzyme inhibition; kinetics; stereochemistry; antiviral chemotherapy. *Mailing Add:* 123 Bruce Dr Cary NC 27511-6303

SCHAEFFER, JAMES ROBERT, ORGANIC CHEMISTRY, MICROBIOLOGY. *Current Pos:* RETIRED. *Personal Data:* b Rochester, NY, Aug 2, 33; m 67, Nancy Palcic; c Christopher, Paul, Susan & Daniel. *Educ:* Univ Notre Dame, BS, 55; Univ Pa, PhD(org chem), 59. *Prof Exp:* Res chemist, Synthetic Chem Div, Eastman Kodak Co, 60-62, from res chemist to sr res chemist, Chem Div, 62-69, res assoc, Res Labs, 69-94; res fel J&J, 94-97. *Concurrent Pos:* US Army Off Ord Res fel, Northwestern Univ, 59-60. *Mem:* Am Chem Soc. *Res:* Chelate, dye and microbiological chemistry; organic sulfur compounds; development laboratory studies in organic synthesis; application of fermentation techniques to the synthesis of organic compounds; preparation of biocatalysts; development of thin films for use in clinical analysis. *Mailing Add:* 49 Jackson Rd Exten Penfield NY 14526

SCHAEFFER, JOHN FREDERICK, EPITHELIAL TRANSPORT. *Current Pos:* ASSOC PROF PHYSIOL & BIOPHYSICS, SCH MED, IND UNIV, 78- *Educ:* Syracuse Univ, PhD(physiol), 70. *Mailing Add:* Ind Univ Sch Med 8600 University Blvd Evansville IN 47712-3534

SCHAEFFER, LEE ALLEN, ORGANIC CHEMISTRY. *Current Pos:* RES ASSOC, CROMPTON & KNOWLES CORP, 73- *Personal Data:* b Allentown, Pa, June 20, 43; m 70. *Educ:* Lehigh Univ, BS, 65, MS, 69, PhD(org chem), 72. *Prof Exp:* Chemist, Lubrizol Corp, Cleveland, Ohio, 65-67. *Mem:* Am Chem Soc; Am Asn Textile Chemists & Colorists; Sigma Xi. *Res:* Preparation of dyes and related chemicals. *Mailing Add:* 16 Stoney Ridge Dr Mertztown PA 19539-9228

SCHAEFFER, LEONARD DAVID, HEALTHCARE. *Current Pos:* CHMN & CHIEF EXEC OFFICER, BLUE CROSS CALIF, 86-; CHMN & CHIEF EXEC OFFICER, WELLPOINT HEALTH NETWORKS INC, 92- *Personal Data:* b Chicago, Ill, July 28, 45; m 68, Pamela L Sidford; c David & Jacqueline. *Educ:* Princeton Univ, BA, 69. *Honors & Awards:* Outstanding Serv Citation, Am Acad Pediat, 81. *Prof Exp:* Mgt consult, Arthur Andersen & Co, 69-73; dep dir mgt, Ill Ment Health/Develop Disability, Springfield, 73-75; dir, Ill Bur Budget, 75-76; vpres, Citibank NAm, New York, 76-78; asst secy mgt & budget, Dept Health & Human Servs, 78, adminr, Health Care Finance Admin, 78-80; exec vpres & chief operating officer, Student Loan Mkt Asn, Washington, 80-82; pres & chief exec officer, Group Health Inc, Minneapolis, 83-86. *Concurrent Pos:* Bd dirs, Allergan Inc & Metra Biosysts; Kellogg Found fel, 81-89; mem, Cong Prospective Payment Assessment Comn, 87-93; bd counrs, Sch Pub Admin, Univ Calif, 88-; mem, PEW Health Professions Comt, Philadelphia, 90-93; int fel, Kings Fund Col, London, 90; chmn, Nat Inst Health Care Mgt, 93-; mem, Coun Econ Impact Health Systs Change, 96- *Mem:* Inst Med-Nat Acad Sci. *Mailing Add:* Blue Cross Calif 21555 Oxnard St Woodland Hills CA 91367-4943

SCHAEFFER, MORRIS, medicine, microbiology, for more information see previous edition

SCHAEFFER, PETER VIKTOR, REGIONAL & COMMUNITY ECONOMIC DEVELOPMENT, LABOR MIGRATION. *Current Pos:* DIR & PROF RESOURCE ECON, WVA UNIV, 93-; FAC ASSOC, REGIONAL RES INST, 93- *Personal Data:* b Zurich, Switz, 1949; US & Swiss citizen; m 76, Patricia M Dresler; c Joseph V. *Educ:* Univ Zurich, Licentiate, 75; Univ Southern Calif, MA, 79, PhD(econ), 81. *Prof Exp:* Consult, Carl Fingerhuth & Partners, Urban & Regional Planners, 74-76; asst prof urban & regional planning, Univ Ill, Urbana-Champaign, 82-88; assoc prof, Univ Colo, Denver, 87-93, dir, 88-93. *Concurrent Pos:* Vis scholar, Int Labour Off, UN, 90; adj prof, Union Inst, 90-92. *Mem:* Am Econ Asn; Am Asn Univ Profs; Regional Sci Asn Int (treas, 87-97); Am Agr Econ Asn; Soc Labor Economists. *Res:* Labor migration; international labor migration; local and regional economic development; human capital. *Mailing Add:* Div Resource Mgt WVa Univ Morgantown WV 26506-6108. *Fax:* 304-293-3752; *E-Mail:* pschaef@wvu.edu

SCHAEFFER, RILEY, INORGANIC CHEMISTRY. *Current Pos:* PROF & CHMN, DEPT CHEM, UNIV NMEX, 81- *Personal Data:* b Michigan City, Ind, July 3, 27; m 50; c 4. *Educ:* Univ Chicago, BS, 46, PhD(chem), 49. *Prof Exp:* Res chemist, Univ Chicago, 49-52; from asst prof to assoc prof chem, Iowa State Univ, 52-58; from assoc prof to prof, Ind Univ, Bloomington, 58-75, chmn dept, 67-72; dean arts & sci, Univ Wyo, 76-77, prof chem, 76-81. *Concurrent Pos:* NSF sr fel, 61-62; Guggenheim fel, 65-66; bd mem, Petrol Res Found, 70-72; vis comt inorg mat, Nat Bur Standards, 73-79; mem adv comt, NSF, 77-83. *Mem:* Am Chem Soc; fel AAAS; Am Asn Univ Professors; Sigma Xi; hon fel Royal Soc Chem. *Res:* Inorganic and physical inorganic chemistry of hydrides; chemistry of covalent inorganic compounds; archaeology; metal-oxygen clusters; structural inorganic chemistry; x-ray diffraction. *Mailing Add:* 2065 Hillsdale Circle Boulder CO 80303-5617

SCHAEFFER, ROBERT L, JR, plant taxonomy, for more information see previous edition

SCHAEFFER, WARREN IRA, BACTERIOLOGY, CELL BIOLOGY. *Current Pos:* assoc prof, Univ Vt, 67-77, actg chmn, 77-79, chmn, 79-88, PROF MED MICROBIOL, COL MED, UNIV VT, 77- *Personal Data:* b Newark, NJ, Aug 13, 38. *Educ:* Rutgers Univ, BS, 60, MS, 62, PhD(bact), 64. *Prof Exp:* Res assoc cell biol, Mass Inst Technol, 64-66; asst prof med microbiol, Univ Calif-Calif Col Med, 66-67. *Concurrent Pos:* Chair Terminology Comt, Tissue Cult Asn, Terminology Comt, Int Asn Cell Cult; chair mem comt, Tissue Cult Asn, counr-at-large. *Mem:* AAAS; Am Soc Microbiol; Sigma Xi; Tissue Cult Asn (secy, 84-88). *Res:* Tissue culture; effects of biologically active agents in cell cultures; expression and maintenance of the carcinogenic state; in vitro aging of epithelial cells; mycoplasmology. *Mailing Add:* 24 Southwind Dr Burlington VT 05401-5470. *Fax:* 802-656-8749; *E-Mail:* wschaeff@moose.uvm.edu

SCHAEFFER, WILLIAM DWIGHT, COLLOID CHEMISTRY. *Current Pos:* EXEC DIR, ENVIRON CONSERV BD GRAPHIC COMMUN INDUSTS INC, 86- *Personal Data:* b Reading, Pa, Dec 4, 21; m 46; c 3. *Educ:* Lehigh Univ, BS, 43, MS, 47, PhD(chem), 67. *Prof Exp:* Asst instr chem, Lehigh Univ, 44-47; chemist & group leader, Res & Develop Dept, Godfrey L Cabot, Inc, 47-55; assoc res dir, Nat Printing Ink Res Inst, Lehigh Univ, 55-69; res dir, Graphic Arts Tech Found, 69-89. *Concurrent Pos:* Vchmn, Int Asn Res Insts Graphic Arts Indust, 71-77; exec dir, Environ Conserv Bd, Graphic Commun Industs Inc, 86- *Mem:* Am Chem Soc; Tech Asn Pulp & Paper Indust; NY Acad Sci; Tech Asn Graphic Arts (pres, 69-70); Inter-Soc Color Coun (pres, 81-82); Sigma Xi. *Res:* Physical colloid and surface chemistry; carbon blacks; printing and printing inks; dispersions of pigments; environmental science. *Mailing Add:* 128 Woodshire Dr Pittsburgh PA 15215-1714

SCHAEFGEN, JOHN RAYMOND, POLYMER CHEMISTRY, MATERIALS SCIENCE ENGINEERING. *Current Pos:* CONSULT, ELJAY ASSOC, INC, 83- *Personal Data:* b Wilmette, Ill, Apr 9, 18; m 45, Laura McConathy; c John Jr, Elizabeth, Susan, Robert, Madelyn, Mary, Kathryn, Caroline & Peter. *Educ:* Northwestern Univ, Ill, BS, 40; Ohio State Univ, PhD(phys org chem), 44. *Prof Exp:* Sr chemist, Res Lab, Goodyear Tire & Rubber Co, 44-51; jr res assoc, Textile Fibers Dept, Pioneering Res, E I DuPont de Nemours & Co, Inc, 51-58, res assoc, 58-77, res fel, 77-82. *Mem:* Am Chem Soc. *Res:* Physical organic chemistry; mechanisms of organic reactions; synthesis and study of properties of high polymers; fiber technology. *Mailing Add:* 129 Cambridge Dr Wilmington DE 19803

SCHAER, JONATHAN, MATHEMATICS. *Current Pos:* ASSOC PROF MATH, UNIV CALGARY, 67- *Personal Data:* b Bern, Switz, Oct 1, 29; m 63; c 2. *Educ:* Univ Bern, dipl educ, 52 & 57, Dr Phil(theoret physics), 62. *Prof Exp:* Pub sch teacher, Bern, Switz, 55-56; asst physics, Univ Bern, 56-57; asst math, Swiss Fed Inst Technol, 57-58; asst physics, Univ Bern, 58-62; asst prof math, Univ Alta, 62-67. *Mem:* Can Math Soc; Am Math Soc; Math Asn Am. *Res:* Geometry; convexity; combinatorics; theory of relativity. *Mailing Add:* Dept Math Univ Calgary 2500 University Dr NW Calgary AB T2N 1N4 Can

SCHAERF, HENRY MAXIMILIAN, MEASURE THEORY, INTEGRATION THEORY. *Current Pos:* from asst prof to assoc prof, 47-75, EMER ASSOC PROF MATH, WASH UNIV, 75- *Personal Data:* b Rohatyn, Poland, Mar 17, 07; nat US. *Educ:* Univ Lwow, MA, 29; Univ Goettingen, actuary's cert, 31; Swiss Fed Inst Technol, DSc, 43. *Prof Exp:* Head, Actuarial Dept, Der Anker Ins Co, Poland, 31-37; chief actuary, Vita-Kotwica Life Ins Co, 37-39; lectr math, Polish mil internees, Switz, 41-44; privat docent, Swiss Fed Inst Technol, 45-48; instr, Mont State Col, 46-47. *Concurrent Pos:* Ford Found fel, Inst Advan Study, NJ & Denmark, 53-54; mem, US Army Math Res Ctr, Univ Wis, 58 & 61, vis prof, Ctr, 62-64; assoc prof, McGill Univ, 64-72. *Mem:* Am Math Soc; Swiss Math Soc; Swiss Asn Actuaries; Polish Math Soc. *Res:* Actuarial theory; real variables; measure and integration theory; structure and cardinality of bases; topological properties of maps; invariant measures; mathematical foundations of actuarial theory. *Mailing Add:* 600 W Olympic Pl Apt 507 Seattle WA 98119-3659

SCHAETZL, RANDALL J, PHYSICAL GEOGRAPHY OF MICHIGAN, SOIL GENESIS. *Current Pos:* asst prof, 87-92, ASSOC PROF, DEPT GEOG, MICH STATE UNIV, 92-, PROF DEPT GEOL SCI, 94- *Personal Data:* b Wausau, Wis, Apr 12, 57; m 91, Julia Brixie; c Madeline, Annika & Heidi. *Educ:* Univ Wis, Madison, BS, 80; Univ Kans, MA, 83; Univ Ill, Urbana, Champaign, PhD(geog), 87. *Prof Exp:* Res asst, Ill State Water Surv, 85-86. *Mem:* Am Quaternary Asn; Am Soc Agron; Asn Am Geographers; Geol Soc

Am; Soil Sci Soc Am. *Res:* Spatial interactions among soil/surficial physical systems, geomorphology, climate and hydrology or biola; problems related to soil geomorphology and geography; surficial processes; soil genesis and soil water; plant geography. *Mailing Add:* Mich State Univ 315 Natural Sci East Lansing MI 48824-1115. *Fax:* 517-432-1671; *E-Mail:* schaetzl@pilot.msu.edu

SCHAETZLE, WALTER J(ACOB), MECHANICAL ENGINEERING. *Current Pos:* RETIRED. *Personal Data:* b Pittsburgh, Pa, Feb 17, 34; m 65; c 2. *Educ:* Carnegie Inst Technol, BS, 57, MS, 58; Wash Univ, DSc(mech eng), 62. *Prof Exp:* Propulsion engr, McDonnell Aircraft Corp, 58-62; from asst prof to assoc prof, Univ Ala, Tuscaloosa, 62-66, prof mech eng, 66- *Concurrent Pos:* Mem staff, Col Petrol, Saudi Arabia, 69-71. *Mem:* Am Soc Mech Engrs; Am Soc Heating, Refrig & Air Conditioning Engrs; Am Soc Eng Educ; Int Solar Energy Soc. *Res:* Rarefied gas flow; experiments in molecule surface interactions; thermal energy storage; community energy systems; man produced energy tornado correlations; heating and cooling systems; heat pump systems; home energy conservation; solar energy. *Mailing Add:* Oak Bluff Dr Northport AL 35476

SCHAFER, ALICE TURNER, ABSTRACT ALGEBRA, MATHEMATICS. *Current Pos:* RETIRED. *Personal Data:* b Richmond, Va, June 18, 15; m 42, Richard; c John Dickerson & Richard Stone. *Educ:* Univ Richmond, BA, 36; Univ Chicago, MS, 40, PhD(math), 42. *Hon Degrees:* DSc, Univ Richmond, 64. *Prof Exp:* High sch teacher math, Va, 36-39; instr, Conn Col, 42-44; mathematician, Off Sci Res & Develop, Appl Physics Lab, Johns Hopkins Univ, 45; instr, Univ Mich, 45-46; lectr, Douglass Col, 46-48; asst prof, Swarthmore Col, 48-51 & Drexel Inst Technol, 51-53; from asst prof to prof, Conn Col, 54-62; prof, Wellesley Col, 62-69, Helen Day Gould prof math, 69-80; prof, Marymount Univ, 89-96. *Concurrent Pos:* NSF sci fac fel, 58-59; mem, Inst Advan Study, 58-59; co-ed, Asn Women Math Newslett, 75-76; consult, Radcliffe Col Sem, Harvard Univ, 80-85; lectr math, Simmons Col, 80-88. *Mem:* Asn Women Math (pres, 73-75, co-treas, 75-76); Am Math Soc; Am Asn Univ Prof; Math Asn Am; AAAS; Int Cong Mathematicians; Sigma Xi. *Res:* Group theory; projective differential geometry. *Mailing Add:* 2725 N Pollard St Arlington VA 22207-5038. *Fax:* 703-284-3859

SCHAFER, DAVID EDWARD, MEDICAL RESEARCH. *Current Pos:* LECTR PHYSIOL, SCH MED, YALE UNIV, 73- *Personal Data:* b Wichita, Kans, Mar 8, 31; m 49; c 2. *Educ:* Friends Univ, AB, 48; Univ Minn, PhD, 59. *Prof Exp:* Asst English, Univ Minn, 48-51, asst physiol, 53-56, instr, 57-58; from instr to asst prof, Sch Med, NY Univ, 58-63; asst prof pathobiol, Johns Hopkins Univ Ctr Med Res & Training, Calcutta, India, 64-66; mem field staff, Rockefeller Found, 66-68; res physiologist, Exp Surg Lab, Vet Admin Hosp, Minneapolis, 68-73; res psychologist, Vet Admin Hosp, West Haven, 73- *Concurrent Pos:* Fulbright lectr, Sci Col, Calcutta Univ, 63-64; vis prof physiol & actg head dept, Fac Med Sci, Bangkok, 66-68; asst prof physiol, Med Sch, Univ Minn, Minneapolis, 68-73. *Mem:* AAAS; Biophys Soc; Soc Math Biol; Sigma Xi. *Res:* Cell physiology; perfusion; membrane permeability; gastrointestinal physiology; cholera. *Mailing Add:* Med Serv Vet Admin Hosp West Haven CT 06516. *Fax:* 203-230-1329

SCHAFER, IRWIN ARNOLD, PEDIATRICS, GENETICS. *Current Pos:* assoc prof, 67-74, PROF PEDIAT, SCH MED, CASE WESTERN RES UNIV, 74-, PROF GENETICS, 88- *Personal Data:* b Pittsburgh, Pa, Mar 22, 28; m 48; c 3. *Educ:* Univ Pittsburgh, BS, 48, MD, 53; Am Bd Pediat, dipl, 59; Am Bd Med Genetics, dipl, 84. *Prof Exp:* Intern, Montefiore Hosp, Pittsburgh, 53-54; epidemic intel off & chief hepatitis invest unit, Commun Dis Ctr, USPHS, 54-56; jr asst resident, Children's Hosp Med Ctr, Boston, 56-58; from instr to asst prof pediat, Stanford Univ, 61-67. *Concurrent Pos:* Res fel med, Children's Hosp Med Ctr, Boston, 58-61; res fel prev med, Harvard Med Sch, 58-61; dir premature infant res ctr, USPHS, 63-64, dir birth defects study ctr, 64-69; pediatrician, Case Western Univ Hosp & Cleveland Metrop Gen Hosp; dir, Genetics Prog, Cleveland Metrop Gen Hosp. *Mem:* Am Pediat Soc; Am Soc Pediat Res; Am Soc Human Genetics; Am Soc Cell Biol; Tissue Cult Asn. *Res:* Metabolism of cells in culture; cell differentiation and biology; embryonic organogenesis; biochemical genetics. *Mailing Add:* Metro Health Med Ctr 3395 Scanton Rd Rm H457 Cleveland OH 44109-1998. *Fax:* 330-456-4223

SCHAFER, JAMES A, MATHEMATICS. *Current Pos:* ASSOC PROF MATH, UNIV MD, COLLEGE PARK, 70- *Personal Data:* b Rochester, NY, Dec 11, 39; m 61; c 2. *Educ:* Univ Rochester, BA, 61; Univ Chicago, MS, 62, PhD(math), 65. *Prof Exp:* Asst prof math, Univ Mich, Ann Arbor, 65-70. *Concurrent Pos:* Vis lectr, Aarhus Univ, 69-71 & 78-79. *Mem:* Am Math Soc. *Res:* Algebraic topology; homological algebra. *Mailing Add:* Dept Math Univ Md College Park MD 20742-0001

SCHAFER, JAMES ARTHUR, KIDNEY EPITHELIA. *Current Pos:* from asst prof to assoc prof physiol, 70-76, from asst prof to assoc prof med, 70-80, PROF PHYSIOL, UNIV ALA, 76-, PROF MED, 80-, SR SCIENTIST, NEPHROLOGY RES & TRAINING CTR, 77- *Personal Data:* b Buffalo, NY, Oct 10, 41; m 64, Margaret Shiefer; c James A Jr & Kirsten A. *Educ:* Univ Mich, BS, 63, PhD(physiol), 68. *Honors & Awards:* Estab Investr Award, Am Heart Asn, 71; Robert F Pitts Mem Award for Outstanding Res Kidney Physiol; Int Cong Physiol Sci, Austrailia, 83; Homer W Smith Award, 94; Max Planck Prize, Von Humboldt Foud & Max Planck Soc Ger, 94. *Prof Exp:* Fel biochem, Gustav-Embden Ctr, WGer, 68-69; fel physiol, Duke Univ, 69-70. *Concurrent Pos:* Ed bd, J Gen Physiol, 79-, ed, Am J Physiol, 83-89; Welcome vis prof, Dartmouth, 86; chmn res comt, Nat Kidney & Urol Dis Adv Bd, 87-90; invited prof, Dept Pharmacol & Toxicol, Univ Lansanne, Switz, 91; mem coun, Am Physiol Soc, 91-; bd mem, Fedn Am Socs Exp Biol, 96- *Mem:* Am Physiol Soc (pres-elect, 95-96, pres, 96-97); Am Soc Nephrol (secy-treas, 89-92); Biophys Soc; Am Fedn Clin Res; Am Heart Asn; hon mem Am Soc Clin Invest. *Res:* Regulation of transport process in renal tubules by intracellular second messengers and gene expression. *Mailing Add:* Dept Physiol & Biophys Univ Ala Birmingham 1918 University Blvd Rm 958 Birmingham AL 35294-0005. *Fax:* 205-934-5787; *E-Mail:* jschafer@uab.edu

SCHAFER, JOHN FRANCIS, PLANT PATHOLOGY. *Current Pos:* RETIRED. *Personal Data:* b Pullman, Wash, Feb 17, 21; m 47, Joyce Marcks; c Patricia, Janice & James. *Educ:* Wash State Univ, BS, 42; Univ Wis, PhD(plant path, agron), 50. *Prof Exp:* Agt, Bur Plant Indust, USDA, 39-42; asst plant path, Univ Wis, 46-49; from asst prof to prof, Purdue Univ, 49-68; prof & head dept, Kans State Univ, 68-72; prof & chmn dept, Wash State Univ, 72-80; integrated pest mgt coordr, Sci & Educ Admin, Univ Minn, USDA, 80-81, actg nat res prog leader plant path & nematol, Agr Res Serv, 81-82, dir, 82-87, collabr, Cereal Rust Lab, Agr Res Serv, 87-95. *Concurrent Pos:* Vis res prof, Duquesne Univ, 65-66; adj prof plant path, Univ Minn, 82-92. *Mem:* Fel AAAS; fel Am Phytopath Soc (pres, 78-79); Am Soc Agron. *Res:* Diseases of cereal crops; cereal breeding; plant disease resistance. *Mailing Add:* 4949 Snyder Lane Apt 108 Rohnert Park CA 94928-4851

SCHAFER, JOHN WILLIAM, JR, SOIL SCIENCE, SOIL GEOGRAPHY. *Current Pos:* Assoc prof, 68-80, PROF AGRON, IOWA STATE UNIV, 80- *Personal Data:* b Mt Pleasant, Mich, May 18, 37; m 67; c 3. *Educ:* Mich State Univ, BS, 59, PhD(soil sci), 68; Kans State Univ, MS, 60. *Honors & Awards:* Wilton Park Award; Agron Educ Award, Am Soc Agron. *Concurrent Pos:* Vis prof, Shenyang Agr Col, People's Repub China. *Mem:* Am Soc Agron; Soil Sci Soc Am; fel Nat Asn Cols & Teachers Agr; Soil Conserv Soc Am. *Res:* Relationships of soils to landscapes and their influence on land use and food production; new methods for effective teaching of undergraduate soil science; use of indigenous, knowledge of soils in decision making. *Mailing Add:* Dept Agron 1126 Agron Iowa State Univ Ames IA 50011-1201

SCHAFER, LOTHAR, PHYSICAL CHEMISTRY, INORGANIC CHEMISTRY. *Current Pos:* from asst prof to assoc prof phys chem, 68-75, PROF PHYS CHEM, UNIV ARK, FAYETTEVILLE, 75- *Personal Data:* b Dusseldorf, WGer, May 5, 39; m 65; c 2. *Educ:* Univ Munich, dipl, 62, PhD(inorg chem), 65. *Honors & Awards:* IR-100 Award, 85. *Prof Exp:* NATO fel chem, Oslo, 65-67; res assoc, Ind Univ, Bloomington, 67-68. *Concurrent Pos:* Teacher-scholar grant, Dreyfus Found, 71. *Mem:* Am Chem Soc; Royal Soc Chem; Am Inst Physics. *Res:* Structural studies by abinitio calculations, electron diffraction and spectroscopy; theoretical investigations of biophysical phenomena. *Mailing Add:* Dept Chem Univ Ark Fayetteville AR 72701

SCHAFER, MARY LOUISE, FOOD CHEMISTRY. *Current Pos:* RETIRED. *Personal Data:* b Shelburn, Ind, Nov 4, 15. *Educ:* Purdue Univ, BS, 38, PhD(chem), 55; Columbia Univ, MS, 49. *Prof Exp:* Intern, Univ Hosp, Western Reserve Univ, 39, dietitian, 40-42; asst nutrit, Teachers Col, Columbia Univ, 47-51; asst chem, Purdue Univ, 51-54; chemist, USPHS, Ohio, 55-69; chemist, Cincinnati Res Labs, Food & Drug Admin, 69-84. *Mem:* Am Chem Soc; Am Dietetic Asn; Sigma Xi. *Res:* Detection and assay methods for organomercury compounds in the environment; gas chromatographic methods for microbiological assessment of canned foods. *Mailing Add:* 6522 Sherman St Cincinnati OH 45230-2846

SCHAFER, RICHARD DONALD, MATHEMATICS. *Current Pos:* dep head dept, 59-68, prof, 59-88, EMER PROF MATH, MASS INST TECHNOL, 88- *Personal Data:* b Buffalo, NY, Feb 25, 18; m 42, Alice Turner; c John D & Richard S. *Educ:* Univ Buffalo, BA, 38, MA, 40; Univ Chicago, PhD(math), 42. *Prof Exp:* Instr math, Univ Mich, 45-46; mem, Inst Advan Study, 46-48; asst prof math, Univ Pa, 48-53; prof & head dept, Univ Conn, 53-59. *Concurrent Pos:* NSF sr fel, Inst Advan Study, 58-59; mem, Sci Manpower Comn, 59-63; vis lectr, Math Asn Am, 57-58. *Mem:* Am Math Soc (assoc secy, 54-58); Math Asn Am. *Res:* Nonassociative and Lie algebras. *Mailing Add:* Dept Math Rm 2-263 Mass Inst Technol Cambridge MA 02139

SCHAFER, ROBERT LOUIS, AGRICULTURAL ENGINEERING, ENGINEERING MECHANICS. *Current Pos:* Agr engr, Agr Res Serv, Ames, Iowa, 59-64, agr engr, Nat Tillage Mach Lab, 64-85, AGR ENG, NAT SOIL DYNAMICS LAB, AGR RES SERV, USDA, 85- *Personal Data:* b Burlington, Iowa, Aug 1, 37; m 59, Carolyn Henn; c Elizabeth D. *Educ:* Iowa State Univ, BS, 59, MS, 61, PhD(agr eng, eng mech), 65. *Concurrent Pos:* Res lectr, Auburn Univ, 70-81, adj prof, 81- *Mem:* Fel Am Soc Agr Engrs; Int Soc Terrain Vehicle Systs; Inst Elec & Electronics Engrs Comput Soc. *Res:* Soil dynamics as a mechanics of the actions of tillage tools and traction devices in soil. *Mailing Add:* PO Box 57 Loachapoka AL 36865-0057. *Fax:* 800-468-6144; *E-Mail:* ris@poka.la.com

SCHAFER, ROLLIE R, NEUROSCIENCE. *Current Pos:* asst grad dean, Univ NTex, 78-82, assoc dean sci & technol, 86-87, assoc vpres res & dean, Grad Sch, 87-97, PROF BIOL SCI, UNIV NTEX, 84-, VPROVOST RES, 97- *Personal Data:* b Denver, Colo, Feb 17, 42; m 64, Sue Pestotnik; c Anthony & Benjamin. *Educ:* Univ Colo, Boulder, BA, 64, MA, 67, PhD(zool), 69. *Prof Exp:* Asst prof biol, Metrop State Col Colo, 68-69 & NMex Inst Mining & Technol, 69-73; asst prof biol sci, Div Biol Sci, Univ Mich, Ann Arbor, 73-76. *Concurrent Pos:* NSF res grants, 72-73, 74-76, 81-83 & 85-88; Dept Energy grants, 93-96. *Mem:* AAAS; Sigma Xi; Am Soc Neurochem; Soc Neurosci; Asn Chemoreception Sci. *Res:* Sensory mechanisms; olfactory reception/information processing; isotopes for research in medicine and the life sciences. *Mailing Add:* Provost's Off Univ NTex Box 13707 Denton TX 76203-6707. *Fax:* 817-565-4438; *E-Mail:* schafer@acad.admin.unt.edu

SCHAFER, RONALD W, ELECTRICAL ENGINEERING. *Current Pos:* REGENT'S PROF, SCH ELEC ENG, GA INST TECHNOL, 74- *Personal Data:* b Tecumseh, Nebr, Feb 17, 38; m 60; c 3. *Educ:* Univ Nebr, Lincoln, BSc, 61, MSc, 62; Mass Inst Technol, PhD(elec eng), 68. *Honors & Awards:* Emanuel R Piore Award, Inst Elec & Electronics Engrs, 80, Centennial Medal, 84. *Prof Exp:* Instr elec eng, Univ Nebr, Lincoln, 62-63 & Mass Inst Technol, 64-68; mem tech staff, Bell Tel Labs, 68-74. *Mem:* Nat Acad Eng; fel Acoust Soc Am; Acoust, Speech & Signal Processing Soc (pres, 77-79); fel Inst Elec & Electronics Engrs. *Res:* Digital signal processing for speech and image processing. *Mailing Add:* 1920 Mercedes Ct Atlanta GA 30345

SCHAFF, JOHN FRANKLIN, SCIENCE EDUCATION, PLANT PHYSIOLOGY. *Current Pos:* from assoc prof to prof, 72-91, assoc dean, Col Educ, 77-84, EMER PROF SCI EDUC, UNIV TOLEDO, 91- *Personal Data:* b Elgin, Ill, Mar 2, 31; m 54, Joanne Doris; c Cheryl, Steven, Bruce & Michael. *Educ:* Ill State Univ, BS, 53; Kans State Univ, MS, 55; Fla State Univ, EdD(sci educ), 68. *Prof Exp:* Teacher bot & gen sci, Proviso Twp High Sch, Maywood, Ill, 56-58, chem, Maine Twp High Sch E, Park Ridge, Ill, 58-61 & chem & biol, Deerfield High Sch, Ill, 61-65; nat teaching fel chem, NFla Jr Col, Madison, 65-67; asst prof sci educ, Syracuse Univ, 68-72. *Concurrent Pos:* Vis prof, State Univ NY, Geneseo, 70, Univ Wyo, 71 & Owens Tech Col, Ohio, 72-74, Ohio State Univ, 87; dir, Grants Prog for Teachers, NSF, 71-86. *Mem:* Sigma Xi; Am Chem Soc; fel AAAS; Nat Asn Res in Sci Teaching; Asn Educ Teachers Sci (pres, 78-79). *Res:* Semimicro experiments for high school chemistry; middle and junior high school science curriculum development; computer applications to high school science teaching; brain physiology and learning science. *Mailing Add:* 7633 Gillcrest Sylvania OH 43560. *E-Mail:* jschaff@uoft02.utoledo.edu

SCHAFFEL, GERSON SAMUEL, CHEMISTRY, RESEARCH ADMINISTRATION. *Current Pos:* RETIRED. *Personal Data:* b Braddock, Pa, Mar 17, 18; m 43; c 3. *Educ:* Carnegie Inst Technol, BS, 39, MS, 40, DSc(org chem), 42. *Prof Exp:* Fel, Westinghouse Res Lab, 42-43, group leader, Plastics Sect, 43-46; instr chem, Carnegie Inst Technol, 45-46; dir plastics res & develop, Gen Tire & Rubber Co, 46-50, mgr mfg & develop, Chem Div, 50-54, dir res, Brea Chem, Inc, 54-56; dir res, Sci Design Co, Inc, 56-60, asst vpres, 60-63, vpres, New York, 63-73; dir technol mgmt, Badger Co, Inc, Cambridge, 73-83; consult, 83-88. *Mem:* Am Chem Soc; fel Am Inst Chemists; NY Acad Sci. *Res:* Kinetics and mechanisms of organic reactions; mechanism of formation of condensation polymers; polymerization of vinyl compounds; new polyesters; petrochemicals; research administration; process licensing. *Mailing Add:* 63 Country Club Lane Belmont MA 02178

SCHAFFER, ARNOLD MARTIN, PHYSICAL & ANALYTICAL CHEMISTRY, INFORMATION SCIENCE. *Current Pos:* mgr catalytic cracking, 81-88, mgr anal chem, 88-91, SR RES CHEMIST, PHILLIPS PETROL CO, 74- *Personal Data:* b New York, NY, Sept 24, 42; m 63, Susan Kramer; c Scott, Mark & Jamie. *Educ:* Polytech Inst Brooklyn, BS, 63; Univ Wash, PhD(chem), 70. *Prof Exp:* Fel chem, Univ Houston, 71-74. *Concurrent Pos:* Instr, Univ Houston, 73-74; mgr tech info, 91- *Mem:* Am Chem Soc; Am Phys Soc; Am Inst Chem Eng; Indust Res Inst; Am Soc Qual Control. *Res:* Properties of heterogeneous catalysts; development of spectroscopic techniques; molecular spectroscopy; advanced mathematic techniques; development of new analytical techniques. *Mailing Add:* Phillips Petrol Co 264 RF PRC Bartlesville OK 74004. *Fax:* 918-661-7353; *E-Mail:* amsc@ppco.com

SCHAFFER, BARBARA NOYES, NEURO PEPTIDE CHEMISTRY, MOLECULAR BIOLOGY. *Personal Data:* b St Louis, Mo, June 15, 47; m 76; c 2. *Educ:* Beloit Col, BS, 69; Wash Univ, PhD(biochem), 73. *Prof Exp:* Asst prof, Univ Chicago, 77-86, Dept Psychiat, Univ Tex, 86-93. *Mem:* Am Soc Biochem & Molecular Biol; Protein Soc. *Res:* Structure and function of insect neuropeptides and their genes. *Mailing Add:* 7220 Briar Cove Dallas TX 75240

SCHAFFER, ERWIN LAMBERT, STRUCTURAL ENGINEERING, FOREST PRODUCTS & APPLICATIONS. *Current Pos:* ASST DIR RES MGT, FOREST PROD LAB, FOREST SERV, USDA, 87- *Personal Data:* b Milwaukee, Wis, Nov 26, 36; m 60; c 1. *Educ:* Univ Wis, BS, 59, MS, 61, PhD(eng mech), 71. *Honors & Awards:* Presidential Design Award, Nat Endowment for the Arts, 84; Tech Transfer Award, Fed Lab Consortium, 85; L J Markwardt Award, Am Soc Testing & Mat, 86. *Prof Exp:* Struct eng, concrete dam destruction/anal, Bur Reclamation, US Dept Interior, 61-63, res engr fire performance, 63-73, res proj leader, wood prod processing, 73-77; res proj leader fire performance, Forest Prod Lab, Forest Serv, USDA, 77-81, wood construct specialist, State & Pvt Forestry, 81-84; vpres res & develop, consult & mgt, PFS Corp, 84-87. *Concurrent Pos:* Exec secy, Soc Wood Sci & Technol, 70-73; vis scientist, Nat Bur Stand, US Dept Com, 76-77; chmn & proc ed, Residential Fire & Wood Prod Sem, Forest Prod Res Soc, 79-80; tech adv, Tech Adv Comt, Nat Forest Prod Asn, 87-; vchmn, Comt D7, Am Soc Testing & Mat, 87-; chmn, Comt Fire Protection, Struct Div, Am Soc Civil Engrs, 89-; res team leader, Forest Prod Lab, Forest Serv, USDA; chmn, Comt D7, Am Soc Testing & Mat, 90-93. *Mem:* Int Acad Wood Sci; fel Am Soc Civil Engrs; Soc Wood Sci & Technol (pres-elect, 76-77, pres, 77-78); Forest Prod Res Soc; Am Soc Testing & Mat. *Res:* Conducted and directed wood product and wood engineering research including structural fire performance; author of over 70 publications; editor, author, or contributor to several books in above fields. *Mailing Add:* 12445 W Firebird Dr Sun City West AZ 85375

SCHAFFER, ERWIN MICHAEL, PERIODONTOLOGY. *Current Pos:* Clin prof & chmn div, 57-64, dean, 64-80, PROF PERIODONTICS, SCH DENT, UNIV MINN, MINNEAPOLIS, 64- *Personal Data:* b Dumont, Minn, July 9, 22; m 47; c 4. *Educ:* Univ Minn, DDS, 45, MSD, 51. *Honors & Awards:* William J Gies Award Periodont, 74. *Mem:* Am Dent Asn; fel Am Col Dent; Am Acad Periodont; Am Acad Oral Med; Int Asn Dent Res. *Res:* Bone regeneration in periodontal disease; cartilage or cementum and dentine grafts; etiology of periodontal disease; root curettage; circadian periodicity. *Mailing Add:* Periodont/17-172 Moos Tower Univ Minn Sch Dent 515 Delaware St SE Minneapolis MN 55455

SCHAFFER, FREDERICK LELAND, VIROLOGY, BIOCHEMISTRY. *Current Pos:* RETIRED. *Personal Data:* b Kingsburg, Calif, July 5, 21; m 45, Lee Guffey; c Glenn, William, James, Liane, Daniel & Carol. *Educ:* Univ Calif, Berkeley, BA, 43, PhD(biochem), 50. *Prof Exp:* Asst, Univ Calif, Berkeley, 47-50, from asst res biochemist to res biochemist, 54-85. *Concurrent Pos:* Res fel, Univ Calif, Berkeley, 50-53, lectr med microbiol, 64-77; mem, Int Comt Taxon Viruses, 81-90. *Mem:* Fel AAAS; Am Soc Microbiol; Soc Vitro Biol; Am Soc Virol. *Res:* Tissue culture; microanalysis; purification, properties and molecular biology of viruses. *Mailing Add:* 38 Hardie Dr Moraga CA 94556

SCHAFFER, HENRY ELKIN, GENETICS. *Current Pos:* AT COMPUT CTR, NC STATE UNIV. *Personal Data:* b New York, NY, May 4, 38; m 64; c 2. *Educ:* Cornell Univ, BS, 59; NC State Univ, MS, 62, PhD(genetics), 64. *Prof Exp:* NIH fel gen med studies, Cornell Univ, 64-65; asst prof biol, Brandeis Univ, 65-66; from asst prof to assoc prof genetics, NC State Univ, 66-80, prof genetics, 74-, prof biomath, 80- *Mem:* AAAS; Biomet Soc; Genetics Soc Am; Soc Study Evolution; Am Soc Naturalists; Sigma Xi. *Res:* Population and mathematical genetics; biometrics; computing and bioinstrumentation. *Mailing Add:* NC State Univ Raleigh NC 27695-0001

SCHAFFER, JUAN JORGE, MATHEMATICS. *Current Pos:* assoc dean, 86-93, PROF MATH, CARNEGIE MELLON UNIV, PITTSBURGH, PA, 68- *Personal Data:* b Vienna, Austria, Mar 10, 30; m 59, Inge Kalbermann; c Alejandro. *Educ:* Univ Pa, MS, 51; Univ Repub Uruguay Ing Ind, 53, MS, 57; Swiss Fed Inst Technol, DrScTech, 56; Univ Zurich, DrPhil(math), 56. *Prof Exp:* Prof math & gen mech, Univ Repub Uruguay, 57-68. *Concurrent Pos:* Guggengeim fel, Univ Chicago & Res Inst Advan Study, 60; vis Carnegie prof, Carnegie Inst Technol, 64-65; vis fel, Australian Nat Univ, 76. *Mem:* Am Math Soc; Am Asn Univ Prof; Uruguayan Asn Adv Sci. *Res:* Differential equations; functional analysis; author and co-author of four books. *Mailing Add:* Dept Math Sci Carnegie Mellon Univ Pittsburgh PA 15213-3890. *Fax:* 412-268-6380; *E-Mail:* js6n@andrew.cmu.edu

SCHAFFER, PRISCILLA ANN, VIROLOGY. *Current Pos:* assoc prof, 76-81, PROF MICROBIOL, DEPT MICROBIOL & MOLECULAR GENETICS, HARVARD MED SCH, 81- *Personal Data:* b St Louis, Mo, Dec 28, 41. *Educ:* Hobart & William Smith Cols, BA, 64; Cornell Univ, PhD(microbiol), 69. *Prof Exp:* Asst prof virol, Dept Virol & Epidemiol, Baylor Col Med, 71-76. *Concurrent Pos:* Fel, Baylor Col Med, 69-71; Found lectr, Am Soc Microbiol, 81-82. *Mem:* AAAS; Am Soc Microbiol; Am Soc Trop Med & Hyg; Brit Soc Gen Microbiol. *Res:* Genetics of DNA tumor viruses, especially herpesviruses. *Mailing Add:* Dana-Farber Cancer Inst 44 Binney St Boston MA 02115-6084

SCHAFFER, ROBERT, analytical chemistry, bio-organic chemistry, for more information see previous edition

SCHAFFER, SHELDON ARTHUR, BIOLOGICAL CHEMISTRY. *Current Pos:* DIR, ATHEROSCLEROSIS RES, CIBA-GEIGY CO, 85- *Personal Data:* b Salt Lake City, Utah, June 12, 43; m 66; c 3. *Educ:* Univ Calif, Berkeley, BS, 65; Univ Ill, Urbana, PhD(chem), 70. *Prof Exp:* NIH res fel biol chem, Med Sch, Harvard Univ, 70-72, teaching fel biochem, 72-73; res biochemist immunol, Am Cyanamid Co, 73-74, group leader atherosclerosis res, 74-81, head, dept metab & endocrinol res, med res div, 81-85. *Mem:* Am Chem Soc; Am Heart Asn; Royal Soc Chem. *Res:* Lipids chemistry and metabolism; atherosclerosis; platelet structure and function; membrane biochemistry. *Mailing Add:* 1934 Rosecrest Dr Oakland CA 94602. *Fax:* 510-732-7227

SCHAFFER, STEPHEN WARD, BIOCHEMISTRY. *Current Pos:* assoc prof, 80-88, PROF PHARMACOL, UNIV SALA, 88- *Personal Data:* b San Diego, Calif, Oct 15, 44; m 67; c 2. *Educ:* Buena Vista Col, BS, 66; Univ Minn, PhD(biochem), 70. *Prof Exp:* Vis prof biochem, Univ El Salvador, 70-71; fel, Johnson Found, Univ Pa, 71-73; from asst prof to assoc prof biochem, Lehigh Univ, 73-80; res assoc prof physiol, Hahnemann Med Col, 78-80. *Concurrent Pos:* Pres, Southeast Pharmacol Soc. *Mem:* Am Chem Soc; Int Soc Heart Res; Am Soc Biol Chemists; Am Soc Pharmacol & Exp Therapeut; Am Col Clin Pharmacol. *Res:* Regulation of myocardial calcium, effects of taurine and sulfonylureas, and diabetic cardiomyopathy. *Mailing Add:* Dept Pharmacol Col Med Univ SAla Mobile AL 36688-0001. *Fax:* 334-460-6798

SCHAFFER, WILLIAM MORRIS, ECOLOGY. *Current Pos:* asst prof, 75-77, assoc prof biol, 77-80, ASSOC PROF ECOL & EVOLUTIONARY BIOL, UNIV ARIZ, 80- *Personal Data:* b Elizabeth, NJ, May 11, 45; m 70. *Educ:* Yale Univ, BS, 67; Princeton Univ, MS, 71, PhD(biol), 72. *Prof Exp:* Asst prof biol, Univ Utah, 72-75. *Mem:* AAAS; Sigma Xi; Soc Study Evolution; Ecol Soc Am; Am Soc Naturalists. *Res:* Evolutionary and ecological aspects of reproductive strategies; plant-pollinator interactions. *Mailing Add:* Dept Ecol Univ Ariz 1600 E University Blvd Tucson AZ 87521-0001

SCHAFFNER, CARL PAUL, BIOCHEMISTRY. *Current Pos:* Fel microbiol, Univ, 53-54, from instr to assoc prof, Inst, 54-72, PROF MICROBIOL, WAKSMAN INST MICROBIOL, RUTGERS UNIV, 72-, PROF BIOCHEM, 80- *Personal Data:* b Bayonne, NJ, Feb 13, 28. *Educ:* Columbia Univ, AB, 50; Univ Ill, PhD, 53. *Honors & Awards:* Pres Medal Honor, Philippines, 73. *Mem:* AAAS; Am Soc Microbiol; Am Soc Biol Chemists; Am Chem Soc; Royal Soc Chem; Sigma Xi; fel Philippine Soc Microbiol. *Res:* Antibiotic chemistry; chemotherapy mechanism of action; biosynthesis. *Mailing Add:* Waksman Inst Rutgers Univ PO Box 759 Piscataway NJ 08855-0759

SCHAFFNER, FENTON, MEDICINE, LIVER DISEASES. *Current Pos:* from assoc prof to prof, 66-73, actg chmn dept, 72-74, PROF PATH, MT SINAI SCH MED, 66-, GEORGE BAEHR PROF MED, 73- *Personal Data:* b Chicago, Ill, Dec 8, 20; m 43, 78; c 4. *Educ:* Univ Chicago, BS, 41, MD, 43; Northwestern Univ, MS, 49; Am Bd Internal Med, dipl, 52 & 77; Am Bd Gastroenterol, dipl, 59. *Prof Exp:* Asst path, Med Sch, Northwestern Univ, 48-53, instr med, 55-57; assoc med, Col Physicians & Surgeons, Columbia Univ, 58-61, assoc prof path, 61-66. *Concurrent Pos:* Chmn dept med, Woodlawn Hosp, Chicago, 50-57; from asst attend physician to attend physician, Mt Sinai Hosp, 58- *Mem:* Am Asn Path; Am Gastroenterol Asn; fel Am Col Physicians; Am Asn Study Liver Dis (secy, 58-72, vpres, 75-76, pres, 76-77); Int Asn Study Liver. *Res:* Liver disease, especially electron microscopy of liver, primary biliary cirrhosis. *Mailing Add:* 596 Heritage Hills Dr Somers NY 10589

SCHAFFNER, GERALD, ELECTRICAL ENGINEERING. *Current Pos:* opers mgr microwave semiconductor devices, 66-69, eng mgr microwaves & microelectronics, 69-90, TECH DIR ENG, TELEDYNE RYAN ELECTRONICS, 90-, ENG MGR MICROWAVES & MICROELECTRONICS, TELEDYNE RYAN ELECTRON CO, 69- *Personal Data:* b Chicago, Ill, May 14, 27; m 52; c 3. *Educ:* Purdue Univ, BS, 49, MS, 50; Northwestern Univ, PhD(electronics), 56. *Prof Exp:* Asst, Purdue Univ, 49-50; design engr, Thordarson Elec Co, 50-51; proj engr, Stewart-Warner Corp, 51-57 & Motorola, Inc, 57-66. *Mem:* Inst Elec & Electronics Engrs. *Res:* Microwave applications of solid state devices; microwave radar systems; impatt diodes. *Mailing Add:* 10325 Caminito Cuervo No 193 San Diego CA 92108-1809

SCHAFFNER, JOSEPH CLARENCE, ENTOMOLOGY. *Current Pos:* asst prof, 63-68, assoc prof, 68-80, PROF ENTOM, TEX A&M UNIV, 80- *Personal Data:* b Paducah, Ky, Mar 20, 30; m 60; c 2. *Educ:* Iowa Wesleyan Col, BS, 51; Iowa State Univ, MS, 53, PhD(entom), 64. *Prof Exp:* Instr entom, Ind Univ, 61 & Iowa State Univ, 61-62. *Mem:* Entom Soc Am; Soc Syst Zool; Royal Entom Soc London. *Res:* Systematic entomology; insect taxonomy. *Mailing Add:* 908 Lazy Lane Bryan TX 77802

SCHAFFNER, WILLIAM ROBERT, AQUATIC ECOLOGY. *Current Pos:* RES ASSOC AQUATIC SCI, CORNELL UNIV, 71- *Personal Data:* b Winthrop, Mass, Feb 29, 36; m 59; c 2. *Educ:* Univ Hartford, BS, 64; Cornell Univ, MS, 66, PhD(aquatic ecol), 71. *Concurrent Pos:* Lectr, Cornell Univ, 79- 84, 88- *Mem:* Am Soc Limnol & Oceanog; Ecol Soc Am; Sigma Xi; Int Asn Great Lakes Res; AAAS. *Res:* Plankton ecology. *Mailing Add:* 108 Warwick Pl Ithaca NY 14850-1731

SCHAFFRATH, ROBERT EBEN, ORGANIC CHEMISTRY, ANALYTICAL CHEMISTRY. *Current Pos:* chmn dept, Long Island Univ, 60-65, assoc prof, 60-75, prof chem, 75-92, EMER PROF, C W POST COL, LONG ISLAND UNIV, 92- *Personal Data:* b Syracuse, NY, Feb 19, 22; m 61, Sylvia I Kiener; c Robert G, Sybil T (Marshall) & Jeannette M (Field). *Educ:* Bates Col, BS, 44; Syracuse Univ, MS, 48, PhD(chem), 58. *Prof Exp:* Instr chem, New Eng Col, 48-51; instr org chem, Univ Mass, 51-54; vis lectr chem, State Univ NY Teachers Col, New Paltz, 58-59, assoc prof, 59-60. *Concurrent Pos:* Adj prof, State Univ New York, Old Westbury, 82-85, 90, 93 & 94-96. *Mem:* AAAS; Am Chem Soc; NY Acad Sci; Sigma Xi. *Res:* Mannich reaction; hindered rotation in organic compounds; nitrogen-sulfur heterocycles; hydrazines; organic synthesis. *Mailing Add:* 2 Todd Dr Glen Head NY 11545-1431

SCHAFFT, HARRY ARTHUR, ELECTRONICS. *Current Pos:* PHYSICIST, NAT INST STANDARDS & TECHNOL, 58- *Personal Data:* b New York, NY, May 21, 32; m 62, Gretchen Engle; c Kai A & Soren O. *Educ:* NY Univ, BS, 54; Univ Md, MS, 58. *Honors & Awards:* Bronze & Silver Medals, Dept Com. *Mem:* Fel Inst Elec & Electronics Engrs; Am Phys Soc. *Res:* Materials, process, assembly, and device characterization and measurement for power transistors, integrated circuits, solar cells; technology transfer and information dissemination. *Mailing Add:* Nat Inst Standards & Technol Bldg 225 Rm B360 Gaithersburg MD 20899

SCHAFRIK, ROBERT EDWARD, MANAGEMENT & APPLICATION OF ADVANCED TECHNOLOGY, INTERMETALLIC COMPOUND MATERIALS. *Current Pos:* assoc dir, 91-93, DIR, NAT MAT ADV BD, NAT RES COUN, 93- *Personal Data:* b Feb 6, 46; m 69, Mary L Schuhmann; c Catherine M (Spage), Frances J, Robert E Jr & Steven J. *Educ:* Case Western Res Univ, BS, 67; Air Force Inst Technol, MS, 74; Ohio State Univ, PhD(metall eng), 79; George Mason Univ, MS, 96. *Prof Exp:* Appln engr, Am Air Filter Co, 67-68; chief prog develop sect civil eng, Hanscom AFB, 68-72; mat res engr, Air Force Aerospace Res Lab, 74-76; asst br chief metals, Air Force Mfg Technol Prog, 76-77; br chief comp integrated mfg, 79-80; br chief syst support, Air Force Mat Lab, 80-81; F-16 engine prog mgr, Aeronaunt Syst Div, 81-84; div chief air superiority, Air Force Syst Command, 84-87; Strategic Defense Initiative Off, 87-88; vpres res & develop, Technol Assesment & Transfer, Inc, 88-91. *Concurrent Pos:* Dir, Bd Mfg & Eng Design, Nat Res Coun, 95- *Mem:* Fel Am Soc Metals Int; Inst Elec & Electronics Engrs; Eng Mat Soc; Am Asn Advan Sci; Int Soc Optical Eng. *Res:* Synthesis and characterization of titanium aluminides; damage accumulation mechanisms for low cycle fatigue in superalloys; development of unit processes and computer architecture for computer-integrated manufacturing; design and production incorporation of new technology. *Mailing Add:* 2101 Constitution Ave NW Washington DC 20418. *Fax:* 202-334-3718; *E-Mail:* rschafri@nas.edu

SCHAIBERGER, GEORGE ELMER, ECOLOGY. *Current Pos:* from instr to asst prof, 62-69, assoc prof, 69-77, PROF MICROBIOL, SCH MED, UNIV MIAMI, 77- *Personal Data:* b Saginaw, Mich, Oct 27, 28; m 50; c 2. *Educ:* Univ Fla, BS, 50, MS, 51; Univ Tex, PhD(microbiol), 55. *Honors & Awards:* Outstanding Res Award, Merck & Co, 61. *Prof Exp:* Asst, Univ Fla, 50-51 & Univ Tex, 51-52; instr microbiol, Univ Ark, 55-57; sr res scientist, Merck & Co, 57-61. *Concurrent Pos:* Del, Int Cong Microbiol, 61; NASA & NIH grants, 66-67; res career develop award, USPHS, 67-72. *Mem:* Am Soc Microbiol; fel Geront Soc. *Res:* Microbial ecology; radiation biology; nucleic acid and protein synthesis; metabolic changes associated with aging; environmental effects on cells; environmental virology. *Mailing Add:* 6601 SW 122nd Ave Miami FL 33183

SCHAIBLE, ROBERT HILTON, COMPARATIVE MEDICAL GENETICS, FOREST MANAGEMENT. *Current Pos:* ENVIRON SCIENTIST, DEPT ENVIRON MGT, STATE IND, 91- *Personal Data:* b Horton, Kans, Apr 30, 31; m 73, Catherine Hirn; c Laura A & David K. *Educ:* Colo State Univ, BS, 53; Iowa State Univ, MS, 59, PhD(genetics, embryol), 63. *Prof Exp:* Res assoc, Hall Lab Mammalian Genetics, Univ Kans, 62-63; fel, Biol Dept, Yale Univ, 63-64; asst prof genetics, NC State Univ, 64-68; USPHS spec res fel, Dept Zool, Ind Univ, Bloomington, 68-70; asst prof biol, Ind Univ-Purdue Univ, Indianapolis, 70-73; asst prof, Dept Med Genetics, Ind Univ Sch Med, 73-89. *Concurrent Pos:* Adj asst prof, Sch Vet Med, Purdue Univ, 77- *Mem:* AAAS; Am Genetic Asn; Am Soc Human Genetics; Sigma Xi; Nat Asn Environ Prof. *Res:* Comparative genetics of vertebrates; genetic control of morphogenesis; proliferation, migration, mutation and differentiation of pigment cells in the clonal development of the pigmentation of the integument. *Mailing Add:* 9142 N Buskirk Rd Gosport IN 47433-9527

SCHAICH, KAREN MARIE, LIPID CHEMISTRY & OXIDATION, FREE RADICALS. *Current Pos:* asst prof lipid chem, Dept Food Sci, 88-94, ASST PROF, TOXICOL GRAD PROG, RUTGERS UNIV, 90-, ASSOC PROF LIPID CHEM, 94- *Personal Data:* b Hamilton, Ohio, Nov 21, 47. *Educ:* Purdue Univ, BS, 69; Mass Inst Technol, ScD(food sci), 74. *Prof Exp:* Res assoc, Brookhaven Nat Lab, 74-76, from asst scientist to assoc scientist, 76-80, scientist, 80-86, guest scientist, Med Dept, 86-95. *Mem:* Am Chem Soc; Inst Food Technologists; AAAS; NY Acad Sci; Sigma Xi; Am Oil Chemists Soc; Oxygen Soc. *Res:* Oxidizing lipids: especially free radical reactions, interaction with proteins and nucleic acids; oxygen radical species, production and roles in toxicity mechanisms; electron spin resonance studies; free radicals in food and biological systems; antioxidant chemistry; electron paramagnetic resonance. *Mailing Add:* Dept Food Sci Rutgers Univ New Brunswick NJ 08903-0231. *E-Mail:* schaich@aesop.rutgers.edu

SCHAICH, WILLIAM LEE, THEORETICAL SOLID STATE PHYSICS. *Current Pos:* from asst prof to assoc prof, 73-80, PROF PHYSICS, IND UNIV, BLOOMINGTON, 80- *Personal Data:* b Springfield, Mass, Oct 15, 44; m 66; c 2. *Educ:* Denison Univ, BS, 66; Cornell Univ, MS, 68, PhD(theoret physics), 70. *Prof Exp:* Fel physics, Air Force Off Sci Res, 70-71; res assoc, Univ Calif, San Diego, 71-73. *Mem:* Am Phys Soc. *Res:* Fundamental problems in theory of electronic structure and processes. *Mailing Add:* 202 S Hillsdale Dr Bloomington IN 47408. *Fax:* 812-855-5533

SCHAIRER, G(EORGE) S(WIFT), AERONAUTICAL ENGINEERING. *Current Pos:* RETIRED. *Personal Data:* b Wilkinsburg, Pa, May 19, 13; m 35; c 4. *Educ:* Swarthmore Col, BS, 34; Mass Inst Technol, MS, 35. *Hon Degrees:* DEng, Swarthmore Col, 58. 58. *Honors & Awards:* Reed Award, Am Inst Aeronaut & Astronaut, 49; Am Soc Mech Engrs Medal, 58; Daniel Guggenheim Medal; Mus Flight Pathfinders Award, 85. *Prof Exp:* Aeronaut engr, Bendix Prod Corp, 35-37 & Consol Aircraft Corp, 37-39; from aerodynamicist to dir res, Boeing Co, 39-59, vpres res & develop, 59-71, vpres, 71-78; consult, 78-89. *Concurrent Pos:* Mem sci adv group, USAF, 44-45; sci adv bd, 56-59; mem aerodyn comt, Power Plant Comt & chmn subcomt propellers for aircraft, Nat Adv Comt Aeronaut; mem steering comt, Adv Panel Aeronaut, US Dept Defense, 57-61; mem comt aircraft operating prog, NASA, 59-60; mem panel sci & tech manpower, President's Sci Adv Comt, 63-64; mem sci adv comt, Defense Intel Agency, 65-71; trustee, Univ Res Asn, 66-76; mem aeronaut & space eng bd, Nat Res Coun, 76-78. *Mem:* Nat Acad Sci; Nat Acad Eng; Int Acad Astronaut; hon fel Am Inst Aeronaut & Astronaut; Am Helicopter Soc; mem Soc Naval Architects & Marine Engrs. *Res:* Aerodynamic design of large aircraft. *Mailing Add:* 4242 Hunts Point Rd Bellevue WA 98004

SCHAIRER, ROBERT S(ORG), AERONAUTICS. *Current Pos:* RETIRED. *Personal Data:* b Plum Twp, Pa, Sept 7, 15; m 47; c 6. *Educ:* Swarthmore Col, BS, 36; Calif Inst Technol, MS, 37, PhD(aeronaut), 39. *Prof Exp:* Aerodynamicist & asst chief airborne vehicles sect, Proj Rand, Douglas Aircraft Co, 39-48; asst chief aircraft div, Rand Corp, 48-53, chief, 53-56; tech asst to corp dir develop planning, Lockheed Aircraft Corp, 56-60, asst dir, 60-61; chief scientist, Pac Missile Range, Dept Navy, Calif, 61-62; asst corp dir develop planning, Lockheed Aircraft Corp, 62-63, corp dir, 63-67, assoc dir corp plan, 76-81. *Mem:* Am Inst Aeronaut & Astronaut; Sigma Xi. *Res:* Unsymmetrical lift distribution on a stalled monoplane wing; stability and control in flight testing; airplane performance. *Mailing Add:* 11750 Chenault St Los Angeles CA 90049

SCHAKE, LOWELL MARTIN, ANIMAL SCIENCE. *Current Pos:* PROF & HEAD, DEPT ANIMAL SCI, UNIV CONN, 84- *Personal Data:* b Marthasville, Mo, June 6, 39; m 59; c 2. *Educ:* Univ Mo, BS, 60, MS, 62; Tex A&M Univ, PhD(animal nutrit), 67. *Prof Exp:* Asst prof animal sci, Tex A&M Univ, 65-72, area livestock specialist, 67-69, mem grad fac, 67-80, from assoc prof to prof, 72-84. *Concurrent Pos:* Prof consult, Feed Co, Oil Co & Feedlots; expert witness. *Mem:* Am Soc Animal Sci. *Res:* Feedlot management; cow body weight and compositional changes; beef cattle behavior and grain processing. *Mailing Add:* Dept Animal Sci Tex Tech Univ Lubbock TX 79409-0001

SCHALEGER, LARRY L, ORGANIC CHEMISTRY. *Current Pos:* AT BROWN & CALDWELL, GLENDALE. *Personal Data:* b Milwaukee, Wis, Nov 24, 34; m 58, 78; c 3. *Educ:* Grinnell Col, BA, 57; Univ Minn, PhD(org chem), 61. *Prof Exp:* Res assoc phys chem, Cornell Univ, 61-62, vis asst prof, 62-63; asst prof, Univ Hawaii, 63-67, assoc prof org chem, 67-75; vis assoc prof chem, Calif State Univ, Long Beach, 75-76; NSF fac fel, 76-77, specialist wood chem, Forest Prod Lab, Univ Calif, 77-78, STAFF SCIENTIST, LAWRENCE BERKELEY LAB, UNIV CALIF, 78- *Concurrent Pos:* Res assoc, Univ Pittsburgh, 70-71. *Mem:* Am Chem Soc; AAAS; fel Am Inst Chem. *Res:* Development of methods for trace analysis of organic compound in environmental media. *Mailing Add:* 1321 Holman Rd Oakland CA 94610

SCHALK, JAMES MAXIMILLIAN, ENTOMOLOGY. *Current Pos:* RETIRED. *Personal Data:* b New York, NY, Dec 19, 32; m 61; c 4. *Educ:* Univ Ga, BSA, 60; Cornell Univ, MS, 63; Univ Nebr, PhD(entom), 70. *Prof Exp:* Res asst entom, Cornell Univ, 61-63; res entomologist, Birds Eye Div, Gen Foods Corp, 63-65; res entomologist, Grain & Forage Div, USDA, 65-71, res entomologist, Plant Genetics & Germplasm Inst, Sci & Educ Admin-Agr Res, 71-78; res leader entomol, US Veg Breeding Lab, 78-85, res entomologist, 85- *Concurrent Pos:* Res entomologist, USAID, 71 & Int Proj Div, USDA, 71-76. *Mem:* Entom Soc Am; Am Soc Hort Sci; Sigma Xi. *Res:* Developing vegetable germplasm with resistance to insects and mites and investigating the nature of arthropod resistance in these plants. *Mailing Add:* 7 Oakland Dr Patchogue NY 11772

SCHALK, MARSHALL, geology; deceased, see previous edition for last biography

SCHALK, TERRY LEROY, B & C QUARTZ PHYSICS, COMPUTER ENVIRONMENT FOR PHYSICS. *Current Pos:* ADJ PROF PHYSICS, UNIV CALIF, SANTA CRUZ, 75- *Personal Data:* b Eldora, Iowa, Aug 3, 43; m 65, Rosemary Allen; c Troy & Andrea. *Educ:* Iowa State Univ, BS, 65, PhD(high energy physics), 69. *Prof Exp:* Res assoc, Univ Calif, Riverside, 69-72; Stanford Linear Accelerator Ctr, 72-75. *Concurrent Pos:* Consult, 78- *Mem:* Am Phys Soc; AAAS; Am Asn Physics Teachers. *Res:* Electroweak physics and charmonium violation; computer environment for physicists. *Mailing Add:* SLAC PO Box 4349 Sanford CA 94305. *Fax:* 650-926-2923; *E-Mail:* tas@scipp.ucsc.edu

SCHALL, ELWYN DELAUREL, ANALYTICAL CHEMISTRY. *Current Pos:* RETIRED. *Personal Data:* b Montpelier, Ohio, May 6, 18; m 42, Odella Rigg; c Janet, Jean, James & Judy. *Educ:* Ohio State Univ, BS, 40, Purdue Univ, MS, 42, PhD(biochem), 49. *Prof Exp:* From asst prof to prof, Purdue Univ, West Lafayette, 49-83, Emer Prof biochem, 83. *Concurrent Pos:* State chemist & seed comnr, Ind, 65-82. *Mem:* Am Chem Soc; Asn Off Analytical Chemists. *Res:* Analytical methods. *Mailing Add:* 108 Jordan Lane West Lafayette IN 47906

SCHALL, JOSEPH JULIAN, EVOLUTIONARY ECOLOGY, PARASITE-HOST ECOLOGY. *Current Pos:* From asst prof to assoc prof, 80-93, PROF ZOOL, UNIV VT, 93- *Personal Data:* b Philadelphia, Pa, June 18, 46; m 72. *Educ:* Pa State Univ, BS, 68; Univ RI, MS, 72; Univ Tex, Austin, PhD(zool), 76. *Concurrent Pos:* NIH res serv award, Univ Calif, Berkeley, 77-80. *Res:* Interface between evolutionary theory and ecology, behavior and physiology; interspecific associations such as the parasite-host and plant-herbivore relationships; ecology of lizard malaria. *Mailing Add:* Dept Zool Univ Vt Marsh Life Sci Burlington VT 05405-0001

SCHALL, ROY FRANKLIN, JR, radioimmunology, for more information see previous edition

SCHALLA, CLARENCE AUGUST, MAGNETOTHERMOELECTRIC CRYOGENICS CONDITIONING DESIGN. *Current Pos:* CONSULT, 92- *Personal Data:* b Cleveland, Ohio, May 25, 18; m 43, Mildred Bulan; c Donald & Janet. *Educ:* Case Western Res Univ, ME, 41. *Honors & Awards:* Achievement Award & Commendations, US War Dept, (Manhattan Proj), US Navy Dept (Fleet Ballistic Missile Progs) & US Nuclear Defense Agency (Underground Tests). *Prof Exp:* Asst plant engr, Cleveland Diesel Engine Div, Gen Motors Corp, 41-43, physicist, 46-50; jr scientist, Univ Calif, Los Alamos, 44-46; res prod eng, Pesco Prod Div, Borg-Warner Corp, 50-59; res scientist, Lockheed Missiles & Space Co, Inc, 59-75, design specialist, 76-81, proj engr, 82-91. *Mem:* Am Soc Mech Engrs; Am Nuclear Soc; Am Vacuum Soc. *Res:* Energy conversion; combustion gas liquefaction; aerospace nuclear liquid metal and liquid hydrogen pumping; undergound nuclear testbeds; in-space materials outgrassing; seawater desalination; coal gasification; missiles and spacecraft facilities; author of over 30 papers and articles. *Mailing Add:* 3540 Louis Rd Palo Alto CA 94303-4405

SCHALLENBERG, ELMER EDWARD, PETROLEUM CHEMISTRY, RESEARCH ADMINISTRATION. *Current Pos:* RETIRED. *Personal Data:* b Rome, NY, Dec 30, 29; m 57, Thea Stauber; c 2. *Educ:* Cornell Univ, AB, 51; Univ Calif, PhD(chem), 54. *Prof Exp:* Mem staff lubricants res & develop, Texaco Inc, Beacon, NY, 54-80, sci planning, 80-81, sr coordr res, Texaco Serv Europ-London, 81-82, sr coordr res & asst to mgr dir, 82-88, geschaftsfuehrer, Texaco Serv-Deutschland, 88-91. *Mem:* Am Chem Soc; Sigma Xi. *Res:* Lubricant additives and product development. *Mailing Add:* 363 Sunset Hill Rd E Fishkill NY 12524-2820

SCHALLER, CHARLES WILLIAM, AGRONOMY. *Current Pos:* RETIRED. *Personal Data:* b Holmen, Wis, June 8, 20; m 42; c 3. *Educ:* Univ Wis, BS, 41, MS, 43, PhD(agron), 46. *Prof Exp:* Asst agron, Univ Wis, 41-46; from jr agronomist to assoc aronomist, Exp Sta, Univ Calif, Davis, 46-61, from instr to prof agron, Univ, 46-87, agronomist, Exp Sta, 61-87. *Mem:* Am Phytopath Soc; Am Soc Agron; Genetics Soc Am. *Res:* Genetics of disease resistance in wheat and barley; production of disease resistant varieties of barley. *Mailing Add:* 7 Parkside Dr Davis CA 95616-8515

SCHALLER, DARYL RICHARD, FOOD SCIENCE. *Current Pos:* CONSULT, 97- *Personal Data:* b Milwaukee, Wis, Oct 21, 43; m 66; c 2. *Educ:* Univ Wis, BS, 64, MS, 66, PhD(food sci), 69. *Prof Exp:* Res fel, Dept Food Sci, Univ BC, 69-72; group leader cereal chem, Kellogg Co, 72-77, dir res serv, 77-79, dir res, 79-81, vpres, 81-85, sr vpres, Sci & Technol, 86-90, sr vpres res qual & nutrit, 90-96. *Concurrent Pos:* Res bd visitors, Univ Wis; bd trustees, Mich Biotechnol Inst. *Mem:* Am Chem Soc; Am Asn Cereal Chemists. *Res:* Ultrastructural changes in meat; chemistry of plant polyphenols, pigments; chemistry and analysis of dietary fiber; food chemistry. *Mailing Add:* 1709 York Island Dr Naples FL 34112-4272

SCHALLER, EDWARD JAMES, COATINGS CHEMISTRY, COLLOID CHEMISTRY. *Current Pos:* sr chemist, Rohm & Haas Co, 65-73, proj leader, 73-80, sect mgr archit coatings res, 80-89, SECT MGR ARCHIT COATINGS TECH SERV, ROHM & HAAS CO, SPRING HOUSE, 89- *Personal Data:* b Philadelphia, Pa, Mar 28, 39; m 68, Arlene Shaheen; c Geoffrey. *Educ:* Villanova Univ, BE, 61; Univ Pa, PhD(chem eng), 65. *Honors & Awards:* Roon Award, 87. *Mem:* Am Chem Soc. *Res:* Development of binders, thickeners, dispersants and other additives for water based coatings (especially architectural), adhesives and sealants. *Mailing Add:* 1831 Canterbury Rd Abington PA 19001. *E-Mail:* rohvm1.rscejs@rohmhaas.com

SCHALLER, GEORGE BEALS, ZOOLOGY NATURAL HISTORY LARGE VERTEBRATES. *Current Pos:* dir, Int Conserv Prog, 79-88, RES ZOOLOGIST, NY ZOOL SOC, BRONX, 66- *Personal Data:* b Berlin, Ger, May 26, 33; m 57, Kay S Morgan; c Eric & Mark. *Educ:* Univ Alaska, BS & BA, 55; Univ Wis, PhD(zool), 62. *Honors & Awards:* Gold Medal, World Wildlife Fund, 80; Cosmos Prize, Japan, 96; Tyler Prize, 97. *Prof Exp:* Res assoc, Johns Hopkins Univ, 63-66. *Concurrent Pos:* Res assoc, Am Mus Nat Hist; fel, Ctr Advan Study Behav Sci, Stanford Univ, 62, Guggenheim Found, 71; adj assoc prof, Rockefeller Univ, 66-; adj prof, Peking Univ, Beijing, & E China Normal Univ, Shanghai. *Mem:* Explorers Club. *Res:* Research and consertion of large vertebrates, particularly mammal, with emphasis of endangered species in Africa and Asia. *Mailing Add:* Int Progs Wild Conserv Soc Bronx Park 185th & Southern Bronx NY 10460

SCHALLER, JANE GREEN, PEDIATRIC MEDICINE. *Current Pos:* DAVID & LEONA KARP PROF & CHMN, DEPT PEDIAT, SCH MED, NEW ENG MED CTR, TUFTS UNIV, 83-; PEDIATRICIAN-IN-CHIEF, BOSTON FLOATING HOSP, 83- *Personal Data:* b Cleveland, Ohio, June 26, 34; c Robert T, George C & Margaret M. *Educ:* Hiram Col, AB, 56; Harvard Univ, MD, 60. *Prof Exp:* Resident pediat, Childrens Hosp, Univ Wash, Seattle, 60-63; sr fel immunol & arthritis, 63-65, from instr to prof pediat, Med Sch, 65-83, head, Div Rheumatic Dis, 68-83, prof pediat, 75-83. *Concurrent Pos:* Vis physician, Med Res Coun, Taplow, Eng, 71-72; vis sr scientist & vis prof rheumatology, Dept Med, Univ Ala, 79-82; lectr pediat, Harvard Univ, 85-; bd visitor, Sch Med, Univ Pittsburgh, 89-; spec consult, Int Pediat Asn, 95; UNICEF rep, Am Acad Pediat, 96- *Mem:* Inst Med-Nat Acad Sci; AAAS; Soc Pediat Res; Am Pediat Soc; Am Acad Pediat; Am Col Rheumatology; NY Acad Sci; Am Pub Health Asn; Soc Irish & Am Rheumatologists. *Res:* Pediatric medicine; rheumatology. *Mailing Add:* Tufts Univ Sch Med New Eng Med Ctr Floating Hosp 750 Washington St Box 286 Boston MA 02111. *Fax:* 617-350-8388

SCHALLERT, WILLIAM FRANCIS, ENGINEERING. *Current Pos:* dean acad affairs, 82-88, prof aero eng, 82-88, prof elec eng, 88, CHMN ELEC ENG DEPT, PARKS COL, ST LOUIS UNIV, 88- *Personal Data:* b Maplewood, Mo, Sept 3, 27; m 54; c 2. *Educ:* Washington Univ, St Louis, BS, 53; St Louis Univ, MS, 55, MBA, 60, PhD, 76. *Prof Exp:* Asst prof aeronaut eng & head elec prog, Parks Col Aeronaut Technol, St Louis, 53-61, asst prof basic eng, St Louis Univ, 61-64; assoc prof eng, Florissant Valley Community Col, 64-67, chmn div eng & eng technol, 64-78, prof eng, 67-82. *Concurrent Pos:* Consult, Emerson Elec Mfg Co, 55-64, Electro-Core, Inc 69- & Sch Eng, Univ Mo, Columbia, 72-76; comnr higher educ, NCent Asn, 71-76; co-dir, NSF grant, 72-76; consult & examr, NCent Asn, 76- *Mem:* Inst Elec & Electronics Engrs; Am Soc Eng Educ; Nat Soc Prof Engrs; Am Soc Cert Eng Technicians. *Res:* Avionics and systems engineering; behavioral and educational systems; electrical power system; pulsed energy systems. *Mailing Add:* Parks Col St Louis Univ Cahokia IL 62206

SCHALLES, ROBERT R, ANIMAL BREEDING, POPULATION GENETICS. *Current Pos:* asst prof animal husbandry & asst animal husbandman, 66-70, assoc prof, 70-80, PROF ANIMAL SCI & ASSOC, AGR EXP STA, KANS STATE UNIV, 80- *Personal Data:* b Durango, Colo, Mar 25, 35; m 56; c 4. *Educ:* Colo State Univ, BS, 63; Va Polytech Inst, MS, 66, PhD(animal breeding), 67. *Prof Exp:* Mgr, Feedlot Serv, Inc, Colo, 61-62. *Mem:* Am Soc Animal Sci; Am Genetic Asn. *Res:* Genetic and environmental influences on growth and development of animals. *Mailing Add:* Animal Sci Kans State Univ Call Hall Manhattan KS 66506

SCHALLHORN, CHARLES H, PHOTOGRAPHIC CHEMISTRY. *Current Pos:* Sr res chemist, Eastman Kodak, 70-79, res assoc, 79-84, dir photo technol, Kodak Japan, 84-88, prog dir Strategic Info, 88-91, DIR BUS RES, EASTMAN KODAK, 91- *Personal Data:* b Saginaw, Mich, Mar 26, 44; m 73; c 1. *Educ:* Univ Mich, Ann Arbor, BS, 66; Univ Calif, Berkeley, PhD(chem), 70. *Concurrent Pos:* Lectr chem, Univ Rochester, 73-82; chmn comt IT9-3, Image Stability, Am Nat Stand Inst. *Mem:* Am Chem Soc; Soc Imaging Sci & Technol. *Res:* Photographic and imaging chemistry. *Mailing Add:* 527 Pinegrove Ave Rochester NY 14617

SCHALLIOL, WILLIS LEE, MATERIALS SCIENCE, ELECTRICAL ENGINEERING. *Current Pos:* RETIRED. *Personal Data:* b Elkhart, Ind, Dec 20, 19; m 42, Ilyff B Williams; c John, Dennis & Gregory. *Educ:* Purdue Univ, BS, 42; Stanford Univ, PhD(metall eng), 50. *Prof Exp:* Mat engr, Westinghouse Elec Corp, Calif, 48-50; actg instr x-ray tech, Stanford Univ, 49-50; supvr pile fuels, Hanford Works, Gen Elec Co, 50-53; mgr br, Nibco Inc, 53-54, dir eng, 55-59; dir res aerospace div, Bendix Corp, 59-63; proj engr, CTS Corp, 63-64; dir res, CTS Res, Inc, 64-69; mem staff, Dept Chem, 69-75, assoc prof mat eng, 76-80, assoc coordr coop eng educ, 76-80, mgr indust rels, Sch Elec Eng, 80-85; vis asst prof mech eng technol, Purdue Univ, West Lafayette, 85-86. *Concurrent Pos:* Dir critical needs prog, Purdue Univ, 76-80. *Res:* Microtranspiration for protection of rocket nozzle throats; chromium-magnesia composites; high-power precision cermet resistor modules; thermoset polymers for mechanical applications; computer-aided cooperative engineering education administration; profile of graduates from the engineering co-op program. *Mailing Add:* 172 Pathway Lane West Lafayette IN 47906-2156. *Fax:* 765-494-3544; *E-Mail:* schallio@ecn.purdue.edu

SCHALLY, ANDREW VICTOR, ENDOCRINOLOGY. *Current Pos:* CHIEF, ENDOCRINOL & POLYPEPTIDE LABS, VET ADMIN HOSP, 62-, SR MED INVESTR, 73-; PROF MED, SCH MED, TULANE UNIV, 66- *Personal Data:* b Wilno, Poland, Nov 30, 26; US citizen; m 56, 76, AnaMaria Comaru; c 2. *Educ:* McGill Univ, BSc, 55, PhD(biochem), 57. *Hon Degrees:* Seventeen from various foreign & Can univs. *Honors & Awards:* Nobel Prize in Med, 77; Award, Am Thyroid Asn, 69; Ayerst Squibb Endocrine Soc Award; Gardner Found Award, 74; Edward T Tyler Award, 75; Borden Award, 75; Albert Lasker Award, 75. *Prof Exp:* Asst protein chem, Nat Inst Med Res, Eng, 49-52; assoc endocrinol, Allan Mem Inst Psychiat, Can, 52-57; asst prof & res assoc protein chem & endocrinol, Col Med, Baylor Univ, 57-62; assoc prof med, Tulane Univ, 62-66. *Concurrent Pos:* NIH fel, 60-62; consult indust, 57- *Mem:* Nat Acad Sci; Am Soc Biol Chem; Am Physiol Soc; AAAS; Endocrine Soc. *Res:* Chemistry and biology of protein and peptide hormones; control of release; determination of structure and synthesis of thyrotropin releasing hormone, luteinizing hormone and follicle-stimulating hormone-releasing hormone; pro-somato statin; endocrine dependent cancers. *Mailing Add:* Vet Admin Hosp 1601 Perdido St New Orleans LA 70146

SCHAMBERG, RICHARD, AERODYNAMICS, SYSTEMS ANALYSIS. *Current Pos:* CONSULT, 87- *Personal Data:* b Frankfurt, Germany, Dec 18, 20; nat US; m 47, 69, Giovanna Castelfranco; c Linda Markell, Ellen Burley (deceased) & Robert. *Educ:* Calif Inst Technol, BS, 43, MS, 44, PhD(aeronaut), 47. *Prof Exp:* Asst, Calif Inst Technol, 43-47, asst aerodyn, 46-47; aerodyn engr, Proj Rand, Douglas Aircraft Co, 47-48; assoc engr, Rand Corp, Calif, 48-50, tech asst to chief, Aircraft Div, 50-55, assoc head, Aero-astronaut Dept, 56-63, head, 63-68; mem sr tech staff-corp, Northrop Corp, 68-71, corp dir technol appls, 71-87. *Concurrent Pos:* Consult tech adv panel on aeronaut, Off Asst Secy Defense Res & Eng, 57-63; mem advan technol panel, Defense Advan Res Proj Agency, 73-75. *Mem:* Opers Res Soc Am; Am Inst Aeronaut & Astronaut; Unmanned Vehicles Soc. *Res:* Aerodynamics of rarefied gases; research and development planning operations research. *Mailing Add:* 10630 Bradbury Rd Los Angeles CA 90064

SCHAMBERGER, ROBERT DEAN, B-QUARK SPECTROSCOPY, P-P INTERACTIONS. *Current Pos:* Postdoctoral asst, 77-85, SR SCIENTIST PHYSICS, STATE UNIV NY, 86- *Personal Data:* b Rochester, NY, June 28, 48. *Educ:* State Univ NY, BA, 70, PhD(physics), 76. *Mem:* Am Phys Soc. *Res:* Quark and hadron interactions at high energies. *Mailing Add:* 7 Sycamore Dr Stony Brook NY 11790

SCHAMBRA, PHILIP ELLIS, BIOPHYSICS. *Current Pos:* DIR, FOGARTY INT CTR, 88- *Personal Data:* b Saginaw, Mich, Nov 8, 34; m 90, Denita Bartels; c Eric, Kirsten & Heidi. *Educ:* Rice Univ, BA, 56; Yale Univ, PhD(biophys), 61. *Honors & Awards:* Superior Serv Award, USPHS, 89. *Prof Exp:* Grants assoc, NIH, 67-68; budget examr, Off Mgt & Budget, Exec Off of the President, 68-71; staff mem, Coun Environ Qual, 71-74; assoc dir interagency progs, Nat Inst Environ Health Sci, NIH, 74-80; chief int coord & liaison br, Fogarty Int Ctr, NIH, Bethesda, Md, 81-84; sci attache & Int Health Rep, Dep Chief Sci Off, US Embassy, New Delhi, India, 84-88. *Mem:* AAAS. *Mailing Add:* Fogarty Int Ctr Bldg 31 Rm B2C02 NIH Bethesda MD 20892. *Fax:* 301-402-2173

SCHAMP, HOMER WARD, JR, HIGH PRESSURE PHYSICS. *Current Pos:* from asst prof to prof, Inst Molecular Physics, 52-71, dir, Inst, 64-65, dean fac, 65-71, RES PROF EDUC, UNIV MD, BALTIMORE COUNTY, 71- *Personal Data:* b St Marys, Ohio, June 23, 23; c 2. *Educ:* Miami Univ, AB, 44; Univ Mich, PhD(physics), 52. *Prof Exp:* Physicist, Mound Lab, Monsanto Chem Co, 51-52. *Mem:* Fel Am Phys Soc. *Res:* Self-diffusion and ionic conductivity in alkali halides; experiments in high pressure physics; thermodynamics. *Mailing Add:* 521 Overdale Rd Baltimore MD 21229-2413

SCHANBACHER, FLOYD LEON, BIOCHEMISTRY, DIFFERENTIATION. *Current Pos:* from asst prof to assoc prof dairy sci, 70-87, PROF DAIRY SCI, OHIO AGR RES & DEVELOP CTR, OHIO STATE UNIV, 87- *Personal Data:* b Cherokee, Okla, Dec 19, 41; m 64; c 1. *Educ:* Northwestern State Col, BS, 64; Okla State Univ, MS, 67, PhD(biochem), 70. *Prof Exp:* Res assoc biochem & entom, Okla State Univ, 70. *Mem:* Am Dairy Sci Asn; Am Chem Soc; Am Soc Microbiol; AAAS. *Res:* Milk protein characterization, biosynthesis and function; control and initiation of mammary differentiation; immunobiology of mammary differentiation; immunotoxicology; biochemical responses to toxic agents. *Mailing Add:* Dept Dairy Sci OH Agr Res Develop Ctr Ohio State Univ 1680 Madison Ave Wooster OH 44691

SCHANBERG, SAUL M, NEUROPHARMACOLOGY. *Current Pos:* asst prof clin pharmacol, 67-69, asst prof neurol & chief sect neuropharmacol, 69-87, PROF PHARMACOL, SCH MED, DUKE UNIV, 69-, PROF BIOL PSYCHIAT & ASSOC DEAN MED SCH, 87- *Personal Data:* b Clinton, Mass, Mar 22, 33; m 55; c 2. *Educ:* Clark Univ, BA, 54, MA, 56; Yale Univ, PhD(pharmacol), 61, MD, 64. *Honors & Awards:* Rehme-Anna Monika Prize, Ger, 67. *Prof Exp:* Teaching asst bot & zool, Clark Univ, 54-55 & physiol, 55-56; res assoc pharmacol, Yale Univ, 61-62, univ scholar, 61-64; intern pediat, Albert Einstein Col Med, 64-65; res assoc pharmacol, Lab Clin Sci, NIMH, 65-67. *Concurrent Pos:* Res consult psychoneuropharmacol, Inst Behav Res, Silver Spring, Md, 65-68; Neurosci Res Prog award, Cent Nerv Syst Intensive Study Unit, 66, NIMH res scientist award, 68. *Mem:* Am Fedn Clin Res; Am Soc Pharmacol & Exp Therapeut; Int Soc Biochem Pharmacol; Am Col Neuropsychopharmacol; Am Soc Neurochem. *Res:* Pharmacologic and toxic effects of drugs, hormones and environmental influences on the metabolism of biogenic amines in the central nervous system; the role biogenic amines play in controlling cell metabolism and in mediating the effects of drugs and hormones on brain metabolism and development in normal and disease states; assessment of multiple molecular and physiological parameters in developing organ systems as indices of altered function maturation; chemical mechanisms in the CNS mediating growth and maturation in the mammalian neonate as regulated by mother-infant interactions and early experiences, effects of endocrines, neuropeptides and drugs, and sympathetic and endocrine physiology as mediators of the stress response. *Mailing Add:* Dept Pharmacol Box 3813 Med Ctr Duke Univ Durham NC 27710-0001

SCHANEFELT, ROBERT VON, FOOD SCIENCE, CEREAL CHEMISTRY. *Current Pos:* Food technologist, A E Staley Mfg Co, 70-73, group leader, 73-76, dir food & agr prod res & develop, 76-85, dir food & indust prod, 85-88, VPRES, A E STALEY MFG CO, 88- *Personal Data:* b Abilene, Kans, Sept 21, 42; m 63; c 2. *Educ:* Kans State Univ, BS, 66, MS, 67, PhD(food sci), 70. *Mem:* Am Asn Cereal Chem; Inst Food Technologists. *Res:* Research and applications development of modified food starches and corn sweetness. *Mailing Add:* 6 Allen Bend Pl Decatur IL 62521

SCHANFIELD, MOSES SAMUEL, FORENSIC GENETICS, PATERNITY TESTING. *Current Pos:* LAB DIR, ANALYTICAL GENETIC TESTING CTR INC, 85- *Personal Data:* b Minneapolis, Minn, Sept 7, 44; m 77; c Sara & Amanda. *Educ:* Univ Minn, Minneapolis, BA, 66; Harvard Univ, MA, 69; Univ Mich, Ann Arbor, PhD(human genetics), 71. *Honors & Awards:* Gold Medal, 1st Latin Am Cong Hemother & Immunohemat. *Prof Exp:* Res fel genetics, Univ Calif, San Francisco, 71-72, NIH fel, 72-74, asst res geneticist, 74-75; dir, Transfusion Serv & Ref Lab, Milwaukee Blood Ctr, 75-78; asst sci dir, Am Red Cross Blood Serv, 79-83; lab dir, Genetic Testing Inst, 83-85. *Concurrent Pos:* Asst clin prof, Dept Med, Med Col Wis, 76-78; consult immunohemat, Vet Admin Ctr, Wood, Wis, 76-78; adj assoc prof genetic prog, George Washington Univ, 79-83; adj assoc prof, dept pediat, Emory Univ Atlanta, Ga, 84-89; adj assoc prof, Dept Anthrop, Lawrence, Kans, 92-; affiliated fac, Biol Dept, Colo State Univ, Ft Collins, 92-; Nat Forensic DNA Rev Panel on Blind Proficiency testing. *Mem:* Am Soc Human Genetics; Am Asn Phys Anthropologists; Int Soc Haemogenetics; Am Acad Forensic Sci; Am Soc Crime Lab; Sigma Xi. *Res:* Development of DNA and non-DNA technologies for parentage and forensic identification using biohazard free technologies; evolution of immunoglobulin attotypes at the molecular and serological level. *Mailing Add:* Analytical Genetic Test Ctr 7808 Cherry Creek Dr S No 201 Denver CO 80231. *Fax:* 303-750-2171; *E-Mail:* moses@geneticid.com

SCHANK, STANLEY COX, CYTOGENETICS, PLANT BREEDING. *Current Pos:* From asst prof to assoc prof, 61-72, PROF GENETICS, UNIV FLA, 72- *Personal Data:* b Fallon, Nev, Oct 31, 32; m 54; c Colleen, David, Gary, Linda & Rodney. *Educ:* Utah State Univ, BS, 54; Univ Calif, PhD(genetics), 61. *Concurrent Pos:* Consult, IRI Res Inst, Brazil, 66; vis res prof, Brazil-Fla Contract, 73-75; fac develop leave, Commonwealth Sci & Indust Res Orgn, Australia, 70 & 78; nat crop adv comt, Genetics Soc Can, 85-; consult, Holstein Asn, Thailand, 90, IICA/Embrapa, Brazil, 93. *Mem:* Am Soc Agron; Genetics Soc Am; Genetics Soc Can; Crop Sci Soc Am. *Res:* General genetics; forage grass cytogenetics and breeding, primarily Pennisetums, Brachiarias and Hemarthrias; biomass production of Napiergrass hybrids for methane. *Mailing Add:* 60 NW 44th St Gainesville FL 32607

SCHANKER, JACOB Z, WIRELESS COMMUNICATIONS, DIGITAL COMMUNICATIONS. *Current Pos:* ENG MGR, MICROWAVE DATA SYSTS, 95- *Personal Data:* b Brooklyn, NY; m 65; c 2. *Educ:* City Col City Univ New York, BEE, 63, ME, 67. *Honors & Awards:* Centennial Medal, Inst Elec & Electronics Engrs, 84. *Prof Exp:* Sr engr, Gen Dynamics-Electronics Div, 63-69 & Harris Corp, RF Commun Div, 69-71; vpres & dir eng Community Music Serv Inc, 71-76; chief engr, Sci Radio Systs Inc, 77-86, dir, prod planning & develop, 86-89; prin engr, Metscoun Inc, 89-95. *Concurrent Pos:* Res asst, Dept Elec Eng, City Col New York, 65-66; adj prof, Rochester Inst Technol, 69-79. *Mem:* Inst Elec & Electronics Engrs; Appl Comput Electromagnetics Soc; Inst Engrs (Australia). *Res:* The application of meteor burst propagation to data communications systems; packet data techniques in HF, VHF and meteor burst systems; broadband HF antenna design and broadband matching network synthesis. *Mailing Add:* 65 Crandon Way Rochester NY 14618. *E-Mail:* j.schanker@ieee.org

SCHANNE, OTTO F, BIOPHYSICS, CARDIAC ELECTROPHYSIOLOGY. *Current Pos:* from asst prof to assoc prof, 66-71, chmn dept, 70-78, assoc dean res, 81-83 PROF, UNIV SHERBROOKE, 71- *Personal Data:* b Stuttgart, Ger, Feb 21, 32; div; c 2. *Educ:* Univ Heidelberg, Dr med, 60; Univ Paris, Dr Etat, 79. *Prof Exp:* Res asst physiol, Univ Heidelberg, 58-60, instr, 60-64; assoc prof pharmacol, Univ Southern Calif, 64-65; asst prof biophys, Univ Montreal, 65-66. *Concurrent Pos:* Med Res Coun Can scholar, 66-70, mem comt physiol & pharmacol, 73-76, mem core comt heart res develop grants, 77-79; mem assoc comt biophys, Nat Res Coun Can, 68-69, mem nat comt biophys, 77-81; Edwards prof cardiol, 85- *Mem:* Biophys Soc; Am Physiol Soc; Can Physiol Soc; Inst Elec & Electronics Engrs. *Res:* Antiarrhythmic drugs and cellular cardiac electrophysiology; membrane properties of cultured cardiac cells; pacemaker mechanisms. *Mailing Add:* Dept Physiol & Biophysics Univ Sherbrooke Fac Med 3001 12th Ave N Sherbrooke PQ J1H 5N4 Can. *Fax:* 819-564-5399

SCHANO, EDWARD ARTHUR, POULTRY HUSBANDRY. *Current Pos:* RETIRED. *Personal Data:* b Buffalo, NY, Oct 8, 18; m 42, 67; c 15. *Educ:* Cornell Univ, BS, 51; Mich State Univ, MS, 58. *Prof Exp:* Prof poultry husb & exten specialist, Cornell Univ, 52- *Mem:* Poultry Sci Asn; World Poultry Sci Asn. *Res:* Youth poultry science projects. *Mailing Add:* 513 Dryden Rd Ithaca NY 14850

SCHANTZ, EDWARD JOSEPH, BIOCHEMISTRY. *Current Pos:* prof, 72-80, EMER PROF BIOCHEM, FOOD RES INST, UNIV WIS-MADISON, 80- *Personal Data:* b Hartford, Wis, Aug 27, 08; m 40; c 5. *Educ:* Univ Wis, BS, 31, PhD(biochem), 39; Iowa State Col, MS, 33. *Prof Exp:* Res asst, Wis Agr Exp Sta, 36-40; biochemist, Res Labs, Carnation Milk Co, 40-42; res chemist, US Army Biol Ctr, 46-72. *Concurrent Pos:* Consult, USPHS, 54-72. *Mem:* Fel AAAS; Am Chem Soc; Am Soc Biol Chem; fel NY Acad Sci. *Res:* Isolation and characterization of toxins and poisons produced by microorganisms; diffusion of substances in gels and various biological systems; studies on poisons produced by certain dinoflagellates and other algae. *Mailing Add:* Food Res Inst Univ Wis 1925 Willow Dr Madison WI 53706-1131

SCHANTZ, PETER MULLINEAUX, VETERINARY PUBLIC HEALTH, PARASITOLOGY. *Current Pos:* VET EPIDEMIOLOGIST, CTR DIS CONTROL, USPHS, 74- *Personal Data:* b Camden, NJ, Oct 22, 39; c 2. *Educ:* Univ Pa, AB, 61, VMD, 65; Univ Calif, Davis, PhD(comp path), 71. *Prof Exp:* Epidemiologist, Pan-Am Zoonosis Ctr, Pan-Am Health Orgn-WHO, Arg, 69-74. *Mem:* Am Vet Med Asn; Am Soc Parasitol; Am Soc Trop Med & Hyg; Sigma Xi. *Res:* Epidemiology, immunodiagnosis and pathology of parasitic zoonoses. *Mailing Add:* 2569 Circlewood Rd Atlanta GA 30345

SCHANUEL, STEPHEN HOEL, MATHEMATICS. *Current Pos:* ASSOC PROF MATH, STATE UNIV NY, BUFFALO, 72- *Personal Data:* b St Louis, Mo, July 14, 33; m 58; c 2. *Educ:* Princeton Univ, AB, 55; Univ Chicago, MS, 56; Columbia Univ, PhD(math), 63. *Prof Exp:* Instr math, Ill Inst Technol, 59-61; instr, Columbia Univ, 61-63; instr, Johns Hopkins Univ, 63-65; asst prof, Cornell Univ, 65-69; assoc prof, State Univ NY, Stony Brook, 69-72. *Concurrent Pos:* Mem, Inst Advan Study, 65-66. *Mem:* Am Math Soc. *Res:* Algebra and number theory, especially transcendental numbers. *Mailing Add:* 106 Diefendorf Hall State Univ NY Buffalo Buffalo NY 14214

SCHAPER, LAURENCE TEIS, SOLID WASTE MANAGEMENT. *Current Pos:* PARTNER, CIVIL ENG, BLACK & VEATCH, 62- *Personal Data:* b Beloit, Kans, Oct 6, 36; m 60; c 2. *Educ:* Kans State Univ, BS, 59; Stanford Univ, MS, 62. *Mem:* Nat Soc Prof Engrs; fel Am Soc Civil Engrs; Am Water Works Asn; Water Pollution Control Asn; Am Pub Works Asn; Am Acad Environ Engrs. *Res:* Solid waste management. *Mailing Add:* 8421 Briar Shawnee Mission KS 66207

SCHAPERY, RICHARD ALLAN, CONTINUUM MECHANICS, FRACTURE MECHANICS. *Current Pos:* PROF AEROSPACE ENG & ENG MECH, UNIV TEX, 90- *Personal Data:* b Duluth, Minn, Mar 3, 35; m 57; c 1. *Educ:* Wayne State Univ, BS, 57; Calif Inst Technol, MS, 58, PhD(aeronaut), 62. *Prof Exp:* From asst prof to prof aeronaut & eng sci, Purdue Univ, 62-69; prof Aerospace Eng & Civic Eng, Tex A&M Univ, 69-80, alumni prof, 80-85, distinguished prof, 80-85, Eng Exp Sta Chair, 85-90, dir, Mech & Math Ctr, 71-90. *Concurrent Pos:* Indust consult, Struct Anal & Mat Characterization, 60-; mem, solid propellant struct integrity comt, 66-72, comts Nat Mat Adv Bd, 78-87; Cockrell Family Regents Chair, Eng, 90- *Mem:* Am Inst Aeronaut & Astronaut; Am Ceramic Soc. *Res:* Elasticity; viscoelasticity; fracture mechanics; thermodynamics; composite materials. *Mailing Add:* 7133 Valburn Dr Austin TX 78731

SCHAPPELL, FREDERICK GEORGE, organic chemistry, marketing; deceased, see previous edition for last biography

SCHAPPERT, GOTTFRIED T, LASER PHYSICS, LASER-MATTER INTERACTIONS. *Current Pos:* MEM STAFF & GROUP LEADER, LOS ALAMOS NAT LAB, 71- *Personal Data:* b Mannheim, Ger, Sept 10, 34; US citizen; m 64, Linda; c Michael. *Educ:* Mass Inst Technol, BS, 56, MS, 58, PhD(physics), 61. *Prof Exp:* Fel, Max Planck Inst Astrophysics, 61-62; instr, Dept physics, Mass Inst Technol, 62-63; consult, Cambridge Res Labs, USAF, 63-65; res assoc, Brandeis Univ, 65-67; physicist, Electronics Res Ctr, NASA, 67-71. *Concurrent Pos:* Fel, Los Alamos Nat Lab. *Mem:* Am Phys Soc; AAAS; Sigma Xi; Optical Soc Am. *Res:* Laser fusion physics; laser physics and engineering; laser matter interaction physics. *Mailing Add:* 145 San Juan St Los Alamos NM 87544. *E-Mail:* gts@lanl.gov

SCHAR, RAYMOND DEWITT, POULTRY SCIENCE. *Current Pos:* RETIRED. *Personal Data:* b Butler, Pa, Apr 9, 23; m 43; c 3. *Educ:* Pa State Univ, BS, 50. *Prof Exp:* Instr voc agr, Pub Schs, Pa, 45-49; sr poultry inspector, Pa Dept Agr, 50-59; poultry coordr, USDA, 59-71, proj leader random sample poultry testing, Animal Improv Progs Lab, Animal Physiol & Genetics Inst, Sci & Educ Admin-Agr Res, 60-79, sr poultry coordr, 71-83, poultry scientist, Animal & Plant Health Inspection Serv, 84-88. *Concurrent Pos:* Adv mem & secy, Nat Comt Random Sample Poultry Testing, 60-79. *Mem:* Poultry Sci Asn; World Poultry Sci Asn (secy-treas, 80-85). *Res:* Poultry production and diseases; study trends; measures to combat diseases through blood testing of breeder flocks. *Mailing Add:* 11711 Roby Ave Beltsville MD 20705

SCHARBER, SAMUEL ROBERT, JR, PHYSICAL CHEMISTRY. *Current Pos:* PROF CHEM, SAN DIEGO COMMUNITY COLS, 60- *Personal Data:* b Winchester, Tenn, Mar 23, 33; m 54, 77, Betty Brinkmeier; c M Pauli (Martin), Joseph Robert, Catherine (Angula) & Betsy Martin (Sulivan). *Educ:* Univ Notre Dame, BS, 55; Harvard Univ, EdM, 63; Univ Tex, Austin, PhD(chem), 70. *Prof Exp:* High sch teacher, Ill, 56-59; consult & reseacher, Bud Toye Co, El Cajon, 71-80. *Concurrent Pos:* Consult & researcher, 80-; acad year inst fel & summer fel, NSF. *Mem:* Am Chem Soc; Optical Soc Am. *Res:* Solid waste recycle, chiefly plastics, metals and rubber; air pollution, palladium deuterium system. *Mailing Add:* 10058 Pandora Dr La Mesa CA 91941. *Fax:* 619-698-2396

SCHARENBERG, ROLF PAUL, NUCLEAR PHYSICS. *Current Pos:* assoc prof, 65-70, PROF PHYSICS, PURDUE UNIV, WEST LAFAYETTE, 71- *Personal Data:* b Hamburg, Ger, Mar 11, 27; m 55; c 2. *Educ:* Univ Mich, Ann Arbor, BS, 49, MS, 50, PhD(physics), 55. *Prof Exp:* From instr to asst prof physics, Mass Inst Technol, 55-60; assoc prof, Case Inst Technol, 61-65. *Mem:* Fel Am Phys Soc. *Res:* Magnetic and electric structure of nuclei. *Mailing Add:* 144 E Navajo St West Lafayette IN 47906

SCHARER, JOHN EDWARD, ELECTRICAL ENGINEERING, APPLIED PHYSICS. *Current Pos:* From asst prof to assoc prof, 66-78, assoc chmn grad studies, 80-82, PROF ELEC ENG, UNIV WIS-MADISON, 78- *Personal Data:* b Monroe, Wis, Oct 11, 39; m 65; c 2. *Educ:* Univ Calif, Berkeley, BS, 61, MS, 63, PhD(elec eng), 66. *Concurrent Pos:* NSF grant, Univ Wis-Madison, 67-, Dept Energy res contract, 67-; Fr AEC vis scientist, Ctr Nuclear Studies, Fontenay-aux-Roses, France, 69-70. *Mem:* Am Phys Soc; Inst Elec & Electronics Engrs. *Res:* Plasma physics, particularly linear and nonlinear wave propagation and instabilities; microwave and RF heating of plasmas; lasers. *Mailing Add:* 842 Prospect Pl Madison WI 53703

SCHARF, ARTHUR ALFRED, BIOLOGY, BIOPHYSICS. *Current Pos:* from asst prof to assoc prof biol & bot, 57-65, chmn natural sci div, 62-63, chmn dept biol, 63-65, prof bot, 65-80, PROF BIOL, NORTHEASTERN ILL UNIV, 65- *Personal Data:* b Chicago, Ill, July 27, 27; m 56; c 4. *Educ:* Northwestern Univ, BS, 48, MS, 50, PhD(bot), 53. *Prof Exp:* Bacteriologist, NShore Sanit Dist, Ill, 48; res asst, Arctic Res Lab, Alaska, 52; instr biol & bot, Ill Teachers Col Chicago-North, 53-56; asst prof biol, Elmhurst Col, 56-57. *Mem:* AAAS. *Res:* History of science. *Mailing Add:* Dept Biol Northeastern Ill Univ 5500 N St Louis Ave Chicago IL 60625-4625

SCHARF, BERTRAM, PSYCHOACOUSTICS. *Current Pos:* PROF PSYCHOL, NORTHEASTERN UNIV, 58- *Personal Data:* b New York, NY, Mar 3, 31; m 65; c Jonathan L & Riitta L. *Educ:* City Col New York, BA, 53; Univ Paris, dipl, 55; Harvard Univ, PhD(exp psychol), 58. *Honors & Awards:* Fechner Medal, Int Soc Psychophys, 95. *Concurrent Pos:* Res assoc, Tech Hochschule Stuttgart, 62; vis res assoc, Sensory Res Lab, Syracuse Univ, 66; vis scientist, Med Sch, Helsinki Univ, 71-72; chmn, Working Group, US Stand Inst, 71-78; assoc ed, J Acoust Soc Am, 77-80; vis prof, Univ Provence, Marseille, 78-79, 85-86, 88; vis scientist, Nat Ctr Sci Res, France, 82-83, 90-91 & 93. *Mem:* Fel Acoust Soc Am; fel AAAS; Psychonomics Soc; Am Psychol Asn; Int Audiol Soc; hon mem Finnish Acoust Soc. *Res:* Effects of noise on people; sensory psychology; psychophysics; psychoacoustics; loudness; frequency analysis; sound localization; normal and pathological hearing; auditory attention. *Mailing Add:* 22 Chestnut Pl Brookline MA 02146. *Fax:* 617-373-3467; *E-Mail:* scharf@neu.edu

SCHARF, WALTER, GEMOLOGY. *Current Pos:* ASSOC PROF CHEM & CHMN DEPT NATURAL SCI, BARUCH COL, 68- *Personal Data:* b Vienna, Austria, July 19, 29; nat US. *Educ:* City Col New York, BS, 52; Columbia Univ, MA, 54, PhD(chem), 57. *Prof Exp:* Asst chem, Columbia

Univ, 52-53; lectr, City Col New York, 53-58, from instr to asst prof, 58-68. *Concurrent Pos:* Proj leader, Evans Res & Develop Corp, 57-58; vis lectr, Columbia Univ, 65. *Mem:* Royal Soc Chem; Am Chem Soc; Sigma Xi; fel Gemol Asn Gt Brit. *Res:* Isolation, purification and mechanism of action of polyphenol oxidases and flavorese enzymes; effects of gamma radiation on proteins; biodegradation of ascorbic acid; contraceptive plant estrogens; crystal growth from melts and solutions. *Mailing Add:* Dept Natural Sci Box A-0506 Baruch Col CUNY 17 Lexington Ave New York NY 10010-5526

SCHARFETTER, D(ONALD) L, ELECTRICAL ENGINEERING. *Current Pos:* MGR PROCESSER MODEL, INTEL CORP, 87- *Personal Data:* b Pittsburgh, Pa, Feb 21, 34; m 55; c 3. *Educ:* Carnegie Inst Technol, BS, 60, MS, 61, PhD(elec eng), 62. *Prof Exp:* Mem tech staff, Bell Labs, 62-76; prof elec eng, Carnegie-Mellon Univ, 76-80; mem staff, Palo Alto Res Ctr, Xerox Corp, 78-83; at Fastek, San Carlos, Ca, 84-87; prof elec eng, Univ Calif, Berkeley, 84-87. *Mem:* Inst Elec & Electronics Engrs. *Res:* Analysis of device characteristics; device physics as applied to semiconductors. *Mailing Add:* Intel 2250 Mission College Blvd PO Box 58125 Santa Clara CA 95052

SCHARFF, MATTHEW DANIEL, CELL BIOLOGY, IMMUNOLOGY. *Current Pos:* assoc cell biol, Albert Einstein Col Med, 63-64, from asst prof to assoc prof, 64-71, chmn dept, 71-83, dir, Div Biol Sci, 74-82, dir, Cancer Ctr, 86-95, PROF CELL BIOL, ALBERT EINSTEIN COL MED, 71- *Personal Data:* b New York, NY, Aug 28, 32; m 54, Carol Held; c Karen, Thomas & David. *Educ:* Brown Univ, AB, 54, New York Univ, MD, 59. *Hon Degrees:* DMedSci, Brown Univ, 94. *Honors & Awards:* Harvey lectr, 74; Dyer lectr, NIH, 80; NY Acad Med Medal, 90. *Prof Exp:* Intern & resident, Boston City Hosp, Mass, 59-61; res assoc, Nat Inst Allergy & Infectious Dis, 61-63. *Mem:* Nat Acad Sci; Harvey Soc; Am Asn Immunol; Am Soc Clin Invest; Am Acad Arts & Sci. *Res:* Molecular and cellular basis of the generation of antibody diversity, the origins of autoantibodies and the role of the monclonal antibodies in preventing and treating infections. *Mailing Add:* Dept Cell Biol Albert Einstein Col Med Bronx NY 10461

SCHARFF, THOMAS G, PHARMACOLOGY. *Current Pos:* RETIRED. *Personal Data:* b Paterson, NJ, Mar 9, 23; m 46; c 5. *Educ:* Trinity Col, Conn, BS, 48, MS, 51; Univ Rochester, PhD(pharmacol), 56. *Prof Exp:* Lab supvr, Bigelow-Sanford Carpet Co, 48-49; res assoc, US AEC Proj, Trinity Col, Conn, 51-52; from instr to prof pharmacol, Sch Med & Dent, Univ Louisville, 56-85. *Concurrent Pos:* Prin investr, Am Heart Asn, 63-68. *Mem:* AAAS; Am Soc Pharmacol & Exp Therapeut; Soc Exp Biol & Med; Soc Toxicol; Am Chem Soc. *Res:* Cellular pharmacology and biochemistry; cell metabolism and transport. *Mailing Add:* 3623 Windwar Way Louisville KY 40220-1817

SCHARFSTEIN, LAWRENCE ROBERT, CHEMICAL METALLURGY. *Current Pos:* GROUP LEADER, MAT ENG, MOBIL RES & DEVELOP CORP, 76- *Personal Data:* b New York, NY, July 21, 27; m 55; c 3. *Educ:* Pa State Univ, BS, 46; NY Univ, PhD(phys chem), 53. *Prof Exp:* Supvr phys chem res, Goodyear Atomic Corp, 53-55; lead engr, Bettis Plant, Westinghouse Elec Corp, 55-59; supvr corrosion res, Carpenter Steel Corp, 59-65, asst mgr chem res, 65-68, mgr chem technol res, Carpenter Technol Corp, 68-71, dir nuclear mat, 71-76. *Mem:* Am Soc Metals; Am Soc Testing & Mat; Nat Asn Corrosion Engrs; Am Chem Soc; Am Nuclear Soc. *Res:* Corrosion; chemistry of metals and surfaces; electrochemistry; plating; nuclear chemistry; physical metallurgy of stainless steels; gas-metal reactions; heat treating. *Mailing Add:* 40 Clover Lane Princeton NJ 08540

SCHARLEMANN, MARTIN G, MATHEMATICS. *Current Pos:* from asst prof to assoc prof, 76-83, PROF, UNIV CALIF SANTA BARBARA, 83- *Personal Data:* b Carlisle, Penn, Dec 6, 48. *Educ:* Princeton Univ, BA, 69; Univ Calif Berkeley, PhD, 74. *Honors & Awards:* Spitalfields lectr, London Math Soc, 87. *Prof Exp:* Vis mem, Inst Advan Study, Princeton, 74-75; asst prof, Univ Ga, 75-76. *Concurrent Pos:* Woodrow Wilson fel, 69-70; NSF res award, 74-; vis lectr, Univ Tex, 81; invited prof, Univ Paris-Sud, 86-87, Univ Marseille, 89; Alexander von Humboldt Found res fel, 89. *Mailing Add:* Univ Calif Santa Barbara Santa Barbara CA 93106-3080

SCHARN, HERMAN OTTO FRIEDRICH, MATHEMATICS, PHYSICS. *Current Pos:* RETIRED. *Personal Data:* b Germany, July 20, 11; US citizen; m 40; c 4. *Educ:* Univ Gottingen, MS, 48; Darmstadt Tech Univ, Dr rer nat(math, physics), 66. *Prof Exp:* Aeronaut engr, Aeronaut Res Inst, Ger, 40-45; high sch teacher, Hanover, 48-57; astronaut engr, Holloman AFB, USAF, 57-71 & Kirtland AFB, 71-73. *Res:* Theory of optimal trajectories in space navigation. *Mailing Add:* 8100 Connecticut St NE Albuquerque NM 87110

SCHARNHORST, KURT PETER, ACOUSTICS. *Current Pos:* Physicist superconductivity, 60-70, RES PHYSICIST SOLID STATE PHYSICS, NAVAL SURFACE WARFARE CTR, 70- *Personal Data:* b Hamburg, Ger, Apr 19, 36; US citizen; m 62; c 2. *Educ:* City Col New York, BS, 61; Univ Md, PhD(physics), 69. *Mem:* Acoust Soc Am. *Res:* Electro-optics; superconductivity; wave propagation phenomena; solid state device physics; acoustics. *Mailing Add:* 10734 Judy Lane Columbia MD 21044

SCHARPEN, LEROY HENRY, PHYSICAL CHEMISTRY, SURFACE SCIENCE. *Current Pos:* exec vpres, 76-85, PRES, SURFACE SCI LABS, INC, 85- *Personal Data:* b Red Wing, Minn, Oct 15, 35; m 63; c 2. *Educ:* Harvard Univ, AB, 61; Stanford Univ, PhD(chem), 66. *Prof Exp:* Res scientist, McDonnell Douglas Corp, 66-68; appln chemist, Sci Instruments Div, Hewlett Packard Co, 68-73, mgr electron spectros, Chem Anal Appln Lab, 73-76. *Mem:* AAAS; Am Chem Soc. *Res:* Application of surface analysis techniques to industrial research; materials and process problem solving. *Mailing Add:* 10145 McLaren Pl Cupertino CA 95014

SCHARPF, LEWIS GEORGE, JR, FERMENTATION, FLAVOR CHEMISTRY. *Current Pos:* dir develop & vpres res & develop, 77-80, vpres tech dir flavors, 80-84, INT FLAVORS & FRAGRANCES, 80-84, VPRES & DIR FLAVOR RES, 84- *Personal Data:* b Springfield, Mo, Sept 15, 40; m 65, Marian Grismore; c Sara S & Laura E. *Educ:* Southwest Mo State Univ, BS, 61; Iowa State Univ, MS, 63, PhD(biochem), 65. *Prof Exp:* Res chemist, Monsanto Co, 65-70, res specialist, Monsanto Indust Chem Co, 70-74, mgr res & develop, 74-77. *Concurrent Pos:* Mem adv coun, Inst Food Sci, Cornell Univ. *Mem:* Flavor & Extract Mfrs Asn; Am Chem Soc; Inst Food Technol; Sigma Xi. *Res:* Food and fermentation chemistry; food ingredient development; flavor chemistry. *Mailing Add:* 35 Lewis Point Rd Fair Haven NJ 07701

SCHARPF, ROBERT F, PLANT PATHOLOGY. *Current Pos:* PLANT PATHOLOGIST, PAC SOUTHWEST FOREST & RANGE EXP STA, US FOREST SERV, 60- *Personal Data:* b St Louis, Mo, June 22, 31; m 57; c 2. *Educ:* Univ Mo, BS, 54; Univ Calif, Berkeley, MS, 57, PhD(plant path), 63. *Mem:* Am Phytopath Soc. *Res:* Forest diseases; epidemiology; hyperparasites. *Mailing Add:* 8548 Mosquito Rd Placerville CA 95667-8362

SCHARPF, WILLIAM GEORGE, ORGANIC CHEMISTRY, PESTICIDE CHEMISTRY. *Current Pos:* RETIRED. *Personal Data:* b Baltimore, Md, Aug 24, 25; m 57; c Eric W & Carl D. *Educ:* Univ Md, BS, 50; Rider Col, MBA, 81. *Honors & Awards:* Thomas A Edison Patent Award, Res & Develop Coun NJ, 79. *Prof Exp:* Res chemist pesticides, US Indust Chem, 43-52; res chemist med, Johnson & Johnson, 53-56; plant chemist, Gen Elec Co, 57-58; sr process chemist boron fuels, Thiokol, 58-59; sr res chemist pesticides, FMC Corp, 59-78, res assoc, 78-86; abstracter, Inst Sci Info, 86-87; chemist, Huels Am, 87-89. *Mem:* Am Chem Soc; Org Reactions Catalysis Soc. *Res:* Structure biological activity correlations; process research related to organic pesticides, particularly carbamate and pyrethroid insecticides. *Mailing Add:* 24 Mesquite Pl Palmyra VA 22963

SCHARRER, BERTA VOGEL, neuroendocrinology, neuroimmunology; deceased, see previous edition for last biography

SCHARTON, TERRY DON, VIBRATIONS, TESTING & ACOUSTICS. *Current Pos:* TECH STAFF, JET PROPULSION LAB, CALIF INST TECHNOL, 87- *Personal Data:* b York, Nebr, May 12, 39; m 64, Mildred Harris; c Tanya, Tara, Marina, Lorna & Carla. *Educ:* Mass Inst Technol, BS, 62, MS, 64. *Hon Degrees:* ScD(mech eng), Mass Inst Technol, 66. *Prof Exp:* Regional mgr acoust, Bolt, Beranck & Newman, 66-77; prin scientist vibrations, ANCO Engrs Inc, 77-87. *Concurrent Pos:* Independent inventor, Automobile Accident Camera. *Mem:* Acoust Soc Am; Am Inst Aeronaut & Astronaut; Am Inst Automotive Engrs. *Res:* Force limited vibration testing; space craft acoustics and vibration; pressure pulse cleaning of tube bunble heat exchangers. *Mailing Add:* 1102 Stanford Santa Monica CA 90403

SCHARVER, JEFFREY DOUGLAS, ORGANIC CHEMISTRY. *Current Pos:* Res chemist, 74-81, SECT HEAD, CHEM DEVELOP LABS, BURROUGHS WELLCOME CO, USA, 81- *Personal Data:* b Massillon, Ohio, Nov 3, 47; m 70; c 2. *Educ:* Bowling Green State Univ, BS, 69; Duke Univ, PhD(chem), 75. *Mem:* Am Chem Soc. *Res:* The development of new organic processes and their application to pharmaceutical research. *Mailing Add:* 13208 Quarterhorse Run Rougemont NC 27572-9343

SCHATTEN, GERALD PHILLIP, CELL BIOLOGY, DEVELOPMENTAL BIOLOGY. *Current Pos:* dir, Integrated Micros Resource Biomed Res, 86-92, PROF, MOLECULAR BIOL, ZOOL & OBSTET-GYNEC & DIR, GAMETE & EMBRYO BIOL PROG, UNIV WIS-MADISON, 86- *Personal Data:* b New York, NY, Nov 1, 49; m 95, Heather Aronson; c Daniel. *Educ:* Univ Calif, Berkeley, BS, 71, PhD(cell biol), 75. *Honors & Awards:* Micrograph Award, Exp Cell Res, Stockholm, 76; Boehringer Ingelheim Professorship, 84. *Prof Exp:* Instr zool, Univ Calif, Berkeley, 75; fels reproduction, Rockefeller Found, NY, 76, 77 & 78; guest researcher, Ger Cancer Res Ctr, Heidelberg, 76-77; from asst prof to prof biol sci, Fla State Univ, 77-86, dir, Electron Micros Lab, Inst Molecular Biophys, 81-86. *Concurrent Pos:* Prin investr res grants, fertil, NSF, 78, 79 & 81, NIH, 79 & 81, Am Cancer Soc, 80, Environ Protection Agency, 81 & Fla State Univ Found; NIH career develop award, 80-85; core scientist, Wis Regional Primate Res Ctr, 89- *Mem:* AAAS; Am Soc Cell Biol; Soc Develop Biol; Soc Study Reproduction; Am Soc Zoologists. *Res:* Fertilization; cancer; egg activation; cell transformation; movement of sperm; pronuclear movements and fusion; intracellular calcium localization; mitosis; cytokinesis; mitotic apparatus; nuclear envelope; in vitro fertilization; reproduction in humans; video microscopy; ion localization; membranes; electron microscopy. *Mailing Add:* Univ Wis-Madison 1117 W Johnson St Madison WI 53706. Fax: 608-262-7319; E-Mail: schatten@facstaff.wisc.edu

SCHATTEN, HEIDE, CELL BIOLOGY, CANCER. *Current Pos:* SR SCIENTIST CELL BIOL, DEPT MOLECULAR BIOL & ZOOL, UNIV WIS-MADISON, 86- *Personal Data:* b Niederweidbach, WGer, Sept 24, 46; m 77. *Educ:* Ger Cancer Res Ctr, Inst Cell Res, dipl, 74, Dr rer nat, 77. *Prof Exp:* Fel cell biol, Univ Calif, Berkeley, 77; fac res assoc cell biol, Fla State Univ, 77-81, from asst res scientist to assoc res scientist cell biol, 81-86. *Concurrent Pos:* Co prin investr, NSF grant, 79; sr investr res grants, NIH, 80- & Environ Protection Agency, 81-; travel grant, Am Soc Cell Biol, 81. *Mem:* Am Soc Cell Biol; Ger Soc Cell Biol. *Res:* Fertilization; pronuclear movements; mitotic apparatus; cell division; microtubules; protein chemistry; mitosis; synchronization; cell culture; transformation; activation; cancer drugs; reproduction; electron microscopy. *Mailing Add:* Dept Zool Inst Microbiol Res Univ Wis 1117 W Johnson St Madison WI 53706-1705. Fax: 608-262-7319

SCHATTEN, KENNETH HOWARD, SOLAR PHYSICS. *Current Pos:* ASTROPHYSICIST, NASA GODDARD SPACE CTR, 79- *Personal Data:* b New York, NY, Feb 1, 44; m 70. *Educ:* Mass Inst Technol, SB, 64; Univ Calif, Berkeley, PhD(physics), 68. *Prof Exp:* Researcher space physics, Univ Calif, Berkeley, 68-69; Nat Acad Sci fel, Goddard Space Flight Ctr, NASA, 69-70, researcher, 70-72; sr lectr physics, Victoria Univ, Wellington, 72-76; vis assoc prof physics, Bartol Res Found, 76; sr res assoc, Stanford Univ, 77-78; sr res assoc, Boston Univ, 78-79. *Concurrent Pos:* Dir, Solar-Terrestrial, NSF, 91-93. *Res:* Solar terrestrial relationships; sun, solar corona, interplanetary space, geophysics; planetary physics; electric and magnetic fields; plasma physics. *Mailing Add:* Code 914 NASA Goddard Space Ctr Greenbelt MD 20771

SCHATTENBURG, MARK LEE, X-RAY LITHOGRAPHY, MICRO-NANO STRUCTURE FABRICATION. *Current Pos:* Postdoctoral assoc, 84-85, sci res staff, 85-90, RES SCIENTIST, MASS INST TECHNOL CTR SPACE RES, 90- *Personal Data:* b Colo, Apr 12, 56. *Educ:* Univ Hawaii, BS, 78; Mass Inst Technol, PhD(physics), 84. *Concurrent Pos:* Res staff, Mass Inst Technol Submicron Structures Lab, 84-; instrument scientist, NASA AXAF High Energy Transmission Gratings Spectrometer, 85- *Mem:* Am Vacuum Soc; Am Astron Soc; Int Soc Optical Eng. *Mailing Add:* Mass Inst Technol 37-421 70 Vassar St Cambridge MA 02139

SCHATTNER, ROBERT I, PHARMACEUTICAL CHEMISTRY, PESTICIDE CHEMISTRY. *Current Pos:* RES DIR, R SCHATTNER CO, 63-, OFFICER & DIR, R SCHATTNER FOUND MED RES, 64-; OFFICER & RES DIR, SPORICIDIN CO, WASHINGTON, DC, 77- *Personal Data:* b New York, NY, June 4, 25; c 2. *Educ:* Univ Pa, DDS, 48; City Univ New York, BS, 49. *Prof Exp:* Dent surgeon, USPHS, 48-49; pvt pract, 49-59. *Concurrent Pos:* Res dir, Chloraseptic Co, 52-63; consult, Norwich Pharmacal Co, 63-65. *Mem:* Am Soc Microbiol; Royal Soc Health; Int Dent Fedn; Am Dent Asn; Am Chem Soc; Dent Mfg Asn; Am Dent Trade Asn. *Res:* Chemical development of new sterilizing solution; aerosol disinfectant spray; antimicrobial additive and preservative; antiseptic and analgesic pharmaceutical preparation for skin, lips and vagina. *Mailing Add:* 7101 Pyle Rd Bethesda MD 20817

SCHATTSCHNEIDER, DORIS JEAN, DISCRETE GEOMETRY, CURRICULUM MATERIALS DEVELOPMENT. *Current Pos:* PROF MATH, MORAVIAN COL, 68- *Personal Data:* b New York, NY, Oct 19, 39; m 62, David A; c Laura E. *Educ:* Univ Rochester, AB, 61; Yale Univ, MA, 63, PhD(math) 66. *Honors & Awards:* Allendoerfer Award, Math Asn Am, 79, Cert Meritorious Serv, 91; Distinguished Teaching Col Math Award, Math Asn Am, 94. *Prof Exp:* Instr math, Northwestern Univ, 64-65; asst prof math, Univ Ill Chicago, 65-68. *Concurrent Pos:* Chair, Math Dept, Moravian Col, 71-74, 85-91; gov, Math Asn Am, 81-89; ed, Math Mag, 81-85; sr assoc, Visual Geometry Proj, NSF, 86-91; prin investr, Humanities, Sci & Technol Proj, NEH, 88-90; proj dir, Pre-calculus & Calculus Proj, Fund Improv Post-Sec Educ, 91-93 & 95-97. *Mem:* Math Asn Am (vpres, 94-96); Am Math Soc; Asn Women Math; Nat Coun Teachers Math. *Res:* Geometry, especially tiling and polyhedra; teaching of geometry; geometry and art; art of M C Escher. *Mailing Add:* Math Dept Moravian Col 1200 Main St Bethlehem PA 18018. *Fax:* 215-861-1462; *E-Mail:* schattdo@moravian.edu

SCHATZ, EDWARD R(ALPH), electrical engineering; deceased, see previous edition for last biography

SCHATZ, GEORGE CHAPPELL, QUANTUM REACTIVE SCATTERING. *Current Pos:* from asst prof to assoc prof, 76-82, PROF CHEM, NORTHWESTERN UNIV, 82- *Personal Data:* b Watertown, NY, Apr 14, 49; m 75, Margaret E Kimmett; c Paul, Albert & Jonathan. *Educ:* Clarkson Univ, BS, 71; Calif Inst Technol, PhD(chem), 75. *Honors & Awards:* Dreyfus Award, 81-86; Fresenius Award, 83; Max Planck Award, 93. *Prof Exp:* Res assoc, Mass Inst Technol, 75-76. *Concurrent Pos:* Consult, Argonne Nat Lab, 78-82 & staff scientist appointee, 83-86, vis scientist, 86-; consult, Battelle Columbus Lab, 79-80, Signal Res Ctr, 85-86 & Pac Northwest Lab, 92-; Sloan Res Fel, 80-82; vis fel, Joint Inst Lab Astrophys, 88-89; sr ed, J Phys Chem, 93- *Mem:* Am Chem Soc; Fel Am Phys Soc; Combustion Inst; AAAS. *Res:* Theoretical chemistry; quantum reactive scattering; classical trajectory simulations; collision induced energy transfer; potential energy surfaces; combustion kinetics; state to state chemistry; surface enhanced spectroscopy; electrodynamics near rough metal surfaces. *Mailing Add:* Dept Chem Northwestern Univ Evanston IL 60208-3113. *Fax:* 847-491-7713; *E-Mail:* g-schatz@nwu.edu

SCHATZ, IRWIN JACOB, INTERNAL MEDICINE, CARDIOVASCULAR DISEASES. *Current Pos:* PROF MED & CHMN DEPT, JOHN A BURNS SCH MED, UNIV HAWAII, HONOLULU, 75- *Personal Data:* b St Boniface, Man, Oct 16, 31; m 67; c 4. *Educ:* Univ Man, MD, 56. *Prof Exp:* Fel, Mayo Clin, 58-61; chief sect peripheral vascular dis, Henry Ford Hosp, Detroit, 61-68; chief sect cardiovasc dis, Sch Med, Wayne State Univ, 68-72; assoc prof cardiol, Med Ctr, Univ Mich, Ann Arbor, 72-75, assoc dir div cardiol, 72-75, prof med, 73-75. *Concurrent Pos:* Fel coun circulation & clin cardiol, Am Heart Asn; spec consult health manpower, Dept HEW, 68-69; past gov, Am Col Cardiol; past pres, Hawaii Health Asn; chmn, Residency Rev Comt Int Med, 93-94. *Mem:* Master Am Col Physicians; fel Am Col Cardiol. *Res:* Ischemic heart disease; atherosclerosis; orthostatic hypotension; ciguatera poisoning. *Mailing Add:* Dept Med Univ Hawaii Med Sch 1356 Lusitana St Honolulu HI 96813

SCHATZ, JOSEPH ARTHUR, MATHEMATICS. *Current Pos:* ASSOC PROF MATH & COMPUT SCI, UNIV HOUSTON, 72- *Personal Data:* b US, June 23, 24; m 48; c 4. *Educ:* Va Polytech Inst, BS, 47; Brown Univ, PhD(math), 52. *Prof Exp:* Draftsman, E I du Pont de Nemours & Co, Inc, 41-42; inspector, Signal Corps, US Dept Army, 42-43, engr, Manhattan Proj, 46; ed asst, Math Rev, Am Math Soc, 48-52; instr math, Lehigh Univ, 52-55 & Univ Conn, 55-57; mem staff, Sandia Corp, 57-72. *Mem:* Am Math Soc; Math Asn Am; Asn Comput Mach; Asn Symbolic Logic; Sigma Xi. *Res:* Applied mathematics; computer sciences; logic. *Mailing Add:* Dept Math Univ Houston Houston TX 77004

SCHATZ, PAUL NAMON, PHYSICAL CHEMISTRY. *Current Pos:* from asst prof to assoc prof, 56-65, PROF CHEM, UNIV VA, 65- *Personal Data:* b Philadelphia, Pa, Oct 20, 28; m 54; c 3. *Educ:* Univ Pa, BS, 49; Brown Univ, PhD(chem), 52. *Prof Exp:* Jewett fel, Calif Inst Technol, 52-53; res assoc chem, Brown Univ, 53-54. *Concurrent Pos:* NSF sr fel, Oxford Univ, 63-64, Guggenheim fel, 74-75; vis sr res fel, St Johns Col, Oxford, 88; vis Erskine fel, Univ Canterbury, NZ, 93. *Mem:* Am Chem Soc; Am Phys Soc. *Res:* Molecular structure, especially spectroscopy and quantum mechanics. *Mailing Add:* Dept Chem Univ Va Chem Bldg 134 Charlottesville VA 22903. *E-Mail:* pns@virginia.edu

SCHATZKI, THOMAS FERDINANT, CHEMICAL PHYSICS, IMAGE ANALYSIS. *Current Pos:* LEAD SCIENTIST, WESTERN REGIONAL LAB, USDA, 72- *Personal Data:* b Berlin, Ger, Oct 20, 27; nat US; m 52; c 2. *Educ:* Univ Mich, BS, 49; Mass Inst Technol, PhD(chem), 54. *Prof Exp:* Res assoc, Univ Wis, 54-55 & Univ Ill, 55-57; chemist, Shell Develop Co, Calif, 57-72. *Mem:* Am Soc Agr Engrs; Inst Elec & Electronics Engrs. *Res:* Image analysis; polymer physics; real-time inspection systems. *Mailing Add:* USDA Western Regional Lab Albany CA 94710. *E-Mail:* tom@pw.usda.gov

SCHATZLEIN, FRANK CHARLES, invertebrate physiology; deceased, see previous edition for last biography

SCHAUB, FRED S, MECHANICAL ENGINEERING. *Current Pos:* PROF ENGR, COOPER-BESSEMER DIV, 52- & MGR RES & DEVELOP, COOPER ENERGY SERVICES, MT VERNON, 68- *Educ:* Antioch Coll, BSME, 52. *Honors & Awards:* Internal Combustion Engine Award, Am Soc Mech Engrs, 91. *Mem:* Combustion Inst. *Res:* Nitrous oxide reduction for spark-ignited engines, nitrous oxide reduction for duel fuel engines; cylinder scavenging and combution-diagnostic techniques; granted patents for nitrous oxide reduction for spark-ignited engines. *Mailing Add:* Cooper Energy Servs-Bessemer Div N Sandusky St Mt Vernon OH 43050

SCHAUB, JAMES H(AMILTON), CIVIL ENGINEERING. *Current Pos:* prof, 69-84, chmn dept, 84-87, DISTINGUISHED SERV PROF CIVIL ENG DEPT, UNIV FLA, 84- *Personal Data:* b Moundsville, WVa, Jan 27, 25; m 48. *Educ:* Va Polytech Inst, BS, 48; Harvard Univ, SM, 49; Purdue Univ, PhD(civil eng), 60. *Honors & Awards:* William H Wisely Award, Am Soc Civil Engrs, 86. *Prof Exp:* Soils engr, State Hwy Dept, Ore, 49-50 & 51-52; lab dir, Palmer & Baker, Inc, Ala, 52-55; asst prof civil eng, Va Polytech Inst, 55-58; instr & res engr, Purdue Univ, 58-60; prof & chmn dept, Univ WVa, 60-67, assoc dean eng, 67-69. *Concurrent Pos:* Fel, NSF, 75-76; conquest prof humanities, Va Mil Inst, 86; vis prof eng, Swarthmore Col, 88. *Mem:* Fel Am Soc Civil Engrs; Am Soc Eng Educ; Nat Soc Prof Engrs; Am Pub Works Asn. *Res:* Soil mechanics; highway engineering; professional ethics. *Mailing Add:* 4401 NW 15th Pl Gainesville FL 32605

SCHAUB, ROBERT GEORGE, VASCULAR BIOLOGY, THROMBOSIS. *Current Pos:* head res pharmacol, 90-91, dir pre clin biol, 91-93, DIR PHARMACOL RES, GENETICS INST, 93- *Personal Data:* b Belleuvue, Pa, Dec 16, 47; m 83; c 1. *Educ:* Univ Nev, BS, 70; Wash State Univ, PhD(physiol), 73. *Prof Exp:* Fel thrombosis, Wash State Univ, 73-75 & SCOR Thrombosis Temple Univ, 75-77; from asst prof to assoc prof physiol, Univ Tenn, 77-82; sr res scientist, Upjohn Co, 82-86, sr scientist thrombosis, 86-90. *Mem:* Am Physiol Soc; Soc Exp Biol & Med; Int Soc Thrombosis & Haemostasis; NY Acad Sci; Sigma Xi; Am Asn Pathologists; Am Soc Hemat. *Res:* Animal models of vascular injury; thrombosis and coagulation; pathophysiology of peripheral circulation; electron microscopy of blood vessels and blood formed elements; hematopoiesis. *Mailing Add:* Pre Clin Res & Develop Genetics Inst 87 Cambridge Park Dr Cambridge MA 02140-2387. *E-Mail:* rschaub@genetics.com

SCHAUB, STEPHEN ALEXANDER, VIROLOGY & PUBLIC HEALTH, EPIDEMIOLOGY & RISK ASSESSMENT. *Current Pos:* SR MICROBIOLOGIST, OFF WATER, US ENVIRON PROTECTION AGENCY, 92- *Personal Data:* b Walla Walla, Wash, Sept 29, 40; m 65; c 2. *Educ:* Wash State Univ, BS, 64; Univ Tex, Austin, MA, 70, PhD(microbiol), 72. *Prof Exp:* Scientist, USPHS, 64-66; res microbiologist, Biomed Res & Develop Lab, US Army, 72-73, survry microbiologist, 74-92. *Concurrent Pos:* Consult, US Justice Dept. *Mem:* Am Soc Microbiol; Sigma Xi; AAAS; Am Water Works Asn. *Res:* Virus concentration and enumeration from water and wastewater; aerobiology of spray irrigation of wastewater; infiltration of viruses in land systems by wastewater application; mechanisms of microbial disinfection, point of use water purification; rapid toxicity testing; microbiol risk assessment; protozoa asaltical methods; drinking water regulation development. *Mailing Add:* 3526 Rippling Way Laurel MD 21784

SCHAUBERT, DANIEL HAROLD, ANTENNAS, MICROWAVE ENGINEERING. *Current Pos:* assoc prof, 82-88, PROF ELEC ENG, UNIV MASS, AMHERST, 88- *Personal Data:* b Galesburg, Ill, Feb 15, 47; m 68, Joyce M Conard; c Karen L. *Educ:* Univ Ill, BS, 69, MS, 70, PhD(elec eng), 74. *Prof Exp:* Sr res & develop eng, Harry Diamond Labs, 74-80; sr res & develop eng & prog mgr, US Bur Radiol Health, 80-82. *Concurrent Pos:* Chmn, Inst Elec & Electronics Engrs Antenna & Propagation Soc, 79-81, newslett ed, 82-84, secy-treas, 84-89, assoc ed, 90-93; mem, Nat Res Coun Comt US Army Basic Res, 85-88; vis researcher, Plessey Res & Technol, 89-90. *Mem:* Fel Inst Elec & Electronics Engrs; Int Radio Sci Union. *Res:* Printed circuit antennas and phased array design and analysis; cellular and PCS antennas; scattering and absorption by dielectric and metallic bodies; antenna and scattering characteristics for transient applications. *Mailing Add:* 149 Aubinwood Rd Amherst MA 01002

SCHAUBLE, J HERMAN, ORGANIC CHEMISTRY. *Current Pos:* assoc prof org chem, 65-80, PROF CHEM, VILLANOVA UNIV, 80- *Personal Data:* b Macomb, Ill, Jan 18, 32; m 58; c 2. *Educ:* Western Ill Univ, BS, 54, MS, 56; Univ Ill, PhD(org chem), 64. *Prof Exp:* Instr chem, Springfield Jr Col, 56-59; res assoc, Mass Inst Technol, 63-65. *Mem:* Am Chem Soc; Royal Soc Chem. *Res:* Synthesis and conformational analysis of four and five membered ring heterocycles; organosulfur and selenium chemistry; synthetic photochemistry in the crystal state and in solution; complex metal hydride reduction of carbon-carbon multiple bonds. *Mailing Add:* 13 Chetwynd Rd Paoli PA 19301-1817

SCHAUER, JOHN JOSEPH, MECHANICAL ENGINEERING. *Current Pos:* PROF MECH ENG, UNIV DAYTON, 68-, CHMN DEPT, 85- *Personal Data:* b Dayton, Ohio, Aug 5, 36; m 70; c 4. *Educ:* Univ Dayton, BME, 58; Carnegie-Mellon Univ, MS, 59; Stanford Univ, PhD(mech eng), 64. *Prof Exp:* Assoc prin res engr, Technol, Inc, Ohio, 65-67. *Res:* Convective heat and mass transfer; acoustics. *Mailing Add:* 209 Telford Ave Dayton OH 45419

SCHAUER, RICHARD C, MOLECULAR ENDOCRINOLOGY. *Current Pos:* ASSOC PROF, GANNON UNIV, ERIE, 78- *Personal Data:* b Pittsburgh, Pa, July 21, 37; m 69; c 2. *Educ:* Univ Pittsburgh, BS, 60; NC State Univ, MS, 68, PhD(physiol zool), 72. *Prof Exp:* From instr to asst prof physiol, Univ NC, Greensboro, 71-78. *Mem:* AAAS; Sigma Xi. *Res:* Effects of estrogen on rat uterus and heart; molecular endocrinology. *Mailing Add:* 4139 Harvard Rd Erie PA 16509. *E-Mail:* schauer__r@cluster.gannon.edu

SCHAUF, CHARLES LAWRENCE, physiology, biophysics, for more information see previous edition

SCHAUF, VICTORIA, infectious diseases, immunology, for more information see previous edition

SCHAUFELE, ROGER DONALD, ENGINEERING DESIGN, AERODYNAMICS. *Current Pos:* CORP CONSULT, 89- *Personal Data:* b Woodbridge, NJ, Mar 30, 28; m 49, Barbara Harkness; c Margaret Roger Jr. *Educ:* Rensselaer Polytech Inst, BAE, 49; Calif Inst Technol, MS, 52. *Honors & Awards:* Frank Kolk Award, Soc Automotive Engrs. *Prof Exp:* Dir technol, Douglas Aircraft Corp, 71-76, dir advan eng, 76-79, dir aircraft design, 79-81, vpres eng, 81-87, vpres & gen mgr com advan prods, 87-89. *Concurrent Pos:* Prof, aircraft design, Calif State Univ, Long Beach. *Mem:* Fel Am Inst Aeronaut & Astronaut; fel Soc Automotive Eng; fel Inst Advan Engr; Nat Aeronaut Asn; Exp Aircraft Asn. *Res:* Engineering design; aerodynamics; commercial advanced design. *Mailing Add:* 13112 Wheeler Pl Santa Ana CA 92705

SCHAUFELE, RONALD A, PROBABILITY. *Current Pos:* RETIRED. *Personal Data:* b Calgary, Alta, Oct 5, 30; m 53, Mary R Houston. *Educ:* Univ Alta, BEd, 56; Univ Wash, BSc, 57, MSc, 62, PhD(math), 63. *Prof Exp:* Asst prof statist, Stanford Univ, 63-64 & Columbia Univ, 64-66; from asst prof to assoc prof math, York Univ, 66-96. *Concurrent Pos:* Can Nat Res Coun grant, 68-69. *Mem:* Am Math Soc; Math Asn Am; Inst Math Statist; Can Math Soc; Can Statist Asn; Am Statist Asn. *Res:* Probability; stochastic processes. *Mailing Add:* 36 S Turner St Apt 201 Victoria BC V8V 2J6 Can

SCHAUMANN, ROLF, FILTER DESIGN, INTEGRATED CIRCUITS. *Current Pos:* PROF & CHAIR ELEC ENG, PORTLAND STATE UNIV, 88- *Personal Data:* b Nuremberg, Ger, July 29, 41; m 69. *Educ:* Univ Stuttgart, DiplIng, 67; Univ Minn, Minneapolis, PhD(elec eng), 70. *Prof Exp:* Prof elec eng, Univ Minn, Minneapolis, 70-88. *Mem:* Inst Elec & Electronics Engrs. *Res:* Theory of active and passive networks; distributed networks; analog integrated circuits; analog filters. *Mailing Add:* 1580 NW 102nd Ave Portland OR 97229-5256

SCHAUMBERG, GENE DAVID, ENVIRONMENTAL CHEMISTRY. *Current Pos:* from asst prof to assoc prof, 65-72, chmn, Div Natural Sci, 69-78, PROF ORG CHEM, SONOMA STATE UNIV, 72- *Personal Data:* b Rochester, Minn, Oct 3, 39; m 88, Terrie Defiesta; c Jason, Nathan, Jocelyn & Tara. *Educ:* Pac Lutheran Univ, BS, 61; Wash State Univ, PhD(chem), 65. *Concurrent Pos:* Fulbright lectr, 71-72, 80-81, 91, 92 & 94; Scientists & Engrs in Econ Develop & NSF grant, 75; vis prof, Univ Calif, Riverside, 79-80 & Univ Hawaii, 85-86; Indo Am fel, 81-82. *Mem:* Am Chem Soc; Sigma Xi; AAAS. *Res:* Synthesis of new organoboron compounds of possible biological interest; soil and environmental chemistry. *Mailing Add:* Dept Chem Sonoma State Univ Rohnert Park CA 94928. *E-Mail:* gene.schaumberg@sonoma.edu

SCHAUMBERGER, NORMAN, MATHEMATICS. *Current Pos:* RETIRED. *Personal Data:* b Brooklyn, NY, May 2 8, 29; m 54; c 2. *Educ:* City Col New York, BS, 51, MA, 52; Brooklyn Col, MA, 58; Columbia Univ, EdD(math educ), 62. *Prof Exp:* Teacher, NY Pub Schs, 51-57; instr math, Cooper Union, 57; prof math, Bronx Community Col, 59-92. *Concurrent Pos:* Lectr, City Col New York, 55-63; instr, Teachers Col, Columbia Univ, 63; NSF acad year inst sec math teachers, Dominican Col, NY, 66-67. *Mem:* Math Asn Am; Am Math Soc. *Res:* Problems in number theory and complex variables. *Mailing Add:* 62-59 Douglaston Pkwy Flushing NY 11362-1532

SCHAUMBURG, HERBERT HOWARD, NEUROLOGY, EXPERIMENTAL NEUROPATHOLOGY. *Current Pos:* assoc prof, 72-76, PROF NEUROL, ALBERT EINSTEIN COL MED, 77-, VCHMN DEPT, 78- *Personal Data:* b Houston, Tex, Nov 6, 32; m 66; c 2. *Educ:* Harvard Univ, AB, 56; Wash Univ, MD, 60. *Honors & Awards:* Moore Award, Am Asn Neuropath, 77. *Prof Exp:* Fel neurol, Albert Einstein Col Med, 67-69; instr path, Harvard Med Sch, 69-71. *Mem:* Am Soc Neurol; Am Neurol Asn; Am Asn Neuropathologists. *Res:* Experimental neuropathology of myelin disease and effects of toxic chemicals on nervous system. *Mailing Add:* 1300 Morris Park Ave Bronx NY 10467

SCHAWLOW, ARTHUR LEONARD, LASERS. *Current Pos:* chmn, Dept Physics, 66-70 & 71-78, prof physics, 71-83, J G Jackson-C J wood prof, 78-91, EMER PROF PHYSICS, STANFORD UNIV, 91- *Personal Data:* b Mt Vernon, NY, May 5, 21; m 51, Aurelia Townes (deceased); c Arthur K, Helen & Edith. *Educ:* Univ Toronto, BA, 41, MA, 42, PhD, 49. *Hon Degrees:* DSc, State Univ Ghent, 68, Univ Bradford, 70, Univ Ala, 84, Trinity Col, Dublin, 86; LLD, Univ Toronto, 70; DTech, Lund Univ, 88; DSL Victoria Univ, Toronto, 93. *Honors & Awards:* Nobel Prize Physics, 81; Nat Medal of Sci, 91; Thomas Young Medal & Prize, Brit Inst Physics, 63; Liebmann Mem Prize, Inst Elec & Electronics Engrs, 64; Frederick Ives Medal, Optical Soc Am, 76; Ballantine Medal, Franklin Inst, 62; Schawlow Medal, Laser Inst Am, 82; Nat Inventors Hall Fame, 96; Ronald H Brown Am Innovator Award, US Dept Com, 96. *Prof Exp:* Demonstr physics, Univ Toronto, 41-44; physicist microwave develop, Res Enterprises, Ltd, 44-45; demonstr physics, Univ Toronto, 45-49; fel & res assoc, Columbia Univ, 49-51; res physicist, Bell Tel Labs, Inc, 51-61. *Concurrent Pos:* Vis assoc prof, Columbia Univ, 60; Marconi int fel, 77. *Mem:* Nat Acad Sci; fel AAAS; fel Am Phys Soc (pres, 81); hon mem & fel Optical Soc Am (pres, 75); fel Inst Elec & Electronics Engrs; fel Am Acad Arts & Sci; fel Am Philos Soc; hon mem Am Soc Laser Med & Surg. *Res:* Radio frequency, optical and microwave spectroscopy; lasers and quantum electronics. *Mailing Add:* Dept Physics Stanford Univ Stanford CA 94305-4060. *Fax:* 650-725-2376; *E-Mail:* alschawl@pacbell.net

SCHAY, GEZA, MATHEMATICAL PHYSICS. *Current Pos:* assoc prof, 66-70, PROF MATH, UNIV MASS, BOSTON, 70- *Personal Data:* b Budapest, Hungary, June 22, 34; US citizen. *Educ:* Eotvos Lorand Univ, Budapest, BA, 56; Princeton Univ, PhD(math physics), 61. *Prof Exp:* Instr physics, Tufts Univ, 58-59; staff mathematician, Int Bus Mach Corp, 60-63; from asst prof to assoc prof math, George Washington Univ, 63-66. *Mem:* Am Math Soc; Inst Math Statist. *Res:* Stochastic processes; diffusion theory; relativistic mechanics. *Mailing Add:* 298 Waltham St Newton MA 02165-1721

SCHAYER, RICHARD WILLIAM, BIOCHEMICAL PHARMACOLOGY. *Current Pos:* RETIRED. *Personal Data:* b Sydney, Australia, Feb 3, 15; US citizen; m 39; c 2. *Educ:* George Washington Univ, BS, 40; Columbia Univ, PhD(biochem), 49. *Hon Degrees:* MD, Univ Lund, 75. *Prof Exp:* Chemist, USPHS, 36-42; asst, Columbia Univ, 46-49; res assoc, Rheumatic Fever Res Inst, Med Sch, Northwestern Univ, 49-57; Merck Inst Therapeut Res, 57-64; USPHS spec fel, 64-65; prin res scientist, Rockland Res Inst, 65-80. *Mem:* Am Soc Biol Chemists; Am Soc Pharmacol & Exp Therapeut; Am Physiol Soc; Soc Exp Biol & Med; Brit Pharmacol Soc. *Res:* Histamine; metabolism; physiological and pathological significance; mechanism of action of glucocorticoids. *Mailing Add:* 250 Main St Apt 19A Spring Valley NY 10977

SCHEAFFER, RICHARD LEWIS, STATISTICS. *Current Pos:* From asst prof to assoc prof statist, 67-77, PROF STATIST & CHMN DEPT, UNIV FLA, 77- *Personal Data:* b Williamsport, Pa, July 13, 40; m 63; c 2. *Educ:* Lycoming Col, AB, 62; Bucknell Univ, MA, 64; Fla State Univ, PhD(statist), 68. *Mem:* Fel Am Statist Asn; Inst Math Statist; Biomet Soc; Int Statist Inst. *Res:* Sampling theory; applied probability, especially in the areas of reliability and two and three dimensional sampling problems. *Mailing Add:* 907 NW 21st Terr Gainesville FL 32603

SCHEARER, LAIRD D, atomic physics; deceased, see previous edition for last biography

SCHEARER, SHERWOOD BRUCE, POPULATION STUDIES. *Current Pos:* EXEC DIR, SYNERGOS INST, 87- *Personal Data:* b Reading, Pa, Jan 27, 42; m 63; c 2. *Educ:* Lafayette Col, AB, 63; Columbia Univ, PhD(biochem), 71. *Prof Exp:* From res assoc to staff scientist, Pop Resource Ctr, 71-74, asst dir, Biomed Div, 71-76, from assoc to sr assoc, Int Progs Div, Pop Coun, 76-81, pres, 81-87. *Concurrent Pos:* Mem, Bd Dir, Western Hemisphere Region, Int Planned Parenthood Fedn, 77-81, Planned Parenthood New York, Pop Resource Ctr, Adv Bd, Margaret Sanger Ctr; chmn, Western Hemisphere Res/Int Planned Fedn Info & Educ Panel, 79-81. *Mem:* AAAS. *Res:* Development, transfer, absorption, implementation and monitoring of contraceptive technology; design and evaluation of epidemiological studies of drugs and devices; social science research into attitudes and practices of populations; analysis and development of population policy. *Mailing Add:* Synergos Inst 100 E 83rd St New York NY 10028

SCHEARER, WILLIAM RICHARD, NATURAL PRODUCTS CHEMISTRY, CHEMISTRY OF NUTRITION. *Current Pos:* assoc prof, 68-92, EMER PROF CHEM, DICKINSON COL, 92- *Personal Data:* b Kutztown, Pa, July 19, 35; m 58; c 3. *Educ:* Ursinus Col, BS, 57; Princeton Univ, MA, 59, PhD(org chem), 63. *Prof Exp:* From asst prof to assoc prof chem, Hartwick Col, 61-65; sr chemist, Ciba Pharmaceut Co, 65-68. *Concurrent Pos:* Vis prof, Lehigh Univ, 81-82. *Mem:* Am Chem Soc. *Res:* Natural products; chemical education; applied chemistry. *Mailing Add:* 1010 Rockledge Dr Dickinson Col Carlisle PA 17013-9127

SCHECHTER, ALAN NEIL, MEDICAL RESEARCH, MOLECULAR BIOLOGY. *Current Pos:* res assoc, Nat Inst Diabetes, Digestive & Kidney Dis, NIH 65-67, USPHS vis fel, 67-68, med officer, 68-72, CHIEF, SECT MACROMOLECULAR BIOL, LAB CHEM BIOL, NAT INST DIABETES, DIGESTIVE & KIDNEY DIS, NIH, 72-, CHIEF, LAB CHEM BIOL, 81- *Personal Data:* b New York, NY, June 28, 39; m 65, Geraldine Poppa; c Daniele & Andrew. *Educ:* Cornell Univ, AB, 59; Columbia Univ, MD, 63. *Prof Exp:* Intern med, Bronx Munic Hosp Ctr, 63-64; asst resident, 64-65. *Concurrent Pos:* Sr asst surgeon, USPHS, 65-67 & med dir, 83- *Mem:* Asn Am Physicians; Am Fedn Clin Res; Am Soc Biol Chemists; Am Soc Clin Invest; Biophys Soc; Am Soc Human Genetics. *Res:* Structure-function relations in proteins; hemoglobin chemistry; molecular genetics; genetic disease; hemoglobin biochemistry and diseases, molecular genetics, pathophysiology and treatment of genetic disease. *Mailing Add:* Lab Chem Biol NIDDK NIH Bldg 10 Rm 9N307 Bethesda MD 20892. *Fax:* 301-402-0101; *E-Mail:* caschecht@helix.nih.gov

SCHECHTER, GERALDINE POPPA, HEMATOLOGY. *Current Pos:* resident med & hemat, 65-67, res assoc hemat, 68-69, asst chief, 70-74, CHIEF HEMAT, VET ADMIN HOSP, WASHINGTON, DC, 74- *Personal Data:* b New York, NY, Jan 16, 38; m 65; c 2. *Educ:* Vassar Col, AB, 59; Columbia Univ, MD, 63. *Prof Exp:* Intern & asst resident med, Columbia-Presby Hosp, 63-65. *Concurrent Pos:* From asst prof to assoc prof, George Washington Univ, 70-81, prof med, 81- *Mem:* Am Fedn Clin Res; Am Soc Hemat; Am Soc Clin Oncol; Am Asn Immunol. *Res:* Lymphocyte biology; immunological response to blood transfusion; hematological malignancies. *Mailing Add:* Hemat Div 688/1516 Vet Admin Med Ctr 50 Irving St Washington DC 20422-0001

SCHECHTER, JOEL ERNEST, CELL BIOLOGY, ELECTRON MICROSCOPY. *Current Pos:* asst prof, 69-73, assoc prof histol, 73-80, ASSOC PROF ANAT, SCH MED, UNIV SOUTHERN CALIF, 73- *Personal Data:* b Detroit, Mich, Apr 18, 39; div; c 2. *Educ:* Wayne State Univ, BA, 61; Johns Hopkins Univ, MA, 63; Univ Calif, Los Angeles, PhD(anat), 68. *Prof Exp:* Instr med art, Sch Med, Johns Hopkins Univ, 63-64. *Concurrent Pos:* Univ Calif, Los Angeles ment health trainee & fel, Brain Res Inst, Los Angeles, 68-69; instr exten art prog, Univ Calif, Los Angeles, 69- *Mem:* AAAS; Am Soc Cell Biol; Tissue Cult Asn; Am Asn Anatomists. *Res:* Developmental cell biology; ultrastructural histochemical studies of human pituitary tumors. *Mailing Add:* Dept cell & Neurobiol Univ Southern Calif 1333 San Pablo St Los Angeles CA 90033. *Fax:* 213-342-3158

SCHECHTER, JOSEPH M, PHYSICS. *Current Pos:* from asst prof to assoc prof, 67-74, PROF PHYSICS, SYRACUSE UNIV, 75- *Personal Data:* b New York, NY, Sept 28, 38. *Educ:* Cooper Union, BEE, 59; Univ Rochester, PhD(physics), 65. *Prof Exp:* Res assoc physics, Fermi Inst, Univ Chicago, 65-67. *Mem:* Am Phys Soc. *Res:* Theoretical elementary particle physics. *Mailing Add:* Dept Physics Syracuse Univ Syracuse NY 13244-1130. *E-Mail:* schechte@suhep.phy.syr.edu

SCHECHTER, MARSHALL DAVID, CHILD PSYCHIATRY. *Current Pos:* PROF PSYCHIAT & DIR DIV CHILD & ADOLESCENT PSYCHIAT, SCH MED, UNIV PA, PHILADELPHIA, 76- *Personal Data:* b Sept 4, 21; US citizen; div; c 4. *Educ:* Univ Wis, BS, 42; Univ Cincinnati, MD, 44. *Hon Degrees:* MA, Univ Pa, 77. *Prof Exp:* Pvt pract, 49-64; clin instr psychiat, Sch Med, Univ Calif, Los Angeles, 53, asst clin prof, 57, assoc clin prof, 63-64; prof psychiat, vchmn & head div child psychiat, Health Sci Ctr, Univ Okla, 69-73, consult prof pediat, 64-73; prof biol psychol, 66-73; prof & dir div child & adolescent psychiat, State Univ NY Upstate Med Ctr, 73-76. *Concurrent Pos:* Consult, Vet Admin Hosp, Oklahoma City, 64-73, Children's Med Ctr, Tulsa, 64-73, Okla State Dept Pub Health, 64-73, Okla State Dept Ment Health, 64-73, Wilford Hall, Lackland AFB, 66-, Head Start, Off Econ Opportunity, Hutchings Psychiat Ctr, 73-, Vet Admin Hosp, NY, 74-76, Off Child Develop, 75, Nat Inst Ment Hyg, 75-76 & Vet Admin Hosp, Philadelphia, 76-; distinguished vis prof, Wilford Hall Lackland Air Force Base, 72- *Mem:* Am Psychiat Asn; Am Psychoanal Asn; Soc Res & Child Develop. *Res:* Adoption; adolescence; autism; learning disabilities. *Mailing Add:* 1142 Morris Rd Univ Pa Wynnewood PA 19096-2313

SCHECHTER, MARTIN, PARTIAL DIFFERENTIAL EQUATIONS. *Current Pos:* PROF MATH, UNIV CALIF, 83- *Personal Data:* b Philadelphia, Pa, Mar 10, 30; m 57; c 4. *Educ:* City Col New York, BS, 53; NY Univ, MS, 55, PhD(math), 57. *Prof Exp:* Assoc res scientist, NY Univ, 57-58, from instr to asst prof math, 58-61; vis assoc prof, Univ Chicago, 61-62; from assoc prof to prof, NY Univ, 62-66; prof math, 65-85, Yeshiva Univ, chmn dept, 66-69. *Concurrent Pos:* NSF sr fel, 65-66; mem, Inst Advan Study, 65-66, mem, Asn, 74-; vis prof math, Hebrew Univ, 73 & Univ Mex, 79. *Mem:* Am Math Soc; Inst Adv Studies. *Res:* Partial differential equations; functional analysis; operator theory; quantum mechanics; scattering theory; spectral theory. *Mailing Add:* Dept Math Univ Calif Irvine CA 92717-3875. *Fax:* 714-856-7993; *E-Mail:* mschecht@math.uci.edu

SCHECHTER, MARTIN DAVID, PHARMACOLOGY. *Current Pos:* PROF & CHMN PHARMACOL, COL MED, NORTHEASTERN OHIO UNIV, 78- *Personal Data:* b Brooklyn, NY, Feb 28, 45; m 68, Audrey; c Jason. *Educ:* Brooklyn Col, BS, 65; State Univ NY Buffalo, PhD(pharmacol), 70. *Prof Exp:* Res assoc pharmacol, Med Col Va, 70-72; sr res fel, Univ Melbourne, 72-74; from asst prof to assoc prof pharmacol, Eastern Va Med Sch, 74-78. *Concurrent Pos:* Fel, NIMH, 68-70; fel, AMA Educ & Res Found, 70-72, sr res fel, 72-74. *Mem:* Sigma Xi; Soc Neurosci; Behav Pharmacol Soc; Am Soc Pharmacol & Exp Therapeut; Am Chem Soc. *Res:* Psychopharmacology with special interest in correlations between behavioral and biochemical events associated with centrally-active drugs; operant conditioning; stimulus properties of drugs; drug abuse; conditioned place preference; genetic control of addiction. *Mailing Add:* Dept Pharmacol Northeastern Ohio Univ Col Med PO Box 95 Rootstown OH 44272. *E-Mail:* mds@neoucom.edu

SCHECHTER, MILTON SEYMOUR, ORGANIC CHEMISTRY, AGRICULTURAL CHEMISTRY. *Current Pos:* RETIRED. *Personal Data:* b Brooklyn, NY, Aug 9, 15; m 46; c 2. *Educ:* Brooklyn Col, BS, 35. *Honors & Awards:* Harvey W Wiley Award, Asn Off Agr Chem, 62; Burdick & Jackson Int Award, Am Chem Soc, 80. *Prof Exp:* Chemist, Insecticide Div, Bur Entom & Plant Quarantine, USDA, Northeastern Region, 37-53 & Pesticide Chem Res Br, Entom Res Div, 53-72, chief chem & biophys control lab, Agr Environ Qual Inst, Beltsville Agr Res Ctr, 72-75, consult, Chem & Biophys Control Lab, Beltsville, Agr Res Ctr, Sci & Educ Admin-Agr Res, 75-88. *Concurrent Pos:* Chmn pesticide monitoring subcomt, Fed Comt Pest Control, 66-67; mem fed working group pest mgt, Monitoring Panel; US mem, Collab Int Pesticide Anal Coun, 65-75. *Mem:* Fel AAAS; Am Chem Soc; NY Acad Sci; Entom Soc Am. *Res:* Synthesis of organic insecticides; pyrethrin-type esters and allethrin; methods of analysis for traces of organic pesticides; disinsection of aircraft; insecticide formulation; photoperiodism; biological rhythms; diapause; effects of light on insects; analytical chemistry. *Mailing Add:* 10909 Hannes Ct Silver Spring MD 20901-1718

SCHECHTER, MURRAY, MATHEMATICS. *Current Pos:* asst prof, 63-68, assoc prof, 68-80, PROF MATH, LEHIGH UNIV, 80- *Personal Data:* b New York, NY, Dec 6, 35; m 59; c 2. *Educ:* Brooklyn Col, BA, 57; NY Univ, PhD(math), 63. *Prof Exp:* Staff mathematician, Kollsman Instrument Corp, 62-63. *Mem:* Am Math Soc; Soc Indust & Appl Math. *Res:* Convexity and its applications to optimization problems. *Mailing Add:* Dept Math Lehigh Univ Bethlehem PA 18015

SCHECHTER, NISSON, BIOCHEMISTRY. *Current Pos:* RES ASST BIOCHEM, STATE UNIV NY, STONY BROOK, 75- *Personal Data:* b Detroit, Mich, May 11, 40. *Educ:* Western Mich Univ, BA, 63, MS, 67, PhD(biochem), 71. *Prof Exp:* Fel biochem, Col Med, Univ Cincinnati, 71-73 & Weizmann Inst Sci, 73-75. *Concurrent Pos:* Weizmann fel, Weizmann Inst Sci, 73-74, Ahron Katzir fel, 74-75. *Mem:* Am Chem Soc; AAAS; Royal Soc Chem. *Res:* Protein synthesis in brain and neural tissue. *Mailing Add:* Dept Psychiat State Univ NY Box 8101 Stony Brook NY 11794-8101. *Fax:* 516-444-7534; *E-Mail:* nschechter@ccmail.sunysb.edu

SCHECHTER, ROBERT, ELECTRONICS ENGINEERING. *Current Pos:* PRES, RAS LTD, 93-; CHMN, USIMCO, INC, 93- *Educ:* Israel Inst Technol, BSc, 72. *Honors & Awards:* John Franklin Carll Award, Soc Petrol Engrs, 94. *Prof Exp:* Staff res & develop, Imod Res & Develop, 72-79; engr & mgt, Elta Elec Indust Ltd, 79-88; vpres mkt & bus develop, Israel Aircraft Indust Int 88-93. *Mailing Add:* 5826 Tudor Lane Rockville MD 20852-2851

SCHECHTER, ROBERT SAMUEL, CHEMICAL ENGINEERING. *Current Pos:* From asst prof to assoc prof chem eng, Univ Tex, Austin, 56-63, chmn dept, 70-73, dir, Ctr Thermodyn & Statist Mech, 68-74, chmn petrol eng, 75-78, Ernest Cockrell, Jr prof chem & petrol eng, 75-81, Dula & Ernest Cockrell Sr chair, 81-84, Getty Oil Co centennial chair petrol eng, 84-89, PROF CHEM ENG, UNIV TEX, AUSTIN, 63-, W A MONTY MONCRIEF CENTENNIAL ENDOWED CHAIR PETROL ENG, 89- *Personal Data:* b Houston, Tex, Feb 26, 29; m 53; c 3. *Educ:* Agr & Mech Col, Tex, BS, 50; Univ Minn, PhD(chem eng), 56. *Honors & Awards:* Donald P Katz lectr, Univ Mich, 79; Chevalier Order of Palmes Academiques, Prime Minister France, 80. *Concurrent Pos:* Vis prof, Univ Edinburgh, Scotland, 65-66 & Univ Brussels, Belg, 69; sr res award, Am Soc Eng Educ, 91. *Mem:* Nat Acad Eng; Am Inst Chem Engrs; Soc Petrol Engrs; Am Inst Mining Engrs; Am Chem Soc; Sigma Xi. *Res:* Surface phenomena; applied mathematics; surfactants; adsorption, micelles, and microemulsions; oil well stimulation, oil recovery and mass transfer; author of 6 books and more than 190 technical publications. *Mailing Add:* Dept Chem Eng Univ Tex Austin TX 78712

SCHECHTER, SAMUEL, NUMERICAL ANALYSIS, LINEAR ALGEBRA. *Current Pos:* CONSULT, 88- *Personal Data:* b Rozwadow, Poland, Mar 28, 23; nat US; m 44, Doris Goldberg; c Martha, Paul & Ruth. *Educ:* Brooklyn Col, AB, 44; Syracuse Univ, PhD(math), 52. *Prof Exp:* Asst mathematician, Brown Univ, 45; instr math, Univ Wis-Madison, 46-47; res asst & instr, Syracuse Univ, 47-50; instr math, Lehigh Univ, Bethlehem, Pa, 50-54; sr res scientist & adj assoc prof, Courant Inst, NY Univ, 54-65; actg assoc prof comput sci, Stanford Univ, 65-66; sr res mathematician, SRI Int, 66-88. *Concurrent Pos:* Consult, Sandia Corp, Albuquerque, NMex, 63-64. *Mem:* Sigma Xi; Am Math Soc; Soc Indust & Appl Math. *Res:* Partial differential equations; automatic digital computers; matrix analysis; mathematical programming; computer science; author or co-author of 14 publications. *Mailing Add:* 12734 Alto Verde Lane Los Altos Hills CA 94022

SCHECHTMAN, BARRY H, SOLID STATE PHYSICS, ENGINEERING. *Current Pos:* Mem tech staff & chief scientist, San Jose Res Lab, IBM Corp, 75-76, mgr org solids, 76-79, appl sci, 79-84, advan record technol, 85-90, MGR STORAGE MFG RES, SAN JOSE RES LAB, IBM CORP, 90-, OEM HEADS ACCT EXEC, 94- *Personal Data:* b New York, NY, Jan 23, 43; m 63; c 2. *Educ:* Cooper Union, BEE, 63; Stanford Univ, MS, 64, PhD(elec eng), 69. *Mem:* Am Phys Soc; Sigma Xi. *Res:* Electronic properties of organic solids; materials and device research for semiconductor fabrication, optical technologies, computer printing, display and data storage; electronic states of molecular solids; charge generation and transport in insulators. *Mailing Add:* NSIC 9888 Carroll Ctr Rd Suite 115 San Diego CA 92126

SCHECKLER, STEPHEN EDWARD, MORPHOLOGY, PALEOBOTANY. *Current Pos:* asst prof, 77-83, ASSOC PROF BOT, VA POLYTECH INST & STATE UNIV, 83- *Personal Data:* b Irvington, NJ, Mar 17, 44; m 68; c 3. *Educ:* Cornell Univ, BSc, 68, MSc, 70, PhD(bot), 73. *Honors & Awards:* Dimond Fund Award, Bot Soc Am. *Prof Exp:* Asst prof, Univ Alta, 75-76. *Concurrent Pos:* Nat Res Coun Can fel, Dept Bot, Univ Alta, 73-75 & 76-77; prin investr, Nat Geog Soc, NSF, Va Ctr Coal & Energy & Sigma Xi grants. *Mem:* Bot Soc Am; Can Bot Asn; Geol Soc Belgium; Geol Soc Am; Sigma Xi. *Res:* Structure and patterns of organization, phylogenies of biocharacters and paleoecology of early land plants, especially early ferns, lycopods, progymnosperms and gymnosperms. *Mailing Add:* Dept Biol Va Polytech Inst & State Univ Blacksburg VA 24061-0406

SCHECTER, ARNOLD JOEL, OCCUPATIONAL MEDICINE, ENVIRONMENTAL HEALTH. *Current Pos:* PROF PREV MED, UPSTATE MED CTR, CLIN CAMPUS, STATE UNIV NY, HEALTH SCI CTR, BINGHAMTON, 79- *Personal Data:* b Chicago, Ill, Dec 1, 34; m 64, Martha J Berenson; c Benjamin S, David A & Anna B. *Educ:* Univ Chicago, BA, 54, BS, 57; Howard Univ, MD, 62; Columbia Univ, MPH, 75. *Prof Exp:* Fel anat, Harvard Med Sch, 62-64, instr med, Harvard Med Sch & Mass Gen Hosp, 64-65; intern surg, Beth Israel Hosp, 66; med officer & aviation med officer, US Army, 67-69; physician med, West Pt Med Ctr, Ky, 69-70; exec dir Health Care Delivery, Floyd County Comprehensive Health Serv Prog, Inc, Ky, 70-71; med dir drug & alcohol dependence, inpatient rehab prog, Region 8 Ment Health Ctr, State Univ NY, 71-72, asst prof psychiat, 72-75; assoc prof prev med, NJ Med Sch, Newark, 75-79. *Mem:* AAAS; Am Soc Cell Biol; Micros Soc; Am Pub Health Asn; Am Occup Med Asn; fel Am Col Physicians; fel Am Col Prev Med; fel Am Col Physicians. *Res:* Biological markers of exposure to chemicals; measurement of human tissue levels of chlorinated dibenzo-p-dioxins and ultrastructural subcellular response as a means of understanding mechanisms of action. *Mailing Add:* 88 Aldrich Ave Binghamton NY 13903-1451. *Fax:* 607-770-8623

SCHECTER, LARRY, NUCLEAR PHYSICS. *Current Pos:* RETIRED. *Personal Data:* b Montreal, Que, Nov 21, 20; US citizen; m 51; c 2. *Educ:* Univ Calif, AB, 48, MA, 51, PhD, 53. *Prof Exp:* Res physicist, Radiation Lab, Univ Calif, 52, Calif Res & Develop Co, Stand Oil Co, Calif, 53-54 & Radiation Lab, Univ Calif, 54-55; from asst prof to prof physics, Ore State Univ, 55-88, chmn dept, 71-77. *Mem:* Am Phys Soc; Am Asn Physics Teachers. *Res:* Particle scattering; intermediate energy nuclear physics. *Mailing Add:* 1536 NW Dixon St Corvallis OR 97330

SCHECTMAN, RICHARD MILTON, ATOMIC PHYSICS. *Current Pos:* Asst prof eng physics, 61-64, assoc prof physics & astron, 64-71, PROF PHYSICS & ENG PHYSICS, UNIV TOLEDO, 71- *Personal Data:* b Wilkes-Barre, Pa, Apr 9, 32; m 60, Devera Hillman; c 2. *Educ:* Lehigh Univ, BS, 54; Pa State Univ, MS, 56; Cornell Univ, PhD(physics), 62. *Honors & Awards:* Clement O Miniger Outstanding Res Award, Sigma Xi, 84. *Concurrent Pos:* Consult, Lawrence Radiation Lab, Univ Calif, 63-65; vis assoc prof, Univ Ariz, 68 & Hebrew Univ, 69; vis scientist, Argonne Nat Lab, 72 & 75, Weizmann Inst Sci, 82-83 & 93, & Universite Libre de Bruxelles, 89. *Mem:* Am Phys Soc; Sigma Xi. *Res:* Particle accelerators; atomic transition probability measurements; beam foil spectroscopy; high-lying Rydberg states; ion-solid interaction. *Mailing Add:* Dept Physics & Astron Univ Toledo Toledo OH 43606. *Fax:* 419-537-2723; *E-Mail:* rms@utphya.phya.utoledo.edu

SCHEDL, HAROLD PAUL, MEDICINE. *Current Pos:* from res asst prof to res assoc prof med, 59-67, PROF MED, COL MED, UNIV IOWA, 67- *Personal Data:* b St Paul, Minn, Sept 17, 20; m 45; c 3. *Educ:* Yale Univ, BS, 42, MS, 44, PhD(chem), 46; Univ Iowa, MD, 55. *Prof Exp:* Res chemist, J T Baker Chem Co, 45-46 & Calco Chem Co, 46-49; intern, Res & Educ Hosp, Univ Ill, 55-56; responsible investr, Nat Heart Inst, 56-59. *Concurrent Pos:* Commonwealth Found overseas fel, Churchill Col, Cambridge, 65; mem clin res fel panel, NIH, 67-70; ed, J Lab Clin Med, 70-74; Macy fac scholar, Westminster Hosp Med Sch, London, 77-78. *Mem:* AAAS; Am Chem Soc; Am Physiol Soc; Am Gastroenterol Asn; Endocrine Soc. *Res:* Small intestinal transport mechanisms for hexose, amino acids and peptides and their regulation through gene expression in the gastrointestinal tract; gastroenterology; calcium metabolism and vitamin D, diabetes and the gastrointestinal tract. *Mailing Add:* Dept Internal Med Univ Iowa Hosp 4574JCP Iowa City IA 52242. *Fax:* 319-353-6399

SCHEEL, CARL ALFRED, ENTOMOLOGY. *Current Pos:* RETIRED. *Personal Data:* b LaCrosse, Wis, May 4, 23; m 46; c 4. *Educ:* Wis State Univ, LaCrosse, BS, 48; Univ Wis, MS, 49, PhD(entom), 56. *Prof Exp:* Instr biol, Wis State Univ, Platteville, 50; asst prof, Cent Mich Univ, 51-52 & Mt Union Col, 52-54; asst entom, Univ Wis, 54-56; from asst prof to assoc prof biol, Cent Mich Univ, 56-64, prof biol, 64-86. *Mem:* Entom Soc Am; Am Inst Biol Sci; Nat Asn Biol Teachers. *Res:* Nutritional physiology of insects. *Mailing Add:* 9711 E School Section Lake Dr Mecosta MI 49332

SCHEEL, KONRAD WOLFGANG, CARDIOVASCULAR PHYSIOLOGY. *Current Pos:* PROF PHYSIOL & MED, TEX COL OSTEOP MED. *Personal Data:* b Mougden, China, Dec 26, 32; US citizen; m 59; c 2. *Educ:* Tulane Univ, BS, 62; Univ Miss, PhD(physiol), 68. *Prof Exp:* Res instr physiol, Med Ctr, Univ Miss, 63-64, res assoc surg, 67-68, asst prof physiol & med, 68-72; asst prof, Univ Tenn, Memphis, 72-75, assoc prof physiol, biophys & med, Ctr Health Sci, 75-80; prof & chmn physiol, Kirksville Col Osteop Med, 81- *Concurrent Pos:* Volkswagen grant, Univ Kiel, 70-71; Tenn Heart investr, Ctr Health Sci, Univ Tenn, Memphis, 72-74 & USPHS grant, 72-75; guest lectr cardiol, Univ Kiel, 70-71; consult, Vet Admin, 73-75 & NIH, 74. *Mem:* Am Physiol Soc; Am Heart Asn; Biomed Eng Soc. *Res:* Coronary and coronary collateral hemodynamics; computer simulations; mechanisms of coronary collateral formation. *Mailing Add:* Dept Physiol Univ N Tex Health Sci Ctr 3500 Camp Bowie Ft Worth TX 76107-2690. *Fax:* 817-735-2283

SCHEEL, NIVARD, SCIENCE EDUCATION. *Current Pos:* prof, 82-93, EMER PROF PHYSICS, TRINITY COL, WASHINGTON, DC, 93- *Personal Data:* b Baltimore, Md, Nov 8, 25. *Educ:* Cath Univ Am, AB, 49, MS, 51, PhD(physics), 61. *Prof Exp:* Instr physics, Xaverian Col, Silver Spring, Md, 50-54 & 58-60, pres, 60-66; actg pres, Cath Univ Am, 68-69, vpres, 69-80. *Mem:* Sigma Xi; Am Asn Physics Teachers. *Mailing Add:* 1066 Pilgrim Pkwy Elm Grove ND 53122

SCHEELE, ROBERT BLAIN, BIOPHYSICS, MOLECULAR BIOLOGY. *Personal Data:* b New York, NY, Dec 23, 40; m 63; c 2. *Educ:* Yale Univ, BS, 62; Univ Pittsburgh, PhD(biophys), 68. *Prof Exp:* NIH fel biophys, State Univ NY, Buffalo, 68-70; res assoc biophys, Univ Conn, 70-75; res assoc molecular biol, Univ Wis-Madison, 75-77, asst scientist molecular biol, Lab Moleculalr, 77-84. *Mem:* Biophys Soc. *Res:* Protein-protein interactions, self-assembly of protein polymers, virus self-assembly and molecular aspects of motility. *Mailing Add:* 1206 Frisch Rd Madison WI 53711

SCHEELINE, ALEXANDER, EMISSION SPECTROSCOPY, OSCILLATING REACTIONS. *Current Pos:* asst prof, 81-87, ASSOC PROF CHEM, UNIV ILL, 87- *Personal Data:* b Altoona, Pa, June 6, 52; m 84, Alice Berkson; c Dorothy. *Educ:* Mich State Univ, BS, 74; Univ Wis, Madison, PhD(chem), 78. *Honors & Awards:* W F Meggers Award, Soc Appl Spectros, 79, 92. *Prof Exp:* Nat Res Coun fel anal chem, Nat Bur Standards, 78-79; asst prof chem, Univ Iowa, 79-81. *Concurrent Pos:* Consult, Spectral Sci Inc, 82-84, 88 & Nat Bur Standards, 82-; asst ed, Spectrochimica Acta, Part B, 89-92; prog officer, Chem Div, NSF, 90-91. *Mem:* Am Chem Soc; Soc Appl Spectros; Optical Soc Am; Soc Electroanal Chemists. *Res:* Spectroscopy and simulation of oscillating reactions for chemical analysis. *Mailing Add:* 61 Roger Adams Lab Box 48 600 S Mathews St Urbana IL 61801

SCHEER, ALFRED C(ARL), CIVIL ENGINEERING. *Current Pos:* RETIRED. *Personal Data:* b Center, Nebr, Feb 1, 26; m 46; c 4. *Educ:* Iowa State Univ, BS, 48, MS, 50. *Prof Exp:* Instr civil eng, Iowa State Univ, 48-50; from asst prof to assoc prof, SDak Sch Mines & Technol, 50-58; assoc prof, Mont State Univ, 58-72, prof civil eng, 72- *Concurrent Pos:* Mem, Hwy Res Bd, Nat Acad Sci-Nat Res Coun. *Mem:* Am Soc Eng Educ; Am Soc Civil Engrs. *Res:* Soil mechanics; highway engineering. *Mailing Add:* 10001 Thomas Dr Bozeman MT 59715

SCHEER, BRADLEY TITUS, PHYSIOLOGY. *Current Pos:* assoc prof biol, 50-53, head dept, 58-64, prof, 54-77, EMER PROF BIOL, UNIV ORE, 77- *Personal Data:* b Los Angeles, Calif, Dec 17, 14; m 36. *Educ:* Calif Inst Technol, BS, 36; Univ Calif, PhD(comp physiol), 40. *Prof Exp:* Asst physiol, Scripps Inst, Univ Calif, 36-37, Med Sch, 37-38 & Inst, 38-40; instr zool, WVa Univ, 40-42; asst biochem, Col Physicians & Surgeons, Columbia Univ, 42-43; instr biol, Calif Inst Technol, 43-45; asst prof biochem, Univ Southern Calif, 45-48, lectr zool, 46-48; assoc prof, Univ Hawaii, 48-50. *Concurrent Pos:* Vis asst prof, Hopkins Marine Sta, Stanford, 47; vis prof, Univ Calif, 52; Fulbright fel, Italy, 53-54; Guggenheim fel, France, 57-58; instr, Westmont Col, 78-82, adj prof biol, 82-86. *Mem:* AAAS; Am Physiol Soc; Soc Gen Physiol; Am Soc Zoologists. *Res:* Comparative biochemistry of carotenoids; isolation of enzymes; blood proteins of invertebrates; ecology of marine fouling organisms; physiology of fertilization; hormones of crustaceans; ion transports; thermodynamics in biology; systems analysis of salt and water balance; science and religion. *Mailing Add:* 93 Quarterdeck Way Pacific Grove CA 93950-2146

SCHEER, DONALD JORDAN, ELECTRICAL ENGINEERING. *Current Pos:* From instr to assoc prof, 59-72, chmn dept elec eng, 78-87, PROF ELEC ENG, UNIV LOUISVILLE, 72- *Personal Data:* b Louisville, Ky, July 25, 34; m 66, Renate Bleckmann; c Stephanie & Christina. *Educ:* Univ Louisville, BEE, 57, MEE, 58, MEng, 72; Ohio State Univ, PhD(elec eng), 66. *Mem:* Inst Elec & Electronics Engrs; Am Astron Soc; Sigma Xi. *Res:* Antennas; microwave engineering; radio astronomy. *Mailing Add:* Dept Elec Eng Univ Louisville Louisville KY 40292. *Fax:* 502-852-6807

SCHEER, MILTON DAVID, PHYSICAL CHEMISTRY. *Current Pos:* CONSULT, 88- *Personal Data:* b New York, Dec 22, 22; m 45, Emily Hirsch; c Jessica, Richard & Julia. *Educ:* City Col New York, BS, 43; NY Univ, MS, 47, PhD, 51. *Prof Exp:* Chemist, US Bd Econ Warfare, Guatemala, 43-44; res asst, NY Univ, 47-50, phys chemist, US Naval Air Rocket Test Sta, 51-52, US Bur Mines, 52-55 & Gen Elec Co, 55-58; phys chemist, 58-68, chief photochem sect, Nat Bur Stands, 68-70, chief, Phys Chem Div, 70-77, dir, Ctr Thermodyn & Molecular Sci, 77-80, chem physicist, Chem Kinetics Div, 81-85; consult assoc, McNesby & Scheer Res Assoc, Inc, 85-88. *Concurrent Pos:* Vis prof, Chem Dept, Univ Md, 80-81; Sr Fulbright fel; vis prof, Univ

Rome, Italy, 82-83. *Mem:* Fel AAAS; Am Chem Soc; Am Phys Soc. *Res:* Reaction kinetics and photochemistry; surface chemistry and physics; low temperature chemistry; high temperature thermodynamics; excited state chemistry; plasma chemistry. *Mailing Add:* 15100 Interlachen Dr No 512 Silver Spring MD 20906-5605

SCHEERER, ANNE ELIZABETH, mathematics, for more information see previous edition

SCHEETZ, HOWARD A(NSEL), MATERIALS SCIENCE, ENGINEERING MECHANICS. *Current Pos:* CONSULT, 89- *Personal Data:* b Sturgis, Mich, Mar 20, 27; m 52, A Betty Rinwaldon; c Robert A & Karen E. *Educ:* Mich State Univ, BS, 50; Pa State Univ, MS, 59. *Prof Exp:* Process engr, Pilot Plant, Corning Glass Works, 50-52; sr engr, Res & Develop Lab, 52-56; res assoc shock & vibration, Pa State Univ, 57-58; res engr, Physics Dept, Cornell Aeronaut Lab, 58-60, Mat Dept, 60-62 & Physics Dept, Armstrong Cork Co, 62-69; res assoc, Packaging Prod Div, Kerr Glass Mfg Corp, 69-73; dir res, Sonobond Corp, 73-77; develop mgr, Tech Ctr, Polymer Corp, 77-89, DSM Engr Plastics, 89- *Concurrent Pos:* Lectr grad fac, Pa State Univ, 66-67; corp rep, Am Ceramic Soc. *Mem:* Inst Elec & Electronics Engrs; Acoust Soc Am; Am Soc Mech; Soc Plastic Engrs. *Res:* Analytical modeling and computer-aided studies of composite physical properties of glass, ceramic, polymeric and mixed composite material systems; applications of ultrasonic techniques to materials research and glass technology. *Mailing Add:* DSM Eng Plastics Tech Ctr 501 Crescent Ave PO Box 15051 Reading PA 19612

SCHEFER, ROBERT WILFRED, COMBUSTION & FLUID MECHANICS, CHEMICAL KINETICS. *Current Pos:* SR MEM TECH STAFF, SANDIA NAT LAB, LIVERMORE, CALIF, 81- *Personal Data:* b San Francisco, Calif, July 7, 46; m 74, Jade Carroll. *Educ:* Univ Calif, Berkeley, BS, 68, MS, 70, PhD(mech eng), 76. *Prof Exp:* Res Eng Combustion, Lawrence Berkeley Lab, 76-81. *Concurrent Pos:* NSF energy fel, 76-77. *Mem:* Combustion Inst; Sigma Xi; Am Inst Aeronaut & Astronaut. *Res:* Combustion; combustion generated air pollution; chemistry (chemical kinetics); fire research; high temperature catalysis; coal utilization. *Mailing Add:* Sandia Nat Lab Div 8351 Livermore CA 94551. *E-Mail:* rwsche@ca.sandia.gov

SCHEFF, BENSON H(OFFMAN), SOFTWARE ENGINEERING, SOFTWARE PRODUCTIVITY & RISK. *Current Pos:* mgr comput analysis & appln, Software Dept, Missile Systs Div, Bedford, 66-73, MGR DATA PROCESSING, EQUIP DIV, RAYTHEON CO, WAYLAND, MASS, 73- *Personal Data:* b New York, NY, May 16, 31; m 53; c 4. *Educ:* Oberlin Col, BA, 51; Columbia Univ, MA, 52. *Prof Exp:* Training instr electronic data processing mach, Nat Security Agency, 52-55; res engr, Servomechanisms Lab, Mass Inst Technol, 55-59; head adv comput control systs implementation, Group Data Systs Eng, Radio Corp Am, Mass, 59-66. *Mem:* Asn Comput Mach; Am Mgt Asn. *Res:* Integrated software engineering methodology; software research and development. *Mailing Add:* Concord Rd Lincoln MA 01773

SCHEFFE, RICHARD DONALD, PHOTOCHEMICAL MODELING OF OZONE, DESIGN OF OZONE PRECURSOR CONTROL STRATEGIES. *Current Pos:* environ engr, Off Air Qual Planning & Stand, 87-90 & 91-93; supvry environ engr, Region I Air Div, 90-91; ENVIRON ENGR, OFF AIR QUAL PLANNING & STAND, US ENVIRON PROTECTION AGENCY, 93- *Personal Data:* b Amityville, NY, June 12, 52; m 79, Debra Hill; c Jonathan, Rachel & Gretchen. *Educ:* State Univ NY, Potsdam, BA, 74; Univ Mich, MS, 78; Clarkson Univ, MS, 84, PhD(environ eng), 87. *Prof Exp:* Sr environ engr, IT Corp, 86-87. *Mem:* Air & Waste Mgt Asn. *Res:* Development of ozone precursor control strategies using modeling and monitoring approaches and quantifying atmospheric deposition of metals and toxic compounds on major United States water bodies. *Mailing Add:* 6 Brown Bark Ct Durham NC 27712. *Fax:* 919-541-2357

SCHEFFER, JOHN R, ORGANIC CHEMISTRY. *Current Pos:* ASSOC PROF CHEM, UNIV BC, 67- *Personal Data:* b Missoula, Mont, Feb 28, 39; m 63; c 2. *Educ:* Univ Chicago, BS, 62. Univ Wis, PhD(chem), 67. *Concurrent Pos:* Nat Res Coun Can grant, 67-; Res Corp grant, 68-; Petrol Res Fund grant, 70-73 & 75-77; Guggenheim fel, 73-74. *Mem:* Am Chem Soc; Royal Soc Chem; Chem Inst Can. *Res:* Organic photochemistry, including new sources and reactions of singlet oxygen. *Mailing Add:* Dept Chem Univ BC 2036 Main Mall Vancouver BC V6T 1Y6 Can

SCHEFFER, ROBERT PAUL, PLANT PHYSIOLOGY. *Current Pos:* from asst prof to assoc prof bot & plant path, 53-63, PROF BOT & PLANT PATH, MICH STATE UNIV, 63- *Personal Data:* b Newton, NC, Jan 26, 20; m 51, Bea Spoolman; c Thomas & Karen. *Educ:* NC State Col, BS, 47, MS, 49; Univ Wis, PhD(plant path), 52. *Prof Exp:* Asst plant path, NC State Col, 47-49; asst, Univ Wis, 49-52, proj assoc, 52-53. *Concurrent Pos:* NIH fel & guest investr, Rockefeller Univ, 60-61; NSF consult, Panel Regulatory Biol, 65-68; distinguished prof, Mich State Univ, 85; assoc ed, Phytopath, 72-75; mem press bd, Am Phytopath Soc, 80-85. *Mem:* Fel Am Phytopath Soc; Am Soc Plant Physiol; fel Explorer's Club. *Res:* Physiology of disease development and disease resistance; toxins in plant disease; chemical ecology of plant diseases. *Mailing Add:* 912 Gainsborough Dr East Lansing MI 48823

SCHEFFER, THEODORE COMSTOCK, FOREST PRODUCTS. *Current Pos:* COURTESY PROF, FOREST RES LAB, ORE STATE UNIV, 69- *Personal Data:* b Manhattan, Kans, Feb 10, 04; m 27; c 2. *Educ:* Univ Wis, BS, 26, MS, 29; Univ Wis, PhD(forest path), 34. *Prof Exp:* Nat Res Coun fel, Johns Hopkins Univ, 34-35; pathologist, Forest Prod Lab, US Forest Serv, 35-65, in chg fungus & insect invests, 65-69. *Mem:* Forest Prod Res Soc; Soc Am Foresters. *Res:* Fundamental and applied control of fungus damage to wood and wood products; effects of fungi on physical-chemical properties; testing fungus resistance; preservation of wood with volatile fungicides; bioassay techniques for appraising quality of preservative treatment. *Mailing Add:* Dept Forest Prod Forest Res Lab Ore State Univ Corvallis OR 97331-7402

SCHEFFER, VICTOR B, MARINE MAMMALOGY. *Current Pos:* SCI WRITER, 69- *Personal Data:* b Manhattan, Kans, Nov 27, 06; wid; c 3. *Educ:* Univ Wash, Seattle, BS, 30, MS, 32, PhD(zool), 36. *Honors & Awards:* John Burroughs Medal, 70; John Wood Krutch Medal, 75. *Prof Exp:* Biologist, US Bur Biol Surv, 37-40, US Fish & Wildlife Serv, 40-56 & US Bur Com Fisheries, 56-69; lectr ecol, Univ Wash, Seattle, 66-72. *Concurrent Pos:* Chmn, Marine Mammal Comn, 73-76. *Mem:* Hon mem Am Soc Mammalogists; Wildlife Soc; AAAS; hon mem Soc Marine Mammal; Am Inst Biol Sci. *Res:* Natural history of marine mammals; wildlife management; ethical treatment of animals; history of environmentalism. *Mailing Add:* 1750 152nd Ave NE Apt C-214 Bellevue WA 98007

SCHEFFLER, IMMO ERICH, MOLECULAR BIOLOGY, SOMATIC CELL GENETICS. *Current Pos:* from asst prof to assoc prof, 71-81, chmn, Dept Biol, 90-92, PROF BIOL, UNIV CALIF, SAN DIEGO, 81- *Personal Data:* b Dresden, Ger, Dec 17, 40; Can citizen; m 65; c 1. *Educ:* Univ Manitoba, BSc, 63, MSc, 64; Stanford Univ, PhD(biochem), 69. *Prof Exp:* Helen Hay Whitney fel, Harvard Med Sch, 68-70; fel, Pasteur Inst, Paris, 70-71. *Concurrent Pos:* NIH 71-74, 74-77 & 77-82, 82-87, 87-92 & 90-95; chmn biol, Univ Calif, San Diego, 90-92; Am Cancer Soc grant, 74-76 & 76-78; NSF grants, 78-81 & 81-84; mem adv panel genetic biol, 77-80; mem adv panel personnel res, Am Cancer Soc; Alexander von Humboldt Sr US Scientist Award, Ger, 84-85. *Mem:* AAAS; Am Soc Cell Biol; fel Am Soc Exp Biol. *Res:* Selection of mutants of mammalian cells grown in tissue culture; mammalian cell genetics; biogenesis of mitochondrion; regulation of ornithine decarboxylase. *Mailing Add:* Dept Biol Univ Calif San Diego La Jolla CA 92093-0322. *Fax:* 619-534-0555

SCHEIB, RICHARD, JR, PHYSICS. *Current Pos:* RETIRED. *Personal Data:* b New York, NY, May 24, 14; m 42, Catherine Liese; c Richard A (deceased). *Educ:* Columbia Univ, AB, 36, MA, 39. *Prof Exp:* Engr & sr engr, Sperry Gyroscope Co, 41-49, eng dept head, 49-62, planning mgr, 62-64, prog mgr, 64-69; assoc prof basic sci, Acad Aeronaut, NY, 70-83, chmn dept, 73-83. *Mem:* Am Phys Soc; Sigma Xi. *Mailing Add:* 29 Crest Rd New Hyde Park NY 11040

SCHEIBE, MURRAY, PHYSICS. *Current Pos:* PHYS RES CORP, 87- *Personal Data:* b Bronx, NY, Feb 28, 32; m 55; c 3. *Educ:* Brooklyn Col, BS, 53; Univ Md, College Park, PhD(physics), 59. *Prof Exp:* Staff scientist, Lockheed Palo Alto Res Lab, Lockheed Aircraft Co, 58-71; staff mem, Mission Res Corp, 71-87. *Mem:* Am Phys Soc. *Res:* Atmospheric physics and chemistry; high temperature gas dynamics; optical radiation phenomena. *Mailing Add:* 1133 Palomino Rd Santa Barbara CA 93105

SCHEIBE, PAUL OTTO, ELECTRICAL ENGINEERING, SYSTEM ANALYSIS & DESIGN. *Current Pos:* PRIN CONSULT, IXZAR, INC, 86- *Personal Data:* b Marion, NDak, Apr 7, 34; m 54; c 3. *Educ:* Univ NDak, BS, 58, MS, 59; Stanford Univ, PhD(elec eng), 62. *Prof Exp:* Instr, NDak State Sch Sci, 53-56; from instr to asst prof elec eng, Univ NDak, 58-60; mem eng staff, Sylvania Electronic Defense Labs, 62-64; mem sr eng staff & dir technol, ESL, Inc, Calif, 64-70; vpres & tech dir, Adac Labs, 70-84; vpres & tech dir, Sterling Networks, 84-89. *Concurrent Pos:* Lectr, Univ Santa Clara, 62- *Mem:* Inst Elec & Electronics Engrs; Soc Nuclear Med; Asn Comput Mach. *Res:* Characterization and bounds on the performance of time-variant systems; automatic design and analysis of electrical networks; statistical parameter estimation; mathematical modeling of physiological systems. *Mailing Add:* Three Still Creek Rd Woodside CA 94062-9731

SCHEIBEL, ARNOLD BERNARD, NEUROPHYSIOLOGY, PSYCHOPHYSIOLOGY. *Current Pos:* from asst prof to assoc prof, 55-68, PROF PSYCHIAT & ANAT, SCH MED, UNIV CALIF, LOS ANGELES, 68- *Personal Data:* b New York, NY, Jan 18, 23; m 50, Marian Clieves. *Educ:* Columbia Univ, BA, 44, MD, 46; Univ Ill, MS, 53; Am Bd Psychiat & Neurol, dipl, 52. *Prof Exp:* Intern, Mt Sinai Hosp, New York, 46-47; resident psychiat, Barnes Hosp, St Louis, 47-48; from asst prof to assoc prof psychiat & anat, Sch Med, Univ Tenn, 51-55. *Concurrent Pos:* Guggenheim fel, Inst Physiol, Italy, 53-54 & 60-61; consult physician, Brentwood Vet Admin Hosp, Calif & Sepulveda Vet Admin Hosp; from actg dir to dir, Brain Res Inst, 90. *Mem:* Fel AAAS; fel Am Psychiat Asn; Am Acad Neurol; Am Neurol Asn; fel Am Acad Arts & Sci; Norweg Acad Sci. *Res:* Distortions of perception and memory in psychoses; experimental study of structural patterns of neuropil in the central nervous system and its relation to functional activity; aging in human brain; neuropsychiatry; neuroscience. *Mailing Add:* Dept Neurobiol Univ Calif Box 951763 Los Angeles CA 90095-1763

SCHEIBEL, EDWARD G(EORGE), CHEMICAL ENGINEERING. *Current Pos:* RETIRED. *Personal Data:* b Ridgewood, NY, Jan 15, 17; m 45; c 4. *Educ:* Cooper Union, BS, 37; Polytech Inst Brooklyn, MChE, 40, DChE, 43. *Prof Exp:* From asst chemist to plant supt, H C Bugbird Co, NJ, 37-42; chem engr, M W Kellogg Co, NY, 42-43; res assoc, Polytech Inst Brooklyn, 43-44; chem engr, Hydrocarbon Res, Inc, 44-45 & Hoffmann-LaRoche, Inc, 45-55; dir eng, York Process Equip Corp, 55-63; prof chem eng & head dept, Cooper Union, 63-70; mgr process technol, Gen Elec Co, Mt Vernon, Ind, 69-73; res engr, Suntech Inc, 74-81; mem staff, E G Scheibel, Inc, 81-84. *Concurrent Pos:* Instr & adj prof, Polytech Inst Brooklyn, 42-52; adj prof, Newark Col Eng, 53-63. *Mem:* Am Chem Soc; Am Inst Chem Eng. *Res:* Distillation, absorption and liquid extraction; liquid oxygen production; fractional liquid extraction; extractive distillation of petroleum; heavy and fine chemicals. *Mailing Add:* 410 Notson Terr Port Charlotte FL 33952

SCHEIBEL, LEONARD WILLIAM, BIOCHEMICAL PHARMACOLOGY, CLINICAL PHARMACOLOGY. *Current Pos:* from asst prof to assoc prof, 81-86, PROF PREV MED & PHARMACOL, SCH MED, UNIFORMED SERV UNIV HEALTH SCI, BETHESDA, MD, 86- *Personal Data:* b Hays, Kans, Jan 18, 38; m 76, Melania P Valdes; c Leonard W Jr & Raymond P. *Educ:* Creighton Univ, Omaha, Nebr, BS, 60, MS, 62; Johns Hopkins Univ, PhD(biochem), 67; Univ Fla, Gainesville, MD, 73. *Prof Exp:* Capt res biochem, Walter Reed Army Inst Res, Washington, DC, 67-70; res assoc pharmacol, Univ Fla, Gainesville, 70-73; intern med, Gorgas Hosp, Balboa Heights, Canal Zone, Panama, 73-74; resident internal med, 74-77; asst prof trop med, Rockefeller Univ, NY, 77-81. *Concurrent Pos:* Guest prof, USN Bur Med & Surg Med Trop, Gorgas Mem Hosp, Panama, 73 & 77; vis asst prof, Div Infectious Dis, Dept Int Med, Cornell Med Sch, 77-81; mem, US Army Med Res & Develop Adv Comt, 82-85; mem, Drug Adv Bd, Food & Drug Admin Anti-Infective Dis, 82-85; adj assoc prof, Dept Immunol Infectious Dis, Johns Hopkins Univ & Dept Microbiol, Sch Med, Univ Md, 82-86; dir, Residency Training Prog, Gen Prev Med, 93-; mem, Human Use Comt, Walter Reed Army Inst Res, 93- *Mem:* Fel Am Col Physicians; fel Am Col Prev Med; Fedn Am Soc Exp Biol; Am Soc Pharmacol & Exp Therapeut; Am Soc Trop Med; Am Soc Parasitologists; Undersea Med Soc; Walter Reed Army Inst Res Asn; fel Infectious Dis Soc Am; Am Soc Clin Pharmacol & Therapeut. *Res:* Tropical medicine emphasizing metabolism and chemotherapy of parasitic diseases; rational design of new pharmacologic agents, testing and employment in the field, working extensively throughout Central and South America; international health and tropical medicine. *Mailing Add:* Dept Prev Med Sch Med Univ Ill 1 Illini Dr Box 1649 Peoria IL 61656-1649. *Fax:* 301-295-3860

SCHEIBER, DAVID HITZ, POLYMER CHEMISTRY. *Current Pos:* RETIRED. *Personal Data:* b Cleveland, Ohio, Aug 16, 31; m 56; c 5. *Educ:* Univ Notre Dame, BS, 53, PhD, 56. *Prof Exp:* Res chemist, Electrochem Dept, E I du Pont de Nemours & Co, Inc, 56-61, staff scientist, 61-62, res assoc, 62-64, res supvr, 64-68, res assoc, Photosysts & Electronics Dept, 68-90. *Mem:* Am Chem Soc. *Res:* Electronic materials. *Mailing Add:* 710 Cardiff Rd Wilmington DE 19803

SCHEIBER, DONALD JOSEPH, UNDERWATER ACOUSTICS, MECHANICS. *Current Pos:* SR STAFF ENGR, MAGNAVOX CO, 62- *Personal Data:* b Ft Wayne, Ind, Jan 24, 32; m 54; c 8. *Educ:* St Procopius Col, 53; Univ Notre Dame, 53-57, PhD(physics), 57. *Prof Exp:* Nat Res Coun res assoc, Nat Bur Standards, 57-58, physicist, 58-62. *Mem:* Nat Security Indust Asn. *Res:* Underwater sound; directional sensors; dynamics of buoy systems; oceanographic sensors. *Mailing Add:* 1299 N 650 W Columbia City IN 46725

SCHEIBNER, RUDOLPH A, ENTOMOLOGY. *Current Pos:* RETIRED. *Personal Data:* b Escanaba, Mich, Oct 22, 26; m 61; c 3. *Educ:* Mich State Univ, BS, 51, MS, 58, PhD(entom), 63. *Prof Exp:* Instr natural sci, Mich State Univ, 63-65; from asst prof to assoc prof entom, Univ Ky, 65-77, exten prof, 78-89. *Mem:* Am Entom Soc; Sigma Xi. *Res:* Taxonomy and ecology of insects. *Mailing Add:* 1007 N Bracewell Dr Plant City FL 33566

SCHEID, CHERYL RUSSELL, CELL PHYSIOLOGY, SMOOTH MUSCLE PHYSIOLOGY. *Current Pos:* asst prof, 80-87, ASSOC PROF MED PHYSIOL, SCH MED, UNIV MASS, 87- *Personal Data:* b Leonardtown, Md, 1948. *Educ:* Boston Univ, PhD(biol), 76. *Prof Exp:* Asst prof med physiol, Tufts Univ Med Sch, Boston, Ma, 79-80. *Mem:* Am Physiol Soc; AAAS. *Res:* Calcium handling in smooth muscles. *Mailing Add:* Dept Physiol Sch Med Univ Mass 55 Lake Ave Worcester MA 01655-0127. *Fax:* 508-856-5997

SCHEID, FRANCIS, MATHEMATICS. *Current Pos:* RETIRED. *Personal Data:* b Plymouth, Mass, Sept 24, 20; wid; c Betsy, Lisa & Sarah. *Educ:* Boston Univ, BS, 42, AM, 43; Mass Inst Technol, PhD(math), 48. *Prof Exp:* From instr to prof math, Boston Univ, 48-86, chmn dept, 56-69. *Concurrent Pos:* Fulbright lectr, Univ Rangoon, 61-62; TV lectr, 61-66. *Res:* Numerical analysis; problems of measuring golfing ability and golf course difficulty and golf related problems. *Mailing Add:* 135 Elm St Kingston MA 02364

SCHEID, HAROLD E, PET FOOD NUTRITION RESEARCH, PET FOOD PRODUCT DEVELOPMENT. *Current Pos:* RETIRED. *Personal Data:* b Whiting, Kans, May 12, 22; m 48; c 6. *Educ:* Sterling Col, BS, 47; Kans State Univ, MS, 49. *Prof Exp:* Asst biochemist, Am Meat Inst Fedn, 49-52; chief chemist & nutritionist, Honeggers & Co, 54-59; proj leader, Quaker Oats Co, 60-75; dir res & develop, Theracon Inc, 75-, consult, 75- *Concurrent Pos:* Mem, Gordon Res Conf, 63-70. *Mem:* Inst Food Technol; Am Chem Soc; Am Asn Feed Micros; Am Asn Clin Chem. *Res:* Biological function and methods of analysis of vitamin B12, B2 and B6; the role of vitamin B12 in the regeneration of liver tissue. *Mailing Add:* 1931 Baintree Davis IL 61019

SCHEIDELMAN, RONALD JEROME, PATENT SEARCHING, LICENSING OF INVENTIONS. *Current Pos:* PRES, SEARCHLINE INC, 68- *Personal Data:* b Utica, NY, Oct 13, 34; m 59, Khalida Bunnie; c Huda, Edward, John, Amaal, Layla & Ronald. *Educ:* LeMoyne Col, BS, 57; Georgetown Univ, MS, 61; Ill Inst Technol, PhD(environ eng), 81. *Prof Exp:* Prof chem, Georgetown Univ, 57-59, Univ Windsor, 63-65; sr scientist, Continental Can Co, 65-67. *Concurrent Pos:* Res fel, Shering-Plough, 59-61, Marine Colloids, 59-61, NIH, 59-61, Petrol Res Found, 63-64 & NSF, 65-66; prof chem, Ill Benedictine Univ, 65-66, Kennedy-King Col, 68-71 & Rosary Col, 82; chmn, Org Topical Group, Chicago Sect, Am Chem Soc, 70-74. *Mem:* AAAS; AMA; Am Chem Soc; Asn Independent Info Prof; Licensing Execs Soc. *Res:* Evaluation of inventions for patentability and marketability; develop and optimize prototypes before filing and pursuing patents. *Mailing Add:* Searchline Inc 4914 Columbia Ave Lisle IL 60532-2202. *Fax:* 630-515-4430; *E-Mail:* searchln@mcs.com

SCHEIDT, FRANCIS MATTHEW, ORGANIC CHEMISTRY. *Current Pos:* RETIRED. *Personal Data:* b Streator, Ill, Mar 2, 22; m 52. *Educ:* Univ Ill, BS, 50, MS, 54, PhD(org chem), 56. *Prof Exp:* Res asst chem, State Geol Surv, Ill, 50-54; chemist, Dow Chem Co, 56-66, sr res chemist, 66-72, res specialist, 72-77, sr res specialist, Britton Res Lab, 77-80, res assoc, 80-88. *Concurrent Pos:* Sect ed, Chem Abstr, 68- *Mem:* Fel Am Inst Chemists; Am Chem Soc; Sigma Xi; NY Acad Sci. *Res:* Synthetic organic chemistry; heterogeneous catalysis. *Mailing Add:* 1906 Norwood Dr Midland MI 48640-6755

SCHEIDT, WALTER ROBERT, CHEMISTRY, X-RAY CRYSTALLOGRAPHY. *Current Pos:* assoc prof, 70-80, PROF CHEM, UNIV NOTRE DAME, 80- *Personal Data:* b Richmond Heights, Mo, Nov 13, 42; m 64, Kathryn S Barnes; c Karl A & David M. *Educ:* Univ Mo, Columbia, BS, 64; Univ Mich, Ann Arbor, MS, 66, PhD(chem), 68. *Prof Exp:* Res fel, Cornell Univ, 68-70. *Concurrent Pos:* Vis prof, Univ Wash, 80, Univ Paris, Orsay, 91. *Mem:* Fel AAAS; Am Chem Soc; Am Crystallog Asn. *Res:* Structure and chemistry of metalloporphyrins, including relating physical and chemical properties to structure; structure of inorganic complexes. *Mailing Add:* PO Box 339 Notre Dame IN 46556-0339. *Fax:* 219-631-6652; *E-Mail:* w.r.scheidt.1@nd.edu

SCHEIE, CARL EDWARD, ENGINEERING PHYSICS. *Current Pos:* dir prod develop, 82-89, VPRES GOLF TECHNOL, WILSON SPORTING GOODS, 90- *Personal Data:* b Fosston, Minn, July 14, 38; m 59; c 3. *Educ:* Concordia Col, Moorhead, Minn, BA, 60; Univ NMex, MS, 62, PhD, 65. *Prof Exp:* Res assoc physics, Univ NMex, 62-65; res aide, Inst Paper Chem, 65-68; from asst prof to assoc prof physics, Concordia Col, Moorhead, Minn, 68-73; prod eval engr, MacGregor Div, Brunswick Corp, 73-79, staff scientist, 79-82. *Concurrent Pos:* Vis scientist, Argonne Nat Lab, 72-73. *Res:* Molecular motion in solids using nuclear magnetic resonance techniques; physics of gulf. *Mailing Add:* 1113 Dawes St Libertyville IL 60048

SCHEIE, HAROLD GLENDON, OPHTHALMOLOGY. *Current Pos:* From intern to resident, Hosp Univ Pa, 35-40, from instr to prof, Grad Sch Med, 46-60, chmn dept ophthal, 60-75, William F Norris & George E Deschweinitz prof ophthal, Sch Med, Grad Sch Med, Univ Pa, 60-75, dir, Scheie Eye Inst, 72-75, EMER WILLIAM F NORRIS & GEORGE E DE SCHWEINITZ PROF OPHTHAL, UNIV PA & FOUNDING DIR, SCHEIE EYE INST, 75- *Personal Data:* b Brookings, SDak, Mar 24, 09; m 52; c 2. *Educ:* Univ Minn, BS, 31, MB & MD, 35; Univ Pa, DSc(med ophthal), 40; Am Bd Ophthal, dipl, 40. *Honors & Awards:* Howe Award, AMA, 64; Distinguished Serv Award for Excellence in Ophthal, Am Soc Contemporary Ophthal, 74; Horatio Alger Award, Am Schs & Cols Asn, 74; Golden Plate Award, Am Acad Achievement, 75. *Concurrent Pos:* From instr to prof, Med Sch, Univ Pa, 40-60, prof & chmn dept, Div Grad Med, 64; ophthal consult to many hosps, labs & govt agencies, 44-; lectr, US Naval Hosp, Philadelphia; chief ophthal serv, Philadelphia Gen Hosp & Children's Hosp, 49-70; chief ophthal serv & consult, Vet Admin Hosp; numerous name lectureships, 52-74; mem adv coun reserve affairs, Surgeon Gen, US Army, 44; mem nat adv comt, Eye-Bank Sight Restoration, Inc & Nat Coun Combat Blindness; mem bd examr, Am Bd Ophthal, 59-66; mem med adv comt, Medic Alert Found Int, 66. *Mem:* AAAS; Am Acad Ophthal & Otolaryngol (vpres, 60-61); Am Asn Ophthal (3rd vpres, 70); fel Am Col Surg (vpres, 61-62); AMA. *Res:* Infantile glaucoma; anesthesia in ophthalmic surgery; ACTH and cortisone; arteriosclerosis; retrolental fibroplasia. *Mailing Add:* 1024 Keith Ave Berkeley CA 94708-1605

SCHEIE, PAUL OLAF, PHYSICS, BIOPHYSICS. *Current Pos:* assoc prof, 73-80, PROF PHYSICS & CHMN DEPT, TEX LUTHERAN COL, 80- *Personal Data:* b Minn, June 24, 33; m 63, Mary A Harrison; c Eric & Maren. *Educ:* St Olaf Col, BA, 55; Univ NMex, MS, 57; Pa State Univ, PhD(biophys), 65. *Prof Exp:* Asst prof physics, Oklahoma City Univ, 58-63, chmn dept, 58-61; asst prof biophys, Pa State Univ, 66-73. *Concurrent Pos:* Vis prof, Med Fac, Univ Bergen, Norway, 80-81 & 90-91. *Mem:* AAAS; Am Asn Physics Teachers; Biophys Soc; Royal Micros Soc; Am Phys Soc. *Res:* Properties of solid-liquid interfaces; physical properties of bacteria; capillarity. *Mailing Add:* 207 Leonard Lane Seguin TX 78155. *E-Mail:* scheie__p@txlutheran.edu

SCHEIG, ROBERT L, INTERNAL MEDICINE, GASTROENTEROLOGY. *Current Pos:* HEAD, DEPT MED, BUFFALO GEN HOSP, 81- *Personal Data:* b Warren, Ohio, Mar 16, 31; m 52; c 1. *Educ:* Yale Univ, MD, 56. *Prof Exp:* From intern to sr asst resident med, Grace-New Haven Hosp, Conn, 56-61; from instr to assoc prof med, Sch Med, Yale Univ, 63-73, assoc dir liver study unit, 63-73, assoc dean regional affairs, 71-73; prof med & head, Div Gastroenterol, Sch Med, Univ Conn,

Farmington, 73-81, actg chmn, Dept Med, 78-79; prof med, State Univ NY, Buffalo, 81- *Concurrent Pos:* Fel, Sch Med, Yale Univ, 61-62; res fel, Harvard Med Sch, 62-63; from assoc physician to attend physician, Yale-New Haven Med Ctr, 63-73, dir adult clin res ctr, 69-71; attend physician, West Haven Vet Admin Hosp, Conn, 66-73, John Dempsey Hosp, Conn, 73-81 & Buffalo Gen Hosp, Erie County Med Ctr, Buffalo & Buffalo Vet Admin Med Ctr, 81-; consult, Hosp of St Raphael, New Haven, 69-73 & Waterbury Hosp, 72-73; attend physician & chief med, Newington Vet Admin Med Ctr, 73-81. *Mem:* Fel Am Col Physicians; Am Gastroenterol Asn; Am Asn Study Liver Dis; Am Fedn Clin Res; Sigma Xi. *Res:* Toxic liver injury; effect of ethanol on lipid metabolism and biochemical and histopathological correlation with clinical disease. *Mailing Add:* State Univ NY 28 Clarendon Place Buffalo NY 14209-1008. *Fax:* 716-845-1491

SCHEIM, DAVID E, MATHEMATICS. *Current Pos:* RETIRED. *Personal Data:* b New York, NY, Dec 26, 48. *Educ:* Univ Rochester, BS, 69, MA, 71; Mass Inst Technol, PhD(math), 75. *Prof Exp:* Dir, Mgt Info Systs, Nat Eye Inst, 81-96. *Mem:* Math Asn Am; Am Math Soc. *Mailing Add:* 3300 Old Farm Rd Blacksburg VA 24060-1534. *E-Mail:* 73750.3305@compuserve.com

SCHEIN, ARNOLD HAROLD, biochemistry, physiology, microbiology; deceased, see previous edition for last biography

SCHEIN, BORIS M, SEMIGROUPS OF TRANSFORMATIONS & RELATIONS. *Current Pos:* DISTINGUISHED PROF MATH, UNIV ARK, 80- *Personal Data:* b Moscow, Russia, June 22, 38; US citizen; m 66, Eugenia Lewenton; c Dina & Michael. *Educ:* Saratov State Univ, BSc, 59, MSc, 60; Russ Pedag Univ, St Petersburg, Russia, PhD(math), 62, DSc, 66. *Prof Exp:* Prof math, Saratov State Univ, 62-79, Tuland Univ, New Orleans, La, 80. *Concurrent Pos:* Managing ed, Semigroup Forum, Springer Int, NY, 70-; ed, Algebra Universalis, Birkhauser-Verlag, Basel, 74-, J Aequationes Mathematicae, 76-82 & 96-, Simon Stevin, Univ Ghent, Belgium, 78-93, Math Social Sci, 80-93, Algebra Colloquium, 93-97; vis prof, Technol Univ, Clausthal, WGer, 81; sr res fel, Univ St Andrews, Scotland, 84, Bar-Ilan Univ, Israel, 93, Politech Milano, Italy, 93, Univ Porto, Port, 93; chmn, Transl Comt, Am Math Soc, 85-87; vis prof, Tel-Aviv Univ, Israel, 86, Polytech Univ Catalonia, Spain, 86, Univ Siena, Italy, 86, Univ Calgary, Can, 86 & Shimane Univ, Japan, 90. *Mem:* Am Math Soc. *Res:* Relation algebra, systems of transformations (everywhere defined or partial, single- or multi-valued) closed under composition; other natural operations, semigroups, ordered sets, lattices, universal algebras, and algebraic automats. *Mailing Add:* Dept Math Sci Univ Ark SE-307 Fayetteville AR 72701. *Fax:* 501-575-8630; *E-Mail:* bschein@comp.uark.edu

SCHEIN, JEROME DANIEL, SENSORY REHABILITATION. *Current Pos:* Peikoff chair deafness res, 89-92, ADJ PROF, UNIV ALTA, 92- *Personal Data:* b Minneapolis, Minn, May 27, 23; m 82; c 2. *Educ:* Univ Minn, PhD(psychol), 58. *Prof Exp:* Instr psychol, Univ Wis, 58-59; asst prof, Fla State Univ, 59-60; prof, Gallaudet Col, 60-68, Powire Vaux Doctor chair, 86-87; dean educ, Univ Cincinnati, 68-70; emer prof sensory rehab, NY Univ, 70- *Concurrent Pos:* Chair sensory panel, Vet Admin Rehab Res & Develop, 81- *Mem:* Fel Am Psychol Asn. *Res:* Education and rehabilitation of persons with impaired vision, hearing and both deaf-blindness. *Mailing Add:* 1703 Andros Isle Apt J-2 Coconut Creek FL 33066. *Fax:* 954-968-3970

SCHEIN, LAWRENCE BRIAN, EXPERIMENTAL SOLID STATE PHYSICS. *Current Pos:* SHEIN CONSULT, 94- *Personal Data:* b Brooklyn, NY, Jan 31, 44; m 69, Edna Biehl; c Daniel & Benjamin. *Educ:* Pa State Univ, BS, 65; Columbia Univ, MA, 67; Univ Ill, PhD(physics), 70. *Honors & Awards:* Chester Carlson Award, 93. *Prof Exp:* Mem tech staff solid state res, RCA Corp, 65-67; David Sarnoff res fel, Univ Ill, 69-70; mem tech staff, Xerox Res Labs, IBM Res Div, 70-79, mgr, Explor Making Area, 79-83, mem staff & mgr electrophotog physics, San Jose, 83-94. *Mem:* Am Phys Soc; Sigma Xi; fel Soc Imaging Sci & Technol; sr mem Inst Elec & Electronics Engrs Electrostatic Soc. *Res:* Metal-semiconductor tunneling; physics of electrophotography; transport properties of molecular crystals and molecularly doped polymers; static electricity. *Mailing Add:* 7026 Calcaterra Dr San Jose CA 95120. *Fax:* 408-927-2100; *E-Mail:* schein@almaden.ibm.com

SCHEIN, MARTIN WARREN, ETHOLOGY, EDUCATIONAL ADMINISTRATION. *Current Pos:* clin prof behav med & psychiat, WVa Univ, 73-84, chmn, dept biol, 80-86, centennial prof biol, 68-88, EMER CENTENNIAL PROF BIOL, WVA UNIV, 88-; CONSULT, NAT DEFENSE MED COL, SAITAMA, JAPAN, 88- *Personal Data:* b Brooklyn, NY, Dec 23, 25; m 61, Maxine Kennedy; c Lonnie G, Michel R & Josh L. *Educ:* Univ Iowa, AB, 49; Johns Hopkins Univ, ScD(vert ecol), 54. *Prof Exp:* Biol aide, USPHS, 47-48; animal climatologist, Exp Sta, La State Univ & USDA, 51-55; from asst prof to assoc prof animal behav, Pa State Univ, 55-65, prof zool, 65-68. *Concurrent Pos:* Comnr undergrad educ in biol sci, George Washington Univ, 62-64, vchmn comn, 64-65, dir, 65-68, vis prof biol, univ, 65-68; vis lectr, Univ Southern Ill, 64; vis prof biol, Banaras Hindu Univ, Varanasi, India, 82-83; Fulbright fel, India, 82-83; teacher, Tokyo Metrop Kokusai High Sch, 90-91. *Mem:* Fel AAAS; Am Soc Zoologists; fel Animal Behav Soc (secy, 55-62, pres-elect, 66, pres, 67); Sigma Xi. *Res:* Behavior of domestic animals; sexual, social and feeding behavior; education in biology. *Mailing Add:* 5800 Nicholson Lane Apt 1001 Rockville MD 20852

SCHEIN, PHILIP SAMUEL, PHARMACOLOGY, ONCOLOGY. *Current Pos:* CHMN & CHIEF EXEC OFF, US BIOSCI INC, 87- *Personal Data:* b Asbury Park, NJ, May 10, 39; m 67; c 2. *Educ:* Rutgers Univ, AB, 61; State Univ NY Upstate Med Ctr, MD, 65; Am Bd Internal Med, dipl, 72, 73; FRCPS(G), 81. *Hon Degrees:* Dr, Nat Univ Rosario, Argentina, 80. *Prof Exp:* Intern med, Beth Israel Hosp, Boston, Mass, 65-66; res assoc pharmacol, Nat Cancer Inst, 66-68; asst resident med, Beth Israel Hosp, Boston, 68-69; res physician Radcliffe Infirmary, Oxford, 69-70; instr, Harvard Med Sch, 70-71; sr investr oncol, Nat Cancer Inst, 71-74; head clin pharmacol, 73-74; chief med oncol, Georgetown Univ Hosp & Lombardi Cancer Res Ctr, 74-; vpres World Wide Clin Res & Develop, Smith, Kline & French Labs, Philadelphia, Pa, 83-86, chief exec officer & pres US Biosci, 86-87. *Concurrent Pos:* Chief resident med, Beth Israel Hosp, Boston, 70-71; clin asst prof, 71-74, assoc prof med & pharmacol, 74-77, prof med & pharmacol, Med Sch, Georgetown Univ, 77-; consult, Walter Reed Army Hosp, 71 & Clin Ctr, NIH, 74; chmn, Gastrointestinal Tumor Study Group, 74-, Oncol Comt Adv Comt, Food & Drug Admin, 78-81, Med Oncol Comt, Am Bd Int Med, 80-; prof med & pharm, Univ Pa, 83. *Mem:* Am Asn Cancer Res; Am Soc Clin Oncol; fel Am Col Physicians; Am Soc Hemat; fel Royal Soc Med; Sigma Xi; Am Soc Clin Invest; Am Assoc Physicians. *Res:* Laboratory and clinical investigations in cancer chemotherapy and endocrinology. *Mailing Add:* US Bioscience Inc 1 Tower Bridge 100 Front St Suite 400 West Conshohocken PA 19428

SCHEIN, RICHARD DAVID, PLANT PATHOLOGY, ECOLOGY. *Current Pos:* RETIRED. *Personal Data:* b East St Louis, Ill, Nov 18, 27; m 55; c 3. *Educ:* DePauw Univ, BA, 48; Univ Calif, PhD(plant path), 52. *Prof Exp:* Asst, Univ Calif, 48-52; asst plant pathologist, Ill Natural Hist Surv, 52-53; from asst prof to assoc prof plant path, Pa State Univ, 55-63, assoc prof bot, 63-66, asst dean coi sci, 64, assoc dean, 65-71, prof bot, 66-76, dir, Off Environ Qual Progs, 71-75, prof plant path, 76-85, emer prof, 85- *Concurrent Pos:* Sr res fel, Agr Univ Neth, 75-76. *Mem:* AAAS; Am Inst Biol Sci; Am Phytopath Soc. *Res:* Plant disease epidemiology; parasitic ecology; influences of physical environment on plant disease development; instrumentation for plant disease study; research and education; economic botany. *Mailing Add:* 526 W Nittany Ave State College PA 16801

SCHEINBERG, ISRAEL HERBERT, MEDICINE. *Current Pos:* assoc prof, 55-57, PROF MED, ALBERT EINSTEIN COL MED, 58-, HEAD DIV GENETIC MED, 73- *Personal Data:* b New York, NY, Aug 16, 19; m 52, 57; c 3. *Educ:* Harvard Univ, AB, 40, MD, 43; Am Bd Internal Med, dipl. *Honors & Awards:* Asn Res Nerv & Ment Dis Award, 59. *Prof Exp:* Intern & asst resident med, Peter Bent Brigham Hosp, 43-44; res assoc chem, Mass Inst Technol, 47-51; instr med, Harvard Med Sch, 51-53, assoc, 53; asst prof, Columbia Univ, 53-55. *Concurrent Pos:* Commonwealth Fund fel, 63-64; jr fel, Soc Fellows, Harvard Univ, 47-50; consult, WHO, 52, 67; prin res scientist, NY State Psychiat Inst, 53-55; vis physician, Bronx Munic Hosp Ctr, 55-; res collabr, Med Dept, Brookhaven Nat Lab, 58-; Miller lectr, Dartmouth Med Sch, 61; vis prof physics, Univ Calif, San Diego, 63-64; chmn subcomt copper, Comn Biol & Med Effects Atmospheric Pollutants, Nat Res Coun, 72-77; vis physician, Children's Hosp, Harvard Med Sch, 77- *Mem:* Am Soc Clin Invest (vpres, 64-65); Asn Am Physicians. *Res:* Protein chemistry; chemistry and genetics of copper metabolism. *Mailing Add:* Wilson's Dis Ctr 432 W 58th St Suite 614 New York NY 10019. *Fax:* 212-523-8708

SCHEINBERG, LABE CHARLES, NEUROLOGY. *Current Pos:* PROF NEUROL, MT SINAI MED CTR, NY, 93- *Personal Data:* b Memphis, Tenn, Dec 11, 25; m 52, Louise Goldman; c Susan, David, Ellen & Amy. *Educ:* Univ NC, AB, 45; Univ Tenn, MD, 48. *Prof Exp:* Intern, Wesley Mem Hosp, 49; resident psychiat, Elgin State Hosp, 50; resident & asst physician, Neurol Inst, NY, 52-56; mem fac, Albert Einstein Col Med, 56-93, prof neurol & asst dean, 68-69, assoc dean, 69-70, prof rehab med & psychiat & dean, 70-72; dir, Dept Neurol & Psychiat, St Barnabas Hosp, NY, 74-79. *Concurrent Pos:* Ed-in-chief, J Neurologic Rehab, Rehab Reports & Mult Sclerosis Res Reports. *Mem:* Fel Am Acad Neurol; Am Neurol Asn; Am Asn Neuro-Path; Am Soc Exp Path. *Mailing Add:* Mt Sinai Med Ctr Neurol SE 98th St 7th Floor New York NY 10029-6574

SCHEINBERG, PERITZ, NEUROLOGY. *Current Pos:* res assoc, Med Res Univ, 50-51, res asst prof physiol, Sch Med, 51-55, assoc prof neurol & chief div, 55-59, PROF NEUROL, SCH MED, UNIV MIAMI, 59-, CHMN DEPT, 61- *Personal Data:* b Miami, Fla, Dec 21, 20; m 42; c 3. *Educ:* Emory Univ, AB, 41, MD, 44; Am Bd Internal Med, dipl, 51; Am Bd Psychiat & Neurol, dipl, 54. *Prof Exp:* Instr med neurol, Duke Univ, 49-50. *Concurrent Pos:* Res fel med neurol, Am Col Physicians, Med Sch, Duke Univ, 48-49, Am Heart Asn res fel, 49-50; consult, Vet Admin Hosp; med adv bd, Nat Multiple Sclerosis Soc & Myasthenia Gravis Found; consult, Surgeon Gen US; examr, Am Bd Psychiat & Neurol; trustee, Asn Univ Prof Neurol; mem stroke coun, Am Heart Asn. *Mem:* Am Asn Res Nerv & Ment Dis; Am Neurol Asn (pres); fel Am Col Physicians; fel Am Acad Neurol; Am Fedn Clin Res; Asn Univ Prof Neurol (pres). *Res:* Medical neurology; blood flow and metabolism of the brain. *Mailing Add:* Mt Sinai Hosp 4300 Alton Rd Miami Beach FL 33140-2849

SCHEINBERG, SAM LOUIS, GENETICS. *Current Pos:* LEADER, PIONEERING RES LAB, 70- *Personal Data:* b New York, NY, June 15, 22; m 45, Helen Schwartz; c Daniel M, Jerry M & Judith A (Berg). *Educ:* Cornell Univ, BS, 49; Iowa State Univ, MS, Univ Wis, PhD(genetics, poultry husb & zool), 54. *Prof Exp:* Fel immunogenetics, NIH, Univ Wis, 54-56; res biologist immunogenetics & immunochem, Oak Ridge Nat Lab, 56-58; geneticist & group leader, USDA, 58-70. *Mem:* Genetics Soc Am. *Res:* Immunogenetics; cellular and serum antigens in birds and mammals; somatic variation in birds and man; immunochemistry. *Mailing Add:* Pioneering Res Lab 7409 Wellesley Dr College Park MD 20740

SCHEINDLIN, STANLEY, PHARMACEUTICAL CHEMISTRY. *Current Pos:* RETIRED. *Personal Data:* b Philadelphia, Pa, July 8, 26; m 54, Phyllis Brooks; c Lewis, Neal & Benjamin. *Educ:* Temple Univ, BS, 45; Philadelphia Col Pharm, MS, 47, DSc(pharmaceut chem), 55. *Prof Exp:* Res fel, Philadelphia Col Pharm, 47-48, asst pharm, 48-49, instr, 49-55; res assoc labs, Nat Drug Co, 55-64, dir pharmaceut res labs, 64-70 & pharmaceut res & develop, 70-71; independent pharmaceut consult, 71-72; dir res, Lemmon Pharmacol Co, 72-77, dir tech affairs, 78-84, dir regulatory affairs, 85-93, sr dir regulatory projs, 93-96. *Concurrent Pos:* Lectr, Philadelphia Col Pharm, 68-69 & Spring Garden Col, 79-80; assoc adj prof, Sch Pharm, Temple Univ, 90-92. *Mem:* Am Soc Pharmacog; Am Chem Soc; Am Pharmaceut Asn; Acad Pharmaceut Sci; Regulatory Affairs Prof Soc. *Res:* Plant constituents; interactions of vitamins; stability; compatibility and incompatibility of drugs; formulation of parenterals; cancer chemotherapy. *Mailing Add:* 3011 Nesper St Philadelphia PA 19152

SCHEINER, BERNARD JAMES, METALLURGY, CHEMISTRY. *Current Pos:* RETIRED. *Personal Data:* b Atlantic City, NJ, Mar 12, 38; m 59; c 2. *Educ:* Univ Nev, Reno, BS, 61, PhD(org chem), 69. *Prof Exp:* Proj leader & res chemist, Reno Metall Res Sta, US Bur Mines, 66-79, supv metallurgist, Fine Particle Technol Group, Tuscaloosa Res Ctr, 79-95. *Mem:* Am Inst Mining, Metall & Petrol Engrs. *Res:* Development of processes for the recovery of metals from low-grade, refractory, and sulfide ores by means of innovative hydrometallurgical techniques; development of dewatering techniques for mineral processing waste slurries. *Mailing Add:* 2802 Union Chapel Rd Northport AL 35476

SCHEINER, DONALD M, BIOCHEMISTRY, MICROBIOLOGY. *Current Pos:* asst prof, 63-71, ASSOC PROF CHEM, RUTGERS UNIV, 71- *Personal Data:* b New York, NY, Mar 12, 32; m 54; c 2. *Educ:* Cornell Univ, BS, 53, MFS, 54, PhD(biochem), 60. *Prof Exp:* Res chemist, Rohm and Haas Co, 60-63. *Mem:* AAAS; Am Chem Soc; NY Acad Sci. *Res:* Analytical biochemistry; microbial metabolism; plant pigments; immunology. *Mailing Add:* Dept Chem Rutgers Univ Camden Campus 311 N Fifth St Camden NJ 08102-1205

SCHEINER, PETER, ORGANIC CHEMISTRY. *Current Pos:* CONSULT, DEPT AIR RESOURCES, NEW YORK, 71- *Personal Data:* b Brooklyn, NY, Mar 13, 35; m 60; c 4. *Educ:* Cornell Univ, AB, 57; Univ Mich, MS, 60, PhD(chem), 61. *Prof Exp:* NIH fel, Mass Inst Technol, 61-62; asst prof chem, Carleton Col, 62-64; from res chemist to sr res chemist, Mobil Oil Corp, 64-69; from assoc prof to prof chem, York Col, NY, 69-76, chmn Dept Natural Sci, 73-76. *Concurrent Pos:* NIH res grant, Carleton Col, 62-64; NY Col, 79-82 & York Col, NY, 79-85; Am Chem Soc-Petrol Res Fund res grant, York Col, NY, 71-73. *Mem:* Am Chem Soc; Sigma Xi. *Res:* Organic photochemistry; heterocycles; air pollution; atmospheric chemistry; nucleoside chemistry. *Mailing Add:* York Col CUNY Jamaica NY 11451-0001

SCHEINER, STEVE, PHYSICAL CHEMISTRY, QUANTUM CHEMISTRY. *Current Pos:* from asst prof to assoc prof, 78-86, PROF CHEM, SOUTHERN ILL UNIV, CARBONDALE, 86- *Personal Data:* b New York, NY, Feb 27, 51. *Educ:* City Col New York, BS, 72; Harvard Univ, AM, 74, PhD(chem physics), 76. *Prof Exp:* Weizmann Found fel chem, Ohio State Univ, 76-78. *Concurrent Pos:* Chair, Gordon Conf, 94. *Mem:* Int Soc Quantum Biol; Biophys Soc; Am Chem Soc; Am Phys Soc. *Res:* Proton transfer; hydrogen bonding; protein structure. *Mailing Add:* Dept Chem & Biochem Southern Ill Univ Mailcode 4409 Carbondale IL 62901. *Fax:* 618-453-6408

SCHEINOK, PERRY AARON, RESEARCH ADMINISTRATION, MATHEMATICS. *Current Pos:* RETIRED. *Personal Data:* b The Hague, Neth, Sept 21, 31; nat US; m 53, 71, Malka Gerstel; c Diane R (Engel) & Nancy L (Giller). *Educ:* City Col New York, BS, 57; Ind Univ, PhD(math, statist), 60. *Prof Exp:* Asst math, Ind Univ, 52-54 & 56-59; mathematician, Burroughs Corp, 56; vis res assoc, Brookhaven Nat Lab, 59; instr comput & math, Wayne State Univ, 59-60, asst prof math, 60-62; sr systs engr, Radio Corp Am, 62-64; res asst prof pharmacol, Hahnemann Med Col, 64-68, res assoc prof, 68-70, res prof physiol & biophys, 70-72, dir comput ctr, 64-72, div biomet & comput, 70-72; exec dir, Del Health Serv Authority, 72-74; proj dir, University City Sci Ctr, 74-77; sr dir med data control, CIBA-GEIGY Corp, 77-82; assoc prof, Dept Math, NJ Inst Technol, 83-87 & Univ Judaism, 87-92. *Concurrent Pos:* Consult, Henry Ford Hosp, 61-62; Pa Hosp, 65-66; free-lane statist consult, 82-; prin investr, NIH grant biomed res, Comput Ctr, 65-72. *Mem:* Am Statist Asn; Math Asn Am. *Res:* Application of probabilistic models to medical diagnosis; computerization of clinical hospital functions; electrocardiogram; clinical labs; time series analysis; large scale biological data bases; health services research. *Mailing Add:* 10141-2 Valley Circle Blvd Chatsworth CA 91311

SCHEIRER, DANIEL CHARLES, BOTANY, ELECTRON MICROSCOPY. *Current Pos:* Asst prof, 74-80, ASSOC PROF BIOL, NORTHEASTERN UNIV, 80-; DIR, ELECTRON MICROSCOPY CTR, 78- *Personal Data:* b Lebanon, Pa, Dec 10, 46; c 2. *Educ:* Wheaton Col, Ill, BS, 68; Pa State Univ, MS, 71, PhD(bot), 74. *Concurrent Pos:* Vis scholar, Harvard Univ, 81-82; vis assoc prof, Molecular Biol Dept, Mass Gen Hosp, 89-90. *Mem:* AAAS; Am Bryol & Lichenol Soc; Bot Soc Am; Microscopy Soc Am; Am Soc Plant Physiol. *Res:* Plant development; biology of asabidopsis. *Mailing Add:* Dept Biol Northeastern Univ 360 Huntington Ave Boston MA 02115-5096. *Fax:* 617-373-3724; *E-Mail:* daniels@neu.edu

SCHEIRER, JAMES E, ELECTROCHEMISTRY. *Current Pos:* chair, Chem Dept, 87-90, PROF CHEM, ALBRIGHT COL, 72- *Personal Data:* b Harrisburg, Pa, Dec 3, 43. *Educ:* Ursinus Col, BS, 65; Univ Pa, PhD(phys chem), 71. *Prof Exp:* Fel chem, State Univ NY Buffalo, 70-72. *Concurrent Pos:* Vis scientist, Victoria Univ, Wellington, NZ, 84-85 & Southampton Univ, Eng, 92. *Mem:* Am Chem Soc. *Res:* Affect of high pressure, temperature, and viscosity on ion conductance in both aqueous and non aqueous solutions. *Mailing Add:* PO Box 15234 Reading PA 19612-5234

SCHEIRING, JOSEPH FRANK, ENTOMOLOGY, ECOLOGY. *Current Pos:* ASST PROF, DEPT BIOL, UNIV ALA, 76- *Personal Data:* b Puchbach, Austria, Apr 18, 45; m 69; c 1. *Educ:* Kent State Univ, BS, 68, MA, 70; Univ Kans, PhD(entom), 75. *Prof Exp:* Res assoc, Dept Entom, Mich State Univ, 75-76. *Concurrent Pos:* Prin investr, Geol Surv Ala, 78-79 & Res Grants Comt, Univ Ala, 77 & 78. *Mem:* Ecol Soc Am; Entom Soc Am; NAm Benthol Soc; Sigma Xi. *Res:* Ecology of aquatic and semi-aquatic insects; niche relations in insects; applications of multivariate statistical methods to biology. *Mailing Add:* Dept Biol Univ Ala Box 870344 Tuscaloosa AL 35487

SCHEITER, B JOSEPH PAUL, institutional research, enrollment projection models, for more information see previous edition

SCHEKEL, KURT ANTHONY, ORNAMENTAL HORTICULTURE, FLORICULTURE. *Current Pos:* Assoc prof ornamental hort, 71-80, ASSOC PROF DEPT HORT & LANDSCAPE ARCHIT, WASH STATE UNIV, 80- *Personal Data:* b Colorado Springs, Colo, Jan 3, 43; m 68; c 1. *Educ:* Colo State Univ, BS, 65, PhD(floricult), 71; Univ Nebr, Lincoln, MS, 68. *Mem:* Am Soc Hort Sci. *Res:* Nutrition and growing temperatures of greenhouse crops. *Mailing Add:* 1001 Armstrong Rd Pullman WA 99163

SCHEKMAN, RANDY W, CELL BIOLOGY. *Current Pos:* from asst prof to assoc prof, 76-83, head, Div Biochem & Molecular Biol, 90-94, PROF, UNIV CALIF, BERKELEY, 83-, INVESTR, HOWARD HUGHES MED INST, 90- *Personal Data:* b St Paul, Minn, Dec 30, 48; m 73, Nancy Walls; c Joel & Lauren. *Educ:* Univ Calif, Los Angeles, BA, 70; Stanford Univ, PhD(biochem), 75. *Honors & Awards:* Eli Lilly Res Award, 87; Lewis S Rosenstiel Award, 94; Gairdner Int Award, 96. *Prof Exp:* Fel, Univ Calif, San Diego, 74-76. *Concurrent Pos:* Fel, Cystic Fibrosis Found, 74; sabbatical fel, John S Guggenheim Found, 82. *Mem:* Am Soc Microbiol; Am Soc Biochemists & Molecular Biologists; Am Soc Cell Biol. *Res:* Molecular mechanism of secretion and membrane assembly in eucaryotic cells. *Mailing Add:* Dept Biochem & Molecular Biol 401 Barker Hall Univ Calif Berkeley CA 94720-3202

SCHELAR, VIRGINIA MAE, CHEMICAL EDUCATION. *Current Pos:* CONSULT, 80- *Personal Data:* b Kenosha, Wis, Nov 26, 24. *Educ:* Univ Wis, BS, 47, MS, 53; Harvard Univ, EdM, 62; Univ Wis, PhD, 69. *Prof Exp:* Instr chem, Univ Wis-Milwaukee, 47-51; info specialist, Abbott Labs, Ill, 53-56; instr phys sci, Wright Jr Col, 57-58; asst prof chem, Northern Ill Univ, 58-63; prof, St Petersburg Jr Col, 65-67; asst prof chem, Chicago State Col, 67-68; prof chem, Grossmont Col, 68-80. *Concurrent Pos:* Mem adv panel eval proposals, NSF, Washington DC, dir summer prog, 61. *Mem:* Am Chem Soc; fel Am Inst Chem. *Res:* Analytical instrumentation computers; protein requirement in nutrition. *Mailing Add:* 5702 Baltimore Dr 282 LaMesa CA 91942

SCHELBERG, ARTHUR DANIEL, PHYSICS. *Current Pos:* STAFF MEM, EG&G INC, E MERCK LABS, LOS ALAMOS, 82- *Personal Data:* b New York, NY, Mar 8, 21; wid; c 5. *Educ:* Princeton Univ, AB, 42; Ind Univ, MS, 48, PhD(physics), 51. *Prof Exp:* Asst, Princeton Univ, 42-43; Los Alamos Sci Lab, 43-46, Ind Univ, 46-50 & Radiation Lab, Univ Calif, 51-52; asst, Los Alamos Sci Lab, 52-82. *Mem:* Sigma Xi. *Res:* Nuclear physics; resonance capture of neutrons in U-238 and Th-232; low level radiography using channel plate image intensifiers; neutron flux measurements on downhole events at the Nevada test site. *Mailing Add:* 470 Camino Encantado Los Alamos NM 87544-2507

SCHELD, WILLIAM MICHAEL, INFECTIOUS DISEASES. *Current Pos:* Intern med, 73-74, resident, 74-76, fel, 76-79, from asst prof to assoc prof med, 79-88, PROF MED, UNIV VA, 88- *Personal Data:* b Middletown, Conn, Aug 15, 47; m 69; c 1. *Educ:* Cornell Univ, BS, 69; Cornell Univ Med Col, MD, 73. *Honors & Awards:* Young Clin Investr Award, Am Fed Clin Res, 86. *Concurrent Pos:* Ed, Europ J Clin Microbiol, 84, mem, ACP MKSAP II, Infectious Dis, 86-88. *Mem:* NY Acad Sci; AAAS; Infectious Dis Soc Am; Asn Clin Path; Am Soc Microbiol; Am Fed Clin Res; Am Soc Clin Invest. *Res:* Basic pathogenesis; pathophysiology of the central nervous system infections. *Mailing Add:* Div Infectious Dis Dept Med Univ Va Sch Med Charlottesville VA 22908

SCHELDORF, JAY J(OHN), CHEMICAL ENGINEERING. *Current Pos:* assoc prof, 66-74, PROF CHEM ENG & ENG SCI, UNIV IDAHO, 74- *Personal Data:* b Camden, NJ, Jan 22, 32; m 53; c 2. *Educ:* Univ Ill, BS, 53; Kans State Univ, MS, 54; Univ Colo, PhD(chem eng), 58. *Prof Exp:* Res chemist, Chem Div, Corn Prod Refining Co, 54-55; instr chem eng, Univ Colo, 55-58, asst prof, 58-66. *Mem:* Am Inst Chem Engrs; Am Chem Soc; Am Soc Eng Educ. *Res:* Fluid dynamics and heat transfer; physical chemistry; thermodynamics. *Mailing Add:* Dept Chem Eng Univ Idaho Moscow ID 83843

SCHELL, ALLAN CARTER, ELECTROMAGNETISM. *Current Pos:* CHIEF SCIENTIST, AF MAT COMMAND, 87- *Personal Data:* b New Bedford, Mass, Apr 14, 34; m 57; c 2. *Educ:* Mass Inst Technol, SB & SM, 56, ScD(elec eng), 61. *Honors & Awards:* J J Bolljahn Award, 66; Centennial Medal, Inst Elec & Electronics Engrs, 84; Meritorious Serv Award, USAF, 88. *Prof Exp:* Res physicist, Microwave Physics Lab, Air Force Cambridge Res Labs, 56-76; dir, electromagnetics, Rome Air Develop Ctgr, 76-87. *Concurrent Pos:* Guenter Loeser Mem lectr, 65; vis assoc prof, Mass Inst Technol, 74; ed press, Inst Elec & Electronics Engrs, 76-79, dir, 81-82; ed, Proc Inst Elec & Electronics Engrs, 90- *Mem:* Fel Inst Elec & Electronics Engrs; Int Union Radio Sci. *Res:* Electromagnetic theory; antennas; angular resolution enhancement. *Mailing Add:* 639 S 19th St Arlington VA 22202

SCHELL, ANNE MCCALL, PSYCHO-PHYSIOLOGY. *Current Pos:* asst prof, 71-78, PROF PSYCHOL, OCCIDENTAL COL, 78-; RES ASSOC, NAT CTR HYPERACTIVE CHILDREN, 80- *Personal Data:* b Waco, Tex, Apr 23, 42; c 2. *Educ:* Baylor Univ, BS, 63; Univ Southern Calif, MA, 68, PhD(psychol), 70. *Prof Exp:* Vis asst prof psychol, Univ Southern Calif, 70-71. *Concurrent Pos:* Statist consult, Pasadena Unified Sch Dist, 73-75; res consult, Gateways Hosp, 75-80. *Mem:* Am Psychol Asn; Soc Psychophysiol Res. *Res:* Study of physiological components and concommitants of cognitive and affective processes in humans; physiological aspects of psychopathology. *Mailing Add:* Occidental Col Dept Psychol 1600 Campus Rd Los Angeles CA 90041-3384

SCHELL, FRED MARTIN, SYNTHETIC ORGANIC CHEMISTRY. *Current Pos:* ASSOC PROF CHEM, UNIV TENN, KNOXVILLE, 72-, ASSOC HEAD, DEPT CHEM. *Personal Data:* b Cincinnati, Ohio, Oct 6, 43; div; c Christopher & Gregory. *Educ:* Univ Cincinnati, BS, 66, MS, 68; Ind Univ, PhD(chem), 72. *Concurrent Pos:* Oak Ridge Nat Lab, 78-93. *Mem:* Am Chem Soc. *Res:* Development of new synthetic reactions and their application to synthesis of natural products; development of expert systems for organic synthesis; neural net development and applications; identification of chemosensory agents. *Mailing Add:* Dept Chem Univ Tenn Knoxville TN 37996-1600. *Fax:* 423-974-3454; *E-Mail:* fschell@utk.edu

SCHELL, GEORGE W(ASHINGTON), CHEMICAL ENGINEERING. *Current Pos:* RETIRED. *Personal Data:* b Easton, Pa, June 25, 21; m 46, Constance Hall; c Helen & Elizabeth. *Educ:* Lafayette Col, BS, 43. *Prof Exp:* Jr chem engr, Atlantic Refining Co, Pa, 44; asst chem, Univ Southern Calif, 44-45; jr chem engr, Atlantic Refining Co, Philadelphia, 45-46, asst chemist, 46-47, asst prod foreman, 47-57, foreman, 57-66, prod technologist, Atlantic Richfield Co, Pa, 66-71; supv chemist, Qual Control Lab, Pennzoil United, Inc, 71-73, chief chemist, Pennzoil Co, 73-77, supt oil movements, 77-79, mgr packaging, 79-84. *Mem:* Am Chem Soc. *Res:* Petroleum technology. *Mailing Add:* 301 E Main Ave Myerstown PA 17067-1124

SCHELL, JOSEPH FRANCIS, GEOMETRY, PROGRAMMING LANGUAGES. *Current Pos:* from assoc prof to prof math, 64-84, chmn dept, 68-80, PROF COMPUT SCI, UNIV NC, CHARLOTTE, 84- *Personal Data:* b Miamisburg, Ohio, Dec 24, 28; m 54, Irene Duzey; c Veronica, Michael, Kevin, Patrick, Mary, Renee, Joseph C & Edmund. *Educ:* Univ Dayton, BS, 50; Ind Univ, MA, 52, PhD(math), 57. *Prof Exp:* Asst, Ind Univ, 50-54; instr math, Univ Dayton, 54-56; res mathematician, Wright-Patterson AFB, Ohio, 56-61; asst prof math, Fla State Univ, 61-64. *Concurrent Pos:* Resident dir, Eglin Grad Ctr, Eglin AFB, 63-64. *Mem:* Am Math Soc; Math Asn Am; Soc Indust & Appl Math; Asn Comput Mach; Inst Elec & Electronics Engrs Comput Soc. *Res:* Differential geometry; relativity theory; topology; programming languages. *Mailing Add:* 712 Mount Vernon Ave Charlotte NC 28203. *E-Mail:* jfs@mosacc.uncc.edu

SCHELL, STEWART CLAUDE, PARASITOLOGY. *Current Pos:* From asst prof to prof, 49-78, chmn dept, 74-78, EMER PROF ZOOL, UNIV IDAHO, 78- *Personal Data:* b Reading, Pa, Feb 4, 12; m 41; c 2. *Educ:* Kans State Univ, BS, 39; NC State Col, MS, 41; Univ Ill, PhD(zool, parasitol), 50. *Mem:* Am Soc Parasitologists. *Res:* Life histories, development and taxonomy of parasitic helminths especially the trematodes. *Mailing Add:* 609 N Almon 4028 Moscow ID 83843

SCHELL, WILLIAM JOHN, MEMBRANE TECHNOLOGY, SEPARATIONS SCIENCE. *Current Pos:* mgr opers, Air Prod Separex Div, 86-90, bus dir, Separations Prod Div, 90-92, TECHNOL DIR, SEPARATIONS PRODS BUS UNIT, HOECHST CELANESE CORP, 92- *Personal Data:* b Buffalo, NY, Oct 19, 40; m 76, Bette Beebe; c Emily & Amelia. *Educ:* State Univ NY Col Forestry, Syracuse Univ, BS, 64, MS, 66; Univ Southern Calif, PhD(polymer chem), 69. *Prof Exp:* Mgr spec membrane prod, Envirogenics Systs Co, 69-78; partner, KS&W Consult, 78-79; pres, Spectrum Separations Inc, 79-86. *Mem:* Am Chem Soc; Am Inst Chem Engrs. *Res:* Membrane systems for fluid separations; pollution control processes; polymer characterization; relaxation behavior of polymers; high performance battery separators, blood oxygenator membranes. *Mailing Add:* Hoechst Celanese Corp 13800 South Lakes Dr Charlotte NC 28273-6737. *Fax:* 704-588-5319; *E-Mail:* bschell@stphccl.hcc.com

SCHELL, WILLIAM R, ENVIRONMENTAL, EARTH & MARINE SCIENCES. *Current Pos:* DEPT RADIATION HEALTH, GRAD SCH PUB HEALTH, UNIV PITTSBURGH. *Personal Data:* b Portland, Ore, Apr 17, 32; m 59; c 1. *Educ:* Ore State Univ, BS, 54; Univ Idaho, MS, 56; Univ Wash, PhD(inorg chem, nuclear chem), 63. *Prof Exp:* Res technician soils chem, Univ Idaho, 54-56; independent investr, US Naval Radiol Defense Lab, 56-59; res asst chem, Univ Wash, 60-63; sr radiochemist, Hazleton-Nuclear Sci Corp, Isotopes, Inc, Calif, 64-65, head div atmospheric & oceanog sci, 65-68; vis scientist, Radiochem Div, Lawrence Radiation Lab, Univ Calif, 68; with div res & labs, Int Atomic Energy Agency, 68-71; res assoc prof with lab radiation ecol, Col Fisheries, Univ Wash, 71-77, assoc prof fisheries, 78-79, prof, 79- *Concurrent Pos:* Guest lectr, Colo State Col, 66; adj prof oceanog, Dept Oceanog & radiol scientist, Dept Environ Health, Univ Wash, 79-82; vis scientist, Gas & Particulate Sci Div, Ctr Anal Chem, Nat Bureau Standards, 81-82; fel, Fulbright Found, Spain, 88. *Mem:* AAAS; Am Chem Soc; Sigma Xi; Health Physics; NY Acad Sci. *Res:* Environmental radiochemistry; colloidal chemistry; fallout studies; radiotracer techniques; chemical and radiochemical instrumentation; gas technology; carbon-14 dating; geophysics; nuclear debris in meteorology; oceanography and air pollution; radiation ecology. *Mailing Add:* 103 Schenley Rd Pittsburgh PA 15214

SCHELLENBERG, CARL B, SYSTEM CAPACITY. *Current Pos:* regional adminr, Western-Pac Region, DIR SYSTS CAPACITY, OFF SYST CAPACITY, DEPT TRANSP, FED AVIATION ADMIN. *Educ:* Occidental Col, BA; Univ Ariz, JD; Northwestern Univ, MA. *Prof Exp:* Staff, IBM Corp. *Mailing Add:* ASC-1 Rm 600W 800 Independence Ave SW Washington DC 20591

SCHELLENBERG, GERARD DAVID, GENETICS. *Current Pos:* sr res fel med genetics, Univ Wash, 78-79, sr res fel neurol, 79-82, sr res fel genetics, 82-83, res asst prof neurol, 83-90, RES ASSOC PROF NEUROL, UNIV WASH, 90- *Personal Data:* b Reedly, Calif, Sept 29, 51; m 86, Mary T Ensek; c Zachary D & Sierra M. *Educ:* Univ Calif, BS, 73, PhD(biochem), 78. *Prof Exp:* Res asst biochem, Univ Calif, Riverside, 73-78. *Res:* Identification of chromosome 14 alzheimers disease locus. *Mailing Add:* 7031 19th Ave NW Seattle WA 98117

SCHELLENBERG, KARL A, BIOCHEMISTRY. *Current Pos:* PROF BIOCHEM & CHMN DEPT, EASTERN VA MED SCH, 73- *Personal Data:* b Hillsboro, Kans, July 13, 31; m 55; c 4. *Educ:* Col William & Mary, BS, 53; Johns Hopkins Univ, MD, 57; Harvard Univ, PhD(biochem), 64. *Prof Exp:* Intern med, Grace-New Haven Community Hosp, Conn, 57-58; biochemist, NIH, 58-60; from asst prof to assoc prof physiol chem, Johns Hopkins Univ, 63-73. *Concurrent Pos:* Markle Found scholar med sci, 65-70. *Mem:* Am Chem Soc; Am Soc Biol Chem; NY Acad Sci. *Res:* Biochemical reaction mechanisms. *Mailing Add:* EVa Med Sch PO Box 1980 Norfolk VA 23501-1980

SCHELLENBERG, PAUL JACOB, BLOCK DESIGNS, GRAPH DECOMPOSITIONS. *Current Pos:* lectr, Univ Waterloo, 71, asst prof, 71-79, dept chmn, 82-88, assoc prof, 79-91, PROF COMBINATORICS & OPTIMIZATION, UNIV WATERLOO, 91-, ASSOC DEAN, FAC MATH, 95- *Personal Data:* b Leamington, Ont, Can, Dec 31, 42; m 66, Sandra L Clifford; c Amy L, Brian J, Scott A, Laura J & Mary J. *Educ:* Univ Waterloo, BSc, 65, MA, 66, PhD(math), 71. *Prof Exp:* Lectr math, Univ Waterloo, 66-67; systs programmer, Comput Ctr, Indian Inst Technol, Kanpur, 67-69. *Mem:* Can Math Soc; Math Asn Am. *Res:* Combinatorial mathematics and designs; room squares, balanced room squares, Latin squares, pairwise balanced designs, and decompositions of graphs. *Mailing Add:* Dept Combinatorics & Optimization Univ Waterloo Waterloo ON N2L 3G1 Can. *E-Mail:* pjschell@math.uwaterloo.ca

SCHELLER, W(ILLIAM) A(LFRED), CHEMICAL ENGINEERING, BIOCHEMICAL ENGINEERING. *Current Pos:* assoc prof, 63-69, chmn dept, 71-78, PROF CHEM ENG, UNIV NEBR, LINCOLN, 69- *Personal Data:* b Milwaukee, Wis, June 6, 29; m 51, Emily Jones; c William L II & Katherine E (Price). *Educ:* Northwestern Univ, BS, 51, PhD(chem eng), 55. *Prof Exp:* Res engr, Calif Res Corp, Stand Oil Co, Calif, 55-60, group supvr, 60-63. *Concurrent Pos:* Du Pont fac fel, 64; Univ Res Coun fac fel, 65; consult, Northern Natural Gas Co & Brunswick Corp, 65-75, NE Ethanol Bd, 71 & IRAS Develop Corp, NY, 76-91; Off Water Resources res grant, Univ Nebr, Lincoln, 66-69; guest prof, Univ Erlangen, 69-70, Ger Res Asn grant, 70; pres & chief exec officer, Scheller & Assoc, Inc, 80- *Mem:* Am Chem Soc; Am Inst Chem Engrs; Am Soc Eng Educ; Sigma Xi. *Res:* Phase equilibrium; direct energy conversion; reaction kinetics; thermodynamics; computer aided design; process economics; alcohol blended fuels, gasohol; fermentation. *Mailing Add:* Dept Chem Eng Univ Nebr Lincoln NE 68588-0126. *Fax:* 402-472-6989

SCHELLING, GERALD THOMAS, NUTRITION, METABOLISM. *Current Pos:* PROF & HEAD DEPT ANIMAL SCI, UNIV IDAHO, 88- *Personal Data:* b Sterling, Ill, Mar 24, 41; m 63; c 2. *Educ:* Univ Ill, BS, 63, MS, 64, PhD(nutrit), 68. *Prof Exp:* Res assoc nutrit, Univ Ill, 68; nutritionist, Smith, Kline & French Labs, 68-70; prof nutrit, Univ Ky, 70-79; prof nutrit, Tex A&M Univ, 79-88. *Mem:* Am Soc Animal Sci; Am Inst Nutrit. *Res:* Ruminant and nonruminant nutrition, with emphasis on growth regulation and nitrogen metabolism. *Mailing Add:* Dept Animal Sci Univ Idaho Moscow ID 83843. *Fax:* 208-885-6420

SCHELLMAN, JOHN ANTHONY, PHYSICAL CHEMISTRY. *Current Pos:* assoc prof, 58-62, PROF CHEM, UNIV ORE, 62- *Personal Data:* b Philadelphia, Pa, Oct 24, 24; m 54, F Charlotte Green; c Heidi M & Lise C. *Educ:* Temple Univ, AB, 48; Princeton Univ, MA, 49, PhD(phys chem), 51. *Hon Degrees:* Dr, Chalmers Univ, Sweden, 83; Univ Padua, Italy, 90. *Prof Exp:* USPHS fel, Univ Utah, 51, res assoc, 52; USPHS fel, Carlsberg Lab, Denmark, 53-55; Du Pont fel, Univ Minn, 55-56; asst prof chem, 56-58. *Concurrent Pos:* Sloan fel, 59-64; mem NIH study sect biophys & biophys chem, 62-67; sr fel, USPHS, Lab des Hautes Pressions, Bellevue, France, 63-64; Guggenheim fel, Weizmann Inst, 69-70; vis scientist, Lab Chem Physics, Bethesda, Md, 80. *Mem:* Nat Acad Sci; Am Chem Soc; Am Soc Biol Chemists; Am Acad Arts & Sci; fel Am Phys Soc; Biophys Soc. *Res:* Optical rotation and thermodynamics of biochemical molecules. *Mailing Add:* 780 Lorane Hwy Eugene OR 97405-2340

SCHELL-SOROKIN, ANITA J, NONLINEAR OPTICS. *Current Pos:* RETIRED. *Educ:* Univ Calif, Santa Barbara, BS, 69; Harvard Univ, PhD(physics), 77. *Prof Exp:* Res scientist, IBM T J Watson Res Ctr, 77-95. *Mem:* Am Phys Soc. *Mailing Add:* 5 Ashwood Dr South Salem NY 10590

SCHELLY, ZOLTAN ANDREW, PHYSICAL CHEMISTRY, COLLOIDAL DYNAMICS. *Current Pos:* actg chmn, 90-91, PROF PHYS CHEM, UNIV TEX, ARLINGTON, 77-, DIR, CTR COLLOIDAL & INTERFACIAL DYNAMICS, 87- *Personal Data:* b Budapest, Hungary, Feb 15, 38; m 67; c 3. *Educ:* Vienna Tech Univ, BS, 62, DSc(phys chem), 67. *Honors & Awards:* Wilfred T Doherty Award, Am Chem Soc, 86. *Prof Exp:* AEC fel, Lab Surface Studies, Univ Wis-Milwaukee, 68; Air Force Off Sci Res fel, Univ Utah, 69-70; asst prof phys chem, Univ Ga, 70-76. *Concurrent Pos:* Alexander von Humboldt lectr fel, Max-Planck Inst Biophys Chem, 74. *Mem:* Am Chem Soc; Austrian Chem Soc; Am Phys Soc; Royal Soc Chem. *Res:* dynamics of fast colloidal processes; relaxation spectrometry; diffusion; laser techniques; chemical instabilities and bifurcations; deterministic chaos; phase transitions. *Mailing Add:* Dept Chem & Biochem Univ Tex Arlington TX 76019-0065. *Fax:* 817-272-3808; *E-Mail:* schelly@uta.edu

SCHELP, RICHARD HERBERT, MATHEMATICS. *Current Pos:* from asst prof to assoc prof, 70-79, PROF MATH, UNIV MEMPHIS, 79- *Personal Data:* b Kansas City, Mo, Apr 21, 36; m 58, Billie M Swopes; c Lisa M (Martin) & Richard J. *Educ:* Cent Mo Univ, BS, 59; Kans State Univ, MS, 61, PhD(math), 70. *Prof Exp:* Assoc math missile scientist, Appl Physics Lab, Johns Hopkins, 61-66; instr math, Kans State Univ, 66-70. *Concurrent Pos:* Managing ed, J Graph Theory, 81-83; vis res, Hungarian Acad Sci, Math Inst, 85, 90 & Univ Paris-Sud, 93. *Mem:* Am Math Soc; Math Asn Am; NY Acad Sci. *Res:* Graph theory and lattice theory; Ramsey theory and Hamiltonian graph theory. *Mailing Add:* Dept Math Sci Univ Memphis Memphis TN 38152. *Fax:* 901-678-2480; *E-Mail:* schelpr@hermes.msci.memst.edu

SCHELPER, ROBERT LAWRENCE, MICROGLIA, NEUROIMMUNOLOGY. *Current Pos:* asst prof, 82-87, ASSOC PROF PATH, SCH MED, UNIV IOWA, 87-, DIR AUTOPSY SERV, 87- *Personal Data:* b San Antonio, Tex, Oct 28, 48; m 84, Ruth N Holliday; c Elizabeth A. *Educ:* St Mary's Univ, San Antonio, Tex, BA, 71; Univ Tex, San Antonio, MD, 75, PhD(anat), 78. *Honors & Awards:* Weil Award, Am Asn Neuropathologists, 85. *Prof Exp:* Instr, Dept Anat, Univ Tex, San Antonio, 76-78. *Concurrent Pos:* Vis prof, Univ SDak. *Mem:* Am Asn Pathologists; Fed Am Socs Exp Biol; Am Asn Anatomists; Soc Neurosci; Reticuloendothelial Soc. *Res:* The origin, functions and pathologic reactions of microglia; studies of inflammatory reactions in nervous tissues injuries; lectin histochemistry for cell identification; blood brain barrier dysfunction and Alzheimer's disease. *Mailing Add:* Dept Path Sch Med Univ Iowa 107 Med Labs Iowa City IA 52242-1087. *Fax:* 319-335-8348; *E-Mail:* robert_schelper@uiowa.edu

SCHELSKE, CLAIRE L, AQUATIC ECOLOGY, LIMNOLOGY. *Current Pos:* CARL S SWISHER PROF WATER RESOURCES, DEPT FISHERIES & AQUATIC SCI, UNIV FLA, 87- *Personal Data:* b Fayetteville, Ark, Apr 1, 32; m 57, Betty Breukelman; c 3. *Educ:* Kans State Teachers Col, AB, 55, MS, 56; Univ Mich, PhD(zool), 61. *Prof Exp:* Res assoc, Univ Ga Marine Inst, 60-62; fishery biologist, Radiobiol Lab, Bur Com Fisheries, 62-63; supvry fishery biologist, 63, chief estuarine ecol prog, 63-66; tech asst, Off Sci & Technol, Exec Off Pres, 66-67; from asst res limnologist to assoc res limnologist, Univ Mich, Ann Arbor, 67-71; asst prof radiol health, Sch Pub Health, 67-68; lectr, Biol Sta, 70; from asst dir to actg dir, Great Lakes Res Div, 70-76, res limnologist, Great Lakes Res Div, 71-72, assoc prof limnol, Dept Atmospheric & Ocean Sci & assoc prof, Natural Resources, Sch Natural Resources, Univ Mich, Ann Arbor, 76-87. *Concurrent Pos:* Adj asst prof, NC State Univ, 64-66; consult to Ill Atty Gen, US Dept Justice. *Mem:* Fel AAAS; Am Soc Limnol & Oceanog (secy, 76-85, vpres, 87-88, pres, 88-90); Int Asn Great Lakes Res; fel Am Inst Fishery Res Biologists. *Res:* Eutrophication limnology and paleolimnology of the Great Lakes, fresh-water ecosystem ecology; relationships among silica, nitrogen, phosphorus and phytoplankton production; nutrients and other factors limiting primary productivity; biogeochemistry of silica. *Mailing Add:* 2738 SW Ninth Dr Gainesville FL 32601

SCHELTEMA, AMELIE HAINS, SYSTEMATICS, MARINE BIOLOGY. *Current Pos:* CONSULT, 70-; VIS INVESTR, WOODS HOLE OCEANOG INST, 80- *Personal Data:* b Boston, Mass, Apr 26, 28; m 55, Rudolf S; c Charles T & Konrad E. *Educ:* Bryn Mawr Col, AB, 50; Univ Oslo, DPh(marine biol), 92. *Prof Exp:* Jr Geologist, US Geol Surv, 51-54; ed, Univ NC Press, 56-58; sci fel, Radcliffe Inst Independent Study, 65-67. *Mem:* Sigma Xi; Am Malacol Union; Am Asn Zool Nomenclature; Unitas Malacologica; Western Soc Naturalists. *Res:* Systematics, taxonomy and anatomy of Aplacophora (Mollusca); zoogeography and ecology of the deep sea; evolution and phylogeny of Mollusca. *Mailing Add:* Woods Hole Oceanog Inst Woods Hole MA 02543. *Fax:* 508-457-2169; *E-Mail:* ascheltema@whoi.edu

SCHELTEMA, RUDOLF S, MARINE BIOLOGY, BIOGEOGRAPHY. *Current Pos:* res assoc marine biol, 60-63, from asst scientist to assoc scientist, 63-85, SR SCIENTIST, WOODS HOLE OCEANOG INST, 85- *Personal Data:* b Madison, Wis, May 27, 26; m 55, Amelie D Hains; c Charles T & Konrad E. *Educ:* George Washington Univ, BS, 51, MS, 54; Univ NC, PhD(zool), 60. *Prof Exp:* Marine biologist, Chesapeake Biol Lab, Md, 51-54; res assoc, Oyster Res Lab, Rutgers Univ, 59-60. *Concurrent Pos:* Fac mem, Cape Cod Community Col, 61-62; sr Fulbright-Hays Scholar, James Cook Univ, NQueensland, Australia, 77-78; assoc ed, Proc Nat Shellfish Asn, 66-68; sr ed adv, Marine Ecol Prog Ser, 80-96 & Zool Scripta, 82-; Mellon Study Award, 80-81; lectr deep-sea & oceanog biol, Woods Hole Oceanog Inst. *Mem:* Am Soc Zool; Soc Syst Zool; Am Soc Naturalists; Am Malacog Union; Systs Asn UK; Sigma Xi. *Res:* Invertebrate zoology; morphology, ecology and comparative physiology of the larvae of marine benthic invertebrates; biogeography and evolution; reproduction of deep-sea invertebrate benthos; life history and settlement of fouling organisms; larval ecology. *Mailing Add:* Dept Biol Woods Hole Oceanog Inst Woods Hole MA 02543. *Fax:* 508-457-2169

SCHELTGEN, ELMER, BIOPHYSICS, MOLECULAR GENETICS. *Current Pos:* RETIRED. *Personal Data:* b Limerick, Sask, Feb 5, 30; m 53; c 2. *Educ:* Univ BC, BA, 55; Ind Univ, Bloomington, AM, 65; Univ Tex, Houston, PhD(biomed sci), 68. *Prof Exp:* Lectr & instr physics, Univ BC, 54-60; NASA grant, Univ Houston, 68-69; USPHS fel, Univ Tex M D Anderson Hosp & Tumor Inst Houston, 69; asst prof cancer res, Univ Sask, 69-71, res assoc bact, 71-77, res assoc microbiol, 78-93. *Mem:* Am Chem Soc; Am Inst Biol Sci. *Mailing Add:* 511 Ave DS Saskatoon SK S7M 1R5 Can

SCHEMENAUER, ROBERT STUART, CLOUD PHYSICS, ARID LANDS WATER. *Current Pos:* Meteorologist, 67-69, res scientist cloud physics, 72-97, EMER SCIENTIST, ATMOSPHERIC ENVIRON SERV, ENVIRON CAN, 97- *Personal Data:* b Prince Albert, Sask, Nov 3, 46; m 70. *Educ:* Univ Sask, BA, 67; Univ Toronto, MSc, 69, PhD(meteorol), 72. *Concurrent Pos:* Assoc ed, J Appl Meteorol, 82, 89, J Climate & Appl Meteorol, 83-88 & J Atmos & Oceanic Technol, 89-; prin investr, Environ Can Chem High Elevation Fog Prog, Int Develop Res Ctr, Can, Inter-Am Comt Agr Develop Fog Collection Projs, Inte-Am Comt Agr Develop, Chile & Peru, 87-90; consult, UN Develop Prog, World Meteorol Asn, Inter Am Comt Agr Develop & Int Develop Res Ctr, Can, 87- *Mem:* Can Meteorol & Oceanog Soc; Am Meteorol Soc; Int Water Resources Asn. *Res:* Laboratory and airborne studies of the microphysical processes responsible for precipitation formation; weather modification; fog as an arid lands water resource; precipitation chemistry; acidic deposition to forests. *Mailing Add:* 92 Caines Ave Willowdale ON M2R 2L3 Can

SCHEMM, CHARLES EDWARD, NUMERICAL MODELING, TURBULENCE. *Current Pos:* SR OCEANOGR, APPL PHYSICS LAB, JOHNS HOPKINS UNIV, 77- *Personal Data:* b Baltimore, Md, Oct 30, 47; m 77, Jae-Kyung Eom; c Elizabeth R. *Educ:* Loyola Col, Md, BS, 69; Princeton Univ, PhD(geophys fluid dynamics), 74. *Prof Exp:* Res assoc, Inst Phys Sci & Technol, Univ Md, 74-77. *Concurrent Pos:* Vis lectr, dept meteorol, Univ Md, 76-81. *Mem:* Am Meteorol Soc; Sigma Xi; AAAS; Am Phys Soc. *Res:* Ocean boundary layer modeling; planetary boundary layer modeling; experimental and numerical studies of submarine hydrodynamics. *Mailing Add:* 11314 Old Hopkins Rd Clarksville MD 21029-1842

SCHEMMEL, RACHEL A, NUTRITION. *Current Pos:* instr food & nutrit, 55-63, from asst prof to assoc prof, 68-76, PROF NUTRIT, MICH STATE UNIV, 77- *Personal Data:* b Farley, Iowa, Nov 23, 29. *Educ:* Clarke Col, BA, 51; State Univ Iowa, MS, 52; Mich State Univ, PhD(nutrit), 67. *Honors & Awards:* Borden Award, 1986; Sr Res Award, Sigma Xi, 86. *Prof Exp:* Dietitian, Childrens Hosp Soc, Calif, 52-54; adminr, St Joseph's Hosp, Calif, 54-55. *Concurrent Pos:* Res fel, Dunn Nutrit Lab, Cambridge, 68; Sabbatic endocrinol, UCLA, 78; Sabbatic diabetes, NIDDK, 88. *Mem:* AAAS; Am Soc Nutrit Sci; Soc Exp Biol & Med; Brit Nutrit Soc; Am Dietetic Asn; Asn Family & Consumer Sci; Inst Food Tech; Soc Nutrit Educ. *Res:* Obesity and lipid and carbohydrate metabolism; hypertension; nutritional status of human subjects; dental caries; nutrition and exercise. *Mailing Add:* Dept Food Sci & Human Nutrit Mich State Univ East Lansing MI 48824

SCHEMNITZ, SANFORD DAVID, WILDLIFE RESEARCH, WILDLIFE ECOLOGY. *Current Pos:* head dept, 76-81, PROF WILDLIFE, DEPT FISHERY & WILDLIFE SCI, NMEX STATE UNIV, 76- *Personal Data:* b Cleveland, Ohio, Mar 10, 30; m 58, Mary Newby; c Ellen, Steven & Stuart. *Educ:* Univ Mich, BS, 52; Univ Fla, MS, 53; Okla State Univ, PhD(wildlife zool), 58. *Prof Exp:* Res game biologist, Bur Res & Planning, State Dept Conserv, Minn, 58-59; asst prof wildlife resources, Univ Maine, Orono, 60; asst prof wildlife mgt, Pa State Univ, 61; from asst prof to prof wildlife resources, Sch Forest Resources, Univ Maine, Orono, 63-75. *Concurrent Pos:* With sub group 108-wildlife habitat mgt, Int Union Forest Res Orgn; res partic, NSF, 62, 64 & 66; Fulbright prof ecol, Tribhuvan Univ, Nepal, 83-84; Fulbright prof wildlife mgt, Moi Univ, Kenya, 90. *Mem:* Ecol Soc Am; Wildlife Soc; Am Soc Mammalogists; Sigma Xi; Wilson Ornith Soc. *Res:* Wildlife conservation; ecology of birds and mammals; forest zoology and ecology; effects of off-road vehicles on environment. *Mailing Add:* Dept Fish & Wildlife Sci NMex State Univ Las Cruces NM 88003-0003

SCHEMPP, ELLORY, CHEMICAL PHYSICS, TECHNICAL MANAGEMENT. *Current Pos:* OWNER, HARVARD CONSULT GROUP, 89-; MGR BUS DEVELOP, AM SUPERCONDUCTOR CORP, WESTBOROUGH, MASS, 91- *Personal Data:* b Philadelphia, Pa. *Educ:* Tufts Univ, BS, 62; Brown Univ, PhD(physics), 68. *Prof Exp:* Fel physics,

Brown Univ, 67-68; res physicist, Bell Tel Labs, NJ, 68-70; asst prof crystallog & res asst prof physics, Univ Pittsburgh, 70-77; vis prof physics, Univ Ill, Champaign-Urbana, 77-78; vis prof, Univ Geneva, Switz, 77-79; sr scientist, Lawrence Berkeley Lab, 80-83; sr scientist, Gen Elec Med Systs, 83-87; vpres opers, Auburn Int, 87-89. *Concurrent Pos:* Course coordr, George Washington Univ, 83-89. *Mem:* Am Phys Soc; Sigma Xi; Instrument Soc Am; Soc Magnetic Resonance Med; Soc Magnetic Resonance Imaging. *Res:* Nuclear quadrupole resonance studies of chemical bonds; molecular and ionic field gradients in crystals; hydrogen bonding and lattice dynamics; nuclear magnetic resonance; applications of magnetic resonance imaging to ground water assessment, hazardous waste mitigation, and oil well drill cores; applications of high-temperature superconductors. *Mailing Add:* 24 Boston Ave Medford MA 02155-6722. *Fax:* 978-436-4248

SCHEMSKE, DOUGLAS WILLIAM, POPULATION BIOLOGY. *Personal Data:* b Chicago, Ill, Sept 8, 48. *Educ:* Univ Ill, BS, 70, PhD(ecol), 77. *Prof Exp:* Fel, Smithsonian Trop Res Inst, 77-78; asst prof evolution & ecol, Amherst Col, 78-79; asst prof evolution & ecol, Univ Chicago, 79-89. *Concurrent Pos:* Vis instr, Field Sta, Univ Minn, 79-80. *Mem:* AAAS; Am Soc Naturalists; Asn Trop Biol; Ecol Soc Am; Soc Study Evolution. *Res:* Evolutionary processes in plant populations, with particular emphasis on breeding systems, population structure, gene flow and the assessment of selection intensities. *Mailing Add:* 407 N 42nd St Seattle WA 98103

SCHENA, FRANCESCO PAOLO, NEPHROLOGY, IMMUNOLOGY. *Current Pos:* Med asst internal med, Univ Bari, 70-71, asst prof internal med, 72-82, assoc prof med ther, 83-85, PROF NEPHROLOGY, UNIV BARI, 86-, CHMN, 89- *Personal Data:* b Foggia, Italy, Mar 24, 40; m 69; c 2. *Educ:* Univ Bari, MD, 64. *Concurrent Pos:* Fel, Dept Nephrology, Univ Louvain-Belg, 68-70; vis prof, Inst Path-Case Western Reserve Univ, Cleveland, 85 & Renal Unit-Guy's Hosp, London, UK, 86; prin investr, CNR-Bilateral Proj, Italy-USA, 85- & CNR- Biotechnol Proj, Rome-Italy, 89-; nephrology consult, IRCCS Sci Res Inst-Bari, 90-; chmn, Regional Comt Organ Transplant, 90- *Mem:* Europ Renal Asn; Int Soc Nephrology; Am Kidney Asn; Am Soc Nephrology; Am Asn Immunologists; NY Acad Sci. *Res:* Principal investigator in the immunological research of human glomerulonephritis; developed new hypothesis on the pathogenesis of IgA nephropathy as the permanence in the blood of circulating immune complexes, which are not solubilised for the presence of increased amount of polymeric IgA; high production of interleukin-2 by peripheral blood mononuclear cells evidences the presence of unknown antigen in the blood which is able to activate continuously lymphocyte T helper. *Mailing Add:* Via Delle Murge 59/A Dept Nephrology Univ Bari Bari 70124 Italy. *Fax:* 39-80-5575188

SCHENCK, HARRY ALLEN, ACOUSTICS. *Current Pos:* OWNER, CHIEF CONSULT CO, 95- *Personal Data:* b San Diego, Calif, May 29, 38; m 59; c 4. *Educ:* Pomona Col, BA, 59; Harvard Univ, SM, 60, PhD(appl physics), 64. *Prof Exp:* Lectr & res fel acoust, Harvard Univ, 64; res physicist, USN Electronics Lab, Naval Ocean Systs Ctr, 64-69, surveillance systs prog mgr, Naval Undersea Ctr, 69-75, head, Undersea Surveillance Dept, 75-84, assoc undersea surveillance, 85-93, sr tech staff, 93-95. *Concurrent Pos:* Vis prof, US Naval Acad, 84-85; assoc ed, USN J Underwater Acoust, 86- *Mem:* Acoust Soc Am. *Res:* Electroacoustic transducers; acoustic radiation and scattering theory. *Mailing Add:* Chief Consult 3855 Talbot St San Diego CA 92106

SCHENCK, HILBERT VAN NYDECK, JR, PHYSICS, MECHANICAL ENGINEERING. *Current Pos:* RETIRED. *Personal Data:* b Boston, Mass, Feb 12, 26; m 50; c 4. *Educ:* Williams Col, BA, 50; Stanford Univ, MS, 52. *Prof Exp:* Test engr, Pratt & Whitney Aircraft Div, United Aircraft Corp, Conn, 52-56, from asst prof to prof mech eng, Clarkson Col Technol, 56-67; prof mech eng & appl Mech & Ocean Eng, Univ RI, 7-83, Dir Scuba Safety Proj, 71-80. *Concurrent Pos:* NSF grant, 63-64, res grant, 65-; Food & Drug Admin res grant scuba safety, 69-71; US Coast Guard grant scuba safety, 71-72; Manned Undersea Sci & Technol grants, 72- *Mem:* Am Phys Soc. *Res:* Engineering heat transfer; statistics of experimentation; instrumentation; underwater photography and oceanographic optics; diving technology and safety; scuba tank corrosion. *Mailing Add:* 343 Delano Rd Marion MA 02738

SCHENCK, JAY RUFFNER, BIOCHEMISTRY. *Current Pos:* RETIRED. *Personal Data:* b Geneva, Ill, Jan 10, 15; m 48; c 2. *Educ:* Univ Ill, BS, 36, MS, 37; Cornell Univ, PhD(biochem), 41. *Prof Exp:* Sci asst, Soybean Res Lab, USDA, 36-37; asst biochem, Sch Med, George Washington Univ, 37-38 & Cornell Univ, 38-40; res biochemist, Abbott Labs, 41-83. *Mem:* Am Chem Soc; Am Soc Biol Chem; Sigma Xi. *Res:* Microbiological assay; intermediary metabolism; isolation and chemistry of antibiotics; immunochemistry. *Mailing Add:* 403 Hull St Waukegan IL 60085

SCHENCK, JOHN FREDERIC, MEDICAL RESEARCH, SOLID STATE PHYSICS. *Current Pos:* consult scientist, Gen Elec Electronics Lab, 65-70, SR SCIENTIST, CORP RES & DEVELOP CTR, GEN ELEC CO, 73- *Personal Data:* b Decatur, Ind, June 7, 39; m 62, 94, Susan Kalia; c Brooke, Kimberley, David & Tania. *Educ:* Rensselaer Polytech Inst, BS, 61, PhD(solid state physics), 65; Albany Med Col, MD, 77. *Honors & Awards:* S S Greenfield Award, Am Asn Physicists Med, 93. *Prof Exp:* Assoc prof elec eng, Syracuse Univ, 70-73. *Concurrent Pos:* Adj asst prof radiol, Univ Pa, 87- *Mem:* Am Phys Soc; Inst Elec & Electronics Engrs; Sigma Xi; Am Asn Physicists Med; AAAS. *Res:* Electrical and electronic technology applied to clinical medicine; nuclear magnetic resonance and solid state devices in medical diagnosis; electric potentials at biological interfaces; social implications of technology; magnetic resonance imaging. *Mailing Add:* Gen Elec Corp Res & Develop Ctr 1 Res Circle Schenectady NY 12309. *Fax:* 518-387-6923; *E-Mail:* schenckalia@msu.com

SCHENCK, NORMAN CARL, PLANT PATHOLOGY, VA MYCORRHIZAE. *Current Pos:* From asst plant pathologist to assoc plant pathologist, 56-69, plant pathologist, Agr Res Ctr & prof plant path, 69-90, EMER PROF PLANT PATH, UNIV FLA, 91- *Personal Data:* b Oak Park, Ill, July 8, 28; m 51; c 4. *Educ:* Univ Ill, BS, 51, PhD(plant path), 55. *Honors & Awards:* Fel Award, Am Phytopath Soc, 86. *Mem:* Am Phytopath Soc; Mycol Soc Am. *Res:* Soil-borne plant disease; endomycorrhizal fungi; VA mycorrhizal fungi collection. *Mailing Add:* PO Box 90190 Gainesville FL 32607-0190

SCHENGRUND, CARA-LYNNE, BIOCHEMISTRY, GLYCOSPHINGOLIPIDS. *Current Pos:* res assoc, Pa State Univ, 69-72, from asst prof to assoc prof biochem, 72-92, actg dept chmn, 86-87, PROF BIOCHEM & MOLECULAR BIOL, HERSHEY MED CTR, PA STATE UNIV, 92- *Personal Data:* b New York, NY, Feb 18, 41; m 61, David M; c Kevin & Karin. *Educ:* Upsala Col, BS, 62; Seton Hall Univ, MS, 65, PhD(chem), 66. *Prof Exp:* Instr, Upsala Col, 67; res worker, Col Physicians & Surgeons, Columbia Univ, 67-68, res assoc biochem, 68-69. *Concurrent Pos:* Mem, Am Soc Neurochem Coun, 95- *Mem:* Am Soc Biochem & Molecular Biol; Am Chem Soc; Am Soc Neurochem. *Res:* Biological roles of gangliosides; neural cell differentiation; mechanism of action of the neurotoxins produced by clostridium botulinum and clostridium tetani. *Mailing Add:* Pa State Univ Col Med Hershey PA 17033. *E-Mail:* cschengr@bcmic.hmc.psu.edu

SCHENK, ERIC A, cardiovascular research; deceased, see previous edition for last biography

SCHENK, H(AROLD) L(OUIS), JR, ELECTROMAGNETIC ANALYSIS, APPLIED MAGNETICS. *Current Pos:* RETIRED. *Personal Data:* b Columbus, Ohio, Jan 27, 29; div; c 2. *Educ:* Ohio State Univ, BSc, 51, MSc, 52. *Prof Exp:* Res physicist, Gen Motors Corp, 52-55; sr engr, Westinghouse Sci & Technol Ctr, 57-94. *Mem:* Am Phys Soc; Inst Elec & Electronics Engrs. *Res:* Magnetic phenomena and technology. *Mailing Add:* 412 Edgetree Dr Murrysville PA 15668

SCHENK, JOHN ALBRIGHT, FOREST ENTOMOLOGY. *Current Pos:* RETIRED. *Personal Data:* b Stevens Point, Wis, Oct 22, 24; m 55, 74, Judene Rae Zabel; c Jonathan D, Cynthia D, Lori L, Gary D & Lisa R(Huber). *Educ:* Univ Mich, BS, 50; Univ Wis, MS, 56, PhD(entom), 61. *Prof Exp:* Relief model aid cartog, Relief Model Div, Army Map Serv, 51-53; forester, US Forest Serv, 53-54; res fel forest entom, Univ Wis, 54-59, Area Forest Entom, Wis Conserv Dept, 59-61; from asst prof to assoc prof, Univ Idaho, 61-66, prof forest entom, 71-83, asst dept head, 83-88. *Mem:* Entom Soc Am; Entom Soc Can; Entom Soc Brit. *Res:* Forest entomological research with emphasis on biology and ecology of forest pests and their control by silvicultural and biological methods; cone and seed insects; bark beetles. *Mailing Add:* 33801 S Baoger Lake Rd Cheney WA 99004

SCHENK, PAUL EDWARD, PETROLOGY, STRATIGRAPHY. *Current Pos:* From asst prof to assoc prof, Dalhousie Univ, 63-75, chmn dept, 81-83, prof geol, 75-85, CARNEGIE PROF GEOL, DALHOUSIE UNIV, 85- *Personal Data:* b Stratford, Ont, Feb 26, 37; m 60; c Margaret E & Catherine R. *Educ:* Univ Western Ont, BSc, 59; Univ Wis, MS, 61, PhD(geol), 63. *Concurrent Pos:* Can leader, IGCP Proj Caledonian Orogeny, 74-85; comnr, NAm Comn Stratig Nomenclature, 75-78. *Res:* Petrology and stratigraphy of evaporites; paleoecology and petrology of carbonate sediments; stratigraphy and sedimentology; paleocurrent study of deep-sea fans; sedimentology in Paleozoic Atlantic of southeastern Atlantic Canada and Northwestern Africa. *Mailing Add:* Earth Sci Dalhousie Univ Halifax NS B3H 4H6 Can. *Fax:* 902-494-6889; *E-Mail:* pschenk@ac.dal.ca

SCHENK, ROY URBAN, BIOCHEMISTRY, HEALTH SCIENCES. *Current Pos:* PRES, BIOENERGETICS, INC, 73-; EXEC DIR, DOMESTICS ABUSE PROF, 93- *Personal Data:* b Evansville, Ind, Nov 18, 29; div; c 10. *Educ:* Purdue Univ, BS, 51; Cornell Univ, MS, 53, PhD, 54. *Prof Exp:* Instr chem, Evansville Col, 54-55; chemist, Northern Regional Res Lab, Ill, 55-57; asst chemist, Univ Ga Exp Sta, 57-60; asst prof chem, Univ Ky, 60-62; mem staff org chem, Mat Lab, Wright-Patterson AFB, Ohio, 62-64; sr res chemist, Drackett Co, Ohio, 64-65; assoc prof pharmaceut chem, Univ Cincinnati, 65-67; res assoc, Univ Wis-Madison, 67-70; biochemist, Bjorksten Res Labs, 70-90. *Mem:* Am Chem Soc; Inst Food Technologists; Sigma Xi; Am Acad Forensic Sci. *Res:* Male perspective on gender issues; nutritional aspects of health and disease; biochemistry; road de-icing alternatives; chemistry related issues for automotive intoxication defense. *Mailing Add:* 1129 Drake St Madison WI 53715-1627. *Fax:* 608-251-0658

SCHENK, WORTHINGTON G, JR, SURGERY. *Current Pos:* Assoc, State Univ NY, 54-56, from asst prof to assoc prof, 56-66, prof surg, 66-84, actg chmn dept, 69-72, chmn dept, 72-84, EMER PROF SURG, SCH MED, STATE UNIV NY, 84- *Personal Data:* b Buffalo, NY, Feb 10, 22; m 46; c 7. *Educ:* Williams Col, BA, 42; Harvard Med Sch, MD, 45; Am Bd Surg, dipl, 54. *Concurrent Pos:* Attend surgeon, E J Meyer Hosp, 54-66, from assoc dir to dir surg res labs & dir surg, 54-; Buswell fel surg res, State Univ NY, Buffalo, 56-60; mem, Surg Study Sect, NIH, 69-73. *Mem:* Soc Vascular Surg (treas, pres); Soc Surg Alimentary Tract; Soc Univ Surg; Soc Clin Surg (secy); Am Surg Asn. *Res:* Biophysics of surgical problems in hemodynamics. *Mailing Add:* 38 Front St Silver Creek NY 14136-9622

SCHENKEL, ROBERT H, PARASITOLOGY, IMMUNOBIOLOGY. *Current Pos:* DIR ANIMAL HEALTH RES & DEVELOP, FT DODGE ANIMAL HEALTH AGRIC RES CTR, 96- *Personal Data:* b New York, NY, June 12, 44; m 71; c 2. *Educ:* Lafayette Col, BS, 65; Adelphi Univ, MS, 67; Univ Ill, PhD(zool), 71. *Prof Exp:* Res assoc immunoparasitol, Univ Ill, Urbana, 71-72; res scientist, Univ NMex, 72-75; sr res parpaitologist, Am Cyanamid Co, 75-77, group leader parasitol res, 77-80, group leader chemother & immunol, 80-82, mgr, animal indust discovery, 82-84, dir global animal prod develop, 85-, dir, animal indust discovery & tech acquisitions. *Mem:* Am Soc Parasitologists; AAAS. *Res:* Development of new drugs for use in treating parasitic infections; development of new host-parasite systems for testing drugs; monoclonal antibodies for antigen identification. *Mailing Add:* Ft Dodge Animal Health/Agr Res Ctr PO Box 400 Princeton NJ 08540-0400

SCHENKEN, JERALD R, PATHOLOGY. *Current Pos:* PATHOLOGIST, DEPT PATH, NEBR METHODIST HOSP & CHILDREN'S MEM HOSP, 65- *Personal Data:* b Detroit, Mich, Oct 11, 33; m 59; c 3. *Educ:* Tulane Univ, MD, 58. *Concurrent Pos:* Clin prof path, Univ Nebr Med Ctr, 75- & Creighton Univ, 78- *Mem:* AMA; Col Am Pathologist; Am Soc Clin Path; Am Col Physicians; Am Med Asn. *Mailing Add:* Pathol Ctr PO Box 14424 Omaha NE 68124-0424

SCHENKENBERG, THOMAS, NEUROPSYCHOLOGY. *Current Pos:* CHIEF PSYCHOL SERV, VET ADMIN HOSP, 70- *Personal Data:* b St Louis, Mo, Nov 3, 43; m 81. *Educ:* Rockhurst Col, AB, 65; Univ Utah, MA, 69, PhD(clin psychol), 70; Am Bd Prof Psychol, dipl & cert clin psychol, 82, dipl & cert clin neuropsychol, 85. *Prof Exp:* Asst prof, Univ Utah, 73-80, assoc prof, Dept Neurol, 80-, res assoc prof, Dept Psychol, 82- *Concurrent Pos:* Nat Inst Aging grant, 77; adj assoc prof, dept psychol, Brigham Young Univ, 73; adj asst prof, Dept Psychiat, Univ Utah, 77- *Mem:* Am Psychol Asn; Nat Register Health Serv Providers Psychol. *Res:* Clinical neuropsychology; electrophysiology; medical psychology. *Mailing Add:* Dept Neurol Univ Utah Sch Med 50 N Medical Dr Salt Lake City UT 84132-1001

SCHENKER, HENRY HANS, TEXTILE CHEMISTRY. *Current Pos:* RETIRED. *Personal Data:* b Vienna, Austria, June 19, 26; nat US; m 55; c 3. *Educ:* City Col, BS, 49; Rutgers Univ, PhD(chem), 53. *Prof Exp:* Asst, Rutgers Univ, 51-52; res chemist, E I du Pont de Nemours & Co, Inc, 52-56, supvr, Anal Lab, 56-61, sr res chemist, 61-91, res assoc, 91-92. *Mem:* Am Chem Soc; NY Acad Sci; Soc Automotive Engrs; Tech Asn Pulp & Paper Indust. *Res:* Ion-exchange; textile chemistry; polymer chemistry; friction products. *Mailing Add:* 1419 Bucknell Rd Wilmington DE 19803

SCHENKER, MARC B, PREVENTIVE MEDICINE, EPIDEMIOLOGY. *Current Pos:* from asst prof to assoc prof, 83-92, PROF & CHAIR OCCUP, ENVIRON MED & EPIDEMIOL, UNIV CALIF, DAVIS, 92- *Personal Data:* b Los Angeles, Calif, Aug 25, 47; m, Heath Massey; c Yael, Phoebe & Hilary. *Educ:* Univ Calif, Berkeley, BA, 69; Univ Calif, San Francisco, MD, 73; Harvard Sch Pub Health, MPH, 80. *Prof Exp:* Fel, Am Col Physicians, 86. *Concurrent Pos:* Prin investr, NIH, 79; dir, Emp Health Serv, Univ Calif Med Ctr, Davis, 83-88, Occup & Environ Med Clin, 83-88, Occup Med Residency Prog, 84-93; vis prof, Univ Occup & Environ Health, Japan, 88; Fulbright vis scholar, NIH & Med Res, France, 93; Fulbright vis scientist, Int Union Against Tuberc & Lung Dis, Paris, France, 93; Fulbright sr scientist award, France, 93; med officer, Sacramento Vet Admin Outpatient Clin, 89-; dir, Univ Calif Agr Health & Safety Ctr. *Mem:* Int Union Against Tuberc & Lung Dis; Soc Occup Environ Health; Int Epidemiol Asn; Am Thoracic Soc; AAAS. *Res:* Occupational respiratory and reproductive health hazards; respiratory diseases include asthma, COPD and lung cancer; hazards in agriculture and the semi-conductor industry; occupational cancer. *Mailing Add:* TB168 Dep Epidemiol & Prev Med Univ Calif Davis CA 95616-8638. *Fax:* 530-752-3239; *E-Mail:* mbschenker@ucdavis.edu

SCHENKER, STEVEN, INTERNAL MEDICINE, GASTROENTEROLOGY. *Current Pos:* PROF MED & PHARMACOL & CHIEF DEP, MED DIV GASTROENTEROL & NUTRIT, UNIV TEX HEALTH SCI CTR. *Personal Data:* b Krakow, Poland, Oct 5, 29; US citizen; c 5. *Educ:* Cornell Univ, BA, 51, MD, 55. *Honors & Awards:* Alcoholism Res Award, 87. *Prof Exp:* From intern to sr resident, Harvard Med Serv, Boston City Hosp, 55-57; clin assoc gastroenterol, Nat Inst Allergy & Infectious Dis, 59-61; asst prof, Col Med, Univ Cincinnati, 61-63; from asst prof to assoc prof internal med, Univ Tex Southwestern Med Sch, 64-69; prof med biochem & head div gastroenterol, Sch Med, Vanderbilt Univ, 69- *Concurrent Pos:* Fel gastroenterol, Col Med, Univ Cincinnati, 58-59; res fel med, Thorndike Mem Lab, Harvard Med Sch, 61-63; Markle scholar acad med, 63-68; USPHS res career develop award, 68; mem alcoholism & alcohol probs rev comt, NIMH, 67-71, chmn, 80-81, VA merit review comt, drugs & alcohol, 85-88, chmn, 87-88; ed, Hepatol, 85- *Mem:* Am Asn Study Liver Dis (pres, 80); Am Fedn Clin Res; Am Soc Clin Invest; Am Gastroenterol Asn; Asn Am Physicians; Clin Climat Asn. *Res:* Liver disease, especially bilirubin metabolism in maturation; metabolic encephalopathies, especially hepatic coma, drug metabolism in liver disease and thiamine deficiency; placental drugs and nutrient transport. *Mailing Add:* Dept Med/GI & Nutrit Univ Tex Health Sci Ctr 7703 Floyd Curl Dr San Antonio TX 78284-7878

SCHENKMAN, JOHN BORIS, BIOCHEMISTRY, PHARMACOLOGY. *Current Pos:* prof & head, 78-87, PROF PHARMACOL, SCH MED, UNIV CONN, FARMINGTON, 87- *Personal Data:* b New York, NY, Feb 10, 36; m 60. *Educ:* Brooklyn Col, BS, 60; State Univ NY, PhD(biochem), 64. *Prof Exp:* Phys biochemist, Johnson Res Found, Sch Med, Univ Pa, 64-66; NSF vis scientist, Osaka Univ, 67-68; from asst prof to assoc prof pharmacol, Sch Med, Yale Univ, 68-78. *Concurrent Pos:* NIH fel, Sch Med, Univ Pa, 66-67; res assoc, Inst Toxicol, Univ Tubingen, Ger, 68, pharmacol study sect, 74-78; mem Flex Comn, Nat Bd Med Examiners, 82-86, pharmacol rev comt, Nat Inst Gen Med Sci, NIH, 82-86; ed, Int Encycl Pharmacol Therapeut, 74-82; assoc ed, Biochem Pharmacol, 75-84. *Mem:* Am Soc Biol Chem; Am Soc Pharmacol & Exp Therapeut; Brit Biochem Soc; Int Soc Study Xenobiotics. *Res:* Biological oxidations; microsomal mixed function oxidations; hemoprotein oxidases; lipid peroxidation. *Mailing Add:* Dept Pharmacol Univ Conn Health Ctr MC 1505 Farmington CT 06030-1505. *Fax:* 860-679-2473

SCHENNUM, WAYNE EDWARD, ECOLOGY, POPULATION BIOLOGY. *Current Pos:* NATURAL RESOURCE MGR, MGENRY COUNTY CONSERV DIST, 85- *Personal Data:* b Elgin, Ill, Aug 23, 49; m 90, Susan Board. *Educ:* Univ Ill, Chicago Circle, BS, 71, PhD(biol), 79. *Prof Exp:* Teaching asst, Univ Ill, Chicago Circle, 74-75, asst prof biol, 76; asst prof, Judson Col, 76-77 & Wheaton Col, 77-78; environ consult, The Nature Conservancy & Ill Natural Land Inst, 78-81, land steward, 81-83; community ecologist, Iowa Conserv Comn, 83-84. *Concurrent Pos:* Vis asst prof, Judson Col, 76 & 78-79, Concordia Teacher's Col, 76, 92, 94, & 96, Wheaton Col, 79, Barat Col, 80-81, Gov's State Univ, 82-83 & Northeastern Ill Univ, 87 & 95. *Mem:* Ecol Soc Am; Natural Areas Asn; Soc Ecol Restoration & Mgt, conserv biol. *Res:* Monitoring of long-term ecological changes in managed and restored natural communities of the Midwest; study of ecological relationships of insects in Midwestern ecosystems; natural areas management, management planning, and inventory; fish and wildlife science; environmental sciences. *Mailing Add:* 136 Wagner Dr Cary IL 60013

SCHENTER, ROBERT EARL, NUCLEAR PHYSICS. *Current Pos:* res assoc, 70-76, mgr nuclear anal, 76-80, FEL SCIENTIST, WESTINGHOUSE HANFORD CO, 80- *Personal Data:* b St Louis, Mo, Jan 4, 37; c 4. *Educ:* Calif Inst Technol, BS, 58; Univ Colo, Boulder, PhD(physics), 63. *Prof Exp:* Res assoc nuclear physics, Case Inst Technol, 63-65; sr res scientist, Nuclear Physics & Fast Reactor Cross Sections, Battelle Mem Inst Pac Northwest Labs, 65-70. *Concurrent Pos:* Lectr, Joint Ctr Grad Study, 66-67. *Mem:* Am Phys Soc. *Res:* Theoretical calculations of the nucleon-nucleus optical model potential in terms of the nucleon-nucleus interaction; calculation of neutron reaction cross sections for reactor analyses. *Mailing Add:* 2240 Davison Ave Richland WA 99352

SCHENZ, ANNE FILER, FLAVOR TECHNOLOGY, SENSORY EVALUATION. *Current Pos:* SR GROUP LEADER, MED NUTRIT BUS UNIT, ROSS PROD DIV, ABBOTT LABS, 87- *Personal Data:* b Sharon, Pa, Sept 16, 45; m 68, Timothy. *Educ:* Westminster Col, Pa, BS, 67; Kent State Univ, PhD(phys chem), 74. *Prof Exp:* Teacher chem, Springfield Sch Dist, Akron, Ohio, 67-68; vis prof anal chem, King's Col, NY, 75-76; prin develop chemist laundry detergents, Lever Bros Co, NJ, 76-78; proj specialist, Gen Foods Corp, 78-81, group leader texture group, flavors & natural prods, tech appln, Culinova Meals Div, 81-87. *Concurrent Pos:* Vis prof phys chem, King's Col, NY, 79; adj asst prof, Food Sci, Ohio State Univ, 89- *Mem:* Am Chem Soc; Asn Chemoreception Sci; Inst Food Technologists. *Res:* Liquid crystals; surfactant and bleach chemistry; texture of liquid foods; surface rheology; artificial sweeteners and salt substitutes; physical preservation of foods; refrigerated meals (Culinova); flavor technology; sensory evaluation. *Mailing Add:* 485 Retreat Lane W Powell OH 43065-9768. *Fax:* 614-624-7262

SCHENZ, TIMOTHY WILLIAM, PHYSICAL CHEMISTRY. *Current Pos:* sr res scientist, 87-90, assoc res fel, Ross Prods Div, 90-95, RES FEL, ABBOTT LABS, 95- *Personal Data:* b Washington, DC, Jan 2, 46; m 68, Anne Filer. *Educ:* Westminster Col, Pa, BS, 68; Kent State Univ, PhD(phys chem), 73. *Prof Exp:* Sr chemist, Gen Food Corp, 74-76, proj specialist, 76-79, res specialist phys chem, 79-87. *Concurrent Pos:* Adj asst prof, Food Sci Dept, Ohio State Univ, 89- *Mem:* Am Chem Soc; Sigma Xi; Inst Food Technologists; Soc Rheology. *Res:* Physical adsorption from solution; interactions with proteins in disperse systems; instrumentation and automation; foams and emulsions; thermal analysis; image analysis. *Mailing Add:* 485 Retreat Lane W Powell OH 43065-9768. *Fax:* 614-624-7262; *E-Mail:* timothy.schenz@rossnutrition.com

SCHEPARTZ, ABNER IRWIN, BIOCHEMISTRY. *Current Pos:* res chemist, 62-65, RES LEADER LEAF RES, TOBACCO LAB, USDA, 65- *Personal Data:* b New York, NY, July 29, 22; m 49; c 2. *Educ:* Purdue Univ, BS, 43; Univ Pittsburgh, PhD(chem), 50. *Prof Exp:* Asst chem, Univ Pittsburgh, 43-44; res assoc, Manhattan proj, Univ Rochester, 44-46; Nat Heart Inst fel, Univ Wis, 50-51; res biochemist, Vet Hosp, Pittsburgh, Pa, 51-56; sr res fel, USDA, Pa, 56-60; res assoc in charge biochem & biophys, Merck Inst Therapeut Res, 60-62. *Concurrent Pos:* Asst chem, Univ Pittsburgh, 46-49, instr, 54-55; consult, Children's Hosp, Pittsburgh, 56. *Mem:* Am Chem Soc; Am Soc Biol Chem; AAAS. *Res:* Uranium toxicology; fat chemistry; isolation of natural products; allergens; electrophoresis of proteins; chemistry of tobacco smoke; biochemistry and biophysics of viruses; electron microscopy; enzymology; tobacco biochemistry. *Mailing Add:* 110 Sandstone Ct Athens GA 30605-3430

SCHEPARTZ, ALANNA, BIOLOGICAL CHEMISTRY. *Current Pos:* NIH fel, 87-88, asst prof, 88-92, ASSOC PROF, DEPT CHEM, YALE UNIV, 92- *Personal Data:* b New York, NY, Jan 9, 62. *Educ:* State Univ NY, Albany, BS, 82; Columbia Univ, PhD(chem), 87. *Honors & Awards:* Presidential Young Investr Award, NSF, 91. *Concurrent Pos:* Fel sci & eng, David & Lucille Packard Found, 91. *Mem:* Am Chem Soc. *Res:* Bioorganic chemistry. *Mailing Add:* Dept Chem Yale Univ PO Box 208107 New Haven CT 06520-8107

SCHEPARTZ, BERNARD, HISTORY OF BIOCHEMISTRY. *Current Pos:* from instr to assoc prof biochem, 48-65, prof, 65-80, EMER PROF BIOCHEM, JEFFERSON MED COL, 80- *Personal Data:* b New York, NY, Nov 9, 18; m 44. *Educ:* Ohio Wesleyan, BA, 41; Univ Mich, MS, 42; Univ Pa, PhD(biochem), 49. *Prof Exp:* Asst, Comt Med Res War Proj, Dept Surg Res, Univ Pa, 42-44, chemist, Nat Defense Res Comt War Proj, Towne Sci Sch, 44-46. *Mem:* AAAS; Am Soc Biol Chem; Am Chem Soc; Sigma Xi. *Res:* Intermediary metabolism of amino acids; dimensional analysis; historical and biographical writing on chemistry and biochemistry. *Mailing Add:* 1901 JF Kennedy Blvd No 704 Philadelphia PA 19103

SCHEPARTZ, SAUL ALEXANDER, DRUG DISCOVERY & DEVELOPMENT. *Current Pos:* biochemist, Sect on Screening, Cancer Chemother, Nat Serv Ctr, Nat Cancer Inst, 58-61, head biochem sect, Drug Eval Br, 61-64, asst chief drug eval br, 64, asst chief cancer chemother, Nat Serv Ctr, 64-66, chief, 66-72, assoc sci dir, Drug Res & Develop Chemother, 72-73, assoc dir drug res & develop, 73-76, actg dep dir, 76-78, actg dir, 80-81, dep dir, Div Cancer Treat, 78-84, cancer expert 89-91, DEP ASSOC DIR, DEVELOP THERAPEUT PROG, DIV CANCER TREAT, NAT CANCER INST, 91- *Personal Data:* b Nutley, NJ, Mar 18, 29; m 56; c 3. *Educ:* Ind Univ, AB, 51; Univ Wis, MS, 53, PhD(biochem), 55. *Prof Exp:* Res assoc, Wistar Inst, Univ Pa, 55-57; biochemist, Microbiol Assocs, Inc, 57-58. *Concurrent Pos:* Assoc vpres acad-indust relations, Univ Med & Dent NJ, 84-89. *Mem:* Am Chem Soc; Am Soc Microbiol; Am Asn Cancer Res. *Res:* Cancer chemotherapy; cancer and aids drug discovery and development; mode of action of antibiotics. *Mailing Add:* 20304 Butterwick Way Gaithersburg MD 20879

SCHEPLER, KENNETH LEE, LASER PHYSICS, BIOPHYSICS. *Current Pos:* Res biophysicist, Laser Effects Br, Sch Aerospace Med, 75-79, nuclear physicist, McClellan AFB, 79-81, LASER PHYSICIST, WRIGHT LAB, WRIGHT-PATTERSON AFB, USAF, 81- *Personal Data:* b Clinton, Iowa, Apr 1, 49; m 72, Shirley R Hartline; c Daniel, Andrew & Emily. *Educ:* Mich State Univ, BS, 71; Univ Mich, MS, 73, PhD(physics), 75. *Honors & Awards:* Avionics Directorate Burka Award, 96. *Concurrent Pos:* Chmn, Tech Coop Prog, Joint Tech Panel Ten (Lasers). *Mem:* Optical Soc Am; Am Phys Soc. *Res:* Optical spectroscopy of laser crystals; tunable lasing of solid state materials; excited state absorption of transition metal doped crystals; computer modeling of laser performance and laser damage; non linear frequency conversion; mechanisms of biological interactions with laser radiation, cataractogenesis. *Mailing Add:* WL/AAJL Wright-Patterson AFB OH 45433-7405. *Fax:* 937-255-7312; *E-Mail:* scheplkl@aa.wpafb.af.mil

SCHEPPERS, GERALD J, ANALYTICAL CHEMISTRY. *Current Pos:* Asst prof, 66-67, assoc prof, 67-77, PROF CHEM, UNIV WIS-PLATTEVILLE, 78-, CHMN DEPT, 80- *Personal Data:* b North Bend, Nebr, Apr 11, 33; m 60; c 5. *Educ:* Nebr State Teachers Col, Wayne, BA, 62; Iowa State Univ, MS, 65, PhD(anal chem), 67. *Mem:* Am Chem Soc. *Res:* Fluorescent indicators; complex formation in non-aqueous solvents. *Mailing Add:* 920 W Madison St Platteville WI 53818-1521

SCHER, ALLEN MYRON, PHYSIOLOGY. *Current Pos:* From instr to assoc prof, 50-62, PROF PHYSIOL, UNIV WASH, 62- *Personal Data:* b Boston, Mass, Apr 17, 21; m 52; c 2. *Educ:* Yale Univ, BA, 42, PhD, 50. *Concurrent Pos:* Mem comput study sect, NIH, 63-67 & cardiovasc A study sect, 67-71. *Mem:* AAAS; Am Physiol Soc; Am Heart Asn. *Res:* Cardiovascular control systems; cardiac electrophysiology. *Mailing Add:* Dept Physiol & Biophys SJ-40 Univ Wash Box 357290 Seattle WA 98195-0001. *Fax:* 206-545-0619

SCHER, CHARLES D, GROWTH CONTROL, REGULATION. *Current Pos:* MEM STAFF, TULANE UNIV SCH MED, NEW ORLEANS, 94- *Personal Data:* b Newark, NJ, July 25, 39; m 64; c 2. *Educ:* Brandeis Univ, BA, 61; Univ Pa, MD, 65. *Prof Exp:* Intern, Bronx Munic Hosp, 65-66, asst resident, 66-67; res assoc, Nat Cancer Inst, 67-71; asst resident, Children's Hosp Med Ctr, 71-72, fel hemat, 72-74; from asst prof to assoc prof, Med Sch, Harvard Univ, 74-82; prof, Children's Hosp Philadelphia, Med Sch, Univ Pa, 82-94. *Concurrent Pos:* Spec fel, NIH, 72-74; scholar, Leukemia Soc Am, 77-82; mem staff, Sidney Farber Cancer Inst, 77-82. *Mem:* Soc Pediat Res; AAAS; Am Soc Cell Biol; Am Soc Microbiol; Am Soc Clin Invest. *Res:* Control of cell replication by growth factors. *Mailing Add:* Tulane Univ Sch Med 1430 Tulane Ave SL37 New Orleans LA 70112

SCHER, HERBERT BENSON, PHYSICAL CHEMISTRY, COLLOID CHEMISTRY. *Current Pos:* SR SCIENTIST, CONTROLLED RELEASE PESTICIDES & PESTICIDE DISPERSIONS, STAUFFER CHEM CO, 68- *Personal Data:* b New York, NY, Dec 11, 37; m 59; c 4. *Educ:* Cornell Univ, BChEng, 60; Univ Minn, MS, 62, PhD(phys chem), 64. *Prof Exp:* Res chemist rheology, Chem Res & Develop Lab, US Army, Edgewood Arsenal, 64-66; sr res chemist, Res Lab, Eastman Kodak Co, 66-68. *Concurrent Pos:* Instr, Univ Calif, Berkeley, 71-77; adj assoc prof, dept chem, Univ San Francisco, 78-80, vis lectr, dept pharm, 81- *Mem:* Am Chem Soc; Controlled Release Soc. *Res:* Controlled release pesticides; microencapsulation; interfacial polymerization; coating technology; diffusion of organic molecules through polymers; pesticide formulations; emulsions and dispersions; rheology; organic molecule-clay interactions; kinetics of pesticide degradation; stabilization of pesticides. *Mailing Add:* 1028 Wickham Dr Moraga CA 94556-2039

SCHER, MARYONDA E, PSYCHIATRY. *Current Pos:* From clin asst to clin instr, 55-65, clin asst prof to clin assoc prof, 65-76, ASSOC PROF PSYCHIAT, UNIV WASH SCH MED, 76- *Personal Data:* b Oakland, Calif, Feb 26, 31; m 52, Allen; c Celia & John. *Educ:* Univ Wash, BS, 50, MD, 54. *Concurrent Pos:* Staff psychiatrist, Vet Admin Hosp, Seattle, 59-80; active mem med staff, Harborview Hosp, Seattle, 65- *Mem:* Fel Am Psychiat Asn. *Res:* Medical education; women. *Mailing Add:* Harborview Med Ctr Dept Psychiat 325 9th Ave Seattle WA 98104-2499

SCHER, ROBERT SANDER, OPTICAL ENCODER DESIGN. *Current Pos:* PRES, ENCODER DESIGN ASSOC, 93- *Personal Data:* b Cincinnati, Ohio, May 24, 34; m 61, Audrey Gordon; c Sarahh, Alexander & Aaron. *Educ:* Mass Inst Technol, SB, 56, SM, 58, Mech Eng, 60, ScD(mech eng), 63. *Prof Exp:* Engr aerospace, Astro Electronics Div, RCA Corp, 63-65; dept mgr optical encoders, Sequential Info Syst, 65-70; tech dir, Teledyne Gurley, 70-77, vpres eng, 77-86, pres, 86-92. *Mem:* Am Soc Mech Engrs; Optical Soc Am. *Res:* Design and development of precision measuring instruments, particularly optical encoders. *Mailing Add:* 2 Laurel Oak Lane Clifton Park NY 12065-4712. *E-Mail:* 74123.1066@compuserve.com

SCHER, WILLIAM, HEMATOLOGY, CELL DIFFERENTIATION. *Current Pos:* Asst prof cell biol, 68-78, ASSOC PROF MED & MEDICAL ONCOLOGY, MT SINAI SCH MED, NEW YORK, 86-95; ASSOC PROF, MT SINAI GRAD SCH BIOL SCI, DEPT CELLULAR & MOLECULAR PATHOL, CITY UNIV NEW YORK, 86- *Personal Data:* b Cleveland, Ohio; m, Barbara Messina. *Educ:* Yale Univ, BS, 55, MS, 57; Univ Va, MD, 61. *Concurrent Pos:* Reviewer, study sect differential agents in human malignancies, NIH, 86. *Mem:* Am Asn Cancer Res; Am Soc Cell Biol; Am Soc Microbiol; Soc Exp Biol & Med; Tissue Cult Asn; Sigma Xi. *Res:* Molecular basis of cell differentiation and its relationship to malignancy; model system for study of synthesis of a differentiation marker, hemoglobin, in an in vitro system: dimethyl sulfoxide-induced mouse erythroleukemia cells. *Mailing Add:* Dept Path Mt Sinai Med Ctr 1 Gustave L Levy Pl Box 1194 New York NY 10029

SCHERAGA, HAROLD ABRAHAM, BIOPHYSICAL CHEMISTRY. *Current Pos:* from instr to prof, 45-58, chmn dept, 60-67, Todd prof, 65-92, EMER TODD PROF CHEM, CORNELL UNIV, 92- *Personal Data:* b Brooklyn, NY, Oct 18, 21; m 43, Miriam Kurnow; c Judith A (Stavis), Deborah R & Daniel M. *Educ:* City Col New York, BS, 41; Duke Univ, AM, 42, PhD(chem), 46. *Hon Degrees:* ScD, Duke Univ, 61, Univ Rochester, 88. *Honors & Awards:* Lilly Award, Am Chem Soc, 57, Nichols Medal, 74, Kendall Award, 78, Pauling Medal, 85, Mobil Award, 90, IBM Award Comput & Chem Pharmaceut Res, 97; Welch Found lectr, Univ Tex, 62; Harvey lectr, 68; Gallagher lectr, 68-69; Lemieux lectr, 73; Hill lectr, 76; Linderstrom-Lang Medal, Carlsberg Lab, 83; Kowalski Medal, Int Soc Thrombosis & Hemostasis, 83; Repligen Award, Chem Biol Processes, 90; Stein & Moore Award, Protein Soc, 95. *Prof Exp:* Am Chem Soc fel, Harvard Med Sch, 46-47. *Concurrent Pos:* Guggenheim fel & Fulbright scholar, Carlsberg Lab, Denmark, 56-57; vis lectr, Div Protein Chem, Wool Res Lab, Commonwealth Sci & Indust Res Orgn, Australia, 59; mem adv panel molecular biol, NSF, 60-62; co-ed, Molecular Biol, 61-86; co-chmn, Gordon Res Conf Proteins, 63; mem, Biochem Training Comt, NIH, 63-65 & Career Develop Comt, 67-71; Guggenheim fel & Fulbright scholar, Weizmann Inst Sci, 63, NIH spec fel, 70, mem bd gov, 70-; mem adv bd, Biopolymers, 63- & Biochem, 69-74, 85-; mem-at-large coun, Gordon Res Conf, 69-71; mem, Tech Adv Panel, Xerox Corp, 69-71 & 74-79; vis prof, Japan Soc Prom Sci, 77; distinguished invited lectr, Univ Calgary, 79; Fogarty scholar, NIH, 84, 86, 88, 89-91. *Mem:* Nat Acad Sci; AAAS; Am Acad Arts & Sci; Am Soc Biol Chem; hon mem NY Acad Sci; Am Chem Soc. *Res:* Physical chemistry of proteins and other macromolecules; structure of water and dilute aqueous solutions; blood clotting. *Mailing Add:* 212 Homestead Terr Ithaca NY 14850-6220. *Fax:* 607-254-4700; *E-Mail:* has5@cornell.edu

SCHERB, FRANK, SPACE PHYSICS. *Current Pos:* assoc prof, 65-69, PROF PHYSICS, UNIV WIS-MADISON, 69- *Personal Data:* b Union City, NJ, Sept 17, 30; m 64; c 4. *Educ:* Mass Inst Technol, SB, 53, PhD(physics), 58. *Prof Exp:* Res staff assoc space physics, Mass Inst Technol, 58-61, from asst prof to assoc prof physics, 61-65. *Mem:* Fel Am Phys Soc; Am Geophys Union; Am Astron Soc. *Res:* Cosmic rays; physics of interplanetary medium, especially the solar wind. *Mailing Add:* Dept Physics Univ Wis 1150 Univ Ave Madison WI 53706

SCHERBA, GERALD MARRON, ZOOLOGY. *Current Pos:* RETIRED. *Personal Data:* b Chicago, Ill, Feb 9, 27; m 51; c 3. *Educ:* Univ Chicago, BS, 50, MS, 52, PhD(zool), 55. *Prof Exp:* From instr to assoc prof biol, Chico State Col, 55-62; prof & chmn, Natural Sci Div, Calif State Univ, San Bernardino, 62-66, dean acad affairs, 66-68, vpres, 68-84, dir, Desert Studies Ctr, 85-92. *Concurrent Pos:* Res grants, NY Zool Soc, 55-56 & 59, Am Acad Arts & Sci, 57 & NSF, 62-64. *Res:* Animal ecology; animal behavior; biology of ants. *Mailing Add:* 3320-C Via Carrizo Laguna Hills CA 92653

SCHERBENSKE, M JAMES, PHYSIOLOGY, BIOCHEMISTRY. *Current Pos:* health scientist adminr, Nat Heart Inst, 68-69, HEALTH SCIENTIST ADMINR KIDNEY & UROL, NAT INST DIABETES & DIGESTIVE & KIDNEY DIS, NIH, 69-, PROG DIR, RENAL PHYSIOL & CELL BIOL. *Personal Data:* b Jamestown, NDak, Jan 13, 37; m 59; c 4. *Educ:* Jamestown Col, BS, 59; Univ SDak, MA, 64, PhD(physiol), 66. *Prof Exp:* Fel renal physiol, Med Ctr, Kans Univ, 66-68. *Concurrent Pos:* Consult, Coordr Coun Urol, Am Urol Asn, 71-79. *Mem:* Am Soc Nephrology; Soc Univ Urologists. *Res:* Renal physiology and transport. *Mailing Add:* NIH/NIDDK/DKUHB Natcher Bldg Rm 6A519 45 Center Dr MSC6600 Bethesda MD 20892-6600

SCHERBERG, NEAL HARVEY, MOLECULAR BIOLOGY, BIOCHEMISTRY. *Current Pos:* From asst prof to assoc prof med, Univ Chicago, 71-80, res assoc, 76-80, tech dir, Thyroid Function Lab, 80-92, TECH DIR, ADULT ENDOCRINOL, UNIV CHICAGO, 92- *Personal Data:* b Minneapolis, Minn, Nov 10, 39; c 2. *Educ:* Oberlin Col, AB, 61; Tufts Univ, PhD(biochem), 66. *Concurrent Pos:* Fel molecular biol, Univ Chicago, 66-71, Am Cancer Soc fel, 66-68; Sr Int Fogarty fel, 86. *Mem:* Am Soc Biochem; Int Isotope Soc. *Res:* Protein synthesis; detection of mutations in DNA. *Mailing Add:* Univ Chicago Thyroid Study Unit 584 S Maryland Ave Chicago IL 60637. *Fax:* 773-702-6940

SCHERER, GEORGE ALLEN, CHEMISTRY. *Current Pos:* RETIRED. *Personal Data:* b Kokomo, Ind, Apr 3, 07; m 29; c 3. *Educ:* Earlham Col, BS, 27; Cornell Univ, MS, 28; Purdue Univ, PhD(chem), 33. *Prof Exp:* Asst chem, Cornell Univ, 27-28 & Purdue Univ, 28-33; prof, Pac Col, 33-34 & McKendree Col, 34-36; from instr to prof, Earlham Col, 36-57; admin secy, Am Friends Bd Missions, 57-60; prof chem & head dept, Western Col, 60-72; adj prof chem, Ind Univ East, 72-77; chem technician, Earlham Col, 72-86. *Concurrent Pos:* Vis prof, Univ Col Women, Hyderabad, India, 65-66. *Mem:* Am Chem Soc. *Res:* Electrode potentials; free energy measurements. *Mailing Add:* 567 Earl Ham Dr Richmond IN 47374-1215

SCHERER, GEORGE WALTER, MATERIALS SCIENCE, CERAMICS. *Current Pos:* PROF, DEPT CIVIL ENG & OPERS RES, PRINCETON UNIV, 96- *Personal Data:* b Teaneck, NJ, Apr 27, 49; m 71. *Educ:* Mass Inst Technol, SB, 72, SM, 72, PhD(mat sci), 74. *Honors & Awards:* George W Morey Award, 85 & Ross Coffin Purdy Award, Am Ceramic Soc, Robert Sosman Award, 94; Woldemar Weyl Award, Int Cong on Glass, 86; W H Zachariasen Award, J Non-Crystal Solids, 87; Fulrath Pac Award, 90; Ralph K Iler Award, Am Chem Soc, 95. *Prof Exp:* Sr ceramist, Corning Glass Works, 74-85. *Mem:* Nat Acad Eng; Am Ceramic Soc; Mat Res Soc. *Res:* Kinetics of crystallization and glass formation; viscous sintering; thermal stress analysis; optical waveguide fabrication; sol-gel processing. *Mailing Add:* Eng Quad Room E-319 Princeton Univ Princeton NJ 00544. *Fax:* 609-258-1563; *E-Mail:* scherer@princeton.edu

SCHERER, HAROLD NICHOLAS, JR, TRANSMISSION LINE ENGINEERING, SUBSTATION ENGINEERING. *Current Pos:* PRES, US NAT COMT CIGRE CONF INT RES ELECS, 93- *Personal Data:* b Plainfield, NJ, Apr 5, 29; m 52, 74, Patricia Condon; c 7. *Educ:* Yale Univ, BE, 51; Rutgers Univ, MBA, 55. *Honors & Awards:* William Habirshaw Award & Medal, Inst Elec & Electronics Engrs, 86. *Prof Exp:* Var engr positions, Pub Serv Elec & Gas Co. 51-63; sect mgr, Am Elec Power Serv Corp, 65-68, asst chief, 68-69, chief, 69-73, vpres, 73-83, sr vpres, Elec Eng, 83-90; pres, Commonwealth Elec Co, 90-93. *Concurrent Pos:* Dir & vchmn, Am Nat Standards Inst, 80-87; mem US-USSR Working Group High Voltage Power Transmission, 75-81, US-Italy Working Group Ultra High Voltage Power Transmission, 79-88; engr review bd, Bonneville Power Admin, 84-94; pres, Inst Elec & Electronics Engrs Power Eng Soc, 90-91; pres, Elec Engrs, Int Power Eng Educ Found, 92-96; consult engr, 93-; mem, Int Admin Coun & exec comt, Conf Int Des Grands Reseaux Elec a Haute Tension; mem, Blue Ribbon Panel Pac Coast Blackout, Bonneville, Power Admin, 96- *Mem:* Nat Acad Eng; fel Inst Elec & Electronics Engrs; distinguished mem Int Conf Large High Voltage Elec Systs. *Res:* Ultra high voltage power transmission. *Mailing Add:* 467 Bay Lane Centerville MA 02632-3352

SCHERER, JAMES R, PHYSICAL CHEMISTRY, VIBRATIONAL SPECTROSCOPY. *Current Pos:* RES CHEMIST, UNIV CALIF, BERKELEY, 92- *Personal Data:* b Kansas City, Mo, Dec 31, 31; div; c 6. *Educ:* St Mary's Col, Calif, BS, 53; Univ Minn, PhD(phys chem), 58. *Prof Exp:* Res chemist, Chem Physics Res Lab, Dow Chem Co, Mich, 58-63, Western Regional Res Lab, Sci & Educ Admin-Agr Res, USDA, 63-87, Univ Calif, San Francisco, 87-90. *Mem:* Am Inst Chemists; Am Chem Soc; Am Phys Soc; Coblentz Soc (pres, 71-72); Am Optical Soc. *Res:* Molecular infrared and Raman spectroscopy; biophysics vibrational assignments; force constant calculations and application of normal coordinate calculations to group frequencies; laboratory data acquisition with digital computers; DNA sequencing; biophysical instrumentation. *Mailing Add:* 1309 Arch St Berkeley CA 94708

SCHERER, KIRBY VAUGHN, JR, ORGANIC CHEMISTRY. *Current Pos:* RETIRED. *Personal Data:* b Evansville, Ind, Feb 7, 36; m 61; c 3. *Educ:* Harvard Univ, AB, 58, AM, 59, PhD(chem), 63. *Prof Exp:* Asst prof chem, Univ Calif, Berkeley, 62-67; assoc prof chem, Univ Southern Calif, 67-93. *Concurrent Pos:* Sr scientist, Jet Propulsion Lab, 75- *Mem:* AAAS; Am Chem Soc; Royal Soc Chem. *Res:* Organofluorine chemistry; synthesis and properties of strained ring systems; chlorocarbon derivatives; organic chemistry of nitrogen. *Mailing Add:* 1912 Marsh Rd Wilmington DE 19810

SCHERER, NORBERT FRANZ, CHEMISTRY. *Current Pos:* PROF CHEM, UNIV CHICAGO, 97- *Personal Data:* b Milwaukee, Wis, July 9, 60; m, Seung-Eun Choi; c Matthew, Amanda & Amber. *Educ:* Univ Chicago, BS, 82; Calif Inst Technol, PhD, 89. *Prof Exp:* NSF fel, Univ Chicago, 89-91, res assoc, 91-92; asst prof chem, Univ Pa, 92-97. *Concurrent Pos:* David & Lucile Packard fel, 93-98; Nat Young Investr award, NSF, 93-98; Arnold & Mabel Beckman fel, 94-96. *Mem:* Am Chem Soc; Am Phys Soc; Optical Soc Am; AAAS. *Res:* Chemical reaction dynamics in condensed phases, ultrafast laser spectroscopy, dynamics at interfaces and time-resolved scanning probe microscopy. *Mailing Add:* Dept Chem Univ Chicago 5735 S Ellis Ave Chicago IL 60637. *Fax:* 773-702-0805; *E-Mail:* nscherer@rainbow.uchicago.edu

SCHERER, PETER WILLIAM, RESPIRATORY PHYSIOLOGY, BIOFLUID MECHANICS. *Current Pos:* From asst prof to assoc prof bioeng, 76-90, PROF BIOENG, UNIV PA, 90- *Personal Data:* b Palmerton, Pa, May 15, 42; m 72; c 1. *Educ:* Haverford Col, BS, 64; Yale Univ, PhD(eng & appl sci), 71, MD, 73. *Concurrent Pos:* Prof, Dept Anesthesia, Univ Pa, Med Sch, 89- *Mem:* Sr mem Biomed Eng Soc; Am Physiol Soc. *Res:* Respiratory fluid mechanics; mass; heat transfer; gas exchange; aerosol transport; heating and humidification of air in the lung; interaction of the respiratory system with the environment. *Mailing Add:* Dept Bioeng Univ Pa 120 Hayden 240 S 33rd St Philadelphia PA 19104-6316. *Fax:* 215-898-1130, 573-2071

SCHERER, ROBERT C, ANIMAL ECOLOGY. *Current Pos:* RETIRED. *Personal Data:* b Jersey Shore, Pa, Apr 26, 31; m 54; c 3. *Educ:* Haverford Col, BS, 53; Pa State Univ, MS, 63, PhD(zool), 65. *Prof Exp:* Assoc prof, Lock Haven State Col, 65-71, prof zool, 71- *Mem:* Am Fisheries Soc; Ecol Soc Am. *Res:* Population dynamics as applied to fish populations. *Mailing Add:* RR 4 Box 203-8 Jersey Shore PA 17740

SCHERER, RONALD CALLAWAY, SPEECH & VOICE SCIENCE. *Current Pos:* SR SCIENTIST, DENVER CTR PERFORMING ARTS, 88-; ASST CLIN PROF OTOLARYNGOL, SCH MED, UNIV COLO, BOULDER, 88- *Personal Data:* b Akron, Ohio, Sept 11, 45; m 71; c 2. *Educ:* Kent State Univ, BS, 68; Ind Univ, MA, 72; Univ Iowa, PhD(speech sci), 81. *Prof Exp:* Res scientist, Denver Ctr Performing Arts, 83-88. *Concurrent Pos:* Prin investr, grants from NIH, Voice Found, Duke Univ, 80-; rev consult, 12 jour & orgn, 82-; consult, 8 univ & book publ, 83-; adj asst prof & consult, Univ Iowa, 83-88, adj assoc prof & consult, 88-; lectr, Prof Voice: Use & Abuse, 84-; adj prof, Dept Speech Path & Audiol, Univ Denver, 84-86; adj asst prof speech sci, Univ Colo, Boulder, 84-93, adj assoc prof, Dept Commun Dis & Speech Sci, 93-; auditor, Int Soc Phonetic Sci, 88-; exec & legis bd, Nat Ctr Voice & Speech, 90-; lectr voice & speech sci, Nat Theatre Conserv, 90-; adj assoc prof, Dept Commun Dis, Univ, 92-; affil clin prof, Dept Commun Dis, Univ Northern Colo, 93- *Mem:* Am Speech Lang Hearing Asn; fel Int Soc Phonetic Sci; Int Arts Med Asn; Acoust Soc Am; Can Voice Care Foun. *Res:* Acoustics, aerodynamics and biomechanics of the larynx and speech production in general; author of numerous scientific publications. *Mailing Add:* Commun Disorders South Hall Rm 337 Bowling Greene Univ Bowling Green OH 43403

SCHERFIG, JAN W, ENVIRONMENTAL & CHEMICAL ENGINEERING. *Current Pos:* from asst prof to assoc prof, 67-77, chmn environ & resources eng, 70-77, PROF CIVIL & ENVIRON ENG, UNIV CALIF, IRVINE, 77- *Personal Data:* b Copenhagen, Denmark, Apr 24, 36. *Educ:* Danish Tech Univ, MS, 59; Univ Calif, Berkeley, PhD(sanit eng), 68. *Prof Exp:* Res engr, Danish Defense Res Bd, 60-61; prod engr, Danish Mineral Oil Refinery, 61-63; teacher chem, Technol Inst, Copenhagen, 62-63; res engr, Eng Sci, Inc, Calif, 63-66; res asst, Univ Calif, Berkeley, 66-67. *Concurrent Pos:* Consult, City of Calexico, Calif, Irvine Ranch Water Dist, Lowry Eng-Sci, Santa Ana, Encibra, Rio de Janeiro & Lowry & Assocs, Santa Ana, 67, City of Laguna Beach, 71. *Mem:* Am Soc Civil Engrs; Am Inst Chem Engrs. *Res:* Eutrophication; marine waste disposal, planning and optimization of water and waste. *Mailing Add:* Dept Civil Environ Eng Univ Calif Irvine CA 92697

SCHERGER, DALE ALBERT, ENVIRONMENTAL ENGINEERING, HYDROLOGY & WATER RESOURCES. *Current Pos:* Engr, Environ Control Technol Corp, 71-73, sr engr, 73-75, chief engr, 75-77, dir eng, 77-82, VPRES, ENVIRON CONTROL TECHNOL CORP, 82- *Personal Data:* b Toledo, Ohio, Aug 22, 49. *Educ:* Univ Mich, BSE, 71, MSE, 72. *Mem:* Water Pollution Control Fedn; Am Water Resources Asn; Nat Prof Eng Soc. *Res:* Advanced waste treatment technology for industrial and municipal wastes; methods development and implementation for control, cleanup and disposal of hazardous substances; development of techniques for controlling urban non-point source runoff. *Mailing Add:* 28 Stonebridge Dr Hockessin DE 19707

SCHERGER, JOSEPH E, FAMILY PRACTICE MEDICINE. *Current Pos:* Clin instr, Sch Med, Univ Calif, 78-80, from asst clin prof to assoc prof, 80-90, dir, Dept Family Pract, 93, CLIN PROF, SCH MED, UNIV CALIF, DAVIS, 90-; VPRES & DIR FAMILY PRACT & PRIMARY CARE EDUC, GROSSMONT HOSP, 93- *Personal Data:* b Delphos, Ohio, 1950. *Educ:* Univ Dayton, BS, 71; Univ Calif, Los Angeles, MD, 75. *Honors & Awards:* Family Physician of yr, Am Acad Family Physicians, 89, Thomas W Johnson Award, 94. *Concurrent Pos:* Family pract residency, Univ Wash, 75-78; med ed, Family & Pract Mgt; clin prof family med, Stanford Univ, Univ Calif, San Diego & Univ Calif, Davis. *Mem:* Inst Med-Nat Acad Sci; Am Asn Family Physicians; Soc Teachers Family Med (pres, 86). *Mailing Add:* Univ Calif Col Med Dean's Off Irvine Hall Irvine CA 92697-3950

SCHERLAG, BENJAMIN J, CARDIOVASCULAR PHYSIOLOGY. *Current Pos:* PROF MED & ADJ PROF PHYSIOL, UNIV OKLA HEALTH SCI CTR, 78-, CARDIOVASC PHYSIOLOGIST, VET ADMIN HOSP, OKLAHOMA CITY, 78- *Personal Data:* b Brooklyn, NY, Oct 31, 32; m 60, Eleanor Kuffman; c Nancy, William, Ronald & Michael. *Educ:* City Col New York, BS, 54; Brooklyn Col, MA, 61; State Univ NY, PhD(physiol), 63. *Honors & Awards:* Pioneers in Cardiac Pacing & Electrophysiol, NAm Soc Pacing & Electrophysiol, 89. *Prof Exp:* Asst physiol, State Univ NY Downstate Med Ctr, 56-63; res physiologist, Cardiopulmonary Lab, USPHS Hosp, NY, 65-68; res physiologist, Sect Cardiovasc Dis, Mt Sinai Hosp Greater Miami, 68-74. *Concurrent Pos:* NIH fel pharmacol, Col Physicians & Surgeons, Columbia Univ, 63-65; NIH fel pharmacol, Col Physicians & Surgeons, Columbia Univ, 63-65, res assoc, 65-67; prof med, Med Sch, Univ

Miami, 74-78; res physiologist, Vet Admin Hosp, Miami, 74-78; med investr, Vet Admin Med Ctr, 80-86, res career scientist, 85. *Mem:* Am Physiol Soc; Am Fedn Clin Res; fel Am Col Cardiol; Am Heart Asn; NY Acad Sci; NAm Soc Pacing & Electrophysiol. *Res:* Cardiac electrophysiology; pharmacology; our major research interest is disordered rhythms of the heart; abnormal impulse formation and conduction due to cardiac ischemia and infarction. *Mailing Add:* Dept Med Univ Okla Health Sci Ctr Vet Admin Med Ctr 151-F 921 NE 13th St Oklahoma City OK 73104. Fax: 405-270-5132; E-Mail: benjamin_scherlag@uokhsc.edu

SCHERMER, EUGENE DEWAYNE, ENVIRONMENTAL CHEMISTRY. *Current Pos:* RETIRED. *Personal Data:* b Spokane, Wash, June 21, 34; m 58; c 2. *Educ:* Eastern Wash State Col, BA, 58; Ore State Univ, MS, 62; La State Univ, PhD(chem), 71. *Prof Exp:* Teacher high schs, Wash, 58-61; instr chem, Grays Harbor Col, 62-84, dean instr, 84-92. *Concurrent Pos:* Investr, Wash State Dept Ecol, 74-76, co-investr with US CEngrs, 75, 79-80. *Mem:* Am Chem Soc. *Res:* The effects of woodwaste leachate on quality of ground and surface waters; effects of dredging on the Grays Harbor Estuary; water quality effects of ocean disposal of dredge spoils. *Mailing Add:* 522 W Scott St Aberdeen WA 98520

SCHERMER, LLOYD G, SCIENCE. *Honors & Awards:* Joseph Henry Medal, Smithsonian Inst, 94. *Mailing Add:* 210 Lake Ave Aspen CO 81611

SCHERMER, ROBERT IRA, CRYOGENICS, SUPERCONDUCTING MAGNETS. *Current Pos:* group leader, 89-93, GUEST SCIENTIST, LAWRENCE BERKELEY LAB, 93- *Personal Data:* b Brooklyn, NY, Sept 10, 34; m 58; c 4. *Educ:* Cornell Univ, BEngPhys, 56; Mass Inst Technol, PhD(nuclear eng), 61. *Prof Exp:* Res assoc nuclear cryogenics, Brookhaven Nat Lab, 60-62, assoc physicist, 62-65, physicist, 65-70; chmn, Dept Pysics, Springfield Tech Community Col, 70-74; mem staff, Los Alamos Nat Lab, 74-80, asst group leader, 80-87; chief scientist, Magnet Div, SSC, 90-93. *Mem:* Am Phys Soc. *Res:* Low temperature physics; magnetic measurements; design of superconducting magnets. *Mailing Add:* Los Alamos Nat Lab Eng Dept One Cyclotron Rd MS 46-161 Berkeley CA 94720. E-Mail: scheamer@lbl.gov

SCHERMERHORN, JOHN W, PHARMACY, BIONUCLEONICS. *Current Pos:* PROF HEALTH CARE SCI & DEAN SCH ALLIED HEALTH SCI, HEALTH SCI CTR, UNIV TEX, 71-, ACTG CHMN, DEPT HEALTH CARE SCI, 74- *Personal Data:* b NJ, Sept 1, 20; m 45; c 4. *Educ:* Rutgers Univ, BS, 42; Univ Minn, PhD(pharmaceut chem), 49. *Prof Exp:* Assoc prof pharmaceut chem, George Washington Univ, 49-S3; prof pharm & chmn dept, Mass Col Pharm, 53-66; prof, Col Pharm, Northeastern Univ, 66-71, dean div health sci, 69-71. *Concurrent Pos:* Consult, 53- *Mem:* AAAS; Am Pharmaceut Asn; Sigma Xi. *Res:* Pharmaceutical product development. *Mailing Add:* 3788 Townsend Dr Dallas TX 75229

SCHERPEREEL, DONALD E, MATERIALS SCIENCE, ENGINEERING MANAGEMENT. *Current Pos:* Sr mat scientist, Whirlpool Corp, 69-76, dir mech syst res, Res & Eng Ctr, 76-85, dir eng serv, 85-86, dir prod line eng, 86-87, DIR PROD ENG, WHIRLPOOL CORP, LA VERGNE DIV, 87- *Personal Data:* b South Bend, Ind, Dec 21, 37; m 60; c 3. *Educ:* Univ Notre Dame, BS, 59, MS, 61, PhD(metall, mat sci), 64. *Prof Exp:* Instr metall, Univ Notre Dame, 60-62; asst prof metall & mat sci, Mich State Univ, 64-69. *Mem:* Am Soc Metals; Am Soc Mech Engrs; Sigma Xi. *Res:* X-ray diffraction; electron microscopy; research management; product simulation; automated design; structural analysis. *Mailing Add:* 21318 Sail Bay Dr Cassopolis MI 49031

SCHERR, ALLAN L, BUSINESS PROCESS REENGINEERING & AUTOMATION, SOFTWARE DEVELOPMENT PROCESS & PROJECT MANAGEMENT. *Current Pos:* INDEPENDENT CONSULT, BUS PROCESS REENG & AUTOMATION, INFO TECHNOL STRATEGY, SOFTWARE PROJ MGT, SOFTWARE DESIGN, 93- *Personal Data:* b Baltimore, Md, Nov 18, 40; m 80, Linda R Martin; c Elise Scherr-Frejka, Stephanie L & Katherine M. *Educ:* Mass Inst Technol, BS & MS, 62, PhD (elec eng), 65. *Honors & Awards:* Grace Murray Hopper Award, Asn Comput Mach, 75. *Prof Exp:* Res asst, Proj MAC, Mass Inst Technol, 63-65; staff engr, Systs Archit Syst Develop Div, IBM Corp, Poughkeepsie, NY, 65-66, mgr TSO design & performance, Syst Develop Div, 67-70, mgr, MVS Prog, 71-74, mgr advan systs prog design, 75-76, mgr, Distrib Systs Prog, Syst Develop Div, Kingston, 77-79, mem, Corp Tech Comt, Armonk, NY, 80, dir, Commun Prog, Systs Commun Div, Kingston, 80-81, dir commun systs, corp staff, Valhalla, NY, 82-83, dir advan systs, Systs Prods Div, Rochester, Minn, 84-85, dir integrated applns, Applns Systs Div, Milford, Conn, 86-88, vpres develop & integration, 88-91, vpres technol & chief exec officer, IBM Consult Group. *Concurrent Pos:* IBM fel, 84. *Mem:* Fel Inst Elec & Electronics Engrs; Sigma Xi. *Res:* Business process re-engineering and automation; distributed processing structures and the software development process; special work on managing technical projects so as to deliberately produce extraordinary, unprecedented results. *Mailing Add:* EMC Corp 171 South St Hopkinton MA 01748. Fax: 203-454-1801

SCHERR, CHARLES W, PHYSICS. *Current Pos:* from asst prof to assoc prof, 56-66, PROF PHYSICS, UNIV TEX, AUSTIN, 66- *Personal Data:* b Philadelphia, Pa, Mar 19, 26; m 52, 70; c 2. *Educ:* Univ Pa, BS, 49; Univ Chicago, MS, 51, PhD(chem phys), 54. *Prof Exp:* Res assoc physics, Univ Chicago, 54-56. *Mem:* Am Phys Soc. *Res:* Quantum mechanical investigation of atomic and molecular structure. *Mailing Add:* Dept Physics Univ Tex Austin TX 78712. Fax: 512-471-9637

SCHERR, DAVID DELANO, ORTHOPEDIC SURGERY, MICROBIOLOGY. *Current Pos:* RETIRED. *Personal Data:* b Columbia, Mo, Oct 15, 34; m 58, 77; c 3. *Educ:* Univ Mo-Columbia, BA, 56, MD, 59; Univ Iowa, MS, 63, PhD(microbiol), 66; Am Bd Orthop Surg, dipl, 69. *Prof Exp:* Staff orthop surg, David Grant Med Ctr, Travis AFB, Calif, 67-69; from asst prof to assoc prof orthop surg & microbiol, Sch Med, Univ Mo, Columbia, 69-75; pvt pract orthop, 75-97. *Mem:* Am Soc Microbiol; Am Acad Orthop Surg; Orthop Res Soc; Asn Acad Surg; AMA; Am Rheumatism Asn; Int Col Surgeons. *Res:* Activity of antibiotics in clinical uses; role of autoimmune mechanisms in rheumatic diseases. *Mailing Add:* 725 Kaylyn Dr Jefferson City MO 65109-0550

SCHERR, GEORGE HARRY, MICROBIOLOGY. *Current Pos:* PRES, TECHNAM, INC, 72- *Personal Data:* b New York, NY, Dec 30, 20; m 44; c 3. *Educ:* Queens Col, NY, BS, 41; Univ Ky, MS, 49, PhD(bact), 51. *Prof Exp:* Bacteriologist, City Dept Health, New York, 41-42; chemist, Calco Chem Div, Am Cyanamid Co, 43-48; asst prof microbiol, Sch Med, Creighton Univ, 51-54; asst prof bact, Col Med, Univ Ill, 54-59; vpres & dir res, Consol Labs, Inc, Ill, 59-69; dir, Colab Labs, Inc, Ill, 69-71; pres, Mat & Technol Systs, Inc, 71-72. *Concurrent Pos:* Community prof environ sci, Governors State Univ, 73- *Mem:* AAAS; Am Soc Microbiol; Soc Indust Microbiol; Genetics Soc Am; Mycol Soc Am. *Res:* Immunology and infectious disease; effect of carcinogens on microorganisms; effect of hormones on infectious diseases; microbial genetics. *Mailing Add:* PO Box 234 Chicago Heights IL 60411. Fax: 708-758-3276; E-Mail: jir@interaccess.com

SCHERR, LAWRENCE, INTERNAL MEDICINE. *Current Pos:* From asst prof to prof, 58-71, ASSOC DEAN, NY UNIV SCH MED, 94-, DAVID V GREENE PROF MED, 96- *Personal Data:* b New York, NY, Nov 6, 28; m 54, Peggy Binenkorb; c Cynthia E & Robert W. *Educ:* Cornell Univ, AB, 50, MD, 57. *Concurrent Pos:* From intern to chief resident, Cornell Med Div, Bellevue Hosp & Mem Ctr, 57-61, co-dir cardiorenal lab & asst vis physician, 61-63, assoc vis physician, 63-65, vis physician, 66-67, dir cardiol & renal unit, 63-67; NY Heart Asn fel, Med Col, Cornell Univ, 59-60, assoc dean, 69-96, prof med, 75-96; physician to outpatients, NY Hosp, 61-63, from asst attend to attend, 63-; career scientist, Health Res Coun New York, 62-66; attend, Manhattan Vet Admin Hosp, 64-69; asst attend, Mem Hosp, 66-69, consult, 69-; Am Heart Asn teaching scholar, 66-67; chmn, Dept Med, N Shore Univ Hosp, 67-, sr vpres med affairs, 69-; fel coun clin cardiol, Am Heart Asn; chmn, NY State Bd Med, 73-75; chmn, Res Review Comt, Int Med, 80-82; chmn bd regents, Am Col Physicians, 85-86, pres, 87-88; White House Health Prof Group, 93. *Mem:* Master Am Col Physicians (pres, 87-88); Am Fedn Clin Res; AMA; Am Bd Internal Med (secy-treas, 79-86); Am Clin & Climat Asn; fel NY Acad Med. *Res:* Internal medicine, including cardiovascular and renal disease and fluid and electrolyte problems; medical education; health and public policy; quality and medical staff structure; graduate medical education. *Mailing Add:* North Shore Univ Hosp 300 Community Dr Manhasset NY 11030. Fax: 516-562-2981; E-Mail: 76336.3135@compuserve.com

SCHERRER, JOSEPH HENRY, POLYMER CHEMISTRY. *Current Pos:* RES CHEMIST, COOK PAINT & VARNISH CO, 64- *Personal Data:* b Chicago, Ill, Sept 5, 31; m 60; c 3. *Educ:* DePaul Univ, BS, 53; Univ Kans, PhD(org chem), 57. *Prof Exp:* Res chemist, Spencer Chem Co, 57-64. *Mem:* Am Chem Soc; Royal Soc Chem. *Res:* Synthesis of organic nitrogen compounds. *Mailing Add:* 5726 Floyd Shawnee Mission KS 66202

SCHERRER, RENE, MICRO & MOLECULAR BIOLOGY, BIOPHYSICS. *Current Pos:* RES SCIENTIST, ECOGENETIKA, 92- *Personal Data:* b Boulogne-sur-Seine, France, June 15, 32. *Educ:* Univ Lausanne, dipl med, 58; Univ Basel, Dr Med, 61. *Prof Exp:* Third asst, Inst Microbiol, Univ Basel, 59-60, second asst, 60-63; res assoc microbiol, Univ Mich, 63-65; from instr to asst prof, Mich State Univ, 65-72; contrib scientist, Western Regional Res Ctr, Agr Res Serv, USDA, Berkeley, 74-84; vis scientist molecular genetics, Univ Calif, Irvine, 85-88; contrib scientist, Western Regional Res Ctr, USDA, Berkeley, 87-92. *Concurrent Pos:* Supvr clin diag lab, Inst Microbiol, Univ Basel, 59-63; vis scientist, Univ Calif, Irvine, 75-76. *Mem:* AAAS; Am Soc Microbiol; Am Soc Cell Biol; Electron Micros Soc Am; Brit Soc Gen Microbiol; NY Acad Sci. *Res:* Molecular and cell biology and biophysics of bacteria; chromosome structure; DNA replication; cell division and cell cycle; morphogenes; molecular cell wall structure; endospore formation, dormancy and heat resistance; water properties of bacteria. *Mailing Add:* Ecogenetika 2609 Martin Luther King Jr Way Berkeley CA 94704-3218

SCHERRER, ROBERT ALLAN, ORGANIC CHEMISTRY, ION-PAIR PARTITIONING. *Current Pos:* res specialist, 69-72, sr res specialist, Riker Labs Div, 72-86, DIV SCIENTIST, 3M PHARMACEUT DIV, 3M CO, 86- *Personal Data:* b Sacramento, Calif, Nov 21, 32; m 54; c 4. *Educ:* Univ Calif, BS, 54; Univ Ill, PhD(chem), 58. *Prof Exp:* From assoc res chemist to res chemist, Parke Davis & Co, 58-66; sr med chemist, Minn Mining & Mfg Co, 66-69. *Concurrent Pos:* Sr ed, J Med Chem, 86 & 87. *Mem:* Am Chem Soc. *Res:* Synthetic medicinal chemistry; antiarthritic agents; regression analysis; antiasthmatic agents; antioxidants; applications of ion-pair partitioning to drug design. *Mailing Add:* 3M Pharmaceut 3M Co 3M Ctr 270-2S06 St Paul MN 55144-1000. Fax: 612-737-5886; E-Mail: rascherrer@mmm.com

SCHERTZ, CLETUS E, AGRICULTURAL ENGINEERING. *Current Pos:* RETIRED. *Personal Data:* b El Paso, Ill, Apr 12, 30; m 58; c 5. *Educ:* Univ Ill, Urbana, BS(agr sci) & BS(agr eng), 54; Iowa State Univ, PhD(agr eng & theoret & appl mech), 62. *Prof Exp:* Asst prof agr eng, Univ Calif, Davis, 62-67; from assoc prof to prof, Univ Minn, St Paul, 67-95. *Mem:* Am Soc Agr Engrs. *Res:* Machines for harvest of food and fiber crops. *Mailing Add:* 2579 Orchard Lane White Bear Lake MN 55110-5618

SCHERTZ, KEITH FRANCIS, CYTOGENETICS. *Current Pos:* RETIRED. *Personal Data:* b El Paso, Ill, Feb 25, 27; m 54; c 6. *Educ:* Univ Ill, BS, 49, MS, 50; Cornell Univ, PhD(plant breeding), 57. *Prof Exp:* Geneticist, Fed Exp Sta, Agr Res Serv, USDA, 57-59, geneticist, Dept Soil & Crop Sci, Tex A&M Univ, 60-96. *Mem:* Fel Am Soc Agron; fel Crop Sci Soc. *Res:* Genetics and cytogenetics of sorghum, apomixis, reproductive behavior and sterility systems. *Mailing Add:* Dept Soil & Crop Sci Tex A&M Univ College Station TX 77843

SCHERVISH, MARK JOHN, FOUNDATIONS OF INFERENCE, STATISTICAL COMPUTING. *Current Pos:* From asst prof to assoc prof, 79-89, PROF STATIST, CARNEGIE MELLON UNIV, 89- *Personal Data:* b Detroit, Mich, Oct 10, 53; m 79. *Educ:* Mich State Univ, BS, 74; Univ Mich, MS, 75; Univ Ill, PhD(statist), 79. *Concurrent Pos:* Vis asst statistician, Statist Lab, Univ Calif, Berkeley, 79; researcher, OEIV, US Dept Energy, Washington, DC, 80; hon res fel, dept statist sci, Univ Col London, 85; vis lectr, Inst Statist Economet, Univ Basel, 89; vis mem math, Sci Res Inst, Berkeley, 92. *Mem:* Fel Am Statist Asn; Royal Statist Soc; fel Inst Math Statist. *Res:* Foundations of inference; statistical computing; comparison of forecasters. *Mailing Add:* Dept Statist Carnegie-Mellon Univ Pittsburgh PA 15213

SCHERY, STEPHEN DALE, ATMOSPHERIC RADIOACTIVITY, NUCLEAR PHYSICS. *Current Pos:* from asst prof to assoc prof, 79-90, RES PHYSICIST, NMEX INST MINING & TECHNOL, 79-, PROF PHYSICS, 90- *Personal Data:* b Rio de Janeiro, Brazil, July 1, 45; US citizen; m 86, Pat Cooksey. *Educ:* Ohio State Univ, BS, 67; Univ Ark, MS, 70; Univ Colo, PhD(physics), 73. *Prof Exp:* Asst prof physics, Kenyon Col, 73-74, marine sci, Tex A&M Univ, Galveston, 74-79. *Concurrent Pos:* Vis prof & consult, Cyclotron Lab, Mich State Univ, 75-78; vis sr scientist, Australian AEC, 86; vis scientist, Dept Geol & Geophys, Yale Univ, 87; vis scholar, Australian Nuclear Sci & Tech Orgn, 90. *Mem:* Am Phys Soc; Am Geophys Union; Health Physics Soc; Sigma Xi. *Res:* Experimental nuclear physics; natural radioactivity in Earth and atmospheric science applications; transport of radon and thoron, aerosols and atmospheric radioactivity. *Mailing Add:* Dept Physics NMex Inst Mining & Technol Socorro NM 87801

SCHERZ, JAMES PHILLIP, CIVIL ENGINEERING. *Current Pos:* Instr civil eng, 65-66, res asst, 66-67, from asst prof to assoc prof, 67-77, PROF CIVIL & ENVIRON ENG, INST ENVIRON STUDIES, UNIV WIS-MADISON, 77- *Personal Data:* b Rice Lake, Wis, May 12, 37; m 62; c 1. *Educ:* Univ Wis, BS, 59, MS, 61, PhD(civil eng), 67. *Concurrent Pos:* Aerial monitoring systs consult, 71- *Res:* Remote sensing to include water quality analysis, especially with special photography; surveying of prehistoric calendon sites. *Mailing Add:* Dept Civil Eng 1201 Eng Bldg Univ Wis 1415 Enginerring Dr Madison WI 53706-1607

SCHETKY, LAURENCE MCDONALD, SHAPE MEMORY ALLOY TECHNOLOGY, SMART MATERIALS & ADAPTIVE STRUCTURES. *Current Pos:* CHIEF SCIENTIST, MEMORY METALS, INC, STAMFORD, CONN, 83- *Personal Data:* b Baguio, Philippines, July 15, 22; US citizen; m 95, Margarita A; c Mark C. *Educ:* Rensselaer Polytech Inst, BChE, 43, MMetE, 48, PhD(physics & metall), 53. *Prof Exp:* Instr metall, Rensselaer Polytech Inst, 46-53; fel, Mass Inst Technol, 53-56, dir mat res, Instrumentation Lab, 56-59; vpres & tech dir, Alloyd Electronics Corp, Mass, 59-63; tech dir metall, Int Copper Res Asn, Inc, 63-83. *Concurrent Pos:* Lectr, Rensselaer Polytech Inst & Mass Inst Technol; US rep, Int Metall Cong, 53; World Exchange Lectr, Am Foundrymen's Soc, 67. *Mem:* Fel Am Soc Metals; Am Inst Mining, Metall & Petrol Engrs; fel Inst Mat UK; Am Inst Aeronaut & Astronaut; Int Soc Optical Eng. *Res:* Physical metallurgy; materials problems in instrumentation; metrology; vapor phase theory; welding and joining; copper research technology; shape memory alloy technology. *Mailing Add:* 77 Rock House Rd Easton CT 06612. *Fax:* 203-740-7311; *E-Mail:* macdee@gnn.com

SCHETTLER, PAUL DAVIS, JR, PHYSICAL CHEMISTRY. *Current Pos:* assoc prof, 67-78, chmn dept, 75-85, PROF CHEM, JUNIATA COL, 76- *Personal Data:* b Salt Lake City, Utah, Mar 31, 37; m 66; c 2. *Educ:* Univ Utah, BS, 58; Yale Univ, PhD(phys chem), 64. *Prof Exp:* Fel, Univ Utah, 63-66; teaching intern chem, Antioch Col, 66-67. *Concurrent Pos:* Consult, Columbia Gas Corp, 81-82. *Mem:* Am Chem Soc. *Res:* Natural gas production from microporous rocks; measurements of isotherms and degassing rates of microporous solids and calculations of their implications for production from natural gas; Devonian shale. *Mailing Add:* RD#4 Box 285 Juniata Col Huntingdon PA 16652

SCHETZ, JOSEPH A, AEROSPACE & OCEAN ENGINEERING. *Current Pos:* chmn dept, 69-93, J BYRON MAUPIN PROF AEROSPACE & OCEAN ENG, VA POLYTECH INST & STATE UNIV, 69- *Personal Data:* b Orange, NJ, Oct 19, 36; m 59; c 4. *Educ:* Webb Inst Naval Archit, BS, 58; Princeton Univ, MSE, 60, MA, 61, PhD(mech eng), 62. *Honors & Awards:* Pendaray Aerospace Literative Award, Am Inst Aeronaut & Astronaut, 97. *Prof Exp:* Sr scientist, Gen Appl Sci Lab, NY, 61-64; assoc prof aerospace eng, Univ Md, Col Park, 64-69. *Concurrent Pos:* Consult, Appl Physics Lab, Johns Hopkins Univ, 64- *Mem:* Fel Am Inst Aeronaut & Astronaut; fel Am Soc Mech Engrs; Soc Naval Architects & Marine Engrs. *Res:* Fluid dynamics; ocean engineering; combustion; jet populsion and turbulent flows. *Mailing Add:* Dept Aerospace & Ocean Eng Va Polytech Inst & State Univ Blacksburg VA 24061. *Fax:* 540-231-9632; *E-Mail:* ptiger@vtvm1.cc.ut.edu

SCHETZEN, MARTIN, NONLINEAR SYSTEM THEORY. *Current Pos:* assoc prof, 65-69, PROF ELEC ENG, NORTHEASTERN UNIV, 69- *Personal Data:* b New York, NY, Feb 10, 28; m 84. *Educ:* NY Univ, BEE, 51; Mass Inst Technol, SM, 54, ScD(elec eng), 61. *Honors & Awards:* Apollo Achievement Award, Apollo Certificate of Commendation. *Prof Exp:* Electronic scientist, Nat Bur Stand, 51-52; asst microwaves, Res Lab Electronics, Mass Inst Technol, 52-54; engr, Appl Physics Lab, Johns Hopkins Univ, 54-56; asst elec eng, Mass Inst Technol, 56-58, commun & nonlinear theory, Res Lab Electronics, 58-60, instr elec eng, 60-61, asst prof elec eng, Mass Inst Technol, 61-65, staff mem, Res Lab Electronics, 61-65. *Concurrent Pos:* Consult, Atlantic Refining Co, Tex, 61-66, Instrumentation Lab, Mass Inst Technol, 64-71 & RCA, Mass, 68-72; vis prof elec eng, Univ Calif, Berkeley, 77-78; vis scientist, Dept Math, Weizmann Inst Sci, Rehovot, Israel, 82 & 84-85. *Mem:* AAAS; Inst Elec & Electronics Engrs; Sigma Xi. *Res:* Nonlinear and communication theory; analysis and synthesis of nonlinear systems; determination of optimum nonlinear systems. *Mailing Add:* Dept Elec & Comput Eng Dana Res Bldg Northeastern Univ Boston MA 02115. *Fax:* 617-373-8970; *E-Mail:* schetzen@neu.edu

SCHETZINA, JAN FREDERICK, PHYSICS. *Current Pos:* asst prof, 70-75, ASSOC PROF PHYSICS, NC STATE UNIV, 75- *Personal Data:* b Moundsville, WVa, Nov 29, 40; m 68; c 1. *Educ:* Gannon Col, BA, 63; Pa State Univ, MS, 65, PhD(physics), 69. *Prof Exp:* Res assoc solid state physics, Pa State Univ, 69-70. *Mem:* Am Phys Soc; Am Vacuum Soc. *Res:* Optical and electrical properties of semiconductors. *Mailing Add:* Dept Physics NC State Univ 316 Cox Hall Box 8202 Raleigh NC 27695. *Fax:* 919-515-7667

SCHEUCH, DON RALPH, ELECTRICAL ENGINEERING. *Current Pos:* PVT CONSULT, 80- *Personal Data:* b Seattle, Wash, Sept 12, 18; m 50; c 3. *Educ:* Univ Calif, BS, 43; Stanford Univ, MA, 46, PhD(elec eng), 49. *Prof Exp:* Res assoc, Radio Res Lab, Harvard Univ, 43-45; sr res engr, SRI Int, 49-51, supvr, 51-53, group head, 53-55, lab mgr, 55-59, asst dir eng, 59-60, exec dir electronics & radio sci, 60-68, vpres eng, 68-69, vpres & chmn, Off Res Opers, 77-80, sr vpres, 77-80. *Concurrent Pos:* Spec consult, USAF, 42-45. *Mem:* Sigma Xi; Inst Elec & Electronics Engrs. *Res:* Weapons systems evaluation; lasers; antennas; communications. *Mailing Add:* 430 Golden Oak Dr Portola Valley CA 94028

SCHEUCHENZUBER, H JOSEPH, BIOMECHANICS, PHYSICAL EDUCATION. *Current Pos:* asst prof, 74-80, PROF BIOMECH, SPRINGFIELD COL, 80- *Personal Data:* b Lancaster, Pa, June 4, 44; m 68. *Educ:* West Chester State Col, BS, 68; Pa State Univ, MS, 70; Ind Univ, PhD(human performance), 74. *Prof Exp:* Phys dir, York YMCA, Pa, 68; instr scuba, Pa State Univ, 69-70; instr aquatics, York Col, Pa, 70-72. *Concurrent Pos:* Spec consult acad appln comput sci, Springfield Col, 74- *Mem:* Am Asn Health Phys Educ & Recreation; Am Col Sports Med. *Res:* Biomechanical study of kinetic and kinematic factors present during normal human locomotive movements, and modification of similar abnormal motions based on that information. *Mailing Add:* Springfield Col 263 Alden St Springfield MA 01109-3707

SCHEUER, ERNEST MARTIN, STATISTICS, OPERATIONS RESEARCH. *Current Pos:* RETIRED. *Personal Data:* b Germany, July 28, 30; US citizen; m 53, 72, Mary Jean Aura; c Susan & Michael. *Educ:* Reed Col, BA, 51; Univ Wash, MS, 54; Univ Calif, Los Angeles, PhD(math), 60. *Prof Exp:* Math statistician, Control Data Corp, Rand Corp, Space Technol Labs & US Naval Ord Test Sta, 51-70; assoc prof, Calif State Univ, Northridge, 70-72, prof mgt sci, 72-91, prof math, 76-91; emer prof mgt sci, Jet Propulsion Lab, Calif Inst Tech, Pasadena, 91-93, emer prof math, 91-93. *Mem:* Fel Am Statist Asn. *Res:* Reliability, theory and applications; statistical distributions; generating random variables for simulations; testing goodness-of-fit; statistical and economic analysis of warranties. *Mailing Add:* 2443 E Oneida St Unit 2 Pasadena CA 91107. *Fax:* 626-577-4962; *E-Mail:* ernest.scheuer@csun.edu

SCHEUER, JAMES, PHYSIOLOGY, BIOCHEMISTRY. *Current Pos:* assoc prof physiol, 72-78, vchmn med, 80-90, chmn med, 90, PROF MED, ALBERT EINSTEIN COL MED, 72-, PROF PHYSIOL, 78- *Personal Data:* b New York, NY, Feb 21, 31. *Educ:* Univ Rochester, BA, 55; Yale Univ, MD, 56. *Prof Exp:* Res assoc, Res Inst Muscle Dis, New York, 62-63; trainee metab & nutrit, Grad Sch Pub Health, Univ Pittsburgh, 63-64, from instr to assoc prof med, Sch Med, 64-72, assoc prof biochem, Fac Arts & Sci, 70-72; chief cardiol, Montefiore Hosp & Med Ctr, 72-87, interim chmn dept med, 87-90. *Concurrent Pos:* USPHS fel cardiol, Mt Sinai Hosp, New York, 59; USPHS fel myocardial metab, Cornell Univ, 62-63; USPHS fel biochem, Univ Pittsburgh, 64-65, career develop award myocardial metab, 68-; mem coun circulation, Rosie Sci Coun, Am Heart Asn; mem, Int Study Group Res Cardiac Metab. *Mem:* Am Soc Clin Invest; Am Physiol Soc; Soc Exp Biol & Med; Asn Am Physicians. *Res:* Correlation of biochemistry, metabolism and mechanical function of the heart, with emphasis on cardiac hypertrophy, the effects of physical condition aging, and the effects of diabetes. *Mailing Add:* Dept Med Physiol & Biophys Albert Einstein Col Med Montefiore Hosp & Med Ctr 111 E 210th St Bronx NY 10467-2490. *Fax:* 718-920-8375

SCHEUER, PAUL JOSEF, ORGANIC CHEMISTRY, MARINE NATURAL PRODUCTS. *Current Pos:* From asst prof to prof, 50-85, chmn dept, 59-62, EMER PROF CHEM, UNIV HAWAII, 85- *Personal Data:* b Heilbronn, Ger, May 25, 15; nat US; m 50, Alice E Dash; c Elizabeth, Deborah, David & Jonathan. *Educ:* Northeastern Univ, BS, 43; Harvard Univ, MA, 47, PhD(chem), 50. *Honors & Awards:* P J Scheuer Award, Marine Natural Prod, 92; Lilly Lectr, Kans Univ, 93; Ernest Guenther Award, Am Chem Soc, 94; Res Award, Am Soc Pharmacog, 94. *Concurrent Pos:*

Barton lectr, Univ Okla, 67; vis prof, Univ Copenhagen, 77, 89; J F Toole lectr, Univ NB, 77; ed, Marine Natural Prod, 78-83, Bio Org Marine Chem, 87-92; Toyo Suisan vis prof, Univ Tokyo, 92. *Mem:* AAAS; Am Chem Soc; Royal Soc Chem; Swiss Chem Soc; Am Soc Pharmacog. *Res:* Structure and biosynthesis of natural products; secondary metabolites of marine organisms; marine toxins; marine ecology. *Mailing Add:* Dept Chem Univ Hawaii Manoa 2545 The Mall Honolulu HI 96822-2275

SCHEUERMANN, W JAMES, DIGITAL SIGNAL PROCESSING, PARALLEL PROCESSORS. *Current Pos:* SR SCIENTIST, AGROSYSTS INC, 84- *Personal Data:* b San Jose, Calif, Oct 24, 39. *Educ:* Stanford Univ, BS, 61, MS, 62. *Prof Exp:* Sr engr, Ford Aeronutronic, 63-65, Raytheon Comput, 65-67; sr mem tech staff, ESL Inc, 67-80; sr systs engr, Adac Labs, 80-84. *Res:* Digital signal processing; massively parallel computer architectures; reconfigurable processing and computing hardware architectures; reconfigurable, high capacity telecommunication systems architectures. *Mailing Add:* Argosysts Inc PO Box 3452 Sunnyvale CA 94088-3452. *Fax:* 408-524-2029; *E-Mail:* jim.scheuermann@argosys.boeing.com

SCHEUING, RICHARD A(LBERT), AERONAUTICAL ENGINEERING. *Current Pos:* RETIRED. *Personal Data:* b Lynbrook, NY, Aug 19, 27; m 50; c 3. *Educ:* Mass Inst Technol, SB & SM, 48; NY Univ, PhD, 71. *Prof Exp:* Aerodyn res eng, Grumman Aerospace Corp, 48-52, aerodyn res group leader, 52-56, head fluid mech sect, 56-70, dep dir, Res Dept, 61-77, dir, Res Dept, 77-90. *Mem:* AAAS; assoc fel Am Inst Aeronaut & Astronaut. *Res:* Fluid dynamics; hypersonics; shock tunnels; magnetohydrodynamics. *Mailing Add:* 8534 SE Banyan Tree St Hobe Sound FL 33455

SCHEUSNER, DALE LEE, EDUCATION, FOOD MICROBIOLOGY. *Current Pos:* HEAD SCI DEPT, CHRISTIAN LIFE SCH, 87- *Personal Data:* b Watertown, SDak, Feb 10, 44; m 71, Tommy; c 2. *Educ:* SDak State Univ, BS, 66; NC State Univ, MS, 68; Mich State Univ, PhD(food sci), 72. *Prof Exp:* Res microbiologist, S C Johnson & Son Inc, 72-83. *Concurrent Pos:* Consult, 83- *Mem:* Am Soc Microbiol; Inst Food Technologists. *Res:* Methods development and application of environmental microbiology and microbial decontamination, especially as applied to health care and food processing facilities. *Mailing Add:* 2506 S Blackman Rd Springfield MO 65809

SCHEVE, BERNARD JOSEPH, PHOTOCHEMISTRY, RADIATION CHEMISTRY. *Personal Data:* b Cincinnati, Ohio, July 2, 45; m 69; c 2. *Educ:* Xaiver Univ, Ohio, BS, 67, MS, 68; Mich State Univ, PhD(photochem), 74. *Prof Exp:* Asst chemist drug chem, Merrell Nat Labs, Richardson Merrell Inc, 71-73; res chemist, Hercules Inc, 74-80, sr res chemist, 80-90. *Mem:* Am Chem Soc; AAAS; NY Acad Sci. *Res:* Polymer modification; free radical chemistry; photo polymers; polysaccharides; polyole fins; terpenes. *Mailing Add:* 3863 Maywood Ct Cincinnati OH 45211-4424

SCHEVE, LARRY GERARD, BIOCHEMISTRY. *Current Pos:* lectr, 77-79, from asst prof to assoc prof, 79-86, PROF CHEM, DEPT CHEM, CALIF STATE UNIV, 87- *Personal Data:* b Palo Alto, Calif, Mar 1, 50; m 83, Gail J Bergner. *Educ:* Seattle Pac Univ, BS, 72; Univ Calif, Riverside, PhD(biochem), 76. *Prof Exp:* Res asst biochem, Dept Surg, Vet Admin Hosp, Martinez, Calif, 77. *Mem:* Am Chem Soc; Sigma Xi; AAAS. *Res:* Biochemistry of peroxidases (thyroid peroxidase and myeloperoxidase of the leukocyte); isolation and purification of membrane-bound proteins. *Mailing Add:* Dept Chem Calif State Univ Hayward CA 94542

SCHEVING, LAWRENCE EINAR, ANATOMY, CHRONOBIOL. *Current Pos:* REBSAMEN PROF ANAT SCI, COL MED, UNIV ARK, LITTLE ROCK, 70- *Personal Data:* b Hensel, NDak, Oct 20, 20; m 49; c 4. *Educ:* DePaul Univ, BS, 49, MS, 50; Loyola Univ Ill, PhD(anat), 57. *Honors & Awards:* Alexander von Humboldt Sr Scientist Prize, 73. *Prof Exp:* Asst embryol, DePaul Univ, 49-50; from instr to assoc prof biol sci & chmn dept, Lewis Col, 50-57; from instr to prof anat, Chicago Med Sch, 57-66; prof, Sch Med, La State Univ, New Orleans, 67-70. *Concurrent Pos:* Instr, Sch Nursing, Garfield Park Hosp, 49-50; vis prof, med Hochschule, Hanover, Ger & Univ Bergan Bergan, Norway,73; mem, Army Med Res & Develop Adv Comt, Wash, DC, 83- *Mem:* Int Soc Chronobiol (secy-tres, pres, 85-); Am Asn Anat. *Res:* Chronobiology; author of over 300 publications. *Mailing Add:* Dept Anat Univ Ark Med Sci 4301 W Markham St Little Rock AR 72205

SCHEWE, PHILLIP FRANK, HIGH ENERGY PHYSICS. *Current Pos:* WITH AM INST PHYSICS, 79- *Personal Data:* b Evanston, Ill, July 7, 50; m 81; c 2. *Educ:* Univ Ill, BS & MS, 72; Mich State Univ, BA, 77, PhD(physics), 78. *Prof Exp:* Asst physicist, Brookhaven Nat Lab, 78-79. *Concurrent Pos:* Ed, Physics News, Physics News Update. *Mem:* Am Phys Soc. *Res:* Deep inelastic lepton scattering; development of superconducting magnets. *Mailing Add:* Am Inst Physics One Physics Ellipse College Park MD 20740. *Fax:* 301-209-0846; *E-Mail:* pschewe@aip.acp.org

SCHEXNAYDER, MARY ANNE, ORGANIC CHEMISTRY, PHOTOCHEMISTRY. *Current Pos:* asst to vpres res, 84-87, mgr res admin, 89-94, MGR INTELLECTUAL PROPERTY, MINOT, 95- *Personal Data:* b La, Nov 6, 48. *Educ:* La State Univ, BS, 70; Rice Univ, PhD(chem), 74. *Prof Exp:* NIH trainee, Inst Lipid Res, Baylor Col Med, 75; res chemist, Hercules Inc, 75-84. *Mem:* Am Chem Soc. *Res:* Free radical chemistry; ziegler catalyst and polymerization. *Mailing Add:* 1712 Dahlia St Baton Rouge LA 70808-8825. *Fax:* 504-267-3629

SCHEY, HARRY MORITZ, BIOSTATISTICS. *Current Pos:* ASSOC PROF MATH, ROCHESTER INST TECHNOL, 84- *Personal Data:* b Chicago, Ill, Feb 20, 30. *Educ:* Northwestern Univ, BS, 50; Harvard Univ, AM, 51; Univ Ill, PhD, 54. *Prof Exp:* Asst physics, Univ Ill, 52-54; sr physicist, Theoret Physics Div, Lawrence Livermore Lab, 54-66; physicist, Educ Res Ctr, Mass Inst Technol, 66-73, co-dir, Proj, CALC, 73-75; fel, Dept Biostatist, Univ NC, Chapel Hill, 75-77; asst prof biostatist, Bowman Gray Sch Med, Wake Forest Univ, 78-84. *Mem:* Am Statist Asn; Biomet Soc. *Res:* Kolmogorov-Smirnov goodness-of-fit tests; clinical studies; renal disease epidemiology; statistical methods in psychiatric diagnosis; obesity in children; leukemia clustering; blood pressure measurement techniques; statistical computing; geometric aspects of linear regression. *Mailing Add:* Dept Math Rochester Inst Tech One Lomb Memorial Dr Rochester NY 14623-5603

SCHEY, JOHN ANTHONY, METAL DEFORMATION PROCESSES. *Current Pos:* prof, 74-88, DISTINGUISHED EMER PROF MECH ENG, UNIV WATERLOO, ONT, 88- *Personal Data:* b Sopron, Hungary, Dec 19, 22; US citizen; m 48, Margit M Sule; c John F. *Educ:* Jozsef Nador Tech Univ, Hungary, dipl, 46; Acad Sci, Budapest, Hungary, PhD(metall), 53. *Hon Degrees:* Dr, Univ Stuttgart, Ger, 87, Univ Heavy Indust, Miskolc, Hungary, 89. *Honors & Awards:* W H A Robertson Medal, Inst Metals, London, Eng, 66; Gold Medal Award, Soc Mfg Engrs, 74; Dofasco Award, Can Inst Mining & Metall, 84. *Prof Exp:* Supt metal works, Steel & Metal Works, Csepel, Budapest, 47-51; reader metals technol, Tech Univ, Miskollc, Hungary, 51-56; supvr fabrication, Res Lab, Brit Aluminum Co, 56-62; metall adv, IIT Res Inst, Chicago, 62-68; prof metall eng, Univ Ill, Chicago Circle, 68-74. *Concurrent Pos:* Mem, Metalworking Processes Comt, Mat Adv Bd-Nat Acad Sci, 67-70; consult, 16 indust orgns, 68-; NAm ed, J Mech Working Technol, 77-87; course dir, Forging Indust Asn, Die Design Inst, 78-86; assoc ed, J Lubrication Technol, Am Soc Mech Engrs, 81-87. *Mem:* Nat Acad Eng; fel Am Soc Metals; fel Soc Mfg Engrs; Can Inst Mining & Metall; Hungarian Acad Scis; Hungarian Acad Eng. *Res:* Interactions between material properties and process conditions in metalworking processes, friction, lubrication and wear; development of new manufacturing processes; social implications of technology; tribology of metalworking. *Mailing Add:* Dept Mech Eng Univ Waterloo Waterloo ON N2L 3G1 Can. *Fax:* 519-888-6197; *E-Mail:* jschey@surya.vwaterloo.ca

SCHIAFFINO, SILVIO STEPHEN, BIOCHEMISTRY, RESEARCH ADMINISTRATION. *Current Pos:* scientist adminr, Nat Cancer Inst, 61-64, asst chief, Res Grants Rev Br, 64-69, chief, 69-72, assoc dir sci rev, 72-78, dep dir, 78-83, ACTG DIR, DIV RES GRANTS, NIH, 83- *Personal Data:* b Brooklyn, NY, Nov 1, 27; m 54; c 2. *Educ:* Georgetown Univ, BS, 46, MS, 48, PhD(biochem), 56. *Prof Exp:* Lab instr chem, Georgetown Univ, 46-48; biochemist, Div Nutrit, US Food & Drug Admin, Washington, DC, 48-50 & 54-60 & Chem Sect, Hazleton Labs, Inc, 60-61. *Mem:* AAAS; Soc Res Adminrs. *Res:* Biochemistry and microbiology of nutritionally important substances, especially vitamins, amino acids and proteins; stability of vitamins; clinical chemistry; food additives. *Mailing Add:* 1732 Ladd St Silver Spring MD 20902-3523. *Fax:* 301-571-1892

SCHIAGER, KEITH JEROME, ENVIRONMENTAL HEALTH, HEALTH PHYSICS. *Current Pos:* RETIRED. *Personal Data:* b Hot Springs, SDak, Mar 29, 30; m 75, Janet Albrecht; c 4. *Educ:* Colo Agr & Mech Col, BS, 56; Univ Mich, MPH, 62, PhD(environ health), 64. *Prof Exp:* Health physicist, Argonne Nat Lab, 57-61; assoc prof radiation biol, Colo State Univ, 64-73; alt group leader environ studies, Los Alamos Sci Lab, 73-75; prof health physics, Univ Pittsburgh, 75-78; dir, Radiol Health, Univ Utah, 82-94. *Concurrent Pos:* Pres, Am Acad Health Physics, 90. *Mem:* Am Nuclear Soc; Sigma Xi; Health Physics Soc (pres-elect, 91). *Res:* Radiological health; environmental radiation; inhalation exposure from radon progeny; radiation risk assessment. *Mailing Add:* 690 E 4149 S Salt Lake City UT 84107

SCHIAVELLI, MELVYN DAVID, PHYSICAL ORGANIC CHEMISTRY. *Current Pos:* from asst prof to assoc prof, Col William & Mary, 68-80, chmn dept, 78-84, dean fac arts & sci, 84-86, provost, 86-93, PROF CHEM, COL WILLIAM & MARY, 80- *Personal Data:* b Chicago, Ill, Aug 8, 42; m 66; c 2. *Educ:* DePaul Univ, BS, 64; Univ Calif, Berkeley, PhD(chem), 68. *Prof Exp:* Res assoc chem, Mich State Univ, 67-68. *Concurrent Pos:* Hon res fel, Univ Aberdeen, Scotland, 83- *Mem:* Am Chem Soc; Royal Soc Chem. *Res:* Secondary isotope effects; acid-catalysis; vinyl cations. *Mailing Add:* Provost/Univ Del 129 Hullihen Hall Newark DE 19716. *E-Mail:* mdschi@chem1.chem.wm.edu

SCHICK, JEROME DAVID, CHEMISTRY, PHYSICS. *Current Pos:* SR ENGR SEMICONDUCTOR DEVICES, IBM CORP, HOPEWELL JUNCTION, 69- *Personal Data:* b Pontiac, Mich, Jan 23, 38; m 66; c Roderic D & Darin W. *Educ:* Wheaton Col, BS, 60; Wayne State Univ, MS, 65, PhD(phys chem), 68. *Prof Exp:* Res chemist, Henry Ford Hosp, Detroit, Mich, 60-63; proj chemist, Bendix Res Labs, 66-68; res chemist, Air Force Avionics Lab, Wright-Patterson AFB, 68-69. *Mem:* Am Chem Soc; Electrochem Soc; Creation Res Soc; Microbeam Anal Soc. *Res:* Semiconductor devices and materials; electron spectroscopy; scanning electron microscopy; auger spectrometry; integrated circuits processing and failure studies; electron beam induced current; transistor and junction charaterization. *Mailing Add:* 26 Kuchler Dr Lagrangeville NY 12540. *Fax:* 914-223-7393

SCHICK, KENNETH LEONARD, SOLID STATE PHYSICS, BIOPHYSICS. *Current Pos:* from asst prof to assoc prof, 59-74, chmn dept, 71-77, PROF PHYSICS, UNION COL, NY, 74- *Personal Data:* b New York, NY, Feb 20, 30; m 57; c 3. *Educ:* Columbia Univ, BA, 51; Rutgers Univ,

PhD(physics), 59. *Prof Exp:* Physicist, US Naval Air Missile Test Ctr, 51-52. *Concurrent Pos:* Vis res prof, State Univ Leiden, 65-66 & 72-73; NATO & NSF sr fel, 67; fel, Weizmann Inst, Israel, 79-80. *Mem:* Am Asn Physics Teachers. *Res:* Magnetic resonance; membrane structure in living systems; dynamic light scattering. *Mailing Add:* Dept Physics Union Col 807 Union St Schenectady NY 12308-3103

SCHICK, LEE HENRY, THEORETICAL NUCLEAR PHYSICS. *Current Pos:* assoc prof, 70-74, PROF PHYSICS, UNIV WYO, 74- *Personal Data:* b Philadelphia, Pa, Nov 23, 35; m 61; c 3. *Educ:* Univ Pa, BS, 56; Univ Colo, MA, 58, PhD(theoret nuclear physics), 61. *Prof Exp:* Lectr math, Univ Birmingham, 61-63; res assoc, Univ Minn, 63-65; asst prof, Univ Southern Calif, 65-70. *Concurrent Pos:* Assoc dean, Col Arts & Sci, 83-91; chair, Dept Physics & Astron, Univ Wyo, 91-97. *Mem:* Am Phys Soc; Am Asn Phys Teachers. *Res:* Application of information-theory and scattering theory to geophysical and quantum mechanical problems. *Mailing Add:* Dept Physics & Astron Phys Sci Bldg Rm 204 Univ Wyo Laramie WY 82070. *Fax:* 307-766-2652

SCHICK, LLOYD ALAN, BIOCHEMISTRY, CHEMISTRY. *Current Pos:* PEHRING DIAGNOST INC, 95- *Personal Data:* b Bluffton, Ohio, Mar 7, 45; m 75; c Rachel & Daniel. *Educ:* Ohio Northern Univ, BA, 66; Purdue Univ, MS, 68; Univ Notre Dame, PhD(biochem), 74. *Prof Exp:* Anal chemist, Ind State Chemist's Lab, 66-68; from asst res scientist to sr res scientist, Miles Labs, 68-83, staff scientist, Diag Div, 83-92; group leader, Reagent Res & Develop, Abaxis, Inc, 92-95. *Concurrent Pos:* Res Award, Ohio Heart Asn, 65-66. *Mem:* Am Chem Soc; Am Asn Clin Chem. *Res:* Medical diagnostics; immunoassay; protein purification techniques; thyroid diagnostics; enzymology; hemolytic and fibrinolytic pathways; dry-phase chemistries; reagent-instrument systems. *Mailing Add:* 179 Granada Dr Mountainview CA 94040. *Fax:* 408-734-2874

SCHICK, MARTIN J, COLLOID CHEMISTRY. *Current Pos:* CONSULT, 83- *Personal Data:* b Prague, Czech, Oct 20, 18; nat US; div; c 2. *Educ:* Carnegie Inst Technol, BS, 42; Polytech Inst Brooklyn, PhD(chem), 48. *Honors & Awards:* Cert Merit, Div Colloid & Surfactant Chem, Am Chem Soc, 84; Merit Award, Am Oil Chemist Soc, 88. *Prof Exp:* Res chemist, Shell Develop Co, 42-45 & 48-58; sr res assoc, Res & Develop Ctr, Lever Bros Co, 58-66; prin scientist, Cent Res Lab, Interchem Corp, Clifton, 66-69; res mgr, Surfactant & Org Chem Lab, Diamond Shamrock Corp, 69-78, sr scientist, process chem div, 78-83. *Concurrent Pos:* Adj prof, Lehigh Univ, 84. *Mem:* Am Chem Soc; Fiber Soc; Am Oil Chemists Soc. *Res:* Surface and polymer chemistry; nonionic surfactants; surfactant synthesis; friction and lubrication of synthetic fibers. *Mailing Add:* 12 W 72nd St New York NY 10023-4163

SCHICK, MICHAEL, STATISTICAL MECHANICS, SURFACE PHYSICS. *Current Pos:* from asst prof to assoc prof, 69-78, PROF PHYSICS, UNIV WASH, 78- *Personal Data:* b Philadelphia, Pa, Mar 17, 39; m 81. *Educ:* Tufts Univ, BA & BS, 61; Stanford Univ, MS, 64 & PhD(physics), 67. *Prof Exp:* Postdoctoral fel, Case Western Res Univ, 67-69. *Concurrent Pos:* Vis prof, Lab Nat Technol, 77-78, Cen Saclay, 84-85 & 89, Nordita, 85, Univ Oslo, 90, Univ Munich, 92 & Univ Ax-Marseille, 94. *Mem:* Fel Am Phys Soc. *Res:* Application of renormalization group to adsorbed systems; classification of order-disorder transitions in adsorbed systems; exact renormalization group; solution of two-dimensionalising model; theories of multilayer growth and wetting; theory of microemulsions; polymer self-assembly. *Mailing Add:* Dept Physics Univ Wash Box 351560 Seattle WA 98195-1560. *E-Mail:* schick@phys.washington.edu

SCHICK, PAUL KENNETH, HEMATOLOGY, ONCOLOGY. *Current Pos:* assoc prof, 79-82, PROF MED, SCH MED, TEMPLE UNIV, 82- *Personal Data:* b Czech, Oct 12, 32; US citizen; m 62; c 2. *Educ:* Boston Univ, MD, 61. *Prof Exp:* Intern & resident med, Kings County Hosp, Brooklyn, NY, 61-63; resident med, New York Med Col, 63-65; pvt pract, 65-69; hemat trainee, Montefiore Hosp, Bronx, 69-71; asst prof, Med Col Pa, 71-76, assoc prof med, 76-79, assoc prof biochem, 79- *Mem:* Int Soc Thrombosis & Hemostasis; fel Am Col Physicians; Am Soc Hemat; Sigma Xi; Am Fedn Clin Res; Am Soc Physiol. *Res:* Understanding the structure and function of platelet membranes in order to define the role of platelets in hemostasis and to develop anti-platelet drugs for the prevention of thrombosis; investigation of megakaryocyte maturation and biochemistry. *Mailing Add:* Cardeza Found Hematol Res Jefferson Med Col Thomas Jefferson Univ 1015 Walnut St Philadelphia PA 19107-5099

SCHICKEDANTZ, PAUL DAVID, ORGANIC CHEMISTRY. *Current Pos:* SR RES CHEMIST, LORILLARD TOBACCO CO, DIV LOEWS INC, 67- *Personal Data:* b Columbus, Ohio, Aug 20, 31; m 57; c 4. *Educ:* Oberlin Col, AB, 53; Ohio State Univ, PhD(org chem), 59. *Prof Exp:* Res chemist, Am Cyanamid Co, 59-61; res chemist, Consumer Prod Div, Union Carbide Co, WVa, 61-63 & Chem & Plastics Div, 63-67. *Mem:* Am Chem Soc; Sigma Xi. *Res:* Synthesis and properties of bridgehead nitrogen compounds; stain repellant and wash and wear textile finishes; synthesis of S-triazines, insect repellents, and condensation polymers; liquid chromatographic analysis of polycyclic aromatic hydrocarbons in tobacco smoke; analysis of urinary drug metabolites; cigarette flavor chemistry; analytical biochemistry. *Mailing Add:* 2809 Watauga Dr Greensboro NC 27408-5228

SCHIDLOW, DANIEL, PEDIATRICS, MEDICAL ADMINISTRATION. *Current Pos:* fel pediat pulmonary med, St Christopher's Hosp, Temple Univ, 76-78, dir fel training & educ proj Sect Pediat Pulmonol, 79-91, assoc dir, Pediat Pulmonary & Cystic Fibrosis Ctr, 81-83, med dir, Dept Ther, 82-88, proj dir, Philadelphia Pediat Pulmonary Ctr, 83-86, DIR, CYSTIC FIBROSIS CTR, ST CHRISTOPHER'S HOSP CHILDREN, SCH MED, TEMPLE UNIV, 83-, CHIEF SECT PEDIAT PULMONOL, 83-; PROF PEDIAT, SCH MED, TEMPLE UNIV, 90- *Personal Data:* b Santiago, Chile, Oct 23, 47; m, Sally Rosen; c David, Michael & Jessica. *Educ:* Univ Chile, dipl, 72; Am Bd Pediat, dipl. *Prof Exp:* Rotating intern, Univ Chile Hosp, Sch Med, Univ Chile, 71-72, resident internal med & instr phys diag, 72-73; resident & emergency rm physician pediat, E G Cortes Hosp Children, Univ Chile, 73-74; resident pediat, Lebanon Hosp Ctr, Albert Einstein Col Med, NY, 74-76; from asst prof to assoc prof pediat, Sch Med, Temple Univ, 78-90. *Concurrent Pos:* Counr, Div Rehab, Pa Dept Health, 83-, Nat Ctr Youth Disabilities, 87-; mem promotions comt, Dept Pediat, Sch Med, Temple Univ, 86-; attend staff, N Div, Albert Einstein Med Ctr, 87-; chair, capital campaign comt, Dept Pediat, St Christopher's Hosp Children, 87, mem exec comt med staff, 88-; mem, med adv coun, Cystic Fibrosis Found, Bethesda, 87-, trustee, 90-, med dir home care svcs, 91-; consult staff, Temple Univ Hosp, 88-; mem org comt, NAm Cystic Fibrosis Conf, 90-93, co-chmn, 92- *Mem:* Fel Am Acad Pediat; fel Am Col Chest Physicians; AAAS; Am Thoracic Soc; Am Fedn Clin Res; hon mem Chilean Pediat Soc. *Mailing Add:* Pediat Pulmonary & Cystic Fibrosis Ctr St Christopher's Hosp Children Erie Ave at Front St Philadelphia PA 19134

SCHIEBLER, GEROLD LUDWIG, MEDICINE, PEDIATRIC CARDIOLOGY. *Current Pos:* From asst prof to prof pediat, 60-92, chmn, Dept Pediat Cardiol, 68-85, ASSOC VPRES, HEALTH AFFAIRS EXTERNAL RELS, UNIV FLA, 85-, DISTINGUISHED SERV PROF, DIV PEDIAT CARDIOL, COL MED, 92- *Personal Data:* b Hamburg, Pa, June 20, 28; m 54; c 6. *Educ:* Franklin & Marshall Col, BS, 50; Harvard Med Sch, MD, 54. *Honors & Awards:* William Wiley Jones Lectr, Children's Hosp, Denver, 77; Claud Batson Mem Lectr, Univ Miss, 84; George Armstrong Award, Nat Ambulatory Pediat Asn, 85; Nat Award, Am Acad Pediat, 89; Award of Merit, AMA, 91, Dr Benjamin Rush Award, 93; Abraham Jacobs Award, Am Acad Pediat & AMA, 93. *Concurrent Pos:* Teaching fel med, Harvard Med Sch, 55-56; med fel pediat, Univ Minn Hosp, 56-57; med fel specialist, Med Ctr, Univ Minn, 57-58, med fel, Mayo Clin & Found, 59-60; Nat Heart Inst res fel, 59-60; mem study sect, Coun Rheumatic Fever & Congenital Heart Dis, Am Heart Asn, 61-64; dir, Cardiovasc Lab, Shands Teaching Hosp, 68-73; asst med dir, Children's Med Serv, 75-83, med dir, 83- *Mem:* Inst Med-Nat Acad Sci; Am Acad Pediat; Am Col Cardiol; Am Heart Asn (vpres, 71-72, pres-elect, 72-73, pres, 73-74); AAAS; NY Acad Sci; AMA; emer mem Soc Pediat Res; Am Pediat Soc. *Res:* Heart disease in infants and children; cardiovascular physiology. *Mailing Add:* Off Assoc Vpres Health Affairs External Rel PO Box 100014 J Hills Millers Health Ctr Gainesville FL 32610-0014. *Fax:* 352-846-0242

SCHIEBOUT, JUDITH ANN, VERTEBRATE PALEONTOLOGY, PALEOECOLOGY. *Current Pos:* asst prof, 76-79, ADJ ASSOC PROF GEOL, LA STATE UNIV, 79-, ASSOC CUR, MUS NATURAL SCI, 93- *Personal Data:* b Tampa, Fla, Oct 16, 46. *Educ:* Univ Tex, Austin, BA, 68, MA, 70, PhD(geol), 73. *Prof Exp:* Lectr, San Diego State Univ, 74-76. *Mem:* Soc Vertebrate Paleont; Geol Soc Am; Sigma Xi; Paleont Soc; Soc Econ Paleontologists & Mineralogists. *Res:* Analysis of early Tertiary mammal distribution and paleogeography; relationship between vertebrate taphonomy and fluvial sedimentation; miocene mammals of southern North America. *Mailing Add:* Mus Natural Sci La State Univ Baton Rouge LA 70803. *Fax:* 504-388-2302; *E-Mail:* naschi@lsuvm.sncc.lsu.edu

SCHIEFERSTEIN, ROBERT HAROLD, PLANT PHYSIOLOGY, AGRONOMY. *Current Pos:* RETIRED. *Personal Data:* b Klamath Falls, Ore, May 18, 31; m 50, Joyce Gnos; c Bradley G, Raylene (Pak), Terry (Wilfley), Karen (Schieferstein) & Craig R. *Educ:* Ore State Univ, BS, 54; Iowa State Univ, MS, 55, PhD(plant physiol), 57. *Prof Exp:* Asst plant physiol, Iowa State Univ, 54-56, res assoc, 56-57; tech rep agr chem, Chipman Chem Co, Inc, 57-61, tech mgr, 61-62; plant physiologist, Shell Develop Co, 62-65, supvr herbicides res, 65-67, chief plant physiologist, 67-68, dept head plant physiol, 68-70, supvr pesticide develop, 71, res & develop proj mgr agron prods, 71-72, prod rep, 72-73, tech support rep, 73-77, staff tech serv rep, Shell Chem Co, 77-85, field develop & tech serv rep & coordr, Field Res Resources, Shell Develop Co, 85-89. *Concurrent Pos:* Consult, 89- *Mem:* Am Soc Plant Physiol; fel Weed Sci Soc Am. *Res:* Herbicides; defoliants; plant growth regulators; plant surface wax and cuticle; research and development administration with agricultural chemicals; weed science; contaminated soils remediation. *Mailing Add:* PO Box 1291 Twain Harte CA 95383. *E-Mail:* schief@mlode.com

SCHIERMAN, LOUIS W, IMMUNOGENETICS. *Current Pos:* PROF, UNIV GA, 77- *Personal Data:* b Carlyle, Ill, Feb 16, 26; m 57; c 2. *Educ:* Univ Ill, BS, 51; Iowa State Univ, MS, 61, PhD(genetics, immunol), 62. *Prof Exp:* Res assoc immunogenetics, Iowa State Univ, 62-64, asst prof, 64-65; res assoc, Mt Sinai Hosp, New York, 65-66, asst prof, Mt Sinai Sch Med, 66-68; assoc prof path, New York Med Col, 68-77. *Mem:* AAAS; Genetics Soc Am; Am Asn Immunol. *Res:* Relationships of blood groups to histocompatibility; tumor immunology; genetic control of immune responses. *Mailing Add:* 2940 La Vista Ct Decatur GA 30033-1100

SCHIESSER, ROBERT H, PHYSICAL CHEMISTRY, SURFACE CHEMISTRY. *Current Pos:* RES SCIENTIST, SCOTT PAPER CO, 76- *Personal Data:* b Niagara Falls, NY, Jan 12, 37; m 65; c 3. *Educ:* Clarkson Tech, BChE, 58, MChE, 60; Lehigh Univ, PhD(phys chem), 66. *Prof Exp:* Sr res chemist, Rohm & Haas Co, 65-68; sr res chemist, Betz Labs, Inc, 68-76. *Mem:* Am Chem Soc; Tech Asn Pulp & Paper Indust. *Res:* Adsorption at solid-liquid interface; polymer solution properties; stability of lyophobic colloids; structure and properties of polyelectrolytes. *Mailing Add:* 1834 Mare Rd Warrington PA 18976

SCHIESSER, W(ILLIAM) E(DWARD), CHEMICAL ENGINEERING. *Current Pos:* From asst prof to prof, 60-76, MCCANN PROF CHEM ENG, LEHIGH UNIV, 76-, MGR USER SERV, COMPUT CTR, 69- *Personal Data:* b Willow Grove, Pa, Jan 9, 34; m 58; c 2. *Educ:* Lehigh Univ, BS, 55; Princeton Univ, MA, 58, PhD(chem eng), 60. *Concurrent Pos:* Consult, Indust & Govt; mem, Am Automatic Control Coun. *Mem:* Am Inst Chem Engrs; Inst Elec & Electronics Engrs. *Res:* Applied mathematics; systems analysis. *Mailing Add:* Iacocca Hall Rm D307 Lehigh Univ 111 Research Dr Bethlehem PA 18015-4791

SCHIESSL, H(ENRY) W(ILLIAM), INORGANIC CHEMISTRY, CHEMICAL ENGINEERING. *Current Pos:* Process design engr, 50-56, asst to dir res & develop, 56-61, res assoc, 64-70, RES MGR, OLIN CORP, 70- *Personal Data:* b Ingolstadt, Ger, Dec 1, 24; nat US. *Educ:* Cornell Univ, BChE, 50; Univ Heidelberg, DSc, 64. *Concurrent Pos:* Mem fac, Univ New Haven. *Mem:* Am Chem Soc; Nat Asn Corrosion Engrs; Sigma Xi. *Res:* Inorganic chemistry; heavy chemicals; statistical analysis of experimental data; thermochemistry; kinetics; hydrazine chemistry. *Mailing Add:* PO Box 477 Northford CT 06472-1446

SCHIEVE, WILLIAM, THEORETICAL PHYSICS, STATISTICAL MECHANICS. *Current Pos:* ASSOC PROF PHYSICS, UNIV TEX, AUSTIN, 67- *Personal Data:* b Portland, Ore, Apr 28, 29; m 52; c 2. *Educ:* Reed Col, AB, 51; Lehigh Univ, MS, 57, PhD(physics), 59. *Honors & Awards:* Silver Medal, US Naval Radiol Defense Lab, 64. *Prof Exp:* Asst physics, Lehigh Univ, 51-57; res fel, Bartol Res Found, 57-60; res physicist, US Naval Radiol Defense Lab, 61-67; actg dir statist mech & thermodyn, 69-77. *Concurrent Pos:* Study fel with Prof Prigogine, Free Univ Brussels, 64-65. *Mem:* Am Phys Soc. *Res:* Thermal conductivity of insulating crystals; statistical mechanics of phonons; fundamental theory of statistical mechanics; perturbation theory; reversibility; molecular dynamics. *Mailing Add:* 5914 Fairlane Dr Austin TX 78757

SCHIEWETZ, D(ON) B(OYD), TECHNOLOGY LICENSING & TRANSFER. *Current Pos:* RETIRED. *Personal Data:* b Dayton, Ohio, Nov 15, 27; div; c Mark. *Educ:* Northwestern Univ, BS, 50; Univ Cincinnati, MS, 52, PhD(chem eng), 54. *Prof Exp:* Res engr, E I du Pont de Nemours & Co, Inc, 54-59, tech supvr, 59-63, area supvr, 63-65, plant supt, 66-70, tech supt, 70-73, mfg supt, 73-75, capacity mgr, 75-76, mfg & res mgr, 76-86, technol sales mgr, Polymer Prod Dept, 86-90, opers mgr, Chem Dept, 90-92; pres opers, Enpac Ltd, 92-94. *Mem:* Am Inst Chem Engrs; Sigma Xi. *Res:* Polymer science and processing technology; chemical kinetics; process economics; venture analysis. *Mailing Add:* Five West Ct Beacon Hill Wilmington DE 19810

SCHIFERL, DAVID, HIGH PRESSURE PHYSICS, SOLID STATE PHYSICS. *Current Pos:* STAFF SCIENTIST, UNIV CALIF, LOS ALAMOS SCI LAB, 77- *Personal Data:* US citizen. *Educ:* Univ Chicago, BS, 66, MS, 69, PhD(physics), 75. *Prof Exp:* Res physicist, Dept Geophys Sci, Univ Chicago, 74-75, x-ray consult, 77; vis scientist, Max Planck Inst Solid Body Res, Stuttgart, WGer, 75-77. *Concurrent Pos:* NATO fel, Max Planck Inst Solid Body Res, Stuttgart, 75-76 & German Acad Exchange Serv, 76-77. *Res:* Experimental high pressure physics primarily with diamond-anvil cells; theoretical and experimental studies on crystal structure stability; materials, non-destructive testing. *Mailing Add:* 459 Grand Canyon Dr Los Alamos NM 87544. *Fax:* 505-665-4311

SCHIFF, ANSHEL J, EARTHQUAKE ENGINEERING. *Current Pos:* CONSULT & PROF CIVIL ENGR, STANFORD UNIV, STANFORD, CA, 85- *Personal Data:* b Chicago, Ill, Sept 24, 36. *Educ:* Purdue Univ, Lafayette, BSME, 58, MSESc, 61, PhD(eng sci), 67. *Prof Exp:* Res asst aeronaut, astronaut & eng sci, Purdue Univ, WLafayette, 59-67, from asst prof to prof mech eng, 66-85. *Concurrent Pos:* Prin, Precision Measurement Instruments, 83-; instr, Indust Courses Instrumentation & Measurements, 74- *Mem:* Instrument Soc Am; Am Soc Eng Educ; Am Soc Mech Engrs; Am Soc Civil Engrs; Earthquake Eng Res Inst. *Res:* Design of instumentation for structural dynamics; experimental and analytical studies of dynamic systems; system identification; evaluation of the impact of natural disasters on community services. *Mailing Add:* Dept Civil Eng Stanford Univ Stanford CA 94305

SCHIFF, ERIC ALLAN, AMORPHOUS SEMICONDUCTORS, PHOTOCONDUCTIVITY. *Current Pos:* from asst prof to assoc prof, 81-95, PROF, DEPT PHYSICS, SYRACUSE UNIV, 95- *Personal Data:* b Los Angeles, Calif, Aug 29, 50; m 73, Nancy R Mudrick; c Nathan & Evan. *Educ:* Calif Inst Technol, BS, 71; Cornell Univ, PhD(physics), 79. *Prof Exp:* Res assoc, James Franck Inst, Univ Chicago, 78-81. *Concurrent Pos:* Vis prof, Brown Univ, 88-89; vis scientist, Xerox Palo Alto Res Ctr, 95. *Mem:* Am Phys Soc; Mat Res Soc; Sigma Xi. *Res:* Electrical and optical properties of amorphous silicon; amorphous silicon based solar cells. *Mailing Add:* Dept Physics Syracuse Univ Syracuse NY 13244-1130. *Fax:* 315-443-9103; *E-Mail:* easchiff@syr.edu

SCHIFF, GILBERT MARTIN, INFECTIOUS DISEASES, VIROLOGY. *Current Pos:* pres, 84-95, DIR, GAMBLE PROG, INFECTIOUS DIS DIV, JAMES N GAMBLE INST MED RES, 95- *Personal Data:* b Cincinnati, Ohio, Oct 21, 31; m 55; c 2. *Educ:* Univ Cincinnati, BS, 53, MD, 57. *Prof Exp:* Intern, Univ Hosp, Iowa City, 57-58, resident internal med, 58-59; med officer, Lab Br, Commun Dis Ctr, Ga, 59-61; head, Tissue Cult Invest Unit, Sect Virol, Perinatal Res Br, Nat Inst Neurol Dis & Blindness, 61-64; dir, Clin Virol Lab, Col Med, Univ Cincinnati, 64-78, asst prof med & microbiol, 64-67, assoc prof med, 67-71, asst prof microbiol, 67-71, prof med, 71- *Concurrent Pos:* Attend physician, Dept Med, Emory Univ, Atlanta, Ga, 59-61; prin investr, USPHS grant, 64-67 & Nat Found res grant, 65-67; consult, Comt Maternal Health, Ohio State Med Asn, 64-70, Hamilton Co Neuromuscular Diag Clin, 66 & 75, Contract Immunization Status in US, 75-77, Vet Admin Comt Viral Hepatitis Among Dent Personnel; Nat Inst Child Health & Human Develop career res develop award, 70-74; dir, Christ Hosp Inst Med Res, Cincinnati, Ohio, 74-83 & Comt Cancer Prog, 79-, human res, 80-, infection control, 81- & chairperson, Libr Comt, 74-; mem, NIH Study Sect, adv comt & rev comt; chairperson, Animal Care Comt, James N Gamble Inst Med Res, 74-; mem comt, Rubella Immunization, Ohio Dept Health, Rubella Control, Cincinnati Dept Health, Surgeon's Gen Adv Comt, Immunization Pract, 71-75, Subcomt Antimicrobial Agents, US Pharmacopeia, 77-80; mem, Univ Liaison Comt, Christ Hosp, 82-, res comt bd trustees, Children's Hosp Med Ctr, 85-, Hoxworth Community Adv Bd, Hoxworth Blood Ctr, 91-; Comt Animal Care, Univ Cincinnati Col Med, 67-77, human res, 75-78, continuing educ, 77-; chmn, Search Comt & dir radiother, Christ Hosp, 80-82. *Mem:* AAAS; Am Soc Microbiol; Sigma Xi; Am Fedn Clin Res (secy-treas, 67-70); Am Pub Health Asn; Sci Res Soc Am; Cent Soc Clin Res (secy-treas, 77-81, vpres, 83, pres, 84); Infectious Dis Soc Am; Am Soc Clin Invest; fel Am Col Physicians. *Res:* Clinical virology. *Mailing Add:* Childrens Hosp Med Ctr 3333 Burnet Ave CH-1 Cincinnati OH 45229-0339

SCHIFF, HAROLD IRVIN, PHYSICAL CHEMISTRY, ATMOSPHERIC CHEMISTRY. *Current Pos:* prof & chmn, Dept Chem & dir nat sci, 64-66, dean sci, 66-72, PROF CHEM, YORK UNIV, 72-, UNIV PROF, 80-, EMER UNIV PROF & DIR, CAN INST RES ATMOSPHERIC CHEM; PRES, UNISEARCH ASSOCS, INC. *Personal Data:* b Kitchener, Ont, June 24, 23; m 48, Daphne; c Michael & Sherry. *Educ:* Univ Toronto, BA, 45, MA, 46, PhD(chem), 48. *Prof Exp:* Asst chem, Univ Toronto, 45-48; fel, Nat Res Coun Can, 48-50; from asst prof to prof, McGill Univ, 50-65, dir, Upper Atmosphere Chem Group, 59-65. *Concurrent Pos:* Nuffield fel, Cambridge Univ, 59-60; Eskine prof, Univ Canterbury, NZ, 73-74; reporter, Working Group VII-Lab Data, Int Asn Geomagnetism & Aeronomy; mem, Comt Stratospheric Pollution, Govt Can; mem bd dirs, Scintrex, Ltd; chmn panel, Atmospheric Chem & Transp, US Acad Sci, 78-80; adv panel, Fed Aviation Admin High Altitude Pollution Prog; pres, Unisearch Assoc, Inc; titular mem, Atmospheric Chem Comm, Int Union Pure & Appl Chem, 85-90. *Mem:* Fel Chem Inst Can; fel Royal Soc Can; Am Geophys Union. *Res:* Mass spectrometry; chemical kinetics; atomic physics; upper and lower atmosphere; excitation processes; atmospheric measurements; acid deposition; photo oxidation; instrument development; collisions. *Mailing Add:* Dept Chem York Univ 4700 Keele St Downsview ON M3J 1P6 Can

SCHIFF, HARRY, THEORETICAL PHYSICS. *Current Pos:* RETIRED. *Personal Data:* b Boryslaw, Poland, May 17, 22; Can citizen; m 52, Sara Adelstein; c Linda Hanna. *Educ:* McGill Univ, BSc, 49, MSc, 50, PhD(physics), 53. *Prof Exp:* Lectr, Univ Alta, 53-54, from asst prof to prof physics, 54-87, chmn dept, 64-67, dir, Theoret Phys Inst, 80-83. *Mem:* Am Phys Soc; Can Asn Physicists. *Res:* Unitary field theories, particularly modified Maxwell fields with application to elementary particle structure; solitons. *Mailing Add:* 13004 66th Ave Edmonton AB T6H 1Y7 Can. *E-Mail:* hschiff@euclid.phys.ualberta.ca

SCHIFF, JEROME A, plant physiology; deceased, see previous edition for last biography

SCHIFF, JOEL D, MUSCLE PHYSIOLOGY, NEUROPHYSIOLOGY. *Current Pos:* asst prof, 73-79, ASSOC PROF PHYSIOL, NEW YORK UNIV, 79- *Personal Data:* b New York, NY, July 17, 43; m 68; c 2. *Educ:* Columbia Univ, AB, 64, MA, 65, PhD(biophys), 72. *Prof Exp:* Res Assoc physiol, Naval Med Res Inst, 72-73. *Mem:* Sigma Xi; Am Physiol Soc; AAAS; Am Inst Biol Sci; NY Acad Sci. *Res:* Mechanisms that regulate contraction of smooth muscle organs in mammals, including the pharmacological-physiological regulation and intracellular mechanisms involved. *Mailing Add:* Dept Basic Sci NYU Dent Ctr 345 E 24th St New York NY 10010-9401

SCHIFF, LEON, INTERNAL MEDICINE. *Current Pos:* Asst bact, 22-23, asst med, 25-26, from instr to assoc prof, 26-55, prof clin med, 55-58, prof med, 58-70, EMER PROF MED, COL MED, UNIV CINCINNATI, 70- *Personal Data:* b Riga, Latvia, May 1, 01; nat US; m 25; c 3. *Educ:* Univ Cincinnati, BS, 22, MD, 24, MS, 27, PhD(med), 29. *Honors & Awards:* Friedenwald Medal, Am Gastroenterol Asn, 73; Nat Comn Digestive Dis Award, 77; Leon Schiff Ann lectr, Univ Cincinnati, 81; Distinguished Serv Award, Am Asn Study Liver Dis, 81; Doris Faircloth Averbach Award, 85. *Concurrent Pos:* Prof med, Sch Med, Univ Miami, 70-72, clin prof, 73-; attend physician, Med Serv, Cincinnati Gen Hosp; consult, US Vet Hosp. *Mem:* Am Soc Clin Invest; Am Gastroenterol Asn; master Am Col Physicians; Am Asn Study Liver Dis; Int Asn Study Liver Dis; Asn Francaise pour l'etude de Foie. *Res:* Diseases of the digestive tract; liver disease and jaundice; clinical research. *Mailing Add:* Dept Med R760 Sch Med Univ Miami 1600 NW Tenth Ave Miami FL 33136-1015

SCHIFF, LEONARD NORMAN, COMMUNICATIONS ENGINEERING. *Current Pos:* DIR COMMUN RES LAB, DAVID SARNOFF RES CTR, 87- *Personal Data:* b New York, NY, Dec 7, 38; m 62; c 2. *Educ:* City Col New York, BEE, 60; NY Univ, MSc, 62; Polytech Inst Brooklyn, PhD(elec eng), 68. *Prof Exp:* Mem tech staff, Bell Tel Labs, Inc, 60-67; mem tech staff, RCA Labs, 67-78, head commun and res, 78-83, dir commun res lab, 83-87. *Mem:* Sr mem Inst Elec & Electronics Engrs; Sigma Xi. *Res:* Communications theory; systems science; satellite communications. *Mailing Add:* Qual Comm Inc 6455 Lusk Blvd Suite 310L San Diego CA 92121

SCHIFF, NATHAN MARK, MOLECULAR POPULATION GENETICS, MOLECULAR SYSTEMATICS. *Current Pos:* res entomologist, Agr Res Ctr, Bee Res Lab, 91-95, Albany, Calif, 95-97, FOREST ENTOMOLOGIST, STONEVILLE HARDWOOD LAB, USDA, 97- *Personal Data:* b New York, NY, Mar 26, 58. *Educ:* Univ Calif, BA, 79; Univ Ariz, MS, 83; Univ Ill, PhD(entom), 88. *Prof Exp:* Fel, Vanderbilt Univ, 88-91. *Mem:* AAAS; Entom Soc Am; Soc Study Evolution. *Res:* Population genetics of honey bees in the US using molecular markers; molecular systematics of the primative Hymenoptera; dietary self selection by lepidoptera larvae. *Mailing Add:* USDA Forest Serv Stoneville Hardwood Lab PO Box 227 Stoneville MS 38776

SCHIFF, PAUL L, JR, PHARMACOGNOSY, NATURAL PRODUCTS CHEMISTRY. *Current Pos:* assoc prof, 70-74, PROF PHARMACOG, SCH PHARM, UNIV PITTSBURGH, 74-, CHMN DEPT, 70- *Personal Data:* b Columbus, Ohio, Feb 3, 40; m 61; c 2. *Educ:* Ohio State Univ, BSc, 62, MSc, PhD(pharmacog). *Prof Exp:* Asst prof pharmacog, Col Pharm, Butler Univ, 67-69, Dept Pharmacog, Sch Pharm, Univ Miss, 70. *Mem:* Am Soc Pharmacog; Acad Pharmaceut Sci; Am Pharmaceut Asn; Am Chem Soc; Phytochem Soc Am; Sigma Xi. *Res:* Isolation and identification of plant metabolites with potential pharmacological activity and in particular with the isolation and identification of benzylisoquinoline-derived alkaloids. *Mailing Add:* 1103 Salk Hall Univ Pittsburgh Sch Pharm Pittsburgh PA 15260-0001

SCHIFF, SIDNEY, ORGANIC CHEMISTRY. *Current Pos:* AT CITGO PETROL CORP, 86- *Personal Data:* b Chicago, Ill, June 9, 29; m 54; c 2. *Educ:* Ill Inst Technol, BS, 51; Ohio State Univ, MS, 54, PhD(chem), 58. *Prof Exp:* Res chemist, 58-77; supvr, Phillips Petrol Co, 77-86. *Mem:* Soc Automotive Engrs; Am Chem Soc; Soc Tribologists & Lubrication Engrs. *Res:* Lubricating oil additives; fuels and lubricants; synthetic lubricants; catalytic cracking catalysts; metals passivation. *Mailing Add:* 2401 Cherokee Hills Circle Bartlesville OK 74006-4738

SCHIFF, STEFAN OTTO, RADIATION BIOLOGY. *Current Pos:* asst prof, 64-71, assoc prof, 71-77, chmn, Dept Biol Sci, 77-87, PROF ZOOL, GEORGE WASHINGTON UNIV, 77-, CHMN GRAD PROG GENETICS, 71- *Personal Data:* b Braunschweig, Ger, July 22, 30; US citizen; wid; c 2. *Educ:* Roanoke Col, BS, 52; Univ Tenn, PhD(radiation biol), 64. *Prof Exp:* Instr zool, Univ Tenn, 63-64. *Mem:* Radiation Res Soc; Sigma Xi; AAAS. *Res:* Effects of microwave radiation on mammalian sensory structures. *Mailing Add:* Dept Biol Sci George Washington Univ 2034 H St NW Washington DC 20052-0001

SCHIFFER, JOHN PAUL, NUCLEAR PHYSICS. *Current Pos:* from asst physicist to assoc physicist, 56-65, from assoc dir to dir, Physics Div, 64-82, SR PHYSICIST, ARGONNE NAT LAB, 65-, ASSOC DIR, PHYSICS DIV, 82-; PROF PHYSICS, UNIV CHICAGO, 69- *Personal Data:* b Budapest, Hungary, Nov 22, 30; nat US; m 60, Marianne Tsuk; c Celia A & Peter E. *Educ:* Oberlin Col, BA, 51; Yale Univ, MS, 52, PhD(physics), 54. *Honors & Awards:* Tom W Bonner Prize, Am Phys Soc, 76; Wilbur Cross Medal, Yale Univ, 85. *Prof Exp:* Asst physics, Yale Univ, 51-54; res assoc, Rice Inst, 54-56. *Concurrent Pos:* Guggenheim fel, 59-60; vis assoc prof, Princeton Univ, 64; vis prof, Univ Rochester, 67-68 & Tech Univ Munich, 73-74; ed, Comments on Nuclear & Particle Physics, 71-75 & Physics Letters, 78-; assoc ed, Revs Modern Physics, 72-77; sr US scientist award, Alexander von Humboldt Found, 73-74; mem, Panel Future Nuclear Sci, Nat Acad Sci-Nat Res Coun, 75-76; mem, Nuclear Sci Adv Comt, Dept Energy, NSF, 80-85, chmn, 83-85. *Mem:* Nat Acad Sci; fel Am Phys Soc; fel AAAS. *Res:* Experimental nuclear physics; nuclear reactions and structure; heavy ion reactions, pion reactions in nuclei; crystallization of cold plasmas. *Mailing Add:* Argonne Nat Lab 9700 S Argonne IL 60439. *Fax:* 630-252-2864; *E-Mail:* schiffer@anlphy.gov

SCHIFFER, MARIANNE TSUK, X-RAY CRYSTALLOGRAPHY. *Current Pos:* Res assoc biochem, Biol & Med Res Div, Argonne Nat Lab, 65-67, asst biochemist, 68-74, biophysicist, 74-87, SR BIOPHYSICIST, BIOL, ENVIRON & MED RES DIV, AGRONNE NAT LAB, 87- *Personal Data:* b Budapest, Hungary, June 28, 35; US citizen; m 60, John P; c 2. *Educ:* Petrik Lajos Chem Indust Tech Sch, Hungary, BS, 55; Smith Col, MA, 58; Columbia Univ, PhD(biochem), 65. *Concurrent Pos:* Vis scientist, Max Planck Inst Biochem, 73-74, Univ Tenn Med Ctr, Knoxville, 90-; lectr, Northwestern Univ, 82-90. *Mem:* Am Crystallog Asn; Am Asn Immunologists. *Res:* Determination of protein structure by x-ray with special emphasis on the structures of immunoglobulins and the photosynthetic reaction center diffraction; correlation of amino acid sequence, conformation and function of protein molecules. *Mailing Add:* Ctr Mech Biol Argonne Nat Lab Argonne IL 60439-4833. *E-Mail:* schiffer@anlcmb.bim.anl.gov

SCHIFFER, MENAHEM MAX, MATHEMATICAL ANALYSIS. *Current Pos:* chmn dept, 53-60, prof, 51-76, EMER PROF MATH, STANFORD UNIV, 76- *Personal Data:* b Berlin, Ger, Sept 24, 11; nat US; m 37; c 1. *Educ:* Hebrew Univ, Israel, MA, 34, PhD(math), 38. *Hon Degrees:* DS, Israel Inst Technol, 73. *Prof Exp:* Instr, Hebrew Univ, Israel, 34-38, sr asst, 38-43, lectr, 43-46, prof, 50-51; res lectr, Harvard Univ, 46-49; vis prof, Princeton Univ, 49-50. *Concurrent Pos:* Fulbright fel, 65-66. *Mem:* Nat Acad Sci; Am Math Soc; Am Acad Arts & Sci; foreign mem Finnish Acad Sci; Am Math Asn. *Res:* Theory of functions; partial differential equations; calculus of variations; applied mathematics. *Mailing Add:* 3748 Laguna Ave Palo Alto CA 94306

SCHIFFMACHER, E(DWARD) R(OBERT), ELECTRICAL ENGINEERING. *Current Pos:* CONSULT ENGR, 82- *Personal Data:* b Lawrence, NY, July 8, 24; m 56, Zetta Whitson; c Robert & Kim. *Educ:* Union Col, NY, BS, 45; Cornell Univ, MS, 52. *Prof Exp:* Instr elec eng, Union Col, NY, 46-47; instr, Cornell Univ, 48-52, res assoc, 52-57; electronic scientist, Nat Bur Standards, 57-60, supvry electronic engr, 60-65; supvry electronic engr, Environ Sci Serv Admin, Nat Oceanic & Atmpheric Admin, 65-70, supvry electronic engr, 70-80, electronic engr, 80-82. *Mem:* Am Astron Soc; Inst Elec & Electronics Engrs. *Res:* Ionospheric studies using radio astronomy techniques and several earth satellite experiments; solar radio astronomy; ground-based ionospheric sounding; geomagnetism. *Mailing Add:* 2155 Emerald Rd Boulder CO 80304-0909

SCHIFFMAN, GERALD, IMMUNOLOGY, BACTERIAL VACCINES. *Current Pos:* PROF MICROBIOL & IMMUNOL, HEALTH SCI CTR, STATE UNIV NY, 70- *Educ:* New York Univ, PhD(biochem), 54. *Mailing Add:* Dept Microbiol & Immunol State Univ NY Health Sci Ctr Brooklyn 450 Clarkson Ave PO Box 44 Brooklyn NY 11203-2098. *Fax:* 718-270-2656

SCHIFFMAN, LOUIS F, TECHNOLOGY TRANSFER, LICENSING. *Current Pos:* PRES & CONSULT, TECHNI RES ASSOCS, INC, WILLOW GROVE, 70- *Personal Data:* b Poland, July 15, 27; nat US; m 63, Mina R Hankin; c Howard & Laura. *Educ:* NY Univ, BChE, 48, MS, 52, PhD(phys chem), 55. *Prof Exp:* Res chem engr, Pa Grade Crude Oil Asn, 48-50; teaching fel chem, NY Univ, 50-54; res chemist, E I du Pont de Nemours & Co, Inc, 54-56 & Atlantic Refining Co, 56-59; res chemist, Amchem Prods Inc, 59-67, head, Corrosion Group, 67-70. *Concurrent Pos:* Publ & ed, Patent Licensing Gazette, World Technol & Guide to Available Technols. *Mem:* Am Chem Soc; fel Am Inst Chem; NY Acad Sci; Licensing Exec Soc; Sigma Xi. *Res:* Enhanced recovery, petroleum production; combustion; barrier separations; corrosion; surface treatment of metals; electroplating; industrial chemistry; radiochemistry; technology transfer. *Mailing Add:* Techni Res Assocs Inc PO Box T Willow Grove PA 19090-0922. *Fax:* 215-576-7924

SCHIFFMAN, ROBERT A, HIGH TEMPERATURE SCIENCE, MICROGRAVITY SCIENCE. *Current Pos:* PRES, RS RES INC, 90- *Personal Data:* b New York, NY, July 4, 45; m, Martine Benhayoun; c Isaac. *Educ:* Long Island Univ, BA, 68; NMex Inst Mining & Technol, MS, 73, PhD(chem metall), 78. *Prof Exp:* Metall consult, 69-79; res assoc, high temperature sci, Ames Labs, 79-81; res assoc fac, high temperature containerless sci, Yale Univ, 81-84; sr mat scientist, containerless mat sci, Midwest Res Inst, 84-87; dir res, Intersonics Inc, 87-90. *Concurrent Pos:* Pres, Robert Schiffman Res Inst, 82- *Mem:* Am Chem Soc; fel Am Soc Metals; Minerals, Metals & Mat Soc. *Res:* High temperature containerless environments for materials research and processing; temperature measuring; high temperature thermodynamics and phase diagrams of multicomponent systems; microgravity experimental methods; non-contact property measurements. *Mailing Add:* Crystal Lake Barton VT 05822. *Fax:* 847-566-6762

SCHIFFMAN, ROBERT L, SOIL MECHANICS, COMPUTER SCIENCE. *Current Pos:* lectr civil eng & fac res assoc, Comput Ctr, 69-70, assoc dir res, 70-77, PROF CIVIL ENG, UNIV COLO, BOULDER, 70- *Personal Data:* b New York, NY, Oct 27, 23; m 47; c 2. *Educ:* Cornell Univ, BCE, 47; Columbia Univ, MS, 51; Rensselaer Polytech Inst, PhD(soil mech), 60. *Honors & Awards:* Hogentogler Award, Am Soc Testing & Mat, 60. *Prof Exp:* Asst civil engr, New York Dept Hosps, 47-49; res assoc, Columbia Univ, 49-54, instr civil eng, 54-55; asst prof, Lehigh Univ, 55-57 & Rensselaer Polytech Inst, 57-60, assoc prof, 60-63, prof, 63-66 & theoret soil mech, Univ Ill, Chicago Circle, 66-70. *Concurrent Pos:* Prin investr, Res Projs, Am Iron & Steel Inst-Pa State Hwy Dept, 55-57, Off Naval Res, 58-66, land locomotion lab, Army Mat Command, 59-65, NSF, 61-, US Geol Surv, 61-64 & US Bur Pub Rds, 64-66; mem comt stress distrib in earth masses, Hwy Res Bd, Nat Acad Sci-Nat Res Coun, 56-63, dept soils, found & geol, comt composite pavements & res needs comt, 64-70, mem comt on mech of earth masses & layered systs, 64-, chmn, 64-70, mem comt theories of pavement design, 65-, comt design of composite pavements & struct overlays & task force on comt interaction on pavement design, 70-; vis assoc prof civil eng, Mass Inst Technol, 62-63, lectr, 63-65, vis prof, 65-66; ed, newsletter, Inst Soc Terrain-Vehicle Systs, 65-67; ed, Soil Mech & found div newslett, 66-68; lectr, Northwestern Univ, 67-68; indust consult; lectr. *Mem:* Am Soc Civil Engrs; Int Soc Terrain-Vehicle Systs; Am Soc Cybernetics; Asn Comput Mach; Am Soc Testing & Mat. *Res:* Theoretical soil mechanics; theory of consolidation; elasticity; computer science. *Mailing Add:* 490 Erie Dr Boulder CO 80303

SCHIFFMAN, SANDRA, BIOCHEMISTRY. *Current Pos:* From instr to asst prof biochem, 61-75, assoc prof, 75-83, PROF MED & BIOCHEM, SCH MED, UNIV SOUTHERN CALIF, 83- *Personal Data:* b Minneapolis, Minn, Feb 26, 37; m 57; c 2. *Educ:* Univ Calif, Berkeley, AB, 58; Univ Southern Calif, PhD(biochem, blood clotting), 61. *Concurrent Pos:* Estab investr, Am Heart Asn, 71-76, mem, Thrombosis Coun, Am Heart Asn. *Mem:* Am Soc Biol Chemists; Am Soc Hemat; Am Heart Asn; NY Acad Sci; AAAS; Sigma Xi. *Res:* Chemistry of proteins of blood coagulation. *Mailing Add:* Dept Med Univ Southern Calif Sch Med 2025 Zonal Ave RMR 308 Los Angeles CA 90033-1089. *Fax:* 213-224-6687; *E-Mail:* misschif@umusc.edu

SCHIFFMAN, SUSAN S, PSYCHOPHYSICS, ELECTROPHYSIOLOGY & CHEMORECEPTION. *Current Pos:* Fel aging & obesity, Duke Med Ctr, 70-72, from asst prof to assoc prof, 72-81, DIR, WEIGHT CONTROL UNIT, DEPT PSYCHIAT, DUKE MED CTR, 76-, PROF PSYCHIAT, 82- *Personal Data:* b Chicago, Ill, Aug 24, 40; m 89, H Troy Nagle; c Amy. *Educ:* Syracuse Univ, BA, 65; Duke Univ, PhD(psychol), 70. *Hon Degrees:* Maestro

Ilustre, La Universidad Autonoma de Guadalajara, Mex, 92. *Honors & Awards:* Finaliste Prize, Sci Pour L'Art-Moet Hennessy-Louis Vuitto; Fred W Tanner Award, Inst Food Technologists. *Concurrent Pos:* Mem, Salt & Water Subgroup, Nat Hypertension Task Force, 76; Comt Sodium Restricted Diets, Food & Nutrit Bd, 74-79; vis scientist biochem, Oxford, 80-81. *Mem:* Sigma Xi; Asn Chemoreception Sci; Am Chem Soc; Europ Chemoreception Sci; Inst Elec & Electronics Engrs. *Res:* Physicochemical properties that relate to perception of taste and smell; changes of taste and smell with age, obesity and disease state. *Mailing Add:* Dept Psychiat Med Sch Duke Univ Durham NC 27710. *E-Mail:* sss@acpub.duke.edu

SCHIFFMANN, ELLIOT, BIOCHEMISTRY, ORGANIC CHEMISTRY. *Current Pos:* RES BIOCHEMIST, LAB PATH, NAT CANCER INST, NIH. *Personal Data:* b Newark, NJ, Apr 23, 27; m 60. *Educ:* Yale Univ, BA, 49; Columbia Univ, PhD(biochem), 55. *Prof Exp:* Scientist, Nat Heart Inst, 55-61; scientist, 61-64, biochemist, Nat Inst Dent Res, 64- *Concurrent Pos:* Lectr, Grad Biochem Lab, Georgetown Univ, 57-58. *Res:* Antimetabolites and cholesterol biosynthesis; mechanisms of calcification in non osseous tissue; chemotaxis in leucocytes; biosynthesis of connective tissue components; recognition processes in cells. *Mailing Add:* Lab Path Nat Cancer Inst NIH Bldg Ten Rm 2A33 Bethesda MD 20892-0001

SCHIFFMANN, ROBERT F, FOOD SCIENCE, MICROWAVE HEATING ENGINEERING. *Current Pos:* PRES, R F SCHIFFMANN ASSOC, CONSULT MICROWAVE, 78- *Personal Data:* b New York, NY, Feb 11, 35; m 56, Marilyn Schneider; c Carla, Erica & Robert Jr. *Educ:* Columbia Univ, BS, 55; Purdue Univ, MS, 59. *Honors & Awards:* Putman Award, Putman Publ Co, 72. *Prof Exp:* Anal develop chemist, DCA Food Industs, Inc, 59-60, res proj leader, 60-61; dir lab radiochem, Nucleonics Corp Am, Inc, 61-62, vpres & tech dir radiochem & health physics, 62-63; res scientist microwave processing & foods, DCA Food Industs, Inc, 63-68, sr proj mgr, 68-71; partner new prod res & develop consult, Bedrosian & Assocs, 71-78. *Concurrent Pos:* Secy & mem exec directorate, Int Microwave Power Inst, 69-71; mem bd gov, 69-; pres, 73-81, chmn, 81-83; assoc ed foods, J Microwave Power, 70-; vpres, Natural Pak Systs, 77-; pres, Innovative Opportunities Ltd, Inc, 84-; nat sci lectr, Inst Food Tech, 87- *Mem:* Inst Food Technologists; Sigma Xi; fel Int Microwave Power Inst; Soc Plastics Indust; hon mem UK Microwave Asn. *Res:* New product and process research and development; microwave processing applications; food processing; microwave oven, food, packaging development; physical chemistry of food systems; fruit and vegetable storage; bakery and dairy production. *Mailing Add:* R F Schiffmann Assoc 149 W 88th St New York NY 10024. *Fax:* 212-769-4630; *E-Mail:* mcirowaves@juno.com

SCHIFFRIN, ERNESTO LUIS, HYPERTENSION, CARDIOVASCULAR MEDICINE. *Current Pos:* asst prof, 81-86, assoc prof 86-91, PROF MED, SCH MED, UNIV MONTREAL, 91- *Personal Data:* b Buenos Aires, Arg, Aug 8, 46; Can citizen; m 71; c 2. *Educ:* Univ Buenos Aires, MD, 69; McGill Univ, PhD(exp med), 80; FRCP(C), 82. *Hon Degrees:* FACP, 84. *Honors & Awards:* Astra Young Investr Award, Can Hypertension Soc, 85; Prix Marcel-Piche, 91. *Prof Exp:* Resident, internal med, Inst Investr Med, Buenos Aires, Argentina, 70-74, atten physician, 74-76; res fel, Clin Res Inst Montreal, 76-80, sr investr, 80-83; attend physician, Hotel-Dieu Hosp, Univ Montreal, 81. *Concurrent Pos:* Lab dir, Exp Hypertension, Clin Res Inst Montreal, 83-, dir MRC Multidisciplinary Res Group on Hypertension, 90-, lab dir, Exp Hypertension, Clin Res Inst Montreal, 83-; mem, Sci Rev Comt, Can Heart Found, 84-87, prog comt, Coun High Blood Pressure Res, Am Heart Asn, 87-89 & Nat Meeting Am Heart Asn, 92-95. *Mem:* Can Hypertension Soc (pres, 91-92); Inter Am Hypertension Soc; Am Fedn Clin Res; Can Soc Clin Invest; Soc Exp Biol & Med; Int Soc Hypertension; Can Soc Internal Med; Am Hypertension Soc. *Res:* Investigation of mechanisms involved in experimental and clinical hypertension; role of vasoactive peptides in hypertension; vascular remodeling in hypertension; endothelium in hypertension. *Mailing Add:* 110 Pine Ave W Montreal PQ H2W 1R7 Can. *Fax:* 514-987-5602; *E-Mail:* schiffe@ircm.umontreal.ca

SCHIFFRIN, MILTON JULIUS, DRUG DEVELOPMENT, ANALGESICS. *Current Pos:* PRES, WHARRY RES ASN, INC, 79- *Personal Data:* b Rochester, NY, Mar 23, 14; m 42, Dorothy E Wharry; c David W & Hilary A. *Educ:* Univ Rochester, BA, 37, MS, 39; McGill Univ, PhD(physiol), 41. *Prof Exp:* Instr physiol, Northwestern Univ, 41-42; dir clin res, Hoffman-LaRoche, 46-64, dir drug regulatory affairs, 64-79, asst vpres, 71-79. *Concurrent Pos:* Porter fel, Am Physiol Soc, 41; lectr pharmacol, Sch Med, Univ Ill, 49-56, clin asst prof anesthesiol, 56-61; vis lectr, Rush Med Col, 70-79. *Mem:* Am Med Writer's Asn (pres, 73); Am Physiol Soc; Int Col Surgeons; Am Col Clin Pharmacol; Drug Info Asn; Pharmacol Soc Can. *Res:* Gastrointestinal physiology; pain; clinical research and regulation of new drugs. *Mailing Add:* Wharry Res Asn Inc 1001 Second Ave W Unit 401 Seattle WA 98119-3560

SCHIFREEN, RICHARD STEVEN, CLINICAL CHEMISTRY, ANALYTICAL CHEMISTRY. *Current Pos:* MEM STAFF, E I DU PONT DE NEMOURS & CO, INC, 80- *Personal Data:* b Trenton, NJ, Mar 17, 52. *Educ:* Muhlenberg Col, BS, 74; Univ Ga, PhD(chem), 78. *Prof Exp:* Fel clin chem, Hartford Hosp, 78-80. *Concurrent Pos:* Mem area comt clin chem, Nat Comt Clin Lab Standards. *Mem:* Am Chem Soc; Am Asn Clin Chem; Sigma Xi. *Res:* Immunoassay development; fibrinolysis; cancer diagnostics. *Mailing Add:* Life Tech Inc PO Box 6482 Rockville MD 20850

SCHILB, THEODORE PAUL, biophysics, physiology, for more information see previous edition

SCHILD, ALBERT, OPERATIONS RESEARCH. *Current Pos:* from instr to prof math, 50-90, chmn dept, 63-79, EMER PROF, TEMPLE UNIV, 90- *Personal Data:* b Hessdorf, Mar 3, 20; nat US; m 46, Clara Shekter; c Hannah, Ruth, Rebecca, Chava, Bracha, Judy & Batsheva. *Educ:* Univ Toronto, BA, 46; Univ Pa, MA, 48, PhD(math), 51. *Prof Exp:* Asst instr math, Univ Pa, 46-50. *Concurrent Pos:* Consult, ETS, Princeton, NJ, 56-; lectr, 60- *Mem:* Am Math Soc; Math Asn Am. *Res:* Theory of functions; complex variables; operations research. *Mailing Add:* 1515 Ripley St Philadelphia PA 19111

SCHILD, RUDOLPH ERNEST, GRAVITATIONAL LENSES, QUASARS. *Current Pos:* ASTROPHYSICIST, SMITHSONIAN ASTROPHYS OBSERV, 69- *Personal Data:* b Chicago, Ill, Jan 10, 40; m 82, Jane Hooper. *Educ:* Univ Chicago, BS, 62, MS, 63, PhD(astrophys), 66. *Prof Exp:* Res assoc, Calif Inst Technol, 66-69. *Concurrent Pos:* Res consult, Mass Inst Technol, 73-74; lectr astron, Harvard Univ, 73-83. *Mem:* Am Astron Soc; Int Astron Union. *Res:* Extragalactic energetic, especially quasars and x-ray sources; gravitational lenses. *Mailing Add:* 99 Hesperus Ave Gloucester MA 01930. *Fax:* 617-495-7467; *E-Mail:* rschild@cfa.harvard.edu

SCHILDCROUT, MICHAEL, PHYSICS, ELECTRICAL ENGINEERING. *Current Pos:* ELEC ENGR, NAVAL SECURITY GROUP, 79- *Personal Data:* b New York, NY, Feb 6, 43. *Educ:* Hunter Col, BS, 66; Univ Pittsburgh, PhD(physics), 75; George Washington Univ, MS, 85. *Prof Exp:* Engr, Naval Intel Support Ctr, 77-79. *Mem:* Am Phys Soc; Inst Elec & Electronics Engrs. *Res:* Evaluating the performance of spread spectrum communication systems; their low probability of intercept; anti-jam capabilities. *Mailing Add:* 2307 Greenery Lane Silver Spring MD 20906

SCHILDCROUT, STEVEN MICHAEL, PHYSICAL INORGANIC CHEMISTRY, MASS SPECTROMETRY. *Current Pos:* from asst prof to assoc prof, 69-81, PROF CHEM, YOUNGSTOWN STATE UNIV, 81- *Personal Data:* b Grand Rapids, Mich, July 18, 43; m 64, Antonia Herz; c Douglas & Jordan. *Educ:* Univ Chicago, SB, 64; Northwestern Univ, PhD(chem), 68. *Prof Exp:* Res fel chem, Rice Univ, 68-69. *Mem:* Am Chem Soc; Am Soc Mass Spectrometry; Sigma Xi. *Res:* Mass spectrometry and chemistry of gaseous ions in organic and inorganic systems. *Mailing Add:* Dept Chem Youngstown State Univ Youngstown OH 44555-3663. *E-Mail:* smschild@cc.ysu.edu

SCHILDKRAUT, CARL LOUIS, BIOLOGICAL CHEMISTRY. *Current Pos:* asst prof, 64-70, assoc prof, 71-76, PROF CELL BIOL, ALBERT EINSTEIN COL MED, 76- *Personal Data:* b Brooklyn, NY, June 20, 37. *Educ:* Cornell Univ, AB, 58; Harvard Univ, AM, 59, PhD(chem), 61. *Honors & Awards:* Hirschl Career Scientist Award, 75. *Prof Exp:* NSF fel, 61-63. *Concurrent Pos:* Kennedy scholar, 66-69; NIH career develop award, 69-74; mem molecular biol adv panel, NSF, 70-73. *Mem:* AAAS; Am Chem Soc; Am Soc Cell Biol; Am Soc Biol Chem & Molecular Biol; Genetics Soc Am. *Res:* Physical chemistry and enzymology of DNA; analysis of the organization and replication of the DNA of mammalian cells; regulatory mechanisms in mammalian cells. *Mailing Add:* Dept Cell Biol Albert Einstein Col Med 1300 Morris Park Ave Bronx NY 10461

SCHILDKRAUT, JOSEPH JACOB, PSYCHIATRY, NEUROPSYCHOPHARMACOLOGY. *Current Pos:* resident psychiat, 60-63, chief resident res unit, 61-63, SR PSYCHIATRIST & DIR NEUROPSYCHOPHARMACOL LAB, MASS MENTAL HEALTH CTR, 67-; PROF PSYCHIAT, HARVARD MED SCH, 74- *Personal Data:* b Brooklyn, NY, Jan 21, 34; m 66; c 2. *Educ:* Harvard Col, AB, 55; Harvard Med Sch, MD, 59. *Honors & Awards:* Anna-Monika Found Prize, Dortmund, Ger, 67; McCurdy-Rinkel Prize, Am Psychiat Asn, 69, Hofheimer Prize, 71; William C Menninger Mem Award, Am Col Physicians, 78. *Prof Exp:* Intern med, Univ Calif Hosp, San Francisco, 59-60; teaching fel, Harvard Med Sch, 60-63; clin assoc, Lab Clin Sci, NIMH, 63-65, spec fel, 65-66, res psychiatrist, 66-67; asst prof, Harvard Med Sch, 67-70, assoc prof, 70-74. *Concurrent Pos:* Prin investr numerous grants; consult comts & orgns. *Mem:* Am Psychiat Asn; Am Col Psychiatrists; World Psychiat Asn; Am Col Neuropsychopharmacol; Am Soc Pharmacol & Exp Therapeut. *Res:* Neuropsychopharmacology, biochemistry, and biology of psychiatric disorders, particularly the affective disorders (depressions and manias) and the schizophrenic disorders. *Mailing Add:* Mass Ment Health Ctr 74 Fenwood Rd Boston MA 02115-6106

SCHILE, RICHARD DOUGLAS, ENGINEERING MECHANICS, MATERIALS & POLYMER ENGINEERING. *Current Pos:* PROF MECH ENG, UNIV BRIDGEPORT, 83-, CHMN MECH ENG DEPT, 88- *Personal Data:* b New Haven, Conn, Apr 3, 31; m 53; c 3. *Educ:* Rensselaer Polytech Inst, BAeroE, 53, MS, 57, PhD(mech), 67. *Prof Exp:* Res engr, Res Labs, United Aircraft, 57-59, group supvr, 59-62, sr mat scientist, 62-69; assoc prof eng, Dartmouth Col, 69-76; eng res dir, Ciba-Geigy Corp, 76-82. *Concurrent Pos:* Pres, Ardes Enterprises, 82- *Mem:* Am Soc Mech Engrs. *Res:* Engineering research and development of thermoplastic and thermosetting; polymers and additives for high performance applications. *Mailing Add:* 22 Bloomer Rd Ridgefield CT 06877

SCHILLACI, MARIO EDWARD, RADIATION PHYSICS, PARTICLE PHYSICS. *Current Pos:* Fel, 67-69, STAFF SCIENTIST, MEDIUM-ENERGY PHYSICS DIV, LOS ALAMOS SCI LAB, UNIV CALIF, 70- *Personal Data:* b Philadelphia, Pa, Feb 18, 40; m 62; c 3. *Educ:* Drexel Univ, BS, 62; Brandeis Univ, MA, 64, PhD(physics), 68. *Concurrent Pos:* Prof physics, Univ NMex, Los Alamos. *Mem:* Am Phys Soc; Radiation Res Soc. *Res:* Medium energy particle physics; medical radiation physics. *Mailing Add:* MS E546 Los Alamos Nat Lab Los Alamos NM 87545. *Fax:* 505-665-1712

SCHILLER, ALFRED GEORGE, veterinary medicine; deceased, see previous edition for last biography

SCHILLER, CAROL MASTERS, BIOCHEMICAL TOXICOLOGY. *Current Pos:* LAWYER, 85-; CONSULT TOXICOL, 86- *Personal Data:* b St Augustine, Fla, Dec 31, 40; m 64; c 2. *Educ:* State Univ NY, Cortland, BSc, 62; Univ NC, Chapel Hill, MAT, 63, JD, 84; Univ Tex, Dallas, PhD(biochem), 70. *Prof Exp:* Instr chem & physics, Barlow High Sch, Redding, Conn & Jordan High Sch, Durham, NC, 63-65; fel med & tutor chem, Univ Toronto, 71-73; res assoc biochem, Univ NC, 73-75; sr staff fel, NIH, 75-78, res chemist, 79-85. *Concurrent Pos:* Alt tech mgr, Nutrit Coord Comt, NIH, 75-, coordr, Fed Women's Prog, 77-78, mem, Digestive Dis Coord Comt, 78-; adj asst prof biochem, Univ NC, 76-80, adj assoc prof, 80-, mem fac, Med Sch, 78-, mem grad fac toxicol, 80-; mem fac, W A Jones Cell Sci Ctr, 77-78, chmn, In Vitro Res & Human Values Comt, Tissue Cult Asn, 74-78; Cong fel, 85-86; expert witness, 86-; chair, Sect Toxicol, Regulatory Affairs & Legal Asst Ctr, 89-92. *Mem:* Am Chem Soc; AAAS; Asn Women Sci; Soc Toxicol; NY Acad Sci. *Res:* Effects of environmental chemicals/causation; premarket product development. *Mailing Add:* 434 Fayetteville St Mall No 1250 Raleigh NC 27601-1767. *Fax:* 919-787-0601

SCHILLER, JOHN JOSEPH, MATHEMATICS. *Current Pos:* from instr to asst prof, 59-71, ASSOC PROF MATH, TEMPLE UNIV, 71- & RES ASSOC PROF PHYSIOL & BIOPHYS, 78- *Personal Data:* b Philadelphia, Pa, Dec 10, 35; m 57; c 3. *Educ:* La Salle Col, BA, 57; Temple Univ, MA, 60; Univ Pa, PhD(math), 66. *Prof Exp:* Physicist, US Naval Res & Develop Ctr, 57-59. *Concurrent Pos:* Mathematician, John D Kettele Corp, 69. *Mem:* Am Math Soc. *Res:* Riemann surfaces; artificial intelligence. *Mailing Add:* 3630 Salina Rd Philadelphia PA 19154-2615

SCHILLER, NEAL LEANDER, MEDICAL MICROBIOLOGY, INFECTIOUS DISEASES. *Current Pos:* from asst prof to assoc prof, 79-96, CHAIR GRAD PROG, MICROBIOL, DIV BIOMED SCI, UNIV CALIF RIVERSIDE, 94-, ASSOC DEAN, GRAD DIV, 95-, PROF MED MICROBIOL, DIV BIOMED SCI, 96- *Personal Data:* b Lowell, Mass, Nov 5, 49; m 73, Kathleen M Pratt; c Matthew N, Kevin V & David E. *Educ:* Boston Col, BS, 71; Univ Mass, Amherst, PhD(microbiol), 76. *Prof Exp:* Res fel, Div Infectious Dis, Cornell Med Ctr, New York Hosp, 76-78, clin lab tech trainee, Diag Microbiol Lab, 77-78. *Concurrent Pos:* Sabbatical leave, Lab Clin Invest, Nat Inst Allergy & Infectious Dis, NIH, Bethesda, Md, 85-86; chmn, div gen med microbiol, Am Soc Microbiol, 86-87. *Mem:* Am Soc Microbiol; AAAS; Am Asn Immunologists; Fedn Am Soc Exp Biol. *Res:* The interaction of pathogenic bacteria with host defense mechanisms; characterization of bacterial virulence factors; genetics, immunobiology and pathogenesis of bacterial pathogens, examination of host defenses including chemotaxis, serum killing, opsonization, complement activation, phagocytic uptake and intracellular killing. *Mailing Add:* Div Biomed Sci Univ Calif 900 University Ave Riverside CA 92521-0121. *Fax:* 909-787-5504; *E-Mail:* neal. schiller@ucr.edu

SCHILLER, PETER WILHELM, PEPTIDE CHEMISTRY, MOLECULAR PHARMACOLOGY. *Current Pos:* from asst prof to prof, Dept Med, 75-92, PROF, DEPT PHARMACOL, UNIV MONTREAL, 92-; DIR, LAB CHEM BIOL & PEPTIDE RES, CLIN RES INST MONTREAL, 75- *Personal Data:* b Frauenfeld, Switz, Feb 9, 42; Swiss & Can citizen. *Educ:* Swiss Fed Inst Technol, Zurich, dipl, 66, DSc, 71. *Honors & Awards:* Kern Prize & Silver Medal, Swiss Fed Inst Technol, Zurich, 71; Max-Bergmann Medal for Achievements in Peptide Res, 87; Marcel-Piché Prize, 87; Galen Award Can, Excellence Pharmaceut Res, 95. *Prof Exp:* Res fel, dept biol, Johns Hopkins Univ, Baltimore, 71-72 & lab chem biol, Nat Inst Arthritis, Metab, & Digestive Dis, NIH, Bethesda, Md, 73-74. *Concurrent Pos:* Vis scholar, dept biochem, Univ Wash, Seattle, 69; vis prof, dept molecular biol, Swiss Fed Inst Technol, Zurich, 79; mem, Sci Rev Comt, Can Heart Found, 81-84, planning comt, Am Peptide Symposia, 81-87; consult, Inst Armand-Frappier, Laval, Que, Can, 84-; mem, Res Rev Comt, Nat Inst Drug Abuse, 86-; assoc mem, Dept Exp Med, McGill Univ, Montreal, 78-89, adj prof, 89-; mem coun, Am Peptide Soc, 93- *Mem:* AAAS; Am Chem Soc; Am Soc Biochem & Molecular Biol; Can Biochem Soc; NY Acad Sci; Swiss Biochem Soc; Protein Soc; Am Peptide Soc (pres-elect, 93-95, pres, 95-97); Am Soc Hypertension; fel Royal Soc Can. *Res:* Molecular pharmacology of peptide hormones and neurotransmitters; chemical synthesis; structure-activity relationships; conformational aspects of peptide-receptor interactions; characterization of receptors and peptide drug-development; chemistry and pharmacology of opioids; development of analgesics. *Mailing Add:* Clin Res Inst Montreal 110 Pine Ave W Montreal PQ H2W 1R7 Can. *Fax:* 514-987-5513; *E-Mail:* schillp@ircm.umontreal.ca

SCHILLER, RALPH, THEORETICAL PHYSICS. *Current Pos:* from asst prof to prof physics, 54-90, head dept, 75-86, EMER PROF, STEVENS INST TECHNOL, 90- *Personal Data:* b New York, NY, July 8, 26; m 50; c 3. *Educ:* Brooklyn Col, BA, 48; Syracuse Univ, MS, 50, PhD(physics), 52. *Prof Exp:* Asst physics, Syracuse Univ, 48-52; asst prof, Univ Sao Paulo, 52-54. *Concurrent Pos:* Res assoc, Syracuse Univ, 60-61; vis prof, Weizmann Inst, 80. *Mem:* Am Phys Soc; Sigma Xi. *Res:* Optics. *Mailing Add:* 519 Wyndham Rd Teaneck NJ 07666

SCHILLER, WILLIAM R, SURGERY, SURGICAL CRITICAL CARE. *Current Pos:* DIR, BURN & TRAUMA CTR, MARICOPA MED CTR, PHOENIX, ARIZ, 89- *Personal Data:* b Bennett, Colo, Jan 14, 37; m 60, 92, Beverlee Fisher; c Julie & Lisa. *Educ:* Drury Col, BS, 58; Northwestern Univ, MD, 62. *Prof Exp:* Prof surg, Univ NMex, 78-83; dir, Trauma Ctr, St Joseph Hosp, Phoenix, Ariz, 83-89. *Concurrent Pos:* Bd dirs, Am Trauma Soc, 84-90; clin prof surg, Univ Ariz, 89-91. *Mem:* Am Trauma Soc; Am Col Surgeons; Am Asn Surg Trauma; Int Soc Surg; Am Burn Asn. *Res:* Investigation into the metabolic effects of injury; clinical aspects of burn and trauma. *Mailing Add:* Burn & Trauma Ctr Maricopa Med Ctr 2601 E Roosevelt Phoenix AZ 85008

SCHILLETTER, JULIAN CLAUDE, HORTICULTURE. *Current Pos:* From instr to assoc prof, 22-45, prof hort & dir residence, 45-67, residence analyst, 67-72, EMER PROF HORT, IOWA STATE UNIV, 72- *Personal Data:* b Clemson, SC, Nov 1, 01. *Educ:* Clemson Univ, BS, 22; Iowa State Univ, MS, 23, PhD, 30. *Concurrent Pos:* Mem, Int Hort Cong, 30; horticulturist, Nat Res Proj, Works Progress Admin, 38. *Res:* Differentiation of flower bud in Dunlap strawberries; growth of Dunlap strawberries; general horticulture. *Mailing Add:* 111 Lynn Ames IA 50014

SCHILLING, CHARLES H(ENRY), CIVIL ENGINEERING. *Current Pos:* CIVIL ENGR, 81- *Personal Data:* b Louisville, Ky, June 3, 18; m 45; c 5. *Educ:* US Mil Acad, BS, 41; Univ Calif, MS, 47; Rensselaer Polytech Inst, PhD(civil eng), 59. *Prof Exp:* US Army, 41-80, engr combat battalion, France & Ger, 44-45, engr aviation battalion, Ger, 47-50, instr mil art & eng, US Mil Acad, 51-52, assoc prof, 52-55, area engr, Eastern Ocean Dist, Corps Engrs, 55-56, prof mil art & eng, US Mil Acad, 56-69, head dept, 63-69, prof eng & head dept, US Mil Acad, 69-80. *Concurrent Pos:* Vis prof, Univ Mich, 65 & Univ Stuttgart, 68-69. *Mem:* Am Soc Eng Educ; Soc Am Mil Engrs; Am Soc Civil Engrs; Nat Soc Prof Engrs. *Res:* Structural engineering; vibrations in suspension bridges; application of computers in engineering and education. *Mailing Add:* 4 Trahern Terr Clarksville TN 37040-3551

SCHILLING, CURTIS LOUIS, JR, POLYMER & ORGANOSILICON CHEMISTRY. *Current Pos:* res chemist, 68-75, proj scientist, 76-79, res scientist, 80-84, SR RES CHEMIST, SPECIALTY CHEM DIV, UNION CARBIDE CORP, 84 - *Personal Data:* b Goshen, NY, May 19, 40; m 61; c 2. *Educ:* Syracuse Univ, BS, 61, MS, 64; Univ Ariz, PhD(org chem), 67. *Prof Exp:* US Army Res Off grantee, Univ Iowa, 67-68. *Mem:* Am Chem Soc; Am Ceramic Soc. *Res:* Organosilicon chemistry; silicone surfactant stabilization of polyurethane foams; organosilicon routes to silicon carbide; organofunctional silanes. *Mailing Add:* Wynnwood Dr Marietta OH 45750-9697

SCHILLING, EDWARD EUGENE, PLANT SYSTEMATICS, CHEMOTAXONOMY. *Current Pos:* from asst prof to prof, 79-92, PROF & HEAD BOT, UNIV TENN, 92- *Personal Data:* b Los Angeles, Calif, Sept 23, 53. *Educ:* Mich State Univ, BS, 74; Ind Univ, PhD(biol), 78. *Prof Exp:* Instr bot, Univ Tex, 78-79. *Concurrent Pos:* Ed, Syst Bot, 91-92. *Mem:* AAAS; Am Soc Plant Taxonomists; Bot Soc Am; Sigma Xi. *Res:* Systematics and evolution of sunflowers; molecular systematics and evolution; systematics of black nightshades. *Mailing Add:* Dept Bot Univ Tenn 1345 Circle Pk Knoxville TN 37996-0001. *Fax:* 423-974-0978; *E-Mail:* botany@utkvx.utk.edu

SCHILLING, EDWARD GEORGE, QUALITY CONTROL. *Current Pos:* assoc prof, Rochester Inst Technol, 67-69, Paul A Miller prof hd & chmn, Grad Statist Dept, 83-92, dir, Ctr Qual & Appl Statist, 92-96, PROF, CTR QUAL & APPL STATIST, ROCHESTER INST TECHNOL, 96- *Personal Data:* b Lancaster, NY, Nov 9, 31; m 59, Jean Bork; c Elizabeth & Kathryn. *Educ:* Univ Buffalo, BA, 53, MBA, 54; Rutgers Univ, MS, 62, PhD(statist), 65. *Honors & Awards:* Brumbaugh Award, Am Soc Qual Control, 74, 78, 79 & 81, Shewhart Medal, 83; Ellis R Ott Award, 84; Harold F Dodge Award, Am Soc Testing & Mat, 93. *Prof Exp:* Instr statist, Univ Buffalo, 57-59; engr, RCA, 59-61; teaching asst statist, Rutgers Univ, 61-62; sr engr, Carborundum Corp, 62-64; instr statist, Rutgers Univ, 64-67; consult statistician, Lamp Bus Div, Gen Elec Co, 69-74, mgr statist & qual systs oper, 75-80, mgr lighting qual oper, Lighting Bus Group, 80-83. *Concurrent Pos:* Consult, 68-69, 83-; series ed, Marcel Dekker, Inc, NY, 84-; mem, Comt ASCZ-1 Qual Assurance, Am Nat Stand Inst, TC-69 Statist Methods, Int Stand Inst & E-11 Qual & Statist, Am Soc Testing & Mat. *Mem:* Fel Am Statist Asn; fel Am Soc Qual Control; Inst Math Statist; Am Soc Testing & Mat; Am Econ Assn; Sigma Xi. *Res:* Mathematical statistics with applications in the physical and engineering sciences, quality control, business and economics. *Mailing Add:* Rochester Inst Technol Rochester NY 14623-5604. *Fax:* 716-475-5959; *E-Mail:* egscta@rit.edu

SCHILLING, GERD, PLASMA HEATING, NEUTRAL BEAM TECHNOLOGY. *Current Pos:* RES PHYSICIST, PLASMA PHYSICS LAB, PRINCETON UNIV, 77- *Personal Data:* b Hanover, Ger, Oct 6, 39; m 69; c 2. *Educ:* Mass Inst Technol, BS, 61; Case Inst Technol, MS, 63, PhD(physics), 67. *Prof Exp:* Res assoc, Notre Dame Univ, 68-70; res physicist, Max Planck Inst Plasma Physics, WGer, 70-74 & Oak Ridge Nat Lab, Fusion Energy Div, 74-77. *Mem:* Am Phys Soc. *Res:* Controlled thermonuclear fusion and plasma physics. *Mailing Add:* Plasma Physics Lab Princeton Univ PO Box 451 Princeton NJ 08543. *Fax:* 609-243-3248

SCHILLING, JEAN-GUY, OCEANOGRAPHY. *Current Pos:* PROF OCEANOG, UNIV RI. *Honors & Awards:* MAURICE EWING AWARD, AM GEOPHYS UNION, 95. *Mailing Add:* Dept Oceanog Univ RI 15 S Ferry Rd Narragansett RI 02882

SCHILLING, JOHN ALBERT, SURGERY. *Current Pos:* PROF SURG, MED SCH, UNIV WASH, 74-, CHMN DEPT, 75- *Personal Data:* b Kansas City, Mo, Nov 5, 17; m 43; c 4. *Educ:* Dartmouth Col, AB, 37; Harvard Univ, MD, 41; Am Bd Surg, dipl, 48. *Prof Exp:* Resident, Roosevelt Hosp, Columbia Univ, 44; instr surg, Univ Rochester, 44-48, asst prof surg & surg anat, Sch Med & Dent, 48-56; prof surg & head dept, Med Ctr, Univ Okla, 56-74. *Concurrent Pos:* Mem, Boyd-Bartlett Exped, Arctic, 41; mem adv bd, Am J Surg, 58-; mem surg study sect, Div Res Grants, NIH, 60-64, mem bd sci counr, Nat Cancer Inst, 66-71, chmn, 69-71, mem diag subcomt, Breast Cancer Task Force, 71-; mem, Am Bd Surg, Inc, 63-69, chmn, 68-69; mem comt metab in trauma, Surgeon Gen, US Army, 63-71, chmn, 67-71; consult, Div Hosp & Med Facil, Dept Health, Educ & Welfare, 66-; mem comt trauma, Div Med Sci, Nat Res Coun, 69-72; consult, Off Surgeon Gen, USAF. *Mem:* Am Soc Exp Path; Am Surg Asn; Soc Exp Biol & Med; Am Cancer Soc; Soc Univ Surg; Sigma Xi. *Res:* Intestinal obstruction; circulation of liver; transplantation of cancer; paper chromatography; peptic ulcer; visualization of biliary tract; wound healing; respiratory physiology; shock. *Mailing Add:* Dept Surg Univ Wash 9807 Lake Washington Blvd NE Bellevue WA 98004

SCHILLING, JOHN H(AROLD), geology, mining; deceased, see previous edition for last biography

SCHILLING, ROBERT FREDERICK, MEDICINE. *Current Pos:* from asst prof to assoc prof, 51-62, PROF MED, UNIV WIS-MADISON, 62- *Personal Data:* b Adell, Wis, Jan 19, 19; m 46; c 5. *Educ:* Univ Wis, BS, 40, MD, 43; Am Bd Nutrit, dipl; Am Bd Internal Med, dipl, 51. *Prof Exp:* Asst med, Harvard Med Sch, 49-51. *Concurrent Pos:* Commonwealth Fund res fel, London Hosp, Eng, 59; consult, NIH, Food & Drug Admin, Vet Admin & Nat Res Coun. *Mem:* Am Soc Clin Invest; Soc Exp Biol & Med; Am Fedn Clin Res; Asn Am Physicians; Am Soc Hemat. *Res:* Hematology; nutrition. *Mailing Add:* 7276 Med Sci Ctr Univ Wis 1300 University Ave Madison WI 53706-1532. *Fax:* 608-263-4689; *E-Mail:* rfsmd@macc.wisc.edu

SCHILLINGER, EDWIN JOSEPH, PHYSICS, SCIENCE EDUCATION. *Current Pos:* From instr to prof, Depaul Univ, 50-88, chmn dept, 52-68 & 76-79, dean, Col Lib Arts & Sci, 66-70 & 80-81, EMER PROF PHYSICS, DEPAUL UNIV, 88- *Personal Data:* b Chicago, Ill, July 14, 23; m 49, Carmelita Larocco; c Rosemarie, Mary, Ann, Edwin III, Jerome & Elizabeth. *Educ:* DePaul Univ, BS, 44; Univ Notre Dame, MS, 48, PhD(physics), 50. *Concurrent Pos:* Consult, NSF, 62-67 & Off Supt Pub Instr, State Ill, 69-72. *Mem:* AAAS; fel Am Phys Soc; Am Asn Physics Teachers. *Res:* Development of courses and curricula in physics and interdisciplinary science for general students, with emphasis on history, philosophy and methodology of science and its interaction with society and public policy. *Mailing Add:* 7724 W Peterson Ave Chicago IL 60631-2246

SCHILLINGER, JOHN ANDREW, JR, AGRONOMY, CROP BREEDING. *Current Pos:* SOYBEAN & ALFALFA PROJ LEADER, 73-, DIR, AGRON RES, ASGROW SEED CO. *Personal Data:* b Severn, Md, June 17, 38; m 59; c 2. *Educ:* Univ Md, College Park, BS, 60, MS, 62; Mich State Univ, PhD(plant breeding), 65. *Prof Exp:* Assoc instr plant breeding, Mich State Univ, 63-65; res entomologist, Entom Res Div, USDA & Mich State Univ, 65-67; from asst prof to assoc prof plant breeding, Univ Md, College Park, 67-73. *Mem:* Am Soc Agron; Entom Soc Am. *Res:* Development of improved varieties of alfalfa and soybeans with resistance to pests and with high yield potential. *Mailing Add:* 645 E Ridge Circle Kalamazoo MI 49009-9107

SCHILSON, ROBERT E(ARL), CHEMICAL ENGINEERING. *Current Pos:* RETIRED. *Personal Data:* b Keokuk, Iowa, May 25, 27; m 52, Mildred J Ham; c David. *Educ:* Univ Ill, BS, 50; Univ Minn, PhD(chem eng), 58. *Prof Exp:* Chem engr, Hanford Works, Gen Elec Co, Wash, 50-53; res engr, Marathon Oil Co, 58-61, adv res engr, 61-65, sr res engr, Denver Res Ctr, 65-73, mgr eng dept, 73-77, adv sr refining engr, La Refining Div, 77-82; lectr math, Univ Sierra Leone, WAfrica, US Peace Corps, 87-89. *Mem:* Am Inst Mining, Metall & Petrol Engrs; Am Inst Chem Eng. *Res:* Thermal methods of oil recovery; catalysis and chemical kinetics; refining and petrochemicals; coke and carbon technology. *Mailing Add:* 14 Anchorage Lane Salem SC 29676

SCHILT, ALFRED AYARS, ANALYTICAL CHEMISTRY. *Current Pos:* CHEM CONSULT, 89- *Personal Data:* b Haigler, Nebr, Aug 30, 27; m 49; c 4. *Educ:* Univ Colo, BA, 50, MA, 52; Univ Ill, PhD(chem), 56. *Prof Exp:* Anal chemist, Eastman Kodak Co, 51-53; asst, Univ Ill, 53-56; from instr to asst prof chem, Univ Mich, 56-62; from assoc prof to prof chem, Northern Ill Univ, 62-89. *Concurrent Pos:* Vis res prof, Ind Univ, 70-71. *Mem:* Am Chem Soc. *Res:* Coordination compounds and their application in chemical analysis; analytical separations; spectroscopy; general analytical methods; perchloric acid and perchlorates. *Mailing Add:* 7704 NW 44th Pl Gainesville FL 32606

SCHIMA, FRANCIS JOSEPH, NUCLEAR PHYSICS, RADIOACTIVITY METROLOGY. *Current Pos:* PHYSICIST, NAT BUR STANDARDS, 66- *Personal Data:* b Chicago, Ill, Apr 15, 35; m 67; c 2. *Educ:* Ill Benedictine Col, BS, 57; Univ Notre Dame, PhD(physics), 64. *Prof Exp:* Res assoc, Ind Univ, 64-66. *Concurrent Pos:* Consult, Nat Coun Radiation Protection & Measurements, 75- *Mem:* Am Phys Soc; Sigma Xi. *Res:* Study nuclear structure through measurement of radioactive decay; prepare standards of radioactivity; low level radioactivity measurements for neutrino detectors. *Mailing Add:* Radioactivity Group 846 Nat Inst Stands & Tech Gaithersburg MD 20899

SCHIMEK, ROBERT ALFRED, MEDICINE. *Current Pos:* assoc prof, 57-76, CLIN PROF OPHTHAL, SCH MED, TULANE UNIV, 76- *Personal Data:* b Beaver Falls, Pa, May 1, 26; m 50; c 2. *Educ:* Franklin & Marshall Col, BS, 45; Johns Hopkins Univ, MD, 50. *Prof Exp:* Asst instr, Johns Hopkins Univ & house officer & resident, Hosp, 50-53; staff ophthalmologist, Henry Ford Hosp, Mich, 53-57; head dept ophthal, Ochsner Clin & Found Hosp, 57-77. *Concurrent Pos:* Clin prof, Sch Med, La State Univ, 78; mem vis staff, Eye, & Ear Inst, Charity, Touro & E Jefferson Hosp, 57- *Mem:* AMA; Asn Res Vision & Ophthal; Am Col Surgeons; Am Acad Ophthal. *Res:* Ophthalmology. *Mailing Add:* 4224 Houma Blvd Suite 110 Metairie LA 70006-2934

SCHIMELPFENIG, CLARENCE WILLIAM, ORGANIC CHEMISTRY, CHEMISTRY EDUCATION. *Current Pos:* CONSULT CHEM EDUC, 92- *Personal Data:* b Dallas, Tex, Apr 8, 30; m 56, Dorothy M Massey; c Laurel A, Gretchen M & Michael W. *Educ:* NTex State Col, BS, 53, MS, 54; Univ Ill, PhD, 57. *Prof Exp:* Asst prof chem, George Washington Univ, 57-59 & NTex State Univ 59-62; res chemist, E I du Pont de Nemours & Co, Inc, 62-73; asst prof chem, State Univ NY Buffalo, 73-75 & Erskine Col, 75-76; from asst prof to assoc prof chem, Tex Wesleyan Col, 76-81; assoc prof chem, NTex State Univ, 81- 82; prof chem, Dallas Baptist Univ, 82-91. *Concurrent Pos:* Robert A Welch Found grantee, 60-62, 77-81. *Mem:* Am Chem Soc; Royal Soc Chem; Sigma Xi. *Res:* Organic and polymer chemistry. *Mailing Add:* 2008 Silver Leaf Dr Pantego TX 76013

SCHIMERT, GEORGE, CARDIOVASCULAR SURGERY. *Current Pos:* RETIRED. *Personal Data:* b Raemismuehle-Zell, Switz, Feb 19, 18; US citizen; m 56; c 8. *Educ:* Univ Friedrich Wilhelm, Berlin, MD, 42; Pazmany Peter Univ, Budapest, MD, 43; Univ Minn, MSc, 60; Am Bd Surg, dipl, 61; Am Bd Thoracic Surg, dipl, 62. *Prof Exp:* Asst surg, Univ Md, 54-55; adv surg & chief thoracic surg, Med Col, Seoul Univ, 58-59; from instr to asst prof surg, Univ Minn, 60; from asst prof to prof surg, State Univ NY, Buffalo, 60-90. *Concurrent Pos:* Fel cardiovasc surg, Univ Md, 55-56; fel med, Hosps, Univ Minn, 56-58; attend thoracic surgeon, Vet Hosp, Buffalo, 61-; assoc surg, Buffalo Gen Hosp, 65-68; chief cardiovasc surg, Buffalo Gen Hosp, 65-90, surgeon, 68-90; assoc attend cardiovasc surgeon, Children's Hosp, 67-; assoc prof, Sch Med, NY Univ, 69- *Mem:* AMA; fel Am Col Chest Physicians; fel Am Col Surg; fel Soc Thoracic Surg; fel Soc Vascular Surg. *Res:* Development of cardiopulmonary bypass equipment; design of prosthetic heart valves; multivalvular replacement; determination of myocardial sodium potassium ratios; correction of overwhelming heart failure by cardiac surgical procedures. *Mailing Add:* Ocean Point Rd East Boothbay ME 04544

SCHIMITSCHEK, ERHARD JOSEF, PHYSICAL CHEMISTRY, PHYSICS. *Current Pos:* PHYSICIST, NAVAL OCEAN SYSTS CTR, 62- *Personal Data:* b Neutitschein, Czech, Dec 8, 31; m 56; c 2. *Educ:* Univ Munich, Dr rer nat, 57. *Prof Exp:* Sr res engr, Convair Gen Dynamics Corp, 58-60, staff scientist, 60-62. *Mem:* Am Phys Soc. *Res:* Electrooptics; quantum electronics; liquid and gas discharge lasers. *Mailing Add:* 3930 Point Loma Ave San Diego CA 92106

SCHIMKE, ROBERT T, BIOCHEMISTRY, MOLECULAR BIOLOGY. *Current Pos:* chmn, Dept Pharmacol, 70-73, Dept Biol, 78-82, PROF BIOL, STANFORD UNIV, 66- *Personal Data:* b Spokane, Wash, Oct 25, 32; div; c 4. *Educ:* Stanford Univ, AB, 54, MD, 58. *Honors & Awards:* Charles Pfizer Award Enzyme Chem, Am Chem Soc, 69; Boris Pregal Award Res Biol, NY Acad Sci, 74; W C Rose Biochem Award, 83; A P Sloan Jr Prize, Gen Motors Cancer Res Found, 85. *Prof Exp:* Biochemist, NIH, 60-65, chief, Sect Biochem Regulation, 65-66. *Mem:* Nat Acad Sci; Inst Med-Nat Acad Sci; Am Soc Biol Chemists; Am Acad Arts & Sci. *Res:* Mechanisms of actions of hormones in metabolic regulation and development; significance and control mechanisms of protein turnover in animals; gene amplification and resistance phenomena. *Mailing Add:* Dept Biol Sci Stanford Univ Stanford CA 94305. *Fax:* 650-723-0155

SCHIMMEL, ELIHU MYRON, MEDICINE. *Current Pos:* PROF MED, SCH MED, BOSTON UNIV, 64-; LECTR, DEPT MED, TUFTS UNIV. *Personal Data:* b Bayonne, NJ, Dec 14, 29; m 55, Edith Stavisky; c Mindy & Benedict. *Educ:* Univ Ill, Urbana, AB, 50; Yale Univ, MD, 54. *Prof Exp:* Instr med, Sch Med, Yale Univ, 60-64. *Concurrent Pos:* USPHS res fel, Mass Gen Hosp, Harvard Univ, 58-60; vis scientist, Dept Nutrit Biochem, Mass Inst Technol, 76-77, USDA Human Nutrit Res Ctr, Tufts, 86-87; contrib ed, Nutrit Reviews, 89-95. *Mem:* Am Fedn Clin Res. *Res:* Gastroenterology; nutrition. *Mailing Add:* 150 S Huntington Ave Boston MA 02130-4893. *Fax:* 617-278-4505

SCHIMMEL, HERBERT, BIOMATHEMATICS, BIOPHYSICS. *Current Pos:* RETIRED. *Personal Data:* b New York, NY, Sept 12, 09; m 34, 71; c 6. *Educ:* Univ Pa, BA, 30, MS, 32, PhD(physics), 36. *Prof Exp:* Engr-economist, US Nat Res Proj, Philadelphia, 36-41; staff dir & consult, US Cong, Washington, DC, 41-47; sr officer sci, technol & econ, UN, 48-52; independent consult, 53-63; assoc math & physics, Albert Einstein Col Med, 64-70, organizer & dir, Sci Comput Ctr, 67-71, assoc prof, 74-78, emer prof neurol & consult, 78-87. *Mem:* Inst Elec & Electronics Engrs. *Res:* Applications of math and physics to medicine and biology. *Mailing Add:* Hunthouse Monroe 218 10 Allids St Nashua NH 03060

SCHIMMEL, KARL FRANCIS, POLYMER SYNTHESIS, ORGANIC SYNTHESIS. *Current Pos:* SR RES ASSOC, PPG INDUSTS, 64- *Personal Data:* b Allentown, Pa, Mar 24, 36; m 61; c 4. *Educ:* Muhlenberg Col, BS, 57; Duquesne Univ, PhD(org chem), 61. *Prof Exp:* Res chemist, E I du Pont de Nemours & Co, Inc, 62-64. *Mem:* Am Chem Soc. *Res:* Coating and resins end uses. *Mailing Add:* PPG Industs Rosanna Dr PO Drawer 9 Allison Park PA 15101-0009

SCHIMMEL, PAUL REINHARD, BIOPHYSICS, BIOCHEMISTRY. *Current Pos:* from asst prof to assoc prof, 67-76, PROF BIOL, MASS INST TECHNOL, 76-, JOHN D & CATHERINE T MACARTHUR PROF BIOCHEM & BIOPHYSICS, 92- *Personal Data:* b Hartford, Conn, Aug 4, 40; m 61, Cleo Ritz; c Katherine & Leyla. *Educ:* Ohio Wesleyan Univ, AB, 62; Mass Inst Technol, PhD(phys biochem), 66. *Honors & Awards:* Pfizer Award, Am Chem Soc, 78. *Prof Exp:* Res assoc chem, Stanford Univ, 66-67. *Concurrent Pos:* Alfred P Sloan fel, 70-72; consult, NIH, 75-79; chmn, Div Biol Chem, Am Chem Soc, 84-85; dir, Repligan Corp, 81-, Alkermes Inc, 87- & Cubist Pharmaceut, Inc, 92- *Mem:* Nat Acad Sci; Am Chem Soc; fel AAAS; fel Am Acad Arts & Sci; Am Soc Biochem & Molecular Biol; RNA Soc; Protein Soc. *Res:* Gene, protein structure and function; aminoacyl acid synthetases; molecular recognition of transfer RNA; directed mutagenesis approach to structure-function relationships; operational RNA code for amino acids. *Mailing Add:* Dept Biol Mass Inst Technol Cambridge MA 02139

SCHIMMEL, WALTER PAUL, AERONAUTICAL & ASTRONAUTICAL ENGINEERING. *Current Pos:* AREA MGR, MAT & ADVAN MFG PROD, TECH TRAFFIC & COMMUN CTR, 94- *Personal Data:* US citizen. *Educ:* Purdue Univ, BS, 65; Univ Notre Dame, MS, 66, PhD(appl phys), 69. *Prof Exp:* Div supvr syst anal, Sandia Nat Labs, Albuquerque, NMex, 69-82; assoc dir electrothermal, Inst Res Hydro, Que, Montreal, 82-85; dept head, Embry Riddle Univ, Daytona Beach, Fla, 85-88, prof, 88- *Concurrent Pos:* NDEA fel, Univ Notre Dame, 65-68. *Mem:* Fel Am Soc Mech Engrs; Accreditation Bd Eng Technol; Am Inst Aeronaut & Astronaut; Am Soc Eng Educ; Can Elec Asn. *Res:* Author of over 100 publications; thermophysical properties; aerothermodynamics and plasma applications; laser measurement techniques; holographic interparometry. *Mailing Add:* 549 Pelican Bay Dr Daytona Beach FL 32119

SCHIMMER, BERNARD PAUL, ENDOCRINOLOGY, MEDICAL RESEARCH. *Current Pos:* from asst prof to assoc prof, 69-80, PROF MED RES & PHARMACOL, UNIV TORONTO, 80- *Personal Data:* b Newark, NJ, June 14, 41; m 65; c 2. *Educ:* Rutgers Univ, BS, 62; Tufts Univ, PhD(pharmacol), 67. *Honors & Awards:* Upjohn Award, Pharmacol Soc Can, 94. *Prof Exp:* Fel endocrinol & biochem, Brandeis Univ, 67-69. *Mem:* Am Soc Biol Chem & Molecular Biol; Can Soc Biol Chemists; AAAS; Endocrine Soc. *Res:* Regulation of differentiated functions in mammalian somatic cell cultures, with principal emphasis on mechanism of adrenocorticotrophic hormone action in adrenal cortex; hormone action studied through use of biochemistry and molecular genetics in cell culture systems. *Mailing Add:* Banting & Best Dept Med Res Univ Toronto 112 College St Toronto ON M5G 1L6 Can

SCHIMMERLING, WALTER, PHYSICS, BIOPHYSICS. *Current Pos:* PROG SCIENTIST, SPACE RADIATION HEALTH PROG, LIFE SCI DIV, NASA, 94- *Personal Data:* b Milan, Italy, Mar 10, 37; div; c 3. *Educ:* Univ Buenos Aires, MS, 62; Rutgers Univ, PhD(radiation sci), 71. *Prof Exp:* Instr physics & Ger, Univ Buenos Aires, 59-62; res assoc physics, AEC, Arg, 62-65; health physicist, Princeton Univ, 65-66, mem prof staff, Princeton-Pa Accelerator, 66-68, head radiation measurements, 68-71, asst dir, 71-72; res sr scientist, Lawrence Berkeley Lab, Univ Calif, Berkeley, 72-93; chief scientist, Space Life Sci Div, Univs Space Res Asn, 93-94. *Concurrent Pos:* Lectr, Univ Calif Exten, 78-80; prin investr, NASA, 75- & Nat Cancer Inst, 78-; vis sci, Ctr Nuclear Studies, Saclay, France, 84-85 & 87; vis sr scientist, NASA, 90-91. *Mem:* Am Phys Soc; Radiation Res Soc; Am Soc Gravitational & Space Biol; AAAS. *Res:* High energy heavy ions; nuclear physics and applications to cancer radiotherapy, space shielding and dosimetry. *Mailing Add:* NASA Hq Code UL Washington DC 20546-0001

SCHIMPF, DAVID JEFFREY, PLANT ECOLOGY. *Current Pos:* Asst prof, 79-85, dept head, 89-93, ASSOC PROF BIOL, UNIV MINN, DULUTH, 85- *Personal Data:* b Chicago, Ill, Oct 10, 48; div; c Brian T & Sally E. *Educ:* Iowa State Univ, BS, 70; Utah State Univ, PhD(biol), 77. *Concurrent Pos:* Dir, Olga Lakela Herbarium, 94- *Mem:* AAAS; Am Inst Biol Sci; Ecol Soc Am. *Res:* Autecology, population ecology, and community ecology of vascular plants; vegetation of the Lake Superior region; ecological concepts. *Mailing Add:* Dept Biol Univ Minn Duluth MN 55812-2496. *E-Mail:* dschimpf@d.umn.edu

SCHIN, KISSU, CELL BIOLOGY, DEVELOPMENTAL BIOLOGY. *Current Pos:* PROF BIOL, STATE UNIV NY, PLATTSBURGH, 70- *Educ:* Univ Gottingen, Ger, PhD(biol), 62. *Mailing Add:* Dept Biol Sci State Univ NY Col Plattsburgh 95 Broad St Plattsburgh NY 12901-2601

SCHINAGL, ERICH F, ALLERGY, AUTO IMMUNE DISEASE. *Current Pos:* med dir, Pharmacia Inc, 65-67, dir clin res, 67-69, med dir, 69-85, proj dir, 85-90, med dir, 91-93, dir urol, gynec & auto immunity, 93-96, CONSULT DRUG DEVELOP & SAFETY, PHARMACIA INC, 96- *Personal Data:* b Vienna, Austria, Sept 18, 32; m 57, Cynthia Stokes; c Catherine, Robert & Helen. *Educ:* Univ Vienna, MD, 61. *Prof Exp:* Intern, 61-62 & resident, Dept Internal Med, 62-65. *Mem:* AAAS; Am Heart Asn; Am Physiol Soc. *Res:* Preclinical and clinical development of drugs and devices in allergy, auto immune disease, cardiology, dermatology, oncology and ophthalmology. *Mailing Add:* 6970 Harriott Rd Powell OH 43065. *E-Mail:* schinagl@qn.net

SCHINDLER, ALBERT ISADORE, PHYSICS, CONDENSED MATTER PHYSICS. *Current Pos:* CONSULT, 92- *Personal Data:* b Pittsburgh, Pa, June 24, 27; m 51, Phyllis L Liberman; c Janet M (Strauss), Jerald S & Ellen S (Balfour). *Educ:* Carnegie Inst Technol, BS, 47, MS, 48, DSc(physics), 50. *Honors & Awards:* Hulburt Award, 56; Nat Capital Award, 62; Naval Res Lab-Sci Res Soc Am Award, 65. *Prof Exp:* Asst physics, Carnegie Inst Technol, 47-50, res physicist, 50-51; supvry res physicist, Naval Res Lab, Washington, DC, 51-75, assoc dir res mat sci & component technol, 75-85; prof mat eng & physics, Purdue Univ, West Lafayette, Ind, 85-92. *Concurrent Pos:* Dir, Div Mat Res, NSF, 88-90; dir, Ind Innovative Superconductor Technol, Purdue Univ, 88-91 & Midwest Superconductivity Consortium, 90-91. *Mem:* Fel Am Phys Soc; Sigma Xi. *Res:* Condensed matter physics; electronic magnetic and superconducting properties of metals, alloys and oxides. *Mailing Add:* 6615 Sulky Lane Rockville MD 20852

SCHINDLER, CHARLES ALVIN, MICROBIOLOGY, BIOCHEMISTRY. *Current Pos:* INDEPENDENT CONSULT MICROBIOL, 94- *Personal Data:* b Boston, Mass, Dec 27, 24; m 55, Barbara Francois; c Marian, Susan & Neal. *Educ:* Rensselaer Polytech Inst, BS, 50; Univ Tex, MA, 56, PhD(microbiol), 61. *Prof Exp:* Res & develop officer, Radiobiol Lab, Atomic Warfare Div, USAF, 52, asst prog dir, Armed Forces Spec Weapons Proj, 52-53, res scientist microbiol, Army Biol Warfare Lab, 56-58, Univ Tex, 61 & Armed Forces Inst Path, 62-68; asst prof microbiol, Univ Okla, 68-72; prof natural sci, Flagler Col, 72-73; sci teacher, Norman Pub Schs, 74-86; sci supvr, Okla City Pub Schs, 89-91, sci consult, 92-94. *Concurrent Pos:* Charles E Lewis fel, 58. *Mem:* Am Soc Microbiol; Am Chem Soc; Brit Soc Gen Microbiol; NY Acad Sci; Sigma Xi. *Res:* Antibiotics and bacteriolytic enzymes, especially their production and mode of action on the bacterial cell; relationship of action of bacteriolytic enzymes to structure of microorganisms; recipient of United States and foreign patents; awarded US and foreign patents. *Mailing Add:* 2000 Morgan Dr Norman OK 73069. *E-Mail:* 104123.771@compuserve.com

SCHINDLER, DAVID WILLIAM, LIMNOLOGY, BIOGEOCHEMISTRY. *Current Pos:* dir, Exp Lakes Area Proj, 70-87, RES SCIENTIST, FRESHWATER INST, CAN DEPT FISHERIES & OCEANS, 68- *Personal Data:* b Fargo, NDak, Aug 3, 40; m 64, 79; c 3. *Educ:* NDak State Univ, BS, 62; Oxford Univ, DPhil(ecol), 66. *Hon Degrees:* DSc, NDak State Univ, 78. *Honors & Awards:* Frank Rigler Mem Award, Soc Can Limnologists, 84; G E Hutchinson Medal, Am Soc Limnol & Oceanog, 85; Ken Doan Medal, Can Dept Fisheries & Oceans, 85. *Prof Exp:* Asst prof biol, Trent Univ, 66-68. *Concurrent Pos:* Res grants, Can Nat Res Coun, Ont Dept Univ Affairs, 66-68 & NSF, 67-68; adj prof zool, Univ Man, 72-, adj prof bot, 81-; vis sr res assoc, Lamont-Doherty Geol Observ, Columbia Univ, 76-; chmn, US Nat Acad Sci Comt Atmosphere & Biosphere, 79-81; chmn, Int Joint Comn Comt Ecol & Oceanog; fel, Royal Soc Can, 83- *Mem:* Am Soc Limnol & Oceanog (vpres, 81-82, pres, 82-83); Brit Ecol Soc; Int Asn Theoret & Appl Limnol; Am Geophys Union; Ecol Soc Am; Am Inst Biol Sci. *Res:* Ecosystems; biological and chemical ecology; biogeochemistry; experimental mainpulation of whole ecosystems. *Mailing Add:* Dept Biol Sci Univ Alta Edmonton AB T6G 2M7 Can. *Fax:* 403-492-7033

SCHINDLER, GUENTER MARTIN, MATHEMATICS. *Current Pos:* RETIRED. *Personal Data:* b Ebersdorf, Ger, Sept 15, 28; nat US; m 57, Helga M Breitenstein; c Nicoline & Christoph. *Educ:* Univ Gottingen, dipl, 53; Univ Kiel, Vor-dipl, 51, Dr rer nat, 56. *Prof Exp:* Assoc math, Univ Gottingen, 53-56; res mathematician, Kernreactor, Karlsruhe, 56-57; sr mathematician, USAF Missile Develop Ctr, NMex, 57-58; sr scientist, Aerophys Develop Corp, Calif, 58-59; chief mathematician, Adv Tech Corp, 59-61; proj mgr, Gen Elec Co, 61-65; sr tech specialist, NAm Rockwell Corp, 65-68; prin scientist, Douglas Aircraft Co, Long Beach, Calif, 68-74; vis prof, Univ Southern Calif, 74-75; independent consult, 75-77; mem tech staff, Rockwell Int-Nam Aircraft Opers, El Segundo, 77-89. *Concurrent Pos:* Lectr, Univ NMex, 58; assoc prof, Univ Calif, 58-59; consult, Avco-Crosley Corp, 59, Astro-Res Corp, 61-65 & US Navy Marine Eng Lab, 65. *Mem:* Am Math Soc; NY Acad Sci. *Res:* Pure and applied mathematics; theoretical physics. *Mailing Add:* 28026 Beechgate Dr Rancho Palos Verdes CA 90275-3817

SCHINDLER, HANS, PETROLEUM CHEMISTRY. *Current Pos:* CONSULT, 76- *Personal Data:* b Vienna, Austria, Sept 2, 11; nat US; wid, Marianne Stern. *Educ:* Prague Ger Univ, DSc(org chem), 34. *Prof Exp:* Asst chief chemist, Julius Schindler Oil Works, Ger, 35-38; sr res chemist, Pure Oil Co, 38-46; sr res chemist, Witco Corp, 46-52, mgr petrolia ref, 53-60, vpres, Sonneborn Div, 60-76. *Concurrent Pos:* Mem, Tech Oil Mission, 45. *Mem:* NY Acad Sci; Am Inst Chem; Am Chem Soc. *Mailing Add:* 1 Wash Sq Village New York NY 10012

SCHINDLER, JAMES EDWARD, ZOOLOGY. *Current Pos:* ASSOC PROF ZOOL, CLEMSON UNIV, 76- *Personal Data:* b Fargo, NDak, Apr 20, 44; m 67; c 2. *Educ:* NDak State Univ, BS, 66; Queen's Col, Oxford Univ, DPhil(zool), 69. *Prof Exp:* Asst prof, Univ Ga, 69-76. *Mem:* Am Soc Limnol & Oceanog; Sigma Xi. *Res:* Aquatic ecology; limnology. *Mailing Add:* Bio Sci Clemson Univ Clemson SC 29632-0001

SCHINDLER, JOE PAUL, ELECTRONICS ENGINEERING, TECHNICAL MANAGEMENT. *Current Pos:* CONSULT, MICROWAVE & ELECTRONICS CO, 86-; MKT CONSULT, SCHINDLER COMMUN. *Personal Data:* b Berlin, Ger, Apr 8, 27; US citizen; m 55, Jane Hoffberg; c 3. *Educ:* Polytech Inst, Brooklyn, BEE, 50, MEE, 58. *Prof Exp:* Eng develop dept head, Polarad Electronics Corp, 50-62, vpres mkt, 62-65; vpres mkt, Narda Microwave Corp, 65-79, Gen Microwave Corp, 87-89 & Bertan Assocs, 90-91; pres & chief exec officer, Rohde & Schwarz, Polarad Inc,

79-87; pres, Chestec Corp, 91-92. *Concurrent Pos:* Dir, N Hills Electronics, 81-91; dir, Safety First Systs, Ltd, 87-, secy & treas, 90- *Mem:* Sigma Xi; Am Mach Asn; Inst Elec & Electronics Engrs. *Res:* Electronics; microwave instrumentation and components; tutorial articles published in microwave journal and microwaves magazines. *Mailing Add:* 118 Old Mill Rd Great Neck NY 11023

SCHINDLER, JOEL MARVIN, developmental biology, cell biology, for more information see previous edition

SCHINDLER, JOHN FREDERICK, FRESH WATER BIOLOGY. *Current Pos:* RETIRED. *Personal Data:* b Chicago, Ill, Aug 23, 31; m 55, Erna Zehtner; c Lynn & Laura. *Educ:* Mich State Univ, BS, 53, MS, 54. *Prof Exp:* Res asst phycol, Mich State Univ, 53, 54, 59-60; test design aide & off biol warfare, US Army, Dugway Proving Ground, Utah, 56-57; chief foreman mining, Minnas Cerro Colo, Mex, 58; asst dir, Naval Arctic Res Lab, Univ Alaska-Off Naval Res, 60-71, dir, 71-73; chief scientist & environ eng, Alaskan Resource Sci Corp, 73-76; dir environ affairs, Husky Oil NPR Opers Inc, 76-83; chief, Environ Assessment Sect, Alaska OCS, Minerals Mgt Serv, Dept Interior, 84-94. *Concurrent Pos:* Mem, NSF Chihuahua Biol Exped, 55; mem, Scott Polar Res; arctic consult & vpres, Pac Alaska Assoc Ltd, 73-, environ consult, Pipeline Coordr Off, State Alaska, 75-76. *Mem:* AAAS; fel Arctic Inst NAm; Explorers Club. *Res:* Arctic logistics and science support in the Arctic; Arctic oceanography; freshwater algae of the Flathead Basin, Montana; genus Staurastrum. *Mailing Add:* 2473 Captain Cook Dr Anchorage AK 99517-1254

SCHINDLER, MAX J, COMPUTER SCIENCE, MICROWAVES. *Current Pos:* PRES, PRIME TECHNOL INC, 80- *Personal Data:* b Warnsdorf, Czech, June 21, 22; US citizen; m 55, Dudy Curry; c Christian, Manfred & Norbert. *Educ:* Vienna Tech Univ, Dipl Ing, 51, Dr Tech Sc, 53. *Honors & Awards:* Inst Elec & Electronics Engrs Award, 76 & Centennial Medal, 84; Jesse Neal Award, 86 & 88. *Prof Exp:* Asst solid-state physics, Vienna Tech Univ, 51-54; engr, Tungsram-Watt, Austria, 54-57; res scientist, Aeronaut Res Lab, Wright Air Develop Ctr, Ohio, 57-58; engr, Phys Lab, RCA Microwave, NJ, 58-61, sr engr, 62-67, mem tech staff, RCA Labs, David Sarnoff Res Ctr, 67-69, lead engr solid state & TWT subsysts eng, RCA Microwave, Harrison, 69-75; comput consult, 76; comput ed, Electronic Design, 76-79. *Concurrent Pos:* Eng physics consult, Nat Corp Sci, NY, 77-81; Microwave consult, Photovolt, NY, 78-82; software corresp, Elektronic, Munich 78-92. *Mem:* Life mem Inst Elec & Electronics Engrs. *Res:* Magnetic materials and measurements; magnetic focusing structures; high-efficiency traveling-wave tubes; microwave solid state amplifiers; electronic delay devices; computer-aided design; computer system design; software design methodologies; book author. *Mailing Add:* 4 S Rockaway Dr Boonton Township NJ 07005

SCHINDLER, STEPHEN MICHAEL, ASTROPHYSICS. *Current Pos:* SR SCIENTIST & MEM PROF STAFF PHYSICS, CALIF INST TECHNOL, 79- *Personal Data:* b New York, NY, Apr 9, 40; m 61; c 2. *Educ:* Long Island Univ, BS, 68; Colo State Univ, PhD(physics), 74. *Prof Exp:* Sr scientist physics, Bettis Atomic Power Lab, 73-74; res assoc physics, Case Western Res Univ, 74-78. *Mem:* Am Phys Soc. *Res:* High energy astrophysics, with emphasis in gamma-ray astronomy, cosmic ray origin theory, and solar particle production. *Mailing Add:* 220-47 Downs Lab Calif Inst Technol Pasadena CA 91125

SCHINDLER, SUSAN, MATHEMATICS. *Current Pos:* PROF MATH, BARUCH COL, 77- *Personal Data:* b Brooklyn, NY, June 4, 42. *Educ:* Mt Holyoke Col, AB, 63; Univ Wis, MA, 65, PhD(math), 69. *Prof Exp:* Asst prof math, Long Island Univ, 69-70; asst prof, 70-77. *Mem:* Am Math Soc; Math Asn Am; Soc Indust & Appl Math. *Res:* Decompositions of group representations. *Mailing Add:* Dept Math Baruch Col 17 Lexington Ave New York NY 10010-5526

SCHINDLER, WILLIAM JOSEPH, ENDOCRINOLOGY. *Current Pos:* RETIRED. *Personal Data:* b Cleveland, Ohio, Dec 11, 31; m 72; c 3. *Educ:* Univ Calif, Los Angeles, BA, 55, PhD(anat), 59; Baylor Col Med, MD, 74. *Prof Exp:* Asst physiol, Sch Med, Univ Calif, Los Angeles, 55-56, asst anat, 56-57, interdisciplinary trainee neurol sci, 58-59; from instr to assoc prof physiol, Baylor Col Med, 59-76; pvt pract, 76-97. *Concurrent Pos:* NSF fel neuroendocrinol, Maudsley Hosp, London, 60-61, Found Fund for Res in Psychiat fel, 61-62; Nat Inst Arthritis & Metab Dis res career develop award, 66- *Mem:* AAAS; Endocrine Soc; Am Physiol Soc; Soc Exp Biol & Med; NY Acad Sci. *Res:* Neuroendocrinology; developmental endocrinology, especially pituitary-thyroid maturation and function; human infertility; growth hormone secretion and control. *Mailing Add:* 3210 Hickory Brook Lane Kingwood TX 77345

SCHINGOETHE, DAVID JOHN, DAIRY NUTRITION. *Current Pos:* From asst prof to assoc prof, 69-80, PROF DAIRY SCI & NUTRIT, SDAK STATE UNIV, 80- *Personal Data:* b Aurora, Ill, Feb 15, 42; m 64, Darlene Wennlund; c Darcy & Deanna. *Educ:* Univ Ill, Urbana, BS, 64, MS, 65; Mich State Univ, PhD(nutrit), 68. *Honors & Awards:* Am Feed Indust Asn Award, Am Dairy Sci Asn, 89, Nutrit Prof Inc Appl Dairy Nutrit Award, 96. *Concurrent Pos:* Actg dept head dairy sci, SDak State Univ, 86; dir, Am Dairy Sci Asn, 96- *Mem:* Am Dairy Sci Asn; Am Soc Animal Sci; Coun Agr Sci & Technol; Am Soc Nutrit Sci. *Res:* Nutritional biochemistry of rumen metabolism; gastrointestinal digestion and absorption; milk synthesis; protein, energy, and vitamin E nutrition of dairy cattle; whey utilization; sunflower product utilization. *Mailing Add:* Dept Dairy Sci Box 2104 SDak State Univ Brookings SD 57007-0647. *Fax:* 605-688-6276; *E-Mail:* schingod@ur.sdstate.edu

SCHINK, CHESTER ALBERT, ORGANIC CHEMISTRY. *Current Pos:* RETIRED. *Personal Data:* b Portland, Ore, Feb 17, 20; m 47, Hannah L Johnson; c 2. *Educ:* Reed Col, BA, 41; Ore State Col, MA, 43, PhD(org chem), 47. *Prof Exp:* Chemist, Exp Sta, Hercules Powder Co, Del, 43-44; Radford Ord Works, Va, 44-45; asst, Ore State Col, 45-47; res chemist, E I du Pont de Nemours & Co, Inc, 47-51; mgr, Krishell Labs, Inc, 51-56; mgr, Chem Support Lab, Tektronix, Inc, 56-70, sr chemist, 70-71, corp chemist, 71-85; consult, 85-97. *Mem:* Am Indust Hyg Asn; Am Chem Soc; Am Soc Safety Eng. *Res:* Identification of constituents of natural products; biologically active compounds; synthetic resins and plastics primarily of the vinyl type; research chemicals, especially purines, pyrimidines and enzymes; air and water quality; water pollution control, industrial hygiene and chemical safety. *Mailing Add:* 3943 SE Cooper St Portland OR 97202

SCHINK, DAVID R, CHEMICAL OCEANOGRAPHY. *Current Pos:* assoc prof, 72-76, assoc dean geosci, 84-88, PROF OCEANOG, TEX A&M UNIV, 76- *Personal Data:* b Los Angeles, Calif, Aug 3, 31; m 51; c 4. *Educ:* Pomona Col, BA, 52; Univ Calif, Los Angeles, MS, 53; Univ Calif, San Diego, PhD(oceanog), 62; Stanford Univ, MS, 58. *Prof Exp:* Res geochemist, Scripps Inst, Calif, 60-62; asst prof oceanog, Narragansett Marine Lab, Univ RI, 62-66; mgr air-ocean studies, Palo Alto Labs, Teledyne-Isotopes, 66-71. *Concurrent Pos:* Admin judge, Atomic Safety & Licensing Bd Panel, Nuclear Regulatory Comn, 74-; assoc ed, J Geophys Res, 80-86, Progress Oceanog, 81- US Nat Report to Int Union Geod & Geophys (chem oceanog), 82-86; mem, expert group, methods, standards & intercalibration, Intergovt Oceanog Comn, UN, 82-87; mem, adv comt ocean sci, NSF, 84-88 & adv comt earth sci, 85-88. *Mem:* AAAS; Am Geophys Union; Am Chem Soc; Oceanog Soc. *Res:* Oceanic silicon budgets and behavior; air-ocean gas exchange; radon/radium in sea water; diagenesis of marine sediments; chemistry of warm-core rings; applications of accelerator mass spectrometry to oceanography. *Mailing Add:* Dept Oceanog Tex A&M Univ College Station TX 77843-3146

SCHINK, F E, ELECTRICAL ENGINEERING. *Current Pos:* RETIRED. *Personal Data:* b Brooklyn, NY, May 4, 22; m 46, Barbara J McCally; c Stephen & Thomas. *Educ:* Polytech Inst, BEE, 52, MEE, 55. *Honors & Awards:* Elec Eng Mgt, Inst Elec & Electronics Engrs, 83, Centennial Medal, 84. *Prof Exp:* Elec engr, Anaconda Co, 46-59; engr, Anaconda-Jurden Assoc, 59-61; sr engr, M W Kellogg Co, 61-62; sr engr, Port Authority NY & NJ, 62-76, asst chief, 76-84, chief elec eng, 84-88. *Concurrent Pos:* Dir, Electro, 76-79; lectr, Int Elec Expos & Congr, 86, 87. *Mem:* Power Eng Soc; fel Inst Elec & Electronics Engrs; Indust Applns Soc. *Mailing Add:* 14 Middlebury Lane Cranford NJ 07016

SCHINZINGER, ROLAND, OPERATIONS RESEARCH. *Current Pos:* RETIRED. *Personal Data:* b Osaka, Japan, Nov 22, 26; nat US; m 94, Shirley Barrows Price; c Stefan, Annelise & Barbara. *Educ:* Univ Calif, BS, 53, MS, 54, PhD, 66. *Honors & Awards:* Centennial Medal, Inst Elec & Electronics Engrs, 84. *Prof Exp:* Engr, Westinghouse Elec Corp, Pa, 54-58; from asst prof to assoc prof elec eng, Robert Col, Istanbul, 58-63; from asst prof to prof elec eng, Univ Calif, Irvine, 66-93, assoc dean, 79-83 & 85-86. *Concurrent Pos:* NSF fel, 64-65; indust consult, 67-; acad visitor, Inst Sci & Technol, Univ Manchester, 72-73, Imp Col, London, 72-73, Univ Karlsruhe, Ger, 85 & Fed Univ Santa Maria, Brazil, 93; lectr & researcher Brazil, Fulbright Comn, 93. *Mem:* Fel AAAS; fel Inst Elec & Electronics Engrs; Opers Res Soc Am; Sigma Xi; Am Soc Eng Educ; Soc Philos & Technol. *Res:* Power systems; utility networks; operations research; failure analysis; contingency planning; engineering ethics. *Mailing Add:* Dept Elec & Comput Eng Univ Calif Irvine CA 92697-2625. *Fax:* 714-824-2321

SCHIPMA, PETER B, INFORMATION SCIENCE. *Current Pos:* PRES, IS GRUPE, INC, 84- *Personal Data:* b Chicago, Ill, Oct 24, 41; m 62; c 3. *Educ:* Ill Inst Technol, BS, 65, MS, 67. *Prof Exp:* Res asst physics, R R Donnelley & Sons Co, 62-66; from asst to assoc scientist info sci, ITT Res Inst, 67-70, res scientist, 70-72, mgr info sci, 72-84. *Concurrent Pos:* Adj assoc prof, Ill Inst Technol, 67-74; consult, WHO, 77-, Czechoslovaki, 78, Saudi Arabia, 81; instr, Trinity Christian Col, 77-86; chmn finance comt, Asn Info & Dissemination Ctrs, 78-79. *Mem:* Am Soc Info Sci; Asn Info & Dissemination Ctrs (secy-treas, 77). *Res:* Machine-readable data base design; application of video technology to information retrieval; artificial intelligence; CD-ROM. *Mailing Add:* IS Grupe Inc 415 E Plaza Dr Westmont IL 60559

SCHIPPER, ARTHUR LOUIS, JR, PLANT PATHOLOGY, PLANT PHYSIOLOGY. *Current Pos:* Plant physiologist, NCent Forest Exp Sta, USDA, 68-78, staff res plant pathologist, Wash Off, 79-84, asst sta dir, PNW Res Sta, Forest Serv, 84-90, ASSOC AREA DIR, NATLANTIC AREA, AGR RES SERV, USDA, 90- *Personal Data:* b Bryan, Tex, Apr 8, 40; m 64; c 2. *Educ:* Univ of the South, BS, 62; Univ Minn, St Paul, MS, 65, PhD(plant path), 68. *Concurrent Pos:* Adj asst prof, Dept Plant Path, Univ Minn, 68-75, adj assoc prof, 75-78. *Mem:* Sigma Xi. *Res:* Biochemical and physiological changes in plants infected with plant parasitic fungi. *Mailing Add:* 119 Rosewood Dr Lansdale PA 19446

SCHIPPER, EDGAR, ORGANIC CHEMISTRY. *Current Pos:* GROUP LEADER, ETHICON INC, 65- *Personal Data:* b Vienna, Austria, Sept 12, 20; nat US; m 51; c 2. *Educ:* City Col New York, BS, 47; Univ Pa, MS, 48, PhD(chem), 51. *Prof Exp:* Pharmaceut chemist, Gold Leaf Pharmaceut Co, 41-42; assoc chemist, Ethicon, Inc, 51-61; mgr org & med chem, Shulton, Inc, 61-65. *Mem:* Am Chem Soc. *Res:* Medicinal organic chemistry; biomedical devices research. *Mailing Add:* 44 Nomahegan Ct Cranford NJ 07016

SCHIPPER, LEE (LEON JAY), ENERGY ANALYSIS, ENERGY POLICY. *Current Pos:* LECTR ACOUST, SAN FRANCISCO CONSERV MUSIC, 71-; STAFF SCIENTIST ENERGY ANALYSIS, LAWRENCE BERKELEY LAB, UNIV CALIF, 77- *Personal Data:* b Santa Monica, Calif, Apr 7, 47; m 71; c 2. *Educ:* Univ Calif, Berkeley, AB, 68, MA, 71, PhD(physics), 82. *Concurrent Pos:* Specialist energy anal, Energy & Resources Group, Univ Calif, 74-77; mem, Demand Panel, Study Nuclear & Alternative Energy Syst, Nat Acad Sci, 76-78; energy consult to var int orgn, 76-; guest researcher, Beijer Inst, Royal Swed Acad Sci, 77- *Mem:* Soc Heating & Air Conditioning Engrs, Sweden; AAAS; Int Asn Energy Economists. *Res:* Conservation; policy; economics of energy systems; energy use in developing countries; structure of clusters of galaxies; life and recordings of Wilhelm Furtwaengler, conductor; acoustics. *Mailing Add:* 631 Vincente Ave Berkeley CA 94707

SCHIRBER, JAMES E, SOLID STATE PHYSICS. *Current Pos:* staff mem, 62-64, div supvr solid state physics, 64-68, MGR SOLID STATE RES DEPT, SANDIA LABS, 68- *Personal Data:* b Eureka, SDak, June 9, 31; m 55, Catherine A Nolan; c Carol, Leo, Peter, Andrew, Mary J, Michael & Mark. *Educ:* Iowa State Univ, BA, 53, PhD(physics), 60. *Prof Exp:* Weather officer, USAF, 53-57; Nat Acad Sci-Nat Res Coun fel, Bristol, 61-62. *Mem:* Fel Am Phys Soc; fel AAAS; Mat Res Soc. *Res:* Low temperature high pressure metal physics; Fermi surface of metals under hydrostatic pressure; magnetism and superconductivity studies under pressure; high temperature organic and fuleerene superconductivity. *Mailing Add:* HC 89 PO Box 94 Hermosa SD 57744. *Fax:* 505-844-4045

SCHIRCH, LAVERNE GENE, BIOCHEMISTRY, ORGANIC CHEMISTRY. *Current Pos:* ASSOC PROF BIOCHEM, MED COL VA, VA COMMONWEALTH UNIV, 78- *Personal Data:* b Chenoa, Ill, Aug 9, 36; m 58; c 3. *Educ:* Bluffton Col, BS, 58; Univ Mich, PhD(biochem), 63. *Prof Exp:* From asst prof to prof chem, Bluffton Col, 63-78. *Concurrent Pos:* Res consult, Ente Nazionale Idrocarburi, Rome, 69-70. *Mem:* Am Chem Soc; Am Soc Biol Chemists. *Res:* Mechanism of action of serine and threonine aldolases, especially the role of pyridoxal phosphate in these enzymes. *Mailing Add:* Biochem Dept Va Commonwealth Univ PO Box 614 Richmond VA 23298. *Fax:* 804-786-1473; *E-Mail:* Bitnet: %schirch@vcuvax

SCHIRMER, HELGA H, MATHEMATICS. *Current Pos:* from assoc prof to prof, 66-93, EMER PROF MATH, CARLETON UNIV, 93- *Personal Data:* b Chemnitz, Ger, Oct 18, 27. *Educ:* Univ Frankfurt, MSc, 53, Dr rer nat(math), 54. *Prof Exp:* Brit Coun res scholar math, Univ Oxford, 54-56; asst lectr, Univ Wales, 56-59; from asst prof to assoc prof, Univ NB, 59-66. *Concurrent Pos:* Vis prof, Univ Calif, Los Angeles, 83, Delhi Univ, 86. *Mem:* Am Math Soc; Can Math Soc. *Res:* General and algebraic topology; theory of fixed points and coincidences; multifunctions. *Mailing Add:* Dept Math & Statist Carleton Univ 1125 Colonel By Dr Ottawa ON K1S 5B6 Can

SCHIRMER, HOWARD AUGUST, JR, CIVIL ENGINEERING. *Current Pos:* chmn geotech eng comn, 76-78, CHMN PROF LIABILITY COMN, AM CONSULT ENGRS COUN, 84- *Personal Data:* b Oakland, Calif, Apr 21, 42; m 65, Leslie M Mecum; c Christine C, Amy K & Patricia L. *Educ:* Univ Calif, Berkeley, BS, 64, MS, 65. *Honors & Awards:* Edmund Friedman Young Engr Award, Am Soc Civil Engrs, 74. *Prof Exp:* Engr, Training Mat & Res Dept, Calif Div Hwys, Sacramento, 60-64; eng analyst, Dames & Moore, San Francisco, 64-67; asst staff engr, 67-68, chief engr, 69-72, assoc, Honolulu, 72-75, partner & managing prin-in-charge, 75-78, regional mgr, Pac Far East & Australia, 78-81, chief oper officer, Los Angeles, 81-83, managing dir, Dames & Moore Int, Los Angeles, 83-89; managing dir, CH2M Hill Int Ltd, 89-90, pres, 91. *Concurrent Pos:* Past chmn, adv comt eng tech, Honolulu Community Col; chmn eng sect & mem budget comt, Aloha United Way, 74. *Mem:* Fel Am Soc Civil Engrs; Fedn Int des Ingenieurs-Conseils; Int Soc Soil Mech & Found Eng; Am Soc Prof Engrs; Am Pub Works Asn (secy, 77-78); Soc Am Mil Engrs. *Mailing Add:* 40100 East Quincy Ave Englewood CO 80110-5051

SCHIROKY, GERHARD H, CHEMICAL VAPOR DEPOSITION, COMPOSITES. *Current Pos:* scientist, 86, MGR MFG TECHNOL, LANXIDE CORP, 87- *Educ:* Friedrich-Alexander Univ, Ger, dipl, 78;Univ Mo, MS, 79; Univ Utah, PhD(mats sci & eng), 82. *Prof Exp:* Sr scientist, Gen Atomics, 82-86. *Mem:* Am Ceramic Soc. *Res:* Ceramic matrix composites; coatings; chemical vapor deposition; metal matrix composites; high temperature processing equipment; development of manufacturing technology; process scale-up; flexible manufacturing. *Mailing Add:* 37 Michaelangelo Ct Hockessin DE 19707

SCHIRRA, WALTER MARTY, JR, ASTRONAUTICS. *Current Pos:* RETIRED. *Personal Data:* b Hackensack, NJ, Mar 12, 23; m 46, Josephine C Fraser; c Walter M III & Suzanne K. *Educ:* US Naval Acad, BS, 45. *Hon Degrees:* D Astronautics, Lafayette Coll, Univ Southern Calif & NJ Inst Technol. *Prof Exp:* From comdr to capt, 45-65, co-develop, Sidewinder Missle, USN, 52-54, suitability develop proj F4H, 58-59, NASA Project Mercury, 59, pilot spacecraft, Sigma 7, 62, Astronaut Office, 64-69, command pilot, Gemini 6, 65, comdr 11 day flight, Apollo 7, 68; pres, Regency Investors, Inc, 69-70; chmn & chief exec off, ECCO Corp, 70-73; chmn, Sernco, Inc, 73-74; staff mem, Johns-Manville Corp, 74-77; vpres develop, Goodwin Cos, Inc, 78-79; consult, 79-80. *Concurrent Pos:* dir, Kimberly Clark, 83-91. *Mem:* Fel Am Astronaut Soc; fel Soc Exp Test Pilots. *Mailing Add:* PO Box 73 Rancho Sante Fe CA 92067

SCHISLA, ROBERT M, ORGANIC CHEMISTRY. *Current Pos:* CONSULT, 85- *Personal Data:* b Indianapolis, Ind, Mar 30, 30; m 53; c 5. *Educ:* Purdue Univ, BS, 52, MS, 54, PhD(org chem), 57. *Prof Exp:* Asst, Purdue Univ, 52-54; res chemist, Monsanto Co, 57-61, sr res chemist, Monsanto Indust Chem Co, 61-65, res specialist, 65, group leader, 66-71, res specialist for fine chems, 71-85. *Res:* Synthetic organic chemistry related to functional fluids and fine chemicals; process development for fine chemicals. *Mailing Add:* 1333 Woodgate St Louis MO 63122

SCHISLER, LEE CHARLES, MYCOLOGY. *Current Pos:* prof, 64-88, EMER PROF PLANT PATH, PA STATE UNIV, 89- *Personal Data:* b Northampton, Pa, June 25, 28; m 51; c 2. *Educ:* Pa State Univ, BS, 50, MS, 52, PhD(bot), 57. *Prof Exp:* Dir res, Butler Co Mushroom Farm, Inc, 57-64. *Mem:* Am Soc Plant Physiol; Mycol Soc Am; Am Phytopath Soc; Sigma Xi; fel AAAS; Am Inst Biol Sci. *Res:* Physiology and pathology of cultivated mushrooms; fungus physiology and mycology. *Mailing Add:* 317 S Sparks St State College PA 16801

SCHIVELL, JOHN FRANCIS, PLASMA DIAGNOSTICS, IMAGE RECONSTRUCTION. *Current Pos:* COMPUT PROGRAMMER, CAMBRIDGE HYDRODYN, 97- *Personal Data:* b Cleveland, Ohio, Sept 5, 42; m 66; c 2. *Educ:* Harvard Univ, AB, 63, AM, 64, PhD(physics), 68. *Prof Exp:* Physicist, Nat Accelerator Lab, 68-73; mem tech staff, Princeton Plasma Physics Lab, 73-95. *Mem:* Am Phys Soc. *Res:* Photoproduction of elementary particles; design and development of particle accelerators; design, construction, and basic measurements on tokamak plasma confinement devices; software systems for experiment control and analysis. *Mailing Add:* Cambridge Hydrodyn PO Box 1403 Princeton NJ 08542

SCHJELDERUP, HASSEL CHARLES, ENGINEERING MECHANICS. *Current Pos:* RETIRED. *Personal Data:* b Vernon, BC, June 18, 26; US citizen; m 53, Rose Khatchadourian; c William Hassel, Mia (Garoon), Kim Elizabeth, Christine (Dovvian), Robert Kevork, Roger Dovian, Katherine (Seroon). *Educ:* Univ BC, BASc, 49; Stanford Univ, MSc, 50, PhD(eng mech), 53. *Prof Exp:* Asst, Stanford Univ, 49-52; group leader struct eng, Northrop Aircraft Corp, 53-55; tech asst strength & dynamics, Douglas Aircraft Corp, 55-59; assoc prof eng, Nat Eng Sci Co, 59-64; dir eng, Dynamic Sci Corp, 64-65; mgr advan technol, Douglas Aircraft Corp, Long Island, 65-67, asst dir res, 67-68, dir res, 68-72, dep dir mat & process eng, 72-79, dir mat & process eng, 79-86; prog mgr, Advan Prod, 86-87. *Concurrent Pos:* Instr, Exten, Univ Calif, Los Angeles, 53-58; struct & dynamics consult, 53- *Mem:* Am Inst Aeronaut & Astronaut; Soc Advan Mat & Process Engrs. *Res:* Random vibrations; structural vibration and fatigue caused by jet engine noise; advanced composite materials. *Mailing Add:* 1630 West Dr San Marino CA 91108-2257. *Fax:* 626-458-8418; *E-Mail:* hcsemail@aol.com

SCHLABACH, T(OM) D(ANIEL), METALLURGY, NON-FUEL MINERAL RESOURCES. *Current Pos:* RETIRED. *Personal Data:* b Cleveland, Ohio, July 4, 24; m 48; c 2. *Educ:* Baldwin-Wallace Col, BS, 48; Mich State Col, PhD(chem), 52. *Prof Exp:* Mem tech staff & res chemist, AT&T Bell Labs Inc, 52-59, supvr, 59-65, dept head metall, 65-89. *Mem:* Fel AAAS; fel Am Inst Chemists; fel Am Soc Metals Int; Minerals Metals & Mat Soc; Mat Res Soc. *Res:* Alloy development; materials conservation and substitution; high-temperature superconductors. *Mailing Add:* 4 Adams Dr Whippany NJ 07981-2050

SCHLACHTER, ALFRED SIMON, ATOMIC PHYSICS, ATOMIC & MOLECULAR PHOTOIONITATION. *Current Pos:* PHYSICIST, LAWRENCE BERKELEY LAB, UNIV CALIF, 75-, HEAD, USER LIAISON GROUP, ADVAN LIGHT SOURCE, 89- *Personal Data:* b Cedar City, Utah, Feb 18, 42. *Educ:* Univ Calif, Berkeley, AB, 63; Univ Wis, Madison, MA, 65, PhD(physics), 69. *Prof Exp:* Asst physics, Univ Wis, 63-68; prin res scientist, Honeywell Corp Res Ctr, 68-70; res assoc, Faculty Sci, Inst Fundamental Electronics, Univ Paris & researcher, Saclay Nuclear Res Ctr, 71-75. *Concurrent Pos:* Nat Ctr Sci Res fel, Univ Paris, 71-72; Joliot-Curie Fel, Saclay Nuclear Res Ctr, 72-73; vis scientist, Justus-Liebig Univ, Giessen, WGer, 80-81; Alexander von Humboldt Found travelling fel, 80-81; adj assoc prof, NC State Univ, 86-95; vis prof, Univ Paris, 92. *Mem:* Fel Am Phys Soc; Optical Soc Am. *Res:* Atomic collisions; sources of negative ions; particle beams; multiply charged ion-atom collisions; fusion energy; synchrotron radiation; photoionization; fundamental experiments on atomic and molecular physics using high-brightness synchrotion radiation; photoionization. *Mailing Add:* Lawrence Berkeley Nat Lab MS 80-101 Univ Calif Berkeley CA 94720. *Fax:* 510-486-6499; *E-Mail:* fred_schlachter@lbl.gov

SCHLAEGER, RALPH, RADIOLOGY. *Current Pos:* from instr to assoc prof, 54-71, prof clin radiol, 71-92, EMER PROF, COLUMBIA UNIV, 92- *Personal Data:* b Milwaukee, Wis, Nov 24, 21. *Educ:* Univ Wis, BS, 42, MD, 45; Univ Pa, 48-49. *Prof Exp:* Asst instr radiol, Temple Univ, 51, instr, 52-54. *Mem:* Radiol Soc NAm; fel Am Col Radiol; Soc Gastrointestinal Radiol; Am Asn Hist Med; Sigma Xi. *Res:* Radiology, especially the gastrointestinal tract. *Mailing Add:* 622 W 168th St New York NY 10032

SCHLAFER, DONALD H, PATHOPHYSIOLOGY. *Current Pos:* dir, Bovine Health Res Ctr, 82-83 & 83-90, from asst prof to assoc prof, 88-97, PROF VET PATH, NY STATE COL VET MED, CORNELL UNIV, 97- *Personal Data:* b Sidney, NJ, July 15, 48; m 80, Judith Appleton; c Nathan J & Russell M. *Educ:* Cornell Univ, BS, 71, DVM, 74, MS, 75; Univ Ga, PhD(vet path), 82. *Prof Exp:* Assoc vet, Guilderland Animal Hosp, 75-77; relief vet, Ft Hill Animal Hosp, 79-80 & Aquebogue Vet Hosp, 80-82. *Concurrent Pos:* Res,

Plum Island Animal Dis Ctr. *Mem:* Am Col Vet Pathologists; Am Col Vet Theriogenologists; Am Col Vet Microbiologists; Am Vet Med Asn; Soc Study Reprod; Soc Theriogenology. *Res:* Pathophysiology of diseases of pregnancy of domestic animals; transplacental infections by viruses, bacteria and protozoan; effects on the fetus and placenta by toxins; in vitro studies utilizing cultured trophoblast cells. *Mailing Add:* NY State Col Vet Med 221 VRT Dept Path Cornell Univ Ithaca NY 14853. *Fax:* 607-253-3317; *E-Mail:* dhs2@cornell.edu

SCHLAFLY, ROGER, SOFTWARE SYSTEMS. *Current Pos:* PRES, REAL SOFTWARE, 90- *Personal Data:* b Ill, Oct, 56. *Educ:* Princeton Univ, BSE, 76; Univ Calif, PhD(math), 80. *Prof Exp:* Instr math, Univ Chicago, 80-83; programmer, Borland Inst, 85-90. *Mem:* Am Math Soc; Soc Indust Appl Math. *Res:* Optimization; differential geometry; computer software; encryption; finance. *Mailing Add:* PO Box 1680 Santa Cruz CA 95073

SCHLAG, EDWARD WILLIAM, PHYSICAL CHEMISTRY. *Current Pos:* dean fac chem, biol & geosci, 82-84, PROF PHYS CHEM, MUNICH TECH UNIV, 71- *Personal Data:* b Los Angeles, Calif, Jan 12, 32; m 55, Angela Grafin zn Castell; c Katherine, Karl & Elisabeth. *Educ:* Occidental Col, BS, 53; Univ Wash, PhD(phys chem), 58. *Hon Degrees:* PhD, Hebrew Univ Jerusalem, 88. *Honors & Awards:* Woodward lectr, Yale Univ, 87; Fritz Haber lectr, Hebrew Univ, Jerusalem, 88; Ames lectr, Univ Edinburgh, 90; Gold Hon J Heyrovsky Medal, Acad Sci Czech Repub, Prague, 93. *Prof Exp:* Res asst, Univ Wash, 54-58; Wissenschaftlicher asst, Inst Phys Chem, Univ Bonn, 58-59; res chemist, Yerkes Lab, E I du Pont de Nemours & Co, NY, 59-60; from asst prof to prof chem, Northwestern Univ, Evanston, 60-71. *Concurrent Pos:* Alfred P Sloan res fel, 65-67; selection comt, US Sr Award Prog, Alexander von Humboldt Found & Ger-Israeli Fel Prog, Minerva Found; mem, Ger-Israel Sci Prog Comt Minerva, Nat Fulbright Comt Geo, Int Orgn Comt Int Cong Photochem, Gov Comt Ger Phys Chem Soc; mem ed bd, Chem Physics, Chem Physics Lett, intern J Mass Spectrometry & Ion Processes, J Phys Chem & Laser Chem. *Mem:* Fel Am Phys Soc; Bavarian Acad Sci; Am Chem Soc. *Res:* Multiphoton ionization mass spectrometry; high resolution sub-Doppler molecular spectroscopy and dynamics; spectroscopy and kinetics molecular ions in a fast beam; dynamics of photoexcited states and van der Waals molecules; synchrotron radiation experiments on molecular ions, inner shell excitations; advances in ion chemistry and physics; trends in chemical physics; accounts of chemical research; ZEKE-spectroscopy. *Mailing Add:* Inst Phys Chem Lichtenbergstr 4 85747 Garching Germany. *Fax:* 49-89-3209-3389; *E-Mail:* schlag@tuch.phys.chemie.tu_muenchen.de

SCHLAG, JOHN, NEUROPHYSIOLOGY. *Current Pos:* asst res anatomist, 61-63, from asst prof to assoc prof, 63-69, PROF ANAT, UNIV CALIF, LOS ANGELES, 69- *Personal Data:* b Liege, Belg, Feb 13, 27; US citizen; m 53; c 2. *Educ:* Univ Liege, MD, 52. *Honors & Awards:* Theophile Gluge Prize, Royal Acad Belg, 61. *Prof Exp:* Asst exp therapeut, Univ Liege, 53-61, lectr psychophysiol, 60-61. *Concurrent Pos:* Fulbright grant, Univ Wash, 53-54; NIH res career develop award, 64-; secy, Belg Nat Ctr Anesthesiol, 59-61. *Mem:* Am Physiol Soc; Fr Asn Physiol; Belg Asn Physiol; Int Brain Res Orgn; corresp mem Royal Acad Med Belg. *Res:* Cerebral control of motor functions; spontaneous activity of cerebral neurons; mechanisms of cortical evoked potentials. *Mailing Add:* Dept Neurobiol Univ Calif Los Angeles Sch Med Los Angeles CA 90005-1763

SCHLAGENHAUFF, REINHOLD EUGENE, NEUROLOGY. *Current Pos:* RETIRED. *Personal Data:* b Amsterdam, Neth, Aug 14, 23; US citizen; m 55; c 2. *Educ:* Univ Wurzburg, MD, 51. *Prof Exp:* Dir, EEG, Electromyography & Echoencephalography Dept, Meyer Mem Hosp, Buffalo, 63-81, assoc dir, Dept Neurol, 69-81; assoc prof neurol, State Univ NY Buffalo, 72-85, clin prof, 85-89; dir, Dept Neurol, Erie County Med Ctr, 81-86. *Concurrent Pos:* Consult neurol & EEG, Vet Admin Hosp, Buffalo, Buffalo Psychiat Ctr & Gowanda Psychiat Ctr, 68- & West Seneca Develop Ctr, 70-91. *Mem:* Acad Neurol; Am Med EEG Asn; Am Inst Ultrasonics in Med; AMA; Am Psychiat Asn. *Res:* Clinical neurology, electroencephalography, electromyography and ultrasound (Doppler-flow). *Mailing Add:* Dept Neurol Erie Co Med Ctr 462 Grider St E Buffalo NY 14215

SCHLAGER, GUNTHER, GENETICS. *Current Pos:* assoc prof, Univ Kans, 69-72, chmn dept, 72-79, chmn, Div Biol Sci, 79-92, PROF SYSTS & ECOL, UNIV KANS, 72- *Personal Data:* b New York, NY, Jan 14, 33; m 56, Ann A Prater; c Karen, Michael & Patrick. *Educ:* Univ Denver, BA, 56; Univ Kans, MA, 59, PhD(entom), 62. *Prof Exp:* USPHS fel, Hall Lab, Mammalian Genetics, Univ Kans, 61-62; assoc staff scientist, Jackson Lab, 62-65, staff scientist, 65-69. *Concurrent Pos:* Lectr, Univ Maine, 64-69; vis prof genetics, Sch Med, Univ Hawaii, 75; mem genetic subgroup Hypertension Task Force, Nat Heart Lung & Blood Inst, NIH, 76-78; consult, Med Dept, Brookhaven Nat Lab, 77-80; fel Coun High Blood Pressure Res. *Mem:* Genetics Soc Am; Am Genetic Asn; Biomet Soc; Soc Exp Biol Med. *Res:* Quantitative and biometrical genetics; genetics of blood pressure in rodents. *Mailing Add:* Div Biol Sci Univ Kans Lawrence KS 66045-0001

SCHLAIKJER, CARL ROGER, PRIMARY & RECHARGEABLE LITHIUM BATTERIES, HIGH ENERGY DENSITY BATTERIES BASED ON CALCIUM OR ALUMINUM. *Current Pos:* CHIEF SCIENTIST, BATTERY ENG, INC, 87- *Personal Data:* b Boston, Mass, Mar 3, 40; m 70; c Katherine & Andrew. *Educ:* Harvard Univ, AB, 61; Mass Inst Technol, PhD(inorg nuclear chem), 66. *Prof Exp:* Staff scientist, Arthur D Little, Inc, Cambridge, 65-67; staff scientist, Lab Phys Sci, P R Mallory & Co, 68-75; group mgr, GTE Lab, Waltham, 75-82; res fel, Duracell Res Ctr, 82-87. *Mem:* Am Chem Soc; Electrochem Soc; Sigma Xi. *Res:* Development of primary and rechargeable inorganic and organic electrolyte lithium cells, and in nonaqueous aluminum, or calcium negative electrode cells intercalating negative and positive elctrodes. *Mailing Add:* 1636 Hyde Park Ave Hyde Park MA 02136. *Fax:* 617-361-1835

SCHLAIN, DAVID, CHEMICAL ENGINEERING. *Current Pos:* RETIRED. *Personal Data:* b Philadelphia, Pa, July 21, 10. *Educ:* Univ Pa, BS, 32, MS, 37; Univ Md, PhD(chem eng), 51. *Prof Exp:* Metallurgist & chemist, US Bur Mines, 37-48, electrochemist, 48-52, chief, Galvanic Corrosion Sect, 52-55, supvry chem res engr, 55-58, proj coordr, 58-70, res supvr, 70-74, res chem engr, 74-81. *Mem:* Electrochem Soc; Am Inst Mining, Metall & Petrol Engrs; Nat Asn Corrosion Engrs; fel Am Inst Chemists; Am Chem Soc. *Res:* Electrowinning and electrorefining of metals; metallic corrosion; electrodeposition of coatings from molten salts and aqueous baths; effects of ultrasonics on metallurgical processes; electrometallurgy; crystallization. *Mailing Add:* 2 Greenway Pl Greenbelt MD 20770

SCHLAM, ELLIOTT, FLAT PANEL DISPLAYS, INTERACTIVE DISPLAY SYSTEMS. *Current Pos:* PRES, ELLIOTT SCHLAM ASSOCS, 89- *Personal Data:* b New York, NY, Oct 7, 40; m 66; c 2. *Educ:* NY Univ, BEE, 61, MEE, 64, PhD(elec eng), 66; Fairleigh Dickinson Univ, MS, 74. *Prof Exp:* Design engr, RCA, 61-62, mem tech staff, 64; proj engr, Ecom, US Army, 68-73, team leader, 73-75, br chief, Eradcom, 75-85, div dir, Labcom, 85-87. *Concurrent Pos:* Instr, George Wash Univ, 75-83, State Univ NY, Stony Brook, 79, Univ Calif, Los Angeles, 83-84 & Univ Wis, 83-85; assoc ed, Inst Elec & Electronics Engrs Trans Elec Devices, 78-80; lectr & course dir, Ctr for Prof Advan, 81-86; conf dir, Soc Photo-Optical Instrumentation Engrs, 83-86. *Mem:* Fel Soc Info Display; Soc Info Display; sr mem Inst Elec & Electronics Engrs. *Res:* Operation and fabrication techniques for thin film electroluminescent displays; high definition displays for commercial and military applications. *Mailing Add:* Elliott Schlam Assocs Four Mahoras Dr Wayside NJ 07712

SCHLAMEUS, HERMAN WADE, ORGANIC CHEMISTRY. *Current Pos:* Technician chem, Southwest Res Inst, 60-62, res chemist, 62-70, sr res chemist, 70-87, PRIN SCIENTIST, SOUTHWEST RES INST, 87- *Personal Data:* b Blanco, Tex, Nov 27, 37; m 84. *Educ:* Southwest Tex State Univ, BS, 60. *Mem:* Sigma Xi; Controlled Release Soc. *Res:* Mainly concerned in research and development in the field of microencapsulation. *Mailing Add:* Southwest Res Inst 6220 Culebra Rd San Antonio TX 78228-0510

SCHLAMOWITZ, MAX, BIOCHEMISTRY, IMMUNOCHEMISTRY. *Current Pos:* RETIRED. *Personal Data:* b New York, NY, Nov 13, 19; m 44, Hannah Katz; c Linda Beverly. *Educ:* City Col New York, BS, 40; Univ Mich, MS, 41, PhD(biochem), 46. *Prof Exp:* Res assoc, Manhattan Dist, Rochester Univ, 44-45; instr biochem, Univ Calif, 47-50; asst, Sloan-Kettering Inst Cancer Res, 51-54; assoc cancer res scientist, Roswell Park Mem Inst, 54-62; assoc prof microbiol, Baylor Col Med, 62-64; assoc biologist, Grad Sch Biomed Sci, Univ Tex, Houston, 64-67, assoc biochemist, 67-71, chief sect immunochem & immunol, 67-78, biochemist, Syst Cancer Ctr, Univ Tex M D Anderson Hosp & Tumor Inst, Houston, 71-85, assoc prof biochem, 67-78, prof biochem, Grad Sch Biomed Sci, Univ Tex, Houston, 79-85. *Concurrent Pos:* Markle Found fel, Univ Calif, 46-47; USPHS & Du Pont fels, Ohio State Univ, 50-51. *Mem:* AAAS; Am Soc Biol Chemists; Am Asn Immunol; NY Acad Sci; Reticuloendothelial Soc; Sigma Xi. *Res:* Carbohydrate chemistry; enzymes; ribonuclease; immunoglobulin chemistry and membrane transport; hormone receptors; phospho-glucomutase-phosphatase; pepsin; glycoproteins; Fc receptors. *Mailing Add:* 5503 Wigton Dr Houston TX 77096-4007

SCHLANT, ROBERT C, INTERNAL MEDICINE, CARDIOLOGY. *Current Pos:* from asst prof to assoc prof, 58-67, PROF MED, SCH MED, EMORY UNIV, 67- *Personal Data:* b El Paso, Tex, Apr 16, 29; m 80, Ellingsen-Honnef; c E Stephanie. *Educ:* Vanderbilt Univ, BA, 48, MD, 51; Am Bd Internal Med, dipl, 58; Am Bd Cardiovasc Dis, dipl, 62. *Honors & Awards:* Distinguished Serv Award, Am Heart Asn. *Prof Exp:* House officer, Peter Bent Brigham Hosp, Mass, 51-52, from jr asst resident med to asst, 52-58. *Concurrent Pos:* Res fel med, Harvard Med Sch, 56-58; mem, Subspecialty Bd Cardiovasc Dis, 71-; fel coun clin cardiol, Am Heart Asn. *Mem:* Fel Am Col Physicians; fel Am Col Cardiol; Am Fedn Clin Res; Asn Univ Cardiol; Am Physiol Soc. *Res:* Cardiovascular physiology. *Mailing Add:* Dept Med Emory Univ Sch Med 69 Butler St SE Atlanta GA 30303-3056

SCHLAPFER, WERNER T, NEUROBIOLOGY, NEUROSCIENCES. *Current Pos:* CHIEF, WESTERN RES & DEVELOP OFF, VET ADMIN MED CTR, LIVERMORE, CALIF, 80-; DEPT BIOL/PHYSICS, OHLONE COL, FREMONT, CALIF, 80- *Personal Data:* b Zurich, Switz, July 19, 35; US citizen; m 65; c 3. *Educ:* Univ Calif, Berkeley, BA, 63, PhD(biophys), 69. *Prof Exp:* Instr med physics, Univ Calif, Berkeley, 69-70; asst res physiologist, Dept Psychiat, Univ Calif, San Diego, 70-72; res physiologist, psychiat serv, Vet Admin Hosp, San Diego, 72-80. *Concurrent Pos:* Lectr, Univ Calif, San Diego, 74-78, asst prof in residence, 78-80. *Mem:* AAAS; Soc Neurosci. *Res:* Mechanisms of the modulation of synaptic transmission, depression, facilitation, post-tetanic potentiation, heterosynaptic facilitation and heterosynaptic inhibition; presynaptic pharmacological regulation of neurotransmitter economics and release in molluscan central nervous systems. *Mailing Add:* Ohlone Col 43600 Mission Blvd Fremont CA 94539-5847

SCHLARBAUM, SCOTT E, FOREST TREE IMPROVEMENT. *Current Pos:* asst prof, 84-88, ASSOC PROF, UNIV TENN, 88- *Personal Data:* b Des Moines, Iowa, July 7, 51; m 80; c 1. *Educ:* Colo State Univ, BS, 74, PhD(cytogenetics), 80; Univ Nebr, MS, 77. *Prof Exp:* Asst cytogenetics & tissue cult, Kans State Univ, 81-83. *Mem:* Am Soc Human Genetics. *Res:* Genetic improvement of softwood and hardwood trees; tree cytogenetics; somatic cell genetics in trees; chromosome transfer for gene mapping and tree improvement; cytotaxonomy and phylogeny of Coniferales. *Mailing Add:* Univ Tenn 1345 Circle Park Knoxville TN 37996-0001

SCHLATTER, JAMES CAMERON, CHEMICAL ENGINEERING, CHEMISTRY. *Current Pos:* tech dir eng, 80-, RES ENGR, CATALYTICA, 80- *Personal Data:* b Madison, Wis, Feb 5, 45; m 67; c 2. *Educ:* Univ Wis, Madison, BS, 67; Stanford Univ, MS & PhD(chem eng), 71. *Prof Exp:* Sr res engr, Gen Motors Res Labs, 71-80. *Concurrent Pos:* Lectr, Stanford Univ, 83- *Mem:* Am Chem Soc; Am Inst Chem Engrs; Catalysis Soc. *Res:* Heterogeneous catalysis; automotive emission control. *Mailing Add:* Catalytica 430 Ferguson Dr Bldg 3 Mountain View CA 94043-5272

SCHLAUDECKER, GEORGE F(REDERICK), CHEMICAL ENGINEERING. *Current Pos:* RETIRED. *Personal Data:* b Erie, Pa, Feb 10, 17; m 80, Betty B Rumpf; c 2. *Educ:* Univ Notre Dame, BS, 38; Mass Inst Technol, MS, 39. *Prof Exp:* Develop engr, Am Locomotive Co, NY, 39; jr engr, E I du Pont de Nemours & Co, Del, 39-41, eng group leader, 41-45; secy-treas, Maumee Develop Co, 46-50, pres, 50-53, pres, Maumee Chem Co, 53-69; gen mgr, Sherwin-Williams Chem, 69-70, dir & group vpres, Sherwin-Williams Co, Cleveland, 70-78; pres, Erie Isles Assocs Inc, Port Clinton, Ohio, 79-83. *Concurrent Pos:* Asst prof, Univ Toledo, 47-49; dir, Indust Nucleonics Corp, 75-80, Energy Utilization Systs, 79-83 & Accuray Corp, 80-87. *Mem:* Am Inst Chem Engrs; Am Chem Soc. *Res:* Diffusional operations; organometallic reactions; organic chemical reaction rates; sublimation; precipitation and filtration; drying. *Mailing Add:* 23 Exmoor Toledo OH 43615-2156

SCHLAUG, ROBERT NOEL, COMPUTATIONAL RADIATION-HYDRODYNAMICS. *Current Pos:* SR STAFF SCIENTIST RADIATION HYDRODYNAMICS SCI, APPLINS INT CORP, 72- *Personal Data:* b Jamaica, NY, Dec 21, 39; m 60, Virginia A Smith; c Erica & Monica. *Educ:* Case Inst Technol, BS, 61; Univ Calif, Berkeley, PhD(nuclear eng), 65. *Prof Exp:* Staff mem high energy fluid dynamics, Gen Atomic Div, Gen Dynamics Corp, 65-68; staff mem radiation hydrodynamics, Systs, Sci & Software, Inc, 68-72. *Mem:* Am Nuclear Soc; Sigma Xi. *Res:* Interactions of radiation and atomic particles with materials and development of computer methods for describing those interactions. *Mailing Add:* 3705 Sioux Ave San Diego CA 92117-5722

SCHLAX, T(IMOTHY) ROTH, ELECTRICAL ENGINEERING, COMPUTER TECHNOLOGY. *Current Pos:* develop engr, Gen Motors Corp, 72-75, proj mgr eng staff, 75-87, mgr comput systs, 88-92, MGR CRASH AVOIDANCE, GEN MOTORS CORP, 92- *Personal Data:* b Kenosha, Wis, Mar 19, 38; m 65, Gunther; c Christine, Gregory, David & Laura. *Educ:* Marquette Univ, BSEE, 60, MSEE, 63; Mass Inst Technol, PhD(solid state electronics), 68, Rensselaer Polytech Inst, MS, 93. *Honors & Awards:* 1975 SAE Vincent Bendix Automotive Electronics Award, Soc Automotive Engrs, 76. *Prof Exp:* Elec engr, Delco Electronics, 67-71. *Mem:* Inst Elec & Electronics Engrs; Soc Automotive Engrs. *Res:* Automotive control computer applications; custom computer approaches for fuel, ignition, and other engine control functions; advanced aids for refining control algorithms; accident analysis; accident countermeasure development. *Mailing Add:* Gen Motors Corp GM Eng Staff GM Tech Ctr Warren MI 48090. *Fax:* 313-986-7517

SCHLECH, BARRY ARTHUR, PHARMACEUTICAL MICROBIOLOGY, ANTIMICROBIALS. *Current Pos:* Sr scientist, Alcon Labs Inc, 70, head microbiol, 70-76, corp microbiologist, 76-81, dir res & develop microbiol, 81-89, sr dir res & develop microbiol, 89-94, VPRES, PHARMACEUT SCI, ALCON LABS, INC, 94- *Personal Data:* b Bayonne, NJ, June 7, 44; m 63; c 5. *Educ:* Univ Tex, Austin, BA, 65, MA, 68, PhD(microbiol), 70. *Mem:* Am Soc Microbiol; Parenteral Drug Asn; Soc Indust Microbiol; Ocular Microbiol & Immunol Group; Pharmaceut Mfrs Asn Biol Sect. *Res:* Pharmaceutical microbiology; antibiotics; contact lens disinfection; opthalmic and cosmetic preservatives; sterilization; ocular infections; microbiological control; microbial limit testing; ultraviolet sterilization; biological indicators. *Mailing Add:* 5113 Dewdrop Lane Ft Worth TX 76123

SCHLECHT, MATTHEW FRED, MEDICINAL CHEMISTRY, AGROCHEMICALS. *Current Pos:* sect res chemist, 88-93, SR RES CHEMIST, DUPONT AGR PROD, 93- *Personal Data:* b Milwaukee, Wis, Nov 26, 53; m 86, Meryl Gardner; c Isaac A. *Educ:* Univ Wis-Madison, BS, 75; Columbia Univ, PhD(chem), 80. *Prof Exp:* Res fel chem, Univ Calif, Berkeley, 80-82; asst prof chem, Polytech Univ, 82-88. *Mem:* Am Chem Soc; AAAS; Am Soc Pharmacog; Int Soc Meterocyclic Soc. *Res:* Agricultural chemistry; organic synthetic methods; molecular modeling; oxidation reactions & mechanisms; medicinal chemistry. *Mailing Add:* E I DuPont De Nemours & Co Stine-Haskell Lab PO Box 30 Newark DE 19714-0030. *E-Mail:* schlecmf@esvax.dnet.dupont.com

SCHLEE, FRANK HERMAN, NAVIGATION. *Current Pos:* RETIRED. *Personal Data:* b New York, NY, Apr 22, 35; m 58; c 3. *Educ:* Polytech Inst Brooklyn, BS, 56; Univ Mich, MS, 49, PhD(instrumentation eng), 63. *Prof Exp:* Engr, Sperry Gyroscope Co, 56-58; res assoc navig, Inst Sci & Technol, Univ Mich, 62-63; sr engr, IBM Corp, 63-66, sr eng, Inst Navig, Fed Systs Dir, 66-92. *Mem:* Am Inst Navig; Am Inst Aeronaut & Astronaut. *Res:* Space guidance; space and aircraft navigation, particularly using optimal filtering techniques. *Mailing Add:* 614 Ivory Foster Rd Owego NY 13827

SCHLEE, JOHN STEVENS, GEOLOGY. *Current Pos:* RETIRED. *Personal Data:* b Detroit, Mich, Sept 27, 28; div; c Louisa E. *Educ:* Univ Mich, BS, 50; Univ Calif, Los Angeles, MA, 53; Johns Hopkins Univ, PhD(geol), 56. *Honors & Awards:* Meritorious Serv Award, Dept Interior, 83. *Prof Exp:* Geologist, US Geol Surv, 56-58, res geologist, 62-95; asst prof geol, Univ Ga, 58-62. *Concurrent Pos:* NSF grant, 60-62; distinguished lectr, Am Asn Petrol Geologists, 78-79. *Mem:* Fel Geol Soc Am; Soc Econ Paleont & Mineral; Sigma Xi. *Res:* Texture, composition and structures in sediments and sedimentary rocks; structure and stratigraphy of continental margins; bathymetry of Southern Lake Michigan; wide angle deep water side-scan sonar systems. *Mailing Add:* US Geol Surv Woods Hole MA 02543. *Fax:* 508-457-2310; *E-Mail:* jschlee@nobska.er.usgs.gov

SCHLEEF, DANIEL J, mechanical engineering, for more information see previous edition

SCHLEGEL, DAVID EDWARD, PLANT PATHOLOGY. *Current Pos:* Jr specialist, Univ Calif, Berkeley, 53-54, instr plant path & jr plant pathologist, 54-56, asst prof & asst plant pathologist, 56-62, assoc prof & assoc plant pathologist, 62-69, Miller prof, 66-67, prof plant path, 69-91, chmn, Dept Plant Path, 70-76, assoc dean res, 76-78, actg dean, Col Natural Resources, 77-78, dean, Col Nat Resources, 78-85, asst dir, Agr Exp Sta, 85-94, EMER PROF PLANT PATH, UNIV CALIF, BERKELEY, 91-,. *Personal Data:* b Fresno, Calif, Sept 3, 27; m 48; c 4. *Educ:* Ore State Univ, BS, 50; Univ Calif, PhD(plant path), 54. *Mem:* AAAS; Am Phytopath Soc. *Res:* Plant virology; plant pathology. *Mailing Add:* 3995 Pasco Grande Moraga CA 94556

SCHLEGEL, DONALD LOUIS, PIPE JOINTING SYSTEMS, PIPE DESIGN. *Personal Data:* b Dayton, Ohio, July 27, 34; m 52; c 5. *Educ:* Univ Payton, BS, 52; Wright State Univ, MBA, 85. *Prof Exp:* Res engr, Univ Dayton Res Inst, 56-58; design engr, Alden Sticson & Assoc, 58-59, Bur Struct City Dayton, 59-65; struct engr, Felexible Co, 65-69; develop engr, Price Bros Co, 69-74, mgr res & develop, 74-93. *Concurrent Pos:* Chmn, Comt Concrete Consolidation, Am Concrete Inst, 80-85, Subcomt Use Flyash in Concrete, 79-86; mem, Comt Admixtures, Am Concrete Inst, 75-, Comt Concrete Coatings, 78- *Mem:* Am Concrete Inst. *Res:* Product and process improvements for pipe, including reinforced concrete, prestressed concrete and fiber reinforced plastic pipe. *Mailing Add:* 2035 Hamlet Dr Kettering OH 45440

SCHLEGEL, JAMES M, PHYSICAL CHEMISTRY. *Current Pos:* asst prof, 62-69, assoc prof, 69-76, PROF PHYS CHEM, RUTGERS UNIV, NEWARK, 76- *Personal Data:* b Ogden, Utah, Aug 24, 37; m 62; c 1. *Educ:* Univ of the Pac, BS, 59; Iowa State Univ, PhD(phys chem), 62. *Prof Exp:* Res asst phys chem, Iowa State Univ, 59-62. *Mem:* Am Chem Soc. *Res:* Stoichiometry and kinetics of reactions in fused salt media. *Mailing Add:* Dept Chem Rutgers State Univ Newark NJ 07102

SCHLEGEL, ROBERT ALLEN, BIOMEMBRANES, APOPTOSIS. *Current Pos:* from asst prof to assoc prof, 76-88, PROF MOLECULAR & CELL BIOL, PA STATE UNIV, 88-, DEPT HEAD, 91- *Personal Data:* b Chicago, Ill, Feb 17, 45; m 68, Peggy. *Educ:* Univ Iowa, BS, 67; Harvard Univ, AM, 68, PhD(biochem & molecular biol), 71. *Prof Exp:* Fel, Walter & Eliza Hall Inst Med Res, Melbourne, 71-74; res asst prof immunol, Univ Utah, 74-76. *Concurrent Pos:* Prin investr res grants, NIH, Nat Cancer Inst, Am Cancer Soc & Am Heart Asn, 76-; estab investr, Am Heart Asn, 83-88. *Mem:* Am Soc Cell Biol. *Res:* Membrane structure and function; blood cell surfaces; recognition of apoptotic cells by phagocytes transbilayer phospholipid movements. *Mailing Add:* Dept Biochem & Molecular Biol Pa State Univ 101 S Frear University Park PA 16802. *Fax:* 814-863-7024; *E-Mail:* ur3@psu.edu

SCHLEGEL, ROBERT JOHN, pediatrics, genetics; deceased, see previous edition for last biography

SCHLEGELMILCH, REUBEN ORVILLE, ENGINEERING MATHEMATICS, PHYSICS. *Current Pos:* CONSULT, 86- *Personal Data:* b Green Bay, Wis, Mar 8, 16; m 43, Margaret E Roberts; c Janet R, Raymond J, Joan C & Margaret A. *Educ:* Univ Wis, BS, 38; Rutgers Univ, MS, 40; Mass Inst Technol, MS, 54. *Prof Exp:* Eng instr, Rugters Univ, 38-40, Cornell Univ, 40-41; res engr, Exp Sta, Univ Ill, 41-42; proj engr & chief engr, Radar Lab, US Army/Air Materiel Command, Eatontown, NJ, 42-51; chief, Radar Lab/Electronic Warfare & Tech Div, Rome Air Develop Ctr, USAF Air Systs Command, Rome, NY, 51-55, dir res & develop, 55-59; tech dir, Defense & Space Corp Hq, Westinghouse Elec Corp, Washington, DC, 59-63; mgr, Advan Technol & Missile Prog, Fed Systs Div, IBM, Owego, NY, 63-68; gen mgr & pres, Shilling Indust, 68-71; mgr, Preliminary Eng Design Directorate, US Army Advan Concepts Agency, Alexandria, Va, 71-74; mgr, Gun Fire Control Systs Develop, Naval Sea Systs Command, Washington, DC, 74-80; tech dir, Off Res & Develop, USCG Hq, Washington, DC, 80-86. *Concurrent Pos:* Govt consult, Res & Develop Bd, Comt Electronics, Dept Defense, 49-54; Alfred P Sloan fel, Sch Indust Mgt, Mass Inst Technol, 54-55; mem, Nat Prof Comt on Eng Mgt, Inst Elec & Electronics Engrs, 56-59, vchmn & chmn, Rome/Utica Sect, 56-59; indust consult, Guided Missile & Space Coun, Aerospace Indust Asn, 59-63; chmn, Southern Tier Empire Post, Am Defense Preparedness Asn, 67-68; mem, Univ Res Rev Bd, Dept Transp,

82-86, Small Bus Innovated Res Prog Rev Bd, 82-86; mem, Comt Visibility, Nat Transp Res Bd, 82-86; mem, Marine Facil Panel, US/Japan Coop Prog in Natural Resources, 82-86; mem, Tech Adv Comt, Great Lakes Comn, 82-86. *Mem:* Sr mem Inst Elec & Electronics Engrs; NY Acad Sci; Nat Soc Prof Engrs. *Res:* Electronics engineering; author of numerous technical articles and reports; recipient of one patent. *Mailing Add:* 8415 Frost Way Annandale VA 22003

SCHLEICH, THOMAS W, BIOCHEMISTRY, PHYSICAL CHEMISTRY. *Current Pos:* from asst prof to assoc prof, 69-79, PROF CHEM, UNIV CALIF, SANTA CRUZ, 79-, CHMN CHEM & BIOCHEM, 91-, PROF PHARMACEUT CHEM, SAN FRANCISCO, 86- *Personal Data:* b Staten Island, NY, May 29, 38; m 62, 70, Priscilla; c Spaulding. *Educ:* Cornell Univ, BS, 60; Rockefeller Univ, PhD(biochem), 66. *Prof Exp:* Res assoc biochem, Dartmouth Col, 66-67; res assoc chem, Univ Ore, 67-69. *Concurrent Pos:* Helen Hay Whitney Found fel, 68-69; adj prof biol & chem, Univ Calif, Davis, 84- *Mem:* AAAS; Am Chem Soc; Biophys Soc; Am Soc Biol Chemists; Soc Magnetic Resonance Med. *Res:* Biophysical chemistry; eye lens metabolism (cataractogenesis); in vivo nuclear magnetic resonance spectroscopy; lens protein structure and function; nucleic acid structure. *Mailing Add:* Dept Chem & Biochem Univ Calif Santa Cruz CA 95064. *Fax:* 408-459-2935; *E-Mail:* yoti@aku.ucsc.edu

SCHLEICHER, DAVID LAWRENCE, TECHNICAL WRITING, SCIENCE MANAGEMENT. *Current Pos:* GEOLOGIST, US GEOL SURV, 65- *Personal Data:* b Palmerton, Pa, July 22, 37; m 61, Ella L Lininger; c Christopher. *Educ:* Pa State Univ, BS, 59, PhD(geol), 65; Calif Inst Technol, MS, 62. *Mem:* Fel Geol Soc Am; Asn Earth Sci Ed. *Res:* Mechanics of tuffisite intrusion; seismicity induced by reservoirs in grabens; preparation of environmental impact statements; quaternary atlas of the United States. *Mailing Add:* 802 Swede Gulch Rd Golden CO 80401. *Fax:* 303-236-0214

SCHLEICHER, JOSEPH BERNARD, CELL BIOLOGY, VIROLOGY. *Current Pos:* RETIRED. *Personal Data:* b Nanticoke, Pa, Apr 4, 29; m 58, Evelyn Warmund; c Joel, Nathan, Leslie & Sanford. *Educ:* Wilkes Col, BS, 51; Miami Univ, MS, 55; Kans State Univ, PhD(microbiol), 61. *Prof Exp:* Res asst immunol, Kans State Univ, 56-58; sr scientist, Develop Dept, Pitman-Moore Co, Ind, 58-62; head virus res sect, Alcon Labs, Inc, Tex, 62-63, head virus & microbiol res sect, 63-64; virologist, Virus Res Dept, Abbott Labs, Inc, 64-69, head antiviral tissue cult screening prog, 67-69, head res of biochem prod from tissue cult cells, Molecular Biol Dept, 69-71, res scientist, Biochem Develop Dept, 71-81 & Infectious Dis Immunol Diag Dept, 81-85, sr res scientist, Hepatitis/AIDS Res Dept, 85-95. *Concurrent Pos:* Consult tissue culture, Falcon Labs, Oxnard, Calif. *Mem:* AAAS; Am Soc Microbiol; Sigma Xi; NY Acad Sci; Tissue Cult Asn. *Res:* Research and development in virus vaccines for humans and animals, primarily in the area of respiratory diseases; antiviral chemotherapy and prophylaxis; interferon; tissue culture mass scale methodology and physiology; production of biochemicals by tissue culture cells; immunology; viral diagnostics. *Mailing Add:* 311 Green Bay Rd Lake Bluff IL 60044-2338

SCHLEIF, FERBER ROBERT, ELECTRICAL ENGINEERING. *Current Pos:* CONSULT ELEC POWER, 74- *Personal Data:* b Oroville, Wash, Mar 6, 13; m 37; c 2. *Educ:* Wash State Univ, BS, 35. *Prof Exp:* Mem staff construct & oper eng, Coulee Dam, Wash, US Bur Reclamation, 36-48, syst planning work, Mo River Basin Proj, 48-50, oper & maintenance eng, 50-62, chief elec power br, 62-74. *Concurrent Pos:* Mem, NAm Power Systs Interconnection comt, Colo, 65, mem spec sessions, North-South Intertie Task Force, 65. *Mem:* Fel Inst Elec & Electronics Engrs. *Res:* Power system stabilization; hydraulic turbine governing; excitation control for stability; generator insulation test techniques; power system tests. *Mailing Add:* 3455 S Corona St Apt 637 Englewood CO 80110

SCHLEIF, ROBERT FERBER, MOLECULAR BIOLOGY, BIOCHEMISTRY. *Current Pos:* from asst prof to assoc prof, 71-81, PROF BIOCHEM, BRANDEIS UNIV, 81- *Personal Data:* b Wenatchee, Wash, Nov 22, 40; m 67; c 1. *Educ:* Tufts Univ, BS, 63; Univ Calif, Berkeley, PhD(biophys), 67. *Prof Exp:* Helen Hay Whitney fel, Harvard Univ, 67-71. *Concurrent Pos:* res grant, USPHS, 71- & NSF, 82-; ed, Proteins, assoc ed, J Molecular Biol. *Mem:* Am Soc Biol Chemists. *Res:* Regulatory mechanisms governing gene activity; genetic, physical and physiological studies; structure of proteins and nucleic acids. *Mailing Add:* Dept Biol Johns Hopkins Univ 3400 N Charles St Baltimore MD 21218-2685. *Fax:* 301-338-5213; *E-Mail:* biozrfs@jhuvms.bitnet

SCHLEIF, ROBERT H, INDUSTRIAL PHARMACY. *Current Pos:* DIR MFG & QUAL ASSURANCE, GEN DERM CORP, 84- *Personal Data:* b Watertown, Wis, Apr 20, 23; m 48; c 3. *Educ:* Univ Wis, BS, 47, PhD(pharm), 50. *Prof Exp:* Asst prof pharm, St Louis Col Pharm, 50-54, from assoc prof to prof, 54-62; res pharmacist, Nutrit Abbot Int, North Chicago, 62-65, mgr prof specifications & stability, 65-70, dir qual assurance, Consumer Div, Abbott Labs, 70-79, mgr qual assurance, 79-84. *Concurrent Pos:* Consult, Vet Admin Hosp. *Mem:* AAAS; Am Pharmaceut Asn; Am Soc Qual Control. *Res:* Arabic acid; ophthalmic solutions; antacids. *Mailing Add:* 917 Vose Dr Gurnee IL 60031

SCHLEIFER, STEVEN JAY, PSYCHO-IMMUNOLOGY. *Current Pos:* assoc prof, 87-92, PROF PSYCHIAT, UNIV MED & DENT NJ, 92-, CHMN, DEPT PSYCHIAT, NJ MED SCH, 92- *Personal Data:* b New York, NY, Mar 10, 50; m 71, Sarah Rosenberg; c 4. *Educ:* Columbia Univ, BA, 71; Mt Sinai Sch Med, MD, 75. *Prof Exp:* Resident psychiat, Los Angeles County Hosp, Univ Southern Calif, 75-76; resident, Mt Sinai Sch Med, 76-79, instr, 78-81, asst prof psychiat, 82-87. *Concurrent Pos:* Prin investr, NIMH grants, 82-; chair, NIMH IRG Study Sect. *Mem:* Am Psychiat Asn; AAAS; Am Psychosomatic Soc; Soc Biol Psychiat; Psychoneuroimmunol Res Soc; Res Soc Alcoholism. *Res:* Effect of brain and behavior on the immune system; effects of bereavement and other life stresses on immunity; major depressive disorder and immunity; neuroendocrine mechanisms in stress effects on immunity; depression in patients with medical disorders; compliance; behavioral aspects of AIDS risk; alcoholism and immunity. *Mailing Add:* MSB-E561 Univ Med & Dent NJ 185 S Orange Ave Newark NJ 07103. *E-Mail:* schleife@umonj.edu

SCHLEIGH, WILLIAM ROBERT, ORGANIC CHEMISTRY. *Current Pos:* RES CHEMIST, EASTMAN KODAK CO, 67- *Personal Data:* b Olean, NY, Feb 26, 41; m 62; c 2. *Educ:* Clarkson Col Technol, BS, 62, PhD(org chem), 66. *Prof Exp:* Fel, Univ Wis, Madison, 65-67. *Mem:* Am Chem Soc; Royal Soc Chem; Sigma Xi. *Res:* Heterocyclic chemistry; synthesis and reactions of heterocyclic compounds; organic reaction mechanisms; photochemistry of heterocyclic compounds. *Mailing Add:* 112 Argyle St Rochester NY 14607-2304

SCHLEIMER, ROBERT P, IMMUNOLOGY, PHARMACOLOGY. *Current Pos:* from prof to assoc prof, 82-93, PROF MED, SCH MED, JOHNS HOPKINS UNIV, 93- *Personal Data:* b New York, NY, Apr 8, 52; m 81, Barbara Sattler; c Lea & Erica. *Educ:* Univ Calif, Davis, PhD(pharmacol), 80. *Res:* Immunopharmacology of inflammation. *Mailing Add:* Johns Hopkins Univ Asthma & Allergy Ctr 5501 Hopkins Bayview Circle Baltimore MD 21224-6801. *Fax:* 410-550-2090

SCHLEIN, HERBERT, ORGANIC CHEMISTRY. *Current Pos:* RETIRED. *Personal Data:* b New Haven, Conn, Nov 7, 27; m 52, Janet Bloom; c Robert & Marilyn. *Educ:* Harvard Univ, BS, 50; Boston Univ, PhD, 54. *Prof Exp:* Chemist, Children's Cancer Res Found, Boston, Mass, 53-58; chemist, Chem & Plastics div, Qm Res & Eng Command, US Dept Army, 58-60: head, Org Chem Sect, Explor Chem & Physics Div, Itek Corp, 60-63; vpres & dir res, Rahn Labs, 63-66; res group leader, Polaroid Corp, 66-85, sr scientist, 86-91. *Mem:* Am Chem Soc. *Res:* Diffusion transfer processes; product design; image-forming systems; electrophotography; photoconductors. *Mailing Add:* 106 Lothrop St Beverly MA 01915

SCHLEIN, PETER ELI, PHYSICS. *Current Pos:* res assoc, 61-62, from asst prof to assoc prof, 61-68, PROF PHYSICS, UNIV CALIF, LOS ANGELES, 68- *Personal Data:* b New York, NY, Nov 18, 32; m 62; c 2. *Educ:* Union Col, NY, BS, 54; Northwestern Univ, PhD, 59. *Prof Exp:* Res assoc physics, Johns Hopkins Univ, 59-61. *Concurrent Pos:* Vis physicist, Saclay, France, 63-64 & European Orgn Nuclear Res, 63-64 & 69-74; J S Guggenheim fel, 69-70; consult, Space Tech Labs, 66. *Mem:* Fel Am Phys Soc. *Res:* Experimental particle physics; properties of elementary particle interactions using electronic techniques. *Mailing Add:* 22A Ave Bouchet Univ Calif 405 Hilgard Ave Geneva CH-1209 Switzerland. *Fax:* 41-22-734-1384

SCHLEITER, THOMAS GERARD, SAFETY ENGINEERING, TECHNICAL APPRAISAL & INSPECTION. *Current Pos:* NUCLEAR ENGR, ARGONNE NAT LAB, 88- *Personal Data:* b Evanston, Ill. *Educ:* Univ Detroit, BME, 52; Univ Mich, MS, 54, MS, 55. *Prof Exp:* Nuclear engr reactor licensing, US Atomic Energy Comn, 56-61, reactor develop, 61-74; nuclear engr reactor develop, US Energy Res & Develop Admin, 74-77; nuclear engr facil develop, US Dept Energy, 77-85, team leader design & safety assessments, 85-88. *Concurrent Pos:* Instr, Montgomery Col, 87-90. *Mem:* Am Nuclear Soc; Am Soc Mech Engrs. *Res:* Conceptual design of an advanced nuclear test reactor, as a thesis-type effort; managed design and safety reviews of major United States reactor facilities and other nuclear facilities. *Mailing Add:* 10011 Wedge Way Gaithersburg MD 20879

SCHLEMMER, FREDERICK CHARLES, II, PHYSICAL OCEANOGRAPHY. *Current Pos:* asst prof, 80-85, ASSOC PROF, MARINE SCI, TEX A&M UNIV, GALVESTON, 85- *Personal Data:* b Watts Bar Dam, Tenn, Aug 10, 43; m 67; c 1. *Educ:* US Naval Acad, BS, 65; Univ SFla, MA, 71; Tex A&M Univ, PhD(oceanog), 78. *Prof Exp:* Asst prof marine sci & asst to pres, Moody Col, 78-80. *Concurrent Pos:* Consult, Encyclopedia Britannica Film Rev Bd. *Mem:* Am Meteorol Soc; Am Geophys Union; Nat Geosci Hon Soc; Oceanog Soc. *Res:* Assessment of circulation patterns and hydrographic property distributions to evaluate pathways for water movement over large areas. *Mailing Add:* 2518 Azalea Ct Galveston TX 77551

SCHLEMPER, ELMER OTTO, inorganic chemistry; deceased, see previous edition for last biography

SCHLENDER, KEITH K, BIOCHEMISTRY, PHARMACOLOGY. *Current Pos:* From asst prof to assoc prof, 69-81, PROF PHARMACOL & THERAPEUT, MED COL OHIO, 81-, DEAN GRAD SCH, 91- *Personal Data:* b Newton, Kans, Oct 3, 39; m 63; c 2. *Educ:* Westmar Col, BA, 61; Mich State Univ, MS, 63, PhD(biochem), 66. *Concurrent Pos:* NIH, res fel biochem, Univ Minn, Minneapolis, 66-69; NIH Res Career Develop Award, 78-83. *Mem:* Am Chem Soc; Am Heart Asn; Am Soc Pharmacol & Exp Therapeut; Am Soc Biochem & Molecular Biol; Sigma Xi. *Res:* Regulation of cellular processes by protein phosphorylation; protein kinases, protein phosphatases, glycogen metabolism. *Mailing Add:* Dept Pharmacol & Therapeut Med Col Ohio CS 10008 Toledo OH 43699-0008

SCHLENK, FRITZ, BIOCHEMISTRY, MICROBIOLOGY. *Current Pos:* RETIRED. *Personal Data:* b Munich, Ger, 1909; nat US; m 40, Tilde Eberle; c Margaret K (Symonds) & Edward F. *Educ:* Univ Berlin, PhD(chem), 34. *Prof Exp:* Asst, Univ Stockholm, 34-37, res assoc, 37-40; asst prof biochem, Sch Med, Univ Tex, 40-43; assoc prof nutrit, Sch Med, prof biochem, Sch Dent & biochemist in charge, M D Anderson Hosp & Tumor Inst, 43-47; prof bact, Iowa State Univ, 47-54; sr biochemist, Argonne Nat Lab, 54-74; res prof biol, Univ Ill, Chicago, 75-90. *Concurrent Pos:* Res assoc prof, Univ Chicago, 54-74. *Mem:* Am Soc Biol Chem; Am Soc Microbiol; Am Acad Microbiol. *Res:* Enzymes, coenzymes intermediate metabolism; transmethylation; yeast cytology. *Mailing Add:* 3460 Saratoga Ave Apt 4 Downers Grove IL 60515-1199

SCHLENK, HERMANN, ORGANIC CHEMISTRY, BIOCHEMISTRY. *Current Pos:* from asst prof org chem to prof biochem, 53-85, asst dir, Inst, 67-75, EMER PROF, HORMEL INST, UNIV MINN, 85- *Personal Data:* b Jena, Ger, July 28, 14; nat US; m 46; c 2. *Educ:* Univ Berlin, dipl, 36; Univ Munich, Dr rer nat(chem), 39. *Prof Exp:* Res chemist, Baden Anilin & Soda Works, Ger, 39-42; res assoc org chem, Univ Munich, 44-46; teaching asst & lectr, Univ Wuerzburg, 46-49; from asst prof to assoc prof biochem, Agr & Mech Col Tex, 49-52. *Mem:* Am Chem Soc; Am Soc Biol Chem; Am Oil Chem Soc. *Res:* Chemistry and biochemistry of lipids. *Mailing Add:* Hormel Inst 801 NE 16th Ave Austin MN 55912-3698

SCHLENKER, EVELYN HEYMANN, RESPIRATORY PHYSIOLOGY. *Current Pos:* asst prof, 80-88, ASSOC PROF PHYSIOL, UNIV SDAK, 88- *Personal Data:* b La Paz, Bolivia, May 30, 48; US citizen; m; c 1. *Educ:* City Col New York, BS, 70; State Univ NY, Buffalo, MA, 73, PhD(biol), 76. *Prof Exp:* Vis asst physiol, Rochester Inst Technol, 76-77; fel respiration physiol, Univ Fla, 78-80. *Mem:* Am Soc Zoologist; Sigma Xi; Am Physiol Soc. *Res:* Control of respiration in animal models of respiratory-muscular diseases; factors affecting airway reactivity in human subjects, including air pollution, smoking and agricultural pollution. *Mailing Add:* Dept Physiol & Pharmacol Med Sch Univ SDak 414 E Clark St844 57069-2390 Vermillion SD 57069. *Fax:* 605-677-5124

SCHLENKER, JAMES D, HAND SURGERY, PLASTIC & RECONSTRUCTIVE SURGERY. *Current Pos:* CHIEF SECT PLASTIC & RECONSTRUCTIVE SURG, LITTLE CO MARY HOSP, 92- *Personal Data:* b Mar 16, 44; m 69, Kathleen E Miller; c James D, Christene M & Robert E. *Educ:* Harvard Univ, AB, 65, MD, 69. *Prof Exp:* Asst prof surg, plastic & reconstructive surg & chief combined hand servs, Univ Chicago, 79-81; asst clin prof surg, Sect Plastic & Reconstructive Surg, Univ Ill, Chicago, 89-; med dir, Ctr Reconstructive Surgery, 88- *Concurrent Pos:* Internship, Cleveland Metrop Gen Hosp, 69-70; residency gen surg, Univ Hosp Cleveland, 70-74; major, McDonald Army Hosp, US Army, 74-76; residency plastic surg, Vanderbilt Univ Hosp, 76-78; fel hand surg, Univ Louiseville, 78-79; assoc ed, Hand Chirurgie, 81-; lectr, Cook Co Grad Sch, 81-, Northwestern Univ, 81-82 & Osler Inst, 92- *Mem:* AMA; Am Soc Plastic & Reconstructive Surg; Asn Acad Surg; Am Asn Hand Surg. *Res:* Hand, plastic and reconstructive surgery. *Mailing Add:* 6311 W 95th St Oak Lawn IL 60453

SCHLENKER, ROBERT ALISON, RADIATION PHYSICS, HEALTH EFFECTS OF RADIATION. *Current Pos:* asst physicist, Argonne Nat Lab, 70-75, biophysicist radiation dosimetry, 75-91, assoc mgr, Environ, Safety & Health Dept, 90-91, ASSOC DIR, ENVIRON, SAFETY AND HEALTH DIV, ARGONNE NAT LAB, 91- *Personal Data:* b Rochester, NY, Oct 25, 40; m 68; c Martin & Laura. *Educ:* Mass Inst Technol, SB, 62, PhD(nuclear physics), 68. *Prof Exp:* Res assoc, Radioactivity Ctr, Mass Inst Technol, 68-69. *Concurrent Pos:* mem, Sci Comt, Nat Coun Radiation Protection & Measurements, 57 & 78-92, mem, Task Group Prob Bone, 78-92; math instr, Col DuPage, 75-78; assoc ed, Radiation Res, 83-86; mem, Comt Biol Effects Internally Deposited Radio Nuclides, Nat Res Coun, 85-89; mem coun, Nat Coun Radiation Protection & Measurements; expert consult, Picillo, Harvery, Bromberg & Caruso, 90-92, Schmeltzer, Aptaker & Shepard, 95-; consult, Ctrs Dis Control, 91-92; pres, Madison Res Group. *Mem:* Am Asn Physicists Med; Health Physics Soc; Radiation Res Soc; AAAS; Soc Risk Anal. *Res:* Cellular radiation biology; radiation dosimetry; radiation epidemiology; radiations risk assessment; environmental sample analysis; bioassay; contaminated site evaluation; occupational and environmental radiation protection. *Mailing Add:* Argonne Nat Lab 9700 S Cass Ave Argonne IL 60439. *Fax:* 630-252-5778; *E-Mail:* raschlenker@anl.gov

SCHLEPPNIK, ALFRED ADOLF, synthetic organic chemistry, chemoreception, for more information see previous edition

SCHLESINGER, ALLEN BRIAN, EMBRYOLOGY, ENVIRONMENTAL BIOLOGY. *Current Pos:* Instr, Creighton Univ, 52-54, from asst prof to assoc prof, 54-61, dir dept, 58-72, chmn dept, 77-85 & 88-90, PROF BIOL, CREIGHTON UNIV, 61- *Personal Data:* b New York, NY, Feb 18, 24; m 47, Julie Manning; c Mary, Sue, Lucy & Amy. *Educ:* Univ Minn, BA, 49, MS, 51, PhD(zool), 57. *Concurrent Pos:* Consult, Omaha Pub Power Dist. *Mem:* Soc Develop Biol; Am Soc Zool; Am Chem Soc; Am Asn Anat; Soc Nuclear Med; Am Fisheries Soc; Sigma Xi; fel AAAS. *Res:* Embryonic growth control; morphogenetic movement; environmental influences on development; effects of discharges of generating plants on river biota. *Mailing Add:* Dept Biol Creighton Univ 2500 California St Omaha NE 68178. *Fax:* 402-280-5595; *E-Mail:* aschles@creighton.edu

SCHLESINGER, DAVID H, peptide synthesis, protein sequencing; deceased, see previous edition for last biography

SCHLESINGER, EDWARD BRUCE, NEUROSURGERY. *Current Pos:* Res asst neurol, Col Physicians & Surgeons, Columbia Univ, 46-47, res assoc neurol surg, 47-49, assoc, 49-52, from asst prof clin neurol surg to prof clin neurol surg, 52-73, chmn dept, 73-80, Byron Stookey prof neurol surg, 73-80, BYRON STOOKEY EMER PROF, COL PHYSICIANS & SURGEONS, COLUMBIA UNIV, 80- *Personal Data:* b Pittsburgh, Pa, Sept 6, 13; m 41, Mary Eddy; c Jane, Mary, Ralph & Prudence. *Educ:* Univ Pa, BA, 34, MD, 38; Am Bd Neurol Surg, dipl, 49. *Concurrent Pos:* Teagle fel, Col Physicians & Surgeons, Columbia Univ, 46-47; jr asst neurologist, Presby Hosp, NY, 45-47, from asst attend neurol surgeon to attend neurol surgeon, 47-73; consult, Monmouth Mem Hosp, NJ, 47-49, Walter Reed Army Hosp, DC, 47-50 & Knickerbocker Hosp, NY, 47-49; attend neurol surgeon, Inst Crippled & Disabled, NY, 47-58 & White Plains Hosp, NY, 54-73; trustee, Wm J Matheson Found, 75, Int Ctr for the Disabled, 83 & Sharon Hosp, Conn; pres, med bd Presby Hosp, 76-79, consult neurosurg, 80-; chmn, Elsberg Fel Comt, NY Acad Med, 78-96. *Mem:* AAAS; Neurosurg Soc Am (vpres, 59-70, pres, 70-71); Am Asn Neurol Surg; Harvey Soc; fel NY Acad Sci; Soc Neurol Surgeons; NY Acad Med. *Res:* Use of radioisotopes in neurology; pharmacology and biogenetics of tumors of the central nervous system; genetic markers of neurological and orthopedic disorders. *Mailing Add:* 710 W 168th St New York NY 10032

SCHLESINGER, ERNEST CARL, MATHEMATICAL ANALYSIS. *Current Pos:* from asst prof to assoc prof, 62-73, PROF MATH, CONN COL, 73- *Personal Data:* b Hildesheim, Germany, Nov 25, 25; nat US; m 58; c 2. *Educ:* Univ Wash, BS, 47, MA, 50; Harvard Univ, PhD, 55. *Prof Exp:* Instr philos, Univ Wash, 49-50; instr math, Yale Univ, 55-58; asst prof, Wesleyan Univ, 58-62. *Concurrent Pos:* Fulbright lectr, Univ Col, Dublin, 68-69. *Mem:* Am Math Soc; Math Asn Am. *Res:* Functions of a complex variable. *Mailing Add:* Box 5566 Conn Col 270 Mohegan Ave New London CT 06320-4196

SCHLESINGER, JAMES WILLIAM, MATHEMATICS. *Current Pos:* From instr to asst prof, 60-67, chmn dept, 69-73, ASSOC PROF MATH, TUFTS UNIV, 67- *Personal Data:* b Salina, Kans, June 20, 31; m 52; c 4. *Educ:* Mass Inst Technol, BS, 55, PhD(math), 64. *Mem:* Am Math Soc. *Res:* Homotopy groups of spheres; semi-simplicial topology; homotopy theory. *Mailing Add:* Dept Math Tufts Univ Medford MA 02155-5555

SCHLESINGER, JUDITH DIANE, PARALLEL COMPUTING, COMPILER & LANGUAGE DESIGN. *Current Pos:* MEM RES STAFF, CTR COMPUT SCI, 90- *Personal Data:* b New York, NY. *Educ:* Brooklyn Col, BS, 67; Ohio State Univ, MS, 69; Johns Hopkins Univ, PhD(comput sci), 76. *Prof Exp:* Comput programmer, Honeywell Info Systs, 69-71; systs scientist, Mgt Adv Serv, 74-75; asst prof comput sci, Dept Math & Comput Sci, Univ Denver, 76-81; consult comput sci, JDS Consult Serv, 81-90. *Concurrent Pos:* Adj assoc prof comput sci, Dept Math & Comput Sci, Univ Denver, 87-90. *Mem:* Asn Comput Mach; Inst Elec & Electronics Engrs Comput Soc; Am Asn Artificial Intel. *Res:* Compiler design and development; artificial intelligence and expert systems; case and productivity tools; languages and programming environments for parallel computers; performance prediction; software reverse engineering. *Mailing Add:* PO Box 3926 Crofton MD 21114. *E-Mail:* judith@super.org

SCHLESINGER, LEE, engineering, soils; deceased, see previous edition for last biography

SCHLESINGER, MARTIN D(AVID), CHEMICAL ENGINEERING. *Current Pos:* PRES, WALLINGFORD GROUP LTD, 77- *Personal Data:* b New York, NY, Aug 9, 14; m 45, Janet Katz; c Jo A, Deborah & Michael. *Educ:* Univ Okla, BS, 41; NY Univ, MChE, 44. *Honors & Awards:* Distinguished Serv Award, Am Chem Soc, 89. *Prof Exp:* Chem engr, M W Kellogg Co, 41-48; asst chief, Gas Synthesis Sect, US Bur Mines, 48-56, asst chief, Coal Hydrogenation Sect, 56-62, res coordr, 62-67, proj coordr process technol, 67-71, staff coordr, 71-74; dep res dir, Pittsburgh Energy Res Ctr, ERDA, 74-77. *Concurrent Pos:* Consult coal conversion, UN & US Agency Int Develop; arbitrator, Am Arbit Asn. *Mem:* Am Chem Soc; Am Inst Chem Engrs; Am Soc Pub Admin; AAAS. *Res:* Conversion of coal to synthetic fuels and chemicals; utilization of waste materials; research management. *Mailing Add:* Wallingford Group Ltd 4766 Wallingford St Pittsburgh PA 15213-1712. *Fax:* 412-681-1655

SCHLESINGER, MILTON J, BIOCHEMISTRY, MICROBIOLOGY. *Current Pos:* from asst prof to assoc prof, 64-72, PROF MICROBIOL & IMMUNOL, SCH MED, WASHINGTON UNIV, 72- *Personal Data:* b Wheeling, WVa, Nov 26, 27; m 55, Sondra Orenstein. *Educ:* Yale Univ, BS, 51; Univ Rochester, MS, 53; Univ Mich, PhD(biochem), 59. *Prof Exp:* Res assoc, Univ Mich, 53-56 & 59-60; vis scientist, Int Ctr Chem Microbiol, Superior Inst Health, Italy, 60-61; res assoc biol, Mass Inst Technol, 61-64. *Concurrent Pos:* Vis scientist, Imp Can Res Fund, London, 74-75; vis scholar, Harvard Univ, Cambridge, Mass, 89-90 & 95-96. *Mem:* Am Soc Biol Chemists; Am Chem Soc; Am Soc Microbiol; Am Soc Virol; AAAS. *Res:* Protein structure and function; molecular biology of animal viruses; protein-lipid interactions; heat-shock; antivirals. *Mailing Add:* Dept Molecular Microbiol Sch Med Washington Univ St Louis MO 63110-1093. *Fax:* 314-362-1232; *E-Mail:* milton@borcim.wustl.edu

SCHLESINGER, MORDECHAY, CONDENSED MATTER, SURFACE PHYSICS. *Current Pos:* head dept, 83-93, PROF PHYSICS, UNIV WINDSOR, 68- *Personal Data:* b Budapest, Hungary, Sept 2, 31; m 57, Sarah H Putterman; c T Ed & Michelle. *Educ:* Hebrew Univ, Jerusalem, Israel, MSc, 59, PhD(physics), 63. *Prof Exp:* NASA fel physics, Univ Pittsburgh, 63-65;

from asst prof to assoc prof, Univ Western Ont, 65-68. *Concurrent Pos:* Div ed, J Electrochem Soc, 79-90, assoc ed, 90-; ed, Can J Physics, 97- *Mem:* Fel Am Phys Soc; Can Asn Physicists; fel Electrochem Soc; fel Inst Physics UK. *Res:* Crystal field studies; angular momentum algebra; thin films; magneto-optical and electrical properties of condensed media; electron microscopy; electrochemistry. *Mailing Add:* Dept Physics Univ Windsor Windsor ON N9B 3P4 Can. *E-Mail:* msch@uwindsor.ca

SCHLESINGER, R(OBERT) WALTER, VIROLOGY. *Current Pos:* prof & chmn microbiol, Rutgers Med Sch, 63-83, EMER DISTINGUISHED PROF MOLECULAR GENETICS & MICROBIOL, ROBERT WOOD JOHNSON MED SCH, UNIV MED & DENT NJ, 83- *Personal Data:* b Hamburg, Ger, Mar 27, 13; US citizen; m 42, Adeline P Sacks; c Robert E & Ann B (Youmans). *Educ:* Univ Basel, MD, 37. *Honors & Awards:* Selman Waksman Award, Am Soc Microbiol, 79; Humboldt Medal, Humboldt Found, Ger, 89; A von Graefe Medal, Berlin Med Soc, 81. *Prof Exp:* Fel bact & path, Rockefeller Inst Med Res, NY, 40-42, asst, 42-46; assoc res prof virol, Univ Pittsburgh, 46-47; assoc mem virol; prof & chmn microbiol, St Louis Univ Sch Med, 55-63. *Concurrent Pos:* Mem, Army Epidemiol Bd, US Army Med Corps, 44-46; prin investr/prog dir, res or training grants, 49-91; vis investr at numerous insts & orgn, 56-81; mem & chmn, numerous govt & insts rev & adv comt, 60-90; asst dean, Rutgers Med Sch, 63-67, acting dean, 70-71; ed, Virol, 63-83; prof, Rutgers Univ Grad Fac, 63-; Guggenheim fel, Guggenheim Found, 72-73. *Mem:* Fel & emer mem AAAS; emer mem Am Asn Immunologists; emer mem Am Soc Microbiol; emer mem Am Soc Virol; emer mem Am Asn Cancer Res; emer mem Soc Exp Biol & Med. *Res:* Various basic aspects of many different viruses from 1937 to the present; replication mechanisms, host adaptation, immunological and molecular aspects of arboviruses, picornaviruses, herpesviruses, adenoviruses, influenza viruses, and factors determining pathogenesis. *Mailing Add:* 7 Langley Rd Falmouth MA 02540

SCHLESINGER, RICHARD B, INHALATION TOXICOLOGY, PULMONARY PHYSIOLOGY. *Current Pos:* Assoc res scientist, Univ NY Med Ctr, 75-78, from asst prof to prof, 78-87, DIR, LAB PULMONARY BIOL & TOXICOL, DEPT ENVIRON MED, NY UNIV MED CTR, 86-, DIR, SYSTEMIC TOXICOL PROG, 88- *Personal Data:* b Mt Kisco, NY, Dec 19, 47; m, Jo-Ann; c 1. *Educ:* Queens Col, NY, BA, 68; NY Univ, MS, 71, PhD(biol), 75. *Honors & Awards:* Kenneth Morgareidge Award, 87. *Concurrent Pos:* Consult, Sci Adv Bd, US Environ Protection Agency, 85-; mem, Panel Pulmonary Toxicol, Bd Environ Studies & Toxicol, Nat Res Coun, 86-89, Respiratory Modelling Group, Nat Coun Res & Planning, 84-; consult, US Environ Protection Agency, 87-; res career develop award, NIH, 83-88. *Mem:* Am Thoracic Soc; Soc Toxicol; Am Indust Hyg Asn. *Res:* Analysis of the effects of ambient air pollutants upon the structure and physiology of the defense mechanisms of the lungs; development of lung disease due to defense mechanism dysfunction. *Mailing Add:* Dept Environ Med NY Univ Med Ctr 550 First Ave New York NY 10016. *Fax:* 914-351-5472

SCHLESINGER, RICHARD CARY, SILVICULTURE. *Current Pos:* CONSULT, 94- *Personal Data:* b Oberlin, Ohio, Apr 27, 40; m 61; c 2. *Educ:* Middlebury Col, BA, 63; Yale Univ, MF, 65; State Univ NY Col Forestry, PhD(forest micrometeorol), 70. *Honors & Awards:* Walnut Res Award. *Prof Exp:* Forester, Nat Forest Admin, US Forest Serv, 65-66, res forester, NCENT Forest Exp Sta, 69-94. *Concurrent Pos:* Adj prof, Univ Mo, Columbia, 92-94. *Mem:* Soc Am Foresters; Sigma Xi. *Res:* Ecology and silviculture of oak-hickory forests. *Mailing Add:* 860 Stratton Rd Williamstown MA 01267

SCHLESINGER, ROBERT JACKSON, MATHEMATICAL MODELING, TECHNOLOGY TRANSFER. *Current Pos:* PROF INFO & DECISION SYSTS, SAN DIEGO STATE UNIV, 84- *Personal Data:* b New York, NY, Dec 5, 27; m 80, Sylvia Tiersten; c Lisa & Kira. *Educ:* Univ Conn, BS, 53; W Coast Univ, MS, 72; Brunel Univ, UK, PhD(mgt systems), 84. *Prof Exp:* Vpres marketing, Data & Info Systs Div, ITT, 61-65; staff mem, Jet Propulsion Lab, Calif Inst Technol, 65-70; founder & chief exec officer, RHO Sigma Inc, 70-80; pres & chief exec officer, Compulaser Inc, 80-82. *Concurrent Pos:* Guest lectr physics, Kyonggi Univ, Seoul, Korea, 79; lectr, Int Solar Conf, Peoples Repub China, Xian, 79, AAAS, 79, Moscow Aeronaut Inst, 90, Seminar Econ Conversion, Ruppin Inst, Israel, 93; vis prof, Nat Econs Univ, Hanod, 95-96. *Mem:* Inst Elec & Electronics Engrs; Sigma Xi; Decision Sci Inst. *Res:* Modeling of production throughput for industrial operations as a result of utilization of various types of automation; granted 8 US patents and published 57 articles. *Mailing Add:* 9291 Wister Dr La Mesa CA 91941. *E-Mail:* robert.schlesinger@sdsu.edu

SCHLESINGER, S PERRY, MILLIMETER-SUBMILLIMETER WAVES, FREE ELECTRON LASERS. *Current Pos:* from asst prof to prof, 56-87, EMER PROF ELEC ENG, COLUMBIA UNIV, 87- *Personal Data:* b New York, NY, Oct 9, 18; m 43, 79, Zipora Bronstein; c Richard S & Joanna L (Grimm). *Educ:* Mich State Univ, BA, 41; Union Col NY, MS, 50; Johns Hopkins Univ, DEng(elec eng), 57. *Prof Exp:* Prin investigator, NSF grants, Office Naval Reserve, Air Force Off Sci Res, 58-87, engr, Res Sect, Turban Generator Div, Gen Elec Co, 46-47; asst prof elec eng, Union Col NY, 47-50 & US Naval Acad, 50-53; res assoc microwaves, Radiation Lab, Johns Hopkins Univ, 53-56. *Concurrent Pos:* Vis res assoc, Plasma Physics Lab, Princeton Univ, 62-63, consult, 63-64; pres, Faculties Assoc Consults Inc, 63-69; vis prof, Israel Inst Technol, 69-70, Tel Aviv Univ, 76-77, 83-84; consult, Naval Res Lab, 74-85; chmn, dept elec eng, Columbia Univ, 80-83. *Mem:* Fel Inst Elec & Electronics Engrs; Am Phys Soc. *Res:* Plasma physics in general with emphasis on electromagnetic wave-plasma interaction; relativistic electron beam coherent sources of high power millimeter waves, in particular development of Raman free electron laser. *Mailing Add:* Dept Elec Eng Columbia Univ New York NY 10027. *Fax:* 212-932-9421; *E-Mail:* perry@ctr.columbia.edu

SCHLESINGER, SONDRA, VIROLOGY, MICROBIOLOGY. *Current Pos:* from asst prof to assoc prof microbiol, 64- 76, PROF MOLECULAR MICROBIOL, SCH MED, WASHINGTON UNIV, 76- *Personal Data:* b Long Branch, NJ, July 10, 34; m 55. *Educ:* Univ Mich, BS, 56, PhD(biochem), 60. *Prof Exp:* Res assoc microbiol, Mass Inst Technol, 61-64. *Concurrent Pos:* Nat Found fel, Inst Superiore Sanita, Italy, 60-61; USPHS grant, 65- *Mem:* Fedn Am Scientists Exp Biol; Am Soc Microbiol; Am Soc Virol; fel AAAS. *Res:* Synthesis and structure of enveloped RNA viruses. *Mailing Add:* Dept Microbiol Box 8230 Wash Univ Sch Med St Louis MO 63110-1093. *Fax:* 314-362-1232; *E-Mail:* sondra@borcim.wustl.edu

SCHLESINGER, STEWART IRWIN, COMPUTER SCIENCE, MATHEMATICS. *Current Pos:* dir, Math & Comput Ctr, 63-69, gen mgr, Info Processing Div, 69-80, gen mgr, Mission Info Systs Div, 80-81, GEN MGR, SATELLITE CONTROL DIV, AEROSPACE CORP, 81- *Personal Data:* b Chicago, Ill, Apr 22, 29; m 51; c 2. *Educ:* Ill Inst Technol, BS, 49, MS, 51, PhD(math), 55. *Prof Exp:* Staff mem, Los Alamos Sci Lab, 51-56; mgr math & comput, Aeronutronic Div, Ford Motor Co, 56-63. *Mem:* Soc Indust & Appl Math; Asn Comput Mach; Soc Comput Simulation (vpres, 78-79, pres, 79-82); Sigma Xi. *Res:* Real-time computing systems; applied mathematics, numerical analysis, data reduction, simulation, interactive computing, and management of software development, particularly involving large scale digital computers. *Mailing Add:* 12131 Skyway Dr Santa Ana CA 92705

SCHLESINGER, WILLIAM HARRISON, PLANT ECOLOGY, BIOGEOCHEMISTRY. *Current Pos:* from asst prof to prof, 80-94, JAMES B DUKE PROF, DUKE UNIV, 94- *Personal Data:* b Cleveland, Ohio, Apr 30, 50; m 88, Lisa Dellwo. *Educ:* Dartmouth Col, AB, 72; Cornell Univ, PhD(biol), 76. *Prof Exp:* Asst prof ecol, Univ Calif, Santa Barbara, 76-80. *Concurrent Pos:* Div Earth Sci, Nicholas Sch Environ, Duke Univ. *Mem:* Ecol Soc Am; fel AAAS; Sigma Xi; Soil Sci Soc Am. *Res:* Ecosystem ecology including nutrient cycling in natural systems and global geochemical cycles; plant community structure. *Mailing Add:* Dept Bot Duke Univ Durham NC 27708-0340. *Fax:* 919-660-7425; *E-Mail:* schlesin@acpub.duke.edu

SCHLESINGER, ZACK, CORRELATED SYSTEMS. *Current Pos:* PROF PHYSICS, UNIV CALIF, SANTA CRUZ, 95- *Personal Data:* US citizen; m 75, Cathy; c Jillian. *Educ:* Univ Calif, Santa Barbara, BA, 75; Cornell Univ, PhD(physics), 82. *Prof Exp:* Postdoctoral staff mem, Bell Labs, 81-83; res scientist, IBM Res, 83-95. *Concurrent Pos:* Guest lectr physics, Ettore Majorana Ctr Sci Culture, Erice, Italy, 95. *Mem:* Fel Am Phys Soc. *Res:* Fundamental properties of correlated election systems, including high-temperature superconductors, Kondo, heavy-Fermion, mixed-valent and two dimensional electron systems. *Mailing Add:* Dept Physics Univ Calif Santa Cruz CA 95064. *E-Mail:* zack@physics.ucsc.edu

SCHLESINGER, BERNARD S, INFORMATION SCIENCE. *Current Pos:* RETIRED. *Personal Data:* b Mar 19, 30; m 52, June Hirsch; c Rashelle, Jill & Joel. *Educ:* Roosevelt Univ, BS, 50; Miami Univ, Ohio, MS, 52; Univ Wis, PhD(phys chem), 55; Univ RI, MSLS, 75. *Prof Exp:* Res chemist, Am Can Co, 55-56; res supvr, USAF Sch Aviation Med, 56-58; indexer & dept head indexing, Chem Abstracts, 58-66; info scientist, Olin-Mathieson Chem Corp, 66-68; prof libr sci & asst dir div, Southern Conn State Col, 68-75; prof librarianship, Univ SC, 75-77; dean, Grad Libr Sch, Univ RI, 77-82; prof libr sci & assoc dean, Tex Women's Univ, Denton. *Mem:* Am Chem Soc; Am Libr Asn; Spec Libr Asn. *Res:* Electrophoresis; cardiovascular disease diagnosis; indexing; abstracting; search strategy; library statistical data. *Mailing Add:* 15707 Hamilton St Omaha NE 68118

SCHLESINGER, DAVID, MOLECULAR BIOLOGY, MICROBIOLOGY. *Current Pos:* from instr to assoc prof, 62-72, PROF MICROBIOL, SCH MED, WASH UNIV, 72- *Personal Data:* b Toronto, Ont, Sept 20, 36; US citizen; m 60; c 2. *Educ:* Univ Chicago, BA, 55, BS, 57; Harvard Univ, PhD(biochem), 60. *Prof Exp:* NSF fel, Pasteur Inst, Paris, France, 60-62. *Concurrent Pos:* Macy fel, 81. *Mem:* Am Chem Soc; Am Soc Microbiol. *Res:* Cell physiology; biochemistry. *Mailing Add:* Dept Molecular Microbiol Genetics & Med Wash Univ Sch Med 660 S Euclid Ave Box 8230 St Louis MO 63110-1093. *Fax:* 314-362-3203; *E-Mail:* Bitnet: davids@wugenmailwustledu

SCHLESINGER, GERT GUSTAV, WATER CHEMISTRY. *Current Pos:* SR ENVIRON CHEMIST, STATE OF CONN, HARTFORD, 79- *Personal Data:* b Karlsruhe, Ger, Mar 20, 33; nat US; m 59, Ina Swade; c Marla & Reva. *Educ:* City Col New York, BS, 53; Case Inst Technol, MS, 55; Univ Pa, PhD, 57. *Prof Exp:* Asst, Case Inst Technol, 53-55; asst instr chem, Univ Pa, 55-57; res assoc inorg chem, Univ Fla, 58-59; asst prof chem, Pace Col, 59-60; sr res chemist, Evans Res & Develop Corp, 60-61; assoc prof chem, Gannon Col, 61-66, Newark Col Eng, 66-68 & US Coast Guard Acad, 68-71; chief clin chemist, Fairfield Hills State Hosp, Conn, 71-73. *Mem:* Am Chem Soc; Am Inst Chemists; Royal Soc Chem; Water Pollution Control Fedn. *Res:* Coordination complexes; kinetics; application of inorganic reagents to organic syntheses; wastewater analysis. *Mailing Add:* 8 Norton Ct Norwich CT 06360. *Fax:* 860-566-8650

SCHLESINGER, JOSEPH, RESEARCH ADMINISTRATION. *Current Pos:* CHMN & PROF DEPT PHARMACOL, NY UNIV MED CTR, 90- *Personal Data:* b Mar 26, 45; m 70; c 2. *Educ:* Hebrew Univ, Jerusalem, BSc, 68, MSc, 69; Weizmann Inst Sci, Israel, PhD, 74. *Honors & Awards:* Hestrin Prize, Biochem Soc Israel, 83. *Prof Exp:* Fel assoc, dept chem, Sch Appl & Eng Physics, Cornell Univ, 74-77; vis scientist, immunol br, Nat Cancer Inst,

77-78, sr scientist, dept chem immunol, Weizmann Inst Sci, Israel, 78-80, assoc prof, 80-83, prof, 83-84, dir, div molecular biol, Biotechnol Res Ctr, Meloy Lab Inc, Md, 85-86, dir Biotechnol Res Ctr, 86-87; res dir & adv, Rorer Biotechnol Inc, 87-90. *Concurrent Pos:* Teaching asst, Hebrew Univ, Jerusalem, 68-69; Ruth & Leonard Simon Prof Cancer Res, dept chem immunol, Weizmann Inst Sci, 83- *Mem:* European Molecular Biol Org. *Res:* Growth factor receptors. *Mailing Add:* Dept Pharmacol NY Univ Sch Med 550 First Ave New York NY 10016-6402. *Fax:* 212-263-7113

SCHLESSINGER, MICHAEL, ALGEBRA. *Current Pos:* assoc prof, 73-79, PROF MATH, UNIV NC, CHAPEL HILL, 79- *Personal Data:* b July 2, 37; m 58; c 3. *Educ:* Johns Hopkins Univ, BA, 59; Harvard Univ, PhD(math), 64. *Prof Exp:* Lectr math, Princeton Univ, 64-66; asst prof, Univ Calif, Berkeley, 66-73. *Concurrent Pos:* Res assoc, Inst Math, Pisa, 69 & Harvard Univ, 72; NSF res grants, 73-81. *Res:* Deformation theory in algebraic geometry, singularities. *Mailing Add:* Dept Math Univ NC Chapel Hill NC 27599-0001

SCHLESSINGER, RICHARD H, ORGANIC CHEMISTRY. *Current Pos:* from asst prof to assoc prof, 66-74, PROF ORG CHEM, UNIV ROCHESTER, 74- *Personal Data:* b Greeley, Colo, Sept 20, 35. *Educ:* Edinboro State Col, BSEd, 57; Ohio State Univ, PhD(org chem), 64. *Prof Exp:* Fel org chem, Harvard Univ, 64-65 & Columbia Univ, 65-66. *Res:* Total synthesis of natural products; synthetic methods. *Mailing Add:* Dept Chem Univ Rochester 404 Hutchison Hall Rochester NY 14627

SCHLEUSENER, RICHARD A, METEOROLOGY, ENGINEERING. *Current Pos:* dir inst atmospheric sci, 65-74, vpres & dean eng, 74-75, actg pres, 75-76, PRES, SDAK SCH MINES & TECHNOL, 76- *Personal Data:* b Oxford, Nebr, May 6, 26; m 49; c 5. *Educ:* Univ Nebr, BS, 49; Kans State Univ, MS, 56; Colo State Univ, PhD(irrig eng), 58. *Prof Exp:* Instr agr eng, Kans State Univ, 49-50; assoc prof civil eng, Colo State Univ, 58-64. *Mem:* Am Soc Civil Eng; Am Meteorol Soc; Am Soc Agr Eng; Am Geophys Union; Sigma Xi. *Res:* Development in weather modification. *Mailing Add:* 315 S Berry Pine Rd Rapid City SD 57702-1923

SCHLEUSNER, JOHN WILLIAM, MATHEMATICS. *Current Pos:* Asst prof, 69-74, ASSOC PROF MATH, WVA UNIV, 74- *Personal Data:* b Birmingham, Ala, Jan 16, 43; m 71. *Educ:* Univ Ala, BS, 65, MA, 66, PhD(math), 69. *Mem:* Am Math Soc. *Res:* Special functions; analysis. *Mailing Add:* Dept Math & Comput Sci Valdosta State Col 1500 N Patterson Valdosta GA 31698-0001

SCHLEYER, HEINZ, BIOPHYSICS, ENZYMOLOGY. *Current Pos:* Fel biophys, 61-64, res assoc, 64-69, ASST PROF BIOPHYS & BIOPHYS IN SURG, JOHNSON RES FOUND, SCH MED, UNIV PA, 69- *Personal Data:* b Pforzheim, Ger, Oct 29, 27; m 63; c 1. *Educ:* Karlsruhe Tech Univ, Diplom chem, 54, Dr rer nat(chem), 60. *Mem:* Biophys Soc; Soc Ger Chem; Am Soc Biol Chem; AAAS. *Res:* Electron transfer systems of photosynthesis; photochemistry of bacteriochlorophyll; structure and function of the hemeprotein P-450 in steroid metabolism; chemical carcinogenesis; application of magnetic resonance and spectroscopic techniques to biologically important compounds. *Mailing Add:* Biophysics 314 Med Educ Bldg Univ Penn Sch Med Philadelphia PA 19104-6070

SCHLEYER, PAUL VON RAGUE, PHYSICAL ORGANIC CHEMISTRY. *Current Pos:* INST CO-DIR & PROF, UNIV ERLANGEN-NURNBERG, WGER, 76- *Personal Data:* b Cleveland, Ohio, Feb 27, 30; m 69, Inge Venema; c Betti, Laura & Karen. *Educ:* Princeton Univ, AB, 51; Harvard Univ, MA, 56, PhD(chem), 57. *Hon Degrees:* Dr, Univ Lyon, 71. *Honors & Awards:* Von Baeyer Medal, Ger Chem Soc, 86; Kahlbaum lectr, Univ Basel, 75; Ingersoll Mem lectr, Vanderbilt Univ, 83; J Musher Mem lectr, Israel, 85; J F Norris Award Phys Org Chem, Am Chem Soc, 87; Cope Scholar Award, 91; Heisenberg Medal, World Asn Theoret Org Chemists, 87; Christopher K Ingold Medal & Lectureship, Royal Soc Chem, London, 88. *Prof Exp:* From instr to prof, Princeton Univ, 54-69, Eugene Higgins prof org chem, 69-76. *Concurrent Pos:* A P Sloan res fel, 62-66; Guggenheim fel, 65-66; Fulbright res fel, Univ Munich, 65-66; vis & guest prof, Univ Colo, 63, Univ Wurzburg, 67, Univ Mich, 69, Univ Munich, 69 & 74-75, Carnegie-Mellon Univ, 69, Kyoto Univ, 70, Univ Munster, 71, Iowa State Univ, 72, Univ Geneva, 72, Univ Groningen, Neth, 72-73, Hebrew Univ Jerusalem, 73, Univ Paris-Sud, 73, Univ Lausanne, Switz, 74, Univ Louvain, Belg, 74, Univ Liege, 74, Univ Western Ont, 78, Univ Copenhagen, 79-80 & Univ Utrecht, 82; consult, Hoffmann-La Roche, 71-72 & Hoechst AG, 80-; DuPont lectr, Clemson Univ, 71; Alexander von Humboldt Found sr US scientist award, 74-75; adj prof, Case Western Res Univ, 76-77 & Carnegie-Mellon Univ, 77-78; sr fel, Hydrocarbon Inst, Univ Southern Calif, 78-; co-ed, J Comput Chem, 80-; distinguished vis prof, Univ Ga, 90- *Mem:* Fel Am Inst Acad Quantum Chem Sci; World Asn Theoret Org Chemists (pres); fel NY Acad Sci; fel Am Inst Chemists; fel Bavarian Acad Sci. *Res:* Bridged ring systems; adamantane and diamondoid molecules; structure, stability and rearrangements of carbonium ions; spectroscopy and hydrogen bonding; conformational analysis; theoretical calculations applied to organic intermediates and the exploration of new molecular structures; lithium and other electron deficient compounds. *Mailing Add:* Inst Org Chem Henkestr 42 91054 Erlangen Germany. *Fax:* 49-9131-859132; *E-Mail:* pvrs@organik.uni_erlangen.de

SCHLEYER, WALTER LEO, BIOPHYSICAL CHEMISTRY. *Current Pos:* RETIRED. *Personal Data:* b Berlin, Ger, June 4, 19; nat US; m 51; c 2. *Educ:* Rutgers Univ, AB, 48; Columbia Univ, AM, 50, PhD(phys chem), 52. *Prof Exp:* Res assoc, Col Physicians & Surgeons, Columbia Univ, 52-54; chemist, Res & Develop Dept, PQ Co, 54-63, tech field serv mgr, 63-66, mkt develop mgr, 66-67, commercial develop mgr, 67-69, tech serv mgr, 69-71, govt & indust rels mgr, 71-83. *Res:* Physical chemistry of biological processes; fundamental properties and industrial applications of alkali silicates; effects of silica and silicates on health and environment; predictive biomedical testing for regulatory purposes. *Mailing Add:* 8333 Seminole Blvd No 325 Seminole FL 33772

SCHLEZINGER, NATHAN STANLEY, NEUROLOGY, PSYCHIATRY. *Current Pos:* Prof, 52-83, EMER PROF CLIN NEUROL, JEFFERSON MED COL, 83- *Personal Data:* b Columbus, Ohio, June 2, 08; m 40; c 3. *Educ:* Ohio State Univ, BA, 30; Jefferson Med Col, MD, 32; Columbia Univ, ScD(med), 38. *Concurrent Pos:* Dir, Neuro-Ophthal Clin, Wills Eye Hosp, 39-; dir, Myasthenia Gravis Clin, Jefferson Hosp, 45-; consult, Vet Admin Hosp, Coatesville & Grandview Hosp, Sellersville. *Mem:* Am Neurol Asn; fel Am Acad Neurol; Asn Res Nerv & Ment Dis; Am Psychoanal Asn; fel Am Psychiat Asn. *Mailing Add:* Wyncote House Apt 813 25 Washington Ave Wyncote PA 19095-1414

SCHLICHT, RAYMOND CHARLES, SYNTHETIC ORGANIC CHEMISTRY. *Current Pos:* RETIRED. *Personal Data:* b North Bergen, NJ, Oct 13, 27; m 48, Annabelle Rinehart; c Charles A, John E, Marilyn A (Faxon), Robert W & Eric J. *Educ:* Cent Col, Iowa, BS, 48; Univ Maine, MS, 50; Ohio State Univ, PhD(org chem), 52. *Honors & Awards:* Award for Innovation, Texaco Res Ctr, 84. *Prof Exp:* Chemist, Texaco, Inc, 52-62, res chemist, 62-70, sr res chemist, 70-84, res assoc, 84-87, sr res assoc, 87-89. *Mem:* Am Chem Soc. *Res:* Reaction chemistry of higher olefins; phosphorus chemistry; nitrogen chemistry; synthesis of lubricating oil additives and fluids; granted 46 US patents. *Mailing Add:* 108 Lyndon Rd Fishkill NY 12524

SCHLICHTING, HAROLD EUGENE, JR, PHYCOLOGY, ALGAL ECOLOGY. *Current Pos:* PRES, BIOCONTROL CO, INC, 73-; ADJ PROF BIOL, ST MARY'S COL, ORCHARD LAKE, 88- *Personal Data:* b Detroit, Mich, Mar 19, 26; m 49, Mary Southworth; c Walter, Thomas, Anne, Arthur, Daniel & Joseph. *Educ:* Univ Mich, BS, 51; Mich State Univ, MS, 52, PhD(bot). 58. *Prof Exp:* Instr natural sci & bot, Mich State Univ, 52-54; fishery res biologist, US Fish & Wildlife Serv, 54-62; asst bot, Mich State Univ, 56-57; asst prof biol, Cent Mich Univ, 57-59; res biologist, 59-60; assoc prof biol, NTex State Univ, 60-68; Fulbright-Hayes lectr, Univ Col Cork, 68-69; assoc prof bot, NC State Univ, 69-73. *Concurrent Pos:* Res grants, NIH, 59-68 & Sigma Xi, 63-64; vis prof, Univ Okla Biol Sta, 64, 66, 68, 70 & 72; NSF fel, Marine Lab, Duke Univ, 66; State of Tex res grant, 66-68; sea grant, 70-72; vis prof bot, Univ Minn Biol Sta, 73, 75, 76 & 77. *Mem:* Int Asn Aerobiol; Sigma Xi; Phycol Soc Am; Int Phycol Soc; PanAm Aerobiol Asn; Brit Freshwater Biol Asn. *Res:* Dispersal of algae and protozoa; algal ecology; mass culturing of algae; biological monitoring; organic waste handling. *Mailing Add:* PO Box 43 Port Sanilac MI 48469

SCHLICK, SHULAMITH, PHYSICAL CHEMISTRY, THERMODYNAMICS & MATERIAL PROPERTIES. *Current Pos:* PROF PHYS & POLYMER CHEM, UNIV DETROIT, MERCY, 83- *Personal Data:* b Yassy, Romania; US citizen; m; c 3. *Educ:* Israel Inst Technol, BS, 55, Eng Dipl, 56, MS, 59, DS (phys chem), 63. *Prof Exp:* Guest scientist, Ford Res Labs, Dearborn, Mich, 65-67; sr lectr, Israel Inst Technol, Haifa, 70-73; sr res assoc magnetic resonance, Wayne State Univ, Detroit, 73-80. *Concurrent Pos:* Sabbatical, Ctr Study Nuclear Energy, Grenoble, France & Weitmann Inst Sci, Rehovot, Israel, 89-90; foreign temp collabr, CENG, Grenoble, France, 89; Varon vis prof, Weizmann Inst Sci, Rehovot, Israel, 90. *Mem:* Am Chem Soc; Am Phys Soc; AAAS; Int Environ Syst Resources Soc; Am Asn Univ Women. *Res:* Multifrequency electron spin resonance (MESR) of polymers; morphology of ionomers, polymer blends and interpenetrating polymer networks; trapped electrons in organic crystals; polymer-supported cotalepis; electron spin resonance impoing of polymeric materials. *Mailing Add:* Dept Chem Univ Detroit Mercy Detroit MI 48219-0900

SCHLICKE, HEINZ M, ELECTRONICS ENGINEERING, APPLIED PHYSICS. *Current Pos:* CONSULT ENGR, 75- *Personal Data:* b Dresden, Ger, Dec 13, 12; US citizen; m 39; c 2. *Educ:* Dresden Tech Univ, BS, 35, MS, 37, DSc(elec eng), 39. *Honors & Awards:* Stoddart Award, Electromagnetic Compatibility Soc of Inst Elec & Electronics Engrs. *Prof Exp:* Res engr, Telefunken, Ger, 38-40; dept head submarine commun, Naval Test Fields, 40-43, naval coun, High Command of Navy, 43-44, proj engr & spec consult, Paperclip scientist, Spec Devices Ctr, Off Naval Res, NY, 46-50; mgr, Electronics Labs, Allen-Bradley Co, 50-68, chief scientist, 68-75. *Concurrent Pos:* Teaching electromagnetic compatibility courses, univs & indust; expert witness elec accident cases; US deleg, Sci Exchange US/USSR. *Mem:* Fel AAAS; fel Inst Elec & Electronics Engrs. *Res:* Electromagnetic interference and hazard control in civilian systems; author of 2 books and co-author of 4 books; over 60 scientific articles published; 20 patents. *Mailing Add:* Interference Control Co 8220 N Poplar Dr Milwaukee WI 53217

SCHLIESSMANN, D(ONALD) J(OSEPH), ENVIRONMENTAL HEALTH. *Current Pos:* CONSULT ENGR, 77- *Personal Data:* b Colome, SDak, Aug 15, 17; m 44, Johnimae Sherrod; c D J Jr, Michael, Pat & Roberta. *Educ:* Univ Ill, BS, 41; Harvard Univ, MS, 49; Environ Eng Intersoc Bd, dipl, 70. *Prof Exp:* Mem staff malaria & typhus control, USPHS, 41-46, training off environ sanit & vector control, 47-48, engr & epidemiologist, 49-53, chief, Cumberland Field Sta, 54-57, dir & chief sanit eng, State Aids Sect, 57-61, dept chief, Tech Br, 61-63, chief aedes aegypti eradication br, 63-66, chief malaria eradication prog, Ga, 66-67, dep dir, Pan Am Health Orgn, Washington, DC, 67-77. *Concurrent Pos:* Consult comn enteric disease, US Armed Forces Epidemiol Bd, 51, mem comn environ sanit, 60-63, comn environ hyg, 63-72; consult, WHO, 58-63, 77, USAID, 78, APHA, 80, mem expert comt control enteric diseases, 63-68. *Mem:* Am Acad Environ Eng. *Res:* Public health engineering; epidemiology and control of diarrheal diseases; control of vectors and reservoirs of communicable diseases. *Mailing Add:* 3813 Savannah Sq E Atlanta GA 30340-4337

SCHLIMM, GERARD HENRY, CIVIL ENGINEERING, STRUCTURES. *Current Pos:* RETIRED. *Personal Data:* b Baltimore, Md, May 26, 29; m 56; c 3. *Educ:* Univ Md, BS, 57, PhD(structures), 70; NJ Inst Technol, MS, 60. *Prof Exp:* Mech engr compressors, Exxon Res & Eng Co, 57-60; instr civil eng, Univ Md, 60-62; asst prof mech eng, US Naval Acad, 62-66; dir, div eng & phys sci, Eve Col, Johns Hopkins Univ, 66-87, sr lectr civil eng, 88-94. *Concurrent Pos:* Consult, Trident Eng Asn, 62-68 & Ellicott City Eng Co, 71-73; mem bd dirs continuing eng studies div, Am Soc Eng Educ, 72-75, mem eng manpower comt, 77-; mem, Gov's Sci Adv Coun, State Md, 75- *Mem:* Am Soc Civil Engrs; Am Soc Eng Educ (secy, 71-72); Nat Soc Prof Engrs; Sigma Xi. *Res:* Engineering manpower; continuing education for engineers. *Mailing Add:* 18 Cedar Lane Lancaster PA 17601-3924

SCHLINGER, EVERT IRVING, ENTOMOLOGY, SYSTEMATICS. *Current Pos:* jr entomologist, Univ Calif, Riverside, 56-57, asst entomologist, 57-61, assoc prof entom & assoc entomologist, 61-68, chmn dept, 68-69, chmn, Div Entomol & Parasitol, 75-76, chmn, Dept Entom Sci, 76-79, chmn, Dept Conserv & Res Studies, 82-83, prof, 69-86, EMER PROF ENTOM, UNIV CALIF, BERKELEY, 86- *Personal Data:* b Los Angeles, Calif, Apr 17, 28; m 88, Marion Buegler; c 4. *Educ:* Univ Calif, Berkeley, BS, 50; Univ Calif, Davis, PhD(insect taxon), 57. *Prof Exp:* Lab asst entom, Univ Calif, 46-50, asst, 50-54 & 55-56; prof collector, Calif Acad Sci, 54-55. *Concurrent Pos:* Prof collector, Assocs Trop Biogeog, 53, 54; Guggenheim fel, 66-67; NSF award, 63-68. *Mem:* Entom Soc Am; Assoc Syst Collections; Sierra Club; Nature Conservancy; Wilderness Soc. *Res:* Insect (diptera) biosystematics; biogeography; insect ecosystems and land use management; spider ecology; arthropod non-target studies; biological control; biology of insect parasitoids. *Mailing Add:* 1944 Edison St Santa Ynez CA 93460

SCHLINGER, W(ARREN) G(LEASON), MECHANICAL ENGINEERING. *Current Pos:* RETIRED. *Personal Data:* b Los Angeles, Calif, May 29, 23; m 47, Katharine Stewart; c Michael, Norman & Sarah L. *Educ:* Calif Inst Technol, BS, 44, MS, 46, PhD(chem & mech eng), 49. *Honors & Awards:* Tech Achievement Award, Am Inst Chem Engrs, 76, Chem Eng Pract Award, 81; KFA Achievement Award, Elec Power Res Inst, 85. *Prof Exp:* Res fel, Calif Inst Technol, 49-53; chem engr, Texaco Inc, 53-57, sr chem engr, 57-60, suprv res, 60-68, dir, 68-70, mgr, Montebello Res Lab, 70-81, assoc dir gasification, 81-87. *Mem:* Nat Acad Eng; Am Chem Soc; fel Am Inst Chem Engrs; AAAS. *Res:* Fluid flow; heat transfer; coal gasification; hydrogen production and hydrogenation reactions; hydrocarbon gasification. *Mailing Add:* 3835 Shadow Grove Pasadena CA 91107

SCHLINK, F(REDERICK) J(OHN), physics, mechanical engineering; deceased, see previous edition for last biography

SCHLIPF, JOHN STEWART, MATHEMATICAL LOGIC. *Current Pos:* asst prof math, 83-84, asst prof computer sci, 84-87, ASSOC PROF COMPUTER SCI, UNIV CINCINNATI, 87- *Personal Data:* b Fargo, NDak, Oct 29, 48; m 70. *Educ:* Carleton Col, BA, 70; Univ Wis-Madison, MA, 72, PhD(math), 75. *Prof Exp:* Instr math, Calif Inst Technol, 75-77; vis lectr math, Univ Ill, 77-79; asst prof math, St Mary's Col Md, 79-81; mem staff, Environ Control Inc, 81-83. *Mem:* Asn Symbolic Logic; Am Math Soc; Asn Comput Mach. *Res:* Logic programming and non-monotonic reasoning; computability and computational complexity; model theory. *Mailing Add:* 1465 Larrywood Lane Cincinnati OH 45224-2133

SCHLISELFELD, LOUIS HAROLD, BIOCHEMISTRY. *Current Pos:* RETIRED. *Personal Data:* b Chicago, Ill, Sept 15, 31. *Educ:* Univ Ill, Urbana, BS, 53, MS, 55; Vanderbilt Univ, PhD(biochem), 64. *Prof Exp:* Res assoc contractile proteins, Inst Muscle Dis, Inc, 66-74; asst res prof, Dept Biol Chem, Univ Ill Med Ctr, Chicago, 74-85; res affil, Dept Neurosurg, Roswell Park Mem Inst, Buffalo, 85-89. *Concurrent Pos:* Adj asst prof, Dept Path, NY Med Col, 91-; biochemist, Neuromuscular Dis Biochem Lab, Dept Anat & Path, Westchester Co Hosp, NY, 93- *Mem:* Am Chem Soc; Am Soc Biol Chemists; Biophys Soc. *Res:* Enzymes and diseases involved in muscle glycogen breakdown; interaction of myosin and actin with adenosine triphosphate; mechanism of muscle contraction; metabolism of anti-cancer drugs in mouse leukemia cells. *Mailing Add:* 63 Chattertown Ave No 4 White Plains NY 10606. *E-Mail:* louis_schliselfeld@nymc.edu

SCHLISSEL, ARTHUR, COMPUTER SCIENCES, INFORMATION SCIENCES. *Current Pos:* from instr to assoc prof, 70-80, chmn dept, 75-84, PROF MATH, JOHN JAY COL CRIMINAL JUSTICE, CITY UNIV NEW YORK, 80- *Personal Data:* b Austria, July 7, 31; US citizen; div; c 2. *Educ:* Brooklyn Col, BS, 54; NY Univ, MS, 58, PhD(math), 74. *Prof Exp:* Lectr math, Brooklyn Col, 57-60, Hunter Col, 60-63 & NY Univ, 63-64; asst prof, Fairleigh Dickinson Univ, 64-67 & Manhattan Col, 67-70. *Concurrent Pos:* Vis prof math, King-Kennedy Prog, Albert Einstein Med Sch, 68-69. *Mem:* Am Math Soc; Math Asn Am; Sigma Xi; Soc Indust Appl Math. *Res:* Asymptotic behavior of the solutions of ordinary and partial differential equations; development of analysis in the 19th and 20th century, with special reference to differential equations; computer science, with special reference to computer graphics and data bases. *Mailing Add:* 2679 E 21st St Brooklyn NY 11235. *E-Mail:* dmejj@cunyvm.cuny.edu

SCHLITT, DAN WEBB, THEORETICAL HIGH ENERGY PHYSICS. *Current Pos:* from asst prof to assoc prof, 64-77, PROF PHYSICS, UNIV NEBR, LINCOLN, 77- *Personal Data:* b Lincoln, Nebr, Nov 2, 35; m 57; c 4. *Educ:* Mass Inst Technol, BS, 57; Univ Wash, PhD(physics), 63. *Prof Exp:* Vis asst prof physics, Univ Md, 63-64. *Concurrent Pos:* NSF grant, 65-69; vis scientist, Inst Theoret Physics, State Univ Utrecht, 72-73. *Mem:* Am Phys Soc; Am Asn Physics Teachers; Soc Indust & Appl Math; Asn Comput Mach; Am Asn Univ Professors. *Res:* Elementary particle theory; mathematical physics; foundations of statistical mechanics; numerical analysis and computation. *Mailing Add:* Dept Physics City Col NY New York NY 10031-9100

SCHLITT, WILLIAM JOSEPH, III, HYDROMETALLURGY, SOLUTION MINING. *Current Pos:* MGR, PROCESS TECHNOL, KVAERNER DAVY, 94- *Personal Data:* b Columbus, Ohio, June 12, 42; m 94, Anne M Ritchie. *Educ:* Carnegie Inst Technol, BS, 64; Pa State Univ, PhD(metall), 68. *Prof Exp:* Scientist, Kennecott Minerals Co, 68-75, sr scientist, 75-76, mgr, Hydrometall Dept, 77-81, prin prog mgr, Process Technol Group, 81-82; process staff mgr, Brown & Root Inc, 82-83, mgr technol, 83-93, prod line mgr chems, 93-94. *Concurrent Pos:* Mem, Oversight Comt Solution Mining Grant, NSF, 77-79, Oversight Comt Treatment Smelter Flue Dust Grant, Environ Protection Agency, 78-79; bd dirs, Soc Mining Engrs Int, 84-94; chmn, Mining & Explor Div, 87-88. *Mem:* Sigma Xi; Can Inst Mining & Metall; Soc Mining Engrs; Metall Soc. *Res:* Processes for extraction and refining of metal values contained in ores and other source materials including approaches involving hydrometallurgy and solution mining. *Mailing Add:* Kvaerner Davy 2440 Camino Ramon, No 100 San Ramon CA 94583. *Fax:* 510-866-6520

SCHLITTER, DUANE A, MAMMALOGY. *Current Pos:* assoc cur mammal, 73-84, CUR MAMMALS, CARNEGIE MUS NATURAL HIST, 85- *Personal Data:* b Monona, Iowa, Apr 2, 42; m 63, Judith E Spratt; c Tamara L & Tanya S. *Educ:* Wartburg Col, BA, 65; Univ Kans, MA, 69; Univ Md, PhD, 76. *Prof Exp:* Res & curatorial asst mammal, African Mammal Proj, Smithsonian Inst, 67-72. *Mem:* Am Soc Mammal (secy-treas, 77-80); Soc Syst Zool; Sigma Xi; AAAS; Zool Soc SAfrica. *Res:* Systematics, evolution, biogeography and ecology of mammals of Africa and Southwest Asia; relationship of diseases, ectoparasite vectors and mammal host in old world medical zoological problems; systematics and biogeography of mammals of eastern North America; conservation of endangered species of mammals in Africa and Southern Asia. *Mailing Add:* Carnegie Mus Natural Hist Annex 5800 Baum Blvd Pittsburgh PA 15206-3706. *Fax:* 412-665-2751; *E-Mail:* schlitterd@clpz.clpgh.org

SCHLIWA, MANFRED, CELL MOTILITY, ELECTRON MICROSCOPY. *Current Pos:* AT INST CELL BIOL, UNIV MUNICH, GERMANY. *Personal Data:* b Kulmbach, WGer, Dec 6, 45; m 78. *Educ:* Univ Frankfurt, MS, 72, PhD(zool), 75. *Prof Exp:* Res assoc zool, Univ Frankfurt, WGer, 76-78; Heisenberg fel cell biol, Univ Colo, Boulder, 79-81; prof zool, Univ Calif, Berkeley, 81-90, dir, Electron Microscope Lab, 84-90. *Mem:* Am Soc Cell Biol; Ger Soc Cell Biol; Ger Zool Soc; Int Pigment Cell Soc. *Res:* Cell biology; subfield cell motility; structure and function of the cytoskeleton. *Mailing Add:* Inst Cell Biol Ludwig-Maximilians Univ Schillerstr 42 80336 Munich Germany. *Fax:* 49 89 5996 882

SCHLOEMANN, ERNST, MAGNETIC MATERIALS, MAGNETIC DEVICES. *Current Pos:* CONSULT, 95- *Personal Data:* b Borgholzhausen, Ger, Dec 13, 26; nat US; m 94, Sally Duren Heatter; c Susan, Sonia & Barbara. *Educ:* Univ Gottingen, BS, 51, MS, 53, PhD(theoret physics), 54. *Honors & Awards:* TL Phillips Award for Excellence in Technol, 92. *Prof Exp:* Asst, Inst Theoret Physics, Univ Gottingen, 52-53; Fulbright fel solid state physics, Mass Inst Technol, 54-55; mem res staff, Raytheon Co, 55-60, proj dir, 60-64, sci fel, 64-95. *Concurrent Pos:* Vis assoc prof, Stanford Univ, 61-62 & Univ Hamburg, 66. *Mem:* Fel Am Phys Soc; fel Inst Elec & Electronics Engrs; Sigma Xi. *Res:* Solid state physics; magnetic phenomena; ferromagnetic resonance; lattice dynamics; thermal conductivity of solids; microwave physics and technology; statistical mechanics; environmental science; resource recovery from waste. *Mailing Add:* 38 Brook Rd Weston MA 02193. *E-Mail:* efschloem@aol.com

SCHLOEMER, ROBERT HENRY, VIROLOGY. *Current Pos:* ASST PROF MICROBIOL, SCH MED, IND UNIV, 75- *Personal Data:* b New York, NY, July 3, 46; m 69; c 2. *Educ:* Boston Col, BS, 68; Univ Va, MS, 72, PhD(biol), 73. *Prof Exp:* Fel, Sch Med, Univ Va, 73-75. *Mem:* Am Soc Microbiol; Sigma Xi. *Res:* Biochemical and biological analysis of viral membrane proteins; structure and assembly of viruses; mechanisms of virus persistence. *Mailing Add:* Dept Microbiol Ind Univ Sch Med 1120 South Dr Indianapolis IN 46202-5135

SCHLOER, GERTRUDE M, MICROBIOLOGY, MOLECULAR BIOLOGY. *Current Pos:* FINANCIAL PLANNER, 92- *Personal Data:* b Milwaukee, Wis, May 16, 26. *Educ:* Marquette Univ, BS, 48, MS, 53; Univ Wis-Madison, PhD(virol), 65. *Prof Exp:* Res assoc virol, Univ Wis-Madison, 66-67; NIH fel, Inst Virol, Univ Giessen, 67-69; instr microbiol, Mt Sinai Sch Med, 69-70, assoc, 70-71, asst prof, 71-73; mem staff, Molecular Biol Lab & Plum Island Animal Dis Lab, USDA, 73- *Mem:* AAAS; Am Soc Microbiol; Am Soc Virol. *Res:* Structure and genetics of influenza virus proteins; virulence and transmission of Newcastle Disease virus; epizootiology of adenovirus 127; structure and protein composition of malignant catarrhal fever virus and African swine fever virus. *Mailing Add:* 3060 Little Neck Rd Cutchogue NY 11935

SCHLOERB, PAUL RICHARD, SURGERY, NUTRITION. *Current Pos:* PROF SURG & DIR, NUTRIT SUPPORT SERV, UNIV KANS MED CTR, KANSAS CITY, KS, 88- *Personal Data:* b Buffalo, NY, Oct 22, 19; m 50, Louise Grimmer; c Ronald G, Patricia (Johnson), Marilyn (Hock), Dorothy (Hoban) & P Richard. *Educ:* Harvard Univ, AB, 41; Univ Rochester, MD, 44; Am Bd Surg, dipl, 52. *Prof Exp:* Asst surg, Peter Bent Brigham Hosp, Boston, 51; instr, Sch Med, Univ Rochester, 52; from asst prof to assoc prof, Med Ctr, Univ Kans, 52-64, res prof, 64-72, asst dean res, 70-72, dean res, 72-78, prof surg, 72-79; prof surg, Sch Med & Dent, Univ Rochester, 79-88; surgeon, Strong Mem Hosp, Rochester, 79-88. *Concurrent Pos:* AEC fel med sci, Nat Res Coun, 48-49; USPHS & NIH career develop award, 62-67; consult, Vet Admin Hosps, Wichita, Kans, 55- & Kansas City, Mo, 59-79; adj prof surg, Sch Med & Dent, Univ Rochester, 88-90. *Mem:* AAAS; Am Physiol Soc; Soc Univ Surg; Am Surg Asn; fel Am Col Surgeons; Am Asn Cancer Res; Am Asn Surg Trauma; Am Soc Parenteral & Enteral Nutrit; Am Inst Nutrit; Am Soc Clin Nutrit. *Res:* Postoperative care; surgical physiology; renal disorders; shock; water and electrolytes; transplantation; nutrition. *Mailing Add:* Univ Kans Med Ctr Dept Surg 39th and Rainbow Blvd Kansas City KS 66160. *Fax:* 913-588-6195; *E-Mail:* pschloer@kumc.edu

SCHLOM, JEFFREY, MOLECULAR BIOLOGY, BIOCHEMISTRY. *Current Pos:* chmn breast cancer virus segment, Nat Cancer Inst, 73-77, head, Tumor Virus Detection Sect, 77-80, chief, Exp Oncol Sect , 80-82, CHIEF, LAB TUMOR IMMUNOL & BIOL, NAT CANCER INST, 82- *Personal Data:* b Brooklyn, NY, June 22, 42; c 2. *Educ:* Ohio State Univ, BS, 64; Adelphi Univ, MS, 66; Rutgers Univ, PhD(microbiol), 69. *Honors & Awards:* Director's Award, NIH, 77 & 90; Leona Kopman Mem Award, 83; Rosenthal Found Award, Am Asn Cancer Res, 85 & 92. *Prof Exp:* Guest worker oncol, Nat Cancer Inst, 67-69; from instr to asst prof virol, Col Physicians & Surgeons, Columbia Univ, 69-73. *Concurrent Pos:* Adj prof, Grad Fac, George Washington Univ. *Mem:* AAAS; Harvey Soc; NY Acad Sci; Am Asn Cancer Res; Tissue Cult Asn; Int Asn Breast Cancer Res; Int Asn Comp Res Leukemia Related Dis. *Res:* Tumor immunology; molecular biology; viral oncology. *Mailing Add:* 10301 Sorrel Ave Potomac MD 20854. *Fax:* 301-496-2756

SCHLOMIUK, DANA, MATHEMATICS. *Current Pos:* Fel, Univ Montreal, 67-68, res assoc, 69, from asst prof to assoc prof, 69-89, PROF MATH, UNIV MONTREAL, 89- *Personal Data:* b Bucharest, Romania, Jan 5, 37; Can citizen; m 58, Norbert. *Educ:* Univ Bucharest, dipl math, 58; McGill Univ, PhD, 67. *Concurrent Pos:* Invited prof, Univ Rome, 73 & 75; vis prof, Sci Univ Tokyo, Noda-Chiba, Japan, 86. *Mem:* Am Math Soc; Can Math Soc. *Res:* Dynamical systems; bifurcations of plane vectorfields with special emphasis on algebraic and global geometric aspects of the theory of polynomial vector fields. *Mailing Add:* Dept Math & Statist Univ Montreal CP 6128 Succ Centre-Ville Montreal PQ H3C 3J7 Can. *Fax:* 514-343-5700; *E-Mail:* dasch@mathcn.umontreal.ca

SCHLOMIUK, NORBERT, MATHEMATICS, HISTORY & PHILOSOPHY OF SCIENCE. *Current Pos:* asst prof, 68-72, ASSOC PROF MATH, UNIV MONTREAL, 72- *Personal Data:* b Cernauti, Rumania, Apr 23, 32; Can citizen; m 58, Dana Tautu. *Educ:* Univ Bucharest, MA, 55; McGill Univ, PhD(math), 66. *Prof Exp:* Instr math, Univ Bucharest, 54-58; lectr, Dalhousie Univ, 61-62, asst prof, 62-63; res asst, Univ Calif, Berkeley, 63-64; lectr, McGill Univ, 64-66, asst prof, 66-68. *Concurrent Pos:* Vis prof, Math Inst, Univ Perugia, 71-72 & Math Res Inst, Swiss Fed Inst Technol, 71-72; vis res fel, Cornell Univ, 85, Kyoto Univ, 86. *Mem:* Am Math Soc; Math Soc France; Ital Math Union; Can Math Soc; NY Acad Sci. *Res:* Algebraic topology and homotopy theory; history of mathematics. *Mailing Add:* Dept Math Univ Montreal Montreal PQ H3C 3J7 Can

SCHLOSBERG, RICHARD HENRY, ORGANIC CHEMISTRY. *Current Pos:* sr staff chemist coal sci, 73-80, res assoc fuels sci, Exxon Res & Eng Co, 80-84, res assoc, 84-93, SR RES ASSOC, EXXON CHEM CO, 93- *Personal Data:* b New York, NY, May 23, 42; m 67, Pamela A Graham; c Laura J (Joseph). *Educ:* City Univ New York, BS, 63; Mich State Univ, PhD(chem), 67. *Prof Exp:* Fel org chem, Case Western Res Univ, 67-69; asst prof chem, Univ Wis-Whitewater, 69-73. *Concurrent Pos:* Ed, Chem of Coal Conversion & assoc ed, Liquid Fuels Technol, 82. *Mem:* Am Chem Soc; Am Inst Chem Engrs; Soc Tribology & Lubrication Engrs. *Res:* Chemistry of synthetic fuels; coal science; heavy oil science; thermal hydrocarbon chemistry; strong acid chemistry; friedel crafts chemistry; environmental chemistry; esterification chemistry; new product development. *Mailing Add:* Exxon Res & Eng Rm LB270 Rte 22 E Clinton Twp Annandale NJ 08801. *Fax:* 908-730-3058; *E-Mail:* rhschlo@erenj.com

SCHLOSS, JOHN VINTON, ENZYMOLOGY. *Current Pos:* prin investr, 81-87, RES SUPVR, E I DU PONT DE NEMOURS & CO, 87- *Personal Data:* b St Louis, Mo, May 11, 51; m 72; c 2. *Educ:* Univ Tulsa, BS, 73; Univ Tenn, PhD(biomed sci), 78. *Prof Exp:* Res fel, Univ Wis, 78-81. *Mem:* Am Chem Soc; Am Soc Biochem & Molecular Biol; Sigma Xi; AAAS; NY Acad Sci; Am Inst Chem. *Res:* Elucidation of enzymic reaction mechanisms; design and utilization of mechanism-based inhibitors of enzymes, primarily for enzymes of agronomic importance. *Mailing Add:* 9269 Reeder Dr Overland Park KS 66214

SCHLOSSER, HERBERT, CONDENSED MATTER THEORY, MOLECULAR BIOPHYSICS. *Current Pos:* assoc prof, 68-72, PROF PHYSICS, CLEVELAND STATE UNIV, 72- *Personal Data:* b Brooklyn, NY, Nov 18, 29; m 60, Martha Chiterer; c Rachelle & Arthur. *Educ:* Brooklyn Col, BS, 50; Polytech Univ New York, MS, 52; Carnegie-Mellon Univ, PhD(physics), 60. *Prof Exp:* Proj supvr, Res Lab, Horizons Inc, 53-55; proj physicist, Carnegie Inst Technol, 59-60; sr physicist, Bayside Res Lab, Gen Tel & Electronics, 60-62; specialist physicist, Repub Aviation Corp, 62-63; asst prof, Polytech Inst Brooklyn, 63-68. *Concurrent Pos:* Consult, Repub Aviation Co, 63; Fulbright-Hays Lectr, Univ Sao Paulo, 66-67; sr Weizmann res fel, Weizmann Inst Sci, Israel, 73-74; res assoc & vis prof, Dept Macromolecular Sci, Case Western Res Univ, 78-79. *Mem:* Am Phys Soc. *Res:* Universality theory, high pressure physics, surface physics; condensed matter theory; electronic structure of macromolecules; molecular biophysics. *Mailing Add:* Dept Physics Cleveland State Univ 1983 W 24th St Cleveland OH 44115-2403. *E-Mail:* fsherb@scivax.lerc.nasa.gov

SCHLOSSER, JON A, MATHEMATICS, PHYSICS. *Current Pos:* assoc prof, 72-78, PROF MATH, NMEX HIGHLANDS UNIV, 78- *Personal Data:* b Houston, Tex, July 26, 37; m 64; c 2. *Educ:* Univ Tex, PhD(physics), 63. *Prof Exp:* Res assoc relativity theory, Univ Tex, 63-64; instr appl math, Univ Chicago, 64-66; asst prof math, La State Univ, Baton Rouge, 66-70. *Mem:* Opers Res Soc Am; Am Math Soc; Math Asn Am. *Res:* Functional analysis; relativity theory; operations research. *Mailing Add:* NMex Highlands Univ Las Vegas NM 87701-4302

SCHLOSSMAN, IRWIN S, ORGANIC CHEMISTRY. *Current Pos:* CONSULT, 90- *Personal Data:* b New York, NY, July 2, 30; m 51, Linette Kerzner; c Beryl & Mark. *Educ:* City Col New York, BS, 51; Polytech Inst Brooklyn, MS, 59; Xavier Univ, Ohio, MBA, 71. *Prof Exp:* Chemist, Nopco Chem Co, NJ, 51-54; Gallowhur Chem Co, NY, 54-55; proj leader res & develop, Halcon Int, Inc, NJ, 55-66; group leader res, Emery Industs, Inc, 66-85, chem syst coordr, 85-88, coordr, Safety Regulatory Affairs, Info Serv, Quantum Chem Corp, 88-89; coordr, Safety, Regulatory Affairs, Info Serv, Henkel-Emery Group, 89-90. *Mem:* Am Chem Soc. *Res:* Liquid and vapor phase oxidation; catalysis; free radical chemistry; hydrogenation; polymer intermediates. *Mailing Add:* 4480 Deer Trail Blvd Sarasota FL 34238-5606

SCHLOSSMAN, MARK LOREN, CONDENSED MATTER PHYSICS OF SOFT MATERIALS. *Current Pos:* ASST PROF PHYSICS, UNIV ILL, CHICAGO, 94- *Personal Data:* b New York, NY, Nov 4, 58. *Educ:* Mass Inst Technol, SB, 80; Cornell Univ, MS, 83, PhD(physics), 87. *Prof Exp:* Fel, Harvard Univ, 87-90; res scientist, Univ Chicago, 90-94. *Mem:* Am Phys Soc. *Res:* Experimental studies of phase transitions in soft condensed matter occurring near or at surfaces. *Mailing Add:* Dept Physics M/C 273 Univ Ill 845 W Taylor St Rm 2236 Chicago IL 60607-7059. *E-Mail:* schloss@rainbow.uchicago.edu

SCHLOSSMAN, MITCHELL LLOYD, COSMETIC CHEMISTRY. *Current Pos:* EXEC DIR, PRESPERSE INC, 85-; DIR, KOBO PROD INC. *Personal Data:* b Brooklyn, NY, Dec 30, 35; m 56, Barbara Nadeil; c David S, Edye G & Julie I. *Educ:* NY Univ, BS, 56. *Honors & Awards:* Merit Award, Soc Cosmetic Chemists, 71. *Prof Exp:* Group leader skin treat prod, Revlon Inc, 57-63; mgr res & develop, Leeming/Pacquin Div, Pfizer & Co, 64-69; dir tech opers, Paris Cosmetics Inc, 69-70; vpres res & develop, Prince Indust Ltd, 70-74; vpres mkt & res, Malmstrom Chem Div, Emery Indust Inc, 74-78; vchmn, Tevco Inc, 78-94. *Concurrent Pos:* Chmn, NY Chap, Soc Cosmetic Chemists, 66, nat dir, 67-68; lectr & instr, Continuing Educ Ctr, South Hackensack, NJ, 85- *Mem:* Fel Soc Cosmetic Chemists; Am Chem Soc; fel Am Inst Chemists; AAAS. *Res:* Lanolin and cosmetic ester research; cosmetic product development; nail lacquers; several US and foreign patents in the cosmetic field. *Mailing Add:* 164 Dezenozo Lane West Orange NJ 07052. *Fax:* 973-669-0647

SCHLOSSMAN, STUART FRANKLIN, IMMUNOLOGY, HEMATOLOGY. *Current Pos:* from instr to assoc prof, 65-77, CHIEF, DIV TUMOR IMMUNOL, DANA FARBER CANCER INST, HARVARD MED SCH, 73-, PROF MED, 77- *Personal Data:* b New York, NY, Apr 18, 35; m 58; c 2. *Educ:* NY Univ, BA, 55, MD, 58. *Prof Exp:* Intern med, Ill Med Div, Bellevue Hosp, 58-59, asst resident, 59-60; res assoc, Lab Biochem, Nat Cancer Inst, 63-65. *Concurrent Pos:* Nat Found fel microbiol, Col Physicians & Surgeons, Columbia Univ, 60-62; asst physician, Med Serv, Vanderbilt Clin, Presby Hosp, 60-62; Ward hemat fel internal med, Sch Med, Wash Univ, 62-63; clin instr med, Sch Med, George Washington Univ, 64-65; dir, Blood Bank, Beth Israel Hosp, Mass, 65-66, assoc med, 65-67, from asst physician to assoc physician, 67-73; Guggenheim fel, 71; chief clin immunol, Beth Israel Hosp, Mass, 71-73; sr assoc med, Peter Bent Brigham Hosp, Mass, 76- *Mem:* Nat Acad Sci; Am Asn Immunol; Am Soc Clin Invest; Am Soc Hemat. *Res:* Internal medicine. *Mailing Add:* One Fox Pl Newton MA 02159-3025. *Fax:* 617-632-2690

SCHLOTFELDT, ROZELLA M, NURSING. *Current Pos:* EMER DEAN, SCH NURSING, CASE WESTERN RES UNIV. *Personal Data:* b 14. *Mem:* Inst Med-Nat Acad Sci. *Mailing Add:* 1111 Carver Rd Cleveland OH 44112

SCHLOTTER, NICHOLAS EDWARD, FABRICATION OF POLYMER FILMS & COATINGS. *Current Pos:* PRES, SCCS TECHNOLOGIES, INC, 95- *Personal Data:* m 80, Gail Anne Cederberg; c Sarah Catherine. *Educ:* Carleton Col, BA, 74; Stanford Univ, MS, 78, PhD(chem), 80. *Prof Exp:* Mem tech staff, Bellcore, 84-91; dir res & develop, Electronic Concepts Inc, 91-95. *Concurrent Pos:* Counr, Am Chem Soc, 96- *Mem:* Am Chem Soc; Am Phys Soc; Coblentz Soc; Soc Appl Spectros. *Res:* Technical consulting on materials issues; surface properties and coatings with the ability to provide clients with state-of-the-art testing and research; provide coatings and products through sub-contractors. *Mailing Add:* 37 Bucks Mill Rd Colts Neck NJ 07722. *E-Mail:* schlotter@scctech.com

SCHLOTTMANN, PEDRO U J, HIGHLY CORRELATED ELECTRON SYSTEMS, LOW DIMENSIONAL MAGNETISM. *Current Pos:* PROF PHYSICS, DEPT PHYSICS, FLA STATE UNIV, 90- *Personal Data:* b Buenos Aires, Arg, Mar 28, 47; Ger citizen; m 77; c 1. *Educ:* Universidad de Cuyo, Bariloche, Licenciado, 70; Tech Univ Munich, Dr rer nat(physics), 73. *Hon Degrees:* Habilitation, Freie Univ Berlin, 78. *Prof Exp:* Postdoctoral researcher physics, Max-Planck Inst, Munich, 73-74; asst, Dept Physics, Freie Univ Berlin, 74-77, asst prof, 77-83; researcher, Inst Festkorperforschung KFA Julich, 82-86; prof, Temple Univ, Philadelphia, 85-90. *Concurrent Pos:* Postdoctoral researcher, Univ Calif, Berkeley, 75-76; Heisenberg fel, DFG, Ger, 82-86; vis prof, Univ Gottingen, 85. *Mem:* Am Phys Soc. *Res:* Condensed matter theory and quantum statistical mechanics of systems with highly correlated states; heavy fermions, high temperature superconductors, narrow band phenomena and low dimensional magnetism and conductors. *Mailing Add:* Dept Physics Keen Bldg Fla State Univ Tallahassee FL 32306

SCHLOUGH, JAMES SHERWYN, ANIMAL PHYSIOLOGY, ENDOCRINOLOGY. *Current Pos:* From instr to assoc prof, 65-76, from asst dean to assoc dean, Col Letters & Sci, 69-74, PROF BIOL, UNIV WIS-WHITEWATER, 76-; CONSULT, NASCO INC, WIS, 67- *Personal Data:* b Wheeler, Wis, Sept 14, 31; m 63; c 2. *Educ:* Wis State Univ-River Falls, BS, 60; Univ Wis, MS, 63, PhD(zool), 66. *Mem:* AAAS; Soc Study Reproduction; Am Soc Mammal. *Res:* Early embryonic development in mammals; estrogen antagonism. *Mailing Add:* 958 W Walworth Ave Whitewater WI 53190

SCHLUB, ROBERT LOUIS, SUGARCANE PATHOLOGY. *Current Pos:* EXTEN PLANT PATHOLOGIST, UNIV GUAM, MANGILAO, 95- *Personal Data:* b Springfield, Ohio, Jan 22, 51; m 75, Joanne DiLucca; c Hala, Karl & Susanna. *Educ:* Ohio State Univ, BS, 73, MS, 75; Mich State Univ, PhD(plant path), 79. *Prof Exp:* Asst, Plant Dis Clinic, Ohio State Univ, 74; asst slide-tape teaching aids gen path, Mich State Univ, 76-78; fel, Soilborne Dis Lab, USDA, Beltsville, Md, 79-80; asst prof sugarcane dis, Depr Plant Path & Crop Physiol, LA State Univ, 80-83; adminr, Our Children's House, Baton Rouge, 84-94. *Mem:* Am Phytopath Soc. *Res:* Development of science and math educational materials for 4-9 year old children; etiology; epidemiology; environmental stress. *Mailing Add:* PO Box 5206 UOG Station Mangilao GU 96923

SCHLUEDERBERG, ANN ELIZABETH SNIDER, VIROLOGY, CHRONIC FATIGUE SYNDROME. *Current Pos:* RETIRED. *Personal Data:* b Detroit, Mich, May 31, 29; m 51, Richard F; c 5. *Educ:* Ohio State Univ, BS, 50; Johns Hopkins Univ, ScM, 54, ScD(microbiol), 59. *Prof Exp:* Instr med, Sch Med, Univ Md, 59-61; res assoc, Sch Med, Yale Univ, 62-69, sr res assoc epidemiol, 69-76; assoc prof, Sch Hyg & Pub Health, Johns Hopkins Univ, 76-78; exec secy, Epidemiol Dis Control Study Sect, Div Res Grants, NIH, 78-87; virol prog officer Nat Inst Allergies & Infectious Dis, NIH, 87-90, chief, Virol Br, 90- *Concurrent Pos:* USPHS fel, 61-62, USPHS grants, 61-78; mem, Scholars Adv Panel, Fogarty Int Ctr, NIH, 80-84. *Mem:* Am Soc Virol; fel Infectious Dis Soc Am; Am Asn Immunol. *Res:* Measles and rubella virus characterization; evaluation of measles and rubella vaccines and vaccine regimens; viral immunity. *Mailing Add:* NIH Solar Bldg Rm 3A16 Bethesda MD 20892. *Fax:* 301-496-8030

SCHLUETER, DONALD JEROME, NUCLEAR PHYSICS & STRUCTURE, SPECTROSCOPY & SPECTROMETRY. *Current Pos:* From instr to asst prof, 62-68, ASSOC PROF PHYSICS, PURDUE UNIV, WEST, 68- *Personal Data:* b Oak Park, Ill, Nov 14, 31; c 1. *Educ:* Northwestern Univ, BS, 53, MS, 57; Univ Kans, PhD(physics), 64. *Concurrent Pos:* NSF consult, AID, India, 67; Midwest Univ Consortium Int Activ/ITM, Malaysia, 86-89. *Mem:* Am Asn Physics Teachers. *Res:* Optical interferometry; nuclear structure. *Mailing Add:* 804 Woodmere Dr Lafayette IN 47905

SCHLUETER, DONALD PAUL, INTERNAL MEDICINE. *Current Pos:* MED LEGAL CONSULT, 96- *Personal Data:* b Milwaukee, Wis, July 24, 27; m 53; c 1. *Educ:* Marquette Univ, BS, 51, MD, 59; Ga Inst Technol, MS, 56. *Prof Exp:* Chemist, E I du Pont de Nemours & Co, 51-52; instr chem, Ga Inst Technol, 53-55; intern med, Milwaukee County Hosp, Wis, 59-60, resident, 60-63; from instr to assoc prof, Med Col Wis, 64-75, prof med, 75-96. *Concurrent Pos:* NIH res fel, 62-63; NIH res fel pulmonary physiol, Med Col Wis, 63-64; consult, Vet Admin Hosp, Wood, Wis, 63-; staff physician, Muirdale Sanatorium, 64-66, clin dir pulmonary dis, 66-68; chief med chest serv, Milwaukee County Hosp, 68-96. *Mem:* Am Fedn Clin Res; Am Thoracic Soc; Am Col Chest Physicians; Am Med Asn; Am Occup Med Asn; Sigma Xi. *Res:* Inorganic paper chromatography; flame spectroscopy; pulmonary physiology-respiratory mechanics; hypersensitivity lung disease. *Mailing Add:* 1091 Kelton Blvd Gulf Breeze FL 32561-5525. *Fax:* 850-934-6130

SCHLUETER, EDGAR ALBERT, ZOOLOGY, PARASITOLOGY. *Current Pos:* RETIRED. *Personal Data:* b Milwaukee, Wis, Sept 23, 18; m 57; c Cynthia, Thomas & Susan. *Educ:* Univ NTex, BS, 42; Univ Wis, MS, 49, PhD, 62. *Prof Exp:* Instr biol & natural sci, Mich State Univ, 49-55 & 57-59; asst prof, Wis State Univ-Superior, 59-62; from asst prof to prof, Univ NTex, 62-83. *Mem:* Am Soc Parasitol; Am Micros Soc; Sigma Xi. *Res:* Host-parasite relationships; parasitology; biochemistry of diseases of parasitic origin. *Mailing Add:* 1105 Piping Rock Lane Denton TX 76205

SCHLUETER, ROBERT J, BIOCHEMISTRY, PHARMACEUTICAL. *Current Pos:* Technician, Res & Develop biol Control, Armour & Co, 48-51, anal chemist, Res Control Lab, 51, biochemist, Pharmaceut Res Dept, 51-52, biochemist, Res Div, 54-60, sr res biochemist, 63-68, assoc res scientist, 68-76, prin scientist, 76-78, mgr biochem processes, 78-82, sr develop assoc, 82-84, mgr biochem develop, 84-88, SR RES BIOCHEMIST, ARMOUR PHARMACEUT CO, KANKAKEE, 88- *Personal Data:* b Chicago, Ill, Feb 28, 29; m 59, Mary A Pomrenke; c Annette, John & Carol. *Educ:* Valparaiso Univ, BA, 51; Northwestern Univ, PhD(biochem), 63. *Concurrent Pos:* US Army Chem Corp, 52-54. *Mem:* Am Soc Pharmacol & Exp Therapeut; Am Soc Biol Chem & Molecular Biol; Soc Exp Biol & Med; Am Chem Soc; Endocrine Soc; Protein Soc. *Res:* Isolation, purification and characterization of biologically active natural products and synthetic polypeptides; analytical and physical biochemistry; enzymology; collagen chemistry; bioassay development; calcitonin; insulin; insulin-like growth factor; biologicals; ACTH; human plasma proteins. *Mailing Add:* 4735 W 98th St Oak Lawn IL 60453-3127

SCHLUTER, ROBERT ARVEL, ELEMENTARY PARTICLE PHYSICS, EXPERIMENTAL HYDRODYNAMICS. *Current Pos:* PROF PHYSICS, NORTHWESTERN UNIV, 91- *Personal Data:* b Salt Lake City, Utah, Aug 27, 24; div; c 1. *Educ:* Univ Chicago, BS, 47, PhD(physics), 54. *Prof Exp:* Res assoc physics, Enrico Fermi Inst Nuclear Studies, Chicago, 54-55; from instr to asst prof, Mass Inst Technol, 55-60. *Concurrent Pos:* Guest scientist, Brookhaven Nat Lab, 57-; vis physicist, Lawrence Radiation Lab, Univ Calif, 58; assoc scientist, Argonne Nat Lab, 60-72; vis scientist, Fermi Nat Accelerator Lab, 75-87. *Mem:* Sigmi Xi; Am Phys Soc; Nat Asn Scholars. *Res:* Interactions of fundamental particles; high energy and elementary particle physics; fluid film dynamics. *Mailing Add:* 2300 Sherman Ave Apt 2C Evanston IL 60201. *Fax:* 847-491-9982; *E-Mail:* schulter@nwu.edu

SCHMAIER, ALVIN HAROLD, KININOGENS, CI INHIBITOR. *Current Pos:* fel thrombosis, Thrombosis Res Ctr, 79-80; from asst prof to assoc prof med, 80-91, PROF MED, TEMPLE UNIV SCH MED, 91-; PROF HEMAT, UNIV MICH MED CTR, 91- *Personal Data:* b Neptune, NJ, Jan 6, 49; m 70; c 1. *Educ:* Univ Va, BA, 70; Med Col Va, MD, 74; Am Bd Internal Med, dipl, 77, Hemat dipl, 80, Oncol dipl, 81. *Prof Exp:* Resident internal med, Temple Univ Sch Med, 74-77; fel hemat/oncol, Hosp Univ Pa, 77-79. *Concurrent Pos:* Clin instr, Temple Univ Hosp, 79-80; dir, Temple Univ Hosp Coagulation Lab, 82-; clin investr award, NIH, 80, res career develop award, 87; mem Coun Thrombosis, Am Heart Asn; dir, Univ Mich Med Ctr Coagulation Lab. *Mem:* Am Fedn Clin Res; Am Soc Hemat; Int Soc Hemostasis & Thrombosis; Am Soc Clin Invest; Cent Soc Res. *Res:* Vascular biology of kinins, thrombin and amyloid B-protein precursor. *Mailing Add:* Univ Mich Med Ctr 102 Observatory St Simpson Mem Bldg Ann Arbor MI 48109. *Fax:* 313-647-5669; *E-Mail:* aschmaie@medmail.med.umich.edu

SCHMALBERGER, DONALD C, ASTROPHYSICS. *Current Pos:* RETIRED. *Personal Data:* b Union City, NJ, Oct 24, 26; m 47. *Educ:* Okla State Univ, BS, 58; Ind Univ, MA, 59, PhD(astrophys), 62. *Prof Exp:* From instr to asst prof astron, Univ Rochester, 62-67; asst prof astron, State Univ NY, Albany, 67-70, asst prof astron & space sci, 70-72, assoc prof astron & space sci, 72-77. *Mem:* AAAS; Am Astron Soc; fel Royal Astron Soc; NY Acad Sci; Int Astron Union. *Res:* Solar physics; theory of stellar atmospheres; physical structure of variable stars; turbulent energy transport in astrophysical media. *Mailing Add:* 75 Lenox Ave Albany NY 12203

SCHMALE, ARTHUR H, JR, MEDICINE, PSYCHIATRY. *Current Pos:* from instr to assoc prof med & psychiat, 56-73, PROF PSYCHIAT, SCH MED & DENT, UNIV ROCHESTER, 73- *Personal Data:* b Lincoln, Nebr, Mar 14, 24; m 54; c 3. *Educ:* Pa State Col, 45; Univ Md, MD, 51. *Prof Exp:* Med intern, Univ Hosp, Baltimore, Md, 51-52, asst resident med & psychiat, 52-53, asst resident psychiat, 53-54; asst resident med & psychiat, Strong Mem Hosp, 54-56. *Concurrent Pos:* NIMH Teaching fel psychiat, Sch Med, Univ Md, 53-54; Hochstetter fel med & psychiat, Sch Med & Dent, Univ Rochester, 54-55, USPHS res fel, 55-57, Markle scholar med sci, 57-62, Buswell fac fel, 60-; Found Fund Res Psychiat fel psychoanal training, 59-63. *Mem:* AAAS; Am Psychosom Soc; Am Asn Univ Prof. *Res:* Psychosomatic medicine; emotions; cancer. *Mailing Add:* 70 Bradford Rd Rochester NY 14618

SCHMALSTIEG, FRANK CRAWFORD, MOLECULAR MECHANISMS OF HOST DEFENSE DEFECTS. *Current Pos:* From asst prof to assoc prof, 77-85, PROF ALLERGY-IMMUNOL, HUMAN BIOCHEM & GENETICS IMMUNOL, UNIV TEX MED BR, 86- *Personal Data:* b Corpus Christi, Tex, Jan 30, 40. *Educ:* Tex A&M Univ, PhD(phys-org chem); Univ Tex, Galveston, MD, 72. *Mem:* Am Asn Immunologists; Reticuloendothelial Soc; Soc Pediat Res; Sigma Xi; Am Pediat Soc. *Res:* Molecular mechanisms of congenital immunodeficiencies including leukocyte adherence defects. *Mailing Add:* Dept Pediat Univ Tex Med Br Rm C236 Children's Hosp Galveston TX 77555-0369

SCHMALTZ, LLOYD JOHN, GEOMORPHOLOGY, GLACIAL GEOLOGY. *Current Pos:* from asst prof to prof, Western Mich Univ, 59-88, head dept, 65-71, chmn, Dept Geol, 74-88, EMER PROF GEOL, WESTERN MICH UNIV, 88- *Personal Data:* b Chicago, Ill, Apr 10, 29; m 52; c 4. *Educ:* Augustana Col, AB, 53; Univ Mo, AM, 56, PhD(geol), 59. *Prof Exp:* Instr geol, Augustana Col, 54-55 & Univ Mo, 56-59. *Mem:* Fel Geol Soc Am; Nat Asn Geol Teachers; Am Quaternary Asn. *Res:* Pediments in central Arizona; Pleistocene geology in southwestern Michigan. *Mailing Add:* 3719 Middlebury Dr Kalamazoo MI 49006

SCHMALZ, ALFRED CHANDLER, ORGANIC CHEMISTRY. *Current Pos:* RETIRED. *Personal Data:* b Dedham, Mass, June 30, 24; m 47, 89, C Gail Hopkins; c Robert C & William D. *Educ:* Bowdoin Col, AB, 47; Middlebury Col, MS, 51; Univ Va, PhD(org chem), 54. *Prof Exp:* Res chemist, Hercules Inc, Del, 54-61, Va, NC & Ga 61-62, group leader fiber develop, 62-63, res supvr fibers & film, 63-71, mgr, Prod Develop, 71-73, mgr, appl res, polymers-fibers, 73-78; res scientist develop & fibers, Hercules Inc, 78-89. *Mem:* Am Chem Soc; Sigma Xi; Am Asn Textile Chem & Colorists; Tech Asn Pulp & Paper Indust. *Res:* Synthetic organic chemistry; paper chemicals; wet strength resins; water soluble polymers; antioxidants; light stabilizers; polyolefin fiber development; dyeing mechanisms. *Mailing Add:* 2594 Harvest Dr Conyers GA 30208-2406

SCHMALZ, PHILIP FREDERICK, ELECTROPHYSIOLOGY. *Current Pos:* Lead technician, 75-81, instr, 81-82, ASSOC PHYSIOL, MAYO FOUND, 82- *Personal Data:* b Buffalo, NY, Nov 15, 41; m 75; c 2. *Educ:* Northern Ill Univ, MS, 69. *Mem:* Am Physiol Soc; Am Motility Soc. *Mailing Add:* Dept Physiol & Biophys Mayo Clin & Found 821C Guggenheim Rochester MN 55905-0001. *Fax:* 507-284-0266; *E-Mail:* schmalz@mayo.edu

SCHMALZ, ROBERT FOWLER, REEF ENVIRONMENT CHEMISTRY, EVAPORITE DEPOSITION. *Current Pos:* from asst prof to prof, Pa State Univ, 58-91, head geol prog, 71-74, coordr, undergrad prog geol, 74-77, EMER PROF GEOL, PA STATE UNIV, 91- *Personal Data:* b Ann Arbor, Mich, May 29, 29; m 64, Barbara Leetch; c Timothy F & Dorothy L. *Educ:* Harvard Col, AB, 51, AM, 54, PhD(geol), 59. *Prof Exp:* Asst marine sedimentation, Oceanog Inst, Woods Hole, 57-58. *Concurrent Pos:* Assoc ed, Sedimentol, 59-61. *Mem:* Am Asn Petrol Geologists; fel Geol Soc Am; Geochem Soc; Soc Econ Paleont & Mineral; fel AAAS. *Res:* Low temperature aqueous geochemistry, chemical oceanography and chemical sedimentation in reef and evaporite environments; chemistry of reduced marine basins and petroleum genesis; radioactive waste management. *Mailing Add:* 536 Deike Bldg University Park PA 16802. *E-Mail:* rfs3@psu.edu

SCHMALZ, ROSEMARY, MATHEMATICS EDUCATION, PSYCHOLOGY OF MATHEMATICAL ACTIVITY. *Current Pos:* PROF MATH, EASTERN ILL UNIV, 87- *Personal Data:* b Evansville, Ind, Dec 17, 40. *Educ:* St Mary-of-the-Woods Col, BA, 63; Univ Ill, MA, 69; Fla State Univ, PhD(math educ), 72. *Prof Exp:* Teacher math, Robstown, Tex, 64-68; prof math, St Mary-of-the-Woods Col, 72-81, Univ Scranton, 81-87. *Mem:* Nat Coun Teachers Math; Math Asn Am; Asn Women Math. *Res:* Role of intuition in mathematics and how it is facilitated. *Mailing Add:* Math Dept Eastern Ill Univ Charleston IL 61920-3099. *E-Mail:* cfrms@eiu.edu

SCHMALZ, THOMAS G, ELECTRONIC STRUCTURE OF ORGANIC POLYMERS. *Current Pos:* asst prof, 81-85, ASSOC PROF MARINE SCI, TEX A&M, GALVESTON, 85- *Personal Data:* b Springfield, Ill, July 12, 48. *Educ:* Mont State Univ, BS, 70; Univ Ill, Urbana, PhD(chem physics), 75. *Prof Exp:* Res assoc, James Franck Inst, Univ Chicago, 76-79; asst prof chem, Rice Univ, 79-81. *Mem:* Am Phys Soc; Am Chem Soc. *Res:* Understanding large conjugated pi-electron systems such as recently discovered carbon cage molecules and electrically conductive carbon polymers; aromatic stabilization in these systems is examined with various AB initio and semiempirical tools; Theory of Aromaticity in conjugated systems. *Mailing Add:* Dept Marine Sci Tex A&M Univ PO Box 1675 Galveston TX 77553-1675

SCHMALZER, DAVID KEITH, CHEMICAL ENGINEERING. *Current Pos:* MGR, FOSSIL ENERGY PROG, ARGONNE NAT LAB. *Personal Data:* b Baltimore, Md, Aug 20, 42; m 65. *Educ:* Johns Hopkins Univ, BES, 64, MS, 65; Univ Pittsburgh, PhD(chem eng), 68. *Prof Exp:* Assoc engr, Com Atomic Power Div, Westinghouse Elec Co, 67; proj engr, Gulf Res & Develop Co, Pa, 68-77; res mgr, Pittsburgh & Midway Coal Mining Corp, 77-80; mem staff, Gulf Mineral Resources Co, 80-85; vpres & mgr res, Solvant Refined Coal Int, 81-85. *Mem:* Am Chem Soc; Am Inst Chem Engrs. *Res:* Performance and management of energy production and conversion research and development based on conventional (oil and gas) feedstocks and nonconventional feedstocks including coal, oil shale, tar sands and biomass. *Mailing Add:* 955 L'Enfant Plaza N Suite 6000 Washington DC 20024. *Fax:* 202-488-2413

SCHMANDT, JURGEN, ENVIRONMENTAL POLICY RESEARCH, GLOBAL ISSUES POLICY RESEARCH. *Current Pos:* DIR, CTR GLOBAL STUDIES, HOUSTON ADVAN RES CTR, 85- *Personal Data:* b Munster, Ger, Mar 4, 29; US citizen; m, Denise Besserat; c Alex, Phillip & Chris. *Educ:* Univ Bonn, PhD(philos), 56. *Prof Exp:* Dep dir & head scholarship dept, Ger Acad Exchange Serv, 58-60; head, Nat Sci Policies, Orgns Econ Coop & Develop, 60-65; assoc dir, Prog Technol Sci, Harvard Univ, 65-70; sr environ fel, US Environ Protection Agency, 80-81. *Concurrent Pos:* Prof pub affairs, LBJ Sch Pub Affairs, Univ Tex, 71-; mem, Comt Risk Perception & Commun, NSF, 87-89. *Mem:* Sigma Xi. *Res:* Public policy related to environmental issues regionally and internationally; sustained development, global warming, natural resources management (especially water), acid rain, desertification and others. *Mailing Add:* Houston Advan Res Ctr 4800 Research Forest Dr The Woodlands TX 77381. *E-Mail:* schmandt@harc.edu

SCHMARS, WILLIAM THOMAS, ELECTRON OPTICS, ELECTRICAL ENGINEERING. *Current Pos:* RETIRED. *Personal Data:* b Lockport, Ill, Jan 10, 38. *Educ:* Univ Ill, BS, 61. *Prof Exp:* Res engr, Autonetics Div, Rockwell Int, 61-66, sr res engr, 66-68, sr engr, 68-93. *Mem:* Nat Soc Prof Engrs. *Res:* Navigation instruments, especially photoelectric autocollimators, precision shaft angle encoders and vibrating string gyro and accelerometer; electrochemical tiltmeter; laser gyro and micro sensor accelerometer research. *Mailing Add:* 1509 Beechwood Ave Fullerton CA 92685

SCHMECKENBECHER, ARNOLD F, INORGANIC CHEMISTRY. *Current Pos:* RETIRED. *Personal Data:* b Allendorf, Ger, Feb 15, 20; US citizen; m 53, Rose Zettler; c Eva (Stephenson). *Educ:* Univ Heidelberg, dipl, 50; Univ Kiel, PhD(chem), 53. *Prof Exp:* Instr inorg chem, Univ Kiel, 53-54; chemist, Gen Aniline & Film Corp, NJ, 55-58; sr chemist, Remington Rand Univac, Pa, 58-60; assoc chemist, Components Div, IBM Corp, 60-61, staff chemist, 61-64, adv chemist, 64-69, sr chemist, 69-89. *Concurrent Pos:* Ger Res Asn scholar, 53-54. *Mem:* Am Chem Soc; Sigma Xi. *Res:* Magnetics materials, particularly materials for use in computer memories and phase locked oscillators; multilayered ceramic substrates for integrated circuit chips. *Mailing Add:* 54 Freedom Pond Lane North Chili NY 14514

SCHMEDTJE, JOHN FREDERICK, ANATOMY. *Current Pos:* ASSOC PROF ANAT, SCH MED, IND UNIV, INDIANAPOLIS, 66- *Personal Data:* b St Louis, Mo, July 9, 19; m 56; c 3. *Educ:* Columbia Univ, AB, 41; Rutgers Univ, PhD(zool), 51. *Prof Exp:* Instr anat, Sch Med, St Louis Univ, 51-53, asst prof, 53-56; instr, Harvard Med Sch, 56-58; asst prof, Sch Med, Tufts Univ, 58-66. *Mem:* AAAS; Am Asn Anat; Electron Micros Soc Am; Histochem Soc; Am Soc Cell Biologists. *Res:* Immunocytochemistry; electron microscopy; cellular aspects of immune reactions in lymphatic tissue and epithelium. *Mailing Add:* Dept Anat Ind Univ Sch Med 635 Barnhill Dr Indianapolis IN 46223-0001

SCHMEE, JOSEF, STATISTICS, QUALITY CONTROL. *Current Pos:* from asst prof to assoc prof, 72-80, dir, 80-86, PROF MGT, GRAD MGT INST, UNION COL, NY, 80-, KENNETH B SHARPE PROF MGT, 93- *Personal Data:* b Grieskirchen, Austria, Feb 13, 45; m 67, Marilyn Restifo. *Educ:* Univ Com, Vienna, Magister, 68; Union Col, NY, MSc, 70, PhD(stat), 74. *Honors & Awards:* Wilcoxon Award, Am Soc Qual Control, 80, Brumbaugh Award, 81. *Prof Exp:* Res asst sociol, Col Com, Vienna, 67-68; analyst finance, Gen Elec Co, 69. *Concurrent Pos:* Asst prof mgt, Univ Munich, 75; dir, Bur Health Mgt Stand, NY Dept Health, 78-79; Fulbright-Hays res scholar, Ger, 80-81; adj prof path, Albany Med Col, 81-; vis res fel, Gen Elec Res & Develop, 88-89. *Mem:* Am Soc Qual Control; Inst Math Statist; Am Statist Asn; Biomet Soc; fel Am Statist Asn. *Res:* Exact confidence intervals on mean, variance, percentiles and range of normal distribution with single censoring; sequential analysis t-test and estimation; semi-Markov models in health care systems; statistics in dentistry; censored data regression analysis; atherosclerosis in swine due to dietary effects; audit sampling; quality management. *Mailing Add:* Bailey Hall Grad Mgt Inst Union Col Schenectady NY 12308. *Fax:* 518-388-6686; *E-Mail:* jschmee@worldnet.att.net

SCHMEELK, JOHN FRANK, APPLIED MATHEMATICS. *Current Pos:* ASST PROF MATH, VA COMMONWEALTH UNIV, 75- *Personal Data:* b Newark, NJ, July 19, 39; m 67. *Educ:* Seton Hall Univ, BS, 62; NY Univ, MS, 65; George Washington Univ, PhD(math), 76. *Prof Exp:* Instr math, Seton Hall Univ, 63-65 & NC State Univ, 65-66; teaching asst math, George Washington Univ, 71-73; instr math, Middlesex County Col, 74-75. *Mem:* Am Math Soc; Math Asn Am; Soc Indust & Appl Math; Am Asn Univ Professors. *Res:* Development of an infinite-dimensional generalized function, for example, continuous linear functionals on test functions that are infinitely differentiable on an infinite dimensional vector space. *Mailing Add:* 1916 Sweetwater Lane Richmond VA 23229-3811

SCHMEER, ARLINE CATHERINE, CELL BIOLOGY, SYNTHETIC ORGANIC & NATURAL PRODUCTS CHEMISTRY. *Current Pos:* RETIRED. *Personal Data:* b Rochester, NY, Nov 14, 29. *Educ:* Col St Mary, Ohio, BA, 51; Univ Notre Dame, MS, 61; Univ Colo Med & Grad Sch, Denver, PhD(cell biol), 69. *Hon Degrees:* DSc, Albertus Magnus Col, 74, State Univ NY, Potsdam, 90. *Honors & Awards:* St Joachim Award, Mercy Hosp, Watertown, NY. *Prof Exp:* Chmn high sch sci dept, Ohio, 54-59 & NY, 59-63; asst prof biol & co-dir med res lab, Ohio Dominion Col, 63, chmn dept, 63-68, assoc prof biol & dir med res lab, 64-72, dir, St Thomas Inst Res Lab, 69-72; res scientist, Cancer Res Ctr & Hosp, Am Med Ctr, Denver, 72-73, dir med res fel prog & anticancer agents of marine origin, 72-82; dir, Mercenene Cancer Res Inst, Hosp St Raphael, New Haven, Conn, 82-93. *Concurrent Pos:* NSF res fels, 59-64; USPHS Nat Cancer Inst & Am Cancer Soc grants; Nat Cancer Inst spec res fel; chmn biol educ sec schs, Archdiocese of New York; partic, NSF High Sch Biol Sci Curric Study & Comn Undergrad Educ Biol Sci Comt Col Biol Teacher Training, DC, 62-63; sr investr & mem cell biol specialty panel, Marine Biol Lab, Woods Hole, 62-, corp mem, 65-; partic, Int Cancer Cong, Tokyo, Japan, 66 & Houston, Tex, 70, Buenos Aires, Argentina, 78, Seattle, Wash, 82 & Budapest, Hungary, 86, Hamburg, Ger, 90; res scientist, Inst Med Biophys, Univ Wurzburg & res prof, Univ Wurzburg Med Sch, Ger, 69-70; vis scientist, Am Med Ctr Cancer Res; consult, Sch Trop Med, Univ Sydney; scholar & fel, Nat Cancer Inst, NIH, NSF, Med Sch, Univ Wurzburg, WGer & Grad & Med Sch, Univ Colo; numerous grants, fel doctoral studies. *Mem:* Am Soc Cell Biol; NY Acad Sci; Electron Micros Soc Am; Am Physiol Soc; fel Royal Micros Soc Eng. *Res:* Cellular biology; developmental drugs cancer; pharmacology toxicology and experimental therapeutics in use of growth inhibitors and biologically active moieties from naturally occurring products and effects of these products on abnormal growth such as cancer, AIDS, viral & bacterial activity; developmental therapeutics. *Mailing Add:* Mercenene Cancer Res Inst 790 Prospect St New Haven CT 06511

SCHMEHL, WILLARD REED, SOILS, INTERNATIONAL AGRICULTURE. *Current Pos:* assoc prof & assoc agronomist, 48-56, prof agron & agronomist, 56-86, EMER PROF AGRON, COLO STATE UNIV, 86- *Personal Data:* b Arlington, Nebr, Apr 16, 18; m 43; c 2. *Educ:* Colo State Univ, BS, 40; Cornell Univ, PhD(soil sci), 48. *Prof Exp:* Asst, Cornell Univ, 40-42; supvr, Hercules Powder Co, 42-43. *Concurrent Pos:* Proj assoc, Univ

Wis, 54-55. *Mem:* Soil Sci Soc Am; Am Soc Agron; Am Soc Sugar Beet Technologists. *Res:* Soil acidity and fertility; availability of phosphates to plants; farming systems; sugar beet nutrition. *Mailing Add:* 1727 Hillside Dr Ft Collins CO 80524

SCHMEISSER, GERHARD, JR, ORTHOPEDIC SURGERY. *Current Pos:* From instr to prof, 57-90, EMER PROF ORTHOP SURG, SCH MED, JOHNS HOPKINS UNIV, 90- *Personal Data:* b Baltimore, Md, Mar 27, 26; m 57. *Educ:* Princeton Univ, AB, 49; Johns Hopkins Univ, MD, 53. *Honors & Awards:* IR 100 Award, 71. *Concurrent Pos:* Vis surgeon, Children's Hosp, 58-; orthop surgeon, Johns Hopkins Hosp, 58-; chief orthop surg, Baltimore City Hosps, 59-; consult, USPHS Hosp, 64-65. *Mem:* Fel Am Acad Orthop Surg. *Res:* External power and control of limb prostheses and braces. *Mailing Add:* Gibson Island MD 21056

SCHMELING, SHEILA KAY, WILDLIFE DISEASE, TROPICAL VETERINARY MEDICINE. *Current Pos:* WILDLIFE VET, COROZAL VET CLIN, 83- *Personal Data:* b Brookings, SDak, May 5, 49. *Educ:* Univ Mass, Amherst, BS, 71; Colo State Univ, MS & DVM, 77. *Prof Exp:* Wildlife vet, Nat Wildlife Health Lab, 79-82. *Concurrent Pos:* Vet, Belize Zoo. *Mem:* Wildlife Disease Asn; Am Asn Wildlife Vets; Am Vet Med Asn; Sigma Xi; Soc Trop Vet Med. *Res:* Determination of the causes of mortality in free-flying raptors, especially the bald and golden eagle. *Mailing Add:* PO Box 196 Corozal Town Belize

SCHMELL, ELI DAVID, IMMUNOCHEMISTRY, REPRODUCTIVE BIOLOGY. *Current Pos:* sci officer biochem, 81-83, PROG MGR MOLECULAR BIOL, OFF NAVAL RES, 84- *Personal Data:* b Baltimore, Md, Jan 5, 50; m 71; c 2. *Educ:* City Univ NY, BS, 71; Johns Hopkins Univ, PhD(cellular & molecular biol), 76. *Honors & Awards:* Forum Prize, Am Fertility Soc, 81. *Prof Exp:* Teaching fel biol, Johns Hopkins Univ, 76-79; staff fel reproductive biol, NIH, 79-81, sr staff fel, 81. *Concurrent Pos:* Teacher asst, Johns Hopkins Med Sch, 74-75, res assoc, 80-81, adj asst prof, 82-83, adj assoc prof, 83-; vis scientist, Israel Inst Technol, 83 & Weizmann Inst Sci, 85; adminr, Mgt Res Progs in Biochem, Microbiol & Molecular Biol, US Navy. *Mem:* Am Soc Biol Chem; Am Soc Cell Biol; AAAS; Am Fertility Soc; Soc Study Reproduction. *Res:* Biochemical and immunochemical studies on the structure and function of human acetylcholinesterase. *Mailing Add:* Indust Park Int Lab Ltd Kiryat Weizmann Nes Ziona 76110 Israel. *Fax:* 972-8-407-566

SCHMELLING, STEPHEN GORDON, HYDROLOGY & WATER RESOURCES. *Current Pos:* RES SCIENTIST, US ENVIRON PROTECTION AGENCY, RS KERR ENVIRON RES LAB, 80- *Personal Data:* b Kenosha, Wis, Mar 21, 40; m 66; c 2. *Educ:* Mass Inst Technol, BS, 62; Univ Calif, Berkeley, PhD(physics), 67. *Prof Exp:* Res physicist, Lawrence Berkeley Lab, 67-70; asst prof physics, State Univ NY, Buffalo, 70-75; assoc prof physics, Univ Cent Univ, 75-88. *Concurrent Pos:* Sr lectr, Univ Ife, Ile-Ife, Nigeria, 74. *Mem:* Am Phys Soc; Am Geophys Union. *Res:* Subsurface contaminant transport particularly in fractured rock geological formations; remediation of ground-water contamination. *Mailing Add:* US Environ Protection Agency PO Box 1198 Ada OK 74821. *Fax:* 580-436-8536

SCHMELTEKOPF, A, ATMOSPHERIC SCIENCE. *Current Pos:* RETIRED. *Personal Data:* b Kyle, Tex, Feb 24, 32. *Educ:* Univ Tex, BS, 59, PhD(physics), 62. *Honors & Awards:* Gold Medal, Dept Com. *Prof Exp:* Staff scientist, Nat Oceanic & Atmospheric Admin, 63-88. *Mem:* Am Phys Soc. *Mailing Add:* 410 E Fork Rd Marshall NC 28753

SCHMELTZ, IRWIN, BIO-ORGANIC CHEMISTRY. *Current Pos:* DIR, US CUSTOMS LAB, NY, 87- *Personal Data:* b New York, NY, Feb 26, 32; m 62; c 4. *Educ:* City Col New York, BS, 53; Univ Utah, PhD(org biochem), 59. *Prof Exp:* Teaching fel chem, 55-59, fel biochem, Univ Utah, 59-60; Cigar Mfrs Asn sr res fel, Eastern Regional Lab, 60-62, res chemist tobacco invests, 62-65, head pyrolysis invests, tobacco lab, 65-70, head smoke invests, 70-71, lubricant invests, Animal Fat Prod Lab, USDA, 71-73; head bio-org chem, Div Environ Carcinogensis, Naylor-Dana Inst Dis Prev, Am Health Found, 73-79; tech fel, Hoffmann-LaRoche, Nutley, NJ, 79-87. *Concurrent Pos:* Consult, Nat Cancer Inst, 73- & Princeton Univ, 74- *Mem:* Am Oil Chemists Soc; Soc Environ Geochem & Health; AAAS; Am Chem Soc; Am Asn Cancer Res. *Res:* Chemical carcinogenesis, environmental chemistry; organic synthesis; biosynthesis of pteridines; chemical composition of tobacco and tobacco smoke; pyrolysis of organic compounds; products from animal fats; analytical organic chemistry. *Mailing Add:* Three Miriam Lane Monsey NY 10952

SCHMELZ, DAMIAN VINCENT, OLD GROWTH FORESTS. *Current Pos:* from instr to assoc prof, 65-75, prof & acad dean, 75-93, PROF & PROVOST-VRECTOR, ST MEINRAD COL, 93- *Personal Data:* b Georgetown, Ind, May 7, 32. *Educ:* St Meinrad Col, BA, 58; Purdue Univ, Lafayette, MS, 64, PhD(ecol), 69. *Prof Exp:* Teacher high sch, Ind, 59-67. *Concurrent Pos:* Mem, Ind Natural Areas Surv, Purdue Univ, 67-69; mem, Ind Natural Resources Comn, 75- *Mem:* Ecol Soc Am; Sigma Xi. *Res:* Forest ecology. *Mailing Add:* Dept Biol St Meinrad Col One Archabbey St Meinrad IN 47577-1022

SCHMERGEL, GABRIEL, INDUSTRIAL BIOTECHNOLOGY. *Current Pos:* RETIRED. *Personal Data:* b 1940. *Educ:* Rensselaer Polytechnic Inst, BSMe, 62; Harvard Bus Sch, MBA, 67. *Hon Degrees:* Dr, Worcester Polytechnic Inst, 88. *Prof Exp:* Pres & chief exec officer, Genetics Inst Inc, 81-97. *Concurrent Pos:* Mem, Bd Dir, Indust Biotechnol Asn, 81-87 & 89, pres, 85-86. *Mem:* Nat Acad Eng. *Mailing Add:* Genetics Inst Inc 87 Cambridge Park Dr Cambridge MA 02140

SCHMERL, JAMES H, LOGIC MODEL THEORY. *Current Pos:* PROF MATH, UNIV CONN, STORRS, 72- *Personal Data:* b Storrs, Conn, April 7, 40. *Educ:* Univ Calif, Berkeley, AB, 62, MA, 63, PhD(math), 70. *Mem:* Am Math Soc; Asn Symbol Logic. *Mailing Add:* Dept Math Univ Conn Storrs CT 06269-3009

SCHMERLING, ERWIN ROBERT, SPACE PHYSICS, DATA SYSTEMS. *Current Pos:* chief data syst scientist, Off Space Sci & Appln, 86-87, MGR, ASTROPHYS DATA SYST, NASA-HQ, 88- *Personal Data:* b Vienna, Austria, July 28, 29; m 57, Esther M Feldman; c Susan & Elaine. *Educ:* Cambridge Univ, BA, 50, MA, 54, PhD(radio physics), 58. *Honors & Awards:* Soviet Geophys Comt Medal, 85. *Prof Exp:* Vis asst prof elec eng, Pa State Univ. 55-57, from asst prof to assoc prof, 57-64; prog chief magnetospheric physics, 64-76, Off Space Sci, NASA Hq, 76-83; vis scholar, Stanford Univ, Calif, 83; asst dir space & earth sci, Goddard Space Flight Ctr, Greenbelt, Md, 84-86. *Concurrent Pos:* Mem comns G & H, Int Sci Radio Union, 58, secy, US Comn III, 66-69, chmn, 69-72; mem, Wave Propagations Stand Com, Inst Elec & Electronics Engrs, 70-; mem comt space res, 82, Adv Group Aerospace Res & Dev, 81-87. *Mem:* AAAS; fel Inst Elec & Electronics Engrs; Am Geophys Union; Sigma Xi. *Res:* Ionospheric and radio physics; physics of the ionosphere; radio wave propagation; electron densities and sounding of ionized regions from the ground and from space vehicles; atmospheric and space physics, environment of earth, planets and interplanetary space; scientific data systems; interactive computers for science education; widely distributed heterogeneous computer systems for access to scientific data and computations. *Mailing Add:* Astrophys Info Syst 9917 La Duke Dr Kensington MD 20895. *Fax:* 202-358-3096; *E-Mail:* eschmerling@gnr.ossa.hq.nasa.gov

SCHMERR, MARY JO F, IMMUNOCHEMISTRY, MOLECULAR BIOLOGY. *Current Pos:* RES CHEMIST BIOCHEM ANIMAL DIS, NAT ANIMAL DIS CTR, USDA, 75- *Personal Data:* b Dubuque, Iowa, Nov 4, 45; m 72; c 3. *Educ:* Clarke Col, Iowa, BA, 68; Iowa State Univ, PhD(biochem), 75. *Mem:* Am Soc Microbiol; Am Chem Soc; Sigma Xi; NY Acad Sci. *Res:* Biochemistry and immunochemistry of animal diseases caused by viruses; study of the function of viral proteins. *Mailing Add:* 1327 325th St Woodward IA 50276-7505

SCHMERTMANN, JOHN H(ENRY), GEOTECHNICAL ENGINEERING. *Current Pos:* PRIN, SCHMERTMANN & CRAPPS CONSULT GEOTECH ENGRS, 78- *Personal Data:* b New York, NY, Dec 2, 28; m 56; c 4. *Educ:* Mass Inst Technol, BSCE, 50; Northwestern Univ, MS, 54, PhD(civil eng), 62. *Honors & Awards:* Collingwood Prize, Am Soc Civil Engrs, 56, Norman Medal, 71, State-of-the-Art Award, 77. *Prof Exp:* Soils engr, Moran, Proctor, Mueser & Rutledge, NY, 51-54; geotech engr, US Army Corps Engrs, 54-56; from asst prof to prof civil eng, Univ Fla, 56-78. *Concurrent Pos:* Prin investr, NSF res grants, 56-; NSF fel, Norweg Geotech Inst, Oslo, 62-63; Nat Res Coun Cross-Can lectr, 71; vis scientist, Nat Res Coun Can, 71-72. *Mem:* Nat Acad Eng; Am Soc Civil Engrs; Am Soc Testing & Mat. *Res:* Soil mechanics and foundation engineering; consolidation and shear strength; methods for field exploration; special soil mechanics problems. *Mailing Add:* Schmertmann & Crapps Inc 4509 NW 23 Ave Suite 19 Gainesville FL 32606

SCHMID, CARL WILLIAM, BIOPHYSICAL CHEMISTRY. *Current Pos:* ASSOC PROF CHEM, UNIV CALIF, DAVIS, 73- *Personal Data:* b Philadelphia, Pa. *Educ:* Drexel Inst Technol, BS, 67; Univ Calif, Berkeley, PhD(chem), 71. *Prof Exp:* Chemist, Eastern Regional Res Labs, 63-67; res asst biophys chem, Univ Calif, Berkeley, 67-71; res fel, Calif Inst Technol, 71-73. *Concurrent Pos:* Jane Coffin Childs Found Fel, 71-73. *Mem:* AAAS; Am Chem Soc. *Res:* Determining the biological function of different DNA sequence classes which comprise the eukaryotic genome. *Mailing Add:* Dept Molec & Cell Biol Univ Cal Davis CA 95616-5224. *Fax:* 530-752-8995

SCHMID, CHARLES ERNEST, ACOUSTICS. *Current Pos:* EXEC DIR, ACOUST SOC AM, WOODBURY, NY, 90- *Personal Data:* b Jamaica, NY, Oct 30, 40; m 66, Linda Dexter; c Andrew & Jenny. *Educ:* Cornell Univ, BSEE, 63; Univ Conn, MSEE, 68; Univ Wash, PhD, 77. *Prof Exp:* Systs engr, Gen Dynamics/Electric Boat, Conn, 63-66; fel, Honeywell, Seattle, 66-90. *Concurrent Pos:* Cong fel sci & eng, Acoust Soc Am, 85-86; bd dirs, Wash State Diversification Comn, 93-95. *Mem:* Fel Acoust Soc Am; Am Inst Physics; AAAS; Coun Eng & Sci Soc Execs. *Res:* Simulation and analysis of underwater sound; computer pattern recognition of musical instruments. *Mailing Add:* Acoust Soc Am 500 Sunnyside Blvd Woodbury NY 11797-2924. *Fax:* 206-842-6012; *E-Mail:* charles@aip.org

SCHMID, DONALD SCOTT, CELL-MEDIATED IMMUNITY, ANTI-VIRAL IMMUNE RESPONSES. *Current Pos:* staff fel, 86-87, res microbiologist, 87-88, CHIEF, VIRAL IMMUNOL SECT, CTRS DIS CONTROL, 88- *Personal Data:* b Canton, Ohio, Apr 26, 51; m 83, Monika Kopp; c Emily E & Elias W. *Educ:* Kent State Univ, BA, 74; Ariz State Univ, MS, 81; Univ Tenn, PhD(microbiol), 82. *Prof Exp:* Fel, Yale Univ Sch Med, 82-85, res assoc, 85. *Mem:* Am Asn Immunologists. *Mailing Add:* Ctrs Dis Control 1600 Clifton Rd MS G 18 Atlanta GA 30333. *Fax:* 404-639-0049

SCHMID, FRANK RICHARD, MEDICINE. *Current Pos:* from assoc to assoc prof, 57-69, PROF MED, MED SCH, NORTHWESTERN UNIV, CHICAGO, 69- *Personal Data:* b New York, NY, June 25, 24; m 54; c 9. *Educ:* NY Univ, MD, 49. *Prof Exp:* From asst to resident to chief resident, Bellevue Hosp, NY, 50-51 & 52-54; asst med, Col Med, NY Univ, 54-57. *Concurrent Pos:* Fel, Arthritis & Rheumatism Found, 56-59; Markle scholar med sci, 60-65; trainee, Med Div, NIH, 54-56; asst vis physician, Bellevue Hosp, 54-57; attend physician, Vet Admin Res Hosp, 57-, Northwestern Mem Hosp, 61- & Cook Co Hosp, 66-69; consult, Rehab Inst Chicago, 67- Mem: Am Rheumatism Asn; Am Fedn Clin Res; Cent Soc Clin Res. Res: Immunological considerations in rheumatic diseases. Mailing Add: 222 E Superior St Chicago IL 60611-2914

SCHMID, FRANZ ANTON, CANCER. Current Pos: RETIRED. Personal Data: b Hermersdorf, Czech, Sept 21, 22; US citizen; m 55; c 1. Educ: Univ Munich, DVM, 51; Fordham Univ, MS, 54. Prof Exp: Res asst surg physiol, Sloan-Kettering Inst Cancer Res, 54-56; vet meat inspector, USDA, 56-58; res assoc, Walker Lab, Sloan-Kettering Inst Cancer Res, 58-84, assoc, 66-84, assoc mem, Exp Cancer Chemother, 84-92. Mem: Am Asn Cancer Res. Res: Experimental chemotherapy of cancer; chemical cancerigenesis; mouse genetics. Mailing Add: 122 Sterling Ave Harrison NY 10528

SCHMID, GEORGE HENRY, ORGANIC CHEMISTRY. Current Pos: from asst prof to prof, 63-94, EMER PROF CHEM, UNIV TORONTO, 94- Personal Data: b Madison, Wis, Aug 6, 31; m 57, 87; c 2. Educ: Univ Southern Calif, BS, 53, PhD(org chem), 61. Prof Exp: Fel, Harvard Univ, 61-63. Mem: Am Chem Soc. Res: The elucidation of the mechanism of electrophilic additions to unsaturated carbon-carbon bonds. Mailing Add: Dept Chem Univ Toronto 80 St George St Toronto ON M5S 1A1 Can

SCHMID, GERHARD MARTIN, ELECTROCHEMISTRY. Current Pos: asst prof, 64-70, assoc prof chem, 70-92, EMER PROF CHEM, UNIV FLA, 92- Personal Data: b Ravensburg, Ger, Oct 26, 29; m 58, Waltraud Menges; c K Peter & Michael R. Educ: Innsbruck Univ, PhD(phys chem), 58. Prof Exp: Fel, Univ Tex, 58-62; temp asst prof, Univ Alta, 62-64. Concurrent Pos: Sr res chemist, Tracor, Inc, 60-62. Mem: Am Chem Soc; Electrochem Soc; Sigma Xi. Res: Structure of the electrical double layer; adsorption on solid electrodes; passivity of metals; corrosion and corrosion inhibition. Mailing Add: Chem Dept Univ Fla PO Box 117200 Gainesville FL 32611

SCHMID, HARALD HEINRICH OTTO, BIOCHEMISTRY. Current Pos: From res fel biochem to res assoc, Univ Minn, 62-66, from asst prof to assoc prof, 66-74, actg dir, 85-86, PROF BIOCHEM, HORMEL INST, UNIV MINN, 74-, EXEC DIR, 87- Personal Data: b Graz, Austria, Dec 10, 35; m 77, Patricia C Igou. Educ: Graz Univ, MS, 58, PhD, 64. Concurrent Pos: Ed, Chem Phys Lipids, 84-; fac mem, Biochem & Molecular Biol Dept, Mayo Grad Sch, Mayo Clin, 93- Mem: Am Chem Soc; AAAS; Am Soc biochem & Molecular Biol; Oxygen Soc. Res: Structure, metabolism and function of complex lipids in biological membranes; lipid turnover and cell signalling; effects of oxygen free radicals on membrane lipids and proteins. Mailing Add: Hormel Inst Univ Minn Austin MN 55912. Fax: 507-437-9606; E-Mail: schmi081@maroon.tc.umn.edu

SCHMID, JACK ROBERT, PHARMACOLOGY, PHYSIOLOGY. Current Pos: RETIRED. Personal Data: b Chicago, Ill, Oct 3, 24; m 48, Jean Beeman; c Jesse R, Jane C (Parr), Jeanette E (Spear) & John S. Educ: Mich State Univ, BS, 52, MS, 54; Univ Ark, Little Rock, PhD(pharmacol), 67. Prof Exp: Assoc pharmacologist, Mead Johnson Res Ctr, Ind, 54-58; high sch teacher, Mich, 59-62; sr pharmacologist, Riker Res Labs, 3M Co, 66-73, pharmacologist specialist, 73-88. Mem: Int Soc Heart Res; NY Acad Sci; Am Chem Soc; Sigma Xi. Res: Cardiopulmonary effects of drugs. Mailing Add: 993 Copper Vista Dr Prescott AZ 86303

SCHMID, JOHN CAROLUS, APPLIED STATISTICS, FACTOR ANALYSIS. Current Pos: prof, 66-84, EMER PROF RES, UNIV NORTHERN COLO, 84- Personal Data: b Milwaukee, Wis, Apr 17, 20; m 48, Jean Parker; c Jean, James & Mary. Educ: Univ Wis, BS, 45, MS, 46, PhD(statist), 49. Prof Exp: Instr math, Univ Wis Exten Div, 46-47; asst prof res, Mich State Univ, 49-52; res psychologist, Air Force Personnel & Training Res Ctr, 52-57; prof statist, Univ Ark, 57-66. Concurrent Pos: Ed, J Educ Res, 63-67 & J Exp Educ, 63-84. Res: Hieraechical factor analysis; multiple regression. Mailing Add: 1212 38th Ave Greeley CO 80634-2716

SCHMID, KARL, BIOCHEMISTRY. Current Pos: assoc prof, 63-66, PROF BIOCHEM, SCH MED, BOSTON UNIV, 66- Personal Data: b Erlinsbach, Switz, July 23, 20; nat US; m 47; c 2. Educ: Swiss Fed Inst Technol, dipl rer nat, 43; Univ Basel, MA & PhD(biochem), 46. Prof Exp: Res assoc, Harvard Med Sch, 48-52; assoc biochemist, Lovett Mem Lab, Mass Gen Hosp, 52-63. Concurrent Pos: Zurich Univ fel chem, Cambridge Univ, 47-48. Mem: Am Chem Soc; Am Soc Biol Chemists; Soc Complex Carbohydrates (pres, 80). Res: Isolation, purification, characterization, chemical structure and biological importance of human plasma proteins, especially glycoproteins; glycosaminoglycans of the tissues of various human organs. Mailing Add: Sch Med Boston Univ 6 Rumford Rd Lexington MA 02173-2394

SCHMID, LAWRENCE ALFRED, THEORETICAL PHYSICS. Current Pos: GUEST SCIENTIST, NAT INST STANDARDS & TECHNOL, 85- Personal Data: b Philadelphia, Pa, Mar 11, 28; m 62, Ursula Hollwig. Educ: Univ Pa, BSEE, 49; Princeton Univ, MA, 51, PhD(physics), 53. Prof Exp: Asst prof physics, Mich State Univ, 53-59; physicist, Goddard Space Flight Ctr, NASA, 59-80; physicist, Nat Bur Standards, 80-85. Mem: AAAS; Am Phys Soc; Am Asn Physics Teachers; Soc Indust & Appl Math; Math Asn Am. Res: Fluid dynamics; thermodynamics; dynamic meteorology; relativity; variational formalism; group theory; surface tension phenomena. Mailing Add: 12 Maplewood Ct Greenbelt MD 20770

SCHMID, LOREN CLARK, ENERGY CONVERSION, TECHNOLOGY TRANSFER. Current Pos: res mgr, Battelle Mem Inst, 65-68, mgr, Reactor Physics Dept, 68-73, dir, Energy prog, 73-75, fusion technol prog mgr, 73-79, energy mission dir, 75-79, mgr planning, 79-83, res & technol appln, 83-85, PROG MGR, ADVAN ENERGY & TECHNOL TRANSFER, BATTELLE NORTHWEST, 85- Personal Data: b Ypsilanti, Mich, Feb 1, 31; m 54; c 3. Educ: Univ Mich, BS, 53, MS, 54, PhD(physics), 58. Honors & Awards: Harold Metcalf Award, Fed Lab Consortium Technol Transfer, 86. Prof Exp: Asst, Eng Res Inst, Univ Mich, 53-56; res assoc, Argonne Nat Lab, 56-58; physicist, Gen Elec Co, 58-65. Concurrent Pos: Actg assoc prof nuclear eng, Univ Wash, 68-74; coordr plutonium recycle short course, Joint Ctr Grad Study, Univ Wash, 73-77, affiliated prof, prog adv & coordr, Nuclear Eng, 74-; Far West Reg Coord, 83-88, nat chmn, Fed Lab Consortium Technol Transfer, 89- Mem: Sigma Xi; Fel Am Nuclear Soc; NY Acad Sci. Res: Fusion reactor technology; nuclear and reactor physics; analysis of radioactive-decay schemes; energy production and conservation; technology transfer. Mailing Add: 2132 Hamilton Ave Richland WA 99352-2008

SCHMID, PETER, MEDICAL SCIENCES, BIOCHEMISTRY. Current Pos: SR PEER COUN OLDER ADULT SERV, CITY MARIN, CALIF, 93- Personal Data: b Signau, Switz, Sept 5, 27; US citizen; m 54; c 2. Educ: Winterthur Tech, Switz, BS, 52; Univ Calif, Berkeley, MS, 59; Univ Calif, San Francisco, PhD(biochem, pharmaceut chem), 64. Prof Exp: Investr org chem, Ciba Pharmaceut Co, Switz, 52-55; res assoc biochem, State Univ NY Upstate Med Ctr, 55-56; fel, Med Ctr, Univ Calif, San Francisco, 63; sr investr radiobiol, US Naval Radiol Defense Lab, 64-67; sr investr & group leader cutaneous hazards, Letterman Army Inst Res, 67-93. Concurrent Pos: Fac mentor, Columbia Pac Univ, San Rafael, Calif. Mem: AAAS; Am Chem Soc; NY Acad Sci; Dermal Clin Eval Soc; Sigma Xi; Am Mgt Asn. Res: Mechanism of cell replication and cell growth; biophysics of skin; medical research in dermatology to include biochemical, biophysical, morphometrics, biostatistics aspects, cosmethology, cell biology, non-invasive measurements, skin protection and dermal toxicology; contract review; budget and program development and management; toxicology, analytical and pharmaceutical chemistry; computer science; environmental science; research administration. Mailing Add: 840 Monticello Rd San Rafael CA 94903

SCHMID, RUDI, INTERNAL MEDICINE, GASTROENTEROLOGY. Current Pos: prof, 66-91, EMER PROF MED, UNIV CALIF, SAN FRANCISCO, 91- Personal Data: b Glarus, Switz, May 2, 22; nat US; m 49; c 2. Educ: Univ Zurich, MD, 47; Univ Minn, PhD, 54; Am Bd Internal Med, dipl, 57. Prof Exp: Intern, Univ Hosp, Univ Calif, San Francisco, 48-49; resident, Univ Hosp, Univ Minn, 49-51; instr med, Sch Med, 52-54; sr hematologist, Nat Inst Arthritis & Metab Dis, 55-57; assoc med, Harvard Med Sch, 57-59, asst prof, 59-62; prof, Univ Chicago, 62-66. Concurrent Pos: USPHS spec res fel biochem, Columbia Univ, 54-55; asst physician, Thorndike Mem Lab, Boston City Hosp, 57-; consult, US Army Surgeon Gen & San Francisco Vet Admin Hosp. Mem: Nat Acad Sci; Am Acad Arts & Sci; Am Soc Exp Path; Am Soc Hemat; Am Soc Biol Chemists; AAAS; Am Soc Clin Invest. Res: Liver physiology and pathophysiology; hepatic enzymes and metabolism; porphyrins; bile pigments; jaundice; porphyria; liver diseases. Mailing Add: 211 Woodland Rd Kentfield CA 94905

SCHMID, SANDRA LOUISE, RECEPTOR-MEDIATED ENDOCYTOSIS, CELL-FREE ASSAYS FOR VESICULAR TRANSPORT. Current Pos: asst mem, 88-94, ASSOC MEM, SCRIPPS RES INST, 94- Personal Data: b Vancouver, BC, Mar 7, 58; m 84, William E Balch; c Jeremy A & Katherine E. Educ: Univ BC, BSc, 80; Stanford Univ, PhD(biochem), 85. Honors & Awards: Jr Career Recognition Award, Am Soc Cell Biol, 90. Prof Exp: Fel, Dept Cell Biol, Yale Univ, 85-88. Concurrent Pos: Lucille P Markey scholar, 87-94; established investr award, Am Heart Asn, 94- Mem: Am Soc Cell Biol; Juv Diabetes Res Found. Res: Development and use of novel cell-free assay systems for the biochemical and enzymological characterization of coated vesicle formation and receptor-mediated endocytosis. Mailing Add: Dept Cell Biol IMM-II Scripps Res Inst 10550 N Torrey Pines Rd La Jolla CA 92037-1027. Fax: 619-784-9126; E-Mail: slschmid@nscsm.scripps.edu

SCHMID, STEVEN, MECHANICAL ENGINEERING. Current Pos: ASST PROF MECH ENG, UNIV NOTRE DAME, 93- Personal Data: b Chicago, Ill, Nov 24, 64. Educ: Ill Inst Technol, BS, 86, MS, 89; Northwestern Univ, PhD(mech eng), 93. Honors & Awards: Excellence Teaching Award, 91; NSF Award, 96. Prof Exp: Sr mech engr, Triodyne Inc, 84-90. Mem: Am Soc Mech Engrs; Soc Mech Engrs; Am Soc Metals; Am Soc Bakery Engrs. Mailing Add: Univ Notre Dame 375 Fitzpatrick Hall Notre Dame IN 46556. Fax: 219-631-8341; E-Mail: schmid.2@nd.edu

SCHMID, WALTER EGID, BOTANY. Current Pos: from asst prof to assoc prof bot, 62-72, assoc dean grad sch, 70-72, PROF BOT, SOUTHERN ILL UNIV, CARBONDALE, 72- Personal Data: b Philadelphia, Pa, Nov 24, 33; m 59; c 1. Educ: Univ Pa, AB, 55; Univ Wis, MS, 58, PhD(bot), 61. Prof Exp: Asst bot, Univ Wis, 55-61; jr res plant physiologist, Univ Calif, Davis, 61-62. Mem: AAAS; Am Soc Plant Physiol; Bot Soc Am; Japanese Soc Plant Physiol; Sigma Xi. Res: Inorganic nutrition of plants. Mailing Add: Dept Plant & Bot Southern Ill Univ Carbondale IL 62901

SCHMID, WERNER E(DUARD), hydrology & water resources; deceased, see previous edition for last biography

SCHMID, WILFRIED, MATHEMATICS. *Current Pos:* PROF MATH, HARVARD UNIV, 78- *Personal Data:* b Hamburg, Ger, May 28, 43. *Educ:* Princeton Univ, BA, 64; Univ Calif, Berkeley, MA, 66, PhD(math), 67; Marina D Bizzarri-Schmid, MD, 77. *Honors & Awards:* Prix Scientifique de UAP, 86. *Prof Exp:* Asst prof math, Univ Calif, Berkeley, 67-70; Sloan fel & vis assoc prof, Columbia Univ, 68-69; vis mem, Inst Advan Study, 69-70; prof math, Columbia Univ, 70-78. *Concurrent Pos:* Vis prof, Univ Bonn, 73-74; John Simon Guggenheim Mem fel, 75-76, 89-90; vis, Inst Advan Study, Princeton Univ, 75-76. *Res:* Representations of Lie groups; complex manifolds. *Mailing Add:* Dept Math Harvard Univ Cambridge MA 02138-2901

SCHMID, WILLIAM DALE, ANIMAL ECOLOGY, COMPARATIVE ANIMAL PHYSIOLOGY. *Current Pos:* from asst prof to assoc prof, 66-74, DIR INST HERMONOGRAPHY, 70-, UNIV MINN, MINNEAPOLIS, 74-, PROF ZOOL, 74, PROF ECOL, EVOLUTION & BEHAV. *Personal Data:* b Santa Ana, Calif, Apr 21, 37; div; c 2. *Educ:* Univ Minn, St Paul, BS, 59; Univ Minn, Minneapolis, PhD(zool), 62. *Hon Degrees:* Dr, Novosibirsk State Univ, Russia, 92. *Honors & Awards:* Fulbright lectr, Coun Int Exchange Scholars, USSR, 89. *Prof Exp:* Asst prof biol, Univ NDak, 62-66. *Concurrent Pos:* Res fel, Nat Res Coun/Nat Acad Sci, USSR, 87; univ affil grant, US Info Agency, Russia, 91-94. *Mem:* AAAS; Ecol Soc Am; Am Soc Zoologists; Am Soc Mammalogists; Wildlife Dis Asn; Sigma Xi. *Res:* Amphibian water balance; vertebrate physiology; comparative animal physiology; winter ecology. *Mailing Add:* Dept Ecol, Evolution & Behav Univ Minn Ecol Bldg 1987 Upper Buford Circle St Paul MN 55108. *E-Mail:* schmi003@maroon.tc.umn.edu

SCHMIDLE, CLAUDE JOSEPH, COATINGS TECHNOLOGY, RADIATION CURING. *Current Pos:* mgr res, 79-81, PRIN SCIENTIST, CONGOLEUM CORP, 81- *Personal Data:* b Buffalo, NJ, June 14, 20; m 45; c 2. *Educ:* Univ Notre Dame, BS, 41, MS, 42, PhD(chem), 48. *Prof Exp:* Sr res scientist, Rohm and Haas Co, 48-62; sect head org & polymers, J T Baker Chem Co, 62-64; sect head coatings res, Gen Tire & Rubber Co, 64-73; supvr radiation curable coatings, Thiokol Corp, 74-78. *Mem:* Am Chem Soc; Soc Plastics Engrs; Nat Asn Corrosion Engrs; Soc Mfg Engrs. *Res:* Aqueous and high solids coatings; radiation curable coatings and inks; acrylic monomers; acrylated urethanes; polyurethane and polyvinyl chloride coatings and foams. *Mailing Add:* 95 Jacobs Creek Rd Trenton NJ 08628-1705

SCHMIDLIN, ALBERTUS ERNEST, TRANSPORTATION CONTAINER SAFETY, AEROSPACE HYDRAULICS & PNEUMATICS. *Current Pos:* CONSULT ENGR, 90- *Personal Data:* b Paterson, NJ, Apr 9, 17; m 43; c 3. *Educ:* Stevens Inst Technol, ME, 39, MS, 41, DSc(mech eng), 62. *Honors & Awards:* Dedicated Serv Award, Am Soc Mech Engrs. *Prof Exp:* Instr mech eng lab, Stevens Inst Technol, 39-41; develop engr, Walter Kidde & Co, Inc, 41-47, proj engr, 47-51, chief proj engr, 51-54, asst mgr develop dept, 54-56, mgr res dept, 56-62, assoc tech dir, 62-63; prin staff scientist & mgr, Fluidics Dept, Singer-Gen Precision Inc, 63-69; indust consult, 69; sr res scientist, Fire Support Armament Ctr, Safety, Security & Survivability Br, US Army Armament Res Develop & Eng Ctr, 69-89. *Mem:* Fel Am Soc Mech Engrs; Soc Automotive Engrs; Am Defense Preparedness Asn. *Res:* Fluid mechanics, heat transfer and mechanical design as related to safety, navigation, guidance and control of aerospace vehicles; internal flow in fluid components; gas dynamics; transient flow; fluid power transmission. *Mailing Add:* 28 Highview Rd Caldwell NJ 07006

SCHMIDLIN, FREDERICK W, SOLID STATE PHYSICS. *Current Pos:* RETIRED. *Personal Data:* b Maumee, Ohio, Aug 28, 25; m 59; c 3. *Educ:* Univ Toledo, BEEP, 50; Cornell Univ, PhD(physics), 56. *Prof Exp:* Asst, Cornell Univ, 50-54; mem tech staff, Ramo-Wooldridge Corp, 56-58; sr mem tech staff, Space Technol Labs, 58-60; sr scientist, Gen Technol Corp, 60-63; prin scientist, Xerox Corp, 63-93. *Mem:* AAAS; Soc Photog Scientists & Engrs; Am Phys Soc; Inst Elec & Electronics Engrs. *Res:* Theory of electrophotography; solid state theory; superconductivity; semiconductivity; photoconductivity; thin film devices; electrostatic printing. *Mailing Add:* Eight Forestwood Lane Pittsford NY 14534

SCHMIDLY, DAVID JAMES, MAMMALIAN SYSTEMATICS, NON-GAME WILDLIFE. *Current Pos:* From asst prof to assoc prof, 71-82, PROF WILDLIFE & FISHERIES SCI, TEX A&M UNIV, 82-, HEAD, DEPT WILDLIFE & FISHERIES, 86- *Personal Data:* b Lubbock, Tex, Dec 20, 43; m 66; c 2. *Educ:* Tex Tech Univ, BS, 66, MS, 68; Univ Ill, PhD(zool), 71. *Concurrent Pos:* Consult, Wildlife Servs. *Mem:* Am Soc Mammalogists; Soc Conserv Biol; Sigma Xi; Southwestern Asn Naturalists. *Res:* Mammalian systematics, natural history and management with special emphasis on non-gamma mammals from the southwestern United States and northern Mexico; preservation management and utilization of biological collections. *Mailing Add:* Tex A&M Univ PO Box 1675 Galveston TX 77553-1675

SCHMID-SCHOENBEIN, GEERT W, MICROCIRCULATION, BIOMECHANICS. *Current Pos:* from asst prof to assoc prof, 79-89, PROF BIOENG, UNIV CALIF, SAN DIEGO, 89- *Personal Data:* b Ebingen, WGer, Jan 1, 48; m 76, Renate E Klein; c 3. *Educ:* Univ Calif, San Diego, MS, 73, PhD(bioeng), 76. *Honors & Awards:* Malphigi Award, Europ Soc Microcirculation, 80; Abott Award, 84; Melville Medal, Am Soc Mech Engrs, 90. *Prof Exp:* Sr staff assoc physiol, Columbia Univ, 76-79. *Concurrent Pos:* Mem, Biomed Sci Grad Prog, Univ Calif, San Diego; mem, Am Venous Forum. *Mem:* Am Physiol Soc; Am Microcirculatory Soc; Biomed Eng Soc; Int Soc Biorheology; Europ Soc Mirocirculation; Am Heart Asn; Am Diabetes Asn; Am Acad Mech; fel Am Inst Med & Biol Eng. *Res:* Biomechanics; microcirculation; bioengineering of cardiovascular diseases; math modeling. *Mailing Add:* Inst Biomed Eng Univ Calif San Diego R-102 La Jolla CA 92093-0412. *Fax:* 619-534-5722

SCHMIDT, ALAN FREDERICK, liquified natural gas technology; deceased, see previous edition for last biography

SCHMIDT, ALFRED OTTO, machine & tool design; deceased, see previous edition for last biography

SCHMIDT, ANTHONY JOHN, embryology; deceased, see previous edition for last biography

SCHMIDT, ARTHUR GERARD, COMPUTER MODELING OF PHYSICAL SYSTEMS. *Current Pos:* SR LECTR & DIR UNDERGRAD LABS, NORTHWESTERN UNIV, 84- *Personal Data:* b Chicago, Ill, Jan 15, 44; m 72; c 5. *Educ:* Depaul Univ, BS, 66; Univ Notre Dame, PhD, 74. *Prof Exp:* Instr physics, LaLumiere Sch, 72-73, physics, chem & biol, 73-74; fel, Oak Ridge Nat Lab, 74-76; instr physics, biol & chem, LaLumiere Sch, 76-78; asst prof physics, Lake Forest Col, 78-84. *Concurrent Pos:* Guest fac fel, Notre Dame Univ, 76-78; instr physics, Ind Univ, South Bend, 77- *Mem:* Am Phys Soc; AAAS; Sigma Xi. *Res:* Measurement of triple admixtures in x-ray techniques in radioactive metals using xx angular correlation techniques; designing and fabrication of lecture demonstrations; writing progs for computers to simulate physical systems; nuclear physics. *Mailing Add:* 3324 Lyons St Evanston IL 60203-1414

SCHMIDT, BARBARA A, ULTRASTRUCTURE, INSECT DEVELOPMENT. *Current Pos:* AT CALIF STATE UNIV. *Educ:* Northwestern Univ, PhD(biol), 76. *Prof Exp:* Kans State Univ, 77- *Res:* Cell developmental biology. *Mailing Add:* Dept Teacher Prep Calif State Univ 6000 JST Sacramento CA 95819

SCHMIDT, BARNET MICHAEL, DIGITAL SIGNAL, ADAPTIVE & STATISTICAL SIGNAL PROCESSING. *Current Pos:* consult mem tech staff, Network Technol Lab, AT&T Bell Labs, 86-90, mem tech staff, Network Systs Analysis Lab, Bell Commun Res, Inc, 90-95, MEM TECH STAFF, NETWORK SURVEILLANCE SYSTS ENG LAB, BELL LABS, 95- *Personal Data:* b New Milford, NJ, June 30, 58. *Educ:* Stevens Inst Technol, BS, 80, MS, 85. *Prof Exp:* Res assoc chem, X-ray Diffraction Lab, Stevens Inst Technol, 79-80; sr engr, Timeplex Div, Open Transport Networks Eng Lab, Unisys Corp, 81-86. *Concurrent Pos:* Sr mem tech staff, Div Commun Systs Develop, Computer Sci Corp Prof Consult Serv, 86-89. *Mem:* Inst Elec & Electronics Engrs; Asn Comput Mach. *Res:* Develop robust, fault-tolerant intelligent communications networks; apply the theory of digital signal processing and statistical signal identification to locating faults in transmission systems to insure the integrity of the international long distance network; granted three US patents; develop video signal and image processing systems. *Mailing Add:* 494 Reis Ave Oradell NJ 07649-2624

SCHMIDT, BERLIE LOUIS, SOIL & WATER CONSERVATION, SOIL & WATER QUALITY. *Current Pos:* NAT PROG LEADER, SOIL & WATER US DEPT AGR, COOP STATE RES, EDUC & EXT SERV, 87-, PROG DIR, US DEPT AGR, NAT RES INITIATIVE COMPETITIVE GRANTS PROG, 94- *Personal Data:* b Treynor, Iowa, Oct 2, 32; m 54, 86, Bonnijane Geisinger-Mehlhop; c Brian, Luanne (Code), Kevin, Kimberly (Nelson) & Christy (Mash). *Educ:* Iowa State Univ, BS, 54, MS, 59, PhD(agron), 62. *Prof Exp:* Soil scientist, Soil Conserv Serv, USDA, 54, 56-57; res assoc soil mgt, Iowa State Univ, 59-62; from asst prof to prof agron, Ohio State Univ, 62-87, assoc chmn, Ohio Agr Res & Develop Ctr, 69-75, chmn dept, 75-86. *Concurrent Pos:* Emer prof agron, Ohio State Univ, 87- *Mem:* Fel Am Soc Agron; fel Soil Sci Soc Am; Int Soil Sci Soc; Sigma Xi; Soil & Water Conserv Soc. *Res:* Soil and water pollution from erosion and runoff; soil and water conservation; wind erosion control; water infiltration into soils; soil science research administration; soil, water and air quality. *Mailing Add:* US Dept Agr Coop Res, Educ & Exten Serv Washington DC 20250-2210. *Fax:* 202-401-1706; *E-Mail:* bschmidt@reeusda.gov

SCHMIDT, BRUNO (FRANCIS), PHYSICS. *Current Pos:* Asst prof, 69-75, assoc prof, 75-81, prof physics, 81-84, PROF COMPUT SCI, SOUTHWEST MO STATE UNIV, 84- *Personal Data:* b Strawberry Point, Iowa, June 10, 42; m 64; c 2. *Educ:* Cornell Col, BA, 64; Iowa State Univ, PhD(physics), 69. *Mem:* Asn Comput Mach; Sigma Xi. *Mailing Add:* VP Acad Affairs Southwest Mo State Univ 901 S National Springfield MO 65804-0027

SCHMIDT, CHARLES WILLIAM, PHYSICS, ACCELERATOR TECHNOLOGY. *Current Pos:* PHYSICIST ACCELERATOR PHYSICS, FERMI NAT ACCELERATOR LAB, 69-, HEAD, LINAC DEPT FERMILAB, 89- *Personal Data:* b St Petersburg, Fla, Aug 11, 42; m 71, Judy K Diport; c Michael C & Brian L. *Educ:* Fla State Univ, BS, 64. *Prof Exp:* Sci asst physics, Argonne Nat Lab, 64-69. *Concurrent Pos:* Vis scientist, Ger Electron-Synchrotron, Hamburg, WGer, 84; Stanford, Calif, 86. *Mem:* Am Phys Soc; Sigma Xi. *Res:* Accelerator physics especially ion source development, magnetic measurements and operation. *Mailing Add:* 60 Oakwood Dr Naperville IL 60540-7314. *E-Mail:* schmidt@admail.fnal.gov

SCHMIDT, CLAUDE HENRI, ENTOMOLOGY. *Current Pos:* proj leader insect physiol & metab sect, Metab & Radiation Res Lab, 64-67, chief insects affecting man & animal res br, Entom Res Div, 67-72, dir, Dakotas-Alaska Area, 72-81, dir, Dakotas Area, N Cent Region, 81-82, dir metals & radiation res lab, 82-88, COLLABR, AGR RES SERV, USDA, 89- *Personal Data:* b Geneva, Switz, May 6, 24; nat US; m 53; c 2. *Educ:* Stanford Univ, BA, 48, MA, 50; Iowa State Univ, PhD(entom), 56. *Prof Exp:* Instr zool, Iowa State

Univ, 55-56; med entomologist, USDA, 56-62; entomologist, Div Isotopes, Int Atomic Energy Agency, Vienna, Austria, 62-64. *Concurrent Pos:* Res consult, USAID, 68; consult, US Army Med Res & Develop Cmnd, 73-77, vol, 89- *Mem:* Fel AAAS; Am Mosquito Control Asn (pres, 81); Am Entom Soc; Am Inst Biol Sci; Am Chem Soc. *Res:* Application of radioisotopes and radiation in entomology; application of the sterile male technique. *Mailing Add:* 1827 Third St N Fargo ND 58102-2335

SCHMIDT, CLIFFORD LEROY, PLANT SYSTEMATICS. *Current Pos:* asst prof natural sci, 60-65, from asst prof to prof biol, 65-90, EMER PROF BIOL, SAN JOSE STATE UNIV, 90-; COURTESY PROF BOT, ORE STATE UNIV, 93- *Personal Data:* b Los Angeles, Calif, Mar 27, 26; m 49, Leona Friesen; c Linda. *Educ:* San Jose State Col, AB, 55, MA, 58; Stanford Univ, PhD(pop biol), 67. *Prof Exp:* Teacher, San Jose Unified Sch Dist, 56-60. *Mem:* Am Inst Biol Sci; Am Soc Plant Taxonomists. *Res:* Biosystematic studies involving chromosomal analysis of Ludwigia sect Dantia; taxonomic studies on Ceanothus. *Mailing Add:* 1745 Skyway St S Salem OR 97302. *E-Mail:* schmidtc@bcc.orst.edu

SCHMIDT, DAVID KELSO, AEROSPACE ENGINEERING, SYSTEMS ENGINEERING. *Current Pos:* asst prof, 74-79, ASSOC PROF AEROSPACE ENG, PURDUE UNIV, 79- *Personal Data:* b Lafayette, Ind, Mar 4, 43; c 3. *Educ:* Purdue Univ, BS, 65, PhD(eng), 72; Univ Southern Calif, MS, 68. *Prof Exp:* Engr & scientist missile design, McDonnell-Douglas Astronaut Corp, 65-69; vis asst prof aerospace eng, Purdue Univ, 72-73; res engr transp eng, Stanford Res Inst, 73-74. *Mem:* Am Inst Aeronaut & Astronaut; Opers Res Soc Am; Am Soc Eng Educ. *Res:* Systems analysis; optimization; control theory and applications; manual control; operations research; flight vehicle dynamics and control. *Mailing Add:* Dept Aerospace & Eng Univ Md College Park MD 20742-0001

SCHMIDT, DENNIS EARL, PSYCHOPHARMACOLOGY. *Current Pos:* instr, 70-71, asst prof, 71-78, ASSOC PROF PHARMACOL, VANDERBILT UNIV, 79- *Personal Data:* b Plymouth, Wis, Jan 23, 40; m 71; c 3. *Educ:* Lakeland Col, BS, 62; Kans State Univ, PhD(biochem), 68. *Prof Exp:* Instr pharmacol, Mt Sinai Sch Med, 69-70. *Concurrent Pos:* NIH fels, Cornell Med Col, 68 & Mt Sinai Sch Med, 68-69; Smith Kline & French fel, Vanderbilt Univ, 70-72. *Mem:* Am Soc Pharmacol & Exp Therapeut; Soc Neurosci; Neurochem Soc. *Res:* Investigation of central cholinergic mechanisms. *Mailing Add:* Dept Pharmacol Vanderbilt Univ Med Ctr N Rm A2127 Nashville TN 37232

SCHMIDT, DONALD ARTHUR, VETERINARY PATHOLOGY, VETERINARY CLINICAL PATHOLOGY. *Current Pos:* instr vet path, Mich State Univ, 53-63, assoc prof path, 63-67, prof, 67-92, EMER PROF VET PATH, UNIV MO, COLUMBIA, 92- *Personal Data:* b Wis, Jan 29, 22; m 51, Lavaune Houser; c Joann, Cheryl L & Katherine M. *Educ:* Univ Wis, BS, 44; Mich State Univ, DVM, 47, PhD, 61; Univ Minn, MS, 50; Am Col Vet Pathologists, dipl, anat, 63, dipl chem, 72. *Prof Exp:* Veterinarian, Chicago Zool Park, Brookfield, Ill, 50-53. *Mem:* Am Vet Med Asn; Am Col Vet Path. *Res:* Food producing animals. *Mailing Add:* Vet Diag Lab Univ Mo A334 Clydesdale Hall Columbia MO 65211

SCHMIDT, DONALD DEAN, PHYSICAL INORGANIC CHEMISTRY. *Current Pos:* tech dir worldwide eng, 94-97, TECH COACH DRILLING, EXPLOR & PROD TECH GROUP, AMOCO CORP, HOUSTON, TEX, 97- *Personal Data:* b Highland. Ill, Dec 21, 42; m 64; c 2. *Educ:* Wabash Col, AB, 65; Ore State Univ, PhD(chem), 70. *Prof Exp:* Res chemist, Dow Chem Co, 70-84; res supvr, Amoco Prod Co, Tulsa, OK, 84-94. *Concurrent Pos:* chmn, Tulsa Sect, Am Chem Soc; chmn elect, API Comt Drilling Fluids. *Mem:* Am Chem Soc; Soc Petrol Engrs. *Res:* Polymer chemistry; rheological behavior and colloidal properties of clays; coordination chemistry; surface chemistry; industrial chemistry; drilling fluids. *Mailing Add:* Amoco Corp 5th Floor W-3 PO Box 3092 Houston TX 77253-3092

SCHMIDT, DONALD HENRY, CARDIOVASCULAR DISEASE, INTERNAL MEDICINE. *Current Pos:* assoc prof, 74-77, PROF MED, UNIV WIS-MILWAUKEE, 77- *Personal Data:* b Rhinelander, Wis, July 20, 35; m 65; c 4. *Educ:* Univ Wis, BS, 57, MD, 60. *Prof Exp:* Asst med, Col Physicians & Surgeons, Columbia Univ, 66-67, instr, 67-68, asst prof clin med, 69-70, asst prof, 70-74. *Concurrent Pos:* Asst vis prof, Harlem Hosp Ctr, 68, dir EKG, 70; asst dir, Cardiovasc Lab, Columbia Presby Hosp, New York, 70, asst attend physician, 71-, dir, 73-; head, cardiovasc sect & attend physician, Mt Sinai Med Ctr, 74- *Mem:* Nuclear Med Soc; Harvey Soc; Am Fedn Clin Res; Cent Soc Clin Res; Am Heart Asn. *Res:* Physiology of the coronary circulation; nuclear cardiology. *Mailing Add:* Mt Sinai Med Ctr Box 342 Milwaukee WI 53201

SCHMIDT, DONALD L, MATERIALS SCIENCE, CHEMISTRY. *Current Pos:* INT MAT CONSULT, 87-; PRES, CARBON FIBER COMPOSITES. *Personal Data:* b Park Falls, Wis, Jan 29, 30; m 62; c John, Jeffrey & Jennifer. *Educ:* Wis State Univ, Superior, BSc, 52; Okla State Univ, MSc, 54. *Honors & Awards:* Res & Develop Award, Am Defense Preparedness Asn, 79. *Prof Exp:* Proj engr, Mat Lab, Air Force Wright Aeronaut Labs, Wright-Patterson AFB, 54-57, mat engr, 57, aeronaut struct mat engr, 57-59, aeronaut struct mat res engr, 59-60, res mat engr mat cent, 60, supvry mat res engr directorate mat, 60-61, tech mgr, Thermal Proj Mat, 61-87; mem, Advan Missile Mat Res Coun, US Dept Defense, 70-87. *Mem:* Sigma Xi; fel Soc Aerospace Mat & Process Engrs. *Res:* Thermal protection materials; high temperature materials sciences, including composites, plastics and glass; carbon-carbon composites. *Mailing Add:* 1092 Lipton Lane Beaver Creek OH 45430-1314

SCHMIDT, DONALD L, ORGANIC POLYMER CHEMISTRY, INTERFACIAL SCIENCE. *Current Pos:* Res chemist, ARPA Lab, Dow Chem Co, 61-63, proj leader aluminum chem, 63-67, sr res chemist, SPL Lab, 67-68, sr res chemist, 68-78, res assoc, Phys Res Lab, 78-88, ASSOC SCIENTIST, DOW CHEM CO, 88-, SR ASSOC SCIENTIST. *Personal Data:* b Sept 10, 31; US citizen; m 63, Julia Ford; c 3. *Educ:* Univ Miami, BS, 56, PhD(org chem), 62. *Honors & Awards:* IR 100 Awards, Indust Res Mag, 69, 72 & 91; A K Doolittle Award, Am Chem Soc, 75. *Mem:* AAAS; Am Chem Soc; Sigma Xi. *Res:* Metal hydride chemistry; inorganic polymer containing Al-O-P bonds; condensation polymerization involving cyclic sulfonium compounds; theory of surfactants and foams; membrane science; interfacial science. *Mailing Add:* 2412 Saint Mary's Dr 1712 Dow Chem Co Midland MI 48640-2534

SCHMIDT, DWIGHT LYMAN, GEOLOGY. *Current Pos:* RETIRED. *Personal Data:* b Fond du Lac, Wis, May 30, 26; m 58; c 2. *Educ:* Univ Wash, BS, 54, MS, 57, PhD(geol), 61. *Prof Exp:* Geologist, US Geol Surv, 61-95. *Concurrent Pos:* Mem comt polar res, Nat Acad Sci. 68-70. *Mem:* AAAS; Geol Soc Am; Mineral Soc Am; Soc Econ Geol; Am Geophys Union. *Res:* Radioactive placer deposits and petrography of the Idaho batholith; geology of Pensacola and Lassiter Coast Mountains, Antarctica; Precambrian and Cenozoic geology of Saudi Arabia; geologic history of the Red Sea; geology of carbonate aquifers of southern Nevada. *Mailing Add:* US Geol Surv Bldg 25 Fed Ctr MS-913 Denver CO 80225

SCHMIDT, ECKART W, PROPELLANTS & EXPLOSIVES. *Current Pos:* RETIRED. *Personal Data:* b Essen, Ger, Apr 16, 35; m 62, Hildegard Breuninger; c Wolfram G & Andreas U. *Educ:* Univ Marburg, BS, 58; Univ Tubingen, Dr rer nat(org chem, astron), 64. *Prof Exp:* Res chemist, Ger Res Inst Aero & Astronaut, 64-66; mgr chem res, Iolin Aerospace Co, 66-78, sr staff scientist, 66-95. *Concurrent Pos:* Consult hazardous mat, 87- *Mem:* Am Inst Aeronaut & Astronaut; Planetary Soc; Am Chem Soc. *Res:* High energy rocket propellants; explosives; fuel technology; astronautics; safety systems; extraterrestrial preparation of rocket propellants; planeto chemistry; energy storage and conversion. *Mailing Add:* 55 151st Pl NE Bellevue WA 98007-5019. *Fax:* 425-746-9468; *E-Mail:* eckarts@isomedia.com

SCHMIDT, EDWARD GEORGE, ASTRONOMICAL PHOTOMETRY VARIABLE STARS. *Current Pos:* from asst prof to assoc prof, 74-80, PROF ASTRON, UNIV NEBR, LINCOLN, 80-, INTERIM ASSOC DEAN, 96- *Personal Data:* b Cut Bank, Mont, Dec 13, 42; m 88; c 7. *Educ:* Univ Chicago, BS, 65; Australian Nat Univ, PhD(astron), 70. *Prof Exp:* Res assoc astron, Univ Ariz, 70-72; sr res fel, Royal Greenwich Observ, 72-74; prog dir, Astron Sci Div, NSF, 92-94. *Mem:* Am Astron Soc; Int Astron Union; Royal Astron Soc. *Res:* Variable stars; application of CCD's to astronomical photometry; automation of instrumentation and data analysis; astronomical instrumentation, space astronomy. *Mailing Add:* Dept Physics & Astron Univ Nebr 116 Brace Lab PO Box 880111 Lincoln NE 68588-0111

SCHMIDT, EDWARD MATTHEWS, BIOENGINEERING. *Current Pos:* SR STAFF SCIENTIST, LAB NEURAL CONTROL, NAT INST NEUROL, DIS & STROKE, 72- *Personal Data:* b Elgin, Ill, Mar 24, 33; m 59, Marilyn A Hatch; c Paul & John. *Educ:* Northwestern Univ, BSEE, 56; Purdue Univ, MSEE, 57, PhD, 65. *Honors & Awards:* Award of Merit, NIH, 93. *Prof Exp:* Asst, Argonne Nat Lab, 53-55; sr res engr, Borg-Warner Res Ctr, 57-61; from instr to assoc prof elec eng & vet anat, bioeng, Purdue Univ, West Lafayette, 61-72. *Concurrent Pos:* Spec fel, Lab Neurol Control, NIH, Bethesda, 69-71; assoc ed, J Neurosci Methods. *Mem:* Inst Elec & Electronics Engrs; Soc Neurosci; Am Physiol Soc. *Res:* Biological control systems; neurophysiology; microelectrode study of cells in the motor cortex of the monkey and their relationship to limb movements; neuroprosthesis; visual prosthesis; control signals from brain structures. *Mailing Add:* Lab Neural Control IRP NINDS NIH Bldg 49 Rm 3A 50 Bethesda MD 20892-4455. *Fax:* 301-402-4836; *E-Mail:* ems@heliz_nih.gov

SCHMIDT, FRANCIS HENRY, PHYSICAL ORGANIC CHEMISTRY. *Current Pos:* Res chemist, E I Du Pont De Nemours & Co, 69-80, sr res chemist, 80-84, res assoc, 84-87, TEACH ASSOC, E I DUPONT DE NEMOURS & CO, 87- *Personal Data:* b Cincinnati, Ohio, Aug 6, 41; m 68, Carol A Wesseler; c Timothy & Lisa. *Educ:* Xavier Univ, BS, 63, MS, 65; Ind Univ, Bloomington, PhD(org chem), 74. *Mem:* Am Chem Soc; Am Soc Testing & Mat. *Res:* Fluoropolymer developments for film production by extrusion; fluoropolymer treatment techniques. *Mailing Add:* 1632 Chippewa Ct Grove City OH 43123-9717

SCHMIDT, FRANCIS J, NUCLEIC ACID BIOCHEMISTRY, MOLECULAR BIOLOGY OF STREPTOMYCES. *Current Pos:* from asst prof to assoc prof, 78-93, PROF BIOCHEM, UNIV MO, COLUMBIA, 93- *Personal Data:* b Minneapolis, Minn, July 9, 47; m 76, Sharon Stevens; c Theresa & Michael. *Educ:* Marquette Univ, BS, 68; Univ Wis, PhD(biochem), 73. *Prof Exp:* Fel, Univ Wis, 74-78. *Concurrent Pos:* Vis scientist, Smith-Kline-Beckman, 85-86; lectr, Am Chem Soc, 85-88; vis prof, Univ Leicester, 86; Sci Adv Bd, Cruachem Ltd, 93-; Bd trustees, Found Biomed Studies, 95-; NIH, spec emphasis study sect, 96. *Mem:* Am Chem Soc; Am Soc Biochem & Molecular Biol; Am Soc Microbiol; AAAS; RNA Soc. *Res:* Structure and function of RNA, especially catalytic RNase p RNA; gene expression and structure in Streptomyces; Bleomycin biosynthesis. *Mailing Add:* Biochem M121 Med Sci Univ Mo Columbia MO 65212. *Fax:* 573-884-4597; *E-Mail:* bcfranks@muccmail.missouri.edu

SCHMIDT, FRANK W(ILLIAM), mechanical engineering, for more information see previous edition

SCHMIDT, FREDERICK ALLEN, MATERIAL SCIENCE, METALLURGY. *Current Pos:* RETIRED. *Personal Data:* b Cincinnati, Ohio, Dec 26, 30; m 51; c 4. *Educ:* Xavier Univ, BS, 51. *Honors & Awards:* Serv Award, Am Inst Aeronaut & Astronaut; Significant Implication for Energy Related Technol in Metall & Ceramics, US Dept Energy, 87. *Prof Exp:* Jr chemist, Iowa State Univ, 51-54, jr res assoc, 54-56, assoc, 56-59, assoc metallurgist, 59-71, metallurgist, 71-76, sr metallurgist, Ames Lab, 76-81, dir, Mat Prep Ctr, 81-93. *Mem:* Am Soc Metals; Am Inst Mining, Metall & Petrol Engrs; Am Inst Aeronaut & Astronaut. *Res:* Methods for preparing high purity refractory metals and thin film solar cells; electrotransport, thermotransport and diffusion of solutes in metals; characterization of refractory metals and alloys. *Mailing Add:* 221 Metals Develop Ames Lab Ames IA 50011-3020

SCHMIDT, GEORGE, CHAOS THEORY, DYNAMICAL SYSTEMS. *Current Pos:* res assoc, 58-59, from asst prof to assoc prof, 59-65, PROF PHYSICS, STEVENS INST TECHNOL, 65- *Personal Data:* b Budapest, Hungary, Aug 1, 26; US citizen; m 55, Katalin Varkonyi; c Franklin R & Ronald W. *Educ:* Budapest Tech Univ, dipl eng, 50; Hungarian Acad Sci, PhD(physics), 56. *Hon Degrees:* MEng, Stevens Inst Technol, 66. *Honors & Awards:* Ottens Res Award, 61. *Prof Exp:* Res assoc physics, Cent Res Inst Physics, Hungary, 55-56; sr lectr, Israel Inst Technol, 57-58. *Concurrent Pos:* Consult, Grumman Aircraft Eng Co, 62, UK Atomic Energy Auth, 65-66 & French AEC, 66; vis prof, Univ Wis, 65, Univ Calif, Los Angeles, 72-73; consult, Exxon Corp, 71, Cornell Univ, 78-79, Appl Sci Inc, 81, Polytechnic Inst NY, 84 & Berkeley Assocs, 85; vis scientist, Polytech, France, 79-80; George Meade Bond Prof Physics & Eng Physics, 83. *Mem:* NY Acad Sci; fel Am Phys Soc. *Res:* Author of more than 100 papers and several books in plasma physics and dynamical systems (chaos) theory; chaos theory. *Mailing Add:* Dept Physics Stevens Inst Technol Hoboken NJ 07030

SCHMIDT, GEORGE THOMAS, GUIDANCE, NAVIGATION & CONTROL. *Current Pos:* DIV LEADER, GUID TECHNOL DEPT, DRAPER LAB, 62- *Personal Data:* b Jersey City, NJ. *Educ:* Mass Inst Technol, BS, 64, MS, 65, ScD(instrumentation), 71. *Concurrent Pos:* Assoc prof systs elec & comput eng, Boston Univ, 71-74, adj prof, 65-70 & 75-82; mem adv group, Aerospace Res & Develop & Guid & Control Panel, NATO, 87-90; lectr, Aeronaut & Astronaut, Mass Inst Technol, 90- *Mem:* Am Inst Aeronaut & Astronaut; Inst Elec & Electronics Engrs; Am Soc Eng Educ; Sigma Xi. *Res:* Control and estimation theory; guidance and navigation systems; guidance, navigation and control; systems engineering. *Mailing Add:* Guid & Navig Div Mgr Draper Lab Cambridge MA 02139

SCHMIDT, GILBERT CARL, PSYCHIATRY, SCIENCE ADMINISTRATION. *Current Pos:* prof pharmacog & biol, col Pharm, 70-81, prof pharmaceut sci & asst dean grad studies & res, 81-89, EMER PROF MED, UNIV SC, 89- *Personal Data:* b Cincinnati, Ohio, Apr 15, 21; m 66, Mary Jo Pitsinger; c Milan, Larry & Nancy. *Educ:* Univ Cincinnati, BS, 46, MS, 49, PhD(biochem), 51. *Prof Exp:* Res assoc, Sperti, Inc, 46-48; asst prof chem, Col Pharm, Univ Cincinnati, 51-52, from assoc prof to prof pharmacog, 52-56, prof biol sci, 56-66, asst prof biochem, Col Med, 59-66; assoc prof biochem & asst prof pediat, Med Col, Univ Ala, 66-68; prof biochem, Northeast La State Univ, 68-70. *Concurrent Pos:* USPHS fel chem, Col Pharm, Univ Cincinnati, 51-52, NSF fel, 52-53; dir, Res Labs, Children's Hosp, Birmingham, Ala, 66-68. *Mem:* AAAS; Am Chem Soc; Am Soc Microbiol; Am Pharmaceut Asn; Am Inst Chemists; Soc Heterocyclic Chem. *Res:* Drug metabolism; biochemical pharmacology; azolesterases; synthesis isotopically labeled drugs; pineal gland metabolism; drug abuse; isolation and properties of natural products. *Mailing Add:* 313 Huntington Rd Summerville SC 29483

SCHMIDT, GLEN HENRY, DAIRY HUSBANDRY. *Current Pos:* prof dairy sci, 74-90, CHMN, DEPT ANIMAL SCI, OHIO STATE UNIV, 91-, EMER PROF, 96- *Personal Data:* b Manning, Iowa, Jan 25, 31; m 52; c 5. *Educ:* Iowa State Univ, BS, 52; Cornell Univ, MS, 56, PhD(dairy sci), 58. *Honors & Awards:* MSD Ag Vet Award, Am Dairy Sci Asn. *Prof Exp:* Asst animal sci, NY State Col Agr, Cornell Univ, 54-57, from instr to prof, 57-74, chmn dept, 74-84. *Mem:* Am Dairy Sci Asn; fel AAAS; Coun Agr Sci & Technol. *Res:* Dairy management. *Mailing Add:* Dept Animal Sci Ohio State Univ 2027 Coffey Rd Columbus OH 43210-1094

SCHMIDT, GLENN ROY, MEAT SCIENCES. *Current Pos:* PROF ANIMAL SCI, COLO STATE UNIV, 79- *Personal Data:* b Two Rivers, Wis, Feb 26, 43; m 66; c 1. *Educ:* Univ Wis, BSc, 65, MSc, 68, PhD(animal sci), 69. *Prof Exp:* Vis scientist meat technol, Meat Indust Res Inst NZ, 69-70; vis scientist animal sci, Res Inst Animal Husb, Zeist, Neth, 70-71; from asst prof to assoc prof, Univ Ill, Urbana, 71-79. *Mem:* Am Soc Animal Sci; Am Meat Sci Asn; Inst Food Technol; Sigma Xi. *Res:* Processed meat technology; swine physiology; muscle biochemistry. *Mailing Add:* Dept Animal Sci Colo State Univ Ft Collins CO 80523-0001

SCHMIDT, GREGORY WAYNE, CELL BIOLOGY, PHOTOSYNTHESIS. *Current Pos:* from asst prof to assoc prof, 79-89, PROF BOT, UNIV GA, 89- *Personal Data:* b Waterloo, Iowa, Mar 25, 47; m 89, Brigitte U Bruns; c Theron, tobias & Nicholas. *Educ:* Grinnell Col, AB, 69; State Univ NY, Stony Brook, PhD(biol), 76. *Prof Exp:* Fel cell biol, Rockefeller Univ, 75-79. *Concurrent Pos:* Asst ed, Plant Physiol, 86-92; prog mgr photosynthesis, USDA, 89-90. *Mem:* Am Soc Plant Physiologists; Int Soc Plant Molecular Biol; Am Soc Photobiol. *Res:* Regulation of chloroplast biogenesis with emphasis on interactions between nucleo-cytoplasmic compartments and organelle in synthesis; maturation and assembly of subunits of photosynthetic complexes; structure of light-harvesting complexes; chloroplast molecular biology. *Mailing Add:* Dept Bot Univ Ga Athens GA 30602. *Fax:* 706-542-1805

SCHMIDT, HARTLAND H, PHYSICAL CHEMISTRY. *Current Pos:* From instr to assoc prof, Univ Calif, Davis & Univ Calif, Riverside, 54-68, PROF CHEM, UNIV CALIF, RIVERSIDE, 68- *Personal Data:* b St Paul, Minn, Nov 22, 29; m 57; c 2. *Educ:* Univ Minn, BA, 51; Univ Calif, Berkeley, PhD(chem), 54. *Mem:* Am Chem Soc; Am Phys Soc; Sigma Xi. *Res:* Thermodynamics; statistical mechanics; critical phenomena. *Mailing Add:* Dept Chem Univ Calif Riverside CA 92521-0001

SCHMIDT, HARVEY JOHN, JR, MATHEMATICS. *Current Pos:* asst prof, 74-76, ASSOC PROF MATH, LEWIS & CLARK COL, 76- *Personal Data:* b Spokane, Wash, June 20, 41; m 69; c 1. *Educ:* Lewis & Clark Col, BA, 63; Univ Ore, MA, 65, PhD(math), 69. *Prof Exp:* Asst prof, Ill State Univ, 69-74. *Concurrent Pos:* Vis fel math, Univ Warwick, 70-71. *Mem:* Am Math Soc; Math Asn Am. *Res:* Finite group theory; representation theory of finite groups. *Mailing Add:* Campus Box 110 Lewis & Clark Col 0615 SW Palatine Hill Rd Portland OR 97219-7899

SCHMIDT, HELMUT, PHYSICS, PARAPSYCHOLOGY. *Current Pos:* INDEPENDENT CONSULT, 94- *Personal Data:* b Danzig, Ger, Feb 21, 28; m 55; c 3. *Educ:* Univ Goettingen, MA, 53; Univ Cologne, PhD(physics), 54. *Honors & Awards:* Outstanding Contrib Award, Parapsychol Asn, 89; Dinsdale Award, Soc Sci Explor, 92. *Prof Exp:* Asst prof physics, Univ Cologne, 54-55 & 58-59, docent, 60-63; vis lectr, Univ BC, 64-65; sr res physicist, Boeing Sci Res Lab, 66-69; res assoc, Inst Parapsychol, 69-70, dir, 70-73; res assoc, Mind Sci Found, 74-94. *Concurrent Pos:* Nat Acad Sci fel, Univ Calif, Berkeley, 56-57; NATO exchange prof, Southern Methodist Univ, 62. *Mem:* Am Phys Soc; Parapsychol Asn. *Res:* Quantum physics; cosmology; solid state physics; study of parapsychological effects with modern electronic equipment. *Mailing Add:* PO Box 296 Mora NM 87732

SCHMIDT, JACK RUSSELL, RESEARCH ADMINISTRATION. *Current Pos:* chief, Int Coord Liaison Br, NIH, 84-88, actg dep dir, 88-89, dir, scholars in residence prog, 89-95, DIR, DIV INT ADVAN STUDIES, FOGARTY INT CTR, NIH, 96- *Personal Data:* b Milwaukee, Wis, July 23, 26; m 58, Mary L Morrow. *Educ:* Univ Wis, BS, 48, MS, 50, PhD(med microbiol), 52. *Prof Exp:* Asst microbiol & immunol, Med Sch, Univ Wis, 49-52; virologist, Walter Reed Army Inst Res, 52-56; head, Viral Immunol Lab, Walter Reed Army Inst Res & Vet Admin Cent Lab Clin Path & Res, 56-57; head dept virol, US Naval Med Res Unit 3, 58-66, tech dir field facil, Ethiopia, 66-72, tech dir res & sci adv, Bur Med & Surg, Navy Dept, 72-74, dir progs & sci adv, Naval Med Res Develop Command, 74-83. *Mem:* Am Soc Trop Med & Hyg; Royal Soc Trop Med & Hyg. *Res:* Ecology and epidemiology of arboviral infections; viral immunology; medical entomology and parasitology; tropical diseases. *Mailing Add:* Fogarty Int Ctr NIH Bldg 16 Rm 202 Bethesda MD 20892

SCHMIDT, JANE ANN, PROTEIN CHEMISTRY, IMMUNOCHEMISTRY. *Current Pos:* sr res & develop assoc 88-91, scientist, 91-96, SENIOR SCIENTIST SANOFI DIAGNOSTICS PASTEUR INC, 96- *Personal Data:* b Minneapolis, Minn, May 25, 51. *Educ:* Macalester Col, BA, 73; Iowa State Univ, PhD(biochem), 80. *Prof Exp:* Assoc, Dept Chem, Univ Iowa, 78-81; fel, Dept Chem, Univ Del, 81-86; assoc, Dept Biochem, Univ Minn, 86-88. *Mem:* Am Chem Soc; AAAS. *Res:* Immunodiagnostics research and development. *Mailing Add:* 430 Saratoga St S St Paul MN 55105-2545

SCHMIDT, JEAN M, BACTERIOLOGY. *Current Pos:* from asst prof to assoc prof, 66-79, PROF MICROBIOL, ARIZ STATE UNIV, 79- *Personal Data:* b Waterloo, Iowa, June 5, 38. *Educ:* Univ Iowa, BA, 59, MS, 61; Univ Calif, Berkeley, PhD(bact), 65. *Prof Exp:* NIH fel, Univ Edinburgh, 65-66. *Concurrent Pos:* NIH res grants, 67-70, 71-74; NSF res grant, 79-82. *Mem:* AAAS; Am Soc Microbiol; Brit Soc Gen Microbiol. *Res:* Cancer research: detection of new anticancer drugs using in vitro tumor cell assays; microbiol ultrastructure and differentiation. *Mailing Add:* Dept Microbiol Ariz State Univ Box 872701 Tempe AZ 85287-2701

SCHMIDT, JEROME P(AUL), MEDICAL MICROBIOLOGY, BIOSAFETY. *Current Pos:* RETIRED. *Personal Data:* b Nortonville, Kans, Feb 1, 28; m 58, Pamela Messer; c Amber B & Ashley B. *Educ:* St Benedict's Col, Kans, BS, 49; Univ Kans, MA, 52; Univ NH, PhD(microbiol), 63. *Honors & Awards:* Pres Award, Am Biol Safety Asn, 88. *Prof Exp:* Bacteriologist, Arctic Aeromed Lab, Fairbanks, Alaska, 56-61; chief, Infectious Processes Unit, USAF Sch Aerospace Med, 63-68, chief microbiol, 68-90. *Concurrent Pos:* Instr, Univ Alaska, 60-61; vis prof, Tex A&M Univ, 65- & NTex State Univ, 68-; mem, Hibernation Info Exchange; chmn, Nat Acad Sci, Subcomt Infectious Agts, 86-; mem, Am Bd Med Microbiol, 88-92; consult, Ctrs Dis Control, 90- *Mem:* AAAS; Am Soc Microbiol; Am Biol Safety Asn (secy-treas, 85-91, pres, 92-93); Soc Exp Biol & Med; fel Am Acad Microbiol; Sigma Xi. *Res:* Epidemiology and etiology of acute upper respiratory diseases; microbiological aspects of mammalian hibernation; effect of environmental factors on infectious processes. *Mailing Add:* 6015 Woodwick San Antonio TX 78239-2147. *Fax:* 216-653-0200

SCHMIDT, JOHN ALLEN, PLASMA PHYSICS. *Current Pos:* res assoc physics, Princeton Univ, 69-78, co-head, Tokamac Fusion Test Reactor, 78-80, head, Appl Physics Div, Plasma Physics Lab, 80-91, proj dir, Tokawac Physics Exp, 92-95, head Adv Projs Dept, 95-97, SR RES PHYSICIST, PRINCETON UNIV, 78-, INTERIM DIR, PLASMA PHYSICS LAB, 97- *Personal Data:* b Aberdeen, SDak, Dec 31, 40; m 68, Kathryn; c Michael. *Educ:* SDak State Univ, BS, 62; Univ Wis, MS, 64, PhD(physics), 69. *Prof Exp:* Res assoc, Univ Wis, 69. *Mem:* Fel Am Phys Soc. *Res:* Use of low plasma pressure toroidal magnetic field geometrics to confine plasmas for thermonuclear energy sources. *Mailing Add:* Plasma Physics Lab Princeton Univ Princeton NJ 08544

SCHMIDT, JOHN LANCASTER, WILDLIFE ECOLOGY, WILDLIFE MANAGEMENT. *Current Pos:* SR REGIONAL DIR, DUCKS UNLIMITED. *Personal Data:* b McPherson, Kans, Sept 19, 43; m 68; c 2. *Educ:* Ottawa Univ, BA, 66; Colo State Univ, MS, 68, PhD(wildlife biol). *Prof Exp:* Exten specialist wildlife, SDak State Univ, 70-72; exten prog leader, Colo State Univ, 72-75, asst dean natural resources, 75-78, assoc prof wildlife, 74-84. *Concurrent Pos:* Consult, City Littleton, Colo, 73, Rogers Nagel Langhart Inc, 74-, Thorne Ecol Inst, 75-, Rocky Mountain Energy Co, Int Environ Consults & Dept Army. *Mem:* Wildlife Soc; Nat Wildlife Fedn; Nat Geog Soc. *Res:* Reintroduction of desert bighorn sheep in Colorado National Monument; feeding ecology at Cape Buffalo in Kruger National Park. *Mailing Add:* 9887B Grove St Westminster CO 80030

SCHMIDT, JOHN P, CHEMICAL ENGINEERING. *Current Pos:* CONSULT, 85- *Personal Data:* b Northhampton, Mass, Apr 17, 33; m 63; c 3. *Educ:* Rensselaer Polytech Inst, BChE, 55; Mass Inst Technol, ScD(chem eng), 63. *Prof Exp:* Mem staff, Eng Dept, E I du Pont de Nemours & Co, Inc, 55-58; vpres res & develop, Halcon Int, Inc, 63-73; exec vpres, Oxirane Int, 73-80; sr vpres, Arco Chem, 80-85. *Concurrent Pos:* Chmn bd, Acad Nat Sci Philadelphia. *Res:* Organic and petrochemical processing. *Mailing Add:* 11 Honey Lake Dr Princeton NJ 08540

SCHMIDT, JOHN RICHARD, agricultural economics, operations research, for more information see previous edition

SCHMIDT, JOHN THOMAS, NEUROBIOLOGY, NEURAL CONNECTIONS. *Current Pos:* from asst prof to assoc prof, 80-94, PROF BIOL SCI, SCH PUB HEALTH SCI, STATE UNIV NY, ALBANY, 94- *Personal Data:* b Louisville, Ky, Sept 25, 49; m 79, Marilyn J Gough; c Sarah & Benjamin. *Educ:* Univ Detroit, BS, 71; Univ Mich, PhD(biophysics & neurosci), 76. *Prof Exp:* Fel, Nat Inst Med Res, London, Eng, 76-77; fel, Anat Dept, Vanderbilt Univ, 77-80. *Concurrent Pos:* Prin investr grant, NIH, 81-; fel, Sloan Found, 81-85; dir, Neurobiol Res Ctr, 87- *Mem:* Soc Neurosci; Asn Res Vision & Opthal; NY Acad Sci. *Res:* Development and regeneration of retinotopic projections in the nervous system; role of activity in the stabilization of synaptic connections; role of MLCK in growth cone motility. *Mailing Add:* Dept Biol Sci State Univ NY 1400 Washington Ave Albany NY 12222. *Fax:* 518-442-4767

SCHMIDT, JOHN WESLEY, AGRONOMY. *Current Pos:* RETIRED. *Personal Data:* b Moundridge, Kans, Mar 13, 17; m 43, Olene L Hall; c Karen, Vicki, Wesley, Loren & Jerold. *Educ:* Tabor Col, BA, 47; Kans State Univ, MSc, 49; Univ Nebr, PhD(agron), 52. *Hon Degrees:* DSc, Kans State Univ, 84. *Honors & Awards:* Crop Sci Award, 75. *Prof Exp:* Assoc prof agron, Kans State Univ, 51-54; assoc agronomist, Univ Nebr, Lincoln, 54-62, prof agron, 62-80, Regents prof, 81-85. *Concurrent Pos:* NSF-US-Japan Coop Sci Prog vis scientist, Japan, 66. *Mem:* Fel Am Soc Agron; fel Crop Sci Soc Am. *Res:* Breeding, genetics and cytogenetics of wheat and related species and genera. *Mailing Add:* 1130 North 37th Univ Nebr Lincoln NE 68503

SCHMIDT, JUSTIN ORVEL, ENTOMOLOGY, BIOLOGY. *Current Pos:* RES ENTOMOLOGIST & TOXINOLOGIST, BEE RES LAB, TUCSON, 80- *Personal Data:* b Rhinelander, Wis, Mar 23, 47; m 92, Li Shen; c Krista & Scott. *Educ:* Pa State Univ, BS, 69; Univ BC, MSc, 72; Univ Ga, PhD(entom), 77. *Honors & Awards:* Technol Transfer Award, USDA, 90. *Prof Exp:* Fel biol, Univ NB, 77-78; res scientist, Univ Ga, 78-80. *Concurrent Pos:* Adj prof, Nutrit Sci Dept, Univ Ariz, Tucson, 92- *Mem:* Am Chem Soc; Entom Soc Am; Int Soc Toxinol; Int Soc Chem Ecol; AAAS; Animal Behav Soc; Sigma Xi; Int Soc Hymenopterists. *Res:* Defensive behaviors of organisms; insect venoms; chemical ecology; insect physiology and biochemistry; Africanized honey bees. *Mailing Add:* Carl Hayden Bee Lab 2000 E Allen Rd Tucson AZ 85719. *Fax:* 520-670-6493; *E-Mail:* jschmidt@ccit.arizona.edu

SCHMIDT, KLAUS H, RADIATION CHEMISTRY, PHOTOCHEMISTRY. *Current Pos:* RETIRED. *Personal Data:* b Stuttgart, Ger, Oct 9, 28; m 55; c 1. *Educ:* Univ Tubingen, Dipl physics, 54; Univ Frankfurt, Dr phil nat(biophys), 60. *Prof Exp:* Res assoc biophys & radiation chem, Max Planck Inst Biophys, 60-63; resident res assoc radiation chem, Argonne Nat Lab, 63-66, assoc physicist, Chem Div, 66-76, physicist, 76-94. *Mem:* Radiation Res Soc. *Res:* Kinetics of radiation or ultra violet induced chemical reactions with optical and electrical methods; developing techniques and equipment for radiation chemistry research; using radiation chemical techniques to study chemical mechanisms or structures. *Mailing Add:* 2815 SE 19th Pl Cape Coral FL 33904

SCHMIDT, KURT F, ANESTHESIOLOGY. *Current Pos:* PROF ANESTHESIOL & CHMN DEPT, TUFTS-NEW ENG MED CTR, 75- *Personal Data:* b New York, NY, Feb 25, 26; m 55; c 3. *Educ:* Univ Munich, MD, 51. *Prof Exp:* Instr anesthesiol, Harvard Med Sch, 55; instr, Sch Med Yale Univ, 55-61, asst prof anesthesiol, 63-68; prof anesthesiol & chmn dept, Albany Med Col, 68-73; assoc prof anesthesiol, Harvard Med Sch, 73-75. *Concurrent Pos:* NIH spec fel neuropharmacol, 61-63. *Mem:* Am Soc Anesthesiol, AMA; NY Acad Sci; Int Anesthesia Res Soc; Asn Univ Anesthetists. *Res:* Neuropharmacology. *Mailing Add:* New Eng Med Ctr Hosp 171 Harrison Ave Boston MA 02111-1854

SCHMIDT, LANNY D, CHEMICAL ENGINEERING, PHYSICAL CHEMISTRY. *Current Pos:* assoc prof, 65-69, PROF CHEM ENG & MAT SCI, UNIV MINN, MINNEAPOLIS, 69- *Personal Data:* b Waukegan, Ill, May 6, 38; m 62; c 2. *Educ:* Wheaton Col, BS, 60; Univ Chicago, PhD(phys chem), 64. *Prof Exp:* Res assoc phys chem, Univ Chicago, 64-65. *Mem:* Nat Acad Eng; Am Chem Soc; Am Vacuum Soc; Am Phys Soc. *Res:* Surface chemistry and physics; adsorption; catalysis; electron microscopy; auger electron spectrometry; kinetics. *Mailing Add:* Dept Chem Eng & Mat Sci Univ Minn Minneapolis MN 55455

SCHMIDT, MAARTEN, ASTRONOMY. *Current Pos:* assoc prof, Calif Inst Technol, 59-64, mem staff, Hale Observ, 59-80, prof astron, 64-81, mem staff, Owens Valley Radio Observ, 70-78, exec officer, 72-74, chmn, Div Physics, Math & Astron, 75-78, dir, 78-80, Francis L Mosley prof, 81-96, EMER PROF ASTRON, ROBINSON LAB, CALIF INST TECHNOL, 96- *Personal Data:* b Groningen, Neth, Dec 28, 29; m 55; c 3. *Educ:* Groningen, BSc, 49; Univ Leiden, PhD, 56. *Hon Degrees:* ScD, Yale, Univ, 66; Wesleyan Univ, 82. *Honors & Awards:* Helen B Warner Prize, Am Astron Soc, 64; Watson Medal, Nat Acad Sci, 91. *Prof Exp:* Sci officer, Leiden Observ, Neth, 53-59. *Concurrent Pos:* Carnegie fel, 56-58. *Mem:* Foreign assoc Nat Acad Sci; Am Astron Soc; fel Am Acad Arts & Sci; assoc Royal Astron Soc. *Res:* Structure, dynamics and evolution of the galaxy; radio astronomy; redshifts and cosmic distribution of quasars. *Mailing Add:* Dept Astron 105-24 Calif Inst Technol Pasadena CA 91125-0002

SCHMIDT, MARK THOMAS, MUSEUM EDUCATION URBAN GEOLOGY. *Current Pos:* STAFF GEOLOGIST, WOODWARD-CLYDE CONSULT, 91- *Personal Data:* b New York, NY, Apr 17, 58. *Educ:* Ky State Univ, BS, 81 & MS, 86. *Prof Exp:* Instr earth sci, Cleveland Mus Nat Hist, 84-85, coordr, Sci Resource Ctr, 86-89; asst to dir educ, Am Geol Inst, 89-91. *Concurrent Pos:* Dir, Northeastern Ohio Sci & Eng Fair, 86-88; mem educ adv comt, Am Geol Inst, 87-88. *Mem:* Geol Soc Am; Nat Asn Geol Teachers; Nat Earth Sci Teachers Asn; Nat Sci Teachers Asn. *Res:* Rock types used for building and monuments; petrology of metasedimentary rocks from Taylor Valley, South Victoria Land, Antarctica. *Mailing Add:* 1586 Maywood Rd South Euclid OH 44121

SCHMIDT, NORBERT OTTO, CIVIL ENGINEERING, SOILS. *Current Pos:* RETIRED. *Personal Data:* b Highland Park, Mich, Nov 15, 25; m 53; c 5. *Educ:* US Mil Acad, BS, 49; Harvard Univ, MS, 55; Univ Ill, PhD(civil eng), 65. *Prof Exp:* From asst prof to assoc prof mil sci, Mo Sch Mines, 59-62; asst civil eng, Univ Ill, 63-65, from instr to asst prof, 65-66; from asst prof to prof civil eng, Univ Mo, Rolla, 75-79. *Concurrent Pos:* Consult, tailings dams & recreational lake dams, 79- *Mem:* Am Soc Civil Engrs; Am Soc Testing & Mat; Nat Soc Prof Engrs; US Comn Large Dams. *Res:* Geotechnical engineering; dams; foundations; testing, dewatering and instrumentation. *Mailing Add:* 970 Loggerhead Island Dr Satellite Beach FL 32937. *Fax:* 573-364-2546

SCHMIDT, P(HILIP) S(TEPHEN), MECHANICAL ENGINEERING, HEAT TRANSFER. *Current Pos:* from asst prof to prof mech eng, 70-90, DONALD J DOUGLAS PROF ENG, UNIV TEX, AUSTIN, 90- *Personal Data:* b Houston, Tex, Feb 26, 41; m 66; c 3. *Educ:* Mass Inst Technol, SB, 62; Stanford Univ, MS, 65, PhD(mech eng), 69. *Honors & Awards:* Ralph R Teetor Award, Soc Automotive Engrs, 72; Distinguished Serv Citation, Am Soc Mech Engrs, 86. *Prof Exp:* Res engr, Bell Helicopter Co, 62-64; Woodrow Wilson teaching intern & assoc prof mech eng, Prairie View Agr & Mech Col, 68-70. *Concurrent Pos:* Consult, Elec Power Res Inst & var corps. *Mem:* Am Soc Eng Educ; Am Soc Mech Engrs. *Res:* Fluid mechanics; thermodynamics and industrial energy utilization. *Mailing Add:* Dept Mech Eng Univ Tex Austin TX 78712-1063

SCHMIDT, PARBURY POLLEN, CHEMICAL PHYSICS. *Current Pos:* PROG OFFICER, OFF NAVAL RES, ARLINGTON, VA, 88- *Personal Data:* b Norwalk, Conn, Sept 4, 39; m 61; c 3. *Educ:* Kalamazoo Col, BA, 61; Wake Forest Col, MA, 64; Univ Mich, Ann Arbor, PhD(chem), 66. *Prof Exp:* NSF fel, Univ Col, Univ London, 66-67; NSF fel & vis res fel, Australian Nat Univ, 67-68; asst prof chem, Univ Ga, 68-70; from asst prof to prof chem, Oakland Univ, 70-88. *Concurrent Pos:* Spec lectr, Gen Studies Sch, Australian Nat Univ, 68; Fulbright res scholar & vis prof, Southampton Univ, UK. *Mem:* Royal Soc Chem London; Am Chem Soc; Sigma Xi; Inst Navig; Electrochem Soc. *Res:* Theory of electron transfer reactions; theory of nerve impulse conduction; theory of nonradiative transitions in molecules. *Mailing Add:* Chem Div Off Naval Res 800 N Quincy St Arlington VA 22217

SCHMIDT, PAUL GARDNER, BIOPHYSICAL CHEMISTRY. *Current Pos:* VPRES DRUG DELIVERY RES, NEXSTAR PHARMACEUT, 95- *Personal Data:* b Pasadena, Calif, June 9, 44; m 66; c 2. *Educ:* Pomona Col, BA, 66; Stanford Univ, PhD(chem), 70. *Prof Exp:* Asst prof chem & biochem, Univ Ill, Urbana, 70-77; assoc prof biochem, Univ Okla, Oklahoma City, 77-83; assoc mem, Okla Med Res Found, Oklahoma City, 77-83; vpres res & develop, Vestar Res Inc, 89-92, exec vpres res, 92-95. *Concurrent Pos:* USPHS res grant, 70-; res career develop award, USPHS, 79-84. *Mem:* AAAS; Am Chem Soc; Biophys Soc; Am Soc Biochem & Molecular Biol. *Res:* Nuclear magnetic resonance; enzyme structure and function; transfer RNA structure; liposones; therapeutic oligonucleotides. *Mailing Add:* Nexstar Pharmaceut Inc 2860 Wilderness Pl Boulder CO 80241

SCHMIDT, PAUL J, ORGANIC CHEMISTRY. *Current Pos:* GEN MGR, ORG CHEM DIV, HILTON DAVIS CO, 88- *Personal Data:* b Cincinnati, Ohio, May 26, 43; m 69; c 2. *Educ:* Xavier Univ, BS, 65; Univ Cincinnati, PhD(chem), 69. *Prof Exp:* Res chemist, 69-74, asst dir chem res, 74-75, dir chem res, 75-80, vpres res & develop, Hilton-Davis Div, Sterling Drug, Inc, 80-87. *Mem:* Am Chem Soc. *Res:* Platinum complexes; organic synthetics. *Mailing Add:* 3590 Concerto Dr Sharonville Cincinnati OH 45241-2715

SCHMIDT, PAUL JOSEPH, MEDICINE, CLINICAL PATHOLOGY. *Current Pos:* dir, 75-90, HEAD TRANSFUSION MED, SOUTHWEST FLA BLOOD BANK INC, 91- ; PROF PATH, COL MED, UNIV SFLA, 75-; CLIN PROF PATH, SCH MED SCI, UNIV, PR, 93- *Personal Data:* b New York, NY, Oct 22, 25; m 53, Louise Kern; c Damien, Matthew, Thomas & Maria. *Educ:* Fordham Univ, BS, 48; St Louis Univ, MS, 52; NY Univ, MD, 53; Am Bd Path, cert clin path, 64, cert blood banking, 73. *Honors & Awards:* Silver Medal, Red Cross Spain; Emily Cooley Mem Award, Am Asn Blood Banks, 74; John Elliott Award, Am Asn Blood Banks, 93. *Prof Exp:* Intern, St Elizabeth's Hosp, Boston, 53-54; physician, Clin Ctr Blood Bank & chief blood bank sect, NIH, 55-60, resident, Clin Path Dept, 61-62, asst chief, 62-64, chief blood bank dept, 65-74. *Concurrent Pos:* From clin assoc prof to clin prof path, Sch Med, Georgetown Univ, 65-74. *Mem:* Col Am Path; Am Soc Clin Path; Int Soc Blood Transfusion; Am Soc Blood Banks (pres, 88). *Res:* Immunohematology; physiology of the formed elements of blood and the effects of storage on their viability; hepatitis; administration and education in blood banking and clinical pathology. *Mailing Add:* Southwest Fla Blood Bank PO Box 2125 Tampa FL 33601. *Fax:* 813-975-1457

SCHMIDT, PAUL WOODWARD, PHYSICS. *Current Pos:* From asst prof to assoc prof, 53-66, PROF PHYSICS, UNIV MO, COLUMBIA, 66- *Personal Data:* b Madison, Wis, May 8, 26; m 50; c 5. *Educ:* Carleton Col, BA, 49; Univ Wis, MS, 50, PhD(physics), 53. *Mem:* Fel Am Phys Soc; Am Crystallog Asn; Sigma Xi; Mat Res Soc. *Res:* Small angle x-ray scattering, both theory and experiment; chemical physics; liquids; biophysics; colloids; fractals. *Mailing Add:* 503 S Garth Ave Columbia MO 65203-3425

SCHMIDT, RAYMOND LEROY, PETROLEUM ENGINEERING, ENHANCED OIL RECOVERY. *Current Pos:* sr res chemist, 78-84, sup thermal recovery, 86-92, SR RES ASSOC, CHEVRON OIL FIELD RES CO, 84-, MGR, TECHNOL TRANSFER INDONESIA, CHEVRON PETROL TECHNOL CO, 92- *Personal Data:* b Tiffin, Ohio, July 7, 42; m 65, Sarah E Oberst; c Elizabeth L & Christopher R. *Educ:* Fla Presby Col, BS, 64; Emory Univ, PhD(phys chem), 67. *Prof Exp:* Instr chem, Emory Univ, 67-68; res fel chem eng, Calif Inst Technol, 68-70; from asst prof to assoc prof chem, Univ New Orleans, 70-78. *Concurrent Pos:* Fel Emory Univ, 67-68; vis assoc, Calif Inst Technol, 77-80. *Mem:* Am Chem Soc; Soc Petrol Engrs. *Res:* Laser scattering spectroscopy from fluid media; adsorption phenomena; surface chemistry of geologic materials; high pressure physical property measurements; thermal methods of enhanced oil recovery including tar sands; phase behavior of petroleum reservoir fluids; technology transfer processes and technology management in international oil industry operations. *Mailing Add:* 7751 Bowen Dr Whittier CA 90602. *Fax:* 562-694-7228; *E-Mail:* scrl@chevron.com

SCHMIDT, REESE BOISE, ANALYTICAL CHEMISTRY. *Current Pos:* chemist, 46-62, mgr appl res, 62-69, mgr process & test, W A Sheaffer Pen Co, 70-78, CONSULT, SHEAFFER EATON, DIV TEXTRON INC, 78- *Personal Data:* b Knoxville, Iowa, May 16, 13; m 49; c 5. *Educ:* Cent Col, Iowa, BS, 34. *Prof Exp:* Technician exp canning, Calif Packing Corp, Ill, 39-40, foreman, 40-43; chemist, US Rubber Co, Iowa, 44-45; teacher pub sch, Iowa, 45-46. *Mem:* Am Chem Soc. *Mailing Add:* 2109 Ave H Ft Madison IA 52627-4145

SCHMIDT, RICHARD, CERAMICS ENGINEERING. *Current Pos:* RETIRED. *Personal Data:* b Pa, May 12, 25. *Educ:* Temple Univ, BS, 46; Am Univ, MA, 77. *Honors & Awards:* Von Karmen Mem Award, 83; Burgess Mem Award, Am Soc Metals. *Prof Exp:* Head, Metals Br, Bur Naval Weapons, 51-60; mgr mat res & develop, Naval Air Systs Command, Washington, DC, 80, dep dir, Aircraft Div, 80-83; mgr aerospace & defense technol, Alcoa, 85-93. *Concurrent Pos:* Chmn, Aerospace Mat Div, Soc Automotive Engrs, 87. *Mem:* Fel Am Soc Metals; Soc Automotive Engrs. *Res:* Metal composites. *Mailing Add:* 272 White Oak Dr New Kensington PA 15068

SCHMIDT, RICHARD ARTHUR, ECONOMIC GEOLOGY, MINERAL ECONOMICS. *Current Pos:* FUELS EVAL, COMMONWEALTH EDISON, 96- *Personal Data:* b Elizabeth, NJ, Mar 18, 35; m 55, 81, Nancy A Carlson; c Cathy (Stillman), Ellen (Silky), Duncan Carlson & Eric Carlson. *Educ:* Franklin & Marshall Col, BS, 57; Univ Wis-Madison, MS, 59, PhD(geol), 63. *Prof Exp:* Nat Acad Sci resident res assoc, Ames Res Ctr, NASA, 63-65; proj scientist, Aerospace Systs Div, Bendix Corp, 65-67; sr geologist, Stanford Res Inst, 67-74; tech mgr fossil fuel resources, Elec Power Rest Inst, 74-79; prin, Booz, Allen & Hamilton, 79-82; independent consult, 82-88; vpres corp plan, Constain Holdings, Inc, 88-93; independent consult, Energy & Environ, 93-95. *Mem:* Am Inst Mining, Metall & Petrol Engrs; fel Geol Soc Am. *Res:* Coal; mining; environmental assessment; resources management and planning; strateic evaluation; business diversification; fuels evaluation. *Mailing Add:* 804 Wildrose Springs Dr St Charles IL 60174. *Fax:* 312-394-7571; *E-Mail:* umdrs@ccmail.ceco.com

SCHMIDT, RICHARD EDWARD, AGRONOMY. *Current Pos:* from instr to assoc prof, 58-86, PROF AGRON, VA POLYTECH INST & STATE UNIV, 86- *Personal Data:* b Detroit, Mich, Sept 3, 31; m 56; c 2. *Educ:* Pa State Univ, BS, 54, MS, 58; Va Polytech Inst, PhD(agron), 65. *Honors & Awards:* Fel, Crop Sci Soc Am. *Prof Exp:* Asst agron, Pa State Univ, 56-58. *Concurrent Pos:* Consult, Weblite Corp, Va, 65- & US Mkt Group, 81- *Mem:* Am Soc Agron; fel Crop Sci Soc Am. *Res:* Turfgrass ecology, particularly environmental influences on the physiological affects of grasses. *Mailing Add:* Crop & Soil Sci Va Polytech Inst & State Univ PO Box 0404 Blacksburg VA 24063-0001

SCHMIDT, RICHARD RALPH, TERATOLOGY. *Current Pos:* INSTR GROSS ANAT, DANIEL BAUGH INST ANAT, JEFFERSON MED COL, 74- *Personal Data:* b Milwaukee, Wis, Mar 28, 44; m 65; c 2. *Educ:* Univ Wis-Madison, BA, 68; Med Col Wis, PhD(anat), 74. *Res:* Biochemical alterations in fetuses with multiple congenital skeletal malformations. *Mailing Add:* Dept Anat Jefferson Med Col 1025 Walnut St Philadelphia PA 19107-5001

SCHMIDT, ROBERT, MECHANICS, ENGINEERING. *Current Pos:* chmn, Civil Eng Dept, 78-80, PROF ENG MECH, UNIV DETROIT, 63- *Personal Data:* b Ukraine, May 18, 27; US citizen; m 78, Irene H B Bongartz; c Ingbert Robert. *Educ:* Univ Colo, BS, 51, MS, 53; Univ Ill, PhD(civil eng), 56. *Honors & Awards:* First Gold Award, Indust Math Soc. *Prof Exp:* Asst prof mech, Univ Ill, 56-59; assoc prof, Univ Ariz, 59-63. *Concurrent Pos:* NSF res grants, 60-63, 64-67, 70-72 & 76-78; ed, Indust Math, Indust Math Soc, 68- *Mem:* Am Soc Civil Engrs; Am Soc Mech Engrs; Indust Math Soc (pres, 66-67 & 81-84); Am Acad Mech; Sigma Xi. *Res:* Theories of plates and shells, sandwich plates and shells and multilaminate plates and shells; nonlinear theories of arches and rods; elastic stability & postbuckling analysis; direct variational methods; biosophy. *Mailing Add:* 2437 Windemere Birmingham MI 48009

SCHMIDT, ROBERT GORDON, GEOLOGY OF METALLIC MINERAL DEPOSITS. *Current Pos:* RETIRED. *Personal Data:* b Minneapolis, Minn, Nov 9, 24; m 52, Alice Hankins; c David J & Leonard E. *Educ:* Univ Wis, MS, 51. *Prof Exp:* Geologist, US Geol Surv, 51-90. *Concurrent Pos:* Res assoc, Dept Anthrop, Nat Mus Natural Hist, Smithsonian Inst. *Mem:* AAAS; Geol Soc Am. *Res:* Economic deposits of iron, copper, gold & silver, mineral resource supplies for ancient civilizations; satellite remote sensing for mineral exploration; mineral resources available to roman and earlier metallurgists. *Mailing Add:* 3732 N Nelson St Arlington VA 22207-4836

SCHMIDT, ROBERT MILTON, PREVENTIVE MEDICINE, GERONTOLOGY. *Current Pos:* DIR, CTR PREV MED & HEALTH RES, 83-, DIR, HEALTH WATCH, 83-; ATTEND PHYSICIAN, DEPT MED, CALIF PAC MED CTR, SAN FRANCISCO, 83- *Personal Data:* b Milwaukee, Wis, May 7, 44; c Eric W & Edward H. *Educ:* Northwestern Univ, AB, 66; Columbia Univ, MD, 70; Harvard Univ, MPH, 75; Emory Univ, PhD(law, med & pub policy), 82; Am Bd Prev Med, dipl. *Honors & Awards:* Award in Pharmacol, Am Soc Pharmacol & Exp Therapeut, 70; Borden Res Award, Col Physicians & Surgeons, 70; Commendation Medal, USPHS, 73. *Prof Exp:* Resident, internal med, Univ Hosp, Univ Calif, San Diego, 70-71; dir, Hemat Div, Nat Ctr Dis Control, Atlanta, 71-78, spec asst to dir, 78-79; attending physician, Dept Med, Wilcox Mem Hosp, Hawaii, 79-82. *Concurrent Pos:* Fel, NSF, 64-66, USPHS, 67-70; scholar, Northwestern Univ, 64-66, health prof, 66-70; comndg med officer, USPHS, 71, adv to comdr, 73; clin asst prof med, Med Sch, Emory Univ, 71-81, clin asst prof community health, 76-86; resident prev med, Ctrs Dis Control, Atlanta, 71-74; clin asst prof pediat, Med Sch, Tufts Univ, 74-86; clin assoc prof humanities in med, Morehouse Med Sch, 77-79; dir, Int Health Resource Ctr, Lihue, Hawaii, 79-82; alumni regent, Col Physicians & Surgeons, Columbia Univ, 80-; sr scientist, Inst Epidemiol & Behav Med, Inst Cancer Res, Calif Pac Med Ctr, San Francisco, 83-88; prof hemat & geront, dir, Ctr Prev Med & Health Res & chair health professions prog, San Francisco State Univ, 83-; consult, WHO, Food & Drug Admin, NIH, Govt China, Mayo Clin, Northwestern Univ, Univ RI, Pan Am Health Orgn, Inst Pub Health (Italy), Nat Inst Aging Res Ctr and others; assoc ed, Contemp Geront, 93- *Mem:* Fel Am Col Physicians; fel AAAS; fel Geront Soc Am; fel Am Geriat Soc; fel Am Col Prev Med; fel Am Soc Clin Path; AMA; Am Pub Health Asn; Am Soc Hemat; Am Asn Blood Banks; Am Soc Microbiol; NY Acad Sci; Sigma Xi; Am Soc Aging; Acad Clin Lab Physicians & Scientists; Am Med Asn. *Res:* Healthy aging and preventive medicine; application of clinical laboratory, health status and health behavioral person-specific data; physician health behavior prescriptions; counseling to enhance healthy aging intervention in primary care. *Mailing Add:* Calif Pac Med Ctr PO Box 7999 San Francisco CA 94120-7999. *Fax:* 415-923-0536

SCHMIDT, ROBERT REINHART, BIOCHEMISTRY. *Current Pos:* MEM FAC, UNIV FLA, 80- *Personal Data:* b St Louis, Mo, Feb 18, 33; m 56; c 4. *Educ:* Va Polytech Inst, BS, 55, PhD(biochem), 61; Univ Md, MS, 57. *Prof Exp:* From asst prof to assoc prof, Va Polytech Inst & State Univ, 61-67, prof biochem, 67-80. *Concurrent Pos:* Res grants, NIH & NSF, 61- *Mem:* Am Soc Microbiol; Am Soc Biol Chemists; Am Soc Plant Physiol. *Res:* Use of synchronized cultures of microorganisms, plant and animal cells to study operation and control of metabolic pathways and enzymes located therein during cellular growth and division. *Mailing Add:* Univ Fla Bldg 981 Museum Rd Gainsville FL 32611-0700. *Fax:* 904-392-8479

SCHMIDT, ROBERT W, BIOCHEMISTRY. *Current Pos:* assoc prof, 61-67, PROF CHEM, BETHEL COL, KANS, 67- *Personal Data:* b Enid, Okla, Feb 16, 30; m 53; c 4. *Educ:* Bethel Col, AB, 52; Univ Okla, MSc, 55, PhD(chem), 60. *Prof Exp:* Instr math & sci high sch, Kans, 52-53; asst prof chem, Simpson Col, 58-61. *Concurrent Pos:* Assoc marine scientist, Va Inst Marine Sci, 69-70; vis prof, Biochem, State Univ Iowa Col Med, 76-77; vis prof, Chem Dept, Univ Okla, 83-84. *Mem:* Am Chem Soc; Am Sci Affil; Midwestern Asn Chem Teachers; Am Asn Univ Professors; Sigma Xi. *Res:* Natural products of plants. *Mailing Add:* Dept Chem Bethel Co North Newton KS 67117

SCHMIDT, ROBERT W, PATHOLOGY, CYTOPATHOLOGY. *Current Pos:* Intern, Univ Hosp, Univ Mich, Ann Arbor, 54-55, resident path, 55-59, from instr to prof, 59-90, EMER PROF PATH, UNIV HOSP, UNIV MICH, ANN ARBOR, 90-; SR ATTEND PATHOLOGIST, TOLEDO HOSP, OHIO, 90- *Personal Data:* b Toledo, Ohio, July 22, 26; m 63; c 4. *Educ:* Univ Toledo, BS, 50; Ohio State Univ, MD, 54. *Concurrent Pos:* Dir path, Wayne Co Gen Hosp, Eloise, Mich, 64-85. *Mem:* Am Soc Cytol; Int Acad Path. *Res:* Clinical and anatomical pathology; gynecologic pathology; exfoliative and fine needle aspirate cytology. *Mailing Add:* Univ Mich Med Ctr Box 0054 Ann Arbor MI 48109

SCHMIDT, ROGER PAUL, PARASITOLOGY, BIOLOGY. *Current Pos:* CHMN, DEPT BIOL, COLUMBIA COL. *Personal Data:* b Abilene, Kans, Jan 16, 44; m 74, Linda McCord; c Dorothy & Melinda. *Educ:* Univ Kans, BA, 66, MA, 72; Kans State Univ, PhD(parasitol), 78. *Concurrent Pos:* Mem, SC Acad Sci. *Mem:* Sigma Xi; AAAS; Am Inst Biol Sci. *Res:* Effects and interactions between pesticides and parasites in poultry. *Mailing Add:* Dept Biol Columbia Col 1301 Columbia Col Dr Columbia SC 29203

SCHMIDT, RONALD GROVER, HYDROGEOLOGY. *Current Pos:* dir, Off Environ Studies, 70-74, Wright State Univ, dir, Brehm Lab, 72-75, chmn, Dept Geol, 74-83, PROF GEOL & ENG, WRIGHT STATE UNIV, 70-, DIR, CTR GROUND WATER MGT, 86- *Personal Data:* b Bloomfield, NJ, Oct 13, 31; m 55; c 2. *Educ:* Columbia Univ, AB, 53, MA, 55; Univ Cincinnati, PhD(geol), 57; Am Inst Prof Geol & Calif Bd Regist, cert & regist geol. *Prof Exp:* Geologist, USAEC Contr NMex, 52; tech officer, Geol Surv Can, 53-54; asst geol, Columbia Univ, 54; instr Hunter Col, 55; asst, Univ Cincinnati, 55-57; geologist, Stand Oil Co, Tex, 56; asst prof, Univ Cincinnati, 57-63; pres & geol consult, Earth Sci Labs, Inc, 60-70. *Mem:* AAAS; Am Geophys Union; Amer Water Res Asn; Geol Soc Am; Water Pollution Control Fed. *Mailing Add:* Dept Geol Wright State Univ 3640 Colonel Glenn Dayton OH 45435-0002

SCHMIDT, RUTH A M, GEOLOGY, ENVIRONMENTAL SCIENCE. *Current Pos:* RETIRED. *Personal Data:* b Brooklyn, NY, Apr 22, 16. *Educ:* NY Univ, AB, 36; Columbia Univ, AM, 39, PhD(geol), 48. *Prof Exp:* Asst paleont, Columbia Univ, 39-42; geologist, US Geol Surv, 43-56, dist geologist, Alaska, 56-63; consult geologist, 64-97. *Concurrent Pos:* Environ consult, Off Pipeline Coordr, Off of Gov, Alaska, 75-77; chmn, Geol Dept, Anchorage Community Col, Univ Alaska, 70- 84, Elder Hostel lectr, 85-86 & 88-89. *Mem:* Fel AAAS; Fedn Am Scientists; fel Geol Soc Am; Am Inst Prof Geol; fel Arctic Inst NAm; Sigma Xi; Am Asn Petrol Geol. *Res:* Cretaceous and tertiary micropaleontology in Alaska; instructional television delivery of earth science to rural Alaska; general geology of Alaska; application of x-rays to paleontology. *Mailing Add:* 1402 W 11th Ave Anchorage AK 99501

SCHMIDT, S K, ENVIRONMENTAL MICROBIOLOGY, MICROBIAL ECOLOGY. *Current Pos:* Asst prof, 86-93, ASSOC PROF BIOL, DEPT ENVIRON, POP & ORGANISM BIOL, UNIV COLO, 93- *Personal Data:* b Spokane, Wash, Dec 6, 55. *Educ:* Boise State Univ, BS, 79; Colo State Univ, MS, 81; Cornell Univ, PhD(microbiol), 86. *Mem:* Soil Ecol Soc; Am Soc Microbiol; Sigma Xi. *Res:* Role of microorganisms in nutrient cycling, biodegradation of toxic chemicals and plant nutrition. *Mailing Add:* Dept Environ Pop & Organism Biol Univ Colo Boulder CO 80309-0334. *Fax:* 303-492-8699

SCHMIDT, STEPHEN PAUL, FESCUE TOXICITY, PROTEIN METABOLISM. *Current Pos:* ASSOC PROF ADVAN NUTRIT & INTRODUCTORY ANIMAL SCI, AUBURN UNIV, 76- *Educ:* Univ Wis, PhD(ruminant nutrit), 72. *Mailing Add:* Auburn Univ Dept Animal & Dairy Sci Auburn AL 36849. *Fax:* 334-844-1519; *E-Mail:* sschmidt@ads.auburn.edu

SCHMIDT, STEPHEN PAUL, INSECT TOXICOLOGY. *Current Pos:* RES BIOCHEMIST, RHONE POULENC AGR CO, 82- *Personal Data:* b San Diego, Calif, Feb 8, 47; m 68; c 2. *Educ:* San Diego State Univ, BS, 73, MS, 75; Univ Calif, Riverside, PhD(entom), 79. *Prof Exp:* Res assoc entom, Okla State Univ, 79-82. *Mem:* Entom Soc Am; AAAS. *Res:* Toxicology and biochemistry of novel pesticides in insects. *Mailing Add:* Rhone Poulenc Agr Co 2 Alexander Dr PO Box 12014 Research Triangle Park NC 27709. *Fax:* 919-549-3946; *E-Mail:* sschmidt@rp

SCHMIDT, STEVEN PAUL, IN VITRO FERTILIZATION, VASCULAR RESEARCH. *Current Pos:* ASSOC DIR VASCULAR RES & DIR, IN VITRO FERTIL LAB, VASCULAR RES LAB, AKRON CITY HOSP. *Mailing Add:* Falor Ctr Vasc Studies Samma Health Syst Akron City Hosp 525 E Market St Akron OH 44309-2090. *Fax:* 330-375-4648

SCHMIDT, THOMAS JOHN, ENDOCRINOLOGY, CELLULAR PHYSIOLOGY. *Current Pos:* ASST PROF, DEPT PHYSIOL & BIOPHYS, UNIV IOWA. *Personal Data:* b Mt Holly, NJ, Dec 13, 46. *Educ:* Univ Del, BA, 69; Cornell Univ, MS, 73, PhD(physiol), 76. *Honors & Awards:* Scholar, Leukemia Soc Am. *Prof Exp:* Biochem & endocrinol, Nat Cancer Inst, 76-79; sr fel, Fels Res Inst, 79- *Mem:* Sigma Xi; Endocrine Soc; NY Acad Sci; Am Asn Cancer Res; Am Physiol Soc; Am Soc Biol Chemists. *Res:* Mode of action of steroid hormones; function of receptors, particularly for glucocorticoids, in normal and neoplastic cells. *Mailing Add:* Dept Physiol & Biophys Univ Iowa 5-610 Bowen Sci Bldg Iowa City IA 52242-1109. *Fax:* 319-335-7330

SCHMIDT, THOMAS WILLIAM, CHEMICAL PHYSICS. *Current Pos:* PROG MGR TECHNOL TRANSFER, OAK RIDGE NAT LAB, MARTIN MARIETTA ENERGY SYSTS, 93- *Personal Data:* b Evansville, Ind, Aug 9, 38; m 61, Janice Elmendorf; c Allison G (Walters) & Christopher T. *Educ:* Univ Evansville, BA, 60; Univ Fla, MS, 63; Univ Tenn, PhD(chem), 67. *Honors & Awards:* IR-100 Award, Res & Develop Mag, 79. *Prof Exp:* Sr res chem physicist, Phillips Petrol Co, 67-77, sect supvr, Eng Data, 77-82, br mgr, Alt Energy, 82, br mgr, Planning & High Tech, 82-83, br mgr, Safety Div, 83-85, br mgr, fuels & lubes, crude oil, Environ Incineration Technol, 85-90, dir environ planning & technol, 90-92. *Mem:* Am Phys Soc; Sigma Xi; Soc Automotive Engrs; Am Chem Soc; Am Inst Chem Engrs. *Res:* Molecular beams; mass spectroscopy; chemical kinetics; ultra high vacuum; vapor-liquid equilibrium. *Mailing Add:* Oak Ridge Nat Lab PO Box 2008 Oak Ridge TN 37831-6273. *Fax:* 423-574-7229; *E-Mail:* schmidttw@ornl.gov

SCHMIDT, VICTOR A, geophysics, paleomagnetism; deceased, see previous edition for last biography

SCHMIDT, VICTOR HUGO, SOLID STATE PHYSICS. *Current Pos:* assoc prof, 64-73, PROF PHYSICS, MONT STATE UNIV, 73- *Personal Data:* b Portland, Ore, July 10, 30; m 58, Shirley Schmidt; c Harold, Lawrence, Marie & Gloria. *Educ:* Wash State Univ, BS, 51; Univ Wash, PhD(physics), 61. *Prof Exp:* Mech design engr, Gilfillan Bros, Inc, 53-54; assoc res engr, Boeing Airplane Co, 55-57; asst prof physics, Valparaiso Univ, 61-64. *Mem:* Fel Am Phys Soc; Am Asn Physics Teachers; Sigma Xi; sr mem Inst Elec & Electronics Engrs. *Res:* Nuclear magnetic resonance, light scattering, dielectric and high pressure studies of ferroelectric phase transitions and proton glass; physical properties and applications of piezoelectric polymers; wind generation of electric power; liquid crystals. *Mailing Add:* Dept Physics Mont State Univ Bozeman MT 59717

SCHMIDT, VOLKMAR, CARBONATE DIAGENESIS, SANDSTONE DIAGENESIS. *Current Pos:* PRES, PETROSCAN INT PETROLOGY CONS INC, CAN, 86- *Personal Data:* b Heidelberg, Ger, Aug 27, 32; m 71, Sylvia Desa; c Carmen & Fiona. *Educ:* Univ Heidelberg, BS, 56; Univ Kiel, PhD(geol), 61. *Prof Exp:* Sr res geologist, Mobil Oil Corp, Tex, 61-69, head, Geol Lab, Mobil Oil Can, Ltd, 68-76; mgr geol res, Petrol Can, 76-86. *Concurrent Pos:* Consult, Petrol Can, 86- *Mem:* Am Asn Petrol Geologists; Soc Econ Paleontologists & Mineralogists; Int Asn Sedimentologists; Can Soc Petrol Geologists. *Res:* Sandstone diagenesis and evolution of reservoir quality; carbonate diagenesis and reservoir quality evolution; sedimentary processes; sediment geochemistry; petroleum reservoir petrography; evaporite facies and petrography; facies and paleoenvironmental studies; sedimentary petrography. *Mailing Add:* 4187 Varsity Rd NW Calgary AB T3B 2Y6 Can

SCHMIDT, WALDEMAR ADRIAN, surgical pathology, cytopathology, for more information see previous edition

SCHMIDT, WALTER, GEOLOGY & EARTH SCIENCES APPLIED FOR POLICY & DECISION MAKERS, PALEOENVIRONMENTAL STUDIES. *Current Pos:* STATE GEOLOGIST & CHIEF, FLA GEOL SURV, DEPT NATURAL RESOURCES-DEPT ENVIRON PROTECTION, 85- *Personal Data:* b Philadelphia, Pa, June 28, 50; m 72, Cheryl Blake; c David W & Amber M. *Educ:* Univ SFla, BA, 72; Fla State Univ, MS, 77, PhD(geol), 83. *Prof Exp:* Res asst, Sedimentation Lab, Fla State, 73-74; asst geologist, NW Fla Water Mgt Dist, 74-75, geologist II, Fla Bur Geol, Dept Neutral Resources, 75-79, geologist III, 79-81, adminr, Geol Invest Sect, 81-85. *Concurrent Pos:* Adj prof, Geol Dept, Fla State Univ. *Mem:* Geol Soc Am; Soc Sedimentary Geol; Am Inst Prof Geologists; Asn Am State Geologists (pres, 95-96). *Res:* Geologic mapping and stratigraphic interpretations including paleontology and mineralogy; geology for public service. *Mailing Add:* Fla Geol Surv 903 W Tennessee St Tallahassee FL 32304. *Fax:* 850-488-8086; *E-Mail:* schmidt_w@dep.state.fl.us

SCHMIDT, WALTER HAROLD, CROP PRODUCTION & MANAGEMENT. *Current Pos:* from asst prof to assoc prof, 65-76, PROF AGRON, OHIO STATE UNIV EXTEN, 76- *Personal Data:* b Gordon, Nebr, Sept 19, 35; m 59, Alyce A; c Lori, Paul, Nancy & Mark. *Educ:* Univ Nebr, Lincoln, BS, 57, MS, 60, PhD(crop prod), 65. *Prof Exp:* Asst county exten agent, Nebr Coop Exten Serv, 57. *Concurrent Pos:* Res scientist, Ohio Agr Res & Develop Ctr. *Mem:* Am Soc Agron; Nat Asn Coop Agr Agents; Am Soc Sugar Beet Technol; Sigma Xi. *Res:* Crop production techniques for corn, forages, grain, soybeans, sugar beets and canola. *Mailing Add:* 1708 Oak Dr Fremont OH 43420-4935. *Fax:* 419-422-7595

SCHMIDT, WERNER H(ANS), CHEMICAL ENGINEERING. *Current Pos:* RETIRED. *Personal Data:* b Frankfurt, Ger, Sept 24, 14; nat US; m 41, Martha F Woitscheek; c Marsha Anne & Paul Werner. *Educ:* Tufts Univ, BS, 36. *Prof Exp:* Chemist foods, Johnson-Salisbury Co, 36; chemist edible oils, Lever Bros Co, 36-39, res chemist, 39-45, res supvr foods, 45-52, chief foods processing sect, 52-60, develop mgr, 60-64, develop mgr foods & toiletries, 64-73, dir develop foods, Foods Div, 73-78. *Concurrent Pos:* Consult, Lever Bros Foods Div, 78-80. *Mem:* Am Chem Soc; Am Oil Chem Soc; Inst Food Technologists. *Res:* Edible oil processing; shortening and margarine formulation and manufacture; catalytic hydrogenation; esterification. *Mailing Add:* 23 Forest Gate Yarmouth Port MA 02675

SCHMIDT, WILLIAM EDWARD, ANALYTICAL CHEMISTRY. *Current Pos:* from asst prof to assoc prof, 53-61, PROF CHEM, GEORGE WASHINGTON UNIV, 61- *Personal Data:* b Pittsburgh, Pa, Sept 7, 20; m 47; c 5. *Educ:* George Washington Univ, BS, 43, MS, 50; Princeton Univ, MA & PhD(chem), 53. *Prof Exp:* Asst chem, George Washington Univ, 41-43, res assoc, Nat Defense Res Comt, 43-44, assoc, 46-50; asst anal chem, Princeton Univ, 50-53. *Concurrent Pos:* Consult, US Vet Admin, 57-59; ed consult, Am Chem Soc, 65- *Mem:* AAAS; Am Chem Soc; Electrochem Soc; Am Inst Chemists. *Res:* Measurement of electrode potentials; mercury cathode electrolysis; electroanalysis; redox proteins; electroplating; radio tracers; reagent chemicals. *Mailing Add:* Dept Chem George Washington Univ Washington DC 20006

SCHMIDT, WOLFGANG M, MATHEMATICS. *Current Pos:* assoc prof, 64-65, PROF MATH, UNIV COLO, BOULDER, 65- *Personal Data:* b Vienna, Austria, Oct 3, 33; m 60, Patricia C Meyer; c Michael, Johannes & Elizabeth. *Educ:* Univ Vienna, PhD(math), 55. *Hon Degrees:* Hon Dr, Univ Ulm, Ger, 88, Univ Paris VI, 94. *Honors & Awards:* Cole Prize Number Theory, Am Math Soc, 72. *Prof Exp:* Asst docent math, Univ Vienna, 55-56; instr, Univ Mont, 56-57; asst docent, Univ Vienna, 57-58 & 59-60; asst prof, Univ Mont, 58-59, Univ Colo, 60-61; res assoc, Columbia Univ, 61-62; docent, Univ Vienna, 62-64. *Concurrent Pos:* Univ Colo, Boulder fac fel, Univ Cambridge, 66-67; grant & invited address, Int Cong Mathematicians, Nice, 70; mem, Inst Advan Study, 70-71. *Mem:* Am Math Soc; Austrian Math Soc; corresp mem Austrian Acad Sci; Am Acad Arts & Scis. *Res:* Number theory, especially geometry of numbers and diophantine approximations. *Mailing Add:* Dept Math Univ Colo Boulder CO 80309-0395

SCHMIDT, WYMAN CARL, SILVICULTURE. *Current Pos:* from res forester to res silviculturist, 60-75, RES UNIT LEADER, INTERMOUNTAIN FOREST & RANGE EXP STA, FORESTRY SCI LAB, MONT STATE UNIV, 75-, EMER PROF, 97- *Personal Data:* b Ocheyedan, Iowa, Sept 9, 29; m 53; c 5. *Educ:* Univ Mont, BS, 58, MS, 61, PhD, 80. *Honors & Awards:* USDA Award; Sci Tech Award, Soc Am Foresters. *Prof Exp:* Forester, Black Hills Nat Forest, 59-60. *Mem:* Soc Am Foresters; Ecol Soc Am. *Res:* Autecological, synecological and silvicultural research in the coniferous forests of the northern Rocky Mountains, including forest regeneration, stand development, cone production, soil moisture, phenology and tree growth relationships; silviculture and forest ecology of subalpine forest ecosystems. *Mailing Add:* Forestry Sci Lab Mont State Univ Bozeman MT 59717-0228

SCHMIDTKE, JON ROBERT, immunology, for more information see previous edition

SCHMIDTKE, R(ICHARD) A(LLEN), MECHANICAL ENGINEERING. *Current Pos:* RETIRED. *Personal Data:* b Benton Harbor, Mich, July 27, 25; m 48, 71, Marjorie Erickson; c John, David, Terry, Joni & Nina. *Educ:* Univ Mich, BS, 48, MS, 49; Ill Inst Technol, PhD(mech eng), 53. *Honors & Awards:* Engr of the Yr, Am Soc Mech Engrs, 76. *Prof Exp:* Instr mech eng, Ill Inst Technol, 49-53, asst prof, 53; mem tech staff, Melpar, Inc, Westinghouse Air Brake Co, 53, sr mem tech staff, 53-54, sr engr, 54-55, proj engr, 55-57, res br leader, 57-58, asst to vpres res & eng, 58-60, spec asst adv develop, 60; dir appl res, Gov Prod Div, Pratt & Whitney Aircraft Div, United Technol Corp, West Palm Beach, 60-70, sr prog mgr 70-76, vpres laser progs, 76-80, vpres engine progs, 80-82. *Mem:* Am Soc Mech Engrs; Am Astronaut Soc; Am Inst Aeronaut & Astronaut; Sigma Xi. *Res:* Free-piston, turbojet, ramjet and rocket engines; heat transfer; aerodynamics; thermodynamics; applied mathematics; marine propulsion; high energy lasers. *Mailing Add:* 372 Fairway N Tequesta FL 33469. *Fax:* 561-746-6891; *E-Mail:* schmidtker@aol.com

SCHMIDT-KOENIG, KLAUS, ZOOLOGY. *Current Pos:* zool, 59-71, adj assoc prof, 71-75, PROF ZOOL, DUKE UNIV, 75- *Personal Data:* b Heidelberg, Ger, Jan 21, 30; m 59; c 3. *Educ:* Univ Freiburg, PhD(zool), 58. *Honors & Awards:* Ornithol Prize, Dutch Ornithol Soc, 95. *Prof Exp:* Fel, Max Planck Inst Physiol of Behav, Ger, 55-57, mem staff, 58-63. *Concurrent Pos:* Pvt docent, Univ Gottingen, 63-71, appl prof, 71-75; prof zool, Univ Tubingen, 75-96. *Mem:* Sigma Xi; hon fel Am Ornith Union; Deutsche Ornithol-Gesellschaft (pres); Int Soc Neurol. *Res:* Animal orientation; behavioral ecology; sensory physiology; biostatistics. *Mailing Add:* Martin Crusiusstr 7 72076 Tubingen Germany

SCHMIDT-NIELSEN, BODIL MIMI, PHYSIOLOGY. *Current Pos:* adj prof, 86-97, EMER PROF, DEPT PHYSIOL, SCH MED, UNIV FLA, GAINESVILLE, 97- *Personal Data:* b Copenhagen, Denmark, Nov 3, 18; nat US; m 39, 68; c 3. *Educ:* Copenhagen Univ, DDS, 41, DOdont, 46, PhD, 55. *Hon Degrees:* DSc, Bates Col, 83. *Honors & Awards:* Bowditch Lectr, 58. *Prof Exp:* Instr, Copenhagen Univ, 41-44, secy, res assoc & asst prof, 44-46; res assoc, Swarthmore Col, 46-48; res assoc, Stanford Univ, 48-49; res assoc, Col Med, Univ Cincinnati, 49-52, asst prof, 52; res assoc zool, Duke Univ, 52-54, sr res assoc, 54-57, assoc res prof, 57-61, assoc res prof zool & physiol, 61-64; prof biol, Case Western Res Univ, 64-71, chmn, Dept Biol, 70-71; res scientist, Mt Desert Island Biol Lab, 71-86. *Concurrent Pos:* Guggenheim fel, 52-53; established investr, Am Heart Asn, 54-62; trustee, Mt Desert Island Biol Lab, 55-69 & 76-, vpres, 79-81, dep dir, 79-, pres, 81-85; NIH career award, 62-64; mem, Physiol Training Grant Comt, Nat Inst Gen Med Sci, 67-71; adj prof, Case Western Univ, 71-75 & Brown Univ, 71-78; assoc ed, Am J Physiol, 76-81. *Mem:* Fel AAAS; Am Physiol Soc (pres, 75-76); Soc Exp Biol & Med; Am Soc Nephrology; Am Soc Zoologists; Int Soc Nephrology; Int Soc Lymphology. *Res:* Biochemistry of saliva; water metabolism of desert animals; osmoregulation; comparative physiology of cellular volume and ion regulation; comparative renal physiology; physiology of the mammalian renal pelvis. *Mailing Add:* 4426 SW 103rd Gainesville FL 32608. *Fax:* 352-371-7290

SCHMIDT-NIELSEN, KNUT, PHYSIOLOGY. *Current Pos:* prof, 52-63, JAMES B DUKE PROF PHYSIOL, DUKE UNIV, 63- *Personal Data:* b Trondheim, Norway, Sept 24, 15; m 39; c 3. *Educ:* Copenhagen Univ, Mag Sc, 41, PhD(zoophysiol), 46. *Hon Degrees:* DM, Lund Univ, 85; PhD, Univ Trondheim, Norway, 93. *Honors & Awards:* Brody Mem lectr, Univ Mo, 62; Hans Gadow lectr, Univ Cambridge, 71; Int Prize Biol, Japan Soc Prom Sci, 92. *Prof Exp:* Res assoc, Swarthmore Col, 46-48; res assoc, Stanford Univ, 48-49; asst prof, Col Med, Univ Cincinnati, 49-52. *Concurrent Pos:* Docent, Univ Oslo, 47-49; Guggenheim fel, Univ Algeria, 53-54; consult, NSF, 57-61; trustee, Mt Desert Island Biol Lab, 58-61; sect ed, Am J Physiol & J Appl Physiol, 61-64; mem sci adv comt, New Eng Regional Primate Res Ctr, Harvard Med Sch, 62-66; regent's lectr, Univ Calif, 63; nat adv bd, Physiol Res Lab, Scripps Inst, Univ Calif, 63-69, chmn, 68-69; USPHS res career award, 64-85; mem subcomt environ physiol, US Nat Comt Int Biol Prog, 65-67; mem comt res utilization uncommon animals, Div Biol & Agr, Nat Acad Sci, 66-68; US Nat Comt Int Union Physiol Sci, 66-73, vchmn, 69-78; animal resources adv comt, NIH, 68; biomed eng adv comt, Duke Univ, 68-85; sect ed, Am J Physiol & J Appl Physiol, 61-64; ed, J Exp Biol, 75-79, 83-86; vis Agassiz prof, Harvard Univ, 77, vis prof, Nairobi, 77, Wellcome vis prof, Univ SDak, 88. *Mem:* Nat Acad Sci; fel AAAS; Am Acad Arts & Sci; Am Physiol Soc; fel NY Acad Sci; Royal Norweg Acad Arts & Sci; foreign mem Physiol Soc London; French Acad Sci; Norweg Acad Sci; Royal Danish Acad; Int Union Physiol Soc (pres, 80-86). *Res:* Comparative physiology, respiration and oxygen supply; water metabolism and excretion; temperature regulation, physiology of desert animals. *Mailing Add:* Dept Zool Duke Univ Durham NC 27708-0325

SCHMIEDER, ROBERT W, ATOMIC PHYSICS, MARINE SCIENCES. *Current Pos:* MEM TECH STAFF, SANDIA NAT LABS, 72-; FOUNDING DIR & EXPED LEADER, CORDELL EXPEDS, 77- *Personal Data:* b Phoenix, Ariz, July 10, 41; m 63; c 3. *Educ:* Occidental Col, AB, 63; Calif Inst Technol, BS, 63; Columbia Univ, MA, 65, PhD(physics), 68. *Prof Exp:* Staff researcher, Lawrence Berkeley Lab, 69-72. *Concurrent Pos:* Instr, Univ Calif, Berkeley, 71-72; NATO Summer Inst, Cargese, France, 87; ed, Defense Res Rev, 86-; prog comm, Int Comb Symp, 82, 84 & 88. *Mem:* Am Phys Soc; Am Geophys Union; Am Inst Biol Sci. *Res:* Physics of highly ionized atoms; combustion physics and chemistry; marine biology and ecology; author of numerous technical articles and 5 books; expeditions to remote locations (Antarctica, Easter Island, Heard Island, etc); radio science. *Mailing Add:* Sandia Nat Labs MS 9214 Livermore CA 94551. *Fax:* 510-294-2234; *E-Mail:* cordell@ccnet.com

SCHMIEDESHOFF, FREDERICK WILLIAM, research administration, applied mechanics; deceased, see previous edition for last biography

SCHMIEDESHOFF, GEORGE M, CONDENSED MATTER PHYSICS, MAGNETISM. *Current Pos:* asst prof, 92-96, ASSOC PROF PHYSICS, OCCIDENTAL COL, 96- *Personal Data:* b Bridgeport, Conn, Nov 8, 55. *Educ:* Univ Bridgeport, BS, 79; Univ Mass, MS, 82, PhD(physics), 85. *Prof Exp:* Int Bus Mach postdoctoral fel physics, Mass Inst Tech, 85-87; lectr physics, Tufts Univ, 87; vis asst prof physics, Bowdoin Col, 87-92. *Concurrent Pos:* Vis scientist, Nat High Magnetic Field Lab, 96-; consult, Los Alamos Nat Lab, 96- *Mem:* Am Phys Soc; Am Asn Physics Teachers; Coun Undergrad Res. *Res:* Experimental studies of magnetic properties of novel superconducting and magnetic materials at low temperatures and in high magnetic fields. *Mailing Add:* Physics Dept Occidental Col Los Angeles CA 90041. *Fax:* 213-259-2958; *E-Mail:* gms@oxy.edu

SCHMIEG, GLENN MELWOOD, PUBLIC SCIENCE LECTURES, SCIENTIFIC TESTIMONY. *Current Pos:* DISTINGUISHED LECTR SCI, OPPORTUNITIES IN SCI, INC, BEMIDJI, MN, 91- *Personal Data:* b Detroit, Mich, Aug 25, 38; div; c Kirk M & Rhiannon E. *Educ:* Univ Mich, BSE, 60, MS, 62; Univ NC, PhD(physics), 67. *Prof Exp:* Physics prof, Univ Wis-Milwaukee, 67-90. *Concurrent Pos:* Expert witness. *Mem:* Am Asn Physics Teachers; Electrostatics Soc Am. *Res:* Classical field theory; electrostatics; mathematical physics. *Mailing Add:* 3224A N Oakland Milwaukee WI 53211

SCHMIEGEL, WALTER WERNER, RUBBER CHEMISTRY, FLUOROELASTOMER CHEMISTRY. *Current Pos:* Res chemist, E I du Pont De Nemours & Co Inc, 69-80, res assoc, 80-88, sr res assoc, 88-96, SR RES ASSOC, DUPONT-DOW ELASTOMERS, 96- *Personal Data:* b Chemnitz, Ger, Jan 13, 41; US citizen; m 71, Karol A Grubbs. *Educ:* Univ Mich, Ann Arbor, BS, 63; Dartmouth Col, AM, 65; Johns Hopkins Univ, PhD(chem), 70. *Mem:* Am Chem Soc. *Res:* Synthetic elastomers; Ziegler catalysis; fluoroelastomer synthesis and reactivity; vulcanization chemistry; polymer nuclear magnetic resonance. *Mailing Add:* DuPont Dow Elastomers ESL 293/206 Wilmington DE 19880-0293

SCHMIR, GASTON L, BIOCHEMISTRY, ORGANIC CHEMISTRY. *Current Pos:* from instr to assoc prof biochem, 60-69, from assoc prof to prof, 69-85, EMER PROF MOLECULAR BIOPHYS, YALE UNIV, 85- *Personal Data:* b Metz, France, June 8, 33; US citizen; m 60, Barbara Chesney; c Miriam, Lisa & Nina. *Educ:* Harvard Univ, AB, 54; Yale Univ, PhD(biochem), 58. *Prof Exp:* Asst scientist, USPHS, 58-60. *Mem:* Am Chem Soc; Am Soc Biol Chemists. *Res:* Bio-organic reaction mechanisms; enzyme models. *Mailing Add:* Dept Molecular Biophys & Biochem Yale Univ Sch Med 260 Whitney Ave PO Box 6666 New Haven CT 06511

SCHMISSEUR, WILSON EDWARD, FARM MANAGEMENT, PRODUCTION ECONOMICS. *Current Pos:* Res assoc, 71-79, asst prof, 79-81, ASSOC PROF AGR ECON, ORE STATE UNIV, 81- *Personal Data:* b East St Louis, Ill, July 17, 42; m 69; c 2. *Educ:* Univ Ill, BS, 64; Purdue Univ, MS, 66, PhD(agr econ), 73. *Concurrent Pos:* Consult, Ethanol Int, Inc, 79. *Mem:* Am Asn Artificial Intel. *Res:* Economics of livestock production; expert systems for commercial livestock management. *Mailing Add:* 321 NW 33rd St Corvallis OR 97330

SCHMIT, JOSEPH LAWRENCE, PHYSICS, CRYSTAL GROWTH. *Current Pos:* CONSULT, 90- *Personal Data:* b Cold Springs, Minn, July 22, 33; m 56, Marilyn Scholl; c Theresa (Stergios), Stephen, Mary (Manning), Thomas, Timothy & Christopher. *Educ:* St John's Univ, BA, 57. *Prof Exp:* Res scientist physics, Honeywell Sensors & Signal Processing Lab, 59-89; staff scientist, Loral, 89-90. *Concurrent Pos:* Co-chair, MCT Workshop, 88; sr Gledden fel, Univ Western Australia, 93. *Mem:* Am Phys Soc; AAAS; Fedn Am Scientists. *Res:* Growth and evaluation of HgCdTe suitable for infrared detectors; growth by Bridgman, by open tube slider LPE and metal-organic chemical vapor deposition; developed technique to measure composition, measurement of the band gap and calculation of the intrinsic carrier concentration of HgCdTe; growth of HgCdTe by MOCVD on GaAs; growth and characterization of HgCdTe. *Mailing Add:* 3607 Farmington Rd Minnetonka MN 55305. *Fax:* 612-935-1005

SCHMIT, LUCIEN A(NDRE), JR, STRUCTURAL SYNTHESIS, DESIGN OPTIMIZATION. *Current Pos:* prof eng & appl sci, 70-91, chmn, Dept Mech & Struct, 76-79, EMER ROCKWELL PROF AEROSPACE ENG, UNIV CALIF, LOS ANGELES, 91- *Personal Data:* b New York, NY, May 5, 28; m 51, Eleanor C Trabish; c Lucien A III. *Educ:* Mass Inst Technol, SB, 49, SM, 50. *Honors & Awards:* Walter L Huber Civil Eng Res Prize, 70; Struct Design Lect Award, Am Inst Aeronaut & Astronaut, 77, Struct Dynamics & Mat Award, 79. *Prof Exp:* Struct engr, Grumman Aircraft Eng Corp, 51-53; res engr, Aeroelastic & Struct Res Lab, Mass Inst Technol, 54-58; from asst prof to prof struct, Case Western Res Univ, 58-69, Wilbert J Austin distinguished prof eng, 69-70, head div solid mech, struct & mech design, 66-70. *Concurrent Pos:* Mem, Sci Adv Bd, USAF, 77-84. *Mem:* Nat Acad Eng; fel Am Inst Aeronaut & Astronaut; fel Am Soc Civil Engrs; fel Am Acad Mech. *Res:* Analysis and synthesis of structural systems; design optimization; finite element methods; nonlinear analysis; design methods for fiber composite structures; control augmented structural synthesis. *Mailing Add:* 545 Third Ave S Edmonds WA 98020

SCHMITENDORF, WILLIAM E, ENGINEERING. *Current Pos:* CHMN MECH ENG & AEROSPACE DEPT, UNIV CALIF, 88- *Personal Data:* b Oak Park, Ill, Aug 6, 41; m 64; c 2. *Educ:* Purdue Univ, BS, 63, MS, 65, PhD(optimization tech), 68. *Prof Exp:* From asst prof to prof, Mech Eng, Northwestern Univ, 67-88. *Concurrent Pos:* Assoc ed, Inst Elec & Electronics Engrs, Transactions Automatic Control, 80- & J Optimization Theory, 80- *Mem:* Inst Elec & Electronics Engrs. *Res:* Optimal control problems; zero-sum and nonzero-sum differential games; optimization problems with vector-valued criteria; controllability problems; minmox problems. *Mailing Add:* Mech & Aerospace Eng Univ Calif Irvine CA 92717

SCHMITT, CHARLES RUDOLPH, APPLIED CHEMISTRY. *Current Pos:* SR SCIENTIST, BECHTEL CORP, OAK RIDGE, TENN, 81- *Personal Data:* b New York, NY, Mar 31, 20; m 45, Alma Peters; c Charles J & Katherine A. *Educ:* Queens Col, NY, BS, 42. *Prof Exp:* Supvr, Plum Brook Ord Works, Sandusky, Ohio, 42-43; pross mech, Spec Eng Detachment, US Army, Oak Ridge, Tenn, 44-45; tech engr, K-25 Plant, Union Carbide Corp, Oak Ridge, Tenn, 46-49, develop engr & specialist, 50-75, supvr develop, Y-12 Plant, 75-80. *Concurrent Pos:* Consult, Rust Eng Co, 70-75. *Mem:* Am Chem Soc; Nat Asn Corrosion Engrs; Am Nuclear Soc. *Res:* Polymerization of polyfurfuryl alcohol resins; dezincification of brass in sea water; metallurgy studies of high purity tungsten; uranium solubility and corrosion studies; water treatment for scale and corrosion control, treatment of chemical and radioactive wastes. *Mailing Add:* 110 Adelphi Rd Oak Ridge TN 37830

SCHMITT, DONALD PETER, AGRICULTURE, BOTANY & PHYTOPATHOLOGY. *Current Pos:* PLANT PATHOLOGIST & NEMATOLOGIST, DEPT PLANT PATH, UNIV HAWAII, 90- *Personal Data:* b New Hampton, Iowa, Oct 29, 41; m 67, Mary A Correa; c Julia M, Peter, Anna M & Cecilia M. *Educ:* Iowa State Univ, BS, 67, MS, 69, PhD(plant path), 71. *Prof Exp:* Plant pathologist & nematologist plant disease, Div Plant Industs, Tenn Dept Agr, 71-75; plant pathologist & nematologist soybeans, Dept Plant Path, NC State Univ, 75-90. *Mem:* Am Phytopath Soc; Soc Nematologists; Sigma Xi; Orgn Trop Am Nematologists. *Res:* Ecology of nematodes on tropical crops; epidemiology of diseases of tropical crops caused by nematodes; management of diseases caused by nematodes. *Mailing Add:* Dept Plant Path Univ Hawaii Manoa Honolulu HI 96822-2270. *Fax:* 808-956-2832

SCHMITT, ERICH, COMPUTER SCIENCE. *Current Pos:* ASSOC PROF COMPUT SCI, STATE UNIV NY, BUFFALO, 68- *Personal Data:* b Sandhausen, Ger, Jan 7, 28; m 56; c 1. *Educ:* Univ Karlsruhe, Dipl Ing, 60, Dr Ing(elec eng), 64, Venia legendi, 67. *Prof Exp:* Dir res dept, Inst Info Processing, Univ Karlsruhe, 64-67; chief adv avionics, Bell Aerosysts Co, 67-68. *Mem:* Asn Comput Mach; Inst Elec & Electronics Engrs. *Res:* Adaptive computing methods; pattern recognition; automatic design; theory of adaptive automata; information theory and coding. *Mailing Add:* Dept Elec/Comput Eng State Univ NY Buffalo Buffalo NY 14214

SCHMITT, FRANCIS OTTO, molecular neurobiology; deceased, see previous edition for last biography

SCHMITT, GEORGE FREDERICK, JR, EROSION OF MATERIALS DUE TO IMPINGEMENT, RESPONSE OF MATERIALS TO HIGH ENERGY LASERS. *Current Pos:* Lt high temperature coatings, USAF, 63-66, proj eng erosion res mat, Mat Lab, 66-81, group leader coatings & protective mat, 81-83, tech area mgr laser hardened mat, 83-86, prog mgr space survivability, 86-90, actg chief plans & progs, 90-91, ASST DIR NONMETALLIC MAT, MAT LAB, USAF, 91- *Personal Data:* b Louisville, Ky, Nov 3, 39; m 65, Ann Cheatham; c Galen & Brandon. *Educ:* Univ Louisville, Ky, BChE, 62, MChE, 63; Ohio State Univ, MBA, 66; Air War Col, dipl strategy, 69. *Honors & Awards:* Merit Award, Am Soc Testing Mat. *Concurrent Pos:* Chmn, Comt G-2, Am Soc Testing & Mat, 77-80; mem, Comt Erosion in Energy Systs, Nat Mat Adv Bd, 79-80; rep, USAF & Govt Int Exchange Agreements, 83- *Mem:* Fel Soc Advan Mat & Process Engrs (pres, 81-82); Am Inst Aeronaut & Astronaut; fel Am Soc Testing & Mat (secy, 72-76); Am Chem Soc; Soc Photo-Optical Instrumentation Engrs. *Res:* Response of materials to impingement of rain, dust and ice at subsonic to hypersonic velocities, materials included plastics, composites, ceramics, elastomers and metals; published 30 technical reports and 60 articles; polymer materials applications; nonmetallic materials for aerospace. *Mailing Add:* 1500 Wardmier Dr Dayton OH 45459-3354. *Fax:* 937-255-9020

SCHMITT, GEORGE JOSEPH, POLYMER CHEMISTRY. *Current Pos:* res dir, Corp Struct Polymer Lab, 81-93, RES DIR COMPOSITES, METALS, CERAMICS, ALLIED-SIGNAL CORP, 93- *Personal Data:* b Farmingdale, NY, June 21, 28; m 52, Christine Schneider; c Paul, Carol, Mark & David. *Educ:* Polytech Inst Brooklyn, BS, 50; State Univ NY Col Forestry, Syracuse Univ, PhD(chem), 60. *Prof Exp:* Develop chemist, Am Cyanamid Co, 53-57; sr res chemist, cent res lab, Allied Chem Corp, 60-61, res supvr polymer chem, Allied Corp, 61-62, dir lab res, 62-64, asst dir, Cent Res Lab, 64-68, mgr polymer sci, Corp Res Lab, 68-80. *Concurrent Pos:* Mem bd dirs, Res & Develop Coun, NJ, 81-84. *Mem:* Am Chem Soc; Sigma Xi; Soc Advan Mat & Process Eng. *Res:* Free radical, ionic and condensation polymerization; fibers; polymer composites; membranes; electrically conducting polymers; biopolymers. *Mailing Add:* 104 Green Ave Madison NJ 07940-2534

SCHMITT, HAROLD WILLIAM, ATOMIC PHYSICS, TECHNOLOGY MANAGEMENT. *Current Pos:* PROF ENG MGT, UNIV TENN, 90-, DIR INDUST PROG TECHNOL TRANSFER, 95- *Personal Data:* b Sequin, Tex, Aug 11, 28; m 52, Jonell Britsch; c Carol (Behm), Laine (Harrington) & Joy D. *Educ:* Univ Tex, BA, 48, MA, 52, PhD(physics), 54. *Prof Exp:* Asst physics, Los Alamos Sci Lab, 52-54; physicist, Oak Ridge Nat Lab, 58-73, group leader, Physics of Fission Group, 60-73; pres, Environ Systs Corp, 73-81, Atom Sci Inc, 81-89. *Concurrent Pos:* Founding pres & chmn bd dirs, Ortec, Inc, 60-64; guest scientist, Nuclear Res Ctr, Karlsruhe, Ger, 66-67; guest prof, Munich Tech Univ, 69 & Univ Frankfurt, 70; consult, 89- *Mem:* AAAS; fel Am Phys Soc; Sigma Xi; Am Soc Eng Mgt; Am Soc Eng Educ. *Res:* Fission physics; neutron physics; nuclear reactions; accelerators; reactors; detectors; instrumentation; atomic physics; elemental analysis; energy and environmental sciences; technology management; technology strategy. *Mailing Add:* 121 Canterbury Rd Oak Ridge TN 37830. *Fax:* 423-974-2805; *E-Mail:* hschmitt@utn.edu

SCHMITT, HARRISON HAGAN, GEOLOGY, ASTRONAUTICS. *Current Pos:* CONSULT, 83- *Personal Data:* b Santa Rita, NMex, July 3, 35. *Educ:* Calif Inst Technol, BA, 57; Harvard Univ, PhD, 64. *Honors & Awards:* Gilbert Award, Geol Soc Am, 89. *Prof Exp:* Fulbright fel, Univ Oslo, 57-58; geologist, US Geol Surv, 64-65; astronaut, NASA, 65, lunar module pilot, Apollo 17, 72, spec asst to adminr, 74; asst adminr, Off Energy Prog, 74; mem, US Senate, NMex, 77-83. *Concurrent Pos:* Bd dir, Nord Resources, Sunwest Fin Servs, Orbital Scis Corp; mem, Press Ethics Comn, 89, Army Sci Bd, 85- *Mem:* Am Inst Aeronaut & Astronaut; AAAS; Geol Soc Am; Am Geophys Union; Petrol Geologists. *Res:* Geology; astronautics. *Mailing Add:* PO Box 14338 Albuquerque NM 87191-4338

SCHMITT, JOHANNA, PLANT POPULATION BIOLOGY, ECOLOGICAL GENETICS. *Current Pos:* asst prof, 82-87, ASSOC PROF BIOL, BROWN UNIV, 87- *Personal Data:* b Philadelphia, Pa, Mar 12, 53; m 83. *Educ:* Swarthmore Col, BA, 74; Stanford Univ, PhD(biol sci), 81. *Prof Exp:* Postdoctoral res assoc, Duke Univ, 81-82. *Concurrent Pos:* Prin investr, NSF, 84-; assoc ed, Evolution, 90-92; coun mem, Soc Study Evolution, 90-92. *Mem:* Soc Study Evolution; Ecol Soc Am; Am Soc Naturalists; Bot Soc Am; Soc Conserv Biol; AAAS. *Res:* Plant population biology; ecological genetics; breeding system evolution; density-dependent phenomena; gene flow and population structure; evolutionary and ecological consequences of maternal effects. *Mailing Add:* Biol Dept Brown Univ Box G-W Providence RI 02912

SCHMITT, JOHN ARVID, JR, medical mycology; deceased, see previous edition for last biography

SCHMITT, JOHN LEIGH, INSTRUMENTATION, NUCLEATION. *Current Pos:* vis asst prof, Univ Mo, Rolla, 74-76, res asst prof physics, 76-85, res assoc prof physics & cloud physics, 85-90, ASSOC PROF PHYSICS, UNIV MO, ROLLA, 90- *Personal Data:* b Newberry, Mich, July 30, 41; m 66; c 1. *Educ:* Mich Col Mining & Technol, BS, 63; Univ Mich, MS, 64, PhD(astron), 68. *Prof Exp:* Fel & part-time lectr astron, Univ Toronto, 68-69; asst prof physics, Southwestern at Memphis, 69-74. *Mem:* Am Astron Soc; Am Meteorol Soc; Am Chem Soc. *Res:* Vapor to liquid nucleation, cloud chambers and optical instrumentation. *Mailing Add:* Cloud & Aerosol Sci Lab Univ Mo Rolla MO 65401. *E-Mail:* Jschmitt@physics.umr.edu

SCHMITT, JOSEPH LAWRENCE, JR, PHYSICAL CHEMISTRY. *Current Pos:* DIR, CYTEC INDUST, 93-, DIR, CORP RES, 96- *Personal Data:* b Cumberland, Md, Sept 22, 41; m 63; c 2. *Educ:* Shippensburg State Col, BS, 63; Bowling Green State Univ, MA, 67; Pa State Univ, PhD(fuel sci), 70. *Prof Exp:* Teacher pub sch, Pa, 63-67; res chemist, Am Cyanamid Co, 70-74, sr res chemist, 74-77, proj leader, 77-85, mgr, 85-86, dir, 86-93. *Mem:* Am Chem Soc; AAAS; Sigma Xi. *Res:* Heterogeneous catalysis; surface chemistry; carbon chemistry. *Mailing Add:* Four Settlers Rd Bethel CT 06801

SCHMITT, JOSEPH MICHAEL, POLYMER CHEMISTRY. *Current Pos:* RETIRED. *Personal Data:* b Louisville, Ky, Feb 9, 30; m 52; c 6. *Educ:* Univ Louisville, BS, 51, PhD(chem), 57. *Prof Exp:* Res chemist, Am Cynamid Co, 57-62, sr res chemist, 62-67, prin chemist, 67-92. *Mem:* Am Chem Soc. *Res:* Plastics; homopolymers, copolymers, multipolymer blends and properties; flocculants; polymers for water treatment. *Mailing Add:* PO Box 336 Ridgefield CT 06877

SCHMITT, KLAUS, MATHEMATICS. *Current Pos:* from asst prof to assoc prof, 67-75, chmn dept, 88-91, PROF MATH, UNIV UTAH, 75- *Personal Data:* b Rimbach, Ger, May 14, 40; US citizen; m 85, Claudia Memoli; c Susan E & Michael K. *Educ:* St Olaf Col, BA, 62; Univ Nebr, MA, 64, PhD(math), 67. *Honors & Awards:* Alexander von Humboldt Prize, 79. *Prof Exp:* Asst prof math, Nebr Wesleyan Univ, 66-67. *Concurrent Pos:* Res grants, NASA, 67, NSF, 69-71, 78-; & US Army, 71-78; vis prof, Univ Wurzburg & Univ Karlsruhe, Ger, 73-74, Univ Bremen, T U Berlin, Univ Louvain, Univ Heidelberg, Univ Zurich. *Mem:* Math Asn Am; Am Math Soc. *Res:* Differential equations; nonlinear analysis; functional differential equations. *Mailing Add:* Dept Math Univ Utah Salt Lake City UT 84112. *Fax:* 801-581-4148

SCHMITT, MICHAEL A, AGRONOMY. *Current Pos:* PROF, SOIL SCI DEPT, UNIV MINN, ST PAUL. *Honors & Awards:* Ciba-Geigy Agronomy Award, Am Soc Agron, 92. *Mailing Add:* Soil Sci Dept Univ Minn 439 Borlaug Hall St Paul MN 55108

SCHMITT, NEIL MARTIN, BIOMEDICAL ENGINEERING. *Current Pos:* assoc prof, 70-80, PROF ELEC ENG, UNIV ARK, FAYETTEVILLE, 80- *Personal Data:* b Pekin, Ill, Oct 25, 40; m 63; c 2. *Educ:* Univ Ark, Fayetteville, BSEE, 63, MSEE, 64; Southern Methodist Univ, PhD(elec eng), 69. *Prof Exp:* Systs engr, IBM Corp, 64-67; engr, Tex Instruments, Inc, 67-70. *Concurrent Pos:* NSF res grant elec eng, Univ Ark, Fayetteville, 71-72. *Mem:* Inst Elec & Electronics Engrs; Biomed Eng Soc; Asn Advan Med Instrumentation; Am Soc Eng Educ. *Res:* Health care delivery systems; early detection of heart disease. *Mailing Add:* Eng Ctr 4185 Univ Ark Fayetteville AR 72701

SCHMITT, OTTO HERBERT, BIOPHYSICS, BIOMEDICAL ENGINEERING. *Current Pos:* from instr to prof zool & physics, Univ Minn, Minneapolis, 39-80, prof biophys, 49-80, prof elec eng, 68-80, prof biomed eng, 73-87, EMER PROF BIOMED ENG, UNIV MINN, MINNEAPOLIS, 87- *Personal Data:* b St Louis, Mo, Apr 6, 13; m 37. *Educ:* Wash Univ, AB, 34, PhD(physics, zool), 37. *Honors & Awards:* Lovelace Award, 60; Morlock Award, Inst Elec & Electronics Engrs, 63, Centennial Medal, 87; Wetherill Medal, Franklin Inst, 72, Franklin Inst Medal, 84. *Prof Exp:* Nat Res Coun fel, Univ Col, London, 38 & Sir Halley Stewart fel, 39. *Concurrent Pos:* Off investr, Nat Defense Res Comt Contract, 40-42; res engr, Columbia Univ, 42-43; supvr engr, Spec Devices Div, Airborne Instruments Lab, NY, 43-47; consult, USPHS & Inst Defense Anal; chmn, Exec Coun Bioastronaut, Joint Armed Forces-Nat Acad Sci, 58-61. *Mem:* Nat Acad Eng; fel Am Phys Soc; Biophys Soc; Am Physiol Soc; Am Inst Aeronaut & Astronaut. *Res:* Nerve impulse mechanisms; tridimensional oscilloscopic displays; bivalent computers; biological tissue impedance analyses; direct current transformers; trigger circuits; electronic plethysmography; antenna radiation pattern measurements; stereo vector electrocardiography; phase space displays; bioastronautics; biomimetics; electromagneto biology; technical optimization of biomedical communication and control systems; strand epidemiology; development of biometric science and technology; personally portable whole life medical history; computerized electrosurgery. *Mailing Add:* 1912 Como Ave SE Minneapolis MN 55414-2525

SCHMITT, RAYMOND W, JR, PHYSICAL OCEANOGRAPHY, FLUIDS. *Current Pos:* fel, Woods Hole Oceanog Inst, 78-79, investr, 79-80, from asst to assoc scientist, 80-94, SR SCIENTIST, WOODS HOLE OCEANOG INST, 94- *Personal Data:* b Pittsburgh, Pa, Mar 18, 50; m 81; c 3. *Educ:* Carnegie-Mellon Univ, BS, 72; Univ RI, PhD(oceanog), 78. *Prof Exp:* Res assoc, Grad Sch Oceanog, Univ RI, 77-78. *Concurrent Pos:* Vis scientist, Div Oceanog, CSIRO, Hobart, Tasmania, 87-88. *Mem:* Am Geophys Union; AAAS; Am Meteorol Soc. *Res:* Oceanic mixing and microstructure; double-diffusive convection (salt fingers); geophysical fluid dynamics; ocean circulation and climate; global water cycle. *Mailing Add:* Woods Hole Oceanog Inst Clark Rm 349 B MS 21 Woods Hole MA 02543

SCHMITT, ROLAND WALTER, SOLID STATE PHYSICS. *Current Pos:* RETIRED. *Personal Data:* b Seguin, Tex, July 24, 23; m 51, 57; c 4. *Educ:* Univ Tex, BA & BS, 47, MA, 48; Rice Inst, PhD(physics), 51. *Hon Degrees:* Dr, Univ Pa, Worcester Polytech Inst & Union Col, 85, Lehigh Univ, 86 & Univ SC, 88; DSC, Union Col, 92, Rensselaer Polytech Inst, 88-93. *Prof Exp:* Res assoc physics, Res Lab, Gen Elec Co, 51-57, mgr, Mat Studies Sect, 57-65; res assoc, Div Eng & Appl Physics, Grad Sch Pub Admin, Harvard Univ, 65; mgr, Metall & Ceramics Lab, Gen Elec Res & Develop Ctr, 66-68, res & develop mgr phys sci & eng, 68-74, energy sci & eng, from vpres to sr vpres corp res & develop, 78-86, sr vpres sci & technol, 86-88; pres, Rensselaer Polytech Inst, 88-93. *Concurrent Pos:* Mem, Liaison Subcomt Mgt & Technol, Nat Acad Sci Adv Comt IIASA, Panel Condensed Matter, Physics Surv Comt & Comt on Surv Mat Sci & Eng; mem, Energy Adv Bd, Walt Disney Enterprises; past mem, adv bds, Univ Tex & Univ Va; chmn eval panel, Inst Basic Stands, Nat Bur Stands; mem, Nat Res Coun Solid State Sci Comt & Comt Nat Progs, Numerical Data Adv Bd; mem coun, Nat Acad Eng, 83-89; pres elect & mem bd dirs, Indust Res Inst; chmn, Nat Sci Bd, NSF, 84-88 & Coun Res & Technol; dir & mem bd dirs, Gen Signal Corp; dir, Coun Superconductivity Am Competitiveness; chmn, Res Priority Panel Future Space Sci, Nat Res Coun, 94-95. *Mem:* Nat Acad Eng; fel Am Phys Soc; fel AAAS; fel Am Acad Arts & Sci; fel Inst Elec & Electronics Engrs; foreign mem Royal Swed Acad Eng Sci; foreign assoc Eng Acad Japan. *Mailing Add:* 776 Riverview Rd Rexford NY 12148-1340

SCHMITT, ROMAN A, COSMO-CHEMISTRY, GEOCHEMISTRY. *Current Pos:* assoc prof, 66-69, prof chem, 69-93, prof geol & oceanog, 85-93, EMER PROF CHEM, GEOL & OCEANOG, ORE STATE UNIV, 93- *Personal Data:* b Johnsburg, Ill, Nov 13, 25; m 54, Jean Vertovec; c Joseph, Mary, Peter & Katherine. *Educ:* Univ Chicago, MS, 50, PhD(nuclear chem), 53. *Honors & Awards:* George P Merrill Award, Nat Acad Sci, 72. *Prof Exp:* Instr nuclear chem, Univ Ill, 53-54, res assoc, 54-56; res scientist chem, Gen Atomic Div, Gen Dynamics Corp, 56-66. *Concurrent Pos:* Consult, NASA, 71-75. *Mem:* Fel AAAS; Geochem Soc; fel Meteoritical Soc. *Res:* Neutron activation analysis of rare earth elements and other elements in meteorites; terrestrial and lunar matter; cosmochemistry; geochemistry. *Mailing Add:* Radiation Ctr Ore State Univ Corvallis OR 97331

SCHMITTER, RUTH ELIZABETH, CELL BIOLOGY, PHYCOLOGY. *Current Pos:* ASSOC PROF BIOL, ALBION COL, 82- *Personal Data:* b Detroit, Mich. *Educ:* Mich State Univ, BS, 64; Univ Edinburgh, MSc, 66; Harvard Univ, PhD(biol), 73. *Prof Exp:* Sr technician electron micros, AEC Plant Res Lab, Mich State Univ, 66-67; res fel biol, Harvard Univ, 73-74; Brown fel bot, Yale Univ, 74-75; asst prof biol, Univ Mass, Boston, 75-82. *Concurrent Pos:* Fulbright scholar, Inst Educ, 64-66; vis assoc prof, Univ Okla, 88. *Mem:* Am Soc Cell Biol; Am Phycol Soc; Electron Micros Soc Am; Brit Phycol Soc; Int Soc Protozoologists; Hastings Ctr. *Res:* Cell ultrastructure, especially functional correlates of dinoflagellate fine structure, and organelle development; algal physiology, including algal nutrition; biochemistry of bioluminescence. *Mailing Add:* Dept Biol Albion Col 611 E Porter St Albion MI 49224-1831. *Fax:* 517-629-0509

SCHMITTHENNER, AUGUST FREDRICK, PLANT PATHOLOGY. *Current Pos:* From instr to assoc prof, 52-66, PROF PLANT PATH, OHIO AGR RES & DEVELOP CTR & OHIO STATE UNIV, 66- *Personal Data:* b Kotagiri, SIndia, Apr 16, 26; US citizen; m 54; c 2. *Educ:* Gettysburg Col, BA, 49; Ohio State Univ, MSc, 51, PhD(bot), 58. *Mem:* Am Phytopath Soc; Sigma Xi. *Res:* Forage crop, soybean and root rot diseases; physiology of oomycetes and parasitism; photobiology; bean diseases. *Mailing Add:* 311 Elm Dr Wooster OH 44691-2209

SCHMITZ, EUGENE H, INVERTEBRATE ZOOLOGY. *Current Pos:* from asst prof to assoc prof, 65-74, prof, 74-94, EMER PROF ZOOL, UNIV ARK, FAYETTEVILLE, 94- *Personal Data:* b Wamego, Kans, Aug 13, 34; m 62, Doris A Geisler; c Eugene & Harold. *Educ:* Univ Kans, AB, 56; Univ Colo, MA, 58, PhD(zool), 61. *Prof Exp:* Instr biol, Univ Colo, 59-60; from asst prof to assoc prof zool, La State Univ, 61-65. *Concurrent Pos:* Ed, Trans Am Micros Soc, 79-95. *Mem:* Soc Integrative & Comp Biol; Am Micros Soc (pres, 97). *Res:* Invertebrate microscopic anatomy. *Mailing Add:* Dept Biol Sci Univ Ark Fayetteville AR 72701. *Fax:* 501-575-4010; *E-Mail:* eschmitz@mercury.uark.edu

SCHMITZ, FRANCIS JOHN, NATURAL PRODUCTS CHEMISTRY, MARINE CHEMISTRY. *Current Pos:* from asst prof to assoc prof, 63-71, PROF CHEM, UNIV OKLA, 71- *Personal Data:* b Raymond, Iowa, Jan 18, 32; m 61, Phoebe E Chapman; c 3. *Educ:* Maryknoll Sem, BA, 54; Loras Col, BS, 58; Univ Calif, Berkeley, PhD, 61. *Prof Exp:* NIH fel, Stanford Univ, 61-62, NSF fel, 62-63. *Mem:* Am Chem Soc; The Chem Soc; Am Soc Pharmacog. *Res:* Structure determination of natural products, emphasis on marine natural products; synthesis of natural products. *Mailing Add:* Dept Chem Univ Okla 620 Parrington Oval Norman OK 73019

SCHMITZ, GEORGE WILLIAM, AGRONOMY. *Current Pos:* assoc prof, 66-72, prof agron, 72-87, EMER PROF PLANT & SOIL SCI, CALIF STATE POLYTECH UNIV, POMONA, 87- *Personal Data:* b Minneapolis, Minn, Dec 15, 19. *Educ:* Univ Ariz, BS, 48; Ohio State Univ, MS, 50, PhD(soils), 52. *Prof Exp:* Sr agronomist, Zonolite Res Lab, 52-56; res agronomist, Calif Spray Chem Corp Div, Stand Oil Co, Calif, 56-60; asst prof agron, Fresno State Col, 60-66. *Res:* Soil fertility; plant physiology. *Mailing Add:* Dept Hort Plant & Soil Sci Calif State Polytech Univ 3801 W Temple Ave Pomona CA 91768

SCHMITZ, HAROLD GREGORY, ELECTRICAL ENGINEERING. *Current Pos:* CONSULT, 91-; SOFTWARE ENG MGR, FMC CORP. *Personal Data:* b Helena, Mont, Aug 31, 43; m 66; c 4. *Educ:* Carroll Col, Mont, BA, 65; Mont State Univ, BS, 66, MS, 67, PhD(elec eng), 70. *Prof Exp:* Res engr, Mont State Univ, 69-70; prin investr comput technol, Honeywell Systs & Res Ctr, 70-76, sect chief comput systs technol, Honeywell, Inc, 76-89; vpres & gen mgr, Secure Comput Technol Corp, 89-91. *Mem:* Inst Elec & Electronics Engrs. *Res:* Research and advanced development in the area of computer architecture and organization. *Mailing Add:* FMC Corp 4800 E River Rd MS M233 Minneapolis MN 55421

SCHMITZ, HENRY, ORGANIC CHEMISTRY. *Current Pos:* RETIRED. *Personal Data:* b Vienna, Austria, Oct 2, 17; nat US; m 40; c 2. *Educ:* NY Univ, BA, 47; Rutgers Univ, MS & PhD(org chem), 50. *Prof Exp:* Res chemist, J T Baker Chem Co, Vick Chem Co, 50-55; sr res scientist, Bristol Labs Div, Bristol-Myers Co, 55-81. *Concurrent Pos:* Adj prof, Onondaga Community Col, Syracuse, 80-88. *Mem:* Am Chem Soc; Sigma Xi. *Res:* Steroids; antibiotics; natural products. *Mailing Add:* 323 DeForest Rd Syracuse NY 13214-2002

SCHMITZ, JOHN ALBERT, VETERINARY PATHOLOGY & MICROBIOLOGY. *Current Pos:* HEAD, DEPT VET & BIOMED SCIS, UNIV NEBR, LINCOLN, 84- *Personal Data:* b Silverton, Ore, Oct 21, 40; m 71, M Charlene Busch. *Educ:* Colo State Univ, DVM, 64; Univ Mo-Columbia, PhD(path), 71. *Prof Exp:* Res assoc path, Col Vet Med, Univ Mo, 68-71; asst prof, Univ Nebr, 71-72; assoc prof, Ore State Univ, 72-78, prof, 78-84, dir vet diag lab, 76-84, dir path serv, environ health sci ctr, 78-84. *Mem:* Am Col Vet Pathologists; Int Acad Path; Am Vet Med Asn; AAAS; Am Asn Vet Lab Diagnosticians. *Res:* Infectious diseases of food-producing animals; congenital, infectious, nutritional, and toxicological conditions found in animals. *Mailing Add:* Sch Bio Sci 345 Manter Univ Nebr-Lincoln PO Box 880118 Lincoln NE 68588-0118. *Fax:* 402-472-9690; *E-Mail:* vets001@unlvm.unl.edu

SCHMITZ, KENNETH STANLEY, BIOPHYSICAL CHEMISTRY, THEORETICAL CHEMISTRY. *Current Pos:* from asst prof to assoc prof, 75-86, PROF CHEM, UNIV MO, KANSAS CITY, 86- *Personal Data:* b St Louis, Mo, Sept 6, 43. *Educ:* Greenville Col, BA, 66; Univ Washington, PhD(chem), 72. *Honors & Awards:* Univ Kans City Fac Fel, 84. *Prof Exp:* NIH fel, Univ Wash, 72 & Stanford Univ, 72-73; asst prof chem, Fla Atlantic Univ, 73-75. *Concurrent Pos:* Univ Mo, Kansas City fac fel, 84; Am Soc Eng Educ fel, 85. *Mem:* Am Chem Soc; Am Phys Soc. *Res:* Statistical mechanics. *Mailing Add:* Dept Chem Univ Mo 5100 Rockhill Rd Kansas City MO 64110. *Fax:* 816-235-5802; *E-Mail:* ksschmitz@cctr.umrc.edu

SCHMITZ, NORBERT LEWIS, ELECTRICAL ENGINEERING. *Current Pos:* from instr to prof, 47-83, EMER PROF ELEC ENG, UNIV WIS-MADISON, 83- *Personal Data:* b Green Bay, Wis, May 18, 21; m 50; c 4. *Educ:* Univ Wis, BS, 42, MS, 47, PhD, 51. *Prof Exp:* Instr, Eve Tech Div, Milwaukee Voc Sch, 44-45; instr elec eng, Marquette Univ, 45-46. *Concurrent Pos:* Elec engr, Cutler Hammer Inc, 42-46, consult, 46-47; consult, Gisholt Mach Co, 51, John Oster Mfg Co, 55-57, Sundstrand Aviation Co, 57-, Caterpillar Tractor Co, 61-70 & Marathon Elec Mfg Corp, 64-72. *Mem:* Inst Elec & Electronics Engrs; fel NY Acad Sci. *Res:* Electric machine theory and control; industrial control; power semiconductor applications. *Mailing Add:* 4717 Co Tr M Middleton WI 53562

SCHMITZ, ROBERT L, CANCER. *Current Pos:* PROF SURG, UNIV ILL, 72- *Personal Data:* b Chicago, Ill, Mar 10, 14; c 5. *Educ:* Univ Chicago, BS, 36, MD, 38; Am Bd Surg, dipl, 48. *Prof Exp:* From assoc clin prof to clin prof surg, Stritch Sch Med, Loyola Univ Chicago, 46-72. *Concurrent Pos:* Assoc attend surgeon, Mercy Hosp, Chicago, 46-58, sr attend surgeon, 58- *Mem:* Am Cancer Soc; AMA; fel Am Col Surg. *Res:* Surgical oncology. *Mailing Add:* Mercy Hosp & Med Ctr Chicago IL 60616

SCHMITZ, ROGER A(NTHONY), CHEMICAL ENGINEERING. *Current Pos:* chmn dept, Univ Notre Dame, 79-81, dean eng, 81-87, vpres & assoc provost, 87-95, KEATING-CRAWFORD PROF CHEM ENG, UNIV NOTRE DAME, 79- *Personal Data:* b Carlyle, Ill, Oct 22, 34; m 57, Ruth Kuhl; c Jan, Joy & Joni. *Educ:* Univ Ill, BS, 59; Univ Minn, PhD(chem eng), 62. *Honors & Awards:* Colburn Award, Am Inst Chem Engrs, 70, Wilhelm Award, 81; Westinghouse Award, Am Soc Eng Educ, 77. *Prof Exp:* Instr chem eng, Univ Minn, 60-62; from asst prof to prof chem eng, Univ Ill, 62-79. *Concurrent Pos:* Guggenheim fel, 68-69. *Mem:* Nat Acad Eng; Am Inst Chem Engrs; Am Soc Eng Educ. *Res:* Ecological modelling; technologies for education. *Mailing Add:* 301 Cushing Hall Univ Notre Dame Notre Dame IN 46556. *Fax:* 219-631-8366; *E-Mail:* roger.a.schmitz.1@nd.edu

SCHMITZ, WILLIAM JOSEPH, JR, PHYSICAL OCEANOGRAPHY. *Current Pos:* from asst scientist to sr scientist, 67-97, EMER SR SCIENTIST, WOODS HOLE OCEANOG INST, 97- *Personal Data:* b Houston, Tex, Dec 20, 37; m 59; c 4. *Educ:* Univ Miami, ScB, 61, PhD(phys oceanog), 66. *Prof Exp:* Res aide, Univ Miami, 59-61; instr, Univ Miami, 64-66; fel, Nova Univ, 66-67. *Mem:* Am Geophys Union. *Res:* Low-frequency ocean circulation. *Mailing Add:* Dept Phys Oceanog Woods Hole Oceanog Inst Woods Hole MA 02543

SCHMITZ, WILLIAM ROBERT, LIMNOLOGY, FISH BIOLOGY. *Current Pos:* Asst zool, Univ Wis, 52-54, proj asst, 54-58, proj assoc, 58-59, instr biol, Ctr Syst, 59-60, asst prof, 60-66, chmn dept bot & zool, Ctr Syst, 67-70, assoc prof, 66-76, asst dir, Trout Lake Res Sta, 67-77, prof zool, 76-89, EMER PROF, CTR SYST, UNIV WIS, 89- *Personal Data:* b Wauwatosa, Wis, Jan 24, 24; m 51, Joan Scheffler; c Gregory & Geoffrey. *Educ:* Univ Wis, BS, 51, MS, 53, PhD(zool), 58. *Mem:* Am Soc Limnol & Oceanog; Soc Int Limnol. *Res:* Hydrobiology; limnology, especially of ice-bound lakes; fisheries biology. *Mailing Add:* Univ Wis 518 S Seventh Ave Wausau WI 54401-5396

SCHMUCKLER, JOSEPH S, SCIENCE EDUCATION. *Current Pos:* assoc prof sci, 68-73, PROF CHEM & SCI, TEMPLE UNIV, 73-, CHMN DEPT SCI EDUC, 69- *Personal Data:* b Philadelphia, Pa, Feb 15, 27; m 50; c 4. *Educ:* Univ Pa, BS, 52, MS, 54, EdD(chem educ), 68. *Honors & Awards:* James Bryant Conant Award, 68; Benjamin Rush Medal, Chem Indust Coun, 68; Lindbach Award, 76. *Prof Exp:* Instr sci educ, Univ Pa, 64-67. *Concurrent Pos:* Chem Teacher, Haverford Twp High Sch, 53-68; partic, Chem Educ Mat Study Prog; consult, Sadtler Res Lab, 54-62; mem bd gov, Chem Educ Proj Corp, 64-67; pres, Chem Proj Corp, 80-81; prof chem educ, Tianjin Normal Univ, People's Rep China, 80- *Mem:* Am Chem Soc; Nat Sci Teachers Asn; Franklin Inst; fel Am Inst Chemists; Sigma Xi. *Res:* Chemistry; organic synthesis; science education at the secondary school level; chemistry education. *Mailing Add:* 864 Beechwood Rd Havertown PA 19083-2622

SCHMUDE, KEITH E, PHYSICAL CHEMISTRY. *Current Pos:* RETIRED. *Personal Data:* b Rockford, Ill, Feb 10, 34; m 55; c 2. *Educ:* Carroll Col, BS, 55; Univ Rochester, PhD(chem), 59. *Prof Exp:* Assoc physicist, Armour Res Found, 59-61; from asst prof to assoc prof chem, Parsons Col, 61-64; res chemist, Dacron Res Lab, E I Du Pont De Nemours & Co, Inc, 64-68, sr res chemist, Textile Res Lab, 68-83, res assoc, 83-92. *Mem:* AAAS. *Res:* Synthetic fibers; kinetics; radiation and nuclear chemistry. *Mailing Add:* 131 School Rd Wilmington DE 19803

SCHMUGGE, THOMAS JOSEPH, REMOTE SENSING, EVAPOTRANSPIRATION. *Current Pos:* PHYSICIST, HYDROL LAB, AGR RES SERV, USDA, BELTSVILLE, MD, 86- *Personal Data:* b Chicago, Ill, Oct 18, 37; m 61, Susan McCall; c Timothy, Nancy, Andrew & Jonathan. *Educ:* Ill Inst Technol, BS, 59; Univ Calif, Berkeley, PhD(physics), 65. *Prof Exp:* Asst prof physics, Trinity Col, Conn, 64-70; sr res assoc, Nat Acad Sci, 70-71; physicist, NASA-Goddard Space Flight Ctr, 71-86. *Concurrent Pos:* Assoc ed, J Geophys Res, 79-83; res fel, Avignon, France, 94. *Mem:* AAAS; Am Geophys Union; Inst Elec & Electronics Engrs; Europ Geophys Union. *Res:* Magnetic resonance of rare earth ions; low temperature physics; remote sensing of the environment and interaction of electromagnetic waves with natural materials; microwave and infrared emission from natural surfaces; soil moisture; soil physics; snow; hydrology; evapotranspiration and the atmospheric boundary layer; surface temperature. *Mailing Add:* Hydrol Lab-007 USDA Beltsville MD 20705-2350. *Fax:* 301-504-8931; *E-Mail:* schmugge@hydrolab.arsusda.gov

SCHMUKLER, SEYMOUR, ORGANIC CHEMISTRY, POLYMER CHEMISTRY. *Current Pos:* CONSULT, 88- *Personal Data:* b Baltimore, Md, Oct 27, 25; m 57; c 2. *Educ:* Johns Hopkins Univ, AB, 48; Columbia Univ, AM, 50, PhD(chem), 54. *Prof Exp:* Asst, Col Physicians & Surg, Columbia Univ, 53; res chemist, E I du Pont de Nemours & Co, 53-54; res chemist, Colgate-Palmolive Co, 54-57; develop chemist, Merck & Co, Inc, 57-59; res & develop chemist, Nopco Chem Co, 59-63; develop chemist, Gen Elec Co, Mass, 63-67; res assoc, Quantum-USI Chem Div, 67-88. *Mem:* Am Chem Soc; Tech Asn Pulp & Paper Indust. *Res:* Molecular rearrangements; synthetic organic and polymer chemistry; polymer modification, evaluation and process development; polymer extrudable and coextrudable adhesives; flexible packaging, rigid packaging and peelable seals. *Mailing Add:* 449 S Elm St Palatine IL 60067

SCHMULBACH, CHARLES DAVID, INORGANIC CHEMISTRY. *Current Pos:* assoc prof, 65-70, chmn dept, 75-82, PROF CHEM & BIOCHEM, SOUTHERN ILL UNIV, CARBONDALE, 70- *Personal Data:* b Belleville, Ill, Feb 2, 29; m 55; c 3. *Educ:* Univ Ill, PhD, 58. *Prof Exp:* Asst prof chem, Pa State Univ, 58-65. *Mem:* Am Chem Soc. *Res:* Stabilization of uncommon oxidation states; electrochemical synthesis of inorganic compounds; homogeneous catalysis by transition metal complexes. *Mailing Add:* 104 S Lark Lane Carbondale IL 62901-2021

SCHMULBACH, JAMES C, FISH BIOLOGY. *Current Pos:* asst prof, 59-65, PROF BIOL, UNIV SDAK, 65- *Personal Data:* b New Athens, Ill, July 5, 31; c 2. *Educ:* Southern Ill Univ, BA, 53, MA, 57; Iowa State Univ, PhD(fisheries biol), 59. *Prof Exp:* Asst, Southern Ill Univ, 55-57; asst, Iowa State Univ, 57-59. *Concurrent Pos:* Fel, Marine Lab, Miami, 63. *Mem:* AAAS; Am Fisheries Soc; Am Inst Biol Sci; Sigma Xi. *Res:* Limnology; bionomics of fishes; macrobenthos of lotic environments. *Mailing Add:* 922 Ridgecrest Dr Vermillion SD 57069-3531

SCHMUTTENMAER, CHARLES A, CHEMISTRY. *Current Pos:* PROF, CHEM DEPT, YALE UNIV. *Concurrent Pos:* Chem grantee, Camille & Henry Dreyfus Found, 94. *Mailing Add:* Dept Chem Yale Univ New Haven CT 06520

SCHMUTZ, ERVIN MARCELL, RANGE MANAGEMENT, ECOLOGY. *Current Pos:* res assoc weed control, 55-56, from instr to prof range mgt, 56-81, EMER PROF RANGE MGT, UNIV ARIZ, 82- *Personal Data:* b St George, Utah, Oct 26, 15; m 36; c 1. *Educ:* Utah State Univ, BS, 39, MS, 41; Univ Ariz, PhD(plant sci), 63. *Honors & Awards:* Commendation Award, Soil Conserv Soc Am, 74. *Prof Exp:* Range exam, Agr Adjust Admin, 37, 39-40 & 41; sr fire guard, US Forest Serv, 38; range exam, Bur Animal Indust, 40; range conservationist, Soil Conserv Serv, USDA, 41-48 & 50-52, dist conservationist, 48-50, work unit conservationist, 52-55. *Concurrent Pos:* Res scientist, Ariz Agr Exp Sta; mem, Range Mgt Educ Coun; consult, range mgt. *Mem:* Fel Soc Range Mgt; fel Soil Conserv Soc Am; Sigma Xi. *Res:* Range ecology, evaluation, conservation and management; reseeding, poisonous, allergenic and landscaping plants; book publisher. *Mailing Add:* 1811 N Highland Ave Tucson AZ 85719

SCHMUTZ, JOSEF KONRAD, RAPTOR BIOLOGY, WATERFOWL BIOLOGY. *Current Pos:* res assoc wildlife mgt, 83-84, asst prof biol, Dept Biol, 84-87, ASSOC PROF BIOL, UNIV SASK, 87- *Personal Data:* b Ulm, WGer, Oct 5, 50; Can citizen; m 72. *Educ:* Univ Wis-Stevens Pt, BSc, 74; Univ Alta, MSc, 77; Queen's Univ, PhD(biol), 81. *Honors & Awards:* J H Albertson Award, Univ Wis-Stevens Point, 73. *Prof Exp:* Res assoc wildlife mgt, Arctic Inst NAm, 82-83. *Concurrent Pos:* Scholar, Nat Res Coun, Govt Can, 77-79, Ont Grad Scholar, Govt Ont, 79-81; wildlife biologist resource mgt, Webb Environ Serv Ltd, 82. *Mem:* AAAS; Am Ornith Union; Can Soc Zoologists; Cooper Ornith Soc; Wildlife Soc. *Res:* Evolutionary biology of birds; wildlife management. *Mailing Add:* Dept Biol Univ Sask Saskatoon SK S7N 5E2 Can

SCHNAAR, RONALD LEE, MEMBRANE BIOCHEMISTRY, CELL-CELL INTERACTIONS. *Current Pos:* asst prof pharmacol, 79-83, assoc prof pharmacol & neurosci, 84-90, PROF PHARMACOL & NEUROSCI, SCH MED, JOHNS HOPKINS UNIV, 90- *Personal Data:* b Detroit, Mich, Nov 1, 50; m 72, Cynthia Roseman; c Melissa, Stephen & Gregory. *Educ:* Univ Mich, BS, 72; Johns Hopkins Univ, PhD(biochem), 76. *Prof Exp:* Res fel biochem, Johns Hopkins Univ, 77; fel neurobiol, Nat Heart, Lung & Blood Inst, NIH, 77-79. *Concurrent Pos:* Fac Res Award, Am Cancer Soc, 84-89; mem, Sci Adv Bd, Glycomed Inc, 89-93; mem, NIH Study Sect, 90-91, chair, 92-93. *Mem:* Am Soc Cell Biol; Soc Neurosci; Am Soc Biochem & Molecular Biol; Am Soc Neurochem; Soc Complex Carbohydrates. *Res:* The role of cell membrane carbohydrate (glycolipids and glycoproteins) in the control of cell-cell interactions; metabolism of cell surface carbohydrates during neuronal differentiation; neurotransmitter and neurotoxin mechanisms. *Mailing Add:* 9094 Goldamber Garth Columbia MD 21045. *Fax:* 410-955-3023; *E-Mail:* rschnaar@welchlink.welch.jhu.edu

SCHNAARE, ROGER L, PHARMACEUTICS, PARENTERALS. *Current Pos:* from asst prof to assoc prof, 68-77, PROF PHARM, PHILADELPHIA COL PHARM & SCI, 77- *Personal Data:* b Staunton, Ill, June 24, 38; m 60; c 3. *Educ:* St Louis Col Pharm, BS, 60; Purdue Univ, MS, 63, PhD(pharm), 65. *Prof Exp:* Asst prof pharm, St Louis Col Pharm, 65-68. *Mem:* Am Pharmaceut Asn; Sigma Xi; Am Asn Pharmaceut Scientists. *Res:* Suspension, emulsion and parenteral dosage form design and development. *Mailing Add:* 230 Hutchinson Ave Haddonfield NJ 08033-3914

SCHNABEL, GEORGE JOSEPH, NON-DESTRUCTIVE ANALYSIS, PIPING SYSTEMS STRESS ANALYSIS. *Current Pos:* RETIRED. *Personal Data:* b Bornet, Tex, May 7, 16; m 40; c 2. *Educ:* Newark Col Eng, BSME, 61. *Prof Exp:* Tech, Pub Serv Elec & Gas Co, 39-47, draftsman, Eng Dept, 47-50, designer, 50-52, from asst engr to sr engr, 52-71, asst chief mech engr, 71-81, consult mech engr, 81-88. *Concurrent Pos:* Mem, Tech Adv Comt, Mat Properties Coun, 60-88 & A-1 Comt on Ferrous Mat, Am Soc Testing & Mat, 65-92; chmn, Steam Power Panel, Am Soc Mech Engrs-Am Soc Testing & Mat, 65-67, Edison Elec Inst Metall & Piping Task Force, 65-69, Metal Properties Coun, Nuclear Mat Comt, 68-74 & Nuclear Regulatory Comn Steam Generator Task Force, 72-78; consult, Elec Power Inst, Power Plant Mat, 70-82; elec utility adv, Elec Power Inst, 75-81; pres, NJ Soc Prof Engrs & Land Surveyors, 78-79. *Mem:* Fel Am Soc Mech Engrs; Mat Properties Coun; Am Soc Testing & Mat. *Res:* Materials in high temperature steam and nuclear power plants; evaluating extension of productive life of existing power plants; publications include economics, safety and reliability of power plants. *Mailing Add:* 70 Woodbridge Ave Metuchen NJ 08840

SCHNABEL, ROBERT B, NUMERICAL COMPUTATION, PARALLEL LANGUAGES. *Current Pos:* From asst prof to assoc prof, 77-88, PROF COMPUTER SCI, UNIV COLO, BOULDER, 88-, CHAIR, 90- *Personal Data:* b New York, NY, Dec 18, 50; m 81; c 2. *Educ:* Dartmouth Col, BA, 71; Cornell Univ, MS, 75, PhD(computer sci), 77. *Concurrent Pos:* Coun mem, Math Programming Soc, 85-88; vchair, Activ Group Optimization, Soc Indust & Appl Math, 86-88; assoc ed, Math Programming B, 88-, Soc Indust & Appl Math J Optimization, 90-, co-ed, Math Programming A, 89-; chair, Spec Interest Group Numerical Math, Asn Comput Mach, 89- *Mem:* Math Programming Soc. *Res:* Numerical computation; numerical solution of unconstrained and constrained optimization problems; systems of nonlinear equations and nonlinear least squares problems; parallel numerical languages and algorithms. *Mailing Add:* Dept Computer Sci Univ Colo Campus Box 430 Boulder CO 80309-0430

SCHNABEL, TRUMAN GROSS, JR, INTERNAL MEDICINE. *Current Pos:* instr physiol, 48-49, from asst instr to prof med, 49-73, vchmn dept med, 73-77, C MAHLON PROF MED, SCH MED, UNIV PA, 77-, STAFF PHYSICIAN CARDIOVASC SERV, 77- *Personal Data:* b Philadelphia, Pa, Jan 5, 19; m 47; c 4. *Educ:* Yale Univ, BS, 40; Univ Pa, MD, 43; Am Bd Internal Med, dipl, 52, recert, 74. *Honors & Awards:* Alfred E Stengel Mem Award, Am Col Physicians, 78. *Prof Exp:* Intern med, Hosp Univ Pa, 44; asst resident, Mass Gen Hosp, 47-48; asst resident, Hosp Univ Pa, 48. *Concurrent Pos:* Am Heart Asn fel, Sch Med, Univ Pa, 49-52, Markle scholar, 52-57; mem staff, Hosp Univ Pa, 52-; with Prof Lars Werko, St Erick's Hosp, Stockholm, Sweden, 55-56; asst ward chief, Philadelphia Gen Hosp, 56-59, ward chief, 59-73, coordr, Univ Pa Med Serv, 65-71, chief, 66-72; consult, Walston Gen Hosp, Ft Dix, NJ, 60-65; mem, Am Bd Internal Med, 63-72, secy-treas, 71-72; mem med educ adv comt, Rehab Serv Admin, HEW, Washington, DC, 68-71; mem clin res fel rev comt, Career Develop Rev Br, Div Res Grants, NIH, 68-71; D V Mattia lectr, Rutgers Med Sch, 75; Neuton Stern lectr & vis prof, Univ Tenn, 77. *Mem:* Am Soc Clin Invest; Am Physiol Soc; AMA; Am Clin & Climat Asn (vpres, 68-69 & 76-77); Am Col Physicians (pres-elect, 73-74, pres, 74-75). *Res:* Cardiovascular physiology. *Mailing Add:* Univ Pa Hosp Ralston House 3615 Chestnut St Philadelphia PA 19104-6006

SCHNABLE, GEORGE LUTHER, RELIABILITY PHYSICS, MICROELECTRONICS. *Current Pos:* SCI/TECH CONSULT, SCHNABLE ASSOCS, 91- *Personal Data:* b Reading, Pa, Nov 26, 27; m 57, Peggy J Butera; c Joseph & Lee Ann. *Educ:* Albright Col, BS, 50; Univ Pa, MS, 51, PhD(chem), 53. *Prof Exp:* Asst chem, Univ Pa, 53; proj engr, Microelectronics Div, Philco Corp, 53-57, eng specialist, 57-59, eng group supvr, 59-62, head, Mat & Processes Develop Group, 62-68, mgr, Advan Mat & Processes Dept, 68-71; head, Process Res Group, RCA Labs, 71-79, head, Device Physics & Reliability Group, 79-87; head device physics & reliability, David Sarnoff Res Ctr, 87-91. *Concurrent Pos:* Div ed, J Electrochem Soc, 79-91. *Mem:* Fel AAAS; Am Chem Soc; fel Electrochem Soc; fel Am Inst Chem; sr mem Inst Elec & Electronics Engrs. *Res:* Semiconductor devices; materials and processes for fabrication of transistors and integrated circuits; silicon chemistry and metallurgy; reliability of electronic devices; granted 39 US patents; authored 76 publications. *Mailing Add:* Schnable Assocs 619 Knoll Dr Lansdale PA 19446-2925

SCHNABLE, PATRICK S, MOLECULAR GENETICS OF MAIZE & ARABIDOPSIS. *Current Pos:* asst prof, 88-94, ASSOC PROF, DEPTS AGRON, ZOOL & GENETICS, IOWA STATE UIV, 94- *Personal Data:* b Rochester, NY, Mar 10, 59; m 82, Katharine B Chamberlin; c James C & Benjamin D. *Educ:* Cornell Univ, BS, 81; Iowa State Univ, PhD(plant breeding & cytogenetics), 86. *Prof Exp:* NIH fel, Max Planck Inst Plant Res, Kiln, WGer, 86-88. *Mem:* AAAS; Am Soc Plant Physiologists; Bot Soc Am; Genetics Soc Am; Int Soc Plant Molecular Biol; Maize Genetics Coop. *Res:* Molecular analysis of meiotic recombination; genetics of cuticular wax biosynthesis; isolation and characterization of nuclear restorers of the maize male-sterile T cytoplasm; molecular basis of dominant mutations. *Mailing Add:* G405 Agron Iowa State Univ Ames IA 50011-1010. *Fax:* 515-294-2299

SCHNACK, LARRY G, ORGANIC CHEMISTRY. *Current Pos:* asst prof, Univ Wis, 65-69, assoc prof, 69-81, asst to vchancellor, 70-75, PROF ORG CHEM, UNIV WIS-EAU CLAIRE, 81-, ASST VCHANCELLOR ACAD AFFAIRS, 76- *Personal Data:* b Harlan, Iowa, Mar 19, 37; m 55; c 4. *Educ:* Iowa State Univ, BS, 58, PhD(org chem), 65. *Prof Exp:* Teacher, Minn High Sch, 58-61. *Mem:* Am Chem Soc. *Res:* Stereochemistry and rearrangements. *Mailing Add:* Univ Wis PO Box 4004 Eau Claire WI 54702-4004

SCHNAIBLE, H(AROLD) W(ILLIAM), CHEMICAL ENGINEERING. *Current Pos:* RETIRED. *Personal Data:* b Lafayette, Ind, Apr 5, 25. *Educ:* Purdue Univ, BS, 50, MS, 53, PhD(chem eng), 55. *Prof Exp:* Res engr, Gulf Res & Develop Co, 55-58; technologist, US Steel Corp, 59-63, sr res engr, Appl Res Lab, 63-78. *Mem:* Am Chem Soc; Am Inst Chem Engrs; Am Inst Mining, Metall & Petrol Engrs; Iron & Steel Soc; Sigma Xi. *Res:* Thermodynamics; kinetics, particularly hydrocarbon reactions; heat transfer; ingot solidification; computer simulation of processes. *Mailing Add:* 115 Highland Rd Verona PA 15147

SCHNAPER, HAROLD WARREN, MEDICINE, CARDIOVASCULAR PHYSIOLOGY. *Current Pos:* exec vchmn dept med, 69-72, PROF MED & SR SCIENTIST, CARDIOVASC RES & TRAINING CTR, MED CTR, UNIV ALA, BIRMINGHAM, 69-, PROF PUB HEALTH & EPIDEMIOL & DIR DIV GERONT & GERIATR MED, 72-, DIR ALL UNIV CTR AGING, 76- *Personal Data:* b Boston, Mass, Nov 11, 23; m 51; c 5. *Educ:* Harvard Univ, AB, 45; La State Univ, cert, 44; Duke Univ, MD, 49. *Prof Exp:* Intern med, Boston City Hosps, 49-50; chief med, US Army 7th Evacuation Hosp, Ger, 51-53; resident, Mt Sinai Hosp, New York, 53-54; asst chief med serv, Vet Admin Hosp, DC, 54-60, chief internal med res, Vet Admin Cent Off, 60-64, assoc dir res serv, 64-66, actg dir, 66-67. *Concurrent Pos:* Fel neurol & dermat, Sch Med, Duke Univ, 49; fel cardiovasc dis, Sch Med, Georgetown Univ, 50-51; fel path, Mt Sinai Hosp, NY, 53; instr, Sch Med, Georgetown Univ, 54-58, asst prof, 58-66; attend physician, DC Gen Hosp, 54-66; vis prof, Mercy Hosp, Buffalo, NY, 59-66; co-dir cardiovasc res & training ctr, Med Ctr, Univ Ala, Birmingham, 66-70; assoc dir for heart & stroke, Ala Regional Med Prog, 69-76; chief, Vet Admin Cardiovasc Res Prog, 69-80. *Mem:* AAAS; AMA; fel Am Col Physicians; Am Fedn Clin Res; fel Geront Soc. *Res:* Clinical hypertension; aging mechanisms; multicenter clinical trials. *Mailing Add:* 3215 Sterling Rd Mountain Brook AL 35213-3507

SCHNAPF, ABRAHAM, MECHANICAL ENGINEERING, SPACECRAFT SYSTEMS. *Current Pos:* PRES, AEROSPACE SYSTS ENG, 82- *Personal Data:* b New York, NY, Aug 1, 21; m 43; c 2. *Educ:* City Col New York, BSME, 48; Drexel Univ, MSME, 53. *Honors & Awards:* Ann Award, Am Soc Qual Control, 68; David Sarnoff Award Outstanding

Achievements Eng, 71; Cert Appreciation Award, Dept Com; Dept Com Medal Mgt, US Weather Satellite Prog, 85; Space Technol Hall Fame, 92. *Prof Exp:* Develop engr aeronaut eng, Goodyear Aircraft Corp, Ohio, 48-50; leader develop eng, Airborne-Navig Systs, Defense Electronic Prod, Radio Corp Am, Camden, 50-55, mgr airborne weapon systs, 55-58, proj mgr Tiros, Astro-Electronics Div, 58-70, mgr prog mgt, 70-76, mgr satellite prog, 77-79, prin scientist, Astro-Electronics Div, RCA Corp, 79-82. *Concurrent Pos:* Mem, Comn on Aerospace Applns, Nat Res Coun, 82- *Mem:* Nat Acad Sci; NY Acad Sci; fel Am Inst Aeronaut & Astronaut; Am Meteorol Soc; AAAS. *Res:* Development, design and testing of spacecraft, ground stations and field operations; management of satellite programs; remote sensing of earth from space. *Mailing Add:* Aerospace Systs Eng PO Box 160 Willingboro NJ 08046

SCHNAPPINGER, MELVIN GERHARDT, JR, AGRONOMY. *Current Pos:* RES REP FIELD RES & DEVELOP, AGR DIV, NOVARTIS, 70- *Personal Data:* b Baltimore, Md, Oct 29, 42; m 67; c 2. *Educ:* Univ Md, College Park, BS, 65, MS, 68; Va Polytech Inst & State Univ, PhD(agron), 70. *Mem:* Am Soc Agron; Soil Sci Soc Am; Weed Sci Soc Am. *Res:* Field testing of herbicides, insecticides and micronutrient fertilizers. *Mailing Add:* 930 Starr Rd Centreville MD 21617

SCHNARE, PAUL STEWART, APPLIED MATHEMATICS. *Current Pos:* ASSOC PROF MATH, EASTERN KY UNIV, 80- *Personal Data:* b Berlin, NH, Oct 16, 36; m 60, Dorothy G Hopkins; c Sigmund & Col. *Educ:* Univ NH, BA, 60, MS, 61; Tulane Univ, La, PhD(math), 67. *Prof Exp:* Instr math, La State Univ, New Orleans, 61-66; asst prof, Univ Fla, 67-74; asst prof, Colby Col, 74-75 & Fordham Univ, 75-76; asst prof math, Univ Petrol & Minerals, Dhahran, Saudi Arabia, 76-80. *Concurrent Pos:* NSF sci fac fel, Tulane Univ, 66-67. *Mem:* AAAS; London Math Soc; Math Asn Am; Am Math Soc; Nat Comput Graphics Asn; Asn Comput Mach. *Res:* Applied and computational mathematics; numerical methods; analytic inequalities; operations research. *Mailing Add:* Dept Math Comput Sci WAL 420 Eastern Ky Univ Richmond KY 40475. *Fax:* 606-622-1020

SCHNATHORST, WILLIAM CHARLES, PLANT PATHOLOGY. *Current Pos:* LAB VASCULAR PLANT DIS, DAVIS CALIF, 88- *Personal Data:* b Ft Dodge, Iowa, May 8, 29; m 51, Rosemarie A Meyer; c Diana L, William J & Douglas A. *Educ:* Univ Wyo, BS, 52, MS, 53; Univ Calif, PhD(plant path), 57. *Prof Exp:* Asst & lab instr plant physiol & bot, Univ Wyo, 52-53; asst plant path, exp sta, Univ Calif, Davis, 54-56, assoc, 56-85, lectr, 70-85, plant pathologist, 86-88; plant pathologist, Agr Res Serv, USDA, 56-85. *Mem:* Bot Soc Am; Mycol Soc Am; Am Phytopath Soc; Int Soc Plant Path; Sigma Xi. *Res:* Nature of disease resistance of plants; physiology of fungi; verticillium wilt; ecology of plant pathogens; diseases of field and tree crops; vascular fungal diseases. *Mailing Add:* 647 Cleveland Davis CA 95616-3127

SCHNATTERLY, STEPHEN EUGENE, SOLID STATE PHYSICS. *Current Pos:* chmn, Physics Dept, 83-86, F H SMITH PROF PHYSICS, UNIV VA, 77-, VPROVOST GRAD STUDIES, 96- *Personal Data:* b Topeka, Kans, Oct 2, 38; m 63, Patricia Tingley; c Karen & John. *Educ:* Univ Wash, BS, 60, MS, 61; Univ Ill, PhD(physics), 65. *Prof Exp:* From instr to prof physics, Princeton Univ, 65-77. *Concurrent Pos:* Res Corp res grant, 66-67; AP Sloan Found fel, 70-71; prin investr, NSF grant, Univ Va, 77- *Mem:* Am Phys Soc. *Res:* Optical properties of solids; inelastic electron scattering spectroscopy; soft x-ray emission spectroscopy. *Mailing Add:* Physics Dept Univ Va Charlottesville VA 22901. *Fax:* 804-924-4576, 986-2920; *E-Mail:* ses5u@virginia.edu

SCHNECK, LARRY, PEDIATRIC NEUROLOGY, NEUROCHEMISTRY. *Current Pos:* asst prof neurol, 60-73, PROF NEUROL, STATE UNIV NY, DOWNSTATE MED CTR, 74- *Personal Data:* b New York, NY, May 15, 26; m 59; c 3. *Educ:* NY Univ, BS, 49; Chicago Med Sch, MD, 53. *Prof Exp:* Resident pediat, Brooklyn Jewish Hosp, 54-56 & neurol, Bronx Munic Hosp, 57-60. *Concurrent Pos:* NIH fel, Albert Einstein Col Med, 67-70; dir neurol, Kingsbrook Jewish Med Ctr, 70-; dir, Albert Isaac Res Inst, 70-; attend physician, Vet Admin Hosp, Brooklyn, 71- *Mem:* Am Acad Pediat; Am Acad Neurol; Am Soc Neurochem; Int Soc Neurochem. *Res:* Neurochemistry and sphingolipidosis. *Mailing Add:* 1126 E 22nd St Brooklyn NY 11210

SCHNECK, PAUL BENNETT, HIGH PERFORMANCE COMPUTER ARCHITECTURES & COMPUTER SECURITY, OPTIMIZING COMPILERS & LANGUAGES. *Current Pos:* fel, Washington C3 Ctr, Mitre Corp, 93-96, FEL & DIR INFO SYSTS, MITRETEK SYSTS, 96- *Personal Data:* b New York, NY, Aug 15, 45; m 67; c 2. *Educ:* Columbia Univ, BS, 65, MS, 66; NY Univ, PhD(comput sci), 79. *Prof Exp:* Mgr systs prog, Comput Appln, Inc, 67-69; sr comput scientist, Inst Space Studies, Goddard Space Flight Ctr, NASA, 69-76, asst dir res, Mission & Data Opers, 76-79, asst to dir, Info Extraction Div, 80-81, asst dir comput & info sci, 81-83; head, Info Sci Div, Off Naval Res, 83-85; founding dir, Supercomput Res Ctr, Inst Defense Anal, 85-93. *Concurrent Pos:* Adj prof, Comput Sci Dept, Univ Md, 81-82; mem, Sci Supercomput Subcomt, Inst Elec & Electronics Engrs/ USAB, 82-90, distinguished visitor, Comp Soc, 88-89, chair, Tech Comt Supercomput Applns, 94-95; panel mem, Off Technol Assessment, 83-86; adj lectr, Johns Hopkins Univ, 91-; chmn bd, Nat Info Technol Ctr Md, 93-94; chair, Tech Comt Supercomput Applns, Inst Electronics Engrs, 94-95. *Mem:* Fel Inst Elec & Electronics Engrs; fel Asn Comput Mach; Brit Comput Soc; Armed Forces Comn & Electronics Asn. *Res:* High performance computer architecture; optimizing compilers and languages for obtaining peak efficiency; algorithms directed towards parallel architectures; information security. *Mailing Add:* Mitretek Systs 7525 Colshire Dr Mc Lean VA 22102

SCHNEEBERGER, EVELINE E, CELL BIOLOGY, ULTRASTRUCTURAL CYTOCHEMISTRY. *Current Pos:* Instr path, Harvard Med Sch, 67-68, assoc, 68-70, from asst prof to assoc prof, 70-88, PROF PATH, HARVARD MED SCH, 88- *Personal Data:* b The Hague, Holland, Oct 2, 34; US citizen. *Educ:* Univ Colo, BA, 56, MD, 59. *Hon Degrees:* MA, Harvard Univ, 90. *Concurrent Pos:* Asst pathologist, Children's Hosp, Boston, Mass, 72-73, pathologist, 73-79; assoc pathologist, Mass Gen Hosp, Boston, 79- *Mem:* Fel AAAS; Sigma Xi; Am Soc Cell Biol; Am Asn Pathologists; Am Thoracic Soc; Microcirculatory Soc. *Res:* Cell biology of the lung; immunology of the lung. *Mailing Add:* Dept Path Mass Gen Hosp Fruit St Cox Bldg 5 Boston MA 02114-2696

SCHNEEMAN, BARBARA OLDS, NUTRITION, FOOD SCIENCE. *Current Pos:* from asst prof to assoc prof, 76-87, PROF, 88-, CHMN, DEPT NUTRIT, UNIV CALIF, DAVIS, 88- *Personal Data:* b Seattle, Wash, Oct 3, 48; m 74; c 1. *Educ:* Univ Calif, Davis, BS, 70; Univ Calif, Berkeley, PhD(nutrit), 74. *Honors & Awards:* Farma Int Fibre Prize, 89. *Prof Exp:* Fel gastroenterol, Bruce Lyon Mem Res Lab, Children's Hosp, 74-76. *Concurrent Pos:* NIH fel, 74-76, 77; mem, dietary guidelines adv comt, 90. *Mem:* Am Inst Nutrit; Am Physiol Soc; Soc Exp Biol & Med; AAAS; Inst Food Technologists. *Res:* Dietary regulation of digestion; impact of processed foods on nutrition and digestion. *Mailing Add:* Col Agr & Envrn Sci Univ Cal Davis CA 95616-8571. *Fax:* 530-752-4789

SCHNEEMEYER, LYNN F, SOLID STATE CHEMISTRY & CRYSTAL GROWTH, INORGANIC SYNTHESIS & HIGH TEMPERATURE SUPERCONDUCTIVITY. *Current Pos:* mem tech staff, 80-87, DISTINGUISHED MEM TECH STAFF RES, AT&T BELL LABS, 87- *Personal Data:* b Baltimore, Md, July 17, 51; m 76, William K Hagmann; c Joseph A & Diane F. *Educ:* Col Notre Dame, Md, BA, 73; Cornell Univ, MS, 76, PhD(inorg chem), 78. *Prof Exp:* Postdoctoral res assoc chem, Mass Inst Technol, 78-80. *Concurrent Pos:* Chair inorg subdiv, N Jersey Am Chem Soc, 82-84; assoc ed, J Crystal Growth, 88-; chair, Solid State Subdiv, Inorg Div, Am Chem Soc, 94. *Mem:* Am Chem Soc; fel Am Phys Soc; Electrochem Soc; Mat Res Soc; Am Asn Crystal Growth. *Res:* Preparation and characterization of interesting inorganic materials, typically in the form of single crystals; electrochemical, flux growth techniques and standard ceramic techniques have used to prepare new inorganic phases with interesting structures and physical properties. *Mailing Add:* AT&T Bell Labs Rm 1A-363 600 Mountain Ave Murray Hill NJ 07974-2070. *E-Mail:* schneemeyer@belllabs.com

SCHNEER, CECIL J, GEOLOGY. *Current Pos:* from asst prof to prof, 54-87, EMER PROF GEOL & HIST SCI, UNIV NH, 87- *Personal Data:* b Far Rockaway, NY, Jan 7, 23; m 43, Mary B Temple; c Jean (Silverman) & David B. *Educ:* Harvard Univ, AB, 43, AM, 50; Cornell Univ, PhD(geol), 54. *Honors & Awards:* Hist Geol Award, Geol Soc Am, 85; Hawley Medal, Mineral Soc Can, 88. *Prof Exp:* Mining geologist, Cerro de Pasco Co, SAm, 43-44; instr geol, Univ NH, 50; instr, Hamilton Col, 50-52; asst mineral, Cornell Univ, 52-54. *Concurrent Pos:* Pres, US Nat Comt Hist Geol, 75-79; vpres, Int Comt Hist Geol, 76-84; assoc ed, Isis (J Hist Sci Soc), 77-80; nat lectr, Sigma Xi, 81-83; chmn, Hist Geol Div, Geol Soc Am, 82. *Mem:* Fel Geol Soc Am; fel Mineral Soc Am; Hist Sci Soc; Nat Asn Geol Teachers; fel London Geol Soc; Hist Earth Sci Soc (pres, 86). *Res:* Dilational symmetry; snowflake morphology; history of science; history of international union of geological sciences. *Mailing Add:* 12 N River Rd Epping NH 03042. *E-Mail:* cjs1@christa.unh.edu

SCHNEID, EDWARD JOSEPH, NUCLEAR PHYSICS, ASTROPHYSICS. *Current Pos:* res scientist, Grumman Aerospace Corp, 68-76, br head, 76-78, lab head, 78-84, sr lab head, 84-88, dir, 88-95, TECH MGR, NORTHROP GRUMMAN CORP, 95- *Personal Data:* b Syracuse, NY, Apr 1, 40; m 67, Mary K; c Megan. *Educ:* LeMoyne Col, BS, 61; Univ Pittsburgh, PhD(physics), 66. *Prof Exp:* NSF res fel nuclear physics, Rutgers Univ, New Brunswick, 66-68. *Mem:* Am Nuclear Soc; Inst Elec & Electronics Engrs; Am Phys Soc. *Res:* Ion beam analysis; advanced nuclear sensor development; gamma ray astronomy. *Mailing Add:* 28 Harvard Lane Commack NY 11735

SCHNEIDAU, JOHN DONALD, JR, medical mycology; deceased, see previous edition for last biography

SCHNEIDER, ALAN M(ICHAEL), SYSTEMS & SIGNALS ENGINEERING, AUTOMATION. *Current Pos:* assoc prof aerospace & mech eng sci, 65-68, PROF APPL MECH & ENG SCI, UNIV CALIF, SAN DIEGO, 68- *Personal Data:* b Milwaukee, Wis, Feb 28, 25; m 48; c 4. *Educ:* Villanova Univ, BEE, 45; Univ Wis, MS, 48; Mass Inst Technol, ScD(instrumentation), 57. *Honors & Awards:* Samuel M Burka Award, 62. *Prof Exp:* Res engr, Hughes Aircraft Co, 48-49; engr, AC Spark Plug Div, Gen Motors Corp, 50-53; res engr, Instrumentation Lab, Mass Inst Technol, 53-55; eng scientist, Airborne Systs Lab, Radio Corp Am, 57-59, sr eng scientist, Missile Electronics & Control Div, 59-61, mgr, Systs Anal, Aerospace Systs Div, 61-65. *Concurrent Pos:* Consult, Gen Dynamics, Convair, 65, Aerospace Systs Div, Radio Corp Am, 65, Aerospace Corp, 65-68, Gen Micro-Electonics Div, Philco Corp, 66, TRW Systs, 67-70, Teledyne Ryan Aeronaut, 68-80, Naval Ocean Systs Ctr, 73-87, Air Pollution Technol Inc, 77, Linkabit Corp, 77-88, Pac Aerosyst, 83, Titan Systs, 83-86, Visutek, 83-84, Qualcomm, 85-86 & Teledyne Ryan Electronics, 85-89; vis assoc, Environ Qual Lab, Calif Inst Technol, 73; vis prof, Stanford Univ, 81; sr vis, Oxford Univ, 84. *Mem:* Assoc fel Am Inst Aeronaut & Astronaut; Inst Navig. *Res:* Vehicle navigation, guidance, and control; automatic and manual rendezvous guidance; inertial systems astrodynamics; systems theory and applications; modeling of physiological systems. *Mailing Add:* Dept Appl Mech & Eng Sci 0411 Univ Calif San Diego 9500 Gilman Dr La Jolla CA 92093

SCHNEIDER, ALFRED, NUCLEAR ENGINEERING, CHEMICAL ENGINEERING. *Current Pos:* prof, 75-90, EMER PROF NUCLEAR ENG, GA INST TECHNOL, 90-, PRES, SCHNEIDER LABS, INC, GA, 90- *Personal Data:* b Ger, Dec 17, 26 ; US citizen; m 50, Tosia Lehrer; c James, George & David. *Educ:* Cooper Union, BChE, 51; Polytech Univ NY, PhD(chem eng), 58. *Honors & Awards:* Antarctica Medal, USN, 63; Robert E Wilson Award, Am Inst Chem Engrs, 86; Gano Dunn Medal, Cooper Union, Advan Sci & Art, 93. *Prof Exp:* Chemist, US Testing Co, 51-52; develop proj mgr, Celanese Corp Am, 52-56; assoc chem engr, Argonne Nat Lab, 56-61; mgr nuclear res & develop, Martin Marietta Co, 61-64; mgr mat & processes, Nuclear Utility Serv, Washington, DC, 64-65; res assoc to dir nuclear technol, Allied Chem Corp, NJ, 65-71, dir nuclear technol, Allied-Gen Nuclear Serv, SC, 71-75. *Concurrent Pos:* Consult, Allied-Gen Nuclear Serv, 75-83, NY State Energy Res & Develop Authority, 76- & Martin Marietta Energy Systs, Inc, 83-95, Westinghouse Elec Co, 89-96; vis prof & res affil, Mass Inst Tech, 91-; secy, Energy Adv Bd, 91-93. *Mem:* Am Chem Soc; Am Inst Chem Engrs; Am Nuclear Soc; AAAS. *Res:* Reprocessing of nuclear fuels; nuclear materials; radioactive waste management; nuclear power reactors; nuclear fuel cycles; isotope separation; energy systems. *Mailing Add:* Ga Inst Technol 5005 Hidden Branches Dr Atlanta GA 30338. *Fax:* 770-391-0446; *E-Mail:* alfred.schneider@me.gatech.edu

SCHNEIDER, ALFRED MARCEL, MATHEMATICAL STATISTICS, OPERATIONS RESEARCH. *Current Pos:* RETIRED. *Personal Data:* b Vienna, Austria, Nov 7, 25; US citizen; m 53; c 2. *Educ:* Univ London, BSc, 48. *Prof Exp:* Res chemist, Vitamins, Ltd, Eng, 48-52; chem engr, Cyanamid Can, 53-55, exp statistician, Am Cyanamid Co, 55-57, leader math anal group, 58-61; mgr, Math Anal Dept, Dewey & Almy Chem Div, W R Grace & Co, 61-66, dir math sci, Tech Group, 66-71, dir opers res, 71-86; consult, 86-90. *Mem:* Am Statist Asn; Opers Res Soc Am; Royal Soc Chem. *Res:* Experimental design; computer applications to chemistry and chemical engineering; simulation. *Mailing Add:* Seven Carleen Ct Summit NJ 07901

SCHNEIDER, ALLAN FRANK, GLACIAL GEOLOGY. *Current Pos:* from assoc prof to prof, 70-93, EMER PROF GEOL, UNIV WIS, PARKSIDE, 93- *Personal Data:* b Chicago, Ill, Feb 7, 26; m 50, Betty-Lou Dorn; c David, Doris & James. *Educ:* Beloit Col, BS, 48; Pa State Univ, MS, 51; Univ Minn, PhD(geol), 57. *Prof Exp:* Asst geol, Pa State Univ, 48-50, instr, 50-51; instr, Univ Minn, 51-54; from instr to asst prof, Wash State Univ, 54-59; geologist, Ind Geol Surv, 59-70, assoc map ed, 60-61, map & field ed, 61-65. *Concurrent Pos:* Geologist, US Geol Surv, 49, Minn Geol Surv, 51-54 & Wis Geol Surv, 76 & 90, lectr, Ind Univ, 69; chair geol dept, Univ Wis, Parkside, 73-75, 80-83, 85-86, 92-93; dist geologist, Lake Mich dist, Wis Dept Natural Resources, 86- *Mem:* Fel Geol Soc Am; Nat Asn Geosci Teachers; Am Quaternary Asn; Sigma Xi. *Res:* Geomorphology; glacial geology; sedimentary petrography; Pleistocene geology of Minnesota, Indiana and Wisconsin; late Quaternary history of Lake Michigan basin. *Mailing Add:* Dept Geol Univ Wis Parkside Box 2000 Kenosha WI 53141-2000. *Fax:* 414-595-2056

SCHNEIDER, ALLAN STANFORD, ADRENAL CHROMAFFIN CELL BIOLOGY, CALCIUM SIGNALLING IN NEUROTRANSMISSION. *Current Pos:* assoc prof, 85-86, dir grad studies, 87-92, PROF PHARMACOL & TOXICOL, ALBANY MED COL, NY, 87-; ADJ PROF BIOMED SCI, SCH PUB HEALTH, STATE UNIV NY, ALBANY, 88- *Personal Data:* b New York, NY, Sept 26, 40; m 68, Mary J Tunis; c Henry & Joseph. *Educ:* Rensselaer Polytech Inst, BChemE, 61; Pa State Univ, MS, 63; Univ Calif, Berkeley, PhD(chem), 68. *Prof Exp:* Inst fel biomembranes, Weizman Inst Sci, Rehovot, Israel, 69-71; staff fel neurobiol, NIH, 71-73; from assoc to assoc mem cell regulation, Sloan Kettering Inst Cancer Res & from asst prof biochem to assoc prof biochem & cell biol, Cornell Univ Grad Sch Med Sci, 73-85, chmn, Biochem Unit, 82-83. *Concurrent Pos:* Mem, Int Sci Adv Comt Chromaffic Cell Biol & Peripheral Catecholamines, 87-93; vis res scholar, Norweg Res Coun, Univ Bergen, Norway, 89; res grants, NIH, Am Heart Asn, Am Cancer Soc & NSF; estab investr award, Am Heart Asn. *Mem:* Am Soc Biochem Molecular Biol; Biophys Soc; Soc Neurosci; Am Heart Asn. *Res:* Hormone and neurotransmitter secretion and action at cell surface receptors; nicotine addiction; cell calcium signaling; adrenal chromaffin cell biology. *Mailing Add:* Dept Pharmacol & Neuro Sci Albany Med Col A-136 Albany NY 12208. *Fax:* 518-262-5799; *E-Mail:* allans@albnyvm1.bitnet

SCHNEIDER, ARTHUR LEE, PROTEIN CHEMISTRY. *Current Pos:* group leader clin chem, 73-84, RES SCI, INSTRUMENTATION LAB, DADE DIV, AM HOSP SUPPLY CORP, 84- *Personal Data:* b St Louis, Mo, Feb 11, 39; m 64; c 2. *Educ:* Univ Mo, Columbia, BS, 61, PhD(biochem), 66. *Prof Exp:* Res assoc biochem, Albert Einstein Col Med, Yeshiva Univ, 66-68; res assoc, Col Physicians & Surgeons, Columbia Univ, 69-70; assoc med, Albert Einstein Col Med, 71-73. *Concurrent Pos:* USPHS fel, NIH, 67-69. *Mem:* Am Chem Soc; Am Asn Clin Chemists; AAAS. *Res:* Use of plasma proteins for clinical chemistry control materials; development of clinical chemistry control materials. *Mailing Add:* 14 Windmill Lane New City NY 10956

SCHNEIDER, ARTHUR SANFORD, PATHOLOGY, HEMATOLOGY. *Current Pos:* PROF & CHMN PATH, UNIV HEALTH SCI, CHICAGO MED SCH, 75- *Personal Data:* b Los Angeles, Calif, Mar 24, 29; m 50, Edith Kadison; c Jo Ann (Farris), William S & Lynnellen. *Educ:* Univ Calif, Los Angeles, BS, 51; Chicago Med Sch, MD, 55. *Prof Exp:* Intern & resident, Vet Admin Hosp, Los Angeles, 55-59; chief med serv, USAF Hosp, Mather AFB, Calif, 59-61; instr med, Univ Calif, Los Angeles Med Sch, 61-64, asst prof med & path, 65-68; chief clin path, Vet Admin Hosp, Los Angeles, 62-68; dir clin path, City of Hope Med Ctr, 68-70, chmn clin path, 70-75; actg chief lab serv, Vet Admin Med Ctr, 75-86, chief, Lab Hemat, 86-94. *Concurrent Pos:* Hemat trainee, Univ Calif, Los Angeles Sch Med, 61-62, res assoc, 62-66, asst clin prof med & path, 68-72, assoc clin prof, 72-75; attend specialist, Wadsworth Vet Admin Ctr, Los Angeles, 68-75. *Mem:* Asn Path Chmn; Am Soc Hemat; Am Soc Clin Pathologists; Acad Clin Lab Physicians & Scientists; Am Fedn Clin Res; Am Col Pathologists; Col Am Pathologists; AMA; Asn Hematopath; Am Soc Investigative Pathol; Asn Molecular Pathol. *Res:* Inherited erythrocyte biochemical abnormalities; computer applications in laboratory medicine; immunofluorescent clinical chemistry analysis; Molecular basis of hereditary erythrocyte enzyme deficiencies with special emphasis on triosephosphate isonerase deficiency. *Mailing Add:* Dept Path Chicago Med Sch 3333 Green Bay Rd North Chicago IL 60064. *Fax:* 847-578-5002; *E-Mail:* schneidr@mis.finchcms.edu

SCHNEIDER, BARBARA G, IMMUNOCYTO CHEMISTRY, MEMBRANE PROTEIN BIOGENESIS. *Current Pos:* ASST PROF PATH, TEX HEALTH SCI CTR, 89. *Educ:* Univ Tex, MA, 75. *Prof Exp:* Res assoc, dept path, Yale Sch Med, 75-86, res coordr, 86-89. *Res:* Retinal cell biology. *Mailing Add:* Dept Path Univ Tex Health Sci Ctr 7703 Floyd Curl Dr San Antonio TX 78284-7750

SCHNEIDER, BARRY I, MOLECULAR PHYSICS, THEORETICAL CHEMISTRY. *Current Pos:* AT NSF, VA, 94- *Personal Data:* b Brooklyn, NY, Nov 16, 40; m 62; c 2. *Educ:* Brooklyn Col, BS, 62; Yale Univ, MS, 64; Univ Chicago, PhD(theoret chem), 68. *Honors & Awards:* Fel, Am Phys Soc; Sr Scientist Humboldt Award, 86. *Prof Exp:* Fel chem, Univ Southern Calif, 68-69; mem tech staff, Gen Tel & Electronics Lab, 69-72; mem tech staff physics, Los Alamos Sci Lab, 72- *Concurrent Pos:* Prog dir atomic, molecular & optical physics, NSF, 89-90. *Mem:* Fel Am Phys Soc. *Res:* Scattering theory, photoionization; many-body theory; structure of molecules. *Mailing Add:* Physics Div NSF Rm 1015 4201 Wilson Blvd Arlington VA 22230

SCHNEIDER, BERNARD ARNOLD, PLANT PHYSIOLOGY, AGRONOMY. *Current Pos:* plant physiologist, Plant Biol Lab, Environ Protection Agency, 72-74, radioisotope safety officer, 74-77, supvry plant physiologist, 77-79, PLANT PHYSIOLOGIST, ENVIRON PROTECTION AGENCY, 79- *Personal Data:* b Washington, DC, June 8, 44; m 68; c 3. *Educ:* Univ Md, College Park, BS, 66, MS, 68, PhD(forage physiol, biochem), 71. *Prof Exp:* Asst agron, Univ Md, 66-71. *Concurrent Pos:* Rep, Plant Growth Regulator Soc Nomenclature Comt, Am Nat Stand Inst-K62, 74-; leader pesticide prod performance guidelines, Am Soc Testing & Mat, Terminology Subcomt, Chemigation Info Exchange Group, Environ Protection Agency; mem, Terminology Comt, Weed Sci Soc. *Mem:* Am Soc Agron; Weed Sci Soc Am; Am Soc Hort Sci; Am Soc Testing & Mat; Am Chem Soc; Plant Growth Regulator Soc Am. *Res:* Develop methods for determining the biological effectiveness of algaecides, herbicides and plant regulators for public protection; author of handbook on toxicology and plant growth regulators; determine the fate and metabolism of pesticides in the environment using radioisotopes of pesticides; plant metabolism studies benefit risk assessments of pesticides; pesticide residue analyst; 30 publications. *Mailing Add:* 9517 Farewell Rd Columbia MD 21045-4327

SCHNEIDER, BRUCE ALTON, AUDITORY PSYCHOPHYSICS, AUDITORY DEVELOPMENT. *Current Pos:* assoc prof, 74-81, PROF PSYCHOL, UNIV TORONTO, 81- *Personal Data:* b Detroit, Mich, July 17, 41; m 67; c 2. *Educ:* Univ Mich, Ann Arbor, BA, 63, Harvard Univ, PhD(psychol), 68. *Prof Exp:* Lectr psychol, Columbia Univ, 67-68, asst prof, 68-72, assoc prof, 72-74. *Concurrent Pos:* Distinguished vis prof, Univ Alta, 81. *Mem:* Soc Math Psychologists. *Res:* Infant and adult auditory perception; how the ear processes sound and how the nature of this auditory processing system changes from infancy to adulthood. *Mailing Add:* Dept Psychol Erindale Col Univ Toronto 3359 Mississauga Rd N Mississauga ON L5L 1C6 Can

SCHNEIDER, BRUCE E, BIOSTATISTICS. *Current Pos:* Group leader, Wyeth Labs, Wyeth-Ayerst Res, 72-75, supvr, 76-77, mgr biostatist, 77-81, assoc dir, biostatist & data systs, 81-85, dir clin info, 85-86, asst vpres clin opers, 87-90, vpres clin opers, 90-92, SR VPRES, RES & DEVELOP OPERS & PLANNING, WYETH-AYERST RES, 92- *Personal Data:* b Sacramento, Calif, July 4, 50; m 75; c 3. *Educ:* Brown Univ, BSc, 72; Villanova Univ, MS, 73; Temple Univ, PhD(appl statist), 77. *Concurrent Pos:* Steering comt, PMA Biostatist subsect, 84-86, chmn steering comt, 87-88, adv, 89-92. *Mem:* Am Statist Asn; Biometrics Soc; Drug Info Asn. *Res:* Nonparametrics; statistical computing; pharmacokinetics. *Mailing Add:* Wyeth-Ayerst Res PO Box 8299 Philadelphia PA 19101

SCHNEIDER, BRUCE SOLOMON, HORMONES-DISEASES OF HYPOTHALAMIC-PITUITARY AXIS, HORMONE PRODUCTION BY TUMORS. *Current Pos:* CHIEF, ENDOCRINOL & METAB, LONG ISLAND JEWISH MED CTR, 83-; PROF MED, ALBERT EINSTEIN COL MED, 89- *Personal Data:* b New York, NY, Feb 23, 42; m 69, Susan Weidman; c Benjamin, Rachel & Yael. *Educ:* Harvard Col, AB, 64; Harvard Med Sch, MD, 68. *Honors & Awards:* Career Scientist Award, Irma T Hirschl Trust, 81. *Prof Exp:* Intern, MT Sinai Hosp, NY, 68-69, resident, 71-73; res assoc endocrinol, Solomon Berson Res Lab, Bronx Vet Admin Hosp, 73-75; asst prof & assoc physician, Rockefeller Univ, NY, 75-83. *Mem:* Harvey Soc; Sigma Xi; Endocrine Soc; Fedn Am Socs Exp Biol; Am Diabetes Asn. *Res:* Physiology, biochemistry, molecular biology of neuropeptides; role of neuropeptides in nutritional homeostasis; expression of neuropeptides by brain and tumor cells. *Mailing Add:* Endocrinol & Metab Neuroencocrinol Lab Long Island Jewish Hillside Med Ctr New Hyde Park NY 11042

SCHNEIDER, CARL STANLEY, SOLID STATE PHYSICS. *Current Pos:* From asst prof to assoc prof physics, 68-81, dir res, 86-89, PROF PHYSICS, US NAVAL ACAD, 81-, ASSOC DEAN, 89- *Personal Data:* b Baltimore, Md, Dec 20, 42; m 71; c 2. *Educ:* Johns Hopkins Univ, BA, 63; Mass Inst Technol, SM, 65, PhD(physics), 68. *Concurrent Pos:* Naval Acad Res Coun grant, US Naval Acad-Nat Bur Stand, 69-75, NSF res grants neutron diffraction, 74-76; affil, David Taylor Res Ctr, 77-; pres, US Naval Acad, 80-81. *Mem:* Am Phys Soc; Sigma Xi (pres, 80-81); Am Asn Physics Teachers. *Res:* Neutron diffraction; prism refraction of thermal neutron for the determination of scattering amplitudes; nonlinear theory of magnetoelasticity; closed loop degaussing. *Mailing Add:* Dept Physics 9-C US Naval Acad 572 Holloway Rd Annapolis MD 21402-5026

SCHNEIDER, CRAIG WILLIAM, PHYCOLOGY. *Current Pos:* From asst prof to assoc prof, 75-87, PROF BIOL, TRINITY COL, 87- *Personal Data:* b Manchester, NH, Oct 23, 48; m 72; c 3. *Educ:* Gettysburg Col, BA, 70; Duke Univ, PhD(bot), 75. *Mem:* Phycol Soc Am; Int Phycol Soc; Brit Phycol Soc; Sigma Xi. *Res:* Benthic algal studies on the Southeastern United States continental shelf and in Bermuda; benthic algal ecology in Connecticut; life-history cultural studies; red-algal morphological studies. *Mailing Add:* Dept Biol Trinity Col 300 Summit St Hartford CT 06106-3100

SCHNEIDER, DAVID EDWIN, PHYSIOLOGICAL ECOLOGY, MARINE ECOLOGY. *Current Pos:* From instr to asst prof, 66-71, assoc prof, 71-92, PROF BIOL, WESTERN WASH UNIV, 92- *Personal Data:* b Philadelphia, Pa, Mar 16, 37; m 82, Bunny Richardet. *Educ:* Bates Col, BS, 59; Duke Univ, PhD(zool), 67. *Mem:* AAAS; Am Soc Zoologists; Am Soc Limnol & Oceanog; Ecol Soc Am; Pac Estuarine Res Soc. *Res:* Temperature and desiccation adaptations of marine intertidal animals; trophic relationships and physiological responses of Arctic marine species. *Mailing Add:* Dept Biol Western Wash Univ Bellingham WA 98225. *Fax:* 360-650-3148; *E-Mail:* dschneid@henson.cc.wwu.edu

SCHNEIDER, DENNIS RAY, MICROBIOLOGY ECOLOGY, INDUSTRIAL PRODUCT DEVELOPMENT. *Current Pos:* RES & DEVELOP DIR, MICRO-BAC INT, 88-, VPRES, 94- *Personal Data:* b Sinton, Tex, June 10, 52; m 76; c 2. *Educ:* Univ Tex, Austin, BA, 73, PhD(microbiol), 78. *Prof Exp:* Fel, Behringwerke AG Marburg/Lahn WGer, 78-79, Univ Mo Med Sch, 80-81; res microbiologist, New Eng Nuclear Dupont, 81-82; res & develop dir, Austin Biol Labs, 82-88. *Concurrent Pos:* Adj assoc prof, Microbiol Dept, Univ Tex, Austin, 86-; prin investr, Nat Agronaut & Space Admin, 92-94. *Mem:* Am Soc Microbiol; AAAS; Soc Petrol Engr. *Res:* Development of microbial products for the treatment of environmentally important waste products; development of microbial products to improve oil and natural gas production. *Mailing Add:* 2200 Creekview Round Rock TX 78681

SCHNEIDER, DONALD LEONARD, BIOCHEMISTRY. *Current Pos:* HEALTH SCI ADMINR, NIH, 90- *Personal Data:* b Muskegon, Mich, Jan 15, 41; m 79; c 1. *Educ:* Kalamazoo Col, BA, 63; Mich State Univ, PhD(biochem), 69. *Prof Exp:* Fel biochem, Cornell Univ, 69-71; res assoc biochem cytol, Rockefeller Univ, 71-72, asst prof, 72-73; asst prof biochem, Univ Mass, Amherst, 73-76; from asst prof to assoc prof, Dartmouth Med Sch, 77-90. *Mem:* AAAS; Am Chem Soc; Am Soc Cell Biol; Am Soc Biochem & Molecular Biol. *Res:* Lysosomes; proton pump ATPases; white blood cell defenses; sugar transport. *Mailing Add:* NIH/DRG 6701 Rockledge Dr MSC 7852 Bethesda MD 20892-7852

SCHNEIDER, DONALD LOUIS, BIOCHEMISTRY, NUTRITION. *Current Pos:* RETIRED. *Personal Data:* b Ft Wayne, Ind, Apr 9, 19; m 41; c 2. *Educ:* Evansville Col, BA, 52; Univ Ariz, MS, 60, PhD(biochem), 63. *Prof Exp:* Chemist, Mead Johnson Res Ctr, 52-58; res assoc biochem & nutrit, Ariz Agr Exp Sta, 58-62; sr scientist, Mead Johnson Res Ctr, 62-63, group leader, 63-68, prin investr, 68-73, sect leader nutrit, 73-76, prin res assoc, 76-81. *Mem:* AAAS; Am Inst Nutrit; NY Acad Sci; Am Inst Biol Sci; Am Inst Chemists. *Res:* Cyclopropenoid fatty acids, biochemical and physiological effects; lipid, cholesterol and bile salt metabolism; baby pig and infant nutrition. *Mailing Add:* 11701 Oak Trail Dr Evansville IN 47711

SCHNEIDER, DONALD P, OBSERVATIONAL COSMOLOGY. *Current Pos:* ASSOC PROF ASTRON, PA STATE UNIV, 94- *Personal Data:* b Hastings, Nebr, Feb 8, 55. *Educ:* Univ Nebr, BS, 76; Calif Inst Technol, PhD(astron), 82. *Prof Exp:* Res fel, Calif Inst Technol, 82-85; mem, Inst Advan Study, 85-94. *Mem:* Am Astron Soc; Int Astron Union. *Res:* Observational cosmology, in particular measuring the properties of high-redshift quasars. *Mailing Add:* Dept Astron Pa State Univ University Park PA 16802. *E-Mail:* dps@astro.psu.edu

SCHNEIDER, E GAYLE, STRUCTURE & FUNCTION OF MEMBRANE. *Current Pos:* ASST PROF BIOCHEM, MED CTR, UNIV NEBR, 79-; PROF OBSTET & GYNEC, ECU SCH MED, GREENVILLE, NC. *Personal Data:* b St Louis, Mo, Aug 1, 46. *Educ:* Harvard Univ, PhD(biochem), 74. *Mem:* Soc Develop Biol; Am Soc Cell Biol; Sigma Xi; AAAS. *Mailing Add:* Obstet-Gynec Dept E Carolina Univ Sch Med Greenville NC 27858

SCHNEIDER, EDWARD GREYER, PHYSIOLOGY. *Current Pos:* ASSOC PROF PHYSIOL, HEALTH SCI CTR, UNIV TENN, MEMPHIS, 73- *Personal Data:* b Indianapolis, Ind, Sept 2, 41; m 83; c 4. *Educ:* DePauw Univ, BA, 63; Ind Univ, Indianapolis, PhD(physiol), 67. *Prof Exp:* Fel physiol, Univ Mo, 67-70, asst prof, 70-71; asst prof, Mayo Grad Sch Med, Univ Minn, 71-73. *Concurrent Pos:* Estab investr, Am Heart Asn, 72-77; consult, Nova Pharm Corp, 86- *Mem:* Am Physiol Soc; Am Fedn Clin Res; Am Soc Nephrology; Sigma Xi; Int Soc Nephrology; Endocrin Soc. *Res:* Examination of the control of renal sodium excretion and the effects of alteration in fluid balance on the excretion of electrolytes by the kidney and the secretron of aldosterone by the adrenal. *Mailing Add:* Dept Physiol & Biophys Univ Tenn Col Med 894 Union Ave Memphis TN 38163-0001. *Fax:* 901-577-4948

SCHNEIDER, EDWARD LEWIS, GERIATRICS, HUMAN GENETICS. *Current Pos:* DEAN & EXEC DIR, ANDRUS GERONT CTR, 88- *Personal Data:* b New York, NY, June 22, 40. *Educ:* Rensselaer Polytech Inst, BS, 61; Boston Univ, MD, 66. *Honors & Awards:* Roche Award, Am Soc Clin Invest. *Prof Exp:* Intern med, Cornell Univ-New York Hosp, 66-67; resident med, 67-68; res assoc, Lab Biol Viruses, Nat Inst Allergy & Infectious Dis, NIH, 68-70; res fel human genetics, Univ Calif Med Ctr, San Francisco, 70-73, prof med & biochem, 79-80; prog coordr, LCCP Res Ctr, NIH, 73-79, assoc dir to dep dir, Nat Inst Aging, 84-88. *Concurrent Pos:* Asst prof human genetics, Johns Hopkins Univ Sch Med, 73-76; adj prof biochem, George Washington Univ, 83-; clin prof med, Georgetown Univ, 85- *Mem:* Am Soc Cell Biol; Geront Soc; Am Soc Human Genetics; Tissue Cult Asn. *Res:* Studies on cellular aging utilizing human diploid cell cultures in vitro and animal systems to examine cell replication, nucleic acid metabolism and repair of DNA damage; molecular genetics. *Mailing Add:* Andrus Geront Ctr Univ Southern Calif MC 0191 3715 McClintock Los Angeles CA 90089-0191

SCHNEIDER, EDWIN KAHN, CLIMATE MODELLING, ATMOSPHERE & ATMOSPHERIC OCEAN DYNAMICS. *Current Pos:* SR RES SCIENTIST, CTR OCEAN LAND ATMOSPHERE STUDIES, UNIV MD, 93- *Personal Data:* b Philadelphia, Pa, May 6, 48; m 79, Penelope L Ganzel; c Andrew & Thomas. *Educ:* Harvard Col, AB, 70; Harvard Univ, MS, 73, PhD(appl physics), 76. *Prof Exp:* Res assoc, Mass Inst Technol, 74-77 & 81-83, prin res scientist, 84; NATO fel, Reading Univ, Eng, 77-78; res fel, Harvard Univ, 78-81; assoc res scientist, Univ Md, 84-90, sr res scientist, 90-93. *Mem:* Am Meteorol Soc. *Res:* Atmospheric general circulation and climate modelling; tropical meteorology; coupled ocean atmospheric climate modelling. *Mailing Add:* 4041 Powder Mill Rd Suite 302 Calverton MD 20705-3106. *Fax:* 301-595-9743; *E-Mail:* schneide@cola.iges.org

SCHNEIDER, ERIC DAVIS, marine geology, marine pollution, for more information see previous edition

SCHNEIDER, ERIC WEST, NUCLEAR CHEMISTRY. *Current Pos:* Assoc res scientist, 78-81, sr res scientist, 81, staff res scientist, 81-87, SR STAFF RES SCIENTIST, RES LABS, GEN MOTORS CORP, 87- *Personal Data:* b Wilkes-Barre, Pa, Sept 1, 52; m 74; c 3. *Educ:* Rensselaer Polytech Inst, BS, 74; Univ Md, PhD(nuclear chem), 78. *Mem:* Am Chem Soc; Am Phys Soc; Sigma Xi. *Res:* Development of radioisotopic methods for industrial applications including, radiotracer methods for measuring wear, radioisotopic gauging and radiographic inspection of materials, and neutron activation and x-ray fluorescence elemental analysis. *Mailing Add:* GM R&D Ctr R406 30500 Mound Rd PO Box 9055 Warren MI 48090-9055

SCHNEIDER, FRANK L, ANALYTICAL CHEMISTRY. *Current Pos:* from instr to prof, 39-72, EMER PROF CHEM, QUEENS COL, NY, 72- *Personal Data:* b New York, NY, May 26, 06; m 45; c 1. *Educ:* Polytech Inst Brooklyn, BS, 28; NY Univ, MS, 30; Rutgers Univ, PhD(chem), 36. *Honors & Awards:* Benedetti-Pichler Award. *Prof Exp:* Asst, Rutgers Univ, 33-34, instr, 34-37, exten div, 36-37; instr chem, Trinity Col, Conn, 37-39. *Mem:* Am Chem Soc; fel Am Inst Chemists; Sigma Xi; hon mem Austrian Microchem Soc. *Res:* Microchemistry; organic analysis; air and water pollution control. *Mailing Add:* 8 Round Hill Lane Port Washington NY 11050

SCHNEIDER, FRED BARRY, COMPUTER SCIENCE. *Current Pos:* ASSOC PROF COMPUT SCI, CORNELL UNIV, 78- *Personal Data:* b NY, Dec 7, 53. *Educ:* Cornell Univ, BS, 75; State Univ NY, Stony Brook, MS, 77, PhD(comput sci), 78. *Mem:* Am Asn Comput Mach; Inst Elec & Electronics Engrs. *Res:* Operating systems; programming languages; concurrency; software engineering. *Mailing Add:* Dept Comput Sci Cornell Univ Upson Hall Ithaca NY 14853

SCHNEIDER, FREDERICK HOWARD, PHARMACOLOGY. *Current Pos:* SR VPRES TECH & MEM BD DIR, DYNAGEN, 91- *Personal Data:* b Detroit, Mich, Nov 19, 38; m 61; c 2. *Educ:* Ariz State Univ, BS, 60, MS, 61; Yale Univ, PhD(autonomic pharmacol), 66. *Prof Exp:* Jr chemist, Merck Sharp & Dohme Res Labs, 61-62; asst prof pharmacol, Sch Med, Univ Colo, Denver, 67-73; assoc prof, Sch Med, Emory Univ, 73-75; pres, Bioassay Syats Corp, Cambridge, Mass, 75-86, chief scientist officer; dir & sr vpres, Bogart Delafield Ferrier, 85-91. *Concurrent Pos:* NSF fel pharmacol, Oxford Univ, 66-67; estab investr, Am Heart Asn, 69-74. *Mem:* AAAS; Am Soc Pharmacol & Exp Therapeut; Tissue Cult Asn. *Res:* Effects of drugs on responses to sympathetic nerve stimulation; neurotransmitter secretion; lysosomal secretion mechanisms; nerve cells in tissue culture; toxicology; in vitro cytotoxicity. *Mailing Add:* 21 Centre St Yarmouth Port MA 02675-1309

SCHNEIDER, G MICHAEL, SOFTWARE ENGINEERING. *Current Pos:* PROF COMPUT SCI, DEPT MATH & COMPUT SCI, MACALESTER COL, 82- *Personal Data:* b Detroit, Mich, May 28, 45. *Educ:* Univ Mich, BS, 66; Univ Wis, MSc, 68, PhD(comput sci), 74. *Prof Exp:* asst prof comput sci, Univ Minn, 74-82. *Concurrent Pos:* Vis prof, Univ Calif, Berkeley, 79 & Imp

Col, Univ London, 80; Fulbright scholar, Univ Mauritius, 95. *Mem:* Asn Comput Mach; Inst Elec & Electronics Engrs. *Res:* Interface between the user and the computer system. *Mailing Add:* Dept Math & Comput Sci Macalester Col St Paul MN 55105. *Fax:* 612-696-6492; *E-Mail:* schneider@macalester.edu

SCHNEIDER, GARY, FOREST ECOLOGY. *Current Pos:* PROF & HEAD DEPT FORESTRY, WILDLIFE & FISHERIES, UNIV TENN, 77-, ASSOC DEAN, SCI & NATURAL RESOURCES, COL AGR, 86- *Personal Data:* b Milwaukee, Wis, Feb 6, 34; m 56, Joretta Jasper; c Gwen & Jennifer. *Educ:* Univ Mich, BS, 56, MF, 57; Mich State Univ, PhD(forest ecol), 63. *Prof Exp:* Asst dist ranger forest admin, US Forest Serv, 57; asst prof, Stephen F Austin State Univ, 62-65; from asst prof to prof forestry fisheries & wildlife, Mich State Univ, 65-77. *Concurrent Pos:* Consult, AEC-Oak Ridge Assoc Univs, 66-72, US Forest Serv and var forest indust, 66- *Mem:* AAAS; fel Soc Am Foresters; Soil Sci Soc Am; Am Forestry Asn; Ecol Soc Am; Am Inst Biol Sci. *Res:* Production ecology; biomass and nutrient analysis of tree species; environmental factors influencing tree growth and development; nutrient cycle in the forest ecosystem; forest soil moisture relations. *Mailing Add:* Col Agr Sci & Nat Resources 125 Morgan Hall Univ Tenn Knoxville TN 37901. *Fax:* 423-974-9329; *E-Mail:* gschneid@utk.edu

SCHNEIDER, GARY BRUCE, CELL BIOLOGY OF BONE DISEASES-BONE LOSS, IMMUNOLOGY OF BONE DISEASE. *Current Pos:* PROF CELL BIOL & ANAT, FINCH UNIV HEALTH SCI, CHICAGO MED SCH, 93- *Personal Data:* b Chicago, Ill, Sept 25, 46; m 70, Barbara Pedian; c Jennifer & Peter. *Educ:* Univ Wis, BS, 69; Coop 5-Col Prog (Amherst, Hampshire, Mt Holyoke, Smith Cols & Univ Mass), PhD(biochem), 73. *Prof Exp:* From asst prof to assoc prof anat, Univ Mass, Med Sch, 74-81; assoc prof cell biol neurobiol & anat, Loyola Univ, Med Sch, 81-85, prof, 85-92, prof orthop surg, 91-92; dir res, Western Pa Res Inst, 91-92. *Concurrent Pos:* Prin investr, Nat Inst Dent Res, NIH, 78-; fel assoc prog, Nat Res Coun, 85- *Mem:* Am Asn Anatomists; Am Asn Immunologists; Am Soc Bone & Mineral Res; Am Soc Cell Biol; Int Asn Dent Res; Int Conf Calcium Regulating Hormones. *Res:* Bone cell biology and immunology; investigated the role of the immune system in the regulation of both normal and pathological bone loss, these relationships have had considerable impact on the understanding of osteolytic diseases such as arthritis and periodontal diseases and metobolic bone diseases such as osteopetrosis and osteoporosis. *Mailing Add:* Dept Cell Biol & Anat Finch Univ Health Sci Chicago Med Sch 3333 Green Bay Rd North Chicago IL 60064-3095. *Fax:* 847-578-3253

SCHNEIDER, GEORGE RONALD, CHEMICAL ENGINEERING, CHEMISTRY. *Current Pos:* MEM TECH STAFF, ADVAN PROGS DEPT, ROCKETDYNE DIV, ROCKWELL INT CORP, 61- *Personal Data:* b Chicago, Ill, Mar 6, 32. *Educ:* Ill Inst Technol, BS, 53; Mass Inst Technol, SM, 56, ScD(chem eng), 61. *Prof Exp:* Chem engr, Gen Elec Co, 53-54. *Mem:* Am Chem Soc; Am Inst Chem Engrs; Combustion Inst. *Res:* Chemical lasers and laser related diagnostics; chemical kinetics of combustion. *Mailing Add:* 3824 Calle Linda Vista Newbury Park CA 91320-3371

SCHNEIDER, GERALD EDWARD, NEUROSCIENCE. *Current Pos:* Res assoc, 66-67, from asst prof to assoc prof, 67-78, PROF NEUROSCI, MASS INST TECHNOL, 78- *Personal Data:* b Libertyville, Ill, Aug 20, 40; m 62, 77; c 4. *Educ:* Wheaton Col, BSc, 63; Mass Inst Technol, PhD(psychol), 66. *Concurrent Pos:* Prin investr, Nat Eye Inst, NIH, 70-; co-investr, Nat Inst Neurol Dis & Stroke, 75-78 & Nat Eye Inst, 78; mem, Biopsychol Study Sect, 78-82, Basic Sci Task Force, Long-term Res Strategies, Nat Inst Neurol & Commun Dis & Stroke, 78; Vision Res Rev Comt, Nat Eye Inst, 89- *Mem:* Soc Neurosci; Cajal Club. *Res:* Nervous system plasticity and regeneration in context of development; development, organization and function of the visual system. *Mailing Add:* Mass Inst Technol 77 Massachusetts Ave Cambridge MA 02139-4307

SCHNEIDER, HANS, LINEAR ALGEBRA, MATRIX THEORY. *Current Pos:* from asst prof to prof, 59-88, James Joseph Sylvester prof, 88-93, EMER PROF MATH, UNIV WIS, 93- *Personal Data:* b Vienna, Austria, Jan 24, 27; m 48, Miriam Wieck; c Barbara, Peter & Michael. *Educ:* Edinburgh Univ, MA, 48, PhD, 52. *Prof Exp:* Asst lectr, Queen's Univ, Belfast, 52-54, lectr, 54-59. *Concurrent Pos:* Vis prof, Wash State Univ, Pullman, 56-57, Univ Calif, Santa Barbara, 64-65, Univ Tubingen, 70, Tech Univ Munich, 72 & 74, Univ Montreal, 77, Univ Wurzburg, 80-81, Technion, Lady Davis vis prof, Haifa, Israel, 85 & 86; ed, H Wielandt's collected works, Linear & Multilinear Algebra, 72-, J Algebraic & Discrete Methods, 79-87, ed-in-chief, Linear Algebra & Its Appl, 72-92; assoc chmn math dept, Univ Wis, 65-66, chmn, 66-68, mem grad sch admin comt, 77-79; NSF res grants, 67- *Mem:* Am Math Soc; Math Asn Am; Soc Indust & Appl Math; Int Linear Algebra Soc (pres, 89-96). *Res:* Linear algebra, including nonnegative matrices and generalizations such as M-matrices and operators leaving a cone invariant in finite dimensional space (Perron-Frogenius theory), inertia theory, diagonal scaling; contributions to semi-groups and universal algebra; author of two books. *Mailing Add:* Univ Wis 213 Van Vleck 480 Lincoln Dr Madison WI 53706-1313. *Fax:* 608-263-8891; *E-Mail:* hans@math.wisc.edu

SCHNEIDER, HAROLD O, PHYSICS, MATHEMATICS. *Current Pos:* MEM STAFF, LOCKHEED CORP, SUNNYVALE, CALIF, 78- *Personal Data:* b Cincinnati, Ohio, Apr 8, 30; m 60; c 2. *Educ:* Univ Cincinnati, BS, 51, MS, 54, PhD(physics), 64. *Prof Exp:* Aeronaut res scientist, Lewis Res Ctr, NASA, 51-61; mathematician, Rand Develop Corp, Ohio, 61-62; staff mem, Lincoln Lab, Mass Inst Technol, 62-72; sr systs analyst, Dynamics Res Corp, Wilmington, Mass, 72-78. *Mem:* Am Inst Aeronaut & Astronaut; Sigma Xi; Soc Indust & Appl Math. *Res:* Spline method, general, analytical, optimal, nonlinear, parameter and state estimation/systems identification technique; 3-degrees-of-freedom (3DOF) application to aerodynamic modeling; multiple radar reentry estimation; systems identification with simulation, analytical covariance error analyses, extension to 6DOF and onboard instrumentation. *Mailing Add:* 855 Clara Palo Alto CA 94303-3910

SCHNEIDER, HAROLD WILLIAM, TOPOLOGY, ACTUARIAL SCIENCE. *Current Pos:* ACTUARIAL ASST, METROP LIFE INS CO, 95- *Personal Data:* b Rochester, NY, Oct 8, 43; m 69, Ellyn Silverstein; c Melissa, Rachelle & Amy. *Educ:* Univ Rochester, AB, 65; Univ Chicago, MS, 66, PhD(math), 72. *Prof Exp:* Teaching asst math, Univ Chicago, 66-69; from instr to prof math, Roosevelt Univ, 69-86; assoc dir, Lincoln Nat Life Ins Co, Ft Wayne, 86-89; dir financial proj, Columbus Life Ins Co, Columbus, Ohio, 90-95. *Mem:* Math Asn Am; Soc Actuaries. *Res:* Differential topology; algebraic topology. *Mailing Add:* 68 Farms Rd Circle East Brunswick NJ 08816-2913. *Fax:* 908-253-2951; *E-Mail:* xmathprof@aol.com

SCHNEIDER, HENRY, plant pathology & anatomy; deceased, see previous edition for last biography

SCHNEIDER, HENRY, BIOCHEMISTRY, TOXICOLOGY. *Current Pos:* from asst res officer to assoc res officer, 66-78, SR RES OFFICER, NAT RES COUN CAN, 78- *Personal Data:* b Montreal, Que, Dec 5, 33; m 62; c 3. *Educ:* Sir George Williams Univ, BSc, 55; Univ Western Ontario, MSc, 57; McGill Univ, PhD(phys chem), 63. *Prof Exp:* Res assoc, Cornell Univ, 62-64; res chemist, Miami Valley Labs, Procter & Gamble Co, 64-66. *Mem:* Chem Inst Can; Int Soc Study Xenobiotics. *Res:* Etiology and therapy of free radical diseases. *Mailing Add:* Nat Res Coun Can Ottawa ON K1A 0R6 Can. *Fax:* 613-941-4475; *E-Mail:* henry.schneider@nrc.ca

SCHNEIDER, HOWARD ALBERT, NUTRITION, BIOCHEMISTRY. *Current Pos:* prof & dir, Inst Nutrit, 70-78, EMER PROF NUTRIT & BIOCHEM, SCH MED, UNIV NC, CHAPEL HILL, 78- *Personal Data:* b Milwaukee, Wis, Dec 25, 12; m 37, Marie Gugler; c Susan C & Cynthia A. *Educ:* Univ Wis, BS, 34, MS, 36, PhD(biochem), 38. *Prof Exp:* Asst biochem, Univ Wis, 36-39; Rockefeller Found fel natural sci, Hosp, Rockefeller Inst, 39-40, from asst to assoc, 40-57, assoc prof nutrit & microbiol, 58-65; mem, Inst Biomed Res, Am Med Asn, 65-70, actg dir, 67-68, dep dir, 69-70. *Concurrent Pos:* Chmn, Inst Lab Animal Resources, Nat Acad Sci-Nat Res Coun, 66-69; mem pub affairs comt, Fedn Am Soc Exp Biol, 68-74, chmn, 70-72; prof, NC State Univ, Greensboro, 70-78 & Univ NC, Greensboro, 70-78; chief ed, Nutrit Support Med Pract, 77-; vis distinguished scholar residence, Fredrik Wachmeister prof sci & eng, Va Mil Inst, 79; mem, Pres Comn World Hynger, 79-80. *Mem:* Fel AAAS; fel Am Inst Chemists; fel Am Inst Nutrit; Soc Nutrit Educ; fel NY Acad Sci; Am Chem Soc. *Res:* Nutrition; resistance to infection; discoverer of the pacifarins, a class of ecological ectocrines; mediating infectious disease. *Mailing Add:* 6 Carolina Meadows Apt 306 Chapel Hill NC 27514-8525. *E-Mail:* hass@med.unc.edu

SCHNEIDER, IMOGENE PAULINE, PARASITOLOGY. *Current Pos:* RETIRED. *Personal Data:* b Milwaukee, Wis, June 6, 34. *Educ:* Ohio State Univ, BS, 56, MS, 58; Univ Chicago, PhD(genetics), 61. *Prof Exp:* NSF fel, Univ Zurich, 61-62; res biologist, Yale Univ, 62-65, Walter Reed Army Inst Res, 65-95. *Mem:* AAAS; Am Soc Trop Med & Hyg; Am Soc Parasitol; Tissue Cult Asn. *Res:* Developmental genetics of Drosophila; insect tissue culture; nutritional requirements of malarial parasites in vitro. *Mailing Add:* 19046 Capehart Dr Gaithersburg MD 20879

SCHNEIDER, IRWIN, SOLID STATE PHYSICS, OPTICS. *Current Pos:* RETIRED. *Personal Data:* b New York, NY, Aug 17, 32; m 59; c 2. *Educ:* Univ Ill, BS, 54, MS, 56; Univ Pa, PhD(physics), 63. *Prof Exp:* Fel physics, Lab Insulation Res, Mass Inst Technol, 63-64; res physicist, US Naval Res Lab, 64-94. *Concurrent Pos:* Nat Acad Sci-Nat Res Coun fel, 64-65. *Mem:* Fel Am Phys Soc; fel Sigma Xi. *Res:* Color centers in alkali halide crystals; holography; color center lasers. *Mailing Add:* 2402 Daphne Lane Alexandria VA 22306-2551

SCHNEIDER, JACOB DAVID, EXPERIMENTAL ATOMIC PHYSICS, PROTOTYPE ENGINEERING. *Current Pos:* Physicist, Los Alamos Sci Lab, 74-80, dep group leader, 86-88, group leader, 88-95, PROJECT LEADER, LOS ALAMOS SCI LAB, 95- *Personal Data:* b St Louis, Mo, Apr 14, 46; m 72, Constance Matthews; c Michael & Matthew. *Educ:* Univ Mo, Rolla, BS, 68; Kans State Univ, MS, 70. *Prof Exp:* Res asst, Los Alamos Sci Lab, 68-69; assoc physicist, Appl Physics Lab, Johns Hopkins Univ, 70-74. *Mem:* Am Inst Physics. *Res:* Project leader for development of a 20 MeV, 100 mA, CW proton accelerator. *Mailing Add:* 675 Totavi Los Alamos NM 87544. *Fax:* 505-667-4344; *E-Mail:* jdschneider@lanl.gov

SCHNEIDER, JAMES CARL, POPULATION DYNAMICS & ECOLOGY OF LAKE FISHES, MANAGEMENT OF SPORT FISHERIES. *Current Pos:* Fisheries res biologist, Mich Dept Natural Resources, 64-77, supvr warmwater Unit, 77-92, actg prog mgr, Res Sect, Fisheries Div, 92, BIOLOGIST IN CHARGE, INST FISHERIES RES, MICH DEPT NATURAL RESOURCES, 92- *Personal Data:* b Detroit, Mich, Jan 17, 40; m 62, Alice Bormann; c Laura & Ann. *Educ:* Univ Mich, BS, 62, MS, 63. *Concurrent Pos:* Assoc ed, NAm J Fisheries Mgr, 89-91. *Mem:* Am Fisheries Soc. *Res:* Population dynamics of freshwater fishes, ecology of lakes; management of fishes. *Mailing Add:* Inst Fisheries Res Mich Dept Natural Resources Ann Arbor MI 48109-1084. *Fax:* 313-663-9399

SCHNEIDER, JOHN ARTHUR, ORGANIC CHEMISTRY, POLYMER CHEMISTRY. *Current Pos:* RETIRED. *Personal Data:* b Saginaw, Mich, Feb 27, 40; m 63; c 2. *Educ:* Albion Col, AB, 62; Mass Inst Technol, PhD(org chem), 66. *Prof Exp:* Res chemist, Dow Chem Corp, 66-69, proj leader latex res, 69-72, develop specialist org chem, 72-73, group leader org chem develop, 73-77, NY dist sales mgr, 77-79, mgr, Chem & Metals Dept Brazil, 79-82, mgr new opportunity develop mkt res, 82-83, proj dir comt opportunity develop, 83-85, tech dir electronic prod, 85-89. *Concurrent Pos:* Instr, Delta Col, 67-69 & Cent Mich Univ, 74-77; vis industr scientist, Univ Wis-Superior, 67. *Mem:* Am Chem Soc (secy, 62-); Sigma Xi. *Res:* Cephalosporin C synthesis; bromine chloride; styrene-butadiene latexes; unsaturated polyesters; oxonium chemistry; polyamines; fire retardancy; peptide synthesis; electronic chemicals. *Mailing Add:* Purdue Res Found 1021 Houde Hall Rm 322A West Lafayette IN 47906

SCHNEIDER, JOHN H, INFORMATION SCIENCE, BIOCHEMISTRY. *Current Pos:* RETIRED. *Personal Data:* b Eau Claire, Wis, Sept 29, 31; c 2. *Educ:* Univ Wis, BS, 53, MS, 55, PhD(exp oncol), 58. *Prof Exp:* Asst prof biochem, Am Univ Beirut, 58-61 & Vanderbilt Univ, 61-62; ed-in-chief, Biol Abstr, 62-63; mem staff scientist-adminr training prog, NIH, 63-64, sci & prog info specialist, 64-67, sci & tech info officer, 67-73, dir, Int Cancer Res Data Bank Prog, 73-84, exec secy, Spec Rev Comt, Grants Rev Br, Nat Cancer Inst, 85-96. *Mem:* AAAS; Am Soc Info Sci. *Res:* Previously stressed development of large automated data bank for collection, processing and dissemination of all technical documents dealing with cancer and descriptions of all current cancer research projects; decimal classifications of biomedicine for use in program analysis; information retrieval and selective dissemination of information; design and development of computer systems for using hierarchical classifications in information systems; automating steps in processing research grants applications; biomedical research administration; cancer research. *Mailing Add:* Div Cancer Prev & Control Bldg EPN Rm 520 Nat Cancer Inst Bethesda MD 20892

SCHNEIDER, JOHN MATTHEW, ELECTROHYDRODYNAMICS, PHYSICAL ELECTRONICS. *Current Pos:* CONSULT. *Personal Data:* b Coulterville, Ill, Apr 27, 35; m 60; c 3. *Educ:* Univ Ill, BS, 59, MS, 60, PhD(elec eng), 64. *Prof Exp:* Instr elec eng, Univ Ill, 60-64, asst prof, 64-66; prof scientist res lab, Xerox Corp, 66-68, mgr res lab, 69-81; dir, Adv Technol Labs, Mead Digital Systs, Dayton, Ohio, 81-97; vpres & prin scientist, Scitex Digital Printing, 97. *Res:* Electrostatics research dealing with the interaction of fields and liquids. *Mailing Add:* 9421 Tanglewyck Pl Dayton OH 45458

SCHNEIDER, JOSEPH, CHEMISTRY. *Current Pos:* RETIRED. *Personal Data:* b Jersey City, NJ, June 25, 18. *Educ:* Columbia Univ, BS, 39; NY Univ, MS, 41; Polytech Inst Brooklyn, PhD(org chem), 62. *Prof Exp:* From instr to asst prof chem, Long Island Univ, 46-55; lectr, Polytech Inst Brooklyn, 56-62; from assoc prof to prof chem, St Francis Col, NY, 63-88. *Concurrent Pos:* Adj prof, Polytech Inst Brooklyn, 64-69, Hunter Col, 70-71; US Off Educ fel, NY Univ, 71-72. *Mem:* AAAS; Am Chem Soc; Royal Soc Chem. *Res:* Enzyme model systems; decarboxylase models; reaction mechanisms; Diels-Alder reaction and its catalysis; formation of carbohydrates from formaldehyde; catalysis by metal ions. *Mailing Add:* 3281 Cypress Ct Monmouth Junction NJ 08852

SCHNEIDER, JURG ADOLF, PHARMACOLOGY. *Current Pos:* EMERGENCY PHYSICIAN, DEPT EMERGENCY MED, MED CTR DEL, 71- *Personal Data:* b Basle, Switz, May 27, 20; nat US; m 46; c 4. *Educ:* Univ Basle, MD, 45. *Prof Exp:* Resident surg, Hosp, Basle, Switz, 46-47; resident, Univ Hosp, Univ Basle, 48-51; res assoc cardiol, Sch Med, Univ Calif, 47-48; sr pharmacologist, Ciba Pharmaceut Prod, Inc, 52-54, dir physiol res, 54-57; dir macrobiol res dept, Chas Pfizer & Co, Inc, 57-62; dir pharmaceut res, E I du Pont de Nemours & Co, Inc, 62-72, dir prod lic, 72-85. *Concurrent Pos:* Res fel, Res Lab, Ciba, Ltd, 45-46; lectr, Col Physicians & Surgeons, Columbia Univ, 57-65, adj prof, 70-; consult, 85- *Mem:* Am Physiol Soc; Am Soc Pharmacol & Exp Therapeut; fel Am Col Clin Pharmacol & Chemother; fel Am Col Neuropsychopharmacol; NY Acad Sci; Am Col Emergency Physicians. *Res:* Central nervous system and cardiovascular pharmacology; research administration. *Mailing Add:* 520 Rothbury Rd Wilmington DE 19803

SCHNEIDER, KENNETH JOHN, CHEMICAL ENGINEERING. *Current Pos:* mgr process evaluations, 72-78, STAFF ENGR, PAC NORTHWEST LAB, BATTELLE MEM INST, 78- *Personal Data:* b Denver, Colo, Nov 5, 26; m 55; c 3. *Educ:* Colo Sch Mines, PRE, 50. *Prof Exp:* Process engr, Gen Elec Co, 50-58, develop engr, 58-61, sr engr, 61-65; Pac Northwest Lab, Battelle Mem Inst, 65-67, res assoc process develop & prog planning, 67-71; eng assoc, Process Develop & Prog Planning, Westinghouse-Hanford Co, 71-72. *Concurrent Pos:* Prin engr, Int Atomic Energy Agency, Vienna, Austria, 78-80. *Mem:* Am Inst Chem Engrs; Am Nuclear Soc. *Res:* Process and equipment development in reprocessing of spent nuclear fuels; development of methods for solidification of highly radioactive wastes for safe storage; project engineering; development program planning and management; evaluation of nuclear fuel cycles. *Mailing Add:* Dept Mech Eng Calif State Polytech Univ 3801 W Temple Ave Pomona CA 91768-4062

SCHNEIDER, LAWRENCE KRUSE, ANATOMY. *Current Pos:* assoc prof anat & head dept, Univ Nev, 73-75, dir div biomed sci, 75-76, dir med admis & asst dean basic sci, 76-77, asst dean acad affairs, 77-78, PROF ANAT & HEAD DEPT, SCH MED SCI, UNIV NEV, RENO, 76- *Personal Data:* b Portland, Ore, Dec 17, 36; m 61; c 3. *Educ:* Univ Wash, BA, 60, PhD(cytochem), 66. *Prof Exp:* Instr biol struct, Univ Wash, 65-66; asst prof anat, Univ NDak, 66-68; asst prof anat & dir grad training, Dept Anat, Col Med, Univ Ariz, 68-73. *Concurrent Pos:* Instnl res grant, Univ NDak, 66-68; Gen Res Support, NASA & Am Cancer Soc instnl res grants, Col Med, Univ Ariz, 68-72. *Mem:* Am Asn Anat; Am Soc Cell Biol; Sigma Xi. *Res:* Radioautography of DNA and RNA synthesis in chromosomes of mammalian lymphocytes in vitro; cell kinetics; effects of various agents on cell growth in tissue culture; cytogenetics. *Mailing Add:* Univ Nev Sch Med Reno NV 89557-0001

SCHNEIDER, LON S, GERIATRICS. *Current Pos:* PROF PSYCHIAT & NEUROL, SCH MED, UNIV SOUTHERN CALIF, 83- *Educ:* Sarah Lawrence Col, AB, 74; Hahnemann Med Col, Md, 78. *Mem:* Am Asn Geriat Psychiat (secy, 87-88); Am Psychiat Asn. *Res:* Geriatric psychiatry; psychopharmacology, biological markers; Alzheimer's disease, depression. *Mailing Add:* Dept Psychiat Sch Med Univ Southern Calif 1975 Zonal Ave KAM-400 Los Angeles CA 90033

SCHNEIDER, MARC H, WOOD SCIENCE & TECHNOLOGY. *Current Pos:* from asst prof to assoc prof, 67-80, PROF WOOD SCI & TECHNOL, UNIV NB, 80- *Personal Data:* b Rochester, NY. *Educ:* State Univ NY, BS, 65, MS, 67, PhD(wood & polymer sci), 78. *Prof Exp:* Fel wood coating, Paint Res Inst, 65-67. *Mem:* Soc Wood Sci & Technol; Forest Prods Res Soc. *Res:* Wood-chemical interactions such as sorption, adhesion and interdiffusion; wood as fuel; wood-polymer composites. *Mailing Add:* Dept Forestry Univ NB Box 4400 Fredericton NB E3B 5A3 Can

SCHNEIDER, MARTIN V, PHYSICS. *Current Pos:* RETIRED. *Personal Data:* b Bern, Switz, Oct 30, 30; m 55. *Educ:* Swiss Fed Inst Technol, MS, 55, PhD(physics), 59. *Prof Exp:* Res assoc,Mmicrowave Res Lab, Swiss Fed Inst Technol, 60-62; mem tech staff radio res, AT&T Bell Labs, 63-68, supvr, Radio Res Dept, 68-96. *Mem:* Am Phys Soc; Am Vacuum Soc; Inst Elec & Electronics Engrs; Sigma Xi. *Res:* Microwave active and passive devices and circuits; optical and thin film active devices; photodetectors. *Mailing Add:* 46 Line Rd Holmdel NJ 07733

SCHNEIDER, MAXYNE DOROTHY, PHYSICAL CHEMISTRY. *Current Pos:* instr, 73-81, asst prof chem, 81-83, ACAD DEAN, COL OUR LADY OF THE ELMS, 83- *Personal Data:* b North Adams, Mass, Nov 4, 42. *Educ:* Col Our Lady of the Elms, AB, 65; Boston Col, PhD(chem), 75. *Prof Exp:* Teacher chem, Cathedral High Sch, Springfield, Mass, 65-69. *Mem:* Am Chem Soc; Inst Theol Encounter with Sci & Technol; Am Asn Higher Educ. *Res:* Science education; science, technology, society, religion. *Mailing Add:* 20 Barthel Ave Gardner MA 01440

SCHNEIDER, MEIER, INDUSTRIAL HYGIENE, HAZARDOUS MATERIALS MANAGEMENT. *Current Pos:* RETIRED. *Personal Data:* b Worcester, Mass, Dec 8, 15; m 44; c 3. *Educ:* Univ Rochester, NY, BA, 40; Calif State Univ, Northridge, MS, 73. *Prof Exp:* Sr chemist, Los Angeles County Air Pollution Control Dist, 48-52; res specialist, Los Angeles Div, Rockwell Int, 55-68; safety & industr hyg coordr, Lockheed-Calif Co, Burbank, 68-70; sr indust hyg engr, Environ Health Serv Prog, Occup Health Sect, Calif State Dept Health, 70-73; indust hyg engr, Dept Personnel, Med Serv Div, City of Los Angeles, 74-81; chief occup safety & health, Metropolitan Water Dist Southern Calif, 81-87. *Concurrent Pos:* Assoc & prof environ & occup health, Health Sci Dept, Calif State Univ, Northridge, 74-88; Calif indust hyg rep, Chem Agents Threshold Limit Value Comt, Am Conf Govt Indust Hygienists, Cincinnati, Ohio, 75-; field prof, Norton AFB Satellite Campus, Univ Southern Calif, 76-86; lectr, air pollution, occup & environ health & safety, indust hyg; expert witness, toxic tort & prod liability litigation; prof rep, Task Force Appl Competitive Technol-Hazardous Mat Technol, Calif Community Cols, 89-90. *Mem:* Am Indust Hyg Asn; Am Conf Govt Indust Hygienists; Sigma Xi. *Res:* Toxicology of industrial chemicals; conducted an environmental study of mercury contamination in dental offices involving risk assessment of dentists and staff. *Mailing Add:* 1208 Point View St Los Angeles CA 90035-2621

SCHNEIDER, MICHAEL CHARLES, GEOLOGY. *Current Pos:* prof geol, 68-76, PROF EARTH SCI, EDINBORO STATE COL, 76- *Personal Data:* b Chicago, Ill, May 7, 29; m 54; c 2. *Educ:* Cornell Col, BA, 52; Miami Univ, MS, 56; Brigham Young Univ, PhD(geol), 67. *Prof Exp:* From instr to assoc prof geol, DePauw Univ, 59-68. *Mem:* AAAS; Geol Soc Am; Soc Econ Paleontologists & Mineralogists; Nat Asn Geol Teachers. *Res:* Water pollution; acid mine drainage; stratigraphic correlation and age dating; science education. *Mailing Add:* Dept Geol Sci Edinboro Univ Pa 219 Meadville St Edinboro PA 16444-0001

SCHNEIDER, MICHAEL J, PLANT PHYSIOLOGY, PHOTOBIOLOGY. *Current Pos:* chmn dept natural sci, 75-80, 83-90, assoc provost, 90-91, PROF BIOL, UNIV MICH, DEARBORN, 77-, INTERIM PROVOST & VCHANCELLOR ACAD AFFAIRS, 91- *Personal Data:* b Saginaw, Mich, Apr 21, 38; m 67, Janet M Dotler; c Michael L. *Educ:* Univ Mich, BS, 60; Univ Tenn, MS, 62; Univ Chicago, PhD(bot), 65. *Honors & Awards:* Sigma Xi. *Prof Exp:* Nat Acad Sci-Nat Res Coun fel, Plant Physiol Lab, USDA, Beltsville, Md, 65-67; USPHS fel bot, Univ Wis-Madison, 67-68; asst prof biol sci, Columbia Univ, 68-73. *Concurrent Pos:* Dept Energy vis prof, Plant Res Lab, Mich State Univ, 80-81. *Mem:* AAAS; Am Soc Plant Physiol; Bot Soc Am; Am Soc Photobiol. *Res:* Physiology and biochemistry of plant growth and development. *Mailing Add:* Natural Sci Dept Univ Mich-Dearborn 4901 Evergreen Rd Dearborn MI 48128-1491. *Fax:* 313-593-4937; *E-Mail:* mschneid@umich.edu

SCHNEIDER, MORRIS HENRY, INDUSTRIAL ENGINEERING. *Current Pos:* RETIRED. *Personal Data:* b Sutton, Nebr, Nov 26, 23; m 52; c 1. *Educ:* Univ Nebr, BS, 51 & 59; Kans State Univ, MS, 61; Okla State Univ, PhD(indust eng), 66. *Prof Exp:* Instr mech eng, Univ Nebr, 54-60; asst prof indust eng, Kans State Univ, 60-62 & Tex Tech Col, 62-64; assoc prof mech eng, Univ Nebr, Lincoln, 65-70, prof indust eng & chmn dept, 70-93. *Concurrent Pos:* Am Soc Tool & Mfg Eng res grant, 66-67; NSF sci equip prog grant, 66-68. *Mem:* Am Soc Eng Educ; Am Inst Indust Engrs; Nat Soc Prof Engrs; Sigma Xi. *Res:* Production design and processes. *Mailing Add:* 175 Nebraska Hall Univ Nebr Lincoln NE 68588

SCHNEIDER, NANCY REYNOLDS, CLINICAL CYTOGENETICS, CANCER CYTOGENETICS. *Current Pos:* resident path, 82-85, from instr to asst prof, 86-92, ASSOC PROF PATHOL, UNIV TEX, SOUTHWESTERN MED CTR, 92-, DIR, CYTOGENETICS LAB. *Personal Data:* b Schenectady, NY, July 27, 42; m 68, John S. *Educ:* Ohio Wesleyan Univ, BA, 63; Univ Mich, MA, 64; Cornell Univ, MD, 81, PhD(human genetics), 81. *Prof Exp:* Fel, Mem Sloan-Kettering Cancer Ctr, 86. *Concurrent Pos:* Mem, Cytogenetic Resource Comt, Col Am Pathologists, 92- *Mem:* AAAS; fel Am Col Med Genetics; Am Soc Clin Pathologists; Am Soc Human Genetics; Am Med Asn; fel Col Am Pathologists. *Res:* Cancer cytogenetics, clinical and case studies. *Mailing Add:* Univ Tex Southwestern Med Ctr Dept Path 5323 Harry Hines Blvd Dallas TX 75235-9072

SCHNEIDER, NORMAN RICHARD, TOXICOLOGY, DIAGNOSTIC MEDICINE. *Current Pos:* ASSOC PROF & VET TOXICOLOGIST, DEPT VET & BIOMED SCI, UNIV NEBR, LINCOLN, 79- *Personal Data:* b Ellsworth, Kans, Mar 28, 43; m 68, Karen M Nelson; c Nelson R. *Educ:* Kans State Univ, BS, 67, DVM, 68; Ohio State Univ, MSc, 72. *Prof Exp:* Chief vet serv, Goose AFB, Labrador, 68-70, Air Force Inst Technol fel, Ohio State Univ, 70-72; vet scientist, Armed Forces Radiobiol Res Inst, Md, 72-76; vet toxicologist, Aerospace Med Res Lab, Wright-Patterson AFB, Ohio, 76-79. *Concurrent Pos:* Consult, Mid-Plains Poison Control Ctr, Nebr, 79-; assoc courtesy prof, Dept Pharmacodynamics & Toxicol, Col Pharm, Med Ctr, Univ Nebr, 82-85; Dept Pharmaceut Sci, 86-; vet prof rep, Nebr State Bd Health, 85-87. *Mem:* Am Bd Vet Toxicol (pres, 88-91); Am Vet Med Asn; Am Acad Vet & Comp Toxicol; Am Asn Vet Lab Diagnosticians; Asn Mil Surgeons US; Asn Off Anal Chemists. *Res:* Nitrite-nitrate pharmacokinetics and pathophysiology; maternal-fetal pharmacokinetics; mycotoxicoses related to fusariotoxins and ergot alkaloids, and chemical detoxification-decontamination; pesticide degradation in rendered animal byproducts; trace elements in nutritional-metabolic disorders. *Mailing Add:* Vet Diag Ctr Dept Vet & Biomed Sci Rm 140A Univ Nebr Lincoln NE 68583-0907. *Fax:* 402-472-3094

SCHNEIDER, PHILIP ALLEN DAVID, INFORMATION SCIENCE, LOGICAL SYSTEMS. *Current Pos:* chief, Manpower Statist Div, 73-75, assoc dir workforce info, Bur Personnel Mgt Info Systs, US Civil Serv Comn, 75-80, ASST DIR WORKFORCE INFO, SR EXEC SERV, US OFF PERSONNEL MGT, 80- *Personal Data:* b St Louis, Mo, Oct 26, 38; m 63, Mary L Brown; c 6. *Educ:* Cornell Univ, AB, 61; Duke Univ, PhD(methodology sci), 68. *Prof Exp:* Mathematician, Abbott Labs, 61-62; plans officer info sci, US Army Security Agency, 62-64; group leader, Defense Commun Agency, 64; consult, Dept Math, Duke Univ, 64-68, Dept Philos, Univ NC, 67-68; dir sci serv, US Army Syst Analysis Group, 68-73. *Concurrent Pos:* NDEA fel, 64-67; NSF fel, 67-68; assoc prof, Sch Gen Studies, Univ Va, 68-73 & Northern Va Community Col, 73-; prof logic, George Mason Univ, 86- *Mem:* Am Statist Asn; Am Philol Asn. *Res:* Proof procedure for systems of logic, theories of truth, conformation criteria for physical theories, foundational criteria for ethical truth; applied statistics. *Mailing Add:* 1516 Chevelle Dr Richmond VA 23235. *Fax:* 202-606-1719; *E-Mail:* pschneid@gmuvax.gmu.edu

SCHNEIDER, PHILLIP WILLIAM, JR, FISHERIES, TOXICOLOGY. *Current Pos:* fish & wildlife biologist, River Basins Studies, US Fish & Wildlife Serv, res toxicologist, 75-78, CHIEF, CHRONIC INVEST, TOXICOLOGY, HASKELL LAB, E I DU PONT DE NEMOURS & CO, 78- *Personal Data:* b Corvallis, Ore, Sept 2, 44; m 69; c 2. *Educ:* Ore State Univ, BS, 66, PhD(fisheries, pharmacol), 74; Univ Maine, MS, 71. *Prof Exp:* Fisheries biologist, US Environ Protection Agency, 68-71. *Mem:* Am Soc Testing & Mat; Am Fisheries Soc; AAAS. *Res:* Neuromuscular physiology, pharmacology and detoxification mechanisms in fish as compared with other vertebrates. *Mailing Add:* 128 Stoney Ridge Rd Landenberg PA 19350

SCHNEIDER, RALPH JACOB, ELECTRONICS, ELECTRICAL ENGINEERING. *Current Pos:* CONSULT, 88- *Personal Data:* b Oxford, Ohio, Sept 2, 22; m 45; c 3. *Educ:* Clarkson Col Technol, BEE, 49. *Prof Exp:* Instrumentation engr, Bell Aircraft Corp, 49-54, preliminary design engr, 54-57; engr, Melpar Div, Westinghouse Air Brake Co, 57-58, proj engr, 58-60; electronics engr, Anal Serv, Inc, 60-85. *Mem:* Sr mem Inst Elec & Electronics Engrs. *Res:* Evaluation of research aircraft and missile components such as storage batteries, critical mechanical components, and radar subsystems; analysis of airborne radar, communications and electronic penetration aids and fire control systems. *Mailing Add:* 718 N Overlook Dr Alexandria VA 22305

SCHNEIDER, RICHARD THEODORE, plasma physics, spectroscopy, for more information see previous edition

SCHNEIDER, ROBERT, HYDROGEOLOGY, HYDROGEOLOGY OF CONTAMINANTS IN GROUND WATER. *Current Pos:* CONSULT HYDROGEOLOGIST, 84- *Personal Data:* b Brooklyn, NY, Apr 7, 21; m 46; c 3. *Educ:* Brooklyn Col, AB, 41. *Prof Exp:* Photogrammetrist, US Geol Surv, 41-43, geologist, 43-44, groundwater geologist, Tenn, 45-50, dist geologist, Minn, 50-60, asst to chief res sec, Groundwater Br, 60-62, actg chief res sect, 62-64, staff geologist, Gen Hydrol Br, 64-65, res geologist, 65-67, chief off radiohydrol, 67-71; water res scientist, Off Water Resources Res, US Dept Interior, 71-75; staff hydrologist, US Geol Surv, 75-84. *Concurrent Pos:* Consult, Govt Brazil, 60 & Govt Israel, 62; assoc ed, J Ground Water, 96- *Mem:* Geol Soc Am; Am Geophys Union; Nat Ground Water Asn; Int Asn Hydrogeologists (secy-treas, 75-77); Am Inst Prof Geologists. *Res:* Thermal characteristics of aquifers; subsurface movement of hazardous wastes; geohydrology of glacial deposits. *Mailing Add:* 6212 N 31st St Arlington VA 22207. *E-Mail:* rschnei@erols.com

SCHNEIDER, ROBERT FOURNIER, CHEMICAL PHYSICS. *Current Pos:* asst prof, 60-68, assoc vprovost, 73-95, ASSOC PROF CHEM, STATE UNIV NY, STONY BROOK, 68-, DIR, INFORMATICS & COMPLIANCE, 95- *Personal Data:* b New York, NY, Feb 24, 33; div; c 3. *Educ:* Columbia Univ, AB, 54, MA, 56, PhD(chem), 59. *Prof Exp:* Res assoc chem, Brookhaven Nat Lab, 59-60. *Concurrent Pos:* Actg vprovost, Comput & Commun, 86-88; vpres, NY State Educ Res Net. *Mem:* AAAS; Soc Res Admin; Nat Coun Univ Res Admin. *Res:* Research administration; computerization of administrative environments. *Mailing Add:* Off Vpres Res State Univ NY Stony Brook NY 11794-3368. *Fax:* 516-632-9839; *E-Mail:* rschneider@wotes.cc.sunysb.edu

SCHNEIDER, ROBERT JULIUS, ACCELERATOR PHYSICS, RADIATION PHYSICS. *Current Pos:* SR RES SPECIALIST, WOODS HOLE OCEANOG INST, 89- *Personal Data:* b Troy, NY, Mar 9, 39; m 61; c 2. *Educ:* Oberlin Col, BA, 60; Wesleyan Univ, MA, 63; Tufts Univ, PhD(physics), 68. *Prof Exp:* Staff assoc physics, Columbia Univ, 68-73; res fel physics, Harvard Univ, 73-80; physicist, Gen Ionex Corp, 80-84; sr scientist, Am Sci & Eng, Inc, 84-88. *Concurrent Pos:* Lectr physics, Harvard Univ, 79-80. *Mem:* Am Phys Soc; Am Asn Physicists Med; Sigma Xi; Am Geophys Union. *Res:* Radiation applied to cancer therapy; accelerators; isotopes; nuclear physics; oceanography. *Mailing Add:* 8 Braebrook Rd Acton MA 01720. *E-Mail:* rschneider@whoi.edu

SCHNEIDER, ROBERT W(ILLIAM), mechanical engineering, for more information see previous edition

SCHNEIDER, RONALD E, THEORETICAL PHYSICS, NUCLEAR PHYSICS. *Current Pos:* RETIRED. *Personal Data:* b Akron, Ohio, Sept 14, 28; m 53; c 4. *Educ:* Univ Akron, BS, 51; Va Polytech Inst, MS, 53; John Carroll Univ, MS, 58; Case Inst Technol, PhD(physics), 64. *Prof Exp:* Engr, Goodrich Tire & Rubber Co, 53-54; sr engr, Goodyear Aerospace Corp, 56-58; instr math, John Carroll Univ, 58-60; from asst prof to assoc prof physics, Univ Akron, 62-93. *Res:* Nuclear forces. *Mailing Add:* 389 Willard Rd Aurora OH 44202

SCHNEIDER, ROSE G, MEDICINE. *Current Pos:* RETIRED. *Personal Data:* b Minsk, Russia, July 19, 08; US citizen; m 41; c 3. *Educ:* Barnard Col, Columbia Univ, AB, 29; Harvard Med Sch, MA, 32; Cornell Med Col, PhD, 37. *Prof Exp:* Instr path, Med Br, Univ Tex, Galveston, 42-43; asst pathologist, Robert B Green Hosp, San Antonio, 44-45; res assoc, Tissue Cult Lab & Tissue Metab Res Lab, Med Br, Univ Tex, Galveston, 48-62, asst res prof surg, 62-63, asst res prof pediat, 63-65, assoc res prof, 65-69, res prof pediat & prof human biol chem & genetics, 69- *Mem:* Int Soc Hemat; Soc Exp Biol & Med; Am Soc Human Genetics; Am Soc Hemat; Sigma Xi. *Res:* Abnormal hemaglobins. *Mailing Add:* 123 Tarpon Ave Galveston TX 77550

SCHNEIDER, SANDRA LEE, IMMUNOHEMATOLOGY, IMMUNOLOGY. *Current Pos:* res scientist immunol & immunohemat, 73-90, RES ASSOC PROF, SOUTHWEST FOUND RES & EDUC, 90- *Personal Data:* b Pueblo, Colo, July 10, 44; m 73. *Educ:* Southern Colo State Col, BS & Univ Colo, MT, 66. *Prof Exp:* Med technologist immunohemat, Belle Bonfils Mem Blood Band, 66-68; supvr blood bank, East Tenn Baptist Hosp, 68-69; med technologist II hemat, Med Ctr, Univ Kans, 69-70; med technologist immunol, Knoxville Blood Bank & Reagents, 70-71. *Concurrent Pos:* Tech transfusion consult, ETenn Baptist Hosp, Knoxville, Tenn, 68-69 & Knoxville Blood Ctr, 70-71. *Mem:* AAAS; Am Soc Primatologists; Am Soc Clin Pathologists; Am Asn Blood Banks; Am Soc Microbiol. *Res:* Design and development of techniques to determine alveolar macrophage and lymphocyte interactions, particularly in the baboon exposed to anti-cancer drugs, cigarette derived smoke and chemically defined environmental agents. *Mailing Add:* PO Box 3 Helotes TX 78023-0003

SCHNEIDER, SOL, PULSE POWER, POWER SWITCHES. *Current Pos:* CONSULT, 81-; STAFF SCIENTIST, BERKELEY RES ASN, 96- *Personal Data:* b New York, NY, Feb 24, 24; m 50, Rhoda Botwinik; c Sandra & Barry. *Educ:* Brooklyn Col, BA, 46; NY Univ, MS, 49. *Honors & Awards:* Res & Develop Achievement Awards, 63 & 78, US Army & Secy Army Spec Act Award, 63; Bronze Medallion, Army Sci Conf, 78; High Voltage Award, Inst Elec & Electronics Engrs, 91 & Germeshausen Award, 92. *Prof Exp:* Chief, Res Unit Power & Gas Tube Sect, Electronics Technol & Devices Lab, US Army, 48-55, chief, Plasma & Pulse Power Br, Electronics Technol & Devices Lab, 56-81; adj prof, Southeastern Ctr Elec Eng Educ, 81-87. *Concurrent Pos:* Army mem, Power & Gas Tubes Panel, Adv Group Electrontubes, Dept Defense, 56-62, assoc army mem Adv Group Electron Devices, 74-81,

Steering Comt, Pulsed Power Workshop, 76; chmn, Power Modulator Symp, Inst Elec & Electronics Engrs, 58-80, emer chmn, 81-, co-chmn, High Voltage Workshop, 88-89, mem, exec comt, 90-, mem, exec comt, Int Pulsed Power Conf, 76-80; mem, exec comt, Gaseous Electronics Conf, Am Phys Soc, 61-66, Electron & Atomic Physics Div, 65-66, AF Panel Educ in Pulsed Power, 78-80, USN Pulsed Power Tech Adv Group, 78-80, Pulsed Power Tech Adv Panel, Strategic Defense Initiative, 84-92; consult, Los Alamos Sci Lab, 80-81, Rockwell Int, 81, SRI Int, 83-91, Vitronics, 88-; consult, Pulse Power Ctr, US Army, 83-, tech studies, Res Off, Battelle, 81-88. *Mem:* Am Phys Soc; fel Inst Elec & Electronics Engrs. *Res:* Modulators, pulse power; plasma devices; power semiconducter devices; research studies and design. *Mailing Add:* 100 Arrowwood Ct Red Bank NJ 07701

SCHNEIDER, STANLEY, PHYSICS. *Current Pos:* STAFF SCIENTIST, MCDONALD DOUGLAS CORP, 65- *Personal Data:* b Brooklyn, NY, Nov 20, 31. *Educ:* Polytech Inst Brooklyn, BS, 53, MS, 56; Harvard Univ, MS, 57. *Mem:* Am Phys Soc. *Mailing Add:* 26628 Fond du Lac Rd Rancho Palos Verdes CA 90275

SCHNEIDER, STEPHEN HENRY, CLIMATOLOGY, ENVIRONMENTAL SCIENCE & TECHNOLOGY & POLICY. *Current Pos:* advan study prog fel, Nat Ctr Atmospheric Res, Stanford Univ, 72-73, sci & dep head, climate proj, 73-78, actg leader, Climate Sensitivity Group, 78-80, head, vis progs & dep dir, advanced study prog, 80-87, head, Interdisciplinary Climate Systs Sec, 87-92, PROF BIOL SCI & SR FEL INST INT STUDIES, STANFORD UNIV, 92- *Personal Data:* b New York, NY, Feb 11, 45; m 90, Terry Root; c Rebecca & Adam. *Educ:* Columbia Univ, BS, 66, MS, 67, PhD(mech eng), 71. *Hon Degrees:* DSc, NJ Inst Technol, 90 & Monmouth Col, 91. *Prof Exp:* Nat Acad Sci-Nat Res Coun res assoc, Goddard Inst Space Studies, NASA, NY, 71-72. *Concurrent Pos:* Mem, Comt Paleoclimatol & Climatic Change, Am Meteorol Soc, 73, mem global atmospheric res prog working group for numerical experimentation, 74-78; ed, Climatic Change, 75-; mem climate dynamics panel, Nat Acad Sci, 76-81; mem, Carter-Mondale Task Force on Sci Policy & Coun Sci & Technol Develop, 76; Univ Corp Atmospheric Res Affil Prof, Lamont-Doherty Geol Observ, Columbia Univ, 76-; mem, Nat Acad Sci, Subcom Resources & Environ, Int Inst Appl Systs Anal, 78-80, Adv & Planning Comt, Social Indicators, Social Sci Res Coun, 79-, US Nat Climate Prog Adv Comt, 80-, Comt Pub Understanding Sci, NSF, 80-81, Sci Adv Comt, World Climate Studies Prog, UN Environ Prog, 80-; co-ed, Food-Climate Interactions, 81, Social Sci Res, An Interdisciplinary Appraisal, 82; ed, Climatic Change, 76-; mem, Comt Policy Greenhouse Buffet, Nat Res Coun, 90-91. *Mem:* Fel AAAS; Am Meteorol Soc; Am Geophys Union; Soc Conserv Biol; Soc Biol Econ. *Res:* Theoretical investigations of climatic changes arising from both natural and possible man-made causes; impact of human activities on climate; impact of climatic change on environment and society; science policy; science popularization; science education; effect of nuclear war on society and environment. *Mailing Add:* Dept Biol Sci Gilbert Bldg Stanford CA 94305-5020. *Fax:* 650-725-4387

SCHNEIDER, SUSAN MARGUERITE, EXPERIMENTAL PSYCHOLOGY, HISTORY OF PSYCHOLOGY. *Current Pos:* ASST PROF PSYCHOL, AUBURN UNIV, 92- *Personal Data:* b Chicago, Ill, Aug 20, 58. *Educ:* Ill Inst Technol, BS, 80; Brown Univ, MS, 81; Univ Kans, PhD(psychol), 89. *Prof Exp:* Asst prof, St Olaf Col, 89-92. *Mem:* Am Psychol Asn; Asn Behav Anal. *Res:* Quantitative analysis of behavior; history and philosophy of psychology. *Mailing Add:* Dept Psychol St Marys Col St Marys City MD 20686

SCHNEIDER, VERNE, HYDROLOGY. *Current Pos:* ASST CHIEF HYDROLOGIST TECH SUPPORT, US GEOL SURV, 95- *Personal Data:* b St Joseph, Mich, Apr 19, 41. *Educ:* Valparaiso Univ, BS, 63; Colo State Univ, MS, 65, PhD(civil eng), 68. *Mem:* Am Soc Civil Engrs; Am Geophys Union; Int Asn Hydrol Sci. *Mailing Add:* US Geol Surv 414 Nat Ctr Reston VA 20192. *Fax:* 703-648-5722; *E-Mail:* vrschnei@usgs.gov

SCHNEIDER, WALTER CARL, NUCLEIC ACIDS, CYTOCHEMISTRY. *Current Pos:* RETIRED. *Personal Data:* b Cedarburg, Wis, Sept 26, 19; m 42, Edith M Janot; c James C, Susan J & Walter C Jr. *Educ:* Univ Wis, BS, 41, PhD(physiol chem), 45. *Prof Exp:* Res asst oncol, McArdle Mem Lab, Univ Wis, 41-45, instr, 47-48; res fel, Jane Coffin Childs Mem Fund, 45-47; chemist, Nat Cancer Inst, 48-52, head, Nucleic Acids Sect, 62-80. *Concurrent Pos:* Assoc ed, J Nat Cancer Inst, 52-54; res consult, George Washington Univ, 58-59. *Mem:* Sigma Xi; Am Soc Biol Chemists; Am Asn Cancer Res; Am Chem Soc. *Res:* Methods for nucleic acid analysis and for isolation of subcellular organelles such as nuclei and mitochondria from animal tissues; composition and function of subcellular organelles in normal and cancer tissues. *Mailing Add:* 15301 Barningham Ct Silver Spring MD 20906

SCHNEIDER, WILLIAM C, AEROSPACE ENGINEERING. *Current Pos:* CONSULT AEROSPACE, 90- *Personal Data:* b New York, NY, Dec 24, 23; m 64; c 4. *Educ:* Mass Inst Technol, SBAero, 49; Univ Va, MS, 52; Cath Univ, DEng(aero eng), 76. *Honors & Awards:* Collier Trophy, 73. *Prof Exp:* Dep dir, Gemini, NASA, 63-65, mission dir, Gemini, 65-66 & Apollo, 66-68, prog dir Skylab, 68-74, dep assoc adminr, manned flight, 74-78, assoc adminr, tracking & data, 78-80; vpres, Computer Sci Corp, 80-90. *Concurrent Pos:* Mem, Aerospace Med Adv Comt, NASA, 83-, Life Sci Adv Comt, 84- & Space Sta Adv Comt, 86-, vpres finance, Alumni League, 86-; chmn, Honors & Awards Comt, Am Inst Aeronaut & Astronaut. *Mem:* Int Astron Asn; Am Astron Soc; Planetary Soc. *Mailing Add:* 11801 Clintwood Pl Silver Spring MD 20902. *Fax:* 301-681-7677

SCHNEIDER, WILLIAM CHARLES, SOLID MECHANICS, ENGINEERING MECHANICS. *Current Pos:* Aerospace engr, 62-85, chief, Mech Design & Analysis Br, 85-95, ASST DIR ENG, JOHNSON SPACE CTR, NASA, HOUSTON, 95- *Personal Data:* b New Orleans, La, Jan 22, 40; m 68; c 3. *Educ:* La State Univ, BS, 62; Univ Houston, MS, 68; Rice Univ, PhD(mech eng), 72. *Concurrent Pos:* Consult mech, 77-; eng consult, DiCaro & Assocs, 77-78; eng consult & vpres, Accident Anal Consult Engrs, 78- *Mem:* Sigma Xi. *Res:* Thermoelasticity; elasticity; fluid-filled porous elastic solids. *Mailing Add:* 1723 Festival Dr Houston TX 77058

SCHNEIDER, WILLIAM GEORGE, PHYSICAL CHEMISTRY. *Current Pos:* RES CONSULT, 80- *Personal Data:* b Wolseley, Sask, June 1, 15; m 40, Jean F Purves; c Judith A & Joanne F. *Educ:* Univ Sask, BSc, 37, MS, 39; McGill Univ, PhD(phys chem), 41. *Hon Degrees:* DSc, York Univ, 66, Mem Univ Newf, 68, Univ Moncton, 69, Univ Sask, 69, McMaster Univ, 69, Laval Univ, 69, Univ NB, 70, Univ Montreal, 70, McGill Univ, 70; LLD, Univ Alta, 68, Laurentian Univ, 68 & Ottawa Univ, 78. *Honors & Awards:* Medal, Chem Inst Can, 61; Henry Marshall Tory Medal, Royal Soc Can, 69; Montreal Medal, Chem Inst Can, 73; Order of Can, 77. *Prof Exp:* Royal Soc Can traveling fel, Harvard Univ, 41-43; res physicist, Woods Hole Oceanog Inst, 43-46; head gen phys chem sect, div pure chem, Nat Res Coun Can, 43-63, dir div pure chem, 63-65, vpres sci, 65-67, pres, 67-80. *Concurrent Pos:* Pres, Int Union Pure & Appl Chem, 83-85. *Mem:* Am Chem Soc; Am Phys Soc; fel Chem Inst Can; fel Royal Soc Can; fel Royal Soc London; Int Union Pure & Appl Chem. *Res:* Intermolecular forces; critical phenomena; ultrasonics; nuclear magnetic resonance; organic semiconductors. *Mailing Add:* 65 Whitemarl Dr Unit No 2 Ottawa ON K1L 8J9 Can

SCHNEIDER, WILLIAM PAUL, ORGANIC CHEMISTRY. *Current Pos:* RETIRED. *Personal Data:* b Marietta, Ohio, Mar 25, 21; m 44; c 4. *Educ:* Marietta Col, AB, 44; Univ Wis, MS, 46, PhD(chem), 50. *Prof Exp:* Instr chem, Marietta Col, 46-47, fel, Harvard Univ, 50-51; chemist, Upjohn Co, 51-83. *Mem:* Am Chem Soc. *Res:* Synthetic organic chemistry; steroids; prostaglandins; natural products. *Mailing Add:* 5539 Hwy 187 Anderson SC 29625-8961

SCHNEIDER, WOLFGANG JOHANN, MOLECULAR BIOLOGY & BIOCHEMISTRY OF CELL SURFACE RECEPTORS. *Current Pos:* CHAIR MOLECULAR GENETICS, BIOCTR VIENNA, 91- *Personal Data:* b Vienna, Austria, Apr 5, 49; m 74, Lieselotte; c Jeannine. *Educ:* Tech Univ Vienna, Austria, BS, 70, MS, 73, PhD(biochem), 75; Univ Graz, Austria, Dozent(med biochem), 86. *Honors & Awards:* Gabor Szasz Prize, Ger Soc Clin Invest, 87; Kurt Adam Prize, Ger Cong Soc, 87; Wieland Heinrich Prize, Heinrich Wieland Found, 91. *Prof Exp:* Fel, Univ BC, 76-78; res assoc, Univ Tex Health Sci Ctr, Dallas, 78-80, asst prof molecular genetics, 81-85; from assoc prof to prof biochem, Univ Alta, Edmonton, 85-91. *Concurrent Pos:* Lectr, Univ Graz, Austria, 86-; mem, Lipid & Lipoprotein Res Group, 87-; ed, Biochem Biophys Acta, 89-; vis prof, Wihuri Res Inst, Helsinki, 90- *Mem:* Am Soc Cell Biol; Am Soc Biochem & Molecular Biol; Can Biochem Soc; Ger Soc Clin Invest; Austrian Atherosclerosis Soc. *Res:* Regulation of oocyte growth through receptor-mediated endocytosis; role of lipoprotein receptors and apolipoproteins in etiology of lipid disorders. *Mailing Add:* Dept Molecular Genetics Biocenter Vienna Dr Bohr Gasse g 2 A 1030 Vienna Austria. *Fax:* 43-1-79515-2013; *E-Mail:* wjs@mol.univie.ac.at

SCHNEIDER, WOLFGANG W, HOMOGENEOUS CATALYSIS, HETEROGENEOUS CATALYSIS. *Personal Data:* b Oberhausen, Ger, Mar 25, 35; c B Patricia. *Educ:* Aachen Tech Univ, BS, 57, MS, 59; Max Planck Inst Coal Res, PhD(org chem), 62. *Prof Exp:* Asst metal-organics, Max Planck Inst Coals Res, 59-61, fel org chem, 61-62; res chemist, B F Goodrich Co, 63-65, sr res & develop chemist, 65-78, res & develop assoc, 78-80, sr res & develop assoc, 80-93. *Mem:* Am Chem Soc. *Res:* Heterogeneous and homogenous catalysis of monomers and polymers from invention to scale-up involving organic chemistry, polymerization and chemical engineering. *Mailing Add:* 3934 Harris Rd Broadview Heights OH 44147

SCHNEIDERMAN, JACOB HARRY, EPILEPSY, ELECTROENCEPHALOGRAPHY. *Current Pos:* asst prof med, 82-89, assoc prof, 89-93, PROF NEUROL & PHYSIOL, UNIV TORONTO, 93- *Personal Data:* m 73, Anne Guth; c Adam & Aimee. *Educ:* Univ Toronto, BSc, 71, MD, 74, FRCP(c), 79. *Prof Exp:* Attend neurologist, Harborview Hosp, Wash, 79-81. *Concurrent Pos:* Vis scholar & med res coun fel, Univ Wash, Seattle, 79-81; attend neurologist, Wellesley Hosp, 82-; mem, Univ Toronto Med Sci, 90; assoc mem, Med Res Coun Group, 92, Excitable Cells & Synapses, Play Fair Neurosci, 93. *Mem:* Am Acad Neurol; Soc Neurosci; Am Soc Neurol Invest; Can Soc Neurosci; Can Soc Clin Neurophysiol. *Res:* Basic and clinical neurophysiology and neuropharmacology with a specific interest in the mechanisms underlying the development of epileptic foci and the initiation and spread of seizures. *Mailing Add:* Rm 116 EK Jones Bldg Wellesley Hosp 160 Wellesley St E Toronto ON M4Y 1J3 Can

SCHNEIDERMAN, JILL STEPHANIE, ENVIRONMENTAL SCIENCE. *Current Pos:* ASST PROF GEOL, POMONA COL, 87- *Personal Data:* b New York, NY, May 13, 59. *Educ:* Yale Col, BS, 81; Harvard Univ, AM, 85, PhD(geol), 87. *Concurrent Pos:* Steele fel, Pomona Col, 91. *Mem:* Geol Soc Am; Nat Asn Geol Teachers; Coun Undergrad Res. *Mailing Add:* Dept Geol Pomona Col Claremont CA 91711

SCHNEIDERMAN, LAWRENCE J, INTERNAL MEDICINE, MEDICAL ETHICS. *Current Pos:* assoc prof community med, 70-80, PROF, SCH MED, UNIV CALIF, SAN DIEGO, 80- *Personal Data:* b New York, NY, Mar 24, 32; m 56; c 4. *Educ:* Yale Univ, BA, 53; Harvard Med Sch, MD, 57. *Prof Exp:* Intern path, Boston City Hosp, Mass, 57-58, intern med, Strong Mem Hosp, Rochester, NY, 58-59; clin assoc, Sect Human Genetics, Nat Inst Dent Res, 59-61; med resident, Sch Med, Stanford Univ, 62-64, from instr to asst prof med, 64-70. *Concurrent Pos:* Nat Heart Inst sr fel, Galton Lab, London, 61-62; vis scholar, Hastings Ctr; vis prof, Albert Einstein Sch Med & Montefiore Hosp, 80-81; vis prof, Dept Med Hist & Ethics, Univ Wash, 89. *Mem:* Am Col Physicians; Physicians for Social Responsibility; Am Soc Health & Human Values. *Res:* Medical ethics. *Mailing Add:* Dept Community/Family Med Sch Med Univ Calif San Diego La Jolla CA 92093-0622

SCHNEIDERMAN, MARTIN HOWARD, RADIATION BIOLOGY, CELL BIOLOGY. *Current Pos:* assoc prof radiol, 90-92, courtesy assoc prof radiation sci & technol, 90-92, PROF RADIOL, UNIV NEBR MED CTR, 92-, COURTESY PROF RADIATION SCI & TECHNOL, 92- *Personal Data:* b Brooklyn, NY, Dec 24, 41; m 72, G Sue Warren; c Tamara G. *Educ:* Cornell Univ, BS, 63; Colo State Univ, MS, 67, PhD(physiol & biophys), 70. *Prof Exp:* Picker Found fel, Univ Fla, 70-72; res scientist, Battelle Mem Inst, 72-75; from asst prof to assoc prof radiation biol, Thomas Jefferson Univ, 75-84; courtesy prof biol, Fla State Univ, 85-90. *Concurrent Pos:* Mem exp combined modalities study group, Nat Cancer Inst, 76-78. *Mem:* Radiation Res Soc; Biophys Soc; Cell Kinetics Soc. *Res:* Effects of radiation, drugs and other challenges on the kinetics and survival of mammalian cells in culture; mechanisms related to observed changes; radioiodinated deoxyuridine in cancer treatment, imaging and therapy. *Mailing Add:* Dept Radiol 600 S 42nd St Omaha NE 68198-1045. *Fax:* 402-559-8112; *E-Mail:* mhschnei@unmcvm.unmc.edu

SCHNEIDERMAN, MARVIN ARTHUR, ENVIRONMENTAL HEALTH, PUBLIC HEALTH & EPIDEMIOLOGY. *Current Pos:* RETIRED. *Personal Data:* b New York, NY, Dec 25, 18; m 41; c 3. *Educ:* City Col New York, BS, 39; Am Univ, MA, 53; Am Univ, PhD(math statist), 61. *Honors & Awards:* Distinguished Serv Medal, US Dept Health & Human Serv; Townsend Harris Award Medal; Rockefeller Pub Serv Award; Samuel Wilkes Lectr, Princeton Univ. *Prof Exp:* Jr statistician, Bur Census, US Dept Com, DC, 40-41; statistician, US War Dept, 41-43, Wright-Patterson AFB, Ohio, 46-48; statistician, Nat Cancer Inst, 48-60, assoc chief, Biomet Br, 60-70, assoc dir field studies & statist, 70-79; prin scientist, Clement Assoc, 80-83; assoc dir sci policy, Environ Law Inst, 79-80, sr scientist, 83-84; prin starr scientist, bd environ studies & toxicol, Nat Res Coun Nat Acad Sci, 84-96. *Concurrent Pos:* Adj prof, Georgetown Univ; adj prof, Grad Sch Pub Health, Univ Pittsburgh, Uniformed Serv Univ Health Sci. *Mem:* Fel AAAS; hon fel Am Statist Asn; Am Asn Cancer Res; fel Royal Statist Soc; Int Statist Inst; Soc Occup & Environ Health; Am Soc Prev Oncol. *Res:* Design of experiments; sequential analysis; risk analysis; environmental health. *Mailing Add:* 6503 E Halbert Rd Bethesda MD 20817

SCHNEIDERMAN, NEIL, PSYCHOPHYSIOLOGY. *Current Pos:* From asst prof to assoc prof, 65-74, PROF PSYCHOL, UNIV MIAMI, 74-, MEM STAFF, LAB QUANT BIOL, 65- *Personal Data:* b Brooklyn, NY, Feb 24, 37; m 60; c 3. *Educ:* Brooklyn Col, BA, 60; Ind Univ, PhD(psychol), 64. *Concurrent Pos:* Asst, Physiol Inst, Univ Basel, 64-65; NSF res grant, 66-72; NIH training grant, 67- *Mem:* Psychonomic Soc; Am Psychol Asn; Sigma Xi. *Res:* Physiological psychology; psychopharmacology; conditioning; role of central nervous system in autonomic conditioning and cardiovascular regulation. *Mailing Add:* Psychol Univ Miami PO Box 248106 Miami FL 33124-8106

SCHNEIDERMAN, STEVEN S, ENVIRONMENTAL STUDIES. *Current Pos:* ASSOC PROF ENVIRON ENG TECHNOL, MURRAY STATE UNIV, 89- *Personal Data:* b Chicago, Ill, Jan 19, 48. *Educ:* Southern Univ, Carbondale, BS, 70, MS, 74, PhD(environ eng & molecular sci), 76. *Prof Exp:* Sr engr, UNL Indust Inc, 74-79; asst prof environ eng, Southern Ill Univ, 79-89. *Mem:* Nat Soc Prof Engrs; fel Am Inst Chemists. *Mailing Add:* Dept Indust & Eng Murray State Univ 1 Murray St Murray KY 42071-3310

SCHNEIDERWENT, MYRON OTTO, PHYSICS, SCIENCE EDUCATION. *Current Pos:* PROF PHYSICS, UNIV WIS-SUPERIOR, 67- *Personal Data:* b Milwaukee, Wis, Jan 8, 35; m 54, Marian Kolbeck; c 2. *Educ:* Univ Wis-Stevens Point, 60; Western Mich Univ, MA, 63; Univ Miss, MSCS, 64; Univ Northern Colo, DEd(sci educ), 70. *Prof Exp:* Teacher, Muskegon Pub Schs, 60-63; instr physics, Interlochen Arts Acad, 64-67. *Concurrent Pos:* Field consult, Harvard Proj Physics, 65-67, mgr, 67; dir proj AWARE, Univ Wis-Superior, 74-76; fac, Defense Equal Opportunity Mgt Inst. *Mem:* Am Asn Physics Teachers; Nat Sci Teachers Asn. *Res:* Classroom use of behavioral objectives; heavy metal uptake in aquatic flora due to coal leachate. *Mailing Add:* Dept Chem & Physics Univ Wis Superior WI 54880-2898. *E-Mail:* mschneid@staff.uwsuper.edu

SCHNEIDKRAUT, MARLOWE J, PROSTAGLANDINS. *Current Pos:* ASSOC PROF, BAXTER HEALTHCARE, DUARTE, CALIF, 90- *Personal Data:* b New York, NY, Oct 27, 54. *Educ:* Albany Med Col, PhD(physiol), 81. *Prof Exp:* Fel, Sch Med, Georgetown Univ, 81-84, res instr physiol, 84-87; asst prof, Sch Med, Wayne State Univ, 87-90. *Mem:* Am Physiol Soc; NY Acad Sci; Am Fedn Clin Researchers; AAAS. *Mailing Add:* Dept Cell Biol Baxter Biotech 9 Parker Irvine CA 92718

SCHNEIR, MICHAEL LEWIS, COLLAGEN METABOLISM, DIABETES COMPLICATIONS. *Current Pos:* from asst prof to assoc prof, 67-85, PROF BIOCHEM, UNIV SOUTHERN CALIF SCH DENT, 86- *Personal Data:* b Chicago, Ill, Nov 17, 37; m 65, Nanette Brizman; c Adam & Aaron. *Educ:* Univ Ill, Urbana, BS, 59, Med Sch, Chicago, MS, 62, PhD(biochem), 66. *Prof Exp:* Fel, Dept Biochem, Tufts Sch Med, 65-66, Univ Pittsburgh Sch Med, 66-67. *Concurrent Pos:* Sabbatical leave, Univ Ala Dent Res Inst, 75. *Mem:* Am Asn Dent Schs; Am Med Writers Asn; Am Chem Soc. *Res:* Strategies for teaching effective research writing. *Mailing Add:* DEN 4348 Univ Southern Calif Sch Dent Los Angeles CA 90089-0641. *Fax:* 213-740-7560; *E-Mail:* schneir@hsc.usc.gov

SCHNEITER, GEORGE, MECHANICAL ENGINEERING. *Current Pos:* Dir stratig & space systs, 88-94, DIR STRATEG & TACTICAL SYSTS, DEPT DEFENSE, 94- *Personal Data:* b Oct 30, 37. *Educ:* Purdue Univ, PhD(mech eng), 66. *Mailing Add:* Dept Defense 3090 Defense Pentagon Rm 3E130 Washington DC 20301

SCHNEIWEISS, JEANNETTE W, PHYSIOLOGY, BIOMETRICS. *Current Pos:* asst prof, 68-73, ASSOC PROF BIOL & PHYSIOL, HOFSTRA UNIV, 73- *Personal Data:* b Corona, NY, Apr 14, 20; m 41; c 3. *Educ:* Brooklyn Col, BS, 58; NY Univ, MA, 61, PhD(biol), 63. *Honors & Awards:* Founders Day Award, NY Univ, 62. *Prof Exp:* NY State Regents col teaching scholar, 59-61; teaching fel sci, NY Univ, 61-63; instr biol, Nassau Community Col, 63-64; asst prof, Adelphi Univ, 64-68. *Mem:* Fel AAAS; Nat Asn Biol Teachers; Nat Sci Teachers Asn. *Res:* Determination of endocrinological effects of high fat diets in weaning, female and albino rats. *Mailing Add:* 217 Oakford St West Hempstead NY 11552

SCHNELL, GARY DEAN, SYSTEMATICS, EVOLUTION. *Current Pos:* from asst prof to assoc prof, Okla Mus Natural Hist, 70-80, head cur, Stovall Mus Sci & Hist, 72-74; interim dir, 79-80, PROF ZOOL, UNIV OKLA, 83-, CUR BIRDS, OKLA MUS NATURAL HIST, 71-, HEAD CUR LIFE SCI, 74-, DIR, OKLA BIOL SURV, 78- *Personal Data:* b Lyons, Kans, July 30, 42; m 65, Mary S Garner; c Steven M & Philip J. *Educ:* Cent Mich Univ, BS, 64; Northern Ill Univ, MS, 66; Univ Kans, PhD(zool), 69. *Prof Exp:* Res assoc zool, Univ Tex, Austin, 69-70. *Concurrent Pos:* Coordr biol, Origin & Struct Ecosysts Integrated Res Prog, US Partic Int Biol Prog, 69-70; vis res assoc, Dept Biol & Ctr Evolution & Paleobiol, Univ Rochester, 77-78; ed, Syst Zool, Soc Syst Zool, 83-86 & Auk, Am Ornith Union, 91-96; prog coordr, Am Ornith Union, 88-91; vpres, Consortium State Biol Surv, 93-96. *Mem:* Fel AAAS; fel Am Ornith Union; Asn Syst Collections (secy, 83-86); Soc Study Evolution; Soc Syst Biol; Am Soc Mammal. *Res:* Systematic biology and ornithology; application of numerical techniques to the classification of organisms; evolutionary biology; conservation biology. *Mailing Add:* Dept Zool Univ Okla Norman OK 73019. *Fax:* 405-325-7702; *E-Mail:* gschnell@ou.edu

SCHNELL, GENE WHEELER, MICROBIOLOGY, BIOCHEMISTRY & BIOTECHNOLOGY. *Current Pos:* RETIRED. *Personal Data:* b Wapakoneta, Ohio, Jan 27, 24; m 46, Janet Berg; c Gary S, Bruce C & Christine J. *Educ:* Ohio State Univ, BSc, 47, MSc, 48, PhD(microbiol), 57. *Prof Exp:* Microbiologist, Ft Detrick, Md, 49-57; sr scientist, Res Ctr, Mead Johnson & Co, 57-61; group leader, 61-63; sect leader, 63-69; prin investr, 69-73; mgr microbiol dept, Kraft Res & Develop, 73-79; prin consult, Bernard Wolnak & Assoc, 79-84, vpres, 84-86. *Concurrent Pos:* Consult biotechnol, 86-; tech adv sr environ employ prog, 86- *Mem:* Am Soc Microbiol; Am Chem Soc. *Res:* Fermentation processes and products; enzymes; genetic engineering; molecular biology; plant genetics; tissue culture; monoclonal antibodies; diagnostics; pharmaceuticals; food ingredients; agricultural chemicals; market research; microbial physiology; biotechnology. *Mailing Add:* 1203 Shermer Rd Glenview IL 60025

SCHNELL, GEORGE ADAM, GEOGRAPHY OF POPULATION & SPORT, THE AGED. *Current Pos:* From asst prof to assoc prof, 62-68, found chmn dept & chmn, 68-94, PROF GEOG, STATE UNIV NY, NEW PALTZ, 68- *Personal Data:* b Philadelphia, Pa, July 13, 31; m 58, Mary L Williams; c David A, Douglas P & Thomas E. *Educ:* West Chester Univ, BS, 58; Pa State Univ, MS, 60, PhD, 65. *Honors & Awards:* Excellence Award, NY State & United Univ Prof, 94; Distinguished Geographer Award, Pa Geographical Soc, 94. *Concurrent Pos:* Vis assoc prof, Univ Hawaii, 66; found & found bd mem, Inst Develop Planning & Land Use Studies, 86-; consult, Mid-Hudson Pattern for Prog, 86, Open Space Inst, 87, Mid-Hudson Regional Econ Develop Coun, 89, Urban Develop Corp, 89-90, 93, Tech Develop Ctr, 91, Catskill Ctr, 91, Educ Testing Serv, 93, 96 & 97; assoc ed, J Pa Acad Sci, 88- *Mem:* Asn Am Geogr; Nat Coun Geog Educ. *Res:* Aged population in Pennsylvania, components of change (especially migration patterns) and regional distribution; physiography and cultural landscape. *Mailing Add:* Dept Geog State Univ NY Hamner House Rm 1 New Paltz NY 12561-2499. *Fax:* 914-257-3009; *E-Mail:* schnellg@npvm.newpaltz.edu

SCHNELL, JAY HEIST, RAPTORS, REMOTE SENSING INSTRUMENT DESIGN. *Current Pos:* CONSULT BIOL, 76- *Personal Data:* b Philadelphia, Pa, Nov 21, 32. *Educ:* Earlham Col, AB, 55; Univ Calif, Berkeley, MA, 57; Univ Ga, PhD(zool), 64. *Prof Exp:* Res asst ecol, Savannah River Plant, Univ Ga, 62-63; fel pop ecol, 64-65; fel radio tracking tech, Cedar Creek Radio-Tracking Sta, Univ Minn, Minneapolis, 65-69; res biologist, Tall Timbers Res Sta, Fla, 69-72; wildlife telemetry consult, Ill, 72-73; dir, Res Ranch, 73-74; dir, George Whittell Wildlife Preserve, Ariz, 74-76. *Mem:* Raptor Res Found. *Res:* Population ecology of small mammals; behavior and ecology of birds of prey; radio-tracking techniques aiding studies in animal and bird behavior; black hawks nesting in Aravaipa Canyon, Arizona; designing, testing digital computer instruments used in eco-behavioral research. *Mailing Add:* Box 54 Klondyke Rural Sta Wilcox AZ 85643

SCHNELL, ROBERT CRAIG, PHARMACOLOGY. *Current Pos:* DEAN GRAD STUDIES & RES, NDAK STATE UNIV, 85- *Personal Data:* b Sturgis, SDak, Oct 14, 42; m 65; c 2. *Educ:* SDak State Univ, BS, 65; Purdue Univ, MS, 67, PhD(pharmacol-toxicol), 69. *Honors & Awards:* Burroughs-Wellcome Toxicol Scholar Award, 83. *Prof Exp:* Asst prof pharmacol-toxicol, Wash State Univ, 71-72; assoc prof, Purdue Univ, 72-79; prof & chmn dept, Med Ctr, Univ Nebr, 79-85. *Concurrent Pos:* Mem bd trustees, Am Asn Accreditation Lab Animal Care, 76-85; Safe Drinking Water Comt, Nat Acad Sci, 79-82; assoc ed, Fundamental & Appl Toxicol, 86- *Mem:* Soc Toxicol; Am Soc Pharmacol & Exp Ther; Am Asn Pharmaceut Sci; Am Asn Col Pharm. *Res:* Drug metabolism; circadium rhythms; toxicology of heavy metals. *Mailing Add:* Col Pharm NDak State Univ Fargo ND 58105-5727

SCHNELLE, K(ARL) B(ENJAMIN), JR, AIR POLLUTION CONTROL, ATMOSPHERIC DIFFUSION MODELLING. *Current Pos:* assoc prof air resources eng, Vanderbilt Univ, 66-70, prof environ & air resources eng, 70-80, chmn, Dept Environ Eng & Policy Mgt & dir environ & water resources eng prog, 76-80, chmn dept, chem eng, 80-88, PROF CHEM & ENVIRON ENG, VANDERBILT UNIV, 80- *Personal Data:* b Canton, Ohio, Dec 8, 30; m 54, Mary Dabbey; c Karl D & Kathryn C. *Educ:* Carnegie Inst Technol, BS, 52, MS, 57, PhD(chem eng), 59. *Prof Exp:* Chem engr, Columbia-Southern Chem Corp, 52-54; from asst prof to assoc prof chem eng, Vanderbilt Univ, 58-64; mgr ed & res, Instrument Soc Am, 64-66. *Concurrent Pos:* Fulbright chair, Univ Liege, Belg, Comn Int Exchange Scholars, 77. *Mem:* Am Soc Eng Educ; Instrument Soc Am; fel Am Inst Chem Engrs; Air & Waste Mgt Asn; Am Soc Environ Engrs. *Res:* Process dynamics and control; dynamic testing; air pollution control; atmospheric diffusion modeling; control of sulfur oxides and nitrogen oxides in coal fired boilers; soil remediation by superictal extraction. *Mailing Add:* 5408 Camelot Rd Brentwood TN 37027-4113. *Fax:* 615-343-7951

SCHNELLER, EUGENE S, MEDICAL SOCIOLOGY, HEALTH POLICY. *Current Pos:* dir, Sch Health Admin & Policy, Ariz State Univ, 85-91, assoc dean admin & res, 91-93, prof health admin & counr to pres health professions educ, 93-96, DIR, SCH HEALTH ADMIN & POLICY, ARIZ STATE UNIV, 96- *Personal Data:* b Cornwall, NY, Apr 9, 43; m, Ellen Stauber; c Andrew Jon & Lee Stauber. *Educ:* CW Post Col, BA, 68; New York Univ, PhD(sociol), 73. *Prof Exp:* Asst prof med sociol, Duke Univ Med Ctr, 72-75; assoc prof sociol, 75-78, assoc prof health admin, Union Col, 78-85; res scholar health policy, Columbia Univ, 83-84. *Concurrent Pos:* Accrediting comn on educ for Health Servs Admin; vis assoc prof, State Univ NY, Albany, 81-82 & Albany Med Col, 83-85; clin prof, Dept Family & Community Med, Univ Ariz, 94-; mem, Calif Comn Future Med Educ, 96- *Mem:* Am Sociol Asn; Am Pub Health Asn; Am Col Healthcare Execs; Asn Univ Progs Health Admin. *Res:* Changes in health occupations and professions; the role of the physician in management; comparative health systems; Acquired Immunodeficiency Syndrome policy; managed care systems. *Mailing Add:* Sch Health Admin & Policy Col Bus Admin Ariz State Univ Tempe AZ 85287-2803

SCHNELLER, STEWART WRIGHT, PHARMACEUTICAL CHEMISTRY. *Current Pos:* asst prof, Univ SFla, 71-75, asst chmn dept, 72-74, actg chmn dept 74-75, assoc prof, 75-78, PROF ORG CHEM, UNIV SFLA, 78-, CHMN, 86- *Personal Data:* b Louisville, Ky, Feb 27, 42; m 66; c 2. *Educ:* Univ Louisville, BS, 64, MS, 65; Ind Univ, Bloomington, PhD(org chem), 68. *Prof Exp:* NIH fel, Stanford Univ, 68-69, res assoc org chem, 69-70; res assoc, Univ Mass, 70-71. *Concurrent Pos:* Petrol Res Fund-Am Chem Soc fel, Univ SFla, 71-74; NIH & Dept Army Support, 74- *Mem:* AAAS; Am Chem Soc; Royal Soc Chem; Int Soc Heterocyclic Chem (pres). *Res:* Heterocyclic synthetic methods; synthetic medicinal chemistry, nucleosides. *Mailing Add:* Col Sci & Math Auburn Univ Auburn AL 36849-5319

SCHNEPFE, MARIAN MOELLER, INORGANIC CHEMISTRY, ANALYTICAL CHEMISTRY. *Current Pos:* RETIRED. *Personal Data:* b San Pedro de Macoris, Dominican Repub, Nov 15, 23; US citizen; m 54. *Educ:* George Washington Univ, BS, 53, MS, 60, PhD(chem), 66. *Prof Exp:* Analytical chemist, US Geol Surv, 54-80. *Concurrent Pos:* Consult, Indonesian Geol Surv Anal Labs, Bandung, Java, 81-82. *Mem:* Am Chem Soc; Sigma Xi. *Res:* Testing of natural materials with a view to their potential for fixation of some of the problem radio-nuclides; development of various analytical procedures; development of spectrophotometric and atomic absorption procedures for the determination of platinum, palladium, rhodium iridium and spectrophotometric procedures for the determination of antimony, arsenic, bromine, germanium, iodine, selenium and thallium in sub-microgram quantities. *Mailing Add:* Potomac Towers Apt 640 2001 N Adams St Arlington VA 22201

SCHNEPP, OTTO, PHYSICAL CHEMISTRY, CHEMICAL PHYSICS. *Current Pos:* PROF CHEM, UNIV SOUTHERN CALIF, 65-, DEPT CHMN, 89- *Personal Data:* b Vienna, Austria, July 7, 25; m 50, 79; c 2. *Educ:* St John's Univ, China, BS, 47; Univ Calif, Berkeley, AB, 48, PhD(chem), 51. *Honors & Awards:* Assocs Award Creative Scholar & Res, Univ Southern Calif, 78; Super Honor Award, US Dept State, 82. *Prof Exp:* Res asst chem, Univ Calif, Berkeley, 51-52; from lectr to sr lectr, Israel Inst Technol, 52-59, from assoc prof to prof, 59-65. *Concurrent Pos:* Res assoc, Duke Univ, 57-58; res physicist, Nat Bur Stand, DC, 58-59; sci counr, US Embassy, Beijing, 80-82. *Mem:* Am Phys Soc; AAAS; Asn Asian Studies. *Res:* Molecular and solid state spectroscopy; coherent raman spectroscopy; lattice vibrations of molecular solids; circular dichroism and magnetic circular dichroism spectroscopy; vacuum ultraviolet spectroscopy; science and technology of China; science policy. *Mailing Add:* Dept Chem Univ Southern Calif Playa Del Rey CA 90293

SCHNEPS, JACK, ELEMENTARY PARTICLE PHYSICS. *Current Pos:* From asst prof to assoc prof, 56-63, dept chmn, 80-89, PROF PHYSICS, TUFTS UNIV, 63- *Personal Data:* b New York, NY, Aug 18, 29; m 60, Lucia DeMarchi; c Loredana, Melissa & Leila. *Educ:* NY Univ, BA, 51; Univ Wis, MS, 53, PhD(physics), 56. *Concurrent Pos:* NSF fel, 58-59; vis scientist, Europ Orgn Nuclear Res, 65-66; vis res fel, Univ Col, Univ London, 73-74; co-prin investr, 76-; vis res fel, Ecole Polytechnique, 82-83; vis prof, Technion, 89-90 & Col France, 97. *Mem:* Europ Phys Soc; fel Am Phys Soc; Sigma Xi. *Res:* Elementary particle research in neutrino and hadron interactions and proton decay. *Mailing Add:* Dept Physics Tufts Univ Medford MA 02155. *Fax:* 617-627-3744; *E-Mail:* jacob@tuhep3.phy.tufts.edu

SCHNETTLER, RICHARD ANSELM, MEDICINAL CHEMISTRY, ORGANIC CHEMISTRY. *Current Pos:* SR RES CHEMIST, MERRELL DOW RES INST, 81- *Personal Data:* b St Nazianz, Wis, May 3, 37; m 65; c 2. *Educ:* Univ Wis, BS, 61; Univ Kans, PhD(med chem), 65. *Prof Exp:* Sr res chemist, Lakeside Labs Inc, 65-75; sr develop chemist, Merrell-Nat Labs, 75-81. *Mem:* Am Chem Soc. *Res:* Reaction mechanisms; natural product synthesis; biogenesis of natural products; cardiovascular and psychopharmacologic agents. *Mailing Add:* Marion Merrell Dow Inc 2110 E Gailbraith Rd Cincinnati OH 45215-6300

SCHNEUR, RINA, NETWORK OPTIMIZATION, TRANSPORTATION. *Current Pos:* RES SCIENTIST, PTCG-SABRE DECISION TECHNOL, 93- *Personal Data:* b Israel. *Educ:* Technion Inst Israel, BSc, 86; Mass Inst Technol, MSc, 88, PhD(opers res), 91. *Prof Exp:* Postdoctoral fel, IBM/Watson Res Ctr, 91-92. *Mem:* Math Prog Soc; Inst Opers Res & Mgt Sci; Soc Indust & Appl Math. *Res:* Developing algorithms for operations-research based software application, mainly in the transportation area; network optimization and mathematical programming. *Mailing Add:* PTCG 22 Third Ave Burlington MA 01803. *Fax:* 781-229-1121; *E-Mail:* rina_schneur@ptcg.com

SCHNIEDERJANS, MARC JAMES, GOAL PROGRAMMING, JUST-IN-TIME. *Current Pos:* from asst prof to assoc prof, 81-90, PROF MGT SCI, UNIV NEBR, LINCOLN, 90- *Personal Data:* b Pocahontas, Ark, Oct 8, 50; m 71, Jill Goehler; c Xan, Ashlyn & Dara. *Educ:* Univ Mo, St Louis, BSBA, 72; St Louis Univ, MBA, 74, PhD(mgt sci),78. *Prof Exp:* Asst prof decision sci, Univ Nebr, Omaha, 78-79, Univ Mo, St Louis, 79-80, Univ Hawaii, Hilo, 80-81. *Concurrent Pos:* Pres, Quickship Leasing Corp, 78-79; consult, Blue Hills Home Corp & Truck Transp Corp, 79, Ralston Purina Corp, 80, Union Diversified Enterprises, Inc, 83-84, Am Nat Bank, 87-88, Am Tool Co, Inc, 90; asst dir, Pac Bus Res Ctr, 80-81; chairperson, Dept Bus & Econ, Univ Hawaii, Hilo, 80-81; CBA fac res fel award, Outstanding Res, Univ Nebr, 86. *Mem:* Opers Res Soc Am; Inst Decision Sci; Inst Mgt Sci; Am Prod & Inventory Control Soc; Prod & Opers Mgt Soc. *Res:* Applied mathematics and statistics in business, health care and education planning. *Mailing Add:* Dept Mgt Univ Nebr Lincoln NE 68588-0491. *Fax:* 402-472-5855

SCHNIEWIND, ARNO PETER, FOREST PRODUCTS. *Current Pos:* Sr lab technician, Univ Calif, 56, asst specialist wood sci & technol, 56-59, lectr forestry, 59-65, from assoc prof to prof, 66-91, EMER PROF FORESTRY, UNIV CALIF, BERKELEY, 91- *Personal Data:* b Cologne, Ger, June 1, 29; US citizen; m; c 3. *Educ:* Univ Mich, BS, 53, MWT, 55, PhD(wood technol), 59. *Honors & Awards:* Wood Award, 59. *Concurrent Pos:* NSF fel, 63-64. *Mem:* Soc Wood Sci & Technol (pres, 73-74); Int Acad Wood Sci; Forest Prod Res Soc; Am Soc Testing & Mat; Am Inst Conserv Hist & Artistic Works. *Res:* Mechanical behavior and physical properties of wood; application of wood science to conservation of wood artifacts. *Mailing Add:* 217 Cambridge Ave Berkeley CA 94708

SCHNITKER, DETMAR, MICROPALEONTOLOGY, PALEOCEANOGRAPHY. *Current Pos:* asst prof, 69-72, assoc prof, 72-79, PROF OCEANOG & GEOL SCI, UNIV MAINE, ORONO, 79- *Personal Data:* b Wilhelmshaven, Ger, July 5, 37; m 64; c 2. *Educ:* Univ NC, Chapel Hill, MS, 66; Univ Ill, Urbana, PhD(geol), 67. *Prof Exp:* Geologist, Soc Nat Petrol Aquitaine, 67-69. *Concurrent Pos:* Fulbright exchange scholar, 60-61; assoc prof, Submarine Geol & Geophys Prog, NSF, 80-81; co-chief scientist, Deep Sea Drilling Proj-Int Prog Ocean Drilling Leg, 81. *Mem:* Paleont Soc; Paleont Res Inst; Paleontologische Ges; Int Paleont Asn; Am Geophys Union. *Res:* Foraminiferal ecology; paleoecology; paleoceanography. *Mailing Add:* Dept Oceanog Coburn Hall Univ Maine Orono ME 04469-0001

SCHNITKER, JURGEN H, SOLVATED ELECTRONS, LIQUID WATER. *Current Pos:* asst prof chem, 89-95, RES SCIENTIST, UNIV MICH, 95- *Personal Data:* b Bremen, Ger, Mar 12, 58; m 96, Susannah Bryant. *Educ:* Univ Aachen, Ger, MS, 82, PhD(chem), 86. *Prof Exp:* Postdoctoral fel, Univ Tex, 86-88; tech staff, AT&T Bell Labs, 88-89. *Mem:* Am Chem Soc. *Res:* Computational chemistry: classical and quantum molecular dynamics simulations of materials, liquids and chemical reactivitiy. *Mailing Add:* Dept Mat Sci Univ Mich Ann Arbor MI 48109-2136. *Fax:* 313-763-4788; *E-Mail:* moldyn@umich.edu

SCHNITTMAN, STEVEN MARC, INFECTIOUS DISEASE CLINICAL RESEARCH ON HUMAN IMMUNODEFICIENCY VIRUS & ACQUIRED IMMUNE DEFICIENCY SYNDROME. *Current Pos:* from med staff fel to sr staff fel, 85-91, CHIEF, MED BR, DIV ACQUIRED IMMUNE DEFICIENCY SYNDROME, NAT INST ALLERGY & INFECTIOUS DIS, INTERNAL MED, INFECTIOUS DIS & IMMUNOL,

NIH, 91- *Personal Data:* b Brooklyn, NY, Apr 3, 56; m 80, Elyse G Stock; c Rachel & Samuel. *Educ:* NY Univ, BA, 78, MD, 82. *Honors & Awards:* Young Investr Award, Am Soc Microbiol, 89. *Prof Exp:* Intern resident internal med, NY Hosp, Cornell Med Ctr, 82-85. *Concurrent Pos:* Clin instr & asst clin prof internal med, Dept Infectious Dis, Georgetown Univ Sch Med, 89- *Mem:* Am Col Physicians; Infectious Dis Soc Am; Am Med Asn; Am Fedn Clin Res. *Res:* Laboratory research on immunopathogenesis of human immunodeficiency virus; clinical research on human immunodeficiency virus/acquired immune deficiency syndrome. *Mailing Add:* 6003 Executive Blvd Rm 2C22 Rockville MD 20852

SCHNITZER, BERTRAM, HEMATOPATHOLOGY, IMMUNOPATHOLOGY. *Current Pos:* from instr to assoc prof, 66-72, PROF PATH, UNIV MICH HOSP, 72-, DIR HEMAT, 76- *Personal Data:* b Frankfurt, Ger, June 21, 29; m 59; c 3. *Educ:* NY Univ, BA, 52; Univ Basle, Switzerland, MD, 58. *Prof Exp:* Resident physician path, Georgetown Univ Hosp, 59-63; pathologist, US Armed Forces Inst Pathol, 63-66. *Concurrent Pos:* Consult, US Vet Admin Hosp; ed bd, Am J Clin Path, 83-, coun mem, Am Soc Clin Path, 88-, pres elect, Exec Comt, Soc Hematopath, 88; mem, path comt, Children Cancer Study Group, 74-; pres, Soc Hematopath, 90- *Mem:* Am Soc Clin Path; Am Soc Hemat; Int Acad Path; Int Soc Exp Hemat. *Res:* Immunophenotypic analysis in the diagnosis of lymphomas and leukemias by flow cytometry; DNA analysis. *Mailing Add:* Dept Path Univ Mich Med Sch Box 0602 1301 Catherine Rd Ann Arbor MI 48109-0602

SCHNITZER, HOWARD J, QUANTUM FIELD THEORY, ELEMENTARY PARTICLE PHYSICS. *Current Pos:* res assoc, Brandeis Univ, 61-62, from asst prof to assoc prof, 62-68, chmn dept, 81-83, PROF PHYSICS, BRANDEIS UNIV, 68-, GERTRUDE & EDWARD SWARTZ PROF THEORET PHYSICS, 92- *Personal Data:* b Newark, NJ, Nov 12, 34; m 66, Phoebe Kazdin; c Mark J & Elizabeth K. *Educ:* Newark Col Eng, BS, 55; Univ Rochester, PhD(physics), 60. *Prof Exp:* Res assoc physics, Univ Rochester, 60-61. *Concurrent Pos:* Alfred P Sloan Found fel, 64-66; vis prof, Rockefeller Univ, 69-70; vis res assoc, Harvard Univ, 74-; assoc ed, Phys Rev Lett, 78-80; John S Guggenheim Found fel, 83-84. *Mem:* Fel Am Phys Soc; Sigma Xi. *Res:* Elementary particle theory; quantum field theory; string theory; conformal field theory. *Mailing Add:* Dept Physics Brandeis Univ Waltham MA 02254-9110. *Fax:* 781-736-2915; *E-Mail:* schnitzer@binah.cc.brandeis.edu

SCHNITZER, JAN EUGENEUSZ, BIOPHYSICS. *Current Pos:* SR ASST PROF PATH, HARVARD MED SCH, BOSTON, 94- *Personal Data:* b Pittsburgh, Pa, June 24, 57. *Educ:* Princeton Univ, BSE, 80; Univ Pittsburgh, MD, 85. *Prof Exp:* Assoc res scientist, Sch Med, Yale Univ, 85-90; asst prof path, physiol, cell biol & med, Univ Calif, San Diego, 90-93. *Concurrent Pos:* Prin investr, NIH grant, 89-94, Nat Am Heart Asn, 91-94; estab investr award, Am Heart Asn, 93- *Mem:* AAAS; Microcircuitry Soc; Am Soc Cell Biol; Am Physiol Soc. *Res:* Vascular endothelial biology; capillary permeability; receptor-mediated trascytosis; biophysics of membrane transport; steric & electrostatic effects on membrane transport; theoretical modeling; cavcolae endocytosis. *Mailing Add:* Dept Path Res Pathol Beth Israel Hosp Harvard Med Sch 330 Brookline Ave Boston MA 02215. *Fax:* 617-735-2943

SCHNITZER, MORRIS, SOIL CHEMISTRY, ORGANIC CHEMISTRY. *Current Pos:* RETIRED. *Personal Data:* b Bochum, WGer, Feb 4, 22; Can citizen; m 48; c 1. *Educ:* McGill Univ, BSc, 51, MSc, 52, PhD(agr chem), 55. *Honors & Awards:* Soil Sci Award, Soil Sci Soc Am, 84. *Prof Exp:* Res scientist, Aluminum Labs Ltd, 55-56; prin res scientist, Land Resource Res Ctr, Agr Can, 56-92. *Concurrent Pos:* Sabbatical fel, Imp Col, Univ London, 61-62. *Mem:* Fel Can Soil Sci; Int Soc Soil Sci; fel Soil Sci Soc Am. *Res:* Chemical structure and reactions of humic substances in soils and waters; chemistry of soil nitrogen. *Mailing Add:* 241 Sherwood Dr Ottawa ON K1Y 3W1 Can

SCHNITZLEIN, HAROLD NORMAN, NEUROANATOMY. *Current Pos:* chmn dept, 73-78, prof anat, 73-, PROF ANAT & RADIOL, COL MED, UNIV SFLA, 85-, PROF ANAT RADIOL & NEUROL, 88- *Personal Data:* b Hannibal, Mo, Aug 24, 27; m 49; c 4. *Educ:* Westminster Col, Mo, AB, 50; St Louis Univ, MS, 52, PhD, 54. *Prof Exp:* From instr to prof anat, Sch Med, Univ Ala, Birmingham, 54-73. *Concurrent Pos:* USPHS spec fel, 60-61. *Res:* Autonomic nervous system; comparative vertebrate neuroanatomy; imaging anatomy. *Mailing Add:* Dept Anat Univ SFla 10902 Janiperus Pl Tampa FL 33618

SCHNITZLER, RONALD MICHAEL, PHYSIOLOGY, EDUCATIONAL ADMINISTRATION. *Current Pos:* dir, Math Sci Div, 85-95, PROF BIOL SCI, NAUGATUCK VALLEY COMMUNITY-TECH COL, 95- *Personal Data:* b Providence, RI, Jan 13, 39; m 68, Ute Vogel; c Micaela A & Alettac. *Educ:* Brown Univ, AB & ScB, 62; Univ Vt, MS, 64, PhD(physiol), 69. *Prof Exp:* Instr physiol, Med Col, Univ Vt, 69-70; Alexander von Humboldt scholar & res assoc, Microbiol Labs, Luisenhosp, Aachen, WGer, 70-71; res assoc physiol, Med Col, Univ Vt, 71-75; from asst prof to prof biol, Sci Dept, Bay Path Col, 75-85. *Concurrent Pos:* NIH spec fel, 71-74. *Mem:* AAAS; Nat Sci Teachers Asn; Sigma Xi; Alexander von Humboldt Asn Am. *Res:* Physiology and pharmacology of neuromuscular transmission, especially mechanism of drug desensitization at the motor end plate; effects of ultrasound on biological tissue. *Mailing Add:* Div Math/Sci Naugatuck Valley Community Tech Col Waterbury CT 06708. *E-Mail:* rschnitzler@nuctc5.commnet.edu

SCHNIZER, ARTHUR WALLACE, ORGANIC CHEMISTRY. *Current Pos:* RETIRED. *Personal Data:* b Des Plaines, Ill, Jan 16, 23; m 47; c 3. *Educ:* Baylor Univ, BS, 43; Northwestern Univ, PhD(chem), 51. *Prof Exp:* Develop chemist, Columbia Chem Div, Pittsburgh Plate Glass Co, 43-46; asst, Northwestern Univ, 47-50; res chemist, Celanese Corp, 50-52, res group leader, 52-55, res sect head, 55-61, dir chem res, 61-66, dir eng res, 66, mgr tech ctr, Celanese Chem Co, Tex, 66-69, dir chem & polymer res, Celanese Res Co, NJ, 69-71; tech dir, Day & Zimmermann, Inc, Philadelphia, 71-76; vpres res & develop, Bird & Son, Inc, 76-80. *Mem:* Am Chem Soc; AAAS; Am Inst Chem Engrs; Soc Chem Indust. *Res:* Reactions of alkyl sodiums, lithiums, magnesium bromides with methoxyl groups; reactions and synthesis of ketene; derivatives of oxygenated petrochemicals; asphalt roofing and plastics extrusion; organic synthesis and process development. *Mailing Add:* 333 University Dr Corpus Christi TX 78412-2741

SCHNOBRICH, WILLIAM COURTNEY, ENGINEERING MECHANICS, STRUCTURAL ENGINEERING. *Current Pos:* Res asst, 53-55, 58-62, from asst prof to assoc prof, 62-68, PROF CIVIL ENG, UNIV ILL, URBANA, 68- *Personal Data:* b St Paul, Minn, Nov 26, 30; m 56. *Educ:* Univ Ill, Urbana, BS, 53, MS, 55, PhD(thin shells), 62. *Concurrent Pos:* Summer res engr, Space Technol Labs, Calif, 62 & 63; consult, John R Gullaksen, Struct Engr, Ill, 64-, Whitman Reguardt & Assocs, Greeley & Hansen Engrs, 76, Beaulieu Poulin, Robitaille & Assocs, 80, Klein & Hoffman, Argonne Nat Lab, 81, Kajima Corp, 84 & Lockwood Greene Engrs, 85; Humboldt sr US scientist award, Alexander von Humboldt-Found, 77 & 84. *Mem:* Am Soc Civil Engrs; Am Soc Mech Engrs; Int Asn Bridge & Struct Engrs; fel Am Concrete Inst; Int Asn Comput Mech; Int Asn Shell Struct. *Res:* Structural mechanics, particularly thin shell structures; nuclear reactor vessels; earthquake resistant design; cooling towers; finite element specialist. *Mailing Add:* 1419 Mayfair Rd Champaign IL 61821

SCHNOES, HEINRICH KONSTANTIN, NATURAL PRODUCTS, MASS SPECTROMETRY. *Current Pos:* from asst prof to assoc prof, 67-74, PROF BIOCHEM, UNIV WIS-MADISON, 74- *Personal Data:* b Knetzgau, Ger, July 12, 39; m 69; c 1. *Educ:* Long Island Univ, BS, 61; Mass Inst Technol, PhD(org chem), 65. *Prof Exp:* Asst res chemist, Space Sci Lab, Univ Calif, Berkeley, 65-67. *Mem:* AAAS; Am Chem Soc; Am Soc Biol Chemists; Royal Soc Chem; Am Soc Mass Spectrometry. *Res:* Natural products chemistry and biochemistry; mass spectrometry and its application to structural and biochemical problems. *Mailing Add:* Dept Biochem Univ Wis 420 Henry Hall Madison WI 53706-1569. *Fax:* 608-262-3453

SCHNOOR, JERALD L, WATER QUALITY MODELING, GLOBAL CLIMATE CHANGE. *Current Pos:* from asst prof to assoc prof, 77-83, chmn, 85-90, PROF ENVIRON ENG TEACHING & RES, COL ENG, UNIV IOWA, 83-85, 90- *Personal Data:* b Davenport, Iowa, Aug 26, 50; m 72; c 2. *Educ:* Iowa State Univ, BS, 72; Univ Tex, MS, 74, PhD(environ eng), 75. *Honors & Awards:* Merit Award, Am Chem Soc, 80; Walter L Huber Res Prize, Am Soc Civil Engrs, 85. *Prof Exp:* NSF postdoctoral res, NSF-Manhattan Col, 76-77. *Concurrent Pos:* Vis prof, Swiss Fed Technol-Z06rich, 82 & 88; mem, Nat Res Coun Panel Lake Acidification, 83-84, Environ Protection Agency Global Climate Res Subcomt, 89-90, assoc ed, Water Resources Res, 85-87, Environ Sci & Technol, 91-; ed, Res J Water Pollution Control Fedn, 89-; prin investr, Hazardous Substances Res Ctr, 89-; co-dir, Ctr Global & Regional Environ Res, 90-; comt chair, Water Pollution Control Fedn, 89-90. *Mem:* Am Soc Civil Engrs; Am Inst Chem Eng; Am Geophys Union; Am Chem Soc. *Res:* Water quality modeling; environmental engineering science; global climate change; lake eutrophication; pesticide fate and movement in the environment; author of two books and over 60 publications. *Mailing Add:* Environ Eng Univ Iowa Iowa City IA 52242-1000a

SCHNOPPER, HERBERT WILLIAM, ASTROPHYSICS, X-RAY ASTRONOMY. *Current Pos:* DIR, DANISH SPACE RES INST, 80- *Personal Data:* b Brooklyn, NY, Mar 13, 33; wid; c Patti J Griffith, Joey Griffith & Rachel Griffith. *Educ:* Rensselaer Polytech Inst, 54; Cornell Univ, MS, 58, PhD(physics), 62. *Prof Exp:* Sr scientist, Jet Propulsion Lab, 62-63; instr & res assoc physics, Cornell Univ, 63-66; from asst prof to assoc prof physics, Mass Inst Technol, 66-73, physicist, 73-74; physicist, Smithsonian Astrophys Observ & lectr, Dept Astron, Harvard Univ, 74-80. *Concurrent Pos:* Consult, Jet Propulsion Lab, 63-80 & Am Sci & Eng, 69-80; vis prof, Steward Observ, Univ Ariz, 70-73; guest physicist, Brookhaven Nat Lab, 71-80; consult, Quartz et Silice, Paris, 72-80; mem, Space Sci Comt, ESA, 80- & Europ Sci Found, 87-; sr res associateship, Nat Res Coun, 94; dep chmn, Space Sci Comt, Europ Sci Found, 94- *Mem:* Danish Phys Soc; Int Astron Union; Am Phys Soc; Am Astron Soc; Royal Danish Acad Sci; Europ Phys Soc. *Res:* Astrophysics; x-ray astronomy; diagnostics of high temperature plasmas; x-rays from heavy ion collisions; x-ray spectroscopy; x-ray optics. *Mailing Add:* Danish Space Res Inst Gl Lundtoftevej 7 DK 2800 Lyngby Denmark. *Fax:* 45 45 93 02 83; *E-Mail:* hs@dsri.dk

SCHNUR, JOEL MARTIN, BIOLBICAL & MOLECULAR ENGINEERING. *Current Pos:* Head, Molecular Optics Sect, Naval Res Lab, 73-79, dept head, Optic Probes Br, 79-84, head, Picosecond Spectros Sect, 79- 84, dep coordr, Energetic Mat Progs, 80-85, head, Biol Molecular Eng Br, 84-89, DIR CTR BIOMOLECULAR SCI & ENG, NAVAL RES LAB, 89- *Personal Data:* b Washington, DC, Feb 5, 45; m 71, Sara Lee; c Tatiana. *Educ:* Rutgers Univ, BS, 66; Georgetown Univ, PhD(phys chem), 71. *Honors & Awards:* Superior Civilian Serv Award, US Gov, Technol Transfer Award. *Concurrent Pos:* Vpres, Concepts Unlimited, 71-; res assoc, Nat Res Coun, Naval Res Lab, 71-72; vis prof, Univ Paris, 83-; assoc prof, Univ Paris VII, 83 & 84; chmn, Gordon Conf on Thin Films, 90. *Mem:* Sigma Xi; Am Chem Soc; Am Phys Soc; AAAS. *Res:* Development of receptor based biosensors, energy transduction systems and hybrid devices; assess potential of self assembled and biologically derived microstructures for technological applications; study fundamentals of self organization in heterogeneous systems; study of chirality in molecular architectures. *Mailing Add:* Code 6900 Naval Res Lab Washington DC 20375-5000. *Fax:* 202-404-6000

SCHNUR, RODNEY CAUGHREN, medicinal chemistry, synthetic organic chemistry; deceased, see previous edition for last biography

SCHNUR, SIDNEY, MEDICINE. *Current Pos:* clin prof, 62-76, EMER CLIN PROF MED, BAYLOR COL MED, 76-; EMER CLIN PROF MED, POSTGRAD SCH MED, UNIV TEX GRAD SCH BIOMED SCI, HOUSTON, 75-, MED SCH, 80- *Personal Data:* b New York, NY, June 23, 10; m 44; c 1. *Educ:* City Col New York, BS, 30, MS, 31; NY Univ, MD, 35; Am Bd Internal Med & Am Bd Cardiovasc Dis, dipl, 44. *Prof Exp:* Intern, Morrisania City Hosp, New York, 35-37; resident internal med, Kings County Hosp, 37-38; resident path, Jefferson Davis Hosp, Houston, 38-39; from clin asst prof to clin assoc prof med, Baylor Col Med, 46-62; coordr cardiol courses, Postgrad Sch Med, Univ Tex Grad Sch Biomed Sci, Houston, 53-75. *Concurrent Pos:* Pvt pract internal med, Houston, 39-; assoc physician, Jefferson Davis Hosp, 40-, chief dept electrocardiol, 45-50, chief cardiac clin, 45-51, chief 4th div med, 58-60; consult, USPHS, 46-50, St Luke's Hosp, 54- & Polly Ryan Mem Hosp, Richmond, 57-59; assoc physician, Methodist Hosp, 46-53, attend physician, 54-66, consult cardiologist, 66-; attend specialist, Vet Admin Regional Off & Hosp, 46-61; clin asst prof med, Univ Tex Grad Sch Biomed Sci Houston, 50-52, clin assoc prof, 52-57; ed consult, Heart Bull, 51-70; contrib ed, Med Rec & Am, 52-62; consult cardiologist, San Jacinto Mem Hosp, Baytown, 54-58; consult cardiologist & electrocardiologist, South Pac Hosp, 54-61; chief med & electrocardiol dept, St Joseph Hosp, Houston, 54-, pres med staff, 62-65; chief electrocardiol, Med Arts Hosp, 58-60, chief med, 63, pres staff, 62-63; mem coun clin cardiol, Am Heart Asn, 63; attend physician, Ben Taub Hosp, 64-; emer trustee, Houston Mus Natural Sci; clin prof med, Sch Med, Univ Tex Biomed Sci, Houston, 57-76. *Mem:* Am Heart Asn (vpres, 77); fel Am Col Physicians; emer fel Am Col Chest Physicians; emer fel Am Col Cardiol; sr mem Am Fedn Clin Res. *Res:* Clinical cardiology; internal medicine. *Mailing Add:* 2139 Sunset Blvd Houston TX 77005

SCHOBER, CHARLES COLEMAN, PSYCHIATRY, PSYCHOANALYSIS. *Current Pos:* prof, 78-94, EMER PROF PSYCHIAT, MED SCH, LA STATE UNIV, 94- *Personal Data:* b Shreveport, La, Nov 30, 24; m 47, 72; c 3. *Educ:* La State Univ, Baton Rouge, BS, 46; La State Univ, New Orleans, MD, 49. *Prof Exp:* Intern, Philadelphia Gen Hosp, 49-51; resident psychiat & Nat Inst Ment Health residency training grant, Norristown State Hosp, Pa, 53-56, staff physician, 56-57; assoc clin dir, Pa Hosp Ment & Nerv Dis, 57-59; instr psychiat, Med Sch, Univ Pa, 58-62, assoc, 62-70, asst prof clin psychiat, 65-71; prof psychiat & head dept, Sch Med, La State Univ, Shreveport, 71-73; prof psychiat, Sch Med, St Louis Univ & mem fac, St Louis Psychoanal Inst, 73-78. *Concurrent Pos:* Attend psychiatrist, Pa Hosp Inst, 63-68, sr attend psychiatrist, 68-71; chief psychiat serv, Vet Admin Hosp, Shreveport, La, Confederate Mem Hosp, 71-73 & Schumpert Med Ctr, 82-84; consult, Brentwood Neuropsychiat Hosp, 71-73; consult, Vet Admin Hosps, St Louis, Mo, 73-78; staff, Brentwood Psychiat Hosp, Schumpert Med Ctr & La State Univ Med Ctr Hosp, 78-; chief, Psychiat Serv, Schumpers Med Ctr, Shreveport, La, 82-84; med & clin dir, Psychiat Serv, Willis Knighton Med Ctr, Shreveport, La, 86-89; psychiat serv, Charter Forest Hosp, Shreveport, La, 89-94. *Mem:* Fel Am Col Psychiat; fel Am Psychiat Asn; Am Psychoanal Asn; AMA. *Res:* Follow-up studies in psychotherapy of schizophrenia; evaluation of effectiveness of clinical teaching methods in psychiatric training of medical students and residents. *Mailing Add:* 626 Wilder Shreveport LA 71104-4326

SCHOBERT, HAROLD HARRIS, COAL CHEMISTRY. *Current Pos:* ASSOC PROF FUEL SCI, PA STATE UNIV, 86-, CHMN, 88- *Personal Data:* b Wilkes-Barre, Pa, Nov 13, 43; m 68; c 2. *Educ:* Bucknell Univ, BS, 65; Iowa State Univ, PhD(chem), 70. *Prof Exp:* Instr chem, Iowa State Univ, 70-72; res chemist, Deepsea Ventures Inc, 72-76; res chemist, Grand Forks Energy Tech Ctr, US Dept Energy, 76-78, supvr, anal chem, 78, mgr, anal res, 78-86. *Mem:* Am Chem Soc; Sigma Xi. *Res:* Studies of the chemistry of coal liquefaction and co-processing; studies of the structure of coal as it influences coal conversion processes; studies of the physical chemistry of coal ash slags; studies of thermal stability of jet fuels. *Mailing Add:* 230 Oakley Dr State College PA 16803-1350

SCHOCH, DANIEL ANTHONY, PRESS & DIE TESTING & ANALYSIS, PRESS VIBRATION SEVERITY & PRODUCTIVITY. *Current Pos:* Design engr, Minster Mach Co, 70-73, res proj engr, 73-77, advan eng supvr, 77-80, appl res mgr, 80-96, ENG DIR, APPL RES CTR, MINSTER MACH CO, 96- *Personal Data:* b Piqua, Ohio, July 25, 48; m 69, Terry McGowan; c Philip, Andrew & Brian. *Educ:* Ohio State Univ, BS, 70. *Concurrent Pos:* Secy & treas, Ohio Soc Prof Engrs, Midwest Chapter, 71-72; mem, Tech Res Comt, Precision Metal Forming Asn, 90- *Mem:* Am Soc Mech Engrs; Nat Soc Prof Engrs; sr mem Soc Mfg Engrs. *Res:* Vibration severity; performance, reliability, part quality, productivity and accuracy of low and high speed mechanical metalforming presses and die tooling; granted 11 patents; authored over 135 research reports. *Mailing Add:* 47 Crestwood Dr Minster OH 45865. *Fax:* 419-628-4226

SCHOCHET, CLAUDE LEWIS, MATHEMATICS. *Current Pos:* assoc prof, 76-80, assoc dean, Col Lib Arts, 87-91, PROF MATH, WAYNE STATE UNIV, 80- *Personal Data:* b Minneapolis, Minn, Aug 5, 44; m 92, Rivka; c 3. *Educ:* Univ Minn, BA, 65; Univ Chicago, MS, 67, PhD(math), 69. *Prof Exp:* Asst prof math, Roosevelt Univ, 69-70; amanuensis, Aarhus Univ, Denmark, 70-71; fel, Hebrew Univ, Jerusalem, 71-72; asst prof math, Ind Univ, Bloomington, 72-76. *Concurrent Pos:* Vis assoc prof, Univ Calif, Los Angeles, 79-80; vis prof, State Univ NY, Stoney Brook, 83-84; mem Math Sci Res Inst, Berkeley, 84-85; fac res award, Bd Gov, Wayne State Univ. *Mem:* Am Math Soc; Math Asn Am; London Math Soc; Europ Math Union. *Res:* Functional analysis; algebraic and differential topology. *Mailing Add:* Dept Math-FAB Wayne State Univ Detroit MI 48202. *Fax:* 313-577-7596; *E-Mail:* claude@math.wayne.edu

SCHOCHET, SYDNEY SIGFRIED, JR, PATHOLOGY, NEUROPATHOLOGY. *Current Pos:* PROF PATHOL, COL MED, WVA UNIV, 81- *Personal Data:* b Chicago, Ill, Feb 7, 37; m 61; c 1. *Educ:* Tulane Univ, BS, 58, MD, 61, MS, 65. *Prof Exp:* Assoc prof pathol, Univ Tex Med Br, 73-79, prof, 79-81. *Concurrent Pos:* Nat Inst Neurol Dis & Blindness spec fel, Armed Forces Inst Path, 66-67; prof path, Univ Okla, 79-81. *Mem:* Am Asn Neuropath; Am Asn Path & Bact; Am Asn Pathologists; Soc Exp Biol & Med; Int Acad Path; Sigma Xi. *Res:* Reactions of the neuron to injury; ultrastructural neuropathology; neuromuscular diseases. *Mailing Add:* Dept Pathol WVa Univ Hlth Sci Ctr PO Box 9203 Morgantown WV 26506-9203

SCHOCK, ROBERT NORMAN, HIGH PRESSURE PHYSICS, ENERGY RESEARCH & DEVELOPMENT. *Current Pos:* sr res scientist high pressure physics, Lawrence Livermore Nat Lab, Univ Calif, 68-72, group leader, 72-74, geosci sect leader, 74-76, earth sci div leader, 76-87, energy prog leader, DEP ASSOC DIR FOR ENERGY, LAWRENCE LIVERMORE NAT LAB, UNIV CALIF, 92- *Personal Data:* b Monticello, NY, May 25, 39; m 59, Susan Esther Benton; c Pamela Ann, Patricia Elizabeth & Christina (Benton). *Educ:* Colo Col, BSc, 61; Rensselaer Polytech Inst, MSc, 63, PhD(geophys), 66. *Prof Exp:* Res assoc, Univ Chicago, 66-68. *Concurrent Pos:* Instr, Univ Chicago, 68 & Chabot Col, 69-71; sr Fulbright fel, Univ Bonn, 73; assoc ed, J Geophys Res, 78-80, J Physics & Chem Minerals, 84-87; vis res fel, Australian Nat Univ, 80-81; bd dir, Alameda County Flood Control & Water Conserv Dist, 84-86, chmn, 84-85; mem, Nat Res Coun, Continental Sci Drilling Comt, 84-86, Sci Adv Comt, Deep Observations & Sampling Earth's Continental Crust, Inc, 85-87, Solid Earth Sci panel, Energy Res Adv Bd, US Dept Energy, 85-87; res coord coun, Gas Res Inst, 95-; tech planning comt, World Energy Coung, 95- *Mem:* AAAS; Am Geophys Union; Sigma Xi. *Res:* High pressure physics; solid state processes; equation of state of solids; rock deformation; energy research and development. *Mailing Add:* Lawrence Livermore Nat Lab Univ Calif L-640 PO Box 808 Livermore CA 94550. *Fax:* 510-423-0618; *E-Mail:* schock1@llnl.gov

SCHODT, KATHLEEN PATRICIA, POLYMER SCIENCE. *Current Pos:* RES CHEMIST, E I DU PONT DE NEMOURS & CO, INC, 77-, SR TECH SPECIALIST. *Personal Data:* b Erie, Pa, Jan 27, 50. *Educ:* Case Western Reserve Univ, BS, 72, MS, 74, PhD(macromolecular sci), 77. *Mem:* Am Chem Soc. *Res:* Physical and mechanical properties of polymers, elastomers; polymer blends. *Mailing Add:* Polymer Prod Chestnut Run Plaza PO Box 80713 Wilmington DE 19880-0713

SCHOEBERL, MARK R, ATMOSPHERIC SCIENCES, ATMOSPHERIC DYNAMICS. *Current Pos:* SR SCIENTIST ATMOSPHERIC SCI, GODDARD SPACE FLIGHT CTR, NASA, 83- *Personal Data:* b Dec 7, 46. *Educ:* Iowa State Univ, BS, 70; Univ Ill, MS, 72, PhD, 76. *Honors & Awards:* Charney Lectr, Am Geophys Union, 96. *Prof Exp:* Staff scientist, Sci Applns Inc, Va, 76-77; staff, Naval Res Lab, Washington, DC, 77-83. *Concurrent Pos:* Adj prof, Fla State Univ, 80-82, Univ Mich, 96; assoc ed, J Geophys Res Letters, 86-88, J Geophys Res, 88-96; chmn, Comt Middle Atmosphere, Am Meteorol Soc, 86-87; scientist, Upper Atmospheric Res Satellite Proj, 93- *Mem:* Fel Am Geophys Union (pres-elect, 96); fel AAAS; fel Am Meteorol Soc. *Res:* Atmospheric dynamics, stratospheric physics, numerical modeling. *Mailing Add:* NASA Goddard Space Flight Ctr Code 910 Greenbelt MD 20771. *E-Mail:* schom@zephyr.gsfc.nasa.gov

SCHOEBERLE, DANIEL F, engineering mechanics, mechanical engineering; deceased, see previous edition for last biography

SCHOECH, WILLIAM JOSEPH, MANUFACTURING PROCESSES & SYSTEMS, PRODUCT & PRODUCTION SYSTEM DESIGN. *Current Pos:* Asst prof elec eng, 70-74, from asst prof to assoc prof mech mfg eng, 74-88, PROF MECH/MFG ENG, VALPARAISO UNIV, 88- *Educ:* Valparaiso Univ, BSEE, 66; Pa State Univ, MSIE, 69; Purdue Univ, PhD(indust eng), 71. *Mem:* Soc Mfg Engrs. *Res:* Manufacturing processes especially metal cutting and manufacturing systems. *Mailing Add:* Valparaiso Univ 102 Gellersen Eng Ctr Valparaiso IN 46383. *E-Mail:* wschoech@exodus.valpa.edu

SCHOEFER, ERNEST A(LEXANDER), METALLURGICAL ENGINEERING, MATHEMATICAL STATISTICS. *Current Pos:* METALL CONSULT, 70- *Personal Data:* b Brooklyn, NY, Sept 15, 08; m 37, Doris Bergen; c Nancy, Janice & Peter. *Educ:* Rensselaer Polytech Inst, CE, 32; Polytech Inst Brooklyn, MMetE, 57. *Prof Exp:* Statistician, Equity Corp, NY, 32-34; res engr, Repub Steel Corp, Ohio, 35-36; field engr, Distributors Group, Inc, NY, 36-37; secy, Alloy Casting Res Inst, 38-40, exec vpres, 40-70. *Concurrent Pos:* Mem, Tech Adv Comt High Alloy Castings, War Prod Bd, 42-45 & Nickel Conserv Panel, Metall Adv Bd, Nat Acad Sci, 52-53, High Alloys Comt, Welding Res Coun, 56- & Int Coun Alloy Phase Diagrams, 79-83. *Mem:* Am Soc Metals; Am Soc Testing & Mat; Am Inst Mining, Metall & Petrol Engrs. *Res:* Metallurgy of stainless steels and other heat and corrosion resistant casting alloys. *Mailing Add:* PO Box 537 Shelter Island NY 11964-0537

SCHOELLMANN, GUENTHER, BIOCHEMISTRY, ORGANIC CHEMISTRY. *Current Pos:* Res assoc, 59-61, from instr to asst prof, 61-67, ASSOC PROF BIOCHEM, SCH MED, TULANE UNIV, 67-, ASSOC PROF OPHTHAL, 76- *Personal Data:* b Stuttgart, Ger, Nov 17, 28; m 58; c 4. *Educ:* Stuttgart Tech Univ, dipl, 55, PhD(org chem), 57. *Mem:* Am Chem Soc; NY Acad Sci; Ger Chem Soc; Ger Biol Soc. *Res:* Chemistry and function of proteins and amino acids; active site of enzymes; enzyme mechanism; peptide synthesis. *Mailing Add:* Tulane Univ La Med Sch 1430 Tulane Ave New Orleans LA 70112-2699

SCHOEN, FREDERICK J, CARDIOVASCULAR PATHOLOGY, BIOMATERIALS. *Current Pos:* from asst prof to assoc prof, Harvard Med Sch, 80-96, prof path, 96-; PATHOLOGIST/DIR, DEPT PATH, DIV CARDIAC PATH, BRIGHAM & WOMEN'S HOSP, 80- *Personal Data:* b New York, NY, Feb 13, 46; m 75, Angeline E Warner; c Mariel & Bryana. *Educ:* Univ Mich, Ann Arbor, BSE, 66; Cornell Univ, PhD(mat sci), 70; Univ Miami, MD, 74. *Hon Degrees:* Am, Harvard Univ, 96. *Honors & Awards:* Ebert Prize, Am Pharmaceut Asn, 88; Clemson Award Appl Biomat Res, Soc Biomat, 94. *Prof Exp:* Assoc scientist, Gulf Gen Atomic Co, San Diego, Calif, 70-72; dir, Autopsy Div, Brigham & Women's Hosp, 88-93. *Concurrent Pos:* Mem, Spec Rev & Site Visit Comts, NIH, 83; lectr appl biol sci, Mass Inst Technol, 85; Lawrence J Henderson assoc prof health sci & technol, Div Health Sci & Technol, Harvard/Mass Inst Technol, 91-95. *Mem:* AAAS; Fedn Am Scientists; Am Soc Artificial Internal Organs; Int Acad Path; Soc Cardiovasc Path; Soc Biomat (pres, 89-90, treas, 86-90); Sigma Xi. *Res:* Clinicopathologic correlations in complications of cardiologic interventions; cardiovascular surgery and associated medical devices (including acute and chronic myocardial injury, angioplasty, endomyocardial biopsy, aortocoronary bypass, cardiac transplantation, heart valve prostheses, cardiac asst devices, and vascular grafts). *Mailing Add:* Dept Path Brigham & Women's Hosp 75 Francis St Boston MA 02115-6195. *Fax:* 617-232-9820

SCHOEN, HERBERT M, chemical engineering; deceased, see previous edition for last biography

SCHOEN, JOHN WARREN, FOREST WILDLIFE ECOLOGY. *Current Pos:* ALASKA AUDUBON, 97- *Personal Data:* b Anacortes, Wash, Apr 17, 47; m 70; c 1. *Educ:* Whitman Col, BA, 69; Univ Puget Sound, MS, 72; Univ Wash, PhD(wildlife ecol), 77. *Prof Exp:* Game biologist II, Alaska Dept Fish & Game, 76-77, Game Biologist III, 77-89, Res Supvr, 89-91; sr conserv biol, 91-97. *Mem:* Wildlife Soc; Ecol Soc Am; Am Soc Mammalogists. *Res:* Wildlife habitat relationships principally black-tailed deer, mountain goats and brown bear; home range patterns and habitat selection to understand the value of old-growth forests as wildlife habitats. *Mailing Add:* Alaska Audubon 308 G Street Suite 217 Anchorage AK 99501

SCHOEN, KENNETH, MATHEMATICS. *Current Pos:* PROF MATH, WORCESTER STATE COL, 71- *Personal Data:* b Bronxville, NY, Jan 18, 32; m 54, Diane E Brechbuhler; c Steven H, Scott J, Kevin J, John L & Robert K. *Educ:* Univ Conn, BA, 54; Yale Univ, AM, 55; Rensselaer Polytech Inst, 61; Univ Pittsburgh, PhD(math), 68. *Prof Exp:* Anal engr, Hamilton Stand Div, United Technologies, 55-62; prof math, Wheeling Jesuit Univ, 62-66; instr, Univ Pittsburgh, 67-68; prof, Worcester Polytech Inst, 68-71. *Concurrent Pos:* Lectr, Univ Conn, 55-62; prof, WLiberty State Col, 65-66 & Clark Univ, 71-72. *Mem:* Soc Indust & Appl Math; Math Asn Am. *Res:* Numerical analysis; taxes. *Mailing Add:* 618 Salisbury St Worcester MA 01609-1311

SCHOEN, KURT L, CHEMISTRY, FLAVOR CHEMISTRY. *Current Pos:* flavor chemist, 56-61, vpres & tech dir, 61-80, SR VPRES, DAVID MICHAEL & CO, INC, 80- *Personal Data:* b Dec 14, 27; US citizen; m 56; c Marcia, Michael & Karen. *Educ:* City Col New York, BS, 49; Polytech Inst Brooklyn, MS, 56. *Prof Exp:* Chemist, Felton Chem Co, 49-52; flavor chemist, H Kohnstamm & Co, Inc, 52-55. *Mem:* Am Chem Soc; Inst Food Technol; Soc Flavor Chemists. *Res:* Synthetic and natural flavorings; development and production of flavorings and synthetic food adjuncts to be used in comestibles. *Mailing Add:* 681 Meetinghouse Rd Elkins Park PA 19117

SCHOEN, MAX H, public health; deceased, see previous edition for last biography

SCHOEN, RICHARD ISAAC, SCIENCE ADMINISTRATION, MOLECULAR PHYSICS. *Current Pos:* prog dir aeronomy, 71-73, prog mgr energy, 73-75, dep div dir energy & resources res, 75-78, SECT HEAD, APPL PHYS, MATH, BIOL SCI & ENG, DIV APPL RES, NAT SCI FOUND-RES APPLN NAT NEEDS, 78- *Personal Data:* b New Rochelle, NY, Aug 13, 27; m 51; c 2. *Educ:* Calif Inst Technol, BS, 49; Univ Southern Calif, MS, 54, PhD(physics) 60. *Prof Exp:* Asst prof physics, Mo Sch Mines, 55-59; asst, Univ Southern Calif, 59-60, res assoc, 60-61; staff mem, Boeing Sci Res Labs, 61-71. *Mem:* AAAS; Am Phys Soc; Am Geophys Union; Sigma Xi. *Mailing Add:* 6419 Cavalier Corridor Falls Church VA 22044-1206

SCHOEN, RICHARD M(ELVIN), MATHEMATICAL DIFFERENTIAL GEOMETRY, PARTIAL DIFFERENTIAL EQUATIONS. *Current Pos:* PROF MATH, STANFORD UNIV, 87- *Personal Data:* b Celina, Ohio, Oct 23, 50. *Educ:* Univ Dayton, BS, 72; Stanford Univ, PhD(math), 76. *Honors & Awards:* MacArthur Prize Fel, MacArthur Found, 83-88; Boscher Prize, Am Math Soc, 89. *Prof Exp:* Prof math, Univ Calif, Berkeley, 80-85 & Univ Calif, San Diego, 85-87. *Concurrent Pos:* Sloan Found fel, 79-81. *Mem:* Nat Acad Sci; Am Acad Arts & Sci; Am Math Soc; Math Asn Am. *Mailing Add:* Math Dept Stanford Univ Stanford CA 94305

SCHOEN, ROBERT, HYDROLOGY. *Current Pos:* FREELANCE SCI WRITER & CONSULT, 92- *Personal Data:* b New York, NY, Nov 2, 30; m 57, Jean Rogers; c Wendy, Paula, Roxana & Peter. *Educ:* Brooklyn Col, BS, 52; Univ Wyo, MA, 53; Harvard Univ, PhD(geol), 63. *Prof Exp:* Geologist, US AEC, 53-58; hydrologist, US Geol Surv, 62-92. *Concurrent Pos:* Asst chief off, Water Qual US Geol Surv, 85-90. *Mem:* Clay Minerals Soc. *Res:* Application of solid-phase analysis to geochemical interpretation of water quality problems; practical applications of science theory for the literate layman; health aspects of water quality. *Mailing Add:* 2716 Calkins Rd Herndon VA 20171

SCHOENBERG, DANIEL ROBERT, MOLECULAR ENDOCRINOLOGY. *Current Pos:* ASSOC PROF PHARMACOL, UNIFORMED SERV UNIV HEALTH SCI, 81 - *Personal Data:* b Chicago, Ill, Aug 14, 49; m 74. *Educ:* Univ Ill, Urbana, BS, 71; Univ Wis-Madison, PHD(oncol), 77. *Prof Exp:* Fel cell biol, Baylor Col Med, 78-80, instr, 80-81. *Mem:* AAAS; Am Soc Cell Biol; Sigma Xi; Endocrine Soc. *Res:* Hormonal regulation of RNA stability; estrogen regulation of mammary tumor cell growth. *Mailing Add:* Dept Pharmacol Ohio State Univ 333 W 10th Ave Columbus OH 43210-1234. *Fax:* 301-295-3220; *E-Mail:* Bitnet: @schoenberg@usuhs

SCHOENBERG, LEONARD NORMAN, ELECTRONIC PACKAGING, PRINTED CIRCUIT BOARDS. *Current Pos:* Mem tech staff, AT&T Bell Labs, 66-91, MEM TECH STAFF, AT&T MICROELECTRONICS, 92- *Personal Data:* b Erie, Pa, Nov 29, 40; m 67, Roberta; c Joshua & Amy. *Educ:* Univ Rochester, BS, 62; Univ Mich, MS, 64, PhD(chem). 66. *Mem:* Am Chem Soc. *Res:* Coordination chemistry; printed circuit board fabrication; electrodeposition; electroless copper and nickel deposition; electroplating of nickel, copper, and gold; PWB design for manufacture; advanced electronic packaging technology. *Mailing Add:* Six Kathay Dr Livingston NJ 07039-4712. *Fax:* 973-386-6576; *E-Mail:* leonard.schoenberg@att.com

SCHOENBERG, MARK, PHYSIOLOGY. *Current Pos:* MED OFFICER RES, NAT INST ARTHRITIS & MUSCULOSKELETAL & SKIN DIS, 86- *Personal Data:* b New York, NY, Sept 3, 43; c 1. *Educ:* Mass Inst Technol, SB, 64; NY Univ, MD, 68. *Honors & Awards:* Res Award in Med, Borden Inc, 68. *Prof Exp:* Intracurricular res fel, Mass Inst Technol-NY Univ, 66-67; intern pediat, Cleveland Metrop Gen Hosp, 68-69; resident internal med, Univ Chicago Hosps & Clins, 69-70; res assoc, 70-72, sr staff fel, 72-75, med officer res, Nat Inst Arthritis, Diabetes, Digestive & Kidney Dis, NIH, 75-86. *Concurrent Pos:* Res assoc, dept med, Univ Chicago, 69-70. *Mem:* Am Soc Clin Invest; Biophys Soc. *Res:* Molecular basis of muscle contraction. *Mailing Add:* Bldg 6 Rm 108 NIH Bethesda MD 20892. *Fax:* 301-402-0009; *E-Mail:* mark@lpb.niams.nih.gov

SCHOENBERG, THEODORE, CHEMICAL ENGINEERING. *Current Pos:* DIR OPERS, TEXTRON SPECIALTY MAT, 65- *Personal Data:* b Brooklyn, NY, Aug 11, 39. *Educ:* City Col New York, BChE, 60; Mass Inst Technol, SM, 62, ScD(chem eng), 65. *Mem:* Am Inst Chem Engrs; Am Chem Soc; Nat Soc Prof Engrs. *Res:* Composite materials; high temperature chemical processes. *Mailing Add:* 120 Park Ave Medford MA 02155-1155

SCHOENBERGER, JAMES A, CLINICAL MEDICINE. *Current Pos:* pres hosp staff, 87-89, PROF PREV MED & MED, RUSH-PRESBY-ST LUKES MED CTR, 75- *Personal Data:* b Cleveland, Ohio, July 16, 19; m 43, Sally Cotter; c James A Jr, John S & Karl L. *Educ:* Univ Chicago, BS, 42, MD, 43. *Prof Exp:* Asst med, Univ Chicago, 46; fel med, Univ Ill Med Ctr 49-50, from instr to asst prof, 50-60, from assoc clin prof to clin prof med, 60-71. *Concurrent Pos:* Pres, Chicago Heart Asn, 74-76; chmn, Dept Prev Med, Rush Med Col, 74-92. *Mem:* Fel Am Col Physicians; Am Fedn Clin Res; Sigma Xi; fel Am Col Cardiol; Cent Soc Clin Res; Am Heart Asm (pres, 80-81). *Res:* Renal function; capillary permeability; body water and electrolytes; therapy of hypertension; epidemiology and prevention of coronary heart disease; systems management of hypertension. *Mailing Add:* PO Box 1514 Rancho Santa Fe CA 90267

SCHOENBERGER, MICHAEL, SEISMIC SIGNAL ANALYSIS. *Current Pos:* sr res engr, Exxon Prod Res Co, 67-71, sr res specialist, 71-76, res assoc, 76-81, sr res assoc, 81-82, Explor Systs Div, geophys adv, 82-84, geophys scientist, Exxon USA, 84-85, sr res supvr, 85-87, res adv, 87-90, sr res supvr, 90-91, supvr, 91-92, RES ADV, EXXON PROD RES CO, 92- *Personal Data:* b McKeesport, Pa, Jan 5, 40; m 64, Lynn Zinner; c Lee, Susan & Robert. *Educ:* Carnegie Inst Technol, BS, 61; Univ Ill, MS, 63, PhD(elec eng), 66. *Prof Exp:* From teaching asst to instr & res assoc elec eng & control theory, Univ Ill, 61-66; sr engr, Surface Div, Westinghouse Elec Corp, 66-67. *Concurrent Pos:* Spec ed proceedings, Inst Elec & Electronics Engrs, 84; ed, Soc Explor Geophys, 87-89, Geophys 88-89. *Mem:* Inst Elec & Electronics Engrs; Europ Asn Geoscientists & Engrs; Soc Explor Geophys (pres, 93-94). *Res:* Geophysical data analysis; optimization and implementation of system parameters; seismic data enhancement. *Mailing Add:* Subsurface Imaging Div Exxon Prod Res Co Box 2189 Houston TX 77252-2189. *E-Mail:* mike.schoenberger@exxon.sprint.com

SCHOENBERGER, ROBERT J(OSEPH), environmental engineering, for more information see previous edition

SCHOENBORN, BENNO P, MOLECULAR BIOLOGY, BIOPHYSICS. *Current Pos:* SR FEL, LOS ALAMOS NAT LAB, 92- *Personal Data:* b Basel, Switz, May 2, 36; m 62, Catherine Kay. *Educ:* Univ Calif, Los Angeles, BA, 58; Univ NSW, PhD(physics), 62. *Hon Degrees:* DSc, NJ Inst Technol, 82. *Honors & Awards:* E O Lawrence Award, 80. *Prof Exp:* NIH fel molecular biol, Med Ctr, Univ Calif, San Francisco, 62-63, asst physicist, 63-64; res fel molecular biol, Cambridge Univ, 64-66; assoc prof pharmacol, Univ Calif, San Francisco, 66-67; from assoc biophysicist to sr biophysicist, Brookhaven Nat Lab, 67-78, assoc chmn & head, Ctr Struct Biol, Dept Biol, 83-92. *Concurrent Pos:* Adj prof biochem, Columbia Univ Med Sch, 78-93; staff, Biophys Prog, State Univ NY, Stony Brook, 88-92. *Mem:* Biophys Soc; assoc mem Australian Inst Physics; Am Crystallog Asn. *Res:* Molecular mechanism of anesthesia; x-ray and neutron scattering of biological structures; biophysics; hydrogen bonding & solvent structure; instrumentation for neutron scattering. *Mailing Add:* Life Sci Div M 888 Los Alamos Nat Lab Los Alamos NM 87545. *Fax:* 505-665-6894; *E-Mail:* schoenborn@lanl.gov

SCHOENBRUNN, ERWIN F(REDERICK), CHEMICAL ENGINEERING. *Current Pos:* group leader, Am Cyanamid Co, 61-66, head explor res & process develop, 66-68, sr chem engr, 68-91, CONSULT, AM CYANAMID CO, STAMFORD, 91- *Personal Data:* b Newark, NJ, July 15, 21; m 48; c Carol, Mary, Laura & Frederick. *Educ:* Princeton Univ, BS, 47; Univ Pa, MS, 49. *Prof Exp:* Res engr, Sharples Corp, 47-51; proj mgr, Petrochem Dept, Nat Res Corp, 51-58; proj mgr, Res Labs, Escambia Chem Corp, Conn, 58-61. *Mem:* Am Chem Soc; Am Inst Chem Engrs. *Res:* Ion exchange; hydrocarbon oxidation; process development; polymerization kinetics; catalysis. *Mailing Add:* 22 Christopher Rd Ridgefield CT 06877. *Fax:* 203-438-3391

SCHOENDORF, WILLIAM H(ARRIS), ELECTRICAL ENGINEERING. *Current Pos:* VPRES, NICHOLS RES CORP, 84- *Personal Data:* b New York, NY, Jan 21, 36; m 58, Ellen; c Kenneth, Jacqueline, Linda & Jay. *Educ:* Mass Inst Technol, BSEE, 57; Univ Pa, MSEE, 58; Purdue Univ, PhD(elec eng), 63. *Prof Exp:* Instr elec eng, Purdue Univ, 58-62; assoc res engr, Conductron Corp, 63-65; radio astron observ, Univ Mich, Ann Arbor, 65-70; group leader, Lincoln Lab, Mass Inst Technol, 70-84. *Concurrent Pos:* Head, Pattern Recognition Div, Inst Elec & Electronics Engrs. *Mem:* Inst Elec & Electronics Engrs; Sigma Xi. *Res:* Scattering of electromagnetic waves by conductors, dielectrics, plasmas and random objects; wave propagation in plasmas and other random media; antenna theory; astrophysical processes; pattern recognition; neural networks; signal processing. *Mailing Add:* 16 Ledgewood Dr Bedford MA 01730

SCHOENE, NORBERTA WACHTER, BIOCHEMISTRY, NUTRITION. *Current Pos:* RES CHEMIST, LIPID NUTRIT LAB, NUTRIT INST, SCI & EDUC ADMIN-AGR RES, USDA, 71- *Personal Data:* b Pittsburg, Kans, July 9, 43. *Educ:* Pittsburg State Univ, BA, 65; George Washington Univ, PhD(biochem), 71. *Mem:* Sigma Xi; AAAS. *Res:* Essential fatty acid and prostaglandin metabolism; phospholipases; effect of dietary essential fatty acids on platelet function and development of hypertension. *Mailing Add:* USDA ARS Beltsville Human Nutrit Res Ctr Bldg 308 Rm 114 BARC-E Beltsville MD 20705-2350. *Fax:* 301-504-9192

SCHOENE, ROBERT B, RESPIRATORY PHYSIOLOGY, HIGH ALTITUDE PHYSIOLOGY. *Current Pos:* Asst prof, 81-85, ASSOC PROF PHYSIOL, UNIV WASH, 85- *Personal Data:* b Columbus, Ohio, Dec 4, 46. *Educ:* Columbia Univ, MD, 72. *Mem:* Am Physiol Soc; Am Thoracic Soc; Am Col Chest Physicians. *Mailing Add:* Dept Med Div Resp Dis Univ Wash Harbor Med Ctr 325 Nineth Ave ZA-62 Seattle WA 98104-2420

SCHOENER, EUGENE PAUL, NEUROPHARMACOLOGY, NEUROPHYSIOLOGY. *Current Pos:* asst prof, 74-78, ASSOC PROF PHARMACOL, SCH MED, WAYNE STATE UNIV, 78-, DIR, ADDICTION RES INST, 85- *Personal Data:* b New York, NY, Oct 22, 43; m 65; c 2. *Educ:* City Col New York, BS, 64; Rutgers Univ, MS, 65, PhD(physiol), 70. *Honors & Awards:* Award, Pharmaceut Mfg Asn Found, 75. *Prof Exp:* Res assoc neuropharmacol, Col Physicians & Surgeons, Columbia Univ, 73-74. *Concurrent Pos:* NIH training grant, Col Physicians & Surgeons, Columbia Univ, 70-73; vis asst prof, State Univ NY Col Purchase, 72-73; career teacher substance abuse, Nat Inst Alcohol Abuse & Alcoholism, Wayne State Univ, 79-82. *Mem:* Am Phys Soc; Soc Neurosci; Int Asn Study Pain; Res Soc Alcoholism; Asn Med Educ Res Substance Abuse. *Res:* Pharmacodynamics of alcohol and abused drugs; mechanisms of pain and analgesia; drug action on neural control systems. *Mailing Add:* Dept Pharmacol Sch Med Wayne State Univ 540 E Canfield Ave Detroit MI 48201-1908

SCHOENER, THOMAS WILLIAM, ECOLOGY. *Current Pos:* PROF, UNIV CALIF, DAVIS, 80-, CHAIR, SECT EVOLUTION & ECOL, 93- *Personal Data:* b Lancaster, Pa, Aug 9, 43; m 86, Susan L Keen. *Educ:* Harvard Univ, BA, 65, PhD(biol), 69. *Honors & Awards:* MacArthur Prize, Ecol Soc Am. *Prof Exp:* Jr fel, Harvard Univ, 69-71, from asst prof to assoc prof biol, 72-74; from assoc prof to prof zool, Univ Wash, 75-80. *Mem:* Nat Acad Sci; Am Soc Ichthyologists & Herpetologists; Am Soc Naturalists; Am Arachnol Soc; Ecol Soc Am; Soc Study Reptiles & Amphibians; Am Ornith Union; Cooper Ornith Soc; Wilson Ornith Soc; Am Acad Arts & Sci. *Res:* Feeding strategies; resource partitioning and the diversity of ecological communities; population dynamics; island ecology; biogeography; theoretical ecology; biology of lizards and spiders; food webs. *Mailing Add:* Div Biol Sci Univ Calif Storer Hall Davis CA 95616. *Fax:* 530-752-1449

SCHOENEWEISS, DONALD F, PLANT PATHOLOGY. *Current Pos:* from asst plant pathologist to plant pathologist, 58-89, EMER PROF, STATE NATURAL HIST SURV, ILL, 89- *Personal Data:* b Columbus, Ohio, July 27, 29; m 64; c 2. *Educ:* Ohio State Univ, BA, 51, MSc, 53, PhD(bot), 58. *Prof Exp:* Asst plant path, Ohio Agr Exp Sta, 55-58; inspector plant parasitic nematodes, USDA, 58. *Mem:* Am Soc Hort Sci; Am Phytopath Soc; Sigma Xi. *Res:* Diseases of shade and ornamental trees and shrubs, especially nursery plants; influence of environmental stresses on disease susceptibility. *Mailing Add:* 800 Ben Franklin Dr No 502 Sarasota FL 34236

SCHOENFELD, ALAN HENRY, PROBLEM SOLVING. *Current Pos:* assoc prof, 84-87, PROF EDUC & MATH, UNIV CALIF, BERKELEY, 87-, CHAIR, FAC EDUC, 94- *Personal Data:* b New York, NY, July 9, 47; m 70, Jean Snitzer; c Anna. *Educ:* Queens Col, NY, BA, 68; Stanford Univ, MS, 69, PhD(math), 73. *Honors & Awards:* Lester R Ford Award, Math Asn Am, 80. *Prof Exp:* Lectr math, Univ Calif, Davis, 73-75, lectr sci educ, Berkeley, 75-78; asst & assoc prof, Hamilton Col, 78-81; assoc prof math & educ, Univ Rochester, 81-84. *Concurrent Pos:* Consult, Xerox Corp, 79; prin investr res grants, NSF, 79-89 & 90-, Spencer Found, 83-, Sloan Found, 84, 87-; vis lectr, Math Asn Am, 81-, chmn, Comt on Teaching Undergrad Math, 82-92; mem math panel, Nat Bd Prof Teaching Stand, 90-; mem, Comt Educ, Am Math Soc, 92-; mem, Nat Res Coun Bd Testing & Assessment, 93-; writing group leader, Nat Coun Teachers Math, Stand 2000, 96- *Mem:* Math Asn Am; Am Educ Res Asn; Cognitive Sci Soc; AAAS; Nat Coun Teachers Math. *Res:* Psychology of mathematical problem solving, metacognition, belief systems. *Mailing Add:* Dept Educ & Math Univ Calif Berkeley CA 94720-1670. *E-Mail:* alans@violet.berkeley.edu

SCHOENFELD, CY, MEDICAL & HEALTH SCIENCES, MOLECULAR BIOLOGY. *Current Pos:* sr res tech lab path, Sch Med, NY Univ, 63-64, sr res tech lab prev med, 64-66, from asst res scientist lab to teaching asst prev med, 66-73, res asst prof urol, Urol Dept, 73-79, RES ASSOC PROF UROL, UROL DEPT, SCH MED, NY UNIV, 79- *Personal Data:* b Brooklyn, NY, Nov 13, 39; m 76; c 2. *Educ:* Brooklyn Col, BS, 62; Long Island Univ, MSc, 65; NY Univ, PhD(biol), 72. *Prof Exp:* Tech lab, Margaret Sanger Res Bur, 62-63; lab supv, Infertil Clin, Belevue Hosp, 63-72. *Concurrent Pos:* Dir res, Fertil Lab Inc, New York, NY, 72-; consult, Universal Diag Lab, Brooklyn, NY, 74-; adj assoc prof, Obstet-Gynec Dept, Univ Med & Dent NJ, Newark, 86- *Mem:* Am Fertil Soc; Soc Study Reproduction; Am Soc Andrology; Am Soc Reproductive Immunol & Microbiol; Am Soc Microbiol; Am Soc Trop Med & Hyg; Sigma Xi. *Res:* Sperm physiology; hormone regulation in humans. *Mailing Add:* 137 E 36th St New York NY 10016

SCHOENFELD, DAVID ALAN, BIOSTATISTICS. *Current Pos:* asst prof, 78-81, ASSOC PROF BIOSTATIST, HARVARD SCH PUB HEALTH, 81-, HARVARD MED SCH, 84- *Personal Data:* b Ft Monmouth, NJ, Apr 19, 45; m; c 3. *Educ:* Reed Col, BA, 67; Univ Ore, MA, 68, PhD(math statist), 74. *Prof Exp:* Statistician, Sch Med, Univ Ore, 71-72; fel, Dept Statist, Stanford Univ, 74-75; res asst prof statist sci, State Univ NY, Buffalo, 75-78. *Concurrent Pos:* Dir, Biostatist Ctr, Mass Gen Hosp. *Mem:* Biomet Soc; Am Statist Asn; Inst Math Statist. *Res:* Clinical trials of AIDS therapies with the AIDS Clinical Trials Group; development and application of statistical methodologies for clinical data; isotonic regression techniques for toxicology experiments. *Mailing Add:* 41 Brook Rd Sharon MA 02067

SCHOENFELD, LAWRENCE STEVEN, CLINICAL PSYCHOLOGY, CHRONIC PAIN. *Current Pos:* PROF PSYCHIAT, ANESTHESIOL & REHAB MED, UNIV TEX HEALTH SCI CTR, SAN ANTONIO, 69- *Personal Data:* b New York, NY, Dec 22, 41; m 67, Heidi Buchbinder; c Jennifer & Jessica. *Educ:* Ohio Wesleyan Univ, BA, 63; Univ Fla, MA, 65 & PhD(psychol), 67; Am Bd Prof Psychol, dipl, 76. *Prof Exp:* Sr asst scientist, USPHS, 67-69. *Concurrent Pos:* Exec dir & founder, Crisis Ctr San Antonio Area Inc, 72-79; consult, San Antonio Police Dept, 73-85, San Antonio Park Rangers, 75-85, SW Res Inst, 78-90, San Antonio Fire Dept, 79-89, Univ Tex San Antonio Police, 79-, City New Baunfels Police Dept & City Seguin Police Dept, 82-; liaison officer, Tex Psychol Asn, 87-88; Tex State Bd Exams Psychologists, 88-94. *Mem:* Fel Am Psychol Asn; Int Asn Study Pain. *Res:* More than 75 publications involving training of psychologists, ethics, clinical psychology and chronic pain. *Mailing Add:* Univ Tex Health Sci Ctr 7703 Floyd Curl Dr San Antonio TX 78284-7792. *Fax:* 210-567-6941; *E-Mail:* schoenfeldl@uthscsa.edu

SCHOENFELD, ROBERT GEORGE, TOXICOLOGY. *Current Pos:* RETIRED. *Personal Data:* b Topeka, Kans, Nov 29, 26; m 46; c 5. *Educ:* Univ Okla, BS, 49, MS, 56, PhD(biochem), 58; Am Bd Clin Chemists, dipl; Am Asn Clin Chemists, cert toxicol chem, 72. *Prof Exp:* Asst chemist, State Hwy Res Lab, Okla, 45-48; asst chief chemist, Wilson & Co, 49-51; clin biochemist, Vet Admin Hosp, 58-65; dir, Schoenfeld Clin Lab, Inc, 61-88; staff, La Mesa Med Lab, Albuquerque, NMex. *Mem:* Am Chem Soc; fel Am Asn Clin Chemists; Am Acad Forensic Sci; fel Asn Off Racing Chemists (pres, 74-75 & 77-79); Sigma Xi. *Res:* Clinical chemistry, toxicology and methodology; drug and narcotic assays; GC-MS analyses. *Mailing Add:* 7204 Aztec Rd NE Albuquerque NM 87110-2252. *Fax:* 505-883-7480

SCHOENFELD, ROBERT LOUIS, ELECTRONICS, COMPUTER SCIENCE. *Current Pos:* asst prof electronics & comput sci, Rockefeller Univ, 57-63, assoc prof, 63-90, head Electronics & Comput Lab, 71-90, EMER PROF, ELECTRONICS & COMPUT SCI, ROCKEFELLER UNIV, 90- *Personal Data:* b New York, NY, Apr 1, 20; m 90, Shulamith Stechel; c David, Paul, Nedda & Bethany. *Educ:* NY Univ, BA, 42; Columbia Univ, BS, 44; Polytech Inst NY, MEE, 49, DEE, 56. *Honors & Awards:* Centennial Medal, Inst Elec & Electronics Engrs, 84. *Prof Exp:* Electronic engr, Allied Lab

Instrument Co, NY, 46-47; res assoc neurol, Col Physicians & Surg, Columbia Univ, 47-51; sr physicist, NY Dept Hosps, 51-52; res fel physics, Sloan-Kettering Inst, 52-57. *Concurrent Pos:* From instr to assoc prof, Polytech Inst Brooklyn, 47-59, adj prof, 59-68, 77-83. *Mem:* Fel Inst Elec & Electronics Engrs; Asn Comput Mach; Sigma Xi; fel Am Inst Med & Biol Eng. *Res:* Electronic instrumentation for biophysics and neurophysiology; bioelectric signals; application of network and communication theory to physical systems; application of computer techniques in biology; microprocessor based instruments; laboratory applications of computer languages; history of philosophy of science. *Mailing Add:* 500 E 63rd St Apt 15C New York NY 10021

SCHOENFELD, RONALD IRWIN, NEUROPHARMACOLOGY, BEHAVIORAL PHARMACOLOGY. *Current Pos:* Asst br chief, 77-91, dept dir, Intermural Res, 91-, DEP DIR, SCI POLICY, NIMH. *Educ:* Univ Chicago, PhD(pharmacol), 68. *Mailing Add:* Rm 17C26 NIMH 5600 Fishers Lane Rockville MD 20857-8030

SCHOENFELD, THEODORE MARK, SAFETY FROM HAZARDOUS CHEMICAL FLUID SPRAYOUTS, MATERIAL PERFORMANCE OF CHEMICALS. *Current Pos:* pres, 50-74, PRES, T M SCHOENFELD SERV, 89- *Personal Data:* b New York, NY, July 10, 07; m 46; c Edward L. *Educ:* Col City New York, BS, 30; Stevens Inst Technol, cert indust engr. *Prof Exp:* Asst dir, Systs Dept, City New York, 33-42; admin officer, US Dept State, 44-46; chief indust engr, MGM Int Corp, 46-49; vpres & chief engr, Ramco Mfg Co, 74-89. *Concurrent Pos:* Nat div dir, Inst Indust Engrs, 75; mem, Nat Ethics Comt, Am Inst Chemists, 86-, Ethics Comt & gov bd, NJ Inst Chemists, 88- *Mem:* Inst Indust Engrs; Am Soc Plastics Engrs; fel Am Inst Chemists. *Res:* Safety devices to prevent sprayouts of hazardous chemicals during production; inventor and developer of hazardous chemical safety shields for US military and major chemical processing plants. *Mailing Add:* 86C Empress Plaza Cranbury NJ 08512

SCHOENFIELD, LESLIE JACK, GASTROENTEROLOGY, INTERNAL MEDICINE. *Current Pos:* assoc prof, 71-72, PROF MED, UNIV CALIF, LOS ANGELES, 72-; DIR, DEPT GASTROENTEROL, CEDARS-SINAI MED CTR, LOS ANGELES,71- *Personal Data:* b Bronx, NY, Feb 20, 32; c 6. *Educ:* Temple Univ, BA, 52, MD, 56; Univ Minn, Minneapolis, PhD(med physiol), 64. *Prof Exp:* From instr to assoc prof internal med, Mayo Grad Sch Med, Univ Minn, 63-70. *Concurrent Pos:* Res assoc, Fells Inst Gastrointestinal Res, Temple Univ, 63; consult internal med & gastroenterol, Mayo Clin, 63-70, assoc dir, Res Unit & Gastrointestinal Training Prog, 66-70; NIH spec fel, Karolinska Inst, Stockholm, 65; res grant, Mayo Clin & Cedars-Sinai Med Ctr, 66-; rev, Gen Med Study Sect, NIH, 70; mem, Res Eval Comt, Vet Admin, 70 & Merit Rev Bd, 72; dir, Nat Coop Gallstone Study, 73-83; chmn, AASLD Res Comt, 75-78; vchmn, Nat Sci Adv Comt, Nat Found Ileitis & Colitis, Inc, 78-; dir, Dornier Nat Biliary Lithotripsy Study, 86-91. *Mem:* AAAS; Am Gastroenterol Asn; Am Asn Study Liver Dis; Int Asn Study Liver; Am Soc Clin Invest. *Res:* Bile flow and composition; hepatic conjugation and secretion; cholestasis biliary lipids and cholelithiasis; acute and chronic hepatitis. *Mailing Add:* Cedars-Sinai Med Ctr 8700 Beverly Blvd Los Angeles CA 90048-0750

SCHOENHALS, ROBERT JAMES, MECHANICAL ENGINEERING. *Current Pos:* From asst prof to assoc prof, 60-68, PROF MECH ENG, PURDUE UNIV, WEST LAFAYETTE, 68- *Personal Data:* b Petoskey, Mich, Apr 29, 33; m 56; c 2. *Educ:* Univ Mich, BSE, 56, MSE, 57, PhD(mech eng), 61. *Concurrent Pos:* Consult, Bendix Energy Controls Div, 63-69; vis prof, Ariz State Univ, 69-70; dir heat transfer prog, Eng Div, NSF, 73-74, energy res coordr, 74-75. *Mem:* AAAS; Am Soc Mech Engrs; Am Soc Eng Educ; Am Soc Heating, Refrig & Air-Conditioning Engrs; Sigma Xi. *Res:* Heat and mass transfer; fluid mechanics; dynamics and automatic control. *Mailing Add:* 2849 Barlow St West Lafayette IN 47906-1515

SCHOENHERR, ROMAN UHRICH, CHEMICAL ENGINEERING, PHYSICAL CHEMISTRY. *Current Pos:* Sr engr, 3M Co, 59-68, eng specialist, 68-72, sr eng specialist, 72-75, CORP ENG SCIENTIST, 3M CO, 75- *Personal Data:* b St Henry, Ohio, Jan 2, 34; m 65; c 3. *Educ:* Univ Dayton, BS, 56; Iowa State Univ, PhD(chem eng), 59. *Mem:* Am Inst Chem Engrs. *Res:* Research and development in heat, mass and momentum transfer with emphasis on mathematical modeling. *Mailing Add:* 3296 Glen Oaks Ave St Paul MN 55110

SCHOENINGER, MARGARET J, NUTRITIONAL ECOLOGY, PREHISTORIC HUMAN DIET. *Current Pos:* assoc prof, 89-94, PROF BIOL ANTHROP, UNIV WIS, 94- *Educ:* Univ Fla, BA, 70; Univ Cincinnati, MA, 73; Univ Mich, PhD(biol anthrop), 80. *Prof Exp:* Instr human anat, Johns Hopkins Univ Sch Med, 80-82, asst prof, 82-84; asst prof anthrop, Harvard Univ, 85-88, assoc prof, 88-89. *Concurrent Pos:* Fel geol sci, Univ Calif, Los Angeles, 80-82. *Mem:* AAAS; Am Asn Phys Anthropologists; Sigma Xi; Soc Am Archaeol; Human Biol Coun. *Res:* Paleodiet and nutrition using stable isotope ratios of carbon and nitrogen in bone; paleoecology using stable isotope ratios of oxygen in bone phosphate; nutritional ecology of Hadza foragers. *Mailing Add:* Dept Anthrop Univ Wis 1180 Observatory Dr Madison WI 53706. *Fax:* 608-265-4216; *E-Mail:* mschoen@macc.wisc.edu

SCHOENLEIN, ROBERT W, OPTICAL ENGINEERING. *Current Pos:* STAFF SCIENTIST, LAWRENCE BERKELEY LAB, CALIF. *Honors & Awards:* Adolf Lomb Medal, Optical Soc Am, 94. *Mailing Add:* Lawrence Berkeley Lab One Cyclotron Rd Berkeley CA 94720

SCHOENLY, KENNETH GEORGE, INSECT ECOLOGY, FORENSIC ENTOMOLOGY. *Current Pos:* DEPT BIOL SCI, LA TECH UNIV. *Personal Data:* b Selma, Ala, Sept 20, 56. *Educ:* Univ Tex, BS, 78, MS, 81; Univ NMex, PhD(biol), 89. *Prof Exp:* Res asst, Univ Tex, El Paso, 78, teaching asst biol, 79-81, vis lectr biol, 82; environ biologist, Univ Tex, El Paso & White Sands Nat Monument, 78-79; biol instr biol, Angelo State Univ, 81-84; grad teaching asst biol, Univ NMex, 85-89, asst cur entom, 89; postdoctoral assoc, Rockefeller Univ, 89-93. *Concurrent Pos:* Teaching assoc, Univ NMex, 85-89, adj asst prof, 89-; forensic entomologist, Ctr Medico Legal Res & Consult, NMex, 88- *Mem:* Am Soc Naturalists; Ecol Soc Am; Entom Soc Am; Am Acad Forensic Sci. *Res:* Community and ecosystem ecology; structure and dynamics of arthropod-dominated communities including statistical analyses of successional communities and food webs; mathematical modelling of ecological systems. *Mailing Add:* Dept Biol Sci La Tech Univ 305 Wisteria St Ruston LA 71272-0001

SCHOENSTADT, ARTHUR LORING, APPLIED MATHEMATICS. *Current Pos:* PROF MATH, NAVAL POSTGRAD SCH, 70-, ASSOC DEAN COMPUT & INFO SERV. *Personal Data:* b New York, NY, Nov 8, 42; m 64; c 2. *Educ:* Rensselaer Polytech Inst, BS, 64, MS, 65, PhD(math), 68. *Mem:* Soc Indust & Appl Math; Sigma Xi. *Res:* Ordinary and partial differential equations; numerical methods. *Mailing Add:* 22402 Montera Pl Salinas CA 93908

SCHOENWETTER, JAMES, ARCHAEOLOGICAL PALYNOLOGY. *Current Pos:* from asst prof to assoc prof, 67-78, PROF ANTHROP, ARIZ STATE UNIV, 78- *Personal Data:* b Chicago, Ill, Jan 2, 35; m 60; c 1. *Educ:* Univ Chicago, BA, 55, BA, 56; Univ Ariz, MA, 60; Southern Ill Univ, PhD(anthropol), 67. *Prof Exp:* Res cur, Mus NMex, 63-67. *Concurrent Pos:* Instr, NMex Highlands Univ, 65-66 & Eastern NMex Univ, 66-67; vis prof, Univ Liverpool, 82-83. *Mem:* Soc Am Archaeol; Am Anthropol Asn; Am Asn Stratig Polynologists; Sigma Xi; Soc Ethnobiol. *Res:* Study of the pollen contained in sediment samples recovered from archaeological excavations to provide estimates of sample antiquity, paleoenvironmental reconstructions, and/or reconstructions of ancient cultural behaviors. *Mailing Add:* Dept Anthropol Ariz State Univ Tempe AZ 85287

SCHOENWOLF, GARY CHARLES, MORPHOGENESIS, DEVELOPMENTAL BIOLOGY. *Current Pos:* from asst prof to assoc prof, 79-89, PROF, ANAT & EMBRYOL, SCH MED, UNIV UTAH, 95- *Personal Data:* b Chicago, Ill, Nov 22, 49; m 71; c 2. *Educ:* Elmhurst Col, BA, 71; Univ Ill, Urbana Champaign, MS, 73, PhD(zool), 76. *Honors & Awards:* Fogarty Award, NIH, 88. *Prof Exp:* Vis lectr embryol, Univ Ill, 76-77; fel anat, Sch Med, Univ NMex, 77-79. *Concurrent Pos:* Postdoctoral fel, Nat Res Serv Award - NIH, 78-79; assoc ed, The Anat Record, 81-; ed adv bd, Scanning Electron Micros, Inc, 81-86. *Mem:* Am Soc Zoologists; Am Asn Anatomists; Soc Develop Biol; Am Soc Cell Biol; AAAS; Int Soc Develop Biol; Soc Neurosci; Teratology Soc. *Res:* Analysis of the mechanisms of morphogenesis, especially those mechanisms involved in the formation of the early rudiments of the nervous system (neurulation); gastrulation. *Mailing Add:* Dept Neurobiol & Anat Univ Ut Sch Med 50 N Medical Dr Salt Lake City UT 84132-0001. *Fax:* 801-581-6453; *E-Mail:* gcschoen@ccutah.edu

SCHOEPFER, ARTHUR E(RIC), CHEMICAL ENGINEERING, CHEMISTRY. *Current Pos:* RETIRED. *Personal Data:* b Chicago, Ill, Apr 28, 31; m 53; c 3. *Educ:* Univ Ill, BS, 52. *Prof Exp:* Process engr, Olin-Mathieson Chem Corp, 52-55, asst proj supvr, High Energy Fuel Div, 55-57, proj supvr, 57-59; develop engr, A E Staley Mfg Co, 59-61, sr develop engr, 61-65, group leader eng res, 65-77, prod mgr, 77-79, plant mgr, 79-85, dir mgr, 85-91. *Mem:* Am Inst Chem Engrs. *Res:* High energy fuels; fused salt electrolysis; solvent extraction; economic evaluation; crystallization; fermentation; ion exchange; process development and design. *Mailing Add:* 4332 Leslie Lane Decatur IL 62526

SCHOEPFLE, GORDON MARCUS, PHYSIOLOGY. *Current Pos:* prof, 69-85, EMER PROF NEUROBIOL IN PSYCHIAT, PHYSIOL & BIOPHYS, SCH MED, UNIV ALA, BIRMINGHAM, 85- *Personal Data:* b Louisville, Ky, June 11, 15; m 42; c 4. *Educ:* DePauw Univ, AB, 37; Princeton Univ, AM, 39, PhD(biol), 40. *Prof Exp:* Asst physiol, Princeton Univ, 39-40; from instr to prof, Sch Med, Wash Univ, 41-69. *Mem:* AAAS; Soc Neurosci; Am Physiol Soc; Biophys Soc; Soc Exp Biol & Med; Sigma Xi. *Res:* Neurophysiology; muscle physiology; interfacial tensions; bioluminescence; mathematics of excitation. *Mailing Add:* Dept Psychol Univ Ala University Sta Birmingham AL 35294

SCHOEPKE, HOLLIS GEORGE, PHARMACOLOGY. *Current Pos:* VPRES RES & DEVELOP, ANAQUEST DIV, BOC GROUP, INC, 87- *Personal Data:* b Kenosha, Wis, Feb 22, 29; m 54; c 2. *Educ:* Univ Wis, BS, 51, PhD(pharmacol), 60. *Prof Exp:* Res asst, Univ Wis, 56-60; res pharmacologist, Abbott Labs, 60-65, head dept pharmacol, 65-69, dir div exp pharmacol, 69-71, dir prod planning & develop div, 71-73, vpres res & develop, Hosp Prod Div, 73-78; dir res & develop, Pharmaceut Div, E I du Pont de Nemours & Co, 78-80; sr vpres, Preclin Res & Develop, G D Scarle & Co, 80-87. *Mem:* Am Soc Pharmacol & Exp Therapeut; Am Heart Asn; Sigma Xi. *Res:* Cardiovascular and autonomic pharmacology; cardiotonic drugs. *Mailing Add:* 307 Indian Pt LBS Barrington IL 60010. *Fax:* 908-604-7650

SCHOESSLER, JOHN PAUL, OPTOMETRY, VISUAL PHYSIOLOGY. *Current Pos:* From instr to prof optom & physiol optics, Ohio State Univ, 68-75, asst dean, 73-77, assoc dean, Col Optom, 92-95, DEAN, OHIO STATE UNIV, 95- *Personal Data:* b Denver, Colo, May 9, 42; m 64, Jane Roberts; c Paul, Kristen, & Rachael. *Educ:* Ohio State Univ, BScOpt, 65, OD, 66, MSc, 68, PhD(physiol optics), 71. *Honors & Awards:* May Schapero Mem Award, Am Acad Optom. *Mem:* Am Acad Optom; Am Optom Asn; Asn Res Vision & Ophthal. *Res:* Corneal physiology; contact lenses; glaucoma detection; visual field defects. *Mailing Add:* Col Optom Ohio State Univ 320 W Tenth Ave Columbus OH 43210. *Fax:* 614-292-7493; *E-Mail:* schoessler.1@osu.edu

SCHOETTGER, RICHARD A, FISH BIOLOGY, ENVIRONMENTAL BIOLOGY. *Current Pos:* Physiologist, Fish Control Lab, 62-67, asst dir lab, 67-69, dir, Fish-Pesticide Res Lab, 69-80, DIR, NAT FISHERIES CONTAMINANT RES CTR, US FISH & WILDLIFE SERV, 80- *Personal Data:* b Arlington, Nebr, Oct 24, 32; m 54, Lorraine L Nelson; c David S & Lisa M. *Educ:* Colo State Univ, BS, 54, MS, 59, PhD(zool), 66. *Honors & Awards:* Award of Excellence, Am Fisheries Soc, 86; Meritorious Serv Award, Dept Interior, 88. *Concurrent Pos:* Res assoc, Dept Natural Resources, Univ Mo-Columbia, 71-; adv comt water qual criteria, Nat Acad Sci, 71-72; co-proj leaders, Effects of Pollutants on Aquatic Organisms & Ecosysts, Develop Water Qual Criteria, Assessment of Complex Anthropogenic Impacts on Ecosysts, Reservoirs & Rivers, US/USSR Environ Exchange Agreement, 79-,. *Mem:* Am Fisheries Soc; Sigma Xi; Soc Environ Toxicol & Chem. *Res:* Toxicity, physiology and ecological effects of pesticides and other contaminants in aquatic organisms. *Mailing Add:* 1900 N Lake of the Woods Rd Columbia MO 65202. *Fax:* 573-876-1896

SCHOFFSTALL, ALLEN M, ORGANIC CHEMISTRY. *Current Pos:* AT DEPT CHEM, EMORY UNIV. *Personal Data:* b Harrisburg, Pa, Mar 20, 39; m 61; c 2. *Educ:* Franklin & Marshall Col, BS, 60; State Univ NY Buffalo, PhD(org chem), 66. *Prof Exp:* NIH fel, Univ Ill, 66-67; from asst prof to prof chem, Univ Colo, Colo Springs, 67-87. *Concurrent Pos:* Consult, Kaman Sci Corp, Colo. *Mem:* AAAS; Am Chem Soc; Sigma Xi. *Res:* Nitrogen heterocyclic and organophosphorus chemistry; chemical evolution. *Mailing Add:* Dept Chem Univ Colo Colorado Springs CO 80933

SCHOFIELD, DEREK, PHYSICS. *Current Pos:* RETIRED. *Personal Data:* b Oldham, Eng, Feb 14, 28; m 55, Penelope Grohmann; c 3. *Educ:* Univ Sheffield, BSc, 49, PhD(physics), 52. *Prof Exp:* Sci off, H M Underwater Detection Estab, Royal Navy, 52-55; sci off, Underwater Physics Sect, Naval Res Estab, 55-56, group leader transducer group, 56-58, head, Elec Sect, 59-61, head, Physics & Math Sect, 61-64, supt physics wing, 64-68, sci adv to vchief Defence Staff, Can Forces Hq, 68-72, chief, Defence Res Estab Atlantic, 72-77; dep chief, Res & Develop Labs, Dept Nat Defence, 77-83, chief res & develop, 83-92. *Res:* Underwater acoustics; electroacoustics. *Mailing Add:* 1795 Rhodes Crescent Ottawa ON K1H 5T1 Can

SCHOFIELD, EDMUND ACTON, JR, ENVIRONMENTAL SCIENCES, CONSERVATION. *Current Pos:* FOUNDER & PRES, THOREAU COUNTRY CONSERV ALLIANCE, CONCORD, MASS, 88- *Personal Data:* b Worcester, Mass, Nov 26, 38. *Educ:* Clark Univ, BA, 62, MA, 64; Ohio State Univ, PhD(bot), 72. *Prof Exp:* Tech ed, Battelle Mem Inst, 65-67; res asst, Dept Bot, Ohio State Univ, 67-71, res assoc plant ecol, 67-72, asst to dir, Inst Polar Studies, 72; NASA Nat Res Coun resident res assoc biol, Calif Inst Technol, 72-73; environ scientist, Ohio Dept Natural Resources, 73-76; dir res, Sierra Club, 76-77; staff ecologist, Inst Ecol, Butler Univ, 77-80; asst publ officer, Arnold Arboretum, Harvard Univ, 85-88. *Concurrent Pos:* Partic, US Antarctic Res Prog, Cape Hallett, Ross Island and southern Victoria Land, Antarctica, Clark Univ, 63-64 & Ohio State Univ, 67-68 & 68-69; res assoc, Inst Polar Studies, Ohio State Univ, 73-76; adj asst prof bot, Butler Univ, 78-80. *Res:* Ecology of Antarctic and Arctic lichens and blue-green algae; history of ecology; history of conservation movement; delineation, characterization and restoration of the Walden ecosystem. *Mailing Add:* 21 James St Worcester MA 01603. *Fax:* 978-287-4301

SCHOFIELD, JAMES ROY, ACADEMIC ADMINISTRATION, HISTORY OF MEDICINE. *Current Pos:* VIS DISTINGUISHED PROF HIST MED, BAYLOR UNIV, 92- *Personal Data:* b Spring, Tex, July 12, 23. *Educ:* Baylor Univ, BS, 45, MD, 47. *Hon Degrees:* LLD, Queens Univ, Can, 88. *Prof Exp:* From instr to asst prof anat, Baylor Col Med, 47-53, assoc prof admin med, 59-66, prof anat, 66-71, from asst dean to acad dean, 53-71; dir div accreditation, Asn Am Med Cols, 71-87, secy, Liaison Comt Med Educ, 74-87. *Concurrent Pos:* Trustee, Baylor Med Found, 52-62, exec vpres, 52-56; Nat coordr, Med Educ Nat Defense, 55-58; consult, Surgeon Gen, US Army, 60 & Div Gen Med Sci, NIH, 61; mem transitional coun, Col Med, Univ United Arab Emirates, 86-91; external auditor, Col Med, Sultan Qahoos Univ, Oman, 86-97. *Mem:* Am Socs Exp Biol & Med; Asn Am Med Cols (asst secy, 59-66); AMA. *Res:* Medical education; pre medical education; history of medicine-impact of disease on history. *Mailing Add:* 700 Greenwood Ct Georgetown TX 78628. *Fax:* 512-869-0304

SCHOFIELD, RICHARD ALAN, PATHOLOGY. *Current Pos:* RETIRED. *Personal Data:* b Royersford, Pa, June 30, 24; m 49, Rosemarie Euker; c Joanne C & William A. *Educ:* Jefferson Med Col, MD, 48. *Prof Exp:* Instr path, Med Col & resident, Univ Hosp, Univ Ala, 50-51; instr & resident, Sch Med & Univ Hosp, Duke Univ, 53-55; pathologist & dir lab, Pottstown Mem Med Ctr, 57-89. *Mem:* Am Soc Clin Path; AMA; Col Am Path. *Res:* Mycology; hemoglobinopathies. *Mailing Add:* 1025 Briar Lane Pottstown PA 19464

SCHOFIELD, ROBERT EDWIN, CULTURAL HISTORY, HISTORY OF CHEMISTRY. *Current Pos:* prof, 79-94, EMER PROF HIST, SCI & TECHNOL, IOWA STATE UNIV, 94- *Personal Data:* b Milford, Nebr, June 1, 23; m 59, Mary-Peale Smith; c Charles S. *Educ:* Princeton Univ, BA, 44; Univ Minn, MS, 48; Harvard Univ, PhD(hist sci), 55. *Honors & Awards:* Pfizer Prize, Hist Sci Soc, 64. *Prof Exp:* Res asst, Ferclevve Corp, 44-45, Clinton Labs, 45-46; res assoc, Knolls Atomic Power Lab, Gen Elec, 48-51; from asst prof to assoc prof hist sci, Univ Kans, Lawrence, 55-60; assoc prof hist sci, Case Inst Technol, 60-72; Lynn Thorndike prof hist sci, Case Western Res Univ, 72-79. *Concurrent Pos:* Guggenheim fel, 59-60, 67-68; mem, Inst Advan Study, 67-68, 74-75; Sigma Xi nat lectr, 78-80; dir, Grad Prog Hist Technol & Sci, Iowa State Univ, Ames, 79-94; chair, Hist Physics Div, Am Phys Soc, 85-86. *Mem:* Hist Sci Soc; fel Am Phys Soc; Soc Hist Technol; Royal Soc Arts; Int Acad Hist Sci; Am Soc Eighteenth Century Studies. *Res:* Eighteenth century natural philosophy; science, theology and society, eighteenth century Britain life and work of Joseph Priestley; author of various publications. *Mailing Add:* 44 Sycamore Rd Princeton NJ 08540

SCHOFIELD, WILFRED BORDEN, BOTANY, BRYOLOGY. *Current Pos:* from instr to prof, 60-92, EMER PROF BOT, UNIV BC, 93- *Personal Data:* b NS, July 19, 27; m 56, Margaret Bledsoe; c 3. *Educ:* Acadia Univ, BA, 50; Stanford Univ, MA, 56; Duke Univ, PhD, 60. *Hon Degrees:* DSc, Acadia Univ, 90. *Honors & Awards:* G E Lawson Medal, Can Bot Asn, 86. *Prof Exp:* Instr bot, Duke Univ, 58-60. *Mem:* Am Bryol & Lichenol Soc (vpres, 65-67, pres, 67-69); Int Asn Bryologists (vpres, 94-); Brit Bryol Soc; Nordic Bryol Soc. *Res:* Taxonomy, ecology, phytogeography and evolution of vascular plants and bryophytes. *Mailing Add:* Dept Bot Univ BC Vancouver BC V6T 1Z4 Can. *Fax:* 604-822-6089

SCHOFIELD, WILLIAM, PSYCHOTHERAPY, HEALTH PSYCHOLOGY. *Current Pos:* From instr to prof, 47-88, EMER PROF PSYCHOL, UNIV MINN, 88- *Personal Data:* b Springfield, Mass, Apr 19, 21; m 46; c 2. *Educ:* Springfield Col, BS, 42; Univ Minn, MA, 46 & PhD(psychol), 48. *Honors & Awards:* Outstanding Contrib Award, Am Psychol Asn, 86. *Concurrent Pos:* Vis prof psychol, Univ Wash, 60 & Univ Colo, 65; exec secy, Minn Psychol Asn, 54-59; mem, Med Policy Adv Comt, Minn, 60-68, Ment Health Serv Rev Comt, NIMH, 68-73; bd examrs psychologist, 83-86; bd dirs, Prof Exam Serv, NY, 76-81; instr & examr, USCG Aux, 67-; consult psychol, Vet Admin, Minneapolis, 53-, Episcopal Diocese of Minn, 69- *Mem:* Am Psychol Asn (secy-treas, 69-72); AAAS. *Res:* Psychodiagnostics and family history in mental illness; health psychology, professional issues in clinical psychology and social factors in psychotherapy. *Mailing Add:* 4300 W River Pkwy Minneapolis MN 55406

SCHOKNECHT, JEAN DONZE, BIOMINERALIZATION, ULTRASTRUCTURE. *Current Pos:* vis asst prof electron micros, 73-74, from asst prof to assoc prof mycol & microbiol, 78-88, SUPVR ELECTRON MICROSCOPE FACIL, SCH DENT, IND UNIV, 89- *Personal Data:* b Urbana, Ill. *Educ:* Univ Ill, Urbana-Champaign, BS, 65, MS, 67, PhD(bot), 72. *Prof Exp:* Res assoc life sci, Univ Ill, 72-73. *Concurrent Pos:* Adj mycologist, Ill Natural Hist Surv, 81, vis assoc prof vet microbiol, 84. *Mem:* Mycol Soc Am; Brit Mycol Soc; Brit Lichen Soc; Bot Soc Am; Sigma Xi; Electron Micros Soc Am; Med Mycol Soc Am; Am Micros Soc. *Res:* Biomineralization, in cell development, and mineral translocation; dental and medical applications; cytology, development and systematics of the fungi. *Mailing Add:* 1218 Downhill Run Goshen KY 40026. *Fax:* 317-274-2419

SCHOLAR, ERIC M, METASTASIS, CHEMOTHERAPY. *Current Pos:* asst prof, 75-82, ASSOC PROF PHARMACOL, MED SCH, UNIV NEBR, 82- *Personal Data:* b New York, NY, Aug 28, 39; m 65, Jacqueline; c Eric, Theresa & Rosetta. *Educ:* Rutgers Univ, BS, 61; Univ Ill, PhD(pharmacol), 68. *Prof Exp:* Res assoc biomed sci, 67-70, instr, 70-72, asst prof biochem pharmacol, Brown Univ, 72-75. *Mem:* Am Soc Exp Pharmacol & Therapeut; Am Asn Cancer Res; AAAS. *Res:* Mechanism of action of anti-neoplastic and immunosuppressive drugs; therapy of tumor metastasis; anti-serum therapy of metastasis. *Mailing Add:* Dept Pharmacol Univ Nebr Med Ctr 600 S 42nd St Omaha NE 68198-6260. *Fax:* 402-559-7495

SCHOLER, CHARLES FREY, CONCRETE, HIGHWAYS & STREETS. *Current Pos:* from instr to assoc prof, 60-89, PROF CIVIL ENG, PURDUE UNIV, WEST LAFAYETTE, 89- *Personal Data:* b Manhattan, Kans, May 31, 34; m 57; c 3. *Educ:* Kans State Univ, BS, 56; Purdue Univ, MS, 57, PhD(civil eng mat), 65. *Prof Exp:* Engr, Burgwin & Martin Consult Engrs, 57-58; asst hwy engr, Riley County, Kans, 60. *Concurrent Pos:* Consult portland cement; dir, Highway Exten Res Project, Indiana Cities & Counties, Purdue Univ, West Lafayette; Concrete Materials Res Coun; mem bd dirs, Am Concrete Inst, 84-87. *Mem:* Am Soc Civil Engrs; Am Concrete Inst; Am Soc Testing & Mat; Am Pub Works Asn. *Res:* Construction materials, especially portland cement; concrete durability, physical and mechanical properties of concrete material and construction applications; low volume roads especially maintenance and construction; aggregates, soils and bituminous materials. *Mailing Add:* 807 Essex St West Lafayette IN 47906

SCHOLES, CHARLES PATTERSON, BIOPHYSICS. *Current Pos:* from asst prof to assoc prof, 73-84, PROF PHYSICS, STATE UNIV NY, ALBANY, 84- *Personal Data:* b Auburn, NY, Oct 31, 42; m 66; c 2. *Educ:* Cornell Univ, AB, 64; Yale Univ, PhD(biophys), 69. *Prof Exp:* NSF fel, Oxford Univ, 69-70; NIH fel, Univ Calif, San Diego, 70-73. *Concurrent Pos:* NIH fel, 76-81; vis prof biochem & biophys, Chalmers Univ, Goteborg, Sweden, 85-86. *Mem:* Biophys Soc; Am Phys Soc; Am Chem Soc. *Res:* Study of biological molecules by techniques of electron paramagnetic resonance and electron nuclear double resonance. *Mailing Add:* Dept Chem State Univ NY Albany NY 12222. *Fax:* 518-442-3462; *E-Mail:* cpsi4@alanyums

SCHOLES, NORMAN W, PHARMACOLOGY, PHYSIOLOGY. *Current Pos:* RETIRED. *Personal Data:* b Ogden, Utah, June 9, 30; m 50, 74; c 3. *Educ:* Univ Utah, BS, 53; Univ Calif, Los Angeles, MS, 56, PhD(pharmacol), 59; Univ Southern Calif, MS Ed, 74; Creighton Univ, BPh, & RPh, 84. *Prof Exp:* Res chemist, Wasatch Chem Corp, Utah, 53-54; Giannini-Bank Am fel, 59-61; res neuropharmacologist, City of Hope Med Ctr, Duarte, Calif, 60-64; asst prof pharmacol, Univ Calif, Davis, 64-68; prof pharmacol, Sch Med, Creighton Univ, 68-86; Pharm Consult Serv Inc, 86-90. *Concurrent Pos:* Electronics for scientists, NSF, 65; educ health sci prof, United Soc Pharmacol Health Sci, 73; vis prof, Australian Nat Univ, Canberra, Australia, 76. *Mem:* AAAS; Soc Exp Biol & Med; Am Soc Pharmacol & Exp Therapeut. *Res:* Synaptic mechanisms in the central nervous system and their physiological significance; mode and site of action of drugs acting upon the central nervous system; neurochemical and electrophysiological correlates of learning; alcohol testing in humans, blood and breath ratio. *Mailing Add:* RR 2 Box 737 Evington VA 24550-9523

SCHOLES, SAMUEL RAY, JR, CHEMISTRY. *Current Pos:* from assoc prof to prof, 46-80, chmn dept, 55-70, EMER PROF CHEM, ALFRED UNIV, 80- *Personal Data:* b Pittsburgh, Pa; wid; c Susan F & Jean A. *Educ:* Alfred Univ, BS, 37; Yale Univ, PhD(phys chem), 40. *Prof Exp:* Asst quant anal, Yale Univ, 37-40; instr chem, Alfred Univ, 40-41 & phys chem, Tufts Col, 41-46. *Mem:* Am Chem Soc; Sigma Xi. *Res:* Properties of solutions of electrolytes; analysis of microgram quantities of fluorine; analysis of water in transformer oils. *Mailing Add:* 45 W University St Alfred NY 14802-1115

SCHOLL, JAMES FRANCIS, SIGNAL-IMAGE PROCESSING, WAVELETS. *Current Pos:* SR RES ASSOC, ROCKWELL INT, 89- *Personal Data:* b Albion, NY, Oct 4, 57. *Educ:* Univ Rochester, BS, 80, MS, 89; Univ Nev, Las Vegas, MS, 84. *Prof Exp:* Assoc scientist, Lockheed Eng & Mgt Serv Co, 83-85. *Mem:* Optical Soc Am; Am Astron Soc; Am Math Soc; Soc Appl & Indust Math; Am Statist Asn. *Res:* Applied mathematical and computational methods in signal and image processing; symbolic computing; numerical mathematics. *Mailing Add:* Rockwell Int Sci Ctr 1049 Camino Dos Rios PO Box 1085 Thousand Oaks CA 91358-0085

SCHOLL, MARIJA STROJNIK, lasers, infrared optics, for more information see previous edition

SCHOLL, PHILIP JON, LIVESTOCK ENTOMOLOGY, LIVESTOCK PARASITOLOGY. *Current Pos:* PROD DEVELOP MGR, AM CYANAMID, ARD, 92- *Personal Data:* b Madison, Wis, Jan 25, 45; m 75, Heloisa. *Educ:* Univ Wis-Madison, BS, 70, MS, 73, PhD(entom), 78. *Prof Exp:* Res asst parasitol & entom, Univ Wis, 71-78, res assoc med entom, 78; res entomologist livestock insects, Agr Res Serv, USDA, 79-92. *Concurrent Pos:* Consult med entom, Univ Federal Rural do Rio de Janeiro, Brazil, 78; grad fac, Univ Nebr Syst, 79-82; asst prof, Univ Nebr, Lincoln, 79-82; US proj leader, US-Can Joint Cattle Grub Pilot Test Proj, 82-86; adj assoc prof, Montana State Univ, Bozeman, 82-86; prof consult, 5th Int Course Trop Myiasis, Rio de Janeiro, Brazil, 87; vis fac, NDak State Univ, Fargo, 90, Tex A&M Univ, College Station, 90; vis lectr, Univ Wis-Madison, 89-91. *Mem:* Sigma Xi; Entom Soc Am; Am Asn Vet Parasitologists; World Asn Advan Vet Parisitol. *Res:* Ecology and population parameters of blood-feeding and myiasis producing Diptera of veterinary and medical importance, especially livestock pests including gonotrophic age-grading, population sampling, seasonal distribution, and the effects of integrated control strategies on population characteristics. *Mailing Add:* Ft Dodge Animal Health Princeton NJ 08543-0400. *Fax:* 609-275-5237

SCHOLLENBERGER, CHARLES SUNDY, POLYMER CHEMISTRY, ORGANIC CHEMISTRY. *Current Pos:* RETIRED. *Personal Data:* b Wooster, Ohio, Aug 8, 22; m 49; c 2. *Educ:* Col Wooster, AB, 43; Cornell Univ, PhD(org chem), 47. *Honors & Awards:* Melvin K Mooney Distinguished Technol Award, Am Chem Soc, 90. *Prof Exp:* Lab asst, Col Wooster, 42-43; lab asst, Cornell Univ, 44, asst org chem, 44-47; res chemist & sect leader, B F Goodrich Res & Develop Ctr, 47-75, res & develop fel, 75-84. *Concurrent Pos:* Chem analyst, Ohio Exp Sta, 42-44; polyurethane specialist & consult. *Mem:* Am Chem Soc; Polyurethane Mfg Asn. *Res:* Polyurethanes; stereo rubbers; polymers; environmental resistance. *Mailing Add:* 46 Hamden Dr Hudson OH 44236-2722

SCHOLLER, JEAN, toxicology, environmental health; deceased, see previous edition for last biography

SCHOLNICK, FRANK, ORGANIC CHEMISTRY. *Current Pos:* ORG RES CHEMIST, EASTERN REGIONAL RES CTR, USDA, 59- *Personal Data:* b Philadelphia, Pa, Apr 17, 25; m 57, Myra Lester; c Faith & Lisa. *Educ:* Temple Univ, BA, 46, MA, 48; Univ Pa, PhD(chem), 55. *Honors & Awards:* Technol Transfer Award, USDA, 90. *Prof Exp:* Org chemist, E F Houghton & Co, 48-49 & Plastics & Coal Chems Div, Allied Chem Corp, 55-59. *Mem:* Am Chem Soc; Am Oil Chem Soc; Am Leather Chem Asn. *Res:* Polymers; coal tar chemistry; organic synthesis; detergents; coatings. *Mailing Add:* 2345 Pine Ridge Dr Lafayette Hill PA 19444-2310

SCHOLNICK, STEVEN BRUCE, GENETICS, BIOLOGY. *Current Pos:* ASST PROF BIOL, WASH UNIV, 89- *Personal Data:* b New York, NY, June 4, 55. *Educ:* Columbia Univ, BA, 76; Cornell Univ, PhD(genetics), 82. *Prof Exp:* Res fel, Dept Biol Chem, Harvard Med Sch, 82-84; asst prof biol, Carnegie-Mellon Univ, 85-89. *Res:* Analysis of developmental regulation of gene expression in Drosophila melanogaster by recombinant DNA techniques. *Mailing Add:* Wash Univ Sch Med 660 S Euclid Ave St Louis MO 63110-1010

SCHOLTEN, PAUL DAVID, SOLID STATE PHYSICS, THERMAL PHYSICS. *Current Pos:* asst prof, 78-82, ASSOC PROF PHYSICS, MIAMI UNIV, 82- *Personal Data:* b Grand Haven, Mich, Apr 17, 49. *Educ:* Kalamazoo Col, BA, 71; Fla State Univ, PhD(physics), 76. *Prof Exp:* Res assoc, Tex A&M Univ, 76-77, vis asst prof, 77-78. *Mem:* Am Phys Soc; Sigma Xi. *Res:* Magnetism; Monte Carlo methods (computational physics). *Mailing Add:* Dept Physics Miami Univ Oxford OH 45056

SCHOLTENS, ROBERT GEORGE, EPIDEMIOLOGY, PARASITOLOGY. *Current Pos:* CONSULT, 88- *Personal Data:* b Grand Rapids, Mich, Feb 11, 29; m 52; c 3. *Educ:* Mich State Univ, BS, 57, DVM, 59; Univ Ill, MS, 61; London Sch Hyg & Trop Med, dipl, 66. *Prof Exp:* Dir animal care, Biochem Res Found, 60-61; asst chief rabies, Nat Rabies Lab, Commun Dis Ctr, USPHS, 61-62, vet epidemiologist, 63-65, chief parasitic dis br, Ctr for Dis Control, 66-67, dep dir malaria prog, 67-73, dir vector biol & control div, Ctr Dis Control, 72-76; assoc prof, Univ Tenn, 76-80, prof dept pathobiol, Col Vet Med, 80-85; dir, Training & Res, Int Livestock Ctr for Africa, 84-88. *Concurrent Pos:* Mem subcomt animal dis surveillance, Animal Health Comt, Nat Acad Sci-Nat Res Coun, 64-; epidemiologist, London Sch Hyg & Trop Med, 65-66. *Mem:* Am Soc Trop Med & Hyg; Royal Soc Trop Med & Hyg; Am Soc Parasitol. *Res:* Epidemiology of parasitic diseases. *Mailing Add:* 5504 Sunset Rd PO Box 1071 Knoxville TN 37914

SCHOLTES, WAYNE HENRY, SOIL SCIENCE. *Current Pos:* from asst prof to assoc prof, Iowa State Univ, 51-55, prof soils 55-, prof forestry & distinguished prof agr 77-, DISTINGUISHED EMER PROF, IOWA STATE UNIV. *Personal Data:* b Clinton, Iowa, Dec 3, 17; m 41; c 3. *Educ:* Iowa State Col, BS, 39, PhD(soil classification), 51; Duke Univ, MS, 40. *Prof Exp:* Jr soil scientist, Soil Conserv Serv, USDA, 41-45, assoc soil scientist, 45-46, soil scientist, Bur Plant Indust, 46-51. *Concurrent Pos:* Vis prof, Univ Ill, 58, Univ Ariz, 66 & 69 & San Carlos Univ Guatemala, 68 & 69; soils specialist, Fac Agron, Univ of the Repub, Uruguay, 63-65. *Mem:* Soil Sci Soc Am; Am Soc Agron; Soil Conserv Soc Am. *Res:* Soil classification and genesis. *Mailing Add:* 2430 Hamilton Dr Ames IA 50014

SCHOLTZ, ROBERT A, ELECTRICAL ENGINEERING. *Current Pos:* res assoc, 63-65, from asst prof to assoc prof, 65-74, PROF ELEC ENG, UNIV SOUTHERN CALIF, 74-, CHAIR ELEC ENG SYSTS, 94- *Personal Data:* b Lebanon, Ohio, Jan 26, 36; m 62, Laura E McKeon; c Michael W & Paul A. *Educ:* Univ Cincinnati, EE, 58; Univ Southern Calif, MSEE, 60; Stanford Univ, PhD(elec eng), 64. *Honors & Awards:* Leonard G Abraham Award, Inst Elec & Electronics Engrs, 83 & Donald G Fink Award, 84. *Prof Exp:* Mem tech staff, Hughes Aircraft Co, 58-63, staff engr, 63-68, sr staff engr, 68-78. *Concurrent Pos:* Consult, Lincom, 76-80, Axiomatix Inc, 79-87, JPL, 86 & 94, Technol Group, 87-89, TRW, 89 & Pulson Commun, 92-; vis colleague, Univ Hawaii, 69 & 78; dir, Commun Sci Inst, Univ Southern Calif, 82-89; Qualcomm Inc, 95. *Mem:* Fel Inst Elec & Electronics Engrs. *Res:* Communication and information theory; synchronization techniques; transmitter optimization and signal design; spread spectrum systems. *Mailing Add:* Dept Elec Eng Univ Southern Calif Los Angeles CA 90089-2565. *E-Mail:* scholtz@milly.usc.edu

SCHOLZ, CHRISTOPHER HENRY, GEOPHYSICS. *Current Pos:* res assoc, 68-71, assoc prof, 73-76, SR RES ASSOC GEOPHYS, LAMONT-DOHERTY EARTH OBSERV, COLUMBIA UNIV, 71-, PROF, 76- *Personal Data:* b Pasadena, Calif, Feb 25, 43; div; c 2. *Educ:* Univ Nev, BS, 64; Mass Inst Technol, PhD(geol), 67. *Prof Exp:* Res fel, Seismol Lab, Calif Inst Technol, 67-68. *Concurrent Pos:* Mem Nat Acad Sci Comn rock mech, 75-78 & Comn seismol; Sloan fel, 75-77 & Green fel, 80-81. *Mem:* Fel Am Geophys Union; Seismol Soc Am. *Res:* Mechanics of rock fracture and flow; earthquake mechanism and seismicity. *Mailing Add:* Lamont-Doherty Earth Observ Palisades NY 10964. *E-Mail:* scholz@ldeo.columbia.edu

SCHOLZ, DAN ROBERT, MATHEMATICS. *Current Pos:* from instr to assoc prof, 46-63, PROF MATH, LA STATE UNIV, BATON ROUGE, 63-, PROF MECH ENG, 77- *Personal Data:* b Marysville, Kans, Sept 17, 20; m 34; c 1. *Educ:* Southwest Tex State Teachers Col, BS, 41, MA, 42; Calif Inst Technol, MS, 43; Washington Univ, PhD(math), 51. *Prof Exp:* Asst math, Washington Univ, 48-50; asst prof, Southwestern La Inst, 51-52. *Mem:* Am Math Soc; Math Asn Am; Soc Indust & Appl Math. *Res:* Functions of a complex variable; numerical analysis. *Mailing Add:* 1245 Pickett Ave Baton Rouge LA 70808

SCHOLZ, EARL WALTER, HORTICULTURE, PLANT PHYSIOLOGY. *Current Pos:* RETIRED. *Personal Data:* b Marysville, Kans, Sept 24, 25; m 47; c 5. *Educ:* Kans State Col, BS, 50; Iowa State Univ, MS, 55, PhD(hort, plant physiol), 57. *Prof Exp:* Horticulturist, Agr Mkt Serv, USDA, 57-63; horticulturist, NDak State Univ, 63-80, assoc prof Hort & Forestry, 80-88. *Mem:* Am Soc Hort Sci. *Res:* Vegetable and strawberry culture. *Mailing Add:* 1133 Ninth St N Fargo ND 58102

SCHOLZ, JOHN JOSEPH, JR, PHYSICAL CHEMISTRY. *Current Pos:* from asst prof to assoc prof, 57-68, vchmn dept, 74-81, PROF CHEM, UNIV NEBR, LINCOLN, 68- *Personal Data:* b Parshall, NDak, June 11, 26; m 50; c 2. *Educ:* Univ NDak, BS, 48; Univ Ill, PhD, 55. *Prof Exp:* Res chemist, Minn Mining & Mfg Co, 53-55; res assoc, Univ Ill, 55-57. *Concurrent Pos:* Consult, Isco Inc, Lincoln, NE, 84- *Mem:* Am Chem Soc; Am Phys Soc. *Res:* Physical absorption; intermolecular forces. *Mailing Add:* 1311 North 37th St Lincoln NE 68503-2015

SCHOLZ, LAWRENCE CHARLES, SOFTWARE ENGINEERING, SYSTEMS ENGINEERING. *Current Pos:* div fel & mgr, SE&I, Space Sta Platform Proj, GE Astro Space Div, 87-89, div fel, Sci & Appl Progs, 87-90, DIV FEL, CIVIL SPACE PROG, MARTIN MARIETTA ASTROSPACE, 90- *Personal Data:* b New York, NY, Aug 8, 33; m 54, Claire Seidner; c Richard & Karen. *Educ:* City Col New York, BEE, 54. *Prof Exp:* Engr electron tube design, Tube Div, RCA Corp, 54-60; res physicist elastic physics, IIT Res Inst, 60-65; group leader nuclear effects, Vitro Labs, 65-69; dir advan systs, Mantech, 69-70; mgr software eng, Astro Electronics Div, RCA Corp, 70-80, mgr mission opers, Satcom Satellite Proj, 80-84, div fel, 84-85, mgr systs eng, Space Sta Proj, 85-87. *Mem:* Sr mem Inst Elec & Electronics Engrs; Comput Soc; AAAS; Am Inst Aeronaut & Astronaut. *Res:* Systems engineering methodology and applications; software reliability; the relation between specification, implementation and testability; software organization for critical applications; spacecraft autonomy and fault tolerance. *Mailing Add:* Martin Marietta Astrospace PO Box 800 Princeton NJ 08543. *E-Mail:* lscholz@ob10.eos.ge.com

SCHOLZ, RICHARD W, NUTRITIONAL BIOCHEMISTRY. *Current Pos:* asst prof, 68-75, assoc prof, 75-81, PROF VET SCI, PA STATE UNIV, UNIVERSITY PARK, 81- *Personal Data:* b Ft Riley, Kans, Apr 1, 42. *Educ:* Cornell Univ, BS; Purdue Univ, MS, 66, PhD(nutrit), 68. *Prof Exp:* Res asst nutrit, Purdue Univ, 64-65, NASA fel, 66-68. *Mem:* Am Inst Nutrit. *Res:* Lung metabolism; metabolic adaptation to alterations in diet and other environmental factors. *Mailing Add:* Dept Vet Sci 122 ASI Bldg University Park PA 16802-0001

SCHOLZ, ROBERT GEORGE, ANALYTICAL CHEMISTRY. *Current Pos:* RETIRED. *Personal Data:* b Chicago, Ill, July 3, 30; m 54, Anita M Gobel; c Robert S, Thomas D & Patricia L (Cohen). *Educ:* Univ Ill, BS, 54; Purdue Univ, PhD(anal chem), 61. *Prof Exp:* Res chemist, Continental Can Co, 61-64 & IIT Res Inst, 64-71; mgr anal chem, Beatrice Foods, Chicago, 71-82; res chemist, Kendall Co, Barrinton, Ill, 82-83; tech support specialist, Varian Assocs, Park Ridge, Ill, 83-88; group leader, Waste Mgt, Inc, 88-93. *Concurrent Pos:* Lectr, Roosevelt Univ, 68-72. *Mem:* Am Chem Soc. *Res:* Technical support in atomic absorption and UV/VIS spectrophotometry; gas and liquid chromatography. *Mailing Add:* 376 Western Clarendon Hills IL 60514

SCHOLZ, WILFRIED, PARTICLE SOLID INTERACTIONS, NUCLEAR & ATOMIC PHYSICS. *Current Pos:* from asst prof to assoc prof, 70-82, PROF PHYSICS, STATE UNIV NY, ALBANY, 82- *Personal Data:* b Landau, Ger, Sept 14, 36; US citizen; m 66, Angela Li; c 2. *Educ:* Univ Freiburg, dipl physics, 60, PhD(physics), 62. *Prof Exp:* Asst nuclear physics, Univ Freiburg, 61-64; res assoc, Yale Univ, 64-67; asst prof physics, Univ Pa, 67-70. *Concurrent Pos:* Consult ed, Atomic Data & Nuclear Data Tables, 82- *Mem:* Am Phys Soc. *Res:* Nuclear spectroscopy and reactions; theory of nuclear structure; electron atom collisions; superconductivity; elastic properties of materials. *Mailing Add:* Dept Physics State Univ NY Albany NY 12222

SCHOMAKER, VERNER, PHYSICAL CHEMISTRY, STRUCTURAL CHEMISTRY. *Current Pos:* prof, 65-84, chmn dept, 65-70, EMER PROF CHEM, UNIV WASH, 84- *Personal Data:* b Nehawka, Nebr, June 22, 14; wid; c 3. *Educ:* Univ Nebr, BSc, 34, MSc, 35; Calif Inst Technol, PhD(chem), 38. *Honors & Awards:* Award, Am Chem Soc, 50. *Prof Exp:* Hale fel chem, Calif Inst Technol, 38-40, sr fel, 40-45, from asst prof to prof, 45-58; chemist, Union Carbide Res Inst, 58-59, from asst dir to assoc dir, 59-65. *Concurrent Pos:* Guggenheim Mem Found fel, 47-48; consult, Shell Develop Co, 48-73, Brookhaven Nat Lab, 48-49, Oak Ridge Nat Lab, 52-55, US Naval Ord Testing Sta, Calif, 55-58 & Union Carbide Corp, 57-58 & 65-80; mem ad hoc comt comput, Int Union Crystallog, 57, Nat Comt Crystallog, 61-64 & 71-74, subcomt molecular struct, Nat Acad Sci-Nat Res Coun, 61-63, adv comt math & phys sci, NSF, 67-69 & eval panel, Reactor Radiation Div, Nat Bur Stand, 74-77; vis assoc, chem, Calif Inst Technol, 84-91, fac assoc, 92- *Mem:* Fel AAAS; Am Crystallog Asn (pres, 62); fel NY Acad Sci; Am Chem Soc. *Res:* Structural chemistry; determination of crystal and molecular structures by x-ray and electron diffraction; crystallographic computations; zeolite catalysis. *Mailing Add:* 12506 26th Ave NE No 103 Seattle WA 98125

SCHOMAN, CHARLES M, JR, RESEARCH & DEVELOPMENT. *Current Pos:* SR ADV TO PRES, LSA, INC, 89- *Personal Data:* b Rochester, NY, Dec 24, 24; m 46. *Educ:* US Naval Acad, BS, 46; Rutgers Univ, MS, 57, PhD(sci), 60. *Honors & Awards:* Jump Award, 58 & Isker Award, 62. *Prof Exp:* Equip engr, US Naval Supply Res & Develop Facil, 54, asst to tech dir, Res Div, 54-55, head Planning, Surv & Coordr Br, 55-57, asst tech dir, 57-58, asst tech dir & head eng planning & surv team, 58-59, sr staff tech consult & asst to officer in chg, 59-61, chief scientist, 61-64, tech dir, 64-66, head advan planning & systs anal, US Naval Ord Lab, 66-73; head advan planning, Naval Surface Weapons Ctr, 73-76; dir plans & progs, David W Taylor Naval Ships Res & Develop Ctr, 76-86, assoc tech dir, David Taylor Res Ctr, 86-89. *Concurrent Pos:* sr exec assoc, Nat Conf Advan Res Conf Comt, 80-84, vpres, Nat War Col Alumni, 74-75, nat pres, Fed Prof Asn, 72-76. *Mem:* Inst Food Technol; Fed Prof Exec Asn (nat pres, 72-76); Sr Execs Asn; Sigma Xi. *Res:* Scientific and engineering research management; technology transfer; food science. *Mailing Add:* 3600 Pimlico Pl Silver Spring MD 20906

SCHOMER, DONALD LEE, NEUROPHYSIOLOGY. *Current Pos:* instr, Harvard Univ, 80-86, asst prof, 86-93, ASSOC PROF NEUROL, HARVARD UNIV, 93-; DIR, CLIN NEUROPHYSIOL, BETH ISRAEL HOSP, BOSTON, 80-, NEUROLOGIST, 93- *Personal Data:* b Chicago, Ill, July 11, 46; m 70; c 4. *Educ:* Mich State Univ, BS, 68; Univ Mich, MD, 72. *Prof Exp:* From asst neurologist to assoc neurologist, Beth Israel Hosp & Childrens Hosp, Boston, 80-93; asst neurologist, 80-85, assoc neurologist, Beth Israel Hosp & Childrens Hosp, Boston, 85-93. *Concurrent Pos:* Actg dir, Clin Neurophysiol, Childrens Hosp, Boston, 86-89; vis physician, Clin Res Ctr, Mass Inst Technol, 85- & vis lectr neurol, 85-; prin investr, NIH grant, 86- *Mem:* Am Acad Neurol; Am Epilepsy Soc; fel Am EEG Soc; Am Acad Clin Neurophysiol. *Res:* The development of technology in neurophysiology; research approaches to epilepsy including experimental anticonvulsants and surgical techniques. *Mailing Add:* Beth Israel Hosp Harvard 330 Brookline Ave Boston MA 02215-5491

SCHONBAUM, EDUARD, PHARMACOLOGY, PHYSIOLOGY. *Current Pos:* CONSULT PHARMACOLOGIST, 88- *Personal Data:* b Vienna, Austria, Sept 18, 23; Neth citizen; m 53. *Educ:* Univ Amsterdam, ChemCand, 50; McGill Univ, PhD(biochem), 55. *Prof Exp:* Res assoc physiol, 55-57, asst prof med res, 57-60, asst prof pharmacol, 60-63; head cent nerv syst pharmacol, Organon Int BV, OSS, Neth, 73-79, head gen pharmacol, 79-81, int coordr pharmacol res, Res & Develop Labs, 81-88. *Concurrent Pos:* Assoc prof pharmacol, Univ Toronto, 63-89; assoc med dir pharmacol, Ciba-Geigy Can Ltd, 68-73. *Mem:* AAAS; Can Physiol Soc; Can Pharmacol Soc; Am Physiol Soc; Dutch Soc Pharmacol; Brit Pharmacol Soc; Ger Pharmacol Soc. *Res:* Temperature regulation. *Mailing Add:* Peelkensweg 4 Venhorst 5428 NM Netherlands. *Fax:* 31 4925 1504

SCHONBECK, NIELS DANIEL, BIOENERGETICS, ENZYMOLOGY. *Current Pos:* from asst prof to assoc prof, 78-85, PROF CHEM, METROP STATE COL, DENVER, 85- *Personal Data:* b Baltimore, Md, Nov 1, 45; m 91, Margaret Bennett; c Dominica & Nicolas. *Educ:* Swarthmore Col, BA, 67; Univ Mich, Ann Arbor, PhD(biochem), 73. *Prof Exp:* Res technician biochem, Univ Mich, Ann Arbor, 69-71, fel, 73-74; Nat Cancer Inst fel, Univ Calif, Berkeley, 74-75, lectr biochem, 75-78. *Concurrent Pos:* Lectr health & med sci prog, Univ Calif, Berkeley, 75-; lectr, Div Natural Sci II, Univ Calif, Santa Cruz, 76; vis scientist, Nat Ctr Atmospheric Res, Boulder, Colo, 85-89 & 96-; vchair, Rocky Flats Environ Monitoring Coun, 88-92, mem health adv panel, 90- *Mem:* AAAS; Sigma Xi; Union Concerned Scientists; Fedn Am Scientists; Am Chem Soc. *Res:* Science and public policy issues concerning environmental and public health effects of nuclear weapons facilities; development of undergraduate programs in biochemistry; radiation-induced diseases. *Mailing Add:* Dept Chem Metropolitan State Col PO Box 173362 Denver CO 80217-3362. *Fax:* 303-556-4941; *E-Mail:* schonben@clem.mscd.edu

SCHONBERG, RUSSELL GEORGE, ENGINEERING, RESEARCH MANAGEMENT. *Current Pos:* FOUNDER & PRES, SCHONBERG RADIATION CORP, 70- *Personal Data:* b Minneapolis, Minn, Sept 15, 26; m 48; c 6. *Educ:* Calif State Polytech Col, BS, 50. *Prof Exp:* Engr, US Air Force, McClellan Field, Calif, 50-51, Calif Res & Develop Co, 51-53 & Radiation Lab, Univ Calif, 53-55; engr, Varian Assocs, 55-58, proj engr, 58-60, mgr elec eng, 60-64, mgr lab opers, 64-68; vpres opers, SHM Nuclear Corp, 68-70. *Mem:* Sr mem Inst Elec & Electronics Engrs; Am Nuclear Soc; Am Soc Non-Destructive Testing. *Res:* Radiation research on polymerization; free radical chemistry and process techniques; development of new and improved radiation sources; design and development of miniature 3.5 million electron volt electron linear accelerator; development of real time x-ray imaging systems, automatic inspection devices and microprocessor controlled remote handling devices; development of 1.5 million electron volt and 6 million electron volt lightweight portable accelerators. *Mailing Add:* 3300 Keller St Bldg 101 Santa Clara CA 95054. *Fax:* 408-980-8605

SCHONBERGER, LAWRENCE B, INFECTIOUS DISEASES. *Current Pos:* epidemic intelligence serv officer, 71-74, chief, Epidemiol Off, 83-88, asst dir med sci, 88-94, ASST DIR PUB HEALTH, DIV VIRAL & RICKETTSIAL DIS, NAT CTR INFECTIOUS DIS, CTR DIS CONTROL & PREV, 94- *Personal Data:* b Chicago, Ill, Mar 15, 43. *Educ:* Oberline Col, BA, 65; Case Western Res Univ, MD, 69; Johns Hopkins Univ, MPH, 74; Am Bd Prev Med, dipl. *Prof Exp:* Actg chief, Div Communicable Dis, Md State Dept Health & Ment Hyg, 74-76. *Mem:* Sigma Xi; Am Epidemiol Soc; fel Am Col Epidemiol; Am Pub Health Asn; Soc Epidemiol Res. *Res:* Epidemiology of virus diseases and possible virus relate illnesses of unknown etiology. *Mailing Add:* Nat Ctr Infectious Dis Ctr Dis Control MS-A39 Atlanta GA 30333

SCHONBRUNN, AGNES, RECEPTOR MECHANISMS, NEUROPEPTIDE ACTION. *Current Pos:* assoc prof, 88-89, PROF PHARMACOL, MED SCH, UNIV TEX, 89- *Personal Data:* b Budapest, Hungary, Oct 29, 49; US citizen; m 74; c 2. *Educ:* McGill Univ, BSc, 70; Brandeis Univ, PhD(biochem), 75. *Prof Exp:* Fel Harvard, Harvard Sch Dent Med, 75-79; from asst prof to assoc prof physiol, Sch Pub Health, Harvard Univ, 79-87. *Concurrent Pos:* Assoc ed, Endocrinol, 93- *Mem:* Am Soc Cell Biol; Endocrine Soc; Am Soc Biol Chemists; Soc Neurosci; Am Soc Pharmacol & Exp Therapeut. *Res:* Structure, function and regulation of membrane receptors in eukaryotic cells; mechanisms of neuropeptide and neurotransmitter action. *Mailing Add:* Dept Pharmcol Univ Tex Health Sci Ctr PO Box 20708 Houston TX 77225. *Fax:* 713-792-5985

SCHONE, HARLAN EUGENE, PHYSICS. *Current Pos:* from asst prof to assoc prof, 65-74, actg grad dean, 70-71, PROF PHYSICS, COL WILLIAM & MARY, 74- *Personal Data:* b Bluffs, Ill, Feb 14, 32; m 56; c 3. *Educ:* Univ Calif, PhD(physics), 61. *Prof Exp:* Physicist, Sci Res Lab, Boeing Airplane Co, 60-65. *Mem:* Am Phys Soc. *Res:* Nuclear magnetic resonance; metal physics. *Mailing Add:* 320 Indian Springs Rd Williamsburg VA 23185. *Fax:* 757-221-3540

SCHONEFELD, STEVEN A, FUNCTIONAL & NUMERICAL ANALYSIS. *Current Pos:* asst prof, 78-92, ASSOC PROF MATH, TRI-STATE UNIV, 92- *Personal Data:* b Ft Wayne, Ind, Apr 16, 42; m 85, Maryellen Wright; c Byron, Tanya, Nola & Cora. *Educ:* Purdue Univ, BS, 64, MS, 66, PhD(math), 69. *Prof Exp:* Asst prof math, Fla State Univ, 69-74. *Mem:* Math Asn Am. *Res:* Use of technology, especially computers in the teaching of mathematics; use of computer algebra systems to enhance the student's understanding of mathematics and numerical analysis. *Mailing Add:* 1105 W Ensley Auburn IN 46706

SCHONEWALD-COX, CHRISTINE MICHELINE, CONSERVATION OF PARKS, CONSERVATION BIOLOGY. *Current Pos:* biol, conserv, 78-82, coop unit coord, 82-87, RES SCIENTIST, CONSERV BIOL, US NAT PARK SERV, 82- *Personal Data:* b Paris, France; m 81; c 1. *Educ:* Univ Calif, Davis, BA, 72; Univ MD, MS, 74, PhD(biol), 78. *Prof Exp:* Asst prof biol, George Mason Univ, 78-79. *Concurrent Pos:* Adj prof, Div Environ Studies, Univ Calif, Davis, 82-; Dept Biol Sci, Mont State Univ, 86-; res assoc, Ecol Inst, Univ Calif, Davis, 82-; mem, grad group ecol, fac, Univ Calif, Davis, 82- *Mem:* Evolution Soc; Sigma Xi; Am Inst Biol Sci. *Res:* Interdesciplinary synthesis to develop means of measuring effectiveness of boundaries of protecting parks and reserves; studies on mammalian carnivores and herbivores. *Mailing Add:* 1816 Poplar Lane Davis CA 95616

SCHONFELD, EDWARD, MEDICAL ADHESIVES, CONTROLLED RELEASE GEL SYSTEMS. *Current Pos:* SR RES SCIENTIST, JOHNSON & JOHNSON, 68- *Personal Data:* b New York, NY, Oct 23, 30; m 76; c 2. *Educ:* Brooklyn Col, BS, 52; Syracuse Univ, MS, 55, PhD(polymer & org chem), 57. *Prof Exp:* Chemist, Thiokol Chem Corp, 57-59; chemist & group leader, Nopco Chem Co, 59-64; chemist & lab mgr, Adhesives Prods Div, PPG Industs, 64-68. *Concurrent Pos:* Instr, Brooklyn Col, 61-62, Bloomfield Col, 78-80; co-adj instr, New York City Tech Col, City Univ NY, 80-86 & Mercer County Community Col, 89- *Mem:* Am Chem Soc; Sigma xi. *Res:* Medical and surgical adhesives; pressure sensitive adhesives; sealants; urethane polymers; polymerization and characterization of polymers; bactericidal polymers; synthesis of quaternaries; UV and EB curing of polymers; gel dressings with controlled release properties for wound dressing applications; pharmaceutical development. *Mailing Add:* 85 Dodds Lane Princeton NJ 08540-4103

SCHONFELD, GUSTAV, INTERNAL MEDICINE, METABOLISM. *Current Pos:* assoc prof, actg chmn dept, 83-87, PROF PREV MED & MED, SCH MED, WASH UNIV, 77-, KOUNTZ PROF MED, 87- *Personal Data:* b Mukacevo, Czech, May 8, 34; m 61; c 3. *Educ:* Wash Univ, BA, 56, MD, 60. *Prof Exp:* Asst prof internal med, Sch Med, Wash Univ, 68-70; assoc prof metab & human nutrit, Mass Inst Technol, 70-72. *Concurrent Pos:* Asst dir, Mass Inst Technol Clin Res Ctr, 70-72; dir, Lipid Res Ctr, Sch Med, Wash Univ, 72-; mem, Adv Comt, Food & Drug Admin, 82-; NIH, Study Sect, 83- *Mem:* Endocrine Soc; Am Soc Clin Invest; Am Physiol Soc; Asn Am Physicians; Am Heart Asn; Am Soc Biochem Chemists. *Res:* Lipoproteins; hyperlipidemia; atherosclerosis; diabetes mellitus. *Mailing Add:* Wash Univ Sch Med Box 8046 660 S Euclid Ave St Louis MO 63110

SCHONFELD, HYMAN KOLMAN, PUBLIC HEALTH. *Current Pos:* RETIRED. *Personal Data:* b New York, NY, Aug 5, 19; m 44, Muriel E Kleiman; c Warren & Judith. *Educ:* Brooklyn Col, BA, 40; NY Univ, DDS, 43; Univ NC, MPH, 60, DrPH(epidemiol), 62. *Prof Exp:* Pvt dent pract, 47-56; dentist, Cent State Hosp, Petersburg, Va, 57-59; clin res assoc, Warner Lambert Res Inst, 62-64, biometrician, 64; sr res assoc med care, Dept Epidemiol & Pub Health, Sch Med, Yale Univ, 64-69, assoc prof pub health, Health Serv Admin, 69-74; sr staff officer, Nat Res Coun, Nat Acad Sci, 74-76; private consult, 76-81; staff mem, Dept Med & Surg, Vet Admin, 77-83. *Res:* Quality of medical and dental health care; evaluation of dental care systems. *Mailing Add:* 1116 Caddington Ave Silver Spring MD 20901

SCHONFELD, STEVEN EMANUEL, periodontal immunology, for more information see previous edition

SCHONHOFF, THOMAS ARTHUR, COMMUNICATIONS THEORY. *Current Pos:* MEM TECH STAFF, SPERRY RES CTR, 80- *Personal Data:* b Quincy, Ill, July 11, 47; m 69; c 3. *Educ:* Mass Inst Technol, BSEE, 69; Johns Hopkins Univ, MSEE, 72; Northeastern Univ, PhD(elec eng), 80. *Prof Exp:* Engr, Johns Hopkins Appl Physics Lab, 69-73; advan res engr, Gen Tel & Electron Sylvania, Inc, 73-78; mem tech staff, MITRE Corp, 78-80. *Concurrent Pos:* Adj prof, Worcester Polytech Inst, 82- *Mem:* AAAS; Inst Elec & Electronics Engrs; Sigma Xi; Planetary Soc. *Res:* Using communication theory and principles to improve the performance of radio communications systems and digital magnetic recording systems. *Mailing Add:* 13 Heatherwood Dr Shrewsbury MA 01545-1620

SCHONHORN, HAROLD, PHYSICAL CHEMISTRY, SURFACE CHEMISTRY. *Current Pos:* CONSULT, 93- *Personal Data:* b New York, NY, Apr 2, 28; m 54, Esther Majesky; c Deborah & Jeremy. *Educ:* Brooklyn Col, BS, 50; Polytech Inst Brooklyn, PhD(phys chem), 59. *Honors & Awards:* Union Carbide Chem Prize, Am Chem Soc, 66. *Prof Exp:* USAEC fel, Polytech Inst Brooklyn, 59-60; res scientist phys chem, Am Cyanamid Co, 60-61; mem tech staff surface chem, Bell Labs, Inc, 61-67, supvr surface chem, 67-84; vpres, Res & Develop Labs, Kendall Co, 84-93. *Mem:* Am Chem Soc; Sigma Xi. *Res:* Surface chemistry and adhesion; adhesive, structural and pressure sensitive. *Mailing Add:* 12 Heathwood Lane Chestnut Hill MA 02167

SCHONHORST, MELVIN HERMAN, AGRONOMY, PLANT BREEDING. *Current Pos:* From asst agronomist to assoc agronomist, 56-64, agronomist plant breeder alfalfa improv, 56-83, prof, 64-83, EMER PROF PLANT SCI, UNIV ARIZ, 83- *Personal Data:* b Slater, Iowa, Jan 21, 19; m 49; c 4. *Educ:* Iowa State Univ, BS, 51, MS, 53; Purdue Univ, PhD(agron, plant breeding), 58. *Honors & Awards:* Pac Seedsmen Award, 72. *Concurrent Pos:* Sabbatical leave, Mex Fed Alfalfa Breeding Prog, 76-77; consult int agr, 84-; mem, Nat Alfalfa Improv Conf. *Mem:* Am Soc Agron; Crop Sci Soc Am. *Res:* Hybrid alfalfa; development of insect, nematode, and disease resistant varieties of alfalfa; pest resistance and tolerance to environmental stresses in alfalfa; also tolerance to high soil salinity, chloride concentration, high temperatures, increased nodulation and association with mycorrhizal fungi; use of organic mulches, mini catchments with limited rainfall for growing food crops in arid and semi-arid environments. *Mailing Add:* 6172 N Camino Almonte Tucson AZ 85718

SCHONING, ROBERT WHITNEY, FISHERIES. *Current Pos:* RETIRED. *Personal Data:* b Seattle, Wash, Sept 29, 23; m 52, 82, Sandra C Wahlberg; c Randall, Kerry, James & Kip. *Educ:* Univ Wash, BS, 44. *Honors & Awards:* Bronze Star Medal. *Prof Exp:* Res biologist, Ore Fish Comn, 47-52, in-charge Columbia River invests, 52-54, from asst dir to dir res, 54-58, from asst state fisheries dir to state fisheries dir, 58-71; dep dir, Nat Marine Fisheries Serv, US Dept Com, 71-73, dir, 73-78; vis prof, Dept Fisheries & Wildlife, Ore State Univ, 78-82; sr policy adv, Nat Marine Fisheries Serv, US Dept Com, 82-86. *Concurrent Pos:* Mem, Fishing Indust Adv Comt, US Dept State, 65-78; comnr, Int Pac Halibut Comn, 72-83 & Int NPac Fish Comn, 74-79; fish scientist, Am Fisheries Soc. *Mem:* Am Fisheries Soc; fel Am Inst Fishery Res Biol. *Res:* Research and management of fish and shellfish. *Mailing Add:* 1775 NW Arbol Pl Corvallis OR 97330-1770

SCHONWALDER, CHRISTOPHER O, ENVIRONMENTAL HEALTH SCIENCES & TOXICOLOGY. *Current Pos:* grants assoc, NIH, 75-76, prog adminr, Environ Toxicol Res Grants & Training Grants Prog, 76-84, prog adminr, Centers & Training Prog, 84-87, chief, Sci Prog Br, Div Extramural Res & Training, Nat Inst Environ Health, 87-92, ASST TO DIR, NIH, 92- *Personal Data:* b Jan 31, 43; m 84, Rebecca; c Matthew. *Educ:* Univ Vt, BS, 64; Pa State Univ, PhD(org chem), 68; Purdue Univ, MS, 73. *Prof Exp:* Res chemist, E I du Pont de Nemours & Co, Inc, 71-73; scientist admin, Off Assoc Comnr Sci, Food & Drug Admin, Rockville, 74-75. *Mem:* AAAS; Am Chem Soc; Soc Res Adminr. *Res:* Environmental health; toxicology; organic chemistry. *Mailing Add:* 9712 Rock Creek Rd Raleigh NC 27613-5302

SCHOOLAR, JOSEPH CLAYTON, PSYCHIATRY, PHARMACOLOGY. *Current Pos:* PROF PHARMACOL, BAYLOR COL MED, 74-, PROF PSYCHIAT, 75-, CHIEF DIV PSYCHOPHARMACOL, 85- *Personal Data:* b Marks, Miss, Feb 28; m 60; c 5. *Educ:* Univ Tenn, AB, 50, MS, 52; Univ Chicago, PhD, 57, MD, 60. *Prof Exp:* Asst zool, Univ Tenn, 50-52, instr biochem, Univ Tenn-AEC Lab, Oak Ridge, 53-54; res asst pharmacol, Univ Chicago, 54-57, res assoc, 57-60; resident & asst in psychiat, Baylor Col Med, 61-64, assoc prof psychiat & pharmacol, 63-74; asst dir, Tex Res Inst Ment Sci, 68-72, dir, 74-85; assoc prof ment sci, Univ Tex Grad Sch Biol Sci, Houston, 68- *Mem:* AAAS; Am Psychiat Soc; AMA. *Res:* Psychopharmacology; drug abuse and addiction; effects of drugs on metabolic topography of the central nervous system; alcohol and substance abuse; adult and adolescent psychiatry; closed head injury. *Mailing Add:* Dept Pharmacol Rm 311D Baylor Col Med One Byalor Plaza Houston TX 77030

SCHOOLEY, ARTHUR THOMAS, CHEMICAL PROCESS ECONOMICS. *Current Pos:* RETIRED. *Personal Data:* b Plymouth, Pa, July 4, 32; m 55, Dorothy V Ward; c Jay, David & Linda. *Educ:* Carnegie Mellon Univ, BS, 54; Univ Akron, MS, 59. *Prof Exp:* Mat engr, Res Ctr, B F Goodrich Co, 54-56, res engr, 56-66, sr res engr, 66-68, res assoc, 68-79, sr res assoc, 79-89. *Mem:* Am Inst Chem Engrs. *Res:* Process modeling and simulation; microplants; process economics; process research. *Mailing Add:* 2015 Burlington Rd Akron OH 44313

SCHOOLEY, CAROLINE NAUS, ELECTRON MICROSCOPY. *Current Pos:* RETIRED. *Personal Data:* b San Francisco, Calif, Feb 15, 32; m 53, John Campbell; c 3. *Educ:* Univ Calif, Berkeley, BA, 53, MA, 58. *Honors & Awards:* Distinguished Serv Award, Micros Soc Am. *Prof Exp:* Res asst zool, Univ Calif, Berkeley, 53-55, cancer res, 56-59, lab technician, 68-83, facil supvr, Electron Microscope Lab, 83-93. *Concurrent Pos:* Dir, Electron Micros Soc Am, 84-87, Educ Outreach Coordr, 93- *Mem:* Royal Micros Soc; Am Soc Cell Biol; Am Women Sci; hon fel AAAS. *Res:* Biological ultrastructural research. *Mailing Add:* PO Box 117 Caspar CA 95420. *Fax:* 707-964-9460; *E-Mail:* schooley@mcn.org

SCHOOLEY, DAVID ALLAN, BIOLOGICAL & ANALYTICAL CHEMISTRY, PROTEIN SCIENCE. *Current Pos:* PROF BIOCHEM, UNIV NEV, RENO, 88- *Personal Data:* b Denver, Colo, Apr 17, 43; m 68, M Eleanor Dobbins; c Christine, Steve & Anna. *Educ:* NMex Highlands Univ, BSc, 63; Stanford Univ, PhD(org chem), 68. *Honors & Awards:* Baxter, Burdick & Jackson Int Award, Agrochem Div, Am Chem Soc, 90. *Prof Exp:* Fel bio-inorg chem, Univ Fla, 68-69; fel bio-org chem, Columbia Univ, 69-71; sr biochemist, Zoecon Corp, 71-74, dir biochem res, 74-88. *Concurrent Pos:* NSF fel, Stanford Univ, 63-66; adv panel, NSF, 86-89; consult, Sandoz Agro, 89-91. *Mem:* Am Chem Soc; Am Soc Biol Chem; AAAS; Protein Soc. *Res:* Biosynthesis and identification of insect juvenile hormones; insect hormone biochemistry; isolation and identification of neuropeptides in insects; analysis for hormones at physiological levels; intermediary metabolism. *Mailing Add:* Dept Biochem Univ Nev 160 Howard Med Sci Reno NV 89557-0014. *E-Mail:* schooley@unr.edu

SCHOOLEY, JAMES FREDERICK, THERMAL PHYSICS. *Current Pos:* RETIRED. *Personal Data:* b Auburn, Ind, Aug 24, 31; m 53; c 7. *Educ:* Ind Univ, AB, 53, Univ Calif, Berkeley, MS, 55, PhD(nuclear chem), 61. *Prof Exp:* Physicist, Cryogenic Physics Sect, Nat Bur Stand, 60-74, chief, 74-82, physicist, Temperature Div, 82-90. *Concurrent Pos:* Nat Acad Sci-Nat Res Coun fel, 60-62. *Mem:* Sigma Xi. *Res:* Study of temperature reference points based on superconductive transitions in pure metals. *Mailing Add:* 13700 Darnestown Rd Gaithersburg MD 20878

SCHOOLEY, JOHN C, PHYSIOLOGY. *Current Pos:* Physiologist, Donner Lab, PHYSIOLOGIST, LAWRENCE BERKELEY LAB, UNIV CALIF, BERKELEY, 71- *Personal Data:* b Chicago, Ill, Apr 24, 28; m 53; c 3. *Educ:* Univ Calif, AB, 51, PhD, 57. *Mem:* AAAS; Am Physiol Soc; Soc Exp Biol & Med; Int Soc Hemat; Am Asn Immunologists; Am Soc Cell Biol. *Res:* Physiology of lymphoid tissue and bone; experimental hematology; production and differentiation of red blood cells; production of erythropoietin and action mechanism of the hormone in normal & pathphysiological conditions; role of stromal cells in modulating hematopoesis. *Mailing Add:* Rural Box 117 Casper CA 95420

SCHOOLEY, ROBERT T, HERPES GROUP VIRUSES, IMMUNOLOGY. *Current Pos:* PROF MED & HEAD, DIV INFECTIOUS DIS, UNIV COLO HEALTH SCI CTR, 90- *Personal Data:* b Nov 10, 49; m 72, Pamela Cook; c Kimberley & Elizabeth. *Educ:* Johns Hopkins Univ, MD, 74. *Prof Exp:* From instr to prof med, Harvard Med Sch, 79-90. *Mem:* AAAS; Am Asn Immunologists; Infectious Dis Soc Am; Am Soc Microbiol; Am Soc Clin Invest; Asn Am Physicians. *Res:* AIDS, immunology, antiviral chemotherapy. *Mailing Add:* Univ Colo Health Sci Ctr Box B178 4200 E Ninth Ave Denver CO 80262. *Fax:* 303-270-8681

SCHOOLMAN, HAROLD M, MEDICINE. *Current Pos:* spec asst to dir med prog develop & eval, 70-72, asst dep dir, Nat Libr Med, 72-77, DEP DIR RES & EDUC NAT LIBR MED, 77- *Personal Data:* b Chicago, Ill, Jan 14, 24; m 59; c 2. *Educ:* Univ Ill, MD, 50; Am Bd Internal Med, dipl, 57. *Prof Exp:* Resident med, Cook Co Hosp, Ill, 51-53; assoc prof med, Cook Co Grad Sch Med, 54-59; instr, Univ Ill, 57-59, clin asst prof, 59-65, assoc prof, 65-67; dir educ serv, Vet Admin Cent Off, Washington, DC, 67-70. *Concurrent Pos:* Fel hemat, Cook Co Hosp, Ill, 53-54; NIH spec res fel, Div Med Sci, London Sch Trop Med, 59-60; assoc attend physician, Res & Educ Hosp & Cook Co Hosp, 54-57; med educ, Cook Co Hosp, 57-59, attend physician, 59, res assoc, Hektoen Inst Med Res, 54-59; chief, Hemat Res Labs, Vet Admin Hosp, Hines, Ill, 61-67 & biostatist res support ctr, 63-67; clin prof, Sch Med, Georgetown Univ, 70- *Mem:* Fel Am Col Med Informatics; fel Am Col Physicians; assoc Royal Soc Med. *Res:* Hematology; biostatistics. *Mailing Add:* Nat Lib Med 8600 Rockville Pike Bethesda MD 20894

SCHOON, DAVID JACOB, CHEMICAL ENGINEERING, ELECTRONICS. *Personal Data:* b Luverne, Minn, May 6, 43; m 69. *Educ:* Univ Minn, Minneapolis, BS, 65, PhD(chem eng), 69. *Prof Exp:* Sr chem engr, 3M CO, 69-86; res specialist, Printware Inc, 86-91. *Res:* Electrooptical object detection and counting systems; biomedical electronics. *Mailing Add:* 871 Mendakota Ct St Paul MN 55120

SCHOONEN, MARTIN A A, HYDROGEOCHEMISTRY, EXPERIMENTAL HYDROTHERMAL GEOCHEMISTRY. *Current Pos:* ASST PROF GEOCHEM, STATE UNIV NY, STONY BROOK, 89- *Personal Data:* b Hoogerheide, Neth, Aug 3, 60; m 90, Josephine Connolly. *Educ:* Univ Utrecht, Neth, BS, 81, MS, 84; Pa State Univ, PhD(geochem & mineral), 89. *Mem:* Am Mineral Soc; Geochem Soc. *Res:* Geochemistry of sulfur and metal sulfides in aqueous systems at temperatures up to 300 degrees celcius; conduct both field studies and experiments in lab; study the geochemistry of waters in pine barrens ecosystem; examine the incorporation of chloride, sodium and sulfate into carbonate minerals. *Mailing Add:* Dept ESS State Univ NY Stony Brook NY 11794-2100. *Fax:* 516-632-8240

SCHOONMAKER, GEORGE RUSSELL, GEOLOGY. *Current Pos:* RETIRED. *Personal Data:* b Chicago, Ill, Dec 1, 16; m 44; c 2. *Educ:* Univ Chicago, BS, 38. *Prof Exp:* Asst inspector core drilling, Corps Engrs, US Dept Army, 39-40; geologist, Marathon Oil Co, 40-53, dist mgr, Can, 53-55, from asst mgr to explor mgr foreign dept, 55-60, explor mgr & vpres, Marathon Int Oil Co, 61-62, explor mgr, Marathon Oil Co, 62-80, vpres, 64-80. *Mem:* Am Asn Petrol Geol; Soc Explor Geophys. *Res:* General oil exploration. *Mailing Add:* 119 E Edgar Findlay OH 45840

SCHOONMAKER, RICHARD CLINTON, CATALYSIS, MATERIAL PROPERTIES. *Current Pos:* from asst prof to assoc prof, 60-69, chmn dept, 67-73 & 78-79, PROF CHEM, OBERLIN COL, 69- *Personal Data:* b Schenectady, NY, Dec 21, 30; m 56; c 4. *Educ:* Yale Univ, ChEng, 52; Cornell Univ, PhD(chem), 60. *Prof Exp:* Asst phys chem, Cornell Univ, 56-58; res physicist, Columbia Univ, 59-60. *Concurrent Pos:* NSF sci fac fel, Math Inst, Oxford Univ, 66-67; vis sr res fel, Dept Physics, Univ York, York Eng, 73-74; NSF prof develop fel; vis prof, Dept Chem, Univ Calif, Berkeley, 80-81; Max Planck fel, Fritz Haber Inst, Max Planck Soc, Berlin, 87-88. *Mem:* Am Phys Soc; Am Chem Soc; Sigma Xi. *Res:* Thermochemistry; thermochemical properties of gaseous molecules; phase equilibria; high temperature chemistry; mass spectrometry; thermodynamics and kinetics of vaporization and condensation processes; surface physics; molecular beams. *Mailing Add:* 270 E College St Oberlin OH 44074

SCHOOR, W PETER, BIOPHYSICAL CHEMISTRY, COMPARATIVE BIOCHEMISTRY. *Current Pos:* br chief, 70-80, MEM STAFF BIOCHEM, GULF BREEZE ENVIRON RES LAB, ENVIRON PROTECTION AGENCY, 80- *Personal Data:* b Frankfurt, WGer, June 4, 36; US citizen; m 70; c 1. *Educ:* Auburn Univ, PhD(biochem), 66. *Prof Exp:* Fel, Inst Molecular Biophys, Fla State Univ, 66-68; asst prof pharmacol, Sch Med, La State Univ, 68-70. *Concurrent Pos:* Adj prof, Univ WFla, 75- *Mem:* Am Chem Soc; Sigma Xi. *Res:* Biochemical molecular mechanisms; metabolism of chemical carcinogens by aquatic organisms; mechanism of osmoregulation and membrane transport. *Mailing Add:* Gulf Breeze Environ Res Lab Environ Protection Agency Gulf Breeze FL 32561

SCHOPF, JAMES WILLIAM, PALEOBIOLOGY, ORGANIC GEOCHEMISTRY. *Current Pos:* from asst prof to assoc prof geol, 68-73, vchair, Dept Earth & Space Sci, 82-83, dean, Div Honors, Col Lett & Sci, 83-85, PROF PALEOBIOL, UNIV CALIF, LOS ANGELES, 73-, DIR, CTR STUDY EVOLUTION & ORIGIN OF LIFE, INST GEOPHYS & PLANETARY PHYSICS, 84-, MEM, MOLECULAR BIOL INST, 91- *Personal Data:* b Urbana, Ill, Sept 27, 41; m 65; c 1. *Educ:* Oberlin Col, AB, 63; Harvard Univ, AM, 65, PhD(biol), 68. *Honors & Awards:* NY Bot Garden Award, Bot Soc Am, 66; Outstanding Paper Award, Soc Econ Paleontologists & Mineralogists, 71; Schuchert Award, Paleont Soc, 74; Alan T Waterman Award & Medal, NSF, 77; G Hawk Award, Univ Kans, 79; Golden Plate Award, Am Acad Achievement, 80; Mark Clark Thompson Medal, Nat Acad Sci, 86; A I Oparin Medal, Int Soc Study Origin of Life, 89; Group Achievement Award, NASA, 97. *Concurrent Pos:* Vis res chemist, Ames Res Ctr, NASA, 67; mem lunar sample preliminary exam team, NASA, 68-71, prin investr lunar samples, 69-74, mem, space sci adv comt, Space Prog Adv Coun, 69-82; mem, Inst Evolutionary & Environ Biol, 70-73 & Inst Geophys & Planetary Physics, 73-, Guggenheim fel, 73 & 88; assoc ed, Origins of Life, 73-87 & Paleobiol, 74-80; Nat Acad Sci vis scientist, Soviet Union, 75; mem working groups Cambrian-Precambrian boundary, UNESCO Int Geol Correlation Prog, 75- & Precambrian biostratigraphy, 76-; mem terrestrial bodies sci working group, NASA, 75-76 & life sci comt, Space Prog Adv Coun, 76-78; vis scientist, Bot Soc Am, China, 78; vis prof, fac sci, Univ Nijmegen, Neth, 80-81; Acad Chem vis scientist, People's Repub China, 81 & 82; vis distinguished lectr, Third World Acad Sci, Trieste, Italy, 92; Hans Vilberth fel, Univ Regensburg, Ger, 96; sr res fel, Alexander von Humboldt Found, 97- *Mem:* Paleont Soc; fel Geol Soc Am; Bot Soc Am; fel Int Soc Study Origin Life (treas, 77-); Phycol Soc Am; Paleont Asn; Am Soc Microbiol; Am Philos Soc; fel AAAS; fel Am Acad Arts & Sci. *Res:* Precambrian paleobiology; optical and electron microscopy of fossil and modern microorganisms; origin of life; paleobotany; organic geochemistry of ancient sediments; interrelationships of atmospheric and biotic evolution. *Mailing Add:* Dept Earth & Space Sci Univ Calif Geol Bldh Rm 5687 Los Angeles CA 90095

SCHOPLER, HARRY A, BIOENGINEERING & BIOMEDICAL ENGINEERING. *Current Pos:* PROF CHEM & PHYSICS, MILWAUKEE SCH ENG, 82- *Personal Data:* b Fuerth, Bavaria, Ger, Jan 5, 26; US citizen; m 49; c 2. *Educ:* Univ Wis-Madison, BS, 50, Milwaukee, MS, 85. *Prof Exp:* Engr, Milwaukee Gas Co, Div Am Natural Resources, 50-56; regional mgr consult eng, Allstates Design & Develop Co, Inc, 56-82. *Concurrent Pos:* Tech translator, Ger, 60-; lectr chem, Univ Wis-Milwaukee, 70-86. *Mem:* Fel Am Inst Chemists. *Res:* Applied research in the area of polymers and composites; instrumentation and equipment for biomedical applications such as percutaneous & transluminal angioplasty. *Mailing Add:* 1600 W Green Tree Rd Milwaukee WI 53209

SCHOPP, ROBERT THOMAS, PHYSIOLOGY. *Current Pos:* PROF PHYSIOL & CHMN DEPT, SCH DENT MED, SOUTHERN ILL UNIV, EDWARDSVILLE, 69- *Personal Data:* b Pontiac, Ill, Nov 5, 23; m 50; c 4. *Educ:* Univ Ill, BS, 50, MS, 51; Univ Wis, PhD(physiol), 56. *Prof Exp:* Instr biol, St Norbert Col, 51-52; asst physiol, Univ Wis, 52-55, instr, 55-56; from instr to asst prof, Sch Med, Univ Colo, 56-67; assoc prof, Kirksville Col Osteop & Surg, 67-69. *Mem:* AAAS; Am Physiol Soc; Am Soc Pharmacol & Exp Therapeut; Am Inst Biol Sci; Am Soc Zoologists. *Res:* Neuromuscular research; autonomic nervous systems; reflex regulation of circulation and respiration. *Mailing Add:* 2934 E Exeter Tucson AZ 85716-5530

SCHOPPER, HERWIG FRANZ, ELEMENTARY PARTICLE PHYSICS. *Current Pos:* RETIRED. *Personal Data:* b Landskron, Czech, Feb 28, 24; Ger citizen; m 49; c 2. *Educ:* Univ Hamburg, dipl, 49, PhD(physics & natural sci), 51. *Hon Degrees:* Dr, Univ Erlangen, 82, Univ Moscow, Univ Genève, Univ London, 89. *Honors & Awards:* Physics Award, Gottingen Acad Sci, 57; Carus Medal, Acad Leopoldina, Halle, 59; Ritter-von-Gerstner Medal, 78; Golden Plate Award, Am Acad Achievement, 84- *Prof Exp:* Assoc prof & lectr, Univ Erlangen, 54-57; prof & dir, Nuclear Phys Inst, Univ Karlsruhe, 57-60; res assoc, Europ Ctr Nuclear Res, Geneva, Switz, 64-67, head particle physics dept & mem directorate, 70-73, chmn intersecting storage ring comt, 73-76, mem sci policy comt, 79-80, dir gen, 81-88. *Concurrent Pos:* Res assoc, Tech Univ, Stockholm, 50-51, Cavendish Lab, Cambridge, Eng, 56-57 & Cornell Univ, 60-61; chmn, Sci Coun Nuclear Physics Ctr, Karlsruhe, 67-69; chmn directorate, German Electron-Synchrotron Particle Physics Lab, Hamburg, 73-80, & Asn Ger Nat Res Ctr, 78-80; prof, Univ Hamburg, 73-; mem expert comn, Ger Res Ministry, Max Planck Inst & var foreign insts; mem, Leopoldina Acad Sci, Halle & Joachim-Jungius Soc, Hamburg, Bayr Acad Sci, Munchen. *Mem:* Ger Phys Soc; Am Phys Soc; Europ Phys Soc. *Res:* Elementary particle physics; nuclear physics; optics; science and society; science and philosophie. *Mailing Add:* CERN Geneva CH 1200 Switzerland

SCHOR, JOSEPH MARTIN, BIOCHEMISTRY. *Current Pos:* vpres, 77-95, EMER SR VPRES SCI AFFAIRS, FOREST LABS, 95- *Personal Data:* b New York, NY, Jan 10, 29; m 90, Laura Struminger; c Esther Helen, Joshua David, Gideon Alexander, Eric & Neil. *Educ:* City Col New York, BS, 51; Fla State Univ, PhD(chem), 57. *Prof Exp:* Sr res chemist, Armour Pharmaceut Co, 57-59; res chemist, Lederle Labs, Am Cyanamid Co, 59-64; dept head biochem, Endo Labs, 64-70, E I du Pont de Nemours & Co Inc, 70-77. *Mem:* Am Chem Soc; fel Am Inst Chemists; Int Soc Thrombosis & Hemostasis; Int Soc Hemat; AAAS; Sigma Xi. *Res:* Absorption, metabolism and disposition of drugs; blood clot lysis; blood coagulation; isolation and characterization of proteins; immunology; cardiovascular drugs; analgetic drugs; controlled release technology; central nervous system drugs. *Mailing Add:* 28 Meleny Rd Locust Valley NY 11560. *Fax:* 212-750-9152

SCHOR, NORBERTO AARON, PATHOLOGY. *Current Pos:* asst prof, 70-74, assoc prof, 74-79, PROF PATH, SCH MED, TULANE UNIV, 79- *Personal Data:* b Cordoba, Arg, Dec 24, 29; m 58; c 2. *Educ:* Nat Univ Litoral, Arg, MD, 55; Am Bd Path, dipl & cert anat path, 72. *Prof Exp:* Vis pathologist, Hosp Ramos Mejia, Buenos Aires, 55; asst prof histol, Nat Univ Litoral, 56-58; Brit Coun res fel, Postgrad Med Sch, Univ London, 58-59; Nat Res Coun Arg res fel, Dept Histol, Gothenburg Univ, Sweden, 59-60; from asst prof to assoc prof cell biol, Nat Univ Cordoba, 60-63; Guggenheim res assoc path, Stanford Univ, 64-67 & res fel, Univ Wis, 67-70. *Mem:* AAAS; Am Asn Pathologists & Bacteriologists; Histochem Soc; Int Acad Path. *Res:* Metabolic pathways of neoplastic cells; transfer of reducing equivalents in neoplastic cells; early activation and transformation of chemical carcinogens by lung and liver; response of lymphoid organs to the action of carcinogens. *Mailing Add:* Dept Path Tulane Univ Sch Med 1430 Tulane Ave New Orleans LA 70112-2699. *Fax:* 504-587-7389

SCHOR, ROBERT, BIOPHYSICS, SOLID STATE PHYSICS. *Current Pos:* from instr to prof physics, 58-92, EMER PROF PHYSICS, UNIV CONN, 92- *Personal Data:* b New York, NY, Oct 25, 29; m 49; c 2. *Educ:* Mass Inst Technol, BS, 50; Univ Mich, MS, 52, PhD(physics), 58. *Prof Exp:* Asst, Univ Mich, 54-58. *Concurrent Pos:* Res fel, Inst Chemico-Phys Biol, Sorbonne, France, 66-67; vis scientist, Mass Inst Technol, 77-78. *Mem:* Am Phys Soc; Biophys Soc; Am Asn Physics Teachers; NY Acad Sci. *Res:* Structure and physical properties of fibrous proteins; chemical thermodynamics; crystal physics; phase transformations in magnetic systems; theory of diffusion coefficient of charged spherical macromolecules in solution. *Mailing Add:* Dept Physics Univ Conn Storrs CT 06269

SCHOR, STANLEY, biostatistics, for more information see previous edition

SCHORE, NEIL ERIC, ORGANIC CHEMISTRY, ORGANOMETALLIC CHEMISTRY. *Current Pos:* PROF CHEM, UNIV CALIF, DAVIS, 76- *Personal Data:* b Newark, NJ, Mar 6, 48; m 78; c 2. *Educ:* Univ Pa, BA, 69; Columbia Univ, PhD(org chem), 74. *Prof Exp:* Fel chem, Calif Inst Technol, 74-76. *Concurrent Pos:* Camille & Henry Dreyfus teacher scholar, 81-85. *Mem:* Am Chem Soc; NY Acad Sci; Sigma Xi. *Res:* Preparation and organic synthesis applications of new organometallic compounds; properties of compounds possessing intramolecular metal-metal interactions. *Mailing Add:* Dept Chem Univ Calif Davis CA 95616

SCHORER, CALVIN E, PSYCHIATRY. *Current Pos:* PROF PSYCHIAT, SCH MED, WAYNE STATE UNIV, 68- *Personal Data:* b Sauk City, Wis, June 29, 19; m 61, Marilyn Parish; c Anna, Joseph, John & Mary (Peers). *Educ:* Univ Wis, BA, 39, MD, 55; Univ Chicago, MA, 42, PhD(eng), 48. *Prof Exp:* Intern, Detroit Receiving Hosp, 55-56; resident psychiat, Lafayette Clin, 56-59; staff psychiatrist, 59-67, dir med staff serv psychiat, 67-92. *Mem:* Am Psychiat Asn; AMA. *Res:* Hypnosis; psychotherapy; teaching of psychiatry; psychopharmacology. *Mailing Add:* 770 Bedford Grosse Pointe Park MI 48230. *Fax:* 313-993-3421; *E-Mail:* cshort@cms.wayne.edu

SCHORI, RICHARD M, NEURAL NETWORKS. *Current Pos:* PROF MATH, ORE STATE UNIV, 78- *Personal Data:* b Tiskilwa, Ill, Oct 30, 38; m 79; c 1. *Educ:* Kenyon Col, BA, 60; Univ Iowa, MS, 62, PhD(math), 64. *Prof Exp:* From asst prof to prof math, La State Univ, Baton Rouge, 64-78. *Concurrent Pos:* NSF res grant math, 68-78. *Mem:* Math Asn Am; Am Math Soc. *Res:* Inverse limits; hyperspaces and infinite dimensional topology; chaotic dynamical systems. *Mailing Add:* Math Dept Ore State Univ Corvallis OR 97331-4605

SCHORK, MICHAEL ANTHONY, BIOSTATISTICS. *Current Pos:* From instr to assoc prof, 62-72, PROF BIOSTATIST, UNIV MICH, ANN ARBOR, 72- *Personal Data:* b Elyria, Ohio, June 11, 36; m 85; c 7. *Educ:* Univ Notre Dame, BA, 58, MS, 60; Univ Mich, MPH, 61, PhD(biostatist), 63. *Concurrent Pos:* Visitor, Inst Human Genetics, Univ Heidelberg, 69-70. *Mem:* Am Statist Asn; Biomet Soc. *Res:* Applications of biostatistical design and analysis techniques to biomedical problems. *Mailing Add:* Dept Biostatist Univ Mich Sch Pub Health Ann Arbor MI 48109

SCHORNO, KARL STANLEY, ORGANIC GEOCHEMISTRY. *Current Pos:* DIR, MASS SPECTROMETRY, KANS CITY ANAL SERV, 93- *Personal Data:* b Berkeley, Calif, Nov 28, 39; m 67, Karen S Baker; c Kristine S & Kevin K. *Educ:* Univ Calif, Berkeley, BA, 62, Okla State Univ, PhD(chem), 67. *Prof Exp:* Res chemist org chem, Univ Calif, 62; teaching asst, Okla State Univ, 62-67, fel, 67; fel med chem, Univ Kans, 67-68; res chemist, Phillips Petrol Co, 68-86; environ GC/MS sect leader, US Pollution Control, 86-87; res mgr geosci, US Dept Energy, 87-88; sr staff scientist, Univ Kans, 88-93. *Concurrent Pos:* Consult, Univ Kans Ctr Bioanal Res, 86-; adj prof, Johnson Co Community Col, 92-93, Univ Kans, 92-94. *Mem:* Europ Geochem Soc; Geochem Soc Am; Am Chem Soc; Sigma Xi; Soc Appl Spectros; Am Soc Mass Spectrometry. *Res:* Medicinal chemistry in the study of drug design; physical organic chemistry, the study of mechanism of several reactions; organic geochemistry, the genesis of petroleum; environmental organic pollutants GC/MS, LC/MS in bioanalytical research. *Mailing Add:* 1036 College Blvd Lawrence KS 66049-3300

SCHORR, HERBERT, ELECTRICAL ENGINEERING. *Current Pos:* EXEC DIR, INFO SCI INST, UNIV SOUTHERN CALIF, 88- *Personal Data:* b New York, NY, Jan 20, 36; m 62; c 3. *Educ:* City Col New York, BEE, 57; Princeton Univ, MA, 60, MS, 61, PhD(elec eng), 62. *Prof Exp:* Instr elec eng, Princeton Univ, 61-62; NSF fel math, Cambridge Univ, 62-63; asst prof elec eng, Columbia Univ, 63-64; mgr archit & prog, IBM Corp, Calif, 64-68, dir comput sci, NY, 68-72, vpres prod & serv planning, Advan Systs Develop Div, 73-75, mgr subsysts anal, Systs Prod Div, 75, mem corp tech comt, CHQ, 75-77, mgr systs technol, Res Div, 77-81, vpres systs, 80-84, group dir, Advan Systs, 84-88. *Concurrent Pos:* Adj asst prof, Columbia Univ, 64-65; lectr, Univ Calif, Berkeley, 65-70; res prof computer sci, Univ Southern Calif, 89- *Mem:* Asn Comput Mach; Inst Elec & Electronics Engrs. *Res:* Computer architecture and systems software. *Mailing Add:* USC-Information Sci Inst 4676 Admiralty Way 10th Floor Marina Del Rey CA 90292

SCHORR, LISBETH BAMBERGER, SOCIAL MEDICINE. *Current Pos:* LECTR SOCIAL MED, SCH MED, HARVARD UNIV, 84-, DIR, PROJ EFFECTIVE INTERVENTIONS, 87- *Personal Data:* b Munich, Ger, Jan 20, 31; m 52. *Educ:* Univ Calif, Berkeley, BA, 52. *Hon Degrees:* LHD, Wilkes Univ, 91, Univ Md, 94. *Honors & Awards:* Dale Richmond Mem Award, Am Acad Pediat, 77; Molly & Sidney Zubrow Award, Pa Hosp, 89; Nelson Cruikshank Award, Nat Coun Sr Citizens, 90; Porter Prize, Health Educ Ctr, Pittsburgh, 93; Reginald S Lourie Awaard, Nat Ctr Clin Infant Progs, 95. *Prof Exp:* Staff, Labor Ed, Proj Health Plans, Inst Indust Rels, Univ Calif, Los Angeles, 52-55, Joint Legis Comt Health Ins, State, NY, 55-56; med care consult, United Auto Workers AM, 56-58; asst dir, Dept Social Sci, Am Fed Labor & Cong Indust Orgns, 58-65; actg chief, Health Servs, Community Action Prog, Econ Opportunity, 65-66, chief, Prog Planning Develop, 67; consult, Dept Social Sci, Children's Defense Fund, 73-79. *Concurrent Pos:* Bd dirs, Group Health Asn Am, 58-62, Found Child Develop, 76-84, 86-92, 93-94, Nat Ctr Clin Infant Progs, 81-90, City Lights, Washington, DC, 86-91, Eureaka Communities, 92-, Pub Educ Fund, 92-93, City Year, 94-; mem, Comn Study Health Care Women, Am Col Obstetricians & Gynecologists, 70-73; mem adv bd, Nat Serv Study Proj, 83-84; mem nat adv comt, Healthy Tomorrows Partnership Children Prog, Bur Maternal & Child Health, HEW, 89-; mem, Task Force Children at Risk, United Way Am, 91. *Mem:* Inst Med-Nat Acad Sci. *Mailing Add:* 3113 Woodley Rd NW Washington DC 20008

SCHORR, MARVIN GERALD, PHYSICS. *Current Pos:* assoc tech dir, 51-57, exec vpres & treas, 57-62, pres, 62-88, CHMN, TECH OPERS, INC, 88- *Personal Data:* b New York, NY, Mar 10, 25; m 57, Rosalie Yorshis; c Eric & Susan. *Educ:* Yale Univ, BS, 44, MS, 47, PhD(electromagnetics), 49. *Prof Exp:* Physicist, Tracerlab, Inc, 49-51. *Concurrent Pos:* Mem nuclear adv comt, Univ Lowell & AEC adv comt isotope & radiation develop, 64-66; chmn, Mass Technol Develop Corp, 74- *Mem:* Fel AAAS; Am Phys Soc; Opers Res Soc Am; Inst Elec & Electronics Engrs. *Res:* Wound ballistics; electromagnetic radiation; radioactivity and nuclear measurement; electronics; operations research. *Mailing Add:* 330 Beacon St Boston MA 02116

SCHOTLAND, RICHARD MORTON, METEOROLOGY. *Current Pos:* PROF ATMOSPHERIC PHYSICS, UNIV ARIZ, 73- *Personal Data:* b Irvington, NJ, Feb 11, 27; m 52; c 2. *Educ:* Mass Inst Technol, SB, 48, SM, 50, ScD(meteorol), 52. *Prof Exp:* Asst, Mass Inst Technol, 50-52; res assoc, Oceanog Inst, Woods Hole, Mass, 52; from asst prof to prof meteorol, NY Univ, 52-73. *Concurrent Pos:* Consult, Brookhaven Nat Lab, chmn, Group Laser Atmospheric Probing; mem, Army Basic Res Comt, Nat Res Coun, 74-, Adv Panel, Nat Ctr Atmospheric Res, 75- & adv panel, Wave Propagation Lab, Nat Oceanic & Atmospheric Admin, 78- *Mem:* Am Meteorol Soc; Am Geophys Union; Royal Meteorol Soc; Optical Soc Am; Sigma Xi. *Res:* Meteorological instrumentation; atmospheric physics; radiowave propagation; atmospheric radiation; remote sensing laser radar. *Mailing Add:* Dept Atmospheric Sci Univ Ariz Tucson AZ 85721-0001

SCHOTT, FREDERICK W(ILLIAM), ELECTROMAGNETICS, ELECTROMECHANICS. *Current Pos:* from asst prof to assoc prof, 48-69, PROF ENG, UNIV CALIF, LOS ANGELES, 69- *Personal Data:* b Phoenix, Ariz, Oct 2, 19; m 46, Mary Peter; c Christopher. *Educ:* San Diego State Col, AB, 40; Stanford Univ, PhD(elec eng), 48. *Prof Exp:* Jr engr, San Diego Gas & Elec Co, 43-44; instr physics, San Diego State Col, 46-47. *Concurrent Pos:* Physicist, US Naval Electronics Lab, 49-50; res physicist, Hughes Aircraft Co, 56; consult, 78- *Mem:* Inst Elec & Electronics Engrs; Am Soc Eng Educ. *Res:* Rotating electric machines; applied electromagnetics. *Mailing Add:* 56-125B Engr IV Univ Calif Los Angeles CA 90024-1594

SCHOTT, GARRY LEE, PHYSICAL CHEMISTRY. *Current Pos:* staff mem, 56-91, AFFIL, LOS ALAMOS NAT LAB, 93- *Personal Data:* b Detroit, Mich, Dec 20, 31; m 60, Irene Dahle; c Thomas & Nancy. *Educ:* Univ Mich, BS, 52; Calif Inst Technol, PhD(chem), 56. *Mem:* Am Chem Soc; Combustion Inst. *Res:* Shock wave processes in condensed matter and gases; chemical kinetics; gaseous combustion; detonation. *Mailing Add:* 120 Monte Vista Dr Los Alamos NM 87544

SCHOTT, HANS, PHYSICAL CHEMISTRY, PHARMACEUTICS. *Current Pos:* from assoc prof to prof, 69-93, EMER PROF PHARMACEUT & COLLOID CHEM, SCH PHARM, TEMPLE UNIV, 94- *Personal Data:* b Ger, Oct 25, 22; US citizen; m 58. *Educ:* Univ Sao Paulo, 43; Univ Southern Calif, MS, 51; Univ Del, PhD(phys chem), 58. *Prof Exp:* Res chemist, Cent Lab, Matarazzo Industs, Brazil, 43-44, head, Chem Lab, Viscose Rayon Plant, 44-47, plant adminstr, 49; res chemist, Thiokol Chem Corp, 47-48 & Textile Fibers Dept, Pioneering Res Div, E I du Pont de Nemours & Co, 51-56; res assoc, Film Div, Olin Mathieson Chem Corp, 58-60; sr res assoc, Phys Chem Sect, Res Ctr, Lever Bros Co, 61-67; res chemist, US Forest Prod Lab, 67-68. *Concurrent Pos:* Geigy vis prof pharm, Univ Manchester, Eng, 85. *Mem:* Am Chem Soc; fel Acad Pharmaceut Sci. *Res:* Effect of electrolytes on nonionic surfactants; physical chemistry of gelatin and interaction with organic drugs; solubilization of cholesterol and derivatives; colloidal and rheological properties of aqueous dispersions of drugs, clays and bacteria; colloid, surface and polymer chemistry. *Mailing Add:* Temple Univ Sch Pharm 3307 N Broad St Philadelphia PA 19140. Fax: 215-707-3678

SCHOTT, JAMES ROBERT, MULTIVARIATE ANALYSIS. *Current Pos:* from asst prof to assoc prof, 82-93, PROF STATIST, UNIV CENT FLA, 93- *Personal Data:* b Cincinnati, Ohio, Jan 9, 55; m 79, Susan Cromartie; c Adam & Sarah. *Educ:* Xavier, BS, 77; Univ Fla, MS, 79, PhD(statist), 81. *Mem:* Am Statist Asn; Inst Math Statist. *Res:* Canonical variate analysis, principal components analysis and other analysis of covariance and correlation matrices. *Mailing Add:* Dept Statist Univ Cent Fla Orlando FL 32816-2370. E-Mail: schott@longwood.cs.ucf.edu

SCHOTT, JEFFREY HOWARD, CHEMICAL ENGINEERING, RESEARCH ADMINISTRATION. *Current Pos:* MGR, SIGMA CHEM CO, 90- *Personal Data:* b Angola, Ind, Feb 4, 47; m 66. *Educ:* Univ Minn, BChemE, 70, MS, 74, PhD(chem eng), 78; Univ Chicago, MBA, 83. *Prof Exp:* Inst unit opers, Dept Chem Eng, Univ Minn, 72-75; res engr, Amoco Chem Corp, 75-78; dir res & develop, Eschem, Inc, subsid, Esmark, Inc, 78-84; exec dir, Tile Coun Am, Inc, 84-87; dir adhesive technol, Avery Dennison, 87-90. *Mem:* Am Inst Chem Engrs; Am Chem Soc; Sigma Xi; Nat Soc Prof Engrs. *Res:* Application of chemical engineering principles to the development and production of adhesives, coatings, and related specialty chemicals. *Mailing Add:* 6320 N Lake Dr Whitefish Bay Milwaukee WI 53217

SCHOTTE, WILLIAM, CHEMICAL ENGINEERING. *Current Pos:* res engr, E I Du Pont de Neumours & Co Inc, 54-58, res proj engr, 58-61, sr res engr, 61-69, sr res specialist, 69-78, SR RES ASSOC, ENG TECH LAB, EXP STA, E I DU PONT DE NEMOURS & CO, INC, 78- *Personal Data:* b Burlington, Iowa, July 3, 27; m 50; c 3. *Educ:* Columbia Univ, BS, 50, MS, 51, EngScD, 55. *Prof Exp:* Res assoc, Columbia Univ, 51-54. *Mem:* Am Chem Soc; Am Inst Chem Engrs. *Res:* Pollution abatement; chemical reactors; separation technology. *Mailing Add:* 2014 Wildwood Dr Wilmington DE 19805

SCHOTTEL, JANET L, MESSENGER RNA STABILITY, MICROBIAL PLANT INTERACTIONS. *Current Pos:* Asst prof, 81-87, ASSOC PROF BIOCHEM, MOLECULAR BIOL & MICROBIOL, UNIV MINN, 87- *Educ:* Wash Univ, St Louis, PhD(biol), 77. *Mem:* Am Soc Microbiol; AAAS; Am Soc Biol Chemists. *Res:* Mechanism of MRNA turnover in Escherichia coli; mechanism of pathogenicity of stretomycin scabies in potato. *Mailing Add:* Dept Biochem Univ Minn 1479 Gortner Ave St Paul MN 55108-1041. Fax: 612-625-5780

SCHOTTELIUS, DOROTHY DICKEY, BIOCHEMISTRY. *Current Pos:* res assoc radiation, 59-71, res assoc neurol & physiol, 71-75, ASST PROF NEUROL, UNIV IOWA, 75- *Personal Data:* b Lohrville, Iowa, Oct 9, 27; m 49. *Educ:* Univ Iowa, BA, 49; State Col Wash, MS, 51; Univ NC, PhD, 57. *Prof Exp:* Res asst biochem, Univ Iowa, 52-54; res asst, Univ NC, 54-57. *Mem:* Am Physiol Soc; Am Epilepsy Soc; Biophys Soc; Am Asn Clin Chem; Sigma Xi. *Res:* Neurochemistry; biochemistry of normal and diseased muscle; pharmacology of anticonvulsant drugs; protein and nucleic acid chemistry. *Mailing Add:* Dept Neurol Univ Iowa 1450 Grand Ave Iowa City IA 52246-1912

SCHOTTENFELD, DAVID, EPIDEMIOLOGY. *Current Pos:* JOHN G SEARLE PROF, CHMN EPIDEMIOL SCH PUB HEALTH & PROF INTERNAL MED, UNIV MICH, ANN ARBOR, 86- *Personal Data:* b New York, NY, Mar 25, 31; m, Rosalie C Schaeffer; c Jacqueline & Stephen. *Educ:* Hamilton Col, AB, 52; Cornell Univ, MD, 56; Harvard Univ, MS, 63; Am Bd Internal Med, dipl; Am Bd Prev Med, dipl. *Honors & Awards:* W G Cosbie lectr, Can Oncol Soc, 87. *Prof Exp:* Intern internal med, Duke Univ, 56-57; resident internal med, Mem Sloan-Kettering Cancer Ctr, Med Col, Cornell Univ, 57-59, Craver fel med oncol, 61-62; clin instr, Dept Pub Health, Cornell Univ, 63-67, from asst prof to prof, 65-86. *Concurrent Pos:* Vis prof epidemiol, Univ Minn, 68, 71, 74, 82 & 86; acad career award prev oncol, Nat Cancer Inst, 80-85. *Mem:* Fel AAAS; fel Am Col Physicians; fel Am Col Prev Med; fel Am Col Epidemiol. *Res:* Cancer epidemiology, prevention and control. *Mailing Add:* Univ Mich 109 Observatory St Ann Arbor MI 48109-2029

SCHOTTMILLER, JOHN CHARLES, IMAGING MATERIALS, TECHNICAL MANAGEMENT. *Current Pos:* PRES & TOTAL QUAL CONSULT, R M CONSULT, INC, 89- *Personal Data:* b Rochester, NY, Aug 6, 30; m 56; c 2. *Educ:* Univ Rochester, BA, 53; Syracuse Univ, PhD(chem), 58. *Prof Exp:* Asst, AEC, Syracuse Univ, 57-58; res chemist, Union Carbide Metals Co, 58-61; staff chemist, Components Div, Int Bus Mach Corp, 61-62; sr scientist, Spec Mat Mfg, Xerox Corp, 62-71, mgr photoreceptor develop & eng, 71-77, mgr process eng, Europ Opers, 77-79, mgr tech serv, 79-82, mgr phys & chem anal, 82-84, mgr qual & bus effectiveness, 84-89. *Mem:* Sigma Xi; Am Soc Qual Control. *Res:* Photoconductivity; solid state and metallurgical chemistry; vacuum deposition; electrophotography; x-rays; microcircuitry; thermodynamics; phase diagrams; reactive metals; metal-metal oxide equilibria; analytical chemistry; total quality control. *Mailing Add:* 48 Hampshire Lane Mendon NY 14506

SCHOTTSTAEDT, WILLIAM WALTER, MEDICINE, PUBLIC HEALTH. *Current Pos:* RETIRED. *Personal Data:* b Fresno, Calif, Mar 28, 17; m 47; c 4. *Educ:* Univ Calif, BA, 47, MD, 48; Univ Mich, BMus, 40, MMus, 41. *Prof Exp:* From asst prof to assoc prof med, prev med & pub health, Sch Med, Univ Okla, 53-60, assoc prof psychiat, 56-60, prof prev med & pub health & chmn dept & consult prof psychiat, neurol & behav sci, 60-68, dean, Col Health, 68-73; prof prev med & community health, Med Br Univ Tex, Galveston, 74-86, dir, Health Educ Ctr, 76-79, assoc dean continuing educ, 79-86. *Concurrent Pos:* Commonwealth fel psychosom med, NY Hosp, 51-53. *Mem:* Am Psychosom Soc; AMA; Am Pub Health Asn. *Res:* Renal excretion. *Mailing Add:* 18 E Wildflower Dr Santa Fe NM 87501-8502

SCHOTZ, LARRY, ELECTRICAL ENGINEERING. *Current Pos:* PRES, L S RES, INC, 80- *Personal Data:* b Milwaukee, Wis, Dec 26, 49; m. *Educ:* Milwaukee Sch Eng, BS, 73. *Honors & Awards:* Eng Design Graphics Award, Am Soc Eng, 72. *Prof Exp:* Proj engr, Sherwood Electronics, 73-75; pres, Draco Labs, Inc, 75-80. *Mem:* Inst Elec & Electronics Engrs; Audio Eng Soc. *Res:* Development of FM tuner controlled by a microprocessor; development of stereo TV decoder. *Mailing Add:* LS Res Inc W66N220 Commerce Ct Cedarburg WI 53012

SCHOTZ, MICHAEL C, BIOCHEMISTRY. *Current Pos:* BIOCHEMIST, LIPID RES LAB, VET ADMIN WADSWORTH MED CTR, UNIV CALIF, LOS ANGELES, 60-, PROF MED, 74- *Personal Data:* b New York, NY, June 30, 28; m 51; c 2. *Educ:* Marietta Col, BS, 47; Univ Southern Calif, MS, 50, PhD(biochem), 53. *Prof Exp:* Harvard Univ res fel cholesterol metab, Huntington Res Labs, Mass Gen Hosp, 53-54; USPHS officer, Res Div, Cleveland Clin Ohio, 55-57, asst staff mem, 57-60. *Concurrent Pos:* Asst prof, Ctr Health Sci, Univ Calif, Los Angeles, 60-68, assoc prof, 68-72, adj assoc prof, 72-74; USPHS grant, 60. *Mem:* AAAS; Am Heart Soc; Am Chem Soc; Am Soc Biol Chem. *Res:* Role of lipoprotein lipase in the deposition of lipids in adipose tissue and heart tissue; determination of antibiotics using high-pressure liquid chromatography; the role of endotoxin in gram-negative septicemia. *Mailing Add:* Dept Med Bldg 113 Rm 312 Va Wadsworth Med Ctr UCLA Los Angeles CA 90073. Fax: 310-478-4538

SCHOULTIES, CALVIN LEE, PLANT PATHOLOGY. *Current Pos:* DIR, REGULATORY SERV, CLEMSON UNIV, 87- *Personal Data:* b Dayton, Ky, Nov 18, 43. *Educ:* Univ Ky, BS, 65, PhD(plant path), 71. *Prof Exp:* Staff res assoc plant path, Univ Calif, Berkeley, 71-75; plant pathologist, Fla Dept Agr & Consumer Serv, 75- *Mem:* Sigma Xi; Am Phytopath Soc. *Res:* Soil microbiology and ecology; biological control of plant pathogens. *Mailing Add:* 212 Barre Hall Clemson Univ Box 340390 Clemson SC 29634-0390

SCHOULTZ, TURE WILLIAM, NEUROSCIENCES. *Current Pos:* ASSOC DEAN, ACAD STUDENT AFFAIRS, ALA, 89- *Personal Data:* b Alhambra, Calif, June 6, 40; m 59; c 3. *Educ:* Colo State Univ, BS, 65; Univ Colo, Boulder, MA, 67; Univ Colo Med Ctr, Denver, PhD(anat), 71. *Prof Exp:* Instr physiol, Med Sch, NY Univ, 71-72; asst mem neurobiol, Pub Health Res Inst, City of New York, 71-72; asst prof anat, Col Med, Univ Ark, Little Rock, 73-89, asst dean, 77-89. *Mem:* Soc Neurosci; Am Asn Anatomists. *Res:* The acute phase of mammalian spinal cord injury; determination of the role of catecholamines in trauma-induced progressive spinal cord destruction and determination of changes in dissolved oxygen concentration after injury. *Mailing Add:* Univ SAla Med Ctr 2451 Fillingim St Mobile AL 36617-2238

SCHOWALTER, WILLIAM RAYMOND, FLUID MECHANICS, POLYMER RHEOLOGY. *Current Pos:* DEAN COL ENG, UNIV ILL URBANA-CHAMPAIGN, 90- *Personal Data:* b Milwaukee, Wis, Dec 15, 29; m 53, Jane Gregg; c Katherine, Mary & David. *Educ:* Univ Wis, BS, 51; Univ Ill, MS, 53, PhD(chem eng), 57. *Hon Degrees:* Dr, Nat Inst Polytech, Lorraine, France, 96. *Honors & Awards:* Lectureship Award, Am Soc Eng Educ, 71; William H Walker Award, Am Inst Chem Engrs, 82; Bingham Medal, Soc Rheology, 88. *Prof Exp:* From asst prof to prof chem eng, Princeton Univ, 57-89, actg chmn, Dept Chem Eng, 71, assoc dean, Sch Eng & Appl Sci, 72-77, chmn dept, 78-87. *Concurrent Pos:* Mem adv bd for chem eng series, McGraw-Hill Book Co; vis sr fel, Brit Sci Res Coun, Cambridge, 70; mem, US Nat Comt Theoret & Appl Mech, 72-81, Nat Res Coun Comn Eng & Tech Systs, 83-88; Sherman Fairchild distinguished scholar, Calif Inst Technol, 77-78. *Mem:* Nat Acad Eng; Am Chem Soc; Am Inst Chem Engrs; Soc Rheology (pres, 81-83); Am Acad Arts & Sci. *Res:* Fluid mechanics; non-Newtonian flow; rheology; colloids. *Mailing Add:* 103 Eng Hall Univ Ill 1308 W Green St Urbana IL 61801. Fax: 217-244-7705

SCHOWEN, RICHARD LYLE, MECHANISM CHEMISTRY. *Current Pos:* from asst prof to prof, 63-77, SUMMERFIELD PROF CHEM, UNIV KANS, 77-, BIOCHEM, 86- *Personal Data:* b Nitro, WVa, Aug 29, 34; m 63; c 2. *Educ:* Univ Calif, Berkeley, BS, 58; Mass Inst Technol, PhD(org chem), 62. *Hon Degrees:* Dr rer nat, Martin Luther Univ, Halle-Wittenberg, Ger. *Honors & Awards:* Dolph Simons Sr Award Biomed Res, 82. *Prof Exp:* Res assoc, Mass Inst Technol, 62-63. *Concurrent Pos:* NIH res career develop award, 68-73; Syntex lectr, Can, 88. *Mem:* Fel AAAS; fel Am Inst Chemists;

Am Chem Soc; Am Soc Biochem & Molecular Biol. *Res:* Reaction mechanisms; biodynamics; isotope effects; enzyme mechanisms. *Mailing Add:* Dept Chem Univ Kans Lawrence KS 66045-0046. *Fax:* 785-864-5349; *E-Mail:* rschowen@ukanvax

SCHOWENGERDT, FRANKLIN DEAN, ATOMIC PHYSICS, SOLID STATE PHYSICS SURFACES. *Current Pos:* assoc prof, 73-80, head Physics Dept, 76-89, PROF PHYSICS, COLO SCH MINES, 80-, VPRES ACAD AFFAIRS, 90- *Personal Data:* b Bellflower, Mo, Mar 8, 36; m 62, Ellen J Johnson; c Anna & John. *Educ:* Univ Mo-Rolla, BS, 66, MS, 67, PhD(physics), 69. *Prof Exp:* Res assoc physics, Univ Nebr, 69-71, vis asst prof, 71-73. *Concurrent Pos:* Chmn, Advan Mats Inst, 85-90; distinguished vis scientist, Jet Propulsion Lab, Calif Technol Inst, 87-88; pres, Rocky Mountain Chap, Am Vacuum Soc, 90-91 & Colo Sch Mines Chap, Sigma Xi, 92- *Mem:* Sigma Xi; Am Phys Soc; Mats Res Soc; Am Vacuum Soc. *Res:* Electron and ion collisions; ion energy loss spectroscopy; low energy electron spectroscopy; cloud physics applied to control of respirable coal dust; auger electron spectroscopy; surface science. *Mailing Add:* Vpres Acad Affairs Colo Sch Mines Golden CO 80401

SCHOWENGERDT, ROBERT ALAN, DIGITAL IMAGE PROCESSING, REMOTE SENSING. *Current Pos:* Res assoc, Optical Sci Ctr, 72-77, asst prof remote sensing, Off Arid Lands & Elec Eng, 77-84, ASSOC PROF ELEC & COMPUT ENG, ARID LANDS, OPTICAL SCI, UNIV ARIZ, 84- *Personal Data:* b St Charles, Mo, Oct 10, 46; m 74; c 2. *Educ:* Univ Mo, BS, 68; Univ Ariz, PhD(optical sci), 75. *Honors & Awards:* H J E Reid Award, NASA Langley Res Ctr, 83. *Concurrent Pos:* Physical scientist, Earth Resources Observation Syst, US Geol Surv, Va, 75-80; Am Soc Eng Educ-NASA summer fac fel, Langley Res Ctr, NASA, 83; Fulbright sr scholar, Univ NSW, Canberra, Australia, 89. *Mem:* Optical Soc Am; Am Soc Photogram; Inst Elec & Electronics Engrs; Int Soc Optical Eng. *Res:* Computer image enhancement; pattern recognition of satellite and aerial remote sensing images; sensor design and performance analysis; automated cartography; computer vision. *Mailing Add:* Dept Elec/Comput Eng Univ Ariz Tucson AZ 85721. *E-Mail:* schowengerdt@ece.arizona.edu

SCHRAAD, MARK WILLIAM, FLUID-SOLID INTERACTION MODELING, MATERIAL MODELING. *Current Pos:* RES ASSOC, LOS ALAMOS NAT LAB, 96- *Personal Data:* b St Paul, Minn, Mar 13, 68; m 92, Kristen Lynn Pallansch. *Educ:* Univ Minn, BS, 90, MS, 91; Univ Mich, MS, 95, PhD(aerospace eng), 96. *Mem:* Am Acad Mech; Am Inst Aeronaut & Astronaut. *Res:* Continuum mechanics; structural mechanics; mechanics of composite materials; micromechanics; constitutive modeling for solid materials; homogenization methods for composite materials; material failure criteria; material stability; material failure; material damage. *Mailing Add:* Los Alamos Nat Lab MS B216 Los Alamos NM 87545. *Fax:* 505-665-5926; *E-Mail:* schraad@lanl.gov

SCHRACK, ROALD AMUNDSEN, PHYSICS. *Current Pos:* Physicist, 49-56, NUCLEAR PHYSICIST, NAT BUR STANDARDS, 56- *Personal Data:* b Ft Meade, Fla, Aug 26, 26; m, Pat Awtenger; c Alan & Bonnie. *Educ:* Univ Calif, Los Angeles, BS, 49, MS, 50; Univ Md, PhD, 61. *Honors & Awards:* Silver Medal, Dept Com, 82; I-R 100 Award. *Mem:* Am Phys Soc; Inst Elec & Electronics Engrs. *Res:* Measurement of nuclear matter distribution by neutral meson photoproduction; nuclear structure physics; neutron cross sections; isotopic assay and distribution by resonance neutron radiography. *Mailing Add:* Div 846 Nat Inst Stand & Technol Gaithersburg MD 20899. *Fax:* 301-869-7682; *E-Mail:* roald.schrack@nist.gov

SCHRADER, DAVID HAWLEY, ELECTRICAL ENGINEERING. *Current Pos:* RETIRED. *Personal Data:* b Syracuse, NY, Dec 9, 25; m 68; c 4. *Educ:* Univ Kans, BS, 51; Univ Wash, MS, 59, PhD(fading of radio waves), 63. *Prof Exp:* Assoc engr, Hazeltine Electronics Corp, 51-55; instr, Univ Wash, 55-63; prof elec eng, Wash State Univ, 63-96. *Mem:* Inst Elec & Electronics Engrs; Sigma Xi. *Res:* Physics of the magnetosphere and the ionosphere-propagation of radio waves. *Mailing Add:* Rte 1 Box 232 Pullman WA 99163

SCHRADER, DAVID MARTIN, PHYSICAL CHEMISTRY. *Current Pos:* PROF CHEM, MARQUETTE UNIV, 68- *Personal Data:* b Minneapolis, Minn, Sept 24, 32; m 55, Janet Davis; c 3. *Educ:* Iowa State Univ, BS, 54; Univ Minn, Minneapolis, PhD(theoret chem), 62. *Prof Exp:* Res fel theoret chem, Columbia Univ, 61-62 & IBM Watson Lab, 62-63; asst prof phys chem, Univ Iowa, 63-67; asst prof chem, Univ Minn, Minneapolis, 67-68. *Concurrent Pos:* Univ res fel & sr vis fel, Sci Res Coun, math dept, Univ Nottingham, UK. *Mem:* Am Phys Soc; Am Chem Soc. *Res:* Atomic and molecular quantum mechanics; positron annihilation. *Mailing Add:* Dept Chem Marquette Univ PO Box 1881 Milwaukee WI 53201-1881. *Fax:* 414-288-3300; *E-Mail:* 6031schrader@vms.csd.mu.edu

SCHRADER, DOROTHY VIRGINIA, MATHEMATICS. *Current Pos:* assoc prof, 61-64, chmn dept, 69-76, PROF MATH, SOUTHERN CONN STATE COL, 64- *Personal Data:* b Boston, Mass, Jan 2, 21. *Educ:* Mass State Col Bridgewater, BS, 42; Boston Col, MA, 46; Univ Wis, PhD(math, hist sci), 61. *Prof Exp:* Instr math, Col St Teresa, Minn, 46-52; asst prof, Dominican Col, Wis, 52-61. *Mem:* Math Asn Am; Hist Sci Soc; Sigma Xi. *Res:* History of medieval mathematics; mathematics education. *Mailing Add:* Seven Valley Brook Rd Branford CT 06405-6032

SCHRADER, GEORGE FREDERICK, INDUSTRIAL ENGINEERING, RESEARCH ADMINISTRATION. *Current Pos:* chmn, Dept Indust Eng & Mgt Systs, Univ Cent Fla, actg chmn, Dept Eng Math & Comput Systs, actg dir, Transp Systs Inst, Univ Cent Fla, 69-77, assoc dean, 77-86, assoc vpres res, 86-88, PROF INDUST ENG & MGT SYSTS, UNIV CENT FLA, 69-, EMER ASSOC DEAN, COL ENG, 88- *Personal Data:* b Mattoon, Ill, July 21, 20; m 44, Joyce Aspinall; c David & Julie. *Educ:* Univ Ill, BS, 47, MS, 51, PhD(indust eng), 60. *Prof Exp:* Instr mech eng, Univ Ill, 47-51, asst prof indust eng, 53-61; prof, Okla State Univ, 61-62; prof & head dept, Kans State Univ, 62-66; dir tech serv, Univ Nebr, Lincoln, 66-67; dir indust res, 67-69. *Concurrent Pos:* Consult, Joliet Ord & Ammunition Ctr, 53, Caterpillar Tractor Co, 54, Champion Paper & Fibre Co, 56-57, Ill Bell Tel Co, 59-60, Bayer & McElrath, Inc, 64-66 & Air Force Oper Anal Group, 63-71. *Mem:* Fel Inst Indust Engrs; Am Soc Eng Educ; Nat Soc Prof Engrs. *Res:* Manufacturing processes; management systems; research and development administration. *Mailing Add:* 2805 Sugarhill Ct Orlando FL 32822

SCHRADER, KEITH WILLIAM, MATHEMATICS. *Current Pos:* from asst prof to assoc prof, 66-78, chmn dept, 79-82 & 85-88, PROF MATH, UNIV MO, COLUMBIA, 78- *Personal Data:* b Apr 22, 38; US citizen; div; c Jeffrey & Melinda. *Educ:* Univ Nebr, BS, 59, MS, 61, PhD(math), 66. *Prof Exp:* Engr electronic warfare, Sylvania Electronic Defense Lab, Gen Tel & Electronics Corp, 63-64. *Concurrent Pos:* NASA study grant, 66-68; NSF study grant, 68-70. *Mem:* Am Math Soc; Soc Indust & Appl Math. *Res:* Differential equations; boundary value problems; oscillation; convergence theorems. *Mailing Add:* Univ Mo 202 Math Sci Columbia MO 65211-0001

SCHRADER, LAWRENCE EDWIN, PHYSIOLOGICAL GENETICS. *Current Pos:* DEAN, WASH STATE UNIV, 89- *Personal Data:* b Atchison, Kans, Oct 22, 41; m 63, 81, Elfriede J Massier; c Kimberly, Kristin & Kara. *Educ:* Kans State Univ, BS, 63; Univ Ill, PhD(agron), 67. *Honors & Awards:* Distinguished Serv Award in Agr, Kans State Univ, 87. *Prof Exp:* Res biochemist, US Army Med Res & Nutrit Lab, Denver, Colo, 67-69; from asst prof to prof, Univ Wis-Madison, 69-84; prof & head admin, Univ Ill, Urbana-Champaign, 84-89. *Concurrent Pos:* Vis prof, NC State Univ, Raleigh, 75-76; mem, bd dirs, Crop Sci Soc Am, 77-79, AAAS, 91-94; chief, USDA Competitive Res Grants Off, Wash, 80-81; consult, Agracetus, Middleton, Wis, 81-89. *Mem:* Am Soc Plant Physiologists (secy, 83-85, pres, 87-88); fel AAAS; Am Chem Soc; fel Am Soc Agron; fel Crop Sci Soc Am. *Res:* Nitrogen and carbon metabolism of higher plants; physiological genetics; translocation and source-sink relations; effect of environmental stress on plant growth and metabolism. *Mailing Add:* 1100 N Western Ave Wenatchee WA 98801-1230. *E-Mail:* schrader@wsuvm1.csc.wsu.edu

SCHRADER, R(OBERT) J, CHEMICAL ENGINEERING. *Current Pos:* RETIRED. *Personal Data:* b South Bend, Ind, Oct 27, 18; m 42, Lois B Kreighbaum; c 3. *Educ:* Purdue Univ, BS & MS, 40; Mass Inst Technol, ScD(chem eng), 43. *Prof Exp:* Instr chem eng, Mass Inst Technol, 42-43; asst supt chem prod plant, Clinton Eng Works, 43-45, head dept chem eng, 45-46; sr engr, Tenn Eastman Corp, 46-52, in charge develop & process improv dept, 52-53, supt polyethylene dept, 53-60, asst to supt to gen supt, Plastics Div, 60-75, works mgr, Div Eastman Kodak Co, 75-81, vpres, 81-83. *Mem:* Am Chem Soc; Am Inst Chem Engrs; Soc Plastics Engrs. *Res:* Development and pilot plant work on new chemical processes; effect of pressure on enthalpy of hydrocarbons and their mixtures; synthetic resins and plastics; petroleum, natural gas and textile products; direct hydration of ethylene to ethyl alcohol; flame cracking of hydrocarbons to acetylene and ethylene. *Mailing Add:* 21 Palisades Blvd Longview TX 75605

SCHRADER, WILLIAM THURBER, ENDOCRINOLOGY, MOLECULAR BIOLOGY. *Current Pos:* VPRES ENDOCRINOL, LIGANT PHARMACEUT, 95- *Personal Data:* b Mineola, NY, Oct 12, 43; m 67. *Educ:* Johns Hopkins Univ, BA, 64, PhD(biol), 69. *Prof Exp:* Res assoc obstet & gynec, Med Sch, Vanderbilt Univ, 71, asst prof, 71-72; from asst prof to prof cell biol, Baylor Col Med, 72-95. *Mem:* Endocrine Soc. *Res:* Molecular mechanisms of hormone action; gene regulation in eukaryotic cells. *Mailing Add:* Ligant Pharmaceut 10255 Science Center Dr San Diego CA 92121

SCHRADIE, JOSEPH, PHARMACOGNOSY. *Current Pos:* Asst prof, 66-70, ASSOC PROF PHARMACOG, COL PHARM, UNIV TOLEDO, 70-, CHMN, DEPT MED CHEM & PHARMACOG, 81- *Personal Data:* b Los Angeles, Calif, July 19, 33; m 60; c 3. *Educ:* Univ Southern Calif, PharmD, 57, MS, 61, PhD(pharmaceut chem, pharmacog), 66. *Mem:* Am Pharmaceut Asn; Acad Pharmaceut Sci; NY Acad Sci; Am Soc Pharmacog. *Res:* Isolation of natural products from marine organisms, also their cultivation; biosynthesis and intermediary metabolism of carbohydrates in lower and higher plants; isolation of antibiotics; biological and phytochemical screens of higher plants. *Mailing Add:* Dept Pharmacog Univ Toledo Toledo OH 43606

SCHRADY, DAVID ALAN, OPERATIONS RESEARCH. *Current Pos:* asst prof opers res, Naval Postgrad Sch, 65-70, assoc prof, 71-74, chmn, Dept Opers Res & Admin Sci, 74-76, dean info & policy sci, 76-80, actg provost, 80-82, provost, 82-87, ACAD DEAN, NAVAL POSTGRAD SCH, 80-, PROF OPERS RES, 88- *Personal Data:* b Akron, Ohio, Nov 11, 39; m 62, Mary Hilt; c 3. *Educ:* Case Inst Technol, BS, 61, MS, 63, PhD(opers res), 65. *Honors & Awards:* Wanner Award Mil, Opers Res Soc, 84, Kimball Medal, 94; Goodeve Medal, Oper Res Soc, UK, 92. *Prof Exp:* Assoc dir, Off Naval Res, 70-71. *Concurrent Pos:* Consult, Decision Studies Group, 67-69, Litton-Mellonics, 67-70 & Naval Supply Systs Command, 70-73, Singapore Ministry Defense, 83. *Mem:* Opers Res Soc Am (treas, 76-79, vpres, 82-83, pres, 83-84); fel Mil Opers Res Soc (pres, 78-79); Inst Mgt Sci; Int Fedn Oper Res Socs (treas, 88-). *Res:* Command and control; logistics. *Mailing Add:* Naval Postgrad Sch Monterey CA 93943-5000. *Fax:* 408-656-2595

SCHRAER, HARALD, CELL BIOLOGY. *Current Pos:* RETIRED. *Personal Data:* b Boston, Mass, June 10, 20; m 52; c 1. *Educ:* Syracuse Univ, AB, 48, MA, 49; Cornell Univ, PhD(biol), 54. *Prof Exp:* Res assoc radiol, Albert Einstein Med Ctr, Pa, 52-56; res assoc physics, Pa State Univ, University Park, 56-58, sr res assoc biophys, 58-61, assoc prof, 61-67, prof, 67-85. *Concurrent Pos:* Vis scientist, NIH, 61; res assoc, Dept Anat, Med Sch, Harvard Univ, 67-68. *Mem:* AAAS; Am Physiol Soc; Soc Exp Biol & Med; Am Soc Cell Biol; Sigma Xi; Am Soc Bone & Mineral Res. *Res:* Structural-functional aspects of metal transport; electron microscopy; skeletal physiology; mineral physiology. *Mailing Add:* 830 Box Spring Mountain Rd Moreno Valley CA 92557

SCHRAG, JOHN L, POLYMER CHEMISTRY. *Current Pos:* Proj assoc chem, 67-70, asst prof chem & eng, 70-71, asst prof chem, 71-75, ASSOC PROF CHEM, UNIV WIS-MADISON, 75- *Personal Data:* b Siloam Springs, Ark, Apr 14, 37; m 60; c 1. *Educ:* Univ Omaha, BA, 59; Okla State Univ, MS, 61, PhD(physics), 67. *Concurrent Pos:* Alfred P Sloan Found res fel, 73-74. *Mem:* Am Chem Soc; Am Phys Soc; Sigma Xi; AAAS; NY Acad Sci. *Res:* Optical and mechanical properties of macromolecules. *Mailing Add:* Dept Chem Univ Wis 1101 University Ave Madison WI 53706. *Fax:* 608-262-0381

SCHRAG, ROBERT L(EROY), ELECTROMAGNETIC FIELDS. *Current Pos:* PROF ELEC ENG, WICHITA STATE UNIV, 57- *Personal Data:* b Moundridge, Kans, Nov 10, 24; m 66; c 2. *Educ:* Kans State Univ, BSEE, 45; Calif Inst Technol, MSEE, 46; Pa State Univ, PhD(ionosphere res), 54. *Prof Exp:* Res analyst, Douglas Aircraft Co, 46-48; instr elec eng, Pa State Univ, 48-53; mem tech staff, Bell Tel Labs, 54-57. *Concurrent Pos:* NSF res grants, 62-64. *Mem:* Inst Elec & Electronics Engrs. *Res:* Electro-impulse deicing. *Mailing Add:* Dept Elec Eng Wallace Hall Box 44 Wichita State Univ 1845 Fairmount Ave Wichita KS 67208

SCHRAGE, F EUGENE, PLASTIC FILMS DEVELOPMENT, AUTOMOTIVE ANTIFREEZE DEVELOPMENT. *Current Pos:* RETIRED. *Personal Data:* b Oak Park, Ill, July 13, 34; m 56; c 3. *Educ:* Univ Ill, BA, 56; Northwestern Univ, MS, 57. *Prof Exp:* Group leader res & develop, Films Dept, Union Carbide, 63-69, tech mgr, Films & Packaging Div, 69-73, opers mgr, Home & Auto Div, 73-77, dir res & develop, 77-86; dir, res & develop, First Brands Corp, 86-93. *Mem:* Soc Plastics Indust. *Res:* Development of plastic wrap and bags, antifreeze, automobile wax, and oil and gas additives. *Mailing Add:* 35 Harwtch Lane West Hartford CT 06117

SCHRAGE, ROBERT W, PETROLEUM & CHEMICAL INDUSTRY ECONOMIC RESEARCH. *Current Pos:* RETIRED. *Personal Data:* b Brooklyn, NY, July 1, 25; m 65, Rosemarie Criscuoli. *Educ:* Columbia Univ, BA, 46, BS & MS, 48, PhD(chem eng), 50. *Prof Exp:* Engr, East Coast Tech Serv Div, Esso Standard Oil Co, 50-58, sect head tech div, Mfg Dept, 58-61, sect head, Econ Coord Dept, Esso Standard Eastern Inc, 62-66, mgr econ & planning, Esso Eastern Chem Inc, 66-71, mgr corp affairs, Essochem Eastern Ltd, Hong Kong, 71-73, econ res adv, Exxon Chem Am, 73-86. *Mem:* Am Chem Soc. *Res:* Petroleum and chemical industry economics. *Mailing Add:* 1752 S Gessner Houston TX 77063

SCHRAM, ALFRED C, BIOCHEMISTRY. *Current Pos:* assoc prof, 65-70, PROF CHEM, WTEX STATE UNIV, 70- *Personal Data:* b Brussels, Belg, Sept 17, 30; US citizen; m 57; c 2. *Educ:* Polytech Inst Brooklyn, BS, 54; Univ Tex, Austin, MA, 56, PhD(chem), 58. *Prof Exp:* Res biochemist, St Barnabas Hosp, Minneapolis, Minn, 58-59; clin instr biochem, Southwestern Med Sch, Univ Tex, 59-62, clin asst prof, 62-65. *Concurrent Pos:* Res biochemist, Vet Admin Hosp, Dallas, 59-65; NIH grant cancer res, 63-65; abstractor, Chem Abstr, 63-; Welch Found res grant, 67-69. *Mem:* AAAS; Am Chem Soc; affil AMA. *Res:* Immunochemistry of synthetic antigens. *Mailing Add:* Hix Rd Canyon TX 79015

SCHRAM, EUGENE P, INORGANIC CHEMISTRY. *Current Pos:* asst prof, 64-69, ASSOC PROF CHEM, OHIO STATE UNIV, 69- *Personal Data:* b Milwaukee, Wis, Apr 19, 34; m 56; c 1. *Educ:* Carroll Col, BS, 56; Purdue Univ, PhD(inorg chem), 62. *Prof Exp:* Res technician, Allis Chalmers Mfg Co, 54-55, res chemist, 56-58; res chemist, Carbon Prod Div, Union Carbide Corp, 62-64. *Mem:* AAAS; Am Chem Soc. *Res:* Chemistry of aluminum heterocycles and molecular compounds containing metal-metal bonds. *Mailing Add:* 4770 Teter Ct Columbus OH 43220-3133

SCHRAM, FREDERICK R, INVERTEBRATE ZOOLOGY, CARCINOLOGY. *Personal Data:* b Chicago, Ill, Aug 11, 43; div; c 1. *Educ:* Loyola Univ, Ill, BS, 65; Univ Chicago, PhD(paleozool), 68. *Prof Exp:* Asst prof, 68-73, assoc prof zool, Eastern Ill Univ, 73-78; chief cur earth & marine sci, Natural Hist Mus, San Diego, 78-87, cur paleont, 78-91; cur paleont, Los Angeles Co Mus Natural Hist, 91-92. *Concurrent Pos:* Res assoc, Scripps Inst Oceanog; adj prof, San Diego State Univ; gen ed, Crustacean Issues, 83-; ed, Contrib Zool, 95- *Mem:* Crustacean Soc; Paleont Soc; fel Linnean Soc London; Soc Integrative Comp Biol; Crustacean Soc China; Palaeont Asn; Brazilian Crustacean Soc; Carcinol Soc Japan. *Res:* Late Paleozoic history of the Malacostraca; comparative anatomy of crustaceans; arthropod relationships and evolution; morphology and systematics of remipede crustaceans; invertebrate morphology and evolution. *Mailing Add:* Inst Syst Biol Box 94766 Amsterdam 1090GT Netherlands

SCHRAMEL, ROBERT JOSEPH, SURGERY. *Current Pos:* From instr to prof surg, 55-76, prof clin surg, 76-89, EMER PROF CLIN SURG, SCH MED, TULANE UNIV, 89- *Personal Data:* b St Louis, Mo, Sept 6, 24; m 47; c 5. *Educ:* Tulane Univ, BS, 45, MD, 48. *Concurrent Pos:* Prin investr, NIH, 57- *Mem:* AAAS; Am Asn Thoracic Surg; NY Acad Sci; Asn Hosp Med Educ; Asn Am Med Cols. *Res:* Pulmonary function in disease states; trauma; extracorporeal circulation; shock; hyperbaric oxygenation; surgical treatment of cardiovascular disease. *Mailing Add:* 518 Fern St New Orleans LA 70118-3830

SCHRAMM, DAVID N, COSMOLOGY, THEORETICAL ASTROPHYSICS. *Current Pos:* assoc prof astrophys, Univ Chicago, 74-76, actg chmn dept, 77, chmn, Dept Astron & Astrophys, 78-84, prof comt conceptual found sci, 84-96, PROF ASTRON & ASTROPHYS, ENRICO FERMI INST & COL, UNIV CHICAGO, 77-, PROF PHYS, 77-, LOUIS BLOCK PROF PHYS SCI, 82-, VPRES RES, 95-, LOUIS BLOCK DISTINGUISHED SERV PROF PHYS SCI, 96- *Personal Data:* b St Louis, Mo, Oct 25, 45; m 86; c D Cary & D Brett. *Educ:* Mass Inst Technol, BS, 67; Calif Inst Technol, PhD(physics), 71. *Honors & Awards:* Gunnar Kullen Mem Lectr, Lund, Sweden, 81; Richtmeyer Mem Award, Am Asn Physics Teachers, 84; Vollmer Fries Lectr, Rensselaer Polytech Inst, 84; John C & Nettie V David Mem Lectr, Univ Nebr, 85; Chelsey Lectr, Carlton Col, 86; Lawson Lectr, Univ Calif, Riverside, 88; William Law SPS award lectr, Colo Sch Mines, 88; Francis W Bartlett Lectr, Linda Hall Libr Sci & Technol, Kans City, Mo, 91; Spencer Lectr, Univ Kans, 92; Julius Edgar Lilienfeld Prize, Am Phys Soc, 93; Monts Lectr, Mont State Univ, 94; 12th Ann William F Marlor Lectr, Rice Univ, 94; Herzberg Lectr, Carlton Univ, Ottawa, ON, 95; Frontier Lectr, Los Alamos Nat Lab, 95; Wallace Distinguished Lectr, Macalester Col, St Paul, Minn, 96. *Prof Exp:* Res fel physics, Calif Inst Technol, 71-72; asst prof astron & physics, Univ Tex, Austin, 72-74. *Concurrent Pos:* Vis fel, Inst Theoret Astron, Cambridge Eng, 72, Japan Soc Prom Sci, 79; consult, Aerospace Corp, Los Angeles, Calif, 74-78, Lawrence Livermore Lab, Livermore, Calif, 75-, Fermilab, Batavia, Ill, 82-, Los Alamos Nat Lab, 92-; sr vis fel, Inst Astron, Cambridge, Eng, 75; vis prof, Stanford Accelerator Ctr, Stanford Univ, 77; assoc ed, Am J Physics, 78-81, Particle World, 92-; adj prof physics, Univ Utah, 81-; distinguished lectr, Col Sci, Tex A&M Univ, 82; bd trustees, Aspen Ctr Physics, 84-90, chmn, 92-; distinguished vis scientist, Carnegie-Mellon Univ, 85; Alexander von Humboldt Award, Fed Repub Ger, 86; sci assoc, CERN, Geneva, Switz, 90; bd physics & astron, Nat Res Coun, 89-, exec comt, 91-, vchmn, 92-93, chmn, 93-; vis prof, Miller Inst, Univ Calif, Berkeley, 92; vis scholar, Univ Ctr Ga, 93; bd govs, Argonne Nat Lab, 96-; bd dirs, Arch Develop Corp,96- *Mem:* Nat Acad Sci; Am Astron Soc; Int Astron Union; fel AAAS; fel Am Acad Arts & Sci; fel Am Phys Soc. *Res:* Theoretical studies of astrophysics with particular emphasis on: cosmology, the origin of the elements, cosmic rays, stellar evolution and supernova, neutrino astrophysics; nucleochronology, the early solar system and black holes; particle physics; author of over 300 published articles and numerous books. *Mailing Add:* Dept Astron Astrophys AAC-140 Univ Chicago 5640 S Ellis Chicago IL 60637. *Fax:* 773-834-0287; *E-Mail:* dns@oddjob.uchicago.edu

SCHRAMM, JOHN GILBERT, ELECTROCHEMICAL ENGINEERING, BIOCHEMICAL ENGINEERING. *Current Pos:* PRES BIO & ELECTRO CHEM ENG, NEXIAL INC, 88- *Personal Data:* b Cincinnati, Ohio, Sept 15, 51; m 80; c 2. *Educ:* Univ Mich, Ann Arbor, BGS, 77. *Prof Exp:* Chemist, energy develop assoc, Gulf & Western, 78-82; sr instr assoc chem eng, dept chem eng, Col Eng, Univ Mich, 82-87; vpres oper, res & develop, Diamond Gen Develop Corp, 87-88. *Mem:* AAAS; Am Inst Chem Engrs; Am Chem Soc. *Res:* Bio-sensors for use in biological or medical environments; electrochemical detectors for oxygen, hydrogen, pH, CO2 or bio-organic molecules of interest. *Mailing Add:* 1505 Pear St Ann Arbor MI 48105

SCHRAMM, LAWRENCE PETER, AUTONOMIC NERVOUS SYSTEM, SPINAL CORD NEUROPHYSIOLOGY. *Current Pos:* PROF BIOMED ENG, JOHNS HOPKINS UNIV, 70- *Personal Data:* b Westchester, Pa, Dec 3, 38; m 60, Diana Campuzano; c Christopher. *Educ:* Haverford Col, BS, 61; Univ Rochester, PhD(physiol), 70. *Prof Exp:* Asst prof biomed eng, Case Western Res Univ, 69-70. *Mem:* Am Physiol Soc; Soc Neurosci; Biomed Eng Soc. *Res:* Modulation of sympathetic activity by spinal cord systems; anatomy, physiology and function of the uterine innervation and circulation. *Mailing Add:* Dept Biomed Eng Johns Hopkins Univ Sch Med 720 Rutland Ave Traylor 606 Baltimore MD 21205-2195. *Fax:* 410-955-9826; *E-Mail:* lschramm@eureka.wbme.jhu.edu

SCHRAMM, LEE CLYDE, PHARMACOGNOSY. *Current Pos:* sr regional med assoc, 81-96, MGR SCI AFFAIRS, CLIN TRIALS CTR, SMITHKLINE BEECHAM CLIN LABS, 96- *Personal Data:* b Portsmouth, Ohio, July 20, 34; m 64, Linda Christine Schade; c John, George & Elizabeth. *Educ:* Ohio State Univ, BSc, 57; Univ Conn, MS, 59, PhD(pharmacog), 62. *Honors & Awards:* Kilmer Prize, Am Pharmaceut Asn, 57. *Prof Exp:* Asst prof, Col Pharm, Univ Minn, Minneapolis, 61-67; assoc prof pharmacog & head dept, Sch Pharm, Univ Ga, 67-81. *Concurrent Pos:* Chmn pharmacog & natural prod sect, Acad Pharmaceut Sci, 79-80; chmn sect teachers biol sci, Am Asn Cols Pharm, 75-76. *Mem:* Am Soc Heath Syst Pharmacists; Am Asn Clin Chem; Am Soc Pharmacog (treas, 75-81); Am Soc Microbiol. *Res:* Phytochemistry, particularly plants and fungi with potential medicinal or toxic activity. *Mailing Add:* 266 Deerhill Dr Bogart GA 30622. *Fax:* 706-546-0217

SCHRAMM, MARTIN WILLIAM, JR, PETROLEUM GEOLOGY. *Current Pos:* PRES, SCHRAMM & ASSOC CONSULTS, 85- *Personal Data:* b Pittsburgh, Pa, Apr 21, 27; m 53; c 4. *Educ:* Univ Pittsburgh, BS, 54, MS, 55; Univ Okla, PhD(geol), 63. *Prof Exp:* Explor geologist, Gulf Oil Corp,

55-57; consult petrol, A W McCoy Assocs, 57-59; proj supvr explor res, Cities Serv Oil Co, Okla, 59-69; mgr, Foreign Div, White Shield Explor Corp, 69-70 & explor & exploitation, White Shield Oil & Gas Corp, 70- 72, consult geologist, 72-74; exec vpres, Geoquest Int, Inc, 74-82; pres & chief exec officer, Seagull Int Explor, Inc, 82-85. *Mem:* Am Asn Petrol Geologists; Am Inst Prof Geologists; fel Geol Soc Am. *Res:* Middle Ordovician stratigraphy and paleogeology; basin analysis; environments of deposition; seismic stratigraphy. *Mailing Add:* 1922 Anvil Dr Houston TX 77090

SCHRAMM, MARY ARTHUR, NURSE ANESTHESIA. *Current Pos:* RETIRED. *Personal Data:* b Yankton Co, SDak, Mar 20, 32. *Educ:* Mt Marty Col, BA, 65; Univ SDak, Vermillion, PhD(physiol), 77. *Honors & Awards:* James Award, 88; Helen Lamb Award, 91. *Prof Exp:* Instr anesthesia, Sch Nurse Anesthesia, Sacred Heart Hosp, 56-69, prog dir & dept head, 65-69; instr physiol, Univ SDak, Vermillion, 69-72; asst prof, Mt Marty Col, Yankton, SDak, 71-76, div head, Health Sci, 72-73 & 84-86, assoc prof & prog dir, 77-81, prof anesthesia, 81-93, prog dir, 88-93; nurse anesthesia educ consult, Jamaica, Wis, 80-84, Guyana, SA, 94. *Concurrent Pos:* Nursing serv dir & anesthetist, St Michael's Hosp, Tyndall, SDak, 56-; educ consult, St Scholastica Col, Duluth, 75, St Cloud Hosp, Minn, 76 & Jamaica Sch Nurse Anesthesia, Proj Hope, 81-84; biomed sci lectr, Am Asn Nurse Anesthetists, 78-81. *Mem:* Am Asn Nurse Anesthetists; Am Asn Respiratory Care; AAAS; Am Nurses Asn. *Res:* Taurine in dog heart slices; respiratory and renal liver physiology; anesthesia research, practice and education. *Mailing Add:* Sacred Heart Monestery Mt Marty Col Yankton SD 57078

SCHRAMM, RAYMOND EUGENE, MATERIALS SCIENCE, PHYSICS. *Current Pos:* PHYSICIST MAT, MAT RELIABILITY DIV, NAT INST STANDARDS & TECHNOL, 67- *Personal Data:* b St Charles, Mo, Aug 11, 41. *Educ:* Regis Col, Colo, BS, 64; Mich Technol Univ, MS, 65. *Honors & Awards:* Bronze Medal, Dept Com, 90. *Prof Exp:* Jr physicist nuclear physics, Ames Lab, Iowa State Univ, 65-66. *Mem:* Am Asn Physics Teachers; AAAS. *Res:* Microstructural properties of deformed metals; cryogenic mechanical properties of composites; ultrasonic non-destructive evaluation of metals using long-wavelength electromagnetic acoustic transducers. *Mailing Add:* Mat Reliability Div Nat Inst Stand & Technol Boulder CO 80303-3328. *Fax:* 303-497-5030

SCHRAMM, ROBERT FREDERICK, CHEMISTRY. *Current Pos:* asst prof to assoc prof, 70-75, PROF CHEM, EAST STROUDSBURG STATE COL, 75- *Personal Data:* b Philadelphia, Pa, Feb 23, 42; m 68; c 2. *Educ:* St Joseph's Col, Pa, BS, 64; Univ Pa, PhD(chem), 69. *Prof Exp:* Advan Res Projs Agency fel, Univ Pa, 69-70. *Concurrent Pos:* Lectr, St Joseph's Col, Pa, 70. *Mem:* AAAS; Am Chem Soc; Sigma Xi. *Res:* Synthesis and characterization of coordination complexes of palladium, platinum and gold; molecular orbital calculations; application of computers to scientific instruction. *Mailing Add:* Three Smithfield Village East Stroudsburg PA 18301-9046

SCHRAMM, ROBERT WILLIAM, NUCLEAR SPECTROSCOPY. *Current Pos:* RETIRED. *Personal Data:* b Wheeling, WVa, Nov 13, 34; m 67; c Adriane & Darian. *Educ:* Liberty State Col, BS, 58; Univ WVa, MS, 59. *Prof Exp:* From instr to assoc prof physics, West Liberty State Col, 58-97, head dept, 66-71. *Concurrent Pos:* Dir, Regional Sci Fair, 58-88; archivist, West Liberty State Col, 77-; adj prof photog, 95-97. *Mem:* Am Asn Physics Teachers; Am Phys Soc. *Res:* Nuclear spectroscopy. *Mailing Add:* Dept Math & Physics West Liberty State Col West Liberty WV 26074. *Fax:* 304-336-7893; *E-Mail:* schrammr@wlsvax.wvnet.edu

SCHRAMM, VERN LEE, BIOCHEMISTRY. *Current Pos:* PROF & CHMN BIOCHEM, ALBERT EINSTEIN COL MED, NY, 87- *Personal Data:* b Howard, SDak, Nov 9, 41; m 64, Deanna Hogarth; c Julie & Nara. *Educ:* SDak State Col, BS, 63; Harvard Univ, SM, 65; Australian Nat Univ, PhD(biochem), 69. *Prof Exp:* Nat Res Coun-NSF res assoc, NASA Ames Res Ctr, 69-71; from asst prof to prof biochem, Sch Med, Temple Univ, 76-87. *Concurrent Pos:* Mem biochem study sect, NIH, 81-85. *Mem:* AAAS; Am Chem Soc; Am Soc Biol Chem. *Res:* Mechanism of enzymes of nucleotide degradation and biosynthesis; transition state analysis of enzyme-catalyzed reactions; logical inhibitor design for the production of novel antibiotics. *Mailing Add:* Dept Biochem A Einstein Col Med 1300 Morris Park Ave Bronx NY 10461-1975

SCHRANK, AULINE RAYMOND, PHYSIOLOGY, BIOPHYSICS. *Current Pos:* From instr to assoc prof physiol, Univ Tex, Austin, 39-58, chmn, Dept Zool, 63-70, actg dean, 72-74, assoc dean, 74-78, dean, 78-80, prof, 58-, EMER PROF PHYSIOL, UNIV TEX, AUSTIN, 89- *Personal Data:* b Hamilton, Tex, Aug 15, 15; m 42; c 2. *Educ:* Tarleton Agr Col, AS, 37; Southwest Tex State Col, AB, 37; Univ Tex, PhD(physiol, biophys), 42. *Mem:* AAAS; Am Soc Plant Physiol; Soc Gen Physiol; Biophys Soc; Scand Soc Plant Physiol. *Res:* Bioelectrical fields in relation to growth phenomena and cell correlation; tropisms, regeneration and active transport. *Mailing Add:* Dept Zool Pathol Lab 334 Univ Tex Austin Austin TX 78712

SCHRANK, GLEN EDWARD, PHYSICS. *Current Pos:* RETIRED. *Personal Data:* b Omaha, Nebr, Aug 6, 26; m 47. *Educ:* Univ Calif, Los Angeles, BA, 47, MA, 50, PhD, 53. *Prof Exp:* Res assoc physics, Univ Calif, Los Angeles, 53; from instr to asst prof, Princeton Univ, 53-61; res physicist, Lawrence Radiation Lab, Univ Calif, 61-63; assoc prof physics, Univ Calif, Santa Barbara, 63-89. *Concurrent Pos:* Guest physicist, Brookhaven Nat Lab, 59-; consult, AEC; consult, Giannini Sci Corp, 59. *Mem:* Am Phys Soc; Ital Phys Soc. *Res:* Nuclear and elementary particle physics. *Mailing Add:* 25202 Butler Rd Junction City OR 97448

SCHRANK, GORDON DABNEY, MICROBIOLOGY. *Current Pos:* from asst prof to assoc prof, 81-87, PROF BIOL, ST CLOUD STATE UNIV, 87- *Personal Data:* b San Angelo, Tex, Aug 11, 48; m 75; c 1. *Educ:* Angelo State Univ, BS, 70; Univ Tex Med Br Galveston, PhD(microbiol), 74. *Prof Exp:* Med technologist bact & serol, Univ Tex, Med Br Galveston, 74-75; instr microbiol, Ctr Health Sci, Univ Tenn, Memphis, 75-77, asst prof, 77-81. *Concurrent Pos:* USDA Res Agreement, 78-81 & 93; USAF res fel, Isolation Tech for Legionellae, 84-85; Air Force Off Sponsored Res, Res Contract, 86-87; NSF Instrumentation Grants, 89-91, 90-92. *Mem:* Am Soc Microbiol; Sigma Xi; Micros Soc Am. *Res:* Area of host-parasite relationships in infectious diseases and how immunity may alter these relationships; plasmid fingerprinting in medically significant bacteria. *Mailing Add:* Dept Biol Sci MS 228 St Cloud State Univ 720 Fourth Ave S St Cloud MN 56301. *Fax:* 320-255-4262; *E-Mail:* schrank@tigger.stcloud.msus.edu

SCHRANKEL, KENNETH REINHOLD, TOXICOLOGY, ENVIRONMENTAL HEALTH. *Current Pos:* from res toxicologist to sr res toxicologist, 81-85, dir, 85-91, US VPRES, US FLAVOR & FRAGRANCE SAFETY ASSURANCE, INT FLAVORS & FRAGRANCES, 92- *Personal Data:* b Rice Lake, Wis, Mar 26, 45; m 70, Dawn Porter; c Peter & Stephan. *Educ:* Wartburg Col, BS, 67; Ill State Univ, MS, 73, PhD(biol), 78. *Prof Exp:* Vis asst prof biol, Tex A&M Univ, 78-79; fel trainee, Univ Wis, 79-81. *Concurrent Pos:* Mem, Flavor & Extract Mfr Asn US; mem, Int Regulatory Affairs Comt, 85-, Flavor Ingredient Comt, 85-, Safety Eval Coord Comt, 87- *Mem:* Sigma Xi; Soc Toxicol. *Res:* Mammalian toxicology; biochemical aspects of insect oogenesis; ultrastructural aspects of insect reproduction; dermatoxicology and phototoxicology of fragrance materials; safety and regulatory assessment of flavor and fragrance ingredients. *Mailing Add:* Corp Safety Assurance Int Flavors & Fragrances 1515 Highway 36 Keyport NJ 07735

SCHRANS, THOMAS, SEMICONDUCTOR LASERS, FIBER OPTIC COMMUNICATIONS. *Current Pos:* STAFF SCIENTIST, ORTEL CORP, 95- *Personal Data:* b Gent, Belg, May 23, 64. *Educ:* State Univ Gent, Belg, engr, 87; Calif Inst Technol, MS, 88, PhD(elec eng), 94. *Prof Exp:* Post-doctoral fel, T J Watson Res Labs, IBM, 94-95. *Mem:* Inst Elec & Electronics Engrs. *Res:* Semiconductor and distributed feedback lasers for analog and digital fiber optic communications. *Mailing Add:* Ortel Corp 2015 W Chestnut St Alhambra CA 91803. *E-Mail:* tschrans@ortel.com

SCHRAUT, KENNETH CHARLES, MATHEMATICS. *Current Pos:* From instr to prof, 40-72, head dept math, 54-72, DISTINGUISHED SERV PROF MATH, UNIV DAYTON, 72- *Personal Data:* b Hillsboro, Ill, May 19, 13; m 52; c Marilyn Szora. *Educ:* Univ Ill, AB, 36; Univ Cincinnati, AM, 38, PhD(math), 40. *Concurrent Pos:* Lectr, Wright Field Grad Ctr, Ohio State Univ, 48-52; dir, USAF Proj, Univ Dayton, 52-54; actg prof, Grad Sch, Univ Cincinnati, 58-60; pres, Honor Sem Metrop Dayton, Inc, 65-67, vchmn & bd dir, 85-88, chmn, 88-93, bd mem emer, 93. *Mem:* Am Math Soc; Am Soc Eng Educ; Math Asn Am; Sigma Xi; Nat Asn Adv Health Prof. *Res:* Infinite series; mathematical analysis. *Mailing Add:* 448 Mirage Dr Kokomo IN 46901

SCHRAUZER, GERHARD N, INORGANIC CHEMISTRY. *Current Pos:* PROF CHEM, UNIV CALIF, SAN DIEGO, 66- *Personal Data:* b Franzensbad, Czech, Mar 26, 32; m 57; c 4. *Educ:* Univ Munich, BS, 53, MS, 54, PhD(chem), 56. *Prof Exp:* Res asst chem, Univ Munich, 55-57; res assoc, Monsanto Chem Co, 57-59; res asst chem, Univ Munich, 59-63, lectr inorg chem, 63-64; res supvr, Shell Develop Co, 64-66. *Concurrent Pos:* Ed & Founder, Bioinorg Chem J, 70-; pres & founder, Int Asn Bioinorg Scientists, Inc. *Mem:* Am Chem Soc; NY Acad Sci; Soc Ger Chem. *Res:* Organometallic coordination and enzyme chemistry; homogeneous catalysis; trace element, vitamin and cancer research. *Mailing Add:* Biotrace Element Res Inst 11526 Sorrento Valley Rd Suite A San Diego CA 92121. *Fax:* 619-534-5743; *E-Mail:* schrau@ucsd.edu

SCHRAY, KEITH JAMES, BIO-ORGANIC CHEMISTRY, IMMUNOASSAYS. *Current Pos:* assoc prof, 72-80, PROF CHEM, LEHIGH UNIV, 80- *Personal Data:* b Portland, Ore, Nov 25, 43; m 63; c 7. *Educ:* Univ Portland, BS, 65; Pa State Univ, PhD(phys org chem), 70. *Prof Exp:* NIH fel, Inst Cancer Res, Philadelphia, 70-72. *Mem:* Am Chem Soc. *Res:* Model and enzyme reaction mechanisms; anomerases; enzyme immunoassays; protein-surface binding. *Mailing Add:* Dept Chem Lehigh Univ 27 Memorial Dr W Bethlehem PA 18015-3044

SCHRECK, CARL BERNHARD, FISH BIOLOGY. *Current Pos:* asst unit leader, 75-78, asst prof fisheries, 75-78, LEADER ORE COOP & ASSOC PROF FISHERIES, FISHERIES RES UNIT, 78- *Personal Data:* b San Francisco, Calif, May 18, 44; m 66; c 2. *Educ:* Univ Calif, Berkeley, AB, 66; Colo State Univ, MS, 69, PhD(fish physiol), 72. *Prof Exp:* Asst prof, Va Polytech Inst & State Univ, 72-75. *Mem:* AAAS; Am Fisheries Soc; Am Inst Fishery Res Biologists; Am Soc Zoologists; Sigma Xi. *Res:* Biology of freshwater and anadromous fish with special emphasis on physiology, endocrinology, genetics and organism-environment interactions. *Mailing Add:* 3060 NW Seneca Pl Corvallis OR 97330

SCHRECK, JAMES O(TTO), ORGANIC CHEMISTRY. *Current Pos:* from asst prof to assoc prof, 66-74, chmn dept, 75-81, PROF CHEM, UNIV NORTHERN COLO, 74- *Personal Data:* b Houston, Tex, Nov 6, 37; m 66; c 2. *Educ:* St Thomas Univ, Tex, BA, 59; Tex A&M Univ MS, 62, PhD(chem), 64. *Prof Exp:* Res assoc chem, Ga Inst Technol, 64-65; vis asst prof & fel, La State Univ, 65-66. *Mem:* Am Chem Soc; Sigma Xi. *Res:* development of reduced scale procedures for the organic chemistry laboratory; chemical education. *Mailing Add:* Dept Chem Univ Northern Colo Greeley CO 80639

SCHRECKENBERG, MARY GERVASIA, NEUROBIOLOGY, DEVELOPMENTAL BIOLOGY. *Current Pos:* prof neurobiol, Fairleigh Dickinson Univ, 74-86, DEPT BIOL, GEORGIAN COURT COL, NJ, 86- *Personal Data:* b Paderborn, Germany, Jan 4, 16; US citizen. *Educ:* Cath Univ Am, BS, 52, MS, 54, PhD(zool), 57. *Prof Exp:* Pres & dean, Tombrock Col, Paterson, NJ, 56-62; prof mod biol, Cheng Kung Nat Univ, Tainan, Taiwan, 63-70. *Concurrent Pos:* Trustee, Tombrock Col, 72-74; fel, Columbia Univ, 70; NSF res grants, Univ Tex, Austin, 71; group leader, Eng Profs, Hua Zhang Univ Sci & Technol, Wuhan, China. *Mem:* Soc Neurosci; Soc Develop Biol; Soc Am Zoologists; Sigma Xi; AAAS. *Res:* Problems dealing with developmental neurobiology; brain opiates; neural plasticity. *Mailing Add:* 510B Portsmouth No ORLV Lakewood NJ 08701-6521

SCHREIBEIS, WILLIAM J, INDUSTRIAL HYGIENE, ENVIRONMENTAL ENGINEERING. *Current Pos:* CONSULT, 89- *Personal Data:* b Pittsburgh, Pa, Oct 28, 29; m 80, Arline Stinemire; c Robert L, Joan (Mansfield), Janis (Rickley), Jeffrey (Wakeham). *Educ:* Univ Pittsburgh, BS, 51, MPH, 56. *Prof Exp:* Sanit engr, USPHS, 51-54; pub health engr, City of Pittsburgh Dept Pub Health, 54-56; indust hyg engr, Indust Health Found, Carnegie-Mellon Univ, 56-65; indust hyg engr, Bell Labs, 65-84, mgr, indust hyg & safety, 85-88, prod safety, 88-89. *Concurrent Pos:* Eng comt, Indust Health Found. *Mem:* Am Indust Hyg Asn; Brit Occup Hyg Soc; Semiconductor Safety Asn. *Res:* Evaluation of environmental health and safety hazards. *Mailing Add:* 75 Dogwood Lane Berkeley Heights NJ 07922-2325

SCHREIBER, ALAN D, IMMUNOHEMATOLOGY, ONCOLOGY. *Current Pos:* PROF MED, CANCER CTR, UNIV PA HOSP, 82- *Personal Data:* b Newark, NJ, Feb 26, 42. *Educ:* Albert Einstein Col Med, MD, 67. *Mem:* Am Soc Hemat; Am Asn Physicians; Am Asn Immunologists; Am Soc Clin Invest. *Mailing Add:* Dept Med Cancer Ctr Univ Penn Sch Med 3400 Spruce St Silverstein Pav 7th Fl Philadelphia PA 19104-4274. *Fax:* 215-662-7617

SCHREIBER, B CHARLOTTE, SEDIMENTARY PETROLOGY, STRATIGRAPHY. *Current Pos:* RETIRED. *Personal Data:* b Brooklyn, NY, June 27, 31; wid; c Christie R & Sue A. *Educ:* Wash Univ, AB, 53; Rutgers Univ, New Brunswick, MS, 66; Rensselaer Polytech Inst, PhD(geol), 74. *Honors & Awards:* Levorsen Award, Am Asn Petrol Geologists, 75. *Prof Exp:* Sedimentologist & oceanogr, Alpine Geophys Assoc, 66-68; instr geol, Lehman Col, City Univ New York, 68-69; instr, Barnard Col, Columbia Univ, 69-71; instr, Rensselaer Polytech Inst, 71-72, res asst, 72-74; from asst to prof geol Queens Col NY, 74-94. *Concurrent Pos:* Teaching fel, Rutgers Univ, 63-66; consult sedimentologist, Johnson Soils Inc, 68-70; teaching fel, Rensselaer Polytech Inst, 71-72; NSF res fel, 72-74; NSF energy related res, Imp Col, London, 76-77; assoc ed, Soc Econ & Petrol Geologists J, 77-; res assoc, Lamont-Doherty Geol Observ, Columbia Univ, 78-81, sr res assoc, 81-97. *Mem:* Geol Soc Am; Soc Econ & Petrol Geologists; Am Asn Petrol Geologists. *Res:* Origin and diagenesis of evaporites and associated carbonates; sedimentologic and stratigraphic sequences as developed on continental margins; deformation and tectonics of the Mediterranean; organic matter in evaporative environments. *Mailing Add:* Dept Geol Appalachain State Univ 130 Rankin Sci Bldg Boone NC 28608. *Fax:* 704-675-4537; *E-Mail:* geologo@aol.com

SCHREIBER, DAVID LAURENCE, HYDRAULIC ENGINEERING, HYDROLOGIC ENGINEERING. *Current Pos:* RETIRED. *Personal Data:* b Klamath Falls, Ore, Nov 15, 41; m 63; c 3. *Educ:* Ore State Univ, BS, 63; Wash State Univ, MS, 65, PhD(eng sci), 70. *Honors & Awards:* Robert E Horton Award, Am Geophys Union, 75. *Prof Exp:* Res asst agr & civil eng, Wash State Univ, 63-67, instr, 68-69; asst prof civil eng, Univ Wyo, 67-68; res hydraul engr, Northwest Watershed Res Ctr, Agr Res Serv, USDA, 69-72; sr res engr, Water & Land Resources Dept, Pac Northwest Lab, Battelle Mem Inst, 72-74; hydraul engr, Hydrol-Meteorol Br, Off Nuclear Reactor Regulation, US Nuclear Regulatory Comn, 74-78; consult hydrol engr, 78-80; pres, Schreiber Consult, Inc, 80-89; vpres, Grant Schreiber & Assocs, 89-95. *Concurrent Pos:* Groundwater dispersion honorarium, Argonne Nat Lab, 81. *Mem:* Am Geophys Union; Am Soc Agr Engrs; Am Soc Civil Engrs; Nat Soc Prof Engrs; Nat Water Well Asn; Am Water Resources Asn. *Res:* Hydraulics and hydrology of surface water and ground water; water resources planning and environmental impact analyses; radionuclide and pollutant dispersion in surface water and ground water; radioactive and hazardous waste management and disposal. *Mailing Add:* 303 Park Dr Coeur d'Alene ID 83814

SCHREIBER, ERIC CHRISTIAN, PHARMACOLOGY, ORGANIC CHEMISTRY. *Current Pos:* RETIRED. *Personal Data:* b Frankfurt, Germany, Aug 16, 21; US citizen; m 74; c 4. *Educ:* Polytech Inst Brooklyn, BS, 51, MS, 53; Univ Conn, PhD(pharmacol), 63. *Prof Exp:* Chemist, Nat Dairy Res Lab, 49-51; chemist, Chas Pfizer & Co, NY, 51-58, head radioisotope lab, Conn, 58-63; dept head drug metab, Wm S Merrell Co, 63-66; dir biopharmaceut res, E R Squibb & Sons, Inc, 66-67, dir drug metab, 67-75, assoc dir, Squibb Inst, 75-77, dir Squibb Int Res Ctr, Regensburg, WGer, 75-77; prof pharmacol & dir toxicol & drug metab, 77-83, adj prof med chem, Ctr Health Sci, Univ Tenn, 83-77. *Mem:* Emer fel Am Inst Chem; Am Pharmaceut Asn; Am Soc Pharmacol & Exp Therapeut; fel Acad Pharmaceut Sci. *Res:* Metabolism of drugs; pharmacokinetics; transfer of chemicals from mother to offspring, central nervous system deficits. *Mailing Add:* 830 Harrison Ferry Rd White Pine TN 37890-9550

SCHREIBER, HANS, IMMUNOLOGY OF CANCER, BIOLOGY OF CANCER. *Current Pos:* res assoc oncol, 74-77, from asst prof to assoc prof, 77-85, PROF PATH, UNIV CHICAGO, 86- *Personal Data:* b Quedlinburg, Ger, Feb 5, 44; m 69, Karin Kugler; c Dorothee K, Ute & Maya. *Educ:* Univ Freiburg, MD, 69; Univ Chicago, PhD, 77. *Honors & Awards:* Goedecke Res Prize, 69. *Prof Exp:* Staff mem oncol, Oak Ridge Nat Lab, 70-74. *Concurrent Pos:* Prin investr, 77-; res career develop award, 78-83; prog dir, 85- *Mem:* Am Asn Cancer Res; Am Soc Invest Path; Am Soc Cytol; Am Asn Immunol; Clin Immunol Soc. *Res:* Regulation of immune responses to antigens, particularly to transplants and cancer cells; biology and genetics of tumor specific molecules; cancer immunology. *Mailing Add:* Univ Chicago MC 1089 5841 S Maryland Ave Chicago IL 60637. *Fax:* 773-702-3701; *E-Mail:* hszz@midway.uchicago.edu

SCHREIBER, HENRY DALE, PHYSICAL CHEMISTRY, MATERIALS SCIENCE. *Current Pos:* from asst prof to assoc prof, 76-85, PROF CHEM, VA MIL INST, 86- *Personal Data:* b Lebanon, Pa, Nov 13, 48; m 81, Charlotte Wagner; c Terri & Lea. *Educ:* Lebanon Valley Col, BS, 70; Univ Wis-Madison, PhD(phys chem), 76. *Concurrent Pos:* Res asst, Johnson Space Ctr, NASA, 73-76; dir, Ctr Glass Chem, 85- *Mem:* Am Chem Soc; Am Ceramic Soc; Am Geophys Union; Geochem Soc. *Res:* Oxidation-reduction processes of multivalent elements and gas solubility transport in silicate melts which simulate basaltic magmas as well as simple glass-forming systems; development of "high-tech" glass. *Mailing Add:* Dept Chem Va Mil Inst Letcher Ave Lexington VA 24450. *Fax:* 540-464-7169

SCHREIBER, HENRY PETER, PHYSICAL CHEMISTRY. *Current Pos:* PROF CHEM ENG, POLYTECH SCH MONTREAL, 74- *Personal Data:* b Brunn, Czech, Nov 3, 26; nat Can; m 54; c 4. *Educ:* Univ Manitoba, BSc, 49, MSc, 50; Univ Toronto, PhD(phys chem), 53. *Honors & Awards:* Protective Coatings Award, Chem Inst Can, 77; Medaille Archambault & Alcan Prize, Asn Can-Francaise pour L'Advan Sci, 80; Dunlop Lectr Award, 83. *Prof Exp:* Fel phys chem, Nat Res Coun Can, 53-55; res chemist high polymer systs, Can Industs, Ltd, 55-74. *Mem:* Soc Rheology; Chem Inst Can; Soc Plastics Eng; Adhesion Soc. *Res:* Rheology of high polymer melts; thermodynamics of liquids; structure of macromolecules; polymer properties of surfaces, interfaces. *Mailing Add:* Dept Chem Eng Ecole Polytech Cp 6079 Succursale Centre Ville Montreal PQ H3C 3A7 Can. *Fax:* 714-340-4159; *E-Mail:* schreiber@crasp.polymtl.ca

SCHREIBER, JOSEPH FREDERICK, JR, GEOLOGY. *Current Pos:* assoc prof, 59-66, PROF GEOL, UNIV ARIZ, 66- *Personal Data:* b Baltimore, Md, June 2, 25; m 51; c 2. *Educ:* Johns Hopkins Univ, AB, 48, MA, 50; Univ Utah, PhD, 58. *Prof Exp:* Asst geol, Johns Hopkins Univ, 48-49, jr instr, 49-50; geologist, Chesapeake Bay Inst, Md, 51 & Calif Co, La, 54-55; asst prof geol, Okla State Univ, 55-59. *Concurrent Pos:* Jr geologist, Atlantic Refining Co, Tex, 49, 50 & Shell Oil Co, Wyo, 52. *Mem:* Soc Econ Paleontologists & Mineralogists; Am Asn Petrol Geol; Geol Soc Am; Int Asn Sedimentologists; Am Quaternary Asn. *Res:* Sedimentology; stratigraphy; marine geology. *Mailing Add:* 850 N Citadel Ave Tucson AZ 85748

SCHREIBER, KURT CLARK, PHYSICAL ORGANIC CHEMISTRY. *Current Pos:* from asst prof to assoc prof, Duquesne Univ, 51-58, head dept, 58-72, assoc dean, Col Arts & Sci, 62-66, actg dean, grad sc,, 81-84, PROF CHEM, DUQUESNE UNIV, 58- *Personal Data:* b Vienna, Austria, Feb 23, 22; nat US; m 51, Lillian Berger; c Emanuel, Celia & Samuel. *Educ:* City Col New York, BS, 44; Columbia Univ, AM, 47, PhD(chem), 49. *Honors & Awards:* Pittsburgh Award, Am Chem Soc, 85; Lifetime Achievement Award, Pa Acad Sci, 96. *Prof Exp:* Asst, Columbia Univ, 46-49; res assoc chem, Univ Calif, Los Angeles, 49-51. *Concurrent Pos:* Ed, Pa Acad Sci Newsletter, 79-86; dir, Pa Sci Talent Search, 78-88; pres, Pa Acad Sci, 88-90. *Mem:* Am Chem Soc; Soc Appl Spectros; AAAS. *Res:* Mechanism of organic reactions. *Mailing Add:* 1812 Wightman St Pittsburgh PA 15217

SCHREIBER, LAWRENCE, PLANT PATHOLOGY. *Current Pos:* RETIRED. *Personal Data:* b Chicago, Ill, June 15, 31. *Educ:* Northwestern Univ, BS, 53; Purdue Univ, MS, 59, PhD, 61. *Prof Exp:* Plant pathologist, Sci & Educ Admin-Agr Res, USDA, 61-94. *Res:* Soil microbiology; vascular wilt diseases; general diseases of shade trees and ornamental plants. *Mailing Add:* 724 Hyatts Rd Delaware OH 43015

SCHREIBER, MARVIN MANDEL, AGRONOMY, PLANT PHYSIOLOGY. *Current Pos:* assoc prof, 59-73, PROF WEED SCI, PURDUE UNIV, 73- *Personal Data:* b Springfield, Mass, Oct 17, 25; m 49, Phyllis Altman; c Michelle. *Educ:* Univ Mass, BS, 50; Univ Ariz, MS, 51; Cornell Univ, PhD(agron, plant physiol), 54. *Prof Exp:* Asst prof agron, Cornell Univ, 54-59. *Concurrent Pos:* Res agronomist, Agr Res Serv, USDA, 56- *Mem:* Fel AAAS; fel Am Soc Agron; fel Weed Sci Soc Am; Int Weed Sci Soc (pres, 79-81); Sigma Xi; Controlled Release Soc. *Res:* Phenology of weed species; integrated weed management; weed control in field crops; weed competition in field crops; microenvironment of weed competition; controlled release pesticides; weed science. *Mailing Add:* 106 Dogwood Ct West Lafayette IN 47906

SCHREIBER, MELVYN HIRSH, RADIOLOGY. *Current Pos:* From instr to assoc prof, 59-67, PROF RADIOL, UNIV TEX MED BR GALVESTON, 67-, CHMN RADIOL, 76- *Personal Data:* b Galveston, Tex, May 28, 31; m 77; c 4. *Educ:* Univ Tex, BA, 53, MD, 55. *Concurrent Pos:* Markle Found scholar, 63-68; mem bd trustees, Am Bd Radiol. *Mem:* Asn Univ Radiol; fel Am Col Radiol; Am Roentgen Ray Soc; Radiol Soc NAm; Soc Chmn Acad Radiol Depts; Am Bd Radiol. *Res:* Cardiovascular and renal disease. *Mailing Add:* Dept Radiol Univ Tex Med Br Galveston TX 77555

SCHREIBER, PAUL J, MOMENTUM SPACE WAVE FUNCTION. *Current Pos:* PHYSICIST INFRARED DETECTORS & ELECTRO-OPTICS, AVIONICS LAB, ELECTRONICS TECHNOL DIV, AIR FORCE WRIGHT AERONAUT LAB, 62- *Personal Data:* b Buffalo, NY, June 23, 40; m 62; c 2. *Educ:* Univ Rochester, BS, 62; Univ Dayton, MS, 69; State Univ NY, Buffalo, PhD(physiol), 79. *Mem:* Am Phys Soc. *Res:* Atomic structure of multi-electron atoms in momentum space; developing helium atom mometum space wave function; infrared heterodyne dectors and special properties of infrared detectors; helium compton profile; electro optics. *Mailing Add:* 2000 Stayman Dr Dayton OH 45440

SCHREIBER, R E, NUCLEAR PHYSICS. *Current Pos:* RETIRED. *Personal Data:* b McMinnville, Ore, Nov 11, 10. *Educ:* Linfield Col, BS, 31; Univ Ore, MS, 32; Purdue Univ, PhD(physics), 41. *Prof Exp:* Res scientist, Los Alamos Nat Lab, 43-74. *Mem:* Fel Am Phys Soc. *Mailing Add:* 4429 Trinity Dr Los Alamos NM 87544

SCHREIBER, RICHARD WILLIAM, BOTANY, CELL BIOLOGY. *Current Pos:* RETIRED. *Personal Data:* b Lawrence, Mass, Apr 4, 17; m 47; c 1. *Educ:* Univ NH, BS, 51, MS, 52; Univ Wis, PhD(bot), 56. *Prof Exp:* Instr biol, Exten Ctr, Univ Wis-Green Bay, 55-57; from asst prof to assoc prof bot, Univ NH, 57-67, prof, 67-87. *Mem:* AAAS; Sigma Xi; NY Acad Sci; Am Soc Cell Biol. *Res:* Metabolic autonomy and evolution of chloroplasts; structure and function of the kinetochore. *Mailing Add:* 42 Cherry Lane Madbury NH 03820

SCHREIBER, ROBERT ALAN, BIOLOGICAL PSYCHOLOGY, BEHAVIORAL GENETICS. *Current Pos:* asst prof, 74-80, ASSOC PROF BIOCHEM, UNIV TENN CTR HEALTH SCI, 80- *Personal Data:* b Brooklyn, NY, Feb 11, 40; m 67; c 2. *Educ:* Univ NC, Chapel Hill, BA, 65; Univ Colo, Boulder, MA, 69, PhD(psychol), 70. *Prof Exp:* Fel dept biochem, Med Univ SC, 70-74. *Concurrent Pos:* NIMH fel, Med Univ SC, 72-73. *Mem:* Soc Neurosci; Behavior Genetics Asn; Int Soc Develop Psychobiol; Sigma Xi. *Res:* Central nervous system hyperreactivity, using mice susceptible to sound-induced seizures; brain energy reserves which are immediately available; physical dependence on ethanol. *Mailing Add:* 10910 Dunbrook Dr Houston TX 77070-3940

SCHREIBER, SIDNEY S, PHYSIOLOGY, NUCLEAR MEDICINE. *Current Pos:* instr clin med, 59-64, from asst prof to assoc prof med, 64-74, PROF CLIN MED, SCH MED, NY UNIV, 74- *Personal Data:* b NY, May 1, 21; m 45, Freda Glass; c John & Hope. *Educ:* City Col New York, BS, 41; NY Univ, MS, 45, MD, 49. *Honors & Awards:* Linder Surg Prize. *Prof Exp:* Instr physics, Townsend Harris, 41-42; instr biol, City Col NY, 42 & NY Univ, 45; instr histol, Hunter Col, 50. *Concurrent Pos:* Clin asst, Mt Sinai Hosp, 52-58, sr clin asst, 58-; consult internist, Radioisotope Unit, Vet Admin Hosp, Bronx, sr consult, Dept Nuclear Med, 52- & New York, 56-; instr, Hunter Col, 60-61; assoc ed, Alcoholism J. *Mem:* AAAS; fel Am Col Physicians; Int Study Group Res Cardiac Metab; Int Soc Heart Res; Sigma Xi; Am Col Nuclear Physicians. *Res:* Nerve regeneration; endocrinology; effect of hormones on tissue growth; effect of anti-folic acid substance on tissue growth; electrolyte metabolism of heart muscle; use of radioactive isotopes in physiology; cation exchange of heart muscle; protein metabolism in heart muscle in stress, hypertension, alcohol and ischemia. *Mailing Add:* Dept Nuclear Med NY Vet Admin Hosp 423 E 23rd St New York NY 10010-4004

SCHREIBER, STUART L, CHEMICAL BIOLOGY. *Current Pos:* PROF, DEPT CHEM & CHEM BIOL, HARVARD UNIV, 88- *Personal Data:* b Fairfax, Va, Feb 6, 56; m 81, Mimi Suzanne Packman. *Educ:* Univ Va, BA, 77; Harvard Univ, PhD(org chem), 81. *Honors & Awards:* Presidential Young Investr Award, NSF, 85; Arthur C Cope Scholar Award, Am Chem Soc, 86; Ciba-Geigy Drew Award, Biomed Res, 92; Merit Award, NIH, 92; Rhone-Poulenc Silver Medal, Royal Soc Chem, 92; Eli Lilly Award, Am Chem Soc, 93; DuPont Merck Young Investr Award, Protein Soc, 95. *Prof Exp:* From asst prof to assoc prof, Yale Univ, 81-86, prof, 86-88. *Concurrent Pos:* Consult, Pfizer, 83-91; investr, Howard Hughes Med Inst, 94- *Mem:* Nat Acad Sci; AAAS; Am Soc Microbiol; Am Soc Biochem & Molecular Biol; Am Chem Soc; Fedn Am Socs Exp Biol; Am Acad Arts & Sci; Am Soc Cell Biol; Clin Immunol Soc; Protein Soc. *Res:* Chemical biology; synthesis and use of cell permeable ligands that function as equivalents to conditional alleles, providing a loss or gain of cellular function, and the discovery of such ligands using protein structure based combinatorial chemistry. *Mailing Add:* Biol Dept Harvard Univ 12 Oxford St Cambridge MA 02138

SCHREIBER, THOMAS PAUL, ELECTRON MICROSCOPY. *Current Pos:* RETIRED. *Personal Data:* b Detroit, Mich, Mar 5, 24; m 53; c 4. *Educ:* Univ Notre Dame, BS, 46; Univ Mich, MS, 48. *Prof Exp:* Qual control engr, US Rubber Co, 46; jr physicist, Phys Instrumentation Dept, Gen Motors Corp, 47-49, from res physicist to sr res physicist, 49-59, staff res scientist, Anal Chem Dept, 59-87, sr staff res scientist & group leader microstruct characterization, 85-87, sr tech staff, 87-89. *Mem:* AAAS; Microbeam Anal Soc. *Res:* Electron probe microanalysis; scanning electron microscopy; surface analysis by electron spectroscopy; analytical electron microscopy. *Mailing Add:* 650 Country Club Dr St Clair Shores MI 48082-1063

SCHREIBER, WILLIAM F(RANCIS), ELECTRONICS. *Current Pos:* RETIRED. *Personal Data:* b New York, NY, Sept 18, 25. *Educ:* Columbia Univ, BS, 45, MS, 47; Harvard Univ, PhD(appl physics), 53. *Honors & Awards:* Honors Award, Tech Asn Graphic Arts, 83; David Sarnoff Gold Medal, Soc Motion Picture & TV Engrs, 90; Gold Medal, Int Soc Optical, Eng, 91. *Prof Exp:* Jr engr, Sylvania Elec Prod, Inc, 47-49; res assoc, Harvard Univ, 53; res physicist, Technicolor Corp, 53-59; from assoc prof to prof elec eng, Mass Inst Technol, 59-90, Bernard Gordon prof, 79-83, dir, Advan TV Res Prog, 83-89. *Concurrent Pos:* Consult, Sylvania Elec Prod, Inc, 53, 60, Technicolor Corp, 59-62, Smithsonian Astrophys Observ, 61-64, Raytheon Corp, 62-64, ECRM, Inc, 68-78 & Addressograph-Multigraph, 78-; dir, Shintron Corp, 62- & ECRM, Inc, 68-78; vis prof, Indian Inst Technol, Kanpur, 64-66, Univ Que & Nat Inst Sci Res, 80-81; consult, Assoc Press, Electronic Image Systs, Inc, Shintron Co, Inc, Am Int, Inc, Scitex, Inc, Comugraphic, Inc, Harris, Inc & EFI, Inc. *Mem:* Nat Acad Eng; Fel Inst Elec & Electronics Engrs; Sigma Xi. *Res:* Application of information theory to image transmission systems; image processing for the graphic arts; laser scanners; author of 12 publications. *Mailing Add:* Mass Inst Technol 36-545 Cambridge MA 02139. *Fax:* 617-253-7302; *E-Mail:* wfs@image.mit.edu

SCHREIBER, WILLIAM LEWIS, ORGANIC CHEMISTRY. *Current Pos:* PROJ CHEMIST ORG SYNTHESIS, INT FLAVORS & FRAGRANCES INC, 71- *Personal Data:* b New York, NY, Aug 10, 43; m 66; c 2. *Educ:* Mass Inst Technol, BS, 65; Univ Rochester, PhD(chem), 70. *Prof Exp:* Res assoc org chem, Rockefeller Univ, 69-71. *Mem:* Am Chem Soc; Sigma Xi. *Res:* Fragrance chemical synthesis; terpene chemistry. *Mailing Add:* Int Flavors & Fragrances Inc R&D 1515 State Rte 36 Union Beach NJ 07735-3542

SCHREIBMAN, MARTIN PAUL, ZOOLOGY, COMPARATIVE ENDOCRINOLOGY. *Current Pos:* RES ASSOC FISH ENDOCRINOL, NEW YORK AQUARIUM, NY ZOOL SOC, 66- *Personal Data:* b New York, NY, Sept 18, 35; m 60; c 1. *Educ:* Brooklyn Col, BS, 56; NY Univ, MS, 59, PhD(biol), 62. *Prof Exp:* From instr to assoc prof, 62-72, prof biol, Brooklyn Col, 72- *Concurrent Pos:* NSF res grants, 65-70 & 77-80; City Univ New York res grant, 77-81; res collabr, Brookhaven Nat Lab, 77-; NIH grants, 80- *Mem:* AAAS; Am Soc Zoologists; Endocrine Soc; Sigma Xi. *Res:* Comparative endocrinology of lower vertebrates, especially teleosts and relating to pituitary cytology and function; osmoregulation; melanogenesis; effects of hypophysectomy on endocrine functions; genetic control of sexual maturation and aging; hypothalamic-pituitary-gonadal axis. *Mailing Add:* Dept Biol City Univ NY Brooklyn Col 2901 Bedford Ave Brooklyn NY 11210-2813

SCHREIDER, BRUCE DAVID, CLINICAL PHARMACOLOGY, PHYSIOLOGY. *Current Pos:* Res assoc toxicol, Dept Pharmacol & Physiol Sci, 75-81, asst prof, 81-90, ASSOC PROF, ANESTHESIA & CLIN PHARMACOL, UNIV CHICAGO, 90- *Personal Data:* b Denver, Colo, Mar 8, 46. *Educ:* Univ Chicago, BS, 68, MD & PhD(pharmacol & physiol), 75. *Mem:* AAAS; Sigma Xi. *Res:* Hepatic microsomal enzyme induction and inhibition by various therapeutic and environmental agents and the interactions between these agents. *Mailing Add:* 1417 W Barry Ave Chicago IL 60657-4205

SCHREIER, ETHAN JOSHUA, ASTROPHYSICS, ASTRONOMY. *Current Pos:* chief data & oper scientist, 81-88, ASSOC DIR OPER, SPACE TELESCOPE SCI INST, 88- *Personal Data:* b New York, NY, Sept 22, 43. *Educ:* City Univ New York, BS, 64; Mass Inst Technol, PhD(physics), 70. *Prof Exp:* Sr scientist, Am Sci & Eng, 70-73; physicist, Smithsonian Astrophys Observ, 73-81. *Concurrent Pos:* Mem, Comt Data Mgt & Comput, 81-86 & Earth Observ Syst Data & Info Syst, Performance Anal Networks Elec, 91-93. *Mem:* Am Astron Soc; Int Astron Union. *Res:* X-ray astronomy; active galaxies and jets; space science operations; information systems. *Mailing Add:* Space Telescope Sci Inst 3700 San Martin Dr Baltimore MD 21218. *Fax:* 410-338-2519; *E-Mail:* schreier@stsci.edu

SCHREIER, HANSPETER, SOIL & WATER CHEMISTRY, GEOGRAPHIC INFORMATION SYSTEMS. *Current Pos:* fel terrain sci, 77-79, asst prof, 79-90, PROF, DEPT SOIL SCI, INST RESOURCES & ENVIRON, WESTWATER RES CTR, UNIV BC, 90- *Personal Data:* b Basel, Switz, Nov 3, 41; Can citizen; m 70; c 1. *Educ:* Univ Colo, BA, 70; Univ Sheffield, MSc, 73; Univ BC, PhD(geomorphol), 76. *Honors & Awards:* Int Develop Res Ctr Award, 96. *Prof Exp:* Res chem, Sandoz Pharmaceut, 61-64. *Mem:* Am Soc Photogram; Int Soc Soil Sci. *Res:* Water chemistry and sediments in river systems; terrain analysis, land evaluation, geographic information systems; watershed evaluations. *Mailing Add:* 2831 W 29th Vancouver BC V6L 1Y2 Can. *E-Mail:* star@unixg.ubc.ca

SCHREINER, ALBERT WILLIAM, INTERNAL MEDICINE, HEMATOLOGY. *Current Pos:* Inst internal med, 55-59, from asst clin prof to assoc prof, 59-67, PROF MED, COL MED, UNIV CINCINNATI, 67- *Personal Data:* b Cincinnati, Ohio, Feb 15, 26; m 53, Jean Tellestrom; c David. *Educ:* Univ Cincinnati, BS, 47, MD, 49. *Prof Exp:* Dir, Dept Internal Med, Christ Hosp, 68-94. *Concurrent Pos:* Fel hemat, Cincinnati Gen Hosp, Ohio, 51-52, attend physician, 57-, clinician, Outpatient Dept, 57-62, chief clinician, 62-65; clin investr leukemia res, Vet Admin Hosp, Cincinnati, 57-59, chief med serv, 59-68, consult, 68-; consult to med dir, Ohio Nat Life, 66-80; dir, dept internal med residency prog, Christ Hosp, 78-87. *Mem:* Am Col Physicians; Am Fedn Clin Res; NY Acad Sci; Am Soc Internal Med; Asn Prog Dirs Internal Med; Soc Res & Educ Primary Care Internal Med. *Res:* Experimental viral oncogenesis in rodents. *Mailing Add:* 8525 Given Rd Cincinnati OH 45243

SCHREINER, ANTON FRANZ, INORGANIC CHEMISTRY. *Current Pos:* from asst prof to assoc prof, 68-76, grad adminr, 74-77, PROF CHEM, NC STATE UNIV, 76-, CHMN ANALYTIC-INORG CHEM, 78- *Personal Data:* b Apr 29, 37; US citizen; m 66; c 1. *Educ:* Univ Detroit, BS, 61, MS, 63; Univ Ill, PhD(inorg chem), 67. *Honors & Awards:* Outstanding Young Scientist Award, Sigma Xi, 73. *Prof Exp:* Res assoc, Univ Ill, 67-68. *Mem:* Am Chem Soc; Sigma Xi; Royal Soc Chem. *Res:* Chemistry and magnetic circular dichroism of transition metals; magnetic circular luminescence; luminescence; crystal field, linear combination of atomic orbitals-molecular orbital, and normal coordinate theory applications; spectroscopy of inorganic materials; laser-optical semiconductor; 4d and 5d metal chemistry. *Mailing Add:* Dept Chem NC State Univ Box 8204 Raleigh NC 27695-0001

SCHREINER, CEINWEN ANN, IMMUNOLOGY, ANIMAL PATHOLOGY. *Current Pos:* VPRES & MGR MAMMALIAN & BIOCHEM TOXICOL, STONYBROOK LABS INC, 94- *Personal Data:* b Philadelphia, Pa, May 27, 43. *Educ:* Muhlenberg Col, BS, 65; Univ NH, MS, 67, PhD(genetics), 72. *Prof Exp:* Res assoc teratol, E R Squibb & Sons Inc, 67-69; prin scientist mutagenicity, McNeil Labs Inc, 72-79; supvr genetic toxicol, Mobil Oil Corp, 79-87, mgr path-immunotoxicol, 87-88, mgr biochem toxicol, 88-93. *Concurrent Pos:* Vchmn, Gordon Conf Genetic Toxicol, 81, chmn, 83; sect ed, Cell Biol & Toxicol, 86-; mem coun, Environ Mutagen Soc, 86-89 & Am Col Toxicol, 86-89; fel, Acad Toxicol Sci, 87- *Mem:* Environ Mutagen Soc; Genetics Soc Am; Teratol Soc; Am Col Toxicol; Genetic Toxicol Asn (treas, 76-82); Soc Risk Anal; Am Chem Soc. *Res:* Development of genetic toxicology immunotoxicology program for petroleum; management of pathological evaluation of dermal and inhalation toxicity studies, analytical chemistry, dermal sensitization, and research into mechanisms of toxicity. *Mailing Add:* Mobil Bus Resources Corp PO Box 310 Paulsboro NJ 08066-0310. *Fax:* 609-737-5570

SCHREINER, FELIX, PHYSICAL CHEMISTRY, INORGANIC CHEMISTRY. *Current Pos:* RETIRED. *Personal Data:* b Hamburg, Ger, Sept 28, 31; m 60, 69; c 2. *Educ:* Univ Hamburg, Vordiplom, 54, dipl, 57, PhD(chem), 59. *Prof Exp:* Asst prof phys chem, Univ Kiel, 59-61; resident res assoc & fel, Argonne Nat Lab, 61-63, asst chemist, 63-65, assoc chemist, 65-88. *Mem:* Am Chem Soc. *Res:* Thermodynamics; low-temperature calorimetry; noble gas chemistry; inorganic fluorine chemistry; energy research; nuclear waste management. *Mailing Add:* 19809 S 116th Ave Mokena IL 60448-1281

SCHREINER, GEORGE E, MEDICINE, PHYSIOLOGY. *Current Pos:* clin instr, Georgetown Univ, 51-52, from instr to assoc prof, 52-61, prof med, 61-87, DISTINGUISHED PROF, GEORGETOWN UNIV, 87- *Personal Data:* b Buffalo, NY, Apr 26, 22; m 48, Joanne Baker; c George, Mary, Meredith (Maclay), William, Sara (Wendull), Peter, Lisa & Salmon. *Educ:* Canisius Col, AB, 43; Georgetown Univ, MD, 46; Am Bd Internal Med, dipl, 55. *Hon Degrees:* DHL, Canisius Col; DSc, Georgetown, 86; FRCPS(Glas). *Honors & Awards:* Davidson Award, Nat Kidney Found, David Hume Award; President's Award; V Bologna Nettons Argento Award; Walton lectr, Royal Col Physician & Surgeons (Glas); Peters Award, Am Soc Nephrology. *Prof Exp:* Intern, Med Serv, Boston City Hosp, 46-47; asst physiol, Sch Med, NY Univ-Bellevue Med Ctr, 47-48, instr, 48-50; sr resident med, Mt Alto Hosp, 50-51. *Concurrent Pos:* Fel physiol, NY Univ-Bellevue Med Ctr, 49-50; dir, Renal Clin, Georgetown Univ Hosp, 52-59, Nephrol Div, 59-72 & Clin Study Unit, 61-72; mem, Nat Res Coun, 60-63 & Nat Coun Regional Med Progs, HEW; chmn, Nat Drug Res Bd Comt for Armed Forces Inst Path Registry Adverse Reactions, 63, mem subcomt drug efficacy, 66; Secy-Gen, Int Cong Nephrology, 63-66; mem, Nat Kidney Found Sci Adv Bd & chmn, DC Chap, 63-68, pres, 68-70, chmn, Nat Adv Bd, 70-; chmn comn res in nephrology, Vet Admin, 72-76, mem merit rev bd, nephrology; consult, NIH, Walter Reed Army Med Ctr, Vet Admin Hosp & Nat Naval Med Ctr; ed-in-chief, Trans, Soc Artificial Internal Organs, 55-85 & Nephron, Int Soc Nephrology, 63-72; nephrology registry, 78- *Mem:* Am Fedn Clin Res (secy-treas, 58-61, pres elect, 61-62, pres, 62-63); Soc Artificial Internal Organs (secy-treas, 56-58, pres elect, 58-59, pres, 59-60); Am Soc Nephrology (secy, 66, pres, 71); AAAS; Int Soc Nephrology (pres-elect, 75, pres, 78-81); Am Soc Clin Invest; Asn Am Physicians; Clin & Climat Soc; Am Soc Hypertension; Am Soc Transplant Physicians; Renal Physicians Asn. *Res:* Clinical nephrology; internal medicine; renal physiology; hemodialysis; dialysis of poisons; renal homotransplantation, biopsy and pathology; pyelonephritis; nephrotic syndrome; ethics of nephrology; hemoperfusion; history of dialysis. *Mailing Add:* Georgetown Univ Hosp 3800 Reservoir Rd NW Washington DC 20007-2197

SCHREINER, HEINZ RUPERT, ENZYME & CLINICAL CHEMISTRY. *Current Pos:* VPRES REAGENT TECHNOL, MILES INC, 89- *Personal Data:* b Apr 13, 30; US citizen; m; c 5. *Educ:* Univ Nebr, BS, 51, MS, 54, PhD(phys & biol chem), 56. *Honors & Awards:* Albert R Behnke Jr Award, Undersea Med Soc, 89. *Prof Exp:* Res chemist, Linde Div, Ocean Systs, Inc, 56-60, group leader, 60-63, res supvr, 63-68, dir res & develop, Ocean Systs, Inc, 68-71; prog mgr, Med Prod Div, Union Carbide Corp, 71-76, assoc dir corp res, 76-77, dir, 77-78, vpres technol, 78-80, dir, bus planning & prod develop, 80-81; vpres clin diagnostics, Technicon Instruments Corp, 81-89. *Concurrent Pos:* Councilor, Am Chem Soc, 63-66. *Mem:* Fel Aerospace Med Asn (vpres, 71); fel AAAS; Am Asn Clin Chem; Am Chem Soc; Am Inst Chemists; Am Soc Pharmacol & Exp Therapeut; Soc Nuclear Med; Undersea Med Soc (pres, 69); Sigma Xi. *Res:* Biotechnology; forty-five publications and patents in the Life Science Field. *Mailing Add:* Hedgehog Hill 196 Ridgefield Ave South Salem NY 10590-9420. *Fax:* 914-763-6024

SCHREINER, LAWRENCE JOHN, RADIATION DOSIMETRY, MAGNETIC RESONANCE. *Current Pos:* PHYSICIST, VANCOUVER ISLAND CANCER CTR, 96- *Personal Data:* b 54; m 85, Heather Ragg; c Beth, Katie & Christine. *Educ:* McGill Univ, BSc, 76; Univ Waterloo, MSc, 78, PhD(physics), 85. *Prof Exp:* Res assoc, Univ Waterloo, 85; med physicist, Dept Med Physics, Montreal Gen Hosp, 85-86; from asst prof to assoc prof radiation oncol, McGill Univ, 86-96. *Concurrent Pos:* Med physicist, Dept Radiation Oncol, Montreal Gen Hosp, 86-; H E Johns travel award for young investrs, Can Col Physicists in Med, 90. *Mem:* Fel Can Col Physicists Med; Can Orgn Med Physicists; Am Asn Physicists Med; Soc Magnetic Resonance Med. *Res:* Use of nuclear magnetic resonance to probe radiation dose; development of three-dimensional dosimetry with magnetic resonance imaging; dosimetry and imaging computer modelling studies in diagnostic radiology; investigation of nuclear magnetic resonance relaxation in heterogeneous systems. *Mailing Add:* Vancouver Island Cancer Ctr 1900 Fort St Victoria BC V8R 1J8 Can

SCHREINER, PHILIP ALLEN, EXPERIMENTAL HIGH ENERGY PHYSICS. *Current Pos:* MEM TECH STAFF, BELL LABS, 81- *Personal Data:* b Duluth, Minn, Sept 29, 43. *Educ:* Univ Calif, Los Angeles, BS, 65, MS, 66, PhD(physics), 70. *Prof Exp:* Fel, Argonne Nat Lab, 71-73, asst physicist high energy physics, 73-77, physicist, 77-81. *Mem:* Am Phys Soc. *Res:* Neutrino interactions. *Mailing Add:* 1534 Chickasaw Dr Naperville IL 60563

SCHREINER, ROBERT NICHOLAS, JR, TEST & EVALUATION, DESIGN & DEVELOPMENT. *Current Pos:* RETIRED. *Personal Data:* b New York, NY, Jan 12, 35; m 56, Anne L Wendt; c Sue A (Mosler), Wendy L (Taylor), Robert E, Kurt N, Martha E & David P. *Educ:* Capital Univ, BS, 56. *Prof Exp:* Engr, Fluid Dynamics Dept, Norair Div, Northrop Corp, Hawthorne, Calif, 56-59; mem tech staff, Dynamics Sect, TRW Inc, 59-64, staff engr, Dynamics Dept, 64-66, Eng Mech Lab, 66-69, Appl Mech Lab, 69-71, Res & Technol Opers, 71-72, head, Tracking Algorithm Design & Develop Sect, 72-78, subproj mgr, BETA Test Prog, 78-79, dept asst prog mgr, 79-81, staff engr, 81-82, design eng & develop, 82-83, field site test dir, Proj 9646, 83, dept asst prog mgr, 83-84, Proj 5810, 84-85, Proj 8524, 85-87, dept mgr test eng & integration, 87-90, mgr systs develop staff & field serv, 90-92. *Concurrent Pos:* Lectr mech eng & adv comput technol, var univs & indust firms, 65-72; substitute teacher math, Torrance Unified Sch Dist, Calif. *Res:* Author of 8 technical articles published in professional journals on dynamics of solid propellants, mechanical shock and vibration, viscoelasticity, nuclear effects and advanced computer technology. *Mailing Add:* 30520 Via Rivera Rancho Palos Verdes CA 90275

SCHREINER, ROGER PAUL, plant root physiology & biochemistry, vesicular arbuscular mycorrhizae symbiosis, for more information see previous edition

SCHREIWEIS, DONALD OTTO, COMPARATIVE ANATOMY, VERTEBRATE EMBRYOLOGY. *Current Pos:* DIR PREPROFESSIONAL HEALTH STUDIES, ST LOUIS UNIV, 81- *Personal Data:* b Tacoma, Wash, July 27, 41; m 73, Jo Christianson. *Educ:* Univ Puget Sound, AB, 63, MS, 66; Wash State Univ, PhD(zool), 72. *Prof Exp:* Asst prof biol, Univ Puget Sound, 71-72; asst prof biol, Univ Nev, Las Vegas, 72-77; chairperson & assoc prof biol, Gonzaga Univ, 77-81. *Mem:* Am Ornith Union; Am Soc Mammal; Sigma Xi. *Res:* Comparative myological studies of birds and bats using numerical methods; comparative vertebrate morphology; teratogenic effects of herbicides, pesticides and heavy metals on vertebrate development. *Mailing Add:* 548 Braebridge Rd Manchester MO 63021. *Fax:* 314-977-3660; *E-Mail:* schreiweisdo@sluvca.slu.edu

SCHREMP, EDWARD JAY, SCIENCE & TECHNOLOGY POLICY, OCEANIC ENGINEERING. *Current Pos:* CONSULT PHYSICIST, 70-; PRES, E J SCHREMP & CO, 75- *Personal Data:* b Newark, NJ, Aug 20, 12; m 47, Magdalene Corbett; c Magdalene G (Liquori). *Educ:* Mass Inst Technol, SB, 34, PhD(theoret physics), 37. *Prof Exp:* Teaching fel physics, Mass Inst Technol, 35-37, instr physics, 37; instr physics, Wash Univ, St Louis, 37-41; asst prof physics, Univ Cincinnati, 41-46; sci liasion officer, Off Asst Naval Attache Res, Am Embassy, London, 46-48; head, Theory Br, Nucleonics Div, US Naval Res Lab, Wash, 48-66, consult theoret physics, 66-70. *Concurrent Pos:* Mem staff, Radiation Lab, Mass Inst Technol, 41-46; off Sci Res & Develop, 41-46; vis scientist, Theoret Study Div, Europ Orgn Nuclear Res, Geneva, Switz, 65-66, Int Ctr Theoret Physics, Trieste, Italy, 67, 68, 69, 70 & 71. *Mem:* Fel Am Phys Soc; NY Acad Sci; Inst Elec & Electronics Engrs; Inst Elec & Electronic Engrs Oceanic Eng Soc; Marine Technol Soc. *Res:* Oceanic engineering implications of a key and major "new ocean technology"; ultimate quantum theoretical implications, for fields and space-time geometry, of simply transitive non-Abelian 4-Parameter subgroups of the Poincare group, when examined in terms of the group-space of any such subgroup. *Mailing Add:* 226 S Fairfax St Alexandria VA 22314

SCHREMP, FREDERIC WILLIAM, PHYSICAL CHEMISTRY. *Current Pos:* RETIRED. *Personal Data:* b Utica, NY, Aug 14, 16; m 48, 58; c 4. *Educ:* Rensselaer Polytech Inst, BS, 42; Univ Wis, PhD(phys chem), 50. *Prof Exp:* Res elec engr, Am Steel & Wire Co, 42-44; res chemist, Oak Ridge Nat Lab, 44-45; sr res assoc, Chevron Oil Field Res Co, Standard Oil Co, Calif, 50-81. *Concurrent Pos:* Consult. *Mem:* Am Chem Soc; Nat Asn Corrosion Engrs. *Res:* Rheology of high polymers; oil field drilling fluid; corrosion. *Mailing Add:* 3225 Arbol Dr Fullerton CA 92635-1713

SCHRENK, GEORGE L, ENGINEERING. *Current Pos:* PRES, SHRENK ASSOC, 92- *Personal Data:* b Seymour, Ind, Nov 28, 37; div. *Educ:* Ind Univ, BS, 55, MS, 56, PhD(theoret physics), 59. *Hon Degrees:* MA, Univ Pa, 71. *Prof Exp:* Eng consult, 59-; sr res assoc, Inst Direct Energy Conversion, Univ Pa, 63-65, chief, Plasma Eng Br, 64-66, asst dir, Comput Ctr, 66-69, assoc prof eng, Towne Sch Civil & Mech Eng, 68-80, assoc prof eng, 70-80; pres, Comp Comm, Inc, 75- *Concurrent Pos:* Fel, NSF, 58-60; adj assoc prof eng, Univ Pa, 80-; expert witness telecommun indust. *Mem:* Am Phys Soc; Am Soc Mech Engrs; sr mem Inst Elec & Electronics Engrs; Asn Comput Mach; Sigma Xi. *Res:* Electromagnetic propagation; telecommunications engineering; computational engineering physics; mathematical modeling and simulation. *Mailing Add:* Shrenk Assoc 3 Red Oak Rd Wilmington DE 19806

SCHRENK, WALTER JOHN, POLYMERIC OPTICAL THIN FILMS, MULTILAYER PACKAGING MATERIALS. *Current Pos:* RETIRED. *Personal Data:* b Toledo, Ohio, Feb 12, 33. *Educ:* Univ Mich, BS, 55. *Honors & Awards:* IR-100 Award, 77; Polymer Processing Hall of Fame, 86; Fred O Conley Award for Plastics Eng & Jack Barney Award for Contrib to Plastics, Soc Plastics Engrs, 87. *Prof Exp:* Sr res scientist, Dow Chem Co, 55-94. *Mem:* Nat Acad Eng; fel Soc Plastics Engrs; Soc Optical Eng; Polymer Processing Soc; Am Soc Mech Engrs. *Res:* Fabrication of polymers and polymer processing with emphasis on multilayer coextrusion of polymer films and sheets, orientation and enhanced properties by control of supramolecular structure thru processing. *Mailing Add:* 1307 Timber Dr Midland MI 48640

SCHRENK, WILLIAM GEORGE, CHEMISTRY. *Current Pos:* RETIRED. *Personal Data:* b Hiawatha, Kans, July 13, 10; m 32; c 2. *Educ:* Western Union Col, AB, 32; Kans State Col, MS, 36, PhD(chem), 45. *Prof Exp:* Teacher high schs, Iowa, 32-38; from instr to assoc prof, Kans State Univ, 38-51, asst chemist, Exp Sta, 43-51, prof chem & chemist, 51-76. *Mem:* AAAS; Am Chem Soc; Soc Appl Spectros. *Res:* Minor elements in plants; physical methods in chemical analysis; spectroscopy for analytical purposes; instrumental techniques in analysis; atomic absorption spectroscopy; flame emission spectroscopy. *Mailing Add:* Dept Chem Kans State Univ Manhattan KS 66506

SCHREUDER, GERARD FRITZ, FOREST ECONOMICS. *Current Pos:* assoc prof, 71-75, prof forestry, 75-77, PROF FORESTRY RESOURCES & DIR FOREST RESOURCES MGT STUDIES, UNIV WASH, 77- *Personal Data:* b Medan, Indonesia, Apr 4, 37; US citizen; m 61; c 2. *Educ:* State Agr Univ Wageningen, MS, 60; NC State Univ, MS, 67; Yale Univ, PhD(econ), 68. *Prof Exp:* Asst expert aerial photos, Orgn Am States, 61-64; asst prof opers res, Yale Univ, 67-70. *Concurrent Pos:* Dir res, Univ Wash, 72-; mem, Comt Renewable Resources Indust Mat, Nat Acad Sci, 75-76. *Mem:* AAAS; Neth Inst Agr Engrs; Sigma Xi. *Res:* Forest resource modelling; aerial photo interpretation as related to environmental impacts and animal damage; forest resource economics. *Mailing Add:* Univ Wash Anderson Hall AR 10 PO Box 932994 Seattle WA 98195

SCHREUDERS, PAUL D, BIOMEDICAL ENGINEERING. *Current Pos:* ASST PROF BIOL RES ENG, UNIV MD, COLLEGE PARK, 95- *Personal Data:* b Des Moines, Iowa, Sept 21, 59. *Educ:* Clemson Univ, BS, 82, MS, 85; Univ Tex, Austin, PhD(biomed eng), 89. *Prof Exp:* Trainee fel biomed sci, Univ Tenn, 90-95. *Mem:* Am Inst Chem Engrs; Biomed Eng Soc; Soc Cryobiol. *Mailing Add:* Bio Resources Eng Ctr Univ Md ANSCI/AGENGR Bldg Rm 1460 College Park MD 20742-5711

SCHREUR, PEGGY JO KORTY DOBRY, NEUROPHARMACOLOGY, BEHAVIORAL PHARMACOLOGY OF PSYCHOACTIVE DRUGS. *Current Pos:* SR RES SCIENTIST, THE UPJOHN CO, 74- *Personal Data:* b Washington, DC, June 18, 43; m 83, Eric J; c Emily J. *Educ:* Col William & Mary, BS, 65; Univ Mich, PhD(physiol), 71. *Prof Exp:* Asst prof biol, Nazareth Col, Kalamazoo, 71-74; instr, Kalamazoo Valley Community Col, 74. *Mem:* Soc Neurosci; Am Physiol Soc; AAAS. *Res:* Behavioral neuropharmacology of serotonin, dopamine and benzodiazepine; related compounds for anxiety, insomnia, depression, pain, schizophrenia and Parkinsons disease. *Mailing Add:* CNS Res Pharmacia & Upjohn Inc 2324 Bronson Blvd Kalamazoo MI 49008-2402. *Fax:* 616-385-4525

SCHREURS, JAN W H, PHYSICAL CHEMISTRY, MAGNETIC RESONANCE. *Current Pos:* RETIRED. *Personal Data:* b Winterswijk, Neth, Feb 10, 32; m 56, Martha Bonjernoor; c Jolanda, Marja (Wallach), Miranda & Peter. *Educ:* Free Univ, Amsterdam, BSc, 53, MSc, 57, PhD(phys chem), 62. *Prof Exp:* Res assoc chem, Columbia Univ, 57-59; res fel, Nat Res Coun Can, 60-62; sr res assoc, Phys Properties Res Dept, Corning Inc, 62-95. *Mem:* Am Phys Soc. *Res:* Electron spin resonance and magnetic susceptibility of glasses and glass ceramics. *Mailing Add:* 345 Field St Corning NY 14830

SCHREYER, RALPH COURTENAY, ORGANIC POLYMER CHEMISTRY. *Current Pos:* RETIRED. *Personal Data:* b Washington, DC, July 27, 19; m 44; c 2. *Educ:* Cath Univ Am, BA, 41; Purdue Univ, PhD(chem), 46. *Prof Exp:* Res chemist, Polychem Dept, Exp Sta, E I du Pont de Nemours & Co, Inc, Del, 46-60, tech assoc, Eastern Lab, Explosives Dept, NJ, 60-68, sr res chemist, Polymer Intermediates Dept, 68-73, staff chemist, 73-76, patent assoc, 76-78, patent assoc, Petrochem Dept, 78-84. *Concurrent Pos:* Patent agent, 76. *Mem:* Am Chem Soc. *Res:* Synthesis of flurocarbons; reactions of carbon monoxide and carbon monoxide and hydrogen with organic compounds; synthesis of nylon intermediates; polymerization of ethylene and fluoro-olefins. *Mailing Add:* 54 Ulverston Dr Cartmel Kennett Square PA 19348-2044

SCHRIBER, STANLEY OWEN, ACCELERATOR PHYSICS. *Current Pos:* dep div leader, Los Alamos Nat Lab, 84-87, div leader, 87-93, div dir, 93-97, DEP DIV DIR, LOS ALAMOS NAT LABS, 97- *Personal Data:* b St Boniface, Man, July 20, 40; m 62, Evelyn Tyson; c Kathleen & Craig. *Educ:* Univ Man, BSc, 62, MSc, 63; McMaster Univ, PhD(physics), 67. *Prof Exp:* From asst res off to sr res off, Chalk River Nuclear Labs, Atomic Energy Can Ltd, 66-84. *Concurrent Pos:* Guest scientist, Los Alamos Nat Lab, 77 & 78-79 & Kek Lab High Energy Physics, Japan, 81; consult, Argonne Nat Lab, 80, Inst Fur Kernphysik, Karlspruhe, Ger, 80. *Mem:* Am Phys Soc; Inst Elec & Electronics Engrs. *Res:* Design, construction, operation and testing of pulsed and continuous wave linear accelerations; charged particle beam dynamics; beam diagnostics; radio frequency systems and beam dynamics; practical uses of accelerator beams. *Mailing Add:* Neutron Sci Div Los Alamos Nat Lab Los Alamos NM 87545. *Fax:* 505-665-8604; *E-Mail:* sos@lanl.gov

SCHRIBER, THOMAS J, SIMULATION MODELING, SIMULATION OUTPUT ANALYSIS. *Current Pos:* from asst prof to assoc prof, 66-72, PROF MGT SCI, UNIV MICH, ANN ARBOR, 72- *Personal Data:* b Flint, Mich, Oct 28, 35; m 67; c 3. *Educ:* Univ Notre Dame, BS, 57; Univ Mich, MSE, 58, AM, 59, PhD(chem eng), 64. *Prof Exp:* Asst prof math, Eastern Mich Univ, 63-66. *Concurrent Pos:* Consult, Ford Motor Co, 66, 71 & 74, Stanford Res Inst, 73, Int Tel & Tel, 74, CPC Int, 77 & 80, Occidental Petrol, 82, Gen Motors, 84-85 & Exxon, 84-85; vis scholar, Stanford Res Inst, 72-73; prin investr, Off Naval Res grant, 81-83. *Mem:* Inst Mgt Sci; fel Decisions Sci Inst; Soc Comput Simulation; Asn Comput Mach. *Res:* Computer applications in management science, especially discrete-event simulation, numerical methods and optimization. *Mailing Add:* Comput Info Systs Dept Univ Mich Bus Sch 701 Tappan St Ann Arbor MI 48109-1234

SCHRICKER, ROBERT LEE, VETERINARY MEDICINE, MICROBIOLOGY. *Current Pos:* RETIRED. *Personal Data:* b Davenport, Iowa, June 28, 28; m 56; c 3. *Educ:* Iowa State Univ, DVM, 52; Univ Ill, Urbana, MS, 58, PhD(vet sci), 61; Am Col Vet Microbiol, dipl. *Prof Exp:* Pvt pract, 52-54; res vet, US Army Biol Labs, 61-71; mem vet biol staff, USDA, 71-81. *Mem:* Am Vet Med Asn. *Res:* Precipitating antigens of leptospires; pathogenesis of zoonotic infectious diseases in primates; pathology and clinical biochemistry; veterinary biologics. *Mailing Add:* 1512 Rockcreek Dr Frederick MD 21702

SCHRIEFFER, JOHN ROBERT, THEORETICAL CONDENSED MATTER PHYSICS. *Current Pos:* CHIEF SCIENTIST & UNIV PROF, NAT HIGH MAGNETIC FIELD LAB, UNIV FLA. *Personal Data:* b Oak Park, Ill, May 31, 31; m 60; c 3. *Educ:* Mass Inst Technol, BS, 53; Univ Ill, MS, 54, PhD(physics), 57. *Hon Degrees:* Dr rer nat, Munich Tech Univ, 68; Dr es Sci, Univ Geneva, 68; DSc, Univ Pa, 73, Univ Ill, 74, Univ Cincinnati, 77, Univ Tel Aviv, 86, Univ Ala, 90. *Honors & Awards:* Nobel Prize in Physics, 72; Comstock Prize, Nat Acad Sci, 68; Oliver E Buckley Solid State Physics Prize, Am Phys Soc, 68; John Ericsson Medal, Am Soc Swed Engrs, 76; Nat Medal Sci, 84. *Prof Exp:* NSF fel, Univ Birmingham & Inst Theoret Physics, Univ Copenhagen, 57-58; asst prof physics, Univ Chicago, 57-60; from asst prof to assoc prof, Univ Ill, 59-62; prof, Univ Pa, 62-64, Mary Amanda Wood prof, 64-80; prof, Univ Calif, Santa Barbara, 80-97, dir, Inst Theoret Physics, 84-89, chancellor's prof, 84-97. *Concurrent Pos:* Guggenheim fel, 67-68; Andrew D White prof-at-lg, Cornell Univ, 67-73; Exxon fac fel, 79-; mem, Class I Mem Comt, Nat Acad Sci, 84-86, mem coun, 90-; mem, Space Sci & Applns Adv Comt, NASA, 88-89; fel, Los Alamos Nat Lab, 88-, dir, Advan Study Prog High Temperature Superconductivity Theory, 88-; consult, IBM, STI, Exxon. *Mem:* Nat Acad Sci; Am Acad Arts & Sci; Am Philos Soc; fel Am Phys Soc; Danish Royal Acad Sci; Sigma Xi. *Res:* Theoretical solid state physics, especially superconductivity; surface physics; general theory of many body problem; magnetism; low dimensional conductors; nonlinear phenomena. *Mailing Add:* Nat High Magnetic Field Lab Univ Fla 1800 E Paul Darick Dr Tallahassee FL 32306-4005

SCHRIEMPF, JOHN THOMAS, SOLID STATE PHYSICS. *Current Pos:* vpres, 84-91, SR VPRES, PHYS SCI INC, ALEXANDRIA, VA, 93- *Personal Data:* b Sandusky, Ohio, July 6, 34; m 57, Tatyana Schramko; c Alexa T. *Educ:* Carnegie Inst Technol, BS, 56, MS, 60, PhD(physics), 64. *Honors & Awards:* Navy Meritorious Civilian Serv Award, 74 & 79. *Prof Exp:* Instr physics, Carnegie Inst Technol, 60-63; res physicist, US Naval Res Lab, 63-81, supt, condensed matter & radiation sci div, 81-84; vpres & chief operating officer, Res Support Instruments Inc, Hunt Valley, Md, 91-93. *Concurrent Pos:* Vis res scholar, Univ Calif, Irvine, 68-69; vis prof, Naval Postgrad Sch, Monterey, Calif, 73. *Mem:* AAAS; Sigma Xi; fel Am Phys Soc; Am Inst Aeronaut & Astronaut; Am Astronaut Soc. *Res:* Transport properties, especially thermal conductivity of metals and alloys; transport properties of metals at high temperatures, especially in the liquid state; interaction between laser radiation and metallic systems. *Mailing Add:* 217 S Royal St Alexandria VA 22314

SCHRIER, DENIS J, IMMUNOPHARMACOLOGY. *Current Pos:* ASSOC RES FEL, WARNER LAMBERT CO, 82- *Personal Data:* b Grand Rapids, Mich, Oct 29, 55; m 77; c 2. *Educ:* Med Col Wis, PhD(path), 80. *Prof Exp:* Fel, Univ Mich, 80-82. *Mem:* Am Thoracic Soc; Am Asn Path; Am Asn Immunol; fel Parker Francis Pulmonary; Soc Leukocyte Biol. *Res:* Direct multidisciplinary team which is involved in the identification of novel antiinflammatory and antiarthritic drugs; arachidonic acid metabolism; protein kinase c; cellular adhesion. *Mailing Add:* Dept Exp Therapeut Warner Lambert Parke-Davis 2800 Plymouth Rd Ann Arbor MI 48105-2430. *Fax:* 313-996-4333

SCHRIER, MELVIN HENRY, CHEMISTRY. *Current Pos:* RETIRED. *Personal Data:* b Brooklyn, NY, Dec 13, 27; m 50; c 2. *Educ:* Brooklyn Col, BS, 51. *Prof Exp:* Chemist, Pittsburgh Testing Lab, 51-53; chemist, Otto B May Inc, Newark, NJ, 53-59, head chemist, Anal Sect, 59-70, mgr, Anal Dept, 70-79; group leader, US Testing Co, Hoboken, NJ, 80-93. *Mem:* Am Chem Soc. *Res:* Analytical research in dyestuff and intermediates. *Mailing Add:* 10 Windham Loop Staten Island NY 10314

SCHRIER, ROBERT WILLIAM, NEPHROLOGY, RENAL DISORDERS. *Current Pos:* prof med & head, Div Renal Dis & Hypertension, 72-92, PROF & CHMN, DEPT MED, SCH MED, UNIV COLO, 76- *Personal Data:* b Indianapolis, Ind, Feb 19, 36; m, Barbara Lindley; c David, Deborah, Douglas, Derek & Denise. *Educ:* DePauw Univ, BA, 57; Sch Med, Ind Univ, MD, 62; Am Bd Internal Med, dipl, 68. *Hon Degrees:* DSc, DePauw Univ, 91, Univ Colo, 96. *Honors & Awards:* John Peters Distinguished Lectr, Yale Univ, 79; Chandros Lectr, Brit Renal Physicians Asn, 84; David M Hume Mem Award, Nat Kidney Found, 87; Sau Win-Lam Lectr, State Univ NY, 89; William Goldring Lectr, NY Univ, 89; John C Merrill Mem Lectr, Harvard Univ, 89; Eduardo Slatupolsky Lectr, Wash Univ, 89; Mayo Soley Award, Western Soc Clin Invest, 89; Robert W Schrier Young Investr Award, 91; John Phillips Mem Award, Am Col Physicians, 92; Francis Blake Award, Asn Am Physicians, 95. *Prof Exp:* Med intern, Marion Co Gen Hosp, 62-63; med resident, Univ Wash Sch Med, 63-65; med asst, Sch Med, Harvard Univ, 65-66; endocrine-metab res fel, Peter Brent Brigham Hosp, 65-66; consult, Walter Reed Gen Hosp & Army Inst Res, 66-67, 68-69; res fel, Charing Cross Hosp Med Sch, London Univ, Eng, 67-68; from asst prof to assoc prof med & Cardiovasc Res Inst, Med Ctr, Univ Calif, San Francisco, 69-72, assoc mem, 70-72, assoc dir, Renal Div, 71-72. *Concurrent Pos:* Fulbright scholar, Gutenberg Univ, Ger, 57-58, Guggenheim fel, 86-87; estab investr, Am Heart Asn, 71-73; mem, Hypertension Task Force, NIH, 75-76, Nephrol/Urol Surv Comt, 75-76, consult, Nat Heart, Blood & Lung Inst, 72-74; lectr, Int Cong Nephrol, Montreal, 78, Athens, 81, London, 87; vis prof, Australian Nat Kidney Found, 83, Howard H Hiatt, Harvard Med Sch, 85, Mrs Ho Tam Kit Hing vis prof, Univ Hong Kong, 87; chmn, Health & Sci Affairs Comt, Nat Kidney Found, 84-86; Pfizer fel, Clin Res Inst, Montreal, 86; hon prof, Univ Paris, 86-87 & Univ Beijing, 88; panel mem, Conf Geriat Assessment Methods Clin Decisionmaking, NIH, 87, chmn, End-Stage Renal Dis Comt, 90; ed, Advan Internal Med, 91; Mr & Mrs I G Bromberg vis prof, Univ Tex, 94. *Mem:* Inst Med-Nat Acad Sci; Int Soc Nephrology (treas, 81-90, vpres, 90-93, pres elect, 93-95, pres, 95-); Am Soc Nephrol (secy-treas, 79-81, pres, 83); Int Soc Physiol; master Am Col Physicians; emer mem Am Soc Clin Invest (vpres, 80-81); Am Clin & Climatol Asn (vpres, 86); Asn Am Physicians (vpres, 93-94, pres, 94-95); fel Am Col Clin Pharmacol; AAAS; Am Soc Renal Biochem & Metab; Am Physiol Soc; Am Fedn Clin Res; Am Heart Asn; fel Molecular Med Soc. *Res:* Kidney diseases; author of numerous technical publications. *Mailing Add:* Dept Med Div Renal Dis Univ Colo Health Sci Ctr 4200 E 9 Ave Box B178 Denver CO 80262

SCHRIER, STANLEY LEONARD, MEDICINE, HEMATOLOGY. *Current Pos:* From instr to assoc prof, 59-72, PROF MED, MED CTR, STANFORD UNIV, 72-, HEAD DIV HEMAT, 68- *Personal Data:* b New York, NY, Jan 2, 29; m 53; c 3. *Educ:* Univ Colo, AB, 49; Johns Hopkins Univ, MD, 54; Am Bd Internal Med, dipl. *Honors & Awards:* Markle Scholar, 61; Eleanor Roosevelt UICC Award, 75; Lady Davis Award, Hebrew Univ, 82; NSF/CNRS Award, France, 83. *Mem:* Am Fedn Clin Res; Am Soc Hemat; Int Soc Hemat; Am Soc Clin Invest; Asn Am Physicians. *Res:* Metabolism and transport of red cell membranes; properties of erythrocyte membranes in health, disease and aging; pathophysiology of human and marine thalassemih. *Mailing Add:* Div Hemat S-161 Stanford Univ Med Ctr 300 Pasteur Dr Stanford CA 94305. *Fax:* 650-723-1269

SCHRIESHEIM, ALAN, RESEARCH ADMINISTRATION, ORGANIC CHEMISTRY. *Current Pos:* sr dep dir & chief oper officer, 83-84, dir & chief exec officer, 84-96, DIR EMER, ARGONNE NAT LAB, 96- *Personal Data:* b NY, Mar 8, 30; m 53; c 2. *Educ:* Polytech Inst Brooklyn, BS, 51; Pa State Univ, PhD(phys org chem), 54. *Honors & Awards:* Petrol Chem Award, Am Chem Soc, 69; Karcher Silver Medalist Lectr. *Prof Exp:* Res chemist, Nat Bur Standards, 54-56; res chemist, Exxon Res & Eng Co, 56-58, sr chemist, 58-59, res assoc, 59-63, sect head, 63-65, asst dir, 65-66, asst mgr, 66-69, dir chem sci lab, Corp Res Labs, 69-75, dir corp res labs, 75-78, gen mgr technol dept, 78-83. *Concurrent Pos:* Mem adv bd, Corp Vis Comt for Dept Chem, Mass Inst Technol, Chemtech & Stanford Energy Inst; co-chmn, Assembly Math & Phys Sci Comt on Chem Sci, Nat Res Coun, Indust Adv Comt-Rutgers Univ, Solid State Sci Adv Panel & Pure & Appl Chem Deleg to the People's Republic of China, Nat Acad Sci, 78; consult & prin, Wash Adv Group, 96- *Mem:* AAAS; Am Chem Soc; Sigma Xi; fel NY Acad Sci; fel Am Inst Chemists. *Res:* Kinetics and mechanism of acid and base catalyzed organic reactions including alkylation, isomerization, hydrogenation and polymerization. *Mailing Add:* Argonne Nat Lab 9700 S Cass Ave Argonne IL 60439-4832

SCHRIEVER, BERNARD ADOLF, AERONAUTICAL ENGINEERING. *Current Pos:* CONSULT, 71- *Personal Data:* b Ger, Sept 14, 10; nat US; m 38; c 3. *Educ:* Tex Agr & Mech Col, BS, 31; Stanford Univ, MS, 42. *Hon Degrees:* DSc, Rider Col & Creighton Univ, 58, Adelphi Col, 59, Rollins Col, 61; LLD, Loyola Univ, Calif, 62, C W Post Col, Long Island, 65; DrAeroSci, Univ Mich, 62; DrEng, Polytech Inst Brooklyn, 62, PMC Cols, 66. *Honors & Awards:* Aviation Medal, Rome, 80; James Forrester Mem Award, 86. *Prof Exp:* USAF, 32-66, chief staff, Far East Air Serv Command, 43-44, comdr adv echelon, 44-45, chief, Plans & Policy Div Res & Develop, 45-49, asst opers, Develop Planning, 50-54, asst to comdr, Air Res & Develop Command, 54-59, comdr, Air Force Systs Command, 59-66; indust consult, 66-71. *Concurrent Pos:* Dir, Am Med Int, Control Data Corp, Emerson Elec, Wackenhut Corp, Rockwell Int, Aerojet. *Mem:* Nat Acad Eng; hon fel Inst Aeronaut & Astronaut. *Res:* Advanced technology in aerospace missions. *Mailing Add:* 2300 M St NW No 900 Washington DC 20037-1434

SCHRIRO, GEORGE R, APPLIED MATHEMATICS, AERODYNAMICS. *Current Pos:* STRUCT ANALYST, DYNAMICIST & SR ENGR, GRUMMAN AEROSPACE CORP, 56- *Personal Data:* b New York, NY, Sept 3, 21; m 48; c 4. *Educ:* NY Univ, BS, 47, MA, 50. *Prof Exp:* Night mgr, Western Union Tel Co, NY, 36-42; instr math, Wash Univ, St Louis, 48-49; teacher high sch, NJ, 49-51; chmn math dept, NY, 51-56. *Concurrent Pos:* Adj asst prof math, C W Post Col, Long Island Univ, 62-80, adj assoc prof, 80- *Mem:* Math Asn Am; Am Inst Aeronaut & Astronaut. *Res:* Stability and control; aeroelastic effects; dynamic analysis; stress and fatigue. *Mailing Add:* 121 Prospect St Farmingdale NY 11735

SCHROCK, GOULD FREDERICK, BOTANY, MYCOLOGY. *Current Pos:* PROF BOT, INDIANA UNIV PA, 68- *Personal Data:* b Rockwood, Pa, Apr 23, 36; m 57; c 2. *Educ:* Indiana Univ Pa, BS, 57, MEd, 61; Univ Chicago, PhD(bot), 64. *Prof Exp:* Joint high sch teacher, Ind, 58-61; assoc prof bot, Kutztown State Col, 64-68. *Mem:* Mycol Soc Am; Bot Soc Am; Int Soc Human & Animal Mycol; Am Inst Biol Sci; Am Hort Soc. *Res:* Factors influencing growth and development of human pathogenic fungi; succession of fungi in selected natural environments. *Mailing Add:* Indiana Univ Pa Indiana PA 15705-0001

SCHROCK, RICHARD ROYCE, ORGANOMETALLIC CHEMISTRY. *Current Pos:* from asst prof to assoc prof, 75-80, PROF CHEM, MASS INST TECHNOL, 80-, FREDERICK G KEYES PROF CHEM, 89- *Personal Data:* b Berne, Ind, Jan 4, 45. *Educ:* Univ Calif, Riverside, AB, 67; Harvard Univ, PhD(chem), 71. *Honors & Awards:* Organometallic Chem Award, Am Chem Soc, 85; Harrison Howe Award, Am Chem Soc, 91; Humboldt Sr Res Award, Humboldt Soc, 95; Inorg Chem Award, Am Chem Soc, 96. *Prof Exp:* NSF fel, Cambridge Univ, 71-72; res chemist, Cent Res & Develop Dept, E I Du Pont de Nemours & Co, Inc, 72-75. *Concurrent Pos:* A P Sloan fel, 76-80; Dreyfus teacher-scholar, 78-83. *Mem:* Am Chem Soc; Am Acad Sci; Nat Acad Sci. *Res:* Synthetic and mechanistic organo-transition metal chemistry; homogeneous catalysis; early transition metal chemistry; metal-alkyl, metal-carbene and metal-carbyne complexes; reduction of carbon monoxide; olefin metathesis; olefin polymerization; acetylene metathesis. *Mailing Add:* Mass Inst Technol 6-331 77 Massachusetts Ave Cambridge MA 02139. *E-Mail:* rrs@mit.edu

SCHROCK, VIRGIL E(DWIN), NUCLEAR POWER, NUCLEAR REACTOR SAFETY. *Current Pos:* lectr mech eng, Univ Calif, Berkeley, 48-51, asst prof, 54-60, assoc prof, 60-68, asst dean res, 68-74, PROF NUCLEAR ENG, UNIV CALIF, BERKELEY, 68- *Personal Data:* b San Diego, Calif, Jan 22, 26; m 46; c 2. *Educ:* Univ Wis, BS, 46, MS, 48; Univ Calif, ME, 52. *Honors & Awards:* Glenn Murphy Award, Am Soc Eng Educ, 83; Heat Trans Mem Award, Am Soc Mech Eng, 85, 50th Anniversary Award, 88. *Prof Exp:* Instr mech eng, Univ Wis, 46-48; US Navy, Eng Off, USS O'Brien DD 725, 52-53. *Concurrent Pos:* Vis res fel, Ctr Info, Studies & Exp, Milan, Italy, 62-63 & 74-75; consult to indust & govt; tech ed, J Heat Transfer, Am Soc Mech Engrs, chmn, Heat Transfer Div, 78-79 & Nat Heat Transfer Conf Coord Comn, 80-81; chmn, Thermal Hydraulics Div, Am Nuclear Soc, 82-83; Japan Soc Prom Sci res fel, 84. *Mem:* Fel Am Nuclear Soc; fel Am Soc Mech Engrs; Am Soc Eng Educ; Sigma Xi. *Res:* Thermodynamic and transport properties of fluids; heat transfer and fluid dynamics; boiling and two-phase flow; thermal design of nuclear power plants; environmental aspects of nuclear power; safety analysis of nuclear systems; resources conservation and planning. *Mailing Add:* 258 Orchard Rd Orinda CA 94563

SCHRODER, DAVID JOHN, FOOD SAFETY & QUALITY, ADMINISTRATION. *Current Pos:* dir, 90-92, HEAD FOOD QUAL BR, ALTA AGR FOOD LAB SERV, 92- *Personal Data:* b Edmonton, Alta, Oct 29, 41; m 65; c 2. *Educ:* Univ Alta, BSc, 64, MSc, 69; Univ Minn, PhD(food microbiol), 73. *Prof Exp:* Res scientist, Agr Can, 73-78; supvr, Alta Agr Food Res, 78-84; head, Alta Agr Food Processing Develop Ctr, 84-90. *Concurrent Pos:* Adj prof, Univ Alta, 80-; exec, Bd Dirs, POS Pilot Plant Corp, 81-90; chmn, Nat Ann Conf, Can Inst Food Sci & Technol, 86; Prov rep, Can Comt Food, 88- *Mem:* Can Inst Food Sci & Technol; Inst Food Technologists. *Res:* Food microbiology, safety, quality, product development and processing development. *Mailing Add:* Food Qual Br 6909 116 St Edmonton AB T6H 4P2 Can

SCHRODER, DIETER K, ELECTRICAL ENGINEERING, SOLID STATE PHYSICS. *Current Pos:* PROF ENG, ARIZ STATE UNIV, 81- *Personal Data:* b Lubeck, Ger, June 18, 35; US citizen; m 61, Beverley; c Mark & Derek. *Educ:* McGill Univ, BEng, 62 & MEng, 64; Univ Ill, PhD(elec eng), 68. *Prof Exp:* Sr engr, Westinghouse Res Labs, 68-72, fel eng, 72-76, adv engr, 76-79, mgr, 79-81. *Concurrent Pos:* Vis engr, Inst Appl Solid State Physics, Freiburg, Ger, 78-79; nat lectr, Inst Elec & Electronics Engrs, 93-94. *Mem:* Fel Inst Elec & Electronics Engrs; Electrochem Soc; Sigma Xi. *Res:* Solid state electronics, especially semi-conductor materials, defects, and material and device characterization. *Mailing Add:* Elec Eng Dept Ariz State Univ Tempe AZ 85287-5706. *Fax:* 602-965-8118

SCHRODER, EDUARDO C, RHIZOSPHERE MICROBIAL ECOLOGY. *Current Pos:* PROF MICROBIOL, UNIV PR, 89- *Personal Data:* b Montevideo, Uruguay, Feb 15, 45; US citizen; m 92; c Lara. *Educ:* Univ Republica, BS, 70; NC State Univ, PhD(microbiol), 80. *Honors & Awards:* Award of Recognition Sigma Xi, 88. *Mem:* Sigma Xi; Am Soc Microbiol; Am Soc Agron. *Res:* Biological nitrogen fixation by tropical legumes, including the genetic and ecological aspects. *Mailing Add:* Dept Agron & Soils BNF Lab Univ PR Mayaguez PR 00681-5000. *Fax:* 787-265-0860; *E-Mail:* e_schroder@rumac.upr.clu.edu

SCHRODER, GENE DAVID, ECOLOGY. *Current Pos:* Asst prof, 74-80, ASSOC PROF ECOL, SCH PUB HEALTH, UNIV TEX, HOUSTON, 80- *Personal Data:* b Atascadero, Calif, Oct 25, 44. *Educ:* Rice Univ, BA, 67, MA, 70; Univ NMex, PhD(ecol), 74. *Concurrent Pos:* Adj assoc prof ecol, Rice Univ, Houston, 79- *Mem:* Ecol Soc Am; Am Soc Mammalogists. *Res:* Dynamics of species interactions with particular interests in competition among desert rodents and factors regulating urban rodent populations. *Mailing Add:* 3814 Oakwick Forrest Rd Rosharon TX 77583

SCHRODER, JACK SPALDING, internal medicine; deceased, see previous edition for last biography

SCHRODER, JOHN L, MINING, ENGINEERING. *Current Pos:* RETIRED. *Personal Data:* b Martinsburg, WVa. *Educ:* WVa Sch Mines, BS, MS, 41. *Honors & Awards:* Howard N Evanson Award, Soc Mining, Metall & Explor, 91; Erskine Ramsay Medal, Am Inst Mech Engrs, 92. *Prof Exp:* Jr engr, HC Firck Coke Co, US Steel, 41-44, asst engr, Mine Planning, 49-51, asst chief engr, 51-53, chief engr, 53-58, gen supt, 58-70, gen mgr, Coal Opers, 70-79, vpres, Coal Opers Resource Develop, 79-81, pres, Subsid US Steel Mining Co Inc, 81-83; safety engr, Gay Coal & Coke & Gay Mining Co, 46-69; spec asst to pres, Am Mining Cong, 83-84; dean, Col Mineral & Energy Resources, WVa Univ, 84-91. *Concurrent Pos:* Chmn, Mine Inspection Exam Bd; mem, Govs Moorels Energy Task Force. *Mem:* Am Inst Mech Engrs; Nat Mine Rescue Asn. *Mailing Add:* 228 Maple Ave Morgantown WV 26505-6666

SCHRODER, KLAUS, SOLID STATE PHYSICS, MATERIALS SCIENCE. *Current Pos:* from assoc prof to prof, 61-95, RES PROF METALL, SYRACUSE UNIV, 95- *Personal Data:* b Celle, Ger, Nov 1, 28; m 57; c 2. *Educ:* Univ Marburg, Vordiplom, 51; Univ Gottingen, Dr rer nat, 54- *Prof Exp:* Res officer, Commonwealth Sci & Indust Res Orgn, Univ Melbourne, 55-58; res assoc mining & metall eng, Univ Ill, 58-60, res asst prof, 60-61. *Mem:* Am Soc Metals; Am Phys Soc. *Res:* Magnetic memory; plastic properties of metals; specific heat; Hall and Seebeck effects of transition element alloys; optical properties of alloys; crack studies; magnetic thin films. *Mailing Add:* 409 Link Syracuse Univ Syracuse NY 13244. *E-Mail:* kschrode@syr.edu

SCHRODER, PETER, COMPUTER GRAPHICS. *Current Pos:* ASST PROF COMPUT SCI, CALIF INST TECHNOL, 95- *Personal Data:* b Hanover, Ger, Mar 30, 60. *Educ:* Univ Berlin, Ger, Univ Dipl, 87; Mass Inst Technol, MS, 90; Princeton Univ, PhD(comput graphics), 94. *Honors & Awards:* Career Award, NSF, 96. *Prof Exp:* Mem tech staff, Thin King Machs Corp, 90-91; vis res fel, GMD, 92-94. *Concurrent Pos:* Sloan Found fel, 96. *Mem:* Asn Comput Mach. *Res:* Multi resolution methods. *Mailing Add:* Calif Inst Technol 1200 E California Blvd MS 256-80 Pasadena CA 91125. *Fax:* 626-792-4257; *E-Mail:* ps@cs.caltech.edu

SCHRODER, VINCENT NILS, PLANT PHYSIOLOGY. *Current Pos:* Asst prof, 55-69, ASSOC PROF AGRON, UNIV FLA, 69- *Personal Data:* b Chicago, Ill, Dec 8, 20; m 59; c 4. *Educ:* Univ Ga, BSA, 48; Duke Univ, PhD(plant physiol), 56. *Mem:* Am Soc Agron; Am Soc Plant Physiologists. *Res:* Plant mineral nutrition; effects of environment on photosynthesis; soil temperature effects on plant growth. *Mailing Add:* 1630 NW 23rd St Gainesville FL 32605-3878

SCHRODT, JAMES THOMAS, CHEMICAL ENGINEERING, MATHEMATICS. *Current Pos:* asst prof, 66-72, ASSOC PROF CHEM ENG, UNIV KY, 72- *Personal Data:* b Louisville, Ky, Oct 7, 37; m; c 2. *Educ:* Univ Louisville, BChE, 60, PhD(chem eng), 66; Villanova Univ, MChE, 62. *Prof Exp:* Jr engr, Tenn Eastman Co, 60; instr chem eng, Univ Louisville, 62-65; sr res engr, Tenn Eastman Co, 65-66. *Mem:* Am Chem Soc; Am Inst Chem Engrs. *Res:* Simultaneous heat and mass transfer; thermodynamics; electrodialysis. *Mailing Add:* Dept Chem & Mat Eng Univ Ky Lexington KY 40506-0046

SCHRODT, VERLE N(EWTON), CHEMICAL ENGINEERING. *Current Pos:* prof & dept head, Chem Eng, 88-89, PROF & ASST DEAN RES & GRAD STUDIES, UNIV ALA, TUSCALOOSA, ALA, 89- *Personal Data:* b Muscatine, Iowa, Apr 26, 33; m 55; c 8. *Educ:* Univ Ill, Urbana, BS, 55; Pa State Univ, MS, 58, PhD(chem eng), 61. *Prof Exp:* Supvr, Appl Sci Labs, Inc, 56-61; sr res engr, Monsanto Co, St Louis, 61-67, eng fel, 67-77, sr eng fel, 77-85; chief, Chem Eng Sci Div, Nat Bur Standards, Boulder, Co, 86-88. *Mem:* Am Inst Chem Engrs; Am Chem Soc. *Res:* Mathematical modeling of chemical and biological systems; design of agricultural growth facilities; image processing; x-ray analysis. *Mailing Add:* 1704 Hollow Lane Tuscaloosa AL 35406-3040

SCHROEDER, ALFRED C(HRISTIAN), ELECTRICAL ENGINEERING, COLORIMETRY. *Current Pos:* RETIRED. *Personal Data:* b West New Brighton, NY, Feb 28, 15; m 81, Dorothy Bleloc; c Carol A. *Educ:* Mass Inst Technol, BS & MS, 37. *Honors & Awards:* David Sarnoff Gold Medal Award, Soc Motion Picture & TV Engrs, 65; Vladimir K Zworykin Award, Inst Elec & Electronics Engrs, 71; Karl Ferdinand Braun Prize, Soc Info Display, 89. *Prof Exp:* Mem tech staff, David Sarnoff Res Ctr, RCA Corp, 37-80. *Mem:* AAAS; fel Inst Elec & Electronics Engrs; Soc Motion Picture & TV Engrs; Optical Soc Am; Sigma Xi. *Res:* Sequential, simultaneous, and simultaneous subcarrier color television systems; tri-color tubes; mechanism of color vision. *Mailing Add:* 114 Pennswood Village Apt I Newtown PA 18940-0909

SCHROEDER, ALICE LOUISE, GENETICS. *Current Pos:* NIH fel, Wash State Univ, 69-70, lectr genetics, 71, asst prof, 71-78, ASSOC PROF GENETICS, WASH STATE UNIV, 78-, ASSOC COORDR, PREMED/PREDENT PROG, 94- *Personal Data:* b Knoxville, Tenn, June 22, 41; m 66; c 2. *Educ:* Univ Colo, Boulder, BA, 63; Stanford Univ, PhD(biol, genetics), 70. *Concurrent Pos:* NIH res grants, 71-74, 78-80, 79-82, 85 & NSF, 85. *Mem:* AAAS; Genetics Soc Am; Asn Women Sci. *Res:* DNA maintenance systems; recombination; genetics of radiation sensitivity; fungal, bacterial and viral genetics. *Mailing Add:* Dept Genetics & Cell Biol Wash State Univ Pullman WA 99164-4234. *E-Mail:* alschroe@wsu.edu

SCHROEDER, ANITA GAYLE, APPLIED STATISTICS. *Current Pos:* MEM STAFF, DEPT STATE, 84- *Personal Data:* b Wichita, Kans. *Educ:* Baker Univ, BS, 66; Kans State Univ, MS, 68; Ore State Univ, PhD(statist), 72. *Prof Exp:* Proj dir, Ark Health Statist Ctr, 72-73; dir, Emergency Med Serv Data & Eval, Ark Health Systs Found, 73-74; pres, Schroeder & Assocs, 74-75; statistician, Westat, Inc, 75-84, dir, Social Sci Serv, 79-84. *Concurrent Pos:* Asst prof biomet, Med Ctr, Univ Ark, 72-74. *Mem:* Sigma Xi; Am Statist Asn; Biomet Soc. *Res:* Surveys in social services and health; evaluation. *Mailing Add:* 6558 River Tweed Lane Alexandria VA 22312-3140

SCHROEDER, DANIEL JOHN, astronomy, optics, for more information see previous edition

SCHROEDER, DAVID HENRY, BIOCHEMICAL PHARMACOLOGY. *Current Pos:* RETIRED. *Personal Data:* b Indianapolis, Ind, Feb 16, 40; m 62; c 2. *Educ:* Purdue Univ, West Lafayette, BS, 62, MS, 66, PhD(biochem), 68. *Prof Exp:* Res assoc chem pharmacol, NIH, 68-70; res biochemist, Wellcome Res Labs, 70-95. *Mem:* Am Chem Soc. *Res:* Development of analytical methods for detection and quantitation of drugs and metabolites; computerization of data; pharmacokinetics, bioavailability of drugs; use of computer spread sheet software for pharmacokinetics analyses. *Mailing Add:* 1425 Harris Ct Cary NC 27511

SCHROEDER, DAVID J DEAN, PERSONNEL RESEARCH, DRUG & ALCOHOL EFFECTS ON PERFORMANCE. *Current Pos:* supvr, Clin Psychol Res Unit, Aviation Psychol Lab, Fed Aviation Admin, 80-87, Clin Psychol Res Sect, Human Resources Br, 87-89; Field Performance Res Sect, Human Resources Res Div, 89-90, mgr, Human Factors Res Lab, 90-91, MGR, HUMAN RESOURCES RES DIV, FED AVIATION ADMIN, 91- *Personal Data:* b Hutchinson, Kans, Mar 21, 42; m 64, Nevonna J Thomas; c Taryn D & Anita J. *Educ:* Tabor Col, BA, 64; Kans State Teachers Col Emporia, MS, 67; Univ Okla, PhD(exp/soc psychol), 71. *Prof Exp:* Res psychologist, Civil Aeromed Inst, 70-72; clin psychol intern, Norfolk Regional Ctr & Northeast Ment Health Clin, Nebr, 72-73; clin psychologist, Vet Admin Hosp, Murfreesboro, Tenn, 73-75; adj asst prof psychol, Mid Tenn State Univ, 74-75; clin psychologist, Vet Admin Med Ctr, Topeka, Kans, 75-80; adj asst prof psychol, Washburn Univ, Topeka, Kans, 75-80. *Concurrent Pos:* Adj asst prof psychol, Washburn Univ, Topeka, Kans, 75-80; comt mem, Aerospace Med Asn, 77-79, Arrangements Comt, 77, Regist Comt, 77-, chair elect, Assoc Fel Group, 81-82, chair, 82-83, mem, Aviation Comt, 82-89, Sci Prog Comt, 82-, Educ Training Comt, 83-, chair, Poster Sessions Subcomt, 85, 86 & 87, Sci & Technol Comt, 85-, Long Range Planning Comt, 86, 87 & 88, Human Factors Comt, 89-, dep chair, Sci Prog Comt, 89-, chair, 90-91 & numerous other comts; pres-elect, Okla Psychol Asn, 91, pres, 92, past-pres, 93; pres-elect, Aerospace Human Factors Asn, 93-94, pres, 94-95; mem, Aerospace Med Asn Coun, 92-95, vpres, 96-97. *Mem:* Sigma Xi; fel Aerospace Med Asn; fel Am Psychol Asn. *Res:* The use of survey methodology to determine employee job satisfaction, well-being/stress and reactions to job change/automation; assessment of factors associated with air traffic controller selection and performance; short and long term effects of alcohol and drugs on performance and the vestibular system; author and co-authorof numerous publications. *Mailing Add:* Human Resources Res Div Fed Aviation Admin Aeronaut Ctr Civil Aeromed Inst PO Box 25082 Oklahoma City OK 73125. *Fax:* 405-954-4852; *E-Mail:* david_schroeder@mmacmail.jccbi.gov

SCHROEDER, DOLORES MARGARET, NEUROANATOMY. *Current Pos:* assoc prof, 75-80, TENURED ASSOC PROF MED SCI, SCH MED, IND UNIV, BLOOMINGTON, 80- *Personal Data:* b New York, NY, July 30, 37; c 1. *Educ:* Notre Dame Col, BS, 58; John Carroll Univ, MS, 63; Case Western Res Univ, PhD(anat), 70. *Prof Exp:* Fel neurosurg, Med Sch, Univ Va, 70-72, from instr to asst prof, 72-75. *Mem:* Soc Neurosci; Am Asn Anat; AAAS; Int Brain Res Orgn. *Res:* Comparative neuroanatomy; development and organization of brainstem and spinal cord. *Mailing Add:* Med Sci Prog Univ Ind Myers Hall Bloomington IN 47405-4401

SCHROEDER, DUANE DAVID, BIOCHEMISTRY. *Current Pos:* MGR PROJ, SCI, PLANNING & ADMIN, BAYER CORP, 91- *Personal Data:* b Newton, Kans, Nov 4, 40; m 61; c 3. *Educ:* Bethel Col, AB, 62; Tulane Univ, PhD(biochem), 67. *Prof Exp:* Damon Runyon fel, Mass Inst Technol, 67-69; sr res biochemist, Miles Inc, 69-71, biochem res supvr, 71-73, mgr biochem res, 73-80, assoc dir biochem res & develop, 80-83, assoc dir biochem res, 83-87, dir res & develop planning & admin, 87-90. *Concurrent Pos:* Res fel, Bayer AG, Ger, 75. *Mem:* AAAS. *Res:* Enzyme active sites and structure/function relationships; biologicals from plasma and recombinant DNA sources; hepatitis transmission; intravenous therapeutic immunoglobulins. *Mailing Add:* Bayer Corp 800 Dwight Way PO Box 1986 Berkeley CA 94710

SCHROEDER, FRANK, JR, NUCLEAR REACTOR SAFETY, REACTOR REGULATION. *Current Pos:* RETIRED. *Personal Data:* b Bartlesville, Okla, Sept 8, 27; m 49; c 2. *Educ:* Univ Ill, BS, 49, MS, 51. *Prof Exp:* Asst physics, Univ Ill, 49-51; physicist, Atomic Energy Div, Phillips Petrol Co, 51-57, supvr Spert-3 reactor exps, 57-60, mgr, Spert Proj, 60-66, reactor safety prog officer, 66-68; dep dir div reactor licensing, US AEC, 68-72, asst dep tech rev directorate of licensing, 72-75; dep dir, Div Tech Rev, Off Nuclear Reactor Regulation, US Nuclear Regulatory Comn, 75-76, dep dir, Div Systs & Safety, 76-80, asst dir, Generic Projs, Div Safety Technol Off, 80-85, dep dir, Div Pressurized Water Reactor Licensing-B, 85-86, asst dir, Div Reactor Projs, 86-87. *Mem:* Fel Am Nuclear Soc. *Res:* Nuclear reactor safety and kinetics; reactor physics; nuclear engineering. *Mailing Add:* 802 S Belgrade Rd Silver Spring MD 20902

SCHROEDER, FRIEDHELM, MEMBRANE LIPID ASYMMETRY, ATHEROSCLEROSIS. *Current Pos:* ASST PROF PHARMACOL, SCH MED, UNIV MO, 76- *Personal Data:* b Kastorf, Ger, July 16, 47; US citizen; m 79. *Educ:* Univ Pittsburgh, BS, 70; Mich State Univ, PhD(biochem), 74. *Prof Exp:* NSF fel biochem, Mich State Univ, 70-74; Am Cancer Soc fel biol chem, Med Sch, Wash Univ, 74-76. *Concurrent Pos:* Prin investr grants, Am Heart Asn, 77-, Nat Cancer Inst, 78-, Pharmaceut Mfg Asn, 78-80, & Hereditary Dis Found, 80-; consult, Miles Res Labs, 76, Hemotropic Dis Group, 80-, & Hormel Inst, 81; mem, Am Heart Asn Arteriosclerosis Coun, 78- *Mem:* Am Soc Pharmacol & Exp Therapeut; Am Soc Biol Chemists; Soc Neurosci; Am Oil Chemists Soc. *Res:* Structure and function of lipids in membranous particles (plasma membranes and lipoproteins) from cancer cell, blood, brain, liver and skin fibroblasts; biochemical, biophysical (fluorescence and differential scanning calorimetry), and pharmacological methods. *Mailing Add:* Dept Phys & Pharmacol Texas A & M Univ TVMC College Station TX 77843-4466. *Fax:* 513-558-4372

SCHROEDER, HANSJUERGEN ALFRED, ORGANIC CHEMISTRY. *Current Pos:* RETIRED. *Personal Data:* b Lautawerk, Ger, Jan 21, 26; nat US; m 53. *Educ:* Univ Berlin, BS, 49, MS, 50; Univ Freiburg, PhD(chem), 53. *Prof Exp:* Asst chem, Univ Berlin, 48-50, instr, 51; res assoc, Olin Corp, 52-56, sr res chemist, 57-58, res specialist, 59-63, sect mgr, 64-69, venture mgr, 7-72, mgr res & develop, 73-74, dir prod res, 75-81, dir res & develop, 82-85. *Mem:* Am Chem Soc; Ger Chem Soc. *Res:* Organic synthetic chemistry; nitrogen heterocycles; fluorine, boron and phosphorous compounds; pesticides; lubricants; high temperature polymers, biocides; pool chemicals; product development. *Mailing Add:* 609 Mix Ave Apt 3 Hamden CT 06514

SCHROEDER, HARTMUT RICHARD, BIOCHEMISTRY. *Current Pos:* DIR IMMUNOL DEVELOP, EX OXEMIS INC, 90- *Personal Data:* b Hitzdorf, Ger, Aug 29, 42; US citizen; m 72; c 3. *Educ:* Youngstown Univ, BS, 66; Pa State Univ, MS, 70, PhD(biochem), 72. *Prof Exp:* Res assoc biochem, Mich State Univ, 72-74; from res scientist to sr res scientist biochem, Ames Div, Miles Lab, Inc, 74-85, sr staff scientist, 85-90. *Concurrent Pos:* NAm ed, J Bioluminescence & Chemiluminescence, 86- *Mem:* Am Chem Soc; Am Soc Photobiol; Am Asn Clin Chem. *Res:* Bioluminescence, chemiluminescence and fluorescence, competitive protein binding reactions, enzyme assays, electrochemistry and immunochemistry; biosensors. *Mailing Add:* 44 Jackson Circle Franklin MA 02038

SCHROEDER, HERBERT A(UGUST), ORGANIC CHEMISTRY, WOOD & PULPING CHEMISTRY. *Current Pos:* assoc prof, 68-79, PROF WOOD CHEM, CHEM & BIORESOURCE ENG, COLO STATE UNIV, 79- *Personal Data:* b Cleveland, Ohio, Feb 26, 30; div; c Rolf, Kurt & Ingrid. *Educ:* Univ Idaho, BS, 52, MS, 54; Univ Hamburg, DSc(org chem), 60. *Prof Exp:* Res chemist, Forest Prod Lab, US Forest Serv, 61-63; asst prof forest prod chem, Forest Res Lab, Ore State Univ, 63-68. *Mem:* Am Chem Soc; Soc Wood Sci & Technol; Tech Asn Pulp & Paper Indust; Sigma Xi. *Res:* Chemistry of wood carbohydrates, wood polyphenolics and pulping processes; chemical treatment of wood; wood adhesives; biomass conversion to energy and chemicals. *Mailing Add:* Dept Chem & Bioresource Eng Eng Res Ctr Colo State Univ Ft Collins CO 80523. *Fax:* 970-491-8671

SCHROEDER, HERMAN ELBERT, ORGANIC CHEMISTRY, POLYMER CHEMISTRY. *Current Pos:* PRES, SCHROEDER SCI SERV INC, 80- *Personal Data:* b Brooklyn, NY, July 6, 15; m 38, Elizabeth Barnes; c Nancy C (Tarczy), Edward L, Peter H & Martha L (Lewis). *Educ:* Harvard Univ, AB, 36, AM, 37, PhD(chem), 39. *Honors & Awards:* Gen Award, Int Inst Rubber Producers; Goodyear Medal, Rubber Div, Am Chem Soc; Lavoisier Medal, Du Pont. *Prof Exp:* Res chemist, Exp Sta, E I du Pont de Nemours & Co, Inc, 38-45, res chemist, Jackson Lab, 45-46, group leader, 46-49, head miscellaneous dyes div, 49-51, asst dir lab, 51-57, asst dir res, Elastomer Chem Dept, 57-63, res dir, 63-65, dir res & develop, 65-80. *Concurrent Pos:* Chmn res comt & trustee & vpres, Univ Del Res Found; sci consult, Metrop Mus Art, 80-84, Winterthor Mus, 81-, Smithsonian, 84-88. *Mem:* Fel AAAS; Am Chem Soc; Soc Chem Indust; NY Acad Sci. *Res:* Catalysis; resins; adhesives; polymers; rubber chemicals; color photography; vat dyes; pigments; application of dyes; fluorine chemicals; textile chemicals; elastomers; discovery and development of new elastomeric polymers and intermediates; fluoropolymers, art conservation. *Mailing Add:* No 74 Stonegates 4031 Kennett Pike Greenville DE 19807-2037

SCHROEDER, JOHN, HIGH PRESSURE PHYSICS. *Current Pos:* assoc prof, 82-90, PROF PHYSICS, RENSSELAER POLYTECH INST, 90- *Personal Data:* b Pardan (Banat), Yugoslavia, Aug 31, 38; US citizen; m 64, Mary Pfenninger; c Stephan C & Erika E. *Educ:* Univ Rochester, BS, 62, MS, 64; Cath Univ Am, PhD(physics), 74. *Prof Exp:* Res & develop officer, Atmospheric Effects Div, Defense Atomic Support Agency, USN, 67-70; res asst, Cath Univ Am, 70-74; physicist, Acoust Div, Naval Res Lab, 74-75; res assoc, Dept Chem, Univ Ill, 75-78; physicist, Corp Res & Develop, Gen Elec Co, 78-81. *Concurrent Pos:* Sr staff mem, Mats Res Lab, Univ Ill, 76-78; staff mem, Ctr Glass Sci & Technol, Rensselaer Polytech Inst, 85- *Mem:* Am Phys Soc; Optical Soc Am. *Res:* Brillouin, raman and rayleigh spectroscopy with emphasis on amorphous solids (glasses) and liquids; high pressure research; behavior of materials under extreme conditions of pressure and temperature; optical properties of glasses, fiber optics; magnetic properties of disordered solids; nonlinear optics; wave propagation in solids; photoluminescence; semiconductor nanocrystallites. *Mailing Add:* Dept Physics SC-1C18 Rensselaer Polytech Inst Troy NY 12180-3590. *Fax:* 518-276-6680; *E-Mail:* schroj@rpi.edu

SCHROEDER, JOHN SPEER, CARDIOLOGY. *Current Pos:* Intern, Med Ctr, Standord Univ, 62-63, resident internal med, 65-67, asst prof med & cardiol, 70-77, dir, Intensive Cardiac Care Unit, 76-91, actg chief, 87-90, ASSOC PROF MED & CARDIOL, MED CTR, STANFORD UNIV, 77- *Personal Data:* b South Bend, Ind, May 6, 37; m 91, Jennifer Jones. *Educ:* Univ Mich, MD, 62; Am Bd Internal Med, dipl, 69; Am Bd Cardiovasc Dis, dipl, 73. *Concurrent Pos:* Fel cardiol, Med Ctr, Stanford Univ, 67-69. *Mem:* Am Fedn Clin Res; fel Am Col Cardiol; NY Acad Sci; fel Am Col Physicians. *Res:* Cardiac transplantation; coronary artery spasm; calcium antagonists; coronary artery disease. *Mailing Add:* Cardiol Div Stanford Univ Hosp 300 Pasteur Dr Stanford CA 94304-2203. *Fax:* 650-725-1597; *E-Mail:* hf.cxv@stanford.edu

SCHROEDER, LAUREN ALFRED, ECOLOGY. *Current Pos:* From asst prof to assoc prof, 68-76, PROF BIOL, YOUNGSTOWN STATE UNIV, 76- *Personal Data:* b Long Prairie, Minn, Feb 24, 37; m 60; c 2. *Educ:* St Cloud State Col, BS, 60; Univ SDak, MA, 65, PhD(zool), 68. *Mem:* AAAS; Am Inst Biol Sci; Ecol Soc Am; Entom Soc Am. *Res:* Ecological energetics of Lepidoptera especially as related to plant defense mechanisms and growth performance of larvae; population dynamics; ecosystem structure; PAH metabolism by aquatic vertebrates. *Mailing Add:* Youngtown State Univ 410 Wick Ave Youngstown OH 44555-0001

SCHROEDER, LEE S, ELEMENTARY PARTICLE PHYSICS, RELATIVISTIC NUCLEAR COLLISIONS. *Current Pos:* res physicist, Lawrence Berkeley Lab, 71-76, from staff scientist to sr staff scientist, 76-92, Bevalac sci dir, 87-92, DEP PROJ DIR, LAWRENCE BERKELEY LAB, 93- *Personal Data:* b Braddock, Pa, Apr 11, 38; m 57; c 4. *Educ:* Drexel Inst, 61; Ind Univ, Bloomington, MS, 63, PhD(physics), 66. *Prof Exp:* Assoc physics, Iowa State Univ, 65-67, asst prof, 67-71. *Concurrent Pos:* Assoc, Ames Lab, AEC, 65-67, assoc physicist, 67-71; US Dept Energy, Nuclear Physics Div, 87-89; asst dir, Phys Sci & Eng Off Sci & Technol Policy, Exec Off Pres, 92-93. *Mem:* Fel, Am Phys Soc. *Res:* Experimental elementary particle physics, particularly the use of bubble chamber, counters, and spark chambers to study the strong interactions of the elementary particles; high energy ions; streamer chambers; spectrometers to measure dilepton production, also kinematically forbidden processes; search for the quark-gluon plasma. *Mailing Add:* 50D-37 Lawrence Berkeley Lab Univ Calif Berkeley Berkeley CA 94720

SCHROEDER, LEON WILLIAM, astrophysics, astronomy education; deceased, see previous edition for last biography

SCHROEDER, LEROY WILLIAM, PHYSICAL CHEMISTRY, POLYMER CHEMISTRY. *Current Pos:* proj scientist, Div Chem & Physics, 77-80, res chemist, 80-90, CHIEF, MAT CHEM, FOOD & DRUG ADMIN, 90- *Personal Data:* b Watertown, Wis, July 18, 43; m 67, Kay Marshek; c Heidi. *Educ:* Wartburg Col, BA, 64; Northwestern Univ, Evanston, PhD(phys chem), 69. *Prof Exp:* Nat Res Coun-Nat Bur Stand assoc, 69-71, res assoc, Am Dent Asn Res Div, 71-74, head dent crystallog, Am Dent Asn Health Found, Nat Bur Stan, 74-77. *Mem:* Am Chem Soc; Am Crystallog Asn; Sigma Xi. *Res:* Molecular structure and dynamics; thermodynamics; chemical processes; hydrogen bonding; diffusion in solids. *Mailing Add:* 23000 Timber Creek Lane Clarksburg MD 20871. *Fax:* 301-443-5259; *E-Mail:* lws@fdadr.cdrh.fda.gov

SCHROEDER, MANFRED ROBERT, ACOUSTICS, NUMBER THEORY. *Current Pos:* EMER PROF PHYSICS & DIR, THIRD PHYSICS INST, UNIV GOETTINGEN. *Personal Data:* b Ahlen, Ger, July 12, 26; nat US; m 56; c 3. *Educ:* Univ Goettingen, dipl, 51, Dr rer nat(physics), 54. *Honors & Awards:* Gold Medal, Audio Eng Soc, 72; W R G Baker Prize Award, Inst Elec & Electronics Engrs, 75, Sr Award Speech & Signal Processing, 79; Lord Rayleigh Gold Medal, Brit Inst Acoustics, 86; Gold Medal, Acoust Soc Am, 91; Helmhotz Medal, 95. *Prof Exp:* Sci asst microwaves & acoust, Univ Goettingen, 52-54; mem tech staff, Bell Tel Labs, Inc, 54-58, head acoust res, 58-63, dir, Acoust & Speech Res Lab, 63-64, dir, Acoust, Speech & Mech Res Lab, 64-69. *Concurrent Pos:* Ed, Speech & Speech Recognition, 85. *Mem:* Nat Acad Eng; fel Acoust Soc Am; fel Inst Elec & Electronics Engrs; fel Audio Eng Soc; fel Am Acad Arts & Scis; Europ Phys Soc; fel NY Acad Sci. *Res:* Speech synthesis and recognition; room acoustics; psycho-acoustics; electro-acoustics; coherent optics; spatial stochastic processes; digital signal processing; number theory; neural networks; chaos; author of 2 books. *Mailing Add:* Univ Goettingen Third Physics Inst Buergerstrasse 42/44 37073 Goettingen Germany. *E-Mail:* mrs17@aol.com

SCHROEDER, MARK EDWIN, insect physiology, for more information see previous edition

SCHROEDER, MELVIN CARROLL, GEOLOGY. *Current Pos:* from asst prof to prof, 54-83, EMER PROF GEOL, TEX A&M UNIV, 87- *Personal Data:* b Saskatoon, Sask, July 19, 17; nat US; m 83; c 2. *Educ:* Wash State Univ, BS, 42, MS, 47, PhD(geol), 53. *Prof Exp:* Geologist, US Geol Surv, 49-54. *Concurrent Pos:* Counr, Geol Soc Am, 85-87; hon life mem, Sci Teachers Assoc Tex. *Mem:* Fel Geol Soc Am; Nat Asn Geol Teachers; Am Asn Petrol Geologists; hon mem Nat Sci Teachers Asn. *Res:* Ground water; radiohydrology; water contamination. *Mailing Add:* Dept Geol Tex A&M Univ College Station TX 77843-3115

SCHROEDER, MICHAEL ALLAN, ORGANIC CHEMISTRY, PHYSICAL CHEMISTRY. *Current Pos:* RES CHEMIST, US ARMY BALLISTIC RES LABS, 68- *Personal Data:* b Little Falls, NY, Nov 13, 38. *Educ:* Union Col, NY, BS, 61; Johns Hopkins Univ, PhD(chem), 68. *Prof Exp:* Res chemist, Naval Weapons Ctr, 67-68. *Concurrent Pos:* Resident res assoc, Nat Res Coun, 67-68. *Mem:* AAAS; Am Chem Soc; Am Defense Preparedness Asn; Sigma Xi. *Res:* Organic mechanisms; chemistry of organic nitro and nitroso compounds; heteroaromatic chemistry; explosive and propellant chemistry; laser spectroscopy; chemistry of high-nitrogen compounds; deamination chemistry. *Mailing Add:* Dir US Army Res Labs Attn AMSRL-WT-PC Aberdeen Proving Ground MD 21005. *Fax:* 410-278-6150

SCHROEDER, MICHAEL ALLEN, POPULATION DYNAMICS, BEHAVIORAL ECOLOGY. *Current Pos:* UPLAND BIRD RES BIOLOGIST, WASH DEPT WILDLIFE, 92- *Personal Data:* b Mission, Tex, Dec 12, 57; m 86, Leslie A Robb; c James E & Katherine E. *Educ:* Tex A&M Univ, BS, 80; Univ Alta, MSc, 85; Colo State Univ, PhD(wildlife biol), 90. *Mem:* Am Ornithologists Union; Wildlife Soc; Soc Conserv Biol; Ecol Soc Am; Wilson Ornith Soc; Cooper Ornith Soc. *Res:* Population dynamics and behavioral ecology of grouse; population regulation, dispersal, migration, recruitment and the evolution of mating sytems. *Mailing Add:* Wash Dept Wildlife PO Box 1077 Bridgeport WA 98813

SCHROEDER, PAUL CLEMENS, EXPERIMENTAL ZOOLOGY. *Current Pos:* from asst prof to assoc prof, Wash State Univ, 68-82, assoc chmn, 83-87, chmn, 87-91, PROF ZOOL, WASH STATE UNIV, 82- *Personal Data:* b Brooklyn, NY, Aug 13, 38; m 66, Alice L Andersen; c Lianne & Lisa. *Educ:* St Peter's Col, NJ, BS, 60; Stanford Univ, PhD(biol sci), 66. *Prof Exp:* NSF fel zool, Univ Calif, Berkeley, 66-67, USPHS fel, 67-68. *Concurrent Pos:* Vis prof, Univ Southern Calif, 73; Alexander von Humboldt Found fel, Zool Inst, Univ Cologne, 74-75, Univ Mainz, 89, & Fogarty Int fel, NIH & Fulbright fel, Dept Anat, Univ Queensland, Brisbane, Australia, 82; prin investr, NIH, 74-77 & 79-82; ed, Marine Biol, 85-89, J Exp Zool, 86-89; vis scientist, Bioctr, Univ Basle, Switz, 89. *Mem:* Fel AAAS; Am Soc Zool; Coleopterists Soc; Int Soc Invert Reproduction (secy, 89-). *Res:* Hormonal control of developmental and reproductive processes primarily in polychaete worms, echinoderms and amphibians; ovulatory mechanisms in vertebrates to provide evolutionary perspective on mammalian ovary. *Mailing Add:* Dept Zool Wash State Univ Pullman WA 99164-4236. *Fax:* 509-335-3184

SCHROEDER, PETER A, LOW TEMPERATURE PHYSICS, ELECTRON TRANSPORT PROPERTIES. *Current Pos:* from asst prof to assoc prof, 61-69, PROF PHYSICS, MICH STATE UNIV, 69- *Personal Data:* b Dunedin, NZ, Dec 6, 28; m 53, M Gwyneth Taylor; c Judith & Christopher. *Educ:* Univ Canterbury, MSc, 50; Bristol Univ, PhD(physics), 55. *Prof Exp:* Asst lectr physics, Univ Canterbury, 54-56, lectr, 56-59; fel, Nat Res Coun Can, 59-60, asst res officer, 60-61. *Concurrent Pos:* Vis prof, Univ Sussex, Eng, 67, Univ Leeds, Eng, 74, Cath Univ Nijmegen, Neth, 82, Univ Paris-Sud, Orsay, France, 90, Max Planck Inst, High Magnetic Field Lab, Grenoble, France, 90. *Mem:* Fel Am Phys Soc; Mat Res Sco. *Res:* Electron transport properties of metals, alloys and layered metallic systems; dielectric properties of clays; magnetic multilayers. *Mailing Add:* Dept Physics Mich State Univ East Lansing MI 48824. *Fax:* 517-353-4500; *E-Mail:* Bitnet: %schroede@msupa

SCHROEDER, ROBERT SAMUEL, PESTICIDE CHEMISTRY, ORGANIC BIOCHEMISTRY. *Current Pos:* mgr qual assurance, 82-87, admin asst, 87-89, TOXICOL SPECIALIST, MOBAY CORP, 90- *Personal Data:* b Chicago, Ill, July 9, 43; m 65; c 2. *Educ:* Iowa State Univ, BS, 64; Ind Univ, Bloomington, PhD(chem), 70. *Prof Exp:* Res chemist, Gulf Oil Chem Co, 69-75, actg sect supvr, 74-75, sect supvr, 76-80. *Mem:* Am Chem Soc; Soc Qual Assurance; Sigma Xi; Coun Agr Sci & Technol. *Res:* Pesticide metabolism and disposition in plants, animals, soil and water; development of residue methods for pesticides; application of instrumental analysis for structure determinations; direction of analytical biochemistry and environmental research; development of computer systems for data collection and reporting; dermal absorption and disposition of xenobiotics. *Mailing Add:* 17210 W 70th St Shawnee Mission KS 66217-9523

SCHROEDER, RUDOLPH ALRUD, PHYSICAL CHEMISTRY. *Current Pos:* RETIRED. *Personal Data:* b Evansville, Minn, Oct 11, 23; m 66. *Educ:* NDak Agr Col, BS, 52, MS, 53; Univ Md, PhD(chem), 57. *Prof Exp:* Asst prof chem, Univ Ky, 57-58; from asst prof to assoc prof, Southwestern Univ, La, 58-74, prof chem, 74- *Mem:* Am Chem Soc. *Res:* Infrared and Raman spectroscopy; hydrogen and interatomic bonding; bond energies; metal chelates; quantum mechanics. *Mailing Add:* 220 W Ardenwood Baton Rouge LA 70806

SCHROEDER, STEVEN A, INTERNAL MEDICINE. *Current Pos:* PRES, ROBERT WOOD JOHNSON FOUND & CLIN PROF MED, MED SCH, UNIV MED & DENT NJ, 91- *Personal Data:* b New York, NY, July 26, 39; m 71, Sally Ross; c David & Alan. *Educ:* Stanford Univ, BA, 60; Harvard Univ, MD, 64; Am Bd Internal Med, dipl, 71 & 80. *Hon Degrees:* LHD, Ruch-Presby-St Luke's Med Ctr, Rush Univ, 94; DSc, Boston Univ, 96. *Honors & Awards:* Pinnacle Award, UniHealth Found, 93; Robert J Glaser Award, Soc Gen Internal Med, 96. *Prof Exp:* Assoc prof health care sci & med, George Washington Med Ctr, 74-76; prof med & chief, Div Gen Internal Med, Univ Calif, San Francisco, 80-90. *Concurrent Pos:* Vis prof, Dept Community Med, St Thomas's Hosp Med Sch, London, 82-83; mem, US Prospective Payment Comn, 83-88, chmn, 84-88; mem, Comt Implications For-Profit Enterprise Health Care, Inst Med, 83-85, Adv Panel Off Technol Assessment Study Physicians & Med Technol, 84-85, Prev Med & Pub Health Sect, Nat Bd Med Examrs, 86-90 & Health & Pub Policy Comt, Am Col Physicians, 87-89; ed, Western J Med, 86-90; chmn, Spec Study Qual Rev & Assurance Medicare, Inst Med, Nat Acad Sci, 87-90; Dozor vis prof, Ben Guiron Univ Negev, Israel, 87; Mack Lipkin vis prof, NY Hosp & Cornell Med Sch, 89; lectr, State Univ NY, Stony Brook, 91. *Mem:* Inst Med-Nat Acad Sci; Soc Gen Int Med; master Am Col Physicians; Am Fedn Clin Res; Am Pub Health Asn; Asn Am Physicians. *Res:* Authored over 100 publications. *Mailing Add:* Robert Wood Johnson Found PO Box 2316 Princeton NJ 08543-2316. *Fax:* 609-987-8746

SCHROEDER, THOMAS DEAN, ANALYTICAL CHEMISTRY. *Current Pos:* ASSOC PROF CHEM, SHIPPENSBURG STATE COL, 69- *Personal Data:* b Reedsburg, Wis, May 2, 39; m 63; c 2. *Educ:* Univ Wis-Platteville, BS, 65; Univ Iowa, MS, 68, PhD(anal chem), 69. *Concurrent Pos:* Pa teaching fel, 81. *Mem:* Am Chem Soc; Sigma Xi. *Res:* Chemical instrumentation; gas chromatographic-mass spectrometry of biochemicals; construction of specific electrodes; flameless atomic absorption. *Mailing Add:* 9785 Forest Ridge Rd Shippensburg PA 17257-9221

SCHROEDER, WALTER ALBERT, PRESETTLEMENT PRAIRIES. *Current Pos:* instr geog, 64-80, chmn dept, 80-88, ASST PROF, UNIV MO, COLUMBIA, 80- *Personal Data:* b Jefferson City, Mo, Sept 9, 34; m 62, Pat Renner; c Paul R & Julianna M. *Educ:* Univ Mo, Columbia, AB, 56; Univ Chicago, MA, 58. *Prof Exp:* Instr geog, Cent Mich Univ, 58-63; lectr, Univ Southern Ill, Carbondale, 63-64. *Mem:* Asn Am Geogr; Am Name Soc. *Res:* Reconstruction of past environments in Missouri especially prairies and natural vegetation before European settlements; use by and impact of settlers from different cultures on the environment. *Mailing Add:* Geog Univ Mo 3 Stewart Hall Columbia MO 65211-0001

SCHROEDER, WARREN LEE, SOILS, CIVIL ENGINEERING. *Current Pos:* From asst prof to assoc prof, 67-77, asst dean eng, 71-85, PROF CIVIL ENG, ORE STATE UNIV, 77-, ASSOC DEAN ENG, 85- *Personal Data:* b Longview, Wash, Jan 3, 39; m 61; c 3. *Educ:* Wash State Univ, BS, 62, MS, 63; Univ Colo, Boulder, PhD(civil eng), 67. *Honors & Awards:* Thomas Fitch Rowland Prize, Am Soc Civil Engrs, 88. *Concurrent Pos:* Staff engr, McDowell & Assocs, Consult Engrs, 66-67 & CH2M/Hill, Consult Engrs, 67-70; pres, Willamette Geotechnical, Inc, 78- *Mem:* Am Soc Civil Engrs; Int Soc Soil Mech & Found Engr. *Res:* Deep foundations; retaining structures; behavior of submerged cohesionless soils; cofferdams and docks. *Mailing Add:* Financial Adm 640 Kerr Adm Bldg Ore State Univ Corvallis OR 97331-2156

SCHROEDER, WILLIAM, JR, ORGANIC CHEMISTRY. *Current Pos:* RETIRED. *Personal Data:* b New York, NY, Apr 9, 27; m 58; c 3. *Educ:* Purdue Univ, BS, 55, PhD(chem), 58. *Prof Exp:* Res assoc org chem, Upjohn Co, 58-65; dir res, Burdick & Jackson Labs, 65-66, vpres res, 66-75, secy, 68-75, vpres, 75-78, dir, Burdick & Jackson Labs, 75-86, pres, 78-86; vpres & gen mgr, Baxter Healthcare, 86-90; pres, Casadonte Res Labs, Muskegon, Mich, 88-90. *Mem:* Am Chem Soc. *Res:* Structures; natural products; carbohydrates; organic synthesis. *Mailing Add:* 3825 Harbor Pt Dr Muskegon MI 44944-2673

SCHROEDER, WILLIAM HENRY, TRACE ELEMENT DETERMINATIONS, MERCURY ENVIRONMENTAL ASPECTS. *Current Pos:* head, Abstracting Sect, Environ Can, Air Pollution Control Directorate, Ottawa, 73-75, phys scientist, Technol Develop & Demonstr, Water Pollution Control Directorate, Burlington, 75-77, res scientist atmospheric chem, Atmospheric Environ Serv, 77-87, head, Chem Processes Sect, 88-91, SR RES SCIENTIST, AIR QUAL RES BR, ATMOSPHERIC ENVIRON SERV, 92- *Personal Data:* b Breslau, Ger, Apr 27, 44; Can citizen; m 75, Claire; c Melanie. *Educ:* Univ Alta, Calgary, BSc, 66; Univ Colo, PhD(chem), 71. *Prof Exp:* Res fel, Fresenius Inst, Wiesbaden, Fed Repub Ger, 71-72. *Concurrent Pos:* Sci liaison officer, Energy Recovery Demonstration Proj, Environ Can contract, St Lawrence Cement Co, Mississauga, Ont, 76-77; sci authority, Environ Can Contract, Barringer Res Inc, 80-82; mem, Great Lakes Toxic Chem Comt, 82-87. *Mem:* Am Chem Soc; Chem Inst Can; Air & Waste Mgt Asn; Am Soc Testing & Mat; NY Acad Sci; Can Stand Asn. *Res:* Atmospheric pathways (sources, transport, transformation and fate); characteristics (physico-chemical, toxicological) of toxic trace elements and organic substances; environmental analytical chemistry; atmospheric chemistry. *Mailing Add:* 90 Bedford Pk Ave Richmond Hill ON L4C 2N8 Can

SCHROEDER, WOLF-UDO, NUCLEAR CHEMISTRY. *Current Pos:* res assoc, Univ Rochester, 75-79, sr res assoc, 79-80, prof nuclear sci, 81-83, assoc prof, 83-87, PROF CHEM, UNIV ROCHESTER, 87- *Personal Data:* b Stralsund, Ger, May 25, 42; m 68. *Educ:* Univ Gottingen, Free Univ Berlin, dipl, 67; Tech Univ Darmstadt, PhD(nuclear physics), 71. *Prof Exp:* Res assoc nuclear physics, Univ Darmstadt, 68-75. *Concurrent Pos:* Fel, Ger Acad Exch Serv; Sci Vis, CERIV, 68-72. *Mem:* Fel Am Phys Soc; Am Chem Soc; Sigma Xi. *Res:* Heavy-ion and light-ion reactions; muon-induced reactions. *Mailing Add:* Dept Chem Univ Rochester Rochester NY 14627. *Fax:* 716-473-5384

SCHROEER, DIETRICH, ARMS-RACE ISSUES. *Current Pos:* asst prof, 66-73, assoc prof, 73-79, PROF PHYSICS, UNIV NC, CHAPEL HILL, 79- *Personal Data:* b Berlin, Ger, Jan 24, 38; US citizen; m 64; c Karsten & Alison. *Educ:* Ohio State Univ, BSc, 60, PhD(physics), 65. *Honors & Awards:* Am Inst Physics-US Steel Sci Writing Award, 72. *Prof Exp:* NATO fel, Munich Tech Univ, 65-66. *Concurrent Pos:* Fulbright fel & Nat Endowment for Humanities fel, Munich, Ger, 72-73; res assoc, Int Inst Strategic Studies, London, 84-85; vis prof, Dept War Studies, Kings Col, London. *Mem:* AAAS; Am Asn Physics Teachers; fel Am Phys Soc; Soc Social Studies Sci, Arms Control Asn; Fedn Am Scientists. *Res:* Crystal-defect and radiation-damage studies by Mossbauer effect; science policy; arms-control issues. *Mailing Add:* Dept Physics & Astron Univ NC Chapel Hill NC 27599-3255. *Fax:* 919-962-0480; *E-Mail:* schroeer@physics.unc.edu

SCHROEER, JUERGEN MAX, MASS SPECTROMETRY, PHYSICS TEACHING. *Current Pos:* assoc prof, 69-74, PROF PHYSICS, ILL STATE UNIV, 74- *Personal Data:* b Berlin, Ger, Oct 2, 33; US citizen; m 64; c Meredith Savale; c William, Christopher, Linnaea & Andrew. *Educ:* Ohio State Univ, BS & MS, 58; Cornell Univ, PhD(physics), 64. *Prof Exp:* Res assoc quantum electronics, Sch Elec Eng, Cornell Univ, 64-65; asst prof physics, Univ Wyo, 65-69. *Concurrent Pos:* Vis prof & Fulbright travel grant, Univ Munster, 75; vis scientist, Mat Res Lab, Univ Ill, 83 & Univ Kaiserslautern, Ger, 91-92; vis prof, Ore Grad Inst, 83-84 & Univ Ill, 85, 86, 90. *Mem:* Am Vacuum Soc; Am Soc Mass Spectrometry. *Res:* Surface physics; secondary ion mass spectrometry. *Mailing Add:* Dept Physics Ill State Univ Campus Box 4560 Normal IL 61790-4560. *Fax:* 309-438-5413

SCHROEN, WALTER H, INDUSTRIAL & MANUFACTURING ENGINEERING, TECHNICAL MANAGEMENT. *Current Pos:* RETIRED. *Personal Data:* b Munich, Ger, June 3, 30; m 67, Hinre Meijer; c Anneke T (Younger), Thorid A, Hans H & Wolfgang J. *Educ:* Univ Munich, BS, 52, MS, 56; Clausthal Tech Univ, PhD(atomic physics), 62. *Prof Exp:* Physicist, Cent Res Labs, Siemens Corp, 53-55 & Semiconductor Div, 56-58; res asst physics, Clausthal Tech Univ, 58-62; sr scientist semiconductor res, Int Tel & Tel Semiconductors, Calif, 62-65; sect head, Semiconductor Res & Develop Labs, Tex Instruments Inc, 65-75, semiconductor group process control, 75-79, mgr semiconductor assembly & packaging, 80-87. *Concurrent Pos:* Ger co-rep, Int Seminar Nuclear Sci, Saclay, France, 59; chmn, Electrochem Soc Symp, 75; fel, Tex Instruments Inc, 87; NATO Advan Study Inst Process & Device Modeling IC Design, 77. *Mem:* Am Phys Soc; Ger Phys Soc; Electrochem Soc; Inst Elec & Electronics Engrs. *Res:* Semiconductor and surface physics; physics of failure in electronics; analysis and modeling; thin films physics; superconductivity and physics of ionization; bipolar and metal-oxide semiconductor devices; semiconductor process control, semiconductor reliability; semiconductor packaging; multichip modules; water-scale assembly; electrical, thermal and stress modeling; semiconductor wafer fab process modeling and device simulation; preparation and properties of superconducting josephson functions; all silicon manufacturing plants; developing a germanium power transistor; shockley transistor research laboratory; silicon surface effects, second breakdown; phenomenon, hi-power 4-layer diode; author of over 80 scientific papers; granted several US and European patents. *Mailing Add:* 6620 Churchill Way Dallas TX 75230. *E-Mail:* whschroen1@aol.com

SCHROEPFER, GEORGE JOHN, JR, BIOCHEMISTRY, CHEMISTRY. *Current Pos:* prof biochem & chem & chmn dept biochem, 72-83, RALPH & DOROTHY LOONEY PROF BIOCHEM, RICE UNIV, 83- *Personal Data:* b St Paul, Minn, June 15, 32; c 5. *Educ:* Univ Minn, BS, 55, MD, 57, PhD, 61. *Prof Exp:* Intern med, Univ Minn, 57-58, Nat Heart Inst res fel, 58-61, res assoc, 61-63, asst prof biochem, 63-64; asst prof, Univ Ill, Urbana, 64-67, from assoc prof to prof biochem & org chem, 67-72, dir sch basic med sci, 68-70. *Concurrent Pos:* USPHS res career develop award, 62-64; fel, Harvard Univ, 62-63; fel, Coun Arteriosclerosis, Am Heart Asn, 64-; mem panel Biochem Nomenclature, Nat Acad Sci, 65-68; assoc ed, Lipids, 69-78; mem biochem training comt, NIH, 70-73; distinguished vis prof sci & technol, Agency Japan, NIH, 93. *Mem:* Fel AAAS; Am Chem Soc; Am Soc Biol Chem; Am Soc Mass Spectrometry; Am Heart Asn. *Res:* Sterol biosynthesis and metabolism; intermediary metabolism of lipids; stereochemistry and mechanism of enzymatic reactions; inhibitors of cholesterol biosynthesis. *Mailing Add:* Dept Biochem PO Box 1892 Rice Univ Houston TX 77251. *Fax:* 713-285-5154

SCHROER, BERNARD J, SYSTEM SIMULATION. *Current Pos:* dir, Johnson Res Ctr, 72-91, chmn, Dept Indust & Systs Eng, 91-95, PROF COL ENG, UNIV ALA, HUNTSVILLE, 88-, DIR, CTR ROBOTICS, 91-, ASSOC VPRES RES, 95- *Personal Data:* b Seymour, Ind, Oct 11, 41; m 63, Kathleen Dittman; c Shannon & Bradley. *Educ:* Western Mich Univ, BSE, 64; Univ Ala, MSE, 67; Okla State Univ, PhD(eng), 72. *Honors & Awards:* Energy Innovation Award, US Dept Energy, 84. *Prof Exp:* Designer, Sandia Labs, 61-62; engr, Teledyne Brown Eng, 64-67; proj engr, Boeing, 67-70 & Comput Sci Corp, 70-71. *Concurrent Pos:* Mem, Gov Ala State Solar Comt, 76, Gov Cabinet, 82; mem bd dirs, Southern Solar Energy Ctr, 80-85; mem energy coun, Ala Dept Energy, 80-89. *Mem:* Nat Soc Prof Engrs; Am Inst Indust Engrs; Am Soc Eng Educ; Technol Transfer Soc; Soc Comput Simulation; Am Soc Qual Cont. *Res:* System simulation of automated manufacturing-production systems. *Mailing Add:* 716 Owens Dr Huntsville AL 35801

SCHROER, RICHARD ALLEN, CLINICAL PATHOLOGY, PROJECT MANAGEMENT. *Current Pos:* SR CRO MONITOR, WYETH-AYERST RES, 95- *Personal Data:* b Celina, Ohio, July 10, 44; div; c Michael & Arthur. *Educ:* Kent State Univ, BS, 66, PhD(chem), 70. *Prof Exp:* Res assoc biochem, Univ Calif, Irvine-Calif Col Med, 71-73; dir biol, Nelson Res & Develop, 73-75; sr res biologist, Lederle Labs, 75-76, group leader clin chem-hemat, 76-88; mgr clin path, Med Res Div, Am Cyanamid Co, 89-93, toxicol proj mgr, 93-95. *Concurrent Pos:* NIH fel, Univ Calif, Irvine-Calif Col Med, 71-73. *Res:* Toxicology; clinical pathology of laboratory animals. *Mailing Add:* 19 Strawberry Hill Lane West Nyack NY 10994

SCHROETER, GILBERT LOREN, GENETICS, CYTOGENETICS. *Current Pos:* Asst prof, 68-77, ASSOC PROF BIOL, TEX A&M UNIV, 77- *Personal Data:* b Reedley, Calif, May 24, 36; m 63; c 1. *Educ:* Fresno State Col, BA, 63; Univ Calif, Davis, PhD(genetics), 68. *Mem:* AAAS; Genetics Soc Am. *Res:* Population cytology; chromosome evolution; cytotaxonomy of orthopteroid insects. *Mailing Add:* Dept Biol Tex A&M Univ College Station TX 77843-0100

SCHROF, WILLIAM ERNST JOHN, ORGANIC POLYMER CHEMISTRY. *Current Pos:* Res chemist, 63-71, sr res chemist, 71-85, sr tech mkt rep, 85-87, SR INF SPEC, E I DU PONT DE NEMOURS & CO, INC, 87- *Personal Data:* b Cincinnati, Ohio, June 5, 31; m 58, Janet Seilkop; c William Jr, Stephen, Peter, Robert & Henry. *Educ:* Univ Cincinnati, AB, 58, PhD(org chem), 64. *Concurrent Pos:* Patent searching, corp level. *Mem:* Am Chem Soc; Am Inst Chem; Sigma Xi. *Res:* Synthesis of anticancer compounds such as coumarins and furoquinolines; polymerization of polyamides for textile and industrial end uses; product development of textile and industrial yarns. *Mailing Add:* 954 Wawaset Rd Kennett Square PA 19348

SCHROFF, PETER DAVID, life sciences, clinical pathology, for more information see previous edition

SCHROHENLOHER, RALPH EDWARD, PROTEIN CHEMISTRY, IMMUNOCHEMISTRY. *Current Pos:* from asst prof to assoc prof, 64-87, PROF MED, SCH MED, UNIV ALA, BIRMINGHAM, 87- *Personal Data:* b Cincinnati, Ohio, Aug 6, 33; m 60, Sandra J Welch; c Robin & John. *Educ:* Univ Cincinnati, BS, 55, PhD(biochem), 59. *Prof Exp:* Res chemist, Nat Cancer Inst, 58-60; asst prof arthritis res, Med Col Ala, 61-63; guest investr, Rockefeller Inst, 63-64. *Concurrent Pos:* Nat Inst Arthritis & Metab Dis grants, 65-78; Nat Cancer Inst res contract, 75-78. *Mem:* Am Col Rheumatology; AAAS; Am Chem Soc; Am Asn Immunol. *Res:* Immunoglobulin structure and function; autoantibodies and immune complexes in rheumatic diseases; laboratory assessment of rheumatic diseases. *Mailing Add:* Dept Med Div Clin Immunol & Rheumatol Univ Ala LHRB415 Birmingham AL 35294-0007. *Fax:* 205-934-1564

SCHROTER, STANISLAW GUSTAW, CHEMICAL ENGINEERING, INORGANIC CHEMISTRY. *Current Pos:* CONSULT, 87- *Personal Data:* b Katowice, Poland, May 8, 17; US citizen; m 46; c 5. *Educ:* Polish Univ Col Eng, Dipl Eng, 49. *Prof Exp:* Tech officer, Steatite & Porcelain Prod Ltd, Eng, 49-52; engr, Can Radio Mfg Corp, Can, 52-56; sr engr, Raytheon Co, Quincy, 56-61, sr engr, 61-87. *Concurrent Pos:* Consult, Georgetown Porcelain Ltd, 53-54. *Res:* Electron emissive materials; high temperature electrical insulation; ferromagnetic porcelains; potting and encapsulation; microelectronics. *Mailing Add:* 103 High New St Newton MA 02164

SCHROTH, MILTON NEIL, PLANT PATHOLOGY. *Current Pos:* From instr to assoc prof plant path, Univ Calif, 61-71, asst dean res, Col Agr Sci, 68-73, assoc dean res, Col Natural Resources & actg asst to vpres agr sci, 73-76, asst dir, Div Agri Sci, 76-79, PROF PLANT PATH, UNIV CALIF, BERKELEY, 71-, CHAIR, PLANT PATH DEPT, 89- *Personal Data:* b Fullerton, Calif, June 25, 33; m 59; c 3. *Educ:* Pomona Col, BA, 55; Univ Calif, Berkeley, PhD(plant path), 61. *Honors & Awards:* Campbell Award, Am Inst Biol Sci, 64. *Mem:* Am Soc Microbiol; fel Am Phytopath Soc; Sigma Xi. *Res:* Root disease research, especially plant bacterial diseases; biological control. *Mailing Add:* Env Sci Univ Calif Berkeley CA 94720-0001

SCHROTT, HELMUT GUNTHER, ENDOCRINOLOGY, MEDICAL GENETICS. *Current Pos:* ASSOC PROF INTERNAL & PREV MED, UNIV IOWA, 73- *Personal Data:* b Wein, Austria, Jan 23, 37; m 61; c 2. *Educ:* Western Reserve Univ, BA, 62; State Univ NY, Buffalo, MD, 66. *Prof Exp:* Intern & resident internal med, Buffalo Gen Hosp, 66-68; resident & fel internal med & endocrinol, Univ Utah Med Ctr, 68-70; fel med genetics, Univ Wash, 70-72; assoc consult med genetics, Mayo Clin, 72-73. *Res:* Conduct clinical trials to determine the efficacy of intervening on disease states: hyperchol esterolemia, diabetes, menopause; conduct community health screening and intervention trials as related to hypercholesterolemia. *Mailing Add:* Univ Iowa Newton Rd S 231 Westlawn Iowa City IA 52240

SCHROY, JERRY M, CHEMICAL TRANSPORT & FATE, WORKPLACE EXPOSURE CONTROL. *Current Pos:* Engr, Detergents & Heavy Chem Sect, Inorg Chem Div, Monsanto, St Louis, Mo, 63-65, engr, Phosphorus Sect, Inorg Chem Process Eng, 65-67, supvr, Plant Tech Serv Group, Inorg Chem Phosphorus Technol Dept, Columbia, Tenn, 67-69, eng specialist, Monsanto Biodize Syst Inc, Long Island, NY, 69-71, eng specialist, Indust Water Pollution Control Dept, Monsanto Environ-Chem Systs, Inc, Chicago, Ill, 71-72, process eng mgr, 72-73, eng specialist, Water Pollution Control Dept, St Louis, Mo, 73-75, eng specialist, Environ Control Group CED, 75-76, prin eng specialist, 76-80, Monsanto fel, 81-85, Monsanto fel, Environ

Technol Group MCC Opers, 85-89, MONSANTO SR FEL, ENVIRON TECHNOL GROUP MCC OPERS, MONSANTO CHEM CO, ST LOUIS, MO, 89- *Personal Data:* b Dayton, Ohio, Nov 6, 39; m 69, Barbara Meyrose; c Catherine, David & Mark. *Educ:* Univ Cincinnati, ChE, 63. *Concurrent Pos:* Mem, sci adv bd, Ctr Excellence Intermedia Transport, Univ Calif, Los Angeles, 84-87, tech adv bd, Cur Catastrophe Prev, NJ Dept Environ Protection, 86-87 & tech adv group, South Coast Air Qual Mgt Dist, Calif/ Environ Protection Agency, 86-90; mem, task group, Am Inst Chem Engrs, 86- & tech rev panel, US Environ Protection Agency Coop Res Prog, 86-90; mem, Comt on Human Exposure Assessment, Nat Acad Sci/Nat Res Coun, 88-90; chmn, Design Inst for Phys Properties Res, Am Inst Chem Engrs, 90; chair, Safety & Health Div, Am Inst Chem Engrs, 92. *Mem:* Fel Am Inst Chem Engrs; Water Pollution Control Fedn; Am Chem Soc; AAAS; Soc Risk Anal; Nat Asn Environ Professionals; Sigma Xi; Am Waste Mgt Asn; Am Acad Environ Engrs; Int Soc Exposure Anal (pres, 92-93). *Res:* Transport and fate of chemicals in the environment; physical chemical properties of 2, 3, 7, 8 Tetrachloropdioxin; mobility of low volatility chemicals in the soil; volatility/vaporization of chemicals from spills and wastewater systems. *Mailing Add:* 5 Springlake Ct Ballwin MO 63011-3549. *Fax:* 314-694-6178; *E-Mail:* 5690044@mcimail.com

SCHRUBEN, JOHANNA STENZEL, mathematics, optics; deceased, see previous edition for last biography

SCHRUBEN, JOHN H, BUILDING CONSTRUCTION, SYSTEMIZATION ARCHITECTURAL-ENGINEERING PRACTICE. *Current Pos:* RETIRED. *Personal Data:* b Stockton, Kans, Jan 19, 26; m 48; c 8. *Educ:* Kans State Univ, BS, 48; Ill Inst Technol, MS, 53. *Prof Exp:* Staff engr, Stand Oil Co, Ind, 48-55; proj mgr, Skidmore, Owings & Merrill, 55-69; pres, Prod Systs Archit & Eng, 69-82; exec mgr, Am Inst Architects, 82-89; PERSONAL CONSULT, US Dept State Foreign Bldg Oper-Bldg Design & Engr, 89-91. *Concurrent Pos:* Master spec develop & consult, US Dept State, Foreign Bldg Oper, Bldg Design & Engr, Engr Support Br, Criteria & Specif, 87- *Mem:* Fel Am Inst Architects. *Res:* Principal developer, author, producer of master specification system. *Mailing Add:* 6200 Meadow Ct Rockville MD 20852

SCHRUM, MARY IRENE KNOLLER, BIOCHEMISTRY, INFORMATION SCIENCE. *Current Pos:* RETIRED. *Personal Data:* b New York, NY, Apr 18, 26; m 69, James H. *Educ:* Col Notre Dame, Md, AB, 48; Georgetown Univ, MS, 56. *Prof Exp:* Sr org chemist, Crown Cork & Seal Co, 48-50; chemist, Dept Med, Johns Hopkins Univ, 50-52; biochemist cellular physiol & metab, Nat Heart Inst, NIH, 52-55, supvr metab, 55-59, biochemist Nat Inst Arthritis & Metab Dis, 59-62, sci reference analyst, Div Res Grants, 62-63; chemist, Food & Drug Admin, Washington, DC, 63-66, head, Cent Retrieval Index Group, Sci Info Facil, 66-68, sr systs analyst, tech opers staff, 68-82. *Res:* Arteriosclerosis; physical-chemical studies of proteins; amino acid chemistry; information storage and retrieval of scientific information and data; research and development; chemical notations; automatic and electronic data processing. *Mailing Add:* 5528 Warwick Pl Chevy Chase MD 20815

SCHRUM, ROBERT WALLACE, petroleum chemistry, for more information see previous edition

SCHRUMPF, BARRY JAMES, RANGE ECOLOGY, REMOTE SENSING. *Current Pos:* Actg dir, 73-75, dir, Environ Remote Appln Lab, 75-88, ASSOC PROF, ORE STATE UNIV, 80-, SEED CERT ASST, 88- *Personal Data:* b San Francisco, Calif, July 13, 43; m 72; c 1. *Educ:* Willamette Univ, BA, 66; Ore State Univ, MS, 68, PhD(rangeland resources), 75. *Res:* Multispectral, multiseasonal and multistage remote sensing for natural vegetation inventory and analysis. *Mailing Add:* 24908 Llewellyn Rd Corvallis OR 97333

SCHRYER, NORMAN LOREN, APPLIED MATHEMATICS. *Current Pos:* MEM TECH STAFF, BELL TEL LABS, 69- *Personal Data:* b Detroit, Mich, Jan 16, 43; m 65. *Educ:* Univ Mich, BS, 65, MS, 66, PhD(math), 69. *Mem:* Asn Comput Mach; Soc Indust & Appl Math. *Res:* Numerical solution of elliptic and parabolic partial differential equations. *Mailing Add:* 122 Sulfrian New Providence NJ 07974-1229

SCHRYVER, HERBERT FRANCIS, VETERINARY PHYSIOLOGY, VETERINARY PATHOLOGY. *Current Pos:* assoc prof, 66-90, EMER PROF VET NUTRIT, NY STATE VET COL, CORNELL UNIV. *Personal Data:* b New York, NY, Oct 15, 27; m 64. *Educ:* Cornell Univ, DVM, 54; Univ Pa, MS, 60, PhD(path), 64; Hofstra Col, BA, 61. *Prof Exp:* From instr to asst prof path, Univ Pa, 58-66. *Concurrent Pos:* Arthritis Found fel, 64-65; charter & emer dipl, Am Col Vet Nutrit. *Mem:* AAAS; Am Soc Cell Biol; Am Vet Med Asn; Int Acad Path; Am Inst Nutrit. *Res:* Mineral nutrition and metabolism; connective tissue physiology and pathology; bone diseases; diseases of domestic animals and wildlife. *Mailing Add:* 547 Ellis Hollow Creek Rd Ithaca NY 14850

SCHTEINGART, DAVID E, INTERNAL MEDICINE. *Current Pos:* resident, 59-60, instr, 60-61 & 62-63, asst prof, 63-67, assoc prof, 67-73, PROF MED, UNIV HOSP, UNIV MICH, ANN ARBOR, 73- *Personal Data:* b Buenos Aires, Arg, Oct 17, 30; m 60; c 3. *Educ:* Nat Col 6, Buenos Aires, BA, 47; Univ Buenos Aires, MD, 54. *Prof Exp:* Resident med, Hosp Nat Clin, Buenos Aires, 56-57. *Concurrent Pos:* Fel med, Mt Sinai Hosp, New York, 57-58; fel endocrinol, Maimonides Hosp, Brooklyn, 58-59 & Univ Hosp, Univ Mich, Ann Arbor, 61-62. *Mem:* Am Fedn Clin Res; NY Acad Sci; Endocrine Soc; Sigma Xi; Am Col Physicians. *Res:* Endocrinology; clinical abnormalities of adrenal cortical steroids; secretion and metabolism; obesity. *Mailing Add:* 5700 MSRB II Box 0678 Univ Mich Med Ctr 1150 W Med Ctr Dr Ann Arbor MI 48109-0001. *Fax:* 313-763-4151

SCHUBEL, JERRY ROBERT, MARINE GEOLOGY. *Current Pos:* PRES & CHIEF EXEC OFFICER, NEW ENG AQUARIUM, BOSTON, 94- *Personal Data:* b Bad Axe, Mich, Jan 26, 36; m 58; c 2. *Educ:* Alma Col, BS, 57; Harvard Univ, MAT, 59; Johns Hopkins Univ, PhD(oceanog), 68. *Prof Exp:* From asst res scientist to res scientist, Chesapeake Bay Inst, Johns Hopkins Univ, 67-74, adj res prof & assoc dir, 73-74; prof marine sci, State Univ NY, Stony Brook, 74-84, actg vprovost, Res & Grad Studies, 85-86, provost, 86-89, dir, Marine Sci Res Ctr, 74-94, dean & leading prof, 84-94. *Concurrent Pos:* Vis assoc prof, Univ Del, 69, lect prof, Univ Md, 69-71; vis prof, Franklin & Marshall Col, 70-71; sci dir & vpres, Hydrocon Inc, 71-74; mem, Univ-Nat Oceanog Lab Syst Adv Coun, 77-80, vchmn, 80; mem bd trustees, Stony Brook Found, State Univ NY, 78-84; panel chmn & partic workshop, Eng Found Conf Offshore Indust, Nat Oceanic & Atmospheric Admin, 79; partic workshop, Sci Comt Ocean Res, Intergovt Oceanog Comn, 79, chmn, 80; mem oversight review team, Off Oceanog Facil, NSF, 80; sr ed, Coastal Ocean Pollution Assessment, 80-84; mem sci work group, Nat Oceanic Satellite Syst, NASA, 80-86; chmn, Outer Continental Shelf Sci Comt, Minerals Mgt Serv, US Dept Interior, 85-86; hon prof, EChina Normal Univ, 85-; chmn bd dir, Marine Div Nat Asn, State Univ & Land Grant Col, 86-88, Nat Res Coun Marine Bd, 89- & NY Gov Task Force Coastal Resources, 90- *Mem:* Am Soc Limnol & Oceanog; AAAS; Nat Asn Geol Teachers; NY Acad Sci; Estuarine Res Fedn (vpres, 81-85, pres, 85-87). *Res:* Estuarine and shallow water sedimentation; suspended sediment transport; interactions of sediment and organisms; pollution; continental shelf sedimentation; marine geophysics; thermal ecology; coastal zone management; marine policy. *Mailing Add:* New Eng Aquarium Cent Wharf Boston MA 02110-3399

SCHUBERT, BERNICE GIDUZ, PLANT TAXONOMY. *Current Pos:* RETIRED. *Personal Data:* b Boston, Mass, Oct 6, 13. *Educ:* Univ Mass, BS, 35; Radcliffe Col, MS, 37, PhD, 41. *Prof Exp:* Tech asst taxon bot, Gray Herbarium, Harvard Univ, 41-50; Guggenheim fel, 50-51; consult plant taxon, Pedobot Proj, Econ Coop Admin, Brussels, Belg, 51-52; plant taxonomist, New Crops Res Br, Agr Res Serv, USDA, 52-61; assoc cur, Harvard Univ, 62-69, lectr biol, 71, cur, Arnold Arboretum, 69-84, sr lectr biol, 75-84. *Concurrent Pos:* Ed, J Arnold Arboretum, 63-78. *Mem:* Am Soc Plant Taxon; Soc Econ Bot; Bot Soc Am; Am Inst Biol Sci; hon mem Soc Bot Mex. *Res:* Desmodium; American species of Dioscorea and Begonia. *Mailing Add:* Harvard Univ Herbaria 22 Divinity Ave Cambridge MA 02138

SCHUBERT, CEDRIC F, MATHEMATICS. *Current Pos:* from assoc prof to prof, 69-94, EMER PROF MATH, QUEEN'S UNIV, ONT, 94- *Personal Data:* b Murray Bridge, Australia, Oct 20, 35; Can citizen; div; c Conrad & Carl. *Educ:* Univ Adelaide, BSc, 57, Hons, 58, MSc, 60; Univ Toronto, PhD(math), 62. *Prof Exp:* Lectr math, Univ Toronto, 61-62; asst prof, Univ Calif, Los Angeles, 62-69. *Mem:* Can Math Soc; AAAS; Am Math Soc. *Res:* Operator and function theoretic properties of linear elliptic partial differential equations. *Mailing Add:* Dept Math & Statist Queen's Univ Kingston ON K7L 3N6 Can. *Fax:* 613-547-0466

SCHUBERT, DANIEL SVEN PAUL, PSYCHIATRY, PSYCHOLOGY. *Current Pos:* asst prof, 72-77, ASSOC PROF PSYCHIAT, CASE WESTERN RES UNIV, 77- *Personal Data:* b Buffalo, NY, Sept 28, 35; m 69, Nancy Lapham; c Alexander W. *Educ:* State Univ Buffalo, BA, 55, MD, 65; Univ Chicago, PhD(psychol), 69. *Prof Exp:* Resident psychiat, Yale Univ, 69-72. *Concurrent Pos:* Consult ed, J Creative Behav, 71-, J Psychiat Treat Eval, 79, ed, Int J Psychiat Med, 87- *Mem:* Am Psychol Asn; fel Am Psychiat Asn; Sigma Xi; fel Am Col Psychiat; fel Acad Psychosom Med. *Res:* Depression in the medical patient; psychosomatic medicine; consultation psychiatry. *Mailing Add:* Dept Psychiat Case Western Res Univ 2500 Metrohealth Dr Cleveland OH 44109-1998. *Fax:* 216-778-8412

SCHUBERT, DAVID CRAWFORD, LASERS. *Current Pos:* RETIRED. *Personal Data:* b Shillington, Pa, Jan 8, 25; m 49; c 3. *Educ:* Lehigh Univ, BS, 49, MS, 50; Univ Md, PhD(physics), 61. *Prof Exp:* Asst physics, Lehigh Univ, 49-50; res physicist, Nat Bur Stand, 50-66; res physicist, Westinghouse Elec Corp, 66-92, sr engr. *Mem:* Am Phys Soc; Inst Elec & Electronics Engrs. *Res:* Physics of the free electron; electron optical study of gas flow at extremely low pressures; plasma physics; quantum optics. *Mailing Add:* 2644 Shadow Cove Annapolis MD 21401

SCHUBERT, EDWARD THOMAS, biochemistry, for more information see previous edition

SCHUBERT, GERALD, GEOPHYSICS, PLANETARY SCIENCES. *Current Pos:* from asst prof planetary & space sci to assoc prof planetary physics, 66-74, PROF GEOPHYS & PLANETARY PHYSICS, UNIV CALIF, LOS ANGELES, 74- *Personal Data:* b New York, NY, Mar 2, 39; m 60, Joyce E Slotnick; c Todd S, Michael E & Tamara S. *Educ:* Cornell Univ, BEngPhys & MAE, 61; Univ Calif, Berkeley, PhD(eng), 64. *Honors & Awards:* James B Macelwane Award, Am Geophys Union, 75. *Prof Exp:* Nat Acad Sci-Nat Res Coun res fel, Dept Appl Math & Theoret Physics, Univ Cambridge, 65-66. *Concurrent Pos:* Alexander von Humboldt fel & Fulbright grant, 69; John Simon Guggenheim Mem Found fel, 72. *Mem:* AAAS; fel Am Geophys Union. *Res:* Geophysical and astrophysical fluid dynamics; planetary physics. *Mailing Add:* Dept Earth & Space Sci Univ Calif Los Angeles CA 90095-1567. *Fax:* 310-825-2779; *E-Mail:* schubert@ucla.edu

SCHUBERT, JACK, ENVIRONMENTAL & TOXICOLOGICAL CHEMISTRY, CHELATION. *Current Pos:* prof, Mich State Univ, 86-, ADJ PROF BIOCHEM, 87- *Personal Data:* b Sept 14, 17; m 47, Mary Naeseth; c Ann (Purdy), Catherine (Weiss) & Amy (Draxler). *Educ:* Univ Chicago, BS, 40, PhD(phys chem), 44. *Prof Exp:* Asst prof physiol chem, Univ Minn, 47-48; sr scientist, Div Biol & Med Res, Argonne Nat Lab, 48-58; prof chem, Univ Buenos Aires, 61-64; prof radiation chem, Grad Sch Pub Health, Univ Pittsburg, 65-77; prof environ health sci, Hope Col, 77-80; Prof chem, Univ Md, Baltimore Co Campus, 80-86. *Concurrent Pos:* Lectr chem, Univ Chicago, 51-55, Univ Calif, Davis, 81; US deleg, First Int Conf Peaceful Uses Atomic Energy, Geneva, 55; sr fel, NSF, Zurich, 56-57; vis prof & consult, Wallenberg Lab, Univ Stockholm, 72; vis prof, Dept Food Sci & Nutrit, Univ Hawaii, Manoa, 88, Dept Environ Biochem, 93. *Mem:* Fel AAAS; Radiation Res Soc; Am Chem Soc; Health Physics Soc; Am Soc Biol Chemists. *Res:* Surface thermodynamics; ion exchange, stability of chelates and complex ions, radiobiology, log-normal distributions; radio and radiation chemistry; decorporation radioisotopes, synergism, genotoxicity; sensitization of bacteria and enzymes by radical anions, irradiated foods and computer simulations; published 160 research papers. *Mailing Add:* Dept Biochem Mich State Univ East Lansing MI 48824-1319. *Fax:* 517-353-9334

SCHUBERT, JOHN ROCKWELL, NUTRITIONAL BIOCHEMISTRY & CLINCAL NUTRITION. *Current Pos:* RETIRED. *Personal Data:* b East Orange, NJ, Aug 1, 25; m 48, Miriam Choate; c Mark W, Virginia C, Marjorie A & John H. *Educ:* Pa State Univ, BS, 48; Ore State Univ, MS, 51, PhD(nutrit), 56. *Prof Exp:* Res asst agr chem, Ore State Univ, 50; mem prod staff, Cutter Labs, Calif, 51; res asst agr chem, Ore State Univ, 51-57, asst prof, 57-63; exec secy nutrit study sect, Res Grants Rev Br, Div Res Grants, NIH, 63-85, referral off, 67-85. *Concurrent Pos:* Spec res fel, Exp Liver Dis Sect, Nat Inst Arthritis & Metab Dis, 60-61. *Mem:* Fel Am Inst Nutrit; fel Am Soc Clin Nutrit. *Res:* Agricultural chemistry; animal nutrition; bacterial physiology; metabolic diseases of nutritional origin; science administration. *Mailing Add:* RR 1 Box 241 B Baker WV 26801-9801

SCHUBERT, KAREL RALPH, PLANT BIOCHEMISTRY, CELL BIOLOGY. *Current Pos:* GEORGE LYNN CROSS PROF, UNIV OKLA, 90- *Personal Data:* b Urbana, Ill, Oct 12, 49; m 67; c 2. *Educ:* WVa Univ, BS, 71; Univ Ill, MS, 73, PhD(biochem), 75. *Prof Exp:* Fel bot & plant path, Ore State Univ, 75-76; from asst prof to assoc prof biochem, Mich State Univ, 76-83; res mgr, Monsanto, 83-85; dir, Plant Genetic Resources Ctr, Mo Bot Garden, 88-89; asst dir, ctr plant sci & biotechnol, Wash Univ, 88-90. *Concurrent Pos:* Adj assoc prof, Wash Univ, 83-85, vis assoc prof, 85-90, adj prof, 90-; consult, Mo Bot Garden, 87-89; pvt consult, 87- *Mem:* Am Soc Plant Physiologists; Am Chem Soc; Sigma Xi; Am Soc Biochem & Molecular Biol; AAAS; Int Soc Plant Molecular Biol. *Res:* Biochemical, physiological and molecular factors involved in the establishment of effective symbiotic association between leguminosa and actinoriza plants and nitrogen-fixing bacteria including Rhizobium and Frankia; biochemical energetics; conservation of plant diversity; wheat tissue culture/transformation; mechanisms of plant defenses against insects; tropical genetic resources; research administration; resource management. *Mailing Add:* Bot/Microbiol Dept Univ Okla 770 Van Vleet Oval Norman OK 73019-0245. *Fax:* 580-327-7619

SCHUBERT, LENHART K, ARTIFICIAL INTELLIGENCE. *Current Pos:* PROF, COMPUT SCI DEPT, UNIV ROCHESTER, 88- *Personal Data:* b Vienna, Austria, 1941; m 68, Marina Blinoff. *Educ:* Univ Toronto, BASc, 63, MASc, 65, PhD(aerospace studies), 70. *Prof Exp:* Postdoctoral fel & lectr mech & comput sci, Johns Hopkins Univ, 70-71; Nat Res Coun postdoctoral fel & lectr, Dept Comput Sci, Univ Alta, 71-73, from asst prof to assoc prof, 73-84, prof, 84-88. *Concurrent Pos:* Alexander Von Humboldt fel, Univ Karlsruhe, Ger, 78-79; adj prof, Dept Comput Sci, Univ Alta, 89-96. *Mem:* Fel Am Asn Artificial Intel. *Res:* Artificial intelligence; language understanding and dialogue, knowledge representation, inference and planning. *Mailing Add:* Dept Comput Sci Univ Rochester Rochester NY 14627

SCHUBERT, ROY W, BIOMEDICAL ENGINEERING, PHYSIOLOGICAL SYSTEMS. *Current Pos:* assoc prof biomed eng, 78-82, PROF ELEC ENG, LA TECH UNIV, 77-, PROF BIOMED ENG, 82- *Personal Data:* b Cleveland, Ohio, Jan 13, 41. *Educ:* Case Inst Technol, BS, 64; Case Western Res Univ, MS, 66, PhD(biomed eng), 76. *Honors & Awards:* James M Todd Award, La Eng Soc; Distinguished Res Award, La Tech Found. *Prof Exp:* Mgr, Bioeng Group, Penn Cent Transp Co, 68-70. *Mem:* Microcirculatory Soc; Inst Elec & Electronics Engrs; Biomed Eng Soc; Sigma Xi. *Mailing Add:* PO Box 1603 Ruston LA 71273-1603

SCHUBERT, RUDOLF, ELECTRICAL CONTACTS, GAS-METAL INTERACTIONS. *Current Pos:* mem tech staff, 84-95, SR CONSULT, BELL COMMUN RES, 96- *Personal Data:* b New York, NY, Sept 28, 40; m 63, 85; c 2. *Educ:* Fairleigh Dickinson Univ, BS, 62, MS, 64; Univ Del, PhD(physics), 69. *Prof Exp:* Mem tech staff, Bell Tel Labs, 69-83. *Concurrent Pos:* Prin investr, Bell Tel Labs, 69-83 & Bell Commun Res, 84-; instr, Am Vacuum Soc, 75-; comt chmn, Am Soc Testing & Mat & Inst Elec & Electronics Engrs. *Mem:* Am Vacuum Soc; Am Soc Testing & Mat; Inst Elec & Electronics Engrs Computer Soc; Electrochem Soc. *Res:* Interaction of the environment with electronics equipment and metal surfaces and specifically as to the corrosion of electrical contacts; restoration of electronic equipment due to damage from fires and contaminants. *Mailing Add:* Bell Commun Res Inc Rm 3x285 331 Newman Springs Rd Red Bank NJ 07701-7040. *Fax:* 732-758-2804; *E-Mail:* andys@nutes.cc.bellcore.com

SCHUBERT, WALTER L, PHYSICS. *Current Pos:* CONSULT TECH WRITER, AVIONIC & COMMUN ELECTRONICS, DATA COMMUN TEACHING & DOC ASSOC, 87- *Personal Data:* b New York, NY, Dec 17, 42; m 83. *Educ:* Hofstra Univ, BA, 64. *Mem:* Am Asn Physics Teachers; Soc Tech Commun. *Res:* Industrial commercial and defense electronics systems. *Mailing Add:* PO Box 20368 Cherokee Sta New York NY 10028

SCHUBERT, WILLIAM K, PEDIATRICS. *Current Pos:* chmn dept, 79-93, PROF PEDIAT, UNIV CINCINNATI, 69- *Personal Data:* b Cincinnati, Ohio, July 12, 26; m 48; c 4. *Educ:* Univ Cincinnati, BS, 49, MD, 52; Am Bd Pediat, dipl, 57. *Prof Exp:* Intern, Med Ctr, Ind Univ, 52-53; resident pediat, Cincinnati Children's Hosp, 53-55; instr pediat, Med Ctr, Univ Cincinnati, 56-59, sr res assoc, 58-63, assoc prof, 63-69; dir, Clin Res Ctr, Med Ctr Children's Hosp, 63-76, Div Gastroenterol & Gastroenterol Clin, 68-79, assoc chief staff, 71-72, physician exec dir, 79-83, pres & chief exec officer, 83-96. *Mem:* Soc Pediat Res; Am Fedn Clin Res; Am Asn Study Liver Dis; Am Gastroenterol Asn; Am Pediat Soc. *Res:* Gastroenterology; metabolism. *Mailing Add:* Children's Hosp Med Ctr 3333 Burnet Ave Cincinnati OH 45229-2899

SCHUBERT, WOLFGANG MANFRED, ORGANIC CHEMISTRY. *Current Pos:* from instr to assoc prof, 47-58, PROF ORG CHEM, UNIV WASH, 58- *Personal Data:* b Hanover, Ger, Feb 16, 20; nat US; m 41, 64; c 2. *Educ:* Univ Ill, BS, 41; Univ Minn, PhD(org chem), 47. *Prof Exp:* Res chemist, Am Cyanamid Co, Conn, 44-46. *Concurrent Pos:* Guggenheim fel & Fulbright res scholar, 60-61. *Mem:* Am Chem Soc; Royal Soc Chem. *Res:* Mechanisms of organic chemical reactions; solvent effects; substituent effects; acid base catalysis. *Mailing Add:* 5809 NE 57th St Seattle WA 98105

SCHUBRING, NORMAN W(ILLIAM), MICROWAVES, FERROELECTRICS. *Current Pos:* jr engr, Gen Motors Res Labs, 52-54, from res engr & group leader to sr res engr & group leader, 54-72, supvry res engr, 72-81, STAFF RES ENGR, GEN MOTORS NAO RES & DEVELOP CTR, 81- *Personal Data:* b Port Hope, Mich, June 1, 24; m 48, Nancy A Postage; c Robert. *Educ:* Wayne State Univ, BSEE, 52, MSEE, 59. *Honors & Awards:* Charles L McCuen Spec Achievement Award, Gen Motors Res Labs, 78. *Prof Exp:* Res asst, Willow Run Res Ctr, Univ Mich, 52. *Concurrent Pos:* Sr Award, Inst Elec & Electronics Engrs, 58-59. *Mem:* Inst Elec & Electronics Engrs; Soc Automotive Engrs. *Res:* Electronics; microwaves; automobile radar; antennas; guided missile countermeasures; instrumentation; ultrasonics; sonics; nondestructive testing; pyroelectrics, piezoelectrics and ferroelectrics; microwave sintering of cermaics. *Mailing Add:* 2723 Avonhurst Dr Troy MI 48084-1062. *Fax:* 810-986-0886; *E-Mail:* nschubri@cm52.gmt.com

SCHUCANY, WILLIAM ROGER, MATHEMATICAL STATISTICS, APPLIED STATISTICS. *Current Pos:* lab mgr statist consult, Southern Methodist Univ, 68-70, asst prof math statist, 70-74, assoc prof, 74-80, Chmn, 84-87, PROF STATIST, SOUTHERN METHODIST UNIV, 80- *Personal Data:* b Dallas, Tex, Sept 7, 40; m 61, Carol Young; c Scott, Gregory & Susan. *Educ:* Univ Tex, BA, 63, MA, 65; Southern Methodist Univ, PhD(statist), 70. *Honors & Awards:* Res Award, Sigma Xi, 79. *Prof Exp:* Engr-scientist, Tracor, Inc, Tex, 63-66; sr engr, LTV Electrosyst, Inc, 66-68. *Concurrent Pos:* Assoc ed, Commun Statist, 71-, J Educ Statist, 81-83, J Am Statist Asn, 83-86; consult, numerous bus & attys. *Mem:* Fel Am Statist Asn; Inst Math Statist. *Res:* Extensions and applications of techniques for improvement of estimators and the construction of approximate statistical tests and interval estimation; nonparametric ranking statistics; computer simulation variance reductions; minimum distance, robustness and resampling plans. *Mailing Add:* Dept Statist Sci Southern Methodist Univ Dallas TX 75275-0001. *Fax:* 214-768-4035; *E-Mail:* schucany@vm.cis.smu.edu

SCHUCHAT, ANNE, EPIDEMIOLOGY. *Current Pos:* epidemic intel serv officer, Ctr Dis Control, 88-90, med epidemiologist, 88-93, asst sect chief, Foodborne Dis Epidmiol Sect, 93, MEDICAL EPIDEMIOLOGIST, CHILDHOOD & RESPIRATORY DIS BR, DIV BACT & MYCOTIC DIS, NAT CTR INFECTIOUS DIS, CTR DIS CONTROL & PREV, 93-, ACTG BR CHIEF, 96- *Personal Data:* b Washington, DC, June 15, 59. *Educ:* Swarthmore Col, BA, 80; Dartmouth Col, MD, 84; Am Bd Internal Med, cert, 87. *Prof Exp:* Intern & resident internal med, Manhattan Vet Admin Hosp, NY Univ Med Ctr, 84-87, chief resident, 87-88. *Concurrent Pos:* Clin asst prof med, Dept Med, Emory Univ Sch Med, 93-; assoc ed, Am J Pub Health, 96-; consult, WHO, Food & Drug Admin. *Mem:* Am Col Physicians; Am Soc Microbiol; Am Med Women's Asn; Am Pub Health Asn; Sigma Xi. *Res:* Published over 50 articles on infectious disease, epidemiology and public health. *Mailing Add:* 785 Houston Mill Rd Apt 6 Atlanta GA 30329

SCHUCHER, REUBEN, clinical chemistry, biochemistry, for more information see previous edition

SCHUCK, JAMES MICHAEL, mammalian cell culture, protein chemistry, for more information see previous edition

SCHUCKER, GERALD D, ANALYTICAL CHEMISTRY. *Current Pos:* sr res chemist, 68-92, TECH SPECIALIST, CORNING INC, 96- *Personal Data:* b McConnellstown, Pa, Oct 29, 36. *Educ:* Juniata Col, BS, 58; Univ Mo, Rolla, MS, 67. *Prof Exp:* Chemist, Pa RR Test Dept, 58-62; res technician anal chem, Cornell Univ, 63-65; teaching asst, Univ Mo, Rolla, 66-67. *Mem:* Am Chem Soc; Soc Appl Spectros. *Res:* Development of new analytical methods for characterization of inorganic materials. *Mailing Add:* Box 129 Big Flats NY 14814-0129

SCHUCKER, ROBERT CHARLES, PETROLEUM CHEMISTRY, CATALYSIS. *Current Pos:* staff engr, 80-84, RES ASSOC, EXXON RES & DEVELOP LABS, BATON ROUGE, LA, 87- *Personal Data:* b Altoona, Pa, Jan 10, 45; m 68; c 2. *Educ:* Univ SC, BS, 68, MS, 70; Ga Inst Technol, PhD(chem eng), 74. *Prof Exp:* Res engr, Procter & Gamble Co, 74-77; mem, Exxon Corp Res Lab, 77-80; Esso Petrol Res Dept, Can, 85-86. *Mem:* Am Chem Soc; Am Inst Chem Engrs; NAm Membrane Soc; Soc Advan Mat & Process Eng. *Res:* Chemistry of heavy petroleum feedstocks with focus on macromolecular structure and reactivity; enhance yield of desirable product via catalytic reactions; separation of petroleum compounds for fuels refining. *Mailing Add:* Exxon Res & Develop Labs PO Box 2226 Baton Rouge LA 70821-2226

SCHUDER, DONALD LLOYD, ENTOMOLOGY. *Current Pos:* From assoc prof to prof, 49-87, EMER PROF ENTOM, PURDUE UNIV, WEST LAFAYETTE, 88- *Personal Data:* b Bartholomew Co, Ind, Mar 4, 22; m 45, Mary Ricketts; c Phillip R & David L. *Educ:* Purdue Univ, BSA, 48, MS, 49, PhD, 57. *Concurrent Pos:* Ed, Ind Nursery News, 54-87; exec secy, Ind Asn Nurserymen, Inc, 54-87; chmn, Nat Insect Photo Salon; chmn, North Cent Insect Photo Salon. *Mem:* Hon mem Entom Soc Am; Int Soc Arboriculture; Am Asn Nurserymen. *Res:* Coccidae; insect pests of ornamental trees, shrubs and Christmas trees. *Mailing Add:* 2319 Sycamore Lane West Lafayette IN 47906-1927

SCHUDER, JOHN CLAUDE, BIOPHYSICS. *Current Pos:* from assoc prof to prof, 60-85, EMER PROF SURG, UNIV MO, COLUMBIA, 85- *Personal Data:* b Olney, Ill, Mar 2, 22; m 46, Retha Sumner; c Linda (Brown), Charles & Jonna. *Educ:* Univ Ill, BSEE, 43; Purdue Univ, MSEE, 51, PhD(elec eng), 54. *Prof Exp:* Instr elec eng, Purdue Univ, 49-54, asst prof, 54-56; assoc prof physics, Doane Col, 56-57; asst prof eng in surg res, Univ Pa, 59-60. *Concurrent Pos:* Fel eng in surg res, Univ Pa, 57-59; res engr, Hosp Univ Pa, 57-60; estab investr, Am Heart Asn, 65-70. *Mem:* Inst Elec & Electronics Eng; Am Soc Artificial Internal Organs; Inst Elec & Electronics Engrs Eng in Med & Biol Soc. *Res:* Application of physics to medical problems, in particular, cardiac pacing, cardiac defibrillation, artificial hearts, electromagnetic energy transport through biological tissue. *Mailing Add:* Dept Surg DC011-00 Univ Mo Columbia MO 65212. *Fax:* 573-884-4585; *E-Mail:* john__schuder@hsc.surg4.missouri.edu

SCHUE, JOHN R, ALGEBRA. *Current Pos:* assoc prof, 62-69, PROF MATH, MACALESTER COL, 69- *Personal Data:* b Gaylord, Minn, Feb 6, 32; m 57, Barbara James; c Martha, Daniel, Stephen & Paul. *Educ:* Macalester Col, AB, 53; Mass Inst Technol, PhD(math), 59. *Honors & Awards:* Thomas Jefferson Award, 89. *Prof Exp:* Instr math, Mass Inst Technol, 58-59; asst prof, Oberlin Col, 59-62. *Concurrent Pos:* NSF sci faculty fel, 68-69. *Mem:* Am Math Soc; Math Asn Am. *Res:* Lie algebras and functional analysis. *Mailing Add:* Dept Math Macalester Col 1600 Grand Ave St Paul MN 55105. *E-Mail:* schue@macalester.edu

SCHUEGRAF, ERNST JOSEF, INFORMATION RETRIEVAL, LIBRARY AUTOMATION. *Current Pos:* From asst prof to assoc prof, 68-89, PROF COMPUT SCI, ST FRANCIS XAVIER UNIV, 89- *Personal Data:* b Bamberg, Ger, Mar 24, 43; Can citizen; m 76, Karen Harrison; c Paul, Monica, Mark & Angela. *Educ:* Univ Erlangen, Ger, MSc, 68; Univ Alta, PhD(comput sci), 74. *Mem:* Asn Comput Mach; Can Asn Info Sci (pres, 92-93). *Res:* Automatic indexing systems using artificial intelligence techniques. *Mailing Add:* PO Box 5000 Antigonish NS B2G 2W5 Can. *Fax:* 902-867-2448; *E-Mail:* eschuegr@stfx.ca

SCHUEL, HERBERT, CELL BIOLOGY, DEVELOPMENTAL BIOLOGY. *Current Pos:* assoc prof, 77-89, PROF ANAT, STATE UNIV NY, BUFFALO, 89- *Personal Data:* b New York, NY, Apr 8, 35; wid; c Victor M & Barbara E. *Educ:* NY Univ, BA, 56; Univ Pa, PhD(zool), 60. *Prof Exp:* Res assoc develop biol, Oceanog Inst, Fla State Univ, 60-61; res assoc chem, Northwestern Univ, 63-65; asst prof biol, Oakland Univ, 65-68; asst prof anat, Mt Sinai Sch Med, 68-72; assoc res prof, 72-73; assoc prof biochem, State Univ Downstate Med Ctr, 73-77. *Concurrent Pos:* NIH fel, Oak Ridge Nat Lab, 61-63; NIH res career develop award, Oakland Univ & Mt Sinai Sch Med, 68-73; mem, Corp Marine Biol Labs; instr comt mem, Marine Biol Lab, 83-86; prin investr grants, Am Cancer Soc, 70-75, Pop Coun, 74-75, NIH, 69-72 & 83-86, NSF, 65-70 & 75-88 & Nat Inst Drug Abuse, 88-93; contribr to sci jour. *Mem:* fel AAAS; Am Physiol Soc; Int Cannabis Res Soc; Am Soc Cell Biol; Biophys Soc; Am Soc Zool; Sigma Xi; Soc Gen Physiologists; Soc Study Reprod; Am Inst Biol Sci. *Res:* Sub-cellular biochemistry; fertilization, prevention of polysperm secretion and cell division; acrosome reaction; cannabinoids. *Mailing Add:* Dept Anat & Cell Biol State Univ NY Sch Med & Biomed Sci Buffalo NY 14214-3000

SCHUELE, DONALD EDWARD, SOLID STATE PHYSICS, LIQUID CRYSTALS. *Current Pos:* from instr to assoc prof, Case Western Res Univ, 62-74, actg dean, 72-73, dean, 73-76, chmn dept, 76-78, vdean, 78-83, vpres, 83-84, dean, 84-86, dean sci, 88-89, actg chmn elec eng & appl physics, 92-93, PROF PHYSICS, CASE WESTERN RES UNIV, 74-, MICHELSON PROF PHYSICS, 89- *Personal Data:* b Cleveland, Ohio, June 16, 34; m 56, Clare A Kirchner; c Donna, Karen, Melanie, Judy, Rachel & Ruth. *Educ:* John Carroll Univ, BS, 56, MS, 57; Case Inst Technol, PhD(physics), 63. *Prof Exp:* Instr math & physics, John Carroll Univ, 56-57; instr physics, Case Inst Technol, 57-59. *Concurrent Pos:* Mem tech staff, Bell Tel Lab, 70-72; Univ rep, Argonne Univ Assocs, 78-82; mem bd overseers, St Mary Sem, 74-81 & bd trustees, 82-; mem Alumni Coun, Case Alumni Asn, 86-; mem, bd trustees, Newman Found, 81- *Mem:* Am Inst Physics; Am Asn Physics Teachers; Sigma Xi. *Res:* Low frequency dielectric constant of ionic crystals, their pressure and temperature dependence; lattice dynamics; thermal expansion at low temperatures; elastic constants of single crystals; equation of state of solids; high pressure physics; electrical and mechanical properties of polymers and liquid crystals. *Mailing Add:* Inst Tech Case Western Res Univ 10900 Euclid Ave Cleveland OH 44106. *Fax:* 216-368-4671; *E-Mail:* des3@po.cwru.edu

SCHUELE, WILLIAM JOHN, INORGANIC CHEMISTRY. *Current Pos:* RETIRED. *Personal Data:* b Philadelphia, Pa, Apr 27, 23; m 52, Ethel M Schaele; c Stewart S & Eric G. *Educ:* Univ Pa, PhD(chem), 56. *Prof Exp:* Sr res chemist, Res Lab, Franklin Inst, 55-65; adv chemist, IBM Corp, 65-92. *Mem:* AAAS; Sigma Xi; Am Chem Soc; NY Acad Sci. *Res:* Fine particles; ferromagnetism; photolithography; semiconductor chemistry; chemical conservation. *Mailing Add:* 33 Clover St South Burlington VT 05403

SCHUELER, BRUNO OTTO GOTTFRIED, ORGANIC CHEMISTRY, CHEMICAL ENGINEERING. *Current Pos:* Res engr process develop, Exp Sta, E I du Pont de Nemours & Co, Inc, Del, 60-66, sr res engr, 66-69, asst div supt, Plastics Dept, Tex, 69-73, staff engr, 73-81, tech fel, plastics dept, 81-87, sr tech fel, 87-92, DU PONT FEL, PACKAGING & INDUST POLYMERS, E I DU PONT DE NEMOURS & CO, INC, 92- *Personal Data:* b Estcourt, SAfrica, Apr 21, 32; m 60; c 2. *Educ:* Univ Natal, BSc, 53, Hons, 54, MSc, 55, PhD(org chem), 57; Cambridge Univ, PhD(chem eng), 60. *Res:* Indole alkaloids, especially voacangine and ibogaine; bubble formation at submerged orifices; effect of chemical structure on distribution coefficients; polymer manufacturing. *Mailing Add:* 1801 N 21 Orange TX 77630

SCHUELER, DONALD G(EORGE), ELECTRICAL ENGINEERING, ENERGY CONVERSION. *Current Pos:* staff mem electronics, Sandia Labs, 63-67 & 69-70, supvr, Solid State Electronics Res, 70-75, supvr, Photovoltaic Projs, 75-81, mgr, Solar Energy Dept, 81-92, mgr admin progs, 92-94, MGR INTEGRATED MGT SYSTS, SANDIA NAT LABS, 94- *Personal Data:* b Harvard, Nebr, Oct 22, 40; m, Joyce Frye; c Daniel & Alyssa. *Educ:* Univ Nebr, Lincoln, BS, 62, MS, 63, PhD(elec eng), 69. *Prof Exp:* Instr elec eng, Univ Nebr, 67-68. *Mem:* Inst Elec & Electronics Engrs; Am Solar Energy Soc; Sigma Xi. *Res:* Solid state microwave devices; ferroelectric ceramic optical devices; energy conversion; photovoltaic devices; solar energy. *Mailing Add:* 13224 Circulo Largo NE Albuquerque NM 87112

SCHUELER, PAUL EDGAR, PHYSICAL ORGANIC CHEMISTRY. *Current Pos:* PROF CHEM, RARITAN VALLEY COMMUNITY COL, 87- *Personal Data:* b New York, NY, Apr 18, 45; m 72; c 2. *Educ:* Univ Rochester, BS, 65; NY Univ, PhD(chem), 73. *Prof Exp:* Fel org chem, Rutgers Univ, 72-73; res assoc hot-atom chem, Brookhaven Nat Lab, 73-75; lectr chem, Rutgers Univ, New Brunswick, 75-77; from asst prof to assoc prof chem, Somerset County Col, 77-87. *Concurrent Pos:* Coordr, NJ Master Fac Prog, 87-90. *Mem:* Am Chem Soc; AAAS; Sigma Xi; NY Acad Sci. *Res:* Mechanistic physical organic chemistry, with emphasis on reactive intermediates in polar aprotic solvents; chemistry education. *Mailing Add:* 426 Harvard Ave South Plainfield NJ 07080

SCHUELLEIN, ROBERT JOSEPH, GENETICS. *Current Pos:* CONSULT SCI ADMIN, 84- *Personal Data:* b NY, Feb 22, 20; m 70, Wilma Linkins. *Educ:* Univ Dayton, BS, 43; Univ Pittsburgh, MS, 48, PhD(genetics), 56. *Prof Exp:* Teacher parochial high sch, Pa, 43-49; teacher, Ohio Univ, 49-53; instr, Univ Dayton, 53, assoc prof biol, 59-64; fel, Columbia Univ, 56; mem staff, Training Grants & Awards Br, Nat Heart Inst, NIH, 64-65, exec secy, Grants Assoc Prog, Div Res Grants, 65-68, chief, Periodontal Dis & Soft Tissue Prog, 68-70, chief, Soft Tissue Stomatol Prog, 70-74, spec asst res manpower, Nat Inst Dent Res, 74-83. *Concurrent Pos:* Consult, Nat Inst Dent Res, 83-97. *Mem:* Genetics Soc Am; Am Soc Human Genetics; Am Genetic Asn. *Res:* Genetics of Drosophila; population and human genetics; evolution and biometrical analysis. *Mailing Add:* 5626 Larmar Rd Bethesda MD 20816

SCHUERCH, CONRAD, SYNTHETIC ORGANIC & NATURAL PRODUCTS CHEMISTRY. *Current Pos:* from asst prof to prof, State Univ NY, 49-78, chmn dept, 56-72, distinguished prof, 78-83, EMER DISTINGUISHED PROF CHEM, STATE UNIV NY, COL ENVIRON SCI & FORESTRY, 83- *Personal Data:* b Boston, Mass, Aug 2, 18; m 48, Margaret C Pratt; c Barbara M, Conrad III, William E & Peter H. *Educ:* Mass Inst Technol, BS, 40, PhD(org chem), 47. *Honors & Awards:* Anselme Payen Award, Am Chem Soc, 72. *Prof Exp:* Res assoc inorg war res, Mass Inst Technol, 42-43; chemist, Res Lab, Nat Adv Comt Aeronaut, Ohio, 45; sessional lectr, McGill Univ, 47-48, Hibbert fel, 48-49. *Concurrent Pos:* Guggenheim fel, 60-61; hon mem, Soc Fiber Sci & Technol, Japan, 90. *Mem:* Am Chem Soc; Tech Asn Pulp & Paper Indust. *Res:* Chemical synthesis of stereoregular polysaccharides; glycoside synthesis and synthetic carbohydrate antigens; solvent effects, accessibility phenomena and structural studies on lignin and wood; stereochemistry of vinyl polymerization; experimental pulping methods. *Mailing Add:* Dept Chem State Univ NY Col Environ Sci & Forestry Syracuse NY 13210

SCHUERMANN, ALLEN CLARK, JR, INDUSTRIAL ENGINEERING. *Current Pos:* asst prof, 71-78, ASSOC PROF INDUST ENG, WICHITA STATE UNIV, 78-, CHMN DEPT, 79- *Personal Data:* b Denver, Colo, Sept 28, 43; m 65; c 2. *Educ:* Univ Kans, BA, 65; Wichita State Univ, MS, 68; Univ Ark, PhD(indust eng), 71. *Prof Exp:* Oper res analyst, Boeing Co, 65-69; sr oper res analyst, Boeing Comput Serv, 71. *Concurrent Pos:* Prin investr, Rehab Serv Admin, 76-81; consult, Boeing Co, 72-73, Kans Gas & Elec Co, 78- & Kans Power & Light Co, 79- *Mem:* Am Inst Indust Engrs; Inst Mgt Sci;

Oper Res Soc Am; Am Soc Eng Educ. *Res:* Modeling of the economic factors, incentives and disincentives which have an impact on the successful rehabilitation and employment of the severely physically disabled. *Mailing Add:* 2723 N Husband St Stillwater OK 74075

SCHUESSLER, HANS A, ATOMIC PHYSICS. *Current Pos:* assoc prof, 69-81, PROF PHYSICS, TEX A&M UNIV, 81- *Personal Data:* b Mannheim, Ger, June 25, 33. *Educ:* Univ Heidelberg, MS, 61, PhD(physics), 64. *Prof Exp:* Asst prof physics, Tech Univ, Berlin, 63-66; from res asst prof to res assoc prof, Univ Wash, 66-69. *Concurrent Pos:* Mem, Nat Comt on Fundamental Constants, 82-88; founding mem, APS Topical Group on Precision Measurements & Fundamental Constants, 88- *Mem:* Am Phys Soc; Europ Phys Soc. *Res:* Radio frequency spectroscopy; optical pumping; ion storage; atomic clocks; lasers; photodissociation of ion molecules; polarized atomic beams; nuclear moments; level crossing; laser generated plasmas; on-line laser spectroscopy of short-lived isotopes; spectroscopy of highly-charged ions. *Mailing Add:* 10292 River Rd College Station TX 77845. *Fax:* 409-845-2590

SCHUETTE, OSWALD FRANCIS, PHYSICS. *Current Pos:* head dept, 63-80, prof, 63-92, EMER DISTINGUISHED PROF PHYSICS, UNIV SC, 92- *Personal Data:* b Washington, DC, Aug 20, 21; wid; c Patrick T, Mary K & Elizabeth A. *Educ:* Georgetown Univ, BS, 43; Yale Univ, MS, 44, PhD(physics), 49. *Prof Exp:* Instr physics, Yale Univ, 43-44, asst instr, 46-48; assoc prof, Col of William & Mary, 48-53; Fulbright scholar, Ger, 53; sci liaison officer, Sci & Tech Unit, US Dept Navy, Ger, 54-58; mem staff, Nat Acad Sci, 59-60; dep spec asst space, Off Secy Defense, 60-63. *Concurrent Pos:* Guest prof, Univ Vienna, Austria, 80. *Mem:* Am Phys Soc; Am Asn Physics Teachers; fel AAAS; Sigma Xi. *Res:* Separation of isotopes; underwater sound; mass spectroscopy; history of science. *Mailing Add:* Dept Physics & Astron Univ SC Columbia SC 29208. *Fax:* 803-777-3065

SCHUETZ, ALLEN W, EMBRYOLOGY, PHYSIOLOGY ANIMAL. *Current Pos:* From instr to prof pop dynamics, obstet & gynec, 66-75, PROF POP DYNAMICS, SCH HYG & PUB HEALTH, JOHNS HOPKINS UNIV, 75- *Personal Data:* b Monroe, Wis, July 8, 36; m 65; c 2. *Educ:* Univ Wis, BS, 58, PhD(endocrinol), 65. *Concurrent Pos:* Fels steroid biochem, Univ Minn, 64-65, 65-66; fel, Marine Biol Lab, Woods Hole, 65, corp mem, 80; Fogarty Found sr int fel, Cambridge Univ. *Mem:* Cell Biol Soc; Soc Study Reprod; Am Soc Zoologists; Soc Develop Biol. *Res:* Cell-cell communication, cycle nucleotide-hormone interactions; specific role of gonadotrophic hormones in regulating gametogenesis and follicular maturation; control mechanisms in oocyte growth and meiotic maturation; nuclear-cytoplasmic interactions in fertilization and early development-cell cycle regulation. *Mailing Add:* Popul Dynamics Johns Hopkins Univ 615 N Wolfe St Baltimore MD 21205-2103. *Fax:* 410-955-0792

SCHUETZLE, DENNIS, ANALYTICAL CHEMISTRY. *Current Pos:* MGR ANALYTICAL SCI DEPT, FORD MOTOR CO, 73- *Personal Data:* b Sacramento, Calif, July 21, 42; m 68; c 2. *Educ:* Calif State Univ, San Jose, BS, 65; Univ Wash, MS, 70, PhD(chem & eng), 72. *Prof Exp:* Technician, Stoner Labs, 64-65; res chemist, Stanford Res Inst, 65-68; res assoc, Univ Wash, 68-72, res assoc prof anal chem, 72-73. *Concurrent Pos:* Consult, Calif Air Resources Bd, Environ Protection Agency, WHO, 70-75; R&D 100 award, 85 & 88. *Mem:* Am Chem Soc; Sigma Xi. *Res:* New analytical techniques for environmental monitoring, process monitoring, quality control and materials properties. *Mailing Add:* 5443 Crispin Way West Bloomfield MI 48323

SCHUFLE, JOSEPH ALBERT, PHYSICAL CHEMISTRY, HISTORY OF SCIENCE. *Current Pos:* head dept chem & dir inst sci res, 64-70, prof, 64-83, EMER PROF CHEM, NMEX HIGHLANDS UNIV, 83- *Personal Data:* b Akron, Ohio, Dec 21, 17; m 42, Lois Mytholar; c Joseph A Jr & Jean A (Fagerstrom). *Educ:* Univ Akron, BS, 38, MS, 42; Western Res Univ, PhD(chem), 48. *Honors & Awards:* John Dustin Clark Medal, Am Chem Soc, 82. *Prof Exp:* Chemist, Akron, Ohio, 39-42; instr math, Western Res Univ, 46-47; from asst prof to prof chem, NMex Inst Mining & Technol, 48-64. *Concurrent Pos:* Vis prof, Univ Col, Dublin, 61-62; vis scholar, Univ Uppsala, Sweden, 77. *Mem:* Fel AAAS; fel Am Inst Chemists; Am Chem Soc; Inst Chem Ireland; Hist Sci Soc; Am Soc Eighteenth Century Studies. *Res:* Biographies of Torbern Bergman, eighteenth century Swedish chemist and Juan Jose D'Elhuyar, eighteenth century Spanish and Colombian chemist. *Mailing Add:* 1301 Eighth St Las Vegas NM 87701

SCHUG, JOHN CHARLES, PHYSICAL CHEMISTRY. *Current Pos:* from asst prof to assoc prof, 64-73, PROF CHEM, VA POLYTECH INST & STATE UNIV, 73- *Personal Data:* b New York, NY, Mar 31, 36; m 58; c 3. *Educ:* Cooper Union, BChE, 57; Univ Ill, MS, 58, PhD(chem), 60. *Prof Exp:* Res chemist, Gulf Res & Develop Co, 60-64. *Concurrent Pos:* Consult, Philip Morris Res Ctr, 66- *Mem:* Am Chem Soc. *Res:* Quantum chemistry; high-resolution nuclear magnetic resonance; mass spectrometry. *Mailing Add:* Dept Chem Va Polytech Inst & State Univ PO Box 0212 Blacksburg VA 24063-0001

SCHUG, KENNETH, INORGANIC CHEMISTRY. *Current Pos:* from instr to assoc prof, 56-75, chmn dept, 76-82 & 85-87, PROF CHEM, ILL INST TECHNOL, 75- *Personal Data:* b Easton, Pa, Aug 27, 24; m 48; c 3. *Educ:* Stanford Univ, BA, 45; Univ Southern Calif, PhD, 55. *Prof Exp:* Res assoc chem, Univ Wis, 54-56. *Concurrent Pos:* Consult, Argonne Nat Lab, 61-63; Fulbright res fel, Kyushu Univ, 64-65. *Mem:* AAAS; Am Chem Soc. *Res:* Inorganic, coordination and solution chemistry; inorganic mechanisms. *Mailing Add:* Dept Chem Ill Inst Technol 3300 S Federal St Chicago IL 60616-3732

SCHUGAR, HARVEY, INORGANIC CHEMISTRY, BIOINORGANIC CHEMISTRY. *Current Pos:* asst prof, 68-73, ASSOC PROF CHEM, RUTGERS UNIV, NEW BRUNSWICK, 73- *Personal Data:* b Pittsburgh, Pa, Dec 2, 36; m 63. *Educ:* Carnegie Inst Technol, BS, 58; Columbia Univ, MA, 59, PhD(chem), 61. *Prof Exp:* Res chemist, Esso Res & Eng Co, 61-63; res chemist, Sci Design Co, 63-65; res assoc & lectr chem, Columbia Univ, 65-67; res assoc, Calif Inst Technol, 67-68. *Mem:* Am Chem Soc. *Res:* Aquo chemistry of ferric complexes; metal ions in biological systems. *Mailing Add:* Dept Chem Box 939 Rutgers Univ Piscataway NJ 08855-0939

SCHUGART, KIMBERLY A, ATMOSPHERIC CHEMISTRY, AMINO ACID INTERACTIONS. *Current Pos:* lectr, 88-89, asst prof, 89-94, ASSOC PROF CHEM, CALIF STATE UNIV, LONG BEACH, 94- *Personal Data:* b Woodstock, Ill, July 12, 59; m 91, Eric Remelmeyer. *Educ:* Northwestern Univ, BA, 81; Univ Wis-Madison, PhD(chem), 85. *Prof Exp:* Fel, Calif Inst Technol, 85-88. *Concurrent Pos:* Dept Energy fac fel, Sandia Nat Lab, 93. *Mem:* Am Chem Soc; Sigma Xi. *Res:* Use of electronic structure theory methodologies to discern chemical and physical properties of molecular substances. *Mailing Add:* Dept Chem Calif State Univ 3903 Csulb Long Beach CA 90840-0004

SCHUH, FRANK J, RESEARCH ADMINISTRATION. *Current Pos:* PRES, DRILLING TECHNOL, INC, 86- *Educ:* Ohio State Univ, BS & MS, 56. *Honors & Awards:* Petrol Eng Award, Nat Eng Asn, 80; Drilling Eng Award, Soc Petrol Engrs, 86. *Prof Exp:* Field drilling engr, Atlantic Richfield Co, Oil & Gas Co, S La Dist, 57-58, res engr, Prod Res Dept, 58-62, staff drilling engr, Drilling Eng Group, 62-72, Drilling Technol Sect, 72-82, dir drilling & prod mech res, 82-85 & sr res adv drilling & opers res, Prod Res Ctr, 85-86. *Concurrent Pos:* Chmn, Drilling Reprints Ser, Soc Petrol Engrs, 73, distinguished lectr, 81-82, nat dir, Region VI, 83-86, co-chmn, Drilling Reprint Ser Comt, 86-89; founder & first chmn, Drilling Eng Asn, 83-84, dir, 85-86; mem, Tech Eng & Develop Comt, Ocean Drilling Prog, NSF, 86-91; co-founder, Supreme Resources Corp, 88-95. *Mem:* Nat Acad Eng; Soc Petrol Engrs; Am Petrol Inst; Drilling Eng Asn; Soc Independent Prof Earth Scientists. *Res:* Author of various publications; granted several patents. *Mailing Add:* Drilling Technol Inc 5808 Wavertree Suite 1000 Plano TX 75093

SCHUH, JAMES DONALD, ANIMAL NUTRITION. *Current Pos:* RETIRED. *Personal Data:* b Chicago, Ill, Oct 9, 28; m 54; c 5. *Educ:* Kans State Univ, BS, 53; Okla State Univ, MS, 57, PhD(animal nutrit), 60. *Prof Exp:* Exten dairy specialist, Univ Nev, 60-64; from assoc prof to prof dairy sci, Univ Ariz, 64-89. *Mem:* Am Dairy Sci Asn. *Res:* Dairy herd management; calf nutrition and immunity; water quality for dairy cattle; dairy heifer management. *Mailing Add:* 1660 Roller Coaster Rd Tucson AZ 85704

SCHUH, JOSEPH EDWARD, cytology, for more information see previous edition

SCHUH, MERLYN DUANE, PHYSICAL CHEMISTRY, BIOCHEMISTRY. *Current Pos:* from asst prof to assoc prof, 75-86, PROF PHYS CHEM & BIOCHEM, DAVIDSON COL, 86-, JAMES G MARTIN CHAIRED PROF CHEM, 92- *Personal Data:* b Avon, SDak, Feb 21, 45; m 69, Judy Swigart. *Educ:* Univ SDak, BA, 67; Ind Univ, Bloomington, PhD(phys chem), 71. *Honors & Awards:* Sci Fac Prof Develop Awardee, NSF, 81. *Prof Exp:* Asst prof phys chem & biochem, Middlebury Col, 71-75. *Concurrent Pos:* Dreyfus scholar, 92-94. *Mem:* Inter-Am Photochem Soc; Am Chem Soc; Sigma Xi; Am Soc Photobiol. *Res:* Lasers used to study the photophysics and spectroscopy of electronic excited state molecules; fluorescent and phosphorescent probes of proteins. *Mailing Add:* PO Box 704 Davidson NC 28036. *Fax:* 704-892-2005; *E-Mail:* meschuh@davidson.edu

SCHUH, RANDALL TOBIAS, SYSTEMATICS, BIOGEOGRAPHY. *Current Pos:* Chmn dept, 80-87, CUR ENTOM, AM MUS NATURAL HIST, 74- *Personal Data:* b Corvallis, Ore, May 11, 43; m; c 1. *Educ:* Ore State Univ, BS, 65; Mich State Univ, MS, 67; Univ Conn, PhD(entom), 71. *Concurrent Pos:* Adj prof biol, City Univ New York, 78-; ed, J NY Entom Soc, 83-89, Cladistics, 91; adj prof entomol, Cornell Univ, 89- *Mem:* Entom Soc Am; Soc Syst Zool. *Res:* Taxonomy, phylogeny and biogeography of Hemiptera of the class Insecta, especially Miridae and semiaquatic families. *Mailing Add:* 150 W 82nd St New York NY 10024

SCHUHMANN, R(EINHARDT), JR, metallurgical engineering; deceased, see previous edition for last biography

SCHUHMANN, ROBERT EWALD, PHYSIOLOGY, ENGINEERING. *Current Pos:* RETIRED. *Personal Data:* b El Paso, Tex, Sept 27, 24; m 53; c 1. *Educ:* Univ Tex, Austin, BS, 49, MS, 52; Baylor Col Med, PhD(physiol), 69. *Prof Exp:* Instr eng, Univ Tex, Austin, 50-51; engr, Tenn Gas Transmission Co, 51-54; supvry engr, Trunkline Gas Co, 54-62; asst to chief engr, Bovay Engrs, Inc, 62-63, mgr dept mech eng, 63-64; sr res physiologist, Southwest Res Inst, 69-74; prof & dean, Univ Houston, Clear Lake, 74-78, prof physiol, Sch Natural & Appl Sci, 74-90. *Concurrent Pos:* Asst prof, Univ Tex Health Sci Ctr, San Antonio, 72-74; vis prof biomed eng, Baylor Col Med, 80-87. *Mem:* Am Physiol Soc; Sigma Xi; Am Heart Asn. *Res:* Cardiovascular and respiratory physiology and central nervous system control of respiration; transvalvular heart assist, left ventricular bypass without thoracotomy by ventricular catheterization; bioinstrumentation; biological control system theory; physiology of human stress; physiology of human aging. *Mailing Add:* Dept Nat Sci Univ Houston-Clear Lake PO Box 645 La Grange TX 78945

SCHUIT, KENNETH EDWARD, anatomy, cell biology; deceased, see previous edition for last biography

SCHUKNECHT, HAROLD FREDERICK, otolaryngology; deceased, see previous edition for last biography

SCHULDINER, SIGMUND, PHYSICAL CHEMISTRY, ELECTROCHEMISTRY & ANALYTICAL CHEMISTRY. *Current Pos:* RETIRED. *Personal Data:* b Chicago, Ill, June 12, 13; m 46, Virginia Lawson; c Anne, Susan & Barbara. *Educ:* NY Univ, BA, 38; Columbia Univ, MA, 39. *Honors & Awards:* William Blum Award, Electrochem Soc, 60; Pure Sci Award, Sci Res Soc Am, 66. *Prof Exp:* Phys sci aide, Glass Sect, Nat Bur Standards, 40-41; asst head metals sect, Norfolk Naval Shipyard, 41-45, head indust probs sect, 45-46; phys chemist, Corrosion Br, US Naval Res Lab, 46-48, head electrode mech sect, Electrochem Br, 48-71, head, Electrochem Br, 71-75; consult, Bur Mines, Avondale Res Ctr, 75-87. *Mem:* Am Chem Soc; Sigma Xi; Electrochem Soc. *Res:* Electrochemistry; kinetics of electrode processes; adsorption; gases in metals; catalysis; corrosion. *Mailing Add:* 12705 Prestwick Dr Ft Washington MD 20744

SCHULDT, MARCUS DALE, COMPUTER SCIENCE. *Current Pos:* RETIRED. *Personal Data:* b Geneva, Ill, Aug 31, 30; m 50; c 2. *Educ:* Aurora Col, BS, 60. *Prof Exp:* Draftsman, Geneva Kitchens, 46-51; engr, Burgess Norton Mfg Co, 55-60; oceanogr, US Coast & Geod Surv, 60-65 & Inst Oceanog, Environ Sci Serv Admin, 65-66; supvry res phys scientist, Environ Protection Agency, 66-76, environ scientist, 76-79, oceanographer, 79-86. *Res:* Application of automation; limnology; oceanography. *Mailing Add:* 2918 Pioneer Rd Ellensburg WA 98926-9404

SCHULDT, SPENCER BURT, THEORETICAL PHYSICS, APPLIED MATHEMATICS. *Current Pos:* STAFF SCIENTIST, HONEYWELL CORP RES CTR, 57- *Personal Data:* b St Paul, Minn, July 1, 30; m 57, 72; c 5. *Educ:* Univ Minn, BA, 51, MS, 57. *Mem:* Am Phys Soc. *Res:* Submicron physics; heat transfer; process control; mathematical programming methods; reliability physics. *Mailing Add:* 8830 Normandale Blvd Minneapolis MN 55437

SCHULENBERG, JOHN WILLIAM, ORGANIC CHEMISTRY. *Current Pos:* RETIRED. *Personal Data:* b Passaic, NJ, Sept 7, 30; m 52, 82, Patsy Lodge; c David, Janet, Ted & Richard. *Educ:* Queens Col, NY, BS, 51; Columbia Univ, MA, 52, PhD(org chem), 56. *Prof Exp:* Res assoc, org chem, Sterling-Winthrop Res Inst, 56-60, sr res chemist, 60-89. *Mem:* Am Chem Soc. *Res:* Heterocyclic synthesis; medicinal chemistry. *Mailing Add:* 187 Adams St Delmar NY 12054. *E-Mail:* 73623.1441@compuserve.com

SCHULER, ALAN NORMAN, POLYMER SCIENCE. *Current Pos:* scientist polymerization, Polaroiod Corp, 78-79, sr scientist, 79-81, res group leader, 81-84, sr res group leader, 84-89, mgr, Polymer Res Lab, 87-89, PROJ MGR, POLAROID CORP, 89- *Personal Data:* b Arlington, Mass, Dec 8, 49; m 71, Karen; c 2. *Educ:* Univ Mass, BS, 71, MS, 74, PhD(polymer sci & eng), 76. *Prof Exp:* Sr chemist emulsion polymer, Union Carbide Corp, 75-78. *Mem:* Am Chem Soc. *Res:* Emulsion polymerization and polymer colloid characterization structure; properties correlations. *Mailing Add:* 15 Dee Rd Lexington MA 02173

SCHULER, GEORGE ALBERT, food science, microbiology; deceased, see previous edition for last biography

SCHULER, MATHIAS JOHN, DYEING TECHNOLOGY, COLOR SCIENCE. *Current Pos:* RETIRED. *Personal Data:* b New York, NY, Apr 29, 18; m 42, Marion Randall; c Jan, Robert, Betty & Susan. *Educ:* Brooklyn Col, BA, 38. *Honors & Awards:* Olney Medal, Am Asn Textile Chemists & Colorists. *Prof Exp:* Asst, Mem Hosp, New York, 38-39; chemist, Continental Baking Co, 39-40; res chemist, Ansbacher Siegle Corp, 40-41; instr, Bd Educ, New York, 41-44; supvr, Kellex Corp, 44-45; res chemist, E I Du Pont de Nemours & Co, Inc, 45-59, sr res chemist, 59-65, res assoc, 65-70, div head, 70-79, environ mgr, 79-82. *Mem:* Am Chem Soc. *Res:* X-rays and chemical reactions; instrumentation; mass spectrometry; physics of interaction of light on dyes and pigments; color and color specification; mechanisms of dyeing hydrophobic fibers; organometallic compounds. *Mailing Add:* 102 Cyrus Ave Pitman NJ 08071

SCHULER, ROBERT FREDERICK, organic chemistry, for more information see previous edition

SCHULER, ROBERT HUGO, PHOTOCHEMISTRY, RADIATION CHEMISTRY. *Current Pos:* PROF RADIATION CHEM & DIR RADIATION LAB, UNIV NOTRE DAME, 76-, ZAHM PROF, 85- *Personal Data:* b Buffalo, NY, Jan 4, 26; m 52; c 5. *Educ:* Canisius Col, BS, 46; Univ Notre Dame, PhD(phys chem), 49. *Honors & Awards:* Notre Dame Centennial Award, 65; Maria Sklodowska-Curie Medal, 92. *Prof Exp:* Asst prof chem, Canisius Col, 49-53; from assoc chemist to chemist, Brookhaven Nat Lab, 53-56; staff fel & dir radiation res labs, Mellon Inst Sci, Carnegie-Mellon Univ, 56-76, prof chem, 67-76. *Concurrent Pos:* Mem adv comt, Mellon Inst Sci, 62-; mem adv comt, Radiation Chem Data Ctr, 65-76, chmn, 73-75; vis prof, Hebrew Univ, Israel, 80; Sir CV Raman prof, Univ Madras, India, 85-86; distinguished lectr, Univ Cordoba, Arg, 88. *Mem:* AAAS; Am Chem Soc; Am Phys Soc; Radiation Res Soc (pres, 75-76); Royal Soc Chem; Sigma Xi. *Res:* Radiation chemistry; kinetics of ionic reactions in the radiolysis of hydrocarbons; electron spin resonance and pulse radiolysis methods to study the nature and reaction kinetics of radiation produced radicals heavy particle radiation chemistry; Raman spectroscopy. *Mailing Add:* Radiation Lab Univ Notre Dame Notre Dame IN 46556-0768

SCHULER, RONALD THEODORE, AGRICULTURAL ENGINEERING. *Current Pos:* PROF AGR ENGR, UNIV WIS-MADISON, 84- *Personal Data:* b Manitowoc, Wis, Dec 26, 40; m 67, Barbara Howell; c 2. *Educ:* Univ Wis-Madison, BS, 63, MS, 67, PhD(agr eng), 72. *Prof Exp:* Res asst agr eng, Univ Wis-Madison, 65-69, instr, 69-70; from asst prof to assoc prof, NDak State Univ, 70-76; assoc prof agr eng, Univ Minn, St Paul, 76-81; prof agr eng & chmn dept, Univ Wis-Platteville, 81-84. *Mem:* Am Soc Agr Engrs; Soil Conserv Soc Am; Sigma Xi; Am Soc Engr Educ; Am Asn Agr Sci; Soc Automotive Engrs. *Res:* Agricultural engineering instrumentation; reduced tillage for soil, water and energy conservation, sunflower seed drying; cattail harvesting; soil compaction; agricultural safety. *Mailing Add:* 926 Arden Lane Madison WI 53711. *Fax:* 608-262-1228; *E-Mail:* schuler@wisplan.uwex.wisc.edu

SCHULER, RUDOLPH WILLIAM, CHEMICAL ENGINEERING. *Current Pos:* res engr, Monsanto Co, 51-55, res group leader, 55-57, asst dir res, 57-64, dir eng & mat res, 64-70, dir technol, New Enterprise Div, 70-76, RES DIR, NEW ENTERPRISE DIV, MONSANTO RES CTR, MONSANTO CO, 76- *Personal Data:* b Stuttgart, Ger, Sept 2, 19; US citizen; m 44; c 2. *Educ:* Purdue Univ, BS, 48, PhD, 51. *Prof Exp:* Res engr, Colgate-Palmolive-Peet Co, 50-51. *Mem:* Am Chem Soc; Am Inst Chem Engrs. *Res:* Reaction kinetics; reactor design; mass transfer. *Mailing Add:* 38 Shady Valley Dr Chesterfield MO 63017

SCHULER, VICTOR JOSEPH, ECOLOGICAL SCIENCES, ENVIRONMENTAL & MARINE CONSULTING. *Current Pos:* PRES, ENVIRON CONSULT SERV, INC, 88- *Personal Data:* b New York, NY, Mar 9, 33; m 56. *Educ:* Cornell Univ, BS, 66, MS, 69. *Prof Exp:* Lab instr, Ithaca Col, 64-65; res asst, Cornell Univ, 66-68; sr res biologist, Ichthyological Assoc Inc, 67-68, vpres proj dir, 75-78, sr vpres, 78-83, pres, V J Schuler Assocs, Inc, 83-88. *Mem:* Am Fisheries Soc; Am Inst Fishery Res Biologists. *Res:* Fisheries population studies; environmental impact studies; fish screening studies; ecological consultant, research program initiation and administration; engineering and design of water-screens for power plants; population-community studies of major East Coast estuaries and rivers; resign design; data analysis; expert testimony before regulating agencies; marine development wetlands and water quality responsibilities; marina setting, design, and permitting. *Mailing Add:* 100 S Cass St PO Box 138 Middletown DE 19709

SCHULERT, ARTHUR ROBERT, chemistry; deceased, see previous edition for last biography

SCHULKE, HERBERT ARDIS, JR, ELECTRONICS, COMMUNICATIONS. *Current Pos:* RETIRED. *Personal Data:* b New Ulm, Minn, Nov 12, 23; m 49, Delores; c Herbert A III & Judd B. *Educ:* US Mil Acad, BS, 46; Univ Ill, Urbana, MS, 52, PhD(electronics), 54. *Prof Exp:* Assigned adv develop long range radio, Signal Res & Develop Labs, Signal Corps, US Army, Ft Monmouth, NJ, 54-56 & Signal Sch Regiment, 57-58, assoc prof elec eng, US Mil Acad, 58-61, chief staff, Signal Res & Develop Labs, 61-63, commun-electronics proj officer, Adv Res Projs Agency, Vietnam, 64-65, mil asst tactical warfare, Off Dir Defense Res & Eng, Off Secy Defense, Washington, DC, 66-69, commanding officer, 29th signal group, US Army Strategic Commun Command, Thailand, 69-70, dep dir plans, Defense Commun Agency, Washington, DC, 70-76; gen mgr & exec dir, Inst Elec & Electronics Engrs, 75-77; dir telecommun, Chase Manhattan Bank, 77-84. *Concurrent Pos:* Pres, Aero-Tele-Com, Inc. *Mem:* Fel Inst Elec & Electronics Engrs; Sigma Xi. *Res:* Military electronics equipment research and development; management of all types of military research and development efforts. *Mailing Add:* 5307 Churususco Dr San Antonio TX 78239-3071

SCHULKE, JAMES DARRELL, PLANT GENETICS, AGRONOMY. *Current Pos:* RETIRED. *Personal Data:* b Aurelia, Iowa, June 25, 32; m 56, Lois A Olin; c Lisa (Wolven), Jill (Lynch) & Suzanne (Andrews). *Educ:* Iowa State Univ, BS, 58; Univ Calif, MS, 60, PhD(genetics), 63. *Prof Exp:* Plant breeder, Spreckels Sugar Co Inc, 63- *Mem:* Am Soc Sugar Beet Technol; Crop Sci Soc Am; Am Inst Biol Sci; Sigma Xi. *Res:* Genetics and plant breeding of sugar beets. *Mailing Add:* PO Box 7442 Spreckels CA 93962

SCHULKIN, MORRIS, ACOUSTICS, REMOTE SENSING. *Current Pos:* assoc to dir, & prin physicist, 76-85, SR FEL, APPL PHYSICS LAB, UNIV WASH, 76- *Personal Data:* b Brooklyn, NY, Feb 6, 19; m 40, 64, 70, Irene Cohen; c Peter, Kenneth, Mindy & Michael. *Educ:* Brooklyn Col, BA, 39; George Washington Univ, MS, 48; Cath Univ Am, PhD, 69. *Prof Exp:* Sci aide, US Weather Bur, 40-41; physicist & engr, Nat Bur Stand, 41-47 & 48-50; physicist, Naval Res Lab, US Dept Navy, 47-48, Underwater Sound Lab, 50-56; chief engr, Martin Co, 56-59; chief scientist, Marine Electronics Off, Avco Corp, 59-63; adv engr, Underseas Div, Westinghouse Elec Corp, 63-66; dir performance anal, Antisubmarine Warfare, Spec Proj Off, 66-67; res physicist, Naval Res Lab, 68; consult physicist, Naval Underwater Systs Ctr, 68-72; assoc sci & tech dir, Naval Oceanog Off, 72-75; vpres, Mar Assoc, Inc, 75-76. *Concurrent Pos:* Assoc, George Washington Univ & asst, Univ Md, 47-48; lectr, Drexel Inst, 59; instr, USDA Grad Sch, 61-65; consult, US Off Naval Res, 61 & 73-75; lectr ocean acoust & eng, Cath Univ Am, 73-77; pres & consult, Ocean Acoust Inc, 76-96; adj prof ocean eng, Univ Miami, 86-90. *Mem:* Am Geophys Union; fel Acoust Soc Am; fel Inst Elec & Electronics Engrs. *Res:* Remote sensing; underwater sound; seismo-acoustics; wave propagation; oceanic variabilities; scales of motion and energy in the ocean and their acoustic effects. *Mailing Add:* 9325 Orchard Brook Dr Potomac MD 20854

SCHULL, WILLIAM JACKSON, HUMAN GENETICS. *Current Pos:* PROF HUMAN GENETICS, UNIV TEX GRAD SCH BIOMED SCI, HOUSTON, 72- *Personal Data:* b Louisiana, Mo, Mar 17, 22; m 46. *Educ:* Marquette Univ, BS, 46, MS, 47; Ohio State Univ, PhD(genetics), 49. *Honors & Awards:* Centennial Award, Ohio State Univ, 70. *Prof Exp:* Head dept genetics, Atomic Bomb Casualty Comn, Japan, 49-51; jr geneticist, Inst Human Biol, Univ Mich, 51-53, asst geneticist, 53-56, from asst prof to prof human genetics, Med Sch, 56-72, prof anthrop, 69-72. *Concurrent Pos:* Vis fel, Australian Nat Univ, 69; consult, Atomic Bomb Casualty Comn, Japan, 54 & 56; consult, NIH, 56-, chmn genetics study sect, 69-72; dir, Child Health Surv, Japan, 59-60; vis prof, Univ Chicago, 63; Ger Res Asn guest prof, Univ Heidelberg, 70; vis prof, Univ Chile, 75; mem comt atomic casualties, Nat Res Coun, 51 & subcomt biol, Comt Dent, 51-55; mem comt on collab proj, Nat Inst Neurol Dis & Stroke, 57-; mem panel in genetic effects of radiation, WHO, 58- & panel of experts human heredity, 61-; mem nat adv comt radiation, USPHS, 60-64 & bd sci counsrs, Nat Inst Dent Res, 66-69; dir, Radiation Effects Res Found & head dept epidemiol & Japan, 78-80; adv, Nat Heart & Lung Inst; mem subcomt biol & med, AEC; mem human biol coun, Soc Study Human Biol. *Mem:* AAAS; USMex Border Health Asn; hon mem Japanese Soc Human Genetics; hon mem, Peruvian Soc Human Genetics; hon mem Genetic Soc Chile; Sigma Xi. *Res:* Biometry. *Mailing Add:* Univ Tex PO Box 20334 Houston TX 77025

SCHULLER, IVAN KOHN, PHYSICS. *Current Pos:* PROF, UNIV CALIF, SAN DIEGO, 87- *Personal Data:* b Cluj, Rumania, June 8, 46; US citizen; m 74, Scheibel; c Daniel & Jonathan. *Educ:* Univ Chile, Licenciado, 70; Northwestern Univ, MS, 72, PhD(physics), 76. *Honors & Awards:* Outstanding Sci Accomplishment in Solid State Physics, US Dept Energy, 87. *Prof Exp:* Res asst physics, Univ Chile, 66-70; res asst, Northwestern Univ, 70-74; sr res aide, Argonne Nat Lab, 74-76; adj asst prof, Univ Calif, Los Angeles, 76-78; sr physicist & group leader, Argonne Nat Lab, 78-87. *Concurrent Pos:* Consult. *Mem:* Fel Am Phys Soc; Sigma Xi; Inst Elec & Electronics Engrs; Soc Explor Geophysicists; Chilean Acad Sci. *Res:* Low temperature physics; solid state physics; prospecting geophysics; superconducting electronics; microelectronics. *Mailing Add:* Physics Dept 0319 Univ Calif San Diego La Jolla CA 92093-0319. *Fax:* 619-534-0173; *E-Mail:* schuller@ucsd.bitnet

SCHULLERY, STEPHEN EDMUND, LIPID MEMBRANES, HYDROGEN BONDING & MOLECULAR MODELING. *Current Pos:* From asst prof to assoc prof, 70-80, PROF CHEM, EASTERN MICH UNIV, 80- *Personal Data:* b Harrisonburg, Va, June 8, 43; m 68, Nancy M Doud; c Daniel S. *Educ:* Eastern Mich Univ, BA, 65; Cornell Univ, PhD(phys chem), 70. *Concurrent Pos:* Summer intern polymers, Gen Motors Res, 65. *Mem:* AAAS; Am Chem Soc. *Res:* Physical chemistry of biological macromolecules; structure and function of model biological cell membranes; thermodynamics of solution phase hydrogen bonding; molecular modeling. *Mailing Add:* 2117 Collegewood Ypsilanti MI 48197

SCHULMAN, HAROLD, OBSTETRICS & GYNECOLOGY. *Current Pos:* PROF OBSTET & GYNEC, STATE UNIV NY, STONY BROOK, 84- *Personal Data:* b Newark, NJ, Oct 26, 30; m 54; c 3. *Educ:* Univ Fla, BS, 51; Emory Univ, MD, 55; Bd Maternal Fetal Med, cert, 75. *Prof Exp:* From instr to asst prof obstet & gynec, Temple Univ, 61-65; from asst prof to assoc prof, 65-71, prof obstet & gynec, Albert Einstein Col Med, 71-83. *Concurrent Pos:* Am Cancer Soc fel, 59-60; USPHS fel, 68. *Mem:* AAAS; Am Col Obstet & Gynec; Soc Gynec Invest; Am Gynec Obstet Soc. *Res:* Obstetric physiology. *Mailing Add:* 4650 NA1A Vero Beach FL 32963

SCHULMAN, HERBERT MICHAEL, CELL BIOLOGY, BIOCHEMISTRY. *Current Pos:* RETIRED. *Personal Data:* b New York, NY, Feb 7, 32. *Educ:* Bard Col, BA, 55; Yale Univ, PhD(microbiol), 62. *Prof Exp:* Asst prof biol, Univ Calif, San Diego, 63-69; staff investr exp hemat, Lady Davis Inst, Jewish Gen Hosp, Mont, 69-97, actg dir, 88-90. *Concurrent Pos:* NIH fel, Univ Calif, San Diego, 62-63 & res grant, 63-69; vis prof, Univ Helsinki, 68-69 & Univ WI, 85; Can Dept Agr grants; vis scientist, John Innes Inst, Norwich, Eng, 77-78; Nuffield Found Travel Grant, 77-78; consult nitrogen fixation res, Can Dept Agr, 76-; vis prof, Nat Univ Mex, 87; assoc prof med, McGill Univ. *Mem:* Can Soc Cell Biol; Int Soc Develop Biol. *Res:* Control of hemoglobin synthesis and development of erythrocytes; biochemistry of iron metabolism; synthesis of leg-hemoglobin; differentiation of root nodules; nitrogen fixation in the high arctic. *Mailing Add:* 3935 St Hubert St Montreal PQ H2L 4A6 Can

SCHULMAN, HOWARD, NEUROSICENCES, BIOCHEMISTRY. *Current Pos:* ASSOC PROF PHARMACOL, SCH MED, STANFORD UNIV, 78- *Personal Data:* b Holon, Israel, Feb 5, 49. *Educ:* Univ Calif, Los Angeles, BS, 71; Harvard Univ, PhD(biochem), 76. *Prof Exp:* Fel, Med Sch, Yale Univ, 76-78. *Res:* Calcium and cyclic adenosine monophosphate-dependent protein phosphorylation in brain function; regulation of the cytoskeleton. *Mailing Add:* Dept Neurobiol Stanford Univ Sch Med Stanford CA 94305-5401. *Fax:* 650-725-2952

SCHULMAN, IRVING, MEDICINE, PEDIATRICS. *Current Pos:* PROF PEDIAT & CHMN DEPT, SCH MED, STANFORD UNIV, 72- *Personal Data:* b New York, NY, Feb 17, 22; m 50; c 2. *Educ:* NY Univ, BA, 42, MD, 45. *Honors & Awards:* Mead-Johnson Award, 60. *Prof Exp:* Instr pediat, Sch Med, NY Univ, 49-50; from instr to assoc prof, Cornell Univ, 52-58; prof, Med Sch, Northwestern Univ, 58-61; prof & head dept, Univ Ill Col Med, 61-72. *Concurrent Pos:* USPHS res fel, Med Col, Cornell Univ, 50-52; consult, Nat Inst Child Health & Human Develop, 64-; ed-in-chief, Advances in Pediat. *Mem:* Soc Pediat Res (pres, 66); Am Pediat Soc; Am Soc Clin Invest; Am Acad Pediat; Am Soc Hemat. *Res:* Pediatric hematology; coagulation physiology. *Mailing Add:* Stanford Univ Med Ctr Stanford CA 94305

SCHULMAN, JAMES HERBERT, SOLID STATE PHYSICS, OPTICAL PHYSICS. *Current Pos:* CONSULT, 91- *Personal Data:* b Chicago, Ill, Nov 15, 15; m 40, Doris Greenfield; c Norma, Barbara & Michael. *Educ:* Mass Inst Technol, SB, 39, PhD(inorg chem), 42. *Honors & Awards:* Sigma Xi Award, 57; Distinguished Achievement Sci Award, US Govt, 72. *Prof Exp:* Instr, Suffolk Univ, 40-41; asst, Div Indust Coop, Mass Inst Technol, 41-44; sr engr, Sylvania Elec Prod, 44-46; head dielectrics br, US Naval Res Lab, 46-60, dep sci dir, Off Naval Res, London, 60-61, head dielectrics br, US Naval Res Lab, 62-64, chair mat sci, US Naval Res Lab, 64-65, supt, Optical Physics Div, 65-67, assoc dir res, US Naval Res Lab, 67-74, sci dir & chief scientist, London Br Off, US Off Naval Res, 74-77, chair mat sci, US Naval Res Lab & actg tech dir, US Off Naval Res, 77-79; res prof, George Wash Univ, 79-81; consult, Nat Mat Adv Bd, Nat Acad Sci-Nat Res Coun, 81-91. *Concurrent Pos:* Assoc ed, J Opt Soc Am, 71-80; US mem, Res Grants Prog Panel, NATO, 79-81; consult, sci & tech mgt, 79-; mem, Panel on Reevaluation of Radiation Doses from Hiroshima & Nagasaki A-Bombs, Nat Acad Sci, 82-86; mem, Comt on US Army Thermoluminescent Dosimetry Syst, Nat Res Coun, 85-87, consult, Technol Issues Comt, Nat Acad Eng, 87-88. *Mem:* Fel AAAS; fel Am Phys Soc; fel Optical Soc Am; Sigma Xi. *Res:* Luminescent materials; radiation sensitive solids; dosimetry; crystal chemistry and physics; glass; color centers; materials science. *Mailing Add:* 4615 N Park Ave Chevy Chase MD 20815-4509

SCHULMAN, JEROME LEWIS, PSYCHIATRY. *Current Pos:* asst prof pediat, psychiat & neurol, 57-65, PROF PEDIAT & PSYCHIAT & CHIEF PSYCHIAT, MED SCH, NORTHWESTERN UNIV, CHICAGO, 65- *Personal Data:* b New York, NY, Nov 15, 25; m 49; c 3. *Educ:* Univ Rochester, BA, 46; Long Island Col Med, MD, 49. *Prof Exp:* Intern med, Jewish Hosp, Brooklyn, 49-50; resident pediat, 50-51 & 53-54; resident psychiat, Johns Hopkins Hosp, 54-57. *Concurrent Pos:* Dir child guid & develop clins & attend pediatrician & psychiatrist, Children's Mem Hosp, 57-; consult, Joseph P Kennedy Jr Found, 58-; asst prof, Med Col, Cornell Univ, 68-69. *Mem:* Am Psychiat Asn; Am Asn Ment Deficiency; Am Pediat Soc; Soc Biol Psychiat; Am Acad Pediat. *Res:* Child psychiatry and development; mental retardation; child psychotherapy. *Mailing Add:* 2300 Childrens Plaza Chicago IL 60614

SCHULMAN, JEROME M, CHEMICAL PHYSICS, MOLECULAR PHARMACOLOGY. *Current Pos:* assoc prof chem, 71-74, PROF CHEM, QUEENS COL, NY, 74- *Personal Data:* b New York, NY, Oct 21, 38; m 83. *Educ:* Rensselaer Polytech Inst, BChE, 60; Columbia Univ, MA, 61, PhD(chem), 64. *Prof Exp:* Res assoc theoret chem, NY Univ, 64-66, asst prof chem, 66-67; sr res assoc, Yeshiva Univ, 67-68; from asst prof to assoc prof chem physics, Polytech Inst Brooklyn, 68-71. *Concurrent Pos:* Alfred P Sloan fel, Polytech Inst Brooklyn & Queens Col, NY, 71-73. *Mem:* Am Chem Soc. *Res:* Quantum theory of atoms and molecules; perturbation theory; electromagnetic properties of atoms and molecules; theoretical organic chemistry; molecular pharmacology; chemistry of organoboron compounds. *Mailing Add:* Dept Chem & Biochem Queens Col Flushing NY 11367. *Fax:* 718-997-5531; *E-Mail:* schulman@qcuaxa.acc.qc.edu

SCHULMAN, JOSEPH DANIEL, HUMAN GENETICS, OBSTETRICS. *Current Pos:* head human genetics sect, 74-79, dir, IVF Inst, genetics training prog, 79-82, DIR, GENETICS & IVF INST, NIH, 84- *Personal Data:* b Brooklyn, NY, Dec 20, 41; m 64; c 2. *Educ:* Brooklyn Col, BA, 61; Harvard Univ, MD, 66. *Prof Exp:* Intern & resident pediat, Mass Gen Hosp, 66-68; clin assoc genetics, NIH, 68-70; resident obstet, Cornell Med Ctr, 70-73; fel develop biochem, Cambridge Univ, Eng, 73-74. *Concurrent Pos:* Prof obstet & gynec, George Washington Univ, Sch Med, 75-84, Med Col Va, 85- *Mem:* Soc Pediat Res; Soc Gynec Invest; Am Soc Human Genetics; Am Soc Clin Invest; Sigma Xi. *Res:* Human biochemistry, genetics and development; human genetic diseases; in vitro fertilization. *Mailing Add:* Genetics & IVF Inst 3020 Javier Rd Fairfax VA 22031-4609

SCHULMAN, LAWRENCE S, PHYSICS, STATISTICAL MECHANICS. *Current Pos:* PROF PHYSICS & CHMN DEPT, CLARKSON UNIV, 85- *Personal Data:* b Newark, NJ, Nov 21, 41; c 3. *Educ:* Yeshiva Univ, BA, 63; Princeton Univ, PhD(physics), 67. *Prof Exp:* From asst prof to prof physics, Ind Univ, Bloomington, 67-78; assoc prof, Israel Inst Technol, 72-77, prof physics, 77- *Concurrent Pos:* Consult, Los Alamos Sci Labs, 64, Lawrence Radiation Lab, Livermore, 65 & 68, IBM Corp, 75-; vis scientist, Israel Inst Technol, 70-71, Fr Atomic Energy Comn, Saclay; NATO fel, 70-71 & CNR, Italy, 93; vis prof, Univ Paris, Norweg Inst Technol, Trondheim; Donders prof, State Univ Utrecht; vis prof, Columbia Univ, 92-96. *Mem:* Am Phys Soc; Israel Phys Soc. *Res:* Mathematical physics; phase transitions; elementary particles; quantum mechanics; statistical physics. *Mailing Add:* Clarkson Univ Potsdam NY 13699-5820

SCHULMAN, MARVIN, ENGINEERING, LIFE SUPPORT EQUIPMENT. *Current Pos:* VPRES, LME, INC, 87- *Personal Data:* b Brooklyn, NY, Nov 13, 27; m 54; c 4. *Educ:* Brooklyn Col, BA, 54. *Prof Exp:* Supvry gen engr, Aircraft & Crew Systs Technol Directorate, US Dept Navy, 54-85; sr staff adv, Ketron Inc, 85-86. *Concurrent Pos:* Mem occupant restraint systs comt, Soc Automotive Engrs; consult, human factors & systs eng, 85- *Mem:* Instrument Soc Am; SAFE. *Res:* Design and development of aircraft escape and fixed seating systems; restraint, occupant protective devices, energy management on impact and protection during high acceleration exposure. *Mailing Add:* 448 Candlewood Rd Broomall PA 19008

SCHULMAN, MARVIN DAVID, ENZYMOLOGY, SECONDARY METABOLISM. *Current Pos:* res fel, 73-79, sr res fel, 79-86, SR INVESTR, MERCK SHARP & DOHME RES LABS, 86- *Personal Data:* b New York, NY, Oct 6, 39; m 63; c 2. *Educ:* Cornell Univ, BA, 61, PhD(biochem), 67. *Prof Exp:* Res & teaching fel, dept biochem, Sch Med, Case Western Reserve Univ, 67-70, instr, 70-73. *Mem:* Am Soc Biol Chemists; Am Chem Soc; Am Soc Microbiol; Soc Indust Microbiol; Am Soc Pharmacog. *Res:* Biochemistry and enzymology of the biosynthesis secondary metabolites, particularly the avermectins; mechanism of action of anthelmintics; bioconversion of natural products. *Mailing Add:* Merck Sharp & Dohme Res Labs PO Box 2000 Rahway NJ 07065. *Fax:* 732-594-1399; *E-Mail:* marv_schulman@merck.com

SCHULMAN, SIDNEY, NEUROLOGY. *Current Pos:* From asst prof to prof, 52-75, Ellen Manning Prof, Div Biol Sci, 75-93, EMER PROF, UNIV CHICAGO, 93- *Personal Data:* b Chicago, Ill, Mar 1, 23; m 45, Mary J Diamond; c Samuel, Patricia & Daniel. *Educ:* Univ Chicago, BS, 44, MD, 46. *Mem:* Am Acad Neurol; Am Neurol Asn. *Res:* Neuropathology; clinical neurology; behavioral effects of experimental lesions in the thalamus. *Mailing Add:* Dept Biol Sci/Ch 405A Univ Chicago 1025 E 57th Chicago IL 60637

SCHULMAN, STEPHEN GREGORY, ANALYTICAL CHEMISTRY, PHOTOCHEMISTRY. *Current Pos:* From asst prof to prof, 70-77, PROF PHARMACEUT, COL PHARM, UNIV FLA, 77- *Personal Data:* b Brooklyn, NY, June 11, 40; div; c Christina, Barbara & Joanna. *Educ:* City Col New York, BS, 61; Univ Ariz, PhD(chem), 67. *Prof Exp:* Asst chemist, Boyce Thompson Inst Plant Res, 62-64, phys chemist, 67-68; mem tech staff, Bellcomm Inc, 68-69. *Concurrent Pos:* Fel, dept chem, Univ Fla, 69-70; vis prof, Univ Ky, 76, State Univ Utrecht, 79, 81 & 83, Univ Stratheclyde, 85, Kumamoto Univ, 86-87, Acad Sinica, 87, Karl Franzens Univ, Graz, 89; comt revision, USP, 80-90; Food Chemicals Codex, Nat Acad Sci, 89-; consult, Futuretech, Inc, Teltech, Inc, Molecular Measurement Technol Ctr, Cranfield Univ, UK. *Mem:* Am Chem Soc; Am Asn Pharmaceut Scientists; Sigma Xi. *Res:* Molecular electronic spectroscopy, mixed ligand chelates; analytical chemistry in biological fluids and living tissues; binding of drugs to proteins and nucleic acids; fast reaction kinetics; fluorescence optical sensors. *Mailing Add:* Col Pharm JHMHC Univ Fla Box 100485 Gainesville FL 32610-0485. *Fax:* 352-392-9455; *E-Mail:* schulman@grove.ufl.edu

SCHULSON, ERLAND MAXWELL, INTERMETALLIC COMPOUNDS, ICE MECHANICS. *Current Pos:* assoc prof, 78-84, PROF ENG, DARTMOUTH COL, 84-, DIR, ICE RES LAB, 83- *Personal Data:* b Ladysmith, BC, May 28, 41; m 64, Sandra K; c 4. *Educ:* Univ BC, BASc, 64, PhD(metall eng), 68. *Hon Degrees:* MA, Dartmouth Col, 87. *Prof Exp:* Sr res fel, Univ Oxford, 68-69; res officer, Chalk River Nuclear Labs, Atomic Energy Can Ltd, 69-78. *Concurrent Pos:* Prin investr, NSF, Dept Energy, NASA, ARO, ONR; consult, pvt indust & govt labs; vis res fel, GE Corp Res & Develop Ctr, 88; vis prof, Univ Grenoble, 89. *Mem:* Am Inst Mining, Metall & Petrol Engrs; Am Geophys Union; Mat Res Soc; Am Soc Metals; Int Glaciol Soc. *Res:* Materials science; relationship between the microstructure and the plastic flow and fracture of materials; structure and mechanical properties of ice; mechanical behavior of intermetallic components; ice mechanics; over 200 published papers. *Mailing Add:* Thayer Sch Eng Dartmouth Col Hanover NH 03755. *Fax:* 603-646-3856; *E-Mail:* erland.schulson@dartmouth.edu

SCHULT, ROY LOUIS, THEORETICAL PHYSICS. *Current Pos:* RETIRED. *Personal Data:* b Brooklyn, NY, Aug 31, 34; m 58, 77, Candace Young; c Frederick, Daniel & Julia. *Educ:* Univ Rochester, BS, 56; Cornell Univ, PhD(theoret physics), 61. *Prof Exp:* Res assoc, Univ Ill, Urbana, 61-63, res asst prof, 63-64, asst prof, 64-69, assoc prof physics, 69-96. *Concurrent Pos:* Vis assoc physicist, Brookhaven Nat Labs, 69-70; assoc mem, La Jolla Inst, Calif, 85- *Mem:* Am Phys Soc. *Res:* Weak interactions; theory of elementary particles; nonlinear systems. *Mailing Add:* 540 Orpheus Ave Leucadia CA 92024. *E-Mail:* r-schult@uiuc.edu

SCHULTE, ALFONS F, PROTEIN DYNAMICS, SPECTROSCOPY. *Current Pos:* ASSOC PROF PHYSICS & CTR RES & EDUC OPTICS & LASERS, UNIV CENT FLA, 90- *Personal Data:* b Wulmeringhauser, WGer; m 90, Cinderella Gayoso; c Ingrid & Friedrick. *Educ:* Tech Univ Munich, dipl, 80 & PhD(physics), 85. *Prof Exp:* Res assoc, Tech Univ Munich, 85-86, Univ Ill, 86-87; vis res prof, Univ Ill, Urbana, 86-88; vis scientist, IBM Almaden Res Ctr, 89-90. *Mem:* Am Phys Soc; Ger Phys Soc; Biophys Soc. *Res:* Dynamic structure and function of proteins; connections between proteins, glasses and spinglasses; ligand binding and relaxation in hemeproteins using time resolved spectroscopic techniques over a wide range of temperature and pressure; applications of Raman spectroscopy. *Mailing Add:* Dept Physics Univ Cent Fla PO Box 25000 Orlando FL 32816-0001. *E-Mail:* afs@physics.ucf.edu

SCHULTE, DANIEL HERMAN, ASTRONOMY, OPTICS. *Current Pos:* RETIRED. *Personal Data:* b Osceola, Iowa, Aug 3, 29; m 55; c Robert Daniel, Marta Sue & Aden Benot. *Educ:* Phillips Univ, AB, 51; Univ Chicago, PhD(astron), 58. *Prof Exp:* Asst, Yerkes Observ, Univ Chicago, 51-56; optical engr, Perkin-Elmer Corp, 56-59; asst astronomer, Kitt Peak Observ, Ariz, Asn Univs Res in Astron, 59-65; staff physicist, Optical Design Dept, Itek Corp, 65-81; from res scientist to sr staff scientist, Lockheed Palo Alto Res Labs, 81-93. *Concurrent Pos:* Consult, Haneman Assocs, Tex, 61 & Tropel, Inc, NY, 62-63. *Mem:* Am Astron Soc; Optical Soc Am; Int Astron Union. *Res:* Observational astronomy; astronomical spectroscopy and photometry; optical design; computer applications to astronomical problems. *Mailing Add:* 118 Mercy Mountain View CA 94041

SCHULTE, HARRY FRANK, industrial hygiene; deceased, see previous edition for last biography

SCHULTE, HARRY JOHN, JR, experimental physics; deceased, see previous edition for last biography

SCHULTE, ROBERT LAWRENCE, NUCLEAR DETECTOR DEVELOPMENT, ION BEAM ANALYSIS OF MATERIALS. *Current Pos:* LAB HEAD, GRUMMAN CORP, CORP RES CTR, 74- *Personal Data:* b Covington, Ky, Apr 16, 45; m 70; c 1. *Educ:* Thomas More Col, AB, 65; Univ Ky, MS, 67, PhD(physics), 71. *Prof Exp:* Res assoc, Univ Toronto, 71-74. *Concurrent Pos:* Adj prof, Long Island Univ, C W Post Ctr, 82- *Mem:* Am Phys Soc; Am Nuclear Soc; Inst Elec & Electronics Engrs. *Res:* Effects of solute & trace element concentrations on the properties of materials using nuclear reaction analysis techniques; design and development of specialized nuclear detection systems for radioisotope measurements. *Mailing Add:* Res & Develop A01-26 Northrop Grumman Corp Bethpage NY 11714

SCHULTE, WILLIAM JOHN, JR, SURGERY. *Current Pos:* CHIEF SURG INTENSIVE CARE UNIT, VET ADMIN CTR, 70-, CHIEF SURG SERV, 80- *Personal Data:* b Stryker, Ohio, Nov 6, 28; m 61; c 7. *Educ:* Univ Toledo, BS, 52; Ohio State Univ, MD, 56; Am Bd Surg, dipl, 64. *Prof Exp:* Asst clin instr, 59-63, from instr to assoc prof, 63-77, prof surg, Med Col Wis, 77- *Concurrent Pos:* Gastrointestinal res fel, 64-65; attend staff, Milwaukee County Gen Hosp, 64- & Wood Vet Admin Hosp, 65-; Vet Admin clin investr, 65-68; staff attend, St Joseph's Hosp & Mt Sinai Hosp, Milwaukee, Wis; asst chief surg serv, Vet Admin Ctr, Milwaukee, 78-80. *Mem:* Am Fedn Clin Res; fel Am Col Surg; Am Gastroenterol Soc; Asn Acad Surg; Cent Surg Asn. *Res:* General surgery; parenteral nutrition; gastrointestinal motility; gastric and pancreatic physiology. *Mailing Add:* Vet Admin Ctr Milwaukee WI 53295

SCHULTER-ELLIS, FRANCES PIERCE, ANATOMY, PHYSICAL ANTHROPOLOGY. *Current Pos:* RETIRED. *Personal Data:* b Helena, Ala, Sept 22, 23; m 42, 77, Spencer P; c Jenny (Varden) & Peter Alan. *Educ:* Birmingham Southern Col, BS, 52; Emory Univ, MS, 54; George Washington Univ, PhD(anat), 72. *Prof Exp:* Instr biol, Chamblee High Sch, Ga, 60-61; instr zool, anat & physiol, Marjorie Webster Jr Col, 61-65; from asst prof to assoc prof anat, Sch Med, Univ Md, Baltimore, 72-87; vis prof, George Washington Univ, 87-88. *Concurrent Pos:* Res collabr, Div Phys Anthropol, Smithsonian Inst, 80-; vis prof anat, St George Univ, WI, 80-87 & 89-92. *Mem:* Human Biol Coun; Am Asn Phys Anthropologists; Am Acad Forensic Sci; NY Acad Sci; Am Asn Anatomists; Am Asn Univ Prof. *Res:* Craniometry, with special emphasis on temporal bone and cranial base variations, middle and inner ear disease, otitis media, human variation and asymmetry; bone aging, morphology of human hand skeleton; human skeleton race and sex identification. *Mailing Add:* 3465 Lochwood Dr Q76 Ft Collins CO 80525

SCHULTES, RICHARD EVANS, BOTANY, AMAZONIAN ETHNOBOTANY. *Current Pos:* RETIRED. *Personal Data:* b Boston, Mass, Jan 12, 15; m 59; c 3. *Educ:* Harvard Univ, AB, 37, MA, 38, PhD(biol), 41. *Hon Degrees:* MH, Univ Nac Colombia, 53; DSc, Mass Col Pharm, 87. *Honors & Awards:* Orden de la Victoria Regia, Colombian Govt; Lindbergh Award, 81; Gold Medal, World Wildlife Fund, 84; Gold Medal, Sigma Xi, 85; Tyler Prize Environ Achievements, 87; Ann Gold Linnean Medal, 92. *Prof Exp:* Collabr, Inst Bot, Nat Univ Mex, 38, 39 & 41; hon res fel, Bot Mus, Harvard Univ, 41-54, cur, Ames Orchid Herbarium, 54-58, lectr econ bot, 58-70, dir Mus, 67-85, prof biol, 70-72, Mangelsdorf prof natural sci, 73-80, Jeffrey prof biol, 80-85. *Concurrent Pos:* Nat Res Coun fel, Inst Natural Sci, Nat Univ Colombia, 41; jungle explor & botanist, USDA, 43-54, collbr, Nat Sci Inst, Bogota, 41-; Guggenheim fel, 50; ed, Bot Mus Leaflets, Harvard Univ, 58-85 & Econ Bot, 63-80; adj prof pharmacog, Sch Pharm, Univ Ill, 75-; collabr, Malaysian Rubber Res Inst, 90- *Mem:* Nat Acad Sci; Col Acad Sci Ecuador; Acad Sci Arg; fel Am Acad Arts & Sci; Linnean Soc; fel Am Col Neuropsychopharmacol; fel Third World Acad Sci; Nat Acad Sci India. *Res:* Latin American ethnobotany, especially narcotics, medicines and poisons used by natives of Amazonas; orchid taxonomy; taxonomy of rubber plants. *Mailing Add:* Bot Mus Harvard Univ Oxford St Cambridge MA 02138

SCHULTHEIS, JAMES J, PHYSICS. *Current Pos:* RETIRED. *Personal Data:* b Rochester, NY, Aug 22, 32; m 55; c 5. *Educ:* John Carroll Univ, BS, 54; Univ Rochester, MS, 56. *Prof Exp:* Engr, Atomic Power Div, Westinghouse Elec Corp, 55-56; asst physicist, Argonne Nat Lab, 56-58; nuclear engr, Knolls Atomic Power Lab, Dept Energy, 58-67, nuclear consult, 67-71, mgr mat syts reliability, Energy Res & Develop Admin, 71-77, mgr steam generator-coolant technol, 77-80, mgr, Ceramic Development Lab, 80-86, proj eng, advan steam generator, 86-93. *Mem:* Am Nuclear Soc. *Res:* Radiological physics; reactor physics; advanced reactor engineering; heat transfer; reactor control; steam generators; materials engineering; ceramic engineering. *Mailing Add:* 1139 Fernwood Dr Niskayuna NY 12309

SCHULTHEISS, PETER M(AX), ELECTRICAL ENGINEERING. *Current Pos:* From instr to assoc prof, 48-64, PROF ENG & APPL SCI, YALE UNIV, 64- *Personal Data:* b Munich, Ger, Oct 18, 24; nat US; m 59; c 3. *Educ:* Yale Univ, BE, 45, MEng, 48, PhD(elec eng), 52. *Mem:* Inst Elec & Electronics Engrs; Acoust Soc Am. *Res:* Communication theory; automatic control; applied mathematics; underwater acoustics. *Mailing Add:* Dept Elec Eng Becton Ctr Yale Univ New Haven CT 06520

SCHULTZ, ALBERT BARRY, GERIATRIC BIOMECHANICS, MUSCULOSKELETAL BIOMECHANICS. *Current Pos:* VENNEMA PROF MECH ENG RES SCIENTIST, INST GERONTEOL UNIV MICH, ANN ARBOR, 83- *Personal Data:* b Philadelphia, Pa, Oct 10, 33; m 55, Susan

Reshikov; c Carl, Adam & Robin. *Educ:* Univ Rochester, BS, 55; Yale Univ, MEng, 59, PhD(mech eng), 62. *Honors & Awards:* Javits Neuroscientist Award, NIH, 85-92; Lissner Award, Am Soc Mech Engrs, 90; Borelli Award, Am Soc Biomech, 96. *Prof Exp:* Lectr mech eng, Yale Univ, 61-62; asst prof, Univ Del, 62-65; from asst prof to prof mat eng, Univ Ill, Chicago Circle, 65-83. *Concurrent Pos:* NIH spec res fel, Stockholm, 71-72; res career award, NIH, 75-80; assoc ed, J Biomech Eng, 76-82; vis prof, Sahlgren Hosp, Gothenburg, Sweden, 78-79; chmn, Bioeng Div, Am Soc Mech Engrs, 81-82; chmn, US Nat Comn Biomech, 82-85. *Mem:* Nat Acad Eng; Int Soc Study Lumbar Spine (pres, 81-82); Am Soc Biomech (pres, 82-83); Am Geriat Soc; Geront Soc Am; Am Soc Mech Engrs. *Res:* Biomechanics; mobility impairment in the elderly; mechanical behavior of human spine. *Mailing Add:* 3112 G G Brown Univ Mich Ann Arbor MI 48109-2125. *Fax:* 313-763-9332

SCHULTZ, ALVIN LEROY, INTERNAL MEDICINE, ENDOCRINOLOGY. *Current Pos:* RETIRED. *Personal Data:* b Minneapolis, Minn, July 27, 21; m 47, Martha Grahaw; c Susan K, David M, Peter J & Michael G. *Educ:* Univ Minn, BA, 43, MD, 46, MS, 52. *Honors & Awards:* Frances M Greenwalt Pharmacol Award, 75; Charles Bolles Bolles-Rogers Award, 92; Shatwell Award, 92. *Prof Exp:* Intern med, Ohio State Univ Hosp, 46-47; resident med, Univ Minn Hosps, 49-52; from instr to assoc prof, Univ Minn, Minneapolis, 52-65, lectr, 52-94, chief med, Hennepin Co Med Ctr, 65-88, prof med, 65-88. *Concurrent Pos:* Assoc dir, Radioisotope Lab, Minneapolis Vet Admin Hosp, 52-53, asst chief med serv, 53-54, consult, Radioisotope Lab & Med Serv, 54-; attend physician, Endocrine Clin, Univ Minn Hosps, 52-60, chief clin, 60-65; dir radioisotope Lab, Methodist Hosp, 55-59; dir med educ & res, Mt Sinai Hosp, 59-65; gov for Minn, Am Col Physician, 84-87 & chmn elect, bd gov, 86, chmn, 87, regent, 88-; chmn bd dir, Coun Med Specialty Soc, 88-92 & pres, 91; endowed vis prof, Univ Minn & Hennegin Co Med Ctr; sr vpres med affairs, Health One Corp, 88-94. *Mem:* Endocrine Soc; Cent Soc Clin Res; Am Fedn Clin Res; fel Am Col Physicians; Am Thyroid Asn. *Res:* Diseases of metabolism and endocrinology, especially of the thyroid gland; hormonal control of lipid metabolism; effects of thyroid function. *Mailing Add:* 5127 Irving Ave S Minneapolis MN 55419. *Fax:* 612-926-4915

SCHULTZ, ANDREW, JR, ENGINEERING. *Current Pos:* from actg dean to dean, Cornell Univ, 63-72, actg dean, 78, Spencer T Olin prof, 72-80, EMER PROF ENG, COL ENG, CORNELL UNIV, 80- *Personal Data:* b Harrisburg, Pa, Aug 14, 13; m 39, Mary S Mory; c 2. *Educ:* Cornell Univ, BS, 36, PhD(admin eng), 41. *Prof Exp:* From instr to asst prof admin eng, Cornell Univ, 38-41, assoc prof, 46-50, prof & head dept, 50-61; vpres & dir res, Logistics Mgt Inst, Washington, DC, 61-63. *Concurrent Pos:* Dir, Chicago Pneumatic Tool Co, S I Handling Systs, Inc, Logistics Mgt Inst, Zurn Indust. *Mem:* Am Soc Eng Educ; Am Inst Indust Engrs. *Res:* Statistical applications in engineering; operations research; industrial engineering. *Mailing Add:* 1000 Vicars Landing Way PH 1 Ponte Vedra Beach FL 32082

SCHULTZ, ARNOLD MAX, PLANT ECOLOGY. *Current Pos:* from asst specialist to specialist forestry, Univ Calif, Berkeley, 49-66, ecologist, 66-77, prof, 77-97, EMER PROF FORESTRY & RESOURCE MGT, AGR EXP STA, UNIV CALIF, BERKELEY, 97- *Personal Data:* b Altura, Minn, Sept 9, 20; m 49; c 5. *Educ:* Univ Minn, BSc, 41, MSc, 42; Univ Nebr, PhD(bot), 51. *Prof Exp:* Jr range conservationist, Soil Conserv Serv, USDA, 42. *Mem:* AAAS; Soc Gen Systs Res; Ecol Soc Am. *Res:* Sampling and biometric techniques in range ecology; nutrient cycles and productivity in arctic tundra ecosystems; ecology of high mountain meadows; ecosystem management; interdisciplinary undergraduate programs. *Mailing Add:* Dept Environ Sci Policy & Mgt 145 Mulford Hall Univ Calif Berkeley CA 94720-3114

SCHULTZ, ARTHUR GEORGE, ORGANIC CHEMISTRY. *Current Pos:* from assoc prof to prof, 78-88, WILLIAM WEIGHTMAN WALKER PROF CHEM, RENSSELAER POLYTECH INST, 88- *Personal Data:* b Chicago, Ill, Sept 14, 42; m 69, Marcia D; c Daniel A & Rebecca L. *Educ:* Ill Inst Technol, BSc, 66; Univ Rochester, PhD(chem), 70. *Prof Exp:* Res fel chem, Columbia Univ, 70-72; asst prof chem, Cornell Univ, 72-78. *Mem:* Am Chem Soc; Am Soc Pharmacog. *Res:* Natural products synthesis; synthetic and mechanistic organic photochemistry; asymmetric organic synthesis. *Mailing Add:* Dept Chem Rensselaer Polytech Inst Troy NY 12180-3590. *Fax:* 518-276-4045; *E-Mail:* schula@rpi.edu

SCHULTZ, ARTHUR JAY, NEUTRON & X-RAY DIFFRACTION, SUPERCONDUCTORS. *Current Pos:* res assoc, 76-78, asst chemist, 78-82, CHEMIST, ARGONNE NAT LAB, 82- *Personal Data:* b Brooklyn, NY, July 15, 47; m 84, Ruth A Pearl; c Michael. *Educ:* State Univ NY Stony Brook, BS, 69; Brown Univ, PhD(inorg chem), 73. *Prof Exp:* Res assoc chem, Univ Ill, Urbana, 73-76. *Mem:* Am Chem Soc; Am Crystallog Asn; AAAS; Sigma Xi. *Res:* Time-of-flight single-crystal neutron diffraction; structural studies by x-ray and neutron diffraction; organic superconductors; high-Tc superconductors; structure-property relationships. *Mailing Add:* IPNS Div Argonne Nat Lab Argonne IL 60439. *Fax:* 630-252-4163; *E-Mail:* ajschultz@anl.gov

SCHULTZ, BLANCHE BEATRICE, MATHEMATICS. *Current Pos:* from instr to prof, 46-86, asst dean, 77-83, EMER PROF MATH, URSINUS COL, 86- *Personal Data:* b Palm, Pa, Aug 23, 20. *Educ:* Ursinus Col, BS, 41; Univ Mich, MS, 49. *Prof Exp:* Teacher high sch, Pa, 41-42. *Concurrent Pos:* Cryptographer & aerial navig instr, USN, 42-46. *Mem:* Am Math Soc; Math Asn Am. *Mailing Add:* 2354 Pleasant Ave Glenside PA 19038-4315

SCHULTZ, CRAMER WILLIAM, PHYSICS. *Current Pos:* RETIRED. *Personal Data:* b Laurel, Mont, May 2, 26; m 49; c 4. *Educ:* Univ Calif, BA, 48; Univ Southern Calif, PhD(physics), 55. *Prof Exp:* Assoc prof, Calif State Univ, Long Beach, 53-64, prof physics, 64-93. *Res:* Cryogenics; solid state physics. *Mailing Add:* 16832 Morse Circle Huntington Beach CA 92649

SCHULTZ, DAVID HAROLD, NUMERICAL ANALYSIS. *Current Pos:* co-supvr data processing, Surv Res Lab, Univ Wis, 65-70, res asst numerical anal, Comput Sci Dept, 68-70, from asst prof to assoc prof, 70-93, PROF MATH, UNIV WIS-MILWAUKEE, 93-, ASSOC CHAIR MATH, 96- *Personal Data:* b Park Falls, Wis, Sept 10, 42; m 65, Marion Olson; c Sigrid & Christine. *Educ:* Univ Wis-Madison, BS, 65, MS, 67, PhD(comput sci & numerical anal), 70. *Concurrent Pos:* Reviewer, Math Rev; grantee, NIH, 73-74, NSF, 89; consult, Argonne Nat Lab, 77-78; ed, Comput Fluid Dynamics, Int J Appl Sci & Comput. *Mem:* Soc Indust & Appl Math. *Res:* Numerical analysis; fluid flow problems; numerical solutions of differential equations. *Mailing Add:* Dept Math Univ Wis Milwaukee WI 53202. *E-Mail:* schultz@csd.csduw.uwm.edu

SCHULTZ, DONALD GENE, ELECTRICAL ENGINEERING. *Current Pos:* RETIRED. *Personal Data:* b Milwaukee, Wis, Aug 28, 28; m 53; c 3. *Educ:* Univ Santa Clara, BSEE, 52; Univ Calif, Los Angeles, MS, 55; Purdue Univ, PhD(automatic control), 62. *Prof Exp:* Assoc prof elec eng, Univ Ariz, 62-66, prof, 66, head, Dept Systs & Indust Engr, 74. *Concurrent Pos:* Consult, Los Alamos Sci Lab. *Mem:* Inst Elec & Electronics Engrs. *Res:* Automatic control; stability. *Mailing Add:* 3005 Cerrado Los Palitos Tucson AZ 85718

SCHULTZ, DONALD PAUL, ENVIRONMENTAL CONTAMINATION EVALUATION. *Current Pos:* RETIRED. *Personal Data:* b Detroit, Mich, Feb 7, 30; m 51; c 4. *Educ:* Concordia Teachers Col, BS, 54; Auburn Univ, PhD(plant physiol), 67. *Prof Exp:* Prin & teacher, St Stephen Lutheran Sch, 54-62; fel, Pesticide Metab, Univ Mo, Columbia, 67-70; chemist herbicide metab, Fish Pesticide Res Lab, US Dept Interior, Mo, 70-71, chemist chief, Southeastern Fish Control Lab, Ga, 71-80; mem staff, Environ Contamination Eval, Fish & Wildlife Serv, Atlanta, 80-92. *Mem:* AAAS; Aquatic Plant Mat Soc; Sigma Xi. *Res:* Uptake and metabolism of pesticides; influence of pesticides on metabolic processes. *Mailing Add:* 1046 Robert Williams Rd Pine Mountain GA 31822

SCHULTZ, DONALD RAYMOND, INORGANIC CHEMISTRY. *Current Pos:* RETIRED. *Personal Data:* b North Tonawanda, NY, Nov 2, 18; m 42, 68; c 4. *Educ:* Univ Mich, BS, 40, MS, 52, PhD(chem), 54. *Prof Exp:* Anal chemist, Pa Salt Mfg Co, 40; anal res chemist, McGean Chem Co, 40-42; res engr, Trojan Powder Co, 42-44; res engr, Inorg Res Brine Prods, Mich Chem Corp, 46-50; res engr, Boron Hydrides Eng Res Inst, Univ Mich, 51-54; sr patent liaison, Cent Res Dept, 3M Co, 54-82. *Concurrent Pos:* Lectr, Bethel Col, 65-66. *Mem:* AAAS; Am Chem Soc; Am Inst Chemists; Sigma Xi. *Res:* Preparation properties and uses of magnesia; inorganic bromides; thermography; coordination chemistry of copper, nickel, cobalt; patent literature; boron hydrides in liquid ammonia; vinyl polymerization with boron alkyls; photoconductivity. *Mailing Add:* Butterfield Trail Village 1923 E Joyce St Apt 332 Fayetteville AR 72703-5173

SCHULTZ, DUANE ROBERT, IMMUNOLOGY, PROTEIN CHEMISTRY. *Current Pos:* staff immunologist, 66-71, assoc prof med, 71-82, PROF, SCH MED, UNIV MIAMI, 82- *Personal Data:* b Bay City, Mich, June 24, 34; m 61; c 1. *Educ:* Univ Mich, BS, 57, MS, 60, PhD(microbiol), 64. *Prof Exp:* Staff immunologist, Cordis Labs, 66-72. *Concurrent Pos:* NIH fel immunol, Walter Reed Army Inst Res, 64-66. *Res:* Isolation, purification and function of the nine components of complement. *Mailing Add:* Dept Med Div Immunol R-102 Univ Miami Sch Med PO Box 016960 Miami FL 33101-6960

SCHULTZ, EDWARD, CELL BIOLOGY. *Current Pos:* From asst prof to assoc prof, 75-92, PROF ANAT, UNIV WIS-MADISON, 92- *Personal Data:* b Suffern, NY, Dec 4, 40; m 66, Jeanne; c Wendi & Kimberley. *Educ:* Ithaca Col, BA, 62, BS, 65; Temple Univ, PhD(anat), 73. *Mem:* Am Asn Anatomists; Am Soc Gravitational Space Biol; Am Soc Cell Biol. *Res:* Skeletal muscle regeneration; skeletal muscle growth; satellite cells; aging. *Mailing Add:* Dept Anat Univ Wis Med Sch 353 Bardeen Lab 1300 University Avenue Madison WI 53706. *Fax:* 608-262-7306; *E-Mail:* eschult1@facstaff.wisc.edu

SCHULTZ, EDWIN ROBERT, STABILITY & CONTROL, DESIGN & ANALYSIS VTOL AIRCRAFT. *Current Pos:* RETIRED. *Personal Data:* b Detroit, Mich, July 24, 27; m 63; c 3. *Educ:* Wayne State Univ, BS, 51; State Univ NY, MS, 58. *Prof Exp:* Flight test engr, McDonnell Aircraft Corp, 51-52; res engr, Cornell Aero Lab, 52-59; mem tech staff, Space Technol Lab, 59-61; supvr, advan res, Kaman Aerospace Corp, 61-64; supvry opers analyst, USAF Hq, Europe, 64-76; tech dir, Technol Assessment Div, WL-TXA, Wright Patterson AFB, 76-91. *Mem:* Am Inst Aeronaut & Astronaut. *Res:* Design and performance analyses of advanced conceptual aircraft for the United States Air Force; integrate emerging technologies into advanced aircraft configurations; development of life cycle cost modeling applied to future combat aircraft. *Mailing Add:* 5400 Lytle Rd Waynesville OH 45068

SCHULTZ, EVERETT HOYLE, JR, MEDICINE, RADIOLOGY. *Current Pos:* RETIRED. *Personal Data:* b Winston-Salem, NC, Sept 13, 27; m 55, Nancy Jansson; c Susan C, Frank E, Janet L & Sally L. *Educ:* Bowman Gray Sch Med, MD, 52. *Prof Exp:* Asst prof radiol, Univ Fla, 58-61; assoc prof, Univ NC, 61-67; radiologist, St Anthony's Hosp, 67-84; assoc prof, Med Col

Ga, 87-96. *Concurrent Pos:* Ed consult, Yearbk Cancer, 64-82. *Mem:* Am Roentgen Ray Soc; Radiol Soc NAm; fel Am Col Radiol. *Res:* Clinical research in human gastrointestinal diseases, particularly pancreatic diseases. *Mailing Add:* 608 Aumond Rd Augusta GA 30909-3308

SCHULTZ, FRANKLIN ALFRED, analytical chemistry, electrochemistry, for more information see previous edition

SCHULTZ, FRED HENRY, JR, ginseng research; deceased, see previous edition for last biography

SCHULTZ, FREDERICK HERMAN CARL, PHYSICS. *Current Pos:* RETIRED. *Personal Data:* b Hanks, NDak, June 11, 21; m 49, Lila Fay Gregory; c 3. *Educ:* Univ NDak, PhB, 42; Univ Idaho, MS, 50; Wash State Univ, PhD(physics), 67. *Prof Exp:* Instr physics, Univ NDak, 42-44 & 46-48, NDak State Univ, 44 & Mont Sch Mines, 50-55; asst prof, Mont State Univ, 55-61; assoc prof, Minot State Col, 61-63; asst prof, Wash State Univ, 63-68; chmn dept, Univ Wis-Eau Claire, 68-77, prof physics, 68-93. *Concurrent Pos:* Dir seismog sta, US Coast & Geod Surv, 55-61; energy consult, 77-; physicist, US Naval Ord Lab Corona, 57, 59, 61 & 63. *Mem:* Am Asn Physics Teachers; Seismol Soc Am; Optical Soc Am; Sigma Xi; NY Acad Sci. *Res:* Seismology; small Montana earthquakes; interaction of polarized infrared radiation with materials and surfaces. *Mailing Add:* 3834 Nimitz St Eau Claire WI 54701

SCHULTZ, FREDERICK JOHN, ORGANIC CHEMISTRY, RESEARCH ADMINISTRATION. *Current Pos:* RETIRED. *Personal Data:* b Davenport, Iowa, Oct 12, 29; m 55; c 4. *Educ:* Augustana Col, Ill, BA, 52; DePauw Univ, MA, 56; Univ Iowa, PhD(chem), 60. *Prof Exp:* Res chemist, Lorillard Inc, 59-62, sr res chemist, 62-65, prod develop mgr, 65-68, mgr res, Res Div, 68-75, dir, 75-78, vpres res & develop, 78-94. *Mem:* AAAS; Am Chem Soc; NY Acad Sci; Am Inst Chemists. *Res:* Composition of tobacco and tobacco smoke; relation of composition to biological activity and organoleptic properties; selective filtration of tobacco smoke; analytical methods development; new products in areas of tobacco and food products. *Mailing Add:* 815 Plummer Dr Greensboro NC 27410

SCHULTZ, GEORGE ADAM, ISOPOD CRUSTACEANS-ECOLOGY. *Current Pos:* ASSOC PROF, JERSEY CITY STATE COL, 70- *Personal Data:* b Phillipsburg, NJ, Apr 10, 32. *Educ:* Univ Chicago, BA, 53; Univ Mont, MA, 58; Duke Univ, PhD(zool), 64. *Concurrent Pos:* Dir, Isopod Study Group. *Mem:* Crustacean Soc; Soc Syst Zool; Am Soc Zoologists; Am Asn Zool Nomenclature. *Res:* Isopod crustaceans, marine, freshwater and terrestrial; systematics; distribution and biology. *Mailing Add:* 15 Smith St Hampton NJ 08827

SCHULTZ, GERALD EDWARD, VERTEBRATE PALEONTOLOGY & BIOSTRATIGRAPHY. *Current Pos:* From asst prof to assoc prof geol, 64-74, PROF GEOL, WTEX STATE UNIV, 74- *Personal Data:* b Red Wing, Minn, Sept 2, 36; div; c Katherine. *Educ:* Univ Minn, BS, 58, MS, 61; Univ Mich, PhD(geol), 66. *Concurrent Pos:* NSF res grant Pleistocene vert, Tex Panhandle, 70-72. *Mem:* Soc Vert Paleont; Am Soc Mammal; Paleont Soc; Am Quaternary Asn; Sigma Xi. *Res:* Vertebrate paleontology, especially late Cenozoic vertebrates and stratigraphy of the High Plains; late Tertiary and Pleistocene microvertebrate faunas and paleoecology. *Mailing Add:* Dept Life Earth & Environ Sci WTex A&M Univ Canyon TX 79016. *Fax:* 806-656-2928

SCHULTZ, GILBERT ALLAN, DEVELOPMENTAL BIOLOGY, MOLECULAR BIOLOGY. *Current Pos:* from asst prof to assoc prof, 72-83, PROF MED BIOCHEM, FAC MED, UNIV CALGARY, 83-, HEAD DEPT, 93- *Personal Data:* b Camrose, Alta, Nov 25, 44; m 69, Frances C Tucker; c Thomas C & Toby D. *Educ:* Univ Alta, BSc, 65, MSc, 66; Univ Calgary, PhD(biol), 70. *Prof Exp:* Nat Res Coun Can fel, Weizmann Inst Sci, 70 & Med Ctr, Univ Colo, Denver, 71-72. *Mem:* Can Soc Cell Biol; Am Soc Cell Biol; Soc Develop Biol; Soc Study Reproduction. *Res:* Study of gene expression during early development of mammalian embryos. *Mailing Add:* Dept Med Biochem Univ Calgary 3330 Hospital Dr NW Calgary AB T2N 4N1 Can. *Fax:* 403-270-0737; *E-Mail:* gschultz@acs.ucalgary.ca

SCHULTZ, HARRY PERSHING, ORGANIC CHEMISTRY. *Current Pos:* from asst prof to prof chem, 47-84, chmn dept, 72-84, EMER PROF CHEM, UNIV MIAMI, 84- *Personal Data:* b Racine, Wis, Mar 9, 18; m 43; c 3. *Educ:* Univ Wis, BS, 42, PhD(org chem), 46. *Prof Exp:* Res chemist, Nat Defense Res Comt, Univ Wis, 42-45 & Merck & Co, Inc, NJ, 46-47. *Mem:* Am Chem Soc. *Res:* Synthesis organic nitrogen heterocycles; organic reduction; chemical topology; polypeptides. *Mailing Add:* PO Box 262 Big Horn WY 82833

SCHULTZ, HARRY WAYNE, PHARMACEUTICAL CHEMISTRY. *Current Pos:* Asst prof, 59-66, ASSOC PROF PHARMACEUT CHEM, ORE STATE UNIV, 66- *Personal Data:* b Burlington, Iowa, June 13, 30; m 55; c 3. *Educ:* Univ Iowa, BS, 52, MS, 57, PhD(pharmaceut chem), 59. *Mem:* Am Pharmaceut Asn; Am Chem Soc. *Res:* Organic pharmaceutical chemistry; relationship of chemical structure to pharmacological activity. *Mailing Add:* 2137 NW Robin Hood Corvallis OR 97330-1152

SCHULTZ, HILBERT KENNETH, SYSTEMS ANALYSIS, COMPUTER SYSTEMS. *Current Pos:* PROF MIS, UNIV WIS-OSHKOSH, 71-, CHAIR, INFO SYSTS OPERS MGT DEPT, 93- *Personal Data:* b Butternut, Wis, Oct 27, 35; m 57; c 4. *Educ:* Univ Wis, Oshkosh, BS, 59; Univ Wis-Madison, MS, 62, PhD(comput sci), 71. *Prof Exp:* Comput analyst supvr, AC Electronics, Inc, 59-61; consult, Info Syst & Modeling, 66-68. *Concurrent Pos:* Consult govt & indust, 75-94. *Mem:* Am Prod & Inventory Control Soc; Decisions Sci Inst. *Res:* Use of fourth generation languages; microcomputer applications; theoretical and practical analysis of transportation problems; experts systems development; systems analysis and design of computer systems for retail, construction, nursing homes and physicians; business process reengineering; workgroup software. *Mailing Add:* Col Bus Admin Univ Wis Oshkosh WI 54901

SCHULTZ, HYMAN, COAL CHEMISTRY, TRACE ANALYSIS. *Current Pos:* res supvr anal res & serv, Pittsburgh Energy Res Ctr, US Bur Mines, 71-75, BR CHIEF ANALYSIS RES, PITTSBURGH ENERGY TECHNOL CTR, DEPT ENERGY, 77- *Personal Data:* b Brooklyn, NY, July 11, 31; m 57, Befferman; c Richard & Daniel. *Educ:* Brooklyn Col, BS, 56; Pa State Univ, PhD(anal chem), 62. *Prof Exp:* Sr res engr, Rocketdyne Div, NAm Aviation, Inc, Calif, 62-67; scientist & head, Gas Anal Sect, Isotopes, Teledyne, Inc, NJ, 67-71. *Concurrent Pos:* Mem, Organizing Comt, Pittsburgh Conf & Expo, 80- *Mem:* AAAS; Sigma Xi; Am Chem Soc. *Res:* Determination of trace materials in complex natural matrices; analysis of coal and the products of coal research; trace toxic materials in coal and their fate when coal is utilized; standardization of analytical methods for coal conversion materials. *Mailing Add:* 111 Camino Ct Jefferson Boro Clairton PA 15025. *Fax:* 412-892-6024; *E-Mail:* schultz@orion.pejc.doe.gov

SCHULTZ, IRWIN, MEDICINE. *Current Pos:* ASSOC CLIN PROF MED, COL MED, ST LOUIS UNIV, 69- *Personal Data:* b New York, NY, July 29, 29; m 55; c 5. *Educ:* NY Univ, BA, 49, MD, 54; Harvard Univ, MSH, 60, ScD(trop med), 64. *Prof Exp:* Asst prof microbiol & med, Med Sch, Northwestern Univ, 61-64; asst prof med, Sch Med, Wash Univ, 65-69. *Concurrent Pos:* Mem, Nat Inst Allergy & Infectious Dis, 59-61. *Mem:* AAAS; Am Fedn Clin Res; Am Col Physicians; Am Soc Microbiol. *Res:* Infectious diseases; epidemiology; pathogenesis of viral infections; host defense mechanisms in infectious disease; vaccine effectiveness. *Mailing Add:* 2865 Netherton Dr St Louis MO 63136-4674. *Fax:* 314-355-5716; *E-Mail:* ischultz@po.com

SCHULTZ, J(EROME) S(AMSON), CHEMICAL ENGINEERING, BIOENGINEERING. *Current Pos:* DIR CTR BIOTECHNOL & BIOENG, UNIV PITTSBURGH, 87- *Personal Data:* b Brooklyn, NY, June 25, 33; m 55; c 3. *Educ:* Columbia Univ, BS, 54, MS, 56; Univ Wis, PhD(biochem), 58. *Prof Exp:* Chem engr, Lederle Labs, Am Cyanamid Co, 58-59, in chg fermentation pilot plant, 59-61, group leader biochem res, 61-64; from asst prof to assoc prof, Univ Mich, Ann Arbor, 64-70, chmn dept, 77-85, prof chem eng, 70-87. *Concurrent Pos:* Res Career Develop Award, NIH, 70-75; sect head emerging technol, 85-86, dep dir; cross-disciplinary res, NSF, 86-87. *Mem:* Nat Acad Eng; AAAS; Am Chem Soc; Am Inst Chem Engrs; Am Soc Artificial Internal Organs. *Res:* Biochemical engineering; production of chemicals and pharmaceuticals by fermentation; kinetics; transport phenomena in membranes; compatibility of biomaterials; artificial organs; transport in blood and tissues; photochemical processes. *Mailing Add:* Univ Pittsburgh 300 Technology Dr Pittsburgh PA 15219

SCHULTZ, JACK C, INSECT ECOLOGY, PLANT-INSECT ECOLOGY. *Current Pos:* from asst prof to assoc prof, Dept Entom, 83-93, PROF ENTOMOL RES LAB, PA STATE UNIV, 93- *Personal Data:* b Chicago, Ill, Jan 4, 47. *Educ:* Univ Chicago, AB, 69; Univ Wash, PhD(zool), 75. *Prof Exp:* Res instr, Dartmouth Col, 75-80, res asst prof, Dept Biol Sci, 81-83. *Concurrent Pos:* Vis fel, Dept Entom, Cornell Univ, 78-79. *Mem:* Ecol Soc Am; Entom Soc Am; Soc Study Evolution. *Res:* Coevolutionary interactions among trees, insects and natural enemies; chemical and physiological responses of trees to insects; foraging and predator-avoidance behavior of insects; tropical ecology. *Mailing Add:* Pesticide Res Lab Pa State Univ University Park PA 16802

SCHULTZ, JAMES EDWARD, MATHEMATICS. *Current Pos:* admin assoc, 68-71, asst prof, 71-78, ASSOC PROF MATH, OHIO STATE UNIV, 78- *Personal Data:* b Sheboygan, Wis, Dec 25, 39; m 63; c 1. *Educ:* Univ Wis-Madison, BS, 63; Ohio State Univ, MS, 67, PhD(math educ), 71. *Prof Exp:* Instr math, high sch, Wis, 63-68. *Concurrent Pos:* Vis asst prof math, Mich State Univ, 73-74; vis asst prof educ, Univ Chicago, 74-75. *Mem:* Math Asn Am. *Res:* Mathematics preparation of elementary teachers. *Mailing Add:* 1332 Lincoln Rd Columbus OH 43212

SCHULTZ, JANE SCHWARTZ, IMMUNOGENETICS. *Current Pos:* dir res admin health sci, Univ Pittsburgh, 88-93, integrity officer, 92-93, res dir, 94-95, RES ASSOC CHEM ENG, UNIV PITTSBURGH, 93-; DIR & CHIEF EXEC OFFICER, BIOMATION, LTD, 93-; SPEC PROJ DIR, NAT DIS RES INTERCHANGE, 96- *Personal Data:* b New York, NY, July 28, 32; m 55, Jerome S; c Daniel S, Judith S (Nyquist) & Kathryn S (Hubbard). *Educ:* Hunter Col, BA, 53; Columbia Univ, MS, 55; Univ Mich, MS, 67, PhD(human genetics), 70. *Honors & Awards:* Dirs Award, NIH, 86, Spec Achievement Award, 88. *Prof Exp:* Res chemist, Gen Foods Corp, 54-55 & Forest Prod Lab, USDA, 55-58; sci teacher, Pearl River High Sch, NY, 58-59; res assoc, Univ Mich, Ann Arbor, 70-71 & 72-75, asst prof human genetics, 75-82, asst dean curric, 79-81, asst dean student affairs, 81-83, assoc prof human genetics, 82-83; chief, Genetics & Transp Biol Br, Nat Inst Allergic & Infectious Dis, 83-88, assoc prof path, 88-93. *Concurrent Pos:* Sr res investr, Dept Immunohaemetology, State Univ Leiden, 71-72; geneticist, Vet Admin Ctr, 72-83; vet admin rep, Genetics Study Sect, NIH, 73-77, Nat Inst Gen Med Sci Coun, 77-81; chief, Div Prog Develop & Rev, Vet Admin Res Serv, 76-79. *Mem:* Am Asn Immunologists; Genetics Soc Am; Am Soc Human Genetics; Am Soc Histocompatibility & Immunogenetics; Soc Res Admin. *Res:* Elucidation of the immunological functions controlled by genetically determined transplantation antigens in mouse, rat and man; major histocompatibility complex-disease associations in man. *Mailing Add:* Univ Pittsburgh-CBB 300 Technology Dr Pittsburgh PA 15219

SCHULTZ, JEROLD M, POLYMER SCIENCE, CRYSTALLIZATION. *Current Pos:* from asst prof to assoc prof, 65-73, PROF METALL, UNIV DEL, 73- *Personal Data:* b San Francisco, Calif, June 21, 35; m 60, Peggy June Ostrom; c Carrie M, Timothy J, Peter A & Anna C. *Educ:* Univ Calif, Berkeley, BS, 58, MS, 59; Carnegie Inst Technol, PhD(metall), 65. *Honors & Awards:* Humboldt Sr Scientist Award, 77; Kliment Ohridski Medal, Bulgaria, 86. *Prof Exp:* Intermediate engr mat res, Westinghouse Res Labs, 59-61. *Concurrent Pos:* Vis asst prof, Stanford Univ, 68; vis prof, Univ Mainz, 74-75 & 82, Univ Sofia, 85, Univ Calif, Berkeley, 96 & Univ Bristol, 97; Humboldt sr scientist, Univ Saarbrucken, 77-78, 82-83 & Univ Bochum, 82-83; vis scientist, Du Pont Exp Sta, 85 & 91, Nat Chem Lab, India, 89-90. *Mem:* Am Phys Soc; Polymer Processing Soc. *Res:* Polymeric materials; phase transformations; diffraction and scattering; composites; failure of materials. *Mailing Add:* Dept Chem Eng Univ Del Newark DE 19716. *Fax:* 302-831-1048; *E-Mail:* schultz@che.udel.edu

SCHULTZ, JOHN E, ORGANIC CHEMISTRY. *Current Pos:* From asst prof to assoc prof, Westminster Col, 64-70, chmn dept, 74-77 & 90-93, asst acad dean, 77-89, PROF CHEM, WESTMINSTER COL, MO, 70- *Personal Data:* b Nowata, Okla, Mar 5, 36; m 55, Mary L Love; c 3. *Educ:* Westminster Col, Mo, BA, 58; Univ Ill, PhD, 63. *Mem:* Am Chem Soc; Sigma Xi. *Res:* Small ring carbocyclic compounds and free radical reactions; information retrieval; computers in education. *Mailing Add:* 2330 N Bluff St Fulton MO 65251-2707

SCHULTZ, JOHN LAWRENCE, INFORMATION SCIENCE. *Current Pos:* RETIRED. *Personal Data:* b Brooklyn, NY, June 22, 32. *Educ:* St John's Univ, BS, 54; Univ Minn, PhD(chem), 59. *Prof Exp:* Asst inorg chem, Univ Minn, 54-56; res chemist, Pigments Dept, E I Du Pont de Nemours & Co, Inc, 57, info chemist, Patent Div, Textile Fibers Dept, 58-64, sr info specialist, Secy Dept, 64-73, sr info specialist, Info Systs Dept, 74-86, sr info consult, Human Resources Dept, 86-92. *Res:* Solution calorimetry; heats of formation of metal ion complexes in aqueous solution; heats of ion exchange processes; storage and retrieval of chemical information. *Mailing Add:* 703 Sonora Ave Wilmington DE 19809

SCHULTZ, JOHN WILFRED, PHYSICAL CHEMISTRY. *Current Pos:* ASSOC PROF CHEM, NAVAL ACAD, 75- *Personal Data:* b Portland, Ore, Sept 15, 31. *Educ:* Ore State Col, BS, 53; Brown Univ, PhD(phys chem), 57. *Prof Exp:* Instr chem, Univ Wash, 56-58; from asst prof to assoc prof chem, Naval Postgrad Sch, 66-75. *Concurrent Pos:* Soc Appl Spectros; Coblentz Soc; Am Phys Soc; Am Chem Soc. *Res:* Molecular spectroscopy; infrared and Raman intensities; spectra of solids. *Mailing Add:* 642 Shore Acres Rd Arnold MD 21012

SCHULTZ, JONAS, ELEMENTARY PARTICLE PHYSICS. *Current Pos:* assoc prof, 66-70, dean grad div, 73-76, PROF PHYSICS, UNIV CALIF, IRVINE, 70- *Personal Data:* b Brooklyn, NY, Mar 15, 35; m 58, Viviane Bornstein; c Lisa Rose, Gregory Mark & Laura Suzanne. *Educ:* Columbia Univ, AB, 56, MA, 59, PhD(physics), 62. *Prof Exp:* Physicist, Nevis Cyclotron Labs, Columbia Univ, 61-63 & Lawrence Radiation Lab, Univ Calif, 63-66. *Concurrent Pos:* Assoc prog dir elem particle physics, NSF, 71-72. *Mem:* Fel Am Phys Soc; fel AAAS; Sigma Xi. *Res:* Elementary particle physics; studies of high energy phenomena. *Mailing Add:* Dept Physics & Astron Univ Calif Irvine CA 92697. *Fax:* 714-824-7478; *E-Mail:* jschultz@uci.edu

SCHULTZ, LANE D, GEOPHYSICS, EDUCATION ADMINISTRATION. *Current Pos:* VPRES, OFF MGR, DUNN GEOSCI CORP, 85- *Personal Data:* b Sellersville, Pa, Oct 20, 44. *Educ:* Franklin & Marshall Col, BA, 66; Lehigh Univ, MS, 72, PhD(geol), 74. *Prof Exp:* Instr, Dickinson Col, 70-71; teaching asst, Lehigh Univ, 71-74; geol sect supvr, Gilbert Assoc Inc, 74-81; mgr geol, Western Geophys Corp, 81-84; mgr geotech, ERT, 84-85. *Mem:* Am Inst Prof Geol; Asn Eng Geol; Am Asn Petrol Geol; Am Soc Photogram. *Res:* Application of geology to engineered structure and characterization of subsurface geological and hydrogeological conditions. *Mailing Add:* 271 Shady Nook Rd Harleysville PA 19438-2617

SCHULTZ, LINDA DALQUEST, ANALYTICAL CHEMISTRY. *Current Pos:* PROF, TARLETON STATE UNIV, 78-, DEPT HEAD DEPT PHYS SCI, 95- *Personal Data:* b Yakima, Wash, Feb 23, 47; m 69, F Michael Schultz; c Michele & Steven. *Educ:* Southern Methodist Univ, BA, 67, MS, 71; NTex State Univ, PhD(chem), 75; Registry Med Technologists, cert, 71; Tarleton State Univ, MBA, 93. *Prof Exp:* Res technologist biochem, Univ Tex Southwestern Med Sch Dallas, 67-69; med technologist, Parkland Mem Hosp, 69-71; teaching asst chem, NTex State Univ, 71-74; res assoc sci, Howard Payne Univ, 75-76; fel, Tex Christian Univ, 76-78. *Mem:* Am Chem Soc. *Res:* Liquid ammonia chemistry. *Mailing Add:* Rte 4 Box 187H Brownwood TX 76801

SCHULTZ, LORIS HENRY, DAIRY SCIENCE. *Current Pos:* prof, 57-85, EMER PROF DAIRY SCI, UNIV WIS-MADISON, 85- *Personal Data:* b Mondovi, Wis, Feb 9, 19; m 49; c David, Mark & Steven. *Educ:* Univ Wis, BS, 41, PhD, 49; Univ Minn, MS, 42. *Honors & Awards:* Res Award, Am Feed Mfr Nutrit, 73; Award Honor, Am Dairy Sci Asn, 89. *Prof Exp:* From asst prof to prof animal husb, Cornell Univ, 49-57. *Concurrent Pos:* Moorman travel award, 75. *Mem:* Am Soc Animal Sci; Am Dairy Sci Asn (pres, 82); Nat Mastitis Coun (pres, 80). *Res:* Physiology of lactation; intermediary metabolism; metabolic disorders. *Mailing Add:* Dept Dairy Sci Univ Wis 266 Animal Sci Bldg Madison WI 53706

SCHULTZ, MARTIN C, SPEECH & HEARING SCIENCES, AUDIOLOGY. *Current Pos:* PROF, SOUTHERN ILL UNIV, 86- *Personal Data:* b Philadelphia, Pa, Aug 29, 26; m 51, Beatrice Golder; c Claudia, Richard, Jeffrey & Amy. *Educ:* Temple Univ, BA, 50; Univ Mich, MA, 52; Univ Iowa, PhD, 55. *Honors & Awards:* Editors Award, J Speech & Hearing Dis, Am Speech & Hearing Asn, 74. *Prof Exp:* Res assoc, Univ Iowa, 53-54; instr, Sch Speech, Northwestern Univ, 54-55; assoc otolaryngol, phys med & psychol, Univ Pa, 55-58, dir, Speech & Hearing Ctr, Univ Hosp, 55-58; supvr, Res Lab, Cleveland Hearing & Speech Ctr, 58-60; asst prof, Univ Mich, 60-65; assoc prof speech, Ind Univ, Bloomington, 65-73; dir training speech path & audiol, Develop Eval Clin, 72-77, dir, Hearing & Speech Div, Childrens Hosp Med Ctr, 73-85; prof commun dis, Emerson Col, 72-85. *Concurrent Pos:* Off Voc Rehab grant, Univ Pa, 55-58; consult, State Dept Health, Pa, 57 & Woods Schs Except Children, 57-58; NIH grant, Cleveland Hearing & Speech Ctr, 59-60, Univ Mich, 60-64; adj prof, Sch Educ, Boston Univ, 72-85; assoc otolaryngol, Harvard Med Sch, 74-86; res affil, Res Lab Electronics, Mass Inst Technol, 74-85; prin investr & res grant, US Dept Educ, 80-84; dir, Audiological Eng Corp. *Mem:* AAAS; Acoust Soc Am; Am Speech & Hearing Asn; Int Soc Phonetic Sci; Sigma Xi; fel Am Acad Audiol. *Res:* Speech and hearing sciences; design methodology; clinical processes and models; hearing and language development in children. *Mailing Add:* Commun Dis & Sci Southern Ill Univ Carbondale IL 62901-4399. *Fax:* 618-453-7714

SCHULTZ, MARTIN H, COMPUTER SCIENCE. *Current Pos:* PROF COMPUT SCI, YALE UNIV, 70-, CHMN DEPT, 74- *Personal Data:* b Boston, Mass, Dec 6, 40; m 65. *Educ:* Calif Inst Technol, BS, 61; Harvard Univ, PhD(math), 65. *Prof Exp:* Asst prof math, Case Western Res Univ, 65-68; assoc prof, Calif Inst Technol, 68-70. *Mem:* Am Math Soc; Soc Indust & Appl Math; Asn Comput Mach. *Res:* Numerical analysis; computational complexity. *Mailing Add:* Dept Comput Sci Yale Univ PO Box 208285 New Haven CT 06520-8285

SCHULTZ, MYRON GILBERT, EPIDEMIOLOGY. *Current Pos:* epidemic intel serv officer, 63-65, chief, Parasitic Dis Br, 67-, MED OFFICER, AGENCY TOXIC SUBSTANCES & DIS REGISTRY, NAT CTR DIS CONTROL, USPHS, 97- *Personal Data:* b New York, NY, Jan 6, 35; m 59; c 3. *Educ:* NY State Vet Col, Cornell Univ, DVM, 58; Albany Med Col, MD, 62; London Sch Hyg & Trop Med, DCMT, 67. *Prof Exp:* Pvt pract vet med, 58-62. *Concurrent Pos:* Clin assoc prof prev med, Emory Univ, 67-, clin asst prof med, 71- *Mem:* Fel Am Col Physicians; Am Soc Trop Med & Hyg; Royal Soc Trop Med & Hyg. *Res:* Epidemiology, clinical tropical medicine; clinical drug evaluation. *Mailing Add:* Agency Toxic Substance & Dis Registry Nat Ctr Dis Control 4 Exec Park Suite 2300 MS E-31 Atlanta GA 30329

SCHULTZ, PETER BERTHOLD, ENTOMOLOGY. *Current Pos:* PROF ENTOM, VA POLYTECH INST & STATE UNIV, 85- *Personal Data:* b Bucharest, Romania, Oct 24, 46; m 88; c 2. *Educ:* Univ Calif, Davis, BS, 68; Midwestern Univ, MS, 72; Va Polytech Inst & State Univ, PhD(entom), 78. *Prof Exp:* Instr entom, USAF, 69-73; regulatory inspector, Va Dept Agr, 73-78; entomologist, Va Truck & Ornamentals Res Sta, 78-85. *Mem:* Entom Soc Am. *Res:* Insect research on ornamental plants. *Mailing Add:* Hampton Rd Agr Res Exten Ctr 1444 Diamond Springs Rd Virginia Beach VA 23455

SCHULTZ, PETER FRANK, EXPERIMENTAL HIGH ENERGY PHYSICS, TELECOMMUNICATIONS. *Current Pos:* MEM TECH STAFF, AT&T BELL LABS, NAPERVILLE, ILL, 81- *Personal Data:* b Oshkosh, Wis, Mar 23, 40; m 66, Lois W Beebe; c Peter, Kristin & Carl. *Educ:* Univ Wis-Madison, BS, 62; Univ Ill, Urbana, MS, 64, PhD(physics), 69. *Prof Exp:* Res assoc physics, Univ Ill, Urbana, 69-72; res assoc, Argonne Nat Lab, 72-76, asst physicist, 76-81. *Mem:* Am Phys Soc. *Res:* Elementary particle physics; acceleration technology; ion sources; telecommunications. *Mailing Add:* 501 Andrus Rd Downers Grove IL 60516

SCHULTZ, PETER G, CHEMISTRY. *Current Pos:* assoc prof, 85-89, PROF, DEPT CHEM, UNIV CALIF, BERKELEY, 89- *Educ:* Calif Inst Technol, PhD, 83. *Honors & Awards:* Alan T Waterman Award, NSF, 88; Denkewalter Lectr Award, Loyola Univ, 90; Ernest Orlando Lawrence Award, US Dept Energy, 91. *Prof Exp:* NIH fel, Mass Inst Technol. *Mem:* Nat Acad Sci. *Mailing Add:* Dept Chem Univ Calif Berkeley CA 94720-0001. *Fax:* 510-643-6890

SCHULTZ, PETER HEWLETT, PLANETARY GEOLOGY. *Current Pos:* ASSOC PROF & DIR NE PLANETARY DATA CTR, BROWN UNIV, 84- *Personal Data:* b New Haven, Conn, Jan 22, 44; m 67. *Educ:* Carleton Col, BA, 66; Univ Tex, PhD(astron), 72. *Prof Exp:* Resident res assoc, Nat Acad Sci-Nat Res Coun, Univ Santa Clara, 73-75, res assoc physics, NASA Ames Res Ctr, 75-76; sr staff scientist, Lunar & Planetary Inst, 76-84. *Concurrent Pos:* Prin investr & assoc ed, Geophys Revs. *Mem:* Sigma Xi; Am Geophys Union; AAAS. *Res:* Morphology of impact craters on planets; impact cratering mechanics; degradational processes on planetary surfaces; volcanic modification of planetary surfaces; atmospheric effects on impact crater formation; lunar and Martian geologic history. *Mailing Add:* Geol Brown Univ Providence RI 02912-9127

SCHULTZ, PHYLLIS W, DEVELOPMENTAL BIOLOGY. *Current Pos:* res assoc & vis instr, Med Ctr, 59-61, asst prof zool, 61-70, fac fel, 64-65, PROF BIOL & ASST DEAN NATURAL & PHYS SCI, MED CTR, UNIV COLO, DENVER, 71- *Personal Data:* b Connersville, Ind, Mar 9, 25; m 54. *Educ:* Univ Cincinnati, BA, 47, MS, 50; Univ Wis, PhD(zool), 57. *Prof Exp:* Preparator zool, Univ Wis, 54-55; chemist med ctr, Univ Colo, 55-57; res assoc embryol, Univ Ore, 57-59. *Concurrent Pos:* Res grants, USPHS, 58-64 & NSF, 64-66. *Mem:* Am Soc Cell Biol. *Res:* Effects of teratogenic agents or antimetabolites on protein formation, ultrastructure and cytochemistry of the chick and mammalian embryo and mammalian placenta. *Mailing Add:* 7243 Costilla St Littleton CO 80120

SCHULTZ, R JACK, POPULATION BIOLOGY, ICHTHYOLOGY. *Current Pos:* from asst prof to prof, 63-74, PROF BIOL, UNIV CONN, 75- *Personal Data:* b Caro, Mich, Aug 17, 29; m 57; c 2. *Educ:* Mich State Univ, BS, 52, MS, 53; Univ Mich, PhD, 60. *Prof Exp:* Res assoc, Mus Zool, Univ Mich, 60-63. *Concurrent Pos:* Ed, Copeia, Am Soc Ichthyologists & Herpetologists, 70-73; prog dir syst biol, NSF, 74-75; head ecol, Univ Conn, 79-85. *Mem:* Am Soc Ichthyologists & Herpetologists; Soc Study Evolution; Ecol Soc Am; Am Genetic Asn (pres, 88-89); Am Soc Naturalists. *Res:* Role of hybridization and polyploidy in the evolution and ecology of fishes; genetics of cancer in fishes. *Mailing Add:* Dept Ecol U-42 Univ Conn 75 N Eagleville Storrs Manfield CT 06269-0002

SCHULTZ, RAY KARL, POLYELECTROLYTES. *Current Pos:* from asst prof to assoc prof, 65-82, PROF CHEM, URSINUS COL, 82- *Personal Data:* b Hereford, Pa, Aug 23, 37; m 64; c 4. *Educ:* Muhlenberg Col, BS, 59; Lehigh Univ, MS, 61, PhD(rheology), 65. *Prof Exp:* Instr quant anal, Muhlenberg Col, 63. *Mem:* Am Chem Soc. *Res:* Equilibrium constants for formation of boratediol complexes; properties of polyelectrolytes; properties of poly(acrylic acid)-co-4-vinyl pyridine. *Mailing Add:* 3902 Yerkes Rd Collegeville PA 19426-3211. *E-Mail:* rschultz@acad.ursinus.edu

SCHULTZ, REINHARD EDWARD, TOPOLOGY, MATHEMATICS. *Current Pos:* From instr to asst prof, 68-74, assoc prof, 74-80, PROF MATH, PURDUE UNIV, WEST LAFAYETTE, 80- *Personal Data:* b Chicago, Ill, Sept 13, 43; m 70; c 1. *Educ:* Univ Chicago, SB, 64, PhD(math), 68. *Concurrent Pos:* Purdue Res Found grant, 69, NSF res grant, 70-72. *Mem:* Am Math Soc. *Res:* Algebraic topology, differential topology; transformation groups. *Mailing Add:* Dept Math Purdue Univ West Lafayette IN 47907-1395

SCHULTZ, RICHARD MICHAEL, BIOCHEMISTRY, MOLECULAR BIOLOGY. *Current Pos:* From asst prof to assoc prof, 71-84, PROF & CHMN BIOCHEM, STRITCH SCH MED, LOYOLA UNIV CHICAGO, 84- *Personal Data:* b Philadelphia, Pa, Oct 28, 42; m 65, Rima Lunin; c Carl M & Eli J. *Educ:* State Univ NY Binghamton, BA, 64; Brandeis Univ, MA, 67, PhD(org chem), 69. *Concurrent Pos:* NIH res fel biol chem, Harvard Med Sch, 69-71; prin investr, NIH grants. *Mem:* Am Chem Soc; Am Soc Biol Chemists; AAAS. *Res:* Mechanism of enzyme action, particularly the hydrolytic enzymes; cancer cell metastasis; protease gene regulation by oncogenes in cancer; association of aldehyde transition-state analogs to protease enzymes; molecular biology. *Mailing Add:* Dept Molecular & Cellular Biochem Loyola Univ Stritch Sch Med 2160 S First Ave Maywood IL 60153. *Fax:* 708-216-8523

SCHULTZ, RICHARD MORRIS, MAMMALIAN DEVELOPMENT, GENE EXPRESSION. *Current Pos:* PROF BIOL, UNIV PA, 78- *Personal Data:* b Malden, Mass, Mar 20, 49; m 79. *Educ:* Harvard Univ, PhD(biochem), 75. *Honors & Awards:* Jan Purkinje Medal Sci, Czech Acad Sci. *Mem:* Fel AAAS; Am Soc Cell Biol; Soc Develop Biol; Soc Study Reproductive Biol. *Res:* Developmental biology; signal transduction; gene expression. *Mailing Add:* Dept Biol Univ Pa Philadelphia PA 19104-6018. *Fax:* 215-898-8780; *E-Mail:* rschultz@mail.sas.upenn.edu

SCHULTZ, RICHARD OTTO, MEDICINE, OPHTHALMOLOGY. *Current Pos:* assoc prof, 64-68, CHMN OPHTHAL, MED COL WIS, PROF OPHTHAL, 68-; DIR OPHTHAL, MILWAUKEE REGIONAL MED CTR, 64- *Personal Data:* b Racine, Wis, Mar 19, 30; m 52, 90, Diane Haldane; c Henry, Richard & Karen. *Educ:* Univ Wis, BA, 50, MSc, 54; MD, Albany Med Col, 56; Univ Iowa, MSc, 60. *Prof Exp:* Instr ophthal, Univ Iowa, 59-60; assoc, Proctor Found, Sch Med, Univ Calif, San Francisco, 63-64. *Concurrent Pos:* NIH spec fel ophthal microbiol, Proctor Found Sch Med, Univ Calif, San Francisco, 63-64; consult, US Vet Admin Hosp, Wood, Wis & Milwaukee Children's Hosp, 64-; Nat Adv Eye Coun, NIH, 84-88. *Mem:* Fel Am Acad Ophthal; fel Am Col Surg; AMA; Asn Res Vision & Ophthal; Am Ophthal Soc; Assoc Univ Prof Ophthal. *Res:* Ocular microbiology; corneal disease; glaucoma screening. *Mailing Add:* Dept Opthamol Med Col Wis Eye Inst 925 N 87th St Milwaukee WI 53226-3512

SCHULTZ, ROBERT GEORGE, PROCESS DEVELOPMENT. *Current Pos:* Res specialist, Monsanto Co, 58-69, group leader, 69-85, mgr technol, 86-89, TECHNOLOGIST, MONSANTO CO, 89- *Personal Data:* b Rahway, NJ, Jan 11, 33; m 58; c 3. *Educ:* Mass Inst Technol, SB, 54; Univ Ill, PhD, 58; Northeast Mo State Univ, MA, 80. *Mem:* Am Chem Soc. *Res:* Homogeneous catalysis; heterogeneous catalysis; process development. *Mailing Add:* 755 Gascogne Dr St Louis MO 63141-7318

SCHULTZ, ROBERT JOHN, MEDICINAL CHEMISTRY. *Current Pos:* indust fel, Starks Assoc, Inc, 73, supvr, 73-75, prin investr, 75-79, co-prin investr, 79-80, PRIN INVESTR, STARKS C P, 80- *Personal Data:* b Detroit, Mich, Apr 19, 44; m 67; c 2. *Educ:* Wayne State Univ, BSc, 66; Brown Univ, PhD(org chem), 71. *Prof Exp:* Res assoc, Univ Mich, 70-73. *Mem:* Am Chem Soc; Sigma Xi. *Res:* Potential chemotherapeutic agents for anticancer screening programs. *Mailing Add:* 6406 Gleason Ct Edina MN 55436-1848

SCHULTZ, ROBERT LOWELL, ANATOMY. *Current Pos:* Asst instr, 53-57, from instr to assoc prof, 57-74, PROF ANAT, SCH MED, LOMA LINDA UNIV, 74- *Personal Data:* b Moscow, Idaho, Mar 18, 30; m 51; c 3. *Educ:* Walla Walla Col, BA, 51, MA, 53; Univ Calif, Los Angeles, PhD(anat), 57. *Concurrent Pos:* USPHS spec fel, Univ Calif, Los Angeles, 63-64. *Mem:* Electron Micros Soc Am; Am Asn Anat; Am Soc Cell Biol. *Res:* Electron microscopy and microanatomy of the nervous system. *Mailing Add:* Dept Pathol & Human Anat Loma Linda Univ Loma Linda CA 92350

SCHULTZ, RODNEY BRIAN, APPLIED PHYSICS, NUMERICAL SIMULATION. *Current Pos:* staff mem, Appl Theoret Physics Div, Los Alamos Nat Lab, 74-88, group leader, Thermonuclear Applns Group, 88-92, prog mgr nuclear counter proliferation, 93, DEP DIV DIR, APPL THEORET & COMPUT PHYSICS DIV, LOS ALAMOS NAT LAB, 94- *Personal Data:* b Enid, Okla, Nov 2, 46; div; c Emily A & Ted B. *Educ:* Okla State Univ, BS, 68; Univ Colo, MS, 71, PhD(astrophys), 74. *Honors & Awards:* Recognition Excellence Award, US Dept Energy, 90. *Prof Exp:* Asst solar physics, High Altitude Observ, 68-74. *Concurrent Pos:* Los Alamos liaison, Defense Intel Agency, Washington, DC, 86-87. *Mem:* Am Inst Aeronaut & Astronaut. *Res:* Thermonuclear weapons research; nuclear weapons nonproliferation and counterproliferation. *Mailing Add:* 2196 Loma Linda Dr Los Alamos NM 87544

SCHULTZ, RONALD DAVID, IMMUNOLOGY, VETERINARY VIROLOGY. *Current Pos:* MEM FAC, NY STATE VET COL, CORNELL UNIV, 80- *Personal Data:* b Freeland, Pa, Apr 21, 44; m 66; c 3. *Educ:* Pa State Univ, BS, 66, MS, 67, PhD(microbiol), 70. *Prof Exp:* Res asst microbiol, Pa State Univ, 66-70; res assoc immunol, NY State Vet Col, 71-73, from asst prof to assoc prof, Vet Virus Res Inst, Cornell Univ, 73-78, assoc dir, Dept Health Serv, Microbiol & Clin Lab, 73-78; prof, Dept Microbiol, Col Vet Med, Auburn Univ, 78-80. *Concurrent Pos:* Consult, Nat Cancer Inst, 72-78, Miles Lab, 75-, Corning Glass, 78- & Hybridoma Sci, 78-; res grants, NIH, USDA & Food & Drug Admin. *Mem:* Am Soc Microbiol; Conf Res Workers Animal Dis; Am Asn Vet Immunologists (pres, 75-80); US Animal Health Asn. *Res:* Developmental aspects of the immune response; cell-mediated immunity; immunoglobulins; clinical immunology; immunopathology; viral infections and the immune response; leukemia. *Mailing Add:* Dept Pathobiol Sci Sch Vet Med Univ Wis 2015 Linden Dr W Madison WI 53706-1102. *Fax:* 608-263-6573

SCHULTZ, RONALD G(LEN), ELECTRICAL ENGINEERING. *Current Pos:* prof elec eng & chmn dept, Cleveland State Univ, 68-73, dean, Col Grad Studies, 73-81, assoc vpres acad affairs, 75-78, vprovost, 78-81, PROF ELEC ENG, CLEVELAND STATE UNIV, 81- *Personal Data:* b Hammond, Ind, Nov 15, 31; m 56, Eunice Rosset; c 3. *Educ:* Valparaiso Univ, BSEE, 53; Northwestern Univ, MS, 54; Univ Pittsburgh, PhD(elec eng), 59. *Prof Exp:* From instr to assoc prof elec eng, Univ Pittsburgh, 54-68. *Concurrent Pos:* Consult, 59- *Mem:* Sigma Xi. *Res:* Computers and control systems; nonlinear control systems. *Mailing Add:* 589 Welshire Dr Bay Village OH 44140

SCHULTZ, RUSSELL THOMAS, AMYIOIDOSIS, EXPERIMENTAL ARTHRITIS. *Current Pos:* Prof med, 73-94, EMER PROF MED, UNIV OKLA, 94- *Educ:* Univ Minn, MD, 53. *Res:* Experimental arthritis. *Mailing Add:* 1840 E Somnolent Way Tucson AZ 85737-8676

SCHULTZ, SHELDON, SOLID STATE PHYSICS. *Current Pos:* from asst prof to assoc prof, 60-71, PROF PHYSICS, UNIV CALIF, SAN DIEGO, 71-, DIR, CTR MAGNETIC RECORDING RES, 90- *Personal Data:* b New York, NY, Jan 21, 33; m 53; c 3. *Educ:* Stevens Inst Technol, ME, 54; Columbia Univ, PhD(physics), 59. *Prof Exp:* Res asst physics, Radiation Lab, Columbia Univ, 59-60. *Concurrent Pos:* Alfred P Sloan Found fel, 62-64. *Mem:* Am Phys Soc; Am Vacuum Soc; Inst Elec & Electronics Engrs; Mat Res Soc. *Res:* Solid state physics; magnetic resonance in metals; magnetic recording particles; surface magnetism; high temperature superconductors; electron paramagnetic resonance; near field optical microscopy; photonic boudgap structures. *Mailing Add:* Dept Physics 0319 Univ Calif San Diego 9500 Gilman Dr La Jolla CA 92093

SCHULTZ, STANLEY GEORGE, PHYSIOLOGY. *Current Pos:* PROF PHYSIOL & CHMN DEPT, MED SCH, UNIV TEX, HOUSTON, 79- *Personal Data:* b Bayonne, NJ, Oct 26, 31; m 60; c 2. *Educ:* Columbia Col, BA, 52; NY Univ, MD, 56. *Honors & Awards:* Hoffman-LaRoche Prize, Outstanding Contrib Gastroenterol. *Prof Exp:* Intern, Bellevue Hosp, NY, 56-57, resident internal med, 57-58; instr biophys, Harvard Med Sch, 64-65, assoc, 65-67; from assoc prof to prof physiol, Sch Med, Univ Pittsburgh, 70-79. *Concurrent Pos:* USPHS res fel cardiol, Lenox Hill Hosp, 58-59; Nat Acad Sci-Nat Res Coun res fel biophysics, Harvard Med Sch, 59-62; estab investr, Am Heart Asn, 64-69; USPHS res career award, 69-72; res career develop award, NIH, 69-72; consult, NIH & Nat Bd Med Examrs; overseas fel, Churchill Col, Cambridge Univ, 76; ed, Am J Physiol, Physiol Rev & Ann Rev Physiol, Handbk Physiol, News in Physiol Sci. *Mem:* AAAS; Asn Am Physicians; Biophys Soc; Am Physiol Soc; Soc Gen Physiol; hon fel Am Soc Gynec-Obstet; Sigma Xi. *Res:* Membrane physiology; epithelial transport. *Mailing Add:* Dept Integrative Biol Univ Tex Med Sch PO Box 20708 Houston TX 77225-0708

SCHULTZ, TERRY WAYNE, TERATOGENESIS. *Current Pos:* ASST PROF HISTOL, DEPT ANIMAL SCI, COL VET MED, UNIV TENN, 82-, PROF. *Personal Data:* b Beloit, Wis, Feb 26, 46; m 68; c 1. *Educ:* Austin Peay State Univ, BS, 68; Univ Ark, MS, 72; Univ Tenn, PhD(zool), 75. *Prof Exp:* Fel, Biol Div, Oak Ridge Nat Lab, 75-77; asst prof histol & cell biol, Dept Biol, Pan Am Univ, 77-80; res assoc, Biol Div, Oak Ridge Nat Lab, 80-82. *Concurrent Pos:* Fac partic, Biomed & Environ Sci, Inst Lawrence Livermore Lab, 78; consult, Biol Div, Oak Ridge Nat Lab, 79. *Mem:* Am Micros Soc; Soc Environ Toxicol & Chem; Electron Micros Soc Am. *Res:* In vitro teratogenesis testing and screening using frog embryos; structure activity relationships of industrial chemicals and environmental toxicity; short-term cytotoxicity testing. *Mailing Add:* Dept Animal Sci Univ Tenn 1345 Circle Pk Knoxville TN 37996-0001

SCHULTZ, THEODORE DAVID, SOLID STATE PHYSICS. *Current Pos:* NAT RES CTR, SMITHSONIAN INST. *Personal Data:* b Chicago, Ill, Jan 6, 29; m 57; c 2. *Educ:* Cornell Univ, BEngPhys, 51; Mass Inst Technol, PhD(physics), 56. *Prof Exp:* NSF fel math physics, Univ Birmingham, 56-58; res assoc physics, Univ Ill, 58-59, res asst prof, 59-60; physicist, Watson Res Ctr, IBM Corp, 60- *Concurrent Pos:* Adj prof, Syracuse Univ, 61-62; vis assoc prof, NY Univ, 64-65; vis prof, Univ Munich, 79-80. *Mem:* Fel Am Phys Soc. *Res:* Theory of solids. and quantum statistical mechanics; quantum field theory. *Mailing Add:* Nat Sci Res Ctr Capital Gallery Bldg 600 Maryland Ave SW Suite 880 Washington DC 20024. *Fax:* 202-287-2970

SCHULTZ, THEODORE WILLIAM, ECONOMICS. *Current Pos:* prof, Univ Chicago, 43-72, chmn, Dept Econs, 46-61, Charles L Hutchinson distinguished serv prof, 52-72, EMER PROF ECONS, UNIV CHICAGO, 72- *Personal Data:* b Arlington, SDak, Apr 30, 02; m, Esther F Werth; c Elaine, Margaret & T Paul. *Educ:* SDak State Col, BS, 27; Univ Wis, MS, 28, PhD, 30. *Hon Degrees:* Numerous from var US & foreign univs, 59-84. *Honors & Awards:* Nobel Prize in Econs, 79; Walker Medal, Am Econ Asn, 72. *Prof Exp:* Mem fac, Iowa State Col, 30-43, prof & head, Dept Econs & Sociol, 34-43. *Concurrent Pos:* Chmn, Am Famine Mission, India, 46; dir, Nat Bur Econ Res, 49-67; res fel, Ctr Advan Study Behav Sci, 56-57. *Mem:* Nat Acad Sci; Am Farm Econs Asn; fel Am Acad Arts & Sci; Am Agr Econ Asn; Am Econ Asn (pres, 60); Am Philos Soc; Royal Econ Soc; Nat Acad Educ. *Mailing Add:* 5620 S Kimbark Ave Chicago IL 60637-1606

SCHULTZ, THOMAS J, COMBUSTION, MANAGEMENT. *Current Pos:* DIR INDUST RES & DEVELOP, SURFACE COMBUSTION INC, 88- *Personal Data:* b Toledo, Ohio, July 22, 41; m 65; c 1. *Educ:* Univ Toledo, BS, 64, MS, 65 & 68. *Prof Exp:* Proj engr, Midland Ross, 65-70, mgr chem eng, 70-80, asst dir develop, 80-88. *Mem:* Am Inst Chem Engrs; Air & Waste Mgt Asn. *Res:* Reactions of natural gas; combustion catalytic oxidation; pyrolysis applied to waste disposal and recycling; heat transfer; several US patents. *Mailing Add:* 1268 Cass Maumee OH 43537

SCHULTZ, VINCENT, ANIMAL ECOLOGY. *Current Pos:* RETIRED. *Personal Data:* b Lakewood, Ohio, Mar 7, 22; m 48, Patricia L Johnson; c 3. *Educ:* Ohio State Univ, BSc, 46, MSc, 48, PhD(zool), 49; Va Polytech Inst, MSc, 54. *Prof Exp:* Wildlife biologist, US Fish & Wildlife Serv, 49-50; sr biologist, State Game & Fish Comn, Tenn, 50-52; asst prof wildlife mgt, Va Polytech Inst, 52-54; res fel biostatist, USPHS, Johns Hopkins Univ, 54-56; assoc prof biostatist & agr statistician, Univ Md, 56-59; ecologist, Environ Sci Br, Div Biol & Med, US AEC, 59-66; prof zool, Wash State Univ, 66-85. *Concurrent Pos:* Consult, Dept Energy, Sandia & Nuclear Regulatory Comn. *Mem:* Int Union Radioecol. *Res:* Application of statistical techniques to ecological research; radiation ecology. *Mailing Add:* NE 630 Oak Pullman WA 99163

SCHULTZ, WARREN WALTER, TECHNICAL MANAGEMENT, ENVIRONMENTAL REMEDIATION. *Current Pos:* VPRES TECHNOL OPERS, SBP TECHNOL, INC, 96- *Personal Data:* b Emporia, Kans, Sept 3, 41; m 79; c 3. *Educ:* Kans State Univ, Emporia, BA, 64, MS, 66; Johns Hopkins Univ, ScD(virol), 72. *Prof Exp:* Teaching asst microbiol, Kans State Univ, Emporia, 64-66; res microbiologist, Naval Med Res Inst, 66-68, head, Div Pathobiol, 71-78; teaching asst pop biol, Johns Hopkins Univ, 69; prof chem & assoc chmn dept, US Naval Acad, 78-82; dep dir, Biol Sci Div, Off Naval Res, 82-84, dep dir life sci, 84-86; biotechnol progs mgr, Naval Res Lab, 86-96. *Concurrent Pos:* Spec asst undersecy defense, Res & Advan Technol. *Mem:* Soc Microbiol; Soc Armed Forces Med Lab Scientists; Am Chem Soc; Soc Am Military Engrs. *Res:* Remediation of soil and ground water. *Mailing Add:* 4056 Cadle Creek Rd Edgewater MD 21037. *Fax:* 410-798-4404; *E-Mail:* 104621.1242@compuserve.com, sbpwarren@aol.com

SCHULTZ, WILLIAM C(ARL), ELECTRICAL ENGINEERING. *Current Pos:* ASSOC PROF TECHNOL, STATE UNIV COL NY, BUFFALO, 75- *Personal Data:* b Sheboygan, Wis, July 30, 27; m 51; c 3. *Educ:* Univ Wis, BS, 52, MS, 53, PhD(elec eng), 58. *Prof Exp:* Asst, Univ Wis, 52-53, instr elec eng, 55-58; asst engr, Computer Lab, Allis-Chalmers Mfg Co, Wis, 53-55; asst engr, Cornell Aeronaut Lab, Inc, 58-70, head computer ctr, 70-75. *Mem:* Inst Elec & Electronics Engrs; assoc fel Am Inst Aeronaut & Astronaut. *Res:* Computer sciences; computer facility management; administrative data processing; flight control systems; cockpit displays; human factors engineering. *Mailing Add:* State Univ Col Buffalo 1300 Elmwood Ave 201 Chasehall Buffalo NY 14222

SCHULTZ, WILLIAM CLINTON, SYNTHETIC ORGANIC CHEMISTRY. *Current Pos:* SR DEVELOP CHEMIST, SYNTHETIC CHEM DIV, EASTMAN KODAK CO, 63- *Personal Data:* b Bainbridge, NY, Sept 19, 37; m 61; c 2. *Educ:* Dartmouth Col, AB, 59; Rutgers Univ, PhD(org chem), 63. *Mem:* Am Chem Soc; Soc Photog Scientists & Engrs. *Res:* Development of economical manufacturing processes for specialty organic chemicals. *Mailing Add:* 67 Tulip Tree Lane Rochester NY 14617-2004

SCHULTZE, CHARLES L, EDUCATION ADMINISTRATION. *Current Pos:* EMER SR FEL, BROOKINGS INST, 97- *Personal Data:* b Alexandria, Va, Dec 12, 24. *Educ:* Georgetown Univ, BA, 48, MA, 50; Univ Md, PhD(econ), 60. *Prof Exp:* Lect & assoc prof econ, Ind Univ, 59-61; from asst prof to prof, Univ Md, 61-88. *Concurrent Pos:* Asst dir, US Bur Budget, 62-64, sr fel, 68-77 & 81-87; sr fel, Brookings Inst, 68; chmn, Coun Econ Advsr, 77-80; distinguished vis prof res, Grad Sch Bus, Stanford Univ, 82-83; Lee Kuan Yew distinguished vis, Nat Univ Singapore, 85; dir, Econ Studies Prog, 87-90. *Mem:* Inst Med-Nat Acad Sci; fel Nat Asn Bus Economists; Nat Acad Pub Admin; Am Econ Asn. *Res:* Author of 11 books and 7 articles. *Mailing Add:* Brookings Inst 1775 Massachusetts Ave NW Washington DC 20036

SCHULTZE, HANS-PETER, VERTEBRATE PALEONTOLOGY. *Current Pos:* from asst prof to assoc prof, 78-87, PROF DEPT SYST & ECOL, UNIV KANS, 87-, CUR, MUS NATURAL HIST, 78- *Personal Data:* b Swinemuende, Ger, Aug 13, 37; m 65; c 3. *Educ:* Univ Freiburg, BSc, 58; Univ Tuebingen, MSc, 62, PhD(paleont), 65. *Prof Exp:* Fel, Ger Sci Found, Naturhistoriska Rikmuseet, Stockholm, 65-67; asst prof, Dept Paleont, Univ Goettingen, 67-70; fel, Ger Acad Exchange, Am Mus Natural Hist, NY & Field Mus, Chicago, 70-71; from asst prof to assoc prof, Univ Goettingen, Ger, 71-78. *Concurrent Pos:* Chmn, Dept Syst & Ecol, Univ Kans, 88-90. *Mem:* Paleont Soc, Ger; Soc Vertebrate Paleont; Sigma Xi; Paleont Asn Eng; Soc Syst Biol. *Res:* Morphology and evolution of fossil fishes and early tetrapods; histology of hard tissue; paleoenvironment of Paleozoic Lagerstatten. *Mailing Add:* Palaontologisch-Geol Inst & Mus Naturkunde der Humboldt Invalidenstr 43 10115 Berlin Germany

SCHULTZE, LOTHAR WALTER, SCIENCE EDUCATION. *Current Pos:* DIR INSTNL RES, STATE UNIV NY COL FREDONIA, 66-, EMER FAC. *Personal Data:* b Berlin, Ger, Dec 5, 20; US citizen; m 47; c 3. *Educ:* State Univ NY Albany, BA, 42; Pa State Univ, MS, 52, DEd(higher educ), 55. *Prof Exp:* Proj engr, US Rubber Co, 42-45; assoc prof sci, State Univ NY Albany, 52-58, dir admis, 58-66. *Mem:* Am Chem Soc; Asn Inst Res. *Res:* Science education for non-science majors; non-academic predictors of college success; mobility of students in transfer. *Mailing Add:* 38 Birchwood Dr Fredonia NY 14063

SCHULZ, ARTHUR R, BIOCHEMISTRY, NUTRITION. *Current Pos:* assoc prof, 69-80, PROF BIOCHEM, IND UNIV, 80- *Personal Data:* b Brighton, Colo, Oct 9, 25; m 56, Marian Maas. *Educ:* Colo State Univ, BS, 50; Univ Calif, PhD, 56. *Prof Exp:* Res assoc biochem, Univ Minn, 57-58; asst prof, Okla State Univ, 58-61; asst prof chem, Colo State Univ, 61-62; biochemist, Vet Admin Hosp, 62-69. *Concurrent Pos:* NSF fel biochem, Swiss Fed Inst Technol, 56-57. *Res:* Steady-state enzyme kinetics, simulation of energy metabolism in the whole animal, biochemistry of exercise; metabolic control. *Mailing Add:* Dept Biochem Ind Univ Sch Med 635 Barnhill Dr Indianapolis IN 46202

SCHULZ, CHARLES EMIL, MOLECULAR BIOPHYSICS. *Current Pos:* ASSOC PROF PHYSICS, KNOX COL, 81- *Personal Data:* b Blue Island, Ill. *Educ:* Knox Col, BA, 72; Univ Ill, MS, 73, PhD(physics), 79. *Prof Exp:* Postdoctoral res assoc molecular biophys & biochem, Yale Univ, 79-81. *Concurrent Pos:* Vis prof, Univ Iowa, 85 & Univ Ill, 90-91; prin investr, NIH grant, 87-90. *Mem:* Am Phys Soc; Am Asn Physics Teachers; Sigma Xi; Biophys Soc. *Res:* Spectroscopic studies of metalloproteins. *Mailing Add:* Knox Col Box K-74 Galesburg IL 61401. *Fax:* 309-343-9816; *E-Mail:* cschulz@knox.bitnet

SCHULZ, DALE METHERD, PATHOLOGY. *Current Pos:* RETIRED. *Personal Data:* b Fairfield, Ohio, Oct 20, 18; m 47, Dorothy Hartman; c Ann (Huston) & Stephen M. *Educ:* Miami Univ, BA, 40; Wash Univ, MS, 42, MD, 49. *Prof Exp:* Res chemist, Tretolite Co, 42-45; from intern to resident path, Barnes Hosp, St Louis, Mo, 49-51; from instr to prof path, Sch Med, Ind Univ, Indianapolis, 52-85. *Concurrent Pos:* Fel, Med Ctr, Ind Univ, Indianapolis, 51-52; pathologist, Methodist Hosp, Indianapolis, 66-85. *Mem:* Am Asn Path & Bact; Int Acad Path. *Res:* Trace metals; fungus diseases; kidney diseases. *Mailing Add:* 9540 Copley Dr Indianapolis IN 46260

SCHULZ, DAVID ARTHUR, MATERIALS SCIENCE, CERAMIC ENGINEERING. *Current Pos:* Sr res scientist, 86-90, SR RES ASSOC, AMOCO PERFORMANCE PROD, INC, ALPHARETTA, GA, 90- *Personal Data:* b Cleveland, Ohio, June 30, 34; m 57, Patricia A Wehner; c Dolores, Diana, Douglas, Dawn & David Jr. *Educ:* Ga Inst Technol, BCerE, 55; Univ Calif, Berkeley, MS, 57, PhD(eng sci), 61. *Prof Exp:* Develop engr, Niagara Develop Lab, Nat Carbon Co, Union Carbide Corp, 55-56; res engr, Inst Eng Res, Univ Calif, Berkeley, 59-60, engr, Inorg Mat Div, Lawrence Radiation Lab, 60-61; develop engr, Adv Mat Lab, Nat Carbon Co, 61-63, develop engr, Nuclear Prod Dept, Carbon Prod Div, 63-66, proj engr, Lawrenceburg Tech Opers, Tenn, 66-67, proj coordr, 67; proj engr, Union Carbide Corp, 68-73, staff engr, 73-76, sr engr, 76-79, sr res scientist, 79-81, sr group leader, Parma Tech Ctr, 81-86. *Mem:* AAAS; Am Chem Soc; fel Am Ceramic Soc; Nat Inst Ceramic Engrs; Sigma Xi. *Res:* Process and product development relating to high-strength, high-modulus carbon fibers and carbon fiber reinforced composites. *Mailing Add:* 6429 Paradise Point Rd Flowery Branch GA 30542-3142. *Fax:* 770-772-8332

SCHULZ, DONALD NORMAN, ORGANIC CHEMISTRY, POLYMER CHEMISTRY. *Current Pos:* group head & res assoc water soluable polymers, Exxon Res & Eng Co, 81-84, group head & sr res assoc polymer synthesis, corp res, 84-86, sect head, Polymer Sci Group, Exxon Chem, 86-89, SECT HEAD, CORP RES, EXXON RES & ENG CO, 90- *Personal Data:* b Buffalo, NY, May 24, 43; m 67, Kathleen Ware; c Heidi A & Katherine A. *Educ:* State Univ NY Buffalo, BA, 65; Univ Mass, PhD(org chem), 71. *Prof Exp:* Res scientist, Cent Res Lab, Firestone Tire & Rubber Co, 71-75, group leader org-polymer chem, 75-81. *Concurrent Pos:* Asst ed, Isotopics, 79, ed, 80-; assoc ed, Rubber Chem Technol, 84-93. *Mem:* Sigma Xi; Am Chem Soc; Am Inst Chemists; fel Am Inst Chem. *Res:* Organometallic chemistry; anionic and cationic polymerizations; polymer synthesis and modification; polymer characterization; heteroatom chemistry. *Mailing Add:* 36 Valley Crest Rd Annandale NJ 08801. *Fax:* 908-730-2536

SCHULZ, HELMUT WILHELM, GENERATION OF ELECTRIC POWER FROM URBAN REFUSE & TOXIC WASTE, NOVEL PROCESS FOR ENHANCED OIL RECOVERY. *Current Pos:* PRES & CHIEF EXEC OFFICER, DYNECOLOGY INC, 74- *Personal Data:* b Berlin, Ger, July 10, 12; US citizen; m 54, Colette Prieur; c Raymond A, Caroline P, Roland W, Robert B & Thomas F. *Educ:* Columbia Univ, BS, 33, ChE, 34, PhD(chem eng), 42. *Honors & Awards:* Atomic Energy Prize, US Dept Energy, 84. *Prof Exp:* Dir res & develop chem & plastics, Union Carbide, 34-64, managing dir, Union Carbide Europ Res, 67-69; spec asst, Secy Defense, 64-67, US Comnr Educ, 70-71; sr res scientist, Columbia Univ, 72-83. *Concurrent Pos:* Chmn, Brandenburg Energy Corp, 79- *Mem:* Fel Am Inst Chem Engrs; emer mem Am Chem Soc; NY Acad Sci. *Res:* Centrifugation process for enrichment of uranium isotopes; reinforced solid rocket motors for high accelleration missiles; laser catalysis; waste to energy conversion processes: simplex, bioplex and toxiplex. *Mailing Add:* 611 Harrison Ave Harrison NY 10528. *Fax:* 914-967-8530; *E-Mail:* hwschulz@msn.com

SCHULZ, HORST H, LIPID BIOCHEMISTRY, ENZYMOLOGY. *Current Pos:* from asst prof to assoc prof, 70-80, PROF BIOCHEM, CITY COL NY, 80-, EXEC OFFICER GRAD SCH, 84- *Personal Data:* b Berlin, Ger, Sept 16, 36. *Educ:* Tech Univ Berlin, Dipl-Ing, 61, Dr-Ing, 64. *Honors & Awards:* Hon Prof, Zhengzhou Grain Col, China, 85. *Prof Exp:* Res assoc, Cornell Univ Med Col, 64-65; instr, Tech Univ Berlin, 65-68; res assoc, Duke Univ Med Ctr, 68-70. *Concurrent Pos:* Prin investr, NIH, 75-; vis assoc prof, Cornell Univ, 78-79. *Mem:* Am Soc Biochem & Molecular Biol; Am Chem Soc; AAAS; NY Acad Sci. *Res:* Beta oxidation of saturated and unsaturated fatty acids, including pathways, enzymology and regulation. *Mailing Add:* Dept Chem City Col NY Convent Ave & 138th St New York NY 10031. *Fax:* 212-650-8322

SCHULZ, JAN IVAN, IMMUNOLOGY, INTERNAL MEDICINE. *Current Pos:* ASSOC PROF IMMUNOL & INTERNAL MED, MCGILL UNIV, 78- *Personal Data:* b Bratislava, Czech, Feb 3, 46; Can citizen; m 75, Mary N Grossman; c Caroline & Matthew. *Educ:* Univ Western Ont, MD, 70; FRCP Can, 74; FACP, 80. *Prof Exp:* Res fel immunol, Montreal Gen Hosp Res Inst, 74-77 & Inst de Cancerologie et d'immunogenetique, France, 77-78. *Concurrent Pos:* Affil staff, Dept Immunol, Montreal Gen Hosp, 78-; mem staff, Dept Med, St Mary's Hosp, Montreal, 78-; assoc physician, Dept Med, Royal Victoria Hosp, Montreal, 79- *Mem:* Fel Am Col Physicians; Am Acad Allergy; Can Soc Allergy & Clin Immunol. *Res:* Experimental and clinical immunotherapy of cancer; therapy of atopic diseases. *Mailing Add:* 687 Pine Ave Montreal PQ H3A 1A1 Can

SCHULZ, JOHANN CHRISTOPH FRIEDRICH, organic chemistry; deceased, see previous edition for last biography

SCHULZ, JOHN C, OPHTHAL. *Current Pos:* Researcher, autonomic pharmacol, 79-82, RESIDENT OPHTHAL, UNIV LOUISVILLE, 87- *Personal Data:* b Peoria, Ill, Dec 4, 55. *Educ:* Univ WVa, PhD(pharmacol), 82, MD, 86. *Mem:* Am Med Asn; Fedn Am Soc Exp Biol. *Res:* Currently engaged in residency training. *Mailing Add:* Wenatchee Valley Clin 820 N Chalan Wenatchee WA 98801

SCHULZ, JOHN HAMPSHIRE, PAPER CHEMISTRY. *Current Pos:* mgr res & develop, 75-80, TECH DIR, KRAFT DIV, ST REGIS PAPER CO, 80- *Personal Data:* b New York, NY, Apr 10, 34; m 63; c 3. *Educ:* Brooklyn Polytech Inst, BChemE, 55; Lawrence Univ, MS, 57, PhD(physics), 61. *Prof Exp:* Asst prof paper technol, Western Mich Univ, 61-63; mgr process develop, Paper & Bd Div, Continental Can Co, Ga, 63-69, tech dir, Hodge, 69-72, gen supt, 72-75. *Mem:* Am Chem Soc; Tech Asn Pulp & Paper Indust. *Res:* Reaction of paper to stress; paper mill quality control; clay coating of paper; paper machine performance analysis. *Mailing Add:* 47 Demarest Mill Rd West Nyack NY 10994-1515

SCHULZ, JOHN THEODORE, ENTOMOLOGY. *Current Pos:* From asst prof to assoc prof entom, NDak State Univ, 57-67, actg chmn dept, 73-74, prof & chmn dept, 74-, EMER PROF ENTOM, NDAK STATE UNIV. *Personal Data:* b Ames, Iowa, June 15, 29; m 53; c 5. *Educ:* Iowa State Univ, PhD(entom), 57. *Mem:* AAAS; Entom Soc Am; Phytopath Soc; Sunflower Asn Am. *Res:* Insect transmission of plant diseases; economic entomology. *Mailing Add:* Entom Dept NDak State Univ Hultz Hall 202 Fargo ND 58105

SCHULZ, KEVIN JON, ELECTRONIC PACKAGING, MAGNETIC RECORDING. *Current Pos:* sr adv engr, 94-97, staff engr, SEAGATE TECHNOL, 97- *Personal Data:* b Valley Forge, Pa, Nov, 1, 60; m 83, Lynne A Roso; c Katharine, Elizabeth & Zachary. *Educ:* Univ Wis-Madison, BS, 83, PhD(metal eng), 88. *Prof Exp:* From assoc engr to staff engr, Storage Systs Div, IBM, 83-93, adv engr, AS/400 Div, 93-94. *Mem:* Am Soc Metals Int. *Res:* Flexible circuit design for magnetic head interconnects; head suspension design; microactuators and disk drive electronic packaging and materials. *Mailing Add:* 7801 Computer Ave S Minneapolis MN 55435-5489

SCHULZ, LESLIE OLMSTEAD, NUTRITION, BIOCHEMISTRY. *Current Pos:* Asst prof, 83-88, ASSOC PROF HEALTH SCI, UNIV WIS, MILWAUKEE, 88- *Personal Data:* b Milwaukee, Wis. *Educ:* Univ NDak, BA, 74; NDak State Univ, MS, 77; Cornell Univ, PhD(nutrit biochem), 83. *Concurrent Pos:* Mem, Nat Coun Against Health Fraud. *Mem:* Am Diabetes Asn; Am Dietetic Asn; Bangladesh Biochem Soc; Sigma Xi. *Res:* Metabolic regulation; hepatic glucose six phosphatase system and lipid metabolism in brown fat tissue; sports nutrition. *Mailing Add:* PO Box 413 Univ Wis Milwaukee WI 53201. *Fax:* 414-229-4666

SCHULZ, MICHAEL, SPACE PHYSICS, PLASMA PHYSICS. *Current Pos:* SR STAFF SCIENTIST, LOCKHEED PALO-ALTO RES LABS, 93- *Personal Data:* b Petoskey, Mich, July 14, 43. *Educ:* Mich State Univ, BS, 64; Mass Inst Technol, PhD(physics), 67. *Prof Exp:* Mem tech staff, Bell Tel Labs, 67-69; mem tech staff, Aerospace Corp, 69-93, sr scientist, 82-93. *Concurrent Pos:* Secy, Magnetospheric Physics, Am Geophysics Union, 80-84; assoc ed, J Geophys Res, 76-78; ed, space res books, Am Geophys Union, 87- *Mem:* Am Phys Soc; Am Geophys Union. *Res:* Dynamics of partially ionized gases; theoretical plasma physics; adiabatic theory of charged particle motion; magnetospheric and radiation belt physics; solar wind; solar-terrestrial relationships. *Mailing Add:* 1037 Twin Oak Ct Redwood City CA 94061

SCHULZ, RICHARD BURKART, ELECTROMAGNETIC COMPATIBILITY. *Current Pos:* ELECTROMAGNETIC COMPATIBILITY CONSULT, 87- *Personal Data:* b Philadelphia, Pa, May 21, 20; m 38, Jeannette Vollmer; c Steven E. *Educ:* Univ Pa, BSEE, 42, MSEE, 51. *Honors & Awards:* L G Gumming Award, 80; Centennial Medal, Inst Elec & Electronics Engrs, 84; R R S Stoddard Award, 88. *Prof Exp:* Res assoc, Univ Pa, 42-45; owner, Electro-Search, 47-55; prog develop coordr, Armour Res Found, 55-61; chief electro-interference, United Control Corp, 61-62; chief electro-compatibility, Boeing Corp, 62-70; staff eng, Southwest Res Inst, 70-74; scientific adv, ITT Res Inst, 74-8374; mgr electromagnetic compatibility, Xerox Corp, 83-87. *Mem:* Fel Inst Elec & Electronics Engrs Electromagnetic Compatability Soc (treas, 67, pres, 68); Soc Aeronaut Eng. *Res:* Electromagnetic shielding; shielding enclosures. *Mailing Add:* 2030 Cologne Dr Carrollton TX 75007. *Fax:* 972-492-1018; *E-Mail:* rschulz248@aol.com

SCHULZ, ROBERT J, MEDICAL PHYSICS. *Current Pos:* RETIRED. *Personal Data:* b Brooklyn, NY, Jan 12, 27; m 51; c 3. *Educ:* Queens Col, NY, BS, 50; Cornell Univ, MS, 57; NY Univ, PhD, 67. *Prof Exp:* Asst physicist radiol physics, Mem Hosp, Sloan Kettering Inst, 52-56; asst prof, Albert Einstein Col Med, Yeshiva Univ, 56-70; prof radiol physics, Yale Univ, 70- *Concurrent Pos:* Attend physicist, Montefiore Hosp, 57-68; chief physicist, Yale-New Haven Hosp. *Mem:* Asn Physicists Med; Am Col Radiol. *Res:* Applications of x-rays and radioactive materials to medical diagnostic and therapeutic problems. *Mailing Add:* 95 Dromara Rd Gilford CT 06437

SCHULZ, WALLACE WENDELL, INORGANIC CHEMISTRY. *Current Pos:* CONSULT, W2S CO, 88- *Personal Data:* b Basil Mills, Nebr, Feb 24, 26; m 89, Kathleen M Gamet; c 2. *Educ:* Univ Nev, BS, 49, MS, 50. *Prof Exp:* From res chemist to sr scientist, Hanford Atomic Prod Oper, Gen Elec Co, 50-65; sr res scientist, Battelle Northwest Labs, 65-69; staff chemist, Atlantic Richfield Hanford Co, 69-77, prin chemsit, Rockwell Hanford Co, 77-80, chief scientist, 80-88. *Mem:* Am Chem Soc; Am Inst Mining, Metall & Petrol Engrs; Am Nuclear Soc; Sigma Xi. *Res:* Solvent extraction chemistry; uranium-plutonium separations processes; fission product separations processes; electrochemistry; nuclear waste management. *Mailing Add:* 5314 Arbustos Ct Albuquerque NM 87111. *Fax:* 505-299-4854; *E-Mail:* 103574.3620@compuserve.com

SCHULZ, WILLIAM, CHROMATOGRAPHY, MASS SPECTROMETRY. *Current Pos:* asst prof, 68-76, assoc prof, 76-, PROF CHEM, EASTERN KY UNIV. *Personal Data:* b Lakefield, Minn, Oct 14, 35; m 73, Judith Hirst; c Sigrid, Morgan & Darvin. *Educ:* Mankato State Col, BS, 61, MS, 65; La State Univ, PhD(anal org chem), 75. *Prof Exp:* Instr chem, Wis State Univ-La Crosse, 65-68. *Concurrent Pos:* Vis assoc prof chem, Collo Sch Mines, 81-82; vis prof chem, Univ Louisville, 84-85 & 89-90; summer fac fel & consult, USAF, 86-92. *Mem:* Am Chem Soc; Asn Off Anal Chemists. *Res:* Mechanism and products of jet fuel oxidation; products of flaming combustion and exhaust; trace environmental organic analysis. *Mailing Add:* Moore 337 Eastern Ky Univ Richmond KY 40475-3101

SCHULZE, DAN HOWARD, MOLECULAR IMMUNOLOGY-B CELL DEVELOPMENT, SODIUM-CALCIUM EXCHANGER FUNCTION IN CELLS. *Current Pos:* asst prof, 89-92, ASSOC PROF MOLECULAR IMMUNOL, UNIV MD SCH MED, 92- *Personal Data:* b Fresno, Calif, Feb 6, 47; m, Susan Hunter; c Duncan & Mark. *Educ:* Ind Univ, BA, 65; Miami Univ, MS, 72; Univ Tex, Austin, PhD(zool), 78. *Prof Exp:* Teaching asst biol & zool, Miami Univ, 70-72; teaching asst zool, Univ Tex, Austin, 72-73; fel,

Univ Minn, St Paul, 78-80 & Albert Einstein Col Med, 80-84; asst prof, Univ Tex Med Br, 84-89. *Mem:* Biophys Soc. *Res:* Study gene expression in developing antibody producing cells; study the structure and function of the sodium-calcium exchange antiporter protein in cells. *Mailing Add:* Dept Microbiol & Immunol Univ Md Sch Med 655 W Baltimore Baltimore MD 21201-1559. *Fax:* 410-706-2129; *E-Mail:* dschulze@cosy.umd.ab.edu

SCHULZE, GENE EDWARD, NEUROTOXICOLOGY, NEUROPHARMACOLOGY. *Current Pos:* staff scientist toxicol, Hazleton Labs Am Inc, 88-91, SR STAFF SCIENTIST, HAZLETON-WASH INC, 91- *Personal Data:* b Louisville, Ky, May 8, 59. *Educ:* Univ Ky, BS, 81, MS, 82, PhD(toxicol), 85; Am Bd Toxicol, cert & dipl, 89. *Honors & Awards:* First Ann Hazleton-Washington Award, 90. *Prof Exp:* Res assoc toxicol, Tex A&M Univ, 85-86; vis scientist toxicol, Nat Ctr Toxicol Res, 86-88. *Concurrent Pos:* Adj instr, dept pharmacol, Univ Ark Med Sci, 87-; adj asst prof, dept biol, Univ Ark, Pine Bluff, 88- *Mem:* Soc Neurosci; Behav Toxicol Soc; Behav Pharmacol Soc; AAAS; NY Acad Sci. *Res:* Behavioral toxicity of drugs and pesticides; interaction between central nervous system and the immune system; the effect of drugs and chemicals on cognitive function using primate models of cognition. *Mailing Add:* Dept Toxicol Bristol Meyers Squibb Co 6000 Thompson Rd Bldg 32A Syracuse NY 13221. *Fax:* 703-759-6947

SCHULZE, IRENE THERESA, VIROLOGY, BIOCHEMISTRY. *Current Pos:* asst prof, 70-73, assoc prof, 73-80, PROF MICROBIOL, SCH MED, ST LOUIS UNIV, 80- *Personal Data:* b Washington, Mo, Feb 8, 29. *Educ:* St Louis Univ, BS, 52, PhD(microbiol), 62. *Prof Exp:* Res asst enzym & biochem, Pub Health Res Inst City New York, Inc, 65-68, assoc virol, 68-70. *Concurrent Pos:* Fel microbiol, Vanderbilt Univ, 62-65; USPHS res grant, Sch Med, St Louis Univ, 71- *Mem:* AAAS; Am Soc Microbiol; Am Soc Biol Chemists. *Res:* Structure and chemical composition of large RNA-containing viruses, for example, influenza and oncogenic viruses; relationships between viral structure and biological activities; viral synthesis and virus-host relationships. *Mailing Add:* Dept Molecular Microbiol & Immunol St Louis Univ Sch Med 1402 S Grand St Louis MO 63104-1080. *Fax:* 314-773-3403; *E-Mail:* schulzeit@sluvca

SCHULZE, KARL LUDWIG, environmental engineering; deceased, see previous edition for last biography

SCHULZE, WALTER ARTHUR, MATERIALS SCIENCE, FERROELECTRICS. *Current Pos:* Res assoc, 74-80, SR RES ASSOC, MAT RES LAB, PA STATE UNIV 80-, AT NY STATE COL CERAMICS, ALFRED UNIV. *Personal Data:* b Philadelphia, Pa, Dec 8, 43; m 71; c 1. *Educ:* Pa State Univ, BS, 65, MS, 68, PhD(solid state sci), 73. *Mem:* Am Ceramic Soc; Inst Elec & Electronics Engrs. *Res:* Preparation and characterization of ferroelectric materials and devices; electrical properties of piezoelectric and high dielectric constant ceramics. *Mailing Add:* NY State Col Ceramics Alfred Univ 2 Pine St Alfred NY 14802

SCHUMACHER, BERTHOLD WALTER, ENGINEERING-PHYSICS, HIGH POWER ELECTRON BEAM TECHNOLOGY. *Current Pos:* CONSULT, 87- *Personal Data:* b Karlsruhe, WGer, Apr 15, 21; US citizen; m 55, Maja M Grun; c Reihard A & Thomas W. *Educ:* Univ Stuttgart, dipl, 50, Dr rer nat, 53. *Prof Exp:* Design engr, Electronics Indust, WGer, 53-54; res fel, Ont Res Found, Toronto, Can, 54-58, dir, Dept Physics, 58-66; mgr electron beam technol, Westinghouse Res Labs, 66-77; prin engr res, Ford Motor Co, 77-87. *Mem:* Am Phys Soc; Phys Soc Eng; Am Welding Soc; Ger Physics Soc; NY Acad Sci. *Res:* Vacuum and electron beam physics and technology; electron beam attenuation, fluorescence and single-scatter probes for measuring gas parameters; high power electron guns with beam transfer to the atmosphere for welding, cutting and face hardening with electron beam and workpiece in air; closed-loop control for welding processes with high energy beams, as well as for resistance welding; basic theories without the relativity concept. *Mailing Add:* 15161 Ford Rd Apt 407 Dearborn MI 48126-4652

SCHUMACHER, DIETMAR, petroleum geology, paleontology, for more information see previous edition

SCHUMACHER, GARY E, DENTISTRY. *Current Pos:* CHIEF RES SCIENTIST CLIN PROG, PAFFENBARGER RES CTR, AM DENT ASN HEALTH FOUND, 96- *Personal Data:* b Dover, Ohio, May 14, 49. *Educ:* Ohio Univ, BS, 71; NY Univ, MS, 71; Ohio State Univ, DDS, 74. *Prof Exp:* Dent officer, USCG, 74-89; chief, Dent Clin, NIH, 89-96. *Mem:* Int Asn Dent Res; Am Asn Dent Res. *Mailing Add:* ADAHF/PRC-NIST Bldg 224 Rm A-153 Gaithersburg MD 20899. *E-Mail:* gary.schumacher@nist.gov

SCHUMACHER, GEBHARD FRIEDERICH B, OBSTETRICS & GYNECOLOGY, REPRODUCTIVE MEDICINE IMMUNOLOGY. *Current Pos:* assoc prof, Univ Chicago, 67-73, prof obstet & gynec, 73-91, chief sect reproductive biol, 71-91, EMER PROF OBSTET & GYNEC, PRITZKER SCH MED, UNIV CHICAGO, 91- *Personal Data:* b Osnabruck, WGer, June 13, 24; m 58, Anne R Zanker; c Michael A & Marc M. *Educ:* Univ Gottingen, MD, 51. *Prof Exp:* Intern gen med, Med Sch, Univ Tubingen, 51-52; resident in biochem, Max Planck Inst Biochem, 52-53 & Max Planck Inst Virus Res, 53-54; resident obstet & gynec, Med Sch, Univ Tubingen, 54-59, sci asst, 59-62, docent, 62 & 64-65; res assoc immunol, Inst Tuberc Res, Col Med, Univ Ill, 62-63; res assoc & asst prof obstet & gynec, Univ Chicago, 63-64; assoc prof obstet & gynec & asst prof biochem, Albany Med Col, 65-67; res scientist, Div Labs & Res, NY State Dept Health, 65-67. *Concurrent Pos:* Ger Sci Found grant, 55-62; NIH grants; Ford Found funds; app fac mem, Div Comt on Immunol, 72-; consult & task force mem, World Health Orgn, Human Reprod Unit, 72-77; mem med adv bd, Int Fertil Res Prog, Triangle Park, NC, 77-; reviewer & ad hoc consult, Nat Inst Child Health & Human Develop, Bethesda, Md, 73-91; prof, Div Comt Immunol, Univ Chicago Pritzker Sch Med, 74, emer prof, 91-; prof, Biol Sch Col Div, Univ, Chicago, 82-91, emer prof & lectr, 91- *Mem:* Ger Soc Biol Chemists; Am Asn Pathologists; Soc Study Reprod; Am Soc Andrology; Europe Soc Immunol; fel Am Col Obstet & Gynec. *Res:* Biology of human reproduction; birth control; infertility; endocrinology-protein metabolism; serum proteins; immunology; inflammation and nonspecific resistance; trauma. *Mailing Add:* Dept Obstet & Gynec Sch Med Univ Chicago Pritcker Sch Med 557 Hamilton Wood Homewood IL 60430

SCHUMACHER, GEORGE ADAM, MEDICINE NEUROLOGY. *Current Pos:* chmn div neurol, 50-68, prof neurol, 50-78, EMER PROF NEUROL, UNIV VT, 79- *Personal Data:* b Trenton, NJ, Sept 22, 12; wid; c 4. *Educ:* Pa State Univ, BS, 32; Cornell Univ, MD, 36. *Prof Exp:* From asst to assoc prof clin med neurol, Cornell Univ Med Ctr, New York, 46-50, dir neurol serv, Bellevue Hosp, 49-50. *Concurrent Pos:* From asst attend neurologist to dir neurol serv, Bellevue Hosp, New York, 46-50; mem med adv bd, Nat Multiple Sclerosis Soc, 49-, chmn, 64-66; attend neurologist, Med Ctr Hosp, VT, 50-78; consult, Hosps, NY & Vt, 50-78; mem prog proj comt, Nat Inst Neurol Dis & Blindness, 62-64; vis scientist, Arctic Health Res Lab, USPHS, 67-68; vis prof human ecol, Inst Arctic Biol, Univ Alaska, 67-68. *Mem:* Am Neurol Asn; Asn Res Nerv & Ment Dis; fel Am Acad Neurol; Am Med Asn. *Res:* Headache; pain; multiple sclerosis; spinal cord physiology. *Mailing Add:* 59 Bilodeau Ct Burlington VT 05401

SCHUMACHER, GEORGE JOHN, PHYCOLOGY. *Current Pos:* from instr to assoc prof biol, 53-61, chmn dept, 59-66, PROF BIOL, STATE UNIV NY, BINGHAMTON, 61- *Personal Data:* b Lindenwold, NJ, Dec 19, 24; m 49; c 3. *Educ:* Bucknell Univ, BS, 48; Cornell Univ, MS, 49, PhD(bot, vert zool), 53. *Prof Exp:* Instr, Cornell Univ, 52-53. *Mem:* Am Phycol Soc; Int Phycol Soc. *Res:* Ecology and taxonomy of freshwater algae, populations and eutrophication. *Mailing Add:* Sci 3 Biol Dept Rm 391 Binghamton Univ PO Box 6000 Binghamton NY 13902-6000

SCHUMACHER, H RALPH, JR, INTERNAL MEDICINE, RHEUMATOLOGY. *Current Pos:* from asst prof to assoc prof, 67-79, PROF MED, SCH MED, UNIV PA, 79- *Personal Data:* b Montreal, Que, Feb 14, 33; m 65, Elizabeth Swisher; c Heidi & Kaethe. *Educ:* Ursinus Col, Collegeville, Pa, BS, 55; Univ Pa, MD, 59. *Honors & Awards:* Hench Award, 85; Van Breeman Award, 89. *Prof Exp:* Intern, Denver Gen Hosp, 59-60; resident, Wadsworth Vet Admin Hosp, Los Angeles, 60-62, fel rheumatol, 62-63; fel, Robert Brigham Hosp, Boston, 65-67. *Concurrent Pos:* Staff physician & chief, Arthritis Sect, Vet Admin Hosp, 67-, dir, Rheumatol-Immunol Ctr, 77-; actg chief, Arthritis Sect, Sch Med, Univ Pa, 78-80 & 90-95. *Mem:* Am Col Rheumatology; Am Fedn Clin Res; Electron Micros Soc Am; AAAS. *Res:* Pathogenesis studies in the rheumatic diseases using light and electron microscopy, electron probe analysis, tissue culture, immunoelectron microscopy in situ hybridization; crystal induced arthritis, rheumatoid arthritis; spondylarthropathies, rehabilitation and arthritis. *Mailing Add:* Vet Admin Med Ctr Univ & Woodland Ave Philadelphia PA 19104. *Fax:* 215-823-6032; *E-Mail:* schumacher.ralph@philadelphia.va.gov

SCHUMACHER, IGNATIUS, ORGANIC CHEMISTRY, MEDICINAL CHEMISTRY. *Current Pos:* PRES, IGNATUS SCHUMACHER CONSULT INC, 86- *Personal Data:* b Munjor, Kans, Apr 1, 28; m 54; c 7. *Educ:* Univ Kans, BS, 58; Univ Mich, PhD(med chem), 62. *Prof Exp:* Org researcher, 62-64; sr org chemist, 64-73, res specialist, 73-77, sr specialist, 77-82, fel, Monsanto Co, 82-86. *Mem:* Am Chem Soc. *Mailing Add:* PO Box 6433 Chesterfield MO 63006

SCHUMACHER, JOSEPH CHARLES, INDUSTRIAL CHEMISTRY. *Current Pos:* RETIRED. *Personal Data:* b Peru, Ill, Sept 15, 11; m 33, 85, Mary M Mohen; c Kathleen J, John C Stephen J & Paul J. *Educ:* Univ Southern Calif, AB, 46. *Honors & Awards:* Gold Medal, Electrochem Technol, Electrochem Soc. *Prof Exp:* Res chemist & prod suprv, Carus Chem Co, Ill, 31-40; mem res develop & orgn staff, Fine Chem, Inc, Calif, 40-41, co-founder, vpres & dir res, Western Electrochem Co, 41-54; dir res, Am Potash & Chem Corp, 54-66, vpres rare earth div, 66-68; vpres electrochem, Vanadium & Rare Earth Div, Kerr-McGee Chem Corp, 68-72; pres, J C Schumacher Co, 72-77, chmn bd, 77-85. *Concurrent Pos:* Trustee, Whittier Col, 68-77. *Mem:* Am Chem Soc; Electrochem Soc; Sigma Xi. *Res:* Industrial electrochemistry; chlorates, perchlorates and electrolyte manganese dioxide and manganese metal chloride process tetanuim dioxide; organic chemistry; photochemicals; boron; hydroquinore. *Mailing Add:* 2220 Ave of the Stars 704 W Tower Los Angeles CA 90067-5656

SCHUMACHER, JOSEPH NICHOLAS, ORGANIC CHEMISTRY. *Current Pos:* RETIRED. *Personal Data:* b Downers Grove, Ill, May 2, 28; m 50; c 9. *Educ:* St Procopius Col, BS, 50; Ohio State Univ, MSc, 52, PhD(org chem), 54. *Prof Exp:* Asst res found, Ohio State Univ, 50-51, asst univ, 51-54; res chemist, R J Reynolds Tobacco Co, 54-68, group leader, 68-78, sect head, 78-82, master scientist, 82-87. *Mem:* Am Chem Soc. *Res:* Natural products; carbohydrates; chromatography. *Mailing Add:* 212 Cascade Ave Winston-Salem NC 27127

SCHUMACHER, RICHARD WILLIAM, AGRICULTURAL & FOOD CHEMISTRY. *Current Pos:* field res scientist, 76-79, MGR, AGR CHEM RES & DEVELOP, MONSANTO AGR PROD CO, 79- *Personal Data:* b Chicago, Ill, 46; m 69; c 1. *Educ:* Univ Ill, BS, 69; Va Polytech & State Univ, MS, 71; Univ Ky, PhD(plant physiol), 74. *Prof Exp:* Res leader, Agr Res Serv, USDA, 74-76. *Mem:* Sigma Xi. *Mailing Add:* 12 Heathercroft Ct Chesterfield MO 63017

SCHUMACHER, ROBERT E, AQUATIC BIOLOGY, FISHERIES MANAGEMENT. *Current Pos:* RETIRED. *Personal Data:* b Heron Lake, Minn, Oct 14, 18; m 45; c 4. *Educ:* Univ Minn, BS, 50. *Prof Exp:* Aquatic biologist, Fisheries Res Unit, State Dept Conserv, Minn, 50-57, res biologist, 57-65; dist fisheries mgr, Mont Dept Fish & Game, 65-71, regional fisheries mgr, 71-82. *Mem:* Am Fisheries Soc. *Res:* Fisheries management and research; aquatic ecology; trout population levels and dynamics. *Mailing Add:* 1227 Fifth St W Kalispell MT 59901

SCHUMACHER, ROBERT THORNTON, MUSICAL ACOUSTICS. *Current Pos:* from asst prof to prof, 57-96, EMER PROF PHYSICS, CARNEGIE-MELLON UNIV, 96- *Personal Data:* b Berkeley, Calif, Sept 29, 30; m 54; c 2. *Educ:* Univ Nev, BS, 51; Univ Ill, MS, 53, PhD(physics), 55. *Prof Exp:* Instr physics, Univ Wash, 55-57. *Concurrent Pos:* Sloan Found fel, 58-62, NSF sr fel, 65-66. *Mem:* Fel Am Phys Soc; AAAS. *Res:* Musical acoustics; measurements, theory, and computer simulations of oscillations of musical instruments, particularly bowed string instruments. *Mailing Add:* Dept Physics Carnegie-Mellon Univ 5000 Forbes Ave Pittsburgh PA 15213. *E-Mail:* rts@andrew.cmu.edu

SCHUMACHER, ROY JOSEPH, ORGANIC CHEMISTRY. *Current Pos:* Chemist, 71-75, res group leader, MC/B Mfg Chemists, 74-78, mkt mgr, 78-81, SR ANALYTICAL CHEMIST, MONSANTO RES CORP, 81- *Personal Data:* b Covington, Ky, Mar 15, 42; m 65; c 2. *Educ:* Xavier Univ, Ohio, BS, 64, MS, 67; Univ Cincinnati, PhD(chem), 71. *Mem:* Am Chem Soc. *Res:* Ylide chemistry; organic synthesis and product development. *Mailing Add:* 3518 Grandview Ave Cincinnati OH 45241

SCHUMACHER, WILLIAM JOHN, ENERGY ECONOMICS, ENERGY SUPPLY PLANNING. *Current Pos:* DIR, ENERGY PRACT, SRI INT, 71- *Personal Data:* b Jersey City, NJ, Mar 11, 36; m 69; c 2. *Educ:* Cornell Univ, BChE, 58, PhD(chem eng), 64. *Prof Exp:* Prof chem eng, Nat Univ Trujillo, 65-70. *Mem:* Am Inst Chem Engrs; Am Chem Soc. *Res:* Energy economics and planning. *Mailing Add:* 1003 Almanor Ave Menlo Park CA 94025

SCHUMAKER, JOHN ABRAHAM, HISTORY OF MATHEMATICS. *Current Pos:* dir, NSF in-serv insts, 62-68, prof & chmn dept, 61-92,EMER PROF & ADJ PROF MATH, ROCKFORD COL, 92- *Personal Data:* b Marshall, Ill, July 24, 25. *Educ:* Univ Ill, BS, 46, AM, 47; NY Univ, PhD(math educ), 59. *Honors & Awards:* Distinguished Serv Award, Math Asn Am. *Prof Exp:* Instr math, Univ Ill, 46-47; from instr to asst prof, MacMurray Col, 47-53; instr, Grinnell Col, 53-55; from asst prof to assoc prof, Montclair State Col, 55-61. *Concurrent Pos:* Vis prof, NSF Inst, Univ Vt, 62-73. *Mem:* AAAS; Am Math Soc; Math Asn Am; Fedn Am Scientists. *Res:* Number theory; history of mathematics; statistics. *Mailing Add:* 911 Woodridge Dr Rockford IL 61108-4012

SCHUMAKER, LARRY L, MATHEMATICS. *Current Pos:* PROF MATH, VANDERBILT UNIV, 88- *Personal Data:* b Aberdeen, SDak, Nov 5, 39; m 63, Gerda Boguszewsui; c Annabel. *Educ:* SDak Sch Mines & Technol, BS, 61; Stanford Univ, MS, 62, PhD(math), 66. *Honors & Awards:* Humbolt prize, 90. *Prof Exp:* Lectr comput sci, Stanford Univ, 66; vis asst prof math, Math Res Ctr, Univ Wis-Madison, 66-68; from asst prof to prof math, Univ Tex, 68-79; prof math, Tex A&M Univ, College Station, 80-88. *Concurrent Pos:* Vis assoc prof, Math Res Ctr, Univ Wis, 73-74; vis prof math, Univ Munich, 74-75 & 89-90, Free Univ Berlin, Hahn Meitner Atomic Energy Inst, 78-79, Univ Sao Paulo, Brazil, 81 & Univ Wurzburg, 87. *Mem:* Am Math Soc; Soc Indust & Appl Math; Math Asn Am. *Res:* Classical approximation theory; total positivity; spline functions; investigating theoretical spaces of multivariate splines and their applications to solving data fitting problems and in computer-aided design. *Mailing Add:* Vanderbilt Univ 1326 Stevenson Ctr Nashville TN 37240-0001. *Fax:* 615-343-0215; *E-Mail:* s@mars.cas.vanderbilt.edu

SCHUMAKER, MARK FRANKLIN, MATHEMATIC MODELING OF BIOPHYSICAL SYSTEMS, OPEN PORE PERMEATION OF ION CHANNELS. *Current Pos:* asst prof, 90-96, ASSOC PROF MATH, WASH STATE UNIV, 96- *Personal Data:* b Berkeley, Calif, Sept 21, 53; m 90, Ann Strehler; c Eric & Richard. *Educ:* Univ Calif, San Diego, BA, 75; Univ Tex, Austin, PhD(physics), 87. *Prof Exp:* Postdoctoral res assoc, Brandeis Univ, 87-90. *Concurrent Pos:* Vis scientist, Dept Physics, Univ Montreal, 97-98. *Mem:* Biophys Soc; Soc Indust & Appl Math; AAAS. *Res:* Construct intermediate models of ion channels which use free energies calculated by molecular dynamics to compute quantities that may be directly compared with experiment. *Mailing Add:* Dept Pure & Appl Math Wash State Univ Pullman WA 99164-3113. *Fax:* 509-335-1188; *E-Mail:* schumaker@wsn.edu

SCHUMAKER, ROBERT LOUIS, physics, mathematics; deceased, see previous edition for last biography

SCHUMAKER, VERNE NORMAN, PHYSICAL BIOCHEMISTRY. *Current Pos:* assoc prof chem, 65-66, PROF CHEM, UNIV CALIF, LOS ANGELES, 66- *Personal Data:* b McCloud, Calif, Sept 16, 29; m 51; c 2. *Educ:* Univ Calif, AB, 52, PhD(biophys), 55. *Prof Exp:* Jr res biophysicist, Virus Lab, Univ Calif, 54-55, assoc res biophysicist, 55-56; Am Cancer Soc fel, Lab Animal Morphol, Brussels, Belg, 56-57; from asst prof to assoc prof biochem, Univ Pa, 57-65. *Concurrent Pos:* John Simon Guggenheim fel, 64-65. *Mem:* AAAS; Biophys Soc; Am Soc Biol Chemists. *Res:* Immunochemistry, structure and function of lipoproteins, chromatin structure; hydrodynamic theory and methodology. *Mailing Add:* Dept Chem & Biochem Univ Calif Los Angeles 405 Hilgard Ave Los Angeles CA 90095-1569

SCHUMAN, GERALD E, SOIL-PLANT RELATIONSHIPS, RECLAMATION OF DISTURBED LANDS. *Current Pos:* Soil scientist, USDA-Agr Res Serv, Reno, Nev, 66-69, Lincoln, Nebr, 69-75, Cheyenne, Wyo, 75-77, soil scientist & res leader, 77-91, SOIL SCIENTIST, RES LEADER & LOCATION LEADER, RANGELAND RESOURCES RES, USDA-AGR RES SERV, CHEYENNE, WYO, 91- *Personal Data:* b Sheridan, Wyo, July 5, 44; m 65, Mabel Kaisler; c William G & Kara L. *Educ:* Univ Wyo, BS, 66; Univ Nev, Reno, MS, 69; Univ Nebr, PhD(agron), 74. *Honors & Awards:* Reclamation Researcher Award, Am Soc Surface Mining Reclamation, 91; Outstanding Achievement Award, Soc Range Mgt, 95. *Concurrent Pos:* Adj prof plant soil & insect sci, Univ Wyo, Laramie, 75-; chmn energy resources div, Soil Conserv Soc Am, 79-81; fac affil dept soil & plant sci, Colo State Univ, Ft Collins, 80-; chmn environ qual div, Am Soc Agron, 84-85; pres, Wyo Sect, Soc Range Mgt, 91; vis fel, Univ Western Australia, 96. *Mem:* Fel Soil & Water Conserv Soc; fel Am Soc Agron; Soc Range Mgt; Am Soc Surface Mining Reclamation (pres, 92-93); Int Soc Soil Sci; fel Soil Sci Soc Am. *Res:* Evaluation of soil-plant relationships on disturbed rangeland soils and highly erodible marginal soils; long term management of reclaimed lands; utilization of municipal, industrial and animal wastes on rangelands; research administration. *Mailing Add:* USDA-Agr Res Serv High Plains Grasslands Res Sta 8408 Hildreth Rd Cheyenne WY 82009. *Fax:* 307-637-6124; *E-Mail:* gschuman@lamar.colostate.edu

SCHUMAN, LEONARD MICHAEL, EPIDEMIOLOGY. *Current Pos:* assoc prof pub health, Univ Minn, Minneapolis, 54-57, prof epidemiol, 57-83, Mayo prof, 83-93, EMER MAYO PROF PUB HEALTH, UNIV MINN, MINNEAPOLIS, 93- *Personal Data:* b Cleveland, Ohio, Mar 4, 13; m 54, Marie T Romich; c Lowell M & Judith F. *Educ:* Oberlin Col, AB, 34; Western Res Univ, MSc, 39, MD, 40; Am Bd Prev Med, dipl, 50. *Honors & Awards:* John Snow Award, Am Pub Health Asn, 83, Sedgwick Mem Medal, 96; Samuel Harvey Award, Am Asn Cancer Educ, 83; Abraham H Lilienfeld Award, Am Col Epidemiol, 89; Outstanding Contrib to Epidemiol Award, Soc Epidemiol Res, 92. *Prof Exp:* Asst epidemiologist, Ill Dept Pub Health, 41-42, dist health supt, 43, asst chief, Div Local Health Admin, 43-45, chief, Div Venereal Dis Control, 47-49, actg chief, Div Commun Dis, 49-50, dep dir in-chg, Div Prev Med, 50-51 & 53-54; epidemiologist, Cold Injury Res Team, US Dept Defense, Korea, 51-53. *Concurrent Pos:* Rockefeller Found fel nutrit, Vanderbilt Univ, 46; vis lectr, Sch Med, Univ Ill, 47-54; lectr, Sch Nursing, Mem Hosp, Springfield, Ill, 47-54, guest lectr, 52-; comn officer, USPHS, 41-47; officer-in-charge, SE Nutrit Res Univ, USPHS, 45-47, consult, Commun Dis Ctr, 55-83; adv comt polio vaccine field trials, Nat Found Infantile Paralysis, 52-55; adv, Polio Vaccine Eval Ctr, Univ Mich, 53-55; Minn State Health Dept, 55-90, Hennepin Coun Gen Hosp, 55-, Air Pollution Med Prog, Nat Cancer Inst, 58-79, Div Radiol Health, 61-69, USDA, 61-83,, Calif State Health Dept, 62, Chronic Dis Div, 64-72; chmn, Coun on Res, Am Col Prev Med, 59-64, Epidemiol Sect, Am Pub Health Asn, 67; mem, Adv Nat Cancer Control Comt, NIH, 59-62, Accident Prev Res Study Sect, 63-66; mem, Adv Field Studies Bd, Nat Adv Cancer Coun, 61-62; mem, Nat Adv Comt Bio-Effects Radiation, USPHS, 66-69, task force smoking & health, 67-68; mem, Nat Adv Urban & Indust Health Coun, 68-69, Nat Adv Environ Control Coun, 69-71; mem, Comt Health Protection & Dis Prev Adv, Secy, HEW, 69-71; fel coun epidemiol, Am Heart Asn, chmn, Conf Chronic Dis Training Prog Dirs, 60-72; panel biomet & epidemiol, Nat Cancer Inst, 61-62, Nat Conf Res Methodology in Community Health & Prev Med, 62 & Surgeon Gen Adv Comt Smoking & Health, 62-64. task group on smoking, Nat Heart, Lung & Blood Inst, 78-79; task group on interstitial lung dis, Nat Heart, Lung & Blood Inst/NIH, 78-79; policy bd, Mid-Career Med Fels, Bush Found, 78-84; mem, Epidemiol & Dis Control Study Sect, NIH, 80-83; mem, Prev Ctrs Grant Rev Comt, Ctr Dis Control, 86-93, vchmn, Health & Environ Network Gov Bd, Freshwater Soc, 87-, bd dir, Smoke Free Generation, 86-92. *Mem:* Am Epidemiol Soc (vpres, 78); Am Thoracic Soc; Am Venereal Dis Asn; Asn Teachers Prev Med; NY Acad Sci; Am Asn Pub Health Physicians; Am Col Prev Med; Asn Mil Surgeons US; Int Epidemiol Soc; Soc Epidemiol Res; Am Pub Health Asn (vpres, 93); Am Col Epidemiol. *Res:* Epidemiology of communicable disease, non-communicable disease including cancer. *Mailing Add:* Epidemiol Div Sch Pub Health Univ Minn PO Box 197 Mayo 420 Delaware St SE Minneapolis MN 55455. *Fax:* 612-626-6931

SCHUMAN, ROBERT PAUL, NUCLEAR CHEMISTRY, PHYSICAL CHEMISTRY. *Current Pos:* RETIRED. *Personal Data:* b Milwaukee, Wis, May 17, 19; m 49, Ellen Bruner; c Barbara, Nancy & Elizabeth. *Educ:* Univ Denver, BS, 41; Ohio State Univ, MS, 44, PhD(chem), 46. *Prof Exp:* Chemist metall lab, Univ Chicago, 44-45; Knolls Atomic Power Lab, Gen Elec Co, 47-57, Atomic Energy Div, Phillips Petrol Co, 57-66 & Idaho Nuclear Corp, 66-69; assoc prof chem, Robert Col, Istanbul, 69-71 & Bogazici Univ, Turkey, 71-77; vis prof, Nuclear Eng, Iowa State Univ, 77-78; sr phys chemist, Idaho Nat Eng Lab, Allied Chem Corp, 78-79, Exxon Nuclear, 79-80 & EG&G Idaho, Inc, 80-84. *Concurrent Pos:* Fulbright grant, Sri Venkateswara Univ, India, 65-66. *Mem:* Am Nuclear Soc; Am Chem Soc; Am Phys Soc; Sigma Xi. *Mailing Add:* 751 Masters Dr Idaho Falls ID 83401-3142

SCHUMAN, STANLEY HAROLD, EPIDEMIOLOGY, PUBLIC HEALTH. *Current Pos:* MED DIR, AGROMED PROG, CLEMSON MED UNIV SC, 84- *Personal Data:* b St Louis, Mo, Dec 29, 25; m 52; c 8. *Educ:* Washington Univ, MD, 48; Univ Mich, MPH, 60, DrPH, 62; Am Bd Pediat, dipl, 60. *Prof Exp:* Clin instr pediat, Sch Med, Washington Univ, 54-59; from asst prof to prof epidemiol, Sch Pub Health, Univ Mich, Ann Arbor, 62-73; prof epidemiol in family pract col med, Med Univ SC, 74-, prof pediat, 76- *Concurrent Pos:* Proj dir, SC Pesticide Study Ctr, Environ Protection Agency, 81-84; author, text Epidemiology, 86. *Mem:* Am Pub Health Asn; Am Acad Family Pract; Am Epidemiol Soc; Soc Epidemiol Res; Coun Agr Sci Technol; Sigma Xi. *Res:* Epidemiology of heat waves in United States' cities; human sweat studies in population survey; screening for cystic fibrosis; population surveys of injuries due to accidents; accident prevention; field trials with young drivers; epidemiology in family practice; computers in medicine; toxicology; cancer of the esophagus agricultural medicine. *Mailing Add:* Mt Pleasant Charleston SC 29425

SCHUMAN, WILLIAM JOHN, JR, MECHANICS. *Current Pos:* sr res scientist, 85-89, vpres, 89-94, PRES, USAF SI, DIV SPECTRUM 39, 94- *Personal Data:* b Baltimore, Md, Jan 23, 30; m 52, Kathleen E Sisson; c Todd L, Craig L & Grant W. *Educ:* Univ Md, BS, 52; Pa State Univ, MS, 54, PhD(eng mech), 65. *Prof Exp:* Asst prof mech, USAF Inst Tech, 54-57; sr engr, Martin Co, Martin Marietta Corp, 57; aero res engr, Ballistic Res Lab, US Army, 57-62, res physicist, 62-83, physicist, Harry Diamond Labs, 83-85. *Concurrent Pos:* Consult, 138 US & foreign govt & indust orgn. *Mem:* Am Soc Mech Engrs; Am Acad Mech; Soc Advan Mat Processes; Sigma Xi. *Res:* Dynamic response of structures, including determination of high explosive blast parameters and details of loading; primary structures; design of blast/thermal and ballistically hardened electronic shelters; light weight armor systems. *Mailing Add:* SI Div Spectrum 39 PO Box 10970 Baltimore MD 21234-0970. *Fax:* 410-661-2418

SCHUMANN, EDWARD LEWIS, ORGANIC CHEMISTRY, MEDICINAL CHEMISTRY. *Current Pos:* RETIRED. *Personal Data:* b Indianapolis, Ind, Aug 1, 23; m 47; c 3. *Educ:* Ind Univ, BS, 43; Univ Mich, MS, 49, PhD(pharmaceut chem), 50. *Prof Exp:* Chemist, Linde Air Prods Co, 43-44; res chemist, Wm S Merrell Co, 49-57; res assoc prod res & develop, Upjohn Co, 57-65, mgr clin drug regulatory affairs, 65-68, dir drug regulatory affairs, 68-85. *Concurrent Pos:* Consult, drug regulatory affairs, 85- *Mem:* Am Chem Soc; Sigma Xi. *Res:* Antispasmodics; histamine antagonists; central nervous system agents; cardiac-cardiovascular drugs; enzyme inhibitors; hormone antagonists; local anesthetics. *Mailing Add:* 809 Dukeshire Ave Portage MI 49024-3619

SCHUMANN, THOMAS GERALD, ELEMENTARY PARTICLE PHYSICS. *Current Pos:* lectr, 71-74, from asst prof to assoc prof, 74-85, PROF PHYSICS, CALIF POLYTECH STATE UNIV, SAN LUIS OBISPO, 85- *Personal Data:* b Los Angeles, Calif, Mar 15, 37. *Educ:* Calif Inst Technol, BS, 58; Univ Calif, Berkeley, MA, 60, PhD(physics), 65. *Prof Exp:* Res assoc physics, Brookhaven Nat Lab, 65-67; asst prof, City Col New York, 67-71. *Mem:* Am Phys Soc. *Res:* Experimental high energy physics using bubble chambers. *Mailing Add:* Dept Physics Calif Polytech State Univ San Luis Obispo CA 93407

SCHUMER, DOUGLAS BRIAN, ACOUSTO-OPTICS, COMMUNICATIONS. *Current Pos:* vpres res & develop, 90-93, vpres res & technol, 93,94, DIR TECHNOL DEVELOP, CARDIAC PACEMAKERS, INC, 94- *Personal Data:* b Passaic, NJ, Mar 22, 51; m 76, Barbara L Witte; c Ariel & Suzanne. *Educ:* Carnegie-Mellon Univ, BS, 73, MS, 74; Rensselaer Polytech Inst, PhD(electroph & elec & syst eng), 77. *Prof Exp:* Mem tech staff, Bell Tel Labs, 77-80; mgr res, Ohaus Scale Corp, 80-83, dir res, 83-84, dir, 84-88, vpres eng & res, 88-90. *Mem:* Am Phys Soc; Optical Soc Am; Inst Physics Eng; Inst Elec & Electronics Engrs; NY Acad Sci; Soc Exp Mech. *Res:* Acousto-optics and surface acoustic waves for signal processing; data compression for graphics transmission; force-frequency quartz resonator sensors; cardiac arrhythmia research; development of electronics technology and sensors and applications. *Mailing Add:* Cardiac Pacemakers Inc 4100 Hamline Ave N St Paul MN 55112

SCHUMER, WILLIAM, SURGERY, BIOCHEMISTRY. *Current Pos:* PROF & CHMN, DEPT SURG, UNIV HEALTH SCI, CHICAGO MED SCH, 75-, DISTINGUISHED PROF BIOCHEM, 90- *Personal Data:* b Chicago, Ill, June 29, 26; m 85; c 2. *Educ:* Ill Inst Technol, 44-45; Chicago Med Sch, MB, 49, MD, 50; Univ Ill, MS, 66; Am Bd Surg, dipl, 54. *Prof Exp:* Asst prof surg, Chicago Med Sch, 59-65, asst prof cardiovasc res, 64-65; dir, surg serv, Univ Calif, Davis, 65-67; from assoc prof to prof surg, Univ Ill, Vet Admin West Side Hosp, 67-75, chief, 67-75. *Concurrent Pos:* Mem attend staff, Mt Sinai Hosp, Chicago, Ill, 62-65, asst chief surg, 63-64, chief dept surg, 90; mem attend staff, Vet Admin Hines Hosp, 60-63 & Vet Admin West Side Hosp, 63-64; dir surg serv, Sacramento County Med Ctr & Univ Calif, Davis, 65-67; mem, Am Bd Surg; mem med staff, Highland Park Hosp, Naval Reg Med Ctr, Great Lakes, 76- & St Mary's Nazareth Hosp Ctr, Chicago, 78; Morris L Parker Res Award, 76; chief surg serv, Va Med Ctr, NChicago, 75-79, chief gen surg sect, 79-82, attend, 82-88 & consult, 88- *Mem:* Am Col Surg; Am Physiol Soc; Shock Soc (pres, 78); Cent Surg Asn; Cent Soc Clin Res; Sigma Xi; Am Surg Asn; AAAS; Am Asn Univ Professors; AMA; Am Soc Contemporary Med & Surg; Am Soc Microbiol; Am Soc Biol Chemists; Am Trauma Soc; Asn Surg Educ; Asn Am Med Cols; Cent Soc Clin Res; Fedn Am Scientists; Fedn Am Socs Exp Biol; Intl Fedn Surg Cols. *Res:* Effect of trauma or shock on cell metabolism; correlation of cell biochemistry, physiology genetics and anatomy in humans and animals in shock. *Mailing Add:* Dept Surg Finch Univ Health Sci Chicago Med Sch Mt Sinai Hosp Med Ctr California Ave at 15th St North Chicago IL 60608. *Fax:* 773-257-6548

SCHUMM, BROOKE, JR, ELECTROCHEMICAL & CHEMICAL ENGINEERING. *Current Pos:* PRES, EAGLE-CLIFFS, INC, 89- *Personal Data:* b Shanghai, China, Oct 8, 31; US citizen; m 55; c 4. *Educ:* Rensselaer Polytech Inst, BS, 53; Univ Rochester, MS, 62, PhD(chem eng), 66. *Prof Exp:* Team leader chem warfare, US Army, 53-55; indust methods engr film processing, Eastman Kodak Co, 55-57, develop engr coatings, 57-58; fel chem engr, Univ Rochester, 58-62; sr technol assoc batteries, Union Carbide Corp, 62-89. *Concurrent Pos:* Union Carbide fel, Univ Rochester, 60-62, sr tech assoc. *Mem:* Electrochem Soc; Am Inst Chemists. *Res:* Industrial coatings, fuel cell batteries, primary electrochemical cells and energy conversion. *Mailing Add:* Eagle Cliffs Inc 31220 Lake Rd Bay Village OH 44140-1001

SCHUMM, BRUCE ANDREW, PHYSICS. *Current Pos:* ASST PROF PHYSICS, UNIV CALIF, SANTA CRUZ, 95- *Personal Data:* b Washington, DC, Oct 23, 58; m, Margo Ross; c Laurel C & Gretchen R. *Educ:* Haverford Col, BA, 81; Univ Chicago, PhD(physics), 88. *Prof Exp:* Postdoctoral fel, Lawrence Berkeley Lab, 88-94, staff scientist, 94-95. *Mem:* Am Phys Soc. *Res:* Experimental particle physicist with broad interests, including precision tests of the standard model, heavy quark physics and CP violation, and quantum chromodynamics. *Mailing Add:* SCIPP Col 10 Rm 150 Univ Calif Santa Cruz CA 95064. *Fax:* 408-459-5777; *E-Mail:* schumm@slac.stanford.edu

SCHUMM, DOROTHY ELAINE, BIOCHEMISTRY. *Current Pos:* res assoc, 71-73, clin instr, 73-74, from instr to assoc prof biochem, 74-79, ASSOC PROF PHYSIOL CHEM, SCH MED, OHIO STATE UNIV, 79- *Personal Data:* b Dayton, Ohio, Aug 4, 43; m 87. *Educ:* Earlham Col, BA, 65; Univ Chicago, MS, 66, PhD(biochem), 69. *Prof Exp:* Res assoc biochem, Ben May Lab Cancer Res, Univ Chicago, 69-70. *Mem:* AAAS; Am Asn Cancer Res; NY Acad Sci; Asn Women Sci; Am Soc Biochem & Molecular Biol. *Res:* Chemical carcinogenesis; oncogenesis; RNA synthesis and transport; aging. *Mailing Add:* Dept Med Biochem Ohio State Univ 364 Hamilton Hall 1645 Neil Ave Columbus OH 43210-1218

SCHUMM, STANLEY ALFRED, FLUVIAL GEOMORPHOLOGY, HYDROLOGY & WATER RESOURCES. *Current Pos:* from assoc prof to prof geol, 67-86, assoc dean, 73-74, UNIV DISTINGUISHED PROF GEOL, COLO STATE UNIV, 86-; SR ASSOC, AYRES ASSOC; PRIN GEOMORPHOLOGIST, MUSSETTER ENG. *Personal Data:* b Kearny, NJ, Feb 22, 27; m 50, Ethel Radli; c Brian M, Mary T & Christine A. *Educ:* Upsala Col, AB, 50; Columbia Univ, PhD(geol), 55. *Honors & Awards:* Horton Award, Am Geophys Union, 59; Kirk Bryan Award, Geol Soc Am, 79; David Linton Award, Brit Geomorphol Res Group, 82; G K Warren Prize, US Nat Acad Sci. *Prof Exp:* Geologist, US Geol Surv, 54-67; vpres, Water Eng & Technol, 80-87. *Concurrent Pos:* Vis lectr, Univ Calif, 59-60; prof affil, Colo State Univ, 63; mem nat comt, Int Union Quaternary Res, 63-69; fel, Univ Sydney, 64-65; cor mem comn hillslope evolution & mem comn appl geomorphol, Int Geog Union, 65; vis geol scientist, Am Geol Inst, 66; vis scientist, Polish Acad Sci, 69; distinguished lectr, Univ Tex, 70; vis prof, Univ de los Andes, Venezuela, 72, Econ Geol Res Univ, Univ Witwatersrand, SAfrica, 75, Univ Canterbury, NZ, 84 & Univ Tsukuba, Japan, 85, Taiwan Nat Normal Univ, 88, Univ New South Wales, Australia, 88; prin investr res projs, Nat Sci Found, US Army Res Off, Nat Park Serv, Off Water Res & Technol, US Geol Surv & Colo Agr Exp Sta; co-investr, US Army CEngr, Bur Sports Fisheries & Wildlife & Fed Hwy Admin; consult, Reg Transp Dist, Denver, Cameron Eng Co, Atlantic Richfield Oil Co & DDI Explor, Paris, Integral Ltd, Medellin, Manawatu bd, NZ, corp engrs, Ohio River Dist, Vicksburg Dist & Sacramento Dist, Rock Island DIst, US Dept Justice, Can Int Develop Agency, Atty Gen, States Colo, Wyo, Mont, Idaho. *Mem:* AAAS; Geol Soc Am; Am Geophys Union; Am Soc Civil Engrs; Am Quaternary Asn. *Res:* Sedimentology, morphology and dynamics of rivers; experimental geomorphology. *Mailing Add:* Dept Earth Resources Colo State Univ Ft Collins CO 80523. *Fax:* 970-223-5578

SCHUNDER, MARY COTHRAN, GROSS ANATOMY, CYTOHISTOCHEMISTRY. *Current Pos:* ASSOC PROF, HEALTH SCI CTR, UNIV N TEX, 72-, ASSOC GRAD FAC MEM BASIC HEALTH SCI, 78- *Personal Data:* b Tulsa, Okla, Sept 28, 31; m 56; c 3. *Educ:* Tex Christian Univ, BA, 53, MA, 70; Baylor Univ, PhD(anat), 76. *Prof Exp:* Staff microbiol, Univ Dallas, 64-69; instr biol, Tex Christian Univ, 69-70; assoc prof anat & chmn dept, Tex Col Osteop Med, 70-75. *Concurrent Pos:* HEW training grant, Bur Health Prof, 72-75; consult anat, Nat Bd Examrs Osteop Physicians & Surgeons, 75-85; rep, Anat Bd State Tex, 70-82, vpres, 78. *Mem:* Sigma Xi. *Res:* Calcium metabolism; histochemical localization of calcium and lipid in calcified tissue and gut. *Mailing Add:* 4627 Washburn Ave Ft Worth TX 76107-3730

SCHUNK, ROBERT WALTER, PLASMA TRANSPORT, NUMERICAL SIMULATIONS. *Current Pos:* assoc prof, 76-79, PROF PHYSICS, UTAH STATE UNIV, 79-; DIR, CTR ATMOSPHERIC & SPACE SCI, 83- *Personal Data:* b New York, NY. *Educ:* NY Univ, BS, 65; Yale Univ, PhD(phys fluids), 70. *Honors & Awards:* Governor's, Medal Sci & Technol, Utah, 88. *Prof Exp:* Inst Sci & Technol fel space physics, Univ Mich, 70-71; res assoc geophys, Yale Univ, 71-73; res assoc space physics, Univ Calif, San Diego, 73-76. *Concurrent Pos:* Assoc ed, J Geophys Res, 77-80; mem, Comt Solar Terrestrial Res, Geophys Res Bd, Nat Acad Sci, 79-85; mem, Nat Ctr Atmospheric Res Comput Divisions Adv Panel, 80-83; prin investr, Solar Terrestrial Theory Prog, 80- *Mem:* Am Geophys Union; AAAS. *Res:* Planetary atmospheres, ionospheres and magnetospheres; solar wind; plasma physics; numerical analysis. *Mailing Add:* Dept Physics Utah State Univ Logan UT 84322-0001. *Fax:* 435-797-2992; *E-Mail:* s-hunk@cc.usu.edu

SCHUNN, ROBERT ALLEN, INORGANIC CHEMISTRY. *Current Pos:* Res chemist, 63-81, training supv, 81-83, PERSONNEL ADMINR, CENT RES DEPT, E I DU PONT DE NEMOURS & CO, INC, 83- *Personal Data:* b Martins Ferry, Ohio, July 15, 36; m 59; c 3. *Educ:* Univ Ohio, BS, 58; Mass Inst Technol, PhD(inorg chem), 63. *Mem:* Am Chem Soc. *Res:* Preparative inorganic chemistry, especially of transition metal compounds; heterogeneous catalysis; organometallic chemistry. *Mailing Add:* 432 East Ave Point Pleasant Beach NJ 08742

SCHUPF, NICOLE, PHYSIOLOGICAL PSYCHOLOGY. *Current Pos:* PROF, NY STATE INST BASIC RES, 88- *Personal Data:* b New York, NY, Jan 20, 43; m 68; c 1. *Educ:* Bryn Mawr Col, BA, 64; NY Univ, PhD(psychol), 70. *Hon Degrees:* MPH, Univ Calif, Berkeley, 84. *Prof Exp:* Res assoc, Rockefeller Univ, 69-71; instr neurol, Med Sch, NY Univ, 74-77; from asst prof to assoc prof psychol, Manhattanville Col, 77-89. *Concurrent Pos:* Adj asst prof neurol, Med Sch, NY Univ, 77-78; res assoc, Siergievsky Ctr, Columbia Univ, 84- *Mem:* AAAS; NY Acad Sci. *Res:* Neuroimmunology; neuroepidemiology. *Mailing Add:* 275 Central Park W New York NY 10024

SCHUPP, GUY, MOSBAUER SCATTERING. *Current Pos:* from asst prof to assoc prof, 64-89, PROF PHYSICS, UNIV MO, COLUMBIA, 89- *Personal Data:* b Blackwater, Mo, Oct 20, 33; m 62; c 2. *Educ:* Mo Valley Col, BS, 54; Iowa State Univ, PhD(physics), 62. *Prof Exp:* Res scientist, Indust Reactor Labs, US Rubber Co, NJ, 62-64 & Res Ctr, 64. *Concurrent Pos:* Sabbatical, Argonne Nat Lab, 71-72; bd trustee, Missouri Valley Col, 88- *Mem:* AAAS; Am Phys Soc; Am Asn Physics Teachers. *Res:* Mossbauer scattering; nuclear spectroscopy; atomic excitation and ionization phenomena. *Mailing Add:* 208 W Ridgely Rd Columbia MO 65203-3524

SCHUPP, PAUL EUGENE, MATHEMATICS. *Current Pos:* from asst prof to assoc prof, 67-75, assoc mem, Ctr Advan Study, 73-74, PROF MATH, UNIV ILL, URBANA, 75- *Personal Data:* b Cleveland, Ohio, Mar 12, 37; m 66. *Educ:* Case Western Reserve Univ, BA, 59; Univ Mich, Ann Arbor, MA, 61, PhD(math), 66. *Prof Exp:* Asst prof math, Univ Wis-Madison, 66-67. *Concurrent Pos:* Vis mem, Courant Inst, 69-70; John Simon Guggenheim mem fel, 77-78. *Mem:* Am Math Soc; London Math Soc. *Res:* Theory of infinite groups and decision problems in algebraic systems; automate theory. *Mailing Add:* 2007 Vawter St Urbana IL 61801

SCHUR, PETER HENRY, INTERNAL MEDICINE, RHEUMATOLOGY & IMMUNOLOGY. *Current Pos:* Assoc, 67-69, from asst prof to assoc prof, 69-77, PROF MED, HARVARD MED SCH, 78- *Personal Data:* b Vienna, Austria, May 9, 33; US citizen; div; c Diana & Erica. *Educ:* Yale Univ, BS, 55; Harvard Univ, MD, 58. *Honors & Awards:* H Aladien Award, Lupus Found, 96. *Concurrent Pos:* Helen Hay Whitney fel, Rockefeller Univ, 64-67; NIH grant, 67-; hon prof, Univ del Norte, Columbia, 88; ed, Arthritis & Rheumatism, 90-95. *Mem:* Am Soc Clin Invest; Am Asn Immunol; Am Col Physicians; Am Col Rheumatism; Am Fedn Clin Res; Asn Am Phys. *Res:* Rheumatology; systemic lupus; immunology; genetics. *Mailing Add:* Brigham & Women's Hosp 75 Francis St Boston MA 02115

SCHURIG, JOHN EBERHARD, LICENSING. *Current Pos:* assoc dir exp therapeut, 82-87 & anticancer res, 87-91, ASSOC DIR LICENSING, BRISTOL-MYERS SQUIBB PHARM GROUP, 91- *Personal Data:* b Morristown, Tenn, Mar 16, 45. *Educ:* Univ Tenn, BS, 67, BS, 69, PhD(pharmacol), 73. *Prof Exp:* Sr res scientist pharmacol, Bristol Labs, 73-78 & antitumor biol, 78-90, asst dir, 80-82. *Mem:* Am Asn Cancer Res; Am Soc Pharmacol & Exp Therapeut; Licensing Exec Soc. *Res:* Anticancer therapies. *Mailing Add:* BTG USA Inc 2200 Renaissance Blvd Gulph Mills PA 19406. *Fax:* 203-284-7503

SCHURLE, ARLO WILLARD, MATHEMATICS. *Current Pos:* PROF STATIST, UNIV GUAM, 91- *Personal Data:* b Clay Center, Kans, Oct 30, 43; m 63. *Educ:* Univ Kans, BA, 64, MA, 66, PhD(math, topology), 67. *Prof Exp:* Asst prof math, Ind Univ, Bloomington, 67-71; assoc prof math, Univ NC, Charlotte, 71-78; Fulbright prof math, Univ Liberia, 78-80; assoc prof math, Univ NC, Charlotte, 80-91. *Mem:* Math Asn Am; Am Math Soc. *Res:* Geometric topology, including decompositions of three-space; compactifications and dimension theory. *Mailing Add:* Div Math Sci Univ Guam UOG Sta Mangilao GU 96923

SCHURMAN, GLENN AUGUST, AERODYNAMICS, GEOPHYSICS. *Current Pos:* RETIRED. *Personal Data:* b La Center, Wash, Sept 6, 22; m 44, Patricia Harper; c Valerie, Christy & Lee. *Educ:* State Col Wash, BS, 44; Calif Inst Technol, MS, 47, PhD(mech eng), 50. *Prof Exp:* Res engr, Am Air Comt Aeronaut, 44-47; from res engr to sr res engr, Calif Res Corp, 50-60, mgr producing res, 60-63, sr staff engr, 63-65, dist supt, Calif Co Div, Chevron Oil Co, 65-69; div prod supt, Standard Oil Co Tex, 69-71; asst gen mgr prod, Calco Div, Chevron Corp, 71-74, vpres & gen mgr prod, Denver, 74-75, managing dir, Chevron Petrol UK Ltd, 75-82, vpres prod, Chevron Corp, 82-87. *Concurrent Pos:* Distinguished lectr, Soc Petrol Engrs, 78; dir, Marine Spill Response Corp. *Mem:* Nat Acad Eng; Soc Petrol Engrs; Am Soc Mech Engrs. *Res:* Auto-ignition of gases near heated surface; aerodynamics and fluid dynamics of gas turbines; oil production and geophysics. *Mailing Add:* 840 Powell St Apt 302 San Francisco CA 94108

SCHURMEIER, HARRIS MCINTOSH, AERONAUTICAL ENGINEERING. *Current Pos:* AEROSPACE CONSULT, 85- *Personal Data:* b St Paul, Minn, July 4, 24; m 49, Bettye Jo; c Harris Jr, Sydne, Dennis & Alan. *Educ:* Calif Inst Technol, BS, 45, MS, 48, AeroE, 49. *Honors & Awards:* Medal for Except Sci Achievement, NASA, 65, Exceptional Serv Medal, 69, Distinguished Serv Medal, 81; Astronaut Engr Award, Nat Space Club, 65 & 81; Von Karman Lectr, Am Inst Aeronaut & Astronaut, 75. *Prof Exp:* Sr res engr, Jet Propulsion Lab, Calif Inst Technol, 49-53, chief, Wind Tunnel Sect, 53-56, chief, Aerodyn Div, 56-58, dep prog mgr, Sergeant Missile, 58-59, mgr, Systs Div, 59-62, proj mgr, Ranger, 62-65, Mariner Mars 1969, 65-69, Voyager, 70-76, dep asst lab dir, Flight Projs, 69-76, asst lab dir, Energy & Technol Appln, 76-81, assoc dir, Defense & Civil Progs, 81-85. *Concurrent Pos:* Chmn, Supersonic Tunnel Asn, 54-56; mem, Res Steering Comt on Manned Space Flight, NASA, 59, Res Adv Comt Missile & Space Vehicle Aerodyn, 60-62, Comt Proj Mgt, 80-81; chmn, W M Keck Observ Proj Rev Bd, 86-95, Galileo Proj Standing Rev Bd, 86-95, Soaring Soc Am Tech Rev Bd, 89-94. *Mem:* Nat Acad Eng; Supersonic Tunnel Asn; fel Am Inst Aeronaut & Astronaut; AAAS; Sigma Xi. *Res:* Space exploration. *Mailing Add:* 6552 Indian Hill Way Fallbrook CA 92028. *Fax:* 760-941-6435

SCHURR, AVITAL, NEUROPHYSIOLOGY, NEUROCHEMISTRY. *Current Pos:* from asst prof to assoc prof, Sch Med, Univ Louisville, Ky, 81-92, actg dir res, Dept Anesthesiol, 83-84, dir, Anal Lab, Anesthesia & Crit Care Res Unit, 83-87, PROF ANESTHESIOL, SCH MED, UNIV LOUISVILLE, KY, 92- *Personal Data:* b Jerusalem, Israel, Aug 23, 41; m 65, Maureen McCabe; c Barak, Hila & Ori. *Educ:* Hebrew Univ, Jerusalem, BSc, 67; Tel Aviv Univ, MSc, 70; Ben Gurion Univ, Beer Sheva, PhD(biochem pharmacol), 77. *Prof Exp:* Researcher biochem, Tel Aviv Univ, Israel, 67-70; researcher photosynthesis, Negev Inst Arid Zone Res Beer Sheva, Israel, 70-72; res assoc biomembranes, Ben Gurion Univ, Beer Sheva, Israel, 72-77; neurochemist neuropharmacol, Tex Res Inst Ment Sci, Houston, 77-79; res assoc neurobiol, Med Sch, Univ Tex, 79-81. *Concurrent Pos:* Lectr biochem, Dept Biol, Ben Gurion Univ, Beer Sheva, Israel, 73-77; lectr neuropharmacol, Baylor Col Med Grad Sch, Houston. *Mem:* Soc Neurosci; AAAS; NY Acad Sci; Am Soc Anesthesiologists; Sigma Xi; Int Soc Neurochem. *Res:* Studies of cerebral ischemia using an in vitro model for the better understanding of the consequences of stroke and brain injury; assessment of pharmacological agents for their potential as protectants against cerebral ischemia; studies on brain energy metabolism; mechanisms of epilepsy. *Mailing Add:* Dept Anesthesiol Univ Louisville Sch Med 2301 S Third St Louisville KY 40292-0001. *Fax:* 502-852-6056

SCHURR, GARMOND GAYLORD, RESEARCH ADMINISTRATION. *Current Pos:* CONSULT, 82- *Personal Data:* b Almont, NDak, Sept 7, 18; m 45; c 4. *Educ:* NDak State Univ, BS(chem), 40. *Prof Exp:* Group leader, Paint Res, Sherwin-Williams Co, 46-58, asst dir, 58-66, dir, 66-74, dir, Res Ctr, 74-79, tech advr, 79-82. *Mem:* Am Chem Soc; Am Soc Testing & Mat; Nat Asn Corrosion Eng; Fedn Socs Coatings Technol. *Res:* Applications of polymeric resins in protective coatings; corrosion control by means of protective coatings. *Mailing Add:* 11210 Sycamore Lane 61A Palos Hills IL 60465-2578

SCHURR, JOHN MICHAEL, PHYSICAL CHEMISTRY, MOLECULAR BIOPHYSICS. *Current Pos:* from asst prof to assoc prof, 66-78, PROF CHEM, UNIV WASH, 78- *Personal Data:* b Pittsfield, Mass, Nov 10, 37; m 58, Karen Martin; c Kerstin S (Longabaugh) & Rebecca S (Hartley). *Educ:* Yale Univ, BS, 59; Univ Calif, Berkeley, PhD(biophys), 64. *Prof Exp:* NIH fel chem, Univ Ore, 64-66. *Concurrent Pos:* Vis scientist, Swiss Fed Water Inst, 74; vis scholar, Kyoto Univ, Japan, 87. *Mem:* Biophys Soc; Am Phys Soc; Am Chem Soc. *Res:* Coherent dynamic light scattering, pulsed laser optical techniques and NMR relaxation; DNA dynamics, including deformational brownian motions; polyelectrolyte phenomena, diffusion, and electrophoresis; energetics of supercoiling. *Mailing Add:* Dept Chem Univ Wash BG-10 Seattle WA 98195

SCHURR, KARL M, ENTOMOLOGY, POLLUTION BIOLOGY. *Current Pos:* from asst prof to assoc prof, 61-95, EMER PROF BIOL, BOWLING GREEN STATE UNIV, 95- *Personal Data:* b Logan Co, Ohio, Feb 28, 32; m 56; c 3. *Educ:* Bowling Green State Univ, BA, 56, MA, 58; Univ Minn, PhD(entom, bot), 61. *Prof Exp:* Res asst, Univ Minn, 58-61. *Concurrent Pos:* Grants, Fed Res, 58-61, NSF, 63-, US Dept HEW, 66-; consult, Ohio State Univ, 63, Greeley & Hansen Co, Ill, 65, Columbus Labs, Battelle Mem Res Inst, 70- & Holmes Co Pub Health Dept & Regional Planning Comn, 71-; res consult marine pollution, Col Law, Univ Toledo & J&S Steel Co; res consult maricult, toxicol & water resources, Auburn Univ; adj prof, Med Col Ohio. *Mem:* Int Asn Advan Earth & Environ Sci (vpres, 77-78); World Maricult Soc; AAAS; Entom Soc Am; Marine Technol Soc; Sigma Xi. *Res:* Invertebrate physiology; water resources; toxicology. *Mailing Add:* PO Box 134 Fisher PA 16225

SCHURRER, AUGUSTA, MATHEMATICS. *Current Pos:* PROF MATH, UNIV NORTHERN IOWA, 50- *Personal Data:* b New York, NY, Oct 11, 25. *Educ:* Hunter Col, AB, 45; Univ Wis, MA, 47, PhD(math), 52. *Prof Exp:* Computer, Off Sci Res & Develop, 45. *Concurrent Pos:* NSF fac fel, Univ Mich, 57-58; mem panel suppl pub, Sch Math Study Group, 61-65. *Mem:* Am Math Soc; Math Asn Am. *Res:* Mathematical analysis; zeros of polynomials; mathematics education; teacher education. *Mailing Add:* 1224 W 20th St Cedar Falls IA 50613-3511

SCHUSSEL, LEONARD J, WATER PURIFICATION, SOLID WASTE. *Current Pos:* LAB SUPVR, GLENBROOK NICKEL CO, 95- *Personal Data:* b New York, NY, Feb 15, 58; m 86, Louise Ackerman; c Kirby W & Daniel K. *Educ:* Washington & Jefferson Col, BA, 80; Ore State Univ, PhD(inorg chem), 88. *Prof Exp:* Postdoctoral assoc, Brandeis Univ, 87-89; res chemist, Umpqua Res Co, 90-95. *Concurrent Pos:* Prof intro chem, Umpqua Community Col, 94. *Mem:* Am Chem Soc. *Res:* Water purification; analytical operations for a nickel smelter and mine operation. *Mailing Add:* PO Box 85 Riddle OR 97469. *E-Mail:* lenny.schussel@cominco.com

SCHUSTEK, GEORGE W(ILLIAM), JR, CHEMICAL ENGINEERING. *Current Pos:* RETIRED. *Personal Data:* b Oak Park, Ill, May 10, 15; m 44; c 3. *Educ:* Univ Chicago, BS, 37, MBA, 51. *Prof Exp:* Res chemist, US Gypsum Co, 37-42; chem engr, Standard Oil Co (Ind), 46-48, group leader, 48-53, sect leader, Res Dept, 54-62, res supvr res & develop, Am Oil Co, 62-69, sr res scientist, 69-74. *Mem:* Am Chem Soc; Am Inst Chem Engrs. *Res:* Petroleum processes. *Mailing Add:* 1080 Prairieview Dr West Des Moines IA 50265-7207

SCHUSTER, CHARLES ROBERTS, JR, PSYCHOLOGY, PHARMACOLOGY. *Current Pos:* PROF PSYCHIAT, WAYNE STATE UNIV, 95- *Personal Data:* b Woodbury, NJ, Jan 24, 30; m 72, Chris-Ellyn Johanson; c Alyson, Charles, Lyzbett & Rebecca. *Educ:* Gettysburg Col, AB, 51; Univ NMex, MS, 53; Univ Md, PhD(psychol), 62. *Honors & Awards:* Nathan B Eddy Award, Col Probs Drug Dependence; Distinguished Sci Award, Am Psychol Asn. *Prof Exp:* Asst instr endocrinol & res biologist, Temple Med Sch, 53-55; jr scientist, Smith, Kline & Fr Labs, 55-57; res assoc psychopharmacol, Univ Md, 61-63; from asst prof to assoc prof pharmacol & psychol, Med Sch, Univ Mich, Ann Arbor, 63-69, lectr psychol, 66-68; assoc prof pharmacol & psychiat, Univ Chicago, 69-72; prof psychiat, pharmacol & physiol sci, 72-91; dir, Nat Inst Drug Abuse, 86-92; sr res scientist, 92-95. *Concurrent Pos:* Ed, Am Psychol Asn J: Exp & Clin Psychopharmacol; assoc dir, Ill Drug Abuse Rehab Prog, 68-72; actg chmn, Dept Psychiat, Univ Chicago, 85-86. *Mem:* Inst Med-Nat Acad Sci; fel Am Psychol Asn; Am Soc Pharmacol; fel Am Col Neuropsychopharmacol; fel AAAS. *Res:* Psychological and physiological dependence on drugs; role of interoceptive processes in the control of behavior; author or co-author of over 150 publications. *Mailing Add:* 2751 E Jefferson PO Box 5180 Detroit MI 48207. *Fax:* 313-993-1372

SCHUSTER, DAVID ISRAEL, ORGANIC CHEMISTRY, CHEMICAL DYNAMICS. *Current Pos:* from asst prof to assoc prof, 61-69, dir grad studies, Dept Chem, 74-78, PROF CHEM, NY UNIV, 69- *Personal Data:* b Brooklyn, NY, Aug 13, 35; m 62; c 1. *Educ:* Columbia Univ, BA, 56; Calif Inst Technol, PhD(chem, physics), 61. *Prof Exp:* Fel org photochem, Univ Wis, 60-61. *Concurrent Pos:* Alfred P Sloan fel, 67-69; vis fel, Royal Inst Gt Brit, 68-69; NSF sci fac fel, 75-76; vis prof, Yale Univ, 75-76. *Mem:* Am Soc Photobiol; Sigma Xi; Am Chem Soc; Inter-Am Photochem Soc; AAAS; Royal Inst Chem. *Res:* Mechanistic organic photochemistry; organic reaction mechanisms; spectroscopy and magnetic resonance; free radical chemistry; flash photolysis; biochemistry of Schizophrenia; mechanism of action of anti-psychotic drugs; characterization of dopamine receptors in the brain; photobiological processes; synthesis of prostaglandins. *Mailing Add:* Dept Chem NY Univ New York NY 10003

SCHUSTER, DAVID J, PEST MANAGEMENT & BIOLOGICAL CONTROL, HOST PLANT RESISTANCE. *Current Pos:* from asst prof to assoc prof, 81-85, PROF ENTOM, GULF COAST RES & EDUC CTR, UNIV FLA, BRADENTON, 85- *Personal Data:* b Memphis, Tenn, Aug 29, 47; m 71, Jan M Dreiling; c Brian, Scott & Amy. *Educ:* Kans State Univ, BS, MS, 70; Okla State Univ, PhD(entom), 73. *Honors & Awards:* Coun Mem Tomato Res Award, 81, 84, 90. *Prof Exp:* Res assoc entom, Okla State Univ, 73-75. *Mem:* Entom Soc Am. *Res:* Pest management of insect and mite pests of vegetables; interactions of insecticides, biological control and host plant resistance are emphasized. *Mailing Add:* Gulf Coast Res & Educ Ctr 5007 60th St E Bradenton FL 34203. *Fax:* 941-751-7639; *E-Mail:* djs@gnv.ifas.ufl.edu

SCHUSTER, DAVID MARTIN, COMPUTATIONAL AERODYNAMICS, AEROELASTICITY. *Current Pos:* STAFF ENGR, LOCKHEED MARTIN ENG & SCI, 91- *Personal Data:* b Cincinnati, Ohio, Dec 8, 57; m 85, Lee Henderson. *Educ:* Univ Cincinnati, BS, 81; Ga Inst Technol, MS, 84, PhD(aerospace eng), 92. *Prof Exp:* Scientist, Lockheed-Ga Co, 77-89; res engr II, Ga Tech Res Inst, 89-91. *Mem:* Assoc fel Am Inst Aeronaut & Astronaut; Soc Automotive Engrs. *Res:* Computational fluid dynamics methods to problems in aerodynamics, aeroelasticity and flight controls; geometry modeling, grid generation, computer graphics and development of numerical algorithms. *Mailing Add:* Lockheed Martin Eng & Sci Langley Res Ctr NASA MS371 Hampton VA 23681-0001. *E-Mail:* dim.schuster@larc.nasa.gov

SCHUSTER, EUGENE F, NONPARAMETRIC STATISTICS, STATISTICAL COMPUTING. *Current Pos:* from asst prof to assoc prof math, 70-76, chmn dept, 79-81 & 83-86, PROF MATH, UNIV TEX, EL PASO, 76- *Personal Data:* b Tintah, Minn, June 6, 41; m 63; c 6. *Educ:* St John's Univ, BA, 63; Univ Ariz, MA, 65, PhD(math statist), 68. *Prof Exp:* Instr math, Univ Ariz, 68; sr analyst opers res, US Army Engr's Strategic Studies Group, 68-70. *Concurrent Pos:* Vis assoc prof, Univ Ariz, 74-75, statist consult, hydrol dept, 75; statist consult, US Army Sci Serv, 81-83. *Mem:* Inst Math Statist; Math Asn Am; Am Statist Asn. *Res:* Large sample theory; nonparametric estimation of density, distribution and regression functions; statistical computing and stochastic simulation. *Mailing Add:* Dept Math Sci Univ Tex El Paso TX 79922-0514

SCHUSTER, FREDERICK LEE, PROTOZOOLOGY, MICROBIOLOGY. *Current Pos:* from assoc prof to assoc prof, 66-74, PROF BIOL, BROOKLYN COL, 74- *Personal Data:* b Brooklyn, NY, Jan 23, 34; m 60, Jean Glickman; c Debbie & Michael. *Educ:* Brooklyn Col, BS, 56; Univ Calif, Berkeley, MA, 58, PhD(protozoan ultrastruct), 62. *Prof Exp:* Res specialist electron micros, Langley Porter Neuropsychiat Inst, 62-63; res assoc biol, Argonne Nat Lab, 63-66. *Mem:* Soc Protozool; Am Soc Cell Biol; Am Soc Microbiol. *Res:* Pathogenic free-living Protozoa; chemotaxis; morphogenesis of Protozoa. *Mailing Add:* Dept Biol Brooklyn Col Brooklyn NY 11210. *E-Mail:* fscbc@cunyvm.cuny.edu

SCHUSTER, GARY BENJAMIN, CHEMISTRY. *Current Pos:* DEAN & PROF CHEM, GA INST TECHNOL, 94- *Personal Data:* b New York, NY, Aug 6, 46; m 68, Anita Rodire; c Eric & Andy. *Educ:* Clarkson Col, BS, 68; Univ Rochester, PhD(chem), 71. *Honors & Awards:* Arthur C Cope Scholar Award, Am Chem Soc, 94. *Prof Exp:* Res asst chem, Univ Rochester, 68-71; phys sci asst radiation chem, US Army, 71-73; res assoc chem, Columbia Univ, 73-75; from asst to assoc prof chem, Univ Ill, 75-81, prof chem 81-94 & dept head 90-94. *Concurrent Pos:* Coun, Am Soc Photobiol; assoc ed, Photochem & photobiol; NIH fel, 74-75; Alfred P Sloan fel, 77-79; John Simon Guggenheim fel, 85-86; Flory fel, 90. *Mem:* Am Chem Soc; Am Soc Photobiol; Interam Photochem Soc; Sigma Xi. *Res:* Photochemistry and photobiology; discovery of optical triggers for liquid crystals; exploration of anthroquimore-based photonucleases. *Mailing Add:* Sch of Chem & Biochem Ga Inst Technol Box 3065 Atlanta GA 30332-0400. *Fax:* 404-894-7452; *E-Mail:* gary.schuster@cos.gatech.edu

SCHUSTER, GEORGE SHEAH, MICROBIOLOGY, CELL BIOLOGY. *Current Pos:* PROF MICROBIOL, CELL BIOL & MOLECULAR BIOL, SCH DENT & MED, MED COL GA, 70- *Personal Data:* b Geneva, Ill, Sept 22, 40; m 63; c 1. *Educ:* Wash Univ, AB, 62; Northwestern Univ, DDS & MS, 66; Univ Rochester, PhD(microbiol), 70. *Mem:* AAAS; Tissue Cult Asn; Sigma Xi. *Res:* Viral carcinogenesis; metabolic functions of cells and the effects of virus infection on these; dental caries. *Mailing Add:* Dept Oral Biol Sch Dent Med Col Ga Augusta GA 30912

SCHUSTER, INGEBORG I M, PHYSICAL ORGANIC CHEMISTRY. *Current Pos:* from asst prof to assoc prof, 73-83, PROF CHEM, OGONTZ CAMPUS, PA STATE UNIV, 83- *Personal Data:* b Frankfurt, Ger, Oct 30, 37; US citizen. *Educ:* Univ Pa, BA, 60; Carnegie Inst Technol, MS, 63, PhD(chem), 65. *Prof Exp:* Huff fel org chem, Bryn Mawr Col, 65-67. *Concurrent Pos:* Eloise Gerry fel, Grad Women Sci, 82. *Mem:* Am Chem Soc. *Res:* Nuclear magnetic resonance spectroscopy elucidation of organic structures with emphasis on electronic effects. *Mailing Add:* Dept Chem Pa State Univ 1600 Woodland Rd Abington PA 19001

SCHUSTER, JAMES J(OHN), CIVIL ENGINEERING, TRANSPORTATION. *Current Pos:* From instr to assoc prof, 58-70, PROF CIVIL ENG, VILLANOVA UNIV, 70-, DIR INST TRANSP STUDIES, 65- *Personal Data:* b Pottsville, Pa, Dec 13, 35; m 58; c 3. *Educ:* Villanova Univ, BCE, 57, MCE, 61; Purdue Univ, PhD(civil eng), 64. *Concurrent Pos:* Consult, Northern Calif Transit Demonstration Proj, 65-66; mem origin & destination comt, Hwy Res Bd, Nat Acad Sci-Nat Res Coun, 65- *Mem:* Inst Traffic Engrs; Am Soc Civil Engrs; Am Soc Eng Educ. *Res:* Origin-destination; vehicular trip prediction; modal split analysis; generation; distribution; assignment. *Mailing Add:* Dept Civil & Environ Eng Villanova Univ 139 Folentino Hall Villanova PA 19085-1672

SCHUSTER, JOSEPH L, RANGE MANAGEMENT, ECOLOGY. *Current Pos:* head dept, 72-93, prof, 93-97, EMER PROF RANGE SCI, TEX A&M UNIV, 97- *Personal Data:* b Teague, Tex, May 21, 32; m 57, Sylvia Needham; c David, Stanley, James & Suzanne. *Educ:* Tex A&M Univ, BS, 54, PhD(range mgt), 62; Colo State Univ, MS, 59. *Prof Exp:* Range conservationist, US Soil Conserv Serv, 54-59 & US Forest Serv, 61-64; asst prof range mgt, Tex Tech Univ, 64-69, prof & chmn dept, 69-72. *Concurrent Pos:* Range mgt consult. *Mem:* Fel Soc Range Mgt (pres, 84); Soil Conserv Soc Am; Wildlife Soc. *Res:* Forest overstory-understory relations; research technique development; range improvement practices; wildlife habitat development. *Mailing Add:* Dept Rangeland Ecol & Mgt Tex A&M Univ College Station TX 77843. *Fax:* 409-845-6430; *E-Mail:* jschuster@tamu.edu

SCHUSTER, MICHAEL FRANK, ECONOMIC ENTOMOLOGY, PHYTOPATHOLOGY. *Current Pos:* OWNER, BISTONE AGR CONSULTS. *Personal Data:* b Mexia, Tex, May 29, 29; m 51; c 7. *Educ:* Tex A&M Col, BS, 55, MS, 61; Miss State Univ, PhD(entom), 71. *Prof Exp:* Asst entomologist, Tex Agr Exp Sta, Weslaco, Tex, 55-71; from asst prof to assoc prof entom, Miss Agr & Forest Exp Sta, 71-78; prof, Agr Exp Sta, Tex A&M Univ, 78-89; adj prof environ sci, Univ Tex, Dallas, 82-90. *Concurrent Pos:* Consult entomologist, USAID, Brazil, 67; guest lectr, Biol Control, Trop Sch Agr, Cardinas Tabasco, Mex, 77; collabr, Centro de Investigaciones Agricoles del Gulfo Norte, INIA, Tampico, 78-; explor parasites of Lygusbugs, Egypt, Sudan, Kenya & Rep SAfrica, 81-85. *Res:* Development of insect controls based on natural regulating factors, such as host plant resistance and biological control; resistance in plants is identified, evaluated and utilized; natural enemies are evaluated for effectiveness; development of citlon insect management egg tenis for USA and interiction. *Mailing Add:* RR 2 No 130 Mexia TX 76667

SCHUSTER, ROBERT LEE, GEOLOGY & CIVIL ENGINEERING. *Current Pos:* chief, Eng Geol Br, 74-79, geologist, 79-95, EMER SCIENTIST, US GEOL SURV, 95- *Personal Data:* b Chehalis, Wash, Aug 29, 27; m 55; c 4. *Educ:* State Col Wash, BS, 50; Ohio State Univ, MS, 52; Purdue Univ, MS, 58, PhD(civil eng), 60; Imp Col, London, dipl, 65. *Honors & Awards:* Richard H Jahns Distinguished Lectr, Geol Soc Am-Asn Eng Geol, 90; Distinguished Prac Award, Eng Geol Div, Geol Soc Am, 90; Int Meritorious Serv Award, Japan Landslide Soc, 93. *Prof Exp:* Geologist, Snow, Ice & Permafrost Res Estab, Corps Engrs, US Army, 52-55; instr civil engr & eng geol, Purdue Univ, 56-60; from assoc prof to prof civil eng, Univ Colo, 60-67; prof civil eng & chmn dept, Univ Idaho, 67-74. *Concurrent Pos:* NSF sci fac fel, Imp Col, London, 64-65; NATO sr fel sci, Imp Col, Univ London, 74; chmn, Joint Am Soc Civil Engrs-Geol Soc Am-Asn Eng Geol Comt on Eng Geol, 74-78; chmn eng geol comt, Transp Res Bd, Nat Res Coun-Nat Acad Sci, 77-81; mem exec comt, Geotech Eng Div, Am Soc Civil Engrs,

78-82, chmn, 80-81, US Nat Soc Int Soc Soil Mech & Found Eng, 78-82, chmn, 80-81; mem, Eng Geol Div, Geol Soc Am, 82, chmn, 84-85; mem, Nat Res Coun Bd Geotech Eng, 91-94. *Mem:* Asn Eng Geol; Geol Soc Am; Am Soc Civil Engrs; Geol Soc London; Int Asn Eng Geol. *Res:* Slope stability; soil and rock properties; engineering geology; natural dams. *Mailing Add:* Cent Geol Hazards Team MS 966 Box 25046 Denver CO 80225-0046

SCHUSTER, RUDOLF MATHIAS, BOTANY. *Current Pos:* from assoc prof to prof bot, 57-90, dir herbarium, 64-70, EMER PROF BOT, UNIV MASS, AMHERST, 83- *Personal Data:* b Altmuehldorf, Ger, Apr 8, 21; nat US; m 43, Olga M Schutay; c Erica C (Watson) & Hilde M (McNeil). *Educ:* Cornell Univ, BSc, 45, MSc, 46; Univ Minn, PhD(entom, bot), 48. *Honors & Awards:* Award, Arctic Inst NAm, 60 & 66; Engler Medal, Int Asn Plant Taxonomy, 93. *Prof Exp:* Instr bot, Univ Minn, 48-50; asst prof, Univ Miss, 50-53 & Duke Univ, 53-56; asst prof bot & cur bryophyta, Univ Mich, 56-57. *Concurrent Pos:* NSF grants, 53-72 & 76-84; Guggenheim fel, 55-56 & 67; Fulbright prof, Univ Otago, NZ, 61-62; fel, Field Mus Natural Hist; Nat Geog Soc grant, 95. *Mem:* Am Bryol & Lichenological Soc; Brit Bryol Soc; fel Linnean Soc. *Res:* Systematics, ecology and distribution patterns of North American, Arctic and Antipodal Hepaticae; phylogeny of the Archegoniates; plant geography; taxonomy of Mutillid wasps. *Mailing Add:* Breckenridge Rd Hadley MA 01035

SCHUSTER, RUSTY, RESOURCE MANAGEMENT. *Current Pos:* MGR, LANDS RECREATION & CULT RESOURCES, BUR RECLAMATION, 96- *Personal Data:* b East Chicago, Ind, Nov 30, 53. *Educ:* Bose-Hulman Inst Technol, BSCE, 75. *Mailing Add:* Bureau Reclamation MC D5300 PO Box 25007 Denver CO 80225. *Fax:* 303-236-6763; *E-Mail:* rschuster@do.usbr.gov

SCHUSTER, SANFORD LEE, SOLID STATE PHYSICS. *Current Pos:* From asst prof to assoc prof physics, 68-74, PROF PHYSICS, MANKATO STATE UNIV, 74- *Personal Data:* b Hastings, Nebr, Sept 28, 38; m 67; c 2. *Educ:* Univ Nebr, Lincoln, BS, 60, MS, 63, PhD(physics), 69. *Mem:* Am Phys Soc; Am Asn Physics Teachers; Am Crystallog Asn. *Res:* Thermal diffuse scattering of x-rays by metals. *Mailing Add:* Dept Physics & Astron MSU 205 Mankato State Univ PO Box 8400 Mankato MN 56002-8400

SCHUSTER, SEYMOUR, MATHEMATICS. *Current Pos:* prof math, Carleton Col, 68-92, chmn dept, 73-76, William H Laird prof math & lib arts, 92-94, EMER WILLIAM H LAIRD PROF, CARLETON COL, 94- *Personal Data:* b Bronx, NY, July 31, 26; m 54, Marilyn Weinberg; c Paul S & Eve E. *Educ:* Pa State Univ, BA, 47, PhD(math), 53; Columbia Univ, AM, 48. *Prof Exp:* Asst math, Pa State Univ, 49-51, instr, 51-52; from instr to assoc prof, Polytech Inst Brooklyn, 53-58; assoc prof, Carleton Col, 58-63; res fel, Univ Minn, Minneapolis, 62-63, assoc prof math, 63-68. *Concurrent Pos:* Fel, Univ Toronto, 52-53; vis assoc prof, Univ NC, Chapel Hill, 61; dir col geom proj, Minn Math Ctr, 64-74, Acad Year Inst for Col Teachers, 66-67; NSF sci fac fel, 70-71; vis scholar, Univ Calif, Santa Barbara, 70-71; guest scholar, Western Mich Univ, 76 & vis scholar, Western Mich Univ, 81; vis prof, Western Wash Univ, 83, Univ Ore, 86; guest scholar, Univ Ariz, 90. *Mem:* Am Math Soc; Sigma Xi; Math Asn Am; Asn Women Math; Nat Asn Mathematcians; fel Inst Combinatorics & Applns. *Res:* Graph theory; projective and non-Euclidean geometry; mathematical film production. *Mailing Add:* Carleton Col Northfield MN 55057. *Fax:* 507-646-4312; *E-Mail:* sschuste@mathcs.carleton.edu

SCHUSTER, TODD MERVYN, BIOPHYSICAL CHEMISTRY, PROTEIN STRUCTURE & FUNCTION. *Current Pos:* assoc prof, Univ Conn, 70-75, chmn dept, 77-81, dir, Biotech Ctr, 85-90, PROF BIOL, UNIV CONN, 75- *Personal Data:* b June 27, 33; US citizen; m 58, Nancy Barnes; c Lela. *Educ:* Wayne State Univ, AB, 58, MS, 60; Wash Univ, PhD(molecular biol), 63. *Prof Exp:* USPHS fel, Max Planck Inst, 63-66; asst prof biol, State Univ NY, Buffalo, 66-70; chief scientist, Xenogen, Inc, 81-85. *Concurrent Pos:* Consult, NIH, 71-75 & NSF, 85-86); McCollum-Pratt Prof, Johns Hopkins Univ, 79-80; Panel Biol Instrumentation, NSF, 85-, Panel Biol Facil & Sci & Technol Sci, 86-90; dir, Univ Conn Biotechnol Ctr. *Mem:* AAAS; Am Chem Soc; Am Soc Biol Chem; Biophys Soc; Am Soc Virol. *Res:* Physical biochemistry of proteins and protein-nucleic acid interactions; mechanisms of ligand binding to hemeproteins; self-assembly of viruses. *Mailing Add:* Dept Molecular & Cell Biol PO Box V-125 Univ Conn Storrs CT 06269

SCHUSTER, WILLIAM JOHN, STELLAR PHOTOMETRY, GALACTIC EVOLUTION. *Current Pos:* INVESTR, INST ASTRON, MEX NAT UNIV, 73- *Personal Data:* b Elkhart, Ind, Mar 21, 48; c Pilar Citlali. *Educ:* Case Western Res Univ, BS, 70; Univ Ariz, PhD(astron), 76. *Mem:* Am Astron Soc; Astron Soc Pac; Int Astron Union. *Res:* Photometric astronomy; calibration of photometric indices; chemical compositions, evolutionary status and effective temperatures of stars; subdwarf stars; high velocity stars; evolution of the galaxy. *Mailing Add:* PO Box 439027 San Diego CA 92143-9027. *Fax:* 52-61-744607; *E-Mail:* schuster@bufadora.astrosen.unam.mx

SCHUSTERMAN, RONALD JAY, MARINE BIOLOGY. *Current Pos:* prof, 72-94, EMER PROF PSYCHOL & BIOL, CALIF STATE UNIV, HAYWARD, 94-; MARINE BIOLOGIST, INST MARINE SCI, UNIV CALIF, SANTA CRUZ, 85- *Personal Data:* b New York, NY, Sept 3, 32; div; c 3. *Educ:* Brooklyn Col, BA, 54; Fla State Univ, MA, 58, PhD(psychol), 61. *Prof Exp:* NSF res fel, Yerkes Labs Primate Biol, 61-62; asst prof psychol, San Fernando Valley State Col, 62-63; psychobiologist, Stanford Res Inst, 63-71, mgr animal behav, 69-71. *Concurrent Pos:* Prin investr, NSF grant, Stanford Res Inst, 63-70, Off Naval Res Contract, 67-71 & Calif State Univ, Hayward, 71-84, 85-; lectr psychol & biol, Calif State Univ, Hayward, 64-71, Off Naval Res Grants, Santa Cruz, 85-; adj prof biol & marine sci, Univ Calif Santa Cruz, 87- *Mem:* Fel AAAS; fel Animal Behav Soc; fel Am Psychol Asn; Soc Marine Mammol. *Res:* Animal behavior and communication; animal cognition; biomarine mammals; animal psychophysics; bioacoustics. *Mailing Add:* 1629 Mariposa Dr Palo Alto CA 94306. *E-Mail:* rjschust@cats.ucsc.edu

SCHUT, HERMAN A, CARCINOGENESIS. *Current Pos:* from asst prof to assoc prof, 80-93, PROF PATH, MED COL OHIO, 93-; DIR, BILLSTEIN LIGAND LAB, 80- *Personal Data:* b Steenderen, Neth, Mar 23, 43; m 68; c 2. *Educ:* McGill Univ, PhD(biochem), 74. *Mem:* Am Asn Cancer Res; Soc Toxicol; Am Soc Pharmacol & Exp Therapeut; Environ Mutagen Soc; Int Soc Study Xenobiotics. *Res:* Mechanisms of chemical carcinogenesis. *Mailing Add:* Dept Path Med Col Ohio 300 Arlington Ave Toledo OH 43614. *Fax:* 419-381-3089

SCHUT, ROBERT N, MEDICINAL CHEMISTRY. *Current Pos:* Res chemist, 59-62, group leader org chem, 62-65, sr res chemist, 65-66, sect head, 66-71, dir med chem dept, Miles Res Div, 71-75, DIR CHEM DEPT, CORP RES, MILES LABS, INC, 75- *Personal Data:* b Hudsonville, Mich, Mar 6, 32; m 60; c 4. *Educ:* Hope Col, AB, 54; Mass Inst Technol, PhD(org chem), 58. *Mem:* AAAS; Am Chem Soc; Royal Soc Chem; Sigma Xi; fel Am Inst Chemists. *Res:* Synthesis of compounds of potential therapeutic interest. *Mailing Add:* 67100 Ponderosa Dr Edwardsburg MI 49112-9541

SCHUTT, DALE W, INSTRUMENTATION. *Current Pos:* SR RES ASSOC & SUPVR PHYSICS DEPT, VA POLYTECH INST & STATE UNIV, 77- *Personal Data:* b Oak Park, Ill, Oct 1, 38; m 74, Sharon Akers; c Kevin & Ryan. *Educ:* Univ Ill, BS, 61; Univ Notre Dame, MS, 63. *Prof Exp:* Test equip design engr, Missile Div, Bendix Corp, 61-64; res asst, Univ Notre Dame, 64-66, from asst prof specialist to assoc prof specialist, 66-77. *Concurrent Pos:* Consult, Custom Electron Apparatus, Electro-optics. *Mem:* Inst Elec & Electronics Engrs. *Res:* Instrumentation used in basic research studies in the area of intermediate energy physics including detectors, wire chambers, data acquisition. *Mailing Add:* Dept Physics Va Polytech Inst & State Univ Blacksburg VA 24061

SCHUTT, PAUL FREDERICK, NUCLEAR REACTOR THEORY, RADIATION SAFETY. *Current Pos:* CHMN & CHIEF EXEC OFFICER, NUCLEAR FUEL SERV, 87- *Personal Data:* b Toledo, Ohio, Sept 1, 32; m 56; c 5. *Educ:* Ill Inst Tech, BS, 54; Univ Ariz, MS, 59. *Prof Exp:* Res scientist, Owens Corning Fiberglass, 54-55, US Army, 55-57; physicist, Babcock & Wilcox Co, 59-62, res & develop coordr, 62-66; prin consult, Union Carbide Corp, 66-68; vpres, Nuclear Assurance Corp, 68-74, pres, 74-86, vchmn, 86-87. *Mem:* fel Am Nuclear Soc; Sigma Xi. *Res:* The development of remote, precise measurement systems to characterize spent nuclear fuel; the development of systems for the safe transport of spent nuclear fuel and highly radioactive materials; develop of advanced naval nuclear fuel. *Mailing Add:* 995 Windsor Trail Roswell GA 30076-1345

SCHUTTA, JAMES THOMAS, DEVELOPMENT & TRAINING FOR PROBLEM SOLVING SKILLS, PROBLEM ANALYSIS FOR ELECTRONIC CIRCUITS & MECHANICAL STRUCTURE. *Current Pos:* DIR, QUAL ASSURANCE, PMI FOOD EQUIP GROUP, 88- *Personal Data:* b Milwaukee, Wis, Jan 11, 44; m 81, Mary J Davis; c Jamie L & Michael J. *Educ:* Milwaukee Sch Eng, BSEE, 78, MSEM, 88. *Prof Exp:* Technician, Western Elec, 62-65; engr & mgr, Johnson Controls Inc, 65-88. *Concurrent Pos:* Pres, E Troy Jaycees, 73-74; lectr, Milwaukee Sch Eng, 78-88, adv, Acad Adv Bd, 80-88; Milwaukee chamber, Chamber Com, 84-88; consult, Am Soc Qual Control, 86-87; mem, Comt Fire Testing, Nat Fire Prev Soc; lectr, Sinclair Community Col, 90-, Univ Dayton, 91- *Mem:* Soc Reliability Engrs (pres, 78-79). *Res:* Communication techniques; ability to communicate technical information within a management setting; evaluation of engineering disciplines and academic backgrounds that affect communication and the ability to provide information to make decisions. *Mailing Add:* PO Box 105 Kure Beach NC 28449

SCHUTTE, A(UGUST) H(ENRY), chemical engineering; deceased, see previous edition for last biography

SCHUTTE, WILLIAM CALVIN, PHYSICAL CHEMISTRY. *Current Pos:* ASST PROF CHEM, UNIV SDAK, 70- *Personal Data:* b Ponca, Nebr, May 14, 41; m 62; c 3. *Educ:* Wayne State Col, BAE, 62; Univ SDak, MNS, 67, PhD(phys chem), 72. *Prof Exp:* Teacher, South Sioux City Pub Sch, 62-67. *Concurrent Pos:* Grant gen res fund, Univ SDak, 72-73 & 74-75, Exxon Educ Found, 76-77 & NSF, Acad Yr Proj, 77-78 & 78-79. *Mem:* Am Chem Soc; Sigma Xi. *Res:* Study of metal concentrations in walleye, paddlefish and morels. *Mailing Add:* 2912 Tipperary Lane Idaho Falls ID 83404

SCHUTZ, BERNARD FREDERICK, GENERAL RELATIVITY. *Current Pos:* lectr astrophys, 74-76, reader in gen relativity, 76-84, PROF, UNIV WALES, COL CARDIFF, 84- *Personal Data:* b Paterson, NJ, Aug 11, 46; m 83, Sian Pouncy; c Rachel G, Catherine V & Annalie E. *Educ:* Clarkson Col Technol, BSc, 67; Calif Inst Technol, PhD(physics), 72. *Prof Exp:* NSF fel physics, Univ Cambridge, 71-72; res fel physics, Yale Univ, 72-73, instr, 73-74. *Concurrent Pos:* Vis prof, Washington Univ, St Louis, 83; dir, Max Planck Inst Gravitational Physics, Albert Einstein Inst, Potsdam, Ger, 95- *Mem:* Am Phys Soc; Royal Astron Soc; Sigma Xi; Int Astron Union; Soc Gen Relativity & Gravitation; Inst Physics. *Res:* General relativity and relativistic astrophysics; gravitational wave detection; numerical relativity. *Mailing Add:* Dept Physics & Astron Univ Wales Col Cardiff PO Box 913 Cardiff CF1 3TH Wales. *Fax:* 44-22-874056; *E-Mail:* b.schutz@astro.cf.ac.uk

SCHUTZ, BOB EWALD, ASTRODYNAMICS, REMOTE SENSING. *Current Pos:* Teaching asst, 65-69, from asst prof to assoc prof, 69-81, PROF AEROSPACE ENG, UNIV TEX, AUSTIN, 81- *Personal Data:* b Brownfield, Tex, Sept 6, 40; m 68; c 2. *Educ:* Univ Tex, BS, 63, MS, 66, PhD(aerospace eng), 69. *Mem:* Assoc fel Am Inst Aeronaut & Astronaut; Am Astron Soc; Am Geophys Union. *Res:* Rotation of the earth; estimation theory applied to orbit determination and geodynamics; applications of digital computers; global positioning system. *Mailing Add:* 3009 Hatley Dr Austin TX 78746

SCHUTZ, DONALD FRANK, GEOCHEMISTRY. *Current Pos:* scientist, Isotopes, Inc, 64-65, dir, Proj Pinocchio, 65-66, mgr nuclear opers, 66-70, vpres & gen mgr, Westwood Labs, 70-75 pres, Teledyne Isotopes, 75-93, eng group exec, Teledyne, Inc, 89-92, chief scientist, Teledyne Environ Systs, 91-95, VPRES, TELEDYNE ENVIRON INC, 96-, GEN MGR, TELEDYNE ENVIRON SERV, 93- *Personal Data:* b Orange, Tex, Sept 22, 34; m 58, Beatriz Valera; c Delfino & Celita. *Educ:* Yale Univ, BS, 56, PhD(geol), 64; Rice Univ, MA, 58. *Honors & Awards:* Cong Antarctic Serv Medal. *Prof Exp:* Instr geol, Kinkaid Sch, 58-60, res staff geologist, Yale Univ, 64. *Concurrent Pos:* Pres & Mem bd of dir, Am Asn Radon Scientists & Technologists, 86-89; mem radiation health sect, Am Pub Health Asn; mem environ radiation sect, Health Physics Soc; mem, environ sci div, Am Nuclear Soc. *Mem:* Am Inst Mining, Metall & Petrol Engr, Soc Petrol Engrs; Geol Soc Am; Am Asn Petrol Geologists; Sigma Xi; Geochem Soc; Am Nuclear Soc. *Res:* Radiochemical tests for clandestine nuclear weapons tests; neutron activation analysis of trace elements in sea water; nuclear reactor environmental monitoring, isotope geochemistry, geochromometry, nuclear fuel analysis; radiotracer applications in enhanced oil recovery and refining; synfuel processes; radon surveys. *Mailing Add:* 763 Rolling Hill Dr Rivervale NJ 07675. *Fax:* 201-664-4617; *E-Mail:* donald.schutz@pobox.tbe.com

SCHUTZ, WILFRED M, COMPUTING, STATISTICS. *Current Pos:* dir comput, 85-87, PROF STATIST & HEAD, BIOMET & INFO SYSTS CTR, INST AGR & NATURAL RESOURCES, UNIV NEBR, LINCOLN, 68-, ASST VPRES & DIR, UNIV-WIDE COMPUT, 87- *Personal Data:* b Eustis, Nebr, Jan 26, 30; m 57; c 3. *Educ:* Univ Nebr, BS, 57, MS, 59; NC State Univ, PhD(genetics, statist), 62. *Prof Exp:* Res geneticist, NC State Univ & Agr Res Serv, USDA, 62-68. *Mem:* Am Soc Agron; Biomet Soc; Am Statist Asn. *Res:* Quantitative genetics, statistics and computing. *Mailing Add:* 8231 Henry St Lincoln NE 68506

SCHUTZBACH, JOHN STEPHEN, BIOCHEMISTRY, MICROBIOLOGY. *Current Pos:* from asst prof to assoc prof, 73-88, PROF MICROBIOL, UNIV ALA, BIRMINGHAM, 88- *Personal Data:* b Pittsburgh, Pa, Mar 3, 41; m 62; c 4. *Educ:* Edinboro State Col, BS, 63; Univ Pittsburgh, PhD(microbiol), 69. *Prof Exp:* Technician microbiol, Univ Pittsburgh, 65; res assoc, Med Col Wis, 71-72, asst prof biochem, 72-73. *Concurrent Pos:* Fel, Med Col Wis, 69-71. *Mem:* Am Chem Soc; Am Soc Microbiol; Am Soc Biol Chemists. *Res:* Enzyme mechanisms; biosynthesis of macromolecules, particularly cell membrane constituents of mammalian cells; membrane structure and function. *Mailing Add:* Dept Microbiol 309VH Univ Ala Birmingham UAB Sta Birmingham AL 35294-0019

SCHUTZENHOFER, LUKE A, GAS DYNAMICS, ROTORDYNAMICS. *Current Pos:* Aerospace engr struct design, Marshall Space Flight Ctr, NASA, 60-62, aerospace engr struct vibrations, 62-64, aerospace engr unsteady gas dynamics, 64-81, br chief, Servomech & Systs Stability Br, 81-87, br chief, Computational Fluid Dynamics Br, 87-91, chief, Eng Systs Integration Advan Launch Syst, 91-93, DIV CHIEF, STRUCT ANALYSIS, MARSHALL SPACE FLIGHT CTR, NASA, 93- *Personal Data:* b East St Louis, Ill, Feb 14, 39; m 60; c 5. *Educ:* St Louis Univ, BS, 60; Univ Ala, MSE, 70, PhD, 78. *Mem:* Am Inst Aeronaut & Astronaut. *Res:* Structural vibrations; unsteady fluid and gas dynamics; applications of stochastic process theory; aero-structural interaction phenomena; statistical communication theory; stability theory; rotordynamics; computational fluid dynamics; structure analysis. *Mailing Add:* 1005 Toney Dr SE Huntsville AL 35802

SCHUTZMAN, ELIAS, ELECTRICAL ENGINEERING. *Current Pos:* RETIRED. *Personal Data:* b New York, NY, Jan 16, 25; m 60. *Educ:* NY Univ, BEE, 51, MEE, 53. *Prof Exp:* Res asst, NY Univ, 51-52, instr elec eng, 52-56, eng scientist, 56-59, asst dir, Grad Ctr, 59-66, adj assoc prof elec eng, 58-68; actg prog dir eng systs, Eng Res Ctr, NSF, 68; staff assoc, Elec Sci & Analysis Prog, 68-72, prog dir, elec & commun prog, Eng Div, 72-85, prog dir, Eng Res Ctr, 85-88. *Concurrent Pos:* Asst dir lab electrosci res & sr res scientist, NY Univ, 66-68. *Mem:* Am Soc Eng Educ; fel Inst Elec & Electronics Engrs; Sigma Xi. *Res:* Large scale computer communications networks; electronic circuits; digital systems; optical communication systems. *Mailing Add:* 1924 Chapel Hill Rd Silver Spring MD 20906

SCHUUR, JERRY D, MATHEMATICS. *Current Pos:* from asst prof to assoc prof, 63-76, PROF MATH, MICH STATE UNIV, 76- *Personal Data:* b Kalamazoo, Mich, Jan 14, 36; m 62; c 3. *Educ:* Univ Mich, BS, 57, MA, 58, PhD(math), 63. *Prof Exp:* Engr, Boeing Airplane Co, 57; physicist, Cornell Aeronaut Lab, 59; teaching fel math, Univ Mich, 58-62, lectr, 62. *Concurrent Pos:* Off Naval Res fel & consult, 68-69; fel, Ital Nat Res Coun, 70; vis prof, Univ Florence, 77. *Mem:* Am Math Soc; Math Asn Am. *Res:* Ordinary differential equations. *Mailing Add:* Dept Math Mich State Univ East Lansing MI 48824. *E-Mail:* jschuur@math.msu.edu

SCHUURMANN, FREDERICK JAMES, MATHEMATICS. *Current Pos:* Asst prof, 67-76, ASSOC PROF MATH, MIAMI UNIV, 76- *Personal Data:* b East Grand Rapids, Mich, Jan 16, 40; m 64; c 2. *Educ:* Calvin Col, BS, 62; Mich State Univ, MS, 63, PhD(math), 67. *Concurrent Pos:* Vis res assoc, Aerospace Res Labs, Wright-Patterson AFB, Ohio, 73-74. *Mem:* Asn Comput Mach; Math Asn Am; Soc Indust & Appl Math. *Res:* Numerical analysis, especially computational problems of approximation theory; computational problems of multivariate statistical analysis. *Mailing Add:* Dept Math Miami Univ Oxford OH 45056-1604

SCHUURMANS, DAVID MEINTE, INDUSTRIAL MICROBIOLOGY. *Current Pos:* RETIRED. *Personal Data:* b Ithaca, Mich, Apr 11, 28; m 51; c 2. *Educ:* Albion Col, BA, 49; Mich State Univ, MS, 51, PhD(bact), 54. *Prof Exp:* Jr bacteriologist, City Health Dept, Jackson, Mich, 49-50; bacteriologist, Div Antibiotics & Fermentation, Mich Dept Pub Health, 53-55, chief, Tissue Cult Unit, 57-61, chief, Antibiotic Screening Sect, 65-77 & Fermentation Sect, 68-77, chief, Div Antibiotics & Fermentation, 77-80, dep chief, biol prod prog, 80-84. *Mem:* Fedn Am Scientists. *Res:* Development of antitumor antibiotics; development and production of bacterial vaccines. *Mailing Add:* 2620 Wilson Ave Lansing MI 48906

SCHUURMANS, HENDRIK J L, POLYMER CHEMISTRY. *Current Pos:* PRES, SERVOCHEM INC, 82- *Personal Data:* b Malang, Indonesia, Dec 26, 28; US citizen; m 56, 74; c 5. *Educ:* State Univ Leiden, BS, 52, MS, 55, PhD(phys chem), 56. *Prof Exp:* Sr res chemist, Monsanto Co, Tex, 56-61; suprvr, mgr & sr develop assoc, Mobil Chem Co, NJ & NY, 61-67; tech dir, Stein-Hall & Co, Inc, NY, 67-71; res dir, M&T Chem Inc, NJ, 71-74; dir new ventures, 74-75; dir res & develop, Plastics Div, ICI Am Inc, 75-82. *Concurrent Pos:* Consult, Med Br, Univ Tex, 58-59. *Mem:* Soc Plastics Engrs; Am Chem Soc; Photo Mkt Asn Int; Tech Asn Pulp & Paper Indust. *Res:* Natural and synthetic polymer evaluation; polymer synthesis, production and processing; thermodynamics and kinetics of rate processes; catalysis studies. *Mailing Add:* PO Box 13588 Richmond VA 23225

SCHUYLER, ALFRED ERNEST, BOTANY, TAXONOMY. *Current Pos:* Asst cur, 62-69, chmn bot dept, 62-75, ASSOC CUR, ACAD NATURAL SCI, PHILADELPHIA, 69- *Personal Data:* b Salamanca, NY, July 10, 35; m 68, Patricia Rodgers. *Educ:* Colgate Univ, AB, 57; Univ Mich, AM, 58, PhD(bot), 63. *Honors & Awards:* Sci Award, Nature Conservancy, 91. *Concurrent Pos:* Am Philos Soc traveling grants, 63-64, 66 & 72 & res grant, Franklin Inst, 70; fac appointments, W K Kellogs Biol Sta, 66, Swarthmore Col, 67-70, 78, 82, 91 & 94, Univ Mont Biol Sta, 78, 82 & 85, Rutgers Univ, Camden, 81 & 82-91; ed, Bartonia, 70-; res assoc, Morris Arboretum, Univ Pa, 71-; mem adv comt, Syst Resources Bot, NSF, 72-74; care & maintenance bot col, Acad Natural Sci, NSF, 72-77, assoc ed, Sci Publ, 78-87, ed, 92-; chmn, Jessup-McHenry Comt, Acad Nat Sci, 88- *Mem:* Am Soc Plant Taxon; Bot Soc Am; Am Inst Biol Scientists. *Res:* Taxonomic research in the Cyperaceae; biology of aquatic vascular plants; environmental consulting; flora of the Delaware and flathead River basins; ecology. *Mailing Add:* Acad Nat Sci 1900 Benjamin Franklin Pkwy Philadelphia PA 19103-1195. *Fax:* 215-299-1028

SCHUYTEMA, EUNICE CHAMBERS, MEDICAL MICROBIOLOGY. *Current Pos:* ASST PROF MICROBIOL, RUSH PRESBY ST LUKE'S MED CTR, 71- *Personal Data:* b Rochester, NY, Feb 4, 29; m 54; c 1. *Educ:* Cornell Univ, BS, 51, MS, 54; Univ Iowa, PhD, 56. *Prof Exp:* Res biochemist, Abbott Labs, 54-68; asst prof biol chem, Univ Ill Med Ctr, 68-71; Asst Dean Preclin Curric, Rush Med Col, 79-85. *Mem:* Am Soc Microbiol. *Res:* Nucleic acid chemistry; anaerobes; bacteriophage. *Mailing Add:* 4756 Crayton Ct Naples FL 33940

SCHUYTEN, JOHN, METALLURGY. *Current Pos:* METALL & FOUNDRY CONSULT, 86- *Personal Data:* b Seattle, Wash, July 17, 14; m 39, Inez Goding; c Suzanne (McDowell), Meredith (Escudier) & Johanna (Tonore). *Educ:* Univ Wash, BS, 36; Univ Calif, Berkeley, MS, 51. *Prof Exp:* Jr engr, Shell Chem Co, 36-39, metallurgist, 40-42, metallurgist, Shell Develop Co, 43-49; instr eng chem & metall, Contra Costa Col, 50-54; metallurgist, Volcan Foundry Co, 55-57, vpres, 57-69, pres, 70-86. *Concurrent Pos:* Dir, Iron Castings Soc, 74-78 & 80-82. *Mem:* Fel Am Soc Metals; Iron Castings Soc (secy, 79). *Res:* Hydrogen attack and stress corrosion of metals; development of ductile iron and alloys for heat, abrasion and corrosion resistance. *Mailing Add:* 260 Arlington Ave Berkeley CA 94707

SCHWAB, ANDREAS JOSEF, BIOLOGICAL TRANSPORT, ORGAN PHARMACOKINETICS. *Current Pos:* ASSOC PROF, DEPT MED, FAC MED, MCGILL UNIV, 82-; RES ASSOC, DEPT MED, MONTREAL GEN HOSP, 92-, MED SCIENTIST, 93- *Personal Data:* b Athens, Greece, June 11, 43; Ger & Greek citizen; m 70, Rosemarie Gruber; c 2. *Educ:* Univ Munich, Ger, MSc, 68, PhD(biochem), 73. *Prof Exp:* Sci asst, Inst Physiol Chem Biophys Chem & Cell Biol, Univ Munich, 73-83, res assoc, 83-84, fac mem physiol chem, 83-85, sr res fel, Ger Res Asn, 85-87. *Concurrent Pos:* Prin investr, Ger Res Asn, 73-85, Med Res Coun Can, 91-; vis assoc prof, Div Exp Med, Dept Med, McGill Univ, Montreal Gen Hosp, 85-88; vis prof, Univ Toronto, 88; res comt, Found Notre-Dame, Hosp Notre-Dame, 90 & 91. *Mem:* Microcir Soc; Am Phys Soc; Biomed Eng Soc; Can Diabetes Asn. *Res:* Theoretical and experimental work on anion transport and lactate metabolism in the dog liver in vivo, perfused rat liver. *Mailing Add:* Med Clin McGill Univ Montreal Gen Hosp 1650 Cedar Ave Montreal PQ H3G 1A4 Can. *Fax:* 514-937-6961; *E-Mail:* mchw@musica.mcgill.ca

SCHWAB, ARTHUR WILLIAM, ORGANIC CHEMISTRY. *Current Pos:* RES CHEMIST, NORTHERN REGIONAL RES LAB, USDA, 42- *Personal Data:* b Minneapolis, Minn, July 17, 17; m 45; c 4. *Educ:* Univ Minn, BChem, 41; Bradley Univ, PhD(chem), 52. *Prof Exp:* Chemist, WPoint Mfg Co, 41-42. *Mem:* Am Chem Soc; Am Oil Chem Soc. *Res:* Fundamental research on the chemistry of vegetable oils and modification of these oils for industrial utilization. *Mailing Add:* 2223 W Albany Ave Peoria IL 61604

SCHWAB, BERNARD, CLINICAL MICROBIOLOGY. *Current Pos:* RETIRED. *Personal Data:* b Worcester, Mass, Dec 26, 26; m 57; c 3. *Educ:* Clark Univ, AB, 49; Univ Mass, MS, 51; Nat Registry Microbiol, registered, 64, specialist med microbiol, 69, specialist food microbiol, 75. *Prof Exp:* Bacteriologist, Vt State Bur Labs, 52-62; bacteriologist in-chg lab, City of Kingston, NY, 62-64; chief bacteriologist, Erie Co Lab, Buffalo, 63-68; microbiologist in-chg diag & spec probs sect, USDA, 68-73, sr staff officer microbiol staff, Meat & Poultry Inspection Prog, Sci Serv Staff, Food & Safety Qual Serv, 73-77, sr staff officer microbiol div, 77-80, chief, Med Microbiol Br, Microbiol Div, Sci Food Safety & Inspection Serv, 81-92. *Mem:* Am Soc Microbiol; fel Am Asn Vet Lab Diagnosticians. *Res:* Public health microbiology; meat and poultry microbiology related to consumer protection programs; swine mycobacteriology, staphylococcus enterotin, antibiotics, species determination. *Mailing Add:* 123 Hedgewood Dr Greenbelt MD 20770

SCHWAB, DAVID JOHN, NUMERICAL MODELING, COASTAL OCEANOGRAPHY. *Current Pos:* phys scientist, 75-81, OCEANOGR, GREAT LAKES ENVIRON RES LAB, NAT OCEANIC & ATMOSPHERIC ADMIN, 81- *Personal Data:* b Milwaukee, Wis, July 28, 50. *Educ:* Univ Wis-Milwaukee, BS, 72, MS, 74; Univ Mich, PhD(oceanic sci), 81. *Prof Exp:* Res specialist, Ctr Great Lakes Studies, 75. *Concurrent Pos:* Adj asst prof oceanic sci, Univ Mich, 81-82; vis scientist, VAW/ETH, Zurich, 82; adj asst prof meteorol, Ohio State Univ, 93-94. *Mem:* Am Geophys Union; Am Meteorol Soc; Oceanog Soc; Int Asn Great Lakes Res (treas, 86-89). *Res:* Geophysical fluid dynamics problems in the Great Lakes and other shallow enclosed seas including theoretical, numerical and observational investigations of circulation, thermal structure, seiches, storm surges, windwaves, and air-sea interaction. *Mailing Add:* NOAA/GLERL 2205 Commonwealth Blvd Ann Arbor MI 48105. *Fax:* 313-741-2055; *E-Mail:* schwab@glerl.noaa.gov

SCHWAB, ERNEST ROE, NEUROETHOLOGY, BIOACOUSTICS. *Current Pos:* ASST PROF BIOL, LA SIERRA UNIV, RIVERSIDE, CALIF, 90- *Personal Data:* b Denver, Colo, July 19, 50; m 74. *Educ:* Union Col, Lincoln, Nebr, BA, 76; Andrews Univ, Berrien Springs, Mich, MS, 82; Loma Linda Univ, Calif, PhD(biol), 89. *Prof Exp:* Grad asst physiol, Andrews Univ, Berrien Springs, Mich, 75-78 & Univ Notre Dame, Ind, 78-80; sci teacher health & biol, South Bend Jr Acad Ind, 80-81; grad asst res, Loma Linda Univ, Calif, 81-83, instr biol, Riverside, Calif, 83-90. *Concurrent Pos:* Vis res prof, Andrews Univ, Berrien Springs, Mich, 89. *Mem:* Sigma Xi; Entom Soc Am; NY Acad Sci; Am Soc Zoologists; Int Union Study Social Insects; Am Inst Biol Sci. *Res:* Role of individual nevrons in cricket courtship behavior as well as the modulation of that behavior by juvenile hormone. *Mailing Add:* 423 Marilyn Lane Redlands CA 92373

SCHWAB, FREDERICK CHARLES, POLYMER CHEMISTRY. *Current Pos:* ASSOC CHEMIST POLYMERS, MOBIL CHEM CO, 69- *Personal Data:* b Meadville, Pa, Mar 1, 37; m 61; c 3. *Educ:* Cleveland State Univ, BChE, 61; Union Col, NY, MS, 66; Univ Akron, PhD(polymer sci), 69. *Prof Exp:* Chemist insulation develop, Gen Elec Co, 61-66. *Mem:* Am Chem Soc. *Res:* Synthesis, characterization and mechanical properties of block polymers. *Mailing Add:* 34 Spear St Metuchen NJ 08840-2124

SCHWAB, FREDERICK LYON, SEDIMENTOLOGY. *Current Pos:* From asst prof to assoc prof, 67-75, PROF GEOL, WASHINGTON & LEE UNIV, 75- *Personal Data:* b Brooklyn, NY, Jan 8, 40; m 65, Claudia Aaron; c Kimberly, Bryan, Jeffery & Jonathan. *Educ:* Dartmouth Col, AB, 61; Univ Wis, MS, 63; Harvard Univ, PhD(geol), 68. *Concurrent Pos:* NSF sci fac fel, Univ Edinburgh, 71-72; consult ed, McGraw-Hill Dict Sci & Technol, Encycl Geol Sci & Encycl Energy; NATO sr scientist, Univ Grenoble, 77-78; mem adv bd, Petrol Res Fund, 85-91; ed, Geosynclines; assoc ed, J Sedimentary Res, chmn, Grad Rec Exam-Geol, 93-. *Mem:* Int Asn Sedimentologists; Geol Soc London; Geol Soc Am; Soc Econ Mineralogists & Paleontologists. *Res:* Depositional environments, provenance and sedimentary tectonics of precambrian of the Blue Ridge; geochemistry of sedimentary rocks; sedimentation and tectonic history of the Cordilleran belt; sedimentation trends through time; Eocambrian Appalachian sediments; origin-early evolution Appalachian-Caledonide belt; late precambrian clautic sediments, Utah and Montana. *Mailing Add:* 916 Shenandoah Rd Lexington VA 24450. *Fax:* 540-463-8142; *E-Mail:* schwab.f@wlu.edu

SCHWAB, GARY MICHAEL, COMPUTING SUPPORT FOR RESEARCH DEVELOPMENT & MANUFACTURING. *Current Pos:* sr scientist, 84-90, tech comput mgr, Chem Coatings Div, 90-91, SR SCIENTIST TECH COMPUT, AUTOMOTIVE DIV, SHERWIN-WILLIAMS CO, 91- *Personal Data:* b Chicago, Ill, Dec, 24, 50; m 91, Ann Koerber. *Educ:* Univ Ill, Chicago, BS, 72, MS, 75, PhD(info eng), 79. *Prof Exp:* Res assoc, Argonne Nat Lab, 76-77; eng consult, Sci Applns Int Corp, 77-84. *Mem:* Int Asn Great Lakes Res; Nat Data Gen Users Group. *Res:* Design, implementation, and support of computer information systems to support research, development and manufacturing activities. *Mailing Add:* 316 N Oak Park Ave Oak Park IL 60302

SCHWAB, GLENN O(RVILLE), AGRICULTURAL ENGINEERING. *Current Pos:* prof, 56-84, EMER PROF AGR ENG, OHIO STATE UNIV, 85- *Personal Data:* b Gridley, Kans, Dec 30, 19; m 51, Lois A Saul; c Richard, Lawrence & Mary K. *Educ:* Kans State Univ, BS, 42; Iowa State Univ, MS, 47, PhD(agr eng, soils), 51. *Honors & Awards:* Hancock Brick & Tile Drainage Eng Award, Am Soc Agr Engrs, 68, John Deere Gold Medal, 87. *Prof Exp:* From instr to prof agr eng, Iowa State Univ, 46-56. *Concurrent Pos:* Consult, Off State Exp Sta, USDA, 59-62, Sheladia Assoc, 86-88. *Mem:* AAAS; life fel Am Soc Agr Engrs; Am Soc Eng Educ; AAAS; Soil & Water Conserv Soc. *Res:* Agricultural drainage; irrigation; erosion and flood control; agricultural hydrology. *Mailing Add:* 2637 Summit View Rd C637 Summit View Rd Powell OH 43065

SCHWAB, HELMUT, analytical chemistry, physical chemistry, for more information see previous edition

SCHWAB, JAMES JEROME, ATMOSPHERIC CHEMISTRY. *Current Pos:* RES SCIENTIST, ATM SCI RES CTR, 88- *Personal Data:* b St Paul, Minn, Aug 22, 54. *Educ:* Univ Minn, BS, 77; Harvard Univ, MS & PhD(atmospheric chem), 83. *Mem:* Am Phys Soc. *Mailing Add:* ATM Sci Res Ctr 100 Fuller Rd Albany NY 12205

SCHWAB, JOHN HARRIS, BACTERIOLOGY, IMMUNOLOGY. *Current Pos:* from instr to assoc prof, 53-67, PROF BACT & IMMUNOL, MED SCH, UNIV NC, CHAPEL HILL, 67- *Personal Data:* b Minn, Nov 20, 27; m 51; c 4. *Educ:* Univ Minn, BA, 49, MS, 50, PhD(bact), 53. *Prof Exp:* Asst bact, Univ Minn, 49-53. *Concurrent Pos:* NIH fel, Lister Inst, London, Eng, 60-61; mem, Med Res Coun Rheumatism Res Unit, Taplow, Eng, 68-69; Josiah Macy, Jr Found fac scholar, Radiobiol Inst, Rijswijk, Neth, 75-76; Fogarty Int fel exp immunother Inst Pasteur, Paris, 85-86. *Mem:* AAAS; Am Soc Microbiol; Am Asn Immunol. *Res:* Bacterial immunosuppressants; microbial factors in chronic inflammatory diseases; toxicity of bacterial cell walls; experimental models of rheumatic carditis and rheumatoid arthritis. *Mailing Add:* Dept Microbiol & Immunol Sch Med Univ NC CB 7290 635-A FLOB Chapel Hill NC 27599-7290. *Fax:* 919-962-8103

SCHWAB, JOHN J, PSYCHIATRY, PSYCHOSOMATIC MEDICINE. *Current Pos:* chmn & prof psychiat & behav sci, 73-91, prof, 91-93, EMER PROF PSYCHIAT, SCH MED, UNIV LOUISVILLE, 93- *Personal Data:* b Cumberland, MD, Feb 10, 23; m 45, Ruby Baxter; c Mary (Stone). *Educ:* Univ Ky, BS, 46; Univ Louisville, MD, 46; Univ Ill, MS, 49; Am Bd Internal Med, dipl, 55; Am Bd Psychiat & Neurol, dipl, 64. *Honors & Awards:* Laughlin Award, Am Soc Physician Analysts. *Prof Exp:* From asst resident to resident med, Louis Gen Hosp, Ky, 49-50; internist & psychosomaticist, Holzer Clin, Gallipolis, Ohio, 54-59; resident psychiat, Col Med, Univ Fla, 59-61, from instr to asst prof, 62-65, assoc prof, 65-67, prof psychiat & med, 65-74, chief psychosom consult serv, 61-64, dir consult-liaison prog, 64-67, dir residency prog, 66-71. *Concurrent Pos:* Med fel, Col Med, Univ Ill, 48-49; fel psychosom med, Duke Univ, 51-52; NIMH career teacher award, 62-64; internist, Yokohama Army Hosp, Japan, 52-54; state trustee, Ment Health Fedn Ohio, 58-61; proj dir res grant, 65-68; prin investr, NIMH Res Grant, 69-73; chmn epidemiol studies rev comt, Ctr Epidemiol Studies, NIMH, 73-75; chmn coun res & develop, Am Psychiat Asn, 74-75; mem bd regents, Am Col Psychiat, 79-81 & bd dirs, Group Advan Psychiat, 85-87; mem, Psychiatrists for Better Psychiat, 91-, pres, 92- *Mem:* Fel Acad Psychosom Med (pres, 70-71); fel Am Asn Social Psychiat (pres, 71-73); AMA; fel Am Psychiat Asn; fel Am Col Psychiat; Group Advan Psychiat. *Res:* Applicability, both theoretical and practical, of psychiatric concepts to general medicine; establishing guidelines for the identification and management of medical patients whose illnesses are complicated by emotional distress; sociocultural aspects of mental illness; psychiatric epidemiology; risk for depression in the family; epidemilogy of depression; family violence. *Mailing Add:* Dept Psychiat & Behav Sci Sch Med Univ Louisville Louisville KY 40292-0001. *Fax:* 502-852-1115

SCHWAB, LINDA S, MEDICINAL CHEMISTRY. *Current Pos:* lectr, 83-86, from asst prof to assoc prof, 86-95, PROF, DEPT CHEM, WELLS COL, AURORA, NY, 95- *Personal Data:* b St Louis, Mo, Oct 25, 51. *Educ:* Wells Col, BA, 73; Univ Rochester, MS, 75, PhD(chem), 78. *Prof Exp:* Fel, Ctr Brain Res, Sch Med, Univ Rochester, 77-78, assoc neurochem, 78-82. *Concurrent Pos:* Med chem & org chem div, Am Chem Soc. *Mem:* Am Chem Soc; Affil mem, Int Union Pure Appl Chem. *Res:* Chemistry of heterocycles; natural products. *Mailing Add:* Dept Biol & Chem Sci Wells Col Aurora NY 13026

SCHWAB, MICHAEL, MATERIALS SCIENCE. *Current Pos:* PHYSICIST MAT SCI, LAWRENCE LIVERMORE LAB, 69- *Personal Data:* b New York, NY, Aug 9, 39; m 68; c 2. *Educ:* Calif Inst Technol, BS, 61; Univ Calif, Berkeley, PhD(physics), 68. *Prof Exp:* Physicist, Lawrence Berkeley Lab, 68-69. *Mem:* Am Phys Soc; AAAS. *Res:* Spectroscopy; nuclear and electron magnetic resonance; materials science; radiation damage; metallurgy. *Mailing Add:* 6215 Harwood Ave Oakland CA 94618

SCHWAB, ROBERT G, physiology; deceased, see previous edition for last biography

SCHWAB, WALTER EDWIN, NEUROBIOLOGY. *Current Pos:* asst prof neurobiol, Dept Biol, 77-84, DIR COMP SERV, VA POLYTECH INST & STATE UNIV, 84- *Personal Data:* b Mexico City, Mex, Jan 4, 41; US citizen; m 64. *Educ:* Georgetown Univ, BS, 64; Va State Col, MS, 71; Univ Md, MS,

73, PhD(zool), 74. *Prof Exp:* Fel res assoc, Dept Develop & Cell Biol, Univ Calif, Irvine, 74-77. *Mem:* Am Soc Zoologists; AAAS; Am Inst Biol Sci. *Res:* Physiology and morphology of intracellular communication in primitive animals, primarily coelenterates. *Mailing Add:* Va Regional Med Teaching Hosp Duck Pond Dr Blacksburg VA 24061

SCHWABE, ARTHUR DAVID, MEDICINE, GASTROENTEROLOGY. *Current Pos:* From intern to assoc resident, Univ Calif, Los Angeles, 56-59, chief resident, 60-61, from instr to assoc prof, 61-71, actg chmn dept, 72, vchmn dept, 72-74, prof med, Med Ctr, 71-89, chief gastroenterol, Dept Med, 67-88, EMER PROF MED, UNIV CALIF, LOS ANGELES, 89- *Personal Data:* b Varel, Ger, Feb 1, 24; US citizen; m 46. *Educ:* Univ Calif, Berkeley, AA, 51; Univ Chicago, MD, 56. *Honors & Awards:* S M Mellinkoff Award, 83. *Prof Exp:* Chief gastroenterol, Harbor Gen Hosp, Torrance, Calif, 62-67; consult, Vet Admin Ctr, Los Angeles, 64-96. *Concurrent Pos:* Ambrose & Gladys Bowyer fel med, Univ Calif, Los Angeles, 58 & 59, USPHS fel gastroenterol, 59-60. *Mem:* Fel Am Col Physicians; NY Acad Sci; Western Asn Physicians; Am Gastroenterol Asn. *Res:* Intestinal fat absorption; familial Mediterranean Fever; intestinal neoplasia. *Mailing Add:* 16386 Royal Hills Dr Los Angeles CA 91436

SCHWABE, CALVIN WALTER, EPIDEMIOLOGY, PARASITOLOGY. *Current Pos:* chmn dept, epidemiol & prev med, Sch Vet Med, Univ Calif, Davis, 66-70, assoc dean, 70-71, prof epidemiol, Sch Med, 67-81, prof, Sch Vet Med, 66-91, adj prof, Agr Hist Ctr, 84-91, EMER PROF EPIDEMIOL, UNIV CALIF, DAVIS, 91- *Personal Data:* b Newark, NJ, Mar 15, 27; m 51, Gwendolyn Thompson; c Catherine M & Christopher L. *Educ:* Va Polytech Inst, BS, 48; Univ Hawaii, MS, 50; Auburn Univ, DVM, 54; Harvard Univ, MPH, 55, ScD(trop pub health), 56. *Honors & Awards:* K F Meyer Goldheaded Cane Award. *Prof Exp:* Assoc prof parasitol & chmn dept, Sch Med, Am Univ Beirut, 56-57, assoc prof parasitol & trop health & chmn dept trop health, Schs Pub Health & Med, 57-62, prof parasitol & epidemiol & asst dir, Sch Pub Health, 62-66; prof epidemiol, Sch Med, Univ Calif, San Francisco, 67-91. *Concurrent Pos:* USPHS res fel, Harvard Univ, 54-56 & Cambridge Univ, 72-73; Fulbright fel, Makerere Univ Col, Kenya, 61, Cambridge Univ, 72-73 & Univ Khartoum, 79-80; mem, WHO Secretariat, 64-66, consult, 60-; consult, Pan Am Health Orgn, 61- *Mem:* Am Soc Trop Med & Hyg; Am Soc Parasitol; Am Vet Med Asn. *Res:* Tropical public health and agriculture; veterinary medicine and human health; third world development; history of veterinary medicine; beginnings of biomedical science in ancient Egypt. *Mailing Add:* 849 A St Davis CA 95616. *Fax:* 530-756-8290

SCHWABE, CHRISTIAN, BIOLOGICAL CHEMISTRY. *Current Pos:* assoc prof, 71-76, PROF BIOCHEM, MED UNIV SC, 76- *Personal Data:* b Flensburg, Ger, May 10, 30; US citizen. *Educ:* Univ Hamburg, DDS, 55; Univ Iowa, DDS, 60, MS, 63, PhD, 65. *Prof Exp:* Pvt pract, Ger, 55-56; res asst, Clinton Corn Processing Co, Iowa, 56-57; res asst stomatol, Col Dent, Univ Iowa, 57-60, instr biochem, Col Med, 63-65; instr biol chem, Sch Dent Med, Harvard Univ, 65, assoc, 66-67, asst prof, 67-71. *Concurrent Pos:* NIH career develop award, 66. *Mem:* Sigma Xi; Am Chem Soc; Am Soc Biol Chemists; Endocrine Soc; Int Asn Dent. Res. *Res:* Connective tissue; enzymology; protein chemistry; chemical endocrinology. *Mailing Add:* Biochem & Molec Biol Dept Med Univ SC 171 Ashley Ave Charleston SC 29425-2211. *Fax:* 803-792-4322

SCHWABER, JERROLD, ANTIBODY DEFICIENCY DISEASES, MOLECULAR BASIS OF ANTIBODY DIVERSITY. *Current Pos:* Fel pediat, 74-78, instr pediat, 78-81, ASST PROF PATH, HARVARD MED SCH, 81- *Personal Data:* b Evanston, Ill, May 24, 47. *Educ:* Univ Chicago, BA, 69, PhD(biophys & theoret biol), 74. *Concurrent Pos:* Fel, Children's Hosp, Boston, 74-78, res assoc, 78- *Mem:* Am Asn Immunologists; Am Soc Cell Biol. *Res:* Antibody gene rearrangement and expression, especially the failure of gene rearrangement in antibody deficiency diseases; lymphocyte development and differentiation. *Mailing Add:* Dept Path Allegheny Univ Health Sci Broad & Vine Sts MS 435 Philadelphia PA 19102-1178. *Fax:* 617-738-8993

SCHWAIGHOFER, JOSEPH, engineering mechanics, for more information see previous edition

SCHWALB, MARVIN N, MYCOLOGY, MICROBIOLOGY. *Current Pos:* from instr to assoc prof, 69-78, PROF MICROBIOL, NJ MED SCH, UNIV MED & DENT, NJ, 78- *Personal Data:* b New York, NY, May 23, 41; m 62; c 3. *Educ:* State Univ NY Buffalo, BA, 63, PhD(biol), 67. *Prof Exp:* Asst prof biol, Bridgewater State Col, 68-69. *Concurrent Pos:* Fel, Brandeis Univ, 67-68. *Mem:* Am Soc Microbiol; Mycol Soc Am. *Res:* Biochemical and genetic regulation of development in higher fungi; recombinant DNA genetic systems in higher fungi. *Mailing Add:* Dept Microbiol NJ Med Sch Univ Med & Dent NJ 185 S Orange Ave Newark NJ 07103-2714

SCHWALBE, LARRY ALLEN, SOLID STATE PHYSICS. *Current Pos:* fel, 75-77, MEM STAFF PHYSICS, LOS ALAMOS NAT LAB, 77- *Personal Data:* b Austin, Tex, Feb 3, 45; m 68; c 2. *Educ:* Univ Ill, BS, 68, MS, 69, PhD(physics), 73. *Prof Exp:* Fel physics, Tech Univ Munich, 73-75. *Res:* Theoretical and experimental studies of high explosives and explosively-driven metal systems, behavior of materials under conditions of high pressure and high strain rates. *Mailing Add:* 253 Canada Way Los Alamos NM 87544

SCHWALL, RICHARD JOSEPH, DATABASE MANAGEMENT, APPLIED STATISTICS. *Current Pos:* DATABASE ANALYST, AMGEN, INC, 92- *Personal Data:* b Evanston, Ill, Oct 11, 49. *Educ:* Calif Inst Technol, BS, 71; Northwestern Univ, PhD(analytical chem), 77. *Prof Exp:* Prog mgr, Rockwell Int Environ Monitoring & Serv Ctr, 77-84; prin scientist, ABB Environ Serv, 84-92. *Res:* Fast electrochemical measurements (kinetic and analytical) by FFT techniques; visibility degradation measurements and theory; statistical analysis of pollution data; data configuration management; fugitive emission modelling; speculative metaphysics. *Mailing Add:* 2008 Wheelwright Lane Newbury Park CA 91320. *E-Mail:* rick.schwall@amgen.com

SCHWALL, ROBERT E, PHYSICS. *Current Pos:* RES STAFF MEM, THOMAS J WATSON RES CTR, IBM CORP, 88-, MGR LITHOGRAPHIC OPTICS, 90- *Personal Data:* b Detroit, Mich, May 31, 47. *Educ:* St Mary's Univ Tex, BS, 68; Stanford Univ, PhD(appl physics), 73. *Prof Exp:* Mgr, Intermagnetics Gen Corp, 78-84. *Mem:* Am Phys Soc; Mat Res Soc. *Res:* Superconductivity; low temperature physics; semiconductor packaging; cryogenic electronics. *Mailing Add:* Am Superconductor Corp 2 Technology Dr Westborough MA 01581

SCHWALM, FRITZ EKKEHARDT, ZOOLOGY, DEVELOPMENTAL PHYSIOLOGY. *Current Pos:* assoc prof, 82-87, PROF BIOL, TEX WOMENS UNIV, 87-, CHMN DEPT, 82- *Personal Data:* b Arolsen, Ger, Feb 17, 36; m 62; c 3. *Educ:* Univ Marburg, PhD(zool), 64. *Prof Exp:* Lectr Ger, Folk Univ, Sweden, 59-60; res assoc exp embryol, Univ Marburg, 64-65; Anglo Am Corp SAfrica advan res fel electron micros, Univ Witwatersrand, 66-67; trainee, Univ Va, 68; res assoc embryol, Univ Notre Dame, 68-70; from asst prof to assoc prof biol, Ill State Univ, 70-82, actg chmn, 79-81. *Mem:* AAAS; Soc Develop Biol; Ger Zool Soc; Am Soc Zoologists. *Res:* Ultrastructure and biochemistry of oogenesis and embryogenesis in insects. *Mailing Add:* Dept Biol PO Box 425799 Denton TX 76204-5799

SCHWALM, MIZUHO K, SOLID STATE PHYSICS. *Current Pos:* MEM STAFF, PHYSICS DEPT, UNIV NDAK, 82- *Personal Data:* b Tokyo, Japan, Sept 23, 40; m 77. *Educ:* Tokyo Gakugei Univ, BA, 64; Univ Wyo, MS, 70; Mont State Univ, PhD(physics), 78. *Prof Exp:* Asst instr, Univ Utah, 79-80; asst prof physics, Moorehead State Univ, 81-82. *Mem:* Sigma Xi. *Res:* Methods for studying electronic structure and transport in disordered systems; computation of optical selection rules; modest size electron energy band calculations. *Mailing Add:* Dept Physics Univ NDak Box 7129 Grand Forks ND 58202-7129

SCHWALM, WILLIAM A, NONLINEAR DYNAMICS, FRACTAL LATTICES. *Current Pos:* from asst prof to assoc prof, 80-90, PROF PHYSICS, UNIV NDAK, 90- *Personal Data:* b Portsmouth, NH, March 3, 47; m 77, Mizuhu Kawajiri. *Educ:* Univ NH, BS, 69; Mont State Univ, PhD(physics), 78. *Prof Exp:* Fel physics, Univ Utah, 78-79, instr, 79-80. *Concurrent Pos:* Vis asst prof, Univ Minn, Minneapolis, 83; vis assoc prof, Mont State Univ, 90-91. *Mem:* Am Asn Physics Teachers; Am Phys Soc; Math Asn Am; Sigma Xi. *Res:* Explicit orbits of rational dynamical systems; transport properties in fractals; transport in two-dimensional systems; diffusion in microporous media; lattice green functions. *Mailing Add:* Physics Dept Univ Sta Grand Forks ND 58202-7129

SCHWAN, HERMAN PAUL, BIOPHYSICS, BIOMEDICAL ENGINEERING. *Current Pos:* asst prof physics in med, Univ Pa, 50-60, asst prof phys med, 50-52, chmn biomed electronic eng, 61-73, prof bioeng, Sch Eng, 75-83, assoc prof phys med, 52-57, prof elec eng, Moore Sch Elec Eng & prof elec eng in phys med, Sch Med, 57-83, A F MOORE EMER PROF, SCH MED, UNIV PA, 83- *Personal Data:* b Aachen, Ger, Aug 7, 15; nat US; m 49, Anne M DelBorello; c Barbara, Margaret, Steven, Carol & Cathryn. *Educ:* Univ Frankfurt, PhD(biophys), 40, Dr habil, 46. *Hon Degrees:* DSc, NC, Univ Pa, 86. *Honors & Awards:* Cert of Commendation, Dept HEW, 66 & 72; Inst Elec & Electronics Engrs Awards, 53, 63 & 67; Rajewsky Prize for Biophys, 74; Alexander von Humboldt Award Award, 80; Edison Medal, Inst Elec & Electronics Engrs, 83 & Centennial Medal, 84; d'Arsonval Award, Bioelectromagnetics Soc, 85. *Prof Exp:* Asst, Kaiser Wilhelm Biophys, 37-40, res assoc, 40-45, admin dir, 45-47; res specialist, US Naval Base, Pa, 47-50. *Concurrent Pos:* Asst prof, Univ Frankfurt, 46-55, vis prof, 62; vis MacKay prof, Univ Calif, Berkeley, 56; consult, Gen Elec Co 57-76, US Army & USN, 57-71 & NIH, 61-76; mem nat comt C95, Am Nat Stand Inst, 61- & Nat Acad Sci-Nat Res Coun, 67-73; lectr, Johns Hopkins Univ, 62-66; sci mem, Max Planck Inst Biophys, 62-; mem nat adv coun environ health, Dept HEW, 69-71; vis W W Clyde prof, Univ Utah, Salt Lake, 80; vis prof, Univ Wurzburg, Ger, 86-87. *Mem:* Fel AAAS; Biophys Soc; Biomed Eng Soc; fel Inst Elec & Electronics Engrs; Nat Acad Eng; hon mem Ger Biophys Soc. *Res:* Impedance measurement techniques and electrodes for biological dielectric research; biophysics of non-ionizing radiation; biomedical engineering; electrical and acoustical properties of tissues and cells; electrical properties of biological membranes and biopolymers; electrical engineering. *Mailing Add:* 99 Kynlyn Rd Wayne PA 19087-2849

SCHWAN, JUDITH A, chemical engineering; deceased, see previous edition for last biography

SCHWAN, THEODORE CARL, ORGANIC CHEMISTRY, POLYMER CHEMISTRY. *Current Pos:* EMER PROF CHEM, VALPARAISO UNIV, 90- *Personal Data:* b Florida, Ohio, June 17, 18; m 44, Betty A Kelley; c T Carl, Judith A, Kurt P & Margaret A. *Educ:* Valparaiso Univ, AB, 41; Univ Notre Dame, MS, 49, PhD(chem), 53. *Prof Exp:* Phys tester & chem analyst,

US Rubber Co, Ind, 38-39, asst to res chemist, 41-42; chem analyst, Ind Steel Prods Co, 40-41; from instr to assoc prof chem, Valparaiso Univ, 48-62, chmn dept, 57-59, prof chem, 62-84; prof chem, Calif Lutheran Univ, Thousand Oaks, Calif, 84-90 & 91-92. *Concurrent Pos:* Res & develop chemist, Continental-Diamond Fibre Corp, Ind, 53-58; grant, Petrol Res Fund, Am Chem Soc, 59 & 63; Univ Ky prof, Univ Indonesia, Int Coop Admin, 59-61, chief of party, 61-62; UN Educ Sci & Cult Orgn vis prof, Haile Selassie Univ, 68-70; prof chem, Col Med & Med Sci, King Faisal Univ, Dammam, Saudi Arabia, 77-79, chmn dept, 78-79. *Mem:* Emer mem Am Chem Soc. *Res:* Copolymerization of unsaturated organic compounds by free radical and heterogeneous catalyst systems; water as a fuel additive for internal combustion engines. *Mailing Add:* 1263 Vanderburgh St Valparaiso IN 46383. *E-Mail:* tschwan@valpo.edu

SCHWAN, THOMAS JAMES, medicinal chemistry; deceased, see previous edition for last biography

SCHWANDT, PETER, NUCLEAR PHYSICS. *Current Pos:* from asst prof to assoc prof, 69-80, PROF PHYSICS, IND UNIV, BLOOMINGTON, 80- *Personal Data:* b Gottingen, Ger, Apr 7, 39; US citizen; m 63; c 1. *Educ:* Ind Univ, Bloomington, BS, 61; Univ Wis-Madison, MS, 63, PhD(physics), 67. *Prof Exp:* Res assoc nuclear physics, Univ Wis-Madison, 67-68 & Univ Colo, Boulder, 68-69. *Mem:* Am Phys Soc; Sigma Xi. *Res:* Medium-energy physics; reaction mechanisms; spin dependent interactions; potential models for composite particle scattering; heavy-ion interactions. *Mailing Add:* Dept Physics Ind Univ Bloomington IN 47405

SCHWANK, JOHANNES WALTER, CATALYSIS, CHEMICAL SENSORS. *Current Pos:* Postdoctoral scholar & lectr, Univ Mich, 78-80, from asst prof to assoc prof chem eng, 80-90, chmn, Dept Chem Eng, 90-95, ASSOC DIR, ELECTRON MICROBEAM ANAL LAB & PROF CHEM ENG, UNIV MICH, 90- *Personal Data:* m 85, Lynne V DuGuay; c Alexander J, Leonard F & Hanna V. *Educ:* Univ Innsbruck, PhD(chem), 78. *Concurrent Pos:* Vis prof chem, Univ Innsbruck, 87-88; vis prof phys chem, Tech Univ Vienna, 88. *Mem:* Am Chem Soc; Am Inst Chem Engrs; Am Soc Eng Educ; NAm Catalysis Soc. *Res:* Structure and activity correlations in supported bimetallic catalyst; thin-film based microchemical sensors. *Mailing Add:* Dept Chem Eng Univ Mich 3030 H H Dow Bldg Ann Arbor MI 48109. *Fax:* 313-763-0459; *E-Mail:* schwank@engin.umich.edu

SCHWARCZ, ERVIN H, PHYSICS. *Current Pos:* PROF PHYSICS, STANISLAUS STATE COL, 67- *Personal Data:* b Cleveland, Ohio, Aug 22, 24; m 48; c 4. *Educ:* Ohio State Univ, BS, 45; Univ Mich, MS, 48, PhD(physics), 55. *Prof Exp:* Res physicist, Lawrence Radiation Lab, Univ Calif, 54-67. *Mem:* AAAS; Am Asn Physics Teachers; Am Phys Soc. *Res:* Nuclear structure and optical model analysis of elastic and quasi-elastic scattering. *Mailing Add:* 1664 Cervato Circle Alamo CA 94507

SCHWARCZ, HENRY PHILIP, STABLE ISOTOPES, ARCHAEOMETRY. *Current Pos:* from asst prof to assoc prof, 62-72, chmn dept, 88-91, PROF GEOL, MCMASTER UNIV, 72-, UNIV PROF, 96- *Personal Data:* b Chicago, Ill, July 22, 33; m 64, Molly A Robinson; c Joshua A. *Educ:* Univ Chicago, BA, 52; Calif Inst Technol, MSc, 55, PhD(geol), 60. *Honors & Awards:* Archaeol Geol Award, Geol Soc Am, 91. *Prof Exp:* Res assoc isotopic geochem, Enrico Fermi Inst Nuclear Studies, Univ Chicago, 60-62. *Concurrent Pos:* Fulbright fel, Nuclear Geol Lab, Univ Pisa, 68-69; vis prof, Hebrew Univ Jerusalem, 75-76, 82-83; vis scientist, Res Lab Archeol, Oxford Univ, 78; assoc mem, Dept Anthrop, McMaster Univ, 88-; vis fel, Clare Hall, Univ Cambridge, 91-92; coun, Am Quaternary Asn, 90 & Acad Sci, Royal Soc Can; assoc ed, Geochimica of Cosmochimica Acta, J Human Evolution, Geoarchaeol, J Archaeol Sci; chmn, Archaeol Geol Div, Geol Soc Am, 93-94; Killiam res fel, Can Coun, 93- *Mem:* Fel Geol Soc Am; fel Geol Asn Can; Geochem Soc; fel Royal Soc Can; Am Quaternary Asn; AAAS. *Res:* Stable isotope geochemistry; archeology; geochronology of cave deposits; dating of Quaternary; isotopic paleodiet; paleoclimate. *Mailing Add:* Dept Geol McMaster Univ Hamilton ON L8S 4M1 Can. *Fax:* 905-522-3141; *E-Mail:* schwarcz@mcmail.cis.mcmaster.ca

SCHWARK, WAYNE STANLEY, PHARMACOLOGY, TOXICOLOGY. *Current Pos:* from asst prof to assoc prof, 72-87, PROF PHARMACOL, NY STATE COL VET MED, CORNELL UNIV, 87- *Personal Data:* b Vita, Man, May 19, 42; m 63; c 2. *Educ:* Univ Guelph, DVM, 65, MSc, 67; Univ Ottawa, PhD(pharmacol), 70. *Prof Exp:* Lectr physiol & pharmacol, Ont Vet Col, Univ Guelph, 65-67; biologist pharmacol div, Food & Drug Dir, Ont, 67-70, res scientist, 70-71. *Concurrent Pos:* Vet consult med sch, Univ Ottawa, 69-70; vis lectr, NY State Vet Col, Cornell Univ, 71; consult, Food & Drug Admin, 77-; Fogarty Sr Int Fel, 84. *Mem:* Am Soc Vet Physiol & Pharmacol; Can Vet Med Asn; Soc Neurosci; Am Acad Vet Pharmacol & Therapeut; Am Epilepsy Soc. *Res:* Neurochemistry and neuropharmacology; neurochemical and neuropharmacological basis of epileptic disorders; clinical pharmacology in veterinary medicine. *Mailing Add:* 313 Winthrop Dr Ithaca NY 14850

SCHWARTING, ARTHUR ERNEST, pharmacognosy, natural products chemistry; deceased, see previous edition for last biography

SCHWARTING, GERALD ALLEN, NEUROBIOLOGY, DEVELOPMENT. *Current Pos:* from asst biochemist to assoc, 78-85, SR BIOCHEMIST, E K SHRIVER CTR, 86-; BIOCHEMIST NEUROL, MASS GEN HOSP, 89- *Personal Data:* b June 18, 46; m 70; c 2. *Educ:* Univ Conn, BS, 69; Univ Munich, Ger, PhD(biochem), 74. *Prof Exp:* Fel, Albert Einstein Col Med, 74-77. *Concurrent Pos:* Asst biochem, Mass Gen Hosp, 79-84, assoc biochem, 85-88; res fel neurol, Harvard Univ, 83-88; asst prof neurosci, Neurol Dept, Harvard Med Sch, 89-92, assoc prof, 93- *Mem:* Am Asn Immunologists; AAAS; Am Soc Biochem & Molecular Biol; Soc Neurosci; Soc Complex Carbohydrates; Asn Chemoreception Sci. *Res:* Expression of novel adhesion moleculed during development of the mammalian nervous system. *Mailing Add:* Dept Biochem Shriver Ctr Mental Retardation 200 Trapelo Rd Waltham MA 02154-6319

SCHWARTZ, A(LBERT) TRUMAN, CHEMICAL EDUCATION, HISTORY OF CHEMISTRY. *Current Pos:* from asst prof to prof, Macalester Col, 66-83, dean fac, 74-76, chmn dept, 80-86, DEWITT WALLACE PROF CHEM, MACALESTER COL, 83- *Personal Data:* b Freeman, SDak, May 8, 34; m 58, Beverly J Beatty; c Ronald E & Katherine M. *Educ:* Univ SDak, BA, 56; Oxford Univ, BA, 58, MA, 60; Mass Inst Technol, PhD(phys chem), 63. *Hon Degrees:* DSc, Univ SDak, 91. *Honors & Awards:* Catalyst Award, Chem Mfrs Asn, 82; Thomas Jefferson Award, 84; Estee lectr, Univ SDak, 91. *Prof Exp:* Res chemist, Miami Valley Labs, Procter & Gamble Co, Ohio, 63-66. *Concurrent Pos:* Asst, Mass Inst Technol, 58-63; NSF fels & grants, 59, 67, 72, 73, 79; mem, State & Dist Comt Selection Rhodes Scholar, 63-; Arthur Lee Haines lectr & vis scientist, Univ SDak, 65; Macalester fac fel, Thermochem Lab, Univ Lund, 68; vis researcher, Univ Mass, 72-73; vis prof & NSF fel, Univ Wis-Madison, 79-80; lectr, Inst Chem Educ, Univ Wis-Madison, 84, 86 & Univ Calif, Berkeley, 85; dep dir, Div Teacher Prep & Enhancement, NSF, 86-87; hon vis prof, Univ York, UK, 94. *Mem:* Fel AAAS; Am Chem Soc; Nat Sci Teachers Asn; Hist Sci Soc. *Res:* Chemical education; history of chemistry; physiocochemical properties of macromolecules, particularly conformation and aggregation of proteins; solution of calorimetry; preparitive electrophoresis; equilibrium properties of ion exchange resins. *Mailing Add:* Macalester Col St Paul MN 55105. *Fax:* 612-696-6432

SCHWARTZ, ABRAHAM, PHYSICAL CHEMISTRY, BIOMATERIALS. *Current Pos:* PRES, FLOW CYTOMETRY STANDARDS CORP,84- *Personal Data:* b Rockville Centre, NY, Apr 4, 43. *Educ:* Bradley Univ, BA, 65; Case Inst Technol, MS, 67; Case Western Reserve Univ, PhD(phys chem), 69. *Prof Exp:* Biophysicist, Aerospace Med Res Lab, 69-73; instr mat sci, Cornell Univ, 73-77; sr chemist, Res Triangle Inst, 77-79, Becton Dickinson Res Ctr, 79-84. *Mem:* Am Phys Soc; Am Chem Soc. *Res:* Electron microscopy; structure and morphology of natural and synthetic polymers; thrombus formation and hard tissues, microbend synthesis, fluorescence standardization and flow cytometry. *Mailing Add:* PO Box 4344 Hato Rey PR 00919-4344

SCHWARTZ, ALAN LEE, MATHEMATICS. *Current Pos:* Asst prof math, 68-74, ASSOC PROF MATH, UNIV MO, ST LOUIS, 74- *Personal Data:* b Chicago, Ill, Dec 8, 41; m 65; c 2. *Educ:* Mass Inst Technol, BS, 63; Univ Wis-Madison, MS, 64, PhD(math), 68. *Concurrent Pos:* Indust consult. *Mem:* AAAS; Am Math Soc; Math Asn Am; Soc Indust Appl Math; Asn Comput Mach; Am Asn Univ Professors. *Res:* Harmonic analysis; integral transformations; orthogonal expansion; computational fluid dynamics. *Mailing Add:* Dept Math Univ Mo St Louis MO 63121-4499

SCHWARTZ, ALAN WILLIAM, exobiology, chemical evolution, for more information see previous edition

SCHWARTZ, ALBERT, systematic zoology, for more information see previous edition

SCHWARTZ, ALBERT B, TECHNICAL MANAGEMENT. *Current Pos:* CONSULT, 88- *Personal Data:* b Philadelphia, Pa, Dec 26, 22; m 63; c Gail. *Educ:* Univ Pa, BS, 44. *Prof Exp:* Chem engr, Anthracite Industs Ltd, 44-45; chem engr, Mobil Res & Develop Corp, 45-49, group leader, 49-56, supv technologist, 56-62, res assoc, 62-64, supvr, 64-70, group mgr, 70-72, sr scientist, 72-81, sect mgr, 81-84, mgr, Cent Res Div, 84-85, sci adv, 85-87. *Mem:* Am Chem Soc; Catalysis Soc; Am Inst Chem Engrs. *Res:* Petroleum and petrochemical research and development, especially catalysis; development of procedures for commercial manufacture of catalysts; granted 66 US patents and numerous foreign patents. *Mailing Add:* 1091 JFK Blvd Apt 1204 Philadelphia PA 19103-1578

SCHWARTZ, ALLAN JAMES, CLINICAL PSYCHOLOGY. *Current Pos:* asst prof, 71-81, ASSOC PROF PSYCHIAT, SCH MED, UNIV ROCHESTER, 81-, ASSOC PROF PSYCHOL, COL ARTS & SCI, 81- *Personal Data:* b New York, NY, Dec 8, 39; m 87, Sharon Bradley; c Edward & Andrew. *Educ:* Columbia Univ, BA, 61, MA, 66; Rensselaer Polytech Inst, MS, 67; Univ Rochester, PhD(psychol), 73. *Honors & Awards:* Edward Hitchcock Award, Am Col Health Asn, 95. *Prof Exp:* Staff writer, Crowell-Collier Publ Co, 61-62; chmn sci dept, Riverdale Country Sch, 62-68. *Concurrent Pos:* Psychologist, Strong Mem Hosp, 71-; mem & chmn, Ment Health Ann Prog Surv, Am Col Health Asn, 73-90; staff develop consult, Delphi House Drug Treatment Ctr, 73-75; group therapist & supvr, Rochester Ment Health Ctr, 73-76; chief, Ment Health Sect, Univ Health Serv, Sch Med, Univ Rochester, 81-91; dir, coun & metal health serv, 91- *Mem:* Am Col Health Asn; Am Psychol Asn; Am Asn Sex Educr, Counr & Therapists; Int Transactional Anal Asn. *Res:* Epidemiology of mental disorders; non-verbal behavior, communication process and outcome in therapeutic, supervisory and consultative relationships; education in human sexuality and treatment of sexual dysfunction; college mental health and college student suicide. *Mailing Add:* Coun & Ment Health Servs PO Box 270356 Rochester NY 14627-0356. *Fax:* 716-442-0815; *E-Mail:* ajsz@uhura.cc.rochester.edu

SCHWARTZ, ANTHONY, IMMUNOLOGY, VETERINARY MEDICINE. *Current Pos:* assoc prof & head small animal surg, 79-83, actg chmn surg, 81-82, CHMN DEPT, TUFTS UNIV, 82-, PROF SURG, SCH VET MED, 83-, ASSOC DEAN, 84- *Personal Data:* b New York, NY, July 30, 40; m 63; c 2. *Educ:* Cornell Univ, DVM, 63; Ohio State Univ, PhD(med microbiol), 72; Am Col Vet Surg, dipl, 71. *Prof Exp:* Small animal pract, Ft Hill Animal Hosp, NY, 63-66; res vet viral immunol, US Army, Ft Detrick, Md, 66-68; resident surg, New York Animal Med Ctr, 68-69; teaching assoc vet surg & res assoc med microbiol, Ohio State Univ, 69-72; asst prof & head small animal surg, 73; from asst prof to assoc prof comp med, Sch Med, Yale Univ, 73-79. *Concurrent Pos:* Fel, Ohio State Univ, 71-72; consult, US Surg Corp, Norwalk, CT, 74-; Robert Wood Johnson Health Policy fel, Washington, DC, 88-89; mem, legis planning comt, Am Vet Med Asn, 89-; mem, bd regents, Am Col Vet Surg, 89-; chmn, animal welfare comt, Mass Vet Med Asn, 89- *Mem:* AAAS; Am Vet Med Asn; Am Asn Immunol; Am Col Vet Surg. *Res:* Cellular immunology; small animal general veterinary surgery; surgical device development. *Mailing Add:* Dept Surg 15 Gould Rd Waban MA 02168-2120. *Fax:* 508-839-7922

SCHWARTZ, ARNOLD, PHARMACOLOGY, BIOCHEMISTRY. *Current Pos:* DIR DEPT PHARMACOL & CELL BIOPHYS, COL MED, UNIV CINCINNATI, 77- *Personal Data:* b New York, NY, Mar 1, 29; m 56; c 2. *Educ:* Brooklyn Col Pharm, BS, 51; Ohio State Univ, MS, 57; State Univ NY, PhD(pharmacol), 61. *Prof Exp:* From asst prof to assoc prof pharmacol, Baylor Col Med, 62-69, prof & head div myocardial biol, 69-72, prof cell biophys & pharmacol & chmn dept cell biophys, 72-77. *Concurrent Pos:* Nat Heart Inst fel biochem, Inst Psychiat, Maudsley Hosp, Univ London, 60-61 & fel physiol, Univ Aarhus, 61-62; USPHS res career develop award, 64-74; NSF grant, 65-67; mem study sect CV-A, NIH, 72-76. *Mem:* Am Soc Cell Biol; Am Soc Pharmacol & Exp Therapeut; Brit Biochem Soc; Int Study Group Res in Cardiac Metab; Am Soc Biol Chem. *Res:* Mechanism of cardiac glycoside action on a biochemical level; etiology of congestive heart failure and ischemia. *Mailing Add:* Inst Molec Pharmacol & Biophys Univ Cincinnati Col Med 231 Bethesda Ave Cincinnati OH 45267-0828. *Fax:* 513-558-1778

SCHWARTZ, ARNOLD EDWARD, civil engineering, soil mechanics, for more information see previous edition

SCHWARTZ, ARTHUR GERALD, CELL BIOLOGY, CANCER. *Current Pos:* From asst prof to assoc prof, 72-85, PROF MICROBIOL, FELS RES INST, MED SCH, TEMPLE UNIV, 85- *Personal Data:* b Baltimore, Md, Mar 13, 41; m 88, Karen J Bantley; c Daniel P. *Educ:* Johns Hopkins Univ, BA, 61; Harvard Univ, PhD(bact, immunol), 68. *Concurrent Pos:* Jane Coffin Childs grantee, Oxford Univ, 68-71 & Albert Einstein Col Med, 71-72. *Mem:* Am Asn Cancer Res; Geront Soc. *Res:* Cancer chemoprevention; role of adrenal steroids in mediating cancer preventive and age-retarding effects of food restriction in laboratory rodents. *Mailing Add:* Fels Res Inst Dept Microbiol Temple Univ Med Sch Philadelphia PA 19140

SCHWARTZ, ARTHUR HAROLD, PSYCHIATRY, ACADEMIC ADMINISTRATION. *Current Pos:* actg chmn, Dept Psychiat, 91-94, PROF PSYCHIAT, ROBERT WOOD JOHNSON MED SCH, UNIV MED & DENT NJ, 81-; DIR MED STUD EDUC, DEPT PSYCHIAT, 96- *Personal Data:* b New York, NY, Apr 6, 36; div; c Lisa. *Educ:* Columbia Univ, AB, 57; Harvard Med Sch, MD, 61. *Prof Exp:* Intern, Univ Ill Res & Educ Hosps, 61-62; Vet Admin fel, Med Ctr, Yale Univ, 62-64; USPHS fel, 64-65; dir psychiat, Dana Psychiat Clin, Yale-New Haven Hosp, 67-68; chief, In-Patient Serv, Conn Ment Health Ctr, 68-69, assoc dir, Gen Clin Div, 69-71, assoc psychiatrist-in-chief, 71-72, actg psychiatrist-in-chief, 72; assoc prof psychiat, Mt Sinai Sch Med, 72-81, dir, Ambulatory Serv, Dept Psychiat, 72-81. *Concurrent Pos:* Actg clin dir, Newport County Ment Health Clin, 66-67; asst prof psychiat, Sch Med, Yale Univ, 67-71, assoc prof clin psychiat, 71-72; consult, Hosp of St Raphael, New Haven, Conn, 70-71; Vet Admin Hosp, West Haven, Conn, 71-72 & Vet Admin Hosp, Bronx, NY, 72-81; actg chmn, Dept Psychiat, Robert Wood Johnson Med Sch, Univ Med & Dent NJ, 91- *Mem:* Fel AAAS; Am Psychoanal Asn; fel Am Psychopath Asn; fel NY Acad Med; fel Am Psychiat Asn. *Res:* Clinical psychiatry; biological psychiatry and psychopharomacology. *Mailing Add:* Dept Psychiat Robert Wood Johnson Med Sch Univ Med & Dent NJ 675 Hoes Lane Piscataway NJ 08854. *Fax:* 732-235-5158, 4430

SCHWARTZ, BENJAMIN L, OPERATIONS RESEARCH. *Current Pos:* CONSULT, OPERS RES FED AGENCIES & PVT INDUST, 71- *Personal Data:* b Pittsburgh, Pa, Jan 11, 26; m 56, Joan Koslan; c Justin, Beryl, Brita & Mila. *Educ:* Carnegie Mellon Univ, BS, 46, MS, 47; Stanford Univ, PhD(oper res), 65; George Washington Univ, MBA, 81. *Prof Exp:* Asst prof math, Duquesne Univ, 50-53; asst div chief, Battelle Mem Inst, 53-58; suboff tech dir, Monterey Lab, 58-64; mem tech staff, Inst Defense Anal, 65-67; subdept head, Mitre Corp, 67-71; sr tech staff, TASC, 87-93. *Concurrent Pos:* Vis assoc prof, US Naval Postgrad Sch, 63-65; vis prof, George Washington Univ, 66-; prof, Am Univ, 69-, Georgetown Univ, 82-85; adj prof, Marymount Univ, Va, 85-88, Johns Hopkins Univ, 88-90, Averett Col, 91-94 & Southeastern Univ, 92-, George Mason Univ, 96- *Mem:* Fel AAAS; Am Math Soc; INFORMS; Asn Comput Mach; Math Asn Am; Oughtred Soc. *Res:* Mathematics, Computational complexity of optimization processes, e.g. LP solitaire games and competitive games, recreational math. *Mailing Add:* 216 Apple Blossom Ct Vienna VA 22181

SCHWARTZ, BERNARD, OPHTHALMOLOGY, PHYSIOLOGY. *Current Pos:* prof, Sch Med, Tufts Univ & ophthalmologist-in-chief, Tufts-New Eng Med Ctr, 68-90, EMER PROF OPHTHAL, SCH MED, TUFTS UNIV, 90- *Personal Data:* b Toronto, Ont, Nov 12, 27; nat US; m 54; c 4. *Educ:* Univ Toronto, MD, 51; Univ Iowa, MS, 53, PhD(physiol), 59; Am Bd Ophthal, dipl, 56. *Prof Exp:* Assoc prof ophthal, Col Med, State Univ NY Downstate Med Ctr, 58-68. *Mem:* Asn Res Vision & Ophthal; fel Am Col Surg; fel Am Acad Ophthal & Otolaryngol; fel NY Acad Med; French Soc Ophthal. *Res:* Metabolism and permeability of the lens and cornea; physiology of intraocular fluid formation; patho-physiology of cataracts and glaucoma; pharmacology for treatment of glaucoma. *Mailing Add:* 180 Beacon St Boston MA 02116-1455. *Fax:* 617-482-0537

SCHWARTZ, BERTRAM, SURFACE CHEMISTRY. *Current Pos:* RETIRED. *Personal Data:* b New York, NY, Nov 1, 24; m 48; c 2. *Educ:* NY Univ, BS, 49. *Honors & Awards:* Electronics Div Award, Electrochem Soc, 87. *Prof Exp:* Mem tech staff, Interchem Corp, 51-52, Sylvania Elec Prod Co, 52-54 & Hughes Aircraft Co, 54-60; mem tech staff, AT&T Bell Labs, 60-90, consult, 90-95. *Mem:* Am Phys Soc; Electrochem Soc. *Res:* Chemistry of solid surfaces; chemical etching of solids; semiconductor material preparation; semiconductor device fabrication techniques. *Mailing Add:* 321 Ovenda Circle Westfield NJ 07090

SCHWARTZ, BRADFORD S, HEMATOLOGY, BLOOD COAGULATION. *Current Pos:* ASST PROF MED, UNIV WIS, 83- *Personal Data:* b Chicago, Ill, Mar 20, 52. *Educ:* Rush Univ, MD, 77. *Mailing Add:* Dept Med Univ Wis 1300 University Ave Madison WI 53706-1532. *Fax:* 608-263-4969

SCHWARTZ, BRIAN B, THEORETICAL PHYSICS, SCIENCE EDUCATION. *Current Pos:* dean, Sch Sci Brooklyn Col, City Univ NY, 77-80, dean res, 79-82, vpres res & develop, 82-86, PROF PHYSICS, GRAD CTR, BROOKLYN COL, UNIV NY, 77- *Personal Data:* b Brooklyn, NY, Apr 15, 38; m 61; Teri B Geller; c Robin & Adam. *Educ:* City Col NY, BS, 59; Brown Univ, PhD(physics), 63. *Prof Exp:* Teaching asst physics, Brown Univ, 59-61; res assoc, Rutgers Univ, 63-65; leader, Theoret Physics Group, Nat Magnet Lab, Mass Inst Technol, 65-77. *Concurrent Pos:* Assoc prof physics, Mass Inst Technol, 69-74; co-dir, NATO Advan Study Inst Large Scale Appl Superconductivity, Entreve, Italy, 73 & Small Scale Devices, Gardone Riviera, Italy, 77; superconductor mat sci, Sintra, Portugal, 80; educ officer, Am Phys Soc, 87-94, assoc exec secy, 90-94. *Mem:* Fel Am Phys Soc; fel AAAS; Am Asn Physics Teachers. *Res:* Low temperature physics; superconductivity; type II superconductors; Josephson junctions; response of ferromagnetic metals; many-body problem; scientific manpower projection and utilization; physics education for the science and non-science major; small business; high technology. *Mailing Add:* Physics Dept Grad Ctr City Univ 33 W 42 St Rm 900 New York NY 10017. *Fax:* 212-750-8341; *E-Mail:* shwartz@ap5.org

SCHWARTZ, CHARLES LEON, THEORETICAL PHYSICS. *Current Pos:* from asst prof to assoc prof, 60-67, PROF PHYSICS, UNIV CALIF, BERKELEY, 67- *Personal Data:* b New York, NY, June 9, 31; m 52; c 3. *Educ:* Mass Inst Technol, SB, 52, PhD(physics), 54. *Prof Exp:* Res assoc physics, Mass Inst Technol, 54-56; res assoc, Stanford Univ, 56-57, asst prof, 57-60. *Mem:* Am Phys Soc. *Res:* Theoretical studies of atoms, nuclei and elementary particles; interaction of science with human affairs. *Mailing Add:* Dept Physics Univ Calif Berkeley CA 94720

SCHWARTZ, COLIN JOHN, CARDIO VASCULAR DISEASES, EXPERIMENTAL PATHOLOGY. *Current Pos:* RETIRED. *Personal Data:* b Angaston, SAustralia, May 1, 31; div; c 4. *Educ:* Univ Adelaide, MB, BS, 54, MD, 59; FRACP; FRCP(C); FRCPath. *Prof Exp:* Resident med & surg, Royal Adelaide Hosp, Australia, 55; vice master, Lincoln Univ Col, Univ Adelaide, 57, actg master, 58; specialist pathologist, Inst Med Ved Sci, 62-67, head, Div Med Res, 67; prof path, Fac Med, McMaster Univ, 68-76; head, Dept Cardiovasc Dis Res, Cleveland Clin Found, 76-78; prof path, Univ Tex Health Sci Ctr, San Antonio, 78-95. *Concurrent Pos:* Mem, Thrombosis Arteriosclerosis Comt; C J Martin overseas res fel cardiovasc dis, Dept Med, Oxford Univ, 59-61; Med Res Coun Gt Brit fel, 61; Nat Heart Found Australia res grant, 62-66; NIH int fel cardiovascular path, C T Miller Hosp, Univ Minn, 67; fel coun on arteriosclerosis, Am Heart Asn, 67, mem, Exec Comt Coun; Med Res Coun Can res grant, 68-; dir, Southam Labs, Chedoke Hosps, 70-76; mem, Heart, Lung & Blood Res Rev Comt B; vpres, San Antonio Div, Am Heart Asn, 80-81; mem, vascular comt, Am Heart Asn; chmn, Gordon Res Conf. *Mem:* Am Asn Path; AMA; Path Soc Gt Brit & Ireland; Am Heart Asn; Int Acad Path. *Res:* Myocardial infarction and the etiology and pathogenesis of atherosclerosis and thrombosis; endothelial structure and function; lipid transport and metabolism; cellular biology; inflammation; macrophage biology, hemodynamics. *Mailing Add:* The Lodge Penny Hill Farm PO Box 603 McLaren Vale SA 5171 Australia. *Fax:* 512-567-3015

SCHWARTZ, DANIEL ALAN, X-RAY ASTRONOMY, COSMOLOGY. *Current Pos:* PHYSICIST, SMITHSONIAN ASTROPHYS OBSERV, 73- *Personal Data:* b San Antonio, Tex, Oct 21, 42; m 69; c 2. *Educ:* Washington Univ, BS, 63; Univ Calif, San Diego, MS, 66, PhD(physics), 69. *Honors & Awards:* Group Achievement Award, NASA, 78. *Prof Exp:* Lectr physics, Univ Calif, San Diego, 68-70, asst res physicist, 69-70; Nat Res Coun resident res assoc, Goddard Space Flight Ctr, NASA, 70-71; from staff scientist to sr scientist x-ray astron, Am Sci & Eng, Inc, 71-73. *Concurrent Pos:* Lectr Astron Dept, Harvard Univ, 81- *Mem:* Am Astron Soc; Am Phys Soc; Int Astron Union. *Res:* Experiment development and observation of extragalactic x-rays to study isotropy of the x-ray background and mechanism of source emission; development of x-ray imaging systems for spectral studies of cosmic x-rays. *Mailing Add:* Dept High Energy Harvard Univ 60 Garden St MS 3 Cambridge MA 02138

SCHWARTZ, DANIEL K, CHEMISTRY, BIOCHEMISTRY. *Current Pos:* ASST PROF, DEPT CHEM, TULANE UNIV, 94- *Personal Data:* b White Plains, NY, June 15, 63; m 94, Tracey R Rangel. *Educ:* Harvard Univ, AB, 84, AM, 87, PhD(physics), 91. *Prof Exp:* Postdoctoral assoc, Dept Chem & Nuclear Eng, Univ Calif, Santa Barbara, 91-92; postdoctoral assoc, Dept Chem & Biochem, Univ Calif, Los Angeles, 92-94. *Concurrent Pos:* Res grantee, Exxon Educ Found; Stone & Webster fel, Harvard Univ, 85-86; chem grantee, Camille & Henry Dreyfus Found, 94. *Mem:* Am Chem Soc; Am Phy Soc; Mat Res Soc. *Res:* Contributed articles to professional journals. *Mailing Add:* Dept Chem Univ Tulane New Orleans LA 70118

SCHWARTZ, DANIEL M(AX), MECHANICAL ENGINEERING, MANAGEMENT. *Current Pos:* RETIRED. *Personal Data:* b San Francisco, Calif, Mar 22, 13; m 37, 85; c 2. *Educ:* Stanford Univ, AB, 33. *Prof Exp:* Mech engr, Pac Gear & Tool Works, Calif, 33-36 & Dept Water & Power, City of Los Angeles, 36-37; mech design engr, Falk Corp, Wis, 37-40; develop engr, Dravo Corp, Pa, 40-46; vpres in charge eng & dir, Eimco Corp, 46-63, sr vpres, 63-66, gen mgr, Tractor Div, 65-66; sr staff engr, Ground Vehicle Systs, Res & Develop Div, Lockheed Missiles & Space Co, 66-67, mgr construct equip syst, 67-72, prog mgr mil progs, 72-78; pres, Foothill Eng, Inc, 78-92. *Concurrent Pos:* Expert witness, Patents, 86. *Mem:* Fel Am Soc Mech Engrs; Soc Automotive Engrs. *Res:* Government proposals, producibility engineering, engineering management; machine design and development of heavy duty equipment; heavy transmissions, clutches; shipyard cranes; mining and milling machinery; construction equipment; loaders and tractors; numerous patents in material handling equipment and power transmissions. *Mailing Add:* 2190 Washington St Apt 1204 San Francisco CA 94109

SCHWARTZ, DAVID ALAN, INFECTIOUS DISEASE OBSTETRIC & PLACENTAL PATHOLOGY, TROPICAL MEDICINE. *Current Pos:* asst prof, 89-94, ASSOC PROF PATH, SCH MED, EMORY UNIV, 94-, ASST PROF MED INFECTIOUS DIS, 96- *Personal Data:* b Philadelphia, Pa, May 20, 53; m 93, Stephanie Baker. *Educ:* Univ Pittsburgh, BA, 74, MSHYG, 77; Far East Univ, MD, 84; Am Bd Path, cert anat path, 92. *Prof Exp:* Resident path, Hahnemann Univ Sch Med, 84-87, chief resident, 87-88; clin fel, Sch Med, Harvard Univ, 88-89. *Concurrent Pos:* Fel gastrointestinal path, Beth Israel Hosp, 88-89; co-prin investr, NIH, 91-; res scientist, Ctrs Dis Control & Prev, 92-; prin investr, Emory Med Care Found, 92-93 & Am Found AIDS Res, 93-; consult infectious dis & perinatal path, USAID, 92-; vis prof, Univ Mayor San Simon, Bolivia, 93; dir fel training placental path, Mahidol Univ, Bangkok, 93-; consult placental path, Ctrs Dis Control & Thailand Ministry Pub Health, 93-; chmn, Path Subcomt, Women & Infants HIV Transmission Study, NIH, 93- *Mem:* Fel Col Am Pathologists; fel Asn Clin Scientists; Sigma Xi; fel Int Acad Path; Am Soc Trop Med & Hyg. *Res:* Investigation of the pathology, diagnosis and clinico-epidemiologic aspects of pathogenesis of acquired immunodeficiency syndrome-related conditions, including emerging opportunistic infections and transplacental infections; pathology and pathogenesis of congenital infections and placental pathology. *Mailing Add:* Dept Path Grady Mem Hosp 80 Butler St SE Atlanta GA 30335. *Fax:* 404-616-9084

SCHWARTZ, DAVID C, CHEMISTRY, BIOCHEMISTRY. *Current Pos:* ASST PROF, DEPT CHEM & BIOCHEM, NY UNIV, 89- *Personal Data:* b New York, NY, Oct 5, 54; m, Louise Pape. *Educ:* Hampshire Col, BA, 76; Columbia Univ, PhD, 85. *Honors & Awards:* Presidential Young Investigator Award, NSF, 90; Amgen Award, Am Soc Biochem & Molecular Biol, 95. *Prof Exp:* Staff assoc, Carnegie Inst Washington, 85-89. *Concurrent Pos:* Consult, US Biochemical. *Res:* Contributed articles to professional journals. *Mailing Add:* 4 Washington Sq Village Apt 8B New York NY 10012-1905

SCHWARTZ, DONALD, CHEMISTRY OF COAL. *Current Pos:* chancellor, 78-83, PROF CHEM, UNIV COLO, 83- *Personal Data:* b Scarsdale, NY, Dec 27, 27; m 50; c Leane, Mark W, Scott B & Bradley F. *Educ:* Univ Mo, BS, 49; Mont State Col, MS, 51; Pa State Univ, PhD(chem, fuel tech), 55. *Prof Exp:* Chemist, Gen Elect Co, 51-53; asst, Pa State Univ, 53-55; asst prof chem, Villanova Univ, 55-57; res chemist, Esso Res Lab, La, 57-58; asst prof chem, Moorhead State Col, 58-59; prof chem, NDak State Univ, 59-65; reg specialist, Cent Am, NSF-Am Chem Soc, 65-66; prog dir, NSF, 66-68; prof chem & assoc dean, Grad Sch, Memphis State Univ, 68-70; dean advan studies, Fla Atlantic Univ, 70-71; vpres acad affairs, 71-74, actg pres, State Univ NY Col Buffalo, 74; chancellor, Ind Univ-Purdue Univ, 74-78. *Concurrent Pos:* Consult, Baroid Div, Nat Lead Co, 60-64; consult vpres, Mid-South Res Assocs, 68-70; bd dir, Ind Comn Humanities, 74-78, Penrose Cancer Hosp, 80-85, Beth El Sch Nursing, 80-85 & Colo Springs Osteop Found, 88- *Mem:* AAAS; Am Chem Soc (secy-treas, Fuel Div). *Res:* Humic acids; desulfurization of coal; zirconium; science education; elucidation of structure of coal. *Mailing Add:* 21 Sanford Rd Colorado Springs CO 80906

SCHWARTZ, DONALD ALAN, PSYCHIATRY. *Current Pos:* RETIRED. *Personal Data:* b Brooklyn, NY, Mar 5, 26; m 52, Ann M Siena; c Nina, Julia & Steven. *Educ:* Case Western Reserve Univ, MD, 52. *Prof Exp:* From instr to assoc clin prof psychiat, Sch Med, Univ Calif, Los Angeles, 58-69; assoc prof psychiat, Sch Med, Univ Calif, Irvine, 69-71; from assoc prof to prof psychiat & chief adult psychiat, Neuropsychiat Inst, 71-74; prof psychiat, Univ Calif, 74-90. *Concurrent Pos:* Chief inpatient serv, Neuropsychiat Inst, Univ Calif, Los Angeles, 59-61; dep dir, Los Angeles Co Dept Ment Health, 61-69; chief psychiat inpatient serv, Orange Co Med Ctr, 69-71. *Mem:* Life fel Am Psychiat Asn. *Res:* Psychopathology; administrative medicine. *Mailing Add:* 11407 Arroyo Ave Santa Ana CA 92705

SCHWARTZ, DORIS R, NURSING. *Current Pos:* RETIRED. *Prof Exp:* Assoc prof, Sch Nursing, NY Hosp, Cornell Univ, 51-80; sr fel geriat grad studies, Sch Nursing, Univ Pa, 80-90. *Mem:* Inst Med-Nat Acad Sci. *Mailing Add:* 91 Foulkeways Gwynedd PA 19436

SCHWARTZ, DREW, GENETICS. *Current Pos:* prof, 64-90, EMER PROF GENETICS, IND UNIV, BLOOMINGTON, 90- *Personal Data:* b Philadelphia, Pa, Nov 15, 19; wid; c Rena A. *Educ:* Pa State Col, 42; Columbia Univ, MA, 48, PhD(bot), 50. *Prof Exp:* Res assoc cytogenetics, Univ Ill, 50-51; sr biologist, Biol Div, Oak Ridge Nat Lab, 51-62; prof biol, Western Res Univ, 62-64. *Mem:* AAAS; Genetics Soc Am. *Res:* Transposable elements in maize; methylation and gene regulation. *Mailing Add:* Dept Biol Ind Univ Bloomington IN 47401. *Fax:* 812-855-6705; *E-Mail:* schwartz@bio.indiana.edu

SCHWARTZ, EDITH RICHMOND, BIOCHEMISTRY, ORTHOPEDICS. *Current Pos:* PROF ORTHOP SURG, SCH MED, TUFTS UNIV, 78- *Personal Data:* b Karlsruhe, Ger; US citizen; c 3. *Educ:* Columbia Univ, AB, 52, MA, 55; Cornell Univ, PhD(biochem), 64. *Prof Exp:* Res assoc biochem, Univ Tex, 66-69; vis asst prof, Univ Ill, 69-70; res assoc pediat, Sch Med, Univ Va, 70-71, res assoc orthop, 71-72, from asst prof to assoc prof orthop, 75-78. *Concurrent Pos:* Damon Runyon fel, Albert Einstein Col Med, 64-66. *Mem:* Orthop Res Soc; Fedn Am Soc Exp Biol; Rheumatism Asn. *Res:* Connective tissue research; osteoarthritis; sulfated proteoglycon metabolism in articular cartilage; human chondrocyte cultures. *Mailing Add:* 6100 Westchester Pk Dr Unit 1705 College Park MD 20740-2851

SCHWARTZ, EDWARD, PHARMACOLOGY. *Current Pos:* dir, 77-81, SR DIR PATH & TOXICOL, SCHERING-PLOUGH CORP, 81- *Personal Data:* b Dec 25, 32; US citizen; m 58; c 3. *Educ:* Philadelphia Col Pharm & Sci, BS, 55; Univ Pa, VMD, 59; Jefferson Med Col, PhD(pharmacol), 63; LaSalle Exten Univ, dipl comput programming, 69; Am Acad Toxicol Sci, dipl. *Prof Exp:* Sr toxicologist, Hoffman-LaRoche, Inc, 62-65; sr res assoc, Warner-Lambert Res Inst, 65-70, head dept toxicol, 70, dir, 70-77, assoc dir, 77. *Mem:* Am Vet Med Asn; Soc Toxicol; Am Soc Pharmacol & Exp Therapeut; Europ Soc Study Drug Toxicity; Can Soc Toxicol; Am Col Toxicol. *Res:* Drug safety evaluation studies in animals. *Mailing Add:* White Eagle Toxicol Labs 2003 Lowee State Rd Doylestown PA 18901. *Fax:* 215-348-5081

SCHWARTZ, ELIAS, PEDIATRICS, HEMATOLOGY. *Current Pos:* DIR MED RES, DU PONT HOSP CHILDREN, 96- *Personal Data:* b New York, NY, Aug, 30, 35; m 60, Esta Rosenberg; c Samuel & Robert. *Educ:* Columbia Col, AB, 56; Columbia Univ, MD, 60. *Hon Degrees:* MA, Univ Pa, 72. *Prof Exp:* Intern, Montefiore Hosp, NY, 60-61; residency, St Christopher's Hosp Children, Philadelphia, 61-63; chief, US Mil Serv, Offut AFB, Nebr, 63-65; fel hemat, Children's Hosp Med Ctr, Boston, 65-67; from asst prof pediat to assoc prof pediat, Jefferson Med Col, Philadelphia, 67-72, dir pediat hemat & oncol, 67-72; dir, Div Hemat, 72-90, physician-in-chief, Children's Hosp Philadelphia, 90-96; prof pediat, Univ Pa, Philadelphia, 72-96, prof human genetics, 79-96, chmn, Dept Pediat, 90-96. *Concurrent Pos:* Instr, Univ Nebr, Omaha, 63-65; chmn, Gov's Comt Sickle Cell Dis, Pa, 74-77; vis sci, Inst Cancer Res, Philadelphia, 75-76 & Weizmann Inst, Rehovot, Israel, 79 & 87. *Mem:* Am Soc Pediat Hemat & Oncol (pres, 88-90); Am Soc Clinic Invest; Soc Pediat Res; Am Pediat Soc; Am Soc Hemat; Asn Am Physicians. *Res:* Molecular biology; hematologic, biochemical, genetic, and clinical studies of sickle cell disease, thalassemia and other hemoglobinopathies; molecular biology of magakaryocyte proteins. *Mailing Add:* 7703 West Ave Elkins Park PA 19027. *Fax:* 302-651-6767; *E-Mail:* eschwart@aidi.nemours.org

SCHWARTZ, ELMER G(EORGE), NUCLEAR ENGINEERING, MATERIALS SCIENCE. *Current Pos:* assoc prof eng, 64-72, PROF ENG, UNIV SC, 72- *Personal Data:* b Pittsburgh, Pa, July 16, 27; m 47; c 5. *Educ:* US Merchant Marine Acad, BS, 50; Carnegie Inst Technol, MS, 60, PhD(nuclear eng), 64. *Prof Exp:* Develop engr, Bettis Atomic Power Lab, Westinghouse Elec Corp, 52-59, develop engr, Atomic Power Div, 60-61. *Concurrent Pos:* Consult, Carolinas-Va Nuclear Power Assocs, 64-68; res partic, Savannah River Lab, 66; vis assoc prof, Carnegie-Mellon Univ, 71-72; tech assoc, E R Johnson Assocs, Inc, 77-78. *Mem:* Am Soc Mech Engrs; Am Soc Metals. *Res:* Nuclear waste management; powder metallurgy compaction; mechanical properties of materials. *Mailing Add:* Dept Mech Eng Univ SC Columbia SC 29208-0001

SCHWARTZ, EMANUEL ELLIOT, MEDICINE, RADIOLOGY. *Current Pos:* ASSOC PROF RADIOL, HAHNEMANN MED COL & HOSP, 71- *Personal Data:* b New York, NY, Oct 14, 23; m 46; c 2. *Educ:* NY Univ, BA, 46; State Univ NY, MD, 50. *Prof Exp:* Intern, Jewish Hosp Brooklyn, 50-51; resident radiol, Yale-New Haven Med Ctr, 51-54; instr, Sch Med, Univ Chicago, 54-55; asst radiother, Hosp Joint Dis, NY, 55-56; asst radiol, Albert Einstein Med Ctr, 57-61, assoc, 61-65; assoc prof & dir div radiation ther & nuclear med, Sch Med, Univ Va, 65-67; radiologist, Coatesville Hosp, 67-71. *Concurrent Pos:* AEC fel, Argonne Cancer Res Hosp, Univ Chicago, 54-55; USPHS fel, Biol Div, Oak Ridge Nat Lab, 56-57; instr, Sch Med, Yale Univ, 53-54. *Mem:* Radiation Res Soc; Am Roentgen Ray Soc; Radiol Soc NAm; AMA; Am Asn Cancer Res. *Res:* Radiographic manifestations of chest disease, particularly in renal patients, and with complications of medical practice. *Mailing Add:* Dept Diag Radiol 230 N Broad St Philadelphia PA 19102-1121

SCHWARTZ, ERNEST, ENDOCRINOLOGY, METABOLISM. *Current Pos:* CHIEF, METAB UNIT, VET ADMIN HOSP, BRONX, 57- *Personal Data:* b New York, NY, May 22, 24; m 51; c 4. *Educ:* Columbia Univ, BA, 45, MA, 50, MD, 51; Am Bd Internal Med, dipl, 57; Am Bd Endocrinol & Metab, dipl, 72. *Prof Exp:* Asst physics, Columbia Univ, 44-46, Jane Coffin Childs fel biochem, 48-49; asst biochem, Sloan-Kettering Inst, 45-46; resident med, Univ Calif Hosp, San Francisco, 51-53, Los Angeles Vet Admin Hosp, 53-54; capt, US Air Force, sect chief med, Wright-Patterson AFB Hosp, Ohio,

54-56; Jane Coffin Child fel endocrinol, Sloan-Kettering Inst, 56-57. *Concurrent Pos:* Asst, Sch Med, Univ Calif, Los Angeles & San Francisco, 52-54; from inst to asst prof, Cornell Univ, 57-68, assoc prof med, 68-; chief, Endocrinol Serv, Our Lady of Mercy Hosp, Bronx, NY, 62-; assoc attend physician, Metab Bone Serv, Hosp Spec Surg, NY, 76- *Mem:* Am Physiol Soc; Endocrine Soc; Soc Exp Biol & Med; Am Fedn Clin Res; fel Am Col Physicians; Am Soc Bone & Mineral Res. *Res:* Effects of thyroid hormone upon protein metabolism; interactions of growth hormone, estrogen and serum somatomedin in normals and in acromegaly; effects of high calcium intake upon radiocalcium kinetics; effects of sodium fluoride upon bone histomorphometry in osteoporosis. *Mailing Add:* Vet Admin Hosp 130 W Kingsbridge Rd Bronx NY 10468. *Fax:* 718-220-2188

SCHWARTZ, FRANK JOSEPH, ICHTHYOLOGY, HERPETOLOGY. *Current Pos:* assoc prof, 68-71, PROF BIOL, INST MARINE SCI, UNIV NC, 71- *Personal Data:* b New Castle, Pa, Nov 20, 29. *Educ:* Univ Pittsburgh, BS, 50, MS, 52, PhD(ichthyol, ecol), 54. *Prof Exp:* Asst zool, Univ Pittsburgh, 50-55; asst prof, Univ WVa, 55-57; Md Dept Res & Educ biologist, Chesapeake Biol Lab, Univ Md, 57-61, res assoc prof, biol, 61-67, prof, 67. *Concurrent Pos:* Assoc ed, Chesapeake Sci, 64-74, J Aquatic Organisms; ed, Trans Am Fisheries Soc, 66-68 & Copeia, Am Soc Ichthyol & Herpet, 68-72; ed, ASB Bull, 86- *Mem:* Int Acad Fishery Scientists; Int Oceanog Found; Am Fish Soc; Am Soc Ichthyologists & Herpetologists; Japanese Soc Ichthyology. *Res:* Taxonomy; distribution, ecology and life histories of marine and freshwater fishes; turtles; crayfishes. *Mailing Add:* Inst Marine Sci 3431 Arendell St Univ NC Morehead City NC 28557. *Fax:* 919-726-2426

SCHWARTZ, GERALD PETER, BIOCHEMISTRY. *Current Pos:* ASST RES PROF BIOCHEM, MT SINAI SCH MED, 66- *Personal Data:* b Cleveland, Ohio, Mar 20, 38; m 63; c 3. *Educ:* John Carroll Univ, BS, 60; Univ Pittsburgh, PhD(biochem), 64. *Prof Exp:* Res assoc biochem, Med Dept, Brookhaven Nat Lab, 64-66, asst scientist, 66-68. *Mem:* AAAS; Am Chem Soc. *Res:* Isolation of enzymes; study of enzyme action; synthesis of peptides of biological interest. *Mailing Add:* 32636 Nantasket Dr No 66 Rancho Palos Verdes CA 90275

SCHWARTZ, GERALDINE COGIN, PHYSICAL CHEMISTRY. *Current Pos:* chemist, 64-71, adv engr, Components Div, 71-78, SR ENGR, GEN TECHNOL DIV, IBM CORP, 78- *Personal Data:* b New York, NY, Apr 4, 23; m 43; c 2. *Educ:* Brooklyn Col, BA, 43; Columbia Univ, MA, 45, PhD(chem), 48. *Prof Exp:* Asst physics, SAM Labs, Manhattan Proj, Columbia Univ, 43; USPHS res fel, Tuberc Res Lab, 48 & Sloan Kettering Inst Cancer Res, 49, inst fel phys chem, 50-52; instr chem, Adelphi Col, 53 & Queens Col, NY, 53-54; asst prof, Bard Col, 58-62. *Mem:* Am Vacuum Soc; Sigma Xi; fel Electrochem Soc. *Res:* Physical chemistry of proteins; thin films; anodic oxidation reactive ion etching and dielectric films. *Mailing Add:* 19 Woodward Rd Poughkeepsie NY 12603-5121

SCHWARTZ, HAROLD LEON, ENDOCRINOLOGY, BIOCHEMISTRY. *Current Pos:* assoc dir, Div Endocrinol & Metab, Dept Med, 81-93, ASSOC PROF MED, UNIV MINN COL MED, 76- *Personal Data:* b Brooklyn, NY, Mar 14, 33; m 56; c 3. *Educ:* Brooklyn Col, BS, 57; NY Univ, MS, 61, PhD(physiol), 64. *Prof Exp:* Res assoc med, Downstate Med Ctr, State Univ NY, 57-64, instr, 64-66; asst prof biochem, Albert Einstein col Med, 67-76. *Concurrent Pos:* USPHS fel, Nat Inst Med Res, London, Eng, 66-67; biochemist, Endocrine Res Lab, Montefiore Hosp & Med Ctr, 67-76. *Mem:* AAAS; NY Acad Sci; Am Thyroid Asn; Endocrine Soc. *Res:* Thyroid hormone biosynthesis and metabolism; mechanisms of hormone action; chemistry of thyroid proteins. *Mailing Add:* Univ Minn Col Med Box 91-UMHC Minneapolis MN 55455. *Fax:* 612-626-3840; *E-Mail:* schwa002@maroon.tc.umn.edu

SCHWARTZ, HEINZ (GEORG), PATHOLOGY. *Current Pos:* RETIRED. *Personal Data:* b Landsberg, Ger, Jan 15, 24; US citizen; m 50; c 1. *Educ:* Rutgers Univ, New Brunswick, BS, 53, PhD(biochem), 57; Temple Univ, MD, 61. *Prof Exp:* Res asst biochem, Merck Inst Therapeut Res, Rahway, 50-57; intern, Abington Hosp, Pa, 61-62; resident path, Temple Univ Hosp, 62-65, instr, 65-66; asst prof & asst dir, Thomas Jefferson Univ Hosp, 66-70, assoc prof path & assoc dir clin labs, 70-78, prof path & dir clin labs, 78-86. *Concurrent Pos:* Consult, Vet Admin Hosp, Coatesville, 67- & Children's Heart Hosp, 78- *Mem:* AMA; Am Asn Clin Path; Am Asn Clin Chem; Col Am Path; Sigma Xi. *Res:* Lipid analysis; immunoglobuline analysis. *Mailing Add:* 1025 Walnut St Philadelphia PA 19107

SCHWARTZ, HENRY GERARD, JR, ENVIRONMENTAL HEALTH ENGINEERING. *Current Pos:* sr engr, 66-76, vpres & mgr, Environ Div, Sverdrup & Pracel & Assoc, Inc, 76-80, VPRES, CORP PRIN, SVERDRUP CORP, 78-, PRES, SVERDRUP ENVIRON, INC, 89- *Personal Data:* b St Louis, Mo, Aug 3, 38; m 60; c 2. *Educ:* Wash Univ, St Louis, BS, 61, MS, 62; Calif Inst Technol, PhD(environ health eng), 66. *Honors & Awards:* Edward Bartow Award, Am Chem Soc, 66; Arthur Sidney Bedell Award, Water Pollution Control Fedn, 76; Kappe Lectr, Am Acad Environ Engrs, 89. *Prof Exp:* Res fel environ health eng, Calif Inst Technol, 65-66. *Concurrent Pos:* Mgt adv group, US Environment Protection Agency, 81-83, 86-88; chmn, Water Pollution Control Fedn Res Found, 88- *Mem:* Nat Acad Eng; Am Soc Civil Engrs; Am Acad Environ Engrs; Water Pollution Control Fedn (pres, 85-86); Air Pollution Control Asn; Sigma Xi; Nat Soc Prof Engrs. *Res:* Adsorption and microbial degradation of pesticides in aqueous solutions; water recovery and reuse in space vehicles; water and air pollution control. *Mailing Add:* 13723 Riverport Dr Maryland Heights MO 63043

SCHWARTZ, HERBERT, BIOLOGICAL ORGANIC CHEMISTRY, APPLIED CHEMISTRY. *Current Pos:* res & develop consult chem, Biovivan Res Inst, 63-87, VPRES RES & DEVELOP, GRAN-TENESCO INC, PHILADELPHIA, PA, 88- *Personal Data:* b Limerick, Pa, Mar 8, 25; m 86, Johanna H Hoar; c David & Simone L (Galletta). *Educ:* Univ Freiburg, Ger, dipl, 55; Univ Utrecht, PhD(chem), 65. *Prof Exp:* Res chemist, Vineland Chem Co, 55-57; chemist anal chem, Food & Drug Admin, Washington, DC, 57-58; chemist biochem, Grad Hosp, Philadelphia, 58-59; res assoc, Inst Org Chem, Univ Utrecht, 59-65. *Concurrent Pos:* Adj prof chem, Cumberland Co Col, 69-75 & Camden Co Col, 77-78. *Mem:* AAAS. *Res:* Biologically active chemistry; investigation into physiologically induced human interactions based upon chronobiology and sociobiology; environmental chemistry; synthetic plant hormones. *Mailing Add:* 161 Rosenhayn Ave Bridgeton NJ 08302-1241. *Fax:* 215-739-0434

SCHWARTZ, HERBERT C, MEDICINE, PEDIATRICS. *Current Pos:* from asst prof to prof, 60-91, chmn dept, 69-71, EMER PROF PEDIAT, SCH MED, STANFORD UNIV, 91- *Personal Data:* b New Haven, Conn, May 8, 26; m 58; c 3. *Educ:* Yale Univ, AB, 48; State Univ NY, MD, 52. *Prof Exp:* Intern med, Vet Admin Hosp, Newington, Conn, 52-53, intern pediat, Grace-New Haven Community Hosp, 53; med resident, Univ Serv, Kings Co Hosp, 53-54 & Stanford Univ Hosp, 54-55; instr, Univ Utah, 58-60. *Concurrent Pos:* Clin & res fel med, Univ Utah, 55-56, res fel, 56-57, res fel biochem, 57-58; Markle scholar acad med, 62. *Mem:* Am Fedn Clin Res; Soc Pediat Res; Am Soc Clin Invest; Am Pediat Soc; Am Soc Hemat. *Res:* Hemoglobin structure and synthesis in mammalian erythrocytes; effects of pregnancy on hemoglobin AIc in diabetic women; structure and function relationship of hemoglobins in deep diving mammals. *Mailing Add:* 1565 Dana Ave Palo Alto CA 94303

SCHWARTZ, HERBERT MARK, NUCLEAR MAGNETIC RESONANCE SPECTROSCOPY, ANALYTICAL. *Current Pos:* DIR NUCLEAR MAGNETIC RESONANCE & SPECTROS, CHEM DEPT, RENSSELAER POLYTECH INST, 81- *Personal Data:* b Philadelphia, Pa, July 30, 48; m 74; c 2. *Educ:* Temple Univ, BA, 70; Univ Del, MA, 74 & PhD(physics), 78. *Prof Exp:* Postdoctoral assoc, nuclear magnetic resonance, Prof G Fasman Biochem Dept, Brandeis Univ, 77-78, Dr S Danyluk Div Biol & Med Res, Argonne Nat Lab, 78-81. *Mem:* Am Phys Soc; Anal Lab Mgrs Asn; Sigma Xi. *Res:* Usage of nuclear magnetic resonance spectroscopy of various systems including nucleosides, biopolymers, polyamides and various types of biological tissues; development of methodologies for academic analytical laboratory management. *Mailing Add:* Chem Dept Rensselaer Polytech Inst Troy NY 12181. *E-Mail:* schwah@rpi.edu

SCHWARTZ, HOWARD F, BOTANY, PHYTOPATHOLOGY. *Current Pos:* PROF, COLO STATE UNIV, FT COLLINS. *Honors & Awards:* Excellence Award, Am Phytopath Soc, 95. *Mailing Add:* Colo State Univ E 207 Plant Sci Bldg Ft Collins CO 80523

SCHWARTZ, HOWARD JULIUS, MEDICINE, ALLERGY. *Current Pos:* USPHS trainee, 68-71, asst prof, 71-74, asst clin prof, 74-77, assoc clin prof med, 77-86, CLIN PROF MED, SCH MED, CASE WESTERN RESERVE UNIV, 86- *Personal Data:* b New York, NY, Nov 24, 36; m 62, Trudy H Blody; c 3. *Educ:* Brooklyn Col, BA, 56; Albert Einstein Col Med, MD, 60. *Prof Exp:* Res fel, Harvard Med Sch, 66-68. *Concurrent Pos:* Clin res fel allergy & immunol, Mass Gen Hosp, 66-68; assoc physician, Univ Hosps, Cleveland, 71-, chief allergy clin, 72-; consult, Hillcrest Hosp, Cleveland & Mt Sinai Hosp, Cleveland; chmn, Comt Insects, Am Acad Allergy. *Mem:* Am Asn Immunologists; fel Am Acad Allergy; fel Am Col Chest Physicians; Am Thoracic Soc; fel Am Col Allergy. *Res:* Allergic respiratory disease, including the interaction of rhinitis and asthma; insect allergy-bee, wasp, hornet and yellow jacket; immunology. *Mailing Add:* 1611 S Green Rd Cleveland OH 44121

SCHWARTZ, ILSA ROSLOW, NEUROANATOMY, AUDITORY SYSTEM. *Current Pos:* assoc prof surg, Sect Otolaryngol & Neuroanat, 87-89, PROF SURG, SECT OTOLARYNGOL, SCH MED, YALE UNIV, 89- *Personal Data:* b Brooklyn, NY, Aug 20, 41; m 64, Alan G; c Leah E & Seth R. *Educ:* Vassar Col, AB, 62; Yale Univ, MS, 64, PhD(molecular biophys), 68. *Prof Exp:* Res assoc, Ctr Neural Sci, Ind Univ, Bloomington, 70-73, asst prof anat & physiol, 73-77; from asst prof to assoc prof surg, div Head & Neck Surg, Sch Med, Univ Calif, Los Angeles, 77-87. *Concurrent Pos:* NIH fel & res fel neuroanat, Albert Einstein Col Med, 68-69; USPHS biomed sci res support grant, Ind Univ, Bloomington, 70-72, NIH res grants, 72; vis res anatomist, Sch Med, Univ Calif, Los Angeles, 76-77; mem, Commun Dis Rev Comt, Nat Inst Neurol & Commun Dis & Stroke, 81-83, chmn, 83-85; panel mem, NIH Consensus Devel Conf on Cochlear Implants, 88; Javits neuroscience investr award, Nat Inst Neurol Commun Dis & Strokes, 88; mem adv coun, Nat Inst Deafness & Other Commun Dis, 88-93; mem, Asn Res Otolaryngol Coun, 87-90; mem bd dir, Friends Nat Inst Deafness & Other Commun Dis, 90-; chair, House Ear Inst Sci Adv Coun, 92-94. *Mem:* Am Asn Anat; Asn Res Otolaryngol (pres, 90-91); Soc Neurosci; Women Neurosci; Asn Women Sci; Cajal Club. *Res:* Synaptic organization; synaptic development; structural and functional correlations of auditory and vestibular neural activity; autoradiographic and immunocytochemical studies of chemical properties of neurons in the auditory system. *Mailing Add:* Dept Surg Div Otolaryngol Yale Univ Sch Med 333 Cedar St PO Box 208041 New Haven CT 06520-8041

SCHWARTZ, IRA, BIOCHEMISTRY, MOLECULAR BIOLOGY. *Current Pos:* from asst prof to assoc prof biochem, 80-89, PROF BIOCHEM & MOLECULAR BIOL, NY MED COL, 89- *Personal Data:* b New York, NY, May 16, 47; m 68; c 3. *Educ:* City Univ New York, BS, 68, PhD(biochem), 73. *Prof Exp:* Lectr, Dept Chem, City Col New York, 68-73; fel, Roche Inst Molecular Biol, 73-75; asst prof biochem, Univ Mass, 75-80. *Concurrent Pos:* Sinsheimer fel, 81-84. *Mem:* AAAS; Am Chem Soc; Am Soc Microbiol; Am Soc Biochem & Molecular Biol. *Res:* Identification of the ribosomal components necessary for binding of nonribosomal protein factors; study of regulation of expression of genes for proteins involved in translation; molecular cloning. *Mailing Add:* Dept Biochem & Molecular Biol NY Med Col Valhalla NY 10595. *Fax:* 914-993-4058; *E-Mail:* schwartz@nymcedu

SCHWARTZ, IRA A(RTHUR), METALLURGY. *Current Pos:* RETIRED. *Personal Data:* b Brooklyn, NY, Mar 8, 15; m 56, Paula Reibel; c David S & Wendy (Sheridan). *Educ:* City Col New York, BS, BME, 42; Stevens Inst Technol, MS, 50. *Prof Exp:* Sr eng draftsman, Hull Design Div, NY Naval Shipyard, USN, 42-46, metallurgist, Mat Lab, 46-52, supvry metallurgist, 52-58, head, Wrought Metals & Radiographic Sect, 58-63, sr task leader, Naval Appl Sci Lab, 63-65, gen metallurgist, Off Chief Engrs, 65-80, res coordr metall & civil eng probs, 69-80. *Concurrent Pos:* Metall consult, Corp Coun, NY, 59-60; consult welding metall & non-destructive testing, 80- *Mem:* Am Soc Metals; Am Foundrymen's Soc. *Res:* Foundry metallurgy involving casting of ferrous and nonferrous alloys by sand, shell and lost-wax methods; physical metallurgy of wrought metals, particularly heat treatment and notch-toughness; nondestructive testing radiography and ultrasonics; metallurgical failures; general metallurgical problems. *Mailing Add:* 8303 The Midway Annandale VA 22003

SCHWARTZ, IRA BRUCE, NONLINEAR DYNAMICS. *Current Pos:* SR RES SCIENTIST APPL MATH, US NAVAL RES LAB, 83- *Personal Data:* b Brooklyn, NY, Dec 3, 50; m 82, Janine Tucker; c Jason & Alexander. *Educ:* Univ Hartford, BS, 73; Univ Conn, MSc, 75; Univ Md, PhD(appl math), 80. *Prof Exp:* NIH fel, NIH, 80-83. *Mem:* AAAS; Soc Indust & Appl Math. *Res:* Applied nonlinear dynamics including theoretical work on coupled nonlinear systems, nonlinear optics, coupled mechanical structures, nonlinear control, and superconductivity. *Mailing Add:* Naval Res Lab Code 6700 1 Washington DC 20375. *Fax:* 202-404-8357; *E-Mail:* schwartz@nls4.nrl.navy.mil

SCHWARTZ, IRVING LEON, PHYSIOLOGY, MEDICINE. *Current Pos:* prof physiol & biophys, chmn, Dept Physiol & dean, Grad Sch Biol Sci, 65-80, Golden & Harold Lamport Distinguished Serv Prof-at-large & dir, Ctr Polypeptide & Membrane Res, 80-89, EMER DEAN, MT SINAI GRAD SCH BIOL SCI, CITY UNIV NY, 89- *Personal Data:* b Cedarhurst, NY, Dec 25, 18; m 46, Felice Nierenberg; c Cornelia Ann, Tony & James. *Educ:* Columbia Col, AB, 39; NY Univ, MD, 43. *Honors & Awards:* Gibbs Mem Award, Rockefeller Inst, 50. *Prof Exp:* Intern, Third Med Div, Bellevue Hosp, NY, 43-44; asst resident, 46-47; from asst physician to assoc physician, Rockefeller Inst, 52-58; sr scientist & attend physician hosp, Med Res Ctr, Brookhaven Nat Lab, 58-61; Joseph Eichberg prof physiol & chmn dept, Col Med, Univ Cincinnati, 61-65. *Concurrent Pos:* NIH fel, Col Med, NY Univ, 47-50; Porter fel, Rockefeller Inst, 50-51, Am Heart Asn fel, 51-52; res collabr, Med Res Ctr, Brookhaven Nat Lab, 61-; exec officer, Biomed Sci Doctoral Prog, City Univ NY, 68-70. *Mem:* Am Physiol Soc; Soc Exp Biol & Med; Am Soc Clin Invest; Biophys Soc; Am Fedn Clin Res; Endocrine Soc; Soc Neurosci. *Res:* Membrane and transport phenomena; mechanism of hormone action; conformation-structure-activity relationships of peptides and proteins. *Mailing Add:* Mt Sinai Med Ctr Box 1022 New York NY 10029

SCHWARTZ, IRVING ROBERT, MEDICINE, HEMATOLOGY. *Current Pos:* from asst prof to assoc prof, 65-86, PROF MED, TEMPLE UNIV, 86- *Personal Data:* b New York, NY, May 7, 23; m 51; c 3. *Educ:* NY Univ, AB, 47; State Univ NY, MD, 51. *Prof Exp:* Intern, Montefiore Hosp, Bronx, NY, 51-52; resident internal med, Bronx Vet Admin Hosp, 52-53 & Ohio State Univ Hosp, Columbus, 53-54; resident hemat, Cardeza Found, Jefferson Med Col, 54-55; from asst dir to dir Sacks Dept Hemat, Albert Einstein Med Ctr, 58-80. *Concurrent Pos:* USPHS res fel, Jefferson Med Col, 55-57; Sacks res fel, Albert Einstein Med Ctr, 57-58; head, dir hemat, Albert Einstein Med Ctr, 80- *Mem:* Am Soc Hemat; AMA; Am Col Physicians; Transplantation Soc; NY Acad Sci. *Res:* Cancer chemotherapy; bone marrow transplantation; radiation effects; hemoglobinopathies; leukoagglutinins; bone marrow preservation. *Mailing Add:* Albert Einstein Med Ctr York & Tabor Rds Philadelphia PA 19141

SCHWARTZ, JACK, COMPUTER MODELING, IMAGE COLOR. *Current Pos:* PRES, TOUCHSTONE TECHNOL, INC, 83- *Personal Data:* b New York, NY, May 4, 31; m 57, Joan D Rosef; c Gary D & Linda G. *Educ:* City Col NY, BS, 53; Harvard Univ, AM, 54, PhD(physics), 58. *Prof Exp:* Res assoc, Brookhaven Nat Lab, 57-60; mem tech staff, RCA Labs, David Sarnoff Res Ctr, NJ, 60-64 & Sanders Assocs, Inc, 64-83. *Concurrent Pos:* Mem tech staff, Mitre Corp, 83-90. *Mem:* Am Phys Soc; Sigma Xi; Soc Imaging Sci & Technol; Inst Elec & Electronics Engrs. *Res:* Twenty US patents, one French patent; nonlinear optics; magnetic resonance phenomena; magnetism in thin ferromagnetic films; atomic beams; system analysis; operations research; solar energy; computer modeling of radar and communications systems; image color correction. *Mailing Add:* 147 Ridge St Arlington MA 02174-1733. *E-Mail:* j.schwartz@ieee.org

SCHWARTZ, JACOB THEODORE, FUNCTIONAL ANALYSIS. *Current Pos:* assoc prof, 57-59, PROF MATH & COMPUT SCI, COURANT INST MATH SCI, NEW YORK UNIV, 59- *Personal Data:* b New York, NY, Jan 9, 30; m 50, 89; c 2. *Educ:* City Col New York, BS, 48; Yale Univ, MA, 49, PhD, 51. *Honors & Awards:* Wilbur Cross Medal, Yale. *Prof Exp:* From instr to asst prof math, Yale Univ, 52-57. *Concurrent Pos:* Dir, Info Sci & Tech Off, DARPA, 87-89. *Mem:* Nat Acad Sci. *Res:* Physics and functional analysis; physical mathematics; probability; computer science; robotics. *Mailing Add:* Dept Math NY Univ New York NY 10003

SCHWARTZ, JAMES WILLIAM, ENGINEERING. *Current Pos:* CONSULT, 86- *Personal Data:* b Elmira, NY, Feb 11, 27; m 45, Anita; c Judith. *Educ:* Cornell Univ, BE, 51, MS, 52. *Prof Exp:* Mem tech staff, RCA Labs, 52-58; vpres, Nat Video Corp, 61-64, Rauland Div, Zenith Rad, 69-79; pres, MD Systs, Inc, 80-86. *Mem:* Sigma Xi; fel Inst Elec & Electronics Engrs. *Res:* Flat panel displays. *Mailing Add:* 2384 Stonebrook Dr Medford OR 97504

SCHWARTZ, JAY W(ILLIAM), SPACE SYSTEMS ENGINEERING, TELECOMMUNICATIONS. *Current Pos:* CHIEF SCIENTIST & VPRES, AVTEC SYSTS INC, ALEXANDRIA, VA, 83- *Personal Data:* b Scranton, Pa, Sept 28, 34; m 92, Rita D Botwin; c Karen B, Michael P, Stephen R, Kenneth P Botwin & Jeffrey E Botwin. *Educ:* Univ Pa, BS, 56; Yale Univ, MEng, 60, PhD(elec eng), 64. *Honors & Awards:* Res Publ Award, Naval Res Lab, 78, 80, & 84. *Prof Exp:* Mem tech staff, Res & Eng Support Div, Inst Defense Anal, 63-67; vis assoc prof elec eng, Polytech Inst Brooklyn, 67-68; sr mem tech staff, Sci & Tech Div, Inst Defense Anal, Va, 68-72; consult to assoc, dir res space & commun sci & technol, Naval Res Lab, 72-83. *Concurrent Pos:* Mem ad hoc sci group, Tactical Satellite Commun, 67-68; chmn, Optical Commun Working group, Navy Laser Technol Prog Off, 72-76; adj assoc prof elec eng, George Washington Univ, 72-76; mem, Mil Man in Space Panel, 78-79. *Mem:* Inst Elec & Electronics Engrs; Int Union Radio Sci. *Res:* Communication satellite systems; military communications; data processing in space vehicles; communication theory; military space systems; timing and synchronization. *Mailing Add:* Avtec Systs Inc 10530 Rosehaven St Fairfax VA 22030. *Fax:* 703-273-1313; *E-Mail:* schwartz@avtec.com

SCHWARTZ, JEFFREY, ORGANOMETALLIC CHEMISTRY. *Current Pos:* ASST PROF CHEM, PRINCETON UNIV, 70-, PROF CHEM. *Personal Data:* b New York, NY, Jan 3, 45; m 70. *Educ:* Mass Inst Technol, SB, 66; Stanford Univ, PhD(chem), 70. *Prof Exp:* NIH fel, Columbia Univ, 70. *Mem:* Am Chem Soc; Royal Soc Chem. *Res:* Applications of organometallic chemistry to organic synthesis; novel organometallic complexes; intramolecular organometallic redox reactions. *Mailing Add:* Dept Chem Princeton Univ Princeton NJ 08540

SCHWARTZ, JEFFREY H, PHYSICAL ANTHROPOLOGY. *Current Pos:* from asst prof to assoc prof, 74-81, PROF PHYS ANTHROP, UNIV PITTSBURGH, 90- *Personal Data:* b Richmond, Va, Mar 6, 48. *Educ:* Columbia Univ, BA, 69, MS, 73, PhD(phys anthrop), 74. *Prof Exp:* Adj lectr, Lehman Col, 73-74. *Concurrent Pos:* Staff osteologist, Am Sch Oriental Res, 70-; res assoc, Carnegie Mus Natural Hist, 76- & Am Mus Nat Hist, 79-; vis scholar, Univ Zurich, 89; Kalbeleisch fel, Am Mus Natural Hist, New York City, 90; sr fel, Japan Soc Prom Sci, 93. *Mem:* Am Asn Phys Anthrop; AAAS; Soc Syst Zool; Soc Vert Paleont; Soc Study Evolution; Sigma Xi. *Res:* Evolutionary theory and systematics; primate phylogeny and paleontology; human and faunal remains of the circum-Mediterranean and Near East; general physical anthropology and vertebrate paleontology. *Mailing Add:* Dept Anthrop Univ Pittsburgh 3401 Forbes Quad Pittsburgh PA 15260

SCHWARTZ, JEFFREY LEE, MICROBIAL BIOCHEMISTRY. *Current Pos:* SECT LEADER & RES INVESTR FERMENTATION, SCHERING-PLOUGH, 79- *Personal Data:* b Far Rockaway, NY, Aug 19, 43. *Educ:* Brooklyn Col Pharm, BS, 66; Univ Wis-Madison, MS, 68, PhD(pharm biochem), 71. *Prof Exp:* Res fel microbial biochem, Wesleyan Univ, 71-73; res fel, Squibb Inst Med Res, 73-74, res investr microbial biochem, 74-79. *Mem:* Am Soc Microbiol; Am Chem Soc. *Res:* Investigating the production of new antibiotics from various microorganisms and the development of novel and sensitive methods for antibiotic detection. *Mailing Add:* 6 Dartmouth Rd West Orange NJ 07052-3906

SCHWARTZ, JEROME LAWRENCE, chemistry, technical management; deceased, see previous edition for last biography

SCHWARTZ, JESSICA, GROWTH HORMONE, GENE REGULATION. *Current Pos:* from asst prof to assoc prof, 79-94, PROF PHYSIOL, MED SCH, UNIV MICH, 94- *Personal Data:* b New Haven, Conn, July 13, 45. *Educ:* Vassar Col, BA, 67; Harvard Univ, PhD(physiol), 74. *Prof Exp:* Asst prof, Sch Med, Emory Univ, 78-79. *Concurrent Pos:* Vis scientist, Mass Inst Technol, 87-88; panel mem, Physiol Processes, Endocrinol, NSF, 90-96; mem, Women Physiol Comm, Am Physiol Soc, 89-92, Prog Adv Comm, E & M, 92-95. *Mem:* Am Diabetes Asn; Am Physiol Soc; Endocrine Soc. *Res:* Molecular and cellular mechanisms of growth factor action- regulation of gene expression. *Mailing Add:* Dept Physiol Med Sci Bldg Two Univ Mich Ann Arbor MI 48109-0622. *Fax:* 313-936-8813; *E-Mail:* jeschwar@umich.edu

SCHWARTZ, JOAN POYNER, NEUROBIOLOGY, NEUROPHARMACOLOGY. *Current Pos:* GROUP HEAD MOLECULAR BIOL, LAB PRECLIN PHARM, NIMH, 76- *Personal Data:* b Ont, Can, Aug 19, 43; m 67. *Educ:* Cornell Univ, AB, 65; Harvard Univ, PhD(biol chem), 71. *Prof Exp:* Instr pharmacol, Dept Pharm, Rutgers Med Sch, 70-71; staff fel, Lab Neuroanat & Neurosci, Nat Inst Neurol & Commun Dis & Stroke, 72-76. *Concurrent Pos:* Mem, Neurol C Study Sect, 85- *Mem:* Am Soc Pharmaceut & Exp Therapeut; Soc Neurosci; Am Soc Neurochem; AAAS. *Res:* Nerve growth factor: regulation of synthesis and mechanism of actions; catecholamine-mediated regulation of gene expression via cyclic adenosine monophosphate levels. *Mailing Add:* MGS CNB NINDS NIH Bldg 10 Rm 3N256 Bethesda MD 20890-1279. *Fax:* 301-402-0117; *E-Mail:* Bitnet: jks@nihcu

SCHWARTZ, JOHN H, MEMBRANE TRANSPORT, RENAL METABOLISM. *Current Pos:* assoc prof, 76-83, PROF MED, SCH MED, BOSTON UNIV, 83- *Personal Data:* m 65, Janice Halpert; c Wendy & Adam. *Educ:* NY Univ, MD, 67. *Mem:* Am Physiol Soc; Am Soc Nephrology. *Res:* Renal physiology. *Mailing Add:* Evans-401 Boston Med Ctr 1 Boston Med Ctr Pl Boston MA 02118-2999. *Fax:* 617-638-8281; *E-Mail:* vhsch@buedu

SCHWARTZ, JOHN T, OPHTHALMOLOGY, EPIDEMIOLOGY. *Current Pos:* PRES, J T SCHWARTZ CONSULT INC, 83- *Personal Data:* b Hazelton, Pa, Aug 28, 26; m 56; c 6. *Educ:* Dartmouth Col, AB, 47; Univ Notre Dame, MS, 50; Jefferson Med Col, MD, 55; Harvard Univ, MPH, 63. *Prof Exp:* Intern med, Madison Gen Hosp, 55-56; head dept ophthal, Naval Base Dispensary, Norfolk, Va, 59-61; asst prof, Sch Med, Univ Mo, Columbia, 61-62; head sect ophthal field & develop res, Nat Inst Neurol Dis & Blindness, 63-68; dep chief dept ophthal, USPHS Hosp, Baltimore, 68-69; head sect ophthal field & develop res, Nat Eye Inst, 69-75; spec asst to dir, Div Hosp & Clin & chief, Dept Ophthal, 76-79, assoc dir med affairs, Bur Med Serv, Health Serv Admin, USPHS, 81-83. *Concurrent Pos:* Clin asst prof ophthal, Sch Med, Univ Mo, 63-64; asst clin prof, George Washington Univ, 65-73; consult ophthal, USPHS Hosp, Baltimore, 69-; Nat Health Exam Surv, Nat Ctr Health Statist, 69-; guest worker, Geront Res Ctr, Nat Inst Aging, 79-80; consult ophthalmoepidemiol, Bur Med Devices, Food & Drug Admin, 80-81; med officer, 82-83. *Mem:* Am Acad Ophthal; Int Soc Twin Studies; Am Eye Study Club; Soc Epidemiol Res. *Res:* Epidemiologic and genetic investigations of etiology of ocular disorders and clinical practice ophthalmology. *Mailing Add:* 18000 Marden Lane Sandy Spring MD 20860

SCHWARTZ, JOSEPH BARRY, PHARMACEUTICAL CHEMISTRY. *Current Pos:* prof pharmaceut, 81-, DIR INDUST PHARM RES, PHILADELPHIA COL PHARM & SCI, 81-, BURROUGHS WELCOME, PROF PHARMACEUT. *Personal Data:* b Richmond, Va, June 11, 41; m 64; c 3. *Educ:* Med Col Va, BS, 63; Univ Mich, MS, 65, PhD(pharmaceut chem), 67. *Prof Exp:* Sr res pharmacist, Merck, Sharp & Dohme Res Labs, West Point, Pa, 67-72, res fel, 72-81. *Concurrent Pos:* Consult, pharmaceut indust firms, 81-; chmn, Pharmaceut Technol Sect, Acad Pharmaceut Sci, 84-85; Linwood F Tice chair pharmaceut, Philadelphia Col Pharm & Sci, 87- *Mem:* AAAS; Am Pharmaceut Asn; fel Acad Pharmaceut Sci; fel Am Asn Pharmaceut Sci; Parentral Drug Asn; Controlled Release Soc; Am Asn Col Pharmacists; Sigma Xi. *Res:* Drug release form wax matrices; physical and chemical properties affecting drug availability; dosage form design and processing; controlled release. *Mailing Add:* 600 S 43rd St Philadelphia PA 19104

SCHWARTZ, JOSEPH ROBERT, physical chemistry, organic chemistry; deceased, see previous edition for last biography

SCHWARTZ, JUDAH LEON, SCIENCE EDUCATION. *Current Pos:* sr res scientist, Educ Res Ctr, 66-72, PROF ENGR SCI & EDUC, MASS INST TECHNOL, 73-; PROF EDUC, HARVARD UNIV, 85- *Personal Data:* b Brooklyn, NY, July 13, 34; m 60; c 3. *Educ:* Yeshiva Univ, BA, 54; Columbia Univ, AM, 57; NY Univ, PhD(physics), 63. *Prof Exp:* Asst physics, Columbia Univ, 54-57; reactor physicist, Am Mach & Foundry Co, 57; instr physics, Israel Inst Technol, 57-58; mem tech staff weapons physics, G C Dewey Corp, 58-61; sr physicist, Autometric Corp, 61-62 & G C Dewey Corp, 62-63; instr physics, NY Univ, 61-63; fel, Lawrence Radiation Lab, 63-64, physicist, 63-66. *Concurrent Pos:* Consult Sci, Tech & World Affairs Prog, Carnegie Endowment for Int Peace, 63- & For Serv Inst, Dept State Educ Develop Ctr; assoc ed, Am J Physics, 72-; assoc ed, Int J Math Educ, 72-; hon res assoc, Dept Psychol, Harvard Univ, 74-75. *Mem:* AAAS; Am Phys Soc. *Res:* Science and mathematics education; computer graphics; computer generated films; cognitive psychology and the development of mathematical competence in children. *Mailing Add:* Grad Sch Educ Harvard Univ Harvard Univ Nichols House Appian Way Cambridge MA 02138

SCHWARTZ, LARRY L, physical chemistry, for more information see previous edition

SCHWARTZ, LAWRENCE B, MASS CELLS. *Current Pos:* ASSOC PROF MED, MED COL VA, 83- *Personal Data:* b Oakridge, Tenn, July 1, 49. *Educ:* Wash Univ, MD & PhD(biochem), 76. *Mem:* Am Asn Immunol; Am Fedn Clin Res; Am Acad Allergy & Immunol. *Mailing Add:* Dept Internal Med Va Commonwealth Univ Box 980263 Richmond VA 23298. *Fax:* 804-371-0283

SCHWARTZ, LEANDER JOSEPH, WASTE MANAGEMENT, RESOURCE RECOVERY. *Current Pos:* assoc prof environ sci, Univ Wis-Green Bay, 69-82, chmn, Dept Biol, 72-75, dean natural sci, 85-88, PROF NATURAL & APPL SCI, UNIV WIS-GREEN BAY, 82- *Personal Data:* b Newton, Wis, Jan 10, 32; m 64; c 2. *Educ:* Wis State Univ, Platteville, BS, 57; Univ Wis, MS, 59, PhD(bot), 63. *Prof Exp:* Asst prof bot, Fox Valley Ctr, Univ Wis, 63-69, dean, 69-72. *Mem:* AAAS; Am Inst Biol Sci; Am Soc Microbiol. *Res:* Aquatic microbiology; resource recovery; anaerobic treatment of high strength liquid waste streams; application of sludges on agricultural lands. *Mailing Add:* 159 Appletree Ct Green Bay WI 54302-4464

SCHWARTZ, LELAND DWIGHT, POULTRY PATHOLOGY. *Current Pos:* SR AVIAN PATHOLOGIST, ANIMAL HEALTH DIAG LAB, COL VET MED, MICH STATE UNIV, 84- *Personal Data:* b Enid, Okla, July 26, 25; m 54; c 2. *Educ:* Okla State Univ, DVM, 53; Univ Ga, MS, 63. *Honors & Awards:* Game Bird Indust Award, 84; Wildlife Conserv Award, 84. *Prof Exp:* Vet, pvt pract, 53-55; vet, Hartsel Ranch, 55-56; inspection livestock, Animal & Plant Health Inspection Serv, USDA, 56-59 & poultry, 59-61; instr avian path, Univ Ga, 61-64; vet, exten, Pa State Univ, 64-84. *Mem:* Sigma Xi; Am Vet Med Asn; Am Asn Avian Pathologists; Am Asn Exped Vet. *Res:* Unidentified viral infections of commercial chickens. *Mailing Add:* 3871 Sandlewood Dr Okemos MI 48864

SCHWARTZ, LEON JOSEPH, MATERIALS SCIENCE. *Current Pos:* Chemist, Photoconductors, 70-74, MAT SCIENTIST, PITNEY-BOWES, INC, STAMFORD, CONN, 74- *Personal Data:* b New York, NY, Jan 28, 43; m 67; c 2. *Educ:* City Col New York, BEng, 64; City Univ New York, MEng, 66, PhD(metall), 70. *Mem:* Electrochem Soc; Soc Photog Scientists & Engrs. *Res:* Materials research on a phenomenological level; inorganics, especially metals, semiconductors, ceramics, intermetallic compounds; solid state diffusion and photoconductivity; materials, electronic, paper; graphic arts; design of experiments, human factors. *Mailing Add:* 30 Briarcliff Dr Monsey NY 10952

SCHWARTZ, LEONARD H, CHEMISTRY. *Current Pos:* From asst prof to assoc prof, 63-71, PROF CHEM, CITY COL NEW YORK, 71- *Personal Data:* b New York, NY, Nov 25, 32; m 93, Jennifer Fung; c Robert, Bonnie & David. *Educ:* City Col New York, BS, 54; NY Univ, PhD(chem), 61. *Concurrent Pos:* Exec officer PhD prog chem, City Univ New York, 71-78. *Mem:* Am Chem Soc; Royal Soc Chem. *Res:* Organic chemistry. *Mailing Add:* 9060 Palisade Ave No 826 North Bergen NJ 07047. *Fax:* 212-650-6107

SCHWARTZ, LEONARD WILLIAM, FLOW BEHAVIOR OF COATINGS, POROUS MEDIA FLOWS. *Current Pos:* PROF MECH ENG & MATH, UNIV DEL, 87- *Personal Data:* b New York, NY, May 21, 43; m 75; c 2. *Educ:* Cornell Univ, BEP, 65, MAE, 66; Stanford Univ, PhD(fluid mech), 72. *Prof Exp:* Aero engr, Lockheed Missiles & Space Co, 65-69; Nat Res Coun fel, Ames Res Ctr, NASA, 73-74; staff scientist, Flow Res Inc, 74-75; sr lectr appl math, Univ Adelaide, Australia, 75-80; sr staff mathematician, Res Lab, Exxon Corp, 80-86. *Concurrent Pos:* Vis prof, Univ Calif, Berkeley, 77, Stanford Univ, 80, Rutgers Univ, 86-87; consult, Failure Anal Assocs, 80-81, Glidden Paints Div, ICI, 90-; ed, J Eng Math, 85-; selector, prin young investr panel, NSF, 85. *Mem:* Am Phys Soc; Soc Indust & Appl Math. *Res:* Fluid mechanics; flow in porous media; coating flows; naval hydrodynamics; aerodynamics; mathematical modelling of fluid flow and heat transfer; nonlinear problems. *Mailing Add:* Dept Mech Eng Univ Del Newark DE 19711

SCHWARTZ, LOWELL MELVIN, PHYSICAL CHEMISTRY. *Current Pos:* from asst prof to assoc prof chem, 65-76, PROF CHEM, UNIV MASS, BOSTON, 76- *Personal Data:* b Brooklyn, NY, Dec 1, 34. *Educ:* Mass Inst Technol, SB, 56, ScD(chem eng), 59; Calif Inst Technol, MS, 57. *Prof Exp:* Chem engr, Dept Appl Physics, Chr Michelsens Inst, Norway, 59-60 & Esso Res & Eng Co, Standard Oil Co NJ, 60-61; res assoc chem, Princeton Univ, 62-63; res instr, Dartmouth Col, 63-65. *Mem:* Royal Soc Chem. *Mailing Add:* 166 Oakleigh Rd Newton MA 02158

SCHWARTZ, LYLE H, MATERIALS SCIENCE, ENGINEERING. *Current Pos:* PRES, ASSOC UNIVS INC, 97- *Personal Data:* b Chicago, Ill, Aug 2, 36; m 73, Celesta S Jurkovich; c 2. *Educ:* Northwestern Univ, BSc, 59, PhD(mat sci), 64. *Prof Exp:* From asst prof to assoc prof, Northwestern Univ, Evanston, 64-72, asst chmn, Dept Mat Sci & Eng, 73-78, dir, Mat Res Ctr, 79-84, prof mat sci; dir, Mat Sci & Eng Lab, Nat Inst Stand & Technol, 84-97. *Concurrent Pos:* Consult, Solid State Sci Div, Argonne Nat Lab, 66-; visitor, Bell Tel Labs, 72-73; mem, Nat Res Coun panel to select NSF doctoral fels in eng, 74-77, chmn, 76 & 77. *Mem:* Nat Acad Eng; Mat Res Soc; Am Crystallog Asn; Am Inst Mining, Metall & Petrol Engrs; fel Am Soc Metals Int; Am Phys Soc. *Res:* X-ray and neutron diffraction; Mossbauer effect; spinodal alloys; alloy catalysts. *Mailing Add:* Assoc Univ Inc 1400 16th St NW Suite 730 Washington DC 20036

SCHWARTZ, M(URRAY) A(RTHUR), MATERIALS SCIENCE ENGINEERING. *Current Pos:* supvr nonmetallic mat res, Tuscaloosa Res Lab, 72-74, staff ceramic engr, 74-90, MAT PROG MGR, US BUR MINES, 90-; DIR, MAT TECHNOL CONSULTS INC. *Personal Data:* b New York, NY, Nov 13, 20; m 44; c 2. *Educ:* Alfred Univ, BS, 43. *Prof Exp:* Ceramic engr, Bendix Aviation Corp, 43-44, Streator Drain Tile Co, 46-47, Fairchild Engine & Airplane Corp, 47-51 & Oak Ridge Nat Lab, 51; supvr ceramics, Aeronaut Res Lab, US Dept Air Force, 51-59; mgr, Aeronutronic Div, Ford Motor Co, 59-60; mat appln, United Tech Ctr, United Aircraft Corp, 60-65; asst dir ceramics div, Ill Inst Technol Res Inst, 65-71; coord engr, Dept Pub

Works, Chicago, 71-72. *Concurrent Pos:* Exec secy, Interagency Comt Mat, 75-79; ed, News from Wash, Bulletin Am Ceramic Soc, 76-86; mats policy analyst, White House Off Sci & Technol Policy, 82-84; deleg eng Affairs Coun, Am Asn Eng Soc, 85-; trustee, Fedn Mat Socs, 83- *Mem:* Fel Am Ceramic Soc (vpres, 81-82); fel Am Inst Chem; Am Soc Metals; Am Inst Ceramic Engrs; AAAS. *Res:* Nonmetallic materials; recycling of waste materials; utilization of mineral resources; industrial ceramics; new materials; basic behavior; refractories; whitewares; glass; aerospace, nuclear and electronic applications; environmental quality; energy conservation; construction materials. *Mailing Add:* Mat Technol Consult Inc 30 Orchard Way N Potomac MD 20854-6128

SCHWARTZ, MARSHALL ZANE, GASTROINTESTINAL PHYSIOLOGY, ORGAN TRANSPLANTATION. *Current Pos:* assoc prof, 81-83, PROF SURG & PEDIAT, 86-, CHIEF PEDIAT SURG, UNIV CALIF, DAVIS, 83- *Personal Data:* b Minneapolis, Minn, Sept 1, 45; m 71; c 2. *Educ:* Univ Minn, BS, 68, MD, 70. *Honors & Awards:* Sam Segal Award, Univ Minn, 66, Boutell Award, 68; James W McLaughlin Award, Univ Tex, 83. *Prof Exp:* Instr & asst surg, Children's Hosp Med Ctr, Med Sch, Harvard Univ, 78-79; from asst prof to assoc prof surg & pediat, Med Br, Univ Tex, 79-81, chief pediat & surg serv, Child Health Ctr, surgeon-in-chief, 80-83. *Concurrent Pos:* Prin investr, Basil O'Connor Starter Res Grant, March of Dimes, 81-86 & Young Investr Award, NIH, 82-85. *Mem:* Soc Univ Surgeons; Am Col Surgeons; Am Pediat Surg Asn; Am Acad Pediat; Soc Surg Alimentary Tract; Asn Acad Surg. *Res:* The relationship of gastrointestinal peptides to the function and adaptation of the small intestine; methods of identifying rejection following small intestine transplantation. *Mailing Add:* Dept Surg 111 Michigan Ave N Washington DC 20010

SCHWARTZ, MARTIN ALAN, ORGANIC CHEMISTRY. *Current Pos:* From asst prof to assoc prof, 66-76, chmn dept, 77-83, PROF CHEM, FLA STATE UNIV, 76- *Personal Data:* b New York, NY, July 5, 40; m 61; c 3. *Educ:* Dartmouth Col, AB, 62; Stanford Univ, PhD(org chem), 66. *Concurrent Pos:* Sr ed, J Org Chem, Am Chem Soc, 71- *Mem:* Am Chem Soc. *Res:* Synthesis of natural products. *Mailing Add:* Chem Fla State Univ 600 W College Ave Tallahassee FL 32306-1096

SCHWARTZ, MARTIN ALEXANDER, CELL BIOLOGY. *Current Pos:* ASSOC MEM, SCRIPPS RES INST, 91- *Personal Data:* b Philadelphia, Pa, Dec 31, 54; m 86, Lenore Jordan; c Sarah & Rebecca. *Educ:* New Col, BA, 75; Stanford Univ, PhD(phys chem), 79. *Prof Exp:* Fel, Mass Inst Technol, 79-82; from asst prof to assoc prof, 91, Harvard Med Sch, 83-91. *Mem:* Am Asn Cell Biol. *Res:* Signaling by integrin cell adhesion receptors, we are studying how these receptors regulate intracellular signaling pathways, and how these pathways influence cell functions. *Mailing Add:* 10666 N Torrey Pines Rd La Jolla CA 92037. *Fax:* 619-554-6408; *E-Mail:* schwartz@scripps.edu

SCHWARTZ, MAURICE EDWARD, THEORETICAL CHEMISTRY. *Current Pos:* asst prof & sr scientist, Radiation Lab, 68-73, ASSOC PROF CHEM, UNIV NOTRE DAME, 73- *Personal Data:* b Laurinburg, NC, Sept 28, 39; m 65; c 2. *Educ:* Presby Col (SC), BS, 61; Vanderbilt Univ, PhD(chem), 66. *Prof Exp:* NSF & Ramsey fels, Oxford Univ, 66; res fel, Princeton Univ, 67-68. *Concurrent Pos:* Vis prof, Univ Calif, Berkeley, 72; NATO sr fel sci, Univ Uppsala, Sweden & Oxford Univ, England, 73; assoc prog dir quantum chem, NSF, 76-77. *Mem:* Am Chem Soc; Am Phys Soc; Am Asn Univ Professors. *Res:* Quantum chemistry; photoelectron spectroscopy; radiation chemistry; surface chemistry and catalysis. *Mailing Add:* 725 Park Ave South Bend IN 46616-1337

SCHWARTZ, MAURICE LEO, COASTAL PROCESSES, COASTAL GEOLOGY. *Current Pos:* from asst prof to prof, 68-93, dean grad studies & res, 87-93, EMER PROF GEOL & EDUC, WESTERN WASH UNIV, 93-; PRES, COASTAL CONSULTS, INC, 83- *Personal Data:* b Ft Worth, Tex, Sept 27, 25; m 50, Norma Sternberg; c Stepanie, Phebe, Philip, Howard & Ivan. *Educ:* Columbia Univ, BS, 63, MA, 64, PhD(geol), 66. *Honors & Awards:* Crismar Award, PanAm Fedn Ocean & Coastal Engrs. *Prof Exp:* Lab instr geol, Columbia Univ, 63-66; lectr, Brooklyn Col, 64-68. *Concurrent Pos:* Fulbright-Hayes res scholar, Inst Oceanog & Fishing Res, Athens, Greece, 73-74; Nat Acad Sci specialist exchange prog visit to USSR, 78 & 86. *Mem:* Geol Soc Am; Coastal Educ & Res Found; Coastal Soc; Am Shore & Beach Preservation Asn. *Res:* Beach processes; sea level changes; earth science education; coastal archeology; barrier islands; artificial beach nourishment. *Mailing Add:* Dept Geol Western Wash Univ Bellingham WA 98225. *Fax:* 360-650-7302

SCHWARTZ, MELVIN, PHYSICS, DATA COMMUNICATION. *Current Pos:* assoc dir high energy & nuclear physics, 91-94, I I RABI PROF PHYSICS, BROOKHAVEN NAT LAB, 94- *Personal Data:* b New York, NY, Nov 2, 32; m 53, Marilyn Fenster; c David N, Diane & Betty. *Educ:* Columbia Univ, AB, 53, PhD(physics), 58. *Hon Degrees:* ScD, Columbia Univ, 91, Adelphi Univ & Weizmann Inst Sci, 95. *Honors & Awards:* Nobel Prize in Physics, 88; Prize, Am Phys Soc, 64. *Prof Exp:* Res assoc, Brookhaven Nat Lab, 56-57, assoc physicist, 57-58; from asst prof to prof physics, Columbia Univ, 58-66; prof physics, Stanford Univ, 66-83; pres, Digital Pathways Inc, 70-91. *Concurrent Pos:* Sloan fel, 59-63; Guggenheim fel, Guggenheim Found, 68. *Mem:* Nat Acad Sci; fel Am Phys Soc. *Res:* High energy experimental particle physics. *Mailing Add:* Dept Physics Columbia Univ New York NY 10027

SCHWARTZ, MELVIN J, THEORETICAL PHYSICS. *Current Pos:* ASSOC PROF PHYSICS, ST JOHN'S UNIV, NY, 66- *Personal Data:* b Brooklyn, NY, Oct 8, 28; m 52; c 2. *Educ:* Brooklyn Col, BS, 51; State Univ Iowa, PhD(physics), 58. *Prof Exp:* Instr physics, Rutgers Univ, 56-57; lectr, Univ Minn, 57-59; res assoc, Syracuse Univ, 59-61; assoc prof, Adelphi Univ, 61-64; res scientist, NY Univ, 64-66. *Concurrent Pos:* Nat Sci Found res grant, 61-64; NASA res grant, 64-66. *Mem:* AAAS; Am Phys Soc; NY Acad Sci; Int Soc Gen Relativity & Gravitation; Sigma Xi. *Res:* Quantum field theory; correspondence principle quantization of electrodynamics; collisionless plasmas; general relativistic kinetic theory of plasmas; social effects of science. *Mailing Add:* 2 Henry St Great Neck NY 11023-1113

SCHWARTZ, MELVIN MARVIN, MATERIALS JOINING, COMPOSITE MATERIALS. *Current Pos:* mgr mfg technol, 78-90, CHIEF METALS/METAL PROCESSES & STAFF SCIENTIST/ENGR, SIKORSKY AIRCRAFT, UNITED TECHNOL CORP, 90- *Personal Data:* b Philadelphia, Pa, Nov 7, 29; m 43, Carolyn Parmer Klein; c Anne-Marie. *Educ:* Temple Univ, BA, 51; Drexel Univ, MS, 65. *Honors & Awards:* C Adams Lectr, Am Welding Soc, 75, R D Thomas Mem Award, 79; G Lubin Award, Soc Advan Mat & Process Eng, 86; Jud Hall Award, Soc Mfg Engrs, 95. *Prof Exp:* Metallurgist, US Bur Mines, 51-52; metallurgist & producibility engr, US Chem Corps, 52-54; tech mfg mgr & lab chief, Martin Marietta, 54-70; mgr & dir, Mfg Res & Develop & prog dir, Rohr Indust, 70-78; mgr & dir, Rohr Indust, 70-78. *Concurrent Pos:* US deleg, Braz & Solder Comt, Roma IV, Int Inst Welding, 67-84; mem, Tech Comt, Am Soc Metals, 85 & 87. *Mem:* Am Welding Soc; fel Soc Advan Mat & Process Eng; fel Am Soc Metals. *Res:* Invention of aluminum dip brazing paste (aluminbraze); development of joining and fabrication methods for metals, ceramics and composites; author of over 100 articles and 13 books. *Mailing Add:* 80 Rolling Meadow Rd Madison CT 06443-2329

SCHWARTZ, MICHAEL AVERILL, PHARMACEUTICAL CHEMISTRY. *Current Pos:* PROF PHARM & DEAN COL, 78-, EMER PROF & DEAN, UNIV FLA. *Personal Data:* b New York, NY, Aug 4, 30; div; c 2. *Educ:* Brooklyn Col Pharm, BS, 52; Columbia Univ, MS, 56; Univ Wis, PhD(pharm), 59. *Prof Exp:* Sr res scientist prod develop, Bristol Labs, Inc, 59-63; from asst prof to prof, State Univ NY, Buffalo, 63-78, 63-70, asst dean, 66-70, dean, Sch Pharm, 70-76. *Concurrent Pos:* USPHS grant, 64-69. *Mem:* Am Pharmaceut Asn; fel Am Asn Pharmaceut Sci; Am Chem Soc; Am Soc Hosp Pharmacists. *Res:* Pharmaceutics; chemistry of penicillins and drug allergy; models for enzymes; drug stability. *Mailing Add:* Col Pharm B100496HSC Univ Fla Gainesville FL 92610

SCHWARTZ, MICHAEL H, QUALITY ASSURANCE, AUDITING. *Current Pos:* qual assurance engr, Pitney Bowes Inc, 81-84, staff qual engr, 84-85, proj mgr, 85-86, qual control mgr, 86-87, SR ENGR, PITNEY BOWES INC, 87- *Personal Data:* b New Haven, Conn, June 16, 59. *Educ:* George Washington Univ, BSEE, 81; Univ New Haven, MBA, 86. *Prof Exp:* Asst proj engr, Raytheon, 80-81. *Mem:* Inst Elec & Electronics Engrs; Am Soc Qual Control; Inst Interconnecting & Packaging Electronic Circuits. *Mailing Add:* Pitney Bowes Inc 2642 Walter Wheeler Dr Stamford CT 06926

SCHWARTZ, MICHAEL MUNI, INDUSTRIAL CHEMISTRY. *Current Pos:* CONSULT, ISOGEN LLC, 96- *Personal Data:* b Chicago, Ill, Aug 30, 43; m 70; c 1. *Educ:* Northwestern Univ, BA, 64; Fla State Univ, MS, 67, PhD(org chem), 70. *Prof Exp:* Sr res chemist, Amoco Oil Co, 70-96. *Mem:* Am Chem Soc. *Mailing Add:* 1208 Hamilton Lane Naperville IL 60540

SCHWARTZ, MISCHA, COMPUTER & DIGITAL COMMUNICATIONS, TELECOMMUNICATIONS. *Current Pos:* prof elec eng & comput sci, Columbia Uni, 74-88, dir, Ctr Telecommun Res, 85-88, Charles Batchelor Prof, 87-96, CHARLES BATCHELOR EMER PROF ENG & COMPUT SCI, COLUMBIA UNIV, 96- *Personal Data:* b New York, NY, Sept 21, 26; m 57, 70, Charlotte Fishman; c David J. *Educ:* Cooper Union, BEE, 47; Polytech Inst Brooklyn, MEE, 49; Harvard Univ, PhD(appl physics), 51. *Honors & Awards:* Educ Medal, Inst Elec & Electronics Engrs, 83, Regional Award, 89; Gano Dunn Award, Cooper Union, 86; Edwin Armstrong Achievement Award, Inst Elec & Electronics Engrs, Commun Soc, 94. *Prof Exp:* Asst proj engr, Sperry Gyroscope Co, 47-49, proj engr, 49-52; from asst prof to prof elec eng, Polytech Inst Brooklyn, 52-74, head dept, 61-65. *Concurrent Pos:* Radiation physicist, Montefiore Hosp, 55-56; NSF sci fac fel, Ecole Normale Superiore, Paris, 65-66; indust consult; chmn comn C, US Nat Comt, Int Union Radio Sci, 78-81; vis scientist, IBM Res, 80 & 94, Nippon Tel & Tel, 81 & NYNEX Corp, 86, Bell Labs, 95; dir, Inst Elec & Electronics Engrs, 78-79; pres Commun Soc, 84-85; vis prof, UCL, London, 95, Univ Calif, San Diego, 97. *Mem:* Nat Acad Eng; Asn Comput Mach; fel Inst Elec & Electronics Engrs; Sigma Xi; Am Asn Univ Professors; fel AAAS. *Res:* Communication systems; computer communications. *Mailing Add:* Dept Elec Eng Columbia Univ 806 Schapiro CEPSR New York NY 10027. *Fax:* 212-316-9068

SCHWARTZ, MORTON ALLEN, drug metabolism, for more information see previous edition

SCHWARTZ, MORTON DONALD, COMPUTERS, INSTRUMENTATION. *Current Pos:* PROF COMPUT ENG & COMPUT SCI, CALIF STATE UNIV, LONG BEACH, 70- *Personal Data:* b Chicago, Ill, Oct 11, 36; m 58, 89, Barbara Siegal; c Karen, Kenneth, Melodie, Patrick, Robert & Michael. *Educ:* Univ Calif, Los Angeles, BS, 58, MS, 60, PhD(eng), 64. *Prof Exp:* Sr engr, NAm Aviation, 64-66; sr scientist, TRW, 66-70. *Concurrent Pos:* Consult, St Mary Med Ctr, Long Beach, Calif, 70-, Hughes

Aircraft Co, 78-; ed, J Clin Eng, 75-; mem, Bd Dir, Am Bd Clin Engrs, 75- *Mem:* Inst Elec & Electronic Engrs; Am Soc Eng Educ; AAAS. *Res:* Computer applications in medicine including instrumentation for cardiac catheterization, pacemaker and firemen paramedic systems. *Mailing Add:* Comput Eng & Comput Sci Calif State Univ 6101 E Seventh Long Beach CA 90840. *E-Mail:* schwartz@engr.csulb.edu

SCHWARTZ, MORTON K, BIOCHEMISTRY, CLINICAL CHEMISTRY. *Current Pos:* From instr to prof biochem, 54-84, prof, Develop Ther Clin Invest, 84-88, PROF, MOLECULAR PHARMACOL & THERAPEUT, SLOAN-KETTERING DIV, MED COL, CORNELL UNIV, 88- *Personal Data:* b Wilkes-Barre, Pa, Oct 22, 25; m 66, Delia Corr; c Gary & Ronald. *Educ:* Lehigh Univ, BA, 48; Boston Univ, MA, 49, PhD(biochem), 52. *Honors & Awards:* Van Slyke Award, Am Asn Clin Chem, Reimer Award, Educ Award; Wiley Medal-Commissioners Citation, Food & Drug Admin. *Concurrent Pos:* Res fel, Sloan-Kettering Div, Med Col, Cornell Univ, 52-54; res fel, Sloan-Kettering Inst Cancer Res, 52-55; asst, Surg Metab Sect, Sloan-Kettering Inst Cancer Res, 55-56, assoc mem, Div Biochem, 57-, mem & lab head, Inst, 69-, assoc field coordr, Human Cancer, 75-81; dir clin res training, Mem Hosp Cancer & Allied Dis, 71-81, vpres lab affairs & dep gen dir, 77-81, attend clin chemist & chmn, Dept Clin Chem, 67-96, chmn, 96-; distinguished scientist, Clin Ligard Assay Soc. *Mem:* Am Soc Biochem & Molecular Biol; Am Chem Soc; Acad Clin Lab Phys & Scientists; Am Asn Clin Chem (pres, 75); Asn Clin Scientists; Am Asn Cancer Res; NY Acad Sci; Int Soc Clin Enzym (pres, 90). *Res:* Enzyme kinetics; serum enzymes; tumor markers; hormone receptor; automation. *Mailing Add:* Mem Sloan Kettering Cancer Ctr 1275 York Ave New York NY 10021. *Fax:* 212-717-3397

SCHWARTZ, NEENA BETTY, PHYSIOLOGY, ENDOCRINOLOGY. *Current Pos:* prof physiol, Med Sch, 73-74, prof biol & chmn dept, 74-77, DEERING PROF NEUROBIOL & PHYSIOL, NORTHWESTERN UNIV, EVANSTON, 81- *Personal Data:* b Baltimore, Md, Dec 10, 26. *Educ:* Goucher Col, BA, 48; Northwestern Univ, MS, 50, PhD, 53. *Hon Degrees:* DSc, Goucher Col, 82. *Honors & Awards:* Williams Distinguished Serv Award, Endocrine Soc, 85; Carl Hartman Award, Soc Study Reproduction, 92. *Prof Exp:* From instr to assoc prof physiol, Col Med, Univ Ill, 53-57; dir, Biol Lab, Inst Psychosom & Psychiat Res & Training, Michael Reese Hosp, 57-61; from assoc prof to prof physiol, Col Med, Univ Ill, 61-70, prof neuroendocrinol, 70-73. *Mem:* Endocrine Soc (pres, 82-83); Am Physiol Soc; Soc Study Reproduction (pres, 77-78); fel AAAS; Am Acad Arts & Sci. *Res:* Endocrinology; reproduction; environmental control of pituitary. *Mailing Add:* Northwestern Univ 2153 Sheridan Rd Rm 2-120 Hogan Hall Evanston IL 60208-3520. *Fax:* 847-491-5521; *E-Mail:* schwartz@casbah.acns.nwu.edu

SCHWARTZ, NORMAN, COMMUNICATION & DEVELOPMENT BETWEEN SCIENTIFIC & LEGAL FIELDS. *Current Pos:* sr med chemist, 64-76, SR INFO SCIENTIST, R W JOHNSON PHARMACEUT RES INST, 76- *Personal Data:* b Philadelphia, Pa, Dec 16, 35; m 59, Leah; c Paul, Raphael & Joel. *Educ:* Univ Pa, BS, 57; Johns Hopkins Univ, MA, 59, PhD(org chem), 62. *Prof Exp:* Res fel, Israel Inst Technol, Haifa, 62-63; Princeton Univ, 63-64. *Res:* Informational interface between lab scientists and patent attorneys employing commercial on-line databases. *Mailing Add:* R W Johnson Pharmaceut Res Inst Welsh & McKean Rd Spring House PA 19477

SCHWARTZ, NORMAN MARTIN, biology, for more information see previous edition

SCHWARTZ, PAUL, DEVELOPMENT OF NEW ANTICANCER DRUGS. *Current Pos:* SR RES SCIENTIST, ANDRULIS RES CORP, 80- *Personal Data:* b New York, NY, Sept 12, 48; m 71; c 2. *Educ:* City Col NY, BS, 69, PhD(chem), 74. *Prof Exp:* Fel biophys, Mich State Univ, 74-75; res chemist, US Vet Admin Med Ctr, Charleston, SC, 75-80. *Mem:* Am Chem Soc. *Res:* Development of new anticancer drugs. *Mailing Add:* 14531 Woodcrest Dr Rockville MD 20853-2371

SCHWARTZ, PAUL HENRY, JR, ENTOMOLOGY, PESTICIDES. *Current Pos:* res entomologist, USDA, 61-69, asst to chief, Fruit Insects Res Br, Entom Res Div, 69-72, staff specialist, 72-73, STAFF SCIENTIST, AGR RES SERV, USDA, 73- *Personal Data:* b Baltimore, Md, Dec 19, 36; m 61, 86, Sandra Palfrey; c Lorrie A, Ken M, Glen W & Timothy B. *Educ:* Univ Md, BS, 59, MS, 61; Univ Fla, PhD(entom), 64. *Prof Exp:* Entomologist, USPHS, 64-65. *Mem:* Entom Soc Am. *Res:* Chemical and other methods for control of insect pests. *Mailing Add:* 8497 Heatherwold Dr Laurel MD 20723

SCHWARTZ, PAULINE MARY, PHARMACOLOGY, BIOCHEMISTRY. *Current Pos:* RES SCIENTIST, DEPT DERMAT, YALE UNIV, 85-; PHARMACOLOGIST & PRIN INVESTR, DERMAT SERV, VET ADMIN MED CTR, WEST HAVEN, 85- *Personal Data:* b Philadelphia, Pa, Aug 8, 47; m 75. *Educ:* Drexel Univ, BS, 70; Univ Mich, MS, 71, PhD(med chem), 75. *Honors & Awards:* Wilson R Earle Award, Nat Tissue Cult Asn, 74. *Prof Exp:* Teaching fel chem, Univ Mich, 70-71; res scholar cancer chemother, Los Angeles Co-Univ Southern Calif Cancer Ctr, 75-76, cancer res training fel, 76; res assoc path, Sch Med, Univ Southern Calif, 76-77; fel, Dept Pharmacol, Yale Univ, 77-80, res assoc, 80-83; res assoc, E I Du Pont Pharmaceut, 83-84. *Concurrent Pos:* NIH, Young Investr award, 81-82; practr-in-residence, Dept Chem, Univ New Haven, distinguished adj prof, 92. *Mem:* Am Chem Soc; Am Asn Cancer Res; Soc Invest Dermat. *Res:* Mechanism of action of anti hyperproliferative drugs; design of chemotherapy; nucleotide metabolism; epidermal differentiation; hyperproliferative skin diseases. *Mailing Add:* 101 Hammonasset Rd Madison CT 06443. *Fax:* 203-937-3829; *E-Mail:* pschwartz@biomed.med.yale.edu

SCHWARTZ, PETER LARRY, CLINICAL BIOCHEMISTRY, MEDICAL EDUCATION. *Current Pos:* lectr clin biochem, Univ Otago, NZ, 71-77, sr lectr, Higher Educ Develop Ctr, 87-92, sr lectr clin biochem, Med Sch, 77-95, PROF PATH, MED SCH, UNIV OTAGO, NZ, 96-, FEL, DIV HEALTH SCI HIGHER EDUC DEVELOP CTR, 96- *Personal Data:* b Chicago, Ill, July 11, 40; NZ & US citizen; m 64, Arleen Halle. *Educ:* Univ Wis-Madison, BS, 62; Wash Univ, MD, 65. *Honors & Awards:* ANZAME-Smith, Kline & French Award, 89. *Concurrent Pos:* Australian Res Grants Comt fel biochem, Monash Univ, Australia, 65-68; external examr, Sch Med Sci, Univ Sains, Malaysia, 84-86; vis prof, Med Sch, Univ Toronto, Can, 86 & Mem Univ, Nfld, 89. *Mem:* Australasian & NZ Asn Med Educ. *Res:* Improved methods of medical and biochemical education; self-learning systems; small group and problem-based learning. *Mailing Add:* Dept Path Univ Otago Med Sch Box 913 Dunedin New Zealand. *Fax:* 64-3-479-7136; *E-Mail:* peter.schwartz@stonebow.otago.ac.nz

SCHWARTZ, RALPH JEROME, SPEECH PATHOLOGY, AUDIOLOGY. *Current Pos:* from asst prof to assoc prof speech, 63-71, assoc prof speech path & audiol, 71-89, EMER PROF, UNIV NORTHERN IOWA, 89- *Personal Data:* b Chicago, Ill, Mar 14, 19; m 66. *Educ:* Northwestern Univ, BS, 41; Marquette Univ, MA, 48; Purdue Univ, PhD(speech path, audiol), 58. *Prof Exp:* Head speech clin, Am Red Cross, McPherson, Kans, 47-52; speech clinician, Inst Logopedics, 52-53; speech therapist & actg head speech & hearing dept, Children's Rehab Inst, Inc, Baltimore, Md, 53-55; asst prof logopedics, Univ Wichita & Inst Logopedics, 57-63. *Mem:* Am Speech & Hearing Asn; Acoust Soc Am; Int Asn Logopedics & Phoniatrics; Am Asn Phonetic Sci; Int Soc Phonetic Sci. *Res:* Voice; diagnosis and appraisal; phonology. *Mailing Add:* 1115 Franklin St Cedar Falls IA 50613

SCHWARTZ, RICHARD DEAN, ASTRONOMY, ASTROPHYSICS. *Current Pos:* ASST PROF ASTRON, UNIV MO, 75- *Personal Data:* b Hutchinson, Kans, Apr 17, 41; m 78. *Educ:* Kans State Univ, BS, 63; Union Theol Sem, MDiv, 66; Univ Wash, MS, 70, PhD(astron), 73. *Prof Exp:* Res asst atomic collision physics, Columbia Radiation Lab, Columbia Univ, 64-68; res teaching asst astron, Univ Wash, 68-73; astronomer pre-main sequence astron, Lick Observ, Univ Calif, Santa Cruz, 73-75. *Concurrent Pos:* Mem user's comt, Kitt Peak Nat Observ, 76-77; Copernicus prin investr, NASA grant, 76-78. *Mem:* Am Astron Soc; Int Astron Union. *Res:* Observational and theoretical pre-main sequence astronomy; T Tauri stars; Herbig-Haro objects; circumstellar dust shells; post-main sequence astronomy; white dwarfs; planetary nebulae. *Mailing Add:* Dept Physics & Astron Univ Mo 8001 Natural Bridge Rd St Louis MO 63121-4499

SCHWARTZ, RICHARD F(REDERICK), ELECTROMAGNETICS, ACOUSTICS. *Current Pos:* prof, 85-95, EMER PROF ELEC ENG, STATE UNIV NY, BINGHAMTON, 95- *Personal Data:* b Albany, NY, May 31, 22; m 45, 82, Margaret O Camp; c Kathryn G, Frederick E (deceased), Karl E, Eric C & Frieda D. *Educ:* Rensselaer Polytech Inst, BEE, 43, MEE, 48; Univ Pa, PhD(elec eng), 59. *Prof Exp:* Asst physics, Rensselaer Polytech Inst, 46, asst elec eng, 46-48, instr, 48; develop engr, Adv Develop Sect, RCA, NJ, 48-51; instr elec eng, Moore Sch Elec Eng, Univ Pa, 51-53, from assoc to res assoc, 53-59, from asst prof to assoc prof, 59-73, chmn grad group elec eng, 68-72; dept head, Mich Technol Univ, 73-79, prof elec eng, 73-85. *Concurrent Pos:* Consult, numerous co & orgn, 57-92; consult elec eng, 95- *Mem:* AAAS; Am Soc Eng Educ; sr mem Inst Elec & Electronics Engrs; Nat Soc Prof Engrs; Acoust Soc Am; Sigma Xi; Audio Eng Soc. *Res:* Microwave theory and techniques; electromagnetic theory; antennas; communication engineering; electromagnetic compatability; musical acoustics; electroacoustics; electrical measurements. *Mailing Add:* Dept Elec Eng Watson Sch Eng-Appl Sci State Univ NY Binghamton NY 13902-6000. *Fax:* 607-777-4464; *E-Mail:* schwartz@bingtow.edum, rschwart@spectra.net

SCHWARTZ, RICHARD JOHN, SOLAR CELLS. *Current Pos:* assoc prof elec eng, Purdue Univ, 64-71, asst head sch, 72-83, head sch, 85-96, PROF ELEC ENG, PURDUE UNIV, LAFAYETTE, 71-, DEAN ENG, 96- *Personal Data:* b Waukesha, Wis, Aug 12, 35; m 57; c 8. *Educ:* Univ Wis, BSEE, 57; Mass Inst Technol, SMEE, 59, ScD(elec eng), 62. *Prof Exp:* Mem tech staff solid state develop, David Sarnoff Res Ctr, RCA Corp, 57-58; sr scientist, Energy Conversion, Inc, 61-64. *Concurrent Pos:* Consult, RCA Corp, 65-77 & Arco Solar, 78-88; gen chmn, Photovoltaic Specialists Conf, Inst Elec & Electronics Engrs; mem, Sci & Technol Comt, Nat Renewable Energy Lab, 92- *Mem:* Fel Inst Elec & Electronics Engrs. *Res:* Solid state devices; direct energy conversion; semiconducting materials. *Mailing Add:* Purdue Univ 1280 Eng Admin Bldg Rm 101 West Lafayette IN 47907-1280

SCHWARTZ, ROBERT, PEDIATRICS. *Current Pos:* PROF MED SCI, BROWN UNIV, 74- *Personal Data:* b New Haven, Conn, Dec 17, 22; m 47; c 3. *Educ:* Yale Univ, BS, 43, MD, 47. *Prof Exp:* Intern, Children's Med Serv, Bellevue Hosp, 47-48; asst pediat, Col Med, NY Univ, 48-49, instr, 49; res fel, Harvard Med Sch, 49-51, res assoc med, 51-53, instr pediat, 53-54, assoc, 55-58; from assoc prof to prof pediat, Sch Med, Case Western Res Univ, 59-74; dir pediat metab & nutrit, RI Hosp, 74-87. *Concurrent Pos:* Fel med, Children's Hosp, Boston, 49-51, NIH fel, 49-51; fel med, Thorndike Mem Lab, Boston City Hosp, 51-53; asst resident, Bellevue Hosp, 48-49, resident physician, 49; asst physician, Children's Hosp, 53-56, chief diabetic clin, 54-58, assoc physician & chief metab, 56-58; sr asst surgeon, Thorndike Mem Lab, Boston City Hosp, 51-53; res collabr, Brookhaven Nat Lab, 59-66; assoc pediatrician, Babies & Children's Hosp, Cleveland, 59-74; staff pediatrician, Metrop Gen Hosp, 59-74; dir, Dept Pediat, Cleveland Metrop Gen Hosp, 67-74. *Mem:* AAAS; Am Soc Pediat Res; Am Fedn Clin Res; Am Acad Pediat; Pediat Soc. *Res:* Pediatrics metabolism; physiology. *Mailing Add:* RI Hosp Eddy Rd Providence RI 02903

SCHWARTZ, ROBERT BERNARD, RADIATION PROTECTION DOSIMETRY, INSTRUMENT CALIBRATION. *Current Pos:* PHYSICIST, NAT INST STAND & TECHNOL, 62- *Personal Data:* b Brooklyn, NY, Sept 2, 29; m 56, Rita Bagley; c David & Sam. *Educ:* Union Univ, NY, BS, 51; Yale Univ, PhD(physics), 55. *Honors & Awards:* Silver Medal Award, Dept Com, 82. *Prof Exp:* Asst physicist, Brookhaven Nat Lab, 55-58; res assoc, Atomic Energy Res Estab, Harwell, Eng, 58-59; asst physicist, Brookhaven Nat Lab, 59-60; physicist, US Naval Res Lab, 60-62. *Mem:* Am Phys Soc; Health Physics Soc. *Res:* Neutron personnel dosimetry. *Mailing Add:* Nat Inst Stand & Technol Gaithersburg MD 20899. *Fax:* 301-926-1604; *E-Mail:* rschwartz@enh.nist.gov

SCHWARTZ, ROBERT DAVID, INDUSTRIAL MICROBIOLOGY, FERMENTATION MICROBIOLOGY. *Current Pos:* SR DEVELOP SCIENTIST, FERMENTATION DEVELOP DEPT, ABBOTT LABS, 87- *Personal Data:* b Brooklyn, NY, Apr 3, 41; m 92, Ellen McDonald; c Jeff, Scott, Adam, Shawn & Peyton. *Educ:* Brooklyn Col, BS, 64; Long Island Univ, MS, 67; Rutgers Univ, PhD(microbial genetics), 69. *Honors & Awards:* Porter Award, Soc Indust Microbiol, 88. *Prof Exp:* Technician metab res, Col Physicians & Surgeons, Columbia Univ, 64-65; med technologist, Middlesex Gen Hosp, New Brunswick, NJ, 68-69; res assoc oncogenic virol, Germfree Life Res Ctr, Life Sci Ctr, Nova Univ Advan Technol, 69-70; res biologist, Exxon Res & Eng Co, 70-76; proj scientist, Union Carbide Corp, 76-79; scientist, Food & Biotechnol Dept, Stauffer Chem Co, 79-87. *Concurrent Pos:* Assoc ed, Enzyme Microbiol Technol, 93-; Soc Indust Microbiol fel, 94; sr ed, J Indust Microbiol Biotechnol, 96- *Mem:* AAAS; Am Soc Microbiol; Soc Indust Microbiol; Sigma Xi. *Res:* Fermentation process development, fermentation microbiology, microbial physiology; enzymatic hydroxylation; biotransformation; pollution control; single cell protein; microbial genetics; microbial energy production. *Mailing Add:* Fermentation Develop Dept 451 Abbott Labs North Chicago IL 60064-4000. *Fax:* 847-938-7509

SCHWARTZ, ROBERT DONALD, GAS CHROMATOGRAPHY, ORGANIC GEOCHEMISTRY. *Current Pos:* RETIRED. *Personal Data:* b New York, NY, Mar 15, 24; m 47, Annette Sterman; c Susan (Hertz), Michael, Donna (Baum) & David. *Educ:* City Univ NY, BS, 43; State Univ NY, Buffalo, PhD(chem), 51. *Prof Exp:* Res chemist, Tonawanda Lab, Linde Air Prods Co, 43-48; asst, Univ Buffalo, 48-51; res chemist, Electro Refractories & Abrasives Corp, 51-52; explor & prod res lab, Shell Develop Co, 52-66; mgr anal res & serv div, Pennzoil Co, 66-86; consult, Gulf States Analytical, 88-93. *Concurrent Pos:* Instr, Fillmore Col, Buffalo, 49-51; coun mem, Am Chem Soc, 74-84 & 86-92. *Mem:* AAAS; Am Soc Testing & Mat; Am Chem Soc; Am Inst Chem. *Res:* Development of analytical techniques for natural gas, petroleum and sedimentary rocks; studies of the origin, migration and transformation of petroleum; separation techniques; gas chromatography. *Mailing Add:* One Wedgewood Forest Dr The Woodlands TX 77381

SCHWARTZ, ROBERT JOHN, NONWOVENS, MELT SPINNING OF FIBERS. *Current Pos:* res engr, 70-72, sr res sci, 72-75, mgr prod develop, 75-78, dir process develop, 78-80 & technol develop, 80-82, vpres, non-wovens res & develop, 82-87, VPRES, LONG RANGE RES & DEVELOP, KIMBERLEY CLARK CORP, 87- *Personal Data:* b Pittsburgh, Pa, Nov 14, 42; m 65, 76; c 1. *Educ:* Univ Md, BS, 64, PhD(chem eng), 68. *Prof Exp:* Res eng, Org Chem Div, FMC Corp, 67-69, sr res engr, 69-70. *Mem:* Am Inst Chem Engrs. *Res:* Development of new filimant spinning and subsequent fabric/web formation technology with emphasis on increasing final product fabric attributes at the lowest cost; exploring novel approaches to fiber formation. *Mailing Add:* 1400 Holcomb Bridge Rd Roswell GA 30076

SCHWARTZ, ROBERT NELSON, PHYSICAL CHEMISTRY, SPECTROSCOPY. *Current Pos:* mem tech staff, 81-86, sr staff physicist, 87-91, SR RES SCIENTIST, HUGHES RES LAB, 92- *Personal Data:* b New Haven, Conn, Feb 4, 40; m 71, Carole A Dallape; c Carrie A & Dana A. *Educ:* Univ Conn, BA, 62, MS, 65; Univ Colo, Boulder, PhD(chem), 69. *Prof Exp:* Fel chem, Univ Ill, Chicago, 69-70; from asst prof to assoc prof, 70-81; vis assoc prof chem, Univ Calif, Los Angeles, 79-81. *Concurrent Pos:* Vis scholar, Univ Calif, Los Angeles, 79-80; adj prof phys & astron, Calif State Univ, Northridge, 81-; vis prof chem, Univ Calif, Los Angeles, 94- *Mem:* Sigma Xi; Am Phys Soc; NY Acad Sci; Optical Soc Am. *Res:* Magnetic resonance; molecular structure and relaxation phenomena; magnetic, linear and nonlinear optical properties of solids. *Mailing Add:* Hughes Res Labs 3011 Malibu Canyon Rd Malibu CA 90265

SCHWARTZ, ROBERT SAUL, ANALYTICAL CHEMISTRY. *Current Pos:* RES CHEMIST ANALYTICAL RES, US CUSTOMS SERV, DEPT TREAS, 75- *Personal Data:* b Brooklyn, NY, Apr 20, 42; m 65; c 2. *Educ:* Brooklyn Col, BS, 63; City Univ New York, PhD(analytical chem), 74. *Prof Exp:* Chemist pharmaceut res, Dept Health & Welfare, Food & Drug Admin, 74-75. *Mem:* Am Chem Soc. *Res:* Analysis and detection of trace quantities of organic vapors; electroanalytical chemistry; instrumentation. *Mailing Add:* 19121 Brooke Grove Ct Gaithersburg MD 20879-2119

SCHWARTZ, ROBERT STEWART, HEMATOLOGY. *Current Pos:* clin fel hemat, 57-58, res fel, 58-60, from instr to assoc prof, 60-71, PROF MED, NEW ENG MED CTR, SCH MED, TUFTS UNIV, 71- *Personal Data:* b East Orange, NJ, Mar 14, 28; m 63; c 1. *Educ:* Seton Hall Col, BS, 50; NY Univ, MD, 54. *Honors & Awards:* Stratton Prize, Am Soc Hemat; John Phillips Award, Am Col Physicians. *Prof Exp:* From intern to resident med, Montefiore Hosp, NY, 54-56; resident, New Haven Hosp, Conn, 56-57. *Concurrent Pos:* Dir blood bank, New Eng Med Ctr Hosp, 61-, chief clin immunol sect, 66-72; chief, Hemat-Oncol Div, 72-90. *Mem:* Am Soc Clin Invest; Am Asn Immunol; Am Fedn Clin Res; Am Soc Hemat; Transplantation Soc. *Res:* Autoimmunity; experimental leukemia. *Mailing Add:* Dept Med New England Univ Med 10 Shattuck St Boston MA 02115

SCHWARTZ, RUTH, NUTRITION. *Current Pos:* RETIRED. *Personal Data:* b Berlin, Ger, Oct 9, 24. *Educ:* Univ London, BSc, 47, PhD(nutrit biochem), 59. *Prof Exp:* Res asst biochem, Postgrad Med Sch, Univ London, 48-49; biochemist, Med Res Coun, Uganda, 50-56; res fel nutrit biochem, Med Sch, Wash Univ, 57-60; lectr nutrit, London Sch Hyg & Trop Med, 60-63; res assoc nutrit biochem, Mass Inst Technol, 64-65; asst nutrit, Univ Conn, 65-70; prof nutrit, Div Nutrit Sci, Cornell Univ, 70-93. *Mem:* AAAS; Am Inst Nutrit; Brit Nutrit Soc; NY Acad Sci; Am Chem Soc. *Res:* Magnesium metabolism; stable isotopes as tracers; absorption and availability of minerals. *Mailing Add:* 3 Sunnyslope Terr Ithaca NY 14850. *Fax:* 607-255-1033

SCHWARTZ, SAMUEL, MEDICAL RESEARCH. *Current Pos:* from asst prof to prof exp med, 48-83, EMER RES PROF, RAPTOR CTR, SCH VET MED, UNIV MINN, MINNEAPOLIS, 90- *Personal Data:* b Minneapolis, Minn, Apr 13, 16; m 37; c 9. *Educ:* Univ Minn, BS, 38, MD, 43. *Prof Exp:* Intern, Univ Minn Hosps, 42-43; group leader res, Manhattan Proj, Univ Chicago, 43-46; staff mem, Minneapolis Med Res Found, 83-89. *Concurrent Pos:* Commonwealth Fund fels, Univ Minn, Carlsberg Lab, Copenhagen & Karolinska Inst, Sweden, 46-48; USPHS Res Career Award Exp Med, Nat Inst Gen Med Sci, 63-; vis prof, Hebrew Univ, Jerusalem, 61-62. *Mem:* Am Soc Biol Chem; Am Soc Clin Invest; Am Asn Cancer Res; Soc Exp Biol & Med. *Res:* Porphyrin and bile pigment metabolism; modification of radiosensitivity by metalloporphyrins. *Mailing Add:* 2341 Texas Ave S Minneapolis MN 55426

SCHWARTZ, SAMUEL, SCIENCE ADMINISTRATION. *Current Pos:* TRUSTEE, HENRY DU PONT WINTERTHUR MUS, WINTERTHUR, DEL, 84-, CHMN, 94- *Personal Data:* b MooseJaw, Sask, Nov 12, 27; nat US; m 56, Margaret Patterson; c Michael R, Thomas R, David C & Janet C. *Educ:* Univ Sask, BA, 48, BC, 50; Harvard Univ, MBA, 53. *Prof Exp:* Res assoc, Harvard Bus Sch, 53-57; staff, Conoco Inc, 57-73, sr vpres coord & planning, 74-75, sr vpres corp planning, 75-78, sr vpres admin, 78-80, group sr vpres admin, 80-83; trustee, Inst Future, Menlo Park, Calif, 75-92; sr vpres admin, EI Du Pont de Nemours & Co, 83-87, sr vpres, Corp Plans Dept, 87-88. *Concurrent Pos:* Dir, Conoco Inc Consol Coal Co, 81-88. *Mailing Add:* Unit 1203 4951 Gulf Shore Blvd N Naples FL 33940-2693

SCHWARTZ, SAMUEL MEYER, MEDICINAL CHEMISTRY, SCIENCE ADMINISTRATION. *Current Pos:* SCI DIR, PEER REV ASSOCS, INC, 86- *Personal Data:* b Winnipeg, Man, Feb 15, 29; m 54, Myra; c Daniel, Gary & Andy. *Educ:* Univ Man, BSc, 52; Univ Minn, PhD(med chem), 56. *Prof Exp:* Assoc prof pharmaceut chem, Sch Pharm, George Wash Univ, 56-64; scientist admin, NIH, 64-78, assoc dir sci rev, Div Res Grants, 78-83; spec asst dir, Nat Inst Arthritis, Diabetes & Degenerative Kidney Dis, NIH, 83-86. *Mem:* AAAS; Am Chem Soc. *Res:* Pharmacology; biochemistry; peer review of grant and contract proposals; biomedical research administrations; technical writing. *Mailing Add:* 4620 N Park Ave Chevy Chase MD 20815

SCHWARTZ, SEYMOUR I, THORACIC SURGERY. *Current Pos:* from instr to assoc prof, 57-66, PROF SURG, UNIV ROCHESTER, 67-, DIR SURG RES, 62- *Personal Data:* b New York, NY, Jan 22, 28; m 49; c 3. *Educ:* Univ Wis, BA, 47; NY Univ, MD, 50; Am Bd Surg & Am Bd Thoracic Surg, dipl. *Prof Exp:* Chief resident, Strong Mem Hosp, Rochester, NY, 56-57. *Concurrent Pos:* From asst surgeon to assoc surgeon, Strong Mem Hosp, Rochester, 57-63, sr assoc surgeon, 63-67, sr surgeon, 67-; Markle scholar acad med, 60-65; mem sci adv comt, Cent Clin Res Ctr, Roswell Park Mem Inst. *Mem:* Fel Am Col Surg; Soc Univ Surgeons; Am Surg Asn; AMA; Am Asn Thoracic Surg. *Res:* Portal hypertension; vascular surgery; platelets. *Mailing Add:* Dept Surg Univ Rochester Med Ctr 601 Elmwood Ave Rochester NY 14642-8410

SCHWARTZ, SHELDON E, MEDICINE. *Current Pos:* AT STATE UNIV NY UPSTATE MED CTR, SYRACUSE. *Personal Data:* b New York, NY, July 21, 19; m 44; c 2. *Educ:* Rensselaer Polytech Inst, BS, 40; NY Univ, MD, 43; Am Bd Internal Med, dipl, 52. *Prof Exp:* assoc prof clin med, Med Ctr, NY Univ, 47- *Concurrent Pos:* Chief arthritis clin, Bellevue Hosp; dir med, Hillcrest Hosp. *Mem:* Am Rheumatism Asn; fel Am Col Physicians. *Res:* Arthritis. *Mailing Add:* 218-65 99th Ave Queens Village NY 11429-1205

SCHWARTZ, SHIRLEY E, LUBRICANT DEGRADATION, ENGINE WEAR. *Current Pos:* staff res scientist, 81-93, SR STAFF RES SCIENTIST, FUELS & LUBRICANTS DEPT, RES & DEVELOP CTR, GEN MOTORS NAM OPERS, 93- *Personal Data:* b Detroit, Mich, Aug 26, 35; m 57, Ronald E; c Steven D, Bradlet A & George B. *Educ:* Univ Mich, BS, 57; Detroit Inst Technol, BS, 78; Wayne State Univ, MS, 62, PhD(phys chem), 70. *Honors & Awards:* Wilbur Deutsch Mem Award, Soc Tribologists & Lubrication Engrs, 87, P M Ku Award, 94; McCuen Award, Gen Motors Res & Develop Ctr, 88 & 93; Arch T Colwell Merit Award, Soc Automotive Engrs, 92, Lloyd L Withrow Distinguished Speaker Award, 95. *Prof Exp:* Res assoc, Wayne County Gen Hosp, 70-71; asst prof, Oakland Community Col, 71-73; asst prof chem, Detroit Inst Technol, 73-78, math & sci div head, 76-78; res staff scientist, BASF Wyandotte Corp, 78-81, sect head, 81. *Concurrent Pos:* Dir, Soc Tribologists & Lubrication Engrs, 85-91; group leader, Coord Res Coun, 90-94; mem pub affairs comt, Soc Automotive Engrs, 91-94. *Mem:* Fel Soc Tribologists & Lubrication Engrs; Soc Automotive Engrs; Sigma Xi; Am Chem Soc; Soc In Vitro Biol. *Res:* Mathematical models of engine oil degradation; development of an automatic engine oil change indicator; engine wear; development of environmentally friendly water-based lubricants; mechanisms of failure of barium enemas and x-ray contrast media. *Mailing Add:* Fuels & Lubricants Dept Gen Motors NAm Oper Res & Develop Ctr 30500 Mound Rd Bldg 1-6 Box 9055 Warren MI 48090-9055

SCHWARTZ, SORELL LEE, PHARMACOKINETICS, RISK ASSESSMENT. *Current Pos:* PROF PHARMACOL, SCH MED, GEORGETOWN UNIV, 68-, SCI DIR, CTR ENVIRON HEALTH & HUMAN TOXICOL, 82- *Personal Data:* b Buffalo, NY, Sept 13, 37; m 63, Marsha Kohlenstein; c Joanne B & Rebecca L. *Educ:* Univ Md, BS, 59; Med Col Va, PhD(pharmacol), 63. *Prof Exp:* Head pharmacol div, US Naval Med Res Inst, 66-68. *Concurrent Pos:* Prin, Int Ctr Toxicol Med. *Mem:* Soc Toxicol; Am Soc Pharmacol & Exp Therapeut; Soc Risk Analysis; Am Col Toxicol; Am Acad Clin Toxicol. *Res:* Pharmacokinetics; exposure analysis; risk analysis; causal inference methods. *Mailing Add:* Dept Pharmacol Georgetown Univ Sch Med Washington DC 20007. *Fax:* 202-687-5015

SCHWARTZ, STANLEY ALLEN, IMMUNODEFICIENCY DISEASES, IMMUNOREGULATION. *Current Pos:* PROF, DEPT MED, STATE UNIV NY, BUFFALO GEN HOSP, 92- *Personal Data:* b Newark, NJ, July 20, 41; m 65, Diane Gottlieb. *Educ:* Rutgers Univ, AB, 63, MS, 65; Univ Calif, San Diego, PhD(cellular biol), 68; Albert Einstein Col Med, MD, 72. *Honors & Awards:* Meller Award, Mem Sloan-Kettering Cancer Ctr, 77; Res Career Develop Award, NIH, 83. *Prof Exp:* Asst prof pediat & biol, Cornell Univ Med Col, 77-78; from assoc prof to prof pediat, microbiol, immunol & epidemiol, Univ Mich, 78-92. *Concurrent Pos:* Asst attend physician pediat, Mem Hosp Cancer & Allied Dis & NY Hosp, 77-78; assoc, Sloan-Kettering Inst Cancer Res, 77-78. *Mem:* Am Soc Clin Invest; fel Am Acad Allergy & Immunol; Am Asn Immunologists; Am Pediat Soc; Soc Pediat Res; Am Fedn Clin Res. *Res:* Analysis of the cellular and molecular immunopathogenic mechanisms underlying human immunodeficiency disorders including AIDS; immunoregulation of cellular cytotoxicity. *Mailing Add:* Div Allergy & Immunol Buffalo Gen Hosp 100 High St Buffalo NY 14023. *Fax:* 716-859-2999; *E-Mail:* sasimmun@acsu.buffalo.edu

SCHWARTZ, STEPHEN EUGENE, ATMOSPHERIC CHEMISTRY & PHYSICS, PHYSICAL CHEMISTRY. *Current Pos:* from assoc chemist to chemist, 75-90, SR CHEMIST, BROOKHAVEN NAT LAB, 90- *Personal Data:* b St Louis, Mo, June 18, 41; m 80; c 2. *Educ:* Harvard Univ, AB, 63; Univ Calif, Berkeley, PhD(chem), 68. *Prof Exp:* Fulbright fel & Ramsay Mem fel, Cambridge Univ, 68-69; asst prof chem, State Univ NY, Stony Brook, 69-75. *Concurrent Pos:* Ed, Advan Environ Sci & Technol, 83; assoc ed, Atmospheric Environ, 84-95 & J Geophys Res, 86-89; mem, Comt Atmospheric Chem, Am Meteorol Soc, 85-91; mem, Comt Atmospheric Res, Nat Res Coun, 88-91; assoc mem, Comn Atmospheric Chem, Int Union Pure & Appl Chem, 91-94; titular mem 95-; adj prof, Inst Terrestrial & Planetary Atmospheres, State Univ NY, Stony Brook. *Mem:* AAAS; Am Geophys Union; Am Chem Soc; Am Phys Soc; Am Meteorol Soc; Am Asn Aerosol Res. *Res:* Physical chemistry; atmospheric chemistry; chemical kinetics; design, conduct and interpretation of measurements of trace atmospheric constituents; laboratory studies of gas and aqueous-phase kinetics; modeling gas-phase and heterogeneous atmospheric reactions; interpretation of residence times and scales of transport; atmospheric aerosols; atmospheric radiation. *Mailing Add:* Dept Appl Sci Brookhaven Nat Lab Upton NY 11973. *Fax:* 516-344-2887

SCHWARTZ, STEPHEN MARK, PATHOLOGY, CARDIOVASCULAR DISEASES. *Current Pos:* from asst prof to assoc prof, 74-87, PROF PATH, UNIV WASH, 84- *Personal Data:* b Boston, Mass, Jan 1, 42; m 64; c 2. *Educ:* Harvard Univ, AB, 63; Boston Univ, MD, 67; Univ Wash, PhD(path), 74. *Hon Degrees:* MD, Goteborg, Sweden, 89. *Prof Exp:* Asst dir labs, Long Beach Naval Regional Med Ctr, 73-74. *Mem:* AAAS. *Res:* Structure, function and pathology of arterial endothelium; cell replication in endothelium and smooth muscle, hypertension. *Mailing Add:* Dept Path Univ Wash Box 357335 Seattle WA 98195-7335. *Fax:* 206-685-3662; *E-Mail:* Bitnet: steve@uwav1acs.washington.edu

SCHWARTZ, STEVEN OTTO, HEMATOLOGY. *Current Pos:* assoc prof, 55-59, prof, 59-79, EMER PROF MED, SCH MED, NORTHWESTERN UNIV, CHICAGO, 79- *Personal Data:* b Hungary, July 6, 11; m 42; c 3. *Educ:* Northwestern Univ, BS, 32, MS, 35, MD, 36; Am Bd Internal Med, dipl, 42. *Honors & Awards:* Solano Medal, Quincy Col, 66. *Prof Exp:* Prof internal med, Cook County Grad Sch Med, 39-68; asst prof med, Univ Ill, 42-47; prof hemat, Chicago Med Sch, 47-55. *Concurrent Pos:* Chief hemat clin, Mandel Clin & assoc hematologist, Michael Reese Hosp, 38-50; attend hematologist & dir hemat dept, Cook County Hosp, 39-68, hematologist, Hektoen Inst Med Res, 45-68; consult, Chicago State Hosp, 41-49, Highland Park Hosp, 50-84, Mother Cabrini Hosp, 51-84, Columbus Hosp, 55-84 & Hines Vet Admin Hosp, 56-84; assoc, Mt Sinai Hosp, 48-51; attend hematologist, West Side Vet Hosp, 55-56; sr attend physician, Northwestern Mem Hosp, 55-84. *Mem:* Am Col Physicians; Int Soc Hemat; Am Soc Hemat; AMA; Am Soc Internal Med. *Mailing Add:* 610 Rice St Highland Park IL 60035-5012

SCHWARTZ, STUART CARL, ELECTRICAL ENGINEERING. *Current Pos:* from asst prof to assoc prof elec eng, 66-74, assoc dean, Sch Eng & Appl Sci, 77-80, PROF ELEC ENG, PRINCETON UNIV, 74- *Personal Data:* b New York, NY, July 12, 39; m 61; c 2. *Educ:* Mass Inst Technol, BS & MS, 61; Univ Mich, PhD(info & control), 66. *Prof Exp:* Res engr, Jet Propulsion Lab, Calif Inst Technol, 61-62. *Concurrent Pos:* Ed, J Appl Math, 70; Guggenheim Mem Found fel, 72. *Mem:* Inst Math Statist; Inst Elec & Electronics Engrs; Soc Indust & Appl Math. *Res:* Application of probability and stochastic processes to problems in statistical communication and systems theory. *Mailing Add:* Dept Elec Eng/Eng Quadrangle Princeton Univ Princeton NJ 08544-0001

SCHWARTZ, THEODORE BENONI, MEDICINE. *Current Pos:* PROF & CHMN DEPT, RUSH MED SCH, 71- *Personal Data:* b Philadelphia, Pa, Feb 14, 18; m 48, Genevieve Bangs; c 6. *Educ:* Franklin & Marshall Col, BS, 39; Johns Hopkins Univ, MD, 43; Am Bd Internal Med, dipl. *Prof Exp:* Intern med, Johns Hopkins Univ, 43-44; resident, Salt Lake Gen Hosp, 46-48; assoc, Duke Univ, 50-52, asst prof, 53-55; from assoc prof to prof, Col Med, Univ Ill, 55-70; chmn dept internal med, Rush-Presby-St Luke's Med Ctr, 70- *Concurrent Pos:* Damon Runyon sr clin fel, 40-52; fel, Duke Univ, 48-50; asst chief med serv, Vet Admin Hosp, Durham, NC, 53-55; dir endocrinol & metab, Presby-St Luke's Hosp, Chicago, Ill, 55-; ed, Yearbk Endocrinol, 64-; mem, Am Bd Internal Med, 70-79 & Am Bd Med Specialties, 71-79. *Mem:* Endocrine Soc; Am Soc Clin Invest; Am Diabetes Asn; fel Am Col Physicians; Am Fedn Clin Res; fel Am Col Endocrinol. *Res:* Endocrinology; protein metabolism; history of medicine. *Mailing Add:* 200 Lee St Evanston IL 60202

SCHWARTZ, THOMAS ALAN, GLASS, GLAZING & CURTAIN WALL CONSTRUCTION. *Current Pos:* Field & lab engr, Simpson Gumpertz & Heger Inc, 73-75, sr engr, 77-79, sr staff engr, 80-82, assoc, 83-85, sr assoc, 86-89, prin, 89-90, PRIN & DEPT HEAD, SIMPSON GUMPERTZ & HEGER INC, 91- *Personal Data:* b Plainfield, NJ, Jan 31, 51; m 79, Mary Morris; c Carolyn A, Trevor A & Kevin L. *Educ:* Tufts Univ, BSCE, 73; Mass Inst Technol, SM, 77. *Prof Exp:* Lectr, Nat Bur Stand, 77, 81, Boston Archit Ctr, 85 & Grad Sch Design, Harvard Univ, 85. *Mem:* Sigma Xi; Am Soc Civil Engrs; Am Soc Testing & Mat. *Res:* Building materials technology in connection with investigation of failures especially roofing, glass, windows, masonry and curtain walls. *Mailing Add:* Simpson Gumpertz & Heger Inc 297 Broadway Arlington MA 02174

SCHWARTZ, TOBIAS LOUIS, BIOPHYSICS, PHYSIOLOGY. *Current Pos:* asst prof biol sci, 68-71, ASSOC PROF BIOL SCI, UNIV CONN, 71- *Personal Data:* b Ft Wayne, Ind, Sept 8, 28; m 49; c 3. *Educ:* City Col New York, BEE, 49; State Univ NY Buffalo, PhD(biophys), 66. *Prof Exp:* Design engr, Niagara Transformer Corp, NY, 54-58; USPHS fel lab neurophysiol, Col Physicians & Surgeons, Columbia Univ, 65-68. *Concurrent Pos:* Nat Inst Neurol Dis & Stroke res grant, 69; master in res, Lab Cellular Neurobiol, Nat Ctr Sci Res, France, 74-75; mem & invited lectr, Marine Biol Lab Corp, Woods Hole, Mass. *Mem:* AAAS; Biophys Soc; Soc Gen Physiol; Soc Neurosci. *Res:* Diffusion phenomena in membranes; active transport; mechanisms of membrane excitability; membrane diffusion theory. *Mailing Add:* Dept Molecular/Cell Biol Univ Conn 75 N Eagleville Rd Storrs CT 06269-3125. *Fax:* 860-486-4331; *E-Mail:* tobias@uconnvm

SCHWARTZ, WILLIAM BENJAMIN, INTERNAL MEDICINE. *Current Pos:* PROF MED, UNIV SOUTHERN CALIF, 92- *Personal Data:* b Montgomery, Ala, May 16, 22; c 3. *Educ:* Duke Univ, MD, 45; Am Bd Internal Med, dipl, 56. *Prof Exp:* Intern & asst resident med, Univ Chicago Clins, 45-46; res fel, Harvard Med Sch, 48-50; from instr to prof, Med Sch, Tufts Univ, 50-80, prof, 58-96, chmn dept, 71-76, Edicott prof, 75-76, Vannevar Bush prof, 76-96. *Concurrent Pos:* Asst, Peter Brent Brigham Hosp, 48-50; fel, Boston Children's Hosp, 49-50; Markle scholar, 50-55; from asst physician to sr physician, New Eng Med Ctr, 50-; estab investr, Am Heart Asn, 56-; chmn, Gen Med Study Sect, NIH, 65-, chmn sci adv bd, Nat Kidney Found, 68-70; chmn health policy adv bd, Rand Corp, 70-, prin adv, Health Sci Prog, 77-; Endicott prof & physician in chief, New Eng Med Ctr Hosps, 71-76; distinguished prof, Dept Vet Affairs, 94-97. *Mem:* Inst Med-Nat Acad Sci; Am Soc Clin Invest; Am Acad Arts & Sci; Asn Am Physicians; Am Soc Nephrology (pres, 74-75). *Res:* Health care policy analysis. *Mailing Add:* Dept Med Univ Southern Calif 1355 San Pablo St Suite 143 Los Angeles CA 90033

SCHWARTZ, WILLIAM JOSEPH, NEUROLOGY, CIRCADIAN RHYTHMS. *Current Pos:* assoc prof, 86-90, PROF NEUROL, MED SCH, UNIV MASS, 90- *Personal Data:* b Philadelphia, Pa, Mar 28, 50; m 79, Randi Eisner; c Aliza J & Jonathan P. *Educ:* Univ Calif, Irvine, BS, 71, San Francisco, MD, 74. *Prof Exp:* Med intern, Moffitt Hosps, Univ Calif, San Francisco, 74-75, neurol resident, 78-81; res assoc, NIMH, 75-78; instr neurol, Mass Gen Hosp, Harvard Med Sch, 81-82, asst prof, 82-86. *Concurrent Pos:* Mem, NIH/ORG Neurol A Study Sect, 89-93; vchmn, Gordon Conf Chronobiol, chmn, 93. *Mem:* Soc Neurosci; AAAS; Am Acad Neurol; Am Neurol Asn; Soc Res Biol Rhythms; Am Sleep Dis Asn. *Res:* Investigation of the neural regulation of circadian rhythms in mammals by the suprachiasmatic nuclei. *Mailing Add:* Dept Neurol Univ Mass Med Ctr 55 Lake Ave N Worcester MA 01655

SCHWARTZ, WILLIAM LEWIS, VETERINARY PATHOLOGY. *Current Pos:* res assoc vet path & toxicol, 67, asst prof, 67-70, PATHOLOGIST, TEX VET MED DIAG LAB, TEX A&M UNIV, 70- *Personal Data:* b Columbus, Ohio, Dec 11, 31; m 53; c 2. *Educ:* Ohio State Univ, BSc, 53, DVM, 57; Tex A&M Univ, MS, 70. *Prof Exp:* Pvt pract, 57-60; dist vet, Ohio Dept Agr, 60-63, vet diagnostician, 63-64; asst prof diag vet med, Ga Coastal Plain Exp Sta, Univ Ga, 64-67. *Concurrent Pos:* Consult mem health adv comt, Tex Specific Pathogen Free Swine Accrediting Agency, Inc, 71-75. *Mem:* Am Vet Med Asn; Am Asn Swine Practitioners; Am Asn Vet Lab Diagnosticians; Sigma Xi. *Res:* Diagnostic veterinary pathology and related fields; diseases of swine. *Mailing Add:* 3008 Broadmoor Bryan TX 77802-2125

SCHWARTZBACH, STEVEN DONALD, ALGAL PHYSIOLOGY, MOLECULAR BIOLOGY. *Current Pos:* from asst prof to assoc prof, 76-87, PROF CELL BIOL, UNIV NEBR, LINCOLN, 88- *Personal Data:* b Bronx, NY, May 24, 47; m 68, Elaine S Lomant; c Lisa, Amy & Ilana. *Educ:* State Univ NY, Buffalo, BA, 69; Brandeis Univ, PhD(biol), 75. *Prof Exp:* Fel molecular biol, Oak Ridge Nat Lab, 74-76. *Mem:* Am Soc Plant Physiol; Japanese Soc Plant Physiol; AAAS. *Res:* Photoregulation of chloroplast development; organelle nucleic acids; regulation of protein synthesis. *Mailing Add:* Sch Biol Sci Univ Nebr E207 Beadle Ctr Lincoln NE 68588-0666

SCHWARTZBART, HARRY, WELDING, FAILURE ANALYSIS. *Current Pos:* CONSULT, 83- *Personal Data:* b Altoona, Pa, Jan 3, 23; m 53; c 3. *Educ:* Pa State Univ, BS, 43, MS, 48. *Prof Exp:* Metallurgist, Revere Copper & Brass, 43-44; aeronaut res scientist, Nat Adv Comt Aeronaut, 48-51; asst dir metals res, Res Inst, Ill Inst Technol, 51-68; dir mat eng, Rockwell Int, 68-83; mgr res, Aerojet Gen, 83. *Mem:* Fel Am Soc Metals Int; Am Welding Soc; Int Soc Air Safety Investrs; Nat Forensic Ctr. *Res:* Mechanical metallurgy; welding; brazing; soldering; shape memory alloys; failure analysis; author of 75 publications. *Mailing Add:* 10951 Oklahoma Ave Chatsworth CA 91311

SCHWARTZBERG, HENRY G, CHEMICAL ENGINEERING, FOOD ENGINEERING. *Current Pos:* prof food process eng, 73-91, EMER PROF FOOD PROCESS ENG, UNIV MASS, 91- *Personal Data:* b New York, NY, Oct 12, 25; m 55, Evelyn Kurdell; c Frances, Pamela & Beverly. *Educ:* Cooper Union, BChE, 49; NY Univ, MChE, 59, PhD(chem eng), 66. *Honors & Awards:* Food Engr Award, Dairy & Food Indust Supply Asn & Am Soc Agr Engrs, 85. *Prof Exp:* Chem engr, Chem & Radiol Labs, Army Chem Ctr, 50-53; res specialist process develop, Tech Ctr, Gen Foods Corp, 54-66; assoc prof chem eng, NY Univ, 66-73. *Concurrent Pos:* Consult, Clairol Co, 66-67, Gen Foods Corp, 66-92, Am Nat Red Cross, 67-74 & Devro, Inc, 68-77; vis lectr Agr, Univ Neth, 80; vis prof, ENSBANA Univ de Dijon, 84, Univ Nacional del Sur, Bahia Blanca, Arg, 84; chmn, Food, Pharm & Biol Div, Am Inst Chem Engrs, 84; vis prof, Tech Res Ctr, Finland, 90; vis researcher, Distam Univ, Milano, 92-93; consult, Ortho Diag & Alliance Pharmaceut. *Mem:* Am Inst Chem Engrs; Inst Food Technol. *Res:* Microwave heating; freeze concentration, food texturization by extrusion; membrane permeation; solid-liquid extraction; expression; freezing and thawing; evaporation; energy storage by brines; drying; preparative chromatography and puffing. *Mailing Add:* Dept Food-Sci Univ Mass Amherst MA 01003. *Fax:* 413-545-1262; *E-Mail:* schwartzberg@foodsi.umass.edu

SCHWARTZKOPF, GEORGE, JR, ELECTRONICS CHEMICALS. *Current Pos:* RES FEL, MALLINCKRODT BAKER INC, 95- *Personal Data:* b Jersey City, NJ, Feb 14, 43; m 62, Mary Krepps; c Wendy & Chad. *Educ:* Rensselaer Polytech Inst, BS, 64; Seton Hall Univ, MS, 69, PhD(org chem), 73. *Prof Exp:* Res chemist, Merck & Co, 64-72; sr org chemist, J T Baker Inc, 73-79, scientist, 79-84, prin scientist, 84-93, Baker fel, 93-95. *Mem:* Am Chem Soc; Electrochem Soc; Soc Photo Optical Instrumentation Engrs. *Res:* Formulation of products used to clean integrated circuits during various fabrication steps. *Mailing Add:* 97 Bickel Rd Washington NJ 07882. *E-Mail:* micro@planet.net

SCHWARTZMAN, JOSEPH DAVID, CLINICAL MICROBIOLOGY. *Current Pos:* asst prof, 80-86, ASSOC PROF PATH, SCH MED, UNIV VA, 86-, ASSOC DIR, CLIN MICROBIOL LAB, UNIV VA HOSP, 80- *Personal Data:* b Washington, DC, Dec 9, 47; m 72; c 2. *Educ:* Dartmouth Col, AB, 70; Dartmouth Med Sch, BMedSc, 72; Harvard Univ, MD, 74. *Prof Exp:* Resident physician path, Univ Colo Affil Hosps, 74-78; res fel path, Sch Med, Univ Colo, 76-78; teaching fel microbiol, Dartmouth Med Sch, 78-80. *Concurrent Pos:* Prin investr, NIH grant. *Mem:* Am Soc Microbiol; Am Soc Trop Med & Hyg; Am Soc Parasitologists; Royal Soc Trop Med & Hyg; Soc Protozoologists; Infectious Dis Soc Am. *Res:* Cell biology of intracellular protozoan parasites; mechanism of parasite motility and host cell invasion of the coccidian Toxoplasma gondii. *Mailing Add:* 1 Med Center Dr Labanan NH 03756

SCHWARTZMAN, LEON, MICROWAVE ENGINEERING, TECHNICAL MANAGEMENT. *Current Pos:* Engr, Sperry Gyroscope, 57-62, sr engr, 62-67, res sect head, 67-70, sr res sect head, 70-73, dept head, 73-82, mgr, ATR Prog, Sperry SFCS, 82-86, DIR PROG DEVELOP, UNISYS- SGSG, 86- *Personal Data:* b Brooklyn, NY, Feb 6, 31; m 54; c 2. *Educ:* Polytech Inst Brooklyn, BEE, 58, MSEE, 63. *Concurrent Pos:* Radar panel, microwave expos, 67; chmn prog comt, Inst Elec & Electronics Engrs, 67-68, vchmn, 69-70, chmn, 70-71. *Mem:* Fel Inst Elec & Electrons Engrs (secy, 68-69); Am Defense Preparedness Asn. *Res:* Antennas and propogation; design and development of advanced microwave antennas; electronic scanning radars; solid state transmitters; gallium arsenide devices and digital signal processing. *Mailing Add:* 1475 Remson Ave Brooklyn NY 11236

SCHWARTZMAN, ROBERT M, DERMATOLOGY, IMMUNOLOGY. *Current Pos:* from asst prof to assoc prof dermat, 59-67, PROF DERMAT, SCH VET MED, UNIV PA, 67-, ASST PROF COMP DERMAT, GRAD SCH MED, 62- *Personal Data:* b New Haven, Conn, Nov 7, 26; m 60; c 3. *Educ:* Univ Pa, VMD, 52; Univ Minn, MPH, 58, PhD(dermatopath), 59. *Honors & Awards:* Morris Animal Found award, 57-59; USPHS res career develop award, 63-72. *Prof Exp:* Instr vet med, Univ Minn, 53-59. *Mem:* Soc Invest Dermat; Am Soc Dermatopath; Am Soc Allergy; Am Vet Med Asn; Am Col Vet Dermat. *Res:* Veterinary and comparative dermatology. *Mailing Add:* 14 Wiltshire Rd Wynnewood PA 19096

SCHWARZ, ANTON, MEDICAL RESEARCH. *Current Pos:* dir corp med res, Int Region II, 77-80, DIR MED SCI, RES DIV, SCHERING-PLOUGH CORP, 81- *Personal Data:* b Munich, Ger, May 26, 27; nat US; m 52; c 2. *Educ:* Maximilian Univ, Ger, MD, 51. *Honors & Awards:* Wolferine Frontiersman Award, 68. *Prof Exp:* Intern internal med, hosp, Munich, Ger, 51-52; intern, St John's Hosp, Long Island, 52-53; resident physician, Dobbs Ferry Hosp, 53-54; sr res assoc pediat, Children's Hosp Res Found, Col Med, Univ Cincinnati, 54-56; asst dir virus res, Res Div, Pitman-Moore Co, 56-63, dir virus res, Res Div, Pitman-Moore Div, 63-65, dir human health res & develop labs, 65-71, dir biol res & develop & biol labs, 71-75, med dir, Europ Area, Dow Chem Co, 75-77. *Mem:* AAAS; Sigma Xi; AMA; NY Acad Sci; Soc Exp Biol & Med; Am Asn Immunol. *Res:* Medical sciences; research administration. *Mailing Add:* 4222 S Minnesota Ave Sioux Falls SD 57105

SCHWARZ, CINDY BETH, ELEMENTARY PARTICLE PHYSICS. *Current Pos:* ASST PROF PHYSICS, VASSAR COL, 85- *Personal Data:* b Bronx, NY, Sept 17, 58; m 87; c 1. *Educ:* State Univ NY, BS, 80; Yale Univ, MPhil, 82, PhD(physics), 85. *Concurrent Pos:* Consult & guest lectr, Int Bus Machines Corp, 89; guest researcher, Brookhaven Nat Lab, 89; prin investr ILI grant, NSF, 91- *Mem:* Am Phys Soc; Am Asn Physics Teachers; Sigma Xi; Am Asn Univ Professors. *Res:* Experimental particle physics. *Mailing Add:* Dept Physics Vassar Col Box 39 Poughkeepsie NY 12604

SCHWARZ, DIETRICH WALTER FRIEDRICH, HEARING SCIENCE. *Current Pos:* assoc prof, 83-85, PROF OTOLARYNGOL, UNIV BC, 85- *Personal Data:* b Stettin, Ger, Nov 22, 39. *Educ:* Univ Freiburg, MD, 67, Dr, 69. *Prof Exp:* Res fel neurophysiol, Univ Toronto, 69-71; clin teadus otolaryngol, 71-75, from asst prof to assoc prof, 75- 83. *Mem:* Soc Neurosci; Can Soc Physiol; Am Soc Physiol; Asn Res Otolaryngol. *Res:* Auditory and vestibular neurophysiology and neuroanatomy. *Mailing Add:* Dept Surg & Physiol R153 Acute Care Unit Univ British Columbia 2211 Wesbrook Mall Vancouver BC V6T 2B5 Can. *Fax:* 604-822-7240

SCHWARZ, ECKHARD C A, POLYMER SCIENCE. *Current Pos:* PRES, BIAX-FIBERFILM CORP, 75- *Personal Data:* b Luebeck, Ger, Nov 13, 30; US citizen; div; c 4. *Educ:* Univ Hamburg, Diplom, 56; McGill Univ, PhD(org chem), 62. *Prof Exp:* Chemist, E B Eddy Co, 57-59; sr res chemist, E I du Pont de Nemours & Co, 62-68, Kimberly-Clark Corp, 68-72 & E I du Pont de Nemours & Co, Ger, 72-73; dir res, Presto Prod, Inc, 73-75. *Mem:* Am Chem Soc; Tech Asn Pulp & Paper Indust. *Res:* Research and development immodification of commodity polymers; design and development of fiber and film processes. *Mailing Add:* 884 Chapman Ave Neenah WI 54956-2019. *Fax:* 920-722-3110

SCHWARZ, FRANK, ELECTRICAL ENGINEERING, OPTICS. *Current Pos:* AT SOS INC, STANFORD, CT. *Personal Data:* b Timisoara, Roumania, June 2, 24; US citizen; m 49; c 2. *Educ:* City Col New York, BEE, 50; Univ Conn, MEE, 61. *Prof Exp:* Develop engr, Spellman TV Co, 50 & Sigma Elec Co, 50-51; proj engr, Sorensen & Co, Inc, 51-53; proj & dept mgr & consult electrooptics, 53-69, MGR ADVAN DEVELOP DEPT, BARNES ENG CO, 69- *Mem:* Sr mem Inst Elec & Electronics Engrs; Optical Soc Am. *Res:* Infrared instruments and electrooptical systems, including infrared horizon sensors, radiometers, trackers, thermal imaging systems. *Mailing Add:* 156 Thunderhill Dr SOS Inc Stamford CT 06902

SCHWARZ, HANS JAKOB, organic chemistry, biochemistry, for more information see previous edition

SCHWARZ, HAROLD A, CHEMICAL DYNAMICS. *Current Pos:* RETIRED. *Personal Data:* b Nebr, Apr 1, 28; m 53; c 4. *Educ:* Univ Omaha, BA, 48; Notre Dame Univ, PhD(chem), 52. *Prof Exp:* From assoc chemist to sr chemist, Brookhaven Nat Lab, 51-96. *Concurrent Pos:* Vis prof, Hebrew Univ, Jerusalem, 68-69. *Mem:* Am Chem Soc; AAAS. *Res:* Radiation and photochemistry. *Mailing Add:* Brookhaven Nat Lab Upton NY 11973. *E-Mail:* schwarz1@bnl.gov

SCHWARZ, JOHN HENRY, THEORETICAL PHYSICS, HIGH ENERGY PHYSICS. *Current Pos:* res assoc, 72-85, PROF THEORET PHYSICS, LAURITSEN LAB, CALIF INST TECHNOL, 85-, HAROLD BROWN PROF, 89- *Personal Data:* b North Adams, Mass, Nov 22, 41; m 86, Patricia Moyle. *Educ:* Harvard Univ, AB, 62; Univ Calif, Berkeley, PhD(physics), 66. *Honors & Awards:* MacArthur Fel Award, 87; Dirac Medal, 89. *Prof Exp:* Instr physics, Princeton Univ, 66-68, lectr, 68-69, asst prof, 69-72. *Concurrent Pos:* Guggenheim fel, 78-79; trustee, Aspen Ctr Physics. *Mem:* Nat Acad Sci; fel Am Phys Soc. *Res:* Theoretical research in particle physics; supersymmetry; superstrings; conformal field theory. *Mailing Add:* Lauritsen Lab Calif Inst Technol MC 452-48 Pasadena CA 91125

SCHWARZ, JOHN ROBERT, MARINE MICROBIOLOGY. *Current Pos:* from asst prof to assoc prof, 76-86, asst dean acad affairs, 78-79, vpres, 79-81, head, 83-87, PROF MICROBIOL, DEPT MARINE BIOL, MOODY COL, TEX A&M UNIV SYST, 86- *Personal Data:* b Passaic, NJ, Oct 8, 44. *Educ:* Rensselaer Polytech Inst, BS, 67, PhD(biol), 72. *Prof Exp:* Res assoc, Univ Md, College Park, 72-75. *Mem:* Am Soc Microbiol; Soc Indust Microbiol; AAAS; Sigma Xi; Am Soc Limnol Oceanog. *Res:* Marine microbial ecology; biodegradation; microbial production on non-conservative gases in the marine environment. *Mailing Add:* Dept Marine Biol Tex A&M Univ PO Box 1675 Galveston TX 77553-1675

SCHWARZ, JOHN SAMUEL PAUL, INDUSTRIAL ORGANIC CHEMISTRY. *Current Pos:* PRES, PURE SYNTHETICS, INC, 73- *Personal Data:* b Chicago, Ill, Mar 6, 32; m 56; c 1. *Educ:* Univ Ill, BS, 54; Univ Calif, PhD(org chem), 58. *Prof Exp:* Res chemist synthetic lubricants, Exxon Res & Eng Co, NJ, 57-58; sr res scientist pharmaceut res, Squibb Inst

Med Res, 60-68; sr res chemist, Nease Chem Co, 68-72. *Mem:* Am Chem Soc; Inst Food Technologists. *Res:* Isolation, structure, stereochemistry of biologically-active natural products; synthesis and chemistry of tetracyclines and penicillins; acyclic isoimide-imide rearrangement; process research, development and production of flavor chemicals; heat capacity, atomic weight relationship. *Mailing Add:* 4954 Via Cinta San Diego CA 92122

SCHWARZ, KLAUS W, SUPERFLUIDS, TURBULENCE. *Current Pos:* res staff mem, 76-85, MGR, DYNAMICAL PHENOMENA GROUP, IBM WATSON RES CTR, 85- *Personal Data:* b Heidelberg, Ger, Mar 12, 38; US citizen; m 62; c 2. *Educ:* Harvard Univ, BA, 60; Univ Chicago, MS, 62, PhD(physics), 67. *Prof Exp:* Asst prof physics, Univ Chicago, 69-76. *Mem:* Fel Am Phys Soc. *Res:* Experimental and theoretical research in quantum liquids and fluid mechanics; computer modeling of dislocation dynamics. *Mailing Add:* TJ Watson Res Ctr IBM PO Box 218 Yorktown Heights NY 10598. *Fax:* 914-945-4506; *E-Mail:* schwarz@watson.ibm.com

SCHWARZ, MARVIN, PHYSIOLOGICAL PSYCHOLOGY, EXPERIMENTAL PSYCHOLOGY. *Current Pos:* assoc prof, Univ Cincinnati, 64-66, prof psychol, 66-96, dir grad studies, 66-76 & 88-96, vprovost, 79-83, EMER PROF, DEPT PSYCHOL, UNIV CINCINNATI, 97. *Personal Data:* b Newark, NJ, Apr 7, 29; m 89, Pamela Raphael; c Barbara (Wasserstrom), Paul J, David F, Michael Raphael & Todd Raphael. *Educ:* Lafayette Col, AB, 51; Yale Univ, MS, 52, PhD(psychol), 55. *Prof Exp:* Exp psychol, US Naval Sch Aviation Med, USNR, 55-58; res asst prof, psychiat, Univ Iowa, 58-64. *Mem:* Am Psychol Soc; fel AAAS; NY Acad Sci; Sigma Xi. *Res:* Recording electrical activity of the brain and relating it to behavior. *Mailing Add:* 11762 Locksley Ct Cincinnati OH 45241. *E-Mail:* marvin.schwarz@uc.edu

SCHWARZ, MAURICE JACOB, ORGANIC CHEMISTRY. *Current Pos:* Develop chemist, Geigy Chem Corp, RI, 67-69, group leader develop, 69-71, develop mgr, Ciba-Geigy Facil, NJ, 71-75, dir chem develop, 75-78, dir prod, 78-83, VPRES, PHARMACEUT RES & DEVELOP, PHARMACEUT DIV, CIBA-GEIGY CORP, 83- *Personal Data:* b Northampton, Eng, Sept 13, 39; US citizen; m 65; c 2. *Educ:* Univ Ore, BA, 62, PhD(chem), 65. *Concurrent Pos:* Mem, Pharmaceut Develop Subsect Steering Comt, 87-; mem bd dir, Res & Develop Coun; vchmn, Res & Develop Coun, NJ, 89- *Mem:* Am Chem Soc; Pharmaceut Mfrs Asn; Am Asn Pharmaceut Scientists; Am Pharmaceut Asn. *Res:* Process development and research; management. *Mailing Add:* Cell Therapeut Inc 201 Elliott Ave W Suite 400 Seattle WA 98119

SCHWARZ, MEYER, ORGANIC CHEMISTRY. *Current Pos:* CHEMIST, AGR ENVIRON QUAL INST, AGR RES SERV, USDA, 64- *Personal Data:* b Amsterdam, Holland, Nov 6, 24; nat US; m 56; c 2. *Educ:* Univ Geneva, BSc, 46, PhD(org chem), 50. *Prof Exp:* Res assoc chem, Fla State Univ, 50-52; res chemist, Sprague Elec Co, Mass, 52-56; chemist, Harry Diamond Labs, 56-64. *Mem:* The Chem Soc; Am Chem Soc. *Res:* Organic synthesis and reaction mechanisms; dielectric materials; polymers; organic fluorine; phosphorus compounds; natural products as related to insect chemistry; insect hormones, pheromones, attractants and repellents. *Mailing Add:* 6612 Isle of Skye Dr Highland MD 20777-9740

SCHWARZ, OTTO JOHN, PLANT PHYSIOLOGY, BIOCHEMISTRY. *Current Pos:* asst prof, 71-77, ASSOC PROF PLANT PHYSIOL, UNIV TENN, KNOXVILLE, 77- *Personal Data:* b Chicago, Ill, Oct 19, 42; m 65; c 2. *Educ:* Univ Fla, BSA, 64; NC State Univ, MS, 67, PhD(plant physiol), 70. *Prof Exp:* NIH fel, Biol Div, Oak Ridge Nat Lab, 69-71. *Concurrent Pos:* NIH biomed sci grant, Univ Tenn, Knoxville, 71-72; vis investr, Comp Animal Res Lab, Oak Ridge Assoc Univ, 79- *Mem:* Am Soc Plant Physiol. *Res:* Regulation of pyrimidine nucleoside phosphorylating enzymes; chemical regulation of secondary product formation in plants; paraquat induced oleoresin synthesis in Pinus; food chain transport of synfuels. *Mailing Add:* Dept Bot Univ Tenn 1345 Circle Pk Knoxville TN 37996-0001

SCHWARZ, RALPH J, ELECTRICAL ENGINEERING. *Current Pos:* From asst to prof elec eng, Columbia Univ, 43-58, chmn, Dept Elec Eng, 58-65, 71-72, assoc dean acad affairs, Sch Eng & Appl Sci, 72-76, Thayer-Lindsey Prof Elec Eng, 76-92, vdean, 76-92, EMER THAYER LINDSLEY PROF, COLUMBIA UNIV, 92- *Personal Data:* b Hamburg, Ger, June 13, 22; nat US; m 51, Irene S Lassally; c Ronald P & Sylvia A (Winik). *Educ:* Columbia Univ, BS, 43, MS, 44, PhD(elec eng), 49. *Honors & Awards:* Centennial Medal, Inst Elec & Electronics Engrs, 84. *Concurrent Pos:* Adv, Inst Int Educ, 51-70; vis assoc prof, Univ Calif, Los Angeles, 56; vis scientist, IBM Res Ctr, 69-70; trustee, Assoc Univs, Inc, 80-92; dir, Armstrong Mem Res Found, 75- *Mem:* Am Soc Eng Educ; fel Inst Elec & Electronics Engrs; AAAS. *Res:* Communication theory; system analysis; pattern recognition. *Mailing Add:* Sch Eng & Appl Sci Columbia Univ 500 W 120th St New York NY 10027. *Fax:* 212-864-0104; *E-Mail:* rjs3@columbia.edu

SCHWARZ, RICARDO, SOLID STATE PHYSICS. *Current Pos:* STAFF MEM, CTR MAT SCI, LOS ALAMOS NAT LABS, 85- *Personal Data:* b Valdivia, Chile, July 5, 42; US citizen; m 66, Fanny; c 2. *Educ:* Univ Chile, MS, 67; Univ Va, PhD(physics), 72. *Prof Exp:* Asst prof physics, Univ Chile, 66-68 & Univ Va, 72; vis asst prof, Univ Ill, Urbana, 73-75; physicist, Argonne Nat Labs, 75-85. *Concurrent Pos:* Vis assoc, Keck Labs Mat Sci, Calif Inst Technol, 82-83; lab fel, Los Alamos Nat Lab, 94. *Mem:* Am Phys Soc; Mat Res Soc; Am Inst Mining Metall & Petrol Engrs; fel Am Soc Metals Int. *Res:* Mechanical properties of solids; ultrasonics; computer modelling of dislocation dynamics in alloys; solid state reactions in thin films; amorphous metallic alloys; dynamic compaction of powders. *Mailing Add:* Ctr Mat Sci Los Alamos Nat Labs Mail Stop K765 Los Alamos NM 87545. *Fax:* 505-665-2992; *E-Mail:* rxzs@lanl.gov

SCHWARZ, RICHARD, CHEMISTRY, ORGANIC & INORGANIC CHEMISTRY. *Current Pos:* PROF, CHEM DEPT, MO WESTERN STATE COL, 76- *Personal Data:* b Kansas City, Mo, Mar 15, 49. *Educ:* Northwestern Mo State Univ, BS, 71; Univ Mo, MS, 74, PhD(chem), 76. *Prof Exp:* Asst chem, Univ Mo, Columbia, 74-76. *Concurrent Pos:* NSF grants, 79 & 81. *Mem:* Am Chem Soc. *Mailing Add:* Dept Chem Mo Western State Col 4525 Downs Dr St Joseph MO 64507

SCHWARZ, RICHARD HOWARD, OBSTETRICS & GYNECOLOGY, MATERNAL FETAL MEDICINE. *Current Pos:* prof obstet & gynec & chmn dept, Downstate Med Ctr, 78-90, PROVOST & VPRES CLIN AFFAIRS, HSCB, STATE UNIV NY, 88-, DISTINGUISHED SERV PROF EMER, 96- *Personal Data:* b Easton, Pa, Jan 10, 31; m 78, Patricia Lewis; c Martha, Nancy (Tedesco), Paul H & Mary (Murray). *Educ:* Jefferson Med Col, MD, 55; Am Bd Obstet & Gynec, dipl, 63, cert, 74. *Prof Exp:* Assoc obstet & gynec, Tulane Univ, 59-63; from instr to assoc prof, Sch Med, Univ Pa, 63-73, prof, 73-78, dir, Jerrold R Giolding Div Fetal Med, 71-78. *Concurrent Pos:* Chmn obstet & gynec, NY Methodist Hosp, 96- *Mem:* AAAS; fel Am Col Obstet & Gynec (pres, 91-92); Am Gynec & Obstet Soc; Infectious Dis Soc Obstet & Gynec (pres). *Res:* Perinatal and placental physiology; high risk obstetrics; diabetes; infectious disease. *Mailing Add:* Chmn Obstet & Gywec NY Methodist Hosp 506 Sixth St Brooklyn NY 11215

SCHWARZ, SIGMUND D, GEOPHYSICS, GEOLOGY. *Current Pos:* PRES, S D SCHWARZ & ASSOC, INC, 90- *Personal Data:* b Portland, Ore, Sept 27, 28; c 3. *Educ:* Ore State Univ, BSc, 52. *Prof Exp:* Photo-radar intelligence officer, USAF Strategic Air Command, Fairchild AFB, 52-54; geologist & geophysicist, Ore State Highway Dept, Salem, 54-58; pres, Geo Recon Inc, Seattle, 58-71; prin & sr geologist & geophysist, Shannon & Wilson, Inc, Seattle, 71-79; pres, Geo-Recon Int Ltd, 79-84; independent consult, 84-94. *Concurrent Pos:* Prin, Geo Recon Ore Ltd, Salem, 56-58; chmn, Wash State Sect, Asn Eng Geologists, 67. *Mem:* Am Inst Mining, Metall & Petrol Engrs; Asn Eng Geologists; Soc Explor Geophysicists; Europ Asn Explor Geophysicists; fel Geol Soc Am; Seismol Soc Am; Am Inst Prof Geologists. *Res:* Author of 20 publications in geophysics. *Mailing Add:* 15317 62nd Pl NE Bothell WA 98011

SCHWARZ, STEVEN E, ELECTRICAL ENGINEERING. *Current Pos:* from asst prof to assoc prof elec eng, 64-74, PROF ELEC ENG, UNIV CALIF, BERKELEY, 74-, ASSOC DEAN, 91- *Personal Data:* b Los Angeles, Calif, Jan 29, 39; m 63, Janet Paschal. *Educ:* Calif Inst Technol, BS, 59, MS, 61, PhD(elec eng), 64; Harvard Univ, AM, 62. *Prof Exp:* Mem tech staff, Hughes Res Labs, 62-64. *Concurrent Pos:* Guggenheim fel, IBM Corp Res Lab, Zurich, 71-72; pres chair undergrad educ, Univ Calif, 90-93. *Mem:* Fel Inst Elec & Electronics Engrs; Am Soc Eng Educ. *Res:* Microwave circuits; electromagnetics; quantum electronics. *Mailing Add:* Dept Elec Eng Univ Calif Berkeley CA 94720

SCHWARZ, WILLIAM MERLIN, JR, ELECTROCHEMISTRY, PHYSICAL CHEMISTRY. *Current Pos:* scientist, 68-70, SR SCIENTIST, XEROX CORP, 70- *Personal Data:* b Hartford, Conn, Nov 13, 34; m 55; c 4. *Educ:* Pa State Univ, 56; Univ Wis, PhD(phys chem), 61. *Prof Exp:* Proj assoc, Univ Wis, 61-63; sr engr, Int Bus Mach Corp, 63-64; chemist, Nat Bur Stand, DC, 64-68. *Mem:* Am Chem Soc; Electrochem Soc; Am Inst Chemists. *Res:* Electrode kinetics; xerographic development; polarography; photoelectrophoresis; xerographic processes and materials. *Mailing Add:* 274 Southboro Dr Webster NY 14580-9742

SCHWARZER, CARL G, ORGANIC CHEMISTRY. *Current Pos:* RETIRED. *Personal Data:* b San Francisco, Calif, Apr 20, 17; m 37; c 1. *Prof Exp:* Chemist, Shell Develop Co, 37-67; dir res & develop, Apogee Chem Co, 67-71; pres, Appl Resins & Technol, 71-73; mgr & chemist, Indust Tank, Inc, J & J Disposal, Inc, 74-76; waste mgt specialist, State Calif Health Serv, Hazardous Mat Mgt Sect, 76-78; tech specialist aerojet gen environ staff & prog mgr hazardous waste mat, Aerojet Energy Conversion Co, 80-87. *Concurrent Pos:* Consult, US, Mex, Europe & China; mem bd dirs, World Asn Solid Waste Transfer & Exchange. *Mem:* Am Chem Soc; Am Civil Eng Asn. *Res:* Synthesis of organic and epoxy resins; hydrocarbon resin surface coatings; manufacture and applications of epoxy, peroxide, phenolic compounds and resins; industrial waste; disposal management in the environmental systems and technology; surveillance and management of hazardous waste materials; resource recovery and reuse of industrials; environmental chemistry disciplines. *Mailing Add:* 7760 Crystal Blvd El Dorado CA 95623

SCHWARZER, THERESA FLYNN, GEOLOGY, GEOCHEMISTRY. *Current Pos:* RETIRED. *Personal Data:* b Troy, NY, Apr 14, 40; m 61; c 1. *Educ:* Rensselaer Polytech Inst, BS, 63, MS, 66, PhD(geol), 69. *Prof Exp:* Instr geol, State Univ NY, Albany, 69; res fel remote sensing, Rice Univ, 69-72; sr res geologist, Exxon Prod Res Co, 72-74, res specialist, 74-76, sr res specialist, 76-78, sr explor geologist, Gulf Coast Div, Exxon, USA, 78-80, proj leader, Tex Offshore, 80-81, dist prod geologist, ETex Div, 81-83, sr supvr, Exxon Prod Res Co, 83-87, geol adv, 87-96. *Concurrent Pos:* Chairwoman, Women Geoscientists Comt, Am Geol Inst, 73-77. *Mem:* Geol Soc Am; Am Asn Petrol Geologists; Soc Explor Geophysicists; Geochem Soc. *Res:*

Inorganic and organic geochemistry; remote sensing; multivariate statistical techniques; interpretation and integration of geophysical, geological and geochemical data for hydrocarbon exploration. *Mailing Add:* 2706 Cottonwood Walk Spring TX 77388

SCHWARZSCHILD, ARTHUR ZEIGER, NUCLEAR PHYSICS. *Current Pos:* res assoc physics, 58-60, assoc physicist, 61-63, physicist, 63-70, dep chmn & head nuclear physics, 78-81, SR PHYSICIST, BROOKHAVEN NAT LAB, 70-, CHMN, PROG ADV COMN, TANDEM USERS GROUP, 75-, CHMN, PHYSICS DEPT, 81- *Personal Data:* b New York, NY, Mar 24, 30; m 52; c 3. *Educ:* Columbia Univ, BA, 51, MA, 56, PhD(physics), 57. *Prof Exp:* Res assoc physics, Columbia Univ, 57-58. *Concurrent Pos:* Consult, NY Univ, 64-80; NATO fel, 66-67; mem, Nuclear Sci Adv Comn, Dept Energy, NSF, 81-83; Argonne Univ Asn rev comt, Physics Div, Argonne Nat Lab, 81-83. *Mem:* Fel Am Phys Soc; AAAS; Sigma Xi; fel NY Acad Sci. *Res:* Heavy ion nuclear reactions; nuclear spectroscopy; measurements of electromagnetic transition probabilities for excited nuclear states; instrumentation for very short lifetime measurements. *Mailing Add:* 31 Howard St Patchogue NY 11772

SCHWARZSCHILD, MARTIN, stellar structure & evolution, stellar dynamics; deceased, see previous edition for last biography

SCHWASSMAN, HORST OTTO, BIOLOGY, PHYSIOLOGY. *Current Pos:* RETIRED. *Personal Data:* b Berlin, Ger, Aug 31, 22; m 60; c 1. *Educ:* Univ Munich, Cand rer nat, 52; Univ Wis-Madison, PhD(zool), 62. *Prof Exp:* Lectr zool, Univ Wis-Madison, 62-63; USPHS fel, Univ Calif, Los Angeles, 63-65, asst res anatomist, 65-67; from asst res physiologist to assoc res physiologist, Scripps Inst Oceanog, 67-70; assoc prof psychol & biol, Dalhousie Univ, 70-72, prof, 72; from assoc prof to prof zool, Univ Fla, 72-95. *Mem:* Asn Trop Biol; Am Soc Ichthyologists & Herpetologists. *Res:* Animal behavior; sensory physiology; visual system; circadian and biological rhythms; neurophysiology of vision in vertebrates. *Mailing Add:* 7214 SW 31st Pl Gainesville FL 32608

SCHWEBEL, SOLOMON LAWRENCE, THEORETICAL PHYSICS. *Current Pos:* ASSOC PROF PHYSICS, BOSTON COL, 64- *Personal Data:* b New York, NY, Oct 21, 16; m 49; c 2. *Educ:* City Col New York, BS, 37; NY Univ, MS, 47, PhD, 54. *Prof Exp:* Instr physics, City Col New York, 46-50; res scientist, Inst Math Sci, NY Univ, 52-54; instr physics, Brooklyn Col, 54-55; staff scientist, Missiles & Space Div, Lockheed Aircraft Corp, 55-61; assoc prof physics, Univ Cincinnati, 61-64. *Mem:* Am Phys Soc; Am Asn Physics Teachers. *Mailing Add:* 14 Kerrydale Rd Needham MA 02192-3732

SCHWEBER, SILVAN SAMUEL, THEORETICAL PHYSICS. *Current Pos:* assoc prof, Brandeis Univ, 55-61, chmn dept, 58-76, chmn sch sci, 62-68 & 73-74, PROF PHYSICS, BRANDEIS UNIV, 61-, PROF HIST SCI, 82-, PROF KORETE & HIST IDEAS, 82- *Personal Data:* b Strasbourg, France, Apr 10, 28; nat US; m 65; c Libby, Howard, Abby & Simone. *Educ:* City Col New York, BS, 47; Univ Pa, MS, 49; Princeton Univ, PhD(physics), 52. *Prof Exp:* Asst instr, Univ Pa, 47-49; instr, Princeton Univ, 51-52; NSF fel, Cornell Univ, 52-54; res physicist, Carnegie Inst Technol, 54-55. *Concurrent Pos:* Vis prof, Mass Inst Technol, 61-62 & 69-70, Hebrew Univ, Jerusalem, 71-72 & Harvard, 87 & 91; assoc hist sci, Harvard Univ, 77- *Mem:* Am Phys Soc; AAAS; Sigma Xi; Hist Sci Soc. *Res:* Field theory; statistical mechanics; history of science. *Mailing Add:* Dept Physics Brandeis Univ MS057 Waltham MA 02254

SCHWEGMANN, JACK CARL, ENTOMOLOGY. *Current Pos:* RETIRED. *Personal Data:* b Denver, Colo, Nov 4, 25; m 47, Nanette Taylor; c Gerard & Michael. *Educ:* Tulane Univ, BS, 48; Univ Okla, MS, 50; La State Univ, PhD(plant path), 53. *Prof Exp:* Plant pathologist, Chalmette Works, Kaiser Aluminum & Chem Corp, 53-54, sr plant pathologist, 54-56, supvr air control, 56-58, supvr fume abatement, Metals Div, 58, coordr air control activ, 58-67, dir environ serv, 67-82, mgr air serv, corp environ affairs, 82-86. *Concurrent Pos:* Univ Calif Coop Exten Master Gardener Prog, Alameda County, 88- *Mem:* AAAS; Sigma Xi; Am Phytopath Soc; NY Acad Sci. *Res:* Air and stream pollution effects on plants and animals; diseases and insect pests of ornamental plants and vegetable crops. *Mailing Add:* 2001 Sandcreek Way Alameda CA 94501-6126

SCHWEICKART, RUSSELL LOUIS, AERONAUTICS, ASTRONAUTICAL ENGINEERING. *Current Pos:* PRES & FOUNDER, ASN SPACE EXPLORERS, 85-; PRES & CHIEF EXEC OFFICER, ALOHA NETWORKS INC, 96- *Personal Data:* b Neptune, NJ, Oct 25, 35; m 90, Nancy K Ramsey; c Vicki Louise, Russell, Randolph, Elin Ashley, Diana Croom Matthew Forbes & David Scot. *Educ:* Mass Inst Technol, BS, 56, MS, 63. *Honors & Awards:* Spec Trustees Award, Nat Acad TV Arts & Sci, 69; De La Vaulx Medal, Fedn Aeronaut Int, 70. *Prof Exp:* Res scientist, Exp Astron Lab, Mass Inst Technol,; astronaut, Johnson Manned Spacecraft Ctr; astronaut, Lunar Module Pilot, Apollo 9, 69; dir user affairs, Off Appln, NASA; sci adv, Gov Edmund G Brown Jr, State Calif, 77-79; chmn, Calif Energy Comn, 79-83, comnr, 79-85; exec vpres, CTA Com Systs, 94-96. *Concurrent Pos:* Consult & lectr; pilot, USAF, 56-61; capt, Mass Air Nat Guard; trustee, Calif Acad Sci; pres, NRS Commun, 91-94. *Mem:* Fel Am Astronaut Soc; Soc Exp Test Pilots; asoc fel Am Inst Aeronaut & Astronaut; Sigma Xi; Asn Space Explorers (pres). *Mailing Add:* Aloha Networks Inc 5718 Geary Blvd San Francisco CA 94121

SCHWEICKERT, RICHARD ALLAN, GEOLOGY, TECTONICS. *Current Pos:* PROF GEOL, UNIV NEV, RENO, 83-, CHMN DEPT, 93- *Personal Data:* b Sonora, Calif, Feb 7, 46; m 67, Susan Parrish; c Torrey & Tiffany. *Educ:* Stanford Univ, BS, 67, PhD(geol), 72. *Prof Exp:* Geologist, Texaco Inc, 71-72 & US Geol Surv, 73; asst prof geol, Calif State Col, Sonoma, 72, Calif State Univ, San Jose, 73 & Calif State Univ, San Francisco, 73; asst prof geol, Columbia Univ, 73-78, assoc prof, 78-82. *Mem:* Geol Soc Am; Am Geophys Union; Soc Econ Paleontologists & Mineralogists. *Res:* Tectonics of orogenic belts and convergent plate boundaries; Paleozoic and Mesozoic tectonic evolution of the western cordillera of the United States; crustal evolution of Sierra Nevada region; origin of melanges. *Mailing Add:* Dept Geol Sci Univ Nev Reno NV 89557-0001. *E-Mail:* richschw@mines.unr.edu

SCHWEIGER, JAMES W, DENTISTRY, PROSTHODONTICS. *Current Pos:* chmn, Div Prosthodontics, 87-91, CLIN PROF PROSTHODONTICS, COLUMBIA UNIV, 83- *Personal Data:* b Osage, Iowa, Oct 13, 29; c 2. *Educ:* Univ Iowa, DDS, 54, MS, 57. *Prof Exp:* Instr prosthetic dent, Dent Sch, Univ Iowa, 57-58, asst prof dent technol, 58-59, asst prof otolaryngol & maxillofacial surg, Sch Med, 59-65, assoc prof, Sch Dent, 65-69; chief, Dent Serv & dir, Maxillofacial Prosthetic Ctr, Vet Admin Ctr, Wilmington, 70-83, coordr res, 81-83; chief, Dent Serv, Mem Sloan Kettering, 83-88. *Concurrent Pos:* Consult, Coun Dent Educ, Thomas Jefferson Univ Hosp, Wilmington Med Ctr Surg & Dent & Children's Hosp Philadelphia, Temple Univ; consult, Bronx Vet Hosp, NY, 88- *Mem:* Fel Am Col Prosthodont; assoc mem Am Acad Ophthal & Otolaryngol; fel Am Acad Maxillofacial Prosthodontics (pres, 81-82); Am Dent Asn; Am Bd Prosthodontics. *Res:* Development of facial plastics for maxillofacial prosthodontics. *Mailing Add:* PO Box 606 Lewes DE 19958

SCHWEIGER, MARVIN I, AERONAUTICAL ENGINEERING. *Current Pos:* INDEPENDENT CONSULT, 86- *Personal Data:* b Middletown, NY, Feb 10, 23; m 80; c 2. *Educ:* Rensselaer Polytech Inst, BAeroE, 48. *Prof Exp:* Asst, Res Labs, Gen Elec Co, 47; res engr, Res Dept, United Aircraft Corp, 48-55, head propulsion sect, Res Labs, 55-61, chief propulsion, 61-62; vpres, Bowles Eng Corp, Md, 62-67; mgr, Aerothermo, 67-71, mgr preliminary design, 71-73, mgr, Internal Aero, 73-78, proj mgr contracted res, Columbus Aircraft Div, 78-80, tech dir res & technol, NAm Aircraft Opers, Rockwell Int Corp, 80-86. *Mem:* Assoc fel Am Inst Aeronaut & Astronaut. *Res:* Aerodynamics; propulsion; control and aircraft. *Mailing Add:* 4765 Powderhorn Lane Westerville OH 43081

SCHWEIGHARDT, FRANK KENNETH, MOLECULAR SPECTROSCOPY, FLUOROCARBON CHEMISTRY. *Current Pos:* MGR & SR RES ASSOC, NEW PROD DEVELOP, AIR PROD & CHEM, INC, 79- *Personal Data:* b Passaic, NJ, May 12, 44; m 68; c Brian & Jennine. *Educ:* Seton Hall Univ, BS, 66; Duquesne Univ, PhD(phys chem), 70. *Prof Exp:* Asst to dean pharmaceut chem, Sch Pharm, Duquesne Univ, 70- 71; fel Nat Res Coun, US Bur Mines, 71-72 res chemist, Dept Energy, 72-79. *Concurrent Pos:* Chemist, Allegheny Co Morgue, 69-71; lectr, Chem Dept, Duquesne, 70; consult anal & forensic chem, 70-; postdoctoral fel, Nat Res Coun, 72; assoc ed, Pa Acad Sci J, 84-85. *Mem:* Am Chem Soc; Spectros Soc; Anal Soc; AAAS; Sigma Xi; Am Soc Testing Mat. *Res:* Development of fluon chemicals and their emulsions for bio-medical applications; development of high purity gases for trace analysis and the electronic's market; analytical chemistry; chromatography. *Mailing Add:* 15 Bastian Ln Allentown PA 18104. *Fax:* 610-481-6517

SCHWEIKER, GEORGE CHRISTIAN, CHEMISTRY, RESEARCH & DEVELOPMENT ADMINISTRATION. *Current Pos:* INDEPENDENT CONSULT, 87- *Personal Data:* b Philadelphia, Pa, Feb 17, 24; m 50, Joyce Gilman; c 4. *Educ:* Temple Univ, AB, 49, AM, 52, PhD(chem), 53. *Prof Exp:* Adj prof chem, Drexel Univ, 50-53; res chemist, Hooker Chem Corp, 53-56, supvr polymer res, 56-57; mgr res, Velsicol Chem Corp, 57-60; mgr plastics res, Celanese Corp, 60-65; dir chem & polymers, Develop Div, Borg-Warner Corp, 65-71; vpres & dir res & develop, PQ Corp, 71-87. *Concurrent Pos:* Mem, corp assoc comt, Am Chem Soc. *Mem:* Fel AAAS; fel Royal Soc Chem; Am Chem Soc; Indust Res Inst; Soc Chem Indust; NY Acad Sci. *Res:* Polymers; organic syntheses; rearrangements; industrial and agricultural chemicals; fire retardants; plastics and plastics additives; inorganic chemicals; research and development management. *Mailing Add:* 12518 Calle Tamega 127 San Diego CA 92128

SCHWEIKER, JERRY W, engineering, for more information see previous edition

SCHWEIKERT, DANIEL GEORGE, ELECTRONIC DESIGN AUTOMATION,. *Current Pos:* SR MGR, CAD, SUN MICROELECTRONICS, 96- *Personal Data:* b Bemidji, Minn, June 15, 37; m 61, Judith Johnson; c Eric, Karl & Kristen. *Educ:* Yale Univ, BE, 59; Brown Univ, ScM, 62, PhD(numerical anal), 66. *Prof Exp:* Res engr, Gen Dynamics/ Elec Boat, 61-64; mem tech staff comput appins, Bell Tel Labs, 66-72, supvr, Bell Labs, 72-80; dir comput-aided design, United Technol Microelectron Ctr, 80-87, dir prog mgt & design methods, 87-88; dir case & tech serv, Cadence Design Systs, 88-91; dir opers & control eng, 92-93; vpres eng, AutoGate Logic, 93-96. *Concurrent Pos:* Mem prog comt, Design Automation Conf, 80-86, exec bd, 86-94, gen chair, 92; mem prog comt, Int Conf Comput Aided Design, 83-88. *Mem:* Fel Inst Elec & Electronics Engrs; Asn Comput Mach; AAAS. *Res:* Development of systems for electronic design automation. *Mailing Add:* 1578 Eddington Pl San Jose CA 95129. *Fax:* 408-774-8047; *E-Mail:* dan.schweikert@eng.sun.com

SCHWEIKERT, EMILE ALFRED, ANALYTICAL CHEMISTRY. *Current Pos:* asst prof analytical chem & asst res chemist, 66-70, assoc prof analytical chem & assoc res chemist, 70-74, PROF CHEM, TEX A&M UNIV, 74-, DIR, CTR CHEM CHARACTERIZATION & ANALYSIS, 72- *Personal Data:* b Flawil, Switz, Sept 10, 39; m 65; c 3. *Educ:* Univ Toulouse, Licensee in sci, 62; Univ Paris, Dr(analytical chem), 64. *Honors & Awards:* George Hevesy Medal, 86. *Prof Exp:* Res asst res ctr metall chem, Nat Ctr Sci Res, Vitry, France, 63-65; sci consult, Europ Nuclear Energy Agency, Orgn Econ Coop & Develop, Paris, 65; scientist, Swiss Govt Deleg, Atomic Energy Matters, Switz, 65-66. *Concurrent Pos:* Adj asst prof grad sch, Col Med, Baylor Univ, 68- *Mem:* Am Chem Soc; NY Acad Sci; Swiss Asn Atomic Energy. *Res:* Analytical chemistry; administration of scientific affairs; secondary ion mass spectrometry; nuclear methods of analysis. *Mailing Add:* Chem Dept Tex A&M Univ College Station TX 77843-3255

SCHWEINLER, HAROLD CONSTANTINE, physics; deceased, see previous edition for last biography

SCHWEINSBERG, ALLEN ROSS, MATHEMATICAL ANALYSIS. *Current Pos:* asst prof, 69-76, ASSOC PROF MATH, BUCKNELL UNIV, 76- *Personal Data:* b Ellwood City, Pa, May 5, 42; m 69. *Educ:* Univ Pittsburgh, BS, 62, MS, 65, PhD(math), 69. *Prof Exp:* Instr math, Univ Pittsburgh, 67-69. *Mem:* Am Math Soc; Math Asn Am. *Res:* Operator theory. *Mailing Add:* Dept Math Bucknell Univ Lewisburg PA 17837-2005

SCHWEISS, JOHN FRANCIS, MEDICINE. *Current Pos:* Asst surg, 52-57, from instr to assoc prof, 57-71, ASSOC PROF PEDIAT & PROF SURG, SCH MED, ST LOUIS UNIV, 71- DIR SECT ANESTHESIOL, 62- *Personal Data:* b St Louis, Mo, June 25, 25; m 50; c 5. *Educ:* St Louis Univ, MD, 48. *Concurrent Pos:* Resident, Presby Hosp, NY, 54-56; chief anesthesiol, Cardinal Glennon Mem Hosp, 56-; pvt pract. *Mem:* Am Soc Anesthesiol; AMA; Int Anesthesia Res Soc. *Res:* Anesthesiology. *Mailing Add:* 3635 Vista Ave St Louis MO 63110

SCHWEISTHAL, MICHAEL ROBERT, FETAL ENDOCRINOLOGY, GROWTH & DEVELOPMENT. *Current Pos:* CLIN PROF & SR LECTR, DEPT SURG, UNIV CALIF SCH MED, SAN DIEGO, 88- *Personal Data:* b Faribault, Minn, June 11, 36; m 65; c 5. *Educ:* Luther Col, Iowa, BA, 58; Univ Minn, PhD(anat), 64. *Prof Exp:* Teaching asst anat, Univ Minn, 60-64; from asst prof to assoc prof, Med Col Va, 64-69; prof biol, ECarolina Univ, 70-71, prof anat & chmn dept, 71-77; assoc dean biomed sci, Oral Roberts Univ, 77, prof anat, 77- 88. *Concurrent Pos:* NSF fel, 60; trainee anat, NIH, 60; lectr, Portsmouth Naval Hosp, 64-69; assoc prof anat & oral biol, Univ Ky, 69-70. *Mem:* AAAS; Am Asn Anatomists; Sigma Xi; Am Physiol Soc; Am Diabetes Asn; Am Asn Clin Anatomists. *Res:* Fetal alcohol syndrome; the effects of ethanol on the endocrine system of the maternal organism, the fetus and the neonate; the effects of ethanol on insulin and carbohydrate metabolism in a developing and growing system. *Mailing Add:* Dept Surg Univ Calif San Diego Sch Med 9500 Gilman Dr La Jolla CA 92093-0604

SCHWEITZER, CARL EARLE, organic chemistry, polymers, for more information see previous edition

SCHWEITZER, DONALD GERALD, THERMODYNAMIC & MATERIALS PROPERTIES. *Current Pos:* Chemist, Dept Nuclear Energy, 55-85, head, High Temperature Gas-Cooled Reactor Safety Div, 74-79, ASSOC CHMN & HEAD RADIOACTIVE WASTE MGT DIV, BROOKHAVEN NAT LAB, 79-, SR SCIENTIST, DEPT ADVAN TECHNOL, 79- *Personal Data:* b New York, NY, Mar 25, 30; m 52; c 2. *Educ:* City Col New York, BS, 51; Syracuse Univ, PhD(chem), 55. *Mem:* Am Inst Mining, Metall & Petrol Eng. *Res:* Reactor safety; graphite research, chemistry of liquid metals; superconductivity; radiation damage; photochemistry; waste management. *Mailing Add:* Dept Advan Technol Brookhaven Nat Lab PO Box 5000 Upton NY 11973-5000

SCHWEITZER, EDMUND OSCAR, III, ELECTRICAL ENGINEERING. *Current Pos:* PRES, SCHWEITZER ENG LABS, 82- *Personal Data:* b Evanston, Ill, Oct 31, 47; m 77; c 3. *Educ:* Purdue Univ, BS, 68, MS, 71; Wash State Univ, PhD(elec eng), 77. *Prof Exp:* Elec engr radar syst, Nat Security Agency, 68-73; elec engr, Probe Syst Inc, 73-74; res asst elec power, Wash State Univ, 74-77; asst prof, Ohio Univ, 77-79; assoc prof elec power, Wash State Univ, 79-84. *Concurrent Pos:* Adj prof elect power, Wash State Univ, 84- *Mem:* Inst Elec & Electronics Engrs. *Res:* Application of microprocessors to electric power systems protection; revenue metering of electric energy; digital signal processing using microprocessors. *Mailing Add:* Attn: K Buxton Schweitzer Eng Labs 2350 NE Hopkins Ct Pullman WA 99163

SCHWEITZER, GEORGE KEENE, INORGANIC CHEMISTRY, PHILOSOPHY OF SCIENCE. *Current Pos:* from asst prof to assoc prof, 48-58, prof, 60-70, DISTINGUISHED PROF CHEM, UNIV TENN, KNOXVILLE, 70- *Personal Data:* b Poplar Bluff, Mo, Dec 5, 24; m 48, Verna L Pratt; c Ruth A, Deborah K & Eric G. *Educ:* Cent Col, Mo, BA, 45; Univ Ill, MS, 46, PhD(inorg chem), 48; Columbia Univ, MA, 59; NY Univ, PhD(philos of sci), 64. *Hon Degrees:* ScD, Cent Col, 64. *Honors & Awards:* Staley lectr. *Prof Exp:* Res fel, Univ Ill, 45-48. *Concurrent Pos:* Fel, Columbia Univ, 59-61; vis prof, Meredith Col, 80 & Eastern Ill Univ, 82, 88; Am Chem Soc lectr. *Mem:* Am Philos Asn; Am Chem Soc; Hist Sci Soc. *Res:* Templated coordination complex matrices; rare earth chelate fluorescence; ion exchanging polymers; history and philosophy of science; transuxanium element separation and determinations; rare earth separations. *Mailing Add:* Dept Chem Univ Tenn Knoxville TN 37996-1600

SCHWEITZER, JEFFREY STEWART, NUCLEAR PHYSICS, NUCLEAR GEOPHYSICS. *Current Pos:* ADJ PROF PHYSICS, STATE UNIV NY, ALBANY, 96- *Personal Data:* b New York, NY, May 6, 46; m 70; c 1. *Educ:* Carnegie Inst Technol, BS, 67; Purdue Univ, MS, 69, PhD(physics), 72. *Prof Exp:* Res fel nuclear physics, Calif Inst Technol, 72-74; sr res physicist, Schlumberger Ltd, 74-87, sci adv, 88-96. *Concurrent Pos:* Reviewer, Sci Fac Prof Develop, NSF, 81; consult, Int Atomic Energy Agency, 85-; ed, Nuclear Geophys, 86-95 & Appl Radiation & Isotopes, 95- *Mem:* Am Phys Soc; Am Nuclear Soc; Inst Elec & Electronics Engrs; Soc Prop Well Log Analysts. *Res:* Experimental work in gamma-ray spectroscopy, neutron and gamma-ray interactions, low energy compound nuclear reactions and development of nuclear well logging tools for spectroscopic analysis; material science of materials for gamma-ray detectors; planetary measurements. *Mailing Add:* 41 Silver Hill Rd Old Quarry Rd Ridgefield CT 06877. *E-Mail:* schweitzer@ridgefield-ct.com

SCHWEITZER, JOHN WILLIAM, MAGNETISM & SUPERCONDUCTIVITY IN STRONGLY CORRELATED SYSTEMS. *Current Pos:* from asst prof to assoc prof, 66-78, PROF PHYSICS, UNIV IOWA, 78- *Personal Data:* b Covington, Ky, Apr 23, 41. *Educ:* Thomas More Col, AB, 60; Univ Cincinnati, MS, 62, PhD(physics), 66. *Mem:* Am Phys Soc. *Res:* Localized magnetic states; itinerant electron magnetism; valence fluctuations; statistical mechanics; solitons in molecular systems; superconductivity; metal-insulator transition in layered ternary sulfides. *Mailing Add:* Dept Physics & Astron Univ Iowa Iowa City IA 52242. *E-Mail:* john__schweitzer@uiowa.edu

SCHWEITZER, LELAND RAY, AGRONOMY, VEGETABLE CROPS. *Current Pos:* PRES, SEED TECH PLUS, 90- *Personal Data:* b Merna, Nebr, July 23, 41; m 71; c 2. *Educ:* Ore State Univ, BS, 66, MS, 69; Mich State Univ, PhD(crop sci), 72. *Prof Exp:* Int Agr Ctr study fel, Off Seed Testing Sta, Wageningen, Neth, 72; seed physiologist, Asgrow Seed Co, 72-90. *Mem:* Am Soc Agron; Asn Off Seed Analysis. *Res:* Seed physiology, technology and testing. *Mailing Add:* 9355 Hopewell Rd Salem OR 97304

SCHWEITZER, MARK GLENN, CARBOHYDRATE CHEMISTRY. *Personal Data:* b Mckeesport, Pa, July 12, 57; m 84, 91. *Educ:* Thiel Col, BA, 79; Ohio State Univ, Columbus, PhD(chem), 84. *Prof Exp:* Prin res chemist, Lever Res, Inc, 84-85; scientist, Rohm & Haas Co, 85-89; dept mgr, Battelle, 89-94. *Mem:* Am Chem Soc. *Res:* Development of new analytical procedures for agricultural products of environmental concern; metabolism of agricultural products; residue analysis and method development. *Mailing Add:* G D Searle Co 4901 Searle Pkwy Skokie IL 60077

SCHWEITZER, PAUL JEROME, operations research, applied mathematics, for more information see previous edition

SCHWEIZER, ALBERT EDWARD, ZEOLITE CHEMISTRY. *Current Pos:* SR STAFF CHEMIST, EXXON RES & DEVELOP LABS, 82- *Personal Data:* b Philadelphia, Pa, Mar 31, 43; m 61, 89, Colette Lajoie; c Catherine, Albert & Susan. *Educ:* West Chester State Col, BS, 64; Rutgers Univ, MS, 68; Calif Inst Technol, PhD(chem), 74. *Prof Exp:* Sr res chemist, Cent Res Labs, Mobil Res & Develop Corp, 64-76, Indust Chem Res & Develop, Air Prod & Chem, Inc, 76-80, ICI Americas, 80-82. *Mem:* Am Chem Soc; Am Ceramic Soc; Sigma Xi. *Res:* Synthesis, mechanistic studies and thermal properties; process development; catalysis; zeolites and transition metal chemistry. *Mailing Add:* 2069 W Magna Carta Baton Rouge LA 70815. *Fax:* 504-359-8034; *E-Mail:* albert.e.schweizer@exxon.sprint.com

SCHWEIZER, BERTHOLD, MATHEMATICS. *Current Pos:* PROF MATH, UNIV MASS, AMHERST, 70- *Personal Data:* b Cologne, Ger, July 20, 29; nat US; m 61; c 1. *Educ:* Mass Inst Technol, SB, 51; Ill Inst Technol, MS, 54, PhD(math), 56. *Prof Exp:* Instr math, Ill Inst Technol, 56-57; asst prof, San Diego State Col, 57-58; vis asst prof, Univ Calif, Los Angeles, 58-60; assoc prof, Univ Ariz, 60-65 & Univ Mass, Amherst, 65-68; prof, Univ Ariz, 68-70. *Mem:* Am Math Soc; Math Asn Am. *Res:* Probabilistic geometry; algebra of functions; functional equations. *Mailing Add:* Dept Math & Statist Univ Mass Amherst MA 01003-0113

SCHWEIZER, EDWARD E, AGRONOMY, WEED SCIENCE. *Current Pos:* PLANT PHYSIOLOGIST, ASN ECOSYST RES CTR, COLO STATE UNIV, USDA, 61- *Personal Data:* b Joliet, Ill, Apr 6, 33; m 53, Marilyn Blatt; c 2. *Educ:* Univ Ill, BS, 56, MS, 57; Purdue Univ, PhD(plant physiol), 62. *Concurrent Pos:* Mem, Coun Agr Sci & Technol. *Mem:* Fel Weed Sci Soc Am; Coun Agr Sci & Technol; Am Soc Sugar Beet Technol. *Res:* Weed research in agronomic crops; integrated pest management; weed crop modeling. *Mailing Add:* 2012 Evergreen Ct Ft Collins CO 80521. *Fax:* 970-491-8247; *E-Mail:* ed@lily.aerc.colostate.edu

SCHWEIZER, EDWARD ERNEST, ORGANIC CHEMISTRY. *Current Pos:* from asst prof to prof, 61-94, EMER PROF CHEM, UNIV DEL, 94- *Personal Data:* b Shanghai, China, Dec 7, 28; US citizen; m 68, Joy Baldwin; c Edward E, Robert A, Paul G, Catherine (McConnell), Kimberley M (Caruso), K Elizabeth (Yaffe) & Sarah E (Wood). *Educ:* NDak State Univ, BS, 51, MS, 53; Mass Inst Technol, PhD(org chem), 56. *Honors & Awards:* Fulbright teaching award, Univ Madrid, 68-69. *Prof Exp:* Sr chemist, Argos Establecimiento de Productos Colorantes, Arg, 51-52; sr res chemist, Minn Mining & Mfg Co, 56-59; res assoc org chem, Univ Minn, 59-60, instr, 60; asst prof chem, Hofstra Col, 60-61. *Res:* Reactions of phosphonium compounds; heterocyclics. *Mailing Add:* Dept Chem Univ Del Newark DE 19716. *Fax:* 302-831-6335

SCHWEIZER, FELIX, OPTICAL RADIATIONS, THEORETICAL PHYSICS. *Current Pos:* CONSULT, 88- *Personal Data:* b Cologne, Ger, Sept 1, 27; US citizen; div; c 3. *Educ:* Rensselaer Polytech Inst, BS, 51, MS, 54; Univ Calif, Los Angeles, PhD(physics), 60. *Prof Exp:* Mem tech staff space physics, Space Technol Labs Inc, 60-62; scientist specialist, Jet Propulsion Lab, Calif Inst Technol, 62-64; asst prof physics, San Fernando Valley State Col, 64-67; physicist, Naval Weapons Sta, Seal Beach, Corona Site, 67-88. *Concurrent Pos:* Mem, Working Group Infrared & Lasers, Joint Dept Defense-Metrol & Calibration Coord Group, 68-88. *Mem:* Am Phys Soc. *Res:* Nuclear physics; electromagnetic theory; radiometry; photometry; lasers; classical mechanics; anomalies in relativity and quantum mechanics. *Mailing Add:* 13330 St Andrews Dr Apt 67K Seal Beach CA 90740

SCHWEIZER, FRANCOIS, OPTICAL ASTRONOMY, EXTRAGALACTIC RESEARCH. *Current Pos:* STAFF ASTRONR, DEPT TERRESTRIAL MAGNETISM & ADJ STAFF MEM, OBSERVATORIES, CARNEGIE INST WASH, 81- *Personal Data:* b Bern, Switz, Aug, 16, 42; m 75, Linda Younker; c Briana, Maia, Rena & Teia. *Educ:* Univ Bern, Switz, licentiate, 68; Univ Calif, Berkeley, MA, 70, PhD(astron), 75. *Prof Exp:* Carnegie fel astron, Hale Observ, Pasadena, Calif, 74-75; staff astronr, Cerro Tololo InterAm Observ, La Serena, Chile, 76-81. *Mem:* Am Astron Soc; Int Astron Union; Swiss Astron Soc; Astron Soc Pac. *Res:* Optical studies of colliding and merging galaxies; structure and formation of elliptical galaxies; surface photometry and structure of spiral galaxies; origin of globular star clusters. *Mailing Add:* Dept Terrestrial Magnetism Carnegie Inst 5241 Broad Branch Rd NW Washington DC 20015-1305

SCHWEIZER, KENNETH STEVEN, THEORETICAL PHYSICAL CHEMISTRY & POLMER SCIENCE, MATERIALS SCIENCE. *Current Pos:* PROF MAT SCI ENG & CHEM, UNIV ILL, URBANA, 91-, CHAIR POLYMER DIV, MAT SCI & ENG, 94- *Personal Data:* b Philadelphia, Pa, Jan 20, 53; m 86, Janis E Pelletier; c Gregory M & Daniel P. *Educ:* Drexel Univ, BS, 75; Univ Ill, MS, 76, PhD, 81. *Honors & Awards:* John H Dillon Medal, Am Phys Soc, 91; Dept Energy Award Sci Achievement Mat Chem, 96. *Prof Exp:* Res assoc fel, AT&T Bell Labs, NJ, 81-83; sr mem tech staff, Sandia Nat Labs, 83-91. *Mem:* Fel Am Phys Soc; Am Chem Soc; Sigma Xi; Soc Rheology. *Res:* Statistical mechanics of liquids, polymers and amorphous materials; structure, thermodynamics, dynamics and phase transitions of polymer solutions, blends, copolymers, molecular fluids and colloidal suspensions. *Mailing Add:* Dept Mat Sci Eng Univ Ill 1304 W Green St Urbana IL 61801-2920. *Fax:* 217-333-2736; *E-Mail:* kschweiz@ux1.cso.uiuc.edu

SCHWEIZER, MALVINA, ENDOCRINOLOGY. *Current Pos:* RETIRED. *Personal Data:* b New Orleans, La, Jan 16, 06. *Educ:* NY Univ, PhD(physiol), 33. *Prof Exp:* Spec asst dir, Nat Heart, Lung & Blood Inst, NIH, 76-89. *Mem:* AAAS; Am Physiol Soc. *Mailing Add:* Collington Retirement Community 10450 Lottsford Rd Mitchellville MD 20721

SCHWEIZER, MARTIN PAUL, IN VIVO NUCLEAR MAGNETIC RESONANCE. *Current Pos:* PROF MED CHEM, UNIV UTAH, 78- *Educ:* Johns Hopkins Univ, PhD(phys biochem), 68. *Res:* In vivo nuclear magnetic resonance studies of aging effects on metabolism and evaluation of pharmaceutical agents. *Mailing Add:* Col Pharm Univ Utah 258 HLS Skaggs Salt Lake City UT 84112-1107

SCHWELB, OTTO, INTEGRATED OPTICS, MICROWAVE DEVICES. *Current Pos:* ASSOC PROF ELEC ENG, CONCORDIA UNIV, 67- *Personal Data:* b Budapest, Hungary, Mar 27, 31; Can citizen; m 66; c 3. *Educ:* Univ Tech Sci, Budapest, dipl, 54; McGill Univ, PhD(elec eng), 78. *Prof Exp:* Mem sci staff, Res & Develop Div, Northern Elec Co, 57-67. *Concurrent Pos:* Lectr, Univ Ottawa, 62-66; consult, Ainslie Antenna Corp, 69-71; Mitec Electronics Ltd, 75-76, Can Elec Asn, 78-80, Com Dev Ltd, 85-87 & Can Marconi Co, 90. *Mem:* Inst Elec & Electronics Engrs; Optical Soc Am; Order Engrs Que; Int Soc Optical Eng. *Res:* Integrated optics; surface acoustic wave devices; microwave components; electromagnetic wave propagation in stratified and periodic media. *Mailing Add:* Concordia Univ 1455 De Maisonneuve Blvd W Montreal PQ H3G 1M8 Can

SCHWELITZ, FAYE DOROTHY, CELL BIOLOGY. *Current Pos:* asst prof biol, 71-78, ASSOC PROF BIOL, UNIV DAYTON, 78- *Personal Data:* b Milwaukee, Wis, June 17, 31. *Educ:* Alverno Col, BA, 53; Purdue Univ, MS, 67, PhD(cell biol), 71. *Prof Exp:* NIH trainee, Purdue Univ, 69-71. *Mem:* Electron Micros Soc Am; Am Soc Plant Physiol; Biophys Soc; Am Soc Cell Biol; Sigma Xi. *Res:* Role of cyclic Adenine Monophosphatase in Euglena; photosynthetic mutants of Euglena; correlation of structural changes with functional and biochemical changes; chloroplast development. *Mailing Add:* 1049 Sherwood Dr Dayton OH 45406-5736

SCHWENDEMAN, JOSEPH RAYMOND, JR, PHYSICAL GEOGRAPHY, RESOURCE GEOGRAPHY. *Current Pos:* chmn dept, Eastern Ky Univ, 66-76, dean undergrad studies & prof geog, 76-83, assoc vpres acad planning & develop, 83-86, VPRES ADMIN AFFAIRS, EASTERN KY UNIV, 86- *Personal Data:* b Fargo, NDak, Dec 13, 30; m 52; c 3. *Educ:* Univ Ky, BA, 56, MS, 57; Ind Univ, PhD(geog), 67. *Prof Exp:* Asst prof phys geog, Univ NDak, 63-64; staff instr, Ind Univ, 63-64; asst prof phys geog & chmn dept geog, Univ NDak, 64-66. *Concurrent Pos:* Co-dir, Geog Studies & Res Ctr, 68- *Mem:* Asn Am Geog. *Res:* Climatology; regional potential studies; planners. *Mailing Add:* 1001 Apple Creek Lane Richmond KY 40475

SCHWENDEMAN, RICHARD HENRY, PHYSICAL CHEMISTRY. *Current Pos:* from asst prof to assoc prof, 57-69, PROF CHEM, MICH STATE UNIV, 69- *Personal Data:* b Chicago, Ill, Aug 26, 29; m 53; c 3. *Educ:* Purdue Univ, BS, 51; Univ Mich, MS, 52, PhD, 56. *Prof Exp:* Res fel chem, Harvard Univ, 55-57. *Mem:* Am Chem Soc; Am Phys Soc. *Res:* Determination of molecular structure and collisional relaxation rates by microwave spectroscopy and infrared laser spectroscopy; theoretical studies in molecular spectra and molecular dynamics. *Mailing Add:* Dept Chem Mich State Univ East Lansing MI 48823

SCHWENDIMAN, JOHN LEO, sand dune control, grass seed production; deceased, see previous edition for last biography

SCHWENK, FRED WALTER, PLANT PATHOLOGY, VIROLOGY. *Current Pos:* asst prof, 69-74, ASSOC PROF PLANT PATH, KANS STATE UNIV, 74- *Personal Data:* b Dickinson, NDak, July 29, 38; m 63; c 2. *Educ:* NDak State Univ, BS, 60, MS, 64; Univ Calif, Berkeley, PhD(plant path), 69. *Prof Exp:* Lab technician plant path, Univ Calif, Berkeley, 64-66. *Mem:* AAAS; Am Phytopath Soc. *Res:* Soybean pathology; teaching of undergraduate plant pathology. *Mailing Add:* Plant Pathol Kans State Univ 4024 Throckmorton Manhattan KS 66506

SCHWENKER, J(OHN) E(DWIN), ELECTRICAL ENGINEERING. *Current Pos:* RETIRED. *Personal Data:* b Bartlesville, Okla, June 27, 28; m 50; c 2. *Educ:* Univ Okla, BS, 52; Rutgers Univ, MS, 56. *Prof Exp:* Mem tech staff, Bell Tel Labs, 52-59, head, Logic Technol Res Dept, 59-68, head, Data Systs Dept, 68-72, head, Data Appln Eng Dept, 72-84. *Mem:* AAAS; Inst Elec & Electronics Engrs. *Res:* Data communications; computers. *Mailing Add:* 10224 S Canton Tulsa OK 74137

SCHWENKER, ROBERT FREDERICK, JR, CELLULOSE CHEMISTRY, POLYMER CHEMISTRY. *Current Pos:* RETIRED. *Personal Data:* b Ann Arbor, Mich, July 3, 20; m 43; c 4. *Educ:* Univ Pa, AB, 48. *Prof Exp:* Asst biol, Wistar Inst, Univ Pa, 46-48; lab asst chem, Rutgers Univ, 48-49, asst instr, 49-51; chemist, Textile Res Inst, 51-55, group leader org chem, 55-60, assoc res dir, 60-66, dir chem & chem processing, 66; assoc dir res & develop, Personal Prod Co, Johnson & Johnson, 66-74, dir res & develop, 74-75, vpres res & develop, 75-82, mem bd dirs, 74-86, vpres sci technol, 82-86. *Mem:* Am Chem Soc; Fiber Soc; Tech Asn Pulp & Paper Indust; fel Am Inst Chemists; Sigma Xi. *Res:* Structure of cellulose derivatives; thermal degradation of high polymers; structure and properties of fibers; chemical specialties. *Mailing Add:* 92 Willow Run Lane Belle Mead NJ 08502

SCHWENSFEIR, ROBERT JAMES, JR, NUCLEAR CRITICALITY SAFETY, CLAD METALS. *Current Pos:* DIR TECH SERVS QUAL ASSURANCE, POLYMETALLURGICAL CORP, 86- *Personal Data:* b Hartford, Conn, June 27, 34; m 67; c Thomas, Michael & Mary. *Educ:* Wesleyan Univ, BA, 56; Trinity Col, Conn, MS, 60; Brown Univ, PhD(physics), 66. *Prof Exp:* Exp physicist, Pratt & Whitney Aircraft Div, United Aircraft Corp, 56-60; res asst solid state physics, Brown Univ, 60-66; res assoc metal physics, Adv Mat Res & Develop Lab, Pratt & Whitney Aircraft Div, United Aircraft Corp, 66-68; asst prof physics, Bucknell Univ, 68-74; nuclear criticality safety engr, Naval Prod Div, United Nuclear Corp, 74-76, nuclear criticality safety specialist, 76-79; mgr nuclear safety & mat, Tex Instruments Inc, 79-82, mem tech staff, 82-85. *Concurrent Pos:* Mem, Tech Adv Comt, Metals Properties Coun. *Mem:* AAAS; Am Asn Physics Teachers; Am Nuclear Soc; Am Phys Soc; Am Soc Metals; NY Acad Sci; Sigma Xi; Soc Automotive Engrs; Am Soc Qual Control. *Res:* Nuclear criticality safety research; mental solid state physics. *Mailing Add:* 54 Marlise Dr Attleboro MA 02703. *Fax:* 508-695-7512

SCHWENTERLY, STANLEY WILLIAM, III, CRYOGENICS, SUPERCONDUCTING MAGNETS. *Current Pos:* RES STAFF MEM PHYSICS, OAK RIDGE NAT LAB, 72- *Personal Data:* b Philadelphia, Pa, Aug 18, 45. *Educ:* Yale Univ, BS, 67; Cornell Univ, PhD(physics), 73. *Concurrent Pos:* Consult, SSC Lab & Nat High Field Magnet Lab. *Mem:* Am Phys Soc; Cryogenic Soc Am. *Res:* Research and development on cryogenic materials and equipment for application in electric power systems; measurements on high-temperature superconducting materials. *Mailing Add:* 1922 Plumb Creek Circle Knoxville TN 37932. *Fax:* 423-574-0584; *E-Mail:* schwenterlsw@ornl.gov

SCHWENZ, RICHARD WILLIAM, PHYSICAL CHEMISTRY. *Current Pos:* asst prof, 84-89, ASSOC PROF PHYS CHEM, UNIV NORTHERN COLO, 89- *Personal Data:* b Portsmouth, Va, June 30, 55; m 81; c 2. *Educ:* Univ Colo, Boulder, BA, 77; Ohio State Univ, PhD(chem), 81. *Prof Exp:* Teaching fel, Univ Ill, Chicago, 81-82 & Northwestern Univ, 82-84; asst prof phys chem, Mundelein Col, 83-84. *Mem:* Am Chem Soc; Am Phys Soc; Sigma Xi. *Res:* Molecular spectroscopy of transition metal oxides and halides; infacing of laboratory instruments. *Mailing Add:* Dept Chem Univ Northern Colo Greeley CO 80639-0001

SCHWEPPE, EARL JUSTIN, COMPUTER SCIENCE, MATHEMATICS. *Current Pos:* PROF COMPUT SCI, SCH BUS, UNIV KANS, 67- *Personal Data:* b Trenton, Mo, Sept 28, 27; m 48; c 3. *Educ:* Mo Valley Col, BS, 48; Univ Ill, MS, 51, PhD(math), 55. *Prof Exp:* Asst math, Univ Ill, 51-55; instr, Univ Nebr, 55-57; asst prof, Iowa State Univ, 57-61; mathematician, Dept Defense, 61-63; res asst prof computer sci & math, Univ Md, College Park, 63-65, assoc prof, 65-67. *Concurrent Pos:* Consult, Fed Systs Div, IBM Corp, 65- *Mem:* Am Math Soc; Math Asn Am; Asn Comput Mach. *Res:* Abstract algebra; projective geometry; graph and network theory; automata theory; information structures; computer language design and translation; machine description and design; simulation; consequent prodecures; computer science curriculum development. *Mailing Add:* 1146 Hilltop Dr Lawrence KS 66044

SCHWEPPE, JOHN S, medicine; deceased, see previous edition for last biography

SCHWEPPE, JOSEPH L(OUIS), ENGINEERING. *Current Pos:* DIR, J K CONTROL SYSTS, INC, 91- *Personal Data:* b Trenton, Mo, Jan 11, 21; m 42; c 3. *Educ:* Univ Mo, BS, 42, MS, 46; Univ Mich, PhD(chem eng), 50. *Prof Exp:* Jr chem engr, Tenn Valley Authority, Ala, 42-43; asst chem eng, Univ Mo, 46; chem enge, E I du Pont de Nemours & Co, Tex, 49-52; res engr, C F Braun & Co, Calif, 52-54, sr chem engr, 54-56, proj engr, 56-58; from assoc prof to prof mech eng, Univ Houston, 58-63, chmn dept, 59-63; pres, Houston Eng Res Corp, 60-90. *Concurrent Pos:* Lectr, Univ Southern Calif, 54-56 & Univ Calif, Los Angeles, 55. *Mem:* Instrument Soc Am; Inst Elec & ElectronicS ENGRS; Am Soc Mech Engrs; Am Inst Chem Engrs. *Res:* Project engineering; process instrumentation; computer control. *Mailing Add:* 4987 Dumfries Dr Houston TX 77092

SCHWERDT, CARLTON EVERETT, virology; deceased, see previous edition for last biography

SCHWERDTFEGER, CARL RICHARD, JR, CRYSTAL GROWTH, MATERIAL SCIENCE. *Current Pos:* MGR CRYSTAL GROWTH, ALPHA SPECTRA, INC, 96- *Personal Data:* b Highland, Ill, July 14, 63; m 86, Gretchen Vera; c Dylan & Luke. *Educ:* Univ Dubuque, BS, 86; Pittsburg State Univ, MS, 87; Colo Sch Mines, PhD(mat sci), 96. *Prof Exp:* Staff scientist, Nat Renewable Energy Lab, 88-96. *Mem:* Am Asn Crystal Growth. *Res:* Crystal growth techniques and material characterization of novel semiconductors and superconductors; large scale production of scintillator crystals. *Mailing Add:* 586 22-5 Rd Grand Junction CO 81503. *E-Mail:* rickspd@alphaspectra.com

SCHWERDTFEGER, CHARLES FREDERICK, PHYSICS. *Current Pos:* from asst prof to assoc prof, 63-73, PROF PHYSICS, UNIV BC, 73- *Personal Data:* b Philadelphia, Pa, July 20, 34; m 63; c 4. *Educ:* Villanova Univ, BSc, 56; Univ Notre Dame, PhD(physics), 61. *Prof Exp:* Res assoc physics, Univ Basel, 61-62 & Ind Univ, 62-63. *Mem:* Am Phys Soc; Can Asn Physicists. *Res:* Electronic properties of solids; electron spin resonance studies in semiconductors. *Mailing Add:* Dept Geophysics & Astron Univ BC 1292219 Main Mall Vancouver BC V6T 1Z4 Can

SCHWERDTFEGER, PETER ADOLF, CHEMISTRY. *Current Pos:* SR LECTR, UNIV AUCKLAND, NZ, 91- *Personal Data:* b Stuttgart, Ger, Sept 1, 55; m 83, Ulrike M Bucher; c Laura M & Roman A. *Educ:* Stuttgart Univ, MSc, 80, BSc, 83, PhD(chem), 86. *Honors & Awards:* Max Planck Award, 91. *Prof Exp:* Sch teacher, Intermediate Sch Stuttgart, 80-81; comput software analyst, Stuttgart Univ, 81-87; Feodor-Lynen fel, Alexander von Humboldt Found, 87-89; res fel, Australian Nat Univ, 89-91. *Mem:* Am Chem Soc; Am Phys Soc; NY Acad Sci; NZ Inst Chem; Ger Chem Asn. *Res:* Relativistic effects in molecules; contributed articles to professional journals. *Mailing Add:* Dept Chem Univ Auckland Private Bag 92019 Auckland New Zealand

SCHWERER, FREDERICK CARL, APPLIED PHYSICS, MATERIALS SCIENCE. *Current Pos:* VPRES, TECHNOL COORD & DIR, COMPUT SCI & PROD DEVELOP, R J LEE GROUP. *Personal Data:* b Pittsburgh, Pa, Feb 1, 41; m 64, Carol Romesburg; c Elizabeth & Eric. *Educ:* Pa State Univ, BS, 62; Cornell Univ, PhD(appl physics), 67. *Prof Exp:* Scientist, Physics Div, US Steel Res Ctr, 67-76, assoc res consult, Basic Res, US Steel Res Lab, 76-85; founder & pres, UE Group, Inc, 85-86; serv tech specialist, Alcoa Tech Ctr, 86-89. *Concurrent Pos:* Prin investr, Apollo Lunar Sci Prog, 71-76. *Mem:* AAAS; Am Inst Mining, Metall & Petrol Engrs; Am Soc Nondestructive Testing; Am Soc Testing & Mat; Am Phys Soc; Inst Elec & Electronics Engrs. *Res:* Experimental and theoretical studies of physical properties of materials; mathematical modeling; electromagnetically induced fluid flows in liquid metals; sensor and measurement technology; applied software and information systems. *Mailing Add:* RJ Lee Group Inc 350 Hochberg Rd Monroeville PA 15146. *Fax:* 412-783-1799; *E-mail:* fred@rjlee.com

SCHWERI, MARGARET MARY, RECEPTOR BINDING, BEHAVIORAL CHARACTERIZATION OF STIMULANT DRUGS IN ANIMALS. *Current Pos:* asst prof, 84-90, ASSOC PROF PHARMACOL, SCH MED, MERCER UNIV, 90- *Personal Data:* b Louisville, Ky, Aug 29, 46. *Educ:* Marquette Univ, BS, 68; Univ Louisville, PhD(pharmacol), 80. *Prof Exp:* Chemist, Brown & Williamson Tobacco Corp, 68-72; res assoc, Biochem Dept, Univ Louisville, 73-76; staff fel, Lab Biorg Chem, Nat Inst Arthritis, Diabetes & Digestive & Kidney Dis, NIH, 80-83, sr staff fel, 83-84. *Concurrent Pos:* Prin investr, New Investr Res Award, Nat Inst Neurol & Commun Dis & Stroke, NIH, 85-88, biomed res support grant, NIH, 88-89, Small Instrument Prog, 88-89 & Acad Res Enhancement Award, 90-93; co-prin investr, Nat Inst Drug Abuse/RO1, 89-92. *Mem:* Soc Neurosci; Am Soc Pharmacol & Exp Therapeut; AAAS. *Res:* Characterization of the structure and function of the stimulant recognition site on the dopamine transport complex; development of affinity labels for this site to act as cocaine antagonists. *Mailing Add:* Mercer Univ Sch Med 1550 College St Macon GA 31207-0001

SCHWERING, FELIX, ELECTRICAL ENGINEERING, THEORETICAL PHYSICS. *Current Pos:* RETIRED. *Personal Data:* b Cologne, Ger, June 4, 30. *Educ:* Aachen Tech Univ, BS, 51, MS, 54, PhD(elec eng), 57. *Prof Exp:* Asst prof theoret physics, Aachen Tech Univ, 56-58; physicist, US Army Signal Res & Develop Lab, NJ, 58-61; proj leader radar res, Telefunken Co, Ulm, Ger, 61-64; res phys scientist, US Army Commun Electronics, Command, 64-91, sr res scientist, 91-96. *Concurrent Pos:* Vis prof, NJ Inst Technol, 86- & Monmouth Univ, 96-; guest researcher, US Army Commun Electronics Command, 96- *Mem:* Fel Inst Elec & Electronics Engrs; Am Geophys Union; Int Sci Radio Union; Armed Forces Commun Electronics Asn. *Res:* Electromagnetic theory, particularly guided and free space propagation of electromagnetic waves; beam wave guides; antenna theory; periodic structures; diffraction and scatter theory; theoretical and electron optics; quasi optical devices; millimeter ware antennas and propagation. *Mailing Add:* US Army Commun Electronics Command Attn: AMSEL-RD-ST-WL Ft Monmouth NJ 07703-5202. *Fax:* 732-532-0456; *E-Mail:* schwerin@doim6.monmouth.army.mil

SCHWERT, DONALD PETERS, QUATERNARY GEOLOGY. *Current Pos:* Asst prof, 78-86, ASSOC PROF GEOL, NDAK STATE UNIV, 86- *Personal Data:* b Wellsville, NY, Dec 12, 49; c 1. *Educ:* Allegheny Col, BS, 72; State Univ NY, MS, 75; Univ Waterloo, PhD(earth sci), 78. *Concurrent Pos:* Fel, Univ Waterloo, 78- *Mem:* Geol Soc Am; Coleopterists Soc; Am Quaternary Asn. *Res:* Use of fossils to determine Quaternary distributions of insects. *Mailing Add:* Geol Sci NDak State Univ Main Campus Fargo ND 58105

SCHWERT, GEORGE WILLIAM, BIOCHEMISTRY. *Current Pos:* chmn dept, 59-74, prof, 59-85, EMER PROF BIOCHEM, COL MED, UNIV KY, 85- *Personal Data:* b Denver, Colo, Jan 27, 19; m 43, 79; c 2. *Educ:* Carleton Col, BA, 40; Univ Minn, PhD(biochem), 43. *Prof Exp:* Asst agr biochem, Univ Minn, 41-42, instr, 42-43; biochemist, Sharp & Dohme, Inc, Pa, 43-44; instr & res assoc biochem, Duke Univ, 46-48, from asst prof to prof, 48-59. *Concurrent Pos:* Markle scholar, 49-54; consult, NIH, 59-64; assoc ed, J Molecular Cell Biol, 83-85. *Mem:* AAAS; Am Chem Soc; Am Soc Biol Chemists; Brit Biochem Soc; Sigma Xi. *Res:* Mechanisms of enzyme action; hydrolases; dehydrogenases; transaminases; relation of protein structure to biological activity. *Mailing Add:* 3316 Braemar Dr Lexington KY 40502-3376

SCHWERZEL, ROBERT EDWARD, PHOTOCHEMISTRY, NONLINEAR OPTICAL MATERIALS. *Current Pos:* res chemist photochem, 73-78, prin res scientist, 78-80, SR RES SCIENTIST PHOTOCHEM, BATTELLE MEM INST, 80- *Personal Data:* b Rockville Center, NY, Dec 14, 43; m 84; c 2. *Educ:* Va Polytech Inst & State Univ, BS, 65; Fla State Univ, PhD(phys org chem), 70. *Honors & Awards:* I R 100 Award, 80. *Prof Exp:* Fel photochem, Cornell Univ, 70-71; fel magnetic resonance, Brown Univ, 71-72; res chemist org chem, Syva Res Inst, 72-73. *Concurrent Pos:* Adj prof, Ohio State Univ, 82- & Bowling Green State Univ, 87- *Mem:* Am Chem Soc; AAAS; Inter-Am Photochem Soc; Int Solar Energy Soc; Sigma Xi. *Res:* Novel applications of photochemistry and spectroscopy, including photochemical utilization of solar energy, optical data storage and processing, photoelectrochemical formation of fuels, development of improved laser dyes and exploratory studies on nonlinear optical materials; use of laser-produced x-ray for x-ray absorption fine structure spectroscopy. *Mailing Add:* 223 Baker Bldg Ga Inst Technol Ga Tech Res Inst/EOEML Atlanta GA 30332-0825

SCHWERZLER, DENNIS DAVID, MECHANICAL ENGINEERING. *Current Pos:* Assoc sr res engr, 71-74, DEVELOP ENGR, ENG STAFF, GEN MOTORS RES LABS, 74- *Personal Data:* b St Louis, Mo, Dec 23, 44; m 67; c 2. *Educ:* Univ Mo-Rolla, BS, 66; Purdue Univ, Lafayette, MS, 68, PhD(mech eng), 71. *Mem:* Am Soc Mech Engrs. *Res:* Vehicle structural dynamics; application of finite element techniques to vehicle structures; experimental dynamic testing of vehicle structures. *Mailing Add:* 2364 London Dr Troy MI 48098

SCHWETMAN, HERBERT DEWITT, ELECTRONICS, PHYSICS. *Current Pos:* RETIRED. *Personal Data:* b Waco, Tex, Aug 1, 11; m 39; c 3. *Educ:* Baylor Univ, BA, 32; Univ Tex, MA, 37, PhD(physics), 52; Harvard Univ, MS, 47. *Prof Exp:* Jr operator, Western Union Tel Co, 28-33; teacher pub schs, Tex, 33-41; instr electronics, Harvard Univ, 41-47; prof physics & chmn dept, Baylor Univ, 47-84. *Mem:* Am Phys Soc; Am Asn Physics Teachers; sr mem Inst Elec & Electronics Engrs; Sigma Xi. *Res:* Mathematics; application of Laplace transforms to analysis of electric circuits and physical problems; electronic analog computers; mechanical harmonic analyzers and synthesizers; ultrasonic and microwave attenuation. *Mailing Add:* 519 Edgewood Ave Waco TX 76708

SCHWETMAN, HERBERT DEWITT, JR, SOFTWARE SYSTEMS. *Current Pos:* PRES & CHIEF EXEC OFFICER, MESQUITE SOFTWARE. *Personal Data:* b Waco, Tex, July 30, 40; m 64, Nanene Hall; c John David & Katherine. *Educ:* Baylor Univ, BS, 61; Brown Univ, MS, 64; Univ Tex, Austin, PhD, 70. *Prof Exp:* Staff, IBM, 64-67, Boole & Babbage, 70-72; prof comput sci, Purdue Univ, 72-84; sr mem tech staff, Microelectronics & Comput Technol Corp, 84-93. *Mem:* Asn Comput Mach; Inst Elec & Electronics Engrs Comput Soc. *Res:* Computer science-simulation of computer systems. *Mailing Add:* 6524 Ladera Norte Austin TX 78731

SCHWETTMAN, HARRY ALAN, PHYSICS. *Current Pos:* Res assoc, 62-64, from asst prof to assoc prof, 64-77, PROF PHYSICS, STANFORD UNIV, 77- *Personal Data:* b Cincinnati, Ohio, Aug 16, 36; m 58; c 3. *Educ:* Yale Univ, BS, 58; Rice Univ, MA, 60, PhD(physics), 62. *Concurrent Pos:* Sloan res fel, 66-72. *Res:* Low temperature physics; development of superconducting accelerator; application of low temperature physics and nuclear physics to medicine. *Mailing Add:* Dept Physics Stanford Univ-Varian Stanford CA 94305-4060

SCHWETZ, BERNARD ANTHONY, TERATOLOGY, DEVELOPMENTAL TOXICOLOGY. *Current Pos:* CHIEF, SYSTS TOXICOL BR, NAT INST ENVIRON HEALTH SCI, 82- *Personal Data:* b Cadott, Wis, Nov 27, 40; m 62; c 2. *Educ:* Univ Wis-Stevens Point, BS, 62; Univ Minn, St Paul, DVM, 67; Univ Iowa, MS, 68, PhD(pharmacol), 70. *Honors & Awards:* Arnold J Lehman Award, Soc Toxicol, 91. *Prof Exp:* Toxicologist, Dow Chem Co, 70-82, dir toxicol res lab, 77-82. *Mem:* Soc Toxicol; Behav Teratology Soc; Teratology Soc. *Res:* Reproduction; developmental toxicology; teratology. *Mailing Add:* 415 N Boundary St Raleigh NC 27604

SCHWIDERSKI, ERNST WALTER, OCEAN TIDES, GEOPHYSICS. *Current Pos:* RETIRED. *Personal Data:* b Satticken, Ger, Feb 24, 24; nat US; m 59; c 1. *Educ:* Karlsruhe Tech Univ, Dipl math, 52, Dr rer nat, 55. *Honors & Awards:* John Adolphus Dahlgren Award. *Prof Exp:* Sci asst & instr math, Math Inst, Karlsruhe Tech Univ, 48-55; head traffic theory br, Stand Elektrik Co, Ger, 55-57; sr res mathematician, Dahlgren Lab, US Naval Surface Warfare Ctr, 58-90. *Concurrent Pos:* Prof lectr, Am Univ, 58-67; adj prof, Va Polytech Inst & State Univ, 68-90. *Mem:* Am Phys Soc; Am Geophys Union. *Res:* Ordinary and partial differential equations; integral equations; real and complex analysis; numerical analysis; mathematical theory of inviscid and viscous fluid flow; ocean tides and currents; marine geodesy; geophysics. *Mailing Add:* 102 Bell St Fredericksburg VA 22405

SCHWIER, CHRIS EDWARD, POLYMER STRUCTURE-PROPERTY RELATIONSHIPS, NEW PRODUCT DEVELOPMENT & COMMERCIALIZATION. *Current Pos:* RES SPECIALIST, MONSANTO CHEM CO, 84- *Personal Data:* b Neenah, Wis, Apr 11, 56. *Educ:* Univ Wis-Madison, BS, 78; Mass Inst Technol, ScD(chem eng), 84. *Mem:* Am Chem Soc; Soc Plastics Engrs. *Res:* Polymer structure-property relationships for ABS and nylon; rubber toughening of polymers; free radical and condensation polymerization kinetics; continuous polymerization reactor design; new product development and commercialization. *Mailing Add:* 1411 Maldonado Dr Pensacola Beach FL 32561

SCHWIESOW, RONALD LEE, REMOTE SENSING, PHYSICAL OPTICS. *Current Pos:* RES ENGR, NAT CTR ATMOSPHERIC RES, 84- *Personal Data:* b Pittsburgh, Pa, May 22, 40; m 62; Nancy C Olson; c Erick J, Paul A & Sara L. *Educ:* Purdue Univ, BS, 62; Johns Hopkins Univ, PhD(physics), 68; Pa State Univ, MS, 74. *Prof Exp:* Jr instr physics, Johns Hopkins Univ, 62-66, res asst crystal spectros, 67-68; Nat Res Coun res fel atmospheric spectros, Res Labs, Environ Sci Serv Admin, 68-70; physicist, Environ Res Labs, Nat Oceanic & Atmospheric Admin, 70-84. *Concurrent Pos:* Guest scientist, Ris Nat Lab, Denmark, 77-79; vis scientist, DLR-Oberpfaffenhofen, Ger, 82-83; committee laser atmospheric studies, Am Meterol Sco, 78-81; consult meteorol instrumentation. *Mem:* Am Meteorol Soc; Sigma Xi; Optical Soc Am; Am Sci Affil. *Res:* Remote measurement of meteorological parameters using lasers; micrometeorology of the boundary layer; inelastic scattering spectroscopy applied to environmental problems; Doppler laser wind instrumentation; cloud dynamics and microphysics; airborne instrumentation for meteorology. *Mailing Add:* 1440 Elder Ave Boulder CO 80304. *E-Mail:* schwies@ncar.ucar.edu

SCHWIMMER, SIGMUND, ENZYMOLOGY, FOOD BIOCHEMISTRY. *Current Pos:* Jr chemist, USDA, Washington, DC, 41-43, from asst chemist to chemist, 43-58, prin chemist, Western Regional Res Lab, 58-65, chief chemist, 65-74, EMER CHIEF RES BIOCHEMIST, WESTERN REGIONAL RES LAB, USDA, 75- *Personal Data:* b Cleveland, Ohio, Sept 20, 17; wid; c 2. *Educ:* George Washington Univ, BS, 41; Georgetown Univ, MS, 41, PhD(biochem), 43. *Honors & Awards:* Guggenheim Found Award, 58; Am Chem Soc Agricultural Food Chem Award, 96. *Concurrent Pos:* NSF sr fel, Carlsberg Found Biol Inst & Royal Vet & Agr Col, Denmark, 58-59; res assoc, Calif Inst Technol, 63-65, head enzyme technol invests, 67-71; sr biochemist, UN Indust Develop Orgn Centre Indust Res, Haifa, Israel, 73-74; guest lectr, Dept Nutrit Sci, Univ Calif, Berkeley, 75-83; ed, J Food Biochem, 77-, Trends in Biotechnol, 83-89; consult, food enzym, 83-; guest ed, Trends in Biochem, 83-84; adj prof, Dept Nutrit Sci, Univ Calif, Berkeley, 84-88; vis scientist, Food Indust Res & Develop Inst, Hsinchu, Taiwan, 92. *Mem:* Am Soc Biochem & Molecular Biol; Inst Food Technol. *Res:* Enzymology; plant and food biochemistry and biotechnology. *Mailing Add:* Western Regional Res Ctr USDA 800 Buchanan St Berkeley CA 94710

SCHWINCK, ILSE, developmental genetics, for more information see previous edition

SCHWINDEMAN, JAMES ANTHONY, SYNTHESIS OF NEW ORGANOLITHIUM REAGENTS. *Current Pos:* sr res chemist agr chem, 81-88, SR RES CHEMIST, FMC LITHIUM DIV, PPG INDUST, 88- *Personal Data:* b Cincinnati, Ohio, Oct 30, 55; m 79. *Educ:* Miami Univ, BS, 77; Ohio State Univ, PhD(org chem), 81. *Prof Exp:* Teaching asst org chem, Ohio State Univ, 77-78, assoc, 78-81. *Mem:* Am Chem Soc; Royal Soc Chem. *Res:* Design and synthesis of new organolithium reagents, organosilicon protecting groups in organic synthesis. *Mailing Add:* FMC Lithium Div PO Box 795 Bessemer City NC 28016-9900

SCHWING, FRANKLIN BURTON, COASTAL PHYSICAL OCEANOGRAPHY, DYNAMICAL PHYSICAL OCEANOGRAPHY. *Current Pos:* PHYS OCEANOGR, PAC FISHERIES ENVIRON GROUP, NAT OCEANIC & ATMOSPHERIC ADMIN, NAT MARINE FISHERIES SERV, 88- *Personal Data:* b Fairmont, WVa, Jan 6, 56; m 85; Holly J Price; c Ryan C & Savannah A. *Educ:* Univ SC, BS, 78, MS, 81; Dalhousie Univ, PhD(phys oceanog), 89. *Prof Exp:* Res coordr, Skidaway Inst Oceanog, 81-85. *Mem:* Am Geophys Union; Am Meteorol Soc; Can Meteorol & Oceanog Soc; Oceanog Soc. *Res:* Dynamics of continental shelf, coastal and shallow water systems; role of circulation on transport of biological organisms; air-sea interactions; remote sensing of the marine environment. *Mailing Add:* Pac Fisheries Environ Group 1352 Lighthouse Ave Pacific Grove CA 93950. *Fax:* 408-656-3319

SCHWING, GREGORY WAYNE, ORGANIC CHEMISTRY, AGRCHEMICALS. *Current Pos:* Res chemist agrchem, 72-77, sr res chemist, 77-78, RES SUPVR HERBICIDES, BIOCHEM DEPT, E I DU PONT DE NEMOURS & CO, INC, 78- *Personal Data:* b Cincinnati, Ohio, Sept 30, 46; m 67; c 3. *Educ:* Purdue Univ, BS, 69; Univ Minn, PhD(organic chem), 72. *Mem:* Am Chem Soc. *Res:* Selective crop herbicides, industrial herbicides, plant growth modifiers, fungicides, insecticides and nematocides; synthesis and evaluation of new classes of compounds for agrichemical utility. *Mailing Add:* 525 E Cypress St Apt 2 Kennett Sq PA 19348-3141

SCHWING, RICHARD C, ENVIRONMENTAL POLICY, CHEMICAL ENGINEERING & TECHNICAL MANAGEMENMT. *Current Pos:* From sr res engr to sr staff res engr, 63-87, PRIN RES ENGR, GEN MOTORS RES LABS, 87- *Personal Data:* b Buffalo, NY, Dec 8, 34; m 56, 71, Stevenson; c 4. *Educ:* Univ Mich, BS, 57, MS, 59, PhD(chem eng), 63. *Honors & Awards:* John M Campbell Award. *Mem:* AAAS; Am Chem Soc; Int Asn Impact Assessment (pres, 84-85); fel Soc Risk Analysis (pres, 88-89). *Res:* Pollution control of internal combustion engines; measurement of corporate externalities; air pollution epidemiology regression analysis; risk-benefit, cost-benefit analyses; risk assessments; technology assessments; forecasting; human behavior and traffic safety. *Mailing Add:* Knowledge Network Develop & Integration Gen Motors ME 480-106-220 Warren MI 48090-9055. *Fax:* 810-986-6017

SCHWINGENDORF, KEITH EUGENE, MATHEMATICS EDUCATION. *Current Pos:* Grad instr, 73-78, math instr & coun coordr, 78-91, PROF MATH, N CENT, PURDUE UNIV, 91- *Personal Data:* b Chicago, Ill, May 9, 48; m 89, Lisa G Mannering; c Karen M, Jeffrey P, Jessica L & Ryan K. *Educ:* Purdue Univ, BS, 70, MS, 71, PhD(math), 78. *Concurrent Pos:* Co-prin investr, NSF, 88-89, 90-94, 94-97, prin investr, 92-95. *Mem:* Am Math Soc; Math Asn Am; Nat Coun Teachers Math; Am Math Asn Two Yr Cols. *Res:* Innovative pedagogical methodologies based on theoretical analyses using learning theories with emphasis on use of technology, cooperative learning and alternatives to lecture method; co-author of over 15 research papers and 7 math texts. *Mailing Add:* 2678 N Van Gogh Trail La Porte IN 46350-8487. *Fax:* 219-785-5507; *E-Mail:* kschwing@purduenc.edu

SCHWINTZER, CHRISTA ROSE, NITROGEN FIXATION, WETLAND ECOLOGY. *Current Pos:* from asst prof to assoc prof, 82-89, PROF BOT, DEPT PLANT BIOL & PLANT, UNIV MAINE, 89- *Personal Data:* US citizen; m 77; c 1. *Educ:* Berea Col, BA, 62; Univ Mich, MA, 63, PhD(bot), 69. *Prof Exp:* Fel, Mo Bot Garden, 69-71; from asst prof to assoc prof ecol, Univ Wis-Green Bay, 71-78; Res Assoc, Harvard Univ Forest, 78-82. *Concurrent Pos:* Res assoc, Biol Sta, Univ Mich, 72-77. *Mem:* Ecol Soc Am; Brit Ecol Soc; Bot Soc Am; Am Soc Plant Physiologists. *Res:* Ecology of actinomycete-nodulated nitrogen fixing plants; ecology of northern bogs, swamps and fens emphasizing vegetation and nutrient status; physiological ecology of wetland plants. *Mailing Add:* Dept Plant Biol & Path Univ Maine Orono Deering Hall Orono ME 04469-0001

SCHWIRZKE, FRED, PHYSICS. *Current Pos:* PROF PHYSICS, NAVAL POSTGRAD SCH, 67- *Personal Data:* b Schwiebus, Ger, Aug 21, 27; m 58; c 4. *Educ:* Karlsruhe Tech Univ, MS, 53, Dr rer nat(physics), 59. *Prof Exp:* Scientist, Max-Planck Inst Physics & Astrophys, 59-61; group supvr plasma physics res, Inst Plasma Physics, Munich, Ger, 61-62; staff mem plasma physics, Gen Atomic Div, Gen Dynamics Corp, San Diego, Calif, 62-67. *Mem:* Am Phys Soc; Inst Elec & Electronics Engrs; Sigma Xi; fel Inst Elec & Electronics Engrs. *Res:* Plasma physics; controlled thermonuclear fusion; turbulence and anomalous diffusion of plasmas confined in magnetic fields; laser produced plasmas; self-generated magnetic fields; plasma diagnostics; impurities and plasma wall effects; plasma sheaths; ionization and charge exchange cross sections; onset of vacuum breakdown and formation of cathode spots. *Mailing Add:* Dept Physics Naval Postgrad Sch Monterey CA 93943

SCHWITTERS, ROY FREDERICK, EXPERIMENTAL HIGH ENERGY PHYSICS. *Current Pos:* S W RICHARDSON FOUND REGENTAL PROF PHYSICS, UNIV TEX, AUSTIN, 94- *Personal Data:* b Seattle, Wash, June 20, 44; m 65, Karen Chrystal; c Marc, Anne & Adam. *Educ:* Mass Inst Technol, SB, 66, PhD(physics), 71. *Hon Degrees:* LLD, Southwest Advent Col, 93. *Honors & Awards:* Alan T Waterman Award, 80. *Prof Exp:* Res assoc exp high energy physics, Stanford Univ, 71-74, from asst prof to assoc prof, Stanford Linear Accelerator Ctr, 74-79; prof physics, Harvard Univ, 79-89; dir, Superconducting Super Collider Lab, 89-93. *Concurrent Pos:* Assoc ed, Ann Rev of Nuclear & Particle Sci, 78-89; div assoc ed, Phys Rev Lett, 79-84. *Mem:* Fel Am Phys Soc; fel AAAS. *Res:* Experimental high energy physics; development of large solid angle detection apparatus for use with high energy colliding beams; study of hadron production in electron-positron collisions. *Mailing Add:* Dept Physics RLM 5-208 Univ Tex Austin Austin TX 78712-1081. *Fax:* 512-471-9637; *E-Mail:* schwitters@physics.utexas.edu

SCHWOEBEL, RICHARD LYNN, PHYSICS & SURFACE PHYSICS, SURFACE STRUCTURE & TRANSPORT. *Current Pos:* RETIRED. *Personal Data:* b New Rockford, NDak, Dec 26, 31; m 54, Jennie; c Paul R & Eric D. *Educ:* Hamline Univ, BS, 53; Cornell Univ, PhD(eng physics), 62. *Prof Exp:* Sr engr, Gen Mills, Inc, 55-57; staff mem, Sandia Nat Labs, 62-65, supvr, 65-69, mgr, Radiation & Surface Physics Res Dept, 78-82, dir components, 88-92, dir surety assessment, 92-95. *Concurrent Pos:* Vis prof, Cornell Univ, 71. *Mem:* Fel Am Phys Soc; sr mem Am Vacuum Soc; Sigma Xi; Mat Res Soc. *Res:* Oxidation of metals; defect nature and transport properties of oxides; microgravimetry; electron microscopy and diffraction; crystal growth processes; surface morphology; nuclear waste management; materials science engineering; research administration; technical management; surety of high consequence systems. *Mailing Add:* 12010 Dusty Rose Rd NE Albuquerque NM 87122. *Fax:* 505-844-0129

SCHWOERER, F(RANK), MECHANICAL ENGINEERING. *Current Pos:* RETIRED. *Personal Data:* b New York, NY, Sept 5, 22; m 49, Lois Green; c 1. *Educ:* Webb Inst Naval Archit, BS, 44; Mass Inst Technol, MS, 47. *Prof Exp:* Develop engr, Aviation Gas Turbine Div, Westinghouse Elec Corp, 47-51, supvr compressor develop, 51-55, mgr adv develop, 55-57, adv engr, Bettis Atomic Power Lab, 57-59, mgr adv reactor develop, 59-64; mgr eng, NUS Corp, 64-65, tech dir, 65-66, vpres, 66-68; assoc, Pickard Lowe & Assocs, 68-75; tech dir, SNUPPS Proj, Nuclear Projs, Inc, 75-84; vpres & tech dir, Neutron Prod Inc, 84-95. *Mem:* Am Soc Mech Engrs; Am Nuclear Soc. *Res:* Nuclear reactor engineering, economics and project management. *Mailing Add:* 7213 Rollingwood Dr Chevy Chase MD 20815

SCHY, ALBERT ABE, AEROSPACE ENGINEERING, SYSTEMS CONTROL THEORY. *Current Pos:* RETIRED. *Personal Data:* b Przemysl, Poland, July 30, 20; m 57; c 4. *Educ:* Univ Chicago, BS, 42. *Prof Exp:* Aerospace engr control eng, NASA Langley Res Ctr, 49-55, sect head, 55-60, asst br head, 60-66, br head, 66-78, asst br head control eng, 78-85, chief scientist, Guid & Control Div, 85-86, distinguished res assoc, 86- *Mem:* Am Inst Aeronaut & Astronaut; Am Automatic Control Coun. *Res:* Dynamics and control of aerospace vehicles; computer aided control system design. *Mailing Add:* 722 Macon Rd Hampton VA 23666

SCHYVE, PAUL MILTON, PSYCHIATRY, MENTAL HEALTH ADMINISTRATION. *Current Pos:* dir stand, 86-89, vpres res & stand, 89-93, SR VPRES, JOINT COMN ACCREDITATION HEALTHCARE ORGN, 93- *Personal Data:* b Rochester, NY, May 16, 44. *Educ:* Univ Rochester, BA, 66, MD, 70, dipl psychiat, 74. *Prof Exp:* Instr psychiat, Univ Rochester, 73-74; chief psychiat, USAF Regional Hosp, 74-75; staff psychiatrist, USAF Med Ctr, Wright-Patterson AFB, 75-76; unit chief, Ill State Phychiat Inst, 76-77, assoc dir, 77-79, clin dir, 79-82, dir, 82-83; assoc dir ment illness, Ill Dept Ment Health & Develop Disabilities, 83-85, dir clin serv, 84-86. *Concurrent Pos:* Regional med consult, USAF Med Corps, 74-75; res assoc, Dept Psychiat, Univ Chicago, 76-80, asst prof, 80-88, assoc prof, 89-92; attend mem, Dept Psychiat, Michael Reese Hosp, 80-94. *Mem:* Am Psychiat Asn; AMA; Am Nat Stand Inst. *Res:* Health systems; outcome measures in healthcare; total quality management. *Mailing Add:* One Renaissance Blvd Villa Park IL 60181

SCIALDONE, JOHN JOSEPH, MECHANICAL ENGINEERING, AEROSPACE ENGINEERING. *Current Pos:* asst mgr advan res, Test & Eval Div, NASA, 64-68, actg off head, 68-70, staff engr, 70-82, staff physicist, 82-87, head polymers sect, 87-96, GROUP LEADER, GODDARD SPACE FLIGHT CTR, NASA, 96- *Personal Data:* b Vitulazio, Italy, July 25, 26; US citizen; m 52, JoAnn Collins; c Anthony M & Gregory J. *Educ:* Univ Naples, dipl eng, 49, DE(mech & aerospace eng), 69; Carnegie Inst Technol, BS, 53; Univ Pittsburgh, MS, 60. *Honors & Awards:* The Space Simulation Award, Inst Environ Sci, 94. *Prof Exp:* Pneumatic engr, Air Brake Div, Westinghouse Air Brake Co, 53-57, analyst, 57-62, sr analyst, Astronuclear Lab, Westinghouse Elec Corp, 62-64. *Concurrent Pos:* Adj prof physics & math, Capitol Col, Laurel, Md, 76; consult, NASA Spacecraft; prin investr, Int Sci Comts on Mat in Space Environ; contamination control vacuum tech. *Mem:* Inst Environ Sci; Am Vacuum Soc; Soc Adv Mat & Process Eng; Am Inst Aeronaut & Astronaut. *Res:* Vacuum research and technology; space technologies; surface physics; kinetic theory; surface contamination; rarified gas dynamics; environmental testing; lubrication in space; instrumentation. *Mailing Add:* 3705 Marlbrough Way College Park MD 20740. *Fax:* 301-286-1646; *E-Mail:* john.j.scialdone.1@gsfc.nasa.gov

SCIAMANDA, ROBERT JOSEPH, NIGHT VISION DEVICES, ELECTRO-OPTICS. *Current Pos:* ASSOC PROF, PHYSICS, EDINBORO UNIV PA, 88- *Personal Data:* b Erie Pa, Aug 11, 31; m 75; c 1. *Educ:* St Bonaventure Univ, BA, 53; Cath Univ Am, MS, 60. *Prof Exp:* Chmn physics, Gannon Univ, 57-75; sr scientist, Idaho Nat Eng Lab, 75-80, Am Sterilizer Co, 80-88. *Mem:* Am Asn Physics Teachers; Am Asn Physicists Med. *Res:* Added color to night vision (patented); design of novel fiber optic image converters. *Mailing Add:* Dept Physics Edinboro Univ Pa 219 Meadville St Edinboro PA 16444-0001

SCIAMMARELLA, CAESAR AUGUST, ENGINEERING MECHANICS. *Current Pos:* PROF APPL MECH, MECH ENG & AEROSPACE & DIR EXP STRESS LAB, ILL INST TECHNOL, 72- *Personal Data:* b Buenos Aires, Arg, Aug 22, 26; m 68, Esther Norbis; c Alejandro, Eduardo & Federico. *Educ:* Univ Buenos Aires, Dipl Eng, 50; Ill Inst Technol, PhD(eng), 60. *Honors & Awards:* Award for Distinguished Res in Field of Eng, Sigma Xi, 66; Frocht Award, Soc Exp Mech, 80, Hetenyi Award, 82 & Lazan Award, 91. *Prof Exp:* Supvr design & stress anal, Hormigon Elastico Inversor, 51-53; spec assignment engr, Ducilo, Inc, 53-54; tech dir, Zofra, Inc, 55-56; sr researcher reactor eng, Arg Atomic Energy Comn, 56-57; assoc res engr, Ill Inst Technol, 58-59, instr, 59-60; prof eng sci & mech, Univ Fla, 61-67; prof appl mech & aerospace eng, Polytech Inst Brooklyn, 67-72. *Concurrent Pos:* Prof, Arg Army Eng Sch, 52-57 & Univ Buenos Aires, 56-57; lectr, Brit Sci Res Coun, 66; NSF vis lectr, Europe, 66; vis prof, Polytech Inst, Milan, Italy, 79; Univ Cagliari, Italy, 79; Polytech Inst Lausanne, Switz, 79; Univ Poitiers, France, 80 & Polytech Bari, Italy, 92; prof, Scoola degli Studi, Nuoro, Italy. *Mem:* Fel Am Soc Mech Engrs; fel Soc Exp Mech; Am Astronaut Soc; Am Soc Testing & Mat; Optical Soc Am; Soc Photo-Optical Instrumentation Engrs. *Res:* Experimental mechanics with particular emphasis in optical techniques; applications of experimental mechanics to the mechanics of materials; studies on the mechanism of failure of materials simple and composite. *Mailing Add:* Dept Mech Eng Ill Inst Technol Chicago IL 60616. *Fax:* 312-567-7230; *E-Mail:* mesciammarella@minna.iit.edu

SCIARINI, LOUIS J(OHN), ORGANIC CHEMISTRY. *Current Pos:* RETIRED. *Personal Data:* b Branford, Conn, June 30, 15; m 53, Maria G Monteggia; c Luisa M & Joseph L. *Educ:* Pavia Univ, Italy, PhD(org chem), 39. *Prof Exp:* Asst chem microbiol, Fordham Univ, 40-45; res asst org chem, Yale Univ, 46-62, res assoc pharmacol, 63-82. *Mem:* AAAS; Am Chem Soc; Sigma Xi. *Res:* Mechanism of enzyme action; fermentation; wood-destroying fungi; chemical control of digitalis therapy; detoxication mechanisms; anti-viral and cancer chemotherapeutic agents. *Mailing Add:* 49 Spring Rock Rd Branford CT 06405-5519

SCIARRA, DANIEL, MEDICINE. *Current Pos:* from instr to assoc prof, 47-67, PROF CLIN NEUROL, COL PHYSICIANS & SURGEONS, COLUMBIA UNIV, 67- *Personal Data:* b Sansevero, Italy, Aug 19, 18; nat US; m 46, 59, 72; c Michael, Dalen, Chetra, Lorraine, Joseph D & Gina-Louise. *Educ:* Harvard Univ, BA, 40, MD, 43; Am Bd Psychiat & Neurol, dipl, 49. *Prof Exp:* Instr neurol, Harvard Med Sch, 44-45. *Concurrent Pos:* Attend neurologist, Neurol Inst. *Mem:* Asn Res Nerv & Ment Dis; Am Neurol Asn; Am Acad Neurol. *Res:* Epilepsy; multiple sclerosis; brain tumors. *Mailing Add:* Neurol Inst 710 W 168th St New York NY 10032

SCIARRA, JOHN J, INDUSTRIAL PHARMACY, AEROSOL TECHNOLOGY. *Current Pos:* prof indust pharm & dean, Brooklyn Col Pharm, Long Island Univ, 75-76, exec dean, Arnold & Marie Schwartz Col Pharm & Health Sci, 77-85, pres, Retail Drug Inst, 85-90, EMER PROF, LONG ISLAND UNIV, 90-; PRES, SCIARRA LABS, 86- *Personal Data:* b Brooklyn, Ny, Dec 28, 27; m 64; c Christopher, John Jay, Gregory & Brian. *Educ:* St John's Univ, NY, BS, 51; Duquesne Univ, MS, 53; Univ Md, PhD(pharm), 57. *Honors & Awards:* Indust Pharm Award, 78. *Prof Exp:* Asst pharm, Duquesne Univ, 51-53; instr, Univ Md, 54-57; from asst prof to prof pharmaceut chem, St John's Univ, NY, 57-75, dir grad div, 66-73, asst dean, Col Pharm & Allied Health Professions, 72-73. *Concurrent Pos:* Consult, 60; mem, Nat Formulary Adv Comt & Adv Panel Pharmaceut, US Pharmacopeia Comt; continuing educ dir, Pharmaceut Soc State NY, 93- *Mem:* Am Pharmaceut Asn; fel Acad Pharmaceut Sci; fel Soc Cosmetic Chem (pres, 80); fel Am Asn Pharmaceut Scientists. *Res:* Pharmacy; physical pharmacy; aerosol science and technology; particle size distribution; metered-dose inhalers; foams for delivery of medication. *Mailing Add:* Sciarra Labs Inc 485-09 S Broadway Hicksville NY 11801. *Fax:* 516-933-7807

SCIARRA, JOHN J, OBSTETRICS & GYNECOLOGY. *Current Pos:* PROF OBSTET & GYNEC & CHMN DEPT, SCH MED, NORTHWESTERN UNIV, 73- *Personal Data:* b West Haven, Conn, Mar 4, 32; m 60; c 3. *Educ:* Yale Univ, BS, 53; Columbia Univ, MD, 57, PhD(anat), 64. *Honors & Awards:* Carl G Hartman Award, Am Fertil Soc, 64. *Prof Exp:* Am Cancer Soc fel, 64-65; asst prof obstet & gynec, Col Physicians & Surgeons, Columbia Univ, 65-68; prof obstet & gynec & head dept, Med Sch, Univ Minn, Minneapolis, 68-73. *Concurrent Pos:* NIH spec fel, 65-68; mem nat med comt, Planned Parenthood-World Pop, 71-74, 87-; mem exec bd, Int Fedn Gynec & Obstet, 86-; chmn, Am Col Obstet & Gynec, comt Int Affairs, 86- *Mem:* Am Col Obstet & Gynec; Am Fertil Soc; Am Col Surgeons; Am Asn Anatomists; Soc Gynec Invest. *Res:* Reproductive physiology and endocrinology. *Mailing Add:* Dept OB/GYN Prentice Womens Hosp Maternity Ctr 333 E Superior St Chicago IL 60611

SCIARRONE, BARTLEY JOHN, PHARMACEUTICS. *Current Pos:* from asst prof to assoc prof, 58-69, asst dean, 81, assoc dean, 83, PROF PHARM, COL PHARM, RUTGERS UNIV, NEW BRUNSWICK, 69- *Personal Data:* b Jersey City, NJ, Nov 24, 26; m 65; c 1. *Educ:* Rutgers Univ, BS, 52, MS, 55; Univ Wis, PhD(phys pharm), 60. *Prof Exp:* Instr pharmaceut chem, Col Pharm, Rutgers Univ, 54-55; asst, Univ Wis, 56-59. *Mem:* Am Pharmaceut Asn. *Res:* Kinetics and mechanisms of interactions in pharmaceutical systems. *Mailing Add:* Sch Pharm Rutgers Univ New Brunswick NJ 08903

SCICLI, ALFONSO GUILLERMO, PHARMACOLOGY. *Current Pos:* MEM SR STAFF, HYPERTENSION RES DIV, HENRY FORD HOSP, DETROIT, 73- *Educ:* Univ Buenos Aires, Arg, PhD(biochem), 63. *Mailing Add:* Hypertension & Vascular Res Div Henry Ford Hosp 2799 W Grand Blvd Detroit MI 48202-2689

SCIDMORE, ALLAN K, ELECTRICAL ENGINEERING. *Current Pos:* Res asst chem eng, Univ Wis-Madison, 51-52, res fel elec eng, 53-54, res asst, 54-55, proj asst, 56-57, asst prof, 58-63, proj head, Digital Computer Lab, 57-59, assoc prof elec eng, 63-69, assoc dir, Univ Indust Res Prog, 76-80, assoc chmn dept, 82-86 & 89-90, PROF ELEC & COMPUTER ENG, UNIV WIS-MADISON, 69- *Personal Data:* b Grafton, NDak, Mar 11, 27; m 53; c 4. *Educ:* Univ NDak, BS, 51; Univ Wis, MS, 53, PhD(elec eng), 58. *Honors*

& *Awards:* AT&T Found Award, ASEE; Polygon Award, outstanding instr, 77, 82, 83, 85, 88; Outstanding Counr Award, Inst Elec & Electronics Engrs; Benjamin Smith Reynolds Award. *Concurrent Pos:* Dir, Nat Eng Consortium, 77-80. *Mem:* Inst Elec & Electronics Engrs; Am Soc Eng Educ. *Res:* Linear and digital circuit design and application. *Mailing Add:* Dept Elec & Computer Eng Univ Wis 750 University Ave Madison WI 53706

SCIDMORE, WRIGHT H, OPTICS. *Current Pos:* CONSULT OPTICAL DESIGN, SCIDMORE & SHEAN, 77- *Personal Data:* b Saratoga Springs, NY, July 20, 25; m 51; c 3. *Educ:* Columbia Univ, BS, 50. *Honors & Awards:* Karl Fairbanks Mem Award, Soc Photo-Optical Instrumentation Engrs, 73. *Prof Exp:* Staff mem, 50-58, chief, Optical Design Lab, Frankford Arsenal, US Army, 58-77. *Concurrent Pos:* Consult mil optical instruments, Int Sci Prog, 68-77. *Mem:* Optical Soc Am; Sigma Xi; Int Soc Optical Eng. *Res:* Geometrical optics; lens design; military optical instruments. *Mailing Add:* Rte 8 Box 160A Brant Lake NY 12815

SCIFRES, CHARLES JOEL, RANGE SCIENCE, WEED SCIENCE. *Current Pos:* PROF, DEPT AGR, UNIV ARK, 87-, DEAN & ASSOC VPRES AGR, DALE BUMPERS COL AGR, FOOD & LIFE SCI, 94- *Personal Data:* b Foster, Okla, June 1, 41; m 61; c 2. *Educ:* Okla State Univ, BS, 63, MS, 65; Univ Nebr, PhD(agron, bot), 68. *Prof Exp:* Asst res agronomist, Range Ecol, Agr Res Serv, USDA, 65-68; asst prof range mgt, Tex A&M Univ, 68-69, assoc prof range ecol & improvements, 69-76, prof range sci, prof range ecol & dept range sci, 76-87. *Mem:* Weed Sci Soc Am; Soc Range Mgt; Sigma Xi. *Res:* Development of vegetation manipulation systems for rangeland resources management for maximum productivity of usable products from the resource while maintaining its ecological integrity; persistence and modes of dissipation of herbicides from the range ecosystem; life history of key range species and community dynamics following vegetation manipulation. *Mailing Add:* Dept Agr Univ Ark Rm 205 Fayetteville AR 72701. *Fax:* 501-575-7273; *E-Mail:* scifres@comp.uark.edu

SCIFRES, DONALD RAY, PHYSICS, ELECTROOPTICS. *Current Pos:* PRES & CHIEF EXEC OFF, SDL INC, 83-, CHMN, 92- *Personal Data:* b Lafayette, Ind, Sept 10, 46; m 69; c 5. *Educ:* Purdue Univ, Lafayette, BS, 68; Univ Ill, MS, 70, PhD(elec eng), 72. *Honors & Awards:* Jack Morton Medal for Contrib to Electron Devices, Inst Elec & Electronics Engrs, 85; Eng Achievement Award, Inst Elec & Electronics Engrs Lasers & Electro-Optics Soc, 94; Edward H Land Medal, Optical Soc Am, 96; George E Pake Prize, Am Phys Soc, 97. *Prof Exp:* Res scientist, res fel & mgr, Xerox Palo Alto Res Ctr, 72-83. *Mem:* Nat Acad Eng; fel Inst Elec & Electronics Engrs; fel Optical Soc Am; Am Phys Soc. *Res:* Integrated optics and electro-optical devices; lasers. *Mailing Add:* SDL Inc 80 Rose Orchard Way San Jose CA 95134

SCIORE, EDWARD, DATABASE SYSTEMS. *Current Pos:* ASST PROF COMPUTER SCI, STATE UNIV NY, STONY BROOK, 80- *Personal Data:* b July 13, 55. *Educ:* Yale Univ, BA, 76; Princeton Univ, PhD(comput sci), 80. *Mem:* Asn Computer Mach. *Res:* Database systems, especially the semantics of data; database design methodologies; improved data description languages. *Mailing Add:* 48 Oxford Rd Newton MA 02159

SCIPIO, L(OUIS) ALBERT, II, SPACE SCIENCES. *Current Pos:* RETIRED. *Personal Data:* b Juarez, Mex, Aug 22, 22; US citizen; m 42, Katherine Jones; c 3. *Educ:* Tuskegee Inst, BS, 43; Univ Minn, BCE, 48, MS, 50, PhD, 54. *Honors & Awards:* Steinman Award, 58. *Prof Exp:* Instr archit & mech drawing, Tuskegee Inst, 46; struct engr, Long & Thorshov, 48-50; lectr aeronaut eng, Univ Minn, Minneapolis, 52-61; assoc prof mech, Howard Univ, 61-62; prof phys sci, Univ PR, 62-63; aerospace eng, Univ Pittsburgh, 63-67; prof aerospace eng & dir grad studies eng & archit, 67-70, prof space sci, 70-88, Emer Distinguished Univ Prof, Howard Univ, 88- *Concurrent Pos:* Fulbright prof, Cairo Univ, 55-56; consult, NASA Knowledge Availability Systs Ctr, Univ Pittsburgh, John Wiley & Sons, Inc & Winzen Res Inc; mem, Army Sci Bd, 78-81; bd vis, Air Force Inst Technol, 79-82. *Mem:* AAAS; Soc Natural Philos; Am Phys Soc; Am Inst Aeronaut & Astronaut; Int Asn Bridge & Struct Engrs; fel Int Biog Asn. *Res:* Continuum mechanics; aerothermoelasticity; shell structures; viscoelasticity; US military history. *Mailing Add:* 12511 Montclair Dr Silver Spring MD 20904

SCITOVSKY, ANNE A, HEALTH ECONOMICS. *Current Pos:* sr res assoc, 63-73, CHIEF, HEALTH ECON DEPT, RES INST, PALO ALTO MED FOUND, 73-; LECTR, INST HEALTH POLICY STUDIES, SCH MED, UNIV CALIF, SAN FRANCISCO, 75- *Personal Data:* b Ludwigshafen, West Ger, Apr 17, 15; US citizen; m 42; c 1. *Educ:* Barnard Col, BA, 37; Columbia Univ, MA, 41. *Prof Exp:* Economist, Bur Res & Statist, Social Security Bd, Washington, DC, 44-46. *Concurrent Pos:* Mem, Publ Adv Bd, Nat Ctr Health Serv Res & Develop, 69-71, consult 75-; mem, Comt Planning Study Costs Environ-related Health Effects, Inst Med, 79-80, Pres Comn Study Ethical Probs Med & Biomed & Behav Res, 79-82, Adv Panel Life-Sustaining Technol & Elderly, Off Technol Assessment, 85-86, Coun Health Care Technol, Inst Med, 86-, Health Adv Comt, 87- & AIDS Adv Comt, 90- *Mem:* Inst Med-Nat Acad Sci; Nat Acad Soc Insurance. *Res:* Empirical studies of the medical care costs of specific illnesses, the effects of changing medical technology on medical care costs, the effect of coinsurance on the demand for physician services, the demand for health care services under prepaid and fee-for-service group practice, and medical care expenses in the last year of life; author of numerous technical publications. *Mailing Add:* 860 Bryant St Palo Alto CA 94301

SCIULLI, FRANK J, EXPERIMENTAL PHYSICS, ELEMENTARY PARTICLE PHYSICS. *Current Pos:* PROF PHYSICS, COLUMBIA UNIV, 81- *Personal Data:* b Philadelphia, Pa, Aug 22, 38; m 65; c 2. *Educ:* Univ Pa, AB, 60, MS, 61, PhD(K-meson decay), 65. *Prof Exp:* Res assoc particle physics, Univ Pa, 65-66; res fel, Calif Inst Technol, 66-68, from asst prof to prof, 69-81. *Mem:* AAAS; fel, Am Phys Soc; Sigma Xi. *Res:* Weak interactions of elementary particles, particularly K-meson decays and neutrino interactions. *Mailing Add:* 1 Deep Hollow Close Irvington NY 10533-2643

SCIULLI, PAUL WILLIAM, BIOLOGICAL ANTHROPOLOGY, DENTAL ANTHROPOLOGY. *Current Pos:* vis asst prof, 74-76, ASST PROF PHYS ANTHROP, OHIO STATE UNIV, 76- *Personal Data:* b Pittsburgh, Pa, Aug 14, 47; m 73. *Educ:* Univ Pittsburgh, BA, 69, PhD(anthrop), 74. *Honors & Awards:* res award, Col Soc & Behav Sci, Ohi State Univ, 75 & 79. *Prof Exp:* Instr phys anthrop, Univ Pittsburgh, 73-74. *Concurrent Pos:* Consult breeding prog, SMI Chinchilla Farm, 75-78. *Mem:* Sigma Xi; Am Asn Phys Anthropologists; Am Asn Human Genetics. *Res:* Biocultural adaptations of prehistoric eastern woodland amerindians and genetic interactions in the production of coat color in the chinchilla. *Mailing Add:* Dept Anthrop Ohio State Univ 124 W 17th Ave Columbus OH 43210-1316

SCIUMBATO, GABRIEL LON, PLANT PATHOLOGY. *Current Pos:* ASST PLANT PATHOLOGIST, MISS STATE UNIV, 76- *Personal Data:* b La Junta, Colo, Sept 12, 45; m 67; c 1. *Educ:* Univ Eastern NMex, BA, 68; La State Univ, MS, 69, PhD(plant path), 73. *Prof Exp:* Technician plant path, La State Univ, 72-73; fel, Tex A&M Univ, 73-75; agronomist res & develop, US Borax Corp, 75-76. *Mem:* Weed Sci Soc; Am Phytopath Soc. *Res:* Control of foliar cotton, soybean and rice diseases. *Mailing Add:* 304 S Deer Creek Dr W Leland MS 38756

SCLAR, CHARLES BERTRAM, PETROLOGY, ORE DEPOSITS. *Current Pos:* chmn dept, 76-85, prof geol, 68-90, EMER PROF GEOL, LEHIGH UNIV, 90- *Personal Data:* b Newark, NJ, Mar 16, 25; m 46, Ruth Choyke; c David A & Philip J. *Educ:* City Col New York, BS, 46; Yale Univ, MS, 48, PhD(geol), 51. *Honors & Awards:* Ward Medalist in Geol, 46. *Prof Exp:* Instr geol, Ohio State Univ, 49-51; res geologist, Battelle Mem Inst, 51-53, prin geologist, 53-57, asst consult, 57-62, res assoc, 62-65, assoc chief chem physics div & dir high-pressure res lab, 65-68. *Mem:* Fel Geol Soc Am; Fel Soc Econ Geol; Geochem Soc; fel Mineral Soc Am; Am Geophys Union. *Res:* Petrology, geochemistry, mineralogy, high-pressure synthesis, phase equilibria, and phase transformations; igneous and metamorphic petrology; shock metamorphism; shock effects in lunar minerals; mineral deposits and industrial applications of mineralogy. *Mailing Add:* 2075 Pleasant Dr Bethlehem PA 18015. *Fax:* 610-758-3677; *E-Mail:* cbs1@lehigh.edu

SCLAR, NATHAN, IR DETECTOR & ARRAY, CRYOGENIC ELECTRONICS. *Current Pos:* RETIRED. *Personal Data:* b New York, NY, Mar 22, 20; m 51, Judith Applebaum; c Douglas, Linda, Eric & Andrew. *Educ:* NY Univ, BS, 48; Syracuse Univ, MS, 52 & PhD(physics), 67. *Honors & Awards:* Cert Recognition, NASA IR Astron Satellite Prog. *Prof Exp:* Res physicist, Naval Res Lab, 52-56; res engr, Dumont Labs, 56-58 & Avion Electronics; 58-59, staff engr, Dumont Labs, 62-64; mgr res, Nuclear Corp Am, 59-62; proj engr, sr scientist, mgr & prin scientist, Rockwell Int, 64-85; CONSULT, Aerojet Electro Systs, 85-90. *Mem:* Fel Am Phys Soc; fel Inst Elec & Electronics Engrs; AAAS. *Res:* Solid state physics; design and development of electron devices and systems; detectors for nuclear, optical and IR radiation and the electronics to condition and to read out arrays of such detectors. *Mailing Add:* 631 Cliff Dr-A3 Laguna Beach CA 92651

SCLATER, JOHN GEORGE, OCEANOGRAPHY, GEOPHYSICS. *Current Pos:* PROF GEOPHYS, SCRIPPS INST OCEANOG, UNIV CALIF, SAN DIEGO, 91- *Personal Data:* b Edinburgh, Scotland, June 17, 40; m 85. *Educ:* Univ Edinburgh, BSc, 62; Cambridge Univ, PhD(geophys), 66. *Honors & Awards:* Rosenstiel Award in Oceanog, 79; Bucher Medal, Am Geophys Soc, 85. *Prof Exp:* NSF res grant, Scripps Inst Oceanog, Univ Calif, San Diego, 65-67, asst geophys res, 67-72, lectr geol, 71-72; from assoc prof oceanog & marine geophys to prof marine geophys, Mass Inst Technol, 72-83; prof geol, Univ Tex, Austin, 83-91. *Concurrent Pos:* Dir, Joint Prog Oceanog Woods Hole Oceanog Inst & Mass Inst Technol, 81-83; Shell Co distinguished prof, 83-88; assoc dir, Inst Geophys, Univ Tex, Austin, 83- *Mem:* Nat Acad Sci; fel Am Geophys Union; fel Geol Soc Am; Am Asn Prof Geologists; fel Royal Soc London. *Res:* Application of the theory of plate tectonics to the ocean environment. *Mailing Add:* Geol Res Div Scripps Inst Oceanog Univ Calif San Diego La Jolla CA 92093-0215

SCLOVE, STANLEY LOUIS, STATISTICS. *Current Pos:* from assoc prof to prof math, 81-82, PROF INFO & DECISION SCI, UNIV ILL, CHICAGO, 82- *Personal Data:* b Charleston, WVa, Nov 25, 40; m 62, 90, Caryl Wertheimer; c Sarabeth, Benjamin & Aaron J. *Educ:* Dartmouth Col, AB, 62; Columbia Univ, PhD(math statist), 67. *Prof Exp:* Res assoc statist, Stanford Univ, 66-68; asst prof, Carnegie-Mellon Univ, 68-72. *Concurrent Pos:* Consult, Alcoa Res Labs, Pa, 69; vis asst prof statist & educ, Stanford Univ, 71-72; vis assoc prof indust eng & mgt sci, Northwestern Univ, 80-81; expert witness, Fed Ct, Chicago, 85; chair-elect, Risk Anal Sect, Am Statist Asn, 97, chair, 98. *Mem:* Am Statist Asn; Inst Math Statist; Classification Soc NAm (secy/treas, 97-). *Res:* Multivariate statistical analysis; cluster analysis; time series analysis; fingerprint probabilities; statistical aspects of protein structure. *Mailing Add:* Dept Info & Decision Sci M/C 294 Col Bus Admin Univ Ill 601 S Morgan St Chicago IL 60607-7124. *Fax:* 312-413-0385; *E-Mail:* u37331@uicvm.uic.edu

SCOBEY, ELLIS HURLBUT, GEOLOGY. *Current Pos:* vpres & treas, 75-92, PRES, MCFARLAND & SCOBEY INC, 92- *Personal Data:* b Kelso, Wash, Sept 15, 11; wid; c John, Michael, Margaret (Putnam) & Jane. *Educ:* Cornell Col, AB, 33; Univ Iowa, MS, 35, PhD(geol), 38. *Prof Exp:* Asst geol, Univ Iowa, 35-38; asst geologist, Gulf Oil Corp, Ind, 38-44; geologist, Bay Petrol Corp, 44-47; dist geologist, Southern Minerals Corp, Tex, 47-51; chief geologist, Guy Mabee Drilling Co, 51-65 & Mabee Petrol Corp, 65-75. *Mem:* Soc Econ Paleontologists & Mineralogists; Am Asn Petrol Geologists. *Res:* Sedimentation; stratigraphy and petroleum geology in Illinois Basin; petroleum geology in West Texas. *Mailing Add:* Two Chatham Ct Midland TX 79705

SCOBEY, ROBERT P, PHYSIOLOGY, NEUROPHYSIOLOGY. *Current Pos:* RETIRED. *Personal Data:* b Providence, RI, Sept 10, 38; m 60; c 3. *Educ:* Worcester Polytech Inst, BSEE, 60; Clark Univ, MA, 62; Johns Hopkins Univ, PhD(physiol), 68. *Prof Exp:* Prof neurol, Sch Med, Univ Calif, Davis, 77-92. *Res:* Neurophysiology of central nervous system; vision. *Mailing Add:* Dept Neurol/Physiol Univ Calif Sch Med Davis CA 95616-5224

SCOBY, DONALD RAY, ENVIRONMENTAL BIOLOGY. *Current Pos:* RETIRED. *Personal Data:* b Sabetha, Kans, Mar 18, 31; m, Glenna J Norrie; c Melodye J. *Educ:* Kans State Univ, BS, 57; Nebr State Teachers Col, MS, 60; NDak State Univ, PhD(bot, ecol), 68. *Prof Exp:* Instr & prin high sch, Kans, 57-60; instr high sch, Colo, 61-65, chmn, Sci Dept, 65-66; instr gen biol & sci methods, NDak State Univ, 67-68, from asst prof to prof, 68-89, emer prof biol & sci educ, 89-96; prof biol, Moorhead State Univ, 89-96. *Mem:* Asn Educ Sci Teachers; Ecol Soc Am; Sigma Xi; Nat Asn Biol Teachers. *Res:* Environmental education procedures; practices for environmental self sufficiency; application of ecological and biological principles to organic farming methods; science education. *Mailing Add:* 3302 Second St No 22 Fargo ND 58102

SCOCCA, JOHN JOSEPH, BIOCHEMISTRY, MOLECULAR BIOLOGY. *Current Pos:* NIH fel, McCollum-Pratt Inst, 66-68, asst prof, Univ, 68-72, assoc prof, 72-86, PROF BIOCHEM, SCH HYG & PUB HEALTH, JOHNS HOPKINS UNIV, 86- *Personal Data:* b Philadelphia, Pa, Mar 23, 40; m 66; c 2. *Educ:* Johns Hopkins Univ, BA, 61, PhD(biochem), 66. *Mem:* Am Soc Biol Chemists; Am Soc Microbiol. *Res:* Mechanism of genetic exchange in gram-negative bacteria; site specific recombination; DNA recognition mechanisms. *Mailing Add:* Dept Biochem Sch Hyg & Pub Health Johns Hopkins Univ 615 N Wolfe St Baltimore MD 21205-2103

SCOFIELD, DILLON FOSTER, PHYSICS, MATERIALS SCIENCE. *Current Pos:* MEM STAFF PHOTO PROD DEPT, EXP STA, E I DUPONT DE NEMOURS & CO, INC, 74- *Personal Data:* b Norfolk, Va, Aug 10, 43; m 71, Patricia Rueling; c M (Nichols) & Jonathan D. *Educ:* George Washington Univ, BS, 65, MS, 66, PhD(solid state physics), 69. *Prof Exp:* Independent syts analyst, 60-67; res analyst solid state & high energy physics, Foreign Technol Div, Air Force Syts Command, 67-70, res physicist solid state physics, Aerospace Res Labs, 70-71; Nat Res Coun assoc, Wright-Patterson AFB, 72-74. *Concurrent Pos:* Pres, Appl Sci, Inc, 77- *Mem:* AAAS; Am Phys Soc; Inst Elec & Electronics Engrs; Asn Comput Mach. *Res:* Physical theory of photographic process, nonlinear mechanics, thin film fluid flow, mechanical and magnetic composites; high level languages for minicomputers; computer architecture; automated laboratory equipment; microprocessor system design; elementary particle physics; gravitation theory. *Mailing Add:* 128 Country Flower Rd Newark DE 19711-2482

SCOFIELD, GORDON L(LOYD), MECHANICAL ENGINEERING. *Current Pos:* PROF MECH ENG & ENG MECH & HEAD DEPT, MICH TECHNOL UNIV, 69- *Personal Data:* b Huron, SDak, Sept 29, 25; m 47; c 2. *Educ:* Purdue Univ, BS, 46; Univ Mo, MS, 49; Univ Okla, PhD, 68. *Prof Exp:* Instr mech eng, SDak State Col, 46-47; asst, Univ Mo, Rolla, 47-48, from instr to prof, 48-69. *Concurrent Pos:* Consult, Naval Ord Test Sta, Calif. *Mem:* Am Soc Mech Engrs; Soc Automotive Engrs (pres, 77); Am Soc Eng Educ; Am Inst Aeronaut & Astronaut. *Res:* Heat transfer and energy conversion. *Mailing Add:* 4302 Carriage Hills Dr Rapid City SD 57702

SCOFIELD, HERBERT TEMPLE, plant physiology; deceased, see previous edition for last biography

SCOFIELD, JAMES HOWARD, THEORETICAL PHYSICS. *Current Pos:* PHYSICIST, UNIV CALIF, LAWRENCE LIVERMORE LAB, 62- *Personal Data:* b Gary, Ind, Oct 10, 33; m 57; c 3. *Educ:* Ind Univ, BS, 55, MS, 57, PhD(theoret physics), 60. *Prof Exp:* Res assoc theoret physics, Stanford Univ, 60-62. *Mem:* Fel Am Phys Soc. *Res:* Atomic structure calculations; interaction of electrons and x-rays with atoms. *Mailing Add:* Lawrence Livermore Lab L-41 UCL PO Box 808 Livermore CA 94551

SCOGGIN, JAMES F, JR, PHYSICS, ELECTRICAL ENGINEERING. *Current Pos:* from assoc prof to prof, 68-83, EMER PROF ELEC ENG, THE CITADEL, 83- *Personal Data:* b Laurel, Miss, Aug 3, 21; m 48, Madeline E Lannelle; c Tracy C (Iannelli), Beryl W (Brown) & James F III. *Educ:* Miss State Univ, BS, 41; US Mil Acad, BS, 44; Johns Hopkins Univ, MA, 51; Univ Va, PhD(physics), 57; Indust Col Armed Forces, grad(nat security), 62. *Honors & Awards:* Centennial Medal, Inst Elec & Electronics Engrs. *Prof Exp:* Physicist, Signal Corps, US Army, 51-53 & 54-55 & Defense Atomic Support Agency, 58-61, engr, Adv Res Proj Agency, 62-65, proj mgr ground surveillance systs, Electronics Command, 66-68. *Mem:* Sr mem Inst Elec & Electronics Engrs; Am Nuclear Soc; fel Radio Club Am. *Res:* Micrometeorology; cellular convection; tropical communications; surveillance systems; artillery sound ranging; nuclear energy; precision electrical measurements. *Mailing Add:* 1310 Pembrooke Dr Charleston SC 29407

SCOGGINS, JAMES R, METEOROLOGY. *Current Pos:* assoc prof, Col Geosci, Tex A&M Univ, 67-69, asst dean opers, 71-73, dir, Ctr Appl Geosci, 73-75, assoc dean res, 75-77, head dept meteorol, 80-90, PROF METEOROL, COL GEOSCI, TEX A&M UNIV, 69-, DIR, COOP INST APPL METEOROL STUDIES, 89- *Personal Data:* b Aragon, Ga, Sept 22, 31; m 52; c 2. *Educ:* Berry Col, AB, 52; Pa State Univ, BS, 54, MS, 60, PhD(meteorol), 66. *Prof Exp:* Mathematician, Lockheed Aircraft Corp, Ga, 57-58, meteorologist, Nuclear Lab, 59-60; meteorologist, Aerospace Environ Div, NASA Marshall Space Flight Ctr, 60-67. *Concurrent Pos:* Consult, Tex Dept Water Resources, 73- *Mem:* Fel Am Meteorol Soc. *Res:* Mesometeorology; applied meteorology. *Mailing Add:* 2505 Whispering Oaks Dr Bryan TX 77802

SCOGIN, RON LYNN, PLANT CHEMISTRY. *Current Pos:* PROF BOT, LAVERNE UNIV, 93- *Personal Data:* b Corpus Christi, Tex, Oct 6, 41; m 67; c 2. *Educ:* Univ Tex, Austin, BA, 64, PhD(bot), 68. *Prof Exp:* Asst prof bot, Ohio Univ, 68-71; from asst prof to assoc prof, Claremont Grad Sch, 72-93, chmn dept, 79-85. *Concurrent Pos:* NSF fel, Univ Durham, Eng, 70-71. *Res:* Biochemical systematics and evolution; biochemical systematics of angiosperms. *Mailing Add:* 1950 Third St LaVerne Univ LaVerne CA 91750-4401

SCOLA, DANIEL ANTHONY, CHEMISTRY, MATERIALS SCIENCE. *Current Pos:* adj prof, 86-93, RES PROF POLYMER CHEM, UNIV CONN, 94- *Personal Data:* b Worcester, Mass, July 11, 29; m 53, Theresa R Batti; c Daniel A Jr, Joan F, Paul M & Christopher J. *Educ:* Clark Univ, BA, 52; Williams Col, MA, 54; Univ Conn, PhD(org & phys chem), 59. *Honors & Awards:* Outstanding Achievement Award, Soc Plastics Engrs, 90. *Prof Exp:* Lab asst chem, Williams Col, 52-54; res chemist, Durez Plastics Co, NY, 55; lab asst, Univ Conn, 55-57, asst instr, 57-58; sr res chemist, Monsanto Res Corp, Mass, 58-64, res group leader, 64-65; sr res scientist, United Aircraft Res Labs, Conn, 65-66; sr res engr, Res Labs, Norton Co, Mass, 66-67; sr res scientist & supvr org mat res, United Technol Res Ctr, East Hartford, 66-74, sr mat scientist, 74-94. *Concurrent Pos:* Adj fac mem, Univ Hartford, 69-; dir & chmn relig educ comt, St Augustine Church, Glastonbury, 69-78; vis prof chem, Trinity Col, Hartford, Conn, 88-; founder, advan polymer composites, Div Soc Plastics Engrs, 87, chmn, 90-91. *Mem:* Am Chem Soc; fel Soc Plastics Engrs; Soc Advan Mat & Process Eng. *Res:* Materials research, especially fiber reinforced polymeric materials; advanced polymer composites, interface effects in composite materials; influence of environment on mechanical and thermal properties of composites; surface effects in adhesive bonding; synthesis of moisture resistant laminating resins, coatings and adhesives; synthesis and evaluation of high temperature polymeric materials for advanced composites and adhesives; development of a family of 3F and 36F polyimides for high temperature applications; characterization of polyimide composites for 370degree C applications; process studies to fabricate void-free polyimide/graphite composites; electropolymerization of monomers onto graphite fiber surface to produce coated fibers. *Mailing Add:* 83 Stone Post Rd Glastonbury CT 06033. *Fax:* 860-486-4745

SCOLARO, REGINALD JOSEPH, PETROLEUM GEOLOGY, EXPLORATION & INVERTEBRATE PALEONTOLOGY. *Current Pos:* GEOL SPECIALIST, SAUDI ARAMCO, 91- *Personal Data:* b Tampa, Fla, Oct 19, 39; m 66, 82, Susan L Fink; c Larra M & Ryan. *Educ:* Univ Fla, BA, 60, BS, 62, MS, 64; Tulane Univ, PhD(paleont), 68. *Prof Exp:* Intern, Smithsonian Inst, 67-68; res fel, Univ Ga, 68-69; assoc prof geol, Radford Col, 69-79, chmn dept, 71-79, prof, 79; proj geologist, Gulf Oil Explor & Prod Co, 79-83; sr geologist I, BP Explor, 83-85, sr geologist II, 85-91. *Concurrent Pos:* Assoc ed, Am Asn Petrol Geologists Bull, 92-94. *Mem:* Geol Soc Am; Paleont Soc; Paleont Res Inst; Am Asn Petrol Geologists. *Res:* Taxonomy and paleoecology of Tertiary and recent Cheilostome Bryozoa. *Mailing Add:* 2055 Jubal Early Hwy Wirtz VA 24184. *Fax:* 966-3-874-2723

SCOLES, GIACINTO, CHEMISTRY. *Current Pos:* DONNER PROF SCI, PRINCETON UNIV, 87- *Personal Data:* b Torino, Italy, Apr 2, 35; m 64, Gioklan Lim; c Gigi. *Educ:* Univ Genoa, Italy, Degree Chem, 59, Libero Docente, 68. *Prof Exp:* Asst prof, Univ Genoa, 60-61 & 64-68, assoc prof, 68-71; res assoc, Univ Leiden, Neth, 61-64; prof chem & physics, Univ Waterloo, Ont, Can, 71-86. *Concurrent Pos:* Killam fel, Sci Coun Can, 86. *Mem:* Fel Chem Inst Can; Can Asn Physicists; Am Phys Soc; Am Chem Soc; Optical Soc Am. *Res:* Chemistry education. *Mailing Add:* Dept Chem Princeton Univ Princeton NJ 08544

SCOLES, GRAHAM JOHN, PLANT BREEDING, CYTOGENETICS. *Current Pos:* ASSOC PROF CYTOGENETICS, UNIV SASK, CAN, 79- *Personal Data:* b Eng; Can citizen. *Educ:* Univ Reading, UK, BSc, 73; Univ Manitoba, MSc, 75, PhD(plant sci), 79. *Mem:* Can Genetics Soc; Am Soc Agron. *Res:* Interspecific hybridization and cross-compatibility in crop species. *Mailing Add:* Crop Sci Dept 51 Campus Dr Univ Sask Saskatoon SK S7N 5A8 Can. *Fax:* 306-966-5015

SCOLLARD, DAVID MICHAEL, IMMUNOLOGY. *Current Pos:* CHIEF RES PATH, G W L HANSENS DIS CTR; CLIN ASSOC PROF PATH, LA STATE UNIV SCH MED. *Personal Data:* b NDak, July 26, 47; m 71; c 2. *Educ:* St Olaf Col, BA, 69; Univ NDak, BS, 71; Univ Chicago, MD &

PhD(path & immunol), 75. *Prof Exp:* Lectr path, Univ Hong Kong, 76-81; asst prof path, Univ Ill, 81-84; asst prof path, Univ Hawaii, 84-89, assoc prof, 89. *Concurrent Pos:* Asst prof path, Univ Chicago, 80; field dir, Chiang Mai-Ill Leprosy Res Proj, 81-84; Fulbright scholar, 90. *Mem:* Am Soc Microbiol; Int Leprosy Asn; US & Can Acad Path; Am Asn Immunologists; Am Soc Invest Path. *Res:* Pathology and immunopathology of infection, with emphasis on mycobacterial diseases. *Mailing Add:* GWL Hansen's Dis Ctr La State Univ PO Box 25072 Baton Rouge LA 70894. *Fax:* 504-346-5786

SCOLMAN, THEODORE THOMAS, NUCLEAR PHYSICS. *Current Pos:* RETIRED. *Personal Data:* b Duluth, Minn, Oct 27, 26; m 55; c 2. *Educ:* Beloit Col, BS, 50; Univ Minn, PhD(physics), 56. *Prof Exp:* Staff mem physics, Weapon Div, Los Alamos Nat Lab, Univ Calif, 56-62, Test Div, 62-66, assoc group leader, 66-69, asst div leader physics, Test Div, 72-78, prog mgr field testing, 78-86, test div leader & prog dir, 86-89. *Mem:* Am Phys Soc. *Res:* Nuclear weapons test and development. *Mailing Add:* 18833 E Latigo Lane Rio Verde AZ 85263

SCOLNICK, EDWARD M, ONCOLOGY. *Current Pos:* sr vpres, 91-93, EXEC VPRES SCI & TECHNOL, MERCK & CO, 93-; PRES, MERCK RES LAB, 90- *Personal Data:* b Boston, Mass, Aug 8, 40; m 65; c 3. *Educ:* Harvard Univ, AB, 61, MD, 65. *Honors & Awards:* Arthur S Flemming Award, 76; Super Award, USPHS, 78; Eli Lilly Award, 80; Indust Res Inst Medal Award, 89. *Prof Exp:* Intern internal med, Mass Gen Hosp, 65-66, asst residency, 66-67; res assoc USPHS Lab Biochem Genetics, Nat Heart Inst, NIH, 67-69, sr staff fel, 69-70 & Viral Lymphoma Br, 70-71, spec adv, Spec Virus Cancer Prog, 73-78, mem, Coord Comt, 75-78, head molecular virol, Virol Sect & Chief Lab, Tumor-Virus Genetics, 75-82; exec dir basic res, Virus & Cell Biol Res, Merck Sharp & Dohme Res Labs, 82-85, vpres, 83-84, sr vpres, 84-85, pres, 85-93. *Concurrent Pos:* Ed-in-chief, J Virol, 82-85; adj prof microbiol, Assoc Fac Sch Med, Univ Pa, 83-86; mem, Study Sect, Prog Excellence Molecular Biol, Nat Heart, Lung & Blood Inst, 88. *Mem:* Nat Acad Sci; Inst Med-Nat Acad Sci; Am Soc Biol Chemists; Am Soc Microbiologists. *Res:* Author or co-author of over 170 publications. *Mailing Add:* Merck Res Lab Bldg 26 West Point PA 19486. *Fax:* 215-652-6413

SCOMMEGNA, ANTONIO, REPRODUCTIVE PHYSIOLOGY. *Current Pos:* PROF OBSTET & GYNEC, PRITZKER SCH MED, UNIV CHICAGO, 69- *Personal Data:* b Barletta, Italy, Aug 26, 31; US citizen; m 58; c 3. *Educ:* Univ Bari, MD, 53; Am Bd Obstet & Gynec, dipl & cert reprod endocrinol, 74. *Honors & Awards:* Franklin Medal, Philadelphia Consortium for Pop Res, 74. *Prof Exp:* Intern, New Eng Hosp, Boston, Mass, 54-55; resident obstet & gynec, 56-59, fel, Dept Human Reproduction, 60-61, res assoc, 61, dir Sect Gynec & Endocrinol, 65-81, attend physician, Dept Obstet & Gynec, Michael Reese Hosp & Med Ctr, 61-, chmn dept, 69- *Concurrent Pos:* Fulbright fel, 54-55; fel, Steroid Training Prog, Worcester Found, Exp Biol & Clark Univ, 64-65; assoc prof, Chicago Med Sch, 65-69; mem ad hoc review group contract proposals, Contraceptive Develop Br, Ctr Pop Res Nat Inst Child Health & Human Develop, 72-77; task force Ovum Transport & Inplantation, World Health Orgn, 72-73; examr, Am Bd Obstet & Gynec, 76-84, 86-; consult, IUD Core Adv Comt, Int Fertility Res Prog, 77-81; mem biomed adv comt, Pop Res Ctr, 78-85; mem scientific adv comt, Prog Appl Res Fertility Regulation, 83-87; mem, Obstet-Gynec Devices Panel, Ctr for Devices & Radiol Health, Food & Drug Admin, 85- *Mem:* Fel Am Col Obstet & Gynec; AMA; Am Fertil Soc; Soc Study Reproduction; hon mem Italian Soc Obstet & Gynec; Soc Gynec Invest; Am Gynec Obstet Soc. *Res:* Infertility and fertility; steroid chemistry; human reproduction; intrauterine contraceptive medication; hormones. *Mailing Add:* 820 S Wood St VI11 Chicago IL 60616-1317

SCOPP, IRWIN WALTER, ORAL MEDICINE, PERIODONTICS. *Current Pos:* PROF PERIODONT, DIR DEPT MED & DIR CONTINUING EDUC, COL DENT, NY UNIV, 54- *Personal Data:* b New York, NY, Dec 8, 09; m 41, Edith Halprin; c Alfred L. *Educ:* City Col NY, BS, 30; Columbia Univ, DDS, 34; State Univ NY, cert pedag, 35. *Honors & Awards:* Hershfeld Medal, Northeastern Soc Periodont; Samuel Charles Miller Mem Award, Am Acad Oral Med, 71. *Prof Exp:* Asst chief, Dent Serv, Vet Admin Hosp, North Little Rock Ark, 44-49, chief, Dent Serv, Vet Admin Regional Off, 49-54, chief, Dent Serv, Vet Admin Hosp, New York, 54-80. *Concurrent Pos:* Consult, Goldwater Hosp, New York, 66-80. *Mem:* Am Acad Periodont; Am Acad Oral Med; fel Am Col Dent; fel Am Pub Health Asn; Sigma Xi (pres, 64-66). *Res:* Dentistry; dental medicine; periodontics and oral medicine; published more than 200 articles in scientific journals. *Mailing Add:* 110 Bleecker St New York NY 10012

SCORA, RAINER WALTER, BOTANY, PHYTOCHEMISTRY. *Current Pos:* from asst botanist to assoc botanist, 64-75, prof bot, 75-95, EMER PROF BOT, UNIV CALIF, RIVERSIDE, 95- *Personal Data:* b Mokre, Silesia, Poland, Dec 5, 28; US citizen; m 71; c 3. *Educ:* DePaul Univ, BS, 55; Univ Mich, MS, 63, PhD(bot), 64. *Honors & Awards:* Cooley Award, Am Inst Biol Sci, 68. *Prof Exp:* Master prep sch, Mich, 58-60. *Concurrent Pos:* NSF res grant, 65-71; germ plasam collection grants, 84-88. *Mem:* Phytochem Soc NAm; Bot Soc Am; Int Asn Bot Gardens; Int Orgn Biosyst; Int Soc Plant Taxon; Sigma Xi. *Res:* Biosystematics of the genus Monarda of Persea and of the subfamily Aurantioideae (Rutaceae); isozymes, phenolics, lipid and essential oil constituents of subfamily Aurantioideae and of family Lauraceae; history, origin and evolution of Citrus and Persea; phytochemistry of asparagus, chrysothamnus, eucalyptus, euphorbia, parthenium, and pedilanthus. *Mailing Add:* Dept Bot & Plant Sci Univ Calif 900 University Ave Riverside CA 92521-0001

SCORDELIS, ALEXANDER COSTICAS, STRUCTURAL ENGINEERING. *Current Pos:* from instr to assoc prof, Univ Calif, Berkeley, 49-61, asst dean, Col Eng, 62-65, vchmn, Div Struct Eng & Struct Mech, 70-73, prof civil & struct eng, 62-90, EMER BYRON C & ELVIRA E NISHKIAN PROF STRUCT ENG, UNIV CALIF, BERKELEY, 90- *Personal Data:* b San Francisco, Calif, Sept 27, 23; m 48; c 2. *Educ:* Univ Calif, Berkeley, BS, 48; Mass Inst Technol, ScM, 49. *Honors & Awards:* Moisseiff Award, Am Soc Civil Engrs, 76 & 81, Howard Award, 89; Western Elec Award, Am Soc Eng Educ, 78; Axion Award, Hellenic Am Prof Soc, 79. *Prof Exp:* Struct designer, Pac Gas & Elec Co, 48. *Concurrent Pos:* Engr, Bechtel Corp, San Francisco, 51-54; consult, eng firms & govt agencies. *Mem:* Nat Acad Eng; hon fel Am Soc Civil Engrs; fel Am Concrete Inst. *Res:* Analysis and design of complex structural systems, especially reinforced and prestressed concrete shell and bridge structures. *Mailing Add:* Univ Calif 729 Davis Hall Berkeley CA 94720

SCORDILIS, STYLIANOS PANAGIOTIS, PROTEIN BIOCHEMISTRY, CELL PHYSIOLOGY. *Current Pos:* from asst prof to assoc prof, 78-91, PROF BIOL, SMITH COL, 91- *Personal Data:* b Bridgeport, Conn, Nov 13, 48; m 83, Gail E Norskey; c Eleni F & Panagiota E. *Educ:* Princeton Univ, AB, 69; State Univ NY, PhD(biophys), 75. *Prof Exp:* Fel, Muscular Dystrophy Asn Am, 75-78. *Mem:* Am Soc Cell Biol; Biophys Soc; Am Chem Soc; Am Soc Biochem & Molecular Biol; AAAS. *Res:* Regulation of and energy transduction in muscle and non-muscle motility; contractile proteins and their interactions; exercise induced changes in human muscle. *Mailing Add:* Dept Biol Sci Smith Col Northampton MA 01063. *Fax:* 413-585-3786; *E-Mail:* scordilis@smith.edu

SCORNIK, JUAN CARLOS, IMMUNOLOGY. *Current Pos:* ASSOC PROF IMMUNOL, COL MED, UNIV FLA. *Educ:* Univ Fla, MD. *Mailing Add:* Dept Path Col Med Univ Fla Box 100275 Gainesville FL 32610-0275. *Fax:* 904-392-6249

SCORSONE, FRANCESCO G, MATHEMATICS. *Current Pos:* assoc prof, 65-66, PROF MATH, EASTERN KY UNIV, 66- *Personal Data:* b Palermo, Italy, June 12, 20; US citizen; m 45; c 2. *Educ:* Univ Palermo, PhD(math), 45. *Prof Exp:* From asst prof to assoc prof math, Hartwick Col, 61-65. *Mem:* Sigma Xi. *Res:* Differential equations; mathematical analysis. *Mailing Add:* 256 Saint Ann Dr Lexington KY 40502

SCOTFORD, DAVID MATTESON, PETROLOGY, STRUCTURAL GEOLOGY. *Current Pos:* Asst prof, 50-60, chmn dept, 60-79, PROF GEOL, MIAMI UNIV, 60- *Personal Data:* b Cleveland, Ohio, Jan 7, 21; m 47; c 4. *Educ:* Dartmouth Col, AB, 46; Johns Hopkins Univ, PhD(geol), 50. *Concurrent Pos:* Fulbright lectr grant, Turkey, 64-65; NSF travel grant, Brazil, 66; consult, Turkish Geol Surv, 65 & Shell Develop Co; fel, Univ Liverpool, 80-81. *Mem:* Fel Geol Soc Am; Mineral Soc Am. *Res:* Metamorphic petrology; structural geology; stratigraphy; shale mineralogy and petrography; feldspar structural and geochemistry studies related to geothermometry. *Mailing Add:* 1029 Cedar Dr Oxford OH 45056

SCOTT, ALASTAIR IAN, ORGANIC CHEMISTRY. *Current Pos:* DAVIDSON PROF SCI, TEX A&M UNIV, 82- *Personal Data:* b Glasgow, Scotland, Apr 10, 28; m 50, Elizabeth Walters; c 2. *Educ:* Glasgow Univ, BSc, 49, PhD(chem), 52, DSc(chem), 63; Yale Univ, MA, 68. *Hon Degrees:* DSc, Univ Coimbra, 90, Univ Paris VI, 92. *Honors & Awards:* Corday Morgan Medal, 64; E Guenther Award, Am Chem Soc, 75; A C Cupe Scholar Award, Am Chem Soc, 94; Centenary Lectr, Royal Soc Chem, 94, Bakesian Lectr, 96. *Prof Exp:* Fel chem, Ohio State Univ, 52-53 & Birkbeck Col, Univ London, 54-56; fel, Glasgow Univ, 56-57, lectr, 57-62; prof, Univ BC, 62-65 & Univ Sussex, 65-68; prof chem, Yale Univ, 68-77 & Tex A&M Univ, 77-80; prof org chem, Univ Edinburgh, 80-82. *Concurrent Pos:* Roche Found fel, 63-65. *Mem:* Fel Royal Soc; Am Chem Soc; Chem Soc; Brit Biochem Soc; hon mem Pharm Soc Japan. *Res:* Chemistry and biochemistry of biologically significant molecules. *Mailing Add:* Dept Chem Tex A&M Univ College Station TX 77843

SCOTT, ALBERT DUNCAN, SOIL CHEMISTRY. *Current Pos:* From asst prof to assoc prof, 50-58, prof soils, 59-90, EMER PROF SOILS, IOWA STATE UNIV, 91- *Personal Data:* b Cupar, Sask, Nov 1, 21; m 47; c 3. *Educ:* Univ Sask, BSA, 43; Cornell Univ, PhD(soils), 49. *Concurrent Pos:* Tech expert soil chem, Food & Agr Orgn, UN, Pakistan, 61-62; vis scientist, Commonwealth Sci & Indust Res Orgn, Adelaide, Australia, 68-69. *Mem:* Clay Minerals Soc; fel Am Soc Agron; fel Soil Sci Soc Am; Int Soc Soil Sci; Int Asn Study Clays. *Res:* Forms, reactions and plant availability of potassium in soils and minerals; clay mineralogy; mica weathering. *Mailing Add:* 1430 Wilson Ave Ames IA 50010

SCOTT, ALEXANDER ROBINSON, ENGINEERING. *Current Pos:* EXEC DIR, MINERALS, METALS & MAT SOC, 73- *Personal Data:* b Elizabeth, NJ, June 15, 41; m 71, Angela J Kendall; c Alexander, Jennifer A & Ashley K. *Educ:* Va Mil Inst, BA, 63; Rutgers Univ, MA, 65. *Prof Exp:* Mem, US Army, 65-67; sales mgr, Hilton Hotels, 67-70; meetings mgr, Am Inst Mining Engrs, 71-73. *Mem:* Am Soc Asn Execs. *Mailing Add:* Minerals Metals & Mat Soc 420 Commonwealth Dr Warrendale PA 15086-7511

SCOTT, ALLEN, ORGANIC CHEMISTRY. *Current Pos:* SCIENTIST ORG CHEM, UPJOHN CO, 77- *Personal Data:* b Louisa, Ky, Jan 22, 48; m 77. *Educ:* Ohio Univ, BS, 69; Purdue Univ, PhD(org chem), 75. *Prof Exp:* Fel, Mass Inst Technol, 75-77. *Concurrent Pos:* NIH Res Serv fel, 75-77. *Mem:* Am Chem Soc. *Res:* Synthesis of pharmaceutical compounds; development of synthetic methods and tools. *Mailing Add:* 5287 Saddle Club Dr Kalamazoo MI 49009-9774

SCOTT, ALWYN C, SOLID STATE ELECTRONICS, APPLIED MATHEMATICS. *Current Pos:* prof comput & elec eng, 84-87, PROF MATH, UNIV ARIZ, 87- *Personal Data:* b Worcester, Mass, Dec 25, 31; m 58, 81; c 3. *Educ:* Mass Inst Technol, BS, 52, MS, 58, ScD(elec eng), 61. *Prof Exp:* Engr, Sylvania Physics Lab, 52-54; from instr to assoc prof elec eng, Mass Inst Technol, 61-65; prof comput & elec eng, Univ Wis-Madison, 65-81; chmn, Ctr Nonlinear Studies, Los Alamos Nat Lab, 81-85. *Concurrent Pos:* Guest prof, Univ Bern, 65-66; Belgian-Am Educ Found guest lectr, Univ Louvain, 66; researcher, Cybernet Lab, Univ Naples, Italy, 69-70; prof, Tech Univ Denmark, 86- *Res:* Experimental and theoretical aspects of solid state device theory and nonlinear wave propagation including semiconductors; superconductors, laser media, high density logic systems and neurophysics. *Mailing Add:* 4233 E Sixth St Univ Ariz 1600 E University Blvd Tucson AZ 85721-0001

SCOTT, ANDREW EDINGTON, ORGANIC CHEMISTRY. *Current Pos:* from asst prof to prof, Univ Western Ont, 63-79, head dept, 65-66, dean fac sci, 66-79, EMER PROF CHEM, UNIV WESTERN ONT, 79- *Personal Data:* b Newport, Scotland, Apr 27, 19; Can citizen; m 46; c 1. *Prof Exp:* Res fel chem, Ont Res Found, 50-52; res chemist, Elec Reduction Co Can, Ltd, 53-55; res fel chem, Ont Res Found, 59-60; lectr, Bristol Univ, 60-62. *Mem:* Fel Can Inst Chem. *Res:* Lignin chemistry; chemistry of condensed phosphates. *Mailing Add:* 451 Westmount Dr London ON N6K 1X4 Can

SCOTT, ARTHUR FLOYD, VERTEBRATE ECOLOGY, HERPETOLOGY. *Current Pos:* from asst prof to assoc prof, 78-90, PROF BIOL, AUSTIN PEAY STATE UNIV, 90- *Personal Data:* b Dickson, Tenn, Jan 10, 44; m 91, Charlie Gregg; c Stuart F & Melissa (McShane). *Educ:* Austin Peay State Col, BS, 66, MAEd, 67; Auburn Univ, PhD(zool), 76. *Prof Exp:* Instr biol, Univ SAla, 67-70; asst prof, Union Col, Ky, 74-77; field rep zool, Ky Nature Preserves Comn, 77-78. *Mem:* Soc Study Amphibians & Reptiles; Herpetologists League. *Res:* Ecology, natural history and distribution of amphibians and reptiles in Kentucky and Tennessee. *Mailing Add:* Dept Biol Austin Peay State Univ 601 College St Clarksville TN 37044-0001

SCOTT, BOBBY RANDOLPH, RADIATION BIOLOGY, RADIATION BIOPHYSICS. *Current Pos:* BIOPHYSICIST, LOVELACE RESPIRATORY RES INST, 77-, EMER PROF. *Educ:* Southern Univ, BS, 66; Univ Ill, MS, 69, PhD(biophys), 74. *Prof Exp:* Postdoctoral partic, Univ Ill, 74-75; Argonne Nat Lab, 75-77. *Concurrent Pos:* Mem, Early Effects Working Group, US Nuclear Regulatory Comn, 84- & Protracted Dose Working Group, US Defense Nuclear Agency, 86-; proj prin investr, Inhalation Toxicol Res Inst, 86-; mem sci comt, 86, Nat Co Radiation Protection & Measurements, 91. *Mem:* Radiation Res Soc; Health Physics Soc; Soc Indust & Appl Math; AAAS; Sigma Xi. *Res:* Developed predictive biomathematical models for stochastic and non-stochastic radiobiological effects including: models for effects of combined exposure to different radiations or exposure to radiation plus genotoxic chemical or exposure to hot particles. *Mailing Add:* Lovelace Respiratory Res Inst PO Box 5890 Albuquerque NM 87185. Fax: 505-845-1250

SCOTT, BRUCE ALBERT, PHYSICAL CHEMISTRY, INORGANIC CHEMISTRY. *Current Pos:* mgr org solid state, 72-82, mgr, Chem Dynamics, 82-89, RES STAFF MEM, SOLID STATE CHEM, THOMAS J WATSON RES CTR, IBM CORP, 67-, SR MGR CHEM & MATS SCI, 89- *Personal Data:* b Trenton, NJ, Feb 23, 40; m 62, 79; c 3. *Educ:* Rutgers Univ, BS, 62; Pa State Univ, PhD(chem), 65. *Prof Exp:* Res chemist, Eastern Lab, E I du Pont de Nemours & Co, 66-67. *Mem:* Am Chem Soc; fel Am Phys Soc. *Res:* Electric and magnetic properties of solids; crystal chemistry; crystal growth; phase equilibria; kinetics and mechanisms of film growth; solid state transformations. *Mailing Add:* Thomas J Watson Res Ctr IBM Corp Box 218 Yorktown Heights NY 10598-0218

SCOTT, BRUCE L, THEORETICAL NUCLEAR PHYSICS, ATOMIC PHYSICS. *Current Pos:* from assoc prof to prof, 65-96, chmn, 88-94, EMER PROF PHYSICS, CALIF STATE UNIV, LONG BEACH, 96- *Personal Data:* b Waco, Tex, Oct 8, 32; wid; c Gregory, Susan & Bradley. *Educ:* Calif Inst Technol, BS, 53; Univ Ill, MS, 55; Univ Calif, Los Angeles, PhD(physics), 60. *Prof Exp:* Consult physics, Atomics Int Div, NAm Aviation Inc, 57-60; asst prof, Univ Southern Calif, 60-65. *Concurrent Pos:* Consult, TRW Systs, Inc, 61-72. *Mem:* Am Asn Physics Teachers. *Res:* Nuclear many-body problem; nucleon-nucleon interaction; electron-hydrogen scattering; 3-body problem; atomic physics. *Mailing Add:* Dept Physics Calif State Univ 1250 Bellflower Blvd Long Beach CA 90840. E-Mail: blscott@csulb.edu

SCOTT, CHARLES COVERT, PHARMACOLOGY. *Current Pos:* RETIRED. *Personal Data:* b Sparta, Ill, Jan 18, 09; m 33; c 2. *Educ:* Mo Valley Col, BS, 29; Univ Mo, BS, 33; Univ Chicago, PhD(physiol) & MD, 37. *Prof Exp:* Prof physiol, Chicago Col Osteop, 34-36; intern med, Billings Hosp, Chicago, 38; asst prof physiol, Sch Med, Univ Tex, 39-40; asst in med, Univ Chicago, 40-41; pharmacologist, Res Labs, Eli Lilly & Co, Ind, 41-47; head dept gen pharmacol, 47-48; internist, Inlow Clin, Ind, 48-50; dir clin pharmacol, Warner-Chilcott Labs, 50-54; pharmacol, 54-57, res, 57-58, vpres basic sci, 58-63, vpres sci affairs, 63-67, dir med regulatory document, Warner-Lambert Res Inst, 67-74. *Mem:* AAAS; Am Soc Pharmacol & Exp Therapeut; AMA; NY Acad Sci; Pharmacol Soc Can. *Res:* Gastrointestinal physiology; secondary shock; pharmacology of analgesic, cardiac, diuretic, antispasmodic and central nervous system drugs. *Mailing Add:* 19419 Spook Hill Rd Freeland MD 21053-9420

SCOTT, CHARLES D(AVID), CHEMICAL ENGINEERING & BIOCHEMICAL ENGINEERING. *Current Pos:* Develop engr, Y-12 Plant, Union Carbide Corp, Oak Ridge Nat Lab, Martin Marietta Corp, 53-57, develop engr, 57-67, group leader bio eng, sect chief, Chem Technol Div, 70-76, assoc div dir, Oak Ridge Nat Lab, 76-83, res fel, 83-87, dir, Bioprocessing Res & Develop Ctr, 91-94, SR RES FEL, CHEM TECH DIV, OAK RIDGE NAT LAB, MARTIN-MARIETTA CORP, 87-; CONSULT ENG RES, 94- *Personal Data:* b Chaffee, Mo, Oct 24, 29; m 56, Alice Bardill; c Timothy, Mary & Lisa. *Educ:* Univ Mo, BS, 51; Univ Tenn, MS, 62, PhD(chem eng), 66. *Honors & Awards:* IR-100 Award, 71, 77, 78 & 79; Am Asn Clin Chem Award, 80; E O Lawrence Mem Award, Dept Energy, 80; Pearlman Award, Am Chem Soc, 94. *Concurrent Pos:* Vis lectr, Univ Tenn, 66-70, adj prof, 70- *Mem:* Nat Acad Eng; Am Inst Chem Engrs; Am Chem Soc; AAAS; Sigma Xi. *Res:* Separations technology, heterogeneous kinetics; biotechnology; energy production; environmental control technology. *Mailing Add:* 109 Danbury Dr Oak Ridge TN 37830

SCOTT, CHARLES EDWARD, CHEMISTRY, REFINING. *Current Pos:* RETIRED. *Personal Data:* b Philadelphia, Pa, Aug 26, 29; m 55; c 3. *Educ:* St Joseph's Col, Pa, BS, 52; Univ Notre Dame, PhD(chem), 57. *Prof Exp:* Res chemist, US Rubber Co, NJ, 55-58; sect chief, Sun Oil Co, 58-63; asst dir carbon & elastomer res, Columbian Carbon Co, 63-72; asst dir petrochem res, Oxy Res & Develop Co, 72-80, vpres, 80- *Concurrent Pos:* Pres, Oxypipeline, Inc, 91- *Mem:* Am Chem Soc. *Res:* Petrochemical processing; carbon black development; new elastomers; petroleum refining; natural gas liquids. *Mailing Add:* 3334 E 100th Pl Tulsa OK 74317

SCOTT, CHARLES JAMES, AERONAUTICAL ENGINEERING. *Current Pos:* Scientist, Rosemount Aeronaut Labs, 52-65, ASSOC PROF MECH ENG, UNIV MINN, MINNEAPOLIS, 65- *Personal Data:* b St Paul, Minn, Apr 16, 29; m 51; c 6. *Educ:* Univ Minn, BS, 51, MS, 54, PhD, 64. *Concurrent Pos:* NATO fel, Univ Naples, 65-66. *Mem:* Am Inst Aeronaut & Astronaut. *Res:* Aerothermodynamics. *Mailing Add:* Dept Mech Eng Univ Minn 111 Church St SE Rm 125 Minneapolis MN 55455

SCOTT, CHARLEY, heat transfer, thermodynamics, for more information see previous edition

SCOTT, DAN DRYDEN, ANALYTICAL CHEMISTRY, SCIENCE EDUCATION. *Current Pos:* from instr to assoc prof, 55-65, PROF CHEM & PHYSICS, MID TENN STATE UNIV, 65-, CHMN, 81- *Personal Data:* b Petersburg, Tenn, Apr 1, 28; m 55; c 2. *Educ:* Middle Tenn State Univ, BS, 50; George Peabody Col, MA, 54, PhD(sci ed, chem), 63. *Prof Exp:* Teacher high sch, Tenn, 52-55. *Concurrent Pos:* Consult chemist, Samsonite, Inc, 64- *Mem:* AAAS; Am Chem Soc; fel Am Inst Chem. *Res:* Curricula for beginning college chemistry; analysis of trace amounts of alkalai metals. *Mailing Add:* Box 320 Mid Tenn State Univ Murfreesboro TN 37132

SCOTT, DANA S, MATHEMATICS, COMPUTER SCIENCE. *Current Pos:* UNIV PROF COMPUT SCI, MATH LOGIC & PHILOS, CARNEGIE-MELLON UNIV, 81-, HILLMAN PROF COMPUT SCI, 89- *Personal Data:* b Berkeley, Calif, Oct 11, 32; m 59; c 1. *Educ:* Univ Calif, Berkeley, BA, 54; Princeton Univ, PhD(math), 58. *Hon Degrees:* Dr, Rijksuniversiteit Utrecht, Neth, 86. *Honors & Awards:* LeRoy P Steele Prize, Am Math Soc, 72; Turing Award, Asn Comput Mach, 76. *Prof Exp:* Bell Tel fel, Princeton Univ, 56-57, instr philos & math, 69-72; instr, Univ Chicago, 58-60; from asst prof to assoc prof math, Univ Calif, Berkeley, 60-63; from assoc prof to prof logic & math, Stanford Univ, 63-69; prof math logic, Oxford Univ, 72-81. *Concurrent Pos:* Miller Inst fel, Univ Calif, Berkeley, 60-61; Alfred P Sloan res fel, 63-65; vis prof math, Univ Amsterdam, 68-69; Guggenheim Found fel, 78-79; vis scientist, Xerox Palo Alto Res Ctr, 78-79. *Mem:* Fel Nat Acad Sci; Asn Symbolic Logic; Am Philos Asn; Am Math Soc; Math Asn Am; Asn Comput Mach; fel Am Acad Arts & Sci; fel NY Acad Sci; fel AAAS; Finnish Acad Sci & Lett. *Res:* Author of various publications. *Mailing Add:* Sch Comput Sci Carnegie Mellon Univ 5000 Forbes Ave Pittsburgh PA 15213-3890

SCOTT, DAVID BYTOVETZSKI, MEDICAL & HEALTH SCIENCES. *Current Pos:* RETIRED. *Personal Data:* b Providence, RI, May 8, 19; m 43, 65; c 4. *Educ:* Brown Univ, AB, 39; Univ Md, DDS, 43; Univ Rochester, MS, 44. *Hon Degrees:* Dr, Col Med & Dent, NJ, Univ Louis Pasteur, France. *Honors & Awards:* Arthur S Flemming Award, 55; Award, Res in Mineralization, Int Asn Dent Res, 68; Birnberg Res Award, Columbia Univ, 83; Callahan Mem Award, 85. *Prof Exp:* Carnegie fel, Univ Rochester, 43-44; mem staff, Nat Inst Dent Res, 44-56, chief lab histol & path, 56-65; Thomas J Hill distinguished prof phys biol, Sch Dent, Case Western Reserve Univ & prof anat, Sch Med, 65-75, dean, Sch Dent, 69-75; dir, Nat Inst Dent Res, NIH, 76-81; consult, 82- *Concurrent Pos:* Cmndg Officer, USPHS, 44-65, asst surgeon gen, 76-82; mem gen res support prog adv comt, NIH, 72- *Mem:* Am Dent Asn; Am Acad Forensic Sci; Electron Micros Soc Am; Am Col Dent; Int Asn Dent Res; Am Bd Forensic Odontol. *Res:* Physical biology; biological mineralization; histology and embryology of tooth structure by physical methods; dental caries; methods for age estimation in forensic odontology. *Mailing Add:* 9100 Belvoir Woods Pkwy Apt 209 Ft Belvoir VA 22060

SCOTT, DAVID EVANS, ANATOMY, NEUROENDOCRINOLOGY. *Current Pos:* from asst prof to assoc prof, 67-76, PROF ANAT, MED SCH, UNIV ROCHESTER, 76- *Personal Data:* b Los Angeles, Calif, June 27, 39; m 61; c 2. *Educ:* Willamette Univ, BA, 60; Univ Southern Calif, MS, 65, PhD(anat), 67. *Prof Exp:* Instr neuroanat & histol, Med Sch, Univ Southern Calif, 65-67. *Concurrent Pos:* NIH grant, 68-; USPHS career develop award,

71-76; NSF grant, 78-80. *Mem:* Soc Neurosci; Am Asn Anat; Am Asn Neuropath; Electron Micros Soc Am. *Res:* Electron microscopy; brain-endocrine interaction. *Mailing Add:* Dept Anat & Neurobiol EVa Med Sch PO Box 1980 Norfolk VA 23501

SCOTT, DAVID FREDERICK, BIOCHEMISTRY. *Current Pos:* asst prof, 71-80, ASSOC PROF CELL & MOLECULAR BIOL, MED COL GA, 80- *Personal Data:* b Watertown, Mass, Mar 18, 40; m 63; c 3. *Educ:* Northeastern Univ, BA, 63; Ind Univ, Indianapolis, PhD(biochem), 68. *Prof Exp:* USPHS fel oncol, Univ Wis, 68-71. *Mem:* Am Asn Dent Res; Am Asn Lab Animal Sci; Sigma Xi; Am Asn Cancer Res; Am Chem Soc; AAAS. *Res:* Intermediary metabolism; metabolic regulation; granulocytic function; biochemical oncology; enzymology; lipid metabolism and obesity; toxic shock syndrome. *Mailing Add:* Dept Biochem & Molec Biol Med Col Ga Augusta GA 30912. *Fax:* 706-721-6608; *E-Mail:* dfscott@uscpcc.uga.edu

SCOTT, DAVID KNIGHT, NUCLEAR PHYSICS. *Current Pos:* CHANCELLOR, UNIV MASS, AMHERST, 93- *Personal Data:* b North Ronaldsay, Scotland, Mar 2, 40; m 66, Kathleen L Smith; c Wendelin, Kelvin & Jeremy. *Educ:* Edinburgh Univ, BSc, 62; Oxford Univ, DPhil(nuclear physics), 67. *Prof Exp:* Res fel nuclear physics, Balliol Col, 67-70, sr res fel, 70-73; res officer, Nuclear Physics Lab, Oxford Univ, 70-73; physicist, Lawrence Berkeley Lab, Univ Calif, 73-75; sr scientist nuclear sci, 75-79; prof physics & chem, Nat Superconducting Cyclotron Lab, Mich State Univ, 79-93, assoc provost, 83-86, provost & vpres acad affairs, 86-93, John Hannah Distinguished prof learning, sci & soc, 92-93. *Mem:* Fel, Am Phys Soc; AAAS; Europ Phys Soc. *Res:* Study of nuclear structure and reaction mechanisms using heavy ion collisions; particularly interested in relation of high energy and low energy phenomena. *Mailing Add:* Off Chancellor Whitmore Admin Bldg Univ Mass Amherst MA 01003. *Fax:* 413-545-2328; *E-Mail:* dkscott@chancellor.umass.edu

SCOTT, DAVID MAXWELL, ZOOLOGY. *Current Pos:* From asst prof to prof, 51-85, EMER PROF ZOOL, UNIV WESTERN ONT, 85- *Personal Data:* b Glasgow, Scotland, Apr 30, 20; Can citizen; m 48, Rosemary; c 3. *Educ:* McGill Univ, BSc, 42, MSc, 47, PhD, 49. *Mem:* Am Ornith Union. *Res:* Ornithology; reproductive biology of passerines, particularly of cowbirds. *Mailing Add:* Dept Zool Univ Western Ont London ON N6A 5B7 Can. *Fax:* 519-661-2014

SCOTT, DAVID ROBERT MAIN, silviculture, for more information see previous edition

SCOTT, DAVID WILLIAM, IMMUNOLOGY. *Current Pos:* DEANS PROF IMMUNOL CANCER CTR, UNIV ROCHESTER SCH MED & DENT. *Personal Data:* b Trenton, NJ, Feb 4, 43; m 67; c 2. *Educ:* Univ Chicago, MS, 64; Yale Univ, PhD(immunol), 69. *Prof Exp:* Jane Coffin Childs Mem Fund fel, Sch Path, Oxford Univ, 69-70; asst prof immunol, 71-74, assoc prof, 74-78, prof immunol, Duke Univ, 79- *Concurrent Pos:* Eleanor Roosevelt fel, 76-77 & 86. *Mem:* AAAS; Am Asn Immunol; Brit Soc Immunol. *Res:* Immunologic tolerance; differentiation of immunologic competence; cellular interactions among lymphocytes. *Mailing Add:* Dept Innunol Holland Lab Am Red Cross 15601 Crabbs Branch Way Rockville MD 20855. *Fax:* 716-273-1042; *E-Mail:* dsct@dbicc.rochester.edu

SCOTT, DON, BIOTECHNOLOGY, FOOD SCIENCE. *Current Pos:* RETIRED. *Personal Data:* b Brooklyn, NY, July 8, 25; m 46, 78, Patricia D Marshall; c Rickie, Keith, Wendy & Greg. *Educ:* Cornell Univ, BS, 44, MS, 45; Univ Chicago, MBA, 70; Ill Inst Technol, PhD, 50. *Prof Exp:* Bacteriologist & biochemist, Vita-Zyme Labs, Ill, 45-46, tech dir, 51-54; instr bact, Ill Inst Technol, 46-50; res bacteriologist, Jackson Lab, E I du Pont de Nemours & Co, 50-51; vpres, Fermco Labs, Inc, 54-66, vpres & gen mgr, Fermco Div, G D Searle & Co, 66-72, pres, Searle Biochemics Div, 72-75, tech dir, New Ventures Div, 73-75; pres, Fermco Biochemics Inc, 75-85 & Fermco Develop Inc, 85-87; tech dir, Scott Biotechnol Inc, 87-90. *Concurrent Pos:* Consult. *Mem:* Am Chem Soc; Am Asn Clin Chemists; Inst Food Technol; Am Inst Chem Engrs; Sigma Xi. *Res:* Microbial enzymes; food stabilization; clinical analytical procedures; research management; organizational structure; regulatory affairs. *Mailing Add:* Scott Biotechnol Inc PO Box 611 Elk Grove IL 60009-0611. *E-Mail:* dscott@mcs.net

SCOTT, DONALD, JR, neurophysiology, for more information see previous edition

SCOTT, DONALD ALBERT, ORGANIC CHEMISTRY. *Current Pos:* assoc prof, 54-57, chmn dept, 54-71, prof, 57-86, EMER PROF CHEM, DREW UNIV, 86- *Personal Data:* b Campville, NY, Nov 20, 17; m 46; c 2. *Educ:* Cornell Univ, AB, 39; Univ Ariz, MS, 41; Univ Iowa, PhD(org chem), 52. *Prof Exp:* Instr chem, Univ Ariz, 41-42 & Cornell Col, 42-43, 46-49; asst prof, Wash & Jefferson Col, 51-54. *Concurrent Pos:* NSF fac fel, Univ Calif, Los Angeles, 60-61, Univ Delft, 79. *Mem:* Am Chem Soc; Nat Sci Teachers Asn. *Res:* Structure of natural organic products; glycosides from bark; electrophilic substitution on carbon attached to sulfur. *Mailing Add:* Dept Chem Drew Univ Madison NJ 07940

SCOTT, DONALD CHARLES, LIMNOLOGY, FISH BIOLOGY. *Current Pos:* from instr to assoc prof zool, 47-65, chmn Div Biol Sci, 67-72, prof, 65-80, EMER PROF ZOOL, UNIV GA, 80- *Personal Data:* b Washington, DC, Jan 6, 20; m 42; c 5. *Educ:* Univ Mich, BS, 42; Ind Univ, PhD(zool), 47. *Prof Exp:* Asst, Ind Univ, 42-47. *Concurrent Pos:* Biologist, USPHS, 51-52; staff assoc, Div Inst Prog, NSF, 64-65. *Mem:* Am Soc Ichthyologists & Herpetologists; Am Fisheries Soc; fel Am Inst Fishery Res Biol. *Res:* Ichthyology. *Mailing Add:* 225 Beech Creek Rd Athens GA 30606

SCOTT, DONALD HOWARD, PLANT DISEASE MANAGEMENT. *Current Pos:* from asst prof to assoc prof, 68-80, PROF & EXTEN PLANT PATHOLOGIST, PURDUE UNIV, LAFAYETTE, 80- *Personal Data:* b Indianapolis, Ind, July 11, 34; m 56; c 4. *Educ:* Purdue Univ, BS, 56; Univ Ill, MS, 64; Purdue Univ, PhD(plant path), 68. *Prof Exp:* Field rep grain dealers, 56-62; res asst plant path, Univ Ill, 62-64, asst exten plant pathologist, 64-68. *Concurrent Pos:* Consult, 78- *Mem:* Am Phytopath Soc; Sigma Xi; Int Soc Plant & Path. *Res:* Diseases and disease control of agronomic crops; effects of crop rotation and tillage practices on disease development; soil-borne disease of soybeans; diseases of turfgrasses. *Mailing Add:* 2197 State Rd 26W West Lafayette IN 47906. *Fax:* 765-494-0363

SCOTT, DONALD RAY, SPECTROSCOPY, CHEMOMETRICS. *Current Pos:* PRES, SCOTT ASSOCS, ROUND ROCK, TEX, 94- *Personal Data:* b Wichita Falls, Tex, Apr 27, 34; m 58, Grace Phillips; c Chris, Laurie & Linda. *Educ:* Univ Tex, Austin, BA, 56; Univ Houston, MS, 60, PhD(phys chem), 65. *Prof Exp:* Res chemist clay & analytical chem, Texaco Res Lab, 56-61; instr & res fel spectros & quantum chem, Dept Chem, Univ Tex, Austin, 64-65; asst prof, Tex Tech Univ, Lubbock, 65-67; scientist polymer photo decomposition, Lockheed-Ga Mat Sci Lab, Atlanta, 67-71; sect chief environ analytical chem, US Environ Protection Agency, Res Triangle Park, NC, 71-73; assoc prof spectros, Dept Chem, SDak Tech, Rapid City, 73-75; br chief environ analytical chem, US Environ Protection Agency, Las Vegas, 75-78; dir & res scientist environ phys & anal chem, Inst Appl Sci, NTex State Univ, Denton, 78-80; res chemist & br chief, US Environ Protection Agency, Research Triangle Park, NC, 80-81; sr sci adv & sr res chemist, 81-94. *Concurrent Pos:* Fel, Theoret Chem Group, Univ Tex, Austin, 64-65; consult, Intersoc Comt Heavy Metals, 74-75 & US Environ Protection Agency, 78-80; ed, US Environ Protection Agency ICP Newsletter, 76-78; adj prof, Chem Dept, NTex State Univ, 78-80; assoc ed, Chemometrics & Intel Lab Systs, 90-97. *Mem:* Sigma Xi; Am Chem Soc; Chemometrics Soc. *Res:* Applications of information theory and pattern recognition to spectral data; environmental analytical chemistry; expert systems for spectral analytical interpretations. *Mailing Add:* 8505 Bobcat Dr Round Rock TX 78681-3667

SCOTT, DONALD S(TRONG), CHEMICAL ENGINEERING, PHYSICAL CHEMISTRY. *Current Pos:* chmn dept, Univ Waterloo, 64-69, actg dean eng, 69-70, prof, 64-87, EMER PROF CHEM ENG, UNIV WATERLOO, 89- *Personal Data:* b Edmonton, Alta, Dec 17, 22; m 45, Dorothy Hensel; c 2. *Educ:* Univ Alta, MSc, 46; Univ Ill, PhD(chem eng), 49. *Honors & Awards:* Plummer Medal, Eng Inst Can, 82; R S Jane award, Can Soc Chem Engrs. *Prof Exp:* Jr petrol engr, Imp Oil, Ltd, 44-45; chem engr, Nat Res Coun Can, 46-47; asst prof chem eng, Univ BC, 49-56, assoc prof, 56-64. *Concurrent Pos:* Vis prof, Univ Cambridge, 63-64; Imp Col, London, 70; assoc dean eng, Univ Waterloo, 80-86. *Mem:* Fel Am Inst Chem Engrs; Am Chem Soc; fel Chem Inst Can; Can Soc Chem Engrs (vpres & pres, 70-72); Sigma Xi; fel Can Acad Eng. *Res:* Three phase bubble column reaction with particular emphasis on hydrotreating of petroleum oils; reactor design; catalysis; conversion of biomass to liquids by use of fluidized bed fast pyrolysis; waste conversion. *Mailing Add:* Dept Chem Eng Univ Waterloo Waterloo ON N2L 3G1 Can

SCOTT, DOUGLAS, COSMOLOGY. *Current Pos:* FAC, DEPT GEOPHYS & ASTRON, UNIV BC, 94- *Personal Data:* b Edinburgh, UK, June 18, 64; m 91, Hilary N Feldman. *Educ:* Univ Edinburgh, BSc(Hons), 86; Univ Cambridge, PhD(astron), 91. *Prof Exp:* Res fel, Univ Calif, Berkeley, 91-94. *Res:* Structure formation; high red shift universe; cosmic microwave background. *Mailing Add:* Dept Geophys & Astron Univ BC 1292219 Main Hall Vancouver BC V6T 1Z4 Can. *Fax:* 510-642-3411

SCOTT, DWIGHT BAKER MCNAIR, biochemistry; deceased, see previous edition for last biography

SCOTT, EARLE STANLEY, INORGANIC CHEMISTRY. *Current Pos:* RETIRED. *Personal Data:* b Bellingham, Wash, Oct 16, 22; m 44; c 7. *Educ:* Reed Col, BA, 49; Univ Ill, PhD(inorg chem), 52. *Prof Exp:* Instr chem, Univ Calif, 52-55; asst prof chem, Amherst Col, 55-60; vis prof, Earlham Col, 60-62; from assoc prof to prof chem, Ripon Col, 62-87, chmn dept, 78-80, May Bumby Severy distinguished serv prof, 82-87. *Mem:* Am Chem Soc. *Res:* Chemical education. *Mailing Add:* 121 W Thorne St Ripon WI 54971

SCOTT, EDWARD JOSEPH, MATHEMATICS. *Current Pos:* from instr to assoc prof, 46-64, PROF MATH, UNIV ILL, URBANA, 64- *Personal Data:* b Chicago, Ill, May 29, 13; m 40; c 1. *Educ:* Maryville Col, Tenn, BA, 36; Vanderbilt Univ, MA, 37; Cornell Univ, PhD(math), 43. *Prof Exp:* Asst math, Univ Md, 37-39; instr, Lawrence Inst Technol, 39-43; instr, Cornell Univ, 43-46. *Res:* Partial differential equations; wave propagation. *Mailing Add:* 101 W Windsor Rd No 4110 Urbana IL 61801-6602

SCOTT, EDWARD ROBERT DALTON, COSMOCHEMISTRY, PLANETOLOGY. *Current Pos:* PROF, UNIV HAWAII, 90- *Personal Data:* b Heswall, Eng, Mar 22, 47; m 80, Anneliese Sullivan; c Victoria & Rosemarie. *Educ:* Univ Cambridge, BA, 68, PhD(mineral), 72. *Prof Exp:* Researcher geophys, Univ Calif, Los Angeles, 72-75; researcher mineral, Univ Cambridge, Eng, 75-78; res fel, Dept Terrestrial Magnetism, Carnegie Inst

Wash, 78-80; sr res scientist, Inst Meteoritics, Univ NMex, 80-90. *Concurrent Pos:* Counr, Meteorit Soc, 77-80; mem, NASA-NSF Antarctic Meteorite Working Group, 83-86; mem, NASA Lunar & Planetary Geosci Rev Panel, 85-87 & 94-95; assoc ed, J Geophys Res, 85-87; assoc ed, Proceedings Lunar Planetary Sci Conf, 87-92, Meteoritics & Planetary Sci, 95- *Mem:* Meteorit Soc; Am Geophys Union; Mineral Soc. *Res:* Origin and evolution of meteorites, asteroids, planets and solar nebula; composition, mineralogy and trace element distributions; analysis by electron probe analysis. *Mailing Add:* Hawaii Inst Geophys Planetology Univ Hawaii Honolulu HI 96822. *Fax:* 808-956-6322; *E-Mail:* escott@kahana.pgd.hawaii.edu

SCOTT, EION GEORGE, plant physiology, plant biochemistry, for more information see previous edition

SCOTT, FRANKLIN ROBERT, FUSION DEVELOPMENT, ENERGY RESEARCH MANAGEMENT. *Current Pos:* RETIRED. *Personal Data:* b Portland, Ore, Aug 23, 22; m 50; c 3. *Educ:* Reed Col, BA, 47; Ind Univ, MS, 49, PhD(physics), 52. *Prof Exp:* Res staff mem, Los Alamos Sci Lab, 51-57; asst dir, Fusion Div, Gen Atomic, 57-67; prof physics, Univ Tenn, 67-73; chief, Open Systs Br, AEC-Energy Res & Develop Agency, 73-75; prog mgr, Elec Power Res Inst, 75-86, consult, 87-96. *Concurrent Pos:* Consult, Oak Ridge Nat Lab, 67-73, Dept Energy, 76-; ed, Rev Sci Instruments, 70-71. *Mem:* Fel Am Phys Soc; Sigma Xi; AAAS. *Res:* Fusion; pulsed power; technical assessments; commercialization. *Mailing Add:* 4805 Terra Grananda Dr Apt 2-B Walnut Creek CA 94595

SCOTT, FRASER WALLACE, NUTRITION, DIABETES. *Current Pos:* RES SCIENTIST NUTRIT, DEPT NAT HEALTH & WELFARE, CAN, 77- *Personal Data:* b Montreal, Que, Nov 21, 46. *Educ:* McGill Univ, BSc, 69, MSc, 72; Queen's Univ, PhD(biochem), 76. *Prof Exp:* Fel cancer res, Cancer Res Unit, Univ Alta, 76-77. *Concurrent Pos:* Adj prof, Dept Biochem, Univ Ottawa. *Mem:* Am Inst Nutrit; Can Soc Nutrit Sci; Can Inst Food Sci & Technol; Am Diabetes Asn. *Res:* Diet as a factor in the pathogenesis of insulin-dependent diabetes; nutrition and immune response; carbohydrate nutrition; diet and health. *Mailing Add:* Nutrit Res Div Health Can 2203C Banting RC Tunney's Pasture Ottawa ON K1A 0L2 Can. *Fax:* 613-941-6182; *E-Mail:* fscott@hpb.ca

SCOTT, FREDERICK ARTHUR, ANALYTICAL CHEMISTRY. *Current Pos:* sr scientist, 71-80, MGR, WESTINGHOUSE HANFORD CO, 80- *Personal Data:* b Albany, NY, Mar 6, 25; m 51; c 2. *Educ:* Rensselaer Polytech Inst, BS, 48, MS, 49, PhD, 52. *Prof Exp:* Sr scientist, Hanford Lab, Gen Elec Co, 52-65; chem div, Pac Northwest Labs, Battelle Mem Inst, 65-70; Wadco, 70-71. *Mem:* Am Chem Soc; Am Nuclear Soc; Sigma Xi. *Res:* Analytical instrument and methods development; sodium technology. *Mailing Add:* 1116 Wright Ave Richland WA 99352-3014

SCOTT, FREDRIC WINTHROP, VETERINARY VIROLOGY, FELINE MEDICINE. *Current Pos:* Nat Inst Allergy & Infectious Dis res fel virol Cornell Univ, 65-68, asst prof, 68-73, assoc prof, 73-78, PROF VET VIROL, COL VET MED, CORNELL UNIV, 78-, DIR, CORNELL FELINE HEALTH CTR, 74- *Personal Data:* b Greenfield, Mass, Nov 22, 35; m 57; Lois E Scott; c Duane D, John G & Raymond C. *Educ:* Univ Mass, BS, 58; Cornell Univ, DVM, 62, PhD(vet virol), 68; Am Col Vet Microbiol, dipl. *Honors & Awards:* Res Award, Am Asn Feline Practitioners; Carnation Award for Excellence in Feline Med, Am Animal Hosp Asn, 90. *Prof Exp:* Vet, Rutland Vet Clin, Vt, 62-64; res vet, Plum Island Animal Dis Lab, Agr Res Serv, 64-65. *Concurrent Pos:* Prin investr res grant, State Agr Exp Sta, 69-79, USPHS Nat Inst Allergy & Infectious Dis, 70-73, Div Res Resources, USPHS, 74-77, Schering Corp, 84-86, 3M Corp, 87 & Morris Animal Found, 86-89; coinvestr res grant, USPHS Nat Inst Child Health & Human Develop, 71-74; prin investr res contract, Nat Inst Allergy & Infectious Dis, 75-81; mem, Int Working Teams on Small Enveloped RNA Viruses, Caliciviruses and Parvoviruses, WHO-Food & Agr Orgn Prog Comp Virol; fel, Mark L Morris Animal Found; mem adv comt, Ctr Vet Med, Food & Drug Admin, 84-86; mem, Am Vet Med Asn Coun Biol & Therapeut Agents, 86-88, chmn, 87-; Rhone Merieux res grant, 90-92; ed-in-chief, Feline Pract J. *Mem:* Am Vet Med Asn; Conf Res Workers Animal Dis; Am Asn Feline Practitioners (pres, 76-78); Am Col Vet Microbiol; Am Animal Hosp Asn; Am Soc Virol; hon first fel Acad Feline Med; Nat Acad Pract. *Res:* Feline and bovine viral diseases; feline infectious pertionitis; feline immunodeficiency virus, feline panleukopenia; feline respiratory diseases; bovine winter dysentery; antiviral compounds; immunology. *Mailing Add:* Dept Microbiol Immunol Col Vet Med Rm C5127 Med Ctr Cornell Univ Ithaca NY 14853

SCOTT, GARLAND ELMO, JR, CERAMICS. *Current Pos:* asst prof ceramics, 77-80, PROF MAT ENG, CALIF STATE POLYTECH INST, 80- *Personal Data:* b Greensboro, NC, Nov 30, 38; m 61; c 2. *Educ:* NC State Univ, BS, 61, MS, 64, PhD, 71. *Prof Exp:* Res asst solid state res, NC State Univ, 61-67; ceramist, Monsanto Co, 67-69; res ceramist, Gen Elec Co, 69-76, mgr, Lamp Div, 76-78. *Concurrent Pos:* Adj prof, dept orthod, Loma Linda Univ. *Mem:* Am Ceramic Soc; Am Soc Metals; Nat Inst Ceramic Engrs. *Res:* Solid state sintering; behavior of glass with low silica content; fracture mechanics; failure analysis; injection molding. *Mailing Add:* 424 Adrian Ct Claremont CA 91711

SCOTT, GARY WALTER, CHEMICAL PHYSICS. *Current Pos:* from asst prof to assoc prof, 74-85, PROF CHEM, UNIV CALIF, RIVERSIDE, 85-, ASSOC DEAN, COL NATURAL & AGR SCIS, 93- *Personal Data:* b Topeka, Kans, Jan 19, 43; m 90, Janet; c 2. *Educ:* Calif Inst Technol, BS, 65; Univ Chicago, PhD(chem physics), 71. *Prof Exp:* NSF fel, Univ Pa, 71-72, NIH fel, 72-74. *Concurrent Pos:* Vis scholar, Wesleyan Univ, 80-81. *Mem:* Am Phys Soc. *Res:* Experimental chemical physics; spectroscopic studies of excited molecular states; photochemical hole burning; degenerate four-wave mixing; low temperature spectroscopy of aromatic molecules, dimers, polymers and novel composite materials. *Mailing Add:* Dept Chem Univ Calif Riverside CA 92521. *Fax:* 909-787-4713; *E-Mail:* garyscott@citrus.ucr.edu

SCOTT, GENE E, PLANT BREEDING. *Current Pos:* RES LEADER, AGR RES SERV, USDA, MISS STATE UNIV, 72- *Personal Data:* b Oberlin, Kans, June 11, 29; m 54; c 2. *Educ:* Kans State Univ, BS, 51, MS, 55, PhD(agron), 63. *Prof Exp:* Agent corn invests, USDA, 54-55, res agronomist, 55-72. *Mem:* Am Soc Agron; Crop Sci Soc Am; Am Phytopath Soc. *Res:* Insect and disease resistance in corn; aspects of corn improvement. *Mailing Add:* Dept Agron Box 9555 Miss State Univ Mississippi State MS 39762-9555

SCOTT, GEORGE CLIFFORD, VETERINARY MEDICINE. *Current Pos:* CONSULT, 89- *Personal Data:* b Shumway, Ill, Dec 6, 26; m 48, Shirley Jacobs; c 7. *Educ:* Univ Ill, BS, 50, DVM, 52. *Prof Exp:* Vet Pract, 52-58; asst vet med dir, Smith Kline & French Labs, 58-64; dir res & develop, Vetco, Johnson & Johnson, 64-66 & Animal Div, Schering Corp, 66-67; dir, Smith-Kline Beckman Corp, 67-74, vpres res & develop, 74-82, vpres sci & technol, 82-86, vpres technol develop, Animal Health Prod Div, 86-89. *Mem:* Am Vet Med Asn; Am Asn Indust Vet; Am Dairy Sci Asn; Am Soc Animal Sci; Am Acad Vet Nutrit; Licensing Execs Soc. *Res:* Parasites of domestic animals, nutrition of ruminants and control of diseases in domestic animals. *Mailing Add:* 800 Hessian Circle West Chester PA 19382. *Fax:* 215-793-2150

SCOTT, GEORGE PRESCOTT, PHILOSOPHY SCIENCE, ORGANIC CHEMISTRY. *Current Pos:* From assoc prof to prof, 49-85, actg head dept, 59-60, EMER PROF CHEM, UNIV SDAK, VERMILLION, 85- *Personal Data:* b Pittsfield, Mass, Sept 17, 21; m 47, M Louise Hampshire; c Laurel, Paula, Beverly, Katherine & Frederick. *Educ:* Worcester Polytech Inst, BS, 43; Univ Rochester, PhD(chem), 49. *Honors & Awards:* Fulbright lectr, UAR, 64-65. *Concurrent Pos:* Res assoc, Univ Ill, 53-55; vis scholar, Univ Tex, Austin, 74, res fel, 85- *Mem:* Am Chem Soc; Sigma Xi. *Res:* Polymers; telomers; free radical kinetics; history and philosophy of science; chemical oscillations. *Mailing Add:* 31 Prentis Vermillion SD 57069

SCOTT, HAROLD GEORGE, PUBLIC HEALTH & EPIDEMIOLOGY. *Current Pos:* CONSULT ENTOMOLOGIST, 90- *Personal Data:* b Williams, Ariz, Aug 20, 25; m 48, Bettie Tabakin; c Jasmine, Lorelei, Rodger, Clifford, Claudius, Curtis, Conrad, Dolores & Gloria. *Educ:* Univ NMex, BS, 50, MS, 53, PhD, 57. *Prof Exp:* Entomologist, Med Field Serv Sch, Ft Sam Houston, US Army, Tex, 50-51, air res & develop Command, Kirtland AFB, USAF, NMex, 51-55, Commun Dis Ctr, USPHS, 55-67, Hosp, New Orleans, 67-69, Environ Health Serv, 69-71 & Environ Protection Agency, 71; prof trop med, Tulane Univ, 71-76, lectr community med, 76-90. *Concurrent Pos:* Dep dir, Senegal River Valley Health Study, 77-80. *Mem:* Entom Soc Am; Asn Mil Surgeons US; Sigma Xi. *Res:* Tropical diseases and systematic entomology. *Mailing Add:* 4 Pats Pl Metairie LA 70001

SCOTT, HENRY WILLIAM, JR, SURGERY. *Current Pos:* prof surg & head dept, Sch Med & surgeon-in-chief, Univ Hosp, Vanderbilt Univ, 52-82, dir, Sect Surg Sci, 75-82, EMER PROF SURG & DIR SECT SURG SCI, VANDERBILT UNIV, 82- *Personal Data:* b Graham, NC, Aug 22, 16; m 42; c 4. *Educ:* Univ NC, AB, 37; Harvard Univ, MD, 41; Am Bd Surg, dipl, 48. *Hon Degrees:* DSc, Univ Aberdeen. *Prof Exp:* Asst surg, Harvard Med Sch, 43-44, Cushing fel neurosurg, 44-45; asst surg, Sch Med, Johns Hopkins Univ, 46, from instr to assoc prof, 47-51. *Concurrent Pos:* Chief surg consult, Vet Admin Hosp, 52-; mem, Am Bd Surg, 56-62, vchmn, 61-62, rep to adv bd, Med Specialties; mem, Nat Bd Med Examr, 65-; mem study sect B, USPHS & chmn, 66-70; hon fel, Royal Australian Col Surg, 76, Swed Surg Soc, 77; H William Scott Jr Chair Surg, Vanderbilt, 82. *Mem:* Soc Clin Surg (pres, 71); Soc Univ Surgeons (pres, 60); Am Surg Asn (treas, 58-65, pres, 73-74); Am Col Surgeons (treas, 67-, pres, 75-76); Soc Surg Alimentary Tract (pres, 70-71). *Res:* Physiology and physiopathology of cardiovascular diseases; gastrointestinal disorders; surgical aspects of cancer. *Mailing Add:* 1161 21st Ave S Nashville TN 37232

SCOTT, HERBERT ANDREW, POLYMERIZATION, HEAT TRANSFER. *Current Pos:* RETIRED. *Personal Data:* b Marion, Va, Mar 29, 24; m 47; c 2. *Educ:* Va Polytech Inst, BS, 44, MS, 47. *Prof Exp:* Chem engr, Tenn Eastman Co, 47-59, supt, Glycol Dept, 59-64 & Polymers Div, 65-68; plant mgr, Holston Defense Corp, Tenn, 68-71; dir systs develop, Tenn Eastman Co, 71-73, dir eng, 73-87. *Mem:* Am Inst Chem Engrs; Sigma Xi; Am Mgt Asn; Nat Soc Prof Engrs. *Res:* Hydrogenation; polyester polymers; polyurethane elastomers. *Mailing Add:* 4512 Chickasaw Rd Kingsport TN 37664-2110

SCOTT, HOWARD ALLEN, VIROLOGY, SEROLOGY. *Current Pos:* RETIRED. *Personal Data:* b Ft Smith, Ark, Aug 12, 26; m 50; c 4. *Educ:* Memphis State Col, BS, 49; Univ Mont, MA, 54; Univ Calif, PhD(plant path), 59. *Prof Exp:* Asst specialist plant path, Univ Calif, 54-59; plant pathologist virol, Crops Res Div, USDA, Md, 59-67; assoc prof plant path, Univ Ark, Fayetteville, 67-69, prof, 69- *Mem:* Am Phytopath Soc; Soc Invert Path. *Res:* Purification; serological studies of plant and insect viruses; vectors of plant viruses. *Mailing Add:* 1029 Eastwood Dr Fayetteville AR 72701

SCOTT, HUBERT DONOVAN, SOIL SCIENCE. *Current Pos:* From asst prof to assoc prof, 71-81, prof, 81-94, UNIV PROF SOIL PHYSICS, UNIV ARK, FAYETTEVILLE, 94- *Personal Data:* b Tarboro, NC, Apr 26, 44; m 68. *Educ:* NC State Univ, BS, 66, MS, 68; Univ Ky, PhD(soil sci), 71. *Honors & Awards:* John W White Award. *Concurrent Pos:* Assoc dir, Ark Water Resource Ctr & Ctr Advan Spatial Technol. *Mem:* Fel Am Soc Agron; Soil Sci Soc Am; Coun Agr Sci & Technol. *Res:* Movement of water and water soluble substances in soil and their subsequent uptake by plants; geographic information systems. *Mailing Add:* Dept Agron Univ Ark Fayetteville AR 72701. *E-Mail:* dscott@cleora.uark.edu

SCOTT, HUGH LAWRENCE, JR, BIOPHYSICS. *Current Pos:* from asst prof to prof physics, 72-85, interim head dept, 85-86, PROF PHYSICS, OKLA STATE UNIV, 86-, HEAD DEPT, 90-; CONSULT, 86- *Personal Data:* b Baltimore, Md, Jan 10, 44; m 66; c 2. *Educ:* Purdue Univ, BS, 65, PhD(physics), 70. *Prof Exp:* Res assoc physics, Univ Utah, 70-72. *Concurrent Pos:* NSF grant, 74-83, 87-; Okla Water Resources Inst grant, 85. *Mem:* Am Phys Soc; Biophys Soc; AAAS. *Res:* Development and analysis of theoretical models, using statistical mechanics and computer simulation for lipid monolayer, lipid bilayer and biological membrane thermodynamic behavior; computer studies of CVD diamond film growth. *Mailing Add:* Dept Physics Okla State Univ Stillwater OK 74078-0444

SCOTT, HUGH LOGAN, III, EXPERIMENTAL NUCLEAR PHYSICS. *Current Pos:* MEM TECH STAFF, SANDIA LABS, 76- *Personal Data:* b Lexington, Ky, Oct 19, 40; m 63; c 2. *Educ:* Univ Ky, BS, 62, MS, 66, PhD(physics), 67. *Prof Exp:* Res fel physics, Bartol Res Found, 67-69; asst prof, Univ Ga, 69-76. *Mem:* Am Phys Soc. *Res:* Nuclear spectroscopy; decay schemes; spin-parities of nuclear states; analog states and elemental analysis via proton-induced x-rays. *Mailing Add:* Sandia Nat Labs Dept 5914 PO Box 5800 Albuquerque NM 87185

SCOTT, J(OHN) D(ONALD), GEOTECHNICAL ENGINEERING, OIL SANDS RESEARCH. *Current Pos:* Aostra prof & chair, 80-85, PROF, UNIV ALTA, 85. *Personal Data:* Can citizen; m 56; c 2. *Educ:* Queen's Univ, Ont, BSc, 54; Univ Ill, Urbana, MSc, 58, PhD(soil mech), 64. *Prof Exp:* Engr, Hardy & Ripley, Consult, 54-57; res asst civil eng, Univ Ill, Urbana, 57-60; asst prof, Univ Waterloo, 60-64, assoc prof, 64-66; prof & chmn dept civil eng, Univ Ottawa, 66-78; sr geotech engr, R M Hardy & Assocs Ltd, 78-80. *Concurrent Pos:* Pvt consult, 57-78; Nat Res Coun res grant, Univ Waterloo, 61-65 & Univ Ottawa, 65-78; Ont Res Coun res grant, Univ Waterloo, 64-65; vis scientist, Nat Res Coun Can, 65-66; dir & consult engr, Fondex Ltd, 71-74; Ont Ministry Transp & Commun res grant, 75-78; Nat Res Coun Can res grant, 78-; adj res prof civil eng, Univ Alta, 78-; Aostra res grant, 80-; geotech engr consult, 80- *Mem:* Eng Inst Can; Can Geotech Soc (treas, 75-78); Can Inst Mining. *Res:* Slope stability; foundation performance; oil sand geotechnique; oil sand mining; tailings dams; oil sands in situ recovery. *Mailing Add:* Dept Civil Eng Univ Alta Edmonton AB T6G 2G7 Can

SCOTT, J(AMES) L(OUIS), MATERIALS SCIENCE, CERAMICS. *Current Pos:* RETIRED. *Personal Data:* b Memphis, Tenn, May 22, 29; m 53; c 2. *Educ:* Univ Tenn, BS, 52, MS, 54, PhD(metall), 57. *Prof Exp:* Instr chem eng, Univ Tenn, 53-56; metallurgist, Oak Ridge Nat Lab, 56-65, head, Ceramics Lab, 65-74, mgr, Fusion Reactor Mat Prog, Metals & Ceramics Div, 74-84, res staff mem, 84- *Concurrent Pos:* Mem, High Temperature Fuels Comt, Atomic Energy Comn, 61-71 & Int Adv Comt, First Int Conf Fusion Reactor Mat, Tokyo, Japan, 84; chmn, Spec Purpose Mat Task Group, Dept Energy, 76-; gen chmn, 5th Topical Meeting Technol Fusion Energy, Knoxville, Tenn, 83. *Mem:* Fel Am Nuclear Soc; fel Am Soc Metals; Am Ceramic Soc. *Res:* Fabrication and irradiation behavior of reactor materials. *Mailing Add:* 8069 Huff Ferry Rd N Loudon TN 37774

SCOTT, JAMES ALAN, ANALYTICAL CHEMISTRY, NYLON POLYMERS. *Current Pos:* From chemist to supvr, E I Du Pont De Nemours & Co, Inc, 65-73, asst chief chemist, Plastics Dept, 73-77, prod mgr, 78-85, sr mkt specialist, 86-90, DEV MGR, E I DU PONT DE NEMOURS & CO, INC, 90- *Personal Data:* b Adrian, Mich, Aug 17, 43; m 65; c 1. *Educ:* Bowling Green State Univ, BS, 64, MS, 65. *Mem:* Am Chem Soc; Soc Plastics Indust; Soc Electroplated Plastics; Am Mgt Asn. *Res:* Analytical chemistry of fluorocarbons and fluorocarbon polymers; atomic absorption spectrophotometry; flame emission spectrophotometry; thermal analysis; analysis automation; flame retardant thermoplastics; nylon polymers; polymer marketing and research. *Mailing Add:* 288 Hogans Valley Way Cary NC 27513

SCOTT, JAMES FLOYD, solid state physics, for more information see previous edition

SCOTT, JAMES HENRY, GEOPHYSICS, GEOLOGY. *Current Pos:* CONSULT GEOPHYSICIST, 86- *Personal Data:* b Marlboro, NY, Apr 19, 30; m 53, Geraldine Foote; c James, Lynda & Sarah. *Educ:* Union Col, NY, BS, 51. *Prof Exp:* Beers & Heroy, 51, Phillips Petrol Co, 51-54, USAEC, 54-62, US Geol Surv, Colo, 62-67 & US Bur Mines, 67-74; geophysicist, US Geol Surv, 74-86. *Mem:* Soc Explor Geophys; Soc Prof Well Log Analysts. *Res:* Well logging and surface geophysics for exploration and evaluation of mineral deposits and construction sites. *Mailing Add:* 12372 W Louisiana Ave Lakewood CO 80228

SCOTT, JAMES J, mining engineering, rock mechanics; deceased, see previous edition for last biography

SCOTT, JAMES MICHAEL, ENDANGERED SPECIES. *Current Pos:* LEADER, FISH & WILDLIFE RES UNIT, UNIV IDAHO, 86- *Personal Data:* b San Diego, Calif, Sept 20, 41; m 66; c 2. *Educ:* San Diego State Univ, BS, 66, MA, 70; Ore State Univ, PhD(zool), 73. *Prof Exp:* Biol aide, US Bur Com Fisheries, 66-68; asst cur vertebrates, Nat Hist Mus, Ore State Univ, 69-73, researcher, Dept Fisheries & Wildlife, 73-74; biologist in charge, Mauna Loa Field Sta, US Fish & Wildlife Serv, 74-84, dir, Condor Field Sta, 84-86. *Concurrent Pos:* Instr ornithol, Malheur Environ Field Sta, Pac Univ, 72 & 73; leader, Maui Forest Bird Recovery Team, 75-79, Hawaii Forest Bird Recovery Team, 75-; mem, Am Ornithologists Union Conserv, 74-75 & 75-76, Sci Adv Bd, Nature Conserv Hawaii Forest Bird Proj, 81-; Richard M Nixon Scholar, Whittier Col; mem, Palila Recovery Team, 75-; mem, Nature Conservancy. *Mem:* Elective Am Ornithologists Union; Ecol Soc Am; The Wildlife Soc; Soc Conserv Biol; Inst Biol Sci. *Res:* Determining limiting factors for endangered species; devising methods for estimating bird numbers which are statistically sound and cost efficient; preserve design for native species and communities. *Mailing Add:* 1130 Kamiaken St Moscow ID 83848-3855

SCOTT, JAMES T, CIVIL ENGINEERING. *Current Pos:* COMDR, CONSTRUCT ENG RES LAB, US ARMY CORPS ENGRS, 95- *Personal Data:* b May 1, 49. *Educ:* Univ Ill, MA, 79. *Mailing Add:* Construct Eng Res Lab US Army Core Engrs PO Box 9005 Champaign IL 61826-9005

SCOTT, JAUNITA SIMONS, BIOLOGY, ZOOLOGY. *Current Pos:* from instr to assoc prof, Benedict Col, 63-80, dir, Biol Study Prog & Pre-Med Adv, 72-80, head, Dept Biol Sci & dir, Health Careers Proj, 81-87, chairperson, Div Math & Natural Sci, 87-92, chair, Biol & Phys Sci Dept, 92-94, chair, Div Arts & Sci, 94-95, interium dean, Sch Arts & Sci, 95-96, PROF BIOL, BENEDICT COL, 81-, ASSOC DEAN, 96- *Personal Data:* b Richland Co, SC, June 13, 36; m 59, Robert L; c R Vincent, Felicia C & Julian C. *Educ:* Livingstone Col, BS, 58; Atlanta Univ, MS, 62; Univ SC, EdD, 79. *Prof Exp:* Teacher biol & sci, Hopkins High Sch, SC, 58-60; instr biol, Morris Col, Sumter, SC, 64-65. *Concurrent Pos:* Prin investr, minority biomed support grant, NIH, 74-79 & 79-84; consult, SC State Dept Educ Progs, SC State Col, Orangeburg, 75; co-investr grant, NIH, 84-87; developer, Middle Sch Summer Lab Sci & Math Enrichment Prog, & dir, 84-; developer & dir, Middle Sch Sci Develop Prog for 5th & 6th grade teachers, 87-90. *Mem:* Am Inst Biol Sci. *Res:* Light and electron microscopic studies on development and regeneration in Rana pipiens as well as heavy metal pollutants on development and ultrastructures in Rana pipiens (spring frog). *Mailing Add:* Benedict Col Harden & Blanding Sts Columbia SC 29204. *Fax:* 803-253-5225

SCOTT, JOHN CAMPBELL, PHYSICS, MATERIALS SCIENCE. *Current Pos:* Res staff mem, San Jose Res Lab, IBM Corp, 80-85, mgr electrophotog mats, IBM Almaden Res Ctr, 86-90, RES STAFF MEM, IBM ALMADEN RES CTR, 90- *Personal Data:* b Edinburgh, Scotland, Oct 5, 49; m 75, Joyce D Wilson. *Educ:* Univ St Andrews, BSc, 71; Univ Pa, PhD(physics), 75. *Prof Exp:* Asst prof physics, Cornell Univ, 75-80. *Mem:* Am Phys Soc; Mat Res Soc; Soc Int Develop. *Res:* Experimental solid state physics; magnetic properties of solids; thin magnetic films; quasi-one-dimensional magnetic materials; electronic and optical properties of polymers; photoconductivity; photorefractive polymers organic light emitting diodes. *Mailing Add:* IBM Almaden Res Ctr K11/D1 650 Harry Rd San Jose CA 95120-6099

SCOTT, JOHN DELMOTH, OPTICS DESIGN FOR VUV THROUGH SOFT X-RAY, SYNCHROTRON RADIATION. *Current Pos:* res fel, 75-78, SR STAFF SCIENTIST, CTR ADVAN MICROSTRUCT & DEVICES, LA STATE UNIV, 88- *Personal Data:* b San Antonio, Tex, Aug 8, 44; m 67, Ann Rootes; c R Ian, Maris & Alyssa. *Educ:* Baylor Univ, BS, 67; NTex State Univ, PhD(chem), 74. *Prof Exp:* Teacher, John Marshall High Sch, 67-69; res fel, NTex State Univ, 75; from asst prof to assoc prof chem, Univ Mont, 78-88. *Concurrent Pos:* Res fel, Robert A Welch Found, 75 & Energy Res & Develop Admin, 75-78; adj prof chem, Northeast La State Univ, 93- *Mem:* Am Chem Soc; Optical Soc Am; Sigma Xi; AAAS. *Res:* Experimental and theoretical investigation of excited electronic states of molecules, principally molecular Rydberg states; development of optics for synchrotron-radiation utilization; x-ray lithography. *Mailing Add:* Ctr Advan Microstruct & Devices La State Univ Baton Rouge LA 70803. *Fax:* 504-388-6954; *E-Mail:* rojohn@lsuvax.sncc.lsu.edu

SCOTT, JOHN E(DWARD), JR, AEROSPACE ENGINEERING. *Current Pos:* assoc prof aeronaut eng, Univ Va, 56-62, res dir, Astronaut Div, 56-60, head aerospace div, Res Labs Eng Sci, 60-67, chmn Dept Aerospace Eng & Eng Physics, 72-77, chmn Dept Mech & Aerospace Eng, 80-82, PROF AEROSPACE ENG, UNIV VA, 62- *Personal Data:* b Portsmouth, Va, Nov 29, 27; m 52; c 4. *Educ:* Va Polytech Inst, BS, 48; Purdue Univ, MS, 50; Princeton Univ, MA, 53, PhD(aeronaut eng), 59. *Prof Exp:* Instr mech eng, Va Polytech Inst, 48; asst, Purdue Univ, 48-50; sr scientist, Exp, Inc, Va, 51; asst, Princeton Univ, 52-54, actg tech dir, Proj Squid, 54-56. *Concurrent Pos:* Dir Proj Squid, 62-67; liaison scientist, Br Off, Off Naval Res, London, 67-68; prog mgr res atomic interactions basic to macroscopic properties of cases, Univ Va, 68- *Mem:* AAAS; Am Phys Soc; Am Inst Aeronaut & Astronaut; Sigma Xi. *Res:* Gas dynamics; propulsion; astronautics; molecular physics. *Mailing Add:* Dept Mech Aerospace Eng Thornton Hall McCormick Rd Charlottesville VA 22903

SCOTT, JOHN FRANCIS, DNA REPLICATION, MOLECULAR GENETICS. *Current Pos:* ASSOC PROF BIOL, UNIV HAWAII, HILO, 86-, ASSOC PROF GENETICS, MANOA, HONOLULU, 89- *Personal Data:* b New Orleans, La, July 29, 44; c John-Michael & Kaymi. *Educ:* Univ Calif, Berkeley, BS, 74; Stanford Univ, PhD(biochem), 79. *Prof Exp:* Asst molecular biologist & spec res fel, Molecular Biol Inst, Univ Calif, Los Angeles, 79-81; asst prof microbiol, Univ Ill, Urbana-Champaign, 81-87. Concurrent Pos: Prin investr, Inst Gen Med Sci res grants, NIH, 79-86, NSF res grant, 83-87; prog dir, NIH MBRS grant, 88- Mem: Sigma Xi. Res: Mechanism of nuclear DNA replication in yeast; chromatin structure and function of yeast chromosomal replicators; further development of yeast as an organism useful for biotechnology and research. Mailing Add: Biol Dept Nat Sci Div Univ Hawaii 200 W Kawili St Hilo HI 96720-4091. Fax: 808-974-7693; E-Mail: jscott@hawaii.edu

SCOTT, JOHN MARSHALL WILLIAM, chemistry, for more information see previous edition

SCOTT, JOHN PAUL, ZOOLOGY, PSYCHOLOGY. Current Pos: res prof, 65-68, Ohio Regents prof psychol, 68-80, EMER REGENTS PROF PSYCHOL, BOWLING GREEN STATE UNIV, 80- Personal Data: b Kansas City, Mo, Dec 17, 09; m 33, 79, Mary-Vesta Marston; c Jean, Vivian, John P & David. Educ: Univ Wyo, BA, 30; Oxford Univ, BA, 32; Univ Chicago, PhD(zool), 35. Honors & Awards: Jordan Prize, 47; Dobzhansky Award, Behav Genetics Asn, 87; Distinguished Animal Behaviorist, Animal Behav Soc, 90. Prof Exp: Asst, Univ Chicago, 32-35; from assoc prof to prof zool, Wabash Col, 35-45, chmn dept, 35-45; res assoc & chmn div behav studies, Jackson Mem Lab, 45-57, sr staff scientist, 57-65, trustee, 46-49. Concurrent Pos: Vis prof, Univ Chicago, 58, Tufts Univ, 81-82; fel, Ctr Adv Study Behav Sci, 63-64. Mem: AAAS; Am Soc Zool; Int Soc Develop Psychobiol (pres, 73-); Int Soc Res Aggression (pres, 73-74); Behav Genetics Asn (pres, 75-76); Animal Behav Soc. Res: Embryology and physiological genetics of the guinea pig; genetics and behavior of Drosophila; sociobiology; genetics and social behavior of dogs, mice and other mammals; development of behavior; evolution of social behavior. Mailing Add: 1052 Pinewood Ct Bowling Green OH 43402

SCOTT, JOHN STANLEY, GEOLOGY. Current Pos: RETIRED. Personal Data: b Hamilton, Ont, July 14, 29; m 56; c 2. Educ: McMaster Univ, BSc, 53; Univ Ill, Urbana, PhD(geol), 60. Prof Exp: Geologist, Photog Surv Corp Ltd, Can, 53-57; geologist, Geol Surv Can, 60-67, res scientist, 69-74, dir, Terrain Sci Div, 74-87, dir gen, Geophys & Terrain Sci Br, 87-89, dir gen, Sedimentary & Cordilleran Geosci Br, 89-92; consult geologist, H G Acres & Co Ltd, Can, 67-69. Concurrent Pos: Mem, Assoc Comt Geotech Res, Nat Res Coun Can, 61-66 & 82-87; counr, Geol Soc Am, 87-89. Mem: Fel Geol Soc Am; fel Geol Asn Can; Can Geotech Soc; Sigma Xi. Res: Engineering geology; hydrogeology as related to construction; stability of slopes in overconsolidated shales; nuclear fuel waste management. Mailing Add: 55 Boyce Ave Ottawa ON K2B 6H8 Can

SCOTT, JOHN W(ALTER), CHEMICAL ENGINEERING, TECHNICAL MANAGEMENT. Current Pos: RETIRED. Personal Data: b Berkeley, Calif, May 27, 19; m 42, Jane Newman; c Nancy, Barbara, James, Charles & Richard. Educ: Univ Calif, BS, 41, MS, 51. Honors & Awards: Award in Chem Eng Pract, Am Inst Chem Eng. Prof Exp: Res chemist, Stand Oil Co, Calif, 46-56, sr res chemist, 56-57, supvr res engr, 57-59, supvr petrol process develop, 60-64, mgr petrol process res & develop div, 64-67, vpres process res, Chevron Res Co, 67-84. Concurrent Pos: Chmn & mem adv bd, Chem Eng Dept, Univ Calif, Berkeley, 72-75; consult, 84-; chmn res, Data Info Serv Comm, Am Petrol Inst, 71-73 & 77-80; awards comt, Am Inst Chem Eng, 79-84; coun mem, Lawrence Hall Sci, 90-96. Mem: Nat Acad Eng; fel Am Inst Chem Eng; fel AAAS; Am Chem Soc. Res: Physical chemistry; adsorption; synthetic fuels; processing; catalytic hydrogenation; hydrocracking; catalysis; technical management. Mailing Add: PO Box 668 Ross CA 94957

SCOTT, JOHN WARNER, HORTICULTURE. Current Pos: asst prof veg crops, 81-91, PROF, HORT SCI, UNIV FLA, 91- Personal Data: b Rochester, NY, Sept 27, 48; m 75; c 2. Educ: Mich State Univ, BS, 70, MS, 74; Ohio State Univ, PhD(hort), 78. Prof Exp: Res technician, Mich State Univ, 70-75; res assoc hort, Ohio State Univ, 75-78, asst prof, 78-81. Concurrent Pos: Mem staff, Gulf Coast Res & Educ Ctr, 81-; consult, DNA Plant Technol, 85- Mem: Am Soc Hort Sci. Res: Breeding, genetics, and culture of vegetable crops, especially tomatoes. Mailing Add: GCREC 5007 60th St E Bradenton FL 34203

SCOTT, JOHN WATTS, JR, NEUROANATOMY, NEUROPHYSIOLOGY. Current Pos: asst prof, 69-76, PROF ANAT, SCH MED, EMORY UNIV, 76- Personal Data: b Oct 5, 38; US citizen; m 66. Educ: Ala Col, AB, 61; Univ Mich, Ann Arbor, PhD(psychol), 65. Prof Exp: NIMH fel, Rockefeller Univ, 65-67, asst prof physiol psychol, 67-69. Concurrent Pos: Nutrit Found grant, Emory Univ, 70-72, NSF grant, 71-73, 78-, NIMH res develop award, 71-76; Nat Inst Neurol & Commun Disorders & Stroke grant, 78-; mem, Behav & Neurosci Study Sect, NIH, 83-86 & Sensory Disorders & Lang Study Sect, 86-87. Mem: Am Asn Anatomists; Soc Neurosci. Res: Olfactory projections to the lateral hypothalamus; physiological properties of feedback circuits of the olfactory bulb; organization of the olfactory projection system. Mailing Add: Dept Anat Sch Med Emory Univ 1440 Clifton Rd NE Atlanta GA 30307-1053

SCOTT, JOSEPH HURLONG, PROCESS DEVELOPMENT, SOLID STATE DEVICE DESIGN. Current Pos: SR SCIENTIST, AEROQUIP CORP, 92- Personal Data: b Atlantic City, NJ, Dec 5, 34; m 76; c 5. Educ: Lincoln Univ, Pa, AB, 57. Honors & Awards: George C Marshall Space Flight Ctr, Nat Aeronaut & Space Admin, 71 & 72, Cert Recognition, 73. Prof Exp: Eng, Solid State Div, RCA, 58, 67, mem tech staff David Sarnoff Res Ctr, 67-70, Head IC Tech, 70-74, dir, 74-79; dir, Res & Develop, Gen Instruments Corp, 79-82; dir, Monsanto Elec Mat, 82-84; pres & chief exec officer, Cadmemic Electronics, 84-85; assoc dir, Olin Chem Res, 85-92. Concurrent Pos: Tech bd dir, Panel Vision Corp, 82-84; co-auth & consult, Nat Acad Sci, 83-84; consult, Rockwell Inst, 84-85. Mem: NY Acad Sci; Sigma Xi; Int Electronic Devices Soc; Am Chem Soc; Elec Chem Soc. Res: Solid State devices and materials while directing efforts in integrated circuit applications; design automation and materials. Mailing Add: 1540 Northbrook Ann Arbor MI 48103

SCOTT, JOSEPH LEE, BOTANY, CYTOLOGY. Current Pos: From asst prof to assoc prof, 70-85, PROF BIOL, COL WILLIAM & MARY, 85- Personal Data: b Delano, Calif, Mar 18, 43; m 64, Donna D Arnold; c Kimberley, Lauren & Brett. Educ: Univ Calif, Santa Barbara, AB, 65, MA, 67; Univ Calif, Irvine, PhD(biol), 71. Mem: Phycol Soc Am; Int Phycol Soc. Res: Development and ultrastructure of algae, particularly cell division and reproductive differentiation in red algae; phycology. Mailing Add: Dept Biol Col William & Mary PO Box 8795 Williamsburg VA 23187-8795. Fax: 757-221-6483; E-Mail: jlscott@mail.wm.edu

SCOTT, JUNE ROTHMAN, MICROBIAL GENETICS. Current Pos: from asst prof to assoc prof, 69-81, PROF MICROBIOL, SCH MED, EMORY UNIV, 81- Personal Data: b New York, NY, Nov 28, 40; m 66, John. Educ: Swarthmore Col, BA, 61; Mass Inst Technol, PhD(microbiol), 64. Prof Exp: Guest investr, Rockefeller Univ, 64-66, res assoc, 66-69. Concurrent Pos: Nat Cancer Inst fel, 65-66; div lectr, Am Soc Microbiol, 88, 90. Mem: Am Soc Microbiol; Genetics Soc Am. Res: Bacterial genetics; gene regulation; bacterial pathogensis. Mailing Add: Dept Microbiol Sch Med Emory Univ 1510 Clifton Rd NE Atlanta GA 30322

SCOTT, KENNETH ELSNER, MECHANICAL ENGINEERING. Current Pos: RETIRED. Personal Data: b Webster, Mass, May 18, 26; m 52, Elizabeth Oldham; c Kenneth E Jr, Cynthia L, Jeffrey A & Donald L. Educ: Worcester Polytech Inst, BS, 48, MS, 54. Honors & Awards: Western Elec Fund Award, Am Soc Eng Educ, 73. Prof Exp: From instr to prof mech eng, Worcester Polytech Inst, 48-65, Alden prof eng & inst dir audiovisual develop, prof mech eng, 72-75, dir instrnl TV, 72-90, dir comput aided design lab, 81-93, acting head, Dept Mech Eng, 88-89. Mem: Fel Am Soc Mech Engrs; Am Soc Eng Educ; Sigma Xi. Res: Education; innovator of teaching methods; pioneer in use of individually prescribed instruction methods and use of audio-visuals in supporting these methods. Mailing Add: 9750 Cypress Lake Dr Ft Myers FL 33919. E-Mail: 76033.3337@compuserve.com

SCOTT, KENNETH RICHARD, MEDICINAL CHEMISTRY, ANALYTICAL CHEMISTRY. Current Pos: from instr to assoc prof, 60-75, PROF PHARMACEUT SCI, COL PHARM, HOWARD UNIV, 75-, ASST DEAN STUDENT AFFAIRS & RECRUITMENT, 71- Personal Data: b New York, NY, Apr 17, 34; m 52; c 2. Educ: Howard Univ, BS, 56; Univ Buffalo, MSc, 59; Univ Md, PhD(pharm chem), 66. Prof Exp: Asst pharm, biochem & anal chem, Univ Buffalo, 56-59. Concurrent Pos: Consult, S F Durst Co, 66-67 & NIH, 67-68; proj dir sem recruitment & retention minority disadvantaged students health professions, Howard Univ, 71; consult, Student Nat Pharmaceut Asn, 72 & Student Health Manpower Conf, 72; actg chmn, Dept Biomed Chem, 76. Mem: Am Chem Soc; Am Asn Cols Pharm; Am Pharmaceut Asn; Nat Pharmaceut Asn; fel Am Inst Chemists; Sigma Xi. Res: Synthetic chemistry, spiranes, carbazoles, steroids and biological testing; analytical chemistry, newer techniques in the development of assay procedures of pharmaceutical preparations. Mailing Add: Pharm Sci Howard Univ 2300 Fourth St NW Washington DC 20059

SCOTT, KENNETH WALTER, POLYMER CHEMISTRY, POLYMER PHYSICS. Current Pos: RETIRED. Personal Data: b Cleveland, Ohio, May 18, 25; m 67, Grace Reginald; c Nancy, Barbara, Robert & John. Educ: Univ Mich, BS, 46; Princeton Univ, AM, 48, PhD(chem), 49. Prof Exp: Sr res chemist, Eastman Kodak Co, 49-55; res scientist, Goodyear Tire & Rubber Co, 55-57, sect head basic rubber res, 57-67, mgr, Basic Polymer Res, 66-73, New Prod Res, 74-77, Transp Prod Res, Res Div, 77-83, Tire & Process Sci, 83-87; vis scientist, Inst Polymer Sci, Univ Akron, 87-94. Mem: Am Phys Soc; Am Chem Soc. Res: Viscoelastic behavior; chemistry and physics of high polymers. Mailing Add: 3030 Oakridge Dr Cuyahoga Falls OH 44224

SCOTT, KEVIN M, GEOLOGY. Current Pos: GEOLOGIST, WATER RESOURCES DIV, US GEOL SURV, 65- Personal Data: b Iowa City, Iowa, Aug 3, 35; m 90, Sally Caylor; c 2. Educ: Univ Calif, Los Angeles, BA, 57, MA, 60; Univ Wis, PhD(geol), 64. Honors & Awards: Kirk Bryan Award, Geol Soc Am, 89. Prof Exp: Geologist, US Geol Surv, 59-60; proj assoc geol, Univ Wis, 61-64; NATO fel, Univ Edinburgh, 64-65. Concurrent Pos: Vis prof, Chinese Acad Sci, 90-93. Mem: Am Asn Petrol Geol; fel Geol Soc Am. Res: Sedimentology of marine and fluvial systems; sedimentary structures and their hydrodynamic interpretation; fluvial morphology; changes in sedimentologic parameters and mineralogy of sediments; environmental geomorphology; sedimentology and hazards assessment of lahars. Mailing Add: US Geol Surv 5400 MacArthur Blvd Vancouver WA 98661

SCOTT, L MAX, HEALTH PHYSICS. Current Pos: ASST PROF NUCLEAR SCI & RADIATION SAFETY OFFICER, LA STATE UNIV, 85- Personal Data: b Sweetwater, Tex, May 9, 34; m 56; c 3. Educ: Tex A&M, BS, 55; Purdue Univ, MS, 59, PhD(genetics), 61. Prof Exp: Internal dosimetry specialist, Union Carbide, 61-77; dir radiation health physics, Gulf Oil Corp, 77-85. Concurrent Pos: Prog chmn, Health Physics Soc, 87-89. Mem: Fel Health Physics Soc; Sigma Xi. Res: Radiation protection; exposure evaluation. Mailing Add: Ctr Energy Studies La State Univ Baton Rouge LA 70803

SCOTT, LAWRENCE TRESSLER, ORGANIC CHEMISTRY. *Current Pos:* PROF, DEPT CHEM, BOSTON COL, 93- *Personal Data:* b Ann Arbor, Mich, June 11, 44; m 66, 93, Dawn Riddle; c 4. *Educ:* Princeton Univ, AB, 66; Harvard Univ, PhD(org chem), 70. *Prof Exp:* Asst prof org chem, Univ Calif, Los Angeles, 70-75; from asst prof to prof, Univ Nev, Reno, 75-85, found prof chem, 85-93, chmn, 88-91. *Concurrent Pos:* Petrol Res Fund grant, 70-73, 75-77, 78-80 & 88-90, Res Corp grant, 74-75; NSF grant, 73-76, 79-85 & 85-88, 88-91, 91-93 & 95-; NIH grant, 79-85 & 85-88; NATO sr scientist award, 81; sr scientist fel, Japan Soc Prom Sci; US-Israel Binat Found grant, 86-89, 91-93 & 95-; Dept Energy grant, 88-92, 93-; NATO grant, 88-90, 93-96. *Mem:* Am Chem Soc; AAAS. *Res:* Synthesis and study of new organic compounds with unusual structures and properties; structural requirements for electron delocalization and the chemical consequences thereof; cyclic conjugation and homoconjugation; aromaticity and pericyclic reactions; cyclic polyacetylenes and nonplanar aromatic hydrocarbons; thermal rearrangements of aromatic compounds. *Mailing Add:* Dept Chem Boston Col Chestnut Hill MA 02167-3860. *E-Mail:* lawrence.scott@bc.edu

SCOTT, LAWRENCE VERNON, VIROLOGY. *Current Pos:* From asst prof to prof, 50-97, chmn dept, 61-, EMER PROF BACT, SCH MED, UNIV OKLA HEALTH SCI CTR, 97- *Personal Data:* b Anthony, Kans, Jan 28, 17; m 45; c 3. *Educ:* Phillips Univ, BA, 40; Univ Okla, MS, 47; Johns Hopkins Univ, ScD, 50. *Concurrent Pos:* Consult, St Anthony & Vet Admin Hosps. *Mem:* Sigma Xi; Am Soc Microbiol; fel Am Acad Microbiol; NY Acad Sci; Am Soc Trop Med & Hyg. *Res:* Viral diseases of man; influenza; herpes simplex; Rous sarcoma; arboviruses. *Mailing Add:* 4125 NW 61st Terr Oklahoma City OK 73112

SCOTT, LAWRENCE WILLIAM, FOOD SCIENCE, ANALYTICAL CHEMISTRY. *Current Pos:* RETIRED. *Personal Data:* b Manhattan, Kans, June 10, 24; m 49; c 3. *Educ:* Kans State Univ, BS, 51, MS, 54; Univ Mo, Columbia, PhD(food sci & nutrit), 70. *Prof Exp:* Res & qual control chemist, Gen Lab, Utah-Idaho Sugar Co, 54-61; assoc prof chem, Univ Wis, River Falls, 61-88. *Mem:* Inst Food Technologists. *Res:* Design of new experiments and modification of old to present interesting science to non-science students; laboratory safety. *Mailing Add:* 521 E Maple River Falls WI 54022

SCOTT, LELAND LATHAM, MATHEMATICS. *Current Pos:* assoc prof, 62-64, PROF MATH, UNIV LOUISVILLE, 64-, PROF GRAD SCH, 69- *Personal Data:* b Elba, Ill, Mar 31, 19; m 46; c 3. *Educ:* Southern Ill Univ, BS, 47; Univ Ill, MS, 48, PhD(math), 51. *Prof Exp:* Asst math, Univ Ill, 47-51; from asst prof to assoc prof, Univ Miss, 51-57; from assoc prof to prof, Southwestern at Memphis, 57-62. *Concurrent Pos:* Ford Found fac fel, 55-56. *Mem:* Am Math Soc; Math Asn Am; Asn Symbolic Logic. *Mailing Add:* 2817 Jermantown Rd No 309 Oakton VA 22124

SCOTT, LEONARD LEWY, JR, ALGEBRA. *Current Pos:* from assoc prof to prof, 71-86, MCCDONNEL-BERNARD PROF MATH, UNIV VA, 87- *Personal Data:* b Little Rock, Ark, Oct 17, 42; m 60; c 2. *Educ:* Vanderbilt Univ, BA, 64; Yale Univ, MA, 66, PhD(math), 68. *Prof Exp:* Instr math, Univ Chicago, 68-70; asst prof, Yale Univ, 70-71. *Concurrent Pos:* Mem ctr advan studies, Univ Va, 71-73; vis assoc prof, Univ Mich, 74-75; vis prof, Yale Univ, 78. *Mem:* Am Math Soc. *Res:* Finite permutation groups; representation theory; cohomology; algebraic groups. *Mailing Add:* Dept Math Univ Va Math & Astronomy Bldg Charlottesville VA 22903-3199

SCOTT, LINUS ALBERT, MECHANICAL ENGINEERING. *Current Pos:* PROF CHEM & MECH ENG & CHMN DEPT, UNIV SFLA, 64-, ASSOC DEAN ACAD AFFAIRS, 82- *Personal Data:* b Jacksonville, Fla, June 8, 23; m 43; c 2. *Educ:* Univ Fla, BME, 48, MSE, 51; Case Inst Technol, PhD(mech eng), 60. *Prof Exp:* From instr to asst prof mech eng, Univ Fla, 48-57; instr, Case Inst Technol, 57-58 & 59-60; assoc prof, Univ Fla, 60-62; prof, Univ Toledo, 63. *Mem:* Am Soc Mech Engrs. *Res:* Instrumentation and automatic control of industrial operations. *Mailing Add:* Col Eng Univ SFla Eng 118 4202 E Fowler Tampa FL 33620-9951

SCOTT, MACK TOMMIE, ANIMAL SCIENCE, VETERINARY MEDICINE. *Current Pos:* ASST PROF RES VET PHYSIOL & DIR EXP ANIMAL HOSP, MEHARRY MED COL, 63- *Personal Data:* b Grand Junction, Tenn, Dec 4, 31; m 58; c 2. *Educ:* Tenn State Univ, BS, 58; Tuskegee Inst, DVM, 62. *Prof Exp:* Instr clin vet med, Tuskegee Inst, 62-63. *Mem:* Am Vet Med Asn; Am Asn Lab Animal Sci. *Res:* Laboratory animal nutrition and diseases; cellular physiology; experimental production of kernicterus and study of the pathogenesis of hemolytic anemia and jaundice in new born rabbits. *Mailing Add:* 6128 Beals Lane Nashville TN 37218

SCOTT, MARION B(OARDMAN), CIVIL ENGINEERING. *Current Pos:* from asst prof to assoc prof, 46-57, head struct eng, 62-64, asst dean, 64-68, PROF CIVIL ENG, PURDUE UNIV, 57-, ASSOC DEAN ENG, 68- *Personal Data:* b Ashland, Nebr, Dec 9, 12; m 42; c 2. *Educ:* Univ Nebr, BSCE, 34; Purdue Univ, MSCE, 44. *Prof Exp:* Engr, State of Nebr Bur Rd & Irrig, 34-37; instr engr drawing, Purdue Univ, 37-41, instr civil eng, 42-44; engr, Third Locks Proj, CZ, 41-42; process engr & asst to head physics dept, Curtiss-Wright Res Lab, 44-46. *Mem:* AAAS; Am Soc Civil Engrs; Rwy Eng Asn; Soc Exp Stress Anal; Am Soc Eng Educ; Sigma Xi. *Res:* Analysis, stress measurement and performance of structural steel bridges, buildings and structural components. *Mailing Add:* 1500 N Grant St West Lafayette IN 47906-2477

SCOTT, MARTHA RICHTER, MARINE GEOCHEMISTRY. *Current Pos:* res assoc, 71-74, vis asst prof oceanog, 74-75, ASSOC PROF OCEANOG, TEX A&M UNIV, 80- *Personal Data:* b Dallas, Tex, July 8, 41. *Educ:* Rice Univ, BA, 63, PhD(geol), 66. *Prof Exp:* NSF fel geol, Yale Univ, 66-67; res assoc geol & oceanog, Fla State Univ, 67-69 & 70-71. *Concurrent Pos:* Assoc prog dir chem oceanog, NSF, 92-93. *Mem:* Am Geophys Union; Am Geol Inst; Am Soc Oceanog; Geochem Soc; AAAS. *Res:* Interaction of land-derived materials with sea water; uranium series isotopes in sea water and sediments; adsorption chemistry in marine environment; incorporation of trace metals into ferromanganese deposits; chemistry of plutonium isotopes in the environment. *Mailing Add:* Dept Oceanog Tex A&M Univ College Station TX 77843-3146. *E-Mail:* Omnet: m.scott.martha

SCOTT, MARVIN WADE, BOTANY, MICROBIOLOGY. *Current Pos:* assoc prof, 66-71, PROF BIOL, LONGWOOD COL, 71-, CHMN DEPT NATURAL SCI, 70- *Personal Data:* b Clifton Forge, Sept 6, 36; m 62; c 2. *Educ:* Hampden-Sydney Col, BS, 59; Va Polytech Inst & State Univ, PhD(bot), 68. *Prof Exp:* Chmn dept sci, Lynchburg Pub Sch Syst, Va, 59-60; res asst bot, Longwood Col, 60-62; instr biol, Hampden-Sydney Col, 62-63. *Mem:* AAAS; Bot Soc Am. *Res:* Isolation and fermentation studies of Streptococcus lactis variety tardus; genetics and cytology studies of species of Illiamn. *Mailing Add:* Stevens Hall Longwood Col Farmville VA 23901

SCOTT, MARY CELINE, DRUG METABOLISM, SCIENTIFIC EDITOR-TECHNICAL WRITER. *Current Pos:* sr scientist, 89-92, SR TECH WRITER, SCHERING-PLOUGH RES INST, 93- *Personal Data:* b Los Angeles, Calif, July 14, 57. *Educ:* Univ Calif, Irvine, BS, 78; Calif State Univ, Long Beach, MS, 80; Purdue Univ, PhD(pharmacol), 85. *Prof Exp:* Teaching asst, Calif State Univ, Long Beach, 79-80; teaching asst, Purdue Univ, 80-82, res asst, 82, David Ross res fel, 83-85, res assoc, 88; fel, Mayo Found, 85-87; Dir, Vision Chem Ctr, Purdue Univ, 88-89. *Concurrent Pos:* Res asst, 77-78, Vet Adm Med Ctr, 78-80; Assoc prin scientist, Schering-Plough Res Inst, 93. *Mem:* AAAS; Am Chem Soc; Am Soc Pharmacol & Exp Therapeut; Soc Neurosci; Int Soc Study Xenobiotics; Sigma Xi. *Res:* Quality and consistency of all reports generated by department of drug metabolism and pharmacokinetics, and assisting in computerization. *Mailing Add:* Schering-Plough Res Inst 2015 Galloping Hill Rd K15-2880 Kenilworth NJ 07033-0569. *Fax:* 908-298-3966

SCOTT, MARY JEAN, MEDICAL PHYSICS, NUCLEAR PHYSICS. *Current Pos:* sr med physicist, 80-90, PRIN MED PHYSICIST, HILLBROW HOSP, JOHANNESBURG, 90- *Personal Data:* b Brooklyn, NY, Nov 8, 31; m 59, Edward C Silk; c John C, Roland H & Carol A. *Educ:* St Lawrence Univ, BS, 52; Johns Hopkins Univ, PhD(physics), 58; Joint Bd Theol Southern Africa, dipl, 90. *Prof Exp:* Vis asst physics, Brookhaven Nat Lab, 55, jr res assoc, 55-58; asst prof, Bryn Mawr Col, 58; vis res assoc nuclear physics, Atomic Energy Res Estab, Eng, 58-60; res assoc, Univ Witwatersrand, 60-61, lectr physics, 61-67; med physicist, Johannesburg Gen Hosp, 67-80. *Mem:* AAAS; Am Phys Soc; SAfrican Asn Physicists Med; SAfrican Inst Physics; SAfrican Soc Nuclear Med (secy-treas, 74-78); Am Asn Physics Teachers; Am Asn Physicists Med. *Res:* Proton polarization; radiobiology; effects of fractionated radiation therapy on cell populations and determination of cell parameters. *Mailing Add:* 15 Meyer St Oaklands Johannesburg 2192 South Africa. *Fax:* 27-11-728-5336

SCOTT, MATTHEW P, MOLECULAR GENETICS, HOMEOTIC GENES. *Current Pos:* PROF DEVELOP BIOL, STANFORD UNIV SCH MED, 90- *Personal Data:* b Boston, Mass, Jan 30, 53; c 1. *Educ:* Mass Inst Technol, BS, 75, PhD(biol), 80. *Prof Exp:* Postdoctoral fel, Ind Univ, 80-83; from asst prof to assoc prof, Univ Colo, Boulder, 83-90. *Concurrent Pos:* Jr fac res award, Am Cancer Soc, 83-84; res career develop award, NIH, 84-89; Searle Scholar's Award, 85-89; Young Investr Award, Passano Found, 90; co-ed, Current Opinions in Genetics & Develop; assoc investr, Howard Hughes Med Inst, 89-90, investr, 93-; vis prof genetics, Harvard Med Sch, 94-95. *Mem:* Genetics Soc Am; Soc Develop Biol (pres, 97-98); Am Soc Cell Biol; Am Soc Biochem & Molecular Biol. *Res:* Research is focused on understanding how genes control animal development; molecular biology is combined with mutants that alter the structures of animals to determine how patterns are formed during embryogenesis. *Mailing Add:* Dept Develop Biol Stanford Univ Sch Med Beckman Ctr B 300 Stanford CA 94305-5427. *Fax:* 650-725-7739; *E-Mail:* hfmps@forsythe.stanford.edu

SCOTT, MECKINLEY, APPLIED MATHEMATICS, STATISTICS. *Current Pos:* PROF MATH & CHAIRPERSON, WESTERN ILL UNIV, 91- *Personal Data:* b Shillong, India, Mar 1, 35; m 65; c 1. *Educ:* Presidency Col Calcutta, India, BS, 55; Gauhati Univ, India, MS, 57; Univ NC, Chapel Hill, PhD(statist), 64. *Prof Exp:* Asst prof math, Colo Sch Mines, 64-65; from asst prof to prof math, Univ Ala, Tuscaloosa, 65-90. *Mem:* Inst Math Statist; Oper Res Soc Am; Nat Coun Teachers Math; Math Asn Am. *Res:* Applied probability; theory of queues. *Mailing Add:* Math Dept Western Ill Univ Macomb IL 61455

SCOTT, MICHAEL DAVID, MARINE MAMMALOGY. *Current Pos:* SR SCIENTIST, INTER-AM TROP TUNA COMN, 79- *Personal Data:* b Minneapolis, Minn, May 12, 50; m 61; c 1. *Educ:* Univ Calif, Los Angeles, BA, 71, MA, 76, PhD(biol), 91. *Prof Exp:* Marine biologist, Univ Fla, 74-75; biol technician, US Fish & Wildlife Serv, 75-79. *Mem:* Marine Mammal Soc; Am Soc Mammal. *Res:* Conduct field studies of the behavior and life history of marine mammals, particularly dolphins; species management and protection programs. *Mailing Add:* Inter-Am Trop Tuna Comn 8604 La Jolla Shores Dr La Jolla CA 92037

SCOTT, MILTON LEONARD, NUTRITION. *Current Pos:* RETIRED. *Personal Data:* b Tempe, Ariz, Feb 21, 15; m 38, Dorothy Jaeger; c Gracie J (Saroka) & June M (Kopald). *Educ:* Univ Calif, AB, 37; Cornell Univ, PhD(nutrit), 45. *Honors & Awards:* Borden Award, 65; NY Farmers Award, 71; Borden Award, Am Inst Nutrit, 77; Klaus Schwarz Award, 80; Earle W Crampton Award, 81. *Prof Exp:* Vitamin chemist, Coop GLF Mills, Inc, Buffalo, NY, 37-42; fel, Cornell Univ, 42-44, res assoc, 44-45, from asst prof to prof nutrit, 45-76, Jacob Gould Schurman prof & chmn, Dept Poultry Sci, 76-79, Jacob Gould Schurman emer prof nutrit, 79- *Concurrent Pos:* Fel, Tech Univ Denmark, 61; consult, feed & pharmaceut industs. *Mem:* AAAS; Am Inst Nutrit; Am Poultry Sci Asn; Soc Exp Biol & Med. *Res:* Biochemistry and nutrition; vitamin E and selenium research. *Mailing Add:* 16 Spruce Lane Ithaca NY 14850

SCOTT, NORMAN JACKSON, JR, HERPETOLOGY, VERTEBRATE ECOLOGY. *Current Pos:* adj assoc prof biol, 75-90, BIOLOGIST, US FISH & WILDLIFE SERV, UNIV NMEX, 74-, ADJ ASSOC PROF BIOL, 90-; BIOLOGIST, NAT BIOL SURV. *Personal Data:* b Santa Monica, Calif, Sept 30, 34; m 56, Mattson; c Brian & Elena. *Educ:* Humboldt State Col, BS, 56, MS, 62; Univ Southern Calif, PhD, 69. *Prof Exp:* Prof zool, Univ Costa Rica, 64-66; course coordr, Orgn Trop Studies, Miami, 66-70; asst prof biol sci, Univ Conn, 58-74. *Concurrent Pos:* Adj prof biol, Univ Calif, Santa Barbara. *Mem:* Am Soc Ichthyologists & Herpetologists; Ecol Soc Am; Soc Syst Zool; Am Soc Zoologists; Asn Trop Biol; Soc Study Reptiles & Amphibians (pres, 87). *Res:* Herpetology; endangered species; tropical biology. *Mailing Add:* Nat Biol Surv Piedras Blancas Res Sta PO Box 70 San Simeon CA 93452-0070. *Fax:* 805-927-3308

SCOTT, NORMAN LAURENCE, CIVIL ENGINEERING. *Current Pos:* PRES & CHMN, CONSULT ENGRS GROUP INC, ILL, 66- *Personal Data:* b Meadow Grove, Nebr, Oct 17, 31; m 56, Joan Culbertson; c Douglas J. *Educ:* Univ Nebr, BS, 54. *Honors & Awards:* Henry C Turner Medal, Am Concrete Inst, 93. *Prof Exp:* first lt, USAF, 54-56; sales engr, RH Wright & Son, Ft Lauderdale, 56-58, mgr, Wright Palm Beach, 58-59; exec secy, Prestressed Concrete Inst, 59-63; gen mgr, Wiss, Janney, Elstner & Assoc, Ill, 63-66. *Mem:* Am Soc Civil Engrs; hon mem Am Concrete Inst (pres, 83-84). *Mailing Add:* 701 Chatham Dr Glenview IL 60025-4403

SCOTT, NORMAN R(OSS), COMPUTER ENGINEERING. *Current Pos:* RETIRED. *Personal Data:* b Brooklyn, NY, May 15, 18; m 50, Marjorie Fear; c Mari, George, Ian & Charles. *Educ:* Mass Inst Technol, BS & MS, 41; Univ Ill, PhD(elec eng), 50. *Prof Exp:* Asst prof elec eng, Univ Ill, 46-50; from asst prof to prof & assoc dean, Col Eng, Univ Mich, Ann Arbor, 51-68, dean, Dearborn Campus, 68-71, prof elec eng & computer sci, 71-87. *Concurrent Pos:* Ed, Trans Electronic Computer, Inst Elec & Electronics Engrs, 61-65; mem, math & computer sci res adv comt, AEC, 62-65. *Mem:* Asn Computer Mach; fel Inst Elec & Electronics Engrs. *Res:* Engineering and logical design of electronic computers; arithmetic systems for computers. *Mailing Add:* Dept Elec Eng & Computer Sci Univ Mich 500 S State St Ann Arbor MI 48109. *E-Mail:* norms@eecs.umich.edu

SCOTT, NORMAN ROY, BIOENGINEERING & BIOMEDICAL ENGINEERING. *Current Pos:* From asst prof to assoc prof agr eng, Cornell Univ, 62-76, chmn dept, 78-84, dir, Cornell Agr Exp Sta, 84-89, actg vpres comput info syst, 87-88, PROF AGR ENG, CORNELL UNIV, 76-, VPRES, RES & ADVAN STUDIES, 89- *Personal Data:* b Spokane, Wash, Sept 6, 36; m 61; c 3. *Educ:* Wash State Univ, BSAE, 58; Cornell Univ, PhD(agr eng), 62. *Honors & Awards:* Henry Giese Award, Am Soc Agr Engrs. *Mem:* Nat Acad Engrs; fel Am Soc Agr Engrs; Am Soc Heat, Refrig & Air-Conditioning Engrs; Instrument Soc Am; NY Acad Sci; Sigma Xi; Am Soc Eng Educ. *Res:* Biological engineering study of poultry involving heat transfer and physiological responses; biomathematical modeling of animal systems; animal calorimetry; electronic instrumentation in biological measurements. *Mailing Add:* 314 Day Hall Cornell Univ Ithaca NY 14853-2801

SCOTT, PAUL BRUNSON, FLUID DYNAMICS, PHYSICS. *Current Pos:* CONSULT, 90- *Personal Data:* b Flint, Mich, Sept 8, 37; m 60; c 1. *Educ:* Mass Inst Technol, SB & SM, 59, ScD(aeronaut eng), 65. *Prof Exp:* Mem staff vehicle anal, Space Tech Labs, 59-60; res staff molecular beam res, Mass Inst Technol, 65, asst prof aeronaut eng, 65-67; asst prof aerospace eng, Univ Southern Calif, 67-72; prin scientist, Xonics, Inc, 72-78; pres, Univ Consults, Inc, 78-80; vpres, Dinet Inc, 85-87; pres, Mammocare, Inc, 87-90. *Concurrent Pos:* Ford Found fel; owner, Touchstone Technol, 90- *Mem:* AAAS; Am Phys Soc; Am Solar Energy Soc; Int Asn Hydrogen Energy. *Res:* Rarefied gas dynamics; molecular beams; intermolecular collisions; x-ray imaging, chemical kinetics; isotope separation, chemical and ultraviolet lasers; photovoltaics; solar water pumping, hydrogen energy. *Mailing Add:* 17500 Lemarsh St Northridge CA 91325

SCOTT, PAUL G, CONNECTIVE TISSUE BIOCHEMISTRY, PROTEIN STRUCTURE. *Current Pos:* Assoc prof, Univ Alta, 81-86, prof oral biol, 86-96, chair, Dept Oral Biol, 93-95, HON PROF EXP SURG, UNIV ALTA, 86-, PROF BIOCHEM, 96- *Personal Data:* b Newcastle-Under-Lyme, Eng, June 11, 47; m 72; c 2. *Educ:* Univ Liverpool, Eng, PhD(biochem), 73. *Mem:* Protein Soc; Am Soc Biochem & Molecular Biol; Biochem Soc; Am Peptide Soc. *Res:* Collagen and proteoglycan structure and function. *Mailing Add:* Dept Biochem Univ Alta Edmonton AB T6G 2H7 Can. *Fax:* 403-492-6361; *E-Mail:* scottp@gpu.siv.ualberta.ca

SCOTT, PETER CARLTON, SCIENCE ADMINISTRATION, GRANT & CONTRACT ADMINISTRATION. *Current Pos:* instr chem, 69-72, chmn Dept Math & Sci, 72-73, DIR DIV SCI & TECHNOL, LINN-BENTON COMMUNITY COL, 73- *Personal Data:* b Seattle, Wash, Mar 20, 40. *Educ:* Ore State Univ, BS, 63; Purdue Univ, Lafayette, PhD(plant physiol), 66. *Prof Exp:* Instr chem, Univ Calif, Santa Cruz, 66-67. *Concurrent Pos:* Herman Frasch Found grant, Ore State Univ, 67-69; res assoc, Ore State Univ, 69- *Mem:* Nat Environ Training Asn; Am Chem Soc; Water Pollution Control Fedn; Am Pub Welfare Asn; Sigma Xi. *Res:* Physiology of plant growth regulators. *Mailing Add:* 3950 NE Me Hwy 20 Corvallis OR 97330

SCOTT, PETER DOUGLAS, BIOMEDICAL ENGINEERING. *Current Pos:* Asst prof, 70-77, ASSOC PROF ELEC ENG, STATE UNIV NY, BUFFALO, 77- *Personal Data:* b Kingston, Pa, Dec 13, 42; m 65; c 2. *Educ:* Cornell Univ, BS, 65, MS, 68, PhD(elec eng), 71. *Concurrent Pos:* Asst prof, Dept Biophys Sci, State Univ NY, Buffalo, 75-; dir, Surg Res Computer Lab, Buffalo Gen Hosp, 75- *Mem:* Sigma Xi; Inst Elec & Electronics Engrs; Am Soc Eng Educ; Comt Social Responsibility in Eng. *Res:* Cardiac electrophysiology; automated intensive care unit monitoring; systems theory; cybernetics. *Mailing Add:* Elec/Comput Eng/136 Bell Hall State Univ NY Buffalo-N Campus Buffalo NY 14260-2050

SCOTT, PETER HAMILTON, CHEMISTRY. *Current Pos:* VPRES TECHNOL, COOLEY INC, 85- *Personal Data:* b Providence, RI, Apr 6, 36; m 60; c 3. *Educ:* Brown Univ, ScB, 60; Lehigh Univ, PhD(chem), 65. *Prof Exp:* Sr res chemist, Olin Res Ctr, Olin Mathieson Chem Corp, 65-67, sr res chemist II, 68-70; closure res mgr, Dewey & Almy Chem Div, W R Grace & Co, 70-75, asst dir res, 75-80, dir res, 80-83; dir technol, Georel Corp, 83-85. *Mem:* Am Chem Soc; Sci Res Soc Am; Soc Plastics Engrs; Am Asn Textile Chem & Colorists; Sigma Xi. *Res:* Reactions of nitrenes and nitrenelike intermediates; mechanisms of oxirane polymerization; organo-sulfur and heterocyclic chemistry; polyurethane chemistry, especially flame retardant polyurethanes; sealant compounds. *Mailing Add:* Cooley Inc PO Box 939 Pawtucket RI 02862-0939

SCOTT, PETER JOHN, TAXONOMY. *Current Pos:* ASSOC PROF BOT & CUR HERBARIUM, MEM UNIV NFLD, 73- *Personal Data:* b Toronto, Can, July 2, 48. *Educ:* Univ Alta, BSc Hons, 70; Mem Univ Nfld, PhD(taxonomy), 73. *Concurrent Pos:* Dir, Bot Garden, Mem Univ Nfld, 94-97. *Mem:* Sigma Xi; Am Soc Plant Taxonomists; Can Bot Asn. *Res:* Flora of Newfoundland: origin, history and relationships with other floras. *Mailing Add:* Biol Dept Mem Univ Nfld St John's NF A1B 3X9 Can. *Fax:* 709-737-3018; *E-Mail:* pscott@plate.ucs.mun.ca

SCOTT, PETER LESLIE, PHYSICS. *Current Pos:* ASSOC PROF PHYSICS, UNIV CALIF, SANTA CRUZ, 66- *Personal Data:* b San Francisco, Calif, May 14, 33; m 77; c 3. *Educ:* Univ Calif, Berkeley, AB, 55, PhD(physics), 62; Univ Mich, MA, 57. *Prof Exp:* NSF fel, 62-63; asst prof physics, Stanford Univ, 63-66. *Concurrent Pos:* Alfred P Sloan fel, 64-68; Fulbright-Hays fel, Galway, Ireland, 70-71, Danforth assoc, 79-85. *Mem:* Fel Am Phys Soc. *Res:* Magnetic resonance; solid state spectroscopy; nonlinear dynamics. *Mailing Add:* Dept Physics Univ Calif Santa Cruz CA 95064-1099

SCOTT, PETER MICHAEL, MYCOTOXINS. *Current Pos:* RES SCIENTIST ANALYTICAL & ORG CHEM, CAN DEPT NAT HEALTH & WELFARE, 65- *Personal Data:* b Blackpool, Eng, Aug 20, 38; UK & Can citizen; m 89, Ellen Volder; c Carol & Susan. *Educ:* Cambridge Univ, BA, 59. PhD(org chem), 62, MA, 63. *Honors & Awards:* Harvey W Wiley Award, Asn Anal Chemist, 89. *Prof Exp:* NATO fel, Univ Calif, Berkeley, 62-64; fel, Univ BC, 64-65. *Concurrent Pos:* Chmn, Joint Mycotoxins Comt, Asn Off Analytical Chemists, 76-92, Gen Referee Mycotoxins, 82-92; Natural toxins methods comt, 92- & off methods Bd, 92-; mem Mycotoxins Working Group, Int Union Pure & Appl Chem, 79-, adv bd, Mycotoxin Res, 84-; ed bd, J Food Protection, 84-, Appl & Environ Microbiol, 86-, Microbiol Aliments & Nutrit, 87-, J Nat Toxins 93-, Regional Ed Can Food Additive Couram, 92- *Mem:* fel Chem Inst Can; fel Can Inst Food Sci & Technol; fel Asn Off Anal Chemists Int; Int Union Pure & Appl Chem. *Res:* Mycotoxins and other fungal metabolites, isolation, identification and analysis in foodstuffs. *Mailing Add:* Health Protection Br Health Can Ottawa ON K1A 0L2 Can. *Fax:* 613-941-4775

SCOTT, RALPH ASA, JR, ANALYTICAL CHEMISTRY, RADIOCHEMISTRY. *Current Pos:* RETIRED. *Personal Data:* b Sterling, Ill, July 23, 30; m 59; c 2. *Educ:* Univ Ill, BS, 52; Univ Okla, MS, 54; Tex A&M Univ, PhD(plant physiol, biochem, org chem), 57. *Honors & Awards:* Patent Award & Eval Awards, US Govt, 65, 88. *Prof Exp:* Radiochemist, Okla Res Inst, 52-53; res plant breeder, W Atlee Burpee Seed Co, Calif, 54-55; prin res chemist & dir waste eval proj, Int Minerals & Chem Corp, Fla, 57-58; res plant physiologist, Olin Mathieson Chem Corp, NY, 58; plant physiologist, Cotton Res Ctr, Crops Res Div, Agr Res Serv, USDA, Phoenix, Ariz, 58-61, sr res plant physiologist, Boll Weevil Res Lab, Starkville, Miss, 61-62; chief chemist, US Dept Defense, USAF, 6571st Aeromed Res Lab, Holloman AFB, NMex, 62-64, sr chemist, Adv Test Tech, Joint Chiefs Staff, Deseret Test Ctr, Ft Douglas, Utah, 65-66; chief div chem, Dept Pub Health, DC, 66-67; chief nationwide aquatic plant control prog, Off Chief Engrs, 67-69, chief phys scientist, Explosives Safety Bd, Dept Defense, 69-88. *Concurrent Pos:* Int sci adv, Secy State, 69-; personal rep Secy Defense, Chem Munition Safety, Okinawa; prog chmn, Chem Health & Safety Div, Am Chem Soc, 78-80 & 83-84, vchmn, 81-82 & chmn, 83-84. *Mem:* Am Chem Soc; Am Soc Plant Physiol; fel Am Inst Chemists. *Res:* Residue analysis, quality control and toxicology; air and water pollution analysis control; allergies; carcinogenic chemicals mode of action; virological and microbiological chemistry as related to chemical ammunition. *Mailing Add:* PO Box 1104 Wickenburg AZ 85358

SCOTT, RALPH CARMEN, INTERNAL MEDICINE, CARDIOLOGY. *Current Pos:* prof, 68-90, EMER PROF MED, COL MED, UNIV CINCINNATI, 90- *Personal Data:* b Bethel, Ohio, June 7, 21; m 45; c 3. *Educ:* Univ Cincinnati, BS, 42, MD, 45; Am Bd Internal Med, dipl; Am Bd Cardiovasc Dis, dipl. *Prof Exp:* Resident & asst path, Col Med, Univ Cincinnati, 48-49, from instr to assoc prof med, 50-68; dir cardiac clin, Cincinnati Gen Hosp, 65-75. *Concurrent Pos:* Fel internal med & cardiol, Univ Cincinnati, 49-57; asst clinician internal med & cardiol, Cincinnati Gen Hosp, 50-51, clinician internal med, 52-, clinician cardiol, 52-55, asst chief clinician, 56-64, from asst attend physician to attend physician, 58-; attend physician, Vet Admin Hosp, 54-61, Holmes Hosp, 57- & Providence Hosp, Cincinnati, 71-; consult, USAF Hosp, Wright-Patterson AFB, 60-, Vet Admin Hosp, 62-85, Good Samaritan Hosp, 67-, Jewish Hosp, 68- & Children's Hosp, 68-85; fel coun clin cardiol, Am Heart Asn; staff, Med Ctr Univ Cincinnati. *Mem:* AMA; Int Cardiovasc Soc; fel Am Col Physicians; fel Am Col Chest Physicians; Am Heart Asn; Sigma Xi. *Res:* Electrocardiography. *Mailing Add:* 2955 Alpine Terr Cincinnati OH 45208-3407

SCOTT, RALPH MASON, RADIOLOGY. *Current Pos:* RETIRED. *Personal Data:* b Leemont, Va, Nov 23, 21; m 46, Alice Francisco; c Susan (Taylor), Ralph M Jr & John T. *Educ:* Univ Va, BA, 47; Med Col Va, MD, 50. *Prof Exp:* Radiotherapist, Robert Packer Hosp, Sayre, Pa, 57-59; asst prof radiol, Univ Chicago, Sch Med, 59-60; assoc prof, Univ Louisville, Col Med, 60-64, prof radiol, 64-77, dir radiation ther, 60-77; prof radiol & chmn, Dept Radiation Ther, Sch Med, Univ Md, 78-80; dir, Dept Radiation Med, Christ Hosp, Cincinnati, Ohio, 83- 92. *Concurrent Pos:* Pres, Am Bd Radiol, 72-74; clin prof radiol, Col Med, Univ Cincinnati, 83-92. *Mem:* Am Radium Soc; Am Col Radiol; Am Roentgen Ray Soc; Radiol Soc NAm; Asn Univ Radiol. *Res:* Clinical radiation therapy. *Mailing Add:* 5516 Tecumseh Circle Louisville KY 40207

SCOTT, RAYMOND PETER WILLIAM, PHYSICAL CHEMISTRY, ANALYTICAL CHEMISTRY. *Current Pos:* dir appl res, 70-85, CONSULT, PERKIN ELMER CORP, 85-; DIR, DEPT PHYS CHEM, HOFFMANN-LA ROCHE INC, 69- *Personal Data:* b Erith, Eng, June 20, 24; m 46; c 2. *Educ:* Univ London, BSc, 46, DSc(chem), 58; FRIC, 58. *Honors & Awards:* Chromatography Award, Am Chem Soc, 77; Tswett Medal Chromatography, Int Chromatography Symp, 78. *Prof Exp:* Lab mgr phys chem, Benzole Prod Res Labs, 50-60; div mgr phys chem, Unilever Res Labs, 60-69. *Concurrent Pos:* Chartered chemist, UK, 76- *Mem:* Royal Soc Chem; Am Chem Soc; Chromatogr Soc; fel Am Inst Chem. *Res:* Separations technology; gas chromatography; liquid chromatography; exclusion chromatography; gas chromatography/mass spectroscopy; liquid chromatography/mass spectroscopy; general physical chemical instrumentation; computer technology and data processing. *Mailing Add:* 2 Sprucewood Lane Avon CT 06001

SCOTT, RICHARD ANTHONY, APPLIED MATHEMATICS. *Current Pos:* from asst prof to assoc prof, 67-77, PROF ENG MECH, UNIV MICH, ANN ARBOR, 77-, ASSOC CHMN, DEPT MECH ENG & APPL MECH, 87- *Personal Data:* b Cork, Ireland, May 5, 36; m 67. *Educ:* Univ Col, Cork, BSc, 57, MSc, 59; Calif Inst Technol, PhD(eng sci), 64. *Prof Exp:* Lectr appl mech, Calif Inst Technol, 64-65, res fel, 65-67. *Concurrent Pos:* Consult, Am Math Soc Math Rev, 68- *Mem:* Am Soc Mech Engrs; Am Acad Mech; Sigma Xi; Soc Indust & Appl Math. *Res:* Wave propagation in solids; elastic wave propagation; linear, nonlinear and random vibrations of solids; dynamics. *Mailing Add:* 118 Auto Lab Univ Mich Dept Mech Eng Ann Arbor MI 48109

SCOTT, RICHARD ROYCE, FLUID MECHANICS. *Current Pos:* ASSOC PROF MECH ENG, UNIV SOUTHWESTERN LA, 75- *Personal Data:* b Fairfield, Ala, Mar 19, 33; m 69; c 1. *Educ:* Univ Miss, BSME, 60; Univ Ala, PhD(eng mech), 68. *Prof Exp:* Proj engr, Procter & Gamble, Inc, 60-62; asst prof systs eng, Wright State Univ, 68-77. *Res:* Supersonic fluidics; pollution control of automotive engines. *Mailing Add:* Dept Mech Eng Univ Southwestern La PO Box 44170 Lafayette LA 70504-4170

SCOTT, RICHARD WALTER, PLANT ECOLOGY, PLANT TAXONOMY. *Current Pos:* instr, 75-86, PROF BIOL, CENT WYO COL, 87- *Personal Data:* b Modesto, Calif, June 30, 41; m 61, Beverly J Wilson; c Suzanne E & Kevin R. *Educ:* Univ Wyo, BS, 64, MS, 66; Univ Mich, MA, 69, PhD(plant ecol), 72. *Prof Exp:* NDEA fel plant ecol, Univ Mich, 66-69; asst prof biol, Albion Col, 69-75. *Concurrent Pos:* Bd mem, Nature Conservancy. *Mem:* Sigma Xi; Am Polar Soc. *Res:* Mountain ecosystems and plant community structure; Alpine plant communities of Western NAmerica biodiversity; alpine flora of the Rocky Mountains; rare and endangered plant species. *Mailing Add:* Div Math Sci & Educ, Dept Biol Cent Wyo Col Riverton WY 82501. *Fax:* 307-855-2094; *E-Mail:* dscott@interserve1.cwc.whecn.edu

SCOTT, ROBERT ALLEN, BIOPHYSICAL CHEMISTRY, BIOINORGANIC CHEMISTRY. *Current Pos:* assoc prof chem & biochem, 87-91, co-dir, Ctr Metalloenzyme Studies, 93-96, PROF CHEM & BIOCHEM, UNIV GA, ATHENS, 91-, HEAD CHEM, 96- *Personal Data:* b Dixon, Ill, Apr 25, 53; c 1. *Educ:* Univ Ill, Urbana, BS, 75; Calif Inst Technol, PhD(chem), 80. *Honors & Awards:* Presidential young investr award, 85-90. *Prof Exp:* NIH fel, Stanford Univ, 79-81; asst prof inorg chem, Univ Ill, Urbana, 81-87. *Concurrent Pos:* Alfred P Sloan Res Fel, 86-88. *Mem:* Am Chem Soc; AAAS; Protein Soc; Am Soc Biochem & Molecular Biol; Soc Biol Inorg Chem. *Res:* Inorganic and physical aspects of biologically important systems; kinetics of electron transfer in metalloenzymes and extended x-ray absorption fine structure studies of metalloproteins and models; site-directed mutagenesis studies of protein determinants of metallo protein stability and redox chemistry. *Mailing Add:* Dept Chem Univ Ga Athens GA 30602-2556. *Fax:* 706-542-9454; *E-Mail:* scott@bscr.uga.edu

SCOTT, ROBERT BLACKBURN, GEOLOGY. *Current Pos:* AT US GEOL SURV. *Personal Data:* b Wilmington, Del, July 22, 37; m 62. *Educ:* Univ Ala, BS, 60; Rice Univ, PhD(geol), 65. *Prof Exp:* Res geologist, Yale Univ, 65-67; asst prof geol, Fla State Univ, 67-71; assoc prof geol, Tex A&M Univ, 71- *Concurrent Pos:* Petrologist, Trans-Atlantic Geotraverse Proj, Nat Oceanic & Atmospheric Admin, 71- *Mem:* AAAS; Geochem Soc; Geol Soc Am; Mineral Soc Am; Am Geophys Union. *Res:* Marine volcanism; oceanic basalt geochemistry and petrology; seawater-basalt reactions and equilibria. *Mailing Add:* Off Regional Geol MS 913 Denver Fed Ctr Denver CO 80225

SCOTT, ROBERT BLACKBURN, JR, organic chemistry; deceased, see previous edition for last biography

SCOTT, ROBERT BRADLEY, GERIATRIC MEDICINE, HEMATOLOGY. *Current Pos:* from asst prof to assoc prof med, 65-74, assoc dean clin activ, 79-82, PROF MED, PATH & BIOCHEM, MED COL VA, VA COMMONWEALTH UNIV, 74- *Personal Data:* b Petersburg, Va, Nov 7, 33; m 58, Harriet Wyche; c 3. *Educ:* Univ Richmond, BS, 54; Med Col Va, MD, 58. *Prof Exp:* From intern to resident internal med, Bellevue & Mem Hosps, NY, 58-61; fel biol, Mass Inst Technol, 63-64, res assoc, 64-65. *Concurrent Pos:* Am Cancer Soc res scholar, 63-65; clin fel med, Mass Gen Hosp, 64-65; dir, Lab Hemat Res, 68-82; chief staff, Med Col Va Hosp, 79-82. *Mem:* Fel Am Col Physicians; Am Fedn Clin Res; Am Soc Hemat; Am Geriat Soc; Gerontological Soc Am. *Res:* Control of differentiation in normal and leukemic blood cell; cell biology; mechanism of cellular aging; geriatrics. *Mailing Add:* Med Col Va 1400 Westwood Ave Suite 106 Med Col Va Richmond VA 23227

SCOTT, ROBERT EDWARD, ANALYTICAL CHEMISTRY. *Current Pos:* res anal chemist & group leader, Chem Div, Pittsburgh Plate Glass Co, 53-65, sr res supvr, Inorg Phys Res Dept, 65-67, SR RES SUPVR CHEM DIV, ANALYTICAL LABS, PPG INDUSTS, INC, 68- *Personal Data:* b Crystal Springs, Miss, Oct 19, 22; m 45; c 3. *Educ:* Univ Tex, BA, 43, MA, 44. *Prof Exp:* Anal chemist, New Prod Develop Lab, Gen Elec Co, Mass, 48-53. *Mem:* Am Chem Soc. *Res:* Wet chemical, ultraviolet-visible-infrared spectrophotometric, polarographic, x-ray, emission spectrographic and gas chromatographic analytical techniques applied to chlorosilanes, silicones, phenolics, autoxidation process hydrogen peroxide, chrome chemicals and chlorinated hydrocarbons. *Mailing Add:* 3214 Kensington Dr Corpus Christi TX 78414-3529

SCOTT, ROBERT EUGENE, EXPERIMENTAL PATHOLOGY, CANCER RESEARCH. *Current Pos:* PROF PATH & HEAD SECT EXP PATH, MAYO CLIN, 80- *Personal Data:* b Terre Haute, Ind, Oct 19, 41. *Educ:* Vanderbilt Univ, MD, 67. *Mem:* Am Asn Pathologist; Am Soc Cell Biol; Am Asn Cancer Res; Int Acad Path; Int Cell Cycle Soc; Int Soc Differentiation. *Mailing Add:* Dept Path Univ Tenn 800 Madison Ave 576 BMH Memphis TN 38163-0001. *Fax:* 901-528-6979

SCOTT, ROBERT FOSTER, PATHOLOGY. *Current Pos:* from asst prof to prof, 59-94, EMER PROF PATH, ALBANY MED COL, 94- *Personal Data:* b Alberta, Can, June 23, 25; m 54; c 3. *Educ:* Univ Alta, BSc, 49, MD, 51; FRCP, 58. *Prof Exp:* Asst prof path, Univ BC, 57-58, clin instr, 58-59. *Concurrent Pos:* Fel, Nat Res Coun Can, 54-55, Life Ins Med Res Found, 56-57; mem, Cardiovasc Study Sect, NIH, 64-68, Path Study Sect, NIH, 73-77; exec mem, Arterrosclerosis Coun, Am Heart Asn, 71-73; asst to dean acad affairs, Albany Med Col, 79-80, assoc to dean, 80- *Res:* Kinetics of arterial wall cells with regard to atherosclerosis utilizing experimental models. *Mailing Add:* Dept Path Albany Med Col 47 New Scotland Ave Albany NY 12208

SCOTT, ROBERT LANE, PHYSICAL CHEMISTRY. *Current Pos:* from asst prof to prof, 48-92, chmn dept, 70-75, EMER PROF PHYS CHEM, UNIV CALIF, LOS ANGELES, 93- *Personal Data:* b Santa Rosa, Calif, Mar 20, 22; m 44, Elizabeth S Hunter; c Joanna I, Jonathan A, David S & Janet H. *Educ:* Harvard Univ, SB, 42; Princeton Univ, MA, 44, PhD(chem), 45. *Honors & Awards:* Fulbright award, 68-69; Joel Henry Hildebrand Award, Am Chem Soc, 84. *Prof Exp:* Asst chem, Princeton Univ, 42-43, Manhattan Proj, 44-45; scientist, Manhattan Proj, Los Alamos Sci Lab, 45-46; Jewett fel, Univ Calif, 46-48. *Concurrent Pos:* Guggenheim fel, 55; NSF sr fel, 61-62. *Mem:* Fel AAAS; Am Chem Soc; fel Am Phys Soc. *Res:* Statistical thermodynamics of liquids and solutions; high polymer solutions; fluorocarbon solutions; hydrocarbon solutions; critical phenomena; tricritical points; solubility and phase equilibria. *Mailing Add:* Dept Chem & Biochem Univ Calif Los Angeles CA 90024-1569. *Fax:* 310-206-5381

SCOTT, ROBERT NEAL, INDUSTRIAL CHEMISTRY. *Current Pos:* Sr res chemist polymer chem, 67-71, group leader org res & develop, 71-75, sect leader org & inorg res & develop, 75-78, sect mgr org & inorg res & develop, 78-82, mgr anal & res & develop admin, 82-84, ASSOC DIR RES, OLIN CORP, 84- *Personal Data:* b Pawtucket, RI, Mar 8, 41; m 63; c 2. *Educ:* Brown Univ, ScB, 63; Northwestern Univ, PhD(chem), 68. *Mem:* Am Chem Soc; Am Soc Lubrication Engrs. *Res:* High temperature polymers; synthetic lubricants; surfactants textile chemicals; hydrazine applications and derivative chemistry; electronic chemicals. *Mailing Add:* Dept Chem Northwestern Univ Evanston IL 60208-3113

SCOTT, ROBERT NELSON, REHABILITATION ENGINEERING, CLINICAL ENGINEERING. *Current Pos:* From asst prof to assoc prof, 56-70, dir, Bioeng Inst, 65-90, PROF ELEC ENG, UNIV NB, 70- *Personal Data:* b St John, NB, Apr 30, 33; m 52; c 5. *Educ:* Univ NB, BSc, 55. *Hon Degrees:* DSc, Acadia Univ, 81. *Mem:* Sr mem Inst Elec & Electronics Engrs; fel Can Med & Biol Eng Soc; Asn Advan Med Instruments. *Res:* Biomedical engineering; myoelectric control of artifical limbs. *Mailing Add:* Dept Elec Eng Univ NB Col Hill PO Box 4400 Fredericton NB E3B 5A3 Can

SCOTT, ROBERT W, geology, paleontology, for more information see previous edition

SCOTT, RONALD E, ELECTRICAL ENGINEERING. *Current Pos:* PROF ENG, NORTHEASTERN UNIV, 83- *Personal Data:* b Leslie, Sask, Mar 25, 21; US citizen; c 1. *Educ:* Univ Toronto, BASc, 43, MASc, 46; Mass Inst Technol, ScD(elec eng), 50. *Prof Exp:* Res assoc elec eng, Mass Inst Technol, 46-50, asst prof, 50-55; prof, Northeastern Univ, 55-60, dean eng, 60-67; dean eng, Col Petrol & Minerals, Dhahran, 67-78; proj head, Nat Inst Elec & Electronics, Algeria, 78-81; dean eng technol, Wentworth Inst Technol, 81-83. *Mem:* Fel Inst Elec & Electronics Engrs; Am Soc Eng Educ; Soc Am Mil Engrs. *Res:* Circuit theory solid state microelectronics reliability and medical electronics. *Mailing Add:* Northeasten Univ 360 Huntington Ave Boston MA 02115

SCOTT, RONALD F(RASER), SOIL MECHANICS. *Current Pos:* from asst prof to prof civil eng, 58-87, DOTTIE & DICK HAYMAN PROF ENG, CALIF INST TECHNOL, 87- *Personal Data:* b London, Eng, Apr 9, 29; m 59; c 3. *Educ:* Glasgow Univ, BSc, 51; Mass Inst Technol, SM, 53, ScD(soil mech), 55. *Honors & Awards:* Walter Huber Res Prize, Am Soc Civil Engrs, 69, Norman Medal, 72, Thomas A Middlebrooks Award, 82, Tersaghi lectr, 83; Newcomb Cleveland Award, AAAS, 76; Rankine lectr, Brit Geotech Soc, 87. *Prof Exp:* Asst soil mech, Mass Inst Technol, 51-55; soil engr, Corps Engrs, US Dept Army, 55-57; div soil engr, Racey, MacCallum & Assocs, Ltd, Can, 57-58. *Concurrent Pos:* Churchill fel, Churchill Col, Eng, 72; Guggenheim fel, 72; prin investr, Jet Propulsion Lab, NASA, mem, Soil Mech Team, Apollo Manned Lunar Missions & Phys Properties Team, NASA Viking; consult, pvt indust & govt agencies. *Mem:* Nat Acad Eng; Am Soc Civil Engrs; Am Geophys Union. *Res:* Soil engineering and mechanics; soil dynamics; earthquake engineering; author of 180 technical publications and 4 books. *Mailing Add:* 2752 N Santa Anita Ave Altadena CA 91001

SCOTT, RONALD MCLEAN, BIOCHEMISTRY, TOXICOLOGY. *Current Pos:* From asst prof to assoc prof, 59-68, PROF CHEM, EASTERN MICH UNIV, 68- *Personal Data:* b Detroit, Mich, Apr 16, 33; m 57; c 3. *Educ:* Wayne State Univ, BS, 55; Univ Ill, PhD(biochem), 59. *Concurrent Pos:* Exchange prof, Coventry Col, Eng, 71-72; vis lectr, Warwick Univ, Eng, 72. *Mem:* Am Chem Soc; Sigma Xi; AAAS. *Res:* Hydrogen bonding in solution, solvation interactions. *Mailing Add:* Dept Chem Eastern Mich Univ Ypsilanti MI 48197

SCOTT, ROY ALBERT, III, PHYSICAL CHEMISTRY, MOLECULAR BIOLOGY. *Current Pos:* ASSOC PROF BIOCHEM & MOLECULAR BIOL, OHIO STATE UNIV, 68- *Personal Data:* b Pottsville, Pa, Mar 22, 34; m 58; c 2. *Educ:* Cornell Univ, AB, 58, PhD(chem), 64. *Prof Exp:* Asst prof chem, Cornell Univ, 63-66; asst prof biophys, Univ Hawaii, 66-68. *Mem:* Am Chem Soc; Am Phys Soc. *Res:* Physical chemistry of biological macromolecules. *Mailing Add:* Dept Biochem Col Med Ohio State Univ 484 W 12th Ave Columbus OH 43210-1214

SCOTT, SHERYL ANN, developmental neurobiology, for more information see previous edition

SCOTT, STEVEN DONALD, ECONOMIC GEOLOGY, MARINE GEOLOGY. *Current Pos:* from asst prof to assoc prof, 69-79, assoc chmn, 80-84, PROF GEOCHEM, UNIV TORONTO, 79-, CHMN GEOL ENG, 88-, DIR, SCOTIABANK MARINE GEOL RES LAB, 89- *Personal Data:* b Ft Frances, Ont, June 4, 41; m 63; c 2. *Educ:* Univ Western Ont, BSc, 63, MSc, 64; Pa State Univ, PhD(geochem), 68. *Honors & Awards:* Waldemar Lindgren Citation, Soc Econ Geologists & Silver Medal Excellence & Innovation Res, 95; Thayer-Lindsley; Bancroft Award, Royal Soc Can, 90. *Prof Exp:* Res assoc geochem, Pa State Univ, 68-69. *Concurrent Pos:* Lectr massive sulfide short courses, Univ Toronto, France, Finland, SAfrica, Ger, Australia, China & Switz; consult mining & marine indust, 70-; tech consult, television, radio, newspapers & magazines, 75-; vis prof, Australia, 76-77, 84, Japan, 77 & France, 85 & 93-; Can leader, US-Japan-Can-Kuroko Res Group, 78-83; second chmn, Mineral Deposits Div, Geol Asn Can, 78-80 & 81-82; vpres, Ocean Explor & Mining Consult, 82-88; prin investr, Can Res Seafloor Hydrothermal Vents & Sulfide Deposits, 83-86; mem, Can Nat Comt Ocean Drilling Prog, 85-90, chmn, 88-90, dir, 95; subj-of-interest, PBS Prog Planet Earth; co-producer, videotape, Explorer Ridge, 85; gov, Earth Sci Sect, Royal Soc Can, 89-90; coun, Int Asn Genesis Ore Deposits, 90-; Soc Geol Appl Ore Deposits, 91-; pres, Can Sci Submercible Facil, 96- *Mem:* Mineral Soc Am; Mineral Asn Can; Geol Asn Can; Soc Econ Geol; Soc Mining Geologists Japan; Am Geophys Union; fel Royal Soc Can; Int Asn Genesis Ore Deposits; Microbiol Asn Can; Int Marine Minerals Soc (pres, 95). *Res:* Modern seafloor hydrothermal systems and deposits; massive copper-zinc sulfide ores; marine geology and tectonics; physical geochemistry; oreforming processes by field and experimental methods; sulfide mineralogy; synthesis and crystal chemistry of metallic sulfides. *Mailing Add:* Dept Geol Earth Sci Ctr Univ Toronto 22 Russell St Toronto ON M5S 3B1 Can. *Fax:* 416-978-3938

SCOTT, STEWART MELVIN, cardiovascular surgery, thoracic surgery; deceased, see previous edition for last biography

SCOTT, THOMAS RUSSELL, NEUROPHYSIOLOGY. *Current Pos:* PROF PSYCHOL, UNIV DEL, 70-, ASSOC DEAN RES & GRAD STUDIES, 92- *Personal Data:* b Ridley Park, Pa, Oct 1, 44; m 67, Bonnie Kime; c Heather S, Ethan K & Heidi C. *Educ:* Princeton Univ, BA, 66; Duke Univ, PhD(biopsychol), 70. *Concurrent Pos:* Vis prof psychol, Rockefeller Univ, 80-82, Oxford Univ, 84, Japanese Inst Physiol, 87-88; prin investr, NIH, 71-93, NSF, 86-96. *Mem:* Fel Am Psychol Asn; Am Psychol Soc; Soc Neurosci; Asn Chemoreception Sci; Soc Study Ingestive Behav; AAAS. *Res:* Neural coding of taste information and the neural and humoral control of feeding in rats and primates. *Mailing Add:* 216 Orchard Rd Newark DE 19711. *Fax:* 302-831-6398; *E-Mail:* thomas.scott@mvs.udel.edu

SCOTT, THOMAS WALLACE, MEDICAL ENTOMOLOGY-INSECT TRANSMITTED DISEASES, ARBOUROLOGY-ARTHROPOD-BORNE DISEASES. *Current Pos:* from asst prof to assoc prof, 83-93, PROF MED ENTOM, UNIV MD, 93- *Personal Data:* b Plainfield, NJ, Nov 29, 50; m 78, Judith M Gramstrup; c Emily M & Valerie E. *Educ:* Bowling Green State Univ, BS, 73, MS, 77; Pa State Univ, PhD(ecol), 81. *Prof Exp:* Fel, Yale Univ, 81-83. *Concurrent Pos:* Sr res assoc, Nat Res Coun, Armed Forces Res Inst Med Sci, Bangkok, Thailand, 90. *Mem:* Entom Soc Am; Am Mosquito Control Asn. *Res:* Role of biting insects in disease transmission; ecological basis and epidemiological significance of details concerning mosquito blood feeding behavior; how mosquito vectors contribute to the evolution and diversification of viral diseases. *Mailing Add:* Dept Entom Univ Md College Park MD 20742-0001

SCOTT, THOMAS WALTER, SOIL FERTILITY. *Current Pos:* From asst prof to assoc prof, 59-74, Ombudsman, 91-93, PROF SOIL SCI, CORNELL UNIV, 74-, MEM DEPT AGRON, 77- *Personal Data:* b Sewickley, Pa, Nov 10, 29; wid; c 4. *Educ:* Pa State Univ, BS, 52; Kans State Univ, MS, 56; Mich State Univ, PhD(soil sci), 59. *Concurrent Pos:* Travel grants from Cornell Univ & NY lime & fertilizer industs to Cambridge Univ, 66-67; USAID assignment to PR, 73-, temp assignment to Panama, 82-83. *Mem:* Am Soc Agron; Soil Sci Soc Am; Soil Conserv Soc Am. *Res:* Undergraduate teaching; animal waste management; soil fertility research and extension; soil fertility research on tropical soils; soil management. *Mailing Add:* Dept Soil Crop & Atmospheric Sci 236 Emerson Hall Cornell Univ Ithaca NY 14853-0001

SCOTT, TOM E, METALLURGY. *Current Pos:* DIR, INST MATS PROCESSING, MICH TECH UNIV, 85- *Personal Data:* b Cleveland, Ohio, Sept 10, 33; m 59; c 4. *Educ:* Case Inst Technol, BS, 56, MS, 58, PhD(phys metall), 62. *Prof Exp:* Res metallurgist, Int Nickel Co, Ind, 61-63; asst prof mech metall, Iowa State Univ, 63-69, assoc prof metall, 69-72, prof metall, 72-81, prof chief, Ames Lab, 75-81; sr tech supvr, Aluminum Co Am, 81-82; from mgr, fabricating technol to mgr, Metal Matrix Composite Develop Dept, Agr Res Ctr Oper, 82-85. *Mem:* Am Soc Metals; Am Inst Mining, Metall & Petrol Engrs; Nat Asn Corrosion Engrs. *Res:* Hydrogen embrittlement; embrittlements; ferrous alloys; deformation; fracture mechanisms. *Mailing Add:* Alcan World Prod 6060 Parkland Blvd Mayfield Heights OH 44124

SCOTT, TOM KECK, PLANT SEEDLING GROWTH & DEVELOPMENT. *Current Pos:* PROF BIOL, UNIV NC, CHAPEL HILL, 82-, PROG MGR, GRAVITATIONAL BIOL, NASA, 94- *Personal Data:* b St Louis, Mo, Aug 4, 31; m 90, Margaret Ray; c David, Stephen, John & Cynthia. *Educ:* Pomona Col, BA, 54; Stanford Univ, MA, 59, PhD(biol), 61. *Prof Exp:* Teaching fel biol, 56-60, res asst, Stanford Univ, 57-61; res assoc, Princeton Univ, 61-63; from asst prof to assoc prof, Oberlin Col, 63-69; from asst prof to prof bot, Univ NC, 69-82, chmn biol curriculum, 70-75, chmn dept, 72-82, dir res serv, 85-90. *Concurrent Pos:* Vis res fel, Univ Nottingham, 67-68; Fulbright lectr, 72-73; assoc, Danforth Found, 73-80; chmn space biol adv panel, NASA, 83-89, plant biol discipline working group, 88-92. *Mem:* Fel AAAS; Bot Soc Am; Am Soc Plant Physiol; Sigma Xi; Am Inst Biol Sci; Am Soc Gravitational & Space Biol; Nat Acad Sci. *Res:* Plant growth and development; auxin relationships and transport; growth regulator interactions; hormone physiology in seedlings. *Mailing Add:* Life Sci Div Code UL NASA Hq Washington DC 20546

SCOTT, VERNE H(ARRY), CIVIL ENGINEERING, HYDROLOGY. *Current Pos:* Res & irrig engr, hydrol, 46-47, assoc prof irrig, 48-63, chmn Dept Water Sci & Eng, 64-71, PROF WATER SCI & CIVIL ENG & HYDROLOGIST, UNIV CALIF, DAVIS, 63- *Personal Data:* b Salem, Ore, June 19, 24; m 48; c 3. *Educ:* Univ Mich, BS, 45, MS, 48; Colo State Univ, PhD(irrig eng), 59. *Concurrent Pos:* Dir, Campus Work-Learn Prog, Univ Calif, Davis, 63- *Mem:* Am Soc Eng Educ; Am Soc Civil Engrs; Am Soc Agr Engrs; Am Geophys Union. *Res:* Ground water and water resources. *Mailing Add:* Dept Land Air & Water Davis CA 95616

SCOTT, W(ILLIAM) RICHARD, SOCIOLOGY OF MEDICINE & ORGANIZATIONS. *Current Pos:* From asst prof to assoc prof, 60-69, PROF, DEPT SOCIOL, STANFORD UNIV, 69-, DIR, STANFORD CTR ORGN RES, 88- *Personal Data:* b Parsons, Kans, 32; m 55; c 3. *Educ:* Univ Kans, BA, 54, MA, 55; Univ Chicago, PhD, 61. *Honors & Awards:* Richard D Irwin Award, Acad Mgt. *Concurrent Pos:* Fel, Ctr Advan Study Behav Sci, 89-90. *Mem:* Inst Med-Nat Acad Sci; Sociol Res Asn; Acad Mgt; Am Sociol Asn. *Res:* Structuring of the field of medical care organizations during the past three decades as they respond to changing technological, professional and policy developments. *Mailing Add:* 940 Lathrop Pl Stanford CA 94305. *Fax:* 650-725-6471; *E-Mail:* scottwr@leland.stanford.edu

SCOTT, WALTER ALVIN, BIOCHEMISTRY, CELL BIOLOGY. *Current Pos:* ASST PROF BIOCHEM, SCH MED, UNIV MIAMI, 75- *Personal Data:* b Los Angeles, Calif, Feb 1, 43; m 70. *Educ:* Calif Inst Technol, BS, 65; Univ Wis, PhD(physiol chem), 70. *Prof Exp:* Fel cell biol dept biophys & biochem, Univ Calif, San Francisco, 70-73; fel tumor virol, Dept Microbiol, Med Sch, Johns Hopkins Univ, 73-75. *Concurrent Pos:* NSF fel, 70-71; Jane Coffin Childs Mem Fund fel, 71-72; NIH fel, 72-73 & 74-75; NIH grant, 75-78 & 78-81; NSF grant, 78-79. *Mem:* Am Soc Microbiol; AAAS; Sigma Xi. *Res:* Structure and function of Simian Virus 40 chromatin; recombination involved in integration and excision of SV40 from cell chromosomes; transformation of pancreatic islet cells by SV40 mutants. *Mailing Add:* Dept Biochem Univ Miami Sch Med PO Box 01629 Miami FL 33101-6129

SCOTT, WALTER NEIL, REGULATION OF HORMONAL TRANSPORT. *Current Pos:* chmn dept, 82-87, PROF BIOL, NY UNIV, 82- *Personal Data:* b Mar 2, 35; m 59; c 2. *Educ:* Univ Louisville, MD, 60. *Prof Exp:* Assoc dean, Mt Sinai Sch Med, 76-82, prof physiol, 79-82. *Mem:* Am Soc Biol Chem; Am Physiol Soc; fel NY Acad Sci (pres, 83); fel NY Acad Med. *Mailing Add:* Dept Biol NY Univ 1009 Main Bldg Washington Sq E New York NY 10003-6607

SCOTT, WILLIAM ADDISON, III, BIOCHEMISTRY, GENETICS. *Current Pos:* Guest investr biochem genetics & USPHS grant, 67-69, res assoc, 69-71, asst prof, 71-77, ASSOC PROF BIOCHEM GENETICS, DEPT CELL PHYSIOL & IMMUNOL, ROCKEFELLER UNIV, 77- *Personal Data:* b Indianapolis, Ind, Apr 27, 40; m 66; c 1. *Educ:* Univ Ill, Urbana, BS, 62; Calif Inst Technol, PhD(biochem), 67. *Mem:* AAAS; Sigma Xi; Harvey Soc. *Res:* Biochemical basis of morphology; membrane structure and function. *Mailing Add:* Bristol-Myers Squibb Co PRI PO Box 4000 Princeton NJ 08543-4000

SCOTT, WILLIAM BEVERLEY, ICHTHYOLOGY. *Current Pos:* EMER PROF ZOOL, UNIV TORONTO, 83- *Personal Data:* b Toronto, Ont, July 7, 17; m 42, Milly G Fairfield; c Paul J & Patricia Louise. *Educ:* Univ Toronto, BA, 42, PhD(zool), 50. *Hon Degrees:* DSc, Univ NB, 85, Queen's Univ, 94. *Honors & Awards:* Centennial Medal, Govt Can, 67, Silver Jubilee Medal, 77. *Prof Exp:* Actg cur, Royal Ont Mus, 48-50, cur, Dept Ichthyol & Herpet, 50-76, assoc dir mus, 73-76; from assoc prof to prof zool, Univ Toronto, 63-83; exec dir, Huntsman Marine Lab, St Andrews, NB, 76-82, sr scientist, 82- *Mem:* Am Soc Ichthyol & Herpet (pres, 73); Can Soc Zool; Am Fisheries Soc; Soc Systs Zool; Fel Am Soc Fish Res Biologists; fel Royal Soc Can; Int Gaomme Fish Asn. *Res:* Systematics and distribution of Canadian freshwater fishes and Northwest Atlantic fishes, particularly salmonids, myctophids and scombrids; food and feeding; commercial fisheries. *Mailing Add:* Huntsman Marine Sci Ctr Brandy Cove Rd St Andrews NB E0G 2X0 Can. *Fax:* 506-529-1212; *E-Mail:* huntsman@nbnetnb.ca

SCOTT, WILLIAM D(OANE), CERAMICS ENGINEERING. *Current Pos:* PROF ENG, UNIV WASH, 65- *Personal Data:* b Lakewood, Ohio, Feb 17, 31; m 59; c 2. *Educ:* Univ Ill, BS, 54; Univ Calif, Berkeley, MS, 59, PhD(eng sci), 61. *Prof Exp:* Res fel, Univ Leeds, 61-63; asst prof eng, Univ Calif, Berkeley & Lawrence Radiation Lab, 64-65. *Mem:* Fel Am Ceramic Soc. *Res:* Nucleation and growth of crystals in glass; mechanical properties of ionic solids and oxides; structure of grain boundaries. *Mailing Add:* Box 352120 Univ Wash Seattle WA 98195-2120

SCOTT, WILLIAM EDWARD, GEOLOGY. *Current Pos:* GEOLOGIST, US GEOL SURV, 74- *Personal Data:* b Middletown, Conn, Sept 6, 47; m 70; c 2. *Educ:* St Lawrence Univ, BS, 69; Univ Wash, MS, 71, PhD(geol), 74. *Mem:* AAAS; Geol Soc Am; Am Quaternary Asn; Am Geophys Union. *Res:* Assessment of volcanic hazards in the Pacific Northwest; late Quaternary eruptive histories of volcanoes in Oregon; Quaternary glaciation and climate change in the Pacific Northwest. *Mailing Add:* David A Johnston Cascades Volcano Observ US Geol Surv 5400 MacArthur Blvd Vancouver WA 98661

SCOTT, WILLIAM EDWIN, CHEMISTRY. *Current Pos:* RETIRED. *Personal Data:* b Rome, NY, Apr 8, 18; m 41; c 3. *Educ:* Hamilton Col, NY, BS; Swiss Fed Inst Technol, DTechSc, 41. *Prof Exp:* Res chemist, Hoffman-La Roche, Inc, 41-56, asst to dir res, 56-59, res coordr, 59-63, dir res admin, 63-69, dir res tech servs, 69- *Mem:* Am Chem Soc; NY Acad Sci; Chem Soc. *Res:* Structure and synthesis of organic medicinal compounds; purification and structure determination of natural products; synthesis of steroid analogs. *Mailing Add:* Three Allen North Caldwell NJ 07006

SCOTT, WILLIAM EDWIN, PEDIATRIC OPHTHALMOLOGY, STRABISMUS. *Current Pos:* from asst prof to assoc prof, 71-79, PROF OPHTHAL, UNIV IOWA COL MED, 79- *Personal Data:* b Iowa City, Iowa, June 23, 37; m 60, Winifred Files; c Christopher & Douglas. *Educ:* Univ Iowa, BA, 59, MS, 62, MD, 64. *Honors & Awards:* Distinguished Serv Award, Am Asn Pediat Ophthal, 82, Honor Award, 90; Honor Award, Am Acad Ophthal, 92. *Prof Exp:* Intern, Wayne State Gen Hosp, Detroit, Mich, 64-65; residency ophthal, Univ Iowa Hosps & Clins, 67-70. *Concurrent Pos:* Fel pediat ophthal, Smith-Kettlewell Inst Visual Sci & Children's Nat Med Ctr, Washington, DC, 71; lectr, Ocular Motility Sect, Univ Tex, 91- *Mem:* Am Acad Ophthal; Am Asn Pediat Ophthal & Strabismus (pres, 88-90); Asn Res Vision & Ophthal; Am Orthoptic Coun. *Res:* Pediatric ophthalmology including the diagnosis and treatment of amblyopia and congenital esotropia, photoscreening for abnormal eye conditions, surgical correction of acquired esotropia and efficacy of oculinum. *Mailing Add:* Ophthal-W249-P Univ Iowa Hosps & Clins Iowa City IA 52242. *Fax:* 319-356-0363

SCOTT, WILLIAM JAMES, JR, TERATOLOGY, DEVELOPMENTAL BIOLOGY. *Current Pos:* Pharmaceut Mfrs Asn Found fel, 69-71, from asst prof res pediat to assoc prof res pediat, 71-78, PROF PEDIAT, CHILDREN'S HOSP RES FOUND, 78- *Personal Data:* b New York, NY, Dec 8, 37; m 62; c 2. *Educ:* Univ Ga, DVM, 61; George Washington Univ, PhD(anat), 69. *Honors & Awards:* Frank R Blood Award, Soc Toxicol, 77. *Prof Exp:* Dir teratol, Woodard Res Corp, 64-68. *Concurrent Pos:* Vet consult, Sch Med, George Washington Univ, 64-69; mem, Human Embryol & Develop Study Sect, NIH, 82-86. *Mem:* Teratol Soc; Am Asn Lab Animal Sci. *Res:* Determination of the mechanisms by which environmental factors interfere with embryonic development to produce congenital malformations. *Mailing Add:* Div Develop Biol Childrens Hosp Res Found 3333 Burnet Ave Cincinnati OH 45229-3039

SCOTT, WILLIAM RAYMOND, algebra; deceased, see previous edition for last biography

SCOTT, WILLIAM TAUSSIG, INTELLECTUAL BIOGRAPHY, ATMOSPHERIC PHYSICS. *Current Pos:* prof, 61-81, EMER PROF PHYSICS, UNIV NEV, RENO, 81- *Personal Data:* b Yonkers, NY, Mar 16, 16; m 42, 61; c 6. *Educ:* Swarthmore Col, BA, 37; Univ Mich, PhD(physics), 41. *Prof Exp:* Instr physics, Amherst Col, 41-44; asst prof math & physics, Deep Springs Jr Col, 44-45; from instr to prof physics, Smith Col, 45-61. *Concurrent Pos:* Res fel, Yale Univ, 59-60; vis prof, Univ Nev, 61-62; dir prog philos inquiry, 70-81; consult, Brookhaven Nat Lab, 47-53, Nat Bur Standards, 54-56; studio physicist, PSSC films, 58-59; res prof, Atmospheric Sci Ctr, Desert Res Inst, 64-; sr mem, Linacre Col, Oxford Univ, 69-70; mem analytical comt, Higher Educ Progs on Sci, Technol & Human Values Res Proj, Univ Mich, 75. *Mem:* Fel Am Phys Soc; Am Asn Physics Teachers; Sigma Xi. *Res:* Biography of Michael Polanyi; philosophy of science; theory of multiple scattering of fast charged particles; interaction of science and religion; theory of cloud droplet growth by condensation and coalescence. *Mailing Add:* 684 Benicia Dr No 64 Santa Rosa CA 95409-3058

SCOTT, WILLIAM WALLACE, MYCOLOGY. *Current Pos:* RETIRED. *Personal Data:* b Utica, NY, Oct 1, 20; m 42; c 4. *Educ:* Univ Vt, AB, 48, MS, 50; Univ Mich, PhD(bot), 55. *Prof Exp:* Res asst plant path, Univ Vt, 48-50; from assoc prof to prof bot, Va Polytech Inst, 55-64; assoc prog dir, NSF, 64-66; dean, Madison Col, Va, 66-68, chmn, Dept Bot, 68-75, assoc dean, Grad Sch, 75-78; prof bot, Eastern Ill Univ, 68-88. *Concurrent Pos:* Vis prof, Univ Wis, 60. *Mem:* Fel AAAS; Bot Soc Am; Mycol Soc Am; Brit Mycol Soc. *Res:* Cryptogamic botany; aquatic fungi; fungus diseases of fish; marine microbiology. *Mailing Add:* 36 Circle Dr Charleston IL 61920

SCOTT, WILLIAM WALLACE, PHYSIOLOGY. *Current Pos:* prof, 46-74, David Hall McConnell Prof urol, 75-78, urologist-in-chg, Hopkins Hosp, 46-74, EMER PROF, SCH MED, JOHNS HOPKINS UNIV, 78- *Personal Data:* b Kansas City, Kans, Jan 27, 13; m 36; c 1. *Educ:* Univ Mo, AB, 34; Univ Chicago, PhD(physiol), 38, MD, 39. *Hon Degrees:* DSc, Univ Mo, 74. *Honors & Awards:* Gold Medal, AMA, 40; Barringer Medal, Am Asn Genito Urinary Surgeons, 71, Keyes Medal, 79; Eugene Fuller Medal, Am Urol Asn, 80; Guiteral Award, Am Urol Asn, 83. *Prof Exp:* Res assoc surg, Univ Chicago, 41-43, from instr to assoc prof urol, 43-46. *Concurrent Pos:* Consult, US Naval Hosp, Bethesda, Clin Ctr, NIH & Walter Reed Gen Hosp, Washington, DC. *Mem:* Am Physiol Soc; Endocrine Soc; Am Asn Cancer Res; Am Asn Genito-Urinary Surg; Am Urol Asn. *Res:* Endocrine relations in prostatic disease; renal circulation. *Mailing Add:* Dept Urol Johns Hopkins Univ Sch Med John Hopkins Hosp Rm 146 Marburg Bldg Baltimore MD 21287

SCOTTER, GEORGE WILBY, ECOLOGY. *Current Pos:* CONSULT, 91- *Personal Data:* b Cardston, Alta, Jan 16, 33; m 59, Etta Pace; c Troy G & Alicia J. *Educ:* Utah State Univ, BSc, 59, MSc, 62, PhD(range sci), 68. *Honors & Awards:* J B Harkin Award. *Prof Exp:* Res scientist ecol, Can Wildlife Serv, 59-66; asst prof range ecol, Utah State Univ, 66-68; res scientist ecol, Can Wildlife Serv, 68-77, prog leader parks res, 77-78, chief, 78-91. *Mem:* Ecol Soc Am; Soc Wildlife Mgt; Soc Range Mgt; Can Bot Asn. *Res:* Wildlife-range relationships and alpine research; wildland management and wilderness recreation research. *Mailing Add:* 399 Okaview Rd Kelowna BC V1W 4K2 Can

SCOUTEN, CHARLES GEORGE, ORGANIC CHEMISTRY. *Current Pos:* SR SCIENTIST, AMOCO OIL RES & DEVELOP, 87- *Personal Data:* b Atlanta, Ga, Nov 21, 40; m 64; c 2. *Educ:* Univ Ga, Athens, BS, 68; Purdue Univ, Lafayette, PhD(org chem), 75. *Prof Exp:* Proj mgr, Xerox, 73-78; sr res chemist, Exxon Res & Eng, 78-87. *Mem:* Am Chem Soc; AAAS; Am Inst Chem Engrs; Am Soc Qual Control; Catalysis Soc. *Res:* Structure and reactivity of heavy fuel materials; new conversion processes for heavy fuels; colloid, interface and surface science. *Mailing Add:* Amoco Oil H-9 150 W Warrenville Rd Naperville IL 60563-8460

SCOUTEN, WILLIAM HENRY, ENZYMOLOGY, PROTEIN CHEMISTRY. *Current Pos:* DIR, BIOTECHNOL CTR, UTAH STATE UNIV, 93- *Personal Data:* b Corning, NY, Feb 12, 42; m 65, Nancy Coombs; c 6. *Educ:* Houghton Col, BA, 64; Univ Pittsburgh, PhD(biochem), 69. *Prof Exp:* NIH fel, State Univ NY, Stony Brook, 69-71; from asst prof to prof, Dept Chem, Bucknell Univ, 71-84; prof & chmn, Dept Chem, Baylor Univ, 84-93. *Concurrent Pos:* Fulbright fel, 76; Dreyfus Teacher-Scholar grant, 76; NSF fac develop fel, Dept Biochem, State Agr Univ, Wageningen & Cambridge Univ, UK, 78; Nat Acad Sci sponsored exchange with Czech Acad Sci, 90; NAm reg ed, BioSeparation, 92-; mem, Fulbright Life Sci Rev Comt, 92-94, chair, 94; assoc ed, Int J BioChromatography, 94-; adj prof, Chem Eng Dept, & mem, Ctr Biopolymers at Interfaces, Univ Utah, 96; bd dirs, Coun Biotehcnol Ctrs, 96; Govt Relations Comt, Coun Chem Res, 96. *Mem:* Am Chem Soc; Am Soc Biochem & Molecular Biol; Am Soc Biol Chemists. *Res:* DNA replication; multienzyme complexes; DNA-binding proteins; protein chemistry; solid state biochemistry; affinity chromatography; author of 75 publications and journal articles. *Mailing Add:* Biotechnol Ctr Utah State Univ Logan UT 84322-4700. *Fax:* 435-750-2766; *E-Mail:* bscouten@cscfs1.usu.edu

SCOVELL, WILLIAM MARTIN, BIOCHEMISTRY & BIOINORGANIC CHEMISTRY, MOLECULAR BIOLOGY. *Current Pos:* assoc prof, 74-78, PROF CHEM, BOWLING GREEN STATE UNIV, 78- *Personal Data:* b Wilkes-Barre, Pa, Jan 16, 44; m 65, Eleanor A Krehely; c Sherry D, William M Jr, Jeffrey J & Christopher M. *Educ:* Lebanon Valley Col, BS, 65; Univ Minn, Minneapolis, PhD(inorg chem), 69. *Prof Exp:* Teaching assoc gen chem, Univ Minn, 65-69, res assoc inorg chem, 69; researcher phys biochem, Princeton Univ, 69-70, instr phys chem, 70-71, gen chem, 71-72; vis asst prof chem, State Univ NY, Buffalo, 72-74. *Concurrent Pos:* Consult, NL Industs, Inc, 74- & Smith, Kline & French Labs, 75; NIH nat individual scholar, dept pathol, Fox Chase Cancer Ctr, 84-85; ed, J Chem Educ, feature entitled Concepts in Biochem; adj prof biochem & molecular biol, Med Col Ohio, Toledo; adj prof Biol Sci Dept, Bowling Green State Univ. *Mem:* Am Chem Soc; AAAS; Sigma Xi (pres, 88-89). *Res:* Interaction of metal ions and complexes of therapeutic value nucleic acids and chromatin; DNA-protein interactions; studies of nucleosome structure; possible biological significance of the interaction of Cis-Pt(NH3)2 Cl2; role of HMG-1 in transcription. *Mailing Add:* Dept Chem Overman Hall Bowling Green State Univ Bowling Green OH 43403. *Fax:* 419-372-9809; *E-Mail:* wscovel@andy.bgsu.edu

SCOVILL, JOHN PAUL, DRUG DESIGN. *Current Pos:* virol div, US Army Med Res Inst Infectious Dis, Ft Detrick, MD, 91-93, STAFF OFF, US ARMY MED RES DEVELOP AQUISITION & LOGISTICS COMMAND PROVISIONAL, 93- *Personal Data:* b Fort Benning, Ga, Jan 16, 48; m 71; c 2. *Educ:* Cent Mich Univ, BSc, 70; Univ Mich, MSc, 73, PhD(med chem), 75. *Prof Exp:* Res chemist, Div Exp Therapeut, Walter Reed Army Inst Res, 75-84; staff officer, Mil Dis Hazards Res Progs, US Army Med Res & Develop Command, 85-86; chem instr, US Mil Acad, 86-87, from asst prof to assoc prof chem, 87-91. *Concurrent Pos:* Vis Fulbright prof chem, Univ Zimbabwe, 90-91. *Mem:* Am Chem Soc. *Res:* Design and preparation of potential chemotherapeutic agents; synthesis and mechanistic studies of organosulfur and organoselenium compounds, nitrogen heterocycles, and transition metal complexes. *Mailing Add:* Div Exp Therapeut Walter Reed Army Inst Res Washington DC 20016

SCOVILL, WILLIAM ALBERT, SURGERY. *Current Pos:* assoc prof surg, 80-, PROF SURG, SCH MED, UNIV MD. *Personal Data:* b Battle Creek, Mich, Nov 26, 40; wid; c 2. *Educ:* Univ Mich, BS, 63, MD, 66; Univ Ill, MS, 73. *Prof Exp:* Instr surg, Sch Med, Univ Ill, 72-74; from asst prof to assoc prof surg & physiol, Albany Med Col, 74-80. *Concurrent Pos:* Dir, Trauma Serv, Albany Med Ctr, 74-80 & Burn Treat Ctr, 75-80; chief gastroenterinal surg, Univ Md Med Syst. *Mem:* Am Col Surgeons; Asn Acad Surg; Am Burn Asn; Reticuloendothelial Soc; Soc Surg Alimentary Tract; Soc Univ Surgeons. *Res:* Influence of trauma, burn injury or surgery on humoral and cellular aspects of reticuloendothelial host defense function. *Mailing Add:* Dept Gen Surg Univ Md Sch Med 22 Green St Baltimore MD 21201

SCOVILLE, RICHARD ARTHUR, MATHEMATICS. *Current Pos:* Asst prof, 61-74, ASSOC PROF MATH, DUKE UNIV, 74- *Personal Data:* b Torrington, Conn, Feb 14, 35. *Educ:* Yale Univ, BA, 56, MA, 57, PhD(math), 62. *Concurrent Pos:* Lectr, Ehime Univ, Japan, 66-67. *Mem:* Am Math Soc. *Res:* Ergodic theory; measure-preserving transformations; sums of dependent random variables. *Mailing Add:* Dept Math Duke Univ Durham NC 27708-0251

SCOW, KATE MARIE, SOIL MICROBIAL ECOLOGY, ENVIRONMENTAL MICROBIOLOGY. *Current Pos:* ASST PROF SOIL MICROBIOL, UNIV CALIF, DAVIS, 89- *Personal Data:* b Washington, DC, Aug 22, 51; m 92, Charles Griffin. *Educ:* Antioch Col, BS, 73; Cornell Univ, MS, 86, PhD(soil sci), 89. *Prof Exp:* Environ biologist, Arthur D Little, Inc, 77-82. *Mem:* Soil Sci Soc Am; Am Soc Microbiol; Soc Environ Toxicol & Chem; Sigma Xi. *Res:* Biodegradation of organic pollutants by microbial populations in soil and the subsurface; kinetics of microbial processes in soil; carbon and nitrogen cycling in agro-ecosystems. *Mailing Add:* Soil Sci Univ Calif Davis Davis CA 95616-5200. *Fax:* 530-752-1552; *E-Mail:* kmscow@ucdavis.edu

SCOW, ROBERT OLIVER, PHYSIOLOGY, ENDOCRINOLOGY. *Current Pos:* from sr asst surgeon to surgeon, 48-59, chief sect endocrinol, lab cellular & develop biol, Nat Inst Diabetes, Digestive & Kiolncy Dis, 61-94, MED DIR, NIH, 59-, EMER SCIENTIST, 94- *Personal Data:* b Dos Cabezas, Ariz, Nov 17, 20; m 48, 77, Elaine Ebner; c John R, Kate M, James W & Ann B. *Educ:* Univ Calif, AB, 43, MA, 44, MD, 46. *Hon Degrees:* Dr, Univ Umea, Sweden, 91. *Honors & Awards:* G Lyman Duff lectr, Am Heart Asn, 74. *Prof Exp:* Intern, San Francisco Hosp, 46 & Presby Hosp, NY, 47-48. *Concurrent Pos:* Guggenheim fel, 55; vis prof exp med & cancer res, Hebrew Univ-Hadassah Med Sch, Israel, 65-66; vis prof pediat, Univ Oulu, 75; vis scientist, Ctr Biochem & Molecular Biol, Nat Ctr Sci Res, France, 77. *Mem:* Am Physiol Soc; Endocrine Soc; Am Asn Anatomists. *Res:* Hormonal influences on growth of striated musculature and bone; hormonal control of fat and carbohydrate metabolism; diabetes; perfusion of isolated organs; role of capillaries and lipoprotein lipase in metabolism of chylomicrons; hormonal regulation and synthesis of lipoprotein lipase; fatty acid transport by lateral movement in cell membranes; discovery and purification of lingual lipase; involvement of fatty acids in bone mineralization; combined lipase deficiency in mice. *Mailing Add:* Rm 127 Bldg 8 NIH Bethesda MD 20892. *Fax:* 301-402-0053; *E-Mail:* rsij@nih.gov

SCOZZIE, JAMES ANTHONY, ORGANIC CHEMISTRY. *Current Pos:* PRES, RICERCA, INC, OHIO 86- *Personal Data:* b Erie, Pa, Nov 3, 43; m 70, Dolores Gardini; c Christopher, Nicole & Cassandra. *Educ:* Gannon Col, AB, 65; Case Western Reserve Univ, MS, 68, PhD(chem), 70. *Prof Exp:* Jr res chemist, Cent Res Dept, Lord Corp, 65; res chemist, Diamond Shamrock Corp, 70-72, sr res chemist, 72-76, res supvr pharmaceut, 76-78, group leader agr chem, 78-81, assoc dir agr chem res, 81-83; dir agr chem res, SDS Biotech Corp, 83-85, dir corp res, 85-86. *Mem:* Am Chem Soc. *Res:* Structure and chemistry of peptide antibiotics; synthesis of biologically active compounds; pesticides; process studies of organic compounds; commercial evaluation; nutrition and animal health; herbicides; plant growth regulants; cardiovascular agents and antiinflammatory agents. *Mailing Add:* Ricerca Inc PO Box 1000 Painesville OH 44077-1000

SCRABA, DOUGLAS G, MOLECULAR BIOLOGY, VIROLOGY. *Current Pos:* RETIRED. *Personal Data:* b Blairmore, Alta, Apr 17, 40. *Educ:* Univ Alta, BSc, 61, BEd, 63, PhD(biochem), 68. *Prof Exp:* Lectr chem, North Alta Inst Technol, 63-64; from asst prof to prof biochem, Univ Alta, 70-97. *Concurrent Pos:* Med Res Coun Can centennial fel, Univ Geneva, 68-70. *Mem:* Can Biochem Soc; Am Soc Microbiol; Soc Gen Microbiol; Micros Soc Can; Am Soc Virol. *Res:* Structure and assembly of mammalian viruses. *Mailing Add:* Dept Biochem Univ Alta Edmonton AB T6G 2E1 Can

SCRANTON, BRUCE EDWARD, MATHEMATICAL ANALYSIS, OPERATIONS RESEARCH. *Current Pos:* MGR, RESOURCE MGT TECHNOL, GEN ELEC, 82- *Personal Data:* b Pittsfield, Ill, May 5, 46; m 68; c 5. *Educ:* Northern Ill Univ, BS, 68; Purdue Univ, MS, 71, PhD(math), 74. *Prof Exp:* Sr assoc opers res, Daniel H Wagner, Assocs, 74-82. *Mem:* Soc Indust & Appl Math; Asn Comput Mach; Inst Elec & Electronics Engrs. *Res:* Systems engineering and design of misson management systems for ground systems. *Mailing Add:* 32 Laurel Circle Malvern PA 19355

SCRANTON, MARY ISABELLE, MARINE BIOGEOCHEMISTRY. *Current Pos:* asst prof, 79-84, ASSOC PROF CHEM OCEANOG, MARINE SCI RES CTR, STATE UNIV NY, STONYBROOK, 84- *Personal Data:* b Atlanta, Ga, Feb 28, 50; m 81; c 1. *Educ:* Mount Holyoke Col, BA, 72; Mass Inst Technol, PhD(oceanog), 77. *Prof Exp:* Nat Acad Sci-Nat Res Coun resident res assoc, US Naval Res Lab, 77-79. *Mem:* Am Geophys Union; Am Soc Limnol & Oceanog; Sigma Xi; Am Soc Microbiol; AAAS. *Res:* Investigations of sources, sinks and distributions of reduced gases in the marine environment; interactions of biological processes and chemical cycles. *Mailing Add:* 101 Van Brunt Manor Rd East Setauket NY 11733-3943

SCRIABINE, ALEXANDER, PHARMACOLOGY. *Current Pos:* PRES, NEVA PRESS INC, 94-; CONSULT, BAYER, PANAX, 95- *Personal Data:* b Yelgava, Latvia, Oct 26, 26; nat US; m 64; c 2. *Educ:* Cornell Univ, MS, 54; Univ Mainz, MD, 58. *Prof Exp:* Res asst pharmacol, Med Sch, Cornell Univ, 51-54; pharmacologist, Res Labs, Chas Pfizer & Co, Maywood, NJ, 54-56, sr pharmacologist, 59-61, supvr, 61-63, mgr, Chas Pfizer & Co, Groton, Conn, 63-66; chief pharmacologist, Div Cardiol, Philadelphia Gen Hosp, 66-67; sr res fel, Merck Inst Therapeut Res, 67-69, dir cardiovasc res, 69-72, sr dir pharmacol, 72-73, exec dir pharmacol, 73-78, assoc dir biol res, Wyeth Labs, Inc, 78-79; assoc prof pharmacol, Sch Med, Univ Pa, 75-99; dir, Miles Inst Preclin Pharmacol, 79-93, actg dir, Int Bone Joint Dis, Miles Inc, 93-94. *Concurrent Pos:* Mem coun thrombosis & coun hypertension, Am Heart Asn; ed, Pharmacol Antihypertensive Drugs, 80, New Cardiovasc Drugs, 85-87, Cardiovasc Drug Rev, 88-; lectr, Yale Univ, 93- *Mem:* Am Soc Pharmacol & Exp Therapeut; Ger Pharmacol Soc; Am Soc Clin Pharmacol & Therapeut; AAAS; Int Soc Heart Res; NY Acad Sci; Am Hypertension Soc; Soc Neurosci. *Res:* Cardiovascular, central nervous system autonomic and renal pharmacology; antihypertensives, neuroprotectives, diuretics, antianginal agents; cardiotonics; pharmacology of tetrahydrozoline, benzthiazide, polythiazide, prazosin, clonidine, timolol, nimodipine, nisoldipine and nitrendipine; calcium channel antagonists. *Mailing Add:* 435 Colonial Rd Guilford CT 06437. *Fax:* 203-458-8428

SCRIBNER, BELDING HIBBARD, NEPHROLOGY. *Current Pos:* from instr to prof, 51-92, head, Div Nephrology, 58-82, EMER PROF MED, UNIV WASH, SEATTLE, 92- *Personal Data:* b Chicago, Ill, Jan 18, 21; m 42; c 4. *Educ:* Univ Calif, AB, 41; Stanford Univ, MD, 45; Univ Minn, MS, 51; Am Bd Internal Med, cert, 51; FRCP, 93. *Honors & Awards:* John Phillips Mem Award, Am Col Physicians, 73; David Hume Mem Award, 75; Mayo Solely Award, Western Soc Clin Res, 82; John Peters Award, Am Soc Nephrology, 86; Jean Hamburger Award, Int Soc Nephrology, 86. *Prof Exp:* From intern to resident med, San Francisco Hosp, 44-47; fel, Mayo Found, Rochester, Minn, 47-50, asst staff mem, 50-51. *Concurrent Pos:* Dir gen med res, Vet Admin Hosp, Seattle, 51-57; Markle scholar, Hammersmith Hosp, London, 57-58; coun mem, Am Soc Nephrology, 74-79, Sci Adv Bd, Nat Kidney Found & Coun, Western Soc Clin Res. *Mem:* Inst Med-Nat Acad Sci; Am Soc Clin Invest; AMA; fel Am Col Physicians; Am Soc Nephrology (pres elect, 77, pres, 78-79); NY Acad Sci; Sigma Xi. *Res:* Fluid and electrolyte balance and kidney disease as pertaining to medicine; nephrology; dialysis; author of numerous technical publications. *Mailing Add:* Dept Med Div Nephrology Rm 11 Univ Wash Sch Med Seattle WA 98195

SCRIGNAR, CHESTER BRUNO, FORENSIC PSYCHIATRY, BEHAVIORAL MEDICINE. *Current Pos:* ADJ PROF LAW & PSYCHIAT, TULANE UNIV SCH MED, DEPT PSYCHIAT & NEUROL, 72-, CLIN PROF, 79- *Personal Data:* b Villa Park, Ill, Oct 15, 34; m 64. *Educ:* Ariz State Univ, Tempe, BA, 57; Tulane Univ Grad Sch, MS, 61; Tulane Univ Med Sch, New Orleans, 61. *Honors & Awards:* John Herr Musser Mem Prize, 61; Milton G Erickson Award, 81. *Concurrent Pos:* Adj prof anxiety treatment, Sch Social Work, 73-; adj prof, Xavier Univ, New Orleans, 84- *Mem:* Am Psychiat Soc; Am Med Asn; Am Acad Psychiat & Law; Am Soc Clin Hypnosis; Am Soc Sex Educators; Asn Advan Behav Therapist. *Res:* Post-traumatic stress disorder and the psychological sequelae of trauma. *Mailing Add:* 2625 General Pershing St New Orleans LA 70115

SCRIMGEOUR, GARRY JOSEPH, ENVIRONMENTAL IMPACT ASSESSMENT, STREAM ECOLOGY. *Current Pos:* FEL, DEPT ZOOL, UNIV ALTA, 92-; SUSTAINABLE FOREST MGT NETWORK CTRS EXCELLENCE. *Personal Data:* b Masterton, NZ, Feb 7, 62; m 88, Shelley Pruss. *Educ:* Univ Canterbury, NZ, BSc, 84, MSc, 87; Univ Calgary, Alta, PhD(ecol), 92. *Honors & Awards:* Wildco Award, NAm Benthological Soc, 92. *Prof Exp:* Environ impact biologist, Waikato Catchment Bd, Hamilton, NZ, 87-88. *Concurrent Pos:* Fel, Nat Sci & Eng Res Coun Can, 92-94; hon fel, Univ Calgary, Alta, 92-93; Izaak Walton Killan fel, Univ Alta, Can, 92. *Mem:* Soc Can Limnologists; NAm Benthological Soc; Can Soc Zoologists; Limnol Soc NZ. *Res:* Environmental impact assessment of pulp mill effluent; benthic ecology; nutrient-herbivore interactions; water quality modelling. *Mailing Add:* Sustainable Forest Mgt Network Ctrs Excellence Biol Sci Bldg Rm G208 Univ Alta Edmonton AB T6G 2E9 Can. *Fax:* 403-492-9234

SCRIMSHAW, NEVIN STEWART, PUBLIC HEALTH. *Current Pos:* head, Dept Nutrit & Food Sci, Mass Inst Technol, 61-79, dir, Clin Res Ctr, 62-66 & 79-85, inst prof human nutrit, 76-88, EMER PROF HUMAN NUTRIT, MASS INST TECHNOL, 88- *Personal Data:* b Milwaukee, Wis, Jan 20, 18; m 41; c 5. *Educ:* Ohio Wesleyan Univ, BA, 38; Harvard Univ, MA, 39, PhD(physiol), 41, MPH, 59; Univ Rochester, MD, 45; Am Bd Nutrit, cert, 64. *Hon Degrees:* DPS, Ohio Wesleyan Univ, 61; ScD, Univ Rochester, 74, Univ Tokushima, 79, Mahidol Univ, 82, Plymouth State Col, 93. *Honors & Awards:* Osborne-Mendel Award, Am Inst Nutrit, 60; Int Award, Inst Food Technol, 69; Joseph Goldberger Award Clin Nutrit, AMA, 69; McCollum Award, Am Soc Clin Nutrit, 75; Bolton Carson Medal, Franklin Inst, 76; Bristol Meyers Award, 88; Feinstein Hunger Award, 91; World Food Prize Laureate, 91. *Prof Exp:* Instr embryol & comp anat, Ohio Wesleyan Univ, 41-42; intern, Gorgas Hosp, CZ, 43-46; asst resident physician obstet & gynec, Strong Mem Hosp & Genesee Hosp, Rochester, NY, 48-49; dir, Inst Nutrit Cent Am & Panama, Guatemala, 49-61. *Concurrent Pos:* Fel nutrit & endocrinol, Dept Vital Econ, Univ Rochester, 42-43, Rockefeller Found fel, Dept Obstet & Gynec, 46-47, Merck Nat Res Coun fel natural sci, 47-49; vis lectr trop pub health, Harvard Univ, 68-86; mem, Food & Nutrit Bd, Nat Acad Sci-Nat Res Coun, 67-77, mem exec comt, 68-75, mem, Comt Int Nutrit Progs, 64-72, chmn, 68-72, mem, Task Force Food-Health-Pop Prob, 73-76; mem adv comt med res, WHO, 71-78, chmn, 73-78; trustee, Rockefeller Found, 71-83; vpres, Int Union Nutrit Sci, 72-, pres, 78-81; mem, US Del Joint Comt, US-Japan Coop Med Sci Prog, 74-; chmn food & nutrit sect, Am Pub Health Asn, 63, mem res comt, 65, chmn ad hoc task force nutrit, 70; mem lectr prog, Inst Food Technol, 69-70, mem, Int Award Jury, 69-72, chmn, 74; mem expert work group on world hunger, UN Univ, 75; sr adv, World Hunger Prog, 75-; vis lectr, Harvard Sch Pub Health, 65-85; dir, Develop Studies Div, 85-86, Div Food & Nutrit Prog, 87-; res assoc, Nat Bur Econ Res, 86-; vis prof, Tufts Univ, 87-, Brown Univ, 88-; dir, Food & Nutrit Prog Human & Social Develop, UN Univ. *Mem:* Fel Am Col Nutrit; fel AAAS; fel Am Inst Nutrit; Am Col Prev Med; Am Physiol Soc. *Res:* Clinical and public nutrition; amino acid protein metabolism; nutrition and infection; diarrhea and malnutrition; single cell protein. *Mailing Add:* PO Box 330 Campton NH 03223

SCRIMSHAW, SUSAN, ANTHROPOLOGY. *Current Pos:* DEAN, SCH PUB HEALTH & PROF COMMUNITY HEALTH SCI & ANTHROP, UNIV ILL, CHICAGO, 94- *Educ:* Columbia Univ, PhD(anthrop), 74. *Honors & Awards:* Margaret Mead Award, Am Anthrop Asn & Soc Appl Anthrop, 85; Spec Recognition Award, Epilepsy Found Am, 87, Distinguished Serv Award, 89. *Prof Exp:* Prof pub health & anthrop & assoc dean acad prog, Univ Calif, Los Angeles, 89-94. *Concurrent Pos:* Mem, Int Health Bd & Comt Pop, Inst Med-Nat Acad Sci. *Mem:* Inst Med-Nat Acad Sci; fel AAAS; fel Am Anthrop Asn; fel Soc Appl Anthrop; Nat Soc Med Anthrop (pres, 85); Am Pub Health Asn; Int Union Anthrop & Ethnol Sci; Soc Med Anthrop; Pop Asn Am; Soc Nutrit Anthrop. *Res:* Developed guidelines for nutrition and primary health care program planning and evaluation; child survival programs, improving pregnancy and childbirth outcomes; medical anthropology, human reproduction; demography; applied anthopology and culture change. *Mailing Add:* Sch Pub Health Univ Chicago 2121 W Taylor St No 116 Chicago IL 60612-7260. *Fax:* 312-996-5939

SCRIVEN, ERIC FRANK VAUGHAN, HETEROCYCLIC CHEMISTRY. *Current Pos:* var res positions, 79-91, DIR RES & DEVELOP, REILLY INDUSTS INC, 91- *Personal Data:* b Milford Haven, Wales, Oct 30, 41; US citizen; m 72, Ursula; c Melanie & Charles. *Educ:* Univ Guelph, Can, MS, 67; Univ E Anglia, UK, PhD(org chem), 69. *Prof Exp:* Lectr, Univ Salford, UK, 71-79. *Mem:* Am Chem Soc; Royal Soc Chem; Int Soc Heterocyclic Chem. *Res:* Heterocyclic chemistry principally pyridiens and pyridines polymers synthesis and applications; mechanistic and synthetic aspects of azide and nitrene chemistry. *Mailing Add:* 512 Lazy Lane Greenwood IN 46142

SCRIVEN, L E(DWARD), (II), ENGINEERING SCIENCE. *Current Pos:* from asst prof to prof, 59-89, assoc head, Dept Chem Eng, 74-77, FEL SUPERCOMPUT INST, UNIV, MINN, 84-, REGENTS PROF CHEM ENG & MAT SCI, 89- *Personal Data:* b Battle Creek, Mich, Nov 4, 31; m 52, Dorene B Hayes; c Ellen D, Teresa A & Mark H. *Educ:* Univ Calif, Berkeley, BS, 52; Univ Del, PhD(chem eng), 56. *Honors & Awards:* Colburn Award, Am Inst Chem Engrs, 60, Walker Award, 77; Gibbs lectr, Am Math Soc, 86; Murphree Award, Am Chem Soc, 89; Tallmadge Award, Am Inst Chem Engrs, 92. *Prof Exp:* Res engr, Shell Develop Co, 56-59. *Concurrent Pos:* Adv ed, Prentice-Hall, Inc; guest investr, Rockefeller Inst, 63; vis prof, Univ Pa, 67, Univ Fed Rio de Janeiro, 69, Univ Nac de La Plata, 72, Univ Witwatersand, 74 & Calif Inst Technol, 89; Guggenheim fel, 69-70; assoc ed, J Fluid Mech, 69-75; fac fel, Exxon Corp Res Labs, 84-89; Amundson Comt, Nat Res Coun, 84-88; mem bd, Chem Sci & Technol, 87-90, co-chair, 90-; sci adv, Packard Found, 88. *Mem:* Nat Acad Eng; fel Am Inst Chem Engrs; Am Phys Soc; Soc Indust & Appl Math; Soc Rheology; Royal Soc Chem. *Res:* Interface, contact line and micellar physics; capillarity and small-scale free-surface flows; coating process fundamentals; porous media science, cryo-electron microscopy, computer-aided analysis, large-scale scientific computation. *Mailing Add:* Cardinal Point 2044 Cedar Lake Pkwy Minneapolis MN 55416

SCRIVER, CHARLES ROBERT, PEDIATRICS, GENETICS. *Current Pos:* lectr pediat, 62-63, from asst prof to assoc prof, 63-69, PROF PEDIAT, MCGILL UNIV, 69-, PROF BIOL & HUMAN GENETICS, 77-; DIR, DEBELLE LAB BIOCHEM GENETICS, MONTREAL CHILDREN'S HOSP, 61- *Personal Data:* b Montreal, Que, Nov 7, 30; m 56, Esther Peirce; c Doellen, Peter, Julie & Paul. *Educ:* McGill Univ, BA, 51, MD, CM, 55; FRCPS(C), 61. *Hon Degrees:* DSc, Univ Manitoba, 92, Glasgow Univ, 93 & Univ Montreal, 93. *Honors & Awards:* Wood Gold Medal, McGill Univ, 55; Royal Col Physicians & Surgeons, Can Medal, 61; F Mead Johnson Award, Am Acad Pediat, 68, Borden Award, 73; Borden Award, Nutrit Soc Can, 69; Allan Award, Am Soc Human Genetics, 78; Gairdner Int Award, 79; Ross Award, Can Pediat Soc, 90; Award of Excellence, Genetics Soc Can, 92. *Prof Exp:* From intern to jr asst resident med, Royal Victoria Hosp, Montreal, 55-56; jr asst resident, Montreal Children's Hosp, 57 & Med Ctr, Boston, Mass, 57-58; McLaughlin traveling fel, Univ Col, London Hosp, 58-60; chief resident pediat, Montreal Children's Hosp, 60-61. *Concurrent Pos:* Markle fel, 61-66; assoc physician, Dept Pediat Med, Montreal Children's Hosp, 63-65, physician, 65-; Med Res Coun assoc, 69- *Mem:* Fel AAAS; Am Soc Clin Invest; Am Soc Clin Nutrit; Am Soc Human Genetics; Am Pediat Soc; Sigma Xi; Asn Am Physicians; British Pediat Asn; fel Royal Soc Can. *Res:* Human genetics; amino acid metabolism; phosphate metabolism; human population genetic variation; treatment of genetic disease; genetic science. *Mailing Add:* Debelle Lab Biochem Genetics Montreal Children's Hosp 2300 Tupper St Montreal PQ H3H 1P3 Can. *Fax:* 514-934-4329; *E-Mail:* mc77@musica.mcgill.ca

SCROGGIE, LUCY E, ANALYTICAL CHEMISTRY. *Current Pos:* RETIRED. *Personal Data:* b Knoxville, Tenn, May 29, 35. *Educ:* Univ Tenn, BS, 57, MS, 59; Univ Tex, PhD(anal chem), 61. *Prof Exp:* Analytical chemist, Analytical Chem Div, Oak Ridge Nat Lab, 61-66; analytical chemist, Res & Develop Dept, Chem & Plastics Div, Union Carbide Corp, 66-69; anal chemist, Indust & Radiol Hyg Br, Div Environ Res & Develop, Tenn Valley Authority, 70-75, res chemist, Lab Br, Div Environ Planning, 75-80, mgt trainee, Off Natural Resources, 80-81, proj mgr, Dis Syst Eng, 81-92. *Mem:* Am Chem Soc; Am Conf Govt Indust Hygienists. *Res:* Analytical methods development; spectrophotometry; industrial hygiene chemistry; analytical chemistry applied to air and water quality and industrial hygiene. *Mailing Add:* 6713 Saddle Creek Pass Knoxville TN 37921-1070

SCROGGS, JAMES EDWARD, MATHEMATICS. *Current Pos:* chmn dept, 66-79, PROF MATH, UNIV ARK, FAYETTEVILLE, 64- *Personal Data:* b Little Rock, Ark, Apr 20, 26; m 48; c 3. *Educ:* Univ Ark, BA, 49; Univ Houston, MA, 54; Rice Inst, PhD(math), 57. *Prof Exp:* From asst prof to assoc prof math, Univ Ark, 57-62; asst prof, Univ Tex, 62-64. *Concurrent Pos:* Fulbright lectr, 80-81. *Mem:* Am Math Soc; Math Asn Am; Soc Indust & Appl Math. *Res:* Functional and complex analysis; Banach and Hilbert spaces. *Mailing Add:* Dept Math Univ Ark Fayetteville AR 72701

SCRUGGS, FRANK DELL, THEORETICAL PHYSICS, COMPUTER ENGINEERING. *Current Pos:* DIR RES & DEVELOP, ADVAN DATA SYST, 85- *Personal Data:* b Los Angeles, Calif, May 18, 39. *Educ:* Cornell Univ, BS, 73; Princeton Univ, MS, 75; Harvard Univ, LLD, 78; Mass Inst Technol, PhD(physics), 81; Calif Inst Technol, ScD, 84. *Prof Exp:* Elem particle physicist, JPL, 62-64; sr comput anal, Dec, 64-66; prin electronic engr, IBM, 66-68; sr comput instr, LA Tech Inst, 70-73; comput engr, Control Data, 73-76; sr res physicist laser, Univ Calif, Los Angeles, 81-83. *Concurrent Pos:* Dir, Ctr Advan Physics, Univ Calif, Los Angeles, 82-83; vpres, Nat Res Coun, 86. *Mem:* Sr fel, Inst Elec & Electronics Engrs (vpres, 71-73); sr fel Soc Cert Data Processors; Am Phys Soc; fel Asn Comput Programmers & Analysts. *Res:* Lasers and optics, and their applications in such areas as atom-field interactions, laser spectroscopy, optical frequency-wavelength standards and sensors, including fiber-optic sensors. *Mailing Add:* Advan Data Syst 932 Newton Ave S St Petersburg FL 33705

SCRUGGS, JACK G, MAN MADE FIBERS, TEXTILES. *Current Pos:* VPRES TECH, PHILLIPS FIBERS CORP, 66- *Personal Data:* b Cullman, Ala, Sept 9, 30; m 54; c 2. *Educ:* Univ Mich, BS, 52; MS, 53; PhD(org chem), 56. *Honors & Awards:* Borden Award, Univ Mich, Lenn & Fink Award. *Prof Exp:* Group leader Monsanto Fibers Div, R&D, 56-66. *Mem:* Am Chem Soc; AAAS; Sigma Xi. *Mailing Add:* 614 Devenger Rd Greer SC 29650

SCUDAMORE, HAROLD HUNTER, medicine; deceased, see previous edition for last biography

SCUDDAY, JAMES FRANKLIN, VERTEBRATE BIOLOGY, WILDLIFE BIOLOGY. *Current Pos:* from asst prof to prof, 69-95, EMER PROF BIOL, SUL ROSS STATE UNIV, 95- *Personal Data:* b Alpine, Tex, Sept 16, 29; m 50; c 3. *Educ:* Sul Ross State Univ, BS, 52; Univ Idaho, MNS, 62; Tex A&M Univ, PhD(wildlife sci), 71. *Prof Exp:* Teacher independent sch dist, Tex, 52-54 & 56-61; instr biol, Sul Ross State Univ, 61-66; res asst wildlife sci, Tex A&M Univ, 67-69. *Concurrent Pos:* NSF res partic syst bot, Okla State Univ, 64; pres, Chihuahuan Desert Res Inst, 84-; prin investr res proj. *Mem:* Herpet League; Am Soc Mammal; Soc Study Amphibians & Reptiles; Cooper Ornith Soc; Wildlife Soc. *Res:* Ecology and systematics of vertebrate animals; desert ecology. *Mailing Add:* 514 Harriet St Alpine TX 79830

SCUDDER, GEOFFREY GEORGE EDGAR, ENTOMOLOGY. *Current Pos:* Instr zool, 58-60, from asst prof to assoc prof, 60-68, PROF ZOOL, UNIV BC, 68-, CUR SPENCER ENTOM MUS, 58- *Personal Data:* b Kent, Eng, Mar 18, 34; m 58. *Educ:* Univ Wales, BSc, 55; Oxford Univ, DPhil(entom), 58. *Honors & Awards:* Gold Medal, Entom Soc Can, 75. *Concurrent Pos:* Royal Soc & Nuffield Found Commonwealth bursary, Imp Col, Univ London, 64-65. *Mem:* Soc Study Evolution; Entom Soc Can; Can Soc Zool; fel Royal Entom Soc London; fel Royal Soc Can. *Res:* Systematics; evolution; entomology of Hemiptera; comparative morphology of insects; freshwater insect ecology and evolution. *Mailing Add:* Dept Zool Univ BC 6720 University Blvd Vancouver BC V6T 1Z4 Can

SCUDDER, HARVEY ISRAEL, PUBLIC HEALTH, BIOLOGY. *Current Pos:* head div biol & health sci, Calif State Univ, Hayward, 67-70, actg head div sci & math, 68-69, actg chmn dept biol sic, 70-71, coordr health sci, 71-72, prof microbiol, 67-80, EMER PROF MICROBIOL, CALIF STATE UNIV, HAYWARD, 80- *Personal Data:* b Elmira, NY, Jan 2, 19; m 45, Florence V Graff; c Paul H & Barbara C (Eikenberry). *Educ:* Cornell Univ, BS, 39, PhD(pub health), 53. *Prof Exp:* Asst entomologist, Boyce Thompson Inst Plant Res, 41; jr entomologist, USPHS, Fla, 42-43, state malaria control entomologist, Ala, 43-44, Carter Mem Lab, Ga, 44-46; chief div malaria control & sanit, Stand-Vacuum Oil Co, Sumatra, 47; tech coordr & officer in chg vector control field sta, State Dept Pub Health, Fresno, Calif, 51-54; res biologist, Tech Develop Labs, Commun Dis Ctr, USPHS, Savannah, Ga, 54-56, asst chief, Health Res Facil, Div Res Grants, NIH, 56-57, exec secy microbiol, virol & rickettsial study sect, 57-59; staff asst, Nat Cancer Inst, 59-61, chief virol res resources br, 61-62; asst to chief div res grants, NIH, 62; chief res training grants, Nat Inst Gen Med Sci, 62-65; manpower consult, Div Community Health Serv, USPHS, 65-66. *Concurrent Pos:* Mem microbiol fel rev panel, NIH, 58-60; mem, Moss Landing Marine Labs, 67-70, chmn policy bd, 69-70; mem, bd trustees, St Rose Hosp, Hayward, 69-83, chmn, 73-74, mem inst rev bd, 83-; trustee, Marine Ecol Inst, Redwood City, 71-, actg chmn, 74-78, chmn, 79-80 & 82-89; mem bd dir, E Bay Found Health Careers Educ, 72-85, chmn, 74-76 & 81-85; mem community adv comt, Fairmont Hosp, San Leandro, 74-83; chmn trustee corp bd, Calif Mosquito & Vector Control Asn, 90-91. *Mem:* AAAS; Am Mosquito Control Asn; Am Soc Trop Med & Hyg; Entom Soc Am; Am Soc Microbiol; Am Pub Health Asn; NY Acad Sci; Soc Vector Ecol; Sigma Xi. *Res:* Environmental sanitation and public health; health manpower; medical entomology; insect paleontology; decision processing systems. *Mailing Add:* 7409 Hansen Dr Dublin CA 94568-2742

SCUDDER, JACK DAVID, SPACE PLASMA PHYSICS. *Current Pos:* PROF PHYSICS & ASTRON, UNIV IOWA, 93- *Personal Data:* b Sao Paulo, Brazil, Sept 28, 47; US citizen; m 69, Eileen Delaney; c Christine. *Educ:* Williams Col, BA, 69; Univ Md, College Park, MS, 72, PhD(plasma physics), 75. *Honors & Awards:* Mariner 10 Sci Award, NASA, 74; Int Sun Earth Explorer Team Award, NASA, 78. *Prof Exp:* Res physicist space plasma physics, Goddard Space Flight Ctr, NASA, 69-93. *Concurrent Pos:* Max Planck fel, Max Planck Soc, 77. *Mem:* Am Geophys Union. *Res:* Kinetic physics of space magneto plasmas with emphasis on transport phenomena. *Mailing Add:* 35 High Circle Dr NE Iowa City IA 52240. *Fax:* 319-335-1753; *E-Mail:* jds@hydra.physics.uiowa.edu, iowasp.scudder

SCUDDER, JEFFREY ERIC, numerical analysis, for more information see previous edition

SCUDDER, WALTER TREDWELL, WEED SCIENCE, VEGETABLE & FIELD CROPS. *Current Pos:* RETIRED. *Personal Data:* b Elmira, NY, Aug 28, 20; div; c 3. *Educ:* Cornell Univ, BS, 41, PhD(veg crops), 51; La State Univ, MS, 43. *Prof Exp:* Asst hort, La State Univ, 41-43; teacher, NY, 43-44; asst veg crops, Cornell Univ, 46-49; instr, 49-50; assoc horticulturist, SC Truck Exp Sta, 50-53; horticulturist, US Marine Corps, 53-55; assoc horticulturist, Univ Fla, 55-68, prof hort & horticulturist, Cent Fla Res & Educ Ctr, 68-86. *Concurrent Pos:* Coun, Agr Sci & Technol. *Mem:* Weed Sci Soc Am; Am Soc Hort Sci; Potato Asn Am; Am Soc Agron; Am Soybean Asn; Crop Sci Soc Am; Sigma Xi. *Res:* Chemical and biological weed control in vegetable and field crops; herbicide evaluation; persistence and degradation of herbicide residues in soil; weed species identification, terminology and distribution; biological nitrogen fixation in legumes. *Mailing Add:* 4001 S Sanford Ave Sanford FL 32773

SCUDERI, LOUIS ANTHONY, CLIMATOLOGY, GEOGRAPHY. *Current Pos:* PROF GEOG, UNIV NMEX, 94- *Personal Data:* b Brooklyn, NY, Sept 13, 54; m 79, Joan E Drake; c Louis & Benjamin. *Educ:* Univ Calif, Los Angeles, BA, 76, MA, 78, PhD(geog), 84. *Prof Exp:* Res scientist, Calif Res & Technol, 84-85; res geogr & database mgr, Earth Technol Corp, 85; res scientist, Itujhes Aircraft Co, 85-88; res assoc, Isotope Lab, Univ Calif, Los Angeles, 86-88; asst prof, Dept Geog, Boston Univ, 88-94. *Mem:* Int Soc Optical Eng; Asn Am Geogrs; Nat Geog Soc; Sigma Xi. *Res:* Solar-climate relationships; effects of volcanic eruptions on climate; creation of three-dimensional computer database for flight simulation and real time infrared simulation. *Mailing Add:* Dept Geog Univ NMex Bandelier W Rm 118 Albuquerque NM 87131

SCULLY, ERIK PAUL, ZOOLOGY, POPULATION BIOLOGY. *Current Pos:* from instr to asst prof, 78-87, ASSOC PROF BIOL, TOWSON STATE UNIV, 87- *Personal Data:* b Ossining, NY, Oct 22, 49; c 1. *Educ:* Fordham Univ, BS, 71; Univ RI, PhD(biol), 76. *Prof Exp:* Lectr ecol, Univ Calif, Irvine, 76-78. *Concurrent Pos:* Dir, Univ Honors Prog. *Mem:* AAAS; Soc Study Evolution; Sigma Xi; Am Soc Naturalists. *Res:* Behavioral ecology and population biology of invertebrates, specifically marine invertebrates; mechanisms of resource utilization and intraspecific competition; use of the computer for instructional purposes. *Mailing Add:* Dept Biol Sci Towson State Univ Towson MD 21204. *E-Mail:* e7b2scu@toe.towson.edu

SCULLY, FRANK E, JR, CHEMISTRY. *Current Pos:* asst prof chem sci, 75-80, ASSOC PROF CHEM, OLD DOMINION UNIV, 80- *Personal Data:* b Brooklyn, NY, Mar 23, 47; m 71. *Educ:* Spring Hill Col, BS, 68; Purdue Univ, PhD(chem), 73. *Prof Exp:* Instr org chem, Yale Univ, 73-75. *Mem:* Sigma Xi. *Res:* Photosensitized oxygenations of cyclopropanes, vinylcyclopropanes, vinylcyclopropanols and norbornyl systems as a probe for an ionic mechanism of dioxetane formation; unsaturated alkoxide systems as an internal trap for intermediates in the reaction of singlet oxygen with olefins; use and effect of crown ethers in singlet oxygenations. *Mailing Add:* 1314 Brunswick Ave Norfolk VA 23508-1345

SCULLY, MARLAN ORVIL, PHYSICS. *Current Pos:* HEAD THEORY GROUP, MAX PLANCK INST QUANTUM OPTICS, 81- *Personal Data:* b Caspar, Wyo, Aug 3, 39; m 58; c 3. *Educ:* Univ Wyo, BS, 61; Yale Univ, MS, 63, PhD(physics), 65. *Honors & Awards:* Adolph Lomb Medal, Optical Soc Am, 70. *Prof Exp:* Physicist, Gen Elec Co, 61-62; instr physics, Yale Univ, 65-67; from asst prof to assoc prof, Mass Inst Technol, 67-71; prof physics & optical sci, Univ Ariz, 70-80; distinguished prof, Dept Physics & Astron, Univ NMex, 80- *Concurrent Pos:* Consult, United Aircraft Res Lab, 65-, Los Alamos Sci Lab, 70- & US Army, Redstone, 71-; mem, Sci Appln Inc, 76-, Litton Indust, 76- & Joint Coun Quantum Electronics; John Simon Guggenheim & Alfred P Sloan fels; Humboldt fel. *Mem:* Fel AAAS; fel Am Phys Soc; fel Am Optical Soc. *Res:* Neutron and low temperature physics; laser physics; quantum statistical mechanics; solid state physics and quantum optics. *Mailing Add:* 3902 Tally Ho Dr Irving TX 75062

SCULLY, ROBERT EDWARD, PATHOLOGY. *Current Pos:* Asst clin prof, Harvard Med Sch, 59-63, assoc prof, 63-69, prof path, 70-92, EMER PROF, HARVARD MED SCH, 92- *Personal Data:* b Pittsfield, Mass, Aug 31, 21. *Educ:* Col of the Holy Cross, AB, 41; Harvard Med Sch, MD, 44. *Hon Degrees:* DSc, Univ Leiden, Neth, 82, Col Holy Cross, Mass, 92. *Honors & Awards:* Fred Waldorf Steward Award, Mem Sloan-Kettering Cancer Ctr, 80; Joanne Vandenberg Hill Award, M D Anderson Hosp, 81; Arthur Purdy Stout Award, Am Soc Clin Pathologists, 83; H P Smith Distinguished Path Educr Award, Am Soc Clin Path, 91; Maude Abbott Lectr, US Can Acad Path, 92. *Concurrent Pos:* From assoc pathologist to pathologist, Mass Gen Hosp, 58- *Mem:* AMA; Int Soc Gynec Pathologists; Soc Gynec Oncol; Int Acad Path; Am Soc Clin Pathologists; Col Am Pathologists; hon fel Royal Col Pathologists. *Res:* Gynecologic and testicular pathology and endocrinology; initial descritption of numerous types of gynecologic and testicular tumors and tumor-like disorders. *Mailing Add:* Mass Gen Hosp Boston MA 02114. *Fax:* 617-726-7474

SCURRY, MURPHY TOWNSEND, MEDICINE, ENDOCRINOLOGY. *Current Pos:* from asst prof to assoc prof, 66-85, CLIN PROF MED, UNIV TEX MED BR, GALVESTON, 85- *Personal Data:* b Houston, Tex, May 25, 33; m 55; c 2. *Educ:* Univ Tex, Austin, BA, 54; Univ Tex Med Br Galveston, MD, 58. *Prof Exp:* Rotating intern, Univ Pa, 59; resident med, Univ Mich, Ann Arbor, 61, NIH fel, 61-63. *Concurrent Pos:* Consult, USPHS Hosp, Galveston, Tex, 70- *Mem:* Endocrine Soc; Am Diabetes Asn; Am Fedn Clin Res; Am Col Physicians. *Res:* Secretion of parathyroid hormone. *Mailing Add:* 1501 Broadway Galveston TX 77550-4906

SCUSERIA, GUSTAVO ENRIQUE, COUPLED CLUSTER METHOD, DENSITY FUNCTIONAL THEORY & LINEAR SCALING ELECTRONIC STRUCTURE METHODS. *Current Pos:* from asst prof to assoc prof, 89-95, ASSOC PROF, DEPT CHEM, RICE UNIV, 95- *Personal Data:* b Buenos Aires, Arg, July 30, 56; m 82, Ana I Ilvento; c Ignacio & Toma's. *Educ:* Univ Buenos Aires, BSc, 79, PhD(physics), 83. *Prof Exp:* Grad asst, Dept Physics, FCEN, Univ Buenos Aires, 79-83, asst prof, 83-85; res assoc, Dept Chem, Univ Calif, Berkeley, 85-87; sr res assoc, Ctr Computational Quantum Chem, Univ Ga, 87-89. *Mem:* Am Chem Soc; Am Phys Soc; AAAS; Mat Res Soc. *Res:* Theoretical chemistry with an emphasis in computational quantum chemistry and development of new methods for molecular electronic structure; fullerene chemistry and applications; density functional theory and molecular dynamics. *Mailing Add:* Dept Chem Rice Univ 6100 Main St Houston TX 77005-1892. *Fax:* 713-285-5155; *E-Mail:* guscus@katzo.rice.edu

SEABAUGH, PYRTLE W, ANALYTICAL CHEMISTRY, APPLIED STATISTICS. *Current Pos:* RETIRED. *Personal Data:* b Millersville, Mo, Sept 14, 35; m 59; c 1. *Educ:* Southeast Mo State Col, BS, 56; Iowa State Univ, PhD(inorg chem), 61; Univ Dayton, MBA, 71. *Prof Exp:* Fel struct chem, Univ Wis, 61-63; sr res chemist, Mound Lab, Monsanto Res Corp, EG&G, 63-67, res specialist, 67-74, sr analytical specialist, 74-95. *Mem:* AAAS; Am

Chem Soc; Am Crystallog Asn; Sigma Xi; Am Inst Physics. *Res:* Development of x-ray fluorescence and diffraction techniques; experimental design; interpretation of research and development data via applied statistics and numerical analysis; financial modeling; structural and pollution chemistry. *Mailing Add:* 9371 Foxburrow Way Spring Valley OH 45370

SEABLOOM, ROBERT W, MAMMALOGY. *Current Pos:* From asst prof to assoc prof biol, 61-75, PROF BIOL, UNIV NDAK, 75- *Personal Data:* b St Paul, Minn, Aug 14, 32; c 2. *Educ:* Univ Minn, BA, 53, MS, 58, PhD(wildlife mgt), 63. *Concurrent Pos:* Vis scientist, Whiteshell Nuclear Res Estab, Atomic Energy Can Ltd, 71-72; fac, Itasca Biol Sta, 68, 70, 82 & 88; vis biologist, Univ Calif, Davis, 82-83. *Mem:* Am Soc Mammal; Wildlife Soc; Sigma Xi. *Res:* Vertebrate population ecology; mammalian ecology, life histories, and distributions; adrenal function in small mammal populations. *Mailing Add:* Dept Biol Univ NDak Grand Forks ND 58201

SEABORG, GLENN THEODORE, NUCLEAR CHEMISTRY. *Current Pos:* Res assoc chem, Univ Calif, Berkeley, 37-39, prof, 39-71, dir nuclear chem res, Lawrence Berkeley Nat Lab, 46-58 & 72-75, assoc dir lab, 54-61, chancellor, 58-61, fac res lectr, 59, UNIV PROF CHEM, UNIV CALIF, BERKELEY, 71-, ASSOC DIR AT LARGE, LAWRENCE BERKELEY NAT LAB, 72- *Personal Data:* b Ishpeming, Mich, Apr 19, 12; m 42, Helen L Griggs; c Peter G, Lynn A (Cobb), David M, Stephen K, John E & Dianne K. *Educ:* Univ Calif, Los Angeles, AB, 34; Univ Calif, Berkeley, PhD(chem), 37. *Hon Degrees:* Numerous from US & foreign univs & cols, 51-96. *Honors & Awards:* Nobel Prize in Chem, 51; Nat Medal of Sci, 91; Award Pure Chem, Am Chem Soc, 47, Nichols Medal, 48, Parsons Award, 64, Gibbs Medal, 66, Marshall Madison Award, 72; Ericsson Gold Medal, Am Soc Swed Engrs, 48; Perkin Medal, Am Sect, Brit Soc Chem Indust, 57; Edison Found Award, 58; Enrico Fermi Award, AEC, 59; Priestley Mem Award, Dickinson Col, 60 & 79; Sci & Eng Award, Fedn Eng Socs, Drexel Inst, 62; Swed Am Yr, Vasa Order Am, 62; Franklin Medal, Franklin Inst, 63; Leif Erikson Found Award, 64; Arches of Sci Award, Pac Sci Ctr, 68; Chem Pioneer, Am Inst Chemists, 68, Gold Medal Award, 73; Prometheus Award, Nat Elec Mfrs Asn, 69; Oliver Townsend Award, Atomic Indust Forum, 71, Vannevar Bush Award, 89. *Concurrent Pos:* Sect chief, Metall Lab, Univ Chicago, 42-46; mem, Gen Adv Comt, AEC, 46-50, mem, Hist Adv Comt, 58-61, chmn, 61-71; mem, Joint Comn Radioactivity, Int Coun Sci Unions, 46-56; mem sc adv bd, Robert Welch Found, 57-; mem, President's Sci Adv Comt, 59-61; mem, Pac Coast Comt, Am Coun Educ, 59-61; mem, Exec Comt & chmn, Steering Comt Chem Educ Mat Study, NSF, 59-74, mem bd, 60-61 & Adv Coun Col Chem, 62-67; trustee, Educ Serv, Inc, 61-67 & Pac Sci Ctr Found, 62-77; mem, Fed Coun Sci & Technol, 61-71; mem, Fed Radiation Coun, 61-71; mem, Nat Aeronaut & Space Coun, 61-71; mem, Comn Humanities, Am Coun Learned Socs & Coun Grad Schs, 62-65; mem, Sci Adv Comt, Pac Sci Ctr Found, 63-77; trustee, Sci Serv, 65-, pres, 66-; mem, Nat Coun Marine Res & Eng Develop, 66-71; bd trustees, Swed Coun Am, 76-; dir, Lawrence Hall Sci, Univ Calif, Berkeley, 82-84, chmn, 84- *Mem:* Nat Acad Sci; fel AAAS (pres, 72); Am Chem Soc (pres, 76); fel Am Nuclear Soc; fel Am Phys Soc; Am Inst Chemists; hon mem Chem Soc London; hon Royal Soc Edinburgh; Royal Acad Exact Phys & Natural Scis Spain; Soc Nuclear Med; Sigma Xi; Chem Soc. *Res:* Heavy ion reactions; transuranium elements. *Mailing Add:* Lawrence Berkeley Nat Lab Univ Calif 1 Cyclotron Rd Berkeley CA 94720. *Fax:* 510-486-4515; *E-Mail:* gtseaborg@lbl.gov

SEABORN, JAMES BYRD, THEORETICAL NUCLEAR PHYSICS. *Current Pos:* assoc prof, 70-83, PROF PHYSICS, UNIV RICHMOND, 83-, CHMN DEPT, 82- *Personal Data:* b Panama City, Fla, Dec 15, 32; m 53; c Jill, Carol, Richard, Thomas & Katrina. *Educ:* Fla State Univ, BS, 60, MS, 62; Univ Va, PhD(nuclear theory), 65. *Prof Exp:* Asst prof physics, Univ Richmond, 65-66; res assoc, Univ Frankfurt, 66; asst prof, NTex State Univ, 67-69; vis lectr, Iowa State Univ, 69-70. *Concurrent Pos:* Consult, Lawrence Livermore Labs, 78-82; sabbatical leaves, Lawrence Livermore Labs, 78 & Univ Mainz, WGer, 85, 93. *Res:* Nuclear structure studies; electromagnetic interactions in atomic nuclei; electromagnetic structure of the nucleon. *Mailing Add:* Dept Physics Univ Richmond Richmond VA 23173. *E-Mail:* seaborn@urvax.urich.edu

SEABROOK, WILLIAM DAVIDSON, INSECT NEUROPHYSIOLOGY. *Current Pos:* PROF BIOL, UNIV NB, FREDERICTON, 67-, RES CONSULT, BIO-ENG INST, 67- *Personal Data:* b Ottawa, Ont, Apr 2, 35; m 60; c 2. *Educ:* Carleton Univ, Can, BSc, 60, MSc, 64; Univ London, PhD(zool), 67. *Prof Exp:* Biologist, Govt Can, 60-62. *Concurrent Pos:* Dean grad studies, Univ NB, 84-89. *Mem:* Can Soc Zool; fel Can Entom Soc; Am Entom Soc. *Res:* Sensory physiology and behavior of insects, particularly chemical senses; use of insect pheromones in population management. *Mailing Add:* Dept Biol Univ NB Bag Serv No 45111 Fredericton NB E3B 6E1 Can. *Fax:* 506-453-3583; *E-Mail:* seabrook@unb.ca

SEADEN, GEORGE, CIVIL ENGINEERING, CONSTRUCTION PLANNING. *Current Pos:* DIR GEN, INST RES CONSTRUCT, 85-; CHIEF CONSTRUCT TECH GROUP, NAT RES COUN, 95- *Personal Data:* b KraKow, Poland, Apr 26, 36; Can citizen; m 78, Linda H Mutch; c Amy E & Maia C. *Educ:* McGill Univ, BE, 58; Harvard Univ, MS, 68; Northwestern Univ, advan mat dipl, 92. *Prof Exp:* Engr, Gatineau Power, 58-59; mgr, Warnock Hersey Ltd, 59-60; engr, Enterprise Fougerolle, 60-62; assoc, Cartier, Cote, Piette, 62-67; sr adv, Ministry Urban Affairs, 69-71; pres, Archer, Seaden & Assoc Inc, 71-84. *Concurrent Pos:* Vis prof, Univ Ottawa, 69-73; chmn bd dirs, St Andrews Sch, Westmount, Que, 75-82; mem, Can Construct Res Bd, 85-91, Construct Indust Develop, 88-93, Civil Eng Res Found, 93-, Res Bd, Am Pub Works Asn, 94-; pres, Conseil Int Atiment, Neth, 89-92; co-chair, Eng & Construct in Sustainable Develop, Washington, 96. *Mem:* Am Soc Civil Engrs; Inst Civil Engrs UK. *Res:* American and international construction technology; numerous publications on innovation issues. *Mailing Add:* Inst Res Construct Montreal Rd Bldg M-20 Ottawa ON K1A 0R6 Can. *Fax:* 613-941-0822; *E-Mail:* george.seaden@nrc.ca

SEADER, J(UNIOR) D(EVERE), APPLIED MATHEMATICS. *Current Pos:* chmn dept, 75-78, PROF CHEM ENG, UNIV UTAH, 66- *Personal Data:* b San Francisco, Calif, Aug 16, 27; m 50, 61, Sylvia Bowen; c Steven F, Clayton M, Gregory R, Donald J, Suzanne M (Swallow), Robert Clark, Kathleen M (Rugg) & Jennifer A (West). *Educ:* Univ Calif, BS, 49, MS, 50; Univ Wis, PhD(chem eng), 52. *Honors & Awards:* 35th Ann Inst Lectr, Am Inst Chem Engrs, 83, Comput in Chem Eng Award, 88. *Prof Exp:* Instr chem eng, Univ Wis, 51-52; res engr, Calif Res Corp, Stand Oil Co, Calif, 52-57, group supvr chem process design, 57, supvr eng res, 58-59; sr res engr, Rocketdyne Div, NAm Aviation, Inc, 59-60, res specialist, 60-61, prin scientist, 60-65; prof chem eng, Univ Idaho, 65-66. *Concurrent Pos:* Eve instr, Eng Exten, Univ Calif, 54-59; dir, Am Inst Chem Engrs, 83-85. *Mem:* Am Inst Aeronaut & Astronaut; fel Am Inst Chem Engrs, 83; Am Chem Soc. *Res:* Heat, mass and momentum transport; chemical kinetics; thermodynamics; physical properties; flammability; process synthesis and design; fuel processes; separation operations. *Mailing Add:* Dept Chem Eng Univ Utah Salt Lake City UT 84112. *E-Mail:* seader@ute.cc.utah.edu

SEAGER, SPENCER LAWRENCE, PHYSICAL CHEMISTRY. *Current Pos:* From asst prof to assoc prof chem, 61-69, PROF CHEM, WEBER STATE COL, 69-, CHMN DEPT, 68- *Personal Data:* b Ogden, Utah, Mar 10, 35; m 60; c 4. *Educ:* Univ Utah, BS, 57, PhD(phys chem), 62. *Mem:* Am Chem Soc; Sigma Xi; Nat Sci Teachers Asn. *Res:* Gas chromatography; gas phase diffusion. *Mailing Add:* Dept Chem 2503 Weber State Col Ogden UT 84408-0001

SEAGLE, EDGAR FRANKLIN, OCCUPATIONAL SAFETY & HEALTH. *Current Pos:* CONSULT ENGR, 78- *Personal Data:* b Lincolnton, NC, June 27, 24; m 58, Doris Long; c Rebecca, Elaine, Craig & William. *Educ:* Univ NC, Chapel Hill, AB, 49; Univ Fla, BCE, 61; Univ NC, MSPH, 54; Univ Tex, DrPH(environ & occup health), 74; Am Acad Environ Engrs, dipl, 75. *Honors & Awards:* Commendation Medal, USPHS. *Prof Exp:* Sanit consult, Div Epidemiol, NC State Bd Health, 54-56; chief, Indust Hyg Sect, Charlotte City Health Dept, NC, 56-59; engr, Div Radiol Health, USPHS, 61-66, chief, Prog Planning Off, 66-68, dir, Off Planning Strategy, 68-69, sr indust hyg engr, 69-75, dir occup safety, 75-78; asst dir, Fels Off Nat Nucl Sci, 78-85; pub health engr, Md State Dept Health, 85-88. *Mem:* Am Soc Civil Engrs; Am Pub Health Asn. *Res:* Radiological health; industrial hygiene; occupational safety; sanitation. *Mailing Add:* 14108 Heathfield Ct Rockville MD 20853

SEAGLE, STAN R, ALLOYS. *Current Pos:* RETIRED. *Personal Data:* b Dec 30, 33; m 55, Joyce A Smith; c Dennis, David, Jeff, Cari & Deborah. *Educ:* Purdue Univ, BS & MS. *Prof Exp:* Vpres technol, RMI Titanium Co, 79-94. *Mem:* Am Inst Mining Metall & Petrol Engrs; fel Am Soc Metals Int; Tech Asn Pulp & Paper Indust; Nat Asn Corrosion Engrs. *Res:* All aspects titanium research and development; numerous publications; 13 US patents. *Mailing Add:* 3376 E Market St Warren OH 44484. *E-Mail:* cfkd97a@prodigy.com

SEAGO, JAMES LYNN, JR, ROOT DEVELOPMENT IN AQUATIC PLANTS. *Current Pos:* From asst prof to assoc prof, 68-91, PROF BIOL, STATE UNIV NY, OSWEGO, 91- *Personal Data:* b Alton, Ill, June 2, 41; m 82, Marilyn A Meiss; c Kirstjan E & Robert M. *Educ:* Knox Col, BA, 63; Miami Univ, MA, 66; Univ Ill, Urbana, PhD(bot), 69. *Concurrent Pos:* Struct sect chair, Bot Soc Am, 77-78; teaching equip grant, NSF, 80, symposium grant, 92; adj prof, State Univ NY, Plattsburgh, 90-92. *Mem:* Bot Soc Am; Torrey Bot Club; Sigma Xi; Nature Conservancy; Nat Wildlife Soc; Wilderness Soc. *Res:* Development of plant roots with emphasis on origin of aerenchyma tissue in aquatic plants and origin of lateral roots; role of student research in undergraduate courses. *Mailing Add:* Dept Biol State Univ NY Oswego NY 13126

SEAGONDOLLAR, LEWIS WORTH, PHYSICS. *Current Pos:* head dept, 65-75, prof, 65-91, EMER PROF PHYSICS, NC STATE UNIV, 91- *Personal Data:* b Hoisington, Kans, Sept 30, 20; m 42; c 3. *Educ:* Kans State Teachers Col, AB, 41; Univ Wis, PhM, 43, PhD(physics), 48. *Prof Exp:* Instr physics, Univ Kans, 47-48, from asst prof to prof, 48-65. *Concurrent Pos:* Civilian with Manhattan proj, Los Alamos Sci Lab, 59-60 & Hanford Lab, 62-64. *Mem:* Health Physics Soc; fel Am Phys Soc; Am Asn Physics Teachers. *Res:* Low energy nuclear physics; nuclear spectroscopy; Van de Graaff generators. *Mailing Add:* Dept Physics NC State Univ Raleigh NC 27695-8202. *E-Mail:* seagondo@tunl

SEAGRAVE, JEANCLARE, SIGNAL TRANSDUCTION, DEVELOPMENTAL BIOLOGY. *Current Pos:* ASSOC SCIENTIST, INST FOR BASIC & APPL MED RES, LOVELACE INSTS, 89-, PROG DIR, SECY PHYSIOL PROG, 93- *Personal Data:* b Los Alamos, NMex, Mar 8, 54; m 89, William H Rahe. *Educ:* Calif Inst Technol, BS, 76; Univ NMex, PhD(med sci/biochem), 81. *Prof Exp:* Fel, Los Alamos Nat Lab, 81-84; res assoc, Sch Med, Univ NMex, 85, res asst prof, 85-89. *Concurrent Pos:* Adj res prof path, Univ NMex Sch Med, 89- *Mem:* Sigma Xi; AAAS; Am Soc Cell Biol; NY Acad Sci; Am Physiol Soc. *Res:* Signal transduction: the mechanisms by which the binding of hormones and neurotransmitters to cell surface receptors induce changes in intracellular biochemical events and cellular functions. *Mailing Add:* Lovelace Insts 2425 Ridgecrest Dr SE Albuquerque NM 87108-5127. *Fax:* 505-262-7043; *E-Mail:* jinkle@lucy.tli.org

SEAGRAVE, JOHN DORRINGTON, NUCLEAR PHYSICS, OPTICAL PHYSICS. *Current Pos:* RETIRED. *Personal Data:* b Bronxville, NY, Jan 23, 26; m 51, Sara H Gibson; c Jean Clare & Charles G. *Educ:* Calif Inst Technol, BS, 46, MS, 48, PhD(physics), 51. *Prof Exp:* Mem staff physics, Los Alamos Nat Lab, 51-90. *Concurrent Pos:* Consult, Los Alamos Nat Lab, 90-93; sci demonstrations children, 90-; co-producer, Arts Alive! & Well, 93- *Mem:* Fel AAAS; Am Optical Soc; fel Am Phys Soc; Sigma Xi. *Res:* Optical physics and detectors; interactive image processing and pattern recognition; structure of very light nuclei and fast neutron scattering. *Mailing Add:* 3514 Arizona Ave Los Alamos NM 87544. *Fax:* 505-662-3422; *E-Mail:* agvadon@rt66.com

SEAGRAVE, RICHARD C(HARLES), CHEMICAL ENGINEERING. *Current Pos:* assoc prof, 66-71, PROF CHEM ENG, IOWA STATE UNIV, 71- *Personal Data:* b Westerly, RI, Dec 31, 35; m 59; c 1. *Educ:* Univ RI, BS, 57; Iowa State Univ, MS, 59, PhD(chem eng), 61. *Prof Exp:* Asst prof chem eng, Univ Conn, 61-62; res fel, Calif Inst Technol, 62-63, asst prof, 63-66. *Mem:* Am Inst Chem Engrs. *Res:* Transport phenomena; reactor dynamics; biomedical engineering. *Mailing Add:* 318 Westbrook Lane Ames IA 50014

SEALANDER, JOHN ARTHUR, JR, ANIMAL PHYSIOLOGY. *Current Pos:* RETIRED. *Personal Data:* b Detroit Lakes, Minn, Dec 9, 17; wid; c 3. *Educ:* Luther Col, AB, 40; Mich State Univ, MS, 42; Univ Ill, PhD(zool), 49. *Prof Exp:* Asst zool, Mich State Univ, 40-42; asst zool & physiol, Univ Ill, 46-48; from asst prof to prof zool, Univ Ark, Fayetteville, 49-88. *Concurrent Pos:* USPHS spec fel, Inst Arctic Biol, Univ Alaska, 63-64; mem staff, Rocky Mt Biol Lab, 57; investr biol sta, Queen's Univ, Ont, 58; res assoc, Univ Ga, 68. *Mem:* AAAS; Am Soc Zool; Ecol Soc Am; Am Soc Mammal; Am Physiol Soc. *Res:* Comparative physiology; acclimatization of mammals to environmental temperature changes; natural history and ecology of mammals. *Mailing Add:* Dept Biol Sci Univ Ark Fayetteville AR 72703

SEALE, DIANNE B, ECOSYSTEMS & POPULATIONS, AMPHIBIANS. *Current Pos:* CTR SCIENTIST, CTR GREAT LAKES STUDIES, UNIV WIS, MILWAUKEE, 80-, FAC MEM BIOL SCI, 84-, ASSOC PROF, 89- *Personal Data:* b Birmingham, Ala, Apr 15, 45; m 73, Martin Boraas. *Educ:* Washington Univ, St Louis, PhD, 73. *Prof Exp:* Fel, Nat Endowment Humanites, Pa State Univ, 73-74, instr environ sci, 73; res scientist, Ill Inst Technol, 74-75; res assoc, Dept Biol, Pa State Univ, 75-80. *Concurrent Pos:* Vis instr, Northwestern Univ, 74-75; prin investr, NSF grants, 75-78 & 78-80; Nat Oceanic & Atmospheric Admin Sea grants, 82-87; Environ Protection Agency grant, 84-86; Johnson Wax Co Career Develop Fel, 93. *Mem:* Sigma Xi; Am Soc Limnol & Oceanog; Ecol Soc Am; Am Soc Ichthyologists & Herpetologists; Int Asn Great Lakes Res; Herpetologists' League. *Res:* Impact of suspension feeders on ecosystem processes; factors regulating suspension feeding dynamics; plant animal interactions; amphibian breeding behavior and larval community structure; nutrient release by amphibians and by Mysis relicta; phytoplankton ecology; animal energetics; microbiology. *Mailing Add:* Dept Biol Sci Univ Wis Box 413 Milwaukee WI 53201. *Fax:* 414-229-3926

SEALE, MARVIN ERNEST, ANIMAL BREEDING. *Current Pos:* RETIRED. *Personal Data:* b Edmonton, Alta, June 7, 22; m 53; c 4. *Educ:* Univ Alta, BSc, 48; Univ Minn, MS, 51, PhD(animal breeding), 65. *Prof Exp:* From asst prof to prof animal sci, Univ Man, 51-85, head dept, 73-80, assoc dean & dir, Glenlea Res Sta, 80-85. *Mem:* Am Soc Animal Sci; Can Soc Animal Prod; Genetics Soc Can. *Res:* Development of new breeds of livestock; inheritance of quantitative traits; evaluation of heterosis. *Mailing Add:* 195 Lyndel Dr Winnipeg MB R2H 1K5 Can

SEALE, RAYMOND ULRIC, ANATOMY, EXPERIMENTAL EMBRYOLOGY. *Current Pos:* assoc prof, 71-80, PROF ANAT, RUSH MED COL, 80- *Personal Data:* b Snyder, Tex, Aug 19, 34; m 55; c 1. *Educ:* Eastern NMex Univ, BS, 56; Wash Univ, AM, 58; Univ Minn, PhD, 63. *Prof Exp:* Asst prof anat, Col Dent, Baylor Univ, 63-65; instr, Univ Tex Southwestern Med Sch, 65-66; asst prof, Sch Med, Univ Colo, Denver, 66-71. *Concurrent Pos:* Vis instr, Southern Methodist Univ, 65-66; spec instr, Med Ctr, Baylor Univ, 63-66; AMA consult gross anat, Fac Med, Univ Saigon, 70. *Mem:* AAAS; NY Acad Sci; Am Asn Anat. *Res:* Developmental aspects of acquired immunological tolerance; morphogenetic movement in chick embryos in vitro; role of catecholamines in differentiation; mosaic and regulative capacity of organ primordia. *Mailing Add:* Dept Anat Rush Med Col 600 S Paulina Chicago IL 60612

SEALE, ROBERT L(EWIS), NUCLEAR ENGINEERING. *Current Pos:* head dept, 69-90, PROF NUCLEAR ENG, UNIV ARIZ, 61- *Personal Data:* b Rosenberg, Tex, Mar 18, 28; m 47, Lina G John; c Katherine, Linda, James & Anne. *Educ:* Univ Houston, BS, 47; Univ Tex, MS, 51, PhD(physics), 53. *Prof Exp:* Nuclear engr, Gen Dynamics Corp, Tex, 53-57, proj engr, 57-59, chief nuclear opers, 59-61. *Concurrent Pos:* Lectr, Southern Methodist Univ, 55-60; consult, Los Alamos Sci Lab, 61 & Sandia Corp, NMex, 66-; mem bd dir, Eng Coun Prof Develop, 72-79 & Inst Nuclear Power Opers Accreditation Bd, 81-90. *Mem:* Am Asn Physics Teachers; Am Phys Soc; Am Nuclear Soc; Nat Soc Prof Engrs; Sigma Xi. *Res:* Radiation shielding; nuclear reactor operations and safety; use of nuclear reactors. *Mailing Add:* 8815 E Calle Bogota Tucson AZ 85715-5524

SEALS, JONATHAN ROGER, INSULIN ACTION, GROWTH CONTROL. *Current Pos:* ASST PROF BIOCHEM, SCH MED, UNIV MASS, 82- *Educ:* Wash Univ, St Louis, PhD(cell biol), 79. *Mailing Add:* Dept Biochem Univ Mass Med Sch 55 Lake Ave N Worcester MA 01655-0103. *Fax:* 508-797-4014

SEALS, RUPERT GRANT, DAIRY INDUSTRY. *Current Pos:* assoc dean & prof, 77-89, EMER PROF ANIMAL SCI, COL AGR, UNIV NEV, 89- *Personal Data:* b Shelbyville, Ky, Aug, 32; m 54; c 4. *Educ:* Fla Agr & Mech Univ, BS, 53; Univ Ky, MS, 56; Wash State Univ, PhD(dairy chem), 60. *Prof Exp:* Instr dairying, Fla Agr & Mech Univ, 54-55; res asst dairy sci, Wash State Univ, 55-59; assoc prof dairy mfg, Tenn Agr & Ind State, 59-64; res assoc, Iowa State Univ, 64-66, asst prof, 66-69; prof food chem & dean sch agr & home econ, Fla A&M Univ, 69-77; dir, Int Prog, Fla A&M Univ, 89-94. *Concurrent Pos:* Coordr spec prog, Coop State Res Serv, USBA, 74- *Mem:* Inst Food Technologists. *Res:* Amino acids in peanuts; milk proteins; lipid and flavor chemistry. *Mailing Add:* 925 E Magnolia Apt M-5 Tallahassee FL 32301

SEAMAN, EDNA, BIOLOGY. *Current Pos:* assoc prof biol, Univ Mass, Harbor Campus, 74-80, chmn dept, 78-80, assoc dean arts & sci, 80-92, PROF BIOL, UNIV MASS, HARBOR CAMPUS, 92- *Personal Data:* b Warsaw, Poland, July 2, 32; nat US; m 56; c 3. *Educ:* Brooklyn Col, BS, 56; Univ Ill, PhD(microbiol), 60. *Prof Exp:* Fel biochem, Brandeis, 60-68; asst prof biol, 68-73. *Res:* Molecular biology; interrelations of DNA, RNA and proteins; bacterial transformations; synthesis of nucleic acids in subcellular systems. *Mailing Add:* Dept Biol Univ Mass Boston 100 Mornssey Blvd Boston MA 02125-3393

SEAMAN, GEOFFREY VINCENT F, PHYSICAL BIOCHEMISTRY, BIOMATERIALS. *Current Pos:* PROF NEUROL & BIOCHEM, WESTERN BIOMEDICAL RES INST, 92- *Personal Data:* b Uxbridge, Eng, Nov 24, 32; m 58, 81; c 7. *Educ:* Royal Col Sci, London, BSc, 55; Cambridge Univ, PhD(biophys), 58. *Prof Exp:* Fel med, Univ Cambridge, 57-60; Beit Mem res fel, Univ Cambridge, 60-61 & Univ Cologne, 61-62; sr asst radiotherapeut, Univ Cambridge, 62-66; asst prof neurol, Ore Health Sci Univ, 66-68, from assoc prof to prof neurol & biochem, 68-88. *Concurrent Pos:* Res fel neurol, Med Sch, Univ Ore, 63-64; ed newslett, Int Soc Biorheology, 69; ed, Biorheology, 72; mem adv comt to NASA, Univ Space Res Asn, 72; ed, Thrombosis Res, 77-81, Clin Hemorheol, 80; NIH, Cardiovasc & Renal Study Sect. *Mem:* Am Soc Biol Chemists; Am Chem Soc; Biophys Soc; Int Soc Biorheology (secy gen, 69); NY Acad Sci; Am Soc Hemorheol; fel NY Acad Sci; Soc Biomats. *Res:* Surface properties of biological cells, especially blood cells; flow properties of blood and cell suspensions; composition and molecular structure of the glycoprotein components of cellular membranes; biocompatibility of surfaces. *Mailing Add:* Emerald Diagnostics Inc PO Box 22510 Eugene OR 97402-0419

SEAMAN, GREGORY G, ENVIRONMENTAL PHYSICS. *Current Pos:* prod specialist, Canberra Industs, 76-78, appln mgr, 79-80, proj mgr, 81-84, MGR SYSTS ENG, INSTRUMENTATION DIV, CANBERRA INDUSTS, 84- *Personal Data:* b Alma, Mich, Jan 6, 38; m 80; c 3. *Educ:* Col Wooster, AB, 59; Yale Univ, MS, 60, PhD(physics), 65. *Prof Exp:* Appointee nuclear physics, Los Alamos Sci Lab, 64-66; fel, Rutgers Univ, 66-68; from asst prof to assoc prof nuclear physics, Kans State Univ, 68-76. *Mem:* Am Phys Soc; Am Asn Physics Teachers. *Res:* Coulomb excitation; Ericson fluctuations; Doppler shift attenuation measurements of nuclear lifetimes; trace element analysis of foods by x-ray fluorescence. *Mailing Add:* Canberra Industs 800 Research Pkwy Meriden CT 06450-7169

SEAMAN, LYNN, CIVIL ENGINEERING, STRUCTURES. *Current Pos:* Civil engr, 61-67, physicist, 67-, SR RES ENGR, STANFORD RES INST INT. *Personal Data:* b De Queene, Ark, Aug 28, 33; m 89, Renate C Ehleben; c Peggy, Mark, Ellen & Tanya. *Educ:* Univ Calif, Berkeley, BS, 59; Mass Inst Technol, PhD(civil eng), 61. *Mem:* Am Soc Civil Engrs; Am Phys Soc. *Res:* Structural mechanics, shell buckling, structural dynamics; materials science, equations of state for soil and other porous media, crack growth and fracturing; wave propagation. *Mailing Add:* Stanford Res Inst 333 Ravenswood Ave Menlo Park CA 94025. *Fax:* 650-859-2260; *E-Mail:* micro2.seaman@crvax.sri.com

SEAMAN, RONALD L, BIOENGINEERING & BIOMEDICAL ENGINEERING. *Current Pos:* SR BIOMED RES SCIENTIST, MCKESSON BIOMED SERV, 94- *Personal Data:* b Seaman, Ohio, Feb 10, 47; m 77; c 5. *Educ:* Univ Cincinnati, BS, 70; Duke Univ, PhD(biomed eng), 75; Georgia Tech, MS(Mgt), 87. *Prof Exp:* Res assoc, Duke Univ, 74; res fel, Univ Tex Health Sci Ctr, Dallas, 75-76, instr physiol, 76-79; res engr, Ga Tech Res Inst, 79-82, sr reg engr, 82-86; assoc prof, La Tech Univ, 86- *Concurrent Pos:* Res teaching asst, Duke Univ, 70-74; teaching asst, Univ Southern Calif, Santa Catalina Marine Biol Lab, 72; adj fac & adv bd, DeKalb Area Tech Voc Sch, 81-85; adj fac, Oglethorpe Univ, 83-84; teacher, Col Mgt, Ga Inst Tech, 84. *Mem:* Inst Elec & Electronics Engrs; AAAS; Soc Neurosci; Bioelectromagnetics Soc; NY Acad Sci. *Res:* Microwave biological effects, primarily neural systems; electromagnetic field interactions with biological tissues; vestibular and auditory transduction; microwave exposure devices; modeling of physiological systems. *Mailing Add:* McKesson Biomed Serv PO Box 35460 Brooks AFB TX 78235-5460

SEAMAN, WILLIAM B, RADIOLOGY. *Current Pos:* prof & chmn dept, 56-82, J PICKER EMER PROF RADIOL, COL PHYSICIANS & SURGEONS, COLUMBIA UNIV, 82- *Personal Data:* b Chicago, Ill, Jan 5, 17; m 44; c 2. *Educ:* Harvard Med Sch, MD, 41. *Honors & Awards:* Gold Medal, Am Col Radiol, 83; W B Cannon Medal, Soc Gastrointestinal Radiol. *Prof Exp:* Instr radiol, Sch Med, Yale Univ, 48-49; from instr to prof, Sch Med, Wash Univ, 49-56. *Concurrent Pos:* Dir radiol serv, Presby Hosp, New York, 56-82; chmn comt radiol, Nat Acad Sci-Nat Res Coun, 69-73; mem bd chancellors, Am Col Radiol, 75-78. *Mem:* Am Roentgen Ray Soc (pres, 73-74); Soc Gastrointestinal Radiol (pres, 73-74); Radiol Soc NAm; Asn Univ Radiol (pres, 56). *Res:* Diagnostic roentgenology. *Mailing Add:* 630 W 168th St Suite 440 New York NY 10032

SEAMAN, WILLIAM E, RHEUMATOLOGY. *Current Pos:* ASSOC PROF MED, UNIV CALIF, SAN FRANCISCO, 76-, CHIEF ARTHRITIS & IMMUNOL, VET ADMIN MED CTR, SAN FRANCISCO, CALIF, 82- *Personal Data:* b Washington, DC, May 22, 42. *Educ:* Harvard Univ, MD, 69. *Mem:* Am Asn Immunol; Am Fedn Clin Res; Am Soc Clin Invest. *Mailing Add:* Dept Med & Microbiol VA Med Ctr Ill 4150 Clement St San Francisco CA 94121-1598. *Fax:* 415-386-4357

SEAMAN, WILLIAM LLOYD, PLANT PATHOLOGY. *Current Pos:* res officer, 60-73, RES SCIENTIST, CAN DEPT AGR, 73- *Personal Data:* b Charlottetown, PEI, July 16, 34; m 59; c 3. *Educ:* McGill Univ, BSc, 56; Univ Wis, PhD, 60. *Prof Exp:* Asst plant path, Univ Wis, 56-60. *Mem:* Am Phytopath Soc; fel Can Phytopath Soc. *Res:* Cereal grain diseases; disease survey. *Mailing Add:* Eastern Cereal & Oil Seed Res Ctr Bldg 75 Driveway Ottawa ON K1A 0C6 Can

SEAMANS, DAVID A(LVIN), ELECTRICAL ENGINEERING, COMPUTER ENGINEERING. *Current Pos:* from instr to asst prof, 54-63, ASSOC PROF ELEC ENG, WASH STATE UNIV, 63- *Personal Data:* b Lawrence, Kans, June 13, 27; m 57; c 2. *Educ:* Univ Kans, BS, 50, MS, 56; Ore State Univ, PhD, 68. *Prof Exp:* Jr engr, Black & Veatch, Consult Engrs, 50-52; instr elec eng, Univ Kans, 53-54. *Mem:* Inst Elec & Electronics Engrs; Simulation Coun; Am Soc Eng Educ; Asn Comput Mach. *Res:* Analog and digital computer technology; artificial intelligence. *Mailing Add:* Sch EE/CS Wash State Univ EE/CS Dept Pullman WA 99164-2752

SEAMANS, R(OBERT) C(HANNING), JR, AERONAUTICAL ENGINEERING. *Current Pos:* RETIRED. *Personal Data:* b Salem, Mass, Oct 30, 18; m 42; c 5. *Educ:* Harvard Univ, BS, 39; Mass Inst Technol, MS, 42, ScD(instrumentation), 51. *Hon Degrees:* DSc, Rollins Col, 62, NY Univ, 67; DEng, Norwich Acad, 71, Notre Dame Univ, 74, Rensselaer Polytech Inst, 74, Univ Wyoming, 75, George Washington Univ, 75, Lehigh Univ, 76, Thomas Col, 80 & Curry Col, 82. *Honors & Awards:* Naval Ord Develop Award, 45; Lawrence Sperry Award, Am Inst Aeronaut & Astronaut, 51; NASA Distinguished Serv Medal, 65 & 69; Goddard Trophy, 68; Dept Air Force Exceptional Civilian Serv Award; Dept Defense Distinguished Pub Serv Medal; Gen Thomas D White USAF Space Trophy; Ralph Coats Roe Medal, Am Soc Mech Engrs; Arthur M Bueche Award, Nat Acad Eng, 94, Daniel Guggenheim Award, 96. *Prof Exp:* From instr to assoc prof aeronaut eng, Mass Inst Technol, 41-55, staff engr, Instrumentation Lab, 41-45, proj leader, 45-50, chief engr, Proj Meteor, 50-55, dir, Flight Control Lab, 53-55; mgr, Airborne Systs Lab & chief systs engr, Airborne Systs Dept, Radio Corp Am, 55-58, chief engr, Missile Electronics & Controls Div, RCA Corp, 58-60; assoc adminr, NASA, 60-65, dep adminr, 65-68; Jerome Clarke Hunsaker prof aeronaut & astronaut, Mass Inst Technol, 68-69; Secy of the Air Force, 69-73; adminr, US ERDA, 74-77; Henry R Luce prof environ & pub policy, Mass Inst Technol, 77-84, dean eng, 78-81, sr lectr aeronaut, 84-96. *Concurrent Pos:* Mem, Subcomt Automatic Stabilization & Control, Nat Adv Comt Aeronaut, 48-58 & Group Instrumentation & Spec Comt Space Technol, 58-59; consult, Sci Adv Bd, USAF, 57-59, mem, 59-62, assoc adv, 62-67; nat deleg, Adv Group Aerospace Res & Develop, NATO, 66-69; consult to adminr, NASA, 68-69; mem bd overseers, Harvard Univ, 68-74. *Mem:* Nat Acad Eng (pres, 73-74); fel Am Astronaut Soc; fel Inst Elec & Electronics Engrs; hon fel Am Inst Aeronaut & Astronaut; AAAS. *Res:* Administration; instrumentation. *Mailing Add:* 675 Hale St Beverly MA 01915

SEAMON, KENNETH BRUCE, HORMONE REGULATION, CALCIUM REGULATION. *Current Pos:* SR VPRES, SCI DEVELOP, IMMUNEX CORP, 96- *Educ:* Carnegie-Mellon Univ, PhD(chem), 77. *Prof Exp:* Res chemist, Ctr Drugs & Biologics, Food & Drug Admin, 83-87, lab chief, Lab Molecular Pharmacol, Div Biochem & Biophys, Ctr Biologist Eval & Res, 87-90, assoc dir res, 90-96. *Mailing Add:* 4209 W Bertona St Seattle WA 98199

SEAMON, ROBERT EDWARD, NUCLEAR PHYSICS. *Personal Data:* b Worcester, Mass, May 18, 39. *Educ:* Worcester Polytech Inst, BS, 61; Yale Univ, MS, 63, PhD(physics), 68. *Prof Exp:* Res staff mem nuclear reactor physics, Los Alamos Sci Lab, 69-71, staff nuclear physics, 71-93. *Concurrent Pos:* Staff mem, Nuclear Data Sect, Int Atomic Energy Agency, Vienna, Austria, 77-78. *Res:* Evaluated nuclear data files (ENDF/B) and associated processing codes used in weapons calculations; phase-shift analysis of nucleon-nucleon scattering data; nucleon-nucleon potentials. *Mailing Add:* Box 421 Los Alamos NM 87544

SEANOR, DONALD A, CHEMISTRY. *Current Pos:* scientist res labs div, Xerox Corp, 67-70, scientist info technol group, 70-71, sr scientist spec mat technol ctr, 71-81, prin scientist, 81-86, MGR, ELASTOMER TECHNOL, XEROX CORP, 86- *Personal Data:* b Gatley, Eng, June 10, 36; m 60; c 2. *Educ:* Bristol Univ, BSc, 57, PhD(phys chem), 61. *Prof Exp:* Nat Res Coun Can fel catalysis, 61-63; from res chemist to sr res chemist, Chemstrand Res Ctr, Inc, Monsanto Co, NC, 63-67. *Concurrent Pos:* Guest lectr, NY State Col Environ Sci & Forestry, Syracuse, 75 & Mgt Res & Develop Course, Mitsloan Sch. *Mem:* Chem Soc; Am Chem Soc; Plastics & Rubber Asn. *Res:* Surface chemistry; solid state physics and chemistry; triboelectricity; polymers; photoconductivity and conduction in polymers; tribology; materials development; elastomer technology. *Mailing Add:* 264 Garnsey Rd Pittsford NY 14534-3806

SEAPY, DAVE GLENN, PHYSICAL ORGANIC CHEMISTRY, PHOTOCHEMISTRY. *Current Pos:* Vis asst prof, 83-84, ASST PROF CHEM, FLA INST TECHNOL, 84- *Personal Data:* b Santa Barbara, Calif, Aug 25, 56; m 84. *Educ:* Univ Calif Davis, BS, 78; Univ Colo Boulder, MS, 81, PhD(chem), 83. *Mem:* Am Chem Soc; Sigma Xi. *Res:* Organic photochemistry; the synthesis of rigid bridged ring compounds for the purpose of studying photochemical mechanisms; the process of intramolecular electron transfer. *Mailing Add:* 880 Roosevelt St Kingsburg CA 93631-2335

SEAQUIST, ERNEST RAYMOND, ASTRONOMY. *Current Pos:* Lectr, Univ Toronto, 65-66, from asst prof to assoc prof, 66-78, prof & assoc chmn, 78-88, CHMN, UNIV TORONTO, 88- *Personal Data:* b Vancouver, BC, Nov 19, 38; m 66; c 2. *Educ:* Univ BC, BASc, 61; Univ Toronto, MA, 62, PhD(astron), 66. *Mem:* Am Astron Soc; Can Astron Soc; Int Astron Union; Royal Astron Soc Can. *Res:* Galactic and extragalactic radio sources. *Mailing Add:* Dept Astron Univ Toronto Toronto ON M5S 3H8 Can

SEARCY, A(LAN) W(INN), MATERIALS SCIENCE, CHEMISTRY. *Current Pos:* from assoc prof to prof ceramic eng, Univ Calif, Berkeley, 54-59, prof eng sci, 59-60, prof mat sci, 60-91, fac asst to chancellor, 63-64, vchancellor, 64-67, Miller res prof, 70-71, assoc dir, Lawrence Berkeley Lab & head, Mat & Molecular Res Div, 80-84, EMER PROF MAT SCI, UNIV CALIF, BERKELEY, 91- *Personal Data:* b Covina, Calif, Oct 12, 25; m 45, Gail Vaught; c Gay, William & Anne. *Educ:* Pomona Col, AB, 46; Univ Calif, PhD(chem), 50. *Prof Exp:* Asst chem, Univ Calif, 47-48, chemist, Radiation Lab, 48-49 & 50; from instr to asst prof, Purdue Univ, 49-54. *Concurrent Pos:* Consult, Los Alamos Sci Lab, Calif, 55-59 & Lawrence Radiation Lab, 56-61, assoc div head, Inorg Mat Div, 61-64; consult, adv res proj agency, US Dept Defense, 58-60; Fulbright lectr, Balseiro Physics Inst, Arg, 60-61; prin investr, Lawrence Berkeley Lab, 60-91; mem, Nat Res Coun, Comt High Temperature Chem, 61-70; Guggenhiem fel, 67-68. *Mem:* Fel AAAS; fel Am Ceramic Soc; Am Chem Soc; Mat Res Soc; Int Acad Ceramics. *Res:* Compositions of vapors at high temperatures and low pressures; thermodynamics of high temperature reactions; kinetics of gas-solid reactions and vaporization; thermodynamics of surfaces; thermodynamics and kinetics of sintering. *Mailing Add:* Dept Mat Sci & Mineral Eng Univ Calif Berkeley CA 94720

SEARCY, CHARLES JACKSON, MATHEMATICS. *Current Pos:* CONSULT, 88- *Personal Data:* b Beaver, Okla, Feb 14, 35; m 61; c 2. *Educ:* Panhandle A&M Col, BS, 57; Okla State Univ, MS, 63, EdD(math), 67. *Prof Exp:* Instr math, Cent State Col, Okla, 65-67; from asst prof to prof math, NMex Highlands Univ, 67-88. *Mem:* Math Asn Am; Am Math Soc. *Res:* Topology; algebra. *Mailing Add:* Box 19 HC31 Las Vegas NM 87701

SEARCY, DENNIS GRANT, CELL PHYSIOLOGY, ARCHAE BACTERIA. *Current Pos:* from asst prof to assoc prof, 71-88, PROF ZOOL, UNIV MASS, AMHERST, 88- *Personal Data:* b Portland, Ore, Sept 25, 42; m 66; c 2. *Educ:* Ore State Univ, BS, 64; Univ Calif, Los Angeles, PhD(zool), 68. *Prof Exp:* NIH trainee, Univ Calif, Los Angeles, 68-69; fel, Calif Inst Technol, 69-71. *Concurrent Pos:* Vis scholar, Oxford, 78-79; Nat Ctr Sci Res fel, Nat Mus Natural History, Paris, 84-85. *Mem:* Int Soc Evolutionary Protistology. *Res:* Evolution; origin of eukaryotic cells; histones; physiology of primitive organisms; sulfur respiration. *Mailing Add:* Dept Biol Univ Mass Amherst MA 01003-5810. *E-Mail:* dsearcy@bio.umass.edu

SEARIGHT, THOMAS KAY, GEOLOGY. *Current Pos:* from asst prof to assoc prof, 59-74, PROF GEOL, ILL STATE UNIV, 74- *Personal Data:* b Vermillion, SDak, June 3, 29; m 54; c 2. *Educ:* Univ Mo, AB, 51, MA, 52; Univ Ill, PhD, 59. *Prof Exp:* Geologist, State Geol Surv, Mo, 52-54. *Concurrent Pos:* Res affil, Ill State Geol Surv, 62- *Mem:* Geol Soc Am; Soc Econ Paleont & Mineral; Am Asn Petrol Geologists. *Res:* Pennsylvania stratigraphy and sedimentation of the mid-continent region. *Mailing Add:* Dept Geog & Geol Ill State Univ Campus Box 4400 Normal IL 61790-0001

SEARLE, CAMPBELL L(EACH), ELECTRONICS. *Current Pos:* RETIRED. *Personal Data:* b Winnipeg, Man, July 24, 26; Can citizen; m 53; c 4. *Educ:* Queen's Univ, Ont, BSc, 47; Mass Inst Technol, SM, 51. *Hon Degrees:* DSc, Queen's Univ, Ont, 95. *Prof Exp:* Mem staff, Div Sponsored Res, Mass Inst Technol, 51-56, from instr to prof elec eng, 56-74; prof psychol & elec eng, Queen's Univ, Ont, 74-79; prof elec eng, Mass Inst Technol, 79-93. *Mem:* Inst Elec & Electronics Engrs; Acoust Soc Am. *Res:* Auditory and speech perception. *Mailing Add:* 55 Wellesley St Weston MA 02193

SEARLE, GORDON WENTWORTH, PHYSIOLOGY. *Current Pos:* RETIRED. *Personal Data:* b Providence, RI, Mar 9, 20; m 45; c 3. *Educ:* Univ Ill, BS, 41, MD, 45; Northwestern Univ, MS, 49, PhD(physiol), 51. *Prof Exp:* Asst physiol, Northwestern Univ, 48-51; asst prof, Albany Med Col, Union, NY, 51-52; asst prof, Col Med, Univ Iowa, 52-55, assoc prof physiol, 55- *Concurrent Pos:* Vis res prof, Med Sch, Univ Newcastle, 64-65. *Mem:* AAAS; Am Physiol Soc; Soc Exp Biol & Med; Sigma Xi. *Res:* Intestinal absorption; bile secretion. *Mailing Add:* 345 Koser Ave Iowa City IA 52246-3037

SEARLE, JOHN RANDOLPH, BIOMEDICAL ENGINEERING. *Current Pos:* ASST PROF BIOMED ENG, MED COL GA, 77- *Personal Data:* b Wilmington, Del, Jan 20, 47; m 73; c 2. *Educ:* Wake Forest Univ, BS, 70; NC State Univ, BS, 70; Duke Univ, PhD(biomed eng), 75. *Prof Exp:* Biomed engr, Vet Admin, 75-77. *Mem:* AAAS; Asn Advan Med Instrumentation; Inst Elec & Electronics Engrs; Eng Med & Biol. *Res:* Fetal heart rate analysis by micromputer; flow in collapsible vessels; high rate dilatometry of dental porcelains. *Mailing Add:* Med Col Ga Ai-1025 University Pl Augusta GA 30912

SEARLE, NORMA ZIZMER, WEATHERING & STABILIZATION OF POLYMERS, RADIOMETRY. *Current Pos:* INDEPENDENT CONSULT PLASTICS & CHEM, 82- *Personal Data:* b New York, NY, Jan 26, 25; m 49, Bernard. *Educ:* Hunter Col, BA, 46; NY Univ, PhD(phys chem), 59. *Prof Exp:* Control chemist, Purepac Pharmaceut Co, 46; res chemist, Montefiore Hosp, New York, 47-53; chemist, New York Dept Health, 53-54; chemist, Am Cyanamid Co, 57-69, sr res chemist, 69-74, group head, 74-82. *Concurrent Pos:* Lectr, short courses on weathering of polymers & paints; consult, Atlas Elec Devices Co, Amoco Performance Prod, Borg Warner Chem, Shell Develop Co, Eli Lilly & Co Pharm & Analytical Develop Div. *Mem:* Am Chem Soc; Am Soc Testing & Mat; Am Asn Textile Chemists & Colorists. *Res:* Application of photochemistry, spectroradiometry and spectroscopy (UV, VIS, NIR, IR, MS, Luminescence) techniques to development of light stable polymers and coatings including paint for space vehicles; material property evaluations by physical chemical and analytical techniques; developed techniques for determining wavelength sensitivity of polymers. *Mailing Add:* 114 Ventnor F Deerfield Beach FL 33442. *Fax:* 954-480-8938; *E-Mail:* a001766t@bc.seflin.org

SEARLE, ROGER, ANALYTICAL CHEMISTRY. *Current Pos:* RETIRED. *Personal Data:* b Wilmington, Del, July 24, 36; m 61; c 2. *Educ:* Oberlin Col, BA, 58; Univ Ill, PhD(org chem), 63. *Prof Exp:* Res chemist, Eastman Kodak Co, 63-88; res chemist, Sterling Drug, 88-93. *Mem:* AAAS; Am Chem Soc; Sigma Xi. *Res:* Physical organic chemistry; organic photochemistry. *Mailing Add:* 2061 Angela Rd Wagener SC 29164

SEARLE, SHAYLE ROBERT, LINEAR MODELS, VARIANCE COMPONENTS. *Current Pos:* res asst animal breeding, NY State Col Agr, Cornell Univ, 56-58, res assoc, 58-59, from asst prof to assoc prof biol statist, 62-69, PROF BIOL STATIST, NY STATE COL AGR, CORNELL UNIV, 69. *Personal Data:* b Wanganui NZ, Apr 26, 28; wid; c 2. *Educ:* Victoria Univ Wellington, BA, 49, MA, 50; Cambridge Univ, dipl math stat, 53; Cornell Univ, PhD(animal breeding), 59. *Honors & Awards:* Alexander von Humboldt Sr US Scientist Award, 84. *Prof Exp:* Actuarial asst, Colonial Mutual Life Ins Co, NZ, 50-51; res statistician, NZ Dairy Bd, 53-62. *Concurrent Pos:* Fulbright travel award, 56-59; short course teaching, George Washington Univ, 77- *Mem:* Fel Am Statist Asn; Biomet Soc; fel Royal Statist Soc; Int Statist Inst. *Res:* Matrix algebra; linear models; variance components. *Mailing Add:* 50 S The Parkway Ithaca NY 14850. *Fax:* 607-255-4698

SEARLE, WILLARD F, JR, OCEAN ENGINEERING, NAVAL & SALVAGE ENGINEERING. *Current Pos:* PRES, SEARLE & CO, 93- *Personal Data:* b Columbus, Ohio, Jan 17, 24. *Educ:* US Naval Acad, Annapolis, BS, 48; Mass Inst Technol, MS, 52. *Honors & Awards:* Harold E Saunders Award, Am Soc Naval Engrs, 85. *Prof Exp:* Eng duty officer, USN, 47-56, head eng res, Exp Diving Unit, 56-64, supvr salvage, 64-69, proj mgr ship acquisition, 69-70; instr ocean eng, Marine Maritime Acad, 71-84; sr vis lectr, Mass Inst Technol, 71-90. *Concurrent Pos:* Mem, var studies, comts & panels, Marine Bd, Nat Res Coun, 70-84, var adv panels, Nat Oceanic & Atmospheric Admin, Ocean Thermal Energy Conversion, Dept Energy, UN Environ Prog & UN Relief Oper, Bangladesh; chmn, Standing Panel Salvage & Ocean Towing, Soc Naval Architects & Marine Engrs, Comt Diving & Salvage, Marine Technol Soc & MacKinnon Searle Consortium Ltd, 71- *Mem:* Nat Acad Eng; Inst Nautical Architects; Soc Naval Architects & Marine Engrs; Am Soc Naval Engrs; Royal Inst Naval Engrs; Soc Am Mil Engrs. *Res:* Unique salvage and wreck clearance; deep search and recovery; explosive ordnance disposal; submarine seafloor cable laying; author of more than 100 technical publications. *Mailing Add:* 2121 Eisenhower Ave Suite 210 Alexandria VA 22314-4688

SEARLES, ARTHUR LANGLEY, ORGANIC CHEMISTRY. *Current Pos:* assoc prof chem 56-73, chmn dept, 70-72, PROF CHEM, COL MT ST VINCENT, 74- *Personal Data:* b Nashua, NH, Aug 8, 20. *Educ:* NY Univ, BA, 42, PhD(chem), 46. *Honors & Awards:* Bene Merenti Medal, 81. *Prof Exp:* Asst, Squibb Inst Med Res, 44; from instr to asst prof org chem, NY Univ, 46-56. *Concurrent Pos:* Consult, Roel-Cryston Corp, New York, 50-52; FMC Corp, Princeton, NJ, 55-57 & US Govt, 56; vis prof, Dept Chem, Hunter Col, 57 & NY Univ, 63, 64 & 66. *Mem:* Am Chem Soc; Royal Soc Chem; Sigma Xi. *Res:* Nitrogen heterocycles; organo-metallics; beta-ketoanilides. *Mailing Add:* 48 Highland Circle Bronxville NY 10708-5909

SEARLES, RICHARD BROWNLEE, PHYCOLOGY. *Current Pos:* From asst prof to assoc prof, 65-83, PROF BOT, DUKE UNIV, 83- *Personal Data:* b Riverside, Calif, June 19, 36; m 57, Georgiana Miller; c 3. *Educ:* Pomona Col, BA, 58; Univ Calif, Berkeley, PhD(bot), 65. *Honors & Awards:* Prescott Award, Phycol Soc Am, 93. *Concurrent Pos:* Chair, Bot Dept, Duke Univ, 91- *Mem:* Phycol Soc Am; Int Phycol Soc (secy, 81-86). *Res:* Marine phycology; morphology; taxonomy and ecology of benthic marine algae. *Mailing Add:* Dept Bot Duke Univ Durham NC 27708-0338. *Fax:* 919-660-7293; *E-Mail:* searles@acpub.duke.edu

SEARLES, SCOTT, JR, ORGANIC MECHANISMS. *Current Pos:* prof, 66-85, EMER PROF CHEM, UNIV MO, COLUMBIA, 85- *Personal Data:* b Minneapolis, Minn, Oct 15, 20; wid; c 5. *Educ:* Univ Calif, Los Angeles, BA, 41, MA, 42; Univ Minn, PhD(org chem), 47. *Prof Exp:* Asst chem, Univ Minn, 42-43; res chemist, Am Cyanamid Co, Conn, 44-45; instr chem & Du Pong fel, Univ Minn, 46-47; instr, Univ Ill, 47-49; asst prof, Northwestern Univ, 49-52; assoc prof, Kans State Univ, 52-62, prof, 62-66. *Concurrent Pos:* NSF sr fel, Calif Inst Technol & Cambridge Univ, 62-63. *Mem:* Am Chem Soc. *Res:* Small ring heterocyclic compounds; rearrangements; reaction mechanisms; ionic catalysis. *Mailing Add:* 7709 N Chesley Dr Columbia MO 65202-9661

SEARLS, CRAIG ALLEN, TECHNICAL MANAGEMENT OF GENERAL ELECTROMAGNETIC & ACOUSTIC REMOTE SENSING APPLIED TO GEOPHYSICAL PROBLEMS. *Current Pos:* geophysicist, Western Elec, 81-90, DEPT MGR, MARTIN MARIETTA, SANDIA NAT LAB, 90- *Personal Data:* b Bremerton, Wash, Feb 27, 54. *Educ:* Univ Puget Sound, BS, 76; Univ Calif, Los Angeles, MS, 78, PhD(geophys & space physics), 81. *Prof Exp:* Sci intern, Northwest Asn Col & Univ Advan Sci, Pac Northwest Div, Battelle Mem Inst, 76. *Mem:* Am Geophys Union; Soc Explor Geophysicists. *Res:* Design, monitoring, and analysis of geophysical experiments addressing a broad range of geophysical problems. *Mailing Add:* 1604 California St NE Albuquerque NM 87110. *Fax:* 505-844-7639

SEARLS, JAMES COLLIER, ANATOMY. *Current Pos:* ASST PROF FAMILY DENT & ANAT, UNIV IOWA, 66- *Personal Data:* b Mitchell, SDak, Aug 22, 26; m 47; c 4. *Educ:* Cornell Col, BA, 50; Univ Iowa, DDS, 55, PhD(anat), 66. *Prof Exp:* Fel, Nat Inst Dent Res, 62-66. *Concurrent Pos:* Gen dent practr, 55-62. *Mem:* Am Asn Anatomists; Int Asn Dent Res. *Res:* Radioisotopic studies of the cartilagenous nasal septum and its role in maxillofacial growth. *Mailing Add:* Dept Anat Univ Iowa Col Med Iowa City IA 52242

SEARLS, ROBERT L, BIOCHEMISTRY, EMBRYOLOGY. *Current Pos:* assoc prof, 68-74, PROF BIOL, TEMPLE UNIV, 74- *Personal Data:* b Madison, Wis, Oct 26, 31; m 61; c 4. *Educ:* Univ Wis, BS, 53; Univ Calif, Berkeley, PhD(biochem), 60. *Prof Exp:* Fel embryol, Brandeis Univ, 60-63; asst prof biol, Univ Va, 63-68. *Mem:* AAAS; Am Chem Soc; Soc Develop Biol; Int Soc Develop Biol. *Res:* Oxidative metabolism; chemical basis of morphogenesis and differentiation. *Mailing Add:* Dept Biol Temple Univ Philadelphia PA 19122

SEARS, CHARLES EDWARD, ECONOMIC GEOLOGY, ENGINEERING GEOLOGY. *Current Pos:* RETIRED. *Personal Data:* b Utica, Mich, Feb 3, 11; m 37; c 4. *Educ:* Va Polytech Inst, BS, 32, MS, 35; Colo Sch Mines, DSc, 53. *Prof Exp:* Instr mining eng & from asst prof to assoc prof geol, Va Polytech Inst & State Univ, 46-77, emer prof geol, 77, dir seismol observ, 61-77. *Concurrent Pos:* Consult geologist. *Mem:* Geol Soc Am; Am Geophys Union. *Res:* Hydrothermal alteration and mineralization at the Climax Molybdenum deposit, Climax, Colorado; geology and petrology; kimberlites; geothermal studies of Virginia areas. *Mailing Add:* 604 Airport Rd Blacksburg VA 24060

SEARS, CURTIS THORNTON, JR, INORGANIC CHEMISTRY, ORGANOMETALLIC CHEMISTRY. *Current Pos:* asst prof, 71-77, assoc chair chem, 86-91, ASSOC PROF CHEM, GA STATE UNIV, 77-, ASSOC VPRES RES, 93- *Personal Data:* b Wareham, Mass, Aug 3, 38; m 60, 80, Ronnie Spilton; c Amy E & Leslie E. *Educ:* WVa Wesleyan Col, AB, 61; Univ NC, PhD(chem), 66. *Honors & Awards:* O'Haus Award, Nat Sci Teachers Asn, 73. *Prof Exp:* NATO fel, 66-67; asst prof chem, Univ SC, 67-71. *Concurrent Pos:* Prog dir, NSF, 91-93. *Mem:* Am Chem Soc. *Res:* Chemistry of second and third row transition metals in low oxidation states. *Mailing Add:* Dept Chem Ga State Univ Atlanta GA 30302. *E-Mail:* reocts@gsusgi2.gsu.edu

SEARS, DAVID ALAN, INTERNAL MEDICINE, HEMATOLOGY. *Current Pos:* Herman Brown Teaching prof & vchmn dept med, 80-90, PROF MED, BAYLOR COL MED, HOUSTON, 90- *Personal Data:* b Portland, Ore, Oct 20, 31; m 58, Yvonne Bowles; c Geoffrey, Cameron & Andrea. *Educ:* Yale Univ, BS, 53; Univ Ore, MS, 58, MD, 59; Am Bd Internal Med, dipl, 66, cert hemat, 74. *Honors & Awards:* St George Medal, Am Cancer Soc, 88. *Prof Exp:* Intern, Sch Med & Dent, Univ Rochester, 59-60, resident med, 60-62, trainee hemat, 62-63, asst prof med, 66-69; assoc prof, 69-77, prof med, 77-80, head div hemat, Univ Tex Med Sch San Antonio, 69-79; chief med serv, Harris County Hosp Dist, 80-90. *Concurrent Pos:* Assoc physician, Strong Mem Hosp, Rochester, NY, 66-69; consult, Highland Hosp, Rochester, NY, 66-69 & Audie Murphy Vet Admin Hosp, San Antonio, 73-80. *Mem:* Am Soc Hemat; Am Fedn Clin Res; Int Soc Hemat; fel Am Col Physicians. *Res:* Hemolytic disease; heme pigment metabolism; erythrocyte membrane; anemia. *Mailing Add:* Dept Med Baylor Col Med One Baylor Plaza Houston TX 77030

SEARS, DEREK WILLIAM GEORGE, METEORITES, THERMOLUMINESCENCE. *Current Pos:* from asst prof to assoc prof chem, 81-88, PROF CHEM, UNIV ARK, 88- *Personal Data:* b Maidstone, Eng, Dec 18, 48; m 71, Hazel; c Andrew, Christopher & David. *Educ:* Univ Kent, Eng, BSc, 70; Univ Col London, dipl, 71, Univ Leicester, PhD(geol astron), 74. *Prof Exp:* Res asst, Univ Manchester, 74-77; res fel, Univ Birmingham, 77-79; asst res chemist, Univ Calif, Los Angeles, 79-81. *Concurrent Pos:* Mem, NASA-NSF Meteorite Working Group, 85-89 & NASA Lunar & Planetary Geosci Rev Panel, 85-89; assoc ed, Geochemica Cosmochemica Acta, 89-, Meteoritics, 90- *Mem:* Fel Meteoritical Soc; Am Chem Soc. *Res:* Study of meteorites by thermoluminescence, cathodoluminescence and related techniques; instrumental neutron activation; electron-microprobe analysis; thermodynamic modelling. *Mailing Add:* Dept Chem & Biochem Univ Ark Fayetteville AR 72701. *Fax:* 501-575-7778; *E-Mail:* cosmo@uafsysb

SEARS, DONALD RICHARD, ENVIRONMENTAL SCIENCE & ENGINEERING. *Current Pos:* PROJ MGR ENVIRON ENG, GRAND FORKS ENERGY TECHNOL CTR, 79- *Personal Data:* b Wilmington, Del, July 23, 28; c 1. *Educ:* Lawrence Col, BS, 50; Cornell Univ, PhD(phys chem), 58. *Prof Exp:* Asst chem, Cornell Univ, 50-52; chemist, Inst Paper Chem,

Lawrence Col, 54; asst chem, Cornell Univ, 54-57; res fel chem phys, Mellon Inst, 58-63; res staff mem, Oak Ridge Nat Lab, 63-68; develop specialist, Oak Ridge Y-12 Plant, 68-72; vis scientist, Nat Ctr Atmospheric Res, 72-73; dir, Air Pollution Eng Lab, Civil Eng Dept, WVa Univ, 73-75; res scientist, Lockheed Res & Eng Ctr, 75-79. *Mem:* AAAS; Air Pollution Control Asn; Am Chem Soc; AAAS; Sigma Xi. *Res:* Characterization and control of particulate emissions; analysis of trace element and organic emissions from combustion of low rank western coals. *Mailing Add:* 4831 E Vespucci Dr Sierra Vista AZ 85635-2334

SEARS, DUANE WILLIAM, IMMUNOLOGY, BIOCHEMISTRY. *Current Pos:* ASST PROF IMMUNOL & BIOCHEM, UNIV CALIF, SANTA BARBARA, 77- *Personal Data:* b Denver, Colo, Mar 23, 46; m 69; c 2. *Educ:* Colo Col, BS, 68; Columbia Univ, PhD(biophys chem), 74. *Prof Exp:* Fel, Albert Einstein Col Med, 74-77. *Mem:* Am Asn Immunologists; NY Acad Sci; AAAS; Am Chem Soc. *Res:* Structural analysis of major histocompatibility complex antigens; immunogenetic analysis of cytotoxic T lymphocyte reactivities; biochemical analysis of cytotoxic T lymphocyte target antigens; molecular analysis of K/NK cells. *Mailing Add:* Dept Biol Sci Univ Calif Santa Barbara CA 93106. *Fax:* 805-961-4724; *E-Mail:* sears@molbio.lscf.ucsf.edu

SEARS, ERNEST ROBERT, plant cytogenetics; deceased, see previous edition for last biography

SEARS, HAROLD FREDERICK, BEHAVIORAL BIOLOGY. *Current Pos:* From instr to asst prof, 74-81, ASSOC PROF BIOL, UNIV SC, UNION, 81-, ASSOC DEAN, 84- *Personal Data:* b Wilmington, Del, Feb 20, 47; m 68; c 2. *Educ:* Northwestern Univ, BA, 69; Univ NC, PhD(zool), 76. *Mem:* AAAS; Sigma Xi; Animal Behav Soc; Am Ornithologists Union; Am Soc Zoologists; Wilson Ornithologists Soc; Cooper Ornithologists Soc. *Res:* Vertebrate communication and display behavior; evolution of display; invertebrate homing and orientation. *Mailing Add:* 3590 Glenn Springs Rd Spartanburg SC 29302-6211

SEARS, J KERN, PLASTICS CHEMISTRY. *Current Pos:* RETIRED. *Personal Data:* b Harper, Kans, May 13, 20; m 50, Sarah Kerr; c Sarah, Elizabeth, Ann & Robert. *Educ:* Harding Col, BS, 42; Univ Mo, MA, 45, PhD(org chem), 47. *Honors & Awards:* Contribution to Vinyl Plastics Award, Soc Plastics Engrs, 83. *Prof Exp:* Assoc prof, Harding Col, 47-51; res chemist, Monsanto Co, 51-71, res specialist, 71-84, consult technologist plasticizer applns, 84-85. *Mem:* Soc Plastics Eng. *Res:* Organic chemistry; compatibility and solventability; resin modification by external additives; polymer testing and evaluation, stabilization of polyvinyl chloride, weathering of plasticized polyvinyl chloride; plasticizer chemistry. *Mailing Add:* 485 Hawthorne Ave St Louis MO 63119

SEARS, JACK WOOD, GENETICS. *Current Pos:* RETIRED. *Personal Data:* b Cordell, Okla, Aug 12, 18; m 43; c 3. *Educ:* Harding Col, BA, 40; Univ Tex, MA, 42, PhD(genetics), 44. *Prof Exp:* Instr zool, Univ Tex, 44-45; prof biol & head dept, Harding Univ, 45-86, emer prof & emer head, 86- *Concurrent Pos:* Mem, Ark State Healing Arts Bd, 72- *Mem:* Fel AAAS; Genetics Soc Am; Am Inst Biol Sci; Am Fisheries Soc. *Res:* Cytogenetics and genetics of Drosophila; aquatic ecology; ecological relationships in Little Red River, Arkansas. *Mailing Add:* 920 E Market St Searcy AR 72143

SEARS, JOHN T, CHEMICAL ENGINEERING, BIOFILMS. *Current Pos:* interim dir, Ctr Biofilm Eng, 92-93, CHMN, DEPT CHEM ENG, MONT STATE UNIV, 82- *Personal Data:* b LaCrosse, Wis, Nov 15, 38; m 71, Carolyn Crane; c Aaron, Russell, Cheryl & Karen. *Educ:* Univ Wis, BS, 60; Princeton Univ, PhD(chem eng), 65. *Prof Exp:* Asst chem engr, Nuclear Eng Dept, Brookhaven Nat Lab, 64-68; res engr, Esso Res & Eng Co, NJ, 68-69; from asst prof to assoc prof chem eng, WVa Univ, 69-81, prof, 81- *Mem:* Am Inst Chem Engrs; Am Soc Eng Educ. *Res:* Coal processing and fluidized beds; biofilms and kinetics. *Mailing Add:* Dept Chem Eng Mont State Univ Bozeman MT 59717. *Fax:* 406-994-6098; *E-Mail:* johns@coe.montana.edu

SEARS, KARL DAVID, LIGNIN & CELLULOSE CHEMISTRY, PULPING & BLEACHING TECHNOLOGY. *Current Pos:* Res chemist, ITT Rayonier, 68-78, group leader, 79-82, sr res scientist, 82-85, mgr chem prod res, 86-87, sr res assoc, 88-95, PRIN SCIENTIST, RAYONIER INC, 96- *Personal Data:* b Cedar Falls, Iowa, Mar 31, 41; m 65, Alison; c David & Robert. *Educ:* State Univ Iowa, BA, 63; Univ Wash, PhD(org chem), 68. *Mem:* Am Chem Soc. *Res:* New product and process development of specialty pulp products; lignosulfonates; pulping and bleaching chemistry. *Mailing Add:* Rayonier Res Ctr 4474 Savannah Hwy Jesup GA 31545. *Fax:* 912-588-8300; *E-Mail:* karl.sears@rayonier.com

SEARS, LEO A, CHEMICAL ENGINEERING. *Current Pos:* Chem engr, E I Du Pont de Nemours & Co Inc, 50-62, sr res engr, 62-66, supvr chem eng, 66-69, RES ASSOC, E I DU PONT DE NEMOURS & CO, INC, 69- *Personal Data:* b Teaneck, NJ, Feb 10, 27; m 52; c 4. *Educ:* Cornell Univ, BChE, 50. *Mem:* Am Chem Soc. *Res:* Polymer synthesis and fabrication. *Mailing Add:* 5 Stable Lane Wilmington DE 19803

SEARS, MARKHAM KARLI, INSECT ECOLOGY. *Current Pos:* From res assoc to teaching asst, 72-74, ASST PROF ENTOM, UNIV GUELPH, 75- *Personal Data:* b San Luis Obispo, Calif, May 3, 46; m 69; c 1. *Educ:* Univ Calif, Davis, BSc, 69, PhD(entom), 74. *Concurrent Pos:* Mem subcomt woody ornamentals, flowers & turf, Ont Crop Protection Comt, 75- *Mem:* Sigma Xi; Entom Soc Am; Can Entom Soc. *Res:* Ecology of insects affecting turfgrasses and woody ornamentals; biology and systematics of immature Coleoptera. *Mailing Add:* Dept Environ Biol Univ Guelph Guelph ON N1G 2W1 Can

SEARS, MARVIN LLOYD, OPHTHALMOLOGY, GLACOMA PHYSIOLOGY. *Current Pos:* PROF OPHTHAL & VISUAL SCI & CHMN DEPT, SCH MED, YALE UNIV, 61-, CHIEF, YALE NEW HAVEN MED CTR, 61- *Personal Data:* b New York, NY, Sept 16, 28; m 50; c Anne, David, Jonathan, Edward & Benjamin. *Educ:* Princeton Univ, AB, 49; Columbia Univ, MD, 53; Yale Univ, MA, 61. *Honors & Awards:* New Eng Ophthal Soc Award, 69; Friedenwald Award, Asn Res Vision & Ophthal, 77; Sanford R Gifford Mem Lectureship, 85; Alcon Res Inst Award, 85. *Prof Exp:* Intern, Columbia Bellevue Hosp, 53-54; from asst resident to chief resident, Wilmer Inst Ophthal, 54-61. *Concurrent Pos:* Robert Weeks Kelly fel ophthal, 57-58; NIH trainee, 59-60; consult to Surgeon Gen, USPHS & mem visual sci study sect, Nat Inst Neurol Dis & Blindness, 62-66, Merck, A G Hoechst; mem bd sci coun, Nat Eye Inst, 70-; mem adv panel, US Pharmacopeia, 75-80; merit award, NIH. *Mem:* AMA; Am Acad Ophthal; Am Ophthal Soc; Am Col Surgeons; Asn Res Vision & Ophthal; Int Soc Eye Res. *Res:* Diseases of the eye; membrane transport. *Mailing Add:* 330 Cedar St Yale Eye Ctr PO Box 208061 New Haven CT 06520-8061. *E-Mail:* searsml@maspo1.mas.yale.edu

SEARS, MILDRED BRADLEY, INORGANIC CHEMISTRY, CHEMICAL ENGINEERING. *Current Pos:* res staff mem, 58-70, RES STAFF MEM, OAK RIDGE NAT LAB, 72- *Personal Data:* b New Castle, Pa, Feb 19, 33; c Margaret Kroen. *Educ:* Col Wooster, BA, 54; Univ Fla, PhD(inorg chem), 58. *Mem:* Am Nuclear Soc; Am Chem Soc; Sigma Xi. *Res:* Engineering and environmental assessments of the nuclear fuel cycle, including waste treatment methods; safety analysis reports; environmental assesments including waste treatment methods; waste characterization. *Mailing Add:* 130 Monticello Rd Oak Ridge TN 37830

SEARS, RAYMOND ERIC JOHN, NUCLEAR MAGNETIC RESONANCE. *Current Pos:* asst prof, 67-80, ASSOC PROF PHYSICS, UNIV NTEX, 80- *Personal Data:* b Wellington, NZ, July 2, 34; m 62; c 4. *Educ:* Univ Victoria, NZ, BSc, 57, MSc, 59; Univ Calif, Berkeley, PhD(physics), 66. *Prof Exp:* Res assoc chem, Mass Inst Technol, 66-67. *Mem:* AAAS; Am Phys Soc; Int Soc Magnetic Resonance; Sigma Xi. *Res:* Nuclear magnetic resonance in solids. *Mailing Add:* Dept Physics Univ NTex Denton TX 76203

SEARS, RAYMOND WARRICK, JR, reliability, maintainability, for more information see previous edition

SEARS, RICHARD LANGLEY, ASTROPHYSICS. *Current Pos:* asst prof, 65-70, ASSOC PROF ASTRON, UNIV MICH, ANN ARBOR, 70- *Personal Data:* b Boston, Mass, Mar 27, 31; m 73; c 1. *Educ:* Harvard Univ, AB, 53; Ind Univ, MA, 55, PhD(astrophys), 58. *Prof Exp:* Vis fel astron, Princeton Univ, 58; instr, Ind Univ, 58-59; asst, Lick Observ, Univ Calif, 59-61; res fel physics, Calif Inst Technol, 60-61, sr res fel, 61-64; vis asst prof physics & astron, Vanderbilt Univ, 64-65. *Concurrent Pos:* Mem, Int Astron Union. *Mem:* AAAS; Am Astron Soc; Royal Astron Soc. *Res:* Stellar interiors and evolution; stellar photometry; theoretical astrophysics. *Mailing Add:* Dept Astron Univ Mich 830 Dennison Ann Arbor MI 48109-1090

SEARS, ROBERT F, JR, PHYSICS. *Current Pos:* From asst prof to assoc prof, 68-78, CHMN DEPT, AUSTIN PEAY STATE UNIV, 77-, PROF PHYSICS, 78- *Personal Data:* b Warren Co, Ky, June 13, 41; m 65; c 3. *Educ:* Centre Col, BA, 63; Univ Colo, PhD(physics), 68. *Concurrent Pos:* Scientist 2, Oak Ridge Assoc Univ, 82. *Mem:* Am Am Physics Teachers (treas, 90-96); Astron Soc Pac; Nat Sci Teachers Asn; Am Phys Soc. *Res:* Study of antiproton-proton interactions resulting in the production of a single pion; high energy physics; energy education. *Mailing Add:* Dept Physics Austin Peay State Univ Clarksville TN 37044-4608. *Fax:* 931-648-5996; *E-Mail:* sears@psu01apsu.edu

SEARS, TIMOTHY STEPHEN, BUSINESS DEVELOPMENT, MARKET DEVELOPMENT & RESEARCH. *Current Pos:* TECH BUS DEVELOP MGR, PENOLES METALS & CHEM, 95- *Personal Data:* b Boston, Mass, Sept 29, 45; m 75; c 3. *Educ:* Boston Univ, AB, 67; Univ Calif, Davis, CPhil, 70, PhD(chem), 73; Univ Calgary, MBA, 85. *Prof Exp:* Fel chem, Univ Calgary, 73-74, instr, 74-76, instr mgt, 86; process engr, Kaiser Aluminum & Chem Corp, 76-80; process res scientist, Petro Can, 80-83; mgr res & technol, Travis Chem, 84-85; mkt develop mgr, Baymag, 86-90, mgr res, develop & qual assurance, 90-95. *Mem:* Am Soc Qual Control; Chem Mgt & Resource Asn. *Res:* Applications research for various industrial minerals in the refractories, rubber and plastics, pulp and paper, mining and chemicals industries. *Mailing Add:* 52 Hawksley Crescent NW Calgary AB T3G 3C5 Can

SEARS, VARLEY FULLERTON, SOLID STATE PHYSICS. *Current Pos:* PHYSICIST, ATOMIC ENERGY CAN LTD, 65- *Personal Data:* b Cadomin, Alta, Can, June 29, 37; m 63; c 2. *Educ:* Univ Toronto, BA, 59, MA, 60, PhD(physics), 63. *Prof Exp:* Asst, Oxford Univ, UK, 63-65. *Mem:* Can Asn Physicists; fel Am Phys Soc. *Res:* Theory of thermal neutron scattering in condensed matter; neutron transport phenomena, diffraction, and optical effects. *Mailing Add:* Atomic Energy Can Ltd Chalk River ON K0J 1J0 Can

SEARS, WILLIAM R(EES), AERODYNAMICS. *Current Pos:* prof, 74-85, EMER PROF AEROSPACE & MECH ENG, UNIV ARIZ, TUCSON, 85- *Personal Data:* b Minneapolis, Minn, Mar 1, 13; m 36, Mabel J Rhodes; c David W & Susan C. *Educ:* Univ Minn, BAeroE, 34; Calif Inst Technol, PhD(aeronaut), 38. *Hon Degrees:* DSc, Univ Ariz, 87. *Honors & Awards:* Vincent Bendix Award, 65; Ludwig Prandtl Ring, Deutsche Gesellschaft fur Luft- und Raumfahrt, 74; Reed Aeronaut Medal, Am Inst Aeronaut & Astronaut, 61; G Edward Pendray Award, 75; Am Soc Mech Engrs Medal, 89; ONR Medal, Am Phys Soc, 93. *Prof Exp:* Asst aeronaut, Calif Inst Technol, 34-37, from instr to asst prof, 37-41; chief aerodynamicist, Northrop Aircraft Inc, Calif, 41-46; prof aeronaut eng & dir, Grad Sch Aeronaut Eng, Cornell Univ, 46-74, dir, Ctr Appl Math, 63-67, J L Given prof eng, 63-74. *Concurrent Pos:* Consult, Calspan Corp; ed, J Aerospace Sci, Inst Aerospace Sci, Am Inst Aeronaut & Astronaut, 57-63. *Mem:* Nat Acad Sci; Nat Acad Eng; fel Am Acad Arts & Sci; hon fel Am Inst Aeronaut & Astronaut; fel Int Acad Astronaut. *Res:* Fluid mechanics; wing and boundary layer theory; wind tunnels. *Mailing Add:* Dept Aerospace & Mech Eng Univ Ariz Tucson AZ 85721

SEASE, JOHN WILLIAM, ELECTROCHEMISTRY. *Current Pos:* instr org chem, 46-48, from asst prof to prof chem, 48-88, E B Nye prof, 82-88, EMER PROF CHEM, WESLEYAN UNIV, 88- *Personal Data:* b New Brunswick, NJ, Nov 10, 20; m 43; c 4. *Educ:* Princeton Univ, AB, 41; Calif Inst Technol, PhD(org chem), 46. *Prof Exp:* Asst inorg chem, Calif Inst Technol, 41-42, asst, Nat Defense Res Comt, 42-45. *Mem:* AAAS; Am Chem Soc; Sigma Xi. *Res:* Electrochemistry of organic compounds. *Mailing Add:* Dept Chem Wesleyan Univ Middletown CT 06457

SEATON, JACOB ALIF, INORGANIC CHEMISTRY. *Current Pos:* head dept chem, 66-78, chmn dept, 78-86, PROF CHEM, STEPHEN F AUSTIN STATE UNIV, 66- *Personal Data:* b Wellington, Kans, Jan 2, 31; m 55; c 3. *Educ:* Wichita State Univ, BS, 53, MS, 55; Univ Ill, PhD(inorg chem), 58. *Prof Exp:* Asst chemist chem eng div, Argonne Nat Lab, 57-58; proj engr polymer br mat lab, Wright Air Develop Ctr, 58-60; sr staff mem inorg res, Spencer Chem Co, 60-62; asst prof chem, Sam Houston State Col, 62-66. *Mem:* Fel Am Inst Chem; Am Chem Soc; Sigma Xi. *Res:* Non-aqueous solvents; inorganic polymers; transition and inner-transition metal compounds. *Mailing Add:* Dept Chem Stephen F Austin State Univ Box 13006 1936 N St Nacogdoches TX 75961-3940

SEATON, MICHAEL JOHN, ATOMIC & MOLECULAR PHYSICS, ASTROPHYSICS. *Current Pos:* asst lectr, Univ Col London, 50-53, lectr, 53-59, reader, 59-63, prof, 63-88, EMER PROF, UNIV COL LONDON, 88- *Personal Data:* b Jan 16, 23; m 43, 60, Joy C Balchin; c June, Richard & Anthony. *Educ:* Univ London, BSc, 48, PhD(math), 51. *Hon Degrees:* Dr, Observ de Paris, 76; DSc, Queens Univ, Belfast, 82. *Honors & Awards:* Gold Medal, Royal Astron Soc, 83; Guthrie Medal, Inst Physics, 84; Hughes Medal, Royal Soc, 92. *Concurrent Pos:* Charge de recherche, Inst Astrophys, Paris, 54-55; adj fel, Joint Inst Lab Astrophys, Colo, 64-; sr res fel, Sci Eng Res Coun, UK, 84-88. *Mem:* Foreign Assoc Nat Acad Sci; Royal Astron Soc (pres, 79-81); fel Royal Soc; hon mem Am Astron Soc. *Res:* Fundamental studies in atomic physics; quantum defect theory; computation of atomic data; studies of gaseous nebulae interstellar matter, stellar atmospheres, and hovae; stellar opacities. *Mailing Add:* Dept Phys & Astron Univ Col London Gower St London WC1E 6BT England. *E-Mail:* mjs@star.ucl.ac.uk

SEATON, VAUGHN ALLEN, VETERINARY PATHOLOGY. *Current Pos:* from instr to assoc prof, 55-64, head vet med diag lab, 74-94, PROF VET PATH & HEAD DEPT, COL VET MED, IOWA STATE UNIV, 64- *Personal Data:* b Abilene, Kans, Oct 11, 28; m 54; c 2. *Educ:* Kans State Univ, BS & DVM, 54; Iowa State Univ, MS, 57. *Honors & Awards:* Edward Pope Award Diag Contrib. *Mem:* Am Pub Health Asn; Am Vet Med Asn; Am Col Vet Toxicol; Asn Vet Lab Diagnosticians. *Res:* Pulmonary adenomatosis in Iowa cattle; infectious diseases; veterinary toxicology. *Mailing Add:* 1626 Crestwood Circle Ames IA 50010

SEATON, WILLIAM HAFFORD, CHEMICAL ENGINEERING. *Current Pos:* RETIRED. *Personal Data:* b Black Oak, Ark, Oct 22, 24; m 44, Dorothy L Beard; c William G & Diane (Racht). *Educ:* Univ Ark, BSChE, 50; Ohio State Univ, MS, 55, PhD(chem eng), 58. *Honors & Awards:* Dudley Medal, Am Soc Testing & Mat, 77. *Prof Exp:* Chem engr, Monsanto Chem Co, 50-53; res assoc, Ohio State Res Found, 53-55; sr res engr, Tenn Eastman Co, 58-67, res assoc, 67-80; sr res assoc, Eastman Chem Co, 80-86. *Concurrent Pos:* Thermophys property data specialist. *Mem:* Fel Am Inst Chem Engrs; Nat Soc Prof Engrs; fel Am Soc Testing & Mat. *Res:* Chemical process data; unit operations research and development; energy hazard potential problems related to safety. *Mailing Add:* 1329 Belmeade Dr Kingsport TN 37664. *E-Mail:* 70701.3075@compuserve.com

SEATZ, LLOYD FRANK, SOIL FERTILITY. *Current Pos:* From asst prof to prof, Univ Tenn, 47-55, head dept, 61-84, Clyde B Austin distinguished prof, 68-84, EMER PROF AGR, UNIV TENN, KNOXVILLE, 84- *Personal Data:* b Winchester, Idaho, June 2, 19; m 49, Jane Whittle; c William L. *Educ:* Univ Idaho, BS, 40; Univ Tenn, MS, 41; NC State Univ, PhD(agron), 49. *Concurrent Pos:* Agronomist & asst chief, Soils & Fertilizer Res Br, Tenn Valley Authority, 53-55. *Mem:* Fel Am Soc Agron; fel Soil Sci Soc Am; Sigma Xi. *Res:* Phosphorus and trace element reactions and availability in soils; factors affecting crop response to fertilization. *Mailing Add:* 9729 Tunbridge Lane Knoxville TN 37922

SEAVER, SALLY S, CELL BIOLOGY OF SCALE-UP, ANTIBODIES FOR DIAGNOSTIC TESTS. *Current Pos:* ASSOC DIR RES & DEVELOP, IMMUNOL & CELL BIOL, HYGEIA SCI, 85- *Personal Data:* b Marblehead, Mass, July 27, 46. *Educ:* Harvard Univ, AB, 67, AM, 68; Stanford Univ, PhD(phys chem), 73. *Prof Exp:* Jane Coffin Child fel biochem endocrinol, Inst Chemie Bulogique, Univ Louis Pasteur, Shasbourg, France, 73-75; asst prof molecular endocrinol, Dept Molecular Biol, Vanderbilt Univ, 75-81; sr scientist appln cell & molecular biol, Millipore Corp, 82-83, group leader, 83-85. *Concurrent Pos:* Vis prof, Dept Biol, Univ Calif, San Diego, 81; consult ed, Immunol, 87-89, 91- *Mem:* Endocrine Soc; Am Soc Cell Biol; Am Chem Soc; Tissue Cult Asn; Sigma Xi. *Res:* Development of hybudenia lines and production (scale-up) of neono-clonal and polyclonal antibodies for diagnostic tests; development of equipment and reagents for biotechnology. *Mailing Add:* Seaver & Assoc 174 Hawthorne Lane Concord MA 01742-0001

SEAVEY, MARDEN HOMER, JR, SOLID STATE PHYSICS. *Current Pos:* PRIN ENGR, DIGITAL EQUIP CO. *Personal Data:* b Preston, Cuba, Jan 12, 29; US citizen; m 55, 65; c 5. *Educ:* Harvard Univ, AB, 52; Northeastern Univ, MS, 56; Harvard Univ, PhD, 70. *Prof Exp:* Physicist, Air Force Cambridge Res Ctr, 52-55, Lincoln Lab, Mass Inst Technol, 55-62, Air Force Cambridge Res Labs, 62-70 & Philips Res Lab, Neth, 70-72; PRIN ENGR, EQUIP DIV, RAYTHEON CO, 72- *Mem:* Am Phys Soc; Inst Elec & Electronics Engrs. *Res:* Resonance phenomena and acoustic effects in ordered magnetic systems; laser gyroscopes; radiation effects in large scale integrated circuits. *Mailing Add:* 381 Cross St Carlisle MA 01741

SEAWRIGHT, JACK ARLYN, ENTOMOLOGY, GENETICS. *Current Pos:* RES LEADER/ENTOMOLOGIST, MED & VET ENTOM LAB, USDA, 68- *Personal Data:* b Ware Shoals, SC, Sept 9, 41; m 62, Rebecca Medlin; c David & Amy. *Educ:* Clemson Univ, BS, 64, MS, 65; Univ Fla, PhD(entom), 69. *Concurrent Pos:* Asst prof, 70-80, prof dept entom, Univ Fla, 80- *Mem:* Entom Soc Am; Am Mosquito Control Asn. *Res:* Genetics of insects with emphasis on genetic control mechanisms. *Mailing Add:* 4902 NW 37 Dr Gainesville FL 32605

SEAY, GLENN EMMETT, PHYSICS. *Current Pos:* RETIRED. *Personal Data:* b Tahlequah, Okla, Mar 9, 26; m 59, Erlene E Hren; c Timothy W, Cynthia E & Jeffrey G. *Educ:* Univ Okla, BS, 50, MS(eng physics), 53, PhD (physics), 57. *Prof Exp:* Mem staff, Los Alamos Sci Lab, Univ Calif, 47-62; div supvr, Sandia Corp, 62-64, dept mgr, 64-68; mgr, Dept Exp Physics, Systs Sci & Software, La Jolla, Calif, 68-70, mgr, Systs & Software Div, 70-76; group leader, Los Alamos Sci Lab, Univ Calif, 76-80, prog mgr, 90-93. *Mem:* Am Phys Soc. *Res:* Flash radiography; atomic spectroscopy; shock waves in gases and solids; detonation physics; initiation of detonation. *Mailing Add:* 101 San Ildefonso Rd Los Alamos NM 87544

SEAY, PATRICK H, PHARMACOLOGY. *Current Pos:* EXEC DIR REGULATORY AFFAIRS, MCNEIL PHARMACEUT, 68-, SR REGULATORY AFFAIRS LAISON, 85- *Personal Data:* b Lexington, SC, Jan 31, 20; m 48; c 3. *Educ:* Princeton Univ, PhD(biol), 50. *Mem:* Am Soc Pharmacol & Exp Therapeut. *Mailing Add:* 325 Wenner Way Ft Washington PA 19034-2919

SEAY, THOMAS NASH, ENVIRONMENTAL SCIENCES, ENTOMOLOGY. *Current Pos:* RETIRED. *Personal Data:* b Cincinnati, Ohio, Sept 29, 32; m 58; c 2. *Educ:* Univ Fla, BSA, 55; Univ Ky, MSA, 63, PhD(biol sci), 67. *Prof Exp:* Asst prof, Georgetown Col, 66-70, assoc prof biol, 70-91, dir environ sci, 74-91, actg chmn biol sci, 84-91. *Mem:* Entom Soc Am; NAm Asn Environ Educ. *Res:* Environmental geography. *Mailing Add:* 304 Hiawatha Trail Georgetown KY 40324

SEBALD, ANTHONY VINCENT, ELECTRICAL ENGINEERING, SYSTEMS SCIENCE. *Current Pos:* ASST PROF SYST SCI, UNIV CALIF, SAN DIEGO, 76- *Personal Data:* b US. *Educ:* Gannon Col, BEE, 63; Univ Ill, MSEE, 75, PhD(elec eng), 76. *Prof Exp:* Assoc engr, IBM Corp, 64-68; prof eng, Univ Catolica de Valparaiso, 69-72. *Mem:* Inst Elec & Electronics Engrs. *Res:* Energy and air pollution policy analysis; solar heating and cooling of buildings; estimation and control in systems which are incompletely specified. *Mailing Add:* Dept Elec & Comput Eng Univ Calif 9500 Gilman Dr La Jolla CA 92093-0407

SEBASTIAN, ANTHONY, MEDICINE, NEPHROLOGY. *Current Pos:* From intern internal med to resident, Moffitt Hosp, Univ Calif, San Francisco, 65-68, asst resident physician, 70-71, asst prof, 71-78, assoc prof, 78-84, PROF MED, UNIV CALIF, SAN FRANCISCO, 84- *Personal Data:* b Youngstown, Ohio, July 11, 38; m 64. *Educ:* Univ Calif, Los Angeles, BS, 60; Univ Calif, San Francisco, MD, 65. *Concurrent Pos:* Bank Am-Giannini Found fel renal dis, Univ Calif, San Francisco, 68-70. *Mem:* Am Soc Nephrol; Am Fedn Clin. *Res:* Am Soc Clin Invest; Int Soc Nephrol. *Res:* Renal and acid-base physiology and pathophysiology; renal acidosis; interrelationship of hydrogen ion and electrolyte transport in the kidney; renal tubular disorders. *Mailing Add:* Dept Med 1202 Moffitt Hosp Univ Calif PO Box 0126 San Francisco CA 94143

SEBASTIAN, FRANKLIN W, ELECTRICAL ENGINEERING, CONSULTING. *Current Pos:* RETIRED. *Personal Data:* b Neenah, Wis, June 3, 20; m 48; c 3. *Educ:* Ill Inst Technol, BSME, 45. *Prof Exp:* Staff engr mech, Kimberly Clark Paper Co, 47-49; engr mech, F H McGraw & Co, 49-52; design engr mech, Ingersoll Corp, 52-57; sales mgr sales, Cameron

Mach Co, 63-67; chief engr mgt, Menasha Paper Co, 67-74; eng mgr admin, Phillip Morris Corp, 74-85; proj engr mech & elec, K V P Paper Co, 52-57, consult eng, K V P Paper Div James River, 85-88. *Concurrent Pos:* Consult engr & chmn bd, Artios Eng, 85- *Res:* New products and developed equipment and processes in the paper industry; developed new equipment to produce new products. *Mailing Add:* 2907 Sonora Kalamazoo MI 49004

SEBASTIAN, JOHN FRANCIS, PHYSICAL ORGANIC CHEMISTRY, BIOCHEMISTRY. *Current Pos:* from asst prof chem to assoc prof, 67-81, PROF CHEM, MIAMI UNIV, 81- *Personal Data:* b San Diego, Calif, Nov 20, 39; c 2. *Educ:* San Diego State Col, BS, 61; Univ Calif, Riverside, PhD(org chem), 65. *Prof Exp:* NIH fel enzyme catalysis, Northwestern Univ, 65-67. *Concurrent Pos:* Res Corp grant, 68- *Mem:* AAAS; Am Chem Soc; Royal Soc Chem; Sigma Xi. *Res:* Mechanisms of enzyme catalysis; enzyme model systems; nuclear magnetic resonance spectroscopy; organometallic and heterocyclic chemistry; applications of molecular orbital theory; DNA structure and function; protein-DNA interactions. *Mailing Add:* Dept Chem Miami Univ Oxford OH 45056

SEBASTIAN, RICHARD LEE, SIGNAL PROCESSING, PATTERN RECOGNITION. *Current Pos:* PRES & CHMN, DIGITAL SIGNAL CORP, SPRINGFIELD, VA, 83- *Personal Data:* b Hutchinson, Kans, June 22, 42; m 64; c 2. *Educ:* Princeton Univ, AB, 64; Univ Md, Col Park, PhD(physics), 70. *Prof Exp:* Staff scientist, Ensco, Inc, Springfield, Va, 69-72, chief scientist, 72, div mgr, 72-74, vpres res, 74-83; chmn, Digital Optronics Corp, 84-87. *Mem:* Am Phys Soc; Inst Elec & Electronics Engrs; Soc Explor Geophysics. *Res:* Signal processing and intelligent systems; geophysics including acoustic seismic and electromagnetic waves; source localization and classification and wave propagation. *Mailing Add:* 6128 River Dr Lorton VA 22079

SEBEK, OLDRICH KAREL, MICROBIAL PHYSIOLOGY, INDUSTRIAL MICROBIOLOGY. *Current Pos:* vis res scientist, 85-87, VIS RES PROF DEPT BIOL SCI, WESTERN MICH UNIV, KALAMAZOO, 88- *Personal Data:* b Prague, Czech, July 3, 19; nat US; m 59; c 1. *Educ:* Charles Univ, Prague, DSc(natural sci) 46; Rutgers Univ, New Brunswick, ScD(natural sci), 49. *Prof Exp:* Asst microbiol, Charles Univ, 45-47; int fel fermentation, J E Seagram & Sons, Inc, 47-48; res assoc microbiol, Rutgers Univ, 48-49; fel chem & enzymol, Fordham Univ, 49-50; Muelhaupt scholar biol, Ohio State Univ, 50-52; sr scientist, Upjohn Co, 52-84. *Concurrent Pos:* Abstractor, Chem Abstr, 50-70; vis scientist & res assoc Dept Biochem, Univ Calif, Berkeley, 66-67; ed, Appl Microbiol, 68-71; vis prof, Nat Polytech Inst, Mexico City, 73; US rep, Int Comn Appl Microbial Genetics, Int Asn Microbiol Socs, 74-82; partic foreign projs, Nat Res Coun, Nat Acad Sci, Czech, 80, Ger Dem Repub, 86, Indonesia, 86; ed, Appl Microbiol & Biotechnol, 90- *Mem:* Am Soc Microbiol; Soc Indust Microbiol; fel Am Acad Microbiol. *Res:* Microbial metabolism and biochemistry; fermentations and biosynthesis; biotrans formation of microbial products, antibiotics, carotenoids, prostaglandins, pigments, amino acids, steroids and synthetic chemicals. *Mailing Add:* 1002 Short Rd Kalamazoo MI 49008-1138

SEBESTA, CHARLES FREDERICK, MATHEMATICS. *Current Pos:* assoc prof, 56-65, head dept, 56-74 & 78-79, PROF MATH, DUQUESNE UNIV, 65- *Personal Data:* b North Braddock, Pa, Mar 6, 14; m 45; c 7. *Educ:* Univ Pittsburgh, AB, 34, MA, 38, PhD, 56. *Prof Exp:* Teacher high sch, Pa, 34-43; instr math, Univ Pittsburgh, 46-54, asst prof, 54-56. *Mem:* Math Asn Am; Sigma Xi. *Res:* Abstract algebra; partial differential equations; analytic function theory. *Mailing Add:* 4344 E Barlind Dr Pittsburgh PA 15227

SEBETICH, MICHAEL J, LIMNOLOGY, ECOLOGY. *Current Pos:* assoc prof, 77-92, PROF BIOL, WILLIAM PATERSON COL, 92- *Personal Data:* b Nanty-Glo, Pa, Feb 25, 43. *Educ:* Duquesne Univ, BS, 65; Col William & Mary, MA, 69; Rutgers Univ, PhD(ecol, limnol), 72. *Prof Exp:* Asst prof, William Paterson Col, 72-73; aquatic biologist, US Geol Surv Water Resources Div, 73-77. *Concurrent Pos:* Ecol consult, Am Mus. *Mem:* Ecol Soc Am; Am Soc Limnol & Oceanog; AAAS; Am Inst Biol Sci; Int Asn Theoret & Appl Limnol; Sigma Xi. *Res:* Nutrient cycling in freshwater ecosystems; lake management; land use effects on freshwater ecosystems. *Mailing Add:* Dept Biol William Paterson Col Wayne NJ 07470

SEBO, STEPHEN ANDREW, ELECTRICAL ENGINEERING. *Current Pos:* assoc prof, 68-74, PROF ELEC ENG, OHIO STATE UNIV, 74- *Personal Data:* b Budapest, Hungary, June 10, 34; US citizen; m 68, Eva A Vambery. *Educ:* Budapest Polytech Univ, MS, 57; Hungarian Acad Sci, PhD(elec eng), 66. *Prof Exp:* Elec engr, Budapest Elec Co, Hungary, 57-61; from asst prof to assoc prof elec power eng, Budapest Polytech Univ, 61-68. *Concurrent Pos:* Consult engr, State Power Bd, Hungary, 61-64; Ford Found fel, 67-68; consult & res, electric utility co, 69-; res engr, Elec Power Res Inst, 75-; vis prof, Xian Jiaotong Univ, 84, Wuhan Univ, 84 & Budapest Polytech Univ, 92. *Mem:* Fel Inst Elec & Electronics Engrs; Int Conf Large Elec Systs. *Res:* Electric power systems; high-voltage power transmission; power system analysis; electric power generation; high-voltage engineering; power system economics; environmental effects; electromagnetic fields; noise and interference. *Mailing Add:* Dept Elec Eng Ohio State Univ 2015 Neil Ave Columbus OH 43210. *Fax:* 614-292-7596; *E-Mail:* sebo@ee.eng.ohio_state.edu

SEBOLT-LEOPOLD, JUDITH S, ANTICANCER DRUG DISCOVERY, BIOCHEMICAL PHARMACOLOGY. *Current Pos:* sr scientist, Warner-Lambert Co, 84-88, res assoc, 88-90, sr res assoc, 90-93, ASSOC RES FEL, PARKE-DAVIS PHARMACEUT RES DIV, WARNER-LAMBERT CO, 93- *Personal Data:* b Kokomo, Ind, Aug 30, 52; m 89; c Matthew & Jonathan. *Educ:* Wellesley Col, BA, 74; Purdue Univ, PhD(biol sci), 80. *Prof Exp:* Res assoc, Lab Exp Oncol, Ind Univ, 80-84. *Mem:* Am Asn Cancer Res; Radiation Res Soc; Am Soc Biochem & Molecular Biol; Sigma Xi. *Res:* Anti-cancer drug discovery; design and evaluation of agents for improved chemotherapy and radiotherapy; identification of solid tumor selective DNA intercalators for chemotherapy as well as hypoxic cell radiosensitizers. *Mailing Add:* Dept Cell Biol Warner Lambert Parke-Davis Co 2800 Plymouth Rd Ann Arbor MI 48105-2430. *Fax:* 313-996-1355; *E-Mail:* leopolj@aa.wl.com

SEBORG, DALE EDWARD, CHEMICAL ENGINEERING. *Current Pos:* chmn dept, 78-81, PROF CHEM & NUCLEAR ENG, UNIV CALIF, SANTA BARBARA, 77- *Personal Data:* b Madison, Wis, Mar 29, 41. *Educ:* Univ Wis-Madison, BSc, 64; Princeton Univ, PhD(chem eng), 69. *Honors & Awards:* Meriam-Wiley Textbook Award, Am Soc Eng Educ, 90. *Prof Exp:* Res asst chem eng, Princeton Univ, 64-68; from asst prof to prof chem & petrol eng, Univ Alta, 68-77. *Mem:* Am Inst Chem Engrs; Inst Elec & Electronics Engrs. *Res:* Process control; computer control techniques; applied mathematics. *Mailing Add:* Dept Chem Eng Univ Calif Santa Barbara CA 93106

SEBRANEK, JOSEPH GEORGE, MEAT SCIENCES. *Current Pos:* asst prof meat sci, 75-79, assoc prof, 79-84, PROF ANIMAL SCI & FOOD TECH, IOWA STATE UNIV, 84- *Personal Data:* b Richland Center, Wis, Feb 22, 48; m 70, Annette Marshall; c Amy & Abby. *Educ:* Univ Wis, Platteville, BS, 70; Univ Wis, Madison, MS, 71, PhD(meat sci & food sci), 74. *Honors & Awards:* Meat Processing Award, Am Meat Asn. *Prof Exp:* Fel, Nat Cancer Inst, 74-75. *Concurrent Pos:* Res chemist, USDA, 82-83. *Mem:* Inst Food Technologists; Am Soc Animal Sci; Am Meat Sci Asn. *Res:* Meat processing, food additives, dehydration of processed meats, curing reactions, use of nitrite, color development and processed meat quality. *Mailing Add:* Iowa State Univ 215 Meat Lab Ames IA 50011. *Fax:* 515-294-5066; *E-Mail:* sebranek@iastate.edu

SEBREE, BRUCE RANDALL, FOOD SCIENCE, CHEMICAL ENGINEERING. *Current Pos:* tech dir, 83-86, VPRES RES & QUAL CONTROL, FLEICHMANN-KURTH/ADM, 86- *Personal Data:* b Marion, Kans, Feb 8, 56; m 73, Marcia Bloomer; c 4. *Educ:* Kans State Univ, BS, 78, MS, 81, PhD(cereal technol), 84. *Prof Exp:* Asst prod engr, Western Foods Corp, 78; res asst cereal sci, Dept Grain Sci, Kans State Univ, 78-83. *Mem:* Am Asn Cereal Chemists; Am Soc Brewing Chemists (secy); Master Brewers Asn Am; Inst Food Technologists; AAAS; Inst Brewing. *Res:* Malting of cereal grains including barley, wheat, oats and rye; analysis methodology associated with malting, cereal composition and malt process reactions. *Mailing Add:* ADM Malting PO Box 1470 Decatur IL 62525

SECCO, ANTHONY SILVIO, CRYSTALLOGRAPHY, DNA & PROTEIN STRUCTURE. *Current Pos:* ASSOC HEAD CHEM, UNIV MAN, 94-, PROF CHEM, 96- *Personal Data:* b Antigonish, NS, Aug 10, 56; m 79. *Educ:* St Francis Xavier Univ, BSc, 78; Univ BC, PhD(chem), 82. *Prof Exp:* Fel, Univ Pa, 82-84. *Mem:* Am Crystallog Asn; Chem Inst Can; AAAS. *Res:* Crystallographic investigations of novel nucleosides and nucleotides; structural studies of DNA and proteins and their interactions. *Mailing Add:* Dept Chem Univ Man Winnipeg MB R3T 2N2 Can. *Fax:* 204-275-0905; *E-Mail:* secco@iris.chem.umanitoba.ca

SECCO, ETALO ANTHONY, PHYSICAL CHEMISTRY. *Current Pos:* from asst prof to prof, 55-94, SR RES PROF, ST FRANCIS XAVIER UNIV, 94- *Personal Data:* b Dominion, NS, Nov 8, 28; m 53, Margaret Brehaut; c Monica, Anthony, Diana, Richard, Robert & Stephen. *Educ:* St Francis Xavier Univ, BSc, 49; Laval Univ, DSc, 53. *Prof Exp:* Instr gen chem, St Francis Xavier Univ, 49-50; instr phys chem, Laval Univ, 52-53; res assoc, Ind Univ, 53-55. *Concurrent Pos:* NATO overseas fel, Cavendish Lab, Cambridge Univ, 61-62. *Mem:* Am Chem Soc; NY Acad Sci; fel Chem Inst Can; Royal Soc Chem; fel Am Inst Chemists; Am Ceramic Soc; Mat Res Soc. *Res:* Kinetics of heterogeneous reactions temperatures; phase equilibria at high temperatures; radiotracers; structural problems; solid state decomposition kinetics; electrical conductivity studies; non-traditional glass preparation and studies; computer modeling of ameltropic solid solid solutions, fast cation conductivity dependence on temperahose and pressure. *Mailing Add:* Dept Chem St Francis Xavier Univ Antigonish NS B2G 1C0 Can

SECHLER, DALE TRUMAN, PLANT BREEDING. *Current Pos:* assoc prof, 67-75, PROF AGRON, UNIV MO, COLUMBIA, 75- *Personal Data:* b Pleasant Hope, Mo, Nov 30, 26; m 54; c 3. *Educ:* Univ Mo, BS, 50, MEd, 54, PhD(plant breeding), 60. *Prof Exp:* Teacher high schs, Mo, 50-55; instr field crops, Univ Mo, 55-60; asst prof agron, Univ Fla, 60-67. *Mem:* Am Soc Agron. *Res:* Genetics and improvement of wheat and oats; grain crops production; plant breeding; international agronomy. *Mailing Add:* 1004 Bourn Ave Columbia MO 65203

SECHRIST, CHALMERS FRANKLIN, JR, AERONOMY, IONOSPHERIC PHYSICS & CHEMISTRY. *Current Pos:* from asst prof to assoc prof, 65-71, PROF ELEC ENG, UNIV ILL, URBANA-CHAMPAIGN, 71-; PROG DIR ENG, DIV UNDER GRAD EDUC, NSF, 92- *Personal Data:* b Glen Rock, Pa, Aug 23, 30; m 57, Beatrice Meyers; c Jonathan & Jennifer. *Educ:* Johns Hopkins Univ, BE, 52; Pa State Univ, MS, 54, PhD(elec eng), 59. *Prof Exp:* From asst elec eng to instr, Pa State Univ, 52-55, asst, Ionosphere Res Lab, 55-59; sr engr, HRB-Singer, Inc, 59-63, staff engr, 63-65. *Concurrent Pos:* Mem, Educ Soc Admin Comt, Inst

Elec & Electronics Engrs, 83-89, Educ Activ Bd, 90, 92 & 93, vpres, Educ Soc, 89 & 90, pres, 91 & 92; prin investr on NSF proj to investigate upper atmosphere sodium layer, 77-84; assoc head, Elec & Comput Eng Dept, 84-86; asst dean eng undergrad progs, 86-92. *Mem:* Inst Elec & Electronics Engrs; Am Geophys Union; Am Meteorol Soc; Am Soc Eng Educ. *Res:* Physics and chemistry of the lower ionosphere and the upper atmosphere metallic-vapor layers. *Mailing Add:* The Landings 12767 Yatch Club Circle Ft Myers IL 33919-4589. *Fax:* 941-454-3383; *E-Mail:* csechris@uiuc.edu

SECHRIST, JOHN WILLIAM, NEUROANATOMY, DEVELOPMENTAL NEUROBIOLOGY. *Current Pos:* RES BIOLOGIST, UNIV CALIF IRVINE, 88- *Personal Data:* b Manila, Philippines, Feb 22, 42; US citizen; m 64, Karen Richert. *Educ:* Wheaton Col, Ill, BS, 64; Univ Ill, PhD(anat), 67. *Prof Exp:* From instr to asst prof neuroanat, Sch Med, Univ Pittsburgh, 67-72; asst prof anat, Col Med, Univ Ariz, 72-76; lectr anat, Univ Ibadan, Nigeria, 76-79; assoc prof biol, Wheaton Col, 79-88. *Mem:* AAAS; Am Asn Anatomists; Am Soc Cell Biol; Soc Neurosci. *Res:* Investigation of cytologic and metabolic changes during neuroblast differentiation and the retrograde reaction; comparative studies of earliest neurons in both vertebrates and invertebrates; neural crest development. *Mailing Add:* 18 Morning Star Irvine CA 92715-3762

SECHRIST, LYNNE LUAN, MICROBIOLOGY. *Current Pos:* VPRES ACAD AFFAIRS & DEAN FAC, GREEN MOUNTAIN COL, VT, 95- *Personal Data:* b Milwaukee, Wis, Oct 26, 41; m 88, Homer Broderick; c Roric S. *Educ:* Ohio Wesleyan Univ, BA, 63; Univ Wis-Madison, MS, 65; Ohio State Univ, PhD(bot), 69. *Prof Exp:* Asst prof biol, Ohio Dominican Col, 69-73; res fel, Univ Dayton, 74-76; from asst prof to prof biol, Col Potsdam, State Univ NY, 76-86, assoc dean libr studies, 86-90, sr asst to vpres acad affairs, 90-92, asst vpres academic servs, 93-95. *Mem:* Am Soc Microbiol; Soc Indust Microbiol; Sigma Xi; Nat Asn Acad Advising; Coun Cols Arts & Scis. *Res:* Cellular slime molds; zygotic development, genetics and electron microscopy of Chlamydomonas; microbial metabolism and emulsification of hydrocarbons from freshwater ecosystems; antibiotic resistant bacteria. *Mailing Add:* 2119 Hampshire Hollow Rd Poultney VT 05764. *Fax:* 315-267-3140

SECHZER, JERI ALTNEU, NEUROPSYCHOLOGY, EARLY DEVELOPMENT. *Current Pos:* vis prof, 91-93, RES PROF, PACE UNIV, 93- *Personal Data:* m 48; c Ellen K, Inda M & Selig L. *Educ:* NY Univ, BS, 56; Univ Pa, MA, 61, PhD(psychol), 62. *Honors & Awards:* Creative Talent Award Am, Inst Res, 63. *Prof Exp:* Res fel physiol psychol, Sch Med, Univ Pa, 61-63, USPHS fel, 63-64; asst prof physiol psychol & anat, Col Med, Baylor Univ, 64-66; res scientist, Dept Rehab Med & Anat, NY Univ Med Ctr, 66-70; from asst prof to assoc prof psychiat, Med Col, Cornell Univ, 70-91. *Concurrent Pos:* Mem, Univ Pa Medico Mission Algeria, 62; mem adv comt, NY Acad Sci, 73-, vchmn, 79-82, chmn, Sect Psychol, 82-84, Ad Hoc Comt Animal Res, 77-87, chmn, 77-86, Women in Sci Comt, 76-, co-prog chmn, 76-82; mem, Comt Animal Res & Experimentation, Am Psychol Asn, 80- 83, chmn, 82-83, bd sci affairs, Consultative Subcomt on Human Rights, ad Hoc Comt Nonsexist Res, 84-87; mem, Adv Panel Assessment of Alternatives to the Use of Animals in Testing, Res & Educ, Off Technol Assessments, US Cong, 84-85; mem, Ethical Practice Comt, NY Psychol Asn, 85-, pres, Acad Div, 92-93; mem, Hastings Ctr Task Force Ethics Animal Exp, 88-90; ad hoc consult, Asn Accreditation Lab Animal Care, 88-91; mem, Comt Pain & Distress in Lab Animals, Nat Res Coun-Inst Lab Animal Resources, 89-91; vis scientist minority inst prog, Univ Southern Colo, 89. *Mem:* Fel Am Psychol Asn; fel AAAS; Am Physiol Soc; Soc Neurosci; Asn Women Sci; fel NY Acad Med; fel NY Acad Sci; fel Am Psychol Soc. *Res:* Neuroscience of learning and memory; early development; neurobehavioral toxicology; bioethics and animal research; sex and gender issues in scientific research. *Mailing Add:* 180 East End Ave Apt 11D New York NY 10128

SECHZER, PHILIP HAIM, ANESTHESIOLOGY, MEDICO-LEGAL. *Current Pos:* PROF ANESTHESIOL, DOWNSTATE MED CTR, STATE UNIV NY, 66-; EMER DIR, MAIMONIDES MED CTR, 87- *Personal Data:* b New York, NY, Sept 13, 14; m 48, Jeri Altneu; c Ellen K, Inda M & Selig L. *Educ:* City Col New York, BS, 34; NY Univ, MD, 38; Am Bd Anesthesiol, dipl, 47; FRCS(I). *Prof Exp:* Intern, Harlem Hosp, New York, 38-40; resident, Fordham Hosp, 41-42; dir anesthesiol & asst prof, Postgrad Med Sch, NY Univ, 55-56; asst prof anesthesiol, Sch Med & physician-anesthetist, Hosp Univ Pa, 56-64; from assoc prof to prof anesthesiol, Col Med, Baylor Univ, 64-66. *Concurrent Pos:* Chief anesthesiol, AAF Sch Aviation Med, Randolph Field, Tex, 46; dir anesthesiol, Fordham Hosp, NY, 47-55; Consult, USPHS Marine Hosp, Staten Island, NY, 48-82, Vet Admin Hosps, Philadelphia 60-63 & Houston, 64-66; dir anesthesiol, Seton Hosp, New York, 50-55; attend anesthesiologist, Vet Admin Hosps, New York, 55-56 & Philadelphia, 58-59; chief Baylor anesthesiol sect, Methodist Hosp, Houston; area consult, Vet Admin, DC, 64-; ed, Commun in Anesthesiol, 70-77; hon police surgeon, New York, 74-; mem, Nat Bd Acupuncture Med; ed, Bd Anesthesiol News, Med Malpractice Prev; dir anesthesiol, maimonides Med Ctr, 66-86, med dir 73-86, dir, Pain Ther Ctr, 72-86; consult, EVP, 87-88, pres, 88-89. *Mem:* Fel Am Col Clin Pharmacol; fel Am Col Anesthesiol; Sigma Xi; fel Am Col Physicians; AMA; Am Soc Anesthesiologists; Soc Obstet Anesthesia & Perinatology; Soc Cardiovasc Anesthesiologists; Can Anaesthetists Soc; Int Asn Study Pain Fellow Faculty of Anesthetics Royal College of Surgeons. *Res:* Circulatory and respiratory physiology; statistical methods and experimental design; evaluation of new drugs and anesthetic methods; medico-legal and ethical issues; developed and applied patient controlled analgesia. *Mailing Add:* 180 East End Ave New York NY 10128

SECKEL, GUNTER RUDOLF, OCEANOGRAPHY. *Current Pos:* RETIRED. *Personal Data:* b Osnabruck, Ger, Nov 4, 23; nat US; m 65. *Educ:* Univ Wash, BS, 50, MS, 54. *Prof Exp:* Asst oceanog, Univ Wash, 50-53; oceanogr biol lab, Bur Com Fisheries, US Fish & Wildlife Serv, Hawaii, 53-63, supvry res oceanogr, 63, chief trade wind zone oceanog prog, 63-67, chief oceanog prog, 67-70; res oceanogr, PAC Environ group, Nat Marine Fisheries Serv, Nat Oceanic & Atmospheric Admin, 70-77, chief, 77-83. *Mem:* Am Geophys Union; Am Meteorol Soc; Sigma Xi. *Res:* Physical oceanography; climatic oceanography of Hawaiian waters; mechanisms producing seasonal and longer term changes in distribution of properties in north Pacific; structure of Pacific north equatorial current. *Mailing Add:* PFEG Nat Marine Fisheries Serv NOAA 1352 Lighthouse Ave Pacific Grove CA 93950-2097

SECKLER, BERNARD DAVID, MATHEMATICS. *Current Pos:* RETIRED. *Personal Data:* b New York, NY, Feb 14, 25; m 53, Evelyn Mehler; c 2. *Educ:* Brooklyn Col, BA, 45; Columbia Univ, MA, 48; NY Univ, PhD(appl math), 58. *Prof Exp:* Instr math, Long Island Univ, 48-53; lectr, Brooklyn Col, 47-54, instr, 57-58; asst appl math, NY Univ, 54-58; assoc prof math, Pratt Inst, 58-64; prof math, C W Post Col, Long Island Univ, 64-93, chmn dept, 68-72. *Res:* Asymptotic expansions; geometrical and asymptotical solution of diffraction problems; Russian abstracting and translating of applied mathematics; Russian translating and translation editing of probability journal. *Mailing Add:* 19 Ramsey Rd Great Neck NY 11023. *E-Mail:* bersec@aol.com

SECOMB, TIMOTHY W, CARDIOVASCULAR SYSTEMS, APPLIED MATHEMATICS. *Current Pos:* from asst prof to assoc prof, 81-92, PROF PHYSIOL, UNIV ARIZ, 92- *Personal Data:* b Melbourne, Australia, Jan 2, 54. *Educ:* Univ Melbourne, BS, 75, MS, 76; Univ Cambridge, PhD(appl math), 79. *Prof Exp:* Res assoc civil eng, Columbia Univ, 79-81. *Mem:* Am Physiol Soc; Soc Indust & Appl Math; Microcirculatory Soc. *Res:* Theoretical studies of blood flow and mass transport in microcirculation; applied mathematics; mathematical modeling in biology; fluid mechanics. *Mailing Add:* Dept Physiol Univ Ariz Tucson AZ 85724-5051

SECOR, DONALD TERRY, JR, APPALACHIAN TECTONICS, ROCK MECHANICS. *Current Pos:* From asst prof to assoc prof, 62-81, chmn dept, 66-69, 77-81, PROF GEOL, UNIV SC, 81- *Personal Data:* b Oil City, Pa, Nov 22, 34; m 59, Dorothy Eisenhart; c Beth, Jane & Carol. *Educ:* Cornell Univ, BS, 57, MS, 59; Stanford Univ, PhD(geol), 62. *Mem:* Fel Geol Soc Am; Am Geophys Union; AAAS. *Res:* Mechanics of geological structures; tectonics of the Appalachian Mountains. *Mailing Add:* Dept Geol Sci Univ SC Columbia SC 29208

SECOR, JACK BEHRENT, PHYSIOLOGICAL ECOLOGY. *Current Pos:* from asst prof to assoc prof biol, 67-77, PROF BIOL, EASTERN NMEX UNIV, 77- *Personal Data:* b Indianapolis, Ind, Aug 18, 23. *Educ:* Butler Univ, BS, 48; Wash State Univ, PhD(bot), 57. *Prof Exp:* Botanist, US Geol Surv, 56-57; range conservationist, US Forest Serv, 57-58; Labatt fel bot, Univ Western Ont, 59-60; instr, Dept Natural Sci, Mich State Univ, 60-63; res asst biochem, Va Polytech Inst, 63-65; res scientist assoc, Univ Tex, Austin, 66-67. *Mem:* Ecol Soc Am. *Res:* Gypsumland ecosystems. *Mailing Add:* 1261 Willow Las Cruces NM 88001-2432

SECOR, ROBERT M(ILLER), CHEMICAL ENGINEERING. *Current Pos:* res engr, Eastern Lab, 56-64, sr res engr, Eng Technol Lab, 64-74, RES ASSOC, E I DU PONT DE NEMOURS & CO, INC, 74- *Personal Data:* b New York, NY, Mar 21, 32; c 2. *Educ:* NY Univ, BChE, 52; Yale Univ, DEng, 58. *Prof Exp:* Asst, Yale Univ, 52-55. *Concurrent Pos:* Adj prof, Chem Eng Dept, Univ Del, 88- & Columbia Univ, 90-; Eastman Kodak fel, Yale Univ; res fel, Hagley Mus & Libr, 95- *Res:* Diffusion; mass transfer; chemical kinetics; applied mathematics; polymer processing. *Mailing Add:* 3701 Centerville Rd Wilmington DE 19807-0304

SECORD, ROBERT N, CHEMICAL ENGINEERING. *Current Pos:* Chem engr, 47-51, head appl res sect, New Prods Res Dept, 51-61, eng mgr, Oxides Div, 61-66, dir process develop, 66-70, res dir, 70-77, DIR, CAB-O-SIL RES & DEVELOP, CABOT CORP, 77- *Personal Data:* b Newton, Mass, Dec 20, 20; m 44; c 4. *Educ:* Mass Inst Technol, BS, 42, MS, 47. *Mem:* Am Chem Soc; Am Inst Chem Engrs. *Res:* Processes for high temperature chemical reactions. *Mailing Add:* Box 341 Sunapee NH 03782-0341

SECOY, DIANE MARIE, VERTEBRATE BIOLOGY. *Current Pos:* from asst prof to assoc prof, 68-82, assoc dean, Grad Studies, 84-90, PROF BIOL, UNIV REGINA, 82- *Personal Data:* b Kenton, Ohio, Oct 31, 38; m 70. *Educ:* Ohio State Univ, BS, 60, MS, 62; Univ Colo, PhD(herpet), 68. *Prof Exp:* Asst cur zool & paleont, Mus, Univ Colo, 67-68. *Mem:* Sigma Xi; Am Soc Ichthyologists & Herpetologists; Herpetologists League; Soc Study Amphibians & Reptiles; Can Soc Zoologists; Am Soc Zoolgists; Can Soc Herpetologists. *Res:* Reptilian morphology; ecology of northern reptiles; history of pest control. *Mailing Add:* Dept Biol Sci Univ Regina Regina SK S4S 0A2 Can

SECREST, DONALD H, PHYSICAL CHEMISTRY. *Current Pos:* from asst prof to assoc prof, 61-82, PROF CHEM, UNIV ILL, 81- *Personal Data:* b Akron, Ohio, Jan 3, 32; m 58, Masaka Fujita; c Hideko & David. *Educ:* Univ Akron, BS, 55; Univ Wis, PhD(theoret chem), 61. *Prof Exp:* Instr phys chem, Univ Wis, 60-61. *Concurrent Pos:* Vis scientist, Max Planck Inst, Gottingen, Ger, 71-72; assoc ed, J Chem Physics, 77-79; Humboldt Award, Ger, 85-86. *Mem:* Fel Am Phys Soc; Soc Indust & Appl Math; Sigma Xi. *Res:* Atomic and molecular scattering problems; molecular structure of small systems, especially development of mathematical techniques for handling quantum mechanical problems; on-line application of computing machinery. *Mailing Add:* Dept Chem Univ Ill Urbana IL 61801. *E-Mail:* secrest@uiuc.edu

SECREST, EVERETT LEIGH, RESEARCH ADMINISTRATION, SYSTEMS SCIENCE. *Current Pos:* RETIRED. *Personal Data:* b Tioga, Tex, Jan 5, 28; m 48; c 2. *Educ:* NTex State Col, BS, 47, MS, 48; Mass Inst Technol, PhD(physics), 51. *Prof Exp:* From asst prof to assoc prof physics, NTex State Col, 51-54; chief nuclear physics, Convair Div, Gen Dynamics Corp, 54-57; sect chief proj, Physics Atomic Energy Div, Babcock & Silcox Co, 57-58, asst mgr physics & math, 58-59; chief appl res, Gen Dynamics, Ft Worth, 59-63, chief scientist, 63-64; assoc dean eng grad studies & res, Univ Okla, 64-65; grad dean, Tex Christian Univ, 65-68, pres res found, 65-72, vchancellor advan studies & res, 68-72, continental nat bank prof mgt sci, 72-93, vchancellor finance & planning, 81-93. *Concurrent Pos:* Consult, Gen Dynamics/Ft Worth, 52-54; guest, Inst Syst Dynamics Group & Opers Resctr, Mass Inst Technol, 72. *Mem:* Am Phys Soc; Am Nuclear Soc; Am Soc Eng Educ; Soc Comput Simulation; Sigma Xi. *Res:* Management science with emphasis on applications of systems dynamics to complex social and economic structures; university administration. *Mailing Add:* 322 Hide A Way Lane Cent Lindale TX 75771-5202

SECRIST, JOHN ADAIR, III, NUCLEOSIDE SYNTHESIS, DRUG SYNTHESIS. *Current Pos:* sr chemist, 79-80, head, Bioorg Sect, 80-84, from assoc dir to dir, org chem dept, 84-90, EXEC VPRES, SOUTHERN RES INST, 90- *Personal Data:* b Vincennes, Ind, Sept, 26, 47; m 68; c 2. *Educ:* Univ Mich, BS, 68; Univ Ill, PhD(org chem), 72. *Prof Exp:* Fel, Harvard Univ, 72-73; asst prof chem, Ohio State Univ, 73-79. *Concurrent Pos:* Mem, Exam Comt, Org Chem Subcomt, Am Chem Soc, 75-90; adj scientist, Comprehensive Cancer Ctr, Univ Ala, Birmingham, 84-; mem, Am Chem Soc Nomenclature Comt, 87- *Mem:* Am Chem Soc; Chem Soc; AAAS; Int Soc Antiviral Res. *Res:* Synthetic organic chemistry; medicinal chemistry; chemotherapy and drug development. *Mailing Add:* Southern Res Inst PO Box 55305 Birmingham AL 35255-5305

SEDAR, ALBERT WILLIAM, MICROSCOPIC ANATOMY. *Personal Data:* b Cambridge, Mass, Dec 20, 22; m 53, Jean Dimmitt; c Holly A, David B, Warren D & Emily L. *Educ:* Brown Univ, AB, 43, MS, 48; Univ Iowa, PhD(zool), 53. *Prof Exp:* Asst gen biol, Brown Univ, 46-48; asst histol, Univ Iowa, 50, asst cytol, 51-52; instr zool & histol, Syracuse Univ, 52-53; NIH res fel cytol, Rockefeller Inst, 53-55. *Concurrent Pos:* USPHS career develop award, 66-71; consult, 93- *Mem:* Am Soc Cell Biol; Electron Micros Soc Am; Am Asn Anatomists. *Res:* Histology; cytophysiology; electron microscopy; fine structure of cells; electron histochemistry of cells; ultrastructure of cells and tissues. *Mailing Add:* Dept Anat Baugh Inst Anat Jefferson Med Col 1020 Locust St Philadelphia PA 19107. *Fax:* 215-923-3808

SEDAT, JOHN WILLIAM, MOLECULAR BIOLOGY, CHEMISTRY. *Current Pos:* ASST PROF MOLECULAR BIOL, UNIV CALIF SCH MED, SAN FRANCISCO, 78- *Personal Data:* b Culver City, Calif, Aug 17, 42; m 75. *Educ:* Pasadena Col, BA, 63; Calif Inst Technol, PhD(biol), 70. *Prof Exp:* Fel, Helen Hay Whitney Found, 70-73; staff scientist, Lab Molecular Biol, Med Res Coun, 73-74; vis scientist, Dept Cell Biochem, Hadassah Med Sch, Jerusalem, Israel, 74-75; res assoc, Dept Radiobiol, Yale Univ Sch Med, 75-78. *Res:* Chromosome and interphase nuclear architecture. *Mailing Add:* Dept Biochem & Biophys Univ Calif San Francisco Med Sch 513 Parnassus Ave San Francisco CA 94122-2722

SEDBERRY, JOSEPH E, JR, AGRONOMY, SOIL CHEMISTRY. *Current Pos:* prof agron, 63-88, EMER PROF, LA STATE UNIV, BATON ROUGE, 88-; PRES, JES INC, 80-; CHMN BD, STEEL FORGINGS, 80- *Personal Data:* b Shreveport, La, Sept 18, 25; m 53; c 3. *Educ:* Centenary Col, BS, 49; La State Univ, Baton Rouge, MS, 52, PhD(agron), 54. *Prof Exp:* Agronomist, NLa Exp Sta, La State Univ, Baton Rouge, 54-55; agronomist, Lion Oil Co, Monsanto Chem Co, 55-58; agronomist, Am Potash Inst, 58-63. *Concurrent Pos:* Ford Found consult, Latin Am, 65-66; res grants, Geigy Chem Co, Eagle Picher Co, Sherwin Williams Co & Am Cyanamid Chem Co, 67- *Mem:* Am Soc Agron; Soil Sci Soc Am. *Res:* Soil testing and fertility with major emphasis on effect of major, secondary and micronutrients on yield; chemical composition of food and fiber crops. *Mailing Add:* 190 Lee Dr Suite 3 Baton Rouge LA 70808

SEDELOW, SALLY YEATES, COMPUTER SCIENCE, LINGUISTICS. *Current Pos:* PROF COMPUT SCI, UNIV ARK, LITTLE ROCK, 85- *Personal Data:* b Greenfield, Iowa, Aug 10, 31; m 58. *Educ:* Univ Iowa, BA, 53; Mt Holyoke Col, MA, 56; Bryn Mawr Col, PhD(Eng lit), 60. *Prof Exp:* Instr Eng, Smith Col, 59-60; asst prof, Parsons Col, 60-61 & Rockford Col, 61-62; human factors scientist, Systs Develop Corp, 62-64; asst prof eng, St Louis Univ, 64-66; assoc prof Eng & comput & info sci, Univ NC, Chapel Hill, 66-70; prof comput sci & ling, Univ Kans, 70-85, assoc dean col lib arts & sci, 79-85. *Concurrent Pos:* Off Naval Res res grant automated lang, Univ NC, Chapel Hill & Univ Kans, 64-74; consult, Syst Develop Corp, 64-67; mem, Adv Panel, Instnl Comput Serv Sect, NSF, 68-70, Comput Applns Res Sect, 70-71, Adv Comt Comput Activities, 72-; vis scientist, NSF-Kan Comput Mach Vis Scientist Prog, 69-70; NSF grant, Univ Kans, 71-72; prog dir, Tech & Systs Prog, NSF, 74-76; chmn group comput in lang & lit, Modern Lang Asn Am, 77-78; mem US deleg comput-based natural-lang processing, USSR, 78; adj prof english, Univ Ark, Little Rock, 85-, adj prof electronics & instrumentation, Grad Inst Technol, 85-; adj prof computer sci, Univ Ark, Fayetteville, 88- *Mem:* Asn Comput Mach; Asn Comput Ling; Am Soc Info Sci; Ling Soc Am; Modern Lang Asn Am; Western Social Sci Asn. *Res:* Computer-based language and literature analysis; stylistics; semantics; computing in the humanities. *Mailing Add:* 401 Golf Eden Isle Dr Heber Springs AR 72543

SEDELOW, WALTER ALFRED, JR, computer sciences, history & philosophy of science, for more information see previous edition

SEDENSKY, JAMES ANDREW, CARDIOVASCULAR PHYSIOLOGY, PULMONARY PHYSIOLOGY. *Current Pos:* from instr to asst prof physiol, 69-76, ASSOC PROF PHYSIOL, SCH MED, WAYNE STATE UNIV, 76- *Personal Data:* b Bridgeport, Conn, Aug 6, 36. *Educ:* Fairfield Univ, BS, 58; Univ Tenn, Memphis, PhD(physiol, biophys), 66. *Prof Exp:* NSF trainee biomath, NC State Univ, 66-67, NIH trainee, 67-69. *Concurrent Pos:* NIH fac educ develop award, 73. *Mem:* AAAS; Math Asn Am; Am Statist Asn; Am Physiol Soc; Am Thoracic Soc. *Res:* Computer simulation and statistical analysis of biomedical systems; electrical impedance plethysmography. *Mailing Add:* Dept Physiol Wayne State Univ Sch Med 540 E Canfield Ave Detroit MI 48201-1908

SEDEROFF, RONALD R, MOLECULAR GENETICS OF FOREST TREES. *Current Pos:* assoc prof, Dept Genetics, 78-84, EDWIN F CONGER PROF FORESTRY, NC STATE UNIV, 87-, ASSOC MEM, DEPT GENETICS & DEPT BIOCHEM, 87- DIR, FOREST BIOTECHNOL GROUP, 87- *Personal Data:* b Montreal, Can, Dec 22, 39; US citizen; c 2. *Educ:* Univ Calif, Los Angeles, BA, 61, MA, 63, PhD(zool), 66. *Prof Exp:* Actg asst prof, Dept Zool, Univ Calif, Los Angeles, 67; fel, Lab Biophysics, Inst Molecular Biol, Univ Geneva, 67-69; asst prof, Dept Biol Sci, Columbia Univ, 69-75; from asst prof to assoc prof, Dept Biol, Univ Ore, 75-78; sr scientist & plant molecular geneticist, Genetics Western Forest Trees & Inst Forest Genetics, USDA Forest Serv, Calif, 84-87. *Concurrent Pos:* Assoc ed, Can J Forestry Res, 89- *Mem:* Nat Acad Sci. *Res:* Molecular genetics of forest trees; genetic regulation of lignin biosynthesis; molecular mechanisms in the formation of the plant cell wall; DNA transfer in conifers; gene expression in the differentiating wood; genetic engineering of wood properties; application of genome mapping to tree breeding; molecular basis of resistance to pathogens in forest trees. *Mailing Add:* Dept Forestry 6113 Jordan Hall NC State Univ Box 8008 Raleigh NC 27695-8008

SEDGWICK, ROBERT T, MECHANICS, MATERIALS SCIENCE. *Current Pos:* CONVENTIONAL MUNITIONS PROG MGR, SYSTS, SCI & SOFTWARE, 69- *Personal Data:* b Rome City, Ind, Aug 2, 33; m 66; c 1. *Educ:* Tri-State Col, BSME, 59; Mich State Univ, MS, 60, PhD(mat sci), 65. *Prof Exp:* Asst instr mech, Mich State Univ, 60-65; scientist, Space Sci Lab, Gen Elec Co, Pa, 65-69. *Mem:* Soc Eng Sci. *Res:* Dislocation mechanics; continuum mechanics; elastic-plastic-hydrodynamic material flow; hypervelocity and ballistic impact studies; Eulerian and Lagrangian numerical code development; shaped charge and fragmentation munitions calculations; fuel-air explosives; conventional warhead design. *Mailing Add:* 1515 San Dieguito Dr Del Mar CA 92014

SEDLACEK, WILLIAM ADAM, PLUTONIUM NDA & ACCOUNTABILITY. *Current Pos:* CONSULT, MAT CONTROL & ACCOUNTABILITY, BABCOCK & WILCOX PROTEC, 94- *Personal Data:* b Glendive, Mont, Feb 22, 36; m 63; c 2. *Educ:* Univ Wyo, BS, 58, PhD(phys chem), 65. *Prof Exp:* Res chemist, Shale Oil & Petrol Res Sta, US Bur Mines, 59-60; NSF fel, Univ Fla, 65-66; staff mem, Los Alamos Sci Lab, Univ Calif, 66-93. *Mem:* Sigma Xi. *Res:* Ternary fission, activation analysis; nuclear reactions, nuclear experimental techniques and environmental pollution; atmospheric dynamics; Aitken nuclei; trace elements, ozone, nondestructive assay of SNM and SNM accountability. *Mailing Add:* 48 Timber Ridge Los Alamos NM 87544-2317

SEDLAK, JOHN ANDREW, ORGANIC CHEMISTRY. *Current Pos:* From res chemist to sr res chemist, 60-84, PRIN RES CHEMIST, AM CYANAMID CO, 84- *Personal Data:* b Bridgeport, Conn, May 17, 34; m 87. *Educ:* Wesleyan Univ, BA, 55; Tufts Univ, MS, 56; Ohio State Univ, PhD(org fluorine chem), 60. *Mem:* Am Chem Soc; Tech Asn Pulp & Paper Indust; Sigma Xi. *Res:* Fluorinated monomers; polynuclear aromatic hydrocarbons; polyelectrolytes; paper chemicals; isocyanates; urethanes; coatings crosslinkers; rubber chemicals; chemiluminescence. *Mailing Add:* 249-11 Hamilton Ave Stamford CT 06902-3465

SEDLET, JACOB, PHYSICAL CHEMISTRY, NUCLEAR CHEMISTRY. *Current Pos:* CHEMIST, ARGONNE NAT LAB, 50- *Personal Data:* b Milwaukee, Wis, Apr 4, 22; m 44, 68, Solveig Petersen; c Susan & Steve. *Educ:* Univ Wis, BS, 45; Purdue Univ, PhD(chem), 51. *Prof Exp:* Asst chemist, Metall Lab, Univ Chicago, 44-46; asst, Purdue Univ, 46-48, asst instr, 48-50. *Concurrent Pos:* Consult radiochem, anal chem & environ surveillance. *Mem:* AAAS; Health Physics Soc; Am Chem Soc. *Res:* Analytical chemistry; radiochemistry; environmental chemistry; nuclear waste treatment; chemical separations. *Mailing Add:* Argonne Nat Lab 9700 S Cass Ave Argonne IL 60439

SEDMAN, YALE S, ENTOMOLOGY. *Current Pos:* from asst prof to assoc prof, 55-65, PROF BIOL SCI, WESTERN ILL UNIV, 65- *Personal Data:* b Detroit, Mich, May 22, 29; m 55; c 3. *Educ:* Ariz State Univ, BS, 50; Univ Utah, MS, 52; Univ Wis, PhD(entom), 55. *Prof Exp:* Asst entom, Univ Utah, 50-52; asst, Univ Wis, 52-54. *Mem:* Soc Syst Zool. *Res:* Systematics of Diptera, especially family Syrphidae. *Mailing Add:* 802 S McArthur St Macomb IL 61455

SEDOR, EDWARD ANDREW, ORGANIC CHEMISTRY, CHEMICAL DYNAMICS. *Current Pos:* VPRES PROCESS DEVELOP/QUAL ASSURANCE, SPECIALTY CHEM PROD, 92- *Personal Data:* b East Chicago, Ind, June 24, 39; c 3. *Educ:* Lake Forest Col, Ill, BA, 61; Mich State Univ, PhD(phys org chem), 66. *Prof Exp:* Res chemist, Archer-Daniels-Midland Co, 65-67, sr res chemist, 67-73; mkt coordr, Ashland Chem Co, 73-74, group leader additive chem, 74-79; sect mgr, Sherex Chem Co, 77-79, assoc res dir, 79-92, dir total qual, 90-92. *Concurrent Pos:* Bd dir, United Way Trico, 95-97. *Mem:* Am Chem Soc; Am Oil Chemists's Soc. *Res:* Fundamental chemistry, processing technology and applications research of fatty derivatives including amines, alcohols, quaternaries andesters; applications areas-emulsifiers, surfactants; plasticizers, mining technology, fabric softeners; custom synthesis; ag intermediates; paper chemicals; photoreproductives. *Mailing Add:* 2 Stanton St Marinette WI 54143

SEDRA, ADEL S, MICRO-ELECTRONICS, CIRCUIT THEORY. *Current Pos:* from asst prof to assoc prof, Univ Toronto, 69-78, exec dir, Microelec Develop Ctr, 83-86, chmn dept, 86-93, PROF ELEC ENG, UNIV TORONTO, 78-, VPRES & PROVOST, 93- *Personal Data:* b Egypt, Nov 2, 43; Can citizen; m 73, Doris Barker; c Paul D & Mark A. *Educ:* Cairo Univ, BSc, 64; Univ Toronto, MASc, 68; Univ Toronto, PhD(elec eng), 69. *Honors & Awards:* Darlington Award, Inst Elec & Electronics Engrs, 84, Cauer-Guillemin Award, 87; Frederick Emmons Terman Award, Am Soc Eng Educ, 88; Achievement Award, Info Technol Asn Can, 93. *Prof Exp:* Instr & res engr, Cairo Univ, 64-66. *Concurrent Pos:* Consult, Elec Eng Consociates Ltd, 69-; Nat Sci & Eng Res Coun Can grant, Univ Toronto, 69-; assoc ed, Inst Elec & Electronics Engrs Trans Circuits & Systs, 81-83; ed, Circuits & Devices Mag, 85-86; mem bd dirs, Dicon Systs Ltd, 85-90; fel, Ryerson Polytechnic Univ, 88; founding bd dirs, Info Technol Ctr, 88-93. *Mem:* Fel Inst Elec & Electronics Engrs. *Res:* Electronic circuit design; active network theory and design; active filters; analog and digital instrumentation; filter-theory & design; switched-capacitor networks; computer-aided design. *Mailing Add:* Dept Elec & Comput Sci Univ Toronto 27 King's College Circle Rm 225 Toronto ON M5S 1A1 Can. *Fax:* 416-978-3939

SEDRANSK, JOSEPH HENRY, statistics, for more information see previous edition

SEDRIKS, ARISTIDE JOHN, CORROSION SCIENCE, ELECTROCHEMISTRY. *Current Pos:* PROG MGR, OFF NAVAL RES, ARLINGTON, VA, 85- *Personal Data:* b Riga, Latvia, May 15, 38; US citizen; m 62; c 3. *Educ:* Univ Wales, BSc, 59, PhD(metall), 62. *Honors & Awards:* F N Speller Award, Nat Asn Corrosion Engrs, 89. *Prof Exp:* Res scientist, Defense Stand Labs, Sydney, Australia, 62-65; head, Metall Dept, Res Inst Advan Studies, Martin-Marietta Labs, Baltimore, 65-71; head, Corrosion Sect, Int Nickel Co, Sterling Forest, NY, 71-79, res mgr, Wrightsville Beach, NC, 79-82; br head, Naval Res Lab, Washington, 82-85. *Concurrent Pos:* Mem, Res Comt, Nat Asn Corrosion Engrs, 86- *Mem:* Fel Nat Asn Corrosion Engrs; fel Am Soc Metals Int; Metals Soc; Electrochem Soc. *Res:* Corrosion control by metallurgical modifications; stress corrosion cracking, hydrogen embrittlement, passivity and localized corrosion; coatings for corrosion control; author of three books. *Mailing Add:* Off Naval Res Code 332 800 N Quincy St Arlington VA 22217-5660. *Fax:* 703-696-0934; *E-Mail:* sedrikj@onrhq.onr.navy.mil

SEEBACH, J ARTHUR, JR, MATHEMATICS. *Current Pos:* From asst prof to assoc prof, 65-87, PROF MATH, ST OLAF COL, 87- *Personal Data:* b Philadelphia, Pa, May 17, 38; m 59; c 1. *Educ:* Gettysburg Col, BA, 59; Northwestern Univ, MA, 62, PhD(math), 68. *Concurrent Pos:* Vis assoc prof, Swiss Fed Inst Technol, 71-72; assoc ed, Am Math Monthly, 70-85; ed, Math Mag, 76-80; ETS comt grad rec exam (math), 82-90, chair, 86-90. *Mem:* Am Math Soc; Math Asn Am; Asn Comput Mach. *Res:* Point set topology. *Mailing Add:* Dept Math St Olaf Col Northfield MN 55057-1574

SEEBASS, ALFRED RICHARD, III, AERODYNAMICS, APPLIED MATHEMATICS. *Current Pos:* dean, Col Eng & Appl Sci, 81-94, PROF AEROSPACE ENG SCI, UNIV COLO, 81-, DEPT CHAIR, 94- *Personal Data:* b Denver, Colo, Mar 27, 36; m 58, Nancy Palm; c Erik P & Scott G. *Educ:* Princeton Univ, BSE, 58, MSE, 61; Cornell Univ, PhD(aerospace eng), 62. *Honors & Awards:* Max Planck Res Award, W H Sobieczky, 91; Durand lectr, Am Inst Aeronaut & Astronaut, 94. *Prof Exp:* Fel, res & teaching asst, Cornell & Princeton Univs, 58-62; from asst prof to assoc prof, Grad Sch Aerospace Eng, Cornell Univ, 62-72, actg dir, Ctr Appl Math, 68-69, assoc dean res & grad progs, Col Eng & prof mech & aerospace eng, 72-75; prof aerospace & mech eng & prof math, Univ Ariz, 75-81, actg chmn, Prog Appl Math, 79-80. *Concurrent Pos:* Consult, Inst Defense Analysis, 64-65, Dept Transp, 67-71, Gen Appl Sci Labs, 68-72, Flow Res, Inc, 76, Boeing Co, 76 & 79, Lockheed Co, Ga, 79 & Calif, 79-80; prin investr, NASA grants, 66-82, Off Naval Res grant & Air Force Off Sci Res grant, 75-82 & US-Israel Bi-Nat Sci Fund grant, 79-81; staff mem, Res Div, Off Adv Res & Technol, NASA Hq, 66-67, mem, Res & Technol Subcomt Fluid Mech, 70, Res Panel, 74-77 & Adv Coun, 81-83; consult, Comt SST-Sonic Boom, Nat Acad Sci, 67-71; adv, Interagency Aircraft Noise Abatement Prog, Int Civil Aviation Orgn, 68-70 & US deleg, Sonic Boom Panel, 69; fac assoc, Boeing Sci Res Labs, Seattle, 70; mem, Air Force Studies Bd, Nat Res Coun, 77-79 & Aeronaut & Space Eng Bd, 77-84, chmn & vchmn, 81-83, mem, Comn Eng & Tech Systs, 82-83 & subcomt fluids, Surv Comt Plasma Physics & Fluids, 83-84; assoc ed, Physics of Fluids, 78-80 & Am Inst Aeronaut & Astronaut J, 81-83; vis prof aeronaut & astronaut & actg assoc dir, Aerospace & Energetics Res Prog, Univ Wash, 79; mem, Sci Adv Bd, USAF, 84-88; ed-in-chief, Progress in Aeronaut & Astronaut, 90; mem, Comn Phys Sci, Math & Appln, 92- *Mem:* Nat Acad Eng; fel Am Inst Aeronaut & Astronaut; fel AAAS. *Res:* Aerodynamics and fluid mechanics; engineering education; geophysical fluid dynamics; computational fluid dynamics. *Mailing Add:* Col Eng & Appl Sci Univ Colo Boulder CO 80309. *Fax:* 303-492-2199

SEEBAUER, EDMUND GERARD, SURFACE CHEMISTRY, SEMICONDUCTOR PROCESSING. *Current Pos:* from asst prof to assoc prof, 88-97, PROF CHEM ENG, UNIV ILL, URBANA, 97- *Personal Data:* b Chicago, Ill, May 15, 61, m; c John. *Educ:* Univ Ill, Urbana, BS, 83; Univ Minn, PhD(chem eng), 86. *Honors & Awards:* Presidential Young Investr Award, NSF, 88. *Prof Exp:* Assoc, Sandia Nat Labs, 87. *Concurrent Pos:* Observer, US Deleg Gen Assembly, Int Union Pure & Appl Chem, 89 & 91; Alfred P Sloan res fel chem, 94. *Mem:* Am Inst Chem Engrs; Am Chem Soc; Am Phys Soc; Am Vacuum Soc; Mat Res Soc; Am Geophys Union. *Res:* Focus on developing new experimental methods for examining the surface chemistry of semiconductor growth under real processing temperatures and pressures. *Mailing Add:* 600 S Mathews Urbana IL 61801. *Fax:* 217-333-5052; *E-Mail:* eseebane@uiuc.edu

SEEBOHM, PAUL MINOR, MEDICINE. *Current Pos:* assoc internal med, Univ Iowa, 49-51, dir allergy clin, 49-70, from asst prof to prof internal med, 51-59, exec assoc dean col, 70-86, consult to dean, Col Med, 86-93, EMER PROF INTERNAL MED, COL MED, UNIV IOWA, 86- *Personal Data:* b Cincinnati, Ohio, Jan 13, 16; m 42, Dorothy Eberhart; c Karen E (Jackson). *Educ:* Univ Cincinnati, BA, 38, MD, 41; Am Bd Internal Med, cert allergy. *Prof Exp:* Asst resident physician, Cincinnati Gen Hosp, 46-48; resident allergy, Roosevelt Hosp, NY, 48-49. *Concurrent Pos:* Mem spec med adv group, Vet Admin, 72-76; chmn allergenic extract rev panel, Food & Drug Admin, 74-84; mem, Iowa State Bd Health, 71-83, 76-83; mem bd dirs, Iowa Health Systs Agency, 76-80. *Mem:* Fel Am Col Physicians; Cent Soc Clin Res; fel Am Acad Allergy & Immunol (secy, pres, 66). *Res:* Pulmonary function in chronic respiratory disease. *Mailing Add:* Univ Iowa Col Med Iowa City IA 52242. *Fax:* 319-356-7893

SEEBURGER, GEORGE HAROLD, science education, biology, for more information see previous edition

SEED, JOHN RICHARD, MICROBIOLOGY, PARASITOLOGY. *Current Pos:* prof & chair, Dept Parasitol Lab Prac, 81-89, PROF DEPT EPIDEMIOL, SCH PUB HEALTH, UNIV NC, CHAPEL HILL, 90- *Personal Data:* b Paterson, NJ, Apr 27, 37; m 59, Judith A Mockridge; c Amy R & David R. *Educ:* Lafayette Col, AB, 59; Yale Univ, PhD(microbiol), 63. *Honors & Awards:* Henry Baldwin Ward Medal, Am Soc Parasitol. *Prof Exp:* Res assoc biol, Haverford Col, 62-63; from asst prof to assoc prof, Tulane Univ, 65-73, prof, 73-74; prof biol & head dept, Tex A&M Univ, 74-80. *Concurrent Pos:* Am Cancer Soc fel, 62-63; chair, Fedn Soc Parisitol, 92-94; consult, J Parisitol, 94- *Mem:* Fel AAAS; fel Am Soc Microbiol; Soc Protozool; Am Soc Parasitol (pres); Am Soc Trop Med Hyg. *Res:* Immunological and physiological studies on parasitic protozoan infections, especially African trypanosomiasis. *Mailing Add:* Dept Epidemiol Univ NC Chapel Hill NC 27599-7400

SEED, RANDOLPH WILLIAM, SURGERY, BIOCHEMISTRY. *Current Pos:* ASST PROF SURG, RUSH UNIV MED SCH, 87- *Personal Data:* b Chicago, Ill, May 1, 33; m 68; c 5. *Educ:* Harvard Univ, BA, 54; Univ Chicago, MD, 60, PhD(biochem), 65. *Prof Exp:* Chmn dept surg, Grant Hosp, Chicago, 70-76; asst prof surg, Med Sch, Northwestern Univ, 71-87. *Concurrent Pos:* Attend surg, Vet Admin Res Hosp, Chicago, 68- *Mem:* Am Thyroid Asn. *Res:* Human thyroid cancer; human thyroid tissue culture and biosynthesis of thyroglobulin. *Mailing Add:* 999 N Lakeshore Dr Chicago IL 60611-1347

SEED, THOMAS MICHAEL, HEMATOLOGY, RADIATION BIOLOGY. *Current Pos:* RES BIOLOGIST & GROUP LEADER, RADIATION HEMAT, DIV BIOL ENVIRON & MED RES, ARGONNE NAT LAB, 75- *Personal Data:* b Paterson, NJ, Dec 8, 45; m 68; c 2. *Educ:* Univ Conn, BA, 68; Ohio State Univ, MS, 69, PhD(microbiol), 72. *Prof Exp:* Fel electron micros, Inst Path, Case Western Reserve Univ, 72-73; res assoc, Blood Res Lab, Am Nat Red Cross, 73-75. *Concurrent Pos:* Lectr, dept biol & physics, Cath Univ Am, 74-75; supvr, Electron Micros Ctr, Div Biol Environ & Med Res, Argonne Nat Lab, 75-; consult, Pharmaceut Res Div, Warner-Lambert/Parke-Davis, Detroit, 78-80; guest ed, Int J Scanning Electron Micros, 81-84. *Mem:* AAAS; Am Soc Microbiol; Int Soc Exp Hemat; Electron Micros Soc Am; Am Soc Radiation Res. *Res:* Structural and function studies of radiation-induced hematopathology; cellular mechanisms of preclinical phase leukemogenic processes; mechanistic studies on red cell destruction during infectious hemolytic anemias. *Mailing Add:* 379 Hill Ave Argonne Nat Lab 9700 S Cass Ave Glen Ellen IL 60137

SEEDS, MICHAEL AUGUST, ASTRONOMY. *Current Pos:* PROF ASTRON, FRANKLIN & MARSHALL COL, 70- *Personal Data:* b Danville, Ill, Dec 14, 42; c 1. *Educ:* Univ Ill, Urbana, BS, 65; Ind Univ, Bloomington, MS & PhD(astron), 70. *Mem:* AAAS; Am Astron Soc; Sigma Xi. *Res:* Photometry of short period variable stars and eclipsing binaries; narrow band photometry; undergraduate astronomy instruction, methods and materials; author of 2 books. *Mailing Add:* Dept Math & Astron PO Box 3003 Lancaster PA 17604

SEEDS, NICHOLAS WARREN, DEVELOPMENTAL NEUROBIOLOGY. *Current Pos:* PROF BIOCHEM, BIOPHYS & GENETICS, MED CTR, UNIV COLO, DENVER, 70-, DIR, NEUROSCI CTR, 89- *Personal Data:* b Circleville, Ohio, Dec 25, 42; m 64; c 2. *Educ:* Univ NMex, BS, 64; Univ Iowa, PhD(biochem), 68. *Prof Exp:* NSF fel, NIH, 68-70. *Concurrent Pos:* Jacob Javits distinguished investr neurosci, 89- *Mem:* Am Soc Biol Chemists; AAAS; Am Soc Cell Biol; Soc Neurosci; Am Soc Neurochem. *Res:* Developmental neurobiology; microtubules; plasminogen activators in cell migration, cell-cell recognition and synaptic plasticity. *Mailing Add:* Dept Biochem-Biophys & Genetics Univ Colo Med Sch Denver CO 80262

SEEFELDT, VERN DENNIS, ANATOMY. *Current Pos:* assoc prof, 71-76, PROF PHYS EDUC, MICH STATE UNIV, 76- *Personal Data:* b Lena, Wis. *Educ:* Wis State Univ, La Crosse, BS, 55; Univ Wis, PhD(phys educ), 66. *Prof Exp:* Asst prof phys educ, Mich State Univ, 66-69; asst prof, Univ Wis-Madison, 69-71. *Concurrent Pos:* Dir, Youth Sports Inst. *Mem:* Am Asn Health, Phys Educ & Recreation; Soc Study Human Biol. *Res:* Motor development; interrelationship of physical growth, motor development and academic achievement in pre-school and elementary aged children. *Mailing Add:* 2893 Bonita Circle East Lansing MI 48823

SEEFELDT, WALDEMAR BERNHARD, NUCLEAR ENGINEERING. *Current Pos:* Chem engr, 48-93, STAFF CONSULT, ARGONNE NAT LAB, 93- *Personal Data:* b Milwaukee, Wis, Apr 4, 25; m 50, Marie H Henrickes; c Laurel M (Schilling), Lynn N (Himmelmann) & Lisa K (Funk). *Educ:* Purdue Univ, BS, 47, MS, 48. *Mem:* Am Nuclear Soc; Am Inst Chem Engrs; Inst Nuclear Mat Mgt; AAAS; Res Soc Am. *Res:* Chemical processing of spent nuclear reactor fuels; methods of immobilizing highly radioactive nuclear waste; nuclear waste management systems. *Mailing Add:* 417 S Kensington Ave La Grange IL 60525. *Fax:* 630-252-5246

SEEFRIED, CARL G, JR, GENERAL CHEMISTRY, PHYSICAL CHEMISTRY. *Current Pos:* dir res & develop, 84-91, VPRES TECHNOL, OLIN CORP, 91- *Personal Data:* b Buffalo, NY, Oct 20, 44; m 69, Renee Petrie; c Carl G III. *Educ:* Union Col, BS, 66; Yale Univ, PhD(phys chem), 69. *Prof Exp:* Res chemist & group leader, Union Carbide Corp, 69-81; supvr, Mobil Chem Co, 81-84. *Mem:* Am Chem Soc; fel Am Inst Chemists; Sigma Xi; NY Acad Sci. *Mailing Add:* Olin Corp 350 Knotter Dr Cheshire CT 06410. *E-Mail:* cgseefried@corp.olin.com

SEEFURTH, RANDALL N, ELECTROCHEMISTRY, MOLTEN SALT CHEMISTRY. *Current Pos:* Res chemist, Allison Div, 63-68, STAFF RES SCIENTIST, RES LABS, GEN MOTORS, 68- *Personal Data:* b Milwaukee, Wis, Sept 19, 41; m 70, Carol A Schweinsberg; c Cory, Jody & James. *Educ:* Univ Wis-Milwaukee, BS, 63. *Honors & Awards:* Extraction & Processing Technol Award, Minerals, Metals & Mat Soc, 92. *Mem:* Electrochem Soc; Metall Soc. *Res:* High temperature, molten salt, chemical and electrochemical studies; lithium-alloy, sulfur and metal sulfide electrodes for application in molten salt or solid ionic conductor battery systems; chemical reduction of rare earth oxides and halides in molten salt media. *Mailing Add:* Phys Chem Dept GM R & D Ctr Bldg 1-2 30500 Mound Rd Warren MI 48090-9055

SEEGAL, RICHARD FIELD, NEUROTOXICOLOGY. *Current Pos:* res scientist virol, 74-80, RES SCIENTIST NEUROTOXIC, NY STATE DEPT HEALTH, 80- *Personal Data:* b Newport, RI, Feb 13, 45; m 69; c 2. *Educ:* Brown Univ, AB, 66; Emory Univ, MA, 70; Univ Ga, PhD(physiol psychol), 72. *Prof Exp:* Fel endocrinol biobehav sci, Univ Conn, 72-74; res assoc neurochem, Dept Pharmacol, Mich State Univ, 77-78. *Mem:* AAAS; Soc Neurosci. *Res:* Neurotoxicology of halogeneted hydrocarbons development of in vitro neurochemical test systems. *Mailing Add:* 324 Elm Ave Delmar NY 12054

SEEGER, PHILIP ANTHONY, PHYSICS OF MATERIALS. *Current Pos:* STAFF MEM MANUEL LUJAN NEUTRON SCATTERING CTR, LOS ALAMOS NAT LAB, 64- *Personal Data:* b Evanston, Ill, Feb 19, 37; m 59; c 3. *Educ:* Rice Univ, BA, 58; Calif Inst Technol, PhD(physics), 63. *Prof Exp:* Res fel low energy nuclear physics, Calif Inst Technol, 62-64. *Mem:* Am Phys Soc; Int Astron Union. *Res:* Calculation of stellar nucleosynthesis and the semiempirical atomic mass law; neutron time-of-flight experiments in nuclear physics, materials science and biophysics. *Mailing Add:* 239 Loma Del Escolar Los Alamos NM 87544-2526. *Fax:* 505-665-2676; *E-Mail:* seeger@lansec.lanl.gov

SEEGER, ROBERT CHARLES, IMMUNOLOGY, PEDIATRICS. *Current Pos:* asst prof, 74-77, ASSOC PROF PEDIAT IMMUNOL, UNIV CALIF, LOS ANGELES, 77- *Personal Data:* b Salem, Ore, May 9, 40; m 64; c 1. *Educ:* Willamette Univ, BA, 62; Univ Ore, MS & MD, 66. *Prof Exp:* Pediat intern, Med Sch, Univ Minn, 66-67; resident, 67-68; clin assoc immunol, NIH, 68-72; spec fel tumor immunol, Nat Cancer Inst, Univ Col, Univ London, 72-74. *Concurrent Pos:* Res career develop award, Nat Cancer Inst, 75. *Mem:* Am Asn Cancer Res; Soc Pediat Res; Am Asn Immunologists. *Res:* Pediatric tumor immunology; childhood neuroblastoma with studies of tumor associated antigens; immune responses which kill tumor cells; chemo-immunotherapy in nude mice; human monocyte subsets. *Mailing Add:* Div Hemat & Oncol MS 57 Childrens Hosp 4650 Sunset Blvd Los Angeles CA 90027-6088

SEEGERS, WALTER HENRY, physiology, biochemistry; deceased, see previous edition for last biography

SEEGMILLER, DAVID W, ELECTROCHEMISTRY. *Current Pos:* USAF, 58-, nuclear res officer, 58-60, from assoc prof to prof chem, USAF Acad, 62-76, dep dept head, 75-76, chief scientist, USAF Europ Off Aerospace Res & Develop, London, 76-78, dep dept head, 78-80, PROF & ACTG HEAD, DEPT CHEM & BIOL SCI, USAF ACAD, 80- *Personal Data:* b Nephi, Utah, Jan 6, 34; m 54; c 4. *Educ:* Brigham Young Univ, BS, 56, MS, 58; Univ Calif, Berkeley, PhD(nuclear chem), 63. *Concurrent Pos:* Res & Develop Award, USAF, 71. *Mem:* Am Chem Soc; Sigma Xi. *Res:* Electrochemistry and physical chemistry of fused salt systems; nuclear chemistry and reactions; thermochemical measurements; high energy-density batteries. *Mailing Add:* W J Schaffer Assoc Inc 2000 Randolph Rd SE Albuquerque NM 87106-4267

SEEGMILLER, JARVIS EDWIN, BIOCHEMISTRY, AGING & DEGENERATIVE DISEASES. *Current Pos:* prof, Dept Med & dir, Div Rheumatology, 69-90, dir, Inst Res Aging, 83-90, EMER PROF, DEPT MED, & ASSOC DIR, SAM & ROSE STEIN INST RES AGING, UNIV CALIF, SAN DIEGO, 90- *Personal Data:* b St George, Utah, June 22, 20; m 50, Roberta Eads; c Dale S (Maudlin), Robert E, Lisa S (Taylor) & Richard L. *Educ:* Univ Utah, AB, 42; Univ Chicago, MD, 48. *Honors & Awards:* Gairdner Found Award, 68; Distinguished Serv Award, USPHS, 69; Geigy Award, 69; Philip Hench Award, 69; Balfourvis lectr, Mayo Clin, 74; Malthe lectr, Oslo, Norway, 75; Mayo Soley Award, Western Soc Clin Res, 79. *Prof Exp:* Asst, US Bur Mines, Utah, 41; asst, Nat Defense Res Comt, Northwestern Tech Inst, 42-44, US Army, 44; asst med, Univ Chicago, 47-48; intern, Marburg Div, Johns Hopkins Hosp, 48-49; biochemist, Nat Inst Arthritis & Metab Dis, 49-51; res assoc, Thorndike Mem Lab, Harvard Med Sch, 52-53; vis investr, Pub Health Res Inst, NY, 53-54; chief sect human biochem genetics & asst sci dir, Nat Inst Arthritis & Metab Dis, 54-69. *Concurrent Pos:* Vis scientist, Univ Col Hosp Sch Med, London, 64-65; Harvey Soc lectr, 70; Macy scholar, Basel Inst Immunol, Switz & Sir William Dunn Sch Path, Oxford, Eng, 75-76; Guggenheim fel, Swiss Inst Exp Cancer Res, Lausanne, Switz, 82-83; John Simon Guggenheim Mem Found fel, 82; Fogarty Int fel, Dept Biochem, Oxford, Eng, 89. *Mem:* Nat Acad Sci; hon mem Harvey Soc; Am Soc Biol Chemists; Am Rheumatism Asn; Am Fedn Clin Res; Am Soc Human Genetics; Am Soc Clin Invest; AAAS; Asn Am Physicians; Am Acad Arts & Sci. *Res:* Enzymology; intermediary carbohydrate and purine metabolism; causes and treatment of gout; hereditary metabolic diseases; human biochemical genetics; hereditary bases of arthritis; nature of the aging process; research administration; author of 346 publications. *Mailing Add:* Stein Inst Res Aging 0664 9500 Gilman Dr La Jolla CA 92093. *Fax:* 619-455-9993

SEEGMILLER, ROBERT EARL, DEVELOPMENTAL TOXICOLOGY. *Current Pos:* assoc prof, 72-80, PROF ZOOL, BRIGHAM YOUNG UNIV, 80- *Personal Data:* b Salt Lake City, Utah, July 8, 43; m 63, Barbara Bruderer; c 8. *Educ:* Univ Utah, BS, 65, MS, 67; McGill Univ, PhD(genetics), 70. *Prof Exp:* Res assoc develop biol, Univ Colo, 70-72. *Concurrent Pos:* Dipl, Pharmaceut Mfrs Asn Found, 70-72, res starter grant, 73; Basil O'Connor res starter grant, Nat Found March of Dimes, 74-76; vis res fel, Dept Pediat, Univ Chicago, 76-77 & Dept Pharmacol, Univ Wash, 87-88. *Mem:* Teratology Soc. *Res:* Drug and gene induced defects of the endochondral skeleton in relation to limb, palate and lung development in laboratory animals; epidemiological assessment of birth defects in human populations. *Mailing Add:* Dept Zool Widb 575 Brigham Young Univ Provo UT 84602-2525. *Fax:* 801-378-7423; *E-Mail:* seegmilr@acd1.loyu.edu

SEEHRA, MOHINDAR SINGH, SOLID STATE PHYSICS, SPECTROSCOPY. *Current Pos:* from asst prof to prof, 69-91, EBERLY DISTINGUISHED PROF PHYSICS, WVA UNIV, 92- *Personal Data:* b W Pakistan, Feb 14, 40; m 63, Harbhajan Kaur; c Jasmeet & Parveen. *Educ:* Punjab Univ, India, BSc, 59; Aligarh Muslin Univ, MSc, 62; Univ Rochester, PhD(physics), 69. *Prof Exp:* Lab instr chem, Arya Col, India, 59-60; lectr physics, Jain Col, India, 62-63. *Concurrent Pos:* Alfred P Sloan Found res fel, 73-76; NSF & Dept Energy res grants. *Mem:* Fel Am Phys Soc; Mat Res Soc; Advan Semiconductor Mat Int. *Res:* Phase transitions and critical phenomena; magnetic resonance and spin-spin relaxation; magnetic optical and transport properties; properties of pyrite and other minerals in coal; catalysis and coal liquefaction; magnetic properties of transition metal oxides, fluorides and sulfides using ESR, magnetic susceptibility, optical absorption and dielectric studies; IR spectroscopy of silica particulates; magnetic and structural properties of nanoscale particles; high temperature structural alloys. *Mailing Add:* Dept Physics PO Box 6315 WVa Univ Morgantown WV 26506-6315. *Fax:* 304-293-5732; *E-Mail:* mseehra@wvu.edu

SEELAND, DAVID ARTHUR, GEOLOGY. *Current Pos:* RETIRED. *Personal Data:* b St Paul, Minn, Nov 14, 36; m 61; c 2. *Educ:* Univ Minn, BA, 59, MS, 61; Univ Utah, PhD(geol), 68. *Prof Exp:* Geologist, US Geol Surv, 61-63 & 67-95. *Mem:* Geol Soc Am; Soc Econ Paleont & Mineral; Sigma Xi. *Res:* Sedimentology, particularly early Paleozoic marine shelf paleocurrents and depositional environments of Tertiary fluvial rocks; structure and stratigraphy of the northern Rocky Mountains. *Mailing Add:* 47 Flower St Lakewood CO 80226

SEELBACH, CHARLES WILLIAM, POLYMER CHEMISTRY, INDUSTRIAL CHEMISTRY. *Current Pos:* RETIRED. *Personal Data:* b Buffalo, NY, Dec 13, 23; m 47, Patricia O'Reilly; c 3. *Educ:* Cornell Univ, AB, 48; Case Western Res Univ, MS, 51; Purdue Univ, PhD, 55. *Prof Exp:* Res chemist, Stand Oil Co, Ohio, 48-52; analytical chemist, Purdue Univ, 52-55; res chemist, Esso Res & Eng Co, 55-57, asst sect head, Res Lab, Esso Stand Oil Co, 57-58, sect head explor res, Esso Res & Eng Co, 58-61, chem coordr, Esso Int, Inc, 61-63, mgr, Polymers Div, Esso Chem Co, Inc, NY, 63-66, mgr, Elastomers New Investments & Planning Div, 66-67; dir indust chem develop, US Steel Corp, 67-69, dir hydrocarbon raw mat develop, 69-71, mgr, Com Develop Plastics Dept, 71-77, mgr, Com Develop Petrochem Develop Dept, USS Chem Div, 77-83; consult, Sutro Mgt Adv, 83-87. *Mem:* AAAS; Am Oil Chem Soc; NY Acad Sci; Soc Plastics Indust; Com Develop Asn; Am Chem Soc. *Res:* Hydrocarbon stability; synthesis antioxidants; liquid thermal diffusion; separation of hydrocarbons and lipids; polymerization catalysis; plastic and elastomer synthesis; chemical intermediate syntheses; metal alkyl derivatives; olefin-diolefin derivatives; oxygenated derivatives; plasticizer products; ethylene cracker feed-product relationships. *Mailing Add:* 1945 Grand Cypress Lane Sun City Center FL 33573-4810

SEELEY, JOHN GEORGE, FLORICULTURE. *Current Pos:* head dept, 56-70, prof, 56-83, EMER PROF FLORICULT SCI, CORNELL UNIV, 83- *Personal Data:* b North Bergen, NJ, Dec 21, 15; m 38, Catherine L Cook; c Catherine A, David J (deceased), Daniel H, George B & Thomas D. *Educ:* Rutgers Univ, BSc, 37, MSc, 40; Cornell Univ, PhD(floricult), 48. *Honors & Awards:* Soc Am Florists Outstanding Res Award, 65; Leonard Vaughan Res Award, Am Soc Hort Sci, 50, Carl Bittner Exten Award, 82. *Prof Exp:* Asst, NJ Exp Sta, 37-40, garden supt, 40-41; res instr floricult, Cornell Univ, 41-43 & 45-48; asst agronomist, Bur Plant Indust, Soils & Agr Eng, USDA, Ga, 43-44; chemist in charge rubber mat lab, Wright Aeronaut Corp, NJ, 44-45; res instr floricult, Cornell Univ, 45-48, asst prof, 48-49; prof floricult, Pa State Univ, 49-56. *Concurrent Pos:* Prof hort & D C Kiplinger chair floricult, Ohio State Univ, 84-85; pres, Fred C Gloeckner Found, Inc, 93. *Mem:* Hon mem Am Acad Floricult; fel AAAS; fel Am Soc Hort Sci (pres, 82-83); fel Int Soc Hort Sci; Sigma Xi. *Res:* Nutrition and plant physiology; soils; soil aeration; light and temperature; floriculture crop. *Mailing Add:* 403 Savage Farm Dr Ithaca NY 14850-6506

SEELEY, ROBERT, RESEARCH ADMINISTRATION. *Current Pos:* QUAL CONTROL MGR, MAPLE ISLAND, INC, 72- *Personal Data:* b New York, NY, Dec 20, 36; m 67; c 4. *Educ:* Univ Ga, BSA, 60, MS, 63. *Mem:* Inst Food Technologists. *Mailing Add:* Maple Island Inc Wanamingo MN 55983

SEELEY, ROBERT D, PHYSICAL CHEMISTRY. *Current Pos:* from assoc prof to prof, 65-83, EMER PROF CHEM, CENT MO STATE UNIV, 83- *Personal Data:* b Kansas City, Kans, May 15, 23; m 46, Wilda M Turdy; c Susan L, Nancy L & Robert P. *Educ:* Tex A&I Univ, BS, 50, MS, 51; Wayne State Univ, PhD(phys chem), 59. *Prof Exp:* SQ instr & training officer, USAF, 44-65, civilian air personnel assistance team aerospace observ & SQ instr, 46-65; asst instr chem, Tex A&I Univ, 50-51; instr gen sci & chem, McCook Jr Col, 51-52; asst instr chem, Wayne State Univ, 53-54; mat engr, Tire Div, US Rubber Co, 54-59; sr chemist, Chemstrand Res Ctr, Inc, 59-62; staff mem high polymer res, Sandia Corp, 62-65. *Mem:* Sigma Xi. *Res:* Structural, surface and performance characteristics of high polymers; chemical sorption; reaction kinetics phenomena studies. *Mailing Add:* 613 SE 471st Rd Warrensburg MO 64093

SEELEY, ROBERT T, MATHEMATICAL ANALYSIS. *Current Pos:* PROF MATH, UNIV MASS, BOSTON, 72- *Personal Data:* b Bryn Mawr, Pa, Feb 26, 32; m 58; c 4. *Educ:* Haverford Col, BS, 53; Mass Inst Technol, PhD(math), 58. *Prof Exp:* Instr math, Harvey Mudd Col, 58-59, asst prof, 59-61; NATO fel, 61-62; from asst prof to assoc prof, Brandeis Univ, 63-67, prof, 67-72. *Concurrent Pos:* Sloan Found fel, 65-67. *Mem:* Am Math Soc; Math Asn Am. *Res:* Partial differential equations. *Mailing Add:* Dept Math Univ Mass Boston MA 02125-3393

SEELEY, ROD R, REPRODUCTIVE PHYSIOLOGY. *Current Pos:* Asst prof, 73-77, ASSOC PROF PHYSIOL, IDAHO STATE UNIV, 77-, PROF BIOL, 80- *Personal Data:* b Rupert, Idaho, Dec 29, 45; m 65; c 4. *Educ:* Idaho State Univ, BS, 68; Utah State Univ, MS, 71, PhD(physiol), 73. *Concurrent Pos:* Chmn, Dept Biol Sci, Idaho State Univ. *Mem:* AAAS; Sigma Xi; Soc Study Reproduction. *Res:* The study of neural and endocrine mechanisms that regulate smooth-muscle motility in the testicular capsule and neural and endocrine mechanisms that control reproduction. *Mailing Add:* Dept Biol Idaho State Univ Pocatello ID 83209-0001

SEELEY, SCHUYLER DRANNAN, PLANT CHEMISTRY, POMOLOGY. *Current Pos:* from asst prof to assoc prof, 71-83, PROF PLANT SCI, UTAH STATE UNIV, 83- *Personal Data:* b Huntington, Utah, Aug 5, 39; m 62, Linda S Harrison; c Kevin, Linda, Brent, Lisa, Larry & Ryan. *Educ:* Brigham Young Univ, BS, 64; Utah State Univ, MS, 67; Cornell Univ, PhD(pomol), 71. *Honors & Awards:* J H Gourley Medal, Am Soc Hort Sci, 75, 83. *Prof Exp:* Res assoc pomol, Cornell Univ, 71. *Mem:* Fel Am Soc Hort Sci; AAAS; Am Inst Chemists. *Res:* Hormonal physiology of fruit tree dormancy; mathematical modeling of chill units and growing degree hours for fruit tree physiodates; instrumental ultramicroanalysis of plant hormones. *Mailing Add:* Dept Plant & Earth Sci Utah State Univ Logan UT 84322-4820. *Fax:* 435-797-3376; *E-Mail:* sdseeley@mendel.usu.edu

SEELEY, THOMAS DYER, BEHAVIORAL ECOLOGY, SOCIOBIOLOGY. *Current Pos:* asst prof, 86-88, ASSOC BIOL, CORNELL UNIV, 88- *Personal Data:* b Bellefonte, Pa, June 17, 52; m 79; c 2. *Educ:* Dartmouth Col, AB, 74; Harvard Univ, PhD (biol), 78. *Prof Exp:* Jr fel, Soc Fels, Harvard Univ, 78-80; from asst prof to assoc prof biol, Yale Univ, 80-86. *Concurrent Pos:* Sci leader, Exped Thailand, Nat Geog Soc, 79-80; consult, Univ Oslo, Norway, 88. *Mem:* Animal Behav Soc; Int Union Study Social Insects; Int Bee Res Asn. *Res:* Physiological, behavioral, and ecological studies of the biology of social insects, especially the honeybee. *Mailing Add:* Sect Neurobiol & Behav Mudd Hall Cornell Univ Ithaca NY 14853-2702

SEELIG, JAKOB WILLIAMS, OPERATIONS RESEARCH. *Current Pos:* VPRES, ANALYTICAL SERV INC, 65- *Personal Data:* b Brooklyn, NY, May 21, 37; m 65; c 3. *Educ:* Rensselaer Polytech Inst, BCE, 58, PhD(civil eng), 63; Columbia Univ, MS, 59; George Washington Univ, MEA, 72. *Mem:* Opers Res Soc Am; Am Inst Aeronaut & Astronaut. *Res:* Acquisition of strategic, special operations and airlift systems; design of structures to withstand nuclear weapon effects. *Mailing Add:* 4702 Briar Patch Lane Fairfax VA 22032

SEELKE, RALPH WALTER, MICROBIAL GENETICS. *Current Pos:* ASST PROF MICROBIOL, UNIV WIS, MILWAUKEE, 85- *Personal Data:* b Murfreesboro, Tenn, Nov 25, 51; m 77; c 3. *Educ:* Clemson Univ, BS, 82; Univ Minn, PhD(microbiol), 82. *Prof Exp:* Fel cell biol, Mayo Clin, 81-83; asst prof microbiol, George Washington Univ, 83-85. *Mem:* Am Soc Microbiol. *Res:* Influence of chromosomal genes on plasmid DNA replication control in Escherichia coli; agrobacterium tumefaciens phage to assist its value in plant gene transfer. *Mailing Add:* Dept Biol Sci Univ Wis Superior WI 54880-2898

SEELMAN, KATHERINE D, SCIENCE POLICY. *Current Pos:* DIR, NAT INST DISABILITY & REHAB RES. *Educ:* NY Univ, PhD(pub policy), 82. *Honors & Awards:* Switzer Lectr; Schaeffer Lectr. *Concurrent Pos:* Asst, NSF; chair, Interagency Comt Disability Res; chair, Res Comt, Paralympic Games, 96. *Res:* Telecommunications policy and accessibility issues for persons with disabilities. *Mailing Add:* Nat Inst Disability & Rehab Res Washington DC 20202-2572

SEELY, GILBERT RANDALL, PHOTOCHEMISTRY, ELECTROCHEMISTRY. *Current Pos:* RETIRED. *Personal Data:* b Bellingham, Wash, Jan 18, 29; m 56, 69, Suzanne Hungerford; c David, Paul, Edward & Robert. *Educ:* Harvard Univ, AB, 50; Univ Calif, PhD(chem), 54. *Prof Exp:* Chemist, Gen Elec Co, NY, 53-54; fel boron chem, Univ Wash, Seattle, 56-57; chemist, Phys Chem Dept, Shell Develop Co, 57-62; investr, Battelle-C F Kettering Res Lab, 62, sr res scientist, 62-72, sr investr, 72-83, sr res scientist, 83-86; res prof, Dept Chem, Ariz State Univ, Tempe, 86-93. *Mem:* Am Soc Photobiol. *Res:* Photochemistry of chlorophyll and porphyrins; photochemistry and energy transfer in polymeric systems; environmental applications; model systems of photosynthesis. *Mailing Add:* 567 W Los Lagos Vista Mesa AZ 85210-6839

SEELY, J RODMAN, PEDIATRICS. *Current Pos:* DIR, GENETICS DIAGNOSTIC CTR, PRESBY HOSP, OKLAHOMA CITY, 80- *Personal Data:* b Willard, Utah, July 28, 27; m 55; c 3. *Educ:* Univ Utah, BS, 50, MD, 52, PhD(biol chem), 64. *Prof Exp:* Intern pediat, Salt Lake Gen Hosp, 52-53, asst resident, 53-56; res instr, Col Med, Univ Utah, 57-58; asst prof, Sch Med, Univ Wash, 58-63; assoc prof, Univ Okla, 64-76, prof, 76-79, clin prof pediat, Sch Med, 79- *Concurrent Pos:* Asst pediatrician, Salt Lake Gen Hosp, 55-58; dir premature ctr, Univ Hosp, Univ Wash, 60-63. *Mem:* AAAS; Am Acad Pediat; Endocrine Soc; NY Acad Sci; Am Soc Human Genetics. *Res:* Human biochemical genetics; cytogenetics; intrauterine diagnosis. *Mailing Add:* 711 Stanton Young Blvd Suite 405 Oklahoma City OK 73104

SEELY, JAMES ERVIN, POLYAMINE BIOSYNTHESIS. *Current Pos:* BIOCHEM, SYNERGEN, 92- *Personal Data:* b Marshalltown, Iowa, July 5, 54; m 78; c 1. *Educ:* Univ SDak, Phd(biochem), 80. *Prof Exp:* Post-doctoral fel, Dept Physiol, Hershey Med Ctr, 81-84; res scientist, Pitman-Moore, Inc, 84-89, sr res scientist, Dept Biochem, 89-92. *Concurrent Pos:* Adj fac, Ind Univ Med Sch, 89- *Mem:* Am Soc Biochem & Molecular Biol; Biochem Soc; AAAS; Endocrine Soc. *Res:* Polypeptide growth factors; structure function studies on growth hormone and other polypeptide growth factors; endocrine growth regulation of livestock animals; folding recombinant proteins and polypeptides. *Mailing Add:* Amgen Boulder Inc 3200 Walnut Boulder CO 80301

SEELY, JUSTUS FRANDSEN, STATISTICS, MATHEMATICS. *Current Pos:* PROF STATIST, ORE STATE UNIV, 69- *Personal Data:* b Mt Pleasant, Utah, Feb 11, 41; m 65, Averil Sanson; c 3. *Educ:* Utah State Univ, BS, 63, MS, 65; Iowa State Univ, PhD(statist), 69. *Prof Exp:* Instr appl statist & comput sci, Utah State Univ, 64-65. *Mem:* Fel Inst Math Statist; fel Am Statist Asn; Int Statist Inst. *Res:* linear model theory; experimental design; mathematical statistcs. *Mailing Add:* Dept Statist Ore State Univ 44 Kidder Hall Corvallis OR 97331-4606. *Fax:* 541-737-3489; *E-Mail:* seely@stat.orst.edu

SEELY, ROBERT J, BIOTECHNOLOGY. *Current Pos:* process biochemist, 85-92, PROCESS VALIDATION MGR, SYNERGEN, INC, 92- *Personal Data:* b Beach, NDak, Oct 20, 46; m 72, Glenda E; c Kit & Lisa. *Educ:* Ore State Univ, BS, 69; Univ Colo, MS, 75; Colo State Univ, PhD(biochem), 85. *Prof Exp:* Sr scientist, Great Western Sugar Co, 77-79; dir res, Bio-Gas Colo, 79-82. *Mem:* Am Chem Soc. *Res:* Process validation of pharmaceutical proteins. *Mailing Add:* Amgen 3201 Walnut St Denver CO 80201

SEELY, SAMUEL, physics, electrical engineering; deceased, see previous edition for last biography

SEEMAN, MARY VIOLETTE, SCHIZOPHRENIA. *Current Pos:* assoc prof, 75-80, PROF, UNIV TORONTO, 80-, HEAD SCHIZOPHRENIA PROG. *Personal Data:* b Lodz, Poland, Mar 24, 35; Can citizen; m 59, Philip; c Marc, Bob & Neil. *Educ:* McGill Univ, BA, 55, MD, 60; FRCPCan, 68. *Prof Exp:* Res psychiatrist, Fullbourne Hosp, Cambridge, 65-67; psychiatrist, Toronto Western Hosp, 67-75; chief psychiat, Mt Sinai Hosp, Toronto, 85-93. *Concurrent Pos:* Head, Active Treatment Clin, Clarke Inst Psychiat, 75-81; asst ed, Can J Psychiat. *Mem:* Am Col Psychiat; Can Med Asn; Can Psychiat Asn; Am Psychiat Asn; Am Asn Social Psychiat. *Res:* Clinical research in schizophrenia especially related to gender differences. *Mailing Add:* Clark Inst Psychiat 250 College St Toronto ON M5T 1R8 Can. *Fax:* 416-979-6849

SEEMAN, NADRIAN CHARLES, MOLECULAR BIOPHYSICS, X-RAY CRYSTALLOGRAPHY. *Current Pos:* PROF CHEM, NY UNIV, 88- *Personal Data:* b Chicago, Ill, Dec 16, 45. *Educ:* Univ Chicago, BS, 66; Univ Pittsburgh, PhD(biochem, crystallog), 70. *Honors & Awards:* Sidhu Award, 74; Feynman Prize, 95. *Prof Exp:* Res assoc biol, Columbia Univ, 70-72; Damon Runyon Found fel, Mass Inst Technol, 72-73, NIH fel biophys, 73-76, res assoc biol, 76-77; from asst prof to assoc prof biol, State Univ NY, Albany, 77-88. *Concurrent Pos:* Consult, Lifecodes, Inc, 83-86 & Polyprobe; sr consult, Molecular Biophysics Technol, Inc, 83-87; res career develop award, 82-87. *Mem:* Am Crystallog Asn; Biophys Soc; Am Chem Soc; AAAS; NY Acad Sci; Am Soc Biochem & Molecular Biol. *Res:* Structure, dynamics, thermodynamics and applications of nucleic acid branched junctions; nucleic acid engineering, DNA nanotechnology, single-stranded DNA topology. *Mailing Add:* Dept Chem NY Univ New York NY 10003

SEEMAN, PHILIP, NEUROPHARMACOLOGY, CELL BIOLOGY. *Current Pos:* from asst prof to assoc prof, 67-71, chmn dept, 77-87, PROF PHARMACOL, UNIV TORONTO, 71- *Personal Data:* b Winnipeg, Man, Feb 8, 34; m 59; c 3. *Educ:* McGill Univ, BSc, 55, MSc, 56, MD, 60; Rockefeller Univ, PhD(life sci), 66. *Honors & Awards:* Walter Murphey Lectr & Award, Can Soc Clin Pharmacol, 81; Lieber Prize, Nat Alliance Res Schizophrenia & Depression, 90; Stanley Dean Award, Am Col Psychiatrists, 91. *Prof Exp:* Intern med, Harper Hosp, Detroit, 60-61. *Concurrent Pos:* Med Res Coun Can fel, Univ Cambridge, 66-67; res awards, Clarke Inst Psychiat, Toronto, Can 75 & Clin Res Soc Toronto, 79; Upjohn award res, Can Pharmacol Soc, 80. *Mem:* AAAS; Am Soc Pharmacol & Exp Therapeut; Biophys Soc; Am Soc Cell Biol; Pharmacol Soc Can; Am Col Neuropsychopharmacol; fel Royal Soc Can. *Res:* Membrane biology; cell actions of anesthetics and tranquilizers; brain dopamine receptors; membrane ultrastructure; biology of schizophrenia. *Mailing Add:* Dept Pharmacol Univ Toronto Toronto ON M5S 1A8 Can

SEENEY, CHARLES EARL, TECHNOLOGY DEPLOYMENT & NEW BUSINESS DEVELOPMENT. *Current Pos:* prog mgr, 90-92, PROF MGR TECHNOL, KERR MCGEE CORP, 90-, MGR, NEW PROD DEVELOP, 92- *Personal Data:* b Jefferson City, Mo, Apr 2, 43; m 66, Barbara Blanchard; c Philip, James & Ann M. *Educ:* Lincoln Univ, BS, 70; Univ Akron, MS, 74. *Prof Exp:* Polymer chemist polymer res, Calgon Corp, 74-76 & Ralston Purina Co, 76-78; supvr polymer res, IMC Corp, 78-80, mgr polymer res, 80-82, mgr macromolecular res, 82-84, dir chem res, 84-86, pres, Imcera Bioprod, 86-90. *Concurrent Pos:* Vis lectr, Urban League Beep Prog, 79-82; managing dir, ViCorp Exec, Inc, 89-; indust consult, Phenolic Thermoset Adhesives, 89-; gov appointee, Ind Health Policy Comt, 90, Okla Coun Environ Qual. *Mem:* Am Chem Soc; Soc Plastics Engrs; NY Acad Sci; Prod Develop & Mgt Asn. *Res:* Developing and linking technology to the marketplace; business enterprises from technological concepts in areas of biotechnology polymer adhesives, and inorganic ultraviolet attenuation materials; awarded 16 US patents. *Mailing Add:* OMRF 825 NE 13th St Oklahoma City OK 73104. *Fax:* 405-359-6908

SEERLEY, ROBERT WAYNE, ANIMAL SCIENCE, ANIMAL NUTRITION. *Current Pos:* RETIRED. *Personal Data:* b Indianapolis, Ind, Oct 6, 30; m 51; c 2. *Educ:* Purdue Univ, BS, 52; Mich State Univ, MS, 57, PhD(animal nutrit), 60. *Prof Exp:* Exten swine specialist, Purdue Univ, 62-54; asst, Mich State Univ, 56-60; from asst prof to assoc prof animal sci, SDak State Univ, 60-67; from assoc prof to prof animal sci, Univ Ga, 67-91. *Concurrent Pos:* AID consult, Korea, 65. *Mem:* Am Soc Animal Sci. *Res:* Amino acids, minerals and vitamins in animal nutrition; building design and space requirements for animal environment. *Mailing Add:* 1030 Dogwood Rd White Plains GA 30678

SEERY, DANIEL J, CHEMICAL KINETICS, FUEL SCIENCE. *Current Pos:* res scientist, United Technol Res Ctr, 64-66, sr res scientist, Kinetics & Heat Transfer Group, 66-77, prin scientist, Combustion Sci Sect, 78-81, mgr combustion sci, 81-90, SR PROG MGR, ENVIRON SCI, UNITED TECHNOL RES CTR, 90- *Personal Data:* b Philadelphia, Pa, Dec 17, 33; m 60, Winifred Sullivan; c 3. *Educ:* St John's Univ, BS, 55; Pa State Univ, MS, 58, PhD(fuel technol), 62. *Prof Exp:* Fel chem, Univ Minn, 62-64. *Mem:* Am Chem Soc; Am Phys Soc; Combustion Inst (pres, 96-). *Res:* Chemical kinetics of combustion behind shock waves and in flames; dissociation of simple molecules; heterogeneous combustion in dust flames; catalytic combustion and combustion generated air pollution; coal devolatilization; high performance power generating systems. *Mailing Add:* Silver Lane United Technol Res Ctr East Hartford CT 06108

SEESE, WILLIAM SHOBER, BASIC CHEMISTRY. *Current Pos:* RETIRED. *Personal Data:* b Meyersdale, Pa, June 13, 32; m 58, Ann Reeves; c David & John S. *Educ:* Univ NMex, BS, 54, MS, 59; Wash State Univ, PhD(chem), 65. *Prof Exp:* Instr chem, biol & math, Ft Lewis Col, Durango, Colo, 58-61; res biochemist, Int Minerals & Chem Corp, Wasco, Calif, 65-66; instr chem & pharmacol, Casper Col, Wyo, 66-87; prof chem, Alice Lloyd Col, Pippa Passes, Ky, 89-91; vis consult & Fulbright Lectr, Sultan Qaboos Univ, Oman, 93-94. *Concurrent Pos:* Assoc prof, King Fahd Univ Petrol & Minerals, Dhahran, Saudi Arabia, 73-76; asst prof, Univ NMex, Gallup, 76-77; Fulbright lectr, Omdurman Islamic Univ, Sudan, 87-88. *Mem:* Am Chem Soc. *Res:* Organic synthesis-heterocyclics, steriods, aromatics and carbohydrates. *Mailing Add:* 2915 Ridgecrest Dr Casper WY 82604. *E-Mail:* arseese@aol.com

SEETHARAM, RAMNATH (RAM), PROTEIN CHEMISTRY, PEPTIDE CHEMISTRY. *Current Pos:* sr res biochemist biochem, Du Pont Co, 88-91, SR RES BIOCHEMIST BIOCHEM, DU PONT MERCK PHARMACEUT CO, 91- *Personal Data:* b Kerala, India, Jan 9, 52; US citizen; m 81; c 2. *Educ:* Univ Bombay, India, BSc, 72, MSc, 75; Indian Inst Sci, PhD(biochem), 81. *Prof Exp:* Res assoc protein chem, Rockefeller Univ, 82-84; sr res biochemist biochem, Monsanto Co, 84-88. *Mem:* Am Soc Biochem & Molecular Biol; Protein Soc. *Res:* Structure-function relationships in proteins; protein-protein interactions; protein folding; protein sequencing, peptide synthesis and chemical methods of analyzing proteins. *Mailing Add:* Microbiol Assoc 9900 Blackwell Rd Rockville MD 20850. *Fax:* 215-237-7865

SEEVERS, DELMAR OSWELL, PHYSICS. *Current Pos:* RETIRED. *Personal Data:* b St John, Kans, June 26, 19; m 43, Marcia Hubenett; c 2. *Educ:* Duke Univ, BS, 41, PhD, 51. *Prof Exp:* Physicist, Bur Ord, USN, 41-45; teaching assoc physics, Duke Univ, 46-51; res physicist, Chevron Res Co, 51-55, sr res physicist, 55-56, res assoc, 56-60, sr res assoc physics, 60-84. *Mem:* Am Phys Soc; AAAS; Clay Minerals Soc. *Res:* Cosmic rays; nuclear and neutron physics; nuclear magnetic and electron paramagnetic resonance; physics of solid-liquid interfaces. *Mailing Add:* 57 Forest Duke Dr Durham NC 27705

SEEVERS, ROBERT EDWARD, PHYSICAL CHEMISTRY. *Current Pos:* from asst prof to prof, 67-93, EMER PROF, SOUTHERN ORE COL, 93- *Personal Data:* b Okanogan, Wash, Mar 18, 35; m 56; c 4. *Educ:* Portland State Col, BS, 63; Ore State Univ, PhD(chem), 68. *Prof Exp:* Sr analyst, Reynolds Metals Co, 60-61; chemist, Ore Steel Mills, 61-63; res asst chem, Ore State Univ, 66-67. *Mem:* Am Chem Soc. *Res:* Solid state chemistry, especially electrical properties of alkali-halide crystals and semiconductors; quantum chemistry. *Mailing Add:* 39638 Mohawk Loop Rd Marcola OR 97454

SEFF, KARL, ZEOLITE CRYSTALLOGRAPHY, INTRAZEOLITIC CHEMISTRY. *Current Pos:* from asst prof to assoc prof, 68-73, PROF CHEM, UNIV HAWAII, 75- *Personal Data:* b Chicago, Ill, Jan 23, 38. *Educ:* Univ Calif, Berkeley, BS, 59; Mass Inst Technol, PhD(phys chem), 64. *Prof Exp:* Scholar chem, Mass Inst Technol, 64; scholar, Univ Calif, Los Angeles, 65-67. *Concurrent Pos:* Vis scholar, Princeton Univ, 74, Oxford Univ, 88 & Pusan & Kyungpook Univ, Korea, 96; vis researcher, Univ Mex, 81; chmn, Hawaii Sect, Am Chem Soc, 83; vis prof, Dartmouth Col, 89. *Mem:* Am Crystallog Asn; Am Chem Soc. *Res:* Intrazeolitic chemistry and zeolite complex structure; structures of molecules of organic or biochemical interest; metal sorption into zeolites to give clusters and continua; x-ray and pulsed-neutron crystallography. *Mailing Add:* Dept Chem Univ Hawaii Honolulu HI 96822. *Fax:* 808-956-5908; *E-Mail:* kseff@gold.chem.hawaii.edu

SEFF, PHILIP, FAULTING, EARLY MAN IN CALIFORNIA. *Current Pos:* CONSULT, PHILIP SEFF & ASSOC, 70- *Personal Data:* b New York, NY, Oct 5, 23. *Educ:* Brooklyn Col, BS, 50; Univ Nebr, MS, 53; Univ Ariz, PhD(geol), 62. *Prof Exp:* Prof geol, Univ Redlands, 66-70. *Concurrent Pos:* Res grant, NSF, 69; geol adv, Park Servs Petrified Forest Nat Park. *Mem:* Geol Soc Am; Sigma Xi. *Mailing Add:* 13020 South Lane Redlands CA 92373

SEFFL, RAYMOND JAMES, ORGANIC CHEMISTRY. *Current Pos:* LAB MGR, CHEM DIV, 3M CO, 58- *Personal Data:* b Chicago, Ill, Sept 21, 27; m 51; c 2. *Educ:* Univ Ill, BS, 50; Univ Colo, PhD(org chem), 54. *Prof Exp:* Jr res chemist, Velsicol Corp, 50-51; sr res chemist, M W Kellog Co div, Pullman, Inc, 54-57; chief chemist, Titan Chem Co, 57-58. *Mem:* Am Chem Soc. *Res:* Organic fluorine chemistry; synthesis and commerical product development. *Mailing Add:* 4941 N Olson Lake Trail Lake Elmo MN 55042

SEGA, GARY ANDREW, MOLECULAR GENETICS, MUTATION INDUCTION IN GERM CELLS. *Current Pos:* Investr, 71-73, RES STAFF MEM MOLECULAR GENETICS, BIOL DIV, OAK RIDGE NAT LAB, 73- *Personal Data:* b Cleveland, Ohio, Mar 23, 41; m 71, Marsha White; c Matthew, Drew & Lauren. *Educ:* Case Inst Technol, BS, 63; Univ Tex, Austin, MA, 66; La State Univ, Baton Rouge, PhD(genetics), 71. *Concurrent Pos:* Adj fac, Pellissippi State Tech Community Col. *Mem:* AAAS; Environ Mutagen Soc; Sigma Xi. *Res:* Molecular mechanisms of mutation induction in mammals, including dosimetry of chemical mutagens in the germ cells and DNA repair. *Mailing Add:* 106 Clark Lane Oak Ridge TN 37830

SEGAL, ALAN H, DENTISTRY. *Current Pos:* RETIRED. *Personal Data:* b Pittsburgh, Pa, Dec 5, 21; m 48; c 2. *Educ:* Univ Pittsburgh, BS, 45, DDS, 46, MDS, 70. *Prof Exp:* Assoc prof dent anat, Univ Pittsburgh, 59-70, prof grad periodont, 71-89, emer prof, Sch Dent, 89- *Concurrent Pos:* Res grant, 63-66; mem, Coun Med TV. *Mem:* Am Dent Asn; Am Col Dentists; Am Acad Periodontists. *Res:* Dental anatomy; preclinical operative dentistry. *Mailing Add:* Passavant Prof Bldg 9102 Badcock Blvd Suite 205 Pittsburgh PA 15237

SEGAL, ALEXANDER, ACOUSTICS & ELECTROACOUSTICS. *Current Pos:* environ mgt specialist, 79-86, ACOUST ENGR, CO SAN DIEGO, 86- *Personal Data:* b Novograd-Volynsky, USSR, Oct 10, 34; m 60, Anna; c Svetlana. *Educ:* Polytech Inst Kiev, MS, 58; Inst Textile & Light Indust Leningrad, PhD(noise abatement), 73. *Prof Exp:* Sr elec engr, State Proj Inst Commun Kiev, 66-68; sr sci assoc, Sci Res Inst Labor Hyg, Kiev, 68-76; mem tech staff acoust, Wyle Lab, 78-79. *Concurrent Pos:* Consult acoust eng, Country Kiev Noise Control Dept Kiev, 71-76 & San Diego, 80-; expert, Proj Inst Kievproject, 73-76; adj prof, San Diego State Univ, 82-86. *Mem:* Acoust

Soc Am; Sigma Xi; Inst Noise Control Eng. *Res:* Community and industrial noise standards; effect of noise on worker productivity; aircraft acoustics; hearing protection; community and industrial noise abatement and control; environmental sciences. *Mailing Add:* 10715 Sunset Ridge Dr San Diego CA 92131

SEGAL, ALVIN, BIOCHEMISTRY, CANCER. *Current Pos:* assoc res scientist environ med, 68-70, res scientist, 70-73, sr res scientist, 73-76, res assoc prof, 76-80, RES PROF ENVIRON MED, MED CTR, NY UNIV, 80- *Personal Data:* b New York, NY, Mar 21, 29; m 58, 84, 89; c 2. *Educ:* Long Island Univ, BS, 51 & 58; NY Univ, MS, 61, PhD(org chem), 65. *Prof Exp:* Pharmacist, Univ Hosp, New York, 58-59; org chemist, Ortho Pharmaceut Corp, 59-61; teaching fel chem, NY Univ, 61-63, univ fel, 63-64, USPHS fel environ med, Col Med, 64-66; asst prof pharmacog, Col Pharm, Univ Tenn, Memphis, 66-68. *Mem:* AAAS; Am Chem Soc; Am Asn Cancer Res. *Res:* Steroids; natural products chemistry; mechanisms of chemical carcinogenesis; major research has been in mechanisms of chemical carcinogenesis; minor research interests; steroids; natural products chemistry. *Mailing Add:* 1401 Village Blvd #1913 West Palm Beach FL 33409

SEGAL, ARTHUR CHERNY, MATHEMATICS. *Current Pos:* chmn dept, 75-78, ASSOC PROF MATH, UNIV ALA, BIRMINGHAM, 67- *Personal Data:* b Newark, NJ, July 22, 38; c 2. *Educ:* Univ Fla, BS, 58; Univ Ariz, MS, 62; Tex Christian Univ, PhD(math), 66. *Prof Exp:* Physicist, ARO, Univ Tenn, 58-59; asst prof math, Judson Col, 62-64; Univ Tex, Arlington, 65-66 & Tex A&M Univ, 66-67. *Mem:* Math Asn Am. *Res:* Biomathematics. *Mailing Add:* Dept Math Univ Ala Birmingham AL 35294-1170

SEGAL, BERNARD, ADDICTION STUDIES. *Current Pos:* PROF HEALTH SCI, UNIV ALASKA, ANCHORAGE, 77- *Personal Data:* b New York, NY, May 9, 36; m 62; c 2. *Educ:* City Col NY, BBA, 60, MSE, 63; Univ Okla, PhD(psychol), 67. *Prof Exp:* Asst prof psychol, Univ RI, 67-70; prof psychol, Murray State Univ, 70-77. *Concurrent Pos:* Police psychologist, Anchorage Police Dept, 90- *Mem:* Am Pub Health Asn; Am Soc Circumpolar Health. *Res:* Etiology, epidemiology, and psychsocial correlates of drug-taking behavior; biobehavioral factor in alcoholism. *Mailing Add:* Ctr Alcohol & Addiction Studies 3211 Providence Dr Anchorage AK 99508. *Fax:* 907-786-4558; *E-Mail:* Bitnet: afro51@uaa.alaska.edu

SEGAL, BERNARD L, INTERNAL MEDICINE, CARDIOLOGY. *Current Pos:* assoc med, Hahnemann Med Col & Hosp, 61-62, assoc prof, 62-72, dir, Likoff Cardiovasc Inst, 80-86, PROF MED, HAHNEMANN MED COL & HOSP, 72-; DIR, PHILADELPHIA HEART INST, 86- *Personal Data:* b Montreal, Que, Feb 13, 29; m 63. *Educ:* McGill Univ, BSc, 50, MD, CM, 55; Am Bd Internal Med, dipl, 63; Am Bd Cardiovasc Dis, dipl, 64. *Prof Exp:* Asst med, Sch Med, Johns Hopkins Univ, 56-57; clin asst, St George's Hosp, London, 59-60. *Concurrent Pos:* Teaching fel, Harvard Med Sch, 57-58 & Sch Med, Georgetown Univ, 58-59; USPHS fel, St George's Hosp, London, Eng, 59-60; Southeast Heart Asn Pa grants, 61-63 & 64-65; NIH grant, 62-64, res grant, 65-68; jr attend, Vet Admin Hosp & Hahnemann Med Col & Hosp, 61-; consult, 62-63; ed, Eng & Pract Med & Theory & Prac Auscultation; head, Auscultation Unit, Hahnemann Med Col & Hosp, 66-86; clin prof med Univ Pa. *Mem:* Fel Am Col Physicians; fel AMA; fel Am Col Cardiol; fel Am Col Chest Physicians; fel NY Acad Sci. *Res:* Atherosclerosis and coronary heart disease. *Mailing Add:* 401 City Line Ave Bala Cynwyd PA 19004

SEGAL, DAVID MILLER, MOLECULAR & CELLULAR IMMUNOLOGY, CANCER RESEARCH. *Current Pos:* SR INVESTR, IMMUNOL BR, NAT CANCER INST, 75- *Educ:* Johns Hopkins Univ, PhD(biochem), 66. *Mailing Add:* Exp Immunol Br Nat Cancer Inst-NIH Bldg 10 Rm 4B17 Bethesda MD 20892-1360. *Fax:* 301-496-0887; *E-Mail:* Bitnet: dave@nihceib

SEGAL, DAVID S, NEUROPHARMACOLOGY, NEUROPSYCHOLOGY. *Current Pos:* NIMH fel, 70-72, from asst prof to assoc prof, 72-78, PROF PSYCHIAT, UNIV CALIF, SAN DIEGO, 78- *Personal Data:* b Montreal, Que, Aug 7, 42; US citizen; m 63; c 3. *Educ:* Univ Calif, Santa Barbara, BA, 65; Univ Calif, Irvine, PhD(psychobiol), 70. *Concurrent Pos:* Regional ed, Pharmacol, Biochem & Behav, 73-; NIMH res scientist develop award, 73-78. *Mem:* AAAS; Soc Neurosci. *Res:* Neurochemical substrates of arousal; drug-induced changes in brain biosynthetic enzymes in response to environmental changes; long-term effects of drugs on behavior and neurochemical mechanisms of adaptation. *Mailing Add:* Dept Psychiat Univ Calif San Diego La Jolla CA 92093-0603. *Fax:* 619-534-7653

SEGAL, EARL, environmental physiology; deceased, see previous edition for last biography

SEGAL, GERALD A, THEORETICAL CHEMISTRY. *Current Pos:* from asst prof to assoc prof, 67-75, dean, Col Lett, Arts & Sci, 89-93, PROF CHEM & CHMN DEPT, UNIV SOUTHERN CALIF, 75- *Personal Data:* b Pittsburgh, Pa, Dec 1, 34; m 79, Karen Sviridoff; c 5. *Educ:* Amherst Col, AB, 56; Carnegie Inst Technol, PhD(chem), 66. *Prof Exp:* NSF fel, Bristol Univ, 66-67. *Concurrent Pos:* Sloan Found fel, 71-73; sr Fulbright fel, France, 73-74. *Mem:* Am Phys Soc; Am Chem Soc. *Res:* Molecular orbital theory; theoretical spectroscopy. *Mailing Add:* SGM 417 Univ Southern Calif Los Angeles CA 90089-1062. *E-Mail:* segal@chem1.usc.edu

SEGAL, HAROLD JACOB, PHARMACY ADMINISTRATION. *Current Pos:* PROF PHARM, FAC PHARM, UNIV TORONTO, 70-, FAC MED, DIV COMMUNITY HEALTH, DEPT HEALTH ADMIN, 75- *Personal Data:* b Winnipeg, Man, Mar 6, 41. *Educ:* Univ Man, BScPharm, 62; Purdue Univ, MS, 66, PhD(pharm admin), 68. *Prof Exp:* Pharmacist, Crescentwood Pharm Ltd, 62-65; res assoc, Comn Pharmaceut Serv, Toronto, 68-70. *Res:* Pharmaceutical and health product marketing; health care delivery systems planning; economics of health care. *Mailing Add:* Koffler Inst Pharm Mgt Univ Toronto Toronto ON M5S 1A1 Can. *Fax:* 416-978-1833; *E-Mail:* harold.segal@utoronto.ca

SEGAL, IRVING EZRA, MATHEMATICS, THEORETICAL PHYSICS. *Current Pos:* prof, 60-89, EMER PROF MATH, MASS INST TECHNOL, 89- *Personal Data:* b New York, NY, Sept 13, 18. *Educ:* Princeton Univ, AB, 37; Yale Univ, PhD(math), 40. *Prof Exp:* Instr math, Harvard Univ, 41; res assoc, Princeton Univ, 42-43; asst, Inst Advan Study, 46, Guggenheim fel, 46-47; from asst prof to prof, Univ Chicago, 48-60. *Concurrent Pos:* Guggenheim fel, 51-52 & 67-68; vis assoc prof, Columbia Univ, 53-54; vis prof, Univ Paris, 65; State Univ Col Pisa, 72, Lund Univ & Univ Copenhagen, 71-72; Humboldt Award, 80. *Mem:* Nat Acad Sci; Am Math Soc; Am Phys Soc; Am Astron Asn. *Res:* Harmonic analysis; operator rings in Hilbert space; analysis in infinite-dimensional spaces; quantum field and particle theory; astrophysics; non-linear relativistic partial differential equations. *Mailing Add:* Mass Inst Technol Rm 2-244 Cambridge MA 02139. *Fax:* 617-253-4358; *E-Mail:* les@math.mit.edu

SEGAL, JACK, TOPOLOGY. *Current Pos:* From instr to assoc prof, 60-70, chmn dept, 75-78, PROF MATH, UNIV WASH, 70- *Personal Data:* b Philadelphia, Pa, May 9, 34; m 55, Arlene Stern; c Gregory & Sharon. *Educ:* Univ Miami, BS, 55, MS, 57; Univ Ga, PhD(math), 60. *Concurrent Pos:* NSF fel, 63-64; Fulbright fel, 69-70; exchange prof, NAS, 79-80. *Mem:* Am Math Soc; Soc Indust & Appl Math. *Res:* Point-set topology; manifolds; dimension and fixed point theory; mappings; abstract spaces; inverse limit spaces; shape theory. *Mailing Add:* Dept Math Univ Wash Seattle WA 98195. *E-Mail:* segal@math.washington.edu

SEGAL, MOSHE, OPERATIONS RESEARCH. *Current Pos:* Mem tech staff, 61-64, supvr opers res methodology, 64-77, SUPVR OPERS RES TECH, BELL TEL LABS, INC, 77- *Personal Data:* b Haifa, Israel, June 3, 34; m 61; c 3. *Educ:* Israel Inst Technol, BS, 56, Ing, 56; Johns Hopkins Univ, DEng, 61. *Concurrent Pos:* Vis scientist, Lady Davies fel, tech, Israel Inst Technol, 76-77. *Mem:* Opers Res Soc Am. *Res:* Queueing theory; communications networks; linear and non-linear mathematical programming; optimization techniques for the design of networks. *Mailing Add:* 47 Patridge Lane Eatontown NJ 07724

SEGAL, ROSALIND A, NEUROLOGY. *Current Pos:* Intern, 80-91, CLIN FEL NEUROL, BETH ISRAEL HOSP, BOSTON, 90- *Personal Data:* b New York, NY, June 30, 58. *Educ:* Rockefeller Univ, PhD(cell biol), 85; Cornell Univ, MD, 86. *Mem:* Am Soc Cell Biol. *Mailing Add:* 54 Blake Rd Brookline MA 02146-4502

SEGAL, SANFORD LEONARD, ANALYTIC & ELEMENTARY NUMBER THEORY, ONE COMPLEX VARIABLE. *Current Pos:* From instr to assoc prof math, 63-77, chmn dept, 79-87, PROF MATH, UNIV ROCHESTER, 77- *Personal Data:* b Troy, NY, Oct 11, 37; m 59, Rima Maxwell; c Adam, Joshua & Zoe. *Educ:* Wesleyan Univ, BA, 58; Univ Colo, PhD(math), 63. *Concurrent Pos:* Fulbright res fel, Univ Vienna, 65-66; vis lectr, Univ Nottingham, Eng, 72-73; res grantee, Fed Univ, Rio de Janeiro, Brazil, 82; res grant, Alexander von Humboldt Found, WGer, 88. *Mem:* AAAS; Am Math Soc; Math Asn Am; Hist Sci Soc. *Res:* Elementary and analytic number theory; functional equations; complex functions of one variable; history of science, particularly 20th century German mathematics. *Mailing Add:* 511 Rockingham St Rochester NY 14620. *Fax:* 716-294-6631; *E-Mail:* ssgl@troi.cc.rochester.edu

SEGAL, SHELDON J, UROLOGY. *Current Pos:* DISTINGUISHED SCIENTIST, POPULATION COUN, 91- *Educ:* Dartmouth Col, BA, 47; Univ Iowa, MS, 51, PhD(embryol & biochem), 52. *Hon Degrees:* Hon prof, Peking Union Med Col, 84, Chinese Acad Sci, 85; MD, Univ Tampere, Finland, 85, Univ Uppsala, Sweden, 86. *Honors & Awards:* Prize Humanism Med, Axel Munthe Found, 85; Planned Parenthood Found Am Sci Res Award, 90; Chorafas Found Award, Swiss Acad Sci, 95. *Prof Exp:* Res scientist, William S Merril Co, 52-53; res assoc urol, Univ Iowa, 53-55, res asst prof, 56; dir pop sci, The Rockefeller Found, 78-91. *Concurrent Pos:* Lectr biol, Univ Iowa, 53-55. *Mem:* Nat Acad Sci; Inst Med-Nat Acad Sci; AAAS; Coun on Foreign Rel; World Acad Art & Sci; Endocrine Soc; Am Fertil Soc; Harvey Soc; Soc Study Social Biol; Int Soc Andrology; hon mem Mex Nat Acad Sci; hon mem Royal Col Obstet & Gynec. *Res:* Contributed numerous articles to publications. *Mailing Add:* The Pop Coun One Dag Hammarskjold Plaza 9th floor New York NY 10017

SEGAL, STANTON, MEDICINE, BIOCHEMISTRY. *Current Pos:* PROF PEDIAT & CHIEF LAB MOLECULAR DIS & METAB, SCH MED, UNIV PA, 66-, PROF MED, 70-, ATTEND PHYSICIAN, HOSP, 70- *Personal Data:* b Camden, NJ, Sept 6, 27; m 56; c 2. *Educ:* Princeton Univ, AB, 48; Harvard Med Sch, MD, 52. *Hon Degrees:* MA, Univ Pa, 71. *Prof Exp:* Res assoc, Sch Med, Univ Pa, 49-50; intern, Med Ctr, Cornell Univ, 52-53; resident med, Hosp Univ Pa, 53-54 & 57-58; clin assoc, NIH, 54-57; NIH sr investr, 58-65, chief sect diabetes & intermediary metab, Nat Inst Arthritis & Metab Dis, 65-66. *Concurrent Pos:* Vis scientist, Nat Inst Med Res,

London, Eng, 63-64; mem metab study sect, NIH, 67-71, mem metab & diabetes training comt, Nat Inst Arthritis, Metab & Digestive Dis, 71-73; mem ment retardation comt, Nat Inst Child Health & Human Develop, 75-79; sr physician, Children's Hosp, Philadelphia. *Mem:* Asn Am Physicians; Am Soc Clin Invest; Endocrine Soc; Am Soc Biol Chemists; Brit Biochem Soc. *Res:* Intermediary metabolism; endocrinology; human genetics; inherited metabolic diseases. *Mailing Add:* Dept Pediat & Nutrit Univ Pa Sch Med 34th & Civic Ctr Blvd Children's Hosp Philadelphia Philadelphia PA 19104

SEGAL, WILLIAM, MICROBIOLOGY. *Current Pos:* asst prof microbiol, Univ Colo, Sch Med, 58-66, from assoc prof, to prof biol, 66-90, EMER PROF, UNIV COLO, BOULDER, 90- *Personal Data:* b Montreal, Que, Dec 22, 22; nat US; m 51; c 2. *Educ:* McGill Univ, BS, 43; Univ Wis, MS, 48; Rutgers Univ, PhD(microbiol), 52. *Prof Exp:* Bacteriologist, Clin Bact Lab, Royal Victoria Hosp, 44-45; asst bacteriologist, Univ Wis, 47-48; vis investr, Pub Health Res Inst, NY, 52-57. *Concurrent Pos:* Vis scientist, Sch Med, Hebrew Univ, Israel, 68; NIH spec res fel, Nat Ctr Sci Res, France, 68-69. *Mem:* AAAS; Am Soc Microbiol; Brit Soc Gen Microbiol; Sigma Xi. *Res:* Intermediates in bacterial nitrogen-fixation; bacterial transformation of organic sulfur compounds; biochemistry and genetics of mycobacteria; biochemistry of tuberculous host-parasite interrelationship; pathogenicity and immunogenicity of tubercle bacillus; microbial ecology. *Mailing Add:* 4251 Amber St Boulder CO 80304-0965

SEGALL, BENJAMIN, THEORETICAL PHYSICS. *Current Pos:* PROF PHYSICS, CASE WESTERN RESERVE UNIV, 68- *Personal Data:* b New York, NY, July 23, 25; m 53; c 3. *Educ:* Brooklyn Col, BS, 48; Univ Ill, MS, 49, PhD(physics), 51. *Prof Exp:* Fel, Univ Ill, 51-52; fel, Copenhagen Inst Theoret Physics, Denmark, 52-53; res physicist, Radiation Lab, Univ Calif, 53-54; res physicist, Res & Develop Ctr, Gen Elec Co, NY, 55-68. *Mem:* Fel Am Phys Soc. *Res:* Theoretical solid state and nuclear physics. *Mailing Add:* Dept Physics Case Western Reserve Univ Cleveland OH 44106

SEGALL, PAUL EDWARD, PROFOUND HYPOTHERMIA, AGE-DELAYING EFFECTS OF NUTRITIONAL RESTRICTION & CRYOPROTECTION. *Current Pos:* PRES & CHIEF EXEC OFFICER, BIO TIME INC, BERKELEY, CALIF, 90- *Personal Data:* b New York, NY, Sept 28, 42. *Educ:* State Univ NY, Stony Brook, BS, 63; Hofstra Univ, Hempstead, MA, 65; Univ Calif, Berkeley, PhD(physiol), 77. *Prof Exp:* Post-grad res physiologist, Dept Physiol Anat, Univ Calif, Berkeley, 78-80, asst res physiologist, 86; lectr human develop, Calif State Univ, Hayward, 80-81; res scientist, Biophys Res & Develop, Berkeley, Calif, 82-85; res dir, Cryomed Sci Inc, Bethesda, Md, 87-89, res scientist, 89-90. *Mem:* Am Physiol Soc; Am Aging Asn; Gerontol. *Res:* Hypothermia; cryobiology; gerontology; author of scientific efforts to extend the human life span; blood plasma volume expansion. *Mailing Add:* Bio Time Inc 935 Pardee St Berkeley CA 94710

SEGALL, STANLEY, ORGANIC CHEMISTRY, FOOD TECHNOLOGY. *Current Pos:* ASSOC PROF BIOL & ENVIRON SCI, DREXEL UNIV, 68-, ASSOC PROF NUTRIT & FOOD & HEAD DEPT, 74- *Personal Data:* b Baltimore, Md, May 12, 30; m 54; c 2. *Educ:* Northeastern Univ, SB, 53; Mass Inst Technol, 54-57, PhD(food tech), 57. *Prof Exp:* Chief chemist, Blue Seal Extract Co, Mass, 51-54; dir res, Rudd-Melikian, Inc, 57-68. *Mem:* Am Chem Soc; Inst Food Technol; Sigma Xi. *Res:* Environmental and toxicological studies; taste and odor; flavor chemistry; food processing; public health aspects of automated industrial feeding. *Mailing Add:* Drexel Univ 3141 Chestnut St Philadelphia PA 19104-2816

SEGALL, STEPHEN BARRETT, PHYSICS. *Current Pos:* PRIN SCIENTIST, FREE ELECTRON LASERS & DIR RES, KMS FUSION, INC, 72- *Personal Data:* b Newark, NJ, Oct, 2, 42; m 65; c 4. *Educ:* Columbia Col, BA, 64; Univ Md, MSc, 72, PhD(physics), 72. *Res:* Laser-plasma interaction physics and free electron laser development. *Mailing Add:* 1349 King George Blvd Ann Arbor MI 48108

SEGAR, WILLIAM ELIAS, PEDIATRICS. *Current Pos:* chmn dept, 74-85, PROF PEDIAT, UNIV WIS-MADISON, 70- *Personal Data:* b Indianapolis, Ind, Dec 16, 23; m 54; c 2. *Educ:* Ind Univ, BS, 44, MD, 47; Am Bd Pediat, dipl, 55. *Prof Exp:* Instr pediat, Yale Univ, 51-53; from asst prof to prof, Sch Med, Ind Univ, 55-67; prof, Mayo Grad Sch Med, 67-70. *Mem:* AAAS; Soc Pediat Res; Am Pediat Soc; Am Fedn Clin Res; Asn Am Physicians. *Res:* Water and electrolyte metabolism; renal physiology. *Mailing Add:* 600 Highland Ave Univ Wisc Childrens Hosp Peds Madison WI 53792-0001

SEGATTO, PETER RICHARD, analytical chemistry, physical chemistry; deceased, see previous edition for last biography

SEGEL, IRWIN HARVEY, BIOCHEMISTRY. *Current Pos:* from asst prof to assoc prof, 64-73, PROF BIOCHEM, UNIV CALIF, DAVIS, 73- *Personal Data:* b Staten Island, NY, Dec 29, 35; c 2. *Educ:* Rensselaer Polytech Inst, BS, 57; Univ Wis, MS, 60, PhD(biochem), 62. *Prof Exp:* NSF fel, 62-63; USPHS res fel, 63-64. *Mem:* AAAS; Am Soc Biol Chemists; Am Soc Plant Physiol; Am Chem Soc; Am Soc Microbiol. *Res:* Microbial biochemistry; enzymology and regulation of sulfur and nitrogen metabolism in microorganisms; membrane transport systems; enzyme kinetics; Author of a book,. *Mailing Add:* Molecular & Cell Biol Sect Univ Calif Davis CA 95616. *Fax:* 530-752-3085

SEGEL, L(EONARD), DYNAMIC BEHAVIOR OF MOTOR VEHICLES. *Current Pos:* from lectr to prof, 67-87, head, Eng Res Div, Transp Res Inst, 67-87, EMER PROF MECH ENG, UNIV MICH, ANN ARBOR, 87- *Personal Data:* b Cincinnati, Ohio, Apr 16, 22; m 44, Sylvia Albert; c Judith C, Marilyn R & Lawrence. *Educ:* Univ Cincinnati, BSAE, 47; State Univ NY, Buffalo, MS, 53. *Honors & Awards:* Crompton-Lanchester Medal, Brit Inst Mech Engrs, 58; Sci Contrib Prize, Soc Automotive Engrs Japan, 90. *Prof Exp:* Res engr, Flight Res Dept, Cornell Aeronaut Lab, Inc, 47-56, prin engr, Vehicle Dynamics Dept, 56-57, head res sect, 57-60, asst dept head, 60-63, staff scientist, Appl Mech Dept, 63-66. *Concurrent Pos:* Vis prf, Technion, Israel Inst Technol, 78, Tokyo Univ, 85; foreign scholar grant, Int Asn Traffic & Safety Sci, 85; vis res fel, Japan Soc Prom Sci, 75. *Mem:* Fel Am Soc Mech Engrs; Human Factors Soc; fel Inst Mech Engrs; Int Asn Vehicle Syst Dynamics (pres, 87-95). *Res:* Flight mechanics; vehicle stability and control; man-vehicle relationships; mobility of off-road vehicles; linear systems; tire mechanics; rotary-wing phenomena; tire-vehicle system dynamics. *Mailing Add:* Transp Res Inst Univ Mich Huron Pkwy & Baxter Rd Ann Arbor MI 48109-2150. *Fax:* 313-936-1081; *E-Mail:* leonard_segel@um.cc.umich.edu

SEGEL, LEE AARON, APPLIED MATHEMATICS, THEORETICAL BIOLOGY. *Current Pos:* head dept, 73-78, dean, 78-89, PROF APPL MATH, WEIZMANN INST SCI, ISRAEL, 73-; CONSULT, LOS ALAMOS NAT LAB, 85- *Personal Data:* b Boston, Mass, Feb 5, 32; m 58, Ruth M Gale; c Joel, Susie (Dym), Daniel & Michael. *Educ:* Harvard Univ, AB, 53; Mass Inst Technol, PhD(math), 59. *Prof Exp:* Res fel, Aerodyn Div, Nat Phys Lab, Eng, 58-60; from asst prof to prof math, Rensselaer Polytech Inst, 60-73, res prof, 73-83. *Concurrent Pos:* Vis assoc prof, Mass Inst Technol, 63-64; vis assoc prof, Sch Med, Cornell Univ & vis scientist, Sloan-Kettering Inst, 68-69; Guggenheim fel & vis prof, Weizmann Inst Sci, 71-72; Vinton Hayes sr fel & vis prof appl math, Harvard Univ, 78-79; ed-in-chief, Bull Math Biol; Ulam scholar, Ctr Nonlinear Studies, Los Alamos Nat Lab, 92-93; vis prof, Univ Utrecht, Pasteur Inst, Princeton Univ, Indian Inst Sci & NIH, 96-97. *Mem:* Soc Indust & Appl Math; Israel Math Soc; fel AAAS; Soc Math Biol. *Res:* Theoretical biology, especially immunology neurobiology; general applied mathematics. *Mailing Add:* Dept Appl Math & Comp Sci Weizmann Inst Sci Rehovot IL 76100 Israel. *Fax:* 972-8-9344-122; *E-Mail:* lee@wisdom.weizmann.ac.il

SEGEL, RALPH E, NUCLEAR PHYSICS, ELEMENTARY PARTICLE PHYSICS. *Current Pos:* PROF PHYSICS, NORTHWESTERN UNIV, 66- *Personal Data:* b New York, NY, Aug 29, 28; m 60, Esther L Sprenkel; c 3. *Educ:* Mass Inst Technol, SB, 48; Johns Hopkins Univ, PhD(physics), 55. *Prof Exp:* Res assoc physics, Johns Hopkins Univ, 55; res assoc, Brookhaven Nat Lab, 55-56; physicist, USAF, 56-61; assoc physicist, Argonne Nat Lab, 61-70, sr physicist, 70-76. *Concurrent Pos:* Sr res officer, Oxford Univ, 58-59; Humboldt Found award, Tech Univ Munich, 78. *Mem:* Fel Am Phys Soc. *Res:* Study nucleon structure using deep inelastic scattering; high energy nuclear reactions. *Mailing Add:* Dept Physics Northwestern Univ Evanston IL 60208. *Fax:* 847-491-9982

SEGEL, STANLEY LEWIS, SOLID STATE PHYSICS. *Current Pos:* assoc prof, 67-76, PROF PHYSICS, QUEEN'S UNIV, ONT, 76-, ASSOC PROF ART, 76- *Personal Data:* b Philadelphia, Pa, Aug 23, 32; m 58; c 3. *Educ:* Allegheny Col, BS, 53; Univ Del, MS, 56; Iowa State Univ, PhD(physics, metall), 63. *Prof Exp:* Instr physics, Robert Col, 57-58; asst prof, Kalamazoo Col, 62-67. *Mem:* Am Asn Physics Teachers; Phys Soc Japan. *Res:* Nuclear magnetic and quadrupole resonance. *Mailing Add:* Dept Physics Queens Univ Rm 205 Kingston ON K7L 3N6 Can

SEGELKEN, JOHN MAURICE, HARDWARE SYSTEMS, TECHNICAL MANAGEMENT. *Current Pos:* Mem tech staff, 70-78, develop supvr, 79-89, RES SUPVR, AT&T BELL LABS, 89- *Personal Data:* b Baltimore, Md, Feb 17, 48; m 70. *Educ:* Univ Md, BS, 70; Purdue Univ, MS, 72. *Concurrent Pos:* Session chmn & organizer, Electronic Components & Tech Conf, 88-, Nat Electronic Packaging Conf, 89-; chmn packaging prog comt, Electronics Components & Tech Conf, 89-; consult to chmn, Cong Report, Nat Res Coun, 89-90; elected bd gov, Inst Elec & Electronics Engrs Components, Hybrids & Mfg Technol. *Mem:* Sr mem Inst Elec & Electronics Engrs; Am Soc Mech Engrs; Int Soc Hybrid Microelectronics. *Res:* Electronic packaging: advanced packaging, multichip modules, system level packaging, 3 dimensional packaging, material science, physical design, thermal analysis, shock and vibration, reliability, assembly, connector technology, engineering economics, innovation, patents and engineering management. *Mailing Add:* Lucent Technol PO Box 900 Princeton NJ 08542

SEGELKEN, WARREN GEORGE, MAGNETIC RESONANCE. *Current Pos:* assoc prof, 67-72, PROF PHYSICS, ASHLAND COL, 72- *Personal Data:* b Jamaica, NY, Mar 13, 26; m 57; c 3. *Educ:* Rutgers Univ, BS, 50, PhD(physics), 55. *Prof Exp:* Asst, Rutgers Univ, 50-52; res physicist, Gen Elec Co, 55-67. *Mem:* Am Asn Physics Teachers; Sigma Xi; Am Phys Soc. *Res:* Solid state physics; nuclear and electronic paramagnetic resonance. *Mailing Add:* 711 Chestnut St Ashland OH 44805

SEGELMAN, ALVIN BURTON, PHARMACOGNOSY, PHYTOCHEMISTRY. *Current Pos:* asst prof, 71-74, ASSOC PROF PHARMACOG, RUTGERS UNIV, 74- *Personal Data:* b Boston, Mass, Sept 27, 31; m 72; c 2. *Educ:* Mass Col Pharm, BS, 54, MS, 67; Univ Pittsburgh, PhD(pharmacog), 71. *Prof Exp:* Chief pharmacist, Kenmore Prof Pharm, 54-61; dir pharmaceut serv, Bell Pharm Co, 61-65; fel, Mass Col Pharm, 65-67; instr pharmacog & microbiol, Univ Pittsburgh, 67-71. *Concurrent Pos:* Res dir, Cliniderm Labs, Boston, 57-65; consult pharmaceut, 72-; prin investr, Rutgers Photodynamic Ther Res Group, Fiber Optics Mat Res Prog, 88-

Mem: AAAS; Am Soc Pharmacog; Acad Pharmaceut Sci; Am Asn Pharm Sci. *Res:* Isolation, purification and structure elucidation of biologically active natural products; design of phytochemical screening and isolation methods; alkaloids, antibiotics, anti-tumor and other biodynamic agents in terrestrial and marine plants and animals; microbiology; microbial transformations and fermentations; medicinal plant tissue culture and analytical toxicology. *Mailing Add:* 54 W 680 S Orem UT 84058

SEGELMAN, FLORENCE H, analytical biochemistry, clinical chemistry; deceased, see previous edition for last biography

SEGERS, RICHARD GEORGE, MATHEMATICS, OPERATIONS RESEARCH. *Current Pos:* CONSULT APPL MATH & STATIST, 86- *Personal Data:* b Cincinnati, Ohio, July 4, 28; m 56; c 4. *Educ:* Univ Dayton, BS, 50; Purdue Univ, MS, 52, PhD(math), 56. *Prof Exp:* Mem tech staff, Networks Dept, Bell Tel Labs, Inc, 55-59; sr mathematician, Vitro Labs, 59-63; res consult, Gen Precision Labs, 63-64 & Exxon Corp, 64-86. *Concurrent Pos:* Vis assoc prof, Grad Sch Bus, Univ Chicago, 69-70; adj fac mem, Dept Math & Physics, Fairleigh Dickinson Univ, 71- *Mem:* Am Math Soc; Soc Indust & Appl Math; Sigma Xi. *Res:* Optimal control, statistics, differential equations. *Mailing Add:* 18 Gunther St Mendham NJ 07945-1415

SEGERSTROM, KENNETH, aerial mapping, for more information see previous edition

SEGGERSON, JOHN J, TUBERCULOSIS PREVENTION. *Current Pos:* chief, Prog Serv Br, 77-96, ASSOC DIR EXTERNAL AFFAIRS, DIV TUBERC ELIMINATION, NAT CTR HIV, STD & TB PREV, CTR DIS CONTROL & PREV, 96- *Personal Data:* b Springfield, Ohio, Sept 15, 41; m 66, Kathryn Cullinan; c Betsy & Mary Kate. *Educ:* St Joseph's Col, BA, 63. *Prof Exp:* Venereal dis investr, Chicago Bd Health, 63; pub health adv & chief, Venereal Dis Control Unit, Cook Co Health Dept, Ill, 64-65; pub health adv, tuberc prog mgr, Kinston Pa State Health Dept 65-67; Erie County Health Dept, NY, 67-68; sr tuberc pub health adv, tuberc prog mgr, Bur Tuberc Control, NY State Dept Health, 68-70; supvry pub health adv, Ctr Dis Control, USPHS Region III, Philadelphia, 70-72, actg assoc regional health, dir & prog dir dis control, 72-74, dir, Div Prev, 74-77. *Mailing Add:* Div Tuberculosis Elimination Nat Ctr HIV STD & TD Prev Ctr Dis Control & Prev E-10 1600 Clifton Rd Atlanta GA 30333. *Fax:* 404-639-8604; *E-Mail:* jjs1@cpstb1.em.cdc.gov

SEGHERS, BENONI HENDRIK, ETHOLOGY, ICHTHYOLOGY. *Current Pos:* DOCTOR & PROF, OXFORD UNIV, 89- *Personal Data:* b Willebroek, Belg, Dec 24, 44; Can citizen. *Educ:* Univ BC, BSc, 67, PhD(zool), 73. *Prof Exp:* Lectr, Univ Man, 72-73; lectr, Univ Western Ont, 74-75, asst prof zool, 76-81; vis scientist, Univ Calgary, 81-82, res assoc, 83-89. *Concurrent Pos:* Fel, Univ Man, 72-74. *Mem:* Can Soc Zool; Animal Behav Soc; Int Soc Human Ethology; NAm Lake Mgt Soc; NAm Benthological Soc. *Res:* Behavior, ecology and evolution of fishes; biology of the fishes of Trinidad, West Indies; anti-predator adaptations in vertebrates; zoogeography; limnology; management of hydroelectric reservoirs. *Mailing Add:* Dept Zool Animal Behav Res Gr Oxford Univ S Park Rd Oxford OX1 3PS England

SEGLIE, ERNEST AUGUSTUS, NUCLEAR PHYSICS. *Current Pos:* res analyst, Inst Defense Anal, OSD/DOT, 79-88, SCI ADV & DIR OPER TEST & EVAL, DEPT DEFENSE, 88- *Personal Data:* b New York, NY, Aug 8, 45; c 2. *Educ:* Cooper Union, BS, 67; Univ Mass, PhD(nuclear physics), 73. *Honors & Awards:* Andrew Goodpastor Award Excellence Res, 87. *Prof Exp:* Assoc physics, Rensselaer Polytech Inst, 73-75; res assoc & lectr physics, Yale Univ, 75-79. *Mem:* AAAS; Int Test & Eval Asn. *Res:* Heavy ion physics, nuclear scattering and reaction theories and fusion reactions; defense analysis, operational testing and evaluation. *Mailing Add:* Dir Oper Test & Eval Rm 3E318 1700 Defense Pentagon Washington DC 20301-1700

SEGLUND, JAMES ARNOLD, GEOLOGY. *Current Pos:* PRES, J A SEGLUND INC, 67- *Personal Data:* b Munising, Mich, Jan 31, 23; m 46; c 3. *Educ:* Univ Mich, BS, 48, MS, 49. *Prof Exp:* Dist geologist, Texaco Inc, 49-56; partner, Rodgers, Seglund & Shaw Assoc, 56-67. *Concurrent Pos:* Deleg, Am Asn Petrol Geologists; dir, Soc Independent Petrol Earth Scientist. *Mem:* Soc Geochemists. *Res:* Geological studies on the Michigan portion of the Mid-continent Rift System; geological studies on New Brunswick, Canada; gold deposits for Northern Michigan. *Mailing Add:* 25 Harbor Circle Diamondhead MS 39525

SEGNAN, ROMEO A, MAGNETIC PROPERTIES OF MATERIALS, MOSSBAUER SPECTROSCOPY. *Current Pos:* from asst prof to assoc prof, 67-75, PROF PHYSICS, AMERICAN UNIV, 75-, DEPT CHAIR, 87- *Personal Data:* b Flume, Italy, Aug 31, 32; US citizen; m, Patricia. *Educ:* Univ Turin, Italy, BS, 57, MS, 57; Carnegie Inst Technol, Pittsburgh, PhD(physics), 63. *Prof Exp:* Fel, Brookhaven Nat Lab, 62-64; instr, Univ Pa, 64-67. *Concurrent Pos:* Prin investr, US Army, Ft Belvoir, Va, 71-75; consult, Time-Life Books, 80-83 & Inst Lifetime Learing, 84; vis prof, Univ Parma, Italy, 90-91. *Mem:* Am Phys Soc; Am Asn Physics Teachers; Audio Eng Soc. *Res:* Magnetism, material science, and physical studies of archeological materials; used the Mossbauer spectroscopy technique to measure the magnetic properties of many magnetically ordered compounds; non-linear effects in amorphous magnetic ribbons. *Mailing Add:* 3404 McKinley St NW Washington DC 20015-1649. *Fax:* 202-885-2723; *E-Mail:* segnan@physics.american.edu

SEGNER, EDMUND PETER, JR, STRUCTURAL ENGINEERING & MECHANICS, RESEARCH ADMINISTRATION. *Current Pos:* chmn & prof, 90-95, EMER PROF, DEPT CIVIL & ENVIRON ENG, UNIV ALA, BIRMINGHAM, 96- *Personal Data:* b Austin, Tex, Mar 28, 28; m 52; c 5. *Educ:* Univ Tex, BS, 49, MS, 52; Tex A&M Univ, PhD(struct eng), 62. *Prof Exp:* Engr, United Gas Pipe Line Co, La, 49-50; sr struct engr, Gen Dynamics Corp, Tex, 51-52 & 53-54; engr, Forrest & Cotton, Inc, 53; from instr to assoc prof civil eng, Tex A&M Univ, 54-63; prof civil eng & struct group coordr, Univ Okla, 63-65; prof civil eng, Univ Ala, Tuscaloosa, 65-76, asst dean res & grad studies, 68-71, assoc dean eng, 71-76; assoc vpres, Res & Grad Studies, Memphis State Univ, 76-80, prof civil eng, 76-90, assoc vpres res, 80-90. *Concurrent Pos:* Consult, 54- *Mem:* Am Soc Civil Engrs; Am Soc Eng Educ; Nat Soc Prof Engrs; Am Concrete Inst. *Res:* Design and analysis of structural steel and reinforced concrete structures; openings in flexural members; splices in tensile reinforcing bars; bond in reinforced concrete design and various flexural studies involving reinforced concrete and structural steel. *Mailing Add:* Dept Civil & Environ Eng Univ Ala Birmingham UAB Sta Birmingham AL 35294-4461

SEGOVIA, ANTONIO, GEOLOGY. *Current Pos:* ASSOC PROF GEOL, UNIV MD, COLLEGE PARK, 69- *Personal Data:* b Asuncion, Paraguay, Nov 3, 32; m 60, 81; c 3. *Educ:* Nat Univ Paraguay, BS, 54; Pa State Univ, PhD(geol), 63. *Prof Exp:* Geologist, Ministry Pub Works, Paraguay, 56; field geologist, Bolivian Gulf Oil Corp, 57; geologist, Photogeol Unit, Gulf Oil Corp, NJ, 57-58, consult, Western Explor Div, 58-60; adv photogeol, Nat Geol Surv, Colombia, 60-61; asst prof geol & head dept, Sch Petrol Eng, Eastern Univ Venezuela, 61-64 & Cent Univ Venezuela, 64-66; sr res scientist, Tulsa Res Ctr, Sinclair Oil Corp, 66-69. *Concurrent Pos:* Consult, Skelly Oil Corp, 65-66, Berea Oil, 80-84 & World Bank, 83-84; pres, Geosysts Inc, 72-76; consult archaeol, Cath Univ Am, 73-75 & Am Univ, 74-75; vis res prof, Cent Univ Venezuela, 75 & Simon Bolivar Univ, Venezuela, 77; dir geol surv, PR, 76. *Mem:* AAAS; fel Geol Soc Am; Soc Petrol Engrs; Am Asn Petrol Geologists; Am Inst Mining, Metall & Petrol Engrs. *Res:* Photogeology; geomorphology; engineering geology; petroleum geology; structural geology; seismicity of regmites, especially deformation of Pleistocene surfaces; geological study of nuclear sites; South American geology. *Mailing Add:* Dept Geol Univ Md College Park MD 20742-0001

SEGOVIA, JORGE, SOCIOMEDICAL SCIENCES, HEALTH SERVICES RESEARCH. *Current Pos:* assoc prof, 76-83, assoc dean, Div Community Med, 92-96, PROF SOCIAL MED, MEM UNIV NFLD, 83-,. *Personal Data:* b Martinez, Arg, Mar 2, 34; m 63, Susan E Ravenna; c Andrea M & Jorge P. *Educ:* Univ Buenos Aires, MD, 59, MPH, 61. *Prof Exp:* Head health educ sect sociomed sci, Sch Pub Health, Univ Buenos Aires, 63-66; head med sociol sect, Ctr Educ Med Invest Clin Buenos Aires, 64-68; mem prof staff med sociol, Ctr Latino Am Admin Med Buenos Aires, 68-71; res assoc sociomed sci, Columbia Univ Sch Pub Health, 71-73; asst prof & consult med care prog, Health & Community, Univ Campinas, Brazil, 73-75. *Concurrent Pos:* Short term consult, Can Int Develop Agency, 84-85; mem adv comt, Can Pub Health Asn and occup health proj; counr, Int Health Section, Am Pub Health Asn, 84-87; bd dirs, Can Health Econs Res Asn, 96-98. *Mem:* Can Pub; Am Pub Health Asn; Am Sociol Asn; hon fel Royal Soc Health UK; Can Asn Teachers Community Health (pres, 93-). *Res:* Health practices and medical care utilization; comparative health systems; health services research; health status measurement. *Mailing Add:* Div Community Med Mem Univ Nfld St John's NF A1B 3V6 Can. *Fax:* 709-737-7382; *E-Mail:* jsegovia@kean.ucs.mun.ca

SEGRE, DIEGO, IMMUNOLOGY. *Current Pos:* prof, 60-92, EMER PROF VET PATHOBIOL, COL VET MED, UNIV ILL, URBANA, 92- *Personal Data:* b Milano, Italy, Feb 3, 22; nat US; m 52, Mariangela Bertani; c Carlo & Alberto. *Educ:* Univ Milano, DVM, 47; Univ Nebr, MS, 54; Univ Wis, PhD(vet sci), 57. *Prof Exp:* Asst prof infectious dis, Univ Milano, 47-51; asst animal pathologist, Univ Nebr, 52-55; res asst vet sci, Univ Wis, 55-57, asst prof, 57-60. *Concurrent Pos:* Vis investr, Dept Biochem, Univ Lausanne, Switz, 66-67; Nat Inst Aging, NIH, Bethesda, Md, 88-89. *Mem:* AAAS; Soc Exp Biol & Med; Am Asn Immunologists; Conf Res Workers Animal Dis; Am Col Vet Microbiol; Sigma Xi; Am Gerontol Soc. *Res:* Mechanisms of immunity and immunological tolerance; maturation and cytokinetics of the immune response; immunology of aging. *Mailing Add:* Dept Vet Pathol Col Vet Med Univ Ill 2001 S Lincoln Ave Urbana IL 61801-6178

SEGRE, GINO C, THEORETICAL PHYSICS. *Current Pos:* assoc prof, 69-74, PROF, UNIV PA, 74- *Personal Data:* b Florence, Italy, Oct 4, 38; US citizen; m 62; c 2. *Educ:* Harvard Univ, AB, 59; Mass Inst Technol, PhD(physics), 63. *Prof Exp:* NSF fel physics, Europ Orgn Nuclear Res, Geneva, Switz, 63-65; res assoc, Lawrence Radiation Lab, Univ Calif, 65-69. *Concurrent Pos:* A P Sloan Found fel, 63-71; Guggenheim fel, 75-76. *Mem:* Am Phys Soc. *Res:* Elementary particle physics. *Mailing Add:* Dept Physics 2n1 Drl E1 Univ Pa Philadelphia PA 19104

SEGRE, MARIANGELA BERTANI, IMMUNOBIOLOGY. *Current Pos:* res assoc, 63-73, asst prof, 73-85, ASSOC PROF IMMUNOL, COL VET MED, UNIV ILL, URBANA, 85- *Personal Data:* b Milan, Italy, Oct 4, 27; US citizen; m 52; c 2. *Educ:* Univ Milan, Dr Sc(biol), 49. *Prof Exp:* Res assoc infectious dis, Col Vet Med, Univ Milan, 49-51; vis investr, Animal Dis Res Inst, Weybridge, Eng, 51; bacteriologist, Montecatini Corp, Milan, 51-52 & Nebr State Dept Health, 53-54. *Concurrent Pos:* Vis investr, Lab Immunol, NIH, 89. *Mem:* Am Asn Immunologists; Am Asn Microbiologists; Am Asn Vet Immunologists. *Res:* Mechanism of antibody formation; immunologic tolerance; immunologic aspects of aging; cytokinetics of the immune response; anti-idiotypic vaccines; immunological methods. *Mailing Add:* Vet Path 2001 S Lincoln Ave Univ Ill Urbana IL 61801-6178. *Fax:* 217-333-4628

SEGREST, JERE PALMER, PLASMA LIPOPROTEINS, PROTEIN DESIGN. *Current Pos:* assoc prof path, 74-80, from asst prof to assoc prof biochem, 74-82, asst prof microbiol, 75-79, PROF PATH, MED CTR, UNIV ALA, BIRMINGHAM, 80-, PROF BIOCHEM, 82- *Personal Data:* b Dothan, Ala, Aug 16, 40; m 66; c 3. *Educ:* Vanderbilt Univ, BA, 62, MD, 67, PhD(biochem), 69. *Prof Exp:* Resident path, Univ Hosp, Vanderbilt Univ, 68-70. *Concurrent Pos:* Europ Molecular Biol Orgn fel, Nat Ctr Sci Res, Gif-sur-Yvette, France, 73; mem, NIH Study Sect Molecular Cytol, 78; mem, comt prof training, Am Chem Soc, 78-86; mem, Ed Affairs Comn, Am Soc Biochem & Molecular Biol, 81-87; vis scientist, Div Endocrinol Metab, Dept Med, Univ Wash, Seattle, 83; dir, Atherosclerosis Res Unit, Univ Ala, 83-, Atheroclerosis Detection & Prev Clin, 88-; prin investr, prog proj, Nat Heart Lung Blood Inst & mini prog proj, 85-87; prin investr on five reports of Invest Grant Rev Comn B, 88-; ed, Plasma Lipoproteins, 86; co organizer, Workshop Molecular Interactions Membranes, Ctr Physics, Aspen, Colo, 86; consult, Southern Biotechnol Assoc, Inc, 86; prof med, 84-; pres, Athero Tech, Inc, 87-. *Mem:* Am Chem Soc; Am Chem Soc; Am Soc Cell Biol; Am Heart Asn; Am Soc Biochem & Molecular Biol. *Res:* Protein-lipid interactions in membrane and plasma lipoproteins; structure and function plasma high density lipoproteins; protein design; role of triplycinde-rich lipoprotein in atherogenesis; clinical detection, prevention and treatment of atherosclerosis; cell biology. *Mailing Add:* Univ Ala Birmingham 1808 Seventh Ave S BDB Rm 630 Birmingham AL 35294-0012. *Fax:* 205-934-9627

SEGUIN, JEROME JOSEPH, PHYSIOLOGY. *Current Pos:* Demonstr & asst, 50-57, lectr, 58-60, from asst prof to assoc prof physiol, 60-90, EMER PROF, UNIV WESTERN ONT, 90- *Personal Data:* b North Bay, Ont, Sept 27, 24; m 52; c 6. *Educ:* Univ West Ont, BSc, 50, MSc, 52, PhD(physiol), 56. *Concurrent Pos:* McEachern sr med fel, Muscular Dystrophy Asn Can, 58-63; guest lectr, Inst Muscle Dis, Inc, NY, 62-63, Inst Fisiologia Umana, Pisa, Italy, 71-72, Dept Physiol, Univ Adelaid, Australia, 86-87. *Mem:* Can Physiol Soc; Soc Neurosci; Int Asn Study Pain. *Res:* Muscle receptor physiology; neurophysiology of pain. *Mailing Add:* Dept Physiol Health Sci Ctr Univ Western Ont London ON N6A 5C1 Can

SEGUIN, LOUIS-ROCH, FISHERIES. *Current Pos:* CONSULT FISHERY BIOLOGIST & MGR, JAMES BAY RESERVOIRS, QUE, 76- *Personal Data:* b Rigaud, Que, Apr 26, 20; m 50; c 4. *Educ:* Col Bourget, BA, 43; Univ Laval, BSc, 47; Univ Montreal, MSc, 54. *Prof Exp:* Biologist, Laurentian Fish Hatchery, Que, 47-49; biologist & dir, Eastern Twp Fishery Sta, Que Dept Fish & Game, 50-61, chief biol, 62-63; prof fish culture, Univ Laval, 63; chief wildlife biologist, Can Int Paper Co, 63-71; exec dir, Que Fedn Camping & Caravaning, 71-72; head fishery sect, Appl Res Ctr Feeding Sci, Univ Que, Montreal, 72-76; prof aquacult, Col St Felicien, Que, 80-85; exp trout rearing sta, Baldwin, Que, 85- *Concurrent Pos:* Gen mgr, Que Outfitters Asn, 73-82; prof Aquacult, Col St Felicien, Que, 80-84. *Mem:* Aquacult Asn Can. *Res:* Trout culture; building and management of lakes; closed circuit for fish rearing. *Mailing Add:* 385 Sequin Rd Baldwin PQ J1A 2S4 Can

SEGUIN, MAURICE KRISHOLM, GEOPHYSICS, GEOLOGY. *Current Pos:* from asst prof to assoc prof, 69-82, FULL PLEDGE PROF GEOPHYS, LAVAL UNIV, 82- *Personal Data:* b Cedars, Que, June 30, 37. *Educ:* Univ Montreal, BA, 58, BSc, 62; McGill Univ, MSc, 63, PhD(geophys), 65. *Hon Degrees:* Degree, Royal Inst Technol, Stockholm, 68. *Prof Exp:* Geophysicist, Iron Ore Co, Can, 64-65; lectr, Royal Inst Technol, Stockholm, 65-68; assoc res, Soquem, Que, 68. *Concurrent Pos:* Mem, Comt Geol & Geophys, Nat Res Coun Can, 69. *Mem:* French-Can Asn Advan Sci; Europ Asn Explor Geophys; Europ Asn Geophys; Sigma Xi; Nat Res Coun Can. *Res:* Applied geophysics; paleomagnetism; permafrost; geophysics. *Mailing Add:* Dept Geolg Laval Univ Quebec PQ G1K 7P4 Can. *Fax:* 418-656-7339; *E-Mail:* sequin@ggl.ulaval.ca

SEGUIN, RUSSELL JOSEPH, ELECTROCHEMICAL SENSORS FOR WATER QUALITY. *Current Pos:* SR STAFF SCIENTIST, HYDROLAB CORP, 96- *Personal Data:* b Albany, NY, Mar 18, 57; div; c Sarah, Alex & Jennifer. *Educ:* Tex A&M Univ, BS, 81; Univ Tex, Austin, MS, 84, PhD(analyticl chem), 96; Wright State Univ, Ohio, MBA, 89. *Prof Exp:* Res scientist, YSI Inc, 84-91; consult water qual sensors, Hydrolab Corp, 92-95. *Mem:* Am Chem Soc. *Res:* Development and characterization of sensors for monitoring water quality using electrochemical and optical detection technologies. *Mailing Add:* 406 Suzzanne Pflugerville TX 78660. *Fax:* 512-255-3106; *E-Mail:* rseguin@hydrolab.com

SEGUIN, WARD RAYMOND, METEOROLOGY. *Current Pos:* RES SCIENTIST METEOROL, NAT OCEANIC & ATMOSPHERIC ADMIN, DEPT COM, 73-, DEP CHIEF, 88- *Personal Data:* b Montpelier, Vt, Aug 28, 42; m 67; c 3. *Educ:* Fla State Univ, BS, 65, MS, 67, PhD(meteorol), 72. *Honors & Awards:* Silver Medal, Dept Com. *Prof Exp:* Fel meteorol, Univ Va, 72-73. *Mem:* Am Meteorol Soc; Nat Weather Asn. *Res:* Study of energy and momentum transfers in the tropical marine atmospheric boundary layer; development of hydrometeorological applications for operational meteorology. *Mailing Add:* 16709 Cavalry Dr Rockville MD 20853. *E-Mail:* seguin@tdlvax.nora.gov

SEGUNDO, JOSE PEDRO, NEUROPHYSIOLOGY. *Current Pos:* instr anat, 53-55, PROF ANAT, HEALTH SCI CTR, UNIV CALIF, LOS ANGELES, 60- *Personal Data:* b Montevideo, Uruguay, Oct 6, 22; c 5. *Educ:* Univ Repub Uruguay, BS, 42, MD, 49. *Prof Exp:* Instr physiol, Univ Repub Uruguay, 50-57; head dept electrobiol, Inst Biol Sci, Montevideo, 57-60. *Mem:* Am Physiol Soc; Biophys Soc; Soc Neurosci; LatinAm Ciencias Fisiologicas. *Res:* Functional organization of multisensory areas of the nervous system; interneuronal communication. *Mailing Add:* Dept Neurobiol Univ Calif Los Angeles Los Angeles CA 90095-1763. *Fax:* 310-825-2224; *E-Mail:* lagsjps@mvsoac.ucla.edu

SEGURA, GONZALO, JR, radiochemistry; deceased, see previous edition for last biography

SEHE, CHARLES THEODORE, DEVELOPMENTAL BIOLOGY, ENDOCRINOLOGY. *Current Pos:* prof develop biol & endocrinol, 71-77, MEM BIOL FAC, MANKATO STATE COL, 77- *Personal Data:* b Geneva, Ill, Feb 26, 23; m 53; c 5. *Educ:* N Cent Col, Ill, AB, 50; Univ Iowa, MS, 53, PhD(zool), 57. *Prof Exp:* Asst embryol, Univ Iowa, 52-57; asst prof endocrinol, Univ Ill, Urbana, 57-58; asst prof embryol & endocrinol, Univ Cincinnati, 58-61; assoc prof embryol & comp anat, N Cent Col, Ill, 61-64; res assoc prof develop biol & endocrinol, Stanford Med Ctr, 64-71. *Concurrent Pos:* Resident res assoc, Argonne Nat Lab, 62-63; consult biol, Teacher Training Prog, Inst Nuclear Sci & Eng, Argonne Nat Lab, 64. *Mem:* AAAS; Am Soc Zool. *Res:* Developmental and secretory characteristics of the ultimobranchial body of vertebrates; hormonal factors in sexual behavioral development. *Mailing Add:* 1104 N Sixth St Mankato MN 56001

SEHGAL, LAKSHMAN R, MICROBIOLOGY, IMMUNOLOGY. *Current Pos:* AT NOWAT NORTHFIELD LAB INC. *Personal Data:* b Hyderabad, AP, India, Feb 15, 42; US citizen; m 66; c 2. *Educ:* Sri Aurobindo Int Ctr Educ, BS, 62; Ill Inst Technol, Chicago, PhD(biol), 70. *Prof Exp:* Instr res, Med Sch, Univ Ill, 70-73, asst prof, 73-77; asst res prof, Pritzker Sch Med, Univ Chicago, 80-; dir surg res, Michael Reese Hosp, formerly. *Concurrent Pos:* Biochemist, dept surg, Cook County Hosp, 73-77; prin investr subcontract, Naval Res Labs, Washington, DC, 85- *Mem:* Asn Acad Surg; Am Asn Clin Chem; Asn Clin Scientists; Shock Soc. *Res:* Development of a hemoglobin based red cell substitute; manufacture of a polymerized pyridoxylated hemoglobin solution which has a normal oxygen carrying capacity. *Mailing Add:* 4324 Hammersmith Lane Glenview IL 60025-1072

SEHGAL, OM PARKASH, PLANT PATHOLOGY, VIROLOGY. *Current Pos:* from asst prof to assoc prof, 63-78, PROF PLANT PATH & BIOL SCI, UNIV MO, COLUMBIA, 78- *Personal Data:* b Rawal Pindi, India, July 22, 32; m 62, Santosh Dhody; c Ravi & Ritu. *Educ:* Univ Lucknow, MSc, 53; Univ Wis, PhD(plant path), 61. *Honors & Awards:* Fulbright Lectr, Lucknow Univ, India, 93. *Prof Exp:* Res asst virol, Indian Agr Res Inst, 55-57; res asst plant path, Univ Wis, 58-61; fel virol, Univ Ariz, 61-63. *Concurrent Pos:* Consult, UN/FAO, 90; assoc ed, Virol, Plant Dis. *Mem:* AAAS; Am Phytopath Soc; fel Indian Virol Soc; Am Soc Virol. *Res:* Viral structure and genetics; helper virus-specificity and biology of satellite plant viral RNAs. *Mailing Add:* Dept Plant Path Univ Mo Columbia MO 65211. *Fax:* 573-882-0588; *E-Mail:* om__sehgal@muccmail.missouri.edu

SEHGAL, PRAVINKUMAR B, VIROLOGY & IMMUNOLOGY, CYTOKINES. *Current Pos:* prof microbiol & immunol, 91-94, PROF MED, NY MED COL, 91-, PROF CELL BIOL & ANAT, 94- *Personal Data:* b Bombay, India, Sept 11, 49; c 2. *Educ:* Seth G S Med Col, MB & BS, 73; Rockefeller Univ, PhD(virol & cell biol), 77. *Honors & Awards:* Irma T Hirschi Award, 81. *Prof Exp:* Intern, King Edward Mem Hosp, 71-72; fel, Rockefeller Univ, 77-79, from asst prof to assoc prof virol, 79-91. *Concurrent Pos:* Assoc ed, J Interferon Res, 79-91, & Virol, 83-88; NIH res grant, 79-; estab investr, Am Heart Asn, 83; proj dir, Nat Found Cancer Res, 84- *Mem:* AAAS; NY Acad Sci; Am Soc Microbiol; Am Soc Virol; Am Asn Immunol; Sigma Xi; Harvey Soc; Am Soc Molecular Biol & Biochem. *Res:* Interleukin-6 and other cytokines in health and disease; mechanisms of RNA transcription; plasma protein synthesis in acute infections; genetic sequence analysis. *Mailing Add:* Dept Cell & Biol & Anat NY Med Col Basic Sci Bldg Valhalla NY 10595-1690. *Fax:* 914-993-4825

SEHGAL, PREM P, PLANT PHYSIOLOGY. *Current Pos:* asst prof, 66-69, assoc prof, 69-77, PROF BIOL, ECAROLINA UNIV, 77- *Personal Data:* b Patiala, India, Nov 16, 34; m 61, Nanda Bose; c Ishan. *Educ:* Univ Delhi, BSc, 54, MSc, 56; Harvard Univ, AM, 61; Duke Univ, PhD(bot), 64. *Prof Exp:* Asst prof bot, B R Col, Agra, 56-57; lectr, Ramjas Col, Delhi, 57-58; res asst, Duke Univ, 61-64, NSF res assoc, 64-65; NIH proj assoc biochem, Univ Wis-Madison, 65-66. *Mem:* Int Soc Plant Morphol; Sigma Xi. *Res:* Interaction of hormones with nitrogen compounds, especially in chlorophyll production; biochemistry of plant tissue cultures with special reference to enzymatic changes; urease. *Mailing Add:* Dept Biol ECarolina Univ 1000 W Fifth St Greenville NC 27834-3006

SEHGAL, SURENDRA N, TUMOR BIOLOGY, IMMUNOLOGY. *Current Pos:* sr scientist microbiol, Wyeth-Ayerst Res, 60-69, head microbial technol, 69-74, asst dir, dept microbiol, 74-83, asst dir, dept immunol, 83-88, asst dir, Dept Immunopharmacol, 88-89, sr res fel, 89-96, DISTINGUISHED RES FEL, WYETH-AYERST RES, 96- *Personal Data:* b Khushab, India, Feb 10, 32; Can citizen, US citizen; m 61; c 3. *Educ:* Banaras Hindu Univ, BPharm, 52, MPharm, 53; Bristol Univ, PhD(microbiol), 57. *Honors & Awards:* Lifetime Achievement Award, Indian Soc Organ Transplantation. *Prof Exp:* Asst prof pharm, Birla Col Pharm, 53-55; fel microbiol, Coun Sci & Indust Res, India, 55; Nat Res Coun Can fel, 58-60. *Concurrent Pos:* Adj assoc prof microbiol, Concordia Univ, Montreal. *Mem:* Am Soc Microbiol; Chem Inst Can; Soc Indust Microbiol; AAAS; Transplant Soc; Indian Soc Organ Transplantation. *Res:* Industrial microbiology; bioconversion of organic compounds; antibiotic fermentations; microbial chemistry; tumor biology; genetic toxicology; immunology; mechanisms involved in inumunosuppression and immunopotentiation; autoimmune disease. *Mailing Add:* Four Sayre Dr Princeton NJ 08540. *E-Mail:* sehgals@war.wyeth.com

SEHGAL, SURINDER K, ALGEBRA. *Current Pos:* from teaching asst to asst prof, 63-71, assoc prof, 71-83, PROF MATH, OHIO STATE UNIV, 83- *Personal Data:* b Hoshiarpur, India, Apr 22, 38; m 66; c 2. *Educ:* Panjab Univ, India, BA, 57, MA, 59; Univ Notre Dame, PhD(math), 65. *Prof Exp:* Lectr math, DAV Col, Hoshiarpur, 59-61; teaching asst, Univ Notre Dame, 61-63. *Mem:* Am Math Soc; Math Asn Am. *Res:* Algebra; group theory. *Mailing Add:* Dept Math Ohio State Univ 231 W 18th Ave Columbus OH 43210-1101

SEHMEL, GEORGE ALBERT, CHEMICAL ENGINEERING & AEROSOL PHYSICS, ARMY SMOKE & OBSCURANTS. *Current Pos:* CONSULT, AEROSOL PARTICLE BEHAV & ENVIRON SAMPLING. *Personal Data:* b Puyallup, Wash, Apr 8, 32; m 58, Edna Morrison; c Elizabeth J (Lee), Barbara J (Roetaisoedner) & Thomas A. *Educ:* Univ Wash, Seattle, BS, 55, PhD(chem eng), 61; Univ Ill, MS, 56. *Prof Exp:* Engr, Gen Elec Co, NY, 57-58 & Wash, 61-63; sr res engr, 63-94; staff engr, Pac Northwest Labs, Battelle Mem Inst, 65-83, sr res engr, 83-94. *Concurrent Pos:* Lectr, Ctr Grad Study, Hanford, 64-69. *Mem:* Am Inst Chem Engrs. *Res:* Program management of aerosol physics research; aerosol particulate mass transfer behavior; meteorology; particulate deposition and resuspension; sampling of aerosols; evaluation of nuclear reactor fuel elements; heat transfer technology; smokes and obscurants; environmental assessments. *Mailing Add:* 2030 Howell Richland WA 99352

SEHON, ALEC, IMMUNOLOGY. *Current Pos:* PROF IMMUNOL & HEAD DEPT, FAC MED, UNIV MAN, 69- *Personal Data:* b Romania, Dec 18, 24; Can citizen; m 50; c 2. *Educ:* Univ Manchester, BSc, 48, MSc, 50, PhD(phys chem), 51, DSc, 65. *Prof Exp:* Demonstr chem, Univ Manchester, 48-49 & Nat Res Labs, 51-52; res assoc chem, Calif Inst Technol & Inst Biochem, Univ Uppsala, 52-53; asst prof exp med, McGill Univ, 53-59, from asst prof to prof chem, 56-69, hon lectr biochem, 59-69. *Concurrent Pos:* Co-dir, Div Immunochem & Allergy, Royal Victorian Hosp, Montreal, 53-59; biophys chemist, McGill Univ Clin, Montreal Gen Hosp, 60-69; Nat Res Coun Can sr res fel, John Simon Guggenheim Mem Found fel & res assoc, Harvard Univ, 63-64; mem, Res Grants Comt, Med Res Coun Can, 64-69; chmn, Gordon Res Conf Immunochem & Immunobiol, 66; dir, NATO Advan Studies Insts, Val Morin, Que, 68, Minaki, Ont, 70; RR Inst res award, Univ Man & Shering travel fel, Can Soc Clin Invest, 73; vis scientist, Walter & Eliza Hall Inst, Melbourne Univ Col, London & Med Res Coun Can, 73-74. *Mem:* Fel AAAS; Am Asn Immunologists; fel Am Acad Allergy; fel Am Col Allergists; Can Soc Immunologists (vpres, 67-69, pres, 69-71). *Res:* Antigen-antibody systems involved in common allergies; development of immunosuppressive therapeutic regimens; tumor immunology; immunodiagnostics. *Mailing Add:* Dept Immunol Fac Med Univ Manitoba 730 William Ave Winnipeg MB R3E 0W3 Can. *Fax:* 204-772-7924

SEIB, DAVID HENRY, ELECTRICAL ENGINEERING, INFRARED FOCAL PLANE ARRAYS. *Current Pos:* mem tech staff elec eng, 76-84 & 88-95, MGR, ROCKWELL INT SCI CTR, 84-88 & 95- *Personal Data:* b Exeter, Calif, Jan 23, 43; m 65, Janice J Baker; c Heather E, Catherine J & Christopher D. *Educ:* Calif Inst Technol, BS, 64; Stanford Univ, MS, 65, PhD(elec eng), 70. *Prof Exp:* Staff scientist solid state physics, tech staff, Aerospace Corp, 69-76. *Mem:* Inst Elec & Electronics Engrs. *Res:* Semiconductor device research, specifically cryogenic readout; integrated circuits for very long wavelength infrared detector arrays; design, analysis and measurement of infrared detector arrays. *Mailing Add:* Boeing N Am Inc 3370 Mira Loma Ave PO Box 3105 Mail Code 031-HB18 Anaheim CA 92803-3105. *Fax:* 714-762-0844; *E-Mail:* dave.h.seib@boeing.com

SEIB, PAUL A, ORGANIC CHEMISTRY, BIOCHEMISTRY. *Current Pos:* ASSOC PROF GRAIN SCI, KANS STATE UNIV, 70- *Personal Data:* b Poseyville, Ind, Jan 8, 36; m 58; c 2. *Educ:* Purdue Univ, BS, 58, MS, 63, PhD(biochem), 65. *Prof Exp:* Asst prof org chem, Inst Paper Chem, 65-70. *Mem:* Am Chem Soc; Am Asn Cereal Chemists; Inst Food Technologists. *Res:* Cereal chemistry; chemistry of vitamin C. *Mailing Add:* 836 Dondee Dr Manhattan KS 66502-3220

SEIBEL, ERWIN, OCEANOGRAPHY, EDUCATIONAL ADMINISTRATION. *Current Pos:* prof oceanog & geol & dir, Tiburon Ctr Environ Studies, 78-81, prof & chmn dept geol sci, 81-88, DEAN UNDERGRAD STUDIES, SAN FRANCISCO STATE UNIV, 88- *Educ:* City Univ New York, BS, 65; Univ Mich, MS, 66, PhD(oceanog), 72. *Prof Exp:* Logistics officer, US Army Corps Engrs, 67-69; master instr, US Army Engr Sch, 69-70, sect head, 70-71; assoc res oceanog & asst proj dir, Great Lakes Res Div, Univ Mich, Ann Arbor, 72-78, asst dir, Mich Sea Grant Prog, 75-78. *Concurrent Pos:* Pres, San Franciso Bay chap, Marine Technol Soc, 82-83, exec secy oceans, 83; pres, San Francisco State Univ Chap, Sigma Xi, 82-84 & 90- *Mem:* Fel AAAS; Am Geophys Union; fel Geol Soc Am; Marine Technol Soc; Soc Econ Paleontologists & Mineralogists; Sigma Xi; fel Acad Sci. *Res:* Multidisciplinary approach to the solution of San Francisco Bay Area and adjacent Pacific Ocean environmental problems through monitoring and modeling the physical, economic social and cultural variables involved; investigation of the effect of nuclear power plant operation on the biological, chemical, geological and physical facets of the aquatic environment; study of the formation and breakup of ice using remote sensing techniques; dynamics of shoreline erosion and resultant sediment transport; enhancing retention rates of minority students. *Mailing Add:* 558 Skiff Circle Redwood City CA 94065-1142

SEIBEL, FREDERICK TRUMAN, SOFTWARE SYSTEM DEVELOPMENT. *Current Pos:* SOFTWARE DEVELOP MGR ADV X-RAY ASTROPHYS FACILITE ASTROPHYS OBSERV, 97- *Personal Data:* b Corning, NY, May 30, 41; m 65, Molly Hinson; c Peter. *Educ:* Yale Univ, BS, 63; Duke Univ, PhD(physics), 68. *Prof Exp:* Staff mem, Los Alamos Sci Lab, 68-77; sr prof tech staff, Princeton Plasma Physics Lab, Princeton Univ, 77-81; dir, Automation & Control, Syst & Advan Technol, Merck & Co, Inc, 81-85; dir, com artificial intel applns, Bolt, Beranel & Newman Labs, 85-97. *Mem:* Sigma Xi. *Res:* Manage the development of the AXAF data facility software. *Mailing Add:* 16 Huckleberry Hill Rd Lincoln MA 01773. *E-Mail:* frederick.seibel.bk.63@aya.yale.edu

SEIBEL, HUGO RUDOLF, ANATOMY, ELECTRON MICROSCOPY. *Current Pos:* from asst prof to assoc prof, 67-75, dir electron micros div, 67-86, PROF ANAT, MED COL VA, 75-, ASSOC DEAN MED, 84- *Personal Data:* b Radautz, Rumania, Nov 9, 37; m 64, Edith E Kramer. *Educ:* Brooklyn Col, BS, 60; Univ Rochester, PhD(anat), 67. *Prof Exp:* Col sci asst & instr biol, Brooklyn Col, 60-62; instr anat, Univ Rochester, 66-67. *Concurrent Pos:* A D Williams grant, Med Col Va, 67-69, NIH grant, 68-71. *Mem:* AAAS; Soc Study Reproduction; Am Asn Anatomists; Pan-Am Asn Anatomists; Transplantation Soc; Sigma Xi. *Res:* Kidney and heart transplantation; electron microscopy and functional correlates of thyroid and pineal. *Mailing Add:* Dept Anat Med Col Va Box 565 MCV Sta Richmond VA 23298

SEIBEL, WERNER, GROSS ANATOMY, DENTAL RESEARCH. *Current Pos:* instr, 72-73, asst prof, 73-77, ASSOC PROF DENT ANAT, SCH DENT, UNIV MD, 77- *Personal Data:* b Krenau, WGer, Sept 27, 43; US citizen; m 67; c 2. *Educ:* Brooklyn Col, BA, 65; Hofstra Univ, MA, 68; Med Col Va, Va Commonwealth Univ, PhD(anat), 73. *Prof Exp:* Asst anat, histol & neuroanat, Med Col Va, Va Commonwealth Univ, 68-72. *Concurrent Pos:* NDEA fel, 68; vis prof, Bone Marrow Transplant Unit Dept Oncol, Johns Hopkins Sch Med. *Mem:* Am Asn Anatomists; Sigma Xi; Am Asn Dent Schs; Int Asn Dent Res; Am Asn Dent Res. *Res:* Mechanisms in the development of fibrotic tissue; functional activities of fibroblast cultures from dermis of rat model with chronic-graft-versus-host disease; pathogenesis of gingival overgrowth induced by phenytoin and cyclosporine-A; oral histology. *Mailing Add:* Dept Oral & Cranial Facial Biol Sci Baltimore Col Dent Surg Univ Md Dent Sch 666 W Baltimore St Baltimore MD 21201

SEIBER, JAMES N, ORGANIC CHEMISTRY. *Current Pos:* asst prof, 69-74, ASSOC PROF ENVIRON TOXICOL, UNIV CALIF, DAVIS, 74- *Personal Data:* b Hannibal, Mo, Sept 21, 40; m 67; c 2. *Educ:* Bellarmine Col, Ky, AB, 61; Ariz State Univ, MS, 64; Utah State Univ, PhD(org chem), 66. *Prof Exp:* Res chemist, Dow Chem Co, 66-69. *Concurrent Pos:* Vis scientist, Pesticides & Toxic Substances Effects Lab, US Environ Protection Agency, Fla, 73-74. *Mem:* AAAS; Am Chem Soc. *Res:* Isolation, structure determination, synthesis and reactions of biologically active chemicals, particularly pesticides, insect pheromones and plant-derived poisons; origin and fate of toxic chemicals in the environment; analytical chemistry of pesticides and pollutants. *Mailing Add:* Ctr Environ Sci & Eng Univ Nev Reno GY MS 199 Reno NV 89557-0901

SEIBER, SUSAN M, PHARMACOLOGY. *Current Pos:* Staff fel pharmacol, 71-76, pharmacologist, Lab Chem Pharmacol, 76-84, DEP DIR, DIV CANCER ETIOL, NAT CANCER INST, 84- *Personal Data:* b Hattiesburg, Miss, May 18, 42; m 71. *Educ:* Univ Va, BS, 64; George Washington Univ, MS, 69, PhD(pharmacol), 70. *Mem:* Am Asn Cancer Res; Teratol Soc; AAAS; Am Soc Pharmacol & Exp Therapeut. *Res:* Developmental pharmacology; drug disposition; carcinogenesis; toxicology. *Mailing Add:* Div Cancer Etiol Nat Cancer Inst NIH Bldg 31 Rm 11AO3 Bethesda MD 20892-0001

SEIBERG, NATHAN, STRING THEORY, FIELD THEORY. *Current Pos:* vis mem, 94-95, PROF, INST ADVAN STUDY, 97- *Personal Data:* b Tel Aviv, Israel, Sept 22, 56; US & Israeli citizen; c 2. *Educ:* Tel Aviv Univ, BSc, 77; Weizmann Inst Sci, PhD(physics), 82. *Honors & Awards:* J F Kennedy Prize, 82; Racah Lectr, Weizmann Inst Sci, 85; Oskar Klein Lectr & Oskar Klein Medal, 95; MacArthur Fel, John D & Catherine T MacArthur Found, 96; Morris Loeb Lectr Physics, 97. *Prof Exp:* Mem, Inst Advan Study, 82-85 & 87-89; sr scientist, Weizmann Inst, 85-86, from assoc prof to prof, 86-91; prof, Rutgers Univ, 89-90, prof II, 90-97. *Concurrent Pos:* Distinguished IFT lectr, Univ Fla, 96. *Mailing Add:* Inst Advan Study Princeton NJ 08540. *E-Mail:* seiberg@sns.ias.edu

SEIBERT, J A, RADIOLOGICAL QUALITY ASSURANCE TESTING. *Current Pos:* ASSOC PROF RADIOL PHYSICS, UNIV CALIF, DAVIS, 83- *Personal Data:* b Dayton, Ohio, Oct 21, 53; m 87. *Educ:* Univ Calif, Irvine, BS, 76, MA, 77, MS, 81 & PhD (radiol sci), 83. *Concurrent Pos:* Lectr, Calif State Univ, Sacramento, 87-88. *Mem:* Am Asn Physicists Med; Radiol Soc NAm; Soc Photo-Optical & Instrumentation Engrs; Inst Elec & Electronics Engrs; Asn Univ Radiologists. *Res:* Medical image processing with goals of improving quantitative and qualitative features by removing degradations and artifacts occured during image acquisition process; radiation shielding specifications; radiological imaging physics research. *Mailing Add:* Diag Radiol Univ Calif Davis 2421 45th St Sacramento CA 95817. *Fax:* 916-734-0316; *E-Mail:* jaseibert@ucdavis.edu

SEIBERT, MICHAEL, PHOTOSYNTHESIS, BIOTECHNOLOGY. *Current Pos:* PRIN SCIENTIST, NAT RENEWABLE ENERGY LAB, 96- *Personal Data:* b Lima, Peru, Nov 15, 44; US citizen; m 75; c 3. *Educ:* Pa State Univ, University Park, BS, 66; Univ Pa, MS, 67, PhD(molecular biol & biophys), 71. *Prof Exp:* Scientist, Exp Sta, E I du Pont de Nemours & Co, 65-68; mem tech staff, GTE Labs, 71-77; sr scientist & task leader photobiol, Solar Energy Res Inst, 77-83, mgr, Photoconversion Res Br, Nat Renewable Energy Lab, 84-96. *Concurrent Pos:* Mem, Proj 4, US/USSR Joint Working Group Microbiol, 79; chmn, Biotechnol & Chem Sci Div, Am Solar Energy Soc, 80; res fel, Nat Ctr Sci Res, France, 83; res prof, Dept Biol, Univ Denver, 85-; vis scientist, Inst Phys & Chem Res, Japan, 87; vis prof, Moscow State Univ, USSR, 88; prog chmn, Int Energy Agency, 90. *Mem:* Biophys Soc; AAAS; Am Soc Photobiol; Am Soc Plant Physiologists; Am Solar Energy Soc; Int Asn Plant Tissue Cult. *Res:* Photosynthetic oxygen evolution; membrane surface chemistry; photobiological conversion of solar energy; primary photochemical process in photosynthesis; photomorphogenesis and cryopreservation of plant tissue; horticultural applications of lighting; algal hydrogen production. *Mailing Add:* Nat Renewable Energy Lab 1617 Cole Blvd Golden CO 80401. *Fax:* 303-384-6150; *E-Mail:* seibertm@tcplink.nrel.gov

SEIBOLD, CAROL DUKE, PHOTOGRAPHIC CHEMISTRY. *Current Pos:* MGR & SR CHEMIST, 3M CO, 73- *Personal Data:* b San Francisco, Calif, July 1, 43; m 64, Jon; c J Duke, Krys E & Erika A. *Educ:* Creighton Univ, BS, 65; Univ Nebr, MS, 67, PhD(chem), 72. *Prof Exp:* Assoc prof chem, Bemidji State Col, 68-69; res chemist, Environ Res Corp, 72-73. *Mem:* Am Chem Soc; Soc Imaging Sci. *Res:* Mechanisms and kinetics of photographic development. *Mailing Add:* 3 Chicadee Lane St Paul MN 55127-6301

SEIDAH, NABIL GEORGE, CLINICAL BIOCHEMISTRY, BIOPHYSICAL CHEMISTRY. *Current Pos:* Nat Res Coun Found fel, Dept Chem, Univ Montreal, 73-74, asst prof, 76-80, BIOCHEMIST, CLIN RES INST, SCH MED, UNIV MONTREAL, 74-, PROF, 80- *Personal Data:* b Cairo, Egypt, Feb 1, 49; Can citizen; m 73; c 2. *Educ:* Cairo Univ, BS, 69; Georgetown Univ, PhD(chem), 73. *Honors & Awards:* Clarke Inst of Psychiat Award, Toronto, 77; Harold Piche Award, Montreal, 83. *Mem:* Med Res Coun Can. *Res:* Determination of amino acid sequence of polypeptide hormones both from pituitary gland and from tumor organs; maturation enzymes of pro-hormones and their genes. *Mailing Add:* Clin Res Inst of Montreal 110 Pine Ave W Montreal PQ H2W 1R7 Can. *Fax:* 514-987-5542

SEIDE, PAUL, ENGINEERING MECHANICS. *Current Pos:* prof, 65-91, EMER PROF CIVIL ENG, UNIV SOUTHERN CALIF, 91- *Personal Data:* b Brooklyn, NY, July 22, 26; m 51, Joan C Matalka; c Richard L & Wendy J (Kielsmeier). *Educ:* City Col New York, BCivEng, 46; Univ Va, MAeroE, 52; Stanford Univ, PhD(eng mech), 54. *Prof Exp:* Aeronaut res scientist, Nat Adv Comn Aeronaut, 46-52; res asst eng mech, Stanford Univ, 52-53; res engr, Northrup Aircraft, Inc, 53-55; head methods & theory sect, Space Technol Lab, 55-61; staff engr, Aerospace Corp, 61-65. *Concurrent Pos:* NSF sr fel, 64-65; consult, Aerospace Corp, 65-68, Northrop Corp, 69, Norair Div, 72-77 & Rockwell Int, 82-85; Albert Alberman vis prof, Technion, Israel Inst Technol, 75; invited lectr, Dalian Univ, Peoples Republic China, 82, & Lanzhou Univ, Peoples Republic China, 87; vis prof, Univ Sydney, Australia, 86, Univ Canterbury, NZ, 86. *Mem:* Am Soc Mech Engrs; Am Soc Civil Engrs; Am Acad Mech; Sigma Xi. *Res:* Stability of structures; nonlinear elasticity; shell analysis. *Mailing Add:* 300 Via Alcance Palos Verdes Estates CA 90274

SEIDEHAMEL, RICHARD JOSEPH, PHARMACOLOGY, MEDICAL SCIENCE. *Current Pos:* DIR CLIN RES DEVELOP, GFI PHARMACEUT SERV INC, 94- *Personal Data:* b Cleveland, Ohio, Dec 26, 40; m 63; c 3. *Educ:* Univ Toledo, BS, 63; Ohio State Univ, MSc, 65, PhD, 68. *Prof Exp:* Sr scientist, Mead Johnson Res Ctr, 69-71, sr investr, 71-74, sr res assoc, 74-80, prin res assoc, 80-83, assoc dir, 83-89; med dir, Bristol-Myers Squibb Co, 89-92; dir clin res develop, Mead Johnson Nutritionals, 92-94. *Mem:* Am Soc Pharmacol & Exp Therapeut; AAAS; NY Acad Sci; Am Soc Clin Pharmacol & Therapeut; Am Heart Asn. *Res:* Respiratory, cardiovascular, central nervous system, ocular and autonomic pharmacology; nutrition; clinical research. *Mailing Add:* GFI Pharmaceut Serv Inc 800 St Mary's Dr Evansville IN 47714

SEIDEL, BARRY S(TANLEY), FLUID MECHANICS. *Current Pos:* assoc prof, 65-69, PROF MECH & AEROSPACE ENG, UNIV DEL, 69- *Personal Data:* b Philadelphia, Pa, Aug 27, 32; m 53; c 2. *Educ:* Univ Del, BSME, 53; Mass Inst Technol, SM, 56, ScD(mech eng), 59. *Prof Exp:* Design engr, Aviation Gas Turbine Div, Westinghouse Elec Co, 53-55; asst prof mech eng, Univ Del, 59-64; NSF res fel, Calif Inst Technol, 64-65. *Concurrent Pos:* Vis prof, Cambridge Univ, 76 & Mass Inst Technol, 84-85; consult, Northern Res & Eng Corp. *Mem:* Am Soc Mech Engrs; Am Inst Aeronaut & Astronaut. *Res:* Fluid mechanics of turbomachinery. *Mailing Add:* 244 Orchard Rd Newark DE 19711

SEIDEL, GEORGE ELIAS, JR, REPRODUCTIVE PHYSIOLOGY. *Current Pos:* from asst prof to assoc prof, 71-83, PROF PHYSIOL, COLO STATE UNIV, 83- *Personal Data:* b Reading, Pa, July 13, 43; m 70, Sarah Moore; c Andrew. *Educ:* Pa State Univ, University Park, BS, 65; Cornell Univ, MS, 68, PhD(physiol), 70. *Honors & Awards:* Alexander von Humboldt Award & Nat Asn Animal Breeders Res Award, 83; Upjohn Physiol Award, Am Dairy Sci Asn, 86. *Prof Exp:* NIH fel, Harvard Med Sch, 70-71. *Concurrent Pos:* Vis scientist, Yale Univ, 78-79, Whitehead Inst, 86-87; assoc ed, J Exp Zool, 79-82. *Mem:* Nat Acad Sci; Am Soc Animal Sci; Sigma Xi; AAAS; Soc Study Reproduction; Soc Study Fertil; Int Embryo Transfer Soc (vpres, 78, pres, 79); Am Dairy Sci Asn. *Res:* Superovulation and embryo transfer; in vitro fertilization; oogenesis; microsurgery to mammalian embryos; transgenic technology, cryopreservation of embryos. *Mailing Add:* Animal Reproduction & Biotechnol Lab Colo State Univ Ft Collins CO 80523. *Fax:* 970-491-3557

SEIDEL, GEORGE MERLE, SOLID STATE PHYSICS. *Current Pos:* from asst prof to assoc prof, 62-67, PROF PHYSICS, BROWN UNIV, 67- *Personal Data:* b Springfield, Mass, Aug 14, 30; m 54; c 3. *Educ:* Worcester Polytech Inst, BS, 52; Purdue Univ, MS, 55, PhD(physics), 58. *Prof Exp:* NSF fel, Univ Leiden, 58-59; res assoc & lectr physics, Harvard Univ, 59-62. *Concurrent Pos:* Fulbright lectr, Atomic Ctr, Arg, 73-74. *Mem:* AAAS; Fedn Am Scientist. *Res:* Low temperature physics, electronic properties of metals; magnetism. *Mailing Add:* Dept Physics Brown Univ Providence RI 02912

SEIDEL, HENRY MURRAY, PEDIATRICS. *Current Pos:* From instr to asst prof pediat, Johns Hopkins Univ, 50-68, asst dean student affairs, 68-71, assoc prof pediat, 68-, assoc prof med care & hosps, 69-, assoc dean, 77-, EMER PROF, SCH MED, JOHNS HOPKINS UNIV. *Personal Data:* b Passaic, NJ, July 19, 22; m 45; c 3. *Educ:* Johns Hopkins Univ, AB, 43, MD, 46. *Mem:* Fel Am Acad Pediat. *Res:* Malignancy; maternal attitudes; medical care staffing; delivery systems. *Mailing Add:* 6336 Sunny Spring Columbia MD 21044-3731

SEIDEL, JAMES STEPHEN, PEDIATRICS. *Current Pos:* CHIEF, DIV GEN & EMERGENCY PEDIAT, HARBOR-UNIV CALIF LAS ANGELES MED CTR, 77-; PROF PEDIAT, SCH MED, UNIV CALIF, LOS ANGELES, 93- *Educ:* Mich State Univ, BS, 64; Univ NC, MSPH, 67; Univ Calif, Los Angeles, MD, 73, PhD(microbiol & immunol), 76. *Concurrent Pos:* Mem, Comt Pediat Emergency Med, 85-93; chair, Subcomt Pediat Resuscitation, Am Heart Asn, 87-91; comt mem, Inst Med Emergency Med Servs Comt, 92-93. *Mem:* Ambulatory Pediat Asn; Am Acad Pediat; Am Pediat Soc. *Res:* Development of emergency medical services for children; pre-hospital care of pediatric emergencies; tropical medicine and parasitology. *Mailing Add:* Harbor-Univ Calif Los Angeles Med Ctr 1000 W Carson St Emer Dept Torrance CA 90502-2004

SEIDEL, MICHAEL EDWARD, VERTEBRATE ZOOLOGY, HERPETOLOGY. *Current Pos:* ASST PROF BIOL, MARSHALL UNIV, 74- *Personal Data:* b New York, NY, Jan 20, 45; m 70; c 2. *Educ:* Univ Miami, BS, 67; NMex Highlands Univ, MS, 69; Univ NMex, PhD(biol), 73. *Prof Exp:* Instr, Univ NMex, 73-74. *Mem:* Herpetologists League; Soc Study Amphibians & Reptiles; Am Soc Ichthyologists & Herpetologists. *Res:* Comparative physiology and ecology of reptiles; systematics of amphibians and reptiles. *Mailing Add:* Dept Biol Sci Marshall Univ 400 Hal Greer Blvd Huntington WV 25755-0001

SEIDEL, THOMAS EDWARD, PHYSICS, SOLID STATE ELECTRONICS. *Current Pos:* SR VPRES, TECH BR, J C SHUMACHER CO. *Personal Data:* b Altoona, Pa, Oct 8, 35; m 60; c 3. *Educ:* St Joseph's Col, Pa, BS, 57; Univ Notre Dame, MS, 59; Stevens Inst Technol, PhD(physics), 65. *Prof Exp:* Engr, Semiconductor Div, RCA Corp, 59-60; mem staff, Sarnoff Labs, 61-62 & 65-66; mem staff, Bell Labs, 66- *Mem:* Electrochem Soc; Am Phys Soc; Inst Elec & Electronics Engrs. *Res:* Ion implantation phenomena and applications to semiconductor devices. *Mailing Add:* 1165 Wales Pl Cardiff by the Sea CA 92007

SEIDELMANN, PAUL KENNETH, ASTRONOMY, CELESTIAL MECHANICS. *Current Pos:* Astronr, US Naval Observ, 65-73, asst dir, 73-76, dir, Nautical Almanac Off, 76-90, dir, Orbital Mech Dept, 90-94, DIR ASTROMETRY, US NAVAL OBSERV, 94- *Personal Data:* b Cincinnati, Ohio, June 15, 37; m 60, Roberta Buck; c Holly (Flippen) & Alan. *Educ:* Univ Cincinnati, EE, 60, MS, 62, PhD(dynamical astron), 68. *Honors & Awards:* Norman P Hays Award, Inst Navig, 91; Pub Serv Group Achievement Award, NASA, 92. *Concurrent Pos:* Lectr, Cath Univ, 66; proj officer, Air Standards Coord Comt, 73-81; vis asst prof, Univ Md, 73 & 75, vis assoc prof, 77, 79, 81, 83, 85, 87 & 89, vis prof, 92; ed comn, Celest Mech, 76-80; secy, vchmn & chmn, Div Dynamical Astron, Am Astron Soc; vpres, Comn 4, Int Astron Union, 85-88, pres, 88-91; pres, Celestial Mech Inst, 86- *Mem:* AAAS; Am Astron Soc; Am Inst Navig (vpres, 78-79, pres, 79-80); Am Inst Aeronaut & Astronaut; Int Astron Union; Royal Astron Soc. *Res:* Dynamical astronomy; planetary research; general planetary theories; celestial navigation; CCD astrometry; astrodynamics; reference systems. *Mailing Add:* US Naval Observ Washington DC 20392. *Fax:* 202-762-1516; *E-Mail:* pks@spica.usno.navy.mil

SEIDEMAN, WALTER E, PROCESS & PRODUCT DEVELOPMENT, PLANT LAYOUT & DESIGN. *Current Pos:* OWNER & DIR CONSULT FIRM, WALTER E SIEDEMAN, PHD & ASSOCS, 76-; DIR, OKLABS, INC, 89- *Personal Data:* b Washington Co, Wis, Jan 21, 33; m 88, Ruth E Kramer; c Russell, Keith & Bonnie. *Educ:* Univ Wis, BS, 59; Univ Mo, MS, 62, PhD(food sci & nutrit), 66. *Prof Exp:* Inst food sci, Univ Mo, 63-65; food scientist res & develop, Wilson & Co, 65-70, asst mgr, Wilson-Sinclair, 70-71, mgr, 71-72 & Wilson & Co, Inc, 72-76. *Concurrent Pos:* Mem, Sci Adv Comt, Poultry & Egg Inst Am, 65-70, Nat Cheese Coun, 66-68, Am Meat Inst & Res & Develop Assocs Mil Food & Packaging Systs, Inc, 71-82. *Mem:* Inst Food Technologists; Am Meat Sci Asn; Asn Off Analytical Chemists; Am Asn Cereal Chemists; Am Oil Chemists Soc. *Res:* Food product and process development specializing in futher processed meat, poultry and flour based products; technological control systems for processing; sanitation systems; food forensics. *Mailing Add:* 921 NW 72nd Oklahoma City OK 73116. *Fax:* 405-843-6832; *E-Mail:* oklabs19@idt.net

SEIDEN, ABRAHAM, PARTICLE PHYSICS. *Current Pos:* PROG & DIR, INST PARTICLE PHYSICS, UNIV CALIF, SANTA CRUZ, 76- *Personal Data:* b Berlin, Ger, Sept 8, 46. *Educ:* Columbia Univ, BS, 67; Calif Inst Technol, MS, 79; Univ Calif, PhD(physics), 74. *Mem:* Fel Am Phys Soc. *Res:* Particle physics. *Mailing Add:* Inst Particle Physics Univ Calif Santa Cruz CA 95064

SEIDEN, DAVID, MORPHOLOGY, CELL BIOLOGY. *Current Pos:* assoc prof neurosci & cell biol, 79-96, ASSOC DEAN, ROBERT WOOD JOHNSON MED SCH, 90-, PROF NEUROSCI & CELL BIOL, 96- *Personal Data:* b New York, NY, Apr 14, 46; m 67; c 3. *Educ:* City Univ New York, BS, 67; Temple Univ, PhD(anat), 71. *Prof Exp:* Teaching asst anat, Sch Med, Temple Univ, 68-70; instr, 71-73, asst prof anat, Rutgers Univ Med Sch, 73-79. *Mem:* AAAS; Am Asn Anatomists; NY Acad Sci. *Res:* Electron microscopy and cytochemistry of skeletal muscle and cardiac muscle. *Mailing Add:* Dept Neurosci & Cell Biol Robert Wood Johnson Med Sch 675 Hoes Lane Piscataway NJ 08854. *E-Mail:* seiden@umdnj.edu

SEIDEN, HY, GEOLOGY. *Current Pos:* RETIRED. *Personal Data:* b New York, NY, Feb 12, 15. *Educ:* Univ Calif, Los Angeles, BA, 50, MA, 72. *Prof Exp:* Consult, geol sci, 75-80. *Mem:* Geol Soc Am; Am Asn Petrol Geol. *Mailing Add:* 1401 Ming Ave Bakersfield CA 93304-4636

SEIDEN, LEWIS S, PSYCHOPHARMACOLOGY. *Current Pos:* Res assoc pharmacol, Univ Chicago, 63-64, from instr to asst prof pharmacol & psychiat, 65-72, assoc prof, 72-77, PROF PHARMACOL & PSYCHIAT, UNIV CHICAGO, 77- *Personal Data:* b Chicago, Ill, Aug 1, 34; m 62; c 2. *Educ:* Univ Chicago, BA, 56, BS, 58, PhD(biopsychol), 62. *Concurrent Pos:* USPHS fels pharmacol, Gothenburg Univ, 62-63 & Stanford Univ, 64-65; USPHS res grant, 65-, res career develop award, 67-77; career res scientist, 77-82. *Mem:* Am Soc Pharmacol & Exp Therapeut; Am Psychol Asn; Soc Neurosci; Int Col Neuropsychopharmacol. *Res:* Relationships between behavior, drugs and biogenic amines in the brain. *Mailing Add:* Dept Pharmacol & Physiol Sci Univ Chicago 947 E 58th St Chicago IL 60637-1431

SEIDEN, PHILIP EDWARD, IMMUNE SYSTEM SIMULATION. *Current Pos:* mem staff, IBM Corp, 60-66, mgr coop phenomena group, 66-70, mgr physics group, Res Ctr, 70-72, dir, Phys Dept, Res Ctr, 72-76, dir, Gen Sci Dept, 76-77, STAFF MEM, RES CTR, IBM CORP, NY, 78- *Personal Data:* b Troy, NY, Dec 25, 34; m 54, Lois Gotteiner; c Jeffrey & Mark. *Educ:* Univ Chicago, AB, 54, BS, 55, MS, 56; Stanford Univ, PhD(physics), 60. *Prof Exp:* Asst betatron, Univ Chicago, 55-56; scientist solid state physics, Missiles & Space Div, Lockheed Aircraft Corp, 56-59; NSF fel magnetism, Univ Grenoble, 60. *Concurrent Pos:* Vis prof, Ind Univ, Bloomington, 67-68; mem, Solid State Sci Panel, Nat Acad Sci, 70-74; Lady Davis vis scientist, Technion Inst, Israel, 74-75. *Mem:* Am Astron Soc; AAAS; Sigma Xi; fel Am Phys Soc; Am Asn Immunologists. *Res:* Galactic structure; immunology; theoretical investigations in immunology by means of computer simulation of the immune system using a cellular automaton model; percolation model of magnetic active regions on the sun. *Mailing Add:* Res Ctr IBM Corp PO Box 218 Yorktown Heights NY 10598. *E-Mail:* seiden@watson.ibm.com

SEIDENFELD, JEROME, CELL CYCLE REGULATION, POLYAMINE METABOLISM. *Current Pos:* SR SCIENTIST, DEPT DRUGS, AMA, 89- *Personal Data:* b Chomutov, Czech, Dec 31, 45; US citizen; m 71, Linda A Camras; c Justine. *Educ:* Yeshiva Univ, BA, 67; Univ Chicago, MS, 69; Univ Calif, San Francisco, PhD(med chem), 79. *Prof Exp:* Res assoc, Ben May Lab Cancer Res, Univ Chicago, 79-81; from asst prof to assoc prof, Pharmacol & Cancer Ctr, Med Sch, Northwestern Univ, 81-89. *Concurrent Pos:* Mem res comt, Am Cancer Soc, Ill Div; adv bd, Leukemia Res Found. *Mem:* Am Asn Cancer Res; Am Asn Blood Banks; Am Soc Pharmacol & Exp Therapeut; Am Med Infomatics Asn; AAAS. *Res:* Growth control and cell cycle regulation; cancer chemotherapy; polyamine functions in cell proliferation; oncologic and hematologic drugs; medical informatics. *Mailing Add:* 6115 N Springfield Chicago IL 60659. *Fax:* 312-464-5841; *E-Mail:* 70560.17@compuserve.com

SEIDER, WARREN DAVID, CHEMICAL ENGINEERING, COMPUTER SCIENCE. *Current Pos:* from asst prof to assoc prof, 67-84, PROF CHEM ENG, UNIV PA, 84- *Personal Data:* b New York, NY, Oct 20, 41; m 65, Diane Harwith; c Deborah A & Benjamin H. *Educ:* Polytech Inst Brooklyn, BS, 62; Univ Mich, MS, 63, PhD(chem eng), 66. *Honors & Awards:* Comput Chem Eng Award, Am Inst Chem Engrs, 92. *Prof Exp:* Res assoc chem eng, Univ Mich, 66-67. *Concurrent Pos:* Mem, Comput Aids for Chem Engrs Educ Comt, 69-71, chmn, 71-; vis assoc prof, Mass Inst Technol, 74-75 & Denmark Tech Univ, 83; dir, Am Inst Chem Engrs, 84-86. *Mem:* Am Chem Soc; Am Inst Chem Engrs. *Res:* Process analysis, simulation, design and control; phase and chemical equilibria; chemical reaction systems; azeotropic distillation; heat and power integration; Czachralski crystallization; applied numerical methods. *Mailing Add:* Dept Chem Eng Univ Pa 220 S 33rd St Philadelphia PA 19104-6393. *Fax:* 215-573-2093; *E-Mail:* seider@cheme.seas.upenn.edu

SEIDL, FREDERICK GABRIEL PAUL, mathematical physics, nuclear physics, for more information see previous edition

SEIDL, MILOS, PLASMA & SURFACE PHYSICS. *Current Pos:* prof, 69-94, EMER PROF PHYSICS, STEVENS INST TECHNOL, 94- *Personal Data:* b Budapest, Hungary, May 24, 23; m 61; c 1. *Educ:* Prague Tech Univ, BSc, 47, PhD(phys electronics), 49, DSc(physics), 63. *Hon Degrees:* MEng, Stevens Inst Technol, 79. *Honors & Awards:* Ernest Mach Medal, Acad Sci, Czech Repub, 96. *Prof Exp:* Mem staff, Res Inst Vacuum Electronics, Prague, 49-53, group leader vacuum devices, 53-58; group leader plasma physics, Inst Plasma Physics, Prague, 59-68; vis scientist, Stanford Univ, 68-69. *Concurrent Pos:* Lectr, Prague Tech Univ, 60-68; Int Atomic Energy Agency fel, Culham Lab, UK Atomic Energy Authority, 62-63; Jess Davis Mem Res Award, Stevens Inst Technol, 78. *Mem:* Am Vacuum Soc; AAAS; Sigma Xi; fel Am Phys Soc. *Res:* Surface physics; ion sources; charged particle optics; plasma production. *Mailing Add:* Dept Physics Stevens Inst Technol Castle Point Hoboken NJ 07030

SEIDLER, NORBERT WENDELIN, FREE-RADICALS & DISEASE, BIOCHEMISTRY OF MUSCLE. *Current Pos:* ASST PROF BIOCHEM, UNIV HEALTH SCIS COL OSTEOP MED, 91- *Personal Data:* b Esslingen, Ger, May 25, 56; US citizen; m 88, Cheryl Gunn; c 3. *Educ:* Princeton Univ, AB, 81; Univ Med & Dent NJ, PhD(biochem), 88. *Prof Exp:* Biomed lab technologist, Fairleigh Dickinson Univ, 81-83; teaching asst, Univ Med & Dent NJ, 83-88; res assoc, State Univ NY Health Sci Ctr, 88-91. *Concurrent Pos:* Instr, Univ Med & Dent NJ, 85-87. *Mem:* Sigma Xi; Am Soc Biochem & Molecular Biol; Am Osteop Asn; Oxygen Soc; Biochem Soc London. *Res:* Free-radical biology, examining the effects of reactive oxygen molecules on proteins and lipids; cardiac and skeletal muscle tissue; relationship between free-radicals and gastrointestinal diseases, cancer, aging and blood coagulation. *Mailing Add:* Dept Biochem Univ Health Sci Col Osteop Med 2105 Independence Blvd Kansas City MO 64124-2311

SEIDLER, RAMON JOHN, MICROBIOLOGY & RISK ASSESSMENT. *Current Pos:* PROF & RES MICROBIOLOGIST, US ENVIRON PROTECTION AGENCY, 84- *Personal Data:* b Floral Park, NY, Aug 10, 41; m 62, Katherine L Kiever; c 3. *Educ:* San Fernando Valley State Col, BA, 64; Univ Calif, Davis, PhD(microbiol), 68. *Prof Exp:* Asst prof biol, Calif State Univ, Northridge, 67; USPHS fel, Univ Tex M D Anderson Hosp & Tumor Inst, 68-70; from asst prof to prof microbiol, Ore State Univ, 70-84. *Concurrent Pos:* ed, J Molecular Ecol. *Mem:* Am Soc Microbiol; AAAS; fel Am Acad Microbiol. *Res:* Molecular systematics; environmental biology; risk assessment methods for genetically engineered bacteria; transgenic plants. *Mailing Add:* 7397 NE Peitibone Dr Corvallis OR 97330. *Fax:* 541-754-4711; *E-Mail:* seidler@heart.cor.epa.gov

SEIDLER, ROSEMARY JOAN, ANALYTICAL CHEMISTRY, INORGANIC CHEMISTRY. *Current Pos:* Asst prof, 66-73, ASSOC PROF CHEM, CENTENARY COL LA, 73- *Personal Data:* b New Orleans, La, Oct 4, 39. *Educ:* Loyola Univ, BS, 61; Tulane Univ, PhD(analytical chem), 66. *Concurrent Pos:* Qual control chemist, O J Beauty Lotion, 78-. *Mem:* Sigma Xi; Am Chem Soc. *Res:* Magnetic properties of alpha-amido acid metal complexes; metal complexes of azo dyes. *Mailing Add:* Dept Chem Centenary Col 2911 Centenary Blvd Shreveport LA 71104

SEIDMAN, DAVID N(ATHANIEL), MATERIALS SCIENCE. *Current Pos:* prof mat sci & eng, 85-96, WALTER D MURPHY PROF, NORTHWESTERN UNIV, 96- *Personal Data:* b Brooklyn, NY, July 5, 38; m 73, Shoshanah Cohen-Sabban; c Elie, Ariel & Eytan. *Educ:* NY Univ, BS, 60, MS, 62; Univ Ill, PhD(phys metall), 65. *Honors & Awards:* Robert Lansing Hardy Gold Medal, Am Inst Metall Engrs, 66; Alexander von Humboldt Prize, 88; Max Planck Res Prize, 93. *Prof Exp:* Res assoc mat sci, 64-66; from asst prof to prof mat sci & eng, Cornell Univ, 76-85; prof mat sci, Hebrew Univ, 83-85. *Concurrent Pos:* Vis scientist, Israel Inst Technol, 69-70, CEN, Grenoble & CENET, Meylan, France, 81; John Simon Guggenheim mem found fel, 72-73 & 80-81; vis prof, Tel-Aviv Univ, 72; Lady Davis vis prof, Hebrew Univ, 78 & 80-81; chmn, Gordon Conf Phys Metall, 82; sci consult, Argonne Nat Lab, 85-95; Alexander von Humboldt sr fel, Univ Goettingen, 89 & 92; vis sci, Cen Saclay, 89. *Mem:* Fel Am Phys Soc; Am Ceramic Soc; Mat Res Soc; AAAS; Micros Soc Am; fel Minerals Metals Materials Soc. *Res:* Internal interfaces (experimental and computers imulations); point and line imperfections in metals, semiconductors and ceramics; radiation damage in metals and semiconductors; internal interfaces; analytical electron microscopy. *Mailing Add:* Dept Mat Sci & Eng Northwestern Univ 2225 N Campus Dr Evanston IL 60208-3108. *Fax:* 847-467-2265; *E-Mail:* d-seidman@nwu.edu

SEIDMAN, IRVING, pathology, for more information see previous edition

SEIDMAN, JONATHAN G, IMMUNOGENETICS, HUMAN GENETICS. *Current Pos:* from asst prof to assoc prof, 81-88, PROF, HARVARD MED SCH, 88- *Personal Data:* b New York, NY, April 22, 50; m 73; c 2. *Educ:* Harvard Univ, BA, 72; Univ Wis, PhD(molecular biol), 75. *Prof Exp:* Fel, Nat Inst Child Health & Human Develop, NIH, 75-79; staff fel, Lab Molecular Genetics, 79-81. *Res:* Study of the immune system using molecular biologic and genetic techniques; study of the molecular basis of familial hypertrophic cardiomyopathy. *Mailing Add:* Dept Genetics Harvard Med Sch 20 Shattuck St Boston MA 02115

SEIDMAN, MARTIN, CARBOHYDRATE CHEMISTRY. *Current Pos:* GROUP MGR, M SEIDMAN ASSOCS, 85- *Personal Data:* b Brooklyn, NY, June 20, 21; m 44; c 8. *Educ:* Brooklyn Col, AB, 41; Okla State Univ, MS, 48; Univ Wis, PhD(biochem), 50. *Prof Exp:* Chemist, P J Schweitzer Co, 41-42; asst sci aide, US Dept Navy, 42-43; instr gen & org chem, Okla State Univ, 46; res asst biochem, Univ Wis, 48-50; res chemist, Visking Co Div, Union Carbide Corp, 50-55 & Salvo Chem Co, 55-57; group leader process res, A E Staley Mfg Co, 57-71, sr scientist, Fermentation Lab, 71-73, group mgr, Starch Syrups & Fermentation Lab, 73-85. *Mem:* AAAS; Am Chem Soc; Am Inst Chemists; Royal Soc Chem. *Res:* Syrup, starch and cellulose chemistry; fermentation; enzymes; process research. *Mailing Add:* 610 S Monroe Decatur IL 62522

SEIDMAN, STANLEY, PHARMACEUTICALS, COSMETIC CHEMISTRY. *Current Pos:* MGR RES & DEVELOP, ANDREWS LABS, 91- *Personal Data:* m 40, Estelle Goldstein; c Andrew David & Shari Ellen. *Educ:* Brooklyn Col Pharm, BS, 57; St Johns Univ, MS, 65. *Prof Exp:* Res & develop chemist, Pordue Frederick Pharm Co, 59-68; chemist phrenterals, Endo Lab, 70-75; dir res, Ex Lax Inc, 75-79; asst dir res & develop, Whitehall Int, 80-86; res & develop mgr, Del Labs, 86-88; mgr cosmetic chemist, Felton Labs, 88-91. *Res:* Pharmaceutical and cosmetic dose forms for pharmaceutical and cosmetic industry; hospital IV, chemotherapy and hypernzmentation formulation of pharmaceuticals. *Mailing Add:* 34 Crescent Dr Andrew Lab Old Bethpage NY 11804

SEIDMAN, STEPHEN BENJAMIN, FORMAL METHODS IN SOFTWARE ENGINEERING & PARALLEL COMPUTATION. *Current Pos:* PROF COMPUT SCI & DEPT CHAIR, COLO STATE UNIV, 96- *Personal Data:* b New York, NY, Apr 13, 44; m 69, Barbara H Koppe; c Miriam (Heidrun) & Naomi (Katrina). *Educ:* City Col New York, BS, 64; Univ Mich, Ann Arbor, MA, 65, PhD(math), 69. *Prof Exp:* Asst prof math, NY Univ, 69-72; from asst prof to assoc prof, George Mason Univ, 72-84, prof comput sci, 84-90; prof, computer sci & eng & dept head, 90-96. *Concurrent Pos:* Vis scholar anthrop, Ariz State Univ, 82-83. *Mem:* Asn Comput Mach; Inst Elec & Electronics Engrs; Comput Soc. *Res:* Software architectures; models of software architectural styles. *Mailing Add:* 408 Jackson Ave Ft Collins CO 80521. *Fax:* 970-491-2466; *E-Mail:* seidman@cs.colostate.edu

SEIDMAN, THOMAS I(SRAEL), MODELLING, PARTIAL DIFFERENTIAL EQUATIONS. *Current Pos:* PROF MATH, UNIV MD, BALTIMORE COUNTY, 72- *Personal Data:* b New York, NY, Jan 7, 35; m 69, Marjorie Shrivo; c Gregory. *Educ:* Univ Chicago, AB, 52; Columbia Univ, MA, 53; NY Univ, MS, 54, PhD(math), 59. *Prof Exp:* Res asst, Courant Inst Math Sci, NY Univ, 55-58; mathematician, Lawrence Radiation Lab, Univ Calif, Livermore, 58-60, lectr math, Los Angeles, 60-61; mem, Math Res Ctr, Univ Wis, 61-62; mathematician, Boeing Sci Res Lab, Wash, 62-64; assoc prof math, Wayne State Univ, 64-67 & Carnegie-Mellon Univ, 67-72. *Concurrent Pos:* Vis prof, Univ Nice, 80-81; assoc ed, Soc Indust & Appl Math, J Control & Optimization, 94- *Mem:* Am Math Soc; Soc Indust & Appl Math. *Res:* Author of over 120 papers in control theory, especially boundary control for diffusion processes; computational methods for ill-posed problems; partial differential equations, especially semiconductor models; numerical analysis; hybrid systems; manufacturing systems; inverse problems. *Mailing Add:* Dept Math & Statist Univ Md Baltimore County Baltimore MD 21250. *Fax:* 410-455-1066; *E-Mail:* seidman@math.umbc.edu

SEIELSTAD, GEORGE A, RADIO ASTRONOMY. *Current Pos:* ASST DEAN & PROF SPACE STUDIES, UNIV NDAK, 93- *Personal Data:* b Detroit, Mich, Dec 8, 37; m 65; c 3. *Educ:* Dartmouth Col, AB, 59; Calif Inst Technol, PhD(physics), 63. *Prof Exp:* Asst prof physics, Univ Alaska, 63-64; from res fel to sr res fel, Calif Inst Technol, 64-72, res assoc radio astron, 72-84, staff mem, Owens Valley Radio Observ, 66-84; asst dir & scientist, Nat Radio Astron Observ, 84-93. *Concurrent Pos:* Docent, Chalmers Univ Technol, 69-70; fel, John Simon Guggenheim Mem Found, 69-70; vis assoc prof astron & elec eng, Univ Ill, Urbana-Champaign, 78. *Mem:* AAAS; Am Astron Soc; Astron Soc Pac; Int Astron Union; Int Sci Radio Union. *Res:* Interferometry; polarimetry; extragalactic radio sources; galactic magnetic field; supernovae; galactic nuclei. *Mailing Add:* 823 Oakfield Dr Grand Forks ND 58201. *Fax:* 701-777-3016

SEIF, ROBERT DALE, BIOMETRY. *Current Pos:* From asst prof biomet to assoc prof agron, 56-69, PROF AGRON, UNIV ILL, URBANA, 69- *Personal Data:* b Cincinnati, Ohio, May 25, 27; m 50; c 4. *Educ:* Ohio State Univ, BS, 50, MS, 52; Cornell Univ, PhD, 57. *Concurrent Pos:* HEW grant, Univ Minn, 65. *Mem:* Am Soc Agron; Crop Sci Soc Am; Biomet Soc; fel Nat Asn Col Teachers Agron. *Res:* Biological statistics; data processing applied to agriculture, especially agronomy and horticulture. *Mailing Add:* Three Shuman Circle Urbana IL 61801

SEIFEN, ERNST, CARDIOTONIC AGENTS, CALCIUM AGENTS. *Current Pos:* PROF PHARMACOL, TOXICOL & ANESTHESIOL, UNIV ARK MED SCI, 70- *Personal Data:* b Oct 28, 30; c 3. *Educ:* Univ Saarbruecken, Germany, MD & PhD(shock res), 66. *Mem:* NY Acad Sci; Am Soc Pharmacol & Exp Therapeut. *Mailing Add:* Dept Pharmacol Univ Ark Med Sci Slot 611 4301 Markham St Little Rock AR 72205-7119

SEIFER, ARNOLD DAVID, APPLIED MATHEMATICS, SYSTEM ANALYSIS & DESIGN. *Current Pos:* SR PRIN SYSTS ENGR, LOCKHEED SANDERS, 92- *Personal Data:* b Newark, NJ, Apr 22, 40. *Educ:* Rensselaer Polytech Inst, BS, 62, MS, 64, PhD(math), 68. *Prof Exp:* Res specialist appl math, Elec Boat Div, Gen Dynamics Corp, 67-73; mathematician sr staff, Appl Phys Lab, Johns Hopkins Univ, 73-76; sr staff engr, Electronics & Space Div, Emerson Elec Co, 76-80; prin engr, Equip Develop Labs, Raytheon Co, 80-92. *Mem:* Soc Indust & Appl Math; Inst Elec & Electronics Engrs; Sigma Xi. *Res:* Interdisciplinary analytical problems of radar system design; radar detection and tracking; analysis and systems design of fire control systems. *Mailing Add:* 16 Ledgewood Hills Dr Apt 303 Nashua NH 03062

SEIFERT, DEBORAH ROECKNER, STRATEGIC PLANNING, SYSTEMS ENGINEERING. *Current Pos:* PVT CONSULT, 96- *Personal Data:* b Dayton, Ohio, Sept 10, 49; m 71, Tom; c Jessica, Danielle & Jordan. *Educ:* Univ Dayton, BS, 70; Ohio State Univ, MS, 75, PhD(indust & systs eng), 79. *Prof Exp:* Programmer, Univ Dayton Res Inst, 68-71; sr eng scientist, Wright Patterson AFB, 71-79; proj leader oper planning, Allied Signal Engines, 79-80, mgr facil planning, 80-84, factory modernization, 83-84, mfg systs eng, 84-85, indust eng, 88-92 & opers support, 92-93, chmn, Corp CIM Comt, 84-87, sr proj mgr mkt serv, 85-88, dir strategic planning & bus develop, 93-96. *Concurrent Pos:* Mem, 4th Decade Comt, Nat Acad Eng, 93- *Mem:* Nat Acad Eng; Inst Indust Engrs (pres elect, 94-, pres); sr mem Soc Mfg Engrs; Comput & Automated Systs Asn. *Res:* Design and development of advanced concepts and processes for the systems integration of manufacturing enterprises, including the development of strategic business plans. *Mailing Add:* 43 Canterbury St Andover MA 01810. *Fax:* 978-470-8482

SEIFERT, GEORGE, APPLIED MATHEMATICS. *Current Pos:* assoc prof, 55-62, PROF MATH, IOWA STATE UNIV, 62- *Personal Data:* b Jena, Ger, Mar 4, 21; nat US; m 48; c 2. *Educ:* State Univ NY, AB, 42; Cornell Univ, MA, 48, PhD(math), 50. *Prof Exp:* Asst prof math, Univ Nebr, 50-55. *Concurrent Pos:* Mem staff, Res Inst Advan Study, 59-60. *Mem:* Am Math Soc; Math Asn Am; Soc Indust & Appl Math. *Res:* Nonlinear ordinary differential equations; volterra integral equations; functional differential equations. *Mailing Add:* 2526 Kellogg Ave Ames IA 50010-4863

SEIFERT, JOSEF, BIOCHEMICAL TOXICOLOGY, INSECTICIDE TOXICOLOGY. *Current Pos:* assoc prof pesticide chem, 86-94, PROF PESTICIDE CHEM, ENVIRON BIOCHEM, UNIV HAWAII, 94-, DEPT CHMN, 94- *Personal Data:* b Prague, Czech, Sept 21, 42; US citizen; m 88, Yukari Takeuchi; c Daniela. *Educ:* Prague Inst Chem Technol, MSc, 64, PhD(biochem toxicol), 73. *Prof Exp:* Res specialist biochem toxicol, Prague Inst Chem Technol, 72-77; postdoctoral biochemist, Pesticide Chem & Toxicol Lab, Univ Calif, Berkeley, 77-78, from asst to assoc res specialist, 78-85. *Concurrent Pos:* Mem prog comt, Am Chem Soc, 88-95, exec comt, Agrochem Div, 92-94, chair-elect & chair, Hawaii Sect, 96-97; vis assoc chemist, Dept Avian Sci & Environ Toxicol, Univ Calif, Davis, 92-93. *Mem:* Am Chem Soc; Soc Toxicol. *Res:* Investigation of mechanisms of target and nontarget toxic effects of pesticides; insecticide neurotoxicity, teratogenicity and metabolism pesticide residue analysis method development in analytical biochemistry; author of 60 papers. *Mailing Add:* Dept Environ Biochem Univ Hawaii Honolulu HI 96822. *Fax:* 808-956-5037; *E-Mail:* josef@hawaii.edu

SEIFERT, KARL E, GEOLOGY. *Current Pos:* from asst prof to assoc prof, 65-72, chair, 88-91, PROF GEOL, IOWA STATE UNIV, 72- *Personal Data:* b Orangeville, Ohio, Mar 16, 34; m 81, Carole Aselman; c Keith, Lynne & Kendall. *Educ:* Bowling Green State Univ, BS, 56; Univ Wis, MS, 59, PhD(geol), 63. *Prof Exp:* Phys scientist, Geotech Br, Air Force Cambridge Res Labs, 61-65. *Mem:* Am Geophys Union; Geochem Soc; Geol Soc Am. *Res:* Trace element geochemistry of igneous and metamorphic rocks as a function of their origin, evolution and environment with an emphasis on layered stratiform complexes, anorthosite complexes and oceanic basalts. *Mailing Add:* Dept Geol Sci Iowa State Univ Ames IA 50011. *Fax:* 515-294-6049; *E-Mail:* kseifert@iastate.edu

SEIFERT, KEITH ANTHONY, MYCOLOGY. *Current Pos:* RES SCIENTIST, AGRI-FOOD AGR & CAN, OTTAWA. *Honors & Awards:* Alexopoulos Prize, Mycological Soc Am, 93. *Mailing Add:* Agri-Food Agr & Can Ctr Land & Biol Resources Res Ottawa ON K1A 0C6 Can

SEIFERT, LAURENCE C, COMMUNICATIONS. *Current Pos:* VPRES, GLOBAL MFG & ENG, 92- *Personal Data:* b Jersey City, NJ; c 4. *Educ:* NJ Inst Technol, BS. *Honors & Awards:* M Eugene Merchant Mfg Medal, Am Soc Mech Engrs, 95. *Prof Exp:* Var eng, mfg & prod planning positions, Western Elec Kearny Works, NJ, AT&T, dir eng, Oklahoma City Works & Merrimack Valley Works, North Andover, Mass, vpres mfg res & develop, Eng Res Ctr, Princeton, NJ, vpres eng, 57-89, vpres, Commun Prod Sourcing & Mfg, 89-92. *Concurrent Pos:* Dir, Enhanced Training Opportunities Prog, AT&T & Int Brotherhood Elec Workers & Technol Int Purchasing Co; mem, Mfg Studies Bd, Nat Res Coun. *Mem:* Nat Acad Eng; Inst Elec & Electronics Engrs; Inst Indust Eng. *Mailing Add:* 181 Camelot Gate Park Ridge NJ 07656

SEIFERT, RALPH LOUIS, MATHEMATICS. *Current Pos:* from asst prof to assoc prof, 70-90, PROF MATH, HANOVER COL, 90- *Personal Data:* b Alma, Mich, Jan 4, 43; m 79, Margaret Francis. *Educ:* Ind Univ, AB, 63; Univ Calif, Berkeley, MA, 66, PhD(math), 68. *Prof Exp:* Asst prof math, Ind Univ, Bloomington, 68-70. *Concurrent Pos:* Writer, CEMREL-Comprehensive Sch Math Proj, 70-74. *Mem:* Am Math Soc; Math Asn Am; Sigma Xi. *Res:* Foundations of mathematics; cognition of quantitative concepts. *Mailing Add:* Dept Math Hanover Col Hanover IN 47243. *E-Mail:* seifert@hanover.edu

SEIFERT, ROBERT P, AGRICULTURAL ECONOMICS. *Current Pos:* Staff, Pioneer Hi-Bred Int Inc, 51-77, dir, Dept Corn Breeding, 77-84, Plant Breeding Div, 84-87, Res Region I Plant Breeding Div, 87-89, vpres res, 89-90, SR VPRES RES, PIONEER HI-BRED INT INC, 90- *Educ:* Kans State Univ, BS, 50, MS, 52. *Concurrent Pos:* Div coordr, Cereal Res & Data Mgt Depts, Pioneer Hi-Bred Int Inc, 84. *Mailing Add:* Pioneer Hi-Bred Int 700 Capital Sq 400 Locust St Des Moines IA 50309-2331

SEIFERT, WILLIAM EDGAR, JR, ANALYTICAL BIOCHEMISTRY. *Current Pos:* Supvr, Univ Tex Health Sci Ctr, Houston, 75-76, sr res assoc, 76-77, res scientist, Analytical Chem Ctr, 77-82, asst prof, 78-83, ASST PROF, GRAD SCH BIOMED SCI, UNIV TEX HEALTH SCI CTR, HOUSTON, 79-, ASST DIR, ANAL CHEM CTR, 82-, RES ASST PROF,

DEPT BIOCHEM & MOLECULAR BIOL, MED SCH, 83- *Personal Data:* b Bozeman, Mont, Dec 21, 48; m 69; c 4. *Educ:* Marietta Col, BS, 70; Purdue Univ, West Lafayette, MS, 73, PhD(biochem), 75. *Mem:* Am Soc Mass Spectrometry. *Res:* Biochemical applications of mass spectrometry; stable isotopes to study biochemical reactions; biochemical applications of x-ray energy spectrometry; investigation of neurological disfunction by mass spectrometry. *Mailing Add:* Univ Tex Med Sch Health Sci Ctr 301 University Blvd Galveston TX 77555

SEIFERT, WILLIAM W(ALTHER), ELECTRICAL ENGINEERING, SYSTEMS ANALYSIS. *Current Pos:* mem res staff, Field Sta, Mass Inst Technol, 44-45, from asst to res assoc, Dynamic Analysis & Control Lab, 45-51, mem res staff, 51-57, from assoc prof to prof elec eng, 57-70, asst dir, Dynamic Anal Control Lab, 52-55, actg dir, 56, asst to dean eng, 59-62, asst dean, 62-67, dir proj transport, 64-70, PROF CIVIL ENG, MASS INST TECHNOL, 70- *Personal Data:* b Troy, NY, Feb 22, 20; m 43; c 4. *Educ:* Rensselaer Polytech Inst, BEE, 41; Mass Inst Technol, SM, 47, ScD(elec eng), 51. *Prof Exp:* Instr elec eng, Rensselaer Polytech Inst, 41-44. *Mem:* Sr mem Inst Elec & Electronics Eng. *Res:* Transportation, computation and control; engineering education; computer modelling of socioeconomic systems; transportation problems in developing countries; environmental problems. *Mailing Add:* 7 Longfellow Rd Wellesley MA 02181

SEIFF, ALVIN, SPACE SCIENCE, PLANETARY ATMOSPHERES. *Current Pos:* SR RES ASSOC, DEPT METEOROL, SAN JOSE STATE UNIV, 87- *Personal Data:* b Kansas City, Mo, Feb 26, 22; m 68, Julia G Hill; c David, Deborah, Michael & Geoffrey. *Educ:* Univ Mo, BS, 42. *Honors & Awards:* H Julian Allen Award, 82; Von Karman Medal & lectr, Am Inst Aeronaut & Astronaut, 90- *Prof Exp:* Res engr, Tenn Valley Authority, 42-44; tech supvr mass spectros, Uranium Isotope Separation Plant, Oak Ridge, Tenn, 44-46; instr physics, Univ Tenn, 46-48; aeronaut res scientist & chief supersonic free-flight res br, Ames Res Ctr & Aeronaut Lab, NASA, 48-63, chief vehicle environ div, 63-72, staff scientist, Dir Off, 72-76, sr staff scientist, Space Sci Div, Ames Res Ctr, 76-86. *Concurrent Pos:* Mem adv comt basic res, NASA, 71-73, mem res coun, Off Advan Res & Technol, 71-74, mem sci steering group, Pioneer Venus Proj, 72-82; mem entry sci team, Viking Mission to Mars, 69-76; mem grad fac aerospace eng, Univ Kans, 79; mem proj sci group, Galileo Orbiter-Probe Mission to Jupiter, 79-; mem, comt planetary atmosphere, Comt Space Res, 82- & joint working group study team on outer planets, Nat Res Coun & Europ Sci Found, 83; mem, US team partic in Soviet-French Vega balloon mission on planet Venus, 83-86; co-investr, Titan Atmosphere Struct, Europ Space Agency Huygens Probe, 91-; mem, Sci Definition Team, US Mars Network Mission, 90-94; chmn sci adv team atmosphere struct & meteorol, Pathfinder Mission to Mars, 93- *Mem:* Assoc fel Am Inst Aeronaut & Astronaut; Am Astron Soc; Am Geophys Soc; Planetary Soc. *Res:* Physical structure of atmospheres of Mars and Venus; in-situ measurements in the atmosphere of Jupiter; hypervelocity entry into atmospheres of earth and other planets; boundary layers and viscous flows; physical measurements from entry probes and balloons; dynamics of atmospheres of Mars and Venus. *Mailing Add:* 782 Raymundo Ave Los Altos CA 94024-3138. *Fax:* 650-604-6779

SEIFFERT, STEPHEN LOCKHART, NUCLEAR MATERIALS & METALLURGICAL PHYSICS, INDUSTRIAL APPLIED PHYSICS. *Current Pos:* CONSULT, SEIFFERT CONSULT, 97- *Personal Data:* b Iowa, Nov 16, 42. *Educ:* NMex State Univ, BS, 67; Univ Utah, MS, 72, PhD(mat sci), 74. *Prof Exp:* Physicist nuclear effects, White Sands Missile Range, 67; res asst, Univ Utah, 70-73; postdoctoral researcher metal physics, Dept Res Fund, Centre d'Etude Nucleaires, Grenoble, France, 73-75; sr metallurgist nuclear mat, EG&G Idaho Inc, 76-79, scientist light water safety res, 79-81; prin staff mem, BDM Corp, 81-90; independent consult, 90-91; chief scientist, Benchmark Environ Corp, 92-96. *Concurrent Pos:* Affil prof metal, Idaho Nat Eng Lab Educ Prog, 77-81; mem, Educ & Outreach Adv Bd, Inst Space Nuclear Power Studies, Univ NMex, 86-; chief scientist, Benchmark Environ Corp, 97- *Mem:* Am Phys Soc; Am Inst Physics; Am Nuclear Soc; Am Soc Testing & Mat; Laser Inst Am; sr mem Am Inst Aeronaut & Astronaut; Syst Safety Soc. *Res:* Nuclear materials applications and reactor safety research; mechanical properties changes; radiation damage in metals; laser optical/thin films and metrology; waste management/waste minimization; manufacturing process analysis/environmentally conscious manufacturing. *Mailing Add:* 9437 Thornton NE Albuquerque NM 87109

SEIFRIED, ADELE SUSAN CORBIN, VIROLOGY, ELECTRON MICROSCOPY & DRUG SAFETY. *Current Pos:* res chemist biochem & virol, Food & Drug Admin, 74-84, chemist over-the-counter drug eval, 84-86, consumer safety officer, Regulatory Affairs, 86-93, DEP DIR DRUG ADV & CONSULT STAFF, CTR DRUG EVAL & RES, FOOD & DRUG ADMIN, 93- *Personal Data:* b Chicago, Ill, Nov 16, 47; m 70, Harold; c Stephanie N, Rebecca M & Jeffrey E. *Educ:* Purdue Univ, BS, 68; Cornell Univ, MS, 70. *Prof Exp:* Teaching & res asst textile chem, Cornell Univ, 68-70, researcher food sci, 70-73; textile chemist, textile testing lab, Better Fabrics Testing Bur, 73-74. *Concurrent Pos:* Abstractor toxicol, Tracor Jitco, 82, Macro Systs, 83. *Mem:* AAAS; Am Soc Microbiol; Am Chem Soc; Regulatory Affairs Prof Soc. *Res:* Development of regulations for the marketing of prescription and over-the-counter drugs and biologics; biochemical basis of vaccine virus infections; phosphorylation, capping and polyadenylation of vaccine viruses and effects of interferon on their replication. *Mailing Add:* 9205 Quintana Dr Bethesda MD 20817

SEIFRIED, HAROLD EDWIN, BIOCHEMICAL PHARMACOLOGY, TOXICOLOGY. *Current Pos:* PROG DIR, DIV CANCER ETIOLOGY, CHEM & PHYS CARCINOGENESIS BR, NAT CANCER INST, 90- *Personal Data:* b Suffern, NY, Apr 23, 46; m 70, Adele S Corbin; c Stephanie W, Rebecca M & Jeffrey E. *Educ:* Univ Rochester, BS, 68; Cornell Univ, MS, 71, PhD(biochem), 73; Am Bd Toxicol, dipl, 80 & 84, 90; Am Bd Indust Hyg, 86 & 92. *Prof Exp:* Sr chemist protein & lipid chem & cosmetic ingredient toxicity, Explor Prod Res, Avon Prod Inc, 73-74; Roche fel & guest worker carcinogen metab & enzymology activation deactivation, Nat Inst Arthritis, Diabetes, Digestive & Kidney Dis, NIH, 74-76, guest worker, transmethylation of fluorinated catecholamines & interaction with neurotransmitters, Nat Inst Arthritis, Metab & Digestive Dis, 77-88; biochem toxicologist indust hyg, occup & environ health, Stanford Res Inst, 76-77; prin toxicol, Indust Hygienist, Tech Resources Inc, 87-90. *Concurrent Pos:* Indust hygientist, sr toxicologist & prin investr, Sci Policy in Toxicol, Tracor Jitco, Inc, 77-90; risk assessment, Clorox Co, Fuji, 88-90. *Mem:* Am Col Toxicol; Am Indust Hyg Asn; Am Chem Soc; Soc Toxicol; Int Soc Study Xenobiotics. *Res:* Chemical carcinogenesis; metabolism; toxicology; carcinogen and poly-cyclic aromatic hydrocarbon metabolism and binding to nucleic acid; enzymology of activation-deactivation; lipid biosynthesis; toxic substances relating to occupational exposure and carcinogenesis, industrial hygiene toxicology, asbestos analysis; chemical synthesis. *Mailing Add:* 9205 Quintana Dr Bethesda MD 20817-2001. *Fax:* 301-496-1040; *E-Mail:* seifreh@nihcdcei.gov

SEIFTER, ELI, NUTRITION. *Current Pos:* asst prof, 62-72, ASSOC PROF BIOCHEM, ALBERT EINSTEIN COL MED, 72-, ASSOC PROF SURG, 76- *Personal Data:* b Cleveland, Ohio, Apr 17, 19; m 46; c 1. *Educ:* Ohio State Univ, AB, 48; Univ Pa, PhD(bot), 53. *Prof Exp:* Asst instr bot, Univ Pa, 50-52; res biochemist, Monsanto Chem Co, 52-57; biochemist, Lond Island Jewish Hosp, NY, 57-62. *Mem:* AAAS; Am Chem Soc; Am Inst Nutrit; Sigma Xi. *Res:* Metabolic pathways; amino acids; metabolic effects. *Mailing Add:* Dept Biochem & Surg Albert Einstein Col Med Bronx NY 10461

SEIFTER, SAM, BIOCHEMISTRY. *Current Pos:* from assoc prof to prof biochem, 56-90, from actg chmn to chmn, 75-76, DISTINGUISHED EMER PROF BIOCHEM, ALBERT EINSTEIN COL MED, 90- *Personal Data:* b Cleveland, Ohio, Dec 1, 16; m 43, Eleanor Charms; c Madeleine & Julian. *Educ:* Ohio State Univ, BA, 39; Western Res Univ, MS & PhD(biochem), 44. *Prof Exp:* Asst immunol, Western Res Univ, 40-44, instr, Med Sch, 44-45, sr instr immunochem, 45; asst prof biochem, Long Island Col Med, 45-49; assoc prof, Col Med, State Univ NY Downstate Med Ctr, 49-53; biochemist, Long Island Jewish Hosp, 54-56. *Mem:* Am Chem Soc; Am Soc Biol Chemists; Biophys Soc; AAAS; Harvey Soc. *Res:* Protein chemistry; enzymology; immunochemistry; connective tissues. *Mailing Add:* Dept Biochem Albert Einstein Col Med 1300 Morris Park Ave Bronx NY 10461

SEIGEL, ARNOLD E(LLIOTT), PHYSICS, MECHANICAL ENGINEERING. *Current Pos:* DIR INSTRNL TV, UNIV MD, COLLEGE PARK, 75- *Personal Data:* b Washington, DC, July 16, 23; m 51; c 3. *Educ:* Univ Md, BS, 44; Mass Inst Technol, MS, 47; Univ Amsterdam, ScD, 52. *Prof Exp:* Mech engr, Signal Corps, US Dept Army, 45 & US Naval Res Lab, 45-46; air conditioning engr, William Brown Consult Engrs, 47; mech engr & physicist, US Naval Ord Lab, 48-61, chief Ballistics Dept, 61-74. *Concurrent Pos:* Lectr, Univ Md, 54-; consult, 58- *Mem:* Am Inst Physics; Am Inst Aeronaut & Astronaut; Am Phys Soc. *Res:* Gas dynamics; interior ballistics; thermodynamics; hydrodynamics; high speed flow; stress waves in solids; aeronautical engineering. *Mailing Add:* 3302 Pauline Dr Chevy Chase MD 20815

SEIGEL, HAROLD OASER, INDUCED POLARIZATION & GRAVITY, MAGNETICS. *Current Pos:* pres, 64-92, CHMN BD, SCINTREX LTD, 92- *Personal Data:* b Toronto, Ont, Mar 8, 24; m 68, Marilyn Silver; c Joel, Laurie & Marcie. *Educ:* Univ Toronto, BA, 46, MA, 47, PhD(geophys), 49. *Honors & Awards:* J Tuzo Wilson Medal, Can Geophys Union, 85; A O Dufresne Award, Can Inst Mining & Metall, 88; Maurice Ewing Gold Medal, Soc Explor Geophys, 95; Asn Explor Geophysicists India Medal, 96; Officer Order Can, 97. *Prof Exp:* Asst mgr, Newmont Explor Ltd, 49-52, consult geophys, 52-56; pres, Seigel Assoc Ltd, 56-64. *Mem:* Soc Explor Geophys; Am Geophys Union; Geol Asn Can; Can Inst Mining & Metall; Asn Explor Geophysicists. *Res:* Applied geophysical methods including electrical, gravity, magnetic and luminescence. *Mailing Add:* 9 Oxbow Rd North York ON M3B 1Z9 Can. *Fax:* 905-669-5132; *E-Mail:* scintrex@scintrex1ld.com

SEIGEL, RICHARD ALLYN, EVOLUTIONARY ECOLOGY, CONSERVATION BIOLOGY. *Current Pos:* asst prof, 87-91, ASSOC PROF ECOL, SOUTHEASTERN LA UNIV, 91- *Personal Data:* b Brooklyn, NY, Aug 2, 54; m 76. *Educ:* Rutgers Univ, BA, 77; Univ Cent Fla, 79; Univ Kans, PhD(ecol & systematics), 84. *Prof Exp:* Postdoctoral assoc, Savannah River Ecol Lab, 84-87. *Concurrent Pos:* Consult, Int Wildlife Coalition, 82-91, La Audubon Soc, 88-89; assoc ed, J Herpet, 89-91. *Mem:* Am Soc Naturalists; Soc Study Amphibians & Reptiles; Am Soc Ichthyologists & Herpetologists; Soc Conserv Biol. *Res:* Evolutionary ecology of amphibians and reptiles, with emphasis on evolution of life-history strategies; conservation biology, especially of non-game species. *Mailing Add:* Dept Biol Sci Southeast La Univ 500 Western Ave Hammond LA 70402-0001

SEIGER, HARVEY N, ELECTROCHEMICAL IMPREGNATION, APPLICATION OF KINETICS TO ELECTROCHEMICAL COLLOIDAL. *Current Pos:* PRIN CONSULT, ELECTROCHEM SCI & TECHNOL ASSOCS, 93- *Personal Data:* b New York, NY, June 20, 24; m 48, Gloria; c Kenneth W & Mark B. *Educ:* City Univ NY, BS, 49, MA, 52; Polytech Inst, PhD(chem), 62. *Honors & Awards:* IR-100 Award Indust Res, 67. *Prof Exp:* Dir res, Gulton Industs, 60-69; dir electrochem, Div Textron, Heliotek, 69-75; vpres res, Yardney Elec Corp, 75-79; consult, Harvey N Seiger Assocs, 79-83; prog mgr, Westinghouse Naval Systs Div. *Mem:*

Electrochem Soc. *Res:* Electrode phenomena with respect to energy storage; physical chemistry-kinetics; thermodynamics; irreversible processes-with batteries as the end product; theoretical electrochemistry; charge transfer at interfaces. *Mailing Add:* 6120 Bluegrass Dr Boynton Beach FL 33437. E-Mail: hnseiger@juno.com

SEIGER, MARVIN BARR, GENETICS. *Current Pos:* from asst prof to assoc prof, 65-86, PROF GENETICS, WRIGHT STATE UNIV, 87- *Personal Data:* b New York, NY, Nov 18, 26; m 60; c 3. *Educ:* Duquesne Univ, BS, 50; Univ Tex, MA, 53; Univ Calif, Los Angeles, MA, 59; Univ Toronto, PhD(genetics), 62. *Prof Exp:* Vis asst prof genetics, Purdue Univ, 62-63; res assoc, Univ Notre Dame, 63-64; NIH trainee biol, Univ Rochester, 64-65. *Concurrent Pos:* Vis res prof, Univ Belgrade, Yugoslavia, 87; vis prof, Fed Univ, Brazil, 76-79. *Mem:* Soc Study Evolution; Genetics Soc Am; Am Soc Zool; Animal Behav Soc; Am Soc Naturalists; Sigma Xi. *Res:* Population dynamics; quantitative inheritance; behavior and ecological genetics. *Mailing Add:* Dept Biol Sci Wright State Univ Dayton OH 45435

SEIGLE, L(ESLIE) L(OUIS), PHYSICAL METALLURGY. *Current Pos:* prof, 65-87, EMER PROF MAT SCI, STATE UNIV NY, STONY BROOK, 87- *Personal Data:* b Dumbarton, Scotland, June 13, 17; m 50, Mary Mantanan; c William, Roxanne & Jonathan. *Educ:* Cooper Union, BChE, 41; Univ Pa, MS, 48; Mass Inst Technol, ScD, 52. *Prof Exp:* Res metallurgist, Int Nickel Co, 38-46; proj leader, Univ Pa, 46-48; instr metall, Drexel Inst Technol, 48; res asst labs, Gen Elec Corp, 48 & Mass Inst Technol, 48-51; head fundamental metall sect, Sylvania Elec Prod, Inc, Gen Tel & Electronics Corp, 51-56, mgr metall lab, Res Labs, 56-65. *Concurrent Pos:* Adj prof, NY Univ, 52-60; mem refractory metals panel, Mat Adv Bd, Nat Acad Sci, 55-65 & comt on coatings, 66-69; NY Univ exchange metall deleg, Moscow Steel Inst, USSR, 57; vis prof, Univ Pittsburgh, 64-65. *Mem:* Am Soc Metals; Am Inst Mining, Metall & Petrol Engrs; Sigma Xi. *Res:* Thermodynamics of alloys, diffusion and sintering of metals; protective coatings on metals. *Mailing Add:* One Saywood Lane Stony Brook NY 11790. E-Mail: lseigle@ccmail.sunysb.edu

SEIGLER, DAVID STANLEY, BOTANY, ORGANIC CHEMISTRY. *Current Pos:* asst prof bot, 70-76, assoc prof, 76-80, PROF PLANT BIOL, UNIV ILL, URBANA, 85- *Personal Data:* b Wichita Falls, Tex, Sept 11, 40; m 61, Janice K Cline; c Dava K (Carson) & Rebecca J (Musgrove). *Educ:* Southwestern State Col, Okla, BS, 61; Univ Okla, PhD(org chem), 67. *Honors & Awards:* Fulbright Hays Lectr, 76. *Prof Exp:* Assoc chem, Northern Regional Lab, USDA, 67-68; fel bot, Univ Tex, Austin, 68-70. *Concurrent Pos:* Nat Acad Sci, exchange with Ger Democrat Rep, 80. *Mem:* Bot Soc Am; Am Chem Soc; Soc Econ Bot; Soc Chem Ecol; Am Soc Plant Taxonomists; Phytochem Soc NAm. *Res:* Phytochemistry; study of secondary plant compounds; biochemical systematics; roles of plant secondary compounds in biological interactions; plant-fungus, plant-plant and plant-insert interactions. *Mailing Add:* Dept Plant Biol Univ Ill 505 S Goodwin Urbana IL 61801. *Fax:* 217-244-7246; E-Mail: d-seigler@uiuc.edu

SEIGLER, HILLIARD FOSTER, SURGERY, IMMUNOLOGY. *Current Pos:* NIH res fel immunogenetics, 65-67, asst prof surg, 67-70, asst prof immunol, 69-70, assoc prof surg & immunol, 71-78, CO-PROG DIR, CLIN CANCER RES UNIT, MED CTR, DUKE UNIV, 70-, PROF SURG 78- *Personal Data:* b Asheville, NC, Apr 19, 34; m 61; c 4. *Educ:* Univ NC, BA, 56, MD, 60. *Honors & Awards:* Henry C Fordham Award, 62. *Concurrent Pos:* Clin investr, Vet Admin Hosp, Durham, NC, 67-70, chief surg, 71-72. *Mem:* Transplantation Soc; Am Col Surgeons; Int Primatol Soc; Asn Acad Surgeons; Soc Univ Surgeons. *Res:* Immunogenetics of transplantation; tumor immunology. *Mailing Add:* Duke Univ Med Ctr Durham NC 27710

SEIKEN, ARNOLD, MATHEMATICS. *Current Pos:* ASSOC PROF MATH, UNION COL, 67-, CHMN DEPT, 68- *Personal Data:* b New York, NY, Feb 23, 28; m 55; c 3. *Educ:* Syracuse Univ, BA, 51; Univ Mich, MA, 54, PhD(math), 63. *Prof Exp:* Instr math, Southern Ill Univ, 58-60; asst prof, Oakland Univ, 61-64; assoc prof, Univ RI, 64-67. *Mem:* Am Math Soc; Math Asn Am. *Res:* Differential geometry, particularly theory of connections. *Mailing Add:* Dept Math Union Col Schenectady NY 12308-2311

SEIL, FREDRICK JOHN, NEUROLOGY, NEUROPATHOLOGY. *Current Pos:* PROF NEUROL, ORE HEALTH SCI UNIV, 78-, PROF CELL DEVELOP BIOL, 90-; DIR, VET ADMIN OFF REGENERATION RES PROG, 81- *Personal Data:* b Nove Sove, Yugoslavia, Nov 9, 33; US citizen; m 55, Daryle F Wolfers; c Jonathan F & J P Timothy. *Educ:* Oberlin Col, AB, 56; Stanford Univ, MD, 60. *Prof Exp:* Resident neurol, Stanford Univ, 61-64, fel, 64-65; fel neurol, Mt Sinai Hosp, New York & Albert Einstein Col Med, 65-66; asst prof neurol, Stanford Univ, 69-75; assoc prof, Health Sci Ctr, Univ Ore, 76-78. *Concurrent Pos:* Staff neurologist, Vet Admin Hosp, Palo Alto, 69-76 & clin investr, Portland, Ore, 76-79, staff neurologist, 79-81. *Mem:* Int Brain Res Orgn; Soc Neurosci; Am Neurol Asn; Am Asn Neuropathologists; Int Soc Develop Neurosci; Am Soc Neural Transplantation. *Res:* Tissue culture studies of structure and function of the nervous system, of myelination and demyelination, of the pathophysiology of neurotoxic agents, and of neural development, regeneration, and plasticity. *Mailing Add:* Off Regeneration Res Prog Vet Admin Med Ctr 3710 SW US Vet Hosp Rd Portland OR 97201. *Fax:* 503-721-7906; E-Mail: seilf@ohsu.edu

SEILER, DAVID GEORGE, SOLID STATE PHYSICS. *Current Pos:* DIV CHIEF, PROG MAT RES, NSF, 90- *Personal Data:* b Green Bay, Wis, Dec 17, 40; m 63; c 2. *Educ:* Case Western Res Univ, BS, 63; Purdue Univ, Lafayette, MS, 65, PhD(physics), 69. *Prof Exp:* Physicist, Nat Bur Stand, 72-73; from temp asst prof to assoc prof physics, NTex State Univ, 69- *Mem:* Am Phys Soc; Optical Soc Am. *Res:* Semiconductors; energy band structures; scattering mechanisms. *Mailing Add:* Nat Inst Stand & Technol Bldg 225 Rm B344 Gaithersburg MD 20899

SEILER, FRITZ A, HAZARDOUS MATERIAL MANAGEMENT, RISK ANALYSIS & MANAGEMENT. *Current Pos:* sr tech assoc, 90-92, DISTINGUISHED TECH ASSOC, IT CORP, 92- *Personal Data:* b Basel, Switz, Dec 20, 31; US citizen; m 64; c Monica, Simone & Daniel. *Educ:* Kantonale Handelsschule, Basel, Switz, 51; Univ Basel, Switz, PhD (physics). *Prof Exp:* Res assoc, Univ Wis, Madison, 62-63; sci assoc physics, Univ Basel, Switz, 63-69, from lectr to asst prof, 75-80; sr scientist, Lovelace Inhalation Toxicol Res Inst, 80-90. *Concurrent Pos:* Staff officer, Swiss Army Staff, 64-74; consult, Swiss Dept Defense, 68-74 & Lung Model Task Force, NCRP, 89; cmndg officer, Swiss Army Radiation Labs, 68-74; vis scientist, Lawrence Berkeley Labs, 74-75, consult, 76, guest scientist, 78; mem, Comt NI4, Am Nat Stand Inst, 86-, mgt coun, 87- *Mem:* Fel Am Phys Soc; Health Physics Soc; Soc Risk Analysis; Am Statist Asn. *Res:* Risk assessment and management; dose effect relationships; uncertainty analysis; statistical sampling; health effects of one or more toxicants; route selection for hazardous material transports; methodologies risk analysis and management; risk comparison; risk-cost-benefit analysis; life cycle. *Mailing Add:* 4101 Lara Dr NE Albuquerque NM 87111

SEILER, GERALD JOSEPH, PLANT BREEDING, GERM PLASM. *Current Pos:* res technician agron & crop physiol, 74-80, RES BOTANIST, AGR RES SERV, USDA, BUSHLAND, TEX, 80- *Personal Data:* b New Rockford, NDak, June 4, 49; m 74, Barbara A Meier; c Jody & Jeremy. *Educ:* NDak State Univ, BA, 71, MS, 73, PhD(bot), 80. *Prof Exp:* Fel bot & biol, NDak State Univ, 71-73; asst, State Biol Surv Kans, 73-74. *Concurrent Pos:* Cur wild sunflower germ plasm, Agr Res Serv, US Dept Agr, 80-; US coordr, Food & Agr Orgn, UN, Rome Italy, 81- *Mem:* Am Soc Plant Taxonomist; fel Agron Soc Am; fel Crop Sci Soc Am; Bot Soc Am; Sigma Xi. *Res:* Breeding of native species of sunflowers for specific characters of insect pest and disease resistance for commercial production; incompatibility of the species and development of techniques for interspecific crossing and physiology of stress and drought in wild species. *Mailing Add:* PO Box 5677 Fargo ND 58105. *Fax:* 701-239-1346; E-Mail: seiler@badlands.nodak.edu

SEILER, STEVEN WING, PLASMA PHYSICS. *Current Pos:* SR RES PHYSICIST, R&D ASSOCS, 79- *Personal Data:* b Glen Ridge, NJ, May 31, 50; m 72. *Educ:* Cornell Univ, BA, 72; Princeton Univ, MA, 74, PhD(physics), 77. *Prof Exp:* Res assoc neutron diagnostics, Plasma Physics Lab, Princeton Univ, 77-79. *Mem:* Am Phys Soc; Sigma Xi; Inst Elec & Electronics Engrs. *Res:* Neutron and alpha particle diagnostics on fusion research tokamaks and micro instability research on Q-machines. *Mailing Add:* 7200 Dogue Forest Ct Alexandria VA 22315

SEILHEIMER, JACK ARTHUR, ZOOLOGY, LIMNOLOGY. *Current Pos:* from instr to assoc prof, 63-73, PROF BIOL, SOUTHERN COLO STATE COL, 73- *Personal Data:* b Kalamazoo, Mich, Nov 12, 35; m 54; c 4. *Educ:* Western Mich Univ, BS, 60; Univ Louisville, PhD(zool), 63. *Prof Exp:* Instr limnol, Univ Louisville, 62. *Concurrent Pos:* Vis lectr, Colo-Wyo Acad Sci, 65 & 66; consult water pollution, Pueblo City County Health Dept, 66- *Mem:* AAAS; Am Soc Limnol & Oceanog; Ecol Soc Am; Sigma Xi. *Res:* Stream ecology; algology; plankton; ichthyology; pollution biology; radioecology. *Mailing Add:* 1 Remington Ct Pueblo CO 81008-1812

SEILING, ALFRED WILLIAM, SEMICONDUCTOR ASSEMBLY PROCESSES, FORMULATION OF HIGH PERFORMANCE EPOXY. *Current Pos:* CONSULT, SEILING & ASSOCS, 84- *Personal Data:* b Watseka, Ill, May 28, 36; m 57; c 4. *Educ:* Blackburn Col, BA, 57; Ind Univ, PhD(chem), 62. *Prof Exp:* Res chemist, Morton Chem, Div Morton Int, 61-64, tech serv supvr, 64-67, tech mgr electronics, 67-74, group mgr, 74-77, gen mkt electronic mat, 77-79, vpres gen mkt, 79-83, vpres mkt dynachem, 83-84. *Res:* Development of materials and processes for assembly and packaging of integrated circuits and other electronic components; systems are fabricated from plastics, ceramics and metals by molding, photolithography and adhesive bonding processes; formulation of high performance epoxy, silicone and polyimide adhesives and molding compounds. *Mailing Add:* 2 Windsor Rise Monterey CA 93940. *Fax:* 408-375-0654

SEIM, HENRY JEROME, ANALYTICAL CHEMISTRY. *Current Pos:* RETIRED. *Personal Data:* b Granite Falls, Minn, Mar 20, 19; m 46, Helen Steen; c David J & Carol (Whiteneck). *Educ:* St Olaf Col, BA, 41; Mont Sch Mines, MS, 43; Univ Wis, PhD(chem), 49. *Honors & Awards:* Award Merit, Am Soc Testing & Mat, 85. *Prof Exp:* Asst chem, Mont Sch Mines, 41-43, instr, 45-46; res & analytical chemist, Boeing Airplane Co, 43-45; asst chem, Univ Wis, 46-49; from instr to assoc prof, Univ Nev, 49-62; mgr chem res, Res Div, Allis-Chambers, Wis, 62-67; dir, 67-69; mgr analsis res & serv, Kaiser Aluminum & Chem Corp, 69-82; sr res assoc, Ctr Technol, 82-86. *Mem:* Am Chem Soc; Am Indust Hyg Asn; Am Soc Testing & Mat. *Res:* Instrumental analysis; ion exchange; electrochemistry. *Mailing Add:* 931 Val Aire Pl Walnut Creek CA 94596

SEINER, JEROME ALLAN, POLYMER COATINGS & PAINTS, METAL TREATMENTS & PRETREATMENTS. *Current Pos:* Engr trainee to var positions, 54-84, dir Advan res, 84-94, DIR, DISCOVERY GROUP, PPG INDUST, 95- *Personal Data:* b Pittsburgh, Pa, Aug 21, 32; m 55, Nancy Schor; c Harriet (Litwin), Henry, Robert & David. *Educ:* Carnegie Mellon Univ, BS, 54, BS, 60; Case Western Res Univ, MEND, 70. *Concurrent Pos:* Lectr math & econ, Carnegie Mellon Univ, 61-80; ed, I&EC Prod Res & Develop, Am Chem Soc J, 79-86, sr ed, I&EC Res, 86-; chmn chem & physics coatings & films, Gordon Res Conf , 87 & Vis Comt, Mat Sci & Eng Dept, Univ Pittsburgh, 88-; elected pres, PPG Collegium, 90- *Mem:* Am Chem Soc; Federated Socs Coatings Technol. *Res:* Coatings and metal treatments; synthesis; formulation and testing of conventional and fire retardant materials; granted 85 US patents. *Mailing Add:* PPG Industs Res & Develop Ctr PO Box 9 Allison Park PA 15101-0009. *Fax:* 412-492-5522; *E-Mail:* seiner@ppg.com

SEINER, JOHN MILTON, AEROSPACE ENGINEERING, ACOUSTICS. *Current Pos:* AEROSPACE ENGINEER JET NOISE, NASA LANGLEY RES CTR, 74- *Personal Data:* b Upper Darby, Pa, Feb 23, 44; m 68; c 4. *Educ:* Drexel Univ, BSME, 67; Pa State Univ, MSAE, 69, PhD(aeorspace eng), 74. *Mem:* Sigma Xi. *Res:* Supersonic jet noise; nonlinear acoustics; physics of high speed turbulence; laser velocimetry and raman spectroscopy. *Mailing Add:* 209 Sheffield Rd Williamsburg VA 23188-1518

SEINFELD, JOHN H, CHEMICAL ENGINEERING. *Current Pos:* LOUIS E NOHL PROF CHEM ENG & CHMN, DIV ENG & APPL SCI, CALIF INST TECHNOL, 67- *Personal Data:* b Elmira, NY, Aug 3, 42. *Educ:* Univ Rochester, BS, 64; Princeton Univ, PhD(chem eng), 67. *Honors & Awards:* Donald P Eckman Award, Am Automatic Control Coun, 70; Curtis W McGraw Res Award, Am Soc Eng Educ, 76; Allan P Colburn Award, Am Inst Chem Engrs, 76; Pub Serv Award, NASA, 80; William H Walker Award, Am Inst Chem Engrs; George Westinghouse Award, Am Soc Eng Educ; Creative Advances Environ Sci & Technol Award, Am Chem Soc, 93. *Concurrent Pos:* Camille & Henry Dreyfus Found teacher-scholar grant, 72; Inst lectr, Am Inst Chem Engrs, 80. *Mem:* Nat Acad Eng; Am Inst Chem Engrs; Am Chem Soc; Air Waste Mgmt Asn; Am Soc Eng Educ; Am Acad Arts & Scis. *Res:* Atmospheric chemistry and physics. *Mailing Add:* Div Eng & Appl Sci Calif Inst Technol Pasadena CA 91125

SEIPEL, JOHN HOWARD, NEUROLOGY, LAW, PENOLOGIC MEDICINE. *Current Pos:* CHIEF MED OFFICER, DC DEPT CORRECTIONS, 79- *Personal Data:* b Pittsburgh, Pa, Nov 9, 25; m 59, Janice L Duffney; c Janice, John, Tabitha & William. *Educ:* Carnegie Inst Technol, BS, 46, MS, 47; Harvard Univ, MD, 54; Northwestern Univ, PhD(chem), 58; George Mason Univ, JD, 90; Am Bd Forensic Examr, dipl; Am Bd Forensic Med, dipl. *Honors & Awards:* S Weir Mitchell Award, Am Acad Neurol, 66. *Prof Exp:* Intern, Pa Hosp, Philadelphia, 54-55, resident surg, 55-56; res scientist, Nat Cancer Inst, 56-58; asst resident neurol, Mt Alto Vet Admin Hosp, Washington, DC, 58; chief resident, Georgetown Univ Hosp, 59 & DC Gen Hosp, 60; res fel, Georgetown Univ Hosp, 60-61, from clin instr to asst prof neurol, 61-79; dir neurol res, Friends Med Sci Res Ctr, Inc, 66-78. *Concurrent Pos:* Neurol attending staff, Georgetown Univ Med Ctr, 61-79, Fairfax Hosp, Va, 61-79; Greenwalt fel neuroanat, NY Univ, 61; chief neurol lab, Georgetown Clin Res Inst, Fed Aviation Admin, 61-66, sr aviation med examr, Aviation Med Serv, 61-, consult neurol, 72-92, sr consult, 92-; consult neurol, Res Div, Md State Dept Ment Hyg & Spring Grove State Hosp, 66-78; staff neurologist, Neurol Serv, US Vet Admin Hosp, Washington, DC, 67-69, chief electrodiag sect, 68-69; dir neurol res, Md Psychiat Res Ctr, 69-78; attend neurologist, Nat Children's Rehab Ctr, Leesburg, Va, 72-73, Fauquier Hosp, Warrenton, 76-78; res assoc, Dept Psychiat, Md Psychiat Res Ctr, Baltimore, 77-78. *Mem:* Fel Am Col Clin Pharmacol; Sigma Xi; fel Brit Royal Col Med; fel Am Col Legal Med; fel Am Col Forensic Examiners. *Res:* Application of physical science and technology to the solution of medical and legal problems, particularly in neurology; aerospace medicine; environmental sciences; pharmacology. *Mailing Add:* 5335 Summit Dr Fairfax VA 22030

SEIREG, ALI A, SYSTEMS DESIGN, ROBOTICS. *Current Pos:* PROF MECH ENG, UNIV WIS-MADISON, 65- *Personal Data:* b Mahalla, Egypt, Oct 26, 27; US citizen; m 54; c 2. *Educ:* Univ Cairo, BSc, 48; Univ Wis, PhD(mech eng), 54. *Honors & Awards:* George Washington Award, Am Soc Eng Educ, 70; Richard Mem Award, Am Soc Mech Engrs, 73; E P Connell Award, Am Gear Mfg Asn, 74. *Prof Exp:* Lectr mech eng, Univ Cairo, 54-56; adv engr res & develop, Falk Corp, 56-59; prof theory appl mech, Marquette Univ, 59-65. *Concurrent Pos:* Consult, Falk Corp, 59-, Vet Admin Res, 64-, NSF, 80-82, & Jet Propulsion Lab, 81-82; ed, Comput in Mech Eng, 81- & SOMA, Eng Human Body, 86-; pres, Gear Res Inst, Am Soc Mech Engrs, 84- & chmn, Coun Eng, 85- *Mem:* Am Soc Mech Engrs (sr vpres, 85-); Am Soc Eng Educ; Soc Exp Stress Anal; Am Gear Mfg Asn; hon mem Chinese Mech Eng Soc; int mem USSR Acad Sci. *Res:* Mechanical systems analysis; computer aided design; robotics; biomechanics; rehabilitation devices; underwater systems; gears and power transmission; friction lubrication and wear. *Mailing Add:* Dept Mech Eng 237 Univ Fla Gainesville FL 32611-2002

SEITCHIK, JEROLD ALAN, SOLID STATE PHYSICS. *Current Pos:* SR MEM TECH STAFF, TEX INSTRUMENTS, INC, 75- *Personal Data:* b Philadelphia, Pa, Jan 26, 35. *Educ:* Univ Del, BS, 56; Univ Pa, PhD(physics), 63. *Prof Exp:* Mem tech staff, Physics Res, Bell Tel Labs, 63-65; sr physicist, Univac Div, Sperry Rand Corp, 65-75. *Mem:* Am Phys Soc. *Res:* Nuclear magnetic resonance; transport properties of thin films; acoustic delay lines; magnetic bubble domains; bipolar device simulation. *Mailing Add:* 6927 Echo Bluff Dr Dallas TX 75248

SEITELMAN, LEON HAROLD, COMPUTER AIDED DESIGN, COMPUTER AIDED ENGINEERING. *Current Pos:* Asst proj eng, 67-70, assoc res scientist, 70-73, SR APPL MATHEMATICIAN, PRATT & WHITNEY, 73- *Personal Data:* b New York, NY, May 27, 40; m 62, Brenda Auerbach; c David J & Ellen R. *Educ:* Cooper Union, BEE, 60; Univ Chicago, SM, 63; Brown Univ, PhD(appl math), 67. *Concurrent Pos:* Lectr, Trinity Col, Hartford, Conn, 68-70 & Vis Lectureship Prog, Soc Indust & Appl Math, 76-84, 92-; adj prof, Univ Conn, 75-76; contrib ed, Soc Indust & Appl Math, 78-, mem, Prog Comt, 82-84 & 88-90, Educ Comt, 86- & Joint Comt Employment Opportunities, 89-, chmn, Vis Lectureship Prog, 79-84, 92-, K-12 Panel, 87- & Joint Comt Employment Opportunities, 91; vis prof, Brown Univ, Providence, RI, 84-85; mem adv bd, Proj to Increase Mastory Math & Sci Conn, 80-, Math Contest Modeling, 84-; mem, Sci Policy Comt, Math Asn Am, 95-, Comt Math & Environ, 96-, Comt Indust & Govt Math, 96- *Mem:* Soc Indust & Appl Math; Am Math Soc; Math Asn Am; AAAS; Sigma Xi; NY Acad Sci. *Res:* Development of curve and surface fitting procedures and associated programming systems for the efficient and accurate treatment of data throughout design, development and manufacturing. *Mailing Add:* 110 Cambridge Dr Glastonbury CT 06033. *Fax:* 860-565-9615

SEITZ, ANNA W, DEVELOPMENTAL BIOLOGY. *Current Pos:* ASST PROF BIOL, UNIV MASS, 85- *Personal Data:* b Hong Kong, China, Dec 23, 41; m 69; c 3. *Educ:* Wellesley Col, BA, 63; Univ Pa, PhD(anat), 80. *Prof Exp:* Fel biol, Sloan-Kettering Inst, 80-85. *Mem:* Soc Develop Biol; Am Soc Cell Biol; Europ Soc Develop Biol; Am Soc Microbiol. *Res:* Developmental genetics of mammalian embryos; genetic engineering of animals. *Mailing Add:* 200 N Valley Rd Pelham MA 01002

SEITZ, EUGENE W, MICROBIOL BIOCHEMISTRY, BACTERIOLOGY. *Current Pos:* RETIRED. *Personal Data:* b Regina, Sask, Sept 27, 35; m 63, 85; c 3. *Educ:* Univ Sask, BSA, 57; Ore State Univ, MSc, 59, PhD(microbiol), 62. *Prof Exp:* Res asst bact, Ore State Univ, 57-59; res fel biochem, 59-62; microl res ins, Res Br, Can Dept Agr, 62-63, res officer, 63-64, res scientist, Food Res Inst, 64-67, proj leader flavor res, 67-73, dir, Biol Flavor Tech, 80-88. *Concurrent Pos:* Field day dir, Univ Sask, 57; chmn, Ore SU chap, Phi Sigma Soc, 60-61; chmn, Am Chem Soc, Monmouth Co, 76-77. *Mem:* Am Chem Soc; Am Dairy Sci Asn; Can Soc Microbiol; Am Soc Microbiol; Sigma Xi; Soc Flavor Chemists. *Res:* Creation of and evaluation of natural flavors and fragrances; biogenesis of flavor compounds by micro-organisms, ie fermentation and microbiological enzyme process; design of microbiol and enzymatic processes. *Mailing Add:* N 92 W 28590 Hickory Rd Hartland WI 53029

SEITZ, FREDERICK, PHYSICS. *Current Pos:* pres, 68-78, EMER PRES, ROCKEFELLER UNIV, 78- *Personal Data:* b San Francisco, Calif, July 4, 11; m 35. *Educ:* Stanford Univ, AB, 32; Princeton Univ, PhD(physics), 34. *Hon Degrees:* Thirty-one from US & foreign univs & cols, 57-84. *Honors & Awards:* Nat Medal Sci, 73; Franklin Inst Medal, 65; Hoover Medal, 68; Compton Award, Am Inst Physics, 70; James Madison Award, Princeton Univ, 78; Vannevar Bush Award, NSF, 83; R Loveland Mem Award, Am Col Physicians, 83. *Prof Exp:* Proctor fel, Princeton Univ, 34-35; from instr to asst prof physics, Univ Rochester, 35-37; res physicist, Gen Elec Co, 37-39; from asst prof to assoc prof, Randall Morgan Lab Physics, Univ Pa, 39-42; prof & head dept, Carnegie Inst Technol, 42-49; res prof, Univ Ill, 49-65, dir, Control Systs Lab, 51-52, tech dir, 52-57, head, Dept Physics, 57-64, dean, Grad Sch & vpres res, 64-65; pres, Nat Acad Sci, Washington, DC, 62-69. *Concurrent Pos:* Dir, Training Prog Atomic Energy, Oak Ridge Nat Lab, 46-47; mem gov bd, Am Inst Physics, 54-, chmn gov bd, 54-59; mem, Naval Res Adv Comt, 55-, chmn, 60-62; mem, Defense Sci Bd, 58-72, vchmn, 61-62, chmn, 63-72; mem, Policy Adv Bd, Argonne Nat Lab, 58-; sci adv, NATO, 59-60; vpres, Int Union Pure & Appl Physics, 60-; mem, Statutory Vis Comt, Nat Bur Stand, 62-66; mem, President's Sci Adv Comt, 62-69; mem, President's Comt Nat Medal Sci, 62-, chmn, 62-63; Grad Res Ctr SW, 63-66; mem, Liaison Comt Sci & Technol, Libr Cong, 63-; bd trustees, Nutrit Found, Rockefeller Found, 64-77, Rockefeller Univ, 66-78, Res Corp, 66-, Princeton Univ, 68-72, Inst Int Educ, 71- & Woodrow Wilson Nat Fel Found, 72-; consult, Educ Comn Inquiry, Ministry Educ, India, 64-; chmn, Sci Adv Coun, Ill, 64-; educ & adv bd, Guggenheim Mem Found, 65; mem, Midwest Sci Adv Comt, 65-; mem, Inst Defense Analysis, 70-; bd dirs, Res Corp, Tex Instruments Inc, 71-, Akzona Inc, 73- & Ogden Corp, 77-; mem, Nat Cancer Adv Bd, 72-74 & 77-; mem, Belg Am Educ Found; vchmn, Mem Sloan Kettering Cancer Ctr, 78-83, mem bd overseers, 83-; mem adv bd, Off Strategic Defense Initiative. *Mem:* Nat Acad Sci (pres, 65); Am Acad Arts & Sci; Am Crystallog Asn; Am Soc Metals; fel Am Phys Soc (pres, 61); Am Philos Soc; Optical Soc Am; Am Inst Mining; Metall & Petrol Engrs. *Res:* Theory of solids; nuclear physics. *Mailing Add:* Rockefeller Univ 1230 York Ave New York NY 10021. *Fax:* 212-327-7559

SEITZ, GARY M, MATHEMATICS. *Current Pos:* PROF MATH, UNIV ORE, 70- *Personal Data:* b Santa Monica, Calif, May 10, 43. *Mailing Add:* Univ Ore Eugene OR 97403-1226

SEITZ, JANICE ANN, SPECIAL EDUCATION-TRANSITION, LEADERSHIP DEVELOPMENT. *Current Pos:* assoc exec dir, Coun Teacher Educ, 89-91, ASST PROF & DIR LEADERSHIP DEVELOP PROG, UNIV ILL, URBANA-CHAMPAIGN, 91- *Personal Data:* b Paulding, Ohio, Mar 16, 39; m 64, Wesley D; c Kimberly P & Matthew W. *Educ:* Bowling Green State Univ, BS, 61; Univ Ill, Urbana-Champaign, MS, 87, PhD, (interdisciplinary leadership prog), 89. *Prof Exp:* First grade teacher, Columbus Pub Schs, Ohio, 61-64, Richmond Pub Schs, Calif, 64-67; resource consult teacher visually impaired, Champaign Ill Schs, 74-85; vis instr, San Francisco State Univ, 80-82. *Concurrent Pos:* Prin investr, US Dept Educ Leadership Develop Prog, 91- *Mem:* Am Asn Col Teacher Educ; Am Voc

Asn; Am Educ Res Asn; Asn Educ & Rehab Blind & Visually Impaired; Asn Supv & Curric Develop; Coun Except Children. *Res:* Longitudinal study of a child with life threatening illness; study needs of beginning teacher of visually impaired; collaborative approach to graduate education; component parts of a model continuing education program for practicing educators; impact of journal writing for graduate and undergraduate students. *Mailing Add:* 4014 Pinecrest Dr Champaign IL 61821. *E-Mail:* seitz@uxl.cso.uiuc.edu

SEITZ, LARRY MAX, ANALYTICAL BIOCHEMISTRY, CEREAL CHEMISTRY. *Current Pos:* RES CHEMIST, US GRAIN MKT RES LAB, AGR RES SERV, USDA, 71- *Personal Data:* b Hutchinson, Kans, June 30, 40; m 62; c 2. *Educ:* Kans State Univ, BS, 62; Univ Ill, PhD, 66. *Prof Exp:* Asst prof chem, Kans State Univ, 66-71. *Mem:* Am Asn Cereal Chemists; Am Chem Soc. *Res:* Mycotoxins; fungal metabolites; growth of fungi on cereal grains; composition of cereal grains. *Mailing Add:* 3008 Conrow Dr Manhattan KS 66502-2464

SEITZ, MARTIN GEORGE, NUCLEAR MATERIALS STABILIZATION, SURPLUS NUCLEAR MATERIALS DISPOSITION. *Current Pos:* CHIEF SCIENTIST, DEPT ENERGY, US GOVT, 91- *Personal Data:* b St Louis, Mo, May 12, 44; m 77, Marilyn S; c Christian M & Amy E. *Educ:* Univ Mo, Rolla, BS, 66; Washington Univ, St Louis, PhD(physics), 71. *Prof Exp:* Exp geophys, Geophys Lab, Carnegie Inst, Wash, 71-75; sr engr, Singer Simulation Prods, Singer Co, 74-75; group leader, Argonne Nat Lab, Univ Chicago, 75-87; prin officer, Booz, Allen & Hamilton, Inc, 87-91. *Concurrent Pos:* Dir, Exchange Res, Ger, 82-85, Plutonium Vulnerability Study, 92-94; team leader, Nuclear Mat Inventory Initiative, 94-96. *Mem:* Am Geophys Union; Am Phys Soc; AAAS. *Res:* Formulate research program for stabilization of nuclear materials; manage the stabilization of plutonium solutions; national needs in nuclear safety and waste disposal. *Mailing Add:* Dept Energy 1317 Woodside Pkwy Silver Spring MD 20910-1552. *Fax:* 202-586-5750; *E-Mail:* martin.seitz@em.doe.gov

SEITZ, WENDELL L, HIGH EXPLOSIVES. *Current Pos:* staff mem, 62-85, sect leader, 85-90, ACTG DEP GROUP LEADER, LOS ALAMOS NAT LAB, 90- *Personal Data:* b Mobeetie, Tex, Aug 3, 34; m 59; c 5. *Educ:* WTex State Univ, BS, 60; Univ Ariz, MS, 63. *Honors & Awards:* Award of Excellence, Dept Energy, 89. *Prof Exp:* Teaching asst physics, Univ Ariz, 60-62. *Mem:* Am Phys Soc. *Res:* Performance and characterization of high explosives. *Mailing Add:* 65 San Juan St Los Alamos NM 87544

SEITZ, WESLEY DONALD, AGRICULTURAL ECONOMICS. *Current Pos:* Asst prof bus admin, Univ Ill, Urbana, 68-70, assoc prof agr econ, 68-74, assoc dir, Inst Environ Studies, 74-82 & head, Dept Agr Econ & Prof, 81-87, assoc head acad progs, PROF AGR CONSUMER ECON, UNIV ILL, URBANA, 74- *Personal Data:* b Wapakoneta, Ohio, Sept 29, 40; m 64; c 2. *Educ:* Ohio State Univ, BS, 62, MS, 64; Univ Calif, Berkeley, PhD(agr econ), 68. *Concurrent Pos:* Mem adv comt, Ill Environ Protection Agency Appln Sludge Agr Land, 73-74; Off Water Res & Technol res grants, 73 & 74; chmn, Coun Agr Sci & Technol Task Force Rev Environ Protection Agency Proposed Guidelines for Registering Pesticides, 75; chmn, N Cent Regional Strategy Comt Natural Resources, 75-76; US Environ Protection Agency grants, 76 & 78; mem, Ill Environ Agency Task Force Agr Nonpoint Sources Pollution, 77-78, mem strip mined land reclamation task force, Argonne Nat Lab, 72-73; chmn, Comt Soil Resource Relation Surface Mining Coal, Nat Acad Sci, 78-79, mem, Comt Abandoned Mine Lands, 85-86; chair, Resource Policy Consortium, 92-93. *Mem:* Am Agr Econ Asn; Am Econ Asn; Soil Conserv Soc Am; AAAS; Asn Resource & Environ Economists; Coun Agr Sci & Technol. *Res:* Alternative policies for the control of non-point sources of water pollution from agriculture; development of resource institutions. *Mailing Add:* 4014 Pinecrest Dr Champaign IL 61821

SEITZ, WILLIAM RUDOLF, ANALYTICAL CHEMISTRY. *Current Pos:* from asst prof to assoc prof, 76-84, PROF CHEM, UNIV NH, 84- *Personal Data:* b Orange, NJ, May 5, 43; m 69; c 2. *Educ:* Princeton Univ, AB, 65; Mass Inst Technol, PhD(chem), 70. *Prof Exp:* Res chemist, Environ Protection Agency, 70-73; instr, Univ Ga, 73-75, asst prof chem, 75-76. *Mem:* Am Chem Soc; Soc Appl Spectros. *Res:* Analytical applications of fluorescence; fiber optic sensors. *Mailing Add:* Dept Chem Univ NH Durham NH 03824. *E-Mail:* wrs@christa.unh.edu

SEITZMAN, JERRY MICHAEL, COMBUSTION & FLUID MECHANICS, OPTICAL DIAGNOSTICS. *Current Pos:* ASST PROF, GA INST TECHNOL, 94- *Personal Data:* b Albuquerque, NMex, Apr 30, 60; m 90. *Educ:* Univ Tex, BS, 82; Stanford Univ, MS, 83, PhD(mech eng), 91. *Prof Exp:* Phys sci res assoc, Stanford Univ, 91-94. *Concurrent Pos:* Partner, Cogent Software, 88-93; consult, Metrolaser, 91-92. *Mem:* Am Inst Aeronaut & Astronaut; Am Soc Mech Engrs; Optical Soc Am; Sigma Xi; Combustion Inst. *Res:* Optical techniques as diagnostics or sensors for combustion, propulsion and fluid systems. *Mailing Add:* Sch Aerospace Eng Ga Inst Technol Atlanta GA 30332-0150

SEKA, WOLF, LASER PHYSICS, SPECTROSCOPY. *Current Pos:* SR SCIENTIST, LAB LASER ENERGETICS, UNIV ROCHESTER, NY, 76-, PROF, INST OPTICS, 86- *Personal Data:* b Klagenfurt, Austria, May 15, 39; m 63; c 2. *Educ:* Univ Tex, PhD(physics), 65. *Prof Exp:* Nat Res Coun fel, Univ BC, Can, 65-68; foreign scientist, French Atomic Energy Comn, France, 68-70; vis scientist, Europ Space Res Inst, 70-72; res scientist, Univ Bern, Switz, 72-76. *Mem:* Fel Am Phys Soc. *Res:* High power solid state laser physics; yttrium-aluminum-garnet and glass oscillator development; highly efficient frequency conversion; laser plasma interaction experiments; laser fusion. *Mailing Add:* Lab Laser Energetics 250 E River Rd Rochester NY 14627. *E-Mail:* seka@lle.rochester.edu

SEKANINA, ZDENEK, PLANETARY SCIENCES, PHYSICS OF COMETS. *Current Pos:* SR RES SCIENTIST, JET PROPULSION LAB, CALIF INST TECHNOL, 80- *Personal Data:* b Mlada Boleslav, Czech, June 12, 36; m 66, Jana Soukupova; c S Jason. *Educ:* Charles Univ, dipl physicist, 59, PhD(astron), 63. *Honors & Awards:* Asteroid 1913 Named Sekanina, 76; Exceptional Sci Achievement Medal, NASA, 85. *Prof Exp:* Astronr, Stefanik Observ, Czech, 59-66 & Ctr Numerical Math, Charles Univ, 67-68; physicist, Smithsonian Astrophys Observ, 69-80. *Concurrent Pos:* Assoc, Harvard Col Observ, 69-80. *Mem:* Int Astron Union. *Res:* Physics and dynamics of cometary nuclei and dust; meteors and fireballs; interplanetary dust. *Mailing Add:* 5238 Redwillow Lane La Canada Flintridge CA 91011. *Fax:* 818-354-0966; *E-Mail:* zs@sek.jpl.nasa.gov

SEKAR, RAJ, INTERNAL COMBUSTION ENGINE DESIGN & DEVELOPMENT, TRANSPORTATION VEHICLE & SYSTEMS RESEARCH. *Current Pos:* TECH STAFF, ARGONNE NAT LAB, 85- *Personal Data:* b India, Mar 12, 43; US citizen; m, Revathy; c Priya. *Educ:* Univ Madras, India, BE, 65; Univ Wis, MS, 69; Ind Univ, MBA, 74. *Honors & Awards:* Fed Lab Consortium Award, US Dept Energy, 90. *Prof Exp:* Res & develop mgt staff, Cummins Eng Co, 69-84. *Mem:* Am Soc Mech Engrs; Soc Automotive Engrs. *Res:* Conducted and published extensive research in the areas of advanced engines and systems and alternative fuels. *Mailing Add:* 1304 Galena Ct Naperville IL 60564

SEKELLICK, MARGARET JEAN, ANIMAL VIROLOGY. *Current Pos:* Res asst develop genetics, 67-69, res asst virol, 69-81, res assoc biol, 81-84, ASST PROF IN RESIDENCE, UNIV CONN, 85- *Personal Data:* b New Haven, Conn, Aug 15, 43. *Educ:* Univ Conn, BA, 65, MS, 67, PhD, 80. *Mem:* AAAS; Am Soc Microbiol; Soc Gen Microbiol; Int Soc Interferon Res. *Res:* Animal virus-host cell interactions; mechanisms of cell killing and persistent infection by viruses; mechanisms of induction and action of interferon; relationship of stress response to interferon induction and action. *Mailing Add:* Dept Molecular & Cell Biol Univ Conn U-125 75 N Eaglevil Storrs Mansfield CT 06269-0002

SEKERKA, IVAN, analytical chemistry, corrosion, for more information see previous edition

SEKERKA, ROBERT FLOYD, PHYSICS, APPLIED MATHEMATICS. *Current Pos:* prof & dean, 82-91, UNIV PROF, PHYSICS & MATHS, MELLON COL SCI, CARNEGIE MELLON UNIV, 91- *Personal Data:* b Wilkinsburg, Pa, Nov 27, 37; m 60, 81, Carolyn L Confer; c Lee A & Robert. *Educ:* Univ Pittsburgh, BS, 60; Harvard Univ, AM, 61, PhD(physics), 66. *Hon Degrees:* Dr, Univ W Timisoara, Romania, 96. *Honors & Awards:* A G Worthing Award, 60; Philip M McKenna Mem Award, 80; Frank Prize, 92. *Prof Exp:* Tech metall, Westinghouse Res Labs, 55-58, sr scientist, 65-68, mgr theoret physics dept, 68, mgr mat growth & properties dept, 69-70; lectr, Carnegie-Mellon Univ, 65-66 & 67-69, assoc prof metall & mat sci, 69-72, prof, Dept Metall Eng & Mat Sci, 72-82, dept head, 76-82. *Concurrent Pos:* Consult, Nat Inst Standards & Technol & Bell Tel Labs, 76-79, USRA/NASA, 75 & Europ Space Agency, 88; assoc ed, Metal Trans, 70-76, J Crystal Growth, 71- , ed board, Applied Microgravity Technol, 87-90; mem space studies bd, Nat Res Coun, Nat Acad Sci, 89-91. *Mem:* Fel Am Phys Soc; Sigma Xi; Am Asn Crystal Growth; fel Am Soc Metals; fel NSF; fel The Metals Soc; Int Asn Crystal Growth (co-vpres). *Res:* Magnetism; solidification; crystals; applied mathematics; morphological stability; transport processes; materials science. *Mailing Add:* Dept Physics Carnegie Mellon Univ Pittsburgh PA 15213-3890. *Fax:* 412-681-0648; *E-Mail:* rs07@andrew.cmu.edu

SEKHON, SANT SINGH, zoology, cytology, for more information see previous edition

SEKI, HAJIME, SURFACE VIBRATIONAL SPECTROSCOPY, TRIBOLOGY. *Current Pos:* res staff mem, 61-67, proj mgr, 67-77, RES STAFF MEM, RES DIV, IBM CORP, 77- *Personal Data:* b Nishinomiya, Japan, Feb 11, 29; m 66; c 3. *Educ:* Brown Univ, BS, 54; Univ Pa, PhD, 61. *Prof Exp:* Res asst physics, Metals Res Lab, Brown Univ, 53-54 & Univ Pa, 54-61. *Mem:* AAAS; Am Phys Soc; Phys Soc Japan; Am Chem Soc. *Res:* Solid state physics of semiconductors, junction, surface phenomenon, photoconductivity; cryogenics of liquid helium, superfluidity; superconductivity; ultrasonic attenuation in crystals; molecular solids; organic surface and interface physics; electrochemistry; surface & interfacial optical vibrational spectroscopy; tribology. *Mailing Add:* 6466 Mojave Dr San Jose CA 95120-5306

SEKI, RYOICHI, THEORETICAL NUCLEAR PHYSICS, ATOMIC PHYSICS. *Current Pos:* from asst prof to assoc prof, 69-76, PROF PHYSICS, CALIF STATE UNIV, NORTHRIDGE, 76- *Personal Data:* b Toyama, Japan, Jan 13, 40; m 67. *Educ:* Waseda Univ, Japan, BS, 62; Northeastern Univ, MS, 64, PhD(physics), 68. *Prof Exp:* Res assoc physics & fel, Univ Denver, 67-68; fel, Univ Ga, 68-69. *Concurrent Pos:* Consult, Lawrence Radiation Lab, Univ Calif, Berkeley, 74-; vis assoc, Calif Inst Technol, 78- *Mem:* Am Phys Soc; Phys Soc Japan; Sigma Xi. *Res:* Theoretical intermediate energy physics, including interaction of mesons with nuclei and atoms. *Mailing Add:* Phys-Astron Calif State Univ Northridge CA 91324

SEKIMOTO, TADAHIRO, ELECTRICAL ENGINEERING. *Current Pos:* mgr, Commun Res Lab, Cent Res Labs, Nippon Elec Co, Ltd, 67-72, gen mgr, Transmission Div, 72-74, mem bd dirs, 74-77, sr vpres & dir, 77-78, exec vpres & dir, 78-80, PRES NIPPON ELEC CO, LTD, 80- *Personal Data:* b Nov 14, 26. *Educ:* Tokyo Univ, DEng, 62. *Honors & Awards:* Purple Ribbon Medal, His Majesty Emperor Japan, 82, Blue Ribbon Medal, 89; Edwin Haward Armstrong Achievement Award, Inst Elec & Electronics Engrs, 82. *Prof Exp:* Staff, Nippon Elec Co, Ltd, 48-65, chief, Basic Res Dept, Commun Res Lab, 65; staff, Comsat, 65-67. *Res:* Electrical engineering. *Mailing Add:* NEC Corp 7-1 Shiba 5-chome Minato-Ku Tokyo 108-1 Japan

SEKINE, YASUJI, POWER SYSTEMS ENGINEERING, SYSTEMS THEORY. *Current Pos:* Lectr, Univ Tokyo, 59-60, from assoc prof to prof, 60-92, EMER PROF ELEC ENG SCI, UNIV TOKYO, 92-; VPRES, CENT RES INST ELEC POWER INDUST, 93- *Personal Data:* b Tokyo, Japan, Dec 7, 31; m 64, Hideko; c Yohko. *Educ:* Univ Tokyo, BS, 54, MS, 56, Dr, 59. *Honors & Awards:* Centennial Mem Award, Inst Elec Engrs, Japan, 88, Outstanding Achievement Award, 91. *Concurrent Pos:* Vis prof, Fed Inst Technol, Zurich, Switz, 87, Univ Tex, Arlington; pres, Power Systs Comput Conf, 90; chmn, Japan Nat Comt, 86-, Inst Elec & Radio Engrs, Japan Coun, 93. *Mem:* Inst Elec Engrs Japan (pres, 89-90); fel Inst Elec & Electronics Engrs; Eng Acad Japan; Royal Swed Acad Eng Sci. *Res:* Electric power systems engineering; systems theory; mathematical programming; analysis, planning and operation of power systems. *Mailing Add:* Cent Res Inst Elec Power Indust 1-6-1 Ohtemochi Chiyoda-Ku Tokyo 100 Japan. *Fax:* 81-5261-4805

SEKULA, BERNARD CHARLES, MICROBIAL LIPID BIOCHEMISTRY, FAT REPLACEMENT. *Current Pos:* sr microbiol chemist, 81-86, prin microbiol chemist, 86-93, RES ASSOC, BEST FOODS RES & ENG CTR, 93- *Personal Data:* b Philadelphia, Pa, Dec 29, 51; m 77, Donna Price; c B Jonathan, Daniel & Andrew. *Educ:* Drexel Univ, BS, 74, MS, 76, PhD(biochem), 79. *Prof Exp:* Res asst, Drexel Univ, 74-76, teaching asst biochem, bot, life sci, 76-77, res asst, 77-79; trainee, Fels Res Inst, 79-81. *Mem:* Sigma Xi; Am Oil Chemists' Soc. *Res:* Lipid biochemistry; yeast fermentations; control of microbial metabolic pathways; structure/function relationship of sterols and sterol metabolism in anaerobic yeast; fat replacers substitutes; dressings research and development. *Mailing Add:* Best Foods Tech Ctr 150 Pierce St Somerset NJ 08873

SEKULER, ROBERT W, VISION. *Current Pos:* LOUIS & FRANCES FALVAGE PROF PSYCHOL, BRANDEIS UNIV, 90- *Personal Data:* b Elizabeth, NJ, May 5, 39; m 61; c 3. *Educ:* Brandeis Univ, BA, 60; Brown Univ, ScM, 63, PhD(psychol), 64. *Prof Exp:* Fel, Mass Inst Technol, 64-65; from asst prof to assoc prof psychol, Northwestern Univ, 65-73, prof neurobiol physiol, 81-84, assoc dean, Col Arts & Sci, 84-90, PROF PSYCHOL, NORTHWESTERN UNIV, 77-, PROF OPTHAL, MED SCH, 77- *Concurrent Pos:* Mem, Adv Panel Sensory Physiol, NSF, 74-77, Steering Comt Physiol Optics, Am Acad Optom, 81-; sr vpres, Optronix Corp, 79-82; consult, Nat Inst Aging, 81-90; chmn, Comt on Vision, Nat Acad Sci/Nat Res Coun, 83-85. *Mem:* Am Acad Optom; Soc Neurosci; Asn Res Vision & Ophthal; Optical Soc Am; Geront Soc. *Mailing Add:* 64 Strawberry Hill Rd Concord MA 01742-5502

SEKUTOWSKI, DENNIS G, CATALYSIS, INORGANIC CHEMISTRY. *Current Pos:* sr res chemist, 81-85, RES ASSOC, PIGMENTS & ADDITIVES DIV, ENGELHARD CORP, 85- *Personal Data:* b Hamtramck, Mich, Aug 14, 48; m 75; c 1. *Educ:* Wayne State Univ, BS, 70; Univ Ill, PhD(inorg chem), 75. *Prof Exp:* Res chemist catalysis, Max Planck Inst Coal Res, Muelheim, WGer, 75-77; res assoc, Tex A&M Univ, 77-78; res chemist catalysis, Oxirane Int, 79-81; res chemist catalysis, Arco Chem Co, 81. *Concurrent Pos:* Tech prog chmn, Gen Polymer Modifiers & Additives Div, Soc Plastic Engrs, 89-91. *Mem:* Am Chem Soc; Soc Plastics Engrs; Tech Asn Pulp & Paper Indust. *Res:* Homogeneous and heterogeneous catalysis, especially in relationship to the petrochemical industry; engineering plastic composites, especially relating to surface chemistry of reinforcing fillers; pigment technology related to coating applications. *Mailing Add:* One Edna Horn Dr Stockton NJ 08559-9720

SELANDER, ROBERT KEITH, BACTERIAL POPULATION GENETICS. *Current Pos:* EBERLY PROF BIOL, PA STATE UNIV, 87- *Personal Data:* b Garfield, Utah, July 21, 27; m 51; c 2. *Educ:* Univ Utah, BS, 50, MS, 51; Univ Calif, Berkeley, PhD(zool), 56. *Honors & Awards:* Walker Prize, 69; Painton Award, 70. *Prof Exp:* From instr to prof zool, Univ Tex, Austin, 56-74; prof biol, Univ Rochester, 74-87. *Concurrent Pos:* Res fel, Am Mus Natural Hist, 60-61; Guggenheim fel, 65; Rand fel, 71. *Mem:* Nat Acad Sci; Soc Study Evolution; fel Am Ornith Union; fel AAAS; foreign fel Linnaean Soc London; fel Am Acad Arts & Sci. *Res:* Population genetics; molecular evolution. *Mailing Add:* Dept Biol Pa State Univ University Park PA 16802. *E-Mail:* rks3@psu.edu

SELASSIE, CYNTHIA R, COMPUTER ASSISTED DRUG DESIGN, DRUG RESISTANCE. *Current Pos:* Res assoc chem, Pomona Col, 80-86, adj assoc prof, 86-89, adj assoc prof, 89-90, ASSOC PROF CHEM TEACHING, POMONA COL, 90- *Personal Data:* b Mombasa, Kenya, Aug 28, 51; US citizen; m 79; c 1. *Educ:* Mt St Mary's Col, BA, 74; Duke Univ, MA, 76; Univ Southern Calif, PhD(pharmaceut chem), 80. *Mem:* Am Chem Soc; Am Pharmaceut Asn; Am Asn Cancer Res; Coun Undergrad Res; Asn Women Sci. *Res:* Computer assisted drug design particularly in the area of antifolates; applications of quantitative structure-activity relationship paradigm to resistance in bacteria and neoplastic cells; enzymatic reactions in nonaqueous solvents as models for drug-membrane associated enzymes. *Mailing Add:* 645 N College Ave Claremont CA 91711

SELBERG, ATLE, MATHEMATICS. *Current Pos:* mem, Inst Advan Study, 47-48, permanent mem, 49-51, prof, 51-87, EMER PROF, INST ADVAN STUDY, 87- *Personal Data:* b Langesund, Norway, June 14, 17; m 47, Hedvig Liebermann; c Ingrid Maria & Lars Atle. *Educ:* Univ Oslo, PhD(math), 43. *Hon Degrees:* Dr, Univ Trondheim, Norway & Univ Oslo, Norway. *Honors & Awards:* Fields Medal & Prize, Int Cong Mathematicians, 50; Wolf Prize, 86; Comdr W Star, Royal Norweg Order St Olav, 87. *Prof Exp:* Res fel Math, Univ Oslo, 42-47; assoc prof, Syracuse Univ, 48-49. *Concurrent Pos:* vis prof numerous univs. *Mem:* Royal Danish Soc Sci; Am Acad Arts & Sci; Norweg Acad Sci & Letters; Royal Norweg Soc Sci; Royal Swedish Acad Sci; Indian Nat Sci Acad; hon fel Tata Inst Fundamental Res. *Res:* Number theory; analysis. *Mailing Add:* Seven Maxwell Lane Princeton NJ 08540

SELBIN, JOEL, INORGANIC CHEMISTRY. *Current Pos:* VIS PROF, UNIV COLO, DENVER, 91- *Personal Data:* b Washington, DC, Aug 20, 31; m 55; c Eric A, Jeffrey L, Deborah L & Jonathan D. *Educ:* George Washington Univ, BS, 53; Univ Ill, PhD(chem), 57. *Prof Exp:* From asst prof to prof chem, La State Univ, Baton Rouge, 57- 91, dir grad studies, Chem Dept, 77-81. *Concurrent Pos:* Petrol res fund int fac award, Rome, Italy, 63-64; vis prof, Univ Calif, Berkeley, 72 & Harvard Univ, 82. *Mem:* Am Chem Soc; fel AAAS; Sigma Xi. *Res:* Bioinorganic chemistry; physical chemical studies on complex inorganic compounds, mainly spectral properties of transition metal complexes. *Mailing Add:* 3345 16th St Boulder CO 80304-2211

SELBY, HENRY M, MEDICINE. *Current Pos:* ASST PROF CLIN RADIOL, MED COL, CORNELL UNIV, 51- *Personal Data:* b US, Sept 20, 18; m 51; c 3. *Educ:* La State Univ, MD, 43; Am Bd Radiol, dipl, 50. *Concurrent Pos:* Asst attend radiologist, NY Hosp, 51 & James Ewing Hosp, 51-; assoc attend roentgenologist, Mem Hosp, 51-; dir radiol, Prev Med Inst, Strang Clin, 65- *Mem:* Am Radium Soc; Am Col Radiol. *Res:* Radiology. *Mailing Add:* 57 W 57th St New York NY 10019-2802

SELBY, PAUL BRUCE, MAMMALIAN GENETICS, RISK ANALYSIS & ENVIRONMENTAL SCIENCES. *Current Pos:* SR STAFF SCIENTIST, OAK RIDGE NAT LAB, 75- *Personal Data:* b Owatonna, Minn, Dec 5, 45; m 70, Patricia Ross; c Kari L & Kristi M. *Educ:* Westmar Col, BA, 67; Univ Tenn, PhD(biomed sci), 72. *Honors & Awards:* Ernest Orlando Lawrence Mem Award, Dept Energy, 81. *Prof Exp:* Res assoc radiation genetics, Gesellschaft fur Strahlen-und Umweltforschung, Neuherberg, Ger, 72-75. *Concurrent Pos:* Mem, Comt Biol Effects Ionizing Radiations, Nat Res Coun, 77-80 & Genetic Effects Subcomt, 77-80; sci adv to US deleg, UN Sci Comt Effects Atomic Radiation, 84, 86-, consult, 92-93. *Mem:* Am Soc Human Genetics; Environ Mutagen Soc. *Res:* Radiation and chemical mutagenesis in mice; genetic risk estimation; induction of dominant skeletal and cominant cataract mutations; statistical considerations in environmental restoration efforts. *Mailing Add:* 131 Clemson Dr Oak Ridge TN 37830. *E-Mail:* pbs@ornl.gov

SELDEN, GEORGE, organic chemistry, chemical engineering; deceased, see previous edition for last biography

SELDEN, ROBERT WENTWORTH, DEFENSE APPLICATION OF SCIENCE. *Current Pos:* RETIRED. *Personal Data:* b Phoenix, Ariz, Aug 11, 36; c 1. *Educ:* Pomona Col, BA, 58, Univ Wis, MS, 60, PhD(physics), 64. *Honors & Awards:* Theodore von Karman Award, 89. *Prof Exp:* Staff mem physics, Lawrence Livermore Nat Lab, 67-73, group leader, Nuclear Exp Design Physics, 73-79, asst assoc dir nuclear exps, 78-79; div leader, Appl Theoret Physics Div, Los Alamos Nat Lab, 79-83, dep assoc dir strategic defense res, 83-84, assoc dir theoret & comput physics, 84-86, dir, Ctr Nat Security, 86-88; chief scientist, USAF, 88-91; assoc dir, Lab Develop, Los Alamos Nat Lab, 91-94, consult, 94- *Concurrent Pos:* Sci adv, US Dept Energy Team for Tech Discussion Nonproliferation, 76-77; President's Defensive Technols Adv Team, 83; Ballistic Missile Defense Technols Adv Panel, US Cong, 84-85; mem, USAF Sci Adv Bd, 84-88. *Mem:* Am Phys Soc; AAAS. *Res:* Technical management of basic and applied research in theoretical and computational physics; principal contributions in the areas of advanced computation, fusion energy and application of science to defense needs; development of advanced technologies in response to national security policies and implications of policy and strategy on technology development; mathematical and systems analysis of ballistic missile defense technologies. *Mailing Add:* 624 La Bajeda Los Alamos NM 87544. *Fax:* 505-672-3730

SELDIN, DONALD WAYNE, INTERNAL MEDICINE. *Current Pos:* from asst prof to prof, 51-88, chmn dept, 69-88, WILLIAM BUCHANAN PROF INTERNAL MED, SOUTHWESTERN MED SCH, UNIV TEX, DALLAS, 88-, SYST PROF INTERNAL MED, 88- *Personal Data:* b New York, NY, Oct 24, 20; wid; c Leslie Lynn, Donald Craig & Donna Leigh. *Educ:* NY Univ, AB, 40; Yale Univ, MD, 43. *Hon Degrees:* DHL, S Methodist Univ, 77; DSc, Med Col Wis, 80, Yale Univ, 88, Med Col Ohio, 96; Dr, Univ Paris, 83. *Honors & Awards:* Frederick Von Miller Hon Lectr Med, Univ Munich, 68; David M Hume Award, Nat Kidney Found, 81, Physician of yr, 97; John P Peters Award, Am Soc Nephrol, 83; Kober Medal, Asn Am Physicians, 85; John K Lattimer Award, Am Urol Asn, 89; Jean Hamburger Award, Int Soc Nephrol, 95. *Prof Exp:* From instr to asst prof internal med, Yale Univ, 48-51. *Concurrent Pos:* Alexander Von Humboldt sr US scientist award, 88-92; pres, Southwestern Med Found, 88-93, vchmn, 93- *Mem:* Inst Med-Nat Acad Sci; Am Soc Clin Invest (pres, 66); Asn Am Physicians (vpres, 79, pres, 80); master Am Col Physicians; Am Fedn Clin Res; Royal Soc Med; AMA; Sigma Xi; Am Physiol Soc; Am Soc Nephrol (pres, 68); Nat Kidney Found; Am Heart Asn; Int Soc Nephrol (vpres, 78-81, pres-elect, 81-84, pres, 84-87). *Res:* Electrolyte and water metabolism; renal function; diabetes; adrenal gland. *Mailing Add:* Dept Internal Med Southwestern Med Ctr Univ Tex 5323 Harry Hines Blvd Dallas TX 75235. *Fax:* 214-648-9100

SELDIN, EMANUEL JUDAH, ENGINEERING PHYSICS. *Current Pos:* LECTR PHYSICS, BALDWIN-WALLACE COL, 85- *Personal Data:* b Brooklyn, NY, Mar 20, 27; m 52; c 2. *Educ:* Brooklyn Col, BA, 49; Univ Wis, MS, 51; Univ Buffalo, PhD(physics), 58. *Prof Exp:* Asst physics, Univ Wis, 49-53 & Univ Buffalo, 53-57; physicist, Parma Tech Ctr, Carbon Prod Div, Union Carbide Corp, 57- 83; instr math, Lorain Co Community Col, 84-85. *Concurrent Pos:* Lectr, Baldwin-Wallace Col, 64; instr physics, Cuyahoga Community Col, 85. *Mem:* Am Phys Soc. *Res:* Processing, mechanical and thermal properties of carbon and graphite. *Mailing Add:* 12211 Park Cliff Rd Strongsville OH 44136

SELDIN, JONATHAN PAUL, COMBINATORY LOGIC & LAMBDA-CALCULUS, PROOF THEORY. *Current Pos:* ADJ ASSOC PROF MATH, CONCORDIA UNIV, MONTREAL, 83- *Personal Data:* b New York, NY, Jan 30, 42; div; c Julie A (Gagnon). *Educ:* Oberlin Col, BA, 64; Pa State Univ, MA, 66; Univ Amsterdam, Dr Math, 68. *Prof Exp:* Lectr pure math, Univ Col Swansea, Wales, 68-69; asst prof, Southern Ill Univ, Carbondale, 69-81. *Concurrent Pos:* Researcher, Odyssey Res Assocs, 86-88. *Mem:* Asn Symbolic Logic; Am Math Soc; Math Asn Am; Sigma Xi. *Res:* Combinatory logic and lambda-calculus, theoretical prototypes for functional programming languages and type assignment for these systems; a theoretical prototype for the typing discipline in programming languages. *Mailing Add:* Dept Math Concordia Univ 7141 Sherbrooke St W Montreal PQ H4B 1R6 Can. *Fax:* 514-848-2831; *E-Mail:* seldin@alcor.concordia.ca

SELEGUE, JOHN PAUL, ORGANOMETALLIC CHEMISTRY, COORDINATION CHEMISTRY. *Current Pos:* from asst prof to assoc prof, 80-91, PROF CHEM, UNIV KY, LEXINGTON, 91- *Personal Data:* b Lorain, Ohio, Dec 31, 52; m 83, Edith C Eberhart; c Paul. *Educ:* Miami Univ, Oxford, Ohio, BS, 74; Mass Inst Technol, PhD(chem), 79. *Prof Exp:* Res assoc, Yale Univ, 78-80. *Concurrent Pos:* NSF fel, 74-77; Alexander von Humboldt fel, 87-88. *Mem:* Am Chem Soc; Sigma Xi; Electrochem Soc. *Res:* Synthetic organotransition metal chemistry using spectroscopic and x-ray diffraction techniques; metallacumulene and carbide complexes; metal clusters; reactions of coordinated ligands; fullerenes; intercalation chemistry. *Mailing Add:* 422 Kentucky Ct Lexington KY 40502-2148. *Fax:* 606-323-1069; *E-Mail:* selegue@ukcc.uky.edu

SELF, GLENDON DANNA, operations research, statistics, for more information see previous edition

SELF, HAZZLE LAYFETTE, ANIMAL SCIENCE. *Current Pos:* ALLEE RES CTR, IOWA STATE UNIV. *Personal Data:* b Clairette, Tex, Aug 1, 20; m 43; c 4. *Educ:* Agr & Mech Col, Tex, BS, 48; Tex Tech Col, MS, 50; Univ Wis, PhD(animal husb, genetics), 54. *Honors & Awards:* Animal Mgt award, Am Soc Animal Soc, 78. *Prof Exp:* Asst prof animal husb, Tarleton State Col, 48-52; assoc, Univ Wis, 53-54, asst prof, 54-59; assoc prof animal husb, Iowa State Univ, 59-61, prof, 61-, in chg expt farms, 60- *Mem:* AAAS; Am Soc Animal Sci; Am Forage & Grassland Coun. *Res:* Physiology of reproduction; breeding and artificial insemination; environmental effects on farm animals. *Mailing Add:* Rte 2 Box C-38 Hico TX 76457-9802

SELF, STEPHEN, VOLCANOLOGY. *Current Pos:* ASST PROF GEOL, ARIZ STATE UNIV, 80- *Personal Data:* b London, Eng, Oct 26, 46. *Educ:* Leeds Univ, BSc, 70; Imp Col Sci & Technol, PhD(geol), & DIC, 74. *Prof Exp:* Fel geol, Victoria Univ, NZ, 74-76; higher sci officer, Inst Geol Sci, UK, 76-77; res assoc, Goddard Inst Space Studies, NASA, & Dartmouth Col, 77-79. *Concurrent Pos:* Vis scientist, Los Alamos Nat Lab, 78; vis prof, Mich Technol Univ, 79. *Mem:* Am Geophys Union; Geol Soc Am; Int Unquaternary Res; Int Asn Sedimentologists; NZ Geol Soc. *Res:* Quantitative volcanology; generation of volcanic rocks; quaternary geology; sedimentology. *Mailing Add:* Dept Geol & Geophys Univ Hi-Manoa Honolulu HI 96822-2270

SELFRIDGE, RALPH GORDON, MATHEMATICS, COMPUTER SCIENCES. *Current Pos:* assoc prof math, 61-72, dir comput ctr, 65-72, PROF COMPUT SCI, UNIV FLA, 72- *Personal Data:* b London, Eng, July 30, 27; m 82. *Educ:* Mass Inst Technol, BS, 47; Cornell Univ, MA, 53; Univ Ore, PhD(math), 53. *Prof Exp:* Mathematician, US Naval Ord Test Sta, Calif, 51-59; assoc prof math, Miami Univ, 59-61. *Mem:* Asn Comput Mach; Math Asn Am. *Res:* Numerical and harmonic analysis; computing technology; algorithms for control of mechanisms, for graphics, and for simulation of automobile systems. *Mailing Add:* 300 CSE Univ Fla Gainesville FL 32611

SELGRADE, JAMES FRANCIS, MATHEMATICS. *Current Pos:* From asst prof to assoc prof, 73-87, PROF MATH, NC STATE UNIV, 87- *Personal Data:* b Washington, DC, Apr 25, 46; m 70; c 4. *Educ:* Boston Col, BA, 68; Univ Wis-Madison, MS, 69, PhD(math), 73. *Mem:* Am Math Soc; Soc Indust & Appl Math; Soc Math Biol. *Res:* Qualitative theory of ordinary differential equations, global analysis and biomathematics. *Mailing Add:* NC State Univ Box 8205 Raleigh NC 27695

SELIG, ERNEST THEODORE, GEOTECHNICAL ENGINEERING, RAILWAY ENGINEERING. *Current Pos:* PROF CIVIL ENG, UNIV MASS, 78- *Personal Data:* b Harrisburg, Pa, Nov 25, 33; m 57; c Ted, Tom & Christina. *Educ:* Cornell Univ, BME, 57; Ill Inst Technol, MS, 60, PhD(civil eng), 64. *Honors & Awards:* Gold Medal, Am Soc Mech Engrs; Charles E Dudley Award & Award of Merit, Am Soc Testing & Mat, Woodland Shockley Award. *Prof Exp:* Res engr, Mech Div, IIT Res Inst, 57-66, mgr, Soil Mech Sect, 66-68; from assoc prof to prof civil eng, State Univ NY Buffalo, 68-78. *Concurrent Pos:* Geotech eng consult, govt & private orgn, 68-; chmn, Soil Mech & Found Div Ill sect, Am Soc Civil Engrs, 64, pres, Buffalo sect, 73-74; chmn, Soil Dynamics Comt, Am Soc Testing & Mat, 66-74, Soil- Struct Interaction Comt, Transp Res Bd, 70-76, Soil & Rock Instrumentation Comt, 76-82, Soil Effects Comt, Soc Automotive Engrs, 66-69, Int Comt RR Geotechnol, 89-; ed, Geotech Eng J, 72-76, Geotech Testing J, 77-85; vis engr, Mass Inst Technol, 74-75; sr acad visitor, Oxford Univ, 86; vis prof, Nottingham, Eng, 86, Univ Pretoria, SAfrica, 92; mem, Comt Roadway and Ballast, Am Railway Eng Asn, 79-; mem, Soil Struct Interaction Comt, Transp Res Bd, 64, Comt Railway Maintenance, 83. *Mem:* Fel Am Soc Civil Engrs; fel Am Soc Testing & Mat; Transp Res Bd; Am Railway Eng Asn. *Res:* Behavior of railway ballast and mechanics of track structure performance; analysis of buried flexible and rigid culverts; soil-structure interaction; soil compaction and compaction equipment performance; stress, strain and moisture instrumentation for soils; dynamic behavior of soils. *Mailing Add:* 49 Harkness Rd Amherst MA 01002

SELIG, WALTER S, ANALYTICAL CHEMISTRY, POTENTIOMETRY. *Current Pos:* RETIRED. *Personal Data:* b Frankfurt am Main, Ger, Apr 13, 24; US citizen; div; c 3. *Educ:* Roosevelt Univ, BS, 51; Miami Univ, MS, 52. *Prof Exp:* Chemist, R Lavin & Sons, Inc, Ill, 53-54, Simoniz Co, 54-59 & Sandia Corp, Calif, 59-60; chemist, Lawrence Livermore Nat Lab, Univ Calif, 60-69, group lead org anal, 69-77, researcher, 77-91. *Concurrent Pos:* US AEC res & teaching fel & vis prof, Dept Org Chem, Hebrew Univ, Israel, 72-73. *Res:* Research and development of analytical methods for organic and inorganic materials; applications of ion-selective electrodes to organic and inorganic analysis; potentiometry. *Mailing Add:* 3396 Orchard Valley Lane Lafayette CA 94549

SELIGA, THOMAS A, ATMOSPHERIC SCIENCES, ELECTRICAL ENGINEERING. *Current Pos:* CHMN ELEC ENG & COMPUT SCI, UNIV TOLEDO, 96- *Personal Data:* b Hazleton, Pa, Dec 3, 37; m 63; c 2. *Educ:* Case Inst Technol, BS, 59; Pa State Univ, MS, 61, PhD(elec eng), 65. *Prof Exp:* Instr elec eng, Pa State Univ, 61-65, asst prof, 65-69; prog dir aeronomy, NSF, 67-68; prof elec eng, Ohio State Univ, 69-85, dir atmospheric sci, 71-85; assoc dean grad studies & res & prof elec eng, Col Eng, Pa State Univ, 85-90. *Concurrent Pos:* Mem rep, Univ Corp Atmospheric Res, 73-85; consult, Environ Anal Asn Inc, 73- & 3M, 85- *Mem:* Inst Elec & Electronics Engrs; Am Geophys Union; AAAS. *Res:* Radar meteorology; radar polarimetry and ionospheric wave propagation; air pollution long range transport and effects; climatic variability; acid precipitation. *Mailing Add:* 2609 Amara Dr No 4 Toledo OH 43615-2905

SELIGER, HOWARD HAROLD, PHYSICS, PHOTOBIOLOGY. *Current Pos:* res assoc biophys, 58-63, assoc prof, 63-68, PROF BIOL, JOHNS HOPKINS UNIV, 68- *Personal Data:* b New York, NY, Dec 4, 24; m 44; c 2. *Educ:* City Col New York, BA, 45; Purdue Univ, MS, 48; Univ Md, PhD(physics), 54. *Prof Exp:* Asst instr physics, Purdue Univ, 48; prof leader radioactivity, Nat Bur Standards, 48-58. *Concurrent Pos:* Guggenheim fel, 58-59; consult, Off Naval Res, 63-65; prin scientist, Chesapeake Bay Inst; mem comt biol effects increased solar ultraviolet, Nat Acad Sci, 81. *Mem:* AAAS; fel Am Phys Soc; Am Soc Limnol & Oceanog; Am Soc Biol Chemists; Am Soc Photobiol (pres, 80-81). *Res:* Radioactivity standardization; bioluminescence; excited states of biological molecules; marine biology of bioluminescent dinoflagellates; photometry; estuarine ecology. *Mailing Add:* Dept Biol Johns Hopkins Univ Baltimore MD 21218

SELIGMAN, GEORGE BENHAM, MATHEMATICS. *Current Pos:* from instr to assoc prof, 56-65, chmn dept, 74-77, PROF MATH, YALE UNIV, 65- *Personal Data:* b Attica, NY, Apr 30, 27; m 59, Irene Schwieder; c Barbara & Karen. *Educ:* Univ Rochester, BA, 50; Yale Univ, MA, 51, PhD(math), 54. *Prof Exp:* Fine instr math, Princeton Univ, 54-56. *Concurrent Pos:* Fulbright lectr, Univ Munster, 58-59. *Mem:* Am Math Soc. *Res:* Lie algebras, especially semi-simple Lie algebras. *Mailing Add:* Dept Math Yale Univ PO Box 2155 New Haven CT 06520. *Fax:* 203-432-7316; *E-Mail:* selig@math.yale.edu

SELIGMAN, ROBERT BERNARD, ORGANIC CHEMISTRY. *Current Pos:* RETIRED. *Personal Data:* b Brooklyn, NY, Dec 30, 24; m 51; c 2. *Educ:* Univ NC, BS, 48, PhD(org chem), 53. *Prof Exp:* Res chemist, Phillip Morris USA, 53-54, leader, Org Sect, 54-55, supvr, 55-57, asst mgr tobacco res, 57-58, mgr, 59-64, asst dir tobacco res & develop, 64-66, dir develop, 66-71, com develop, 71-76, vpres res & develop, 76-81, vpres res & develop, Tobacco Tax Guide, 81-88. *Mem:* Am Chem Soc; NY Acad Sci. *Res:* Synthetic tuberculostats; tobacco chemistry; consumer product development. *Mailing Add:* 16 Roslyn Rd Richmond VA 23226-1610

SELIGMAN, STEPHEN JACOB, INFECTIOUS DISEASES. *Current Pos:* assoc prof, 68-81, PROF MED, HEALTH SCI CTR, STATE UNIV NY, BROOKLYN, 81-, PROF ANAT & CELL BIOL, 91- *Personal Data:* b Brooklyn, NY, Feb 4, 31; m 85, Hannelore; c William Glenn & Marc David. *Educ:* Harvard Univ, AB, 52; NY Univ, MD, 56. *Prof Exp:* Fel infectious dis, Univ Calif, Los Angeles, 61-63, asst prof med, 63-68. *Mem:* AAAS; Infectious Dis Soc Am; Am Soc Microbiol; Soc Exp Biol & Med; Am Fedn Clin Res. *Res:* Human immunodeficiency virus-1, antibodies to the V3 loop of gp120. *Mailing Add:* Box 77 State Univ NY Health Sci Ctr Brooklyn NY 11203

SELIGMANN, BRUCE EDWARD, INFLAMMATION, HOST DEFENSE. *Current Pos:* VPRES RES, SELECTIDE CORP, 92- *Educ:* Univ Md, PhD(biochem), 79. *Prof Exp:* Sr staff scientist, Ciba-Geigy, 85-92. *Mailing Add:* Hoechst Marion Roussel Inc 6290 N Nirvana Pl Tucson AZ 85750

SELIGSON, DAVID, PATHOLOGY, BIOCHEMISTRY. *Current Pos:* assoc prof, 59-69, DIR CLIN LABS, NEW HAVEN, YALE UNIV, MED CTR, 58-, PROF MED & PATH, SCH MED, YALE UNIV, 69-, CHMN DEPT LAB MED, 71- *Personal Data:* b Philadelphia, Pa, Aug 12, 16; m 49; c 3. *Educ:* Univ Md, BS, 40; Johns Hopkins Univ, ScD(biochem), 42; Univ Utah, MD, 46. *Hon Degrees:* MA, Yale Univ, 65. *Honors & Awards:* Donald J VanSlyke Award, Am Asn Clin Chemists, 70, Ames Award, 71. *Prof Exp:* Res biochemist, USDA, 42-43; chief, Hepatic & Metab Dis Lab, Walter Reed Army Med Ctr, 43-45; USPHS fel, Univ Pa, 49-51, assoc prof clin chem in med, Grad Sch Med & dir div biochem, Grad Hosp, 53-58. *Concurrent Pos:* Medici Publici & Med Alumni Asn fel, Col Med, Univ Utah, 66. *Mem:* Fel Am Soc Clin Pathologists; fel Col Am Pathologists; fel Am Col Physicians; Am Soc Clin Invest; Am Asn Clin Chemists (pres, 61-62); Sigma Xi. *Mailing Add:* 27 Turtle Bay Dr Branford CT 06405-4970

SELIGSON, FRANCES HESS, REGULATORY AFFAIRS, FOOD SAFETY & TOXICOLOGY. *Current Pos:* MGR, HERSHEY FOODS CORP, 87- *Personal Data:* b Philadelphia, Pa, Sept 6, 49; m 75. *Educ:* Drexel Univ, BS, 71; Univ Calif, Berkeley, PhD(nutrit), 76. *Prof Exp:* Asst prof pub health nutrit, Univ NC, Chapel Hill, 76-77; scientist, Procter & Gamble Co, 77-87. *Mem:* Am Dietetic Asn; Am Inst Nutrit; Inst Food Technologists. *Res:* Protein quality evaluation; calcium bioavailability; calcium-mineral interactions; blood lipid effects of sucrose polyesters and soy protein. *Mailing Add:* Nutrit Food Safety Dept Hershey Foods Corp PO Box 805 Hershey PA 17033-0805. *Fax:* 717-534-5224

SELIGY, VERNER LESLIE, MOLECULAR GENETICS, BIOTECHNOLOGY. *Current Pos:* FED DEPT HEALTH MUTAGENESIS SECT, ENVIRON & OCCUP TOXICOL DIV, 92- *Personal Data:* b Niagara-on-Lake, Ont, Sept 16, 40; m 66; c 3. *Educ:* Univ Toronto, BSc, 65, MSc, 66, PhD(molecular biol), 69. *Prof Exp:* Fel biochem, Nat Res Coun Can, 69-71, asst res officer chromatin struct, 71-75, assoc res officer molecular genetics, 76-82, sr res officer toxicol, Div Biol Sci, 82-92, head sect, 86-90, molecular cell biol, Inst Biol Sci, 90-92. *Concurrent Pos:* Adj prof biol, Carleton-Ottawa Univ Grad Ctr, 78-; assoc mem, Inst Biochem, Carleton Univ, 80-87 & Ottawa Univ, 87-89; group coordr molecular genetics, Div Biol Sci, Nat Res Coun Can, 82-85; sci adv, Indust Develop Off, Nat Res Coun, 80-, contracts res develop, 86-; bd dir, Plant Biotechnol, Univ Toronto, 87-90. *Mem:* Genetics Soc Can; Can Biochem Soc; Genetics Soc Am. *Res:* Cloning, expression, regulation & engineering of genes coding for industrially important enzymes (glycosidases); regulatory proteins that control gene expression & cell development in yeast/fungi & insect/mammalian systems. *Mailing Add:* Environ & Occup Toxicol Div Mutagenisis Sect Tunney Pasture Environ Health Ctr Health Can Ottawa ON K1A 0L2 Can. *Fax:* 613-941-4768; *E-Mail:* vern_seligy@inet.hwc.ca

SELIM, MOSTAFA AHMED, OBSTETRICS & GYNECOLOGY, GYNECOLOGIC ONCOLOGY. *Current Pos:* instur, Case Western Res Univ, 70-71, sr instr, 71-72, from asst prof to assoc prof, 72-85, PROF, REPRODUCTIVE BIOL, CASE WESTERN RES UNIV, 85- *Personal Data:* b Cairo, Egypt, June 11, 35; US citizen; m 64. *Educ:* Alexandria Univ, PNS, 54; Cairo Univ, MBBCH, 59. *Prof Exp:* Intern, Ahmed Maher Hosp, Egypt, 60; house officer, Royal Infirmary, UK, 61-62; Lister Hosp, 62-63 & Fairfield Gen Hosp, 63; residency, Womans Hosp, St Lukes Hosp Ctr, 64-66, chief resident, 66-67; fel pelvic cancer surg & res, Roswell Park Mem Inst, 67-68; pvt pract, Dar El Shiefa Hosp, Egypt, 69-70. *Concurrent Pos:* Intern, St Vincents Hosp, NY, 63-64; dir, Div Gynec Oncol, Cleveland Metrop Gen Hosp, 70- & Div Gynec Serv, 72- *Mem:* Am Col Obstet & Gynec; Am Col Surgeons; Am Fertil Soc. *Res:* Improved methods of early diagnosis of gynecologic cancer and protocols for treatment with irradiation, chemotherapy and radical surgery; improve irradiation response by increasing the blood flow by chemical and physical factors. *Mailing Add:* Metro Health Med Ctr 2500 Metro Health Dr Cleveland OH 44109

SELIN, IVAN, RESOURCE MANAGEMENT. *Current Pos:* UNDER SECY MGT, DEPT STATE, 89-, CHMN-DESIGNATE, NUCLEAR REGULATORY COMN, 91- *Personal Data:* b New York, NY, Mar 11, 37; m 52, Nina Kallet; c Douglas & Jessica. *Educ:* Yale Univ, BE, 57, MS, 58, PhD(elec eng), 60; Univ Paris, DrSci(math), 62. *Honors & Awards:* Distinguished Civilian Serv Medal, Secy Defense, 70. *Prof Exp:* Researcher, Rand Corp, 60-65; analyst & actg asst secy, Off Secy Defense, 65-70; chmn bd, Am Mgt Systs, Inc, 70-89. *Concurrent Pos:* Mem PSAC panel, Conventional Arms Transfers, 75; mem adv panel to Secy Defense B-1, 77; chmn mil econ adv panel to Dir CIA, 78-89. *Mem:* Sigma Xi. *Res:* Information theory, with applications to radar and to communications in a noisy environment. *Mailing Add:* 2905 32nd St NW Washington DC 20008

SELING, THEODORE VICTOR, ELECTRICAL ENGINEERING, RADIO ASTRONOMY. *Current Pos:* CHIEF ENGR RADIO ASTRON, CALIF INST TECHNOL, 82- *Personal Data:* b Lansing, Mich, Mar 27, 28; m 52; c 2. *Educ:* Mich State Univ, BS, 49; Univ Mich, MSE, 60, PhD(elec eng), 69. *Prof Exp:* Engr, Pub Utilities Comn, State Mich, 49-50; ionosphere data anal elec engr, US Army Signal Corp, 50-52; proj engr, AC Spark Plug Div, Gen Motors Corp, 52-54, sr proj engr, 54-60 & Defense Systs Div, 60-62; assoc res engr, Univ Mich, 62-69, res scientist, 82- *Concurrent Pos:* Consult microwave receiving systs, Environ Res Inst-Mich, 73-74 & 81-82, Space Labs, 81-82. *Mem:* Inst Elec & Electronics Engrs; Am Astron Soc. *Res:* Radio astronomy instrumentation; centimeter & mm wave radiometers and associated electronic systems. *Mailing Add:* Dept Radio Astron 105-24 Calif Inst Technol Pasadena CA 91125

SELINGER, PATRICIA GRIFFITHS, DATABASE MANAGEMENT SYSTEMS. *Current Pos:* Mem res staff, IBM Res, San Jose, 75-78, mgr, R Proj, 78-82, Off Systs Lab, 83 & Computer Sci Dept, 83-86, MGR, DATABASE TECHNOL INST, IBM RES, SAN JOSE, 86- *Personal Data:* b Cleveland, Ohio, Oct 15, 49. *Educ:* Harvard Univ, AB, 71, MS, 72, PhD(appl math), 75. *Honors & Awards:* Software Syst Award, Asn Comput Mach, 88. *Concurrent Pos:* Vchair, Spec Interest Group Mgt Data, Asn Comput Mach, 83-85. *Mem:* Asn Comput Mach. *Res:* Database management systems; relational language extensions; distributed data; query optimization; parallel query processing. *Mailing Add:* IBM Corp 650 Harry Rd San Jose CA 95120

SELINSKY, BARRY STEVEN, BIOCHEMISTRY. *Current Pos:* ASST PROF BIOCHEM, DEPT CHEM, VILLANOVA UNIV, 88- *Personal Data:* b Ashland, Pa, June 2, 58; m 81; c 2. *Educ:* Lebanon Valley Col, BS, 80; State Univ NY, Buffalo, PhD(biochem), 84. *Prof Exp:* Postdoctoral fel res, Dept Physiol, Duke Univ, 84-85; staff fel res, Nat Inst Environ Health Sci, 85-88. *Concurrent Pos:* Consult, Otsuka Electronics, 88-90. *Mem:* Biophys Soc; Am Chem Soc. *Res:* Protein-lipid interactions in biological membranes; biophysical measurements of the hepatic metabolism of fluorinated xenobiotics. *Mailing Add:* Dept Chem Villonava Univ Mendel Hall Villanova PA 19085

SELISKAR, DENISE MARTHA, SALT MARSH & SAND DUNE ECOLOGY, HALOPHYTE AGRONOMY. *Current Pos:* assoc res scientist, 86-93, RES SCIENTIST, UNIV DEL, 93- *Personal Data:* b Ft Collins, Colo, Jan 28, 53; m 78, John L Gallagher. *Educ:* Bowling Green State Univ, BS, 75; Ore State Univ, MS, 80; Univ Del, PhD(marine biol), 86. *Prof Exp:* Res technician I, Univ Ga, 75-76, res technician II, 76-78; instr, Salisbury State Univ, 80-81, lectr, 85. *Concurrent Pos:* Consult, Wetlands Ecol Team, 81-; prin investr, Nat Oceanic & Atmospheric Admin, 87-, Del Dept Transp, 89-93, Del Dept Nat Resources, 89-90, Nat Park Serv, 93- *Mem:* Bot Soc Am; Estuarine Res Fedn; Soc Wetland Scientists; Int Asn Ecol; Tissue Cult Asn. *Res:* Salt marsh and sand dune plant physiological ecology; marsh and dune restoration; halophyte tissue culture and biotechnology; mechanisms of salt tolerance in plants. *Mailing Add:* 209 Shipcarpenter St Lewes DE 19958. *Fax:* 302-645-4028; *E-Mail:* seliskar@chopin.udel.edu

SELKE, WILLIAM A, CHEMICAL ENGINEERING, ENVIRONMENTAL ENGINEERING. *Current Pos:* CONSULT, 86- *Personal Data:* b Newburgh, NY, June 16, 22; m 52, Martha W Floyd; c W August Jr, Whitney F & Edward D. *Educ:* Mass Inst Technol, SB, 43, SM, 47; Yale Univ, DEng, 49. *Prof Exp:* Engr, State Water Comn Proj, Yale Univ, 47; assoc chem eng, Columbia Univ, 49-50, asst prof, 50-55, eng mgr, Atomic Energy Comn Proj, 54-55; dir fundamental res, Peter J Schweitzer, Inc, 55-57; dir res, Schweitzer Div, Kimberly-Clark Corp, 58-81, vpres res & develop, tech paper-spec products, 81-85, vpres technol assessment, 85-86. *Concurrent Pos:* Engr, E I du Pont de Nemours & Co, 51; adj prof, Lenox Inst Water Technol, 87- *Mem:* AAAS; Am Chem Soc; Tech Asn Pulp & Paper Indust; Am Inst Chem Engrs; fel NY Acad Sci; Asn Environ Eng Prof. *Res:* Thermodynamics; ion exchange; dielectric materials; tobacco; paper making; sanitary and environmental engineering. *Mailing Add:* Meeting House Stockbridge MA 01262-0506

SELKER, HARRY PAUL, INTERNAL MEDICINE. *Current Pos:* asst prof, 85-91, ASSOC PROF MED, DIV GEN MED & CLIN DECISION MAKING, SCH MED, TUFTS UNIV, 91- *Educ:* Reed Col, BA, 74; Brown Univ, MD, 78; Univ Calif, Los Angeles, MSPH, 84; Am Bd Internal Med, dipl. *Prof Exp:* Intern internal med, Univ Calif Los Angeles/Cedars-Sinai Med Ctr, 78-79; jr resident, Boston City Hosp, 79-80, sr resident, 80-81; chief med resident, Boston Univ Med Ctr/Univ Hosp, 81-82; Robert Wood Johnson clin scholar, Dept Med, Univ Calif Los Angeles Sch Med, 82-84, asst prof med, Div Gen Internal Med & Health Servs Res, 84-85. *Concurrent Pos:* Asst vis physician, Cardiol Dept, Boston City Hosp, 81-84; spec affil attend physician, Div Gen Internal Med & Med Intensive Care, Dept Med, Cedars-Sinai Med Ctr, 84-85; asst attend physician, Div Gen Med & Clin Decision Making, Dept Med, New Eng Med Ctr, 85-91, attend physician, 91-; dir, Ctr Cardiovasc Health Servs Res, 85-, Ctr Health Servs Res & Study Design, 87-; teaching & res scholar, Am Col Physicians, 86-89; mem, Spec Proj Study Sect, Nat Heart, Lung & Blood Inst, NIH, 87-90; assoc ed, Soc Gen Internal Med Newslett, 90-93, ed, 93-; rep, Nat Heart Attack Alert Prog, NIH, 92-; consult, Agency Health Care Policy & Res, Health Care Financial Admin & Inst Med-Nat Acad Sci; mem, Coun Cardiopulmonary & Crit Care, Am Heart Asn & Coun Clin Cardiol. *Mem:* Fel Am Col Physicians; AAAS; AMA; Am Pub Health Asn; Am Fedn Clin Res; Am Heart Asn; Int Soc Comput Electrocardiol; Asn Health Servs Res; Soc Gen Internal Med; Soc Med Decision Making. *Res:* Computerized electrocardiography for diagnosis and treatment of acute cardiac ischemia. *Mailing Add:* New Eng Med Ctr 750 Washington St Boston MA 02111-1533

SELKER, MILTON LEONARD, PHYSICAL ORGANIC CHEMISTRY. *Current Pos:* RETIRED. *Personal Data:* b Detroit, Mich, Nov 2, 15; m 41; c 2. *Educ:* Western Reserve Univ, BS, 36, MA, 37, PhD(phys org chem), 40. *Prof Exp:* Lab asst qual anal, Western Reserve Univ, 35-36, org chem, 37; rubber res chemist, Bell Tel Labs, Inc, 40-46; engr, Kahn Co, 46-52 & Clevite Corp, 52-64, dir, Mech Res Div, 64-69; dir, Gould Mat Technol Lab, Gould Inc, 69-71, vpres, 71-75, vpres res & develop, 76-77, consult, 78-81. *Mem:* Am Chem Soc. *Res:* Physical organic chemistry; rubber-metal bearings; plating of metals; rubber recycling; metal-organic bonding; thin film technology. *Mailing Add:* 3175 Morley Rd Cleveland OH 44122

SELKIRK, JAMES KIRKWOOD, CHEMICAL CARCINOGENESIS, REGULATORY PROTEINS. *Current Pos:* group leader chem carcinogenesis, Oak Ridge Nat Lab, 75-78, sr scientist, Biol Div, 78-85, chief, Carcinogenesis & Toxicol Eval Br, 85-89, assoc dir, Div Toxicol Res & Testing, 89-92, GROUP LEADER, LAB MOLECULAR CARCINOGENESIS, OAK RIDGE NAT LAB, 92- *Personal Data:* b New York, NY, Dec 3, 38; m 61, Carole Bozzone; c James Jr & David. *Educ:* NY State Col Environ Sci Forestry, BS, 64; Syracuse Univ, BS, 64; Upstate Med Ctr Syracuse, PhD(biochem), 69. *Honors & Awards:* Exemplary Serv Award, Environ Protection Agency, 90. *Prof Exp:* Fel, McArdle Lab Cancer Res, Univ Wis, 69-72; staff fel chem, Nat Cancer Inst, 72-75, sr staff fel, 74-75. *Concurrent Pos:* Lectr, Biomed Grad Sch, Univ Tenn, 76-80, sr lectr, 80-; assoc ed, Carcinogenesis, 79-85, Cancer Res, 82-85; mem, Breast Cancer Task Force, NIH, 80-81; mem, Comt Pyrene & Anogs, Nat Acad Sci, 81; mem, Carcinogenesis Study Sect, Am Cancer Soc, 84-87 & 92-96. *Mem:* Am Asn Cancer Res; Sigma Xi; NY Acad Sci; AAAS; Soc Toxicol; Am Soc Biol Chem & Molecular Biol; Am Cancer Soc. *Res:* Mechanism of action of chemical carcinogens in in vivo and in vitro systems; the enzymatic pathways involved in translocation of activated cell cycle regulatory proteins from the cytoplasm to the nucleus. *Mailing Add:* Lab Molecular Carcinogenesis Nat Inst Environ Health Sci PO Box 12233 Research Triangle Park NC 27709. *Fax:* 919-541-2260; *E-Mail:* selkirk@niehs.nih.gov

SELKOE, DENNIS J, NEUROSCIENCES. *Current Pos:* instr, 75-78, from asst prof to assoc prof, 78-90, PROF NEUROL, HARVARD MED SCH, 90-; CO-DIR, CTR NEUROL DIS, BRIGHAM & WOMEN'S HOSP, BOSTON, 85- *Personal Data:* b New York, NY, Sept 25, 43. *Educ:* Columbia Univ, BA, 65; Univ Va Sch Med, MD, 69; Am Bd Psychiat & Neurol, cert, 77. *Hon Degrees:* Dr, Harvard Univ, 91. *Honors & Awards:* Wood Kalb Found Prize for res on Alzheimers Dis, 84; Andrew Floud Mem Lectr, Neurol Inst, Columbia Univ, 84; Potamkin Prize, Am Acad Neurol, 89; Aring Lectr, Univ Cincinnati Med Ctr, 91; Lilly Lectr, Eli Lilly Co, Indianapolis, 91; Rita Hayworth Award, Alzheimer's Asn, 95. *Prof Exp:* Intern med, Hosp Univ Pa, 69-70; res assoc, NIH, 70-72; res neurologist, Peter Bent Brigham, Children's & Beth Israel Hosp, Boston, 72-74, chief res neurologist, 74-75. *Concurrent Pos:* Res assoc neurosci, Children's Hosp Med Ctr, 75-78; asst neuropathologist, Children's, Brigham & Women's Hosp, 75-82, assoc physican, 82-85, physician, 85-92, sr physician, 92-; assoc neuropathologist, McLean Hosp, 78-85; distinguished lectr, Univ Calif, Irvine, 84 & Inst Brain Res, Univ Toyko, 87; award neurosci res, McKnight Found, 88-91; Wellcome vis prof, La State Univ Med Sch, 95. *Mem:* Am Acad Neurol; Soc Neurosci; AAAS; Am Soc Neurochem; Am Asn Neuropathologists; Am Neurol Asn; World Fedn Neurol. *Res:* Biochemistry and cell biology of neurol aging in normal and pathological states, particularly Alzheimer's disease and related experimental models; protein chemistry and molecular biology of CNS amyloidosis; biochemistry of brain fibrous proteins and the neuronal cytoskeleton. *Mailing Add:* Ctr Neurol Dis Brigham & Women's Hosp 221 Longwood Ave-LMRC Boston MA 02115

SELL, GEORGE ROGER, MATHEMATICS. *Current Pos:* assoc head, Sch Math, 70-71, assoc prof, 68-73, PROF MATH, SCH MATH, UNIV MINN, MINNEAPOLIS, 73- *Personal Data:* b Milwaukee, Wis, Feb 7, 37; m 58; c 6. *Educ:* Marquette Univ, BS, 57, MS, 58; Univ Mich, PhD(math), 62. *Prof Exp:* Benjamin Pierce instr math, Harvard Univ, 62-64; asst prof, Univ Minn, Minneapolis, 64-67; assoc prof, Univ Southern Calif, 67-68. *Concurrent Pos:* Mathematician, Inst Defense Analysis, NJ, 66; vis prof, Univ Florence, 71-72, Univ Palermo, 75, Tech Univ Warsaw, 75, Japan Soc Prom Sci, 77 & Australian Nat Univ, 79; prog dir, NSF, 77-78; co-founder & first assoc dir, Inst Math Appln, 81-87. *Mem:* Am Math Soc; Math Asn Am; Soc Indust & Appl Math. *Res:* Dynamical systems, ordinary and partial differential equations; applied mathematics. *Mailing Add:* Sch Math Univ Minn 206 Church St SE Minneapolis MN 55455-0488

SELL, JEFFREY ALAN, SPECTROSCOPY, CHEMICAL PHYSICS & SENSORS. *Current Pos:* Assoc sr res scientist, Gen Motors, 78-80, sr res scientist physics, 80-86, prin res scientist & mgr, advan mat & processing, Gen Motors Res Labs, 86-95, LEADER, TECH RESOURCE CTR EXHAUST SENSORS, POWERTRAIN CONTROL CTR, GEN MOTORS, 96- *Personal Data:* b Anderson, Ind, Sept 18, 52; div, Lynne Johannessen; c Jason & Stephanie. *Educ:* Purdue Univ, BS, 74; Calif Inst Technol, PhD(chem), 79. *Hon Degrees:* LEADER, TECH RESOURCE CTR EXHAUST SENSORS, POWERTRAIN CONTROL CTR, GEN MOTORS, 96- *Honors & Awards:* Campbell Award, 91. *Concurrent Pos:* Lectr physics & math, Lawrence Inst Technol, 81- *Mem:* Optical Soc Am; Am Chem Soc; Am Phys Soc; Soc Automotive Engrs; Mat Res Soc; Sigma Xi. *Res:* Tunable diode laser spectroscopy; ultraviolet photoelectron spectroscopy; visible laser spectroscopy of rare earth crystals; thermodynamics; laser processing of materials; combustion diagnostics; laser deposition and ablation of materials; superconductivity; photothermal deflection spectroscopy; combustion ignition; magnetic and electrochemical sensors. *Mailing Add:* Gen Motors Powertrain Control Ctr Gen Motors Rd Milford MI 48380. *Fax:* 248-685-6374; *E-Mail:* jsell@msa.gmr.com

SELL, JERRY LEE, POULTRY NUTRITION. *Current Pos:* prof animal nutrit, 76-86, C F CURTISS DISTINGUISHED PROF AGR, IOWA STATE UNIV, 86- *Personal Data:* b Adel, Iowa, Feb 6, 31; m 53, M JoAnn Adams; c Roger & Rex (deceased). *Educ:* Iowa State Univ, BS, 57, MS, 58, PhD(poultry nutrit), 60. *Honors & Awards:* Poultry Nutrit Res Award, Am Feed Mfrs, 78; Res Award, Nat Turkey Fed, 90; Merck Poultry Res Award, 96. *Prof Exp:* Assoc prof animal sci, Univ Man, 60-66; assoc prof animal sci, 66-68, prof animal nutrit, NDak State Univ, 68-76. *Concurrent Pos:* Mem sub-comt poultry nutrit, Nat Res Coun, US Nat Acad Sci, 81-84 & 89-93, mem, comt animal nutrit, 93-96. *Mem:* Sigma Xi; Am Poultry Sci Asn (pres, 86-87); World Poultry Sci Asn; Am Inst Nutrit. *Res:* Energy efficiency of chickens and turkeys; functional development of gastro-intestinal tract of turkeys; disease-nutrition interactions. *Mailing Add:* Dept Animal Sci Iowa State Univ Ames IA 50011. *Fax:* 515-294-2401; *E-Mail:* jsell@iastate.edu

SELL, JOHN EDWARD, BIOCHEMISTRY, IMMUNOLOGY. *Current Pos:* RETIRED. *Personal Data:* b Gainesville, Fla, June 14, 41. *Educ:* Mich State Univ, BS, 63; Univ Wis-Madison, MS, 67; Univ Cincinnati, PhD(biochem), 71. *Prof Exp:* Res assoc microbiol, Univ Mich, Ann Arbor, 71-73, res assoc internal med, 73-76; res assoc biochem, Mich State Univ, 80-91. *Mem:* AAAS; Am Chem Soc. *Res:* Biochemistry of neonatal respiration; carcinofetal antigens; cellular fluorescence spectroscopy. *Mailing Add:* 331 Timberlane Ave East Lansing MI 48823-4775

SELL, KENNETH W, BLOOD BANKING. *Current Pos:* PROF & CHMN, DEPT PATH & DIR, CANCER CTR, EMORY SCH MED, 85- *Personal Data:* b Valley City, NDak, Apr 29, 31; m 50; c 4. *Educ:* Univ NDak, BA, 53; Harvard Med Sch, MD, 56; Cambridge Univ, PhD(immunopath), 68. *Prof Exp:* Intern & resident, Bethesda Naval Hosp, 56-59, mem pediat staff, 59-60; dir, Navy Tissue Bank, Md, 60-70; chmn, Dept Clin & Exp Immunol, Navy Med Res Inst, 70-77; sci dir, Nat Inst Allergy & Infectious Dis, NIH, 77-85; clin prof, Dept Pediat, Georgetown Sch Med, 77-85. *Concurrent Pos:* Command officer, Navy Med Res Inst, 74-77; lectr, Found Advan Educ Sci, NIH, 60-77; dir, Transplantation Serv, Nat Naval Med Ctr, 71-77; lectr, Uniformed Serv Univ Health Sci, 77-85. *Mem:* Am Asn Tissue Banks; Soc Cryobiol; Transplantation Soc; Am Acad Pediat; Am Col Path. *Res:* Clinical immunology and transplantation with contributions to immunoparasitology and immune regulation of responses to viral diseases; experimental and clinical study of immunosuppression for organ transplantation. *Mailing Add:* Dept Path & Lab Med Rm 184 EUH Emery Univ Sch Med 1364 Clifton Rd NE Atlanta GA 30322. *Fax:* 404-727-3133

SELL, NANCY JEAN, CHEMICAL PHYSICS. *Current Pos:* From asst prof to assoc prof, 71-82, chmn discipline & coordr, grad prog environ sci, 81-83, PROF PHYSICS & ENG, UNIV WIS, GREEN BAY, 82- *Personal Data:* b Milwaukee, Wis, Jan 18, 45. *Educ:* Lawrence Univ, BA, 67; Northwestern Univ, MS, 68, PhD(chem physics), 72; Inst Paper Chem, MS, 86. *Concurrent Pos:* Consult, numerous industs & law firms; pres, N J Sell & Assocs SC, 84-; secy, Process Simulation Comt, Tech Asn Pulp & Paper Indust, 89-91, vchair & prog chair, 91-93, chair, 93- *Mem:* Tech Asn Pulp & Paper Indust; Am Chem Soc; Am Soc Testing & Mat; Sigma Xi. *Res:* Industrial resource recovery and subsequent industrial energy conservation; industrial pollution control; process simulation; pulp and paper engineering and technology; hazardous waste sorbents and solidifiers. *Mailing Add:* 3244 Peterson Rd Green Bay WI 54311-7238. *Fax:* 920-465-2376

SELL, SARAH H WOOD, PEDIATRICS, PUBLIC HEALTH. *Current Pos:* from instr to prof, 54-78, EMER PROF PEDIAT, SCH MED, VANDERBILT UNIV, 78- *Personal Data:* b Birmingham, Ala, Mar 20, 13; m 52, Charles G; c Charles G & Clive H. *Educ:* Berea Col, AB, 34; Vanderbilt Univ, MS, 38, MD, 48; Am Bd Pediat, dipl, 54, cert pediat infectious dis, 89. *Prof Exp:* Intern pediat, Vanderbilt Univ Hosp, 48-49; resident, Cincinnati Children's Hosp, 49-51; instr microbiol & pediat, Sch Med, La State Univ, 51-53; instr pediat, Sch Med, Tulane Univ, 53-54. *Concurrent Pos:* Res fel microbiol & pediat, Sch Med, La State Univ, 51-53; med consult, Tenn State Dept Pub Health, environ epidemiol, 88, dir, 89-92; consult immunizations, Ctr Dis Control, 63-66; mem adv comt infectious dis, Nat Inst Allergy & Infectious Dis, 73-77, consult meningitis vaccine trial, Finland, 74; consult pediat, US Dept Health & Human Serv, Social Security Admin, 92- *Mem:* Am Pediat Soc; Am Acad Pediat; Am Col Chest Physicians; Infectious Dis Soc Am; Am Soc Microbiol; Pediat Infectious Dis Soc. *Res:* Infectious diseases of infants and children; bacterial meningitis and sequelae, otitis media, respiratory infections and immunizations; life long emphasis on Haemophilus influenzae diseases and prevention; bacterial polysaccharide vaccines. *Mailing Add:* 3804 Woodlawn Dr Nashville TN 37215

SELL, STEWART, PATHOLOGY, IMMUNOLOGY. *Current Pos:* PROF PATH, PATH LAB MED, ALBANY MED CTR, ALBANY, 97- *Personal Data:* b Pittsburgh, Pa, Jan 20, 35; m 90, Ilze Klavins; c Sherri (Phillips), Stacy (Klinke), Sean, Stephanie (Kinzell) & Philip. *Educ:* Col William & Mary, BS, 56; Univ Pittsburgh, MD, 60; Am Bd Path, Dipl, 66, 83; Am Bd Lab Immunol, 81. *Prof Exp:* Intern & asst resident path, Mass Gen Hosp, 60-62; res assoc, NIH, 62-64; from instr to assoc prof, Sch Med, Univ Pittsburgh, 65-70; from assoc prof to prof path, Sch Med, Univ Calif, San Diego, 70-82; prof path, Path Lab Med, Univ Tex Health Sci Ctr, Houston, 82-96. *Concurrent Pos:* Nat Inst Allergy & Infectious Dis spec fel, Univ Birmingham, Eng, 64-65 & res career develop award, 65-70; mem adv path study sect B, NIH, 72-76. *Mem:* AAAS; Brit Soc Immunol; Am Asn Immunologists; NY Acad Sci; Am Soc Invest Path. *Res:* Immunology and pathology; alpha fetoprotein; chemical carcinogenesis; liver stem cells; viral pathogenesis; oncogenes in liver cancer; Hepatitis B Virus trausgenic mice; P53 in experimental liver cancer. *Mailing Add:* Albany Med Col 27 New Scotland Ave Albany NY 12208. *Fax:* 518-262-5927

SELLA, GEORGE JOHN, PHARMACOLOGY. *Current Pos:* Staff, Am Cyanamid Co, 54-76, corp vpres, 77, sr vpres, 77-78, vchmn, 78-79, pres, 79-90, CHIEF EXEC OFFICER, AM CYANAMID CO, 83-, CHMN BD, 84- *Personal Data:* b West New York, NJ, Sept 29, 28; m 55, Janet M Auf-der-Heide; c George C, Jaime A, Lorie J, Michael J & Carlie. *Educ:* Princeton Univ, BS, 50; Harvard Univ, MBA, 52. *Concurrent Pos:* Bd dirs, Union Camp Corp, Equitable Life Assurance Soc US, Multiple Sclerosis Soc. *Mem:* Nat Asn Med; Pharmaceut Mfr Asn. *Mailing Add:* Am Cyanamid Co 1 Cyanamid Plaza Wayne NJ 07470-2012

SELLARS, JOHN R(ANDOLPH), AERONAUTICAL ENGINEERING. *Current Pos:* RETIRED. *Personal Data:* b Ft Stanton, NMex, Mar 1, 25; m 50; c 3. *Educ:* NMex State Univ, BS, 45; Univ Mich, MS, 50, PhD(aeronaut eng), 52. *Prof Exp:* Res assoc, Appl Physics Lab, Johns Hopkins Univ, 45-46; res assoc, Univ Mich, 46-52, asst prof, 52-55; mem tech staff, TRW Systs, 55-58, mgr, Aerodyn Dept, 58-61, dir Aerosci Lab, 61-66, mgr, Systs Labs Eng Oper, 66-69, mgr, res & technol opers, Appl Technol Div, TRW Systs, 69-81, vpres & gen mgr, Energy Technol Div, TRW Energy Develop Group, 81-86. *Mem:* Am Inst Aeronaut & Astronaut; Sigma Xi. *Res:* Reentry systems; stability of flow; heat transfer. *Mailing Add:* 128 Via Los Miradores Redondo Beach CA 90277

SELLAS, JAMES THOMAS, ORGANIC CHEMISTRY. *Current Pos:* RETIRED. *Personal Data:* b Chicago, Ill, Dec 29, 24; m 51; c 3. *Educ:* Univ Ill, BS, 48; Univ Iowa, MS, 51, PhD(chem), 54. *Prof Exp:* Chemist, Stand Oil Co, 53-59, Aerojet-Gen Corp, Gen Tire & Rubber Co, 59-71 & Aerojet Solid Propulsion Co, 71-75, sr chem specialist, Aerojet Solid Propulsion Co, 75-78 & Aerojet Tech Syst Co, 78-85. *Concurrent Pos:* Consult, 85- *Mem:* Am Chem Soc; Sigma Xi. *Res:* Polymer chemistry; development of new and novel class of controllable high burning rate propellants for thrust vector control and controllable solid rocket application; expanding the technology of extinguishable solid propellants and the use of new oxidizers; expanding technology of ultra high burning rate propellants; development of high density-impulse propellants, and high combustion efficiency propellants; development of space storable propellants; additives developed and research carried out to determine methods to control both temperature and pressure sensitivity in the combustion of solid propellants. *Mailing Add:* 3708 Lynwood Way Sacramento CA 95864

SELLE, JAMES EDWARD, METALLURGICAL ENGINEERING, MATERIALS ENGINEERING. *Current Pos:* ASSOC SCIENTIST, EG&G ROCKY FLATS, GOLDEN, COLO, 80- *Personal Data:* b Waukesha, Wis, Sept 1, 31; m 58; c 2. *Educ:* Univ Wis, BS, 55, MS, 56; Univ Cincinnati, PhD(metall eng), 67. *Honors & Awards:* Wilson Award, Am Soc Metals, 72. *Prof Exp:* Res engr, Gen Motors Res Staff, Mich, 56-58 & Dayton Malleable Iron Co, Ohio, 58; sr res chemist, Mound Lab, Monsanto Res Corp, 58-67, group leader, 67-70, sr res specialist, 70-73; res staff mem, Oak Ridge Nat Lab, 74-80. *Mem:* Am Soc Metals. *Res:* Equilibrium diagrams; allotropic transformations; compatibility; nuclear reactor fuels studies; high temperature reactions; liquid metal corrosion; impurity effects on material properties. *Mailing Add:* 4755 W 101st Pl Westminster CO 80030

SELLERS, ALFRED MAYER, MEDICINE, CARDIOLOGY. *Current Pos:* Asst instr, 52-54, instr, 54-56, assoc, 56-59, asst prof, 59-66, chief hypertension clin, Univ Hosp, 61-71, ASSOC PROF MED, UNIV HOSP & MED SCH, UNIV PA, 66- *Personal Data:* b Philadelphia, Pa, Feb 23, 24; wid; c Joseph M & David A. *Educ:* Duke Univ, BS & MD, 51; Am Bd Internal Med, dipl, 58, recert, 75. *Hon Degrees:* MA, Univ Pa, 71. *Concurrent Pos:* Attend physician, Vet Admin Hosp, Philadelphia, 67-; mem coun high blood pressure res & mem med adv bd & fel coun clin cardiol, Am Heart Asn. *Mem:* AAAS; fel Am Col Physicians; Am Fedn Clin Res; fel Am Col Cardiol; fel Am Col Chest Physicians; fel Am Col Clin Pharmacol. *Res:* Internal medicine; cardiology; hypertension. *Mailing Add:* Dept Med Univ Pa Hosp 3400 Spruce St Philadelphia PA 19104

SELLERS, ALVIN FERNER, VETERINARY PHYSIOLOGY. *Current Pos:* prof physiol, 60-, EMER PROF, NY STATE VET COL, CORNELL UNIV. *Personal Data:* b Somerset, Pa, Aug 9, 17; m 42; c 3. *Educ:* Univ Pa, VMD, 39; Ohio State Univ, MS, 40; Univ Minn, PhD, 49. *Prof Exp:* Asst, Ohio State Univ, 39-40; instr animal physiol, Univ Minn, 40-42 & 46-49, assoc prof vet physiol, 49-54, prof vet physiol & pharmacol & head div, 54-60. *Concurrent Pos:* Guggenheim fel, Physiol Lab, Cambridge & Rowett Res Inst, Scotland, 57-58. *Mem:* Am Physiol Soc; Soc Exp Biol & Med; Am Gastroenterol Asn. *Res:* Ruminant digestive tract; absorption; blood flow. *Mailing Add:* Dept Physiol NY State Col Vet Med Cornell Univ Ithaca NY 14853

SELLERS, ALVIN LOUIS, PHYSIOLOGY. *Current Pos:* RETIRED. *Personal Data:* b Philadelphia, Pa, Oct 16, 16; m 42; c 3. *Educ:* Univ Calif, Los Angeles, BA, 40, MD, 43. *Prof Exp:* Intern med, Univ Calif Hosp, 43-44; resident, Permanente Hosp, 44-46; Nat Res Coun res fel, St Mary's Hosp Med Sch, Eng, 47-48; res fel, Cedars of Lebanon Hosp, Los Angeles, 48-49, res assoc, 50-70, sr res assoc, 70-93. *Concurrent Pos:* Assoc clin prof med, Univ Southern Calif, 56-73; clin prof med, Univ Calif, Los Angeles, 79-93. *Mem:* Soc Exp Biol & Med; Am Physiol Soc; Am Heart Asn. *Res:* Physiology of the kidneys; hypertension. *Mailing Add:* 1117 Sierra Alta Way Los Angeles CA 90069

SELLERS, CLETUS MILLER, JR, ENVIRONMENTAL PHYSIOLOGY. *Current Pos:* Asst prof biol, 73-81, ASSOC PROF BIOL, JAMES MADISON UNIV, 81- *Personal Data:* b Harrisonburg, Va, Sept 6, 44; m 70. *Educ:* Hampden-Sydney Col, BA, 66; James Madison Univ, MS, 70; Va Polytech Inst & State Univ, PhD(zool), 73. *Mem:* Sigma Xi. *Res:* Development and implementation of biological monitoring for rapid detection and quantification of environmental toxicant effects. *Mailing Add:* Dept Biol James Madison Univ 800 S Main St Harrisonburg VA 22807-0001

SELLERS, DONALD ROSCOE, TOXIC MATERIALS DETECTION, CLINICAL CHEMISTRY. *Current Pos:* BIOCHEMIST, ABBOTT LABS, 83- *Personal Data:* b Kansas City, Mo, June, 24, 46; m 68; c 2. *Educ:* Univ Mo, AB, 68, MS, 70, PhD(biochem), 72. *Prof Exp:* Head, Stress Biochem Lab, Wright Patterson AFB, Ohio, 72-77; sr biochemist, Midwest Res Inst, 77-83. *Mem:* AAAS. *Res:* Development of methodologies and instrumentation that employ biological mechanisms to detect chemicals of interest in the environment and workplace. *Mailing Add:* 705 Roosevelt Dr Libertyville IL 60048

SELLERS, DOUGLAS EDWIN, analytical chemistry; deceased, see previous edition for last biography

SELLERS, EDWARD MONCRIEFF, CLINICAL PHARMACOLOGY, WOMENS HEALTH. *Current Pos:* assoc prof pharmacol & med, 76-80, assoc dean acad affairs, 84-89, PROF PHARMACOL, MED & PSYCHIAT, UNIV TORONTO, 80-, DIR, PSYCHOPHARMACOL & DEPENDENCE RES UNIT, 96- *Personal Data:* b Victoria, BC, June 12, 41. *Educ:* Univ Toronto, MD, 65; Harvard Univ, PhD(pharmacol), 71; FRCP(C) & Am Bd Internal Med, dipl internal med, 72; FACP, 77. *Honors & Awards:* Rawls Parlmer Award, Am Soc Clin Pharmacol & Exp Therapeut; Serv Award, Can Soc Clin Pharmacol. *Prof Exp:* Head, Clin Pharmacol Prog & Clin Res Unit, Addiction Res Found, 72-81, head med, 79-84, head, Psychopharmacol Res Group, 84-92, dir, Clin Res & Treat Inst, 91-93. *Concurrent Pos:* Dir, Div Clin Pharmacol, Toronto Western Hosp, 75-79; consult, Clarke Inst Psychiat; vpres, Addicted Res Found, 92-94. *Mem:* Am Soc Pharmacol & Exp Therapeut; Am Soc Clin Pharmacol & Therapeut (pres), 81); Can Soc Clin Pharmacol (pres), 86); Col on Probl Drug Dependence (pres), 94); Soc Neurosci; Am Col Neuropsychopharamcol; Res Soc Alcoholism; Int Soc Biomed Res Alcoholism. *Res:* Alcohol and drug abuse; pharmacogenetics; drug metabolism and toxicology; drug treatment of alcohol and substance abuse; women's health. *Mailing Add:* Ctr Res Women's Health 76 Grenville St Toronto ON M5S 1B2 Can. *Fax:* 416-323-7553; *E-Mail:* e.sellers@utoronto.ca

SELLERS, ERNEST E(DWIN), ELECTRICAL ENGINEERING. *Current Pos:* RETIRED. *Personal Data:* b Manhattan, Kans, Aug 17, 25; m 49; c 4. *Educ:* Kans State Univ, BS, 48, MS, 49. *Prof Exp:* Res engr, Res Labs, Radio Corp Am, NJ, 49-51; instr elec eng, Kans State Univ, 51-52; res engr, Univ Mich, Ann Arbor, 52-85, emer engr & managing dir off, Inst Sci & Technol, 85-89. *Concurrent Pos:* Sr engr, Tex Instruments Co, 59; head, Univ Mich Tech Inst Radar Lab, 63-66. *Mem:* AAAS; Inst Elec & Electronics Engrs; Instrument Soc Am. *Res:* Electronics systems analysis; air defense; combat surveillance; detection and control theory; radar; television; countermeasures; navigation; radio astronomy; microwave propagation and reflection; signal handling; data processing; data display; bio-medical engineering. *Mailing Add:* 2105 Copley St Ann Arbor MI 48104

SELLERS, FRANCIS BACHMAN, ATOMIC PHYSICS, NUCLEAR PHYSICS. *Current Pos:* head physicist, 64-80, VPRES RADIATION PHYSICS, PANAMETRICS INC, 81- *Personal Data:* b Washington, NC, Mar 22, 30; m 58; c 2. *Educ:* Wake Forest Col, BS, 54; Univ Kans, PhD(physics), 60. *Prof Exp:* Sr physicist, Phys Res Dept, Allied Res Assocs, Inc, Mass, 60-62, head physics res dept, 62-64. *Mem:* Am Phys Soc; Sigma Xi; Am Geophys Union; Am Meteorol Soc. *Res:* Interaction of nuclear particles with matter; production and measurement of x-radiation; measurement of atmospheric and extraterrestrial parameters; radiation detection techniques for rocket and satellite applications; atmospheric physics. *Mailing Add:* Parametrics Inc 221 Crescent St Waltham MA 02154-3497

SELLERS, FRANK JAMIESON, PEDIATRIC CARDIOLOGY. *Current Pos:* RETIRED. *Personal Data:* b Winnipeg, Man, Mar 10, 28; m 61; c 3. *Educ:* Univ Man, BSc, 54; Queen's Univ, Ont, MD & CM, 55. *Prof Exp:* From asst prof to assoc prof pediat, Univ Sask, 63-70; assoc prof pediat, Univ Ottawa, 70- *Mem:* Can Med Asn; Can Pediat Soc; Can Cardiovasc Soc; Can Soc Clin Invest. *Res:* Congenital heart disease; rheumatic fever. *Mailing Add:* 41 Davidson Dr Gloucester ON K1J 6L7 Can

SELLERS, JAMES ALLEN, STUDY OF PARTITION FUNCTIONS. *Current Pos:* ASST PROF MATH, CEDARVILLE COL, 92- *Personal Data:* b San Antonio, Tex, Sept 1, 65; m 90, Mary L Bressler; c Nathaniel J, David S, Elizabeth C & Michael O. *Educ:* Univ Tex, San Antonio, BS, 87; Pa State Univ, PhD(Math), 92. *Prof Exp:* Casualty actuary, United Servs Automobile Asn, 87. *Mem:* Am Math Soc; Math Asn Am. *Res:* Congruences and recurrences involving partition functions. *Mailing Add:* Cedarville Col PO Box 601 Cedarville OH 45314. *E-Mail:* sellersj@cedarville.edu

SELLERS, JOHN WILLIAM, RUBBER, PLASTICS. *Current Pos:* RETIRED. *Personal Data:* b Wausau, Wis, Apr 13, 16; m 44, Lee King; c Rick & Diane. *Educ:* Univ Ill, BS, 42; Ohio State Univ, PhD(chem), 49. *Prof Exp:* Tech dir foods, Food Mat Corp, 37-40; jr chem engr rubber, Firestone Tire & Rubber Co, 42-45, sr res chemist, 49-51; sr res chemist, Chem Div, PPG Indust, 51-57, supvry org res, 57-58, sr supvr org res, 59-63, Rubber Chem Res, 63-65; head, Org Res Sect, Petrol Chems, Inc, 58-59; tech adv to mgt & dir corp res, Tenneco Chem, Inc, 65-67; dir res & develop, Paterson Paper Co, 67-68, vpres tech, 68-70; mgr indust waste mgt, Procon, Inc, 70-71 & environ control, H J Heinz Co, 71-73; vpres opers, Intersci, Inc, 73-76, exec vpres, 77-82, pres & chief exec officer, 83-87; tech asst to sr vpres, Reeves/Southeastern Corp, 87-89. *Concurrent Pos:* Consult, Intersci, Inc, 87- *Mem:* Sigma Xi; Am Chem Soc; Am Inst Chem Eng. *Res:* Organic synthesis; high polymers; plastics; vulcanization and reinforcement of elastomers; oxidation of hydrocarbons; kinetics and mechanisms; market development; management. *Mailing Add:* 1002 Lake Avoca Dr Tarpon Springs FL 34689

SELLERS, PETER HOADLEY, MATHEMATICS OF NETWORKS. *Current Pos:* res assoc, 66-72, ASSOC PROF MATH, ROCKEFELLER UNIV, 72-, SR RES ASSOC, 74- *Personal Data:* b Philadelphia, Pa, Sept 12, 30; m 58, Lucy Newlin; c Mortimer, Therese, Mary & Lucy. *Educ:* Univ Pa, PhD(math), 65. *Prof Exp:* Programmer math, Johnson Found, Univ Pa, 58-61; master, Kangaru Sch, Embu, Kenya, 61-63; fel math, Johnson Found, Univ Pa, 65-66. *Concurrent Pos:* Ed, Genomics; trustee, Col Atlantic, Bar Harbor, Maine. *Mem:* Am Math Soc; Math Asn Am; Soc Indust & Appl Math. *Res:* Combinatorial analysis; analysis of genetic sequences; chemical kinetics. *Mailing Add:* Lab Math Rockefeller Univ New York NY 10021-6399. *Fax:* 212-327-7974

SELLERS, THOMAS F, JR, PREVENTIVE MEDICINE, INFECTIOUS DISEASES. *Current Pos:* RETIRED. *Personal Data:* b Atlanta, Ga, Apr 9, 27; m 49; c 3. *Educ:* Emory Univ, BS, 47, MD, 50. *Prof Exp:* Res fel infectious dis, Sch Med, Emory Univ, 55-57 & Med Col, Cornell Univ, 57-58; asst prof med, Emory Univ, 58-60, prof prev med, Sch Med, 60-90, emer prof, 90- *Concurrent Pos:* Mem adv comt health, Appalachian Regional Comn, 65-67; staff mem community med, Cent Middlesex Hosp, London, Eng, 74-75. *Mem:* Am Col Physicians; Am Pub Health Asn; Am Col Prev Med; Asn Teachers Prev Med. *Mailing Add:* 4875 Franklin Pond Rd Atlanta GA 30342-2765

SELLGREN, KRISTEN, INFRARED ASTRONOMY, INTERSTELLAR DUST. *Current Pos:* ASST PROF ASTRON, DEPT ASTRON, OHIO STATE UNIV, 90- *Personal Data:* b San Diego, Calif, Nov 14, 55. *Educ:* Univ Calif, San Diego, BA, 76; Calif Inst Technol, PhD(physics), 83. *Honors & Awards:* Newton Lacy Pierce Prize, Am Astron Soc, 90. *Prof Exp:* Postdoctoral res assoc, Space Telescope Sci Inst, 83-84; asst astronr, Inst Astron, Univ Hawaii, 84-89, assoc astronr, 89-90. *Mem:* Am Astron Soc. *Res:* Infrared imaging and spectroscopy of the galactic center, interstellar dust and other astronomical sources. *Mailing Add:* Dept Astron Ohio State Univ 174 W 18th Ave Columbus OH 43210-1106

SELLIN, H A, structual geology; deceased, see previous edition for last biography

SELLIN, IVAN ARMAND, ATOMIC PHYSICS. *Current Pos:* from assoc prof to prof, 70-83, DISTINGUISHED SERV PROF PHYSICS, UNIV TENN, KNOXVILLE, 83-, PROJ DIR, 70- *Personal Data:* b Everett, Wash, Aug 16, 39; m 62, Helen Gill; c Peter & Frank. *Educ:* Harvard Univ, BS, 59; Univ Chicago, SM, 60, PhD(physics), 64. *Honors & Awards:* Sr US Scientist Award, Alexander von Humboldt Found, 77; Jesse Beams Medal, Am Phys Soc, 83; Japanese Soc Promotion Sci Award, 94; Swedish Nat Sci Coun Award, 94. *Prof Exp:* Instr physics, Univ Chicago, 64-65; asst prof, NY Univ, 65-67; res physicist, Oak Ridge Nat Lab, 67-70; consult, NSF, 80-83. *Concurrent Pos:* Lectr, Univ Chicago, 61-64; proj dir & consult, Oak Ridge Nat Lab, 70-; vis prof, Am States, 72; NSF grants; NASA grants, Off Naval Res Contracts, Dept Energy contracts, Univ Tenn, 72-82; mem adv comt atomic & molecular physics, Nat Acad Sci, 73-76, chmn, 80-83; chmn, Fourth Int Conf Beam-Foil Spectros, 75; guest prof, Swed Natural Sci Res Coun, 78; sr Fulbright Hays grant, Ger, 77; guest prof, Cent Atomico Bariloche, Arg, 81; counr coun PLA Am Phys Soc, 79-83; mem panel atomic, molecular & optical physics, NRC-NAS Natural Physics Soc, 83-84; Cecil & Ida Green hon chmn, Tex Christian Univ, 84; Allett fel, Univ Witwatersrand, 85; Humboldt Found award, 86-88. *Mem:* Fel Am Phys Soc; Cosmos Club. *Res:* Physics of ion beams; structure and collisions of heavy ions; physics of highly ionized matter; x-ray interactions with atoms and molecules. *Mailing Add:* 40 Rivers Runway Oak Ridge TN 37830. *Fax:* 423-574-1118; *E-Mail:* selling@utkvx

SELLIN, LAWRENCE C, THREE-DIMENSIONAL STRUCTURAL ANALYSIS, DRUG DEVELOPMENT. *Current Pos:* SR SCI ADV & DIR INTERNET SERV, ASTRA-FINLAND, 92-, ASSOC PROF BIOPHYS, UNIV OULU, 92- *Personal Data:* m 84, Marjukka Molsa; c Michael P & Kira S. *Educ:* Univ Del, BA, 72; Seton Hall Univ, MS, 73; NJ Med Sch, PhD(physiol), 78. *Prof Exp:* Fel, Univ Lund, Sweden, 78-80; res physiologist, US Army Med Res Inst Infectious Dis, 80-84; res neurophysiologist, Alko Res Lab, Finland, 84-85; mgr cardiovasc drug develop, Orion Pharmaceut, Finland, 85-89; prog mgr, NSF, 89-90; sci res adminr, NIH, 90-92. *Concurrent Pos:* Vis scientist, Swed Med Res Coun, 82; res consult, Astra Pharmaceut Group, 90. *Mem:* Biophys Soc. *Res:* Three-dimensional structure activity studies of peptides and natural products using electrophysiology; three-dimensional computer simulations and two-dimensional nuclear magnetic resonance for the purpose of drug development; signal analysis using wavelet transform. *Mailing Add:* Astra PL6 Masala 02431 Finland. *Fax:* 358-9-61365257; *E-Mail:* lawrence.sellin@pp.inet.fi

SELLINGER, OTTO ZIVKO, NEUROCHEMISTRY. *Current Pos:* assoc res pharmacologist, 65-68, RES SCIENTIST, MENT HEALTH RES INST, UNIV MICH, ANN ARBOR, 68- *Personal Data:* b Zagreb, Yugoslavia, Sept 14, 29; nat US; m 55; c 4. *Educ:* Mass Inst Technol, SB, 54; Tulane Univ, PhD(biochem), 58. *Prof Exp:* NIH fel, Lab Physiol Chem, Univ Louvain, Belg, 58-59; NIH fel biochem, Ist Superiore Sanita, Rome, Italy, 59-60; asst prof biochem & med, Med Sch, Tulane Univ, 60-64; Fulbright vis prof biochem, Univ of the Repub, Montevideo, Uruguay, 64-65. *Concurrent Pos:* Fogarty Int Scientist Award, Univ Claude Bernard, Villeurbanne, France, 81-82. *Mem:* Am Soc Neurochem; Int Soc Neurochem. *Res:* Neurochemistry; protein methylation in aging brain. *Mailing Add:* 307 Doty Ave Ann Arbor MI 48103

SELLMER, GEORGE PARK, ZOOLOGY. *Current Pos:* RETIRED. *Personal Data:* b Milwaukee, Wis, Mar 12, 18; m 43; c 2. *Educ:* Upsala Col, AB, 48; Rutgers Univ, MS, 52, PhD(zool), 59. *Prof Exp:* From instr to assoc prof, Upsala Col, 48-61, chmn dept, 58- 79, prof biol, 61- *Mem:* Soc Sci Study Sex; Am Asn Sex Educr, Councr & Therapists. *Res:* Anatomy and ecology of bivalve mollusks; human sexuality; biological control of insect pests. *Mailing Add:* 35 Bergen Blvd Little Falls NJ 07424

SELLMYER, DAVID JULIAN, SOLID STATE PHYSICS, MATERIALS SCIENCE & ENGINEERING. *Current Pos:* assoc prof, Univ Nebr, 72-75, chmn dept, 78-84, prof, 75-87, GEORGE HOLMES DISTINGUISHED PROF PHYSICS, UNIV NEBR, LINCOLN, 87-, DIR CTR MAT RES & ANALYSIS, 88- *Personal Data:* b Joliet, Ill, Sept 28, 38; m 62, Catherine J Zakas; c Rebecca A, Julia M & Mark A. *Educ:* Univ Ill, BS, 60; Mich State Univ, PhD(physics), 65. *Prof Exp:* From asst prof to assoc prof metall & mat sci, Ctr Mat Sci, Mass Inst Technol, 65-72. *Concurrent Pos:* Consult, USAF Cambridge Res Lab, Bedford, Mass, 71-72 & Dale Electron, Norfolk, Nebr, 79-; vis scientist, Nat Mag Lab, MIT-1105-80, Inst phys, Beijing, 85 & 86, Synchrotim Radiation Ctr, Univ Wis, 88- *Mem:* AAAS; fel Am Phys Soc; Sigma Xi; Mat Res Soc. *Res:* Electronic structure and magnetism in metallic compounds and alloys; physics of metallic glasses; amorphous magnetism; physics of thin films and multilayers; magnetic recording materials. *Mailing Add:* Behlen Lab Physics & Ctr Mat Res & Anal Univ Nebr Lincoln NE 68588-0113

SELLNER, KEVIN GREGORY, PLANKTON ECOLOGY. *Current Pos:* asst cur, Dept Limnol, Acad Natural Sci, 78-81, asst cur, 81-86, assoc cur, 86-94, CUR, BENEDICT ESTUARINE RES LAB, ACAD NATURAL SCI, 94- *Personal Data:* b Albany, NY, Oct 11, 49. *Educ:* Clark Univ, BA, 71; Univ SC, MS, 73; Dalhousie Univ, PhD(oceanog), 78. *Prof Exp:* Res asst algal physiol, Univ SC, 71-73. *Concurrent Pos:* Adj asst prof, Chesapeake Biol Lab, Univ Md, 84-87; adj res scientist, Chesapeake Bay Inst, Johns Hopkins Univ, 85-87. *Mem:* Am Soc Limnol & Oceanog; Phycol Soc Am; Estuarine Res Fedn. *Res:* Dynamics of carbon, nitrogen and oxygen in estuarine environmnets; the importance of plankton primary production in carbon, nitrogen and phosphorous flux to secondary producers, for example, bacteria and herbivorous zooplankton and fish; associated effects on carbon deposition and microbial oxidation in partially mixed estuaries. *Mailing Add:* Acad Natural Sci Benedict Estuarine Res Lab 10545 Mackall Blvd St Leonard MD 20685

SELLS, BRUCE HOWARD, MOLECULAR BIOLOGY. *Current Pos:* dean, Col Biol Sci, 83-95, prof, 83-96, EMER PROF MOLECULAR BIOL, UNIV GUELPH, CAN, 96- *Personal Data:* b Ottawa, Ont, Aug 15, 30; m 53, Bernice; c Jennifer, Monica, David & Lisa. *Educ:* Carleton Univ, BSc, 52; Queen's Univ, Ont, MA, 54; McGill Univ, PhD(biochem), 57. *Prof Exp:* Damon Runyon res fels, Lab Animal Morphol, Free Univ Brussels, 57-59 & State Serum Inst, Copenhagen, Denmark, 59-60; cancer res scientist, Roswell Park Mem Inst, 60-61; res scientist, Columbia Univ, 61-62; from asst prof to assoc prof, Lab Biochem, St Jude Children's Res Hosp & Dept Biochem, Univ Tenn, Memphis, 62-73, mem, Hosp, 68-72; prof & dir molecular biol, Med Sch, Mem Univ Nfld, 72-83, assoc dean basic med sci, 79-83. *Concurrent Pos:* Vis res scientist, Inst Animal Genetics, Univ Edinburgh, 69-70; mem, Biochem Grants Comt, Med Res Coun Can, 73 , Grants Comt Molecular Biol & Coun & Centennial Fel Comt; assoc ed, Can J Biochem, 74; Killam sr res fel, Inst Molecular Biol, Univ Paris, 78-79; exchange scientist, Coop Res Prog, Fr Nat Ctr Sci Res, US Nat Res Coun; sci officer, Nat Cancer Inst, 79-81; chmn, Comt Biotechnol Develop Grants, Med Res Coun Can, 83-85; mem, Sub-Comt Biol Phenomena, Nat Res Coun Can, 83-86; rapporteur, Microbiol & Biochem Div, Royal Soc Can, 85-87, convenor, 87-; chmn, Steering Group, assoc, Comt Sci Criteria Environ Qual, Nat Res Coun Can, 86; E W R Steacie Prize Awards comt, 86-88; Med Res Coun vis prof, Inst Pasteur, Paris, France, 89; Ayerst Award Selection Comt, Can Biochem Soc, 90; mem, Life Sci Div Fel Rev Comt, Acad Sci, Royal Soc Can, 90-; mem, Standing Comt, Genetic Basis Human Dis Network, Med Res Coun, 91. *Mem:* Can Biochem Soc (pres); Am Soc Biol Chemists; Am Soc Microbiol; Can Asn Univ Teachers; Am Soc Cell Biol; fel Royal Soc Can. *Res:* Nucleic acids; biosynthesis of ribosomes; studies on growth and differentiation; translational control. *Mailing Add:* Col Biol Sci Univ Guelph Guelph ON N1G 2W1 Can. *E-Mail:* bsells@uoguelph.ca

SELLS, GARY DONNELL, CELL BIOLOGY, GENERAL BIOLOGY. *Current Pos:* assoc prof, 65-71, PROF PHYSIOL, NORTHEAST MO STATE UNIV, 71- *Personal Data:* b New Hartford, Iowa, Aug 5, 32; m 53; c 4. *Educ:* Univ Northern Iowa, BA, 54, MA, 59; Iowa State Univ, PhD(plant physiol), 65. *Prof Exp:* Teacher high schs, Iowa, 54-62. *Mem:* Nat Asn Biol; Am Inst Biol Sci; Sigma Xi. *Res:* Physiology; botany; developmental anatomy; mitochondrial research in plants & animals. *Mailing Add:* 6 Grim Ct S Kirksville MO 63501-4435

SELLS, JACKSON S(TUART), ELECTRICAL ENGINEERING. *Current Pos:* RETIRED. *Personal Data:* b Buffalo, NY, Dec 27, 20; m 41; c 2. *Educ:* Univ Miami, BS, 46, MS, 50; Purdue Univ, BSEE, 52. *Prof Exp:* Asst prof elec eng & physics, Univ Miami, 46-55, from assoc prof elec eng, 55-65, prof, 65- *Concurrent Pos:* Consult, Mercy Hosp, Fla, 53-60 & City of Miami, 60-80. *Mem:* Am Soc Eng Educ; Illum Eng Soc; Inst Elec & Electronics Engrs; Am Sci Affil; Simulations Coun. *Res:* Servomechanisms; radiotelemetry; control and network theories. *Mailing Add:* 8215 Saragoza Ct Orlando FL 32836

SELLS, JEAN THURBER, MATHEMATICS. *Current Pos:* ASSOC PROF MATH, SACRED HEART UNIV, 76-, CHMN, DEPT MATH, 81- *Personal Data:* b Butte, Nebr, May 24, 40; m 62; c 2. *Educ:* Nebr Wesleyan Univ, AB, 61; Univ Minn, Minneapolis, MA, 63, PhD(math), 66. *Prof Exp:* Asst prof math, Tex A&I Univ, 66-67; asst prof, Univ Louisville, 67-70; from asst prof to assoc prof, Frostburg State Col, 70-72; assoc prof, Coker Col, 73-75; asst prof, Fordham Univ, 75-76. *Mem:* Am Math Soc; Math Asn Am; Nat Coun Teachers Math. *Mailing Add:* 36 September Lane Weston CT 06883-1519

SELLS, ROBERT LEE, PHYSICS. *Current Pos:* prof, 63-73, DISTINGUISHED TEACHING PROF PHYSICS & ASTRON & CHMN DEPT, STATE UNIV NY COL GENESEO, 73- *Personal Data:* b Lancaster, Ohio, Oct 14, 25; m 47; c 2. *Educ:* Univ Mich, BS, 48; Univ Notre Dame, PhD(physics), 53. *Prof Exp:* From asst prof to assoc prof physics, Rutgers Univ, 53-63. *Mem:* Am Asn Physics Teachers; Am Phys Soc. *Res:* Theoretical physics; atomic and nuclear physics; solid state physics; teaching physics. *Mailing Add:* 27 Oak St Geneseo NY 14454

SELLSTEDT, JOHN H, MEDICINAL CHEMISTRY. *Current Pos:* Sr res chemist, Wyeth Labs, Inc, 65-69, group leader, 69-77, MGR RES ANALYTICAL CHEM, RES & DEVELOP LABS, WYETH LABS DIV, AM HOME PROD CORP, 77- *Personal Data:* b Minneapolis, Minn, June 11, 40; m 61; c 2. *Educ:* Univ Minn, BS, 62, PhD(org chem), 65. *Res:* Antiallergy and cardiovascular research; mass spectroscopy; cephalosporins and penicillins. *Mailing Add:* 1025 Blvd Marcel Laurin St Laurent PQ H4R 1J6 Can

SELMAN, ALAN L, THEORETICAL COMPUTER SCIENCE. *Current Pos:* prof & chmn, Dept Comput Sci, 90-96, PROF, DEPT COMPUT SCI, STATE UNIV NY, BUFFALO, 96- *Personal Data:* b New York, NY, Apr 2, 41; m 63, Sharon Jevotovsky; c Jeffrey & Heather. *Educ:* City Col Univ NY, BS, 62; Univ Calif, Berkeley, MA, 64; Pa State Univ, PhD(math), 70. *Prof Exp:* Instr math, Pa State Univ, 68-70; lectr, Carnegie-Mellon Univ, 70-72; asst prof, Fla State Univ, 72-77; from assoc prof to prof comput sci, Iowa State Univ, 77-86; prof, Northeastern Univ, 86-90, actg dean, Col Comput Sci, 88-89. *Concurrent Pos:* Res mathematician, Carnegie-Mellon Univ, 70-72; NSF grants, 75-87, 87-90, 90-93; vis scientist, Technician, 81-82; Fulbright award, 81-82. *Mem:* Asn Comput Mach; Europ Asn Theoret Comput Sci; Inst Elec & Electronics Engrs Comput Soc. *Res:* Structural complexity theory-studies of properties of complexity classes. *Mailing Add:* Dept Comput Sci State Univ NY 226 Bell Hall Buffalo NY 14260. *E-Mail:* selman@cs.buffalo.edu

SELMAN, BRUCE R, ENERGY TRANSDUCTION, CHLOROPLAST ATPASE BIOGENESIS. *Current Pos:* PROF BIOCHEM, UNIV WIS, 76- *Educ:* Univ Rochester, PhD(biol), 73. *Mailing Add:* 2022 Kendall Ave Madison WI 53705. *Fax:* 608-262-3453; *E-Mail:* Bitnet: bselman@wiscmacc

SELMAN, CHARLES MELVIN, ORGANIC POLYMER CHEMISTRY, ORGANOMETALLIC CHEMISTRY. *Current Pos:* sr polymerization chemist, 67-78, supvr polyolefins process, 79-82, MGR POLYOLEFINS, PHILLIPS PETROL CO, 83- *Personal Data:* b Brenham, Tex, Jan 18, 37; m 60; c 2. *Educ:* Southwestern Univ, BS, 59; N Tex State Univ, MS, 66, PhD(chem), 68. *Prof Exp:* Res chemist, Dow Chem Co, 60-63. *Mem:* Am Chem Soc; Soc Plastics Engrs. *Res:* Polymerization reactions of organic molecules catalyzed with organometallic compounds. *Mailing Add:* 5120 Parsons Dr Bartlesville OK 74006-5735

SELMAN, KELLY, CELL BIOLOGY, REPRODUCTIVE BIOLOGY. *Current Pos:* asst prof, 74-79, ASSOC PROF ANAT, COL MED, UNIV FLA, 79- *Personal Data:* b Cleveland, Ohio, July 22, 42; m 84, Robin A Wallace. *Educ:* Univ Mich, BA, 64; Harvard Univ, MA, 65, PhD(biol), 72. *Prof Exp:* Instr biol, Simmons Col, 67-68 & Univ Va, 71-72; fel anat, Harvard Univ Med Sch, 72-74. *Mem:* Am Soc Cell Biol; AAAS; Am Asn Anat. *Res:* Oogenesis and fertilization in lower vertebrates. *Mailing Add:* Dept Anat & Cell Biol Univ Fla Col Med PO Box 100235 Gainesville FL 32610-0235. *Fax:* 352-392-3305; *E-Mail:* selman@anatomy.med.ufl.edu

SELMANOFF, MICHAEL KIDD, REPRODUCTIVE NEUROENDOCRINOLOGY. *Current Pos:* from asst prof to assoc prof, 77-91, PROF DEPT PHYSIOL, SCH MED, UNIV MD, 91- *Personal Data:* b Minneapolis, Minn, July 18, 49; m, Amy Doigan; c Lisa M, Justin M & Mollie R. *Educ:* Earlham Col, BA, 70; Univ Conn, PhD(neurobiol), 74. *Prof Exp:* Fel Rockefeller Found, Dept Obstet, Gynec & Reprod Sci, Reprod Endocrinol Ctr, Sch Med, Univ Calif, San Francisco, 74-77. *Concurrent Pos:* Res career develop award, grants for 16 years, NIH, 78- *Mem:* Endocrine Soc; Soc Neurosci; Am Physiol Soc; Int Brain Res Orgn/World Fedn Neuroscientists; AAAS; Soc Study Reprod. *Res:* Role of tuberoinfundibular GABAergic and dopaminergic neurons in the release of prolactin and luteinizing hormone from the anterior pituitary gland. *Mailing Add:* Dept Physiol Sch Med Univ Md 655 W Baltimore St Baltimore MD 20201-1559

SELOVE, WALTER, PARTICLE PHYSICS. *Current Pos:* from assoc prof to prof, 56-92, EMER PROF PHYSICS, UNIV PA, 92- *Personal Data:* b Chicago, Ill, Sept 11, 21; m 55, Fay Ajzenberg. *Educ:* Univ Chicago, BS, 42, MS, 48, PhD(physics), 49. *Prof Exp:* Asst instr electronics, Univ Chicago, 42-43; mem staff, Radiation Lab, Mass Inst Technol, 43-45; from jr physicist to assoc physicist, Argonne Nat Lab, 47-50; from instr to asst prof physics, Harvard Univ, 50-56. *Concurrent Pos:* Mem staff, Radiation Lab, Univ Calif, 53-54; NSF fel, 56; Guggenheim fel, 71-72. *Mem:* Fel Am Phys Soc; Sigma Xi. *Res:* Radar receivers; nuclear and particle physics. *Mailing Add:* Dept Physics Univ Pa 209 S 33rd St Philadelphia PA 19104

SELOVER, JAMES CARROLL, ORGANIC CHEMISTRY. *Current Pos:* PRIN, SELOVER ASSOCS, 91- *Personal Data:* b Los Angeles, Calif, Mar 25, 29; m 81, Peggy Armstrong; c Jay, Scott, Jon, Lee & Lauren. *Educ:* Rutgers Univ, BS, 50; Stanford Univ, MS, 52, PhD(org chem), 53. *Prof Exp:* Res chemist, M W Kellogg Co, Pullman, Inc, 53-55; sr res chemist, Richfield Oil Corp, 55-59; tech dir new prods & qual control, Pilot Chem Co, 59; sr chem economist, Stanford Res Inst, 59-68, dir long range planning serv, 68-69; planning syts mgr, Bechtel Corp, 69-71, exec engr, 73-79; exec vpres, Lurgi Corp, 79-85; mgr corp planning, Bechtel Nat Inc, 71-91, vpres, 85-91. *Mem:* Am Chem Soc; Sigma Xi; Am Inst Chem Engrs. *Res:* Management consulting and corporate research planning. *Mailing Add:* 3911 Avenida Brisa Rancho Santa Fe CA 92091-4221. *Fax:* 619-759-3487; *E-Mail:* drjims135@aol.com

SELOVER, THEODORE BRITTON, JR, THERMODYNAMICS & MATERIAL PROPERTIES, NUMERIC PROPERTY DATA BASES. *Current Pos:* CONSULT CHEMIST, 85- *Personal Data:* b Cleveland, Ohio, Jan 13, 31; m 55, Barbara Allen; c Cynthia (Ingersoll), Mark & Peter. *Educ:* Brown Univ, ScB, 52; Western Res Univ, MS, 57. *Prof Exp:* Jr chemist, Stand Oil Co, Ohio, 52, chemist, 54-57, sr chemist & proj leader basic res, 57-60, tech specialist, 60-62, sr res chemist, 62-69, res assoc, 69-71, info specialist, 71-85; tech dir, Am Inst Chem Engrs, Design Inst Phys Prop Data, 86-95. *Concurrent Pos:* Mem, Eng Soc Libr Bd, 79-92, chmn, 85-87, 91-92; mem tech comt, Design Inst Phys Prop Data, 80-, chmn, 86-95; tech ed, Hemisphere Publ Co, 86-91; mem, Codata Task Group Exp Phys Properties Data Repository, 93-95. *Mem:* Am Chem Soc; Am Soc Testing & Mat; Am Phys Soc; Sigma Xi; Am Inst Chem Eng. *Res:* Plasma chemistry; high temperature materials; fused salt batteries; technical editing of Russian translations of property data; aqueous capacitors; thermodynamic and transport property data; numerical database; information resources. *Mailing Add:* 3575 Traver Rd Shaker Heights OH 44122-4925

SELSKY, MELVYN IRA, BOTANY. *Current Pos:* from asst prof to assoc prof, 60-72, PROF BIOL, BROOKLYN COL, 72- *Personal Data:* b Brooklyn, NY, June 25, 33; m 63; c 2. *Educ:* Brooklyn Col, BA, 54, MA, 56; Univ Ill, PhD(plant virol), 60. *Prof Exp:* Substitute teacher biol, Brooklyn Col, 54-56; asst bot, Univ Ill, 56-57 & plant virol, 57-59, res assoc, 60. *Concurrent Pos:* Nat Cancer Inst grant, 64-66; fel, Yale Univ, 69-70. *Mem:* AAAS; Am Soc Microbiol; NY Acad Sci. *Res:* Organelle transfer RNAs; chloroplast development in Euglena gracilis; blue-green algae. *Mailing Add:* Dept Biol City Univ NY Brooklyn Col 2901 Bedford Ave Brooklyn NY 11210-2813

SELTEN, REINHARD, ECONOMICS. *Current Pos:* RETIRED. *Personal Data:* b Breslau, Ger, Oct 5, 30; m 59, Elisabeth A Laugreiner. *Educ:* Frankfurt Univ, dipl math, 57, PhD, 61. *Honors & Awards:* Nobel Prize in Econs, 94. *Prof Exp:* Asst, Frankfurt Univ, 57-67, pvt docent, 68-69; prof, Free Univ Berlin, 69-72, Univ Bielefeld, Ger, 72-84 & Univ Bonn, Ger, 84-96. *Concurrent Pos:* vis prof, Univ Calif, Berkeley, 67-68. *Mem:* Foreign assoc Nat Acad Sci; fel Econometric Soc; foreign hon mem Am Acad Arts & Sci. *Mailing Add:* Hardtweg 23 53639 Konigswinter Germany

SELTER, GERALD A, ORGANIC CHEMISTRY. *Current Pos:* from asst prof to assoc prof, 68-80, PROF ORG CHEM, SAN JOSE STATE UNIV, 80- *Personal Data:* b Windsor, Ont, May 3, 40; m 63; c 3. *Educ:* Wayne State Univ, BS, 62; Wash State Univ, PhD(chem), 66. *Prof Exp:* Fel, Univ Calif, Berkeley, 66-67 & 68. *Concurrent Pos:* Lectr, Univ Calif, Berkeley, 67-68. *Mem:* Am Chem Soc. *Res:* Reactivity of alpha-pentadienyl esters; solvolytic reactivity of allylic halides and esters, especially the mechanisms of the neighboring group participation in such reactivity. *Mailing Add:* Dept Chem San Jose State Univ 1 Washington Sq San Jose CA 95192-0101

SELTIN, RICHARD JAMES, VERTEBRATE PALEONTOLOGY. *Current Pos:* From instr to assoc prof, 56-69, chmn natural sci, 74-84, PROF NATURAL SCI, MICH STATE UNIV, 69- *Personal Data:* b Chicago, Ill, Nov 4, 27; m 53; c 3. *Educ:* Univ Wyo, BS, 49; Univ Chicago, MA, 54, PhD(paleont), 56. *Concurrent Pos:* Am Philos Soc grants, 58, 60, 62, 64, 66; consult, Mich State Univ, 57- *Mem:* Soc Vert Paleont; Soc Study Evolution; Sigma Xi; Soc Col Sci Teachers. *Res:* Primitive reptiles and amphibians. *Mailing Add:* 919 Collingwood Dr East Lansing MI 48823-3517

SELTMANN, HEINZ, PLANT PHYSIOLOGY. *Current Pos:* from asst prof to assoc prof bot, 56-74, PROF BOT & CROP SCI, NC STATE UNIV, 74; PLANT PHYSIOLOGIST, USDA, 56- *Personal Data:* b Frankfurt am Main, Ger, Sept 8, 24; nat US. *Educ:* Drew Univ, BA, 49; Univ Chicago, MS, 50, PhD(bot), 53. *Prof Exp:* Asst, Univ Chicago, 50-53; asst prof bot, Barnard Col, Columbia Univ, 53-56. *Res:* Physiology of tobacco plant; plant growth regulators. *Mailing Add:* 1324 Brooks Ave Raleigh NC 27607

SELTSER, RAYMOND, PREVENTIVE MEDICINE, PUBLIC HEALTH. *Current Pos:* assoc dir, Ctr Dis Control, 88-89, ASSOC DIR, SPEC POP RES, AGENCY HEALTH CARE POLICY & RES, PUB HEALTH SERV, 90- *Personal Data:* b Boston, Mass, Dec 17, 23; m 46, Charlotte Gale; c Barry J & Andrew D. *Educ:* Boston Univ, MD, 47; Johns Hopkins Univ, MPH, 57; Am Bd Prev Med, dipl, 69. *Prof Exp:* Asst med, Sch Med, Boston Univ, 48-51; asst chief med info & intel br, Off Surgeon Gen, US Dept Army, 53-56; epidemiologist, Div Int Health, USPHS, 56-57; from asst prof to assoc prof epidemiol, Johns Hopkins Univ, 57-66, from assoc prof to prof chronic dis, 63-69, prof epidemiol, 66-81, assoc dean, Sch Hyg & Pub Health, 67-81; dean, 81-87, emer prof & dean Pub Health, Univ Pittsburgh, 87- *Concurrent Pos:* Resident med & infectious dis, Mass Mem Hosp, 48-51; asst med, Sch Med, Harvard Univ, 50-51; consult, NIMH, 58-70, Nat Cancer Inst, 64-71, Fed

Radiation Coun, 66-68, Nat Inst Environ Health Sci, 67-71, Bur Radiol Health, Dept HEW, 68-71 & Off Biomet, Nat Inst Neurol Dis & Stroke, 73-76; fel coun epidemiol, Am Heart Asn, 65-75, mem exec comt coun stroke, 69-72; vis prof, Med Col Pa, 66-69; mem coun pub health consult, Nat Sanit Found, 67-69; secy, Asn Sch Pub Health, 69-71; mem bd overseers, Am J Epidemiol, 71-81; chmn adv comt radiation registry physicians, Div Med Sci, Nat Acad Sci-Nat Res Coun, 72-76; mem, Nat Coun Radiation Protection & Measurements, 73-; chmn biomet epidemiol contract rev comt, Nat Cancer Inst, 73-77; chmn bd Prev Med, 74- Mem: Am Col Occup & Environ Med; fel Am Pub Health Asn; fel Am Col Prev Med; Asn Health Servs Res; Int Epidemiol Asn; Soc Disability Studies. Res: Streptococcal disease; poliomyelitis; hemorrhagic fever; influenza; ionizing radiation effects; cerebral vascular disease. Mailing Add: 4701 Willard Ave Chevy Chase MD 20815-4635. Fax: 301-594-2155

SELTZER, BENJAMIN, BEHAVIORAL NEUROLOGY, NEUROANATOMY. Current Pos: PROF NEUROL & PSYCHIAT, SCH MED, TULANE UNIV, 88-, ADJ PROF ANAT, 88- Personal Data: b Philadelphia, Pa, Aug 5, 45; m 74, Natalie Ross; c Daniel, Jennifer, Peter & Nathan. Educ: Univ Pa, AB, 65; Jefferson Med Col, MD, 69. Prof Exp: Intern, Boston City Hosp, 69-70, resident neurol, 70-73, asst neurologist, 73-75; from asst prof to assoc prof neurol & psychiat, Sch Med, Boston Univ, 78-88. Concurrent Pos: Clin fel neurol, Sch Med, Harvard Univ, 70-73, instr, 73-78, lectr, 78-88; assoc neurol, Beth Israel Hosp, Boston, 75-88; neurologist & clin investr, Geriat Res Ctr, Vet Admin Hosp, Bedford, Mass, 75-88, assoc dir, 84-88; dir prog, Behav Neurol & Clin Neurosci, Sch Med, Tulane Univ, 88-; adj prof psychol, Univ New Orleans, 90- Mem: Fel Am Acad Neurol; fel Royal Soc Med; Soc Neurosci. Res: Anatomy of the cerebral cortex in the monkey: connections and architectonics of association areas; phenomenology and classification of organic mental disorders; diagnosis and treatment of Alzheimers's disease. Mailing Add: 1430 Tulane Ave New Orleans LA 70112. Fax: 504-584-1727

SELTZER, CARL COLEMAN, PHYSICAL ANTHROPOLOGY. Current Pos: Nat Res Coun fel, Harvard Univ, 33-35, res asst, Fatigue Lab, 37-38, res assoc anthrop, 38-39, res assoc phys anthrop, 39-42, res fel, Peabody Mus, 42-63, res grant, Sch Pub Health, 42-47, anthropologist, Dept Hyg, 47-56, res assoc, 63-68, SR RES ASSOC BIOL ANTHROP, SCH PUB HEALTH, HARVARD UNIV, 68-, HON RES ASSOC PHYS ANTHROP, PEABODY MUS, 74- Personal Data: b Boston, Mass, June 1, 08; m 30; c 3. Educ: Harvard Univ, AB, 29, PhD(phys anthrop), 33. Prof Exp: Anthropologist, Constitution Clinic, Presby Hosp, NY, 30-31. Concurrent Pos: Consult, Off Indian Affairs, US Dept Interior, 37-42; res assoc, Robert B Brigham Hosp, Boston, 40-; res assoc, Adolescent Unit, Children's Hosp, 57-; fel, Coun Epidemiol, Am Heart Asn, 64-; consult, Vet Admin Outpatient Clinic, Boston, 65- & Framingham Heart Study, Boston Univ, 71-73; vis prof nutrit, Tufts Univ, 79- Mem: AAAS; Am Asn Phys Anthrop; Am Anthrop Asn; NY Acad Sci; Soc Epidemiol Res. Res: Human constitution; constitutional medicine; growth and development; obesity. Mailing Add: Norumbega Point Weston 99 Norumbega Rd 130 Weston MA 02193

SELTZER, EDWARD, CHEMICAL ENGINEERING, FOOD SCIENCE. Current Pos: prof, 69-84, EMER PROF FOOD PROCESS ENG, COOK COL, RUTGERS UNIV, NEW BRUNSWICK, 84- Personal Data: b Chelsea, Mass, Oct 28, 11; m 41; c 3. Educ: Harvard Univ, BS, 33. Prof Exp: Res chemist & chem engr, Walter Baker Co Div, Gen Foods Corp, Mass, 34-39, res chemist & proj leader, Cent Res Lab, NJ, 39-42, from chem engr to head processing eng div, 41-46; chief res engr, Thomas J Lipton, Inc, NJ, 46-59, asst dir tech res, 59-69. Mem: Am Chem Soc; Am Inst Chem Engr; fel, Inst Food Technologists; Res & Develop Assocs Mil Food & Packaging Systs. Res: Food research; process engineering; spray drying; dehydration; research administration; grant research. Mailing Add: 1175 Sussex Rd Teaneck NJ 07666-2770

SELTZER, JAMES EDWARD, ELECTROMAGNETICS, MATHEMATICAL STATISTICS. Current Pos: RETIRED. Personal Data: b Lebanon, Pa, Apr 15, 36. Educ: US Mil Acad, BS, 58; Purdue Univ, MSE, 63, PhD(eng), 71. Prof Exp: res engr, Harry Diamond Labs, 67- Mem: Inst Elec & Electronics Engrs; Union Radio Scientists. Res: Analysis and simulation of radar systems including backscatter from terrain and complex targets; evaluation of clutter effects. Mailing Add: 22 N Washington St Lebanon PA 17042

SELTZER, JO LOUISE, BIOCHEMISTRY, CELL BIOLOGY. Current Pos: Res assoc, Dept Pharmacol, Washington Univ, 70-72, res instr biochem, 72-78, res asst prof med, 78-96, RES ASSOC PROF MED, DIV DERMAT, DEPT MED, SCH MED, WASHINGTON UNIV, 96- Personal Data: b St Louis, Mo, July 10, 42; m 63, Carl; c Katherine Jenny, Thomas Abraham & Eve Miriam. Educ: Wash Univ, AB, 63, PhD(pharmacol), 69. Mem: Sigma Xi; Am Soc Biol Chem; AAAS. Res: Matrix Metalloproteinases; biochemistry and cell biology with emphasis on gelatinasea (72 kda type IV collagen asg). Mailing Add: Washington Univ Sch Med 600 S Euclid Ave Campus PO Box 8123 St Louis MO 63110-1093. Fax: 314-362-8159

SELTZER, LEON Z(EE), AERONAUTICAL ENGINEERING. Current Pos: RETIRED. Personal Data: b Chicago, Ill, Apr 17, 14; m 40; c 1. Educ: Univ Mich, BSE, 40; Univ Ill, PhC, 34. Prof Exp: Aeronaut engr, Douglas Aircraft Co, Calif, 40-41; prof aeronaut eng & chmn dept, Va Polytech Inst, 41-47 & WVa Univ, 49-63; prof aerospace eng & dean, Parks Col, St Louis Univ, 63-81. Mem: Am Soc Eng Educ; Soc Automotive Engrs; Am Inst Aeronaut & Astronaut; Am Helicopter Soc. Res: Theoretical and applied aerodynamics, including flying and flight testing. Mailing Add: 13045 Avenida Marbella San Diego CA 92128

SELTZER, MARTIN S, SOLID STATE PHYSICS, PHYSICAL METALLURGY. Current Pos: MEM STAFF, PORTER, WRIGHT, MORRIS & ARTHUR, 77- Personal Data: b New York, NY, Apr 8, 37; m 60; c 3. Educ: NY Univ, BMetalEng, 58, Yale Univ, MEng, 60, DEng(metall), 62. Prof Exp: Res scientist, N V Philips Gloeilampenfabrieken, 62-63; fel, Dept Metall, Battelle Mem Inst, 63-77. Mem: AAAS; Am Ceramic Soc. Res: Self diffusion and mechanical properties of inorganic binary compounds. Mailing Add: 41 S High St Columbus OH 43230

SELTZER, RAYMOND, POLYMER CHEMISTRY, ORGANIC CHEMISTRY. Current Pos: assoc dir, 76-80, dir res & develop additives 80-88, RES ASSOC, PLASTICS & ADDITIVES DIV, RES DEPT, CIBA-GEIGY CHEM CO, 68-, VPRES RES, ADDITIVES DIV, 88- Personal Data: b New York, NY, May 27, 35; m 66; c 2. Educ: City Col New York, BS, 56; Purdue Univ, PhD(org chem), 61. Prof Exp: Res chemist, Eastman Kodak Co, 61-63 & M&T Chem, Inc, Am Can Co, NY, 63-68. Mem: Am Chem Soc; Sigma Xi; NY Acad Sci; Soc Plastic Engrs. Res: Synthesis, characterization, evaluation and application of novel polymeric systems; developmental novel epoxy and other thermosetting resins; ultraviolet curable resins; high temperature stable polymers; film, coatings, adhesive, casting and composite applications; stabilizers for polymers; coatings; lubricants. Mailing Add: 11 Angus Lane New City NY 10956-2856

SELTZER, SAMUEL, DENTISTRY. Current Pos: PROF ENDODONT, SCH DENT, TEMPLE UNIV, 67- Personal Data: b Philadelphia, Pa, Feb 3, 14; m 46; c 1. Educ: Univ Pa, DDS, 37. Prof Exp: Assoc prof oral histol & path, Sch Dent, Univ Pa, 59-67. Mem: AAAS; fel Am Col Dent; NY Acad Sci; Sigma Xi. Res: Biological aspects of dental pulp disease; injury of dental pulp and mechanisms of repair. Mailing Add: 1901 John F Kennedy Blvd Philadelphia PA 19103

SELTZER, STANLEY, ORGANIC CHEMISTRY, PHYSICAL CHEMISTRY. Current Pos: from res assoc to chemist, 58-73, SR CHEMIST, BROOKHAVEN NAT LAB, 73- Personal Data: b New York, NY, Feb 25, 30; m 52, Regina Kratzer; c Eric. Educ: City Col, BS, 50; Harvard Univ, AM, 56, PhD(chem), 58. Prof Exp: Phys chem analyst, M W Kellogg Co Div, Pullman, Inc, 50-52. Concurrent Pos: Vis prof, Cornell Univ, 64-65; NIH spec fel, 69-70; vis prof, Brandeis Univ, 69-70; instr, Columbia Univ, 69-73; vis prof, State Univ NY, Stony Brook, 74 & 77, adj prof, 78- Mem: Am Chem Soc; Biophys Soc; Am Soc Photobiol. Res: Mechanisms of reaction in organic and biochemical systems; kinetic isotope effects. Mailing Add: Dept Chem Brookhaven Nat Lab Upton NY 11973. Fax: 516-282-5815; E-Mail: seltzer@bnlchm.bitnet

SELTZER, STANLEY, CHEMICAL ENGINEERING. Current Pos: Chem engr, Chem Mat Dept, Gen Elec Co, Mass, 51-60, process engr, Silicone Prods Dept, Waterford, 60-61, eng leader, 61-65, mgr process eng, 66-69, mgr intermediates mfg, 69-79, mgr advan technol, 79-85, MGR PROCESS SAFETY & TECHNOL, GEN ELEC CO, 86- Personal Data: b Brooklyn, NY, Aug 8, 25; m 51, Joanne Zellman; c 4. Educ: Cooper Union, BChE, 47; Univ Mich, MS, 48, PhD(chem eng), 51. Mem: Am Chem Soc; Am Inst Chem Engrs. Res: Advanced incineration systems; fluidized bed reactions; process control computers. Mailing Add: 2481 McGovern Dr Schenectady NY 12309-2433

SELUND, ROBERT B(ERNARD), CHEMICAL ENGINEERING. Current Pos: RETIRED. Personal Data: b La Crosse, Wis, Jan 25, 07; m 34; c Robert B Jr. Educ: Univ Minn, BS, 30. Prof Exp: Chem engr, Stand Oil Co, 30-40, res group leader, 41-51, res sect leader, 52-61, tech serv sect leader, Am Oil Co, 61-77. Mem: Am Chem Soc; Am Inst Chem Engrs. Res: Asphalt; motor oils; wax; crude oil distillation and coking; petroleum refining. Mailing Add: 250 Seventh Ave S Apt 303 Naples FL 33940-5791

SELVADURAI, A P S, MATERIALS SCIENCE ENGINEERING, ENVIRONMENTAL SCIENCES. Current Pos: chair, Dept Civil Eng & Appl Mech, 93-96, PROF CIVIL ENG & APPL MECH, MCGILL UNIV, CAN, 93- Personal Data: b Matara, Sri Lanka, Sept 23, 42; Can citizen; m 72; c 4. Educ: Brighton Polytech, Sussex, Eng, dipl eng, 64; London Univ, Eng, DIC, 65; Stanford Univ, Calif, MS, 67; Univ Nottingham, Eng, PhD(theoret mech), 71, DSc, 86. Honors & Awards: King George VI Mem Fel, English Speaking Union of the Commonwealth, UK, 65; Davidson Dunton Lectr, Carleton Univ, Ottawa, 87; Res Achievement Award, Carleton Univ, Ottawa, 90; Leipholz Medal, Can Soc Civil Eng, 91. Prof Exp: Lectr civil eng, Univ Aston, Birmingham, UK, 71-75; from asst prof to prof, Carleton Univ, Ottawa, Can, 75-93. Concurrent Pos: Staff res engr, Woodward Clyde Assocs, Oakland, Calif, 66-67; vis sr researcher, Bechtel Group, San Francisco, Calif, 81-82; consult, Atomic Energy Can Ltd, 83- & Ministry Transp Ont, 84-; dir, Am Acad Mech, 84-88 & 90-; vis prof, Dept Theoret Mech, Univ Nottingham, UK, 86; founding chmn, Eng Mech Div, Can Soc Civil Eng, 89; assoc ed, Can J Civil Eng, 90-96; vis prof, Inst de Mecanique de Grenaoble, France, 91; Erskire fel, Univ Conterbury, NZ, 92. Mem: Fel Eng Inst Can; fel Can Soc Civil Eng; fel Am Acad Mech; fel Inst Math & Its Appln. Res: Continuum mechanics and applied mathematics; finite elasticity; contact and interface problems; integral equations in mechanics; fracture and damage mechanics; composite materials mechanics; geomechanics; soil-structure interaction; nuclear waste management; hygrothermal processes in porous media; mechanics of layered systems; ice mechanics and ice structure interaction; environmental geomechanics; continium, computation, solid and experimental geomechanics. Mailing Add: Dept Civil Eng & Appl Mech McGill Univ Montreal PQ K1S 5B6 Can

SELVAKUMAR, CHETTYPALAYAM RAMANATHAN, MICROELECTRONIC DEVICES, MICROELECTRONIC PROCESS TECHNOLOGY. *Current Pos:* fel, 85-87, asst prof, 87-93, ASSOC PROF MICROELECTRONICS, UNIV WATERLOO, 94- *Personal Data:* b Karur, Tamil Nadu, India, Mar 17, 50; m 80, Kumari; c Sivanny & Maruvaracy. *Educ:* Univ Madras, BE, 72; Indian Inst Technol Bombay, MTech, 74; Indian Inst Technol, Madras, PhD(elec eng), 85. *Prof Exp:* Proj assoc microelectronics, Indian Inst Technol, Madras, 78-84. *Concurrent Pos:* Consult, Digital Equip Co, Ottawa & Gennum Corp, Ont, 90-; mem, Tech Prog Comt, Inst Elec & Electronics Engrs Bipolar Circuits & Technol Mgt, 90-, chmn, 94; key assoc researcher, Info Technol Res Ctr, 91-; assoc researcher, Micronet, Fed Ctr Excellence, 91-; vis fac, Stanford Univ, 92. *Mem:* Inst Elec & Electronics Engrs; Mat Res Soc. *Res:* Design, analytical/computer aided modeling and analysis of microelectronic devices and processes; bipolar transistors; polysilicon emitters; heterostructure devices; silicon-germanium alloys; photodetectors; microelectronic process technology; oxidation; ion-beam mixing; dc and ac electrical characterization of devices; microelectronic sensors. *Mailing Add:* Dept Elec & Comput Eng Univ Waterloo Waterloo ON N2L 3G1 Can. *Fax:* 519-746-3077

SELVAVEL, KANDASAMY, ESTIMATION OF PARAMETERS, HALF-LIFE STUDIES. *Current Pos:* Asst prof, 90-95, ASSOC PROF MATH & STATIST, CLAFLIN COL, 96- *Personal Data:* b Jaffna, Sri Lanka, Dec 29, 54. *Educ:* Univ Sri Lanka, BS, 79; Bowling Green State Univ, MA, 86, PhD(math & statist), 90. *Concurrent Pos:* Res assoc, Off Sci Res, USAF, 94, 95 & 96. *Mem:* Math Asn Am. *Res:* Moments of order statistics; estimation of parameters from truncation parameter families and sequential estimation; problem of estimation of half-life of dioxin in Vietnam veterans of operation ranch hand. *Mailing Add:* 115 Mt Gilead Dr Orangeburg SC 29118. *Fax:* 803-531-2860; *E-Mail:* selvard@clafi.claflin.edu

SELVERSTON, ALLEN ISRAEL, NEUROPHYSIOLOGY, COMPARATIVE PHYSIOLOGY. *Current Pos:* assoc prof neurophysiol, 74-76, assoc prof, 76-81, PROF BIOL, UNIV CALIF, SAN DIEGO, 81- *Personal Data:* b Chicago, Ill, Jan 17, 36; m 63; c 4. *Educ:* Univ Ore, MA, 64, PhD(neurophysiol), 67. *Prof Exp:* Res assoc neurophysiol, Stanford Univ, 67-69. *Concurrent Pos:* USPHS fel, 67-69; Alexander von Humboldt sr fel, 82-83. *Mem:* AAAS. *Res:* Animal behavior; neural mechanisms underlying behavior; integrative activity of invertebrate ganglia. *Mailing Add:* Dept Biol Univ Calif San Diego 9500 Gilman Dr La Jolla CA 92093-0322

SELVERSTONE, JANE ELIZABETH, METAMORPHIC PETROLOGY. *Current Pos:* ASSOC PROF, DEPT EARTH & PLANETARY SCI, UNIV NMEX, 95- *Personal Data:* b Cambridge, Mass, July 6, 56; m 84, David Gutzler; c Benjamin & Sonia. *Educ:* Princeton Univ, AB, 78; Univ Colo, MS, 81; Mass Inst Technol, PhD (geol), 85. *Prof Exp:* Adj prof geol, Univ Colo, 85-86; from asst prof to assoc prof, Harvard Univ, 86-92; res assoc prof, Univ Colo, 92-95. *Concurrent Pos:* NSF presidential young investr award, 87-92; chair, Short Course Comt, Mineral Soc Am, 89-91; distinguished lectr, Mineral Soc Am, 92-93; co-ed, J Metamorphic Geol, 93-; comt of visitors, Petrol & Geochem, NSF, 93; Tectonics Panel, NSF, 96- *Mem:* Geol Soc Am; Am Geophys Union; Mineral Soc Am. *Res:* Metamorphic petrology; application of petrologic techniques to interpretation of tectonic processes; determination of pressure-temperature-time-deformation paths of rocks; fluid-rock interactions in high-pressure rocks. *Mailing Add:* Dept Earth & Planetary Sci Univ NMex 200 Yale Blvd Albuquerque NM 87131-1116. *E-Mail:* selver@unm.edu

SELVIDGE, HARNER, ELECTRONICS. *Current Pos:* CONSULT, ALTA ASSOCS, 69- *Personal Data:* b Columbia, Mo, Oct 16, 10; m 33; c 4. *Educ:* Mass Inst Technol, 32, MS, 33; Harvard Univ, SM, 34, SD(commun eng), 37. *Prof Exp:* Instr physics & commun eng, Harvard Univ, 35-38; assoc prof elec eng, Kans State Col, 38-41; sr engr, Carnegie Inst, 41-42; appl physics lab, Johns Hopkins Univ, 42-45; dir spec prods develop, Bendix Aviation Corp, 45-56, staff engr, 56-60; vpres & gen mgr, Meteorol Res, Inc, Calif, 60-69. *Concurrent Pos:* Mem, Harvard-Mass Inst Technol Eclipse Exped, Russia, 36; consult engr, Am Phenolic Corp, 38-42; assoc engr, Taylor Tube Co, Ill, 39-40; dir res, Fournier Inst, 42-45. *Mem:* Am Meteorol Soc; fel Inst Elec & Electronics Engrs; assoc fel Am Inst Aeronaut & Astronaut. *Res:* Antennas; propagation and transmission lines; vacuum tubes; proximity fuses; fire control radar; guided missile control systems; nucleonics; industrial instrumentation and controls; meteorological systems. *Mailing Add:* Alta Assocs Box 1128 Sedona AZ 86336

SELWITZ, CHARLES MYRON, CONSERVATION SCIENCE. *Current Pos:* SR CONSULT, GETTY CONSERV INST, MARINA DEL REY, CALIF, 83- *Personal Data:* b Springfield, Mass, July 20, 27; m 55, Ruth Fineman; c Leslie J & Lisa Ann (Kaufman). *Educ:* Worcester Polytech Inst, BS, 49; Univ Cincinnati, PhD(chem), 53. *Honors & Awards:* Oliver Torrey Fuller Award, Asn Preserv Technol, 96. *Prof Exp:* Asst inorg chem, Univ Cincinnati, 49-50; res chemist, Gulf Res & Develop Co, Pittsburgh, 53-55, group leader, 55-61, res chemist, 61-72, res assoc, 72-74, sect supvr, 74-76, dir synthetic chem, 76-82. *Concurrent Pos:* Mem, Int Comt Monuments & Sites. *Mem:* Am Chem Soc; Mat Res Soc; Asn Preserv Technol. *Res:* Preservation of archaeological sites; disinfestation of historic objects by non toxic means; high temperature polymers; conservation science; stone corrosion and consolidation; preservation of aged adobe; polymers for art conservation. *Mailing Add:* 3631 Surfwood Dr Malibu CA 90265. *Fax:* 310-440-7711

SELWYN, DONALD, REHABILITATION ENGINEERING. *Current Pos:* PRES BD TRUSTEES & EXEC TECH DIR, NAT INST REHAB ENG, 67. *Personal Data:* b New York, NY, Jan 31, 36; m 56, 86, Myra Rowman Markoff; c Laurie, Gerald & Marcia. *Educ:* Thomas A Edison Col NJ, BA, 77. *Honors & Awards:* Humanitarian Award, US House of Rep, 72. *Prof Exp:* Serv engr, Bendix Aviation, 56-59; serv mgr, Bogue Elec Mfg Co, 59; proposal engr, Advan Design Group, Curtiss-Wright Corp, 60-64; indust bioengr & rehab eng consult, NY, 64-67. *Concurrent Pos:* Consult, NY State Off Voc Rehab, 64-, Pres's Comt Employ Handicapped, 66-; trustee, Rehab Res Ctr Trust, Nat Inst Rehab Eng. *Mem:* Am Acad Consult; Inst Elec & Electronics Engrs; Soc Tech Writers & Publs; Nat Rehab Asn; NY Acad Sci. *Res:* Contributed numerous articles on the rehabilitation of severely and totally disabled to professional journals; developer or co-developer of field-expander glasses for hemianopsia, tunnel and monocular vision, electronic speech clarifiers; developer or co-developer of electronically guided wheelchairs, off-road vehicles and cars for quadriplegics, patentee of industrial, military and handicapped rehabilitating inventions. *Mailing Add:* Nat Inst Rehab Eng PO Box T Hewitt NJ 07421-1020

SELWYN, PHILIP ALAN, FLUID MECHANICS, APPLIED RESEARCH MANAGEMENT. *Current Pos:* VPRES, ARETE ASSOC, 93- *Personal Data:* b New York, NY, Feb 12, 45; m 66, Karen Peller; c Eric. *Educ:* Univ Rochester, BS, 65; Mass Inst Technol, PhD(chem physics), 70. *Prof Exp:* Res assoc, Mass Inst Technol, 70, res staff mem geophys fluid mech, Inst Defense Anal, 70-76; prog mgr antisubmarine warfare & hydrodyn, Ocean Monitoring & Control Div, Tactical Technol Off, Defense Advan Res Projs Agency, 76-79; chief scientist, Fleet Ballistic Missile Submarine Security Technol Prog, Strategic Syst Proj Off, 79-82; spec asst vpres, Sci & Technol, Honeywell Inc, 82-83; dir, Off Naval Technol, 83-93. *Mem:* Nat Security Indust Asn; Am Geophys Union. *Res:* Nonequilibrium statistical mechanics; atmospheric and oceanic fluid mechanics; remote sensing technology; operations analysis; signal processing; technical management. *Mailing Add:* 2047 Mayfair Mclean Ct Falls Church VA 22043. *E-Mail:* selwyn@arete-dc.com

SELZER, ARTHUR, MEDICINE, CARDIOLOGY. *Current Pos:* Asst, Stanford Univ, 41-42, clin instr, 42-47, from asst clin prof to clin prof, 47-76, EMER CLIN PROF MED, MED SCH, STANFORD UNIV, 76-; CLIN PROF MED, SCH MED, UNIV CALIF, SAN FRANCISCO, 60- *Personal Data:* b Lwow, Poland, July 3, 11; nat US; m 36; c 2. *Educ:* Univ Lwow, MB, 35; Cracow Univ, MD, 36; Am Bd Internal Med, dipl, 43. *Concurrent Pos:* Chief cardiol & dir cardiopulmonary lab, Pac Med Ctr, 59-84; consult, Letterman Gen Hosp. *Mem:* Am Fedn Clin Res; distinguished fel Am Col Cardiol; master Am Col Physicians. *Res:* Clinical cardiovascular physiology; operable heart disease; coronary artery disease; heart failure; pharmacology of digitalis. *Mailing Add:* 5 Greenview Lane Burlingame CA 94010

SELZER, MELVIN LAWRENCE, PSYCHIATRY. *Current Pos:* CLIN PROF, DEPT PSYCHIAT, UNIV CALIF, SAN DIEGO, 81- *Personal Data:* b New York, NY, Feb 3, 25; m 78; c 3. *Educ:* Tulane Univ, BS, 49, MD, 52; Am Bd Psychiat & Neurol, dipl, 59. *Prof Exp:* Intern, Univ Mich Hosp, 52-53; resident psychiat, Ypsilanti State Hosp, 54-57; assoc psychiatrist, Health Serv, Med Sch, Univ Mich, Ann Arbor, 57-59, from instr to prof psychiat, 59-78. *Concurrent Pos:* Examr, Am Bd Psychiat & Neurol, 62-68; mem comt alcohol & drugs, Nat Safety Coun, 63-72; resource consult, President's Comt Traffic Safety, 64-65; mem fac, Inst Continuing Legal Educ, Univ Mich-Wayne State Univ Law Schs, 65-70; mem criminal code revision comt, State Bar Mich, 66-69; ed referee, J Studies Alcohol, 67- & Am J Psychiat, 69-; mem fac, Pract Law Inst, NY, 68-71; consult, Fed Aviation Admin, 69, US Dept Transp, 69- & Archdiocese of Detroit, 72; consult ed, Life Threatening Behav, 70-78; res psychiatrist, Hwy Safety Res Inst, 70-75; mem res rev comt, Nat Inst Alcohol Abuse & Alcoholism, 76-78. *Mem:* Fel Am Psychiat Asn; Asn Am Med Cols; fel Am Col Psychiat. *Res:* Psychoanalytic therapy; student mental health; alcoholism and drug abuse; psychological aspects of traffic accidents. *Mailing Add:* 6967 Paseo Laredo La Jolla CA 92037

SELZER, MICHAEL EDGAR, MEDICINE. *Current Pos:* dir, Ctr Neurologic Rehab, 91-94, PROF NEUROL, SCH MED, UNIV PA, 86-, PROF REHAB MED, 92- *Personal Data:* b Buenos Aires, Arg, Feb 14, 43; US citizen; m, Mary Morrison; c Molly B & Carl J. *Educ:* Univ Pa, AB, 62; NY Univ, MD & PhD(med), 68. *Concurrent Pos:* Prin investr, NIH, 91- *Mem:* Am Acad Neurol; AAAS; Am Epilepsy Soc; Am Neurol Asn; Soc Neurosci; Am Soc Neurorehab. *Res:* Regeneration in the central nervous system; the sea lamprey is used in electrophysiological, anatomical and molecular biological experiments to determine how the lamprey recovers from spinal cord injury. *Mailing Add:* Dept Neurol Univ Pa Col Med Philadelphia PA 19104. *Fax:* 215-573-2107

SEMAN, GABRIEL, VIROLOGY, CYTOLOGY. *Current Pos:* ASSOC PROF VIROL & ASSOC VIROLOGIST, UNIV TEX M D ANDERSON HOSP & TUMOR INST HOUSTON, 68- *Personal Data:* b Budapest, Hungary, Sept 3, 25; m 52; c 5. *Educ:* Univ Paris, BS, 46, MD, 54. *Prof Exp:* Gen practitioner, France, 54-61; res assoc, Res Ctr Cancerology & Radiobiol, Paris, 61-64; Eli Lilly res fel, Univ Tex M D Anderson Hosp & Tumor Inst Houston, 64-65; sr res assoc & head dept cytol & electron micros, Inst Cancerology & Immunogenetics, Villejuif, France, 65-68. *Mem:* AAAS; Am Asn Cancer Res; Tissue Cult Asn. *Res:* Ultrastructure cytology; normal and leukemic cytohematology; viral oncology; electron microscopy. *Mailing Add:* 7727 Sands Pt Dr Houston TX 77036

SEMAN, GEORGE WILLIAM, ELECTRICAL ENGINEERING. *Current Pos:* VPRES RES CABLE TECHNOL LABS. *Personal Data:* b Pittsburgh, Pa, May 29, 40. *Educ:* Carnegie Inst Technol, BS, 62, MS, 64, PhD(elec eng), 66. *Prof Exp:* Res engr space syst, Avco Corp, 66-67, res engr, nuclear weapons effects, EG&G Inc, 67-68; sr res engr nuclear weapons effects, Ion Physics Corp, 68-69; RES MGR ELEC CABLES, GEN CABLE, PIRELLI CABLE CORP, 69- *Mem:* Sr mem Inst Elec & Electronics Engrs. *Res:* New cable designs; evaluation of electrical and mechanical performance of extruded and laminar dielectric transmission and distribution cables. *Mailing Add:* 205 Raymond Rd Monmouth Junction NJ 08852

SEMANCIK, JOSEPH STEPHEN, PATHOLOGY, VIROLOGY. *Current Pos:* assoc prof, 72-74, chmn dept, 80-83, PROF PLANT PATH, UNIV CALIF, RIVERSIDE, 74- *Personal Data:* b Barton, Ohio, June 9, 38; m 63. *Educ:* Western Res Univ, AB, 60; Purdue Univ, MS, 62, PhD(path), 64. *Honors & Awards:* Alexander von Humboldt Found Prize, 75. *Prof Exp:* Asst plant pathologist & lectr plant path, Univ Calif, Riverside, 64-69; assoc prof plant path, Univ Nebr, Lincoln, 69-72. *Concurrent Pos:* USPHS grants, 65-68 & 69-73; assoc ed, Virol, 71-73 & Phytopathol, 74-76; NSF awards, 73-75, 75-78 & 78-81; Guggenheim fel, 78. *Mem:* AAAS; fel Am Phytopath Soc; Sigma Xi. *Res:* Purification and characterization of pathogenic nucleic acids; cell biology; viroids; viroid-cell interactions. *Mailing Add:* Dept Plant Path Univ Calif Riverside 900 University Ave Riverside CA 92521-0101

SEMBA, KAZUE, PSYCHOBIOLOGY, NEUROSCIENCE. *Current Pos:* res assoc, 84-89, asst prof, 89-94, PROF, UNIV BC, 94- *Personal Data:* b Tsuchiura, Japan, Jan 13, 49; m 72. *Educ:* Tokyo Univ Educ, BEd, 71, MA, 73; Rutgers Univ, PhD(psychobiol), 79. *Honors & Awards:* Murray L Barr Jr Scientist Award, 92. *Prof Exp:* Res asst, Inst Aminal Behav, Rutgers Univ, 75-76, teaching asst physiol & exp psychol, Dept Psychol, 76-77; fel, Dept Vet Physiol & Pharmacol, Iowa State Univ, 79-80; res specialist, Col Med & Dent NJ, 80-81, instr, Rutgers Med Sch, Univ Med & Dent NJ, 81-84. *Mem:* Soc Neurosci. *Res:* Central cholinergic systems; sleep and wakefulness; biological rhythms. *Mailing Add:* Dept Anat & Neurobiol Dalhousie Univ Tuffer Bldg Halifax NS B3H 4H7 Can

SEMEL, MAURIE, ENTOMOLOGY, PLANT PEST MANAGEMENT. *Current Pos:* Grad asst, 49-54, from asst prof to assoc prof, 54-88, EMER PROF ENTOM, CORNELL UNIV, 88- *Personal Data:* b NY, Jan 18, 23; m 50, Marilyn Burley; c Mark, Valerie & Brad. *Educ:* Cornell Univ, PhD(entom), 54. *Concurrent Pos:* Vis sr scientist, Int Potato Ctr, Lima, Peru, 72-73; mem, Adv Coun Agr, NY State Dept Agr & Mkt, 80-88. *Mem:* Entom Soc Am; NY Acad Sci; Sigma Xi. *Res:* Control of insects affecting vegetable and ornamental crops. *Mailing Add:* 4356 Ranchwood Dr Bucyrus OH 44820

SEMELUK, GEORGE PETER, PHYSICAL CHEMISTRY. *Current Pos:* assoc prof, 60-67, PROF CHEM, UNIV NB, 67- *Personal Data:* b Coleman, Alta, Apr 14, 24; m 49; c 3. *Educ:* Univ Alta, BSc, 47, MSc, 49; Ill Inst Technol, PhD(kinetics), 55; Cambridge Univ, PhD(kinetics), 60. *Prof Exp:* Res chemist, Lamp Div, Gen Elec Co, Ohio, 53-55; proj engr, Electrochem Labs, Inc, Okla, 55-58. *Concurrent Pos:* Consult, Dow Chem Can, Ltd, 64- *Mem:* Fel AAAS; fel Chem Inst Can; Am Chem Soc; The Chem Soc. *Res:* Unimolecular decompositions; structure and chemistry of excited states; photosensitized decompositions. *Mailing Add:* 826 Windsor St Fredericton NB E3B 4G5 Can

SEMENIUK, FRED THEODOR, PHARMACEUTICAL CHEMISTRY. *Current Pos:* from asst prof to prof pharmaceut chem, 47-80, EMER PROF, UNIV NC, CHAPEL HILL, 80- *Personal Data:* b Edmonton, Alta, Jan 3, 15; nat US; m 56; c 2. *Educ:* Univ Alta, BSc, 39; Purdue Univ, PhD(pharmaceut chem), 47. *Prof Exp:* Asst instr pharmaceut chem, Purdue Univ, 41-46; instr, Univ Wis, 46-47. *Mem:* AAAS; Am Chem Soc; Am Pharmaceut Asn. *Res:* Organic medicinals; organic chemical nomenclature. *Mailing Add:* 1402 Mason Farm Rd Chapel Hill NC 27514

SEMENUK, NICK SARDEN, ORGANIC CHEMISTRY, INFORMATION SCIENCE. *Current Pos:* dir environ comp anal, 89, market intel, 90-91, DIR COMP INTEL, BRISTOL-MYERS SQUIBB, 91- *Personal Data:* b Nestow, Alta, June 16, 37; US citizen; m 63, Patricia J Webster; c Steven H, David B & Larisa K. *Educ:* Univ Alta, BSc, 58; Purdue Univ, PhD(chem), 64. *Prof Exp:* Sr res chemist org div, Olin Mathieson Chem Co, 63-65, chem div, 65-69; info res scientist, Squibb Inst Med Res, New Brunswick, 69-71, dir sci info dept, 71-76, sect head, 76-87, dir biosci info, Princeton, 87-88. *Mem:* AAAS; Am Chem Soc; Chem Inst Can; Drug Info Asn; NY Acad Sci. *Res:* Pharmaceutical chemistry; cyclic adenosine monophosphate. *Mailing Add:* 2871 Princeton Pike Lawrenceville NJ 08648

SEMERJIAN, HRATCH G, COMBUSTION, LASER DIAGNOSTICS. *Current Pos:* group leader combustion, 77-87, CHIEF, PROCESS MEASUREMENTS DIV, CHEM SCI & TECHNOL LAB, NAT INST STAND & TECHNOL, 87- *Personal Data:* b Istanbul, Turkey, Oct 22, 43; US citizen; m 69, 86; c 2. *Educ:* Robert Col, Turkey, BS, 66; Brown Univ, MSc, 68, PhD(eng), 72. *Honors & Awards:* Silver Medal, Dept Com, 84. *Prof Exp:* Lectr combustion, Univ Toronto, 72-73; res engr, Pratt & Whitney Aircraft, United Technol Corp, 73-77. *Concurrent Pos:* Res fel, Univ Toronto, 71-73. *Mem:* Am Inst Aeronaut & Astronaut; Am Soc Mech Engrs; Combustion Inst; Am Inst Chem Engrs; AAAS. *Res:* Laser diagnostics in reacting flows; combustion modelling and diagnostics; gas turbine combustion; particle sizing techniques; radiative heat transfer; spray combustion. *Mailing Add:* 15008 Good Meadow Ct Gaithersburg MD 20878

SEMKEN, HOLMES ALFORD, JR, VERTEBRATE PALEONTOLOGY. *Current Pos:* from asst prof to assoc prof, 65-73, chmn dept, 86-92, PROF GEOL, UNIV IOWA, 73- *Personal Data:* b Knoxville, Tenn, Jan 28, 35; m 57, Elaine Friedrichs; c Steven H & David A. *Educ:* Univ Tex, BS, 58, MA, 60; Univ Mich, PhD(geol), 65. *Prof Exp:* Mus intern geol, Smithsonian Inst, 60-61. *Concurrent Pos:* Secy, Exec Comt, Am Geol Inst. *Mem:* Fel Geol Soc Am; Paleont Soc; Soc Vert Paleont; Am Soc Mammal; Am Quaternary Asn. *Res:* Paleoecology and biogeography of Pleistocene and Holocene mammals, especially rodents; archaeological geology, especially zooarchaeology; vertebrate paleontology. *Mailing Add:* Dept Geol Univ Iowa Iowa City IA 52242. *Fax:* 319-355-1821

SEMLER, CHARLES EDWARD, HIGH TEMPERATURE MINERALOGY, REFRACTORY TESTING. *Current Pos:* CONSULT, SEMLER MAT SERV, 86- *Personal Data:* b Dayton, Ohio, Dec 27, 40; m 62; c David & Douglas. *Educ:* Miami Univ, BA, 62, MS, 65; Ohio State Univ, PhD(mineral), 68. *Honors & Awards:* Cramer Award, 83. *Prof Exp:* Res engr ceramics, Ferro Corp, 64-65; sr res engr mat res, Monsanto Res Corp, 68-70; asst prof geol, Wash Univ, 70-71; sr res mineral refractories, Dresser Indust, 71-74; from asst prof to assoc prof, Ohio State Univ, 74-86, dir, Refractories Res Ctr, 74-85, adj prof & consult, 85-86. *Concurrent Pos:* Abstractor, Am Chem Soc, 71-74; chmn Spalling Comt, Am Soc Testing & Mat, 75-; chmn refractories comt, Am Foundrymen's Soc, 76-85; ed comt, Interceram, WGer, 78-; NSF Exchange Scientist, India, 76; vis prof, Sydney, Australia, 81; fac consult, Sandia Nat Labs, Albuquerque, 82; guest worker, Nat Bur Standards, Gaithersburg, Md, 83 & 84; chmn, Refractories Div, Am Ceramic Soc, 84-85; fac fel, NASA-Lewis Res Ctr, Cleveland, 85; invited lectr, Japan, 93. *Mem:* Fel Am Ceramic Soc; Am Soc Testing & Mat; Nat Inst Ceramic Eng; Brit Ceramic Soc; Can Ceramic Soc; Australian Ceramic Soc; Int Am Ceramic Soc (vpres, 92-93). *Res:* Refractories testing by destructive and non-destructive methods; high temperature phase equilibrium relations of oxide materials; microstructure of materials; thermal shock of materials; test development; in plant inspection and trouble shooting; refractories failure analysis; incinerator design and evaluation; technical writing, training seminars and video production; technology transfer; refractory lining design; technical marketing. *Mailing Add:* Semler Mat Serv 4160 Mumford Ct Columbus OH 43220

SEMLYEN, ADAM, ELECTRICAL ENGINEERING, POWER SYSTEM ANALYSIS. *Current Pos:* vis assoc prof, Univ Toronto, 69-71, from assoc prof to prof, 71-89, EMER PROF ELEC ENG, UNIV TORONTO, 89- *Personal Data:* b Gherla, Romania, Jan 10, 23; m, Mary; c Georgeta. *Educ:* Timisoara Polytech Inst, Dipl Ing, 50; Iasi Polytech Inst, Dr Ing, 63. *Prof Exp:* Lectr power apparatus, Timisoara Polytech Inst, 50-58, from assoc prof to prof power systs, 58-69. *Concurrent Pos:* Engr, Power Sta Timisoara, Romania, 49-51; consult, Regional Power Authority, Timisoara, 60-69 & Elec Eng Consociates, 70-; Nat Res Coun Can grant, Univ Toronto, 71- *Mem:* Fel Inst Elec & Electronics Engrs. *Res:* Power system dynamics; power system optimization; electro-magnetic transients in high voltage systems. *Mailing Add:* Dept Elec & Comput Eng Univ Toronto Toronto ON M5S 3G4 Can

SEMMELHACK, MARTIN F, ORGANIC CHEMISTRY. *Current Pos:* PROF ORG CHEM, PRINCETON UNIV, 78- *Personal Data:* b Appleton, Wis, Nov 19, 41; m 96, Christina Kraml; c Robert, Julia & Matthew. *Educ:* Univ Wis, Madison, BS, 63; Harvard Univ, AM, 65, PhD(org chem), 67. *Prof Exp:* NIH fel, Stanford Univ, 67-68; from asst prof to prof org chem, Cornell Univ, 68-78. *Concurrent Pos:* Fel, Alfred P Sloan Found, 72-74; teacher-scholar award, Camille & Henry Dreyfuss Found, 73-78; Guggenheim fel, 78-79. *Mem:* Am Chem Soc; The Chem Soc. *Res:* Synthesis of biologically active compounds; organometallic reagents and electrochemical techniques in organic synthesis. *Mailing Add:* Dept Chem Princeton Univ Princeton NY 08540. *Fax:* 609-258-3904; *E-Mail:* mfshack@princeton.edu

SEMMES, STEPHEN WILLIAM, MATHEMATICS. *Current Pos:* PROF MATH, RICE UNIV, 87- *Personal Data:* b Savannah, Ga, May 26, 62. *Educ:* Armstrong State Col, BS, 80; Wash Univ, PhD(math), 83. *Mem:* Am Math Soc. *Mailing Add:* Dept Math Rice Univ MS 136 6100 Main St Houston TX 77005

SEMMLOW, JOHN LEONARD, BIOENGINEERING, BIOMEDICAL ENGINEERING. *Current Pos:* asst prof elec eng, 77-80, PROF SURG, MED SCH & PROF BIO ENG, RUTGERS UNIV, 81- *Personal Data:* b Chicago, Ill, Mar 12, 42. *Educ:* Univ Ill, Champaign, BS, 64; Univ Ill Med Ctr, PhD(physiol), 70. *Prof Exp:* Sr engr, Motorola, Inc, 64-66; instr physiol optics, Univ Calif, Berkeley, 69-70; asst prof bioeng, Univ Ill, Chicago, 71-77; asst prof physiol, Med Sch, Rush Univ, Chicago, 71-77. *Concurrent Pos:* NSF US/France Exchange fel, 85. *Mem:* Fel Inst Elec & Electronics Engrs; Sigma Xi; NY Acad Sci; Biomed Eng Soc. *Res:* Eye movement and other physiological motor control systems; design and development of bioinstrumentation for noninvasive diagnosis, particularly in cardiology and neurology. *Mailing Add:* 81 Louis St New Brunswick NJ 08901. *Fax:* 732-932-3753; *E-Mail:* semmlow@gandolf.rutgers.edu

SEMON, MARK DAVID, PHYSICS, MATHEMATICS. *Current Pos:* from asst prof to assoc prof, 76-88, PROF PHYSICS, BATES COL, 90- *Personal Data:* b Milwaukee, Wis, Mar 27, 50. *Educ:* Colgate Univ, AB, 71; Univ Colo, MS, 73, PhD(physics), 76. *Prof Exp:* Woodrow Wilson fel, 71-72; vis prof physics, Amherst Col, 88-90. *Concurrent Pos:* Res asst, Kitl Peak Nat Observ, Los Alamos Sci Lab, 75; asst ed, Am Physics, 88-90. *Mem:* Am Phys Soc; Sigma Xi; Am Asn Physics Teachers. *Res:* Quantum scattering theory; phase transitions and critical phenomena; aharonov-bohm effect; classical and quantum electrodynamics. *Mailing Add:* Bates Col Dept Physics 44 Campus Ave Lewiston ME 04240. *Fax:* 207-786-8334; *E-Mail:* msemon@bates.edu

SEMON, WARREN LLOYD, mathematics, for more information see previous edition

SEMONIN, RICHARD GERARD, ATMOSPHERIC PHYSICS, PRECIPITATION CHEMISTRY. *Current Pos:* Res asst radar meteorol, 55-56, from res assoc to assoc prof sci, 56-65, prof, 65-71, asst head, 70-80, prin scientist, 71-86, CHIEF, ATMOSPHERIC SCI SECT 86- *Personal Data:* b Akron, Ohio, June 25, 30; m 51; c 4. *Educ:* Univ Wash, Seattle, BSc, 55. *Concurrent Pos:* NSF grants, 58-60 & 61-80; US Army Res & Develop Labs grant, 62-64; Dept Energy contract, 69-; Dept Interior contract, 71-; prof atmospheric sci, Univ Ill, 75- *Mem:* Fel AAAS; fel Am Meteorol Soc; Weather Modification Asn; Nat Weather Asn; Sigma Xi. *Res:* Microphysical processes necessary or attendant to the formation of clouds and precipitation; weather modification, controlled and inadvertent; causes and distribution of acid deposition. *Mailing Add:* 1902 Crescent Dr Champaign IL 61821-5826

SEMRAU, KONRAD (TROXEL), CHEMICAL ENGINEERING. *Current Pos:* chem engr, 50-63, SR CHEM ENGR, SRI INT, 63- *Personal Data:* b Chico, Calif, June 5, 19. *Educ:* Univ Calif, BS, 48, MS, 49. *Prof Exp:* Asst tech engr, Carbide & Carbon Chem Co Div, Union Carbide & Carbon Corp, 46. *Mem:* Am Inst Chem Engrs; Am Chem Soc; Sigma Xi; Air & Waste Management Asn. *Res:* Dust and mist collection; fine particle technology; air pollution control engineering; mass transfer. *Mailing Add:* 806 Coleman Ave Apt 8 Menlo Park CA 94025-2453

SEMTNER, ALBERT JULIUS, JR, OCEANOGRAPHY. *Current Pos:* PROF OCEANOG, NAVAL POSTGRAD SCH, 86- *Personal Data:* b Oklahoma City, Okla, May 25, 41; m 69; c 2. *Educ:* Calif Inst Technol, BS, 63; Univ Calif, Los Angeles, MA, 65; Princeton Univ, PhD(geophys fluid dynamics), 73. *Honors & Awards:* Smithsonian Leadership Award, 93. *Prof Exp:* Lt comdr oceanog, Nat Oceanic & Atmospheric Admin, 68-73; adj asst prof meteorol, Univ Calif, Los Angeles, 73-76; scientist oceanog, Nat Ctr Atmospheric Res, 76-86. *Concurrent Pos:* Consult, Rand Corp, 74-75. *Mem:* Am Geophys Union; Am Meteorol Soc; Oceanog Soc. *Res:* Numerical simulation of ocean circulation; prediction of climatic changes with coupled models of the atmosphere, the ocean and sea ice. *Mailing Add:* 3470 Edgefield Pl Carmel CA 93923

SEMTNER, PAUL JOSEPH, ECONOMIC ENTOMOLOGY, INSECT ECOLOGY. *Current Pos:* ASST PROF ENTOM, VA POLYTECH INST & STATE UNIV, 74- *Personal Data:* b Seminole, Okla, May 9, 45; m 70; c 3. *Educ:* Okla State Univ, BS, 67, MS, 70, PhD(entom), 72. *Prof Exp:* Res assoc entom, Okla State Univ, 72-73; instr, Connors State Col, 73-74. *Mem:* Entom Soc Am; Sigma Xi. *Res:* Pest management of tobacco insect pests and effects of the environment on their abundance. *Mailing Add:* 825 S Main St Blackstone VA 23824

SEMURA, JACK S, STATISTICAL PHYSICS, COMPLEX SYSTEMS. *Current Pos:* from asst prof to assoc prof, 73-82, PROF PHYSICS, PORTLAND STATE UNIV, 82- *Educ:* Univ Hawaii, BA, 63, MS, 65; Univ Wis-Madison, PhD(physics), 72. *Honors & Awards:* Russell B Scott Award, Cryogenic Eng Soc, 85. *Prof Exp:* Res assoc, Univ Pittsburgh, 71-73. *Concurrent Pos:* Vis prof, Univ Wis-Madison, 80; affil, Los Alamos Nat Lab, 93- *Mem:* Am Phys Soc; Sigma Xi; Am Asn Physics Teachers; AAAS; Inst Elec & Electronics Engrs Comput Soc. *Res:* Theoretical physics; statistical physics; maximum entropy analysis; signal processing thermodynamics; phase transitions; acoustic resonance; environmental physics; heat transfer in cryogenic liquids; complex systems. *Mailing Add:* Dept Physics Portland State Univ Portland OR 97207. *Fax:* 503-725-3888; *E-Mail:* semuraj@pdx.edu

SEN, AMAR KUMAR, PHYSIOLOGY, PHARMACOLOGY. *Current Pos:* from asssoc prof to prof, 66-92, coord grad studies, Dept Pharmacol, 84-89, EMER PROF PHARMACOL, FAC MED, UNIV TORONTO, 92- *Personal Data:* b Calcutta, India, Mar 14, 27; m 56; c 2. *Educ:* Univ Calcutta, MSc, 49, MB & BS, 55; Univ London, PhD(physiol), 60. *Honors & Awards:* Res Award Med Res Comm Can, NIH, Cystic Fibrosis Found, Heart & Stroke Found Can. *Prof Exp:* Instr physiol, Sch Med, Vanderbilt Univ, 60-61, asst prof physiol, 63-66; sci pool officer, S K M Hosp, Calcutta, India, 62; dir clin res, Sandoz Ltd, Bombay, India, 62-63. *Concurrent Pos:* Consult pharmacologist, Addiction Res Found, Ont. *Mem:* NY Acad Sci; Can Biochem Soc; Can Pharmacol Soc; Am Physiol Soc; Soc Gen Physiol. *Res:* Transport of electrolytes and non-electrolytes across the cell membrane. *Mailing Add:* Dept Pharmacol Univ Toronto Fac Med Toronto ON M5S 1A8 Can. *Fax:* 416-441-6307

SEN, AMIYA K, ELECTRICAL ENGINEERING, PLASMA PHYSICS. *Current Pos:* from instr to assoc prof, 58-74, PROF ELEC ENG, COLUMBIA UNIV, 74- *Personal Data:* b Calcutta, India, Dec 14, 30; m 63; c 1. *Educ:* Indian Inst Sci, Bangalore, dipl, 52; Mass Inst Technol, SM, 58, PhD(elec eng), 63. *Prof Exp:* Test engr elec eng, Gen Elec Co, 53-54, design anal engr, 54-55; teaching asst, Mass Inst Technol, 56-57, instr, 57-58. *Concurrent Pos:* Various NSF, NASA and Dept Energy grants, 65-; mem, Adv Subcomt, NSF, 80-82; vis prof, Technische Hogeschool, Eindhoven, Holland, 70, Nagoya Univ, Nagoya, Japan, 77, Univ Calif, Berkeley, 84. *Mem:* Fel Am Phys Soc; Am Geophys Union; Inst Elec & Electronics Engrs. *Res:* Energy conversion; plasma and space physics; magnetohydrodynamics; author or coauthor of over 55 scientific journal publications. *Mailing Add:* Dept Elec Eng SW Mudd Bldg Columbia Univ New York NY 10027

SEN, ASIM KUMAR, ALTERNATIVE ENERGY SOURCES, SPACECRAFT DYNAMICS & CONTROL. *Current Pos:* PRES & SCIENTIST, SYNCHROSAT LTD, 73- *Personal Data:* b Calcutta, India, Jan 2, 39; Can citizen; m 66, Tapati Das Gupta; c Devjani. *Educ:* Univ Calcutta, BSc, 58, MSc, 61, PhD(radio physics & electronics), 67. *Prof Exp:* Lectr, Univ Kalyani, India, 65-67; postdoctoral fel, Univ Man, 67-69; postdoctoral res assoc, Goddard Space Flight Ctr, NASA, 69-71; res consult, Commun Res Ctr Govt Can, 72. *Concurrent Pos:* Sessional lectr elec engs, Univ Man, 68; sessional lectr elec eng, Univ Ottawa, 75-84; adj prof elec eng, Univ Ottawa, 84-86. *Mem:* Fel Inst Electronics & Telecommun Engrs; assoc fel Am Inst Aeronaut & Astronaut; sr mem Inst Elec & Electronics Engrs. *Res:* Momentum turbine; gyrolite stabilization; determination of trap modes in spinning satellites. *Mailing Add:* PO Box 1259 Sta B Ottawa ON K1P 5R3 Can. *Fax:* 613-829-4963

SEN, BUDDHADEV, PHYSICAL INORGANIC CHEMISTRY. *Current Pos:* from asst prof to assoc prof, 61-72, PROF CHEM, LA STATE UNIV, BATON ROUGE, 72- *Personal Data:* b India, Aug 7, 23; nat US; m 56; c 2. *Educ:* Univ Calcutta, India, BSc, 45, MSc, 47, DPhil(sci), 54. *Prof Exp:* Lectr chem, City Col Calcutta, India, 48 & Jadavpur Univ, India, 48-56; fel, La State Univ, 54-56, from vis asst prof to asst prof, 56-60; vis asst prof, Univ Alta, 60-61. *Concurrent Pos:* Petrol Res Fund int grant, Univ Col London, 66-67; chmn Freshman Chem Prog, Dept Chem, La State Univ, 76. *Mem:* Am Chem Soc. *Res:* Coordination chemistry of transition and post-transition elements; thermodynamics of chelates; properties of mixed solvents. *Mailing Add:* 774 Baird Dr Baton Rouge LA 70808-5916

SEN, DIPAK KUMAR, MATHEMATICAL PHYSICS. *Current Pos:* From lectr to assoc prof, 58-77, PROF MATH, UNIV TORONTO, 77- *Personal Data:* b Patna, India, Feb 28, 36. *Educ:* Patna Univ, India, MSc, 54; Univ Paris, DresSci(physics), 58. *Mem:* Am Math Soc; Can Math Soc. *Res:* Relativity; cosmology. *Mailing Add:* Dept Math Univ Toronto 100 St George St St George Campus Toronto ON M5S 3G3 Can

SEN, GANES C, MOLECULAR BIOLOGY. *Current Pos:* STAFF MEM, MOLECULAR BIOL, CLEVELAND CLIN, 88- *Personal Data:* b Varanasi, India, Jan 17, 45; m 73, Indira Haldar; c Srisan & Ritu. *Educ:* Calcutta Univ, BSc, 65, MSc, 67; McMaster Univ, PhD(biochem), 74. *Prof Exp:* Fel molecular biol, Yale Univ, 74-76, res assoc, 76-78; asst & assoc mem molecular biol, Sloan-Kettering Cancer Ctr, 78-88, head, Lab Oncogenic Viruses & Interferons, 81-88. *Concurrent Pos:* Asst & assoc prof, Grad Sch Med Sci, Cornell Univ, 79-88; prof physics, biophysics & biochem, Case Western Univ, 89- *Mem:* Am Soc Microbiol; Am Soc Virol; Am Heart Asn; Am Soc Biochem & Molecular Biol; AAAS. *Res:* Mechanisms of interferon actions; host-virus interactions; actions of double-stranded RNA; angiotens in converting enzyme; blood pressure regulation. *Mailing Add:* Dept Molecular Biol Cleveland Clin Found Res Inst Clin Ctr 9500 Euclid Ave NC2-103 Cleveland OH 44195-5285. *Fax:* 216-444-0512; *E-Mail:* beng@cesmtp.ccf.org

SEN, MIHIR, HEAT TRANSFER, FLUID MECHANICS. *Current Pos:* assoc prof, 86-94, PROF AEROSPACE & MECH ENG, UNIV NOTRE DAME, 94- *Personal Data:* b Calcutta, India, Jan 17, 47; m 72, Beatriz Urquidi; c Pradeep & Maya. *Educ:* Indian Inst Technol, Madras, India, BTech, 68; Mass Inst Technol, ScD, 75. *Honors & Awards:* Nat Researcher Award, Gov Mex, 84. *Prof Exp:* From asst prof to prof thermal & fluid sci, Nat Autonomous Univ Mex, Mexico City, 75-85. *Concurrent Pos:* Mech eng coordr, Nat Acad Eng-Mex, 80-83; consult, Dept Solar Energy, Nat Autonomous Univ Mex, 81-83, Inst Eng, 84-85; Sundstrand Heat Transfer, 89; vis prof mech & aerospace eng, Cornell Univ, Ithaca, 85-86. *Mem:* Nat Acad Eng-Mex; Am Soc Mech Engrs; AAAS; Soc Indust & Appl Math; Am Phys Soc; Am Soc Eng Educ. *Res:* Heat transfer and fluid mechanics; mathematical modeling; numerical methods; heat exchangers; porous media flow; natural convection; thermosyphon loops; hydrodynamic stability; bifurcation theory and chaos; numerous technical and nontechnical publications. *Mailing Add:* 52833 Sporn Dr South Bend IN 46635-1228. *Fax:* 219-631-8341; *E-Mail:* mihir.sen.1@nd.edu

SEN, PABITRA NARAYAN, ELECTROMAGNETICS, ACOUSTICS. *Current Pos:* mem prof staff petrophys, Schlumberger-Doll Res, 78-87, prog leader, 81-83 & 94-95, SCI ADV, SCHLUMBERGER-DOLL RES, 87- *Personal Data:* b Calcutta, India, Sept 5, 44; m 84, Susan Shu; c Indra & Maya. *Educ:* Calcutta Univ, BSc, 64, MSc, 67; Univ Chicago, PhD(physics), 72. *Prof Exp:* Res assoc physics, Mich State Univ, 72-73; mem res staff physics, Xerox Palo Alto Res Ctr, 73-76; sr scientist, Xonics Inc, 76-78. *Concurrent Pos:* Vis prof, Univ Provence, France, 85; external examr, Brandeis, 85, Harvard Univ, 86 & 95, Brooklyn Col, 88 & Univ Oslo, 96; adv comt, Int Sch Energy & Develop, Jamaica, 87, 2nd Int Conf Electronic Transport & Optical Properties of Inhomogeneous Media, Paris, 87-88; guest res fel, Dept Theoret Physics, Oxford Univ, Eng, 88-89 & Royal Soc, London, 88; vis scientist, S N Base Nat Ctr Basic Res, India, 89, 91 & 93; distinguished speaker, Soc Prof WellLog Analysts, 91-92; vis fel, Inst Math, Univ Minn, 95. *Mem:* Fel Am Phys Soc; Soc Petrol Engrs; Soc Explor Geophys; Soc Prof Well Log Analysts; Math Asn Am. *Res:* Electromagnetic, vibrational, structural and transport properties of inhomogeneous, amorphous, composite and porous media; statistical mechanics of weakly connected systems; rocks and geological materials; interfacial properties; nuclear magnetic resonance in porous media. *Mailing Add:* Schlumberger-Doll Res Old Quarry Rd Ridgefield CT 06877-4108. *Fax:* 203-438-3819; *E-Mail:* sen@sdr.slb.com

SEN, PRANAB KUMAR, BIOSTATISTICS, STATISTICS. *Current Pos:* from asst prof to prof biostatist, 65-82, adj prof statist, 80-88, CARY C BOSHAME PROF BIOSTATIST, UNIV NC, CHAPEL HILL, 82-, PROF STATIST, 88- *Personal Data:* b Calcutta, India, Nov 7, 37; m 63; c 2. *Educ:* Univ Calcutta, India, BSc, 55, MSc, 57, PhD(statist), 62. *Prof Exp:* Asst prof statist, Univ Calcutta, India, 61-64 & Univ Calif, Berkeley, 64-65. *Concurrent*

Pos: USAF Systs Command contract statist anal, Univ NC, 71-78; Richard Merton guest prof, Univ Freiburg, Ger, 74-75; lect, math sth statist, Conf Bd Math Sci, NSF, 83- *Mem:* Fel Inst Math Statist; fel Am Statist Asn; Int Statist Inst. *Res:* Nonparametric methods; multivariate analysis; order statistics; weak convergence; nonparametric statistics and sequential procedures. *Mailing Add:* 110 Baskerville Circle Chapel Hill NC 27514

SEN, TAPAS K, PSYCHOLOGY, STATISTICS. *Current Pos:* PRES, TRANSFORMATION STRATEGIES INT, INC, 97- *Personal Data:* b Calcutta, India, Mar 1, 33; US citizen; m 66; c 2. *Educ:* Calcutta Univ, India, BS, 51, MSc 54; Johns Hopkins Univ, PhD(psychol), 63. *Prof Exp:* Res scholar statist, Indian Statist Inst, Calcutta, 55-59; assoc psychologist visual res, Appl Physics Lab, Johns Hopkins Univ, 60-63; mem tech staff speech res, Bell Labs, 63-72; dist mgr human resources planning/corp planning, AT&T, 73-78, div mgr human resources, 79-91, human resources dir, Workplace of the Future, 92-96. *Concurrent Pos:* NSF fel, Johns Hopkins Univ, 59-63; chair, Coun Tech Group, Human Factors Soc, 72-77, Mayflower Group, 84-85; mem, Tech Adv Comt Workforce Preparedness, Nat Planning Asn, 88-89; chair, NJ Govs Taskforce Educ & Workforce Qual, 95-96. *Mem:* Am Psychol Asn; fel Human Factors & Ergonomics Soc; Soc Indust & Orgn Psychol. *Res:* Organizational competency; understanding and developing models of effective organization and culture change using employee involvement and quality; macro-ergonomic and leadership dimensions are identified. *Mailing Add:* 29 Arden Rd Morristown NJ 07046

SEN, UJJAL, ELECTRONICS & ELECTRICAL TECHNICAL MANAGEMENT. *Current Pos:* Res & develop engr, Spectronics Corp, 87-89, chief res & develop engr, 89-90, res & develop mgr, 90-92, TECH DIR, SPECTRONICS CORP, 93- *Personal Data:* b Calcutta, India, May 29, 57; m 91, Urmi Choudhury. *Educ:* Indian Inst Technol, BSc, 77, Indian Inst Sci, BE, 80; State Univ NY. *Prof Exp:* Qual control engr, Siemens Ltd, 80-81; teaching asst elec eng, State Univ NY, Buffalo, 81-84, res asst elec eng, 81-87. *Concurrent Pos:* Scientist, Aerospace Mat Spec Nondestructive Testing, Soc Automotive Engrs, 88-; mem, Comt Nondestructive Testing, Am Soc Testing & Mat, 88- *Mem:* Inst Elec & Electronics Engrs; Soc Photo-Optical Instrumentation Engrs; Illum Eng Soc; Am Soc Testing & Mat; Am Soc Nondestructive Testing. *Res:* Optical diagnostics of electric discharges and gas plasmas; optical measurement and instrumentation; electro-optic devices and systems; pulsed power technology; electronic power control; nondestructive techniques and systems; author of numerous publications. *Mailing Add:* 7 Willis Ave Syosset NY 11791

SENAGORE, ANTHONY J, COLON & RECTAL SURGERY. *Current Pos:* SURGEON & DIR RES, FERGUSON-BLODGETT DDI, 89-; INTERIM PROG DIR, G S BUTTERWORTH HOSP, 96- *Personal Data:* b Nov 20, 58; US citizen; m 83, Patricia Kaman; c Antonio & Christina. *Educ:* Wayne State Univ, BSc, 80; Mich State Univ, MD, 81, MSc, 89. *Prof Exp:* Asst prof, Dept Surg, Mich State Univ, 88-89. *Mem:* AMA; assoc fel Am Col Surgeons; Asn Acad Surg; AAAS; Am Soc Colon & Rectal Surgeons; Am Physiol Soc. *Res:* Surgical techniques for the colon and rectum; recurrent colorectal carcinoma; colorectal anastomotic healing; author of 18 publications. *Mailing Add:* Ferguson Clin 75 Sheldon Blvd SE Grand Rapids MI 49503-4240. *Fax:* 616-356-4040

SENAY, LEO CHARLES, JR, PHYSIOLOGY. *Current Pos:* From instr to assoc prof, 57-68, PROF PHYSIOL, SCH MED, ST LOUIS UNIV, 68- *Personal Data:* b Fall River, Mass, Jan 18, 27; m 51, 90; c 7. *Educ:* Harvard Univ, AB, 49; State Univ Iowa, PhD(physiol), 57. *Concurrent Pos:* NIH career develop award, 65-70; Anglo-Am fel, SAfrica, 70-82; vis prof appl physiol, Univ Witwatersrand, 71; consult, NIH. *Mem:* AAAS; Am Physiol Soc; Am Col Sports Med; Sigma Xi. *Res:* Environmental physiology, particularly human responses to heat stress and exercise; body fluid dynamics; pharmocology of blood vessels. *Mailing Add:* Dept Physiol St Louis Univ Sch Med 1402 S Grand Blvd St Louis MO 63104-1080

SENCER, DAVID JUDSON, medicine, for more information see previous edition

SENCIALL, IAN ROBERT, BIOCHEMISTRY. *Current Pos:* RETIRED. *Personal Data:* b Nottingham, Eng, June 2, 38; m 62; c 3. *Educ:* Univ London, BS, 61; Univ Birmingham, PhD(biochem), 67. *Prof Exp:* Org res chemist, Fisons Pest Control Ltd, Eng, 61-64; res biochemist, Mem Univ Nfld, from lectr to prof biochem, Sch Med, 73-96. *Mem:* Can Biochem Soc. *Res:* Studies on the biosynthesis and metabolism of steroid carboxylic acids by the human and by animals; steroid metabolism in essential hypertension; cytochrome P-450. *Mailing Add:* 35 Taylor Pl St John's NF A1A 1L4 Can

SENCINDIVER, JOHN COE, SOIL SCIENCE. *Current Pos:* asst prof, 78-82, ASSOC PROF SOIL SCI, WVA UNIV, 82- *Personal Data:* b Martinsburg, WVa, Aug 21, 48; m 73; c 3. *Educ:* WVa Univ, BS, 70, PhD(agron soil sci), 77. *Prof Exp:* NDEA fel, 71-74; soil scientist reclamation, Forest Serv, 75-78. *Concurrent Pos:* Soil scientist soil surv, USDA Soil Conserv Serv, 71-75. *Mem:* Soil Sci Soc Am; Am Soc Agron; Soil Conserv Soc; Int Soc Soil Sci; Am Soc Surf Mining & Water Reclamation. *Res:* Soil genesis and classification; overburden and minesoil properties; surface mine reclamation. *Mailing Add:* Dept Plant Sci WVa Univ PO Box 6108 Morgantown WV 26506-0001

SENDA, MOTOTAKA, MICROBIOLOGY. *Current Pos:* FEL, INST BIOCHEM & CELL BIOL, SYNTEX DISCOVERY RES. *Personal Data:* b Okayama, Japan, Feb 8, 54; m 87. *Educ:* Okayama Univ, BS, 77, BS, 81, MS, 83; Osaka Univ, PhD, 88. *Prof Exp:* Jr scientist, Dept Microbiol & Chemother, Hoffman-La Roche Japan Res Ctr, 83-85, sr scientist, 86-89; fel, Dept Molecular Genetics & Microbiol, Univ Med & Dent NJ, 89- *Concurrent Pos:* Vis fel, Dept Peptide Res, Hoffman-La Roche US Res Ctr, 85-86. *Mem:* Am Soc Biochem & Molecular Biol. *Res:* Role of lipoprotein lipase in the metabolism of lipoprotein and apo-lipoprotein; interferon receptor and its role by the method of genomeii gene analysis and a signal transduction. *Mailing Add:* Stimmune Biotechnol 5400 Hollis St Emeryville CA 94608-2508

SENDELBACH, ANTON G, DAIRY SCIENCE, GENETICS. *Current Pos:* From instr to assoc prof, 56-75, PROF DAIRY SCI, UNIV WIS-MADISON, 75- *Personal Data:* b Waumandee, Wis, Mar 23, 24; m 56; c 4. *Educ:* Wis State Univ, River Falls, BS, 54; Univ Wis, MS, 56, PhD(dairy sci), 60. *Mem:* Am Dairy Sci Asn; Sigma Xi. *Res:* Dairy sire and cow evaluation for dairy herd improvement. *Mailing Add:* Univ Wis 2655 Chesapeake Dr Madison WI 53719

SENDERS, JOHN W, MAN-MACHINE SYSTEMS ANALYSIS, COGNITIVE SCIENCE & HUMAN RELIABILITY. *Current Pos:* vis prof, 73-74, prof ind eng, 74-85, EMER PROF MECH & IND ENG, UNIV TORONTO, CAN, 85- *Personal Data:* b Cambridge, Mass, Feb 26, 20; m 78, Ann Crichton-Harris; c Warren, Stefan, Daniel Sellen, Abigail Sellen & Adam Sellen. *Educ:* Harvard Univ, AB, 48, Univ Tilburg, Nether, PhD, 83. *Prof Exp:* Consult eng, 48-50; res psychologist, Aero Med Lab, Wright Patterson AFB, 50-56; head, Dept Psychol, Arctic Aero Med Lab, USAF, Fairbanks, 56-57; prin res scientist, Minneapolis-Honeywell Regulator Co, 57-62; prin scientist & consult, Bolt, Beranek & Newman, Inc, 62-70. *Concurrent Pos:* Mem, Comt Bio-Astronaut, Nat Acad Sci-Nat Res Coun, 59-60, Man-in-Space Comt, Space Sci Bd, 60-62, Comt Hearing, Bio-acoust & Bio-mech, 62-85, Highway Safety Comt, Highway Res Bd, 65 & 72-85, Comt Vision, 70-85, Road Characteristics Comt, 72- & Indust Eng Grant Selection Comt, 74-77; lectr & sr res assoc psychol, Brandeis Univ, 65-72; sr lectr mech eng, Mass Inst Technol, 66-67; pres, Senders Assoc, Inc, 68-73; sr res assoc, Univ Calif, Santa Barbara, 79-80; res prof, Univ Maine, 81-83; prof eng & psychol, Dept Mech Eng, 83-90; consult var indust, govt agencies, res co & legal firms; pres, Human Factors North, Inc, 83-, chmn bd, 85-93; mem, Sci Adv Bd, Div Life Sci, Air Force Off Sci Res, 85-90. *Mem:* Sr mem Inst Elec & Electronics Engrs; fel Am Psychol Soc; fel Am Psychol Asn; fel AAAS; Psychonomic Soc; fel Human Factors & Ergonomics Soc. *Res:* Models of visual monitoring behavior; quantification of mental workload; nature and source of human error; cognitive science; human perceptual motor skill; human information processing; medical error & equipment design; human reliability. *Mailing Add:* 295 Indian Rd Toronto ON M6R 2X5 Can. *Fax:* 416-769-6155; *E-Mail:* jw.senders@utoronto.ca

SENDLEIN, LYLE V A, GEOLOGICAL ENGINEERING, GEOPHYSICS. *Current Pos:* actg chmn, Dept Geol Sci, 90-92, DIR INST MINING & MINERAL RES, UNIV KY, 82-, DIR KY WATER RESOURCES RES INST, 92- *Personal Data:* b St Louis, Mo, May 11, 33; m 55, Louise Darr; c Lyle S, Todd L & Erik L. *Educ:* Washington Univ, St Louis, BS, 58, AM, 60; Iowa State Univ, PhD(geol soil eng), 64. *Prof Exp:* From instr to prof geol & geophys, Iowa State Univ, 60-77; dir, Coal Extraction & Utilization Res Ctr, Southern Ill Univ, Carbondale, 77-82. *Concurrent Pos:* Consult, Atlantic Ref Co, Tex, 57 & Alpha Portland Cement Co, Mo, 58; consult engr, H M Reitz, 59-60 & US Gypsum Co, Ill, 60-77; asst div chief, Energy & Minerals Resources Res Inst, Iowa State Univ, 74-75; vis prof, Middle East Tech Univ, Ankara, Turkey. *Mem:* Geol Soc Am; Am Geophys Union; Soc Explor Geophys; Nat Water Well Asn; Sigma Xi. *Res:* Engineering geology related to urban and rural problems; mining and reclamation research in coal mines and the study of groundwater movement in karst systems; ground investigations of pollution from sanitary landfills, coal mines, and other point sources and nonpoint sources. *Mailing Add:* Ky Water Resources Res Inst Univ Ky Lexington KY 40506-0107

SENEAR, ALLEN EUGENE, ANALYTICAL CHEMISTRY. *Current Pos:* RETIRED. *Personal Data:* b Chicago, Ill, Nov 2, 19; m 48, Virginia Koch; c Allen W, Elizabeth A, Donald F & Virginia R. *Educ:* Williams Col, Mass, BA, 41; Calif Inst Technol, PhD(org chem), 46. *Prof Exp:* Asst radiochem, Williams Col, Mass, 40; asst chem, Calif Inst Technol, 41-43, Comt Med Res contract, 43-45; fel, Univ Ill, 46-47; from instr to asst prof chem, Univ Calif, 47-55; res engr, Boeing Co, 55-85. *Concurrent Pos:* Chair, Puget Sound Sect, Am Chem Soc, 86. *Mem:* Am Chem Soc; Soc Appl Spectros; AAAS. *Res:* Synthetic organic chemistry, especially monomer synthesis; polymer preparation. *Mailing Add:* 1446 92nd Ave NE Bellevue WA 98004

SENECA, HARRY, INTERNAL MEDICINE, BACTERIOLOGY. *Current Pos:* ASSOC PROF UROL & COL PHYSICIANS & SURGEONS, COLUMBIA UNIV, 47-, RES ASSOC, 52- *Personal Data:* b Beirut, Lebanon, July 24, 09; m 48. *Educ:* Am Univ Beirut, MD, 33; Tulane Univ, MS, 43; Am Bd Internal Med, dipl. *Honors & Awards:* Henderson Award, 64; Hugh Young Award, 76. *Prof Exp:* Instr bact & parasitol, Med Sch, Am Univ Beirut, 33-37; from asst prof to assoc prof bact & parasitol & lectr trop dis, Royal Col Med, Iraq, 37-40; Rockefeller fel, Tulane Univ, 41; from instr to asst prof trop med, Tulane Univ, 42-43. *Concurrent Pos:* Instr path, Med Sch, Am Univ Beirut, 35-36; dir, Govt Bact, Parasitol & Vaccine Insts, Baghdad, Iraq, 37-40; attend physician, Royal Hosp, Baghdad, 37-40, Charity Hosp, New Orleans, La, 41-44 & Columbia Presby Hosp, 47-; consult, Schering Corp, NJ, 46-51 & Chas Pfizer & Co, Inc, NY, 51-54; mem, Chagos Dis Found, Rio de Janeiro, Brazil, 73-; Gen Consult NJ Hospitals. *Mem:* Am Soc Trop Med & Hyg; Am Soc Parasitol; Am Geriat Soc; Am Soc Microbiol; fel

Am Col Physicians. *Res:* Experimental medicine in relation to treatment and diagnosis; gastrointestinal diseases; bacterial and parasitic diseases; hemoflagellates; sepsis and septic shock; E histolytica; antibacterials and antibiotics; oxysteroids; antihistaminics; bacterial resistance; neoplastic diseases; pyelonephritis. *Mailing Add:* 2165 Lemoine Ave 48 Ft Lee NJ 07024-6017

SENECAL, GERARD, PHYSICS. *Current Pos:* RETIRED. *Personal Data:* b Atwood, Kans, July 27, 29. *Educ:* St Benedicts Col, Kans, BA, 51; Univ Mich, MA, 57; Kans State Univ, PhD(physics), 63. *Prof Exp:* Air Force Cambridge Res Labs res asst, Kans State Univ, 61-62; from instr to assoc prof physics, Benedictine Col, 62-72, actg chmn dept, 66-68 & chmn dept, 68-72, pres, 72-87. *Concurrent Pos:* Lectr-consult, Mobile Lab Prog, Oak Ridge Inst Nuclear Studies, 66-; proj dir, Undergrad Res Participation Grants St Benedicts Col, 66-67 & 68-69; NSF sci fac fel, Univ Calif, Berkeley, 71-72. *Mem:* Am Phys Soc; Am Asn Physics Teachers. *Res:* Electrical and magnetic properties of thin evaporated semiconducting films; electrical properties of polymer materials, particularly polyethylene crystals. *Mailing Add:* St Josephs St Patricks Church 705 Spring Garden Atchison KS 66002

SENECAL, VANCE E(VAN), CHEMICAL ENGINEERING,. *Current Pos:* RETIRED. *Personal Data:* b Phillipston, Pa, Aug 16, 21; m 45; c 4. *Educ:* Slippery Rock State Teachers Col, BS, 43; Carnegie Inst Technol, BS, 47, MS, 48, DSc(chem eng), 51. *Prof Exp:* Develop engr, Pittsburgh Coke & Chem Co, 48; res engr, Exp Sta, E I Du Pont de Nemours & Co, 51-56, res proj engr, 56-59, res proj supvr, 59-60, res supvr, 60-62, res mgr, Polymer Tech, 62-66, develop mgr, 66-67, res mgr chem eng, 67-69, lab dir, Eng Technol Lab, 69-77, dir eng res, 77-83, vchmn & exec dir, Comt Educ Aid, 83-86. *Mem:* Am Inst Chem Engrs; Am Chem Soc; Sigma Xi. *Res:* Solid deformation mechanics; liquid dynamics; heat transfer; fluid distribution; research and education administration. *Mailing Add:* 1309 Grayson Rd Welshire Wilmington DE 19803

SENECHAL, DAVID, QUANTUM FIELD THEORY, ELECTRON SYSTEMS. *Current Pos:* PROF PHYSICS, UNIV SHERBROOKE, 92- *Personal Data:* b Alma, Que, Apr 2, 63; m 96. *Educ:* McGill Univ, BSc, 85; Cornell Univ, MSc, 87, PhD(physics), 90. *Prof Exp:* Nat Sci & Eng Res Coun Can postdoctoral scholar, Univ Laval, 90-92. *Mem:* Can Asn Physicists. *Res:* Electronic and magnetic properties of highly anisotropic solids, in particular, low-dimensional magnets, using the methods of quantum field theory. *Mailing Add:* Dept Physics Univ Sherbrooke Sherbrooke PQ J1K 2R1 Can. *Fax:* 819-821-8046; *E-Mail:* dsenech@physique.usherb.ca

SENECHAL, LESTER JOHN, MATHEMATICS. *Current Pos:* assoc prof, 68-75, PROF MATH, MT HOLYOKE COL, 75- *Personal Data:* b Chicago, Ill, June 10, 34; div; c 2. *Educ:* Ill Inst Technol, BS, 56, MS, 58, PhD(math), 63. *Prof Exp:* Instr math, Ill Inst Technol, 59-60 & Univ Tenn, 60-62; asst prof, Univ Ariz, 63-65 & Univ Mass, Amherst, 66-68. *Concurrent Pos:* Fulbright lectr, Brazil, 65; vis prof, Rijksuniversitijt te Groningen, Neth, 74-75 & Acad Sci USSR, 78-79; vis scholar, Univ Tex, Austin, 87-88; vis prof, Univ NC, Chapel Hill, 90-91. *Mem:* Am Math Soc. *Res:* Differentiability properties of nonlinear operators; descent methods in nonlinear optimization. *Mailing Add:* Dept Math Statist Comput Sci Mt Holyoke Col South Hadley MA 01075-1411

SENECHAL, MARJORIE LEE, MATHEMATICAL CRYSTALLOGRAPHY, DISCRETE GEOMETRY. *Current Pos:* Lectr, 66-67, asst prof, 67-74, assoc prof, 74-78, PROF MATH, SMITH COL, 78- *Personal Data:* b St Louis, Mo, July 18, 39. *Educ:* Univ Chicago, BS, 60; Ill Inst Technol, MS, 62, PhD(math), 65. *Concurrent Pos:* Sabbaticals, Univ Groningen, Netherlands, 74-75; exchange scientist, Inst Crystall Moscow, Nat Acad Sci, 78-79; mem, Adv Comt USSR Eastern Eruop, Comn Int Relations, Nat Acad Sci, 82-85. *Mem:* Am Math Soc; Sigma Xi. *Res:* Application of discrete geometry, including symmetry theory and the theory of tessellations to physical chemical and biological problems; history of the science of structure of matter. *Mailing Add:* Clark Sci Ctr Dept Math Smith Col Northampton MA 01063-0001

SENECHALLE, DAVID ALBERT, MATHEMATICS. *Current Pos:* SR SCIENTIST, TRACOR, INC, 78- *Personal Data:* b Chicago, Ill, July 8, 40; m 63; c 1. *Educ:* Univ Tex, BA, 65, PhD(functional anal), 67. *Prof Exp:* Res sci asst math, Univ Tex, Austin, 62-65; eng scientist, Tracor, Inc, 65-67; asst prof math, Univ Ga, 67-70; asst prof math, Col New Platz, State Univ NY, 70-74, assoc prof, 74-78. *Mem:* Am Math Soc. *Res:* Functional analysis; electronic counter-measures. *Mailing Add:* 4803 Balcones Dr Austin TX 78731

SENFT, JOHN FRANKLIN, FOREST PRODUCTS. *Current Pos:* from instr forestry to asst prof wood sci, 59-71, ASSOC PROF WOOD SCI, PURDUE UNIV, WEST LAFAYETTE, 71- *Personal Data:* b York, Pa, Apr 13, 33; m 58, Kathryn A Glatfelter; c Dan (deceased) & Nancy. *Educ:* Pa State Univ, BS, 55, MF, 59; Purdue Univ, PhD(wood tech), 67. *Prof Exp:* Instr forestry, Pa State Univ, 57-59. *Mem:* Forest Prod Soc; Soc Wood Sci & Technol; Am Soc Testing & Mat. *Res:* Mechanical properties of wood; stress rating of lumber, wood anatomy, mechanical properties and wood quality. *Mailing Add:* Dept Forestry & Nat Resources Purdue Univ West Lafayette IN 47907

SENFT, JOSEPH PHILIP, LAND RECLAMATION, SOLID WASTE MANAGEMENT. *Current Pos:* CONSULT, STATE COLLEGE, 89- *Personal Data:* b York Co, Pa, Oct 2, 36; div; c Miriam, Linda & Brian. *Educ:* Juniata Col, BS, 59; State Univ NY Buffalo, MA, 61, PhD(biol), 65. *Prof Exp:* Fel physiol, Sch Med, Univ Md, 64-65, res assoc, 65-66, instr, 66-67; from asst prof to assoc prof, Rutgers Univ, New Brunswick, 67-72; vis prof, Juniata Col, 72-73, assoc prof, 73-77; res scientist, Rodale Res Ctr, 77-82; inst sci, Germantown Acad, 84-88; vis prof, Juniata Col, 88-89; res assoc, Pa State Univ, 89-96. *Concurrent Pos:* Instr sci, Morristown-Beard Sch, 83-84; mem corp, Marine Biol Lab, Woods Hole. *Mem:* Am Soc Surface Mining & Reclamation; Sigma Xi. *Res:* Nutritional quality of amaranth grain as possible food source; relationships between soil and plant nutrients for optimum nutritional quality of plant food products; conductance mechanisms in squid nerve axon membranes; active transport mechanisms in frog skin, lobster nerve, and rat gut; land reclamation; municipal, agricultural and industrial waste utilization. *Mailing Add:* 107 E Aaron Dr State College PA 16803-3004

SENFTLE, FRANK EDWARD, BOREHOLE NUCLEAR GEOPHYSICS, MAGNETO CHEMISTRY. *Current Pos:* ADJ PROF PHYSICS, HOWARD UNIV, 89- *Personal Data:* b Buffalo, NY, May 4, 21; m 49, Anne Keogh; c Mary, Anne, Joseph, Frank, Theresa & Patrick. *Educ:* Univ Toronto, BS, 42, MA, 44, PhD(geophys), 47. *Honors & Awards:* Distinguished Serv Gold Medal, US Dept Interior, 91. *Prof Exp:* Lectr chem, physics & math, St Michael's Col, Toronto, 40-46; physicist-in-charge, Radiation Lab, Dept Mines & Resources, Ont, Can, 47-49; res assoc, Mass Inst Technol, 49-51; physicist-in-charge, Nucleonics Group, US Geol Surv, 51-60, head, Solid State Physics Group, 60-65, head, Physics Lab, 65-89. *Concurrent Pos:* Lectr, Ottawa Univ, 47-49; vis res prof, Howard Univ, 65-66 & 70-81; prin investr, Lunar Sci Prog, NASA, 70-73; consult, Int Atomic Energy Agency, Vienna, Austria, 72-88. *Mem:* Am Phys Soc. *Res:* Development of instruments and methods in nuclear and solid state physics applied to geochemical processes; magnetic properties of crystalline and amorphous materials. *Mailing Add:* Dept Physics & Astron Howard Univ Washington DC 20059. *Fax:* 202-806-4430

SENFTLEBER, FRED CARL, ANALYTICAL CHEMISTRY. *Current Pos:* AT DEPT CHEM, JACKSONVILLE UNIV. *Personal Data:* b Roslyn, NY, Nov 19, 48; m 71; c 2. *Educ:* Univ Tampa, BS, 70; Southern Ill Univ, PhD(anal chem), 77. *Prof Exp:* Res assoc separation chem, Bucknell Univ, 75-76; instr anal & inorg chem, Providence Col, 76-77, asst prof, 77-78; asst prof anal chem, Murray State Univ, 78- *Mem:* Am Chem Soc. *Res:* Studies into changes in metabolic pathways brought about by various pathological conditions; studies involving the use of transition metal complexes in the catalysis of electrochemical reactions. *Mailing Add:* Math & Sci Jacksonville Univ 2800 University Blvd N Jacksonville FL 32211-3321

SENGAR, DHARMENDRA PAL SINGH, HISTOCOMPATIBILITY ANTIGENS, TISSUE TYPING. *Current Pos:* fel oncol, Dept Med, Univ Ottawa, 72-73, asst prof med, 73-79, from asst prof to assoc prof path & med, 79-90, PROF PATH & MED, UNIV OTTAWA, 90-; DIR RES & TECH, REGIONAL TISSUE TYPING LAB, OTTAWA GEN HOSP, ONT, 74- *Personal Data:* b Aligarh, Uttar Pradesh, India, Jan 2, 41; Can citizen; m 71; c 3. *Educ:* Vikram Univ, Madhya Pradesh, India, BVSc & AH, 61; Agra Univ, Uttar Pradesh, India, MVSc & AH, 63; Univ Guelph, Ont, MSc, 67, PhD(immunogenetics), 69. *Prof Exp:* Asst prof reproductive physiol, Col Vet Med, Uttar Pradesh Agr Univ, India, 63-65; fel immunogenetics, dept surg, Univ Calif, Los Angeles, 69-72. *Mem:* NY Acad Sci; Am Asn Immunologists; Transplantation Soc; Can Transplantation Soc. *Res:* Host immune responses in renal allograft recipients; association of histocompatibility antigens with disease states; mixed leukocyte response; lymphocyte subsets. *Mailing Add:* Dept Path Univ Ottawa Ottawa Gen Hosp 501 Smyth Rd Ottawa ON K1N 6N5 Can. *Fax:* 613-737-8281

SENGBUSCH, HOWARD GEORGE, PARASITOLOGY, ACAROLOGY. *Current Pos:* asst gen biol, State Univ NY, 51-52, from asst prof to assoc prof biol, 52-57, univ res found grant, 56 & 61, dir, Great Lakes Lab, 65-67, dean fac arts & sci, 65-70, res grant, 70, prof biol, 57-81, EMER PROF, STATE UNIV NY, BUFFALO, 81- *Personal Data:* b Buffalo, NY, Dec 14, 17; m 42, Beatrice Ebling; c Craig Howard & Lee Ardell. *Educ:* State Univ NY, BS, 39; Univ Buffalo, EdM, 47; NY Univ, MS & PhD(parasitol), 51. *Prof Exp:* Teacher pub sch, NY, 39-41. *Concurrent Pos:* NSF grant, Mt Lake Biol Sta, Univ Va, 55-56; mem USAEC radiation safety prog, USPHS, Nev, 57, scientist dir, 80-; with Max Planck Inst, 57-58; NIH fel, La State Univ, Cent Am, 60; Fulbright prof, Univ Philippines Univ, 62-63; vis prof, Univ Mysore, 69-70; consult, Roswell Park Mem Inst, NY, 63-; fac exchange scholar, State Univ NY, 74-; res assoc entom, Bishop Mus, 77- & Buffalo Mus Sci, 81-85; adj prof biol, Inst Arthrodology & Parasitol, Ga Southern Univ, Statesboro, Ga, 83-; courtesy prof biol, Fla State Univ, 86- *Mem:* Am Soc Parasitol; Entom Soc Am; fel AAAS; Am Soc Acarology; Soc Syst Zool. *Res:* Physiology, ecology and taxonomy of soil mites; survey of dog heartworm, Dirofilaria immitis, in west New York; survey of toxoplasma antibodies in west New York; survey and epidemiol of hair follicle mites. *Mailing Add:* 2112 Skyland Dr Tallahassee FL 32303

SENGE, GEORGE H, SEQUENTIAL MACHINES. *Current Pos:* SR SCIENTIST ENGR, HUGHES AIRCRAFT CO, 77- *Personal Data:* b Braunschweig, Ger, Oct 10, 37; US citizen. *Educ:* Univ Calif, Berkeley, BA, 60; Univ Calif, Los Angeles, MA, 61, PhD(math), 65; Univ Wis-Madison, MS, 77. *Prof Exp:* Asst prof math, Univ Calif, San Diego, 65-68 & Univ Wis-Milwaukee, 68-74; asst prof math, Lawrence Univ, 75-76. *Mem:* Am Math Soc; Math Asn Am. *Res:* Digital signal processing and synthetic aperture radar systems; interferometric synthetic aperture radar; sequential machines. *Mailing Add:* 314 Gretna Green Way Los Angeles CA 90049-4008

SENGEL, RANDAL ALAN, PSYCHOPATHOLOGY, SCHIZOPHRENIA. *Current Pos:* Res assoc behav sci, Vet Admin Hosp, 77-80, RES HEALTH SCIENTIST, VET ADMIN, 81- *Personal Data:* b Liberal, Kans, Jan 8, 48; m 71; c 1. *Educ:* Univ Okla, BA, 70, MA, 73, PhD(human ecol), 76. *Concurrent Pos:* Consult, Task Force Ecopsychiat Data Base, Am Psychiat Asn, 76-78; Nat Res Serv fel, 80. *Mem:* AAAS; Sigma Xi. *Res:* Cognitive and neuropsychological deficits in schizophrenia. *Mailing Add:* 737 S Lahoma Norman OK 73069

SENGER, CLYDE MERLE, MAMMALOGY, CAVE BIOLOGY. *Current Pos:* from assoc prof to prof, 63-93, chairperson biol, 73-77, EMER PROF BIOL, WESTERN WASH UNIV, 93- *Personal Data:* b Portland, Ore, June 25, 29; m 51, Louise F Cooley; c Robert, David, Stuart, Stanley, Sharon & Penny. *Educ:* Reed Col, BA, 52; Purdue Univ, MS, 53; Utah State Univ, PhD, 58. *Prof Exp:* Co-op agt parasitol, Mont State Univ, 53-55 & Utah State Univ, 55-56; asst prof zool, Univ Mont, 57-63. *Mem:* AAAS; Am Soc Mammal; Am Inst Biol Sci. *Res:* Cave biology-mycetophilid flies of lava tubes; taxonomy of fleas. *Mailing Add:* 1103 Yew St Bellingham WA 98226-8870

SENGERS, JAN V, THERMOPHYSICAL PROPERTIES. *Current Pos:* assoc prof, Univ Md, Col Park, 68-74, affil prof chem eng, 91, PROF, INST PHYS SCI & TECHNOL 74-, PROF & CHAIR CHEM ENG, UNIV MN, COL PARK, 94- *Personal Data:* b Heiloo, Neth, May 27, 31; m 63, Johanna M Levelt; c Rachel T, Adriaan J, Maarten W & Phoebe J. *Educ:* Univ Amsterdam, Drs, 55, PhD(physics), 62. *Hon Degrees:* Dr, Tech Univ Delft, 92. *Honors & Awards:* Nat Bur Stand Awards, 66, 68, 69, 70 & 77; Touloukian Medal, Am Soc Mech Engrs, 91. *Prof Exp:* Res asst physics, Van der Waals Lab, Univ Amsterdam, 53-55, res assoc, 55-63; physicist, Nat Bur Stand, 63-67. *Concurrent Pos:* Physicist, Nat Bur Stand, 68-; Jr Cornelis Gelderman Vis Prof, Delft Technol Univ, Neth, 74-75; corresp, Royal Dutch Acad Sci. *Mem:* Fel AAAS; fel Am Phys Soc; fel Am Soc Mech Engrs; Am Inst Chem Engrs; Am Chem Soc. *Res:* Thermophysical properties of fluids; critical phenomena and fluctuation phenomena in gases and liquids. *Mailing Add:* 110 N Van Buren St Rockville MD 20850-1861. *Fax:* 301-314-9404; *E-Mail:* js45@umail.umd.edu

SENGERS, JOHANNA M H LEVELT, CRITICAL PHENOMENA, FLUID MIXTURES. *Current Pos:* sr fel, 83-95, EMER FEL, THERMOPHYSICS DIV, NAT INST STAND & TECHNOL, 95- *Personal Data:* b Amsterdam, Neth, Mar 4, 29; m 63, Jan V; c Rachel, Arjan, Maarten & Phoebe. *Educ:* Univ Amsterdam, Drs, 54, PhD(physics), 58. *Hon Degrees:* DSc, Delft Univ Technol, 92. *Honors & Awards:* Silver Medal, Dept Com, 72, Gold Medal, 78; Wise Award, 85; Alexander von Humboldt Res Award, 91. *Prof Exp:* Wetenschappelijk ambtenaar, van der Waals Lab, Univ Amsterdam, 54-58; res assoc inst theoret chem, Univ Wis, 58-59; wetenschappelijk ambtenaar, Van Der Waals Lab, Univ Amsterdam, 59-63; physicist, Heat Div, Inst Basic Standards, Nat Bur Standards, 63-78, physicist & supvr, Thermophysics Div, Nat Eng Lab, 78-87. *Concurrent Pos:* Lectr, Cath Univ Louvain, 71; res assoc inst theor physics, Univ Amsterdam, 74-75; Regent's Prof, Dept Chem, Univ Calif, Los Angeles, 82; chair, Working Group A, Int Asn Properties Steam, 86-90; chmn, Int Asn Properties Water & Steam, 91-92. *Mem:* Nat Acad Sci; Nat Acad End; fel Am Phys Soc; Europ Phys Soc; Am Soc Chem Engrs; corresp mem Neth Royal Acad Sci; Am Soc Mech Engrs. *Res:* Thermodynamic properties of fluids and fluid mixtures; critical phenomena in fluids; equation of state, theoretical and experimental; supercritical aqueous systems. *Mailing Add:* Phys & Chem Properties Div Nat Inst Stand & Technol Gaithersburg MD 20899. *Fax:* 301-869-4020

SENGUPTA, ABHIJIT, MATERIAL TESTING & FRACTURE MECHANICS, MICROSCOPY. *Current Pos:* PROCESS DEVELOP ENGR, GEN MOTORS OVONIC BATTERY CO, 95- *Personal Data:* b Silchar, India, Sept 27, 64. *Educ:* Jadarpur Univ, BS, 86; Indian Inst Technol, MS, 88; Wayne State Univ, MS, 91, PhD(metall eng), 93. *Prof Exp:* Res assoc & fel, Wayne State Univ, 94; qual inspector, Quigley Indust, 94; mat engr, Veltec Labs, 94-95. *Concurrent Pos:* Adj fac, Univ Detroit, 95-, Wayne State Univ, 95- *Mem:* Am Soc Mat; Am Soc Qual Control; Am Soc Metals; Am Soc Mining, Metall & Petrochem Engrs; Heat Treating Soc. *Res:* Various journal publications in the areas of fracture mechanics, high temperature fatigue, creep fracture, single crystal nickel based superalloys and electron microscopic work. *Mailing Add:* 32325 Concord 17C Madison Heights MI 48071. *E-Mail:* asen@koole.net

SEN GUPTA, BARUN KUMAR, MICROPALEONTOLOGY, MARINE GEOLOGY. *Current Pos:* PROF GEOL, LA STATE UNIV, 79- *Personal Data:* b Jamshedpur, India, July 31, 31; m 56, Mandira Gupta; c Sagaree & Upal. *Educ:* Calcutta Univ, BSc, 51, MSc, 54; Cornell Univ, MS, 61; Indian Inst Technol, Kharagpur, PhD(geol), 63. *Prof Exp:* From asst lectr to lectr geol, Indian Inst Technol, Kharagpur, 55-66; Nat Res Coun Can fel, Atlantic Oceanog Lab, Bedford Inst, 66-68, temporary res scientist, 68; asst prof geol, Univ Ga, 69-72, from assoc prof to prof, 72-79. *Concurrent Pos:* NSF res grants, 67-72, 75-78, 82-86, 88-90, NATO res grant, 87-91; vis prof, Univ Fed Rio Grande Do Sul, Porto Alegre, Brazil, Univ Bordeaux I, France; pres, Cushman Found Foraminiferal Res, 87-88; Fulbright scholar, Univ Utrech, Neth, 92; Cole Mem Res Award, Geol Soc Am 95; res grant, US Mineral Mgr Serv, 95-98. *Mem:* AAAS; fel Geol Soc Am; fel Cushman Found Foraminiferal Res; Paleont Soc; Soc Sedimentary Geol. *Res:* Stratigraphy, ecology, and paleoecology of Cenozoic benthic foraminifera. *Mailing Add:* Dept Geol & Geophys La State Univ Baton Rouge LA 70803-4101. *Fax:* 504-388-2302; *E-Mail:* glbarun@lsuvm.sncc.lsu.edu

SENGUPTA, BHASKAR, OPERATIONS RESEARCH. *Current Pos:* AT AT&T BELL LABS. *Personal Data:* b New Delhi, India, Feb 7, 44; m 70. *Educ:* Indian Inst Technol, BTech, 65; Columbia Univ, MS, 73, EngScD, 76. *Prof Exp:* Proj engr elec eng, Crompton Greaves Ltd, 65-69; syst engr comp sci, IBM World Trade Corp, 69-71, Serv Bur Co, 71-72; asst prof oper res, State Univ NY, Stony Brook, 76- *Concurrent Pos:* Consult, Turner Construct Co, 76- *Mem:* Inst Mgt Sci; Oper Res Soc Am. *Res:* Stochastic models in inventory, production and health care. *Mailing Add:* NEC USA Four Independence Way Princeton NJ 08540

SENGUPTA, DIPAK L(AL), ELECTRONICS. *Current Pos:* prof & chmn, 86-95, PROF ELEC ENG & PHYSICS, UNIV DETROIT, 95- *Personal Data:* b Batisha, Bangladesh, Mar 1, 31; m 62, Sujata Basu; c Sumit & Mita. *Educ:* Univ Calcutta, BSc, 50, MSc, 52; Univ Toronto, PhD(elec eng), 58. *Honors & Awards:* Fulbright Lectr, India, 92-93. *Prof Exp:* Res fel electronics, Gordon McKay Lab Appl Physics, Harvard Univ, 59; res assoc, Radiation Lab, 59-61, assoc res physicist, 61-63; asst prof elec eng, Univ Toronto, 63-64; asst dir electronics, Cent Electronics Eng Res Inst Pilani, India, 64-65; lectr elec eng, Univ Mich, Ann Arbor, 65-66, assoc res eng, 65-68, res scientist & adj prof elec eng & comput sci, 68-86. *Mem:* Fel Inst Elec & Electronics Engrs; AAAS; Sigma Xi; Int Union Radio Sci. *Res:* Electromagnetic theory; antennas; plasma physics; interaction of electromagnetic waves and plasmas; acoustic and electromagnetic waves; electromagnetic interference. *Mailing Add:* Dept Elec Eng & Physics Univ Detroit Mercy 4001 W McNichols Rd Detroit MI 48219. *Fax:* 313-993-1187

SENGUPTA, DIPENDRA C, ANALYSIS & FUNCTIONAL ANALYSIS, COMPUTER SCIENCES. *Current Pos:* Lectr, Elizabeth City State Univ, 84-85, vis prof, 85-86, asst prof, 86-90, ASSOC PROF MATH, ELIZABETH CITY STATE UNIV, 90- *Personal Data:* m 83, Jharna Dana; c Swarnali & Sohini. *Educ:* Univ Kalyani, BS, 76, MS, 79; State Univ NY, Stonybrook, MA, 81, PhD(math), 84. *Concurrent Pos:* Prin investr, NSF, 90-93. *Mem:* Am Math Soc; Math Asn Am; Coun Undergrad Res. *Res:* Cohomology of Kleinian groups; non-linear dynamics; fractal chaos. *Mailing Add:* Elizabeth City State Univ Elizabeth City NC 27909. *Fax:* 919-335-3487; *E-Mail:* dsengupta@ga.unc.edu

SENGUPTA, GAUTAM, MECHANICAL & AEROSPACE ENGINEERING. *Current Pos:* sr specialist, Boeing Co, 73-80, prin engr noise control, 73-85, lead engr, comput acoust, 86-90, PRIN ENGR, BOEING CO, 90- *Personal Data:* b Gaibandha, Bangladesh, Sept 1, 45; m 72; c 2. *Educ:* Univ Calcutta, BSc Hons, 63; Indian Inst Technol, Kharagpur, BTech Hons, 66; Univ Southampton, PhD(struct acoust), 70. *Honors & Awards:* Outstanding Tech Contrib, Am Inst Aeronaut & Astronaut, 78. *Prof Exp:* Spec engr acoust fatigue, Eng Sci Data Univ, London, 70-71; resident res assoc struct dynamics, Langley Res Ctr, NASA, 72-73. *Concurrent Pos:* Reviewer, J Sound & Vibration, Shock & Vibration Digest, Am Inst Aeronaut & Astronaut J, 70-; resident res assoc, Langley Res Ctr, NASA-Nat Acad Sci, 72-73; dir educ, Pac Northwest Sect, Am Inst Aeronaut & Astronaut, 78-80. *Mem:* Fel Am Inst Aeronaut & Astronaut; Acoust Soc Am. *Res:* Vibration and noise control, especially cabin noise, airframe noise, aeroacoustics, sonic fatigue, wave propagation, periodic structures, matrix methods, correlation techniques and intrinsic structural tuning; computational fluid and structural dynamics; physics. *Mailing Add:* 13514 SE 181st Pl Renton WA 98058

SENGUPTA, JHARNA DANA, ANALYSIS & FUNCTIONAL ANALYSIS, COMPUTER SCIENCES. *Current Pos:* ASST PROF MATH, ELIZABETH CITY STATE UNIV, 86- *Personal Data:* m 83, Dipendra; c Swarnali & Sohini. *Educ:* Univ Kalyani, BS, 76, MS, 79; State Univ NY, Stonybrook, MA, 81, PhD(math), 86- *Prof Exp:* Asst prof, Fordham Univ, 86-87. *Concurrent Pos:* Prin investr, NSF, 88-90 & 90- *Mem:* Am Math Soc; Math Asn Am. *Res:* Projective structures, monodromy map of the fuchsian groups of the second kind. *Mailing Add:* 1712 Aydlett Circle Elizabeth City NC 27909. *Fax:* 919-335-3487

SENGUPTA, SAILES KUMAR, OPERATIONS RESEARCH, SOFTWARE SYSTEMS. *Current Pos:* RES SCIENTIST, LIVERMORE LAB, 92- *Personal Data:* b Bankura, India, Jan 1, 35; US citizen; m 69; c 2. *Educ:* Univ Calcutta, BSc, 53, MSc, 56; Univ Calif, Berkeley, PhD(statist), 69. *Prof Exp:* Lectr math, WBengal Educ Serv, 57-62; teaching res asst statist, Univ Calif, Berkeley, 63-64 & 65-67; asst prof math, Univ Mo, Kansas City, 69-76; from assoc prof to prof math, SDak Sch Mines & Technol, 76-92. *Concurrent Pos:* Fac res partic, Argonne Nat Lab; vis fel, Inst Math & Its Applns, Univ Minn, 87; fac res partic, NASA, Langley, ASD; sr Univ Corp Atmospheric Res fel, Naval Oceanog Atmospheric Res Lab. *Mem:* Sigma Xi; Am Statist Asn; Inst Elec & Electronics Engrs. *Res:* Statistical pattern recognition; satellite data analysis; computing, image understanding; multivariate statistical analysis of geochemical data. *Mailing Add:* 5566 Felicia Ave Livermore CA 94550-8126

SENGUPTA, SUBRATA, FLUID MECHANICS, HEAT TRANSFER. *Current Pos:* DEAN, SCH ENG, UNIV MICH, DEARBORN, 90-, DIR, CTR ENG EDUC & PRACT, 91- *Personal Data:* b Calcutta, India, June 29, 48; US citizen; m, Mala Dasgupta; c Vikram & Vivek. *Educ:* Indian Inst Technol, Kharjpur, BTech, 69; Case Western Res Univ, MS, 72, PhD(fluid thermal sci), 74. *Prof Exp:* Grad prog dir & dir, Resource Recovery Lab, Univ Miami, Fla, 78-86, prof mech ocean eng, 81-90, chmn eng sci. *Concurrent Pos:* Chair mech eng, Miami Univ, 86-90; assoc dir, State Ctr Solid & Hazardous Wastes, Fla, 88-90. *Mem:* Fel Am Soc Mech Engrs; Am Inst Aeronaut & Astronaut; Soc Automotive Engrs; Am Geophys Union; Sigma Xi. *Res:* Experimental and computational phenomenon in fluid mechanics and heat transfer; phase change material slurries to enhance heat transfer is currently being investigated; chemically reacting flows in engines and catalysts. *Mailing Add:* Univ Mich 4901 Evergreen Rd Dearborn MI 48128-2406. *Fax:* 313-593-9967

SENGUPTA, SUMEDHA, COMPUTER SCIENCE, STATISTICS. *Current Pos:* CONSULT STATISTICIAN, 92-, PRES STAT-TECH, CONSULT FIRM STATIST, MPS, 87- *Personal Data:* b India, Feb 17, 43; US citizen; m 69, Sailes Kumar; c Dyuti & Chaitee K. *Educ:* Patna Univ, BS, 62, MS, 64; Indian Inst Technol, PhD(statist), 68. *Prof Exp:* Res fel & lectr, Dept Math & Statist, Indian Inst Technol, India, 65-69; lectr, Nat Col Bus, 76-77; res scientist statist res, Inst Atmospheric Sci, 77-80; sr res statistician, Res Inst Geochem, 80-81; statistician reliability & qual control, MPI-Control Data, 81-84; prin statistician, Defense Systs Div, Honeywell, 85-86, consult, 87-90. *Concurrent Pos:* Consult, Ace Elec Co, Kans, 71, Marion Lab, 76, Jackson County, Kans, 76, & to assoc adminr, Regional Hosp, SDak, 82-, MPI-Control Data, Honeywell, Nat Gould, Alexandria Exter, Lawrence Livermore Nat Lab, 92; vis assoc prof, Dept Math & Comput Sci, SDak Sch Mines & Technol, 89-90. *Mem:* Sigma Xi; Am Statist Asn; sr mem Am Soc Qual Control. *Res:* Bayesian inference in life testing and reliability; statistical methodology in metereology and atmospheric science; quality and process control; statistical methods in uranium research, measurement control in plutonium assay; computer graphics. *Mailing Add:* 5566 Felicia Ave Livermore CA 94550-8126. *Fax:* 510-606-5458; *E-Mail:* 73141.1153@compuserve.com

SENHAUSER, DONALD ALBERT, PATHOLOGY, IMMUNOPATHOLOGY. *Current Pos:* chmn dept, 75-92, PROF PATH, COL MED, OHIO STATE UNIV, 75- *Personal Data:* b Dover, Ohio, Jan 30, 27; m 61; c 2. *Educ:* Columbia Univ, AB, 48, MD, 51. *Prof Exp:* Intern, Roosevelt Hosp, New York, 51-52; asst resident & instr path, Columbia Presby Hosp, 55-56; asst resident, Cleveland Clin Found, Ohio, 56-58, sr resident, 58-59, clin assoc, 59-61, staff physician, 61-63; from assoc prof to prof path, Univ Mo, Columbia, 63-75, vchmn dept, 66-75, asst dean acad affairs, 69-71. *Concurrent Pos:* Fel path, Cleveland Clin Found, Ohio, 56-59; travelling fel immunol res, 60-61; consult, Study Group, WHO, 71- & long range planning comt, Nat Libr Med, 85-86; mem, bd gov, Col Am Path, 80-86; distinguished practitioner, Nat Acad Practise, 85- *Mem:* AAAS; Am Soc Clin Path; Col Am Path (pres, 91-93); Int Acad Path; Asn Am Pathologists. *Res:* Ultrastructural studies of the immunopathology of lymphocyte-target cell interaction; role of lipid molecules in cell membrane structural and antigenic integrity apheresis and immunosuppression; medical information science. *Mailing Add:* Dept Pathol Ohio State Univ Col Med 133 Hamilton Hall 1645 Neil Ave Columbus OH 43210-1238

SENICH, DONALD, SOIL MECHANICS. *Current Pos:* dir div, Energy Resources Res, NSF, 73-78, div dir, Integrated Basic Res, 78-79, dir div, Problem Focused Res, 79-81, div dir, Indust Sci & Technol Innovation, 81-91, DIV DIR, DESIGN MFG & INDUST MFG, NSF, 91- *Personal Data:* b Cleveland, Ohio, Sept 5, 29; m 52; c 4. *Educ:* Univ Notre Dame, BSME, 53; Iowa State Univ, MS, 61, PhD(soil mech), 66. *Prof Exp:* Resident engr, US Army, Frankfurt Am Main, WGer, 61-63; chief nuclear eng, Nuclear Power Field Off, Ft Belvoir, Va, 66-67; officer in chg, US Army Reactor, Ft Greely, Alaska, 67; chief construct engr, Mil Assistance Command, Vietnam, 68-69, staff scientist, Apollo Lunar Explor Off, NASA, 69-73. *Mem:* Sigma Xi. *Res:* Soil mechanics; physical and surface chemistry; development of fundamental knowledge to aid in the solution of major problems in the areas of discipline sciences. *Mailing Add:* NSF 6602 Jenny Dee Pl Springfield VA 22152

SENIOR, BORIS, PEDIATRICS, ENDOCRINOLOGY. *Current Pos:* RETIRED. *Personal Data:* b Priluki, Russia, Apr 24, 23; US citizen; m 54; c 3. *Educ:* Univ Witwatersrand, Mb, BCh, 46; MRCP, 53, FRCP, 70. *Prof Exp:* Res asst, Univ Col Hosp, London, 51-54; Coun Sci & Indust Res sr bursar, Univ Cape Town, 54-55; asst prof pediat, Sch Med, Boston Univ, 62-63; from asst prof to prof & chief pediat endocrinol, Med Ctr, Tufts Univ, 63-96. *Mem:* Endocrine Soc; Am Pediat Soc; Sigma Xi. *Res:* Disorders of carbohydrate metabolism; carbohydrate-lipid interrelationships. *Mailing Add:* 133 Hyde St Newton MA 02161

SENIOR, JOHN BRIAN, INORGANIC CHEMISTRY. *Current Pos:* asst prof, 66-70, ASSOC PROF CHEM, UNIV SASK, 70- *Personal Data:* b Cleveleys, Eng, Oct 11, 36. *Educ:* Univ London, BSc, 58; McMaster Univ, PhD(chem), 62. *Prof Exp:* Sci Indust Res-NATO fel chem, Birkbeck Col, London, 62-63; fel, Univ Western Ont, 63-64; asst prof chem, St Paul's Col, Man, 64-66. *Mem:* The Chem Soc; Chem Inst Can. *Res:* Chemistry of acidic nonaqueous solvent systems; halogen cations and oxycations. *Mailing Add:* Dept Chem & Chem Eng Univ Sask Saskatoon SK S7N 0W0 Can

SENIOR, JOHN ROBERT, INTERNAL MEDICINE, GASTROENTEROLOGY. *Current Pos:* ADJ PROF MED, UNIV PA, 84-; MED REVIEWING OFF GASTROINTESTINAL, FOOD & DRUG ADMIN, HFD-180. *Personal Data:* b Philadelphia, Pa, July 17, 27; m 52, Sara Spedden; c John O, Laura B & Lisa A. *Educ:* Pa State Univ, BS, 50; Univ Pa, MD, 54. *Prof Exp:* Instr med, Univ Pa, 57-59; res fel, Harvard Med Sch, 59-62; asst prof med & assoc biochem, Univ Pa, 62-68, assoc prof med, 68-78, assoc prof community med, 74-76, clin prof med, 78-80; vpres clin affairs, Sterling-Winthrop Res Inst, Rensselaer, NY, 81-; clin prof med, Albany Med Ctr, 81-84. *Concurrent Pos:* Nat Inst Arthritis & Metab Dis res & training grants gastroenterol, Philadelphia Gen Hosp, 62-71; consult, US Naval Reg Med Ctr, Philadelphia, 66-, Nat Bd Med Examr & Am Bd Internal Med, 70-; dir clin invest, Presby-Univ Pa Med Ctr, 71-73; Carnegie Corp & Commonwealth Fund grant comput based exam, Philadelphia, 71-73; dir clin res Clin Res Ctr, Grad Hosp, Univ Pa, 73-74, dir, Emergency Serv & Spec Treat Unit Alcohol-Related Dis & dir, Off Eval, 74-79; dir regulatory proj, E R Squibb & Sons, NJ, 79-81; rear admiral, Med Corps, US Naval Res; independent med consult int pharmaceut res & develop, 84-95; consult, G H Besselaar Assoc, Princeton, NJ, 86-93. *Mem:* Am Soc Clin Invest; Am Soc Clin Pharmacol & Therapeut; Am Asn Study Liver Dis (pres); Am Gastroenterol Asn; fel Am Col Physicians; Am Fedn Clin Res. *Res:* Lipid metabolism; biochemistry; cell physiology; computer science; medical information processing; hepatic and central nervous effects of ethanol; viral and drug-induced hepatitis; evaluation of clinical competence; design analysis of clinical trials; hepatology-effects of ursodiaol in chronic cholestatic liver disease. *Mailing Add:* 54 Merbrook Lane Merion Station PA 19066-1618. *E-Mail:* seniorj@cder.fda.gov

SENIOR, THOMAS BRYAN ALEXANDER, ELECTROMAGNETICS. *Current Pos:* res assoc, Univ Mich, Ann Arbor, 57-58, from assoc res mathematician to res mathematician, 58-61, assoc dir, Radiation Lab, 61-75, dir, Radiation Lab, 75-87, assoc chmn, Elec Eng & Comput Sci Dept, 84-90, actg chmn, 87-88, PROF ELEC ENG & COMPUT SCI, UNIV MICH, ANN ARBOR, 69-, ARTHUR F THURNAU PROF, 90-, ASSOC CHMN ACAD AFFAIRS, 91- *Personal Data:* b Menston, Eng, June 26, 28; m 57, Heather Golby; c Margaret, David, Hazel & Peter. *Educ:* Univ Manchester, BSc, 49, MSc, 50; Cambridge Univ, PhD(appl math), 54. *Honors & Awards:* Van der Pol Gold Medal, Int Union Radio Sci, 93. *Prof Exp:* From sci off to sr sci off, Radar Res & Develop Estab, Ministry of Supply, Eng, 52-57. *Concurrent Pos:* Ed, Radio Sci, 73-79; chmn US Nat Comt, Int Union Radio Sci, 82-84, vchmn comm B, 85-87, chmn, 88-90, vpres, 93-96, pres, 96- *Mem:* Fel Inst Elec & Electronics Engrs; Sigma Xi. *Res:* Theoretical problems in scattering and diffraction of electromagnetic and acoustical waves; radio wave propagation; optics. *Mailing Add:* Radiation Lab Elec Eng & Comput Sci Dept Univ Mich Ann Arbor MI 48109-2122

SENITZER, DAVID, IMMUNOLOGY, MICROBIOLOGY. *Current Pos:* DIR TRANSPLANT IMMUNOL, MONTEFIORE MED CTR, 85-; ASSOC PROF SURG, ALBERT EINSTEIN COL MED. *Personal Data:* b New York, NY, Oct 9, 44; m 66; c 3. *Educ:* City Col New York, BS, 66; La State Univ, PhD(microbiol), 69; Am Bd Med Lab Immunol, dipl. *Prof Exp:* Res assoc immunol, Col Physicians & Surgeons, Columbia Univ, 69-72; asst prof microbiol, Med Col Ohio, 72-77, assoc prof microbiol & path, 78-85. *Mem:* AAAS; Am Soc Microbiol; Am Asn Immunologists; Am Soc Clin Pathologists; Am Soc Histocompatibility & Immunogenetics. *Res:* Transplantation immunology; autoimmune disease mechanisms; regulation of the immune response. *Mailing Add:* Histo Compatibility Lab City Hope Nat Med Ctr 1500 E Duarte Rd Duarte CA 91010

SENITZKY, BENJAMIN, PHYSICS. *Current Pos:* ADJ PROF, UNIV ARIZ, 89- *Personal Data:* b Vilno, Poland, Nov 15, 26; nat US; m 50, W Jeanne Smith; c Susan (Chiarella), Hannah (Weiss) & Ruth (Ellerd). *Educ:* Columbia Univ, BS, 48, PhD, 56. *Prof Exp:* Mem tech staff, Bell Tel Labs, Inc, 56-59; physicist, Tech Res Group, Inc, 59-66; assoc prof, Polytech Univ, 66-75, asst head dept, 74-78, prof electrophys, 75-89. *Mem:* Inst Elec & Electronics Engrs. *Res:* Atomic beam resonance techniques for study of hyperfine structure in atomic spectra; high field breakdown in semiconductors; millimeter wave amplification using resonance saturation effects; interaction of radiation and semiconductors. *Mailing Add:* 618 W Rushwood Dr Tucson AZ 85704. *E-Mail:* senitzky@primenet.com

SENITZKY, ISRAEL RALPH, QUANTUM OPTICS. *Current Pos:* RES PROF PHYSICS, CTR LASER STUDIES, UNIV SOUTHERN CALIF, 85- *Personal Data:* b Vilna, Poland, Feb 28, 20; m 44, Lillian Levitt; c Judith (Reichman) & Naomi (Galili). *Educ:* City Col, BS, 41; NY Univ, MS, 44; Columbia Univ, PhD(physics), 50. *Prof Exp:* Physicist, Inst Explor Res, US Army Electronics Command, 42-72; prof physics, Technion-Israel Inst Technol, 72-83. *Concurrent Pos:* Vis prof physics, Univ Southern Calif, 83-84. *Mem:* Fel Am Phys Soc. *Res:* Quantum mechanics; quantum electronics; lasers; quantum optics; relationship between quantum theory and classical theory; resonance fluoresence; microwaves. *Mailing Add:* Ctr Laser Studies Univ Southern Calif Univ Park Los Angeles CA 90089-1112

SENKAN, SELIM M, COMBUSTION, REACTION ENGINEERING. *Current Pos:* PROF CHEM ENG, UNIV CALIF, LOS ANGELES, 89- *Educ:* Middle E Tech Univ, BS, 72; Mass Inst Technol, MS, 73, PhD(chem eng), 77. *Honors & Awards:* L K Cecil Award, Am Inst Chem Engrs, 91. *Prof Exp:* Dir, Pract Sch, Mass Inst Technol, 78-82; assoc prof, Ill Inst Technol, 82-87, prof chem eng, 87-89. *Mem:* Am Inst Chem Engrs; Am Chem Soc. *Res:* Chemical kinetics and reaction engineering; experimental and computational chemical kinetics; combustion and incineration; air pollution and pollution prevention; real time detection of chemicals in the gas phase. *Mailing Add:* Dept Chem Eng Univ Calif 405 Hilgard Ave Los Angeles CA 90095-1592. *Fax:* 310-206-4107; *E-Mail:* senkan@seas.ucla.edu

SENKLER, GEORGE HENRY, JR, PHYSICAL ORGANIC CHEMISTRY. *Current Pos:* Staff res, E I duPont de Nemours & Co, 74-79, res supvr, 79-81, prod mgr, 81-85, tech mgr, 85-89, tech dir, 89-92, bus dir, 92-96, TECH OPER DIR, E I DUPONT DE NEMOURS, 96- *Personal Data:* b Postville, Iowa, Oct 25, 45; m 72, Carol A Bahn; c Carol & Daniel. *Educ:* Hamline Univ, BS, 67; Princeton Univ, MA, 72, PhD(chem), 75. *Res:* Studies on the stereochemistry of organophosphorus, arsenic and sulfur compounds; development of industrially important processes; inorganic and organic pigment research; engineering plastics; ethylene copolymers. *Mailing Add:* DuPont Printing & Publishing E I du Pont de Nemours & Co Wilmington DE 19898. *E-Mail:* senkler@aol.com

SENKOWSKI, BERNARD ZIGMUND, PHARMACEUTICAL CHEMISTRY, TECHNICAL MANAGEMENT. *Current Pos:* PRIN, BZS CONSULT SERV, 88- *Personal Data:* b Dearborn, Mich, Feb 2, 27; m 52, Anna Eliseo; c Bernard Jr & Andrea. *Educ:* Rutgers Univ, AB, 51, MS, 60,

PhD(chem), 65. *Honors & Awards:* Merit Award, Asn Pharmaceut Asn. *Prof Exp:* Chemist, Hoffmann-La Roche Inc, 51-62, head anal res, 62-65, asst dir qual control, 65-70, dir qual control, 70, asst vpres, 71-77, dir pharmaceut opers, 72-77; vpres mfr & eng, Alcon Labs, 77-88. *Concurrent Pos:* Lectr, Rutgers Univ, 65-70; mem rev comt, US Pharmacopoeia, 70-75; mem, Comt Vitamins, Nat Formulary. *Mem:* Fel AAAS; Sigma Xi; Am Chem Soc; fel Am Inst Chemists; fel Am Asn Pharmaceut Scientists. *Res:* Corporate manufacturing, domestic and international; facilities planning; GMP, OSHA regulatory compliance; analytical research; quality control; pharmaceutical operations. *Mailing Add:* 29462 Clipper Way Laguna Niguel CA 92677-4621

SENKUS, MURRAY, CHEMISTRY. *Current Pos:* dir chem res, R J Reynolds Tobacco Co, 51-60, asst dir res, 60-64, dir res, 64-76, dir sci affairs, 76-79 CONSULT TOBACCO INST, R J REYNOLDS TOBACCO CO, 79- *Personal Data:* b Redberry, Sask, Aug 31, 14; nat US; m 38; c 4. *Educ:* Univ Sask, BSc, 34, MSc, 36; Univ Chicago, PhD(phys org chem), 38. *Prof Exp:* Instr chem, N Park Col, 37-38; chemist, Com Solvents Corp, 38-50; dir res & develop, Daubert Chem Corp, 50-51. *Mem:* AAAS; NY Acad Sci; Am Chem Soc; Sigma Xi. *Res:* Tobacco and synthetic organic chemistry; insecticides; recovery of fermentation products; chemotherapeutic agents; chemistry of flavors. *Mailing Add:* 2516 Country Club Rd Winston-Salem NC 27104-4106

SENN, TAZE LEONARD, HORTICULTURE, SEAWEED. *Current Pos:* prof, 58-81, EMER PROF HORT & HEAD DEPT, CLEMSON UNIV, 81- *Personal Data:* b Newberry, SC, Oct 16, 17; m 39; c 3. *Educ:* Clemson Univ, BS, 39; Univ Md, MS, 50, PhD(hort), 58. *Honors & Awards:* Gold Seal-Silver Seal, Nat Coun of State Garden Clubs. *Prof Exp:* Asst horticulturist, Clemson Col, 39-40, asst botanist, 40-41, assoc prof hort, 46-56; asst plant pathologist, Univ Tenn, 41-43 & 46; agriculturist, Eastern Lab, USDA, 56-58. *Concurrent Pos:* Vpres, res & develop, Southeastern Resources Corp, 90. *Mem:* Fel AAAS; fel Am Soc Hort Sci; Sigma Xi; Am Soc Testing & Mat. *Res:* Active compounds of marine plants; physiological aspects of plant propagation; tobacco chemistry; horticultural physiology; post-harvest physiology of horticultural crops; horticultural therapy; humus chemistry. *Mailing Add:* 201 Strawberry Lane Clemson SC 29631. *Fax:* 864-656-4960

SENNE, JOSEPH HAROLD, JR, CIVIL ENGINEERING. *Current Pos:* PROF CIVIL ENG, UNIV MO, ROLLA, 63-, CHMN DEPT, 65- *Personal Data:* b St Louis, Mo, Nov 9, 19; m 46; c 1. *Educ:* Wash Univ, BS, 48; Univ Mo, MS, 51; Iowa State Univ, PhD, 61. *Prof Exp:* Asst construct engr, Laclede Christy Clay Prod Co, Mo, 41-42; from instr to asst prof civil eng, Mo Sch Mines, 48-54; asst prof, Iowa State Univ, 54-63. *Mem:* Am Soc Eng Educ; Am Soc Civil Engrs; Nat Soc Prof Engrs; Sigma Xi. *Res:* Welded wire fabric in reinforced concrete beams and pipe; structural design; orbital mechanics; satellite tracking. *Mailing Add:* Dept Civil Eng Univ Mo 316 Butler-Carlton Bldg Rolla MO 65401

SENNELLO, LAWRENCE THOMAS, PHARMACOKINETICS, DRUG ANALYSIS. *Current Pos:* group leader, Analytical Chem Res, 69-70, SECT MGR, PHARMACOKINETICS & BIOPHARMACEUT, ABBOTT LABS, ABBOTT PARK, 71- *Personal Data:* b New York City, NY, Feb 4, 37; m 62, Barbara Little; c Lawrence Jr, Alison R, Robert E & Kathleen A. *Educ:* Lake Forest Sch Mgt, Ill, MBA, 80; Univ Ill, Urbana, BS, 59, PhD(chem), 68. *Prof Exp:* Teaching asst chem, Univ Ill, Urbana, 66-67. *Mem:* Am Chem Soc; Sigma Xi; NY Acad Sci; Am Col Clin Pharmacol. *Res:* Analytical chemistry methodology. *Mailing Add:* Drug Anal Dept Abbott Labs Abbott Park IL 60064. *Fax:* 847-938-0299; *E-Mail:* lawrence.t.sennell@abbott.com

SENOFF, CAESAR V, INORGANIC CHEMISTRY. *Current Pos:* RETIRED. *Personal Data:* b Toronto, Ont, Apr 30, 39; m 68; c 1. *Educ:* Univ Toronto, BSc, 61, MA, 63, PhD(chem), 65. *Prof Exp:* Fel chem, Clarkson Col Technol, 65-67 & Univ Tex, Austin, 67-68; asst prof chem, Univ Guelph, 68-73, assoc prof, 73-96. *Mem:* Am Chem Soc. *Res:* Coordination chemistry of transition elements; organometallic chemistry. *Mailing Add:* Dept Chem Univ Guelph Guelph ON N1G 2W1 Can. *E-Mail:* csenoff@uoguelph.ca

SENOGLES, SUSAN ELIZABETH, SIGNAL TRANSDUCTION. *Current Pos:* asst prof, 89-95, ASSOC PROF, UNIV TENN, 95- *Personal Data:* b Latrobe, Pa. *Educ:* Univ Minn, BS, 77, PhD(biochem), 84. *Prof Exp:* Res assoc, Duke Univ, 84-89. *Mem:* Am Soc Biochem & Molecular Biol; Soc Neurosci. *Res:* Transmembrane signal transduction; G protein specificity of effector coupling. *Mailing Add:* 858 Madison Ave G01 Memphis TN 38163-0001. *Fax:* 901-448-7360

SENOZAN, NAIL MEHMET, PHYSICAL CHEMISTRY. *Current Pos:* PROF CHEM, CALIF STATE UNIV, LONG BEACH, 80-, CHAIR, DEPT CHEM & BIOCHEM, 96- *Personal Data:* b Istanbul, Turkey, Sept 13, 36; m 82. *Educ:* Brown Univ, ScB, 60; Univ Calif, Berkeley, PhD(chem), 65. *Concurrent Pos:* Fulbright prof, Izmir, Turkey. *Mem:* AAAS. *Res:* Biophysical chemistry; hemoglobin; hemocyanin. *Mailing Add:* Dept Chem Calif State Univ 3903 Csulb Long Beach CA 90840-0001

SENSABAUGH, GEORGE FRANK, FORENSIC GENETICS, HUMAN GENETICS. *Current Pos:* from asst prof to assoc prof, 72-86, PROF FORENSIC SCI, UNIV CALIF, BERKELEY, 86- *Personal Data:* b Palo Alto, Calif, June 8, 41; m 63, Linda Sallander; c Jeffrey & Laura. *Educ:* Princeton Univ, BA, 63; Univ Calif, Berkeley, Dr, 69. *Honors & Awards:* Paul L Kirk Award, Am Acad Forensic Sci, 87. *Prof Exp:* Fel, Univ Calif, San Diego, 69-71, Nat Inst Med Res, London, 71-72. *Concurrent Pos:* Vis prof forensic sci, Univ Strathclyde, Glasgow, Scotland, 84-89; mem, DNA Comn, Inst Soc Forensic Haemogenetics, 90-91 & Comn DNA Tech Forensic Sci, Nat Res Coun, 91-92 & 94-96. *Mem:* Fel Am Soc Forensic Sci; Am Chem Soc; Am Soc Human Genetics; NY Acad Scis; Int Soc Forensic Haemogenetics. *Res:* Human biochemical genetics and applications thereof in forensic science and public health; forensic science. *Mailing Add:* Sch Pub Health Univ Calif Berkeley CA 94720

SENSEMAN, DAVID MICHAEL, NEUROPHYSIOLOGY, ANIMAL BEHAVIOR. *Current Pos:* asst mem, Monell Chem Senses Ctr, 77-81, RES ASST PROF PHYSIOL, SCH DENT MED, UNIV PA, 78- *Personal Data:* b Dayton, Ohio, Dec 6, 48; m 81. *Educ:* Kent State Univ, BS, 71; Princeton Univ, PhD(biol), 77. *Honors & Awards:* Merck Award, 71. *Concurrent Pos:* NIH fel, 76-78; res grant, Nat Inst Dent Res, 78-81. *Mem:* AAAS; Biophys Soc. *Res:* Biophysics and neuropharmacology of exocrine and endocrine gland function. *Mailing Add:* Dept Life Sci Univ Tex San Antonio 6900 N Loop 1604 W San Antonio TX 78249-1130

SENSEMAN, SCOTT ALLEN, MANAGEMENT OF UNIX-BASED COMPUTER NETWORK, CHROMATOGRAPHY. *Current Pos:* grad asst, 86-90, RES ASST, UNIV ARK, 90- *Personal Data:* b Tipp City, Ohio, Mar 22, 64. *Educ:* Wilmington Col, BS, 86; Univ Ark, MS, 90, PhD(agron), 94. *Prof Exp:* Field technician, Monsanto Agr Div, 86. *Mem:* Sigma Xi; Am Chem Soc; Am Soc Agron; Weed Sci Soc Am. *Res:* Water quality and analytical methodology related to pesticide monitoring of surface and ground water; pesticide stability in water samples as compared to solid phase extraction media. *Mailing Add:* Soil & Crop Sci Dept Tex A&M College Station TX 77843-2474. *Fax:* 501-575-3975; *E-Mail:* senseman@terra.uark.edu

SENSENY, PAUL EDWARD, ENGINEERING MECHANICS, GEOPHYSICS. *Current Pos:* CIVIL ENGR, DEFENSE SPEC WEAPONS AGENCY, 89- *Personal Data:* b Chambersburg, Pa, June 14, 50; m 72, Thersa M Hughes; c Jennifer. *Educ:* Univ Pa, BSME, 72; Brown Univ, ScM, 74, PhD(solid mech), 77. *Honors & Awards:* Stand Develop Award, Am Soc Testing & Mat, 97. *Prof Exp:* Res asst, Brown Univ, 72-76; res engr, SRI Int, 76-79; mgr, Mat Lab, Re/Spec Inc, 79-87, sr staff scientist, 87-89. *Mem:* Fel Am Soc Mech Eng; Am Soc Civil Eng; Am Geophys Union; Soc Exp Stress Anal; Am Acad Mech; Soc Eng Sci; Am Soc Testing & Mat. *Res:* Development of constitutive equations for geologic materials that model the influence of pressure, temperature, loading rate, pore fluids and thermomechanical history on deformation and strength; deformation and damage of structures subjected to dynamic loads. *Mailing Add:* Defense Spec Weapons Agency Attn PMT 6801 Telegraph Rd Alexandria VA 22310-3398. *E-Mail:* senseny@hq.dswa.mil

SENSIPER, S(AMUEL), MICROWAVE ENGINEERING, ANTENNA ENGINEERING. *Current Pos:* CONSULT ANTENNAS, ELECTROMAGNETICS & MICROWAVES, 70- *Personal Data:* b Elmira, NY, Apr 26, 19; m 50, Elaine M Zwick; c Martin, Sylvia & David. *Educ:* Mass Inst Technol, SB, 39, ScD, 51; Stanford Univ, EE, 41. *Prof Exp:* Asst, Stanford Univ, 39-41; from asst proj engr to sr proj engr & res sect head, Microwave Equip, Sperry Gyroscope Co, NY, 41-48, consult, 48-51; mem staff, Res Lab Electronics, Mass Inst Technol, 49-51; res engr & head, antenna sect, Microwave Lab, Hughes Aircraft Co, 51-53, head circuits & anal sect, Electron Tube Lab, 53-58, sr staff engr, Res Lab, 58-60; dir, Command & Control Labs, Space Electronics Corp, 60-63, assoc sr div mgr electronics opers, 63-64, dir eng, Electronic Systs, 64, mgr, Res & Ed Div, Space-Gen Corp, 64-67; mgr antenna syst lab, TRW Systs Group, 67-70. *Concurrent Pos:* indust electronics fel, Mass Inst Technol, 47-49; Instr, Univ Southern Calif, 55-57 & 79-81. *Mem:* AAAS; fel Inst Elec & Electronics Engrs; Sigma Xi; Sci Res Soc Am; Nat Soc Prof Engrs. *Res:* Systems theory and analysis, communications systems and components; electromagnetic theory; microwave electron tubes and devices; antennas and transmission components; microwave test equipment. *Mailing Add:* PO Box 3102 Culver City CA 90231-3102. *E-Mail:* sensiper1@aol.com or 76337.2531@compuserve.com

SENTERFIT, LAURENCE BENFRED, MICROBIOLOGY, IMMUNOLOGY. *Current Pos:* assoc prof microbiol, 70-84, PROF MICROBIOL & PATH, MED COL, CORNELL UNIV, 84-; DIR, LAB MICROBIOL, NEW YORK HOSP, 70- *Personal Data:* b Sarasota, Fla, July 30, 29; m 57; c 3. *Educ:* Univ Fla, BS, 49, MS, 50; Johns Hopkins Univ, ScD(pathobiol), 55; Am Bd Med Microbiol, dipl, 66. *Prof Exp:* Instr ophthal microbiol, Sch Med, Johns Hopkins Univ, 54-58; chief microbiologist & dir, Lab Exp Path, Charlotte Mem Hosp, NC, 58-64; res scientist, Chas Pfizer & Co, Inc, 64-66; assoc prof path & asst prof microbiol, Sch Med, St Louis Univ, 66-70. *Concurrent Pos:* Attend microbiologist, Hosp Spec Surg. *Mem:* Am Soc Microbiol; Am Asn Immunologists; Soc Exp Biol & Med; Am Venereal Dis Soc; Asn Clin Scientist; Int Org Mycoplasmology. *Res:* Immunology of parasitic diseases; vaccines for respiratory agents, particularly parainfluenza, respiratory syncytial virus and mycoplasma pneumonia; immunopathology and hypersensitivity; parasitology. *Mailing Add:* Dept Microbiol Cornell Univ Med Col 1300 York Ave New York NY 10021-4896. *Fax:* 201-825-8466

SENTI, FREDERIC R(AYMOND), FOOD SAFETY ASSESSMENT. *Current Pos:* RETIRED. *Personal Data:* b Cawker City, Kans, Apr 29, 13; m 39; c 3. *Educ:* Kans State Univ, BS, 35, MS, 36; Johns Hopkins Univ, PhD(chem), 39. *Hon Degrees:* DSc, Kans State Univ, 72. *Prof Exp:* Asst chemist, Eastern Regional Res Lab, Bur Agr & Indust Chem, USDA, 41-42, assoc chemist, 42-45, chemist, 45-47, prin chemist, 47-48, chief, Anal Phys

Chem & Physics Sect, Northern Utilization Res & Develop Div, Agr Res Serv, 49-54, Cereal Crops Sect, 54-59, dir, North Region Res Lab, 59-65, Dept Adminr Nutrit, Consumer & Indust Res, Agr Res Serv, 64-72, asst adminr, Nat Prog Staff, 72-74; res assoc, Feds Am Soc Exp Biol, 74-77, assoc dir, 77-84, sr sci consult, Life Sci Res Off, 84-86. *Concurrent Pos:* Lectr phys chem, Grad Sch, Temple Univ, 46-48; mem, Bd Trustees, Am Type Cult Collection, 62-67, chmn, 68-69; chief staff officer, Comt Processed Foods for Develop Countries & Domestic Food Distrib Prog, USDA, 64-74, vchmn, Task Group on Gen Recognized As Safe New Plant Varieties, Food & Drug Admin, 72-74; consult, Agency Int Develop, Govt India, 66-68; mem, Panel World Food Supply, Pres Sci Adv Comt, 66-67; mem, Liaison Panel, Food Protection comt, Nat Res Coun, 71-74. *Mem:* Am Chem Soc; Inst Food Technologists; fel AAAS; Am Crystallog Asn; Am Asn Cereal Chemists. *Res:* Structure and solution properties of starches and microbial polysaccharides; mycotoxins; cereal and oilseed chemistry and technology; development of processed foods for food assistance programs; safety evaluation of food additives. *Mailing Add:* 3134 Piedmont St Arlington VA 22207

SENTILLES, F DENNIS, JR, MATHEMATICS. *Current Pos:* asst prof, 67-70, ASSOC PROF MATH, UNIV MO-COLUMBIA, 70- *Personal Data:* b Donaldsonville, La, Aug 7, 41; m 63; c 2. *Educ:* Francis T Nicholls State Col, BS, 63; La State Univ, MS, 65, PhD(math), 67. *Prof Exp:* Instr math, La State Univ, 66-67. *Mem:* Am Math Soc. *Res:* Abstract functional analysis; application of functional analytic techniques to specific problems in function and measure spaces. *Mailing Add:* Dept Math Univ Mo 202 Columbia MO 65211

SENTMAN, DAVIS DANIEL, MIDDLE ATMOSPHERIC, MAGNETOSPHERIC & SOLAR TERRESTRIAL PHYSICS. *Current Pos:* PROF PHYSICS, UNIV ALASKA, 91- *Personal Data:* b Iowa City, Iowa, Jan 19, 45. *Educ:* Univ Iowa, BA, 71, MS, 73, PhD(physics), 76. *Prof Exp:* Res assoc, Univ Iowa, 76-77; res geophysicist, Inst Geophys & Planetary Physics, Univ Calif, Los Angeles, 78-90; sr res physicist, TRW, Redondo Beach, Calif, 90-91. *Mem:* Am Geophys Union. *Res:* Physics of planetary magnetospheres; solar terrestrial interactions; terrestrial electromagnetic resonances; middle atmosphere electrodynamics. *Mailing Add:* Dept Physics Univ Alaska Fairbanks CA 99775-0001

SENTMAN, LEE H(ANLEY), III, AERONAUTICAL & ASTRONAUTICAL ENGINEERING. *Current Pos:* asst prof, 65-69, assoc prof, 69-79, PROF AERONAUT & ASTRONAUT ENG, UNIV ILL, URBANA, 79- *Personal Data:* b Chicago, Ill, Jan 27, 37. *Educ:* Univ Ill, BS, 58; Stanford Univ, PhD(aeronaut, astronaut), 65. *Prof Exp:* Sr dynamics engr, Lockheed Missiles & Space Co, Calif, 59-65. *Concurrent Pos:* Vis prof aerospace eng, Univ Ariz, 71-72; consult, various aerospace companies. *Mem:* Am Inst Aeronaut & Astronaut; Am Phys Soc; Optical Soc Am. *Res:* Chemical lasers, unstable resonators; rotational nonequilibrium effects, vibrational relaxation of excited molecules, fluid dynamics; kinetic theory and statistical mechanics; supersonic combustion. *Mailing Add:* Dept Aeronaut & Astronaut Eng Univ Ill 306 Talbot Lab 104 S Wright Urbana IL 61801

SENTURIA, JEROME B(ASIL), COMPARATIVE PHYSIOLOGY, ENVIRONMENTAL PHYSIOLOGY. *Current Pos:* Asst prof biol, Cleveland State Univ, 66-71, asst dean, Col Arts & Sci, 77-81 & 83-85, assoc dean, 89-92, ASSOC PROF, BIOL, CLEVELAND STATE UNIV, 71- *Personal Data:* b San Antonio, Tex, Dec 2, 38; M89, Diana Jordan; c Sam J & Harris. *Educ:* Univ Calif, Los Angeles, BA, 60; Rice Univ, MA, 63; Univ Tex, PhD(zool), 67. *Concurrent Pos:* fel, Heart Lab, Nat Heart Inst, Malmo, Sweden, 67-68. *Mem:* Soc Crybiol; Am Inst Biol Sci; Am Soc Zool; Am Physiol Soc; Am Heart Asn; Int Hibernation Soc. *Res:* Cardiovascular physiology in hibernating mammals; seasonal variation in the physiology of hibernating mammals. *Mailing Add:* Dept Biol Cleveland State Univ 1983 E 24th St Cleveland OH 44115-2403. *E-Mail:* senturia@bio4.csuohio.edu

SENTURIA, STEPHEN DAVID, MICROSYSTEMS TECHNOLOGY. *Current Pos:* Mem res staff, from asst prof to assoc prof, 67-81, PROF ELEC ENG, MICROSYST TECHNOL LAB, MASS INST TECHNOL, 81- *Personal Data:* b Washington, DC, May 25, 40; m 61, 92, Margaret Ellickson; c Todd A, Rachel A (Kros) & Samuel E (Dickerman). *Educ:* Harvard Univ, BA, 61; Mass Inst Technol, PhD(physics), 66. *Honors & Awards:* Doolittle Prize, Am Chem Soc, 86. *Mem:* Fel Inst Elec & Electronics Engrs. *Res:* Microsensors and microactuators; computer aided design for microelectromechanical systems. *Mailing Add:* 98 Crowninshield Rd Brookline MA 02146

SENTZ, JAMES CURTIS, PLANT BREEDING & QUANTATIVE GENETICS, TECHNOLOGY TRANSFER & DEVELOPMENT. *Current Pos:* assoc prof & prog officer, 91-95, EMER PROF AGRON & PLANT GENETICS, INT AGR PROGS, UNIV MINN, 95- *Personal Data:* b Littlestown, Pa, Sept 24, 27; div; c 3. *Educ:* Pa State Univ, BS, 49; NC State Univ, MS, 51, PhD(agron), 53. *Prof Exp:* Asst statistician, NC State Univ, 52-54; res agronomist, Agr Res Serv, USDA, 54-57; from asst prof to assoc prof agron & plant genetics, Univ Minn, prof & prog officer, 71-75 & 76-88; agr res liaison, Int Inst Trop Agr, USAID, Ibadan, Nigeria, 88-91. *Concurrent Pos:* Cornell Univ Grad Educ Prog vis prof, Col Agr, Univ Philippines, 66-68; res adv, Tech Asst Bur, USAID, Washington, DC, 75-76; consult, 91- *Mem:* Am Soc Agron; Crop Sci Soc Am; Asn Int Agr Res & Develop; Biomet Soc; Coun Agr Sci & Technol. *Res:* Population and quantitative genetics; maize breeding; experimental research designs; grain legumes; plant breeding methods; technology transfer; agriculture development in third world; project design, management and evaluation. *Mailing Add:* Int Agr Prog Univ Minn 190 Coffey Hall St Paul MN 55108. *Fax:* 612-625-3111; *E-Mail:* james.c.sentz_1@tc.umn.edu

SENUM, GUNNAR IVAR, PHYSICAL CHEMISTRY. *Current Pos:* Asst chemist, 76-78, assoc chemist, 78-81, CHEMIST, BROOKHAVEN NAT LAB, 81 - *Personal Data:* b Kristiansand, Norway, Nov 10, 48; US citizen. *Educ:* Brooklyn Col, BS, 70; State Univ NY, PhD(chem), 75. *Mem:* Am Chem Soc; Am Phys Soc; AAAS. *Res:* Atmospheric chemistry, analytical instrumentation for tracing and tagging using perfluorocarbons; trace analyses of ambient atmospheric constituents; development of new applications of perfluorocarbon tracers, including petroleum reservoir characterizations. *Mailing Add:* Environ Chem Div Bldg 426 Brookhaven Nat Lab Upton NY 11973. *E-Mail:* gsenum@bnl.gov

SENUS, WALTER JOSEPH, SATELLITE GEODESY, ELECTRONIC SURVEYING. *Current Pos:* TECH DIR, ROME AIR DEVELOP CTR, 84- *Personal Data:* b Rome, NY, Feb 5, 46; m 68; c 4. *Educ:* Syracuse Univ, BS, 67, MS, 71; Univ Hawaii, PhD(geodesy/geophys). *Prof Exp:* Staff physicist, Rome Air Develop Ctr, 66-72; electron engr, Res & Develop, USCG, 72-78; chief scientist, Defense Mapping Agency, 78-84. *Concurrent Pos:* Prof math, Northern Va Community Col, 74-; lectr math, George Mason Univ, 76-81 & State Univ NY, Utica-Rome; assoc prof, George Washington Univ, 76-83. *Mem:* Am Geophys Union. *Res:* Application of satellite technology to furthering the fields of geodesy and geophysics; defining the physical fields of the earth and other bodies in our solar system. *Mailing Add:* 3019 Franklin Corner Lane Herndon VA 20171

SENYK, GEORGE, IMMUNOLOGY, MICROBIOLOGY. *Current Pos:* ASSOC SCIENTIST, CETUS IMMUNE CORP, PALO ALTO, CA, 82- *Personal Data:* b Kharkov, Ukraine, May 6, 26; US citizen; m 55; c 2. *Educ:* Univ Frankfurt, 46-49; Univ San Francisco, BS, 66; Univ Calif, San Francisco, PhD(microbiol), 71. *Prof Exp:* Lectr, San Francisco State Col, 70; fel biochem, Univ Calif, San Francisco, 71, trainee, Dept Clin Path & Lab Med & lectr med technol-clin microbiol, 72-73, asst prof clin path & lab med & training coordr curriculum med technol-clin microbiol, 73-77, asst dir, Grad Prog Clin Lab Sci-Clin Microbiol, 74-77, res microbiologist, Dept Microbiol, 77-82. *Mem:* AAAS; Am Soc Microbiol; Am Asn Immunologists. *Res:* Role of cellular immunity in resistance to infections; in vitro correlates of cellular immunity; monoclonal antibodies. *Mailing Add:* 2319 32nd Ave San Francisco CA 94116-2207

SENZEL, ALAN JOSEPH, TOXICOLOGY, ANALYTICAL CHEMISTRY. *Current Pos:* CONSULT ANALYTICAL CHEM, 93- *Personal Data:* b Los Angeles, Calif, May 26, 45; m 69, Phyllis S Abt; c Richard S & Lisa B. *Educ:* Calif State Univ, Long Beach, BS, 67; Univ Calif, Los Angeles, MS, 69, PhD(anal chem), 70. *Honors & Awards:* Commendable Serv Award, US Food & Drug Admin, 78. *Prof Exp:* Assoc ed, Anal Chem & Mem Exec Comt, Div Anal Chem, Am Chem Soc, 70-74; anal methods ed, Asn Off Anal Chemists, 74-78; head info off, Chem Indust Inst Toxicol, 78-79; sr chemist, Del Green Assoc, Inc, Foster City, Calif, 81-84; dep mgr, Environ Systs, Environ Resources Mgt Inc, Exton, PA, 88-89; proj scientist, Residue Chem Dept, Agr Div, Ciba-Geigy Corp, Greensboro, NC, 89-93; contract lab mgr, Entropy, Inc, Raleigh, NC, 95-96. *Concurrent Pos:* Consult environ chem & eng, 78- *Mem:* AAAS; Am Chem Soc; Instrument Soc Am; Asn Off Anal Chemists; Soc Environ Chem & Toxicol; Soc Tech Commun. *Res:* Toxicology of bulk, commodity chemicals; analytical methodology for agricultural products, foods, feeds, beverages, drugs, pesticides, cosmetics, color additives, and other commodities important in public health; chemical literature and journal publication; air pollution measurement; hazardous waste analysis, treatment, storage and disposal; risk assessment of hazardous waste sites; pesticide registration. *Mailing Add:* 7704 Audubon Dr Raleigh NC 27615-3403. *Fax:* 919-878-3803

SEO, EDDIE TATSU, BATTERY ENGINEERING & MANUFACTURING. *Current Pos:* INDEPENDENT CONSULT. *Personal Data:* b Los Angeles, Calif, July 12, 35; m 64, Alice Y Ibaraki; c Audrey Y & Hilary T. *Educ:* Univ Calif, Los Angeles, BS, 59; Univ Calif, Riverside, PhD(chem), 64. *Prof Exp:* Res assoc chem, Univ Kans, 64-65; mem tech staff, TRW Systs Group, 65-77; sr res assoc, Gates Corp, 77-90; sr scientist & engr, Hughes Aircraft Co, 90-93. *Mem:* Am Chem Soc; Electrochem Soc; Sigma Xi. *Res:* Electrochemical energy conversion and storage. *Mailing Add:* 7276 S Highland Dr Littleton CO 80120. *E-Mail:* etseo@netway.net

SEO, STANLEY TOSHIO, CHEMISTRY. *Current Pos:* Chemist, 55-64, SUPVRY RES CHEMIST, HAWAII FRUIT & VEG RES LAB, AGR RES SERV, USDA, 64- *Personal Data:* b Honolulu, Hawaii, Mar 5, 28. *Educ:* Univ Hawaii, BS, 50, MS, 52. *Mem:* AAAS; Am Chem Soc; Entom Soc Am; Am Inst Chemists. *Res:* Commodity treatment by fumigation, heat, low temperatures and use of gamma radiation; chemical factors affecting the infestation of fruit by fruitflies; radiation biology by use of gammaradiation; applications to sterile-insect technology for eradication and control of fruit flies; chemical factors pertaining to radiation biology. *Mailing Add:* 5404 Halapepe St Honolulu HI 96821-1720

SEON, BEN K, IMMUNOLOGY, CANCER. *Current Pos:* from cancer res scientist to sr cancer res scientist, Roswell Park Cancer Inst, 67-75, assoc cancer res scientist, 75-78, cancer res scientist V, 78-85, CANCER RES SCIENTIST VI & PROF, ROSWELL PARK CANCER INST, 85- *Personal Data:* b Fukuoka-Ken, Japan, May 5, 36; m 66, Takako; c Carl Y, Amy Y & Mae Y. *Educ:* Osaka Univ, MS, 63, PhD(biochem), 66. *Prof Exp:* Fel biochem, Osaka Univ, 66-67. *Mem:* Am Asn Immunologists; Am Asn Cancer Res. *Res:* Utilization of hybridoma technology for cancer; application of immunoconjugates for cancer therapy; human B cell antigen receptors. *Mailing Add:* Molecular Immunol Dept Roswell Park Cancer Inst Buffalo NY 14263

SEPERICH, GEORGE JOSEPH, FOOD SCIENCE, MEAT CHEMISTRY. *Current Pos:* dir, Sch Agr & Environ Resources, 82-88, ASSOC PROF AGR, DIV AGR, ARIZ STATE UNIV, 76- *Personal Data:* b Chicago, Ill, Mar 18, 44; m 68; c 1. *Educ:* Loyola Univ, BS, 67; Mich State Univ, MS, 72, PhD(food sci), 76. *Prof Exp:* Dir educ prog, Mich Dept Labor, 75-76. *Mem:* Inst Food Technologists; AAAS; Am Meat Sci Asn; Am Soc Animal Sci. *Res:* Muscle food constituents; muscle turnover and metabolism; isolation and characterization of food and muscle food proteins and muscle cellular physiology and biochemistry related to exercise and pathology. *Mailing Add:* Sch Agr Busn Ariz State Univ Box 873306 Tempe AZ 85287-3306

SEPINWALL, JERRY, PSYCHOPHARMACOLOGY, PHYSIOLOGICAL PSYCHOLOGY. *Current Pos:* Sr scientist, 66-71, res group chief, 71-75, RES SECT HEAD, HOFFMANN-LA ROCHE, INC, 75- *Personal Data:* b Montreal, Que, Dec 14, 40; m 63; c 3. *Educ:* McGill Univ, BA, 61; Cornell Univ, MA, 63; Univ Pa, PhD(psychol), 66. *Concurrent Pos:* Instr, Brooklyn Col, 67 & Montclair State Col, 70. *Mem:* Soc Neurosci; Am Soc Pharmacol & Exp Therapeut; Am Psychol Asn; Behav Pharmacol Soc; NY Acad Sci. *Res:* Pharmacology of antianxiety agents; physiology and neurochemistry of motivation and learning. *Mailing Add:* Dept Pharmacol Hoffmann-La Roche Inc 340 Kingsland St Nutley NJ 07110-1150

SEPKOSKI, J(OSEPH) J(OHN), JR, PALEONTOLOGY. *Current Pos:* RES ASSOC, FIELD MUS NATURAL HIST, 80-; from asst prof to assoc prof, 78-85, PROF GEOL, UNIV CHICAGO, 86- *Personal Data:* b Presque Isle, Maine, July 26, 48; m, Christine M Janis; c David. *Educ:* Univ Notre Dame, BS, 70; Harvard Univ, PhD(geol), 77. *Honors & Awards:* Charles Schuchert Award, Paleont Soc, 83. *Prof Exp:* From instr to asst prof geol, Univ Rochester, 74-78. *Concurrent Pos:* Ed, Paleobiol, 83-86. *Mem:* AAAS; Paleont Soc (pres, 95-96); Sigma Xi; Soc Study Evolution; Soc Syst Biologists; Geol Soc Am. *Res:* Evolutionary paleobiology and paleoecology, with particular emphasis on diversification and distribution of marine invertebrates, especially in the early Paleozoic; geostatistics; mass extinction and periodicity of extinction. *Mailing Add:* Dept Geophys Sci Univ Chicago Chicago IL 60637. *Fax:* 773-702-9515; *E-Mail:* jjsepkos@midway.uchicago.edu

SEPKOSKI, JOSEPH JOHN, SR, ORGANIC CHEMISTRY. *Current Pos:* RETIRED. *Personal Data:* b Cleveland, Ohio, July 30, 21; wid; c J John Jr, Carol M, Diane (Karl), Gregory B (deceased) & Mary D (deceased). *Educ:* John Carroll Univ, BS, 43; Univ Notre Dame, MS, 50; Rutgers Univ, MBA, 56. *Prof Exp:* Prod chemist, Schering Corp, 50-53; develop chemist, Celanese Corp Am, 53-55; sr chemist, Chicopee Mfg Corp, 55-57, res supvr, 57-62; group leader, Thatcher Mfg Co, 62-63; sr res chemist, Indust Chem Div, Allied Chem Corp, 63-67 & Plastics Div, 67-68, group leader, 68-74, tech serv supvr spec chem, Plastics Div, 74-81, tech coordr, Allied Fibers & Plastics Co, 81-82, supvr tech support, Chem Sect, 82-86. *Mem:* Fel Am Inst Chem; Am Chem Soc. *Res:* Thermosetting resins, reinforced and non-reinforced; urethanes; low molecular weight polyethylene. *Mailing Add:* 323 West Shore Trail Sparta NJ 07871

SEPMEYER, L(UDWIG) W(ILLIAM), ELECTRICAL ENGINEERING. *Current Pos:* CONSULT ENGR, 63- *Personal Data:* b East St Louis, Ill, Nov 6, 10; m 36, Inez Hopkins; c Adrienne. *Educ:* Univ Calif, BS, 33. *Prof Exp:* Consult engr, Calif, 34-41; asst, Univ Calif, Los Angeles, 34-37 & 40-41; engr, Lansing Mfg Co, Calif, 39-40; engr, Elec Res Prods Div, Western Elec Co, 41-42; engr, Div War Res, Univ Calif, 42-45 & Calif Inst Technol, 45; elec engr, US Naval Ord Test Sta, 45-51; engr, Rand Corp, 51-56 & Eng Systs Develop Corp, 56-63. *Concurrent Pos:* Consult, 47- & US Naval Ord Test Sta, 51-57. *Mem:* Fel Acoust Soc Am; fel Audio Eng Soc; Am Soc Testing & Mat; Inst Noise Control Eng USA; Inst Elec & Electronics Engrs. *Res:* Architectural acoustics; noise control; acoustical instrumentation; electrical sound recording and reproduction. *Mailing Add:* 1862 Comstock Ave Los Angeles CA 90025. *Fax:* 310-553-1541

SEPPALA, LYNN G, OPTICAL DESIGN. *Current Pos:* OPTICAL ENGR, LAWRENCE LIVERMORE LAB, 76- *Personal Data:* b Watertown, SDak, May 21, 46; m 80. *Educ:* SDak State Univ, BS, 68; Univ Rochester, PhD(optics), 74. *Honors & Awards:* R&D 100 Award, 90. *Prof Exp:* Optical designer, ITEK Corp, 74-76. *Mem:* Optical Soc Am; Int Soc Optical Eng. *Mailing Add:* Lawrence Livermore Nat Lab L-487 Univ Calif PO Box 5508 Livermore CA 94550

SEPPALA-HOLTZMAN, DAVID N, HOMOTOPY THEORY, COHOMOLOGY OPERATIONS. *Current Pos:* PROF MATH, ST JOSEPH'S COL, 81- *Personal Data:* b New York, NY, Aug 31, 50; m 83, Anne Seppala; c Erica. *Educ:* State Univ NY, Stony Brook, BSc, 72; Oxford Univ, UK, MSc, 73, DPhil(math), 79. *Prof Exp:* Assoc prof, Cath Univ Nijmegen, 76-81. *Concurrent Pos:* Mem, Nat Comt Student Chap, Math Asn Am, 86-88, chair, NY Metro Sect, 88-90; vchair, math sect, NY Acad Sci, 94-96, chair, 96-89. *Mem:* NY Acad Sci; Am Math Soc; Math Asn Am; Nat Coun Teachers Math. *Res:* Algebraic topology; systems of higher order cohomology operations and their applications; generate materials to induce and nuture a sense of wonder in future elementary school teachers. *Mailing Add:* Dept Math St Joseph's Col 245 Clinton Ave Brooklyn NY 11205-3688. *E-Mail:* holtzmrd@isz.nyu.edu

SEPPI, EDWARD JOSEPH, PHYSICS, MATHEMATICS. *Current Pos:* mgr med diag inst, Varian Assoc, 74-76, eng mgr, 76-77, div mgr, 77-78, tech dir, 78-80, sr scientist, 80-93, PRIN SCIENTIST, VARIAN ASSOC, 93- *Personal Data:* b Price, Utah, Dec 16, 30; m 53, Betty Stowell; c Duane, Kevin & Cynthia. *Educ:* Brigham Young Univ, BS, 52; Univ Idaho, MS, 56; Calif Inst Technol, PhD(physics), 62. *Prof Exp:* Jr engr, Geneva Steel Co, 51; lab instr, Brigham Young Univ, 51-52; physicist, Hanford Labs, Gen Elec Co, 52-58; res asst physics, Calif Inst Technol, 58-60, Gen Elec fel, 60-62, univ fel, 62; staff physicist, Inst Defense Anal, 62-64; head res area physics group, Stanford Linear Accelerator Ctr, 64-66, res area dept head, 66-68, head exp facil dept, 68-74. *Concurrent Pos:* Consult, Inst Defense Anal, 64-72; sr scientist super conducting collider, Dallas, Tex, 90-91. *Mem:* Am Phys Soc. *Res:* High energy, nuclear and solid state physics; lasers; medical diagnostic instrumentation; research administration; electron accelerator and beam transport, medical imaging instrumentation, fast body CT scanning, amorphous silicon imagers for radiology; basic technology in nuclear, laser and solid state physics; 22 issued patents; author 82 scientific publications & abstracts. *Mailing Add:* 320 Dedalera Dr Portola Valley CA 94028. *Fax:* 650-424-6988

SEPSY, CHARLES FRANK, MECHANICAL ENGINEERING. *Current Pos:* res assoc, Res Found, 51-56, from instr to assoc prof, 56-67, PROF MECH ENG, OHIO STATE UNIV, 67- *Personal Data:* b Rochester, NY, May 19, 24; m 45; c 2. *Educ:* Univ Tenn, Knoxville, BME, 49; Univ Rochester, MSc, 51. *Honors & Awards:* Carrier Award, Am Soc Heating, Refrig & Air-Conditioning Engrs, 67. *Prof Exp:* Asst mech eng, Univ Rochester, 50-51. *Concurrent Pos:* Consult, Owens-Corning Fiberglas, 58-, Bender & Assocs, Consult Engrs, 60-65 & Off Civil Defense, 63-; educ consult, NAm Heating, Air Conditioning Wholesalers Asn, 64-; consult, CVI Corp, 65- *Mem:* Am Soc Heating, Refrig & Air-Conditioning Engrs; Am Soc Eng Educ; Inst Environ Sci. *Res:* Internal control of the environment for man and machines with respect to regulating temperature, humidity, contaminants, noise and distribution; system simulation and energy requirements of building environmental control systems. *Mailing Add:* 3675 Rushmore Dr Columbus OH 43211

SEPUCHA, ROBERT CHARLES, CHEMICAL PHYSICS, PHYSICAL OPTICS. *Current Pos:* SR VPRES & GROUP MGR, SYST GROUP, SPARTA, INC, 91- *Personal Data:* b Salem, Mass, June 12, 43; m 66; c 3. *Educ:* Mass Inst Technol, SB, 65, SM, 67; Univ Calif, San Diego, PhD(eng physics), 71. *Prof Exp:* Sr res scientist, Aerodyne Res Inc, 71-76; physicist, High Energy Laser Syst Proj Off, US Army, 76-78; prof mgr, Space Defense Technol Div, Directed Energy Off, Defense Advan Res Proj Agency, 79-80, dep dir, 80-84; vpres, Space technol, W J Schafer Assoc Inc, 84-91. *Mem:* Am Phys Soc; Optical Soc Am; Sigma Xi. *Res:* Systems analysis and architecture development for defense and information systems. *Mailing Add:* 9790 Kedge Ct Vienna VA 22181. *Fax:* 703-734-9735

SEQUEIRA, JOEL AUGUST LOUIS, PHARMACOKINETICS, PHYSICAL PHARMACY. *Current Pos:* sect leader, 78-87, assoc dir pharmaceut res & develop, 87-96, SR DIR, SCHERING CORP, 96- *Personal Data:* b Bombay, India, July 13, 47; US citizen; m 73; c 1. *Educ:* Univ Bombay, BPharm, 69; Columbia Univ, MS, 72; State Univ NY, Buffalo, PhD(pharmaceut), 76. *Prof Exp:* Sr res scientist, Pharmaceut Res & Develop, Johnson & Johnson Res, 76-78. *Mem:* Acad Pharmaceut Sci; Am Pharmaceut Asn; Soc Invest Dermat; Am Asn Pharm Scientists. *Res:* Topical and transdermal dosage form design; pharmacokinetics; percutaneous absorption; aerosol dosage form design; oral control release dosage form design. *Mailing Add:* Schering Corp 2000 Galloping Hill Rd Kenilworth NJ 07033

SEQUEIRA, LUIS, PLANT PATHOLOGY. *Current Pos:* RETIRED. *Personal Data:* b San Jose, Costa Rica, Sept 1, 27; m 54; c 4. *Educ:* Harvard Univ, BA, 49, MA, 50, PhD(biol), 52. *Prof Exp:* Parker traveling fel from Harvard Univ, Biol Inst, Brazil, 52-53; from asst plant pathologist to dir, Coto Res Sta, United Fruit Co, Costa Rica, 53-60; res assoc plant path, NC State Univ, 60-61; from assoc prof to prof, Univ Wis-Madison, 61-78, prof plant path & bact, 78-86, prof, Plant Asn, 86-87, J C Walker prof plant path, 88-93. *Concurrent Pos:* NSF sr fel, Univ Reading, 70-71; ed-in-chief, Phytopath, 79-81. *Mem:* Nat Acad Sci; fel Am Phytopath Soc (pres, 85-86); Bot Soc Am; Mycol Soc Am; Am Soc Plant Physiol. *Res:* Soil microbiology; root diseases; plant growth regulators; physiology of parasitism. *Mailing Add:* Dept Plant Path Univ Wis Madison WI 53706

SEQUIN, CARLO HEINRICH, COMPUTER AIDED DESIGN, COMPUTER GRAPHICS. *Current Pos:* vis lectr logic design microprocessors, 76-77, vchmn, comput sci div, 80-83, PROF COMPUT SCI, UNIV CALIF, BERKELEY, 77- *Personal Data:* b Winterthur, Switz, Oct 30, 41; m 68, Margareta Frey; c Eveline & Andre. *Educ:* Univ Basel, Switz, dipl, 65, PhD(physics), 69. *Prof Exp:* Mem tech staff MOS integrated circuits, Bell Tel Labs, 70-76. *Concurrent Pos:* consult, Xerox, Computervision & Siemens. *Mem:* Fel Inst Elec & Electronics Engrs; Asn Comput Mach; fel Swiss Acad Eng Sci. *Res:* Computer graphics and geometric modeling; computer-aided design tools for architects and mechanical engineers; interactive visualization of buildings and mechanisms; geometric modeling. *Mailing Add:* Dept Elec Eng & Comput Sci Univ Calif Soda Hall No 1776 Berkeley CA 94720-1776. *E-Mail:* sequin@cs.berkeley.edu

SERAD, GEORGE A, CHEMICAL ENGINEERING. *Current Pos:* res engr, Celanese Res Co, 64-70, res eng, 70-73, tech group leader, 73-75, tech mgr, 75-83, TECH MGR SPECIALTIES OPERS, CELANESE FIBERS CO, 85- *Personal Data:* b Philadelphia, Pa, Feb 26, 39; m 67; c 2. *Educ:* Drexel Inst Technol, BS, 61; Univ Pa, MS, 62, PhD(chem eng), 64. *Prof Exp:* Lab asst chem res, Scott Paper Co, Pa, 58 & 59; engr aide, Texaco Inc, NJ, 60 & 61. *Mem:* Am Inst Chem Engrs; Am Chem Soc. *Res:* Transport phenomena; electrochemistry; catalysis; fibers and polymers processing; product development. *Mailing Add:* 3008 Cutchin Dr Charlotte NC 28210-4816

SERAFETINIDES, EUSTACE A, PSYCHIATRY. *Current Pos:* vis assoc prof, 71-72, prof, Dept Psychiat & Mem, Brain Res Inst, 72-94, EMER PROF, DEPT PSYCHIAT, SCH MED, UNIV CALIF, LOS ANGELES, 94- *Personal Data:* b Athens, Greece, June 4, 30; m 65, Jean Rawlinson. *Educ:* Nat Univ Athens, MD, 53; Royal Col Physicians & Surgeons, dipl psychol med, 59; Univ London, PhD(psychol med), 64. *Prof Exp:* Clin asst-res assoc, Maudsley Hosp, Inst Psychiat, Univ London, 57-65; assoc prof psychiat, neurol & behav sci, Sch Med, Univ Okla, 65-71; assoc chief of staff res, Vet Admin Hosp Brentwood, Los Angeles, 72-95. *Concurrent Pos:* NIMH res scientist development award, 67-72. *Res:* Electro-clinical and psychopharmacological investigations of brain-behavior relationships; epilepsy; cerebral dominance consciousness and schizophrenia. *Mailing Add:* Dept Psychiat Univ Calif Los Angeles CA 90024

SERAFIN, FRANK G, SURFACE CHEMISTRY, MATERIALS SCIENCE. *Current Pos:* Chemist, 60-68, group leader, 68-72, res assoc, 72-82, SR RES ASSOC, W R GRACE & CO, CAMBRIDGE, 82- *Personal Data:* b Passaic, NJ, Oct 8, 35. *Educ:* Wesleyan Univ, Middletown, Conn, BA, 57; Northeastern Univ, Boston, MS, 68 & 76. *Mem:* Am Chem Soc; Soc Appl Spectros; Royal Soc Chem; Sigma Xi. *Res:* Materials analysis and characterization including organic and inorganic compounds, mixtures and polymers. *Mailing Add:* 31 Livingston Dr Peabody MA 01960-3446

SERAFIN, ROBERT JOSEPH, RADAR ENGINEERING, RADAR METEOROLOGY. *Current Pos:* mgr field observ facil radar meteorol instrumentation, 73-81, dir, Atmospheric Tech Div, 81-89, DIR, NAT CTR ATMOSPHERIC RES, 89- *Personal Data:* b Chicago, Ill, Apr 22, 36; m 61, Betsy Furgerson; c Katharine J, Robert J Jr & Elizabeth. *Educ:* Univ Notre Dame, BS, 58; Northwestern Univ, MS, 61; Ill Inst Technol, PhD(elec eng), 72. *Prof Exp:* Engr elec eng radar, Hazeltine Res Corp, 60-62; res engr radar signal process, IIT Res Inst, 60-69, sr engr, 69-73, res assoc radar meteorol, 70-73. *Mem:* Nat Acad Eng; sr mem Inst Elec & Electronics Engrs; Sigma Xi; Am Meteorol Soc. *Res:* Doppler radar signal processing theory and implementation; random signal theory; atmospheric turbulence, severe storms, tornadoes and damaging winds. *Mailing Add:* Nat Ctr Atmospheric Res 1850 Table Mesa Dr PO Box 3000 Boulder CO 80307-3000

SERAFINI, ANGELA, BACTERIOLOGY, CYTOLOGY. *Current Pos:* RETIRED. *Personal Data:* b Sassoferrato, Italy, July 27, 13; nat. *Educ:* Wayne State Univ, BA, 50; Univ Mich, MS, 56. *Prof Exp:* Med technologist, Wayne County Gen Hosp, Eloise, Mich, 33-35, sr bacteriologist, mycologist, parasitologist & instr, 44-55; sr bacteriologist, supvr med technologists & instr med technol, Grace Hosp, Detroit, 35-44; from asst res microbiologist to assoc res microbiologist, Parke, Davis & Co, 56-70; instr med technol, Sch Med, Wayne State Univ, 70-72, res asst, 72-78. *Mem:* Emer mem Am Soc Microbiol; Am Soc Tissue Cult; Am Soc Med Technol. *Res:* Respiratory human viruses; tumor viruses of animals and man; immunology; cytology. *Mailing Add:* 1255 Woodbridge Dr St Clair Shores MI 48080-3304

SERAFINI, JOHN S, FLUID DYNAMICS. *Current Pos:* ASSOC PROF, DEPT MECH ENG, UNIV AKRON, 81- *Personal Data:* b Cleveland, Ohio, Oct 30, 25. *Educ:* Rensselaer Polytech Inst, BS, 47, MS, 47; Case Inst Technol, PhD(aeronaut Eng), 62. *Prof Exp:* Res prog mgr, Lewis Res Ctr, NASA, 49-81. *Mem:* Am Phys Soc. *Res:* Fluid dynamics. *Mailing Add:* 473 Walleyford Dr Berea OH 44017-2224

SERAFY, D KEITH, ECHINODERM BIOLOGY, MARINE BENTHIC INVERTEBRATES. *Current Pos:* PROF BIOL & MARINE SCI, SOUTHAMPTON COL, LONG ISLAND UNIV, 78- *Personal Data:* b St Petersburg, Fla, June 3, 47; m 86; c 1. *Educ:* Univ SFla, BA, 69; Univ Maine, MS, 71, PhD(zool), 73. *Prof Exp:* Assoc res scientist marine sci, NY Ocean Sci Lab, 73-78 & Va Inst Marine Sci, 75-78. *Concurrent Pos:* Asst prof marine sci, Col William & Mary, 75-78. *Mem:* Am Soc Zoologists; Sigma Xi; Union Concerned Scientists. *Res:* Systematics and ecology of the phylum Echinodermata (sea urchins, sand dollars, heart urchin, brittle stars and starfish); environmental surveys of benthic marine invertebrates in the north Atlantic between New York and Virginia. *Mailing Add:* Dept Biol Southampton Col Southampton NY 11968

SERAPHIN, BERNHARD OTTO, SOLID STATE PHYSICS. *Current Pos:* PROF OPTICAL SCI, OPTICAL SCI CTR, UNIV ARIZ, 70- *Personal Data:* b Berlin, Ger, Nov 4, 23; nat US; m 58; c 2. *Educ:* Friedrich Schiller Univ, dipl, 50; Humboldt Univ, PhD(physics), 51. *Prof Exp:* Sci asst, Inst Solid State Res, Ger, 50-52; physicist, Res Lab, Siemens-Schuckertwerke Co, Co, 52-56; chief semiconductor team, Physics Lab, Brown Bovery Co, Switz, 56-59; head, Semiconductor Br, Michelson Lab, US Dept Navy, 59-70. *Concurrent Pos:* Liaison scientist, Off Naval Res, London, 65-67; guest prof, Tech Univ Denmark, 69-70, Univ VI Paris, Univ Strasbourg, Univ Nice, 76-77, Int Ctr Theoret Phys, Trieste, Italy, 82-83; sr Fulbright scholar, Univ Split, Yugoslavia, 82. *Mem:* Fel Am Phys Soc. *Res:* Modulation spectroscopy; electroreflectance; energy band structure and optical properties of solids; material science aspects of solar energy conversion. *Mailing Add:* Optical Sci Ctr Univ Ariz Tucson AZ 85721

SERAT, WILLIAM FELKNER, AGRICULTURAL ENVIRONMENTAL CHEMISTRY. *Current Pos:* PRES, HARTSHORN CO, 79- *Personal Data:* b Chicago, Ill, Nov 14, 29; wid; c 3. *Educ:* Univ Colo, AB, 51; Iowa State Univ, MS, 53; Univ Calif, Los Angeles, PhD(biochem), 58. *Prof Exp:* Res asst biochem, US Atomic Energy proj, 56-58; tech rep, Rohm and Haas Co, 58-62; res chemist, Calif State Dept Health, 62-69, coord & prin investr, Community Studies in Pesticides, 69-79. *Concurrent Pos:* Lectr biol & biochem, St Mary's Col, Calif, 64-72. *Mem:* Am Chem Soc; Sigma Xi. *Res:* Environmental and health aspects of pesticides; physico-chemical aspects of environment. *Mailing Add:* 12 Camelford Ct Moraga CA 94556-2408

SERBER, ROBERT, physics; deceased, see previous edition for last biography

SERBIA, GEORGE WILLIAM, ASEPTIC PROCESSING & LOW ACID FOODS. *Current Pos:* RETIRED. *Personal Data:* b New York, NY, May 28, 28; m 55; c 4. *Educ:* Polytech Inst Brooklyn, BChemE, 54; Pepperdine Univ, MBA, 78. *Prof Exp:* Engr, Gen Foods Cent Labs, Hoboken, NJ, 54-60, admin asst, Jell-o Div, White Plains, NY, 60-61, group leader, Jell-o Div Labs, Tarrytown, NY, 62-66, tech res mgr, Gen Foods Int, Sao Paulo, Brazil, 66-68, sr group leader, Gen Foods Res, Tarrytown, NY, 68-70; assoc dir eng res & develop, Hunt-Wesson Foods, Fullerton, Calif, 70-85, dir prod & process develop, Hunt-Wesson/Beatrice Grocery Res & Develop Ctr Group, 85-89. *Concurrent Pos:* Adj prof, Chapman Col, 89- *Mem:* Inst Food Technol; Am Oil Chemists Asn; Nat Food Processors Asn. *Res:* Management of new product and improved product research and development; edible oils research and development; commercial development of aseptic pudding in plastic packaging and aseptic tomato products; commercial development of quick-cooking rice from benchtop to plant. *Mailing Add:* 248 S Malena Dr Orange CA 92869

SERBIN, LISA ALEXANDRA, PSYCHOLOGY, DEVELOPMENTAL PSYCHOLOGY. *Current Pos:* assoc prof, 78-84, dir, Centre Res Human Develop, 81-91, PROF PSYCHOL, CONCORDIA UNIV, 84- *Personal Data:* b New York, NY, Sept 18, 46; US & Can citizen; m 71; c 2. *Educ:* Reed Col, BA, 68; State Univ NY, Stony Brook, PhD(psychol), 72. *Prof Exp:* Asst prof psychol, State Univ NY, Binghamton, 73-78. *Mem:* Fel Am Psychol Asn; fel Can Psychol Asn; Soc Res Child Develop; Int Soc Study Behav Develop. *Res:* Early sex role development and the development of gender concepts in infants and preschoolers; inkergenetictional transfer of high risk status, a longitudinal study of outcomes for highly aggressive and/or withdrawn children. *Mailing Add:* Centre Res Human Develop Concordia Univ 7141 Sherbrooke St W Montreal PQ H4B 1R6 Can. *Fax:* 514-848-2815; *E-Mail:* lserbin@vax2.concordia.ca

SERCARZ, ELI, IMMUNOLOGY, CELL BIOLOGY. *Current Pos:* From asst prof to assoc prof microbiol, 63-70, PROF BACT, UNIV CALIF, LOS ANGELES, 70- *Personal Data:* b Bronx, NY, Feb 14, 34; m 55; c 4. *Educ:* San Diego State Col, BA, 55; Harvard Univ, MA, 56, PhD(bact, immunol), 60. *Concurrent Pos:* Fel bact, Harvard Med Sch, 60-62; fel virol, Mass Inst Technol, 62-63; grants, NSF, 63-69, NIH, 67-81 & Am Heart Asn, 69-72; consult, Eye Res Lab, Cedars-Sinai Med Ctr, 66-69; Guggenheim fel, Nat Inst Med Res, London, 70-71. *Mem:* Am Soc Microbiol; Am Asn Immunol; Nat Inst Med Res London. *Res:* Cell cooperation; iridium gene control; tritium cell specificity; immune unresponsiveness; idrotyke regulation. *Mailing Add:* Dept Microbiol & Molec Genet Univ Calif 609 Circle Dr E Los Angeles CA 90095-1489. *Fax:* 310-206-5231; *E-Mail:* elis@microbiolifesci.ucla.edu

SERDAREVICH, BOGDAN, BIOCHEMISTRY. *Current Pos:* PRES, SERDARY RES LABS, INC, 72- *Personal Data:* b Vel Bukovica, Yugoslavia, Dec 3, 21; m 64; c 2. *Educ:* Univ Zagreb, MSc, 55; Swiss Fed Inst Technol, PhD(org chem & biochem), 61. *Prof Exp:* Res assoc peptide chem, Univ Pittsburgh, 61-63; sr res assoc org chem, Swiss Fed Inst Technol, 63-64; asst prof lipid chem, Univ Western Ont, 64-75. *Concurrent Pos:* USPHS fel, 61-63; res grants, Swiss Nat Res Coun, 63-64 & Med Res Coun Can, 64- *Mem:* Sr mem Chem Inst Can; NY Acad Sci; Am Oil Chemists Soc; Am Chem Soc. *Res:* Research and synthesis of lipids; lipid metabolism in relation to atherosclerosis and aging process; cell membranes structure and function. *Mailing Add:* Serdary Res Labs Inc 1643 Kathryn Dr London ON N6G 2R7 Can

SERDENGECTI, SEDAT, CONTROL & SYSTEMS ENGINEERING. *Current Pos:* asst prof physics, Harvey Mudd Col, 61-63, asst prof control systs eng, 63-65, assoc prof control systs, 65-71, PROF ENG, HARVEY MUDD COL, 71- *Personal Data:* b Izmit, Turkey, July 28, 27; m 58; c 2. *Educ:* Syracuse Univ, BS, 51; Calif Inst Technol, MS, 52, PhD(mech eng), 55. *Prof Exp:* Fel, Calif Inst Technol, 55-57; res engr, Turkish Gen Staff, 57-58 & Chevron Res Corp, Calif, 58-61. *Concurrent Pos:* Consult, Metaflo Res Corp, Calif, 59-61, Chevron Res Corp, 61-64 & Gen Motors Corp, Mich, 65- *Res:* Applied mathematics and mechanics; rock physics; stress analysis; optimalizing control systems; computer science. *Mailing Add:* Harvey Mudd Col 301 E 12th St Claremont CA 91711

SERDUKE, FRANKLIN JAMES DAVID, NUCLEAR PHYSICS. *Current Pos:* PHYSICIST, LAWRENCE LIVERMORE NAT LAB, 76- *Personal Data:* b Berkeley, Calif, May 23, 42; m 63; c 2. *Educ:* San Francisco State Univ, AB, 64; Univ Calif, Davis, MA, 66, PhD(physics), 70. *Prof Exp:* Asst physicist, Physics Div, Argonne Nat Lab, 73-76. *Mem:* Am Phys Soc; Am Geophys Union. *Res:* Theoretical nuclear physics; nuclear shell theory; few body problems; nuclear matter; pion-nucleus interactions; numerical modeling; Speakeasy computer language. *Mailing Add:* 549 El Pintado Rd Danville CA 94526

SERENE, JOSEPH WILLIAM, LOW TEMPERATURE PHYSICS, SUPERFLUID FERMI LIQUIDS. *Current Pos:* PROF PHYSICS & CHAIR DEPT, GEORGETOWN UNIV, 93- *Personal Data:* b Indiana, Pa, Apr 4, 47; wid; c Peter & Stephen. *Educ:* Dartmouth Col, AB, 69; Cornell Univ, PhD(physics), 74. *Prof Exp:* Fel, Stanford Univ, 74-75; guest prof physics, Nordic Inst Theoret Atomic Physics, 75-76; asst prof, State Univ NY, Stony Brook, 76-79; from asst prof to assoc prof appl physics, Yale Univ, 79-84; prog dir, Condensed Matter Theory, NSF, 84-86, sect head, Condensed Matter Sci, 86-87; res physicist, Naval Res Lab, 87-93, sect head, Complex Systs Theory, 92-93. *Mem:* Am Phys Soc; AAAS. *Res:* Theoretical condensed matter physics; superfluid helium 3, superconductivity and superfluids in neutron stars; strongly-correlated metals, semiconductors, and superconductors; application of massively-parallel computers to condensed matter physics. *Mailing Add:* Dept Physics Georgetown Univ Washington DC 20057-0995. *E-Mail:* serene@ariel.physics.georgetown.edu

SERENO, PAUL C, PALEONTOLOGY. *Current Pos:* ASST PROF, UNIV CHICAGO, 87- *Personal Data:* b 1958. *Educ:* Columbia Univ, PhD(palenot). *Res:* Discoverer of Eoraptor, the earliest known dinosaur, in the Argentine foothills of the Andes mountains. *Mailing Add:* Dept Obstet & Anat 1025 E 57th St Chicago IL 60637-1508

SERFLING, ROBERT JOSEPH, MATHEMATICAL STATISTICS, PROBABILITY. *Current Pos:* chmn, 82-85, 86-88, PROF MATH SCI, JOHNS HOPKINS UNIV, 79- *Personal Data:* b Kalamazoo, Mich, Jan 23, 39; m 61; c 2. *Educ:* Ga Inst Technol, BS, 63; Univ NC, Chapel Hill, PhD(math statist), 67. *Honors & Awards:* Humboldt Prize, Alexander von Humboldt Found, W Germany, 84. *Prof Exp:* Res statistician, Res Triangle Inst, 67; from asst prof to prof statist, Fla State Univ, 67-79. *Concurrent Pos:* Statistician & chmn, Assessment Admin Rev Comn, State Fla, 73-77; vis statist adv, NSF, 77-78; vis scholar, Limburgs Univ, Centrum, Belgium, 82; vis prof, Albert-Ludwigs Univ, Freiburg, WGer, 86. *Mem:* Fel Am Statist Asn; fel Inst Math Statist; Am Math Soc; Math Asn Am; Oper Res Soc Am; fel Int Statist Inst. *Res:* Probability theory; statistical inference; stochastic processes; operations research. *Mailing Add:* Dept Math Univ Tex Dallas Richardson TX 75083

SERFOZO, RICHARD FRANK, OPERATIONS RESEARCH. *Current Pos:* ASST PROF OPER RES, SYRACUSE UNIV, 69-72, 73- *Personal Data:* b Detroit, Mich, Mar 29, 39; m 62; c 1. *Educ:* Wayne State Univ, BS, 61; Univ Wash, MA, 65; Northwestern Univ, PhD(appl math), 69. *Prof Exp:* Prof engr, Ford Motor Co, 62; oper res analyst, Boeing Co, 62-68; vis asst prof oper res, Cornell Univ, 72. *Mem:* Am Math Soc; Oper Res Soc Am; Inst Mgt Sci. *Res:* Applied probability; semi-stationary processes; thinning of point processes, control of queues. *Mailing Add:* Sch Indust & Syst Eng Ga Inst Technol Atlanta GA 30332-0001

SERGEANT, DAVID ERNEST, BIOLOGY, ECOLOGY. *Current Pos:* RETIRED. *Personal Data:* b Hangchow, China, Jan 17, 27; Can citizen; m 54; c 3. *Educ:* Cambridge Univ, BSc, 48, MSc, 49, PhD(zool), 53. *Prof Exp:* Biologist fisheries biol, Fisheries Res Bd, Can Biol Sta, St John's, Nfld, 51-55 & Arctic Unit, Montreal, 55-65; biologist, Can Fisheries & Oceans Dept, Arctic Biol Sta, 65-87. *Concurrent Pos:* Adj prof, Renewable Resources Dept, Macdonald Col, McGill Univ. *Mem:* Soc Marine Mammal. *Res:* Life history, population dynamics of sea mammals and advice towards the management of endangered species. *Mailing Add:* Box 745 Hudson Heights PQ J0P 1J0 Can

SERGOVICH, FREDERICK RAYMOND, CYTOLOGY, CYTOGENETICS. *Current Pos:* RETIRED. *Personal Data:* b Toronto, Ont, Nov 1, 33; m 60; c 2. *Educ:* McMaster Univ, BA, 60; Univ Western Ont, PhD(anat), 64. *Prof Exp:* Dir, Cytogenetics Lab, Childrens Psychiat Res Inst, 64-94. *Concurrent Pos:* Lectr, Med Sch, Univ Western Ont, 64-66, asst prof, 66-72; grants, Med Res Coun Can, 64-71, Ont Ment Health Fedn, 66-69 & 71-72 & Ont Cancer Treatment & Res Fedn, 69-72; consult, Victoria Hosp, London, Ont, 65- *Mem:* Am Soc Human Genetics; Can Asn Anat; Can Soc Cell Biol. *Res:* Human cytogenetics; correlation of clinical expression with chromosomes in lesion in mental retardation syndromes; fluorescence analysis of chromosomes in primary malignancies. *Mailing Add:* 240 Emery St E London ON N6C 2E2 Can

SERIANNI, ANTHONY STEPHAN, NMR SPECTROSCOPY, AB INITIO MOLECULAR ORBITAL CALCULATIONS. *Current Pos:* asst prof, 82-88, ASSOC PROF CHEM, UNIV NOTRE DAME, 88- *Personal Data:* b Chestnut Hill, Pa, Nov 18, 53. *Educ:* Albright Col, BS, 75; Mich State Univ, PhD(biochem), 80. *Honors & Awards:* Horace S Isbell Award, Am Chem Soc, 88. *Prof Exp:* Res assoc biochem, Cornell Univ, 80-82. *Concurrent Pos:* Pres & chief exec off, Omicron Biochems Inc, 82-; chmn-elect, Div Carbohydrate Chem, Am Chem Soc, 90- *Mem:* Am Soc Biochem & Molecular Biol; AAAS; Int Soc Magnetic Resonance; NY Acad Sci. *Res:* Developing improved chemical/enzymic methods to introduce stable isotopes into carbohydrates and their derivatives; meclaristic studies of fundamental reactions of sugars in solution, carbohydrate conformation and in vivo biological metabolism. *Mailing Add:* Dept Chem & Biochem Univ Notre Dame Notre Dame IN 46556. *Fax:* 219-239-6924

SERIF, GEORGE SAMUEL, BIOCHEMISTRY. *Current Pos:* from asst prof to assoc prof, 62-67, prof biochem & molecular biol & chmn fac, 67-71, PROF BIOCHEM & CHMN DEPT, OHIO STATE UNIV, 71- *Personal Data:* b Saskatoon, Sask, Apr 5, 28; m 48; c 3. *Educ:* McMaster Univ, BSc, 51, MSc, 53, PhD(biochem), 56. *Prof Exp:* Mem tech staff, DuPont of Can, 52-54; Hoffmann-La Roche fel, agr biochem, Univ Minn, 56-57; mem staff, Scripps Clin & Res Found, Calif, 57-58; from asst prof to assoc prof biochem, Sch Med, Univ SDak, 58-62. *Mem:* Am Soc Biol Chem; Am Chem Soc; Soc Exp Biol & Med; NY Acad Sci. *Res:* Mechanism of hormone action; carbohydrate metabolism; metabolism of fluoro derivatives; antimetabolites. *Mailing Add:* Dept Biochem Ohio State Univ 484 W 12th Ave Columbus OH 43210

SERKES, KENNETH DEAN, SURGERY. *Current Pos:* assoc clin res, Baxter/Travenol Labs, Inc, 68-70, assoc dir clin res, 70-72, med dir, Artificial Organs Div, 72-83, vpres, Med Reg Affairs, Omnis Surg Div, 83-85, sr med adv, Baxter Labs, 85-87, MED CONSULT, BAXTER/TRAVENOL LABS, 87- *Personal Data:* b St Louis, Mo, Aug 18, 26; m 74; c 3. *Educ:* Yale Univ, BS, 50; Washington Univ, MD, 51; Am Bd Surg, dipl, 57. *Prof Exp:* Assoc surg, Jewish Hosp St Louis, 56-62, asst dir, 62-67; asst to dir, Albert Einstein Med Ctr, Pa, 67-68. *Concurrent Pos:* From instr to asst prof, Sch Med, Wash Univ, 56-57; assoc prof, Sch Med, Temple Univ, 67-68; asst prof, Northwestern Univ, 68-87. *Mem:* Fel Am Col Surg; Am Soc Artificial Internal Organs; Int Soc Peritoneal Dialysis; Int Soc Nephrology; Am Col Surgeons; Cent Surg Asn. *Res:* Shock; blood volume; membrane and bubble oxygenation; artificial kidneys; organ preservation; general surgery; development of artificial kidneys; organ preservation; development of artificial organs; peritoneal dialysis research and development. *Mailing Add:* 860 Ladera Lane Montecito CA 93108

SERLIN, IRVING, POLYMER CHEMISTRY. *Current Pos:* RETIRED. *Personal Data:* b New York, NY, Apr 3, 23; m 50, Marion Wolther; c Bruce S & Fran E. *Educ:* City Col, BS, 43; Columbia Univ, MA, 47, PhD(org chem), 50. *Prof Exp:* Res chemist, Am Diet Aids, Inc, 43-44; lab instr org chem, Columbia Univ, 47-49, res assoc biochem, 51-53; res chemist, Cent Res Labs, Donut Corp Am, 50-51; assoc scientist, Brookhaven Nat Lab, 53-56; res chemist, Shawinigan Resins Corp, 56-65; res specialist, Monsanto Co, 65-70, sr res specialist, 70-85; consult, 85. *Concurrent Pos:* Mem, Int Physiol Cong, Belg, 56. *Mem:* Am Chem Soc; Sigma Xi. *Res:* Organic chemistry; synthesis of new resins for reprographic systems; synthesis of high temperature resins; pressure sensitive adhesive basic research; computerized statistical data analysis of experimental designs. *Mailing Add:* 94 Hadley Springfield MA 01118

SERLIN, OSCAR, SURGERY. *Current Pos:* chief surg serv, Vet Admin Hosp, East Orange, 67-75, chief staff, 75-88, CHIEF STAFF, VET ADMIN MED CTR, 88- *Personal Data:* b New York, NY, Aug 10, 17; m 51; c 2. *Educ:* Dalhousie Univ, MD & CM, 41; Am Bd Surg, dipl, 52. *Prof Exp:* Chief surg serv, Vet Admin Hosp, Lebanon, 56-57 & Philadelphia, 57-67; prof surg, Col Med NJ, Col Med & Dent NJ, 71-91. *Concurrent Pos:* Clin prof, Sch Med, Temple Univ, 58-67. *Mem:* Fel Am Col Surg. *Res:* Chemotherapy in treatment of cancer. *Mailing Add:* 67-75-New Eng Ave #75-E Summit NJ 07901-1801

SERMOLINS, MARIS ANDRIS, RESEARCH ADMINISTRATION. *Current Pos:* DIR PROD TECHNOL, SIKA CORP, 87- *Personal Data:* b Liepaja, Latvia, Sept 4, 44; US citizen; m 76; c 1. *Educ:* City Col CUNY, BChE, 66; Rutgers Univ, MS, 71; Pace Univ, MBA(management), 74. *Prof Exp:* Mgr, pro develop Permacez Div, Johnson & Johnson, 66-77; vpres, res & develop, Arno Tapes Inc, Scholl Corp, 77-80; tech dir, Am Cyanamid - Eng Mat, 80-84, Essex Spec Pro-Essex Chem, 84-87. *Mem:* Soc Advan Mat & Process Eng; Am Concrete Inst; Am Soc Testing Mat; Trans Res Bd; Nat Asn Corrosion Engrs. *Res:* Polyurethane sealants; epoxy & acrylic resins and concrete; cement based products and admixtures used in construction and industrial markets. *Mailing Add:* 31 Willowbrook Rd Freehold NJ 07728

SERNAS, VALENTINAS A, HEAT TRANSFER. *Current Pos:* From asst prof to assoc prof, 66-79, PROF MECH ENG, RUTGERS UNIV, NEW BRUNSWICK, 79- *Personal Data:* b Klaipeda, Lithuania, Nov 3, 38; US citizen; m 62; c 2. *Educ:* Univ Toronto, BASc, 61, MASc, 64, PhD(mech eng), 67. *Hon Degrees:* Dr, Vilnius Tech Univ, 94. *Mem:* Fel Am Soc Mech Engrs; Optical Soc Am; Soc Plastics Eng. *Res:* Heat transfer; boiling and condensation; optical methods applied to heat transfer; food extrusion. *Mailing Add:* Col Eng Rutgers Univ PO Box 909 Piscataway NJ 08855-0909

SERNE, ROGER JEFFREY, GEOCHEMISTRY, ANALYTICAL CHEMISTRY. *Current Pos:* From res scientist to sr res scientist, 69-78, sect mgr, 78, STAFF SCIENTIST EARTH SCI, BATTELLE NORTHWEST LABS, 78- *Personal Data:* b Lakewood, Ohio, Mar 20, 46; m 68; c 2. *Educ:* Univ Wash, BS, 69. *Mem:* Am Soc Agron; Soil Sci Soc Am; Am Geophys Union; Am Soc Testing & Mat. *Res:* Migration of hazardous wastes in geologic environment; adsorption mechanisms of trace constituents onto geomedia. *Mailing Add:* Battelle Northwest Labs PO Box 999 Sigma 5 K6-81 Richland WA 99352

SERNKA, THOMAS JOHN, MEDICAL PHYSIOLOGY, MEDICAL BIOPHYSICS. *Current Pos:* ASSOC PROF PHYSIOL & BIOPHYS, WRIGHT STATE UNIV, 76- *Personal Data:* b Cleveland, Ohio, July 26, 41; div; c 1. *Educ:* Oberlin Col, BA, 63; Harvard Univ, MA, 66; Univ Iowa, PhD(physiol, biophys), 69. *Prof Exp:* NIH fel, Univ Calif, San Francisco, 69-71; from instr to asst prof physiol, Univ Tex Med Sch Houston, 71-74; asst prof, 74-75, assoc prof physiol & biophys, med sch, La State Univ, Shreveport, 75-76. *Mem:* Am Physiol Soc; Biophys Soc; Soc Exp Biol & Med. *Res:* Gastric mucosal transport and metabolism. *Mailing Add:* W Minster Col 1840 S 1300 E Salt Lake City UT 84105-3617

SERNYAK, MICHAEL JOSEPH, BIOPOLAR DISORDER, NOVEL NEUROLEPTICS. *Current Pos:* DIR MENTAL HYGIENE CLIN & DIR SCHIZOPHRENIZ PROG, VA CONN HEALTHCARE SYST, WEST HAVEN CAMPUS, 92- *Personal Data:* b Upper Darby, Pa, Dec 6, 61; m 91, Ismene Petrakis; c Alexander. *Educ:* Amherst Col, BA, 83; Jefferson Med Col, MD, 87. *Prof Exp:* Resident in psychiat, Sch Med Yale Univ, 87-91, asst prof, Dept Psychiat, 92- *Concurrent Pos:* Consult psychopharmacol, Dept Ment Health, Conn, 93- *Mem:* Am Psychiat Asn. *Res:* Investigating novel treatments for acute mania in patients with bipolar disorder; evaluating new neuroleptic medications for the treatment of schizophrenia and other psychotic disorders. *Mailing Add:* Va Conn Healthcare Syst West Haven Campus 950 Campbell Ave West Haven CT 06516. *Fax:* 203-789-7346

SEROVY, GEORGE K(ASPAR), MECHANICAL ENGINEERING, TURBOMACHINERY. *Current Pos:* from asst prof to assoc prof mech eng, Iowa State Univ, 53-60, asst dir eng res inst, 68-72, asst to dean, Col Eng, 72-86, prof, 60-90, EMER PROF MECH ENG, IOWA STATE UNIV, 90- *Personal Data:* b Cedar Rapids, Iowa, Aug 29, 26; m 71, 90; c William, Ann, Mary, David & Dana. *Educ:* Iowa State Univ, BS, 48, MS, 50, PhD(mech eng), 58. *Honors & Awards:* Dedicated Serv Award, Am Soc Mech Engrs, 91. *Prof Exp:* Asst mech eng, Iowa State Univ, 48-49; aeronaut res scientist, Nat Adv Comt Aeronaut, 49-53. *Concurrent Pos:* Mem, Nat Acad Sci propulsion adv panel, USAF Systs Command, 69-76, US mem NATO AGARD Propulsion & Energetics panel, 87-93; Anson Marston distinguished prof, Iowa State Univ; tech ed, J turbomachinery & J Eng for Gas Turbines, 88-93; Prof invite, EPFL, Fed Inst Technol, Lausanne, Switz, 87. *Mem:* Fel Am Soc Mech Engrs; Am Inst Aeronaut & Astronaut. *Res:* Fluid mechanics of turbomachinery; aircraft propulsion; internal flow; heat transfer. *Mailing Add:* Dept Mech Eng Iowa State Univ Ames IA 50011-0001. *Fax:* 515-294-3261

SERPONE, NICK, INORGANIC & ENVIRONMENTAL PHOTOCHEMISTRY, PULSED LASER SPECTROSCOPY. *Current Pos:* assoc prof, 74-80, dir, Can Ctr Laser Spectros, 81-87, PROF PHYS INORG CHEM, CONCORDIA UNIV, 80-, DIR CONCORDIA CTR ASER SPECROS, 95- *Personal Data:* m 68, Linda G Bell; c Caterina J & Lindsey A. *Educ:* Sir George Williams Univ, BSc, 64; Cornell Univ, PhD(phys-inorg chem), 68. *Prof Exp:* Asst prof, Sir George Williams Univ, 68-73. *Concurrent Pos:* Vis prof, Univ Bologna, 75-76; res scholar, Boston Univ, 77-78, vis assoc prof, 79; vis scientist, Brookhaven Nat Lab, 79-81; invited prof, Ecole Polytech Federale Lausanne, 83-84; consult, Graphics Res Lab, 3M Co, 87-95; assoc dir res, Nat Ctr Sci Res, Ecole Centrale Lyon, 90-91, vis prof, 90-91; appointee comt, US Nat Acad Sci, 90-91. *Mem:* Am Chem Soc; Int Am Photchem Soc. *Res:* Modify and examine photophysics of various semiconductors (titanium oxide and cadmium sulfide colloids) by laser spectroscopy to probe features of charge carrier dynamics; apply charge carriers to do redox chemistry; photophysical properties of dyes and silver halides. *Mailing Add:* Dept Chem Concordia Univ Montreal PQ H3G 1M8 Can. *Fax:* 514-848-2868; *E-Mail:* serpone@vax2.concordia.ca

SERR, FREDERICK E, COMPUTER SCIENCES, DATA NETWORKS ANALYSIS. *Current Pos:* NETWORK ANALYST, BBN CORP, CAMBRIDGE, MASS, 88- *Personal Data:* b Minneapolis, Minn, July 7, 52. *Educ:* Mich State Univ, BS, 74; Stanford Univ, PhD(physics), 78. *Prof Exp:* Res assoc, Mich State Univ, 78-80; res assoc physics, Mass Inst Technol, 80-83. *Concurrent Pos:* Vis scientist, Niels Bohr, Denmark, 80-81. *Mem:* Am Phys Soc. *Res:* Wide area data communications; Hatchetts Systems technology. *Mailing Add:* BBN Corp 150 Cambridge Park Dr Cambridge MA 02140

SERRA, JERRY M, ADHESION SCIENCE, PRESSURE SENSITIVE ADHESIVE TECHNOLOGY. *Current Pos:* Res scientist, Polyken Technol Div, Kendall Co, 73-79, group leader anal, 79-82, sect head pipeline coatings, 82-85, mgr res & develop, 85-89, assoc dir res & develop, 89-93, DIR RES & DEVELOP, POLYKEN TECHNOL DIV, KENDALL CO, 93- *Personal Data:* b Boston, Mass, Mar 28, 46; m, Merri Remor; c Jerry J, Glenn P & Shawn M. *Educ:* Univ RI, BS, 68, MS, 71, PhD(biol sci), 75. *Concurrent Pos:* NSF trainee, 68-72. *Mem:* Am Chem Soc; AAAS; Soc Automotive Engrs; Nat Asn Corrosion Engrs; Soc Plastics Engrs. *Res:* Development of pressure sensitive adhesives for use in healthcare and industrial tapes and anti-corrosion coatings for steel, oil, gas and water pipelines. *Mailing Add:* 11 Clydesdale Rd Chelmsford MA 01824-1157

SERRE, JEAN-PIERRE, MATHEMATICS. *Current Pos:* PROF, COL FRANCE, 56- *Personal Data:* b Bages, France, Sept 15, 26; m 48, Josiane Heulot; c Claudine. *Educ:* Lycee de Nimes, France, Baccalaureat, 44; Ecole Normale Superieure, France, agregation, 48. *Hon Degrees:* Several from foreign univs, 78-83. *Honors & Awards:* Medaille Fields Award, Int Cong Mathematicians, 54; Balzan Prize, 85; Leroy P Steele Prize, Am Math Soc, 95. *Mem:* Foreign mem Nat Acad Sci; Neth Acad Sci. *Res:* Contributed numerous articles to professional journals. *Mailing Add:* 6 Ave de Montespan Paris 75116 France

SERRIN, JAMES B, PARTIAL DIFFERENTIAL EQUATIONS, CONTINUUM THERMOMECHANICS. *Current Pos:* from asst prof to regents prof, Univ Minn, 54-97, prof aero eng, 60-97, head, Sch Math, 64-65, EMER REGENTS PROF MATH, UNIV MINN, 97- *Personal Data:* b Evanston, Ill, Nov 1, 26; m 52, Barbara West; c 3. *Educ:* Univ Ind, PhD(math), 51. *Hon Degrees:* DSc, Univ Sussex, 72, Univ Ferrara & Univ Padova, 92. *Honors & Awards:* Birkhoff Prize, Am Math Soc, 73. *Prof Exp:* Instr math, Mass Inst Technol, 52-54. *Concurrent Pos:* Vis prof, Univ Chicago, 64 & 75 & Johns Hopkins Univ, 66; vis fel, Univ Sussex, 67, 72 & 76, Univ Modena, 88 & 90, Ga Inst Tech, 90; NSF Grant, Air Force, 71-75, 77-79, 79-82 & 82-84. *Mem:* Nat Acad Sci; Math Asn Am; Soc Natural Philos; fel AAAS; Am Math Soc; Am Acad Arts & Sci; foreign mem Finnish Acad Sci. *Res:* Partial differential equations; theoretical fluid mechanics; thermodynamics; ordinary differential equations. *Mailing Add:* Dept Math Univ Minn Minneapolis MN 55455. *Fax:* 612-626-2017; *E-Mail:* serrin@math.umn.edu

SERTH, ROBERT WILLIAM, CHEMICAL ENGINEERING. *Current Pos:* assoc prof, 78-85, PROF CHEM ENG, TEX A&M UNIV, KINGSVILLE, 85- *Personal Data:* b Rochester, NY, Aug 30, 41; m 64; c 1. *Educ:* Univ Rochester, BS, 63; State Univ NY, Buffalo, PhD(chem eng), 69; Univ Ariz, MA, 70. *Prof Exp:* Asst prof chem eng, Univ PR, 71-74; sr res engr energy & environ, Monsanto Res Corp, 74-77, res specialist, 77-78. *Mem:* Am Inst Chem Engrs; Air Pollution Control Asn; AAAS. *Res:* Fluid mechanics; rheology; applied mathematics; pollution control. *Mailing Add:* Dept Chem Eng Tex A&I Univ Santa Gertrudis Kingsville TX 78363-3479

SERVADIO, GILDO JOSEPH, FOOD SCIENCE. *Current Pos:* PRES, SERVALL INC, 86- *Personal Data:* b Ridgefield, Conn, Jan 27, 29; m 55, Norma Leard; c Lee, Maria & Carol. *Educ:* Tufts Univ, BS, 52; Univ Mass, MS, 55, PhD(food technol), 61. *Prof Exp:* Proj leader, Pillsbury Co, 55-58; instr packaging, Univ Mass, 58-61; sr scientist, Mead Johnson & Co, 61-63; res mgr, Beech-Nut Life Savers, Inc, NY, 63-65, assoc dir res, 65-67; dir res & develop labs, Heublein Inc, Hartford, 67-75, vpres res & develop labs, 75-86; dir, Baron Resources Inc, 86-93. *Concurrent Pos:* Mem, Wash Lab Comt, Nat Canners Asn, 65-86, Res & Develop Assocs, US Army Natick Labs, 65 & Distilled Spirits Inst, 69-86; chmn tech comt, Vinegar Inst, 70-86; chmn comt food protection, Grocery Mfrs Asn, 70-86. *Mem:* Inst Food Technol; Am Asn Cereal Chemists; Sigma Xi. *Res:* Food and beverage chemistry; food colorimetry; baking, infant nutrition and nutritional products technology; chemistry and processing of fruits, vegetables and formulated foods; technology of wines, beers and distilled spirits; research administration; research consultant, foods, beverages. *Mailing Add:* 10 Sagamore Dr Simsbury CT 06070

SERVAIS, RONALD ALBERT, AEROTHERMOCHEMISTRY, PROCESS MODELING. *Current Pos:* chmn, 74-81 & 87-91, prof, 81-86, PROF CHEM ENG, UNIV DAYTON, 92- *Personal Data:* b La Crosse, Wis, Apr 6, 42; m 64, Sandra K Dwyer; c Vicki & Connie. *Educ:* St Louis Univ, BS, 63, MS, 66; Washington Univ, DSc(chem eng), 69. *Prof Exp:* Assoc engr, McDonnell Aircraft Corp, 63-64, engr, 64-66; asst prof mech eng, Univ Mo, Rolla, 68-72; res scientist, USAF Mat Lab, 73-74. *Concurrent Pos:* Partner, Creative Eng Consult & Assocs, 73- *Mem:* Am Inst Aeronaut & Astronaut; Am Inst Chem Engrs; Nat Soc Prof Engrs; Am Soc Eng Educ. *Res:* Numerical solution of equations describing reacting; viscous, conducting, and diffusing flow fields, including reentry physics and air pollution modeling; aerodynamics of automobiles and trucks; performance of materials exposed to intense radiant heating; computer modeling of manufacturing processing. *Mailing Add:* 2130 Vienna Pky Univ Dayton Dayton OH 45459-1357

SERVAITES, JEROME CASIMER, PLANT PHYSIOLOGY, BIOCHEMISTRY. *Current Pos:* MEM FAC, BIOL DEPT, VA POLYTECH INST & STATE UNIV, 80- *Personal Data:* b Dayton, Ohio, Sept 15, 44. *Educ:* Univ Dayton, BS, 68, MS, 72; Univ Ill, Urbana-Champaign, PhD(biol), 76. *Prof Exp:* Teaching asst, Dept Biol, Univ Dayton, 70-72; res asst, Dept Agron, Univ Ill, 72-75, res assoc, 76; res assoc, Dept Hort, Univ Wis, 76-77, fel agron, 77-78; plant physiologist res, Sci & Educ Admin-Agr Res, USDA, 78-80. *Mem:* AAAS; Am Soc Agron; Am Soc Plant Physiol. *Res:* Photosynthetic carbon metabolism and photorespiration in crop plants; biochemical mechanisms and processes limiting yield of crop plants. *Mailing Add:* 7816 Port Circle Dayton OH 45459

SERVE, MUNSON PAUL, ORGANIC CHEMISTRY, BIOCHEMISTRY. *Current Pos:* asst prof, 65-75, PROF CHEM, WRIGHT STATE UNIV, 75- *Personal Data:* b Medina, NY, Nov 26, 39; m 69. *Educ:* Univ Notre Dame, BS, 61, PhD(org chem), 64. *Prof Exp:* Am Cancer Soc fel, Univ Chicago, 64-65. *Concurrent Pos:* Vis scientist, NIH, 75-76 & Toxic Hazards Br, USAF, 80- *Mem:* Am Chem Soc; Sigma Xi. *Res:* Photochemistry; photolysis of benzotriazoles; shift reagents in organic structure determinations; chemical toxicology of enviromental pollutants. *Mailing Add:* Dept Org Biochem Wright State Univ Dayton OH 45435

SERVI, LESLIE D, PERFORMANCE ANALYSIS. *Current Pos:* sr mem, 83-87, PRIN MEM, TECH STAFF, GTE LABS, 87- *Personal Data:* b Buffalo, NY, July 27, 55; c Amelia & Joseph. *Educ:* Brown Univ, BS & MS, 77; Harvard Univ, MS, 78, PhD(appl sci), 81. *Prof Exp:* Mem tech staff, Mitre Corp, 77, AT&T Bell Labs, 78, Dept Teletraffic Theory & Appln, Bell Labs, 81-83. *Concurrent Pos:* Chmn invited sessions, Oper Res Soc Am & Inst Mgt Sci, 86-93; secy, Telecommun Col, Oper Res Soc Am, 87-89, chair elect, 92, coun mem, Appl Probability Col, 90; vis scientist, Mass Inst Technol & Harvard Univ, 89-90. *Mem:* Oper Res Soc Am; sr mem Inst Elec & Electronics Engrs; Int Reference Orgn Forensic Med & Sci. *Res:* Applied probability; communications; optimal control; performance analysis, operations research. *Mailing Add:* GTE Labs Inc 40 Sylvan Rd Waltham MA 02254. *E-Mail:* lds@gte.com

SERVIS, KENNETH L, PHYSICAL CHEMISTRY, ORGANIC CHEMISTRY. *Current Pos:* from asst prof to assoc prof, 65-84, PROF CHEM, UNIV SOUTHERN CALIF, 84-, DEAN ACAD REC & REGISTR, 89- *Personal Data:* b Indianapolis, Ind, July 27, 39; m 68, Harriet F Struck; c Brian, Pamela & Laura M. *Educ:* Purdue Univ, BS, 61; Calif Inst Technol, PhD(chem), 65. *Prof Exp:* Am-Yugoslavia Cultural Exchange fel, Rudjer Boskovic Inst, Univ Zagreb, Yugoslavia, 64-65. *Concurrent Pos:* Alfred P Sloan fel, 69-71; Guggenheim fel, 73-74; Fulbright Hays Award, Univ Zagreb, 74. *Mem:* Am Chem Soc; Int Soc Magnetic; Croatian Chem Soc. *Res:* Structure and reactivity of organic compounds; molecular rearrangements; nuclear magnetic resonance spectroscopy. *Mailing Add:* 14 Gaucho Dr Rolling Hills Estates CA 90274

SERVIS, ROBERT EUGENE, BIO-ORGANIC CHEMISTRY. *Current Pos:* RES SCIENTIST, DEPT MED RES, BLODGETT MED CTR, 74- *Personal Data:* b Lansing, Mich, June 28, 41; m 69. *Educ:* Univ Mich, BS, 63; NY Univ, MS, 66, PhD(chem), 69, MD, 74. *Prof Exp:* Res scientist, NY Univ, 69-74. *Mem:* AAAS; Am Chem Soc; NY Acad Sci; Am Inst Chemists. *Res:* Natural products; alkaloids; bioorganic chemistry; gas chromatography; mass spectrometry of biological materials. *Mailing Add:* 1275 Essex Dr Luzern MI 48936

SERVOS, KURT, MINERALOGY. *Current Pos:* RETIRED. *Personal Data:* b Anrath, Ger, Dec 20, 28; nat US. *Educ:* Rutgers Univ, BS, 52; Yale Univ, MS, 54. *Prof Exp:* Sr cur geol, NY State Mus, 56-57; asst prof mineral, Stanford Univ, 57-60; independent geologist, 60-67; prof geol, Menlo Col, 67-90. *Concurrent Pos:* Geologist, Stanford Res Inst, 65-67. *Mem:* Mineral Soc Am; Am Crystallog Asn; Mineral Asn Can; Geol Soc Am; Am Geophys Union; Int Asn Geochem and Cosmochen. *Res:* Crystallography. *Mailing Add:* 1281 Mills St No 9 Menlo Park CA 94025-3264. *E-Mail:* kurtseryos@aol.com

SERWAY, RAYMOND A, SOLID STATE PHYSICS. *Current Pos:* prof & head dept, 80-86, PROF PHYSICS, JAMES MADISON UNIV, 86- *Personal Data:* b Frankfort, NY, June 26, 36; m 59; c 4. *Educ:* Syracuse Univ, BA, 59; Univ Colo, MS, 61; Ill Inst Technol, PhD(physics), 67. *Prof Exp:* Teaching asst physics, Univ Colo, 59-61; res physicist, Rome Air Develop Ctr, 61-63; assoc physicist, IIT Res Inst, 63-67; from asst prof to prof physics, Clarkson Univ, 67-80. *Concurrent Pos:* Vis guest scientist, Argonne Nat Lab, 73; vis guest prof, IBM Zurich Res Lab, Switz, 74. *Mem:* AAAS; Am Phys Soc; Am Asn Physics Teachers; Sigma Xi. *Res:* Thin-film solar cells and semiconducting solar cell materials exhibiting the photovoltaic effect; magnetic resonance spectroscopy; electron spin resonance absorption spectroscopy in inorganic systems; paramagnetic defect centers in irradiated solids; crystalline field splitting; structure of inorganic molecules. *Mailing Add:* Dept Physics James Madison Univ Harrisonburg VA 22807

SERWER, PHILIP, VIROLOGY, MACROMOLECULE FRACTIONATION. *Current Pos:* asst prof, 76-81, assoc prof, 81-85, PROF BIOCHEM, UNIV TEX HEALTH SCI CTR, SAN ANTONIO, 85- *Personal Data:* b Brooklyn, NY, Feb 5, 42; m 66; c 3. *Educ:* Univ Rochester, AB, 63; NY Med Col, MS, 68; Harvard Univ, PhD(biophysics), 73. *Prof Exp:* Fel res, Calif Inst Technol, 72-75, sr res fel, 75-76. *Concurrent Pos:* Sci Adv Bd, FMC Prod; Coun Electrophoresis Soc; Human Genome Study Sect, NIH. *Mem:* Am Soc Virologists; Electrophoresis Soc; Biophys Soc; Am Soc Biol Chemists; Electron Micros Soc Am. *Res:* Structure and assembly of viruses; structure and sieving of gels; fractionation of DNA; mutagenesis; detection and isolation of viruses and viral precursors. *Mailing Add:* Dept Biochem Univ Tex Health Sci Ctr 7703 Floyd Curl Dr San Antonio TX 78284-7760. *Fax:* 210-567-6595

SESCO, JERRY ANTHONY, FORESTRY, ECONOMICS. *Current Pos:* From forester to res forester, 63-74, PROJ LEADER, N CENT FOREST EXP STA, US FOREST SERV, 74- *Personal Data:* b Pensacola, Fla, July 26, 39; m 61; c 2. *Educ:* Univ Ga, BS, 61; Auburn Univ, MS, 62; Southern Ill Univ, PhD(econ), 74. *Mem:* Soc Am Foresters; Forest Prod Res Soc; Sigma Xi; Am Econ Asn. *Res:* Forest products marketing and economics. *Mailing Add:* Forest Serv Off of Chief PO Box 960900 Washington DC 20090-6090

SESHADRI, KALKUNTE S, PHYSICAL CHEMISTRY. *Current Pos:* SCIENTIST, EG&G, TECH SERV WVA, 85- *Personal Data:* b Jagalur, India, May 11, 24; m 51, Champaka; c Viji R & Veena. *Educ:* Mysore Univ, BSc, 45, MSc, 47; Ore State Univ, PhD(phys chem), 60. *Prof Exp:* Lectr chem, Cent Col, Bangalore, 45-56; lectr phys chem, Maharani's Col, Mysore, 60; fel Nat Res Coun Can, 60-62; res assoc, Ohio State Univ, 62-66; res chemist, Gulf Res & Develop Co, 66-68, sr res chemist, 68-83; consult, Univ Pittsburgh, 83-85. *Mem:* Am Chem Soc. *Res:* Infrared molecular structure determination, intensity measurement and band shape analysis; surface and catalytic studies by magnetic resonance and optical spectroscopic techniques; study of coal, coal liquids, shale oils, coaltar and polymer by proton, carbon-13, silicon-29, fluorine-19 and nitrogen-15 nuclear magnetic resonance spectroscopy and fourier transform infrared spectroscopy; high performance liquid chromatography, gas chromatography, supercritical fluid chromatography and mass spectroscopy of synthetic and natural fuels. *Mailing Add:* 1244 Parkview Dr Morgantown WV 26505-3245

SESHADRI, RANGASWAMY, MECHANICAL ENGINEERING. *Current Pos:* DEAN FAC, ENG & APPL SCI, MEMORIAL UNIV, NFLD, 93- *Personal Data:* b Madras, India, Aug 27, 45; m 75, Sherry Middleton; c Jagan N & Jana K. *Educ:* Univ Jabalpur, India, BEng, 67; Indian Inst Technol, ThM, 69; Univ Calgary, MSc & PhD, 74. *Prof Exp:* Proj engr, EBA Eng Consults, 74; intermediate engr, Assoc Eng Servs Ltd, 77; sr engr, Syncrude Can Ltd, Edmonton, eng assoc, 78; from assoc prof to prof eng, Univ Regina, 87-93, dean, 89-93. *Concurrent Pos:* Pres & dir, Dynatek Eng Corp. *Mem:* Am Soc Mech Engrs; Can Soc Mech Engrs. *Res:* Group invariance in engineering boundary value problems. *Mailing Add:* Fac Eng & Appl Sci Memorial Univ Nfld St John's NF A1B 3X5 Can. *Fax:* 709-737-8975

SESHADRI, SENGADU RANGASWAMY, APPLIED PHYSICS, ELECTRICAL ENGINEERING. *Current Pos:* PROF ELEC ENG, UNIV WIS-MADISON, 67- *Personal Data:* b Madras City, India, Oct 25, 28; m 59, Susheela. *Educ:* Madras Univ, MA, 51; Indian Inst Sci, Bangalore, dipl, 53; Harvard Univ, PhD(appl physics), 59. *Prof Exp:* Lectr electronics, Madras Inst Tech, 53-55; res fel appl physics, Harvard Univ, 59-60 & 61-63; prin sci officer, Electronics Res & Develop Estab, Bangalore, 60-61; consult, Appl Res Lab, Sylvania Elec Prod Inc, Mass, 62-63, sr eng specialist, 63-67. *Concurrent Pos:* Vis prof, Univ Toronto, 65; NSF sr fel, Calif Inst Technol, 70-71; vis scientist, G A Technologies Inc, 82-83; fel, Japan Soc Prom. *Mem:* Optical Soc Am. *Res:* Surface waves; antennas in anisotropic media; plasma instabilities; nonlinear waves; microsonics; magnetic waves devices; optical waveguide theory; metal surfaces; optics. *Mailing Add:* Univ Wis-Madison 2440 Eng Hall 1415 Engvn Dr Madison WI 53706-1691. *Fax:* 608-262-1267; *E-Mail:* seshadri@engr.wisc.edu

SESHADRI, VANAMAMALAI, MATHEMATICAL STATISTICS. *Current Pos:* assoc prof, 65-70, PROF MATH, MCGILL UNIV, 70- *Personal Data:* b Madras, India, Apr 25, 28; m 49; c 2. *Educ:* Univ Madras, BA, 50, MA, 57; Okla State Univ, PhD, 61. *Prof Exp:* Teacher, Pub Schs, Ceylon, 50-54; asst lectr math, Mandalay Univ, 54-57; asst, Okla State Univ, 57-60; asst prof, Southern Methodist Univ, 60-62; asst prof math statist, 62-64. *Mem:* Am Statist Asn; Inst Math Statist. *Res:* Statistical inference; distribution theory, characterization of distributions; applications of characterization to goodness of fit. *Mailing Add:* Dept Math McGill Univ 805 Sherbrooke St W Rm 1005 Montreal PQ H3A 2K6 Can

SESONSKE, ALEXANDER, NUCLEAR ENGINEERING, CHEMICAL ENGINEERING. *Current Pos:* assoc prof, 54-58, prof, 58-86, EMER PROF, NUCLEAR & CHEM ENG, PURDUE UNIV, 86- *Personal Data:* b Gloversville, NY, June 20, 21; wid; c Michael J & Jana L. *Educ:* Rensselaer Polytech Inst, BChE, 42; Univ Rochester, MS, 47; Univ Del, PhD(chem eng), 50. *Honors & Awards:* Compton Award, Am Nuclear Soc, 87. *Prof Exp:* Chem engr, Chem Construct Corp, 42-43; res assoc, S A M Labs, Columbia Univ, 43; chem engr, Houdaille-Hershey Corp, 43-45; res engr, Columbia Chem Div, Pittsburgh Plate Glass Co, 45-46; mem staff, Los Alamos Sci Lab, Univ Calif, 50-54. *Concurrent Pos:* Mem staff, Los Alamos Sci Lab, 58-59, consult, 60-62; mem rev comt, Argonne Nat Lab, 65-68 & 75-81; consult, Oak Ridge Nuclear Lab, 62-65, United Nuclear Corp, 63 & Elec Power Res Inst, 73; independent consult, 86- *Mem:* Fel Am Nuclear Soc; Am Soc Eng Educ; Am Inst Chem Engrs. *Res:* Nuclear reactor engineering; heat transfer; nuclear fuel cycle analysis. *Mailing Add:* 16408 Felice Dr San Diego CA 92128-2804. *E-Mail:* 72440.371@compuserve.com

SESSA, DAVID JOSEPH, PROTEIN SCIENCE, POLYMER CHEMISTRY. *Current Pos:* Assoc chemist, Agr Res Serv, USDA, 63-68, RES CHEMIST, NAT CTR AGR UTILIZATION RES, 68- *Personal Data:* b Hackensack, NJ, Mar 3, 38; m 86, Virginia L Brand; c Brian, Valerie, Kenneth, Jennifer, Belinda & Michelle. *Educ:* Tufts Univ, BS, 59. *Concurrent Pos:* Chmn, protein & co-prod sect, Am Oil Chemists Soc, 84-85, 85-86. *Mem:* Am Chem Soc; Am Oil Chemists Soc; NAm Thermal Anal Soc. *Res:* Physico-chemical changes in proteins under low moisture; extrusion processing; fundamental and applied research on biobased materials to develop value-added products; molecular basis of functionality; protein interactions and derivitization. *Mailing Add:* Nat Ctr Agr Utilization Res 1815 N University St Peoria IL 61604-3902. *Fax:* 309-681-6686; *E-Mail:* sessadj@ncaur1.ncaur.gov

SESSA, GRAZIA L, BIOCHEMISTRY. *Current Pos:* asst prof pharmacol, 70-75, SPEC TRAINING DIR LAB, MT SINAI HOSP, 75-; DIR, CORE LABELING & COMPLIANCE, JOHNSON PHARM INST, 92- *Personal Data:* b Italy; US citizen; m; c 2. *Educ:* Univ Rome, PhD(biol), 58. *Prof Exp:* Fel, Brit Cancer Campaign, Oxford, 60-63; Fulbright scholar, Res Inst Pub Health, New York, 63-64; res fel, Sch Med, NY Univ, 64-65, asst res scientist, 65-67, asst prof microbiol, 68-70; asst prof pharmacol, 70-75, SPEC TRAINING DIR LAB, MT SINAI HOSP, 75- *Concurrent Pos:* Dir, Clin Lab Training, Mt Sinai Hosp, 70-79; mem staff clin chem, Monmouth Med Ctr, Long Branch, NY, 79-81; mem staff, Merck Int Div, 81-92. *Res:* Interaction of drugs with brain membranes; functions of the blood-brain barrier. *Mailing Add:* Johnson Pharm Inst Rte 202 PO Box 300 Raritan NJ 08869-0602

SESSIONS, JOHN TURNER, JR, MEDICINE, DIGESTIVE DISEASES & NUTRITION. *Current Pos:* from asst prof to assoc prof, 52-64, PROF MED, SCH MED, UNIV NC, CHAPEL HILL, 64- *Personal Data:* b Atlanta, Ga, July 8, 22; m 50, Nina Cataliotte. *Educ:* Emory Univ, BS, 43, MD, 45; Am Bd Gastroenterol, dipl, 68. *Prof Exp:* Intern, Kings County Hosp, Brooklyn, 45-46; intern & resident, Grady Mem Hosp, Atlanta, 48-50; asst med, Sch Med, Boston Univ, 50-52. *Concurrent Pos:* Res assoc, Evans Mem Hosp, Boston, 50-52; mem training comt gastroenterol & nutrit, Nat Inst Arthritis, Metab & Digestive Dis, 68-; ed, Viewpoints Digestive Dis, 68- *Mem:* AAAS; Am Col Physicians; Am Gastroenterol Asn; Am Fedn Clin Res; Am Asn Study Liver Dis; Am Clin & Climat Asn. *Res:* Biochemical and physiologic aspects of gastroenterology and hepatology. *Mailing Add:* Dept Med Burnett-Womack Bldg Rm 318 Univ NC Sch Med Chapel Hill NC 27514. *Fax:* 919-966-6842; *E-Mail:* jts@unc.edu

SESSLE, BARRY JOHN, NEUROPHYSIOLOGY, ORAL BIOLOGY. *Current Pos:* assoc prof dent, Fac Med, Univ Toronto, 71-76, chmn, Div Biol Sci, 77-85, assoc dean res, 85-90, PROF, FAC DENT & PROF PHYSIOL, FAC MED, UNIV TORONTO, 77-, DEAN, 90- *Personal Data:* b Sydney, Australia, May 28, 41; m 67, Mary Baldwin; c Erica & Claire. *Educ:* Univ Sydney, BDS, 63, BSc & MDS, 65; Univ NSW, PhD(physiol), 69. *Honors & Awards:* Oral Sci Award, Int Asn Dent Res, 76, J Pindborg Int Prize Oral Biol, 94. *Prof Exp:* Fel physiol, Med Sch, Univ NSW, 65-68; vis assoc orofacial neurophysiol, Nat Inst Dent Res, 68-70. *Concurrent Pos:* Mem, Dent Sci Grants Comt, Can Med Res Coun, 79-82; prin investr, Can Med Res Coun grants, 71-, NIH grants, 74-; vis prof, Can Med Res Coun, Univ BC, 80, Univ Alta, 85, Univ Montreal, 86, Laval Univ, 86, McGill Univ, 86; Japan

Soc Prom Sci Fel, 80; pres, Can Asn Dent Res, 77-78; secy, Can Pain Soc, 82-87; pres, Neurosci Group, Int Asn Dent Res, 85-86. *Mem:* Int Asn Study Pain; Soc Neurosci; Int Asn Dent Res (vpres, 92-93, pres elect, 93-94, pres, 94-95); Can Physiol Soc; Can Acad Sci; fel Roy Soc Can. *Res:* Neural basis of facial and oropharyngeal function; general sensory and motor neurophysiology; perceptual and behavioral correlates; co-editor of sex books, co-author of one book and author of 177 journal papers. *Mailing Add:* Fac Dent Univ Toronto Toronto ON M5G 1G6 Can

SESSLER, ANDREW M, THEORETICAL PHYSICS. *Current Pos:* theoret physicist, 61-73, dir, 73-80, THEORET PHYSICIST, LAWRENCE BERKELEY LAB, UNIV CALIF, 80-, DISTINGUISHED SR SCIENTIST, 94- *Personal Data:* b Brooklyn, NY, Dec 11, 28; m 51; c 3. *Educ:* Harvard Univ, BA, 49; Columbia Univ, MS, 51, PhD(physics), 53. *Honors & Awards:* E O Lawrence Award, 70; US Particle Accelerator Sch Prize, 88; Leland J Haworth Distinguished Scientist, Brookhaven Nat Lab, 91-92; Nicholson Medal, Am Phys Soc, 94, Wilson Prize, 97. *Prof Exp:* Asst physics, Columbia Univ, 49-52; NSF fel, Cornell Univ, 53-54; from asst prof to assoc prof physics, Ohio State Univ, 54-61. *Concurrent Pos:* Mem high energy physics adv panel, US AEC, 69-72; mem comt on high energy physics, Argonne Univ, 71-73; chmn sci policy bd, Stanford Synchrotron Radiation Lab, 76-78; chmn advan fuels adv comt, Elec Power Res Inst, 78-81; chmn comt on Isabelle, Brookhaven Nat Lab, 80-82; mem review comt, Plasma Physics Lab, Princeton Univ, 81-85; mem comt concerned sci coun, 84-87; Japan Soc Prom Sci Fel, 85; mem Study Directed Energy Weapons, Am Phys Soc, 85-86; mem Fed Am Sci Coun, 79-82, 85-88, vchmn, 87-88, chmn, 88-; chmn panel pub affairs, Am Phys Soc, 88, vchmn, 87; mem comt appln physics, Am Phys Soc, 91-93; mem bd dir, AUI, 91-94; mem sci policy bd, SSRL, 91-96; mem coun, sci soc pres, 97. *Mem:* Nat Acad Sci; fel Am Phys Soc (pres-elect, 97); Sigma Xi; fel AAAS; sr mem Inst Elec & Electronics Engrs. *Res:* Theory of particle accelerators; plasma physics. *Mailing Add:* Lawrence Berkeley Lab Univ Calif MS 71-259 Berkeley CA 94720. *E-Mail:* tbalbl@lbl.gov

SESSLER, DANIEL I, ANESTHESIOLOGY. *Current Pos:* PROF ANESTHESIOL, DIR OUTCOMES RES GROUP, UNIV CALIF, SAN FRANCISCO, 96-; PROF & VCHAIR ANESTHESIOL & INTENSIVE CARE, UNIV VIENNA, 96- *Personal Data:* b Columbus, Ohio, Dec 25, 54. *Educ:* Columbia Univ, NY, MD, 80; Am Bd Pediat, cert, 85; Am Bd Anesthesiol, cert, 87. *Concurrent Pos:* Lectr, 81-96; Fulbright scholar, 96-97. *Mem:* Asn Univ Anesthesiologists; Am Soc Clin Invest. *Mailing Add:* Dept Anesthesia Univ Calif San Francisco CA 94143-0648. *Fax:* 415-476-8444

SESSLER, GERHARD MARTIN, ELECTROACOUSTIC TRANSDUCERS, ELECTRETS. *Current Pos:* PROF ELEC ENG, TECH UNIV DARMSTADT, 75- *Personal Data:* b Rosenfeld, Ger, Feb 15, 31; m 61, Renate Schulz; c Cornelia, Christine & Gunther. *Educ:* Univ Munich, Ger, Vordiplom, 53; Univ Goettingen, Ger, Diplom, 57, Dr rer nat(physics), 59. *Honors & Awards:* Callinan Award, Electrochem Soc, 70; Dakin Award, Inst Elec & Electronics Engrs Dielectrics Soc, 86; Helmholtz Award, Deutsche Gesellschaft Akustik, 93; George R Stibitz Award, AT&T; Helmholtz Rayleigh Interdisciplinary Medal, Acoust Soc Am, 97. *Prof Exp:* Mem tech staff, Bell Labs, Murray Hill, NJ, 59-65, supvr, 66-75. *Concurrent Pos:* Consult, Bell Labs, Murray Hill, NJ, 75-88, 91-92, IBM Res Lab, San Jose, Calif, 84; vis prof, Tongji Univ, Shanghai, China, 81-87, consult prof, 87. *Mem:* Fel Inst Elec & Electronics Engrs; fel Acoust Soc Am; Am Phys Soc. *Res:* Electroacoustic sensors, particularly the capacitive and piezoelectric type; materials research, particularly in organic and inorganic electrets and in piezoelectric polymers. *Mailing Add:* Fichtestrasse 30 B 64285 Darmstadt Germany. *Fax:* 49-6151-165545; *E-Mail:* ses@uet.th-darmstadt.de

SESSLER, JOHN CHARLES, physics, operations research, for more information see previous edition

SESSLER, JOHN GEORGE, MECHANICAL ENGINEERING, METALLURGICAL ENGINEERING. *Current Pos:* consult, 72-76, TECH CONSULT, ENGR PROD LIABILITY & ACCIDENT RECONSTRUCT, 76- *Personal Data:* b Syracuse, NY, Apr 8, 20; m 53, Phyllis Long; c Laurels, Robert, Michael, John & Marita. *Educ:* Syracuse Univ, BS, 50, MS, 62. *Honors & Awards:* NASA Minor Award, 68. *Prof Exp:* Res engr, Syracuse Univ, 50-60, sr res engr, 60-72. *Mem:* Am Soc Testing & Mat; Am Inst Mining, Metall & Petrol Engrs; Am Soc Metals. *Res:* Mechanical behavior of metals and alloys, including creep, fatigue, notch behavior and fracture. *Mailing Add:* 121 Jean Ave Syracuse NY 13210

SESSLER, JONATHAN LAWRENCE, LIGAND DESIGN & SYNTHESIS, MOLECULAR RECOGNITION. *Current Pos:* from asst prof to assoc prof, 84-91, PROF CHEM, UNIV TEX, 92- *Personal Data:* b Urbanna, Ill, May 20, 5e; m 89, Carol Rubel; c Jordan & Chanan. *Educ:* Univ Calif, Berkeley, BS, 77; Stanford Univ, PhD(org chem), 82. *Honors & Awards:* Presidential Young Investr, NSF, 86; Teacher-Scholar Award, Camille & Henry Dreyfus Found, 88; Arthur C Cope Scholar Award, Am Chem Soc, 91. *Prof Exp:* Fel org chem, Univ Louis Pasteur, Strasbourg, 83 & Kyoto Univ, 84. *Concurrent Pos:* Chmn sci adv bd, Pharmacyclics Inc, 91-; vis sr scientist, Japanese Soc Prom Sci, 92; sr scientist, Von Humboldt Stifung, 92-94. *Mem:* Am Chem Soc. *Res:* Ligand design and synthesis; molecular recognition via base pairing; covalent and non-covalent models for electron transfer; development of expanded porphyrin chemistry; radiation and photodynamic therapy sensitizers based on texaphyrins. *Mailing Add:* Dept Chem & Biochem Univ Tex Austin TX 78712. *Fax:* 512-471-7550; *E-Mail:* sessler@mail.utexas.edu

SESTANJ, KAZIMIR, ORGANIC CHEMISTRY, MEDICINAL CHEMISTRY. *Current Pos:* RETIRED. *Personal Data:* b Zagreb, Yugoslavia, Nov 11, 27; Can citizen; wid. *Educ:* Univ Zagreb, dipl, 55, PhD(org chem), 61. *Prof Exp:* Res chemist, Pliva Pharmaceut & Chem Works, Yugoslavia, 54-63; res photochem, Harvard Univ, 63-64; fel synthetic carcinostatics, Children's Cancer Res Found, Boston, Mass, 64-65; res chemist, Ayerst Labs Div, Ayerst, Mckenna & Harrison Ltd, 65-94, sect head, Chem Dept, Wyeth-Ayerst Res, Princeton, NJ, 83-94. *Concurrent Pos:* Sect head chem dept, Ayerst, McKenna & Harrison Ltd, 80-83. *Mem:* Am Chem Soc. *Res:* Synthetic organic chemistry; peptide synthesis; drug metabolism; chemistry of odors; synthetic pharmaceuticals; inhibitors aldose reductase. *Mailing Add:* 6890 E Sunrise Dr 120-204 Tucson AZ 85750-0840

SETCHELL, JOHN STANFORD, JR, ELECTRICAL CONTACTS, COLOR SYSTEMS. *Current Pos:* Physicist mfg technol, Eastman Kodak Co, 69-73, sr physicist, 74-78, proj physicist mfg technol, 79-82, supvr engr copy prod, 83-84, proj engr electronic photog, 85-89, proj mgr printer prod, 90-91, COLOR SYSTS ENGR, EASTMAN KODAK CO, 91- *Personal Data:* b Brooklyn, NY, Dec 4, 42; m 65, Cynthia Andreasen; c Anitra L. *Educ:* Rensselaer Polytech Inst, BS, 63; Univ Ill, MS, 69. *Mem:* Am Soc Testing & Mat; Am Sci Affil. *Res:* Physics of electrical contacts; electrophotographic process control; thermal diffusion dye transfer printing; color science. *Mailing Add:* 376 English Rd Rochester NY 14616. *Fax:* 716-253-1991; *E-Mail:* setchell@ssd.kodak.com

SETH, BRIJ B, STRUCTURE-PROPERTY CORRELATION, MATERIALS BEHAVIOR. *Current Pos:* adv engr, Westinghouse Elec Corp, 69-70, mgr mat develop, 70-74, mat eng, 74-79, L P Disc, 79-83 & diag, 83-86, consult engr, 84-91, mgr mat & comput systs, 91-96, MGR MAT ENG, WESTINGHOUSE ELEC CORP, 96- *Personal Data:* b Udaipur, India, Sept 4, 38; US citizen; m 65, Pushpa; c Monisha A & Naveen B. *Educ:* Univ Rajasthan, India, BSc, 58; Indian Inst Sci, BE, 60; Univ Toronto, Can, MASc, 62 PhD(metall eng), 64. *Prof Exp:* Group leader res & develop, Atlas Steel Co, 64-69. *Concurrent Pos:* Lectr, Univ Toronto, 61-64; prin investr, numerous projs, 65-90; secy comt res, Can Inst Mining & Metall, 68-69; chmn, Power Activ Comt, Am Soc Metals, 79-81. *Mem:* Fel Am Soc Metals; Am Soc Mech Engrs. *Res:* New materials and processes to enhance the reliability of steam turbines and application of quantitative techniques to optimize the use of materials; fracture mechanics; failure investigations; advanced high temperature materials. *Mailing Add:* 1641 Indian Dance Ct Maitland FL 32751. *Fax:* 407-281-5080

SETH, KAMAL KISHORE, NUCLEAR & PARTICLE PHYSICS. *Current Pos:* from asst prof to assoc prof, 61-74, PROF PHYSICS, NWESTERN UNIV, EVANSTON, 74- *Personal Data:* b Lucknow, India, Mar 10, 33; m 62, Frances Phillips; c 3. *Educ:* Univ Lucknow, BSc, 51 & 53, MSc, 54; Univ Pittsburgh, PhD(physics), 57. *Prof Exp:* Lectr, Univ Pittsburgh, 54-56; res assoc, Brookhaven Nat Lab, 56-57 & Duke Univ, 57-61. *Concurrent Pos:* Vis scientist, Saclay Nuclear Res Ctr, France, 67; vis prof, Univ Tokyo, 71, Univ Torino, Italy & Infotron Sys Corp; consult, Oak Ridge Assocs Univs, Lewis Res Lab, NASA & Oak Ridge Nat Lab. *Mem:* Fel Am Phys Soc. *Res:* Nuclear structure, low and medium energy nuclear spectroscopy; pion spectroscopy; antiproton induced reactions; nuclear and particle physics of strong interactions using electron and hadron probes; quark and glluon spectroscopy. *Mailing Add:* Dept Physics Northwestern Univ Evanston IL 60208

SETH, MOHAN S, SIMULATION OF SUB-SURFACE MULTIPHASE FLOW, SOLUTION OF LARGE LINEAR SPARSE EQUATIONS. *Current Pos:* PRES, TECH SOFTWARE & ENG, 73- *Personal Data:* b Udaipur, India, July 22, 36; m 57, Gina L Vlado; c Raju & Rohini. *Educ:* Univ Rajasthan India, BS, 57; Indian Sch Mines, MS, 60; Univ Tex, PhD(petrol eng), 66. *Prof Exp:* Sr res scientist res engr, Arco, Plano, Tex, 66-71; mgr, Europ Opers, Intercomp Resource Develop, 71-73; pres, Tech Software & Eng Inc, 73-92; vpres/mgr petrol technol, Maxwell Labs Inc, 92-93. *Concurrent Pos:* Exec vpres, Arab Petrol Consult, 76-79. *Mem:* Soc Petrol Engrs; Geothermal Res Coun. *Res:* Development of mathematical models for simulating flow of oil, gas and geothermal energy in reservoirs; employing novel gridding and numerical algorithms. *Mailing Add:* 2506 Springwood Lane Richardson TX 75082. *Fax:* 972-699-1211; *E-Mail:* mseth@metronet.com

SETH, RAJINDER SINGH, PULP & PAPER TECHNOLOGY. *Current Pos:* res scientist, 71-77, sr scientist & head, Fibre & Paper Physics Sect, Pointe Claire Lab, 77-86, HEAD, FIBRE & PROD QUAL SECT, PULP & PAPER RES INST CAN, VANCOUVER LAB, 87- *Personal Data:* b Lahore, India, June 11, 37; Can citizen; wid; c Arvind & Anita. *Educ:* Panjab Univ, India, BSc, 57, MSc, 58; Univ Alberta, Can, PhD(physics), 69. *Honors & Awards:* Weldon Medal, Can Paper Asn, 84. *Prof Exp:* Lectr, DAV Col, India, 58-60, Govt Col, India, 60-64; sr res physicist, Consolidated Bathurst Inc, Can, 69-71. *Mem:* Mat Res Soc; fel Tech Asn Pulp & Paper Indust; Can Pulp & Paper Asn; Am Phys Soc. *Res:* Structure and physical properties of wood pulp fibres and paper. *Mailing Add:* Pulp & Paper Res Inst Can 3800 Wesbrook Mall Vancouver BC V6S 2L9 Can. *Fax:* 604-222-3207; *E-Mail:* seth_raj@vanlab.paprican.ca

SETH, SHARAD CHANDRA, COMPUTER SCIENCE, ELECTRICAL ENGINEERING. *Current Pos:* From asst prof to assoc prof, 72-83, PROF COMPUT SCI, UNIV NEBR, LINCOLN, 83- *Personal Data:* b Madhya Pradesh, India, Nov 1, 42. *Educ:* Univ Jabalpur, BE, 64; Indian Inst Technol, Kanpur, MTech, 66; Univ Ill, Urbana, PhD(elec eng), 70. *Concurrent Pos:* Vis prof IIT Kanpur, India, 74-75, 82-83; consult, Bell Labs, GTE, RPI, NIH & US West. *Mem:* Asn Comput Mach; Inst Elec & Electronics Engrs. *Res:* Design and maintenance of reliable digital systems; document analysis of optically scanned images. *Mailing Add:* Dept Comput Sci & Eng Univ Nebr Ferguson Hall Lincoln NE 68588

SETHARES, GEORGE C, MATHEMATICS. *Current Pos:* assoc prof, 73-80, PROF MATH, BRIDGEWATER STATE COL, 80- *Personal Data:* b Hyannis, Mass, Oct 16, 30; m 52; c 4. *Educ:* Boston Univ, BMus, 53; Univ Mass, MA, 59; Harvard Univ, PhD(math), 67. *Prof Exp:* Instr math, Boston Univ, 59-64; res mathematician, Air Force Cambridge Res Labs, 64-73. *Concurrent Pos:* Lectr, Northeastern Univ, 67-68. *Res:* Analytic function theory; Teichmuller mappings; network theory; automata theory; computer science. *Mailing Add:* Dept Math & Comput Sci Bridgewater State Col Bridgewater MA 02325

SETHARES, JAMES C(OSTAS), PHYSICIST, ELECTRICAL ENGINEERING. *Current Pos:* RETIRED. *Personal Data:* b Hyannis, Mass, Dec 13, 28; m 73, Janet Jarvis; c William, Marilyn & Andrea. *Educ:* Univ Mass, BSEE, 59; Mass Inst Technol, SMEE, 62. *Prof Exp:* Teaching asst elec eng, Mass Inst Technol, 59-62, pres, NDE, 78-88; res physicist, Microwave Physics Lab, Air Force Cambridge Res Labs, 62-89. *Concurrent Pos:* Lectr, Boston Univ, 60-63 & Lowell Technol Inst, 63-69; consult, NDE Asn Inc, 78- *Mem:* Inst Elec & Electronics Engrs. *Res:* Microwave magnetics research; liquid crystal displays for microwaves, millimeter waves and infrared. *Mailing Add:* 75 Lake St Cotuit MA 02635. *E-Mail:* jseth@ccsnet.com

SETHER, LOWELL ALBERT, ANATOMY. *Current Pos:* Asst prof, 64-74, ASSOC PROF ANAT, MED COL WIS, 74- *Personal Data:* b Iola, Wis, Aug 5, 31; m 63; c 3. *Educ:* Concordia Col, Minn, BA, 60; Univ NDak, MS, 62, PhD(anat), 64. *Concurrent Pos:* Consult, 25th ed, Dorlands Med Dictionary. *Res:* Cross sectional anatomy and imaging. *Mailing Add:* Dept Anat Med Col Wis 8701 Watertown Plank Milwaukee WI 53226-3548

SETHI, DHANWANT S, PHYSICAL CHEMISTRY. *Current Pos:* LAB DIR, ENVIROANALYTICAL INC, 91- *Personal Data:* b Rawalpindi, WPakistan, Dec 13, 37; m 66; c 2. *Educ:* Delhi Col, BSc, 56; Hindu Col, MSc, 58; NY Univ, PhD(chem), 67. *Prof Exp:* Jr sci officer, AEC, India, 58-59; tech asst chem, Dir Gen Health Servs, India, 59-62; lectr, NY Univ, 66-67; NSF vis scientist, Nat Ctr Atmospheric Res, Colo, 68-69; asst res geophysicist, Inst Geophys, Univ Calif, Los Angeles, 69; prof chem, Univ Bridgeport, 69-91, chmn dept, 80-91. *Concurrent Pos:* Res collab, Brookhaven Nat Lab, 72- *Mem:* AAAS; Am Chem Soc; Air Pollution Control Asn. *Res:* Gas phase kinetics, photochemistry, flash photolysis and kinetic absorption spectroscopy. *Mailing Add:* Enviroanal Inc 627 Main St Monroe CT 06468-2809

SETHI, ISHWAR KRISHAN, COMPUTER VISION & VISUAL INFORMATION SYSTEMS, PATTERN RECOGNITION. *Current Pos:* asst prof, 82-85, assoc prof, 85-92, PROF COMPUT SCI, WAYNE STATE UNIV, 92- *Personal Data:* b India, Jan 30, 48; m 75, Suman; c Rahul & Saurabh. *Educ:* Indian Inst Technol, Kharagpur, BTech, 69, MTech, 71, PhD(electronics), 78. *Prof Exp:* Lectr electronics, Indian Inst Technol, Kharagpur, 71-78, asst prof, 79-82. *Concurrent Pos:* Consult, Comput Maintainance Corp India, Ltd, 82-; UN Develop Prog, 88 & Unisys, 90-; prin investr, NSF grants, 85-86 & 91-93; vis prof, Indian Inst Technol, Delhi, India, 88; assoc ed, Pattern Recognition J, 90-; consult, NIH, 92-; Environ Protection Res Inst, res grant, 94-97; Mach Vision & Applns, 94-; assoc ed, Pattern Recognition Letters, 95-; trans pattern anal & mach intel, Inst Elec & Electronics Engrs, 97- *Mem:* Inst Elec & Electronics Engrs; Int Soc Neural Networks; Int Soc Optical Eng. *Res:* Dynamic scene analysis and object recognition; image processing; artificial neural networks; mobile robots; multimedia computing. *Mailing Add:* Dept Comput Sci Wayne State Univ Detroit MI 48202. *E-Mail:* sethi@cs.wayne.edu

SETHI, JITENDER K, PHARMACY, IMMUNOLOGY. *Current Pos:* sr scientist, 81-83, SR SCIENTIST, MED AFFAIRS DEPT, PARKE-DAVIS DIV, WARNER-LAMBERT CO, NJ, 83- *Personal Data:* b Lahore, India, Oct 16, 39; US citizen; m 64; c 2. *Educ:* Punjab Univ, BS, 60, MS, 62; Univ Iowa, PhD(pharm), 72. *Prof Exp:* Prof serv rep pharmaceut, Pfizer India Ltd, 62-67; res & teaching asst pharm, Univ Iowa, 67-72; fel tumor immunol, Sloan Kettering Inst, NY, 72-74, res assoc immunodiagnosis, 74-81. *Concurrent Pos:* Instr, Cornell Univ Grad Sch Med Sci, 75-81. *Mem:* Am Asn Cancer Res; Tissue Cult Asn; Am Asn Immunolgists. *Res:* Research related to tumor antigens, particularly human sarcomas to determine and to clinically evaluate if these could be of immunodiagnostic value; role and specificity of complement in complement mediated antigen antibody reactions. *Mailing Add:* 76 Chilton St Basking Ridge NJ 07920

SETHI, SATINDER, ANALYTICAL CHEMISTRY. *Current Pos:* prin scientist, 87-90, dir anal sci, 90-97, VPRES ANALYTICAL SCI, GLAXO WELLCOME, 97- *Personal Data:* b Delhi, India, Feb 15, 54; US citizen. *Educ:* Delhi Univ, BSc, 75; Univ Va, PhD(anal chem), 79. *Prof Exp:* Postdoctoral fel, Univ Utah, 79-83; res scientist, Baxter Int, 83-87. *Mem:* Am Chem Soc; Am Asn Pharmaceut Scientists. *Res:* Programming compounds through early pharmaceutical development; integrating the analytical activities throughout the process of drug development from discovery to manufacturing. *Mailing Add:* 5 Moore Dr Research Triangle Park NC 27709

SETHIAN, JOHN DASHO, PLASMA PHYSICS. *Current Pos:* RES PHYSICIST PLASMA PHYSICS, US NAVAL RES LAB, 77- *Personal Data:* b Washington, DC, Mar 20, 50; m 77. *Educ:* Princeton Univ, AB, 72; Cornell Univ, MS, 74, PhD(appl physics), 76. *Prof Exp:* Res assoc plasma physics, Univ Md, 76-77. *Mem:* Am Phys Soc. *Res:* Intense relativistic electron beams; electron beam induced CTR magnetic confinement systems, plasma heating and collective ion acceleration; generation and propagation of intense beams. *Mailing Add:* US Naval Res Lab Code 6730 Washington DC 20375-0001

SETHURAMAN, JAYARAM, MATHEMATICAL STATISTICS, PROBABILITY. *Current Pos:* assoc prof, 65-68, PROF STATIST, FLA STATE UNIV, 68-, ROBERT O LAWTON DISTINGUISHED PROF, 93- *Personal Data:* b Hubli, India, Oct 3, 37; m 65, Brinda Ramachandran; c 2. *Educ:* Madras Univ, MA, 58; Indian Statist Inst, Calcutta, PhD(statist), 62. *Honors & Awards:* Wilks Medal Statist, US Army Res Off. *Prof Exp:* Lectr statist, Indian Statist Inst, 61-62. *Concurrent Pos:* Fels, Univ NC, Chapel Hill, 62-63, Mich State Univ, 63-64 & Stanford Univ, 64-65; mem, Indian Statist Inst, 74-; US Army Res Off res grant, 72-82; vis prof statist, Univ Mich, 74-75; vis prof & actg head, Indian Statist Inst, Bangalore, 79-80; chmn, Dept Statist, Fla State Univ, 86-89; Fulbright fel, 95. *Mem:* Fel Inst Math Statist; fel Am Statist Asn; Int Statist Inst; Sigma Xi. *Res:* Probability; stochastic processes. *Mailing Add:* Dept Statist Fla State Univ Tallahassee FL 32306-3303. *Fax:* 850-644-5271; *E-Mail:* sethu@stat.fsu.edu

SETHURAMAN, S, meteorology, for more information see previous edition

SETHY, VIMALA HIRALAL, NEUROPSYCHOPHARMACY. *Current Pos:* SR RES SCIENTIST, UPJOHN CO, 76- *Educ:* Univ Bombay, India, MD, 63, PhD(pharmacol), 67. *Res:* Mechanism of action of antidepressants; physiology of the central cholinergic system. *Mailing Add:* Cent Nervous Syst Unit Pharmacia & Upjohn Co Kalamazoo MI 49001-0199

SETIAN, LEO, ELECTRICAL ENGINEERING. *Current Pos:* from asst prof to assoc prof, 70-79, PROF ELEC ENG, JOHN BROWN UNIV, 79- *Personal Data:* b Providence, RI, July 22, 30; m 57, Sona Krikorian; c Lynn, Ann, Richard, David & Peter. *Educ:* Brown Univ, AB, 55; Univ RI, MS, 66; Mont State Univ, PhD(elec eng), 71. *Prof Exp:* Electronic engr, Underwater Sound Lab, 57-63 & Electronics Res Lab, 66-68. *Concurrent Pos:* Consult, Underwater Systs Ctr, New London, Conn, Galtronics, Tiberias, Israel, 90, 92. *Mem:* Am Sci Affiliation; Am Soc Eng Educ; Inst Elec & Electronics Engrs. *Res:* Moisture measurement in living foliage using an open-wire transmission line. *Mailing Add:* John Brown Univ Box 3058 Siloam Springs AR 72761

SETLER, PAULETTE ELIZABETH, PHARMACOLOGY, PHYSIOLOGY. *Current Pos:* EXEC DIR, BIOL RES, JANSSEN RES FOUND, 87- *Personal Data:* b Pittsburgh, Pa, Jan 1, 38. *Educ:* Seton Hill Col, BA, 59; Univ Pa, PhD(physiol), 70. *Prof Exp:* Res assoc pharmacol, McNeil Labs, 59-62; pharmacologist, Smith Kline & French Labs, 62-66; instr physiol, Sch Dent Med, Univ Pa, 68; supvr, Churchill Col, Cambridge Univ, 71-72; Smith Kline & French Labs, 72-81; McNeil Pharmaceut, 81-87. *Concurrent Pos:* Res assoc, Physiol Lab, Cambridge Univ, 70-72. *Mem:* Assoc Am Physiol Soc; Soc Neurosci; AAAS. *Res:* Pharmacology of biogenic amines as studied behaviorally and biochemically and the interaction of amine neurotransmitters in regulation of behavior; the pharmacology of psychotropic drugs; control of ingestive behavior and body fluid balance. *Mailing Add:* Athena Neurosci 8001 Gateway Blvd South San Francisco CA 94080

SETLIFF, EDSON CARMACK, FOREST PATHOLOGY, FOREST MYCOLOGY. *Current Pos:* ASSOC PROF, SCH FORESTRY, LAKEHEAD UNIV, ONT, 85- *Personal Data:* b Indianola, Miss, Nov 3, 41; m 69, Dorene Lyon; c Eric J & Alissa E. *Educ:* NC State Univ, BS, 63; Yale Univ, MF, 64; State Col Environ Sci & Forestry, Syracuse Univ, PhD(forest mycol), 70. *Prof Exp:* Res assoc, Dept Plant Path, Univ Wis, 70-73; res scientist forest path, Cary Arboretum, NY Bot Garden, 73-77; res assoc, Dept Environ & Forest Biol, Col Environ Sci & Forestry, State Univ NY, Syracuse, 77-80; mem staff, Forintek Can Corp, Vancouver, BC, 80-85. *Concurrent Pos:* Adj assoc prof, Vassar Col, 75- & Univ BC, 81-85. *Mem:* Am Phytopath Soc; Mycol Soc Am; Sigma Xi; Soc Am Foresters; Tech Asn Pulp & Paper Indust; Brit Mycol Soc. *Res:* Taxonomy of tropical Polyporales; physiology and cultural morphology of wood decay fungi; mushroom culture; etiology of tree root diseases; tree disease diagnosis; cytology and fine structure of Polyporales; wood products pathology; birch decline; forest biotechnology. *Mailing Add:* Sch Forestry Lakehead Univ Thunder Bay ON P7B 5E1 Can. *Fax:* 807-343-8116; *E-Mail:* esetliff@flash.lakeheadu.ca

SETLIFF, FRANK LAMAR, ORGANIC CHEMISTRY. *Current Pos:* assoc prof, 69-74, chmn dept, 73-75, PROF CHEM, UNIV ARK, LITTLE ROCK, 74- *Personal Data:* b Lake Charles, La, Sept 21, 38; m 62, Carolyn Carver; c Christopher & Catherine. *Educ:* McNeese State Univ, BS, 60; Tulane Univ, MS, 62, PhD(org chem), 66. *Prof Exp:* Teaching asst org chem, Tulane Univ, 60-62, res asst, 64-66; asst prof, Little Rock Univ, 66-69. *Mem:* Am Chem Soc; NY Acad Sci; Sigma Xi. *Res:* Small ring compounds; Hammett coorelations of nuclear magnetic resonance data; heterocyclic compounds; fluorination reactions. *Mailing Add:* Dept Chem Univ Ark 33rd University Ave Little Rock AR 72204. *Fax:* 501-569-8838; *E-Mail:* flsetliff@ualr.edu

SETLOW, JANE KELLOCK, BIOPHYSICS. *Current Pos:* BIOLOGIST, BIOL DEPT, BROOKHAVEN NAT LAB, 74- *Personal Data:* b New York, NY, Dec 17, 19; div; c Peter, Michael, Katherine (O'Brien) & Charles. *Educ:* Swarthmore Col, BA, 40; Yale Univ, PhD, 60. *Prof Exp:* Asst biophys, Dept Radiol, Sch Med, Yale Univ, 59-60; biologist, Biol Div, Oak Ridge Nat Lab, 60-74. *Concurrent Pos:* Mem, NIH Recombinant DNA Molecule Prog Adv Comt, 74-78, chmn, 78-80; ed J Genetic Eng, vols 1-13, 79-91. *Mem:* Biophys Soc (pres, 77). *Res:* Molecular biology; ultraviolet action spectra; photoreactivation; cellular repair mechanisms; bacterial recombination; mutagenesis. *Mailing Add:* Biol Dept Brookhaven Nat Lab Upton NY 11973

SETLOW, PETER, BIOCHEMISTRY. *Current Pos:* from asst prof to assoc prof, 71-80, PROF BIOCHEM, UNIV CONN, 80-, INTERIM CHAIR, 95- *Personal Data:* b New Haven, Conn, June 1, 44; m 65, Barbara Cunningham; c Barry & Jennifer. *Educ:* Swarthmore Col, BA, 64; Brandeis Univ, PhD(biochem), 69. *Prof Exp:* NSF fel, Stanford Univ, 68-71. *Mem:* Am Soc Biol Chemists; Am Soc Microbiol. *Res:* Biochemical regulation of differentiation; bacterial sporulation and germination. *Mailing Add:* Dept Biochem Univ Conn Health Ctr Farmington CT 06030. *E-Mail:* setlow@sun.uchc.edu

SETLOW, RICHARD BURTON, CANCER RESEARCH, PHOTOBIOLOGY. *Current Pos:* sr biophysicist, Brookhaven Nat Labs, 74-86, actg assoc dir life sci, 84-86, chmn biol dept, 79-87, ASSOC DIR LIFE SCI, BROOKHAVEN NAT LABS, 86- *Personal Data:* b New York, NY, Jan 19, 21; m 42, 89, Neva Cummings; c Peter, Michael, Katherine (O'Brien) & Charles. *Educ:* Swarthmore Col, AB, 41; Yale Univ, PhD(physics), 47. *Hon Degrees:* DSc, York Univ, 85; Dr, Univ Essen, 93. *Honors & Awards:* Finsen Medal, 80; Fermi Award, 89. *Prof Exp:* Asst physics, Med Sch, Yale Univ, 41-42, from asst instr to assoc prof, 42-61; biophysicist, Oak Ridge Nat Lab, 61-74, group leader biophys, 64-69, sci dir biophys & cell physiol, 69-74. *Concurrent Pos:* Prof biomed sci, Univ Tenn, Oak Ridge, 67-74, dir, Grad Sch Biomed Sci, 72-74; adj prof biochem, State Univ NY, Stony Brook, 75- *Mem:* Nat Acad Sci; Radiation Res Soc; Biophys Soc; Am Soc Photobiol; Environ Mutagen Soc; Am Asn Cancer Res. *Res:* Ionizing and non-ionizing radiation; molecular biophysics; action of light on proteins viruses and cells; nucleic acids; repair mechanisms; environmental carcinogenesis; action spectra; skin cancer. *Mailing Add:* Biol Dept Brookhaven Nat Lab Upton NY 11973. *Fax:* 516-344-3407; *E-Mail:* folleers@bnl.gov

SETLOW, VALERIE PETIT, AIDS POLICY DEVELOPMENT & ANALYSIS, PROGRAM MANAGEMENT & SUPERVISION. *Current Pos:* DIR HEALTH SCI POLICY, INST MED, NAT ACAD SCI, 93- *Personal Data:* b New Orleans, La, Jan 24, 50; m 76; c 2. *Educ:* Xavier Univ, BS, 70; Johns Hopkins Univ, PhD(biol), 76. *Honors & Awards:* Except Achievement Award, USPHS, 90. *Prof Exp:* Fel human genetics, Mt Sinai Hosp, NY, 76-77; fel, Nat Diabetes & Metab Inst, NIH, 77-79 & Nat Heart, Lung & Blood Inst, 79-81, asst prog dir, Diabetes Div, Nat Inst Diabetes & Digestive & Kidney Dis, 81-83, spec asst to dir, 83-86; sr analyst, Health Planning & Eval, 86-88; dir policy, Nat Aids Prog Off, 88-93. *Concurrent Pos:* Prin investr, Sci Children Grant, Am Chem Soc, 87-90; consult, Elem Sch Sci, 89- *Mem:* AAAS; Am Soc Biochem & Molecular Biol. *Res:* Gene regulation in viruses; public health policy analysis; development and management. *Mailing Add:* 609 John Marshall Dr NE Vienna VA 22180. *Fax:* 202-690-7054

SETO, BELINDA P L, VIROLOGY. *Current Pos:* res chemist, Bur Biologics, 80-, SR ADV TO DEP DIR EXTRAMURAL RES, FOOD & DRUG ADMIN, 95- *Personal Data:* b Canton, China, July 25, 48; US citizen; m 75; c 2. *Educ:* Univ Calif, Davis, BS, 70; Purdue Univ, PhD(microbiol), 74. *Prof Exp:* Staff fel, Nat Heart, Lung & Blood Inst, NIH, 74-80. *Concurrent Pos:* Lectr, Howard Univ, 77. *Mem:* Am Soc Biol Chemists. *Res:* Human non-A and non-B hepatitis to isolate the soluble antigen associated with the hepatitis virus, to develop radioimmunoassay for testing, and structural studies of the viral DNA. *Mailing Add:* OMP NIH Bldg 1 Rm 252 NIH Bethesda MD 20892. *Fax:* 301-402-2517, 496-9150

SETO, FRANK, ZOOLOGY. *Current Pos:* asst prof, 64-69, assoc prof, 69-80, PROF ZOOL, UNIV OKLA, 81- *Personal Data:* b Los Angeles, Calif, Mar 12, 25; m 55; c 2. *Educ:* Berea Col, BA, 49; Univ Wis, MS, 50, PhD(zool), 53. *Prof Exp:* Asst prof, Exten Div, Univ Wis, 53-56; asst prof zool, Berea Col, 56-62. *Concurrent Pos:* NSF res grant, Berea Col, 60-61; USPHS spec fel, Oak Ridge Nat Lab, 62-64, USPHS res grant, 75; Am Cancer Soc grant, 65-68. *Mem:* Nat Asn Biol Teachers; Int Soc Develop Comp Immunol; Am Soc Zoologists; Soc Develop Biologists; Soc Exp Hemat. *Res:* Developmental biology and immunology. *Mailing Add:* 613 Shadow Creek Ct Norman OK 73072

SETO, JANE MEI-CHUN, internal medicine, for more information see previous edition

SETO, JOSEPH TOBEY, ELECTRON MICROSCOPY, MOLECULAR BIOLOGY. *Current Pos:* from asst prof to assoc prof microbiol, Calif State Univ, Los Angeles, 60-67, chmn dept, 64-75, prof, 67-88, EMER PROF MICROBIOL, CALIF STATE UNIV, LOS ANGELES, 88- *Personal Data:* b Tacoma, Wash, Aug 3, 24; m 59; c 2. *Educ:* Univ Minn, BS, 49; Univ Wis, MS, 55, PhD(bact), 57. *Honors & Awards:* Alexander von Humboldt Award, 72; Humboldt Medal, 91. *Prof Exp:* Asst bact, Sch Med, Univ Ill, 50-53; res assoc, Fermentation Div, Upjohn Co, Mich, 57; res virologist, Med Ctr, Univ Calif, Los Angeles, 58-59; asst prof biol, San Francisco State Univ, 59-60. *Concurrent Pos:* Consult & res virologist, US Naval Biol Lab, Univ Calif, 60-63; guest prof, Inst Virol, Univ Giessen, 65-66, 72-73, 79-80 & 86-87; Humboldt Found award, 72; WHO res exchange worker, 72; Humboldt Found Reinvitation, 86. *Mem:* AAAS; Am Soc Microbiol; fel Am Acad Microbiol; Electron Micros Soc Am; Sigma Xi. *Res:* Characterization of orthomyxovirus and paramyxovirus glycoproteins; persistent infections of paramyxoviruses in tissue cultures; molecular basis of the pathogenesis of paramyxoviruses. *Mailing Add:* Dept Microbiol Calif State Univ Los Angeles CA 90032-6205

SETSER, CAROLE SUE, FOOD SCIENCE, SENSORY ANALYSIS. *Current Pos:* Instr food sci, Kans State Univ, 64-66, asst to dean, Col Home Econ, 66-68, from asst prof to assoc prof, 74-86, PROF FOOD SCI, KANS STATE UNIV, 86- *Personal Data:* b Warrenton, Mo, Aug 26, 40; m 69, Donald W; c Bradley, Kirk & Brett. *Educ:* Univ Mo, Columbia, BS, 62; Cornell Univ, MS, 64; Kans State Univ, PhD(foods, nutrit), 71. *Mem:* Inst Food Technologists; Sigma Xi; Am Asn Cereal Chemists; Am Chem Soc Food & Agr Div. *Res:* Sensory studies of foods; reduced calorie bakery product development and sensory textural and flavor evaluation; Functionality of macromolecule substitutes in foods. *Mailing Add:* Dept Foods & Nutrit Kans State Univ 213 Justin Hall Manhattan KS 66506-1407. *Fax:* 785-532-3132; *E-Mail:* setser@ksuvm.ksu.edu

SETSER, DONALD W, PHYSICAL CHEMISTRY. *Current Pos:* from asst prof to assoc prof, 63-69, PROF PHYS CHEM, KANS STATE UNIV, 70- *Personal Data:* b Great Bend, Kans, Jan 2, 35; m 69, Carole Schulze; c Brad W, Kirk W & Brett D. *Educ:* Kans State Univ, BS, 54, MS, 56; Univ Wash, PhD(phys chem), 61. *Prof Exp:* Fel phys chem, Univ Wash, 61-62; NSF fel, Cambridge Univ, 62-63. *Concurrent Pos:* Alfred P Sloan fel, 68-70; sr Brit fel, Queen Mary Col, Univ London, 68. *Mem:* Am Chem Soc; fel Am Phys Soc. *Res:* Chemical kinetics; spectroscopy of small molecules; energy transfer; state-to-state reaction dynamics. *Mailing Add:* Dept Chem Kans State Univ Manhattan KS 66502. *Fax:* 785-532-6666; *E-Mail:* setserdw@ksu.edu

SETTERFIELD, GEORGE AMBROSE, CYTOLOGY, CELL BIOLOGY. *Current Pos:* RETIRED. *Personal Data:* b Halifax, NS, Aug 29, 29; m 51, Diana Charter; c Thomas, David, Jennifer, Wayne & Christopher. *Educ:* Univ BC, BA, 51; Univ Wis, PhD(bot), 54. *Prof Exp:* Instr genetics & cytol, Univ BC, 54-56; asst res officer biophys, Nat Res Coun Can, 56-57, assoc res officer, 58-62; from assoc prof to prof biol, Carleton Univ, 62-85, chmn dept, 63-68. *Concurrent Pos:* Vis prof, Laval Univ, 68-69; assoc ed, Can J Botany, 70-78 & Can J Biochem, 77-; mem adv comt biol, Nat Res Coun Can, 72-75, mem grant selection comt plant biol, 72-76, chmn, 74-75; mem adv comt acad planning, Coun Ont Univs, 73-; vis scientist, Nat Res Coun Lab, Saskatoon, Sask, 77-78. *Mem:* AAAS; fel Royal Soc Can; Can Soc Plant Physiologists; hon mem Can Soc Cell Biol (pres, 74-75); Soc Develop Biologists. *Res:* Experimental cytology; relation of structure to function in plant cells; plant hormones and growth processes; somatic cell genetics of plants; physiology of cell division; fine structure of nuclei. *Mailing Add:* 1063 Glen Forest Way Victoria BC V9C 3X8 Can

SETTERGREN, CARL DAVID, FORESTRY, WATERSHED MANAGEMENT. *Current Pos:* From instr ecol to assoc prof forest hydrol, 64-77, PROF FOREST HYDROL, UNIV MO, COLUMBIA, 77- *Personal Data:* b Chicago, Ill, Dec 12, 35; m 65; c 1. *Educ:* Univ Mo, BSF, 58, MS, 60; Colo State Univ, PhD(watershed mgt), 67. *Mem:* Soc Am Foresters; Am Water Resources Asn. *Res:* Forest hydrology; forest influences. *Mailing Add:* 1007 College Park Dr Columbia MO 65203

SETTERSTROM, CARL A(LBERT), CHEMICAL ENGINEERING. *Current Pos:* MANAGING PARTNER, HARRINGTON RES CO, 68- *Personal Data:* b Brooklyn, NY, May 2, 15; m 40, Star Peterson; c Star F & Barbara. *Educ:* Polytech Inst, Brooklyn, BChE, 36. *Prof Exp:* Sci asst plant physiol, Boyce Thompson Inst Plant Res, 36-40; from tech rep to gen mgr, Textile Fibers Dept, Union Carbide Corp, 40-54; spec proj mgr, Chas Pfizer & Co, Inc, 54-58; asst dir, Res & Develop Div, Sun Oil Co, 58-59; asst to pres, Avisun Corp, 59, gen mgr mkt, 60; vpres, Rexall Chem Co, NJ, 60-68. *Concurrent Pos:* Pres, PNC Co, 70-79. *Mem:* Am Chem Soc; AAAS; NY Acad Sci. *Res:* New product development; corporate acquisitions and evaluations; marketing of polymers; corporate profit strategies; plastics and fibers technology. *Mailing Add:* 323 Dogleg Dr 323 Dogleg Dr Williamsburg VA 23188-7412

SETTLE, FRANK ALEXANDER, JR, ANALYTICAL CHEMISTRY. *Current Pos:* From asst prof to prof, 64-95, EMER PROF CHEM, VA MIL INST, 95- *Personal Data:* b Nashville, Tenn, Sept 19, 37; m; c 4. *Educ:* Emory & Henry Col, BS, 60; Univ Tenn, PhD(chem), 64. *Honors & Awards:* Maury Res Award, 83. *Concurrent Pos:* NSF res fel, Va Polytech Inst & State Univ, 72-73; instr, Am Chem Soc Comput & Electronics Short Courses, 72-73 & 75-76; consult, Tenn Eastman Co, 77; instr, Microprocessor Short Courses, Va Mil Inst, 76 & 78; consult, Bendix Environ & Process Instruments Div, 79; proj dir, Sci Instrument Info & Curricula Proj, 80-; vis scientist, Ctr Anal Chem, Nat Bur Stand, Gaithersburg, Md, 87-88, 89 & 90; vis prof, USAF Acad, 91-92. *Mem:* Am Chem Soc. *Res:* Computer interfacing of chemical instrumentation; computer-based information systems; expert systems for chemical analysis; laboratory automation; intelligent system. *Mailing Add:* Dept Chem Va Mil Inst Sci Bldg Lexington VA 24450

SETTLE, RICHARD GREGG, neuropsychology, psychophysics, for more information see previous edition

SETTLE, WILBUR JEWELL, BOTANY. *Current Pos:* asst prof, 70-80, ASSOC PROF BIOL, STATE UNIV NY COL ONEONTA, 80- *Personal Data:* b Barren Co, Ky. *Educ:* Centre Col, Ky, AB, 62; Ohio State Univ, MSc, 65, PhD(bot), 69. *Prof Exp:* Asst prof biol, Bowling Green State Univ, 69-70. *Concurrent Pos:* Res Found State Univ NY fac res fel, 71. *Mem:* AAAS; Bot Soc Am; Am Soc Plant Taxonomists; Soc Econ Bot; Sigma Xi. *Res:* Plant biosystematics, especially the genus Blephilia. *Mailing Add:* Dept Biol State Univ NY Oneonta NY 13820-4015

SETTLEMIRE, CARL THOMAS, BIOCHEMISTRY. *Current Pos:* asst prof biochem, 69-74, ASSOC PROF BIOL & CHEM, BOWDOIN COL, 74- *Personal Data:* b Dayton, Ohio, July 14, 37; m 60; c 3. *Educ:* Ohio State Univ, BS, 59, MS, 61; NC State Univ, PhD(biochem), 67. *Prof Exp:* Instr nutrit, Ohio Agr Res & Develop Ctr, 61-62; NIH trainee biochem, NC State Univ, 62-66; NIH fel, Ohio State Univ, 66-69. *Concurrent Pos:* Mem, Nat Student Support Rev Comt, Dept HEW, 68-70. *Mem:* AAAS; Am Chem Soc. *Res:* Membrane biochemistry and ion transport in whole cells and in mitochondria; membrane changes in cystic fibrosis. *Mailing Add:* Dept Biol Bowdoin Col Brunswick ME 04011

SETTLEMYER, KENNETH THEODORE, TAXONOMIC BOTANY, FLORISTICS. *Current Pos:* from asst prof to assoc prof, 66-72, chmn dept, 78-81 & 86-88, PROF BIOL SCI, LOCK HAVEN UNIV PA, 72- *Personal Data:* b Arnold, Pa, Dec 19, 35; m 64, Joan Empfield; c Kenneth T Jr, Jonathan P & Timothy R. *Educ:* Pa State Univ, BS, 57, MEd, 61, DEd(biol sci), 71. *Prof Exp:* Instr biol, Freeport Area Joint Schs, Pa, 57-66. *Concurrent Pos:* Partic, NSF Inserv Inst, Univ Pittsburgh, 60-61; consult & reviewer, Choice; NSF grant, Pa State Univ, 63, 64 & 65. *Mem:* AAAS; Am Inst Biol Sci; Nat Asn Biol Teachers; Bot Soc Am; Am Soc Plant Taxonomists. *Res:* Taxonomy and floristics of woody plants. *Mailing Add:* Dept Biol Sci Lock Haven Univ 401 N Fairview St Lock Haven PA 17745-2390. *Fax:* 717-893-2432; *E-Mail:* ksettlem@eagle.lhup.edu

SETTLES, F STAN, INDUSTRIAL ENGINEERING, MANUFACTURING. *Current Pos:* PROF & CHAIR, INDUST & SYSTS ENG, 94- *Personal Data:* b Oct, 1938; m 62, Evelyn F Brown; c Frank, Richard, Charles & Michael. *Educ:* LeTourneau Col, BS(indust eng) & BS(prod technol), 62; Ariz State Univ, MSE, 67, PhD(indust eng), 69. *Honors & Awards:* Opers Res Div Award, Am Inst Indust Engrs, 81. *Prof Exp:* Design engr, AiRes Mfg Co, 62-64, develop engr, 64-67, staff asst to mgr, 67-68, sr systs analyst, Mat Dept, 68-70, mat mgr aircraft propulsion engines, 70-74, mgr prod systs anal & design, Mat Dept, 74-78, mgr oper planning, Indust Eng Dept, 78-80, mgr indust eng, Garrett Pneumatic Systs Div, 80-83, mgr indust & mfg eng, Garrett Turbine Engine Co, 83-85, consult, Garrett/AiRes Mfg, Torrance, Calif, 85, div vpres mfg opers, AiRes Mfg Co, 85-87, corp dir indust & mfg eng, Garrett Corp, 87, dir planning, Garrett Engine Div, Allied-Signal Aerospace, 88-92; res prof, Ariz State Univ, 92-94. *Concurrent Pos:* Inst dir, Opers Res Div, Inst Indust Engrs, 76-78, vpres, Systs Eng & Tech Div, 81-83; asst dir, White House Off Sci & Technol Policy, 92-93; prog dir design & integration eng, NSF, 92-94. *Mem:* Nat Acad Eng; fel Am Inst Indust Engrs (pres, 87-88, treas, 90-92); Inst Opers Res & Mgt Sci; Soc Mfg Engrs; Sigma Xi; Am Mgt Asn. *Res:* Total quality management; agile/flexible manufacturing; author of various publications. *Mailing Add:* 1750 E Ocean Blvd No 713 Long Beach CA 90802. *Fax:* 213-740-1120; *E-Mail:* settles@usc.edu

SETTLES, GARY STUART, TURBULENT & SEPARATED FLOWS, FLOW VISUALIZATION. *Current Pos:* assoc prof, 83-88, PROF & DIR, GAS DYNAMICS LAB, MECH ENG DEPT, PA STATE UNIV, 88- *Personal Data:* b Maryville, Tenn, Oct, 9, 49. *Educ:* Univ Tenn, BS, 71; Princeton Univ, PhD(mech & aerospace eng), 76. *Prof Exp:* Res scientist, Princeton Combustion Labs, Div Flow Res Corp, 75-77; res scientist & lectr fluid mech, Mech & Aerospace Eng Dept, Princeton Univ, 77-83. *Concurrent Pos:* Consult, Aerodyn Lab, Boeing Com Airplane Co, 80-81, IBM Corp, 82-83, United Technol Res Ctr, 82-90. *Mem:* Am Inst Aeronaut & Astronaut; Am Soc Mech Engrs; Optical Soc Am; Soc Photo-Optical Instrumentation Engrs; Am Phys Soc; Sigma Xi; Am Soc Metals Int; Am Metal Powder Inst; Steel Struc Painting Coun. *Res:* Fluid mechanics, specializing in experimental methods, high-speed flows, turbulent boundary layers, and shock waves; flow visualization techniques and optical flow diagnostics; advanced materials processing and manufacturing processes. *Mailing Add:* 301D Reber Bldg University Park PA 16802. *Fax:* 814-863-4848; *E-Mail:* g55@ecl.puu.edu

SETTLES, HARRY EMERSON, REGENERATION, ELECTROMYOGRAPHY. *Current Pos:* asst prof, 78-79, ASSOC PROF ANAT, UNIV SDAK, 79- *Personal Data:* b Denver, Colo, Dec 19, 40; m 67; c 3. *Educ:* Wabash Col, AB, 63; Tulane Univ, PhD(anat), 67. *Prof Exp:* From instr to asst prof anat, NY Med Col, 69-78. *Mem:* Sigma Xi; AAAS; Am Asn Anatomists; Am Soc Zoologists. *Res:* Experimental embryology; regeneration; electron microscopy. *Mailing Add:* Dept Anat Univ SDak Sch Med Vermillion SD 57069

SETTLES, RONALD DEAN, PHYSICS, MATHEMATICS. *Current Pos:* SR STAFF PARTICLE PHYSICS, MAX PLANCK INST PHYSICS & ASTROPHYS, 64- *Personal Data:* b Lawrence, Kans, Feb 12, 38; m 63, Reinhilde Steinacker; c Marcus, Erik & Monica. *Educ:* Va Polytech Inst, BS, 59, MS, 61; La State Univ, PhD(physics), 64. *Mem:* Sigma Xi; Ger Phys Soc. *Res:* Elementary particle physics. *Mailing Add:* Max-Planck Inst Physics Fohringer Ring 6 80805 Munich Germany

SETTOON, PATRICK DELANO, BIOCHEMISTRY, FOOD CHEMISTRY. *Current Pos:* RETIRED. *Personal Data:* b Amite, La, Feb 15, 34; m 56; c 3. *Educ:* Southeastern La Univ, BS, 57; La State Univ, Baton Rouge, MS, 61, PhD, 67. *Prof Exp:* Chemist, Union Carbide Corp, 57-58; from instr to assoc prof, Southeastern La Univ, 58-69, prof chem & chmn dept chem & physics, 69-80, dean, Col Sci & Technol, 80-86, provost & vpres, Acad & Student Affairs, 86-90. *Res:* Mechanisms involved in food decomposition; accessory growth factors for microorganisms. *Mailing Add:* 800 Rue Chalet Hammond LA 70403

SETZLER-HAMILTON, EILEEN MARIE, MARINE ECOLOGY, FISH BIOLOGY & ECOLOGY. *Current Pos:* res assoc, 75-87, sr res assoc, 87-89, RES ASSOC PROF FISH ECOL, CTR ENVIRON & ESTUARINE STUDIES, CHESAPEAKE BIOL LAB, UNIV MD, 89- *Personal Data:* b Fremont, Ohio, Apr 28, 43; m 79, Joseph A. *Educ:* Col St Mary of Springs, BA, 65; Univ Del, MS, 69; Univ Ga, PhD(zool), 77. *Prof Exp:* Fisheries biologist, Southwest Fisheries Ctr, Nat Marine Fisheries Serv, Nat Oceanic & Atmospheric Admin, 74. *Mem:* Am Fisheries Soc; Sigma Xi; Estuarine Res Fedn; Atlantic Estuarine Res Soc (secy-treas, 78-79). *Res:* Fish ecology; anadromous fish populations; estuarine ecology; larval fish ecology; benthic community habitat relationships; management of estuarine living resources; exotic species in estuarine environments. *Mailing Add:* Ctr Environ & Estuarine Studies Chesapeake Biol Lab Univ Md PO Box 38 Solomons MD 20688-0038. *Fax:* 410-326-7273; *E-Mail:* hamilton@cbl.cees.edu

SEUBOLD, FRANK HENRY, JR, ORGANIC CHEMISTRY, PUBLIC HEALTH ADMINISTRATION. *Current Pos:* RETIRED. *Personal Data:* b Chicago, Ill, Nov 16, 22; m 42, 90, Helen Winters; c 2. *Educ:* Northwestern Univ, BS, 43; Univ Calif, Los Angeles, PhD(chem), 48. *Prof Exp:* Jr chemist, Shell Develop Co, 43-45, chemist, 47-52; asst prof chem, Northwestern Univ, 52-54; res chemist, Union Oil Co Calif, 54-59; sr chemist, Aerojet-Gen Corp Div, Gen Tire & Rubber Co, 59-63, tech dept mgr, Space-Gen Corp, Calif, 63-71; dir, Proj Mgt & Planning Div, Health Maintenance Orgn Serv, Health Serv & Ment Health Admin, Dept Health & Human Serv, 71-74, assoc bur dir, Health Serv Admin, 74-76, dir, Div Health Maintenance Orgns, Bur Med Serv, Health Serv Admin, 76-77, dir, Div Health Maintenance Develop, Off Asst Secy Health, 77-78, dep dir, Div Intramural Res, Nat Ctr Health Serv Res, 79-81, dir, Health Maintenance Orgns, Off Asst Secy Health, 80-87. *Res:* Mechanisms of organic reactions free radical processes; oxidations of hydrocarbons; reaction of organic peroxides; polymerization; heterogeneous catalysis; solid rocket propellants; encapsulation; immunochemistry; biological and chemical detection systems and instrumentation; health care delivery systems; health maintenance organization; health services research. *Mailing Add:* 731 Gailen Ave Palo Alto CA 94303

SEUFERT, WOLF D, BIOPHYSICS, MOLECULAR BIOLOGY. *Current Pos:* from asst prof to assoc prof, 67-75, PROF BIOPHYS, FAC MED, UNIV SHERBROOKE, 75- *Personal Data:* b Dusseldorf, Ger, Apr 17, 35; Can citizen; m 61; c 2. *Educ:* Univ Dusseldorf, Dr Med, 60. *Hon Degrees:* DSc, Univ Provence Marseille, 79. *Prof Exp:* Intern med, Hosp Nördlingen, Ger, 61-62; res assoc physiol, Univ Heidelberg, 63-64; med res scientist, Dept Basic Res, Eastern Pa Psychiat Inst, 64-65; guest investr biophys, Rockefeller Univ, 66-67. *Concurrent Pos:* Pres, WDS Consults Inc, Sherbrooke, Que, 92- *Mem:* Biophys Soc. *Res:* Physico-chemical characteristics of biological membranes and membrane models; medical instrumentation; biomedical engineering; applied biophysics. *Mailing Add:* Dept Physiol & Biophys Univ Sherbrooke Fac Med Sherbrooke PQ J1H 5N4 Can. *Fax:* 819-564-5399

SEUFZER, PAUL RICHARD, INORGANIC CHEMISTRY, RESEARCH ADMINISTRATION. *Current Pos:* supvr chem dept, 53-63, SUPT DEVELOP LAB, TECH DIV, GOODYEAR ATOMIC CORP, 63- *Personal Data:* b Cleveland, Ohio, Dec 23, 21; m 44. *Educ:* Western Reserve Univ, BS, 43, MS, 49, PhD(inorg chem), 51. *Prof Exp:* Anal chemist, Harshaw Chem Co, 43-44; shift foreman, Tenn Eastman Corp & US Army, CEngrs, Tenn, 44-46; res chemist, Argonne Nat Lab, 51-53. *Mem:* AAAS; Am Chem Soc; Sigma Xi. *Res:* Physical inorganic chemistry of fluorine and uranium. *Mailing Add:* 15 Ridgeway Dr Chillicothe OH 45601

SEUGLING, EARL WILLIAM, JR, PHARMACY, CHEMICAL ENGINEERING. *Current Pos:* CONSULT PHARMACEUT/DENT, COSMETIC, TOILETRIES DEVELOP, QUAL CONTROL/QUAL ASSURANCE PROD, 78-; SALES/TECH SERV, ALPINE AROMATICS INT, INC, 84- *Personal Data:* b Little Falls, NJ, Jan 6, 33; m 68; c 3. *Educ:* Rutgers Univ, BS, 55; Ohio State Univ, MSc, 57, PhD(pharm), 61. *Prof Exp:* Sr pharmaceut scientist, Vick Div Res, Richardson Merrell Inc, 60-63; res mgr, Res Dept, Strong Cobb Arner Inc, 63-65, dir res, 65-69; dir res, Block Drug Co, 69-78. *Mem:* Am Pharmaceut Asn; Acad Pharmaceut Sci; Am Inst Chem Eng; Am Chem Soc; Soc Cosmetic Chem. *Res:* Ionic and adsorptive exchange reactions in pharmaceutical sciences; product and process development, specifically, improved granulation, compression and advanced tablet coating techniques; development of dental, pharmaceutical, cosmetic and toiletry products; research administration; technical management. *Mailing Add:* 44 Courtney Pl Palm Coast FL 32137-8126

SEVACHERIAN, VAHRAM, ENTOMOLOGY, APPLIED STATISTICS. *Current Pos:* res asst entom, 66-70, lectr entom, asst res entomologist, lectr statist & asst res statistician, 71-72, asst prof, 72-81, ASSOC PROF STATIST & ENTOM, UNIV CALIF, RIVERSIDE, 81- *Personal Data:* b Nov 25, 42; US citizen. *Educ:* Univ Calif, Los Angeles, BA, 64; Calif State Univ, Los Angeles, MA, 66; Univ Calif, Riverside, PhD(entom), 70. *Prof Exp:* Asst zool, Calif State Univ, Los Angeles, 64-66. *Mem:* Entom Soc Am; Ecol Soc Am; Entom Soc Can; Am Statist Soc; Sigma Xi. *Res:* Systems analysis; sampling techniques; statistical ecology; integrated pest management; economic thresholds in agriculture. *Mailing Add:* 1200 Country Club Dr Riverside CA 92506

SEVALL, JACK SANDERS, BIOCHEMISTRY. *Current Pos:* RES SCIENTIST, HELICON FOUND. *Personal Data:* b Jan 12, 46; US citizen. *Educ:* Willamette Univ, BA, 67; Purdue Univ, PhD(biochem), 71. *Prof Exp:* Lab instr biochem, Purdue Univ, 69-70; res assoc biol, Calif Inst Technol, 71-74; asst prof biochem, Tex Tech Univ, 74-80; sr scientist, Wadley Insts Molecular Med, 80-; assoc scientist, dept molecular & cell biol, Southwest

Found. *Concurrent Pos:* Damon Runyon Mem Fund Cancer Res fel, Calif Inst Technol, 72-74; NSF res grant, 75, NIH res grants, 76-79 & 81-84, Roger A Welch res grant, 77-80. *Mem:* Soc Cell Biol; Biophys Soc; AAAS; Am Soc Biol Chemists. *Res:* Eukaryotic gene structure; nonhistone chromosomal protein role in gene structure and function. *Mailing Add:* Specialty Labs Inc 2211 Michigan Ave Santa Monica CA 90403. Fax: 310-828-6634

SEVENAIR, JOHN P, SCIENCE EDUCATION. *Current Pos:* from asst prof to assoc prof, 74-86, PROF CHEM, XAVIER UNIV, 86-, CHAIR CHEM, 93- *Personal Data:* b Somerville, NJ, Oct 12, 43. *Educ:* Mass Inst Technol, BS, 65; Univ Notre Dame, PhD(chem), 70. *Prof Exp:* Res assoc chem, Ga Inst Technol, 69-71 & Univ Ala, 71-72; teaching res fel, Tulane Univ, 72-74. *Mem:* Am Chem Soc; Nat Speleol Soc; Sigma Xi. *Res:* Chemistry of humic substances; science education of minorities. *Mailing Add:* Xavier Univ Box 100C New Orleans LA 70125

SEVENANTS, MICHAEL R, FOOD CHEMISTRY. *Current Pos:* CHEMIST, PROCTER & GAMBLE CO, 65-, GROUP LEADER, 70- *Personal Data:* b Two Rivers, Wis, Mar 16, 38; m 62; c 3. *Educ:* Univ Calif, Davis, BS, 61, PhD(agr chem), 65. *Mem:* Am Chem Soc; Am Oil Chemists Soc; Sigma Xi. *Res:* Chemical identification and sensory correlation of natural flavorous components in foods. *Mailing Add:* 324 Overton St Newport KY 41071-1746

SEVER, DAVID MICHAEL, HERPETOLOGY. *Current Pos:* From asst prof to assoc prof, 74-87, chmn dept, 80-89, PROF BIOL, ST MARY'S COL, IND, 87- *Personal Data:* b Canton, Ohio, Feb 21, 48; m 69; c 2. *Educ:* Ohio Univ, BS, 70, MS, 71; Tulane Univ, PhD(biol), 74. *Concurrent Pos:* Res grants, Highlands Biol Sta Ind, 73 & 75, Ind Acad Sci, 75, 82 & 86, Am Philos Soc, 77, Ind Nat Res, 79 & NSF, 86-94. *Mem:* Am Inst Biol Sci; Am Soc Icthyologists & Herpetologists; Herpetologists League; Soc Study Amphibians & Reptiles; Sigma Xi; Am Soc Zoologists. *Res:* Anatomy and evolution of the secondary sexual characters of salamanders; systematics, ecology, behavior and physiology of salamanders; author of 70 publications. *Mailing Add:* Dept Biol St Mary's Col Notre Dame IN 46556. *E-Mail:* dsever@jade.saintmarys.edu

SEVER, JOHN LOUIS, PEDIATRIC & OBSTETRICS & GYNECOLOGY, MICROBIOLOGY & IMMUNOLOGY. *Current Pos:* assoc prof, 63-73, PROF PEDIAT, SCH MED, GEORGETOWN UNIV, 73-, PROF OBSTET & GYNEC, 83-; CONSULT, NIH, 88- *Personal Data:* b Chicago, Ill, Apr 11, 32; m 56, Gerane Werle; c Kimberly (Kempa), Beverly (Rzepka) & Valerie (Kappler). *Educ:* Univ Chicago, BA, 51; Northwestern Univ, BS, 52, MS, 56, MD, PhD(microbiol), 57. *Honors & Awards:* Borden Award; Pasteur Award; Wellcome Award,; Abbott Award, Am Soc Microbiol. *Prof Exp:* Instr microbiol, Med Sch, Northwestern Univ, 54-60; head, Sect Infectious Dis, Nat Inst Neurol Dis & Stroke, 60-71; chief, Infectious Dis Br, Nat Inst Neurol & Commun Disorders & Stroke, 60-88. *Concurrent Pos:* Resident pediat, Chicago Children's Mem Hosp, Ill, 57-60; mem res & clin staff, Nat Children's Med Ctr, 65-; ed, J Teratology, 75-; rep, World Health Org Rotary Int, 84, 92 & 93; mem, Vaccine Develop Comt, WHO, 91-; pres, Asn Med Lab Immunologist, 93-94; Infectious Dis Soc Obstet & Gynec, 93-95, Pan Am Group Rapid Viral Diag, 93-95. *Mem:* Am Soc Microbiol; AMA; Soc Pediat Res; Am Asn Immunologists; Am Epidemol Soc; Am Pediat Soc. *Res:* Infectious diseases; virology; perinatal infections; vaccines; chronic infections of central nervous system; acquired immune deficency syndrome. *Mailing Add:* Dept Child Pediats Obstet & Gynec Microbiol & Immunol George Washington Univ Childrens Nat Med Ctr 111 Michigan Ave Washington DC 20010

SEVERE, JOANNE B, BIOSTATISTICS, CLINICAL TRIALS IN PSYCHIATRY. *Current Pos:* Chief, Res Proj & Publ Br, 93-97, BIOSTATIST GROUP, NIMH, 97. *Personal Data:* b Washington, DC, Nov 17, 50; m, Marty; c 2. *Educ:* Univ Md, BS, 68; Georgetown Univ, MS, 79. *Mem:* Am Statist Asn; Am Col Psychosocial Res. *Res:* Coordination and statistical analysis of data from large-scale multisite clinical trials in the treatment of major mental disorders. *Mailing Add:* NIMH Biostatist Group Rm 10-102 5600 Fishers Lane Rockville MD 20857. *E-Mail:* jsevere@nih.gov

SEVERIN, CHARLES MATTHEW, NEUROANATOMY, ANATOMY. *Current Pos:* ASSOC PROF ANAT, STATE UNIV NY, BUFFALO, 85- *Personal Data:* b Youngstown, Ohio, Dec 4, 48; m, Judith; c Matthew & Amanda. *Educ:* St Louis Univ, BA, 70, MS, 72, PhD(anat), 75. *Prof Exp:* Asst anat, Sch Med, St Louis Univ, 71-73, instr, 73-74. *Mem:* Sigma Xi; Soc Neurosci; Am Asn Clin Anat; Am Asn Anat. *Res:* Connections of the reticular formation; organization of the hippocampus; head injury; educational materials for the blind or visually impaired. *Mailing Add:* Anat Sci 317 Farber State Univ NY Buffalo Sch Med Buffalo NY 14214-3001. Fax: 716-829-2915

SEVERIN, KENNETH PAUL, MICROBEAM ANALYSIS, MICROPALEONTOLOGY. *Current Pos:* RES ASSOC, DEPT GEOL & GEOPHYS, UNIV ALASKA, 90- *Personal Data:* b Monterey, Calif, Mar 7, 55. *Educ:* Calif Inst Technol, BS, 78; Univ Calif, Davis, PhD(geol), 87. *Prof Exp:* Researcher, Univ Calif, Davis, 87-89; asst prof geol, Univ PR, Mayaguez, 89-90. *Res:* Retrieval of environmental-biological information from incrementally grown biological structures such as fish otoliths and mammalian teeth. *Mailing Add:* 2235 Penrose Lane Fairbanks AK 99709

SEVERIN, MATTHEW JOSEPH, MEDICAL MICROBIOLOGY. *Current Pos:* dean students, Sch Med, 75-85, PROF MED MICROBIOL, CREIGHTON UNIV, 72-, PROF PREV MED & PUB HEALTH & EPIDEMIOL. *Personal Data:* b Omaha, Nebr, Aug 7, 33; m 58; c 4. *Educ:* Creighton Univ, BS, 55, MS, 60; Univ Nebr, PhD(med microbiol), 68, JD, 86. *Prof Exp:* Bacteriologist, Clin Labs, Immanuel Hosp, Omaha, 58-60; asst prof biol, Univ Omaha, 61-63; dir labs, Omaha-Douglas County Health Dept, 63-73. *Concurrent Pos:* USPHS grants, 63-; lectr, Col St Mary, Nebr, 67-75; asst prof, Sch Med, Creighton Univ, 68- & Col Med, Univ Nebr, 72-77; asst prof, Col Med, Univ Nebr, 72-77; lectr, St Joseph's Sch Nursing, 72- *Mem:* Fel Am Soc Clin Scientists; Am Soc Microbiol; fel Am Pub Health Asn; Infectious Dis Soc Am; Am Soc Epidemiol. *Res:* Venereal disease agents and streptococcal disease agents and their chemotherapeutic sensitivities; AIDS and legal issues. *Mailing Add:* Dept Med Microbiol Creighton Univ Sch Med California & 24th Omaha NE 68178

SEVERINGHAUS, CHARLES WILLIAM, WILDLIFE MANAGEMENT. *Current Pos:* RETIRED. *Personal Data:* b Ithaca, NY, Sept 3, 16; m 41, 71, Jacqueline D Czerwiec; c Jane R, William D, Charles L & Mark R. *Educ:* Cornell Univ, BS, 39. *Honors & Awards:* Achievement Award, NE Sect, Wildlife Soc, 51; Conserv Award, Am Motors Corp, Wildlife Soc, 62; Wildlife Conserv Award, Nat Wildlife Fed & Sears-Roebuck Found, 65. *Prof Exp:* Conserv worker, State Conserv Dept, 39-41, asst game res investr, 41, game res investr, 41-59, dist game mgr, 41-44, leader deer mgt res, 44-56, leader big game mgt invests, 56-61, supv wildlife biologist, 61-74, prin wildlife biologist, 74-77. *Concurrent Pos:* Consult wildlife biologist, Cornell Univ, 77-86, pvt pract, 86-; dir at large, Am Wildlife Res Found, 92. *Mem:* Hon mem Wildlife Soc; Am Soc Mammalogists. *Res:* Game management; life history, population dynamics, ecology, reproduction and management of white-tailed deer and black bear. *Mailing Add:* 1549 Bea Gull Dr Titusville FL 32796-3777

SEVERINGHAUS, JOHN WENDELL, MEDICINE. *Current Pos:* from asst prof to prof anesthesia, 58-91, dir, anesthesia res, Cardiovasc Res Inst, 58-91, EMER PROF ANESTHESIA, MED CTR, UNIV CALIF, SAN FRANCISCO, 91- *Personal Data:* b Madison, Wis, May 6, 22; m 48; c 4. *Educ:* Haverford Col, BS, 43; Columbia Univ, MD, 49; Am Bd Anesthesiol, dipl, 58. *Hon Degrees:* Dr med, Univ Copenhagen, Denmark, 79. *Prof Exp:* Staff physicist, Radiation Lab, Mass Inst Technol, 43-45; staff physician, Sage Hosp, Ganado, Ariz, 51 & Embudo Hosp, NMex, 51; res assoc physiol, Univ Pa, 51-53; sr asst surgeon, Clin Ctr, USPHS, 53-56, surgeon, 56-58. *Concurrent Pos:* Hon fel, Fac Anesthetists, Royal Col Surgeons, London, 75. *Mem:* Am Soc Anesthesiol; Am Physiol Soc; Am Soc Clin Invest; Asn Univ Anesthetists. *Res:* Pulmonary physiology; control of respiration; physiologic effects in anesthesia; electrodes for blood and tissue oxygen and carbon dioxide tension. *Mailing Add:* Dept Anesthesia Univ Calif Med Ctr San Francisco CA 94143-0542

SEVERN, CHARLES B, PEDIATRICS, NEONATOLOGY. *Current Pos:* Asst prof, 68-70, ASSOC PROF PATH & ANAT, COL MED, UNIV NEBR MED CTR, OMAHA, 70-, ASSOC PROF OBSTET & GYNEC & PEDIAT, 73- *Personal Data:* b Breckenridge, Minn, Apr 11, 39; m 66; c 3. *Educ:* Univ Minn, Minneapolis, BA, 62; Univ Mich, MS, 66, PhD(anat), 68; Univ Nebr, MD, 76. *Concurrent Pos:* Resident gen pediat, Univ Nebr, 76, chief resident, 78, fel neonatol, 78-79. *Mem:* Am Asn Anatomists; Teratology Soc. *Res:* Human embryology; perinatal pathology and development; fetal and newborn pathology. *Mailing Add:* Perinatal Care Ctr PO Box 1658 Bismarck ND 58502

SEVERNS, MATTHEW LINCOLN, OPHTHALMOLOGY, MEDICAL INSTRUMENTATION. *Current Pos:* RES ASSOC OPHTHAL, JOHNS HOPKINS UNIV MED CTR, 87-; VPRES OPERS, VISION REHAB SYSTS, INC, 94- *Personal Data:* b Wilmington, Del, Nov 12, 52; m 92, Amy V Lindsey. *Educ:* Univ Del, BA, 76; Univ Va, ME, 78, PhD(biomed eng), 80. *Prof Exp:* Head field opers, Megonigal Electronics Inc, 75-76; staff engr, Rehab Eng Ctr, Univ Va, 77; asst prof computerized med, George Washington Univ Med Ctr, 80-82; head, Advan Automation Res Group, Am Red Cross Nat Labs, 82-86; dir res & develop, LKC Technologies, Inc, 86-94. *Concurrent Pos:* Consult biomed instrumentation, 76-; NIH consult, 92- *Mem:* Optical Soc Am; AAAS; Inst Elec & Electronics Engrs. *Res:* Techniques and instrumentation for diagnosis of eye diseases; signal processing and neural network analysis and classification of evoked potentials; rehabilitative technology for the visually impaired; design of medical electronic systems. *Mailing Add:* 2211 Weaver Lane Baltimore MD 21207-6656

SEVERS, WALTER BRUCE, PHARMACOLOGY. *Current Pos:* from asst prof to assoc prof, 68-77, PROF PHARMACOL, HERSHEY MED CTR, PA STATE UNIV, 77-, PROF NEUROSCI, 86- *Personal Data:* b Pittsburgh, Pa, June 10, 38; m 70, Anne E Daniels; c Mary, Jane, Steven, William & Katherine. *Educ:* Univ Pittsburgh, BS, 60, MS, 63, PhD(pharmacol), 65. *Honors & Awards:* I M Setchenov Medal, Acad Med Sci, USSR; Blue Medal for Sci, Bulgarian Union Sci Workers; Medallion For Sci, Univ Belgrade. *Prof Exp:* Instr pharmacol, Univ Pittsburgh, 64-65, USPHS fel, 65-66; USPHS fel, Lab Chem Pharmacol, Nat Heart Inst, 66-68. *Concurrent Pos:* Asst prof, Ohio Northern Univ, 65-66. *Mem:* Soc Neurosci; Am Soc Pharmacol & Exp Therapeut; Pavlovian Soc Am; Am Physiol Soc; Sigma Xi. *Res:* Hypertension; renin-angiotensin system; interaction between angiotensin and the central nervous system; salt/water balance; intracranial pressure control; neuropeptides. *Mailing Add:* Dept Pharmacol Pa State Univ Hershey Med Ctr Hershey PA 17033. Fax: 717-531-5013

SEVERSIKE, LEVERNE K, AEROSPACE ENGINEERING. *Current Pos:* Res asst gas dynamics, Eng Exp Sta, 60-63, from instr to asst prof, 63-76, ASSOC PROF AEROSPACE ENG, IOWA STATE UNIV, 76- *Personal Data:* b Des Moines, Iowa, Nov 5, 36; m. *Educ:* Iowa State Univ, BS, 58, MS, 61, PhD(aerospace eng), 64. *Mem:* Am Inst Aeronaut & Astronaut; Am Astronaut Soc; Nat Space Soc; Planetary Soc; Sigma Xi. *Res:* Vehicle flight mechanics; flight and reentry trajectories; optimization techniques; gas dynamics; optimal controls. *Mailing Add:* 2961 N Western Ave Ames IA 50010

SEVERSON, ARLEN RAYNOLD, BIOLOGICAL STRUCTURE, CELL PHYSIOLOGY. *Current Pos:* assoc prof, 72-79, PROF ANAT & CELL BIOL, SCH MED, UNIV MINN, DULUTH, 79- *Personal Data:* b Clarkfield, Minn, Dec 5, 39; m 62, Julianne Berg; c 4. *Educ:* Concordia Col, Moorhead, Minn, BA, 61; Univ NDak, MS, 63, PhD(anat), 65. *Prof Exp:* Res collabr histochem, Brookhaven Nat Lab, 65-67; asst prof anat, Sch Med, Ind Univ, Indianapolis, 67-72, res assoc orthop, 68-69. *Concurrent Pos:* USPHS fel, 65-67, spec fel, 71; guest worker, Nat Inst Dent Res, Md, 71; res collabr hemat, Brookhaven Nat Lab, 76; assoc ed, Anat Rec, 78-; consult ed, Gerodont, 82-90. *Mem:* Am Asn Anatomists; Am Soc Bone & Mineral. *Res:* Histochemistry, biochemistry and cellular physiology of connective tissue, bone and teeth; proteoglycan and collagen metabolism; bone cell origin and metabolism; effects of hormones on connective tissue, bone and cartilage metabolism; osteoinduction; cell biology; neurosciences; calcification of atherosclerotic lesions. *Mailing Add:* Dept Anat & Cell Biol Sch Med Univ Minn Duluth MN 55812. *Fax:* 218-726-6235; *E-Mail:* asevero@d.umn.edu

SEVERSON, DAVID LESTER, BIOCHEMICAL PHARMACOLOGY. *Current Pos:* ASSOC PROF PHARMACOL & BIOCHEM, UNIV CALGARY, 76- *Educ:* Univ BC, PhD(pharmacol), 72. *Res:* Metabolism of heart and blood vessels. *Mailing Add:* Dept Pharmacol Therapeut Univ Calgary Fac Med Calgary AB T2N 1N4 Can. *Fax:* 403-283-4740

SEVERSON, DONALD E(VERETT), CHEMICAL ENGINEERING. *Current Pos:* RETIRED. *Personal Data:* b Minneapolis, Minn, Dec 16, 19; m 47; c 5. *Educ:* Univ Minn, BChE, 41, PhD(chem eng), 58. *Prof Exp:* Res chem engr, Md Res Labs, Ford, Bacon, & Davis Inc, DC, 43-45. *Concurrent Pos:* Asst dir res contract, Univ NDak-US Army Qm Corps, 49-53; dir res contract, NSF grant, 57-59; dir res contracts, Univ NDak-Great Northern Rwy, 59-64 & 65-71; consult, Coal Res Lab, US Bur Mines, 64-; prin investr, Off Coal Res Proj Lignite, 72- *Mem:* Am Chem Soc; Am Inst Chem Engrs; Am Soc Eng Educ; Sigma Xi. *Res:* Food dehydration; mass transfer in evaporation; drying; coal research; gasification; high pressure technology. *Mailing Add:* 107 S Tanager Ct Louisville CO 80027-9700

SEVERSON, HERBERT H, HEALTH PSYCHOLOGY, SCHOOL PSYCHOLOGY. *Current Pos:* asst prof, 75-81, ASSOC PROF EDUC PSYCHOL & SPEC EDUC, UNIV ORE, 81-; RES SCIENTIST & PRIN INVESTR, ORE RES INST, 79-; LIC CLIN PSYCHOLOGIST, ORE, 81-; NAT LIC SCH PSYCHOLOGIST, 87- *Personal Data:* b Madison, Wis, May 27, 44; m 75, Bonnie McQueen; c Karyn & Britt. *Educ:* Wis State Univ, Whitewater, BS, 66; Univ Wis-Madison, MS, 69, PhD(educ psychol), 73. *Prof Exp:* Sch psychologist, Madison Pub Sch-Wis, 69-72; asst prof psychol, Univ Northern Colo, 72-75. *Concurrent Pos:* Regional dir, Nat Asn Sch Psychologists, 79-81; mem, Ore Sch Psychologist Asn; from dir to sci coordr, Ore Res Inst, 79-88; adj prof, Univ Ore, 83- *Mem:* Fel Am Psychol Asn; Nat Asn Sch Psychologists; Asn Adv Behav Ther; Soc Behav Med; Soc Prev Res. *Res:* Smoking and smokeless tobacco prevention with adolescents; drug use prevention; chewing tobacco cessation; worksite health promotion; identification of at risk children; screening for behavior disorders; risk preception; health psychology; smoking cessation with pregnant women; passive smoking; over 100 publications in journals, two books and seven video tapes. *Mailing Add:* Ore Res Inst 1715 Franklin Blvd Eugene OR 97403. *Fax:* 541-484-1108; *E-Mail:* herb@ori.org

SEVERSON, KEITH EDWARD, RANGE SCIENCE, WILDLIFE ECOLOGY. *Current Pos:* RETIRED. *Personal Data:* b Albert Lea, Minn, Dec 22, 36. *Educ:* Univ Minn, BA, 62; Univ Wyo, MS, 64; Univ Wyo, PhD(range mgt), 66. *Prof Exp:* Instr range ecol, SDak State Univ, 66-67, asst prof wildlife ecol, 67-70; range scientist, Rapid City, SDak, 70-77; wildlife biologist, 77-85; proj leader & res wildlife biologist, Rocky Mt Forest & Range Exp Sta, US Forest Serv, Tempe, AZ, 85-93; res biologist, Sch Mines & Technol, 93-95. *Mem:* Soc Range Mgt; Wildlife Soc. *Res:* Effects of grazing by livestock on wildlife habitat; nutrient cycling in pinyon-juniper woodlands; livestock distribution patterns and influences on riparian habitat; small mammals in pinyon-juniper habitats. *Mailing Add:* PO Box 7 Isle MN 56342

SEVERSON, ROLAND GEORGE, ORGANIC CHEMISTRY. *Current Pos:* from instr to assoc prof, 50-58, prof, 58-88, chmn dept, 60-88, EMER PROF CHEM, UNIV NDAK, 88- *Personal Data:* b Malta, Mont, Apr 1, 24; m 45; c 4. *Educ:* Mont State Col, BS, 46; Purdue Univ, MS, 48, PhD(chem), 51. *Prof Exp:* Asst chem, Purdue Univ, 46-48, asst instr, 48-50. *Mem:* Am Chem Soc. *Res:* Organometallics; synthesis of substituted organosilanes; organosilicon chemistry. *Mailing Add:* 2682 Catalina Dr Grand Junction CO 81506-1753

SEVERSON, RONALD CHARLES, GEOCHEMISTRY. *Current Pos:* SOIL SCIENTIST GEOCHEM, BR GEOCHEM, ENVIRON GEOCHEM SECT, US GEOL SURV, 74- *Personal Data:* b Tracy, Minn, Nov 14, 45; m 69. *Educ:* Univ Minn, BS, 67, MS, 72, PhD(pedology), 74. *Prof Exp:* Soil scientist, USDA Soil Conserv Serv, Minn, 65-67; soil analyst, US Cold Regions Res & Eng Lab, NH, 68-69; res asst, Soil Sci Dept, Univ Minn, St Paul, 70-74. *Concurrent Pos:* Instr soil genesis & geog, Dept Plant & Earth Sci, Univ Wis-River Falls, 73. *Mem:* Am Soc Agron; Soil Sci Soc Am; Coun Agr Sci & Technol; Am Soc Surface Mining & Reclamation; Int Affil Land Reclamatrists. *Res:* Spatial distribution of elements in soil materials and their changes with cultural activities. *Mailing Add:* 12520 W Auburn Ave Lakewood CO 80228. *Fax:* 303-236-3200

SEVERUD, FRED N, structural engineering; deceased, see previous edition for last biography

SEVIAN, WALTER ANDREW, APPLIED MATHEMATICS, COMPUTER SCIENCE. *Current Pos:* ADJ INSTR, SUFFOLK COMMUNITY COL, 91- *Personal Data:* b Copiague, NY, Sept 16, 40; m 64; c 3. *Educ:* State Univ NY, Stony Brook, BS, 62, MS, 64, PhD(appl math), 70. *Prof Exp:* Asst prof math, Southhampton Col, 70-71; systs engr energy systs anal, Brookhaven Nat Lab, 72-84; eng analyst, Grumman Data Systs, 84-85; sr engr, All Systs, 85-90. *Concurrent Pos:* Adj asst prof math, State Univ NY, Stony Brook, 74-75. *Mem:* Am Geophys Union; Asn Comput Users. *Res:* Computerized model/data couplings in environmental assessment of energy systems; free surface motion in groundwater hydrology; algorithm development for microcomputers; simulation of aircraft EW systems. *Mailing Add:* 35 Central Ave Miller Place NY 11764

SEVIK, MAURICE M, AEROSPACE ENGINEERING. *Current Pos:* HEAD, SHIP SIGNATURES DIRECTORATE, DAVID TAYLOR MODEL BASIN, 72- *Personal Data:* b Istanbul, Turkey, Mar 19, 23; US citizen; m 53; c 2. *Educ:* Robert Col, BS, 43; Imp Col Sci & Technol, DIC, 45; Pa State Univ, PhD(eng mech), 63. *Honors & Awards:* Gold Medal, Am Soc Naval Engrs, 90; Charles B Martell Award, Nat Security Indust Asn, 92; Rayleigh Lectr, Am Soc Mech Eng, 95; Robert Conrad Dexter Award for Sci Excellence, Off Naval Res, 96; Peter Bruel Gold Medal for Noise Control & Acoust, Am Soc Mech Engrs, 96. *Prof Exp:* Mem staff, aircraft design, Canadair, Arro Aircraft Co, 46-59; Appl Res Lab, Pa State Univ, 59-72. *Concurrent Pos:* Consult, IBM Corp, 64-65 & Off Res Anal, USAF, 65-66; vis prof, Cambridge Univ, 70, fel, Churchill Col, 70; prof & mem grad fac, asst dir, Appl Res Lab, 68; past chmn, Noise Control & Acoust Div, Am Soc Mech Eng, hon chmn; mem, Comt Hydroelasticity, Am Soc Naval Architects; mem, IPAC Comt, Aerospace Eng & Eng Sci Depts, Pa State Univ; adv panel, Instrumentation & Controls Div, Oak Ridge Nat Lab. *Mem:* Nat Acad Eng; fel Am Soc Mech Engrs; fel Acoust Soc Am; Am Soc Naval Engrs; Sigma Xi; Asn Prof Engrs. *Res:* Acoustics; measurement and control of flow and machinary-induced vibrations and noise with specific applications to submarines and surface ships; written approximately 24 publications and granted over 6 patents. *Mailing Add:* 7817 Horsehoe Lane Potomac MD 20854

SEVILLA, MICHAEL DOUGLAS, PHYSICAL CHEMISTRY, BIOPHYSICAL CHEMISTRY. *Current Pos:* from asst prof to assoc prof, 70-83, PROF CHEM, OAKLAND UNIV, 83- *Personal Data:* b San Jose, Calif, Feb 16, 42; m 63, Cynthia; c Lisa, Laura & Jessica. *Educ:* San Jose State Col, BS, 63; Univ Wash, PhD(phys chem), 67. *Prof Exp:* Univ Wash, 67-68; res chemist, Atomics Int Div, NAm Rockwell Corp, 68-70; actg assoc dean, Col Arts & Sci, 94-96. *Concurrent Pos:* Assoc ed, Radiation Res J; res grants, Dept Energy, 73-96, USDOA, 82-84, NIH, 86-, Petrol Res Fund, 87-91; counr, Radiation Res Soc, 89-91; chair radiation chem, Gordon Res Conf, 98. *Mem:* AAAS; Am Chem Soc; Sigma Xi; Radiation Res Soc; Am Soc Photobiol. *Res:* Radiation effects on biological molecules with particular interest in the free radical mechanisms of radiation damage and radioprotection; quantum chemistry. *Mailing Add:* Dept Chem Oakland Univ Rochester MI 48309. *Fax:* 248-370-2321; *E-Mail:* sevilla@oakland.edu

SEVIN, E(UGENE), ENGINEERING. *Current Pos:* RETIRED. *Personal Data:* b Chicago, Ill, Jan 5, 28; m 51; c 3. *Educ:* Ill Inst Technol, BS, 49, PhD(eng mech), 58; Calif Inst Technol, MS, 51. *Prof Exp:* Mem tech staff, Ill Inst Technol, 51-65, dir, Eng Mech Div, 65-70; prof mech eng & head, Mech Eng Dept, Technion Israel Inst Technol, 70-74; chief, Strategic Struct Div, Defense Nuclear Agency, 74-80, asst dep dir, 80-86, dir, Offensive & Space Systs, off dir, Defense Res & Eng, 86-94. *Concurrent Pos:* Eve instr, Ill Inst Technol, 55-63, adj prof, 65-70; mem adv comts, Dept Defense Agencies, 55- *Mem:* Nat Acad Eng; Am Inst Aeronaut & Astronaut; Am Soc Mech Engrs. *Res:* Structural dynamics and shock isolation, with emphasis on numerical methods, and particular application to nuclear weapons effects and the design of hardened military construction; high-explosive testing techniques for simulating nuclear airblast; cratering and ground shock, and developed a number of new and improved hardened facilities concepts, including deep underground constructions and the first superhard silos design; numerical methods; computer applications of structural design; nuclear weapons effects; author of over 30 publications. *Mailing Add:* 1782 Kenton Circle Lyndhurst OH 44124

SEVOIAN, MARTIN, VETERINARY MEDICINE & PATHOLOGY, MICROBIOLOGY. *Current Pos:* PROF VET SCI, UNIV MASS, AMHERST, 55- *Personal Data:* b Methuen, Mass, Mar 28, 19; m 54, Lucile H; c Janna & James. *Educ:* Univ Mass, BS, 49; Univ Pa, VMD, 53; Cornell Univ, MS, 54; Am Col Vet Microbiol, dipl. *Prof Exp:* Asst prof path, Cornell Univ, 54-55. *Concurrent Pos:* Adj prof, Tufts Univ. *Mem:* Am Vet Med Asn. *Res:* Infectious diseases, especially neoplasms; biologic delivery systems using biodegradeable polymers; immunology. *Mailing Add:* Paige Univ Mass Amherst MA 01003-0002

SEVON, WILLIAM DAVID, III, SURFICIAL GEOLOGY, GEOMORPHOLOGY. *Current Pos:* GEOLOGIST, PA GEOL SURV, 65- *Personal Data:* b Andover, Ohio, July 22, 33; m 88, Cecilia L Saccketti; c Douglass W & David H. *Educ:* Ohio Wesleyan Univ, BA, 55; Univ SDak, MA, 58; Univ Ill, PhD(geol), 61. *Prof Exp:* Lectr geol, Univ Canterbury, 61-65. *Mem:* AAAS; Geol Soc Am; Soc Econ Paleontologists & Mineralogists; Am Quaternary Asn; Sigma Xi. *Res:* Surficial geology of Pennsylvania Piedmont; Appalachian landscape development. *Mailing Add:* Pa Geol Surv PO Box 8453 Harrisburg PA 17105-8453. *Fax:* 717-783-7267

SEVY, ROGER WARREN, PHARMACOLOGY. *Current Pos:* asst prof, 54-57, head dept, 57-73, dean, Sch Med, 73-78, PROF PHARMACOL, SCH MED, TEMPLE UNIV, 56- *Personal Data:* b Richfield, Utah, Nov 6, 23; m 48; c 2. *Educ:* Univ Vt, MS, 48; Univ Ill, PhD(physiol), 51, MD, 54. *Prof Exp:* Asst physiol, Col Med, Univ Ill, 48-51, instr, 51-54. *Mem:* AAAS; Am Physiol Soc; Am Soc Pharmacol & Exp Therapeut; Endocrine Soc. *Res:* Cardiovascular pharmacology; vascular smooth muscle; hypertension; adrenal hormones and cardiovascular-renal function; pharmacology of platelets. *Mailing Add:* 242 Mather Rd Jenkintown PA 19046-3129

SEWARD, FREDERICK DOWNING, SUPERNOVA REMNANTS, NEUTRON STARS. *Personal Data:* b Goshen, NY, Dec 28, 31. *Educ:* Princeton Univ, BA, 53; Univ Rochester, PhD(physics), 58. *Prof Exp:* Staff mem res, Lawrence Livermore Lab, 58-77; astrophysicist res, Smithsonian Inst, 77-96. *Concurrent Pos:* Vis fel, Univ Leicester, Eng, 76, Inst Astron, Cambridge, 82; consult, NASA, 75-94. *Mem:* Fel Am Phys Soc; Am Astron Soc. *Res:* X-ray astronomy. *Mailing Add:* 158 Spencer Brook Rd Concord MA 01742. *Fax:* 617-495-7356

SEWARD, THOMAS PHILIP, III, APPLIED PHYSICS, GLASS SCIENCE. *Current Pos:* Res scientist, Corning Glass Works, 67-74, res supvr-mgr, 74-90, mgr, 90-93, SR RES ASSOC, INT TECHNOL, CORNING, INC, 93- *Personal Data:* b Brooklyn, NY, May 2, 39; m 65, 88, Eve Crittenden; c Amy & William. *Educ:* Wesleyan Univ, BA, 61; Harvard Univ, MS, 63, PhD(appl physics), 68. *Concurrent Pos:* Chmn glass div, Am Ceramic Soc, 88-89; chmn, NAm Sect, Soc Glass Technol, 95-97; adj prof glass sci & eng, Alfred Univ, NY, 95- *Mem:* Fel Am Ceramic Soc; Optic Soc Am; Mat Res Soc; Soc Glass Technol. *Res:* Structure, properties and composition of glass and glass ceramics; photochromic glass; interaction of light with glasses and ceramics; properties and manufacturing processes of fused silica glass. *Mailing Add:* 614 Euclid Ave Elmira NY 14901-1917

SEWARD, WILLIAM DAVIS, SOLID STATE PHYSICS. *Current Pos:* DIR, ENG SUPPORT, RAYTHEON E-SYSTS, FALLS CHURCH, 95- *Personal Data:* b Richmond, Va, Mar 14, 38; m 60, Shirley A Stevens; c Benjamin E. *Educ:* Univ Richmond, BS, 60; Cornell Univ, PhD(physics), 65. *Prof Exp:* Res assoc physics, Univ Ill, 65-67; asst prof, Univ Utah, 67-73; asst prof physics, Pomona Col, 73-76, assoc prof, 76-81; tech mgt staff, Eng Res Assocs, Vienna, Va, 81-95. *Mem:* Am Phys Soc. *Res:* Solid helium; computer aided instruction, system development. *Mailing Add:* Raytheon E Systs 7700 Arlington Blvd Falls Church VA 22042. *E-Mail:* wseward@fallschurch.esys.com

SEWELL, CURTIS, JR, ELECTRONICS ENGINEERING, GEOLOGY COMPUTER HARDWARE. *Current Pos:* RETIRED. *Personal Data:* b Iowa Park, Tex, Apr 14, 24; m 45, Wanda Beall; c Curtis E, Jack M & William M. *Educ:* Hardin Col, 41-42; Tex Tech Col, 42-43; Univ NH, 43; Va Polytech Inst, 44. *Prof Exp:* Electronics engr, Los Alamos Sci Lab, 46-57; mgr eng res, Isotopes, Inc, NJ, 57-62; electronics engr, Lawrence Livermore Lab, 62-88. *Concurrent Pos:* Instr, Chabot Col, Livermore, Calif, 78- *Mem:* Creation Res Soc. *Res:* Electronic circuit design; nuclear and laboratory instrumentation; digital computers; feedback amplifiers; microcomputers and systems for control and data processing; evolution vs creation. *Mailing Add:* 1625 Alviso Pl Livermore CA 94550

SEWELL, DUANE CAMPBELL, physics, for more information see previous edition

SEWELL, FRANK ANDERSON, JR, ELECTRONIC PHYSICS. *Current Pos:* SR ENGR, T J WATSON RES CTR, IBM CORP, 83- *Personal Data:* b Atlanta, Ga, June 25, 34; m 58; c 1. *Educ:* Vanderbilt Univ, BA, 56; Emory Univ, MA, 58; Brown Univ, PhD(physics), 66. *Prof Exp:* Instr physics, Emory Univ, 57-58; sr engr, Sperry Gyroscope Co, 58-60, res staff mem, Sperry Rand Corp, 65-73, mgr optoelectronics dept, 73-78, dir, semiconductor lab, Sperry Res Ctr, Sperry Rand Corp, 78- *Mem:* Sr mem Inst Elec & Electronics Engrs; Am Phys Soc; Soc Photog Scientists & Engrs. *Res:* Semiconductor device physics; electrophotography; high resolution x-ray and electron beam lithography. *Mailing Add:* T J Watson Res Ctr IBM Corp PO Box 218 Yorktown Heights NY 10598

SEWELL, HOMER B, ANIMAL NUTRITION. *Current Pos:* County agt, 53-58, from asst prof to assoc prof, 58-72, PROF ANIMAL HUSB, EXTEN, UNIV MO, COLUMBIA, 72- *Personal Data:* b Red Bird, Mo, Aug 4, 20. *Educ:* Univ Mo, BS, 53, MS, 63; Univ Ky, PhD(ruminate nutrit), 65. *Mem:* Am Soc Animal Sci; Sigma Xi. *Res:* Beef cattle feeding; stability of vitamin A liver stores of ruminants. *Mailing Add:* 2606 Highland Dr Columbia MO 65203

SEWELL, JOHN I, AGRICULTURAL WATER QUALITY. *Current Pos:* from asst prof to prof agr eng, Univ Tenn, 62-77, assoc head dept, 73-77, asst dean, 77-87, ASSOC DEAN, AGR EXP STA, UNIV TENN, KNOXVILLE, 87- *Personal Data:* b Cedartown, Ga, Aug 28, 33; m 60, Rebecca Underwood; c Mary & John Jr. *Educ:* Univ Ga, BSAE, 54; NC State Univ, MSAE, 58, PhD(agr eng), 62. *Prof Exp:* Instr agr eng, NC State Univ, 60-62. *Concurrent Pos:* Mem, Tenn Air Pollution Control Bd, 90- *Mem:* Sr mem Am Soc Agr Engrs; Coun Agr Sci & Technol; Soil Conserv Soc Am. *Res:* Land grading in alluvial lands for improved surface drainage; animal waste management; infrared aerial remote sensing; irrigation; pond sealing; farm structures; water quality. *Mailing Add:* Assoc Dean Agr Exp Sta 103 Morgan Hall Univ Tenn Knoxville TN 37916

SEWELL, KENNETH GLENN, ELECTRO-OPTICS, INFRARED. *Current Pos:* ENG PROJ MGR, LOCKHEED MARTIN TACTICAL AIRCRAFT SYSTS, FT WORTH, 89- *Personal Data:* b Sherman, Tex, July 26, 33; m 54; c 2. *Educ:* Okla State Univ, BS, 57; Southern Methodist Univ, MS, 60; Tex Christian Univ, PhD(physics), 64. *Prof Exp:* Aerodyn engr, Chance Vought Aircraft Corp, 57-60; res scientist, LTV Res Ctr, Ling-Tempco Vought Inc, 60-61, sr scientist, 64-67; assoc prof physics, Abilene Christian Col, 67-68; sr scientist, LTV Res Ctr Ling-Tempco Vought, Inc, Dallas, 68-69, tech dir Isoray, 69-70; dir res & develop, Varo Inc, 70-74, engr mgr, 74-78, gen mgr, Tex Div, 78-86; dir res & develop, Recon Optical, 86-89. *Mem:* Am Phys Soc; Optical Soc Am; Inst Elec & Electronics Engrs. *Res:* Photoelectric devices; infrared, x-ray imaging, research and development management; nonlinear optics; atomic physics; electrooptics; infrared techniques. *Mailing Add:* 7661 La Bolsa Dr Dallas TX 75248

SEWELL, WINIFRED, INFORMATION SCIENCE, PHARMACY. *Current Pos:* CONSULT, 70- *Personal Data:* b Newport, Wash, Aug 12, 17. *Educ:* Wash State Univ, AB, 38; Columbia Univ, BS, 40. *Hon Degrees:* DSc, Philadelphia Col Pharm & Sci, 79. *Honors & Awards:* Eliot Prize, Med Libr Asn, 77. *Prof Exp:* Jr asst librn, Columbia Univ, 40-42; librn, Wellcome Res Labs, NY, 42-46; sr librn, Squibb Inst Med Res, NJ, 46-61; med subj heading specialist, Nat Libr Med, 61-62, dep chief bibliog serv div, 62-64, head drug lit prog, 64-70; adj asst prof, Health Sci Ctr, Univ Md, Baltimore City, 70-85. *Concurrent Pos:* Ed, Unlisted Drugs, 49-59 & 61-64; mem comn pharmaceut abstr, Int Fedn Pharm, 58-60; ad hoc comt on patent off steroid code, 59-60; comt current med terminology, AMA, 62-64; consult, Winthrop Labs, 63; comt mod methods handling chem info, Nat Acad Sci-Nat Res Coun, 64-67; adj lectr Col Libr & Info Serv, Univ Md, 69-92; consult, Nat Asn Hosp Develop, Fed Libr Comt, Sheppard & Enoch Pratt Hosps, Biospherics, Nat Libr Med & Indust, acad & govt groups, 70-; ed, health affairs series of Gale Info Guides, 72-81; consult, Nat Health Planning Info Ctr, 75-81; Nat Libr Med res grant, 81-85; consult, US Pharmacopiea, 90- *Mem:* Drug Info Asn (vpres, 65-66, pres, 70-71); Spec Libr Asn (pres, 60-61); Am Libr Asn; Am Soc Info Sci; fel Med Libr Asn; AAAS. *Res:* Coordination of chemical and biomedical terminology, especially in online information retrieval systems; library science; drug information centers; medical information transfer; online searching behavior of pharmacists and pathologists; bibliometrics of molecular biology; working with natural language search engives for use by health professionals. *Mailing Add:* 6513 76th Pl Cabin John MD 20818. *Fax:* 301-229-5009; *E-Mail:* winswell@wam.umd.edu

SEXSMITH, FREDERICK HAMILTON, CHEMISTRY. *Current Pos:* mgr Res & Develop Div, Hughson Chem Co Div, 66-80, dir res, Chem Prod Group, 80-84, div mgr, Elastomer Prod Div, 84-87, mgr, New Bus & Technol, Int Group, 87-90, SR FEL, LORD CORP, 90- *Personal Data:* b Ft Erie, Ont, Mar 30, 29; US citizen; m 64, Joan Mather; c Malcolm H & Katherine A. *Educ:* Queen's Univ, Ont, BA, 51, MA, 53; Princeton Univ, MA, 54, PhD(phys chem), 57. *Prof Exp:* Supvr, Chicopee Mfg Co, 56-62, dir res specialty chem, Refined Prod Co, 62-64 & Refined Prod Co Div, Millmaster-Onyx, 64-65; sect head, Ethicon Inc, 65-66. *Concurrent Pos:* Textile Res Inst fel, Princeton Univ, 57. *Mem:* Am Chem Soc; Chem Inst Can; Fiber Soc; Am Asn Textile Chemists & Colorists; Am Inst Chemists. *Res:* Applied polymer chemistry; colloid science; surface chemistry; emulsion polymerization; textile finishes; adhesives for elastomers; polyurethane coatings; rubber chemicals; granted 22 US patents. *Mailing Add:* 1325 Ponderosa Dr Erie PA 16509. *Fax:* 814-866-6117

SEXSMITH, ROBERT G, STRUCTURAL ENGINEERING. *Current Pos:* ASSOC PROF CIVIL ENG, UNIV BC, 92- *Personal Data:* b Regina, Can, Apr 13, 38; m 64, Sheila Stanley; c 3. *Educ:* Univ BC, BASc, 61; Stanford Univ, MS, 63, Engr, 66, PhD(civil eng), 67. *Prof Exp:* Design engr, Phillips, Barratt & Partners, 63-64; from asst prof to assoc prof struct eng, Cornell Univ, 67-76; res scientist, Western Forest Prod Lab, 76-79; sr engr, 79-81, prin, Buckland & Taylor Ltd, 81-92. *Concurrent Pos:* Mem, Struct Div Exec Comt, Can Soc Civil Eng, 77-83, Can Comt Earthquake Eng. *Mem:* Am Concrete Inst; Am Soc Civil Engrs; Can Soc Civil Eng; Int Asn Bridge & Struct Eng; Earthquake Eng Res Inst. *Res:* Application of probabilistic concepts to structural engineering; structural mechanics; decision analysis for seismic safety. *Mailing Add:* Dept Civil Eng Univ BC 2324 Main Mall Vancouver BC V6T 1Z4 Can

SEXTON, ALAN WILLIAM, PHYSIOLOGY. *Current Pos:* RETIRED. *Personal Data:* b Newark, NJ, Mar 25, 25; m 46; c 3. *Educ:* Mont State Univ, BS, 50; Univ Mo, MA, 52, PhD(physiol), 55. *Prof Exp:* Instr physiol, Med Sch, Univ Mo, 54-55; instr human growth, Med Sch, Univ Colo, Denver Ctr, 55-59, physiologist, Child Res Coun, 55-62, asst prof physiol, Med Sch, 59-63, from asst prof to assoc prof phys med, 63-85. *Concurrent Pos:* Mgt consult, Nat Heart, Lung & Blood Inst. *Mem:* Am Physiol Soc; Soc Exp Biol & Med. *Res:* Physiology of muscle contraction; effects of hormones on muscle contractility. *Mailing Add:* 30163 Canterbury Circle Evergreen CO 80439

SEXTON, KEN, ENVIRONMENTAL RISK ASSESSMENT, TOXIC AIR POLLUTANTS. *Current Pos:* dir, Sci Rev, Health Effects Inst, 85-87, DIR, OFF HEALTH RES, US ENVIRON PROTECTION AGENCY, 87- *Personal Data:* b Moscow, Idaho, Nov 6, 49. *Educ:* USAF Acad, BS, 72; Wash State Univ, MS, 77; Tex Tech Univ, MA, 79; Harvard Univ, PhD(environ health), 83. *Prof Exp:* Comput officer, USAF, 72-74; res asst, Wash State Univ, 75-77, environ engr chem eng, 77-79; environ engr, Acurex Corp, 79-80; prog dir, Calif Dept Health, 83-85. *Mem:* Am Chem Soc; Am Pub Health Asn; Air Pollution Control Asn; NY Acad Sci; AAAS; Am Soc Heating, Refrig & Air-Conditioning Engrs. *Res:* Human exposure to toxic air pollution, particularly health risk assessment; environmental policy analysis; indoor air quality in non-occupational environments. *Mailing Add:* 3746 W Calhoun Pkwy Minneapolis MN 55416

SEXTON, OWEN JAMES, VERTEBRATE ECOLOGY, CONSERVATION BIOLOGY. *Current Pos:* From instr to assoc prof, 55-68, exec officer dept, 64-66, PROF BIOL, WASH UNIV, 68- *Personal Data:* b Philadelphia, Pa, July 11, 26; m 52, Mildred L Bloomsburgh; c Kenneth G, Jean V, Ann V & Carolyn Q. *Educ:* Oberlin Col, BA, 51; Univ Mich, MA, 53, PhD(vert natural hist), 57. *Concurrent Pos:* NSF fel, Univ Chicago, 66-67; trop consult, UNESCO, 74-75; prof zool, Univ Mich Biol Sta, 75-83; vis res fel, Univ New Eng, NSW, Australia, 84. *Mem:* Ecol Soc Am; Am Soc Ichthyologists & Herpetologists; Soc Study Amphibians & Reptiles. *Res:* Studies of factors regulating the distribution of organisms (emphasis upon amphibians and reptiles but including other vertebrates and plants) in space and time. *Mailing Add:* Campus Box 1137 St Louis MO 63130. *Fax:* 314-935-4432

SEXTON, ROBERT FENIMORE, HISTORY. *Current Pos:* EXEC DIR, PRICHARD COM ACAD EXCELLENCE, 83-; FOUNDER & PRES, KY CTR PUB ISSUES, 88- *Personal Data:* b Cincinnati, Ohio, Jan 13, 42; m 85, Pam Peyton Papka; c Rebecca, Robert B, Ouita, Paige & Perry. *Educ:* Yale Univ, BA, 64; Univ Wash, Seattle, MA, 68, PHD(hist), 70. *Hon Degrees:* DHL, Berea Col, 90, Georgetown Col, 93. *Honors & Awards:* Charles A Dana Award, 94. *Prof Exp:* Asst prof hist, Murray State Univ, 68-70; dir, Off Acad Progs, Commonwealth Ky, 70-73; assoc dean & exec dir, Off Exp Educ, Univ Ky, 73-80; dep exec dir, Ky Coun Higher Educ, 80-83. *Concurrent Pos:* Bd dirs, Ky Long Term Policy Res Ctr, Coun Advan Exp Learning, 76-80; mem, Gov Task Force Health Care, 92- *Mem:* Am Asn Higher Educ. *Mailing Add:* 151 Kentucky Ave Lexington KY 40502-1754

SEXTON, THOMAS JOHN, CRYOBIOLOGY, ANIMAL PHYSIOLOGY. *Current Pos:* res physiologist, 71-83, res leader, 83-88, DIR, LIVESTOCK & POULTRY SCI INST, AGR RES SERV, USDA, 88- *Personal Data:* b Mt Holly, NJ, Aug 11, 42; m 64; c 3. *Educ:* Del Valley Col, BS, 64; Univ NH, MS, 66; Pa State Univ, PhD(dairy sci), 72. *Honors & Awards:* Res Award, Poultry Sci Asn, 82. *Prof Exp:* Res asst, Univ NH, 64-66 & Univ Conn, 66-67; res assoc, Pa State Univ, 67-71. *Concurrent Pos:* Adj prof, Auburn Univ, Ala, 84- *Mem:* Poultry Sci Asn; World's Poultry Sci Asn; Sigma Xi; Soc Cryobiol. *Res:* Critical problems that limit the reproductive efficiency of the avian male; cryogenic preservation of semen, artificial insemination and isolation of female gamete. *Mailing Add:* USDA ARS Livestock & Poultry Sci Bldg 200 Rm 17 Barc E 10300 Baltimore Ave Beltsville MD 20705-2350

SEXTRO, RICHARD GEORGE, ENVIRONMENTAL SCIENCES. *Current Pos:* energy assessment, 76-82, STAFF SCIENTIST INDOOR AIR QUAL, LAWRENCE BERKELEY LAB, 82- *Personal Data:* b Odell, Nebr, Dec 31, 44; m 67, Joan Jaques; c Laura & Gregory. *Educ:* Carnegie Inst Technol, BS, 67; Univ Calif, Berkeley, MS, 69, PhD(nuclear chem), 73. *Prof Exp:* Fel nuclear chem, Lawrence Berkeley Lab, 74-75 & energy policy, NSF, 75-76. *Concurrent Pos:* Mem, Radiation Adv Comt, US Environ Protection Agency Sci Adv Bd; Hewlett fel, Princeton Univ, 88-89. *Mem:* AAAS; Int Soc Exposure Anal; Am Asn Aerosol Res; Int Soc Indoor Air Qual. *Res:* Measurement and behavior of indoor air pollutants, with emphasis on concentrations of radon and progeny in indoor air and on the behavior of environmental tobacco smoke and other indoor particles. *Mailing Add:* Lawrence Berkeley Lab Bldg 90-3058 Berkeley CA 94720. *Fax:* 510-486-6658; *E-Mail:* rgsextro@lbl.gov

SEYA, TSUKASA, COMPLEMENT RECEPTORS. *Current Pos:* DIR COMPLEMENT, CTR ADULT DIS, OSAKA, 87- *Personal Data:* b Fukushima Prefecture, Oct 18, 50; m 90; c 2. *Educ:* Hokkaido Univ, Master D, 76, PhD, 84, MD, 87. *Prof Exp:* Resident clotting factors, Dept Internal Med, Sch Med, Hokkaido Univ, 76-79, res fel complement, Fac Pharmaceut Sci, 79-84; res assoc complement, Sch Med, Wash Univ, 84-87. *Concurrent Pos:* Lectr, Osaka Univ. *Mem:* Am Asn Immunologists; NY Acad Sci. *Res:* Complement proteins, receptors, regulatory molecules and adhesion molecules participating in host-defense system which involves host lymphocytes phagocytes and cytokine networks. *Mailing Add:* Dept Immunol Ctr Adult Dis 1-3-3 Nakamichi Higashinari-ku Osaka 537 Japan. *Fax:* 81-6-972-7749; *E-Mail:* tseya@takaipro.jrdc.go.jp

SEYB, LESLIE PHILIP, ENVIRONMENTAL CHEMISTRY. *Current Pos:* RETIRED. *Personal Data:* b Franklin, Iowa, May 11, 15; m 39, Helen Standiford; c Stefan & Stanford. *Educ:* Coe Col, AB, 35; Univ Iowa, MS, 37, PhD(org chem), 39. *Prof Exp:* Chem asst, Patent Dept, Phillips Petrol Co, 39-42; res chemist & group leader, Diamond Alkali Co, 42-50, mgr res, 50-53, assoc dir res, 53-63; chief phys sci, Pac Northwest Water Lab, Environ Protection Agency, 64-67, asst prog dir eutrophication, 67-71, asst dir, 71-78. *Mem:* Am Chem Soc; Sigma Xi. *Res:* Fatty acids; wetting agents; textile bleaching; heterocyclic N-compounds; ethylene derivatives; N-chloro organic; chloro hydrocarbons; textile mothproofing; pesticides; xylene derivatives; metallo organics; acetylene derivatives; water pollution and industrial waste control; water and analytical chemistry. *Mailing Add:* 2960 NW Jackson St Corvallis OR 97330

SEYBERT, DAVID WAYNE, ENZYMOLOGY, LIPID PEROXIDATION. *Current Pos:* asst prof, 79-82, assoc prof chem, 82-96, PROF, DUQUESNE UNIV, 96- *Personal Data:* b Hazleton, Pa, May 2, 50; m 87, Diane Benacquista; c Bryan, Justin & Marissa. *Educ:* Bloomsburg State Col, BA, 72; Cornell Univ, PhD(biochem), 76. *Prof Exp:* Res assoc, Med Ctr, Duke Univ, 76-79. *Concurrent Pos:* NIH prin investr, Duquesne Univ, 80-84, 91-95. *Mem:* Am Chem Soc; AAAS; Sigma Xi; Am Soc Biochem & Molecular Biol. *Res:* Enzymology of biological oxidation, with particular emphasis on hemoproteins and cytochrome P-450 catalyzed steroid hydroxylations, lipid peroxidation, oxidation of low density lipoprotein, iron chelation. *Mailing Add:* Dept Chem & Biochem Duquesne Univ Pittsburgh PA 15282-1503. *Fax:* 412-396-5683; *E-Mail:* seybert@duq3.cc.duq.edu

SEYBOLD, PAUL GRANT, STRUCTURE-PROPERTY RELATIONS, LUMINESCENCE. *Current Pos:* from asst prof to PROF CHEM, WRIGHT STATE UNIV, 70- *Personal Data:* b Camden, NJ, July 11, 37. *Educ:* Cornell Univ, BA, 60; Harvard Univ, PhD(biophys), 68. *Prof Exp:* Postdoctoral fel theoret chem, Univ Uppsala, Sweden, 67-69; postdoctoral fel biochem, Univ Ill, 69-70. *Concurrent Pos:* Vis scientist, Monell Chem Senses Ctr, 73, Univ Wash, 81; vis prof, Stockholm Univ, Sweden, 78-79, Univ Fla, 86; vis scholar, Univ Calif, San Diego, 86-87. *Mem:* Am Chem Soc; AAAS; Sigma Xi. *Res:* Development of molecular structure, property relationships for chemicals; molecular luminescence spectroscopy, especially room-temperature phosphorescence. *Mailing Add:* Dept Chem Wright State Univ Dayton OH 45435

SEYBOLD, VIRGINIA SUSAN (DICK), NEUROSCIENCE, SPINAL CORD. *Current Pos:* from instr to assoc prof, 78-90, PROF, DEPT CELL BIOL & NEUROANAT, UNIV MINN, 90- *Personal Data:* b Milwaukee, Wis, March 23, 51; m 72. *Educ:* Col William & Mary, BS, 72; Univ Minn, PhD(pharmacol), 77. *Mem:* Soc Neurosci. *Res:* Determination of transmitter-coded neuronal cirucitry in the spinal cord using immunohistochemical, labeling via retrograde transport and autoradiographic methods with focus on pathways for pain, analgesia and autonomic function. *Mailing Add:* 4-135 Jackson Hall Univ Minn Sch Med 321 Church St SE Minneapolis MN 55455-0217

SEYDEL, FRANK DAVID, BIOETHICS, BIOCHEMISTRY. *Current Pos:* DIR, BIOCHEM GENETICS LAB, DEPT OBSTET/GYNEC, SCH MED, GEORGETOWN UNIV, 83- *Personal Data:* b Davenport, Iowa, May 15, 44; m 70; c 2. *Educ:* Iowa Wesleyan Col, BS, 66; Iowa State Univ, PhD(biochem, cell biol), 73; Princeton Theol Sem, MDiv, 76; Am Bd Med Genetics, dipl, 90. *Prof Exp:* Asst prof chem, Univ Tenn, 76-80; assoc prof, Friends Univ, Wichita, 80-83. *Concurrent Pos:* Minister, Iowa Conf United Methodist Church, 74- Handicapped. *Mem:* Sigma Xi; Am Soc Human Genetics; Am Asn Ment Retardation. *Res:* Analysis of alfa feto-protein for prenatal diagnosis of neural tube defects. *Mailing Add:* 11134 Oak Leaf Dr Silver Spring MD 20901-1310

SEYDEL, ROBERT E, MATHEMATICS. *Current Pos:* PROF MED, QUINCY COL, 88- *Personal Data:* b Davenport, Iowa, Aug 29, 42. *Educ:* Iowa Wesleyan Col, BS, 65; Univ Iowa, PhD(math), 73. *Prof Exp:* Researcher, Lockheed Space Co, 79-85; sr engr, McDonald Douglas, 85-88. *Res:* Finite projective planes. *Mailing Add:* 48 Spring Way St Peters MO 63376-2699

SEYER, JEROME MICHAEL, BIOCHEMISTRY. *Current Pos:* from asst prof to assoc prof, 74-84, PROF BIOCHEM, UNIV TENN, MEMPHIS, 84- *Personal Data:* b Oran, Mo, Jan 2, 37; m 69; c 2. *Educ:* Univ Mo, Columbia, BS, 59, PhD(biochem), 66. *Prof Exp:* Orthop res fel, Mass Gen Hosp, Boston, 66-69; prof exp res asst biochem, Univ Mo, Columbia, 65-66; res assoc orthop res, Mass Gen Hosp, Boston, 66-71; res assoc orthop res, Children's Hosp, Boston, 71-74. *Concurrent Pos:* Res assoc, Harvard Med Sch, 66-; res chemist, Vet Admin Hosp, Memphis, 74-86, Carrer Scientist, 86- *Mem:* AAAS; Am Chem Soc; Orthop Res Soc. *Res:* Biological mechanism of calcification of bone and dental enamel and development of cartilage collagen; special emphasis of the two above areas along protein sequence analysis; diseases in connective tissues with special reference to fibrosis of lung, liver and scar tissue and amino acid sequence of collagen. *Mailing Add:* Dept Biochem E Virginia Med Sch Hampton VA Med Ctr 100 Emancipation Rd Hampton VA 23667

SEYFERT, CARL K, JR, STRUCTURAL GEOLOGY, PETROLOGY. *Current Pos:* chmn dept, 67-72, assoc prof, 67-72, PROF GEOL, STATE UNIV NY COL BUFFALO, 72- *Personal Data:* b Pecos, Tex, Feb 12, 38; m 60; c 2. *Educ:* Vanderbilt Univ, BA, 60; Stanford Univ, PhD(geol), 65. *Prof Exp:* From instr to asst prof geol, Queens Col, NY, 64-67. *Concurrent Pos:* Geol Soc Am Penrose grant, Stanford Univ, 62-64; Shell grant fundamental res, 62-64; Sigma Xi grant, Queens Col, NY, 65-68; Res Found State Univ NY grant, State Univ NY Col Buffalo, 69-72. *Mem:* AAAS; Geol Soc Am. *Res:* Igneous and metamorphic petrology and structural geology; compositional variation within granitic plutons; paleomagnetism and geotectonics; reconstruction of large scale movements of continents throughout geologic time. *Mailing Add:* Dept Earth Sci State Univ NY 1300 Elmwood Ave Buffalo NY 14222-1095

SEYFERTH, DIETMAR, ORGANOMETALLIC CHEMISTRY. *Current Pos:* from instr to assoc prof, 57-65, PROF CHEM, MASS INST TECHNOL, 65-, ROBERT T HASLAM & BRADLEY DEWEY PROF CHEM, 83- *Personal Data:* b Chemnitz, Ger, Jan 11, 29; nat US; m 56, Helena A McCoy; c Eric S, Karl D & Elisabeth M. *Educ:* Univ Buffalo, BA, 51; Harvard Univ, MA, 53, PhD(inorg chem), 55. *Hon Degrees:* Dr, Univ Aix-Marseille III, Paul

Sabatier Univ, Toulouse, 92. *Honors & Awards:* Frederic Stanley Kipping Award in Organosilicon Chem, 72; Distinguished Serv Award Advan Inorg Chem, Am Chem Soc & Award in Organometallic Chem; Sr Award, Alexander von Humboldt Found. *Prof Exp:* Res chemist, Dow Corning Corp, 55-56; res assoc, Harvard Univ, 56-57. *Concurrent Pos:* Regional ed, J Organometal Chem, 63-81, coord ed, Organometal Chem Rev, 64-81; Guggenheim fel, 68; ed, Organometallics, Am Chem Soc, 81- *Mem:* Am Chem Soc; Royal Soc Chem; fel Ger Acad Scientists Leopoldina; fel AAAS; Ger Chem Soc; fel Inst Mat; Mat Res Soc; Am Ceramic Soc; fel Am Acad Arts & Sci. *Res:* Main group, especially silicon, lithium and mercury and transition metal organometallic chemistry; organophosphorus chemistry; organic synthesis; applications of organometallic chemistry to ceramics. *Mailing Add:* Dept Chem 4-382 77 Massachusetts Ave Mass Inst Technol Cambridge MA 02139-4307. *E-Mail:* seyferrh@wrcf.mit.edu

SEYFRIED, THOMAS NEIL, NEUROBIOLOGY, NEUROGENETICS. *Current Pos:* assoc prof, 85-90, PROF BIOL, BOSTON COL, 90- *Personal Data:* b Flushing, NY, July 25, 46; m 73; c 3. *Educ:* St Francis Col, Maine, BA, 68; Ill State Univ, MS, 73; Univ Ill, PhD(genetics), 76. *Prof Exp:* Fel neurogenetics, Dept Neurol, Sch Med, Yale Univ, 76-79, asst prof, 79-84. *Mem:* Genetics Soc Am; AAAS; Am Soc Neurochem; Int Soc Neurochem; Soc Neurosci; Am Epilepsy Soc. *Res:* Cellular localization and function of brain gangliosides; developmental genetics of inherited epilepsy in mice; genetic control of brain myelinogenesis; cellular adhesion in brain tumors. *Mailing Add:* Dept Biol Boston Col Chestnut Hill MA 02167

SEYFRIED, WILLIAM E, JR, EXPERIMENTAL GEOCHEMISTRY, HYDROTHERMAL ORE DEPOSITS. *Current Pos:* from asst prof to assoc prof geol, 78-85, PROF GEOL, UNIV MINN, 85-, HEAD, DEPT GEOL & GEOPHYSICS, 93- *Personal Data:* b Flushing, NY, July 31, 48; m 71, Carol Coulter; c Erin & Peter. *Educ:* Bridgewater State Col, BSc, 70; La State Univ, MSc, 73; Univ Southern Calif, PhD(geol), 77. *Honors & Awards:* Thayer-Lindsley Distinguished Lectr, Soc Econ Geologists, 89-90. *Prof Exp:* Postdoctoral fel, Stanford Univ, 77-78. *Concurrent Pos:* Vis scientist, US Geol Surv, Reston, Va, 85-86. *Mem:* Geochem Soc; AAAS; Am Geophys Union; Soc Econ Geologists; Geol Soc Am. *Res:* Chemical evolution of aqueous fluids during rockfluid interaction processes; combined experimental and theoretical approaches to constrain the reactivity and solubility of geologically important minerals in aqueous fluids at a wide range of temperatures and pressures. *Mailing Add:* Dept Geol & Geophysics Univ Minn 310 Pillsbury Dr SE Minneapolis MN 55455-0219. *Fax:* 612-625-3819

SEYLER, CHARLES EUGENE, PLASMA PHYSICS. *Current Pos:* PROF PLASMA PHYSICS ELEC ENG, CORNELL UNIV, 81- *Personal Data:* b Eustis Fla, June, 2, 48; c Sean & Kyle. *Educ:* Univ SFla, BA, 70, MA, 72; Univ Iowa, PhD(physics), 75. *Prof Exp:* Res scientist plasma physics, Courant Inst Math Sci, NY Univ, 75-78; staff mem, Los Alamos Nat Lab, 78-81. *Concurrent Pos:* Vis staff mem, Los Alamos Nat Lab, 81- *Mem:* Am Geophys Union. *Res:* Plasma processes and dynamics of terrestrial ionosphere and magnetosphere. *Mailing Add:* 92 Mount Pleasant Rd Ithaca NY 14850

SEYLER, RICHARD G, NUCLEAR PHYSICS. *Current Pos:* Vis asst prof, 61-63, from asst prof to assoc prof, 63-73, PROF PHYSICS, OHIO STATE UNIV, 73- *Personal Data:* b Du Bois, Pa, June 14, 33; m 64. *Educ:* Pa State Univ, BS, 55, MS, 59, PhD(physics), 61. *Mem:* Am Phys Soc. *Res:* Theoretical low-energy nuclear physics. *Mailing Add:* Dept Physics Ohio State Univ Columbus OH 43210

SEYMOUR, ALLYN H, RADIATION ECOLOGY, FISH BIOLOGY. *Current Pos:* asst dir lab radiation biol, Univ Wash, 58-63, prof, 63-79, dir lab radiation ecol, 66-78, EMER PROF FISHERIES, COL FISHERIES, UNIV WASH, 79- *Personal Data:* b Seattle, Wash, Aug 1, 13; m 40, Barbara J Noonan; c Allyn H Jr, Denny R & Gary N. *Educ:* Univ Wash, BS, 37, PhD, 56. *Prof Exp:* Jr scientist, State Dept Fisheries, Wash, 40-41; asst scientist, Int Fisheries Comn, 42-47; res assoc & asst dir appl fisheries lab, Univ Wash, 48-56; marine biologist, Div Biol & Med, US AEC, DC, 56-58. *Concurrent Pos:* Chmn panel radioactivity in the marine environ, 68-71 & mem panel nuclear weapons effects, Nat Res Coun, 74-75; sci adv, Nat Coun Radiation Protection & Measurement, 87- *Mem:* Am Inst Fishery Res Biol; Health Physics Soc; Sigma Xi. *Res:* Biological distribution of radioisotopes; aquatic radioecology. *Mailing Add:* 5855 Oberlin NE Seattle WA 98105-2125

SEYMOUR, BRIAN RICHARD, APPLIED MATHEMATICS, ACOUSTICS. *Current Pos:* from asst prof to assoc prof, Univ BC, 73-81, actg dir appl math, 86-88, dir, Inst Appl Math, 88-93, PROF MATH, UNIV BC, VANCOUVER, 81- *Personal Data:* b Chesterfield, UK, Sept 25, 44; US citizen; m 65, Rosemary Pembleton; c Mark, Jane & Richard. *Educ:* Univ Manchester, UK, BSc, 65; Univ Nottingham, UK, PhD(theoret mech), 69. *Prof Exp:* Asst prof appl math, Lehigh Univ, Bethlehem, Pa, 69-70; asst prof math, NY Univ, 70-73; vis fel math, St Catherine's Col, Oxford, UK, 78-79; vis prof math, Monash & Melbourne Univ, Australia, 84-85, Ctr Water Res, Univ Western Australia, 93-94. *Concurrent Pos:* Sr fel, Sci Res Coun, UK, 78; sr Killam fel, Killam Found, Can, 84. *Mem:* Can Appl Math Soc; Soc Indust & Appl Math. *Res:* Analytical and numerical solutions of problems in fluid mechanics and elasticity; wave propagation in nonlinear and inhomogenesis materials. *Mailing Add:* 2796 W 38th Ave Vancouver BC V6N 2W9 Can. *E-Mail:* seymour@math.ubc.ca

SEYMOUR, EDWARD E, CHEMISTRY, ENGINEERING. *Current Pos:* dep prog dir advan automation, 94-95, dep dir air traffic systs develop, 95-96, DIR AIR TRAFFIC SYSTS DEVELOP, FED AVIATION ADMIN, 96- *Personal Data:* b July 28, 50. *Educ:* Univ Santa Clara, BS, 72; George Washington Univ, MSA, 78; Univ Puget Sound, JD, 83. *Prof Exp:* Chief staff & prog coun, Off Ocean Servs, Nat Ocean Serv, Nat Oceanic & Atmospheric Admin, US Dept Com, 84-86, sr attorney, Off Gen Coun, 86-91, dep dir, Systs Prog Off, 91-94. *Mailing Add:* 701 Pennsylvania Ave NW Suite 200 Washington DC 20004

SEYMOUR, KEITH GOLDIN, PESTICIDE CHEMISTRY, FORMULATIONS. *Current Pos:* RETIRED. *Personal Data:* b Fairfax, Mo, Jan 25, 22; m 43; c 2. *Educ:* Iowa State Univ, BS, 43, MS, 50; Tex A&M Univ, PhD(soil chem), 54. *Prof Exp:* Chemist, Tex Div, Dow Chem Co, 54-59, res specialist, 59-65, group leader, Bioprod Dept, 65-71, res mgr, Agr Prod Dept, Dow Chem Co, 71-82. *Concurrent Pos:* Consult, UN Indust Develop Orgn, 83-84. *Mem:* Sigma Xi; Am Chem Soc. *Res:* Colloid, surface, agricultural and physical chemistry; pesticide formulations and application systems. *Mailing Add:* 1131 S Sunset Maryville MO 64468

SEYMOUR, MICHAEL DENNIS, ANALYTICAL CHEMISTRY. *Current Pos:* From asst prof to assoc prof, 78-92, PROF CHEM, HOPE COL, 93- *Personal Data:* b St Cloud, Minn, May 17, 50. *Educ:* St John's Univ, BA, 72; Univ Ariz, PhD(anal chem), 78. *Concurrent Pos:* Vis scientist, Nat Ctr Atmospheric Res, 85-86; res scientist, Parke-Davis Pharmaceut, 93-94. *Mem:* Am Chem Soc; Sigma Xi. *Res:* Chemical education. *Mailing Add:* Dept Chem Hope Col Holland MI 49423-3698

SEYMOUR, PAUL D, MATHEMATICS. *Honors & Awards:* Delbert Ray Falkerson Fund Award, Am Math Soc, 94. *Mailing Add:* Bellcore 445 South St Marlborough NJ 07690

SEYMOUR, RICHARD JONES, OCEANOGRAPHY. *Current Pos:* HEAD OCEAN ENG RES, SCRIPPS INST OCEANOG, UNIV CALIF, SAN DIEGO, 84- *Personal Data:* b Harrisburg, Pa, Aug 28, 29; c 1. *Educ:* US Naval Acad, BS, 51; Univ Calif, San Diego, PhD(oceanog), 74. *Prof Exp:* Vpres, Wire Equip Mfg Co, Inc, 51-59; head rocket develop, Elkton Div, Thiokol Chem Corp, 59-62; chief engr, United Technol Div, United Aircraft Corp, 62-69; res asst oceanog, Scripps Inst Oceanog, Univ Calif, San Diego, 70-73; staff oceanogr, Calif Dept Boating & Waterways, 74-84. *Mem:* Am Soc Civil Engrs; Am Soc Mech Engrs. *Res:* Sediment transport; wave measurement and analysis; coastal processes. *Mailing Add:* 6530 Manana Pl La Jolla CA 92037

SEYMOUR, ROLAND LEE, mycology, for more information see previous edition

SFAT, MICHAEL R(UDOLPH), BIOTECHNOLOGY. *Current Pos:* EMER PRES, BIO-TECH RESOURCES INC, 69- *Personal Data:* b Timisoara, Rumania, Oct 28, 21; nat US; wid; c Gail (Sergent) & Mary A (Bauer). *Educ:* Cornell Univ, BChE, 43, MChE, 47. *Prof Exp:* Res assoc chem eng, Cornell Univ, 43-44; from asst microbiologist to sr microbiologist, Merck & Co, Inc, 47-52; chem engr, Labs, Pabst Brewing Co, 52-54; res dir, Rahr Malting Co, 54-58, coordr res & develop, 58-60, vpres res & develop, 60-69; pres, Biotech Resources, 62-89, emer pres, 90-96. *Mem:* Fel Nat Acad Eng; Am Soc Brewing Chem (pres, 74); Am Soc Microbiol; Am Inst Chem Engrs; Inst Food Technol; Am Asn Cereal Chem; Am Chem Soc; fel Am Inst Med & Biol Eng; fel Am Acad Microbiol. *Res:* Industrial fermentations; malting; enzymes; bioengineering. *Mailing Add:* Sfat Enterprises 1035 S Seventh St Manitowoc WI 54220

SFERRA, PASQUALE RICHARD, ENTOMOLOGY. *Current Pos:* assoc prof, 63-73, PROF BIOL, COL MT ST JOSEPH, 73- *Personal Data:* b St Louis, Mo, Sept 2, 27; m 50; c 4. *Educ:* Washington Univ, AB, 52; Rutgers Univ, MSc, 55, PhD(entom), 57. *Prof Exp:* Asst prof entom, Exp Sta, State Univ NY Col Agr, Cornell Univ, 56-62, asst prof biol, 62-63. *Concurrent Pos:* Biol sci adv, US Environ Protection Agency. *Mem:* AAAS; Entom Soc Am; Am Inst Biol Sci; Sigma Xi. *Res:* Respiratory pacing in insects; insect toxicology; carbohydrate metabolism in insects; taxonomy of desert insects. *Mailing Add:* 5645 Candlelite Terr Cincinnati OH 45238-1848

SFORZA, PASQUALE M, FLUID MECHANICS. *Current Pos:* res fel, Polytech Univ, 61-62, from res asst to res assoc aerospace eng, 62-65, from asst prof to assoc prof, 65-77, head dept mech & aerospace eng, 83-86, head, Dept Aerospace Eng, 88-95, PROF AEROSPACE & MECH ENG, POLYTECH UNIV, 77-, HEAD DEPT AEROSPACE ENG, 88- *Personal Data:* b New York, NY, Mar 5, 41; m 63, Mary A Aufmuth; c Laura, Michael & Julia. *Educ:* Polytech Inst Brooklyn, BAeE, 61, MS, 62, PhD(astronaut), 65. *Honors & Awards:* Technol Achievement Award, Am Inst Aeronaut & Astronaut, 77. *Concurrent Pos:* Pres, Flowpower, Inc, 78-; assoc ed, J Am Inst Aeronaut & Astronaut, 80-82, book review ed, 83- *Mem:* Assoc fel Am Inst Aeronaut & Astronaut; Am Soc Mech Engrs; NY Acad Sci. *Res:* Theoretical and experimental fluid mechanics; high temperature energy transfer; hypersonic aerodynamics; wind engineering; energy conversion; airplane and engine design. *Mailing Add:* Polytech Univ 6 Metrotech Ctr Brooklyn NY 11201

SFORZINI, RICHARD HENRY, JET PROPULSION. *Current Pos:* vis prof, 66-67, prof, 67-85, EMER PROF AEROSPACE ENG, AUBURN UNIV, 85- *Personal Data:* b Rochester, NY, July 25, 24; m 47, Corinne B Lorenz; c Richard H Jr, Suzanne (Simonelli), Deborah (Pugh), Michael J, Stephen C, Andrew L & Mark A. *Educ:* US Mil Acad, BSc, 47; Mass Inst Technol, MechE, 54. *Honors & Awards:* Wyld Propulsion Award, Am Inst Aeronaut & Astron, 96. *Prof Exp:* Instr ord, US Mil Acad, 54-56, asst prof, 56-57; proj dir missile systs, Res & Develop Div, Army Rocket & Guided Missile Agency, Redstone Arsenal, Ala, 58-59; engr, Huntsville Div, Thiokol Chem Corp, Ala, 59-62, mgr eng dept, 62-64, dir eng, Space Booster Div, Brunswick, Ga, 64-66. *Concurrent Pos:* Chmn solid rocket tech comt, Am Inst Aeronaut & Astronaut, 80-81. *Mem:* Assoc fel Am Inst Aeronaut & Astronaut. *Res:* Aircraft and missile propulsion systems, especially internal ballistics, combustion, ignition, swirling flow through nozzles and problems of very large solid-propellant rockets; aerodynamics. *Mailing Add:* 912 Cherokee Rd Auburn AL 36830-2723

SGOUTAS, DEMETRIOS SPIROS, BIOCHEMISTRY, CLINICAL CHEMISTRY. *Current Pos:* from asst prof to assoc prof path, 70-74, PROF PATH & LAB MED, MED SCH, EMORY UNIV, 75-, DIR, RADIOIMMUNOASSAY LAB, 73- *Personal Data:* b Thessaloniki, Greece, Sept 2, 29; US citizen; m 61; c 2. *Educ:* Univ Thessaloniki, BS, 54; Univ Ill, Urbana, PhD, 63. *Prof Exp:* Res assoc food chem, Univ Ill, Urbana, 63-64, asst prof, 64-65; asst prof chem, Univ Thessaloniki, 65-66; asst prof food chem, Univ Ill, Urbana, 66-70. *Concurrent Pos:* Prin investr, Chicago & Ill Heart Asn grants, 64-69; NIH grants, 67-; prof allied health professions, Emory Univ, 70- *Mem:* Am Chem Soc; Am Oil Chemists Soc; Am Soc Biol Chemists; Am Asn Clin Chemists. *Res:* Lipid metabolism as related to cardiovascular diseases. *Mailing Add:* Dept Path & Lab Med Emory Univ Med Sch 763 WMB Atlanta GA 30322. *Fax:* 404-727-5567

SGRO, J A, HUMAN FACTORS. *Current Pos:* PROF & HEAD PSYCHOL DEPT, VA POLYTECH INST & STATE UNIV, 79- *Personal Data:* b New Haven, Conn, Nov 22, 37; m; c 2. *Educ:* Lehigh Univ, MA, 61; Texas Christian Univ, PhD(psychol), 66. *Prof Exp:* From asst prof to prof psychol, Old Dominion Univ, 67-79. *Mem:* Am Psychol Asn; Psychonomic Soc. *Res:* Factors that contribute to leadership & following, dealing with sexual roles & perception that followers have of leaders & vice versa. *Mailing Add:* Dept Psychol Va Polytech Inst & State Univ PO Box 0436 Blacksburg VA 24063-0001

SHA, WILLIAM T, NUCLEAR ENGINEERING, NUCLEAR SCIENCE. *Current Pos:* sr nuclear engr & dir anal thermal hydraul res prog, Energy & Technol Div, 67-80, sr consult, Thermal Hydraul, 80-83, DIR, MULTIPHASE FLOW RES INST, ARGONNE NAT LAB, 83- *Personal Data:* b Kiangsu, China, Sept 13, 28; US citizen; m 57, Joanne Y; c Andrea, Beverly & William C. *Educ:* Polytech Inst Brooklyn, BS, 58; Columbia Univ, DESc, 64. *Prof Exp:* Engr, Combustion Eng Inc, 57-60; fel scientist, Atomic Power Div, Westinghouse Elec Corp, 60-67. *Mem:* Fel Am Nuclear Soc. *Res:* Reactor design and safety; system stability; nuclear-thermal-hydraulic interaction calculation; multiphase fluid mechanics and heat transfer. *Mailing Add:* Energy & Technol Div Bldg 308 Argonne Nat Lab Argonne IL 60439

SHAAD, DOROTHY JEAN, OPHTHALMOLOGY, PSYCHOLOGY. *Current Pos:* RETIRED. *Personal Data:* b Newton, Mass, Aug 16, 09. *Educ:* Univ Kans, AB, 29; Bryn Mawr Col, MA, 30, PhD(exp psychol), 34; Univ Kans, MD, 44. *Prof Exp:* Asst, Howe Lab Ophthal, Harvard Med Sch, 31-32; instr, St Mary Col, Kans, 34; clin technician, Manhattan Eye, Ear & Throat Hosp, New York, 35-38; intern, Duke Univ Hosp, 44-45; assoc ophthal, Med Ctr, Univ Kans, 45-46, asst prof, 46-77, assoc res vision & ophthal, 71-77. *Concurrent Pos:* Practicing ophthalmologist, 45-69. *Mem:* AMA. *Res:* Light perception and dark adaptation; binocular vision. *Mailing Add:* 2322 W 51st St Shawnee Mission KS 66205-2010

SHA'AFI, RAMADAN ISSA, BIOPHYSICS, PHYSIOLOGY. *Current Pos:* from asst prof to assoc prof, 72-78, PROF PHYSIOL, UNIV CONN HEALTH CTR, 78- *Personal Data:* b Nabi-Rubien, Palestine, June 9, 38; Jordanian citizen; c 2. *Educ:* Univ Ill, BS, 62, MS, 63, PhD(biophys), 65. *Prof Exp:* Fel, Harvard Med Sch, 65-67, instr biophys, 67-69; asst prof physiol, Am Univ Beirut, 69-72. *Mem:* Biophys Soc; Am Physiol Soc; Soc Gen Physiol. *Res:* Mechanism of water and solute transport across mammalian red and white cells. *Mailing Add:* Dept Physiol Univ Conn Health Ctr Farmington CT 06030-0001

SHAAK, GRAIG DENNIS, SCIENCE ADMINISTRATION, PALEONTOLOGY. *Current Pos:* Asst cur paleontol, Fla Mus Natural Hist, 72-78, chmn dept, 78-79, from asst dir to assoc dir, 79-86, actg dir, 86-87, ASSOC DIR, FLA MUS NATURAL HIST, 87- *Personal Data:* b Harrisburg, Pa, Oct 18, 42; m 93, Kris; c Angela J. *Educ:* Shippensburg Univ, BS, 67; Ind Univ, MAT, 69; Univ Pittsburgh, PhD(geol), 72. *Mem:* Soc Econ Paleontologists & Mineralogists; Paleont Soc; Geol Soc Am; Paleont Res Inst; Am Asn Mus. *Res:* Diversity, structure, and evolution of shallow benthic marine communities; succession in late Pleistocene freshwater communities; echinoid evolution, biogeography and biometrics. *Mailing Add:* Fla Mus Natural Hist Univ Fla Gainesville FL 32611. *Fax:* 904-392-8783

SHAATH, NADIM ALI, ORGANIC CHEMISTRY, MEDICINAL CHEMISTRY. *Current Pos:* PRES, KATO WORLD WIDE LTD, 90- *Personal Data:* b Jaffa, Palestine, Dec 10, 45; m 67; c 1. *Educ:* Univ Alexandria, BSc, 67; Univ Minn, PhD(org chem), 73. *Prof Exp:* Teaching assoc chem, Univ Minn, 67-72, res specialist med chem, 72-75; from asst prof to assoc prof chem, State Univ NY, Purchase, 75-81; res dir, Felton Int, 81-90. *Concurrent Pos:* Teaching assoc, Exten Div, Univ Minn, 70-73; prin investr multiple grants, 76- *Mem:* Am Chem Soc; AAAS. *Res:* Neuromuscular junction blocking or paralysing drugs; nuclear magnetic resonance shift reagents; mechanism of organic reactions; metabolism of narcotic stimulants; flavors and fragrances. *Mailing Add:* KATO World Wide Ltd One Bradford Rd Mt Vernon NY 10553

SHABANA, AHMED ABDELRAOUF, KINEMATICS DYNAMICS & CONTROL, COMPUTATIONAL MECHANICS. *Current Pos:* from asst prof to assoc prof, 83-93, PROF MECH ENG, UNIV ILL, CHICAGO, 93- *Personal Data:* b Domiat, Egypt. *Educ:* Cairo Univ, BSc, 74; Ain Shams Univ, MSc, 78; Univ Iowa, PhD (mech eng), 82. *Honors & Awards:* Alexander Von Humboldt Res Award, 95. *Prof Exp:* Teaching asst mech eng, Ain Shams Univ, Egypt, 74-78; res asst mech eng, Univ Iowa, 79-82, fel, 82-83. *Concurrent Pos:* Prin investr, Univ Ill Res Bd, 84-85. *Mem:* Fel Am Soc Mech Engrs; Am Acad Mech. *Res:* Kinematics; dynamics and control of multibody systems; computational mechanics and computer aided design; scientific and technical papers on computational mechanics. *Mailing Add:* Dept Mech Eng Univ Ill Chicago 842 W Taylor St Chicago IL 60607-7022

SHABANOWITZ, HARRY, MATHEMATICS. *Current Pos:* RETIRED. *Personal Data:* b Brooklyn, NY, Nov 11, 18; m 43; c 2. *Educ:* City Col New York, BS, 49; Columbia Univ, MA, 50; Syracuse Univ, PhD(math educ), 74. *Prof Exp:* Sr engr, Westinghouse Elec Corp, 51-65 & Gen Elec Co, 65-66; from assoc prof to prof math, Elmira Col, 66-84. *Concurrent Pos:* Spec lectr, 57-65. *Mem:* Am Math Soc; NY Acad Sci. *Res:* Research and development of high sensitivity television camera tubes; theoretical and experimental investigation of the factors limiting television camera tube performance; study of high quantum efficiency photoemissive surfaces; secondary electron emission; electron optical geometry. *Mailing Add:* 205 Scenic Dr W Horseheads NY 14845

SHABAZZ, ABDULALIM A, INTEGRAL EQUATIONS, COMPLEX ANALYSIS. *Current Pos:* PROF MATH, CLARK ATLANTA UNIV, 86-, CHMN DEPT, 90- *Personal Data:* b Bessemer, Ala, May 22, 27. *Educ:* Lincoln Univ, AB, 49; Mass Inst Technol, MS, 51; Cornell Univ, PhD(math), 55. *Prof Exp:* Asst prof math, Tuskegee Inst, 56-57; assoc prof & chmn, Math Dept, Atlanta Univ, 57-63; dir educ & minister, Masjid Muhammad, Washington, DC, 63-75; dir adult educ, Masjid Elijah Muhammad, Chicago, 75-79; dir adult educ & Imam, Masjid Wali Muhammad, Detroit, 79-82; from assoc prof to prof math, Umm Al Qura Univ, Makkah, 82-86. *Mem:* Sigma Xi; Am Math Soc; Am Soc Eng Educ; Math Asn Am; AAAS; Nat Coun Teachers Math. *Res:* Eigen value problems for certain classes of Hermitian forms and the analytic continuations of functions represented by certain power series, using pade approximants and the method of Borel, and the applications thereof to single-atom frequency-dependent polarizabilities. *Mailing Add:* Dept Math Sci Clark Atlanta Univ PO Box 196 Atlanta GA 30314-4389. *Fax:* 404-880-6152

SHABEL, BARRIE STEVEN, MATERIALS CHARACTERIZATION, NONDESTRUCTIVE TESTING. *Current Pos:* res engr, aluminum alloys, phys metall div, Alcoa Res Labs, 66-74, sr res engr, 74-75, sr res engr, mech & metalworking, eng properties & design div, 75-78, staff engr, mech & aluminum alloys, 80-84, SCI ASSOC, ALLOY TECHNOL DIV, ALCOA LABS, ALCOA TECH CTR, 84- *Personal Data:* b New York, NY, Aug 31, 38; m 62; c 1. *Educ:* Mass Inst Technol, SB, 59; Rensselaer Polytech Inst, MMetE, 61; Syracuse Univ, PhD(solid state sci), 67. *Honors & Awards:* IR-100 Award, 77. *Prof Exp:* Mat engr, zirconium/columbium alloys, Knolls Atomic Power Lab, 59-60, mat engr radiation damage, 60-63. *Mem:* Am Soc Metals; The Metall Soc; Inst Mining, Metall & Petrol Engrs; Mat Res Soc; Sigma Xi. *Res:* Physical and mechanical metallurgy of aluminum alloys; mechanics of sheet metal forming, plasticity; application of statistics to industrial research; nondestructive testing. *Mailing Add:* 3464 Burnett Dr Murrysville PA 15668-1346

SHABICA, ANTHONY CHARLES, JR, ORGANIC CHEMISTRY. *Current Pos:* ADJ PROF, COL VIRGIN ISLANDS, 81- *Personal Data:* b Meadville, Pa, Nov 20, 15; m 40; c 3. *Educ:* Brown Univ, ScB, 38; Pa State Univ, MS, 39, PhD(org chem), 42. *Prof Exp:* Jr chemist, Calco Chem Co, 37 & 39; asst, Pa State Univ, 39-42; sr chemist, Merck & Co, Inc, 42-46; head develop dept, Ciba Pharmaceut Co, 46-48, dir develop res, 48-67, vpres develop & control, 67-81. *Concurrent Pos:* Mem bd, NJ Coun Res & Develop, 68-, chmn, 76-77; res assoc, Woods Hole Oceanog Inst. *Mem:* Am Pharmaceut Asn; Am Chem Soc; fel Am Inst Chemists; fel NY Acad Sci; Int Pharmaceut Fedn; Sigma Xi. *Res:* Heterocyclic chemistry; natural products; mechanism of the polymerization of olefins; steroidal sapogenins and related compounds alkaloids; process research, development and design. *Mailing Add:* Box 1631 Destin FL 32540-1631

SHABICA, CHARLES WRIGHT, COASTAL GEOLOGY & ENGINEERING. *Current Pos:* PROF EARTH SCI, NORTHEASTERN ILL UNIV, 71-; PRES CHARLES SHABICA & ASSOC, COASTAL CONSULTS, 85- *Personal Data:* b Elizabeth, NJ, Jan 2, 43; m 67; c Jon, Andrew & Dana. *Educ:* Brown Univ, AB, 65; Univ Chicago, PhD(geol), 71. *Concurrent Pos:* Kellogg fel, 79; vis prof, Col VI, 80-81; prin investr marine sci curric, earth watch exped, 80-; coastal consult, City Highland Park, Loyola Univ & others, 84-; designer shore protection structures, Great Lakes, 84-; mem, Chicago Shoreline Protection Comn, 86-; res collabr, Nat Park Svc, 89-; chmn bd dirs, Aesti Corp. *Mem:* Sigma Xi; Am Shore & Beach Asn; Coastal Soc; Int Asn Great Lakes Res; fel Inst for Limnology & Ecosystems Res Lab. *Res:* Coastal processes; coastal engineering. *Mailing Add:* 326 Ridge Winnetka IL 60093

SHACK, ROLAND VINCENT, OPTICS. *Current Pos:* res assoc, 64-65, assoc prof, 65-70, PROF OPTICS, UNIV ARIZ, 70- *Personal Data:* b Chicago, Ill, Jan 15, 27; m 57; c 4. *Educ:* Univ Md, BS, 49; Am Univ, BA, 51; Univ London, PhD(physics), 65. *Prof Exp:* Physicist, Nat Bur Stand, 49-57 & Perkin-Elmer Corp, 57-64. *Mem:* Optical Soc Am. *Res:* Optical image evaluation and testing; interferometry; systems analysis. *Mailing Add:* 6918 E Blue Lake Dr Tucson AZ 85715

SHACK, WILLIAM JOHN, APPLIED MECHANICS, ENVIRONMENTAL DEGRADATION OF MATERIALS. *Current Pos:* scientist, 76-85, SR SCIENTIST, ARGONNE NAT LAB, 85-, ASSOC DIR ENERGY TECH DIV, 89- *Personal Data:* b Pittsburgh, Pa, Jan 12, 43; m 75, Nancy Treeger; c Emily. *Educ:* Mass Inst Technol, BS, 64; Univ Calif, Berkeley, MS, 65, PhD(appl mech), 68. *Prof Exp:* From asst prof to assoc prof, Mass Inst Technol, 68-75. *Concurrent Pos:* Mem, USNR Corp Adv Comt, Reactor Safeguards. *Mem:* Am Soc Mech Engrs. *Res:* Solid mechanics; fracture mechanics; environmental degradation of materials. *Mailing Add:* Argonne Nat Lab Bldg 212 Argonne IL 60439. *Fax:* 630-252-4798; *E-Mail:* wjshack@anl.gov

SHACKELFORD, CHARLES DUANE, CIVIL ENGINEERING. *Current Pos:* asst prof, 88-93, ASSOC PROF, DEPT CIVIL ENG, COLO STATE UNIV, 93- *Personal Data:* b Sewickley, Pa, Sept 9, 54; m 84, Anne Marie Lynch; c Kathryn, David & Daniel. *Educ:* Univ Mo, Rolla, BSCE, 80; Univ Tex, MS, 83, PhD, 88. *Honors & Awards:* Walter L Huber Civil Eng Prize, Am Soc Chem Engrs, 95. *Prof Exp:* Civil design engr, Pacific Gas & Elec Co, 80-81; Geotech engr, Ardaman & Assocs Inc, 83-84. *Concurrent Pos:* Consult, David E Daniel, Austin, Tex, 85-89, Shepard & Miller Ins, 90, USAF, 91, Woodward-Clyde Consult, 92 & Dept Energy, 93 & 95; young investr award, NSF, 92. *Mem:* Am Soc Testing Mat; Am Soc Chem Engrs; Asn Ground Water Scientists & Engrs; Int Soc Soil Mechs & Found Eng; Soil Sci Soc Am. *Res:* Contaminant transport through saturated and unsaturated porous media; coupled flow processes; diffusion of contaminants in soils; electrokinetics remediation; environmental geotechnics; in situ soil washing; permeability and compatibility of fine-grained soils; permeable reactive walls; physico-chemical properties of soils; soil and waste stabilization; unsaturated flow through clay liners and cover systems. *Mailing Add:* 2836 Claremont Dr Ft Collins CO 80526-2267

SHACKELFORD, CHARLES L(EWIS), ELECTRONICS. *Current Pos:* SR ENGR, ELECTRON TUBE DIV, INT TEL & TEL CORP, 69- *Personal Data:* b Wagoner, Okla, Oct 19, 18; m 45; c 1. *Educ:* Okla State Univ, BS, 41; Univ Mo, MS, 42. *Prof Exp:* Repairman, Porum Tel Co, 35-40; asst, Univ Mo, 41-42; engr, Westinghouse Elec Corp, Pa, 42, NJ, 42-52; engr, Chatham Electronics Div, Tung-Sol Elec, Inc, 52-66, chief engr, Power Tube Div, NJ, 66-69. *Mem:* Sr mem Inst Elec & Electronics Engrs. *Res:* Electron emission; conduction of electricity through gases and vapors. *Mailing Add:* 3916 Oakland Rd Bethlehem PA 18017

SHACKELFORD, ERNEST DABNEY, BIOMEDICAL ENGINEERING, SUBSONIC AERODYNAMICS. *Current Pos:* ADJ FAC FLUID MECH, NC A&T STATE UNIV, 90- *Personal Data:* b Petersburg, Va, Aug 24, 26; m 51, Joan Hahn; c Cynthia, Dabney, Pamela, Sue & David. *Educ:* Ga Inst Technol, BAE, 46; Med Col Va, MD, 52. *Prof Exp:* Intern, Univ Wis Hosp, Madison, 52-53; physician internal med, NC Mem Hosp, Chapel Hill, 53-55, res physician radiol, 63-67; pvt pract, Asheboro, NC, 55-63; radiologist, diag roentgenol, ultrasound & nuclear med, Randolph Mem Hosp, Inc, 67-90. *Concurrent Pos:* Consult, Hospice Randolph, NC, 84- *Mem:* Am Inst Aeronaut & Astronaut; Soc Indust & Appl Math; Am Col Radiol. *Res:* Central nervous system causation factors in pulmonary edema; nuclear medicine; ultrasonology; radiology; fluid dynamics. *Mailing Add:* 203 Shannon Rd Asheboro NC 27203-5011. *E-Mail:* e.d.s@garfield.ncat.edu

SHACKELFORD, JAMES FLOYD, MATERIALS SCIENCE ENGINEERING, CERAMICS ENGINEERING. *Current Pos:* from asst prof to assoc prof, 73-84, PROF MAT SCI & ENG, UNIV CALIF, DAVIS, 84-, ASSOC DEAN, COL ENG, 84- *Personal Data:* b Springfield, Mo, Sept 1, 44; m 71, Penelope Openshaw; c Scott. *Educ:* Univ Wash, BS, 66, MS, 67; Univ Calif, PhD(mat sci & eng), 71. *Prof Exp:* Postdoctoral fel mat sci & eng, Univ Calif, Berkeley, 71 & McMaster Univ, Hamilton, Can, 72-73. *Concurrent Pos:* Consult, var indust & legal clients, 72- & Lawrence Livermore Nat Lab, 77-; vis prof, Indian Inst Sci, Bangalore, 89 & Indian Inst Technol, Bombay, 89-90. *Mem:* Fel Am Ceramic Soc; Mat Res Soc; Am Soc Mat. *Res:* Author of over 80 publications including an introductory textbook; materials science and engineering; structure of noncrystalline solids; nondestructive testing; biomaterials. *Mailing Add:* Col Eng Univ Calif Davis CA 95616. *Fax:* 530-752-2123; *E-Mail:* jfshackelford@ucdavis.edu

SHACKELFORD, ROBERT G, electrooptics; deceased, see previous edition for last biography

SHACKELFORD, SCOTT ADDISON, ENERGETIC MATERIALS, PERFLUOROCARBON DERIVATIVES. *Current Pos:* PRIN SCIENTIST, ALLIANCE PHARMACEUT CORP, 93- *Personal Data:* b Long Beach, Calif, Aug 11, 44; m 69, Marilyn Coon; c Laura & Vicki. *Educ:* Simpson Col, BA, 66; Northern Ariz Univ, MA, 68; Ariz State Univ, PhD(org chem), 73. *Prof Exp:* res chemist, Frank J Seiler Res Lab, 72-74, prin investr & div chief energetic chem, 74-77; Air Force exchange scientist, Inst Chem Antrieb & Verfahrenstech, WGer, 78-80; chief, Basic Chem Res Sect, Air Force Rocket Propulsion Lab, 80-84; chief, chem & energetics, Europ Off Aerospace Res & Develop, 84-87; sr scientist, Frank J Seiler Res Lab, 87-93. *Concurrent Pos:* Lectr, Dept Chem, USAF Acad, 74-78, instr, 77, asst prof, 78-; secy, Joint Tech Coord Group, 75-77; prin investr org synthesis & thermochem mech, 81-84, propellant chem task mgr, 82-84; mem, Simpson Col Sci Adv Comt, 83-87, Jannaf Combustion Subcomt Panel, chmn on Propellant Combustion Chem, 90-91; dir, Aerospace Res Div, Europ Off Aerospace Res & Develop, 86-87; Nat Alliance Treaty Organ Advan Study Inst Lectr, 89. *Mem:* Am Chem Soc. *Res:* Kinetic deuterium isotope effects in mechanistic decompostion and combustion studies; organic compound deuteration; polynitroaliphatic compound synthesis; xenon difluoride fluorination mechanisms; perfluorocarbon derivative synthesis, characterization, and emulsion behavior; granted several US patents. *Mailing Add:* 672 W Via Rancho Pkwy Escondido CA 92029. *Fax:* 619-558-3625

SHACKELFORD, WALTER MCDONALD, ANALYTICAL CHEMISTRY, HIGH PERFORMANCE COMPUTING. *Current Pos:* res chemist, Athens Environ Res Lab, US Environ Protection Agency, 74-85, sr scientist res systs, Off Info & Res Mgt, 85-92, dir, Sci Comput, 92-96, CHIEF, ENTERPRISE COMPUT SERV, US ENVIRON PROTECTION AGENCY, 96- *Personal Data:* b Birmingham, Ala, Jan 8, 45; m 69, Bonnie Freeman; c Malcolm, Emily & Charles. *Educ:* Univ Miss, BS, 67; Ga Inst Technol, PhD(anal chem), 71. *Prof Exp:* Chemist, E I du Pont de Nemours & Co, Inc, Chattanooga Nylon Plant, 67; res assoc, Univ New Orleans, 73-74. *Concurrent Pos:* Chemist, Edgewood Arsenal, Md, 71-73. *Mem:* Sigma Xi; Am Chem Soc; Am Soc Mass Spectrometry. *Res:* Laboratory information management; computer systems; high performance computing systems. *Mailing Add:* 103 Megan Ct Cary NC 27511-5877

SHACKLE, DALE RICHARD, CHEMISTRY. *Current Pos:* SCIENTIST, VALENCE TECHNOL. *Personal Data:* b Caldwell, Ohio, Oct 4, 41; m 65; c 2. *Educ:* Marietta Col, BS, 63; Ohio Univ, PhD(chem), 69. *Prof Exp:* Chemist process improv, Goodyear Atomic Corp, 63-65; teaching asst chem, Ohio Univ, 65-69; proj leader paper coatings, Mead Corp, 69-74, sect head, 74-77, mgr process eng, 77-79, assoc dir res, 79- *Res:* Specialty coatings for paper and the materials used in these coatings. *Mailing Add:* 17135 Oak Leaf Dr Morgan Hill CA 95037

SHACKLEFORD, JOHN MURPHY, ANATOMY. *Current Pos:* chmn dept, 72-80, PROF ANAT, UNIV S ALA, 72-, ASST DEAN ADMIS, COL MED, 87- *Personal Data:* b Mobile, Ala, Dec 22, 29; m 58; c 2. *Educ:* Spring Hill Col, BS, 57; Univ Ala, PhD(anat), 61. *Prof Exp:* From instr to assoc prof anat, Med Ctr, Univ Ala, 61-72, asst prof dent, 64-72. *Concurrent Pos:* NIH res grants, 62-72. *Mem:* Am Asn Anatomists. *Res:* Cytochemistry and histophysiology of exocrine glands; electron microscopy of bones and teeth. *Mailing Add:* 3763 Claridge Rd S Mobile AL 36608

SHACKLETON, NICHOLAS JOHN, GEOLOGY. *Current Pos:* Asst dir res, 72-85, reader, 87-91, DIR SUB-DEPT QUARTERARY RES, UNIV CAMBRIDGE, 88-, AD HOMINEN PROF, 91- *Personal Data:* b London, Eng, June 23, 37; m 86, Vivien A Law. *Educ:* Univ Cambridge, BA, 61, MA, 64, PhD, 67. *Hon Degrees:* DSc, Univ Cambridge, 84; LLD, Dalhousie Univ, 96. *Honors & Awards:* Shepard Medal, Soc Econ Paleontologists & Mineralogists, 85; Carus Medal, Deutsche Acad Naturforscher Leopoldina, 85; Crafoord Prize, Royal Swed Acad Sci, 95. *Concurrent Pos:* Res fel, Clare Hall, Cambridge, 74-81, off fel, 81-; sr vis res fel, Lamont-Doherty Geol Observ, Columbia, 74-75, sr res assoc, 75-; vis prof, Eidgenoessische Tech Sch, Zurich, 79, Cath Univ Louvain-La-Neuve, 94-95. *Mem:* Fel Am Geophys Union; Acad Europ; fel Royal Soc. *Res:* Contributed numerous articles to professional journals. *Mailing Add:* 12 Tenison Ave Cambridge CB1 2DX England. *Fax:* 44-223-334871; *E-Mail:* njs5@can.ac.uk

SHACKLETT, ROBERT LEE, PHYSICS. *Current Pos:* from asst prof to assoc prof physics, Calif State Univ, 55-65, asst acad vpres, 67-68, asst dean, Sch Grad Studies, 68-75, actg dean, 75-76, prof, 65-79, EMER PROF PHYSICS, CALIF STATE UNIV, FRESNO, 79-; VPRES FOUND MIND-BEING RES, LOS ALTOS, CA, 87- *Personal Data:* b Calif, Apr 5, 26; m 79, Edie Fischer; c 2. *Educ:* Calif State Univ, Fresno, AB, 49; Calif Inst Technol, PhD(physics), 56. *Concurrent Pos:* NSF fel, Univ Uppsala, 61-62; co-inventor, Digital Commun Syst, US Patent Off, 75- *Mem:* Am Phys Soc; Am Asn Physics Teachers; Int Soc Study Subtle Energies & Energy Med; Sigma Xi. *Res:* physics of consciousness; models of mind-matter interface. *Mailing Add:* PO Box 2128 Aptos CA 95001-2128. *E-Mail:* shaklet@ix.netcom.com

SHACKLETTE, LAWRENCE WAYNE, POLYMER PHYSICS, ELECTROCHEMISTRY. *Current Pos:* sr res physicist, 79-82, res assoc, 82-86, SR RES SCIENTIST, RES & TECHNOL, ALLIEDSIGNAL, INC, 86- *Personal Data:* b New York, NY, Feb 26, 45; m 69, Nancy Shipley; c Justin & Jessie. *Educ:* Brown Univ, BS, 67; Univ Ill, MS, 69, PhD(solid state physics), 72. *Prof Exp:* Assoc prof physics, Seton Hall Univ, 72-79. *Mem:* Fel Am Phys Soc; Mat Res Soc. *Res:* Phase transitions and electronic transport in metals, ceramics; optical polymers and devices; applications of conductive polymers as rechargeable batteries; electronic devices and electromagnetic shielding materials; materials physics, of blends, and hovel composites. *Mailing Add:* AlliedSignal Inc PO Box 1021 Morristown NJ 07962. *E-Mail:* shacklet@research.allied.com

SHADDUCK, JOHN ALLEN, COMPARATIVE PATHOLOGY, VIROLOGY. *Current Pos:* PROF VET PATH & HEAD DEPT, COL VET MED, UNIV ILL, 80- *Personal Data:* b Toledo, Ohio, Apr 22, 39; m 60; c 2. *Educ:* Ohio State Univ, DVM, 63, MSc, 65, PhD(vet path), 67; Am Col Vet Pathologists, dipl. *Prof Exp:* Fel vet path, Ohio State Univ, 63-67, from asst prof to assoc prof vet path, 67-73; from assoc prof to prof comp path, Univ Tex Health Sci Ctr, Dallas, 73-80. *Concurrent Pos:* Fel comp virol & neuropath, Univ Munich, 67-68; consult indust, fed govt, Food & Drug Admin & WHO; prin investr grants & contracts; ed, Vet Path. *Mem:* AAAS; Am Vet Med Asn; Am Soc Exp Path; Am Col Vet Path; Sigma Xi. *Res:* Viral oncology; ophthalmic pathology; infectious diseases; host-parasite relationships; immunoregulatory events; comparative and functional aspects of inflammation. *Mailing Add:* Col Vet Med Tex A&M Univ College Station TX 77843-4461. *Fax:* 409-845-5088; *E-Mail:* jshadduck@uthvax.tamu.edu

SHADDY, JAMES HENRY, ECOLOGY, ENTOMOLOGY. *Current Pos:* PROF ECOL, TRUMAN STATE UNIV, 69- *Personal Data:* b Everett, Wash, Aug 30, 38; m 66, Nancy J Stout. *Educ:* Okla State Univ, BS, 62, MS, 64; Mich State Univ, PhD(entom), 70. *Prof Exp:* Res technician, Mich State Univ, 67-68. *Mem:* AAAS; Entom Soc Am (secy/treas, 90-95); Nat Asn Col Teachers Agr; Sigma Xi. *Res:* Environmental assessment; computer assisted instruction; aquatic biology; old field ecology. *Mailing Add:* Sci Div Truman State Univ Kirksville MO 63501. *Fax:* 660-785-4045; *E-Mail:* jshaddy@truman.edu

SHADE, ELWOOD B, FORESTRY, BIOLOGICAL SCIENCES. *Current Pos:* RETIRED. *Personal Data:* b Hollidaysburg, Pa, Aug 9, 13; div. *Educ:* Juniata Col, BA, 35; Pa State Univ, BSF, 46, MF, 47. *Prof Exp:* Pub sch instr, Pa, 41-44 & Md, 44-45; forester, US Forest Serv, 47-55; park forester, City of Portland, Ore, 55-56; naturalist, Nat Park Serv, 56-57; from asst prof to assoc prof forestry, Univ Ark, Monticello, 60-81. *Mem:* Fel Soc Am Foresters. *Res:* Forest and outdoor recreation. *Mailing Add:* 139 Falls Monticello AR 71655

SHADE, JOYCE ELIZABETH, SYNTHETIC INORGANIC CHEMISTRY. *Current Pos:* ASST PROF CHEM, US NAVAL ACAD, 82- *Personal Data:* b Louisville, Ky, Oct 30, 53. *Educ:* Univ Louisville, BA, 75, PhD(chem), 80. *Prof Exp:* Asst chem, Univ Louisville, 75-80; res fel, Ohio State Univ, 80-82. *Concurrent Pos:* Instr chem, Univ Louisville, 79; physics teacher, Presentation Acad, 77-79. *Mem:* Am Chem Soc; Sigma Xi. *Res:* Syntheses and characterization of cyclopentadienyl-type iron complexes; identification of diastereomeric isomers. *Mailing Add:* Dept Chem 572 Holloway Rd Annapolis MD 21402-5026

SHADE, RAY W(ALTON), CHEMICAL ENGINEERING. *Current Pos:* CHEM ENGR, GEN ELEC CO, 77- *Personal Data:* b Souderton, Pa, Jan 11, 27; m 52; c 1. *Educ:* Mass Inst Technol, SB, 49, SM, 51; Rensselaer Polytech Inst, PhD(chem eng), 64. *Prof Exp:* Chem engr, Knolls Atomic Power Lab, Gen Elec Co, 51-53 & Res & Develop Ctr, 53-66, mgr polymer processing, 66-68, mgr chem eng br, 68-70; assoc prof bio-environ eng, Rensselaer Polytech Inst, 70-77, chmn environ eng curriculum, 71-77. *Mem:* Am Chem Soc; Am Inst Chem Engrs. *Res:* Chemical and polymer processing; vacuum technology and thin vacuum deposited films; electroless plating. *Mailing Add:* 19 El Dorado Dr Clifton Park NY 12065-2097

SHADE, ROBERT EUGENE, HYPERTENSION, RENAL PHYSIOLOGY. *Current Pos:* ASSOC SCIENTIST, SOUTHWEST FOUND BIOMED RES, 83- *Personal Data:* b Nov 10, 42; m 79, Linda Freeman; c Steven, Kathryn, Kristin & Jonathan. *Educ:* Ind Univ, PhD(physiol), 70. *Prof Exp:* Asst prof, Health Sci Ctr, Univ Tenn, 72-76, assoc prof, 76-78; assoc prof, Sch Med, Univ SC, 78-83. *Concurrent Pos:* Adj assoc prof, Dept Pharmacol, Health Sci Ctr, Univ Tex, 83-92, adj assoc prof, Dept Physiol, 92-94, adj prof, 94-; fel, Coun High Blood Pressure Res, Am Heart Asn, 92. *Mem:* Am Physiol Soc. *Res:* Interactions between neural and neural mechanisms in the regulation of blood pressure in the non-human primate. *Mailing Add:* Dept Physiol & Med Southwest Found Biomed Res PO Box 760549 San Antonio TX 78245-0549. *Fax:* 210-670-3322; *E-Mail:* bshade@icarus.sfbr.org

SHADER, LESLIE ELWIN, MATHEMATICS. *Current Pos:* from instr to asst prof, 68-73, assoc prof, 73-81, PROF MATH, UNIV WYO, 81- *Personal Data:* b Ft Collins, Colo, July 18, 35; m 58; c 3. *Educ:* Colo State Univ, BS, 57, MS, 61; Univ Colo, Boulder, PhD(math), 69. *Prof Exp:* Teacher math, High Sch, Colo, 57-58 & Wyo, 58-59; asst, Colo State Univ, 59-61; instr, Univ Wyo, 61-65; instr, Univ Colo, Boulder, 65-66 & 67-68. *Mem:* Am Math Soc; Math Asn Am. *Res:* Polynomials over a finite field; matrix theory; combinatorics; number theory. *Mailing Add:* 1120 Mitchell St Laramie WY 82070

SHADER, RICHARD IRWIN, PSYCHOPHARMACOLOGY, PHARMACOLOGY. *Current Pos:* chmn psychiat, Tufts Univ, 79-91, chmn pharmacol, 91-93, CLIN PROF PSYCHIAT, DENT MED, TUFTS UNIV, 79-, PROF PHARMACOL, SCH MED, 89- *Personal Data:* b Mt Vernon, NY, May 27, 35; m 58, Aline Brown; c Laurel B, Jennifer (Hersch) & Robert A. *Educ:* Harvard Univ, Cambridge, Mass, BA, 56; Sch Med, New York Univ, MD, 60; Boston Psychoanal Soc Inst, MD, 70. *Honors & Awards:* Taylor Manor Hosp Psychiat Award, 80; Seymour Vestermark Award, Am Psychiat Asn, 88, 90. *Prof Exp:* Intern, Greenwich Hosp, Conn, 60-61; resident psychiat, Mass Ment Health Ctr, 61-62 & 64-65, dir, Psychopharmacol Res Lab, 68-79, dir training & educ, 75-77, dir continuing educ, 77-79; resident psychiat, NIMH, 62-64; asst prof psychiat, Med Sch, Harvard Univ, 68-70, assoc prof, 70-79; psychiatrist-in-chief, New Eng Med Ctr, 79-91. *Concurrent Pos:* J Michaels Merit Scholar, Boston Psychoanal Soc & Inst, 68-69; dir, Am Bd Psychiat & Neurol, 76-84, pres & dir, Am Bd Emergency Med, 80-90, exec comt, 85-90; bd dirs, Med Found, 80-87; ed-in-chief, J Clin Psychopharmacol, 80-; mem, Nat Adv Ment Health Coun, 84-87, Clin Affairs Coun, Vet Admin, Washington, DC, 85-87; mem, Psychiatry Test Comn, Nat Bd Med Examrs, 87-, chair, 91-92 & Step I Comt, 93-96; mem, Med & Sci Adv Bd, Alzheimer's Dis & Related Disorders Asn, 88-; fel, Ctr Advan Study Behav Sci, Stanford, Calif, 90-91. *Mem:* AMA; Am Soc Pharmacol & Exp Therapeut; Am Col Neuropsychopharmacol (pres, 90); Am Asn Chmn Departments Psychiat (pres, 85-86); Am Soc Clin Pharmacol & Therapeut; Am Bd Psychiat & Neurol (treas, 82-83, pres, 84). *Res:* Pharmacokinetic and pharmacodynamic factors which influence responses to psychoactive drugs, particular emphasis on aging, drug interactions and adverse drug reactions. *Mailing Add:* Dept Pharmacol & Exp Therapeut Tufts Univ Sch Med 136 Harrison Ave Boston MA 02111. *Fax:* 617-956-6738; *E-Mail:* rshader@infonet.tufts.edu

SHADOWEN, HERBERT EDWIN, VERTEBRATE ZOOLOGY. *Current Pos:* PROF BIOL, WESTERN KY UNIV, 61- *Personal Data:* b Fredonia, Ky, Sept 11, 26; m 50; c 3. *Educ:* Berea Col, BA, 50; Univ Ky, MS, 51; La State Univ, PhD(zool), 56. *Prof Exp:* Assoc prof zool, La Polytech Inst, 55-61. *Mem:* Am Soc Mammal; Am Ornith Union. *Res:* Small-mammal population studies; taxonomy of amphibians and reptiles. *Mailing Add:* 1927 Cedar Ridge Rd Bowling Green KY 42101

SHAEFFER, JOSEPH ROBERT, HEMATOLOGY. *Current Pos:* INVESTR, CTR BLOOD RES, 77-; ASSOC PROF MED BIOCHEM, HARVARD MED SCH, 78- *Personal Data:* b New York, NY, June 3, 35; m 57; c 3. *Educ:* Mass Inst Technol, SB, 56; Univ Rochester, PhD(biophys), 62. *Prof Exp:* Res fel biochem, Univ Ky, 62-65; asst physicist, Univ Tex M D Anderson Hosp & Tumor Inst, 65-68, asst biologist, 68-71, assoc biologist, 71-76; vis assoc prof med, Peter Bent Brigham Hosp, Boston, 76-77. *Concurrent Pos:* USPHS fel, 62-64. *Mem:* Biophys Soc; Am Soc Biochem & Molecular Biol; NY Acad Sci; Am Soc Hematol; Sigma Xi. *Res:* Proteolysis in human erythroid cells; human hemoglobin, structure, biosynthesis and degradation; thalassemia. *Mailing Add:* 1 Valley Rd Lexington MA 02173-4218

SHAEIWITZ, JOSEPH ALAN, CHEMICAL PROCESS DESIGN, ENGINEERING EDUCATION. *Current Pos:* ASSOC PROF CHEM ENG, WVA UNIV, 84- *Personal Data:* b Brooklyn, NY, Oct 12, 52. *Educ:* Univ Del, BS, 74; Carnegie-Mellon Univ, MS, 76, PhD(chem eng), 78. *Prof Exp:* Asst prof chem eng, Univ Ill, 78-84. *Mem:* Am Inst Chem Engrs; Am Chem Soc; Am Soc Eng Educ. *Res:* Chemical engineering education; chemical process design; design education and outcomes assessment. *Mailing Add:* Dept Chem Eng PO Box 6102 Morgantown WV 26506-6102. *Fax:* 304-293-4139; *E-Mail:* shaeiwit@cemr.wvu.edu

SHAER, ELIAS HANNA, PHYSICAL & ANALYTICAL CHEMISTRY. *Current Pos:* scientist res & develop, Scott Sani-fresh & Clean Works, 93-96, CHEM TECHNOL LEADER, SANI-FRESH DIV, KIMBERLY-CLARK, 96- *Personal Data:* b Beit-Jala, Israel, Aug 2, 41; US citizen; m 70; c 2. *Educ:* Austin Peay State Univ, BS, 66; Univ Miss, MS, 70, PhD(phys chem), 77. *Prof Exp:* Lab instr chem, Univ Miss, 66-70; dir, Div Contractors, Vulcan Waterproofing Co, 70-73; lab instr, Univ Miss, 73-77; sr res chemist, Drackett Co, 77-80, scientist, Res & Develop, 80-93. *Mem:* Am Chem Soc. *Res:* Kinetics solvent effect on the rate of methyl radicals combination; thermodynamics of liquids and liquid mixtures; cleaning compositions and emulsions. *Mailing Add:* 450 Wilde Green Dr Roswell GA 30075-5599

SHAER, NORMAN ROBERT, COMPUTER SCIENCE, ELECTRICAL ENGINEERING. *Current Pos:* mgr comput sci, AT&T Bell Tel Labs, 72-74, dir develop, Mail Network Serv, 82-88, dir, Systs Appl Develop Lab, 88-92, DIR, INFO TECHNOL & APPL, AT&T BELL TEL LABS, 92- *Personal Data:* b Boston, Mass, Mar 31, 37; m 58; c 2. *Educ:* Tufts Univ, BSEE, 58; NY Univ, MEE, 60. *Prof Exp:* Mem tech staff, Bell Tel Labs, 58-63, supvr systs eng, 63-66, dept head electronic switching, 66-69; vpres bus info systs, Comput Systs Labs, 69-71. *Mem:* AAAS; Inst Elec & Electronics Engrs. *Res:* Use of computers for large scale, real time systems; design and implementation. *Mailing Add:* Lucent Technol Rm 1N424 101 Crawfords Corner Rd PO Box 3030 Holmdel NJ 07733-3030

SHAEVEL, MORTON LEONARD, FOOD FORMULATION & PROCESSING, FROZEN FOOD STABILITY & QUALITY ASSURANCE SYSTEMS. *Current Pos:* GEN MGR PROD DEVELOP & QUAL ASSURANCE SYSTS, SHAEVEL & ASSOCS, LTD, 89- *Personal Data:* b Boston, Mass, June 7, 36; m 61; c 2. *Educ:* Univ Mass, Amherst, BS. *Prof Exp:* Food technologist, B Manischewitz Co, 58-62; res chemist, Nabisco Brands, Inc, 62-64, res mgr, 64-68, dir new prod res, 68-73; vpres res & develop, Freezer Queen Foods, Inc, 73-82, vpres new bus develop, 82-84, gen mgr, 84-85, pres, 85-89. *Concurrent Pos:* Chmn, Prepared Foods Comt, Am Frozen Food Inst, 75-77, res coun, 77-81, Qual Maintenance Comt, 81-85, mem bd dirs, 87-90; mem, Tech & Sci Issues Comt, Off Technol Assessment Food Stability TF, US Cong, 78-79 & Grocery Mfrs Am, 79-80. *Mem:* Inst Food Technologists; Am Soc Qual Control; Am Frozen Food Inst. *Res:* Conceived, developed and automated new product systems in commercial production facilities; state-of-the-art frozen food production, stability and durability; frozen food industry consultant. *Mailing Add:* PO Box 1565 Buffalo NY 14231-1565

SHAEVITZ, MICHAEL H, HIGH ENERY PARTICLE PHYSICS. *Current Pos:* PROF, DEPT PHYSICS, COLUMBIA UNIV, 80- *Personal Data:* b Zanesville, Ohio, Oct 2, 47. *Educ:* Ohio State Univ, BS, 69, MS, 72, PhD(physics), 75. *Mem:* Fel Am Phys Soc. *Res:* High energy particle physics. *Mailing Add:* Columbia Univ N Eng Labs 136 S Broadway Irvington NY 10533

SHAFAI, LOTFOLLAH, MICROWAVES, ELECTRONICS. *Current Pos:* dir, Inst Tech Develop, 85-88, head elec eng, 87-89, PROF ELEC ENG, UNIV MAN, 79-, APPL ELECTROMAGNETIC CHAIR, 89- *Personal Data:* b Maraghen, Iran, Mar 17, 41; Can citizen; m 66, Fateme Tafreshi; c Cyrus & Leili. *Educ:* Univ Tehran, BSc, 63; Univ Toronto, MSc, 66, PhD(elec eng), 69. *Honors & Awards:* Merit Award, Asn Prof Engrs, 83-84; Sr Scientist Award, Sigma Xi, 89; Maxwell Premium Award, Inst Elec Engrs, 90, R W Award, 96. *Prof Exp:* Lectr elec eng, Univ Man, 69-70, from asst prof to assoc prof, 70-76; vis scientist appl electromagnetic, Commun Res Ctr, Ottawa, 76-77; vis prof, Electromagnetic Inst, Tech Univ Denmark, 77-79. *Concurrent Pos:* Res Award, Univ Manitoba, 83, 87 & 89. *Mem:* Fel Inst Elec & Electronics Engrs. *Res:* Antennas; electromagnetic scattering and diffraction; wave guides; computer solution of field problems; optics. *Mailing Add:* Dept & Comput Elec Eng Univ Man Winnipeg MB R3T 2N2 Can. *Fax:* 204-261-4639; *E-Mail:* shafai@ee.umanitoba.ca

SHAFER, A WILLIAM, MEDICINE. *Current Pos:* DIR, SOUTHEASTERN MICH RED CROSS BLOOD CTR, 75- *Personal Data:* b Great Bend, Kans, Nov 1, 27; m 50, June Alefs; c 2. *Educ:* Univ Kans, BA, 50, MD, 54. *Prof Exp:* Assoc hemat, Scripps Clin & Res Found, 59-60, assoc mem, 60-66, head hemat, 64-66; from asst prof to prof med & lab med, , Univ Okla, 66-73; prof path & med, Col Med & dir clin labs, Med Ctr, Univ Ky, 73-75. *Concurrent Pos:* Clin prof med & adj prof allied health, Wayne State Univ, 76-87. *Mem:* Fel Am Col Physicians; Am Bd Internal Med; Am Bd Path; Am Fedn Clin Res; fel Am Soc Clin Path. *Res:* Metabolism of normal, abnormal and stored erythrocytes. *Mailing Add:* Red Cross Blood Ctr Area VI PO Box 33351 Detroit MI 48232-5351

SHAFER, JULES ALAN, PROTEIN CHEMISTRY, ENZYMOLOGY. *Current Pos:* from asst prof to prof, 64-90, EMER PROF BIOL CHEM, UNIV MICH, ANN ARBOR, 90-; EXEC DIR BASIC RES, MERCK RES LAB, 90- *Personal Data:* b New York, NY, Nov 21, 37; m 59; c 3. *Educ:* City Col New York, BChE, 59; Polytech Inst Brooklyn, PhD(chem), 63. *Prof Exp:* Fel chem, Polytech Inst Brooklyn, 62-63 & Harvard Univ, 63-64. *Concurrent Pos:* NIH grants, 65-85. *Mem:* AAAS; Am Chem Soc; Am Soc Biol Chemists; NY Acad Sci; Int Soc Magnetic Resonance; Int Comt Thrombosis & Hemostasis; NY Acad Sci. *Res:* Mechanisms and models of enzyme action, especially thrombin insulin receptor kinase and enzymes requiring pyridoxal phosphate. *Mailing Add:* Merck Sharp & Dohme Res Labs Sunnytown Pike West Point PA 19486

SHAFER, PAUL RICHARD, ORGANIC CHEMISTRY. *Current Pos:* from instr to prof chem, 52-88, EMER PROF CHEM, DARTMOUTH COL, 88- *Personal Data:* b Springfield, Ohio, June 17, 23; m 46; c 3. *Educ:* Oberlin Col, BA, 47; Univ Wis, PhD(chem), 51. *Prof Exp:* Fel, Univ Ill, 51-52. *Concurrent Pos:* NSF fel, Calif Inst Technol, 59-60. *Mem:* Am Chem Soc; Royal Soc Chem. *Res:* Natural products; reaction mechanisms; nuclear magnetic resonance of fast exchange reactions. *Mailing Add:* Ibey Rd Enfield NH 03748

SHAFER, RICHARD HOWARD, BIOPHYSICAL CHEMISTRY. *Current Pos:* from asst prof to assoc prof, 75-87, PROF CHEM & PHARMACEUT CHEM, UNIV CALIF, SAN FRANCISCO, 87- *Personal Data:* b New Rochelle, NY, July 20, 44; m 74; c 2. *Educ:* Yale Univ, BA, 66; Harvard Univ, MA, 69, PhD(chem physics), 72. *Prof Exp:* Fel, Univ Calif, San Diego, 73-75. *Concurrent Pos:* Fulbright scholar, Paris, France, 66-67. *Mem:* Am Chem Soc; Biophys Soc. *Res:* Physical chemistry of nucleic acids; drug-nucleic acid interactions and hydrodynamic properties of high polymers. *Mailing Add:* Dept Pharmaceut Chem Univ Calif San Francisco Sch Pharm B-0446 S-926 San Francisco CA 94143

SHAFER, ROBERT E, HIGH SPEED ELECTRONICS, ACCELERATOR DESIGN. *Current Pos:* PHYSICIST RES & DEVELOP, LOS ALAMOS NAT LAB, 86- *Personal Data:* b San Francisco, Calif, June 2, 36; m 68. *Educ:* Stanford Univ, BS, 58; Univ Calif, Berkeley, PhD(physics), 66. *Prof Exp:* Res assoc, Mass Inst Technol, 66-69; physicist res & develop, Fermi Nat Accelerator Lab, 69-86. *Mem:* Am Inst Physics; AAAS. *Res:* High energy physics experiments; designing and building particle accelerators. *Mailing Add:* 1322 Big Rock Loop Los Alamos NM 87544

SHAFER, SHELDON JAY, ORGANIC CHEMISTRY. *Current Pos:* develop chemist, Plastics Div, Gen Elec Co, 77-79, polymer chemist, 79-83, advan polymer chemist, 83-89, sr scientist, Plastics Div, 89-91, STAFF SCIENTIST, RES & DEVELOP CTR, GEN ELEC CORP, 92- *Personal Data:* b Passaic, NJ, June 17, 48. *Educ:* Fairleigh Dickinson Univ, BS, 70; State Univ NY, Albany, PhD(org chem), 76. *Prof Exp:* Res fel org chem, Univ Calif, Santa Cruz, 76-77. *Mem:* Am Chem Soc. *Res:* Physical organic chemistry; reaction mechanisms; organic electron transfer reactions; organosulfur chemistry; process chemistry in monomers and thermo plastic polymers. *Mailing Add:* 10 Mann Blvd Clifton Park NY 12065-2620

SHAFER, STEPHEN JOEL, BIOCHEMICAL & DEVELOPMENTAL GENETICS. *Current Pos:* from asst prof to assoc prof, 73-85, PROF BIOL, DOWLING COL, 85- *Personal Data:* b Philadelphia, Pa, Dec 28, 39; m 70. *Educ:* Haverford Col, BA, 63; Univ Pa, MS, 65; Temple Univ, PhD(biochem genetics), 72. *Prof Exp:* Res asst genetics, Haverford Col, 65-66; res assoc biochem genetics, Temple Univ, 72-73. *Mem:* NY Acad Sci; AAAS; Am Soc Zool; Nat Asn Advan Health Prof. *Res:* Application of recombinant DNA techniques to mutants of drosophila melanogaster. *Mailing Add:* Dept Math & Sci Dowling Col 1500 Idle Hour Blvd Oakdale NY 11769-1906

SHAFER, STEPHEN QUENTIN, EPIDEMIOLOGY, NEUROEPIDEMIOLOGY. *Current Pos:* clin scholar med, Johnson Clin Scholars Prog, 76-78, asst prof pub health & neurol, 78-89, ASSOC CLIN PROF NEUROL, SERGIEVSKY CTR, COLUMBIA UNIV, 89- *Personal Data:* b Barrytown, NY, Dec 18, 44; m 66; c Elizabeth Jay Stillman. *Educ:* Harvard Univ, BA, 66; Columbia Univ, MD, 70, MPH, 77, MA, 79; Am Bd Internal Med, dipl, 75; Am Bd Psychiat & Neurol, 85. *Prof Exp:* Intern & resident, Harlem Hosp Ctr, 70-72, clin fel neurol, 72-74, resident med, 74-75. *Concurrent Pos:* Resident neurol, Columbia Univ, 81-84. *Mem:* Am Pub Health Asn; Am Acad Neurol. *Res:* Cerebrovascular disease; chronic disease epidemiology; neuroepidemiology; epilepsy. *Mailing Add:* Harlem Hosp Ctr 506 Lenox Ave New York NY 10037. *Fax:* 212-939-4245

SHAFER, STEVEN RAY, POLLUTANT-PARASITE INTERACTIONS, SOIL MICROBIOLOGY. *Current Pos:* RES PLANT PATHOLOGIST, AGR RES SERV, USDA, 83-; ASSOC PROF PLANT PATH & SOIL SCI, NC STATE UNIV, 84- *Personal Data:* b Troy, Ohio, Apr 5, 56; m 91, Rose. *Educ:* Ohio State Univ, BS, 78, MS, 80; NC State Univ, PhD(plant path), 83. *Concurrent Pos:* Assoc ed, Phytopath, Am Phytopath Soc, 88-90 & sr ed, 91-93; mem, Panel on Monitoring & Managing Natural Resources, Nat Acad Sci, 90; vis assoc prof microbiol ecol, Duke Univ, 94; tech co-dir, Environ Monitoring & Assessment Prog Agr Lands Resource Group, 95-97. *Mem:* Am Phytopath Soc; AAAS; Hist Sci Soc. *Res:* Effects of air pollutants on plants and associated soilborne microorganisms, including mycorrhizal fungi, rhizobia, nematodes, and rhizosphere-inhabiting bacteria; development of indicators of agroecosystem health. *Mailing Add:* USDA-NC State Univ Air Qual Res Prog 1509 Varsity Dr Raleigh NC 27606. *Fax:* 919-856-4598

SHAFER, THOMAS HOWARD, DEVELOPMENTAL BIOLOGY, SCIENCE EDUCATION. *Current Pos:* ASST PROF BIOL, UNIV NC, WILMINGTON, 78- *Personal Data:* b Columbus, Ohio, Jan 23, 48; m 70; c 2. *Educ:* Duke Univ, BS, 70; Ohio State Univ, MS, 73, PhD(bot), 75. *Prof Exp:* Res assoc develop plant physiol, Ohio State Univ, 75-76; vis asst prof, Denison Univ, 76-77 & Univ Ill, 77-78. *Mem:* AAAS. *Res:* Relation of plant hormones to the synthesis of gene products; gene activation in early embryogenesis. *Mailing Add:* Dept Biol Sci Univ NC at Wilmington 601 S College Rd Wilmington NC 28403-3201

SHAFER, W SUE, CELL BIOLOGY. *Current Pos:* assoc dir, 89-97, DEP DIR, NAT INST GEN MED SCI, NIH, 97- *Personal Data:* b Alton, Ill, Oct 3, 41. *Educ:* Univ Wis, BS, 63; Univ Fla, PhD(develop biol), 68. *Prof Exp:* Fel, Univ Fla, 68-69; bus mgr, Soc Develop Biol, Inc, 70-74; chief, Off Prog Planning & Eval, Div Res Resources, NIH, 83-87; dep dir, Div Basic Res, Nat Inst Alcohol Abuse & Alcoholism, US Dept Health & Human Serv, 87-89. *Concurrent Pos:* Guest lectr, Kalamazoo Col, 69-72, vis lectr, 72-73. *Mem:* Soc Develop Biol; Am Soc Cell Biol. *Mailing Add:* Nat Inst Gen Med Sci NIH 2AN 32C Natcher Bldg Bethesda MD 20892. *Fax:* 301-480-1852; *E-Mail:* wst@cu.nih.gov

SHAFER, WILLIAM GENE, ORAL PATHOLOGY. *Current Pos:* RETIRED. *Personal Data:* b Toledo, Ohio, Nov 15, 23; m 43. *Educ:* Univ Toledo, BS, 47; Ohio State Univ, DDS, 47; Univ Rochester, MS, 50; Am Bd Oral Path, dipl, 52. *Prof Exp:* From instr to assoc prof, Ind Univ, Indianapolis, 50-59, dent cancer coordr, 52-88, chmn dept, 56-59, prof oral path, Sch Dent, 59. *Concurrent Pos:* Consult, US Vet Admin, 53- & Surgeon Gen, USAF, 60-; secy-treas, Am Bd Oral Path, 61- *Mem:* AAAS; Soc Exp Biol & Med; Am Dent Asn; fel Am Acad Oral Path (vpres, 54, pres, 57); NY Acad Sci. *Res:* Experimental dental caries; salivary glands and endocrines; x-ray irradiation; experimental salivary gland tumors; tissue culture. *Mailing Add:* 3306 Kenilworth Dr Indianapolis IN 46288

SHAFFAR, SCOTT WILLIAM, COMBUSTION RESEARCH, LASER DIAGNOSTICS. *Current Pos:* Sr engr, 84-93, ENG SPECIALIST, NORTHROP CORP, 93- *Personal Data:* b Waukeegan, Ill, Dec 1, 62; m, Renee. *Educ:* Calif Polytech Inst, BS, 84; Univ Calif, Irvine, MS, 93. *Mem:* Am Inst Aeronaut & Astronaut; Am Asn Aerosol Res; Int Soc Optical Eng. *Res:* Combustion; laser based diagnostics; aerosol science; atomization; air pollution; propulsion fluids. *Mailing Add:* Northrop Corp MS 9G23/GS 8900 E Washington Blvd Pico Rivera CA 90660

SHAFFER, BERNARD W(ILLIAM), ENGINEERING, RATIONAL ANALYSIS OF STRESS & MOTION. *Current Pos:* prof, 73-93, EMER PROF MECH & AEROSPACE ENG, POLYTECH UNIV, 93- *Personal Data:* b New York, NY, Aug 7, 24; wid; c Janet I & Roberta (Nordman). *Educ:* City Col New York, BME, 44; Case Inst Technol, MS, 47; Brown Univ, PhD(appl math), 51. *Honors & Awards:* Richards Mem Award Outstanding Achievement, Am Soc Mech Engrs, 68. *Prof Exp:* Aeronaut res scientist, Nat Adv Comt Aeronaut, Ohio, 44-47; res assoc, Grad Div, Appl Math, Brown Univ, 47-50; from asst prof to prof mech eng, NY Univ, 50-73, proj dir, Res Div, 51-73. *Concurrent Pos:* Spec lectr, Case Inst Technol, 46-47; res & consult for govt agencies & pvt enterprises, 50-; vis res prof mech eng, Fla Atlantic Univ, 92, distinguished vis res prof, 93-95. *Mem:* Fel Am Soc Mech Engrs; Am Acad Mech; assoc fel Am Inst Aeronaut & Astronaut. *Res:* Stress analysis; elasticity; plasticity; kinematics; mechanics of metal cutting; analysis of filament reinforced plastics. *Mailing Add:* 18 Old Field Lane Great Neck NY 11020

SHAFFER, CHARLES FRANKLIN, IMMUNOLOGY, TRANSPLANTATION BIOLOGY. *Current Pos:* from asst prof to assoc prof biol, 71-85, PROF BIOL, WITTENBERG UNIV, 85- *Personal Data:* b Pittsburgh, Pa, Oct 9, 40; m 64; c 3. *Educ:* Univ Pittsburgh, BS, 63, MS, 65;

Univ Pa, PhD(biol), 68. *Prof Exp:* Pa scholar exp med, Dept Med Genetics, Sch Med, Univ Pa, 68-71. *Concurrent Pos:* Adj assoc prof microbiol & immunol, Med Sch, Wright State Univ, 77- *Mem:* Transplantation Soc; Am Asn Immunologists. *Res:* Immunologic and genetic aspects of tissue and organ transplantation. *Mailing Add:* Dept Biol Wittenberg Univ PO Box 720 Springfield OH 45501-0720

SHAFFER, CHARLES HENRY, JR, microbiology; deceased, see previous edition for last biography

SHAFFER, CHARLES V(ERNON), ELECTRICAL ENGINEERING, COMPUTER ENGINEERING. *Current Pos:* Asst res prof electronic ord, Univ Fla, 46-51, from assoc prof, to prof, 51-85, grad coord, 65-68, asst dean grad sch, 69-71, EMER PROF ELEC ENG, UNIV FLA, 85- *Personal Data:* b Melbourne, Fla, Feb 22, 22; m 44, Onyx Grubbs; c Charles L, Joy D & Mary O (Jones). *Educ:* Univ Fla, BEE, 44, MSE, 60; Stanford Univ, PhD(elec eng), 65. *Honors & Awards:* Award, NASA, 70; Centennial Medal, Inst Elec & Electronics Engrs, 84. *Concurrent Pos:* Consult, US Army Missile Command, 71-74; dir, Northeast Regional Data Ctr, State Univ Systs Fla, 72-74; mem tech staff, Bell Labs, Denver, Colo, 70, Holmdel, NJ, 76 & IBM, Gen Systs Div, Boca Raton, Fla, 78. *Mem:* Comput Soc; Inst Elec & Electronics Engrs; Sigma Xi. *Res:* Network theory and design; computer communications; system science; microcomputers. *Mailing Add:* 3425 NW Eighth Ave Gainesville FL 32605-4909. *E-Mail:* shaffer@nervm.nerdc.ufl.edu

SHAFFER, DAVID, CHILD PSYCHIATRY. *Current Pos:* AT DEPT PSYCHOL, UNIV GA. *Personal Data:* b Johannesburg, S Africa, Apr 20, 36; Brit citizen; c 2. *Educ:* Univ London, MB, BS, 61; MRCP, 64; FRCPsych, 81. *Prof Exp:* Lectr pediat, Univ Col Hosp, London, 64-65; registr psychiat, Maudsley Hosp, London, 65-69; sr registr & lectr child psychiat, Inst Psychiat, London, 69-74; sr lectr, NY State Psychiat Inst, 74-77, dir, Dept Child Psychiat, 77-; prof clin psychiat & pediat, Col Physicians & Surgeons, Columbia Univ, 77- *Concurrent Pos:* Von Ameringen fel, Found Fund Psychiat, Yale Univ, 67-68. *Mem:* Asn Child Psychiat & Psychol, London (treas, 75-77); Am Acad Child Psychiat; Am Psychiat Asn; Brit Pediat Asn; Royal Col Psychiat, London (secy, 75-77). *Res:* Relationships between brain damage and psychiatric disorder in children; suicide and depression in childhood; psychological aspects of enuresis; classification of child psychiatric disorders. *Mailing Add:* Dept Psychol Univ Ga 1180 E Broad St Athens GA 30601-3040

SHAFFER, DAVID BRUCE, RADIO ASTRONOMY, ANTENNA MEASUREMENTS. *Current Pos:* CONSULT, 93- *Personal Data:* b Berea, Ohio, Feb 17, 46; m 79, Donna Weistrop. *Educ:* Carnegie-Mellon Univ, BS, 68; Calif Inst Technol, PhD(astron), 74. *Prof Exp:* Teaching asst physics, Calif Inst Technol, 71-73; instr astron, Yale Univ, 73-75; asst scientist, Nat Radio Astron Observ, 75-77, assoc scientist, 77-79; staff scientist, Very Long Baseline Interferometer Group, Phoenix Corp, 79-82; chief scientist, Interferometrics, Inc, 82-93. *Concurrent Pos:* Vis assoc prof physics, Univ Nev, Las Vegas, 93- *Mem:* Am Astron Soc; Int Astron Union; Int Sci Radio Union; Royal Astron Soc. *Res:* Long baseline radio interferometry of compact extragalactic radio sources, galaxies and quasars. *Mailing Add:* 1742 Saddleback Ct Henderson NV 89014. *Fax:* 702-451-5562; *E-Mail:* shaffer@nevada.edu

SHAFFER, DOROTHY BROWNE, MATHEMATICS. *Current Pos:* from asst prof to prof, 63-92, EMER PROF MATH, FAIRFIELD UNIV, 92- *Personal Data:* b Vienna, Austria, Feb 12, 23; nat US; m 43, 78; c 3. *Educ:* Bryn Mawr Col, AB, 43; Radcliffe Col, MA, 45, PhD, 62. *Prof Exp:* Mem staff, Dynamic Anal & Control Lab, Mass Inst Technol, 45-47; asst, Harvard Univ, 48; consult, Corning Glass Works, 49-50; assoc mathematician, Cornell Aeronaut Lab, 52-56; staff mathematician, Dunlap & Assocs, Inc, 58-60; lectr, Univ Conn, Stamford Br, 63. *Concurrent Pos:* NSF fac fel, Courant Inst Math Sci, NY Univ, 69-70; Prof develop fel, Res Div, IBM Corp, 79; vis prof, Imp Col Sci & Technol, London 78, Univ Md, College Park & Univ Calif, La Jolla, 81 & 86. *Mem:* Am Math Soc; Math Asn Am; Sigma Xi; Asn Women Math; NY Acad Sci. *Res:* Conformal mapping and level curves of Green's Function; operations research; theoretical aerodynamics; polynomials; univalent functions; potential theory; special functions. *Mailing Add:* Dept Math Fairfield Univ Fairfield CT 06430. *E-Mail:* drshaffer@fair1.fairfield.edu

SHAFFER, DOUGLAS HOWERTH, MATHEMATICS, STATISTICS. *Current Pos:* RETIRED. *Personal Data:* b Danville, Pa, Oct 31, 28; m 52; c 2. *Educ:* Carnegie Inst Technol, BS, 50, MS, 51, PhD, 53. *Prof Exp:* Instr math, Carnegie Inst Technol, 53-54; res mathematician, Westinghouse Elec Corp, 54-63, fel mathematician, 63-65, adv mathematician, 65-75, consult mathematician, 75-79, mgr, 79-90; consult, 90-91. *Res:* Applied and statistical mathematics; design of experiments; mathematics education. *Mailing Add:* 150 Washington St Pittsburgh PA 15218

SHAFFER, HARRY LEONARD, ELECTRICAL ENGINEERING, SECURE SYSTEMS & PUBLIC KEY CRYPTOGRAPHY. *Current Pos:* MEM STAFF, DATA SECURITY, RAYTHEON, 92- *Personal Data:* b Boston, Mass, Dec 15, 33; m 60, Maryann F Anzuoni; c Maryann, Micheal, Jeanne, Wayne, Lorna & Brian. *Educ:* Northeastern Univ, BSEE, 62, MSEE, 64. *Honors & Awards:* Leslie Warner Award, Comput Applns. *Prof Exp:* Sr technologist, GTE Sylvania Appl Res Lab, 64-70, eng specialist digital signal processing res, Eastern Div GTE Sylvania Electronics Systs Group, 70-87, GTE Edcd, 88-92. *Concurrent Pos:* NSF grant, 63-64. *Mem:* Inst Elec & Electronics Engrs. *Res:* Development of algorithms to digitally process speech and modem signals, in real-time on mini-computers and micro-processors; extensive study into algorithms for secure-speech transmission on communications channels; digital signal processing; currently involved with system configuration for electronic distribution of cryptographic keys (aka key management). *Mailing Add:* 55 Howard Ave Lynnfield MA 01940

SHAFFER, JACQUELIN BRUNING, lung molecular biology, for more information see previous edition

SHAFFER, JAY CHARLES, SYSTEMATIC ENTOMOLOGY. *Current Pos:* from asst prof to assoc prof, 68-81, PROF BIOL, GEORGE MASON UNIV, 81- *Personal Data:* b Sunbury, Pa, July 21, 38; m 69; c 3. *Educ:* Bucknell Univ, BS, 61; Cornell Univ, PhD(syst entom), 67. *Prof Exp:* Vis res assoc entom, Smithsonian Inst, 66-67. *Concurrent Pos:* Assoc ed, Biotropica, 72-79; res assoc entom, Smithsonian Inst, 79- *Mem:* Lepidop Soc. *Res:* Systematics and biology of the Pyralidae, Lepidoptera; origin, development and present status of the insect fauna of Aldabra atoll. *Mailing Add:* Dept Biol George Mason Univ 4400 University Dr Fairfax VA 22030-4444. *E-Mail:* jshaffe1@wpgate.gmu.edu

SHAFFER, JOHN CLIFFORD, PHYSICS. *Current Pos:* Asst prof, 65-68, assoc prof, 68-75, PROF PHYSICS, NORTHERN ILL UNIV, 75-, CHMN DEPT, 73- *Personal Data:* b Towanda, Pa, May 3, 38; m 66; c 2. *Educ:* Franklin & Marshall Col, BS, 60; Univ Del, MS, 62, PhD(physics), 66. *Mem:* AAAS; Am Phys Soc. *Res:* Optical properties of solids; luminescence; band structure of solids; disordered solids; surface physics. *Mailing Add:* Dept Physics Northern Ill Univ De Kalb IL 60115-2853

SHAFFER, LAWRENCE BRUCE, X-RAY SCATTERING-SMALL ANGLE & DIFFUSE. *Current Pos:* PROF PHYSICS & CHMN DEPT, ANDERSON UNIV, IND, 70- *Personal Data:* b Delta, Ohio, Oct 14, 37; m 59; c 4. *Educ:* Ohio State Univ, BSc, 59; Univ Wis, MSc, 60, PhD(physics), 64. *Prof Exp:* Asst prof physics, Hiram Col, 63-70, chmn dept, 64-70. *Concurrent Pos:* Res Corp grants, 64-; teaching equip grants, NSF, 65-67 & Kettering Found, 65-; NASA res grants, 66-69; guest scientist, Inst Solid State Res, Nuclear Res Ctr, Julich GmbH, WGer, 77-78, Oak Ridge Nat Lab, 70-75, 84-85 & 91-92, Brookhaven Nat Lab, 85, 86, 87, 88 & 89; Woodrow Wilson fel. *Mem:* AAAS; Am Phys Soc; Am Asn Physics Teachers; Am Crystallog Asn. *Res:* Thermodynamics of liquids and solutions using x-ray methods; measurement of dislocations and interstitial atom content in crystal surfaces by x-ray methods; diffuse scattering using synchrotron radiation. *Mailing Add:* 1821 E 240 N Anderson IN 46012-3462. *E-Mail:* lbs@anderson.edu

SHAFFER, LOUIS RICHARD, CONSTRUCTION ENGINEERING. *Current Pos:* TECH DIR CONSTRUCT ENG RES LAB, US ARMY, 69- *Personal Data:* b Sharon, Pa, Feb 7, 28; m 55; c 3. *Educ:* Carnegie-Mellon Univ, BS, 50; Univ Ill, Urbana, MS, 57, PhD(systs civil eng), 61. *Honors & Awards:* Walter L Huber Res Prize, Am Soc Civil Engrs, 67, Construct Mgt Award, 78, Construct Res Award, 87. *Prof Exp:* Asst to master mech, Nat Castings Co, Pa, 50-52, asst to dir eng, Sharon Steel Corp, 53-54; instr civil eng, 55-61, from asst prof to assoc prof, 61-65, PROF CIVIL ENG, UNIV ILL, URBANA, 65- *Concurrent Pos:* Asst dir, Tech Dir Construct Eng Res Lab, US Army, 69-70 & dep dir, 70-76; coordr, Int Working Comn on Orgn & Mgt Construct, 74-; chmn, Tech Coun Res, Am Soc Civil Engrs, 76-77; chmn US Nat Comt, Int Coun Bldg Res, 77-83. *Mem:* Am Soc Civil Engrs; Soc Am Mil Engrs. *Res:* Modern construction management with emphasis on technical innovation to increase productivity of management on all levels. *Mailing Add:* 2203 Pond St Urbana IL 61801

SHAFFER, MORRIS FRANK, medical microbiology; deceased, see previous edition for last biography

SHAFFER, NELSON ROSS, OIL SHALES, CLAY MINERALOGY. *Current Pos:* RES SCIENTIST GEOL, IND GEOL SERV, 74-, EXEC DIR, IND ACAD SCI, 92- *Personal Data:* b Galion, Ohio, Aug 18, 48; m 67, 80, Kathryn Smith; c 6. *Educ:* Ohio State Univ, BSc, 72, MSc, 74; Ind Univ, PhD, 96. *Prof Exp:* Teaching asst geol, Ohio State Univ, 73-74, res asst geochem, 74. *Concurrent Pos:* Res assoc, Glenn A Black Lab Archaeol, 87-; mem exec comt, IGCP, UN, 87-; prin invest, Basalt Waste Isolation proj, 85-87, US Dept Energy, 84-85; consult, 78- *Mem:* Fel Geol Soc Am; Soc Mining Engrs; Geochem Soc; Mineral Soc Am; Am Chem Soc; Am Asn Petrol Geologists. *Res:* Geochemistry and mineralogy of metalliferous black shales, limestone, phosphates, other sedimentary rocks, and ground water; stable isotope studies of sulfides, shales, archaeological artifacts; mineralogy of meteorites, biominerals; industrial uses of minerals. *Mailing Add:* Ind Geol Surv 611 N Walnut Grove Bloomington IN 47405

SHAFFER, PATRICIA MARIE, BIOCHEMISTRY & MOLECULAR BIOLOGY. *Current Pos:* student counr, 59-78, assoc prof, 71-81, PROF CHEM, UNIV SAN DIEGO, 81- *Personal Data:* b Los Angeles, Calif, June 11, 28. *Educ:* San Francisco Col Women, BA, 52; Stanford Univ, MS, 59; Univ Calif, San Diego, PhD(chem), 75. *Prof Exp:* Asst prof chem, San Diego Col Women, 59-68. *Concurrent Pos:* NATO fel, Univ Newcastle upon Tyne, Eng, 80-81; sabbatical leave, Dept Genetics, Univ Ga, 87-88. *Mem:* Am Soc Biochemists & Molecular Biologists; AAAS; Am Chem Soc; Coun Undergrad Res; Grad Women Sci; Int Asn Women Bioscientists. *Res:* Metabolism of primidine deoxyribonucleosides in Neurospora crassa and aspergillus nidulans; ammonium repressible enzymes; a-ketoglutarate dioxygenases; L-asparaginases. *Mailing Add:* Dept Chem Univ Calif 5998 Alcala Park San Diego CA 92110-2492

SHAFFER, ROBERT LYNN, MYCOLOGY, TAXONOMY. *Current Pos:* from asst prof to prof bot, 60-81, dir, 75-86, CUR FUNGI, HERBARIUM, UNIV MICH, ANN ARBOR, 60-, WEHMEYER PROF FUNGAL TAXON, 81- *Personal Data:* b Long Beach, Calif, Dec 29, 29; m 58; c 1. *Educ:* Kans State Col, BS, 51, MS, 52; Cornell Univ, PhD, 55. *Prof Exp:* From instr to asst prof bot, Univ Chicago, 55-60. *Mem:* Mycol Soc Am (secy-treas, 68-71, vpres, 71-72, pres, 73-74); NAm Mycol Asn; Int Asn Plant Taxon. *Res:* Taxonomy of fungi, especially Agaricales. *Mailing Add:* Herbariem Rm 2006 Univ Mich 830 N University Ave Ann Arbor MI 48109-1048

SHAFFER, RUSSELL ALLEN, THEORETICAL PHYSICS. *Current Pos:* asst prof, 64-67, ASSOC PROF PHYSICS, LEHIGH UNIV, 67- *Personal Data:* b Philadelphia, Pa, Nov 3, 33; m 58, Olga Loginow; c Laura, Andrea, Sandra & Valerie. *Educ:* Drexel Univ, BS, 56; Johns Hopkins Univ, PhD(physics), 62. *Prof Exp:* Res assoc physics, Vanderbilt Univ, 62-64. *Mem:* Am Asn Physics Teachers. *Res:* Theory of elementary particle interactions; electroweak interactions; lepton physics. *Mailing Add:* Dept Physics Lehigh Univ 16 Memorial Dr E Bethlehem PA 18015-3182. *Fax:* 610-758-5730

SHAFFER, THOMAS HILLARD, RESPIRATORY & DEVELOPMENTAL PHYSIOLOGY. *Current Pos:* assoc prof, 77-87, PROF PHYSIOL & PEDIAT, TEMPLE UNIV, 87-, DIR RESPIRATORY, PHYSIOL SECT, 77- *Educ:* Drexel Univ, PhD(appl mech), 72. *Prof Exp:* Asst prof physiol, Univ Pa Sch Med, 74-77. *Mem:* Am Thoracic Soc; Am Physiol Soc; AAAS; NY Acad Sci. *Res:* Biological development of the respiratory system. *Mailing Add:* Dept Physiol & Pediat Sch Med Temple Univ 3420 N Broad St Philadelphia PA 19140-5104

SHAFFER, WAVE H, physics; deceased, see previous edition for last biography

SHAFFNER, RICHARD OWEN, GAS DISCHARGE PHYSICS. *Current Pos:* sr staff scientist discharge plasmas, 78-79, mgr, Daymax Div, 80, sr proj engr, 81, SR STAFF SCIENTIST, ILC TECHNOL, INC. *Personal Data:* b Chicago, Ill, June 12, 38; div; c 2. *Educ:* Ill Inst Technol, BSEE, 60, Mass Inst Technol, SMEE, 62; Case Western Res Univ, PhD(elec eng), 74. *Prof Exp:* Engr discharge lamps, Lighting Bus Group, Gen Elec Co, Ohio, 68-71, sr engr, 71-75, sr design engr, 75-78. *Mem:* Am Phys Soc; Inst Elec & Electronics Engrs; Sigma Xi. *Res:* Radiation from discharge plasmas and physical chemistry associated with discharge; metal halide arc lamp design. *Mailing Add:* ILC Tech 399 Java Dr Sunnyvale CA 94089

SHAFIQ, SAIYID AHMAD, CELL BIOLOGY. *Current Pos:* ASSOC PROF NEUROL, STATE UNIV NY, DOWNSTATE MED CTR, 74- *Personal Data:* b Sitapur, India, Dec 29, 29; m 55; c 3. *Educ:* Oxford Univ, DPhil(cytol), 54. *Prof Exp:* Lectr zool, Univ Dacca, 54-59; Fulbright fel anat, Univ Wash, 59-60; res assoc cell biol, Inst Muscle Dis, 60-63, asst mem, 63-69, assoc mem, 69-74. *Mem:* Am Asn Anatomists. *Res:* Cytology; muscle pathology; electron microscopy. *Mailing Add:* Dept Neurol Downstate Med Ctr State Univ NY 450 Clarkson Ave Box 1213 Brooklyn NY 11203-2012

SHAFIT-ZAGARDO, BRIDGET, HUMAN GENETICS. *Current Pos:* res assoc, dept cell biol, 81-84, ASST PROF, DEPT PATH, ALBERT EINSTEIN COL MED, 84- *Personal Data:* b Bronx, NY, May 6, 52; m 76; c 2. *Educ:* C W Post Col, BS, 73; NY Univ, MS, 78; City Univ New York, MPhil, 80; Mt Sinai Sch Med, PhD(genetics), 81. *Mem:* Am Soc Human Genetics; Am Soc Cell Biol. *Res:* Molecular biology of Alzheimer's disease; inherited disorders in man; brain-specific genes; human gene polymorphisms. *Mailing Add:* Dept Path Albert Einstein Med Col 1300 Morris Park Ave Bronx NY 10461-1975

SHAFRITZ, DAVID ANDREW, MOLECULAR BIOLOGY, MEDICINE. *Current Pos:* from asst prof to assoc prof, 73-81, PROF MED & CELL BIOL, ALBERT EINSTEIN COL MED, 81-, DIR, MARION BESSIN LIVER RES CTR, 85- *Personal Data:* b Philadelphia, Pa, Oct 5, 40; m 64, Sharon C Klemow; c Gregory S, Adam B & Keith M. *Educ:* Univ Pa, AB, 62, MD, 66. *Honors & Awards:* Merrel lectr, Am Asn Study Liver Dis, 78; J Friedenvald Lectr, Univ Md, 83; Grace Kimball Lectr, Wilkes Col, 87; James Gibson Lectr, Univ Hong Kong, 87. *Prof Exp:* Res assoc, Molecular Dis Br, Sect Human Biochem, Nat Heart & Lung Inst, 68-71; from instr to asst prof med, Harvard Med Sch, 71-73. *Concurrent Pos:* spec res fel, Nat Inst Arthritis, Metab & Digestive Dis, Gastrointestinal Unit, Mass Gen Hosp, 71-73; res career develop award, Nat Inst Arthritis, Metab & Digestive Dis, 75-80; assoc ed, Hepat, 81-86; Herman Lapota prof liver dis res, 93. *Mem:* AAAS; Am Asn Study Liver Dis; Int Asn Study Liver; Am Soc Biol Chemists; Am Soc Clin Invest; Harvey Soc; Asn Am Physicians; Am Gastroenterol Asn; Interurban Clin Club. *Res:* Mammalian protein synthesis and messenger RNA metabolism; eukaryotic gene regulation; liver regeneration and regulation of cellular differentiation, liver somatic gene therapy, hepatitis B virus infection, chronic liver disease and primary liver cancer; diseases of liver and intestine. *Mailing Add:* Dept Med & Cell Biol Albert Einstein Col Med 1300 Morris Park Ave Bronx NY 10461-1975. *Fax:* 718-918-0857

SHAFROTH, STEPHEN MORRISON, ATOMIC PHYSICS. *Current Pos:* PROF RES, UNIV NC, 88- *Personal Data:* b Denver, Colo, June 12, 26; m 54; c 3. *Educ:* Harvard Univ, BA, 47; Johns Hopkins Univ, PhD(physics), 53. *Prof Exp:* From instr to asst prof physics, Northwestern Univ, 53-59; res physicist, France, 59 & Bartol Res Found, 60-67; from assoc prof to prof, Univ NC, Chapel Hill, 67-88; prof, Triangle Univs Nuclear Lab, Durham, 70-88; researcher, Oak Ridge Nat Lab, 88. *Concurrent Pos:* Vis lectr, Temple Univ, 65; adv bd, Nuclear Data Sheets, 66-78; lectr & consult, US Naval Res Lab, 66-; assoc ed, Atomic Data & Nuclear Data Tables, 75-; ed, Scintillation Spectros of Gamma Radiation. *Mem:* Fel Am Phys Soc. *Res:* Experimental nuclear physics; high resolution x-ray spectroscopy following atomic excitation by heavy ions accelerated by a tandem Van de Graaff; high resolution projectile electron spectroscopy. *Mailing Add:* Dept Physics Univ NC Chapel Hill NC 27599. *Fax:* 919-962-0480

SHAFTAN, GERALD WITTES, SURGERY. *Current Pos:* STAFF MEM, BROOKDALE HOSP MED CTR, BROOKLYN. *Personal Data:* b New York, NY, Apr 15, 26; m 49; c 2. *Educ:* Brown Univ, AB, 45; NY Univ, MD, 49. *Prof Exp:* Asst instr, State Univ NY Downstate Med Ctr, 56-57, from instr to assoc prof, 57-68, prof surg, 68- *Concurrent Pos:* Consult, Vet Admin Hosp, Brooklyn, 64-; chief surg serv, Kings County Hosp Ctr, Brooklyn, 72- *Mem:* Am Col Surgeons; Asn Acad Surg; Am Soc Surg Hand; Am Asn Surg Trauma; Sigma Xi. *Res:* Management of multiple trauma and shock; control of bleeding and healing of fractures. *Mailing Add:* Dir Dept Surg Linden Blvd Brookdale Plaza Brooklyn NY 11212

SHAFTMAN, DAVID HARRY, MATHEMATICS, NUCLEAR ENGINEERING. *Current Pos:* RETIRED. *Personal Data:* b Philadelphia, Pa, Aug 27, 24; m 44, 75; c 4. *Educ:* Univ Chicago, BS, 48, MS, 49. *Prof Exp:* Asst mathematician, Naval Reactors Div & Reactor Eng Div, Argonne Nat Lab, 50-55, assoc mathematician, Reactor Eng Div & Reactor Physics Div, 55-69, assoc mathematician, Appl Physics Div, 69-74, mathematician, Appl Physics Div, 74-77, mathematician, Reactor Anal & Safety Div, 77-90. *Mem:* AAAS; Am Math Soc; Am Nuclear Soc. *Res:* Reactor design and development; theoretical reactor physics; theory and application of functional analysis. *Mailing Add:* 19 Olympus Dr Apt 3A Naperville IL 60540-7946

SHAH, ASHOK CHANDULAL, PHARMACEUTICS. *Current Pos:* RETIRED. *Personal Data:* b Palanpur, India, Apr 25, 39; m 66; c 1. *Educ:* Univ Bombay, BSc (hons), 59, BSc, 61; Univ Wis, MS, 63, PhD(pharm), 65. *Prof Exp:* Sr scientist, Upjohn Co, 65-94. *Mem:* Am Pharmaceut Asn; fel Acad Pharmaceut Sci. *Res:* Chemical kinetics in solutions; physical properties of solids, including phase behavior, and surface, crystal, thermal, mechanical and dissolution properties; formulation of new solid drug dosage forms. *Mailing Add:* 8338 Phoebe St Kalamazoo MI 49009

SHAH, BABUBHAI VADILAL, STATISTICS. *Current Pos:* statistician, Res Triangle Inst, 66-68, mgr, 68-71, assoc dir, 72-75, CHIEF SCIENTIST, RES TRIANGLE INST, 76- *Personal Data:* b Bombay, India, Feb 6, 35; US citizen; m 66, Ketki B Desai; c Parag & Mona. *Educ:* Univ Bombay, BS, 55, MS, 57, PhD(statist), 60. *Prof Exp:* Res assoc statist, Iowa State Univ, 59-62; res analyst, Karamchand Premchand Ltd, India, 62-66. *Concurrent Pos:* Adj prof biostatist, Univ NC, 79- *Mem:* Fel Am Statist Asn; Royal Statist Soc; Int Statist Inst. *Res:* Data analysis in complex sample surveys, microsimulation models, optimization techniques. *Mailing Add:* Res Triangle Inst PO Box 12194 Res Triangle Park NC 27709

SHAH, BHAGWAN G, ANIMAL SCIENCE & NUTRITION, AGRICULTURAL & FOOD CHEMISTRY. *Current Pos:* RES SCIENTIST & SECT HEAD, MACRO NUTRIT & MINERALS, NUTRIT RES DIV, BUR NUTRIT SCI, HEALTH PROTECTION BR, HEALTH & WELFARE, CAN, 66- *Personal Data:* b Bombay, India, Mar 16, 24; Can citizen; m 55. *Educ:* Bombay Univ, BSc, 45, MSc, 51; Univ Ill, Urbana, PhD(nutrit biochem), 64. *Prof Exp:* Fulbright res fel, US Educ Found, 60. *Concurrent Pos:* Mem, Comt Rev Can Dietary Standard, 73-75; mem, Exec Bd, Can Soc Nutrit Sci, 79-82; reviewer, Nat Health Res & Develop Prog, grant appls, 80- & US Recommended Daily Allowance Comt, 85; assoc ed, Nutrit Reports Int. *Mem:* AAAS; Can Soc Nutrit Sci; Am Inst Nutrit; Int Union Nutrit Sci. *Res:* Role of calcium, phosphorus, fluorine in osteoporosis; role of minerals in cardiovascular disease; bioavailability from foods of mineral nutrients such as iron & zinc. *Mailing Add:* Three Brockington Cres Nepean ON K2G 4K6 Can

SHAH, BHUPENDRA K, STATISTICS & BIOMETRICS, COMPUTER SCIENCE. *Current Pos:* RES SCIENTIST, HELEN HAYES HOSP, 84- *Personal Data:* b Visnagar, India, Dec 8, 35; US citizen; m 58; c 2. *Educ:* Univ Baroda, BS, 55, MS, 57; Yale Univ, PhD(statist), 68. *Prof Exp:* Daxina fel, Gout India, 55-57; lectr statist, Univ Baroda, 57-64; statistician, E I du Pont de Nemours & Co, 68-69; res math statistician, Info Sci Div, Rockland Res Inst, 69-70, assoc res scientist biomet, 70-83; adj prof, State Univ NY, Albany, 82-84. *Concurrent Pos:* Consult med statist, Nat Inst Neurol Dis & Strokes, Washington, DC, 69-71, Impact Nuclear Power Plants; NIMH res grant, 73; Fulbright scholar, US Govt, 62-63. *Res:* Application of statistics and computers to medical research; developing statistical theory to help establish bioequivalence of two pharmaceuticals; least squares theory. *Mailing Add:* 540 Highview Ave Pearl River NY 10965

SHAH, BHUPENDRA UMEDCHAND, METALLURGY. *Current Pos:* RES SPECIALIST METALL, RES DIV, TIMKEN CO, 67- *Personal Data:* b Bombay, India, June 15, 38; m 63; c 2. *Educ:* Birla Eng Col, India, BEng, 59; Mich State Univ, MSc, 61, PhD(metall), 67; Univ Akron, MBA, 76. *Prof Exp:* Proj engr, Bausch & Lomb, NY, 62-63. *Mem:* Am Inst Mining Metall & Petrol Engrs; Am Soc Metals; Am Foundrymen's Soc. *Res:* Development of new steelmaking processes and strand casting. *Mailing Add:* Timken Co HSO-05 PO Box 6925 Canton OH 44706-0925

SHAH, DHARMISHTHA V, clinical nutrition, nutritional biochemistry; deceased, see previous edition for last biography

SHAH, DHIREN B, FOOD SAFETY, MICROBIOL PATHOGENESIS. *Current Pos:* staff, Bacterial Physiol Br, Food & Drug Admin, 79-82, chief, Microbiol Biochem Br, 82-87, chief, Microbiol Ecol Br, 87-94, DIR DIV MICROBIOL, STUDIES, CTR FOOD SAFETY & APPL NUTRIT, FOOD & DRUG ADMIN, 94- *Personal Data:* b Bombay, India, June 7, 36; m 68, Sheela; c Neel & Jai. *Educ:* Univ Bombay, BS, 56; Univ Wis, MS, 59; PhD(microbiol), 62. *Prof Exp:* Postdoctoral res assoc, Johns Hopkins Univ, 68-72; asst prof, Univ Ky Col Med, 72-79. *Mem:* Am Soc Microbiol; Sigma Xi. *Res:* Microbiological food safety issues; methods for detection/quantitation of foodborne pathogens; microbiol ecology; food safety regulations. *Mailing Add:* Ctr Food Safety & Appl Nutrit FDA 200 C St SW HFS-515 Washington DC 20204. *Fax:* 202-401-7740; *E-Mail:* dbs@fdacf.ssw.dhhs.gov

SHAH, DINESH OCHHAVLAL, BIOPHYSICS. *Current Pos:* from asst prof to assoc prof, 70-75, chmn, Dept Chem Eng, 87-91, PROF ANESTHESIOL, BIOPHYS & CHEM ENG, UNIV FLA, 75-, DIR, CTR SURFACE SCI & ENG, 84- *Personal Data:* b Bombay, India, Mar 31, 38; m 68; c 2. *Educ:* Univ Bombay, BS, 59, MS, 61; Columbia Univ, PhD(biophys), 65. *Honors & Awards:* Excellence Teaching Award, Univ Fla, 72, Pres Scholar Award & Outstanding Serv Award, 75; Best Paper Award, Int Cong Chem & Technol, India, 78; Vishwa Gurjari Int Award, 92; Pride India Award, 93. *Prof Exp:* Nat Res Coun-NASA resident res assoc, Ames Res Ctr, NASA, 67-68; res assoc surface chem, Lamont Geol Observ, Columbia Univ, 68-70. *Concurrent Pos:* Consult, Barnes-Hind Pharmaceut, Inc, 72, Sun Oil Co, 73-, Alcoa, Inc, Alcon Labs, Inc, Ampex, Berol Kemi, Sweden, Kraft Gen Foods, Inc, PPG, Inc, Procter & Gamble Co. *Mem:* AAAS; Am Soc Eng Educ; Am Chem Soc; Am Inst Chem Engrs; Am Soc Anesthesiol. *Res:* Surface chemistry of biological systems and processes; lung surfactant; corneal surface; biomembranes; biomaterials; emulsification of fat; lipoproteins and mechanisms of anesthesia. *Mailing Add:* Dept Chem Eng Univ Fla PO Box 116005 Gainesville FL 32611-6005

SHAH, GHULAM M, ANALYTICAL MATHEMATICS, APPLIED MATHEMATICS. *Current Pos:* assoc prof, 70-75, chmn dept, 73-80, PROF MATH, UNIV WIS-WAUKESHA, 75- *Personal Data:* b Srinagar, India, May 22, 37; m 62, Zubeda; c Fasahat H, Sabahat H & Shujahat H. *Educ:* Univ Jammu & Kashmir, India, BA, 56; Aligarh Muslim Univ, India, MA, LLB & dipl statist, 58; Univ Wis-Milwaukee, PhD(math), 66. *Prof Exp:* Lectr math, Amar Singh Col, India, 58-60; jr lectr, Regional Eng Col, Srinagar, 60-61, lectr, 61-63; asst, Univ Wis-Milwaukee, 63-66, asst prof, 66-70. *Res:* Zeros of polynomials in complex variables; differential equations and analytic function theory. *Mailing Add:* Dept Math Univ Wis Waukesha WI 53188. *Fax:* 414-521-5491; *E-Mail:* gshah@uwcmail.uwc.edu

SHAH, HAMISH V, ANALYTICAL CHEMISTRY, INORGANIC CHEMISTRY. *Current Pos:* RES & DEVELOP, MGR ORG CHEM, CARDINAL STABILIZERS, 82- *Personal Data:* B Rajpipla, Gujarat, India, May 18, 53; US citizen; m; c 2. *Educ:* Saurashtra Univ, Rajkot, India, BS, 73, MS, 75. *Prof Exp:* Jr chemist org chem, IPCL, India, 75-77; chemist org chem, Kings Labs Inc, 78; chief chemist org chem, Columbia Organic Chemicals Co, 78-82. *Mem:* Am Chem Soc. *Res:* Organotin compounds, their structure and reactivity; one patent. *Mailing Add:* 835 Knollwood Dr Columbia SC 29209

SHAH, HARESH C, CIVIL ENGINEERING. *Current Pos:* assoc prof, 68-73, dir, John A Blume Earthquake Eng Ctr, 76-85, PROF CIVIL ENG, STANFORD UNIV, 73-, CHMN DEPT, 85- *Personal Data:* b Godhra, India, Aug 7, 37; m 65. *Educ:* Univ Poona, BS, 59; Stanford Univ, MS, 60, PhD(civil eng), 63. *Prof Exp:* Teaching asst civil eng, Stanford Univ, 61-62; actg asst prof, San Jose State Col, 62; from instr to assoc prof civil & mech eng, Univ Pa, 62-68. *Concurrent Pos:* Consult, Local State & Fed Govt Agencies, 68-, UNESCO & var foreign govts, 68- *Mem:* Am Soc Civil Engrs; Earthquake Eng Res Inst; Am Concrete Inst; Seismol Soc Am. *Res:* Structural mechanics; application of theory of probability and statistics to civil engineering problems; earthquake engineering and risk analysis; innovations in engineering education. *Mailing Add:* Dept Technol North Harris Co Col 2700 W Thorne Dr Houston TX 77073-3410

SHAH, HASMUKH N, POLYMER ENGINEERING. *Current Pos:* RES POLYMERS, BRISTOL MYERS SQUIBB CONVATEC, 90- *Personal Data:* b Radhanpur, India, Mar 25, 34; US citizen; m 59, Hansa; c Samil & Viral. *Educ:* Univ Bombay, India, BS Hons, 55, BS, 57, MS, 60. *Hon Degrees:* Degree plastics, SGer Plastic Inst, 70. *Prof Exp:* Proj engr single use clin thermometers, Akzona Inc, Info-chem, 77-81 & insulin pump, Becton Dickinson Advan Bus Develop, 81-83; tech dir polymer powder coating, Plasti-coats & prints, 83-87; proj engr polymer catheter, Johnson & Johnson Interventional Syst, 89. *Concurrent Pos:* Bd dirs, Med Div, Soc Plastics Engrs, 82. *Mem:* Nat Acad Sci; Soc Plastics Engrs. *Res:* Develop new biodegradable polymer films; new adhesives; polymer powder coating; select appropriate materials for medical device. *Mailing Add:* 1906 Mindy Lane Piscataway NJ 08854

SHAH, ISHWARLAL D, METALLURGICAL ENGINEERING. *Current Pos:* RES ASST, DEAN WITTIER, 84- *Personal Data:* b Rangoon, Burma, May 8, 35; m 63. *Educ:* Univ Bombay, BSc, 56; Univ Mo-Rolla, BS, 58; Purdue Univ, MS, 61; Stanford Univ, PhD(metall eng), 67. *Prof Exp:* Res asst metall eng, Purdue Univ, 58-61; res chemist, Delta Res, Ill, 61-63; res asst mineral eng, Stanford Univ, 63-67, res assoc, 67-68; res metallurgist, US Bur Mines, 68-84. *Mem:* Am Inst Mining Metall & Petrol Engr; Am Soc Metals. *Res:* Fundamentals of roasting of copper sulphide ores; solubilities and diffusion of gases in metals at high temperatures; extractive metallurgy of copper-nickel sulfides, production of alumina, iron and steel making. *Mailing Add:* 3912 Grimes Lane Minneapolis MN 55424

SHAH, JAGDEEP C, SOLID STATE PHYSICS. *Current Pos:* mem tech staff, 67-85, DISTINGUISHED MEM TECH STAFF, AT&T BELL LABS, 85- *Personal Data:* b Surat, India, Sept 3, 42; m 67, Shobhana Bhatt; c Roopak & Raina. *Educ:* Univ Bombay, BSc, 62; Mass Inst Technol, PhD(solid state physics), 67. *Honors & Awards:* Humboldt Sr Scientist Award. *Prof Exp:* Teaching asst physics, Rensselaer Polytech Inst, 62-63; res asst, Mass Inst Technol, 63-67. *Mem:* Am Inst Physics; fel Am Phys Soc. *Res:* Optical, electrical, and transport properties of semiconductors; high intensity effects and non-equilibrium phenomena in semiconductors; electron-hole liquids in semiconductors, amorphous solids; ultrafast spectroscopy in semiconductors; semiconductor microstructures; physics of high speed electronic and optoelectronic devices. *Mailing Add:* AT&T Bell Labs Rm 4D-415 Crawfords Corner Rd Holmdel NJ 07733

SHAH, KANTI L, ENVIRONMENTAL SCIENCES, WATER RESOURCES. *Current Pos:* from asst prof to assoc prof, 70-76, PROF CIVIL ENG, OHIO NORTHERN UNIV, 76-, DISTINGUISHED CHAIR HOLDER, 76- *Personal Data:* b Aligarh, India, Jan 6, 35; m 56; c 3. *Educ:* Aligarh Muslim Univ, India, BS, 55; Univ Kans, MS, 63; Univ Okla, PhD(environ sci), 69. *Prof Exp:* Asst engr, Irrig Dept, State of Uttar Pradesh, India, 55-59; city engr, Munic Corp, India, 59-60; lectr civil eng, M G Polytech, Hathras, India, 60-61; sanit engr, Kans State Dept Health, 63-67; res assoc, Univ Okla, 69; sanit engr, Pa Dept Health, 70. *Concurrent Pos:* Consult water qual mgt, Pa Dept Health, 70. *Mem:* Sigma Xi; Am Soc Civil Engrs. *Res:* Interdisciplinary approach to environmental and water resources, especially wastewater and stream water quality. *Mailing Add:* Dept Civil Eng Ohio Northern Univ 525 S Main Ada OH 45810-1555

SHAH, KEERTI V, VIROLOGY. *Current Pos:* res assoc pathobiol, 62-63, from asst prof to assoc prof, 63-74, PROF IMMUNOL & INFECTIOUS DIS, SCH HYG & PUB HEALTH, JOHNS HOPKINS UNIV, 74-, ASSOC CHMN, 85- *Personal Data:* b Ranpur, India, Nov 2, 28; m 67; c 2. *Educ:* B J Med Col, Poona, India, MBBS, 51; Johns Hopkins Univ, MPH, 57, DrPH, 63. *Prof Exp:* From intern to resident gen med, Sassoon Hosp, Poona, India, 51-53; asst res officer virol, Virus Res Ctr, Poona, 53-58, res officer, 58-61. *Mem:* AAAS; Am Soc Microbiol; Am Asn Immunologists; Am Soc Trop Med Hyg. *Res:* Biology of DNA tumor viruses. *Mailing Add:* 9303 Flagstone Dr Baltimore MD 21234-2179

SHAH, MANESH J(AGMOHAN), CHEMICAL ENGINEERING, MATHEMATICS. *Current Pos:* PRES, BLUELINK INT, 92- *Personal Data:* b Bombay, India, July 9, 32; US citizen; m 60, Margarita Sotomayor; c Yasmin & Sheila. *Educ:* Tech Inst Bombay, BS, 53, MS, 55; Univ Mich, MSChE, 57; Univ Calif, Berkeley, PhD(chem eng), 61. *Prof Exp:* Assoc engr phys chem, IBM Corp, 60-62, staff engr process control, 62-65, adv engr, 65-69, sr control systs engr, Data Processing Div, 69-72, sr engr, Gen Systs Div, 72-80, consult engr, Nat Accounts Div & Storage Prod Div, 81-92. *Concurrent Pos:* Adj prof, Univ PR, 78-79, San Jose State Univ, 94; sr lectr, Stanford Univ, 80-87. *Mem:* Fel Am Inst Chem Engrs. *Res:* Process simulation and control; electric birefringence of colloids; heat transfer and fluid mechanics in non-Newtonian fluids; applied mathematics in chemical engineering; expert systems; computer integrated manufacturing; statistical process control/design of experiments. *Mailing Add:* 1788 Frobisher Way San Jose CA 95124. *Fax:* 408-263-9886

SHAH, MIRZA MOHAMMED, MULTIPHASE HEAT TRANSFER & FLOW, HEATING VENTILATING & AIR CONDITIONING. *Current Pos:* MECH ENGR, KING FAISAL SPECIALIST HOSP & RES CTR, RIYADH, SAUDI ARABIA, 94- *Personal Data:* b Delhi, India, Aug 11, 41; US citizen; m 77, Gulrukh Rehman; c Akbar & Alvira. *Educ:* Aligarh Muslim Univ, India, BSc, 59, BSME, 63; Calif State Univ, Los Angeles, MSME, 73. *Prof Exp:* Scientist in chg airconditioning & refrig, Cent Mech Eng Res Inst, India, 65-68; res engr heat transfer, Tech Univ Norway, Trondheim, 68-69; mech engr, Bechtel Power Corp, 73 & United Engrs & Constructors, 74-76; sr engr mech eng, Gilbert-Commonwealth, 76-78; prin engr, EBASCO Serv Inc, 78-89 & 91-93; sr engr, EE Linden Assoc, Darien, CT, 89-91. *Concurrent Pos:* Consult, Kirloskar Pneumatic Co, Poona, India, 68-69 & Gen Elec Co, 82-84. *Mem:* Am Soc Heating, Refrig & Air-Conditioning Engrs; Am Soc Mech Engrs. *Res:* Heat transfer in multiphase flow; general predictive techniques for heat transfer during boiling and condensation; critical heat flux; heat transfer in fluidized beds and other two component systems. *Mailing Add:* Eng Serv MBC-38 King Faisal Hosp & Res Ctr PO Box 3354 Riyadh 11211 Saudi Arabia. *Fax:* 966-1-442-7681; *E-Mail:* mirza@kfshrc.edu.sa

SHAH, PRADEEP L, ELECTRICAL ENGINEERING, QUANTUM ELECTRONICS. *Current Pos:* mgr, metal oxide semiconductors-complementary metal oxide semiconductors technol, 73-80, complementary metal oxide semiconductors develop mgr, 80-83, eprom develop mgr, 83-92, MGR ANALOG & R F DESIGN BR TEX INSTRUMENTS, 92- *Personal Data:* b Poona, India, Oct 17, 44; m 74; c 2. *Educ:* Indian Inst Technol, BTech, 66; Rice Univ, PhD(elec eng), 70. *Prof Exp:* Supvr optics, Hycel Inc, 71-72; adj asst prof, Rice Univ, 72-73. *Concurrent Pos:* Res assoc, Rice Univ, 70-72. *Mem:* Inst Elec & Electronics Engrs. *Res:* Development of very large scale integrated circuits spanning areas of solid state physical electronics such as materials science, device physics and electronic circuit and system design and analysis. *Mailing Add:* Tex Instruments PO Box 655474 MS 446 Dallas TX 75265-5474

SHAH, RAJESH J, LUBRICANTS FUELS & GREASES TESTING, PETROLEUM PRODUCTS. *Current Pos:* TECH SERVS & BUS DEVELOP DIR, KOEHLER INSTRUMENT CO, 95- *Personal Data:* b Bombay, India, Dec 6, 69; m, Niloufar Faridi. *Educ:* Univ Dept Chem Technol, India, BChemE, 91; Pa State Univ, PhD(chem eng), 95. *Concurrent Pos:* Chair, Am Soc Testing & Mat, 95-97, Comt D02-G-07-3 Testing & vchair, D02-G Greases, Nat Lubricating Grease Asn, 97; vchair, Lube Fundamentals, Soc Tribologists & Lubrication Engrs, 97, secy, Grease Comt, 98; res asst prof, Dept Chem, Stevens Inst Technol, 97. *Mem:* Nat Lubricating Grease Asn; Am Soc Testing & Mat; Am Inst Chem Engrs; Am Chem Soc; Soc Tribologists & Lubrication Engrs; Soc Automotive Engrs. *Res:* Specialize in lab scale testing of lubricants, fuels and greases; additive technology development in petroleum products; pilot scale testing and formulation of lubricants and greases; international marketing and business development. *Mailing Add:* 1595 Sycamore Ave Bohemia NY 11716. *Fax:* 516-589-3815; *E-Mail:* rshah@koehlerinstrument.com

SHAH, RAMESH KESHAVLAL, HEAT EXCHANGERS, HEAT TRANSFER. *Current Pos:* CHMN & PROF, DEPT MECH ENG, UNIV KY, 95- *Personal Data:* b Bombay, India, Sept 23, 41; US citizen; m 68, Rekha R Maniar; c Nilay R & Nirav R. *Educ:* Gujarat Univ, India, BE, 63; Stanford Univ, MS, 64, Engr, 70, PhD(mech eng), 72. *Honors & Awards:* Region III Tech Achievement Award, Am Soc Mech Engrs, 79, Valued Serv Award, 87, 91; Outstanding Serv Award, Am Soc Mech Engrs, 86, 50th Anniversay Award, Heat Transfer Div, 88; Charles Russ Richards Mem Award, 89. *Prof Exp:* Proj engr, Air Preheater, 64-66 & Avco Lycoming, 68-69; res engr, Gen Motors Corp, 71-76, tech dir res, 76-83, staff develop engr, 83-89, sr staff res scientist, Harrison Div, 89-95. *Concurrent Pos:* Adj prof, State Univ NY, Buffalo, 78-; tech ed, J Heat Transfer, 81-86; chmn, Heat Transfer Div, Am Soc Mech Engrs, 85-86; chmn, First World Conf Exp Heat Transfer, Fluid Mech & Thermodyn, 87-88; tech prog chmn, Nat Heat Trans Conf, 88-89; ed-in-chief, Int J Exp Thermal & Fluid Sci, 88-; pres, Assembly World Confs Exp Heat Transfer, Fluid Mech & Thermodyn, 88-; tech prog chmn, Nat Heat Transfer Conf, 88-89, co-chmn, 90-91; chmn, First Aerospace Heat Exchange Technol Conf, 93; vpres, Niagara Frontier Asn Res & Develop Dirs, 93-94; co-chmn, First Heat & Mass Transfer Conf, Am Soc Mech Engrs & Indian Soc for Heat & Mass Transfer, 94; invited to lectr & present short courses in 28 countries on five continents. *Mem:* Am Soc Mech Engrs; Soc Automotive Engrs; Am Soc eng Educ; Indian Soc Heat & Mass Transfer. *Res:* Compact and other heat exchangers theory, analysis, design and optimization; internal flow forced convection; brazing of compact heat exchangers; condensation and vaporization in compact heat exchangers. *Mailing Add:* Dept Mech Eng Univ Ky Lexington KY 40506-0108. *E-Mail:* shah@engr.uky.edu

SHAH, RAMESH TRIKAMLAL, MECHANICAL ENGINEERING. *Current Pos:* PROF AERONAUT & MECH ENG, CALIF STATE POLYTECH UNIV, SAN LUIS OBISPO, 68- *Personal Data:* b Padra, India, Sept 13, 34; m 57; c 2. *Educ:* Univ Baroda, BE, 56; Tech Univ Mech Eng, Magdeburg, Ger, DrIng(mech eng), 59. *Prof Exp:* Prof mech eng, Univ Baroda, 56-67 & Ill Inst Technol, 67-68. *Concurrent Pos:* Consult, Jyoti Ltd, Sayaji Iron Works, Metrop Springs & Buganda Steel, Gaskets & Oil Seals, 60-67; consult, Maurey Mfg, Versionall Steel Press & Southern Calif Edison & O'Connar Eng, 67- *Mem:* Am Soc Mech Engrs; Am Soc Heating, Refrig & Air-Conditioning Engrs; Asn Ger Engrs; Indian Inst Engrs. *Res:* Mechanical design; stress analysis. *Mailing Add:* Dept Mech Eng Calif State Polytech Univ San Luis Obispo CA 93407

SHAH, REKHA D, CHROMATOGRAPHIC TECHNIQUES, ENANTIOMERIC SEPARATIONS OF PHARMACEUTICAL DRUGS & RAW MATERIAL. *Current Pos:* sr assoc scientist, 84-92, scientist, 92-97, SR SCIENTIST, R W JOHNSON PHARMACEUT RES INST, 97- *Personal Data:* b India, Apr 10, 46; US citizen; m, Dinubhai H; c Rushi D & Dev D. *Educ:* MS Univ Buredu, India, BSc, 67; Ind State Univ, MS, 71. *Prof Exp:* Anal chemist, FMC Corp, 72-77, Union Carbide, 77-82; scientist, Smith Kline Beecham, 82-84. *Mem:* Am Chem Soc. *Res:* Enantiomeric separations and detection techniques. *Mailing Add:* R W Johnson Pharmaceut Res Inst McKean Rd Rm 409 Spring House PA 19477. *Fax:* 215-628-7067; *E-Mail:* rshah@priusini.com

SHAH, SHANTILAL NATHUBHAI, BIOCHEMISTRY, NEUROCHEMISTRY. *Current Pos:* assoc res biochemist, 73-80, from res biochemist II to res biochemist III, 81-85, res biochemist IV, 85-88, RES BIOCHEMIST V, LANGLEY-PORTER PSYCHIAT INST, UNIV CALIF, SAN FRANCISCO, 88- *Personal Data:* b Dhulia, India, Aug 5, 30; m 56; c 3. *Educ:* Univ Bombay, BS, 51; Univ Nagpur, BSc, 54, MSc, 56; Univ Ill, Urbana, PhD, 60. *Prof Exp:* Res asst, Univ Ill, Urbana, 56-60; Inst Metab Res res fel, Highland Hosp, Oakland, Calif, 60-62; asst res physiologist & Alameda County Heart Asn fel, Univ Calif, Berkeley, 62-65; lectr, Sardar Patel Univ, India, 65-67; res specialist, Sonoma State Hosp, 69-73. *Concurrent Pos:* NIH grants, Sonoma State Hosp, Calif, 68- *Mem:* AAAS; Am Inst Nutrit; Biochem Soc; Int Soc Neurochem; Am Soc Neurochem; Am Soc Biol Chem; Soc Exp Biol. *Res:* Lipid metabolism of the central nervous system and other tissues. *Mailing Add:* 1873 Los Olivos Ave Santa Rosa CA 95404-2015

SHAH, SHEILA, PATHOLOGY, ANATOMIC & CLINICAL. *Current Pos:* ASSOC PATHOLOGIST, HEARTLAND HOSPS, 80- *Personal Data:* b Zanzibar, Tanzania, Mar 14, 45; US citizen; m 73, Upendra Pai; c Sona & Neil. *Educ:* Bombay Univ, MD, 68; Am Bd Pathol, dipl, 75. *Prof Exp:* Intern med, KEM Hosp, Bombay, 68-69; resident, WVa Univ Hosp, 70-74, asst prof & pathologist, 74-78, dir hemat lab path, 78-80, assoc prof path, 79-80; pres, Buchanan Co Med Soc, 93. *Concurrent Pos:* Pathologist, Cancer & Leukemia Group B, 76-; mem, Kans City Soc Pathologists & Mo Soc Path. *Mem:* Int Acad Path; Am Col Path; Am Asn Clin Pathologists; AMA. *Res:* Platelet function abnormalities in myeloproliferative disorders related to morphological abnormalities. *Mailing Add:* Heartland Hosp E 5325 Faraon St Joseph MO 64506

SHAH, SHIRISH, ENVIRONMENTAL SCIENCES, EDUCATION ADMINISTRATION. *Current Pos:* ASSOC PROF CHEM, COL NOTRE DAME, MD, 91-; ADJ PROF PHYS SCI, COPPIN STATE COL, 96- *Personal Data:* b Ahmedabad, India, May 24, 42; US citizen; m 73, Kathleen Long; c Lawrence. *Educ:* Gujarat Univ, BSc, 62; Univ Del, Newark, PhD(phys chem), 68, World Univ, PhD, 86. *Honors & Awards:* Leadership Award, Nat Asn Indust Technol, 90. *Prof Exp:* From asst prof to assoc prof sci, Chesapeake Co, 68-76; coordr acad prog develop, Community Col, Baltimore, 76-78; prog mgr, Md Dept Transp Res Prog, 81-82; prog mgr, MCI/CCB Telecommun Prog, 85-89. *Concurrent Pos:* Dir qual control, Vita Foods Inc, 68-72; adminr Marine & Food Sci Res Projs, Chesapeake Col, 72-76; educ mgr, Baltimore City's Manpower Proj, 80-81; educ consult, Baltimore City's Joint Apprenticeship Comt, 83-91; mem, Baltimore City's Adult Educ Comt, 82-91 & Hazardous Chem Comn, 85-86; Bd Dir, MD Lung Asn, 71-80. *Mem:* Nat Sci Teacher's Asn; Am Chem Soc; Nat Environ Training Asn; Inst Elec & Electronics Engrs; Nat Inst Chemists; Am Tech Educ Asn; Am Pub Health Asn. *Res:* Radiation chemistry of aqueous solutions; food preservation techniques; curriculum development in marine science, food science, electronic communications, traffic engineering, waste water treatment and computers & telecommunications. *Mailing Add:* 5605 Purlington Way Baltimore MD 21212. *Fax:* 410-532-5799; *E-Mail:* sshah@suno.com

SHAH, SHIRISH A, QUALITY AFFAIRS, REGULATORY AFFAIRS. *Current Pos:* MGR RES & DEVELOP, PERRIGO CO, 92- *Personal Data:* b Bombay, India, Apr 26, 38; US citizen; m 66, Portia Dahling; c Sanjay, Kishan & Kinnari. *Educ:* Univ Bombay, India, BPharm, 61; Univ Conn, MS, 64; Univ Iowa, PhD(pharmaceut), 75. *Prof Exp:* Sr scientist res & develop, Revlon Health Care, 63-67 & 75-76; sect head formulations res, Pennwalt Pharmaceut Div, 67-72; asst mgr prod develop, Johnson & Johnson Baby Prod Co, 76-79; dir, Res & Tech Serv, Zenith Labs, 79-85; vpres develop & tech affairs, Lemmon Co, 85-87; dir prod develop, Ciba Consumer Pharmaceut, 88-89; mgr prod develop, DuPont-Merck Pharmaceut Co, 90-92. *Concurrent Pos:* Teaching asst, Col Pharm, Univ Iowa, 72-75. *Mem:* Am Asn Pharmaceut Scientists; Am Pharmaceut Asn; Am Chem Soc; Drug Info Asn; Controlled Release Soc. *Res:* In vitro dissolution kinetics of single and multi-drug systems and its correlation to in vivo bioavailability; preformulation and formulation development of conventional and controlled release pharmaceutical dosage forms. *Mailing Add:* 607 Springwood Dr Kalamazoo MI 49009. *E-Mail:* sshah@perri62.com

SHAH, SURENDRA P, CIVIL ENGINEERING, STRUCTURAL ENGINEERING. *Current Pos:* PROF CIVIL ENG, NORTHWESTERN UNIV, 81-, DIR, CTR CONCRETE & GEOMAT, 89-, WALTER MURPHY PROF, 92-; DIR, SCI & TECHNOL CTR ADVAN CEMENT-BASED MAT, NSF, 89- *Personal Data:* b Bombay, India, Aug 30, 36; US citizen; m 62, Dorothie Crispell; c Daniel & Byron. *Educ:* Col Eng, Bombay, India, BS, BVM, 59; Lehigh Univ, MS, 60; Cornell Univ, PhD(struct eng), 65. *Honors & Awards:* Rilem Gold Medal, 80; Thompson Award, Am Soc Testing & Mat, 83; Vis Sr Scientist Award, NATO, 86; Anderson Award, Am Concrete Inst, 89, Swedish Concrete Award, 93. *Prof Exp:* Design engr, Modjeski & Masters, Pa, 60-62; res asst struct eng, Cornell Univ, 64-65; res assoc, 65-66; asst prof mat eng, Univ Ill, Chicago Circle, 66-73, prof civil eng & mat eng, 73-81. *Concurrent Pos:* Develop engr, Res Labs, Portland Cement Asn, 66; consult, Corning Glass Works, 67, US Gypsum Co, 74-75 & Sci Mus Va, 76-77; vis assoc prof, Mass Inst Technol, 69-70; vis prof, Delft Univ Technol, 76-77; NSF res grants, 78-; consult, Holderbark Mgt, Ltd, Switz; mem tech comt, Hwy Res Bd; mem ad-hoc comt, Nat Acad Sci; consult, Amoco Res; guest prof, Denmark Tech Univ, 84; vis sr NATO scientist, Paris, 86; vis prov, Univ Sidney, 87; Humboldt distinguished vis scientist, Ger, 90-95; ed-in-chief, J Advan Cement-Based Mats, Elseviere. *Mem:* Fel Am Concrete Inst; Am Soc Civil Engrs; Am Ceramic Soc; Soc Exp Mech; Am Soc Testing & Maton. *Res:* Relating macroscopic mechanical behavior of concrete to its microscopic properties; developing fiber-reinforced concrete; micromechanics of composite materials; fracture of brittle solids; application of ferrocement to low cost housing; properties of concrete; nondestructive testing; advanced cement-based materials; materials science and engineering. *Mailing Add:* 921 Isabella St Evanston IL 60201-1773

SHAH, SWARUPCHAND MOHANLAL, mathematical analysis; deceased, see previous edition for last biography

SHAHABUDDIN, SYED, MANAGEMENT INFORMATION SYSTEMS. *Current Pos:* PROF BUS, CENT MICH UNIV, 80- *Personal Data:* b Swat, Pakistan, Mar 2, 39; US citizen; m 67; c 2. *Educ:* Univ Peshawar, Pakistan, BA, 62; Univ Karachi, Pakistan, MBA, 65; Kent State Univ, MBA, 68; Univ Mo, Columbia, PhD(economet), 76. *Prof Exp:* Asst prof bus, Wis State Univ, 68-69, Talladega Col, 69-75 & Univ Notre Dame, 75-80. *Concurrent Pos:* Consult, Off Prod Div, Int Bus Mach, 71-77; prof, Univ Wis-Madison, 76; Fulbright scholar, Univ Karachi, Pakistan, 89-90. *Mem:* Decision Sci Inst; Inst Mgt Sci; Am Statist Asn. *Res:* Forecasting; management information systems; manufacturing. *Mailing Add:* Dept Mgt & Law Cent Mich Univ Smith Hall 200 Mt Pleasant MI 48859. *Fax:* 517-774-2372

SHAHANI, KHEM MOTUMAL, FOOD TECHNOLOGY, BIOCHEMISTRY. *Current Pos:* assoc prof, 57-61, PROF DAIRY & FOOD TECHNOL, UNIV NEBR, LINCOLN, 61- *Personal Data:* b Hyderabad Sind, India, Sept 3, 23; nat US; m 54; c 4. *Educ:* Univ Bombay, BSc, 43; Univ Wis, PhD(dairy technol, biochem), 50. *Honors & Awards:* Borden Award, 64; Gamma Sigma Delta Int Award Distinguished Serv to Agr, 66; Sigma Xi Outstanding Scientist Award, 77; Pfizer Award, 77; Nordica Int Award, 77; Dairy Res Found Award, 83. *Prof Exp:* Instr agr, King George V Agr Col, India, 43-45; fel dairy technol, Univ Ill, 50-51; bus consult chem, Int Bus

Consults, India, 52-53; res assoc dairy technol, Ohio State Univ, 53-57. *Concurrent Pos:* Inst Food Technologists sci lectr; mem adv comt food hyg, WHO. *Res:* Bioprocessing; food enzymes and their immobilzation and application; products; antibiotics in milk; mode of action of antibiotics and milk and microbial lipase; lysozymes; other enzymes; cultured dairy foods; lactase and proteases immobilization and their uses; infant foods, whey utilization and continuous alcohol fermentation by immobilized yeast. *Mailing Add:* 05943127xxxrn St Lincoln NE 68506

SHAHBENDER, R(ABAH) A(BD-EL-RAHMAN), ELECTRICAL ENGINEERING. *Current Pos:* CONSULT, 87- *Personal Data:* b Damascus, Syria, July 23, 24; m 54; c 3. *Educ:* Cairo Univ, BEE, 46; Wash Univ, St Louis, MSEE, 49; Univ Ill, PhD(elec eng), 51. *Honors & Awards:* Indust Res-100 Award, 64 & 69; Mat Design Eng Award, 63; RCA Labs Outstanding Achievement Award, 60, 63, 73 & 82. *Prof Exp:* Engr, Anglo-Egyptian Oilfields, Ltd, Egypt, 46-48; sr res engr, Honeywell Controls Div, Pa, 51-55; develop engr, Radio Corp Am, 55-58, sr staff mem, Res Labs, 58-61, head digital device res, 61-72, head appl electronics res, 72-75, tech staff, RCA Labs, 75-87. *Concurrent Pos:* Univ Ill fel, 50 & 51; chmn dept electronics physics, Evening Div, La Salle Col, 60-67. *Mem:* AAAS; fel Inst Elec & Electronics Engrs; Sigma Xi. *Res:* Behavior of nonlinear automatic control systems and adaptive systems; nondestructive testing by means of ultrasonics; digital computer memory systems; digital video systems; kinescope displays; satellite communication systems. *Mailing Add:* RCA Corp David Sarnoff Res Ctr Princeton NJ 08540

SHAHEEN, DONALD G, ANALYTICAL CHEMISTRY. *Current Pos:* VPRES & TECH DIR, DEGESCH AM INC, 76- *Personal Data:* b Trenton, NJ, Sept 5, 30; m 55; c 3. *Educ:* Rider Univ, BS, 53; NY Univ, MS, 58. *Prof Exp:* Chemist, Callery Chem Co, 55-59; sr chemist, Reaction Motors Div, Thiokol Chem Corp, 59-63; mgr, Chem Dept, Life Systs Div, Hazleton Labs, Inc, Va, 63-69; res mgr, Biospherics, Inc, 69-76. *Mem:* Am Chem Soc; Am Microchem Soc; Am Soc Testing & Mat. *Res:* Organic microanalyses; analytical method development; instrumental trace and functional group analyses; thermal stability; decomposition studies; phase diagram studies. *Mailing Add:* Degesch Am Inc Weyers Cave VA 24486

SHAHIDI, FEREIDOON, MEAT, OILSEEDS. *Current Pos:* assoc prof, 87-92, PROF FOOD CHEM, MEM UNIV NFLD, 92- *Personal Data:* b Tehran, Iran, Apr 13, 51; Iranian & Can citizen; m 74; c 3. *Educ:* Shiraz Univ, BSc, 73; McGill Univ, PhD(chem), 77. *Prof Exp:* Res fel org chem, McGill Univ, 77-78; res fel org & gen chem, Univ Toronto, 77-81, res assoc & lectr food eng, 81-84, adj prof food eng, 84-87. *Concurrent Pos:* Ed, J Food Lipids. *Mem:* Am Chem Soc; Royal Chem Soc; Inst Food Technologists; fel Can Inst Food Sci & Technol; Am Meat Sci Asn; Am Oil Chemists Soc; Chem Inst Can. *Res:* New food processing systems and their chemical characteristics; solute-solvent interaction; flavor chemistry; food chemistry; meat and seafood research; seafoods aquaculture; processing by-products; oilseeds and pulses. *Mailing Add:* Dept Biochem Mem Univ Nfld St John's NF A1B 3X9 Can. *Fax:* 709-737-4000

SHAHIDI, FREYDOON, AUTOMORPHIC FORMS. *Current Pos:* from asst prof to assoc prof, 77-82, PROF MATH, PURDUE UNIV, WEST LAFAYETTE, 86- *Personal Data:* b Tehran, Iran, June 19, 47; m 77, Guity Ravai; c Alireza & Amir. *Educ:* Tehran Univ, BS, 69; Johns Hopkins Univ, PhD(math), 75. *Prof Exp:* Vis mem math, Inst Advan Study, 75-76; vis asst prof math, Ind Univ, Bloomington, 76-77. *Concurrent Pos:* Prin investr, NSF, 77-; vis prof, Univ Toronto, Can, 81-82; vis mem math, Inst Advan Study, 83-84, 90-91; vis prof, Univ Paris 7, 90, Katholishe Univ Eichstatt, Ger, 93, Ecole Normale Superieure, 95; Japan Soc Prom Sci fel, Kyoto Univ, 93, 97. *Mem:* Am Math Soc. *Res:* Theory of automorphic forms, L-functions and group representations. *Mailing Add:* Dept Math Purdue Univ West Lafayette IN 47907. *Fax:* 765-494-0548; *E-Mail:* shahidi@math.purdue.edu

SHAHIDI, NASROLLAH THOMAS, HEMATOLOGY. *Current Pos:* assoc prof, 66-70, PROF PEDIAT, CTR HEALTH SCI, UNIV WIS-MADISON, 70- *Personal Data:* b Meshed, Iran, Dec 11, 26; US citizen; c 3. *Educ:* Univ Montpellier, dipl, 47; Sorbonne, MD, 54. *Prof Exp:* Resident pediat, Hosp for Sick Children, Paris, France, 54-56; asst resident, Baltimore City Hosp, Md, 56-57; instr, Harvard Med Sch, 60-63; asst prof, Children's Hosp, Zurich, Switz, 64-66; dir pediat hemat, Children's Hosp, 70-77. *Concurrent Pos:* Res fel, Harvard Med Sch, 57-60; asst physician, Children's Hosp Med Ctr, Boston, 60-63; vis investr, Swiss Nat Found, 64-66; hematologist, Children's Hosp, Wis, 66. *Mem:* Am Pediat Soc; Am Soc Hemat; Am Soc Pediat Res; affil Royal Soc Med. *Res:* Red cell 2, 3-diphosphoglycerate and oxygen transport; androgens and erythropoiesis; acquired and congenital thrombocytopenic purpura; red cell metabolism, glucose-6-phosphate dehydrogenase deficiency and drug-induced hemolytic anemias. *Mailing Add:* 600 Highland Ave Madison WI 53792-0001

SHAHIN, JAMAL KHALIL, MATHEMATICS. *Current Pos:* assoc prof, 66-68, PROF MATH & CHMN DEPT, SALEM STATE COL, 68- *Personal Data:* b Bethlehem, Jordan, Mar 5, 31; US citizen; m 58; c 3. *Educ:* Univ Calif, Berkeley, BA, 60; Lehigh Univ, MS, 62, PhD(math), 65. *Prof Exp:* Asst math, Lehigh Univ, 60-62, from instr to asst prof, 62-66. *Mem:* Am Math Soc; Math Asn Am. *Res:* Differential geometry in affine space; Euclidean and Riemannian geometry. *Mailing Add:* 59 Box Ford Rd Ipswich MA 01938

SHAHIN, M Y, ENGINEERING. *Honors & Awards:* Fed Engr Yr Award, Nat Soc Prof Engrs, 91. *Mailing Add:* 1207 Wilshire Ct Champaign IL 61821-6916

SHAHIN, MICHAEL M, PHYSICAL CHEMISTRY. *Current Pos:* sr scientist, Res Div, Xerox Corp, 63-68, lab mgr xerographic sci, 68-72 & imaging res, 72-73, mgr phys chem, 73-78, mgr tech planning & corp res, 78-85, mgr mat res, 85-89, MGR TECH ASSESSMENT, XEROX CORP, 89- *Personal Data:* b Isfahan, Iran, Sept 7, 32; m 58; c 2. *Educ:* Univ Birmingham, BSc, 55, PhD(phys chem), 58. *Prof Exp:* res fel phys chem, Nat Res Coun Can, 58-60; res chemist, E I du Pont de Nemours & Co, 60-61; res assoc, Sch Med, Yale Univ, 61-63. *Mem:* Am Chem Soc; Am Phys Soc; Royal Chem Soc (London). *Res:* Photochemistry; gas-phase kinetics; chemical reactions in electrical discharges; radiation chemistry; gas chromatography; mass spectrometry; ion-molecule reactions; ionization phenomena; research management. *Mailing Add:* 12 Widewaters Lane Pittsford NY 14534-1024

SHAHINIAN, PAUL, HIGH TEMPERATURE MECHANICAL BEHAVIOR OF METALS, APPLICATION OF FRACTURE MECHANICS TO CRACK GROWTH AT HIGH TEMPERATURE. *Current Pos:* CONSULT & PRES, PAUDEAN ASSOCS, 83- *Personal Data:* b Richmond, Va, June 17, 21; m 51, Grace Jelalian; c Dean V. *Educ:* Va Polytech Inst, BS, 43; Mass Inst Technol, SM, 47; Univ Md, PhD(metall), 59. *Honors & Awards:* Nat Res Lab Appl Sci Award, 80. *Prof Exp:* Metallurgist, Curtiss-Wright Corp, 43-45; asst prof physics, Richmond Prof Inst, 47-48; res metallurgist, US Naval Res Lab, 48-59, sect head, 59-66, supvry res physicist, 66-72, assoc supt, Eng Mat Div, 72-74, consult, 74-77, sect head thermostruct mat, 77-83. *Concurrent Pos:* Consult, Geo-Centers, Inc, 88-89. *Mem:* Am Soc Metals. *Res:* Effects of metallurgical and environmental factors on high-temperature creep and fatigue of metals; neutron radiation effects on crack growth in reactor steels; applicability of fracture mechanics at high temperature. *Mailing Add:* 8909 Captain's Row Alexandria VA 22308

SHAHN, EZRA, MOLECULAR BIOLOGY, BIOPHYSICS. *Current Pos:* asst prof biol, 66-70, ASSOC PROF BIOL, HUNTER COL, 71- *Personal Data:* b New York, NY, Nov 12, 33; m 85; c 1. *Educ:* Bard Col, AB, 55; Univ Pa, PhD(molecular biol), 65. *Prof Exp:* Biophysicist, Off Math Res, Nat Inst Arthritis & Metab Dis, 58-60; fel bacteriophage, Wistar Inst, 65-66. *Concurrent Pos:* NSF res grant, 67-69, cause grant, 77-80. *Res:* Mathematical models of biological systems; mechanisms of genetic recombination of bacteriophage; effects of ultraviolet light on bacteriophage; thermodynamics of membrane function; science education. *Mailing Add:* Dept Biol Sci City Univ NY Hunter Col 695 Park Ave New York NY 10021-5024

SHAHRIK, H ARTO, CYTOLOGY, ORAL BIOLOGY. *Current Pos:* ASST CLIN PROF, DEPT GEN DENT & ORAL DIAG, SCH DENT MED, TUFTS UNIV, 78- *Personal Data:* b Istanbul, Turkey, June 22, 23; US citizen; m 62, Nina Oganian; c Anahid L & Lilian K. *Educ:* Univ Istanbul, Lic es sc, 47, BDS, 50; Tufts Univ, DMD, 59. *Prof Exp:* Intern pediat dent & res, Forsyth Dent Ctr, Boston, Mass, 55-56, clin fel oral biol, 56-57; sr res fel histochem & cytochem & asst mem, Inst Stomatol Res, 59-63; assoc res specialist, Sci Resources Found, 63-64; assoc res clinician & assoc mem oral biol, 64-67; res specialist, head histochem & cytochem & mem oral biol, 67-76. *Mem:* AAAS; Am Dent Asn; Am Asn Dent Res. *Res:* Tissues of the oral cavity in health and disease, oxidative enzymes; keratinization; salivary fluids and cells; tobacco smoke toxicity on human oral and bronchial cells. *Mailing Add:* 193 Marrett Rd Lexington MA 02173

SHAHROKHI, FIROUZ, AEROSPACE ENGINEERING. *Current Pos:* from asst prof to assoc prof, 66-76, PROF AEROSPACE ENG & DIR SPACE INST, UNIV TENN, 76- *Personal Data:* b Tehran, Iran, July 29, 38; US citizen; c 2. *Educ:* Univ Okla, BSME, 61, PhD(mech eng), 66. *Prof Exp:* Design engr, Boeing Co, Wash, 61-62; res engr, Res Inst, Okla Univ, 62-65; asst prof, La State Univ, New Orleans, 65-66. *Mem:* Am Inst Aeronaut & Astronaut; Am Soc Mech Engrs. *Res:* Sensor technology radiating heat transfer; remote sensing for earth resources; radiative heat transfer in boundary layer flow. *Mailing Add:* Space Inst Univ Tenn B H Goethert Pkwy Tullahoma TN 37388-8897

SHAIKH, A(BDUL) FATTAH, STRUCTURAL ENGINEERING. *Current Pos:* from asst prof to assoc prof, 67-81, PROF STRUCT ENG, UNIV WIS-MILWAUKEE, 81- *Personal Data:* b Sukkur, WPakistan, Aug 13, 37; m 67; c 3. *Educ:* Univ Karachi, BE, 60; Univ Hawaii, MS, 64; Univ Iowa, PhD(struct eng), 67. *Honors & Awards:* Martin P Korn Award, Prestressed Concrete Inst, 71. *Prof Exp:* Asst engr, Water & Power Develop Auth, WPakistan, 60-62; instr struct eng, Univ Iowa, 66-67. *Mem:* Am Concrete Inst; Prestressed Concrete Inst; Am Soc Civil Engrs. *Res:* Deflections of concrete structures; connections in precast-prestressed concrete; behavior of concrete structures. *Mailing Add:* Dept Civil Eng Univ Wis Milwaukee WI 53201. *Fax:* 414-229-6958

SHAIKH, ZAHIR AHMAD, METAL TOXICOLOGY. *Current Pos:* assoc prof, Univ RI, 82-86, prof pharmcol & toxicol, 86-96, chmn dept, 85-96, PROF & CHMN, DEPT BIOMED SCI, UNIV RI, 96- *Personal Data:* b Jullundur, Punjab, India, Mar 31, 45; m 75, Mary Butterfield; c Faraz, Kashan & Summur. *Educ:* Univ Karachi, BSc, 65, MSc, 67; Dalhousie Univ, PhD(biochem), 72. *Prof Exp:* Res assoc environ health, Univ Okla, 72-73; sr fel pharmacol & toxicol, Univ Rochester, 73-75, from asst prof to assoc prof toxicol, 75-82. *Concurrent Pos:* Prin investr, NIH res grants, 75-, mem toxicol study sect, 85-89. *Mem:* Soc Toxicol; Am Soc Pharmacol & Exp Therapeut; Fel Pakistan Acad Med Sci. *Res:* Heavy metal metabolism and toxicity; metallothionein and its role in modulating the effects of metals on liver, kidney and testis; urinary metallothionein as a biological indicator of metal exposure; cellular transport mechanisms for metal ions. *Mailing Add:* Dept Biomed Sci Col Pharm Univ RI Kingston RI 02881-0809. *Fax:* 401-792-2181

SHAIN, ALBERT LEOPOLD, PHYSICAL CHEMISTRY, POLYMER CHEMISTRY. *Current Pos:* RETIRED. *Personal Data:* b Brussels, Belg, Dec 7, 42; US citizen; m 66; c 2. *Educ:* Univ Calif, Los Angeles, BS, 65; Wash Univ, PhD(phys chem), 69. *Prof Exp:* Fel, Inst Phys Chem, Univ Amsterdam, 69-70 & Univ Calif, Los Angeles, 70-71; res assoc chem physics, Univ Del, 71-73; mem staff elaschem, Exp Sta, E I du Pont de Nemours & Co Inc, 73-80, mem staff, Polymer Prod Dept, 80-90. *Concurrent Pos:* Hon fel, Univ Siena, Italy. *Mem:* Am Chem Soc; Soc Plastics Engrs. *Res:* Magnetic resonance and optical spectroscopy of molecular excited states; polymer chemistry and physics, polymer flammability. *Mailing Add:* 1811 Bryce Dr Wilmington DE 19810

SHAIN, IRVING, ELECTROANALYTICAL CHEMISTRY. *Current Pos:* PROF CHEM & CHANCELLOR, UNIV WIS-MADISON, 77- *Personal Data:* b Seattle, Wash, Jan 2, 26; m 47; c 4. *Educ:* Univ Wash, BS, 49, PhD(chem), 52. *Prof Exp:* From instr to prof chem, Univ Wis-Madison, 52-75, chmn dept, 67-70, vchancellor, 70-75; prof chem, provost & vpres acad affairs, Univ Wash, 75-77. *Concurrent Pos:* Dir, Olin Corp. *Mem:* Am Chem Soc; Int Soc Electrochem; Electrochem Soc; fel AAAS. *Res:* Instrumental analysis; polarography; kinetics of electrode reactions. *Mailing Add:* 2820 Marshall Ct No 8 Madison WI 53705-2270

SHAIN, SYDNEY A, CELL BIOLOGY, MOLECULAR BIOLOGY. *Current Pos:* PROF, DEPT OBSTET & GYNEC, UNIV TEX HEALTH SCI CTR, 89-, PROF, DEPT PHYSIOL & CELLULAR & STRUCT BIOL, 89- *Personal Data:* b Chicago, Ill, Aug 31, 40; m 67, Rochelle N; c 2. *Educ:* Univ Ill, BS, 62; Univ Calif, Berkeley, PhD(biochem), 68. *Prof Exp:* Res assoc, Sch Med, Univ Pa, 70-71; from asst to assoc found scientist, Southwest Found Biomed Res, 71-76, found scientist & chmn, Dept Cellular & Molecular Biol, 77-89. *Concurrent Pos:* Pop Coun fel, Weizmann Inst Sci, Rehovoth, Israel, 68-70; res assoc, Audie L Murphy Mem Vet Hosp, 76-; adj assoc prof, Dept Physiol, Health Sci Ctr, Univ Tex, 78-81, adj prof, 81-; mem, Reproductive Endocrinol Study Sect, Asn Health Rec, 86-90. *Mem:* Endocrine Soc; Am Asn Cancer Res; Am Soc Biochem & Molecular Biol; NY Acad Sci; Am Soc Cell Biol. *Res:* Steroid and mitogen modulation of prostate cell function. *Mailing Add:* Univ Tex Health Sci Ctr 7703 Floyd Curl Dr San Antonio TX 78284-7836. *Fax:* 210-567-3013; *E-Mail:* shains@uthscsa.edu

SHAIN, WILLIAM ARTHUR, FORESTRY. *Current Pos:* asst prof forest mensuration, 61-70, assoc prof, 70-79, PROF DEPT FORESTRY, CLEMSON UNIV, 79- *Personal Data:* b Louisville, Ky, Feb 16, 31; div; c 4. *Educ:* Univ Ga, BSF, 53, MF, 56; Mich State Univ, PhD(forestry), 63. *Prof Exp:* Forester, Int Paper Col, 53; instr forestry, Miss State Univ, 56-59. *Mem:* Soc Am Foresters; Am Soc Photogram. *Res:* Forest sampling techniques; aerial photogrammetry. *Mailing Add:* Dept Forestry Clemson Univ Clemson SC 29634-1003

SHAININ, DORIAN, AERONAUTICAL ENGINEERING, QUALITY CONTROL. *Current Pos:* RETIRED. *Personal Data:* b San Francisco, Calif, Sept 26, 14; m 40, Margaret Leach; c 7. *Educ:* Mass Inst Technol, SB, 36. *Honors & Awards:* Brumbaugh Award, Am Soc Qual Control, 51, Edwards Medal, 69, E L Grant Award, 81, Shewhart Medal, 89. *Prof Exp:* Engr, Hamilton Stand Div, United Aircraft Corp, 36-43, chief inspector, 43-52; chief engr, Rath & Strong, Inc, 52-57, vpres & dir statist eng, 57-76; pres, Dorian Shainin Consults, Inc, 75-80; pres, Shainin consult, 80-95. *Concurrent Pos:* Lectr, Univ Conn, 50-83, fac assoc, Sch Bus Admin, 64-; lectr, Am Mgt Asn, 51-78; consult med staff, Newington Children's Hosp, 57-94; lectr, Assoc Bus Progs, London, Eng, 67-70 & Kwaliteitsdienst voor de Industrie, Rotterdam, Neth, 71-76. *Mem:* Fel AAAS; fel Am Soc Qual Control (exec secy, 53-54, vpres, 54-57); Am Statist Asn; Int Acad Qual. *Res:* Plant operating cost reduction; statistical quality control; reliability engineering; accelerated life testing; statistically designed experiments in research and development; creative and analytical methods of problem solving; product liability prevention; management and productivity improvement. *Mailing Add:* 35 Lakewood Circle S Manchester CT 06040-7018

SHAINOFF, JOHN RIEDEN, BIOCHEMISTRY. *Current Pos:* res assoc, Cleveland Clin Found, 57-59, mem asst staff, 60-63, mem staff, 63-75, actg dir atherosclerosis thrombosis res, 75-76, assoc dir, 76-78, DIR, THROMBOSIS RES SECT, RES DIV, CLEVELAND CLIN FOUND, 80- *Personal Data:* b Pittsburgh, Pa, Oct 9, 30; m 59, Joan D Goodyear; c Todd, Chris, Peter & Jon. *Educ:* Univ Pittsburgh, BS, 51, MS, 54, PhD(biophys), 56. *Honors & Awards:* Outstanding Res Award, Int Fibrinogen Res Soc, 96. *Prof Exp:* Asst biophys, Univ Pittsburgh, 51-56; fel chem, Yale Univ, 56-57. *Mem:* Am Soc Biol Chem; Biophys Soc; Am Heart Asn; Int Soc Thrombosis & Haemostasis; Am Asn Invest Path; Int Fibrinogen Res Soc (secy). *Res:* Protein chemistry; blood coagulation; arteriosclerosis; thrombosis; fibrin complexes; profibrin. *Mailing Add:* Res Inst Cleveland Clin Found Cleveland OH 44195-5286. *Fax:* 216-444-7927

SHAIR, FREDRICK H, CHEMICAL ENGINEERING. *Current Pos:* from asst prof to assoc prof, 65-77, PROF CHEM ENG, CALIF INST TECHNOL, 77- *Personal Data:* b Denver, Colo, May 25, 36; m 64; c 3. *Educ:* Univ Ill, Urbana, BS, 57; Univ Calif, Berkeley, PhD(chem eng), 63. *Prof Exp:* Res engr, Space Sci Lab, Gen Elec Co, 61-65. *Mem:* Am Inst Chem Engrs; Am Phys Soc; Am Chem Soc; Sigma Xi. *Res:* Plasma chemistry; monequilibrium electrical discharges relating to chemical synthesis and separations; kinetics and transport associated with ecological systems; dispersion of pollutants; indoor air quality. *Mailing Add:* 2330 Glen Canyon Rd Altadena CA 91001-3540

SHAIR, ROBERT C, CHEMICAL & ENVIRONMENTAL ENGINEERING, PHYSICAL CHEMISTRY. *Current Pos:* RETIRED. *Personal Data:* b New York, NY, Aug 2, 25; m 49, Cecelia Nadel; c 2. *Educ:* City Col New York, BChE, 47; Polytech Inst Brooklyn, MChE, 49, PhD(chem eng), 54. *Prof Exp:* Vpres res & develop, Gulton Industs, Inc, 59-71; mgr energy prod, Motorola, Inc, Ft Lauderdale, Fla, 71-79; mgr eng, Centec Corp, 79-83; water resources develop mgr & wellfield protection officer, Water Resources Mgt Div, Broward Co, Fla, 83-93. *Concurrent Pos:* Mem, Dept Natural Resource Protection Adv Bd, Broward Co, Fla; adj prof, Broward Community Col. *Mem:* Am Soc Civil Engrs; Am Soc Chem Engrs. *Res:* Batteries; energy conversion; electrochemistry; power sources; energy engineering; environmental engineering; surface and groundwater management; water resources management. *Mailing Add:* 4921 Sarazen Dr Hollywood FL 33021

SHAKA, ATHAN JAMES, DOUBLE RESONANCE, PULSE SEQUENCE DEVELOPMENT. *Current Pos:* ASST PROF PHYS CHEM, UNIV CALIF, IRVINE, 88- *Personal Data:* b Newton, Mass, Apr 9, 58. *Educ:* Harvey Mudd Col, BS, 80; Oxford Univ, PhD(phys chem), 84. *Prof Exp:* Jr res fel chem, St Johns Col, Oxford, 84-85; Miller res fel phys chem, Univ Calif, Berkeley, 86-88. *Concurrent Pos:* Dreyfus Found new fac award, 88; NSF presidential young investr, 89. *Mem:* Am Chem Soc; Am Phys Soc. *Res:* New techniques in nuclear magnetic resonance; multiple-pulse nuclear magnetic resonance; two dimensional and three dimensional nuclear magnetic resonance; spatial localization of nuclear magnetic resonance signals; nuclear magnetic resonance in solids; spectrometer hardware and software. *Mailing Add:* Chem Dept Univ Calif Irvine CA 92717-2025

SHAKARJIAN, MICHAEL PETER, IMMUNOPHARMACOLOGY, MAST CELL & LEUKOCYTE BIOLOGY. *Current Pos:* SR RES SCIENTIST ASTHMA/ALLERGY, ARIAD PHARMACEUT, INC, CAMBRIDGE, MASS, 93- *Personal Data:* b Niagara Falls, NY, Nov 30, 55. *Educ:* State Univ NY, Buffalo, BS, 77, MA, 80; Va Commonwealth Univ, PhD(pharmacol), 89. *Prof Exp:* Res tech, Div Clin Pharmacol, Univ NC, Chapel Hill, 82-84; vis scientist, Hosp Nuestra Senora del Mar, Inst Munic d'Investigatio Medica, 84; Nat Res Coun fel, Walter Reed Army Inst Res, 89-91; fel, Bristol-Myers Squibb Pharmaceut Res Inst, 91-93. *Mem:* Fel Am Soc Pharmacol & Exp Therapeut; AAAS. *Res:* Investigation of the pathways involved in the activation of hematopoietic cells; investigation of activation pathways in mast cells/leukocytes; posttranslational modification of signalling proteins. *Mailing Add:* 16 Eliot Crescent Winthrop MA 02152. *Fax:* 617-494-8144; *E-Mail:* shakarji@ariad.com

SHAKE, ROY EUGENE, PLANT ECOLOGY. *Current Pos:* asst prof, 65-67, ASSOC PROF BIOL, ABILENE CHRISTIAN UNIV, 67- *Personal Data:* b Claremont, Ill, July 3, 32; m 57, Bonnie Sargent; c Roger, Gary, Dan, Tim, Linda & Misti. *Educ:* Eastern Ill Univ, BS, 54; Univ Wis-Madison, MS, 56. *Prof Exp:* From instr to asst prof biol, Abilene Christian Col, 58-62; asst, Univ Fla, 62-64; prof, Polk Co Jr Col, 64-65. *Res:* Collecting and identifying reptiles and fish in West Central Texas; actinomycete activity in lake water; succession in lentic environments; arid/semi-arid plants. *Mailing Add:* Dept Biol Abilene Christian Univ Box 27868 Abilene TX 79699

SHAKESHAFT, ROBIN, PHYSICS. *Current Pos:* assoc prof, 81-84, PROF PHYSICS & CHAIR, UNIV SOUTHERN CALIF, 84- *Personal Data:* b Leamington Spa, Eng, June 3, 47. *Educ:* Univ London, BSc, 68; Univ Nebr, PhD(physics), 72. *Prof Exp:* Res assoc, NY Univ, 72-75; from asst prof to assoc prof physics, Tex A&M Univ, 75-81. *Concurrent Pos:* Prin investr, NSF, 77-; vis asst prof physics, NY Univ, 78-79, vis assoc prof, 80-81. *Mem:* Am Phys Soc. *Res:* Theoretical atomic physics, in particular, scattering theory, interactions of atoms with intense fields. *Mailing Add:* Dept Physics Univ Southern Calif University Park Los Angeles CA 90089

SHAKHASHIRI, BASSAM ZEKIN, CHEMISTRY. *Current Pos:* ASST DIR, NSF, 84- *Personal Data:* b Enfeh, Lebanon, Oct 9, 39, US citizen. *Educ:* Boston Univ, AB, 60; Univ Md, College Park, MSc, 65, PhD(chem), 68. *Prof Exp:* Res assoc, Univ Ill, Urbana, 67-68, vis asst prof chem, 68-70; asst prof, 70-76, assoc prof, 76-80, PROF CHEM, UNIV WIS-MADISON, 80- *Concurrent Pos:* Danforth Assoc, 80-; consult, Exxon Educ Found, Chicago Mus Sci & Indust, 81; chmn, Chem Educ Div, Am Chem Soc, 81. *Mem:* AAAS; Am Chem Soc; Royal Soc Chem; Nat Sci Teachers Asn. *Res:* Inorganic reaction mechanisms; innovations in undergraduate and graduate education in chemistry; lecture demonstrations. *Mailing Add:* Dept Chem Univ Wis 1101 Univ Ave Madison WI 53706-1322

SHAKIN, CARL M, NUCLEAR PHYSICS. *Current Pos:* prof, 73-86, DISTINGUISHED PROF PHYSICS, BROOKLYN COL, 86- *Personal Data:* b New York, NY, Feb 17, 34; m 55; c 2. *Educ:* NY Univ, BS, 55; Harvard Univ, PhD(theoret physics), 61. *Prof Exp:* Instr physics, Mass Inst Technol, 60-63, NSF fel, 63-65, from asst prof to assoc prof, 65-70; assoc prof, Case Western Reserve Univ, 70-73. *Mem:* Fel Am Phys Soc. *Res:* Nuclear theory; nuclear structure; nuclear reactions; intermediate energy physics. *Mailing Add:* Dept Physics CUNY Brooklyn Col Bedford Ave & Ave H Brooklyn NY 11210. *Fax:* 718-469-6503; *E-Mail:* casbc@cunyvm

SHAKLEE, JAMES BROOKER, FISH BIOLOGY, BIOCHEMICAL GENETICS. *Current Pos:* BIOLOGIST, WASH DEPT FISH & WILDLIFE, 85- *Personal Data:* b Salina, Kans, Mar 29, 45; m 65; c 2. *Educ:* Colo State Univ, BS, 68, MS, 74; Yale Univ, MPhil, 70, PhD(biol), 72. *Prof Exp:* Res assoc develop genetics, Univ Ill, 72-73 & 74-75; asst prof zool, Univ Hawaii & asst marine biologist, Hawaii Inst Marine Biol, 75-81; sr res scientist, Div

Fisheries Res, Commonwealth Sci & Indust Res Orgn, 81-85. *Concurrent Pos:* NIH fel, Univ Ill, 74-75. *Mem:* Soc Study Evolution; Am Soc Ichthyologists & Herpetologists; Am Soc Zoologists; Sigma Xi; Am Fisheries Soc. *Res:* Study of the population and evolutionary genetics of fishes primarily by analyzing their isozymes and other proteins. *Mailing Add:* 4522 46th Ct NE Olympia WA 98516

SHAKUN, WALLACE, FINANCIAL MANAGEMENT, THERMOECONOMICS. *Current Pos:* SR RES ENGR, ENERGY MAT SCI LAB, ENG EXP STA, GA INST TECHNOL, 80-; DEAN TECHNOL ENG, CLAYTON STATE COL, 88- *Personal Data:* b New York, NY, July, 21, 34; m 58; c 3. *Educ:* City Univ New York, BME, 58; Univ Vt, MS, 65; Univ Glasgow, PhD(math), 69; Univ Louisville, MBA, 76. *Prof Exp:* Advan design engr prod develop, Gen Elec Co, 60-66; sr res engr, Energy Mat Sci Lab, Eng Exp Sta, Ga Inst Technol, 80-87; vpres engr com prod, Modernfold, 78-80. *Concurrent Pos:* Vis asst prof, Univ Vt, 60-65; vis asst prof, Univ Louisville, 72-78; pres, W W Shakun Consults, 80- *Mem:* Assoc fel Royal Aeronaut Soc. *Res:* Program development based on strategic planning requiring a multidisciplinary approach in order to ascertain the impact of new technologies on hardware development. *Mailing Add:* 420 Jefferson Circle NE Atlanta GA 30328

SHAKUR, ASIF MOHAMMED, STABLE ISOTOPE-RATIO MASS SPECTROMETRY, MICROPROCESSOR INTERFACING. *Current Pos:* PROF PHYSICS-MICROELECTRONICS, SALISBURY STATE UNIV, 85- *Personal Data:* b Karachi, Pakistan, Apr 14, 51; Can citizen. *Educ:* Univ Calgary, MS, 79, PhD(stable isotopes), 82. *Prof Exp:* Assoc prof physics, Univ Karachi, 75-77; sr res officer, Alta Res Coun, 82-85. *Concurrent Pos:* Adj prof physics, Univ Calgary, 82-85. *Mem:* Am Asn Physics Teachers; Inst Elec & Electronics Engrs. *Res:* Stable isotope mass spectrometry; hydrogeology; geomicrobiology; geochronology; semiconductor devices-microelectronics. *Mailing Add:* Dept Physics Salisbury State Univ 1101 Camden Ave Salisbury MD 21801

SHALABY, SHALABY W, BIOMATERIALS, POLYMER SCIENCE. *Current Pos:* CORP RES SCIENTIST & PROF BIOENG DEPT & MAT SCI & ENG PROG, US SURG CORP. *Personal Data:* b Dayrut, Egypt, Jan 3, 38; m 65, Joanne E; c Waleed, Tarek, David & Marc. *Educ:* Ain Shams Univ, Egypt, BSc, 58; Univ Lowell, MS, 63, PhD(chem), 66, PhD(polymer sci), 67. *Honors & Awards:* P B Hoffmann Award, 79. *Prof Exp:* Asst forensic chem, Medico-Legal Dept, Egypt, 59-60; instr polymer sci, Univ Lowell, 65-67; instr math, Belvidere Sch, Mass, 66-67; lectr polymer sci, Col Appl Sci, Egypt, 67-68; sr res chemist, Allied Chem Corp, NJ, 69-74; prin scientist, Ethicon, Inc, 74-78, mgr, Polymer Res Sect, 78-83, mgr, Polymer Technol Dept, 83-86; add-mgr, Polymer Chem Ctr, Johnson & Johnson, 84-90, mgr, Polymer Technol Ctr, 90; prof bioeng, Clemson Univ, 90-94. *Concurrent Pos:* Researcher, Nat Res Ctr, Cairo, 67-68; NASA res assoc, Old Dom Univ, Va, 68-69. *Mem:* Sigma Xi; Am Chem Soc; NY Acad Sci; Am Phys Soc; Soc Plastics Engrs; Soc Biomat; Royal Soc Chem; Fiber Soc; Am Asn Pharm Scientists. *Res:* Synthesis and modification of macromolecules; study of structure-properties relationships and assessment of pertinent physical and structural parameters; structural and engineering designs and development of new polymeric materials for biomedical and pharmaceutical applications; organometallic chemistry; thermal analysis; controlled drug delivery. *Mailing Add:* 6309 Hwy 187 Anderson SC 29625

SHALALA, DONNA E, PUBLIC HEALTH. *Current Pos:* US SECY, DEPT HEALTH & HUMAN SERV, 93- *Personal Data:* b Cleveland, Ohio, Feb 14, 41. *Educ:* Western Col Women, BA, 62; Syracuse Univ, PhD, 70. *Prof Exp:* Pres, Hunter Col City Univ NY, 80-88; chancellor, Univ Wis-Madison, 88-93. *Mailing Add:* US Dept Health & Human Serv 200 Independance Ave SW Washington DC 20201

SHALAWAY, SCOTT D, NONGAME WILDLIFE, HABITAT MANAGEMENT. *Current Pos:* vis asst prof biol, Dept Zool, Okla State Univ, 80-81, asst prof ornith, Univ Okla Biol Sta, 81, asst prof wildlife, Dept Zool, Okla State Univ, 81-84. *Personal Data:* b Pottstown, Pa, Aug 13, 52; m 75. *Educ:* Univ Del, BS, 74; Northern Ariz Univ, MS, 77; Mich State Univ, PhD(wildlife ecol), 79. *Prof Exp:* Resource specialist impact statements, Mich Dept Nat Resources, 80. *Concurrent Pos:* Mem, Animal Res Coun, Okla City Zoo, 80- *Mem:* Wildlife Soc; Am Ornithologists Union; Wilson Ornith Soc; Am Soc Mammalogists; Ecol Soc Am. *Res:* Breeding biology, behavior and habitat requirements of nongame and endangered species of wildlife; eastern bluebird biology; black-tailed prairie dog habitat impacts. *Mailing Add:* RR 5 Cameron WV 26033

SHALE, DAVID, MATHEMATICS. *Current Pos:* from asst prof to assoc prof, 64-70, PROF MATH, UNIV PA, 70- *Personal Data:* b Christchurch, NZ, Mar 22, 32; US citizen; m 66; c 2. *Educ:* Univ NZ, MSc, 53; Univ Chicago, PhD(math), 60. *Prof Exp:* Lectr math, Univ Toronto, 59-61; instr, Univ Calif, Berkeley, 61-62, asst prof, 61-64. *Concurrent Pos:* Temp mem, Inst Advan Study, 63-64. *Mem:* Am Math Soc. *Res:* Abstract analysis and applications, especially to quantum theory. *Mailing Add:* Univ Pa Dept Math 209 S 33rd St Philadelphia PA 19104-6935

SHALEK, ROBERT JAMES, BIOPHYSICS. *Current Pos:* from asst physicist to assoc physicist, 54-60, PHYSICIST, UNIV TEX M D ANDERSON HOSP & TUMOR INST, 60-, PROF BIOPHYS, 65- *Personal Data:* b Chicago, Ill, Apr 15, 22; m 51; c 6. *Educ:* Univ Ill, BA, 43; Southern Methodist Univ, MA, 48; Rice Inst, MA, 50, PhD(biophys), 53. *Prof Exp:* Instr radiol physics, Univ Tex M D Anderson Hosp & Tumor Inst, 50-53; USPHS fel, Univ London, 53-54. *Concurrent Pos:* Consult, Oak Ridge Inst Nuclear Studies, 53-61. *Mem:* Am Phys Soc; Radiation Res Soc; Biophys Soc; Am Asn Physicists Med (pres, 66); Brit Inst Radiol; Sigma Xi. *Res:* Radiation chemistry; radiological physics. *Mailing Add:* 5304 Pine St Bellaire TX 77401

SHALER, AMOS J(OHNSON), FAILURE METALLURGY, FORENSIC MATERIALS ENGINEERING. *Current Pos:* PRES, AMOS J SHALER, INC, CONSULTS, 65- *Personal Data:* b Harrow, Eng, July 8, 17; US citizen; m 43, Patricia Bowman; c Louise, Cynthia S (Muzzy) & James L. *Educ:* Mass Inst Technol, SB, 40, ScD(phys metall), 47. *Honors & Awards:* Award, Am Inst Mining, Metall & Petrol Engrs, 51; Cert of Appreciation, US Off Naval Res, 51; Cert of Appreciation, US Mission to NATO, 70. *Prof Exp:* Asst, New Consol Gold Fields, SAfrica, 40-42; heat treatment supt, Cent Ord Factory, 42; res & develop engr, C H Hirtzel & Co, Ltd, 42-43; tech dir, Indust Rys Equip Co, 43-45; mem staff, Div Indust Coop, Mass Inst Technol, 46-47, from asst prof to assoc prof phys metall, 47-53; prof metall & head dept, Pa State Univ, 53-60; vpres, MGD, Inc, 79-91. *Concurrent Pos:* Sci liaison officer, Off Naval Res, 50-51; dir, Belg-Am Educ Found, 58-; consult, 60-65; consult, President's Off Sci & Technol, 61-65; spec consult to asst secy gen, NATO, 69-70. *Mem:* Am Soc Metals; Int Oceanog Found; Nat Fire Protection Asn; Nat Acad Forensic Engrs. *Res:* Waste water recycling; chemical oceanography; water purification; failure prevention in buried pipes; powder metallurgy; refractory materials; new materials systems; new products and processes; residual stress in materials; methods of forensic engineering. *Mailing Add:* 705 W Park Ave State College PA 16803

SHALIT, HAROLD, ORGANIC CHEMISTRY. *Current Pos:* RETIRED. *Personal Data:* b Philadelphia, Pa, May 9, 19; m 42, Mildred Miller; c Ellen P (Laird) & Anne R (Tindall). *Educ:* Univ Pa, AB, 41; Pa State Univ, MS, 43; Polytech Inst Brooklyn, PhD(org chem), 48. *Prof Exp:* Sr res assoc, Polytech Inst Brooklyn, 46-48; res chemist, Stand Oil Co Ind, 48-51; res chemist, Houdry Process Corp, 51-58, sect head explor & fuel cell res, 58-63; dir phys chem res, Assoc Chem Div, Atlantic Richfield Co, 63-72, mgr catalytic res, 72-76, sr res assoc, 76-82, sr res adv, 82-85. *Concurrent Pos:* Adj prof chem, Drexel Univ, 74-76. *Mem:* Am Chem Soc; Catalysis Soc; Sigma Xi. *Res:* Physical, organic, petroleum and electro-organic chemistry; high pressure reactions; kinetics; catalysis. *Mailing Add:* 106 Meetinghouse Pond Wayne PA 19087-5513

SHALITA, ALAN REMI, DERMATOLOGY, BIOCHEMISTRY. *Current Pos:* assoc prof, State Univ NY, 75-79, head, Div Dermat, 75-80, prof med, Downstate Med Ctr, 79-80, med dir, Univ Hosp Brooklyn, 92-96, PROF & CHMN, DEPT DERMAT, STATE UNIV NY HEALTH SCI CTR, 80-, ASSOC VPRES CLIN AFFAIRS, UNIV HOSP BROOKLYN, 93- *Personal Data:* b New York, NY, Mar 22, 36; m 60, Simone Baum; c Judith & Deborah. *Educ:* Brown Univ, AB, 57; Free Univ Brussels, BS, 60; Bowman Gray Sch Med, MD, 64. *Hon Degrees:* DSc, Long Island Univ, 90. *Prof Exp:* Training grant fel dermat, Med Ctr, NY Univ, 68-70, from instr to asst prof dermat, 70-73; asst prof dermat, Col Physicians & Surgeons, Columbia Univ, 73-75. *Concurrent Pos:* USPHS spec fel biochem, Med Ctr, NY Univ, 70-72; dep dir, Div Finance, Nat Prog Dermat, 70-; Dermat Found grant, 76. *Mem:* AAAS; NY Acad Sci; Soc Invest Dermat; Am Fedn Clin Res; fel Am Acad Dermat (vpres, 95-); Am Dermat Asn (secy/treas, 96-); Asn Prof Dermat (pres, 96). *Res:* Factors involved in the pathogenesis of acne vulgaris, including cutaneous lipogenesis and microbial lipids and lipolytic enzymes. *Mailing Add:* 70 E 77th St New York NY 10021-1811. *Fax:* 718-270-2794

SHALLCROSS, FRANK V(AN LOON), PHYSICAL CHEMISTRY, SOLID STATE DEVICE TECHNOLOGY. *Current Pos:* RETIRED. *Personal Data:* b Philadelphia, Pa, Nov 9, 32; m 56, Phoebe Bailey; c Mark & David. *Educ:* Univ Pa, AB, 53; Brown Univ, PhD(chem), 58. *Prof Exp:* Chemist, M & C Nuclear, Inc, Mass, 57-58; mem tech staff, David Sarnoff Res Ctr, RCA Corp, 58-87, SRI Int, 87-95. *Mem:* AAAS; Am Chem Soc; fel Am Inst Chemists. *Res:* Solid state physical chemistry; thin films; photoconductive materials; solid state image sensors; semiconductors; charge-coupled devices; integrated circuit technology; infrared imagers. *Mailing Add:* 12 Jeffrey Lane Princeton Junction NJ 08550-1608

SHALLENBERGER, ROBERT SANDS, FOOD CHEMISTRY, CARBOHYDRATE CHEMISTRY. *Current Pos:* asst prof biochem, 56-60, assoc prof food sci & technol, 60-66, PROF BIOCHEM, CORNELL UNIV, 66- *Personal Data:* b Pittsburgh, Pa, Apr 11, 26; m 51; c 4. *Educ:* Univ Pittsburgh, BS, 51; Cornell Univ, MS, 53, PhD(biochem, hort, plant physiol), 55. *Prof Exp:* Assoc technologist chem, Gen Foods Corp, 55-56. *Mem:* Am Chem Soc. *Res:* Chemical reactions affecting color, flavor, texture and nutritive value in processed foods; carbohydrate structure and reactions. *Mailing Add:* 68 Ridgewood Dr Geneva NY 14456

SHALLOWAY, DAVID IRWIN, COMPUTATIONAL STRUCTURE BASED DRUG DESIGN, PROTEIN FOLDING. *Current Pos:* res assoc physics, Lab Nuclear Studies, 75-77, GREATER PHILADELPHIA PROF BIOL SCI BIOCHEM, CORNELL UNIV, 90- *Personal Data:* b Miami, Fla, Apr 6, 48; m 85, Kelly Lynn Morris; c Phoebe L. *Educ:* Mass Inst Technol, SB, 69, PhD(physics), 75; Stanford Univ, MS, 70. *Prof Exp:* Res fel molecular biol, Dana-Farber Cancer Inst, Harvard Med Sch, 77-81; from asst prof to assoc prof molecular biol, Pa State Univ, 82-90. *Concurrent Pos:* Mem, Pa State Biotechnol Inst, 87-90; vis assoc prof, Univ Calif, San Francisco, 88-89; prof, Dept Path, Vet Sch, Cornell Univ, 90- *Mem:* Am Soc Microbiol. *Res:* Theoretical prediction of protein structure and deformation; molecular mechanisms of proto-oncoprotein signal transduction and their roles in carcinogenesis. *Mailing Add:* Biotechnol Bldg Rm 265 Cornell Univ Ithaca NY 14853. *Fax:* 607-255-2428; *E-Mail:* dis2@cornell.edu

SHALOWITZ, ERWIN EMMANUEL, CIVIL ENGINEERING. *Current Pos:* PROJ MGR, ELECTRONIC ACQUISITION SYST PROJ, GEN SERV ADMIN, WASHINGTON, DC, 59- *Personal Data:* b Washington, DC, Feb 13, 24; m 52, Elaine Langerman; c Ann, Aliza & Jonathan. *Educ:* George Washington Univ, BCE, 47; Am Univ, MA, 54. *Prof Exp:* Consult waterfront struct, chief, Struct Res Eng & head, Defense Res, Navy Dept, Washington, DC, 48-59. *Concurrent Pos:* Adv atomic tests, Navy Dept, Wash, DC, 55-57, mem, Spec Weapons Effects Test Planning, 57-58; spec asst protective construct, proj mgr bldg systs, chief res, chief contract procedures & contract support, Gen Serv Admin, Wash, DC, 59-, chmn, Fire Safety Comt & Fallout Protection Comt, 59-61 & Bldg Eval Comt, 68-70; mem, Interagency Comt Housing Res & Bldg Technol, 68-70 & Nat Eval Bd Archit Eng Selection, 75-77; Gen Serv Admin rep, Procurement Policy Comt, Nat Acad Sci, 76-79. *Mem:* Soc Advan Mgt; fel Am Soc Civil Engrs; fel Am Biog Inst. *Res:* Atomic test reports; protective construction; civil engineering and water power; technical management; building research; contracting techniques and national contract organization staffing model. *Mailing Add:* 5603 Huntington Pkwy Bethesda MD 20814

SHALVOY, RICHARD BARRY, SURFACE PHYSICS, ANALYTICAL CHEMISTRY. *Current Pos:* RES CHEMIST, OLIN CORP, 87- *Personal Data:* b Norwalk, Conn, Apr 26, 49; m 72, Karol A Mihailoff; c Stacy, Joanna & Becky. *Educ:* Rensselaer Polytech Inst, BS, 71; Brown Univ, ScM, 74, PhD(physics), 77. *Prof Exp:* Res fel, Univ Ky, 76-78, sr physicist electron spectros, 78-80; res chemist, Stauffer Chem Co, 80-85, sr res chemist anal res, 85-87. *Mem:* Am Vacuum Soc; Eastern Electron Spectros Soc (pres, 91-). *Res:* Characterization of catalysts and metals using electron spectroscopy; chemical bonding in semiconductors; analytical surface chemistry. *Mailing Add:* 317 Sharon Dr Cheshire CT 06410

SHAM, LU JEU, THEORETICAL PHYSICS, SOLID STATE PHYSICS. *Current Pos:* assoc prof physics, 68-74, dean natural sci, 85-89, PROF PHYSICS, UNIV CALIF, SAN DIEGO, 74- *Personal Data:* b Hong Kong, China, Apr 28, 38; m 65, Georgina Bien; c Kevin Shen & Alisa Shen. *Educ:* Univ London, BSc, 60, Imp Col, ARCS, 60; Cambridge Univ, PhD(solid state physics), 63. *Honors & Awards:* Humboldt Found Award, 81. *Prof Exp:* Physicist, Univ Calif, San Diego, 63-65, asst res physicist & lectr physics, 65-66; asst prof, Univ Calif, Irvine, 66-67; reader appl math, Queen Mary Col, Univ London, 67-68. *Concurrent Pos:* Vis prof, Max Planck Inst Solid State Res, Stuttgart, Ger, 78; Guggenheim fel, 83-84. *Mem:* AAAS; Fel Am Phys Soc. *Res:* Electronic properties in solids; theory of semiconductor heterostructures. *Mailing Add:* 5744 Bellevue Ave La Jolla CA 92037. *Fax:* 619-534-0173; *E-Mail:* lusham@ucsd.edu

SHAMAN, PAUL, STATISTICS. *Current Pos:* assoc prof, 77-85, PROF STATIST, UNIV PA, 85- *Personal Data:* b Portland, Ore, Mar 30, 39; m 64, Susan Slobin; c David & Jeffrey. *Educ:* Dartmouth Col, AB, 61; Columbia Univ, MA, 64, PhD(statist), 66. *Prof Exp:* From asst res scientist to assoc res scientist, NY Univ, 64-67; res assoc, Stanford Univ, 67-68; from asst prof to assoc prof statist, Carnegie-Mellon Univ, 68-77. *Concurrent Pos:* Prog dir statist & probability, NSF, 84-85; managing ed, Inst Math Statist, 86-90. *Mem:* Am Statist Asn; fel Inst Math Statist; Math Asn Am. *Res:* Time series analysis. *Mailing Add:* Dept Statist Univ Pa Philadelphia PA 19104-6302. *Fax:* 215-898-1280; *E-Mail:* shaman@wharton.upenn,edu

SHAMASH, YACOV A, CONTROL SYSTEMS, ROBOTICS. *Current Pos:* PROF & DEAN ENG & APPL ENG, STATE UNIV NY, STONY BROOK, 92- *Personal Data:* b Jan 12, 50; m 76; c 2. *Educ:* Imp Col, BSc, 70, PhD(control systs), 73. *Hon Degrees:* DIC, Imp Col, 73. *Prof Exp:* Lectr elec eng, Tel-Aviv Univ, 73-76; vis asst prof systs eng, Univ Pa, 76-77; prof & chair elec eng, Fla Atlantic Univ, 77-85; prof & chair elec eng, Wash State Univ, 85-92. *Concurrent Pos:* Dir, Ctr Analog/Digital Integrated Circuits, NSF, 89-92 & Keytronics, Inc, 90-; bd gov, Inst Elec & Electronics Engrs Aerospace & Electronics Systs Soc, 91-95; mem, CAD/CAM Tech Comt, Am Inst Aeronaut & Astronaut, 85-90. *Mem:* Fel Inst Elec & Electronics Engrs; Am Inst Aeronaut & Astronaut; Am Soc Eng Educ. *Res:* Control systems; robotics. *Mailing Add:* Col Eng State Univ NY Stony Brook NY 11794-2200

SHAMBAUGH, GEORGE E, III, DEVELOPMENTAL BIOLOGY, NEUROBIOLOGY. *Current Pos:* from asst prof to assoc prof, 69-81, PROF MED, MED SCH, NORTHWESTERN UNIV, 81- *Personal Data:* b Boston, Mass, Dec 21, 31; wid; c George, Benjamin, Daniel, James & Elizabeth. *Educ:* Oberlin Col, BA, 54; Cornell Univ, MD, 58. *Prof Exp:* Gen med intern, Denver Gen Hosp Univ, 58-59; prev med adv, MAAG, Taiwan, 59-61; resident, Walter Reed Gen Hosp, 61-64; res internist, Walter Reed Army Med Ctr, 64-67; fel physiol chem, Univ Wis, 67-69. *Concurrent Pos:* Pres, Taipei Int Med Soc, 60-61; attend staff mem, Northwestern Mem Hosp, 69-; attend & chief endocrinol & metab, Vet Admin Lakeside Med Ctr, 74-, dir geriat eval, 97-; mem, Comt Nutrit Issues, Am Soc Clin Nutrit, 77-82; vis lectr, Sharam Zedek Med Ctr, Jerusalem, Israel, 90. *Mem:* Endocrine Soc; Cent Soc Clin Res; Am Thyroid Asn; Am Inst Nutrit; Am Soc Clin Nutrit; Am Physiol Soc. *Res:* Fetal fuels and growth factors in fetal and neonatal development in the rat with emphasis on metabolism and cellular mechanisms in fetal tissues; proliferation and differentiation; neuroendocrine ontogeny; utilization of altered fuel mixtures by discrete tissues; modulation of cell replication by circulating hormones and growth factors in mother and fetus; neurochemistry; nutrition. *Mailing Add:* Ctr Endocrinol Metab & Nutrit Northwestern Univ Med Sch 303 E Chicago Ave Chicago IL 60611. *Fax:* 312-640-2401; *E-Mail:* martord@nwu.edu

SHAMBAUGH, GEORGE FRANKLIN, ENTOMOLOGY. *Current Pos:* from assoc prof to prof, 62-85, EMER PROF ENTOM, OHIO AGR RES & DEVELOP CTR & OHIO STATE UNIV, 85- *Personal Data:* b Columbus, Ohio, Nov 3, 28; m 53; c 3. *Educ:* Wilmington Col, AB, 50; Ohio State Univ, MSc, 51, PhD(entom), 53. *Prof Exp:* Entomologist & asst chief pesticides br, Natick Qm Res & Eng Command, 55-62. *Mem:* AAAS; Am Soc Zoologists; Am Entom Soc; Sigma Xi. *Res:* Electrophysiology of insect nerves and muscles; insect sense physiology; insect attractants and repellent; insect digestive enzymes. *Mailing Add:* 1574 Sunset Lane Wooster OH 44691-1824

SHAMBELAN, CHARLES, SYNTHETIC FIBERS. *Current Pos:* RETIRED. *Personal Data:* b Philadelphia, Pa, Mar 16, 30; m 56, Kay Promish; c Adele (Kennedy) & Michele (Nathanson). *Educ:* Temple Univ, BA, 51, MA, 55; Univ Pa, PhD(phys chem), 59. *Prof Exp:* Chemist, Frankford Arsenal, 51-55; res chemist, E I DuPont de Nemours & Co, Inc, 58-64, res supvr, 64, res assoc, 73, res fel, 77, sr res fel, 85-90. *Mem:* Am Chem Soc. *Res:* Polymers; nonwoven fabrics; synthetic fibers. *Mailing Add:* 3203 Summerset Rd Wilmington DE 19810

SHAMBERGER, RAYMOND J, BIOCHEMISTRY. *Current Pos:* LAB DIR, KING JAMES MED LAB-OMEGATECH, 91- *Personal Data:* b Munising, Mich, Aug 23, 34; m 70, Barbara Walsh; c Chrissa, Erik, Monica, Kara, Michael & Shannon. *Educ:* Alma Col, BS, 56; Ore State Univ, MS, 60; Univ Miami, PhD(biochem), 63. *Prof Exp:* Asst, Ore State Univ, 57-59 & Univ Southern Calif, 63; dir res, Sutton Res Corp, Calif, 63-64; sr cancer res scientist, Roswell Park Mem Inst, 64-69; sect head enzyme, Cleveland Clin Found, 69-87; sr scientist, Ciba Corn, 87-91. *Concurrent Pos:* Prof, Cleveland State Univ, 70-89; mem, Comts Nutrit & Path, Fedn Am Socs Exp Biol & Med. *Mem:* Am Asn Cancer Res; Am Soc Clin Pathologists; Am Asn Clin Chemists; Fedn Am Soc Exp Biol; fel Am Col Nutrit. *Res:* Chemistry of trace metals; mechanisms of cancer formation; enzyme chemistry. *Mailing Add:* 9865 W Alpine Dr Kirtland OH 44094. *Fax:* 440-835-2177

SHAMBLIN, JAMES E, MECHANICAL ENGINEERING, INDUSTRIAL ENGINEERING. *Current Pos:* from asst prof to assoc prof, 64-69, PROF INDUST ENG, OKLA STATE UNIV, 69-, DIR, CTR LOCAL GOVT TECHNOL, 75- *Personal Data:* b Holdenville, Okla, Mar 24, 32; m 59; c 2. *Educ:* Univ Tex, BSME, 54, MSME, 62, PhD(mech eng), 64. *Honors & Awards:* H B Maynard Innovative Achievement Award, Inst Indust Engrs; Chester F Carlson Award for Innovation in Eng Educ, Am Soc Eng Educ. *Prof Exp:* Test engr, Pratt & Whitney Aircraft Div, United Aircraft Corp, 54-55; res engr, Southwest Res Inst, 55-60; teaching asst mech eng, Univ Tex, 60-62, instr, 62-64. *Mem:* Am Inst Indust Engrs; Am Soc Eng Educ; Am Pub Works Asn; Am Soc Civil Engrs. *Res:* Application of engineering and management technology to problems of local government. *Mailing Add:* 711 W Lakeshore Dr Stillwater OK 74075

SHAMBROOM, W(ILIAM) DAVID, COMPUTER SCIENCE. *Current Pos:* sr mem tech staff, 93-97, PRIN MEM TECH STAFF, GTE LABS, 97- *Personal Data:* b Teaneck, NJ, Jan 18, 49; m 87, Rose M Giaconia. *Educ:* Harvard Univ, AB & AM, 77, PhD(physics), 80. *Prof Exp:* Res assoc physics, Northeastern Univ, 78-81, asst prof physics, 81-84, asst prof physics & comput sci, 84-85, asst prof comput sci, 85-87; prin software eng, Wang Labs, 87-91; prin engr, Charles River Data Systs, 91-93. *Mem:* Am Phys Soc; Digital Equip Comput Users Soc; Asn Comput Mach; Inst Elec & Electronics Engrs. *Res:* Computer security; distributed systems; fault-tolerant computing. *Mailing Add:* 96 Overlook Rd Arlington MA 02174. *E-Mail:* dshambroom@gte.com

SHAMBURGER, JOHN HERBERT, ENGINEERING GEOLOGY. *Current Pos:* CONSULT GEOLOGIST, 86- *Personal Data:* b Meridian, Miss, Nov 22, 25; m 48, Dorothy Coggin; c Marie, Carol, Brenda & Lisa. *Educ:* Univ Miss, BS, 49. *Prof Exp:* Civil engr, 49-51, geologist, 53-62, chief eng geol applications group, geotech lab, Waterways Exp Sta, US Army Corp Engrs, 62-86. *Mem:* Asn Eng Geol; Soc Am Mil Engrs; Int Geog Union. *Res:* Engineering geologic site characterization; alluvial environment of deposition suitability for engineering requirements; groundwater containment at disposal sites; remote imagery interpretation methodology. *Mailing Add:* Eight Briarwood Pl Vicksburg MS 39180

SHAMES, DAVID MARSHALL, NUCLEAR MEDICINE. *Current Pos:* NIH fel, 70-71, asst prof, 71-75, assoc prof radiol, 75-80, ASSOC CLIN PROF, UNIV CALIF, SAN FRANCISCO, 80- *Personal Data:* b Norfolk, Va, Dec 27, 39. *Educ:* Univ Va, BA, 61; Yale Univ, MD, 65. *Prof Exp:* Intern internal med, Yale-New Haven Hosp, 65-66; staff assoc kinetic anal metab systs, Math Res Br, NIH, 66-69; asst resident internal med, Johns Hopkins Hosp, 69-70. *Concurrent Pos:* Nat Insts Gen Med Sci res career develop award, 72-77. *Mem:* Soc Nuclear Med; Am Fedn Clin Res. *Res:* Kinetic analysis of nuclear medicine tracer data using the computer, especially the cardiovascular, cerebrovascular and renal systems. *Mailing Add:* Providence Hosp Box 0628 San Francisco CA 94143

SHAMES, IRVING H, ENGINEERING. *Current Pos:* prof & head, State Univ NY, Buffalo, Div Interdisciplinary Studies & Res Eng, 62-70, fac prof eng & appl sci, 70-73, prof & chmn, Dept Eng Sci, Aerospace Eng & Nuclear Eng, 73, fac prof, Eng & Appl Sci, 79, DISTINGUISHED TEACHING PROF, STATE UNIV NY, BUFFALO, 80- *Personal Data:* b Boston, Mass, Oct 31, 23; m 54; c 2. *Educ:* Northeastern Univ, BS, 48; Harvard Univ, MS, 49; Univ Md, PhD, 53. *Prof Exp:* From instr to asst prof, Univ Md, 49-55; asst prof, Stevens Inst Technol, 55-57; prof eng sci & chmn dept, Pratt Inst, 57-62, actg chmn physics, 60-61. *Concurrent Pos:* Vis lectr, Ord Lab, US Dept

Navy, 52-55 & Res Lab, 53-55; vis prof, Mat Dept, Technion, Israel, 69, Mech Eng Dept, 75; prin investr, Esso grant, Sunyab grant, co-prin investr, NASA grant, NSF grant, 90. *Mem:* Am Soc Eng Educ; Sigma Xi. *Res:* Dynamics and mechanics; author of numerous publications and text books.. *Mailing Add:* Dept Civil, Mech & Environ Eng Rm 716 George Washington Univ 801 22nd St NW Washington DC 20052

SHAMGOCHIAN, MAUREEN DOWD, NEUROENDOCRINOLOGY, NEUROIMMUNOLOGY. *Current Pos:* ASST PROF CELL BIOL & ENDOCRINOL, WORCESTER STATE COL, 93- *Personal Data:* b Clinton, Mass, Feb 11, 48; m, Edward G; c Michael E & Alexander M. *Educ:* Worcester State Col, BS, 80; Univ Mass, PhD(molecular & cellular physiol), 90. *Prof Exp:* Res assoc, Univ Mass Med Sch, 90-93. *Res:* Role of neuropeptides in the regulation of pituitary hormone release; expression and physiological function of prolactin in the brain, in particular its possible role in neuroimmune responses in the brain. *Mailing Add:* Worcester State Col 486 Chandler St Worcester MA 01602

SHAMIR, ADI, computer science, for more information see previous edition

SHAMIS, SIDNEY S, electrical engineering, for more information see previous edition

SHAMMA, MAURICE, NATURAL PRODUCTS CHEMISTRY. *Current Pos:* RETIRED. *Personal Data:* b Cairo, Egypt, Dec 14, 26; nat US; m 55; c 1. *Educ:* Berea Col, AB, 51; Univ Wis, PhD(chem), 55. *Prof Exp:* Fel, Wayne State Univ, 55-56; from asst prof to prof chem, Pa State Univ, University Park, 56-89. *Mem:* Am Chem Soc. *Res:* Isolation, characterization and synthesis of natural products, particularly alkaloids; synthesis of new nitrogen heterocycles. *Mailing Add:* 2036 Highland Dr State College PA 16803

SHAMOIAN, CHARLES ANTHONY, PSYCHIATRY, BIOCHEMICAL PHARMACOLOGY. *Current Pos:* fel psychiat, Cornell Univ-NY Hosp, 67-70, from instr to assoc prof clin psychiat, 70-84, dir, Geriat Serv, Westchester Div, 79-89, PROF CLIN PSYCHIAT, CORNELL UNIV-NY HOSP, 84-, DIR, ACUTE TREAT SERV, WESTCHESTER DIV, 89- *Personal Data:* b Worcester, Mass, Oct 5, 31; m 61; c 2. *Educ:* Clark Univ, AB, 54, MA, 56; Tufts Univ, PhD(physiol), 60, MD, 66. *Prof Exp:* Instr physiol, Med Sch, Tufts Univ, 61-62, res assoc pharmacol, 63-66; intern med, Bellevue Hosp, New York, 66-67. *Concurrent Pos:* Asst attend psychiatrist, Payne Whitney Psychiat Clin, 71-78, assoc attend psychiatrist, 78-; attend psychiatrist, NY Hosp, 84- *Mem:* AAAS; Am Physiol Soc; Am Psychopath Asn; Am Psychiat Asn; NY Acad Med; Am Asn Geriat Psychiat. *Res:* Geriatric psychopharm. *Mailing Add:* Dept Psychiat Cornell Univ Med Col 21 Bloomingdale Rd White Plains NY 10605

SHAMOO, ADIL E, ETHICS IN RESEARCH, BIOPHYSICS. *Current Pos:* prof & chmn, 79-82, PROF, DEPT BIOL & CHEM, UNIV MD, BALTIMORE, 82- *Personal Data:* b Baghdad, Iraq, Aug 1, 41; m 67; c 3. *Educ:* Univ Baghdad, 62; Univ Louisville, MS, 66; City Univ New York, PhD(physiol, biophys), 70. *Prof Exp:* Instr physics, Univ Louisville, 65-68; from asst to assoc biophys, Mt Sinai Sch Med, 68-71, asst prof physiol & biophys, 71-73; from asst prof to assoc prof, Univ Rochester, 73-78. *Concurrent Pos:* Guest worker, Nat Inst Neurol Dis & Stroke, 72-73; guest prof, Max-Planck Inst Biophys, Frankfurt, 77-78; ed-in-chief, Membrane Biochem, 77-, Accountability in Res Policies & Qual Assurance, 88-; adj prof physics, E Carolina Univ, Greenville, NC. *Mem:* Am Asn Biol Chemists; NY Acad Sci; Biophys Soc; Am Physiol Soc; Soc Qual Assurance. *Res:* Physiology and ethics in research; biochemistry of membrane transport; membrane biochemistry-lipid membranes; quality assurance in research. *Mailing Add:* Biochem Dept Univ Md 108 N Greene St Baltimore MD 21201. *Fax:* 410-706-3189; *E-Mail:* ashamoo@umabnet.ab.umd.edu

SHAMOON, HARRY, ENDOCRINOLOGY, DIABETES. *Current Pos:* From asst prof to assoc prof, 80-90, PROF MED, ALBERT EINSTEIN COL MED, 90- *Personal Data:* b Baghdad, Iraq, Apr 11, 48; US citizen; m 71, Rona Levine; c Evan, Mark & Michael. *Educ:* Columbia Univ, BA, 70; Yale Univ, MD, 74. *Mem:* Am Diabetes Asn; Endocrine Soc; Am Fedn Clin Res; fel Am Col Physicians; Am Soc Clin Invest. *Res:* Physiology of glucose regulation in humans; clinical trials of diabetes treatment. *Mailing Add:* Albert Einstein Col Med 1300 Morris Park Ave Bronx NY 10461. *E-Mail:* shamoon@aecom.yu.edu

SHAMOS, MICHAEL IAN, COMPUTATIONAL GEOMETRY, COMPUTER LAW. *Current Pos:* asst prof math & comput sci, 75-90, ADJ SR RES COMPUT SCIENTIST, CARNEGIE-MELLON UNIV, 90- *Personal Data:* b New York, NY, Apr 21, 47; m 73; c 2. *Educ:* Princeton Univ, AB, 68; Vassar Col, MA, 70; Am Univ, MS, 72; Yale Univ, MS, 73, MPhil, 74, PhD(comput sci), 78; Duquesne Univ, JD, 81. *Prof Exp:* Assoc engr comput sci, IBM Corp, 68-70; supvry programmer, Nat Cancer Inst, NIH, 70-72; teaching fel, Yale Univ, 72-75. *Concurrent Pos:* Consult, various law firms; pres, Unus, Inc, 79-, Lunus Inc, 84-; assoc, Webb, Burden Ziesenheim & Webb, PC, 90- *Mem:* Asn Comput Mach; Math Asn Am; Nat Sci Teachers Asn; Sigma Xi; NY Acad Sci. *Res:* Theoretical computer science; graph theory; discrete mathematics; computational geometry; combinatorics; analysis of algorithms; computers and law. *Mailing Add:* 605 Devonshire St Pittsburgh PA 15213-2904

SHAMOS, MORRIS HERBERT, BIOPHYSICS, LABORATORY MEDICINE. *Current Pos:* PRES, M H SHAMOS & ASSOC, 83- *Personal Data:* b Cleveland, Ohio, Sept 1, 17; m 42, Marion Cahn; c Michael I. *Educ:* NY Univ, AB, 41, MS, 43, PhD(physics), 48. *Honors & Awards:* Ness Award, Asn Am Col & Univs, 95. *Prof Exp:* Sr vpres & chief sci officer, Technicon Corp, 75-83. *Concurrent Pos:* Consult, US AEC, 56-69, Nat Broadcasting Co, 57-65 & UN Info Serv, 58; chmn dept physics, Washington Sq Col, NY Univ, 57-70; sr vpres res & educ, Technicon Corp, 70-75; mem adv coun, NY Polytech Inst, 80-, fel, Polytechn Univ. *Mem:* Fel AAAS; Am Phys Soc; sr mem Inst Elec & Electronics Engrs; Nat Sci Teachers Asn (pres-elect, 66-67, pres, 67-68); NY Acad Sci (rec secy, 77-79, vpres, 80-81, pres, 82); Am Chem Soc; Sigma Xi. *Res:* Atomic and nuclear physics; cosmic rays; electron scattering; physical electronics; high energy physics; nuclear detectors and instrumentation; biophysics, electrical properties of hard tissues; biophysical theory of aging. *Mailing Add:* 3515 Henry Hudson Pkwy Bronx NY 10463. *Fax:* 718-884-0852; *E-Mail:* sci4soc@aol.com

SHAMOUN, SIMON FRANCIS, PLANT PATHOLOGY, FOREST BIOTECHNOLOGY. *Current Pos:* RES SCIENTIST BIOCONTROL FOREST PESTS FOREST PATH, CAN FORESTRY SERV, PAC FORESTRY CENTRE, CAN, 88-, PROJ LEADER, MICROBIOL CONTROL FOREST PESTS. *Personal Data:* b Habbaniya, Iraq, July 1, 46; Can citizen; m 79, Marina Thomas; c Martin, Steven & Christina. *Educ:* Mosul Univ, Iraq, BSc, 72; NC State Univ, MSc, 79; Univ Ark, PhD(plant path), 88. *Prof Exp:* Agr engr forestry, Gen Directorate Forests, 72-74; lab instr forestry, Mosul Univ, Iraq, 74-76; res asst plant path, NC State Univ, 76-79 & Univ Ark, 79-88. *Concurrent Pos:* Res scientist & proj leader, Pac Forestry Centre, Victoria; adj prof, Univ Victoria & Simon Fraser Univ. *Mem:* Am Phytopath Soc; Can Phytopath Soc. *Res:* Developing environmentally safe products for biological control of forest pests including weeds and diseases; forest tree diseases and biochemical analysis of fungi by means of biotechnology techniques. *Mailing Add:* Pac Forestry Centre Can Forestry Serv 506 W Burnside Rd Victoria BC V8Z 1M5 Can. *Fax:* 250-363-0775; *E-Mail:* sshamoun@pfc.forestry.ca

SHAMSIE, JALAL, CHILD PSYCHIATRY. *Current Pos:* asst prof, 72-80, PROF PSYCHIAT, UNIV TORONTO, 80- *Personal Data:* b Delhi, India, Jan 29, 30; Can citizen; m 59; c 2. *Educ:* Punjab Univ, India, BSc, 47; Punjab Univ, Pakistan, MBBS, 53; FRCP(C), 62. *Prof Exp:* Dir child & child adolescent serv psychiat, Douglas Hosp, Montreal, Que, 61-71; asst prof, McGill Univ, 67-71. *Concurrent Pos:* Dir Res & Educ, Thistletown Regional Ctr Children & Adolescents, Toronto, 72-80; consult child psychiat, Clarke Inst, 76- *Mem:* Royal Col Psychiatrists Gt Brit; Can Psychiat Asn. *Res:* Adolescent psychiatry; administrative psychiatry. *Mailing Add:* 32 Grovetree Rd Rexdale ON M9V 2Y2 Can. *Fax:* 416-745-3094

SHAMSUDDIN, ABULKALAM MOHAMMAD, CARCINOGENESIS, CHEMOPREVENTION. *Current Pos:* resident path, Univ Md Hosp, 75-77, instr path, Sch Med, Univ Md, 77-79, from asst prof to assoc prof, 80-88, PROF PATH, SCH MED, UNIV MD, 88- *Personal Data:* b Comilla, Bangladesh, Mar 1, 48; m 71, Daliah Salahuddin; c Shomon. *Educ:* Dhaka Univ, Dhaka Med Col, MD, 72; Univ Md, Baltimore, Phd(carcinogenesis), 80. *Prof Exp:* Resident path, Baltimore City Hosp, 73-75. *Concurrent Pos:* Path fel, Johns Hopkins Hosp, 73-75; vis scientist, Cancer Inst Tokyo, 82 & Nat Cancer Ctr Res Inst, Tokyo, 85; reviewer & consult, Nat Cancer Inst, 83-; res fel, Univ Tokyo, Inst Med Sci, 89. *Mem:* AAAS; Am Asn Cancer Res; Am Asn Pathologists; Am Soc Cell Biol. *Res:* Carcinogenesis; tumor markers for early diagnosis of cancer; cancer prevention using dietary substances; new tests for cancer diagnosis. *Mailing Add:* Dept Pathol Univ Md Sch Med Ten S Pine St Baltimore MD 21201-1192. *Fax:* 410-706-8414

SHAN, ROBERT KUOCHENG, AQUATIC ECOLOGY. *Current Pos:* from asst prof to assoc prof, 69-75, PROF BIOL, FAIRMONT STATE COL, 75- *Personal Data:* b Gaoan, China, Nov 9, 27; m 63, Lily Chen; c Tony D. *Educ:* Taiwan Norm Univ, BS, 56; Univ BC, MS, 62; Ind Univ, Bloomington, PhD(zool), 67. *Prof Exp:* Asst fishery biol, Nat Taiwan Univ, 55-56, asst zool, 56-59; res assoc, Ind Univ, Bloomington, 67-69. *Concurrent Pos:* Vis prof, Jinan Univ, China, 80 & 84. *Mem:* Am Inst Biol Sci; Am Soc Limnol & Oceanog; Ecol Soc Am. *Res:* Systematics and ecology of marine copepods; ecology and genetics of chydorid cladocerans. *Mailing Add:* Dept Math & Sci Fairmont State Col 1201 Locust Ave Fairmont WV 26554-2451. *Fax:* 304-366-4870

SHANAHAN, PATRICK, MATHEMATICS. *Current Pos:* From instr to assoc prof, 57-67, PROF MATH, COL OF THE HOLY CROSS, 67- *Personal Data:* b Clyde, Ohio, Aug 4, 31; m 53; c 9. *Educ:* Univ Notre Dame, BA, 53; Ind Univ, PhD(math), 57. *Concurrent Pos:* NSF sci fac fel, Harvard Univ, 66-67. *Mem:* Am Math Soc; Math Asn Am; London Math Soc. *Res:* Differential topology; equivariant version of the Atiyah-singer index theorem, and its applications to geometric and topological problems. *Mailing Add:* 18 Sunset Hill Rd Thompson CT 06277

SHANBERGE, JACOB N, PATHOLOGY, HEMOSTASEOLOGY. *Current Pos:* CHIEF COAGULATION & HEMOSTASIS, WILLIAM BEAUMONT HOSP, 79- *Personal Data:* b Milwaukee, Wis, Jan 14, 22; m 53; c 4. *Educ:* Marquette Univ, BS, 42, MD, 44. *Honors & Awards:* Murray Thelin Award, Nat Hemophilia Found, 77. *Prof Exp:* Assoc dir, Milwaukee Blood Ctr, 48; asst chief lab serv, Vet Admin Ctr Hosp, Wood, Wis, 52-55 & West Roxbury, Mass, 55-60; Nat Heart Inst spec res fel, Zurich, Switz, 60-61; assoc dir path, Michael Reese Hosp & Med Ctr, Chicago, 62-64; dir hemat labs & blood bank & assoc in path, Evanston Hosp, Ill, 64-69; dir dept path & lab med, Mt Sinai Med Ctr, 69-79. *Concurrent Pos:* Res fel biochem, Sch

Med, Marquette Univ, 48; assoc path, Peter Bent Brigham Hosp, Boston, 55-60. *Mem:* Col Am Path; Am Asn Path; Int Soc Thrombosis & Haemostasis; Am Soc Hemat. *Res:* Blood coagulation. *Mailing Add:* Hemostasis & Coag Lab 341 Riverview Dr Ann Arbor MI 48104. Fax: 313-551-3694

SHAND, JULIAN BONHAM, JR, SOLID STATE PHYSICS. *Current Pos:* DANA PROF PHYSICS & CHMN DEPT, BERRY COL, 67-, PROF COMPUT SCI, 73- *Personal Data:* b Columbia, SC, Nov 6, 37; m 63; c 3. *Educ:* Univ SC, BS, 59; Univ NC, Chapel Hill, PhD(physics), 65. *Prof Exp:* Asst prof physics, Univ Ga, 64-67. *Mem:* Am Phys Soc; Am Asn Physics Teachers; Sigma Xi. *Res:* Electrons in metals; pseudopotentials; positron annihilation in solids. *Mailing Add:* 112 Parkway Dr Rome GA 30161-5942

SHAND, MICHAEL LEE, SOLID STATE PHYSICS, OPTICS. *Current Pos:* staff physicist, Allied Chem Corp, 76-80, sr res physicist, 80-85, mgr laser res & develop, 85-93, MGR ELECTRO OPTICS, ALLIEDSIGNAL INC, 94- *Personal Data:* b Stockton, Calif, July 2, 46; m 69; c 1. *Educ:* Princeton Univ, AB, 68; Univ Pa, MSc, 69, PhD(physics), 73. *Prof Exp:* Res assoc physics, Univ Paris, 73-74; vis asst prof, Ariz State Univ, 75-76. *Concurrent Pos:* Res assoc fel, FrForeign Ministry, 73-74. *Mem:* Sigma Xi; Am Phys Soc; Inst Elec & Electronics Engrs; Optical Soc Am. *Res:* Raman scattering; quantum optics; nonlinear optics; laser physics. *Mailing Add:* AlliedSignal Inc 101 Columbia Rd Morristown NJ 07960

SHANDS, HENRY LEE, PLANT GENETICS, PLANT BREEDING. *Current Pos:* nat prog leader plant germplasm, 86-92, assoc dep adminr genetic resources, 92-97, ASST ADMINR GENETIC RESOURCES, AGR RES SERV, USDA, 97- *Personal Data:* b Madison, Wis, Aug 30, 35; m 62, Catherine Ann Miller; c Deborah, Jeanne & James. *Educ:* Univ Wis, BS, 57; Purdue Univ, MS, 61, PhD(plant genetics), 63. *Prof Exp:* Asst prof agron, Purdue Univ-USAID Contract, Minas Gerais, Brazil, 63-65, asst prof plant genetics, Purdue Univ, Lafayette, 65-67; res agronomist, Dekalb Agres, Inc, 67-86. *Concurrent Pos:* Exec secy, Nat Plant Genetic Resources Bd; dir, Nat Genetic Resources Prog. *Mem:* Fel AAAS; fel Am Soc Agron; fel Crop Sci Soc Am; Am Phytopath Soc; Genetics Soc Can. *Res:* Plant breeding through genetics and cytogenetics; disease resistance. *Mailing Add:* Bldg 005 Rm 115 USDA Agric Res Serv-Beltsville Agr Res Ctr-W Beltsville MD 20705-2350

SHANDS, JOSEPH WALTER, JR, MEDICAL MICROBIOLOGY. *Current Pos:* CONSULT, 91- *Personal Data:* b Jacksonville, Fla, Nov 1, 30; m 55; c 4. *Educ:* Princeton Univ, AB, 52; Duke Univ, MD, 56. *Prof Exp:* Fel microbiol, Univ Fla, 61-64, from asst prof to prof immunol & med microbiol, Col Med, 67-76, prof med & chief, Div Infectious Dis, 76-91. *Concurrent Pos:* Ed, J Infection & Immunity, 70-78, ed-in-chief, 79-; mem bacteriol & mycol study sect, NIH. 71-74. *Mem:* Am Soc Microbiologists; Reticuloendothelial Soc; Infectious Dis Soc Am; Am Asn Immunologists. *Res:* Endotoxin; coagulation; host-parasite relationships. *Mailing Add:* 1632 NW 24th St Gainesville FL 32605

SHANE, HAROLD D, MATHEMATICAL STATISTICS. *Current Pos:* from asst prof to assoc prof, 68-75, chmn dept, 71-85, PROF MATH, BARUCH COL, 76- *Personal Data:* b New York, NY, Jan 22, 36; m 62, Mita; c Erica & Lisa. *Educ:* Mass Inst Technol, SB, 57; NY Univ, MS, 62, PhD(math), 68. *Prof Exp:* Engr electronics, Elec Div, Daystrom Inc. 58-61; instr math, Sch Eng, Cooper Union, 62-68. *Mem:* Math Asn Am; Inst Math Statist. *Res:* Nonparametric statistical theory and methodology; inequalities for order statistics; mathematical applications to political science and management. *Mailing Add:* Baruch Col City Univ NY Lexington Ave New York NY 10010-5585. *E-Mail:* hdsbb@cunyvm

SHANE, JOHN RICHARD, MAGNETISM. *Current Pos:* asst prof, Univ Mass, Boston, 68-70, chmn physics dept, 80-82, dir eng prog, 81-83, ASSOC PROF PHYSICS, UNIV MASS, BOSTON, 70-, DIR ENG PROG, 93- *Personal Data:* b San Diego, Calif, Sept 13, 36; m 59; c 2. *Educ:* Univ Maine. BS, 58; Mass Inst Technol, PhD(solid state physics), 63. *Prof Exp:* Mem res staff solid state physics, Sperry Rand Res Ctr, 63-68. *Concurrent Pos:* Consult, Air Force Cambridge Res Lab, Bedford, Mass, 68-70. *Mem:* Am Phys Soc. *Res:* Magnetic properties of matter; antiferromagnetism; antiferromagnetic and paramagnetic resonance; spin-lattice relaxation; magnetic phase transitions. *Mailing Add:* Dept Physics Univ Mass Harbor Campus Boston MA 02125

SHANE, ROBERT S, MATERIALS SCIENCE, TECHNOLOGY TRANSFER. *Current Pos:* PRIN, SHANE ASSOCS, 76-; ED, MAT ENG MARCEL DEKKER, INC, 78- *Personal Data:* b Chicago, Ill, Dec 8, 10; m 36, Jeanne F Lazarus; c 3. *Educ:* Univ Chicago, BS, 30, PhD(chem), 33. *Honors & Awards:* Gold Key Award, Gen Elec Co, 63; Margaret Dana Award, Am Soc Testing & Mat, 83. *Prof Exp:* Res chemist, Nat Aniline Div, Allied Chem & Dye Corp, 34-35; chemist, Stein-Hall Mfg Co, 35-36; chemist, Fuel Antioxidants, Universal Oil Prod Co, 36; tech dir, Western Adhesives Co, 37-40; res chemist, Gelatin Prod Co, 41-42; plant supt, Amecco Chem, Inc, 42-43; group leader, Bausch & Lomb Optical Co, 43-45; owner, dry cleaning bus, 46-52; prog supvr govt contract res, Wyandotte Chem Corp, 52-54; asst dir new prod develop, Am Cyanamid Co, 54-55; mgr chem ceramics, Com Atomic Power Dept, Westinghouse Elec Corp, 55-57; nucleonics specialist, Bell Aircraft Corp, 57-58; consult engr, Light Mil Electronics Dept, Gen Elec Co, 58-64, res engr, Laminated Prod Dept, 64-66, systs specialist radiation effects, Spacecraft Dept, 66-67; mgr design rev, Reentry Systs, 67-69, mgr parts, Mat & Processes Eng, Space Systs Orgn, 69-70; staff scientist & consult, Nat Mat Adv Bd, Nat Acad Sci, 70-76. *Concurrent Pos:* Guest instr, Pa State Univ, 56; consult, US Dept Defense, 76-. *Mem:* Am Chem Soc; fel Am Soc Testing & Mat; fel Am Inst Chem Engrs; Am Soc Metals; AAAS. *Res:* Materials engineering; radiation effects; energy transmission; surface phenomena; plastics fabrication; physical chemistry; technology transfer and innovation. *Mailing Add:* 1904 NW 22nd St Stuart FL 34994-9270. *Fax:* 561-692-3636; *E-Mail:* robtshane@juno.com

SHANE, SAMUEL JACOB, INTERNAL MEDICINE. *Current Pos:* RETIRED. *Personal Data:* b Yarmouth, NS, May 17, 16; m 72; c 4. *Educ:* Dalhousie Univ, BSc, 36, MD, CM, 40; FRCP(C). *Prof Exp:* From asst med dir to med dir, Point Edward Hosp, Sydney, NS, 49-57; from asst prof to assoc prof med, Dalhousie Univ, 57-68; assoc prof med, Fac Med, Univ Toronto, 68-81; dir cardiovasc unit, Sunnybrook Hosp, 68-81; consult cardiologist, Surrey Mem Hosp, Surrey, BC, 81-83. *Concurrent Pos:* Med dir tuberc div, Halifax Tuberc Hosp & Health Ctr, 57-64; cardiologist, Halifax Children's Hosp, 57-68; dir cardiac unit, Victoria Gen Hosp, 58-68; Can Tuberc Asn traveling fel, 60; consult, NS Rehab Ctr, 60-68 & Cardiol Halifax Infirmary, 64-68. *Mem:* Am Col Cardiol; Am Thoracic Soc; Am Col Physicians; Am Col Chest Physicians. *Res:* Diseases of chest and heart; cardiovascular hemodynamics and catheterization; clinical pharmacology. *Mailing Add:* 22 Shallmar Blvd Suite 303 Toronto ON M5N 2Z8 Can

SHANEBROOK, J(OHN) RICHARD, MECHANICAL ENGINEERING. *Current Pos:* From asst prof to assoc prof, 65-75, dept chmn, 74-79, PROF MECH ENG, UNION COL, NY, 75- *Personal Data:* b Syracuse, NY, July 10, 38; m 67, Joan F Eisler; c Jill F & Julie M. *Educ:* Syracuse Univ, BME, 60, MME, 63, PhD(mech eng), 65. *Concurrent Pos:* NSF res grants, 67-72; Eng Found Res grant, 73-75, Cardiac Eng res grants, 75-81, Sloan Found, 83-88, R A Smith res grants, 89- *Mem:* Am Soc Mech Engrs; Union Concerned Scientists; Soc Eng Sci Inc. *Res:* Theoretical analysis of viscous flow fields, both laminar and turbulent; fluid dynamics of artificial heart valves, blood pumps, bypass grafts, and biomedical catheters; energy conservation; societal issues related to nuclear technology; technological literacy for undergraduate liberal arts students. *Mailing Add:* Dept Mech Eng Steinmetz Hall Union Col Schenectady NY 12308. *E-Mail:* shanebrr@union.edu

SHANEFIELD, DANIEL J, ORGANIC CHEMICAL ADDITIVES FOR CERAMICS. *Current Pos:* DISTINGUISHED PROF, CERAMICS ENG DEPT, RUTGERS UNIV, 86- *Personal Data:* b Orange, NJ, Apr 29, 30; m 64, Elizabeth Davis; c Douglas & Alison. *Educ:* Rutgers Univ, BS, 56, PhD(phys chem). 62. *Prof Exp:* Sr tech specialist phys chem, ITT Fed Labs, 62-67; sr res chemist, AT&T Corp, 67-86. *Concurrent Pos:* Assoc ed, J Am Ceramic Soc, 86-; pres, PCA Co, Princeton, NJ, 92- *Mem:* Am Chem Soc; fel Am Inst Chemists; fel Am Ceramic Soc. *Res:* Integrated circuit packaging; ceramic tape casting; additives for ceramics. *Mailing Add:* Rutgers Univ Ceramics Engr Dept PO Box 909 Piscataway NJ 08855. *Fax:* 732-932-3258; *E-Mail:* shanefie@rci.rutgers.edu

SHANER, GREGORY ELLIS, PLANT PATHOLOGY. *Current Pos:* From asst prof to assoc prof, 68-81, head dir grad prog, bot & plant path, 82-87, PROF PLANT PATH, PURDUE UNIV, WEST LAFAYETTE, 81- *Personal Data:* b Portland, Ore, Dec 19, 42; m 64; c 2. *Educ:* Ore State Univ, BS, 64, PhD(plant path), 68. *Concurrent Pos:* Sr ed, Phytopath, 82-84, editor-in-chief, 85-87. *Mem:* Fel Am Phytopath Soc; Crop Sci Soc Am; Am Soc Agron; Soc Econ Bot; Sigma Xi. *Res:* Plant disease epidemiology; development of improved varieties of wheat and oats; nature and genetics of disease resistance in small grains. *Mailing Add:* Dept Bot & Plant Path Purdue Univ 1155 Lilly Hall West Lafayette IN 47907-1155

SHANER, JOHN WESLEY, HIGH PRESSURE PHYSICS, VERY HIGH TEMPERATURE DENSE FLUIDS. *Current Pos:* GROUP LEADER, SHOCKWAVE PHYSICS, LOS ALAMOS NAT LAB, 78- *Personal Data:* b Arlington, MA, June 3, 42; m 66; c 3. *Educ:* Mass Inst Technol, BS, 64; Univ Calif, Berkeley, PhD(physics), 69. *Prof Exp:* Assoc instr physics, Univ Utah Physics Dept, 70-72; group leader exp physics, Lawrence Livermore Lab, 72-78. *Mem:* Fel Am Phys Soc; Int Org High Pressure Sci & Technol (treas, 85-88). *Res:* Physics of materials at very high pressures and or very high temperatures; shock wave physics of explosives and inert materials; dense, non-ideal plasma physics. *Mailing Add:* 155 Piedra Loop Los Alamos NM 87544

SHANEYFELT, DUANE L, polymer chemistry, applied chemistry, for more information see previous edition

SHANFIELD, HENRY, PHYSICAL CHEMISTRY, CHEMICAL ENGINEERING. *Current Pos:* ASSOC PROF CHEM, UNIV HOUSTON, 74- *Personal Data:* b Toronto, Ont, May 17, 23; US citizen; m 50; c 2. *Educ:* Univ Toronto, BASc, 46, MASc, 57, PhD(phys chem, chem eng). 51. *Prof Exp:* Sr res scientist, Nat Res Coun Can, 47-48; res engr, Esso Eng & Res Ctr, Standard Oil Co, 51-53; asst dir res, Paper-Mate Mfg Div, Gillette Co, 53-58; mgr chem lab, Aeronutronic Div, Philco-Ford Corp, Newport Beach, 58-68; dir res & eng, Polymetrics, Inc, 68-71; dir eng, Foremost Water Systs, 71; mgr water systs, KMS Technol Ctr, 71-74. *Mem:* AAAS; Am Chem Soc; Am Inst Aeronaut & Astronaut; Combustion Inst; Sigma Xi. *Res:* Chemical kinetics; thermodynamics; electrochemistry; membrane transport phenomena; thin layer chromatography; semipermeable membranes. *Mailing Add:* 944 Omar St Houston TX 77009

SHANGGUAN, DONGKAI, METAL JOINING, MATERIALS PROCESSING. *Current Pos:* mfg engr, 91-94, TECH SPECIALIST, FORD MOTOR CO, 91- *Personal Data:* b Henan Prov, China, Dec 12, 63; US citizen; m 86, Guilian Gao; c George & Henry. *Educ:* Tsinghua Univ, China, BSc, 84; Univ Oxford, DPhil(metall & sci mats), 89. *Prof Exp:* Res fel, Univ Ala, 89-91. *Concurrent Pos:* Vis fel, Univ Cambridge, 89. *Mem:* Sr mem Soc Mfg Engrs; Am Soc Metals; Soc Automotive Engrs. *Res:* Crystal growth, solidification, metal casting and joining, electronic packaging technology and reliability; computer modeling of microstructural evolution during phase transformations, metal matrix composites, metal corrosion and protection, materials analysis and characterization; development of new materials and processing technologies. *Mailing Add:* 25400 Anthony Dr Novi MI 48375

SHANGGUAN, HANQUN, LIGHT DELIVERY & OPTICAL DIAGNOSIS, LASER-INDUCED CAVITATION BUBBLE DYNAMICS. *Current Pos:* res asst, 91-96, POST-DOCTORAL FEL, ORE MED LASER CTR, 96- *Personal Data:* b Jilin, China, Aug 15, 58; m, Zhenghong Zhu; c Shirley & Julia. *Educ:* Wuhan Inst Surv & Mapping, BEng, 82; Portland State Univ, MS, 93, PhD(elec & comput eng), 96. *Prof Exp:* Engr, China Nuclear Instruments & Equip Co, 82-90. *Mem:* Optical Soc Am; Int Soc OpticalEng; Biomed Optics Soc. *Res:* Laser-tissue interaction; laser-induced cavitation; light delivery; optical diagnosis using laser-induced fluorescence tissue weld using infrared pulsed diode laser. *Mailing Add:* Ore Med Laser Ctr 9205 SW Barnes Rd Portland OR 97225. *Fax:* 503-216-2422; *E-Mail:* hanquan@ee.pdx.edu

SHANGRAW, RALPH F, INDUSTRIAL PHARMACY. *Current Pos:* From asst prof to assoc prof, 58-70, PROF PHARMACEUT DEPT, SCH PHARM, UNIV MD, BALTIMORE, 70-, CHMN DEPT PHARMACEUT, 71- *Personal Data:* b Rutland, Vt, June 11, 30; m 55; c 3. *Educ:* Mass Col Pharm, BS, 52, MS, 54; Univ Mich, PhD(pharmaceut chem), 58. *Concurrent Pos:* Mem, XIX, XX, XI, XXII, XXIII, Comt, US Pharmacopeia, 70-95; distinguished scientist, Am Asn Pharmaceut Sci. *Mem:* Am Pharmaceut Asn; fel Acad Pharmaceut Sci; Soc Cosmetic Chemists; Am Asn Cols Pharm; fel Am Asn Pharmaceut Scientists. *Res:* Direct tablet compression; pharmaceutical excipients; nitroglycerin formulation; vitamins and nutritional supplements. *Mailing Add:* 1313 Biddle Ct Baltimore MD 21228

SHANHOLTZ, VERNON ODELL, AGRICULTURAL ENGINEERING. *Current Pos:* res instr, 66-70, asst prof, 70-78, ASSOC PROF SOIL & WATER CONSERV, VA POLYTECH INST & STATE UNIV, 78- *Personal Data:* b Slanesville, WVa, Apr 22, 35; m 65; c 2. *Educ:* WVa Univ, BS, 58, MS, 63; Va Polytech Inst & State Univ, PhD(civil eng), 70. *Prof Exp:* Hydraul engr, Agr Res Serv, 58-66. *Mem:* Am Geophys Union; Am Soc Agr Engrs; Soil & Water Conserv Soc Am; Sigma Xi. *Res:* Modeling agricultural watershed systems. *Mailing Add:* 300 Dogwood Lane Christiansburg VA 24073

SHANHOLTZER, WESLEY LEE, SOLID STATE PHYSICS. *Current Pos:* From asst prof to assoc prof, 66-82, PROF PHYSICS, MARSHALL UNIV, 82- *Personal Data:* b Cumberland, Md, Jan 25, 38; m 66, Karen McDiffett; c Geneva & Holly. *Educ:* WVa Univ, BS, 62, MS, 64, PhD(physics), 68. *Mem:* Sigma Xi; Am Asn Physics Teachers. *Res:* Electron spin resonance studies of conduction electrons paramagnetic susceptibility in lithium metal; electron spin resonance of doped semiconductor crystals. *Mailing Add:* 2160 Donald Ave Huntington WV 25701

SHANK, BRENDA MAE BUCKHOLD, CELL PHYSIOLOGY. *Current Pos:* CHMN & PROF RADIATION ONCOL, MT SINAI SCH MED, 89-, DIR RADIATION ONCOL, MT SINAI HOSP, 89- *Personal Data:* b Cleveland, Ohio, Sept 25, 39; m 69. *Educ:* Western Res Univ, BA, 61, PhD(biophys), 66; Rutgers Med Sch, MD, 76. *Prof Exp:* Res biophysicist, Lawrence Radiation Lab, Univ Calif, 66-68, NIH fel biophys, Donner Lab Med Physics, 68-69; asst prof radiol, Case Western Reserve Univ, 69; asst prof physiol, Rutgers Med Sch, 69-74; res & fel, Mem Sloan-Kettering Cancer Ctr, 76-80, asst attend, Mem Hosp, 80-85, assoc attend & assoc mem, 85-89; assoc prof Radiation Oncol Med, Cornell Univ Med Sch, 85-89. *Mem:* AAAS; NY Acad Sci; Radiol Soc NAm; Radiation Res Soc; Am Soc Therapeut Radiol & Oncol; Am Soc Clin Oncol. *Res:* Osmotic adaptation in tissue-culture cells; flour beetle, tribolium confusum, regarding effects of radiation and weightlessness in biosatellite; electronic counting of erythrocytes; membrane properties and growth control of cultured cells; radiation kinetics; total body irradiation for marrow transplantation. *Mailing Add:* Mt Sinai Med Ctr 1 Gustave Levy Place Box 1236 New York NY 10029

SHANK, CHARLES PHILIP, POLYMER CHEMISTRY. *Current Pos:* AT DREXEL-HYSOL. *Personal Data:* b Pittsburgh, Pa, Feb 6, 41; m 63; c 4. *Educ:* Univ Dayton, BS, 63, MS, 65; Univ Akron, PhD(polymer sci), 68. *Prof Exp:* Res chemist, NCR Corp, 68-73; DEVELOP CHEMIST, PLASTICS DIV, GEN ELEC CO, 73- *Mem:* Am Chem Soc. *Res:* Characterizations and use of polymers and copolymers, particularly impact modification of polymers and copolymer sequence distribution and its effect on properties. *Mailing Add:* Mallinckrodt Inc PO Box 5439 St Louis MO 63147

SHANK, CHARLES VERNON, ELECTRICAL ENGINEERING. *Current Pos:* DIR, LAWRENCE BERKELEY LAB, 89- *Personal Data:* b Mt Holly, NJ, July 12, 43. *Educ:* Univ Calif, Berkeley, BS, 65, MS, 66, PhD(elec eng), 69. *Prof Exp:* Mem tech staff, AT&T Bell Labs, 69-83, dir, Electronics Res Lab, 83-89. *Mem:* Nat Acad Sci; Nat Acad Eng. *Res:* Quantum electronics. *Mailing Add:* Bldg 50A Rm 4133 Cyclotron Rd Berkeley CA 94720. *Fax:* 510-486-6720; *E-Mail:* cvshank@lbl.gov

SHANK, FRED R, FOOD SCIENCE, NUTRITION. *Current Pos:* dep dir, div nutrit, 78-79, dep dir, off nutrit & food Sci, 79-86, DIR, OFF PHYS SCI, CTR FOOD SAFETY & APPL NUTRIT, FOOD & DRUG ADMIN, WASHINGTON, DC, 86- *Personal Data:* b Harrisonburg, Va, Oct 11, 40; m 67; c 2. *Educ:* Univ Ky, BS, 62, MS, 64; Univ Md, PhD(nutrit), 69. *Prof Exp:* Res asst nutrit, Univ Ky, 62-64 & Univ Md, 64-68; biomed lab officer, USAF, Brooks AFB, San Antonio, Tex, 68-70, proj officer, Dietary Info Serv, Air Force Data Systs Design Ctr, Washington, DC, 70-71; nutritionist, Food & Nutrit Serv, US Dept Agr, Washington, DC, 71-74, chief, eval & tech serv br, Nutrit & Tech Serv Staff, 74-78. *Mem:* AAAS; Am Asn Cereal Chemists; Am Inst Nutrit; Am Soc Clin Nutrit; Inst Food Technologists; Sigma Xi. *Res:* Nutrient sufficiency, nutrient toxicity, assessment of nutritional status; effects of nutritional status, food consumption and food processing on human performance and disease. *Mailing Add:* HFS-1 Ctr Food Safety & Appl Nutrit FDA 200 C St SW Washington DC 20204-0001

SHANK, HERBERT S, MATHEMATICS. *Current Pos:* RETIRED. *Personal Data:* b Orange, NJ, Sept 25, 27. *Educ:* Univ Chicago, BA, 49, MS, 52; Cornell Univ, PhD, 69. *Prof Exp:* Mathematician, Inst Syst Res, Univ Chicago, 54-59 & Labs Appl Sci, 59-65; mem prof staff, Ctr Naval Anal, 65-68; res assoc, Cornell Univ, 68-70; nat res coun fel, Univ Waterloo, 70-71, prof math, 71-78; assoc prof, Univ Mass, Boston, 83-84; prof, Calif State Univ, Hayward, 89. *Concurrent Pos:* Instr, Ill Inst Technol, 57-58; vis prof, Univ Newcastle, NWS, 74 & Queen's Univ, 81, 84-85 & 88; vis scientist, Cornell Univ, 81-82; consult, Loyola Univ, Chicago, 88. *Mem:* Am Math Soc; Math Asn Am; fel Inst Combinatories & its applications. *Res:* Graph theory; combinatorial mathematics; operations research; electrical network theory. *Mailing Add:* 73 Port Watson St Cortland WY 13045

SHANK, KENNETH EUGENE, radiological & environmental health, for more information see previous edition

SHANK, LOWELL WILLIAM, FORENSIC CHEMISTRY. *Current Pos:* From asst prof to assoc prof, 66-82, dept head, 85-90, PROF ANALYTICAL CHEM, WESTERN KY UNIV, 82-, DEPT HEAD, 95- *Personal Data:* b Hagerstown, Md, June 28, 39; m 63, Sharyn; c Jennifer & Kimberly. *Educ:* Goshen Col, BS, 61; Ohio State Univ, MSc, 64, PhD(anal chem), 66. *Mem:* Am Chem Soc; Sigma Xi. *Res:* Chemical education. *Mailing Add:* Dept Chem Western Ky Univ Bowling Green KY 42101. *Fax:* 502-745-5361; *E-Mail:* lowell.shank@wku.edu

SHANK, MAURICE E(DWIN), AERONAUTICAL PROPULSION, MECHANICAL ENGINEERING. *Current Pos:* RETIRED. *Personal Data:* b New York, NY, Apr 22, 21; m 48; c 3. *Educ:* Carnegie Inst Technol, BS, 42; Mass Inst Technol, ScD, 49. *Prof Exp:* Instr metall, Mass Inst Technol, 46-49, from asst prof to assoc prof mech eng, 49-60; dir advan mat, Pratt & Whitney, 60-70, mgr mat eng & res, 70-71, dir eng technol, Com Prods Div, Pratt & Whitney Aircraft Group, United Technologies Corp, 72-85, vpres, 85-87, aerospace consult, Pratt & Whitney of China, Inc, 87-92; independent consult, 87-95. *Concurrent Pos:* Consult ed, McGraw-Hill Bk Co; mem, Comt Res, NSF, 74-77; mem bd, Aeronaut & Space Eng, 89- *Mem:* Nat Acad Eng; fel Am Soc Mech Engrs; fel Am Inst Mining, Metall & Petrol Engrs; fel Am Soc Metals; fel Am Inst Aeronaut & Astronaut. *Res:* Advancing state-of-the-art technology in engine aerodynamic components; noise and emission reduction; fuel systems and controls; materials and structures to assure competitive engine performance weight and cost. *Mailing Add:* 10020 A Main St No 246 Bellevue WA 98004

SHANK, PETER R, VIROLOGY. *Current Pos:* from asst prof to assoc prof, 78-92, PROF MED SCI, BROWN UNIV, 92-, ASSOC DEAN MED & BIOL SCI RES, 93- *Personal Data:* b Ithaca, NY, Feb 17, 46; m 70, Kathleen Ryan; c Jonathan & Jeffrey. *Educ:* Cornell Univ, BS, 68; Univ NC, Chapel Hill, PhD(virol), 73. *Hon Degrees:* MA, Brown Univ, 83. *Prof Exp:* Fel, Univ Calif, San Francisco, 73-78. *Concurrent Pos:* Vis scientist, Lab Molecular Virol, Nat Cancer Inst, NIH, 86-87. *Mem:* Am Soc Microbiol; AAAS; Am Soc Virol. *Res:* Molecular biology of human immunodeficiency virus. *Mailing Add:* Div Biol & Med Brown Univ Providence RI 02912. *Fax:* 401-863-7411; *E-Mail:* peter_shank@brown.edu

SHANK, RICHARD PAUL, NEUROCHEMISTRY, NEUROBIOLOGY. *Current Pos:* FEL BIOL RES, JANSSEN RES FOUND, 87- *Personal Data:* b Indianapolis, Ind, July 29, 41; m 67; c 1. *Prof Exp:* Res physiologist, Vet Admin, 70-72; res trainee chem, Ind Univ, 72-74, res assoc, 74-75; asst prof, Sch Med, Temple Univ, 75-79; sr scientist, Franklin Inst, Philadelphia, Pa, 79-81 & Grad Hosp, 81-82; prin scientist, 82-86, res fel chem, McNeil Pharmaceut, 86-87. *Concurrent Pos:* Adj asst prof, Thomas Jefferson Med Col, 82-; adj assoc prof, Sch Med, Temple Univ, 82- *Mem:* Am Physiol Soc; Soc Neurosci; Am Soc Neurochem; Int Soc Neurochem. *Res:* Neurochemistry of amino acids; neurotransmitter receptors; antidepressants and their mechanisms of action; modulation of synaptic transmission. *Mailing Add:* RW Johnson Pharmaceut Res Inst Spring House PA 19477-0776. *Fax:* 215-628-3297

SHANK, ROBERT ELY, NUTRITION. *Current Pos:* Danforth prof & head dept, 48-83, EMER PROF PREV MED, SCH MED, WASHINGTON UNIV, 83- *Personal Data:* b Louisville, Ky, Sept 2, 14; m 42, Eleanor Caswell; c Jane, Robert & Bruce. *Educ:* Westminster Col, Mo, AB, 35; Washington Univ, MD, 39. *Honors & Awards:* Distinguished Serv Award, Am Heart Asn, 80. *Prof Exp:* From intern to house physician, Barnes Hosp, Mo, 39-41; resident physician, St Louis Isolation Hosp, 41; asst resident physician & asst, Rockefeller Inst Hosp, 41-46; assoc mem, Pub Health Res Inst, New York,

46-48. *Concurrent Pos:* With nutrit surv, Nfld, 48-; spec consult, USPHS, 49-53; mem food & nutrit bd, Nat Res Coun, 50-71; mem adv comt metab, Surgeon Gen, US Dept Army, 56-60 & adv comt nutrit, 60-72; mem sci adv comt, Nat Vitamin Found, 58-61; mem human ecol study sect, NIH, 59-63 & nutrit study sect, 64-68; mem prof adv comt, Nat Found, 61-62 & Nat Adv Coun Child Health & Human Develop, 69-73; mem, Clin Appln & Prev Adv Comt, Nat Heart, Lung & Blood Inst, 76-80. *Mem:* Am Soc Biol Chemists; Am Soc Clin Invest; Soc Exp Biol & Med; Asn Am Physicians; fel Am Inst Nutrit; Am Soc Study Liver Dis. *Res:* Metabolism of progressive muscular dystrophy; cirrhosis of the liver; infectious hepatitis and homologous serum jaundice; appraisal of nutritional status; iron deficiency; relationship between nutrients and hormonal function; Hepatitis B. *Mailing Add:* 1325 Wilton Lane Kirkwood MO 63122-6940

SHANKAR, HARI, MATHEMATICAL MODELING, HARMONIC FUNCTIONS. *Current Pos:* PROF MATH, OHIO UNIV, 63- *Personal Data:* b Aligarh, India, Nov 10, 30. *Educ:* Aligarh Muslam Univ, MS, 56; Univ Cincinatti, MS, 63. *Mem:* Math Asn Am. *Res:* Growth properties, entire functions, harmonic functions & analytical functions. *Mailing Add:* Dept Math Ohio Univ Athens OH 45701-2979

SHANKAR, RAMAMURTI, PHYSICS. *Current Pos:* JW Gibbs instr, 77-79, from asst prof to assoc prof, 79-86, PROF, PHYSICS, YALE UNIV, 86- *Personal Data:* b New Delhi, India, Apr 28, 47; US citizen; m 76; c 4. *Educ:* Indian Inst Sci, BTech, 69; Univ Calif, Berkeley, PhD(theoret phys), 74. *Prof Exp:* Jr fel, Harvard Soc fellows, 74-77. *Res:* Common problems in statistical mechanics and quantum field theory, statistical mechanics of homogeneous and random systems. *Mailing Add:* 55 Sloan Physics Labs Yale Univ New Haven CT 06511. *Fax:* 203-432-6175

SHANKAR, VIJAYA V, AERONAUTICAL & ASTRONAUTICAL ENGINEERING. *Current Pos:* DIR, ROCKWELL INT CORP SCI CTR, THOUSAND OAKS, CALIF. *Honors & Awards:* Hugh L Dryden Res Lectr, Am Inst Aeronaut & Astronaut, 91. *Mailing Add:* Rockwell Int Corp-Sci Ctr PO Box 1085 1049 Camino Dos Rios Thousand Oaks CA 91360-2362

SHANKEL, DELBERT MERRILL, MICROBIAL GENETICS, ANTIMUTAGENUIS & ANTICARCINOGENESIS. *Current Pos:* from asst prof to prof bact, Univ Kans, 59-96, from assoc dean to actg dean arts & sci, 69-74, exec vchancellor, 74-80 & 90-92, actg chancellor, 80-81, prof microbiol & spec counr to chancellor, 81-96, chancellor, 94-95, EMER PROF & EMER CHANCELLOR, UNIV KANS, 96- *Personal Data:* b Plainview, Nebr, Aug 4, 27; m 58, Carol J Mulford; c Merrill, Jill & Kelley. *Educ:* Walla Walla Col, BA, 50; Univ Tex, PhD(bact), 60. *Prof Exp:* Instr sci & math, Walla Walla Col, 50-51; instr chem, San Antonio Col, 54-55; res scientist bact, Univ Tex, 56-59. *Concurrent Pos:* Consult, Cramer Chem Co, 59-96 & NCent Asn Cols & Sec Schs, 73-; NIH sr fel, Univ Edinburgh, 67-68; vis prof, Nat Inst Genetics, Japan, 88. *Mem:* AAAS; Am Soc Microbiologists; Genetics Soc Am; Radiation Res Soc; Environ Mutagen Soc; Sigma Xi. *Res:* Genetic effects of radiations and chemicals and interactions of repair processes; mutagenesis and antimutagenesis. *Mailing Add:* Dept Microbiol Univ Kans Lawrence KS 66045. *Fax:* 785-864-4120

SHANKEY, T VINCENT, GENERIC EVOLUTION IN BLADDER & PROSTATE CANCERS, FLOW & IMAGE CYTOMETRY. *Current Pos:* ASST & ASSOC PROF UROL & PATH & DIR UROL RES, LOYOLA UNIV MED CTR, 86- *Personal Data:* b Nyack, NY, Jan 15, 47. *Educ:* Univ Dayton, Ohio, BS, 69, MS, 71; Univ Fla, PhD(immunol & med micro), 77. *Prof Exp:* Postdoctoral res fel, Univ Pa, 77-81; asst prof path, Pa State Univ Med Ctr, 81-83; sr res scientist, Life Sci Group, Allied Corp, 83-86. *Res:* Understanding genetic and phenotypic changes that occur during the evolution of bladder and prostate cancers with the aim of developing diagnostic markers to aid prognostic and therapeutic decisions; studies of genetic and phenotypic heterogeneity in human cancers using single quantitative analytical techniques to determine which changes are biologically and clinically important. *Mailing Add:* Dept Urol Loyola Univ Med Ctr 2160 S First Ave Maywood IL 60153-5594. *Fax:* 708-216-6585; *E-Mail:* tshanke@luc.edu

SHANKLAND, DANIEL LESLIE, NEUROPHYSIOLOGY, TOXICOLOGY. *Current Pos:* RETIRED. *Personal Data:* b San Diego, Calif, June 18, 24; m 55; c 3. *Educ:* Colo State Univ, BS, 48; Univ Ill, MS, 52, PhD(entom), 56. *Prof Exp:* Salesman, Stauffer Chem Co, 52 & Farm Air Serv, 52-54; res rep, Stauffer Chem Co, 55-57; prof entom, Purdue Univ, West Lafayette, 57-76; prof entom & head dept, Miss State Univ, 76-80; prof entom & head dept, Univ Fla, 80-86, dir, Ctr Environ Toxicol, 86-89. *Mem:* AAAS; Entom Soc Am; Sigma Xi. *Res:* Physiology; neurophysiology, especially neurotoxic action of insecticides. *Mailing Add:* 778 Gunsmoke Dr Bailey CO 80421-1013

SHANKLAND, RODNEY VEEDER, organic chemistry; deceased, see previous edition for last biography

SHANKLE, ROBERT JACK, DENTISTRY. *Current Pos:* from assoc prof to prof oper dent, 51-66, dir admis, 64-75, prof endodont & chmn dept, 66-84, EMER PROF ENDODONT, SCH DENT, UNIV NC, CHAPEL HILL, 84- *Personal Data:* b Ga, Sept 17, 23; m 52; c 2. *Educ:* Emory Univ, DDS, 48; Am Bd Endodontics, dipl. *Prof Exp:* Instr crown & bridge prothodont, Sch Dent, Emory Univ, 49-51. *Concurrent Pos:* Consult, Womack Army Hosp, Ft Knox, Ky, Ft Benning, Ga & Ft Dix, NJ; ed, NC Dent J, 72-77; dir pub rels & develop, 75- *Mem:* Am Dent Asn; fel Am Asn Endodont; fel Am Col Dent; fel Int Col Dent; fel Acad Gen Dent; fel Acad Dent Int. *Res:* Endodontics. *Mailing Add:* 104 Fox Ridge Rd Chapel Hill NC 27514

SHANKLIN, JAMES ROBERT, JR, SYNTHETIC ORGANIC CHEMISTRY, MEDICINAL CHEMISTRY. *Current Pos:* sr res chemist, 73-80, GROUP MGR CARDIOVASC SYNTHESIS, A H ROBINS CO, 80- *Personal Data:* b Bluefield, WVa, Dec 28, 41; m 66; c 2. *Educ:* Yale Univ, BA, 64; Univ Va, PhD(chem), 72. *Prof Exp:* Teacher, Va Episcopal Sch, 64-66; fel, Wayne State Univ, 71-73. *Concurrent Pos:* Adj fac mem, Va Commonwealth Univ, 73- *Mem:* Am Chem Soc; Sigma Xi. *Res:* Organosulfur chemistry; heterocyclic chemistry; medicinal chemistry specializing in the cardiovascular and central nervous system areas. *Mailing Add:* 7459 Hunting Lake Dr Painesville OH 44077

SHANKS, CARL HARMON, JR, ENTOMOLOGY. *Current Pos:* ENTOMOLOGIST, WASH STATE UNIV, 59-, SUPT, SOUTHWESTERN WASH RES UNIT, 80- *Personal Data:* b Martinsville, Ohio, May 20, 32; m 55; c 3. *Educ:* Wilmington Col, BS, 54; Ohio State Univ, MSc, 55; Univ Wis, PhD(entom), 60. *Mem:* Entom Soc Am. *Res:* Biology and control of arthropod pests of small fruits and vegetables; plant resistance to insects and mites; biological control of weeds. *Mailing Add:* 106 N Nashville Way Vancouver WA 98664

SHANKS, JAMES BATES, HORTICULTURE. *Current Pos:* RETIRED. *Personal Data:* b Steubenville, Ohio, June 17, 17; m 43, 74; c 3. *Educ:* Ohio State Univ, PhD, 49. *Prof Exp:* From assoc prof to emer prof hort, Univ Md, Col Park, 49-88. *Mem:* Fel Am Soc Hort Sci; Plant Growth Regulator Soc Am. *Res:* Greenhouse flowering crops. *Mailing Add:* 11340 Frances Dr Beltsville MD 20705

SHANKS, JAMES CLEMENTS, JR, SPEECH PATHOLOGY. *Current Pos:* SCH DENT, IND UNIV, INDIANAPOLIS, IND, 67- *Personal Data:* b Detroit, Mich, Oct 15, 21; m 50; c 3. *Educ:* Mich State Univ, BA, 43; Univ Denver, MA, 49; Northwestern Univ, PhD(speech path), 57. *Prof Exp:* Instr speech, Iowa State Teachers Col, 49-50; asst prof speech path, Syracuse Univ, 52-55; from asst prof to prof speech path & clin dir speech path serv, Sch Med, Ind Univ, Indianapolis, 55-88. *Concurrent Pos:* Consult, New Castle State Hosp, 59. *Mem:* Am Speech & Hearing Asn; Am Cleft Palate Asn. *Res:* Speech disorders involving function of the larynx and valum manifested as deviations of voice quality and vocal resonance. *Mailing Add:* 7501 Sommerset Bay Apt B Indianapolis IN 46240

SHANKS, ROGER D, DAIRY CATTLE BREEDING. *Current Pos:* From asst prof to assoc prof, 79-92, PROF GENETICS, UNIV ILL, 92- *Personal Data:* b Libertyville, Ill, May 30, 51; m 71, Wendy Jones; c Anna & Dea. *Educ:* Univ Ill, BS, 74; Iowa State Univ, MS, 77, PhD(animal sci), 79. *Honors & Awards:* Agway Inc Young Scientist Award in Dairy Prod, Am Dairy Sci Asn, 84. *Mem:* Am Soc Animal Sci; Am Dairy Sci Asn; Am Genetic Asn; Biomet Soc; Genetics Soc Am; AAAS. *Res:* Genetic and economic aspects of dairy cattle improvement programs including evaluation, selection, and mating designs; investigation of genetic abnormalities including deficiency of uridine monophosphate synthase, atresia coli and citrullinemia. *Mailing Add:* Dept Animal Sci 308 Animal Sci Lab Univ Ill 1207 W Gregory Dr Urbana IL 61801. *E-Mail:* r-shanks@uiuc.edu

SHANKS, SUSAN JANE, SPEECH LANGUAGE PATHOLOGY. *Current Pos:* RETIRED. *Personal Data:* b Toledo, Ohio. *Educ:* Univ Toledo, BEd, 57; Bowling Green State Univ, MA, 60; La State Univ, PhD(speech path), 66. *Prof Exp:* Teacher, St Pius X Sch, 57-58; grad asst speech pathologist, Bowling State Univ, 58-59; speech pathologist, Samuel Gompers Rehab Ctr, 60-63; asst prof, Univ SFla, 67-68 & Stephen F Austin State Univ, 68-70; prof speech path, Calif State Univ, Fresno, 70-94. *Mem:* Am Speech & Hearing Asn. *Res:* Voice disorders; language disorders in children and adults. *Mailing Add:* 5330 N Colonial No 101 Fresno CA 93704

SHANKS, WAYNE C, III, GEOCHEMISTRY. *Current Pos:* geologist, Reston, Va, 82-91, GEOLOGIST, US GEOL SURV, LAKEWOOD, COLO, 91- *Personal Data:* b Detroit, Mich, Aug 26, 47; m 70; c 2. *Educ:* Mich State Univ, BS, 69; La State Univ, MS, 71; Univ Southern Calif, PhD(geol), 76. *Prof Exp:* Teaching asst geol, La State Univ, 70-71; res asst, Univ Southern Calif, 71-75; asst prof geol, Univ Calif, Davis, 75-77; from asst prof Geol & Geophys, 77-80, to assoc prof Geol & Geophys, Univ Wis, Madison, 80-82. *Concurrent Pos:* Instr geol, Pierce Col, Calif, 73-75; NSF traineeship, 74. *Mem:* Sigma Xi; Soc Econ Geol; Geochem Soc; Am, Geophys Union. *Res:* Geochemistry of submarine hydrothermal and geothermal ore fluids; origin of ore deposits and stable isotope geochemistry. *Mailing Add:* US Geol Surv PO Box 25046 MS 973 Lakewood CO 80225

SHANLEY, MARK STEPHEN, MICROBIAL PHYSIOLOGY, METABOLIC REGULATION. *Current Pos:* PROF, UNIV N TEX, 87- *Personal Data:* b San Antonio, Tex, Oct 22, 54; m 93, Cobra Smithey; c Ryan A & Nina P. *Educ:* Tex A&M Univ, BS, 77, PhD(biochem), 83. *Prof Exp:* Fel, Yale Univ, 83-86; prof, Southern Methodist Univ, 86-87. *Mem:* Am Soc Microbiol; Sigma Xi. *Res:* Examine the structural basis for the regulation of gene expression in bacteria, especially those microorganisms responsible for the degradation of toxic xenobiotic compounds. *Mailing Add:* Univ NTex PO Box 5218 Denton TX 76203-0218. *Fax:* 817-565-3821; *E-Mail:* quip@sol.acs.unt.edu

SHANMUGAM, KEELNATHAM THIRUNAVUKKARASU, BACTERIAL PHYSIOLOGY, HYDROGEN METABOLISM. *Current Pos:* asst res scientist, 80-81, assoc prof, 81-89, PROF MICROBIOL, UNIV FLA, 89- *Personal Data:* b Keelnatham, India, Oct 15, 41; m 72; c 1. *Educ:*

Annamalai Univ, India, BSc, 63; UP Agr Univ, India, MSc, 65; Univ Hawaii, PhD(microbiol), 69. *Prof Exp:* Assoc res microbiologist cell physiol, Univ Calif, Berkeley, 69-71; asst prof biol, Birla Inst Technol & Sci, India, 71-72; res chemist biochem, Univ Calif, San Diego, 73-75, asst res agronomist microbiol, Davis, 76-80. *Mem:* Am Soc Microbiol. *Res:* Study of the mechanism of regulation of anaerobic processes using hydrogen metabolism in Escherichia coli as a model system; genetic alteration of nitrogen-fixing cyanobacteria for solar energy conversion to hydrogen and ammonia. *Mailing Add:* Dept Microbiol & Cell Sci Univ Fla Box 110700 Gainesville FL 32611

SHANMUGAN, K SAM, COMMUNICATION SYSTEMS, SIGNAL PROCESSING. *Current Pos:* PROF ELEC ENG, UNIV KANS, 80- *Personal Data:* b India, Jan 6, 43; US citizen; m 68; c 2. *Educ:* Madras Univ, India, BE, 64; Indian Inst Sci, ME, 66; Okla State Univ, PhD(elec eng), 70. *Prof Exp:* Res assoc elec eng, Okla State Univ, 70-71 & Univ Kans, 71-73; assoc prof, Wichita State Univ, 73-78; mem tech staff, Bell Labs, NJ, 78-80. *Concurrent Pos:* Consult, Boeing Aircraft, Wichita, 74-75, United Telephone, 80, Tex Instruments, 83-84, Hughes Aircraft, 83-84 & TRW, 85-; assoc dir, Image Processing Lab, Univ Kans, 80-83, dir, Telecommunications Lab, 83- *Mem:* Inst Elec & Electronics Engrs. *Res:* Image processing; general systems theory; modeling and analysis of communication systems. *Mailing Add:* 4412 Turnberry Dr Lawrence KS 66047

SHANNON, BARRY THOMAS, CLINICAL IMMUNOLOGY, FLOW CYTOMETRY. *Current Pos:* DIR, CLIN IMMUNOL LAB & FLOW CYTOMETRY RESOURCE CTR, COLUMBUS CHILDREN'S HOSP, 82-; CLIN ASSOC PROF IMMUNOL, DEPT PEDIAT & PATH, OHIO STATE UNIV, 83-; SCI CONSULT, ROSS LABS, 91- *Personal Data:* b Philadelphia, Pa, Nov 2, 52; m 76, Linda J Trenkamp; c Sean T, Lori M & Heather E. *Educ:* Ursinus Col, BS, 74; Pa State Univ, MS, 76; Wake Forest Univ, PhD(immunol), 80. *Prof Exp:* Fel immunol, Med Univ SC, 80-82. *Concurrent Pos:* Prin investr, Children's Hosp Res Found & Ohio State Univ Comprehensive Cancer Ctr, 89-90,; co-investr, Muscular Dystrophy Asn, 88-90, NIH, 87-92; ed, Lab Immunol Newslett, 85-89; cytometry qualification judge, Bd Registry, Am Soc Clin Path, 93-; mem, Clin Immunol Registry Comt, Am Soc Clin Path, 93- *Mem:* Asn Med Lab Immunologists; Clin Cytometry Soc; Soc Anal Cytol. *Res:* DNA analysis and oncogene expression prognostic indicator of pediatric tumors; characterization of vasoactive intestinal polypeptide receptor on leukemia lympho-blasts; clinical laboratory assays as prognrotic tools in pediatric HIV infection; isolation and cultivation of both human and murine glomerular capillary endothelial cells. *Mailing Add:* Dept Lab Med Children's Hosp 700 Children's Dr Columbus OH 43205. *Fax:* 614-722-5308

SHANNON, CLAUDE ELWOOD, APPLIED MATHEMATICS. *Current Pos:* prof elec eng, 57-78, Donner prof sci, 58-80, EMER DONNER PROF SCI, MASS INST TECHNOL, 80- *Personal Data:* b Gaylord, Mich, Apr 30, 16; m 49; c 3. *Educ:* Univ Mich, BS, 36; Mass Inst Technol, MS & PhD(math), 40. *Hon Degrees:* MSc, Yale Univ, 54; DSc, Univ Mich, 61, Pittsburgh Univ, Princeton Univ, Northwestern Univ, Univ Edinburgh, Oxford Univ, Carnegie-Mellon Univ, Tufts Univ, Univ Pa. *Honors & Awards:* Noble Award, 40; Morris Liebmann Mem Award, 49; Stuart Ballantine Medal, 55; Vanuxem Lectr, Princeton Univ, 58; Steinmetz Lectr, Univ Schenectady, 62; Medal of Hon, Inst Elec & Electronics Engrs, 66, Shannon Lectr, 73; Nat Medal Sci, 66; Chichele Lectr, Oxford Univ, 78; John Fritz Medal, 83. *Prof Exp:* Asst elec eng & math, Mass Inst Technol, 36-39; Nat Res Coun fel, Princeton Univ, 40, res mathematician, Nat Defense Res Comt, 40-41; res mathematician, Bell Tel Labs, Inc, 41-57. *Concurrent Pos:* Fel, Ctr Advan Study Behav Sci, 57-58; dir, Teledyne, Inc, 60-86; vis fel, All Souls Col, Oxford Univ, 78. *Mem:* Nat Acad Sci; Nat Acad Eng; fel Inst Elec & Electronics Engrs; Am Acad Arts & Sci; Sigma Xi; Am Math Soc; Am Philos Soc; Royal Irish Acad. *Res:* Boolean algebra and switching circuits; communication theory; mathematical cryptography; computing machines. *Mailing Add:* 5 Cambridge St Winchester MA 01890

SHANNON, FREDERICK DALE, ORGANIC CHEMISTRY, POLYMER CHEMISTRY. *Current Pos:* instr, 58-60, assoc prof, 60-62 & 64-65, dir summer sch, 71-73, acad dean, 73-85, PROF CHEM, HOUGHTON COL, 65- *Personal Data:* b Akron, Ohio, June 10, 31; m 57; c 1. *Educ:* Univ Akron, BS, 53, MS, 59, PhD(chem), 64. *Prof Exp:* Res chemist, Inst Rubber Res, Univ Akron, 53-54 & 56-58. *Mem:* Am Chem Soc; Am Sci Affil; Am Asn Higher Educ; Am Conf Acad Deans. *Res:* Cyclic dienes; cationic polymerization; molecular structure determination. *Mailing Add:* 7390 Centerville Rd Houghton NY 14744

SHANNON, IRIS R, NURSING. *Current Pos:* chmn dept & assoc prof, Rush-Presby-St Luke's Med Ctr, 66-90, ASSOC PROF, HEALTH SYST MGT, RUSH UNIV, 90- *Educ:* Fisk Univ, BSN, 48; Univ Chicago, MA, 54; Univ Ill, PhD(pub policy anal), 87. *Hon Degrees:* DPS, Elmhurst Col, 93. *Honors & Awards:* Hildrus A Poindexter Distinguished Serv Award, Am Pub Health Asn, 81. *Prof Exp:* Staff nurse, Chicago Bd Health, 48-50; instr pub health nursing, Meharry Col, 51-56; teacher nursing, Head Start Chicago, 57-66. *Concurrent Pos:* Dir nursing, Mile Square Neighborhood Health Ctr, 66-69; co-dir, Nursing Asn, Rush-Presby-St Luke's Hosp, 71-76; mem, Equal Health Opportunity Comt, Am Pub Health Asn, 69-70, Comt Nursing, Am Hosp Asn, 77-78, Nat Adv Coun Nurse Training, HEW, 78-81 & Task Force Credentialing Nursing, Am Nurses Asn, 80-83; adj fac, Sch Pub Health, Univ NC, 77- *Mem:* Inst Med-Nat Acad Sci; Am Nurses Asn; fel Am Pub Health Asn (pres, 88-89); Am Acad Nursing; fel Royal Soc Health. *Res:* Community health; author of numerous technical publications. *Mailing Add:* 3100 S King Dr Chicago IL 60616. *Fax:* 312-842-5732

SHANNON, JACK CORUM, PLANT PHYSIOLOGY. *Current Pos:* from assoc prof to prof hort, 71-87, PROF PLANT PHYSIOL, PA STATE UNIV, 87- *Personal Data:* b Halls, Tenn, Feb 27, 35; m 55, Barbara Miles; c David L & Jackie L. *Educ:* Univ Tenn, BS, 58; Univ Ill, MS, 59, PhD(plant physiol), 62. *Prof Exp:* Asst prof, Purdue Univ, 62-63; plant physiologist, Crop Res Div, Agr Res Serv, USDA, 63-71. *Concurrent Pos:* Chair, Intercol Grad Prog, Plant Physiol, Pa State Univ, 83-96. *Mem:* Am Soc Plant Physiologists; Am Soc Agron; Crop Sci Soc Am; Sigma Xi; Am Soc Hort Sci; Nat Sweet Corn Breeders Asn; Int Plant Tissue Cult Asn. *Res:* Study of sugar movement into Zea mays L kernels and the utilization of these sugars in starch biosynthesis. *Mailing Add:* 1455 Park Hills Ave State College PA 16803. *Fax:* 814-863-6139; *E-Mail:* jack_shannon@agcs.psu.edu

SHANNON, JACK DEE, METEOROLOGY. *Current Pos:* Asst meteorologist, 76-80, METEOROLOGIST, ARGONNE NAT LAB, 80-, DEP MGR ATMOSPHERIC PHYSICS PROG, 81- *Personal Data:* b McAlester, Okla, Oct 18, 43; div. *Educ:* Univ Okla, BS, 65, MS, 72, PhD(meteorol), 75. *Concurrent Pos:* Mem, Interagency Task Force on Acid Precipitation, 84-90; mem, Comt Atmospheric Chem, Am Meteorol Soc, 85-88, Joint Steering Comt Air Qual Monitoring, 86-90 & Comt Meteorol Aspects Air Pollution, 93- *Mem:* Am Meteorol Soc; Royal Meteorol Soc; AAAS; Am Geophys Union; Air Waste Mgt Asn. *Res:* Numerical modeling of regional acid deposition; objective placement of sensors; numerical modeling of regional visibility; modeling of deposition of heavy metals and pesticides. *Mailing Add:* ERD Bldg 203 Argonne Nat Lab Argonne IL 60439. *Fax:* 630-252-5498; *E-Mail:* jack_shannon@anl.gov

SHANNON, JAMES AUGUSTINE, physiology; deceased, see previous edition for last biography

SHANNON, JERRY A, JR, SCIENCE EDUCATION, BIOLOGY. *Current Pos:* assoc prof biol & conserv, 56-64, prof, 64-89, EMER PROF SCI EDUC & BIOL, STATE UNIV NY, COL ONEONTA, 89- *Personal Data:* b Meshoppen, Pa, Mar 31, 24; m 54, Collette J Lake; c Kathleen A, Maureen A (Salzer), Lizabeth A & John A. *Educ:* Pa State Teachers Col, Mansfield, BS, 48; Peabody Col, MA, 49; Cornell Univ, EdD, 57. *Prof Exp:* Supvr biol, Demonstration Sch, Vanderbilt Univ, 49-50; high sch teacher, Ind, 50-51 & NY, 51-52; instr biol & conserv, Wis State Col, Oshkosh, 53; from instr to asst prof elem sch sci, Iowa State Teachers Col, 53-56. *Concurrent Pos:* Grants, State Univ NY, plant taxon, Univ Northern Iowa, 61, NSF, Univ NC, 65, biol educ, Univ Rochester, 68, sci educ, Univ Colo, 72. *Res:* Science and environmental education; local flora. *Mailing Add:* 82 West St Oneonta NY 13820

SHANNON, ROBERT DAY, solid state chemistry, inorganic chemistry, for more information see previous edition

SHANNON, ROBERT RENNIE, OPTICAL ENGINEERING. *Current Pos:* prof, 69-92, dir, Optical Sci, 83-92, EMER PROF OPTICAL SCI, UNIV ARIZ, 92- *Personal Data:* b Mt Vernon, NY, Oct 3, 32; m 54, Helen Lang; c Betsy, Barbara, Jennifer, Amy, John & Robert Jr. *Educ:* Univ Rochester, BS, 54, MA, 57. *Honors & Awards:* Goddard Medal, Soc Photo-Optical Instrument Engrs, 81. *Prof Exp:* Staff physicist, Itek Corp, 59-62, dept mgr optical design, 62-67, dir advan tech labs, 67-69. *Concurrent Pos:* Topical ed, Optical Soc Am, 75-78. *Mem:* Nat Acad Eng; fel Soc Photo-Optical Instrument Engrs (pres, 79-80); fel Optical Soc Am (pres, 85). *Res:* Applied optics, especially lens design, image analysis, optical testing, laser application, and application of computers to engineering problems; atmospheric optics; massive optics design and fabrication. *Mailing Add:* Optical Sci Ctr Univ Ariz Tucson AZ 85721. *Fax:* 520-721-1035; *E-Mail:* shannon@ccit.arizona.edu

SHANNON, ROBERT VIRGIL, AUDITORY PSYCHOPHYSICS, SPEECH PERCEPTION BY THE BRAIN. *Current Pos:* HEAD, DEPT AUDITORY IMPLANTS & PERCEPTION, HOUSE EAR INST, 89- *Personal Data:* b Davenport, Iowa, Oct, 30, 49; m, Elaine H Minehart; c Matt. *Educ:* Univ Iowa, BA, 71; Univ Calif, San Diego, PhD(psychol), 75. *Honors & Awards:* Volta Award, Cochlear Implant Club Int, 95. *Prof Exp:* Asst prof otolaryngol res, Univ Calif, San Francisco, 82-85; coordr, Sensory Aids Lab, Boys Town Nat Res Hosp, 85-89. *Concurrent Pos:* Vis res assoc, Elec Eng Dept, Stanford Univ, 85; assoc prof otolaryngol, Creighton Med Sch, 86-89; adj assoc prof biomed eng, Univ Southern Calif, 92-; consult, Sci & Technol Comn, Henan, China, 93- *Mem:* Fel Acoust Soc Am; AAAS; Asn Res Otolaryngol; Am Auditory Soc; Am Speech Language & Hearing Asn. *Res:* Study of the neurol code for auditory perception and speech; design of prosthetic devices to restore hearing to the deaf; design of first functional implant in human brainstem; design and patent of low cost cochlear implant. *Mailing Add:* House Ear Inst 2100 W Third St Los Angeles CA 90057. *E-Mail:* shannon@hei.org

SHANNON, STANTON, SOIL CHEMISTRY. *Current Pos:* CONSULT, ROGERS BROS SEED CO, 85- *Personal Data:* b Phoenix, Ariz, Dec 28, 28; m 57; c 2. *Educ:* Univ Ariz, BS, 52, MS, 53; Univ Calif, Davis, PhD(plant physiol), 61. *Prof Exp:* Sr lab technician, Citrus Exp Sta, Dept Soils & Plant Nutrit, Univ Calif, Riverside, 56-57; res asst plant anal, Univ Calif, Davis, 57-61; from asst prof to assoc prof veg crops, NY State Col Agr, Cornell Univ, 61-85. *Mem:* Am Soc Plant Physiologists; Am Soc Hort Sci. *Res:* Post harvest physiology of vegetable crops; plant biochemistry; mineral element nutrition; cultural practices for mechanically harvested vegetables, water relations and photosynthetic efficiency. *Mailing Add:* 1413 White Rd Phelps NY 14532

SHANNON, WILBURN ALLEN, JR, MEDICAL RESEARCH, CYTOCHEMISTRY. *Current Pos:* RETIRED. *Personal Data:* b Springfield, Tenn, June 21, 41; m 64. *Educ:* Mid Tenn State Univ, BS, 64; Vanderbilt Univ, MA, 67, PhD(biol), 70. *Prof Exp:* Res assoc path, Harvard Med Sch & Mass Gen Hosp, 70-71; res assoc, Sch Med, Johns Hopkins Univ & Sinai Hosp Baltimore, 71-75; asst prof cell biol, Southwestern Med Sch, 74-83; dir, Res Morph & Cytochem Unit, Gen Med Res Serv, Vet Admin Hosp, 75-83. *Concurrent Pos:* USPHS fel, Harvard Med Sch & Mass Gen Hosp, Boston, 70-71; Nat Cancer Inst fel, Sch Med, Johns Hopkins Univ & Sinai Hosp Baltimore, 71-83. *Mem:* Am Soc Cell Biol; Electron Micros Soc Am; Histochem Soc. *Res:* Ultracytochemistry, especially development of methods and application to normal and pathological tissue studies; endocrinology; mitochondriology. *Mailing Add:* 6710 Meadowcreek Dr Dallas TX 75240-8625

SHANNON, WILLIAM MICHAEL, MICROBIOLOGY. *Current Pos:* res virologist, 69-71, sr virologist, 72-74, HEAD MICROBIOL, VIROL DIV, SOUTHERN RES INST, 75- *Personal Data:* b Mt Holly, NJ, Oct 11, 40; m 64; c 3. *Educ:* Univ Ala, Tuscaloosa, BS, 62; Loyola Univ, La, MS, 65; Tulane Univ, PhD(microbiol), 69. *Prof Exp:* Radioisotope res technician, Vet Admin Hosp, Birmingham, Ala, 62-63; res asst endocrinol, Med Units, Univ Tenn, Memphis, 63-64; res asst virol, Loyola Univ, La, 64-65; res asst, Sch Med, Tulane Univ, 64-66, NASA fel, 66-69. *Mem:* AAAS; Am Soc Microbiol; NY Acad Sci; Am Asn Cancer Res; Brit Soc Gen Microbiol; Am Soc Virol. *Res:* Biochemistry of virus-infected cells; antiviral chemotherapy; retroviruses; herpesviruses; exotic RNA viruses; virus-host cell interactions; molecular virology. *Mailing Add:* 2212 Lime Rock Rd Birmingham AL 35216

SHANNY, RAMY A, RESEARCH & DEVELOPMENT MANAGEMENT. *Current Pos:* pres, Arco Power Technol, 86-94, PRES, ADVAN POWER TECHNOL, 94- *Personal Data:* b Jerusalem, Israel, Nov 6, 35; US citizen; m 77, Laura Hamilton; c Ronnit, Michelle & Emily. *Educ:* Tri State Col, BSME, 61; Princeton Univ, MS & MA, 64, PhD(plasma physics), 66. *Prof Exp:* Res physicist, Missile & Space Div, Gen Elec, 65-69; res physicist, US Naval Res Lab, 69-70, br head theoret physics, 70-71, supt, Plasma Physics Div, 71-75; exec vpres, Int Nuclear Energy Syst Co, 77-82, pres, 82-85. *Mem:* Fel Am Phys Soc; NY Acad Sci; Inst Elec & Electronics Engrs; AAAS; Int Soc Optical Engrs. *Res:* Fusion, theoretical simulation of plasma instabilities; fusion concept and engineering; ionospheric research; design of major high frequency phased array for inospheric modification; trace element detection using laser induced plasmas; subsurface electromagnetic imaging. *Mailing Add:* 1412 21st St NW Washington DC 20036

SHANSKY, ALBERT, PROTEIN CHEMISTRY. *Current Pos:* CONSULT, A SHANSKY CONSULT, 70- *Personal Data:* b Brooklyn, NY, Mar 26, 25. *Educ:* Brooklyn Col, BS, 48, MS, 49; Ill Inst Technol, PhD(biochem), 52. *Prof Exp:* Asst dir res, Helene Curtis Inc, Clairol Corp. *Mem:* Am Chem Soc; fel Am Inst Chemists; fel AAAS; NY Acad Sci. *Mailing Add:* 10 Winfield St Norwalk CT 06856

SHANSKY, MICHAEL STEVEN, VISUAL PHYSIOLOGY, PSYCHOLOGY. *Current Pos:* Asst prof physiol optics, 71-77, ASSOC PROF VISUAL SCI, ILL COL OPTOM, 77-, CHMN DEPT VISUAL SCI & DIR RES, 72- *Personal Data:* b Milwaukee, Wis, May 3, 43; m 68; c 1. *Educ:* Marquette Univ, BA, 66; Syracuse Univ, PhD(psychol), 74. *Concurrent Pos:* Guest lectr, DePaul Univ & Northeastern Ill Univ, 73- *Mem:* AAAS; Asn Res Vision & Ophthal. *Res:* Neurophysiology of vision; information processing in the vertebrate visual system; visual perception; polysensory integration. *Mailing Add:* 15310 157th Ave Big Rapids MI 49307

SHANTARAM, RAJAGOPAL, MATHEMATICAL STATISTICS. *Current Pos:* asst prof, 71-74, ASSOC PROF MATH & STATIST, UNIV MICH, FLINT, 74- *Personal Data:* b Poona, India, Mar 29, 39; m 69. *Educ:* Ferguson Col, India, BS, 59; Univ Poona, MS, 61; Pa State Univ, PhD(math), 66. *Prof Exp:* Asst prof math & statist, State Univ NY, Stony Brook, 66-71. *Mem:* Am Math Soc; Math Asn Am; Am Statist Asn. *Res:* Characteristic functions; limit distributions; mathematical statistics; mathematical modeling; operations research. *Mailing Add:* Dept Comput Sci Univ Mich 214 Murchie Sci Bldg Flint MI 48502-2186

SHANTEAU, ROBERT MARSHALL, HIGHWAY RESEARCH. *Current Pos:* ENG DEPT TRAFFIC & ENG, MONTEREY, CALIF, 90- *Personal Data:* b Los Angeles, Calif, June 24, 47; m 80. *Educ:* San Jose State Univ, BS, 70; Univ Calif, Berkeley, MS, 76, PhD(civil eng), 80. *Prof Exp:* Asst prof civil eng, Purdue Univ, 80-85; res engr, Ind Dept Hwys, 85-90. *Mem:* Opers Res Soc Am; Inst Transp Engrs; Am Soc Civil Engrs. *Res:* Application of mathematical and physical principles to problems in highway engineering and pavement management. *Mailing Add:* 13 Primrose Circle Seaside CA 93955

SHANTHIKUMAR, JEYAVEERASINGAM GEORGE, PRODUCTION SYSTEMS, STOCHASTIC MODELS. *Current Pos:* asst prof mgt sci, 84-88, PROF, MGT SCI, UNIV CALIF, BERKELEY, 88- *Personal Data:* b Sri Lanka, July 1, 50; m 77; c 3. *Educ:* Univ Sri Lanka, BSc, 72; Univ Toronto, MASc, 77, PhD(indust eng), 79. *Prof Exp:* Asst lectr prod & mech eng, Univ Sri Lanka, 73-75; teaching asst indust eng, Univ Toronto, 75-79; asst prof, Syracuse Univ, 79-82; assoc prof, Univ Ariz, 82-84. *Concurrent Pos:* Consult, Syracuse Res Inc, 82. *Mem:* Opers Res Soc Am; Inst Mgt Sci. *Res:* Develop models to understand the behavior to obtain performance measures and to design production systems; develop efficient techniques to derive solutions to stochastic and deterministic models of production systems. *Mailing Add:* 80 Los Balcones Alamo CA 94507

SHANZER, STEFAN, ELECTROENCEPHALOGRAPHY, EYE MOVEMENTS & VISION. *Current Pos:* Prof clin neurol, 77-90, PROF NEUROL, MOUNT SINAI SCH MED, 90-; EMER DIR NEUROL, BETH ISRAEL MED CTR, 94- *Personal Data:* b Krakow, Poland, June 3, 24; US citizen; m 55, Hilda Roy; c Danuta & Marius. *Educ:* Bologna Univ, Italy, MD, 51. *Concurrent Pos:* Dir neurol, Beth Israel Med Ctr, 77-93; consult, Neurologist NY Downtown Hosp. *Mem:* Am Physiol Soc; Am Neurol Soc; Am Electroencephalographic Soc; Am Acad Neurol; Am Epilepsy Soc; Asn Res Nervous & Ment Dis. *Res:* Oculomotor system; electroencephalography. *Mailing Add:* Dept Neurol Beth Israel Med Ctr 140 E 83rd St New York NY 10028

SHAPERE, DUDLEY, PHILOSOPHY OF SCIENCE, HISTORY OF SCIENCE. *Current Pos:* Z SMITH REYNOLDS PROF PHILOS & HIST SCI, WAKE FOREST UNIV, 84- *Personal Data:* b Harlingen, Tex, May 27, 28; m 75; c 2. *Educ:* Harvard Univ, BA, 49, MA, 55, PhD(philos), 57. *Hon Degrees:* Dr, Univ Peruana Cayetano Heredia, Lima, Peru, 95. *Prof Exp:* Instr philos, Ohio State Univ, 57-60; from asst prof to prof, Univ Chicago, 60-72; prof, Univ Ill, Urbana-Champaign, 72-75; prof, Univ Md, College Park, 75-84. *Concurrent Pos:* Vis assoc prof, Rockefeller Univ, 65-66; consult, Comn Undergrad Educ Biol Sci, 65-71; spec consult & prog dir, Hist & Philos Sci Prog, NSF, 66-75; vis prof, Harvard Univ, 68; NSF res grants, 70-72, 73-75, 76-78, 85-86; mem, Inst Advan Study, Princeton, NJ, 78-79, 81. *Mem:* Am Philos Asn; Philos Sci Asn; Hist Sci Soc; AAAS; Am Psychol Asn; Int Acad Philos & Sci. *Res:* Characteristics of explanation; the relations of theory, observation, and experiment and the nature of change and innovation in the development of science. *Mailing Add:* 3125 Turkey Hill Ct Winston-Salem NC 27106

SHAPERO, DONALD CAMPBELL, SCIENCE POLICY. *Current Pos:* US-USSR exchange scientist, Nat Acad Sci, 73, sr staff officer, 75-78, spec asst prog coord, 79-82, DIR BD PHYSICS & ASTRON, NAT ACAD SCI, 82- *Personal Data:* b Detroit, Mich, Apr 17, 42; m 69, 85, Linda J Ravdin; c Stephen B & Daniel R. *Educ:* Mass Inst Technol, BS, 64, PhD(physics), 70. *Prof Exp:* Fel theoret physics, Thomas J Watson Res Ctr, IBM Corp, 70-72; asst prof, Am Univ, 72-73 & Cath Univ, 73-75; exec dir energy res adv bd, US Dept Energy, 78-79. *Concurrent Pos:* Mem, Nat Organizing Comt, 19th Gen Assembly, Int Union Pure & Appl Physics, 85-88 & Nat Organizing Comt, 20th Gen Assembly, Int Astron Union, 86-88; mem, US Deleg 20th & 21st Gen Assemblies, Int Union Pure & Appl Physics, 90 & 93, secy, US Liaison, 87-93. *Mem:* Am Phys Soc; Int Astron Union; Am Astron Soc. *Res:* Many-body theory; quantum field theory; science policy on physical sciences. *Mailing Add:* Nat Acad Sci 2101 Constitution Ave Washington DC 20418. *Fax:* 202-334-3575; *E-Mail:* dshapero@nas.edu

SHAPERO, SANFORD MARVIN, GERONTOLOGY. *Current Pos:* RETIRED. *Personal Data:* b Cincinnati, Ohio, Mar 4, 29; m 82, Evelyn Leavitt. *Educ:* Univ Dayton, BA, 50; Hebrew Union Col, BHL, 52, MHL, 55, DHL, 59. *Hon Degrees:* DD, Hebrew Union Col, 81. *Prof Exp:* Exec vpres, Alliance Med Indust, 68-69; vpres, NAm Biologicals, 69-72; regional dir & nat dir geront, Union Am Hebrew Col, 72-79; pres & chief exec officer, City of Hope, 79-96. *Concurrent Pos:* Mem, Nat Adv Coun Aging. *Res:* Aging. *Mailing Add:* 1568 Gilcrest Dr Beverly Hills CA 90210

SHAPIRA, RAYMOND, BIOCHEMISTRY, NEUROCHEMISTRY. *Current Pos:* from asst prof to assoc prof, 58-71, PROF BIOCHEM, EMORY UNIV, 72- *Personal Data:* b New Bedford, Mass, June 29, 28; m 56; c 3. *Educ:* Univ NMex, BS, 50; Fla State Univ, PhD(chem), 54. *Prof Exp:* Res biochemist, Biol Div, Oak Ridge Nat Lab, 54-57. *Concurrent Pos:* Fulbright lectr, Weizmann Inst Sci, 67. *Mem:* AAAS; Am Chem Soc; Fedn Am Socs Exp Biol; Am Soc Biol Chemists; Am Soc Neurochem; Sigma Xi. *Res:* Studies on the structure, metabolism and function of myelin proteins; induction of tolerance in experimental allergic encephalomyelitis; studies on myelin from patients with multiple sclerosis. *Mailing Add:* Dept Biochem Emory Univ Sch Med Rollins Res Bldg Atlanta GA 30322-3050. *Fax:* 404-727-2738

SHAPIRA, YAACOV, PHYSICS. *Current Pos:* Mem res staff solid state physics, Nat Magnet Lab, 64-85, SR SCIENTIST, PHYSICS DEPT, MASS INST TECHNOL, 85- *Personal Data:* b Haifa, Israel, Jan 9, 38; m 73. *Educ:* Brandeis Univ, BA, 60; Mass Inst Technol, PhD(physics), 64. *Mem:* Am Phys Soc; AAAS. *Res:* Ultrasonic behavior of solids; Fermi surface; high field superconductors; magnetic phase transitions; magnetic semiconductors. *Mailing Add:* Dept Physics Tufs Univ Four Colby St Medford MA 02155

SHAPIRO, ALAN ELIHU, HISTORY OF SCIENCE. *Current Pos:* from asst prof to assoc prof, 72-84, PROF HIST SCI, UNIV MINN, MINNEAPOLIS, 84-, DIR, PROG HIST SCI & TECHNOL, 89- *Personal Data:* b New York, NY, Jan 6, 42; m 72, Linda Roepke. *Educ:* Polytech Inst Brooklyn, BS, 62, MS, 65; Yale Univ, MPhil, 69, PhD(hist sci), 70. *Prof Exp:* Instr physics, St John's Univ, NY, 65-66; NATO fel, Cambridge Univ, 70-71; asst prof hist sci, Oberlin Col, 71-72. *Concurrent Pos:* Assoc ed, Centaurus; mem coun, Hist Sci Soc, 77-80; mem-at-large, Sect L, AAAS, 84-87, nominating comt, 91-94, coun, 94; Guggenheim fel, 85-86; pres, Midwest Junto Hist Sci, 91-92. *Mem:* Fel AAAS; corresp mem Int Acad Hist Sci; Hist Sci Soc; Sigma Xi. *Res:* History of physical sciences from the sixteenth to nineteenth centuries; Newton; optics; mechanics. *Mailing Add:* Univ Minn Sch Physics 116 Church St SE Minneapolis MN 55455. *Fax:* 612-624-4578; *E-Mail:* ashapiro@physics.spa.umn.edu

SHAPIRO, ALVIN, NUCLEAR SCIENCE & ENGINEERING. *Current Pos:* from instr to assoc prof, 62-78, PROF NUCLEAR ENG, UNIV CINCINNATI, 78- *Personal Data:* b Jersey City, NJ, Apr 20, 30; m 71; c 4. *Educ:* Polytech Inst Brooklyn, BME, 51; Univ Cincinnati, MS, 62, PhD(physics), 68. *Prof Exp:* Engr, Allis-Chalmers Mfg Co, 55-58 & Gen Elec Co, 58-62. *Concurrent Pos:* Consult, Mound Lab, Monsanto Res Corp, 70- *Mem:* Am Nuclear Soc; Am Phys Soc; Sigma Xi. *Res:* Methods of neutron and photon transport; nuclear reactor physics and radiation shielding; neutron dosimetry. *Mailing Add:* Mine Dept Univ Cincinnati Cincinnati OH 45221-0072

SHAPIRO, ALVIN PHILIP, INTERNAL MEDICINE, MEDICAL EDUCATION. *Current Pos:* from asst prof to assoc prof, 56-60, assoc dean acad affairs, 71-75, vchmn med, 75-79, actg chmn, 77-79, PROF MED, SCH MED, UNIV PITTSBURGH, 67- *Personal Data:* b Nashville, Tenn, Dec 28, 20; m 51; c 2. *Educ:* Cornell Univ, AB, 41, Long Island Col Med, MD, 44. *Honors & Awards:* Co-recipient, Albert Lasker Spec Pub Health Award, 80. *Prof Exp:* Res fel, Cincinnati Gen Hosp, 48-49; instr internal med, Col Med, Univ Cincinnati, 49-51; asst prof, Univ Tex Southwestern Med Sch Dallas, 51-56. *Concurrent Pos:* Asst clinician, Cincinnati Gen Hosp, 48-49, clinician & asst attend physician, 49-51; Fulbright vis prof, Univ Utrecht, 68; mem, Coun for High Blood Pressure, Am Heart Asn; attend physician, Parkland Mem & Vet Admin Hosps, Dallas, Tex, 51-56 & Presby Hosp, Vet Admin Hosp, Pittsburgh, 56-; attending physician, Shadyside Hosp, 86-, dir, Intern Med Training Prog & assoc chief med. *Mem:* Fel AAAS; Am Psychosom Soc (pres, 75); Acad Behav Med Res (pres, 88); Am Heart Asn; Am Soc Clin Invest. *Res:* Hypertension; experimental hypertension; psychosomatic disorders. *Mailing Add:* Dept Med Shadyside Hospital Pittsburgh PA 15232-1381. *Fax:* 412-623-2555

SHAPIRO, ANATOLE MORRIS, ELEMENTARY PARTICLE PHYSICS, HIGH ENERGY PHYSICS. *Current Pos:* from assoc prof to prof, 58-92, EMER PROF PHYSICS, BROWN UNIV, 92- *Personal Data:* b Syracuse, NY, June 28, 23; div; c 2. *Educ:* Univ Buffalo, BA, 44; Cornell Univ, PhD(physics), 52. *Hon Degrees:* MSc, Harvard Univ, 56. *Prof Exp:* Assoc physicist, Brookhaven Nat Lab, 52-54; res fel & lectr, Harvard Univ, 54-56, asst prof physics, 58-. *Concurrent Pos:* Assoc physicist, Europ Orgn Nuclear Res, Geneva, 64-65, Fermilab, 71-72 & 87, Stanford Linear Accelerator Ctr, Stanford Univ, 80-81, Dept Energy Res Div, 83-87, Gran Sasso Lab, INFN, Italy, 87-89. *Mem:* Am Asn Physics Teachers; fel Am Phys Soc; Italian Phys Soc. *Res:* Nuclear physics; high energy particle interactions; proton-proton and pion-proton elastic and inelastic cross sections; production and decay of K-mesons and hyperons; hybrid systems for interactions above 100 GeV/c. *Mailing Add:* 530 N St SW Apt S705 Washington DC 20024

SHAPIRO, ARTHUR MAURICE, POPULATION BIOLOGY, BIOGEOGRAPHY. *Current Pos:* from asst prof to assoc prof, 72-80, PROF EVOLUTION, ECOL & ENTOMOL, UNIV CALIF, DAVIS, 81- *Personal Data:* b Baltimore, Md, Jan 6, 46; m 69, Adrienne Austin; c Austin & Alexa. *Educ:* Univ Pa, BA, 66; Cornell Univ, PhD(entom), 70. *Prof Exp:* Asst prof biol, Richmond Col, NY, 70-72. *Mem:* Fel AAAS; Ecol Soc Am; Soc Study Evolution; fel Royal Entom Soc London; fel Explorers Club. *Res:* Genetics and ecology of colonizing species; adaptive strategies of weedy insects and plants; coevolution of insect-plant relationships; historical biogeography of the Andean region; phenology; biogeography and systematics of Pieridae and Hesperiidae. *Mailing Add:* Ctr Pop Biol Univ Calif Davis CA 95616. *Fax:* 530-752-1449

SHAPIRO, ASCHER H(ERMAN), FLUID DYNAMICS, BIOMEDICAL ENGINEERING. *Current Pos:* Asst mech eng, Mass Inst Technol, 39-40, from instr to prof, 40-62, Ford prof eng, 62-75, chmn fac, 64-65, head, Dept Mech Eng, 65-74, inst prof, 75-86, EMER INST PROF, MASS INST TECHNOL, 86- *Personal Data:* b Brooklyn, NY, May 20, 16; m 85, Kathleen Larke; c Peter M, Martha A & Bernett M. *Educ:* Mass Inst Technol, SB, 38, ScD(mech eng), 46. *Hon Degrees:* DSc, Univ Salford, Eng, 78, Israel, Inst Technol, 85. *Honors & Awards:* Navy Ord Develop Award, 45; Akroyd Stuart Mem Lectr, Nottingham Univ, 56; Richards Mem Award, Am Soc Mech Engrs, 60, Worcester Reed Warner Medal, 65, Fluids Eng Award, 81; Lamme Award, Am Soc Eng Educ, 77. *Concurrent Pos:* Consult mech engr, 38-; vis prof, Cambridge Univ, 55-56; mem subcomt, Nat Adv Comt Aeronaut, USAF; tech adv panel aeronaut, Off Secy Defense; chmn, Nat Comt Fluid Mech Films, 62-65 & 71-, mem, 65-; mem sci adv bd, USAF, 64-66; mem sci & pub policy comt, Nat Acad Sci, 73-77. *Mem:* Nat Acad Sci; Nat Acad Eng; fel Am Acad Arts & Sci; hon mem Am Soc Mech Engrs; fel Am Inst Aeronaut & Astronaut; fel Am Inst Med Biol Eng. *Res:* Fluid mechanics; supersonic flow of gases; gas turbine power plant; jet and rocket propulsion; dynamics and thermodynamics of compressible fluid flow; biomedical engineering; cardiovascular function; pulmonary function; centrifuges. *Mailing Add:* Dept Mech Eng Mass Inst Technol Cambridge MA 02139. *Fax:* 617-522-4418

SHAPIRO, BENNETT MICHAELS, BIOCHEMISTRY. *Current Pos:* EXEC VPRES, WORLDWIDE BASIC RES, MERCK RES LABS, 90- *Personal Data:* b Philadelphia, Pa, July 14, 39; m 82; c 3. *Educ:* Dickinson Col, BS, 60; Jefferson Med Col, MD, 64. *Prof Exp:* Intern med, Hosp, Univ Pa, 64-65; res assoc, Lab Biochem, Nat Heart Inst, 65-68; vis scientist, Pasteur Inst, Paris, 68-69; chief sect cellular differentiation, Nat Heart & Lung Inst, 69-70; from assoc prof to prof biochem, Univ Wash, 78-90, chmn dept, 85-90. *Concurrent Pos:* Guggenheim fel; Cell Biol Study Sect NIH, 80-83; bd of sci counr, NIH, 87- *Mem:* AAAS; Am Chem Soc; Soc Develop Biol; Am Soc Cell Biol; Am Soc Biol Chemists. *Res:* Regulation of cell behavior; ionic and enzymic regulation; role of the cell surface in fertilization and development. *Mailing Add:* Merck Res Labs PO Box 2000 Rahway NJ 07065-0900

SHAPIRO, BERNARD, NUCLEAR MEDICINE. *Current Pos:* CLIN PROF RADIOL, SCH MED, TEMPLE UNIV, 78- *Personal Data:* b Philadelphia, Pa, May 22, 25; m 49; c 3. *Educ:* Univ Pa, MD, 51; Am Bd Nuclear Med, dipl, 72. *Prof Exp:* From house officer to resident internal med, Hosp, Univ Pa, 51-53; Am Cancer Soc fel, Norweg Hydro Inst, Oslo, 53-54; Southeast Pa Heart Asn fel, Univ Pa, 54-55, Am Heart Asn fel, 55-56; head radioisotope lab, South Div, Albert Einstein Med Ctr, Philadelphia, 56-66, head radiation res lab, 56-90, head dept nuclear med, 66-90. *Concurrent Pos:* Clin assoc prof radiol, Sch Med, Temple Univ, 67-78. *Mem:* AMA; Radiation Res Soc; Soc Nuclear Med; NY Acad Sci; Sigma Xi; fel Am Col Nuclear Physicians. *Res:* Clinical radioisotopes; radiation research. *Mailing Add:* A Einstein Med Ctr York & Tabor Rds Philadelphia PA 19141

SHAPIRO, BERNARD LYON, ORGANIC CHEMISTRY, NUCLEAR MAGNETIC RESONANCE. *Current Pos:* ED & PUBL, NMR NEWSLETT, 87- *Personal Data:* b Montreal, Que, June 16, 32; US citizen; m 60; c 2. *Educ:* McGill Univ, BSc, 52; Harvard Univ, AM, 54, PhD(org chem), 57. *Prof Exp:* Res fel chem, Harvard Univ, 56-58; res fel, Mellon Inst, 58-64; assoc prof, Ill Inst Technol, 64-68; admin officer, Tex A&M Univ, 68-71, prof chem, 68-87. *Concurrent Pos:* Ed, Ill Inst Technol Nuclear Magnetic Resonance Newslett, 58- & Nuclear Magnetic Resonance Abstracts Serv, Preston Tech Abstracts Co, 64-; consult, Res Div, W R Grace & Co, 64- & Shell Develop Co, 66. *Mem:* AAAS; Am Chem Soc; Am Phys Soc. *Res:* Organic chemistry; especially stereochemistry of haloketones; aliphatic fluorine compounds; organophosphorus compounds; nature of coupling constants, especially involving fluorine and phosphorous. *Mailing Add:* 966 Elsinore Ct Palo Alto CA 94303-3410

SHAPIRO, BERT IRWIN, NEUROPHYSIOLOGY, BIOPHYSICS. *Current Pos:* MEM STAFF, NAT INST GEN MED SCI, NIH, 76- *Personal Data:* b New York, NY, Jan 14, 41; m 62; c 2. *Educ:* Swarthmore Col, BA, 62; Harvard Univ, MA, 65, PhD(biol), 67. *Prof Exp:* Instr biol & gen educ, 67-68, from asst prof to assoc prof biol, Harvard Univ, 68-76. *Concurrent Pos:* Mem, Bermuda Biol Sta. *Mem:* Am Soc Cell Biol. *Res:* Neurophysiology, particularly of conduction mechanisms; action of pharmacological compounds, especially toxins; purification and structure of protein toxins, especially from invertebrates. *Mailing Add:* Dept Cell Biol & Biophys Nat Inst Gen Med Sci NIH Bethesda MD 20892-6200

SHAPIRO, BURTON LEONARD, ORAL BIOLOGY, GENETICS. *Current Pos:* Teaching asst, Univ Minn, 61-62, instr, 62-66, assoc prof, 66-70, chmn, Dept Oral Biol, 68, dir grad studies, 71-75, prof, Ctr Humanistic Studies, Col Liberal Arts, 85-88, PROF ORAL PATH, SCH DENT & PROF, DEPT LAB MED & PATH, SCH MED, UNIV MINN, MINNEAPOLIS, 85- *Personal Data:* b New York, NY, Mar 29, 34; m 58; c 3. *Educ:* NY Univ, DDS, 58; Univ Minn, MS, 62, PhD(genetics), 66. *Concurrent Pos:* Consult, lectr & cytologist, Minn Oral Cancer Detection, 63-66 & Wyo State Bd Health, 66-70; geneticist & oral pathologist, Cleft Palate-Maxillofacial Clin, Univ Minn, 65-69; mem, Grad Fac Dent & Genetics, oral biol Grad Sch, Univ Minn, Minneapolis, 66-, mem med staff, Univ Minn Hosp, 67-; chmn health sci policy and rev coun, 74-79; exec comt grad sch, 74-79; mem bd dirs, Minn Chapter Cystic Fibrosis Found, 75-83; spec vis prof, Japanese Min Educ, Sci & Cult, 83; vis scientist, Dept Biol, Univ Miami, 85, 86. *Mem:* Fel AAAS; Am Dent Asn; fel Am Acad Oral Path; Int Asn Dent Res; Am Soc Human Genetics; fel Am Assoc Oral Path; adv fel Am Cancer Soc. *Res:* Down syndrome; cystic fibrosis; genetics and oral disease; cleft palate microforms in American Indians; temporomandibular joint disorders; introduced concept of amplified developmental instability in down syndrome to explain its pathogenesis; ongoing tissue culture studies to determine basic defect in cystic fibrosis: discovered mitochandrial lesion and calcium abnormality. *Mailing Add:* Dept Oral Biol Univ Minn Minneapolis MN 55455. *Fax:* 612-626-2651; *E-Mail:* burt@mailbox.mail.umn.edu

SHAPIRO, CAREN KNIGHT, MEDICAL MICROBIOLOGY, IMMUNOBIOLOGY. *Current Pos:* asst prof biol, 77-82, ASSOC PROF BIOL, D'YOUVILLE COL, NY, 82- *Personal Data:* b Berkeley, Calif, Apr 19, 45; m 72, Stuart C. *Educ:* Univ Calif, Davis, AB, 67; Univ Wis, MS, 71, PhD(med microbiol), 72. *Prof Exp:* Res assoc, Ind Univ, 73-76; res affil, Roswell Park Mem Inst, 77. *Mem:* Sigma Xi; NY Acad Sci; Am Soc Microbiol; AAAS; Asn Women Sci. *Mailing Add:* 142 Viscount Dr Williamsville NY 14221-1770. *Fax:* 716-881-7760; *E-Mail:* cshapiro@ournet.tfnet.org

SHAPIRO, CHARLES SAUL, NUCLEAR RADIATION. *Current Pos:* from asst prof to assoc prof, 67-75, PROF PHYSICS, SAN FRANCISCO STATE UNIV, 75-, SCI ADV COMT, SCOPE-RADPATH, EXEC DIR & CHMN, SCOPE-RADTEST. *Personal Data:* b Brooklyn, NY, June 16, 36; m 56; c David, Terri & Gary. *Educ:* Brooklyn Col, BS, 57; Syracuse Univ, MS, 60, PhD(physics), 65. *Prof Exp:* Assoc physicist, IBM Corp, 57-59; teaching asst physics, Syracuse Univ, 59-60; res assoc reactor physics, Brookhaven Nat Lab, 61-64; staff mem physics, IBM, 64-67. *Concurrent Pos:* Guest researcher, Stockholm Int Peace Res Inst, 73-74; consult, Lawrence Livermore Nat Lab, 84- *Mem:* Am Phys Soc; Am Nuclear Soc; Health Physics Soc; Sigma Xi. *Res:* Radiation transport; shielding and dosimetry; reactor physics; environmental consequences of nuclear war; biogeochemical pathways of radionuclides; relations of science and humanities; science and society; science education; arms control and disarmament; radioactivity; fallout from nuclear test explosions. *Mailing Add:* Dept Physics San Francisco State Univ 1600 Holloway Ave San Francisco CA 94132

SHAPIRO, DAVID, BEHAVIORAL MEDICINE, STRESS PSYCHOPHYSIOLOGY. *Current Pos:* PROF, DEPT PSYCHIAT, UNIV CALIF, LOS ANGELES, 74-, PROF, DEPT PSYCHOL, 75- *Personal Data:* b New York, NY, July 20, 24; m 51, Shirley Walrath. *Educ:* Univ Ill, AB, 48; Univ Mich, AM, 50, PhD(psychol), 53. *Honors & Awards:* Res Recognition Award, Biofeedback Soc Am, 88; Distinguished Contrib Psychophysiol, Soc Psychophysiol Res, 88. *Prof Exp:* Lectr, Dept Social Relations, Harvard Med Sch, 53-55, res assoc, Dept Psychiat, 56-63, assoc in psychol, 63-66, asst prof psychiat, 66-69, assoc prof psychol, 69-71, sr assoc psychiat, 71-74. *Concurrent Pos:* Consult, Nat Res Coun, 55, Dept Psychiat, Boston Univ, 56-60, Vet Admin, Dept Med Surg, 73-, John Wiley & Sons, 73, Ohio State Univ Pres, 73, Acad Press, 78-, New Eng J Med, 80-, NATO Sci Proj, 84-; prin investr, Off Naval Res Contract, 71-75; prin investr, Nat Heart, Lung & Blood Inst Res Grants, 74-; ed, Psychophysiol, 78-87. *Mem:* Soc Psychophysiol Res (pres, 75-76); fel Am Psychol Asn; fel AAAS; fel Soc Behav Med; Am Psychoson Soc; Acad Behav Med Res. *Res:* Human psychophysiological research on stress effects on autonomic response systems; role of behavior in hypertension and other cardiovascular disorders; published numerous articles in various publications. *Mailing Add:* Dept Psychiat UCLA 760 Westwood Plaza Los Angeles CA 90024. *Fax:* 310-825-6792; *E-Mail:* iha3dos@mvs.oac.ucla.edu

SHAPIRO, DAVID JORDON, BIOCHEMISTRY. *Current Pos:* asst prof, 74-78, ASSOC PROF BIOCHEM, UNIV ILL, URBANA, 78-, PROF. *Personal Data:* b Brooklyn, NY, Apr 13, 46. *Educ:* Brooklyn Col, BS, 67; Purdue Univ, PhD(biochem), 72. *Prof Exp:* Helen Hay Whitney Found fel biochem, Med Sch, Stanford Univ, 72-73; biol, 73-74. *Mem:* Am Chem Soc; Sigma Xi; Am Soc Biol Chemists; AAAS. *Res:* Control of gene expression and messenger RNA synthesis in animal cells; nucleic acid hybridization and use of immunologic techniques to isolate specific messenger RNAs in hormone dependent development. *Mailing Add:* Dept Biochem B-4 RAC Univ Ill 600 S Matthews Ave Urbana IL 61801-3792

SHAPIRO, DAVID M, BIOCHEMISTRY. *Current Pos:* asst prof biochem, Health Sci Ctr, 69-92, dir student servs, 73-92, ADJ PROF, FAMILY PRACT, UNIV TEX, SAN ANTONIO, 92- *Personal Data:* b New York, NY, June 9, 29; m 50; c 3. *Educ:* Queens Col, NY, BS, 51; Johns Hopkins Univ, PhD(biochem), 61. *Prof Exp:* Chemist, Sun Chem Co, 51-54; instr chem, Brooklyn Col, 54-55; chemist, Nopco Chem Co, 55-56; res assoc biol chem, Univ Mich, 61-65; asst prof biochem, Woman's Med Col, Pa, 64-69. *Concurrent Pos:* Fel, Inst Sci & Technol, Univ Mich, 61-62; NIH fel, 62-63. *Mem:* AAAS. *Res:* Photosynthesis and electron transport; protein synthesis in bacteriophage-infected systems. *Mailing Add:* Dept Family Prac Univ Tex Health Sci Ctr San Antonio TX 78284-7794

SHAPIRO, DONALD M, APPLIED MATHEMATICS, COMPUTER SCIENCE. *Current Pos:* PROF BIOSTATIST, NY MED COL, 67- *Personal Data:* b Pittsburgh, Pa, Nov 15, 35; m 56; c 3. *Educ:* Univ Pittsburgh, BS, 56; Wash Univ, ScD(appl math), 66. *Prof Exp:* Reactor physicist, United Aircraft Corp, 56 & Internuclear Corp, 57; res assoc appl math, Washington Univ, 63-64; asst prof psychiat, Univ Mo, 64-66; asst prof appl math, Washington Univ, 66-67. *Mem:* AAAS; Asn Comput Mach; Soc Indust & Appl Math; Opers Res Soc Am; Data Processing Mgt Asn. *Res:* Use of computers and statistics in both research and hospital administration. *Mailing Add:* NY Med Col PO Box 31 Valhalla NY 10595-0031

SHAPIRO, DOUGLAS YORK, BEHAVIORAL ECOLOGY. *Current Pos:* PROF & DEPT HEAD, DEPT BIOL, EASTERN MID UNIV, 92- *Personal Data:* b Houston, Tex, July 25, 41; div; c Aidan R A (Shapiro-Leighton). *Educ:* Harvard Univ, BA, 64; Case Western Res Univ, MD, 68; Cambridge Univ, PhD(animal behav), 77. *Prof Exp:* Med intern, New York Hosp & Cornell Med Ctr, 68-69; res assoc neurol, Nat Inst Neurol Dis & Stroke, NIH, 69-71; clin asst psychiat, W Suffolk Hosp, Eng, 73-75; from asst prof to prof animal behav, Dept Marine Sci, Univ PR, 77-92. *Mem:* Animal Behav Soc; Am Soc Ichthyologists & Herpetologists; Ecol Soc Am. *Res:* Behavioral aspects of socially controlled female-to-male sex reversal in coral reef fish; formation and development of fish social groups; sperm allocation strategies of fish. *Mailing Add:* Dept Biol Eastern Mich Univ Ypsilanti MI 48197. *Fax:* 313-487-9235; *E-Mail:* douglas.shapiro@emich.edu

SHAPIRO, EDWARD K EDIK, thermal physics, inorganic chemistry, for more information see previous edition

SHAPIRO, EDWIN SEYMOUR, MATHEMATICS. *Current Pos:* prof, 69-78, PROF QUANT METHODS, UNIV SAN FRANCISCO, 78- *Personal Data:* b Los Angeles, Calif, June 20, 28; m 62; c 2. *Educ:* Univ Calif, MA, 51; Univ Pittsburgh, PhD, 62. *Prof Exp:* Mathematician, US Naval Radiol Defense Lab, Calif, 51-69. *Mem:* Am Math Soc; Opers Res Soc Am; Math Asn Am. *Res:* Military operations; applied mathematics. *Mailing Add:* 3051 Atwater Dr Burlingame CA 94010-5820

SHAPIRO, EUGENE, metallurgical & materials engineering, for more information see previous edition

SHAPIRO, GILBERT, PARTICLE PHYSICS. *Current Pos:* physicist, Lawrence Radiation Lab, 61-63, from asst prof to assoc prof, 63-79, PROF PHYSICS, UNIV CALIF, BERKELEY, 79- *Personal Data:* b Philadelphia, Pa, Mar 17, 34; m 58; c 3. *Educ:* Univ Pa, BA, 55; Columbia Univ, MA, 57, PhD(physics), 59. *Prof Exp:* Res assoc physics, Nevis Cyclotron Lab, Columbia Univ, 59-61. *Concurrent Pos:* NSF sr fel, Saclay Nuclear Res Ctr, France, 65-66. *Mem:* Am Phys Soc. *Res:* Particle and muon physics; polarized proton targets. *Mailing Add:* Dept Physics Univ Calif Berkeley CA 94720. *Fax:* 510-486-6738; *E-Mail:* g.shapiro@lbl.gov

SHAPIRO, HERMAN SIMON, BIOCHEMISTRY, GENETICS. *Current Pos:* ASSOC PROF BIOCHEM, COL MED NJ, 69- *Personal Data:* b New York, NY, Aug 29, 29. *Educ:* City Col New York, BS, 51; Columbia Univ, PhD(biochem), 57. *Prof Exp:* Asst biochem, Col Physicians & Surgeons, Columbia Univ, 51-52, res biochemist, 56-57, from res assoc to asst prof biochem, 58-69. *Mem:* Brit Biochem Soc. *Res:* Elucidation of nucleotide sequences of the DNA of diverse cellular sources, especially the correlation of structure and function of these macromolecules. *Mailing Add:* Dept Biochem UMDNJ 100 Bergen St Newark NJ 07103-2407

SHAPIRO, HOWARD MAURICE, MEDICINE, BIOENGINEERING. *Current Pos:* asst to chmn, Cancer & Leukemia Group B, 76-77, chief cytokinetics, Sidney Farber Cancer Inst, 77-82, RES ASSOC, BETH ISRAEL HOSP, 82-, INVESTR, CTR BLOOD RES, 83-; PRES, HOWARD M SHAPIRO, MD, PC, 76- *Personal Data:* b Brooklyn, NY, Nov 8, 41; m 64; c 2. *Educ:* Harvard Univ, BA, 61; NY Univ, MD, 65. *Prof Exp:* Asst res scientist, NY Univ, 62-65; from intern to asst resident surg, Bellevue Hosp, 65-67; res assoc math statist & appl math, Biomet Br, Nat Cancer Inst, 67-70; sr staff fel, Baltimore Cancer Res Ctr, 70-71; resident surg, Col Med, Univ Ariz, 71-72; from asst dir med systs & instrumentation to dir clin res diag prod, G D Searle & Co, 72-76. *Concurrent Pos:* Lectr path, Harvard Med Sch, 76-; vis prof path, Rush Med Col, 85-89. *Mem:* AAAS; Am Asn Cancer Res; Am Soc Clin Oncol; Am Soc Hemat; Inst Elec & Electronics Engrs. *Res:* Biomedical instrumentation and computing; oncology and hematology; analytical and theoretical biology; medical education and communication. *Mailing Add:* 283 Highland Ave Newton MA 02165

SHAPIRO, IRVING MEYER, BIOCHEMISTRY. *Current Pos:* from asst prof to assoc prof, 69-76, actg chmn dept, 75-80, PROF BIOCHEM, SCH DENT MED, UNIV PA, 76-, CHMN DEPT, 80- *Personal Data:* b London, Eng, Oct 28, 37; m 65; c 1. *Educ:* London Hosp Med Col, LDSRCS BDS, 61; Univ Liverpool, MSc, 64; Univ London, PhD(biochem), 68. *Honors & Awards:* Basic Sci Award, Int Asn Dent Res, 74. *Prof Exp:* Vis scientist biochem, Forsyth Dent Ctr, Boston, 64-66. *Concurrent Pos:* Consult biochem, Koch Light Chem, Ltd, Eng, 67-70; res consult, Vet Admin Hosp, Philadelphia, 76-. *Mem:* AAAS; Biochem Soc; Royal Soc Med; Bone & Tooth Soc; Am Chem Soc. *Res:* Role of mitochondria in the initiation of the mineralization process; use of mineralized tissues in the diagnosis and treatment of lead poisoning. *Mailing Add:* Dept Biochem Univ Pa Sch Dent Med 4001 Spruce St Philadelphia PA 19104-6003

SHAPIRO, IRWIN IRA, PHYSICS, ASTRONOMY. *Current Pos:* SR SCIENTIST, SMITHSONIAN INST, 82-; PAINE PROF PRACT ASTRON & PROF PHYSICS, HARVARD UNIV, 82-, DIR, HARVARD-SMITHSONIAN CTR ASTROPHYS, 83- *Personal Data:* b New York, NY, Oct 10, 29; m 59; c 2. *Educ:* Cornell Univ, AB, 50; Harvard Univ, AM, 51, PhD(physics), 55. *Honors & Awards:* Albert A Michelson Medal, Franklin Inst, 75; Morris Loeb Lectr, Harvard Univ, 75; B A Gould Prize, Nat Acad Sci, 79; Math & Phys Sci Award, NY Acad Sci, 82; Dannie Heineman Prize, Am Astron Soc, 83, Dirk Brouwer Award, 87; John C Lindsay Lectr, NASA Goddard Space Flight Ctr, 86; William Bowie Lectr, Am Geophys Union, 90; Goodspeed-Richards Mem Lectr, Univ Pa, 91; Karl G Jansky Lectr, Nat Radio Astron Observ, 92; Thomas Gold Lectr, Cornell Univ, 93; Charles A Whitten Medal, Am Geophys Union, 93, William Bowie Medal, 93; NASA Group Achievement Award, 93 & 94; Einstein Medal, 94; Gerard P Kuiper Prize, Am Astron Soc, 96. *Prof Exp:* Staff mem physics & astron, Lincoln Lab, Mass Inst Technol, 54-70, prof geophys & physics, 67-80, Schlumberger prof, 80-85. *Concurrent Pos:* Consult, NASA, 67-68, prin investr, 68-73; vchmn, Div Dynamical Astron, Am Astron Soc, 69-70; numerous named & vis lectureships, 69-; John Simon Guggenheim fel, 82; emer Schlumberger prof, Mass Inst Technol, 85- *Mem:* Nat Acad Sci; fel Am Phys Soc; fel Am Geophys Union; Am Astron Soc; Int Astron Union; Am Acad Arts & Sci; Sigma Xi; fel AAAS. *Res:* Radio and radar techniques: applications to astrometry, astrophysics, geophysics, planetary physics and tests of theories of gravity; author or co-author of over 300 publications. *Mailing Add:* Harvard Smithsonian Ctr Astrophys 60 Garden St Cambridge MA 02138. *Fax:* 617-495-7105

SHAPIRO, IRWIN LOUIS, biochemistry; deceased, see previous edition for last biography

SHAPIRO, ISADORE, MATERIALS SCIENCE. *Current Pos:* CONSULT, 82- *Educ:* Univ Minn, BS, 38, PhD(phys chem), 44. *Prof Exp:* Fel, Univ Minn, 44-45; chemist, E I DuPont, 46-47; Naval Ord Test Sta, 47-52; dir, Pascal Lab, Owen Matheson Chem Corp, 52-59; head chem lab, Aircraft Div, Hughes Tool Co, 59-62; part owner, Aerospace Chem Systs, 62-66; dir contract res, Hitco, 66-67; prin scientist, McDonald Douglas Corp, 67-71; head mat processing group, Air Res Mfg, 71-82. *Mem:* Am Chem Soc; Am Phys Soc; Am Ceramic Soc; Nat Inst Ceramic Engrs; Soc Advan Mat & Process Eng; Soc Rheology; Am Inst Aeronaut & Astronaut; Sigma Xi. *Res:* Discovery of carborane series of compounds. *Mailing Add:* 5624 W 62nd St Los Angeles CA 90056-2009

SHAPIRO, JACK SOL, MATHEMATICS. *Current Pos:* Asst prof, 70-78, ASSOC PROF MATH, BARUCH COL, CITY UNIV NEW YORK, 78- *Personal Data:* b Brooklyn, NY, Nov 3, 41; m 70; c 2. *Educ:* Brooklyn Col, BS, 63; Yeshiva Univ, MA, 66, PhD(math), 70. *Mem:* Am Math Soc; Math Asn Am. *Res:* Functional analysis and operator theory. *Mailing Add:* 1824 Ave S Brooklyn NY 11229

SHAPIRO, JACOB, BIOPHYSICS, RADIOLOGICAL HEALTH. *Current Pos:* LECTR BIOPHYS IN ENVIRON HEALTH, SCH PUB HEALTH & UNIV HEALTH PHYSICIST, HARVARD UNIV, 61- *Personal Data:* b New York, NY, Sept 4, 25; m 48; c 2. *Educ:* City Col New York, BS, 44; Brown Univ, MS, 48; Univ Rochester, PhD(biophys), 54. *Prof Exp:* Instr physics, Univ RI, 46-47; tech adv nuclear energy, Opers Off, AEC, NY, 48-50; res assoc radiation biol, Univ Rochester, 53-55; supvr radiation anal, Elec Boat Div, Gen Dynamics Corp, 55-61. *Concurrent Pos:* Consult, US Adv Comt Nuclear Waste. *Mem:* Am Phys Soc; fel Health Physics Soc. *Res:* Evaluation of hazards, setting standards for radioactive surface contamination; radon air pollution; radiation detection and dosimetry. *Mailing Add:* Harvard Sch Pub Health 677 Huntington Ave Boston MA 02115-6023

SHAPIRO, JAMES ALAN, MICROBIOLOGY, MOLECULAR GENETICS. *Current Pos:* from asst prof to assoc prof, 73-82, PROF MICROBIOL, UNIV CHICAGO, 82- *Personal Data:* b Chicago, Ill, May 18, 43; m 64; c 2. *Educ:* Harvard Col, BA, 64; Cambridge Univ, PhD(genetics), 68. *Prof Exp:* Fel, Pasteur Inst, Paris, 67-68 & Harvard Med Sch, 68-70; invited prof genetics, Univ Havana, 70-72; fel, Brandeis Univ, 72-73. *Concurrent Pos:* Mem, Working Group Prod Useful Substances Microbiol Means, US/USSR Sci Exchange Prog, NSF, 75-78; NSF genetic biol panel, 81-84, Int Comn Indust Microorganisms, 82. *Mem:* Genetics Soc Am; Soc Gen Microbiol; Am Soc Microbiol; AAAS; Brit Genetical Soc; Sigma Xi. *Res:* Microbial hydrocarbon metabolism. *Mailing Add:* CLSC 861 Univ Chicago Chicago IL 60637

SHAPIRO, JEFFREY HOWARD, OPTICAL COMMUNICATIONS. *Current Pos:* assoc prof, 73-85, PROF ELEC ENG, MASS INST TECHNOL, 85-, ASSOC HEAD ELEC ENG, 89- *Personal Data:* b New York, NY, Dec 27, 46; m 69, Ellen Kirschenbaum; c Lisa & David. *Educ:* Mass Inst Technol, SB, 67, SM, 68, EE, 69, PhD(elec eng), 70. *Prof Exp:* Asst prof elec eng, Case Western Res Univ, 70-73. *Concurrent Pos:* NSF res grants, 71-77, 81-91; consult, Lincoln Lab, Mass Inst Technol, 77- *Mem:* Fel Inst Elec & Electronics Engrs; fel Optical Soc Am; Soc Photo-Optical Instrumentation Engrs. *Res:* Communication theory for optical systems; quantum noise reduction, coherent laser radars. *Mailing Add:* Dept Elec Eng & Comput Sci Mass Inst Technol Cambridge MA 02139. *Fax:* 617-258-7354; *E-Mail:* jhs@mit.edu

SHAPIRO, JEFFREY PAUL, PLANT-INSECT INTERACTIONS, PROTEIN CHEMISTRY. *Current Pos:* RES ENTOMOLOGIST, AGR RES SERV, USDA, 86- *Personal Data:* b Monterey Park, Calif, Sept 1, 50; m 88, Rita P; c 2. *Educ:* San Diego State Univ, BS, 73, MS, 77; Cornell Univ, PhD(entom), 81. *Prof Exp:* Sr res biologist, Monsanto Co, 83-85. *Concurrent Pos:* Assoc ed, Arch Insect Biochem & Physiol, 86-93. *Mem:* Entom Soc Am; Am Soc Biochem & Molecular Biol; Phytochem Soc NAm. *Res:* Biochemistry; insect biochemistry; chemistry of insect proteins/lipoproteins interacting with plant compounds; phytochemicals affecting insects; plant enzymology and defenses against insects. *Mailing Add:* USDA/Agr Res Serv 2120 Camden Rd Orlando FL 32803-1419. *E-Mail:* jshapiro@asrr.arsusda.gov

SHAPIRO, JOEL ALAN, THEORETICAL HIGH ENERGY PHYSICS. *Current Pos:* from asst prof to assoc prof, 71-88, PROF, HIGH ENERGY PHYSICS, RUTGERS UNIV, 88- *Personal Data:* b New York, NY, Feb 23, 42; m 65; c 2. *Educ:* Brown Univ, ScB, 62; Cornell Univ, PhD(theoret physics), 67. *Prof Exp:* Vis res physicist, Univ Calif, Berkeley, 67-69; res assoc high energy physics, Univ Md, College Park, 69-71. *Concurrent Pos:* Mem, Inst Advan Study, 86-87. *Mem:* Am Phys Soc; Am Asn Physics Teachers. *Res:* Gauge field theories and strings. *Mailing Add:* Dept Physics Rutgers Univ PO Box 849 Piscataway NJ 08855. *E-Mail:* shapiro@physics.rutgers.edu

SHAPIRO, JOSEPH, LIMNOLOGY. *Current Pos:* assoc prof geol & geophys, 64-70, PROF GEOL & GEOPHYS, LIMNOL RES CTR, UNIV MINN, MINNEAPOLIS, 70-, ASSOC DIR, 64- *Personal Data:* b Montreal, Que, May 24, 29; m 52; c 2. *Educ:* McGill Univ, BSc, 50; Univ Sask, MSc, 52; Yale Univ, PhD(limnol), 57. *Prof Exp:* Res assoc limnol, Univ Wash, 56-58, res instr, 58-59; asst prof sanit eng, Johns Hopkins Univ, 59-64. *Mem:* Fel AAAS; Am Soc Limnol & Oceanog; Int Asn Theoret & Appl Limnol. *Res:* Chemical, physical and biological phenomena occurring in natural waters. *Mailing Add:* Ecol 109 Zool Bldg Rm 220B Pillsbury Hall Univ Minn 310 Pillsbury Dr SE Minneapolis MN 55455

SHAPIRO, LARRY JAY, HUMAN GENETICS. *Current Pos:* CHMN, PEDIAT & BIOL CHEM, SCH MED, UNIV CALIF, SAN FRANCISCO, 93- *Personal Data:* b Chicago, Ill, July 6, 46; m 68; c 3. *Educ:* Washington Univ, AB, 68, MD, 71. *Honors & Awards:* Basil O'Connor Award, March of Dimes, 75; E Mead Johnson Award, Am Acad Pediat, 82. *Prof Exp:* Intern & resident pediat, St Louis Children's Hosp, 71-73; res assoc genetics, NIH, 73-75; from asst prof to assoc prof in residence pediat & genetics, 75-81, prof pediat & biol chem, Sch Med, Univ Calif, Los Angeles, 83-93. *Concurrent Pos:* Res career develop award, NIH, 80-85; pres, Soc Inherited Metabol Dis, 86-87; investr, Howard Hughes Med Inst, 87- *Mem:* Inst Med-Nat Acad Sci; Am Soc Human Genetics; Am Fedn Clin Res; fel Am Acad Pediat; Soc Inherited Metab Dis (pres, 86-87); Soc Pediat Res (pres elect, 90-91); Am Pediat Soc; Am Soc Clin Invest; Genetics Soc Am; Asn Am Physicians; Am Bd Med Genetics (vpres, 87-88, pres, 88-89); AAAS. *Res:* Pediatrics, with emphasis on inborn errors of metabolism, disorders of sulfated steroid metabolism, molecular genetics, and biology of sex chromosomes. *Mailing Add:* Univ Calif Dept Pediat Box 0110 San Francisco CA 94143-0110

SHAPIRO, LEE TOBEY, ASTRONOMY. *Current Pos:* AT MOREHEAD PLANETARIUM. *Personal Data:* b Chicago, Ill, Dec 12, 43; m 70; c 2. *Educ:* Carnegie Inst Technol, BS, 66; Northwestern Univ, MS, 68, PhD(astron), 74. *Prof Exp:* assoc prof astron & astrophys & dir Abrams Planetarium, Mich State Univ, 74- *Mem:* Am Astron Soc; Royal Astron Soc; Int Planetarium Soc; Am Asn Mus. *Res:* Late type giants and subgiants in close binaries; membership, size and configuration of the local group of galaxies; development and statistics of planetariums throughout the world. *Mailing Add:* 104 Saddle Ridge Rd Chapel Hill NC 27514-3480

SHAPIRO, LEONARD DAVID, DATABASE MANAGEMENT SYSTEMS, EDUCATION. *Current Pos:* PROF & HEAD COMPUT SCI, PORTLAND STATE UNIV, ORE, 87- *Personal Data:* b San Francisco, Calif, Dec 4, 43; m 70; c 3. *Educ:* Reed Col, BA, 65; Yale Univ, PhD(math), 69. *Prof Exp:* From instr to asst prof math, Univ Minn, Minneapolis, 70-76, vis prof econ, 76-77; chmn, 77-85, prof, Dept Math Sci, NDak State Univ, Fargo, 79-87. *Concurrent Pos:* Vis scholar econ, Univ Calif, Berkeley, 77, comput sci, 83-84. *Mem:* Am Math Soc; Math Asn Am; Econometric Soc; Asn Comput Mach; Int Elec & Electronics Engrs Soc. *Res:* Topological dynamics; minimal sets; diophantine approximation; mathematical economics; database management systems; results on main memory and novel uses of database systems for artificial intelligence and operations. *Mailing Add:* Dept Comput Sci Portland State Univ PO Box 751 Portland OR 97207-0751

SHAPIRO, LUCILLE, MICROBIAL DEVELOPMENT. *Current Pos:* chmn, 89-96, PROF, DEVELOP BIOL DEPT, SCH MED, STANFORD UNIV, 89-, PROF GENETICS, 90- *Personal Data:* b New York, NY, July 16, 40; m 60; c 3. *Educ:* Brooklyn Col, BA, 62; Albert Einstein Col Med, PhD(molecular biol), 66. *Honors & Awards:* Hirschl Career Scientist Award, 76; De Witt Stetten Jr Lectr, NIH, 89; Clayton S White Lectr, Okla Med Res; Krampitz Lectr, Case Western Univ, 94; Sonneborne Lectr, Ind Univ, 96; Lamson Lectr, Univ Tenn, 96; Excellence in Sci Award, Fedn Am Soc Exp Biol, 94. *Prof Exp:* Jane Coffin Childs fel biochem, Albert Einstein Col Med, 66-67, from asst prof to prof molecular biol, 67-86, chmn, Molecular Biol Dept, 77-86, dir biol serv, 81-86; prof & chmn, Molecular Biol Dept, Col Physicians & Surgeons, Columbia Univ, 86-89. *Concurrent Pos:* Am Cancer Soc fac res assoc award, 68-71 & 71-76; Albert & Jane Nerken fel molecular biol, 70-76; mem, Study Sect Cell & Molecular Biol, NIH, 75, Study Sect Develop Biol, NSF, 76-77, Microbial Chem Study Sect, NIH, 78-80, Bd Sci Counr, NIAMKKD, 80-84, Gen Med Sci Coun, NIH, 81, adv bd, NSF Biol & Behav Sci Dir, 82 & 83-87, nat bd, Am Heart Asn, 84-87 & coun, Am Soc Biochem & Molecular Biol, 90-93; co-chmn, adv bd, NSF Biol & Behav Sci Dir, 82 & 83-87; distinguished lectr, Carnegie Mellon Univ, 88, Woods Hole Arts & Sci, 89, Univ Colo, 89 & Southwestern Univ Tex, 90; assoc ed, Molecular Biol of Cell, 92-; Merit award, NIH, 93-; resident scholar, Rockefeller Found, Bellagio, Italy, 96. *Mem:* Nat Acad Sci; Sigma Xi; fel AAAS; Am Soc Biochem & Molcular Biol; Am Soc Microbiol; NY Acad Sci; Am Acad Arts & Sci; Am Acad Microbiol; Am Soc Biol Chemists; Am Soc Cell Biol; Genetics Soc; Inst Med-Nat Acad Sci. *Res:* Unicellular differentiations; developmental biology. *Mailing Add:* Dept Develop Biol Beckman Ctr Stanford Univ Sch Med Stanford CA 94305-5427

SHAPIRO, LYNDA P, MARINE BIOLOGY. *Current Pos:* PROF BIOL & DIR, INST MARINE BIOL, UNIV ORE, 90- *Personal Data:* b Brooklyn, NY, June 11, 38. *Educ:* Univ Ark, BA, 60, MS, 63; Duke Univ, PhD, 74. *Prof Exp:* Instr biol, La State Univ, 63-66; res teaching asst, Columbia Univ, 67-68; tech assoc, Med Ctr, Duke Univ, 68-69; investr, Woods Hole Oceanog Inst, 75, asst scientist, 75-79; res scientist, Bigelow Lab Ocean Sci, 79-90. *Concurrent Pos:* Comnr, S Slough Nat Estuarine Res Reserve, 90- *Mem:* AAAS; Am Soc Limnol & Oceanog; Phycol Soc Am. *Res:* Ecology, biogeography and physiology of marine phytoplankton; distributions of ultraphytoplankton species, effects of environmental factors on those distributions and effects of those distributions on the various marine environments; predation on ultraplankton by pelagic protists. *Mailing Add:* Dept Biol Univ Ore Eugene OR 97403

SHAPIRO, MARK HOWARD, SURFACE PHYSICS, COMPUTER SIMULATION. *Current Pos:* from asst prof to assoc prof, Calif State Univ, Fullerton, 70-78, actg assoc dean, Sch Math, Sci & Eng, 85-86, dept chair, 89-96, ACTG DIR OFF FAC RES & DEVELOP & PROF PHYSICS, CALIF STATE UNIV, FULLERTON, 78- *Personal Data:* b Boston, Mass, Apr 18, 40; m 61, Anita R Lavine; c David, Diane & Lisa. *Educ:* Univ Calif, Berkeley, AB, 62; Univ Pa, MS, 63, PhD(physics), 66. *Prof Exp:* Res fel physics, Kellogg Radiation Lab, Calif Inst Technol, 66-68; res assoc, Nuclear Struct Res Lab, Univ Rochester, 68-70. *Concurrent Pos:* Res Corp grant & fac res grant, 71-72; vis assoc, Kellogg Radiation Lab, Calif Inst Technol, 76-; Calif Inst Technol Pres venture fund grant, 77-78; US Geol Surv grant, 78-85; NSF grant, 84-87 & 90-; actg dir, Off Fac Res & Develop, CSUF, 86-87; rotator, NSF, 87-88; vis scientist, Nat Inst Stand & Technol, 87- *Mem:* AAAS; Am Phys Soc; Am Asn Physics Teachers; Am Geophys Union; NY Acad Sci; Mat Res Soc. *Res:* Nuclear structure physics; nuclear reaction physics; laboratory nuclear astrophysics; applications of nuclear physics in geophysics; nuclear safety; ion-surface interactions; molecular dynamics. *Mailing Add:* Dept Physics Calif State Univ Fullerton CA 92834-6866. *Fax:* 714-449-5810; *E-Mail:* mshapiro@fullerton.edu

SHAPIRO, MARTIN, ENTOMOLOGY, MICROBIOLOGY. *Current Pos:* mem staff, Gypsy Moth Methods Develop Lab, 75-85, INSECT PATH LAB, USDA, 85- *Personal Data:* b New York, NY, Mar 18, 37; m 67; c 2. *Educ:* Brooklyn Col, AB, 58; Cornell Univ, MS, 61; Univ Calif, Berkeley, PhD(entom), 66. *Prof Exp:* Entomologist, USDA, Tex, 65-66; res entomologist, Int Minerals & Chem Corp, 66-70; USPHS fel insect path,

Boyce Thompson Inst Plant Res, 70-72; entomologist, Maag & Easterbrooks, Inc, 72-73; mem staff, Res Unit Vector Path, Mem Univ Nfld, 73-75. *Concurrent Pos:* Consult, Int Minerals & Chem Corp, 70-73. *Mem:* Soc Invert Path; Entom Soc Am; Tissue Cult Asn; Int Orgn Biol Control. *Res:* Insect pathology and tissue culture; photobiology. *Mailing Add:* Agr Res Ctr Bldg 011A Rm 214 Barc-west Beltsville MD 20705

SHAPIRO, MAURICE A, ENVIRONMENTAL HEALTH ENGINEERING, PUBLIC HEALTH. *Current Pos:* prof sanit eng, 51-69, prof 69-82, EMER PROF ENVIRON HEALTH ENG, GRAD SCH PUB HEALTH, UNIV PITTSBURGH, 82- *Personal Data:* b Denver, Colo, June 4, 17; m 45; c 6. *Educ:* Johns Hopkins Univ, AB, 41; Univ Calif, Berkeley, MEng, 49; Am Acad Environ Engr, dipl. *Prof Exp:* Asst sanit engr, USPHS, 41-47, field officer, United Yugoslav Relief Fund Am, 47-48; eng res assoc, Am Pub Health Asn, 49-51. *Concurrent Pos:* Vis prof, Israel Inst Technol, 65-66; found dir, Westernport Bay Environ Study, Victoria, Australia, 73-74; vis mem sci fac, Univ Melbourne, 73-74; vis lectr, Monash Univ, 73-74; Wuhan Univ, 86. *Mem:* Am Soc Civil Engrs; Am Water Works Asn; Am Pub Health Asn; Am Pub Works Asn; Soc Environ & Occup Health. *Res:* Water and air pollution control; health aspects of energy conversion and water quality; radioactive wastes disposal; environmental health aspects of energy conversion, environmental health planning. *Mailing Add:* 5712 Wilkins Ave Pittsburgh PA 15217

SHAPIRO, MAURICE MANDEL, COSMIC RADIATION, NEUTRINO ASTROPHYSICS. *Current Pos:* DIR, INT SCH COSMIC RAY ASTROPHYS, ERICE, ITALY, 77- *Personal Data:* b Jerusalem, Palestine, Nov 13, 15; US citizen; m 42, Inez Weinfield; c Joel N, Elana A (Naktin) & Raquel T (Kislinger). *Educ:* Univ Chicago, SB, 36, SM, 40, PhD(physics), 42. *Honors & Awards:* Edison Lectr; Medal of Hon, Soc Encour Progress, Paris; Victor Hess Mem Lectr,. *Prof Exp:* Assoc physicist, USN, 42-44; group leader, Los Alamos Lab, Univ Calif, 44-46; sr physicist, Oak Ridge Nat Lab & lectr, Nucleonics Sch, 46-49; chief scientist, Lab Cosmic Physics, Naval Res Lab, 49-82, dir, Nucleonics Div, 53-65; consult, NASA, 65-70. *Concurrent Pos:* Chmn, Dept Phys & Biol Sci, Austin Col, 38-41; lectr, George Washington Univ, 43-44, Reactor Dept, Erco Div, ACF Indust, Inc, 56-58; lectr, Grad Sch, Univ Md, 49-50 & 52-55, assoc prof, 50-51; Guggenheim fel & vis prof, Weizmann Inst, 62-63; prin investr, Gemini, Skylab Cosmic-Ray Exposure Facil, NASA, 63-82; mem comt emulsion exp, Space Sci Bd, Nat Acad Sci & mem panel x-ray & gamma ray astron, 65; mem working group space biophys, Coun Europ, 70-; chmn, Div Cosmic Physics, Am Phys Soc, 71-72 & High Energy Astrophys Div, 82; chmn comt interdisciplinary res & consult panel cosmic radiation, US Nat Comt, Int Geophys Year; prin investr, Gemini, Skylab Cosmic-Ray Exp & Long Duration Exposure Facil, NASA, 63-82; deleg, int confs cosmic radiation, Int Union Pure & Appl Physics; deleg, int confs nuclear & high energy physics, nuclear photog & comt on space res; mem, Comn Honor for Celebration of Einstein Centenary, Acad Lincei, 77-79; mem steering comn, DUMAND Consortium; vis prof astron, Northwestern Univ, 78, Univ Iowa & Univ Bonn, WGer, 81-84 & Univ Md, 85-; assoc ed, Phys Rev Lett, 78-84; Humboldt sr US scientist award, 81; vis scientist, Max Planck Inst Astrophys, Munich, 84-85; regents lectr, Univ Calif, Riverside, 85. *Mem:* Fel Am Phys Soc; Sigma Xi; Am Technion Soc; Fedn Am Scientists; Am Astron Soc; Int Astron Union. *Res:* Cosmic rays, especially composition, origin, propagation and nuclear transformations; nuclear-emulsion techniques for high-energy physics and cosmic rays; charged sigma hyperons; physics of underwater explosions; neutron and fission physics; neutrino astrophysics; reactor design; piezoelectricity; editor of 8 volumes on cosmic rays and astrophysics. *Mailing Add:* 205 Yoakum Pkwy No 1514 Alexandria VA 22304. *Fax:* 703-370-1985

SHAPIRO, NATHAN, GENETICS. *Current Pos:* prof, 70-84, EMER PROF BIOL, EASTERN CONN STATE COL, 84- *Personal Data:* b Boston, Mass, July 16, 24; m 51; c 2. *Educ:* Univ Wis, BS, 49, MS, 50; Purdue Univ, PhD(genetics), 63. *Prof Exp:* Mycologist, Mat Testing Lab, NY Naval Shipyard, 51-53; res asst, Biol Dept, Brookhaven Nat Lab, 56-59; asst prof zool, Smith Col, 59-70. *Res:* Radiation genetics; plant growth hormones. *Mailing Add:* 5400 N A1A B21 Vero Beach FL 32963

SHAPIRO, PAUL JONATHON, mechanical engineering, for more information see previous edition

SHAPIRO, PAUL ROBERT, THEORETICAL ASTROPHYSICS, COSMOLOGY. *Current Pos:* from asst prof to assoc prof, 81-92, PROF ASTRON, UNIV TEX, 92- *Personal Data:* b New Haven, Conn, Aug 2, 53; m 93, Cecilia Colome; c Sofia. *Educ:* Harvard Col, AB, 74; Harvard Univ, PhD(astron), 79. *Prof Exp:* Res fel astrophys, Inst Advan Study, 78-81. *Concurrent Pos:* Alfred P Sloan Found res fel physics, 84-88; vis prof, Inst Astron Nat Autonomous, Univ Mex, Mexico City, 97; deans fel, Univ Tex, 97. *Mem:* Am Astron Soc; Am Phys Soc; Sigma Xi. *Res:* Theoretical astrophysics research including the intergalactic medium, cosmology and the formation of galaxies and structure in the universe; interstellar medium; gas dynamics. *Mailing Add:* Dept Astron Univ Tex Austin TX 78712

SHAPIRO, PHILIP, NUCLEAR PHYSICS, RADIATION EFFECTS. *Current Pos:* RETIRED. *Personal Data:* b Brooklyn, NY, Sept 10, 23; wid; c 2. *Educ:* Brooklyn Col, BS, 48; Univ Iowa, PhD(physics), 53. *Prof Exp:* Asst physics, Univ Iowa, 48-53; physicist, Radiation Div, US Naval Res Lab, 53-66, Nuclear Physics Div, 66-71, from Cyclotron Br to Cyclotron Appln Br, 71-85; physicist, SFA Inc, 85-96. *Mem:* AAAS; Am Phys Soc. *Res:* Neutron radiotherapy; dosimetry; nuclear reactions; radiation effects on microelectronics. *Mailing Add:* 496 Naylor Pl Alexandria VA 22304

SHAPIRO, RALPH, DYNAMIC METEOROLOGY. *Current Pos:* CONSULT & EXPERT WITNESS, 94- *Personal Data:* b Malden, Mass, Nov 9, 22; m 45; c 3. *Educ:* Bridgewater Col, BS, 43; Mass Inst Technol, MS, 48, DSc(meteorol), 50. *Prof Exp:* Asst, Pressure Change Proj, Mass Inst Technol, 47-50; meteorologist, Planetary Atmospheres Proj, Lowell Observ, 50-51; proj scientist, Geophys Res Directorate, Hanscom AFB, 51-57, assoc chief, Meteorol Develop Lab & chief, Atmospheric Dynamics Br, Air Force Cambridge Res Ctr, 57-75, chief, Climatol & Dynamics Br, Air Force Geophys Lab, 75-80; sr scientist, S T Systs Corp, 80-94. *Concurrent Pos:* Consult ed, McGraw-Hill Encycl Sci & Technol, 73-80. *Mem:* AAAS; Am Geophys Union; fel Am Meteorol Soc; foreign mem Royal Meteorol Soc; Sigma Xi. *Res:* Mathematical modeling of large-scale atmospheric circulations; numerical weather prediction; numerical analysis of partial differential equations; digital filter design; statistical weather prediction; flux of solar radiation through the atmosphere. *Mailing Add:* 30 Wayne Rd Needham MA 02194

SHAPIRO, RAYMOND E, chemistry; deceased, see previous edition for last biography

SHAPIRO, ROBERT, BIOCHEMISTRY, ORGANIC CHEMISTRY. *Current Pos:* fel biochem, Sch Med, 60-61, from asst prof to assoc prof, 61-70, PROF CHEM, NY UNIV, 70- *Personal Data:* b New York, NY, Nov 28, 35; m 64; c 1. *Educ:* City Col New York, BS, 56; Harvard Univ, AM, 57, PhD(chem), 59. *Prof Exp:* NATO fel chem, Cambridge Univ, 59-60. *Mem:* AAAS; Am Chem Soc; Am Soc Biochem & Molecular Biol. *Res:* Chemistry of nucleic acids; chemical mutagenesis and carcinogenesis; origin of life; human genome project. *Mailing Add:* Dept Chem NY Univ 100 Washington Sq E New York NY 10003-6603. *Fax:* 212-260-7905; *E-Mail:* Bitnet: shapiror@nyuacf

SHAPIRO, ROBERT ALLEN, INDUSTRIAL ENGINEERING. *Current Pos:* ENGR, ACACIA GROUP, 92- *Personal Data:* b Long Branch, NJ, Aug 14, 30; m 53; c 3. *Educ:* Okla State Univ, BS, 53, MS, 64, PhD(indust eng), 65. *Prof Exp:* Div prod engr, Shell Oil Co, 53-61; assoc prof, Univ Okla, 64-72, asst to pres, 67-88, prof indust eng, & assoc vpres admin & finance, 72-92, dir, Sch Eng, 65-92. *Concurrent Pos:* Consult, Okla Mgt Study Comt, 67, US Army & USPHS, 67- *Mem:* Am Inst Indust Engrs; Am Soc Petrol Engrs; Am Soc Eng Educ; Am Soc Qual Control. *Res:* Operations research, including recurrent processes, modern organization theory, econometric models of decisions under uncertainty and statistical quality control. *Mailing Add:* 3750 W Main St Suite 118 Norman OK 73072

SHAPIRO, ROBERT HOWARD, ORGANIC CHEMISTRY. *Current Pos:* ACADEMIC DEAN & PROVOST, US NAVAL ACADEMY, ANNAPOLIS, MD, 89- *Personal Data:* b New Haven, Conn, July 18, 35; m 56; c 3. *Educ:* Univ Conn, BS, 61; Stanford Univ, PhD(chem), 64. *Prof Exp:* NSF fel chem, Royal Vet & Agr Col, Denmark, 64-65; from asst prof to prof chem, Univ Colo, Boulder, 65-80; prof & dept head chem & dean, Coll Lett & Sci, James Madison Univ, 80-89. *Concurrent Pos:* Consult, Criminal Lawyers, 66- *Mem:* Am Chem Soc; Royal Soc Chem. *Res:* Reaction mechanisms; mass spectrometry; environmental chemistry; natural products chemistry. *Mailing Add:* US Naval Academy Annapolis MD 21402-5088

SHAPIRO, RUBIN, ANALYTICAL CHEMISTRY. *Current Pos:* RETIRED. *Personal Data:* b Chicago, Ill, Nov 7, 24; div; c 2. *Educ:* Univ Ill, BS, 48; Univ Wis, PhD(anal chem), 53. *Prof Exp:* Res chemist, Am Nat Can Co, 53-57, supvr, 57-68, res assoc, 68-77, sr res assoc, 77-86, res fel, 86-89. *Mem:* Am Chem Soc; Soc Appl Spectros. *Res:* Emission, mass and atomic absorption spectroscopy; gas chromatography; analytical chemistry. *Mailing Add:* 1215 N Waterman 1-J Arlington Heights IL 60004-5192

SHAPIRO, SAM, EPIDEMIOLOGY, BIOSTATISTICS. *Current Pos:* dir, Health Serv Res & Develop Ctr, Johns Hopkins Med Insts, 73-83, prof, 73-85, EMER PROF HEALTH POLICY & MGT, SCH HYG & PUB HEALTH, JOHNS HOPKINS UNIV, 85- *Personal Data:* b New York, NY, Feb 12, 14; m 38; c 2. *Educ:* Brooklyn Col, BS, 33. *Prof Exp:* Chief, Natality Anal Br, Nat Off Vital Statist, USPHS, 47-54; sr study dir, Nat Opinion Res Ctr, 54-55; assoc dir, Div Res & Statist, Health Ins Plan of Greater New York, 55-59, vpres & dir, 59-73. *Concurrent Pos:* Lectr pub health, Sch Pub Health & Admin Med, Columbia Univ, 61-80; adj prof community med, Mt Sinai Sch Med, 72-78; consult to var insts & orgns. *Mem:* Inst Med-Nat Acad Sci; fel Am Pub Health Asn; fel Am Statist Asn; fel Am Heart Asn; Am Epidemiol Soc; fel AAAS; Am Soc Prev Oncol; Asn Health Serv Res. *Res:* Evaluative research in organization; delivery; economics; quality of health care. *Mailing Add:* Sch Hyg & Pub Health Johns Hopkins Med Insts 624 N Broadway Baltimore MD 21205

SHAPIRO, SAMUEL S, APPLIED STATISTICS. *Current Pos:* PROF STATIST, FLA INT UNIV, 72- *Personal Data:* b Brooklyn, NY, July 13, 30; m 56, Yevette Trieff; c Michael & Bonnie. *Educ:* City Col New York, BBA, 52; Columbia Univ, MS, 54; Rutgers Univ, MS, 61, PhD(statist), 64. *Honors & Awards:* Jack Youdin Prize, 72; Ellis R Ott Award, Am Soc Qual Control, 94. *Prof Exp:* Statist qual control engr, Pittsburgh Plate Glass Co, 56-58; statistician, Res & Develop Ctr, Gen Elec Co, NY, 58-67 & Prog Methodology, Inc, 67-72. *Concurrent Pos:* Lectr, Union Col, 65-66; UN tech adv, Indian Statist Inst, 66. *Mem:* Am Statist Asn; fel Am Statist Asn. *Res:* Testing for distributional assumptions. *Mailing Add:* Dept Statist Fla Int Univ University Park Miami FL 33199-0400. *Fax:* 305-348-4172; *E-Mail:* shapiro@servms.fiu.edu

SHAPIRO, SANDOR SOLOMON, HEMATOLOGY. *Current Pos:* from instr to assoc prof, 64-72, assoc dir, 78-85, PROF MED, CARDEZA FOUND, JEFFERSON MED COL, 72-, DIR, FOUND, 85- *Personal Data:* b Brooklyn, NY, July 26, 33; m 54; c 2. *Educ:* Harvard Univ, BA, 54, MD, 57. *Prof Exp:* Intern, Harvard Med Serv, Boston City Hosp, 57-58; asst surgeon, Div Biol Stand, NIH, USPHS, 58-60; asst resident, Boston City Hosp, 60-61; NIH spec fel, Mass Inst Technol, 61-64. *Concurrent Pos:* Mem hemat study sect, NIH, 72-76 & 78-79; mem med adv coun, Nat Hemophilia Found, 73-75; chmn, Pa State Hemophilia Adv Comt, 74-76. *Mem:* Am Soc Clin Invest; Am Soc Hemat; Am Asn Immunologists; Int Soc Thrombosis & Hemostasis; Am Asn Physicians. *Res:* Hemostasis and thrombosis, prothrombin metabolism, hemophilia; lupus anticoagulants; endothelial cells. *Mailing Add:* Cardeza Found Jefferson Med Col 1015 Walnut St Philadelphia PA 19107-5099

SHAPIRO, SEYMOUR, BOTANY. *Current Pos:* head dept, 64-69, actg dean arts & sci, 69-70, actg head dept, 74-75, dean fac natural sci & math, 75-79, PROF BOT, UNIV MASS, AMHERST, 64- *Personal Data:* b New York, NY, Feb 16, 24; m 47; c 1. *Educ:* Univ Mich, BS, 47, PhD(bot), 52. *Prof Exp:* Instr bot, Univ Mich, 50-51, res assoc, 51-52; res collabr biol, Brookhaven Nat Lab, 53, assoc botanist, NY, 53-61; assoc prof biol, Univ Ore, 61-64. *Concurrent Pos:* Consult, NSF, 62-69, vis scientist, Inst Atomic Sci in Agr, Wageningen, Neth, 70-71; vis prof, Univ Col North Wales, UK, 74. *Mem:* AAAS; Am Soc Plant Physiologists; Am Soc Develop Biol; Bot Soc Am. *Res:* Regeneration; morphogenesis of higher plants. *Mailing Add:* Dept Biol Univ Ma Amhurst Amherst MA 01003-0002

SHAPIRO, SIDNEY, ELECTRONIC DEVICES, SUPERCONDUCTIVITY. *Current Pos:* assoc prof, Univ Rochester, 67-73, assoc dean, Col Eng & Appl Sci, 74-79, chmn dept, 80-89, prof, 73-93, EMER PROF ELEC ENG, UNIV ROCHESTER, 94- *Personal Data:* b Boston, Mass, Dec 4, 31; m 60, Janice Yeutter; c Sara R (Gifford) & Johanna S (Kelley). *Educ:* Harvard Univ, AB, 53, AM, 55, PhD(appl physics), 59. *Prof Exp:* Res asst appl physics, Harvard Univ, 55-59; physicist, Arthur D Little, Inc, 59-64; mem tech staff, Bell Labs, Inc, NJ, 64-67. *Concurrent Pos:* Vis prof, Physics Lab I, Tech Univ Denmark, 72-73. *Mem:* Fel Inst Elec & Electronics Engrs. *Res:* Fast relaxation processes in devices; electron tunneling; Josephson effect; microwave phenomena and devices involving superconducting junctions and weak links. *Mailing Add:* 220 Parkwood Ave Rochester NY 14620-3406. *E-Mail:* shapiro@ee.rochester.edu

SHAPIRO, STANLEY, RESEARCH MANAGEMENT, GENERAL MANAGEMENT. *Current Pos:* CHIEF FINANCIAL OFFICER, METAMOR TECHNOLOGIES, LTD, 93- *Personal Data:* b Brooklyn, NY, Jan 3, 37; m 58; c 3. *Educ:* City Col New York, BChe, 60; Rensselaer Polytech Inst, MS, 64; Lehigh Univ, PhD(metall), 66. *Prof Exp:* Res engr, Pratt & Whitney, 60-61; res engr, Res Lab, United Aircraft Corp, 61-64; instr & res asst, Lehigh Univ, 64-66; res sci supvr, Metals Res Labs, Olin Corp, 66-79; pres, Revere Res, Inc, 70-84; vpres res & develop, Nat Can Co, 84-87; vpres, Res & Develop Oper, Am Nat Can, 87-89; consult, mergers & acquisitions, 89-93. *Mem:* Am Inst Metal Engrs; Am Soc Metals; AAAS; Am Soc Testing & Mats; Sigma Xi. *Res:* Non-ferrous metals research and development; alloy and process research. *Mailing Add:* Metamor Technol 1 North Franklin Chicago IL 60606. *Fax:* 312-943-7703; *E-Mail:* sshapiro@metamor.com

SHAPIRO, STANLEY KALLICK, MICROBIOLOGY, BIOCHEMISTRY. *Current Pos:* head dept, 74-85, PROF BIOL SCI, UNIV ILL, CHICAGO, 69- *Personal Data:* b Montreal, Que, Mar 20, 23; nat US; m 45, Gertrude Luner. *Educ:* McGill Univ, BSc, 44, MSc, 45; Univ Wis, PhD(microbiol), 49. *Prof Exp:* Asst prof bact, Iowa State Univ, 49-54; assoc biochemist, Argonne Nat Lab, 54-69. *Mem:* AAAS; Am Soc Microbiol; Am Soc Biol Chemists; Sigma Xi. *Res:* Microbial physiology and biochemistry; sulfonium biochemistry, transmethylation, polyamine biosynthesis, sulfur amino acid metabolism. *Mailing Add:* Dept Biol Sci Univ Ill 845 W Taylor St M/C 066 Chicago IL 60607-7060

SHAPIRO, STANLEY SEYMOUR, DRUG DISCOVERY, MECHANISM OF ACTION OF DERMATOLOGICAL DRUGS. *Current Pos:* sr biochemist, Hoffmann-La Roche Inc, 68-76, res fel, 76-80, sr res fel, 80-85, dir dermat res, 85-93, asst vpres, 90-93, SR DIR DERMAT RES, HOFFMANN-LA ROCHE, 93- *Personal Data:* b Brooklyn, NY, Sept 22, 40; m 65, Elaine Schwartz; c 3. *Educ:* Brooklyn Col, BS, 63; Univ Del, PhD(biochem), 66. *Prof Exp:* NIH fel molecular biol, Albert Einstein Col Med, 66-68. *Concurrent Pos:* Mem coadj staff, Rutgers Univ, Newark, 69-86. *Mem:* Am Acad Dermat; NY Acad Sci; Am Soc Biol Chemists; Am Chem Soc; Am Inst Nutrit; Soc Invest Dermat. *Res:* Biochemistry and cell biology of retinoids; identify and develop agents for the treatment of dermatological disorders; effect of vitamin D analogs in dermatological disorders. *Mailing Add:* Dermat Res & Drug Discovery Johnson & Johnson Consumer Prod Worldwide 199 Grandview Rd Skillman NJ 08558-9418. *Fax:* 201-237-7010

SHAPIRO, STEPHEN D, COMPUTER & INFORMATION SCIENCE. *Personal Data:* b New York, NY, Feb 18, 41; m 69; c 1. *Educ:* Columbia Univ, BS, 63, MS, 64, PhD(digital syst), 67. *Prof Exp:* Mem tech staff comput software algorithms, Bell Tel Lab, 67-71; prof comput sci, Dept Elec Eng, Stevens Inst Technol, 74-80; prof elec eng, State Univ NY, Stony Brook, 80-92. *Concurrent Pos:* Consult info processing, var comn & indust orgn, 71-; consult dir comput sci educ prog, Bell Labs, 76-; NSF grant, 76-; chmn, Elec Eng Dept, Comput Sci Comn, 78- *Mem:* Sigma Xi; sr mem Inst Elec & Electronics Engrs; Asn Comput Mach. *Res:* Information processing; software engineering; picture processing; telecommunications. *Mailing Add:* 20 Old Post Rd East Setauket NY 11733

SHAPIRO, STEPHEN MICHAEL, NEUTRON SCATTERING STUDIES OF SOLIDS. *Current Pos:* assoc chmn, Physics Dept, 94, PHYSICIST, BROOKHAVEN NAT LAB, 74- *Personal Data:* b Pittsfield, Mass, June 21, 41; div; c Julien & Aurelie. *Educ:* Union Col, BS, 63; Johns Hopkins Univ, PhD(physics), 69. *Honors & Awards:* Award Outstanding Sci Achievement, Dept Energy, 88. *Prof Exp:* Res assoc, Physics Lab, Univ Paris, 69-70; res assoc, Brookhaven Nat Lab, 71-73; vis physicist, Riso Nat Lab, Denmark, 73-74. *Concurrent Pos:* Yamada fel, Osaka Univ, 83; distinguished vis, Lab Leon Brillovin, Saclay, France. *Mem:* Am Phys Soc; Mat Res Soc; AAAS. *Res:* Neutron scattering studies of phase transitions, magnetic phenomenon and heavy fermions; spin glasses. *Mailing Add:* Dept Physics 510B Brookhaven Nat Lab Upton NY 11973

SHAPIRO, STEWART, DENTISTRY, PUBLIC HEALTH. *Current Pos:* PROF FAMILY PRACT & COMMUNITY HEALTH, COLS MED & HEALTH, PROF COMMUNITY DENT, COL DENT & CHMN DIV COMMUNITY DENT, UNIV OKLA, 72- *Personal Data:* b Springfield, Mass, Mar 21, 37; c 2. *Educ:* Boston Col, BA, 58; Tufts Univ, DMD, 62; Harvard Univ, MScH, 69; Century Univ, PhD, 81. *Prof Exp:* Res assoc oral physiol, Dent Sch, Tufts Univ, 62-63, instr oral physiol & oral diag, 64-65; staff mem, Forsyth Dent Ctr, 65-66; asst prof community dent, Sch Dent, Univ Md, 69-72. *Concurrent Pos:* Pvt pract dent, 62-68; lectr epidemiol, Sch Hyg & Pub Health, Johns Hopkins Univ, 69-70, assoc, 70-72; consult, Job Corps Prog, Dept Labor, 70-72; Vet Admin Hosp, Muskogee, Okla, 72- & Head Start, Div Dent Health, Dept HEW, 73- *Mem:* Am Dent Asn; Int Asn Dent Res; Am Pub Health Asn; Am Asn Dent Schs. *Res:* Prevention; gerontology; behavior. *Mailing Add:* Div Community Dent Univ Okla Sch Dent Oklahoma City OK 73190

SHAPIRO, STUART, SECONDARY METABOLISM, QUANTITATIVE STRUCTURE-ACTIVITY RELATIONSHIPS. *Current Pos:* MICROBIOL, ZAHNARTZ INST, UNIV ZURICH, 91- *Personal Data:* b Brooklyn, NY, 1952. *Educ:* Washington Square Col, NY Univ, BA, 71; Univ Ill, Urbana-Champaign, MS, 76; Worcester Polytech Inst, PhD(biomed sci), 81. *Prof Exp:* Fel biol, Dalhousie Univ, 81-83; asst prof chem, Concordia Univ, 83-85; res, Bact Inst Armand-Frappier, 85-86; asst prof & res assoc biol, Dalhousie Univ, 86-87; mgr, Indust Microbiol Dept, Sigma Tau SpA, 88-91. *Concurrent Pos:* Vis scientist, pharm, Univ Wis-Madison, 88; Colgate fel. *Mem:* Soc Indust Microbiol; Swiss Soc Microbiol. *Res:* Microbial biochemistry; natural products chemistry; biofilms; quantitative structure-activity relationships; computational chemistry. *Mailing Add:* Dept Oral Microbiol & Gen Immunol Zahn Inst Univ Zurich Plattenstr 11 CH-8028 Zurich Switzerland. *E-Mail:* toukie@zui.unizh.ch

SHAPIRO, STUART CHARLES, KNOWLEDGE REPRESENTATION & REASONING, NATURAL LANGUAGE PROCESSING. *Current Pos:* from asst prof to assoc prof, 77-83, chmn dept, 84-90, PROF COMPUT SCI, STATE UNIV NY, BUFFALO, 83-; RES SCIENTIST, NAT CTR GEOG INFO & ANAL, BUFFALO SITE, 89- *Personal Data:* b New York, NY, Dec 30, 44; m 72, Caren D Knight. *Educ:* Mass Inst Technol, SB, 66; Univ Wis, MS, 68, PhD(comput sci), 71. *Prof Exp:* From asst prof to assoc prof comput sci, Ind Univ, 71-78. *Concurrent Pos:* Teaching asst, Comput Sci Dept, Univ Wis, 66-67; consult, Ling Group, Rand Corp, 68-71; Anal & Simulation Inc, 83-87; Calspan-UB Res Ctr, Buffalo, 87- & Univ Southern Calif Info Sci Inst, 87-89; NJ Inst Technol, 93; lectr, Comput Sci Dept, Univ Wis, 71; vis res asst prof, Comput Sci Dept, Univ Ill, Urbana, 74; actg chmn, Comput Sci Dept, State Univ NY, Buffalo, 78-79, NSF grant, 78-; external fel, Cognitive Sci Prog, Univ Rochester, 82-83; mem, Eval Panel NSF fels comput sci, Nat Res Coun, 83-85 & Rev Panel Res Prog Math & Info Sci Dir, Air Force Off Sci Res, 86-88; prin lectr & consult, Smart Systs Technol, McLean, Va, 83-85; prin investr, Rome Air Develop Ctr, Air Force Off Sci Res, 84-89 & Defense Adv Res Proj Agency, 87-89. *Mem:* Asn Comput Mach; Asn Comput Ling; Inst Elec & Electronics Engrs; Cognitive Sci Soc; Am Asn Artificial Intel; Sigma Xi. *Res:* Artificial intelligence; representation of knowledge; reasoning; natural language processing; intelligent computer-human interfaces; logic. *Mailing Add:* 142 Viscount Dr Williamsville NY 14221-1770. *E-Mail:* shapiro@cs.buffalo.edu

SHAPIRO, STUART LOUIS, ASTROPHYSICS. *Current Pos:* PROF PHYSICS & ASTRON, UNIV ILL, 96-; SR SCIENTIST, NCSCA, 96- *Personal Data:* b New Haven, Conn, Dec 6, 47; m 71. *Educ:* Harvard Univ, AB, 69; Princeton Univ, MA, 71, PhD(astrophys sci), 73. *Prof Exp:* Lab instr physics, Harvard Col, 67-69; teaching asst astron, Princeton Univ, 73; res assoc, Cornell Univ, 73-75, instr, 74-75, asst prof, 75-77, assoc prof astron, Ctr Radio Phys & Space Sci, 77-95. *Mem:* Am Astron Soc; Int Astron Union; Sigma Xi. *Res:* Theoretical problems in relativistic astrophysics and high-energy astrophysics; black hole physics; the physics of compact objects, such as white dwarfs, neutron stars and black holes; x-ray astronomy; cosmology; dynamical astronomy. *Mailing Add:* Univ Ill Dept Physics Loomis Lab Physics 1110 W Green St Urbana IL 61801

SHAPIRO, VADIM, GEOMETRIC & SOLID MODELING. *Current Pos:* ASST PROF MECH ENG & COMPUT SCI, UNIV WIS-MADISON, 94- *Personal Data:* b Kiev, Ukraine, Mar 10, 59; US citizen; m 81, Larisa; c Gregory & Benjamin. *Educ:* NY Univ, BA, 81; Univ Calif, Los Angeles, MS, 83; Cornell Univ, MS, 89, PhD(mech eng), 91. *Honors & Awards:* Career Award, NSF, 95. *Prof Exp:* From res scientist to sr res scientist, Gen Motors Res, 83-86, staff res engr, Anal Process Dept, 92-94; res assoc, Cornell Univ, 91-92. *Mem:* Soc Indust & Appl Math; Asn Comput Mach; Am Soc Mech Engrs. *Res:* Geometric and solid modeling, applied computational geometry, physical modeling analysis and simulation, design and production automation; granted 1 US patent. *Mailing Add:* Univ Wis 1513 University Ave Madison WI 53706-1572. *Fax:* 608-265-2316; *E-Mail:* vshapiro@engr.wisc.edu

SHAPIRO, VICTOR LENARD, MATHEMATICAL ANALYSIS. *Current Pos:* fac res lectr, 78, PROF MATH, UNIV CALIF, RIVERSIDE, 64- *Personal Data:* b Chicago, Ill, Oct 16, 24; m 48, Florence Gilman; c Pamela, Laura, Charles & Arthur. *Educ:* Univ Chicago, BS, 47, MS, 49, PhD(math), 52. *Prof Exp:* Instr math, Ill Inst Technol, 48-52; from instr to prof, Rutgers Univ, 52-60; prof, Univ Ore, 60-64. *Concurrent Pos:* Asst, Univ Chicago, 51-52; mem, Inst Advan Study, 53-55 & 58-59, NSF fel, 54-55. *Mem:* Am Math Soc; Math Asn Am; Soc Indust Appl Math; AAAS. *Res:* Harmonic analysis; partial differential equations. *Mailing Add:* Dept Math Univ Calif Riverside CA 92521

SHAPIRO, WILLIAM, INTERNAL MEDICINE, CARDIOLOGY. *Current Pos:* DIR, AUTOMATED ELECTROCARDIOGRAM SVCS, VETS ADMIN HOSP, DALLAS, 81- *Personal Data:* b Newark, NJ, Dec 8, 27; m 51; c 3. *Educ:* Duke Univ, AB, 47, MA, 48, MD, 54. *Prof Exp:* Intern, Mt Sinai Hosp, NY, 54-55; jr asst resident internal med, Duke Hosp, Durham, NC, 55-56, res fel cardiol, 56-57, sr asst resident, 57-58; from instr to asst prof, Med Col Va, 60-65; chief cardiovasc sect, Vet Admin Hosp, 68-81; from asst prof to assoc prof, Univ Tex Health Sci Ctr, Dallas, 65-79, prof internal med, 79- *Concurrent Pos:* Consult, Vet Admin Hosp, Dallas, 65-68 & Coronary Care Comt, Am Heart Asn, 68- *Mem:* Am Fedn Clin. *Res:* Am Physiol Soc; fel Am Col Physicians; Am Heart Asn; Am Col Cardiol. *Res:* Clinical cardiology; cardiovascular physiology. *Mailing Add:* Dallas Vet Admin Med Ctr 4500 S Lancaster Rd Dallas TX 75216-7191

SHAPIRO, ZALMAN MORDECAI, URANIUM & ZINCONIUM CHEMISTRY, PROCESS METALLURGY. *Current Pos:* PRES, ASSOC TECH & BUS CONSULTS, 83- *Personal Data:* b Canton, Ohio, May 12, 20; m 45, Evelyn Greenberg; c Joshua, Ezra & Deborah. *Educ:* Johns Hopkins Univ, AB, 42, MA, 45, PhD(phys chem), 48. *Prof Exp:* Res assoc, Johns Hopkins Univ, 42-46, jr instr chem, 46-48; sr scientist res labs, Westinghouse Elec Corp, 48-49; sr scientist, Bettis Atomic Power Div, 49-50, supv scientist, 50-53, mgr phys chem sect, 53-54, mgr chem metall sect, 54-55, asst mgr, Reactor Design Sub-Div, 55-57; pres, Nuclear Mat & Equip Corp, 57-70; exec asst to mgr, Breeder Reactor Div, Westinghouse Elec Corp, 71-73, dir, Fusion Power Systs Dept, 73-81 & Spec Proj, Nuclear Energy Syst, 81-83. *Concurrent Pos:* Chmn, Isotope & Radiation Enterprises, Ltd, 64-68; pres, Nuclear Decontamination Corp, Nuclear Mat Equip Corp & vpres, Arco Chem Co, 68-70; vpres, Kawecki Berylco Industs; dir, Diagnon Corp, Arco-Hanford Co, 68-70, PSM Technologies, 88-, Pressure Chem Co, 92-; hon fel tech, Israel Inst Technol, 88- *Mem:* AAAS; fel Am Nuclear Soc; Am Chem Soc; Am Soc Metals; Sigma Xi. *Res:* Chemical erosion of steel; carbonyl chemistry; flame reactions of metallic halides; zirconium, hafnium, uranium and plutonium chemistry; metallurgy; fusion power systems technology. *Mailing Add:* 1045 Lyndhurst Dr Pittsburgh PA 15206-4535

SHAPLEY, JAMES LOUIS, AUDIOLOGY, SPEECH PATHOLOGY. *Current Pos:* clin assoc prof, 61-86, EMER CLIN ASSOC PROF, UNIV WASH, 86- *Personal Data:* b Asotin, Wash, Mar 9, 20; m 47; c 3. *Educ:* Univ Wash, BA, 47, MA, 52; Univ Iowa, PhD(audiol), 54. *Prof Exp:* Assoc instr speech, Univ Wash, 47-51; chief audiologist, Houston Speech & Hearing Ctr, Tex, 54-56; from instr to asst prof audiol, Univ Iowa, 56-60; chief audiol & speech path, Vet Admin Hosp, Seattle, 60-86. *Mem:* Acoust Soc Am; Am Speech & Hearing Asn; Sigma Xi. *Res:* Psychoacoustics; clinical audiology. *Mailing Add:* 1253 23rd Ave E Seattle WA 98112-3536

SHAPLEY, JOHN ROGER, CATALYSIS. *Current Pos:* from asst prof to assoc prof, 72-79, PROF CHEM, UNIV ILL, URBANA, 79- *Personal Data:* b Manhattan, Kans, Apr 15, 46; m 70, 84, Patricia A Summers; c Rebecca L & Joy R. *Educ:* Univ Kans, BS, 67; Harvard Univ, PhD(chem), 72. *Honors & Awards:* Sr US Scientist Award, Alexander von Humboldt Found, 90. *Prof Exp:* Assoc, Stanford Univ, 71-72. *Concurrent Pos:* NSF fel, 71-72; A P Sloan Found fel, 78-80; teacher-scholar, Camille & Henry Dreyfus Found, 78-83; vis prof chem, Cornell Univ, 79. *Mem:* Am Chem Soc; Royal Soc Chem. *Res:* Organotransition metal chemistry; synthesis and characterization of novel compounds; metal clusters; catalysis; dynamic nuclear magnetic resonance. *Mailing Add:* 204 W Florida Ave Urbana IL 61801. *Fax:* 217-333-2685; *E-Mail:* shapley@c.scs.uiuc.edu

SHAPLEY, LLOYD STOWELL, GAME THEORY, MATHEMATICAL ECONOMICS. *Current Pos:* PROF MATH & ECON, UNIV CALIF, LOS ANGELES, 81- *Personal Data:* b Cambridge, Mass, June 2, 23; m 55; c 2. *Educ:* Harvard Univ, AB, 48; Princeton Univ, PhD(math), 53. *Hon Degrees:* PhD, Hebrew Univ Jerusalem, 86. *Honors & Awards:* Von Neumann Theory Prize, Opers Res Soc Am, 81. *Prof Exp:* Mathematician, Rand Corp, 48-49; Henry B Fine instr math, Princeton Univ, 52-54; mathematician, Rand Corp, 54-55; sr res fel math, Calif Inst Technol, 55-56; mathematician, Rand Corp, 56-81. *Concurrent Pos:* Mem ed bd, Int J Game Theory, 70-, Math Prog, 71-, J Math Econ, 74- & Math Opers Res, 75- *Mem:* Nat Acad Sci; Am Math Soc; Math Prog Soc; fel Economet Soc; fel Am Acad Arts & Sci. *Res:* Game theory and its application to economics and political science. *Mailing Add:* Dept Math & Econ Univ Calif Los Angeles Los Angeles CA 90024

SHAPLEY, ROBERT M, NEUROPHYSIOLOGY, BIOPHYSICS. *Current Pos:* prof psychol & biol, 87-93, SPENCER PROF SCI, CTR NEURAL SCI, NY UNIV, 93- *Personal Data:* b New York, NY, Oct 7, 44; m 66, Laurie Sigal; c Nina & Alice. *Educ:* Harvard Univ, AB, 65; Rockefeller Univ, PhD(biophys), 70. *Prof Exp:* Fel physiol, Northwestern Univ, 70-71 & Cambridge Univ, 71-72; from asst prof to assoc prof neurophysiol, Rockefeller Univ, 72-87. *Concurrent Pos:* assoc ed, J Gen Physiol, 83-95, Visual Neurosci, 87-91; MacArthur fel, 86; mem, Comt Vision, Nat Res Coun, 86-90; sensory physiol ed, Exp Brain Res, 90- *Mem:* Int Brain Res Orgn; Soc Neurosci; Asn Res Vision & Ophthal. *Res:* Visual neurophysiology; mathematical analysis of neural networks; visual perception; brain imaging; dynamics of cerebral cortex. *Mailing Add:* One Washington Sq Village New York NY 10012. *Fax:* 212-995-4011; *E-Mail:* shapley@cns.nyu.edu

SHAPOCHKA, SERGEY N, AUTOMATIC CONTROL FOR MOTION TESTING APPLICATION, MINE HOIST MACHINES. *Current Pos:* PROJ ENGR, INCONTROL INC, 96- *Personal Data:* m 83, Irina Grineva; c Michael. *Educ:* Donetsk State Tech Univ, Ukraine, MD, 81, PhD(mach), 87. *Prof Exp:* Prof elec eng & electronics, Donetsk State Tech Univ, Ukraine, 81-96. *Concurrent Pos:* Leader res group, Donetsk State Tech Univ, Ukraine, 88-92; assoc prof elec eng, Supreme Coun Educ, Moscow, 91; tech dir, Stag, Donetsk, Ukraine, 92-96. *Res:* Automatic control systems for industrial application; author of 62 scientific publications. *Mailing Add:* 2052-G Vestavia Park Ct Birmingham AL 35216. *Fax:* 205-664-9015; *E-Mail:* jim@in-control-inc.com, Internet Home Page: http://www.in-control-inc.com

SHAPPIRIO, DAVID GORDON, PHYSIOLOGY, CELL BIOLOGY. *Current Pos:* from instr to prof zool, Univ Mich, Ann Arbor, 57-75, assoc chmn, Div Biol Sci, 76-83, actg chmn, 76, 77, 78, & 80, actg chmn, Dept Cell & Molecular Biol, 75, dir, Honors Prog, 83-91, PROF BIOL, UNIV MICH, ANN ARBOR, 75-, ARTHUR F THURNAU PROF, 89- *Personal Data:* b Washington, DC, June 18, 30; m 53; c Susan & Mark. *Educ:* Univ Mich, BS, 51; Harvard Univ, AM, 53, PhD(biol), 55. *Honors & Awards:* Bausch & Lomb Sci Award; Amoco Found Award. *Prof Exp:* NSF fel, Molteno Inst, Cambridge Univ, 55-56; Nat Res Coun-Am Cancer Soc fel, Univ Louvain, 56-57. *Concurrent Pos:* Lalor fel, Lalor Found, 53-55; Danforth assoc, Danforth Found, 68-; consult biol textbooks, res grant appl, NIH, NSF; grad training grants, NIH; vis lectr, Am Inst Biol Sci; consult, prof articles & books, various publishers; dir, NSF Sci Educ Prog, Univ Mich; reviewer prof res manuscripts in field. *Mem:* Fel AAAS; Am Soc Cell Biol; Soc Comp & Integrative Biol; Entom Soc Am; Am Inst Biol Sci; Xerces Soc; Asn Biol Lab Educ. *Res:* Physiology and biochemistry of insect diapause; respiratory enzymology; biology of wasps; undergraduate science education, especially honors/independent study experience. *Mailing Add:* Dept Biol Univ Mich 608 Soule Blvd Ann Arbor MI 48103-4625

SHAPTON, WILLIAM ROBERT, VIBRATION, DESIGN. *Current Pos:* PROF MECH ENG, MICH TECHNOL UNIV, 79-, DIR, DESIGN & DYNAMIC SYST AREA. *Personal Data:* b Lansing, Mich, June 25, 41; m 63, Patricia Chapman; c Heather (Berner) & William. *Educ:* Mich State Univ, BS, 62, MS, 63; Univ Cincinnati, PhD(vibrations), 68. *Honors & Awards:* Medal of Hon, Soc Automotive Engrs, 89; Forest R McFarland Award, 86; Ralph Teetor Award, 79. *Prof Exp:* Systs engr, Missile Div, Bendix Corp, 63-64, engr, Automation & Measurement Div, 64-65; assoc prof vibration, Univ Cincinnati, 65-79. *Concurrent Pos:* Consult, Automation & Measurement Div, Bendix Corp, 65-68, Gen Elec Co, 69-70, Mound Lab, Monsanto Res Corp, 72-78, NASA, 76-82 & Cincinnati Milacron, 77-80; pres, Mich Technol Univ Senate, 86-89; mem bd dirs, Soc Automotive Engrs, 90-92; mem bd dirs & vpres, Educ Support Inst Mich Technol Univ, 91-93; chmn, Hon & Awards Comt, Soc Automotive Engrs, 93-98; Ford Motor Co, C3P, 96-97. *Mem:* Soc Automotive Engrs; Am Soc Mech Engrs; Am Soc Eng Educ; Soc Exp Mech. *Res:* Vibration, shock and measurement of mechanical systems; seismic response of structures; machine tool dynamics; experimental engineering; sound quality; noise, vibration and harshness. *Mailing Add:* Dept Mech Engr Mich Technol Univ 1400 Townsend Dr Houghton MI 49931-1295. *Fax:* 906-487-2822; *E-Mail:* wshapton@mtu.edu

SHAR, ALBERT O, ALGEBRAIC TOPOLOGY, STATISTICS. *Current Pos:* EXEC DIR INFO TECHNOL, SCH MED, UNIV PA, 87- *Personal Data:* b Brooklyn, NY, Mar 11, 44. *Educ:* Brandeis Univ, BA, 65; Fordham Univ, MS, 66; Univ Pa, PhD(math), 70. *Prof Exp:* Asst prof math, Univ Colo, 70-71; dir comput serv, Univ NH, 71-76 & 81-87, assoc prof, 76-81. *Concurrent Pos:* Vis prof math, Res Inst Math, Zurich, Switz, 77-78. *Mem:* Am Math Soc. *Res:* Developing educational tools re: software & medical informational basis. *Mailing Add:* Computing & Info Tech Univ Pa 1201 Blockey Hall Philadelphia PA 19104-6021

SHAR, LEONARD E, HIGH SPEED COMPUTER ARCHITECUTRE. *Current Pos:* PRIN, PANASYS INC, 89- *Personal Data:* b SAfrica, 48; US citizen; m 86; c 1. *Educ:* Univ Witwatersrand, BSc, 68; Stanford Univ, MS, 70, PhD(elec eng & comput sci), 72; Santa Clara Univ, MBA, 78. *Honors & Awards:* Archimedes Prize, Nat Sci Coun, 64. *Prof Exp:* Mgr, Hewlett Packard, 72-79; vpres, Elxsi Ltd, 79-88. *Concurrent Pos:* Vis lectr, Stanford Univ, 75. *Mem:* Inst Elec & Electronics Engrs; Asn Comput Mach. *Res:* All aspects of computer architecture & applications with emphasis on achieving highest performance. *Mailing Add:* Panasys Inc 2334 Lundy Pl San Jose CA 95051

SHARA, MICHAEL M, CATACLYSMIC BINARIES, WOLF-RAYET STARS. *Current Pos:* assoc astronr, 82-88, ASTRONR, SPACE TELESCOPE INST, 88- *Personal Data:* b Montreal, Que, Aug 12, 49; m 71; c 2. *Educ:* Univ Toronto, BSc, 71, MSc, 72; Tel-Aviv Univ, PhD(astrophys), 78. *Prof Exp:* Teaching fel, Univ Montreal, 78-80; vis assist prof, Ariz State Univ, 80-82. *Mem:* Am Astron Soc; Can Astron Soc; Int Astron Union. *Res:* Structure and evolution of cataclysmic binary stars; surveys of nearby galaxies for very luminous stars and hydrodynamical simulations of stellar collisions. *Mailing Add:* 12115 Heneson Garth Owings Mills MD 21117

SHARAN, SHAILENDRA KISHORE, STRUCTURE-FLUID INTERACTION, COMPUTATIONAL MECHANICS. *Current Pos:* from asst prof to assoc prof, 81-89, PROF CIVIL ENG, SCH ENG, LAURENTIAN UNIV, 89- *Personal Data:* b Muzaffapur, Bihar, Nov 7, 47; Can citizen; m 72, Asha Sinha; c Niki & Sumit. *Educ:* Bilhar Univ, BSc, 69; Indian Inst Technol, Kanpur, MTech, 70; Queen's Univ, MSc, 75; Univ Waterloo, PhD(civil eng), 78. *Prof Exp:* Lectr civil eng, Indian Inst Technol, Delhi, 78; adj prof civil eng, Univ Estadual Maringa, Brazil, 79-81. *Concurrent Pos:* Vis fac, Indian Inst Technol, Delhi, 87-88. *Mem:* Can Soc Civil Eng; Am Soc Civil Engrs; Eng Inst Can; Can Inst Mining & Metall; Can Asn Earthquake Eng; Asn Comput Mech. *Res:* Seismic response analyses of structure-fluid systems such as dams and offshore structures; development of finite element techniques for infinite solid and fluid media; numerical modelling in geomechanics. *Mailing Add:* Sch Eng Laurentian Univ Sudbury ON P3E 2C6 Can

SHARAWY, MOHAMED, DENTISTRY. *Current Pos:* asst prof, Sch Dent, 70-73, assoc prof, 73-78, PROF ORAL BIOL & ANAT & COORD ANAT DENT, MED COL GA, 78-, DIR, CRANIOFACIAL RES, DENT RES CTR, 90-, PROF ORAL & MAXILLOFACIAL SURG, 92- *Personal Data:* b Cairo, Egypt, Mar 13, 41; US citizen; m 65; c 3. *Educ:* Cairo Univ, PNS, 58, DDS, 62; Univ Rochester, PhD(anat), 70. *Honors & Awards:* Outstanding Contrib to Dent Medal, Egyptian Dent Asn. *Prof Exp:* Intern oral surg, Sch Dent, Cairo Univ, 62, instr, 62-65; Fulbright fel, Inst Int Educ, 65-68; UAR scholar, Univ Rochester, 68-70. *Concurrent Pos:* Consult, US Army; sect ed, Cranio J. *Mem:* Int Asn Dent Res; Am Asn Dent Res; Am Asn Anatomists; Am Asn Dent Sch; Am Dent Asn; Am Acad Implant Prosthodontics. *Res:* Mechanism of bone induction, using demineralized bone powder; development of animal models for TMJ disc dislocation. *Mailing Add:* Dept Oral Biol Sch Dent Med Col Ga Augusta GA 30912. *Fax:* 706-721-6276; *E-Mail:* msharawy.dentistr@mailgw.mcg.edu

SHARBAUGH, AMANDUS HARRY, REACTIONS IN GELS, MICROWAVE ENGINEERING. *Current Pos:* PVT CONSULT, 83- *Personal Data:* b Richmond, Va, Mar 28, 19; m 40; c 2. *Educ:* Western Res Univ, AB, 40; Brown Univ, PhD(chem), 43. *Honors & Awards:* Potter Prize, Brown Univ; Dakin Award, Inst Elec & Electronics Engrs. *Prof Exp:* Res assoc, Res Lab, Gen Elec Co, 42-61, liaison scientist, 61-64, mgr dielec studies, 64-71, mgr, Plasma Physics Br, 71-80, sr consult, 80-83. *Concurrent Pos:* Fel physics, Union Univ, NY, 44-48; secy, Conf Elec Insulation, 54, vchmn, 55, chmn, 56; mem adv comt, US Dept Defense, 56-57; mem conf elec insulation & dielec behav, Nat Acad Sci; US Adv to CIGRE; Holder world's record microwave communication. *Mem:* Electrochem Soc; fel Inst Elec & Electronics Engrs. *Res:* Dielectric behavior; magnetron design; electronic breakdown and conduction; microwave spectroscopy; liesegang rings. *Mailing Add:* 28 Hemlock Dr Clifton Park NY 12065

SHARBER, JAMES RANDALL, SPACE PHYSICS, AURORAL MAGNETOSPHERIC PHYSICS. *Current Pos:* STAFF SCIENTIST, DEPT SPACE SCI, SOUTHWEST RES INST, 84- *Personal Data:* b Clarksville, Tenn, Aug 13, 41; m 74; c 1. *Educ:* Murray State Col, BA, 63; Tex A&M Univ, PhD(physics), 72. *Honors & Awards:* Marcus D O'Day Award, 85. *Prof Exp:* Res asst scientist, Div Atmospheric & Space Sci, Univ Tex, Dallas, 66-72; vis asst prof physics, US Naval Acad, 72-74; assoc prof physics & space sci, Fla Inst Technol, 74-84. *Concurrent Pos:* Consult, Southwest Res Inst, 82-83. *Mem:* Am Geophys Union; Am Asn Physics Teachers; Am Inst Aeronaut & Astronaut. *Res:* Analysis of scientific data taken by earth satellites and ground observatories; descriptions of the electron and ion fluxes incident on the earth's auroral regions to determine the processes responsible for the entry of solar wind particles into the magnetosphere and their subsequent acceleration and precipitation to produce auroras and deposit energy into the atmosphere; instrumentation for particle measurements in the upper atmosphere, geospace and interplanetary space. *Mailing Add:* 309 E Skyview Dr San Antonio TX 78228

SHARDA, RAMESH, NEURAL NETWORK APPLICATIONS, ELECTRONIC COMMERCE. *Current Pos:* From asst prof to prof mgt sci & info systs, 80-91, CONOCO/DUPONT PROF MGT TECH, OKLA STATE UNIV, 91-, INTERIM DIR MGT SYSTS, TELECOMMUN MGT PROG, 94- *Personal Data:* b Bijainagar, India, June 1, 53; US citizen; m 80, Usha; c Rohit & Ruchy. *Educ:* Univ Udaipur, BS, 75; Ohio State Univ, MS, 76; Univ Wis-Madison, MBA, 78, PhD(quant anal), 81. *Concurrent Pos:* Ed, Interactive Trans Opers Res & Mgt Sci, Inst Opers Res & Mgt Sci, 95- *Mem:* Decision Sci Inst; Int Neural Network Soc; Inst Opers Res & Mgt Sci. *Res:* Use of operational research models in management decision making; group information support through knowledge networks; use of the internet in collaborative learning. *Mailing Add:* Col Bus Admin Okla State Univ Stillwater OK 74078. *Fax:* 405-744-7474; *E-Mail:* sharda@okstate.edu

SHARE, GERALD HARVEY, GAMMA-RAY ASTRONOMY. *Current Pos:* Nat Acad Sci-Nat Res Coun resident res assoc cosmic radiation, 66-68, ASTROPHYSICIST, NAVAL RES LAB, 68- *Personal Data:* b New York, NY, Oct 9, 40; m 80; c 2. *Educ:* Queens Col, NY, BS, 61; Univ Rochester, PhD(physics), 66. *Concurrent Pos:* Vis sr staff scientist, Astrophys Div, NASA Hq, 89-91. *Mem:* Am Phys Soc; Am Astron Soc; Sigma Xi. *Res:* Cosmic x-and-gamma radiation; investigation of solar and celestial gamma radiation; measurements of radioactive cobalt in supernova; diffuse Galactic continuum and lines from 26A1 and positron annihilation; spectra of cosmic bursts; space background. *Mailing Add:* Naval Res Lab Code 4152 Washington DC 20375-0001

SHARE, LEONARD, PHYSIOLOGY. *Current Pos:* PROF PHYSIOL & BIOPHYS & CHMN DEPT, UNIV TENN CTR HEALTH SCI, MEMPHIS, 69- *Personal Data:* b Detroit, Mich, Oct 14, 27; m 49; c 3. *Educ:* Brooklyn Col, AB, 47; Oberlin Col, AM, 48; Yale Univ, PhD(physiol), 51. *Prof Exp:* USPHS fel physiol, Sch Med, Western Reserve Univ, 51-52; from instr to prof physiol, 52-69. *Mem:* AAAS; Int Soc Neuroendocrinol; Endocrine Soc; Am Physiol Soc; Neurosci Soc. *Res:* Water and electrolyte metabolism; vasopressin secretion; metabolism. *Mailing Add:* Dept Physiol & Biophys 894 Union Ave Rm 426 Univ Tenn Memphis TN 38163-0001. *Fax:* 901-528-7126

SHARE, NORMAN N, NEUROPHARMACOLOGY. *Current Pos:* VPRES PHARMACOL, PAN LABS INT, INC, 86- *Personal Data:* b Montreal, Que, Dec 25, 30; m 56; c 1. *Educ:* Univ Montreal, BPh, 58; McGill Univ, PhD(pharmacol), 62. *Prof Exp:* Fel, Columbia Univ, 62-64; chief pharmacologist, Charles E Frosst & Co, 64-65, mgr, Dept Pharmacol, 65-71, asst dir res biol, Dept Pharmacol, 71-79, dir pharmacol, 79-81, sr dir neuropsychopharmacol, Merck Inst Therapeut Res, 82-86. *Mem:* Pharmacol Soc Can; Am Soc Pharmacol & Exp Therapeut; NY Acad Sci. *Res:* Chronic obstructive lung disease. *Mailing Add:* Pan Labs 11804 North Creek Pkwy S Bothell WA 98011-8890. *Fax:* 425-487-3787

SHARER, ARCHIBALD WILSON, ZOOLOGY. *Current Pos:* RETIRED. *Personal Data:* b Dayton, Ohio, Sept 19, 19; m 41; c 3. *Educ:* Ohio State Univ, BS, 43; Univ Mich, MS, 48, PhD(zool), 59. *Prof Exp:* Asst zool, Univ Mich, 46-50; instr biol, Fla State Univ, 50-53; instr, Lake Forest Col, 53-56; instr, Duke Univ, 58-60; assoc prof biol, NC Wesleyan Col, 60-63, chmn, Div Sci, 63-77, prof biol, 63-83. *Mem:* Am Arachnological Soc; Am Inst Biol Sci. *Res:* Behavior, ecology and natural history of vertebrates and invertebrates; herpetology; arachnology. *Mailing Add:* 3116 Ridgecrest Dr Rocky Mount NC 27803

SHARER, CYRUS J, ECONOMIC GEOGRAPHY, POPULATION. *Current Pos:* RETIRED. *Personal Data:* b Cleveland, Ohio, Mar 8, 22; m 55; c 2. *Educ:* Univ Pa BS, 43, MA, 49; Univ Mich, PhD(geog), 55. *Prof Exp:* Instr econ geog, Wharton Sch, Univ Pa, 48-50, lectr, 53-54; from instr to prof geog, Villanova Univ, 54-85, chmn dept, 62-81. *Mem:* Soc Hist Discoveries. *Res:* US and world patterns of iron and steel production; resource management and population change in the Bahama Islands and West Indies. *Mailing Add:* 505 E Lancaster Ave Wayne PA 19087

SHARF, DONALD JACK, speech & hearing sciences; deceased, see previous edition for last biography

SHARGEL, LEON DAVID, pharmacology, drug metabolism, for more information see previous edition

SHARGOOL, PETER DOUGLAS, PLANT BIOCHEMISTRY. *Current Pos:* RETIRED. *Personal Data:* b Feb 25, 35; Can citizen; m 61; c 2. *Educ:* Univ London, BSc, 62; Univ Alta, MSc, 65, PhD(plant biochem), 68. *Prof Exp:* Res worker biochem, Wellcome Res Labs, Eng, 54-62; Nat Res Coun Can grant, Univ Sask, 68-73, from assoc prof to prof biochem, 73-94. *Concurrent Pos:* Med Res Coun grant, 75-77, Nat Sci & Engr Res Coun grant, 77-; Nat Res Coun res contract, 82-86. *Res:* Mechanisms regulating the biosynthesis of amino acids and other secondary products in plants. *Mailing Add:* 4798 Fairbridge Dr RR 7 Duncan BC V9L 4W4 Can

SHARIAT, AHMAD, DEVELOPMENT OF CORRELATIONS & SOFTWARE FOR APPLIED ENGINEERING, TEACHING CHEMICAL ENGINEERING. *Current Pos:* RES ENGR, FRACTIONATION-RES INC, 90- *Personal Data:* b Cairo, Egypt, Mar 21, 45; m 73, Homai Jangali; c Mozghan & Zhila. *Educ:* Tenn Technol Univ, BS, 67; La State Univ, MS, 69, PhD(chem eng), 70. *Prof Exp:* Prof chem eng, Sch Eng, Shinaz Univ, 71-84, head, Chem Eng Dept, 75-76; vis prof, Okla State Univ, 76-77; res engr, Chem Eng Consults, 84-87; sr chem engr, Alameda Instruments Inc, 89-90. *Concurrent Pos:* Lectr, Aspen Simulation Package, San Jose State Univ, 88. *Mem:* Am Inst Chem Engrs. *Res:* Distillation; development of softwares which are used in applied chemical engineering. *Mailing Add:* Fractionation Res Inc PO Box 2108 Stillwater OK 74076. *Fax:* 405-744-7732; *E-Mail:* shariat@fri.org

SHARITZ, REBECCA REYBURN, ECOLOGY, BOTANY. *Current Pos:* assoc res ecologist, 77-85, SR RES ECOLOGIST, SAVANNAH RIVER ECOL LAB, UNIV GA, 86-, HEAD, DIV WETLANDS ECOL, 88-, PROF BOT, 89- *Personal Data:* b Wytheville, Va, Aug 10, 44; m 76. *Educ:* Roanoke Col, BS, 66; Univ NC, Chapel Hill, PhD(bot), 70. *Prof Exp:* Asst prof biol, Saginaw Valley Col, 70-71. *Concurrent Pos:* Res assoc, Univ NC, 71; adj asst prof bot, 72-; plant ecologist, US Energy Res & Develop Admin, 75-76; acting div, Savannah River Ecol Lab, 87. *Mem:* Bot Soc Am; Am Inst Biol Sci; Ecol Soc Am (treas, 87-90, vpres 90-91); Int Asn Ecol (secy-gen, 90-). *Res:* Population dynamics of vascular plant species, structure and processes in swamp forest systems, response of wetland communities to environmental disturbance; structure and diversity of plant communities. *Mailing Add:* Dept Botany Univ Ga 1180 E Broad St Athens GA 30601-3040

SHARKAWI, MAHMOUD A, PHARMACOLOGY. *Current Pos:* from instr to assoc prof, 68-80, PROF PHARMACOL, FAC MED, UNIV MONTREAL, 80- *Personal Data:* b Cairo, Egypt, May 26, 35; m 70; c 4. *Educ:* Cairo Univ, BPharm, 57; Univ Minn, Minneapolis, MSc, 61; Univ Calif,

San Francisco, PhD(pharmacol), 64. *Prof Exp:* Lectr pharmacol, Cairo Univ, 64-65; res assoc, Univ Ill, 65-66; res assoc, Stanford Univ, 66-67. *Mem:* AAAS; Int Soc Biochem Pharmacol; Am Soc Pharmacol & Exp Therapeut; Pharmacol Soc Can. *Res:* Interactions between ethanol and centrally acting drugs; factors modifying ethanol elimination. *Mailing Add:* Dept Pharmacol Univ Montreal Fac Med Montreal PQ H3C 3J7 Can

SHARKEY, JOHN BERNARD, INORGANIC CHEMISTRY, INSTRUMENTATION. *Current Pos:* from asst prof to prof chem & phys sci, 70-90, chairperson, 77-90, ASSOC DEAN, PACE UNIV, 90- *Personal Data:* b Elizabeth, NJ, Sept 5, 40; m 63, Dolores Passiatore; c Laura, Ian & Brian. *Educ:* NY Univ, BA, 64, MSc, 68, PhD(phys chem), 70. *Prof Exp:* Anal chemist, Engelhard Industs, NJ, 62-66. *Mem:* Am Chem Soc. *Res:* Polymorphism in inorganic compounds; history of chemistry; microscopy. *Mailing Add:* Dept Chem & Phys Sci Pace Univ New York NY 10038. *Fax:* 212-346-1725

SHARKEY, MARGARET MARY, CELL BIOLOGY. *Current Pos:* RETIRED. *Educ:* Fordham Univ, BS, 54, MS, 60; St John's Univ, NY, PhD(cell biol), 72. *Prof Exp:* Teaching asst cytol, histol & embryol, St John's Univ, NY, 69-70; asst prof cell biol, histol & embryol, St Thomas Aquinas Col, 70-72; sci prog dir training grants, 88-92. *Mem:* Am Asn Cancer Res. *Res:* Administration of cell biology; genetics. *Mailing Add:* 3735 Jones Ferry Lane Alpharetta GA 30202

SHARKEY, MICHAEL JOSEPH, SYSTEMATICS, TAXONOMY. *Current Pos:* ASST PROF ENTOM, UNIV KY, 96- *Personal Data:* b Kitchener, Ont, Nov 2, 53; m 79; c 2. *Educ:* Univ Guelph, BSc, 77; McGill Univ, MSc, 81, PhD(entom), 84. *Prof Exp:* Res scientist, Biosyst Res Inst Agr Can, 82-96. *Concurrent Pos:* Ed, Ichnews, 84- *Mem:* Entom Soc Can; Int Hymenopterists Soc. *Res:* Taxonomy of Hymenoptera, especially Braconidae; biological control; systematic theory; quantitative aspects of phylogenetic reconstruction. *Mailing Add:* Dept Entom S-225 Agr-Sci Ctr N Univ Ky Lexington KY 40546-0091

SHARKEY, THOMAS D, ANALYTICAL GAS EXCHANGE & MODELING, PHOTOSYNTHESIS & ISOPRENE EMISSION. *Current Pos:* from asst prof to assoc prof, Dept Bot, 87-91, chair, 92-94, PROF, DEPT BOT, UNIV WIS-MADISON, 91-, DIR BIOTRON, 93- *Personal Data:* b Detroit, Mich, Jan 28, 53; m 74, Paulette Bochnig; c Jessa S B. *Educ:* Mich State Univ, BS, 74, PhD(bot & plant path), 80. *Prof Exp:* Fel, Res Sch Biol Sci, Australian Nat Univ, 80-82; asst res prof, Biol Sci Ctr, Desert Res Inst, 82-84, assoc res prof & assoc dir, 84-87; assoc prof, Biol Dept, Univ Nev, Reno, 86-87. *Concurrent Pos:* Vis, Dept Plant Biol, Carnegie Inst Wash, 80, Univ Gottingen, 85; mem, Prog Comt, Am Soc Plant Physiologists, 87-88; panel mem, Physiol Processes Prog, NSF, 88-91. *Mem:* AAAS; Am Soc Plant Physiologists; Australian Soc Plant Physiologists; Int Soc Photosynthesis Res. *Res:* Biochemistry and biophysics of the exchange of gases between plant leaves and the atmosphere and environmental effects on plant-atmosphere interactions; photosynthesis and isoprene emission from plants. *Mailing Add:* Dept Bot Univ Wis Madison WI 53706. *Fax:* 608-262-7509; *E-Mail:* tsharkey@facstaff.wisc.edu

SHARKEY, WILLIAM HENRY, PHYSICAL CHEMISTRY. *Current Pos:* RETIRED. *Personal Data:* b Vinita, Okla, Oct 7, 16; m 42; c 2. *Educ:* Okla State Univ, BS, 37; Univ Ill, PhD(org chem), 41. *Prof Exp:* Res chemist, org res, Gen Elec Co, 39; res chemist, Du Pont Co, 40 & 41-53, res supvr chem, 53-80, admin assoc, 81; adj prof chem, Univ Miami, 84-87. *Mem:* Sigma Xi; Am Chem Soc; AAAS. *Res:* Organic synthesis; dye chemistry and dyeing materials; photooxidative processes; four-membered ring chemistry; fluorine chemistry including fluoropolymers; polymerization methods especially anionic and coordination polymerization. *Mailing Add:* 6001 Pelican Bay Blvd Naples FL 34108

SHARKOFF, EUGENE GIBB, GENERAL PHYSICS, SCIENCE ADMINISTRATION. *Current Pos:* RETIRED. *Personal Data:* b Washington, DC, Feb 1, 25; m 59, Maribel Ferrell; c Tammy M & Kimberly G. *Educ:* US Mil Acad, BMAS, 46; Mass Inst Technol, SM, 52, PhD(physics), 53. *Honors & Awards:* Cert Adv Group Aerospace Res & Develop, NAtlantic Treaty Orgn, 59. *Prof Exp:* Assoc prof physics, USAF Inst Technol, 63-66; dir, PPAAR Prog, Res Avionics, Princeton Univ, 66-69; var res & tech mgt, Picatinny Arsenal, USA, 69-80; instr physics, Isothermal Community Col, 84-88; pres, Rutherford County Habitat for Humanity, 89-90. *Mem:* Am Asn Physics Teachers; Sigma Xi. *Res:* Solid state thermal physics-measured thermal conductivity of magnesium at low temperature; structures with asymmetric loading; mechanics; one published manual. *Mailing Add:* 3171 Hwy 221 N Union Mills NC 28167

SHARLOW, JOHN FRANCIS, HARDWARE SYSTEMS, OBJECT-ORIENTED PROGRAMMING. *Current Pos:* dept chair, 86-90, PROF COMPUT SCI & MATH, EASTERN CONN STATE UNIV, 69- *Personal Data:* b Potsdam, NY, Aug 28, 41; m 91, Linda Freeman; c Jacqueline Diane & Jennifer Jo. *Educ:* State Univ NY, Potsdam, BS, 63, MS, 65; Clarkson Col Technol, MS, 67; State Univ NY, Albany, EdD, 71. *Prof Exp:* Asst prof math, State Univ NY Agr & Technol Col, 65-69. *Mem:* Asn Comput Mach; Math Asn Am. *Res:* Mathematics education; computer science education; object-oriented programming. *Mailing Add:* 458 Beaumont Hwy Lebanon CT 06249. *E-Mail:* sharlow@ecsuc.ctstateu.edu

SHARMA, ARJUN D, CARDIOLOGY. *Current Pos:* DIR, INTERVENTIONAL ELECTROPHYSIOL, SUTTER HOSP, 89- *Personal Data:* b Bombay, India, June 2, 53; Can citizen; m 81; c 2. *Educ:* Univ Waterloo, BSc, 72; Univ Toronto, MD, 76. *Prof Exp:* Asst prof med, 83-88, assoc prof med & pharmacol, Univ Western Ont, 88-89. *Mem:* Am Col Cardiol; Am Col Physicians; Can Cardiovasc Soc. *Res:* Cardiac electrophysiology; andrenergic receptors in heart; adenosine effects on heart. *Mailing Add:* 4149 American River Dr Sacramento CA 95864

SHARMA, BHAVENDER PAUL, ENZYME TECHNOLOGY. *Current Pos:* PRES, INTERSPEX PRODS INC, 91- *Personal Data:* b Patiala, Punjab, India, Oct 22, 49; nat US; m 73, Kathryn A Bilinski; c Jana & Neal. *Educ:* Panjab Univ, India, BSc Eng, 69; Syracuse Univ, MBA, 85; Rutgers Univ, PhD(biochem eng), 77. *Prof Exp:* Instr biochem eng, Rutgers Univ, 75-76; sr proj engr & proj mgr, Corning Inc, 76-83; sr scientist process develop, Genencor Inc, 83-88; dir technol & strategic planning, Genencor Int, 88-91. *Mem:* Am Inst Chem Engrs; Am Chem Soc. *Res:* Process development and scale-up of enzyme manufacturing; product development of a semi-automated cell culture apparatus for vaccine and antibody production; application and preparation of free and immobilized enzymes and cells. *Mailing Add:* InterSpex Prods Inc 1155 Chess Dr Suite 114 Foster City CA 94404-1118. *Fax:* 650-570-5215

SHARMA, BHUDEV, CODING THEORY, FUNCTIONAL EQUATIONS. *Current Pos:* PROF MATH & CHAIR, XAVIER UNIV, LA, 88- *Personal Data:* b Bankpur, India, June 21, 38; m 59, Kusum Lata; c Ritu, Swati & Harsh D. *Educ:* Agra Univ, India, BSc, 55, MSc, 57; Univ Delhi, India PhD(math), 71. *Honors & Awards:* Award for Outstanding Contrib, Indian Soc Info Theory & Applns, 97. *Prof Exp:* Lectr math, NAS Col, Meerut, 57-63; head, Dept Math, Munic Degree Col, Mussoorie, 63-64, Vaish Col, Shamli, 64-66; lectr math, Univ Delhi, India, 66-72, reader, 72-79, prof, 79-88. *Concurrent Pos:* Chief ed, J Combinatorics, Info & Systs Sci, 76-; co-chair, Int Conf Combinatorics, Info Theory & Statist, Univ Southern Maine. *Mem:* Am Math Soc; Indian Math Soc; Opers Res Soc India. *Res:* Characterizations of measures of information from functional equations; coding several proposed new types of codes; introduced general way of defining distance and thus expanded the existing studies; rate distortion and response designs; published 100 research papers and authored 21 books. *Mailing Add:* 6300 Ackel St No 265 Metairie LA 70003. *Fax:* 504-482-1561; *E-Mail:* bsharma@mail.xula.edu

SHARMA, BRAHMA DUTTA, DENTAL BIOMATERIALS RESEARCH. *Current Pos:* CONSULT, 95-; PRES, HEALTH FIRST INT, 95- *Personal Data:* b Khurja, India, Sept 20, 47; US citizen; c 3. *Educ:* Agra Univ, India, BS, 66; Allahabad Univ, MS, 68; Queens Univ, Belfast, UK, PhD(chem), 71. *Prof Exp:* dir res, Dent Mat, Coe Labs, Inc, Chicago, 73-89. *Mem:* Am Chem Soc; AAAS; fel Acad Dent Mat; Int Asn Dent Res. *Res:* Dental biomaterial such as impression materials, resins & restoratives. *Mailing Add:* 503 Eisenhower Dr Louisville CO 80027-1180

SHARMA, DINESH C, ENDOCRINOLOGY, SYSTEMS DESIGN. *Current Pos:* HEALTH SCI ADMINR, NAT INST CHILD HEALTH & HUMAN DEVELOP, NIH, 72- *Personal Data:* b Feb 1, 38. *Educ:* Kans State Univ, PhD, 61; Bombay Univ, India, DSc, 67; Univ Mich, MSE, 71. *Concurrent Pos:* Regent's prof, Univ Calif. *Mem:* Inst Elec & Electronics Engrs; fel Royal Soc Chem. *Res:* Biochemistry of steroids; drug delivery systems. *Mailing Add:* PO Box 2188 Rockville MD 20847

SHARMA, GHANSHYAM D, reservoir & marine geology, petroleum engineering, for more information see previous edition

SHARMA, GOPAL CHANDRA, PHARMACOLOGY, CANCER. *Current Pos:* SCI REV ADMINR, DIV RES GRANTS, NIH, 90- *Personal Data:* b Churi-Ajitgarh, India, Apr 18, 32; US citizen; m 60; c 2. *Educ:* Agra Univ, BS, 53, DVM, 58; Univ Mo, Columbia, MS, 66, PhD(med pharmacol), 69. *Prof Exp:* Officer prev immunization, Dept Animal Husb, Govt India, 58-59, vet surgeon asst, 59-61; res asst genetics, Indian Coun Agr Res, 61-65; res asst med pharmacol, Univ Mo, Columbia, 66-67, Nat Cancer Inst spec proj fel, Med Sch, 67-69; asst prof pharmacol, Sch Med, Univ NDak, 69-70; sr res scientist cancer res, Food & Drug Admin, 70-73; dir plant res, Am Med Ctr, Denver, 73-77, pharmacologist, Pharmacol & Toxicol Br, Div Vet Med Res, Bur Vet Med, 77-90. *Res:* Evaluation of anticancer drugs; effect of cancer on disposition of drugs in the body; drug toxicities and prevention; drug distribution and interaction; cyclic adenosine monophosphate; comparative pharmacology; drug interaction and analytical microdetection of drug and chemical residue in the tissue of food animals, effect of drugs on the metabolism of other drugs. *Mailing Add:* 2 Holliben Ct Severna Park MD 21146

SHARMA, GOPAL KRISHAN, ECOLOGY. *Current Pos:* assoc prof, 68-76, PROF BIOL SCI, UNIV TENN, MARTIN, 76- *Personal Data:* b Hoshiarpur, India, Mar 24, 37; m 66. *Educ:* Univ Mo, Columbia, BS, 61, MS, 62, PhD(bot), 67. *Prof Exp:* Teaching asst bot, Univ Mo, Columbia, 62-66; instr, Prestonsburg Community Col, Ky, 66-67, chmn div biol sci, 67-68. *Concurrent Pos:* Instr, Cult Enrichment Prog, Prestonsburg, Ky, 66; NSF fel, Univ Mich, 68-69; res fel econ bot, Harvard Univ, 76-77. *Mem:* AAAS; Am Inst Biol Sci; Bot Soc Am; Ecol Soc Am; Sigma Xi. *Res:* Ecology and ethnobotany of Cannabis; cuticular features as indicators of environmental pollution. *Mailing Add:* Dept Biol Univ Tenn Martin Martin TN 38238-0001

SHARMA, GOVIND C, PLANT SCIENCE. *Current Pos:* assoc prof, 70-73, PROF PLANT SCI & CHMN DEPT PLANT & SOIL SCI, ALA A&M UNIV, 73- *Personal Data:* b Udaipur, India, Mar 3, 44; m 68, Prabha Gupta; c 1. *Educ:* Univ Udaipur, India, BS, 64; Univ Fla, MAgr, 65; Kans State Univ, PhD(veg crops), 70. *Prof Exp:* Res asst, Pesticide Lab, Univ Fla, 65-66; agr coordr, Peace Corps, 66. *Concurrent Pos:* Consult int agr, USAID-sponsored projs; consult inst planning, area univs & cols. *Mem:* Am Soc Hort Sci; Am Soc Agron. *Res:* Plant breeding; tissue culture; host plant resistance; plant transformation; genetic engineering. *Mailing Add:* PO Box 1208 Ala A&M Univ Normal AL 35762

SHARMA, HARI M, MAHARISHI AYUR-VEDA, HERBAL FOOD SUPPLEMENTS. *Current Pos:* prof, Ohio State Univ, 80-95, dir, Anat Path Prog, 81-90, cancer prev & natural prod res, 90-95, EMER PROF PATH, OHIO STATE UNIV, 95- *Personal Data:* b Aligarh, India, Jan 16, 38; m, Indu; c 4. *Educ:* Lucknow Univ, India, MD, 61; Ohio State Univ, MS, 65. *Concurrent Pos:* Maharishi Ayurveda, Health Care Syst, India; fel, Nat Acad Ayurveda, Ministry Health & Family Welfare, Govt India. *Mem:* Int Soc Nephrol; Int Acad Path; Am Col Pathologists; Royal Col Physicians Can; Am Soc Exp Path. *Res:* Maharishi Ayurveda; cancer; atherosclerosis; natural products; free radicals and antioxidants. *Mailing Add:* Dept Path M 368 Starling-Loving Hall Ohio State Univ 320 W Tenth Ave Columbus OH 43210. *Fax:* 614-293-5984; *E-Mail:* sharma.2@osu.edu

SHARMA, JAGADISH, SOLID STATE PHYSICS, ELECTRON SPECTROSCOPY. *Current Pos:* PHYSICIST, NAVAL SURFACE WEAPONS CTR, 80- *Personal Data:* b Calcutta, India, Dec 15, 23; US citizen; m 51; c 2. *Educ:* Calcutta Univ, BS, 44, MS, 47, PhD(physics), 53. *Prof Exp:* Nat Inst Res fel thermoluminescence, Khaira Physics Lab, Calcutta Univ, 53-54; res fel, Color Ctr, Nat Res Coun, Div Elec Eng, Ottawa, Can, 55-57; lectr, dept physics, Indian Inst Technol, Kharagpur, 58-61, asst prof radiation damage, 65-67; res assoc, dept aerospace & mech sci, Princeton Univ, 61-64; res physicist, Div Explosives & Electron Spectros, Energetic Mat Res & Develop Comn, US Army, 67-80. *Mem:* AAAS. *Res:* Fluorescence; thermoluminescence; color centers; radiation damage; solid state physics of explosives and propellants; Auger, uv, x-ray photoelectron spectroscopy of explosives and propellants. *Mailing Add:* Mat Eval Br Naval Surface Weapons Ctr White Oak Lab Silver Spring MD 20903. *Fax:* 301-394-4472

SHARMA, JAGDEV MITTRA, MICROBIOLOGY, VIROLOGY. *Current Pos:* ENDOWED PROF, COL VET MED, UNIV MINN, 88- *Personal Data:* b Punjab, India, June 28, 41; m 69; c 2. *Educ:* Punjab Univ, India, BVSc, 61; Univ Calif, Davis, MS, 64, PhD(comp path), 67. *Honors & Awards:* Upjohn Award, Am Asn Avian Pathologists, 82. *Prof Exp:* Jr specialist avian med, Univ Calif, Davis, 62-66; poultry pathologist, Wash State Univ, 67-71; vet med officer, Regional Poultry Res Lab, Sci & Educ Admin-Agr Res, USDA, 71-88; clin prof, dept path, Mich State Univ, 74-88. *Mem:* Am Vet Med Asn; Am Asn Avian Pathologists; Int Asn Comp Res Leukemia & Related Dis; World Vet Poultry Asn. *Res:* Avian immunology; mechanisms of virus-induced immunosuppression; infectious diseases. *Mailing Add:* Vet Pathobiol Col Vet Med Univ Minn St Paul MN 55108. *Fax:* 612-625-5203; *E-Mail:* sharm001@maroon.tc.umn.edu

SHARMA, KRISHNA, LENS PROTEIN MODIFICATIONS, PROTEASES IN LENS. *Current Pos:* RES ASST PROF BIOCHEM & OPHTHAL, UNIV MO, 93-, ASST PROF, 94- *Personal Data:* b N Mudnur, Karnataka, India, July 18, 55; m 87, Sandhya Noojibail; c Sangita S & Nikhilesh S. *Educ:* Univ Mysore, India, BSc, 74, MSc, 78, PhD(biochem), 82. *Prof Exp:* Jr res fel, Kasturba Med Col India, 78, lectr biochem, 79-82, asst prof, 82-83, reader, 86-90. *Concurrent Pos:* Fel, Univ Mo, 83-86, prin investr, 93-; prin investr, Kasturba Med Col, 88-90. *Mem:* AAAS; Asn Res Vision & Ophthal; Asn Clin Biochemists India; Am Soc Molecular Biol. *Res:* Mechanisms of cataract development; role of protein modifications and proteolytic system in cataractogenesis; role of various peptide hydrolases in lens protein turnover and effect of cross-linking of alpha crystallin on its chaperone like function. *Mailing Add:* Mason Eye Inst Univ Mo Columbia MO 65212. *Fax:* 573-884-4100; *E-Mail:* opthks@showme.missouri.edu

SHARMA, MADAN LAL, ENTOMOLOGY, ECOLOGY. *Current Pos:* RETIRED. *Personal Data:* b Faridkot, India, Aug 28, 34; Can citizen; m 68. *Educ:* Univ Punjab, India, BSc, 54 & 56, MSc, 57; Univ Paris, DSc(entom), 65. *Prof Exp:* Scientist, Agr Dept, French Govt, 65-66; lectr, Univ Sherbrooke, 66-68, from asst prof to prof entom, 68-92. *Concurrent Pos:* French Govt fel, Nat Inst Agron Res, 71; res fel, Quebec-France & France-Can Mission, Nat Inst Agron Res, France, 81. *Res:* Biology and ecology of Aphids and Coccids; bibliography of Aphidoidea. *Mailing Add:* 2510 Belvedere St Ascot PQ G1H 5J9 Can

SHARMA, MANGALORE GOKULANAND, BIOMECHANICS, RHEOLOGY. *Current Pos:* res asst eng mech, Pa State Univ, 57-60, asst prof, 60-64, assoc prof, 64-75, PROF ENG MECH, PA STATE UNIV, 75- *Personal Data:* b Mulki, India, Nov 3, 27; US citizen; m 62; c 2. *Educ:* Univ Mysore, India, BE, 52; Indian Inst Sci, DIISc, 54; Pa State Univ, PhD(eng mech), 60. *Prof Exp:* Design engr, Hindustan Aeronaut, 54-57. *Concurrent Pos:* Vis prof, Indian Inst Sci, 67-68; consult, Gen Tire & Rubber Co, 64-68 & Fed Hgy Admin, 81- *Mem:* Am Soc Rheology; Am Soc Testing & Mat; Am Acad Mech; Am Soc Testing & Mat Comt Composite Mat; Sigma Xi. *Res:* Analysis of hemodynamic flow through blood vessels; fluid dynamical contribution to atherosclerosis; rheology of blood vessels; effect of hypertension on rheological properties; physical properties of biopolymers used in cardiac assist devices; mechanics of composite materials and their failure analysis; viscoplasticity of metals at elevated temperatures. *Mailing Add:* 948 S Sparks St State College PA 16801

SHARMA, MINOTI, SEPARATION TECHNIQUES NUCLEIC ACID SYNTHESIS, INSTRUMENTAL DEVELOPMENT. *Current Pos:* CANCER RES SCIENTIST BIOPHYS, ROSWELL PARK CANCER INST, 81-, ASST RES PROF, 84- *Personal Data:* b India, US citizen. *Educ:* Tufts Univ, MS, 65; Southampton Univ, UK, PhD(org chem), 70. *Prof Exp:* Res asst prof bioenergetics, State Univ NY, Buffalo, 77-80. *Mem:* Am Chem Soc; Soc Biol Chem; AAAS. *Res:* Developing new technology to assay DNA modification using laser-induced flourescence detection. *Mailing Add:* Dept Biophys Roswell Pk Cancer Inst Elm & Carlton Sts Buffalo NY 14263

SHARMA, MOHESWAR, ORGANIC CHEMISTRY. *Current Pos:* CANCER RES SCIENTIST CARBOHYDRATES, ROSWELL PARK MEM INST, 72- *Personal Data:* b Jhanji, India; US citizen; m 62; c 2. *Educ:* Calcutta Univ, BS, 53, MS, 56, PhD(chem), 62. *Prof Exp:* Fel chem, Tufts Univ, 63-65, Univ Alta, 65-67; vis lectr, Univ Southampton, 67-72. *Mem:* Am Chem Soc. *Res:* Carbohydrates; cell membranes. *Mailing Add:* 281 Coronation Dr Amherst NY 14226

SHARMA, NITA, SYSTEM SOFTWARE, TOPOLOGY RELIABILITY. *Current Pos:* SOFTWARE DEVELOP ENGR, NCUBE CORP, 92- *Personal Data:* b Bombay, India, Aug 12, 66; m 90, Ratnesh. *Educ:* Birla Inst Technol & Sci, India, BE, 87; Indian Inst Sci, MTech, 88; NC State Univ, PhD(comput eng), 92. *Concurrent Pos:* Adj fac, Santa Clara Univ, 93- *Mem:* Inst Elec & Electronics Engrs. *Res:* Reliability and design of parallel and distributed systems. *Mailing Add:* Hitachi Data Systs 750 Central Expressway PO Box 54996 MS 32/21 Santa Clara CA 95056. *Fax:* 650-508-5408; *E-Mail:* sharma@ncube.com

SHARMA, OPENDRA K, MOLECULAR BIOLOGY OF HIV & RELATED INFECTIOUS DISEASES. *Current Pos:* Sr scientist, 77-85, CHIEF, LAB MOLECULAR BIOL, CANCER RES CTR, AMA, 85- *Personal Data:* b Dehradun, India, Sept 3, 41. *Educ:* Lucknow Univ, India, PhD(biochem), 66. *Mem:* Am Soc Biol Chemists; Am Asn Cancer Res; Am Chem Soc. *Res:* Nucleotide analogs and anti-viral agents application of urinary toxicity of heavy metals and modified nucleosides in cancer diagnosis and cancer management. *Mailing Add:* 6003 Executive Blvd Rm 2C04 Bethesda MD 20892

SHARMA, PRASANTA, INDUSTRIAL WASTEWATER TREATABILITY, PRODUCT DEVELOPMENT FOR APPLICATION IN INDUSTRIAL WASTEWATER TREATMENT. *Current Pos:* SR ENVIRON CHEMIST, HILL BROS, 90- *Personal Data:* b Assam, India, Mar 7, 40; UK citizen; c 2. *Educ:* Univ Wales, MSc, 64; Univ London, PhD(inorg spectros), 80. *Prof Exp:* Fel, NDak State Univ, 81-82, fel chem, Univ Ala, Birmingham, 82-84, biochem, 84-86, asst prof chem, 86-90. *Mem:* Am Chem Soc. *Res:* Developing clean-up techniques for industrial wastewater effluent. *Mailing Add:* Hill Bros 15017 E Clark Ave City of Industry CA 91745-1409

SHARMA, RAGHUBIR PRASAD, PHARMACOLOGY, TOXICOLOGY. *Current Pos:* from asst prof to assoc prof, 69-79, PROF & TOXICOLOGIST ANIMAL, DAIRY & VET SCI, UTAH STATE UNIV, 79- *Personal Data:* b Bharatpur, India, Sept 9, 40; m 58; c 2. *Educ:* Univ Rajasthan, BVSc, 59; Univ Minn, St Paul, PhD(pharmacol), 68; Am Bd Vet Toxicol, dipl, 74; Am Bd Toxicol, dipl, 81. *Prof Exp:* Clin vet, Govt Rajasthan, India, 59-60; instr pharmacol, Univ Rajasthan, 60-61; asst prof, Uttar Pradesh Agr Univ, India, 61-64. *Concurrent Pos:* NIH grant, Utah State Univ, 69-72 & 91-94, NIMH res grant, 70-71; Food & Drug Admin res grant, 74-77, Nat Inst Environ Health Sci grant, 79-85, March of Dimes Found grant, 87-; mem, Am Conf Indust Hyg, 86- *Mem:* Am Soc Pharmacol & Exp Therapeut; Soc Toxicol; Am Conf Govt Indust Hygienists. *Res:* Pharmacology and toxicology of selected chemicals; mechanisms, metabolism and biochemical alterations; neurochemical alterations and molecular interactions; immunotoxicology. *Mailing Add:* Dept Physiol & Pharmacol Univ Ga Col Vet Med Athens GA 30602-7389. *Fax:* 435-750-3959; *E-Mail:* sharma@cc.usu.edu

SHARMA, RAM ASHREY, MEDICINAL CHEMISTRY. *Current Pos:* CANCER RES SCIENTIST MED CHEM, ROSWELL PARK MEM INST, BUFFALO, 71- *Personal Data:* b Azamgarh, India, Sept 5, 43; m 61, Geeta; c Shashi, Ajay (Kumar) & Manjari. *Educ:* Univ Gorakhpur, India, BS, 63, MS, 66; Univ Roorkee, PhD(chem), 70. *Prof Exp:* Asst prof chem, K N Govt Col Gyanpur, Varanasi, India, 66-68; res assoc, Coun Sci & Indust Res, New Delhi, 68-70; asst prof, Univ Roorkee, 70-71. *Mem:* Am Chem Soc. *Res:* Synthesis and biological evaluation of metabolite analogs of purines and pyrimidines of potential medicinal interest. *Mailing Add:* 99 Valley Brook Lane East Amherst NY 14051

SHARMA, RAM AUTAR, THERMODYNAMICS & MATERIAL PROPERTIES, METALLURGY ENGINEERING. *Current Pos:* SR STAFF SCIENTIST, PHYS CHEM DEPT, GEN MOTORS RES LABS, 69- *Personal Data:* b Narnaul, Haryana, India, Aug 20, 27; US citizen. *Educ:* Banaras Hindu Univ, India, MSc, 52; London Univ, UK, PhD(chem metall), 63. *Honors & Awards:* Extractive Metall & Technol Award, Minerals, Metals & Mat Soc. *Prof Exp:* Sr sci officer, Nat Metall Lab, Jamshedpur, India, 53-59; sr res fel, Univ Pa, Philadelphia, 63-66; res chemist, Argonne Nat Lab, Ill, 66-69. *Mem:* Electrochem Soc; Minerals, Metals & Mat Soc. *Res:* Author about 100 scientific and technical papers; granted 25 patents; inventor of GM Neochem process for producing neodymuim and rare earth metals. *Mailing Add:* 2951 Homewood Dr Warren MI 48098

SHARMA, RAM RATAN, PHYSICS, SOLID STATE PHYSICS. *Current Pos:* assoc prof, 68-72, PROF PHYSICS, UNIV ILL, CHICAGO, 72- *Personal Data:* b Jaipur, India, Oct 6, 36; m 67; c 1. *Educ:* Maharaja's Col, Jaipur, BS, 58; Univ Bombay, MS, 62; Univ Calif, Riverside, MA, 64, PhD(physics), 65. *Prof Exp:* Lectr physics & chem, Indian Inst, Jaipur, 57-58; sci officer physics, Atomic Energy Estab, Bombay, 58-62; asst, Univ Calif, Riverside, 62-65; res assoc, Purdue Univ, West Lafayette, 65-68, Argonne Nat Lab, Argonne, Ill, 71-89. *Concurrent Pos:* Advan Res Proj Agency fel, Purdue Univ, West Lafayette, 65-68; res assoc, Argonne Nat Lab, 71-; vis scientist, Atomic Energy Res Estab, Eng, 74; vis prof, Univ Liverpool, 75. *Mem:* Fel Am Phys Soc; Biophys Soc Am Phys Soc. *Res:* Solid state physics; properties of magnetic ions in solids and biological systems; bound-excitons and biexcitons in semiconductors, bound magnetic polarons in dilute magnetic semiconductors; electron-nuclear interactions in solids; shielding effects; polarizabilities of ions; surface color-centers; nuclear fusion; transport of drugs through blood-brain barrier; recrystallization of amorphous substances; epitaxial growth; high temperature superconductivity; muon spin resonance; author of two book. *Mailing Add:* Dept Physics MC 273 Univ Ill Chicago 845 W Taylor St Rm 2236 Chicago IL 60680. *Fax:* 312-996-9016; *E-Mail:* sharma@uic.edu

SHARMA, RAMESH C, NUCLEAR PHYSICS, SOLID STATE PHYSICS. *Current Pos:* asst prof, 62-69, ASSOC PROF PHYSICS, SIR GEORGE WILLIAMS CAMPUS, CONCORDIA UNIV, 69- *Personal Data:* b Delhi, India, June 5, 31. *Educ:* Univ Delhi, BSc, 50, MSc, 52, MA, 53; Univ Toronto, PhD(nuclear physics), 59. *Prof Exp:* Lectr physics, Ramjas Col, Delhi, 55-56; res asst, Univ Toronto, 56-59; res fel, Ont Cancer Inst, Can, 59-60; lectr, Ramjas Col, Delhi, 60-61; lectr, Col Eng & Technol, Delhi, 61-62. *Concurrent Pos:* Nat Res Coun Can grant, 64-65. *Mem:* Am Soc Eng Educ; Can Asn Physicists; Am Phys Soc. *Res:* Nuclear structure, nuclear fission. *Mailing Add:* Dept Physics Concordia Univ 1455 Boul De Maisonneuve W Montreal PQ H3G 1M8 Can

SHARMA, RAN S, BIOSTATISTICS, MATHEMATICAL STATISTICS. *Current Pos:* RETIRED. *Personal Data:* b Ruppura, Gujarat, India, June 9, 37; nat US; m 67, Sudh Mistry; c Mona & Satyan. *Educ:* Gujarat Univ, India, BA, 59, MA, 61; Univ Calif, Los Angeles, PhD(biostatist), 66. *Prof Exp:* Asst, Univ Calif, Los Angeles, 62-66; biostatistician, Riker Labs, 66; sr statistician, E R Squibb & Sons, Inc, 66-70; asst prof, Sch Med, Temple Univ, 68-74, assoc prof biomet & actg chmn dept, 74-80; dir preclin biostatist, Ortho Pharmaceut Corp, 80-97. *Concurrent Pos:* Res asst, Bur Econ & Statist, Gujarat State, 61-62; part-time biostatist consult, 63-65; sr dir, RWJ-PRI dir ortho pharmaceut, J&J Co, 91-97. *Mem:* Biomet Soc; Am Statist Asn. *Res:* Use of multivariate techniques in repeated measures and in related topics; non-parametrics; bioassay; repeated measures; pair comparisons. *Mailing Add:* 1815 Cynthia Lane Feasterville Trevose PA 19053

SHARMA, SADHANA R, INTERNATIONAL PHYSICS. *Current Pos:* ASSOC PROF, DEPT PHYSICS, BROCK UNIV, 93- *Educ:* Panjab Univ, BS, 76, MS, 77; Northwestern Univ, PhD(physics), 82. *Prof Exp:* Assoc prof, Dept Physics, Univ Guelph, 87-93. *Mem:* Am Phys Soc. *Res:* Physics. *Mailing Add:* Dept Physics Brock Univ St Catherines ON L2S 3A1 Can

SHARMA, SANSAR C, NEUROBIOLOGY. *Current Pos:* assoc prof, 72-78, PROF OPHTHAL, NEW YORK MED COL, 78-, PROF ANAT, 81- *Personal Data:* b Pirthipur, India, Mar 10, 38; m 70, Janet Phillips; c David & Nina. *Educ:* Panjab Univ, India, BSc, 61, MSc, 62; Univ Edinburgh, PhD(physiol), 67. *Prof Exp:* Lectr, DAV Col, Ambala, India, 62-63; fel, Univ Edinburgh, 64-68; fel, Washington Univ, 68-72. *Concurrent Pos:* NSF grant, 74-75 & 92-94; Nat Eye Inst grant, 75-; res career develop award, NIH, 78-83. *Mem:* Fel AAAS; Am Physiol Soc; Soc Neurosci; NY Acad Sci; Brit Soc Develop Biol. *Res:* Formation of specific nerve connections in the visual system; developmental neurophysiology of the spinal cord. *Mailing Add:* Dept Anat & Ophthal New York Med Col Valhalla NY 10595. *Fax:* 914-993-4653; *E-Mail:* sharma@nymc.edu

SHARMA, SANTOSH DEVRAJ, OBSTETRICS & GYNECOLOGY. *Current Pos:* assoc prof, 74-78, PROF OBSTET & GYNEC, JOHN A BURN SCH MED, HONOLULU, 78- *Personal Data:* b Kenya, Feb 24, 34. *Educ:* B J Med Sch, Poona, India, MB & BS, 60; Am Bd Obstet & Gynec, dipl, 77. *Prof Exp:* From lectr to sr lectr obstet & gynec, Med Sch Makerere Univ, Kampala, Uganda, 67-72; asst prof obstet & gynec, Sch Med, Howard Univ, Washington, DC. 72-74. *Mem:* Fel Royal Col Obstetricians & Gynecologists; fel Am Col Obstetricians & Gynecologists; Am Soc Colposcopy & Cervical Path. *Res:* Clinical uses of prostagrandins in obstetrics and gynecology. *Mailing Add:* 1319 Punahou St No 801 Honolulu HI 96826

SHARMA, SHIV KUMAR, RAMAN & FOURIER TRANSFORM INFRARED SPECTROSCOPY, LIDAR FOR ENVIRONMENTAL MONITORING. *Current Pos:* from asst res prof to assoc res prof, 80-86, RES PROF/GEOPHYSICIST, HAWAII INST GEOPHYSICS & PLANETOL, UNIV HAWAII, 86-, ASSOC DIR, 90- *Personal Data:* b Alapur, India, July 2, 46; nat US; m 74, Madhu Malaviya; c Bhavya & Bhavna. *Educ:* Jiwaji Univ, BSc, 66, MSc, 68; Indian Inst Technol, PhD(physics), 73. *Prof Exp:* Res assoc, Univ Leicester, 74-77; postdoctoral fel, Geophys Lab, Carnegie Inst Washington, 77-80. *Concurrent Pos:* Res fel, Int Inst Technol, Delhi, India, 69-74; fac fel, Associated Western Univs, Wash, 94-95. *Mem:* Fel Nat Acad Sci India; Am Geophys Union; Am Electrochem Soc; Mineral Soc Am; Optical Soc Am; Soc Appl Spectros; Am Ceramic Soc. *Res:* Mineral physics; experimental petrology; Raman infrared spectroscopy of solids under high pressure and temperature; development of remote in situ environmental sensors. *Mailing Add:* Hawaii Inst Geophys & Planet 2525 Correa Rd Honolulu HI 96822. *Fax:* 808-956-3188

SHARMA, SHRI C, MEDICAL FOODS, FOOD PROCESSING. *Current Pos:* PRES, NUTRALAB INC, 88- *Personal Data:* b Rewari, Haryana, June 18, 45; US citizen; m 75, Pushp L Kaushik; c Anu, Samar & Rupa. *Educ:* Indian Inst Technol, Kharagpur, India, BTech Hons, 67; Univ Wis-Madison, MS, 71; Rutgers Univ, PhD, 74. *Prof Exp:* Fel food processing, Rutgers Univ, 73-75; sr food scientist, Best Foods CPC Int, 75-77, sect head, 77, prin scientist, 78; mgr mat res, PepsiCo Inc, Res & Technol Ctr, 79-80, assoc dir, 80-82; assoc dir chem res, Warner Lambert Co, 82-83, dir, 83-84, sr dir res & develop, 84-85; vpres technol, Nutrit Technol Corp, 85-88. *Concurrent Pos:* Consult, Sara Lee Corp, 85-87; Procter & Gamble Co, 88-89 & Frito-Lay, Inc, 91- *Mem:* Inst Food Technologists; Am Asn Cereal Chemists; Am Inst Nutrit; Am Soc Parental & Enteral Nutrit; fel Am Col Nutrit. *Res:* Development of novel food products; applied food technologies to pharmaceutical products; polymer technologies for development of food as well as pharmaceutical products; credited with commercialization of over 75 consumer products; 45 patents; author of 25 technical papers. *Mailing Add:* 5400 Indian Heights Dr Cincinnati OH 45243

SHARMA, SOMESH DATT, molecular parasitology & immunology, for more information see previous edition

SHARMA, SURESH C, LOW ENERGY POSITRON ANNIHILATION SPECTROSCOPY, DIAMOND FILMS & DEFECT CHARACTERIZATION. *Current Pos:* from asst prof to assoc prof, 80-89, PROF PHYSICS, UNIV TEX, ARLINGTON, 90- *Personal Data:* b Bulandshahar, India, June 6, 45; US citizen; m 67; c 2. *Educ:* Agra Univ, BSc, 65; Meerut Univ, MSc, 67; Brandeis Univ, PhD(physics), 76. *Honors & Awards:* Outstanding Res Contrib Award, Sigma Xi, 80. *Prof Exp:* Lectr physics, M M H Col, Ghaziabad, 67; res asst nuclear physics, Univ Delhi, India, 68-69. *Concurrent Pos:* Assoc dir, Ctr Positron Studies, Univ Tex, Arlington, 80-82, dir, 83-96; co-chmn, 6th Int Conf Positron Annihilation, 82; mem int adv comt, Int Workshops Positron & Positronium Chem, 85- *Mem:* Am Phys Soc; Mat Res Soc. *Res:* Low energy positron annihilation to investigate positronium localization in density fluctuations, lattice defects, surfaces and fluids; deposition and electronic structure of diamond films; photoemission from negative electron affinity surfaces. *Mailing Add:* Dept Physics Univ Tex Box 19059 Arlington TX 76019. *Fax:* 817-272-3637; *E-Mail:* sharma@albert.uta.edu

SHARMA, UDHISHTRA DEVA, ANIMAL SCIENCE, BIOLOGY. *Current Pos:* PROF BIOL, ALA STATE UNIV, MONTGOMERY, 66- *Personal Data:* b Amritsar, India, Aug 16, 28; m 59, Sarla; c Sadhana. *Educ:* Punjab Univ, BVSc, 48; Univ Ill, Urbana, MS, 54, PhD(reproductive physiol), 57. *Prof Exp:* Res asst animal genetics, Indian Vet Res Inst, 49-53; res assoc germ cell physiol, Am Found Biol Res, Madison, Wis, 57-58; prof animal genetics, Postgrad Col Animal Sci, Indian Vet Res Inst, 58-64; prof animal husb & head dept, Punjab Agr Univ, 64-65; vis prof anat, Med Ctr, Univ Ark, Little Rock, 65-66. *Mem:* Am Vet Med Asn. *Res:* Physiology of reproduction, artificial insemination and preservation of bovine semen; animal sciences and veterinary medicine; biological sciences. *Mailing Add:* 4438 Eley Ct Montgomery AL 36106

SHARNOFF, MARK, MOLECULAR PHYSICS, SOLID STATE PHYSICS. *Current Pos:* from asst prof to assoc prof, 65-74, PROF PHYSICS, UNIV DEL, 74- *Personal Data:* b Cleveland, Ohio, July 26, 35; m 59; c 3. *Educ:* Univ Rochester, BS, 57; Harvard Univ, PhD(physics), 63. *Prof Exp:* Nat Acad Sci-Nat Res Coun resident res assoc, Nat Bur Stand, 63-65. *Concurrent Pos:* Regional ed, J Luminescence, 69-81; NIH spec fel & vis assoc prof biophys, Pa State Univ, 72-73. *Mem:* AAAS; Am Phys Soc; Biophys Soc; Am Chem Soc; Optical Soc Am; Int Soc Optical Eng. *Res:* Dynamic nuclear polarization; electron spin resonance of free radicals and transition metal ions; optical properties of coordination complexes; microwave-optical studies of isomerization and energy transport in organic systems; microdifferential holographic interferometry of activity patterns in biological tissues; biophysics; spectroscopy and spectrometry; optics; fluids. *Mailing Add:* Dept Physics Univ Del Newark DE 19716-2570

SHAROBEAM, MONIR HANNA, FRACTURE MECHANICS, COMPUTATIONAL SOLID MECHANICS. *Current Pos:* ASST PROF ENG SCI, RICHARD STOCKTON COL NJ, 91-, DIR DUAL DEGREE ENG PROG, 91- *Personal Data:* b Fayoum, Egypt, Feb 3, 54; m 85, Nahad E Ayad; c Marina M. *Educ:* Cairo Univ, Egypt, BS, 76, MS, 81; Univ Tenn, Knoxville, PhD(eng sci & mech), 90. *Prof Exp:* Asst lectr mach design, Cairo Univ, 81-86. *Concurrent Pos:* Co-investr, Cairo Univ, Petrogas, 82-84; consult mech engr, Albaric-Sreg, France & Contracto, Egypt, 83-85. *Mem:* Am Soc Mech Engrs; Am Soc Testing & Mat; Syndicate Egyptian Engrs. *Res:* Develop the load separation methodology in elastic-plastic fracture mechanics; develop linear and non-linear computational models for defective structures using the finite element method; develop optimum design kinetic energy storage systems. *Mailing Add:* 704 S Falconcrest Ct Smithville NJ 08201. *Fax:* 609-748-5515; *E-Mail:* msharo@vax002.stockton.edu

SHAROM, FRANCES JANE, MEMBRANE PROTEINS & TRANSPORTERS, CANCER RESEARCH. *Current Pos:* From asst prof to assoc prof, 80-94, PROF BIOCHEM, UNIV GUELPH, 94- *Personal Data:* b Newcastle-upon-Tyne, UK, June 6, 53; Can citizen; wid; c Jeffrey R & Sofia E. *Educ:* Univ Guelph, BSc, 75; Univ Western Ont, PhD(biochem), 78. *Concurrent Pos:* Nat Sci & Eng Res Coun Can res fel, Univ Guelph, 80-84; vis scientist, Dept Oncol, Toronto Gen Hosp, 88, Ont Cancer Inst, 88; dir, Guelph-Waterloo Ctr Grad Work Chem, 91-94. *Mem:* Am Asn Cancer Res; Am Soc Biochem & Molecular Biol; Can Soc Biochem, Cell & Molecular Biol. *Res:* Molecular structure and function of p-glycoprotein, which is responsible for multidrug resistance in human cancers; behavior and interactions of glycosyl-phosphatidytinositol anchored membrane proteins. *Mailing Add:* Dept Chem & Biochem Univ Guelph Guelph ON N1G 2W1 Can. *Fax:* 519-766-1499; *E-Mail:* sharom@chembio.uoguelph.ca

SHARON (SCHWADRON), YITZHAK YAAKOV, NUCLEAR STRUCTURE THEORY, NUCLEAR MODELS. *Current Pos:* assoc prof, 72-75, PROF PHYSICS, STOCKTON STATE COL, 75- *Personal Data:* b Tel Aviv, Israel, Feb 29, 36; m 91, Sandra Brook; c Dina Aurahama. *Educ:* Columbia Univ, AB, 58; Princeton Univ, MA, 60, PhD(physics), 66. *Prof Exp:* Teaching asst, dept physics, Columbia Univ, 57-58; consult, Phys Sci Study Comt, Educ Serv, Inc, 58-59; asst instruction, dept physics, Princeton Univ, 58-59, res asst, 59-60, asst instruction, 60-62, res asst, 63-65, asst, Inst Advan Study, 65-66; asst prof, Northeastern Univ, 66-72. *Concurrent Pos:* Physicist, Lawrence Radiation Lab, Berkeley, Calif, 68; res participant, Oak Ridge Nat Lab, Tenn, 69 & Nat Bur Standards, Washington, DC, 71; vis asst prof, Temple Univ, Philadelphia, 70-71; vis prof, lab nuclear physics, Univ Montreal, 70; vis fel, Princeton Univ, NJ, 80-82 & 91-92; visitor, Rutgers Univ, NJ, 95-96. *Mem:* Am Phys Soc; Am Asn Physics Teachers; Sigma Xi. *Res:* Nuclear theory, especially nuclear models and the connections between them; shell model, collective model, SU(3) models; projected wave functions; systematics of nuclear properties; physics education. *Mailing Add:* Jadwin Hall Princeton Univ Princeton NJ 08554. *Fax:* 609-748-5515; *E-Mail:* sharon@ruthep.rutgers.edu

SHARON, NEHAMA, VIROLOGY. *Current Pos:* ASSOC PROF PATH, SCH MED, NORTHWESTERN UNIV, 72- *Personal Data:* b Tiberias, Israel, Mar 2, 29. *Educ:* Hebrew Univ, Jerusalem, PhD(immunol), 61. *Mem:* Am Soc Microbiol; Am Soc Clin Path; Sigma Xi. *Res:* Abnormal changes in serum protein. *Mailing Add:* 175 E Delaware Pl Chicago IL 60611

SHAROV, ALEXEI A, POPULATION ECOLOGY OF INSECTS, SIMULATION MODELING. *Current Pos:* RES SCIENTIST, VA POLYTECH INST & STATE UNIV, 92- *Personal Data:* b Moscow, Russ, Mar 30, 54; m 75, Lioudmila Larchenkova; c Michael & Olga. *Educ:* Moscow State Univ, Russ, MS, 76, PhD(entom), 80, DSc, 88. *Prof Exp:* Res assoc, Moscow State Univ, Russ, 80-86, res scientist, 87-90; vis scientist, WVa Univ, Morgantown, 91-92. *Concurrent Pos:* Prof biostatist, Moscow Agr Acad, Russ, 89-90. *Mem:* Entom Soc Am; Ecol Soc Am. *Res:* Population dynamics of insects, in particular, forest pests; ecological modelling; theoretical biology, biosemiotics. *Mailing Add:* Dept Entom Va Polytech Inst & State Univ Blacksburg VA 24061-0319. *Fax:* 540-231-9131; *E-Mail:* sharov@vt.edu

SHARP, A C, JR, MAGNETISM. *Current Pos:* PROF PHYSICS, MCMURRY UNIV, 65- *Personal Data:* b Lorenzo, Tex, July 16, 32; m 55; c 3. *Educ:* Tex A&I Univ, BS, 57, MS, 58; Tex A&M Univ, PhD(physics), 65. *Prof Exp:* Instr physics, Univ Tex, Arlington, 58-61; asst prof, Tex Woman's Univ, 64-65. *Concurrent Pos:* Fulbright exchange prof, Univ Liberia, 81-82. *Mem:* Am Phys Soc; Am Asn Physics Teachers; Optical Soc Am. *Res:* Polymer solution theory using polyisobutylene-n-alkane systems; magnetic properties of thin permalloy films. *Mailing Add:* Dept Physics McMurry Univ Box 38 McMurray Station Abilene TX 79697. *Fax:* 915-691-6599

SHARP, A(RNOLD) G(IDEON), MECHANICAL ENGINEERING. *Current Pos:* res engr, Woods Hole Oceanog Inst, 58-63, res assoc, 63-78, res specialist, 78-90, SR ENGR, WOODS HOLE OCEANOG INST, 90- *Personal Data:* b Worcester, Mass, May 16, 23. *Educ:* Tufts Univ, BS, 45; Worcester Polytech Inst, MS, 53. *Prof Exp:* Instr mech eng, Worcester Polytech Inst, 46-53; asst prof civil eng, Univ Mass, 53-58. *Concurrent Pos:* Lectr, Lincoln Col, Northeastern Univ, 60-61. *Mem:* Soc Exp Mech. *Res:* Applied mechanics; stress analysis; structural design; properties of materials; oceanographic instrumentation; deep-submergence vehicle design. *Mailing Add:* PO Box 434 Woods Hole MA 02543-0434. *Fax:* 508-457-2195; *E-Mail:* asharp@whoi.edu

SHARP, AARON JOHN, plant geography; deceased, see previous edition for last biography

SHARP, ALLAN ROY, BIOPHYSICS, APPLIED PHYSICS. *Current Pos:* from asst prof to assoc prof, 75-85, PROF PHYSICS, UNIV NB, 85- *Personal Data:* b Hamilton, Ont, Nov 3, 46; m 71; c 3. *Educ:* McMaster Univ, BSc, 67; Univ Waterloo, MSc, 69, PhD(physics), 73. *Prof Exp:* Fel, Univ Toronto, 72-74; lectr, Univ Natal, 74-75. *Concurrent Pos:* Nat Sci Eng Res Coun Can res grant, 76- *Mem:* Can Asn Physicists. *Res:* Nuclear magnetic resonance studies of interactions of molecules with biopolymers, primarily water with cellulose; effects of these molecules on wood properties; materials science of wood. *Mailing Add:* Dept Physics Univ NB Col Hill Box 4400 Fredericton NB E3B 5A3 Can

SHARP, DAVID HOWLAND, THEORETICAL PHYSICS. *Current Pos:* FEL, LOS ALAMOS SCI LAB, 74- *Personal Data:* b Buffalo, NY, Oct 14, 38; m 65, 83; c 4. *Educ:* Princeton Univ, AB, 60; Calif Inst Technol, PhD(physics), 64. *Prof Exp:* NSF fel physics, Princeton Univ, 63-64, res assoc, 64-65; res fel, Munich Tech Univ, 65-66; res fel, Calif Inst Technol, 66; instr, Palmer Phys Lab, Princeton Univ, 66-67; asst prof physics, Univ Pa, 67-74. *Concurrent Pos:* Consult, Jason Div, Inst Defense Anal, 60-66 & Lawrence Livermore Lab, Univ Calif, Livermore, 64-66; guest partic, Battelle Rencontres Math & Physics, 69; mem, Bd Hons Examrs, Swarthmore Col, 72; mem, J Robert Oppenheimer Mem Comt, 76-, chmn, 78. *Mem:* AAAS; Asn Math Physicists; Int Soc Gen Relativity & Gravitation; fel Am Phys Soc; Soc Indust & Appl Math. *Res:* Elementary particle physics; theory of gravitation; fluid dynamics, neural nets. *Mailing Add:* B285 Los Alamos Net Lab PO Box 1663 Univ Calif Los Alamos NM 87545

SHARP, DEXTER BRIAN, PESTICIDE CHEMISTRY, METABOLISM. *Current Pos:* CONSULT PESTICIDES, DEXTER B SHARP, INC, 85- *Personal Data:* b Chicago, Ill, June 14, 19; m 45, Peggy E Person; c Peggy L, Judith A & Janice K. *Educ:* Carleton Col, BA, 41; Univ Nebr, MA, 43, PhD(chem), 45. *Prof Exp:* Asst chem, Univ Nebr, 41-45; res chemist, Chem Dept, Exp Sta, E I du Pont de Nemours & Co, Inc, 45-46; Am Chem Soc fel & instr, Univ Minn, 46-47; from asst prof to assoc prof chem, Kans State Col, 47-51; res chemist, Monsanto Agr Co, 51-54, group leader, 54-68, mgr residue metab, 68-75, environ sci dir, 75-82, dir environ & formulations technol, 82-85. *Concurrent Pos:* Mem, comt registration pesticides, Nat Acad Sci, 68-, comt sci & regulatory issues underlying pesticide use patterns & agr innovation, 85-86; mem, Comn Pesticide Chem, Int Union Pure & Appl Chem, 84-88; consult, Stewart Pesticide Regist Assocs Inc, 88- *Mem:* Am Chem Soc; Weed Sci Soc Am; Int Union Pure & Appl Chem. *Res:* Mechanisms of organic reactions; oxidation; pesticides; gas-liquid chromatography; pesticide metabolism; plant and animals; residues; environmental fate; applicator and dietary exposure; pharmacokinetics; risk assessment; pesticide registration; residue in environmental sciences. *Mailing Add:* 9817 Foster Overland Park KS 66212-2360

SHARP, EDWARD A, MATHEMATICS, COMPUTER SCIENCE. *Current Pos:* ASSOC PROF MATH, CREIGHTON UNIV, 57-, DIR COMPUT CTR, 66- *Personal Data:* b Milwaukee, Wis, Oct 3, 20. *Educ:* St Louis Univ, AB, 43, AM, 56. *Mem:* Am Math Soc; London Math Soc; Soc Indust & Appl Math. *Mailing Add:* Dept Math Creighton Univ Omaha NE 68178-0001

SHARP, EUGENE LESTER, plant pathology, for more information see previous edition

SHARP, GARY DUANE, CLIMATE-DRIVEN POPULATION BIOLOGY & TIME SERIES ANALYSIS, HIGH RESOLUTION GEOLOCATION. *Current Pos:* SCI DIR, COOP INST RES INTEGRATED OCEAN SCIS, 91- *Personal Data:* b Lubbock, Tex, Feb 22, 44; m, Kathleen T Dorsey. *Educ:* San Diego State Univ, BSc, 67; Calif State Univ, San Diego, MSc, 68; Univ Calif, San Diego, PhD(zool), 72. *Prof Exp:* Sr scientist, Inter-Am Trop Tuna Comn, 69-78; fisheries resources officer, Food Agr Orgn UN, 78-83; vis scientist, Univ Corp Atmospheric Res, 87-90. *Concurrent Pos:* Consult-advisor appl ocean scis, Ctr Climate-Ocean Resources Study, 83- *Mem:* Am Soc Limnologists & Oceanographers; AAAS; Oceanog Soc; Int Soc Ecol Econ; Am Geophys Union. *Res:* Responses of aquatic resource populations to climate-driven ocean variability; data visualization and database development. *Mailing Add:* 780 Harrison Rd Salinas CA 93907. *Fax:* 408-582-3656; *E-Mail:* gsharp@igc.apc.org

SHARP, GERALD DUANE, RUMINANT NUTRITION, LIVESTOCK EVALUATION. *Current Pos:* assoc prof, 76-79, PROF & CHAIR, ANIMAL SCI DEPT, CALIF STATE POLYTECH UNIV, POMONA, 79- *Personal Data:* b Twin Falls, Idaho, July 28, 33; m 54; c 2. *Educ:* Univ Idaho, BS, 55, MS, 62; Wash State Univ, PhD(animal nutrit), 69. *Prof Exp:* Animal scientist, Caldwell Br Exp Sta, Univ Idaho, 62-64, Swine Herdsman, 64-66; asst dairy scientist, Wash State Univ, 69-70; asst prof, Fort Hays Kans State Col, 70-72, prof & farm supt, 72-76. *Mem:* Sigma Xi; Am Soc Animal Sci; Coun Agr Sci & Technol. *Mailing Add:* 1010 Rosemary Lane La Verne CA 91750-1858

SHARP, HENRY, JR, MATHEMATICS. *Current Pos:* PROF MATH, WASHINGTON & LEE UNIV, 83- *Personal Data:* b Nashville, Tenn, Oct 14, 23; m 57; c 2. *Educ:* Vanderbilt Univ, BE, 47; Duke Univ, AM, 50, PhD(math), 52. *Prof Exp:* Res assoc, Johns Hopkins Univ, 52-53; asst prof math, Ga Inst Technol, 53-56; from asst prof to prof, Emory Univ, 58-83. *Concurrent Pos:* NSF fac fel, 64-65, res grant, 68-69. *Mem:* Am Math Soc; Math Asn Am. *Res:* Point-set topology, dimension theory and graph theory. *Mailing Add:* Rte 4 Box 436-A Lexington VA 24450-9804

SHARP, HOMER FRANKLIN, JR, ZOOLOGY, ECOLOGY. *Current Pos:* from instr to assoc prof, 63-79, PROF BIOL, OXFORD COL, EMORY UNIV, 79- *Personal Data:* b Lithonia, Ga, Sept 5, 36; m 61; c 2. *Educ:* Emory Univ, BA, 59; Univ Ga, MS, 62, PhD(zool), 70. *Prof Exp:* Asst prof biol, LaGrange Col, 62-63. *Mem:* Am Soc Mammalogists; Sigma Xi; AAAS. *Res:* Bioenergetics of populations; diversity of benthic communities; secondary succesion; wetland ecology. *Mailing Add:* Dept Biol Oxford Col Emory Univ Oxford GA 30267

SHARP, HUGH T, COST ESTIMATING, TECHNICAL PUBLISHING. *Current Pos:* PRES, STRATEGIC ADVANTAGE, LLC, 94- *Personal Data:* b New York, NY, Sept 6, 29; m 54, Elaine; c 1. *Educ:* Villanova Univ, BChE, 53. *Prof Exp:* Ed & mem sales & mkt staff, Chem Eng, McGraw-Hill Publ Co, 53-68, dir spec proj, Planning & Develop Dept, 68-70, advert sales mgr, 70-72, gen mgr, Sweet's Div, McGraw Hill Info Syst Co, 72-79 & Cost Info Syst Div, 79-80; vpres planning & develop, Sweet's Group, McGraw-Hill, Inc, 80-90; vpres & gen mgr, R S Means Co, Inc, Southern Co, 90-94. *Concurrent Pos:* Vpres, Mfrs Agent Publ Co, Inc, 75-82. *Mem:* Am Inst Chem Engrs; Am Asn Cost Engrs; Info Indust Asn. *Mailing Add:* 4 Van Wyck St Montvale NJ 07645. *Fax:* 201-573-9686; *E-Mail:* 103043.1064@compuserve.com

SHARP, JAMES H, PHYSICAL CHEMISTRY, CHEMICAL PHYSICS. *Current Pos:* scientist, Physics Res Lab, 64-68, mgr, Chem Physics Res Br, Res & Eng Sci Div, 68-71, mgr, Org Solid State Physics, Rochester Corp Res Ctr, 71-72, technol ctr mgr, Info Technol Group, 72-74, RES MGR, XEROX RES CENTRE CAN, XEROX CORP, 74- *Personal Data:* b Moosejaw, Sask,

Apr 20, 34; c 4. *Educ:* Univ BC, BA, 57, MSc, 60; Univ Calif, Riverside, PhD(phys chem), 64. *Prof Exp:* Fel org solid state, Nat Res Coun Can, 63-64. *Mem:* Am Phys Soc; Am Chem Soc; Chem Inst Can; Sigma Xi. *Res:* Photochemistry; photolyses and photophysics of organic materials; electron spin resonance; photoconductivity and transport phenomenon; optical sensitization and energy transfer; spectroscopy of the organic solid state. *Mailing Add:* 2660 Speakman Dr Mississauga ON L5K 2L1 Can

SHARP, JAMES JACK, CIVIL ENGINEERING. *Current Pos:* PROF & ASSOC DEAN ENG & APPL SCI, MEM UNIV NFLD, 70- *Personal Data:* b Glasgow, Scotland, July 22, 39; m 63; c 3. *Educ:* Glasgow Univ, BSc, 61, MSc, 63; Univ Strathclyde, ARCST, 61, PhD(hydraul), 69. *Honors & Awards:* Dagenais Award, Can Soc Civil Eng, 91; Award of Merit, Asn Prof Engrs & Geoscientists, 96. *Prof Exp:* Exec engr, Govt Malawi, 63-66; lectr civil eng, Univ Strathclyde, 66-70. *Concurrent Pos:* Hon prof, Shandong Univ Technol, China; external assessor, Univ Malaya, Malasia. *Mem:* Am Soc Civil Engrs; Brit Inst Civil Engrs; fel Can Soc Civil Eng; fel Eng Inst Can; fel Inst Civil Engrs. *Res:* Hydraulics; densimetric phenomena; energy dissipation. *Mailing Add:* Dept Eng Mem Univ Nfld Elizabeth Ave St John's NF A1C 5S7 Can. *Fax:* 709-737-4042; *E-Mail:* jsharp@engrs.mun.ca

SHARP, JOHN BUCKNER, FORESTRY. *Current Pos:* dist forester, Agr Exten Serv, Univ Tenn, Knoxville, 47-49, assoc exten forester, 52-57, state exten forester, 57-74, PROF FORESTRY, UNIV TENN, KNOXVILLE, 74- *Personal Data:* b Maynardville, Tenn, Nov 5, 20; m 49, Helen Anderson; c Nancy, Paul & Mary J. *Educ:* Univ Tenn, BS, 43, MS, 45; Duke Univ, MF, 47; Harvard Univ, MPA, 50, DPA, 52. *Prof Exp:* Carnegie Corp fel, Harvard Univ, 50-52. *Mem:* Soc Am Foresters. *Res:* Farm forestry; forestry administration; holder of two US patents; author of two books. *Mailing Add:* 5052 Mountain Crest Dr Knoxville TN 37918

SHARP, JOHN GRAHAM, EXPERIMENTAL HEMATOLOGY, TUMOR BIOLOGY. *Current Pos:* from asst prof to prof anat, 73-82, PROF CELL BIOL, ANAT & RADIOL, UNIV NEBR MED CTR, 82- *Personal Data:* b Halifax, Eng, Feb 10, 46; m 73, Sheila Jamison; c John A & Matthew E. *Educ:* Univ Birmingham, Eng, BSc, 67, MSc, 68, PhD(exp hemat), 71. *Prof Exp:* Res fel anat, Univ Birmingham, Eng, 70-71; Damon Runyon res fel, Radiation Res Lab, Univ Iowa, 71-73, asst instr, Dept Anat, 72-73, instr radiol, 73. *Concurrent Pos:* Yamagawa-Yoshida Mem Int Cancer fel, Dept Histopath, Univ London, 81-82; Paul Grange vis cancer res fel, Dept Anat, Monash Univ, Australia, 84. *Mem:* Int Soc Exp Hemat; Am Asn Immunologists; Am Asn Anatomists; Radiation Res Soc; Cell Kinetics Soc; AAAS. *Res:* Cell renewal systems; stromal cell regulation of stem cell proliferation and differentiation in bone marrow, thymus and intestine and its relevance to the development of cancers in these tissues; antisense oligo nucleotide therapy of cancer. *Mailing Add:* Dept Cell Biol Anat & Radiol 3026 Wittson Hall Univ Nebr Med Ctr 600 S 42nd St Omaha NE 68198-6395. *Fax:* 402-559-7328

SHARP, JOHN MALCOLM, JR, HYDROGEOLOGY. *Current Pos:* assoc prof, Univ Tex, 82-84, C E Yager prof, 85-89, Gulf Found Centennial prof, 90-92, CHEVRON CENTENNIAL PROF GEOL, UNIV TEX, 92- *Personal Data:* b St Paul, Minn, Mar 11, 44; m 67, Carol Martin; c Kathryn, John D & Susan. *Educ:* Univ Minn, BGeolE, 67; Univ Ill, MS & PhD(hydrogeol), 74. *Honors & Awards:* O E Meinzer Award, Geol Soc Am, 79. *Prof Exp:* Civil engr, USAF, 67-71; from asst to assoc prof geol, Univ Mo, Columbia, 74-82, chmn dept, 80-82. *Concurrent Pos:* Alexander von Humboldt fel, 81 & 83; chmn Hydrogeol Div, Geol Soc Am, 87-88, mem coun, 90-93, counr, 91-93. *Mem:* Am Inst Mining Engrs; Geol Soc Am; Am Geophys Union; Asn Groundwater Sci & Engrs; Int Water Resources Asn; Int Asn Hydrogeologists; Am Inst Hydrol (vpres, 88-91); Sigma Xi. *Res:* Energy transport in porous media; flood-plain hydrogeology; economics of water resource development; basinal hydrogeology; coastal subsidence; water resources of Trans-Pecos Texas and the Edwards aquifer. *Mailing Add:* Dept Geol Sci Univ Tex Austin TX 78712

SHARP, JOHN ROLAND, AQUATIC TOXICOLOGY, PHYSIOLOGICAL ECOLOGY. *Current Pos:* ASST PROF BIOL, ZOOL & BIOL FISHES, INTRO AQUATIC TOXICOL, SOUTHEAST MO STATE UNIV, 80- *Personal Data:* b Joplin, Mo, Dec 5, 49; m 79; c 1. *Educ:* Southwest Mo State Col, BS, 71; Tex A&M Univ, PhD(biol), 79. *Prof Exp:* Res assoc, Tex A&M Univ, 78-79. *Concurrent Pos:* Instr marine ichthyol, Gulf Coast Res Lab, 76 & 81-82. *Mem:* Sigma Xi. *Res:* Individual and interactive effects of environmental stressors on the physiology and developmental biology of marine and freshwater fishes, particularly the embryo-larval life history stages; ecology of fishes. *Mailing Add:* Dept Biol SE Mo State Univ One University Plaza Cape Girardeau MO 63701-4701

SHARP, JOHN T(HOMAS), RHEUMATOLOGY. *Current Pos:* CLIN PROF MED, EMORY UNIV, 87- *Personal Data:* b Dalhart, Tex, Nov 16, 24; m 49, Marjorie S Gliun; c John R, Thomas G & Jeffrey D. *Educ:* Columbia Univ, NY, MD, 47. *Prof Exp:* Div chief, rheumatology, Baylor Col Med, 62-76, prof med, 64-76; chief, Dept Med, Vet Admin Hosp, Danville, Ill, 76-80; prof med, Univ Ill, Urbana, 76-80 & Univ Colo, 80-86; dir rheumatology, Alpert Arthritis Ctr, Rose Hosp, 80-86. *Mem:* Master Am Col Rheumatology; Am Col Physicians; Am Asn Immunologists; emer mem Soc Am Microbiologists. *Res:* Radiologic assessment of disease progression in rheumatoid arthritis. *Mailing Add:* 712 E 18th St Tifton GA 31794

SHARP, JOHN TURNER, INTERNAL & PULMONARY MEDICINE, CARDIOLOGY. *Current Pos:* prof med, 87-94, EMER PROF MED, PHYSIOL & BIOPHYS, UNIV S FLA, TAMPA, 94- *Personal Data:* b Jamestown, NY, Jan 18, 27; m 49, Susan C; c John, William, Robert, Carolyn & Paul. *Educ:* Univ Buffalo, MD, 49. *Prof Exp:* Intern med, Bellevue Hosp, New York, 49-50; resident internal med, Vet Admin Hosp, Buffalo, 52-54; Am Heart Asn res fel cardiopulmonary physiol & clin cardiol, Buffalo Gen Hosp & Sch Med, State Univ NY, Buffalo, 54-57; Am Heart Asn estab investr, 57-59; prof dir pulmonary dis serv, Vet Admin Hosp, Hines, 59-87. *Concurrent Pos:* Nat Heart Inst res grants, 59-62 & 64-79; from assoc prof to prof med, Univ Ill Col Med, 64-82. *Mem:* Am Soc Clin Invest; Am Col Physicians; fel Am Col Chest Physicians; fel Am Col Cardiol; Am Physiol Soc. *Res:* Cardiopulmonary physiology; respiratory physiology, particularly the mechanics of respiration and respiratory muscle function in normal and diseased man; human hemodynamics in health and disease; epidemiology of chronic respiratory diseases. *Mailing Add:* 623 Concord Lane Holmes Beach FL 34217

SHARP, JONATHAN HAWLEY, CHEMICAL OCEANOGRAPHY, BIOLOGICAL OCEANOGRAPHY. *Current Pos:* assoc prof, 73-87, PROF OCEANOG, COL MARINE STUDIES, UNIV DEL, 87- *Personal Data:* b Bridgeton, NJ, Apr 29, 43; m 73; c 2. *Educ:* Lehigh Univ, BA, 65, MS, 67; Dalhousie Univ, PhD(oceanog), 72. *Prof Exp:* Fel oceanog, Scripps Inst Oceanog, Univ Calif, San Diego, 72-73. *Concurrent Pos:* Consult, Org Am States, 72-74; mem Md Environ Res Guidance Comt, 77-84; panel, Off Naval Res, 79-81; mgr, Del Estuary Res Proj, 81-86; chmn, Sci Tech Adv Comt, Del Estuary Prog, 89- *Mem:* AAAS; Am Soc Limnology & Oceanog; Am Chem Soc; Am Geophys Union; Oceanog Soc. *Res:* Biological chemistry of seawater, interaction between marine micro-organisms and chemistry of sea; dynamics of estuarine and coastal waters. *Mailing Add:* Dept Marine Sci Univ Del Newark DE 19717-0001

SHARP, JOSEPH C(ECIL), NEUROBIOLOGY, EXPERIMENTAL PSYCHOLOGY. *Current Pos:* PROF SCI, SOUTHERN UTAH UNIV, 93- *Personal Data:* b Salt Lake City, Utah, May 30, 34; m 56, Pauline Burnham; c Joseph C & Cindy (Stephenson). *Educ:* Univ Utah, BS, 57, MS, 58, PhD(psychol), 61. *Prof Exp:* Chief behav radiation, Walter Reed Army Inst Res, 60-67, chief exp psychol, 67-68; dep comn environ health, Dept Health, State NY, 69-70; dep dir neuropsychiat, Walter Reed Army Inst Res, 71-74; dep dir life sci, NASA Ames Res Ctr, 74-85, dir space res, 85-93. *Concurrent Pos:* US space rep, UK, 87. *Mem:* Am Psychol Asn; Radiation Res Soc; Int Soc Chronobiol; Sigma Xi. *Res:* Central nervous system and radiation effects; space biology and medicine; experimental psychology, drug abuse and neuroendocrinology; space physiology. *Mailing Add:* Southern Utah Univ Col Sci GC406J Cedar City UT 84721

SHARP, KENNETH GEORGE, INORGANIC CHEMISTRY. *Current Pos:* sr res assoc, Polymers Div, 90-93, SR RES ASSOC, CENT RES DEPT, E I DUPONT DE NEMOURS & CO, 93- *Personal Data:* b Dec 24, 43; US citizen; m 67; c 1. *Educ:* Univ Calif, Riverside, BA, 65; Rice Univ, PhD(chem), 69. *Prof Exp:* Nat Res Coun-Nat Bur Stand fel, Nat Bur Stand, Washington, DC, 69-71; asst prof inorg chem, Univ Southern Calif, 71-80; assoc scientist, Dow Corning Corp, 80-90. *Mem:* Am Chem Soc. *Res:* Inorganic synthesis via energetic intermediates; high-temperature chemistry; silicon and fluorine chemistry. *Mailing Add:* 164 Hamilton Rd Landenberg PA 19350

SHARP, LEE AJAX, range management; deceased, see previous edition for last biography

SHARP, LOUIS JAMES, IV, POLYMER CHEMISTRY. *Current Pos:* DIR SCI AFFAIRS, DEXTER PACKAGING PRODS DIV, DEXTER CORP, 94- *Personal Data:* b Washington, DC, Oct 13, 44; m 68; c 3. *Educ:* Univ Notre Dame, BS, 66; Calif Inst Technol, PhD(chem), 70. *Prof Exp:* Res fel, Radiation Lab, Univ Notre Dame, 69-72; asst prof chem, Marian Col, 72-74; dir resin res & develop, Lily Indust Coatings Inc, 74-80; group leader synthesis, Betz Labs, 80-81; mgr polymer chem, Midland Dexter Corp, 81-87, dir res & admin serv, 87-94. *Mem:* Am Chem Soc; Sigma Xi. *Res:* Synthesis and rheology of resins for coatings, including polyesters, acrylics, urea-formaldehyde resins, silicones, melamines, alkyds, water-based resins, high solids resins and ultraviolet cured resins. *Mailing Add:* Dexter Corp One E Water St Waukegan IL 60085

SHARP, PHILLIP ALLEN, MOLECULAR BIOLOGY, CANCER BIOLOGY. *Current Pos:* assoc prof, 74-79, dir, Ctr Cancer Res, 85-91 PROF DEPT BIOL, MASS INST TECHNOL, 79-, HEAD DEPT BIOL, 91- *Personal Data:* b Falmouth, Ky, June 6, 44; m 64, Ann H; c Christine A, Sarah K & Helena H. *Educ:* Union Col, BA, 66; Univ Ill, Urbana, PhD(chem), 69. *Hon Degrees:* Numerous from US & foreign univs, 91-96. *Honors & Awards:* Nobel Prize in Physiol or Med, 93; Fac Res Award, Am Cancer Soc, 74; Eli Lilly Award, 80; US Steel Award, Nat Acad Sci, 80; Alfred P Sloan Jr Prize, Gen Motors Res Found, 86; Gairdner Found Int Award, Can, 86; Albert Lasker Basic Med Res Award, 88; Louisa Gross Horwitz Prize, Columbia Univ, 88. *Prof Exp:* Fel biophys chem & molecular biol, Calif Inst Technol, 69-71; res staff virol & molecular biol, Cold Spring Harbor Lab, 71-74. *Concurrent Pos:* Consult, Biogen Ltd, 78-, Chmn, Sci Bd; lectr, Univ Ky, 79, Univ Chicago, 80, Loyola Univ Chicago, 81, Univ Ill, Urbana-Champaign, 84, Univ Calif, Los Angeles, 89, Purdue Univ, 89, Univ Calif, Berkeley, 90, NY Univ Med Ctr, 90, Southwestern Med Ctr, Univ Dallas, 90 & Univ Wis-Madison, 90; consult, Bristol-Myers Squibb; mem, Pres Comm Advisors Sci & Technol, 94-; trustee & mem, Alfred P Sloan Found, 95-; mem, Nat Cancer Adv Bd, NIH, 96- *Mem:* Nat Acad Sci; Inst Med-Nat Acad Sci; Am

Soc Microbiol; fel AAAS; Am Chem Soc; Am Philos Soc; Am Asn Cancer Res. *Res:* Molecular biology of gene expression in mammalian cells. *Mailing Add:* Ctr Cancer Res Rm E17-529B Mass Inst Technol Cambridge MA 02139. *Fax:* 617-253-3867; *E-Mail:* sharppa@mit.edu

SHARP, RICHARD DANA, magnetospheric physics, ionospheric physics, for more information see previous edition

SHARP, RICHARD LEE, CHEMICAL TOXICOLOGY. *Current Pos:* RETIRED. *Personal Data:* b Kansas City, Mo, Sept 14, 35; m 64; c 1. *Educ:* William Jewell Col, AB, 61; Purdue Univ, PhD(org chem), 66. *Prof Exp:* Prod chemist, Eastman Kodak Co, 66-67, develop chemist, 67-69, supvr synthetic org chem, Synthetic Chem Div, 69-73, tech assoc Health & Safety Lab, 73-91. *Mem:* Am Chem Soc; Am Indust Hyg Asn. *Res:* Directive effects in the hydroboration of functionally substituted olefins and related compounds; synthesis of fine organic chemicals; toxicity testing of organic chemicals. *Mailing Add:* 135 Apple Creek Lane Rochester NY 14612

SHARP, ROBERT PHILLIP, GEOMORPHOLOGY. *Current Pos:* chmn, Div Geol Sci, 52-68, prof geomorphol, 47-79, EMER ROBERT P SHARP PROF GEOL, CALIF INST TECHNOL, 79- *Personal Data:* b Oxnard, Calif, June 24, 11; m 38, Jean P Todd; c Kristin T (Sharp) & Bruce T. *Educ:* Calif Inst Technol, BS, 34, MS, 35; Harvard Univ, AM, 36, PhD(geol), 38. *Honors & Awards:* Kirk Bryan Award, Geol Soc Am, 64, Penrose Medal, 78, G K Gilbert Award, 96, Distinguished Career Award, 96; Nat Medal Sci, 89; Chas P Daly Medal, Am Geog Soc, 91. *Prof Exp:* Instr geol, Univ Ill, 38-43; prof, Univ Minn, 45-47. *Mem:* Nat Acad Sci; fel Geol Soc Am; Am Geophys Union; Glaciol Soc; fel Am Acad Arts & Sci. *Res:* Glaciology; glacial geology; arid region geomorphology; planetary surfaces. *Mailing Add:* Div Geol & Planetary Sci Calif Inst Technol Pasadena CA 91125. *Fax:* 626-795-1547; *E-Mail:* aleen@gps.caltech.edu

SHARP, ROBERT RICHARD, PHYSICAL CHEMISTRY. *Current Pos:* from asst prof to assoc prof, 69-86, PROF CHEM, UNIV MICH, ANN ARBOR, 86- *Personal Data:* b Newport News, Va, May 15, 41; m 68; c 1. *Educ:* Case Western Res Univ, AB & MS, 65, PhD(chem), 68. *Prof Exp:* NSF fel, Oxford Univ, 67-69. *Mem:* Am Chem Soc; AAAS; Sigma Xi; Am Phys Soc; Int Soc Magnetic Resonance. *Res:* Nuclear magnetic resonance of chemical and biological systems. *Mailing Add:* Dept Chem Univ Mich Ann Arbor MI 48104. *E-Mail:* robert.sharp@um.cc.umich.edu

SHARP, THOMAS JOSEPH, ALGEBRA. *Current Pos:* ASST PROF MATH, W GA COL, 69- *Personal Data:* b Hattiesburg, Miss, Oct 15, 44; m 70; c 2. *Educ:* Univ Southern Miss, BS, 65; Auburn Univ, MS, 66, PhD(math), 71. *Mem:* Am Math Soc; Math Asn Am. *Res:* Characterization of projection-invariant subgroups of abelian groups and their relationship to fully-invariant subgroups; study of big subgroups and little homomorphisms. *Mailing Add:* Dept Math WGa Col Maple St Carrollton GA 30018

SHARP, WILLIAM BROOM ALEXANDER, CORROSION, MATERIALS SCIENCE. *Current Pos:* res engr, Westvaco Res Ctr, 78, sr res engr, 79-82, group leader corrosion & mat, 83-92, GROUP MGR, WESTVACO RES CTR, 93- *Personal Data:* b Glengarnock, Scotland, May 12, 42; m 67; c 3. *Educ:* Univ Cambridge, BA, 64, MA, 68; Univ London, MSc, 68; Univ Ottawa, PhD(chem), 76. *Honors & Awards:* Weldon Medal, Can Pulp & Paper Asn, 78; Eng Div Award & E H Neese Award, Tech Asn Pulp & Paper Indust, 85. *Prof Exp:* Res officer high temperature oxidation res, Cent Elec Res Lab, Eng, 64-69; assoc scientist corrosion res, Pulp & Paper Res Inst, Can, 75-78. *Concurrent Pos:* Chmn, 3rd Int Symp Corrosion in Pulp & Paper Indust, 80; ed, Corrosion Notebook column, Tech Asn Pulp & Paper Indust J, 80-; chmn, Tech Adv Coun, Mat Technol Inst, 87-88; chmn, Tech Adv Comt, NSF Eng Res Ctr, Mont State Univ, 90-; chmn, Eng Div, Tech Asn Pulp-Paper Indust, 92-94, mem, bd dir, 97-; vchmn db dir, Mat Technol Indust, 95- *Mem:* Brit Inst Corrosion Sci & Technol; Brit Inst Metall; Electrochem Soc; Nat Asn Corrosion; fel Tech Asn Pulp & Paper Indust. *Res:* Mechanisms of corrosion in pulp and paper mill equipment. *Mailing Add:* 8524 Moon Glass Ct Columbia MD 21045

SHARP, WILLIAM EDWARD, III, EXPERIMENTAL SPACE PHYSICS, SPECTROSCOPY. *Current Pos:* MGR, ITT AEROSPACE, 97- *Personal Data:* b Del Norte, Colo, Feb 6, 40. *Educ:* William Jewell Col, BA, 62; Univ NH, MS, 65; Univ Colo, PhD(astro-geophys), 70. *Prof Exp:* Instr physics, Stetson Univ, 64-66; res scientist, Univ Mich, 70-97. *Concurrent Pos:* Lectr, Univ Mich, 72-; prin investr, NASA, 74-; assoc ed, J Geophys Res, 81-83; prog dir, NSF, 85-86, asst dir, Space Physics Res Lab, 86-90; vis prof physics, Univ Mich, Dearborn, 90- *Mem:* Am Geophys Union. *Res:* Chemical and physical processes occurring in the aurora and in atmospheric regions above 80 km. *Mailing Add:* ITT Aerospace 1919 W Cook Rd Ft Wayne IN 46801

SHARP, WILLIAM R, CELL BIOLOGY, MICROBIOLOGY. *Current Pos:* DEAN RES, COOK COL, DIR RES, NJAES, RUTGERS UNIV, 93- *Personal Data:* b Akron, Ohio, Sept 13, 36. *Educ:* Univ Akron, BS, 63, MS, 64; Rutgers Univ, PhD(bot), 67. *Prof Exp:* NSF fel & NIH grant, Case Western Res Univ, 67-69; from asst to prof microbiol, Ohio State Univ, 69-78; dir, Pioneer Res, Campbell Soup Co, 78-81; exec vpres & res dir, DNA, Plant Technol Corp, 81-88; exec vpres, DNA Pharmaceut, Inc, 89-90; exec vpres, Phytopharmacol, Inc, 91-93. *Concurrent Pos:* Fulbright Hays fel, Ctr Nuclear Energy in Agr, Univ Sao Paulo, 71, 73, & 74; vis prof, Orgn Am States, 72; foreign corresp, Sao Paulo Acad Sci, 86- *Mem:* AAAS. *Res:* Cellular aspects of plant genetics and breedings; propagation and genetic engineering; phytopharmaceuticals. *Mailing Add:* Martin Hall Rm 104 Rutgers Cook Col Lypman Dr PO Box 231 New Brunswick NY 08903

SHARPE, CHARLES BRUCE, ELECTRICAL ENGINEERING. *Current Pos:* res assoc, Willow Run Res Ctr, 49-50, res assoc electronics defense group, 51-53 & 55-60, from asst prof to assoc prof, 55-60, PROF ELEC ENG, UNIV MICH, ANN ARBOR, 61- *Personal Data:* b Windsor, Ont, Apr 8, 26; nat US; m 54; c 5. *Educ:* Univ Mich, BS, 47, PhD(elec eng), 53; Mass Inst Technol, SM, 49. *Prof Exp:* Asst, High Voltage Lab, Mass Inst Technol, 47-49. *Mem:* Sr mem Inst Elec & Electronics Engrs. *Res:* Network synthesis; microwave circuit theory; theory and application of ferrites; microwave properties of ferroelectrics; synthesis of nonuniform transmission lines; electromagnetic sounding problems in geophysics. *Mailing Add:* Elec Eng & Comput Sci Bldg Univ Mich Ann Arbor MI 48109

SHARPE, DAVID McCURRY, PHYSICAL GEOGRAPHY, LANDSCAPE ECOLOGY. *Current Pos:* chmn, 76-82, FAC GEOG, SOUTHERN ILL UNIV, CARBONDALE, 66-, CHMN, 86- *Personal Data:* b Orange, NJ, Jan 2, 38; m 61, Anne Shepard; c 2. *Educ:* Syracuse Univ, BS, 60, MS, 63; Southern Ill Univ, Carbondale, PhD(geog), 68. *Prof Exp:* Jr forester, Forest Serv, USDA, Mt Hood Nat Forest, 60-61. *Concurrent Pos:* NSF grant, Div Environ Biol, Oak Ridge Nat Lab, 72-74; fac appointee, Environ Assessment Div, Argonne Nat Lab, 94- *Mem:* Asn Am Geog; AAAS; Ecol Soc Am; Sigma Xi; Int Asn Landscape Ecol. *Res:* Ecology and biogeography of regional forest ecosystems including impact of forest resource use and land use change; interaction between relict forest stands separated by nonforest land use; software development for environmental sciences. *Mailing Add:* Dept Geog Southern Ill Univ Carbondale IL 62901

SHARPE, GRANT WILLIAM, FORESTRY. *Current Pos:* prof, 67-90, EMER PROF WILDLAND RECREATION, COL FOREST RESOURCES, UNIV WASH, 90- *Personal Data:* b Kentfield, Calif, May 15, 25; m 48, Wenonah Finch; c Christopher, Kathryn, Charles, Loretta, Paul, Patricia, Frederick, Rosemary & Lena. *Educ:* Univ Wash, BS & MF, 51, PhD, 56. *Prof Exp:* From asst prof to assoc prof forestry, Univ Mich, Ann Arbor, 56-67. *Concurrent Pos:* Soc Am Foresters vis scientist lectr, NSF; Pac Crest Trail Adv Coun, USDA, 78-81. *Mem:* Fel Asn Interpretive Naturalists; Soc Am Foresters; fel Nat Asn Interpretation; Sigma Xi. *Res:* Recreational use of wild lands; park management; author of several books. *Mailing Add:* 241 Mats View Rd Port Ludlow WA 98365

SHARPE, LAWRENCE, PSYCHIATRY. *Current Pos:* MEM STAFF, DEPT NEUROPHARMACOL NIDA ADDICTION RES CTR, 77- *Personal Data:* b London, Eng, Dec 25, 30. *Educ:* Univ London, MB & BS, 54, dipl psychol med, 61. *Prof Exp:* House surgeon & physician, Highlands Hosp, London, Eng, 54-55; registr, Cell Barnes Hosp, St Alban's, 57; sr house officer & registr, Maudsley Hosp, London, 58-61; fel pediat & psychiat, Johns Hopkins Hosp, 62-63, instr pediat & psychiat, Johns Hopkins Univ, 63-65; asst prof psychiat, State Univ NY Downstate Med Ctr, 66-67; asst prof psychiat, Col Physicians & Surgeons, Columbia Univ, 67-76. *Concurrent Pos:* Consult, Md Children's Ctr, Boys Village Md, Barrett Sch for Girls & McKim's Boys Haven, 63-65; psychiatrist, Res Found Ment Hyg, Inc, 67-; res psychiatrist biomet res, NY State Dept Ment Hyg, Inc, 67- *Mem:* Royal Col Psychiat; Royal Soc Med. *Mailing Add:* Columbia Univ Col Phys Surg Dept Psych 722 W 168th St New York NY 10032

SHARPE, LOUIS HAUGHTON, ADHESION, ADHESIVES ENGINEERING. *Current Pos:* CONSULT, 86- *Personal Data:* b Port Maria, Jamaica, WI, Jan 31, 27; m 68, Diane E Schoenig. *Educ:* Va Polytech Inst, BS, 50; Mich State Univ, PhD(phys chem), 57. *Honors & Awards:* Adhesives Award, Am Soc Testing & Mat, 68, Award of Merit, 82; William C Wake Mem lectr, Inst Mat, Gt Brit, 90; Award For Excellence In Adhesion Sci, Adhesion Soc, 93. *Prof Exp:* Engr, State Hwy Dept, Mich, 54-55; mem tech staff, Bell Labs, 55-59, supvr, adhesives & surface chem, 59-65, surface chem appl res, 65-68, adhesives eng & develop, 68-85. *Concurrent Pos:* Ed, J Adhesion, 69-; Robert L Patrick fel, Adhesion Soc, 91. *Mem:* Am Chem Soc; fel Am Inst Chem; fel Am Soc Testing & Mat; fel NY Acad Sci; Adhesion Soc (pres, 86-88). *Res:* Surface chemistry; adhesion; adhesives; mechanical properties of polymers. *Mailing Add:* 28 Red Maple Rd Sea Pines Plantation Hilton Head Island SC 29928. *Fax:* 803-671-4810

SHARPE, MICHAEL JOHN, MATHEMATICS. *Current Pos:* Asst prof, 67-73, assoc prof, 73-77, PROF MATH, UNIV CALIF, SAN DIEGO, 77- *Personal Data:* b Sydney, Australia, Mar 15, 41; m 66; c 1. *Educ:* Univ Tasmania, BSc, 63; Yale Univ, MA, 65, PhD(math), 67. *Concurrent Pos:* Vis prof, Univ Paris, 73-74. *Mem:* Inst Math Statist; Am Math Soc. *Res:* Probability theory; Markov processes; continuous parameter martingales; potential theory. *Mailing Add:* Dept Math Univ Calif San Diego 9500 Gilman Dr La Jolla CA 92093-0112

SHARPE, ROGER STANLEY, ECOLOGY. *Current Pos:* Asst prof, 68-72, ASSOC PROF BIOL, UNIV NEBR, OMAHA, 72-, COORDR, ENVIRON STUDIES, 91- *Personal Data:* b Omaha, Nebr, Mar 31, 41; m 62, Beverly Diimig; c 3. *Educ:* Munic Univ Omaha, BA, 63; Univ Nebr, MS, 65, PhD(zool), 68. *Concurrent Pos:* Environ consult, numerous projs; vis prof, Charles Univ, Prague, Czech, 88, 90. *Mem:* Am Ornith Union; Cooper Ornith Soc; Wilson Ornith Soc. *Res:* Conservation biology; zoogeography of Great Plains avifauna; avian ecology and behavior. *Mailing Add:* Univ Nebr Omaha 6000 Dodge St Omaha NE 68182-0001. *E-Mail:* sharpe@cwis.unomaha.edu

SHARPE, ROLAND LEONARD, DYNAMIC ANALYSIS OF STRUCTURES, EARTHQUAKE ENGINEERING. *Current Pos:* PRES, ROLAND L SHARPE CONSULT STRUCT ENGR, 73-74 & 87- *Personal Data:* b Shakopee, Minn, Dec 18, 23; m 46, Jane Steele; c Douglas R, Deborah

L & Sheryl A. *Educ:* Univ Mich, BSE, 47, MSE, 49. *Honors & Awards:* Earnest Howard Award, Am Soc Civil Engrs, 94. *Prof Exp:* Designer struct eng, Cummins & Barnard, Engrs, 47-48; asst prof struct eng, Univ Mich, 48-50; exec vpres & gen mgr, John A Blume & Assocs, Engrs, 50-73; chmn & chief exec officer, Eng Decision Anal Co, 74-87. *Concurrent Pos:* Mem planning comn, City of Palo Alto, Calif, 55-60; mem bd dirs, Earthquake Eng Res Inst, 71-74; exec dir & managing dir, Appl Technol Coun, 73-82; prin investr, Guidelines for Seismic Design of Buildings, 73-78; chmn & chief exec officer, Calif Eng & Develop Co, 74-84; managing dir, Eng Decision Anal Co, GmbH, 74-82; chmn, Struct Div Exec Comt, Am Soc Civil Engrs, 83, Mgt Group B, 89-93; chmn, US Joint Comt Earthquake Eng, 83-89; mem, Nat Earthquake Hazard Reduction Prog Adv Comt, Fed Emergency Mgt Agency & US Geol Surv, 91-93; mem, Hwy Seismic Res Coun, Nat Ctr Earthquake Eng Res, Buffalo, NY; pres, Struct Engrs World Cong, 95- *Mem:* Am Concrete Inst; hon mem Am Soc Civil Engrs; Earthquake Eng Res Inst; hon mem Japan Struct Consult Asn. *Res:* Development of building code requirements for seismic design of buildings; research on performance of structures subjected to earthquake ground motions; development of world wide organization for structural engineers. *Mailing Add:* 10320 Rolly Rd Los Altos CA 94024-6520. *Fax:* 650-948-9095

SHARPE, THOMAS R, HEALTH CARE ADMINISTRATION, STATISTICS. *Current Pos:* grad res asst health care, Admin Dept, Univ Miss, 71-74, res asst prof, 74-80, res inst pharmaceut scientist & asst dir admin sci res, 80-86, ASSOC DIR RES SERVS, UNIV MISS, 86- *Personal Data:* b Milwaukee, Wis, Nov 25, 44; m 68. *Educ:* Univ Ill, BS, 70; Univ Miss, MS, 73, PhD(health care admin), 75. *Prof Exp:* Staff pharmacist, Northwestern Univ Hosp, 70-71. *Concurrent Pos:* Charles R Walgreen Mem fel, Am Found Pharmaceut Educ, 72-74; consult, Nat Ctr Health Serv Res, 75-, Miss State Bd Health, 76- & Drug Info Designs Inc, 78- *Mem:* Am Pharmaceut Asn; Am Pub Health Asn; Am Soc Hosp Pharmacists; Am Sociol Asn; Am Heart Asn. *Res:* Drug post marketing surveillance; patient compliance; sociology of occupations and professions; epidemiology of hypertension; computer applications to pharmacy; social indicators; rural health, optimum delivery of comprehensive health care. *Mailing Add:* Natural Prods Ctr Rm 1006 Sch Pharm Univ Miss University MS 38677

SHARPE, WILLIAM D, PATHOLOGY, HISTORY OF MEDICINE. *Current Pos:* asst prof, 63-68, CLIN ASSOC PROF PATH, COL MED & DENT NJ, 68- *Personal Data:* b Canton, Ohio, July 18, 27. *Educ:* Univ Toronto, BA, 50; Univ Buffalo, MA, 55; Johns Hopkins Univ, MD, 58. *Prof Exp:* Intern med, Jersey City Med Ctr, 58-59; resident path, Pa Hosp, 59-63. *Concurrent Pos:* Fel path, Pa Hosp, Philadelphia, 59-63; asst instr, Sch Med, Univ Pa, 60-63; dir labs, Cabrini Med Ctr, NY. *Mem:* Int Acad Path; Mediaeval Acad Am; Am Philol Asn; Am Asn Pathologists & Bacteriologists; Col Am Pathologists. *Res:* Chronic radiation intoxication in human beings; ancient, medieval and colonial American medical history. *Mailing Add:* Cabrini Med Ctr 227 E 19th St New York NY 10003-2600

SHARPE, WILLIAM FORSYTH, ECONOMICS. *Current Pos:* prof, 93-95, STANCO 25 PROF FIN, STANFORD UNIV, 95- *Personal Data:* b Cambridge, Mass, June 16, 34; m 54, 86, Kathryn D Peck; c Deborah A & Jonathan F. *Educ:* Univ Calif, Los Angeles, AB, 55, MA, 56, PhD, 61. *Hon Degrees:* DHL, DePaul Univ, 97. *Honors & Awards:* Nobel Prize in Econ Sci, 90; Nicholas Molodovsky Award, 89. *Prof Exp:* Economist, Rand Corp, 57-61; from asst prof to prof econ, Univ Wash, 61-68; prof, Univ Calif, Irvine, 68-70; from Timken prof to emer Timken prof fin, Stanford Univ, 70-92; prin, William F Sharpe Assoc, 86-92. *Concurrent Pos:* Graham & Dodd Award, Financial Analysts Fedn, 72, 73 & 86-88. *Mem:* Am Financial Asn (vpres, 79, pres, 80). *Res:* Author of several books. *Mailing Add:* 25 Doud Dr Los Altos CA 94022-2323

SHARPE, WILLIAM NORMAN, JR, MECHANICAL ENGINEERING. *Current Pos:* DECKER PROF, DEPT MECH ENG, JOHNS HOPKINS UNIV, 83- *Personal Data:* b Pittsboro, NC, Apr 15, 38; m 59; c 2. *Educ:* NC State Univ, BS, 60, MS, 61; Johns Hopkins Univ, PhD(mech), 66. *Prof Exp:* Instr mech, Johns Hopkins Univ, 65-66; asst prof mech, Mich State Univ, 66-70, assoc prof, 70-75, prof, 75-78; prof mech eng & chmn dept, La State Univ, 78-82. *Mem:* Am Soc Mech Engrs; Am Soc Eng Educ; Soc Exp Stress Anal; Am Soc Testing & Mat; Sigma Xi; fel Am Soc Mech Engrs. *Res:* Experimental mechanics, especially strain measurement by laser interferometry; fatigue; fracture. *Mailing Add:* 220 Ridgewood Rd Baltimore MD 21210

SHARPLES, FRANCES ELLEN, ECOLOGY, MAMMALOGY. *Personal Data:* b Brooklyn, NY, Feb 5, 50. *Educ:* Barnard Col, AB, 72; Univ Calif, Davis, MA, 74, PhD(zool), 78. *Prof Exp:* Teaching asst zool & ecol, Univ Calif, Davis, 72-78; res assoc environ impact assessment, Oak Ridge Nat Lab, 78-82, mgr instnl planning, 82-84, cong fel, 84-85, res staff mem, 85-92, head, Environ Anal Sect, 92-96. *Concurrent Pos:* Mem, Comt Sci, Eng & Pub Policy, AAAS, 80-86; mem, Recombinant DNA Adv Comt, NIH, 84-87. *Mem:* Fel AAAS; Ecol Soc Am; Am Inst Biol Sci; Sigma Xi; Nat Asn Environ Profs. *Res:* Environmental law and policy, science policy, management of scientific research staff and research and development activities. *Mailing Add:* Oak Ridge Nat Lab Bldg 1505 Mail Stop 6036 Oak Ridge TN 37831-6036

SHARPLES, GEORGE CARROLL, CITRUS & GRAPE NUTRITION & CULTURE, LETTUCE SEED PHYSIOLOGY. *Current Pos:* Asst horticulturist, Agr Exp Sta, Univ Ariz, 48-58, res assoc hort, 58-62, from asst horticulturist to assoc horticulturist, 62-72, horticulturist, 72-83, EMER PROF, UNIV ARIZ, 83- *Personal Data:* b Toledo, Ohio, Dec 17, 18; m 44, Patricia Durant; c John & Mark. *Educ:* Univ Ariz, BS, 41, MS, 48. *Mem:* Am Soc Hort Sci; AAAS. *Res:* Grape nutrition and culture; citrus nutrition; lettuce seed physiology and precision planting. *Mailing Add:* 1353 Lemon Tempe AZ 85281

SHARPLESS, GEORGE ROBERT, biology, for more information see previous edition

SHARPLESS, K BARRY, HOMOGENEOUS CATALYSIS, ASYMMETRIC TRANSFORMATIONS. *Current Pos:* PROF CHEM, SCRIPPS RES INST, 90- *Personal Data:* b Philadelphia, Pa, Apr 28, 41; m; c 3. *Educ:* Dartmouth Col, BA, 63; Stanford Univ, PhD(chem), 68. *Honors & Awards:* Creative Work Org Synthesis Award, Am Chem Soc, 83, Arthur C Cope Award, 92, Harrison Howe Award & Remsen Award; Paul Janssen Prize, Creative Org Synthesis, Belg, 86; Prelog Medal, Eidgenossiche Technische Hochschule, Zurich; Rolf Sammet Prize, Johann Wolfgang Geothe Universitat, Frankfurt-am-Main; Chem Pioneer Award, Am Inst Chemists; Scheele Medal & Prize, Swed Acad Pharmaceut Sci, 91; Tetrahedron Prize Creativity in Org Chem, 93; King Faisal Int Prize Sci, 95. *Prof Exp:* NIH fel chem, Stanford Univ, 68-69 & Harvard Univ, 69-70; from asst prof to prof, Mass Inst Technol, 70-91. *Concurrent Pos:* Prof, Stanford Univ, 77-80. *Mem:* Nat Acad Sci; fel Am Acad Arts & Sci; fel AAAS. *Res:* Developing new homogeneous catalysts for the oxidation of organic compounds, using inorganic reagents to effect new transformations in organic chemistry, and asymmetric catalysis involving both early and late transition metal-mediated processes. *Mailing Add:* Scripps Res Inst CVN-2 10666 N Torrey Pines Rd La Jolla CA 92037

SHARPLESS, SETH KINMAN, PHARMACOLOGY, PHYSIOLOGICAL PSYCHOLOGY. *Current Pos:* PROF PSYCHOL, UNIV COLO, BOULDER, 69- *Personal Data:* b Anchorage, Alaska, May 21, 25; m 47; c 2. *Educ:* Univ Chicago, MA, 51; McGill Univ, PhD(psychol), 54. *Prof Exp:* Res assoc psychol, McGill Univ, 54-55; asst prof, Yale Univ, 55-57; asst prof pharmacol & sr res fel, Albert Einstein Col Med, 57-64, assoc prof pharmacol, 64-69. *Concurrent Pos:* NIH career develop fel, 61-69; mem rev comt psychol serv fel, NIMH, 71-, mem exp psychol study sect, NIH, 71- *Mem:* Am Psychol Asn; Philos Sci Asn; Asn Symbolic Logic; Am Physiol Soc; Am Soc Pharmacol & Exp Therapeut. *Res:* Neuropharmacology; physiological basis of behavior; drugs on central nervous system. *Mailing Add:* 637 17th St Boulder CO 80302

SHARPLESS, STEWART LANE, ASTRONOMY. *Current Pos:* PROF ASTRON & DIR C E KENNETH MEES OBSERV, UNIV ROCHESTER, 64- *Personal Data:* b Milwaukee, Wis, Mar 29, 26. *Educ:* Univ Chicago, PhB, 48, PhD(astron), 52. *Prof Exp:* Carnegie fel, Mt Wilson & Palomar Observs, 52-53; astronomer, US Naval Observ, 53-64, dir, Astron & Astrophys Div, 63-64. *Concurrent Pos:* Dir-at-large, AURA, Inc, 66-69. *Mem:* AAAS; Am Astron Soc; Int Astron Union. *Res:* Galactic structure; spectroscopy. *Mailing Add:* 3431 Winton Rd S Rochester NY 14623

SHARPLESS, THOMAS KITE, CYTOLOGY, BIOMEDICAL ENGINEERING. *Current Pos:* systs engr, 72-82, MED IMAGING SYSTS ENGR, MEM HOSP CANCER & ALLIED DIS & ASSOC, SLOAN KETTERING INST, 82- *Personal Data:* b Boston, Mass, May 23, 39; c 1. *Educ:* Haverford Col, AB, 62; Princeton Univ, PhD(biochem), 69. *Prof Exp:* Res assoc membrane biochem, Pub Health Res Inst City New York, Inc, 69-70; programmer, Hudson Comput Corp, 70-71; consult, 72-73. *Concurrent Pos:* Res fel, USPHS, 69-70. *Mem:* Asn Comput Mach. *Res:* Automated, high-speed measurement and classification of single cells and cell populations by flow or pulse microphotometry; applications in cell immunology, cytogenetics and diagnostic cytopathology. *Mailing Add:* 6017 Greene St Philadelphia PA 19144

SHARPLEY, ROBERT CALDWELL, APPLIED MATHEMATICS. *Current Pos:* from asst prof to assoc prof, 76-82, PROF MATH, UNIV SC, 83- *Personal Data:* b Chicago, Ill, Jan 31, 46; m 66; c 2. *Educ:* Univ Tex, BA, 68, MA, 69, PhD(math), 72. *Prof Exp:* Vis asst prof math, La State Univ, 72; asst prof, Oakland Univ, 72-76. *Concurrent Pos:* Proj dir & fac fel, Oakland Univ, 73-74 & NSF res grant, 77-88; vis assoc prof math, McMaster Univ, 78-79; vis prof math, Univ Wyo, 86-87; proj dir, Partnership Comput Sci, 91-, Dept Energy & NSF res grants. *Mem:* Am Math Soc; Sigma Xi; Math Asn Am; Soc Indust & Appl Math. *Res:* Fourier analysis; functional analysis; partial differential equations, Sobolev and Besov spaces; numerical analysis; groundwater modeling; geophysical applications; computational science. *Mailing Add:* Dept Math Univ SC Columbia SC 29208. *Fax:* 803-777-3783; *E-Mail:* sharpley@math.scarolina.edu

SHARRAH, PAUL CHESTER, physics; deceased, see previous edition for last biography

SHARRETT, A RICHEY, PUBLIC HEALTH & EPIDEMIOLOGY. *Current Pos:* Med officer, 72-86, CHIEF SOC & ENVIRON EPIDEMIOL RES, EPIDEMIOL & BIOMETRY PROG, NIH, 86- *Personal Data:* b Worcester, Mass, July 15, 37. *Educ:* Oberlin Col, BA, 59; Univ Melbourne, Australia, MA, 61; Univ Pittsburgh, MD, 66; Johns Hopkins Sch Hyg & Pub Health, Dr PH(epidemiol), 79. *Res:* Relationship of biochemical, physiological, life style and other environmental risk factors to atherosclerosis and the incidence of major cardiovascular disease. *Mailing Add:* NHLBI-EB MS 7934 6701 Rockledge Dr Bethesda MD 20892

SHARROW, SUSAN O'HOTT, FLOW CYTOMETRY, T-CELL ONTOLOGY & DIFFERENTIATION. *Current Pos:* CHEMIST, NAT CANCER INST, NIH, 71- *Educ:* Mich State Univ, BS, 71. *Res:* Expression of Class I antigens. *Mailing Add:* Rm 4B-17 EIB Nat Cancer Inst NIH Bldg 10 Bethesda MD 20892-0001

SHARTS, CLAY MARCUS, FLUORINE CHEMISTRY, ORGANIC CHEMISTRY. *Current Pos:* assoc prof, 62-71, PROF CHEM, SAN DIEGO STATE UNIV, 71- *Personal Data:* b Long Beach, Calif, Feb 9, 31; m 52; c Chris, Melora, Kim & Vanessa. *Educ:* Univ Calif, BS, 52; Calif Inst Technol, PhD(chem), 59. *Prof Exp:* Asst, Calif Inst Technol, 55-58; res chemist, Explosives Dept, E I du Pont de Nemours & Co, 58-62. *Concurrent Pos:* NSF sci fac fel, Univ Cologne, 71-72; consult, Technicon Instruments Corp, 73-83, UNESCO, 80 & Alliance Pharmaceut Corp, 90-91. *Mem:* AAAS; Am Chem Soc. *Res:* Small-ring and organic fluorine compounds; spiropolymers; perfluorocarbons as oxygen carriers in artificial blood; perfluoroalkyl substituted steroids and sugars as surfactants for perfluorocarbons; bromoperfluoroalkanes as imagents; methamphetamine synthesis for forensic purposes. *Mailing Add:* Dept Chem San Diego Univ San Diego CA 92182-1030. *E-Mail:* csharts@sciences.sdsu.edu

SHASHA, DENNIS E, DATABASE SYSTEMS, KNOWLEDGE EXPLORATION. *Current Pos:* ASSOC PROF COMPUT SCI, COURANT INST, NEW YORK UNIV, 84- *Personal Data:* US citizen; m 83, Karen Shashoua; c Cloe & Tyler. *Educ:* Yale Univ, BS, 77; Syracuse Univ, MS, 80; Harvard Univ, PhD(appl math), 84. *Prof Exp:* Engr, Int Bus Mach Co, 77-80. *Concurrent Pos:* Expert witness; consult, AT&T, Lucent Bellcore, Union Bank Switz; IBM fel. *Mem:* Asn Comput Mach; Inst Elec & Electronics Engrs. *Res:* Systems and theory for knowledge exploration; parallel algorithms for database systems; algorithms for tree-matching; puzzles; authored four books. *Mailing Add:* 251 Mercer St New York NY 10012. *E-Mail:* shasha@cs.nyu.edu

SHASHIDHARA, NAGALAPUR SASTRY, APPLIED FLUID MECHANICS, HYDROTHERMAL ENGINEERING. *Current Pos:* SUPVR HYDROTHERMAL ENG, EBASCO SERV, INC, 71- *Personal Data:* b Mysore, India, Aug 13, 40; m 71; c 1. *Educ:* Mysore Univ, BS, 61; Indian Inst Sci, MS, 64; Rutgers Univ, MS & PhD(fluid mech), 71. *Prof Exp:* Asst engr fluid mech, Simpson & Group Co, Bangalore, India, 61-62; sr sci officer hydrodynamics, Indian Inst Sci, 62-66; res asst fluid mech, Rutgers Univ & Princeton Univ, 66-71. *Concurrent Pos:* Res scientist rheology, E I du Pont de Nemours & Co, Inc, 67; consult fluid mech & other hydrothermal probs to many US & foreign elec utilities. *Mem:* Int Asn Hydraul Res; Am Geophys Union; Sigma Xi; Asn Sci Workers India (secy, 62-66). *Res:* Dispersion in air and water of thermal, radioactive and chemical effluents from industrial facilities and their effects on the environment. *Mailing Add:* 25 Suffolk Lane Princeton Junction NJ 08550

SHASHOUA, VICTOR E, BIOCHEMISTRY. *Current Pos:* asst prof, 70-75, ASSOC PROF BIOL CHEM, HARVARD MED SCH, 75-, ASSOC BIOCHEMIST, MCLEAN HOSP, 70-, CHIEF SCI OFFICER, NEUROMED DEPT, 92- *Personal Data:* b Kermanshah, Iran, Nov 15, 29; nat US; m 55; c 3. *Educ:* Univ London, BSc, 51; Loughborough Col Tech, Eng, dipl, 51; Univ Del, PhD(org chem), 56. *Prof Exp:* Res chemist, E I du Pont de Nemours & Co, Inc, 51-64, res assoc, 64-68; mem neurosci res prog, Mass Inst Technol, 64-68, res assoc biol, 68-70. *Mem:* Am Chem Soc; Am Neurochem Soc; Int Soc Neurochem; Soc Neurosci; Am Soc Cell Biol. *Res:* Neurochemistry; behavior and biochemistry. *Mailing Add:* 176 Tappan St Brookline MA 02146

SHASTRY, B SRIRAM, HIGH TEMPERATURE SUPERCONDUCTIVITY. *Current Pos:* mem tech staff, AT&T Bell Labs, 88-95, DEPT HEAD, LUCENT TECHNOL, 95- *Personal Data:* b Akola, India, Nov 26, 50; m 75; c 2. *Educ:* Tata Inst Fundamental Res, Bombay, PhD(physics), 76. *Prof Exp:* Lectr physics, Univ Hyderabad, India, 77-79; Royal Soc bursar, Imp Col, London, 79-80; instr, Univ Utah, Salt Lake City, 80-82; fel & reader, Tata Inst, Bombay, 82-89. *Concurrent Pos:* Vis lectr physics, Princeton Univ, 87-88. *Mem:* Am Phys Soc; fel Indian Acad Sci. *Res:* Quantum spin systems; strongly correlated forms systems; high temperature superconductivity; magnetism. *Mailing Add:* Lucent Technol 943 Holmdel Rd Cruz Plaza Holmdel NJ 07733-2103

SHASTRY, BARKUR SRINIVASA, MOLECULAR BIOLOGY, GENETICS. *Current Pos:* ASSOC PROF, OAKLAND UNIV, 86- *Personal Data:* m 74, Premalatha Upadhyaya; c Savitha & Rohith. *Educ:* Univ Mysore, India, PhD(biochem), 74. *Prof Exp:* Fel, Univ Ill, 74-78; sr fel, Wash University, St Louis, 78-82; sr res assoc, Rockefeller Univ, 82-85. *Concurrent Pos:* Prin investr, NIH, 88-91. *Mem:* Am Asn Cancer Res; Am Soc Biochem & Molecular Biol; Am Soc Cell Biol; Int Soc Eye Res; Genetic Soc Am; AAAS. *Res:* Molecular analysis of human genetic eye diseases and molecular basis of tissue specific gene regulation; biology of mutant alleles in the molecular pathogenesis of human eye disorders. *Mailing Add:* Eye Res Inst Oakland Univ 407 Dodge Hall Rochester MI 48309-4401

SHATKIN, AARON JEFFREY, BIOCHEMISTRY, VIROLOGY. *Current Pos:* PROF & DIR, CTR ADVAN BIOTECHNOL & MED, RUTGERS UNIV, 86-, PROF MOLECULAR BIOL & MOLECULAR GENETICS, UNIV MED & DENT NJ, 86- *Personal Data:* b Providence, RI, July 18, 34; m 57, Joan A Lynch; c Gregory M. *Educ:* Bowdoin Col, AB, 56; Rockefeller Univ, PhD(microbiol), 61. *Hon Degrees:* DSc, Bowdoin Col, 79. *Honors & Awards:* US Steel Found Award Molecular Biol, 79; T A Edison Award, 91. *Prof Exp:* Sr asst scientist virol, Cell Biol Sect, NIH, 61-63, res biochemist, 63-68; assoc mem, Roche Inst Molecular Biol, 68-71, mem, 71-77, head, Lab Molecular Virol, 77-83, head, Dept Cell Biol, 77-86. *Concurrent Pos:* Vis prof, Georgetown Univ, 68; guest investr, Salk Inst, Calif, 68-69; mem molecular biol study sect, NSF, 71-74; instr, Cold Spring Harbor Lab, 72-74; ed, J Virol, 73-77, ed-in-chief, Molecular Cell Biol, 80-90, Advan Virus Res, 84-; Inst Comt to Rev Virus Cancer Prog, Nat Cancer Inst, 73, Comt Int Asilomar Conf Recombinant DNA, 74, chair adv comt nucleic acid, Am Cancer Soc, 81-82, chair, Am Cancer Soc Coun, 93-94, adv comt, NY Univ & Am Inst Biologists, 79, McArdle Lab, 78-82, Einstein Med Col, 81, Jones Cell Sci Ctr, 82-, Brookhaven Nat Lab, 83-86, Dept Molecular Biol, Princeton Univ, 86-, Wadsworth Lab, 86, Bowdoin Col Sci, 86-88, Children Hosps Boston, 87, Univ Pa, 89, J Gamble Res Inst, 88-92; vis prof, Univ PR, 78-80, Rockefeller Univ, 78-87, Princeton Univ, 84-87; mem nucleic acid comt, Am Cancer Soc, 79-82, MacArthur Found, 88; mem, Sci Adv Bd, Merck Sharp & Dohme Res Labs, 90-94, Nat Res Adv Bd, Cleveland Clin Found, 88, 90-93, Sci Adv Bd, Worcester Found, 92-95, Spanish Res Coun, 92, Howard Hughes Med Inst, 95- *Mem:* Nat Acad Sci; AAAS; Am Soc Biol Chem; Am Soc Microbiol; fel NY Acad Sci; Harvey Soc; Am Soc Cell Biol; fel Am Acad Microbiol. *Res:* Structure and function of animal cells and viruses; biochemistry of virus replication; gene expression mechanisms. *Mailing Add:* 1381 Rahway Rd Scotch Plains NJ 07076

SHATTES, WALTER JOHN, EXPERIMENTAL PHYSICS. *Current Pos:* RETIRED. *Personal Data:* b Oceanside, NY, May 27, 24; m 60; c 2. *Educ:* Union Col, BS, 50; Rutgers Univ, PhD(physics), 56. *Prof Exp:* Res physicist, Tung-Sol Elec Co, 55-62; sr physicist, Airco, 62-89. *Mem:* Am Vacuum Soc; Am Phys Soc. *Res:* Vacuum technology; physical vapor deposition; superconductors; semiconductors; semiconductor devices and materials; thin films, cryogenics. *Mailing Add:* 70 Beverly Rd Bloomfield NJ 07003

SHATTUCK, THOMAS WAYNE, PHYSICAL CHEMISTRY. *Current Pos:* ASST PROF CHEM, COLBY COL, 76- *Personal Data:* b Denver, Colo, Aug 10, 50; m 78. *Educ:* Lake Forest Col, BA, 72; Univ Calif, Berkeley, PhD(chem), 76. *Concurrent Pos:* Vis asst prof, Univ Maine, Orono, 78. *Mem:* Am Chem Soc; Am Phys Soc; Sigma Xi. *Res:* Solid state nuclear magnetic resonance; nuclear quadrupole resonance of transition metal complexes; liquid crystal phase transitions. *Mailing Add:* Dept Chem Colby Col Waterville ME 04901

SHATZ, CARLA J, NEURAL NETWORKS. *Current Pos:* PROF NEUROBIOL, UNIV CALIF, BERKELEY, 92-, INVESTR, HOWARD HUGHES MED INST, 94- *Personal Data:* b New York, NY, Aug 2, 47. *Educ:* Radcliffe Col, BA, 69; Univ Col London, MPhil, 71; Harvard Univ PhD(neurobiol), 76. *Honors & Awards:* Grass lectr, Ann Meeting, Soc Neurosci, 91; Golgi Award Lectr, Fed Indust Design Inst Australia, 93; Silvo Conte Award, Nat Found Brain Res, 93; Victor Hamburger Award, Int Soc Develop Neurosci, 94. *Prof Exp:* Fel, Dept Neurosci, Harvard Med Sch, 76-78; from asst prof to prof neurobiol, Stanford Univ Sch Med, 78-91. *Concurrent Pos:* Mellon Found fel, 79-84; A P Sloan fel, 79-81; neurosci develop award, McKnight Found, 82-84; res career develop award, Nat Eye Inst, 84-89, merit award, 92-; coun mem, Soc Neurosci, 86-90; sect ed develop neurosci, J Neurosci, 89-93; Stanford Univ fel, 90-92; mem, Comn Life Sci, Nat Res Coun, 90-96; coun, Gordon Res Conf, 91-94. *Mem:* Nat Acad Sci; Europ Acad Scis & Arts; Soc Neurosci (pres-elect, 93, pres, 94); AAAS; Asn Res Vision & Opthal; Sigma Xi; fel Am Acad Arts & Sci. *Res:* Understanding how the adult pattern of precise and orderly connections in the mammalian central nervous system is achieved during development. *Mailing Add:* Div Neurobiol Univ Calif 221 Life Scis Addn Berkeley CA 94720-3200

SHATZ, STEPHEN S, MATHEMATICS. *Current Pos:* from asst prof to assoc prof, 64-69, PROF MATH, UNIV PA, 69- *Personal Data:* b New York, NY, Apr 27, 37; c 2. *Educ:* Harvard Univ, AB, 57, AM, 58, PhD(math), 62. *Prof Exp:* Instr math, Stanford Univ, 62-63, actg asst prof, 63-64. *Concurrent Pos:* Vis lectr, Haverford Col, 66; mem, Res Ctr, Physics & Math, Univ Pisa, 66-67; chmn, Dept Math, Univ Pa, 83-86; mem, MRSI, Berkeley, Calif, 86-87. *Mem:* Am Math Soc. *Res:* Algebraic geometry. *Mailing Add:* Dept Math Univ Pa Philadelphia PA 19104-6395

SHAUB, WALTER M, INFORMATION QUALITY ASSURANCE, CRITICAL ISSUES ANALYSIS. *Current Pos:* TECH DIR INFO TRANSFER, US CONF MAYORS/CORRE, 86- *Personal Data:* b Mt Vernon, NY, Sept 21, 47; m 69; c 2. *Educ:* State Univ NY, BS, 69; Cornell Univ, PhD(phys chem), 75. *Honors & Awards:* Medal, Am Inst Chemists, 69. *Prof Exp:* Post doctoral res assoc laser optics, US Naval Res Lab, 75-76, res chemist chem genetics, 76-81; asst prof chem, George Mason Univ, 76-78; res chemist chem kinetics, US Nat Bur Standards, 81-83, group leader res mgt, 83-86. *Concurrent Pos:* Tech dir, Coalition Resource Recovery & the Environ, 86-; consult, US Environ Protection Agency adv bd, 89, mem bd, 89-; spec ed, Elsevier, Sci of the Total Environ, 89-90. *Mem:* AAAS; NY Acad Sci; Am Chem Soc; Air & Waste Mgt Asn; assoc mem Am Soc Mech Engrs. *Res:* Mathematical theories catalytic formation of dioxins and furans involving fly ash; physical and chemical properties of fly ash; writer/editor technical issues concerned with waste management. *Mailing Add:* 2027 Winged Foot Ct Reston VA 22091-1337

SHAUDYS, EDGAR T, AGRICULTURAL ECONOMICS. *Current Pos:* RETIRED. *Personal Data:* b Washingtons Crossing, Pa, Nov 23, 28; m 52; c 4. *Educ:* Wilmington Col, BS, 50; Ohio State Univ, MS, 52, PhD(agr econ), 54. *Prof Exp:* Teaching asst biol, Wilmington Col, 47-50; res asst, Ohio State Univ, 50-54, prof agr econ, 54-86. *Mem:* Am Soc Farm Mgrs & Rural Appraisers; Am Agr Econ Asn. *Res:* Farm management production and organization; land tenure and farm real estate taxation; cost of production studies for crops and livestock. *Mailing Add:* 1184 Fairview Ave Columbus OH 43212

SHAUGHNESSY, THOMAS PATRICK, SEMICONDUCTOR PROCESSING, MICROLITHOGRAPHY. *Current Pos:* PROCESS ENG DEPT, RATHION, 85- *Personal Data:* b Dedham, Mass, July 12, 42; m 67; c 2. *Educ:* Boston Col, BS, 64, PhD(physics), 70. *Prof Exp:* Asst silicon photovoltaics, Boston Col, 72-75; group leader, Spire Corp, 75-79; mgr process eng, GCA Corp, Burlington, 79-85. *Mem:* Am Vacuum Soc; Electrochem Soc; Inst Elec & Electronics Engrs. *Res:* Silicon integrated process development; photolithography; electron beam lithography; photoresist chemistry; reactive ion etch; ion implantation; anneal techniques; diffusion; depostions; device modeling and testing. *Mailing Add:* 1619 E Silver Wood Phoenix AZ 85048

SHAULIS, NELSON JACOB, VITICULTURE. *Current Pos:* from asst prof to prof pomol, 44-67, prof, 67-78, EMER PROF VITICULT, EXP STA, NY STATE COL AGR & LIFE SCI, CORNELL UNIV, 78- *Personal Data:* b Somerset, Pa, Sept 10, 13; wid; c Catherine S (Santomartino) & Margaret S (Harty). *Educ:* Pa State Col, BS, 35, MS, 37; Cornell Univ, PhD(soils), 41. *Honors & Awards:* Outstanding Achievement Award, E Sect, Am Soc Enol & Viticult, 84, Hon Res Lectr, 85; Award of Merit, Am Wine Soc, 90; Award of Merit, Soc Wine Educators. *Prof Exp:* Asst soil technol, Pa State Col, 35-37, asst county agent, 37-38, instr pomol, 38-44; asst soil conservationist, Soil Conserv Serv, US Dept Agr, 38-44. *Concurrent Pos:* Fulbright res scholar, Australia, 67-68; consult viticult, 79- *Mem:* Fel Am Soc Hort Sci; Am Soc Agron; Soil Sci Soc Am; hon mem Am Soc Enol & Viticult; Crop Sci Soc Am. *Res:* Vineyard sites; grapevine physiology; vineyard mechanization and management including mineral nutrition, rootstocks and canopy microclimate; define attributes of site, canopy and crop affecting attainment of viticultural goals; define attributes of site, growth, canopy and crop affecting attainment of viticultural goals; then management by description of vineyard and vine, diagnosis of limiting factors, and prescription of best practices. *Mailing Add:* Dept Hort Sci NY State Agr Exp Sta Geneva NY 14456

SHAVER, ALAN GARNET, ORGANOMETALLIC CHEMISTRY, INORGANIC CHEMISTRY. *Current Pos:* from asst prof to assoc prof, 75-88, chair chem, 91-95, PROF CHEM, MCGILL UNIV, 89-, DEAN SCI 95- *Personal Data:* b Brockville, Ont, Dec 17, 46. *Educ:* Carleton Univ, BSc, 69; Mass Inst Technol, PhD(chem), 72. *Prof Exp:* Fel, Univ Western Ont, 72-73. *Mem:* Chem Inst Can; Am Chem Soc. *Res:* Synthesis and characterization of new types of complexes; special interest in optically active organometallic complexes and in complexes with catenated sulfur ligands. *Mailing Add:* Dept Chem McGill Univ Montreal PQ H3A 2K6 Can. *E-Mail:* shaver@omc.lan.mcgill.ca

SHAVER, EVELYN LOUISE, CYTOGENETICS, REPRODUCTIVE BIOLOGY. *Personal Data:* b London, Ont, Aug 21, 31. *Educ:* Univ Western Ont, BSc, 54, MSc, 58, PhD(anat), 68. *Prof Exp:* Res asst micro-anat, Univ Western Ont, 54-60; res technician biol, Atomic Energy of Can Ltd, 60-64; demonstr, Univ Western Ont, 64-66, from lectr to emer prof anat, 66-93. *Mem:* Am Asn Anat; Can Asn Anat; Can Soc Cell Biol; Soc Study Reproduction. *Res:* Factors influencing the chromosome complement of pre- and postimplantation embryos; invitro fertilization. *Mailing Add:* 246 Edward St London ON N6C 3J6 Can

SHAVER, GAIUS ROBERT, PLANT ECOPHYSIOLOGY, ECOSYSTEM ECOLOGY. *Current Pos:* asst scientist ecol, 79-84, assoc scientist, 84-89, SR SCIENTIST, ECOSYSTS CTR, MARINE BIOL LAB, 89- *Personal Data:* b Pasadena, Calif, Aug 19, 49; m 84, Eleanore Beale; c Nat & Robbie. *Educ:* Stanford Univ, BS, 72, AM, 72; Duke Univ, PhD(bot), 76. *Prof Exp:* Res assoc ecol, San Diego State Univ & Univ Alaska, 76-78. *Concurrent Pos:* Instr biol, San Diego State Univ, 77-78. *Mem:* Am Ecol Soc; Brit Ecol Soc; Soc Am Naturalists; AAAS; Sigma Xi. *Res:* Ecology of plants; ecology of arctic tundras; mineral nutrition, growth and ecophysiology of plants; N and P cycling in ecosystmes. *Mailing Add:* 50 Upland Ave Falmouth MA 02540

SHAVER, KENNETH JOHN, FOOD CHEMISTRY. *Current Pos:* RETIRED. *Personal Data:* b Auburn, NY, Dec 18, 25; m 48; c 1. *Educ:* Syracuse Univ, BS, 48, PhD(chem), 52. *Prof Exp:* Res chemist, Monsanto Co, 52-82, group leader, 64-82, res mgr, 78-82. *Mem:* Am Chem Soc; Int Asn Dent Res; Inst Food Technologists; Sigma Xi. *Res:* Food phosphates; food preservatives. *Mailing Add:* 32 Millbrook Lane St Louis MO 63122

SHAVER, LEE ALAN, CHEMISTRY, QUALITY SYSTEMS. *Current Pos:* CHEM QUAL CONTROL MGR, FMC CORP, 70- *Personal Data:* b Tucson, Ariz, 1945. *Educ:* Northern Ariz Univ, BS, 67; Ariz State Univ, MS, 70; Seton Hall Univ, PhD(anal chem), 78. *Mem:* Am Chem Soc; Soc Appl Spectros. *Mailing Add:* 3031 Rimrock Dr Lawrence KS 66047-2716

SHAVER, ROBERT HAROLD, GEOLOGY & PALEONTOLOGY, STRATIGRAPHY & SEDIMENTATION. *Current Pos:* RETIRED. *Personal Data:* b North Henderson, Ill, Sept 8, 22; m 45, 87, Marcia Sue Hayes Terrell; c Joanne Lee, Mark Harold, Jill Margaret & Bruce Robert. *Educ:* Univ Ill, BS, 47, MS, 49, PhD(geol), 51. *Prof Exp:* Asst geol, Univ Ill, 47-50; from asst prof to prof, Univ Miss, 51-56, chmn dept, 52-56; head, Geol Sect, Ind Geol Surv, 56-86 & chief, Res & Proj Develop Br, 86-87; assoc prof geol, Ind Univ, Bloomington, 56-64, asst chmn dept, 67-72, prof, 64- *Concurrent Pos:* Co-ed J Paleont, 64-69; actg chmn, Ind Univ, Bloomington, 70; chairperson, Geol Soc Am, Soc Econ Paleontologists & Mineralogists, Am Asn Petrol Geologists & Paleont Soc. *Mem:* Fel Geol Soc Am; Paleont Soc; hon mem Soc Econ Paleontologists & Mineralogists (pres-elect, 75-76, pres, 76-77). *Res:* Silurian and Devonian stratigraphy, paleoecology and sedimentation; Silurian paleoecology (reef faunas); carboniferous paleontology (ostracoda). *Mailing Add:* 2012 Viva Dr Bloomington IN 47401

SHAVER, ROY ALLEN, ORGANIC CHEMISTRY. *Current Pos:* RETIRED. *Personal Data:* b Rushville, Ill, Aug 4, 31; m 59; c William, James & Thomas. *Educ:* Western Ill Univ, BS, 53, MS, 56. *Prof Exp:* From instr to prof chem, Univ Wis-Platteville, 56-91, chmn dept, 77-79,. *Concurrent Pos:* Consult fuels, Shell Oil, 77-81. *Mem:* Am Chem Soc. *Res:* Nonbenzenoid aromaticity-electrophilic reactions of the tropylium ion; time predictions on cheese rancidification. *Mailing Add:* 490 N Washington Platteville WI 53818

SHAVITT, ISAIAH, THEORETICAL CHEMISTRY, QUANTUM CHEMISTRY. *Current Pos:* prof, 81-94, EMER PROF CHEM, OHIO STATE UNIV, 94- *Personal Data:* b Kutno, Poland, July 29, 25; US citizen; m 57, Veronica Neuwirth; c Sharon. *Educ:* Israel Inst Technol, BSc, 50, dipl eng, 51; Cambridge Univ, PhD(theoret chem), 57. *Prof Exp:* Instr chem, Israel Inst Technol, 53-54 & 56-57, lectr, 57-58; res assoc theoret chem, Naval Res Lab, Univ Wis, 58-59; asst prof chem, Brandeis Univ, 59-60; staff chemist, IBM Watson Sci Comput Lab, Columbia Univ, 60-62; sr lectr, Israel Inst Technol, 62-63, assoc prof, 63-67; staff mem theoret chem, Battelle Mem Inst, 67-81. *Concurrent Pos:* Mem nat coun, Info Processing Asn Israel, 66-67; adj prof chem, Ohio State Univ, 68-81; vis scientist, Max Planck Inst Physics & Astrophys, Munich, Ger, 76; chmn, Sub-Div Theoret Chem, Am Chem Soc, 78-79; vis prof chem, Univ Wollongong, Australia, 79; fel, Japan Soc Prom Sci, Inst Molecular Sci, Okazaki, Japan, 80; interim co-dir, Ohio Supercomput Ctr, 88; vis prof chem, Univ Fla, 92; adj prof, Univ Ill, Urbana-Champaign, 94- *Mem:* Am Chem Soc; Int Soc Theoret Chem Physics; fel Am Phys Soc; Int Acad Quantam Molec Sci. *Res:* Molecular quantum mechanics; computational methods. *Mailing Add:* Dept Chem Ohio State Univ Columbus OH 43210-1185. *Fax:* 614-292-1685; *E-Mail:* shavitt@mps.ohio-state.edu

SHAW, A(LEXANDER) J(OHN), CHEMICAL ENGINEERING, SONOCHEMISTRY. *Current Pos:* RETIRED. *Personal Data:* b Vancouver, BC, May 7, 20; m 47, Joyce Bell; c Robert A & John N. *Educ:* Univ BC, BASc, 44, dipl bus mgt, 62. *Prof Exp:* Shift supvr, BC Distillery, 44-46; from res engr to chief chemist & develop engr, Western Chem Industs, Ltd, 46-68; consult engr chem, B H Levelton & Assocs Ltd, 68-90; spec projs, Res & Develop Lab, Chatterton Petrochem Corp, 90-92. *Mem:* Sr mem Chem Inst Can. *Res:* Process and product development, environmental quality studies, waste management; vitamins; proteins, fats, oils; alpha-glyceryl ethers; nucleotides; production biochemicals and medicinal chemicals; air and water quality studies; hazardous chemical disposal; air and water pollution control; energy from biomass; sonochemistry & photochemistry in synthesis of aromatic chemicals. *Mailing Add:* 4427 W Fifth Ave Vancouver BC V6R 1S4 Can. *E-Mail:* ajshaw@unixg.ubc.ca

SHAW, ALAN BOSWORTH, GEOLOGY. *Current Pos:* RETIRED. *Personal Data:* b Englewood, NJ, Mar 28, 22; m 82, Mary Merrem Williams; c 2. *Educ:* Harvard Univ, AB, 46, AM, 49, PhD(geol), 49. *Honors & Awards:* Raymond C Moore Medal, Excellence in Paleont, Soc Sedimentary Geol, 96. *Prof Exp:* Asst prof geol, Univ Wyo, 49-55; area paleontologist, Shell Oil Co, Colo, 55-60; consult paleontologist, 60-61; res assoc, Amoco Prod Res, 61, res sect supvr paleont & palynol, 61-65, spec res assoc, Okla, 65-68, consult geologist, Denver Div Explor, 68-70, district geologist, 70-71, consult geologist, 71-76, chief paleontologist, 76-77, mgr geol, Chicago Br, 77-82, res consult, 82-85. *Concurrent Pos:* Consult, Amoco, Okla, 86-87. *Mem:* Paleont Soc (pres, 68); Soc Sedimentary Geol; Am Asn Petrol Geol. *Res:* Invertebrate paleontology and carbonate stratigraphy. *Mailing Add:* 1315 Kamira Dr Kerrville TX 78028-8805

SHAW, BARBARA RAMSAY, BIOPHYSICAL CHEMISTRY OF DNA, MODIFIED OLIGONUCLEOTIDES. *Current Pos:* from asst prof to assoc prof, 75-92, PROF CHEM, DUKE UNIV, 92- *Personal Data:* b Newton, NJ; m 69, Robert W; c 1. *Educ:* Bryn Mawr Col, AB, 65; Univ Wash, MS, 67, PhD(phys chem), 73. *Honors & Awards:* Fac Career Develop Award, Am Cancer Soc, 86-90. *Prof Exp:* Vis scientist, Princeton Univ, 71-73; res fel biophys chem, Ore State Univ, 73-75. *Concurrent Pos:* Mem, Nuclear Protein rev panel, Am Cancer Soc, 86-90; consult, Chem Indust Inst Toxicol. *Mem:* AAAS; Fedn Am Soc Exp Biol; Am Chem Soc; Am Asn Cancer Res. *Res:* Boronated nucleic acids as pharmaceutical, antisense and gene therapy agents; protein-nucleic acid interactions and chromatin structure; DNA structure and mutagenesis, mechanisms and kinetics of mutations. *Mailing Add:* Dept Chem Duke Univ Box 90346 Durham NC 27708-0346. *Fax:* 919-660-1605

SHAW, BRENDA ROBERTS, ELECTROANALYTICAL CHEMISTRY, MODIFIED ELECTRODES. *Current Pos:* Asst prof, 86-90, ASSOC PROF CHEM, UNIV CONN, 90- *Personal Data:* b Dunkirk, NY, May 12, 56. *Educ:* Earlham Col, AB, 77; Univ Ill, PhD(chem), 83. *Mem:* Am Chem Soc; Sigma Xi. *Res:* Nature and design of electrode surfaces; use of polymers and zeolites to support prospective electrocatalysts. *Mailing Add:* Dept Chem Univ Conn 215 Glenbrook Rd Storrs CT 06269-3060

SHAW, C FRANK, III, INORGANIC BIOCHEMISTRY, PHARMACEUTICAL CHEMISTRY. *Current Pos:* from lectr to assoc prof, 74-86, chmn, 90-92, PROF CHEM, UNIV WIS-MILWAUKEE, 86- *Personal Data:* b Mt Vernon, NY, Mar 17, 44; div; c Jennifer & Bryan. *Educ:* Univ Del, BS, 66; Northwestern Univ, PhD(inorg chem), 70. *Prof Exp:* NSF grant, dept chem, Purdue Univ, Lafayette, 70-72; fel chem, McGill Univ, 72-74. *Concurrent Pos:* Book rev ed, Can J Spectros, 73-77; indust consult; DFG Gast prof, 93-94. *Mem:* Am Chem Soc; Sigma Xi. *Res:* Inorganic biochemistry of essential metals; heavy metal drugs, environmental contaminants, gold, cadmium, zinc and metallo proteins. *Mailing Add:* Dept Chem Box 413 Univ Wis Milwaukee WI 53201-0413. *Fax:* 414-229-5530

SHAW, CHARLES ALDEN, COMPUTER AIDED DESIGN, COMPUTER APPLICATIONS. *Current Pos:* MGR TECHNOL PARTNERSHIPS, CADENCE DESIGN SYSTS INC, SANTA JOSE, CALIF, 89- *Personal Data:* b Detroit, Mich, June 8, 25; m 89, Jeanne Steves; c Amy & Polly. *Educ:* Harvard Univ, BS, 45; Syracuse Univ, MSEE, 58. *Honors & Awards:* Recognition Award, Asn Comput Mach, 88. *Prof Exp:* Test & design engr, Gen Elec Co, Syracuse, NY, 47-51; chief engr, Onondaga Pottery Electronics, NY, 51-61; unit & subsect mgr, Gen Elec Semiconductor Prod Dept, Gen Elec Co, Paris, 61-66, consult to dir gen, Bull Gen Elec, 66-69, mgr comput aided design, Integrated Circuits Prod Dept, Syracuse, 69-71, proj mgr Solid State Appln Oper, 71-73, mgr, Comput Aided Design Ctr, 73- 77, mgr, Solid State Appln Oper, 78-81, dir, comput aided design, Intersil, Gen Elec, Cupertina, Calif, 81-88. *Mem:* Asn Comput Mach; Inst Elec & Electronics Engrs. *Res:* Computer aided design for design of electronic circuits. *Mailing Add:* 4925 Monaco Dr Pleasanton CA 94566-7671. *Fax:* 408-944-9265; *E-Mail:* shaw@cadence.com

SHAW, CHARLES GARDNER, PHYTOPATHOLOGY, MYCOLOGY. *Current Pos:* RETIRED. *Personal Data:* b Springfield, Mass, Aug 12, 17; m 40, Esther Anne Tennant; c Charles Gardner III, Sharon Anne (Taber) & Mark Tennant. *Educ:* Ohio Wesleyan Univ, BA, 38; Pa State Col, MS, 40; Univ Wis, PhD(bot, plant path), 47. *Prof Exp:* Instr, Bot Lab, Ohio Wesleyan Univ, 37-38; lab asst, Pa State Col, 38-40; lab asst, Univ Wis, 41-43, asst, 46-47; instr plant path & jr plant pathologist, Wash State Univ, 47-48, asst prof & asst plant pathologist, 48-51, assoc prof & assoc plant pathologist, 51-57, actg chmn dept, 60-61, chmn dept, 61-72, prof & plant pathologist, 57-84. *Concurrent Pos:* Consult, US Agency Int Develop Pakistan Agr Univ, 69-70 & 72; vis prof plant path, Dept Bot, Univ Auckland, NZ, 75; vis scientist, Govt New Zealand Div Indust & Sci Res, 81-82; chief of party, Wash State Univ-US AID, Univ Jordan, 77-79, Ministry Agr, Govt Jordan, 82-83. *Mem:* Mycol Soc Am; Am Phytopath Soc; Brit Mycol Soc; Int Soc Plant Path; Am Soc Plant Taxon. *Res:* Saprots of conifers; vectoring of wood decay fungi, delignification of wood; taxonomy of Peronosporaceae. *Mailing Add:* NW325 Janet St Pullman WA 99163

SHAW, CHARLES GARDNER, III, forest pathology, for more information see previous edition

SHAW, CHENG-MEI, NEUROPATHOLOGY. *Current Pos:* from res instr to assoc prof, 60-74, PROF PATH, SCH MED, UNIV WASH, 74- *Personal Data:* b Chang-Hua, Taiwan, Oct 24, 26; m 51; c 4. *Educ:* Taihoku Gym, dipl, 46; Nat Taiwan Univ, MD, 50. *Prof Exp:* Resident surg, Nat Taiwan Univ Hosp, 50-53 & neuropsychiat, 53-54; fel neurosurg, Lahey Clin, 54-55; resident neurosurg, Col Med, Baylor Univ, 55-58; res fel path, Col Med, Baylor Univ, 58-60. *Concurrent Pos:* Nat Multiple Sclerosis Soc res fel, 60-63. *Mem:* Am Asn Neuropath; Int Acad Path; Am Asn Path; Sigma Xi. *Res:* Immunopathology; etiology and pathogenesis of experimental allergic encephalitis; mechanisms of immunological adjuvants; morphological studies of malformation of human central nervous system. *Mailing Add:* Univ Wash Hosp Neuropath Lab Box 356480 Seattle WA 98195-6480. *Fax:* 206-543-3644

SHAW, DAVID ELLIOT, COMPUTATIONAL FINANCE, PARALLEL COMPUTATION. *Current Pos:* managing gen partner, 88-90, CHMN, D E SHAW & CO, 90- *Personal Data:* b Chicago, Ill, Mar 29, 51. *Educ:* Univ Calif, San Diego, BA, 72; Stanford Univ, MS, 74, PhD, 80. *Honors & Awards:* Fac Develop Award, IBM, 83. *Prof Exp:* Pres & chief exec officer, Stanford Systs Corp, 76-79; assoc prof comput sci & dir, Non-Von Supercomput Proj, Columbia Univ, 80-86; vpres, Morgan Stanley & Co, 86-88. *Concurrent Pos:* Chmn, New York City Mayor's Comt Technol & Pub Policy, 87. *Mem:* Asn Comput Mach; Inst Elec & Electronics Engrs. *Res:* Parallel computer architectures for artificial intelligence and other applications; computational finance. *Mailing Add:* D E Shaw & Co 120 W 45th St 39 Fl New York NY 10036

SHAW, DAVID GEORGE, CHEMICAL OCEANOGRAPHY, ORGANIC CHEMISTRY. *Current Pos:* asst prof, 73-76, ASSOC PROF, INST MARINE SCI, UNIV ALASKA, 76- *Personal Data:* b Los Angeles, Calif, Apr 20, 45; m 69. *Educ:* Univ Calif, Los Angeles, BS, 67; Harvard Univ, AM, 69, PhD(chem), 71. *Prof Exp:* NSF fel, Harvard Univ, 71-72; res assoc chem oceanog, Marine Sci Inst, Univ Conn, 72-73. *Mem:* AAAS; Geochem Soc; Am Chem Soc; Am Soc Limnol & Oceanog. *Res:* Transport and reactivity of organic chemicals in marine systems; organic trace analysis; environmental quality. *Mailing Add:* Inst Marine Sci Univ Alaska Fairbanks AK 99775

SHAW, DAVID HAROLD, PHYSIOLOGY, PHARMACOLOGY. *Current Pos:* from asst prof to assoc prof, 69-85, PROF & CHAIR ORAL BIOL, COL DENT, UNIV NEBR MED CTR, LINCOLN, 85- *Personal Data:* b Grants Pass, Ore, Jan 18, 41; m 63, JoAnne Morehouse; c Stephen, Richard & Matthew. *Educ:* Univ Nebr, BS, 63, MS, 65; Univ of the Pac, PhD(physiol, pharmacol), 69. *Prof Exp:* Asst physiol, Univ Nebr, 63-64, asst & res assoc cell physiol, 64-65, instr physiol, 65-66; instr & res assoc physiol & pharmacol, Univ of the Pac, 67-69. *Mem:* AAAS; Int Asn Dent Res; Am Asn Dent Res; Sigma Xi. *Res:* The effect of dental plaque extract on cultured cells; gingival retraction material toxicity; catecholamine response to dental treatment. *Mailing Add:* Dept of Oral Biol Univ Nebr Med Ctr Col Dent Lincoln NE 68583-0740. *Fax:* 402-472-5290; *E-Mail:* dshaw@unmc.edu

SHAW, DAVID T, ELECTROMECHANICAL ENGINEERING, MATERIALS SCIENCE ENGINEERING. *Current Pos:* From asst prof to assoc prof, 64-74, co-dir, Ctr for Integrate Process Systs Technol, 86-88, PROF ELEC ENG, STATE UNIV NY BUFFALO, 74-, DIR LAB FOR POWER & ENVIRON STUDIES, 78-, EXEC DIR, NY STATE INST ON SUPERCONDUCTIVITY, 87- *Personal Data:* b China, Mar 13, 38; m 61; c 2. *Educ:* Nat Taiwan Univ, BS, 59; Purdue Univ, MS, 61, PhD(nuclear eng), 64. *Concurrent Pos:* NSF res initiation grant, 65-67; consult, Bell Aerosystem Co, NY, 66-69 & Jet Propulsion Lab, Calif, 68-; vis assoc, Dept Environ Eng Sci, Calif Inst Technol, 70-71; vis prof, Univ Paris, 76; consult, Atomic Energy Comn, Paris, 77- *Mem:* Am Nuclear Soc; Inst Elec & Electronics Engrs; Am Soc Mech Engrs; Am Soc Eng Educ. *Res:* Control of particulate emissions into the atmosphere; acoustic agglomeration; atmospheric nucleation processes; aerosol measurement techniques; aerosol physics; energy conversion; research interests include high temperature synthesis of ultra fine particles; electromagnetic wave interactions with aerosols and superconductivity materials preparation and characterization. *Mailing Add:* State Univ NY Buffalo NY State Inst Superconduct 330 Bonner Hall Amherst NY 14260

SHAW, DENIS MARTIN, GEOCHEMISTRY. *Current Pos:* From lectr to prof geol, McMaster Univ, 48-89, chmn dept, 53-59 & 62-66, dean grad studies, 78-84, EMER PROF GEOL, McMASTER UNIV, 89- *Personal Data:* b St Annes, Eng, Aug 20, 23; m 46, 76, Susan L Evans; c 3. *Educ:* Cambridge Univ, BA, 43, MA, 48; Univ Chicago, PhD(geochem), 51. *Honors & Awards:* Miller Medal, Royal Soc Can, 81. *Concurrent Pos:* Vis prof, Ecole Nat Superieure de Geol, France, 59-60 & Inst Mineral, Univ Geneva, 66-67; exec ed, Geochimica et Cosmochimica Acta, 70-88. *Mem:* Geochem Soc; fel Royal Soc Can; Geol Asn Can; Mineral Asn Can (pres, 64-65); Geol Soc Am; Meteoritical Soc. *Res:* Geochemistry; chemical mineralogy. *Mailing Add:* Dept Geol McMaster Univ Hamilton ON L8S 4M1 Can

SHAW, DEREK HUMPHREY, CARBOHYDRATE CHEMISTRY, MICROBIAL BIOCHEMISTRY. *Current Pos:* head, Marine Prod Div, Nfld Biol Sta, 75-76, head, Microbial Chem Sect, 76-86, HEAD FISH HEALTH & PARASITOL SECT, NORTHWEST ATLANTIC FISHERIES CTR, 87- *Personal Data:* b Maidstone, Eng, Apr 27, 37; Can citizen; m 60; c 2. *Educ:* Univ Cape Town, BSc, 59, PhD(carbohydrate chem), 65. *Prof Exp:* Prod chemist, Seravac Labs Ltd, Cape Town, SAfrica, 60-63; Nat Res Coun Can fel biosci, Ottawa, Ont, 65-67; res scientist marine carbohydrates, Fisheries Res Bd Can, 67-72, div head fisheries technol, St John's, Nfld, 72-74. *Concurrent Pos:* Adj prof chem, Mem Univ Nfld. *Mem:* Fel Chem Inst Can. *Res:* Marine carbohydrates; gas chromatography of carbohydrate derivatives; microbial polysaccharides from bacteria pathogenic to fish; biochemistry of fish diseases. *Mailing Add:* 602 Windward Way Qualicum Beach BC V9K 2K4 Can

SHAW, DON W, PHYSICAL CHEMISTRY, MATERIALS SCIENCE. *Current Pos:* mem tech staff, Tex Instruments, Inc, 65-72, sr scientist, 72-77, head, Explor Mat Br, 78-79, DIR, MAT SCI LAB, TEX INSTRUMENTS, INC, 79- *Personal Data:* b Pecan Gap, Tex, Dec 26, 37; m 59; c 2. *Educ:* East Tex State Univ, BS, 58; Baylor Univ, PhD(phys chem), 65. *Honors & Awards:* Electrochem Soc Electronics Div Award, 83; Gallium Arsenide Symp Award; Heinrich Welker Gold Medal, 89. *Prof Exp:* Instr chem, Dallas Inst, 58-61. *Concurrent Pos:* Assoc ed, J Crystal Growth; div ed, J Electrochem Soc, 81-91; mem, Vis Comt Chem, Univ Tex & Tech Adv Comt, Eng Res Ctr, Univ Ill; dir, Tsukuba Res & Develop Ctr, Japan, 91-93; prin fel, 93-; prin ed, J Mat Res, 97- *Mem:* Nat Acad Eng; Electrochem Soc; Am Asn Crystal Growth; Am Chem Soc; Sigma Xi; Mats Res Soc. *Res:* Electronic materials, crystal growth mechanisms; kinetics of vapor phase epitaxial growth of semiconductors; materials for solid state microwave devices; preparation and properties of gallium arsenide. *Mailing Add:* 10009 Apple Creek Dr Dallas TX 75243

SHAW, EDGAR ALBERT GEORGE, ACOUSTICS. *Current Pos:* from asst res officer to prin res officer, 50-86, head acoust sect, 75-85, EMER RESEARCHER, INST MICROSTRUCT SCI, NAT RES COUN CAN, 86- *Personal Data:* b Middlesex, Eng, July 10, 21; Can citizen; m 45, Millicent Chandler; c Jennifer & Kenneth. *Educ:* Univ London, BSc, 48, PhD(physics), 50. *Honors & Awards:* Rayleigh Medal, Inst Acoust, Brit, 79. *Prof Exp:* Tech officer, UK Ministry Aircraft Prod & Brit Air Comn, US, 40-46. *Concurrent Pos:* Lectr, Univ Ottawa, 58-73; mem, Comt Hearing, Bio-Acoust & Biomech, Nat Res Coun-Nat Acad Sci, 65-95; chmn, Int Comn Acoust, 75-78; co-chmn, Int Comn Biol Effects of Noise, 88-93, mem at large, 93- *Mem:* Fel Acoust Soc Am (pres, 73); fel Royal Soc Can; Brit Inst Physics; Can Asn Physicists; fel Inst Acoust Brit. *Res:* Electroacoustics; psychoacoustics; physiological acoustics; acoustic measurements; wave acoustics; urban and industrial noise; hearing and hearing protection; mechanical vibrations; acoustics of external and middle ear. *Mailing Add:* Inst Microstruct Sci M36 Nat Res Coun Can Ottawa ON K1A 0R6 Can

SHAW, EDWARD IRWIN, RADIATION BIOLOGY, CANCER BIOLOGY. *Current Pos:* from asst prof to prof radiation biophys, Univ Kans, 56-85, chmn dept, 68-78, prof physiol & cell biol, 80-96, EMER PROF PHYSIOL & CELL BIOL, UNIV KANS, 96- *Personal Data:* b New York, NY, Jan 17, 27; m 56, 80, Cynthia Blackhall; c 3. *Educ:* Univ Mo, AB, 48, MA, 50; Univ Tenn, PhD(zool, radiation biol), 55. *Prof Exp:* Asst zool, Univ Mo, 48-51 & Univ Tenn, 52-55; res assoc biol div, Oak Ridge Nat Lab, 55-56. *Concurrent Pos:* Instr, Univ Tenn, 55; consult, Menninger Found, Kans, 57-62 & AAAS, 71-75; dir, Radiation Protection, Energy Res Develop Admin Training Grant, 74-77. *Mem:* Fel AAAS; Radiation Res Soc; Health Physics Soc; Sigma Xi. *Res:* Radiation biophysics; radiation effects at the cell level; health physics; mutation-induction and recovery from pre-mutational lesions; theoretical cancer biology. *Mailing Add:* 1635 Mississippi St Lawrence KS 66044

SHAW, ELDEN K, ELECTRICAL ENGINEERING. *Current Pos:* from asst prof to assoc prof, 66-77, PROF ELEC ENG, SAN JOSE STATE UNIV, 77- *Personal Data:* b Brigham, Utah, Aug 20, 34; m 57; c 4. *Educ:* Utah State Univ, BS, 56; Stanford Univ, MS, 57, PhD(elec eng), 67. *Prof Exp:* Sr res engr, Litton Industs Tube Corp, 60-66. *Concurrent Pos:* Res asst, Stanford Univ, 64-66; consult, S F D Labs, Inc, 66-70. *Mem:* Inst Elec & Electronics Engrs. *Res:* Steady state plasma discharges; crossed field microwave tubes, electron optics. *Mailing Add:* 2320 E San Ramon Ave MS 94 Calif State Univ Fresno CA 93740-8030

SHAW, ELLSWORTH, SOIL SCIENCE, AGRICULTURAL CHEMISTRY. *Current Pos:* PLANT & SOIL SCIENTIST & LAB & FIELD DIR, GAC PRODUCE, MEXICO, 70- *Personal Data:* b Chicago, Ill, Mar 7, 20; m 43; c 6. *Educ:* Univ Chicago, BS, 41; Univ Ariz, PhD(soil chem), 49. *Prof Exp:* Res chemist, Testing Mat, Kellogg Switchboard & Supply Co, 41-42; plant indust sta, US Dept Agr, 49-52; consult agr, 53-70. *Concurrent Pos:* Shell fel, 46-49; independent agr consult, Ariz & Calif; res assoc agr chem & soils, Univ Ariz, 60. *Mem:* Am Chem Soc; Am Soc Agron; fel Am Inst Chem; Sigma Xi. *Res:* Application of radioisotopes to soil and plant nutritional problems; effect of fumigants on soil; availability of soil zinc to plants; soil and fertilizer need to plants through measurement of nitrogen uptake. *Mailing Add:* 3602 E Flower Tucson AZ 85716

SHAW, ELWOOD R, ANALYTICAL CHEMISTRY. *Current Pos:* RETIRED. *Personal Data:* b Clark Co, Ohio, Sept 29, 18; m 56, Pauline; c Lisa. *Educ:* Cedarville Col, AB, 40, BS, 41; Ohio State Univ, MSc, 56. *Prof Exp:* Instr math & chem, Cedarville Col, 40-41, prof chem, 46-54; teacher high schs, Ohio, 41-42, 45-46; asst prof chem & res chemist, Antioch Col, 54-59; from res assoc to sr res assoc chem, C F Kettering Res Lab, 59-84. *Mem:* Am Chem Soc; Am Soc Plant Physiologists. *Res:* Hydrothermal research; germanates and silicates; organic synthesis; substituted hydrazines; metalloporphins; photosynthesis. *Mailing Add:* 1102 Clifton Rd Xenia OH 45385-9458

SHAW, EUGENE, MICROBIOLOGY, VIROLOGY. *Current Pos:* PRES, INST ADVAN BIOTECHNOL, 92- *Personal Data:* b Burlington, Iowa, Aug 3, 25; m 56; c 4. *Educ:* Northwestern Univ, BS, 49; Univ Iowa, MS, 55, PhD(microbiol), 63. *Prof Exp:* With Med Serv Corps, US Army, 51-70; sr scientist, Virol Div, Ortho Res Found, 70-92. *Mem:* Am Soc Microbiol; Tissue Cult Asn; NY Acad Sci. *Res:* Enteroviruses; infectious hepatitis. *Mailing Add:* Off Pres Inst Adv Biotech PO Box 574 Hingham MA 02043

SHAW, FREDERICK CARLETON, INVERTEBRATE PALEONTOLOGY. *Current Pos:* from asst prof to assoc prof, 68-78, chmn, Dept Geol & Geog, 72-81, PROF GEOL, LEHMAN COL, 78-, DEAN NATURAL & SOCIAL SCI, 81- *Personal Data:* b Boston, Mass, July 8, 37; m 58; c 2. *Educ:* Harvard Univ, AB, 58, PhD(geol), 65; Univ Cincinnati, MS, 60. *Prof Exp:* From instr to asst prof geol, Mt Holyoke Col, 63-68. *Concurrent Pos:* Geol Soc Am res grant, 65; instr & dir social sci training prog, Mt Hermon Sch, 65-66; NSF res grant, 68-71; prin investr, MBRS & MISIP training res grants , 85-; Smithsonian Foreign Currency Grant, 85- *Mem:* AAAS; Paleont Soc; Geol Soc Am; Sigma Xi. *Res:* Systematics and paleoecology of Paleozoic invertebrates; Ordovician biostratigraphy. *Mailing Add:* Dept Geol Herbert H Lehman Col Bronx NY 10468

SHAW, GAYLORD EDWARD, ANIMAL PHYSIOLOGY. *Current Pos:* ASSOC PROF ANAT & PHYSIOL MICROBIOL, KENT STATE UNIV, 70- *Personal Data:* b London, Ont, Mar 10, 39; m 65; c 2. *Educ:* Graceland Col, Iowa, BA, 62; Univ Ill, Urbana, MS, 66, PhD(vet med sci), 70. *Prof Exp:* Res asst pathol & hyg, Col Med, Univ Ill, 62-63; instr biol, Graceland Col, 63-64; res asst physiol & pharmacol, Col Vet Med, Univ Ill, 64-69, res asst vet biol structure, 69-70. *Concurrent Pos:* Lab dir, Caries Susceptibility Testing & Res Ctr, 78-82. *Mem:* AAAS; Sigma Xi. *Res:* Oral leukocyte infiltration and phagocytic activity; oral lactobacillus counts as a clinical parameter of caries activity. *Mailing Add:* 300 S Cherry St Lamoni IA 50140-1337

SHAW, GEORGE, II, ROBOTICS, EMBEDDED & REAL-TIME COMPUTER SYSTEMS. *Current Pos:* OWNER & CONSULT SOFTWARE ENGR, SHAW LABS LIMITED, HAYWARD, CALIF, 77- *Personal Data:* b Castro Valley, Calif, Oct 13, 59. *Prof Exp:* Asst mgr & computer tech, Computer Systs Unlimited, San Lorenzo, Calif, 76; warehouse mgr, Tech Rep Assocs-TRA Sales, Hayward, Calif, 76-77; mgr & sr computer tech, Byte Shop Mountain View, Mountain View, Calif, 77; partner & mgr, Acropolis, Hayward, Calif, 81-82; programmer assoc, Am Inst Res, Palo Alto, Calif, 86-88. *Concurrent Pos:* Teaching, Basic Prog, Microcomputer Oper, 77-; consult, Microsysts Anal, Systs & Appln Prog, 77-; chairperson, Asilomar Forth Modification Lab, 82 & 85, publications comt, Forth Int Standards Team, 82-; dir, Forth Modification Lab, 87-88; founder & chairperson, NBay, Forth Interest Group, 88-90, ACM Special Interest Group, SIG Forth, 88-91. *Mem:* Asn Comput Mach; assoc mem Inst Elec & Electronics Engrs; assoc mem Inst Elec & Electronics Engrs Computer Soc. *Res:* Computer software; several inventions. *Mailing Add:* Shaw Labs Ltd PO Box 3909 Hayward CA 94540

SHAW, GLENN EDMOND, ATMOSPHERIC PHYSICS. *Current Pos:* From asst prof to assoc prof, 71-79, PROF PHYSICS, GEOPHYS INST, UNIV ALASKA, 79- *Personal Data:* b Butte, Mont, Dec 5, 38; m 57, Gladys Culner; c Susan, Joseph, Raymond, Glenn Jr & Sarah. *Educ:* Mont State Univ, BS, 63; Univ Southern Calif, MS, 65; Univ Ariz, PhD, 71. *Honors & Awards:* Terris & Katrima Moore Prize, 93. *Mem:* Am Meteorol Soc; Am Geophys Union; Royal Meteorol Soc; AAAS; Royal Inst. *Res:* Atmospheric physics, especially cloud physics; physics of aerosols; nucleation; atmospheric chemistry. *Mailing Add:* Geophys Inst Univ of Alaska Fairbanks AK 99775-0800. *Fax:* 907-474-7290; *E-Mail:* maunaloa@gluaf.gi.alaska.edu

SHAW, GORDON LIONEL, THEORETICAL PHYSICS. *Current Pos:* assoc prof, 65-68, PROF PHYSICS, UNIV CALIF, IRVINE, 68- *Personal Data:* b Atlantic City, NJ, Sept 20, 32; m 58; c 3. *Educ:* Case Inst Technol, BS, 54; Cornell Univ, PhD(theoret physics), 59. *Prof Exp:* Res assoc theoret physics, Ind Univ, 58-60 & Univ Calif, San Diego, 60-62; asst prof physics, Stanford Univ, 62-65. *Mem:* Am Phys Soc. *Res:* Theory of strong interactions of elementary particles. *Mailing Add:* Dept Physics Univ Calif 4129 Frederick Reinus Hall Irvine CA 92697-4575

SHAW, HARRY, JR, APPLIED MATHEMATICS. *Current Pos:* RETIRED. *Personal Data:* b Miami, Fla, Feb 6, 27; m 49; c 2. *Educ:* Emory Univ, BA, 49; Univ Miami, MS, 51. *Prof Exp:* Instr math, Marion Mil Inst, 51-52; asst, Univ NC, 52-54 & Univ Md, 54-56. *Mem:* Asn Comput Mach; Sigma Xi. *Res:* Numerical analysis. *Mailing Add:* 6048 Stevens Forest Rd Columbia MD 21045

SHAW, HELEN LESTER ANDERSON, AMINO ACIDS, TRACE MINERALS. *Current Pos:* prof & chair, Dept Food & Nutrit, 89-94, DEAN & PROF, SCH HUMAN ENVIRON SCI, UNIV NC, GREENSBORO, 94- *Personal Data:* b Lexington, Ky, Oct 18, 36; m 88, Charles Van. *Educ:* Univ Ky, Lexington, BS, 58; Univ Wis-Madison, MS, 65, PhD(nutrit sci), 69. *Prof Exp:* Dietitian, Roanoke Vet Admin Med Hosp, 59-60; Santa Barbara Cottage Hosp & Univ Calif, Santa Barbara, 60-63; from asst prof to prof, Dept Human Nutrit & Food, Univ Mo, Columbia, 69-88. *Concurrent Pos:* Chair, Grad Nutrit Area, Univ Mo, Columbia, 85-88. *Mem:* Am Dietetic Asn; Am Soc Clin Nutrit; Soc Nutrit Educ; Am Soc Parenteral & Enteral Nutrit; Am Asn Family Consumer Sci; Am Soc Nutrit Sci. *Res:* Amino acid requirements and metabolism; zinc bioavailability and requirement; zinc and copper interactions; zinc and histidine interactions. *Mailing Add:* Sch Human Environ Sci Univ NC 235 Stone Bldg Greensboro NC 27412-5001. *Fax:* 910-334-5089

SHAW, HENRY, AIR POLLUTION CONTROL, REACTION KINETICS & CATALYSIS. *Current Pos:* PROF CHEM ENG, NJ INST TECHNOL, 86- *Personal Data:* b Paris, France, Oct 25, 34; US citizen. *Educ:* City Col New York, BChE, 57; Newark Col Eng, MSChE, 62; Rutgers Univ, PhD(phys chem), 67, MBA, 76. *Honors & Awards:* Frank Dittman Excellence Award Outstanding Community Serv & Eng Achievement, Am Inst Chem Engrs. *Prof Exp:* Nuclear engr, Nuclear Design, Babcock & Wilcox Co, 57-61, Nuclear Res, Mobil Oil Co, 61-65; instr radiation sci, Rutgers Univ, 65-67; mgr environ, Exxon Res & Eng Co, 67-86. *Concurrent Pos:* Mem, Workshop on Greenhouse Effect, AAAS/Dept Energy, 79; partic, Nat Comn Air Qual Workshop on Greenhouse Effect, 80; chmn res comt, Am Inst Chem Engrs, 83-86; chmn, Chem Technol Adv Comt, Oak Ridge Nat Lab, 84-86; mem, Study on Chem Eng Frontiers, Nat Res Coun, 85-86; chmn bd, Eng Found, 87-89; mem Comt Alternative Chem Demilitarization Technol, Nat Res Coun, 92-93. *Mem:* Fel Am Inst Chem Engrs; AAAS; Am Chem Soc; Am Soc Eng Educ; Am Geophys Union; Sigma Xi. *Res:* Preventing hazardous waste generation through process modifications; destruction of hazardous wastes using plasma, convention and catalytic incineration, scrubbing and adsorption of acid rain precursors. *Mailing Add:* 2 Gary Ct Scotch Plains NJ 07076-2007

SHAW, HERBERT JOHN, PHYSICS. *Current Pos:* PROF RES, STANFORD UNIV, 88- *Personal Data:* b Seattle, Wash; c 3. *Educ:* Univ Wash, BSEE, 41 MA, 43; Standford Univ, PhD (physics), 48. *Honors & Awards:* Morris N Liebmann Mem Award, Inst Elec & Electronics Engrs, 78. *Prof Exp:* Liaison scientist, US Off Naval Res, London, 68-69. *Concurrent Pos:* Consult govt agencies & electronics firms. *Mem:* Nat Acad Eng; fel Inst Elec & Electronics Engrs. *Res:* Fiber optic device involving sensing and signal processing; microwave antennas, high power microwave tubes, solid state devices. *Mailing Add:* Edward L Ginzton Lab Stanford Univ Stanford CA 94305-4085

SHAW, HERBERT RICHARD, GEODYNAMICS. *Current Pos:* GEOLOGIST, IGNEOUS & GEOTHERMAL PROCESSES BR, US GEOL SURV, 59- *Personal Data:* b San Mateo, Calif, Dec 7, 30; div; c 1. *Educ:* Univ Calif, Berkeley, PhD(geol), 59. *Concurrent Pos:* Vis prof, Univ Calif, Berkeley, 74-75; lectr, 76; Ernst Cloos Scholar, Johns Hopkins Univ, 78; freelance writer, 80-82. *Mem:* Fel Geol Soc Am; fel Am Geophys Union; AAAS; Sigma Xi; Mineral Soc Am. *Res:* Experimental, theoretical and field geologic investigations relating to interpretation of terrestial evolution. *Mailing Add:* US Geol Surv MS 910 Menlo Park CA 94025

SHAW, JAMES HARLAN, WILDLIFE ECOLOGY, WILDLIFE RESEARCH. *Current Pos:* asst prof wildlife ecol, 74-81, ASSOC PROF ZOOL, OKLA STATE UNIV, 81-, PROF WILDLIFE ECOL, 88- *Personal Data:* b Tyler, Tex, May 8, 46. *Educ:* Stephen F Austin Univ, BS, 68; Yale Univ, MFS, 70, PhD(wildlife ecol), 75. *Prof Exp:* Teaching asst biol, Yale Univ, 73-74, teaching fel ecol, 74. *Mem:* Wildlife Soc; Ecol Soc Am; Am Soc Mammalogists; Animal Behav Soc. *Res:* Ecology, behavior and management of large mammals; conservation education. *Mailing Add:* Dept Zool Okla State Univ 415 LSW Stillwater OK 74078-0002

SHAW, JAMES HEADON, DENTISTRY. *Current Pos:* from instr to assoc, Harvard Univ, 45-48, asst prof dent med, 48-55, assoc prof biol chem, 55-65, dir training ctr, clin scholars Oral Biol, 72-84, prof nutrit, 65-84, EMER PROF NUTRIT, SCH DENT MED, HARVARD UNIV, 84. *Personal Data:* b Sharon, Ont, Jan 1, 18; nat US; m 43, Vera Chapman; c Sandra (Eaton) & Stephen. *Educ:* McMaster Univ, BA, 39; Univ Wis, MS, 41, PhD(biochem), 43. *Hon Degrees:* MA, Harvard Univ, 55. *Prof Exp:* Res assoc nutrit, Univ Wis, 43-45. *Concurrent Pos:* Asst ed, Nutrit Rev, 46-89; consult, Forsyth Dent Infirmary Children, 47-63; mem comt dent, Med Sci Div, Nat Res Coun, 53-62, comt diet phosphate & dent caries, food & nutrit bd, Div Biol & Agr, 58-63; career investr, USPHS, 64-84. *Mem:* AAAS; Soc Exp Biol & Med; Am Inst Nutrit; Int Asn Dent Res. *Res:* Oral disease in rodents and subhuman primates; nutritional relationships to the development, calcification, metabolism and disease susceptibility of the oral structures. *Mailing Add:* 10 Stiles Terr Newton Center MA 02159

SHAW, JAMES SCOTT, ASTRONOMY. *Current Pos:* Asst prof, 70-77, assoc prof, 77-96, PROF ASTRON, UNIV GA, 96- *Personal Data:* b Grand Junction, Colo, Oct 13, 42; c 2. *Educ:* Yale Univ, AB, 64; Univ Pa, PhD(astron), 70. *Mem:* Sigma Xi; Int Astron Union; Am Astron Soc. *Res:* Eclipsing binary stars; intrinsic variable stars; photoelectric photometry. *Mailing Add:* Dept Physics & Astron Univ Ga Athens GA 30602

SHAW, JANE E, PHYSIOLOGY, CLINICAL PHARMACOLOGY. *Current Pos:* sr scientist, 70-72, PRIN SCIENTIST, ALZA RES, 72-, PRES, ALZA RES DIV, EXEC VPRES, ALZA CORP & CHMN BD, ALZA LTD, 85-, PRES & CHIEF OPERATING OFFICER, ALZA CORP, 87- *Personal Data:* b Worcester, Eng, Feb 3, 39; m, Peter F Carpenter; c Jonathan. *Educ:* Univ Birmingham, BS, 61, PhD(physiol), 64. *Hon Degrees:* DSc, Worcester Polytech Inst, 92. *Concurrent Pos:* Bd dirs, McKesson Corp, Intel Corp. *Mem:* AAAS; NY Acad Sci; Am Phys Soc; Am Soc Clin Pharmacol & Therapeuts; Am Asn Pharm Sci; Am Pharm Asn. *Res:* Elucidation of the physiological role of the prostaglandins; mechanism of action of analeptics; mechanism of gastric secretion; physiology and pharmacology of skin. *Mailing Add:* One Larch Dr Atherton CA 94027. *Fax:* 650-494-5121

SHAW, JOHN A, PROCESS MEASUREMENT & CONTROL, HUMAN FACTORS. *Current Pos:* SR APPLN ENGR, ABB PROCESS AUTOMATION, 75- *Personal Data:* b Raleigh, NC, Apr 20, 46; m 69; c 1. *Educ:* NC State Univ, BS, 70. *Honors & Awards:* Kates Award, Instrument Soc Am, 84, Pond Award, 89. *Prof Exp:* Engr, Duke Power Co, 70-75. *Concurrent Pos:* Consult, Process Control Solutions. *Mem:* Instrument So Am; Am Inst Chem Engrs. *Res:* Process control; man-machine interface; process safety. *Mailing Add:* 374 Cromwell Dr Rochester NY 14610. *E-Mail:* 73777.3444@compuserve.com

SHAW, JOHN H, PHYSICS. *Current Pos:* RETIRED. *Personal Data:* b Sheffield, Eng, Jan 25, 25; m 49; c 4. *Educ:* Cambridge Univ, BA, 46, MA, 50, PhD(physics), 51. *Prof Exp:* From lectr to prof physics, Ohio State Univ, 53-81. *Mem:* Am Meteorol Soc; fel Optical Soc Am; Royal Meteorol Soc. *Res:* Infrared spectroscopy; infrared studies of atmospheric gaseous constituents. *Mailing Add:* 4940 Sharon Ave N Columbus OH 43231

SHAW, JOHN THOMAS, ORGANIC CHEMISTRY. *Current Pos:* RETIRED. *Personal Data:* b Philadelphia, Pa, Sept 12, 25; m 46, Halina Traczyk; c Laurence, Halina & Alisande. *Educ:* Temple Univ, AB, 50, MA, 52, PhD, 54. *Prof Exp:* Sr res chemist, Org Chem Div, Am Cyanamid Co, 54-63; asst prof chem, Am Int Col, 63-65; from assoc prof to prof chem, Grove City Col, 65-91. *Concurrent Pos:* Res grant, Petrol Res Fund, 73-75, 76-77, 78-80, 85-86 & 89-91. *Mem:* Am Chem Soc; Sigma Xi; Int Soc Heterocyclic Chem. *Res:* Synthesis and reactions of nitrogen heterocycles. *Mailing Add:* 520 Woodland Ave Grove City PA 16127

SHAW, KENNETH C, ZOOLOGY. *Current Pos:* asst prof, 63-76, ASSOC PROF ZOOL, IOWA STATE UNIV, 76- *Personal Data:* b Cincinnati, Ohio, Sept 18, 32; m 55; c 4. *Educ:* Univ Cincinnati, BS, 54; Univ Mich, MS, 58, PhD(zool), 66. *Prof Exp:* Asst zool, Univ Mich, 56-60, instr, 60-61. *Mem:* Am Entomol Soc; Am Soc Zoologists; Orthopterist's Soc; Animal Behav Soc; Sigma Xi; Am Entom Soc. *Res:* Acoustical behavior of Homoptera and Orthoptera; nature and adaptive significance of the "chorusing" behavior of crickets and katydids. *Mailing Add:* Dept Zool Iowa State Univ Ames IA 50011-2010

SHAW, KENNETH NOEL FRANCIS, biochemistry; deceased, see previous edition for last biography

SHAW, LAWRANCE NEIL, CROP TRANSPLANTER DEVELOPMENT, LAND LOCOMOTION. *Current Pos:* from asst prof to assoc prof, 69-79, PROF AGR ENG, UNIV FLA, 79- *Personal Data:* b Hallock, Minn, Mar 15, 34; m 66. *Educ:* NDak State Univ, BS, 56; Purdue Univ, MS, 59; Ohio State Univ, PhD(agr eng), 69. *Prof Exp:* Grad assoc agr eng, Purdue Univ, 57-59; exten engr agr eng, Univ Maine, 59-67; grad assoc agr eng, Ohio State Univ, 67-69. *Concurrent Pos:* Vis prof, Nat Inst Agr Eng, Silsoe, Eng, 76 & Friedrich-Wilhelms Universitat, Bonn, Ger, 86. *Mem:* Am Soc Agr Engrs; Int Soc Horticult Sci. *Res:* Research and development of systems and equipment for the field production of vegetables, including machinery for soil tillage, crop planting, weed and pest control and harvesting; Four United States patents. *Mailing Add:* 8715 NW Fourth Pl Gainesville FL 32607

SHAW, LEONARD G, SYSTEMS ANALYSIS, ELECTRICAL ENGINEERING. *Current Pos:* from asst prof to assoc prof, Polytech Inst NY, 60-75, dept head, 82-90, dean, 90-95, vprovost, 95-96, PROF ELEC ENG, POLYTECH INST NY, 75- *Personal Data:* b Toledo, Ohio, Aug 15, 34; m 61; c 3. *Educ:* Univ Pa, BS, 56; Stanford Univ, MS, 57, PhD(elec eng), 61. *Prof Exp:* Res asst, Dept Elec Eng, Stanford Univ, 59-60. *Concurrent Pos:* Vis prof, Tech Univ Eindhoven, Neth, 70; consult signal processing, Mgt Div, Sperry Syst, 73-; Nat Ctr Sci Res assoc, Automatic Control Lab, Univ Nantes, France, 76-77. *Mem:* Fel Inst Elec & Electronic Engrs; Am Soc Eng Educ. *Res:* Image processing; stochastic control; spectral analysis; control of traffic and message queues; reliability. *Mailing Add:* Dept Elec Eng Polytech Univ Brooklyn NY 11201. *E-Mail:* lshaw@poly.edu

SHAW, LESLIE M J, PATHOLOGY, PHARMACOLOGY. *Current Pos:* res fel clin chem, 70-72, mem staff, 72-74, asst prof, 74-77, ASSOC PROF CLIN CHEM, DEPT PATH & LAB MED, & DIR, TOXICOL LAB, HOSP UNIV PA, 77-, PROF, 87- *Personal Data:* b Newark, NJ, Feb 4, 41; m 67; c 4. *Educ:* LeMoyne Col, BS, 62; Upstate Med Ctr, State Univ NY, PhD(biochem), 68. *Prof Exp:* Res fel molecular biol, Johns Hopkins Univ, 68-70. *Mem:* Am Chem Soc; Am Asn Clin Chem; AAAS; Nat Acad Clin Biochem; Am Asn Pathologists; Am Soc Clin Pharmacol & Therapeut. *Res:* Metabolism and mechanism of action of phosphorothioate radio and chemoprotectors in cancer patients and experimental animal models; clinical significance of unbound drug concentration in serum; pharmacokinetics of cyclosporine, pharmacologic activity of cylosporine metabolites. *Mailing Add:* Toxicol Lab Univ Pa Hosp Wm Pepper Lab 3400 Spruce St Philadelphia PA 19104-4283

SHAW, M(ELVIN) P, SOLID STATE PHYSICS & ELECTRONICS, CLINICAL PSYCHOLOGY. *Current Pos:* prof, 70-96, MER PROF, ELEC & COMPUT ENG, WAYNE STATE UNIV, 96-; CONSULT PSYCHOLOGISTS, BMS CONSULT, 96- *Personal Data:* b Brooklyn, NY, Aug 16, 36; m 59, 87, Bernitta Miller; c Adam & Evan. *Educ:* Brooklyn Col, BS, 59; Case Inst Technol, MS, 63, PhD(physics), 65; Ctr Humanistic Studies, MA, 88. *Prof Exp:* Exp physicist & scientist-in-charge microwave physics, Res Labs, United Aircraft Corp, 64-70; admin dir, Asn Birmingham, 88-93. *Concurrent Pos:* Lectr, Trinity Col, Conn, 65-66; adj asst prof, Rensselaer Polytech Inst, 70; vis lectr, Yale Univ, 69-70; consult, Energy Conversion Devices, 70-85; adv, Nat Res Coun Comt, 75-78. *Mem:* Fel Am Phys Soc; sr mem Inst Elec & Electronic Engrs; Am Psychol Asn. *Res:* Amorphous solar cells; cyclotron resonance; electron spin resonance; superconductivity; solid state microwave sources; crystal growth and purification of metals and semiconductors; switching in crystalline and amorphous semiconductors; scientific creativity. *Mailing Add:* BMS Consult 250 Martin St Suite 207 Birmingham MI 48009

SHAW, MARGARET ANN, pharmacy, for more information see previous edition

SHAW, MARGERY WAYNE, HUMAN GENETICS, LEGAL GENETICS. *Current Pos:* assoc prof, Univ Tex, 67-69, prof biol, Univ Tex, M D Anderson Hosp & Tumor Inst, 69-75, prof genetics & dir, Med Genetics Ctr, Houston, 71-88, EMER PROF GENETICS, UNIV TEX HEALTH SCI CTR, 88- *Personal Data:* b Evansville, Ind, Feb 15, 23; div, Charles R; c Barbara R. *Educ:* Univ Ala, AB, 45; Columbia Univ, MA, 46; Univ Mich, MD, 57; Univ Houston, JD, 73. *Hon Degrees:* ScD, Univ Evansville, 77 & Univ Southern Ind, 86. *Honors & Awards:* Billings Silver Medal, AMA, 66; Achievement Award, Am Asn Univ Women, 70. *Prof Exp:* Instr zool, Univ Alaska, 51-53; from instr to assoc prof human genetics, Univ Mich, 58-67. *Concurrent Pos:* Mem, Genetics Study Sect, NIH, 66-70, training comt, 70-74; mem, Med Adv Bd, Nat Genetics Found, 72-86. *Mem:* Am Soc Human Genetics (pres, 82); Am Soc Cell Biol; Tissue Cult Asn; Genetics Soc Am (pres, 77-78); Environ Mutagen Soc; Am Soc Law & Med. *Res:* Inherited diseases; human chromosomes; legal aspects of medical genetics. *Mailing Add:* 2617 Pine Tree Dr Evansville IN 47711-2117

SHAW, MARY M, SOFTWARE ARCHITECTURE & ENGINEERING, PROGRAMMING LANGUAGES. *Current Pos:* PROF COMPUT SCI, CARNEGIE-MELLON UNIV, 72- *Personal Data:* b Washington, DC, Sept 30, 43; m, Roy Weil. *Educ:* Rice Univ, BA, 65; Carnegie-Mellon Univ, PhD(comput sci), 72. *Honors & Awards:* Warnier Prize, Contrib Software Eng & Syst Develop Methods. *Concurrent Pos:* Mem, Tech Comt Software Eng, Inst Elec & Electronics Engrs, Comput Soc, 81-94, Defense Sci Bd Task Force Software, 85-87, Working Group Syst Implementation Lang, Int Fedn Info Processing Soc, 85-94, Comput Sci & Telecommun Bd, Nat Res Coun, 86-93; assoc ed, Inst Elec & Electronic Engrs Software, 83-87; chief scientist, Software Eng Inst, Carnegie-Mellon Univ, 84-88. *Mem:* Fel Asn Comput Mach; fel Inst Elec & Electronics Engrs; Inst Elec & Electronics Engrs Comput Soc; NY Acad Sci; Sigma Xi; fel AAAS. *Res:* Software architecture; programming language design; abstraction techniques for advanced programming; software engineering; computer science education. *Mailing Add:* Sch Comput Sci Carnegie-Mellon Univ 5000 Forbes Ave Pittsburgh PA 15213-3890. *E-Mail:* mary.shaw@cs.cmu.edu

SHAW, MICHAEL, PLANT PATHOLOGY, PLANT PHYSIOLOGY. *Current Pos:* dean agr sci, 67-75, vpres acad develop, 75-80, prof agr bot, 67-83, vpres & provost, 81-83, univ prof, 83-89, EMER UNIV PROF, UNIV BC, 89- *Personal Data:* b Barbados, BWI, Feb 11, 24; m 48, Jean N Berkinshaw; c Christopher A, Rosemary E, Nicholas R & Andrew L. *Educ:* McGill Univ, BSc, 46, MSc, 47, PhD(bot, plant path), 49; Univ Sask, PhD(ad eundem), 71. *Hon Degrees:* DSc, McGill Univ, 75. *Honors & Awards:* Gold Medal, Can Soc Plant Physiol, 71; Flavelle Medal, Royal Soc Can, 76; Gold Medal, Biol Coun Can, 83. *Prof Exp:* Nat Res Coun Can fel, Bot Sch,

Cambridge Univ, 49-50; from assoc prof to prof plant physiol, Univ Sask, 50-67, head dept biol, 61-67. *Concurrent Pos:* Vis researcher, Hort Res Labs, Univ Reading, 58-59; ed, Can J Bot, 64-79; vpres, Biol Coun Can, 71, pres, 72 & 87-89; mem adv comt biol, Nat Res Coun Can, 71-73; mem, Sci Coun Can, 76-82; mem, Natural Sci & Eng Res Coun Can, 78-80. *Mem:* AAAS; Am Soc Plant Physiol; fel Royal Soc Can; Can Soc Plant Physiol; Can Bot Asn; fel NY Acad Sci; fel Am Phytopathlogy Soc; fel Can Phytopath Soc. *Res:* Host-parasite relations of obligate plant parasites. *Mailing Add:* Dept Plant Sci Univ BC Vancouver BC V6T 1Z4 Can. *Fax:* 604-822-8640

SHAW, MILTON C(LAYTON), MECHANICAL ENGINEERING, TRIBOLOGY. *Current Pos:* PROF ENG, ARIZ STATE UNIV, 77- *Personal Data:* b Philadelphia, Pa, May 27, 15; m 39, Mary J Greeninger; c Barbara J & Milton S. *Educ:* Drexel Inst, BS, 38; Univ Cincinnati, MEngSc, 40, ScD(chem physics), 42. *Hon Degrees:* Dr, Cath Univ Louvain, 70. *Honors & Awards:* Westinghouse Award, Am Soc Eng Educ, 56; Hersey Award, Am Soc Mech Engrs, Medalist, 85; Gold Medal, Am Soc Tool & Mfg Eng, 58; Wilson Award, Am Soc Metals, 71. *Prof Exp:* Res engr, Cincinnati Milling Mach Co, 38-42; chief, Mat Br, Nat Adv Comt Aeronaut, 42-46; from asst prof to prof mech eng, Mass Inst Technol, 46-61, head, Mach Tool Div, 46-61; head, Dept Mech Eng, Carnegie-Mellon Univ, 61-75, dir, Processing Res Inst, 70-71, univ prof, 74-77. *Concurrent Pos:* Guggenheim fel, 56; Fulbright vis prof, Aachen Tech Univ, 57; vis prof, Univ Birmingham, 60, 61 & 64; Springer prof, Univ Calif, Berkeley, 72; distinguished guest prof, Ariz State Univ, 76; consult var co, 46- *Mem:* Nat Acad Eng; hon mem Am Soc Mech Engrs; hon mem Am Soc Lubrication Engrs; hon mem Soc Mfg Eng; fel Am Acad Arts & Sci; hon mem Int Inst Prod Engrs (pres, 61); fel Am Soc Metals. *Res:* Metal cutting; lubrication, friction and wear; behavior of materials; grinding research, brittle fracture. *Mailing Add:* Ariz State Univ ECG 247 Tempe AZ 85287-6106. *Fax:* 602-965-1384

SHAW, MONTGOMERY THROOP, POLYMER SCIENCE. *Current Pos:* assoc prof, 76-82, PROF, DEPT CHEM ENG, UNIV CONN, 82- *Personal Data:* b Ithaca, NY, Sept 11, 43; m 94, Maripaz Nespral; c Steven. *Educ:* Cornell Univ, BChE & MS, 66; Princeton Univ, MA, 68, PhD(chem), 70. *Prof Exp:* Chemist polymer thermodyn, Union Carbide Corp, 70-74, proj scientist polymer rheology, 74-76. *Mem:* Am Chem Soc; Soc Rheology (secy, 77-81); Sigma Xi; Inst Elec & Electronics Engrs; Soc Plastic Engrs; Am Phys Soc. *Res:* Research directed at relating the physical and chemical behavior high-polymers to the structure of the polymer, and developing the theory and experiments to substantiate these relationships. *Mailing Add:* 124 High Meadow Lane Coventry CT 06238. *Fax:* 860-486-4745; *E-Mail:* shawmt@uconnvm.uconn.edu

SHAW, NOLAN GAIL, GEOLOGY, STRATIGRAPHY. *Current Pos:* PRES, NOLAN G SHAW & ASSOCS INC, 85- *Personal Data:* b Forsan, Tex, Oct 2, 29; m 67; c Nolan Jr, Scott, Susan, Michael & Jon. *Educ:* Baylor Univ, AB, 51; Southern Methodist Univ, MS, 56; La State Univ, PhD(paleont), 66. *Prof Exp:* From asst prof to prof, Centenary Col La, 55-78, William C Woolf prof chair geol, 78-85, chmn depts, 74-85. *Mem:* Am Asn Petrol Geologists; fel Geol Soc Am; Sigma Xi; Soc Ecol Paleontologists & Mineralogists. *Res:* Stratigraphy of Arkansas, Louisiana and Texas. *Mailing Add:* 626 Lake Forbing Dr Shreveport LA 71106. *Fax:* 318-865-1110

SHAW, PAUL DALE, BIOCHEMISTRY. *Current Pos:* from asst prof to assoc prof, 60-74, PROF BIOCHEM, UNIV ILL, URBANA, 74- *Personal Data:* b Morton, Ill, Aug 12, 31; m 55; c 2. *Educ:* Bradley Univ, BS, 53; Univ Ill, PhD(biochem), 57. *Prof Exp:* Res fel chem, Harvard Univ, 58-60. *Mem:* Am Chem Soc; Am Soc Biochem & Molecular Biol; AAAS; Am Soc Microbiol; Am Phyopath Soc. *Res:* Chemistry and biochemistry of natural products; metabolism of microorganisms; bacterial molecular biology. *Mailing Add:* Dept Plant Path Univ Ill 360 PABL 1201 W Gregory Dr Urbana IL 61801. *Fax:* 217-244-1230

SHAW, PETER ROBERT, marine geophysics, seismology, for more information see previous edition

SHAW, PHILIP EUGENE, GENERAL CHEMISTRY. *Current Pos:* chemist, 65-72, res leader, 72-85, SUPVRY RES CHEMIST, CITRUS AND SUBTROP PROD LAB, US DEPT AGR, 85- *Personal Data:* b St Petersburg, Fla, July 21, 34; m 59; c 3. *Educ:* Duke Univ, BS, 56; Rice Univ, PhD(chem), 60. *Honors & Awards:* Fel Award, Div Agr & Food Chem, Am ChemSoc, 93; Res & Develop Award, Citrus Prod Div, Inst Food Technologists. *Prof Exp:* Res assoc chem, Sterling-Winthrop Res Inst Div, Sterling Drug, Inc, 60-65. *Concurrent Pos:* Chem instr, Hillsboro Community Col, 83-87. *Mem:* Fel Am Chem Soc; Inst Food Technologists. *Res:* Isolation and identification of natural food flavors and insect attractants; chemistry of nutrients; development of analytical methodology. *Mailing Add:* Citrus & Subtrop Prods Lab US Dept Agr Box 1909 Winter Haven FL 33883-1909

SHAW, RALPH ARTHUR, METABOLISM, ENDOCRINOLOGY. *Current Pos:* resident med, Hahnemann Hosp, 63-65, from sr instr med to assoc prof med & biochem, 66-72, dir clin chem lab, 70-71, PROF MED & RES PROF BIOCHEM, HAHNEMANN MED COL, 72-, ASSOC VPRES HEALTH AFFAIRS, 71- *Personal Data:* b Peoria, Ill, Dec 27, 30; m 55; c 2. *Educ:* Northwestern Univ, BS, 54, MD, 62; Purdue Univ, MS, 56, PhD(biochem), 58. *Prof Exp:* Consult, Children's Mem Hosp, 59-61, fel biochem, 61-62; intern, Evanston Hosp, Ill, 62-63. *Concurrent Pos:* Mem bd, Action for Brain Injured Children, Inc; fel biochem & med, Sch Med, Northwestern Univ, 58-61; USPHS fel, Hahnemann Hosp, 65-66. *Mem:* Am Fedn Clin Res; Am Diabetes Asn; Am Geriat Soc; NY Acad Sci; Am Schizophrenia Found. *Res:* Diabetes mellitus. *Mailing Add:* 1840 Tall Oaks Rd Orwigsburg PA 17961-9540

SHAW, RICHARD FRANCIS, OCEANOGRAPHY. *Current Pos:* res assoc IV, Coastal Ecol Lab, La State Univ, 81-85, interim dir, Coastal Fisheries Inst, 89-90, asst prof, Coastal Fisheries Inst & Dept Marine Sci, Ctr Wetland Resources, 85-89, ASSOC PROF, DEPT OCEANOG & COASTAL SCI, LA STATE UNIV, 89-, DIR, 90- *Personal Data:* b Lawrence, Mass, Feb 22, 52; m 86, Carolyn A Rubino; c Gregory P. *Educ:* Univ Maine, PhD(oceanog), 81. *Prof Exp:* Res asst, Dept Oceanog, Univ Maine, 73-79; consult coordr, Human Sci Res Inc, 79-80; regional coordr & consult, Kathryn Chandler Assocs, Inc & Market Facts, Inc, 81. *Mem:* Am Fisheries Soc; Am Soc Ichthyologists & Herpetologists; Am Soc Limnol & Oceanog; Estuarine Res Soc. *Res:* Ecology, population dynamics, growth rates, condition factors, age determination, recruitment, migration and transport of larval fishes. *Mailing Add:* La State Univ Baton Rouge Baton Rouge LA 70803-0001. *Fax:* 504-388-6513

SHAW, RICHARD FRANKLIN, THEORETICAL GERONTOLOGY, THEORETICAL EVOLUTIONARY GENETICS. *Current Pos:* INDEPENDENT RESEARCHER, 93- *Personal Data:* b Redlands, Calif, May 14, 24; m 49, Lois Banfill; c Rachel, Alan, Sarah & Wayne. *Educ:* Univ Calif, Berkeley, AB, 48, MA, 50, PhD(zool), 55. *Prof Exp:* Proj leader, Dept Animal Husb, Univ PR, 55-56; res fel, Dept Biostatist, Grad Sch Pub Health, Univ Pittsburgh, 56-57; asst prof genetics, Dept Prev Med, Univ Va, 57-63; res assoc, Dept Human Genetics, Univ Mich, 63-65, Sickle Cell Ctr, Univ Chicago, 74-77; asst prof biol, Wayne State Univ, 65-68; asst prof pediat, Dalhousie Univ, Can, 68-72; assoc prof epidemiol, Fac Med, Univ Sherbrooke, Can, 72-74; proprietor, Shaw-Banfill Books, 78-85; adj assoc prof, Grad Sch, Howard Univ, 85-89; guest res, Div Computer Res & Technol, NIH, 88-93. *Concurrent Pos:* Assoc pediat, Wayne State Univ, 65-68, fac res fel, 67; researcher epidemiol, Can Govt, 72-74; consult, Howard Univ Cancer Ctr, 78-88; vis scientist, Nat Biomed Res Found, Georgetown, 85-86. *Mem:* AAAS; Am Soc Naturalists. *Res:* The causes of aging from the viewpoint of evolution and DNA structure of nuclear and mitochondrial genes; methods of computation in population genetics; methods for computer models in evolutionary and ecological genetics. *Mailing Add:* 10201 Grosvenor Pl No 522 Rockville MD 20852

SHAW, RICHARD GREGG, POLYMER CHEMISTRY. *Current Pos:* RETIRED. *Personal Data:* b Wilmington, Del, Nov 21, 29; m 57; c 3. *Educ:* Cornell Univ, AB, 51; Univ Pa, MS, 52; Ind Univ, PhD, 60. *Prof Exp:* Group leader opers div, Union Carbide Corp, 60-75, technol mgr wire & cable, Polyethylene Div, 75-77, mkt mgr wire & cable, Domestic Int Liaison, 77-78; consult, 78-93. *Mem:* Am Chem Soc; Inst Elec & Electronics Engrs; Soc Photog Scientists & Engrs. *Res:* Polymer free radical chemistry; photosensitive systems; polymer property predictions; polymer synthesis and modification; engineered plastic materials design; physics of dielectrics. *Mailing Add:* 10318 Beaver Meadow Rd Remsen NY 13438

SHAW, RICHARD JOHN, FLORICULTURE, HORTICULTURAL THERAPY. *Current Pos:* asst prof, 70-76, ASSOC PROF PLANT & SOIL SCI, UNIV RI, 76- *Personal Data:* b Fall River, Mass, Jan 15, 39; m 65, Loretta Hagemann; c Cynthia & Deborah. *Educ:* Univ RI, BS, 61; Univ Mo, MS, 63, PhD(hort), 66. *Prof Exp:* Asst prof hort, La State Univ, Baton Rouge, 66-70. *Concurrent Pos:* Treas, New Eng Chap, Am Hort Ther Asn, 89-93, pres, 93- *Mem:* Am Soc Hort Sci; Am Hort Soc; Am Hort Ther Asn; Prof Plant Growers Asn. *Res:* Effects of environment, growth regulators, growing media and fertilizers on the production of greenhouse crops. *Mailing Add:* Dept Plant Sci Univ RI Kingston RI 02881-0804. *Fax:* 401-792-4017

SHAW, RICHARD JOSHUA, BOTANY. *Current Pos:* From asst prof to assoc prof bot, 50-69, prof, 69-87, EMER PROF BIOL, UTAH STATE UNIV, 87- *Personal Data:* b Ogden, Utah, June 25, 23; m 47; c 3. *Educ:* Utah State Univ, BS, 48, MS, 50; Claremont Grad Sch, PhD(bot), 61. *Concurrent Pos:* Emer dir intermountain herbarium, Utah State Univ, 84. *Mem:* Am Soc Plant Taxon; Sigma Xi. *Res:* Taxonomic botany; biosystematics. *Mailing Add:* 1561 E 1220 N Logan UT 84341

SHAW, RICHARD P(AUL), ENGINEERING, OCEANOGRAPHY. *Current Pos:* RETIRED. *Personal Data:* b Brooklyn, NY, June 23, 33; m 61, Heather Stern; c Deardre & Melissa. *Educ:* Polytech Inst Brooklyn, BS, 54; Columbia Univ, MS, 55, PhD(appl mech), 60. *Honors & Awards:* Eminent Scientist Award, Comp Mech Inst, 88. *Prof Exp:* Sr instr appl mech, Polytech Inst Brooklyn, 56-57; asst prof eng sci, Pratt Inst, 57-62; from assoc prof to prof eng sci, State Univ NY, Buffalo, 62-80, prof civil eng, 80-96, adj prof geol sci, 92-96. *Concurrent Pos:* Nat Res Coun-Environ Sci Serv Admin fel, Joint Tsunami Res Effort, Univ Hawaii, 69-70, Nat Oceanog & Atmospheric Admin sr res assoc, 73-74; Am Coun Educ Govt exchange fel, Int Decade Ocean Explor, NSF, 77-78; pres, Int Soc Innovative Numerical Anal. *Mem:* Am Soc Civil Engrs; Am Geophys Union; Am Soc Mech Engrs; Acoust Soc Am; Marine Technol Soc; Int Soc Innovative Numerical Anal. *Res:* Numerical methods (boundary integral/element methods); wave motion (acoustic, elastic, water); ocean engineering and oceanography; structures and solid mechanics; oceanography; geophysical solid mechanics. *Mailing Add:* Dept Civil Eng State Univ NY Buffalo NY 14260. *E-Mail:* rshaw@acsu.buffalo.edu

SHAW, ROBERT BLAINE, AGROSTOLOGY, GRASS TAXONOMY. *Current Pos:* PROF, DEPT FOREST SCI, COL NATURAL RESOURCES, COLO STATE UNIV. *Personal Data:* b Commerce, Tex, May 24, 49; m 76; c 1. *Educ:* Southwest Tex State Univ, BS, 74; Tex A&M Univ, MS, 76, PhD(range sci), 79. *Prof Exp:* Res assoc, Range Sci Dept, Tex A&M Univ, 78-79; instr biol, Southwest Tex State Univ, 79-80; asst prof plant taxon, Sch Forestry, Univ Fla, 80-90. *Mem:* Soc Range Mgt; Am Soc Plant Taxonomists; Bot Soc Am. *Res:* Evolution, ecology, anatomy, morphology and systematics of the grasses; distribution, composition and evolution of the North American grasslands. *Mailing Add:* Colo State Univ Ft Collins CO 80523-0001

SHAW, ROBERT FLETCHER, ENGINEERING, EDUCATION ADMINISTRATION. *Current Pos:* RETIRED. *Personal Data:* b Montreal, Que, Feb 16, 10; m 35, Johann a MacInnes; c Robert F (deceased). *Educ:* McGill Univ, BEngr, 33. *Hon Degrees:* DEngr, Tech Univ, NS, 67, DSc, McMaster Univ, 67, Univ New Brunswick, 86, Mcgill Univ, 87. *Honors & Awards:* Companion of the Order of Can, 67; Govt Can Centennial Medal, 67; Julian C Smith Medal, Eng Inst Can, 67; Sir John Kennedy Medal, 79; Syst & Cybernet Award, Inst Elec & Electronics Engrs, 67; Gold Medal, Can Coun Prof Eng, 75. *Prof Exp:* From engr & estimator to asst to vpres, Found Co Can Ltd, 37-43, from shipyard mgr, Pictou, NS, to mgr eng & asst to pres, 43-58, exec vpres, 58-62, pres & dir, 62-63; dep comnr, Gen Expo 67, 63-68; vprin admin, McGill Univ, 68-71; dep minister, Environ Can, 71-75; pres, Monenco Pipeline Consult Ltd, 75-78; consult, Monenco Ltd, 78-90. *Concurrent Pos:* Vpres, dir & chief engr, Defense Construct Ltd, 51-52; with NATO, 52; past mem, Sci Coun Can & Nat Design Coun; past chmn, Fed/Provincial Atlantic Fisheries Comt; past co-chmn, BC Fed/Provincial Fisheries Comt; spec adv, Minister Indust Develop, Nfld, 78-79 & Nfld & Labrador Hydro, 82-85. *Mem:* Eng Inst Can (pres, 75-76). *Mailing Add:* 3980 Cote des Neiges Rd Apt c29 Montreal PQ H3H 1W2 Can

SHAW, ROBERT HAROLD, AGRICULTURAL METEOROLOGY. *Current Pos:* From asst prof to prof, 48-80, DISTINGUISHED PROF, 80-, EMER PROF AGR CLIMAT, IOWA STATE UNIV, 86- *Personal Data:* b Madrid, Iowa, June 26, 19; m 45; c 3. *Educ:* Iowa State Univ, BS, 41, MS, 42, PhD(agr climat), 49. *Honors & Awards:* Outstanding Achievement in Biometeorol, Am Meteorol Soc. *Concurrent Pos:* Mem comt meteorol and climat, Am Soc Agron, 60, 63-66, chmn, 65-66; mem working group biometeorol, Am Meteorol Soc, 63-66; assoc ed climat, Agron J, 64-66; mem comt agr meteorol, Am Meteorol Soc, 65-66; mem panel teaching climat, Am Asn Geographers, 66-67; mem panel natural resource sci, Comn Educ Agr and Nat Resources, Nat Res Coun, 66-68; mem working group, Instructions in Climat, World Meteorol Orgn, 67-68; mem comt meteorol and climat, Agr Bd, Nat Res Coun, 4 yrs. *Mem:* fel AAAS; fel Am Soc Agron; Sigma Xi; fel Soil Sci Soc Am; Am Meteorol Soc. *Res:* Water use; weather statistics; evaluation of microclimate; crop-weather relationships; solar-wind energy climatology. *Mailing Add:* 1431 Duff Ave Ames IA 50010

SHAW, ROBERT R, CONSERVATION. *Current Pos:* Asst state conservationist, Soil Conserv Serv, USDA, Vt, 74-76, state conservationist, 76-79, state conservationist, Ohio, 79-84, dir, Land Treatment Prog Div, 84-86, dir, Conserv Planning & Appl Div, 86, asst chief, 86, dep chief, Assess & Planning, 86-87, DEP CHIEF TECHNOL, SOIL CONSERV SERV, USDA, 87- *Personal Data:* b Ft Fairfield, Maine, Mar 8, 39. *Educ:* Univ Maine, BS, 61; Xavier Univ, MBA, 83. *Mailing Add:* Nat Arboretum Soil Conserv Serv USDA 3501 New York Ave NE Washington DC 20002

SHAW, ROBERT REEVES, MATERIALS SCIENCE, CERAMICS. *Current Pos:* ADV ENGR, IBM CORP, 81- *Personal Data:* b Bokoshe, Okla, June 9, 36; m 62; c 4. *Educ:* Univ Wash, BS, 59, MS, 60; Mass Inst Technol, SM, 65, ScD(ceramics), 67. *Prof Exp:* Res engr, Boeing Corp, 59-60; res trainee, Gen Elec Res Lab, 60-62; res asst ceramics, Mass Inst Technol, 62-67; sr res physicist, Am Optical Corp, 67-77; prog supvr, Phys Sci Lab, P R Mallory & Co, Inc, 77-81. *Mem:* Am Ceramic Soc. *Res:* Glass structure and properties; composite materials; optical phenomena in crystal and glass systems; phase separation; electron microscopy; microstructure-controlled phenomena; battery reactions and systems; eletronic packaging technology. *Mailing Add:* 5 Pine Ridge Rd Poughkeepsie NY 02603

SHAW, ROBERT WAYNE, SPECTROSCOPY. *Current Pos:* RES CHEMIST, ANAL YTICAL CHEM DIV, OAK RIDGE NAT LAB, 75- *Personal Data:* b Davenport, Iowa, Sept 9, 47; m 69. *Educ:* Iowa State Univ, BS, 69; Princeton Univ, PhD(chem), 74. *Prof Exp:* Res chemist, Indust Tape Lab, 3M Co, 68; fel Dept Chem, Univ Calif, Los Angeles, 73-75. *Mem:* Am Chem Soc; AAAS; Sigma Xi; Optical Soc Am. *Res:* New spectroscopic methods and instrumentation for analytical and physical chemical research. *Mailing Add:* Analytical Chem Div Oak Ridge Nat Lab Box 2008 MS6142 Oak Ridge TN 37831

SHAW, ROBERT WAYNE, BIOPHYSICAL CHEMISTRY. *Current Pos:* ASST PROF CHEM, TEX TECH UNIV, 81- *Personal Data:* b Bartlesville, Okla, July 10, 49. *Educ:* WVa Univ, BA, 71; Pa State Univ, PhD(biochem), 76. *Prof Exp:* Fel biochem, Inst Enzyme Res, Univ Wis, 76-81. *Mem:* AAAS; Am Chem Soc; Am Soc Biol Chemists. *Res:* Mechanism of a variety of physiologically important metalloenzymes; electron paramagnetic resonance; optical spectroscopies coupled to rapid kinetic methods. *Mailing Add:* Dept Chem & Biochem Tex Tech Univ MS 1061 Lubbock TX 79409-1061. *Fax:* 806-742-1289; *E-Mail:* Bitnet: pvrws@ttacs

SHAW, ROBERT WILLIAM, JR, PHOTOVOLTAICS, SUPERCONDUCTIVITY & ENERGY SYSTEMS. *Current Pos:* pres, 83-97, PRES, ARETE CORP, 97-, PRES, UTECH VENTURE CAPITAL CORP, 85- *Personal Data:* b Ithaca, NY, Aug 10, 41; m 64, Anne Meads; c Mark A & Christopher M. *Educ:* Cornell Univ, BEP, 64, MS, 64; Stanford Univ, PhD(appl physics), 68; Am Univ, MPA, 81. *Prof Exp:* Fel, Cavendish Lab, Cambridge Univ, 69 & Air Force Off Sci Res; mem tech staff, Bell Labs, 69-72; assoc, Booz, Allen & Hamilton 72-74, res dir, 74-75, vpres, 75-79, sr vpres, 79-83. *Concurrent Pos:* Chmn, Superconductivity Inc, 87-, Evergreen Solar Inc, 94- & Proton Energy Systs, 96- *Mem:* AAAS; Am Phys Soc; Sigma Xi; Int Transactional Anal Asn; Asn Humanistic Psychol. *Res:* Consulting for and financing of energy technology companies; author of many book chapters, articles and research papers on energy technologies and solid state theory. *Mailing Add:* PO Box 1664 Center Harbor NH 03226

SHAW, RODNEY, OPTICS. *Current Pos:* CONSULT, 93- *Personal Data:* b Rotherham, UK, May 9, 37; m 63; c 2. *Educ:* Leeds Univ, BS, 58; Cambridge Univ, PhD(physics), 61. *Prof Exp:* Res scientist, Ilford Ltd, UK, 61-64; lectr appl physics, Hull Univ, UK, 64-67; prin lectr photog sci, Polytech Cent London, 67-70; res scientist, Ciba-Geigy Photochemie, Switz, 70-73; prin scientist physics, Xerox Corp, 73-81; res assoc, Res Labs, Eastman Kodak Co, 82-86; dir, Ctr for Imaging Sci, Rochester Inst Technol, 86-93. *Concurrent Pos:* Ed, J Imaging Sci, 77- *Mem:* Fel Optical Soc Am; fel Soc Photog Scientists & Engrs. *Res:* Application of image evaluation methodologies to unconventional imaging processes. *Mailing Add:* Five Hidden Springs Dr Pittsford NY 14534

SHAW, ROGER WALZ, electronic materials, cryogenics, for more information see previous edition

SHAW, SPENCER, GASTROENTEROLOGY. *Current Pos:* ASST CHIEF SECT LIVER DIS & NUTRIT, VET ADMIN MED CTR, BRONX, 83- *Personal Data:* b New York, NY, Apr 28, 46. *Educ:* Univ Rochester, MD, 70. *Prof Exp:* Assoc prof, Mt Sinai Sch Med, 85- *Mem:* Am Fedn Clin Res; fel Am Col Physicians; Am Soc Clin Nutrit. *Mailing Add:* Bronx Vet Admin Hosp 130 W Kingsbridge Rd Bronx NY 10468-3904

SHAW, STANLEY MINER, NUCLEAR PHARMACY, MEDICAL RESEARCH. *Current Pos:* from asst prof to assoc prof, 62-71, actg head, Sch Health Sci, 90-93, PROF NUCLEAR PHARMACY, PURDUE UNIV, LAFAYETTE, 71-, DIV HEAD, 90-,. *Personal Data:* b Parkston, SDak, July 4, 35; m 62, Excellda J Watke; c Kim, Renee & Elena. *Educ:* SDak State Univ, BS, 57, MS, 59; Purdue Univ, PhD(bionucleonics), 62. *Honors & Awards:* Res Award, Parenteral Drug Asn, 70; Prof Henry Heine Award Outstanding Teaching, Sch Pharm, Purdue Univ, 89 & 93; Distinguishing Pharm Educr Award, Am Asn Col Pharm, 94. *Prof Exp:* Instr pharmaceut chem, SDak State Univ, 60-62. *Concurrent Pos:* Lederle pharm fac awards, 62 & 65; mem, Bd Pharm Specialties, Specialty Coun Nuclear Pharm, 78-82; chmn, Sect Nuclear Pharm, Acad Pharm Pract, 79-80, historian, 81-85; mem, Founder's Award, Sect Nuclear Pharm, Acad Pharm Pract, 81-85. *Mem:* Fel Am Soc Inst Pharmacists; fel Am Pharmaceut Asn; fel Acad Pharm Pract & Mgt; Sigma Xi; fel Am Soc Hosp Pharmacists. *Res:* Use of radioactive isotopes for the diagnosis of disease states; therapeutic drugs and agents that interfere with diagnostic procedures. *Mailing Add:* Sch Pharm Purdue Univ West Lafayette IN 47907-1333. *Fax:* 765-494-6790; *E-Mail:* sshaw@pharmacy.purdue.edu

SHAW, STEPHEN, IMMUNOGENETICS, CELL BIOLOGY. *Current Pos:* SR INVESTR, NIH, 76- *Personal Data:* b May 6, 48; c 2. *Educ:* Harvard Univ, MD, 74. *Honors & Awards:* Commendation Medal, Pub Health Serv. *Mem:* Am Asn Immunologists; AAAS; Am Soc Histocompatibility & Immunogenetics. *Res:* Human T cell recognition. *Mailing Add:* NIH Bldg Ten Rm 4B17 Bethesda MD 20892-1360. *Fax:* 301-496-0887; *E-Mail:* Bitnet: steve@nihceib

SHAW, VERNON REED, ANALYTICAL CHEMISTRY. *Current Pos:* asst prof, 73-77, ASSOC PROF CHEM, UNIV EVANSVILLE, 77- *Personal Data:* b Bellefontaine, Ohio, Apr 10, 37; m 66. *Educ:* Wittenberg Univ, BS, 64; Univ Ill, MS, 66, PhD(chem), 68. *Prof Exp:* Asst, Univ Ill, 64-68; asst prof chem, Adrian Col, 68-73. *Mem:* Am Chem Soc. *Res:* Gas chromatography of metal halide using fused salt liquid phases. *Mailing Add:* Dept Chem 1800 Lincoln Ave Evansville IN 47722-0001

SHAW, WALTER NORMAN, BIOLOGICAL CHEMISTRY. *Current Pos:* RETIRED. *Personal Data:* b Penns Grove, NJ, Dec 12, 23; m 52, Ruth Coulter; c Deborah S (Davisson), Lydia S (Enright) & Susan S (Harrison). *Educ:* Duke Univ, BA, 44; Univ Pa, PhD, 56. *Prof Exp:* Asst instr biochem, Univ Pa, 51-54, instr res med, Univ Hosp, 56-58, assoc, 58-61; sr pharmacologist, Lilly Res Labs, 61-66, sr biochemist, 66-69, res scientist, 69-75, sr res scientist, 75-94. *Concurrent Pos:* Consult, Genetic Models Inc. *Mem:* AAAS; Am Diabetes Asn. *Res:* Hormonal control of lipid and carbohydrate metabolism; study of disease states in genetically determined disease states in laboratory animals; biological activity of various proteins prepared by recombinant methods. *Mailing Add:* Genetic Models Inc 8501 Zionville Rd Indianapolis IN 46268

SHAW, WARREN A(RTHUR), STRUCTURAL & CIVIL ENGINEERING. *Current Pos:* res engr, 52-62, dir Struct Div, 62-72, HEAD CIVIL ENG DEPT, US NAVAL CIVIL ENG LAB, 72- *Personal Data:* b Wichita, Kans, Mar 10, 25; m 50; c 2. *Educ:* Univ Kans, BS, 49, MS, 52; Univ Ill, Urbana, PhD(civil eng), 62. *Prof Exp:* Instr eng mech, Univ Kans, 49-52. *Mem:* Am Soc Civil Engrs; Am Concrete Inst; Sigma Xi. *Res:* Engineering mechanics; structural dynamics; blast resistance of structures and structural elements; nuclear weapons effects research. *Mailing Add:* 1835 Guava Ct Oxnard CA 93033

SHAW, WILFRID GARSIDE, CATALYSIS, ENVIRONMENTAL SCIENCE. *Current Pos:* MGR RES & DEVELOP, BRIT PETROL AM, 88-; CONSULT, 93- *Personal Data:* b Cleveland, Ohio, May 30, 29; m 53; c 2. *Educ:* Oberlin Col, AB, 51; Univ Cincinnati, MS, 53, PhD(phys org chem), 57. *Prof Exp:* Sr chemist, Sohio Chem Co, 56-59, tech specialist, 59-62, sr res chemist, 62-71, res assoc, 71-74, sr res assoc, 75-82, dir res, 85-87, lab site mgr, 82-90; br mgr res & develop, BP AM, 88-93. *Mem:* Am Chem Soc; Catalysis Soc. *Res:* Heterogeneous and homogeneous catalysis; petrochemical processes and catalysts; environmental analysis and control; characterization of solids, liquid crystals; phototropy; molecular structure; petroleum processes. *Mailing Add:* 1028 Linden Lane Lyndhurst OH 44124

SHAW, WILLIAM S, GEOLOGY. *Current Pos:* PRES, CREIGNISH MINERALS LTD, 78-, PRES, SCOTIAROCK LTD, 89- *Personal Data:* b Glace Bay, NS, Oct 20, 24; m 50; c 6. *Educ:* St Francis Xavier Univ, BSc, 45; Mass Inst Technol, PhD(geol), 51. *Honors & Awards:* Distinguished lectr, Can Inst Mining & Metall, 87; Cert Merit Can Eng Centennial Year, Asn Prof Engrs NS, 87. *Prof Exp:* Geologist, Geol Surv Can, 49-52; sr geologist, Dominion Oil Co Div, Stand Oil Co Calif, 52-56, div stratigrapher, Calif Co Div, 56-57; consult geologist, Rodgers, Seglund & Shaw, 57-68; prof geol & chmn dept, St Francis Xavier Univ, 68-90. *Concurrent Pos:* Mem bd dirs, Deuterium of Can, Ltd, 69-81; dep minister, Mines & Energy, NS, 79-80; mem, Vol Econ Planning Bd, NS, 69-80; mem, NS Royal Comn Post-Sec Educ, 83-85; mem bd dirs, Eldorado Nuclear Ltd, 85-89; mem, Nat Adv Bd Sci & Technol, 90-93. *Mem:* Am Asn Petrol Geol; Can Inst Mining & Metall; Geol Soc Am; fel Geol Asn Can; Can Soc Petrol Geologists; Mining Soc NS. *Res:* Oil and gas exploration; geology of evaporites; mineral exploration including metallics, industrial minerals and groundwater. *Mailing Add:* 6 Highland Dr Antigonish NS B2G 1N6 Can

SHAW, WILLIAM WESLEY, WILDLIFE CONSERVATION, RESOURCE MANAGEMENT. *Current Pos:* PROF NATURAL RESOURCES, UNIV ARIZ, 74- *Personal Data:* b Pittsburgh, Pa, May 12, 46; m 69, Darcy; c Reed & Scott. *Educ:* Univ Calif, Berkeley, BA, 68; Utah State Univ, MS, 71; Univ Mich, Ann Arbor, PhD(natural resources), 74. *Honors & Awards:* Leedy Nat Award for Urban Wildlife Conserv, 88. *Concurrent Pos:* Int Wildlife & Nat Parks, Australia, Argentina, Egypt, Kuwait; Nat Res Coun Comt Fed Land Acquisition, 90-91. *Mem:* Wildlife Soc; Soc Conserv Biol. *Res:* Values of wildlife resources and management of wildlife for non-consumptive uses; urban wildlife conservation; wildlife and national parks in developing countries. *Mailing Add:* Sch Renewable Natural Resources Univ Ariz 1600 E University Blvd Tucson AZ 85721-0001. *Fax:* 520-621-8801; *E-Mail:* wshaw@ag.srnr.arizona.edu

SHAWCROFT, ROY WAYNE, SOIL PHYSICS, MICROMETEOROLOGY. *Current Pos:* RETIRED. *Personal Data:* b LaJara, Colo, Aug 17, 38; m 67; c 2. *Educ:* Colo State Univ, BS, 61, MS, 65; Cornell Univ, PhD(soil sci), 70. *Prof Exp:* soil scientist, sci & educ admin-agr res, US Dept Agr, 61-65, 70-82; exten irrigation agronomist, Col State Univ, 82-93. *Mem:* Am Soc Agron; Soil Sci Soc Am. *Res:* Plant, soil, water and atmospheric relations in semi-arid region of central plains United States; dryland and irrigated agriculture; agronomic management of irrigation system, Northeastern Colo; general climatology and weather data analysis. *Mailing Add:* 702 Main Ave Akron CO 80720

SHAWCROSS, WILLIAM EDGERTON, ECONOMIC BOTANY, ANTHROPOLOGY. *Current Pos:* RETIRED. *Personal Data:* b Norfolk, Va, Nov 29, 34. *Educ:* Univ NC, Chapel Hill, AB, 59; Control Data Inst, cert comput prog, 71; Harvard Univ, cert nat sci, 81, MA, 82, 86. *Prof Exp:* Ed asst, Sky Publ Corp, Mass, 56-61, asst ed, 61-63, managing ed, 64-87, dir & vpres, 72-80, pres, 80-91, publisher, 87-91. *Mem:* Am Astron Soc; fel AAAS. *Res:* Astronomy and archaeoastronomy; economic botany; anthropology. *Mailing Add:* 1105 Massachusetts Ave Apt 7A Cambridge MA 02138-5216. *E-Mail:* shawcros@ix.netcom.com

SHAWE, DANIEL REEVES, GEOLOGY, MINERAL DEPOSITS. *Current Pos:* Br chief, Rocky Mt Mineral Resources, 69-72, RES GEOLOGIST, US GEOL SURV, 51- *Personal Data:* b Gardnerville, Nev, May 24, 25; m 51, Helen Cruikshank; c Jill J, Jennifer S & Scott R. *Educ:* Stanford Univ, BS, 49, MS, 50, PhD(geol), 53. *Mem:* Int Asn Genesis Ore Deposits; fel Geol Soc Am; fel Soc Econ Geol; Soc Geol Appl to Ore Deposits. *Res:* Ore deposits; geology uranium in sedimentary rocks; geology beryllium in volcanic rocks; resources fluorine in United States; structure in Great Basin; gold deposits in south-central Nevada; geologic mapping. *Mailing Add:* 8920 W Second Ave Lakewood CO 80226

SHAWL, STEPHEN JACOBS, COOL VARIABLE STARS, GLOBULAR CLUSTERS. *Current Pos:* From asst prof to assoc prof, 72-85, PROF PHYSICS & ASTRON, UNIV KANS, 85- *Personal Data:* b San Francisco, Calif, June 18, 43; m 66; c 2. *Educ:* Univ Calif, Berkeley, AB, 65; Univ Tex, Austin, PhD(astron), 72. *Mem:* Int Astron Union; Am Astron Soc; Astron Soc Pac. *Res:* Cool variable stars; globular clusters. *Mailing Add:* 2904 Oxford Rd Lawrence KS 66049. *Fax:* 785-864-5262; *E-Mail:* shawl@kuphsx.phsx.ukans.edu

SHAWYER, BRUCE L R, PURE MATHEMATICS. *Current Pos:* head, 85-91, PROF MATH & STATIST, MEM UNIV NFLD, 85- *Personal Data:* b Kirkcaldy, Scotland, May 12, 37; m 66; c 4. *Educ:* St Andrews Univ, BSc, 60, PhD(math), 63. *Honors & Awards:* Adrian Pouliot Award, Can Math Soc, 96. *Prof Exp:* Asst lectr math, Univ Nottingham, 62-64, lectr, 64-66; from asst prof to prof prof math, Univ Western Ont, 66-85. *Concurrent Pos:* Alexander von Humboldt res fel, Univ Ulm, 79-80; ed-in-chief, Crux Math Orum, Math Mayhem, 96- *Mem:* Math Asn Am; Can Math Soc; fel Inst Math & Its Appln. *Res:* Summability of series and integrals; approximation of series. *Mailing Add:* Dept Math & Statist Mem Univ Nfld St John's NF A1C 5S7 Can. *E-Mail:* bshawyer@math.mun.ca

SHAY, JERRY WILLIAM, CELL BIOLOGY, CANCER & AGING. *Current Pos:* from asst prof to assoc prof, 75-92, PROF CELL BIOL, UNIV TEX SOUTHWESTERN MED CTR, 92- *Personal Data:* b Dallas, Tex, Nov 7, 45; m 85, Jennifer Cuthbert; c Stephanie, Jennifer, Jessica & Michael. *Educ:* Univ Tex, Austin, BA, 66, MA, 69; Univ Kans, PhD(physiol & cell biol), 72. *Prof Exp:* Fel marine biol, Marine Biol Lab, 72; fel molecular cellular & develop biol, Univ Colo, 72-75. *Concurrent Pos:* NIH fel, 72-73; Muscular Dystrophy Asn fel, 73-75; res grants, NIH, Muscular Dystrophy Asn & Am Heart Asn, 75-80; course coordr med genetics, Southwestern Med Sch 76-87; course dir, W Alton Jones Cell Sci Ctr, 76-77, adj staff mem, 77-78; mem exec comt, Cancer Ctr, 77-78; adj assoc prof, Univ Tex, 77-92; NIH res career develop award, 78-83; Nat Sci Found Res grant, 81-88; NIH res grant, 86-; Am Cancer Soc grant, 86-90; mem, Human Genome Proj Study Sect, 89-90; mem, Mammalian Genetics Study Sect, NIH, 90-94); sci adv bd, Geron Corp, Menlo Park, Ca, 92. *Mem:* Am Soc Cell Biol; Tissue Culture Asn; Am Asn Cancer Res; Sigma Xi; Am Soc Microbiol; Int Soc Differentiation. *Res:* Somatic cell and molecular genetics of aging; molecular mechanisms of cell immortalization; mammalian mitochondrial genetics and molecular biology; breast cancer. *Mailing Add:* Dept Cell Biol & Neurosci Univ Tex Southwestern Med Ctr 5323 Harry Hines Blvd Dallas TX 75235-9039. *Fax:* 214-648-8694; *E-Mail:* shay@utsw.swmed.ed

SHAY, JOSEPH LEO, solid state physics, for more information see previous edition

SHAYEGANI, MEHDI, MEDICAL MICROBIOLOGY. *Current Pos:* DIR, BACTERIOL LABS, NY STATE DEPT HEALTH, ALBANY, 73-, CHIEF LAB LIN MICROBIOL, 87-; ASSOC PROF, DEPT OBSTET & GYNECOL & DEPT MICROBIOL IMMUNOL, ALBANY MED SCH, 81-; PROF, SCH PUB HEALTH, STATE UNIV NY, ALBANY, 95- *Personal Data:* b Rasht, Iran, Apr 2, 26; m 61, Asieh Djabbarzadeh; c Bobeck, Aryan & Susan. *Educ:* Univ Tehran, PharmD, 53; Univ Pa, MS, 58, PhD(med microbiol), 61. *Prof Exp:* Dir, Mobile Unit Lab & Public Health Lab, Iran, 52-56; instr med microbiol, Med Sch, Univ Pa, 58-61; res assoc, Inst Microbiol, Rutgers Univ, 61-62; res assoc, Dept Commun Med, Sch Med, Univ Pa, 62-68, asst prof, Sch Med & Dept Path Biol, Vet Med, 68-72. *Mem:* Fel Am Acad Microbiol; Am Soc Microbiol; Reticuloendothelial Soc; Sigma Xi. *Res:* Host-parasite relationship in selected bacteria; identification of virulent genes in Haemophilus ducreyi, the pathogens of sexually transmitted chancroid infections; development of DNA probes and polymerase chain reaction for identification of H ducreyi in genital ulcers; molecular epidemiology for "fingerprinting" of bacteria involved in outbreaks. *Mailing Add:* 23 Fairway Ave Delmar NY 12054. *Fax:* 518-486-7971

SHAYKEWICH, CARL FRANCIS, SOIL PHYSICS. *Current Pos:* Asst prof, 67-74, ASSOC PROF SOIL PHYSICS, UNIV MAN, 74- *Personal Data:* b Winnipeg, Man, July 18, 41; m 67. *Educ:* Univ Man, BSA, 63, MSc, 65; McGill Univ, PhD(soil physics), 68. *Mem:* Am Soc Agron; Can Soc Soil Sci. *Res:* Soil physics, especially water relations in soil-plant-atmosphere system. *Mailing Add:* Dept Soil Sci Univ Man Winnipeg MB R3T 2N2 Can

SHE, CHIAO-YAO, ATOMIC & MOLECULAR PHYSICS, OPTOELECTRONICS. *Current Pos:* from asst prof to assoc prof, 68-74, PROF PHYSICS, COLO STATE UNIV, 74- *Personal Data:* b Fukien, China, Aug 4, 36; m 64, Lucia S Yein; c Colleen & Camille. *Educ:* Nat Taiwan Univ, BS, 57; NDak State Univ, MS, 61; Stanford Univ, PhD(elec eng), 64. *Prof Exp:* Asst prof elec eng, Univ Minn, 64-68. *Concurrent Pos:* Vis prof, Naval Res Lab, Univ Md, Lawrence Livermore Lab & Nat Ctr Sci Res, France. *Mem:* Am Phys Soc; fel Optical Soc Am; Inst Elec & Electronics Engr; Am Geophys Union. *Res:* Optical properties of solids; lidar application; laser spectroscopy; non-linear optical processes; thermal and dynamical structures of mesopause. *Mailing Add:* Dept Physics Eng Bldg Colo State Univ Ft Collins CO 80523

SHEA, DANIEL FRANCIS, MATHEMATICS, COMPLEX ANALYSIS. *Current Pos:* From asst prof to assoc prof, 65-72, PROF MATH, UNIV WIS-MADISON, 72- *Personal Data:* b Springfield, Mass, Aug 2, 37; m 66, Gail Berkert; c Leslie & Darrell. *Educ:* Am Int Col, BA, 59; Syracuse Univ, MS, 61, PhD(math), 66. *Concurrent Pos:* Vis assoc prof, Purdue Univ, 70-71; vis prof, Calif Inst Technol, 74-75, Univ Hawaii, 78-79 & Univ Wuerzburg, 91. *Mem:* Math Asn Am; Am Math Soc. *Res:* Functions of a complex variable; asymptotics; functional equations. *Mailing Add:* Dept Math Univ Wis Madison WI 53706. *E-Mail:* shea@math.wisc.edu

SHEA, FREDERICKA PALMER, ACQUIRED IMMUNODEFICIENCY SYNDROME RELATED RESEARCH, TEEN RISK-TAKING. *Current Pos:* asst prof, Wayne State Univ Col Nursing, 67-72, asst dir, 69-74, dir, Ctr Health Res, 86-90, ASSOC PROF NURSING, URBAN ENVIRON HEALTH, WAYNE STATE UNIV COL NURSING, 72- *Personal Data:* b Pittsfield, Mass, June 13, 40. *Educ:* Boston Univ, BS, 62, MS 63; Univ Mich, PhD(med care orgn), 86. *Prof Exp:* Staff nurse, Berkshire Med Ctr, 63-64; pub health nurse, Peace Corp, Togo, WAfrica, 64-66; intensive care unit nurse, Berkshire Med Ctr, 66-77. *Concurrent Pos:* Co-proj dir, AIDS Training for GM physicians & nurses, Gen Motors Corp, 88; prin investr, AIDS Training Prog for Health Care Providers, NIMH contract, 88-; co-prin investr, AIDS Educ for Children & Families, Nat Inst Child Health & Human Develop, 89- *Mem:* Am Nurses Asn. *Res:* Psychosocial aspects of Acquired Immunodeficiency Syndrome, clients, families, health care providers, care delivery; adolescent risk-taking behavior; clinical decision making. *Mailing Add:* Wayne State Univ 5557 Cass Ave Detroit MI 48202-3615

SHEA, JAMES H, GEOLOGY. *Current Pos:* assoc prof, 67-74, PROF GEOL, UNIV WIS-PARKSIDE, 74- *Personal Data:* b Eau Claire, Wis, Dec 20, 32; m 60; c 2. *Educ:* Univ Wis, BS, 58, MS, 60; Univ Ill, PhD(geol), 66. *Prof Exp:* Geologist, Texaco, Inc, 60-61; admin asst sec sch curric, Earth Sci Curric Proj, Am Geol Inst, 64-65, asst to dir, 65-66; asst prof geol, Univ Tenn, 66-67. *Mem:* AAAS; fel Geol Soc Am; Am Asn Petrol Geologists; Nat Asn Geol Teachers; Soc Econ Paleont & Mineral. *Res:* Philosophy of science; recent sediments; geological education; history of geology. *Mailing Add:* Dept Geol Univ Wis-Parkside Box 2000 Kenosha WI 53141-2000

SHEA, JOHN RAYMOND MICHAEL, JR, ANATOMY, HISTOLOGY. *Current Pos:* asst prof, 68-74, ASSOC PROF ANAT, JEFFERSON MED COL, 74- *Personal Data:* b Burlington, Vt, Oct 9, 38; m 68. *Educ:* Rensselaer Polytech Inst, BS, 60; McGill Univ, MSc, 62, PhD(anat), 65; Univ Surrey, MSc, 75. *Honors & Awards:* Christian R & Mary F Lindback Award, 70. *Prof Exp:* From sessional lectr to lectr anat, McGill Univ, 65-68. *Mem:* Anat Soc Gr Brit & Ireland; Am Asn Anat. *Res:* Cytology; nuclear morphology; cytophotometric analysis. *Mailing Add:* Dept Anat Jefferson Med Col Jeff Hall 1020 Locust St Rm 568 Philadelphia PA 19107

SHEA, JOSEPH F(RANCIS), ENGINEERING MECHANICS. *Current Pos:* RETIRED. *Personal Data:* b New York, NY, Sept 5, 26; m 74; c 7. *Educ:* Univ Mich, BS, 49, MS, 50, PhD(eng mech), 55. *Honors & Awards:* Arthur S Flemming Award, 65. *Prof Exp:* Instr eng mech, Univ Mich, 48-50 & 53-55; res mathematician, Bell Tel Labs, 50-53, engr, 55-59; dir advan systs, AC Spark Plug Div, Gen Motors Corp, 59-61; space prog dir, Space Tech Labs, Thompson Ramo Wooldridge, Inc, 61-62; dep dir systs eng, Off Manned Space Flight, NASA, 62-63, mgr, Apollo Spacecraft Prog, Manned Spacecraft Ctr, 63-67, dep asst adminr manned space flight, Washington, DC, 67-68; vpres & gen mgr, Equip Div, Raytheon Co, 68-69, sr vpres & gen mgr, 69-75, sr vpres & group exec, 75-81, sr vpres eng, 81-90; Hunsacker prof, Mass Inst Technol, 89, adj prof aeronaut & astronaut, 90-94. *Mem:* Nat Acad Eng; fel Am Astronaut Soc; fel Am Inst Aeronaut & Astronaut; fel Inst Elec & Electronics Engrs. *Res:* Guidance and navigation, both radio and inertial; systems engineering; space technology. *Mailing Add:* 53 Autumn Rd Weston MA 02193

SHEA, KATHLEEN LOUISE, EVOLUTIONARY ECOLOGY, RESTORATION ECOLOGY. *Current Pos:* asst prof biol, 85-91, ASSOC PROF BIOL, ST OLAF COL, 91-, CHAIR DEPT, 94- *Personal Data:* b Denver, Colo, Apr 10, 48; m 83, Michael A Farris; c David W Farris. *Educ:* Grinnell Col, BA, 70; Washington Univ, St Louis, MA, 72; Univ Colo, Boulder, PhD(environ, pop & organismic biol), 85. *Prof Exp:* Res technician biochem, Washington Univ, St Louis, 72-74; lab coordr bot & genetics, Univ Guelph, Ont, 75-77; res technician physiol, Univ Colo Health Sci Ctr, 79-80. *Concurrent Pos:* Chair, Ecol Sect, Bot Soc Am, 92-95, chair, Conserv Comt, 95-96. *Mem:* Bot Soc Am; Ecol Soc Am; Soc Study Evolution. *Res:* Plant evolutionary ecology; patterns of variation in genetic structure, mating systems, reproductive output, growth and demography; to better understand how populations, especially forest/trees, respond to environmental change. *Mailing Add:* Dept Biol St Olaf Col 1520 St Olaf Ave Northfield MN 55057. *E-Mail:* sheak@stolaf.edu

SHEA, MICHAEL FRANCIS, ENGINEERING PHYSICS. *Current Pos:* PHYSICIST, FERMI NAT ACCELERATOR LAB, 69- *Personal Data:* b Henderson, Ill, Sept 22, 33; m 61; c 7. *Educ:* Ill Benedictine Col, BS, 55; Univ Notre Dame, PhD(nuclear physics), 60. *Prof Exp:* Fel, Univ Notre Dame, 60-61; physicist, Midwestern Univs Res Asn, 61-64; res scientist space physics, Lockheed Palo Alto Res Labs, 64-67; assoc physicist, Argonne Nat Lab, 67-69. *Mem:* Am Phys Soc; Inst Elec & Electronics Eng; Comput Soc. *Res:* Bremsstrahlung production; nuclear resonance fluorescence; space radiation measurements; satellite instrumentation; particle accelerator beam diagnostic instrumentation and measurements; computer control systems and microprocessor instrumentation. *Mailing Add:* 4512 Cornell Ave Downers Grove IL 60515. *Fax:* 630-840-8590; *E-Mail:* shea@fnal.gov

SHEA, MICHAEL JOSEPH, EXPERIMENTAL SOLID STATE PHYSICS. *Current Pos:* prof physics, 69-88, chmn dept, 74-79, CHMN DEPT, CALIF STATE UNIV, SACRAMENTO, 88- *Personal Data:* b Eau Claire, Wis, Sept 4, 39; m 66; c 3. *Educ:* Marquette Univ, BS, 61; Univ Minn, Minneapolis, MS, 63; Bryn Mawr Col, PhD(physics), 69. *Mem:* Am Asn Physics Teachers; Int Solar Energy Soc; Sigma Xi. *Res:* Photoproperties of lead monoxide; photoproperties of lead monoxide; holography; Building energy research. *Mailing Add:* Dept Physics Calif State Univ 6000 Jay St Sacramento CA 95819

SHEA, PHILIP JOSEPH, PHARMACOLOGY, PHYSIOLOGY. *Current Pos:* RETIRED. *Personal Data:* b Groton, NY, Dec 11, 21; m 49, Lelia Perry; c Kevin M, Karin (Burks) & Sean T. *Educ:* Syracuse Univ, BS, 52, MS, 56. *Prof Exp:* Pharmacologist, Biochem Lab, Merrell Dow Res Inst, Indianapolis, Ind, 56-62, Human Health Labs, 62-72, Dow Pharmaceut, 72-81, res assoc, 81-88. *Mem:* NY Acad Sci; Am Soc Pharmacol & Exp Therapeut. *Res:* Cardiovascular-renal physiology and pharmacology; autonomic pharmacology; drug screening and evaluation. *Mailing Add:* Four Sycamore Rd Carmel IN 46032-1954

SHEA, RICHARD FRANKLIN, ELECTRONICS, NUCLEAR INSTRUMENTATION. *Current Pos:* RETIRED. *Personal Data:* b Boston, Mass, Sept 13, 03; m 90, Louise Hasseltine; c Doris (Brosseau), Eleanor (Smith) & Carol (Jeffries). *Educ:* Mass Inst Technol, BS, 24. *Honors & Awards:* Nuclear & Plasma Sci Soc Spec Award, 73 & Richard F Shea Award, 86. *Prof Exp:* Radio engr, Am Bosch Corp, 25-28, Amrad, Mass, 28-29, Kolster Radio Co, NJ, 29 & Atwater-Kent, Pa, 29-30; chief engr, Pilot Radio Corp, Mass, 30-31, Freed-Eisemann, NY, 32-34 & Fada Radio Co, 34-37; sect engr, Gen Elec Co, 37-50, mgr adv planning, Labs Dept, 50-54, res liaison, 54-55, consult engr, Knolls Atomic Power Lab, 55-63; consult, 63-80. *Concurrent Pos:* Consult, War Assets Bd; ed consult, John Wiley & Sons, Inc; ed-in-chief, Nuclear & Plasma Sci Soc, Inst Elec & Electronics Engrs. *Mem:* Fel Inst Elec & Electronics Engrs. *Res:* Design of radio receivers; circuits and novel application of new materials; application of electronics in nuclear field; solid state circuits and applications. *Mailing Add:* 6501 17th Ave W I 105 Bradenton FL 34209

SHEA, STEPHEN MICHAEL, PATHOLOGY. *Current Pos:* PROF PATH, ROBERT WARD JOHNSON MED SCH, UNIV MED & DENT NJ, 73- *Personal Data:* b Galway, Ireland, Apr 25, 26. *Educ:* Nat Univ Ireland, BSc, 48, MB & BCh, 50, MSc, 51, MD, 59; Am Bd Path, dipl, 60. *Prof Exp:* Asst lectr pharmacol, Univ Col, Dublin, 53-56; resident path, Mallory Inst Path, Boston City Hosp, 56-59; asst prof, Univ Toronto, 59-61; from instr path to instr math biol, Harvard Med Sch, 61-64, from assoc to assoc prof path, 65-73. *Concurrent Pos:* NIH grants, 62, 73 & 86; assoc pathologist, Mass Gen Hosp, 72-73. *Mem:* Am Asn Invest Path; Electron Micros Soc Am; Am Soc Cell Biol; Soc Math Biol; Biophys Soc; Microcirculatory Soc. *Res:* Morphometric and quantitative aspects of tissue and cellular structure; ultrastructure and microvascular permeability; glomerular blood flow and filtration. *Mailing Add:* Dept Path UMDNS Robert Wood Johnson Med Sch 675 Hors Lane Piscataway NJ 08854

SHEA, TIMOTHY GUY, ENVIRONMENTAL ENGINEERING. *Current Pos:* VPRES, ENG SCI INC, 80- *Personal Data:* b Elmhurst, Ill, Aug 22, 39; m 66; c 1. *Educ:* Loyola Univ Los Angeles, BS, 62; Univ Calif, Berkeley, MS, 63, PhD(environ eng), 68. *Honors & Awards:* Am Water Works Asn Qual Div Res Award, 71. *Prof Exp:* Vpres eng & sci, Toups Corp, 77-80. *Mem:* Water Pollution Control Fedn; Int Asn Water Pollution Res (actg secy-treas, 67-69); Am Water Works Asn. *Res:* All aspects of environmental engineering related to water quality management, waste treatment, aquatic ecosystem modelling, resource allocation institutions, and storm water treatment. *Mailing Add:* 6806 Old Stone Fence Rd Fairfax Sta VA 22039

SHEA, WILLIAM RENE, PHILOSOPHY OF SCIENCE. *Current Pos:* DIR INST SCI, UNIV LOUIS PASTEUR DE STRASBOURG. *Personal Data:* b Gracefield, Que, May 16, 37; m 70, Evelyn Fischer; c Herbert, Joan-Emma, Louisa, Cecilia & Michael. *Educ:* Univ Ottawa, BA, 58; Gregorian Univ, Rome, LPh, 59, LTh, 63; Cambridge Univ, Eng, PhD, 68. *Honors & Awards:* Alexandre Koyre Medal, Int Acad Hist Sci, 93; Knight of the Order of Malta, 93. *Prof Exp:* Assoc prof, Univ Ottawa, 68-73; fel, Harvard Univ, 73-74; prof hist & philos sci, McGill Univ, 74- *Concurrent Pos:* Dir, Sch Advan Study, Paris, 81-82; secy-gen, Int Union Hist & Philos Sci, 83-89, pres, 90-93; mem gen comt, Int Coun Sci Union, Paris, 83-89; consult, Killam Found, Ont, 83-85; mem, McGill Ctr Med, Ethics & Law, 90-, Hydro-Que prof environ ethics, 92-; vis prof, Univ Rome, 92. *Mem:* Fel Royal Soc Can; Hist Sci Soc; Europ Sci Found; Can Nat Comn Hist & Philos Asn; Int Acad Hist Sci. *Res:* History and philosophy of science; environmental ethics. *Mailing Add:* Dir Inst de Sci Univ Louis Pasteur de Strasbourg 7 Rue de la Universite-6700 Strasbourg France

SHEAGREN, JOHN NEWCOMB, INTERNAL MEDICINE, INFECTIOUS DISEASE. *Current Pos:* PROF & ASSOC CHMN DEPT INTERNAL MED & ASSOC DEAN, SCH MED, UNIV MICH, 83- *Educ:* Columbia Univ, MD, 62. *Mailing Add:* Vet Admin Med Ctr Chief Staff II 2215 Fuller Rd Ann Arbor MI 48105-2300

SHEALY, CLYDE NORMAN, HOLISTIC MEDICINE, NEUROSURGERY. *Current Pos:* CLIN & RES PROF PSYCHOL, FOREST INST PROF PSYCHOL, 87- *Personal Data:* b Columbia, SC, Dec 4, 32; m 59; c 3. *Educ:* Duke Univ, BSc & MD, 56; Saybrook Inst, PhD(psychol), 77. *Hon Degrees:* DSc, Ryodoraku Inst. *Prof Exp:* Asst med, Sch Med, Duke Univ, 56-57; asst surg, Wash Univ, 57-58; teaching fel, Sch Med, Harvard Univ, 62-63; sr instr neurosurg, Sch Med, Western Reserve Univ, 63-66, asst prof, 66; chief, Dept Neurosurg, Gundersen Clin & Lutheran Hosp, LaCrosse, Wis, 66-71; clin assoc, Dept Psychol Univ Wis-Lacrosse, 71-82. *Concurrent Pos:* Asst clin prof neurosurg, Sch Med, Univ Wis, 67-74; assoc clin prof, Sch Med, Univ Minn, 70-75; sr dolorologist, Pain & Health Rehab Ctr; pres, Holos Inst Health. *Mem:* Am Holistic Med Asn (pres, 78-80); Am Asn Neurol Surgeons; AMA; Am Asn Study Pain; Am Asn Study Headache. *Res:* Holistic medicine, integration of body, mind, emotion, and spirit; psychophysiologic basis of stress; neurochemical aspects of pain and stress. *Mailing Add:* 1328 E Evergreen St Springfield MO 65803-4400

SHEALY, DAVID LEE, OPTICS. *Current Pos:* from asst prof to assoc prof, 73-84, PROF & CHMN PHYSICS, UNIV ALA, BIRMINGHAM, 84- *Personal Data:* b Newberry, SC, Sept 16, 44; m 69; c 2. *Educ:* Univ Ga, BS, 66, PhD(physics): 73. *Prof Exp:* Syst analyst, Dept Physics, Univ Ga, 73. *Concurrent Pos:* Consult, Dept Physics, Univ Ga, 75-, NASA-Marshall Space Flight Ctr, 78-, Motorola, 79-84, Los Alamos Nat Lab, 88-92. *Mem:* Fel, Optical Soc Am; Acoust Soc Am; Am Asn Physics Teachers; Am Phys Soc; Am Inst Aeronaut & Astronaut; Int Soc Optical Eng. *Res:* Formulation and implementation of new optical design techniques based on analytical expressions for the illuminance and the caustic surface of an optical system; x-ray/EUV optical instrumentation. *Mailing Add:* Dept Physics Univ Ala Birmingham Birmingham AL 35294-1170. *Fax:* 205-934-8042; *E-Mail:* shealy@phy.uab.edu

SHEALY, HARRY EVERETT, JR, BIOLOGY, BOTANY. *Current Pos:* ASSOC PROF BIOL, UNIV SC, 73- *Personal Data:* b Columbia, SC, Oct 24, 42; m 65; c 2. *Educ:* Univ SC, BS, 65, MS, 71, PhD(biol), 72. *Prof Exp:* Fel plant sci, Univ Man, 72-73. *Mem:* Bot Soc Am. *Res:* Biology of reproduction in seed plants; vascular plant systematics. *Mailing Add:* Univ SC Aiken 171 University Pkwy Aiken SC 29801-6309

SHEALY, OTIS LESTER, FIBER MANUFACTURE, TEXTILES. *Current Pos:* CONSULT, 83- *Personal Data:* b Little Mountain, SC, Oct 3, 23; m 50, Harriet Sanders; c Malcolm, Barbara, Glenn & Alan. *Educ:* Newberry Col, AB, 44; Univ NC, PhD(chem), 50. *Hon Degrees:* ScD, Newberry Col, 68.

Prof Exp: Instr org chem, Univ NC, 48-49; res chemist, E I DuPont de Nemours & Co, Inc, 50-52, res supvr, 52-55, res mgr, 55-59, prod develop mgr, 59-64, res dir, 64-66, tech dir, 66-83. *Mem:* Fel Brit Textile Inst; Am Chem Soc; Fiber Soc. *Res:* Polyester and polyamide fibers engineering of sheet structures. *Mailing Add:* 109 Walnut Ridge Rd Wilmington DE 19807

SHEALY, Y(ODER) FULMER, SYNTHETIC ORGANIC CHEMISTRY, MEDICINAL CHEMISTRY. *Current Pos:* sr chemist, Southern Res Inst, 57-59, sect head, 59-66, div head, 66-90, DISTINGUISHED SCIENTIST, SOUTHERN RES INST, 90- *Personal Data:* b Chapin, SC, Feb 26, 23; m 50, Elaine Curtis; c Robin T, Nancy G & Priscilla B. *Educ:* Univ SC, BS, 43; Univ Ill, PhD(chem), 49. *Prof Exp:* Chemist, Off Sci Res & Develop, 43-45; asst chem, Univ Ill, 45-47; Abbot Labs fel, Univ Minn, 49-50; res chemist, Upjohn Co, 50-56; asst prof chem, Univ SC, 56-57. *Mem:* Fel AAAS; NY Acad Sci; Am Chem Soc; Am Pharmaceut Asn; Int Asn Vitamin & Nutrit Oncol; Am Asn Cancer Res. *Res:* Pyrimidines and purines; triazenes; steroids; anticancer agents; carbocyclic analogs of nucleosides; folic acid analogs; chloroethylating agents; antiviral agents; retinoids; cancer chemopreventive agents. *Mailing Add:* Southern Res Inst 2000 Ninth Ave S PO Box 55305 Birmingham AL 35255. *Fax:* 205-581-2705

SHEAR, CHARLES L, PUBLIC HEALTH & EPIDEMIOLOGY. *Current Pos:* RES SCI, MERCK, SHARP & DOHME RES LAB, 86- *Personal Data:* b Baltimore, Md, Apr 3, 53; m 77; c 3. *Educ:* Univ Md, BS, 74; Tulane Univ, MPH, 76, PhD, 79. *Prof Exp:* Asst prof family med, Univ S Ala, 79-80; asst prof epidemiol, Sch Med, Univ Calif Irvine, 80-84 & La State Univ Sch Med, 84-86. *Res:* Cardiovascular disease epidemiology. *Mailing Add:* 14 Bittersweet Dr Gales Ferry CT 06335

SHEAR, CHARLES ROBERT, ANATOMY, NEUROBIOLOGY. *Current Pos:* mem fac dept anat, 76-85, ASSOC PROF ANAT, SCH MED, UNIV MD, BALTIMORE, 85- *Personal Data:* b Chicago, Ill, Jan 20, 42; m 66. *Educ:* Univ Ill, BS, 65; Columbia Univ, MA, 67, PhD(biol sci), 69. *Prof Exp:* Leverhulme Trust vis fel, Univ Hull, 69-70; from instr to assoc prof anat, Emory Univ, 70-76. *Concurrent Pos:* Mem, Nat Adv Coun On Regeneration, Vet Admin. *Mem:* AAAS; Am Asn Anat; Am Soc Cell Biol. *Res:* Ultrastructural aspects of skeletal muscle growth, development and regeneration; cellular organization and function of the neural retina; electron microscopy. *Mailing Add:* Dept Anat Univ Md Sch Med 655 W Baltimore St Baltimore MD 21201-1559

SHEAR, CORNELIUS BARRETT, PLANT PHYSIOLOGY. *Current Pos:* RETIRED. *Personal Data:* b Vienna, Va, Sept 24, 12; m 35; c 3. *Educ:* Univ Md, BS, 34, MS, 38. *Honors & Awards:* J H Gourley Award, 59. *Prof Exp:* Agent, Crops Res Div, Sci & Educ Admin, Agr Res, USDA, 33-35, asst sci aide, 35-39, from jr physiologist to sr plant physiologist, 39-63, prin res plant physiologist, 63-77. *Concurrent Pos:* Consult fruit nutrit, People's Repub China, 81, 83, 85. *Mem:* Int Soc Hort Sci; fel Am Soc Hort Sci. *Res:* Mineral nutrition of fruit trees and tissue analysis as means of determining their nutrient status; physiology of corking and relation of nutrition, especially calcium to quality in apples. *Mailing Add:* 4218 Kenny St Beltsville MD 20705

SHEAR, DAVID BEN, BIOPHYSICS. *Current Pos:* asst prof, 67-73, ASSOC PROF BIOCHEM, UNIV MO, COLUMBIA, 73- *Personal Data:* b Boston, Mass, Jan 26, 38; div; c 2. *Educ:* Swarthmore Col, BA, 59; Brandeis Univ, PhD(biophys), 66. *Prof Exp:* NIH fel, Univ Buffalo, 66-67; asst prof physics, Univ Ga, 67-69. *Mem:* Biophys Soc. *Res:* Applications of thermodynamics, kinetics and statistical mechanics to biology; bioenergetics; muscle contraction; photosynthesis; mathematical models in biology. *Mailing Add:* Dept Biochem 117 Schweitzer Hall Columbia MO 65211

SHEAR, WILLIAM ALBERT, BIOLOGY. *Current Pos:* assoc prof, 74-80, PROF BIOL, HAMPDEN-SYDNEY COL, 81- *Personal Data:* b Coudersport, Pa, July 5, 42; m 80. *Educ:* Col Wooster, BA, 63; Univ NMex, MS, 65; Harvard Univ, PhD(evolutionary biol), 71. *Honors & Awards:* John Peter Mettauer Award, 80; Cabell Award, 85. *Prof Exp:* Asst prof biol, Concord Col, 70-74. *Concurrent Pos:* Res assoc, Am Mus Natural Hist, 78- *Mem:* Sigma Xi; Am Arachnol Soc. *Res:* Behavior, taxonomy and biogeography of arachnids and myriapods; early evolution of land animals; revisions of families and genera of Opiliones and Diplopoda, especially North American forms; web-building behavior of spiders; Devonian fossils of arachnids and myriapods. *Mailing Add:* Dept of Biol Hampden-Sydney Col Hampden-Sydney VA 23943

SHEARD, JOHN LEO, INORGANIC CHEMISTRY. *Current Pos:* RETIRED. *Personal Data:* b Southbridge, Mass, Feb 24, 24; m 47, Doris Mauke; c Christopher, Suzanne, Martha & Samuel. *Educ:* Harvard Univ, AB, 45, AM, 47; Univ Minn, PhD(chem), 53. *Prof Exp:* Instr chem, Northeastern Univ, 46-47; res chemist, Electrochem Div, E I du Pont de Nemours, 52-70, staff scientist, 70-78, res assoc, Electronics Div, 78-85. *Mem:* Am Ceramic Soc; Sigma Xi. *Res:* Fabrication of multilayer capacitors; ferrocyanides and ferricyanides; oxygen fluorides; acrylonitrile and pulp bleaching; precious metal compositions for solid state circuitry. *Mailing Add:* 1549 Waldorf Ave NE Palm Bay FL 32905

SHEARD, MICHAEL HENRY, PSYCHIATRY, NEUROPHARMACOLOGY. *Current Pos:* Res assoc psychiat res, 64-78, prof, 78-92, EMER PROF PSYCHIAT, CONN MENT HEALTH CTR, YALE UNIV, 92- *Personal Data:* b Manchester, Eng, Aug 23, 27; US citizen; m 69, Wendy; c Paul, Russell & Craig. *Educ:* Univ Manchester, MB & ChB, 51, MD, 64; Am Bd Psychiat & Neurol, dipl, 61; Royal Col Physicians, DPM, 62. *Hon Degrees:* MA, Yale, 76. *Concurrent Pos:* NIMH fel psychiat, Yale Univ, 62-64; consult, Conn Dept Corrections, 58- *Mem:* Fel Am Psychiat Asn; fel Royal Col Physicians; Sigma Xi. *Res:* Psychopharmacology. *Mailing Add:* 693 Leetes Island Branford CT 06405

SHEARER, CHARLES M, ANALYTICAL ORGANIC CHEMISTRY, PHARMACEUTICAL ANALYSIS. *Current Pos:* mgr, Wyeth Labs, 68-88, SR RES SCIENTIST, WYETH-AYERST RES, 88- *Personal Data:* b Ashland, Ohio, July 30, 31; m 58. *Educ:* ETenn State Col, BA, 53; Univ Detroit, MS, 64, PhD(chem), 68. *Prof Exp:* Chemist, Columbus Coated Fabrics, 54-55; res chemist, Parke, Davis & Co, 57-66. *Mem:* Am Chem Soc. *Res:* Analysis and determination of rates of degradation of pharmaceuticals. *Mailing Add:* Three Banner Rd Cherry Hill NJ 06003-1514

SHEARER, DUNCAN ALLAN, ANALYTICAL CHEMISTRY. *Current Pos:* RETIRED. *Personal Data:* b Kamsack, Sask, Feb 15, 20; m 46, Muriel Webster; c Cameron & Joanne. *Educ:* Univ Sask, BA, 48, MA, 50; Univ Toronto, PhD(org chem), 54. *Prof Exp:* Res scientist, Can Dept Agr, 54-73, sr res scientist, 73-80. *Mem:* Fel Chem Inst Can; Spectros Soc Can. *Res:* Lignin; organo-mercury chemistry; analytical methods in agriculture; pheromones of the honeybee. *Mailing Add:* 1182 Gateway Rd Ottawa ON K2C 2W9 Can

SHEARER, EDMUND COOK, PHYSICAL CHEMISTRY, ENVIRONMENTAL CHEMISTRY. *Current Pos:* From asst prof to assoc prof, 68-79, PROF CHEM, FT HAYS STATE UNIV, 79- *Personal Data:* b Birmingham, Ala, May 20, 42; m 66, Frances I Lawrence; c Terri, Tammy & Timothy. *Educ:* Ark Polytech Col, BS, 64; Univ Ark, PhD(chem), 69. *Mem:* Am Chem Soc; Sigma Xi. *Res:* Reaction kinetics, atmospheric precipitation studies. *Mailing Add:* Dept Chem Ft Hays State Univ Hays KS 67601. *E-Mail:* ches@fhsuvm.fhsu.edu

SHEARER, J(ESSE) LOWEN, mechanical engineering; deceased, see previous edition for last biography

SHEARER, MARCIA CATHRINE (EPPLE), TAXONOMY OF ACTINOMYCETES, TISSUE CULTURE. *Current Pos:* sr scientist, 86-89, PRIN SCIENTIST, SCHERING CORP, 90- *Personal Data:* b Akron, Ohio, Oct 27, 33; m 58. *Educ:* Ohio State Univ, BS, 56; Wayne State Univ, Detroit, Mich, MS, 63. *Prof Exp:* Microbiologist, Parke, Davis & Co, 56-68; microbiologist, Smith Kline & French Labs, Div Smith Kline & French, 68-72, sr microbiologist, Div Smith Kline Corp, 72-80, assoc sr investr, Div Smith Kline Beckman, 80-85. *Concurrent Pos:* Consult taxon, Var Corps, 85; mem exec bd, US Fedn Cult Collections, 90- *Mem:* Am Soc Microbiol; Soc Indust Microbiol; Am Inst Biol Sci; Sigma Xi; World Fedn Cult Collections; US Fedn Cult Collections. *Res:* Isolation of microorganisms from soils and other natural materials; knowledgeable culture collection curator with experience in preserving a wide variety of microorganisms; preparation of taxonomic descriptions of actinomycetes for patents and publications; tissue culture preparation for virology section. *Mailing Add:* 3 Banner Rd Cherry Hill NJ 08003

SHEARER, NEWTON HENRY, POLYOLEFINS, VINYL POLYMERS. *Current Pos:* RETIRED. *Personal Data:* b Lynchburg, Va, May 29, 20; m 55, Betty Lou Johnson; c Layne & Newton H III. *Educ:* Lynchburg Col, BA, 41; Univ Va, MS, 44, PhD(chem), 46. *Prof Exp:* Mgr, Eastman Res Co, Switz, 61-63, res assoc, Tenn Eastman Co, 63-70, mgr tech info serv, 70-86; pres, Kingsport Inst Continued Learning, ETenn State Univ & Univ Tenn, 93-97. *Mem:* Sigma Xi. *Res:* Synthesis of antimalarials; synthesis and polymerization of vinyl monomers; manufacturing processes for polyolefins. *Mailing Add:* 4535 Preston Ct Kingsport TN 37664

SHEARER, RAYMOND CHARLES, FORESTRY. *Current Pos:* RES SILVICULTURIST, INTERMOUNTAIN RES STA, FOREST SERV, USDA, 57- *Personal Data:* b Anaheim, Calif, June 3, 35; m 56, Barbara B Israelsen; c Scott, Sandra, Susan, Spencer, Sonia, Sylvia, Samuel, Seth, Stella & Stephen. *Educ:* Utah State Univ, BS, 57, MS, 59; Univ Mont, PhD, 85. *Mem:* Soc Am Foresters; Forest Hist Soc. *Res:* Regeneration of Larix occidentalis, Picea engelmannii and Pseudotsuga menziesii, including seed production, seed dissemination, germination, causes of seedling mortality and development; cutting methods and growth and mortality in western larch forests. *Mailing Add:* Forestry Sci Lab PO Box 8089 Missoula MT 59807-8089. *Fax:* 406-543-2663; *E-Mail:* fswals-r.shearer/ou-22lola@mhs.attmail.com

SHEARER, THOMAS ROBERT, BIOCHEMISTRY. *Current Pos:* from asst prof to assoc prof, 69-80, PROF NUTRIT & DIR DIV, DENT & MED SCHS, ORE HEALTH SCI UNIV, 80-, CHMN ORAL MOLECULAR BIOL, 93-, ASST DEAN RES, 96- *Personal Data:* b South Bend, Ind, Aug 11, 42; m 64, Lise Wilson; c Yvette & Matthew. *Educ:* Beloit Col, BA, 64; Univ Wis, MS, 67, PhD(biochem), 69. *Prof Exp:* Fel biochem, Univ Wis, 69. *Concurrent Pos:* Sabbatical biochem, Univ Wis, 76 & Kyoto Univ, Japan, 88-89. *Mem:* Asn Res Vision & Opthal; Am Inst Nutrit; Int Asn Dent Res; Int Cong Eye Res; Am Soc Biochem & Molecular Biol; Am Inst Nutrit. *Res:* Mechanism of selenium-overdose cataract; calpain enzymes. *Mailing Add:* Dept Oral Molecular Biol Ore Health Sci Univ 611 SW Campus Dr Portland OR 97201. *Fax:* 503-494-8918; *E-Mail:* shearert@ohsu.edu

SHEARER, WILLIAM MCCAGUE, SPEECH & HEARING SCIENCE. *Current Pos:* PROF COMMUN DISORDERS, NORTHERN ILL UNIV, 58- *Personal Data:* b Zanesville, Ohio, June 24, 26; m 54; c 2. *Educ:* Ind Univ, BA, 51; Western Mich Univ, MA, 54; Univ Denver, PhD(speech), 58. *Prof Exp:* Asst prof speech path, Minot State Col, 54-56. *Concurrent Pos:* Fel, Sch Med, Stanford Univ, 63-64; vis prof, Commun Sci Lab, Univ Fla, 68-69. *Mem:* Am Speech & Hearing Asn; Am Asn Phonetic Sci; Sigma Xi. *Res:* Anatomy of speech and hearing. *Mailing Add:* Speech/Hearing Clin Northern Ill Univ De Kalb IL 60115

SHEARER, WILLIAM THOMAS, ALLERGY, IMMUNOLOGY. *Current Pos:* CHIEF ALLERGY & IMMUNOL SERV, TEX CHILDREN'S HOSP, HOUSTON, 78-; PROF PEDIAT, MICROBIOL & IMMUNOL, BAYLOR COL MED, HOUSTON, 78-, DIR, AIDS RES CTR, 91- *Personal Data:* b Detroit, Mich, Aug 23, 37. *Educ:* Univ Detroit, BS, 60; Wayne State Univ, PhD(biochem), 66; Wash Univ, MD, 70; Am Bd Pediat, cert, 75; Am Bd Allergy & Immunol, 75. *Prof Exp:* Asst pediat, Wash Univ, 70-72, from instr to prof, 72-78. *Concurrent Pos:* Fel chem, Ind Univ, 66-67; res fel, USPHS, 72-74; res scholar award, Cystic Fibrosis Found, 74-77; dir, Div Immunol, St Louis Children's Hosp, 74-76, dir, Div Allergy & Immunol, 76-78; from assoc pediatrician to pediatrician, Barnes Hosp, 76-78; fac res award, Am Cancer Soc, 77-79; dir, Allergy & Immunol Training Prog, Baylor Col Med, 79-; chmn, Allergy & Immunol Training Prog Dirs Comt, Am Acad Allergy & Immunol, 87-90; chmn, Sect Allergy & Immunol, Southern Med Asn, 90-91; exec comt mem, Sect Allergy & Immunol, Am Acad Pediat, 90-; dir, Am Bd Allergy & Immunol, 90-; numerous positions & comts, NIH, 88-91. *Mem:* Sigma Xi; Am Asn Immunologists; fel Am Acad Pediat; Soc Pediat Res; fel Am Acad Allergy; Am Soc Clin Invest. *Res:* Tumor immunology; interaction of antibody and complement with cell membrane antigens; immunodeficiency diseases of children; allergic disorders of children; cystic fibrosis; signal transduction across cell membranes HIV-1 infection and pediatric AIDS. *Mailing Add:* Tex Children's Hosp 6621 Fannin St Suite A380 MC 1-3291 Houston TX 77030. *Fax:* 713-770-1260; *E-Mail:* wshearer@bcm.tmc.edu

SHEARN, ALLEN DAVID, DEVELOPMENTAL GENETICS. *Current Pos:* from asst prof to assoc prof, 71-81, PROF BIOL, JOHNS HOPKINS UNIV, 81- *Personal Data:* b Chicago, Ill, May 27, 42; m 64, Margaret Moses; c Emily, Eli & Isaac. *Educ:* Univ Chicago, BA, 64; Calif Inst Technol, PhD(genetics), 69. *Prof Exp:* Helen Hay Whitney Found res fel molecular biophys & biochem, Yale Univ, 68-71. *Concurrent Pos:* Consult, Genetic Biol Adv Panel, NSF, 72-75. *Mem:* AAAS; Soc Develop Biol; Genetics Soc Am. *Res:* Applying the techniques of molecular biology to the study of the regulation of development in higher organisms. *Mailing Add:* Dept Biol Johns Hopkins Univ 3400 N Charles St Baltimore MD 21218-2608. *E-Mail:* bio_cals@jhuvms.hcf.jhv.edu

SHEARN, MARTIN ALVIN, internal medicine, rheumatology, for more information see previous edition

SHEASLEY, W(ILLIAM) DAVID, PHYSICAL CHEMISTRY, POLYMER SCIENCE. *Current Pos:* sr chemist, 73-79, RES SECT MGR, ROHM & HAAS CO, 79- *Personal Data:* b Youngstown, Ohio, Oct 31, 46; m 69; c 2. *Educ:* Grove City Col, BS, 68; Ohio State Univ, MS, 70, PhD(phys chem), 72. *Prof Exp:* Fel chem lasers, Cornell Univ, 72-73. *Mem:* Am Chem Soc; Soc Rheology; Electron Micros Soc Am. *Res:* Analytical research and polymer characterization; particular emphasis on surface analysis electron spectroscopy for chemical analysis, morphological studies (electron microscopy and fluorescence techniques), and mechanical, rheological, and dielectric properties; adhesives and adhesion. *Mailing Add:* Rohm & Haas Co Spring House PA 19477. *Fax:* 215-619-1626

SHEATH, ROBERT GORDON, PHYCOLOGY, STREAM BIOLOGY. *Current Pos:* DEAN, COL BIOL SCI & PROF, DEPT BOT, UNIV GUELPH, ON, 95- *Personal Data:* b Toronto, Ont, Dec 26, 50; m 90, Mary D Rardin. *Educ:* Univ Toronto, BSc, 73, PhD(bot), 77. *Honors & Awards:* Bold Award, Phycol Soc Am, 76. *Prof Exp:* From asst prof to prof, Univ RI, 78-91, chair, 87-90; prof & head, Dept Biol, Mem Univ Nfld, 91-95. *Concurrent Pos:* Assoc ed, Phycol Soc Am, 84-89, pres, 91-92; mem, Freshwater Flora Comt, Brit Phycol Soc, 93-97; ed adv, Int Phycol Soc, 93-95. *Mem:* Phycol Soc Am (pres, 91-92); Int Phycol Soc; Brit Phycol Soc; Arctic Inst NAm; Am Soc Limnol Oceanog; NAm Benthol Soc; Japanese Phycol Soc. *Res:* Macroscopic algae of North American streams; freshwater red algae (Rhodophyta) systematics, ecology, biogeography and evolution. *Mailing Add:* Dean's Off Univ Guelph Guelph ON N1G 2W1 Can. *Fax:* 519-767-2044; *E-Mail:* rsheath@uoguelph.ca

SHEATS, GEORGE FREDERIC, physical chemistry, toxicity identification evaluation of effiments; deceased, see previous edition for last biography

SHEATS, JOHN EUGENE, ORGANOMETALLIC CHEMISTRY, PHYSICAL ORGANIC CHEMISTRY. *Current Pos:* assoc prof, 70-78, PROF, RIDER UNIV, 78- *Personal Data:* b Atlanta, Ga, Dec 20, 39; m 72; c 1. *Educ:* Duke Univ, BS, 61; Mass Inst Technol, PhD(chem), 66. *Honors & Awards:* Emmett Reid Award, Am Chem Soc, 84. *Prof Exp:* Asst prof chem, Bowdoin Col, 65-70. *Mem:* Am Chem Soc; Sigma Xi; Coun Undergrad Res. *Res:* Mechanism of decomposition of benzenediazonium ion; synthesis and properties of substituted Cobalticinium salts and other organo-transition metal compounds; preparation of organo-metallic polymers; biomedical applications of organometallic compounds; binuclear maganese complexes as models for photosynthetic oxygen evolution; coordination chemistry of transition metals. *Mailing Add:* Dept Chem Rider Univ Lawrenceville NJ 08648. *Fax:* 609-895-5782; *E-Mail:* sheats@enigma.rider.edu

SHECHMEISTER, ISAAC LEO, MEDICAL MICROBIOLOGY, IMMUNOLOGY. *Current Pos:* RETIRED. *Personal Data:* b Windaw, Latvia, June 11, 13; nat US; m 38; c 2. *Educ:* Univ Calif, AB, 34, MA, 35, PhD(bact), 49; Am Bd Microbiol, dipl. *Prof Exp:* Asst bact, Univ Calif, 36-39, lectr epidemiol, Sch Pub Health, 46, prin bacteriologist, Infectious Dis Proj, 46-50; asst prof bact & immunol, Sch Med, Washington Univ, 50-52, asst prof microbiol, 52-53, assoc prof bact, Sch Dent, 53-57; assoc prof microbiol, Southern Ill Univ, 57-64, prof, 64-81. *Concurrent Pos:* Consult, Radiol Defense Lab, US Dept Navy, Calif, 46-51; spec fel biophys, Statens Seruminstitut, Denmark, 66-67. *Mem:* Am Soc Microbiol; Am Asn Immunol. *Res:* Electron microscopy of antigen-antibody reactions; animal virology and immunology; dental caries. *Mailing Add:* Dept Microbiol Southern Ill Univ Carbondale IL 62901

SHECHTER, HAROLD, ORGANIC CHEMISTRY. *Current Pos:* from asst prof to assoc prof, 46-70, PROF CHEM, OHIO STATE UNIV, 70- *Personal Data:* b New York, NY, July 12, 21. *Educ:* Univ SC, BS, 41; Purdue Univ, PhD(chem), 46. *Prof Exp:* Asst chem, Purdue Univ, 41-42. *Mem:* Am Chem Soc. *Res:* Nitration of saturated hydrocarbons; mechanics of addition reactions of oxides of nitrogen; synthesis of polynitro compounds; kinetics of neutralization of pseudo acids; mechanisms of reactions of hydrazoic acid; homomorphic ring strain; chemistry of small ring compounds; alkylation of ambident ions; decomposition of carbenes. *Mailing Add:* Dept of Chem Ohio State Univ Columbus OH 43210

SHECHTER, LEON, ORGANIC CHEMISTRY, POLYMER CHEMISTRY. *Current Pos:* CONSULT, 77- *Personal Data:* b New York, NY, Dec 19, 12; m 37. *Educ:* Univ SC, BS, 33, MS, 34; Univ Cincinnati, PhD(org chem), 37. *Prof Exp:* Asst, Univ Cincinnati, 34-37; res chemist, Union Carbide Plastics Co, 37-44, head coating resins res, 44-52, sect head plastics res, 52-56, asst dir res, 56-58, resident dir, 58-59, dir, 60-61, dir polymer res & develop, 61-63, dir appln res & develop, 63-64, vpres res & develop, 64-67, vpres res & develop chem & plastics, Union Carbide Corp, 67-74, vpres exploratory technol, Patents & Licensing Chem & Plastics, 74-77. *Mem:* Am Chem Soc. *Res:* Alkyds; vinyl polymers; silicones; epoxy resins; phenolics; research and development management-long range research chemicals and plastics; patent management and licensing. *Mailing Add:* 22 Harvey Dr Summit NJ 07901-1217

SHECHTER, YAAKOV, HUMAN GENETICS, GENETIC COUNSELING. *Current Pos:* from asst prof to assoc prof, 69-76, PROF BIOL SCI, LEHMAN COL, 76- *Personal Data:* b Tel Aviv, Israel, Feb 11, 34; US citizen; m 59, Roberta A; c Mikal R & Batsheva S. *Educ:* Univ Calif, Los Angeles, BSc, 59, PhD(plant sci), 65, cert med mycol, 67. *Prof Exp:* Res asst agr sci, Univ Calif, Los Angeles, 60-65, fel med mycol, Sch Med, 65-66; lectr bot, Univ Southern Calif, 66-67; res biochemist, Sch Med, Univ Calif, Los Angeles, 67-69. *Concurrent Pos:* Adj cur, New York Bot Garden, 69-; consult, Human Affairs Res Ctr, New York; vis assoc prof, Stein-Moore Lab, Rockefeller Univ, 75-76; lectr, Dept Pediat, Div Genetics, Col Physicians & Surgeons, Columbia Univ, 80-; univ asst dean res & sci educ, City Univ New York, 89-94. *Mem:* Sigma Xi; NY Acad Sci; Inst Soc, Ethics & Life Sci; Am Soc Human Genetics. *Res:* Human genetics; genetics of keratins; genetic counseling; science education. *Mailing Add:* Dept Bio Sci City Univ NY Lehman Col 250 Bedford Pk W Bronx NY 10468-1589. *Fax:* 718-960-8236; *E-Mail:* yshlc@cunyvm

SHEDD, DONALD POMROY, SURGERY OF THE HEAD & NECK. *Current Pos:* RES PROF, STATE UNIV NY BUFFALO, 70- *Personal Data:* b New Haven, Conn, Aug 4, 22; m 46; c 4. *Educ:* Yale Univ, BS, 44, MD, 46. *Prof Exp:* Intern surg, Yale Univ, 46-47, from asst resident to resident, 50-53, from instr to assoc prof, 53-67; chief, Dept Head & Neck Surg, Roswell Park Mem Inst, 67-96. *Concurrent Pos:* Harvey Cushing fel surg res, Yale Univ, 49-50; Markle scholar med sci, 53-58; mem head & neck cancer group, Nat Head & Neck Cancer Cadre, 73-76, Organ Site Prog, Nat Cancer Inst, 86-88. *Mem:* Soc Univ Surg; Soc Head & Neck Surg (treas, 71-, pres, 76-77); Am Col Surg; Sigma Xi. *Res:* Oncology, particularly in head and neck cancer; physiology of deglutition; speech rehabilitation; history of surgery. *Mailing Add:* Dept Head & Neck Surg Roswell Park Mem Inst Buffalo NY 14263

SHEDLARSKI, JOSEPH GEORGE, JR, MICROBIAL BIOCHEMISTRY. *Current Pos:* PVT DENT PRACT, 81- *Personal Data:* b Forty Fort, Pa, Mar 15, 39; m 83, Sandra McDonald. *Educ:* King's Col, Pa, BS, 61; St John's Univ, NY, MS, 63; Princeton Univ, MA, 66, PhD(biochem sci), 69; La State Univ, DDS, 81. *Prof Exp:* Instr biol, Col Misericordia, 63-64; asst prof biol, Univ New Orleans, 71-75, assoc prof, 76-77. *Concurrent Pos:* Can Nat Cancer Inst fel, McMaster Univ, 69-71; res award, Am Asn Dent, 81. *Mem:* Acad Gen Dent; Am Soc Geriat Dent; Am Dent Asn. *Res:* Microbial cell wall-sheath structure; biogenesis; regulation; sugar transport in bacteria. *Mailing Add:* 4409 Laudun St Metairie LA 70006

SHEDLER, GERALD STUART, operations research, computer science, for more information see previous edition

SHEDLOCK, KAYE M, SEISMOLOGY, TECTONICS. *Current Pos:* Mathematician, US Geol Surv, 78-87, geophysicist, 86-88, chief, Br Geol Risk Assessment, 88-94, GEOPHYSICIST, US GEOL SURV, 94- *Personal Data:* b Wash, DC, Mar 30, 51. *Educ:* Univ Md, BS, 73; Johns Hopkins Univ, MS, 78; Mass Inst Technol, PhD(geophys), 86. *Concurrent Pos:* Mem, Nat Earthquake Prediction Eval Coun, 90-94, bd trustees, External Vis Comt Geophys Dept, Colo Sch Mines, 91-94, chair, 95-97, bd dirs, Seismol Soc Am, 91-94; expert, NSF Presidential Young Investr Panel, 90-91. *Mem:* Seismol

Soc Am; Am Geophys Union. *Res:* Seismotectonics of intraplate regions; subduction and transform (strike-slip) tectonics. *Mailing Add:* US Geol Surv Denver Fed Ctr MS 966 Box 25046 Denver CO 80225. *Fax:* 303-273-8600; *E-Mail:* shedlock@gldvxa.cr.usgs.gov

SHEDRICK, CARL F(RANKLIN), CHEMICAL ENGINEERING. *Current Pos:* RETIRED. *Personal Data:* b South Bend, Ind, Aug 2, 20; m 46; c 3. *Educ:* Purdue Univ, BS, 42; Columbia Univ, MSE, 48. *Prof Exp:* Res engr, E I duPont de Nemours & Co, Inc, NJ, 42-50, tech economist, Polychem Dept, Del, 50-67, chem eng, Plastics Dept, E I duPont de Nemours & Co, Inc, 67-85. *Mem:* Am Chem Soc; Am Inst Chem Engrs. *Res:* Process development of plastic materials; process and equipment design; applications research; economic evaluation. *Mailing Add:* 2535 Deepwood Dr Wilmington DE 19810

SHEDRINSKY, ALEXANDER M, ORGANIC CHEMISTRY OF ART, ARCHAEOLOGY & CONSERVATION. *Current Pos:* from asst prof to assoc prof, 88-97, PROF CHEM DEPT, LONG ISLAND UNIV, 97-; ADJ PROF CONSERV, CONSERV CTR, INST FINE ARTS, NY UNIV, 97- *Personal Data:* b St Petersburg, Russia, Mar 27, 43; m 82, Maria K Kurbatova; c Michail & Maria-Antonia. *Educ:* Leningrad Univ, MS, 65; NY Univ, MS, 83, PhD(org chem), 86. *Prof Exp:* Asst prof, Leningrad North-West Polytech Inst, 72-75; lectr org chem, Leningrad Pharmaceut Sch, 76-79; postdoctoral fel, Conserv Ctr, Inst Fine Arts, NY Univ, 86-88. *Concurrent Pos:* Andrew W Mellon fel, Objects Conserv Dept, Metrop Mus Art, 88-90; adj assoc prof conserv, Conserv Ctr, Inst Fine Arts, NY Univ, 93-97; Fulbright prof, Dept Conserv, IE Repine Inst Painting, Sculpture & Archit, Acad Art, St Petersburg, Russia, 95; vis scientist, Am Mus Natural His, 96-; Forchheimer vis prof, Sch Appl Sci & Technol, Univ Jerusalem, Israel, 97. *Mem:* Am Chem Soc; NY Acad Sci; Int Inst Conserv. *Res:* Organic chemistry of materials of art; archaeology; conservation. *Mailing Add:* Chem Dept Long Island Univ Univ Plaza Brooklyn NY 11201. *Fax:* 212-772-5851

SHEEHAN, BERNARD STEPHEN, INFORMATION SYSTEMS, TELEMATICS. *Current Pos:* asst to acad vpres, Univ Calgary, 67-69, dir, Off Instnl Res, 69-81, prof fac mgt, 81-90, assoc vpres, priorities & planning, 87-89, EMER PROF FAC MGT, UNIV CALGARY, 90-; ASSOC VPRES INFO & COMPUT SYSTS, UNIV BC, 90- *Personal Data:* b Halifax, NS, July 25, 35; m 59; c 4. *Educ:* Tech Univ NS, BE, 57; Mass Inst Technol, SM, 61; Univ Conn, PhD(elec eng), 65. *Prof Exp:* Engr, Can Gen Elec Co, 57-58; lectr eng, St Mary's Univ, NS, 58-59; teaching asst, Mass Inst Technol, 59-61; instr, Univ Conn, 61-65; dean arts & sci, St Mary's Univ, NS, 65-67. *Concurrent Pos:* Res grants, Can Coun, 73-74 & Social Sci & Humanities Coun Can, 83-85; consult, Alta Advan Educ & Manpower, 75-77; Dept Commun, Can, 84-85; mem bd, Social Sci Fedn Can, 84-86; mem, Nat Adv Comt Educ Statist, 85-88; vchmn, Telematics, Can Higher Educ Res Network, 85-87. *Mem:* Distinguished mem Asn Instnl Res (vpres, 74-75, pres, 75-76); Can Soc Study Higher Educ (vpres, 82-83, pres, 83-84); distinguished mem Can Soc Study Higher Educ (vpres, 82-83, pres, 83-84). *Res:* Analysis in management, including institutional and system-wide problems in planning, resource allocation and decision processes; information technology. *Mailing Add:* 3728 Collingwood St Vancouver BC V6S 2M5 Can

SHEEHAN, DANIEL MICHAEL, ENDOCRINE TOXICOLOGY, DEVELOPMENTAL TOXICOLOGY. *Current Pos:* res chemist, 75-78, chief, Develop Mechanisms Br, 86-91, actg dir, Div Reprod Develop Toxicol, 91-94, RES BIOLOGIST, NAT CTR TOXICOL RES, 78- *Personal Data:* b Boston, Mass, Sept 5, 44; m; Susan Laney; c Catherine & Anne. *Educ:* Univ S Fla, Tampa, BA, 66 & MA, 68; Univ Tenn Oak Ridge Grad Sch Biomed Sci, PhD(biomed sci), 73. *Prof Exp:* Lab instr introd biol, Univ SFla, Tampa, 66-67, lab coordr genetics, 67-68; Nat Defense Educ Act grad fel, Univ Tenn, Oak Ridge, 68-72; fel, Oak Ridge Assoc Univ, 72-73; NIH trainee, Baylor Col Med, 73-74, fel, 74-75. *Concurrent Pos:* From adj asst prof to adj assoc prof biochem, Univ Ark, 76-90, adj asst prof interdisciplinary toxicol, 76-84, adj assoc prof, 84-95, adj prof, 90-; ed bd, Proc Soc Exp Biol & Med, 87-90 & 91-94, coun mem & chmn, Publ Comt, 91-96. *Mem:* Soc Toxicol; Teratol Soc; Endocrine Soc; Soc Study Reproduction; Soc Exp Biol & Med. *Res:* Endocrine toxicology with emphasis on the developmental toxicity of estrogens, including drugs, chemicals, plant and mammalian hormones and endocrine disruptors and application to risk assessment. *Mailing Add:* Div Reprod & Develop Toxicol Nat Ctr Toxicol Res 3900 NCTR Rd Jefferson AR 72079. *Fax:* 870-543-7682; *E-Mail:* dsheehan@nctr.fda.gov

SHEEHAN, DAVID VINCENT, BIOLOGICAL PSYCHIATRY, PSYCHOPHARMACOLOGY. *Current Pos:* PROF PSYCHIAT, UNIV SFLA, COL MED, 85-, DIR, CLIN RES, 85-, OFFICE PSYCHIAT RES, 88- *Personal Data:* b Drogheda, Ireland, Mar 23, 47; m 70, Kathleen E Harnett; c Ivan S, Tara H & Dashiell D. *Educ:* Univ Col, Dublin Med Sch, Nat Univ Ireland, MB, 70; Univ SFla, MBA, 95. *Prof Exp:* Psychiat resident, Boston City Hosp, 72-73, Mass Gen Hosp, 73-75; instr psychiat, Harvard Med Sch, 75-80, asst prof, 80-85. *Concurrent Pos:* Clin & res fel psychiat, Harvard Med Sch, 72-75; dir psychosom med clin, Mass Gen Hosp, 75-83, anxiety res, 83-85; vis prof, Can, Japan, S Korea, Taiwan, Peru, Columbia, New York, San Antonio, 75-; sci adv bd mem, Nat Depressive & Manic Depressive Asn, 86-92; consult, Am Psychiat Asn, 87-89. *Mem:* Am Psychiat Asn. *Res:* Biological basis, treatment and diagnosis of anxiety, phobic and depressive disorders. *Mailing Add:* Univ SFla 3515 E Fletcher Ave Tampa FL 33613. *Fax:* 813-979-3511; *E-Mail:* dsheehan@com1.med.usf.edu

SHEEHAN, DESMOND, ORGANIC CHEMISTRY. *Current Pos:* RETIRED. *Personal Data:* b Aldershot, Eng, Apr 8, 31; m 56; c 4. *Educ:* Univ Reading, BSc, 55; Yale Univ, MS, 61, PhD(chem), 64. *Prof Exp:* Exp officer, Ministry Supply, Eng, 55-56; res chemist, Microcell Ltd, 56-58 & Am Cyanamid Co, Conn, 58-65; dir res, Techni-Chem Co, Conn, 65-70; sr res assoc, Allied Chem Corp, Morristown, 70-72, mgr org res, Corp Res Lab, 72-79, sr scientist, Corp Technol, Off Sci Technol, 80-86. *Mem:* Fel Am Chem Soc; The Royal Chem Soc. *Res:* Synthetic organic chemistry; reaction mechanism. *Mailing Add:* 7406 Admiral Dr Alexandria VA 22307-2011

SHEEHAN, JOHN FRANCIS, GENERAL CYTOPATHOLOGY. *Current Pos:* from instr to prof biol, Creighton Univ, 30-49, res assoc prof exfoliative cytol, 48-67, prof biol, 49-88, prof path, Sch Med, 67-88, prof gynec, 75-88, EMER PROF, PATH & BIOL, CREIGHTON UNIV, 88- *Personal Data:* b Portsmouth, NH, July 28, 06; wid; c John T. *Educ:* Univ NH, BS, 28, MS, 30; Univ Iowa, PhD(biol), 45. *Honors & Awards:* Sheehan Hall lectr, Creighton Univ, 84. *Prof Exp:* Asst zool, Univ NH, 28-30. *Concurrent Pos:* Mem adj med staff, St Joseph Hosp, 72, chief, Cytol Lab, 78-84. *Mem:* Sigma Xi; Am Asn Anat; Am Soc Clin Pathologists; Am Soc Cytopath; fel Am Soc Colposcopy & Cervical Pathol; Am Micros Soc; Am Asn Univ Professors; Am Inst Biol Sci. *Res:* Cytology cancer cell; exfoliative gynecologic cytology; colpomicroscopy; ultracentrifuge; cytoplasm. *Mailing Add:* 7300 Graceland Dr No 307A Omaha NE 68134-4341

SHEEHAN, THOMAS JOHN, ENVIRONMENTAL HORTICULTURE. *Current Pos:* asst ornamental horticulturist, Agr Exten Serv, 54-56 & Exp Sta, Univ Fla, 56-63, from asst ornamental horticulturist to ornamental horticulturist, Exp Sta, 63-67, prof, 67-91, chmn, 86-91, EMER PROF ENVIRON HORT, UNIV FLA, 91- *Personal Data:* b Brooklyn, NY, Apr 13, 24; m 50, Marion E Ruff; c Thomas, Peter (deceased) & Marion. *Educ:* Dartmouth Col, AB, 48; Cornell Univ, MS, 51, PhD(floricult, plant breeding & physiol), 52. *Honors & Awards:* Silver Seal Award, Nat Fedn Garden Clubs, 80; Gold Medal, Am Orchid Soc, 95. *Prof Exp:* Asst floricult, Cornell Univ, 48-52; asst horticulturist, Exp Sta, Univ Ga, 52-54. *Concurrent Pos:* Vis prof, Univ Hawaii, 62-63; consult floricult, Food & Agr Orgn, UN, 71, 74-75 & 80, Jaflex, 71-91 & Cypress Gardens, 85-92, AID-Bolivia, 92. *Mem:* Am Hort Soc; hon life mem Am Orchid Soc; Palm Soc; fel Am Soc Hort Sci. *Res:* Nutrition and other cultural factors of orchids; photoperiod and photoperiod-temperature studies and growth tailoring compounds and their use with floricultural crops; Orchidaceae, Amryllidaceae and Zingiberaceae. *Mailing Add:* Dept Environ Hort Univ Fla Gainesville FL 32611

SHEEHAN, WILLIAM C, POLYMER CHEMISTRY. *Current Pos:* CONSULT, 87- *Personal Data:* b Macon, Ga, Oct 31, 25; m 74, Carol; c Bruce, Weslie R, Laura L, Darin & Paticia L. *Educ:* Mercer Univ, AB, 49; Inst Textile Technol, MS, 51; Univ Tenn, PhD(org chem), 56. *Honors & Awards:* New Tech Prod Award, Indust Res, 63. *Prof Exp:* Res chemist, Bibb Mfg Co, Ga, 49 & 51-53; instr chem, Univ Tenn, 55; res chemist, E I du Pont de Nemours & Co, Va, 56-59; head textile sect, Southern Res Inst, 59-62, asst head phys sci div, 62-64, head polymer div, 64-65; dir fiber res, Phillips Petrol Co, Okla, 65-70, dir res, 70-73, tech vpres, 73-79, vpres mkt, Phillips Fibers Corp, 79-86, mem bd dirs, 75-86. *Concurrent Pos:* Mem comt textile functional finishing, Nat Res Coun, 65-74; fel, Inst Textile Technol & Univ Tenn; mem bd dirs, Textile Res Inst, 75-79; mem, Indust Res Inst, 75-79. *Mem:* Am Chem Soc; Am Mgt Asn; AAAS. *Res:* Fiber and polymer chemistry; textile finishing and auxiliaries; production of supertenacity polypropylene fiber; development of protective military clothing; development of nonwoven process and products; new fiber developments. *Mailing Add:* 10 Skipper Lane Salem SC 29676

SHEEHAN, WILLIAM FRANCIS, PHYSICAL CHEMISTRY, QUANTUM CHEMISTRY. *Current Pos:* prof, 55-91, EMER PROF CHEM, SANTA CLARA UNIV, 91- *Personal Data:* b Chicago, Ill, Oct 19, 26; m 53; c 7. *Educ:* Loyola Univ, Ill, BS, 48; Calif Inst Technol, PhD(chem), 52. *Prof Exp:* Chemist, Shell Develop Co, 52-55, chmn dept, 72-79. *Concurrent Pos:* Sabbatical leaves, Univ Sussex, Louis Pasteur Strasbourg Univ. *Mem:* Sigma Xi. *Res:* Quantum chemistry; structural chemistry; valence; thermodynamics; quantum chemistry. *Mailing Add:* 2614 Via Berrenda Santa Fe NM 87505

SHEEHE, PAUL ROBERT, EPIDEMIOLOGY. *Current Pos:* assoc prof biostatist, 65-69, PROF PREV MED, STATE UNIV NY UPSTATE MED CTR, 69- *Personal Data:* b Buffalo, NY, Dec 8, 25; m 48, Genevieve Richert; c 5. *Educ:* Univ Buffalo, BSBA, 48, MBA, 54; Univ Pittsburgh, ScD(biostatist), 59. *Prof Exp:* Statistician, Erie Co Health Dept, NY, 50-52; teaching fel statist, Univ Buffalo, 52-54; statistician, Pratt & Letchworth, 54-57; assoc biostatistician, Roswell Park Mem Inst, 59-65. *Mem:* Fel Am Col Epidemiol; Am Epidemiol Soc. *Res:* Statistics; epidemiol. *Mailing Add:* Dept Prev Med State Univ NY Health Sci Col Med 750 E Adams St Syracuse NY 13210-2306

SHEEHY, MICHAEL JOSEPH, GENE THERAPY, IMMUNOMODULATION. *Current Pos:* SR SCIENTIST, AGRACETUS, INC, 92- *Personal Data:* b Dayton, Ohio, Mar 3, 47; m 70; c 3. *Educ:* Ohio Wesleyan Univ, BA, 68; Univ Wis, PhD(med genetics), 76. *Prof Exp:* Sci dir, Am Red Cross Blood Servs, Badger Region, 85-92. *Concurrent Pos:* Prin investr, Juv Diabetes Found, 82-87, NIH, 84-91, March of Dimes, 85-87 & 88-90, Am Red Cross, 85-92; from adj asst prof to adj assoc prof med, Univ Wis-Madison, 85-93; consult, Heart Transplant Prog, St Lukes Hosp, Milwaukee, 86-89. *Mem:* Am Asn Immunologists; Am Soc Human Genetics. *Res:* Improvement of technology for delivering genes to mammalian cells and tissues, to achieve immunological effects for fighting cancer and infectious disease. *Mailing Add:* Agracetus Inc 8520 University Green Middleton WI 53562. *Fax:* 608-836-9710

SHEEHY, THOMAS W, MEDICINE, HEMATOLOGY. *Current Pos:* DIR, CAMELLIA PAVILION, UNIV ALA MED CTR, 88- *Personal Data:* b Columbia, Pa, May 20, 21; m 44, H Carolyn Moyer; c 4. *Educ:* St Vincent Col, BS, 47; Syracuse Univ, MD, 51; Baylor Col Med, MS, 55; Am Bd Internal Med, dipl, 58. *Prof Exp:* From intern to resident med, Brooke Gen Hosp, US Army, 51-55, asst chief, Walter Reed Gen Hosp, 56-59, chief med div & hemat, Army Trop Res Lab, PR, 59-62, chief, Dept Gastroenterol Res, Walter Reed Army Inst Res, 62-65, med consult, Vietnam, 65-66, chief gen med & dir educ & med res, Walter Reed Gen Hosp, 66-67; prof med & assoc dir, Div Nutrit & Clin Res, Med Ctr, Univ Ala, Birmingham, 67-72, co-chmn, Dept Med, 69-88; chief med serv, Vet Admin Med Ctr, Birmingham, 69-88. *Concurrent Pos:* Studentship, Walter Reed Army Inst Res, 55-56, fel hemat, 56-57; from asst prof to assoc prof, Sch Med, Univ PR, 59-62; assoc prof, George Washington Univ, 63-65; mem, Hemat Study Sect, NIH, 62-65 & 71-75. *Mem:* Am Fedn Clin Res; Am Soc Hemat; Asn Mil Surg US; fel Am Col Physicians; Am Gastroenterol Asn; Sigma Xi; Asn Am Physicians. *Res:* Study of folic acid metabolism, minimal daily requirements; gastroenterology, small bowel metabolism, absorption, function, enzymes; tropical disease, malaria, scrub typhus, tropical sprue. *Mailing Add:* Camellia Pavillon 615 S 18th St Birmingham AL 35233-1924. *Fax:* 205-975-7319

SHEELER, JOHN B(RIGGS), SOIL ENGINEERING, LOADS ON UNDERGROUND CONDUITS. *Current Pos:* RETIRED. *Personal Data:* b Anita, Iowa, Oct 25, 21; m 45, Mary I Squire; c John R, Daniel, Anne, Diane, Robert, James, William & John E. *Educ:* Iowa State Univ, BS, 50, PhD(chem & soil eng), 56. *Prof Exp:* Res assoc, Iowa State Univ, 50-56, asst prof civil eng, 56-59, assoc prof civil & chem eng, 59-88, emer prof, 88. *Concurrent Pos:* Mem, Hwy Res Bd, Nat Acad Sci-Nat Res Coun, 51. *Mem:* AAAS; Am Inst Chem Engrs; Am Chem Soc; Sigma Xi. *Res:* Soil mechanics, engineering and stabilization; physico-chemical phenomena in soils; further development of Marston-Spangler theory of loads on underground conduits. *Mailing Add:* 505 Bel Aire Dr Marshalltown IA 50158

SHEELEY, EUGENE C, AUDIOLOGY. *Current Pos:* RETIRED. *Personal Data:* b Tiffin, Ohio, Jan 4, 33. *Educ:* Heidelberg Col, BA, 54; Western Res Univ, MA, 55; Univ Pittsburgh, PhD(audiol), 64. *Prof Exp:* Audiologist, Cincinnati Speech & Hearing Ctr, 55-60; asst res audiol, Univ Pittsburgh, 61 & 63-64; dir, Hearing Test & Child Study Ctr, NMex Sch Deaf, 64-67; prof, Dept Communicative Dis, Univ Ala, Tuscaloosa, 67-94. *Concurrent Pos:* Asst clin audiol, Univ Pittsburgh, 62; spec instr, Univ Eastern NMex, 65-67; consult, Partlow State Sch & Hosp, Tuscaloosa, 68-74, chmn, Commun Skills Comt, 74-82; consult, Hearing Conserv Progs, Ala Industs, 72-86. *Mem:* Acad Rehabilitative Audiol; Am Speech-Lang-Hearing Asn; Am Auditory Soc; Am Acad Audiol. *Res:* Central auditory masking; noise exposure. *Mailing Add:* Dept Commun Dis Univ Ala Box 870242 Tuscaloosa AL 35487-0242

SHEELY, W(ALLACE) F(RANKLYN), METALLURGICAL ENGINEERING. *Current Pos:* mgr appl res, Mat & Technol Dept, Westinghouse-Hanford Co, 70-76, mgr, Chem Eng Dept, 76-80, mgr Mat Technol, 80-82, ASST MGR TECHNOL, WESTINGHOUSE-HANFORD CO, 82- *Personal Data:* b Albany, NY, Nov 28, 31; m 55; c 2. *Educ:* Rensselaer Polytech Inst, BMetE, 53, MMetE, 56, PhD, 57. *Prof Exp:* Res assoc, Rensselaer Polytech Inst, 53-57; res metallurgist, Union Carbide Metals Co, 57-60; sr metallurgist, Div Res, USAEC, 60-68; sr staff engr, Chem & Metall Div, Pac Northwest Labs, Battelle Mem Inst, 68-69, assoc div mgr, 69-70. *Concurrent Pos:* Dept Com sci & technol fel, 65-66. *Mem:* Am Soc Metals; Am Nuclear Soc. *Res:* Plasticity and mechanical properties; nuclear metallurgy and chemistry. *Mailing Add:* 2900 S Garfield St Kennewick WA 99337

SHEEN, SHUH-JI, TABACCO GENETICS & CHEMISTRY. *Current Pos:* TABACCO CONSULT, 91- *Personal Data:* b Jiangsu, China, Mar 21, 31; m 59, Rosetina Y Hsu; c Vida, Vernon, Vera, Volney & Vidal. *Educ:* Chung Hsing Univ, Taiwan, BS, 53; NDak State Univ, MS, 58; Univ Minn, PhD(plant genetics), 62. *Honors & Awards:* Hon Prof, Shandong Agr Univ, China, 87. *Prof Exp:* Asst agron, Chung Hsing Univ, Taiwan, 54-56; asst prof biol, Hanover Col, 62-66; from asst prof to assoc prof agron, Univ Ky, 66-74, assoc prof, 74-79, prof plant path, 79-91. *Concurrent Pos:* NSF acad res exten grant, 65-66; USDA contract grants tobacco & health probs, 67-82. *Mem:* AAAS; Am Chem Soc; Inst Food Technologists; Am Phytopath Soc; Soc Green Veg Res. *Res:* Plant biomass utilization with specific interest on the isolation and modification of leaf protein from tobacco and soybean; formulation of safer tobacco products. *Mailing Add:* 404 Lakeshore Dr Lexington KY 40502. *Fax:* 606-266-3274

SHEER, M LANA, PHYSICAL CHEMISTRY, POLYMER CHEMISTRY. *Current Pos:* res chemist, E I Du Pont de Nemours & Co, Inc, 73-77, tech specialist, 77-79, prod specialist, 79-80, financial anal, 81-83, market res, 83-85, market develop, 85-90, ELEC PROGS MGR, E I DU PONT DE NEMOURS & CO, INC, 91- *Personal Data:* b Brooklyn, NY, June 14, 45; m 78. *Educ:* Emory Univ, BS, 65, MS, 67, PhD(phys chem), 69. *Prof Exp:* Res chemist, Stauffer Chem Co, 69-73. *Mem:* Soc Advan Mat Process Eng; Am Chem Soc; Sigma Xi. *Res:* Nuclear magnetic resonance; infrared and ultraviolet spectroscopy; computer applications to molecular spectral theory; Raman spectroscopy; applications of spectroscopy to polymeric materials; development of thermoplastic engineering materials; process development for injection molded engineering plastics; market and product management of injection molded engineering plastics; financial forecasting, advanced composites and engineering polymers market development. *Mailing Add:* E I Du Pont de Nemours PO Box 80713 Wilmington DE 19880-0713

SHEERAN, PATRICK JEROME, PESTICIDE CHEMISTRY. *Current Pos:* res supvr process develop, Biochem Dept, Exp Sta, E I Du Pont De Nemours & Co, Inc, 68-87, PRIN RES SCIENTIST, DU PONT MERCK PHARMACOL, 87- *Personal Data:* b Meade Co, Ky, Aug 29, 42; m 63; c 4. *Educ:* Bellarmine Col, BS, 64; Univ Vt, PhD(chem), 68. *Res:* Organic synthesis involving 4-8 membered heterocycles; biologically active organic compounds. *Mailing Add:* 538 Church Hill Rd Landenberg PA 19350

SHEERS, WILLIAM SADLER, MEDICAL PHYSICS, ENGINEERING. *Current Pos:* ASSOC PROF PHYSICS, WASHINGTON & JEFFERSON COL, 85- *Personal Data:* b Pittsburgh, Pa, Oct 28, 48. *Educ:* Washington & Jefferson Col, BA, 71; WVa Univ, MS, 75; Univ NMex, PhD(physics), 84. *Prof Exp:* Res fel, Baylor Col Med, 83-85. *Concurrent Pos:* Consult. *Mem:* Am Phys Soc; Inst Elec & Electronics Engrs. *Res:* Medical physics/engineering. *Mailing Add:* Dept Physics Washington Jefferson Col 60 S Lincoln St Washington PA 15301-4812. *Fax:* 412-223-5271; *E-Mail:* sheers@cpnsca.psc.edu

SHEETS, DONALD GUY, chemistry, for more information see previous edition

SHEETS, GEORGE HENKLE, PAPER CHEMISTRY, CHEMICAL ENGINEERING. *Current Pos:* RETIRED. *Personal Data:* b Washington Court House, Ohio, Apr 22, 15; m 41, Margaret Muenchow; c Cynthia (Webster) & Karen (Campbell). *Educ:* Ohio State Univ, BChE, 37; Inst Paper Chem, MS, 39, PhD(chem), 41. *Prof Exp:* Develop engr res & develop, Mead Corp, 41-50, div mgr oper mgt, 50-60, managing dir, 60-61, exec vpres corp mgt, 62-80. *Mem:* fel Tech Asn Pulp & Paper Indust (pres, 69-70); Can Pulp & Paper Asn. *Res:* Pulping; papermaking. *Mailing Add:* 60 Harman Terr Dayton OH 45419

SHEETS, HERMAN E(RNEST), MECHANICAL & OCEAN ENGINEERING. *Current Pos:* prof ocean eng & chmn dept, 69-80, EMER PROF, UNIV RI, 80- *Personal Data:* b Dresden, Ger, Dec 24, 08; nat US; m 42, 82, Paulann Hosler; c Lawrence E, Michael R, Arne H, Diana E, Elizabeth J & Karn S (Ryken). *Educ:* Dresden Tech Univ, dipl, 34; Prague Tech Univ, DrTechSci(appl mech), 36. *Prof Exp:* Dir res, St Paul Eng & Mfg Co, Minn, 42-44; proj engr, Elliott Co, Pa, 44-46; eng mgr, Goodyear Aircraft Corp, Ohio, 46-53; dir res & develop, Elec Boat Div, Gen Dynamics Corp, 53-66, vpres eng & res, 66-69. *Concurrent Pos:* Mem marine bd, Nat Acad Eng; mem, Nat Acad Sci-Nat Acad Eng sci & eng adv comt to Nat Oceanic & Atmospheric Admin; consult engr, 80- *Mem:* Nat Acad Eng; fel Am Soc Mech Engrs; Soc Naval Archit & Marine Engrs; Am Soc Naval Engrs-Am Inst Aeronaut & Astronaut. *Res:* Ocean engineering systems; hydrodynamics. *Mailing Add:* 87 Neptune Dr Groton CT 06340. *Fax:* 860-572-8266; *E-Mail:* jcn9000@aol.com

SHEETS, JOHN WESLEY, JR, MEDICAL DEVICES & DIAGNOSIS. *Current Pos:* sr dir develop, 95-97, SR DIR RES & DEVELOP, ALCON LABS INC, 97- *Personal Data:* m 87, Robin Ritchie; c Camille Barbara. *Educ:* Univ Fla, BS, 75, MS, 78, PhD(mat sci), 83. *Prof Exp:* Biomat engr & mgr, Intermedics Intraocular, 82-86; dir res, Pharmacia Opthalmics, 86-88; dir prod & process develop, Johnson & Johnson Co, 88-94. *Concurrent Pos:* Lectr, Calif Polytech, 83; instr, Univ NTex Health Sci Ctr, 96. *Mem:* Am Chem Soc; Soc Biomat; Mat Soc. *Res:* Research and development of medical devices and surgical products, primarily for opthalmic applications. *Mailing Add:* 4001 Sarita Dr Ft Worth TX 76109. *Fax:* 817-551-6977

SHEETS, RALPH WALDO, ENVIRONMENTAL CHEMISTRY. *Current Pos:* from asst prof to assoc prof, 71-82, PROF CHEM, SOUTHWEST MO STATE UNIV, 82- *Personal Data:* b Point Cedar, Ark, Apr 18, 35; m 89, Doris Files; c R Lincoln & Thomas J. *Educ:* Henderson State Col, BS, 66; Univ Ark, MS, 69, PhD(phys chem), 71. *Prof Exp:* Fel surface chem, Ames Lab, AEC, 70-71. *Concurrent Pos:* Sci translr Russ, Consults Bur, Plenum Publ Corp, 71-, Faraday Press Inc, 71-72 & Allerton Press Inc, 72-76. *Mem:* Am Chem Soc; Am Nuclear Soc; Air & Waste Mgt Asn; Water Pollution Control Fedn; Sigma Xi. *Res:* Indoor air pollution; infrared and ultraviolet spectroscopy of adsorbed species; atmospheric radioactivity. *Mailing Add:* Dept Chem Southwest Mo State Univ Springfield MO 65804-0089

SHEETS, ROBERT CHESTER, METEOROLOGY. *Current Pos:* CONSULT METEOROL, 95- *Personal Data:* b Marion, Ind, June 7, 37; m 59; c 3. *Educ:* Ball State Teachers Col, BS, 61; Univ Okla, MS, 65, PhD(meteorol), 72. *Prof Exp:* Chief forecaster, USAF Air Weather Serv, Ft Knox, Ky, 61-64; asst meteorol, Univ Okla, 64-65; res meteorologist, Nat Oceanic & Atmospheric Admin, US Dept Com, 65-74, supvry meteorologist, Environ Res Lab, Nat Hurricane & Exp Meteorol Lab & actg chief Hurricane Group, 75-88; dir, Nat Hurricane Ctr, 88-95. *Mem:* Am Meteorol Soc; Weather Modification Asn. *Res:* Experimental and theoretical research on the formation, motion, intensity, scale interactions and structure of hurricanes and other tropical storms; emphasis on hurricane modification schemes and evaluation techniques. *Mailing Add:* 1726 Lake Clay Dr Lake Placid FL 33852

SHEETS, THOMAS JACKSON, AGRICULTURAL CHEMISTRY, PESTICIDES. *Current Pos:* assoc prof entom & crop sci, NC State Univ, 65-69, prof entom, crop sci, & hort sci, 69-92, toxicol, 89-92, EMER PROF ENTOM, CROP SCI & HORT SCI, NC STATE UNIV, 92- *Personal Data:* b Asheville, NC, Dec 11, 26; m 52; c 2. *Educ:* NC State Col, BS, 51, MS, 54; Univ Calif, PhD, 59. *Prof Exp:* Res instr, NC State Col, 51-54; res agronomist,

Agr Res Serv, USDA, Calif, 54-59, plant physiologist, Delta Br Exp Sta, Miss, 59-60 & Md, 60-65. *Concurrent Pos:* Ed, Weed Sci, 71-73; Ed-in-chief, Weed Sci Soc Am, 74-78; dir, Pesticide Res Lab, 79. *Mem:* Coun Agr Sci & Technol; fel Weed Sci Am (vpres, 80, pres-elect, 81, pres, 82); Sigma Xi; Soil Weed Sci Soc. *Res:* Movement, persistence and modes of detoxification of pesticides; pesticide residues. *Mailing Add:* 1518 Delmont Dr Raleigh NC 27606

SHEETZ, DAVID P, PHYSICAL CHEMISTRY. *Current Pos:* Res chemist, 52-56, proj leader, 56-59, group leader, 59-65, asst lab dir, 65-66, lab dir, 66-67, asst dir res & develop, Midland Div, 67-71, dir res & develop, Mich Div, 71-78, tech dir, 78, vpres & dir, 78-80, corp dir res & develop, 80-85, SR VPRES & CHIEF SCIENTIST, DOW CHEM CO, 86- *Personal Data:* b Colebrook, Pa, Dec 4, 26; m 46; c 3. *Educ:* Lebanon Valley Col, BS, 48; Univ Nebr, MS, 51, PhD(chem), 52. *Concurrent Pos:* Mem, Coun Chem Res. *Mem:* Am Chem Soc; Sigma Xi; Am Inst Chemists; Indust Res Inst; Soc Chem Indust. *Res:* Polymer, colloid and organic chemistry. *Mailing Add:* 1201 W St Andrews Rd Midland MI 48640-9437

SHEETZ, MICHAEL PATRICK, CELL MOTILITY. *Current Pos:* PROF CELL BIOL, SCH MED, WASH UNIV, 85-, CHMN DEPT, 90- *Personal Data:* b Dec 11, 46; m; c Jonathan, Jennifer & Courtney. *Educ:* Calif Inst Technol, PhD(chem), 72. *Concurrent Pos:* Univ Conn Health Ctr, 75-85. *Mem:* Am Soc Cell Biol; Biophys Soc. *Res:* Studying the molecular basis of intracellular organelle motility and the biophysical basis of motor enzyme function. *Mailing Add:* Dept Cell Biol Duke Univ Med Ctr PO Box 709 Durham NC 27710-0001. *Fax:* 919-684-8592; *E-Mail:* mike_sheetz@cellbio.duke.edu

SHEFER, JOSHUA, ELECTRICAL ENGINEERING. *Current Pos:* RETIRED. *Personal Data:* b Leipzig, Ger, Nov 1, 24; US citizen; m 50, Sarah Porath; c Ruth, David & Abigail. *Educ:* Israel Inst Technol, BSc, 48; Univ London, PhD(elec eng), 55. *Prof Exp:* Res engr, Electronics Res Lab, Israeli Ministry Defence, 48-52 & 56-58; sci attache, Israeli Embassy, London, 58-60; res fel, Harvard Univ, 60-62; mem tech staff, Bell Tel Labs, 62-67; mem tech staff, RCA Labs, GE-Astro, 67-86, staff engr, 86-91. *Concurrent Pos:* Lectr microwave theory & technol, Israel Inst Technol, 57-58; consult, Foxbro Co, Mass, 61-62. *Mem:* Inst Elec & Electronics Engrs; Sigma Xi. *Res:* Electromagnetic theory; antenna and propagation studies; microwaves; mobile radio; display devices; television systems; satellite communications. *Mailing Add:* 223 Gallup Rd Princeton NJ 08540. *E-Mail:* sheferj@aol.com

SHEFER, SARAH, LIPID METABOLISM, ARTERIOSCLEROSIS. *Current Pos:* Assoc prof, 79-83, PROF DIGESTIVE DIS, MED SCH, UNIV MED & DENT NJ, 83- *Personal Data:* b Tel Aviv, Israel, Oct 6, 26; US citizen; m; c 3. *Educ:* London Univ, PhD(biochem), 56. *Mem:* Am Heart Asn; Am Inst Nutrit; Am Soc Biol Chemists; AAAS. *Res:* Lipid metabolism. *Mailing Add:* Dept Med MSB-H-534 Univ Med Dent NJ Med Sch 185 S Orange Ave Newark NJ 07103-2714. *Fax:* 973-982-6761

SHEFFER, ALBERT L, CLINICAL IMMUNOLOGY, ALLERGY. *Current Pos:* DIR ALLERGY CLIN, BRIGHAM & WOMEN'S HOSP, BOSTON, 71- *Personal Data:* b Lewistown, Pa, Aug 7, 29; m 54, Barbara Church; c 4. *Educ:* Franklin & Marshall Col, BS, 52; George Washington Univ, MD, 56. *Prof Exp:* Fel pulmonary dis, Grad Hosp & Henry Phipps Inst, Univ Pa, 57-58; res med, Grad Hosp, Univ Pa, Philadelphia, 58-60; fel appl immunol & allergy, Med Ctr, Temple Univ, 61; attend physician, Rockefeller Univ Hosp, 61-62; guest investr, Rockefeller Univ, 62; clin prof, Harvard Med Sch, 66; dir allergy clin, Beth Israel Hosp, Boston, 69-85. *Concurrent Pos:* Allergy sect chief, New Eng Deaconess Hosp, Boston, 72-; asst allergy, Children's Hosp Med Ctr, Boston, 74-; consult, US Pharmacopeia, 75-; dir allergy training prog, Brigham & Women's Hosp, Boston, 76-; chmn, NHCBI/WHO, Global Strategy of Asthma. *Mem:* Am Acad Allergy; Am Fed Clin Res; Asn Am Physicians. *Res:* Pathogenesis and treatment of asthma, anaphylaxis, urticaria, and angioedema. *Mailing Add:* Brigham & Women's Hosp 75 Francis St Boston MA 02115. *Fax:* 617-731-2748; *E-Mail:* alsheffer@bics.bwh.howard.edu

SHEFFER, HOWARD EUGENE, organic chemistry, for more information see previous edition

SHEFFER, RICHARD DOUGLAS, CYTOGENETICS, BIOSYSTEMATICS. *Current Pos:* asst prof, 77-81, ASSOC PROF GENETICS, IND UNIV NORTHWEST, 81- *Personal Data:* b Portland, Ind, Apr 19, 47; m 69; c 1. *Educ:* Purdue Univ, BS, 70; Univ Hawaii, PhD(bot), 74. *Prof Exp:* Res assoc, Univ Hawaii, 74-75; asst prof, Univ NB, 75-76; instr, Montclair State Col, 76-77. *Concurrent Pos:* Res assoc, Mo Bot Garden, 79- *Mem:* AAAS; Am Genetics Asn; Am Bot Soc; Int Asn Plant Taxon; Am Genetics Soc. *Res:* Cytogenetics and cytotaxonomy of the genus anthurium. *Mailing Add:* 208 Shorewood Dr Valparaiso IN 46383-8007

SHEFFI, YOSEF, TRANSPORTATION SYSTEMS, OPERATIONS RESEARCH. *Current Pos:* From asst prof to assoc prof, 78-89, PROF TRANSP SYST, MASS INST TECHNOL, 89- *Personal Data:* b Jerusalem, Israel. *Educ:* Israel Inst Technol, BSc, 75; Mass Inst Technol, SM, 77, PhD(transp), 78. *Concurrent Pos:* Sr oper res analyst, Transp Syst Ctr, US Dept Transp, 78-79; consult, 78-81. *Mem:* Transp Res Bd; Oper Res Soc Am; Inst Transp Engrs. *Res:* Transportation systems analysis; travel demand models; network analysis; performance of transportation facilities. *Mailing Add:* Dept Civil Eng Mass Inst Technol 77 Massachusetts Ave Cambridge MA 02139

SHEFFIELD, ANN ELIZABETH, SURFACE CHARACTERIZATION OF ATMOSPHERIC PARTICLES, TRANSPORT & FATE OF AIR POLLUTANTS. *Current Pos:* ASST PROF CHEM, ALLEGHENY COL, 88- *Personal Data:* b Leicester, UK, Jan 29, 60; US citizen. *Educ:* Johns Hopkins Univ, BA, 81; Univ Md, College Park, PhD(chem), 88. *Prof Exp:* Assoc engr, IBM Corp, 81-83; res asst, Univ Md, College Park, 83-85, teaching asst chem, 88; res chemist, Nat Bur Stand, 85-88. *Mem:* Am Chem Soc. *Res:* Surface properties of atmospheric particles and their interaction with gas-phase organic pollutants; further understanding of how pollutants are transported in the atmosphere and deposited to the Earth's surface. *Mailing Add:* 611 Hickory St Meadville PA 16335-2159. *E-Mail:* asheffie@alleg.edu

SHEFFIELD, HARLEY GEORGE, MEDICAL PARASITOLOGY, ELECTRON MICROSCOPY. *Current Pos:* RETIRED. *Personal Data:* b Detroit, Mich, Jan 10, 32; m 59; c 2. *Educ:* Wayne State Univ, BS, 53, MS, 58; La State Univ, PhD(med parasitol), 62. *Prof Exp:* Res biologist, Parke, Davis & Co, 58-59; from scientist to sr scientist, Nat Inst Allergy & Infectious Dis, NIH, 62-73, scientist dir, Microbiol & Infectious Dis Prog, 73-91. *Mem:* Am Soc Parasitol; Am Soc Trop Med & Hyg; AAAS. *Res:* Electron microscopy of parasitic protozoa, especially toxoplasma and related organisms; electron microscopy of parasitic nematode intestine and other tissues. *Mailing Add:* 11831 Enid Dr Potomac MD 20854

SHEFFIELD, JOEL BENSON, CELL BIOLOGY, DEVELOPMENTAL BIOLOGY. *Current Pos:* from asst prof to assoc prof, 77-89, PROF BIOL, TEMPLE UNIV, 89-, DEPT CHAIR, 90- *Personal Data:* b Brooklyn, NY, Dec 30, 42; m 65; c 1. *Educ:* Brandeis Univ, AB, 63; Univ Chicago, PhD(biol), 69. *Prof Exp:* Guest investr virol, Rockefeller Univ, 63-64; fel cell membranes, Dutch Cancer Inst, 70-71; asst mem virol, Inst Med Res, 71-77. *Concurrent Pos:* Res fel, Int Agency Res Cancer, WHO, 70; Nat Cancer Inst fel, 71; fac assoc, Rutgers Univ, 74- *Mem:* AAAS; Am Soc Cell Biol; Asn Res Vision & Ophthal; Soc Neurosci. *Res:* Structure and biogenesis of cellular and viral membranes; cell-cell interactions in retinal development. *Mailing Add:* Dept Biol Temple Univ Philadelphia PA 19122. *E-Mail:* v5415e@vmm.temple.edu

SHEFFIELD, JOHN, PLASMA PHYSICS. *Current Pos:* assoc dir, 77-88, DIR, FUSION ENERGY DIV, OAK RIDGE NAT LAB, 88- *Personal Data:* b Purley, Eng, Dec 15, 36; m 64, Dace Kancbergs; c 2. *Educ:* London Univ, BSc, 58, MSc, 62, PhD(plasma physics), 66. *Honors & Awards:* Outstanding Achievement Award, Am Nuclear Soc, 90. *Prof Exp:* Exp officer plasma physics, Harwell Lab, UK Atomic Energy Authority, 58-61; Culham Lab, 61-66; asst prof plasma physics, Univ Tex, Austin, 66-71; prin sci officer fusion res, Culham Lab, UK Atomic Energy Authority, 71-77. *Mem:* Fel Am Phys Soc; fel Am Nuclear Soc. *Res:* Magnetic fusion; magnetic confinement schemes; diagnostics and technology for fusion. *Mailing Add:* Oak Ridge Nat Lab PO Box 2008 Oak Ridge TN 37831

SHEFFIELD, L THOMAS, medicine, for more information see previous edition

SHEFFIELD, LEWIS GLOSSON, ENDOCRINOLOGY, REPRODUCTIVE PHYSIOLOGY. *Current Pos:* asst prof, 86-91, DIR, ENDOCRINOL-REPRODUCTIVE PHYSIOL PROG, UNIV WIS-MADISON, 90-, PROF DAIRY SCI, 91- *Personal Data:* b Adel, Ga, Oct 30, 57; m 80, Mary F Tanner. *Educ:* Clemson Univ, MS, 80; Univ Mo, PhD, 83. *Honors & Awards:* First Award, NIH, 88. *Prof Exp:* Assoc, Mich State Univ, East Lansing, 83-86. *Concurrent Pos:* Milk synthesis chair, Am Dairy Sci Asn, 91-92; mem, Comt Mammary Gland Biol. *Mem:* Am Dairy Sci Asn; Endocrine Soc; Sigma Xi. *Res:* Demonstration that epidermal growth factor interacts with estrogen and progesterone to regulate mammary development; demonstration that prolactin causes a decrease in epidermal growth factor-induced growth responses, which appears to be related to mammary gland differentiation. *Mailing Add:* 1675 Observatory Dr Madison WI 53706

SHEFFIELD, RICHARD LEE, FREE-ELECTRON LASERS, ACCELERATOR PHYSICS. *Current Pos:* Staff mem high energy, high-density physics, Los Alamos Nat Lab, 78-82, free electron laser technol, 82-85, dep group leader, 85-89, group leader, accelerator theory & free electron laser technol, 89-93, PROJ LEADER ADV TECH, LOS ALAMOS NAT LAB, 93- *Personal Data:* b Dayton, Ohio, Sept 22, 50; m 79; c 3. *Educ:* Wright State Univ, BS, 72; Mass Inst Technol, PhD(physics), 78. *Honors & Awards:* R&D 100 Award, R&D 100 Mag, 88; Strategic Defense Tech Achievements Award, Strategic Defense Preparedness Asn, 89. *Concurrent Pos:* Adj prof, Physics Dept, Wright State Univ, 86-; partner, Beam Energetics, 86-90; consult, Felcorp, 87-89; lectr, US Accelerator, 89; prin investr, Advan FEL Initiative, Los Alamos Nat Lab, 90-; adv, UV/FEL Adv Panel, Brookhaven Nat Lab, 91- *Mem:* Fel Am Phys Soc. *Res:* Advanced free-electron laser technology initiative; high-brightness electron linac for advanced free-electron laser. *Mailing Add:* MS H851 Los Alamos Nat Lab Los Alamos NM 87545. *E-Mail:* sheff@lanl.gov

SHEFFIELD, ROY DEXTER, MATHEMATICS. *Current Pos:* RETIRED. *Personal Data:* b Dorsey, Miss, Sept 5, 22; m 50. *Educ:* Univ Miss, BA, 48, MA, 49; Univ Tenn, PhD(math), 56. *Prof Exp:* Asst prof math, Univ Miss, 51-56; sr nuclear engr, Gen Dynamics/Convair, 56-57; prof math, Univ Miss, 57-63; prof, Miss State Univ, 63-71; chmn dept math, Univ Miss, 71-77, prof, 71-80. *Concurrent Pos:* Consult, Gen Dynamics/Convair, 57-61. *Mem:* Am Math Soc; Math Asn Am. *Res:* Functional analysis; linear algebra; nonlinear programming. *Mailing Add:* 201 St Andrews Circle Oxford MS 38655

SHEFFIELD, STEPHEN ANDERSON, SHOCK WAVE PHYSICS, HIGH EXPLOSIVE TECHNOLOGY. *Current Pos:* TECH STAFF MEM, LOS ALAMOS NAT LAB, 85- *Personal Data:* b Ogden, Utah, Mar 14, 41; m 62, Cheryl D Nalder; c Sheila, Brett, Craig, Julie, Jannette, Sherry, Rebecca, Allen & Mark. *Educ:* Univ Utah, BS, 65; Univ NMex, MS, 67; Wash State Univ, PhD(eng sci), 78. *Prof Exp:* Mem tech staff, Sandia Nat Labs, 65-71 & 73-85, Ireco Chem, 71-73. *Concurrent Pos:* Consult, Megabar Corp, 85-87. *Mem:* Am Phys Soc; Combustion Inst. *Res:* Relating to shock waves in condensed phase high explosives, reacting liquids and inert materials,; including high explosives initiation and detonation and high pressure equations of state. *Mailing Add:* Group DX-1 MS-P952 Los Alamos Nat Lab Los Alamos NM 87545. *Fax:* 505-667-6372; *E-Mail:* ssheffield@lanl.gov

SHEFFIELD, WILLIAM JOHNSON, PHARMACY. *Current Pos:* RETIRED. *Personal Data:* b Nashua, NH, May 9, 19; m 55; c 3. *Educ:* Univ NC, BS, 42, MS, 49, PhD(pharm), 54. *Prof Exp:* From asst prof to assoc prof, 52-68, prof pharm, Col Pharm, 68-88, asst dean col, 56-58 & 68. *Mem:* AAAS; Acad Pharmaceut Sci; Am Pharmaceut Asn. *Mailing Add:* 1610 Blanchard Dr Round Rock TX 78681

SHEFFY, BEN EDWARD, NUTRITION, MICROBIOLOGY. *Current Pos:* Caspary prof nutrit & asst dir, J A Baker Inst Animal Health, 51-83, EMER PROF, CORNELL UNIV, 83- *Personal Data:* b Luxemburg, Wis, Mar 12, 20; m 48; c 2. *Educ:* Univ Wis, BS, 48, MS, 50, PhD, 51. *Concurrent Pos:* Guggenheim fel, Cambridge Univ, 59-60; NIH spec fel, Univ Munich, 66-67; nutrit consult, NY Zool Soc; consult, Joint Comn Rural Reconstruct, Repub China, 74-75. *Mem:* Brit Nutrit Soc; Am Asn Lab Animal Sci. *Res:* Nutrition and disease interrelationships. *Mailing Add:* James A Baker Inst Animal Health Cornell Univ Ithaca NY 14853

SHEFTER, ELI, DRUG DELIVERY, PHARMACEUTICS. *Current Pos:* ASSOC DIR DEVELOP, CYTEL CORP, 93- *Personal Data:* b Philadelphia, Pa, Sept 10, 36; div; c David & Daniel. *Educ:* Temple Univ, BSc, 58; Univ Wis, PhD(phys pharm & chem), 63. *Prof Exp:* Nat Inst Gen Med Sci fel, 64-65; asst prof, Sch Pharm, State Univ NY, Buffalo, 66-69, assoc prof, 69-81; mgr, Drug Delivery Systs, DuPont, 81-87; sr scientist, Pharm Res & Develop, Genentech Inc, 87-89; prof pharm, Sch Pharm, Univ Colo, 90-92. *Concurrent Pos:* Pfeiffer fel, Am Found Pharmaceut Educ, 72; Norweg Sci Found fel, 80-81. *Mem:* Fel Acad Pharmaceut Sci; Am Pharm Asn; Am Chem Soc; Am Asn Pharmaceut Scientists. *Res:* Correlations of structure and pharmacological activity; phase transformations of solid pharmaceuticals; drug formulation; design of delivery systems for protein and carbohydrates. *Mailing Add:* 2667 Hidden Valley Rd La Jolla CA 92037-4026. *Fax:* 619-552-8801

SHEID, BERTRUM, BIOCHEMISTRY. *Current Pos:* asst prof, 69-75, ASSOC PROF PHARMACOL, STATE UNIV NY, DOWNSTATE MED CTR, 75- *Personal Data:* b Brooklyn, NY, Apr 19, 37. *Educ:* City Col New York, BS, 56; Brooklyn Col, MA, 60; Univ Conn, PhD(biochem), 65. *Prof Exp:* Fel biochem, Col Physicians & Surgeons, Columbia Univ, 65-67; asst prof path, Albert Einstein Col Med, 67-69. *Mem:* AAAS; Am Chem Soc; Am Biol Scientists; NY Acad Sci; Sigma Xi. *Res:* Nucleic acid metabolism in normal and malignant tissues; experimental cancer chemotherapy. *Mailing Add:* Dept Pharmacol State Univ NY Health Sci Ctr Brooklyn Box 29 Brooklyn NY 11203

SHEIKH, MAQSOOD A, PATHOLOGY, MEDICAL SCIENCES. *Current Pos:* LAB DIR & CORP VPRES, NEW YORK LIFE INSURANCE CO, 93- *Personal Data:* b Uttar Pradesh, India, May 7, 47; US citizen; m, Shirin; c Amina & Harris. *Educ:* Punjab Univ, BSc, 70; City Univ NY, MS, 75; PhD(chem), 82. *Prof Exp:* Supvr-mgr, Cabrini Med Ctr, 72-92; fel, City Col NY, 77-78; Queens Col, 78-81; Mt Sinai Sch Med, 82-86 & Rockefeller Univ, 84-86; adj lectr, Hostos Community Col, 81-82; pres & chief exec officer, Clin Path Lab, 86-93. *Mem:* Am Inst Chemists; Am Chem Soc. *Res:* Peptide synthesis and organophosphorus compounds; synthesized peptides and proteins and transforming growth factors. *Mailing Add:* 2 Fulton St Nutley NJ 07110

SHEINAUS, HAROLD, PHARMACY. *Current Pos:* RETIRED. *Personal Data:* b New York, NY, Sept 5, 18; m 49; c 2. *Educ:* City Col New York, BS, 39, Columbia Univ, BS, 49, MS, 51; Purdue Univ, PhD(pharm, pharmaceut chem), 55. *Prof Exp:* Instr pharm, Columbia Univ, 51-52; dir develop & process lab, Carroll Dunham Smith Pharmacol Co, 54-60; sr scientist, Warner-Lambert Res Inst, 61-63; dept head pharmaceut res & develop, 64-70, dir pharmaceut prod develop, 70-79, dir concept develop, Prod Div, Bristol-Myers Co, 79-81. *Concurrent Pos:* Vpres adv coun, County Off on Aging, 84-86; mem & chmn, Educ Comt, 83-91. *Mem:* Am Pharmaceut Asn; Acad Pharmaceut Sci; Sigma Xi. *Res:* Application of new developmental materials and techniques to pharmacy; aerosol pharmaceuticals; emulsions; sustained action formulations; preservatives; effervescent products; solubilization techniques. *Mailing Add:* 132 Wildwood Terr Watchung NJ 07060

SHEINBERG, HASKELL, POWDER METALLURGY, PARTICULATE MATERIAL TECHNOLOGY. *Current Pos:* staff mem, 46-81, LAB FEL, LOS ALAMOS NAT LAB, 82- *Personal Data:* b Houston, Tex, Dec 12, 19; m 46, Beatrice Freeman; c 2. *Educ:* Rice Univ, BS, 41. *Prof Exp:* Fel, Consolidated Steel, 41-43; engr, US Army, 43-45. *Concurrent Pos:* Fel, Los Alamos Nat Lab. *Mem:* Fel Am Soc Metals; Am Powder Metall Inst; emer mem Am Ceramic Soc; Metall Soc. *Res:* Powder metallurgy and particulate materials, ceramics, composites, high temperature superconductor materials, anisotropic materials and cermets; methods of consolidating and fabricating these materials. *Mailing Add:* Los Alamos Nat Lab G770 PO Box 1663 Los Alamos NM 87545. *Fax:* 505-667-5268

SHEINESS, DIANA KAY, RETROVIRUSES, RETROVIRAL ONCOGENES. *Current Pos:* ASST PROF BIOCHEM, LA STATE MED CTR, 81- *Personal Data:* b Corpus Christi, Tex, Oct 1, 47. *Educ:* Univ Tex, Austin, BA, 67; Columbia Univ, MA, 73, PhD(cell biol), 74. *Prof Exp:* Fel genetics, Univ Edinburgh, Scotland, 74-75 & microbiol, Med Sch, Univ Calif, 76-81. *Mem:* Am Soc Microbiol; Sigma Xi. *Res:* Elucidating the function in normal cells of genes that have served as progenitors for retroviral oncogenes. *Mailing Add:* 17608 Clover Rd Bothell WA 98012

SHEINGOLD, ABRAHAM, ELECTRONICS. *Current Pos:* from asst prof to assoc prof, 46-54, dean, Acad Admin, 77-82, PROF ELECTRONICS, US NAVAL POSTGRAD SCH, 54- *Personal Data:* b New York, NY, Feb 17, 17; m 41; c 2. *Educ:* City Col New York, BS, 36, MS, 37. *Prof Exp:* Instr high schs, NY, 36-43; instr elec commun, Mass Inst Technol, 43-46. *Mem:* Inst Elec & Electronics Engrs. *Mailing Add:* 3281 Trevis Way Carmel CA 93923

SHEINGORN, MARK, MATHEMATICS. *Current Pos:* from asst prof to assoc prof, 73-82, PROF MATH, BARUCH COL, 82- *Personal Data:* b New York, NY, Dec 3, 44; m 72, Longhoks. *Educ:* Dartmouth Col, AB, 65; Univ Wis-Madison, MS, 67, PhD(math), 70. *Prof Exp:* Nat Res Coun fel, Nat Bur Standards, 70-72; asst prof math, Hofstra Univ, 72-73. *Concurrent Pos:* NASA fel, Univ Wis, 66-68; NSF grant, 73-84; vis mem, Inst Advan Study, Princeton, 74-75, 81 & 85-86; vis lectr, Univ Ill, Urbana, 78-79; vis prof, State Univ NY, Stony Brook, 82-83, Princeton Univ, 89-90; NAS exchange scientist, Polish Acad, Warsaw, 90; vis fel, Macquarie Univ, Australia, 92. *Mem:* Am Math Soc. *Res:* Analytic number theory; Riemann surfaces. *Mailing Add:* 1200 Broadway New York NY 10001-4317. *Fax:* 212-447-3076; *E-Mail:* mark@gursey.baruch.cuny.edu

SHEININ, ERIC BENJAMIN, PHARMACEUTICAL CHEMISTRY, ANALYTICAL CHEMISTRY. *Current Pos:* Res chemist anal & pharmaceut chem, 71-79, SUPVRY CHEMIST, FOOD & DRUG ADMIN, 79- *Personal Data:* b Chicago, Ill, Dec 23, 43; m 65, 76, Gail Mesmer; c David, Aaron, Todd, Courtney & Melissa. *Educ:* Univ Ill, Urbana, BS, 65; Univ Ill Med Ctr, PhD(pharmaceut chem), 71. *Concurrent Pos:* Adj prof chem, Montgomery Col, Rockville, Md. *Mem:* Am Chem Soc; Am Asn Pharm Sci; Asn Off Anal Chemists. *Res:* Use of nuclear magnetic resonance spectroscopy and mass spectrometry; development of methodology for the analysis of pharmaceutical preparations; laboratory evaluation of analytical methodology included in new drug applications. *Mailing Add:* Food & Drug Admin HFD-160 5600 Fishers Lane Rockville MD 20857. *Fax:* 301-443-9281

SHEININ, ROSE, BIOCHEMISTRY, VIROLOGY. *Current Pos:* PROF BIOL & VICE RECTOR ACAD, CONCORDIA UNIV, 89- *Personal Data:* b Toronto, Ont, May 18, 30; m 51; c 3. *Educ:* Univ Toronto, BSc, 51, MSc, 53, PhD(biochem), 56. *Hon Degrees:* DSc, Mt St Vincent Univ, 85; LHD & DSc, Acadia Univ, 87; DSc, Guelph Univ, 91. *Prof Exp:* Res assoc tumor virol, Ont Cancer Inst, 58-76; from asst prof to assoc prof med biophys, Univ Toronto, 67-75, chmn dept, 75-81, prof microbiol & parasitol, 75-81, prof microbiol, 81-89. *Concurrent Pos:* Fel, Brit Empire Cancer Campaign, 56-58; vis prof, Med Res Coun, 72, sci officer, 74-; Josiah Macy Jr fac scholar award, 81-82; vdean, Sch Grad Studies, Univ Toronto, 84-89. *Mem:* Can Biochem Soc (pres, 75); Can Soc Cell Biol (pres, 73); Am Soc Microbiol; fel Am Acad Microbiol; fel Royal Soc Can; Am Soc Virol. *Res:* Tumor virology; chromatin structure and replication; biochemical genetics; somatic cell genetics; women in medical sciences and medicine. *Mailing Add:* 28 Inglewood Dr Toronto ON M4T 1G8 Can. *Fax:* 514-848-8766

SHEINSON, RONALD SWIREN, COMBUSTION & PHYSICAL CHEMISTRY, ATMOSPHERIC ENVIRONMENTAL SCIENCES. *Current Pos:* RES CHEMIST, US NAVAL RES LAB, NAVY TECHNOL CTR SAFETY & SURVIVABILITY, 70- *Personal Data:* b Philadelphia, Pa, Dec 16, 42; m 68, Harriet Krasnow; c 2. *Educ:* Temple Univ, BA, 64; Mass Inst Technol, PhD(chem physics), 70. *Honors & Awards:* Stratospheric Ozone Protection Award, Environ Protection Agency, 96. *Concurrent Pos:* US Rep, UN Environ Prog, Halon Tech Options Cmt. *Mem:* Sigma Xi; Am Chem Soc; Combustion Inst. *Res:* Combustion suppression; fire extinguishment; halon replacement, gas phase oxidation mechanisms; spectroscopy chemiluminescence; electron paramagnetic resonance. *Mailing Add:* 809 N Belgrade Rd Silver Spring MD 20902-3245. *Fax:* 202-767-1716

SHEKELLE, RICHARD BARTEN, EPIDEMIOLOGY. *Current Pos:* PROF EPIDEMIOL, SCH PUB HEALTH, UNIV TEX, 83- *Personal Data:* b Ventura, Calif, Mar 24, 33; m 52; c 5. *Educ:* Univ Chicago, AB, 52, AM, 58, PhD(human develop), 62. *Prof Exp:* Res assoc psychiat, Univ Ill, Chicago, 59-61, res assoc prev med, 61-65, from instr to assoc prof, 65-74; from assoc prof to prof prev med, Rush-Presby-St Luke's Med Ctr, 74-83. *Mem:* Soc Epidemiol Res; Am Epidemiol Soc. *Res:* Epidemiology of cardiovascular diseases and cancer. *Mailing Add:* 7859 Portal Dr Houston TX 77071. *Fax:* 713-794-4876

SHELANSKI, MICHAEL L, NEUROPATHOLOGY, NEUROSCIENCES. *Current Pos:* DELAFIELD PROF & CHMN, DEPT PATH, COL PHYSICIANS & SURGEONS, COLUMBIA UNIV, 87-; DIR, PATH SERV, PRESBY HOSP, 87-, DIR ALZHEIMER'S DIS RES CTR, 89- *Personal Data:* b Philadelphia, Pa, Oct 5, 41; m 63; c Howard, Samuel & Noah. *Educ:* Univ Pennsylvania, MD, 66, PhD(physiol), 67. *Prof Exp:* Intern path, Albert Einstein Col Med, 67-68, fel neuropath, 68-69, asst prof, 69-71; staff investr neurobiol, Lab Biochem Genetics, Nat Heart & Lung Inst, 71-73; Guggenheim fel, Inst Pasteur, Paris, 73-74; assoc prof neuropath, Harvard Med Sch, 74-78; prof pharmacol & chmn dept, Med Sch, NY Univ, 78-86.

Concurrent Pos: Nat Inst Neurol Dis & Stroke teacher-investr award, 70-71 & 73-74, asst prof in residence, Col, 71-73; mem, Neurol A Study Sect, NIH, 74-78 & Pharmacol Sci Study Sect, Nat Inst Gen Med Sci,86-; mem, Med & Sci Adv Bd, Alzheimer's Dis & Related Dis Asn, 85-93; chmn, Sci Adv Panel, NY Overhead Power Lines Proj, 81-86 & Zenith Awards Comt, Alzheimer's Asn, 93- *Mem:* Am Soc Cell Biol; Am Asn Neuropath; Am Soc Neurochem; Soc Neurosci. *Res:* Microtubule and neurofilaments; physical biochemistry of self-assembly; chemistry of senile and pre-senile dementias; neuronal differentiation. *Mailing Add:* Dept Path Columbia Univ Col P&S 630 W 168th St New York NY 10032-3702. *Fax:* 212-305-5498; *E-Mail:* shelans@cpath.cpmc.columbia.edu

SHELBURNE, JOHN DANIEL, PATHOLOGY. *Current Pos:* intern, Duke Univ, 72-73, from asst prof to assoc prof path, 73-85, dept chmn protem, 89-91, PROF PATH, MED CTR, DUKE UNIV, 85- *Personal Data:* b Washington, DC, Aug 27, 43; m 66, Katherine Parrish; c Mark & Kerri. *Educ:* Univ NC, Chapel Hill, AB, 66; Duke Univ, PhD(path), 71, MD, 72. *Honors & Awards:* William Myles Shelley Mem lectr, 85; Florey Mem lectr, Univ Adelaide, Australia, 88. *Prof Exp:* Assoc dir, Vet Admin Hosp, Durham, 73-77, dir, Diag Electron Micros Lab, 77-93. *Concurrent Pos:* Assoc chief of staff res & develop & chief lab sci, Vet Admin Med Ctr, Durham, NC, 82-91, assoc chief staff opers, 91- *Mem:* Int Acad Path; Am Asn Pathologists; Micros Soc Am; Microbeam Analysis Soc; Col Am Pathologists. *Res:* Lysosomes; autophagy; surgical pathology; x-ray microanalysis; ion microscopy. *Mailing Add:* Dept Path Box 3712 Duke Univ Med Ctr Durham NC 27710. *Fax:* 919-286-6818

SHELBY, JAMES ELBERT, GLASS & GLASS CERAMICS, GAS SOLIDS REACTIONS. *Current Pos:* PROF GLASS SCI, NY STATE COL CERAMICS, ALFRED UNIV, 82-, DIR GLASS SCI LAB, 88- *Personal Data:* b Memphis, Tenn, Mar 11, 43; div; c Stephanie R. *Educ:* Univ Mo, Rolla, BS, 65, MS, 67, PhD(ceramic eng). 68. *Hon Degrees:* Univ Mo, 93. *Honors & Awards:* Morey Award, Am Ceramic Soc, 75. *Prof Exp:* Staff mem, Sandia Nat Lab, Livermore, 68-82. *Concurrent Pos:* Chmn, Gordon Res Conf Glass, 85; consult glass, 82-; mem, NAm Thermal Anal Soc, Keramos. *Mem:* Fel Am Ceramic Soc; Soc Glass Technol. *Res:* Glasses and glass-ceramics: diffusion, properties, phase separation, low melting glasses and solar energy; radiation effects, fluorides, heavy metal oxides, thermal analysis, hydroxyl, gas diffusion controlled reactions, optical properties and gases in glasses and melts; author of over 200 publications and 2 books. *Mailing Add:* 1344 Snyder Rd Alfred Station NY 14803. *Fax:* 607-871-2392

SHELBY, NANCY JANE, NEUROENDOCRINE REGULATION OF IMMUNE RESPONSE FOLLOWING TRAUMA, NEUROENDOCRINE REGULATION OF TRANSPLANT REJECTION. *Current Pos:* From res asst to res assoc, 69-93, ADJ ASSOC PROF SOCIOL, UNIV UTAH, 92; RES ASST PROF PSYCHOL, 94-, ASST PROF SURG, 94- *Personal Data:* b Powell, Wyo, May 2, 50; m 81, James H Martin; c Kassia A & Sara N. *Educ:* Univ Utah, BS, 88, MS, 91, PhD(behav immunol & med sociol), 93. *Honors & Awards:* Robert B Lindberg Award, Am Burn Asn, 90. *Concurrent Pos:* Mem, Res Comt, Am Burn Asn, 90-96; adj asst prof, Dept Sociol, Mont State Univ, 92. *Mem:* Int Transplantation Soc; Am Burn Asn; Surg Infection Soc; Int Immunocompromised Host Soc; Shock Soc; AAAS; Am Psychol Asn; Psychoneuroimmunol Res Soc; Int Cytokine Soc; Am Soc Transplant Physicians; NY Acad Sci. *Res:* Host adaptation to trauma, particularly the neuroendocrine regulation of immune response and cytokine production; circadian dysregulation in trauma; author of numerous publications; granted one US patent. *Mailing Add:* Dept Surg Univ Utah 50 N Medical Dr Salt Lake City UT 84132. *Fax:* 801-581-6612; *E-Mail:* jshelby@msscc.med.utah.edu

SHELBY, ROBERT MCKINNON, OPTICAL PHYSICS, SPECTROSCOPY. *Current Pos:* Fel, 78-76, RES STAFF, ALMADEN RES CTR, IBM RES, 79- *Personal Data:* b Ogden, Utah, Aug 11, 50; m 90; c 4. *Educ:* Calif Inst Technol, BS, 72; Univ Calif, Berkeley, PhD(chem), 78. *Concurrent Pos:* Chmn, Western Spectros Asn, 87-88; mem, Quantum Optics Prog Sub comt, Quantum Electronics & Laser Sci Conf, 90-92. *Mem:* Fel Optical Soc Am; Am Phys Soc. *Res:* Laser physics; quantum optics; generation and application of non-classical light beams; dynamics of non-linear optical systems. *Mailing Add:* Dept K18-D1 IBM 650 Harry Rd San Jose CA 95120. *Fax:* 408-927-4098; *E-Mail:* shelby@almaden.ibm.com

SHELBY, T H, geology; deceased, see previous edition for last biography

SHELDAHL, LOIS MARIE, EXERCISE PHYSIOLOGY, CARDIAC REHABILITATION. *Current Pos:* PHYSIOLOGIST, VET ADMIN MED CTR, 78-; ASSOC PROF, MED COL WIS, 90- *Personal Data:* b Radcliffe, Iowa, Jan 29, 43. *Educ:* Concordia Col, BA, 66; Univ Ariz, MEd, 68; Pa State Univ, PhD(exercise physiol), 78. *Prof Exp:* Instr, Anoka Jr High, 66-67; instr/coach, Univ Ariz, 68-74. *Mem:* Am Heart Asn; fel Am Col Cardiol; Am Col Sports Med; Am Physiol Soc; Am Asn Cardiovasc Pulmonary Rehabilitation. *Res:* Evaluation of work potential in patients with heart disease; influence of central blood volume on cardiovascular and neurohormonal responses to exercise. *Mailing Add:* Vet Admin Med Ctr CPRC 111R Milwaukee WI 53295. *Fax:* 414-382-5319

SHELDEN, HAROLD RAYMOND, II, ORGANIC CHEMISTRY. *Current Pos:* Asst prof, 69-74, assoc prof, 74-79, PROF CHEM, LOMA LINDA UNIV, LA SIERRA CAMPUS, 79-, CHMN DEPT, 80- *Personal Data:* b Indianapolis, Ind, July 7, 42; m 65. *Educ:* Loma Linda Univ, BA, 64; Univ Calif, Irvine, PhD(org chem), 69. *Mem:* Am Chem Soc. *Res:* Mechanisms of organic reactions. *Mailing Add:* Dept Chem La Sierra Univ Riverside CA 92515

SHELDEN, ROBERT MERTEN, REPRODUCTIVE PHYSIOLOGY, EMBRYOLOGY. *Current Pos:* asst prof, 76-83, ADJ ASSOC PROF, DEPT OBSTET & GYNEC, ROBERT WOOD JOHNSON MED SCH, 83- *Personal Data:* b Troy, Mont, Mar 23, 38; m 64; c 3. *Educ:* Univ Mont, BA, 64, PhD(zool), 68. *Prof Exp:* Asst prof biol, Moorhead State Col, 68-71; res assoc, Dept Obstet & Gynec, Ohio State Univ, 73-75. *Concurrent Pos:* Minn State Col Bd res grant, 68-69; NIH fel reproductive endocrinol, Dept Obstet & Gynec, Ohio State Univ, 71-73. *Mem:* AAAS; Soc Study Reproduction. *Res:* Endocrine regulation of the uterine environment; immunogenic potentials of primate reproductive organs. *Mailing Add:* Univ Med Group 303 George St No 250 New Brunswick NJ 08903

SHELDON, ANDREW LEE, ZOOLOGY, ECOLOGY. *Current Pos:* from asst prof to assoc prof, 69-77, PROF ZOOL, 78-, DIR WILDLIFE BIOL PROG, UNIV MONT, 90- *Personal Data:* b Greenfield, Mass, Apr 22, 38; m 90; c 2. *Educ:* Colby Col, BA, 60; Cornell Univ, PhD(zool), 66. *Prof Exp:* Asst res zoologist, Sagehen Creek Field Sta, Univ Calif, 64-67; res assoc, Resources for the Future, Inc, 67-69. *Concurrent Pos:* Vis scientist, Oak Ridge Nat Lab, 77-78, Savannah River Ecol Lab, 85-86. *Mem:* Am Soc Naturalists; Ecol Soc Am; NAm Benthological Soc; Am Fisheries Soc; Soc Conserv Biol. *Res:* Community structure and dynamics; comparative ecology; running water biology; biometrics; fishes, aquatic insects. *Mailing Add:* Div Biol Sci Univ Mont Missoula MT 59812-0001

SHELDON, ELEANOR BERNERT, MEDICAL ADMINISTRATION. *Current Pos:* RETIRED. *Personal Data:* b Hartford, Conn, Mar 19, 20. *Educ:* Univ NC, AB, 42; Univ Chicago, PhD, 49. *Prof Exp:* Assoc dir, Chicago Community Inventory, Univ Chicago, 47-50; res assoc & lectr sociol, Univ Calif Los Angeles, 55-62; sociologist & exec assoc, Russell Sage Found, 61-72; mem bd dirs, UN Res Inst Social Develop, 73-79; trustee, Rockefeller Found, 78-85; trustee, Inst E&W Security Studies, Nat Opionion Res Ctr, 84-89. *Mem:* Inst Med-Nat Acad Sci. *Mailing Add:* 630 Park Ave New York NY 10021

SHELDON, ERIC, THEORETICAL NUCLEAR PHYSICS, ASTROPHYSICS. *Current Pos:* univ prof, 85-88, PROF PHYSICS, 70-96, EMER PROF, UNIV MASS, LOWELL, 96- *Personal Data:* b Oct 24, 30; Brit citizen; m 59, Sheila Harper; c Adrian. *Educ:* Univ London, BSc, 51, Hons, 52, PhD(sci), 55, DSc(physics), 71. *Prof Exp:* Lectr & demonstr physics, Acton Tech Col, Eng, 52-55; assoc physicist, IBM Res Lab, Switz, 57-59; res assoc physics, Swiss Fed Inst Technol, 59-63, pvt dozent, 63-64, prof, 64-69; vis prof, Univ Tex, Austin, 69-70. *Concurrent Pos:* NSF sr foreign scientist fel & vis prof, Univ Va, 68-69; chartered chemist, UK, 81-, chartered physicist, 85-; vis prof, Univ Oxford, UK, 89. *Mem:* Fel AAAS; fel Brit Inst Physics; fel Royal Soc Chem; Royal Inst Gt Brit; fel Am Phys Soc; fel Royal Astron Soc. *Res:* Theoretical nuclear physics involving nuclear reaction mechanism and nuclear structure studies in the low and intermediate energy range; astrophysics; cosmology; relativity. *Mailing Add:* Dept Physics Univ Mass Lowell MA 01854-2881. *Fax:* 978-934-3068; *E-Mail:* sheldone@woods.uml.edu

SHELDON, GEORGE FRANK, HEALTH MANPOWER, TRAUMA CARE. *Current Pos:* PROF & CHMN, DEPT SURG, UNIV NC SCH MED, 84- *Personal Data:* b Salina, Kans, Dec 20, 34; m, Ruth Guy; c Anne (Anderson), Julia & Betsy. *Educ:* Univ Kans, BA, 57, MD, 61. *Honors & Awards:* Nat Safety Coun Award, Am Col Surgeons, 93. *Prof Exp:* Asst instr western civilization, Univ Kans, 56-57; fel internal med, Mayo Clin, 64-65; from asst prof to prof, Univ Calif, San Francisco, 71-84. *Concurrent Pos:* Chmn, Am Bd Surg, 89-90. *Mem:* Inst Med-Nat Acad Sci; Am Bd Surg; Am Asn Surg Trauma (pres, 79-81, secy, 84); Am Surg Asn (secy, 89-93,pres, 94); Am Col Surgeons. *Res:* Internal medicine and surgery; metabolism; nutrition. *Mailing Add:* Dept Surg CB 7050 Univ NC Sch Med Chapel Hill NC 27599-7050

SHELDON, HUNTINGTON, PATHOLOGY, MEDICINE. *Current Pos:* from asst prof to assoc prof, 59-66, PROF PATH, MCGILL UNIV, 66-, STRATHCONA PROF, 80- *Personal Data:* b New York, NY, Jan 14, 30; m 86, Adelaide Keppelman; c Karan, Jennifer, Zoe & Greta. *Educ:* McGill Univ, BA, 51; Johns Hopkins Univ, MD, 55. *Hon Degrees:* LLD, McGill Univ, 96. *Prof Exp:* From asst to instr path, Johns Hopkins Univ, 56-59. *Concurrent Pos:* From intern to asst resident, Johns Hopkins Hosp, 56-59; vis prof, Harvard Univ, 72; trustee, Johns Hopkins Univ. *Mem:* Am Soc Cell Biol; Am Soc Exp Path; Biophys Soc; Int Acad Path. *Res:* Application of electron microscopy to problems in pathology. *Mailing Add:* PO Box 697 Shelburne VT 05482-0697. *Fax:* 802-985-3654

SHELDON, JOHN WILLIAM, CHEMICAL PHYSICS, FLUID DYNAMICS. *Current Pos:* assoc prof phys sci, 72-76, chmn dept, 74-86, PROF PHYS, FLA INT UNIV, 76- *Personal Data:* b Miami, Fla, Nov 21, 33; m 79, Olga del Portillo; c William L, John F, John M, Joseph E, James W & Jeffrey A. *Educ:* Purdue Univ, BS, 55, MS, 59; Tex A&M Univ, PhD(nuclear eng), 64. *Prof Exp:* Res engr, NASA, 55, head, Gaseous Electronics Sect, 64-66; from asst prof to assoc prof eng sci, Fla State Univ, 66-72. *Mem:* Am Phys Soc; Am Vacuum Soc. *Res:* Atomic collision phenomena, measurement of collision cross sections by beam techniques; ionospheric flow and probe theory; electrical phenomena accompanying shock waves in two-phase flows; chemical kinetics of explosives. *Mailing Add:* Dept Phys Fla Int Univ Tamiami Trail Miami FL 33199

SHELDON, JOSEPH KENNETH, INSECT ECOLOGY. *Current Pos:* PROF BIOL, MESSIAH COL, 92- *Personal Data:* b Ogden, Utah, Nov 11, 43; m 65, Donna Zielaskowski; c Jodi & Bret. *Educ:* Col Idaho, BS, 66; Univ Ill, PhD(entom), 72. *Prof Exp:* From asst prof to prof biol, Eastern Col, 71-92. *Concurrent Pos:* Fac mem, Au Sable Inst Environ Studies. *Mem:* AAAS; Ecol Soc Am; Am Entom Soc (vpres, 82, pres, 91-); Am Sci Affil; Soc Conserv Biol. *Res:* Insect ecology in general with a specific focus on the conservation insect populations. *Mailing Add:* Dept Natural Sci Messiah Col Grantham PA 17027

SHELDON, RICHARD P, GEOLOGY. *Current Pos:* RETIRED. *Personal Data:* b Tulsa, Okla, Oct 25, 23; m 66. *Educ:* Yale Univ, BS, 50; Stanford Univ, PhD, 56. *Prof Exp:* Geologist, Lion Oil Co, 57-58; from geologist to asst chief geologist, US Geol Serv, Saudi Arabia, 58-72, chief geologist, 72-77, res geologist, 77-82, geologist, US Mission, 82-84. *Concurrent Pos:* Consult, econ geologist, 82- *Mem:* AAAS; Geol Soc Am; Soc Econ Geol; Am Asn Petrol Geologists; Soc Econ Paleontologists & Mineralogists. *Res:* Sedimentary petrology; physical stratigraphy; sedimentary mineral deposits. *Mailing Add:* 3816 T St NW Washington DC 20007

SHELDON, VICTOR LAWRENCE, SOILS, FERTILIZERS. *Current Pos:* PRES, VLS ASSOC, 76- *Personal Data:* b Maysville, Mo, Sept 24, 21; m 46; c 4. *Educ:* Univ Mo, BS, 43, MA, 48, PhD(soils, plant physiol), 50. *Prof Exp:* Asst prof soils, Univ Mo, 52-55; agronomist & consult, Olin Mathieson Chem Corp, 55-61; mgr agr serv, John Deere Chem Co, 61-66; mgr tech serv, Esso Chem Co, Stand Oil, NJ, 66-67; vpres mkt, Esso Pakistan Fertilizer Co, Karachi, 67-69; prof agr & chmn dept, Western Ill Univ, 69-81. *Concurrent Pos:* Leader deleg to CENTO Agr Conf, US State Dept; consult, VLS Assoc, 72-76, Tenn Valley Authority, Int Inst Trop Agr & Int Fertilizer Develop Ctr. *Mem:* Soil Sci Soc Am; Am Soc Plant Physiol; Am Soc Agron; Sigma Xi. *Res:* Efficiency of phosphorus uptake from various compounds; influence of phosphorus on metabolism of plants; biodegradation of pesticides; fatty acids in soybean oil according to planting site and genotype; fertilizer marketing plan for Nigeria; management systems for fertilizer operaters. *Mailing Add:* 221 Wood Chuck Lane Macomb IL 61455

SHELDON, WILLIAM ROBERT, PHYSICS, STRATOSPHERIC CHEMISTRY. *Current Pos:* assoc prof, 68-73, Chair, Dept Physics, 86-88, PROF PHYSICS, UNIV HOUSTON, 73- *Personal Data:* b Ft Lauderdale, Fla, May 17, 27; m 79; c William R J, J Christopher & Olivia. *Educ:* Univ Mo, BS, 50, MS, 56, PhD(physics), 60. *Prof Exp:* Sr physicist, Rocketdyne Div, NAm Aviation, Inc, 60; res specialist space physics, Aerospace Div, Boeing Co, 60-66; res scientist cosmic ray physics, Southwest Ctr Advan Studies, 66-68. *Concurrent Pos:* Proj leader, Joint French-US Cosmic Ray Exped, Mont Blanc Tunnel; proj leader rocket and balloon measurements of x-rays and electric fields at Roberval and Ft Churchill, Can, Ft Yukon, Alaska, Kiruna, Sweden, Siple Sta, Antarctica and the Kerguelen Islands; leader US team, French-USSR ARAKS experiment, 74-75; dept chmn Dept Physics, Univ Houston, 73-; proj leader, Atmospheric Ozone Measurements, 87- *Mem:* Am Phys Soc; Am Geophys Union; Sigma Xi. *Res:* Cosmic rays; high energy muons; auroral particle precipitation; x-rays in the atmosphere; atmospheric ozone. *Mailing Add:* Dept Physics Univ Houston Houston TX 77204-5506. *E-Mail:* sheldon@uh.edu

SHELDRAKE, RAYMOND, JR, horticulture, for more information see previous edition

SHELDRICK, GEORGE MICHAEL, CHEMISTRY CRYSTALLOGRAPHY. *Current Pos:* PROF INORG CHEM, UNIV GOTTINGEN, 78- *Personal Data:* b Huddersfield, Gt Brit, Nov 17, 42; m 68, Katherine E Herford; c 4. *Honors & Awards:* Al Patterson Award, Am Crystallog Asn, 93. *Prof Exp:* Lectr, Cambridge Univ, Eng, 66-78. *Concurrent Pos:* Staff, Inst Inorg Chem. *Res:* Contributed numerous articles to professional journals. *Mailing Add:* Inst Anorganische Chem Tammannstrasse 4 37077 Goettingen Germany

SHELDRICK, PETER, MOLECULAR BIOLOGY, VIROLOGY. *Current Pos:* Sr researcher, 68-77, DIR RES, NAT CTR SCI RES, FRANCE, 77- *Personal Data:* b Newark, NJ, Jan 22, 36; m 91, Ewa Siwiec; c Hugo. *Educ:* Brown Univ, Providence, RI, BA, 58; Univ Calif, Berkeley, PhD(chem), 62. *Concurrent Pos:* Mem, Herpes Virus Study Group, Int Comt Taxon Viruses, 76-87. *Mem:* Europ Molecular Biol Orgn; Am Soc Microbiol; Soc Gen Microbiol Gt Brit; NY Acad Sci. *Res:* Structure and function of herpes virus genomes: DNA base sequence organization; transcription of RNA; in vivo polypeptide synthesis; enzymatic activities. *Mailing Add:* Inst Rech Sci Sur Le Cancer B P No 8 Villejuif Cedex 94801 France

SHELEF, LEORA AYA, FOOD MICROBIOLOGY, FOOD SAFETY. *Current Pos:* res assoc food microbiol, Dept Biol, Wayne State Univ, 67-71, from asst prof to assoc prof food sci, 71-79, actg chair, Dept Family & Consumers Res, 81-83, chair, 83-86, chair, Dept Nutrit & Food Sci, 86-91, PROF FOOD SCI, WAYNE STATE UNIV, 79- *Personal Data:* b Haifa, Israel; US citizen; m 55, Mordecai; c Roy & Dori. *Educ:* Israel Inst Technol, BSc, 56, MSc, 59, DSc (food eng & biotechnol), 63. *Honors & Awards:* Fulbright Sr Lectr, Tallinn Tech Univ, USSR, 90. *Prof Exp:* Postdoctoral res assoc food rheology, Dept Agr Eng, Pa State Univ, 64-66. *Concurrent Pos:* Vis prof, Mercy Col, Detroit, 73 & 76 & Dept Environ Indust Health, Univ Mich, Ann Arbor, 79; NSF fac prof develop award, 78. *Mem:* Am Soc Microbiol; Int Asn Milk Food Environ Sanit; Inst Food Technologists. *Res:* Effect of indirect antimicrobials on food pathogens and spoilage microorganisms such as sodium lactate, lysozyme, nisin and other naturally occurring substances; growth and virulence characteristics of Listeria monocytogenes in meat, fish and similar foods; chemistry and nutrition of soy products. *Mailing Add:* Dept Nutrit & Food Sci Wayne State Univ 160 Old Main Detroit MI 48202-3940

SHELEF, MORDECAI, CATALYSIS, FUEL SCIENCE. *Current Pos:* prin res scientist, Ford Motor Co, 69-73, staff scientist, 73-77, mgr fuels & lubricants dept, 77-81, mgr chem dept, 81-87, SR STAFF SCIENTIST, RES STAFF, FORD MOTOR CO, 87- *Personal Data:* b Suvalki, Poland, June 28, 31; m 55; c 2. *Educ:* Israel Inst Technol, BSc, 56, MSc, 59; Pa State Univ, PhD(fuel sci), 66. *Prof Exp:* Res scientist, Israel Mining Industs, Haifa, 56-63; res asst, Pa State Univ, 63-66. *Mem:* Am Chem Soc; Catalysis Soc. *Res:* Development of new fuel sources; kinetics and mechanism of surface reactions; chemisorption; carbon gasification; mineral dressing; evaluation of energy systems; control of nitrogen oxide emissions. *Mailing Add:* 3033 Morningview Terr Bloomfield Hills MI 48301. *Fax:* 313-248-5627; *E-Mail:* mshelef@smail.srl.com

SHELINE, RAYMOND KAY, NUCLEAR CHEMISTRY. *Current Pos:* assoc prof, 51-55, PROF CHEM, FLA STATE UNIV, 55-, PROF PHYSICS, 59-, ROBERT O LAWTON DISTINGUISHED PROF CHEM & PHYSICS, 67- *Personal Data:* b Port Clinton, Ohio, Mar 31, 22; m 51; c 7. *Educ:* Bethany Col, BS, 43; Univ Calif, PhD(chem), 49. *Honors & Awards:* Niels Bohr Inst Silver Cup; Egyptian Nat Lectr, Eins Shams Univ, Cairo, 56; Am Inst Physics Citation, 63, Alexander von Humboldt sr scientist award, 76; Fla Award, Am Chem Soc, 80. *Prof Exp:* Asst, Bethany Col, 40-42; chemist, Manhattan Proj, Columbia Univ, 43-45; jr scientist, Los Alamos Sci Lab, Univ Calif, 45-46, asst, Univ, 46-49; instr, Inst Nuclear Studies, Univ Chicago, 49-51; res participant, Oak Ridge Inst Nuclear Studies, 51-52. *Concurrent Pos:* Res chemist, Merck Chem Co, 46; Fulbright res prof & Guggenheim fel, Niels Bohr Inst, Coepnhagen, Denmark, 55-56 & 57-58, Ford res prof, 57-58; Guggenheim fel, 64; Nordita prof, Univ Lund & Copenhagen Univ, 71-72; consult, NSF, Los Alamos Sci Lab, Univ Calif & Lawrence Livermore Nat Lab, 61-; Gillon lectureship, Nat Univ Zaire, Kinshasa, 76; res fel, Australian Nat Univ, 82-83; Fulbright prof, Univ Kinshasa, Zaire, 84- *Mem:* Foreign mem Royal Danish Acad Sci & Lett; Am Chem Soc; fel Am Phys Soc. *Res:* Nuclear spectroscopy by decay scheme studies and Van de Graaff excitation; coulomb excitation; correlation of experimental data with nuclear models; muonic x-ray studies; octupole shapes in nuclei. *Mailing Add:* Dept Physics Fla State Univ 210 Nuclear Res Bldg Tallahassee FL 32306. *Fax:* 850-644-9848

SHELKIN, BARRY DAVID, GEOLOGY. *Current Pos:* RETIRED. *Personal Data:* b Brooklyn, NY, Oct 11, 28; m 52; c 3. *Educ:* Brooklyn Col, BS, 55. *Prof Exp:* Cartog aide, US Coast & Geod Surv, 55-56; geologist, Gulf Oil Corp, 56-60, Span Gulf Oil Co, 60-63 & Nigerian Gulf Oil Co, 63-64; sr photointerpreter, Data Anal Ctr, Itek Corp, 64-65; sr scientist, Autometric Oper, Raytheon Co, 65-69, head terrain sci sect, 69-70; chief, Terrain Sci Div, Defense Nuclear Agency, 70-73, chief, Support Div, 73-82, asst chief, Topog Reg Div, 82-89, asst dir tech info, 90-92. *Mem:* Geol Soc Am; Am Asn Petrol Geologists; Int Soc Optical Eng. *Res:* Geological research, terrain, and environmental analysis through the medium of aerial photography; administration of cartographic contracts; technical information management. *Mailing Add:* 8206 Chancery Ct Alexandria VA 22308

SHELL, DONALD LEWIS, MATHEMATICS. *Current Pos:* RETIRED. *Personal Data:* b Worth Twp, Sanilac Co, Mich, Mar 1, 24; m 46, 73; c 2. *Educ:* Mich Technol Univ, BS, 44; Univ Cincinnati, MS, 51, PhD(math), 59. *Prof Exp:* Instr math, Mich Technol Univ, 46-49; mathematician, Gen Elec Co, 51-52, numerical analyst, 52-53, supvr systs anal & synthesis, 53-54, mgr comput tech develop, 54-56, mgr, Evendale Comput, 56-57, comput consult specialist, 57-59, mgr digital anal & comput, Knolls Atomic Power Lab, 60-61, eng math, adv tech lab, 61-63, mgr comput appln & processing telecommun & info processing opers, 63-66, mgr eng, Info Serv Dept, 66-68, mgr automation studies, Res & Develop Ctr, 68-69, mgr info tech planning, 69-71, mgr info servs qual assurance, 71-72; chmn bd & gen mgr, Robotics, Inc, 72-75; mgr file systs, Gen Elec Info Serv Co, 75-76, mgr technol systs, 76-78, mgr appln systs, 78-80, mgr Mark III Systs, 80-84. *Mem:* Math Asn Am; Asn Comput Mach. *Res:* Numerical computation; applications of digital computers; sorting. *Mailing Add:* Box 1029 Lake Junaluska NC 28745-1029

SHELL, EDDIE WAYNE, FISH BIOLOGY. *Current Pos:* RETIRED. *Personal Data:* b Chapman, Ala, June 16, 30; m 53. *Educ:* Auburn Univ, BS, 52, MS, 54; Cornell Univ, PhD(fishery biol), 59. *Prof Exp:* Asst fisheries, Auburn Univ, 52-54 & Cornell Univ, 56-58; asst fish culturist, Auburn Univ, 59-61, assoc prof fisheries, 61-70, prof, 70-94, head dept, 73-94. *Concurrent Pos:* Dir, Int Ctr Aquacult, 73. *Mem:* AAAS; Am Fisheries Soc. *Mailing Add:* Dept Fisheries Swingle Hall Auburn Univ Auburn AL 36849-3501

SHELL, FRANCIS JOSEPH, PHYSICAL CHEMISTRY. *Current Pos:* RETIRED. *Personal Data:* b Medicine Lodge, Kans, Mar 27, 22; m 44, Helen McKinney; c Barbara (Walker), Frances (Barton) & Robert James. *Educ:* Ft Hays Kans State Col, AB & MS, 49; Univ Ky, PhD(phys chem), 53. *Prof Exp:* Res chemist, Phillips Petrol Co, 52-57, asst dir tech serv div, 57-66, mgr tech serv, 66-81, sr chem assoc, 81-85. *Concurrent Pos:* Chmn, Oil Well Cement Comt, Am Petrol Inst, 76-78. *Mem:* Am Chem Soc; Am Petrol Inst; Soc Petrol Engrs. *Res:* Non-aqueous solutions; oil well cements; drilling fluids; fracturing; colloids. *Mailing Add:* 534 Crestland Dr Bartlesville OK 74006

SHELL, JOHN WELDON, PHARMACOLOGY. Current Pos: FOUNDER, CHMN & CHIEF EXEC OFFICER, DEPOMED SYSTS, INC, 89- Personal Data: b Waxahachie, Tex, Apr 20, 25; m 52, Barbara Schlutius; c John N & Suzanne M. Educ: Univ Colo, BA, 49, BS, 53, PhD(pharmaceut chem), 54. Prof Exp: Asst chem, Univ Colo, 49-53; res assoc physics, Upjohn Co, 54-57, res scientist in prod res, 57-60, sr res scientist, 60-62; dir qual control, Allergan Pharmaceut, 62-64, dir res, 64-68; vpres Alza Corp, 68-87 & IOLAB Div, Johnson & Johnson, 87-89. Concurrent Pos: Vis grad lectr, Univ Southern Calif, 65-66; adj prof, 72-77, adj prof med, Med Ctr, Univ Calif, San Francisco, 77- Mem: Fel Am Asn Pharmaceut Sci; fel Acad Pharmaceut Sci; Asn Res Vision & Ophthal; Controlled Release Soc; Licensing Execs Soc. Res: Crystallography; x-ray analysis; biopharmaceutics; pharmacokinetics; ocular pharmacology; pharmacodynamics. Mailing Add: 952 Tournament Dr Hillsborough CA 94010. Fax: 650-513-0999

SHELLABARGER, CLAIRE J, RADIOBIOLOGY, ENDOCRINOLOGY. Current Pos: RETIRED. Personal Data: b College Corner, Ohio, Oct 23, 24; m 48; c 3. Educ: Miami Univ, AB, 48; Ind Univ, MA, 49, PhD(zool), 52. Prof Exp: Asst, Ind Univ, 50-52; jr scientist, Brookhaven Nat Lab, 52-53, asst scientist, 53-54, assoc scientist, 54-57, scientist, 60-68, asst chmn, 68-70, sr scientist & head, Radiobiol Div, 70-80; prof path, State Univ NY, Stony Brook, 80-89. Concurrent Pos: Lectr, Adelphi Col, 56; USPHS fel, Nat Inst Med Res, Eng, 57-58 & Inst Cancer Res, London, 66-67. Mem: Am Soc Zool; Soc Exp Biol & Med; Am Soc Exp Path; Radiation Res Soc; Am Physiol Soc. Res: Radiation carcinogenesis. Mailing Add: 196 S Country Rd Bellport NY 11713

SHELLENBARGER, ROBERT MARTIN, TECHNICAL MANAGEMENT. Current Pos: TECH MGR, DUPONT-SABANGI, IZMIT, TURKEY, 96- Personal Data: b Sacramento, Calif, June 25, 36; m 59, Betty Wise; c Robert I, Zane A, Michael A, David B & Patricia A. Educ: Col Pac, BS, 57; Univ NC, PhD(phys chem), 63. Prof Exp: Res chemist, EI DuPont De Nemours & Co Inc, 62-71, supvr res & develop, 71-85, Group Mgr, 85-95. Res: Structure and properties of synthetic fibers and nonwoven fabrics. Mailing Add: PO Box 11570 Wilmington DE 19850-1570

SHELLENBERGER, CARL H, PHYSIOLOGY, PHARMACOLOGY. Current Pos: DIR CLIN AFFAIRS, WARNER-LAMBERT CO, 81- Personal Data: b York, Pa, Sept 11, 35; m 84; c 3. Educ: Muhlenberg Col, BS, 58; State Univ NY, PhD(physiol), 68. Prof Exp: Res asst anesthesiol, Med Sch, Univ Pa, 58-61; mem staff pharmacol dept, Endo Labs, Inc, 67-70; sr clin scientist, Consumer Prod Div, Warner-Lambert Co, 70-73; asst dir, Sandoz, Inc, 73-75, assoc dir, 75-78, sr assoc dir clin res, 78-81. Mem: AAAS; NY Acad Sci; Am Acad Dermat. Res: Fibrinolysis; neuropharmacology; glucose and fat metabolism; adrenal gland metabolism; respiratory and analgesic pharmacology; clinical investigation of proprietary and ethical drugs; medical instrumentation. Mailing Add: Four Crestview Ct E Morris Plains NJ 07950

SHELLENBERGER, MELVIN KENT, NEUROPHARMACOLOGY. Current Pos: ADJ ASSOC PROF PHARMACOL & PHYS THER EDUC, 84-, VPRES, INT MED TECH CONSULTS, INC, 84- Personal Data: b Pittsburg, Kans, Oct 29, 36; m 59; c 4. Educ: Kans State Col Pittsburg, BS, 58; Univ Wash, MS, 62, PhD(pharmacol), 65. Prof Exp: Lab technician, Pharmacol Dept, Upjohn Co, 59-60; lab instr dent, med, pharm & pharmacol courses, Univ Wash, 60-65, lectr pharm & pharmacol courses, 62-65; from instr to assoc prof pharmacol, Univ Kans Med Ctr, 67-84. Concurrent Pos: Nat Inst Neurol Dis & Stroke fel pharmacol, Univ Mich, 65-66, NIMH trainee neuropsychopharmacol, 66-67; res assoc, Kans Ctr Ment Retardation & Human Develop, 71-; NIMH career develop res award, Univ Kans Med Ctr, 72-77. Mem: Int Soc Neurochem; Am Soc Pharmacol & Exp Therapeut; Soc Neurosci. Res: Correlating possible chemical mediators in the brain with electrical, physiological and behavioral events. Mailing Add: Athena Neurosci Inc 800F Gateway Blvd San Francisco CA 94080. Fax: 650-877-8370

SHELLENBERGER, PAUL ROBERT, DAIRY SCIENCE. Current Pos: from asst prof to assoc prof, 67-77, PROF DAIRY SCI, PA STATE UNIV, UNIVERSITY PARK, 77- Personal Data: b Dover, Pa, May 28, 35; m 57; c 2. Educ: Pa State Univ, BS, 57, MS, 59; Iowa State Univ, PhD(animal nutrit), 64. Prof Exp: Area dairy specialist, Agr Ext Serv, Tex A&M Univ, 64-66; actg assoc prof agr, Tarleton State Col, 66-67. Concurrent Pos: Mem, Coun Agr Sci & Technol; nat teacher fel award, Nat Asn Cols & Teachers Agr, 77. Mem: Nat Asn Col & Teachers Agr; Am Dairy Sci Asn; Coun for Agr Sci & Technol. Mailing Add: Dept Animal Sci Penn State Univ 324 Henning Bldg University Park PA 16802-3503

SHELLENBERGER, THOMAS E, BIOCHEMISTRY, TOXICOLOGY. Current Pos: CONSULT, 88- Personal Data: b Havre, Mont, May 3, 32; m 53; c 3. Educ: Mont State Univ, BS, 54, MS, 55; Kans State Univ, PhD(biochem), 61. Prof Exp: Res asst chem, Mont State Univ, 54-55; asst instr, Kans State Univ, 55-60; biochemist, Stanford Res Inst, 60-66, mgr biochem toxicol labs, 66; chmn dept toxicol, Gulf S Res Inst, 66-72; actg dep dir, Nat Ctr Toxicol Res, Food & Drug Admin, 77-78, chief div comp pharmacol, 72-88. Concurrent Pos: Assoc prof biochem, Univ Ark, Little Rock, 74- Mem: AAAS; NY Acad Sci; Am Chem Soc; Soc Toxicol; Am Col Vet Toxicologists. Res: Metabolism of carcinogens; comparative endocrinology; reactions and mechanisms of organophosphates; hazards of pesticides to fish and wildlife; poultry nutrition, vitamins and protein. Mailing Add: Laurel Washington Area Ten Laurel MD 20707

SHELLEY, AUSTIN L(INN), ELECTRICAL ENGINEERING. Current Pos: from instr to asst prof, 50-61, ASSOC PROF ELEC ENG, PURDUE UNIV, WEST LAFAYETTE, 61-, EXEC ASST TO HEAD SCH, 64- Personal Data: b New Ross, Ind, Apr 9, 22; m 48; c 2. Educ: Univ Ky, BS, 47; Purdue Univ, MS, 52, PhD(elec eng), 58. Prof Exp: Instr elec eng, Miss State Col, 47-49. Mem: Illum Eng Soc; Inst Elec & Electronics Engrs; Am Soc Eng Educ; Sigma Xi. Res: Circuits; machinery; servomechanisms. Mailing Add: 310 Lawn Ave West Lafayette IN 47906

SHELLEY, EDWARD GEORGE, SPACE PHYSICS. Current Pos: Res scientist, Lockheed Res Labs, 59-73, staff scientist, 73-80, sr staff scientist, 80-84, proj leader, 84-93, MGR, LOCKHEED RES LABS, 93- Personal Data: b Watford City, NDak, Jan 8, 33; m 52, Betty V Brooks; c David W & Suzanne C (Gianuzzi). Educ: Ore State Univ, BS(physics) & BS(math), 59; Stanford Univ, MS, 61, PhD(nuclear physics), 67. Concurrent Pos: Res assoc physics, Stanford Univ, 65-68; vis prof, Univ Bern, Switz, 90-91. Mem: Am Geophys Union; Europ Geophys Soc. Res: Magnetospheric physics, primarily in area of satellite observations of space plasmas. Mailing Add: Villa Nueva Way Mountain View CA 94040. Fax: 650-424-3333

SHELLEY, WALTER BROWN, DERMATOLOGY. Current Pos: PROF DERMAT, DEPT MED, DIV DERMAT, MED COL OHIO, 83- Personal Data: b St Paul, Minn, Feb 6, 17; m 42, 80; c 5. Educ: Univ Minn, BS, 40, PhD(physiol), 41, MB & MD, 43. Hon Degrees: MD, Univ Uppsala, Sweden, 77. Honors & Awards: Soc Cosmetic Chem Award, 55; Pollitzer lectr, NY Univ, 56; Rauschkolb Mem lectr, Univ Chicago, 57; Hellerstrom Medal, Karolinska Inst, Sweden, 71; Am Med Writers Asn Award, 73; Dohi Medalist, Nagoya, Japan, 81; Rose Hirschler Award, Women's Dermat Soc; Rothman Medal; Gold Medal Award, Am Acad Derm, 92. Prof Exp: Asst physiol, Univ Minn, 38-41; instr, Col St Thomas, 42-43; from instr to asst instr dermat, Univ Pa, 46-49; instr, Dartmouth Col, 49-50; from asst prof to prof dermat, Sch Med, Univ Pa, 50-80, chmn dept, 65-80; prof dermat, Peoria Sch Med, Univ Ill, 80-83. Concurrent Pos: Pvt pract; chief clin, Univ Hosp, 51-56 & 65-66; regional consult, US Vet Admin, 55-59; mem comt cutaneous dis, Nat Res Coun, 55-59, mem coun, 61-64; Prosser White Oration, Univ London, 57; consult, Surgeon Gen, US Army, 58-61 & USAF, 58-61; mem comn cutaneous dis, Armed Forces Epidemiol Bd, 58-61, dep dir, 59-61; consult, Philadelphia Gen Hosp, 60-65, chief dermat serv, 65-67; mem & dir, Am Bd Dermat, 60-69, past pres; consult dermatologist, Children's Hosp Philadelphia, 65-80. Mem: Hon mem Soc Invest Dermat (pres, 76); Am Physiol Soc; hon mem Am Dermat Asn (pres, 76); hon mem Am Acad Dermat (pres, 72); Asn Prof Dermat. Res: Physiology of the skin, especially the eccrine and apocrine sweat gland, sebaceous gland and pruritus; allergic states. Mailing Add: Dept Dermat Div Dermat Med Col Ohio PO Box 10008 Toledo OH 43699. Fax: 419-382-0354

SHELLEY, WILLIAM J, CHEMICAL ENGINEERING. Current Pos: RETIRED. Personal Data: b Wichita, Kans, Mar 15, 22; m 54. Educ: Univ Mich, BS, 48, MSE, 49. Prof Exp: Prod engr uranium div, Mallinckrodt Chem Works, 49-50, admin asst, 50-55, prod control mgr, 55-61, vpres & mgr, 61-67; asst to vpres, Kerr-McGee Corp, 67-71, dir & vpres nuclear licensing & regulations, Kerr-McGee Oil Industs, Kerr-McGee Corp, 71-84. Mem: Am Inst Chem Engrs; Am Chem Soc; Am Mgt Asn. Mailing Add: 42 Mayfair Dr Bella Vista AR 72714-5332

SHELLHAMER, DALE FRANCIS, ORGANIC CHEMISTRY. Current Pos: Assoc prof chem, 74-81, PROF CHEM, POINT LOMA COL, 81- Personal Data: b Tamaqua, Pa, Dec 4, 42; m 71; c 2. Educ: Univ Calif, Irvine, BA, 69; Univ Calif, Santa Barbara, PhD(org chem), 74. Concurrent Pos: Am Heart Asn grant, 78. Mem: Am Chem Soc. Res: Electrophilic additions to alkenes, alkynes and dienes; physical organic properties of fluorinated hydrocarbons. Mailing Add: Dept Chem Point Loma Col 3900 Lomaland Dr San Diego CA 92106-2810

SHELLHAMMER, HOWARD STEPHEN, MAMMALS, ECOLOGY. Current Pos: From asst prof to assoc prof, 61-70, PROF BIOL SCI, SAN JOSE STATE UNIV, 70- Personal Data: b Woodland, Calif, Aug 30, 35; m 56; c 1. Educ: Univ Calif, Davis, BA, 57, PhD(zool), 61. Concurrent Pos: Consult, H T Harvey & Assoc, Alviso, Calif. Mem: Am Soc Mammal; Animal Behav Soc; Wildlife Soc; Soc Conserv Biol. Res: Evolution and ecology of salt marsh harvest mice and other California mammals; ecology of large mammals; fire ecology; interactions with prescribed burning; behavior-ethology. Mailing Add: Dept Biol Sci San Jose State Univ One Washington Sq San Jose CA 95192-0001

SHELLOCK, FRANK G, CARDIOVASCULAR PHYSIOLOGY. Current Pos: DIR, FUTURE DIAG, 95- Personal Data: b Glendale, Calif, Dec 16, 54. Educ: Columbia Pac Univ, PhD(physiol), 82. Prof Exp: Res scientist, Cedar's-Sinai Med Ctr, Los Angeles, Calif, 82- Mailing Add: 7511 McConnell Ave Los Angeles CA 90045

SHELLY, DENNIS C, ANALYTICAL CHEMISTRY. Current Pos: ASST PROF, TEX TECH UNIV, 90- Personal Data: b Chambersburg, Pa, Feb 16, 55; m 78; c 2. Educ: Huntington Col, BS, 77; Tex A&M Univ, PhD(anal chem), 82. Prof Exp: Sr chemist, Lilly Res Labs, Eli Lilly & Co, 81-82; postdoctoral fel, Dept Chem, Ind Univ, 83-84; asst prof, Stevens Inst Technol, 84-90. Mem: Am Chem Soc; Soc Appl Spectros; Sigma Xi. Res: Development of bioanalytical instrumentation with unique applicability to the rapid identification of bacteria and metabolic profiling of isolated tissue; behavior of polymers in microenvironments and on-line monitoring of polymer processing. Mailing Add: Tex Tech Univ MS 1061 Lubbock TX 79409-1061

SHELLY, JAMES H, MATHEMATICS, COMPUTER SCIENCE. *Current Pos:* vis lectr, 87-90, LECTR, NC STATE UNIV, 90- *Personal Data:* b Zanesville, Ohio, Nov 28, 32; m 56; c 3. *Educ:* Oberlin Col, BA, 54; Univ Ill, Urbana, AM, 56, PhD(math), 59. *Prof Exp:* Assoc engr, IBM Corp, 59-62, sr assoc engr, 62-64, staff engr, 64-66, proj engr, 66-67, adv engr, 67-73, sr engr, 73-85, mem sr tech staff, 85-87. *Mem:* Asn Comput Mach; Soc Indust & Appl Math; Inst Elec & Electronic Engrs; Inst Elec & Electronics Engrs Comput Soc. *Res:* Processor and systems design and development; logical design; switching theory; combinatorial mathematics. *Mailing Add:* 1008 Bayfield Dr Raleigh NC 27606-1702

SHELLY, JOHN RICHARD, FOREST PRODUCTS MANUFACTURING & WOOD BUILDING DESIGN. *Current Pos:* res asst, Forest Prod Lab, 74-81, res scientist, Wood Bldg Res Ctr, 88-94, HEAD INTERN SERV CTR, UNIV CALIF, BERKELEY, 94- *Personal Data:* b Sellersville, Pa, Jan 19, 49; m 74; c 1. *Educ:* Pa State Univ, BS, 70; Univ Calif, Berkeley, MS, 77, PhD, 88. *Prof Exp:* Asst prof forest prod, Dept Forestry, Univ Ky, 81-86. *Concurrent Pos:* Extension specialist, Coop Extension, Univ Calif, 77-78. *Mem:* Forest Prod Res Soc; Soc Wood Sci & Technol; Sigma Xi. *Res:* Performance of wood products in structures; the theory of the flow of fluids through porous materials; principles and practice of wood drying methods, in particular energy efficiency in commercial lumber drying operations. *Mailing Add:* Forest Prod Lab 1301 S 46th St Richmond CA 94804. *E-Mail:* jrsfpl@nature.berkeley.edu

SHELSON, W(ILLIAM), ENERGY ANALYSIS, SYSTEM PLANNING. *Current Pos:* RETIRED. *Personal Data:* b Toronto, Ont, June 18, 22; m 58, Charlotte Samuels; c Kenneth N & Lorne M. *Educ:* Univ Toronto, BASc, 44, PhD, 52; Pa State Univ, MS, 47. *Prof Exp:* Stress analyst, Curtiss-Wright Corp, 47-48; res assoc appl math, Brown Univ, 48-49; mech engr, Can Stand Asn, 50-51; res engr, Ont Hydro, 52-56, chmn, Opers Res Group, 56-67, mgr opers res, 67-74, mgr fuel resources planning, 75-80, mgr energy resources planning, 80-83. *Concurrent Pos:* Spec lectr, Univ Toronto, 56-57; assoc mem, Coal Indust Adv Bd, Int Energy Agency, 80-83. *Mem:* Can Oper Res Soc. *Res:* Operations research; systems analysis; stress analysis; energy analysis and planning of electric power systems; evaluation and optimization of primary energy supply alternatives. *Mailing Add:* 53 Evanston Dr Downsview ON M3H 5P4 Can

SHELTON, DAMON CHARLES, BIOCHEMISTRY, NUTRITION. *Current Pos:* PRES, DAMON C SHELTON CONSULTS, INC, 87- *Personal Data:* b Richland, Ind, Apr 4, 22; m 43, Virginia M Hall; c Karen S & Sandra K. *Educ:* Purdue Univ, BSA, 47, MS, 49, PhD(agr biochem), 50. *Prof Exp:* Instr agr chem, Purdue Univ, 49-50, fel, 51-52; pvt bus, 52-53; from assoc prof to prof agr biochem, WVa Univ, 53-60, from assoc prof to prof med biochem, Sch Med, 60-67; res mgr, 67-75, res dir, Ralston Purina Co, 75-87. *Concurrent Pos:* Assoc animal nutritionist, Ala Polytech Inst, 50-51. *Mem:* Am Chem Soc; Am Inst Nutrit; Am Soc Biochem & Molecular Biol; AAAS; Am Asn Lab Analytical Sci; Can Asn Lab Anal Sci. *Res:* Blood proteins; amino acids; antibiotics and vitamins in nutrition and pathology; microbiology; mineral and antibiotic interrelationships; lipid-protein interactions; biological transport-peptides and amino acids; nutrition management of research and special animals. *Mailing Add:* 9338 Lincoln Dr St Louis MO 63127

SHELTON, EMMA, CELL BIOLOGY, ELECTRON MICROSCOPY. *Current Pos:* RETIRED. *Personal Data:* b Urbana, Ill, June 10, 20. *Educ:* Brown Univ, PhD(biol), 49. *Honors & Awards:* Superior Serv Award, USPHS, 78. *Prof Exp:* Jr biologist, Nat Cancer Inst, 44-46, res biologist, 49-78; secy, Am Soc Cell Biol, 78-81. *Concurrent Pos:* Vis biologist, Lab Electron Micros, Villejuif, France, 63-64; exec officer, Am Soc Cell Biol, 78-81. *Mem:* Fel AAAS; Am Soc Cell Biol; Am Asn Path; Histochem Soc; Am Asn Cancer Res; Sigma Xi. *Res:* Fine structure of ribosomes, enzymes, immunoglobulins; electron microscopy of cell interactions in the immune response. *Mailing Add:* 8410 Westmont Terr Bethesda MD 20817-6813

SHELTON, FRANK HARVEY, NUCLEAR PHYSICS. *Current Pos:* RETIRED. *Personal Data:* b Flagstaff, Ariz, Oct 4, 24; m 48, Lorene Gregory; c Jill J, Joyce L & Gwen E. *Educ:* Calif Inst Technol, BS, 49, MS, 50, PhD(physics), 52. *Prof Exp:* Res analyst, NAm Aviation, Inc, 50; mem staff, Sandia Corp, 51-55; tech dir, Armed Forces Spec Weapons Proj, US Dept Defense, 55-59; sr scientist, Nuclear Div, Kaman Aircraft Corp, 59-68, vpres & chief scientist, Kaman Sci Corp, 68-89. *Concurrent Pos:* Mem subcomt civil defense, Nat Acad Sci, 57; mem sci adv group effects, Defense Nuclear Agency, Dept Defense, 74- *Mem:* Fel Am Phys Soc. *Res:* Military effects of nuclear weapons and missile applications; peaceful uses of nuclear detonations. *Mailing Add:* 1327 Culebra Ave Colorado Springs CO 80903. *Fax:* 719-599-1942

SHELTON, GEORGE CALVIN, VETERINARY PARASITOLOGY. *Current Pos:* RETIRED. *Personal Data:* b Tex, Apr 26, 23; m 49; c 2. *Educ:* Tex A&M Univ, DVM, 48; Auburn Univ, MS, 52; Univ Minn, PhD(vet microbiol), 65. *Prof Exp:* Asst prof vet bact & parasitol, Univ Mo, 49-51; res assoc, Auburn Univ, 52; from asst prof to prof vet bact & parasitol, Univ Mo-Columbia, 52-59, prof vet microbiol, Sch Vet Med, 59-73, assoc dean, Col Vet Med, 69-73, assoc dean acad affairs, 71-73; prof & emer dean, Col Vet Med, Tex A&M Univ, 73-88. *Concurrent Pos:* NSF fac fel, 61-62. *Mem:* Am Vet Med Asn; Am Soc Parasitol; Conf Res Workers Animal Dis. *Res:* Internal parasites of ruminants. *Mailing Add:* 7851 S Tomlin Hill Rd Columbia MO 65201

SHELTON, JAMES CHURCHILL, MATERIALS & SURFACE SCIENCE, APPLIED PHYSICS. *Current Pos:* mgr, advan technol, 85-90, mgr competitive assessment, 91-92, MGR STRATEGY, AT&T NETWORK SYSTS, 93- *Personal Data:* b Kansas City, Mo; m 63; c 4. *Educ:* Cornell Univ, BEP, 63, PhD, 73. *Prof Exp:* Instr nuclear reactor eng, Rickover's US Naval Nuclear Power Prog, 63-69; mem tech staff mat res & integrated optics, Bell Labs, 72-80; corp prod planning & mkt div, Western Elec Co, 80-85. *Concurrent Pos:* Fel, NSF, 70-72. *Mem:* AAAS; Inst Elec & Electronics Engrs. *Res:* Communications and information network architectures, especially integrated and packet, photonic, broadband; technology assessment and planning; integrated optics, especially semiconductor laser sources, optical waveguides, switches, modulators, polarizers and detectors; surface physics, especially surface segregation, electron beam-solid interactions and diagnostics; general physics; competitive business strategy. *Mailing Add:* 2 Winthrop Dr Holmdel NJ 07733

SHELTON, JAMES EDWARD, SOIL CHEMISTRY, SOIL FERTILITY. *Current Pos:* From instr to asst prof, 59-78, ASSOC PROF SOILS, NC STATE UNIV, 78- *Personal Data:* b Allais, Ky, Sept 26, 29; m 53; c 2. *Educ:* Univ Ky, BS, 53, MS, 57; NC State Univ, PhD(soils), 60. *Mem:* Am Soc Agron; Soil Sci Soc Am; Int Soc Soil Sci; Am Soc Hort Sci. *Res:* Role of fertilizers in soil-plant relationships. *Mailing Add:* Soil Sci NC State Univ Box 7619 Raleigh NC 27695-0001

SHELTON, JAMES REID, ORGANIC & RUBBER CHEMISTRY, POLYMER SCIENCE. *Current Pos:* instr chem, Case Western Res Univ, 36-41, from asst prof to prof org chem, 41-77, dean grad studies, 66-67, prof polymer sci, 68-77, EMER PROF CHEM & MACROMOL SCI, CASE WESTERN RES UNIV, 77- *Personal Data:* b Allerton, Iowa, Jan 16, 11; m 34, Leah E Brown; c Margaret M, James W & Patricia A. *Educ:* Univ Iowa, BS, 33, MS, 34, PhD(org chem), 36. *Honors & Awards:* Charles Goodyear Medal, Rubber Div, Am Chem Soc, 83. *Prof Exp:* Asst org chem, Univ Iowa, 35-36. *Concurrent Pos:* Vis prof org chem, Univ Leiden, Neth, 67-68. *Mem:* AAAS; Am Chem Soc. *Res:* Mechanism of oxidation and antioxidant action in rubber and related systems; mechanism of organic reactions; high polymers; organic sulfur compounds; reaction of free radicals with olefins; reactions of peroxides. *Mailing Add:* Dept Chem Case Western Res Univ Cleveland OH 44106-7078

SHELTON, JOHN C, organic chemistry, for more information see previous edition

SHELTON, JOHN WAYNE, GEOLOGY. *Current Pos:* VPRES, MASARA CORP, 88- *Personal Data:* b China Spring, Tex, Dec 28, 28; m 49; c 2. *Educ:* Baylor Univ, BA, 49; Univ Ill, MS, 51, PhD(geol), 53. *Prof Exp:* Asst, Univ Ill, 50-52; geologist, Shell Oil Co, 53-63; from asst prof to prof geol, Okla State Univ, 63-88. *Concurrent Pos:* Consult, Continental Oil Co, 64- *Mem:* Geol Soc Am; Soc Econ Paleont & Mineral; Am Asn Petrol Geologists. *Res:* Sedimentation; structural geology. *Mailing Add:* Masera Corp 1743 E 71st St Tulsa OK 74136

SHELTON, KEITH RAY, BIOCHEMISTRY. *Current Pos:* from asst prof to assoc prof, 70-90, PROF BIOCHEM, MED COL VA, VA COMMON WEALTH UNIV, 90- *Personal Data:* b Chatham, Va, Jan 11, 41; m 65; c 3. *Educ:* Univ Va, BA, 63; Univ Ill, Urbana, PhD(biochem), 68. *Prof Exp:* Res assoc biochem, Rockefeller Univ, 67-69; Nat Res Coun Can fel, 69-70. *Mem:* Am Soc Cell Biol; Am Soc Biol Chemists; Am Chem Soc. *Res:* Molecular and cellular responses to toxic metals. *Mailing Add:* Dept Biochem & Molec Biophys Med Col Va VCU PO Box 980614 Richmond VA 23298-0614. *Fax:* 804-786-9526

SHELTON, KEVIN L, GEOLOGY. *Current Pos:* PROF GEOL, UNIV MO-COLUMBIA. *Honors & Awards:* Lindgren Award, Soc Econ Geologists, 91. *Mailing Add:* Dept Geol Univ Mo 101 Geol Bldg Columbia MO 65211

SHELTON, ROBERT DUANE, FOREIGN TECHNOLOGIES ASSESSMENT, JAPANESE TECHNOLOGY POLICY. *Current Pos:* PROF & CHAIR ENG, 85-, PROF & DIR ITRI, LOYOLA COL. *Personal Data:* b Dublin, Tex, Sept 14, 38; c Duane E. *Educ:* Tex Tech Univ, BSEE, 60; Mass Inst Technol, SM, 62; Univ Houston, PhD(elec eng), 67. *Honors & Awards:* IEEE Cong fel, 94-95. *Prof Exp:* Engr, Adcom, Inc, Mass, 62 & Tex Instruments Inc, 62-63; aerospace technologist, Manned Spacecraft Ctr, NASA, Tex, 63-64; from instr to asst prof elec eng, Univ Houston, 64-68; assoc prof, Tex Tech Univ, 68-70; from assoc prof to prof elec eng & comput sci, Univ Louisville, 70-84; policy analyst, NSF, 84-85. *Concurrent Pos:* NASA res grants, Univ Houston, Tex Tech Univ & Univ Louisville, 66-72; consult, Houston Res Inc, Gulf Aerospace Corp & Univac Ind, 67-68; NSF grants educ improv, Tex Tech Univ & Univ Louisville, 70-72; dir, Int Technol Res Inst, 90-; chair, Publn Comt, Am Soc Eng Educ. *Mem:* Sr mem Inst Elec & Electronics Engrs; AAAS; Asn Comput Mach. *Res:* Communications; computers; computer software; educational statistics; research on international technologies, particularly in Japan, former Soviet Union and Western Europe. *Mailing Add:* 8998 Watchlight Ct Columbia MD 21045. *Fax:* 410-617-5123; *E-Mail:* rds@loyola.edu

SHELTON, ROBERT NEAL, SOLID STATE PHYSICS. *Current Pos:* vchancellor res, 90-96, PROF PHYSICS, UNIV CALIF, DAVIS, 87- *Personal Data:* b Phoenix, Ariz, Oct 5, 48; m 69, Adrian A (Millar); c 3. *Educ:* Stanford Univ, BS, 70, MS, 73; Univ Calif, PhD(physics), 75. *Prof Exp:* From asst prof to prof physics, Iowa State Univ, 78-87. *Concurrent Pos:* Vprovost res, Univ Calif, Davis. *Mem:* Am Phys Soc; Sigma Xi. *Res:* Experimental condensed matter physics- emphasis on novel materials; superconductivity; magnetism; correlated electron systems. *Mailing Add:* Dept Physics Univ Calif Davis CA 95616

SHELTON, ROBERT WAYNE, ORGANIC CHEMISTRY. *Current Pos:* from assoc prof to prof, 56-85, head dept, 58-66, EMER PROF CHEM, WESTERN ILL UNIV, 85- *Personal Data:* b Springfield, Ill, Dec 3, 23; m 46, Mary E Myers; c Richard M, Barbara Ann (Avraham) & John M. *Educ:* Ill Col, AB, 49; Univ Iowa, PhD(chem), 54. *Prof Exp:* Res chemist, E I du Pont de Nemours & Co, 53-56. *Mem:* Am Chem Soc. *Res:* Synthesis; organophosphorus compounds. *Mailing Add:* 1103 Willow Ct Estes Park CO 80517-7152

SHELTON, RONALD M, MATHEMATICS. *Current Pos:* From asst prof to assoc prof, 60-61, PROF MATH, MILLIKIN UNIV, 71-, CHMN DEPT, 63- *Personal Data:* b Shipman, Ill, July 11, 31; m 53; c 2. *Educ:* Univ Ill, BS, 53, MS, 57, PhD(math educ), 65. *Concurrent Pos:* Consult, Decatur Pub Schs, 67. *Mem:* Math Asn Am. *Res:* Teaching of mathematics at the college level. *Mailing Add:* 71 Montgomery Pl Decatur IL 62522

SHELTON, WILFORD NEIL, ELECTRON PHYSICS. *Current Pos:* From res asst to res assoc, 60-63, from actg asst prof to assoc prof, 63-76, PROF PHYSICS, FLA STATE UNIV, 76- *Personal Data:* b Dalton, Ga, Dec 29, 35; m 65, Faye Beasley; c Douglas N, Gregory L & Janet K. *Educ:* Univ Calif, Los Angeles, AB, 58; Fla State Univ, PhD(physics), 62. *Mem:* Am Phys Soc; Sigma Xi. *Res:* Electron scattering on atoms and molecules; resonant charge exchange between atoms; electron-impact ionization of atoms; electron-photon angular correlations; states of nuclei; fourier transform infrared spectroscopy; electrostatic precipitation. *Mailing Add:* 2012 Sheridan Rd Tallahassee FL 32303. *Fax:* 850-644-6504; *E-Mail:* shelton@phy.fsu.edu

SHELTON, WILLIAM LEE, fisheries, for more information see previous edition

SHELUPSKY, DAVID I, PHYSICS. *Current Pos:* From instr to asst prof, 64-71, ASSOC PROF PHYSICS, CITY COL NEW YORK, 72- *Personal Data:* b New York, NY, Dec 9, 37; m 63. *Educ:* City Col New York, BS, 59; Princeton Univ, MA, 61, PhD(physics), 65. *Mem:* Am Math Soc; Am Phys Soc; Math Asn Am. *Res:* Axiomatic quantum field theory; algebraic methods in statistical mechanics. *Mailing Add:* Dept of Physics City Col New York Convent at 138th St New York NY 10031

SHELVER, WILLIAM H, MEDICINAL CHEMISTRY, ORGANIC CHEMISTRY. *Current Pos:* From asst prof to assoc prof pharmaceut chem, 60-68, PROF PHARMACEUT SCI, NDAK STATE UNIV, 68-,. *Personal Data:* b Ortonville, Minn, May 31, 34; m 89, Weilin Liu. *Educ:* NDak State Univ, BS, 56, MS, 57; Univ Va, PhD(org chem), 62. *Mem:* Am Chem Soc; Am Pharmaceut Asn; Sigma Xi. *Res:* Development of relationships between structure and biological activity by synthesis of new compounds; measurement of physical properties of new and existing compounds, especially in analgesic and hypotensive drugs. *Mailing Add:* Dept of Pharmaceut Chem/BTO NDak State Univ Fargo ND 58102

SHEMANCHUK, JOSEPH ALEXANDER, VETERINARY ENTOMOLOGY. *Current Pos:* ENTOMOLOGIST VET-MED ENTOM, AGR CAN RES STA, LETHBRIDGE, 55- *Personal Data:* b Wostok, Alta, Apr 28, 27; m 51; c 2. *Educ:* Univ Alta, BScAgr, 50, MSc, 58. *Prof Exp:* Entomologist med entom, Household Med Entom Unit, Can Dept Agr, Ottawa, 50-51 & Dominion Entom Lab, Sask, 51-55. *Concurrent Pos:* Scientist exchange fel, Nat Res Coun Can & USSR Acad Sci, 71, Nat Res Coun Can & Czech Acad Sci, 80. *Mem:* Fel Entom Soc Can; Am Mosquito Control Asn; Can Soc Zool. *Res:* Behavior, culture and biological control of blood-sucking flies; development of repellents for protection of man and livestock; epidemiology of insect-borne diseases in livestock. *Mailing Add:* Agr & Agr-Food Can Lethbridge Res Ctr PO Box 3000 Lethbridge AB T1J 4B1 Can

SHEMANO, IRVING, PHARMACOLOGY. *Current Pos:* ASSOC DIR CLIN DEVELOP-ONCOL, ADRIA LABS, 78- *Personal Data:* b San Francisco, Calif, June 23, 28; m 56; c 2. *Educ:* Univ Calif, AB, 50, MS, 51; Univ Man, PhD(pharmacol), 56. *Prof Exp:* Asst pharmacologist, Abbott Labs, 51-53; sr pharmacologist, Smith Kline & French Labs, 56-60; dir macrobiol res labs, Merrell-Nat Labs, 60-70, head dept immunol & endocrinol, 70-74, group dir, Clin Pharmacol Dept, 74-78. *Mem:* Am Soc Pharmacol & Exp Therapeut; Am Soc Clin Pharmacol & Therapeut; Am Soc Clin Oncol. *Res:* Immunopharmacology; gastrointestinal pharmacology; cancer res. *Mailing Add:* Adria Labs PO Box 16529 Columbus OH 43216-6529

SHEMANSKY, DONALD EUGENE, ATMOSPHERIC PHYSICS. *Current Pos:* PPOF, AEROSPACE ENG, UNIV CALIF LOS ANGELES, 91- *Personal Data:* b Moose Jaw, Sask, Apr 28, 36; m 67; c 4. *Educ:* Univ Sask, BE, 58, MSc, 60, PhD(auroral physics), 66. *Honors & Awards:* Exceptional Sci Achievement Medal, NASA, 81, Group Achievement Award, Voyager Sci Instrument Develop, 81, Group Achievement Award, Voyager Sci Invest, 81, 86 & 90. *Prof Exp:* Physicist, Bristol Aero Industs, Ltd, 60-61; res asst, Univ Sask, 61-66; jr physicist, Kitt Peak Nat Observ, Ariz, 66-69; res asst prof physics, Univ Pittsburgh, 69-74; res assoc prof physics, Univ Mich, 74-78; res assoc, Univ Ariz, 78-79; sr res scientist, Tucson Labs, Space Sci Inst, Univ Southern Calif, 79-84; sr res scientist, Lunar Planetary Lab, Univ Ariz, 84-91. *Concurrent Pos:* Assoc ed, J Geophys Res, 81-84; prin investr, NASA, NSF, DOE grants; co-investr, Voyager, Galileo, Cassini Spacecraft Experiments; comt mem, Nat Acad Sci Workshop, 85, NASA Planetary Atmospheres Rev Comts, NASA Saturn-Titan Voyager Workshop, 80, NASA Io Torus Plasma Workshop, 89, NSF CEDAR Workshops, NASA LEXSWG Atmospheric Sci Workshop, 90. *Mem:* Am Geophys Union; Am Astron Soc; Planetary Soc; Am Phys Soc. *Res:* Physics of Io plasma torus and Jupiter, Saturn, Uranus, Neptune and Titan atmosphere-magnetosphere interactions atmosphere-magnetosphere interactions; interstellar medium and cygnus loop study in extreme ultraviolet; theoretical physics of gas-surface interactions; earth atmosphere/magnetosphere; lunar, mercury atmosphere; laboratory astrophysics; atomic, molecular physics and chemistry; accretion disk theory. *Mailing Add:* 650 E Alameda St Altadena CA 91001

SHEMDIN, OMAR H, oceanographic engineering, oceanography, for more information see previous edition

SHEMENSKI, ROBERT MARTIN, METALLURGICAL ENGINEERING. *Current Pos:* sr scientist, Fabric Develop Dept, 70-77, prin metall, 77-, MGR WIRE SCI & TECHNOL, GOODYEAR TIRE & RUBBER CO. *Personal Data:* b Martins Ferry, Ohio, June 17, 38; m 60; c 3. *Educ:* Univ Cincinnati, MetE, 61; Ohio State Univ, PhD(metall eng), 64. *Prof Exp:* Mem tech staff, Bell Tel Labs, 66-67; sr scientist, Battelle Mem Inst, 67-70. *Mem:* Am Soc Metals; Am Inst Mining, Metall & Petrol Engrs; Nat Asn Corrosion Engrs. *Res:* Anger spectroscopy; secondary ion mass spectrometry; iron filamentary single crystals metallic dissolution kinetics; internal friction; properties of beryllium; scanning electron microscopy; failure analyses; fatigue; fiber reenforcement systems; x-ray photoelectron spectroscopy. *Mailing Add:* 204 Sutton Ave NE Canton OH 44720

SHEMER, JACK EVVARD, COMPUTER SCIENCE, ELECTRICAL ENGINEERING. *Current Pos:* RETIRED. *Personal Data:* b Phoenix, Ariz, Aug 22, 40; m 63; c 1. *Educ:* Occidental Col, BA, 62; Ariz State Univ, MS, 65; Southern Methodist Univ, PhD(elec eng), 68. *Honors & Awards:* Spec Award, Comput Soc, 76. *Prof Exp:* Sr engr, Gen Elec Co, Phoenix, 62-67; sect mgr, Sci Data Systs, Santa Monica, Calif, 68-72; prin scientist & area mgr, Xerox Palo Alto Res Ctr, El Segundo, Calif, 72-76; vpres systs eng, Transaction Technol Inc, Citicorp, 76-79; chief exec officer, Teradata Corp, 79-87, chmn, 87-88, vchmn, 88-92. *Concurrent Pos:* Tech ed, Computer, 73-76. *Mem:* Inst Elec & Electronics Engrs; Asn Comput Mach. *Res:* Computer architecture; file and database management, performance analysis; queueing theory and applications; automatic control systems; digital image coding and display. *Mailing Add:* PO Box 522 Nye MT 59061

SHEMILT, L(ESLIE) W(EBSTER), CHEMICAL & ELECTROCHEMICAL ENGINEERING, MASS TRANSFER. *Current Pos:* dean fac eng, 69-79, prof, 69-87, EMER PROF CHEM ENG, MCMASTER UNIV, 87- *Personal Data:* b Souris, Man, Dec 25, 19; m 46, Elizabeth McKenzie; c Roderick & Roslyn (Hanes). *Educ:* Univ Toronto, BASc, 41, PhD(phys chem), 47; Univ Man, MSc, 46. *Hon Degrees:* DHc, St Staszie Univ, 92; DSc, McMaster Univ, 94. *Honors & Awards:* T P Hoar Prize, Inst Corrosion Sci & Technol, 80; R S Jane Mem lect Award, Can Soc Chem Eng, 85; Officer Order of Can, 91; Julian C Smith Medal Eng Inst Can, 93. *Prof Exp:* Lab supvr, Defence Industs, Ltd, 41-42; supvr tech dept & acid plant supvr, 42-44; lectr chem, Univ Man, 44-45; spec lectr, Univ Toronto, 45-47; from asst prof to prof, Univ BC, 47-60; prof chem eng & head dept, Univ NB, 61-69. *Concurrent Pos:* Vis prof, Univ Col, London, 59-60 & Ecole Polytech Lausanne, 75, Indian Inst Technol, Kanpur, 75, Madras, 75, Univ Sydney, 81 & spec vis prof, Yokohama Nat Univ, 87; chmn, NB Res & Productivity Coun, 62-69; sci adv, Prov NB, 64-69; chmn, Atlantic Prov Inter-Univ Comt on Sci, 66-69; mem, Nat Res Coun Can, 66-69; ed, Can J Chem Eng, 67-84, emer ed, 87-; chmn tech adv comt, Nuclear Fuel Waste Mgt, 79-; int ed, Chem Eng Res & Design, 84-89. *Mem:* Am Chem Soc; fel Am Inst Chem Engrs; hon fel Chem Inst Can (pres, 70-71); fel Eng Inst Can; Can Res Mgt Asn; fel Royal Soc Can; fel Can Acad Eng. *Res:* Fundamentals of corrosion; chemical engineering thermodynamics; industrial wastes; mass transfer; process dynamics; radioactive waste management. *Mailing Add:* McMaster Univ Hamilton ON L8S 4L7 Can. *Fax:* 905-522-0058; *E-Mail:* shemilt@tacaecl.eng.mcmaster.ca

SHEN, BENJAMIN SHIH-PING, ASTROPHYSICS, ENGINEERING SCIENCE. *Current Pos:* from assoc prof to prof astron & astrophys, Univ Pa, 66-72, Reese W Flower prof, 72-96, chmn dept, 73-79, dir, Flower & Cook Observ, 73-79, assoc univ provost, 79-80, chmn, Coun Grad Deans, 79-81, Univ provost, 80-81, REESE W FLOWER EMER PROF ASTRON & ASTROPHYS, UNIV PA, 96- *Personal Data:* b Hangzhou, China, Sept 14, 31; nat US; m 71, Lucia E Simpson; c 2. *Educ:* Assumption Col, AB, 54; Clark Univ, AM, 56; Univ Paris, DSc d'Etat (physics), 64. *Prof Exp:* Asst prof physics, State Univ NY Albany, 56-59; assoc prof space sci, aeronaut & astronaut, Sch Eng, NY Univ, 64-66. *Concurrent Pos:* Consult, Space Sci Lab, Gen Elec Co, 61-68; guest staff mem, Brookhaven Nat Lab, 63-64, 65-70; gen chmn, Int Conf Spallation Nuclear Reactions & Their Appln, 75; assoc ed, Comments Astrophys, 79-85; mem, US Nat Sci Bd, 90-94. *Res:* Spallation nuclear reactions in astronomy and space-radiation shielding engineering; galaxies and quasars; science and technology policy. *Mailing Add:* David Rittenhouse Lab Univ Pa Philadelphia PA 19104-6396

SHEN, CHE-KUN JAMES, BIOCHEMISTRY, MOLECULAR BIOLOGY. *Current Pos:* asst prof, 81-83, ASSOC PROF GENETICS, UNIV CALIF, DAVIS, 83- *Personal Data:* b Taipei, Taiwan, 1949. *Educ:* Nat Taiwan Univ, BS, 71; Univ Calif, Berkeley, PhD(biochem), 77. *Prof Exp:* Elec officer electronics & mech radar div, Navy Repub China, 7; NIH res fel biol, Calif Inst Technol, 78-80. *Mem:* Sigma Xi. *Res:* Molecular biology; human molecular genetics. *Mailing Add:* Sec Molec & Cell Biol Univ Calif Davis CA 95616-5224. *Fax:* 530-752-6363

SHEN, CHIH-KANG, SOIL MECHANICS. *Current Pos:* HEAD, DEPT CIVIL & STRUCT ENG, HONG KONG UNIV SCI & TECHNOL, 92-, PROF. *Personal Data:* b Chekiang, China, Sept 21, 32; m 64; c 1. *Educ:* Nat Taiwan Univ, BS, 56; Univ NH, MS, 60; Univ Calif, Berkeley, PhD(soil mech), 65. *Prof Exp:* Asst prof, Loyola Univ, Calif, 65-70; from asst prof to prof civil eng, Univ Calif, Davis, 70-91. *Concurrent Pos:* Res assoc, Univ Calif, Los Angeles, 66-; mem, Hwy Res Bd, Nat Acad Sci-Nat Res Coun, 66- *Mem:* Am Soc Civil Engrs; Int Soc Soil Mech & Found Engrs. *Res:* Soil stabilization and compaction; flexible pavement design; shear strength of unsaturated soils. *Mailing Add:* Dept Civil & Struct Eng Hong Kong Univ Sci & Technol Clearwater Bay Kowloon Hong Kong People's Republic of China. *Fax:* 852-358-1534

SHEN, CHI-NENG, CONTROL SYSTEMS, ENGINEERING SYSTEMS. *Current Pos:* from assoc prof to prof mech eng, 58-67, prof elec & systs eng, 73-91, EMER PROF ELEC & SYSTS ENG, RENSSELAER POLYTECH INST, 91- *Personal Data:* b Peiping, China, July 18, 17; m 47; c 2. *Educ:* Nat Tsing Hua Univ, China, BEng, 39; Univ Minn, MS, 50, PhD(eng), 54. *Prof Exp:* Instr mech eng, Univ Minn, 51-54; asst prof, Dartmouth Col, 54-58. *Concurrent Pos:* Vis prof mech eng, Mass Inst Technol, 67-68; consult. *Mem:* Am Soc Mech Engrs; Am Nuclear Soc; Am Inst Aeronaut & Astronaut; Am Soc Eng Educ; Sigma Xi. *Res:* Martian vehicle navigation, including obstacle detection, terrain modeling and park selection; nuclear reactor stability for kinetics and two-phase flow phenomena; automatic controls, including nonlinear control systems and estimation theory; guidance and navigation. *Mailing Add:* Elec Comput & Syst Eng Dept Rensselaer Polytech Inst Troy NY 12181

SHEN, CHIN-WEN, oil well drilling, enhanced oil recovery; deceased, see previous edition for last biography

SHEN, CHUNG YI, APPLIED MATHEMATICS. *Current Pos:* PROF MATH, SIMON FRASER UNIV, 67- *Personal Data:* b Canton, China, May 23, 37; US citizen; m 82; c 3. *Educ:* Ore State Univ, BS, 60, MS, 63, PhD(math), 68. *Concurrent Pos:* Fel, Carnegie-Mellon Univ, 68-69; vis assoc prof, Nat Taiwan Univ, 74-75; consult, Northrop Corp, 85- *Mem:* Am Math Soc; Can Math Soc; Can Appl Math Soc. *Res:* Electromagnetic scattering; numerical methods. *Mailing Add:* Dept Math & Statist Simon Fraser Univ Burnaby BC V5A 1S6 Can

SHEN, CHUNG YU, FLUIDIZATION, PHOSPHORUS & DERIVATIVES. *Current Pos:* CONSULT, SHEN & SHEN, INC, 86- *Personal Data:* b Dec 15, 21; m, Colleen N Yu; c Sheldon, Vincent & Anthony. *Educ:* Nat Southwestern Asn Univ, Kunming, China, BS, 42; Univ Louisville, MChE, 50; Univ Ill, PhD(chem eng), 54. *Prof Exp:* Sect chief, Cent Chem Works, Shanghai, China, 42-48; int fel, J E Seagram & Sons, Inc, 49-50; sr chem engr, Inst Indust Res, 50-52; sr fel, Monsanto Co, 54-86. *Concurrent Pos:* Mem, Chem Eng Prod Res Panel, 75-86; expert, People's Repub China. *Mem:* Fel Am Inst Chem Eng; Am Oil Chemist Soc; Am Res Soc; Sigma Xi; AAAS. *Res:* Process and product development; 65 US patents in phosphates, phosphonates, detergent processing, chelation and sequestion agents, various chemicals based on cyanides and fatty natural materials; 26 publications. *Mailing Add:* 1033 Cy Ann Dr St Louis MO 63017

SHEN, COLIN YUNKANG, DOUBLE DIFFUSION CONNECTION, NUMERICAL MODELING. *Current Pos:* RES PHYSICIST, NAVAL RES LAB, 84- *Personal Data:* b Taichung, Taiwan. *Educ:* Univ Mass, BS, 71; Univ RI, PhD(phys oceanog), 77. *Prof Exp:* Fel, Univ Wash, 78-81, sr oceanogr, 82-83. *Concurrent Pos:* Vis scientist, Nat Ctr Atmospheric Res, 77-78. *Mem:* Am Geophys Union; Sigma Xi; Am Phys Soc. *Res:* Double diffusive convection, fluid mixing, ocean internal waves, ocean eddies; specialize in numerical modeling of various fluid phenomena. *Mailing Add:* Remote Sensing Hydrodynamics Br Code 7250 Naval Res Lab Washington DC 20375. *E-Mail:* shen@cct.nrl.navy.mil

SHEN, D(AVID) W(EI) C(HI), ELECTRICAL ENGINEERING. *Current Pos:* from asst prof to assoc prof, 55-66, prof elec eng, Moore Sch Elec Eng, 66-, EMER PROF SYSTS ENG, UNIV PA, 72- *Personal Data:* b Shanghai, China, Jan 4, 20; nat US. *Educ:* Nat Tsing Hua Univ, China, BSc, 39; Univ London, PhD(elec eng), 48. *Prof Exp:* Lectr elec eng, Nat Univ Amoy, China, 40-44; with Marconi Wireless & Tel Co, Eng, 44-45; elec engr, Messrs Yangtse, Ltd, 46-48; sr lectr elec eng, Adelaide Univ, 50-53; vis asst prof, Univ Ill, 53-54, Mass Inst Technol, 54 & City Col New York, 55. *Concurrent Pos:* Mem res staff, Stromberg-Carlson Div, Gen Dynamics Corp, NY; consult, CDC Control Serv, Inc, 55-; mem, Franklin Inst. *Mem:* Am Soc Eng Educ; fel Inst Elec & Electronics Engrs; fel Brit Inst Elec Eng; Tensor Soc; fel AAAS. *Res:* Electrical machinery; analogue computers; optimal and adaptive control theory; control in biological systems. *Mailing Add:* Dept Systs Eng Univ Pa 220 S 33rd St Philadelphia PA 19104

SHEN, GLEN T, GEOCHEMISTRY. *Current Pos:* res scientist, 88-89, asst prof, 89-95, ASSOC PROF OCEANOG, UNIV WASH, 95- *Personal Data:* b Rego Park, NY, July 11, 57. *Educ:* Mass Inst Technol, SB, 79, PhD(chem oceanog), 86. *Honors & Awards:* Presidential Young Investr Award, NSF, 91. *Prof Exp:* Res scientist, Lamant-Doherty Geol Observ, 86-88. *Mem:* Am Geophys Union. *Res:* Chemical oceanography; trace element geochemistry; paleochemical indicators of ocean-atmosphere processes and climate change; Carbonate and Sediment Geochemistry; estuarine chemical dynamics; analytical chemistry. *Mailing Add:* Sch Oceanog Univ Wash PO Box 357940 Seattle WA 98195-7940. *E-Mail:* glenshon@ocean.washington.edu

SHEN, HAO-MING, ELECTROMAGNETIC PULSES, ELECTROMAGNETIC MEASUREMENT. *Current Pos:* RETIRED. *Personal Data:* b Changzhou, China, 1933; m 59; c 3. *Educ:* Beijing Univ, China, Bachelor physics, 58; Chiaotung Univ, China, PhD(electronics eng), 66. *Prof Exp:* Teaching asst physics, Beijing Univ, 58-63; lectr, Harbin Civil Eng Col, 66-78, assoc prof elec eng, 78-79; res prof elec eng, Inst Electronics, Acad Sci, China, 83-86; res assoc appl physics, Harvard Univ, 86-93, proj scientist, 93-94; sr eng specialist, Caleb Systs Inc, 94-96. *Concurrent Pos:* Mem, Comn E & var comts, Int Union Radio Sci, 85- *Mem:* Sr mem Inst Elec & Electronics Engrs Electromagnetic Compatibility Soc; sr mem Inst Elec & Electronics Engrs Microwave Theory & Technol Soc; Int Union Radio Sci. *Res:* Electromagnetic theory, antennas, microwaves, specifically in electromagnetic pulses, transient, electromagnetic compatibility. *Mailing Add:* 50 Puritan Rd Somerville MA 02145

SHEN, HSIEH WEN, HYDRAULICS. *Current Pos:* PROF CIVIL ENG, UNIV CALIF, BERKELEY, 85- *Personal Data:* b Peking, China, July 13, 31; m 56. *Educ:* Univ Mich, BS, 53, MS, 54; Univ Calif, Berkeley, PhD(hydraul), 61. *Honors & Awards:* Horton Award, Am Geophys Union; Einstein Award, Am Soc Civil Engrs, 90-91. *Prof Exp:* Hydraul engr, US Army CEngrs, 55-56; struct engr, Giffels & Vallet, Inc, 56; res engr hydraul, Inst Eng Res, Univ Calif, 56-61; hydraul engr, Harza Eng Co, 61-63; from assoc prof to prof hydraul eng, Colo State Univ, Ft Collins, 64-85. *Concurrent Pos:* Freeman fel, Am Soc Civil Engrs, 65-66; Guggenheim fel, 72; Humboldt Found sr res Award, Ger, 90-91. *Mem:* Nat Acad Eng. *Res:* Various aspects of fluvial hydraulics, including meandering, local scour, sediment transport under wind, stable channel shape and change of bed forms. *Mailing Add:* 412 O'Brien Hall Univ Calif Berkeley CA 94720

SHEN, HUNG TAO, COLD REGIONS HYDRAULICS, TRANSPORT PROCESSES IN RIVERS & OIL SLICK TRANSPORT IN SURFACE WATERS. *Current Pos:* from asst prof to assoc prof, 76-83, PROF CIVIL & ENVIRON ENG, CLARKSON UNIV, 83- *Personal Data:* b Shanghai, China, May 4, 44; US citizen; m 73, Hayley H; c Scott P & June P. *Educ:* Chung Yuan Univ, Taiwan, BS, 65; Asian Inst Tech, MEng, 69; Univ Iowa, PhD(mech & hydraul), 74. *Prof Exp:* Eng analyst, Sargent & Lundy, Chicago, 74-76. *Concurrent Pos:* Consult, Cold Regions Res & Eng Lab, US Army, 84-; vis prof, Swed Nat Sci Res Coun, Lulea Univ, 90-91; vis scholar, Comt Scholarly Commun Peoples Repub China, Nat Acad Sci, 91; prin investr, NSF, US Army, World Bank, Dept Trans, Nat Oceanic & Atmospheric Admin. *Mem:* Am Soc Civil Engrs; Int Asn Hydraul Res; Am Geophys Union; Int Asn Great Lakes Res. *Res:* River ice; development of theories on frazil ice transport under ice covers, dynamic transport of surface ice and jamming and the first comprehensive computer model on river ice processes. *Mailing Add:* 213 May Rd Potsdam NY 13676. *Fax:* 315-268-7985

SHEN, JUN, STATISTICAL SIGNAL PROCESSING, CHANNEL CODING & MODULATION. *Current Pos:* SR ENGR, FAVINON DIV, HARRIS CORP, 95- *Personal Data:* b Hetei, Anhui, China, Dec 4, 62; m 89, Lingli Wang; c Roland & Audey. *Educ:* Beijing Univ Aeronaut & Astronaut, China, BS, 84, MS, 87; Univ Southern Calif, PhD(elec eng), 95. *Prof Exp:* Asst prof multichannel signal processing, Beijing Univ Aeronaut & Astronaut, 87-89; res asst, Southern Ill Univ, 89-92. *Mem:* Inst Elec & Electronics Engrs Commun Soc; Inst Elec & Electronics Engrs Signal Processing Soc. *Res:* Developed a new class of robust interference cancellation algorithms for communication receivers and statistical signal processing; designed and implemented a multichannel communications system for rocket use; published more than 15 journal and conference papers. *Mailing Add:* 234 Escuela Ave No 21 Mountain View CA 94040. *Fax:* 650-594-3777; *E-Mail:* jshen@farinon.harris.com

SHEN, KELVIN KEI-WEI, POLYMER & ORGANIC CHEMISTRY. *Current Pos:* res chemist, US Borax Res Corp, 72-80, sr res chemist, 80-88, tech serv mgr, 88-93, prof mgr, 93-95, TECH MGR, US BORAX INC, 95- *Personal Data:* b Liao-pei, China, Sept 29, 41; m 68, Yvonne Shen; c Doris & William. *Educ:* Nat Taiwan Univ, BS, 64; Univ Mass, Amherst, MS, 66, PhD(chem), 68. *Prof Exp:* Guest scientist, Brookhaven Nat Lab, 66-68; res fel, Yale Univ, 68-69; instr chem, Drexel Univ, 69-70; asst prof, Calif State Univ, Los Angeles, 70-72. *Concurrent Pos:* Petrol Res Fund grant, Calif State Univ, Los Angeles, 72. *Mem:* AAAS; Am Chem Soc; Soc Plastics Engrs. *Res:* Chemistry of small ring compounds; organometallic chemistry; fire retardants in plastics; x-ray crystallography; photochemistry; syntheses of herbicides; environmental studies of pesticides; fire retardancy. *Mailing Add:* US Borax Inc 26877 Tourney Rd Valencia CA 91355

SHEN, LESTER SHENG-WEI, HEAT TRANSFER, THERMAL ENVIRONMENTAL ENGINEERING. *Current Pos:* RES ASSOC, UNDERGROUND SPACE CTR, UNIV MINN, 86- *Personal Data:* b St Louis, Mo, Jul 8, 55. *Educ:* Haverford Col, BS, 77; Ga Inst Technol, MSME, 79; Univ Minn, PhD(mech eng), 86. *Res:* Analysis of building thermal performance; evaluation and implementation of weatherization procedures for low-income weatherization programs; development of interactive computer tools for training and education; indoor air quality. *Mailing Add:* 4732 Elliott Ave S Minneapolis MN 55409. *Fax:* 612-824-2412; *E-Mail:* shenx001@maroon.tc.umn.edu

SHEN, LIANG CHI, ELECTRICAL ENGINEERING, WELL LOGGING & SUBSURFACE SENSING. *Current Pos:* Asst assoc prof, 67-77, chmn dept, 77-81, PROF ELEC ENG, UNIV HOUSTON, 77- *Personal Data:* b Chekiang, China, Mar 17, 39; US citizen; m 65, Wei Liu; c Michael & Eugene. *Educ:* Nat Taiwan Univ, BS, 61; Harvard Univ, SM, 63, PhD(appl physics), 67. *Concurrent Pos:* Consult, Gulf Oil, 81-82; res fel, ARCO Oil & Gas Co, 90-91. *Mem:* Fel Inst Elec & Electronics Engrs; Soc Petrol Engrs; Soc Explor Geophysicists; Soc Prof Well Log Analysts; Am Geophys Union. *Res:* Antennas; microwaves; electromagnetic wave propagation in earth; well-logging; subsurface sensing. *Mailing Add:* Univ Houston Dept Elec Engring Houston TX 77204

SHEN, LINUS LIANG-NENE, ENZYME INHIBITION, DRUG DESIGN. *Current Pos:* scientist II res, Corp Res, 75-81, sr scientist res, Pharmaceut Prod Div, 81-87, VOLWILER FEL RES, PHARMACEUT PROD DIV, ABBOTT LABS, 87- *Personal Data:* b Chi-Kiang Prov, China, Aug 28, 41; US citizen; m 78, Alice Ping Lu; c 2. *Educ:* Nat Taiwan Univ, Taipei, Taiwan, BS, 64; NC State Univ, MS, 69; Univ NC, Chapel Hill, PhD(biochem), 71. *Prof Exp:* From res asst to res assoc res Dept Biochem, Univ NC, Chapel Hill, 68-72, instr res & teaching, 72-75, asst prof res & teaching, 75. *Mem:* Am Soc Biochem & Molecular Biol; Am Soc Microbiol. *Res:* Structure, function and inhibitors of microbial and mammalian DNA topoisomerases; molecular mechanisms of the antibacterial activity of quinolones. *Mailing Add:* Antiinfectious Res Div Abbott Labs D47P AP9A Abbott Park IL 60064. *Fax:* 847-938-6603; *E-Mail:* linus.l.shen@abbott.com

SHEN, MEI-CHANG, APPLIED MATHEMATICS. *Current Pos:* from asst prof to assoc prof, 65-70, PROF APPL MATH, UNIV WIS-MADISON, 70- *Personal Data:* b Shanghai, China, Oct 3, 31; m 64; c 2. *Educ:* Taiwan Univ, BSc, 54; Brown Univ, PhD(appl math), 63. *Prof Exp:* Res assoc appl math, Brown Univ, 62-63; vis mem, Courant Inst Math Sci, NY Univ, 63-65. *Concurrent Pos:* Vis prof, Courant Inst Math Sci, NY Univ, 71-72; vis fel, Calif Inst Tech, 76; vis prof, Hong Kong Univ Sci & Technol, 91-92. *Mem:* Am Math Soc; Soc Indust & Appl Math; Acad Mech; Am Phys Soc. *Res:* Asymptotic methods; biofluid-dynamics; nonlinear wave propagation; plasma dynamics; geophysical fluid dynamics. *Mailing Add:* Dept Math Univ Wis Madison WI 53706

SHEN, PETER KO-CHUN, REACTOR PHYSICS. *Current Pos:* assoc prof reactor physics & fuel cycle, Joint Ctr Grad Study, Univ Wash, 75-79, dean, Joint Ctr Grad Study, 77-79, AFFIL PROF NUCLEAR ENG, UNIV WASH, 79-; MGR SYST OPERS, WESTINGHOUSE, HANFORD, 90- *Personal Data:* b China, Oct 28, 38; US citizen; m 65; c 1. *Educ:* Nat Taiwan Univ, BS, 61; Univ Minn, MS, 65; Kans State Univ, PhD(nuclear eng), 70. *Prof Exp:* Res assoc nuclear shielding, Kans State Univ, 69-70; supv nuclear engr reactor physics & fuel mgt, Southern Calif Edison Co, 70-75; technician & dir, Washington Pub Power Supply Syst, 80-85. *Mem:* Am Nuclear Soc. *Res:* Nuclear fuel cycle core physics, thermal hydraulic and nuclear power plant design and operation. *Mailing Add:* 2455 W G Way Apt H269 Richland WA 99352

SHEN, QUANG, GAS-PHASE MOLECULAR STRUCTURE & CONFORMATION. *Current Pos:* from asst prof to assoc prof, 80-94, PROF CHEM, COLGATE UNIV, 94- *Personal Data:* b Shanghai, China, Nov 3, 48; US citizen; m 76, Mary Ellen Mitchell; c Alan & Stephen. *Educ:* Furman Univ, BS, 70, Ore State Univ, PhD(chem), 73. *Prof Exp:* Postdoctoral fel, Univ Windsor, 74-76, Univ Troundheim, 76-78, NDak State Univ, 78-80. *Concurrent Pos:* Res grantee, Am Chem Soc, 85, NATO, 90 & 94 & NSF, 91 & 93. *Res:* Molecular structure; determination of structures and conformations of gaseous molecules via electron diffraction. *Mailing Add:* Colgate Univ 13 Oak Dr Hamilton NY 13346. *Fax:* 315-824-7935; *E-Mail:* mshen@center.colgate.edu

SHEN, S(HAN) F(U), MECHANICAL ENGINEERING. *Current Pos:* prof aeronaut eng, Grad Sch Aeronaut Eng, 61-92, John Edson Sweet prof eng, 78-92, PROF, SIBLEY SCH MECH & AEROSPACE ENG, CORNELL UNIV, 92- *Personal Data:* b Shanghai, China, Aug 31, 21; m 50; c 2. *Educ:* Nat Cent Univ, China, BS, 41. *Hon Degrees:* ScD, Mass Inst Technol, 49. *Honors & Awards:* US Sr Scientist Award, Humboldt Found, WGer, 84. *Prof Exp:* Res assoc math, Mass Inst Technol, 48-50; from asst prof to prof, Univ Md, 50-61. *Concurrent Pos:* Guggenheim fel, 57-58; vis prof, Univ Paris, 64-65 & 69-70, Tech Univ Vienna, 77 & Univ Tokyo, 84-85. *Mem:* Nat Acad Eng; Acad Sinica Repub China; corresp mem Int Acad Astronaut. *Res:* Aerodynamics; rarefied gasdynamics; fluid mechanics. *Mailing Add:* Sibley Sch Mech & Aerospace Eng Cornell Univ Upson Hall Ithaca NY 14853

SHEN, SHELDON SHIH-TA, CELL PHYSIOLOGY, DEVELOPMENTAL BIOLOGY. *Current Pos:* asst prof, 79-83, assoc prof, 84-89, PROF ZOOL, IOWA STATE UNIV, 89- *Personal Data:* b Shanghai, China, Nov 22, 47; US citizen; m 79; c 3. *Educ:* Univ Mo, BS, 69; Univ Calif, Berkeley, PhD(physiol), 74. *Prof Exp:* Fel cancer biol, Univ Calif, Berkeley, 74-77, asst res zoologist cell biol, 77-79. *Concurrent Pos:* NIH fel, 74-76; USPHS, NIH grant, 77-79, NSF grant, 80-92. *Mem:* Sigma Xi; Soc Develop Biol; Am Soc Cell Biol; AAAS; Am Soc Zoologists. *Res:* Ions ca second messengers in signal transduction; cytoplasmic factors controlling chromosome diminution in Ascaris embryos; regulation of sea urchin egg activation. *Mailing Add:* Dept Zool & Genet Iowa State Univ 339 Sci II Bldg Ames IA 50011-3223

SHEN, SINYAN, ENERGY & ENVIRONMENTAL SCIENCE & TECHNOLOGY RESEARCH ADMINISTRATION, SUPERCONDUCTING ENERGY & TELECOMMUNICATION TECHNOLOGY. *Current Pos:* DIR RES ENERGY & ENVIRON, SUPCON INT, 88-; PROF, HARVARD UNIV, 89- *Personal Data:* b Sinagapore, China, Nov 12, 49; US citizen; m 73, Yuan-Yuan Lee; c Jia & Jian. *Educ:* Univ Singapore, BSc, 69; Ohio State Univ, PhD(physics), 73; Harvard Univ, MPA, 88. *Prof Exp:* Prof, Northwestern Univ, 74-82; energy adv, State NY, 82, State Ore, 83. *Concurrent Pos:* Adv, US Dept Energy, 77-, Superconductivity Consortium, 86-, Nat Geog, 86, Int Energy Agency, 86-; ed-in-chief, Chinese Music Int J, 78-, World Resource Rev, 89-; consult, NSF, 79-, USDA, 81-, Gas Res Inst, 82-; sr res leader, US Dept Energy, Argonne Nat Lab, 83-; sci authority, Encyclopedia Britannica, 83; mgr, US Nepal Reforestation, 85; hon prof, Chinese Acad, 86; dir, Global Warming Int Ctr, 91-; sci leader, Global Treeline Prog, 91-, Russia Reforestation Prog, 92-; chmn, Global Warming Sci & Policy Int Cong, Austrian Acad Sci, 96. *Mem:* Inst World Resource Res; AAAS; Am Phys Soc. *Res:* Global warming science and policy, climate and environmental change indicators, international energy and material resource economics, reforestation and biological regeneration of oil and gas fields and superconducting energy and telecommunication technology. *Mailing Add:* Supcon Int One Heritage Plaza PO Box 5275 Woodridge IL 60517-0275. *Fax:* 630-910-1561; *E-Mail:* syshen@megsinet.net

SHEN, TEK-MING, SEMICONDUCTOR LASERS, MICROWAVES. *Current Pos:* mem tech staff, 80-89, DISTINGUISHED MEM TECH STAFF, AT&T BELL LABS, MURRAY HILL, 89- *Educ:* Univ Hong Kong, BSc, 73; Univ Ca, Berkeley, PhD(physics),79. *Prof Exp:* Res asst, Univ Calif, 79-80. *Mem:* Sr mem Inst Elec & Electronics Engrs. *Res:* Studies of dynamic properties of multifrequency and single-frequency semiconductors lasers and their system performance; lightwave systems. *Mailing Add:* AT&T Bell Labs 3B-620 101 Crawfords Corner Rd Holmdel NJ 07733

SHEN, THOMAS T, COMPUTER PROGRAMMING, MATHEMATICAL MODELING. *Current Pos:* RETIRED. *Personal Data:* b Chia-Xing, China, Aug 14, 26; US citizen; m 59; c 2. *Educ:* St John's Univ, Shanghai, BSc, 48; Northwestern Univ, Evanston, MSc, 60; Rensselaer Polytech Inst, PhD(environ eng), 72. *Prof Exp:* Environ engr, Wash State Health Dept, 62-66; sr environ engr, NY State Health Dept, 66-70; sr res scientist, NY State Dept Environ Conserv, 70-93. *Concurrent Pos:* Chmn, NY State Coun, Am Soc Civil Engrs, 79-80, Air Pollution Control Comt, 87-89, Air & Radiation Comt, 89-90 & Air Pollution Control Comt, Am Acad Environ Engrs, 89-; adj fac, Div Environ Sci, Columbia Univ, 81-90; mem & consult, US Environ Protection Agency Sci Adv Bd, 87-; bd mem, NY State Asn Libr Bd & Chinese Am Acad & Prof Soc, 90- *Mem:* Am Soc Civil Engrs; Air & Waste Mgt Asn; Am Acad Environ Engrs. *Res:* Combustion emission control; measurement and monitoring techniques; volatile organic compounds emission assessment and control; multimedia pollution prevention methodologies. *Mailing Add:* 146 Fernbank Ave Delmar NY 12054

SHEN, TSUNG YING, ORGANIC CHEMISTRY. *Current Pos:* A BURGER prof biol & med chem, Chem Dept, 86-96, EMER PROF & RES PROF, UNIV VA, 96- *Personal Data:* b Peking, China, Sept 28, 24; nat US; m 53, Amy Lin; c Bern, Hubert, Theodore, Leonard, Evelyn & Andrea. *Educ:* Nat Cent Univ, China, BSc, 46; Univ London, dipl, 48; Univ Manchester, PhD(org chem), 50, DSc, 78. *Honors & Awards:* Galileo Medal Sci Achievement, Univ Pisa, 76; Rene Descartes Silver Medal, Univ Paris, 77; Medal of Merit, Giornate Mediche Int del Collegium Biol Europa, 77; Burger Award, Am Chem Soc, 80. *Prof Exp:* Fel, Ohio State Univ, 50-52; res assoc, Mass Inst Technol, 52-56; res fel synthetic org chem, Merck Sharp & Dohme Res Labs, 56-67, assoc dir, 67-69, dir synthetic chem res, 69-71, sr dir med chem, 71-74, exec dir med chem, 74-76, vpres membrane & arthritis res, 76-86. *Concurrent Pos:* Vis chem prof, Univ Calif, Riverside, 73; scientific adv, Genelab Tech, T-Cell Sci, OsteaArth Sci, Cyto Med, 90-, & Argonex Pharm, 95- *Mem:* Am Chem Soc; NY Acad Sci; AAAS. *Res:* Medicinal chemistry; anti-inflammatory and immunopharmacological agents, viral and cancer chemotherapy; nucleosides, carbohydrate derivatives and membrane receptor regulators; biomedical applications of natural products and derivatives. *Mailing Add:* 10013 Park Royal Dr Great Falls VA 22066

SHEN, VINCENT Y, computer sciences, software engineering, for more information see previous edition

SHEN, WEI-CHIANG, CELL BIOLOGY, DRUG-PROTEIN CONJUGATES. *Current Pos:* ASSOC PROF PHARMACOL, UNIV SOUTHERN CALIF, SCH PHARM, 87- *Personal Data:* b Chekiang, China, May 3, 42; US citizen; m 68; c 2. *Educ:* Tunghai Univ, Taichung, Taiwan, BS, 65; Boston Univ, PhD(chem), 72. *Prof Exp:* Res fel biol chem, Harvard Med Sch, 72-73; res assoc biochem, Brandeis Univ, 73-76; from asst res prof to assoc res prof, Sch Med, Boston Univ, 76-83, assoc prof path & pharmacol, 83-87. *Concurrent Pos:* Vis lectr biochem toxicol, Brandeis Univ, 80-87; Cancer Res Scholar Award, Mass Div, Am Cancer Soc, 82-85; vis prof, Coal Med Col, N China, 86. *Mem:* NY Acad Sci; Am Soc Cell Biol; Am Soc Pharmacol & Exp Therapeut; AAAS; Am Soc Biol Chemists. *Res:* Endocytosis and lysosomal degradation of macromolecules in mammalian cells; conjugates of drugs and monoclonal antibodies as potential tumor-targeting agents in cancer chemotherapy; development of immunoassay methods. *Mailing Add:* Sch Pharm Univ Southern Calif 1985 Zonal Ave Los Angeles CA 90033-1058. *Fax:* 213-342-1390

SHEN, WU-MIAN, PHOTOELECTROCHEMISTRY & PHOTOCATALYSIS, OPTICAL & DIELECTRIC CHARACTERIZATION OF SEMICONDUCTORS. *Current Pos:* vis scholar, Dept Physics, 83-84, res asst, 84-91, RES ASSOC, APPL SCI INST, BROOKLYN COL, 91- *Personal Data:* b Shanghai, China, Aug 23, 42; m 74, Li-li Yang; c Zong-jing. *Educ:* Shanghai Jiao-Tong Univ, BE, 64, ME, 81; City Univ New York, PhD(physics), 91. *Prof Exp:* Engr, Tianjin Electronic Wire & Cable Co, 64-78; lectr semiconductor physics, Dept Appl Chem, Shanghai Jiao-Tong Univ, 81-83. *Mem:* Am Phys Soc; Electrochem Soc; Sigma Xi. *Res:* Photoelectrochemistry; solar energy conversion; optical and dielectric characterization of semiconductor with liquid junction or solid state junction; electrical insulation and dielectric phenomena; electrochemical deposition of high-temperature superconducting film. *Mailing Add:* Dept Physics Brooklyn Col City Univ New York Brooklyn NY 11210. *Fax:* 718-951-4407; *E-Mail:* wmsbc@cunyum.cuny.edu

SHEN, YUAN-SHOU, PHYSICAL METALLURGY. *Current Pos:* RES SCIENTIST, ENGELHARD INDUSTS, PLAINVILLE, 78- *Personal Data:* b Peking, China, Dec 12, 21; m 48; c 2. *Educ:* Nat Southwest Assoc Univ, BS, 43; Ore State Univ, MS, 64, PhD(mat sci), 68. *Prof Exp:* Assoc prof metall, Cheng Kung Univ, Taiwan, 61-62; res metallurgist, Wah Chang Albany Corp, Ore, 65-67; sr res staff, P R Mallory & Co Inc, Mass, 67-78. *Mem:* Am Soc Metals; Metall Soc; Am Soc Testing & Mat. *Res:* Phase diagram; intermetallic compound; composite material; alloy development; electric contact material; silver alloy; powder metallurgy; brazing alloys. *Mailing Add:* 6 Shackford Rd Reading MA 01867

SHEN, YUEN-RON, SOLID STATE PHYSICS. *Current Pos:* From asst prof to assoc prof, 64-70, PROF PHYSICS, UNIV CALIF, BERKELEY, 70- *Personal Data:* b Shanghai, China, Mar 25, 35; m 64. *Educ:* Nat Taiwan Univ, BS, 56; Stanford Univ, MS, 59; Harvard Univ, PhD(solid state physics), 63. *Honors & Awards:* Outstanding Res Award DOE-MRS Res, 83; Alexander von Humboldt Award, 84; Charles Hard Townes Award, 86; Sustained Outstanding Res Award, 87; Arthur L Schawlow Prize, 92; Max-Planck Res Award, 96. *Concurrent Pos:* Sloan fel, 66-68; Guggenheim Found fel, 72-73. *Mem:* Nat Acad Sci; Optical Soc Am; Photonics Soc Chinese-Ams; AAAS; fel Am Phys Soc; Chinese Acad Scis. *Res:* Quantum electronics. *Mailing Add:* Dept Physics Univ Calif Berkeley CA 94720. *Fax:* 510-643-8923; *E-Mail:* shenyr@physics.berkeley.edu

SHEN, YVONNE FENG, ORGANIC CHEMISTRY. *Current Pos:* chief chemist, 74-84, LAB DIR, ORANGE CO WATER DIST, 84- *Personal Data:* b Hu-Nan, China, Sept 11, 42; US citizen; m 68, Kelvin; c Doris & Bill. *Educ:* Tunghai Univ, Taiwan, BS, 64; Univ Mass, PhD(org chem), 68. *Prof Exp:* Fel, Princeton Univ, 68-69, Drexel Univ, 69-70 & Univ Southern Calif, 70-71; jr res scientist, City Hope Med Ctr, 71-73. *Mem:* Am Chem Soc; Am Water Works Asn. *Res:* Chemistry aspects of water and wastewater treatment. *Mailing Add:* Orange Co Water Dist PO Box 8300 Fountain Valley CA 92728-8300

SHENDRIKAR, ARUN D, ENVIRONMENTAL CHEMISTRY. *Current Pos:* CONSULT, ENVIRON, HEALTH & SAFETY ASSOC, 93- *Personal Data:* b Gulberga, India, July 10, 38; m 66, Rajani; c Rita & Atul. *Educ:* Osmania Univ, India, BS, 57, MS, 61; Durham Univ, PhD(anal chem), 66. *Prof Exp:* Lectr chem, V V Sci Col, India, 61-62; lectr in-chg, 62-63; lectr, Osmania Univ, 62-63; asst prof, Environ Sci Inst, La State Univ, 66-73; sr fel aerosol, Nat Ctr Atmospheric Res, 73-74; sr res chemist, Oil Shale Corp, 74-76; tech dir, O A Labs, Indianapolis, 76-78; tech staff specialist, Meteorol Res Inc, Altadena, 78-80; sr chemist, Res Triangle Inst, Res Triangle Park, 80-82, inorg mgr, Compuchem Labs, 82-86. gen mgr, Beta Labs, 86-88; mgr anal serv, EIRA Inc, St Rose, La, 88-89; dir environ affairs, Litho Indust, Inc, 89-93. *Concurrent Pos:* Mem adv comt, Colo Air Pollution Control Comt, 74- *Mem:* Assoc mem Royal Inst Chem; Sigma Xi; Am Soc Testing & Mat; Am Chem Soc. *Res:* Method development and applications to environmental pollution studies; hazardous wastes characterization and remediation; control technology evaluations and sampling method validations; analytical data validation and interpretation for process performance evaluation; title V permitting, emission inventory, environmental compliance, plant safety, industrial hygiene, Right-To-Know Act and regulatory liaison. *Mailing Add:* 1011 W St Helena Pl Apex NC 27502

SHENEFELT, RAY ELDON, TERATOLOGY, PEDIATRIC PATHOLOGY. *Current Pos:* ASSOC PROF, PATH DEPT, MED SCH, UNIV MISS, 92- *Personal Data:* b Spokane, Wash, Oct 2, 33; m 57; c 4. *Educ:* Univ Wis-Madison, BS, 59, MD, 63. *Prof Exp:* Intern path, Univ Wis Hosps, 63-64; resident, Univ Iowa Hosps, 64-66; fel, Dartmouth Med Sch, 66-69; asst prof pediat & path, Cincinnati Children's Hosp, 69-73; med officer teratol, Nat Ctr Toxicol Res, 74-79; instr pediat & path, Bonheur Children's Hosp, 80-86; assoc pathologist, Duckworth Path Group, Memphis, Tenn, 88-89; pathologist, Cook-Fort Worth Children's Hosp, 89-92. *Concurrent Pos:* Asst prof path, Med Sch, Univ Ark, 73-79. *Mem:* Pediat Path Soc. *Res:* Pathologic sequence in development of malformations. *Mailing Add:* 100 Redbud Trail Jackson MS 39402. *E-Mail:* rshenefelt@pathology.umsmed.edu

SHENEFELT, ROY DAVID, ENTOMOLOGY. *Current Pos:* from asst prof to prof, 46-77, EMER PROF ENTOM FORESTRY, UNIV WIS-MADISON, 77- *Personal Data:* b Evanston, Ill, Jan 27, 09; m 32; c 2. *Educ:* Spokane Col, AB, 32; State Col Wash, MS, 35, PhD(entom), 40. *Prof Exp:* From instr to asst prof zool, State Col Wash, 35-46. *Mem:* Entom Soc Am; Entom Soc Can. *Res:* Taxonomy of Braconidae; forest entomology; cacao insects. *Mailing Add:* 630 N Oak St Oregon WI 53575

SHENEMAN, JACK MARSHALL, MICROBIOLOGY. *Current Pos:* RETIRED. *Personal Data:* b Grand Rapids, Mich, Mar 26, 27; m 57, Hielke Brugman; c Elisa & Eric. *Educ:* Mich State Univ, BS, 52, MS, 54, PhD(microbiol), 57. *Prof Exp:* Asst microbiol, Mich State Univ, 54-57; res assoc, Wis Malting Co, 57-61, asst dir res, 61-63; sr food scientist, Eli Lilly & Co, 63-69; res microbiologist, Basic Veg Prod Inc, 69-75; food & drug scientist, Food & Drug Br, Calif Dept Health Serv, 75-92. *Mem:* AAAS; Am Soc Microbiol; Inst Food Technologists; Asn Food & Drug Officials; Sigma Xi. *Res:* Industrial fermentations; food flavors and preservatives; microbiology of dehydrated vegetable products; new product and process development in vegetable dehydration; food hazard microorganisms; bacterial spores; microbiological quality control methods; food and drug regulation. *Mailing Add:* PO Box 2476 El Macero CA 95618-2476. *Fax:* 530-756-3832

SHENG, HWAI-PING, MEDICAL PHYSIOLOGY, PEDIATRICS. *Current Pos:* asst prof physiol, 75-88, ASSOC PROF PEDIAT & MOLECULAR PHYSIOL & BIOPHYSICS, BAYLOR COL MED, 88- *Personal Data:* b Johore, Malaysia, July 18, 43; US citizen; m 77; c 1. *Educ:* Univ Singapore, BSc, 66, Hons, 67; Baylor Col Md, PhD(physiol), 71. *Prof Exp:* Lectr pharmacol, Univ Hong Kong, 71-74. *Concurrent Pos:* Fulbright Fel, 67-70. *Mem:* Am Physiol Soc; Soc Exp Biol & Med; Am Inst Nutrit. *Res:* Growth, nutrition and body composition. *Mailing Add:* Dept Physiol Fac Med Univ Hong Kong 5 Sassoon Rd Hong Kong People's Republic of China. *Fax:* 852-855-9730

SHENG, PING, SOLID STATE PHYSICS. *Current Pos:* PROF PHYSICS, HONG KONG UNIV SCI & TECHNOL, 94- *Personal Data:* b Shanghai, China, Aug 5, 46; m 70, Deborah Wen; c Ellen & Ada. *Educ:* Calif Inst Technol, BS, 67; Princeton Univ, PhD(physics), 71. *Prof Exp:* Vis mem, Sch Natural Sci, Inst Advan Study, Princeton, NJ, 71-73; mem tech staff physics, RCA David Sarnoff Res Ctr, 73-80; group head, Corp Res Ctr, Exxon Res & Eng, 80-86, sr res assoc, 86-94. *Concurrent Pos:* Consult prof, Fudan Univ & S China Univ Technol; regent lectr, Univ Calif Irvine, 91; prof univ, Univ Pierre et Marie Curie, Paris. *Mem:* Fel Am Phys Soc; Optical Soc Am; Soc Explor Geophysicists. *Res:* Electrical transport in wave propagation inhomogeneous systems; liquid crystals; structure and physical properties of random composites. *Mailing Add:* Dept Physics Hong Kong Univ Sci & Technol Clearwater Bay Kowloon Hong Kong People's Republic of China. *Fax:* 852-2358-1652; *E-Mail:* phsheng@usthk.ust.hk

SHENG, YEA-YI PETER, FLUID MECHANICS, ENVIRONMENTAL SCIENCES. *Current Pos:* assoc prof, 86-88, PROF, COASTAL & OCEANOG ENG, UNIV FLA, 88- *Personal Data:* b Shanghai, China, Aug 3, 46; m 70, Ruth; c David. *Educ:* Nat Taiwan Univ, BS, 68; Case Western Res Univ, MS, 72, PhD(mech & aerospace eng), 75. *Prof Exp:* Res assoc environ, Case Western Res Univ, 75-77, sr res assoc, 77-78; assoc consult, Aeronaut Res Assoc, Princeton, 78-79, consult meteorol & oceanog, 79-93; sr consult & mgr coastal oceanog, 84-86. *Mem:* Am Geophys Union; Am Soc Mech Engrs; Am Soc Civil Engrs. *Res:* Flow and dispersion of contaminants in coastal, estuarine, offshore and atmospheric environments; turbulent transport processes in stratified flows; turbulence modeling; computational fluid dynamics; water quality modeling. *Mailing Add:* 9817 SW First Pl Gainesville FL 32607. *E-Mail:* pete@coastal.ufl.edu

SHENITZER, ABE, MATHEMATICS. *Current Pos:* PROF MATH, ARTS & EDUC, YORK UNIV, 69- *Personal Data:* b Warsaw, Poland, Apr 2, 21; nat US; m 52; c 2. *Educ:* Brooklyn Col, BA, 50; NY Univ, MSc, 51, PhD, 54. *Prof Exp:* Asst, Inst Math Sci, NY Univ, 52-55; mem staff, Bell Tel Labs, Inc, 55-56; from instr to asst prof math, Rutgers Univ, 56-58; assoc prof, Adelphi Univ, 58-63, prof, 63-69. *Mem:* Am Math Soc. *Res:* Group theory; differential equations; approximation theory. *Mailing Add:* Dept Math & Statist York Univ North York ON M3J 1P3 Can

SHENK, JOHN STONER, AGRONOMY, PLANT BREEDING. *Current Pos:* From asst prof to assoc prof, 70-81, PROF AGRON, PA STATE UNIV, 78- *Personal Data:* b Lancaster Co, Pa, July 25, 33; m 52; c 4. *Educ:* Pa State Univ, BS, 65; Mich State Univ, MS, 67, PhD, 69. *Mem:* Am Soc Agron; Am Forage & Grassland Coun; Sigma Xi. *Res:* Plant breeding and genetics; development and utilization of chemical and bioassay technique for the production of new plant varieties with improved nutritional quality; chemical infrared and bioassay; computer analysis of infrared data. *Mailing Add:* Agron 116 Agr Sci Pa State Univ University Park PA 16802-3504

SHENK, THOMAS EUGENE, MOLECULAR BIOLOGY. *Current Pos:* ELKINS PROF MOLECULAR BIOL, PRINCETON UNIV, 84-, CHMN, 96-; PROF, AM CANCER SOC, 86- *Personal Data:* b Brooklyn, NY, Jan 1, 47; m 79, Susan M Hillman; c Christopher T & Gregory T. *Educ:* Univ Detroit, BS, 69; Rutgers Univ, PhD, 73. *Honors & Awards:* Waksman Award Microbiol, Theobald Smith Soc, 80; Eli Lilly Award, Am Soc Microbiol, 82. *Prof Exp:* from asst prof to prof molecular biol, Univ Conn, Farmington, 75-80; prof, State Univ NY, Stony Brook, 80-84. *Concurrent Pos:* Fel, Jane coffin Childs Mem Fund, 73-75; mem, Virol Study Sect, NIH, 82-86, chair, 90-92; bd trustee, Cold Spring Harbor Lab, 82-87; ed, J Virol, 84-94, ed-in-chief, 94-; merit award, NIH, 87-95 & 95-03; investr, Am Heart Asn & Howard Hughes Med Inst, 88. *Mem:* Nat Acad Sci; Inst Med-Nat Acad Sci; Am Soc Microbiol; Am Soc Virol (pres elect, 96-97). *Res:* Molecular biology; viruses and apoptosis; mammary tumors induced by human adenovirus; stem cell biology and gene therapy; author of numerous publications. *Mailing Add:* Dept Molecular Biol Princeton Univ Princeton NJ 08544-0001

SHENKEL, CLAUDE W, JR, GEOLOGY. *Current Pos:* RETIRED. *Personal Data:* b Lyons, Kans, Apr 29, 19; m 41; c 2. *Educ:* Kans State Col, BS, 41; Univ Colo, MS, 47, PhD(geol), 52. *Prof Exp:* From asst prof to prof geol, Kans State Univ, 49-87. *Concurrent Pos:* Consult, Spec Res Proj, East Venezuelan Basin, 56-57, res geol, Andes Mountains, SAm, 65, spec res geol, SAm, 65-66. *Mem:* Fel Geol Soc Am; Am Inst Prof Geol; Am Asn Petrol Geologists. *Res:* Regional stratigraphic analysis of San Juan and Paradox Basins; petroleum and sub-surface geology. *Mailing Add:* 20231 Meadowwood Dr Sun City West AZ 85375

SHENKER, MARTIN, OPTICS. *Current Pos:* inspector, 49-50, jr physicist, 50-51, optical designer, 51-57, asst chief optical designer, 57-60, chief optical designer, 60-73, VPRES OPTICAL DESIGN, FARRAND OPTICAL CO, 73- *Personal Data:* b New York, NY, Aug 12, 28; m 49; c 3. *Educ:* NY Univ, AB, 48, MS, 51. *Prof Exp:* Jr actuary, New York City Teachers' Retirement Bd, 48-49. *Mem:* Fel Optical Soc Am; Soc Photo-Optical Instrument Engrs. *Res:* Optical design; geometrical optics. *Mailing Add:* 5 Ormian Dr Pomona NY 10970

SHENKER, SCOTT JOSEPH, GAME THEORY, COMPUTER NETWORKS. *Current Pos:* MEM RES STAFF, PALO ALTO RES CTR, XEROX CTR, 84- *Personal Data:* b Alexandria, Va, Jan 24, 56; m 80; c 1. *Educ:* Brown Univ, ScB, 78; Univ Chicago, PhD(physics), 83. *Prof Exp:* Res assoc, Dept Physics, Cornell Univ, 83-84. *Mem:* Asn Comput Mach; Inst Elect & Electronics Engrs; Am Econ Asn. *Res:* Analysis of computer network algorithms; analysis of resource allocation mechanisms from a game theoretic point-of-view. *Mailing Add:* Palo Alto Res Ctr Xerox Corp 3333 Coyote Hill Rd Palo Alto CA 94304. *Fax:* 650-812-4471; *E-Mail:* shenker@psic.xerox.com

SHENKER, STEPHEN HART, THEORETICAL PHYSICS. *Current Pos:* PROF PHYSICS, RUTGERS UNIV, 89- *Personal Data:* b Alexandria, Va, Jan 25, 53; m 90, Rebecca Passonneau. *Educ:* Harvard Univ, AB, 75; Cornell Univ, PhD(physics), 80. *Honors & Awards:* Presidential Young Investr Award, NSF, 85; Morris Loeb lectr, Harvard Univ, 94. *Prof Exp:* James Franck fel, Univ Chicago, 79-80, from asst prof to prof, 81-89; fel, Inst Theoret Physics, 80-81. *Concurrent Pos:* A P Sloan Found fel, 83; MacArthur fel, 87; gen mem, Aspen Ctr Physics, 90- *Mem:* Am Phys Soc. *Res:* Quantum field theory; statistical mechanics; quantum gravity; string theory. *Mailing Add:* Dept Physics & Astron Rutgers Univ PO Box 849 Piscataway NJ 08855. *Fax:* 732-445-4993; *E-Mail:* shenker@physics.rutgers.edu

SHENKIN, HENRY A, NEUROSURGERY. *Current Pos:* DIR NEUROSURG, EPISCOPAL HOSP, 58-; PROF NEUROSURG, MED COL PA, 74- *Personal Data:* b Philadelphia, Pa, June 25, 15; m 41, Renee Friedenberg; c Budd, Rober, Katerine & Emily. *Educ:* Univ Pa, AB, 35; Jefferson Med Col, MD, 39. *Prof Exp:* Charles Harrison Frazier traveling fel from Univ Pa to dept physiol & brain tumor registry, Sch Med, Yale Univ, 41-42. *Concurrent Pos:* Assoc prof neurol surg, Div Grad Med, Univ Pa, 60-67; clin prof neurosurg, Sch Med, Temple Univ, 67- *Mem:* Am Asn Neurol Surg; Soc Neurol Surg; Am Col Surg; Sigma Xi. *Res:* Cerebral circulation and the metabolism of the neurosurgical patient. *Mailing Add:* 3300 Darby Rd No 3103 Haverford PA 19041. *Fax:* 610-642-1158; *E-Mail:* hshenkin@aol.com

SHENOI, BELLE ANANTHA, ELECTRICAL ENGINEERING. *Current Pos:* dept chair, 86-92, PROF ELEC ENG, WRIGHT STATE UNIV, 86- *Personal Data:* b Mysore, India, Dec 23, 29; m 61; c 2. *Educ:* Univ Madras, BS, 51; Indian Inst Sci, Bangalore, DIISc, 55; Univ Ill, MS, 58, PhD(elec eng), 62. *Honors & Awards:* Meritorious Serv Award, Inst Elec & Electronics Engrs, Circuits & Systs Soc. *Prof Exp:* From teaching asst to instr elec eng, Univ Ill, 56-62; from asst prof to prof elec eng, Univ Minn, Minneapolis, 62-86. *Concurrent Pos:* NSF grant, 64-68. *Mem:* Fel Inst Elec & Electronics Engrs (pres, Circuits & Systs Soc, 75); fel Inst Electronics & Telecommun Engrs. *Res:* Digital filters and signal processing; theory and design of networks; analysis of systems. *Mailing Add:* Elec Eng Dept 311 Russ Ctr Wright State Univ Dayton OH 45435. *Fax:* 513-873-5009; *E-Mail:* bshenoi@kiwi.cs.wright.edu

SHENOLIKAR, ASHOK KUMAR, SOFTWARE SYSTEMS, COMPUTER SCIENCES. *Current Pos:* SYST ARCHITECT, GRUMMAN DATA SYSTS, 86- *Personal Data:* b Hyderabad, India; US citizen; m 70; c 2. *Educ:* Osmania Univ, Hyderabad, India, BE, 60; Univ Okla, BS, 66, MS, 69. *Prof Exp:* Consult, 69-73; appln engr, Gibbs & Hills, Inc, 73-78; prin engr, Harris Corp, 78-86. *Mem:* Inst Elec & Electronic Engrs; Soc Mfg Engrs; Nat Comput Graphics Asn. *Res:* Technology evaluation and selection for advanced, integrated, large scale information systems; concept definition for strategic system architectures in multi vendor environments. *Mailing Add:* 5464 Ashleigh Rd Fairfax VA 22030

SHENOY, GOPAL K, SYNCHROTRON RADIATION, MOSSBAUER SPECTROSCOPY. *Current Pos:* vis scientist, Argonne Nat Lab, 74-76, physicist, 76-81, assoc dir adv photon source, 88-90, SR PHYSICIST, ARGONNE NAT LAB, 81-, DIV DIR, EXP FACIL ADV PHOTON SOURCE, 90- *Personal Data:* US citizen; m 70, Kasbekar Ravibala; c Shami & Lakshmi. *Educ:* Univ Bombay, BS, 59, MS, 61, PhD(physics), 66. *Prof Exp:* Sci assoc physics, Tech Univ Munich, 70-72; res assoc physics, Centre Recherche Nucleaire, Strasbourg, 72-74. *Concurrent Pos:* Vis scientist, Tech Univ Helsinki, 71; group leader, Argonne Nat Lab, 84-88. *Mem:* Am Phys Soc; Mat Res Soc; AAAS; Sigma Xi. *Res:* Application of Mossbauer spectroscopy and synchrotron radiation to investigate properties of materials such as storage hydrides, rare earth, actinites and superconductors. *Mailing Add:* 1067 Carriage Ct Naperville IL 60540

SHEPANSKI, JOHN FRANCIS, ARTIFICIAL NEURAL SYSTEMS, PATTERN RECOGNITION. *Current Pos:* STAFF SCIENTIST, TRW INC, 84- *Personal Data:* b Rochester, NY, Mar 4, 54; m 76. *Educ:* St Bonaventure Univ, BS, 76; Univ Rochester, MA, 79, PhD(physics), 82. *Prof Exp:* Res fel, Calif Inst Technol, 82-84. *Mem:* Am Phys Soc; Int Neural Network Soc. *Res:* Artificial neural networks and their application to pattern recognition; biophysics (photosynthesis); chemical physics; laser spectroscopy; statistical mechanics. *Mailing Add:* 6627 Noble Ave Van Nuys CA 91405

SHEPARD, ALAN BARTLETT, JR, ASTRONAUTICS. *Current Pos:* RETIRED. *Personal Data:* b East Derry, NH, Nov 18, 23; m 45, Louise Brewer; c Laura & Juliana. *Educ:* US Naval Acad, BS, 44. *Hon Degrees:* MS, Dartmouth Col; DSc, Miami Univ. *Honors & Awards:* Langley Medal, Smithsonian Inst, 64. *Prof Exp:* comndg ensign, USN, 44, designated naval aviator, 47, Fighter Squadron 42, Aircraft Carriers, Mediter, 47-49, Test Pilot Sch, 50-53, 55-57, Fighter Squadron 193, 53-55, test pilot, F4D Skyray, 55, F3H Demon, F84 Crusader & F11F Tigercat, 56, F5D SKylancer, 56, instr, Naval Test Pilot Sch, 57; officer & comdr-in-chief, Atlantic Fleet, 58-59; astronaut, NASA, 59-61, chief, Astronaut Off, 65-74, comdr, Apollo 14 Lunar Landing Mission, 71. *Concurrent Pos:* Pres, Seven Fourteen Enterprises, 86. *Mem:* Fel Soc Exp Test Pilots. *Res:* Became fifth man to walk on moon and hit first lunar golf shot; published author. *Mailing Add:* Seven Fourteen Ent 6225 Vectorspace Blvd Titusville FL 32780-8040

SHEPARD, BUFORD MERLE, ENTOMOLOGY, ECOLOGY. *Current Pos:* PROF ENTOM & RESIDENT DIR, COASTAL RES EDUC CTR, 88- *Personal Data:* b Dexter, Ga, Apr 10, 42; m 60. *Educ:* Mid Tenn State Univ, BS, 66; Univ Ga, MS, 68; Tex A&M Univ, PhD(entom), 71. *Prof Exp:* Entomologist, Hillsborough Co Health Dept, 68-69; asst prof entom, Univ Fla, 71-72; from asst prof to prof entom, Clemson Univ, 72-83; entomologist, Int Rice Res Inst, 83-84, dept head entom, 85-89. *Concurrent Pos:* Consult, Insect Pest Mgt, Brazil, Panama, Seychelles, Australia, Kenya & Costa Rica. *Mem:* Entom Soc Am; Philippine Asn Entomologists. *Res:* Biological control, insect ecology and integrated pest management; developing and evaluating integrated pest management programs in the United States, tropical Asia and South America. *Mailing Add:* Coastal Res Educ Ctr 2865 Savannah Hwy Charleston SC 29111

SHEPARD, DAVID C, BIOLOGY. *Current Pos:* RETIRED. *Personal Data:* b Montpelier, Vt, Mar 13, 29; m 52; c 2. *Educ:* Stanford Univ, AB, 51, PhD, 57. *Prof Exp:* From instr to prof biol, San Diego State Univ, 56-91. *Mem:* AAAS; Am Soc Cell Biol; Sigma Xi. *Res:* Cell growth and division; cell aging. *Mailing Add:* 12008 Wintercrest Dr No 125 Lakeside CA 92040-3755

SHEPARD, EDWIN REED, ORGANIC CHEMISTRY. *Current Pos:* RETIRED. *Personal Data:* b Springfield, Ohio, June 24, 17; m 40; c 5. *Educ:* Wittenberg Col, AB, 38; Ohio State Univ, PhD(org chem), 42. *Prof Exp:* Org chemist, Eli Lilly & Co, 42-51, head dept org chem res, 51-57, head dept appln res, 58-66, res assoc, Prod Develop Div, 66-72, res adv, 73-81. *Mem:* NY Acad Sci; AAAS; Am Chem Soc. *Res:* Chemotherapy, especially antibiotics; cardiovascular drugs; agricultural and food chemicals; product development through new drug application. *Mailing Add:* 2290 Demaret Dr Dunedin FL 34698

SHEPARD, HARVEY KENNETH, NONLINEAR DYNAMICAL SYSTEMS, THEORETICAL HIGH ENERGY PHYSICS. *Current Pos:* from asst prof to assoc prof, 69-79, chmn, 85-88, PROF PHYSICS, UNIV NH, 79- *Personal Data:* b Chicago, Ill, Sept 19, 38; c 2. *Educ:* Univ Ill, Urbana, BS, 60; Calif Inst Technol, MS, 62, PhD(physics), 66. *Prof Exp:* Consult, Rand Corp, Calif, 61-65; lectr & res fel high energy physics, Univ Calif, Santa Barbara, 65-67 & Univ Calif, Riverside, 67-69. *Concurrent Pos:* Mem, Inst Advan Study, 77-78; mem, Mass Inst Technol Ctr Theoret Physics, 84-85. *Mem:* Am Phys Soc; Biophys Soc; Sigma Xi. *Res:* Nonlinear dynamics; high energy theoretical physics; theoretical elementary particle physics; mathematical physics; biophysics. *Mailing Add:* Dept Physics Univ NH Durham NH 03824. *Fax:* 603-862-2998; *E-Mail:* shepard@curie.unh.edu

SHEPARD, JAMES F, plant pathology, plant virology, for more information see previous edition

SHEPARD, JOSEPH WILLIAM, PHYSICAL CHEMISTRY. *Current Pos:* RETIRED. *Personal Data:* b St Paul, Minn, Aug 16, 22; m 43; c 4. *Educ:* Wayne State Univ, BS, 43; Univ Mich, MS, 47, PhD(chem), 53. *Prof Exp:* Res chemist, Eng Div, Chrysler Corp, 47-49; dir, Imaging Res Lab, Minn Mining & Mfg Co, 52-68, tech dir, Microfilm Prod Div, 68-80, tech dir, Duplicating Prod Div, 75-78, div vpres, Eng Syst Div, 82-85. *Mem:* AAAS; Am Chem Soc; Soc Photog Scientists & Engrs; Sigma Xi. *Res:* Surface and crystal chemistry; colloids; solid state; photochemistry. *Mailing Add:* 9821 Admiral Dewey NE Albuquerque NM 87111-1343

SHEPARD, KENNETH LEROY, medicinal chemistry, for more information see previous edition

SHEPARD, KENNETH WAYNE, ACCELERATOR PHYSICS. *Current Pos:* physicist, 75-86, SR PHYSICIST, ARGONNE NAT LAB, 86- *Personal Data:* b Columbus, Ohio, Jan 2, 41; m 62; c 2. *Educ:* Univ Chicago, BS, 62; Dartmouth Col, MA, 64; Stanford Univ, PhD(physics), 70. *Prof Exp:* Res asst, Calif Inst Technol, 70-73, res assoc, 73-75. *Mem:* Am Phys Soc. *Res:* Development of high-field, radio-frequency superconducting devices for use in particle accelerators; investigation of the RF properties of superconductors; development of superconducting devices. *Mailing Add:* 9700 S Cass Ave Argonne IL 60439

SHEPARD, MARION L(AVERNE), MATERIALS SCIENCE, METALLURGICAL ENGINEERING. *Current Pos:* from asst prof to assoc prof, 67-78, PROF MECH ENG, DUKE UNIV, 78-, ASSOC DEAN, SCH ENG, 77- *Personal Data:* b Owosso, Mich, Dec 20, 37; m 62; c 1. *Educ:* Mich Tech, BS, 59; Iowa State Univ, MS, 60, PhD(metall), 65. *Prof Exp:* Anal engr, Pratt & Whitney Aircraft Div, United Aircraft Corp, 60-62, proj metallurgist, 65-67, sr proj metallurgist, 67. *Mem:* Am Soc Mech Engrs; Am Soc Eng Educ. *Res:* Phase equilibria in cryobiological systems; response of materials to chemical and thermal fields; precipitation hardening. *Mailing Add:* 3421 Pinafore Dr Durham NC 27705

SHEPARD, MAURICE CHARLES, MEDICAL BACTERIOLOGY. *Current Pos:* chief div bact, US Naval Med Field Res Lab, 53-75, CONSULT PREV MED, NAVAL REGIONAL MED CTR, 75- *Personal Data:* b River Falls, Wis, Feb 29, 16; wid; c 3. *Educ:* Univ Wis, BS, 39, MS, 40; Duke Univ, PhD(microbiol), 53. *Prof Exp:* Asst bact, Univ Wis, 39-40; instr, Univ Mass, 40-44; coordr field labs, Venereal Dis Div, USPHS, Washington, DC, 45-48, dir spec venereal dis res unit, NC, 49-52 & Ark, 52-53. *Mem:* Am Soc Microbiol; NY Acad Sci; hon mem Int Orgn Mycoplasmol. *Res:* Biology of mycoplasma; ureaplasmas; etiology of nongonococcal urethritis. *Mailing Add:* 1008 River St Jacksonville NC 28540

SHEPARD, PAUL FENTON, PARTICLE PHYSICS. *Current Pos:* from asst prof to assoc prof, 74-85, PROF PHYSICS & ASTRON, UNIV PITTSBURGH, 85- *Personal Data:* b Ann Arbor, Mich, Jan 27, 42; m 63; c 2. *Educ:* Col William & Mary, BS, 63; Princeton Univ, MA, 66, PhD(physics), 69. *Prof Exp:* Adj asst prof physics, Univ Calif, Los Angeles, 69-73. *Mem:* AAAS; Am Phys Soc. *Res:* High energy experimental particle physics; direct photon production and heavy quark spectroscopy; applications of solid state devices to high energy physics. *Mailing Add:* Dept Physics & Astron Univ Pittsburgh 100 Allen Hall Pittsburgh PA 15260

SHEPARD, ROBERT ANDREWS, ORGANIC CHEMISTRY. *Current Pos:* RETIRED. *Personal Data:* b Gaziantep, Turkey, Oct 22, 23; m 49, Eugenia Melzar; c Virginia (Rickeman), Andrew & Marjorie (Knobloch). *Educ:* Yale Univ, BS, 44, PhD(chem), 50. *Prof Exp:* Instr chem, Yale Univ, 46-50; from instr to assoc prof chem, Northeastern Univ, 50-58, chmn, Dept Chem, 58-68, dean, Col Lib Arts, 68-76, prof chem, 58-86. *Concurrent Pos:* Actg dir, Marine Sci Inst, 79-82. *Res:* Organic fluorine chemistry; marine chemistry; diazo compounds. *Mailing Add:* HC 66 Box 125 Samoset Rd Boothbay Harbor ME 04538

SHEPARD, ROBERT STANLEY, PHYSIOLOGY, PHARMACOLOGY. *Current Pos:* RETIRED. *Personal Data:* b Washington, DC, June 19, 27; m 50; c 4. *Educ:* George Washington Univ, BS, 50, MS, 51; Univ Iowa, PhD(physiol), 55. *Prof Exp:* From assoc prof to assoc prof, Wayne State Univ, 55-70, prof physiol, Sch Med, 70-87. *Concurrent Pos:* Lectr, Mercy Col, Mich, 58-61 & Grace Hosp, 62-81. *Mem:* Am Physiol Soc. *Res:* Lathyrism; blood coagulation; muscle and cardiovascular physiology; teaching techniques. *Mailing Add:* 27130 Sylvan Ave Warren MI 48093-7531

SHEPARD, ROGER N, COGNITIVE SCIENCE. *Current Pos:* PROF PSYCHOL, STANFORD UNIV, 68- & RAY LYMAN WILBUR PROF SOCIAL SCI, 89- *Personal Data:* b Palo Alto, Calif, Jan 30, 29; m 52; c 3. *Educ:* Stanford Univ, BA, 51; Yale Univ, MS, 52, PhD(exp psychol), 55. *Hon Degrees:* DSc, Rutgers Univ, 93. *Honors & Awards:* Distinguished Sci Contrib Award, Am Psychol Asn, 76; James McKeen Cattell Fund Award, 79, 80; Howard Crosby Warren Medal, Soc Exp Psychologists, 81; Behav Sci Award, NY Acad Sci, 87; Nat Medal of Sci, 95. *Prof Exp:* Res assoc, Naval Res Lab, 55-56; res fel, Harvard Univ, 56-58, prof psychol, 66-68, dir, Psychol Labs, 67-68; mem tech staff, Bell Tel Lab, 58-66, head dept, 63-66; prof, Harvard Univ, 66-68. *Concurrent Pos:* John Guggenheim fel, 71-72; fel, Ctr Advan Study Behav Sci, 71-72; First Fowler Hamilton vis res fel, Christ Church, Oxford Univ, 87; William James fel, Am Psychol Soc, 89- *Mem:* Nat Acad Sci; fel AAAS; fel Am Acad Arts & Sci; fel Am Psychol Asn; Psychomet Soc (pres, 73-74); Soc Exp Psychologists. *Res:* Originator of the experimental paradigm of "mental rotation"; originator of first method of nonmetric multidimensionol scaling; originator of the auditory illusion of endlessy ascending pitch; formulator of a proposed universal law of generalization; author of over 100 scientific papers and 3 books. *Mailing Add:* Dept Psychol Bldg 420 Stanford Univ Stanford CA 94305-2130. *E-Mail:* roger@psych.stanford.edu

SHEPARD, THOMAS H, PEDIATRICS. *Current Pos:* from instr to assoc prof, 55-68, head, Cent Lab Human Embryol, 69-93, PROF PEDIAT, SCH MED, UNIV WASH, 68-, HEAD, CENT LAB HUMAN EMBRYOL, 62- *Personal Data:* b Milwaukee, Wis, May 22, 23; m 47, Alice Kelly; c 3. *Educ:* Amherst Col, AB, 45; Univ Rochester, MD, 48. *Honors & Awards:* Joseph Warkany Lectr, 88. *Prof Exp:* Asst resident pediat, Albany Med Col, 49-50; chief resident, Univ Rochester, 50-52; fel endocrinol, Med Sch, Johns Hopkins Univ, 54-55. *Concurrent Pos:* Res assoc embryol, Dept Anat & vis asst prof, Col Med, Univ Fla, 61-62; vis investr, Dept Embryol, Carnegie Inst Wash, 62 & fetal lab, Dept Pediat, Copenhagen Univ, 63. *Mem:* AAAS; Am Pediat Soc; Teratology Soc (pres, 68). *Res:* Human embryology and teratology; clinical pediatrics; development of the thyroid; embryo explantation and organ culture; metabolism of achondroplastic dwarfism; author of one book in its 8th edition. *Mailing Add:* Dept Pediat Univ Wash Sch Med Seattle WA 98195. *Fax:* 206-543-3184

SHEPARDSON, JOHN U, ANALYTICAL CHEMISTRY. *Current Pos:* RETIRED. *Personal Data:* b Winchendon, Mass, May 4, 20; wid; c Ann, Sallie & Roy M. *Educ:* Univ Mass, BS, 42; Rensselaer Polytech Inst, MS, 48, PhD(analytical chem), 50. *Prof Exp:* Analyst, Lever Bros Co, 46-47; mgr control dept, Uranium Div, Mallinckrodt Chem Works, 50-59, mgr tech admin, 59-64, dir control, Winthrop Labs, Sterling Drug, 64-76; tech dir, Cis Radiopharmaceut Inc, 76-79; chief chemist, Astro Circuit Corp, 80-84. *Concurrent Pos:* Consult, 84-89. *Mem:* Am Chem Soc. *Res:* Organic analytical reagents; inorganic separations; organic analysis; pharmaceuticals. *Mailing Add:* 11 Hitchinpost Rd Chelmsford MA 01824-1919

SHEPHARD, MARK S, COMPUTATIONAL MECHANICS, COMPUTER ENGINEERING. *Current Pos:* From asst prof to assoc prof civil & mech eng, 79-87, PROF, RENSSELAER POLYTECH INST, 87-, SAMUEL A & ELISABETH C JOHNSON PROF ENG, 93-, PROF COMPUT SCI, 96-; CONSULT, SIMMETRIX CORP, 97- *Personal Data:* m 72, Sharon L Nirschel; c Steven W & Kari L. *Educ:* Clarkson Univ, BS, 74; Cornell Univ, PhD(struct eng), 79. *Honors & Awards:* Comput Eng Award, Asn Comput Mach. *Concurrent Pos:* Assoc dir, Ctr Interactive Comput Graphics, Rensselaer Polytech Inst, 80-90, dir, Sci Comput Res Ctr, 90-, Johnson chair, 93; vis res fel, Gen Elec Corp Res, 85; consult comput aided eng, 80-93; prin investr, NSF & NASA. *Mem:* Fel Asn Comput Mech (vpres, 96-98); Int Asn Comput Mech; Am Soc Mech Engrs; Am Soc Civil Engrs; assoc fel Am Inst Aeronaut & Astronaut; Am Soc Eng Educ. *Res:* Automated and adaptive finite element analysis technologies; advanced computational environments. *Mailing Add:* Sci Comput Res Ctr Rensselaer Polytech Inst 110 Eighth St Troy NY 12180-3590. *E-Mail:* shephard@scorec.rpi.edu

SHEPHARD, ROY JESSE, PHYSIOLOGY, MEDICINE. *Current Pos:* PROF APPL PHYSIOL & PREV MED, UNIV TORONTO, 64-, PROF PHYSIOL, 66-, PROF MED, INST MED SCI, 68-, ASSOC PROF PHYS EDUC, SCH PHYS & HEALTH EDUC, 71- *Personal Data:* b London, Eng, May 8, 29; m 56, Muriel Cullum; c Sarah & Rachel. *Educ:* Univ London, BSc, 49, MB, BS, 52, PhD(sci), 54, MD, 59. *Hon Degrees:* DPE, Univ Gent; Dr, Univ Montreal. *Honors & Awards:* Citation, Am Col Sports Med; Adolph Abrahams Medal, Brit Asn Sport & Med; Philip Noel Baker Res Prize, Int Coun Sport Sci & Phys Educ. *Prof Exp:* Med officer, Res Aviation Facil, Inst Aviation Med, 54-56; asst prof prev med, Univ Cincinnati, 56-58; sr sci officer, Chem Defense Res Estab, UK Ministry Defense, 58-59; prin sci officer, 59-64. *Concurrent Pos:* Fulbright scholar, Univ Cincinnati, 56-58; consult, Toronto Rehab Ctr, 67-, Gage Inst Chest Dis, 71- & Univ Que, Trois Rivieres, 71-; vpres, Int Comt Phys Fitness Res; vis prof, Univ Paris, 85-86; assoc ed, Int J Sport Sci; vis scientist, Defense & Civil Inst of Environ Med, 91- *Mem:* Brit Physiol Soc; Am Physiol Soc; Brit Asn Sports Med (vpres); Am Asn Health, Phys Educ & Recreation; Am Col Sports Med (past pres); Can Asn Sports Sci (past pres); hon fel Belg Asn Sports Med. *Res:* Cardiorespiratory physiology with particular reference to endurance fitness, sport medicine and the environment; exercise immunology. *Mailing Add:* Sch Phys & Health Educ Univ Toronto 320 Huron St Toronto ON M5S 1A1 Can. *Fax:* 416-978-4384; *E-Mail:* roy.shephard@dciem.dnd.ca

SHEPHARD, WILLIAM DANKS, EXPERIMENTAL ELEMENTARY PARTICLE PHYSICS. *Current Pos:* from asst prof to assoc prof, 63-73, PROF PHYSICS, UNIV NOTRE DAME, 73- *Personal Data:* b Gary, Ind, July 8, 33; m 59, Barbara Parker. *Educ:* Wesleyan Univ, BA, 54; Univ Wis, MS, 55, PhD, 62. *Prof Exp:* Asst physics, Univ Wis, 54-60; asst prof, Univ Ky, 60-63. *Concurrent Pos:* Guest jr res asst, Brookhaven Nat Lab, 57-58, guest assoc physicist, 60-72, guest physicist, 73-; Fulbright fel, Max Planck Inst Physics, 62-63; guest physicist & consult, Argonne Nat Lab, 63-80; guest physicist, Nat Accelerator Lab, 71-; consult, Oak Ridge Nat Lab, 61-63; guest prof physics, Fac Math & Natural Sci, Univ Nijmegen, Netherlands, 75-76. *Mem:* Am Phys Soc; Sigma Xi. *Res:* Elementary particle physics; high energy interactions; experiments in hadron-hadron, photon-hadron and hadron-nucleus interactions involving heavy quark production and decay, hadron spectroscopy and multiparticle final states. *Mailing Add:* Dept Physics Univ Notre Dame Notre Dame IN 46556. *Fax:* 219-631-5952; *E-Mail:* shephard@undhep.hep.no.edu

SHEPHERD, ALBERT PITT, JR, PHYSIOLOGY. *Current Pos:* asst prof, 74-77, PROF PHYSIOL, UNIV TEX HEALTH SCI CTR SAN ANTONIO, 77- *Personal Data:* b Lexington, Miss, Dec 29, 43; m 65; c 1. *Educ:* Millsaps Col, BS, 66; Univ Miss, PhD(physiol), 71. *Prof Exp:* Asst instr physiol, Univ Tex Med Sch Houston, 72-73; asst prof, Col Med, Univ Calif, Irvine, 73-74. *Concurrent Pos:* Mem Nat Bd Med Examiners; assoc ed, Am J Physiol. *Mem:* Am Physiol Soc; Microcirc Soc; Int Soc Oxygen Transport to Tissue; Am Heart Asn; Inst Elec & Electronics Engrs; Can Physiol Soc; Europ Microcirculatory Soc. *Res:* Intestinal circulation; control of microcirculation; biomedical instrumentation. *Mailing Add:* Dept of Physiol Univ of Tex Health Sci Ctr San Antonio TX 78284-7756

SHEPHERD, BENJAMIN ARTHUR, ZOOLOGY. *Current Pos:* from instr to asst prof, 69-73, asst chmn dept zool, 76-78, actg chmn, 78, assoc prof, 73-79, PROF ZOOL, SOUTHERN ILL UNIV, CARBONDALE, 79-, ASSOC VPRES ACAD AFFAIRS, 79- *Personal Data:* b Woodville, Miss, Jan 28, 41; c 2. *Educ:* Tougaloo Col, BA, 61; Atlanta Univ, MA, 63; Kans State Univ, PhD(zool), 70. *Prof Exp:* Instr biol, Tougaloo Col, 63-65; asst zool, Kans State Univ, 66-69. *Mem:* Am Soc Zoologists; Soc Study Reproduction; AAAS; Am Asn Anatomists; Sigma Xi. *Res:* Epididymal histophysiology of the mammal including effects of androgens and age on the viability and fertilizing capacity of spermatazoa; influence of olfactory stimulation on estrous induction. *Mailing Add:* Acad Affairs Southern Ill Univ Carbondale IL 62901-4399

SHEPHERD, D(ENNIS) G(RANVILLE), mechanical engineering, aeronautical & astronautical engineering; deceased, see previous edition for last biography

SHEPHERD, DAVID PRESTON, RADIATION BIOLOGY, ZOOLOGY. *Current Pos:* from asst prof to assoc prof biol, 70-80, PROF BIOL, SOUTHEASTERN LA UNIV, 80- *Personal Data:* b Center, Tex, Aug 2, 40; m 88; c 1. *Educ:* Lamar Univ, BS, 63; Tex A&M Univ, MS, 67, PhD(biol), 70. *Prof Exp:* Instr zool, Tex A&M Univ, 69-70. *Mem:* AAAS; Sigma Xi. *Res:* Radiation; physiology; ecology; herpetology; archeology; paleontology. *Mailing Add:* Dept Biol Sci Southeastern La Univ 500 Western Ave Hammond LA 70402-0001

SHEPHERD, FREEMAN DANIEL, JR, PHYSICS, ELECTRONICS. *Current Pos:* Staff scientist, Air Force Cambridge Res Labs, Hanscom AFB, 57-59, group leader, infrared devices, 66-76, br chief electronic devices, 66-81, chief, Electronic Device Technol Div, 82-91, SR SCIENTIST, INFRARED ARRAYS & SENSORS, ROME LAB RL/ESE, HANSCOM AFB, 91- *Personal Data:* b Boston, Mass, June 7, 36; m 59, Carol A Smith; c Freeman III, Suzanne & Mark. *Educ:* Mass Inst Technol, BS & MS, 59; Northeastern Univ, PhD(elec eng), 65. *Honors & Awards:* Tech Achievement Award, USAF Systs Command, 70; Charles E Ryan Award, 78; Harry L Davis Award, 88; Harold E Brown Award, 89; Fed Lab Technol Transition Award, 90; Aviation Week Laurels Award, 90; Harry Diamond Award, Inst Elec & Electronics Engrs, 92. *Concurrent Pos:* Assoc mem adv group electron devices, Spec Devices Working Group, 70-76; mem, Working Group Basic Mech Radiation Effects, 71-76; Air Force rep, Comt Electromagnetic Detection Devices, Nat Mat Adv Bd-Nat Res Coun-Nat Acad Sci, 71-72; fel Rome Lab, 88; mem, DOD Passive Sensing Steering Group, 88-91. *Mem:* Fel Inst Elec & Electronics Engrs; Sigma Xi; fel Soc Photo-Optical Instrumentation Engrs. *Res:* Infrared imaging and passive sensing; over 50 publications and 7 patents. *Mailing Add:* US Air Force Rome Lab RI/Er L G Hanscom AFB MA 01824

SHEPHERD, GORDON GREELEY, AERONOMY, SPACE PHYSICS. *Current Pos:* DIR, SOLAR TERRESTRIAL PHYSICS LAB, INST SPACE & TERRESTRIAL SCI, 88- *Personal Data:* b Sask, Can, June 19, 31; m 53, 87; c 3. *Educ:* Univ Sask, BSc, 52, MSc, 53; Univ Toronto, PhD(molecular spectros), 56. *Prof Exp:* From asst prof to assoc prof physics, Univ Sask, 57-69; prof physics, York Univ, 69- *Concurrent Pos:* Mem ed adv bd, Planetary & Space Sci; Can Coun Killam Res fel, 91- *Mem:* Optical Soc Am; Can Asn Physicists; Am Geophys Union; fel Can Aeronaut & Space Inst; fel Royal Soc Can. *Res:* Interferometric spectroscopy of airglow and aurora from the ground; rockets and satellites; principal investigator for space shuttle and upper atmospheric research satellite investigations of upper atmospheric winds. *Mailing Add:* Centre for Res in Exp Space Sci York Univ 4700 Keele St Downsview ON M3J 1P3 Can. *Fax:* 416-736-5626

SHEPHERD, GORDON MURRAY, NEUROPHYSIOLOGY. *Current Pos:* asst prof physiol, 67-68, assoc prof, 69-79, PROF NEUROSCIENCE, SCH MED, YALE UNIV, 79- *Personal Data:* b Ames, Iowa, July 21, 33; m 59; c 3. *Educ:* Iowa State Univ, BS, 55; Harvard Med Sch, MD, 59; Oxford Univ, PhD(neurophysiol), 62. *Honors & Awards:* R H Wright Award, 86; Freeman Award, 88. *Prof Exp:* Res assoc biophys, NIH, 62-64; vis scientist neurophysiol, Karolinska Inst, Sweden, 64-66. *Concurrent Pos:* USPHS fel, 59-62, spec fel, 64-66 & res grant, 66-; assoc fel, Retina Found, Boston, 66-67 & dept biol, Mass Inst Technol, 67; vis assoc prof, Neurol Inst, Univ Pa, 71-72; mem study sect, NIH, 75-79; chair, Nat Asn Chemorecep Sci, 81-84, comt in hist neuroscience, Soc Neuroscience, 85-; vis prof, Col France, 86-; physiol comt, Nat Bd Examrs, 84-88. *Mem:* Soc Neurosci; Am Physiol Soc; Int Brain Res Orgn; Sigma Xi. *Res:* Synaptic organization of the olfactory system; transduction properties of sensors reactors; interactive properties of neuronal dendrites; mechanisms of cortical integration; computational neurology models. *Mailing Add:* Sect Neuroanat Med Sch Yale Univ New Haven CT 06510. *Fax:* 203-785-6990; *E-Mail:* Bitnet: shepherd@yalemed

SHEPHERD, HURLEY SIDNEY, FUNGAL MOLECULAR BIOLOGY, ORGANELLE GENETICS. *Current Pos:* RES GENETICIST, SOUTHERN REGIONAL RES CTR, USDA, 84- *Personal Data:* b Oxford, NC, Dec 17, 50; m, Connie Yates; c Elizabeth, Matthew & Benjamin. *Educ:* Univ NC, BS, 73; Duke Univ, PhD(bot), 78. *Prof Exp:* Res assoc, Univ Calif, San Diego, 79-81; asst prof bot & biochem, Univ Kans, 81-84. *Mem:* Genetics Soc Am; AAAS; Sigma Xi. *Res:* Control of gene expression in fungi due to environmental and developmental effects and interactions between the nuclear and organelle genomes. *Mailing Add:* 1100 Robert E Lee Blvd New Orleans LA 70124-4305. *Fax:* 504-286-4419

SHEPHERD, JAMES E, ENGINEERING. *Current Pos:* RETIRED. *Personal Data:* b Houston, Tex, May 29, 10. *Educ:* Univ Mo, BA, 32, MA, 33; Harvard Univ, MS, 35, DSc, 40. *Prof Exp:* Sci adv, Sperry Corp, 41-72. *Mem:* Fel Inst Elec & Electronics Engrs; fel AAAS; Am Phys Soc; Sigma Xi. *Mailing Add:* Box 27 210 Park Lane Concord MA 01742-1620

SHEPHERD, JIMMIE GEORGE, physics, for more information see previous edition

SHEPHERD, JOHN PATRICK GEORGE, SOLAR ENERGY. *Current Pos:* assoc prof physics, 69-75, PROF PHYSICS, UNIV WIS-RIVER FALLS, 75- *Personal Data:* b West Wickham, Eng, May 11, 37; m 63; c 2. *Educ:* Univ London, BSc & ARCS, 58, PhD(electron physics) & dipl, Imp Col, 62. *Prof Exp:* Res asst electron physics, Imp Col, Univ London, 61-63; res assoc, Case Inst Technol, 63-65, asst prof, 65-66; sr sci officer, Royal Radar Estab, Eng, 66-69. *Concurrent Pos:* Consult, 3M Co, 71- *Mem:* Am Phys Soc. *Res:* Band structure of solids; deHass van Alphen effect in metals and alloys, pseudo potential models of band structure of same; laser and nonlinear optics; band structure of semiconductors; solar energy; optical design; electro-chemical studies. *Mailing Add:* Dept Physics Univ Wis 410 S Third St River Falls WI 54022

SHEPHERD, JOHN THOMPSON, PHYSIOLOGY. *Current Pos:* assoc prof, Mayo Grad Sch Med, Univ Minn, 57-62, dir res, Mayo Found, 69-77, dir educ, Mayo Clin & Found & dean, Mayo Med Sch, 77-83, PROF PHYSIOL, MAYO GRAD SCH MED, UNIV MINN, 62-, ASSOC DIR, MAYO CLIN GEN CLIN RES CTR, 92- *Personal Data:* b Northern Ireland, May 21, 19; m 45; c 2. *Educ:* Queen's Univ Belfast, MB & BCh, 45, MCh, 48, MD, 51. *Hon Degrees:* DSc, Queens Univ Belfast, 56 & 79; Laurea Honoris Med, Univ Bologna, 84 & Univ Gent Belg, 85. *Honors & Awards:* Carl J Wiggers Award, Am Physiol Soc, 78; Gold Heart Award, Asn Am Physicians, 78. *Prof Exp:* House physician, Royal Victoria Hosp, Belfast, Northern Ireland, 45-46; extern surgeon, 46; lectr physiol, Queen's Univ Belfast, 47-53; Anglo-French Med Exchange bursary, 57. *Concurrent Pos:* Leathem traveling fel & Fulbright scholar, 53-54; consult, Mayo Clin, 57- & Northern Ireland Hosps; chmn, Dept Physiol & Biophys, Mayo Med Sch, 66-74, Bd Develop, Mayo Clin & Found, 83-87; foreign hon mem, Koninklijke Acad, Belg, 82; mem, Cardiovasc Physiol Comn, Int Union Physiol Sci, 82-, chmn, 91- *Mem:* Am Heart Asn (pres, 75-76); Int Union Physiol Sci. *Res:* Heart and peripheral circulation of man and animals in health and disease, especially hemodynamics. *Mailing Add:* Dept Physiol Mayo Clin & Found Plummer 1043 Rochester MN 55905-0001. *Fax:* 507-284-1025

SHEPHERD, JOSEPH EMMETT, COMBUSTION, GAS DYNAMICS. *Current Pos:* ASSOC PROF, CALIF INST TECHNOL, 93- *Personal Data:* b Joliet, Ill, Mar 7, 53; m 79; c 2. *Educ:* Univ SFla, BS, 76; Calif Inst Technol, PhD(appl physics), 81. *Prof Exp:* Mem tech staff, Sardia Nat Labs, 80-86; from asst prof to assoc prof, Rensselaer Polytech, 86-93. *Mem:* Am Phys Soc; AAAS; Sigma Xi; Combustion Inst. *Res:* Rapid evaporation; detonations; gasdynamics; combustion; explosions. *Mailing Add:* Dept Aeronaut Calif Inst Technol MS105-5 Pasadena CA 91125

SHEPHERD, JULIAN GRANVILLE, INVERTEBRATE PHYSIOLOGY. *Current Pos:* asst prof, 75-84, ASSOC PROF BIOL, STATE UNIV NY BINGHAMTON, 84- *Personal Data:* b Lutterworth, Eng, Dec 16, 42; US citizen; m 66, 84; c 1. *Educ:* Cornell Univ, BA, 64; Harvard Univ, PhD(biol), 72. *Prof Exp:* Res scientist insect reproduction, Int Ctr Insect Physiol & Ecol, 72-74; fel, Harvard Univ, 74-75. *Mem:* AAAS; Entom Soc Am; Soc for Invert Reproduction; Lepidopterist Soc; Sigma Xi. *Res:* Development and physiology of invertebrate, mainly insect, spermatozoa. *Mailing Add:* Dept Biol Sci State Univ NY Box 6000 Binghamton NY 13902-6000

SHEPHERD, LINDA JEAN, BIOCHEMISTRY, BIOTECHNOLOGY. *Current Pos:* SCI WRITER, 87- *Personal Data:* b Philadelphia, Pa, May 25, 49; m 93, Paul D Hamilton. *Educ:* Millersville State Col, BA, 71; Pa State Univ, PhD(biochem), 76. *Prof Exp:* Mgr, Prod Develop, Worthington Diag Corp, 76-81; Genetic Systs Corp, 81-87. *Res:* Author in fields of science and spirituality, history and philosophy of science, and science policy and ethics. *Mailing Add:* 14985 256th Ave SE Issaquah WA 98027. *E-Mail:* ljsheprd@halcyon.com

SHEPHERD, MARK, JR, ELECTRICAL ENGINEERING. *Current Pos:* RETIRED. *Personal Data:* b Dallas, Tex, Jan 18, 23; m 45; c 3. *Educ:* Southern Methodist Univ, BS, 42; Univ Ill, Urbana, MS, 47. *Hon Degrees:* PhD, Southern Methodist Univ, 79. *Prof Exp:* Test engr, Gen Elec Co, 42-43; engr, Farnsworth TV & Radio Corp, 47-48; proj engr, Geophys Serv Inc, 48-51, from asst chief engr to chief engr semiconductor design, 52-54, asst vpres, Semiconductor-Components Div,

54-55, gen mgr, 54-61, vpres, 55-61, exec vpres, 61-66, chief oper officer, 61-69, pres, 67-76, chief exec officer, 69-84, chmn, Tex Instruments, 76-88. *Mem:* Nat Acad Eng; Inst Elec & Electronics Engrs; Soc Explor Geophys. *Res:* Solid state control systems. *Mailing Add:* Tex Instruments Inc MS 236 PO Box 655474 Dallas TX 75265

SHEPHERD, RAYMOND EDWARD, PHYSIOLOGICAL CHEMISTRY. *Current Pos:* asst prof, 80-84, ASSOC PROF PHYSIOL, LA STATE UNIV MED CTR, 84- *Personal Data:* b Joliet, Ill, Aug 21, 41; c 1. *Educ:* Bethel Col, BS, 62; Univ Mont, MS, 68; Wash State Univ, PhD(exercise physiol), 74. *Prof Exp:* Instr biol, Graceville High Sch, 64-66; instr physiol, Dakota State Col, 68-70; NIH fel, Brown Univ, 74-76, from instr to asst prof physiol chem, 76-78; assoc prof exercise physiol, Univ Toledo, 78-80. *Concurrent Pos:* Fel, Nat Inst Arthritis Metab & Digestive Dis, 74. *Mem:* NY Acad Sci; AAAS; Am Col Sports Med; Am Physiol Soc; Sigma Xi. *Res:* Regulation of adenylate cyclase, protein kinase, and triglyceride lipase in fat cells by hormones and fatty acids. *Mailing Add:* Dept Physiol La State Univ Med Ctr 1901 Perdido St New Orleans LA 70112-1394

SHEPHERD, RAYMOND LEE, GENETICS, PLANT PATHOLOGY. *Current Pos:* RETIRED. *Personal Data:* b Arkadelphia, Ark, Oct 13, 26; m 50; c 3. *Educ:* Ouachita Baptist Col, 50; Univ Ark, MS, 60; Auburn Univ, PhD(plant breeding), 65. *Prof Exp:* Proprietor retail grocery bus, 54-57; res asst plant breeding, Univ Ark, 57-60; asst agron, 60-65, supvry res agronomist, Auburn Univ, 65-91. *Mem:* Am Soc Agron. *Res:* Genetics and breeding investigations on cotton, especially the development of basic breeding stocks which are resistant to nematodes and diseases. *Mailing Add:* 1424 Ferndale Dr Auburn AL 36830

SHEPHERD, REX E, REDOX REACTIONS, MODELING CATALYTIC REACTIVITIES. *Current Pos:* asst prof, 75-81, ASSOC PROF INORG ANAL, DEPT CHEM, UNIV PITTSBURGH, 81- *Personal Data:* b Greenville, Ohio, Nov 27, 45. *Educ:* Purdue Univ, BS, 67; Stanford Univ, MS, 69, PhD(inorg chem), 71. *Prof Exp:* Fel, Dept Chem, Yale Univ, 71-72 & State Univ NY, Buffalo, 72-73; vis asst prof, Purdue Univ, 73-75. *Concurrent Pos:* Consult, Maynard Metals, Inc, 74-75. *Mem:* Am Chem Soc. *Res:* Mechanistic inorganic chemistry as related to transition metal complexes, bioinorganic systems, catalytic activation of small molecules and photochemistry studied by physical chemical methods. *Mailing Add:* Dept Chem Univ Pittsburgh Pittsburgh PA 15260-0001

SHEPHERD, ROBERT JAMES, PLANT PATHOLOGY, VIROLOGY. *Current Pos:* RETIRED. *Personal Data:* b Clinton, Okla, June 5, 30; m 78; c 3. *Educ:* Okla State Univ, BS, 54, MS, 56; Univ Wis, PhD(plant path), 59. *Honors & Awards:* Ruth Allen Award, Am Phytopath Soc, 81. *Prof Exp:* Asst plant path, Okla State Univ, 54-55; asst, Univ Wis, 56-58, res assoc, 58-59, asst prof, 59-61; asst prof, Univ Calif, Davis, 61-65; assoc prof, Univ Ark, 65-66; from assoc prof to prof, Univ Calif, Davis, 66-84, assoc plant pathologist, 66-72; prof plant path, Univ Ky, 84-96. *Concurrent Pos:* Assoc ed, Phytopath, 65-66; ed, Virol, 71-74; chmn, Plant Virus Subcomt, Int Comt Taxonomy Viruses; assoc ed, J Gen Virol, 78-81; mem sci bd, Calgene, 80-85. *Mem:* Nat Acad Sci; Soc Gen Microbiol; fel Am Phytopath Soc. *Res:* Characterization and description of plant viruses; epidemiology and control of plant virus diseases; recombinant DNA vectors for plants. *Mailing Add:* 16532 SE Main St Portland OR 97233-4045

SHEPHERD, ROBIN, FORENSIC ENGINEERING. *Current Pos:* PROF, STRUCT-EARTH CIVIL ENG, UNIV CALIF, IRVINE, 80- *Personal Data:* b York, Eng, June 18, 33; US citizen; m 86; c 2. *Educ:* Univ Leeds, UK, BS, 55, MS, 65; Univ Canterbury, NZ, PhD(civil eng), 71; Univ Leeds, UK, DSc, 73. *Honors & Awards:* E R Cooper Medal, Royal Soc NZ, 72. *Prof Exp:* Asst eng, DeHavilland Aircraft Co, UK, 55-57, NZ Ministry Works, 58-59; fac mem struct, Univ Canterbury, NZ, 59-71; assoc prof struct, Univ Auckland, NZ, 72-79; dir, NZ Heavy Eng Res Asn, 79-80. *Concurrent Pos:* Vis prof, Calif Inst Technol, 77; vis overseas scholar, St John's Col, Cambridge, UK, 84; Erskine fel, Univ Canterbury, NZ, 87; pres, Forensic Expert Adv Inc, Calif, 90- *Mem:* Fel Am Soc Civil Engrs; fel Nat Acad Forensic Engrs; Earthquake Eng Res Inst; Seismogr Soc Am. *Res:* Application of structural dynamic analysis procedures to the prediction of earthquake-induced loads and movements in civil engineering structures including improved methods of seismic design. *Mailing Add:* PO Box 410 Fawnskin CA 92333

SHEPHERD, VIRGINIA L, CELL BIOLOGY, BIOCHEMISTRY. *Current Pos:* ASST PROF MED & BIOCHEM, UNIV TENN, MEMPHIS, 84- *Educ:* Univ Iowa, PhD(biochem), 75. *Res:* Receptor modulation in macrophages. *Mailing Add:* Dept Med/Biochem Vet Admin Med Ctr & Res Serv Vanderbilt Univ 1310 24th Ave S Rm 506 Nashville TN 37212-2637

SHEPHERD, W(ILLIAM) G(ERALD), ELECTRICAL ENGINEERING. *Current Pos:* prof elec eng, Univ Minn, 47-79, assoc dean, Inst Technol, 54-56, head, Dept Elec Eng, 56-63, vpres acad admin, 63-73, dir, Space Sci Ctr, 74-79, EMER PROF ELEC ENG, UNIV MINN, MINNEAPOLIS, 79- *Personal Data:* b Ft William, Ont, Aug 28, 11; nat US; m 36, 81, Mary Dunlap; c William B, Anne E (Stoddard) & Sara L (Mantis). *Educ:* Univ Minn, BS, 33, PhD(physics), 37. *Honors & Awards:* Citation, Bur Ships, 47; Medal of Honor, Nat Electronics Conf, 65. *Prof Exp:* Mem tech staff, Bell Tel Labs, NJ, 37-47. *Concurrent Pos:* Consult, Bendix Aviation Corp, 49-63, Gen Elec Co, 55-63 & Control Data, 58-63; US Comn VII chmn, Int Sci Radio Union, 53-57 & Int Comn VII, 57-63; mem eng sci panel, NSF, 58-61, eng div adv comt, 64-69; mem adv group electron devices, Dept Defense, 58-68, chmn, 62-68; mem space technol adv comt, NASA, 64-69. *Mem:* Nat Acad Eng; fel Inst Elec & Electronics Engrs (vpres, 65-66, pres, 66-67); Am Phys Soc. *Res:* Microwave electronics; physical electronics, especially electron emission. *Mailing Add:* 103 Shepherd Lab 2197 Falwell Ave St Paul MN 55108-1336

SHEPHERD, WILLIAM LLOYD, MATHEMATICS. *Current Pos:* RETIRED. *Personal Data:* b Okla, Oct 2, 15; m 39; c 1. *Educ:* Okla State Univ, BS, 38, MS, 41. *Prof Exp:* Instr math, Southwestern Col (Kans), 43-45; asst prof, Okla State Univ, 46-47; instr, Univ Tex, 47; instr, Univ Ore, 48-52; asst prof math & physics, Tex Western Col, 52-60; mathematician, White Sands Missile Range, US Dept Army, NMex, 60-73, res mathematician, Res Proj Off, Instrumentation Directorate, 73-80. *Concurrent Pos:* consult, 80-83. *Mem:* Am Math Soc. *Res:* Mathematics for missile range instrumentation problems; digital signal processing; number theoretic considerations in interferometric angle measurements. *Mailing Add:* 10430 Argonaut Lane Jackson CA 95642-9559

SHEPLEY, LAWRENCE CHARLES, COSMOLOGY. *Current Pos:* RETIRED. *Personal Data:* b Washington, DC, Aug 11, 39. *Educ:* Swarthmore Col, BA, 61; Princeton Univ, MA, 63, PhD(physics), 65. *Prof Exp:* Res physicist, Univ Calif, Berkeley, 65-67; from asst prof to assoc prof physics, Univ Tex, Austin, 67-95, assoc dir, Ctr Relativity Theory, 71-95. *Concurrent Pos:* NSF grant, 68-78; vchmn grad affairs, Physics Dept, Univ Tex, Austin, 71-73. *Mem:* Am Phys Soc; Am Asn Physics Teachers. *Res:* Cosmological models; equivalent lagrangians. *Mailing Add:* Dept Physics Univ Tex Austin TX 78712. *E-Mail:* larry@helmholtz.ph.utexas.edu

SHEPP, ALLAN, LASER PHYSICS, IMAGING SCIENCE. *Current Pos:* DIR, BUS PLANNING/LASER PHYSICS, AVCO RES LAB, TEXTRON, 85- *Personal Data:* b New York, NY, Apr 2, 28; m 48; c 2. *Educ:* Oberlin Col, BA, 48; Cornell Univ, PhD(phys chem), 53. *Prof Exp:* Fel div pure chem, Nat Res Coun Can, 53-55; chemist, Tech Opers, Inc, 55-69, dir chem, 65-69; sr scientist, Polaroid Corp, Cambridge, 69-85. *Mem:* Am Phys Soc; sr mem Soc Photog Scientists & Engrs (exec vpres, 71-); Am Chem Soc. *Res:* Photographic theory; color imaging; lasers and optics. *Mailing Add:* 68 Shade St Lexington MA 02173-7721

SHEPP, LAWRENCE ALAN, MATHEMATICS. *Current Pos:* MEM TECH STAFF MATH, LUCENT TECHNOL, 62- *Personal Data:* b Brooklyn, NY, Sept 9, 36; m 62; c 3. *Educ:* Polytech Inst Brooklyn, BS, 58; Princeton Univ, MA, 60, PhD(math), 61. *Honors & Awards:* Paul-Levy Prize, Inst Henri Poincare, Paris, 66 & 89; Distinguished Scientist Award, Inst Elec & Electronics Engrs, 82. *Prof Exp:* Instr probability & statist, Univ Calif, Berkeley, 61-62. *Concurrent Pos:* Mem, Comt Appl Math, Nat Acad Sci, 74-77; adj prof, Columbia Univ & Neurol Inst, 74-; vis scientist, Math Dept, Mass Inst Technol, 75; prof, Statist Dept, Stanford Univ, 84- *Mem:* Nat Acad Sci; Am Math Soc; Math Asn Am; AAAS; Inst Elec & Electronics Engrs; fel Inst Math Statist. *Res:* Probability and statistics; stochastic processes; Gaussian measure theory; analysis; asymptotics; random walk; limit theorems; computered tomography; medical imaging; reconstruction of pictures from projections. *Mailing Add:* Lucent Technol 600 Mountain Ave Rm 2C374 New Providence NJ 07974-2008

SHEPPARD, ALAN JONATHAN, NUTRITIONAL BIOCHEMISTRY, ANIMAL NUTRITION. *Current Pos:* chief lipid res sect, 60-70, RES CHEMIST, DIV NUTRIT, FOOD & DRUG ADMIN, 60-, CHIEF, FATS & ENERGY SECT, 70- *Personal Data:* b Parkersburg, WVa, Oct 11, 27; m 60. *Educ:* Ohio State Univ, BS, 51; Va Polytech, MS, 54; Univ Ill, MS, 56, PhD(animal nutrit), 59. *Prof Exp:* Agronomist, Northern Va Pasture Res Sta, 53; res asst animal sci, Agr Exp Sta, Univ Ill, Urbana, 59-60. *Concurrent Pos:* Instr grad sch, USDA, 60-63; actg chief macronutrient res br, Food & Drug Admin, 67; mem sub comn 9,12 di-cis-linoleic acid, Oils & Fats Sect, Int Union of Pure & Appl Chem, 74-78; adj prof chem, Am Univ, 77-; assoc prof, Human Nutrit Prog, Howard Univ, 77- *Mem:* Am Inst Nutrit; Am Oil Chem Soc; Am Soc Animal Sci; Am Dairy Sci Asn; Asn Off Analytical Chem. *Res:* Gas chromatography of vitamins; nutritional-metabolic studies in the lipid and fatty acid fields; interface between research and application to regulatory problems. *Mailing Add:* 10603 Vickers Dr Vienna VA 22181. *Fax:* 202-205-4594

SHEPPARD, ALBERT PARKER, ELECTRONICS & COMPUTERS, COMPUTER & RESEARCH ADMINISTRATION. *Current Pos:* JENKINS PROF MATH, FLA SOUTHERN COL, 89-, DIR, ACAD COMPUT, 96- *Personal Data:* b Griffin, Ga, June 6, 36; m 96, Marjory Ward; c Frank P & Phillip Hancock. *Educ:* Oglethorpe Univ, BS, 58; Emory Univ, MS, 59; Duke Univ, PhD(elec eng), 65. *Prof Exp:* Instr physics, Univ Ala, 59-60; sr engr, Martin Co, Fla, 60-63; radio physicist, US Army Res Off, NC, 63-65; head, Spec Tech Br, Eng Exp Sta, Ga Inst Technol, 65-71, chief, Chem Sci & Mat Div, 71-72, assoc dean, Col Eng, 72-74, prof elec eng, 72-89, assoc vpres res, 74-88, actg vpres res, 80 & 88, from asst to pres, Info Tech, 86-88, actg vpres, 88-89, vpres, Interdisciplinary Prog, 88-89. *Concurrent Pos:* Lectr, DeKalb Col, 67-71; pres, Microwave & Electronic Consults, Lakeland; chmn, Eng Coun, Univ Space Res Asn, 76-92; Indust Res Inst Univ Comt, 86-90. *Mem:* Sr mem Inst Elec & Electronics Engrs. *Res:* Software applications; microwave engineering; multimedia. *Mailing Add:* 1240 Jefferson Dr Lakeland FL 33803. *Fax:* 941-682-4878; *E-Mail:* asheppard@flsouthern.edu

SHEPPARD, ASHER R, MEMBRANE BIOPHYSICS. *Current Pos:* OWNER, ASHER SHEPPARD CONSULT, 93- *Personal Data:* b Brooklyn, NY, Apr 4, 43; m 65, Ann Schlesinger; c Eva, Julia & Abe. *Educ:* Union Col, BS, 63; State Univ NY Buffalo, MS, 71, PhD(physics), 75. *Prof Exp:* Nat Inst Environ Health Sci fel environ biophys, Inst Environ Med, NY Univ Med Ctr, 74-76; Nat Inst Environ Health Sci fel environ biophys, Brain Res Inst, Univ Calif, Los Angeles, 76-78; res physicist, Pettis Mem Vet Hosp, Loma Linda, Calif, 78-93. *Concurrent Pos:* Asst res prof physiol, Loma Linda, Calif, 79-, Dept Neurosurg, 88-; sci adv to WHO, 80-88, Dept Energy, 80, Calif Dept Health Serv, 89-, Inst Elec & Electronic Engrs Comar, 88-, City Seattle, 84-86

& 88. *Mem:* AAAS; Am Phys Soc; Bioelectromagnetics Soc; Soc Neurosci; Biophys Soc; Bioelectrochem Soc. *Res:* Biological effects of electric and magnetic fields; biophysical modeling of cell environment in fields; determination of health criteria for field exposures at radiofrequencies and extremely low frequency. *Mailing Add:* 108 Orange St Suite 8 Redlands CA 92373-4719. *Fax:* 909-307-5810

SHEPPARD, CHESTER STEPHEN, ORGANIC CHEMISTRY. *Current Pos:* RETIRED. *Personal Data:* b Buffalo, NY, Sept 27, 27; m 52; c 2. *Educ:* Canisius Col, BS, 52; Univ Pittsburgh, MLS, 55, PhD(org chem), 61. *Prof Exp:* Jr fel coal chem, Mellon Inst Indust Res, 52-61; res chemist, Lucidol Div, Wallace & Tiernan, Inc, 62-63; group leader res, Pennwalt Corp, 63-65, supvr res, 66-70, mgr res, Lucidol Div, 71-90, Atochem, 90-91. *Mem:* Am Chem Soc; Am Inst Chem; Royal Soc Chem; Sigma Xi. *Res:* Nitrogen chemistry; free radicals; peroxides; aliphatic azo chemistry; foamed polymers; polymerization; plasticizers; stabilizers; organic blowing agents; hydrazine chemistry. *Mailing Add:* 726 Parkhurst Buffalo NY 14223

SHEPPARD, DAVID CRAIG, INSECTICIDE RESISTANCE MANAGEMENT, AGRICULTURAL WASTE MANAGEMENT & RESOURCE RECOVERY. *Current Pos:* asst prof, 77-84, ASSOC PROF, DEPT ENTOM, UNIV GA, 84- *Personal Data:* b High Point, NC, Feb 18, 47; c David C & Justin M. *Educ:* Clemson Univ, BS, 69, MS, 72; La State Univ, PhD(entom), 75. *Prof Exp:* Asst, Clemson Univ, 69-71; res asst, La State Univ, 72-75; res assoc, 75-76. *Res:* Management of livestock pests, especially insecticide resistance problems and animal manure management with a non-pest fly which reduces waste by half, eliminates pests flies, with 11 percent conversion manure to high protein feed. *Mailing Add:* Entom Dept Univ Ga Coastal Plains Exp Sta Tifton GA 31793-0748. *Fax:* 912-386-3086

SHEPPARD, DAVID E, BIOCHEMICAL GENETICS. *Current Pos:* asst prof, 67-69, ASSOC PROF BIOL, UNIV DEL, 69- *Personal Data:* b Chester, Pa, Jan 16, 38; m 60; c 3. *Educ:* Amherst Col, BA, 59; NIJohns Hopkins Univ, PhD(biochem genetics), 63. *Prof Exp:* Asst prof biol, Reed Col, 63-65; NIH fel, Univ Calif, Santa Barbara, 65-66. *Concurrent Pos:* NIH fel, Univ BC, 73. *Mem:* Genetics Soc Am; Am Soc Microbiol. *Res:* Transduction; feed-back inhibition; genetic control of protein synthesis; arabinose operon. *Mailing Add:* Dept Biol Univ Del Newark DE 19717-0001

SHEPPARD, DAVID W, PHYSICS. *Current Pos:* RETIRED. *Personal Data:* b Quincy, Mass, Dec 28, 27; m 52; c 2. *Educ:* Gordon Col, BA, 52; Andover Newton Theol Sch, BD, 56; Brown Univ, MA, 61; Ohio State Univ, PhD(physics), 68; Univ Pittsburgh, MLS, 77. *Prof Exp:* Pastor, Congregational Church, Dunstable, Mass, 54-57 & Riverpoint Congregational Church, West Warwick, RI, 57-61; instr physics, Defiance Col, 61-64, asst prof, 64-65; chem, Dept Physics, Thiel Col, 75-77, asst prof, 68-80; assoc prof, WVa Wesleyan Col, 80-93. *Mem:* Am Phys Soc; Am Asn Physics Teachers. *Res:* Nuclear magnetic resonance. *Mailing Add:* 41 Bogges St Buckhannon WV 26201

SHEPPARD, DEAN, PULMONARY MEDICINE. *Current Pos:* Asst prof, 81-86, ASSOC PROF MED, UNIV CALIF, SAN FRANCISCO, 86- *Personal Data:* b Bronx, NY, June 13, 49. *Educ:* State Univ NY, Stony Brook, MD, 75. *Mem:* Am Physiol Soc; Am Thoracic Soc. *Mailing Add:* Dept Med Univ Calif Box 0854 San Francisco CA 94143-0854. *Fax:* 415-282-5998

SHEPPARD, DONALD M(AX), MECHANICAL ENGINEERING. *Current Pos:* from asst prof to assoc prof eng sci, 69-77, asst chmn coastal & oceanog eng, 77-78, ASSOC PROF COASTAL & OCEANOG ENG, UNIV FLA, 77-, ACTG CHMN COASTAL & OCEANOG ENG, 78- *Personal Data:* b Port Arthur, Tex, Mar 21, 37; m 58; c 2. *Educ:* Lamar State Univ, BS, 60; Tex A&M Univ, MS, 62; Ariz State Univ, PhD(mech eng), 69. *Prof Exp:* Design engr, Collins Radio Co, 60-61; asst mech eng, Tex A&M Univ, 61-62, Univ Ariz, 62-63 & Southwest Res Inst, 63-64; instr, Ariz State Univ, 64-68, NSF fel, 67-68. *Concurrent Pos:* Instr, San Antonio Col, 63-64. *Res:* Stratified shear flows internal waves coastal hydraulics; nearshore sediment transport; geophysical fluid mechanics. *Mailing Add:* 1656 NW 22nd Circle Gainesville FL 32605

SHEPPARD, EMORY LAMAR, DIGITAL ELECTRONICS & MICROPROCESSORS, ELECTRONIC COMMUNICATIONS. *Current Pos:* ASSOC PROF EET, CLEMSON UNIV, 81- *Personal Data:* b Hendersonville, NC, Sept 18, 42; m 67; c 2. *Educ:* Clemson Univ, BS, 67; NC State Univ, MS, 75. *Prof Exp:* Antenna eng, Radiation, Inc, 67-79; systs eng, Res Triangle Inst, 69-72; head, Dept EET, Spartanburg Tech Col, 73-75; assoc prof EET, Univ NC, Charlotte, 75-78; assoc prin engr, Harris Corp, 78-81. *Concurrent Pos:* Prin investr, impedance matching lens radar proj, Appl Sci Assocs, Inc, 82, pulse detection presence impulse noise proj, Security Tag Systs, Inc, 83, passive subharmonic transponder proj, 84-85 & microstrip patch transponder proj, 85- *Mem:* Inst Elec & Electronics Engrs. *Res:* High gain low noise antennas; phased array radar; broadband autotracking feed systems; signal detection in the presence of noise; remote sensing; digital communications; microprocessor applications; physics. *Mailing Add:* PO Box 2384 Blowing Rock NC 28605

SHEPPARD, ERWIN, PHYSICAL CHEMISTRY. *Current Pos:* RETIRED. *Personal Data:* b New York, NY, May 27, 21; m 43, Hilda Pellis; c Laura & Marianne. *Educ:* City Col, BS, 42; Polytech Inst Brooklyn, PhD(chem), 51. *Prof Exp:* Res assoc phys biochem, Med Col, Cornell Univ, 49-57; staff chemist, S C Johnson & Son, Inc, 57-58, phys res mgr, 58-81; prog developer, Grad Sch, Univ Wis-Milwaukee, 82-85. *Mem:* Am Chem Soc; Electron Micros Soc Am; Soc Appl Spectros; Sigma Xi; AAAS. *Res:* Physical chemistry of polymeric and colloidal systems; organic coatings; surface chemistry; aerosol technology; electrokinetic and light scattering investigations; electron microscopy and corrosion studies. *Mailing Add:* 1108 N Milwaukee St Apt 145 Milwaukee WI 53202-3152

SHEPPARD, HERBERT, biochemistry; deceased, see previous edition for last biography

SHEPPARD, JOHN CLARENCE, RADIOCHEMISTRY, INORGANIC CHEMISTRY. *Current Pos:* assoc nuclear engr, Eng Res Div, 72-77, prof chem eng & anthrop, 77-92, EMER PROF CHEM, WASH STATE UNIV, 92-, ADJ PROF GEOL, 92- *Personal Data:* b San Pedro, Calif, June 4, 23; m 50; c 3. *Educ:* San Diego State Col, AB, 49; Washington Univ, MA, 54, PhD(chem), 55. *Prof Exp:* Chemist, US Naval Radiol Defense Lab, 49-51; asst, Washington Univ, 52-55; chemist, Hanford Labs, Gen Elec Co, 55-57; asst prof chem, San Diego State Col, 57-60; chemist, Hanford Labs, Gen Elec Co, 60-63; sr res scientist chem dept, Battelle Mem Inst, 65-71. *Mem:* Am Chem Soc; AAAS; Sigma Xi. *Res:* Electron transfer reactions between ions in aqueous solution; solvent extraction of actinide elements; activation analysis; atmospheric chemistry; radiocarbon dating. *Mailing Add:* 510 SE Crestview St Pullman WA 99163-2257

SHEPPARD, JOHN RICHARD, cell biology, biochemistry; deceased, see previous edition for last biography

SHEPPARD, KEITH GEORGE, ELECTROCHEMICAL PROCESSES, CORROSION. *Current Pos:* teaching fel, Stevens Inst Technol, NJ, 79-80, res asst prof, 80-81, asst prof math & metall eng, 81-85, assoc prof, 86-91, PROF MAT SCI & ENG, STEVENS INST TECHNOL, NJ, 92-, ASSOC VPRES RES, 92- *Personal Data:* b London, Eng, June 28, 49; m 77; c 3. *Educ:* Leeds Univ, Eng, BS, 71; Univ Birmingham, Eng, PhD(metall), 80. *Prof Exp:* Coordr, Stats (MR) Ltd, Birmingham, Eng, 72-73; exp officer, Metals & Alloys, Birmingham, Eng, 73-75. *Mem:* Electrochem Soc; Nat Asn Corrosion Engrs; Am Electroplaters & Surface Finishers Soc; Mat Res Soc. *Res:* Structure and properties of electrodeposits, electroless deposits and deposits produced by laser-enhanced electrodeposition; corrosion and corrosion testing; electron microscopy; failure analysis; environmental degradation of engineering ceramics. *Mailing Add:* Dept Mat Sci & Eng Stevens Inst Technol Hoboken NJ 07030. *Fax:* 201-216-8306

SHEPPARD, LOUIS CLARKE, MEDICAL PRODUCTS LIABILITY, PATENT INFRINGEMENT. *Current Pos:* asst vpres res, 88-90, PROF PHYSIOL & BIOPHYS, UNIV TEX MED BR, 88-, ASSOC VPRES RES, 90- *Personal Data:* b Pine Bluff, Ark, May 28, 33; m 58; c 3. *Educ:* Univ Ark, BS, 57; Univ London, PhD(elec eng), 76. *Honors & Awards:* Ayrton Premium, Inst Elec & Electronic Engrs. *Prof Exp:* Prof biomed eng & chmn dept, Univ Ala, Birmingham, 79-88, dir acad comput, Med Ctr, 81-83, prof elec eng & biostatist & biomath, 86-88. *Concurrent Pos:* Fac mem, Grad Sch, Univ Ala, Birmingham, 75-88, adj prof, Dept Biomed Eng, 89-; sr scientist, Cystic Fibrosis Res Ctr, 81-88; prof elec & computer eng, Univ Tex, Austin, 89-; adj prof, Dept Elec Eng, Cullen Col Eng, Univ Houston, 89-; mem sci staff, Shriners Burn Inst, Galveston, 89- *Mem:* Am Inst Chem Engrs; sr mem Inst Elec & Electronic Engrs; sr mem Biomed Eng Soc; Brit Computer Soc; Sigma Xi. *Res:* Computer based systems for intensive care; automated blood and drug infusion for closed-loop, feedback control of cardiac and vascular pressures. *Mailing Add:* 20 E Broad Oaks Dr Houston TX 77056-1201

SHEPPARD, MARSHA ISABELL, SOIL PHYSICS, MODELLING SOIL CONTAMINANT TRANSPORT. *Current Pos:* SOIL SCIENTIST & HEAD ECOL RES, ATOMIC ENERGY CAN LTD, 86-, SR SCIENTIST, 90- *Personal Data:* b Smiths Falls, Ont, 47; m 75; c 2. *Educ:* Carleton Univ, BA, 71, MA, 73; Univ Guelph, PhD(soil sci), 77. *Mem:* Am Soc Agron. *Res:* Soil contaminant transport; soil-plant uptake; radionuclide migration; modelling. *Mailing Add:* PO Box 432 Pinawa MB R0E 1L0 Can. *Fax:* 204-753-2638; *E-Mail:* sheppardm@aecl.ca

SHEPPARD, MOSES MAURICE, SCIENCE EDUCATION. *Current Pos:* from asst prof to prof sci educ, 63-85, chmn, Dept Sci Educ, 85-91, EMER PROF SCI EDUC, E CAROLINA UNIV, 91- *Personal Data:* b Hendersonville, NC, Sept 5, 28; m 51, 92, Elizabeth Holland; c Maurice Glen, John Leonard, Frank Layne & Ashley Layne. *Educ:* ECarolina Col, BS, 52, MA, 58; Ohio State Univ, PhD(sci ed, physics), 66. *Prof Exp:* Teacher pub schs, Norfolk Co, 52-53; qual engr, Ford Motor Co, 53-54; teacher pub schs, Norfolk Co, 54-58, sci coordr, 58-61; instr sci educ & math, Ohio State Univ, 62-63. *Concurrent Pos:* Partic, NSF Acad Year Inst, Ohio State Univ, 61-62; fel earth sci, Southwest Ctr Advan Study, Tex, 68. *Mem:* Nat Sci Teachers Asn; Asn Educ Teachers Sci; Nat Asn Res Sci Teaching. *Res:* Science teaching on both the secondary school and college level. *Mailing Add:* 2024 York Rd Greenville NC 27858

SHEPPARD, NORMAN F, JR, BIOSENSORS, BIOMATERIALS. *Current Pos:* ASST PROF BIOMED ENG, JOHNS HOPKINS UNIV SCH MED, 89- *Personal Data:* b Ipswich, Mass. *Educ:* Mass Inst Technol, BS, 78, MS, 79, MS, 82, PhD(elec eng), 86. *Honors & Awards:* Presidential Young Investr, NSF, 90. *Prof Exp:* Postdoctoral fel, chem eng, Mass Inst Technol, 86-89. *Mem:* Am Chem Soc; Inst Elec & Electronic Engrs; AAAS. *Res:* Development of biomedical sensors and devices using microfabrication technology; development of a miniature glucose sensor and devices for the controlled release of medications. *Mailing Add:* Dept Biomed Eng Johns Hopkins Univ 144 Neb 34th & Charles Sts Baltimore MD 21218. *E-Mail:* nsheppar@eureka.wbme.jhu.edu

SHEPPARD, RICHARD A, GEOLOGY. *Current Pos:* geologist, US Geol Surv, 60-75, br chief, 76-79, res geologist, 80-94, PECORA FEL, US GEOL SURV, 95- *Personal Data:* b Lancaster, Pa, May 14, 30; m 57, Evenne Wails. *Educ:* Franklin & Marshall Col, BS, 56; Johns Hopkins Univ, PhD(geol), 60. *Honors & Awards:* Spec Act Award, US Geol Surv, 66 & 93; Meritorious Serv Award, Dept Interior, 86. *Concurrent Pos:* Mem, Int Comt Natural Zeolites, 76- Mem: AAAS; fel Geol Soc Am; fel Mineral Soc Am; Clay Minerals Soc; fel Soc Econ Geol; Int Zeolite Asn. *Res:* Geology of Cascade Mountains, especially petrology of Cenozoic volcanic rocks; distribution and genesis of zeolites in sedimentary rocks; origin of chert and flourite in pacustrine deposits. *Mailing Add:* US Geol Surv Box 25046 Fed Ctr MS-939 Denver CO 80225. *Fax:* 303-236-0459; *E-Mail:* rsheppard@usgs.gov

SHEPPARD, ROGER FLOYD, ENTOMOLOGY, INSECT BEHAVIOR. *Current Pos:* ASSOC PROF BIOL, CONCORD COL, 76 - *Personal Data:* b Barberton, Ohio, July 25, 45; m 70. *Educ:* Ohio Univ, BS, 67; Ohio State Univ, MS, 73, PhD(entom), 76. *Mem:* Am Entom Soc. *Res:* Sexual behavior of insects. *Mailing Add:* Dept Biol Concord Col PO Box 1000 Athens WV 24712-1000

SHEPPARD, RONALD JOHN, MANAGEMENT DEVELOPMENT, BUSINESS & TECHNICAL ANALYSIS. *Current Pos:* DEAN & DIR, OFF ECON DEVELOP & CONTINUING EDUC, CITY UNIV NY, 90- *Personal Data:* b New Rochelle, NY, Apr 13, 39; m 63, Shirl C; c Jeff B & Mark J. *Educ:* Rensselaer Polytech Inst, BS, 61; Howard Univ, MS, 62, PhD(physics), 65; Rochester Inst Technol, MBA, 74. *Prof Exp:* Prin consult, Booz Allen Hamilton Inc, 66-71; prod mgr, Xerox Corp, 71-77; prod planning mgr, Ford Motor Co, 77-79; dir strategic anal, Gen Motors, 79-83; new bus develop mgr, Imp Clevite, 83-84; dean & dir, Ctr Bus & Indust, Univ Toledo, 84-90. *Concurrent Pos:* Assoc prof, Empire State Col, 76-; lectr, Rochester Inst Technol, 74-76, Univ Rochester, 75; vis prof, Southern Univ, Bethune Cookman, 75 & 76; pres bd dir, Montessori Sch, Rochester, NY, 75-77; NASA eval team, Denver, Colo, 81. *Mem:* Planetary Soc; Am Soc Training & Develop. *Res:* Technology assessment; research and development management; technology forecasting; creative process in science and art; issues in aerospace management and strategic defense; Eastern Europe business privatization. *Mailing Add:* Col Staten Island Bldg 2A Rm 202 2800 Victory Blvd Staten Island NY 10314. *Fax:* 718-982-2038

SHEPPARD, STEPHEN CHARLES, ECOTOXICOLOGY, ENVIRONMENTAL EXPOSURE PATHWAYS. *Current Pos:* SR SCIENTIST, ATOMIC ENERGY CAN LTD RES, 82- *Personal Data:* b Sarnia, Ont, Nov 6, 51; m 75, Marsha I Joynt; c 2. *Educ:* Univ Guelph, BSc, 73, MSc, 74; Univ Man, PhD(soil sci & plant physiol), 82. *Prof Exp:* Fac, Univ Guelph, 74-79. *Concurrent Pos:* Ed, Can J Soil Sci, 93-96; assoc ed, J Environ Qual, 96. *Mem:* Am Soc Agron; Agr Inst Can; Int Union Radioecologists; Can Soil Sci Soc; Int Soil Sci Soc. *Res:* Investigation of exposure pathways for contaminants in soils and related ecotoxicology. *Mailing Add:* Atomic Energy Can Ltd Res Pinawa MB R0E 1L0 Can. *Fax:* 204-753-2638; *E-Mail:* sheppards@aecl.ca

SHEPPARD, WALTER LEE, JR, CORROSION ACID & ALKALI PROOF MASONRY MATERIALS. *Current Pos:* PRES & CHIEF EXEC OFFICER, CCRM INC, 78- *Personal Data:* b Philadelphia, Pa, June 23, 11; m 53; c 2. *Educ:* Cornell Univ, BChem, 32; Univ Pa, MS, 33. *Prof Exp:* From field sales to asst sales mgr & advert mgr, Atlas Mineral Prod, 38-48; chief engr & sales instr acid proof cements, Tanks & Linings, Ltd, Droitwich, Eng, 48-49; field sales, asst sales mgr & advert mgr, Electro-Chem Eng & Mfg Co, 49-66 & Interpace Inc, 66-68; nat acct mgr & field sales mgr, Pennwalt Corp, 68-76. *Mem:* Nat Soc Prof Engrs; Am Acad Environ Engrs; Nat Asn Corrosion Engrs; Am Soc Testing & Mat. *Res:* Acid proof cements; all kinds of non-metallic structural and lining materials that are corrosion and chemical resistant; author of 2 textbooks and over 100 articles and technical papers on corrosion and chemical resistant materials. *Mailing Add:* 923 Old Manoa Rd Havertown PA 19083

SHEPPARD, WILLIAM JAMES, CHEMICAL MARKET STUDIES. *Current Pos:* sr chem economist, 64-73, assoc sect mgr, 73-75, SR RES SCI, BATTELLE MEM INST, 75- *Personal Data:* b Boston, Mass, Apr 10, 31; m 55, Eva Kappes; c George & Margaret. *Educ:* Oberlin Col, AB, 52; Harvard Univ, MA, 54, PhD(chem), 59. *Prof Exp:* Instr chem, Swarthmore Col, 58-62, asst prof, 62-64. *Mem:* Am Chem Soc; Sigma Xi. *Res:* Planning of research on chemicals and materials; economic and technical analysis of markets for chemical products and processes; fuel production and environmental control. *Mailing Add:* 505 King Ave Columbus OH 43201. *Fax:* 614-424-3329

SHEPPERD, WAYNE DELBERT, FORESTRY, SILVICULTURE. *Current Pos:* Forestry res technician, Rocky Mountain Forest & Range Exp Sta, 70-76, forest silviculturist, Rio Grande Nat Forest, 76-78, RES FORESTER, ROCKY MOUNTAIN FOREST & RANGE EXP STA, US FOREST SERV, 78- *Personal Data:* b Sterling, Colo, June 28, 47; m 70, Colleen Billings; c Ryan & Marnie. *Educ:* Colo State Univ, BS, 70, MS, 74, PhD, 91. *Concurrent Pos:* Fac affil, Colo State Univ. *Mem:* Sigma Xi; Nature Conservancy. *Res:* Silviculture of sub alpine forests; growth and yield prediction; silviculture of aspen; dendro chronology and disturbance in forest ecosystems. *Mailing Add:* 830 Wagonwheel Ft Collins CO 80521. *E-Mail:* wshep@lamar.colostate.edu

SHEPPERSON, JACQUELINE RUTH, PARASITOLOGY. *Current Pos:* assoc prof, 65-68, chmn Sci Dept, 67-79, PROF BIOL, WINSTON-SALEM UNIV, 68- *Personal Data:* b Hopewell, Va, Feb 10, 35. *Educ:* Va State Univ, BS, 54; NC Cent Univ, Durham, MS, 56; Howard Univ, PhD(zool), 64. *Prof Exp:* Inst biol, Ft Valley State Col, 55-59; asst prof zool, Howard Univ, 64-65. *Res:* Survey studies of helminths in wild mammals; chemical relationships of host and parasite; physiological studies on plant parasitic nematodes. *Mailing Add:* Dept Life Sci Winston-Salem State Univ 601 W ML King Dr Winston-Salem NC 27110-0003

SHEPRO, DAVID, VASCULAR PHYSIOLOGY. *Current Pos:* PROF BIOL, BOSTON UNIV, 68-, ASSOC PROF SURG, 71- *Personal Data:* b Holyoke, Mass, Feb 14, 24; m 48, Marilyn; c Lisa & Douglas. *Educ:* Clark Univ, BA, 48, MA, 50; Boston Univ, PhD, 58. *Honors & Awards:* Landies Award, Am Microcir Soc. *Prof Exp:* Instr biol, Simmons Col, 50-52, from asst prof to prof, 53-68. *Concurrent Pos:* Mem corp, Marine Biol Lab, Woods Hole, 66-, clerk of corp, 72-80; ed-in-chief, J Microvascular Res; pres, Pro Barrier Inc; dir, ComTec; Burroughs Welcome vis prof. *Mem:* Microcirc Soc; fel AAAS; fel Am Physiol Soc; Am Soc Cell Biol. *Res:* Biology of endothelial cells and pericytes; molecular mechanisms in acute inflammation. *Mailing Add:* Microvascular Res Lab Boston Univ Five Cummington St Boston MA 02215. *Fax:* 617-353-6666; *E-Mail:* shepro@bu_biobu.edu

SHEPS, CECIL GEORGE, PREVENTIVE MEDICINE. *Current Pos:* dir, Health Serv Res Ctr, Univ NC, 68-72, prof, 68-79, vchancellor health sci, 71-76, TAYLOR GRANDY DISTINGUISHED EMER PROF SOCIAL MED, UNIV NC, CHAPEL HILL, 86- *Personal Data:* b Winnipeg, Man, July 24, 13; US citizen; m 37; c 1. *Educ:* Univ Man, MD, 36; Yale Univ, MPH, 47; Am Bd Prev Med & Pub Health, dipl, 50. *Hon Degrees:* DSc, Chicago Med Sch, 70, Univ Man, 85; PhD, Ben-Gurion Univ Negev, 83. *Honors & Awards:* Miles Award Sci Achievement, Can Pub Health Asn, 70; Thomas Jefferson Award, 83; Louis Gorin Award, Nat Rural Health Asn, 85; Sedgwick Mem Medal, Am Pub Health Asn, 90. *Prof Exp:* Asst dep minister & actg chmn, Dept Pub Health, Sask, Can, 45-46; Rockefellor Found fel, Yale Univ, 46-47; assoc prof pub health admin, Univ NC, 47-50, dir prog planning & actg chmn, asst dep minister, res prof health planning, 50-53; lectr prev med, Harvard Med Sch, 54-58, clin prof, 58-60; prof med & hosp admin & dir, Grad Sch Pub Health, Univ Pittsburgh, 60-65; prof community med, Mt Sinai Sch Med, 65-68. *Concurrent Pos:* Spec consult, Training Div Commun Dis Ctr, USPHS, 48-51; WHO traveling fel, 51; gen dir, Beth Israel Hosp, Boston, 53-60 & Beth Israel Med Ctr, New York, 65-68; mem & chmn, Health Serv Study Sect, NIH, 55-62; mem, Nat Adv Comt Chronic Dis & Health of Aged, 57-61; nat planning comt, White House Conf Aging, 59-61; consult med affairs, Welfare Admin, Dept Health, Educ & Welfare, Washington, DC; chmn higher educ pub health, Millbank Mem Found Comn, 72-76; mem, Prog Comt, Inst Med, 76-79, Mem Comt, 81-85. *Mem:* Inst Med-Nat Acad Sci; Am Pub Health Asn; Asn Teachers Prev Med. *Res:* Social medicine; medical and hospital administration. *Mailing Add:* 725 Airport Rd Bldg CB No 7590 Univ NC Chapel Hill NC 27599-7590. *Fax:* 919-966-5764

SHER, ALVIN HARVEY, NUCLEAR CHEMISTRY, SEMICONDUCTOR PHYSICS. *Current Pos:* dir, Prog Off, 89-90, DEP DIR, COMPUT & APPL MATH LAB, NAT INST STAND & TECHNOL, 91- *Personal Data:* b St Louis, Mo, Aug 15, 41; m 63, Adrienne Polmer; c 3. *Educ:* Wash Univ, AB, 63, AM, 65; Simon Fraser Univ, PhD(nuclear chem), 67. *Honors & Awards:* Silver Medal, Dept Com, 90. *Prof Exp:* Res chemist, Nat Bur Stand, 68-72, sect chief semi- conductor processing, 72-75, asst chief, Electronic Technol Div, 75-77, dept dir, Ctr Electronics & Elec Eng, 78-83, chief, prog off, 84-87, asst dir, mgt info technol, 87-89, dir prog off, 89-90. *Concurrent Pos:* Analyst, Nat Bur Stand Off Progs, 76. *Mem:* Inst Elec & Electronics Engrs. *Res:* Development of measurement methods relating to reliability of semiconductor microelectronic devices. *Mailing Add:* Comput & Appl Math Lab Bldg 820 Rm 602 Nat Inst Stand & Technol Gaithersburg MD 20899. *E-Mail:* sher@micf.nist.gov

SHER, ARDEN, PHYSICS. *Current Pos:* MEM STAFF, SRI INT, 79- *Personal Data:* b St Louis, Mo, July 5, 33; m 55; c 3. *Educ:* Wash Univ, St Louis, BS, 55, PhD(physics), 59. *Prof Exp:* Res assoc physics, Wash Univ, St Louis, 59; NSF fel, Saclay Nuclear Res Ctr, France, 60; sr engr, Cent Res Labs, Varian Assocs, Calif, 61-67; assoc prof physics, Col William & Mary, 67-72, dir appl sci, 70-76, prof physics, 72-79. *Concurrent Pos:* Consult, Langley Res Ctr, NASA, 68-69 & 72; consult prof mat sci, Stanford Univ, 82-, consult prof elec eng, 85- *Mem:* Fel Am Phys Soc. *Res:* Solid state physics. *Mailing Add:* 707 Crestview Dr San Carlos CA 94070-1510. *Fax:* 650-859-3090

SHER, IRVING HAROLD, information systems, intelligent systems; deceased, see previous edition for last biography

SHER, PAUL PHILLIP, CLINICAL CHEMISTRY, COMPUTER APPLICATION. *Current Pos:* DIR CLIN LABS, NY UNIV MED CTR, 81- *Personal Data:* b Oct 25, 39; m; c 3. *Educ:* Hobart Col, Geneva, NY, BS, 61; Washington Univ, St Louis, MD, 65. *Concurrent Pos:* Ed, Lab Med. *Mem:* fel Col Am Pathologists; fel Asn Clin Scientists; fel Nat Acad Clin Biochem. *Mailing Add:* BICC Ore Health Scis Univ 3181 SW Sam Jackson Park Rd Portland OR 97201-3098

SHER, RICHARD B, TOPOLOGY. *Current Pos:* head dept, 80-86, PROF MATH, UNIV NC, GREENSBORO, 74- *Personal Data:* b Flint, Mich, Jan 21, 39; m 62, Walter M Williams; c Robert & Richard. *Educ:* Mich Technol Univ, BS, 60; Univ Utah, MS, 64, PhD(math), 66. *Prof Exp:* From asst prof to assoc prof math, Univ Ga, 66-74. *Concurrent Pos:* Managing ed, Topology & Its Applns. *Mem:* Math Asn Am; Am Math Soc; Inst Advan Study. *Res:* Point set topology; piecewise linear topology; shape theory; infinite-dimensional manifolds; theory of retracts. *Mailing Add:* RR 1 Box 206-F Union Hall VA 24176-9746. *Fax:* 502-852-7868

SHER, RUDOLPH, NUCLEAR ENGINEERING. *Current Pos:* assoc prof, 61-70, prof, 70-86, EMER PROF MECH ENG, STANFORD UNIV, 86- *Personal Data:* b New York, NY, May 28, 23; m 52, Bonnie Goodman; c Victor & Erica. *Educ:* Cornell Univ, AB, 43; Univ Pa, PhD(physics), 51. *Honors & Awards:* Fel, Am Nuclear Soc, 86. *Prof Exp:* Staff mem radiation lab, Mass Inst Technol, 43-46; assoc physicist nuclear eng, Brookhaven Nat Lab, 51-61. *Concurrent Pos:* Vis scientist, Comm a l'Energie Atomique, France, 58-59 & A B Atomenergi, Sweden, 68-69; consult, Brookhaven Nat Lab, 70-; ed, Progress in Nuclear Energy, 75-80; vis staff mem, Int Atomic Energy Agency, 78-79; consult, Elec Power Res Inst, 83- *Mem:* Am Nuclear Soc. *Res:* Nuclear reactor physics; nuclear data; nuclear safeguards; nuclear aerosols. *Mailing Add:* 740 Mayfield Ave Stanford CA 94305

SHERA, E BROOKS, NUCLEAR PHYSICS, BIOPHYSICS. *Current Pos:* staff mem, 64-93, guest scientist, 94-96, AFFIL, LOS ALAMOS NAT LAB, 96- *Personal Data:* b Oxford, Ohio, Aug 28, 35; m 56, 88, Karen Stoll; c Christopher & Katherine. *Educ:* Case Western Res Univ, BA, 56, PhD(physics), 62; Univ Chicago, MS, 58. *Honors & Awards:* R & D 100 Award. *Prof Exp:* Instr physics, Case Western Res Univ, 61-62; resident res assoc, Argonne Nat Lab, 62-64. *Concurrent Pos:* Consult. *Mem:* Fel Am Phys Soc; AAAS. *Res:* Single molecule detection techniques; laser-induced fluorescence; muonic x-ray studies; neutron-capture gamma ray studies; low energy nuclear physics; nuclear structure; biophysics; advanced techniques for DNA sequencing. *Mailing Add:* Los Alamos Nat Lab 454 Los Alamos NM 87545. *Fax:* 505-665-3644; *E-Mail:* ebs@lanl.gov

SHERALD, ALLEN FRANKLIN, developmental genetics, for more information see previous edition

SHERBECK, L ADAIR, POLYMER CHEMISTRY. *Current Pos:* From res chemist to sr res chemist, E I Du Pont de Nemourss & Co, Inc, 51-59, supvr technol, 59-64, sr supvr nomex technol, 64-80, RES ASSOC, TEXTILE FIBERS DEPT, TECH DIV, E I DU PONT DE NEMOURS & CO, INC, 80- *Personal Data:* b New Norway, Alta, July 24, 22; m 43; c 3. *Educ:* Univ Alta, BSC, 47; McGill Univ, PhD(chem), 51. *Mem:* Am Chem Soc. *Res:* Wood and cellulose chemistry; addition and condensation polymerization; fiber production and properties. *Mailing Add:* 1826 Cherokee Rd Waynesboro VA 22980-2229

SHERBERT, DONALD R, MATHEMATICAL ANALYSIS. *Current Pos:* From instr to asst prof, 62-68, dir undergrad prog, 80-87, ASSOC PROF MATH, UNIV ILL, URBANA, 68- *Personal Data:* b Wausau, Wis, Feb 24, 35; m 81; c 2. *Educ:* Univ Wis, BS, 57; Stanford Univ, PhD(math), 62. *Concurrent Pos:* Mem math fac, Inst Teknologi Mara, Shah Alam, Malaysia, 87-88. *Mem:* Am Math Soc; Math Asn Am. *Res:* Functional analysis. *Mailing Add:* Dept Math Univ Ill 1409 W Green St Urbana IL 61801-2917

SHERBON, JOHN WALTER, DAIRY CHEMISTRY. *Current Pos:* From asst prof to assoc prof, 63-77, PROF FOOD SCI, CORNELL UNIV, 77- *Personal Data:* b Lewiston, Idaho, Oct 31, 33; m 57; c 2. *Educ:* Washington State Univ, BS, 55; Univ Minn, MS, 58, PhD(dairy sci), 63. *Mem:* Inst Food Technol; Am Dairy Sci Asn. *Res:* Physical state of fat in dairy and other food products; analysis for protein content of milk; protein gelation; chemical instrumentation in agricultural chemistry. *Mailing Add:* Food Sci Cornell Univ 114 Stocking Ithaca NY 14853-7201. *Fax:* 607-254-4868; *E-Mail:* jws7@cornell.edu

SHERBOURNE, ARCHIBALD NORBERT, STRUCTURAL ENGINEERING & MECHANICS. *Current Pos:* RETIRED. *Personal Data:* b Bombay, India, July 8, 29; Can citizen; m 59, Jean D Nicol; c Mary, Sarah, Jeffrey, Nicolas, Jonathan & Simon. *Educ:* Univ London, BSc, 53; Lehigh Univ, BSCE, 55, MSCE, 57; Cambridge Univ, MA, 59, PhD(eng), 60; Univ London, DSc, 70. *Honors & Awards:* Eng Medal, Am Prof Engrs, Ont, 75. *Prof Exp:* Engr, Brit Rwys, 48-52; engr, Greater London Coun, 52-54; instr civil & mech eng, Lehigh Univ, 54-57; engr, US Steel Corp, Calif, 56; sr asst res eng, Cambridge Univ, 59-61; assoc prof civil eng, Univ Waterloo, 61-63, chmn, Dept Civil Eng, 64-66, dean fac eng, 66-74, prof, 63-96. *Concurrent Pos:* Vis sr lectr, Univ Col, Univ London, 63-64; Orgn Econ Coop & Develop res fel, Swiss Fed Inst Technol, 64; vis prof, Univ West Indies, 69-70; Nat Res Coun sr res fel, Nat Lab Civil Eng, Portugal, 70; WGer Acad Exchange fel, 75; NATO sr scientist fel & vis lect, Western Europe, 75-76; vis prof, Ecole Polytech Fed, Lausanne, Switz, 75-77, Mich Technol Univ, 80-81 & 81-83, Ocean Eng, Fla Atlantic Univ, 85, Archit & Civil Eng, NC AT&T State Univ, 87, Civil Eng, Kuwait Univ, 89 & Aerospace Eng, IISC, Bangalore, India, 90; consult/adv tech educ, Orgn Am States, Inter Am Develop Bank & Can Int Develop Agency; Gleddon sr vis fel, Univ Western Australia, 78. *Mem:* Fel Brit Inst Struct Engrs; fel Royal Soc Arts; fel Can Acad Eng; fel Can Soc Civil Eng. *Res:* Design of steel structures; structural composites; plasticity. *Mailing Add:* Fac Eng Dept Civil Eng Univ Waterloo Waterloo ON N2L 3G1 Can

SHERBURNE, JAMES AURIL, ECOLOGY. *Current Pos:* DIR, UNIV MAINE INT PROGS, 86- *Personal Data:* b Milo, Maine, Aug 8, 41; m 63; c 2. *Educ:* Univ Maine, BA, 67, MS, 69; Cornell Univ, PhD(ecol), 72. *Prof Exp:* Dir, Peace Corps Environ Prog, Smithsonian Inst, 75-78; unit leader, Coop Wildlife Res Unit, Univ Maine, 78-82; dir, African Oper Wildlife Found, Nairobi, 85-86. *Concurrent Pos:* Var int tech consultancies, Africa, Asia, Latin Am; sci adv, US Agency for Int Develop, US Fish & Wildlife Serv Int Affairs, 82- *Mem:* AAAS; Sigma Xi; Ecol Soc Am; Int Union Conserv Nature & Natural Resources; Entom Soc Am. *Res:* Pesticide residues in vertebrates; chemical interactions between plants and vertebrates, particularly frugivous birds and secondary chemicals, affecting behavior; developing wildlife and natural resource management projects internationally, particularly Africa, South America, and Asia; methods of plant dispersal by vertebrates; international policy studies. *Mailing Add:* PO Box 313 Winterport ME 04496

SHERBY, OLEG D(IMITRI), MATERIALS SCIENCE. *Current Pos:* assoc prof, 58-62, PROF MAT SCI & ENGR, STANFORD UNIV, 62- *Personal Data:* b Shanghai, China, Feb 9, 25; nat US; m 49; c 4. *Educ:* Univ Calif, BS, 47, MS, 49, PhD(metall), 53; Univ Sheffield, DMet, 68. *Honors & Awards:* Dudley Medal, Am Soc Testing & Mat, 58; Centennial Medal, Am Soc Mech Engrs, 80; Gold Medal, Am Soc Metals, 85; Yukawa Mem lectr, Iron & Steel Inst, Japan, 88. *Prof Exp:* Asst metall, Univ Calif, 47-49, res metallurgist, Inst Eng Res, 49-56; NSF fel, Univ Sheffield, 56-57; sci liaison officer metall, US Off Naval Res, Eng, 57-58. *Concurrent Pos:* Consult, Los Alamos Nat Lab, 59-, Lockheed Palo Alto Res Lab, 61-64 & Lawrence Livermore Nat Lab, 65-; fel, Univ Paris, France, 67-68. *Mem:* Nat Acad Eng; Am Inst Mining, Metall & Petrol Engrs; fel Am Soc Metals; Sigma Xi. *Res:* Theoretical and experimental aspects of mechanical behavior of solids and diffusion in solids. *Mailing Add:* Dept Mat Sci & Eng Stanford Univ Stanford CA 94305

SHERCK, CHARLES KEITH, FOOD SCIENCE. *Current Pos:* mgr qual control, 54-59, mgr res opers, 59-64, mgr grocery prod res & develop, 64-69, dir corp res & develop, 70-77, dir, Res & Develop Facil & Tech Serv, 78-81, DIR RES & DEVELOP ADMIN, PILLSBURY CO, 81- *Personal Data:* b Willard, Ohio, July 27, 22; m 46; c 2. *Educ:* Miami Univ, BA, 47. *Prof Exp:* Chemist, Am Home Prod Corp, 47-50, mgr mfg, 50-54. *Concurrent Pos:* Bd dir, AACC, 73-74. *Mem:* Am Asn Cereal Chem; Inst Food Technol. *Res:* Management food research and development. *Mailing Add:* 4805 Markay Ridge Minneapolis MN 55422

SHERDEN, DAVID J, EXPERIMENTAL ELEMENTARY PARTICLE PHYSICS, DATA ACQUISITION SYSTEMS. *Current Pos:* PHYSICIST, STANFORD LINEAR ACCELERATOR CTR, 69- *Personal Data:* b Washington, DC, Oct 26, 40; m 63, Sharon Brady; c David & Robert. *Educ:* Univ San Francisco, BS, 62; Univ Chicago, MS, 64, PhD(physics), 70. *Res:* Experimental elementary particle physics; high energy electron and photon interactions; data acquisition systems. *Mailing Add:* 140 Atherwood Ave Redwood City CA 94061. *E-Mail:* djs@slac.stanford.edu

SHEREBRIN, MARVIN HAROLD, BIOPHYSICS, BIOMEDICAL ENGINEERING. *Current Pos:* Res asst biophys, 60-65, asst prof, 67-73, ASSOC PROF BIOPHYS, FAC MED, UNIV WESTERN ONT, 73- *Personal Data:* b Winnipeg, Man, Mar 23, 37; m 66; c 3. *Educ:* Univ Man, BSc, 60; Univ Western Ont, MSc, 63, PhD(biophys), 65. *Concurrent Pos:* Can Med Res Coun fel, Weizmann Inst Sci, 65-67, Can Med Res Coun res scholar, 67-72. *Mem:* Inst Elec & Electronics Eng; Can Med & Biol Eng Soc; Biophys Soc. *Res:* Mechanical properties of arteries; mechanochemistry of contractile systems; elastin and collagen: function and structure; analysis of peripheral pulse wave; electronics systems in hospitals. *Mailing Add:* Dept Med Biophys Univ Western Ont Health Sci Ctr London ON N6A 5C1 Can. *E-Mail:* sherebrin@uwovax.uwo.ca

SHERER, GLENN KEITH, DEVELOPMENTAL BIOLOGY, CELL BIOLOGY. *Current Pos:* ASSOC PROF BIOL & DEPT CHAIR, UNIV SAINT THOMAS, 84-, DIR, DIV SCI & MATH, 86- *Personal Data:* b Allentown, Pa, May 11, 43; m 70; c 1. *Educ:* Muhlenberg Col, BS, 64; Temple Univ, PhD(biol), 72. *Prof Exp:* Res fel, NIH, 72-73, guest worker cell biol, 73; res assoc med, Col Physicians & Surgeons, Columbia Univ, 73-75; assoc med, Med Univ SC, 75-77, asst prof res med, 77-80; asst prof biol, Bowdoin Col, 80-84. *Concurrent Pos:* NIH res fel, Col Physicians & Surgeons, Columbia Univ, 74-75 & Med Univ SC, 75-76. *Mem:* AAAS; Am Soc Cell Biol; Am Soc Zool; Soc Develop Biol; Tissue Cult Asn; Am Inst Biol Sci. *Res:* Epithelial-mesenchymal interactions in liver development; development of embryonic microvasculature; cell culture; tissue interaction in vertebrate organogenesis; embryonic development of the liver. *Mailing Add:* Dept Biol Sci Univ St Thomas 2115 Summit Ave St Paul MN 55105-1048. *Fax:* 612-647-4378

SHERER, JAMES PRESSLY, ORGANIC CHEMISTRY. *Current Pos:* SR RES ASSOC, E I DU PONT DE NEMOURS & CO, INC, 65- *Personal Data:* b Rock Hill, SC, Aug 25, 39; m 61; c 2. *Educ:* Erskine Col, BA, 61; Duke Univ, MA, 63, PhD(org chem), 66. *Mem:* Am Chem Soc. *Res:* Synthesis and reactions of dicationoid aromatic systems containing one or more quaternary nitrogen atoms at bridgehead positions; research and development of synthetic fibers; synthesis of nitrogen heterocyclic compounds. *Mailing Add:* 2127 Gloucester Pl Wilmington NC 28403-5349

SHERGALIS, WILLIAM ANTHONY, ANALYTICAL & PHYSICAL CHEMISTRY. *Current Pos:* DEAN, ARTS & SCI & PROF CHEM, KING'S COL, 90- *Personal Data:* b Hazleton, Pa, May 25, 41; m 64; c 2. *Educ:* Univ Pa, BS, 62; Drexel Univ, MS, 64; Temple Univ, PhD(phys chem), 69. *Prof Exp:* Assoc prof chem, Widener Col, 68-78, chmn sci, 78-81; prof chem & acad dean, Cardinal Newman Col, 81-85; vpres acad affairs, Ohio Dominican Col, 85-90. *Mem:* Am Chem Soc; Sigma Xi; AAAS. *Res:* Electro-analytical techniques and their applications to chemical and biochemical systems; science education. *Mailing Add:* 47 Walden Dr Mountaintop PA 18707

SHERIDAN, DOUGLAS MAYNARD, BASE & PRECIOUS METAL DEPOSITS, METALLIC MINERAL DEPOSITS. *Current Pos:* RETIRED. *Personal Data:* b Faribault, Minn, Nov 9, 21; m 55, Patricia Loly; c John D & Kathryn P (Osborne). *Educ:* Carleton Col, BA, 43; Univ Minn, Minneapolis, MS(geol), 51. *Prof Exp:* Geologist, US Geol Surv, 48-89. *Mem:* Mineral Soc Am; Soc Econ Geologists; Geol Soc Am. *Res:* Economic geology of precambrian base-metal sulfide deposits in Colorado; economic geology of metallic mineral deposits of all ages in Colorado; precambrian pegmatite deposits in South Dakota. *Mailing Add:* 27334 Mildred Lane Evergreen CO 80439-5421

SHERIDAN, JOHN FRANCIS, IMMUNOLOGY, MICROBIOLOGY. *Current Pos:* asst prof med & dir, Bone Marrow Transplant Lab, 84-87, ASSOC PROF, SECT ORAL BIOL, DEPT MED MICROBIOL & IMMUNOL, OHIO STATE UNIV, 87- *Personal Data:* b Brooklyn, Ny, June 2, 49; m 72; c 4. *Educ:* Fordham Univ, BS, 72; Rutgers Univ, MS, 74, PhD(microbiol), 76. *Prof Exp:* Pub Health Serv fel div immunol, Med Ctr, Duke Univ, 76-78; res assoc immunol, Johns Hopkins Univ, 78-79, instr, 79-82, asst prof, div comp med, 82-84. *Mem:* Am Soc Microbiol; AAAS; Am Asn Immunol; Am Soc Virol; Neurosci Soc. *Res:* Infection and immunity; cellular immunology; virology-herpesviruses, rotaviruses, influenza virus; neuroimmunology. *Mailing Add:* Dept Oral Biol Box 192 Postle Hall Ohio State Univ Col Dent 305 W 12th St Columbus OH 43210-1241. *Fax:* 614-292-7619

SHERIDAN, JOHN ROGER, ATOMIC PHYSICS, CHEMICAL PHYSICS. *Current Pos:* from asst prof to prof, 64-87, head dept, 67-76 & 78-80, EMER PROF PHYSICS, UNIV ALASKA, FAIRBANKS, 87- *Personal Data:* b Helena, Mont, Sept 24, 33; m 59, Carol Buckner; c Lenita & Timothy. *Educ:* Reed Col, BA, 55; Univ Wash, PhD(physics), 64. *Prof Exp:* Res engr, Boeing Co, 55-60; res asst physics, Univ Wash, 60-63, assoc, 63-64. *Concurrent Pos:* Danforth assoc, 66-; vis scientist, Stanford Res Inst, 68-69; vis prof, Queen's Univ Belfast, 75-76; vis fac, Univ Calif, Irvine, 84-85. *Mem:* Sigma Xi; fel Am Phys Soc; Am Asn Physics Teachers; AAAS. *Res:* Use of photon coincidence techniques in laboratory studies of reactions of atoms, molecules; metastable and long-lived atomic, molecular reactions using molecular beams; optical calibration using photon coincidence; quenching and radiative lifetimes of excited atoms and molecules; development of software for computer-based instruction in physics. *Mailing Add:* 5495 Windmill Lane Freeland WA 98249. *E-Mail:* sherisft@whidbey.com

SHERIDAN, JUDSON DEAN, CELL PHYSIOLOGY, CELL BIOLOGY. *Current Pos:* PROF PHYSIOL, BIOL SCI & PROVOST RES & GRAD DEAN, UNIV MO- COLUMBIA, 87- *Personal Data:* b Greeley, Colo, Nov 10, 40; m 63; c 2. *Educ:* Hamline Univ, BS, 61; Oxford Univ, DPhil(neurophysiol), 65. *Prof Exp:* Res assoc neurophysiol & neuropharmacol, Neurophysiol Lab, Harvard Med Sch, 65-66, instr neurobiol, 66-68; from asst prof to assoc prof zool, Univ Minn, Minneapolis, 68-76, prof genetics & cell biol, 76-79, prof anat, Med Sch, 79-87, assoc dean, Grad Sch, 83-87. *Concurrent Pos:* USPHS fel, 65-68; assoc ed develop physiol, Develop Biol, 71-73; Nat Cancer Inst career develop award, 72; consult cell biol study sect, NSF, NIH, 72-; sr res fel, Dept Biochem, Univ Glasgow, Scotland, 74-75; Rhodes scholar, 62-65. *Mem:* AAAS; Am Soc Cell Biol; NY Acad Sci. *Res:* Cellular communication via specialized points of cell-to-cell contacts, especially during development and abnormal cell growth. *Mailing Add:* GRE Prog ETS MS 33V Princeton NJ 08541. *Fax:* 573-884-4078

SHERIDAN, MARK ALEXANDER, COMPARATIVE PHYSIOLOGY & BIOCHEMISTRY, COMPARATIVE ENDOCRINOLOGY. *Current Pos:* asst prof, 85-91, ASSOC PROF, NDAK STATE UNIV, 91- *Personal Data:* b Fullterton, Calif, Nov 8, 58; m 81, Nancy G Ibsen; c Kathleen, Melissa, Matthew & Daniel. *Educ:* Humboldt State Univ, AB, 80, MA, 82; Univ Calif, Berkeley, PhD(zool), 85. *Prof Exp:* Post-grad res scientist, Univ Wash, 85. *Concurrent Pos:* Zool grad prog coordr, NDak State Univ, 86-90, dir, Regulatory Biosci Ctr, 91-; vis scientist, Nat Marine Fisheries Serv, Seattle, Wash, 86 & 88, Dept Biol, Humboldt State Univ, Arcata, Calif, 91, Dept Biol, Hiroshima Univ, 91; vis prof, Univ Gothenburg, 96; panelist, NSF, 97- *Mem:* AAAS; Am Fisheries Soc; Sigma Xi; Soc Integrative & Comp Biol; Am Diabetes Asn. *Res:* Hormonal control of growth, development and metabolism of fish, especially pancreatic physiology; regulation of gene expression. *Mailing Add:* Dept Zool Stevens Hall NDak State Univ Fargo ND 58105. *Fax:* 701-237-7149; *E-Mail:* msherida@plains.nodak.edu

SHERIDAN, MICHAEL FRANCIS, PETROLOGY, VOLCANOLOGY. *Current Pos:* from asst prof to assoc prof, 66-76, PROF GEOL, ARIZ STATE UNIV, 76- *Personal Data:* b Springfield, Mass, Feb 20, 40; m 64; c 3. *Educ:* Amherst Col, AB, 62; Stanford Univ, MS, 64, PhD(geol), 65. *Honors & Awards:* Castaing Award, 83. *Prof Exp:* Geologist, US Geol Surv, 64-74; instr geol, Amherst Col, 65-66. *Concurrent Pos:* Consult geologist, 69-; NASA Surtsey Exped, 70; vis prof, Univ Tokyo, 72-73, Univ Pisa, 79-80 & Univ Calabria, 83; sr Fulbright-Hays scientist, Iceland, 78 & Antarctic Exped, 78. *Mem:* Geol Soc Am; Int Asn Volcanol & Chem Earth's Interior; Mineral Soc Am; Am Geophys Union. *Res:* Physical processes in volcanology; ash-flow tuff field relationships and mineralogy, volcanic risk, geothermal energy. *Mailing Add:* State Univ NY PO Box 600001 State Univ NY-Buffalo 4240 Ridge Lea Rd Buffalo NY 14260-0001

SHERIDAN, PETER STERLING, INORGANIC CHEMISTRY. *Current Pos:* asst prof, 80-84, ASSOC PROF CHEM, COLGATE UNIV, 84- *Personal Data:* b Portland, Maine, Mar 1, 44; m 67. *Educ:* Kenyon Col, Ohio, BA, 66; Northwestern Univ, Evanston, PhD(chem), 71. *Prof Exp:* Lectr chem, Univ Kent, Canterbury, UK, 70-71, fel, 71-72; fel, Univ Southern Calif, 72-74; asst prof, State Univ NY Binghamton, 74-80. *Mem:* Am Chem Soc. *Res:* Photochemical reactions of transition metal complexes. *Mailing Add:* Dept Chem Colgate Univ Hamilton NY 13346-1399

SHERIDAN, PHILIP HENRY, NEUROLOGY & DEVELOPMENTAL NEUROBIOLOGY, EPILEPSY & SLEEP DISORDERS. *Current Pos:* sr surgeon, 85-92, MED DIR, USPHS, 92-; CHIEF, EPILEPSY BR, DIV CONVULSIVE INFECTIOUS & IMMUNE DIS, NAT INST NEUROL DIS & STROKE, NIH, 95- *Personal Data:* b Washington, DC, June 29, 50; m 87, Margaret Mary Williams; c Gerard, Philip, Kathleen, Patrick, Mary Margaret & Mary Anne. *Educ:* Yale Univ, BS, 72; Georgetown Univ, MD, 76. *Honors & Awards:* Pub Health Serv Commendation Medal, NIH, 91. *Prof Exp:* Health scientist adminr, Epilepsy Br, Nat Inst Neurol Dis & Stroke, NIH, 84-89; chief, Develop Neurol Br, Div Convulsive Develop & Neuromuscular Dis, Nat Inst Neurol Dis & Stroke, NIH, 89-94. *Concurrent Pos:* Neurologist, Med Neurol Br, NIH Clin Ctr, 82-; attend physician, Va Dept Health Childrens Specialty Serv Child Neurol Clin, 82-; consult neurologist, Nat Naval Med Ctr, 84-; med monitor & proj officer, Antiepileptic Drug Develop Prog, NIH, 84-; reviewer, J Am Med Asn, Annals Neurol, Pediat Neurol, Epilepsia, 89- & Biol Psychiat, 92-; spec asst to the dir, Nat Inst Neurol Dis & Stroke, NIH, 94- *Mem:* Am Acad Neurol; Soc Neurosci; Child Neurol Soc; Am Epilepsy Soc. *Res:* To establish a nationwide multidisciplinary program of federally funded research to elucidate the functioning of the nervous system and to improve diagnosis and treatment of neurological and neuromuscular disorders. *Mailing Add:* NIH Fed Bldg Rm 516 7550 Wis Ave Bethesda MD 20892-9020. *Fax:* 301-496-9916; *E-Mail:* ps5gi@nih.gov

SHERIDAN, RICHARD COLLINS, CHEMISTRY. *Current Pos:* RETIRED. *Personal Data:* b Trotwood, Ohio, Aug 19, 29; m 57, Carol Moore; c Vicki, Susan, Laura & Jennifer. *Educ:* Murray State Col, BS, 56; Univ Ky, MS, 61. *Honors & Awards:* Wilson Dam Award, Am Chem Soc, 76. *Prof Exp:* Chemist, B F Goodrich Chem Co, 56-58; res chemist, Nat Fertilizer Develop Ctr, Tenn Valley Authority, 60-88; chem instr, Univ NAla, 89-91. *Concurrent Pos:* Counr, Wilson Dam Sect, Am Chem Soc. *Mem:* Am Chem Soc. *Res:* Synthesis of oxamide; pyrolysis of urea phosphate; preparation of ammonium polyphosphates; history of chemistry; preparation of new nitrogen-phosphorus fertilizer compounds; melamine phosphate; recovery of uranium from phosphate rock; ion chromatography; production of phosphoric acid; cleaning and repair of old tombstones. *Mailing Add:* 105 Terrace St Sheffield AL 35660. *E-Mail:* sheridanrc@aol.com

SHERIDAN, RICHARD P, PLANT PHYSIOLOGY, BIOLOGY. *Current Pos:* asst prof, 68-74, ASSOC PROF BOT, UNIV MONT, 74- *Personal Data:* b Detroit, Mich, Mar 10, 39; m 62; c 2. *Educ:* Univ Ore, BA, 62, MA, 63, PhD(biol), 67. *Prof Exp:* NIH fel, Scripps Inst Oceanog, Univ Calif, San Diego, 67-68. *Concurrent Pos:* NSF res grant, 69-71. *Mem:* Phycol Soc Am; Am Soc Plant Physiologists. *Res:* Algal physiology with emphasis on the photosynthetic mechanisms. *Mailing Add:* Dept Biol Sci Univ Mont Missoula MT 59812-0001

SHERIDAN, ROBERT E, GEOLOGY, OCEANOGRAPHY. *Current Pos:* PROF GEOL & GEOPHYSICS, RUTGERS UNIV, 86- *Personal Data:* b Hoboken, NJ, Oct 11, 40; m 66; c 3. *Educ:* Rutgers Univ, BA, 62; Columbia Univ, MA, 65, PhD(geol), 68. *Prof Exp:* Res asst, Lamont Geol Observ, NY, 62-64, res scientist, 68; from asst prof to prof geol, Univ Delaware, 68-86. *Concurrent Pos:* WAE appointment, US Geol Surv, 75-93; coordr, Marine Geol & Geophys Prog, Col Marine Studies, Univ Del, 78-80; vis prof, Rutgers Univ, 79; chair, Joides Passive Margin Panel, 79-81. *Mem:* Geol Soc Am; Am Geophys Union; Am Asn Petrol Geol; Nat Maritime Hist Soc. *Res:* Geology and geophysics of the continental margin off eastern North America; stratigraphy of the Western North Atlantic; discovery of USS Monitor; recovery of oldest oceanic sediments; development of pulsation tectonic theory. *Mailing Add:* Geol Rutgers Univ New Brunswick NJ 08903

SHERIDAN, THOMAS BROWN, MAN-MACHINE SYSTEMS, HUMAN FACTORS. *Current Pos:* res asst mech eng, 54-55, from instr to assoc prof mech eng, 55-70, prof eng, appl psychol, aeronaut & astronaut, 70-, FORD PROF, MASS INST TECHNOL, 95- *Personal Data:* b Cincinnati, Ohio, Dec 23, 29; m 53; c Paul, Richard, David & Margaret. *Educ:* Purdue Univ, BS, 51; Univ Calif, Los Angeles, MS, 54; Mass Inst Technol, ScD, 59. *Hon Degrees:* Dr, Delft Univ Technol, Neth, 91. *Honors & Awards:* Paul Fitts Award, Human Factors Soc, 77; Centennial Medal, Inst Elec & Electronics Engrs, 82, Norbert Wiener Award, 92, Joseph Wohl Award, 95. *Prof Exp:* Res asst eng, Univ Calif, Los Angeles, 53-54. *Concurrent Pos:* Vis prof control eng, Delft Univ Technol, Neth, 72; mem, NIH Study Sects Accident Prev & Injury Control, 73-77; chmn & mem, Comt Human Factors, Nat Res Coun, 78-88; mem, US Cong Off Tech Assessment Comt Appropriate Technol, 81-82; mem, NASA Tech Oversight Comn Flight Telerobot, 87-; mem, Defense Sci Bd Task Force Training, 87-88; mem, Nuclear Regulatory Comn, Nuclear Safety Res Comn, 88-91; mem, Comn Com Espec Develop Space Facil, Nat Res Coun, 88-95, Comm Human Factors, Automation Air Traffic Comt, 95- *Mem:* Nat Acad Eng; fel Inst Elec & Electronics Engrs Systs Man & Cybernet Soc (pres, 73-75); Fel Human Factors Soc (pres, 90-91). *Res:* Man-machine systems control and design for auto, aircraft and space vehicles, nuclear power, deep ocean science; robotics and human-operated remote manipulators; human-computer cooperation and decision-aiding. *Mailing Add:* 32 Sewall St Newton MA 02165. *Fax:* 617-258-6575; *E-Mail:* sheridan@mit.edu

SHERIDAN, WILLIAM, GENETICS. *Current Pos:* RETIRED. *Personal Data:* b Cohoes, NY, Dec 1, 30; m 59; c 3. *Educ:* City Col New York, BA, 54; Univ Stockholm, Fil Lic, 62, Fil Dok(genetics), 68. *Prof Exp:* Instr genetics, Inst Genetics, Univ Stockholm, 60-61; res assoc, Lab Radiation Genetics, Sweden, 62-68; docent, Inst Genetics, Univ Stockholm, 68-73, actg dir inst, 70-71; head mammalian genetics sect, Nat Inst Environ Health Sci, NIH, 73-88, staff mem, off sr sci adv to dir, 88-94. *Concurrent Pos:* Asst ed, Mutation Res, 74- *Mem:* Genetics Soc Am; Environ Mutagen Soc. *Res:* Mammalian genetics; environmental mutagenesis; radiation genetics. *Mailing Add:* 4609 Pemberton Dr Raleigh NC 27609

SHERIDAN, WILLIAM FRANCIS, GENETICS. *Current Pos:* assoc prof, 75-80, PROF BIOL, UNIV NDAK, 80- *Personal Data:* b Lakeland, Fla, Dec 4, 36; m 64; c 2. *Educ:* Univ Fla, BSA, 58, MS, 60; Univ Ill, PhD(cell biol), 65. *Prof Exp:* Teaching asst bot, Univ Fla, 58-61; teaching asst, Univ Ill, 61-63, USPHS trainee biol, 63-65; instr, Yale Univ, 65-66, res fel sch med, 66-68; asst prof, Univ Mo-Columbia, 68-75. *Concurrent Pos:* Fulbright res award, 77-78; vis prof, Dept Physiol, Carlsberg Res Lab, Copenhagen, 77-78, Purdue Univ, 88, Univ Oregon, 89. *Mem:* Genetics Soc Am; Soc Develop Biol. *Res:* Maize genetics and embryo development; maize morphogenesis; tissue culture of cereals and its genetic applications. *Mailing Add:* Dept Biol Univ NDak Box 8238 Grand Forks ND 58202-8238

SHERIDON, NICHOLAS KEITH, DISPLAY DEVICES PHYSICS, PRINTING DEVICES PHYSICS. *Current Pos:* sr physicist, Xerox Webster Res Ctr, Xerox Corp, 67-71, scientist, 71-72, sr scientist, 72-75, prin scientist, Palo Alto Res Ctr, 75-80, res fel, 80-88, SR RES FEL, XEROX CORP, 88- *Personal Data:* b Detroit, Mich, Dec 8, 35; m 61, Kathleen E Sullivan; c Timothy, Jennifer & Amy. *Educ:* Wayne State Univ, BS, 57, MS, 59. *Prof Exp:* Asst physicist systs div, Bendix Corp, 60-62, physicist res labs, 62, sr physicist, 64-67. *Mem:* Inst Elec & Electronics Engrs; Soc Photog Instrumentation Eng; Soc Photog Scientists & Engrs; Soc Info Display. *Res:* Electrography, non-impact printing; display devices, electronic imaging; electrophotography; optical and acoustical holography; optical data processing; electron physics; surface chemistry; gaseous electronics; gas discharge; chemistry fluid dynamics. *Mailing Add:* Xerox Corp Palo Alto Res Ctr 3333 Coyote Hill Rd Palo Alto CA 94304. *E-Mail:* nsheridon.parc@xerox.com

SHERIFF, ROBERT EDWARD, EXPLORATION GEOPHYSICS. *Current Pos:* PROF, UNIV HOUSTON, 80- *Personal Data:* b Mansfield, Ohio, Apr 19, 22; m 45, Margaret Sites; c 6. *Educ:* Wittenberg Univ, AB, 43; Ohio State Univ, MS, 47, PhD(physics), 50. *Honors & Awards:* Kauffman Gold Medal, Soc Explor Geophysicists, 69. *Prof Exp:* Physicist, Manhattan Proj, 44-46; from geophysicist to chief geophysicist, Stand Oil Co, Calif, 50-75; sr vpres, Seiscom-Delta Inc, 75-80. *Concurrent Pos:* Adj prof geophys, Univ Houston, 73-80. *Mem:* Hon mem Soc Explor Geophysicists (1st vpres, 72-73); Europ Asn Explor Geophysicists; Sigma Xi; Am Asn Petrol Geologists; AAAS. *Res:* Techniques of geophysical interpretation, including data acquisition and data processing techniques; applications of geophysics to reservoirs. *Mailing Add:* Dept Geol Univ Houston 4800 Calhoun Rd Houston TX 77204-5503

SHERIFF, STEVEN, PROTEIN CRYSTALLOGRAPHY. *Current Pos:* RES FEL, BRISTOL-MYERS SQUIBB PHARMACEUT RES INST, 88- *Personal Data:* b Washington, DC, Dec 26, 51; m, Michele Alperin; c Jacob M Alperin-Sheriff & Aliza N Alperin-Sheriff. *Educ:* Pomona Col, BA, 73; Univ Wash, Seattle, PhD(biochem), 79. *Prof Exp:* NIH fel, Univ Calif, Los Angeles, 79-81, Naval Res Lab, 81-82; Nat Res Coun-Naval Res Lab fel, Naval Res Lab, 82-84; res scientist, Genex Corp, 84; guest researcher, NIH, 85, sr staff fel, 85-88. *Concurrent Pos:* Consult, Columbia Univ, 85. *Mem:* Am Crystallog Asn; AAAS; Protein Soc. *Res:* Protein Crystallography; anisotropy; structures of antibody-antigen complexes; methods for describing interactions between molecules in complex. *Mailing Add:* Bristol-Myers Squibb Pharm Res Inst PO Box 4000 Princeton NJ 08543-4000. *E-Mail:* sheriff@bms.com

SHERINS, RICHARD J, ENDOCRINOLOGY, ANDROLOGY. *Current Pos:* fel, Nat Cancer Inst, 69-70, sr investr endocrinol, Endocrinol & reproduction res br, 70-77, DEVELOP ENDOCRINOL BR, NAT INST CHILD HEALTH & HUMAN DEVELOP, NIH, 77- *Personal Data:* b Brooklyn, NY, July 6, 37; m 60; c 3. *Educ:* Univ Calif, Los Angeles, BA, 59, San Francisco, MD, 63. *Prof Exp:* Fel endocrinol, Univ Wash, 67-69. *Concurrent Pos:* Assoc clin prof obstet & gynec, Sch Med, George Washington Univ, 75- *Mem:* Am Fedn Clin Res; Endocrine Soc; Am Col Physicians; Am Fertility Soc; Am Soc Andrology (treas, 79-81, pres, 82-83). *Res:* Disorders of male reproduction; control of pituitary gonadotropin secretion. *Mailing Add:* NIH Nat Inst Child Health Bethesda MD 20892

SHERK, FRANK ARTHUR, FINITE GEOMETRY. *Current Pos:* Lectr math, 57-61, from asst prof to prof, 61-94, EMER PROF MATH, UNIV TORONTO, 94- *Personal Data:* b Stayner, Ont, May 20, 32; m 54, Anne B Cressman; c Janet E (Young), Carol A (Blake), Murray W & Donna J (Barker). *Educ:* McMaster Univ, BA, 54, MSc, 55; Univ Toronto, PhD(math), 57. *Mem:* Am Math Soc; Can Math Soc. *Res:* Projective geometry; regular maps; discrete groups. *Mailing Add:* Dept Math Univ Toronto Toronto ON M5S 1A1 Can

SHERMA, JOSEPH A, ANALYTICAL CHEMISTRY. *Current Pos:* From assoc prof to prof, 58-82, CHARLES A DANA PROF ANALYTICAL CHEM, LAFAYETTE COL, 82-, HEAD CHEM DEPT, 85- *Personal Data:* b Newark, NJ, Mar 2, 34; m 61; c 2. *Educ:* Upsala Col, BS, 55; Rutgers Univ, PhD(anal chem), 58. *Concurrent Pos:* researcher, Perrine Primate Lab, Environ Protection Agency, 72; vis researcher, Argonne Nat Lab, Iowa State Univ, Syracuse Univ Res Corp, Hosp Univ Pa, Waters Assocs & Whatman Inc; ed, J Asn Official Anal Chemists. *Mem:* Am Inst Chem; Am Chem Soc; Soc Appl Spectros; Sigma Xi. *Res:* Ion exchange and solution chromatography; analytical separations; pesticide analysis; quantitative thin-layer chromatography; food additive determination; clinical analysis; author of over 350 publications. *Mailing Add:* Dept Chem Lafayette Col Easton PA 18042-1782

SHERMAN, ADRIA ROTHMAN, TRACE ELEMENT NUTRITION, IRON IMMUNITY. *Current Pos:* PROF NUTRIT, RUTGERS UNIV, 87- *Personal Data:* b 1950; m; c 2. *Educ:* Pa State Univ, PhD(nutrit), 77. *Prof Exp:* Assoc prof nutrit, Univ Ill, Urbana, 84-87. *Mem:* Am Inst Nutrit; Am Soc Clin Nutrit. *Res:* Nutritional immunology; iron; developmental nutrition. *Mailing Add:* Dept Nutrit Sci Rutgers Univ Thompson Hall Cook Col 107 Lipman Dr New Brunswick NJ 08903. *Fax:* 732-932-6837; *E-Mail:* sherman_c@aesop.rutgers.edu

SHERMAN, ALBERT HERMAN, ORGANIC CHEMISTRY. *Current Pos:* RETIRED. *Personal Data:* b Philadelphia, Pa, Mar 5, 21; m 44; c 3. *Educ:* Rutgers Univ, BS, 42, MS, 50, PhD(chem), 53. *Prof Exp:* Chemist, Rare Chems Div, Nopco Chem Co, 47-49; asst anal chem, Rutgers Univ, 49-52; sr chemist, Nitrogen Div, Allied Chem Corp, 52-57; res chemist, Atla Powder Co, 57-71 & ICI Am, Inc, 71-80. *Mem:* Am Chem Soc. *Res:* Surfactants; detergents; textile additives; organic synthesis; cosmetic chemistry. *Mailing Add:* 20100 W Country Club Dr No 504 Miami FL 33180

SHERMAN, ALFRED ISAAC, OBSTETRICS & GYNECOLOGY. *Current Pos:* PROF OBSTET & GYNEC, SCH MED, WAYNE STATE UNIV, 67-; DIR, DEPT OBSTET & GYNEC RES & EDUC, SINAI HOSP, DETROIT, 75- *Personal Data:* b Toronto, Ont, Sept 4, 20; US citizen; m 44; c 3. *Educ:* Univ Toronto, MD, 43; Am Bd Obstet & Gynec, dipl; Bd Gynec Oncol, dipl, 74. *Prof Exp:* From sr intern to asst resident obstet & gynec, Hamilton Gen Hosp, Ont, 44-45; fel path, Univ Rochester, 46-47; intern, St Louis Maternity & Barnes Hosps, 47-48, asst resident, 49-50; fel obstet & gynec, Sch Med, Washington Univ, 50-51, from instr to prof obstet & gynec, 51-65. *Concurrent Pos:* Dir, Dept Obstet & Gynec Oncol, Beaumont Hosp, Royal Oak, 75-; resident, Barnard Hosp, 50-51; consult & vis physician, St Louis City Hosp; consult, Mallinckrodt Inst Radiol, Homer G Phillips, St Luke's & Jewish Hosps; civilian consult, USAF; co-dir cytogenetics lab, John Hartford Found, Mo, 62-67. *Mem:* Radium Soc; Am Col Obstet & Gynec; Endocrine Soc; Soc Gynec Invest; Soc Gynec Oncol. *Mailing Add:* 6767 W Outer Dr Detroit MI 48235-2899

SHERMAN, ANTHONY MICHAEL, POLYMER SYNTHESIS & CHARACTERIZATION, POLYMER PROCESSING. *Current Pos:* CONSULT, 93- *Personal Data:* b Barberton, Ohio, Mar 3, 40; m 63; c 4. *Educ:* Univ Akron, BS, 65, MS, 68, PhD(polymer sci), 75. *Prof Exp:* Chemist, Goodyear Res, 63-66; sr chemist, B F Goodrich Chem Co, 66-77; sr res chemist, Mobil Chem Co, 77-85; res mgr, Alcolac, 85-93. *Concurrent Pos:* Lectr, John Carroll Univ, Cleveland, 75-76. *Mem:* Am Chem Soc. *Res:* Specialty monomers and derived specialty polymers. *Mailing Add:* 8 Hampton Circle Newtown PA 18940

SHERMAN, ARTHUR, PLASMA PHYSICS. *Current Pos:* PRES, SHERMAN & ASSOC, INC, 92- *Personal Data:* b Brooklyn, NY, Oct 15, 31; m 56; c 3. *Educ:* Polytech Inst Brooklyn, BME, 53; Princeton Univ, MSE, 58; Univ Pa, PhD(eng), 65. *Prof Exp:* Res engr, Gen Elec Corp, 53-68; pres, Med Diag Ctrs, 68-73; staff engr, RCA Corp, 73-79; vpres eng, Combustion Power Corp, 79-81; sr engr, Appl Mat, Inc, 81-83; sr scientist, Varian Res, 83-91. *Concurrent Pos:* Lectr, Univ Pa, 65-68 & Univ Calif, Berkeley, 82-83. *Mem:* Am Phys Soc; Electrochem Soc; Am Vacuum Soc; Mat Res Soc. *Res:* Chemical vapor deposition; plasma physics; magnetohydrodynamics; fluid mechanics. *Mailing Add:* 600 Sharon Park Dr Suite C-307 Menlo Park CA 94025. *Fax:* 650-328-1987

SHERMAN, BURTON STUART, ANATOMY. *Current Pos:* asst, 56-59, from instr to assoc prof, 60-85, EMER PROF ANAT, STATE UNIV NY DOWNSTATE MED CTR, 85-; PROF ANAT & EMBRYOL, SCH HEALTH SCI, TOURO COL, 85-, EMER DEAN, 89- *Personal Data:* b Brooklyn, NY, Nov 12, 30; m 52, Ellen I Chanin; c Steven, Lisa, Cari & Keith. *Educ:* NY Univ, BA, 51, MS, 56; State Univ NY Downstate Med Ctr, PhD(anat), 60. *Prof Exp:* Res asst leukemia, Sloan-Kettering Inst Cancer Res, 51-52; res chemist, Jewish Hosp Brooklyn, NY, 52-56, res assoc biochem, 59-60. *Concurrent Pos:* Vis scientist, Strangeways Res Lab, Eng, 64-65; dean, Sch Health Sci, Touro Col, 85-89. *Mem:* Am Asn Anat; AAAS; Am Asn Clin Anatomists; Sigma Xi. *Res:* Leukemia research; osteogenesis; calcification of collagen and macromolecules; tissue and organ culture; vitamin A metabolism, biochemistry and effects on growth and proliferation of tissues; developmental anatomy. *Mailing Add:* Touro Col Barry Levine Sch HS Bldg 10 135 Carmen Rd Dix Hills NY 11746

SHERMAN, BYRON WESLEY, ELECTRICAL ENGINEERING. *Current Pos:* instr, 63-66, asst prof elec eng, 66-81, PROF, UNIV MO-COLUMBIA, 81- *Personal Data:* b St Louis, Mo, Sept 20, 35; m 55; c 4. *Educ:* Univ Mo, BS, 57, MS, 59, PhD(elec eng), 66. *Prof Exp:* Asst instr elec eng, Univ Mo, 57-59; eng consult, Columbia Pictures Corp, Calif, 60-61 & Wells Eng, 61-62; electronics engr, McDonnell Aircraft Corp, 62-63. *Concurrent Pos:* Eng consult, Audience Studies, Inc, Calif, 66-67; summer fac fel, NASA Manned Spacecraft Ctr, 67-68, consult, 68-; consult, Lockheed Electronics Corp, Tex, 67-68 & Inst Bioeng Res, Univ Mo, 68-75. *Mem:* Inst Elec & Electronics Engrs. *Res:* Electric field instrumentation. *Mailing Add:* 4321 New Haven Rd Columbia MO 65201

SHERMAN, CHARLES HENRY, PHYSICS, ACOUSTICS. *Current Pos:* RETIRED. *Personal Data:* b Fall River, Mass, Dec 16, 28; wid; Beverly Mae Partridge; c Brett & Kitt (Lee). *Educ:* Mass Inst Technol, BS, 50; Univ Conn, MS, 57, PhD(physics), 62. *Prof Exp:* Physicist, Tracerlab, Inc, 50-53; physicist, USN Underwater Sound Lab, 53-63; assoc dir res, Parke Math Labs, Inc, Mass, 63-71; head appl res br, Transducer Div, New London Lab, Naval Underwater Systs Ctr, 71-74, head Transducer & Arrays Div, 74-81, prog mgr, 81-88. *Concurrent Pos:* Adj prof, Dept Physics, Univ Conn, 62-63, Dept Ocean Eng, Univ RI, 75- *Mem:* Fel Acoust Soc Am; Am Phys Soc; Sigma Xi. *Res:* Acoustics; theoretical physics; nonlinear physics. *Mailing Add:* 22 Champlin Dr Westerly RI 02891

SHERMAN, D(ONALD) R, STRUCTURAL ENGINEERING. *Current Pos:* assoc prof, 66-72, PROF STRUCT, UNIV WIS-MILWAUKEE, 72-, DIR, STRUCT LAB, 87- *Personal Data:* b Cleveland, Ohio, Aug 2, 35; m 60; c 3. *Educ:* Case Inst Technol, BS, 57, MS, 60; Univ Ill, PhD(struct eng), 64. *Prof Exp:* Engr, Pittsburgh Testing Lab, 57-58; design engr, Aerojet-Gen Corp, 63; engr, Esso Res & Eng Co, 64-66. *Mem:* Am Soc Civil Engrs; Soc Exp Stress Anal; Struct Stability Res Coun. *Res:* Stability of structural steel columns; tubular structures; equipment design for seismic loads. *Mailing Add:* Dept Civil Eng & Mech Univ Wis 3200 N Cramer St Milwaukee WI 53211

SHERMAN, DAVID MICHAEL, mineral physics, mineral spectroscopy, for more information see previous edition

SHERMAN, EDWARD, TECHNICAL MANAGEMENT, ORGANIC CHEMISTRY. *Current Pos:* RETIRED. *Personal Data:* b New York, NY, Feb 8, 19; m 45; c 2. *Educ:* Univ Ill, BS, 40; Lehigh Univ, MS, 47, PhD(chem), 49; Northwestern Univ, MBA, 70. *Prof Exp:* Asst org chem lab, Univ Ala, 40-41; jr inspector, US Food & Drug Admin, 41-42; asst oil chem, Lehigh Univ, 46-47; res assoc high nitrogen compounds, Ill Inst Technol, 49-50; group leader chem res, Quaker Oats Co, 50-64, sect leader, 64-71, coordr tech & admin serv, 71-72, asst dir chem res & develop, 72-78, mgr spec projs, 78-80, chem prod mgr, 80-83. *Concurrent Pos:* Consult, 83- *Mem:* AAAS; Am Chem Soc; Polyurethane Mfrs Asn. *Res:* Chemical product development and marketing; environmental sciences; industrial hygiene; furans; tetrahydrofurans; lactones; lactams; aromatics; ring cleavage; polymers; photochemistry; levulinic acid; cycloaliphatics; nitrogen heterocycles; nitroaminoguanidine; nitroguanyl azide; nitroaminotetrazole; pharmaceuticals; oil oxidation; hemin and hemochromogens; resins. *Mailing Add:* 17723 Tiffany Trace Dr Boca Raton FL 33487-1225

SHERMAN, FRED, GENETICS, BIOPHYSICS. *Current Pos:* from sr instr to prof, Sch Med & Dent, Univ Rochester, 61-81, Wilson prof radiation biol & biophys, 81-96, prof & chmn, Dept Biochem, 82-96, ACTG CHMN & PROF BIOCHEM & BIOPHYSICS, SCH MED & DENT, UNIV ROCHESTER, 96- *Personal Data:* b Minneapolis, Minn, May 21, 32; m 58, 94; c Aaron, Mark & Rhea. *Educ:* Univ Minn, BA, 53; Univ Calif, Berkeley, PhD(biophys), 58. *Honors & Awards:* Wander Mem Lectr, 75. *Prof Exp:* Fel genetics, Univ Wash, 59-60 & Lab Physiol Genetics, France, 60-61. *Concurrent Pos:* Instr, Cold Spring Harbor Lab, 70-87; assoc ed, Genetics, 75-82, Molecular & Cellular Biol, 79-88, Yeast, 85-; mem, Comn Chem Environ Mutagens, Nat Res Coun, 79-83; lectr, Fedn Europ Biochem Studies, 82; study sect mem, Am Cancer Soc, 82-88, NIH, 90-95; bd dirs Genetic Soc Am, 84-85. *Mem:* Nat Acad Sci; AAAS; Genetics Soc Am; Am Soc Microbiol. *Res:* Mutational alteration of yeast cytochrome C; yeast genetics; cytoplasmic inheritance; cytochrome deficient mutants of yeast; amino acid changes in cytochrome C; DNA changes in yeast genes; contributed to numerous scientific publications. *Mailing Add:* Dept Biochem & Biophysics Univ Rochester Rochester NY 14642. *Fax:* 716-271-2683; *E-Mail:* fsrm@bphvax.biophysics.rochester.edu

SHERMAN, FREDERICK GEORGE, BIOLOGY. *Current Pos:* prof zool & chmn dept, 60-68, prof biol, 68-82, EMER PROF, SYRACUSE UNIV, 82- *Personal Data:* b McGregor, Mich, Apr 16, 15; m 42, Barbara Tenney; c Susan S (Treffeisen), Martha & Sarah S (Friedman). *Educ:* Univ Tulsa, BS, 38; Northwestern Univ, PhD(physiol), 42. *Prof Exp:* Fel, Sch Med, Wash Univ, St Louis, 46; from instr to prof biol, Brown Univ, 46-60. *Concurrent Pos:* Fel, Picker Found, 51-52; res collabr, Brookhaven Nat Lab, 53-56 & 58-68; vis scientist, NIH, Bethesda, 57, spec fel, 67-68. *Mem:* Am Physiol Soc; Soc Gen Physiol(secy, 57-59); Sigma Xi. *Res:* Biochemical changes associated with aging; regulation of protein synthesis. *Mailing Add:* 106 Dewitt Rd Syracuse NY 13214-2005

SHERMAN, FREDERICK S, MECHANICS. *Current Pos:* asst prof mech eng, Univ Calif, 58-59, assoc prof, 59-65, prof aeronaut sci, 65-70, asst dean, Col Eng, 73-80, prof mech eng, 70-91, EMER PROF, UNIV CALIF, BERKELEY, 91- *Personal Data:* b San Diego, Calif, Apr 14, 28; m 53; c 2. *Educ:* Harvard Univ, BS, 49; Univ Calif, MS, 50, PhD(mech eng), 54. *Prof Exp:* Instr mech eng, Univ Calif, 54-56; aeronaut res engr mech br, Off Naval Res, US Dept Navy, Washington, DC, 56-58. *Concurrent Pos:* Mem fluid mech subcomt, Nat Adv Comt Aeronaut, 57-58. *Mem:* Am Inst Phys. *Res:* Fluid mechanics; mixing in stratified fluid flows; non-linear instability; free convection; unsteady flow separation. *Mailing Add:* 261 Grizzly Peak Blvd Kensington CA 94708

SHERMAN, GARY JOSEPH, MATHEMATICS. *Current Pos:* Asst prof, 71-78, PROF MATH, ROSE-HULMAN INST TECHNOL, 78- *Personal Data:* b Bellaire, Ohio, Dec 18, 41; m 64; c 3. *Educ:* Bowling Green State Univ, BS, 63, MA, 68; Ind Univ, Bloomington, PhD(math), 71. *Mem:* Am Math Soc; Math Asn Am. *Res:* Group theory; partially ordered groups. *Mailing Add:* Dept Math Rose-Hulman Inst Technol Terre Haute IN 47803-3999

SHERMAN, GEORGE CHARLES, physical optics, for more information see previous edition

SHERMAN, GERALD PHILIP, PHARMACOLOGY, PHARMACY. *Current Pos:* dir undergrad studies, 78-80, chmn, Dept Pharmacol, 81-93 univ admin, Off Acad Affairs, 93-94, PROF PHARMACOL, UNIV TOLEDO, 80-, ASST DEAN COL PHARM, 94- *Personal Data:* b Philadelphia, Pa, Mar 20, 40; wid; c Bradley & Rodney. *Educ:* Philadelphia Col Pharm & Sci, BSc, 63, MSc, 65, PhD(pharmacol), 67. *Prof Exp:* NIH fel, Univ Pittsburgh, 67-68; asst prof physiol & pharmacol, Univ Pittsburgh, 68-69; asst prof mat med, Univ Ky, 69-70, from asst prof to assoc prof clin pharm, 70-78. *Mem:* Am Asn Col Pharm; Am Soc Clin Pharmacol & Therapeut. *Res:* Clinical drug efficacy studies; autonomic and cardiovascular pharmacology; sports medicine; drug testing programs. *Mailing Add:* Col of Pharm Univ of Toledo Toledo OH 43606. *Fax:* 419-530-8407

SHERMAN, GORDON R, COMPUTER SCIENCES, OPERATIONS RESEARCH. *Current Pos:* assoc prof math, Univ Tenn, 60-69, prof, 69-73, head, Dept Comput Sci, 70-73, PROF MATH & COMPUT SCI, UNIV TENN, KNOXVILLE, 73-, DIR, COMPUT CTR, 60- *Personal Data:* b Menomonee, Mich, Feb 24, 28; m 51; c 2. *Educ:* Iowa State Univ, BS, 53; Stanford Univ, MS, 54; Purdue Univ, PhD(math), 60. *Prof Exp:* Res assoc, Purdue Univ, 56-60. *Concurrent Pos:* NASA res grant, 62-70, grant data entry systs, 74-75; NSF grant, 63-64 & 69-71; prog dir, NSF, 71-72; chmn, Knoxville/Knox Co Comput Adv Comt, 75. *Mem:* Asn Comput Mach; Soc Indust & Appl Math; Opers Res Soc Am; Am Statist Asn; Sigma Xi; fel Brit Comput Soc; Data Processing Mgt Asn. *Res:* Optimization of discrete functions; application of digital computers; computer installation management. *Mailing Add:* 301 Cheshire Dr Apt 105 Knoxville TN 37919-5849

SHERMAN, HAROLD, PHYSICS, NUCLEAR OIL WELL LOGGING. *Current Pos:* RETIRED. *Personal Data:* b Newark, NJ, Oct 19, 21; m 43; c 2. *Educ:* Brooklyn Col, AB, 42; NY Univ, PhD, 56; Pace Univ, JD, 86. *Prof Exp:* Physicist, Signal Corps, US Dept Army, Ohio, 42-44; electronics engr, Fada Radio, NY, 44; physicist, Premier Crystal Labs, 44-47; asst physics, NY Univ, 48-49, res assoc, 52-56; instr, St Peter's Col, 49-51; sr engr, A B Dumont Labs, NJ, 51-52; sr scientist, Avco Corp, Conn, 56; sr res proj physicist, Schlumberger-Doll Res Ctr, 56-83. *Mem:* Am Phys Soc; Sigma Xi. *Res:* Gas discharges; nuclear instrumentation; nuclear well logging. *Mailing Add:* 24 Webster Rd Ridgefield CT 06877. *Fax:* 203-438-6870

SHERMAN, HARRY LOGAN, BOTANY, ECOLOGY. *Current Pos:* from asst prof to assoc prof biol, 61-69, PROF BIOL SCI & HEAD DEPT, MISS UNIV WOMEN, 69- *Personal Data:* b Anniston, Ala, Dec 5, 27; m 55; c 4. *Educ:* Jacksonville State Univ, BS, 55; Univ Tenn, Knoxville, MS, 58; Vanderbilt Univ, PhD(biol), 69. *Prof Exp:* Instr & res asst bot, Univ Tenn, Knoxville, 57-59. *Mem:* Am Inst Biol Sci; Am Soc Plant Taxon; Int Soc Plant Taxon. *Res:* Biosystematics, including cyto- and chemo-taxonomy and reproductive biology; taxonomy. *Mailing Add:* Dept Math & Sci Miss Univ Women Box 100 Columbus MS 39701-5821

SHERMAN, IRWIN WILLIAM, ZOOLOGY, PARASITOLOGY. *Current Pos:* from asst prof to assoc prof, Univ Calif, Riverside, 62-73, chmn, Dept Biol, 74-79, dean, Col Natural & Agr Sci, 81-88, exec vchancellor, 93-94, PROF ZOOL, UNIV CALIF, RIVERSIDE, 73- *Personal Data:* b New York, NY, Feb 12, 33; m 66, Vilia G Turner; c Jonathan & Alexa. *Educ:* City Col New York, BS, 54; Northwestern Univ, MS, 59, PhD(biol), 60. *Honors & Awards:* Ward Medal Biol, 54; Wellcome Trust Lectr, 88. *Prof Exp:* Asst protozool, Univ Fla, 54; lab technician, US Army, 54-56; teacher, Yonkers Bd Educ, 56-57; asst parasitol, Northwestern Univ, 57-60; NIH fel, Rockefeller Inst, 60-62. *Concurrent Pos:* Guggenheim Mem Found fel, Carlsberg Found, Copenhagen, 67; eve lectr biol, City Col New York, 57, 60-62; spec NIH fel, Nat Inst Med Res, Mill Hill, Eng, 73-74; mem trop med & parasitol study sect, NIH, 70-74 & 79-80; vis prof, Mill Hill, UK, 73-74; chmn ad hoc, Study Group Parasitic Dis, Dept Army, 77-78; mem, Steering Comt Malaria Chemother, World Health Orgn, 78-86; vis scientist, Walter & Eliza Hall Inst, Melbourne, Australia, 86, Scripps Res Inst, La Jolla, Calif, 91-92. *Mem:* AAAS; Soc Protozool; Am Soc Parasitol; Am Soc Tropical Med & Hygiene; Sigma Xi. *Res:* Biochemistry and cell biology of malaria; malaria immunity. *Mailing Add:* Dept Biol Univ Calif Riverside CA 92521. *Fax:* 909-787-4286; *E-Mail:* sherman@mail.ucr.edu

SHERMAN, JAMES H, PHYSIOLOGY. *Current Pos:* From res assoc to asst prof, 63-71, asst dir, Off Allied Health Educ, Dept Postgrad Med, 72-77, ASSOC PROF PHYSIOL, MED SCH, UNIV MICH, ANN ARBOR, 71- *Personal Data:* b Detroit, Mich, Mar 14, 36; m 65; c 2. *Educ:* Univ Mich, BS, 57; Cornell Univ, PhD(cell physiol), 63. *Mem:* Biophys Soc; NY Acad Sci; Am Physiol Soc; Sigma Xi. *Res:* Cell membrane permeability; intracellular pH; active transport of amino acids in tumor cells; surface properties of cell membranes; co-auth Human Physiology the Mechanisms of Body Function. *Mailing Add:* Dept Physiol Univ Mich 7715 Med Sci II Bldg 0622 Ann Arbor MI 48109-0001

SHERMAN, JEROME KALMAN, ANATOMY, CRYOBIOLOGY. *Current Pos:* from asst prof to assoc prof, 59-66, PROF ANAT, MED COL, UNIV ARK MED SCI, LITTLE ROCK, 67- *Personal Data:* b Brooklyn, NY, Aug 14, 25; m 52, Hildegard Schroeder; c Karen, Marc & Keith. *Educ:* Brown Univ, AB, 47; Western Reserve Univ, MS, 49; Univ Iowa, PhD(zool), 54. *Prof Exp:* Asst biol, Western Reserve Univ, 47-49; from asst to res assoc urol, Univ Iowa, 49-54; res assoc, Am Found Biol Res, 54-58. *Concurrent Pos:* Consult,

Am Breeders Serv, 55-56, Winrock Farm, 59-60, Idant Corp, 72-73 & Dow Chem Co, 77-; mem adv bd, Am Type Cult Collections, 73-77; Lederle med fac award, 61-63; Fulbright sr res award, Univ Munich, Ger, 65-66; spec chair prof, Nat Chung-Hsin Univ, Taiwan, 73-74; Nat Sci Award, Taiwan, 73-74. *Mem:* Am Asn Anat; Soc Cryobiol; Sigma Xi; Am Asn Tissue Banks; Soc Exp Biol & Med. *Res:* Effects of cooling, freezing and rewarming on protoplasm of various cells and tissues; low temperature preservation of living cells, especially mammalian gametes; fertility and sterility; cytology; ultrastructural and biochemical cryoinjury of cellular organelles; cryobanking of human semen and cryosurvival of organisms which cause sexually transmitted diseases during crybanking of semen; male infertility. *Mailing Add:* Dept Anat Univ Ark Med Sci 4301 W Markham Little Rock AR 72205-7101

SHERMAN, JOHN EDWIN, SUPERCOMPUTERS TECHNICAL COMPUTING. *Current Pos:* CONSULT, LARGE COMPUT SYSTS, 88- *Personal Data:* b Brooklyn, NY, Jan 18, 22; m 45; c 3. *Educ:* Hofstra Col, BA, 50. *Prof Exp:* Physicst, US Naval Air Missile Test Ctr, 51-53; design engr, McDonnell Aircraft Corp, 53-54; math analyst analog comput, Lockheed Missile & Space Co, 54-56, group engr, 56-57, sect leader, 57-59, dept mgr hybrid comput, 59-66, div mgr, 66-69, div mgr data processing, 69-75, div mgr sci comput, 75-80, dir, Tech Comput Serv, 80-88. *Concurrent Pos:* Pres, Simulation Coun, Inc, 59-60, dir, 60-66, dir pub, 64-74; dir, Am Fedn Info Processing Socs, 62-72. *Mem:* Inst Elec & Electronics Engrs; Soc Comput Simulation. *Res:* Analog and hybrid computing; digital computing; data processing. *Mailing Add:* 1847 Grant Rd Mountainview CA 94040

SHERMAN, JOHN FOORD, PHARMACOLOGY. *Current Pos:* RETIRED. *Personal Data:* b Oneonta, NY, Sept 4, 19; m 44, Deane Murray; c Betsy & Mary A (Small). *Educ:* Albany Col Pharm, NY, BS, 49; Yale Univ, PhD(pharmacol), 53. *Hon Degrees:* ScD, Albany Col Pharm, 70. *Prof Exp:* Pharmacologist, Lab Trop Dis, Nat Microbiol Inst, 53-56, dep chief extramural progs, Nat Inst Arthritis & Metab Dis, 56-61, assoc dir extramural progs, Nat Inst Neurol Dis & Blindness, 61-62, Nat Inst Arthritis & Metab Dis, 62-63 & NIH, 64-68, dep dir, NIH, 68-74; vpres, Asn Am Med Col, 74-87, exec vpres, 87-90. *Concurrent Pos:* Consult. *Mem:* Inst Med-Nat Acad Sci; Sigma Xi; AAAS; Musculoskeletal Transplant Found. *Res:* Pharmacology of the central nervous system; chemotherapy; medical research and education administration. *Mailing Add:* 11016 Ardwick Dr Rockville MD 20852

SHERMAN, JOHN WALTER, PALEOLIMNOLOGY. *Current Pos:* PRES, CREATIONS GALLERY, 92- *Personal Data:* b Auburn, NY, Aug 19, 45; m 70, 80. *Educ:* Hamilton Col, BA, 67; Univ Vt, MS, 72; Univ Del, PhD(geol), 76. *Prof Exp:* Sr scientist, Acad Natural Sci, Philadelphia, 75-92. *Mem:* Am Soc Limnol & Oceanog; Sigma Xi; NAm Lakes Mgt Soc. *Res:* Paleoecological studies involving the use of diatoms as indicators of past water quality; ecological requirements of diatom communities. *Mailing Add:* 122 Kells Ave Newark DE 19711

SHERMAN, JOSEPH E, microbiology, food technology, for more information see previous edition

SHERMAN, KENNETH, BIOLOGICAL OCEANOGRAPHY. *Current Pos:* coord, Marine Resources Monitoring Assessing & Prediction Prog, 71-73, chief resource assessment div, US Dept Com, Nat Oceanic & Atmospheric Admin, Washington, DC, 73-75, LAB DIR & CHIEF, MARINE ECOSYST BR, US DEPT COM, NAT OCEANIC & ATMOSPHERIC ADMIN, NAT MARINE FISHERIES SERV, NARRAGANSETT, RI, 75- *Personal Data:* b Boston, Mass, Oct 6, 32; m 58; c 3. *Educ:* Suffolk Univ, BS, 54; Univ RI, MS, 60; Morski Inst Ryback, DSc, 78. *Hon Degrees:* DSc, Suffolk Univ, 79. *Prof Exp:* Instr conserv educ, Mass Audubon Soc, 54-55; fishery aide, US Bur Com Fisheries, Mass, 55-56; teacher high sch, Mass, 59-60; fishery res biologist zooplankton ecol, US Bur Com Fisheries, Hawaii, 60-63, Maine, 63-71. *Concurrent Pos:* Mem biol oceanog comt, Int Coun Explor Sea, 72-87; US proj officer, Plankton Sorting Ctr, Szczecin, Poland, 73-; adj prof, Grad Sch Oceanog, Univ RI, 80- *Mem:* AAAS; Am Soc Limnol & Oceanog; Ecol Soc Am; Am Soc Zool; Am Soc Ichthyol & Herpet. *Res:* Tuna oceanography; zooplankton ecology; Atlantic herring biology; distribution and abundance of epipelagic marine copepods; estuarine ecology; taxonomy of marine copepods; predator prey relationships of pelagic fishes; plankton in ecosystems; productivity of living marine resources. *Mailing Add:* 28 Tarzwell Dr Narragansett RI 02882

SHERMAN, LARRY RAY, PESTICIDE CHEMISTRY. *Current Pos:* ASST PROF CHEM, UNIV SCRANTON, PA, 81- *Personal Data:* b Easton, Pa, June 26, 34; m 66, Irene Price. *Educ:* Lafayette Col, BSc, 56; Utah State Univ, MSc, 61; Univ Wyo, PhD(anal chem), 69. *Prof Exp:* Res assoc, NC A&T State Univ, Greensboro, 69-71, assoc prof chem, 70-74; dir res, Hillyard Chem Co, St Joseph, Mo, 74-76; asst prof chem, Univ Miss, 76-78; asst prof, Univ Akron, Ohio, 78-81. *Concurrent Pos:* Engr, Gen Elec Co, Cleveland, Ohio, 56-58; chem anal, Weyerhauser Co, Seattle, Wash, 62-64; instr chem, Northern Ill Univ, De Kalb, 64-66; NASA fel, Univ Wyo, Laramie, 67-69; res assoc, NC A&T State Univ, 69-71; NSF fel, Pa State Univ, 72; res assoc, Univ Miss, 76-78; fel, Univ Akron, Ohio, 80, vis prof, 87-88; NASA fel, Lewis Res Ctr, Cleveland, Ohio, 84; guest prof, Univ Dortmund, WGer, 86; fac fel, Brooks AFB, San Antonio, Tex, 88 & 92-95; NATO fel, Vrije Univ, Brussels, Belg, 89. *Mem:* Sr mem Sigma Xi; fel Royal Soc Chem; Am Chem Soc. *Res:* Organotin chemistry: analyses, toxicology and in vitro and in vivo biological activity and fundamental chemistry of di and tri-alkyl/aryl tin compounds; author of approximately 65 publications. *Mailing Add:* Dept Chem Univ Scranton Scranton PA 18510-4626. *Fax:* 717-941-7510; *E-Mail:* ihsinpa@juno.com

SHERMAN, LAURENCE A, PATHOLOGY, HEALTH SCIENCES. *Current Pos:* PROF PATH, NORTHWESTERN UNIV MED SCH, CHICAGO, ILL, 90- *Personal Data:* b Cambridge, Mass, Jan 1, 35; m 65; c 2. *Educ:* Univ Chicago, BA & BS, 56; Albany Med Col, MD, 64; Loyola Univ, Chicago, JD, 94. *Prof Exp:* Intern med, Boston City Hosp, Mass, 64-65; resident, Univ Calif, Los Angeles, 65-66; fel enzym, Sch Med, Wash Univ, 66-68, from instr to prof med path, 69-83; assoc dir, Mo-Ill Regional Red Cross Blood Prog, 73-82, chief med serv, 82-90. *Concurrent Pos:* Dir coagulation lab & chief vascular div, Jewish Hosp, St Louis, 69-73, assoc dir blood bank, 70-73; dir blood bank, Barnes Hosp, St Louis, 73-82, co-dir hemostasis lab, 78-80; dir blood banking, training prog, Nat Heart, Lung & Blood Inst, Wash Univ, 77-85; chmn sci prog, Am Asn Blood Banks, 79-84, bd dirs, 80-90; mem, comt apheresis, Am Red Cross, 85-, dir coun, 86-87; med dir, Blood Bank, Northwestern Mem Hosp, 93- & Children's Mem Hosp, 95- *Mem:* Am Fedn Clin Res; Am Soc Hemat; Am Asn Pathologists; Am Soc Clin Invest; Am Heart Asn; fel Col Am Path; fel Am Col Physicians; Am Asn Blood Banks (pres, 88-89). *Res:* Thrombosis and metabolism of coagulation moieties, particularly fibrinogen and its derivatives; transfusions medicine and blood bank. *Mailing Add:* Dept Path Northwestern Univ Med Sch 303 E Chicago Chicago IL 60611-2950. *Fax:* 312-908-1613

SHERMAN, LINDA ARLENE, IMMUNOLOGY, BIOCHEMISTRY. *Current Pos:* asst mem, 78-85, ASSOC MEM IMMUNOL, RES INST SCRIPPS CLIN, 85- *Personal Data:* b Brooklyn, NY, Feb 27, 50; m 78; c 2. *Educ:* Barnard Col, AB, 71; Mass Inst Technol, PhD(biol), 76. *Prof Exp:* Postdoctoral immunol, Albert Einstein Sch Med, 76-77, Harvard Med Sch, 77-78. *Concurrent Pos:* Consult & panel reviewer, NSF, 85-89. *Mem:* Am Asn Immunologists; AAAS. *Res:* Molecules involved in cytolytic T lymphocyte recognition of alloantigens and foreign antigens and tumor antigens. *Mailing Add:* Dept Immunol IMM15 Scripps Res Inst 10550 N Torrey Pines Rd La Jolla CA 92037-1092. *Fax:* 619-784-8298

SHERMAN, LOUIS ALLEN, PHOTOSYNTHESIS, MEMBRANE STRUCTURE. *Current Pos:* from asst prof to assoc prof, 72-82, dir Biol Sci, 85-89, PROF & HEAD BIOL SCI, PURDUE UNIV, 89- *Personal Data:* b Chicago, Ill, Dec 16, 43; m 69; c 2. *Educ:* Univ Chicago, BS, 65, PhD(biophysics), 70. *Prof Exp:* Fel photosynthesis, Cornell Univ, 70-72. *Concurrent Pos:* Fulbright res fel, Univ Leiden, Netherlands, 79-80. *Mem:* Biophys Soc; Am Soc Microbiol; Am Soc Photobiol; AAAS; Plant Physiol. *Res:* Photosynthesis and the structure of photosynthetic membranes; isolation of photosynthetic mutants in cyanobacteria; isolation of photosynthetic membrane components; cloning of photosynthesis genes on specially designed hybrid plasmids. *Mailing Add:* Dept Biol Sci Purdue Univ Lilly Hall Life Sci West Lafayette IN 47907-1392. *Fax:* 765-494-0876; *E-Mail:* lsherman@bilbo.purdue.edu

SHERMAN, MALCOLM J, MATHEMATICAL STATISTICS. *Current Pos:* asst prof, 68-70, ASSOC PROF MATH, STATE UNIV NY, ALBANY, 70-, ASSOC PROF BIOMET & STATIST, SCH PUB HEALTH, 88- *Personal Data:* b Chicago, Ill, July 28, 39; m 63, Susan Roth; c Barbara L & Michael J. *Educ:* Univ Chicago, SB & SM, 60; Univ Calif, Berkeley, PhD(math), 64. *Prof Exp:* Asst prof math, Univ Calif, Los Angeles, 64-68. *Concurrent Pos:* Asst dir to staff dir, US Comn Civil Rights, 84-85. *Mem:* Math Asn Am; Am Statist Assoc. *Res:* Applied statistics and functional analysis (operator theory). *Mailing Add:* Dept Math & Statist State Univ NY Albany Albany NY 12222. *Fax:* 518-442-4731; *E-Mail:* mjs78@math.albany.edu

SHERMAN, MARTIN, ENTOMOLOGY, INSECTICIDE TOXICOLOGY. *Current Pos:* asst prof entom, Univ & asst entomologist, Agr Exp Sta, 49-52, assoc prof & assoc entomologist, 52-58, prof entom & entomologist, 58-85, EMER ENTOMOLOGIST & PROF, UNIV HAWAII, 85- *Personal Data:* b Newark, NJ, Nov 21, 20; m 43, 75, Ruth Goldsmith; c Laurel (Englehart) & Susan (Kitakis). *Educ:* Rutgers Univ, BSc, 41, MSc, 43; Cornell Univ, PhD(insect toxicol), 48. *Prof Exp:* Res asst entom, Cornell Univ, 45-48; entomologist, Beech-Nut Packing Co, 48-49. *Concurrent Pos:* Fulbright scholar, Univ Tokyo, 56-57 & State Entom Lab & Royal Vet & Agr Col, Denmark, 66; vis prof, Rutgers Univ, 73; mem gov bd, Entom Soc Am, 74-77. *Mem:* Am Chem Soc; Soc Toxicol; Soc Environ Toxicol & Chem; Int Soc Study Xenobiotics; fel Am Inst Chemists; Entom Soc Am. *Res:* Comparative vertebrate and insect toxicology; insecticide residue analysis; insecticide formulation; metabolism of insecticides. *Mailing Add:* 1121 Koloa St Honolulu HI 96816

SHERMAN, MERRY RUBIN, ENDOCRINE BIOCHEMISTRY. *Current Pos:* PROF BIOCHEM, RUTGERS UNIV, 86- *Personal Data:* b New York, NY, May 14, 40. *Educ:* Wellesley Col, BA, 61; Univ Calif, Berkeley, MA, 63, PhD(biophysics), 66. *Prof Exp:* NIH fel, Weizmann Inst, 66-67 & Nat Inst Dent Res, 68-69; res assoc, Sloan-Kettering Inst, 71-76, assoc mem, 76-86. *Concurrent Pos:* Vis investr, Cardiovascular Res Inst, Univ Calif, San Francisco, 75-76; assoc prof biochem, Grad Sch Med Sci, Cornell Univ, 77-86. *Mem:* Am Soc Biol Chemists; Endocrine Soc; Am Asn Cancer Res. *Res:* Steroid hormone receptors; proteolytic enzymes. *Mailing Add:* Mountain View Pharm Inc 871-L Industrial Rd San Carlos CA 94070. *Fax:* 212-752-3121

SHERMAN, MICHAEL IAN, ONCOLOGY, VIROLOGY. *Current Pos:* PRES & CHIEF EXEC OFFICER, PHARMAGENICS, INC, 90- *Personal Data:* b Montreal, Que, Sept 27, 44; m 68, Beatrice Vojtanik. *Educ:* McGill Univ, BS, 65; State Univ NY Stony Brook, PhD(molecular biol), 69. *Prof Exp:* Fel, dept path, Univ Oxford, 69-70 & dept zool, 70-71; from asst mem to mem, Roche Inst Molecular Biol, Roche Res Ctr, 71-86, from dir to sr sir cell biol, 86-90. *Concurrent Pos:* Mem rev panel, NASA, 78; mem, Human

Embryol Develop Study Sect, NIH, 79-81; adj assoc prof human genetics, Columbia Col Physicians & Surgeons, 80-86; secy & trustee, Biotechnol Coun NJ, 95- *Mem:* Am Asn Cancer Res. *Res:* Cancer; virology; genomics. *Mailing Add:* 314 Forest Ave Glen Ridge NJ 07028. *Fax:* 201-818-9044; *E-Mail:* sherman@pharmag.com

SHERMAN, NORMAN K, PHOTONUCLEAR REACTIONS, SUBATOMIC PHYSICS & LASER ACCELERATION. *Current Pos:* assoc res officer, Nat Res Coun Can, 68-75, x-rays & nuclear radiations, 68-84, physicist laser & plasma physics, Div Physics, 84-88, consortium adv, 88-90, planning & prog develop, Sci Affairs Off, 90-95, SR RES OFFICER, NAT RES COUN CAN, 75-, CORP PLANNING & ASSESSMENT, 95-, PROJ OFFICER TRIUME, 95- *Personal Data:* b Kingston, Ont, Jan 28, 35; m 60, Paule Langlois; c Norman P, Louis P, Elisabeth M S, Anne G & Marie P. *Educ:* Royal Mil Col, Can, BSc, 56; Queen's Univ, Ont, BSc, 57, MSc, 59, PhD(physics), 62. *Honors & Awards:* Farrington Daniels Award Achievement Radiation Dosimetry, Am Asn Physicists Med, 75. *Prof Exp:* Lectr physics, Royal Mil Col, Ont, 59-60 & Queen's Univ, Onat, 61-62; foreign fel, CEN Saclay, France, 62-64; NATO fel nuclear physics, Univ Paris, 62-64 & Yale Univ, 64-65; asst prof physics, McGill Univ, 65-68. *Concurrent Pos:* Res assoc, Accelerator Lab, Univ Sask 65; user zero gradient synchrotron, Argonne Nat Lab, 66-68; ed, Youth Sci News, 73-76; mem ad hoc comt synchrotron radiation, Nat Res Coun, 76-78, actg head, Electron Linac Lab, 77-80; secy, comt intermediate physics, NSERC, 78-81; proj mgr, Can Synchrotron Radiation Fac, 78-; secy, Adv Bd TRIUMF, Nat Res Coun Can, 78-81, comt high energy physics, 78-84, comt subatomic physics, 84-85; foreign collabr, Saclay linear accelerator, 82; external user, superconducting Linear Accelerator, MUSL, Univ Ill, Champaign, 83; agreement adminr, Can Audio Res Consortium, 88-95; facilitator, Solid State Optoelectronics Consortium Can, 88-90; adv, Simulated Mfg Res Consortium, 88-90; secy, proj Athena Steering Comt, 89-95; working party, sci merit, KAON, 90, cost benefit, 90; adminr, Nat Res Coun, Queen's Univ contrib agreement Sudbury Neutrino Observ, 91-93 & Carleton Univ agreement high energy physics, 91-; corp coordr, Inst Biodiag Proj Off, 91-92; secy, Nat Res Coun-CRPP Adv Comt, 92-, Nat Res Coun Adv Bd, Herzberg Inst Astrophys, 93-95, Steacie Inst Molecular Sci, 93-95, Inst Biol Sci, 93-95 & Inst Marine Biosci, 93-95. *Mem:* AAAS; Am Phys Soc; NY Acad Sci; Can Asn Physicists; Youth Sci Found (pres, 76-78); Can Inst Synchrotron Radiation. *Res:* Superconducting nuclear particle detector; magnesium photofission; lithium phototritons; proton scattering; shielding; radiation-damage reversal; de-excitation neutrons; bremsstrahlung spectra, radiators, filters, depth dose; photoneutron fine structure by time-of-flight; photoneutron angular distributions; photon total absorption; electron pair cross section of uranium; liquid-deuterium gamma-ray spectrometer; linearly polarized gamma rays; laser photocathodes; laser driven accelerators; laser produced gamma rays; picosecond optical damage to metals; two-temperature heat transport in metals on picosecond time scale; electron-to-lattice coupling constant in metals, synchrotron radiation, photonuclear reactions. *Mailing Add:* Corp Planning & Assessment Rm E-129 M-58 Nat Res Coun 1200 Montreal Rd Ottawa ON K1A 0R6 Can. *E-Mail:* norm.sherman@nrc.ca

SHERMAN, PATSY O'CONNELL, CORPORATE TECHNICAL EDUCATION & DEVELOPMENT, APPLIED CHEMISTRY. *Current Pos:* RETIRED. *Personal Data:* b Minneapolis, Minn, Sept 15, 30; m 53, Hubert T; c Sharilyn (Loushin) & Wendy (HeilÖ. *Educ:* Gustavus Adolphus Col, BA, 52. *Honors & Awards:* Spurgeon Award. *Prof Exp:* Chemist, Cent Res Dept, Minn Mining & Mfg Co, 52-57, chemist chem div, 57-67, res specialist, 67-70, sr res specialist, 70-73, res mgr, Chem Resources Div, 73-81, mgr tech develop, 3M, 82-92. *Concurrent Pos:* Bd dirs, Nat Inventors Hall Fame, Minn State Bd Inventors. *Mem:* Am Chem Soc. *Res:* Fluorine-containing polymers; oil and water repellent textile treatments. *Mailing Add:* 1006 Devonshire Curve Bloomington MN 55431

SHERMAN, PAUL DWIGHT, JR, INDUSTRIAL ORGANIC CHEMISTRY. *Current Pos:* Group leader & technol mgr, Union Carbide Corp, 76-82, info syts mgr, 82-84, bus mgr, 84-86, group leader, 86-89, ASSOC DIR, UNION CARBIDE CORP, 89- *Personal Data:* b San Diego, Calif, May 18, 42; m 63, Marilyn Richards; c Laura L & Karen A. *Educ:* Univ NH, BS, 64; Brown Univ, PhD(org chem), 70. *Mem:* Am Chem Soc. *Res:* Application of analytical techniques for the solution of industrial process problems; organic-analytical chemistry; hydroformylation process development; technical management. *Mailing Add:* 319 Oak Tree Lane South Charleston WV 25309

SHERMAN, PAUL WILLARD, BEHAVIORAL ECOLOGY. *Current Pos:* from asst prof to assoc prof, 80-91, PROF NEUROBIOL & BEHAV, CORNELL UNIV, 91- *Personal Data:* b July 6, 49; US citizen; m 81; c 2. *Educ:* Stanford Univ, BA, 71; Univ Mich, MS, 74, PhD(biol), 76. *Honors & Awards:* A B Howell Award, Cooper Ornith Soc, 74; A M Jackson Award, Am Soc Mammalogists, 77; Clark Award, Cornell Univ, 84. *Prof Exp:* Miller fel zool, Univ Calif, Berkeley, 76-78, asst prof psychol, 78-80. *Concurrent Pos:* Guggenheim fel, 85. *Mem:* Animal Behav Soc; Am Soc Naturalists. *Res:* Evolution of social behavior. *Mailing Add:* 42 Sparrow Crest Ithaca NY 14850

SHERMAN, PHILIP MARTIN, STRATEGIC PLANNING, COMPUTER SCIENCE. *Current Pos:* OWNER & COMPUT CONSULT, SHERMAN DATA SYSTS, 84- *Personal Data:* b Norwalk, Conn, July 10, 30; m 55, Doris Gottlieb; c Judith (Schwartz), Alan & Emily. *Educ:* Cornell Univ, BEPhys, 52; Yale Univ, MEE, 54, PhD(elec eng), 59. *Prof Exp:* Engr, Sperry Gyroscope Co, NY, 52-55; instr elec eng, Yale Univ, 57-59; engr, Bell Tel Labs, 59-63, supvr, 63-67, dept head, 67-69; mgr info syts, Webster Res Ctr, 69-78, mgr technol planning, 78-84. *Concurrent Pos:* Adj lectr, Rochester Inst Technol, 90- *Mem:* Inst Elec & Electronics Engrs; Asn Comput Mach. *Res:* Computer programming and analysis; systems analysis; computer language studies; computer data management. *Mailing Add:* Sherman Data Systs 471 Claybourne Rd Rochester NY 14618

SHERMAN, ROBERT GEORGE, NEUROPHYSIOLOGY, ZOOLOGY. *Current Pos:* PROF ZOOL, MIAMI UNIV, 78- *Personal Data:* b Charlevoix, Mich, Mar 22, 42; m 65; c 2. *Educ:* Alma Col, BS, 64; Mich State Univ, MS, 67, PhD(zool), 69. *Prof Exp:* USPHS fel, Univ Toronto, 69-70, spec fel, 70-71; from asst prof to assoc prof physiol, Clark Univ, 71-78. *Mem:* Soc Gen Physiologists; Soc Neurosci; Electron Microscopy Soc Am. *Res:* Structure and function of synapses in arthropods; ultrastructure of arthropod muscle; cardiac physiology of arthropods; development of nerve and muscle. *Mailing Add:* Dept Zool Miami Univ 500 E High St Oxford OH 45056-1618. *Fax:* 513-529-6900

SHERMAN, ROBERT HOWARD, PHYSICAL CHEMISTRY, CRYOGENICS. *Current Pos:* RETIRED. *Personal Data:* b Chicago, Ill, Nov 18, 29; m; c 3. *Educ:* Ill Inst Technol, BS, 51; Univ Calif, PhD(chem), 55. *Prof Exp:* Staff mem, Los Alamos Nat Lab, 55-96. *Concurrent Pos:* Consult, Argonne Nat Lab, 59-60. *Mem:* Am Chem Soc; Am Phys Soc. *Res:* Thermodynamics, especially at low temperatures; liquid helium; critical point phenomena; hydrogen isotope technology (tritium); isotope separation; Raman spectroscopy. *Mailing Add:* 1931 Canino Manzana Los Alamos NM 87544

SHERMAN, ROBERT JAMES, BOTANY, ECOLOGY. *Current Pos:* RETIRED. *Personal Data:* b Bristow, Iowa, July 28, 40; m 62; c 1. *Educ:* Coe Col, BA, 62; Ore State Univ, MS, 66, PhD(bot), 68. *Prof Exp:* Asst prof biol, Univ Colo, Colorado Springs, 68-70; asst prof, Sonoma State Univ, 70-80, chmn dept, 75-78, prof, 80-94, actg dean, Sch Nat Resource, 90-91. *Concurrent Pos:* Consult grasslands biomed, Int Biol Prog, 69-70; NSF grants; Dept Health, Educ & Welfare grant. *Mem:* Ecol Soc Am. *Res:* Structure and pattern of Pinus ponderosa forests; fire ecology; oak woodlands ecology. *Mailing Add:* 69435 Green Ridge Loop Sisters OR 97759

SHERMAN, ROGER TALBOT, SURGERY. *Current Pos:* prof surg, 83-92, WHITAKER PROF, SCH MED, EMORY UNIV, ATLANTA, GA, 92-; DIR SURG EDUC, PIEDMONT HOSP, ATLANTA, 93- *Personal Data:* b Chicago, Ill, Sept 30, 23; m 52; c 5. *Educ:* Kenyon Col, AB, 46; Univ Cincinnati, MD, 48; Am Bd Surg, dipl, 57. *Honors & Awards:* Curtis P Artz Trauma Soc Award; Sherman lectr, Southeastern Surg Cong. *Prof Exp:* Fel path, St Luke's Hosp, Chicago, 49-50; asst resident surgeon, Cincinnati Gen Hosp, 50-55; instr surg, Col Med, Univ Cincinnati, 55-56; from asst prof to prof, Col Med, Univ Tenn, Memphis, 59-72; prof surg & chmn dept, Col Med, Univ SFla, 72-82; chief surg, Grady Mem Hosp, Atlanta, 83-92. *Mem:* Am Surg Asn; Am Asn Surg of Trauma; Am Col Surgeons; Am Burn Asn. *Res:* Surgical infections, shock and trauma. *Mailing Add:* 1170 Woods Circle NE Atlanta GA 30324

SHERMAN, RONALD, ELECTRICAL ENGINEERING, APPLIED MATHEMATICS. *Current Pos:* Mem tech staff radar systs, Bell Labs, 65-67, mem tech staff ocean systs, 67-70, supvr electromagnetic pulse eng & design principles group, 70-76, supvr systs anal & planning group, 76-80, SUPVR FINANCIAL MODELING STUDIES GROUP, BELL LABS, 80- *Personal Data:* b Philadelphia, Pa, Sept 5, 41; wid; c 2. *Educ:* Univ Pa, BSEE, 62, PhD(elec eng), 65; Columbia, MBA, 82. *Concurrent Pos:* Vis sr lectr, Stevens Inst Technol, 69-71, assoc prof elec eng, 71-77, prof, 77-80. *Mem:* Inst Elec & Electronics Engrs. *Res:* Electromagnetics; effect of pulsed fields on communications systems; estimation and control theory; adaptive tracking; statistics; clustering algorithm development; financial model development. *Mailing Add:* Bell Tel Labs Rm MH 5C 110 600 Mountain Ave Murray Hill NJ 07974

SHERMAN, SAMUEL MURRAY, NEUROSCIENCES, OPHTHALMOLOGY. *Current Pos:* prof anat, Dept Anat Sci, 79-80, PROF NEUROBIOL & BEHAV, STATE UNIV NY, STONY BROOK, 80- *Personal Data:* b Pittsburgh, Pa, Jan 4, 44; m 69, Marjorie Eloken; c Erika Kirsten & Benjamin William. *Educ:* Calif Inst Technol, BS, 65; Univ Pa, PhD(neuroanat), 69. *Hon Degrees:* MA, Univ Oxford, 85. *Prof Exp:* USPHS fel, Australian Nat Univ, 70-72; from asst prof to prof physiol, Sch Med, Univ Va, 72-78. *Concurrent Pos:* NSF res grant, 73-; USPHS res grant, 75-; USPHS res career develop award, 75-80; mem, Visual Sci B Study Sect, NIH, 75-79; AB Sloan fel, 77-80; Newton-Abraham vis profl, Univ Oxford, 85-86; mem & chair Behav & Neurosci Study Sect 1, NIH, 89- *Mem:* Soc Neurosci; Am Physiol Soc; Am Asn Anat; Asn Res Vision & Ophthal; AAAS. *Res:* Functional organization of the mammalian visual system. *Mailing Add:* Dept Neurobiol & Behav State Univ NY Health Sci Col Med Stony Brook NY 11794-5230. *Fax:* 516-632-6661; *E-Mail:* ssherman@brain.bio.sunysb.edu

SHERMAN, THOMAS FAIRCHILD, BIOLOGY. *Current Pos:* from asst prof to assoc prof, 66-79, PROF BIOL, OBERLIN COL, 79- *Personal Data:* b Ithaca, NY, May 25, 34; m 70, Katia Brahemcha; c Catharine L (deceased), Anita S, Elizabeth B (deceased), Caroline R & Claire G. *Educ:* Oberlin Col, AB, 56; Oxford Univ, DPhil(biochem), 60. *Prof Exp:* Vis asst prof zool, Oberlin Col, 60-61; res fel hist sci, Yale Univ, 61-62; vis asst prof zool, Pomona Col, 62-65; res fel math biol, Harvard Univ, 65-66. *Res:* Vascular branching; connective tissue transport; history of science. *Mailing Add:* Dept Biol Oberlin Col 135 W Lorain St Oberlin OH 44074-1076

SHERMAN, THOMAS LAWRENCE, MATHEMATICS. *Current Pos:* from asst prof to assoc prof, 64-74, PROF MATH, ARIZ STATE UNIV, 74- *Personal Data:* b Los Angeles, Calif, Nov 17, 37. *Educ:* Univ Calif, Los Angeles, AB, 59; Univ Utah, MS, 61, PhD(math), 63. *Prof Exp:* Mem, US Army Math Res Ctr, Univ Wis, 63-64. *Mem:* Am Math Soc; Math Asn Am; Soc Indust & Appl Math. *Res:* Ordinary differential equations. *Mailing Add:* Ariz State Univ Box 871804 Tempe AZ 85287-1804

SHERMAN, THOMAS OAKLEY, MATHEMATICS. *Current Pos:* asst prof, 69-70, ASSOC PROF MATH, NORTHEASTERN UNIV, 70- *Personal Data:* b Brooklyn, NY, May 6, 39; m 61; c 3. *Educ:* Mass Inst Technol, BS, 60, PhD(math), 64. *Prof Exp:* Mem staff math, Inst Advan Study, 64-65; asst prof, Brandeis Univ, 65-69. *Res:* Lie groups; harmonic analysis; numerical analysis. *Mailing Add:* Dept Math Northeastern Univ 360 Huntington Ave Boston MA 02115-5096

SHERMAN, WARREN V, RADIATION CHEMISTRY, PHOTOBIOLOGY. *Current Pos:* assoc prof, 68-74, PROF CHEM, CHICAGO STATE UNIV, 74-; DIR, MINORITY BIOMED RES SUPPORT PROG, 91- *Personal Data:* b London, Eng, Jan 7, 37; m 63; c 2. *Educ:* Univ London, BSc, 58, PhD(org chem), 61. *Prof Exp:* Fulbright res fel chem, Brandeis Univ, 61-63; res fel, US Army Natick Lab, 63-64 & Israel Atomic Energy Comn, 64-66; res fel, Radiation Lab, Univ Notre Dame, 66-68. *Concurrent Pos:* NSF fac develop grant, 79-80; vis prof physics, Ill Inst Technol, 79-80. *Mem:* Am Chem Soc; Royal Soc Chem; fel Europ Molecular Biol Orgn; Royal Inst Chem; Am Soc Photobiol. *Res:* Photochemistry and high-energy radiation chemistry of organic and biological compounds; visual pigments. *Mailing Add:* Dept Chem Chicago State Univ 95th St at King Dr Chicago IL 60628. *Fax:* 773-995-3809; *E-Mail:* bij1wvs@uxa.ecn.bgu.edu

SHERMAN, WAYNE BUSH, PLANT BREEDING, HORTICULTURE. *Current Pos:* Asst prof hort, 66-72, assoc prof, 72-78, PROF HORT, UNIV FLA, 78- *Personal Data:* b Lena, Miss, Feb 25, 40; m 63; c 1. *Educ:* Miss State Univ, BS, 61, MS, 63; Purdue Univ, PhD(hort), 66. *Mem:* Am Soc Hort Sci; Am Pomol Soc. *Res:* Fruit crops. *Mailing Add:* PO Box 110690 Univ Fl Gainesville FL 32611

SHERMAN, WILLIAM REESE, BIOCHEMISTRY, MASS SPECTROMETRY. *Current Pos:* res asst, 61-63, res asst prof, 63-69, assoc prof, 69-75, PROF BIOCHEM, DEPT PSYCHIAT, SCH MED, WASHINGTON UNIV, 75-, PROF BIOL CHEM, DEPT BIOL CHEM & MOLECULAR BIOPHYS, 78- *Personal Data:* b Seattle, Wash, Jan 18, 28; m 51; c 2. *Educ:* Columbia Univ, AB, 51; Univ Ill, PhD(org chem), 55. *Prof Exp:* Sr res chemist, Abbott Labs, 55-59, group leader, 59-61. *Mem:* Am Chem Soc; Int Soc Neurochem; Am Soc Neurochem; Am Soc Mass Spectrometry; Fedn Am Socs Exp Biol. *Res:* Biochemistry of the inositols and the phosphoinositides with emphasis on the effects of lithium on the metabolism of these substances; biochemical applications of mass spectrometry. *Mailing Add:* Dept Psych Wash Univ Sch Med 4940 Children's Pl St Louis MO 63110-1002

SHERMAN, ZACHARY, STRUCTURAL & MECHANICAL ENGINEERING, AEROSPACE ENGINEERING. *Current Pos:* DESIGNATED ENG REP, FED AVIATION ADMIN, 86- *Personal Data:* b New York, NY, Oct 26, 22; m 47, Bertha Leikin; c Gene Victor & Carol Beth. *Educ:* City Col New York, BCE, 43; Polytech Inst Brooklyn, MCE, 53, PhD(mech, struct), 69; Stevens Inst Technol, MME, 68. *Prof Exp:* Stress analyst, Gen Dynamics, Calif & Tex, 43-45; sr stress analyst, Repub Aviation Corp, 45-47; struct designer, Cent RR of NJ, 48-49; struct engr, Parsons, Brinckerhoff, Hall & MacDonald, NY, 49-51; designer-in-chg, F L Ehasz, 51-52; engr-in-chg, Loewy-Hydropress Co, 52-54; from assoc prof to prof civil eng, Univ Miss, 54-59; prin engr, Repub Aviation Corp, 59-62; in-chg, Stress Anal Lab, Stevens Inst Technol, 62-67; lectr civil eng, City Col NY, 67-69; assoc prof aerospace eng, Pa State Univ, 69-73; CONSULT ENGR, 73- *Concurrent Pos:* Consult engr, S S Kenworthy Eng & Concrete Eng Co, Tenn, 54-58; independent consult engr, indust & ins, 58-; NSF int travel grant to Int Aeronaut Fedn Cong, 71; adj prof civil eng, Sch Eng, Cooper Union, 78-; adj prof math, Pace Univ, 78- *Mem:* Fel Am Soc Civil Engrs; Am Inst Aeronaut & Astronaut; Sigma Xi; NY Acad Sci. *Res:* Dynamics and vibrations; optimization; tornado resistant construction; design; elasticity; earthquake design. *Mailing Add:* 25 Neptune Blvd Apt 7H Long Beach NY 11561

SHERR, BARRY FREDERICK, AQUATIC MICROBIAL ECOLOGY, PROTOZOOLOGY. *Current Pos:* PROF OCEANOG, ORE STATE UNIV, 90- *Personal Data:* b New York, NY, Mar 9, 44; m 79, Evelyn Brown; c Aaron & Jared. *Educ:* Kans Wesleyan Univ, BA, 65; Univ Kans, MA, 68; Univ Ga, PhD(zool), 77. *Prof Exp:* Res assoc microbiol, Univ Ga, 77-79; res assoc aquatic ecol, Israel Oceanog & Limnol Res, Ltd, 79-81; res assoc, Univ Ga Marine Inst, 82-84, asst marine scientist, 84-87, assoc marine scientist microbiol ecol, 87-90. *Concurrent Pos:* Prin investr, NSF, 83-, Dept Energy, 92-, NASA, 93-; vis scientist overseas labs. *Mem:* Am Soc Microbiol; Am Soc Limnol & Oceanog; Soc Protozoologists; Am Geophys Union. *Res:* Flow of carbon-energy and nutrient cycling in marine pelagic food webs; roles of planktonic protozoa in facilitating these processes via their trophic interactions with components of the microbial community and with metazooplankton. *Mailing Add:* Col Oceanic & Atmospheric Sci Ore State Univ Ocean Admin Bldg 104 Corvallis OR 97331. *Fax:* 541-737-2064; *E-Mail:* sherrb@ucs.orst.edu

SHERR, CHARLES J, BIOLOGY, CANCER. *Current Pos:* MEM & HERRICK FOUND CHMN, DEPT TUMOR CELL BIOL, ST JUDE CHILDRENS RES HOSP; INVESTR, HOWARD HUGHES MED INST. *Educ:* Oberlin Col AB, 66; NY Univ, PhD(immunol) & MD, 72. *Honors & Awards:* Damashek Prize, Am Soc Hemat, 87. *Prof Exp:* Path resident, Bellevue Hosp Ctr, New York; staff, George Todaros Lab, Nat Cancer Inst. *Concurrent Pos:* Outstanding investr grant, Nat Cancer Inst, NIH, 88-95; adj prof biochem, Univ Tenn. *Mem:* Nat Acad Sci; fel Am Soc Microbiol. *Res:* Mitogenic signal transduction; hematopoietic growth factors and their receptor; cell cycle regulation; oncogenes and tumor suppresors. *Mailing Add:* St Judes/Howard Hughes Med Inst 332 N Lauderdale Memphis TN 38105

SHERR, EVELYN BROWN, MICROBIAL ECOLOGY, AQUATIC FOOD WEBS. *Current Pos:* PROF, COL OCEANOG, ORE STATE UNIV, 90- *Personal Data:* b Dublin, Ga, Dec 19, 46; m 79; c 2. *Educ:* Emory Univ, BS, 69; Duke Univ, PhD(zool), 74. *Prof Exp:* Res assoc microbiol, Univ Ga, 74-75, res assoc marine ecol, 75-77, asst marine scientist, 77-82, assoc marine scientist, Marine Inst, 82-90. *Concurrent Pos:* Prin investr NSF, 76-91; vis investr, Kinneret Limnological Lab, Israel, 79-81; ed adv, Marine Ecol Prog Ser, 86. *Mem:* Am Soc Limnol & Oceanog; Am Soc Microbiol; Soc Protozoologists. *Res:* Pathways of carbon flow in aquatic food webs; feeding and growth rates of pelagic ciliates and flagellates; ecological roles of heterotrophic protozoa. *Mailing Add:* Col Oceanic & Atmospheric Sci Oceanog Admin Bldg 104 Corvallis OR 97331. *Fax:* 541-737-2064; *E-Mail:* sherrb@ucs.orst.edu

SHERR, RUBBY, NUCLEAR PHYSICS. *Current Pos:* from asst prof to prof, 46-82, EMER PROF PHYSICS, PRINCETON UNIV, 82- *Personal Data:* b Long Branch, NJ, Sept 14, 13; m 36, Rita P Ornitz; c Elizabeth (Sklar) & Frances (Hess). *Educ:* NY Univ, BA, 34; Princeton Univ, PhD(physics), 38. *Prof Exp:* Asst radioactivity, Harvard Univ, 38-39, instr nuclear physics, 39-42; staff mem radiation lab, Mass Inst Technol, 42-44; staff mem, Manhattan Proj, Los Alamos Sci Lab, Univ Calif, 44-46. *Mem:* Fel Am Phys Soc; Sigma Xi. *Res:* Radar systems; radioactivity; nuclear structure. *Mailing Add:* Dept Physics Princeton Univ-Jadwin Hall Princeton NJ 08540

SHERRARD, JOSEPH HOLMES, ENVIRONMENTAL ENGINEERING. *Current Pos:* PROF & HEAD CIVIL ENG, MISS STATE UNIV, 89- *Personal Data:* b Waynesboro, Va, June 12, 42; m 64, Frances; c Stephanie & Joseph. *Educ:* Va Mil Inst, BS, 64; Sacramento State Col, MS, 69; Univ Calif, Davis, PhD(civil eng), 71. *Honors & Awards:* Fulbright Lectr, Ecuador, 80, 88-89; Walter L Huber Res Prize, 87; Wesley W Horner Award, 90. *Prof Exp:* Jr civil engr, Calif Div Hwy, 64-65; Zurn Industs fel, Cornell Univ, 71-72; asst prof bioeng, Okla State Univ, 72-74; from assoc prof to prof civil eng, Va Polytech Inst & State Univ, 74-89. *Mem:* Am Soc Civil Engrs; Am Water Works Asn; Water Pollution Control Fedn. *Res:* Biological and chemical wastewater treatment. *Mailing Add:* Dept Civil Eng Miss State Univ Starkville MS 39762. *Fax:* 601-325-8573; *E-Mail:* sherrard@civil.msstate.edu

SHERREN, ANNE TERRY, ANALYTICAL CHEMISTRY. *Current Pos:* assoc prof, 66-76, chmn dept, 75-78, 81-84 & 88-90, chmn sci div, 83-87, PROF CHEM, NORTH CENT COL, ILL, 76- *Personal Data:* b Atlanta, Ga, July 1, 36; m 66, William. *Educ:* Agnes Scott Col, BA, 57; Univ Fla, PhD(chem), 61. *Prof Exp:* Instr chem, Tex Woman's Univ, 61-63, asst prof, 63-66. *Mem:* AAAS; Am Chem Soc; Am Inst Chem; fel Nat Sci Teachers Asn (pres, 78-81). *Res:* Turbidity measurements; technetium chemistry; neutron activation analysis; electrochemistry; absorption spectrophotometry. *Mailing Add:* 10 S 108 Meadow Ln Naperville IL 60564

SHERRER, ROBERT E(UGENE), ENGINEERING MECHANICS. *Current Pos:* assoc prof, 60-, EMER PROF MECH ENG, UNIV WASH. *Personal Data:* b Abilene, Kans, Aug 20, 23; m 56; c 2. *Educ:* Univ Kans, BS, 48; Univ Wis, MS, 53, PhD(eng mech), 58. *Prof Exp:* Engr, Allis-Chalmers Mfg Co, 48-52; instr eng mech, Univ Wis, 52-57, asst prof, 57-60. *Concurrent Pos:* Consult, Forest Prod Lab, Madison, Wis, 56-58 & Boeing Co, 60- *Mem:* Am Soc Eng Educ. *Res:* Fluid and solid mechanics; mechanical vibration; structural analysis; materials; dynamics. *Mailing Add:* 18711 Kenik Pl NE Seattle WA 98155

SHERRICK, CARL EDWIN, PSYCHOLOGY. *Current Pos:* res psychologist, Princeton Univ, 62-70, SR RES PSYCHOLOGIST, 70- *Personal Data:* b Carnegie, Pa, Oct 28, 24; m 54; c 3. *Educ:* Carnegie Inst Technol, BS, 48; Univ Va, MA, 50 & PhD(psychol), 52. *Prof Exp:* Asst prof psychol, Washington Univ, St Louis, 53-59; res assoc, Cent Inst for the Deaf, 59-61, Univ Va, 61-62. *Concurrent Pos:* Prin investr psychol, Princeton Univ, 72-; lectr psychol, Princeton Univ, 74-; mem, NANCDS Coun, NIH, 86-89, NADCD Coun, 89-91. *Mem:* Am Psychol Asn; Acoustical Soc Am; Am Pyschol Soc. *Res:* The capacity of the skin for processing information to identify the receptive systems; adaptation of devices that transform visual and auditory signals for the blind and or deaf. *Mailing Add:* Psychol Green Hall Princeton Univ Princeton NJ 08544-0001

SHERRILL, BETTE CECILE BENHAM, BIOCHEMISTRY, SCIENCE ADMINISTRATION. *Current Pos:* ASST PROF LIPOPROTEIN METAB & MEMBRANE TRANSP, DEPTS MED & BIOCHEM, BAYLOR COL MED, 81-; PRES, SHERRILL ENVIRON CONSULT INC, 92- *Personal Data:* b Vernon, Tex, Aug 7, 44; m 63; c 2. *Educ:* NMex State Univ, BS, 66; Tex Christian Univ, PhD(phys chem), 73. *Prof Exp:* Asst scientist rocket telemetry, Phys Sci Lab, White Sands Missile Range, 62-66; res fel membrane transp, Dept Internal Med, Univ Tex Health Sci Ctr, 73-75, instr, 75-77, asst prof cholesterol metab & membrane transp, 77-81; exec dir, Inst Biosci & Bioengr, Rice Univ, 87-92. *Concurrent Pos:* Res asst chem, NMex State Univ, 66-67; res fel, Robert A Welch Res Found, 73 & NIH grant, 73-75; consult, Sherrill Eng Consults, Inc, Irving, Tex, 78-; consult & pres, Sherrill Environ Consult Inc, Houston, 81-; estab investr, Am Heart Asn, 81-84. *Mem:* Fel Am Heart Asn; Am Chem Soc; Am Asn Appl Sci; Sigma Xi; fel Am Inst Chemists. *Res:* Membrane transport; hepatic transport kinetics of intestinal and serum lipoproteins; thermodynamic properties of lipids; liquid diffusion studies. *Mailing Add:* PO Box 871 Alamosa CO 81101-0871

SHERRILL, J(OSEPH) C(YRIL), CHEMICAL ENGINEERING. *Current Pos:* PRES, SHERRILL ASSOCS, INC, 71- *Personal Data:* b Philadelphia, Pa, Nov 18, 17; m 42, Jean Sommerville; c Harry, Rob & Anne. *Educ:* Pa State Univ, BS, 41, MS, 47, PhD(chem), 52. *Prof Exp:* Asst petrol res, Pa State Univ, 41-47, instr textile chem, 47-52; prof detergency res & asst dean, Tex Woman's Univ, 52-57; sect head detergency eval, Armour & Co, 57-58, mgr soap res, 58-59, sales mgr pvt brand detergents, Armour Grocery Prod Co, 59-69; mkt mgr, Darrill Industs, Inc, 69-71. *Mem:* Am Inst Chemists; Am Inst Chem Engrs; Sigma Xi. *Res:* Detergency evaluation; forces bonding soils to surfaces, especially fabric surfaces; ultrasonic methods for evaluation of detergency. *Mailing Add:* 2360 Maple Rd Homewood IL 60430

SHERRILL, MAX DOUGLAS, SOLID STATE PHYSICS. *Current Pos:* RETIRED. *Personal Data:* b Hickory, NC, Jan 2, 30; m 55; c 5. *Educ:* Univ NC, BS, 52, PhD(physics), 61. *Prof Exp:* Physicist, Gen Elec Res & Develop Ctr, 60-67; from assoc prof to prof physics, Clemson Univ, 67-91. *Mem:* Am Phys Soc. *Res:* Electrical and magnetic properties of metals, particularly superconductivity. *Mailing Add:* 326 Woodland Way Clemson SC 29631

SHERRILL, WILLIAM MANNING, RADIOPHYSICS. *Current Pos:* res engr, Southwest Res Inst, 59-63, sr res engr, 63-66, mgr intercept & direction finding res, 66-71, asst dir, Dept Appl Electromagnetics, 71-74, DIR DEPT RADIO LOCATION SCI, SOUTHWEST RES INST, 74- *Personal Data:* b San Antonio, Tex, Feb 23, 36; m 58; c 3. *Educ:* Univ Tex, BA & BS, 57; Rice Univ, MS, 59. *Prof Exp:* Anal engr, Pratt & Whitney Aircraft Div, United Aircraft Corp, Conn, 58-59. *Mem:* Inst Elec & Electronics Eng; Am Astron Soc; Sigma Xi; AAAS. *Res:* Ionospheric propagation and mode angular spectra; radio location research; high frequency radio direction finding; solar system radio astronomy. *Mailing Add:* Southwest Res Inst PO Drawer 28510 San Antonio TX 78228-0510

SHERRIS, JOHN C, MICROBIOLOGY. *Current Pos:* from assoc prof to prof, 59-86, chmn dept, 70-80, EMER PROF, SCH MED, UNIV WASH, 86- *Personal Data:* b Colchester, Eng, Mar 8, 21; m 44; c 2. *Educ:* Univ London, MRCS & LRCP, 44, MB & BS, 48, MD, 50; Am Bd Med Microbiol, cert, 61; Am Bd Path, cert, med microbiol, 66; FRCPath, 68. *Hon Degrees:* Dr med, Karolinska Inst, Sweden, 75. *Honors & Awards:* Becton- Dickinson Award, Am Soc Microbiol, 78. *Prof Exp:* House surgeon & physician med, King Edward VII Hosp, Windsor, Eng, 44-45; trainee path & microbiol, Stoke Mandeville Hosp, 45-48, sr registr, 48-50; sr registr, Radcliffe Infirmary, Oxford, 50-52; lectr bact, Univ Manchester, 53-56, sr lectr, 56-59. *Concurrent Pos:* Chmn, Am Bd Med Microbiol, 71-73; vchmn Am Acad Microbiol, 76-78. *Mem:* Fel Am Acad Microbiol; Am Soc Microbiol (pres 82-83). *Res:* Clinical microbiology; chemotherapy; pathogenesis of infection. *Mailing Add:* Dept Microbiol Univ Wash Box 357242 Seattle WA 98195

SHERRITT, GRANT WILSON, ANIMAL SCIENCE. *Current Pos:* RETIRED. *Personal Data:* b Hunter, NDak, Mar 27, 23; m 52; c 3. *Educ:* Iowa State Univ, BS, 48; Univ Ill, MS, 49; Pa State Univ, PhD(animal husb), 61. *Prof Exp:* Asst animal husb, Univ Ill, 48-49; instr animal husb, 49-61, from asst prof to assoc prof animal sci, Pa State Univ, 81-84. *Concurrent Pos:* Mem comt, Nat Swine Indust, 63. *Mem:* AAAS; Am Soc Animal Sci. *Res:* Crossbreeding and selection experiments in swine breeding; swine management studies, especially as related to the sow. *Mailing Add:* 131 E Lytle Ave State College PA 16801

SHERROD, LLOYD B, ANIMAL NUTRITION, AGRICULTURAL & FOOD CHEMISTRY. *Current Pos:* RETIRED. *Personal Data:* b Goodland, Kans, Mar 5, 31; m 63, Judith E Harms; c Donna J & Barbara E. *Educ:* SDak State Univ, BS, 58; Univ Ark, MS, 60; Okla State Univ, PhD(animal nutrit), 64. *Prof Exp:* Asst animal scientist, Univ Hawaii, 64-67; assoc prof animal sci, Res Ctr, Tex Tech Univ, 67-73, prof, 73-79; prof chem, Frank Phillips Col, Borger, Tex, 79-88. *Concurrent Pos:* Instr nutrit, Amarillo Col, Tex, 89-95. *Mem:* AAAS; Am Inst Biol Sci; Am Soc Agron; Am Dairy Sci Asn; Am Soc Animal Sci; Sigma Xi. *Res:* Ruminant animal nutrition research with emphasis on factors influencing ration component digestibility, nutrient utilization and retention and nutrient requirements. *Mailing Add:* PO Box 1017 Panhandle TX 79068

SHERRY, ALLAN DEAN, BIOINORGANIC CHEMISTRY. *Current Pos:* from asst prof to assoc prof, 72-82, PROF CHEM, UNIV TEX, DALLAS, 82-, HEAD, PROG CHEM, 79- *Personal Data:* b Viroqua, Wis, Oct 13, 45; m 82; c 2. *Educ:* Wis State Univ, LaCrosse, BS, 67; Kans State Univ, PhD(inorg chem), 71. *Prof Exp:* Fel bioinorg chem, NIH, 71-72. *Concurrent Pos:* Sr fel, NIH, 83-84. *Mem:* Am Chem Soc. *Res:* Aqueous lanthanide chemistry; lanthanides as probes of calcium sites in proteins; fluorescence and nuclear magnetic resonance spectroscopy of metalloproteins; biological nuclear magnetic resonance spectroscopy. *Mailing Add:* Dept Chem Univ Tex Dallas PO Box 830688 Richardson TX 75083-0688

SHERRY, CLIFFORD JOSEPH, NEUROPHYSIOLOGY, PSYCHOPHARMACOLOGY. *Current Pos:* SR SCIENTIST, SYSTS RES LABS, 89- *Personal Data:* b Chicago, Ill, Jan 16, 43; m 69; c 3. *Educ:* Roosevelt Univ, BS, 68; Ill Inst Technol, MS, 74, PhD, 76. *Prof Exp:* Res assoc pharmacol, Med Sch, Univ Ill, 74-75; from instr to asst prof biol, Tex A&M Univ, 75-82; biofeedback therapist, Biofeedback & Stress Mgt Consult, 83-87. *Concurrent Pos:* Writer, Word Plus, 83- *Mem:* Neurosci Soc. *Res:* Neurophysiology, especially the relationship between single neuron activity and behavior; behavioral teratology; psychopharmacology, especially hallucinogens and drugs of abuse; psychobiology of reproductive and sexual behavior; biobehavioral effects of electromagnetic fields and potentials. *Mailing Add:* 5811 Echoway St San Antonio TX 78247-1420

SHERRY, HOWARD S, PHYSICAL INORGANIC CHEMISTRY, CHEMICAL ENGINEERING. *Current Pos:* tech mgr, Res & Develop Div, 77-80, gen mgr zeolites, 80-90, VPRES ZEOLITES & CATALYSTS, PQ CORP, 90- *Personal Data:* b New York, NY, Nov 18, 30; m 55; c Alan, Jonathan, Deborah & David. *Educ:* NY Univ, BSChE, 57; State Univ NY Buffalo, MA, 62, PhD(phys chem), 63. *Prof Exp:* Res chem engr, Union Carbide Metals Co, 57-59; Union Carbide fel, 62-63; sr res chem appl res & develop div, Mobil Res & Develop Corp, 63-65; vis lectr chem, Univ Colo, 65-66; sr res chem cent res div, Mobil Res & Develop Corp, 66-69, res assoc, 69-71, res assoc appl res div, 71-77. *Concurrent Pos:* Mem panel rare earths, Nat Acad Sci, 69. *Mem:* Am Chem Soc; Am Inst Chem Engrs; Mineral Soc Am; Catalysis Soc; Int Zeolite Asn; British Zeolite Asn. *Res:* Ion exchange in zeolites; zeolites as catalysts; zeolite science and technology and catalysis; rare earth chemistry. *Mailing Add:* 106 Monte Alto Rd Santa Fe NM 87505. *Fax:* 215-293-7510

SHERRY, JOHN M, METALLURGICAL ENGINEERING. *Current Pos:* RETIRED. *Personal Data:* b Munice, Ind, Oct 11, 13. *Educ:* Ball State Univ, BS, 35. *Prof Exp:* Asst chief spectrogr, Aluminum Res Lab, 41-44; founder & pres, John M Sherry Labs, 47-69; metallurgist, Ont Corp, 69-80. *Mem:* Fel Am Soc Metals. *Mailing Add:* 101 N Riley Rd Muncie IN 47304

SHERSHIN, ANTHONY CONNORS, OPERATIONS RESEARCH, MATHEMATICS. *Current Pos:* asst prof, 72-74, ASSOC PROF MATH, FLA INT UNIV, 74- *Personal Data:* b Clifton, NJ, Oct 16, 39; m 68; c Roxana, Alexandra & Tania. *Educ:* Georgetown Univ, AB, 61; Univ Fla, MS, 63, PhD(math), 67; Fla Int Univ, MSM, 84. *Prof Exp:* Opers res analytical autonetics div, NAm Rockwell Corp, 63-64; asst prof math, Univ SFla, 67-72. *Mem:* Am Math Asn. *Res:* Graph theory; networks; finance & economics; US and Canada trade. *Mailing Add:* Dept Math Fla Int Univ Miami FL 33199. *Fax:* 305-348-3879; *E-Mail:* shershin@servax.fiu.edu

SHERTZER, HOWARD GRANT, TOXICOLOGY, CANCER RESEARCH. *Current Pos:* ASSOC PROF TOXICOL, MED CTR, UNIV CINCINNATI, 79- *Personal Data:* b New York, NY, Oct 9, 45; m 68; c 2. *Educ:* Univ Mich, Ann Arbor, BS, 67; Univ Calif, Los Angeles, PhD(cell biol), 73. *Prof Exp:* Fel biochem, Cornell Univ, 73-75; asst prof cell biol, Tex A&M Univ, 75-79. *Concurrent Pos:* Vis prof, Cornell Univ, 76-; prin investr, Nat Inst Environ Health Sci, 79- & Nat Cancer Inst, 84-; vis prof, Karolinska Inst, Stockholm, Sweden, 89. *Mem:* Am Soc Pharmacol & Exp Therapeut; Int Soc Study Xenobiotics; Soc Toxicol. *Res:* Phenomena and mechanisms associated with chemical protection from environmental toxins, mutagens and carcinogens; chemoprotective dietary constituents, in particular, indole compounds and derivatives. *Mailing Add:* Kettering Lab Univ Cincinnati Med Ctr Cincinnati OH 45267-0056

SHERVAIS, JOHN WALTER, GEOCHEMISTRY, VOLCANOLOGY. *Current Pos:* asst prof, 84-88, ASSOC PROF IGNEOUS PETROL, UNIV SC, 88- *Personal Data:* b Philadelphia, Pa, Mar 9, 48; m; c 2. *Educ:* San Jose State Univ, Calif, BSc, 71; Univ Calif, Santa Barbara, PhD(petrol), 79. *Prof Exp:* Fac assoc petrol & mineral, Univ Calif, Santa Barbara, 75-79, lectr petrol, 81-82; NATO postdoctoral res, Confederate Tech Acad, Zurich, 79-80; res assoc lunar petrol, Univ Tenn, Knoxville, 82-84. *Concurrent Pos:* Regent's fel, Univ Calif, 76-77; prin investr, NASA, 85- & NSF, 85-; assoc ed, Geol Soc Am Bull, 89- *Mem:* Fel Geol Soc Am; Am Geophys Union. *Res:* Petrology and geochemistry of Earth's mantle; evolution of basic and intermediate magma systems; origin and significance of ophiolites, ocean island basalts, arc volcanism, flood basalts, and lunar mare volcanism. *Mailing Add:* Dept Geol Univ SC Columbia SC 29208-0001. *Fax:* 803-777-6610; *E-Mail:* shervais@epoch.geol.scarolina.edu

SHERWIN, ALLAN LEONARD, NEUROLOGY, IMMUNOCHEMISTRY. *Current Pos:* Life Ins Med Res Fund fel, 60-61, lectr neurol, 62-65, asst prof neurol & asst neurologist, 65-71, ASSOC PROF NEUROL & NEUROLOGIST, McGILL UNIV, 72- *Personal Data:* b Montreal, Jan 29, 32; m 64; c 1. *Educ:* McGill Univ, BSc, 53, MD & CM, 57, PhD(immunochem), 65; FRCPS(C), 64. *Concurrent Pos:* Markle scholar acad med, 62-67. *Mem:* Am Acad Neurol; Can Neurol Soc; Can Med Asn. *Res:* Clinical neuropharmacology; antiepileptic drugs. *Mailing Add:* 4043 Marlowe Montreal PQ H3A 2B4 Can

SHERWIN, CHALMERS W, SPECIAL RELATIVITY. *Current Pos:* RETIRED. *Personal Data:* b Two Harbors, Minn, Nov 27, 16. *Educ:* Wheaton Col, BS, 37; Univ Chicago, PhD(physics), 40. *Prof Exp:* Staff scientist, Gen Atomic Co, 68-79. *Mem:* Fel Am Phys Soc. *Mailing Add:* 17166 Pacato Way San Diego CA 92128

SHERWIN, MARTIN BARRY, GENERAL CHEMISTRY, RESEARCH ADMINISTRATION. *Current Pos:* vpres eng res, 80-87, exec vpres, W R Grace & Co, 87-92, gen mgr, 87-91, CORP VPRES, GRACE MEMBRANE SYSTS, 92- *Personal Data:* b New York, NY, July 27, 38; m 64; c 3. *Educ:* City Col New York, BChE, 60; Polytech Inst Brooklyn, MS, 63; City Univ New York, PhD(chem eng), 67. *Prof Exp:* Jr process engr, Sci Design Co, 60-62; process develop engr, Halcon Int, Inc, 62-64; lectr chem eng, City Col New York, 64-66; staff engr, Chem Systs, Inc, 66-68, mgr process develop, 68-69, dir res & develop, 69-71, vpres res & develop, 71-78, managing dir, Chem Systs Int, Ltd, 79-80. *Mem:* Fel Am Inst Chem Engrs; Am Chem Soc. *Res:* Development of new and improved processes and products; chemical engineering. *Mailing Add:* W R Grace & Co One Town Center Rd Boca Raton FL 33486-1010

SHERWIN, RUSSELL P, PATHOLOGY. *Current Pos:* asst prof, 62-63, Hastings assoc prof, 63-69, HASTINGS PROF PATH, SCH MED, UNIV SOUTHERN CALIF, 69- *Personal Data:* b New London, Conn, Mar 11, 24; m 48; c 3. *Educ:* Boston Univ, MD, 48. *Prof Exp:* Instr path, Georgetown Univ, 49-50; from instr to asst prof, Boston Univ, 53-62. *Concurrent Pos:* Asst, Harvard Univ, 56-62; mem path ref panel asbestosis & neoplasia, Int Union Against Cancer, 65-; sci consult oncol, Vet Admin, Washington, DC, 71-74; mem subcomt exp biol, Nat Cancer Inst, 72-75; sci consult, Am Cancer Soc; mem res grants, Am Lung Asn, Air Qual Health Adv Comt State Calif. *Mem:* Am Soc Exp Path; Am Asn Cancer Res; Int Acad Path; AAAS; Sigma Xi. *Res:* Air quality standards and pollutant effects; cancer, specifically breast, lung and adrenal gland cancer; diseases of the lung, especially emphysema and fibrosis; histoculture; pathobiology; tissue culture; electromicroscopy; cinemicrography; histochemistry. *Mailing Add:* 2011 Zonal Ave HMR 201 Los Angeles CA 90033. *Fax:* 213-342-3049

SHERWOOD, A GILBERT, PHYSICAL CHEMISTRY. *Current Pos:* RETIRED. *Personal Data:* b Lloydminster, Sask, June 17, 30; m 53; c 2. *Educ:* Univ Man, BSc, 53, MSc, 58; Univ Alta, PhD(photochem), 64. *Prof Exp:* Fel, Univ Alta, 64-65; Nat Res Coun fel, 65-66; asst prof chem, Simon Fraser Univ, 66-77, assoc prof, 77-90. *Mem:* Chem Inst Can. *Res:* Gas phase photochemistry; free radical kinetics; photoelectrochemistry; electrochemical storage of solar energy. *Mailing Add:* Box 214 Whaletown BC V0P 1Z0 Can

SHERWOOD, ALBERT E(DWARD), CHEMICAL ENGINEERING. *Current Pos:* CONSULT, 85- *Personal Data:* b New Haven, Conn, Sept 19, 30; m 53; c 2. *Educ:* Mass Inst Technol, SB & SM, 57; Univ Calif, Berkeley, PhD(chem eng), 64. *Prof Exp:* Chem engr, Esso Res & Eng Co, 57-58; res assoc molecular physics, Univ Md, 64-65; chem engr, Lawrence Livermore Nat Lab, Univ Calif, 65-85. *Mem:* Am Chem Soc; Am Nuclear Soc; Am Inst Chem Engrs; Sigma Xi. *Res:* Energy and mass transport; industrial applications of nuclear explosions; equations of state; mathematical modeling of in-situ coal gasification; tritium technology; radioactive gas containment and capture systems. *Mailing Add:* 3060 Miranda Ave Alamo CA 94507

SHERWOOD, ARTHUR ROBERT, PLASMA PHYSICS. *Current Pos:* RETIRED. *Personal Data:* b Berkeley, Calif, Sept 6, 36; m 84; c 2. *Educ:* Pomona Col, BA, 58; Univ Calif, Berkeley, PhD(physics), 67. *Prof Exp:* Physicist, Lawrence Radiation Lab, Univ Calif, 67; staff mem physics, Los Alamos Sci Lab, 67-93. *Mem:* Fel Am Phys Soc. *Res:* Experimental plasma physics, especially as related to the controlled thermonuclear reactor program. *Mailing Add:* 15 Whispering Pines Circle Durango CO 81301. *Fax:* 505-665-0154

SHERWOOD, BRUCE ARNE, PHYSICS EDUCATION, SYSTEMS DESIGN. *Current Pos:* PRIN RES SCIENTIST, CTR DESIGN EDUC COMPUT, CARNEGIE MELLON UNIV, 85-, PROF, DEPT PHYSICS, 85- *Personal Data:* b Laporte, Ind, Dec 12, 38; m 90. *Educ:* Purdue Univ, BS, 60; Univ Chicago, MS, 63, PhD(physics), 67. *Prof Exp:* Asst prof physics, Calif Inst Technol, 66-69; from asst prof to prof, Comput Based Educ Res Lab & Dept Physics, Univ Ill, Urbana-Champaign, 69-83, assoc prof to prof, Dept Ling, 82-83. *Concurrent Pos:* Secy, Comn Int Confer Univ, Univ Esperanto Asn, Rotterdam, Neth, 80-91. *Mem:* Am Phys Soc; Am Asn Physics Teachers; AAAS; Ling Soc Am; Esperanto Studies Asn Am; Fel Asn Develop Comput-Based Instruct, 87. *Res:* Physics education research; use of computers in physics education. *Mailing Add:* Dept Physics Carnegie Mellon Univ Pittsburgh PA 15213. *Fax:* 412-268-5646; *E-Mail:* bruce.sherwood@cmu.edu

SHERWOOD, JESSE EUGENE, atomic physics, nuclear properties; deceased, see previous edition for last biography

SHERWOOD, JOHN L, PLANT VIROLOGY. *Current Pos:* Res assoc, 81-82, asst prof, 82-87, ASSOC PROF PLANT PATH, OKLA STATE UNIV, 87- *Personal Data:* b Shreveport, La, Feb 24, 52; m 74. *Educ:* Col William & Mary, BS, 74; Univ Md, MS, 77; Univ Wis-Madison, PhD(plant path), 81. *Mem:* Am Phytopath Soc; Sigma Xi. *Res:* Virus diseases of cereals, peanut and vegetables; use of monoclonal antibodies to address agricultural problems; mechanisms of viral cross-protection. *Mailing Add:* Dept Plant Path Univ Ga Athens GA 30602

SHERWOOD, LOUIS MAIER, ENDOCRINOLOGY, METABOLISM. *Current Pos:* SR VPRES, MED & SCI AFFAIRS, US HUMAN HEALTH, 92- *Personal Data:* b New York, NY, Mar 1, 37; m 66, Judith Brimberg; c Jenniffer Beth & Ari David. *Educ:* Johns Hopkins Univ, AB, 57; Columbia Univ, MD, 61. *Honors & Awards:* Joseph Mather Smith Award, Columbia Univ Outstanding Res, 72. *Prof Exp:* NIH trainee endocrinol & metab, Col Physicians & Surgeons, Columbia Univ, 66-68; assoc med, Harvard Med Sch, 68-69, from asst prof to assoc prof, 69-72; prof med, Div Biol Sci Pritzker Sch Med, Univ Chicago, 72-80; physician-in-chief & chmn dept med, Michael Reese Hosp, 72-80; Baumritter prof & chmn, Dept Med, Albert Einstein Col Med, Yeshiva Univ, NY, 80-87; sr vpres, Med & Sci Affairs, Merck, Sharp & Dohme Int, 87-89, exec vpres, Worldwide Develop, Merck Res Labs, 89-92. *Concurrent Pos:* Chief endocrine unit, Beth Israel Hosp, Boston, Mass, 68-72, assoc physician, 71-72; res career develop award, NIH, 70-72; attend physician, West Roxbury Vet Admin Hosp, 71-72; trustee, Michael Reese Hosp & Med Ctr, 74-77; mem gen med B study sect, NIH, 75-79; Macy Found fel, vis scientist, Weizmann Inst, Israel, 78-79; physician-in-chief, Montefiore Med Ctr, 87-; vis prof med, Yeshiva Univ, NY, 93-; adj prof med, Sch Med, Univ Pa. *Mem:* Endocrine Soc; Am Soc Biol Chem; Am Fedn Clin Res; Asn Profs Med; Am Soc Clin Invest; Asn Am Physicians. *Res:* Protein chemistry, correlations between structure and function; parathyroid hormone; human placental lactogen; correlations of structure-function and factors regulating synthesis and secretion; clinical pharmacology; new drug development; outcomes research. *Mailing Add:* Merck Co Sumneytown Pike PO Box 4 West Point NY 19486. *Fax:* 215-652-7697; *E-Mail:* louis_sherwood@merck.com

SHERWOOD, MARTHA ALLEN, PALEOMYCOLOGY, MYCOLOGY. *Current Pos:* RES ASSOC PALEONT, GEOL DEPT, UNIV ORE, 81- *Personal Data:* b Eugene, Ore, Nov 8, 48; m 83, Miriam S Pike; c 1. *Educ:* Univ Ore, BA, 70; Cornell Univ, PhD(mycol), 77. *Prof Exp:* Cryptogamic botanist, Farlow Herbarium, Harvard Univ, 77-79; res asst mycol, Commonwealth Mycol Inst, Kew, 79-80. *Mem:* Mycol Soc Am. *Res:* Taxonomy and paleoecology of fossil fungi; morphology and taxonomy of living Ascomycetes including lichens; monographic studies in the Phacidiales and Ostropales. *Mailing Add:* 250 E 38th Eugene OR 97405

SHERWOOD, PETER MILES ANSON, SURFACE SCIENCE, CORROSION & OXIDATION INCLUDING CARBON FIBER SURFACES. *Current Pos:* assoc prof, 85-91, PROF CHEM, KANS STATE UNIV, 91- *Personal Data:* b London, Eng, July 12, 45; m 82, Gillian T Taylor. *Educ:* Univ St Andrews, BSc, 67; Univ Cambridge, MA, 70, PhD(chem), 70, ScD, 95. *Prof Exp:* Fel chem, Downing Col, Cambridge, 70-72; lectr, Univ Newcastle Upon Tyne, 72-84, sr lectr, 84-85. *Concurrent Pos:* Vis assoc prof, Univ Calif, Berkeley, 76; vis prof, Univ Bari, Italy, 84; sr res scientist, Eastman Kodak Co, 86; vis scientist, Nat Measurement Lab, Commonwealth Sci & Indust Res Orgn, Australia, 87; prog officer anal & surface chem, NSF, 90-91; ed, Critical Reviews Surface Chem, 91-; dir, State Kans Depscor Prog, 93- *Mem:* Am Chem Soc; fel Royal Soc Chem; Soc Appl Spectros; Am Vacuum Soc; Mat Res Soc; fel Inst Physics. *Res:* Surface science, in particular x-ray photoelectron spectroscopy, applied to materials surfaces and corrosion and oxidation; studies of carbon fiber surfaces and their role in composites, electrode and metal surfaces; valence band photoemission. *Mailing Add:* Dept Chem Willard Hall Kans State Univ Manhattan KS 66506-3701. *Fax:* 785-532-6666; *E-Mail:* escachem@ksuvm.edu

SHERWOOD, ROBERT LAWRENCE, IMMUNOTOXICOLOGY, ANIMAL MODELS OF INFECTIOUS DISEASE. *Current Pos:* res specialist, IIT Res Inst, 83-86, staff scientist, 86-87, sr scientist, 87-96, GROUP LEADER APPL MICROBIOL, IIT RES INST, 88-, MGR RES, 96- *Personal Data:* b Salt Lake City, Utah, Oct 23, 53; m 75, Carol Erickson; c Randall, Scott, Michael & Kristi. *Educ:* Brigham Young Univ, BS, 76, MS, 78; Univ Calif, Davis, PhD(microbiol), 84. *Prof Exp:* Res asst microbiol, Brigham Young Univ, 76-78, immunol, Univ Calif, Davis, 78-83. *Mem:* Am Soc Microbiol; Soc Toxicol. *Res:* Rodent models of mammalian infectious disease; biopesticide safety assessment; drug safety and efficacy studies; immunotoxicology. *Mailing Add:* IIT Res Inst 10 W 35th St Chicago IL 60616. *E-Mail:* rsherwood@iitri.com

SHERWOOD, ROBERT TINSLEY, PLANT PHYSIOLOGY. *Current Pos:* PLANT PATHOLOGIST, USDA, 58- *Personal Data:* b West Orange, NJ, Feb 21, 29; m 55; c 3. *Educ:* Cornell Univ, BS, 52, MS, 54; Univ Wis, PhD, 58. *Prof Exp:* Res asst prof plant path, NC State Univ, 58-69, prof, 69-71. *Concurrent Pos:* Adj prof, Pa State Univ, 71- *Mem:* Am Phytopath Soc; Am Soc Agron. *Res:* Physiology of parasitism; forage crop disease; fungal diseases of plants; regulation of apomictic seed formation. *Mailing Add:* US Pasture Res Lab USDA Pa State Univ University Park PA 16802

SHERWOOD, WILLIAM CULLEN, GEOCHEMISTRY. *Current Pos:* assoc prof geol, 64, 72-73, PROF GEOL, JAMES MADISON UNIV, VA, 73- *Personal Data:* b Washington, DC, Feb 8, 32; m 58; c 3. *Educ:* Univ Va, BA, 54, MA, 58; Lehigh Univ, PhD(geol), 61. *Prof Exp:* Mat res analyst, Va Hwy Res Coun, 61-67; asst prof geol, Univ Va, 67-70, asst prof environ sci, 70-72. *Concurrent Pos:* Mem subcomt on fundamentals of binder-aggregate adhesion, Hwy Res Bd, Nat Acad Sci-Nat Res Coun, 65-67; lectr, Univ Va, 66-67; fac consult, Va Hwy Res Coun. *Mem:* Geochem Soc; Geol Soc Am; Nat Asn Geol Teachers; Am Inst Prof Geologists. *Res:* Erosion and sedimentation control; land use planning; geochemistry of weathering and soils; chemistry of natural waters; environmental geology. *Mailing Add:* Geog & Geol James Madison Univ 800 S Main ST Harrisonburg VA 22807-0001

SHERYLL, RICHARD PERRY, OCEANOGRAPHIC INSTRUMENTATION, BIOLOGICAL OCEANOGRAPHIC. *Current Pos:* RES & DEVELOP ENGR ELECTRONICS, CYCLOPS RES & DEVELOP, 84- *Personal Data:* b Pa, June 18, 56; m 91, Andrea Weber. *Educ:* State Univ NY, BS, 82. *Prof Exp:* Res asst mat anal, Metrop Mus Art, 81-84. *Concurrent Pos:* Res scientist, City Col, 82-84; res & develop engr, World

Wide Wind, 84-85, Seaspec Assocs, 85-86 & VIAC Inc, 88-90. *Mem:* AAAS; NY Acad Sci; Inst Elec & Electronics Engrs; Am Chem Soc. *Res:* Pure and applied research as it pertains to oceanographic and marine studies; design and development of instrumentation for such studies; author of several publications; awarded 2 US and 2 foreign patents. *Mailing Add:* Cyclops Res & Develop 340 W 87th St 3A New York NY 10024

SHESHTAWY, ADEL A, petroleum engineering, earth science, for more information see previous edition

SHESKIN, THEODORE JEROME, NUMERICAL SOLUTION MARKOV CHAINS, MATRIX COMPUTATIONS. *Current Pos:* from asst prof to assoc prof, 74-88, PROF INDUST ENG, CLEVELAND STATE UNIV, 88- *Personal Data:* b New York, NY, June 11, 40. *Educ:* Mass Inst Technol, BS, 62; Syracuse Univ, MS, 65; Pa State Univ, PhD(indust eng), 74. *Prof Exp:* Test equip engr, Int Bus Mach Corp, 62-64; logic design engr, Burroughs Corp, 65-68; digital systs engr, Digital Info Devices, 68-71. *Concurrent Pos:* Summer fac fel, Nat Aeronaut & Space Admin, 79-92. *Mem:* Sr mem Inst Indust Engrs; Am Soc Eng Educ. *Res:* Systems analysis of space stations and satellites; development of new methodologies for the numerical solution of markov chains and matrix computations; science policy. *Mailing Add:* Indust Eng Dept Cleveland State Univ Cleveland OH 44115. *Fax:* 216-687-9330; *E-Mail:* t.sheskin@csuohio.edu

SHESTAKOV, ALEKSEI ILYICH, NUMERICAL ANALYSIS, COMPUTATIONAL PHYSICS. *Current Pos:* PHYSICIST MAGNETIC FUSION ENERGY, LAWRENCE LIVERMORE NAT LAB, UNIV CALIF, 76- *Personal Data:* b Yugoslavia, Feb 8, 49; US citizen. *Educ:* Univ Calif, Berkeley, BS, 70, MA, 73, PhD(appl math), 75. *Mem:* Am Math Soc; Am Phys Soc. *Res:* Developing numerical models for use in problems arising in magnetic fusion energy; calculations; solution of linear systems. *Mailing Add:* Lawrence Livermore Nat Lab PO Box 808 L-477 Livermore CA 94550

SHESTAKOV, SERGEY VASILIYEVICH, GENETICS, BIOTECHNOLOGY. *Current Pos:* Researcher, Moscow State Univ, 61-77, prof, Dept Genetics, 77-80, dep dean fac biol, 78-80, CHMN, DEPT GENETICS, MOSCOW STATE UNIV, 80-, DIR, INT BIOTECHNOL CTR, 91- *Personal Data:* b Leningrad, Russia, Nov 23, 34; m 64, Galina Andreevna Grigorieva; c Alexander Sergeevich. *Educ:* Moscow State Univ, MS, 57, PhD, 64. *Hon Degrees:* DSc, Moscow State Univ, 74. *Honors & Awards:* Award, USSR Min Higher Educ, 81; USSR State Prize, 88; M Lomonosov Premium Prize, 95. *Concurrent Pos:* Postdoctoral scholar, Princeton Univ, NJ, 66-67; vis prof, Pa State Univ, 75, Mich Univ, 92; vis researcher, Pasteur Inst, Paris, 81, Univ Chicago, 94; UNESCO fel, 85; dir, N Vavilov Inst Gen Genetics, Russ Acad Sci, 88-91, chmn, Sci Coun Genetics, 88-; mem, Coun Sci Develop, Int Acad Sci, 89- *Mem:* Russ Acad Sci; Int Acad Sci; Biotechnol Acad Russ. *Res:* Discovery of genetic transformation in blue-green algae; construction of integrative and birepliconic vectors and cloning of different genes in phototrophic bacteria; discovery and molecular analysis of genes involved in photosynthesis and resistance to herbicides; nitrogen fixation and hydrogen metabolism. *Mailing Add:* Dept Genetics Fac Biol Moscow State Univ Moscow 119899 Russia. *Fax:* 7-095-9395022; *E-Mail:* sergey@shest.msk.su

SHETH, ATUL C, ENERGY CONVERSION, POLLUTION CONTROL. *Current Pos:* assoc prof & mgr, Anal & Eng Lab Serv Group, 84-90, assoc prof & mgr, Pollution Control & Environ Sect, 90-93, PROF CHEM ENG, SPACE INST, UNIV TENN, TULLAHOMA, 93-, CO-CHAIR, INDUST SYSTS RES GROUP, 95- *Personal Data:* b Bombay, India, Dec 2, 41; US citizen; m 65, Sheila Amin; c Roma & Archana. *Educ:* Univ Bombay, India, BChemEng, 64; Northwestern Univ, MS, 69, PhD(chem eng), 73. *Honors & Awards:* Anil P Desai Prize, 60. *Prof Exp:* Shift supvr, Esso Stan Eastern Inc, 64-67; chem operator, Riker Labs, 67; process engr, Armour Indust Chem Co, 69; clerk, Charlotte Charles Inc, 71-72; fel chem eng, Argonne Nat Lab, 72-74, chem engr, 74-80; chem engr, Exxon Res & Eng Co, 80-84. *Concurrent Pos:* Murphy fel, 67-71; tech leader, Seed Processing Team, Dept Energy & NASA, 78-80. *Mem:* Am Inst Chem Engrs; Sigma Xi; Air & Waste Mgt Asn. *Res:* Alternate energy fields such as nuclear reactors, high-temp electric batteries, magnetohydrodynamics and coal liquefaction; catalytic coal gasification process with Exxon; seed and sorbent regeneration; pollution control and trace element study; hazardous and non-hazardous waste management; scale-up of high temperature super conducting materials/wires/tapes production. *Mailing Add:* Dept Chem Eng Space Inst Univ Tenn Tullahoma TN 37388-8897. *Fax:* 615-393-7201; *E-Mail:* asheth@utsi.edu

SHETH, BHOGILAL, PHARMACEUTICAL TECHNOLOGY. *Current Pos:* PROF PHARMACEUT, COL PHARM, UNIV TENN, 87- *Personal Data:* b Bombay, India, Sept 18, 31; US citizen. *Educ:* Gujerat Univ, India, BPharm, 52; Univ Mich, MS, 55, PhD(pharmaceut chem), 61. *Prof Exp:* Sect head prod develop, Alcon Labs, 60-64; group leader pharm res, Warner-Lambert Co, 64-68; assoc prof, 68-74, prof pharmaceut, Col Pharm, Univ Tenn, 74-78; area dir, Div Res & Develop, Vicks Health Care, 78-87. *Concurrent Pos:* Consult, var pharmaceut cos, 68-78, 87- *Mem:* Am Pharmaceut Asn; Acad Pharmaceut Sci; Am Soc Hosp Pharmacists; Am Asn Pharm Sci. *Res:* Pharmaceutical research and development; surface chemistry applications to dosage forms; rheology; drug dissolutions; product formulations. *Mailing Add:* 1418 Popular Ridge Dr Memphis TN 38120

SHETH, KETANKUMAR K, FLUID DYNAMICS, TURBO MACHINERY. *Current Pos:* sr assoc engr, 85-87, staff engr, 87-89, ENG SUPVR, CENTRILIFT, 89- *Personal Data:* b Gondal, Gujarat, India, Jan 21, 59; m, Rita; c Dhara & Hardik. *Educ:* Sardar Patel Univ, India, BE, 80; Tex A&M Univ, MS, 85. *Prof Exp:* Maintenance engr, Tata Chem Ltd, India, 80-82; res assoc, Tex A&M Univ, 83-85. *Mem:* Am Soc Mech Engrs; Soc Petrol Engrs. *Res:* Design, prototype testing, development of centrifugal pumps; plant maintenance; granted 4 US patents. *Mailing Add:* 8810 S 73rd E Ave Tulsa OK 74133

SHETLAR, DAVID JOHN, ENTOMOLOGY, LANDSCAPE PEST MANAGEMENT. *Current Pos:* ASSOC PROF EXTEN & RES, DEPT ENTOMOL, OHIO STATE UNIV, 90- *Personal Data:* b Columbus, Ohio, June 30, 46; m 68, R Renee Rice; c Norann R Kliewe. *Educ:* Univ Okla, BS, 69, MS, 75; Pa State Univ, PhD(entomol), 77. *Prof Exp:* Instr & cur, Dept Entomol, Pa State Univ, 75-76, asst prof teaching & res, 77-83; res scientist, Chemlawn Servs Res & Develop, Delaware, Ohio, 84-90. *Mem:* Sigma Xi; Entomol Soc Am. *Res:* Pest management in ornamental plants, turf and Christmas trees. *Mailing Add:* Dept Entom Ohio State Univ 1991 Kenny Rd Columbus OH 43210-1000. *Fax:* 614-292-9783; *E-Mail:* shetlar.1@osu.edu

SHETLAR, MARTIN DAVID, PHOTOCHEMISTRY, PHOTOBIOLOGY. *Current Pos:* from asst prof to assoc prof, 68-84, PROF CHEM & PHARMACEUT CHEM, SCH PHARM, UNIV CALIF, SAN FRANCISCO, 84- *Personal Data:* b Wichita, Kans, Aug 28, 38; m 66; c 1. *Educ:* Kans State Univ, BS, 60; Univ Calif, Berkeley, PhD(chem), 65. *Prof Exp:* Biophysicist, Donner Lab, Univ Calif, Berkeley, 65-68. *Concurrent Pos:* AEC fel, 66-68. *Mem:* AAAS; Am Chem Soc; Am Soc Photobiol; Int-Am Photochem Soc; Sigma Xi; European Soc Photobiol. *Res:* Photochemistry and free radical chemistry in nucleic acid-protein systems; organic photochemistry; photochemical kinetics. *Mailing Add:* Sch Pharm Univ Calif San Francisco CA 94143

SHETLAR, MARVIN ROY, NUTRITION. *Current Pos:* RETIRED. *Personal Data:* b Bayard, Kans, Apr 3, 18; m 40; c 3. *Educ:* Kans State Univ, BS, 40; Ohio State Univ, MS, 43, PhD(biol chem), 46. *Prof Exp:* Asst milling indust, Kans State Univ, 38-40; asst, Ohio State Univ, 41-42, instr agr chem, 44-46; Am Cancer Soc fel, Sch Med, Univ Okla, 46-47, res assoc, 47-50, from asst prof to prof biochem, 53-64, chmn dept, 64, res prof, 64-66; prof, Univ Tex Med Br, Galveston, 66-73; assoc chmn, Dept Biochem, Health Sci Ctr, Tex Tech Univ, 72-75, prof biochem & dermat, 77-88. *Concurrent Pos:* NIH sr res fel, 57-62; vis prof, Univ Calif-Univ Airlangga Proj Med Educ Indonesia, 64-66 & Col Med, Univ King Faisal, Dammam, Saudi Arabia, 79-81; mem, Am Bd Clin Chem; adj prof nutrit, Tex Tech Univ, 85- *Mem:* Am Chem Soc; Am Inst Chem; Soc Exp Biol & Med; Am Asn Biol Chem; Am Asn Clin Chem; Sigma Xi. *Res:* Animal glycoproteins and mucopolysaccharides; wound healing; fetal alcohol syndrome. *Mailing Add:* Dept Nutrit Tex Tech Univ Lubbock TX 79409-1162

SHETLER, ANTOINETTE (TONI), COMPUTER PROGRAMMING TOOLS, COMPUTER SYSTEM PERFORMANCE. *Current Pos:* staff engr, 82-85, ENG MGR, SYSTS DIV, TRW, 86- *Personal Data:* b Ont; US citizen; c 3. *Educ:* Univ Wash, BA, 62. *Prof Exp:* Sci programmer, Boeing Co, 65-66; systs programmer, Pac Northwest Bell, 66-68; systs programmer, Rand Corp, 68-71, assoc dept head, 73-76; sr prog staff mem, Xerox Data Systs, 71-73, comput scientist, Star Proj, 76-82. *Concurrent Pos:* Dep chair conf bd, Asn Comput Mach, 80-86, mem, Facil Planning Comt, 88-90. *Mem:* Asn Comput Mach; Inst Elec & Electronics Engrs. *Res:* Operating systems and computer programming tools; analysis and improvement of the software engineering process; computer system performance; development of technical conferences. *Mailing Add:* Systs Div TRW 1 Federal Systems Park Dr Fairfax VA 22033

SHETLER, STANWYN GERALD, PLANT TAXONOMY. *Current Pos:* asst cur, Smithsonian Inst, Nat Mus Nat Hist, 62-63, assoc cur, 63-81, cur, 81-95, dir, Flora NAm Prog, 71-80, asst dir progs, 84-86, actg dep dir, 86-91, dep dir, 91-94, EMER CUR, DEPT BOT, SMITHSONIAN INST, NAT MUS NATURAL HIST, 96- *Personal Data:* b Johnstown, Pa, Oct 11, 33; m 63, Elaine M Retberg; c Stephen G & Lara S. *Educ:* Cornell Univ, BS, 55, MS, 58; Univ Mich, PhD, 79. *Concurrent Pos:* Pres, Audubon Naturalist Soc Cent Atlantic States, Inc, 74-77; mem bd dirs, Piedmont Environ Coun, Va, 84-86 & 94; mem nat comt, Man & Biosphere Prog, 88-95. *Mem:* Fel AAAS; Am Soc Plant Taxon; Bot Soc Am; Am Inst Biol Sci; Arctic Inst NAm; Int Asn Plant Taxon. *Res:* Taxonomy and ecology of Campanula; flora and vegetation of the Arctic, especially Alaska; history of Russian botany; biological conservation; flora of central Atlantic region. *Mailing Add:* 142 E Meadowland Lane Sterling VA 20164-1144. *Fax:* 202-786-2563; *E-Mail:* shetler.stanwyn@nmnh.si.edu

SHETTERLY, DONIVAN MAX, HEAT TRANSFER, GLASS SCIENCE. *Current Pos:* physicist, 86-89, SR DEVELOP SCIENTIST, GLASS TECH INC, 89- *Personal Data:* b Des Moines, Iowa, Oct 29, 46; wid; c Julia K & Benjamin J. *Educ:* Cent Col, BA, 68; Purdue Univ, MS, 70. *Prof Exp:* Assoc physicist, Owens-Illinois Inc, Toledo, 70-74, physicist, 74-80, sr physicist, Glass Technol Sect, 80-85; eng mgr, Warren Tech Assocs, 85-86. *Mem:* Am Ceramic Soc; Sigma Xi; Soc Mfg Engrs. *Res:* Heat transfer; glass forming; phase separation in glass; glass homogeneity and process control. *Mailing Add:* 3033 Gallatin Rd Toledo OH 43606

SHETTLE, ERIC PAYSON, ATMOSPHERIC PHYSICS, ATMOSPHERIC AEROSOLS. *Current Pos:* PHYSICIST, AIR FORCE GEOPHYS LAB, 73- *Personal Data:* b New York, NY, Nov 23, 43; m 65; c 2. *Educ:* Johns Hopkins Univ, BA, 65; Univ Wis-Madison, MA, 67. *Prof Exp:* Teaching & res asst, Dept Physics, Univ Wis, 66-68, res asst, Dept Meteorol, 68-72; instr & res assoc, Dept Physics, Univ Fla, 72-73. *Mem:* Optical Soc Am; Am Meteorol Soc; Am Geophys Union; AAAS. *Res:* The optical and infrared properties of the atmosphere, especially the atmospheric aerosols and their effects on radiative transfer of light in scattering atmospheres; atmospheric remote sensing, lidor applications. *Mailing Add:* 5504 Uppingham St Chevy Chase MD 20815-5508

SHEVACH, ETHAN MENAHEM, CELLULAR IMMUNOLOGY, IMMUNOGENETICS. *Current Pos:* clin assoc immunol, Lab Clin Invest, NIH, 69-71, sr staff fel, 71-72, lab immunol, 72-73, sr investr, Nat Inst Allergy & Infectious Dis, 73-87, HEAD, CELLULAR IMMUNOL, LAB IMMUNOL, NIH BETHESDA, MD, 87- *Personal Data:* b Brookline, Mass, Oct 16, 43; m 67, Ruth Schneider; c Matthew & Seth. *Educ:* Boston Univ, AB & MD, 67. *Prof Exp:* Intern med, Bronx Munic Hosp Ctr, NY, 67-68, asst resident, 68-69. *Concurrent Pos:* Ed-in-chief, J Immunol, 87-92, Cellular Immunol, 96- *Mem:* Am Asn Immunologists; Am Soc Clin Invest; Am Fedn Clin Res; Asn Am Physicians; Coun Biol Ed. *Res:* Basic mechanisms that control immunocompetent cell interactions; mechanisms of lymphocyte activation, cell surface antigens involved in T cell triggering and growth factor receptors; pathogenesis of autoimnune disease. *Mailing Add:* Lab Immunol Nat Inst Allergy & Infect Dis NIH Bldg 10 Rm 11N315 Bethesda MD 20892. *Fax:* 301-496-0222; *E-Mail:* ems1@box-e.nih.gov

SHEVACK, HILDA N, MECHANICAL ENGINEERING. *Personal Data:* b Brooklyn, NY, Apr 12, 34; div. *Educ:* City Col New York, BSME, 59. *Prof Exp:* Asst to chief engr, Starret TV Corp, NY, 50-52; integrated logistics support mgr, Govt Systs Div, Gen Instrument Corp, Hicksville, NY, 52-94. *Concurrent Pos:* Dir & chmn, Publ Comts, Soc Logistics Engrs, 68- *Mem:* Fel Soc Logistics Engrs; Inst Elec & Electronics Engrs; Am Soc Mech Engrs; Am Inst Indust Engrs; Am Defense Preparedness Asn; Soc Women Engrs. *Mailing Add:* 8672 18th Ave Brooklyn NY 11214

SHEVEL, WILBERT LEE, SYSTEMS DEVELOPMENT, INTEGRATED INFORMATION SYSTEMS. *Current Pos:* MANAGING DIR, EIM, 94- *Personal Data:* b Monessen, Pa, Oct 26, 32; m 54, Faye Johnston; c Lynn, Laurel, Kathleen & Amy. *Educ:* Carnegie-Mellon Univ, BS, 54, MS, 55, PhD(elec eng), 60. *Honors & Awards:* Nation's Outstanding Young Elec Engr, 61 & 64. *Prof Exp:* Vpres & asst gen mgr, Motorola, 73-74; vpres & gen mgr, Rockwell Int, 74-76; pres, Omex, 76-80 & Barrington, 80-82; vpres, Unisys Corp, 82-94, pres, Paramax, 88-92. *Concurrent Pos:* Mem, Long Range Planning Comt, Inst Elec & Electronics Engrs, 83-85 & bd dirs, Aerospace Industs Asn Can, 90-92. *Mem:* Fel Inst Elec & Electronics Engrs; Inst Elec & Electronics Engrs Magnetics Soc (pres, 67-68); Sigma Xi. *Res:* Impact on information systems of technological advances; integration levels, speed, automated assembly, software, security, storage; cooperative computing and processing of information. *Mailing Add:* 12279 Fairway Pointe Row San Diego CA 92128

SHEVELL, RICHARD S, AERODYNAMICS, FLIGHT MECHANICS. *Current Pos:* prof aeronaut & astronaut, 70-89, EMER PROF AERONAUT & ASTRONAUT, STANFORD UNIV, 89- *Personal Data:* b New York, NY, June 6, 20; m 48, Lorraine King; c Steven, Jeanne & Diane. *Educ:* Columbia Col, BA, 40; Calif Inst Technol, MS, 41, AE, 42. *Prof Exp:* Aerodynamicist, Douglas Aircraft Co, 42-47, supvr aero performance, 47-59, dir aerodyn, 59-67, dir com advan design, 67-70. *Concurrent Pos:* Consult design & expert witness, 55-96; chmn, Stanford Transp Res Prog, Stanford Univ, 72-78; mem, Am Inst Aeronaut & Astronaut Aircraft Design Tech Comt, 81-86, AGARD Flight Mechs Panel, NATO, 73-80, Aeronaut & Space Eng Bd, Nat Res Coun, 85-89. *Mem:* Fel Am Inst Aeronaut & Astronaut. *Res:* Aerodynamic design of aircraft; involved with DC-6, DC-7, DC-8, DC-9 and DC-10 transport aircraft; system analysis of transportation systems. *Mailing Add:* 151 Stockbridge Ave Atherton CA 94027-3942. *Fax:* 650-366-3458; *E-Mail:* shevell@leland.stanford.edu

SHEVIAK, CHARLES JOHN, PLANT SYSTEMATICS. *Current Pos:* CUR BOT, NY STATE MUS, 78- *Personal Data:* b Chicago, Ill, May 31, 47; m 68. *Educ:* Univ Ill, Urbana, BS, 70, MS, 72; Harvard Univ, PhD(plant syst), 76. *Prof Exp:* Dir, Ill Endangered Plants Proj, Natural Land Inst, 77-78. *Mem:* AAAS; Am Soc Plant Taxonomists; Sigma Xi. *Res:* Systematics, ecology and biogeography of North American orchids; biogeography, especially forest-grassland relationships; evolution of colonizing species; northeastern floristics. *Mailing Add:* Cur Bot NY State Mus Albany NY 12234-0001

SHEVLIN, PHILIP BERNARD, ORGANIC CHEMISTRY. *Current Pos:* from asst prof to assoc prof, 70-79, PROF CHEM, AUBURN UNIV, 80- *Personal Data:* b Mineola, NY, June 28, 39. *Educ:* Lafayette Col, BS, 61; Yale Univ, MS, 63, PhD(chem), 66. *Prof Exp:* Res assoc chem, Brookhaven Nat Lab, 65-66 & 68-70. *Mem:* Am Chem Soc; fel AAAS. *Res:* Fullerene chemistry; chemistry of atomic carbon and other high energy intermediates. *Mailing Add:* Dept Chem Auburn Univ Auburn AL 36830. *E-Mail:* shevlpb@mail.auburn.edu

SHEW, DELBERT CRAIG, MASS SPECTROMETRY. *Current Pos:* RES CHEMIST, R S KERR ENVIRON RES LAB, ENVIRON PROTECTION AGENCY, 72- *Personal Data:* b Canton, Ohio, Dec 29, 40; m 67. *Educ:* Hanover Col, AB, 62; Ind Univ, MS, 66; Univ Ark, PhD(chem), 69. *Prof Exp:* Res chemist, E I du Pont de Nemours & Co, 68-71; assoc prof math, Washington Tech Inst, 71-72. *Concurrent Pos:* Consult legal aspects environ pollution, various law firms, 74- *Mem:* Am Soc Mass Spectrometry. *Res:* Isolation of organic pollutants from ground water and identification using electron impact and chemical ionization mass spectrometry. *Mailing Add:* 1200 S Constant Dr Ada OK 74820

SHEWAN, WILLIAM, ELECTRICAL ENGINEERING, MATHEMATICS. *Current Pos:* instr electronics, Valparaiso Tech Univ, 46-50, from instr to assoc prof, 52-57, chmn dept, 57-76, actg dean, Col Eng, 78-80, prof, 80-84, EMER PROF ELEC ENG, VALPARAISO UNIV, 84- *Personal Data:* b Chicago, Ill, May 24, 14; m 49; c 6. *Educ:* Valparaiso Univ, BS, 50; Univ Notre Dame, MS, 52; Purdue Univ, PhD(elec eng), 66. *Prof Exp:* Chief electronic technician, US Navy, 42-45; jr eng, Northern Ind Pub Serv Co, 45-46. *Concurrent Pos:* Consult, res & develop, US Navy Crane, 73-76; vis prof, Northern Western Univ Tech Ctr, Evanston, Ill. *Mem:* Sr mem Instrument Soc Am; sr mem Inst Elec & Electronics Engrs; Am Soc Eng Educ; Sigma Xi. *Res:* Nonlinear circuit analysis; variable speed drives for rotating machines-solid state devices; numerical methods in systems engineering. *Mailing Add:* 2154 Ransom Rd Valparaiso IN 46383

SHEWCHUN, JOHN, solid state physics & electronics, for more information see previous edition

SHEWEN, PATRICIA ELLEN, INFECTIOUS DISEASES. *Personal Data:* b Stratford, Ont, Mar 21, 49; m 72, Edward Claude; c Spencer & Katrina. *Educ:* Univ Guelph, BSc, 71, DVM, 75, MSc, 79, PhD(immunol), 82. *Prof Exp:* Vet, Magilvary Vet Hosp, Toronto, 75-77; from asst prof to prof immunol, Univ Guelph, 82-97, asst dean res, 95-96. *Concurrent Pos:* Pres, Int Conf Res Workers Animal Dis, 96. *Mem:* Am Asn Vet Immunologists (pres, 95); Am Soc Microbiol; Can Vet Med Asn; Int Union Immunol Soc. *Res:* Infectious disease focused on the immunologic aspects of bovine pneumonic pasteurellosis and orvine chlamydial infection. *Mailing Add:* Dept Pathobiol Univ Guelph Bldg 46 Guelph ON N1G 2W1 Can

SHEWMAKER, JAMES EDWARD, ENVIRONMENTAL EARTH & MARINE SCIENCES. *Current Pos:* RETIRED. *Personal Data:* b Paragould, Ark, Jan 22, 22; m 46, Reba Fay Nadeau; c James Edward Jr, Cynthia Marie, Ann Emily, Jane Elizabeth & Mary Joyce. *Educ:* Harding Univ, BS, 44; Univ Nebr, MS, 49, PhD(phys chem), 51. *Prof Exp:* Res chemist, Exxon Res & Eng Co, 51-58, sr chemist, 58-61, res assoc, 62-83. *Mem:* Am Chem Soc; NY Acad Sci. *Res:* Surfactants and detergents; biodegradability; demulsification; oil-field chemicals; radiation chemistry; trace metal contaminants in petroleum; pollution control; cleaning cargo spaces of oil tankers. *Mailing Add:* 1370 S Martine Ave Scotch Plains NJ 07076

SHEWMON, PAUL G(RIFFITH), MATERIALS SCIENCE ENGINEERING. *Current Pos:* chmn dept, 75-83, PROF METALL ENG, OHIO STATE UNIV, 75- *Personal Data:* b Rochelle, Ill, Apr 18, 30; m 52; c 3. *Educ:* Univ Ill, BSc, 52; Carnegie Inst Technol, MS & PhD(metall eng), 55. *Honors & Awards:* Alfred Noble Prize, 60; Howe Medal, Am Soc Metals, 77; Mathewson Gold Medal, 82. *Prof Exp:* Res engr, Res Lab, Westinghouse Elec Corp, 55-58; from asst prof to prof metall eng, Carnegie Inst Technol, 58-67; assoc dir, Metall Div, Argonne Nat Lab, 67-68, dir, Mat Sci Div, 69-73; dir, Div Mat Res, NSF, 73-75. *Concurrent Pos:* NSF fel, 64-65; mem, adv com reactor safeguards, US Nuclear Regulatory Comn, 77-, chmn, 82; Alexander von Humboldt Sr Scientist Award, 84. *Mem:* Nat Acad Eng; Am Inst Mining, Metall & Petrol Engrs; Am Nuclear Soc; Am Soc Metals; fel AAAS; fel Metall Soc. *Res:* Physical metallurgy; nuclear materials; kinetics of reactions in solids. *Mailing Add:* Dept Mat Sci & Eng Ohio State Univ Columbus OH 43210

SHI, YUN YUAN, AERONAUTICS, APPLIED MATHEMATICS. *Current Pos:* sr scientist, McDonnell Douglas Astronaut Co, 65-78, prin scientist, 78-80, staff scientist res & develop, 80-87, SR STAFF MGR, ADVAN TECHNOL CTR, MCDONNELL DOUGLAS SPACE SYST CO, 87- *Personal Data:* b Nanking, China, Sept 26, 32; m 60, Man Hwa; c Edmond, Theodore & Monica. *Educ:* Nat Taiwan Univ, BSc, 55; Brown Univ, MSc, 58; Calif Inst Technol, PhD(aeronaut, math), 63. *Prof Exp:* Res asst eng physics, Brown Univ, 57-58; scholar & teaching asst, Calif Inst Technol, 58-62; res specialist, Missile & Space Syst Div, Douglas Aircraft Co, 62-63; asst prof eng & sci, Carnegie Inst Technol, 63-65. *Concurrent Pos:* Vis prof, Natl Taiwan Univ, 92-93. *Mem:* AAAS; fel Am Inst Aeronaut & Astronaut; sr mem Inst Elec & Electronics Engrs. *Res:* Wave propagation in anelastic solids; fluid mechanics; magneto-hydrodynamics; nonlinear oscillations; singular perturbation methods; astronomical science; electromagnetic wave scattering from turbulent plasma; optimal control and estimation; digital signal processing; guidance, control and navigation of launch and space vehicles; Kalman filtering and real time tracking; sensor and space experiments; optimizations and nonlinear programming. *Mailing Add:* 6792 Sunview Dr Huntington Beach CA 92647

SHIAO, DANIEL DA-FONG, PHYSICAL CHEMISTRY, PHYSICAL BIOCHEMISTRY. *Current Pos:* PRES, ROHAI TECHNOL INC, 91- *Personal Data:* b Kiangsi, China, Apr 6, 37; m 74, Jeanne; c Nora, Lena & David. *Educ:* Nat Taiwan Univ, BS, 58; NMex Highlands Univ, MS, 63; Univ Minn, PhD(phys chem), 68. *Prof Exp:* Fel, Yale Univ, 68-70; sr res chemist, Eastman Kodak Co, 70-79, res assoc, 79-91. *Concurrent Pos:* Consult, UNESCO, 87. *Mem:* Am Chem Soc; Soc Photog Sci & Eng. *Res:* Physical chemistry at interfaces of silver halide grains; mathematical modeling of diffusion processes and heterogeneous catalysis; physical-chemical measurements pertaining to product design; product performance optimization via statistical analysis and experimental design. *Mailing Add:* 1009 Whalen Rd Penfield NY 14526. *Fax:* 716-377-7778

SHIAU, YIH-FU, LIPID METABOLISM, G-I PHYSIOLOGY. *Current Pos:* ASSOC PROF MED, UNIV PA, 83- *Personal Data:* b Chang-Hwa, Taiwan, Jan 12, 42; m; c 2. *Educ:* Taipei Med Col, MD, 66; George Washington Univ, PhD(physiol), 71. *Hon Degrees:* MA, Univ Pa, 83. *Prof Exp:* Chief, G-I Sect, Vet Admin Med Ctr, 82-89. *Concurrent Pos:* Assoc ed, Digestive Dis & Sci, 82-87. *Mem:* Am Physiol Soc; Am Soc Gastrointestinal Endoscopy; Am Gastroenterol Asn; Am Fed Clin Res; AAAS. *Res:* Lipid absorption and lipid metabolism; bile salt absorption and bile salt secretion. *Mailing Add:* 850 W Chester Pike Havertown PA 19083. *Fax:* 318-674-7176

SHIBATA, EDWARD ISAMU, EXPERIMENTAL HIGH ENERGY PHYSICS. *Current Pos:* from asst prof to assoc prof, 72-84, PROF PHYSICS, 84-, ASSOC HEAD PHYSICS, PURDUE UNIV, WEST LAFAYETTE, 94- *Personal Data:* b Gallup, NMex, Mar 1, 42; m 73, Frances H. *Educ:* Mass Inst Technol, SB, 64, PhD(physics), 70. *Prof Exp:* Res assoc physics, Northeastern Univ, 70-72. *Mem:* Am Phys Soc; Am Asn Phys Teachers; Inst Elec & Electronics Engrs; NSF & Japan Ctr Global Partnership Int Res fel, 94-95. *Res:* Meson and baryon spectroscopy and decay; electron-positron annihilations at high energy; use of scintillating fibers and visible light counters for charged particle tracking; Measurement of electroweak parametes. *Mailing Add:* Dept Physics Purdue Univ West Lafayette IN 47907-1396. *Fax:* 765-494-0706; *E-Mail:* shibata@physics.purdue.edu

SHIBATA, SHOJI, PHARMACOLOGY. *Current Pos:* assoc prof, 67-69, PROF PHARMACOL, SCH MED, UNIV HAWAII, MANOA, 70- *Personal Data:* b Kyoto, Japan, Nov 12, 27; m 58; c 2. *Educ:* Nara Med Col, Japan, MD, 52; Kyoto Univ, PhD(pharmacol), 57. *Prof Exp:* Japanese Govt fel, 54-57; instr pharmacol, Sch Med, Kyoto Univ, 57-59; asst prof, Sch Med, Univ Miss, 63-66. *Concurrent Pos:* Instr & lectr, Sch Med, Univ Southern Calif, 60-61; assoc prof pharmacol & chmn dept, Col Pharm, Kyoto Univ, 62-63. *Mem:* Am Soc Pharmacol & Exp Therapeut; Am Soc Physiol; Sigma Xi; Int Soc Heart Res, Am Sect. *Res:* Cardiovascular pharmacology and natural products. *Mailing Add:* Dept Pharmacol Univ Hawaii 1960 East-West Rd Biomed T411 Honolulu HI 96822. *Fax:* 808-956-3170

SHIBIB, M AYMAN, HIGH VOLTAGE INTEGRATED CIRCUITS, SEMICONDUCTOR TECHNOLOGY & PRODUCT DEVELOPMENT. *Current Pos:* mem tech staff, AT&T Bell Labs, 80-87, DISTINGUISHED MEM TECH STAFF, BELL LABS, LUCENT TECHNOL, 87- *Personal Data:* b Damascus, Syria, Feb 14, 53; US citizen; m 82, Reem Estwany; c Dena & Kareem. *Educ:* Am Univ Beirut, BS, 75; Univ Fla, Gainesville, MS, 76, PhD(elec eng), 79. *Honors & Awards:* Appreciation Award, Inst Elec & Electronics Engrs Electron Devices Soc, 94; Res & Develop 100 Award, 95 & 96. *Prof Exp:* Grad res asst microelectronics, Elec Eng Dept, Univ Fla, 76-78, grad res assoc, 78-79, vis asst prof, 79-80. *Concurrent Pos:* Vchmn & chmn, Electron Device Group, Inst Elec & Electronics Eng, Lehigh Valley Sect, 84-88, vchmn, Exec Comt, 87-88 & chmn, 88-89; sect chmn, Inst Elec & Electronics Engrs, ISPSD, 91; guest ed, Trans Electron Devices, 91; distinguished lectr, Inst Elec & Electronics Engrs Electron Devices Soc, 94- *Mem:* Sr mem Inst Elec & Electronics Engrs; Am Phys Soc; Electrochem Soc; Sigma Xi; NY Acad Sci. *Res:* Development of silicon device physics and technology development; high voltage integrated circuits used in telecommunication systems; fundamental limitations of performance of silicon solar cells and bipolar transistors; granted 8 US patents. *Mailing Add:* 2525 N 12th St PO Box 13396 Reading PA 19612-3396. *Fax:* 610-939-3769

SHIBKO, SAMUEL ISSAC, BIOCHEMISTRY. *Current Pos:* rev scientist, Food & Drug Admin, 67-72, spec asst to dir toxicol div, 72-76, actg chief SPAL, 76-77, CHIEF CONTAMINANTS & NATURAL TOXICANTS EVAL BR, FOOD & DRUG ADMIN, 77- *Personal Data:* b Bargoed, Wales, Oct 2, 27. *Educ:* Univ Birmingham, BSc, 54; Imp Col, dipl, 58, Univ London, PhD(biochem), 58. *Prof Exp:* Res assoc, McCollum Pratt Inst, Johns Hopkins Univ, 58-60; asst biochemist dept food sci & technol, Univ Calif, Davis, 60-64; instr nutrit & food sci, Mass Inst Technol, 64-65, asst prof, 65-67. *Concurrent Pos:* Gen referee toxicol tests, Asn Off Anal Chemists, 74- *Mem:* AAAS; Soc Exp Biol & Med; NY Acad Sci; Soc Toxicol; Soc Environ Geochem & Health. *Res:* Food toxicology; evaluation of safety of food additives, and hazards associated with contamination of the food supply with heavy metals, industrial chemicals and natural toxicants; techniques for establishing safety of food chemicals. *Mailing Add:* 6634 31 St Pl NW Washington DC 20015

SHIBLES, RICHARD MARWOOD, CROP PHYSIOLOGY, PHOTOSYNTHESIS. *Current Pos:* From asst prof agron to assoc prof agron, 60-69, PROF AGRON, IOWA STATE UNIV, 69- *Personal Data:* b Brooks, Maine, Feb 12, 33; m 64, Evelyn Burleigh; c Elise Ann. *Educ:* Univ Maine, BS, 56; Cornell Univ, MS, 58, PhD(agronomy), 61. *Concurrent Pos:* Lectr fel, Japanese Soc Prom Sci, 88. *Mem:* Fel AAAS; fel Am Soc Agron; fel Crop Sci Soc Am; Am Soc Plant Physiol; Am Asn Univ Profs; Sigma Xi. *Res:* Genotypic and environmental aspects of plant physiology as they relate to crop productivity; photosynthetic and respiratory metabolism. *Mailing Add:* Dept Agron 2101 Ia State Univ Ames IA 50011-1010. *Fax:* 515-294-5506; *E-Mail:* rshibles@iastate.edu

SHIBLEY, JOHN LUKE, ZOOLOGY. *Current Pos:* RETIRED. *Personal Data:* b Gentry, Ark, Apr 12, 19; m 48, Anna Mozley; c Marianna, Joe, Rebecca & Susan. *Educ:* Univ Okla, BS, 41; Univ Ga, MS, 49, PhD(zool), 56. *Prof Exp:* Instr zool, Univ Ga, 49-50; from assoc prof to prof biol, La Grange Col, 50-86. *Res:* Population survival of Euglena with ultraviolet irradiation treatment. *Mailing Add:* 1315 Vernon Rd La Grange GA 30240

SHICHI, HITOSHI, BIOCHEMISTRY, BIOPHYSICS. *Current Pos:* PROF OPHTHAL & DIR RES, WAYNE STATE UNIV, KRESGE INST, 88- *Personal Data:* b Nagoya, Japan, Dec 20, 32; m 62, Asae Nakagawa; c Yukari & Mikaru. *Educ:* Nagoya Univ, BS, 55, MS, 57; Univ Calif, Berkeley, PhD, 62. *Honors & Awards:* US-Japan Eye Res Exchange Prog Award, 76. *Prof Exp:* Res biochemist, Univ Calif, Berkeley, 62; asst prof biochem, Nagoya Univ, 62-63; asst prof, Univ Tokyo, 63-67; res chemist, Nat Inst Neurol Dis & Stroke, 67-69, res chemist, Lab Vision Res, Nat Eye Inst, 69-81; prof & asst dir, Eye Res Inst, Oakland Univ, Rochester, 81-88. *Concurrent Pos:* Fulbright scholarship, 57-62. *Mem:* Am Soc Biol Chem; Asn Res Vision & Ophthal; Asn Ocular Pharmacol & Therapeut; AAAS. *Res:* Drug metabolism; immunology. *Mailing Add:* Dept Ophthal Wayne State Univ 4717 St Antoine Detroit MI 48201. *Fax:* 313-577-7781; *E-Mail:* hshichi@med.wayne.edu

SHICHMAN, D(ANIEL), MECHANICAL ENGINEERING. *Current Pos:* CONSULT, 94- *Personal Data:* b Brooklyn, NY, Aug 20, 28; m 49; c 3. *Educ:* Univ Mich, BS, 50; Stevens Inst Technol, MS, 61. *Prof Exp:* Develop engr, Nylon Div, E I duPont de Nemours & Co, Del, 50-51, develop engr, Atomic Energy Div, Ind, 51-53; res engr, Mech Eng Dept, Res Ctr, Uniroyal, Inc, 53-60, mgr fiber eng res, 60-66, mgr eng res, 66-78; dir res & develop, NRM Corp Div, Condec Corp, 78-80. *Mem:* Sigma Xi; Am Chem Soc; Nat Soc Prof Engrs (vpres, 74-76). *Res:* Process equipment development for chemical, rubber and plastic industry; sprayed metals; synthetic fiber and automation; process equipment for rubber and plastics industry. *Mailing Add:* 20 Copper Kettle Rd Trumbull CT 06611

SHICK, PHILIP E(DWIN), PULP CHEMICAL RECOVERY FURNACE DESIGN & OPERATION. *Current Pos:* tech dir mill div, Owens-Ill Glass Co, 56-60, tech dir forest prod div, 60-63, actg dir res & eng, 63-65, dir res, 65-66, sr res scientist, 66-82, CONSULT, FOREST PROD DIV, OWENS-ILL, INC, 82- *Personal Data:* b Kendallville, Ind, Jan 7, 18; m 63; c 2. *Educ:* Harvard Univ, SB, 39; Lawrence Col, MS, 41, PhD(phys chem), 43. *Prof Exp:* Res chemist, Masonite Corp, Miss, 43-45; res proj leader, WVa Pulp & Paper Co, 45-48; res supvr, Mead Corp, 48-56, tech asst to vpres res, 56. *Mem:* Can Pulp & Paper Asn; Am Chem Soc; fel Tech Asn Pulp & Paper Indust. *Res:* High temperature thermodynamics; chemistry of lignin; pulping and papermaking; neutral sulfite semichemical recovery. *Mailing Add:* 3628 Cavalear Dr Toledo OH 43606-1145

SHIDA, MITSUZO, CHEMISTRY. *Current Pos:* PRES, MS INTERTECH, 86- *Personal Data:* b Hamamatsu, Japan, Oct 2, 35; m 59; c 2. *Educ:* Kyoto Univ, BS, 58; Polytech Inst Brooklyn, PhD(chem), 64. *Prof Exp:* Sr res chemist, W R Grace & Co, 63-66; sr res scientist, Plastic Div, Allied Chem Corp, 66; mgr polymer physics, Chemplex Co, Rolling Meadows, 66-70, polymer res dept, 70-86. *Mem:* Am Chem Soc; Soc Rheol; Chem Soc Japan. *Res:* Polymer physical chemistry, especially solution properties; morphological and rheological aspects of polymer science. *Mailing Add:* 4778 RFD Long Grove IL 60047-6930

SHIDELER, GERALD LEE, sedimentology, marine geology, for more information see previous edition

SHIDELER, ROBERT WEAVER, BIOCHEMISTRY. *Current Pos:* assoc prof chem, 46-50, prof chem & chmn dept chem, 54-77, chmn natural sci area, 66-77, EMER HAROLD & LUCY CABE DISTINGUISHED PROF CHEM, HENDRIX COL, 78- *Personal Data:* b Joliet, Ill, Apr 25, 13; m 48; c 2. *Educ:* Goshen Col, AB, 34; Univ Chicago, MS, 41; Univ Tex, PhD, 56. *Prof Exp:* Teacher high sch, NDak, 35-36, Ind, 36-40; instr sci, Independence Jr Col, Iowa, 41-42; instr, US Army Air Force Training Sch, Wis, 42-44. *Mem:* AAAS; Am Chem Soc; NY Acad Sci. *Res:* Methods in investigating intermediary metabolism; individual differences in mineral metabolism. *Mailing Add:* 1601 Quail Creek Dr Conway AR 72032

SHIEH, CHING-CHYUAN, TELECOMMUNICATION FACILITY NETWORK OPERATIONS, NETWORK OPERATIONS SYSTEMS DESIGN. *Current Pos:* mem tech staff micro-syst, AT&T Bell Labs, 84-85, mem tech staff comput syst, AT&T Info Systs, 85-86, MEM TECH STAFF, TELECOMMUN, AT&T BELL LABS, 87- *Personal Data:* b Pingtung, Taiwan, Repub of China, Oct 20, 50; US citizen; m 77, Miaw M Lin; c Angell, Eric & Luke. *Educ:* Nat Taiwan Univ, BS, 72; Univ Maine, MS, 76; Univ Pa, PhD(elec eng), 84. *Prof Exp:* Digital prod mgr data commun telemetry, Sonex Philmont Electronics Inc, 80-83. *Concurrent Pos:* Lectr, Nat Taiwan Univ, 74-75; syst consult syst design, DazoTron Electronics Assoc, 82-83. *Mem:* Inst Elec & Electronics Engrs; Nat Geog Soc. *Res:* Digital network operations re-engineering and mechanization; integrated operation systems, expert systems and user interface systems architecture design for digital network operations; network core data integrity, central and local database synchronization; real-time control system and data communication system design; 32-bit microprocessor based single board computer design. *Mailing Add:* 44 Providence Ct Princeton Junction NJ 08550

SHIEH, JOHN SHUNEN, COMPUTER SCIENCE. *Current Pos:* ASST PROF COMPUT SCI, DEPT COMPUT SCI, MEM UNIV NFLD, 88- *Personal Data:* b Shanghai, China, Jan 10, 46; Can citizen; m 76; c 2. *Educ:* Univ Sci & Technol China, BSc, 67; Simon Fraser Univ, PhD(computer sci), 86. *Prof Exp:* Technician, Wangching Standard Space Parts Factory, 67-76; lectr computer sci, Cent China Univ Sci & Technol, 76-81; res scientist, Simon Fraser Univ, 87-88. *Concurrent Pos:* Sr res scientist, Nordco Ltd, 88-91. *Res:* Mobile robot vision, scene analysis and object recognition; knowledge based system design. *Mailing Add:* Dept Comput Sci Mem Univ Nfld St John's NF A1C 5S7 Can

SHIEH, KENNETH KUANG-ZEN, INDUSTRIAL MICROBIOLOGY. *Current Pos:* RETIRED. *Personal Data:* b Keelung, Taiwan, Feb 15, 36; US citizen; m 66; c 2. *Educ:* Taiwan Prov Col Agr, BS, 61; Ill Inst Technol, MS, 65, PhD(microbiol), 69. *Prof Exp:* Sr res microbiologist, Cent Res Dept, Corn Prods Sect, Anheuser-Busch Inc, 68-75, res assoc, 75-93. *Mem:* Am Soc Microbiol. *Res:* Production of enzymes from a microbial origin for transformation of one kind of carbohydrate to another. *Mailing Add:* 501 Prince Way Ct Ballwin MO 63011

SHIEH, LEANG-SAN, DIGITAL CONTROL SYSTEMS, NETWORK THEORY. *Current Pos:* from asst prof to assoc prof, 71-78, PROF CONTROL SYSTS, UNIV HOUSTON, 78- *Personal Data:* b Tainan, China, Jan 10, 34; US citizen; m 62; c 2. *Educ:* Nat Taiwan Univ, BS, 58; Univ Houston, MS, 68, PhD(elec eng), 70. *Prof Exp:* Design engr, Taiwan Florescent Lamp Co, 60-61; power systs engr, Taiwan Elec Power Co, 61-65. *Concurrent Pos:* Vis prof, Inst Univ Polit, Venezuela, 76-77; vis scientist, Battelle Columbus Lab, 77 & Math Res Ctr, Univ Wis-Madison, 79. *Mem:* Inst Elec & Electronics Engrs; Am Soc Elec Engrs. *Res:* Model reduction, identification, realization and adaptive control of multivariable control systems. *Mailing Add:* Dept Elec & Comput Eng Univ Houston 4800 Calhoun Houston TX 77204

SHIEH, PAULINUS SHEE-SHAN, nuclear engineering, physics, for more information see previous edition

SHIEH, YUCH-NING, GEOCHEMISTRY, PETROLOGY. *Current Pos:* from asst prof to assoc prof, 72-87, PROF GEOCHEM, PURDUE UNIV, 87- *Personal Data:* b Chan-hua, Taiwan, Feb 15, 40; m 66, Tiee-Leou Ni; c Lisa & Mae-Mae. *Educ:* Nat Taiwan Univ, BS, 62; Calif Inst Technol, PhD(geochem), 69. *Prof Exp:* Fel geochem, McMaster Univ, Can, 68-72. *Concurrent Pos:* Vis scientist, Inst Earth Sci, Acad Sinica, Taipei, China, 80-81, vis prof, 89-90; assoc ed, Isotope Geosci, 82- *Mem:* Geochem Soc; Am Geophys Union; Geol Soc China. *Res:* Oxygen, carbon and hydrogen isotopes in igneous and metamorphic rocks; sulfur isotopes in ore deposits and coals; stable isotope studies of active geothermal systems. *Mailing Add:* Dept Earth & Atmospheric Sci Purdue Univ West Lafayette IN 47907. *Fax:* 765-496-1210

SHIELD, RICHARD THORPE, MECHANICS. *Current Pos:* RETIRED. *Personal Data:* b Swalwell, Eng, July 9, 29; m 58; c 2. *Educ:* Univ Durham, BSc, 49, PhD(appl math), 52. *Prof Exp:* Res assoc appl math, Brown Univ, 51-53; sr res fel, A R E Ft Halstead, Eng, 53-55; from asst prof to prof, Brown Univ, 55-65; prof appl mech, Calif Inst Technol, 65-70; head dept, Univ Ill, Urbana, 70-84, prof theoret & appl mech, 70-91. *Concurrent Pos:* Guggenheim mem fel, Univ Durham, 61-62; co-ed, J Appl Math & Physics, 65-, assoc ed, J Appl Mech, 79-; Alcoa vis prof, Univ Pittsburgh, 70-71; mem comt, US Nat Theoret & Appl Mech, 81-86; distinguished scholar, Calif Inst Technol, 82; Russell Severance Springer vis prof, Univ Calif, Berkeley, 84. *Mem:* Fel AAAS; fel Am Acad Mech (pres, 77-78); fel Am Soc Mech Engrs; fel Soc Eng Sci; Sigma Xi. *Res:* Elasticity, plasticity; stability theory. *Mailing Add:* 1314 Fork Point Lane Oriental NC 28571

SHIELDS, DENNIS, CELL BIOLOGY, BIOCHEMISTRY. *Current Pos:* ASST PROF ANAT, 78-, ASSOC PROF, ALBERT EINSTEIN COL MED. *Personal Data:* b London, Eng, Sept 9, 48; m 75. *Educ:* Univ York, Eng, BA, 71; Nat Inst Med Res, London, PhD(biochem), 74. *Honors & Awards:* Solomon A Berson Award, Am Diabetes Asn, 78. *Prof Exp:* Fel cell biol, Rockefeller Univ, 74-77. *Mem:* Am Soc Cell Biol; Biochem Soc; Endocrine Soc. *Res:* Biosynthesis and subcellular compartmentation of secretory and membrane proteins; pancreatic islet hormone biosynthesis; post-translational modifications of proteins. *Mailing Add:* Dept Develop & Molecular Biol Albert Einstein Col Med 1300 Morris Park Ave Bronx NY 10461-1975. *Fax:* 718-823-5877

SHIELDS, FLETCHER DOUGLAS, PHYSICS. *Current Pos:* assoc dean lib arts, 76-79, PROF PHYSICS, UNIV MISS, 59- *Personal Data:* b Nashville, Tenn, Oct 27, 26; m 48; c 4. *Educ:* Tenn Polytech Inst, BS, 47; Vanderbilt Univ, MS, 48, PhD(physics), 56. *Prof Exp:* Res physicst, Carbide & Carbon Chem Corp, 48-49; from asst prof to assoc prof physics, Middle Tenn State Col, 49-59. *Mem:* Fel Acoust Soc Am; Sigma Xi. *Res:* Thermal relaxation processes in gas by means of sound absorption measurements; energy and mometum accommodation of gas molecules on solid surfaces. *Mailing Add:* Dept Physics Univ Miss NCPA Rm 1065 Coliseium Dr University MS 38677

SHIELDS, FLETCHER DOUGLAS, JR, STREAM CORRIDOR HABITAT RESTORATION, ENVIRONMENTAL DESIGN OF STREAM ALTERATIONS. *Current Pos:* RES HYDRAUL ENGR, NAT SEDIMENTATION LAB, USDA AGR RES SERV, 90- *Personal Data:* b Murfreesboro, Tenn, Oct 15, 53; m 77, Rebecca Bradley; c Sarah, Laura & Bradley. *Educ:* Harding Univ, BS, 75; Vanderbilt Univ, MS, 77; Colo State Univ, PhD(hydraul eng), 87. *Honors & Awards:* Young Civil Engr Govt, Am Soc Civil Engrs, 84. *Prof Exp:* Instr civil eng, Tenn State Univ, 77-78; hydraul engr, US Corps Engrs, 78-80; res civil engr, US Army Engr Waterways Exp Sta, 80-90. *Concurrent Pos:* Mem, Task Comt Aquatic Habitat & Sedimentation, Am Soc Civil Engrs, 87-90. *Mem:* Mem Am Soc Civil Engrs; mem Order of the Engr. *Res:* Restoration of stream and riparian zone habitats damaged by erosion; streambank erosion and its control, especially using woody vegetation; completed projects examining effects of woody vegetation on flood control levees and riprap revetments. *Mailing Add:* USDA Agr Res Serv Nat Sedimentation Lab PO Box 1157 Oxford MS 38655-1157. *Fax:* 601-232-2915; *E-Mail:* shields@gis.sedlab.olemiss.edu

SHIELDS, GEORGE SEAMON, INTERNAL MEDICINE, COMPUTER MEDICINE. *Current Pos:* RETIRED. *Personal Data:* b Bombay, NY, Oct 18, 25; m 48; c 5. *Educ:* Mass Inst Technol, SB, 48; Cornell Univ, MD, 52. *Prof Exp:* Intern, Bellevue Hosp, NY, 52-53, resident, 53-54; USPHS res fel hemat, State Univ NY Downstate Med Ctr, 54-56; resident, Salt Lake Co Gen Hosp, 56-57; Am Cancer Soc fel biochem & hemat, Col Med, Univ Utah, 57-60, instr internal med, 59-61; from asst prof to assoc prof, Col Med, Univ Cincinnati, 61-70; dir med systs, Good Samaritan Hosp, 69-75; vpres, Micro-Med Inc, 80-87. *Concurrent Pos:* Pres, Sycamore Prof Asn Inc, 71-; med dir, Winton Hills Med Ctr, 73-75, Wesley Hall Home, 75-, Riverview Home, 78- & 3 Rivers Home, 78- *Mem:* Biomed Eng Soc; Soc Comput Med; Soc Advan Med Systs; Am Fedn Clin Res; Am Chem Soc. *Res:* Biochemistry, protein, enzymology, nucleic acids, trace metals, copper; hematology, anemias, leukemias, pathogenesis; computer applications. *Mailing Add:* 8830 Hollyhock Dr Cincinnati OH 45231

SHIELDS, GERALD FRANCIS, CYTOGENETICS, MOLECULAR EVOLUTION. *Current Pos:* asst prof, 75-85, PROF ZOOL, INST ARCTIC BIOL, UNIV ALASKA, 85- *Personal Data:* b Anaconda, Mont, Nov 9, 43; m 67; c 2. *Educ:* Carroll Col, BA, 66; Cent Wash State, MS, 70; Univ Toronto, PhD(zool), 74. *Prof Exp:* Teacher biol, Billings Cent High Sch, 66-68; NSF res asst, Cent Wash State Col, 68-70; teaching asst, Dept Zool, Univ Toronto, 70-74. *Concurrent Pos:* Nat Res Coun fel, 72-74. *Mem:* Am Ornith Union; Soc Study Syst Zool; Soc Study Evolution; Can Soc Genetics & Cytol; Sigma Xi. *Res:* Cytogenetics and chromosomal evolution in insects and vertebrates; DNA evolution in vertebrates; rates of chromosome and DNA change. *Mailing Add:* PO Box 81964 Fairbanks AK 99708-1964

SHIELDS, HOWARD WILLIAM, SOLID STATE PHYSICS, BIOPHYSICS. *Current Pos:* from asst prof to assoc prof, 58-66, PROF PHYSICS, WAKE FOREST UNIV, 66-, DEPT CHAIR, 90- *Personal Data:* b Tomotla, NC, May 19, 31; m 60, Anne Kosler; c Carolyn, Burton & John. *Educ:* Univ NC, BS, 52; Pa State Univ, MS, 53; Duke Univ, PhD(physics), 56. *Prof Exp:* Res assoc physics, Duke Univ, 56-57. *Concurrent Pos:* Sloan Found res fel, 63-65; vis prof, Yale Univ, 68-69. *Mem:* Fel Am Phys Soc; Radiation Res Soc; Sigma Xi. *Res:* Electron spin resonance; studies made on irradiation damage in organic solids; phase transitions, and high T superconductors. *Mailing Add:* 3380 Sledd Ct Winston-Salem NC 27106. *Fax:* 910-759-6142; *E-Mail:* shields@wfu.edu

SHIELDS, JAMES EDWIN, BIOCHEMISTRY, ENTOMOLOGY. *Current Pos:* sr biochemist, 68-76, RES SCIENTIST, LILLY RES LABS, ELI LILLY & CO, 77-; FOUNDER & PRES, AMARYLLIS RES INST, 78- *Personal Data:* b Marion, Ind, July 29, 34; m 62; c 1. *Educ:* DePauw Univ, AB, 56; Univ Calif, Berkeley, PhD(biochem), 61. *Prof Exp:* USPHS fel, Univ Zurich, 60-62; asst prof chem, Case Western Reserve Univ, 62-68. *Concurrent Pos:* Adj prof chem, Indiana Univ & Purdue Univ, 79- *Mem:* Am Chem Soc; Lepidopterists Soc; AAAS; Sigma Xi. *Res:* Peptide and protein chemistry; horticulture. *Mailing Add:* 17808 Grassy Branch Rd Noblesville IN 46060-9237

SHIELDS, JIMMIE LEE, environmental physiology, for more information see previous edition

SHIELDS, JOAN ESTHER, ORGANIC CHEMISTRY. *Current Pos:* asst prof, 68-71, ASSOC PROF CHEM, C W POST COL, LONG ISLAND UNIV, 71- *Personal Data:* b Cambridge, Mass, Oct 11, 34. *Educ:* Regis Col, Mass, AB, 56; Tufts Univ, MS, 58; Boston Col, PhD(org chem), 66. *Prof Exp:* Instr chem, Regis Col, Mass, 58-63; fel, Max Planck Inst Coal Res, 66-68. *Mem:* Am Chem Soc; Sigma Xi. *Res:* Organometallic chemistry; organosulfur and nitrogen heterocyclics and photochemical cycloadditions. *Mailing Add:* Dept of Chem C W Post Col Greenvale NY 11548

SHIELDS, LORA MANEUM, biology, for more information see previous edition

SHIELDS, LORAN DONALD, ANALYTICAL CHEMISTRY, ACADEMIC ADMINISTRATION. *Current Pos:* PRES, SOUTHERN METHODIST UNIV. *Personal Data:* b San Diego, Calif, Sept 18, 36; m 57; c 4. *Educ:* Univ Calif, Riverside, BA, 59; Univ Calif, Los Angeles, PhD(chem), 64. *Prof Exp:* From asst prof to assoc prof chem, Calif State Univ, Fullerton, 63-69, chmn fac coun, 67, vpres admin, 67-70, prof 67-, actg pres, 70-71, pres, 71. *Concurrent Pos:* Consult, Calif State Senate for Legis in Support of Res in Calif State Cols, 68-69 & NSF, 70; mem exec comt, Coun of Pres, Calif State Univ & Cols Syst, 73-, chmn, 75-76; resource leader, Res Corp Conf for Pub Univ Sci Dept Chairs, Ala, 74; mem, Nat Sci Bd, 74-80, mem Budget Comt, Progs Comt, Sci Educ Adv Comt, 74- & Nat Comt on Coop Educ; exec dir, Calif Coun Sci & Technol. *Mem:* Am Inst Chemists; Sigma Xi; AAAS; Am Chem Soc; Am Col Pub Rels Asn. *Res:* Transition metal coordination chemistry; instrumental methods of analytical chemistry. *Mailing Add:* 1746 Tattenham Rd Leucadia CA 92024-1033

SHIELDS, PAUL CALVIN, PURE MATHEMATICS. *Current Pos:* assoc prof, 74-76, PROF MATH, UNIV TOLEDO, 76- *Personal Data:* b South Haven, Mich, Nov 10, 33; div; c 6. *Educ:* Colo Col, AB, 56; Yale Univ, MA, 58, PhD(math), 59. *Prof Exp:* CLE Moore instr math, Mass Inst Technol, 59-61; asst prof, Boston Univ, 61-63; asst prof, Wayne State Univ, 63-69; vis scholar & res assoc, Stanford Univ, 70-73; vis lectr, Univ Warwick, Coventry Eng, 73-74. *Concurrent Pos:* Res assoc, Willow Run Lab, Univ Mich, 60; vis prof elec eng, Cornell Univ, 78, Stanford Univ, 80-82; Fulbright Scholar, Math Inst, Budapest, Hungary, 85; prof stat, Univ Toronto, Can, 85-86. *Mem:* Am Math Soc; Sigma Xi. *Res:* Ergodic theory; information theory; statistical mechanics; operator theory; linear algebra. *Mailing Add:* Dept Math Univ Toledo Toledo OH 43606-3390

SHIELDS, ROBERT JAMES, PARASITOLOGY. *Current Pos:* instr biol, 63-65, asst prof, 65-70. assoc prof, 70-76, chmn dept, 78-81, PROF BIOL, CITY COL NEW YORK, 77- *Personal Data:* b Philadelphia, Pa, Apr 23, 34; m 58. *Educ:* East Stroudsburg State Col, BS, 55; Ohio State Univ, MS, 59, PhD(zool), 62. *Prof Exp:* Instr zool, Ohio State Univ, 62-63. *Mem:* Am Soc Parasitol; Am Soc Zoologists; Am Micros Soc. *Res:* Life-histories, ecology and physiology of marine and fresh-water copepods parasitic on fishes. *Mailing Add:* Dept Biol City Col NY 160 Convent Ave New York NY 10031-9198

SHIELDS, THOMAS WILLIAM, THORACIC SURGERY. *Current Pos:* instr, Northwestern Univ, Chicago, 56-57, assoc, 57-62, assoc prof, 64-68, chief surg serv, Vet Admin Lakeside Hosp, 68-86, PROF SURG, NORTHWESTERN UNIV, CHICAGO, 68- *Personal Data:* b Ambridge, Pa, Aug 17, 22; m 48; c 3. *Educ:* Kenyon Col, BA, 43; Temple Univ, MD, 47; Am Bd Surg, dipl, 55; Bd Thoracic Surg, dipl, 56. *Hon Degrees:* DSc, Kenyon, 78. *Prof Exp:* Intern, Allegheny Gen Hosp, Pittsburgh, 47-48; resident, New Eng Deaconess Hosp, Boston, 48-49; resident, Passavant Mem Hosp, Chicago, 49-50 & Vet Admin Res Hosp, Chicago, 54-55; sr resident, Chicago Munic Tuberc Sanitarium, 55-56. *Concurrent Pos:* Allan B Kanavel fel surg, Passavant Mem Hosp, Chicago, 49-50; thoracic surgeon, Vet Admin Res Hosp, 56-57, mem staff thoracic surgeons, 57-; assoc surg staff, Passavant Mem Hosp, 56-57, attend surgeon, 58-72; attend thoracic surgeon, Chicago Munic Tuberc Sanitarium, 56-68 & attend surgeon, Northwestern Mem Hosp, 72-80. *Mem:* Western Surg Asn; Am Col Surg; Am Asn Thoracic Surg; Soc Thoracic Surg; Cent Surg Asn. *Res:* Clinical cancer research; editor and contributor to surgical, thoracic surgical, and cancer literature. *Mailing Add:* 1721 Jenks St Evanston IL 60201-1528

SHIELDS, WILLIAM MICHAEL, DNA TYPING, BEHAVIORAL ECOLOGY OF BIRDS. *Current Pos:* from asst prof to assoc prof, 79-88, PROF BIOL, COL ENVIRON SCI & FORESTRY, STATE UNIV NY, 88- *Personal Data:* b Valley Stream, NY, Nov 23, 47; m 90, Barbara J Hager. *Educ:* Rutgers Univ, AB, 74; Ohio State Univ, MS, 76, PhD(zool), 79. *Concurrent Pos:* Mem prof adv comt, Burnet Park Zoo, 79-93; assoc ed, Wilson Bull, 84-87, Am Midland Naturalist, 84-89; prin investr, NSF, 84-87, Adirondack Wildlife Prog, 85- & US Fish & Wildlife Serv, 93-; dir, Cranberry Lake Biol Sta, 87-94. *Mem:* Fel Am Ornithologists Union; Animal Behav Soc; Am Soc Naturalists; Ecol Soc Am; Soc Study Evolution; Soc Conserv Biol. *Res:* Interface of genetics, ecology and behavior that controls the evolution of sociality in the barn swallow, flamingo and other animals; conservation biology of vertebrates in the Adirondacks and the tropics, especially theoretical issues; evolutionary theory and its applications to human problems (forensic DNA typing). *Mailing Add:* Col Environ Sci & Forestry State Univ NY Syracuse NY 13210. *Fax:* 315-470-6934; *E-Mail:* wms1@syr.edu

SHIER, DOUGLAS ROBERT, OPERATIONS RESEARCH, APPLIED MATHEMATICAL MODELING. *Current Pos:* PROF OPER RES, COL WILLIAM & MARY, 88- *Personal Data:* b Cleveland, Ohio, Oct 16, 46. *Educ:* Harvard Univ, AB, 68; London Sch Econ, PhD(oper res), 73. *Prof Exp:* Res statistician, Ctr Dis Control, USPHS, 68-70; res assoc, Nat Bur Standards, 73-74; asst prof quant methods, Univ Ill, 74-75; mathematician, Nat Bur Standards, 75-80; prof math sci, Clemson Univ, 80-87. *Mem:* Am Statist Asn; Math Asn Am; Opers Res Soc Am. *Res:* Mathematical and statistical modeling; network and location problems; environmental sciences. *Mailing Add:* Dept Math Sci Clemson Univ Clemson SC 29634

SHIER, WAYNE THOMAS, TOXINS, SINGLE CELL PROTEIN. *Current Pos:* assoc prof, Dept Pharmaceut Cell Biol, 80-85, PROF, DEPT MED CHEM, UNIV MINN, 85- *Personal Data:* b Harriston, Ont, Dec 1, 43; m 69, Gloria C Bulan; c John T, Maria T & Anna C. *Educ:* Univ Waterloo, BSc, 66; Univ Ill, Urbana, MS, 68, PhD(chem), 70. *Prof Exp:* Res assoc biochem, Salk Inst, 70-72, asst res prof, 72-80. *Concurrent Pos:* Am Cancer Soc Dernham jr fel, 70-71; consult, Tokyo Tanabe Co, Ltd, 71 & Marcel Dekker, Inc, 79-; USPHS res grant, 72-80, 85-88 & 88-93; Cystic Fibrosis Found res grant, 78-80; NSF res grant, 80-85, 85-87 & 87-90; ed, J Toxicol-Toxins Rev, 82-; Am Cancer Soc res grant, 83-86; USDA res grant, 93-97. *Mem:* AAAS; Am Soc Biol Chemists; Am Soc Biochem & Molecular Biol; Am Chem Soc; Soc Toxicol; Am Soc Cell Biol; Int Soc Toxinol. *Res:* Structure and synthesis of glycoproteins; phospholipases; cystic fibrosis; cyclic nucleotides; lipids; cytotoxic mechanisms; regulation of prostaglandin synthesis; calcium homeostasis; antiviral agents; single cell protein; mycotoxins; tumor promoters; oncogene inhibitors; antibotic resistance. *Mailing Add:* Dept Med Chem Col Pharm Weaver-Densford Hall Minneapolis MN 55455. *Fax:* 612-624-2974; *E-Mail:* shier001@maroon.tc.umn.edu

SHIFFER, JAMES DAVID, NUCLEAR ENGINEERING. *Current Pos:* nuclear engr, Humbolt Bay Power Plant, Pacific Gas & Energy Co, Eureka, Calif, 61-71, tech mgr, Diablo Canyon Power Plant, Avila Beach, Calif, 71-80, mgr nuclear opers, San Francisco, 80-84, vpres nuclear power generation, 84-90, sr vpres & gen mgr, Nuclear Power Generation Bus Unit, 90-91, EXEC VPRES, PACIFIC GAS & ELECTRIC, SAN FRANCISCO, 91- *Personal Data:* b San Diego, Calif, Mar 24, 38; m 86, Esther Zamora; c James II, Elizabeth (Gonzales), Russell, Bryan (Boots), Jeremy (Hellier) & Marisol (Boots). *Educ:* Stanford Univ, BSChemE, 60, MSChemE, 61. *Prof Exp:* Pres & chief exec officer, PG & E Enterprises, 94-95. *Concurrent Pos:* Bd dirs & pres, PG&E Enterprises, Nuclear Energy Inst, US Oper Servs, 94-95. *Mem:* Am Inst Chem Engrs. *Mailing Add:* Pacific Gas & Electric Co 77 Beale St B32 PO Box 77000 San Francisco CA 94177

SHIFFMAN, BERNARD, COMPLEX VARIABLES. *Current Pos:* assoc prof, 73-77, chair, dept math, 90-93, PROF MATH, JOHNS HOPKINS UNIV, 77- *Personal Data:* b New York, NY, 42; m 65; c 2. *Educ:* Mass Inst Technol, BS, 64; Univ Calif, Berkeley, PhD(math), 68. *Prof Exp:* Moore instr math, Mass Inst Technol, 68-70; assoc prof, Yale Univ, 70-73. *Concurrent Pos:* Mem, Inst Advan Study, 75; res fel, Alfred P Sloan Found, 73-75; vis prof, Univ Kaiserslautern, 77; lectr, Inst Math, Acadeimia Sinica, Beijing, 78, Nordic Summer Sch, Joensuu, Finland, 81; mem, Inst des Hautes Etudes Scientifiques, 79; vis prof, Univ Paris, 81 & 85; ed, Forum Math, 88-95; assoc ed, Am J Math, 90-92, ed, 92-93, ed-in-chief, 93-; vis prof, Univ Grenoble, 92 & 95. *Mem:* Am Math Soc; Math Scis Res Inst. *Res:* Meromorphic mappings; value distribution theory; complex manifolds. *Mailing Add:* Dept Math Johns Hopkins Univ Baltimore MD 21218

SHIFFMAN, CARL ABRAHAM, PHYSICS. *Current Pos:* PROF PHYSICS, NORTHEASTERN UNIV, 67- *Personal Data:* b Boston, Mass, Nov 14, 30; m 56; c 2. *Educ:* Mass Inst Technol, BS, 52; Oxford Univ, DrPhil, 56. *Prof Exp:* Physicist, Nat Bur Standards, 56-60 & Mass Inst Technol, 60-67. *Res:* Low temperature physics; superconductivity. *Mailing Add:* Dept Physics Dana Bldg Rm 111 Northeastern Univ Boston MA 02115

SHIFFMAN, MAX, MINIMAX THEORY, AERODYNAMICS. *Current Pos:* RETIRED. *Personal Data:* b New York, NY, Oct 30, 14; div; c Bernard & David. *Educ:* City Col New York, BS, 35; NY Univ, MS, 36, PhD(math), 38. *Prof Exp:* Instr math, St John's Univ, NY, 38-39 & City Col New York 38-42; res mathematician, US Army, US Off Naval Res & Appl Math Panel, US Off Sci Res & Develop, NY Univ, 41-48, assoc prof math, 46-49; prof math, Stanford Univ, 49-66; prof math, Calif State Univ, Hayward, 67-81; mathematician & owner, Mathematico, 70-90. *Concurrent Pos:* Res mathematician, Rand Co, Santa Monica, Calif, 51; consult mathematician, George Washington Univ, 58-61, US Gov't, 61-62. *Mem:* Math Asn Am; Am Math Soc; Soc Indust & Appl Math. *Res:* Minimal surfaces; stationary extremals; groups; conformal mapping; potential theory; complex variable; calculus of variations; hydrodynamics; aerodynamics; partial differential equations; games; probability; topological and linear space methods in analysis; non-measurable and partially measurable sets. *Mailing Add:* 16913 Meekland Ave Apt 7 Hayward CA 94541-1300

SHIFFMAN, MORRIS A, ENVIRONMENTAL HEALTH. *Current Pos:* assoc prof environ sanit, 64-69, PROF ENVIRON HEALTH, UNIV NC, CHAPEL HILL, 69- *Personal Data:* b New York, NY, Oct 12, 22; m 50; c 2. *Educ:* Middlesex Univ, DVM, 44; Univ Mich, MPH, 45; Nat Vet Sch, Alfort, France, DVet, 49; Univ Pa, MGA, 57, PhD, 67. *Prof Exp:* Qual control supvr, Gen Ice Cream Corp, 45; sr veterinarian, UN Relief & Rehab Admin, 46-47; food & drug sanit supvr, Milwaukee Health Dept, 49-53; chief milk & food sanit, Phila Dept Pub Health, 53-64. *Concurrent Pos:* Mem subcomt food sanit, Nat Res Coun, 59-62, chmn, 62-65; mem food estab sanit adv comt, USPHS, 60-63; adv panel zoonoses, WHO, 61-72; mem comt sanit eng & environ, Nat Acad Sci-Nat Res Coun, 62-65; mem adv panel food hyg, WHO, 72- & Sci Adv Comt, Pan-Am Zoonoses Ctr, 72- *Mem:* AAAS; Am Soc Pub Admin; Sigma Xi. *Res:* Administration of environmental health programs; environmental health policy; project-impact studies in developing countries. *Mailing Add:* 201 Ridgecrest Dr Chapel Hill NC 27514

SHIFFRIN, RICHARD M, PSYCHOLOGY. *Current Pos:* Asst prof psychol, 68-70, assoc prof, 71-73, PROF PSYCHOL, IND UNIV, 73-, LUTHER DANA WATERMAN PROF, 80-, DIR, COGNITIVE PROG, 88- *Personal Data:* b New Haven, Conn, Mar 13, 42. *Educ:* Yale Univ, BA, 64; Stanford Univ, PhD(exp & math psychol), 68. *Concurrent Pos:* Grantee, Pub Health Serv, 68-, NIH, 69-72, NSF, 77-78, Luther Dana Waterman Res Award, 80-, Air Force Off Sci Res, 86-90 & 91-93, NIMH Nat Res Serv Awards, 93-98, NSF, 95-98; vis res asst prof psychol, Rockefeller Univ, 70-71, vis prof, 75-76; fel, John Simon Guggenheim, 75-76; ed, J Exp Psychol Learning Memory & Cognition, 81-84; chmn, Soc Math Psychol, 85; vis prof, Univ Queensland, Brisbane, Australia, 88 & Univ Amsterdam, Neth, 94-95; assoc dir, Inst Study Human Capabilities, Ind Univ, 91-; James McKeen Cattell Sabbatical fel, 94-95. *Mem:* Nat Acad Sci; Soc Exp Psychologists; fel Am Psychol Soc; Am Psychol Asn; Soc Math Psychol; Psychonomic Soc; fel AAAS; Cognitive Sci Soc; Inst Psychol Asn; Int Asn Appl Psychol; Am Acad Arts & Sci. *Res:* Mathematical, computer and parallel distributed models of learning, memory, sensory coding, information processing, forgetting, information retrieval, attention and automatism, organization and structure of memory, control processes in memory. *Mailing Add:* Psychol Dept Ind Univ Bloomington IN 47405. *Fax:* 812-855-1086; *E-Mail:* shiffrin@indiana.edu

SHIFLET, THOMAS NEAL, RANGE MANAGEMENT, ECOLOGY. *Current Pos:* RETIRED. *Personal Data:* b Marysville, Tex, July 25, 30; m 53; c 2. *Educ:* Tex A&M Univ, BS, 51; Univ Calif, Berkeley, MS, 67; Univ Nebr, PhD(range mgt), 72. *Prof Exp:* Area range mgt conservationist, Soil Conserv Serv, USDA, 57- 60, state range conservationist, 60-67, staff range conservationist, 67-70, regional range conservationist, 70-74, chief range conservationist, 74-75, dir, Div Ecol Sci, 75-87. *Concurrent Pos:* Range conservationist, Soil Conserv Serv, USDA, 53-54, work unit conservationist, 54-57. *Mem:* Soc Range Mgt; Soil Conserv Soc Am; Coun Agr Sci & Technol; Nat Asn Conserv Districts. *Mailing Add:* 4859 S Crescent Ave Springfield MO 65804

SHIFLETT, LILBURN THOMAS, MATHEMATICS. *Current Pos:* RETIRED. *Personal Data:* b Adamsville, Ala, Feb 4, 21; m 42; c 2. *Educ:* Univ N Ala, BS, 46; George Peabody Col, MA, 48, PhD(math), 63. *Prof Exp:* Teacher high sch, Ark, 46-48; from instr to assoc prof, Southwest Mo State Univ, 48-58, dir div honors, 65-67, prof math, 58-85, head Dept Math, 68-85. *Res:* Geometry; statistics. *Mailing Add:* 829 S Weller Ave Springfield MO 65802

SHIFLETT, RAY CALVIN, MATHEMATICS. *Current Pos:* assoc prof, 75-80, PROF MATH, CALIF STATE UNIV, FULLERTON, 80- *Personal Data:* b Levensworth, Wash, Dec 3, 39; m 59; c 2. *Educ:* Eastern Wash State Col, BA, 63; Ore State Univ, MS, 65, PhD(math), 67. *Prof Exp:* NSF res asst, Ore State Univ, 66-67; asst prof math, Wells Col, 67-75, chmn dept, 69-75. *Mem:* Math Asn Am; Am Math Soc. *Res:* Analysis, especially measure theory, doubly stochastic measures and Markov operators. *Mailing Add:* 2013 E Union Ave Fullerton CA 92631

SHIGEISHI, RONALD A, PHYSICAL CHEMISTRY. *Current Pos:* ASST PROF CHEM, CARLETON UNIV, 67- *Personal Data:* b Vancouver, BC, Apr 5, 39; m 68. *Educ:* Univ Toronto, BSc, 61; Queen's Univ, PhD(chem), 65. *Prof Exp:* Nat Res Coun fel, 65-67. *Concurrent Pos:* Nat Res Coun res grants, 67-69. *Res:* Surface chemistry of gas-metal systems. *Mailing Add:* Dept Chem Carleton Univ Ottawa ON K1S 5B6 Can

SHIGLEY, JOSEPH E(DWARD), mechanical engineering; deceased, see previous edition for last biography

SHIGO, ALEX LLOYD, PLANT PATHOLOGY. *Current Pos:* RETIRED. *Personal Data:* b Duquesne, Pa, May 8, 30; m 54; c 2. *Educ:* Waynesburg Col, BS, 56; Univ WVa, MS, 58, PhD(plant path), 59. *Honors & Awards:* New Eng Logger Award Outstanding Res, 73; Ciba-Giegy Award, Am Phytopath Soc, 75. *Prof Exp:* Plant pathologist, US Forest Serv, 59-74; chief plant pathologist & leader, Pioneer Proj, 74-86. *Concurrent Pos:* Lectr, Univ Maine; adj prof, Univ NH. *Mem:* Mycol Soc Am; Am Phytopath Soc. *Res:* Decay and discoloration in living trees; physiology of wood-inhabiting fungi; diseases of northern hardwoods; fungi parasitic on other fungi; myco-parasites. *Mailing Add:* 4 Denbow Rd Durham NH 03824

SHIH, ARNOLD SHANG-TEH, PHYSICS. *Current Pos:* RES PHYSICIST SURFACE PHYSICS, NAVAL RES LAB, 75- *Personal Data:* b Shanghai, China, May 17, 43; US citizen; m 69; c 2. *Educ:* Univ Calif, Berkeley, AB, 65; Columbia Univ, PhD(physics), 72. *Prof Exp:* Physicist surface chem, Nat Bur Standards, 72-75. *Mem:* Am Phys Soc. *Res:* Electronic and structural properties at the surface of solids; Van der Waals forces between atoms and solid surfaces. *Mailing Add:* Naval Res Lab Code 6840 4555 Overlook Ave Washington DC 20375-5000

SHIH, CHANG-TAI, systematics, biological oceanography, for more information see previous edition

SHIH, CHING-YUAN G, PLANT PHYSIOLOGY, CROP BREEDING. *Current Pos:* PRES, WINDMILL FLORIST, 81-; PRES, GAZEBO FLORIST, 89- *Personal Data:* b Taiwan, China, May 25, 34; m 67; c 2. *Educ:* Chung Hsing Univ, Taiwan, BS, 58; Nat Taiwan Univ, MS, 62; Univ Calif, Davis, PhD(plant physiol), 68. *Prof Exp:* Fel veg crops, Univ Calif, Davis, 68-69; res assoc, Univ Iowa, 60-71; adj asst prof, 78-81, adj assoc prof bot, 81-, dir, Univ Scanning Electron Micros Lab, 71-81. *Mem:* AAAS; Electron Micros Soc Am; Am Soc Cell Biol. *Res:* Structure of phloem cells in relation to translocation; plant hormones in relation to nucleic acid synthesis; virus-host-relationship in cultured cells; scanning electron microscopy in biology; biological microsculptures. *Mailing Add:* 4255 Campus Dr Suite A 118 Irvine CA 92612

SHIH, CORNELIUS CHUNG-SHENG, fluid mechanics, for more information see previous edition

SHIH, FREDERICK F, FOOD SCIENCE & TECHNOLOGY. *Current Pos:* RES CHEMIST, USDA, 76- *Personal Data:* b China, Dec 11, 36; US citizen; m 77, Betty; c 2. *Educ:* Ft Hays State Univ, MS, 66; La State Univ, PhD(chem), 76. *Mem:* Am Chem Soc; Sigma Xi. *Res:* Textile research on the improvement of cotton fabrics with chemical treatments; chemical and enzymatide modification of food proteins for the improvement of functional properties. *Mailing Add:* 4624 David Dr Kenner LA 70065-3331

SHIH, HANSEN S T, LASER PHYSICS, NONLINEAR OPTICS. *Current Pos:* TECH SPECIALIST & PROJ MGR, XEROX CORP, 79- *Personal Data:* b Shanghai, China, April 15, 42. *Educ:* Mass Inst Technol, BS, 65, MS, 68; Harvard Univ, PhD(appl physics), 70. *Prof Exp:* Res assoc, Dept Physics & Optical Sci Ctr, Univ Ariz, Tucson, 71-75; res physicist, Naval Res Lab, 75-76; sr res physicist, Tech Ctr, Libby-Omens-Ford, 77-79. *Mem:* Am Phys Soc. *Res:* Laser physics; nonlinear optics; acoustics; process modelling of physical processes of industrial interests, including vacuum film deposition, color, fluid dynamics and acoustics. *Mailing Add:* 828 Bradford Circle Lynn Haven FL 32444

SHIH, HSIANG, POLYMER CHEMISTRY. *Current Pos:* res chemist, 70-75, SR RES CHEMIST, PIONEERING RES LAB, TEXTILE FIBERS DEPT, E I DU PONT DE NEMOURS & CO, 75- *Personal Data:* b Chungking, China, Nov 11, 43; m 70. *Educ:* Nat Taiwan Univ, BS, 65; Yale Univ, MPh, 68, PhD(chem), 69. *Prof Exp:* Fel chem, Stanford Univ, 69-70. *Mem:* Am Chem Soc. *Res:* Polymer chemistry and its industrial applications; thermodynamics and other physical chemistry fields. *Mailing Add:* 727 Foxdale Rd Wilmington DE 19803

SHIH, HSIO CHANG, PHYSICS. *Current Pos:* lectr, 67-68, actg chmn dept, 71, ASSOC PROF PHYSICS, ROOSEVELT UNIV, 68- *Personal Data:* b Wuchang, Hupei, China, Apr 1, 37; m 71. *Educ:* Ohio Univ, BSME, 58; Ill Inst Technol, MS, 62, PhD(physics), 68. *Prof Exp:* Mech designer, Precision Transformer Corp, 58-60; asst prof physics, Ill Inst Technol, 68. *Concurrent Pos:* Chmn dept physics & eng sci, 73-77. *Mem:* Am Phys Soc; Am Asn Physics Teachers. *Res:* Electrodynamics. *Mailing Add:* 240 N Linden St Westmont IL 60559

SHIH, JAMES WAIKUO, VIRAL HEPATITIS. *Current Pos:* SR INVESTR, DEPT TRANFUSION MED, NIH, 83- *Personal Data:* b China, July 24, 41; US citizen; m 68, Maria C; c Lorena & Kendra. *Educ:* Chung Hsing Univ, Taiwan, BS, 64; Vanderbuilt Univ, PhD, 70. *Prof Exp:* Mem staff, Molecular Anat Prog, Oak Ridge Nat Lab, 71-78; assoc prof microbiol, Div Molecular Virol & Immunol, Georgetown Univ, 78-80; res microbiologist, Hepatitis Br, Div Blood & Prod, Bur Biologics, Food & Drug Admin, 80-83. *Concurrent Pos:* Adj assoc prof, Dept Microbiol, Sch Med & Dent, Georgetown Univ. *Mem:* Am Soc Microbiol; Am Asn Immunologist. *Res:* Characterization of structure-function relationship by molecular and immunochemical procedures; specific application in clinical and diagnostic research of viral hepatitis and infectious disease pathogens; viral vaccine development and evaluation. *Mailing Add:* Transfusion Transmitted Virus Lab Clin Ctr Nat Inst Health Bethesda MD 20892. *Fax:* 301-402-1360; *E-Mail:* jshih@dtm.cc.nih.gov

SHIH, JASON CHIA-HSING, BIOTECHNOLOGY, MICROBIOLOGY. *Current Pos:* from asst prof to assoc prof, 76-88, PROF POULTRY SCI, NC STATE UNIV, 88- *Personal Data:* b Hunan, China, Oct 8, 39; US citizen; m 67, Jane C H Chien; c 2. *Educ:* Nat Taiwan Univ, BS, 63, MS, 66; Cornell Univ, PhD(biochem), 73. *Prof Exp:* Lectr chem, Tunghai Univ, Taiwan, 66-69; res asst nutrit, Cornell Univ, 69-73; res assoc biochem, Univ Ill, 73-75; sr res assoc poultry sci, Cornell Univ, 75-76. *Concurrent Pos:* Adv, NC-China Coun Adv Bd, 79-; vis lectr, Ministry Agr, China, 82; vis fel, Univ Col, Cardiff, Wales, 83; vis prof, Shenyang Agr Col, China, 85; Nat Taiwan Univ, 86 & Bowman Gray Sch Med, Wake Forest Univ, 91; UNDP specialist to China, 87-93; Pew fel, 91; fel, Arteriosclerosis Res Coun, Am Heart Asn, 92- *Mem:* Poultry Sci Asn; Am Inst Nutrit; Am Soc Microbiol; Soc Chinese Bioscientists Am (secy-treas, 85-86); Am Heart Asn. *Res:* Biotechnology of anaerobic digestion; study of basic microbiology, product utilization and environmental benefits of the bioprocess of anaerobic fermentation of poultry waste; experimental atherosclerosis; study of quail atherosclerosis as a model for pathogenesis; prevention and therapy of atherosclerosis in humans; biodegradation and utilization of feather keratin. *Mailing Add:* Dept Poultry Sci NC State Scott Hallx 7608 Raleigh NC 27695-7608. *Fax:* 919-515-2625

SHIH, JEAN CHEN, BIOCHEMISTRY, PHARMACOLOGY. *Current Pos:* from asst prof to assoc prof, 74-85, prof biochem, 85-88, BOYD & ELSIE WELIN PROF BIOCHEM, SCH PHARM, UNIV SOUTHERN CALIF, 88- *Personal Data:* b Yunan, China, Jan 29, 42; US citizen; m 69; c Jeffrey & Jack. *Educ:* Nat Taiwan Univ, Taipei, BS, 64; Univ Calif, Riverside, PhD(biochem), 68. *Honors & Awards:* Achievement Award, Chinese Am Engrs & Scientists Asn. *Prof Exp:* Scholar biochem, Dept Biol Chem & Psychiat, Sch Med, Univ Calif, Los Angeles, 68-70, asst res biochemist, 70-74. *Concurrent Pos:* Vis assoc prof pharmacol, Dept Pharmacol, Sch Med, Univ Calif, Los Angeles, 81; mem, Psychopath & Clin Biol Res Rev Comt, NIMH, Dept Health & Human Serv, 84-88; mem, Cellular Neurobiol & Psychopharmacol Subcomt, Neurosci Res Rev Comt Dept Health & Human Serv, Nat Inst Mental Health, 90-94; res scientist Award, Nat Inst Mental Health, 90-94; Wellcome vis prof, Burroughs Wellcome Fund & Fed Am Soc Exp Biol. *Mem:* Am Soc Biol Chemists; Am Soc Neurochem; Soc Neurosci; Am Asn Col Pharm; AAAS. *Res:* Molecular mechanism of neurotransmission with emphasis on the structure and function relationship of membrane proteins in central nervous systems; regulation of enzymes and receptors, and their implicaition in aging and in disease states, gene and behavior. *Mailing Add:* Sch Pharm Univ Southern Calif 1985 Zonal Ave Los Angeles CA 90033-1058

SHIH, JENN-SHYONG, WATER SOLUBLE POLYMERS SYNTHESES & APPLICATIONS, VINYL PYRROLIDONE HOMOPOLYMERS & COPOLYMERS. *Current Pos:* sr res chemist, 85-89, res scientist, 89-92, SR RES SCIENTIST, INT SPECIALTY PRODS, 92- *Personal Data:* b Taiwan, Repub China, June 18, 52; US citizen; m, Vicki Chen; c Jason & Jimmy. *Educ:* Nat Taiwan Univ, BS, 75, MS, 77; Carnegie-Mellon Univ, MS, 83, PhD(synthetic polymer chem), 84; Fairleigh-Dickinson Univ, MBA, 92, MA, 96. *Prof Exp:* Res chemist, Union Carbide, 84-85. *Mem:* Am Chem Soc. *Res:* Vinyl amides, monomers and polymers syntheses and applications; water soluble polymers used in the personal care, pharmaceutical and industry applications. *Mailing Add:* Int Specialty Prods 1361 Alps Rd Wayne NJ 07470

SHIH, KWANG KUO, solid state devices & physics, for more information see previous edition

SHIH, THOMAS Y, CANCER RESEARCH, HUMAN GENE THERAPY. *Current Pos:* vis scientist, HIH, 71-75, res chemist, 75-82, head, Oncogene Biochem Group, 82-93, BIOTECHNOL PROG ADV, OFF DIR, HIH, 93- *Personal Data:* b Taipei, Taiwan, July 10, 39; m 68; c 2. *Educ:* Nat Taiwan Univ, MD, 65; Calif Inst Technol, PhD(biochem), 69. *Honors & Awards:* Sci Achievement Award, Chinese Med & Health Asn, 89. *Prof Exp:* Asst biol, Calif Inst Technol, 66-69; res assoc biochem, Brandeis Univ, 69-71. *Concurrent Pos:* Mem, Cellular Biol & Physiol Study Sect, NIH, 92-93; pres, Chinese Med & Health Asn, 92. *Mem:* AAAS; Am Chem Soc; Am Soc Microbiol; NY Acad Sci. *Res:* Oncogenes and cancer; molecular biology of tumor viruses; molecular mechanisms of malignant transformation; human gene therapy. *Mailing Add:* 6820 Marbury Rd Bethesda MD 20817

SHIH, TOM I-PING, THERMAL-FLUIDS & COMPUTATIONAL FLUID DYNAMICS, TURBINE BLADE COOLING. *Current Pos:* assoc prof, 88-93, PROF MECH ENG, CARNEGIE MELLON UNIV, 93- *Personal Data:* b Tainan, China, Dec 16, 52; US citizen; m 77, Audrey Chiu-Hsiao Chang; c Marie C & George C. *Educ:* Nat Cheng Kung Univ, China, BSE, 76; Univ Mich, Ann Arbor, MSE, 78, PhD(mech eng), 81. *Honors & Awards:* Ralph R Teetor Award, Soc Automotive Engrs, 86. *Prof Exp:* Mech engr, Lewis Res Ctr, NASA, 81-82; asst prof mech eng, Univ Fla, 82-87, dir, Comput Fluid Dynamics Lab, 83-88, assoc prof, 87-88. *Concurrent Pos:* Consult, Alcoa Tech Ctr, 90-92, Mid-Mich Res, 93-, Westinghouse PGBU, 96 & Ford Sci Res Lab, 96- *Mem:* Am Inst Aeronaut & Astronaut; Am Soc Mech Engrs. *Res:* Develop and apply computational fluid dynamics to study problems in fluid mechanics, heat transfer and combustion; authored and co-authored 9 computational fluid dynamics codes and over 90 technical papers. *Mailing Add:* Dept Mech Eng Carnegie-Mellon Univ Pittsburgh PA 15213. *Fax:* 412-268-3348; *E-Mail:* ts2k@andrew.cmu.edu

SHIH, TSUNG-MING ANTHONY, NEUROPHARMACOLOGY, NEUROTOXICOLOGY. *Current Pos:* pharmacologist, Biomed Lab, Chem Systs Lab, 78-80, chief, Appl Pharmacol Br, 93-94, PHARMACOLOGIST, US ARMY MED RES INST CHEM DEF, ABERDEEN PROVING GROUND, MD, 80-, CHIEF, NEUROTOXICOL, BR, 96- *Personal Data:* b Taipei, Taiwan, Oct 8, 44; US citizen; m 87, Hui-Mei A Wang; c Liane & Jason. *Educ:* Kaohsiung Med Col, Taiwan, BS, 67; Univ Pittsburgh, PhD(pharmacol), 74. *Prof Exp:* Teaching asst, Columbia Univ, 68-69; teaching asst, Dept Pharmacol, Univ Pittsburgh, 69-71, NIH trainee, 72-74, res asst III, Dept Psychiat, 74-76, res assoc, 76-78. *Concurrent Pos:* Fel, Western Psychiat Inst & Clin, Univ Pittsburgh, 74-76, dean Chinese Lang Sch Baltimore, 82-84, prin, 84-87, chmn bd; bd dirs, Orgn Chinese Ams, Northern Md Chap, 92-95, vpres, 94-95. *Mem:* Sigma Xi; Am Soc Neurochem; Soc Toxicol; Soc Neurosci; Am Soc Pharmacol & Exp Therapeut. *Res:* Central neuropharmacological mechanisms of action of anticholinesterases and their treatment compounds; central neurotransmitter system dynamics and interactions; mechanism of action of anticonvulsants in organophosphorus compound poisoning; published numerous articles and chapters in professional journals and books. *Mailing Add:* US Army Med Res Inst Chem Defense Bldg E-3100 Aberdeen Proving Ground MD 21010-5425. *Fax:* 410-671-1960; *E-Mail:* dr.__tony__shih@ftdetrck__ccmail.army.mil

SHIH, VIVIAN EAN, BIOCHEMICAL GENETICS. *Current Pos:* Dir amino acid lab, Joseph P Kennedy Jr Mem Labs, 67-, asst neurol, 68-75, ASSOC PROF NEUROL, MASS GEN HOSP & HARVARD UNIV MED SCH, 75-, PEDIATRICIAN, MASS GEN HOSP, 88- *Personal Data:* b China, Dec 27, 34; US citizen; m 65; c 2. *Educ:* Col Med, Nat Taiwan Univ, MD, 58. *Honors & Awards:* Javits Neurosci Investr Award. *Concurrent Pos:* Consult & co-prin investr, Mass Metab Disorders Prog, Mass Dept Pub Health, 67-80; consult amino acid metab dis, Walter E Fernald State Sch, Waltham, Mass, 68- & Wrentham State Sch, Wrentham, Mass, 68-70; consult pediat, Cambridge Hosp, Cambridge, Mass, 69-; asst prof neurol, Harvard Med Sch, 70-75; assoc, Ctr Human Genetics, 71-80. *Mem:* Soc Pediat Res; Am Acad Pediat; Am Asn Human Genetics; Am Pediat Soc; Soc Inherited Metabolic Disorders. *Res:* Biochemical genetics and hereditary metabolic disorders. *Mailing Add:* Mass Gen Hosp 149 13th St 6th Floor W Bldg Boston MA 02129-2000

SHIH, WEI JEN, NUCLEAR MEDICINE. *Current Pos:* from asst prof to assoc prof, 81-94, PROF, DIV NUCLEAR MED, DEPT DIAG RADIOL, MED CTR, UNIV KY, 94-; CHIEF NUCLEAR MED, VET ADMIN MED CTR, LEXINGOTN, 90- *Personal Data:* b Taiwan, Oct 22, 36; US citizen; m 68, Jamie L; c Jenny & George. *Educ:* Nat Defense Med Ctr, MD, 63; Am Nuclear Med Bd, 82- *Prof Exp:* Fel nuclear med, Am Nuclear Bd Examiners, 76-79, fel pathol,79-81. *Concurrent Pos:* Attending physician nuclear med, Univ Ky Med Ctr, 81-, Vet Admin Med Ctr, Lexington, 81-, asst chief, 81-90; Fulbright scholar, Univ Bonn, Ger, 89. *Mem:* Soc Nuclear Med; Radiol Soc N Am; Am Roentgenology Soc. *Res:* Imaging study using radionuclear tracers in humans and animals; recently interested in brain and lung imaging using new radiopharmaceutical I-123 IMP or HIPDM. *Mailing Add:* Dept Diag Radiol Univ Ky Med Ctr 971 Edgewater Dr Lexington KY 40502

SHILEPSKY, ARNOLD CHARLES, MATHEMATICS, COMPUTER SCIENCES. *Current Pos:* from asst prof to assoc prof, Wells Col, 74-85, chmn, Div Physics & Math Sci, 78-81 & 83-85, Herbert E Ives Prof Sci, 85-91, PROF MATH, WELLS COL, 85- *Personal Data:* b Norwalk, Conn, Dec 10, 44; m 68, Carol Carter; c Lisa R & Beth C. *Educ:* Wesleyan Univ, AB, 66; Univ Wis-Madison, PhD(math), 71. *Prof Exp:* Asst prof, Ark State Univ, 71-74. *Concurrent Pos:* Proj dir, Exxon Comput Literacy grant, 81-82; Pew vis prof, Cornell Univ, 88, vis fel, Math Sci Inst, Cornell Univ, 97; consult, Digicomp Res Corp, 92- *Mem:* Math Asn Am; Am Math Soc; Asn Women Math; Asn Comput Mach. *Res:* Geometric topology; properties of embeddings in Euclidean spaces; mathematics and computer science education. *Mailing Add:* Dept Math Wells Col Aurora NY 13026. *E-Mail:* ashilepsky@wells.edu

SHILLADY, DONALD DOUGLAS, THEORETICAL CHEMISTRY. *Current Pos:* PROF CHEM, ACAD DIV, VA COMMONWEALTH UNIV, 70- *Personal Data:* b Norristown, Pa, Aug 27, 37; m 68; c 3. *Educ:* Drexel Univ, BS, 62; Princeton Univ, MA, 65; Univ Va, PhD(chem), 70. *Prof Exp:* Fel chem, Univ Va, 69-70. *Mem:* Am Chem Soc; Sigma Xi. *Res:* Quantum chemistry, ab initio and semiempirical computational methods applied to chemical bonding and interpretation of circular dichroism and magnetic circular dichroism of lanthanides in polymers. *Mailing Add:* 12302 Thornridge Lane Midlothian VA 23112-4836

SHILLING, WILBUR LEO, ORGANIC CHEMISTRY, POLYMER CHEMISTRY. *Current Pos:* RETIRED. *Personal Data:* b St Joseph, Mo, Aug 30, 21; wid; c 4. *Educ:* Univ Mo, AB, 42; Univ Notre Dame, MS, 47; Ohio State Univ, PhD(chem), 49. *Prof Exp:* Res chemist, Mallinckrodt Chem Works, 42-46; sr res chemist, Crown Zellerbach Corp, 49-69, supvr polymer-fiber res, 69-72, res assoc, 72-77, proj mgr, Pioneering Res, 78-81. *Mem:* Am Chem Soc. *Res:* Cellulose and carbohydrates; lignin and lignans; consumer paper products; applied polymer research; advanced technology assessment. *Mailing Add:* 10615 SW Highland Dr Tigard OR 97224

SHILLITOE, EDWARD JOHN, ORAL CANCER. *Current Pos:* PROF & CHAIR, DEPT MICROBIOL, DENT BR, UNIV TEX, HOUSTON, 83- *Personal Data:* b Hull, Eng, Sept 13, 47; m 77, Edith Rice; c Laura, Diana & Caroline. *Educ:* Univ London, BDS, 71, PhD(immunol), 76. *Prof Exp:* Fel virol, Dept Microbiol, Hershey Med Ctr, Pa State Univ, 76-78; asst prof oral path, Dent Sch, Univ Calif, San Francisco, 78-83. *Concurrent Pos:* Adj prof med, M D Anderson Cancer Ctr, Houston, 93- *Res:* Etiology of oral cancer, utilizing virological methods; gene therapy of cancer. *Mailing Add:* 8380 Turnberry Dr Manlius NY 13104

SHILMAN, AVNER, ANALYTICAL CHEMISTRY, PHYSICAL CHEMISTRY. *Current Pos:* from asst prof to assoc prof chem, 63-68, PROF CHEM, NEWARK COL ENG, 68- *Personal Data:* b Tel Aviv, Israel, Aug 28, 23; US citizen; m 72. *Educ:* Columbia Univ, MS, 53, MA, 57; Polytech Inst Brooklyn, PhD(chem), 61. *Prof Exp:* Mgr pharm, Shilman Pharmacy, 45-48 & 50-51; fel, Polytech Inst Brooklyn, 61-63. *Mem:* Am Chem Soc. *Res:* Analytical methods and physical chemical principles of chromatographic and electrophoresis processes. *Mailing Add:* 150 E 18th St Apt 11D New York NY 10003-2444

SHILS, MAURICE EDWARD, CLINICAL NUTRITION. *Current Pos:* from asst prof to prof, 62-85, EMER PROF MED, MED COL, CORNELL UNIV, 85- *Personal Data:* b Atlantic City, NJ, Dec 31, 14; m 39; c 2. *Educ:* Johns Hopkins Univ, BA, 37, ScD(nutrit, biochem), 40; NY Univ MD, 58. *Honors & Awards:* Goldberger Award Clinical Nutrition, AMA, 83; Rhoads Lectr, Aspen, 87. *Prof Exp:* Asst biochem, Sch Hyg & Pub Health, Johns Hopkins Univ, 40-41, instr, 41-42; asst biochemist, Edgewood Arsenal, US Dept Army, 42-43, food technologist, Off Qm Gen, 43-45; exec secy subcomt nutrit & indust fatigue, Nat Res Coun, 45-46; instr nutrit & indust hyg, Sch Pub Health, Columbia Univ, 46-49, asst prof nutrit, 49-54; res assoc, Sloan-Kettering Inst, 57-59, head, Surg Metab Lab, 59 & metab lab, 61, assoc mem, 60, asst prof biochem, Sloan-Kettering Div, 59-62,. *Concurrent Pos:* Assoc attend physician, Mem Hosp, New York, 67-72, attend physician, 72-85, dir clin nutrit, 77-85,; exec secy, 76-85, Comm Pub Health, NY Acad Med, consult clin nutrit, 85-, res scholar, 85- *Mem:* AAAS; Am Inst Nutrit; Am Soc Clin Nutrit (pres, 85-86); Soc Exp Biol & Med; Harvey Soc; Am Col Physicians; Sigma Xi. *Res:* Clinical nutrition research; nutrition and metabolism; trace elements in man; intravenous nutrition. *Mailing Add:* 3511 Doncaster Rd Winston-Salem NC 27106-5400. *Fax:* 919-748-5425

SHILSTONE, JAMES MAXWELL, JR, QUALITY CONTROL, SOFTWARE DEVELOPMENT. *Current Pos:* VPRES, SHILSTONE & ASSOCS, 77- & SHILSTONE SOFTWARE, 85- *Personal Data:* b New Orleans, La, Feb 19, 55; m 82; c 1. *Educ:* Rice Univ, BA, 77. *Mem:* Am Concrete Inst; Am Soc Concrete Construct. *Res:* Development of computer programs for concrete technical management relating to quality control and production. *Mailing Add:* 2209 Argyle Circle Plano TX 75023

SHIM, BENJAMIN KIN CHONG, NICKEL CATALYSTS, RESEARCH & DEVELOPMENT. *Current Pos:* CONSULT, 87- *Personal Data:* b Honolulu, Hawaii, May 21, 29; m 53, Elizabeth Aldridge; c Michael, Kenneth, Karen, Linda & Matthew. *Educ:* Univ Rochester, BS, 52; Northwestern Univ, PhD(phys chem), 56. *Prof Exp:* Chemist, Esso Res & Eng Co, 56-62; sr chemist, Lord Corp, 62-68; sr res chemist, Calsicat Div, Mallinckrodt, Inc, 68-86; tech dir, Chem Surveys, Inc, 86-87. *Mem:* Am Chem Soc. *Res:* Heterogeneous catalysts-preparation; characterization and process research and development. *Mailing Add:* 901 Hartt Rd Erie PA 16505-3209

SHIM, JUNG P, MANAGEMENT SCIENCE, INFORMATION TECHNOLOGY. *Current Pos:* assoc prof, 84-89, PROF MGT SCI, MGT & INFO SYSTS, MISS STATE UNIV, 89- *Personal Data:* b Korea, Sept 3, 47; m 80; c 2. *Educ:* Yeungnam Univ, BBA, 71; Seoul Nat Univ, MBA, 73; Univ Nebr, Lincoln, PhD(mgt sci), 83. *Prof Exp:* Grad asst mgt sci, Mgt & Info Systs, Univ Nebr, 78-82; asst prof mgt sci, Mgt & Info Systs, Univ Wis-LaCrosse, 82-84; vis prof, Decision Support Systs, Ga State Univ, 90-91. *Concurrent Pos:* Invited lectr, Numerous univs & Res Insts, Korea, 90-; vis prof, Ga State Univ, 90-91; lectr, US Army Masters Bus Admin Prog, 91. *Mem:* Inst Mgt Sci; Acad Mgt. *Res:* Management Information Systems/DDS; expert systems; hypertext/hypermedia; multiple criteria decision making; coauthored several books and software packages. *Mailing Add:* 603 Shadowood Lane Starkville MS 39759

SHIMABUKURO, FRED ICHIRO, RADIO ASTRONOMY. *Current Pos:* mem tech staff, Electronics Res Lab, 62-74, STAFF SCIENTIST, AEROSPACE CORP, 74- *Personal Data:* b Honolulu, Hawaii, Sept 3, 32; m 67; c 1. *Educ:* Mass Inst Technol, BS, 55, MS, 56; Calif Inst Technol, PhD(elec eng), 62. *Prof Exp:* Mem tech staff, Hughes Aircraft Co, 56-58. *Mem:* Am Astron Soc; Inst Elec & Electronics Engrs. *Res:* Solar radio astronomy; millimeter-wave propagation. *Mailing Add:* 26697 Whitehorn Dr Palos Verdes CA 90275

SHIMABUKURO, RICHARD HIDEO, PLANT PHYSIOLOGY. *Current Pos:* EXP CONSULT, INT ATOMIC ENERGY AGENCY, SUDAN, 84- *Personal Data:* b Hakalau, Hawaii, Sept 20, 33; m 65; c 3. *Educ:* Univ Hawaii, BS, 56; Univ Minn, MS, 62, PhD(plant physiol), 64. *Honors & Awards:* Foreign Res Scientist Award, Japanese Govt, 73; Outstanding Res Award, Weed Sci Soc Am, 88. *Prof Exp:* RES PLANT PHYSIOLOGIST, BIOSCI RES LAB, USDA, 64- *Concurrent Pos:* Expert consult, Int Atomic Energy Agency to the Sudan, 84; distinguished vis scholar, Adelaide Univ, Australia, 90. *Mem:* Fel AAAS; Am Soc Plant Physiol; Weed Sci Soc Am; Scand Soc Plant Physiologists. *Res:* Metabolism of chemical pesticides in plants; mechanism of action of herbicidal chemicals in plants and their metabolism in different plant organs. *Mailing Add:* Biosci Res Lab State Univ Sta Fargo ND 58105

SHIMADA, KATSUNORI, ELECTRONICS ENGINEERING. *Current Pos:* RETIRED. *Personal Data:* b Tokyo, Japan, Mar 12, 22; nat US; m 75, Ikuko Ueno; c Karl & Keiko. *Educ:* Univ Tokyo, BS, 45; Univ Minn, MS, 54, PhD(elec eng), 58. *Honors & Awards:* NASA Cert of Recognition, 71, 73, 75, 77, 78, 81, 83, 84, 86, 88, 89. *Prof Exp:* Engr, Tokyo Shibaura Elec Co, Japan, 45-49; instr elec eng, Univ Minn, 54-58; assoc prof, Univ Wash, 58-64; resident res appointee, Jet Propulsion Lab, Calif Inst Technol, 64-65, res group supvr, 64-80, mgr, Photovoltaic Integration Ctr, 80-85, supvr, Celestial Sensors Group, 85-88; consult, Nat Space Develop Agency, La, 88-93. *Concurrent Pos:* Consult, Boeing Co, Wash, 61-63. *Mem:* Inst Elec & Electronics Engrs; Sigma Xi; Am Inst Aeronaut & Astronaut. *Res:* Celential Sensors; energy conversion; articles published in technical journals and conference proceedings in thermionic energy conversion; granted 4 Japanese patents and 2 US patents. *Mailing Add:* 3840 Edgeview Dr Pasadena CA 91107

SHIMAMOTO, YOSHIO, THEORETICAL PHYSICS, MATHEMATICS. *Current Pos:* RETIRED. *Personal Data:* b Honolulu, Hawaii, Oct 4, 24; m 55, Kimie Sato; c Kiyomi S (Camp) & Ken. *Educ:* Univ Hawaii, AB, 48; Harvard Univ, AM, 51; Univ Rochester, PhD(physics), 54. *Honors & Awards:* Sr Scientist Award, Alexander von Humboldt-Stiftung, 72. *Prof Exp:* Assoc physicist, Brookhaven Nat Lab, 54-58, physicist, 58-64, chmn, Dept Appl Math, 64-75, sr scientist, 64-87. *Concurrent Pos:* Vis res prof digital comput lab, Univ Ill, Urbana, 64, consult, Dept Comput Sci, 67-83; mem math & comput sci res adv comt, US AEC, 65-72, chmn, 69-71; adj prof dept math statist, Columbia Univ, 71-72; vis prof math inst, Hanover Tech Univ, 72-73; assoc ed, J Comput Physics, 75-77; pvt consult, 87-91. *Res:* Reactor and particle physics; computer design; graph theory. *Mailing Add:* 158 Donegan Ave East Patchogue NY 11772

SHIMAMURA, TETSUO, PATHOLOGY. *Current Pos:* PROF PATH, ROBERT WOOD JOHNSON MED SCH, UNIV MED & DENT NJ. *Personal Data:* b Yokohama, Japan, Feb 18, 34; m 60, Yoko Ono; c Akiko & Masako. *Educ:* Yokohama Munic Univ, MD, 59, PhD, 88. *Prof Exp:* Intern med, US Army Med Command, Japan, 59-60; residency in path, Sch Med, Washington Univ, 61-64; resident, Methodist Hosp, Houston, Tex, 64-65; res asst, Baylor Sch Med, & resident res assoc, Vet Admin Hosp, Houston, 65-66; asst prof, Baylor Sch Med, 66; asst prof, Univ SDak, 67-68; from asst prof to assoc prof path, Rutgers Med Sch, 68-75, prof, 75- *Mem:* Int Acad Path; Am Soc Nephrol; Int Soc Nephrol; Am Soc Invest Path; AAAS; NY Acad Sci. *Res:* Renal pathology; experimental amyloidosis and hydronephrosis; experimental chronic renal disease; nutrition and glomerular diseases. *Mailing Add:* Robert Wood Johnson Med Sch 675 Hoes Lane Piscataway NJ 08854. *Fax:* 732-235-4825; *E-Mail:* shimamte@umdnj.edu

SHIMAN, ROSS, BIOCHEMISTRY & ENZYMOLOGY, KINETICS. *Current Pos:* PROF BIOL CHEM, M S HERSHEY MED CTR, PA STATE UNIV, 69- *Personal Data:* b Washington, DC, May 22, 38; m 64; c 2. *Educ:* Columbia Col, BA, 60; Univ Calif, Berkeley, PhD(biochem), 65. *Prof Exp:* Res chemist, NIH, 65-68. *Mem:* AAAS; Am Soc Biol Chemists. *Res:* Mechanism of phenylalanine hydroxylase action; regulation of enzyme expression and activity in mammalian cells. *Mailing Add:* Dept Biochem & Molecular Biol Hershey Med Ctr Pa State Univ Hershey PA 17033

SHIMANEK, SCHUYLER EDWYN, INTEGRATED CIRCUIT DESIGN. *Current Pos:* Failure anal engr, 84-90, SR DESIGN ENGR, PHILIPS SEMICONDUCTORS, 90- *Personal Data:* b Eugene, Ore, Aug 12, 59; m 81, JoAnne; c Jared, Rebecca, Julie & Kristen. *Educ:* Brigham Young Univ, BS, 84, MS, 88. *Mem:* Inst Elec & Electronics Engrs. *Res:* Design and development of low power complex programmable logic integrated circuits fabricated using deep submicron complementary metal-oxide semiconductor transistor technology. *Mailing Add:* 9221 Holm Bursun Dr NW Albuquerque NM 87114. *E-Mail:* schuylen.shamanek@abq.sc.philips.com

SHIMANUKI, HACHIRO, INSECT PATHOLOGY, APICULTURE. *Current Pos:* res leader, 85-87, res microbiol, Beneficial Insects Lab, Agr Res Serv, 87-, RES LEADER, USDA. *Personal Data:* b Kahului, Hawaii, July 25, 34; m 58, 83; c 3. *Educ:* Univ Hawaii, BA, 56; Iowa State Univ, PhD(bact), 63. *Honors & Awards:* J I Hambleton Mem Award, 78; First Apicult Res Award, Apiary Insp Am, 78. *Prof Exp:* Res microbiologist, Bioenviron Bee Lab, 63-66, invest leader, 66-72, microbiologist, 72-75, lab chief. *Concurrent Pos:* Ed, Apidologie, 82- *Mem:* Am Soc Microbiol; Entom Soc Am; Soc Invert Path; Am Beekeeping Fedn; Sigma Xi; Am Honey Prod; Am Asn Prof Apicult. *Res:* Diseases of honey bees; computer simulation of honey bee populations; honey bee nutrition; parasitic bee mutes. *Mailing Add:* Bee Res Lab Bldg 476 Barc-E Beltsville MD 20705

SHIMAOKA, KATSUTARO, ONCOLOGY, THYROIDOLOGY. *Current Pos:* FAC, MED CTR, HARBOR-UCLA CALIF, LOS ANGELES, 94- *Personal Data:* b Nara, Japan, Sept 4, 31; m 56, Tomoko Suzuki; c Julia E & Eva E. *Educ:* Keio Univ, Japan, MD, 55. *Prof Exp:* Intern, St Luke's Hosp, Denver, Colo, 56-57; resident med, Louisville Gen Hosp, Ky, 57-58; resident med, Roswell Park Mem Inst, Buffalo, NY, 58-59, fel 59-61; res asst, Univ Col Hosp Med Sch, London, 61-63; sr res assoc, Roswell Park Mem Inst, 63-65, sr cancer res scientist, 65-67, cancer res internist I, 67-69, cancer res internist II, 69-79, assoc chief cancer clinician, 79-86; chief Nagasaki Lab, Radiation Effect Res Found, 87-89, assoc chief res, 89-94. *Concurrent Pos:* From res asst prof to res assoc prof, State Univ NY, Buffalo, 71-81, res assoc prof physiol, 72-86, res prof med, 81-94; chief, Endocrinol Clin, E J Meyer Mem Hosp, Buffalo, 74; mem consult staff med, Erie Co Med Ctr, Buffalo, 75-86; attend & consult physician, Vet Admin Med Ctr, Buffalo, 79-94; lectr, Nagasaki Univ Sch Med, 87-94, Res Inst Environ Med, Nagoya Univ, 88-89. *Mem:* Endocrine Soc; Am Asn Cancer Res; Soc Nuclear Med; Am Soc Clin Oncol; Am Thyroid Asn; Am Soc Bone Mineral Res. *Res:* Thyroid and iodine metabolism; radiation induced cancer; cancer chemotherapy; lymphoma and leukemia; consequences of cancer treatment on endocrine organs. *Mailing Add:* Harbor UCLA Med Ctr 1000 W Carson St Torrance CA 90509. *Fax:* 310-533-0627; *E-Mail:* shimaoka@harbor2.humc.edu

SHIMIZU, HIROSHI, OTOLARYNGOLOGY, AUDIOLOGY. *Current Pos:* asst prof, Johns Hopkins Univ, 63-67, assoc prof, Dept Environ Med, 67-70, assoc prof otolaryngol, Dept Pub Health Admin, 70-90, dir, Hearing & Speech Ctr, 76-90, EMER ASSOC PROF OTOLARYNGOL, SCH MED, JOHNS HOPKINS UNIV, 90- *Personal Data:* b Kyoto, Japan, Aug 21, 24; US citizen; m 51, Tokuko Tokunaga; c Yoji & Keiko (Walker). *Educ:* Kyoto Prefectural Univ Med, MD, 49, MScD, 55. *Honors & Awards:* Clin Achievement Award, Am Speech-Lang-Hearing Found, 83; Distinguished Serv Award, Am Auditory Soc, 89, Carhart Mem Award, 91. *Prof Exp:* Asst otolaryngol, Kyoto Prefectural Univ Med, 50-56, instr, 56-57 & 60-63; clin fel, White Mem Hosp, Los Angeles, 57-58; resident otolaryngol, Hosp, 58; res fel audiol, Johns Hopkins Univ, 58-60. *Concurrent Pos:* Prin investr, NIH grants, 65-70; consult med staff, John F Kennedy Inst Ment Handicapped Child, 71-75; consult, Prog Mult Handicapped Hearing Impaired Children, Baltimore City Schs, 75-76; vis prof, Dept Otolaryngol, Ain Shams Univ, Cairo, Egypt, 79, 81, 83, 88 & 89; bd dirs, Hearing & Speech Agency Metrop Baltimore, 80-90; mem bd examrs, speech pathologists, Md, 80-85; mem, Nat Inst Child Health & Human Develop Prog Proj Site Visit, Univ NC Child Develop Prog Res Inst, 81; mem, Am Speech Lang Hearing Asn, Prof Servs Bd Site Visit, Michael Reese Hosp & Med Ctr, David T Siegel Inst Commun Dis, 81, Montefiore Hosp & Med Ctr Speech & Hearing Ctr, Bronx, NY, 82; mem task force, Md State Dept Health & Ment Hyp, Identification Infant Hearing Impairment, 83-85; prin investr, Johns Hopkins Hosp, Dept Health & Human Servs, 83-88; assoc med staff, Mt Washington Pediat Hosp, Baltimore, 89-90. *Mem:* Am Auditory Soc; Am Speech & Hearing Asn; Japan Soc Otolaryngol; Japan Soc Audiol; Acoust Soc Am; Am Electroencephalographic Soc; Am Acad Audiol. *Res:* Auditory evoked potentials in both normal listeners and patients; electrophysiological studies and assessment of auditory disorders by means of evoked potentials, such as cortical response, auditory brain stem response and electrocochleography. *Mailing Add:* 120 Othoridge Rd Lutherville MD 21093

SHIMIZU, KEN'ICHI, crystallography, electron microscopy, for more information see previous edition

SHIMIZU, NOBUMICHI, TRACE ELEMENT GEOCHEMISTRY, GEOCHEMICAL KINETICS. *Current Pos:* sr res sci geochem, 78-88, VIS PROF GEOCHEM, MASS INST TECHNOL, 88-; SR SCI GEOCHEM, WOODS HOLE OCEANOG INST, 88- *Personal Data:* b Tokyo, Japan, Feb 4, 40; m 65; c 2. *Educ:* Univ Tokyo, BSc, 63, MSc, 65, DSc, 68. *Prof Exp:* Instr geol, Univ Tokyo, 68-75; res assoc geochem, Carnegie Inst, Wash, 71-74; assoc prof geochem, Universite de Paris 6, 74-78. *Mem:* Geochem Soc; fel Am Geophys Union; AAAS; NY Acad Sci. *Res:* Distribution of trace elements among minerals; kinetics of geochemical processes; geochemical evolution of the mantle. *Mailing Add:* Dept Geol & Geophys Clark 102B Woods Hole Oceanog Inst Woods Hole MA 02543. *Fax:* 508-457-2175; *E-Mail:* nshimizu@whoi.edu

SHIMIZU, NOBUYOSHI, CELL BIOLOGY, HUMAN GENETICS. *Current Pos:* from asst prof to assoc prof, 77-82, PROF RES & TEACHING, UNIV ARIZ, 82- *Personal Data:* b Osaka City, Japan, Aug 10, 41; m 67; c 1. *Educ:* Nagoya Univ, BA, 65; Inst Molecular Biol, MSc, 67, PhD(molecular biol), 70. *Prof Exp:* Res assoc, Inst Molecular Biol, 70-71; res biologist, Univ Calif, 71-74 & Yale Univ, 74-76. *Concurrent Pos:* Res biologist, Yale Univ, 74-75, vis asst prof, 77; jr fac res award, Am Cancer Soc, 78-80. *Mem:* NY Acad Sci; AAAS; Tissue Cult Asn; Am Soc Cell Biol; Am Soc Biol Chemists. *Res:* Genetic control of mammalian cell surface functions with emphasis on receptor-mediated hormonal signal transfer mechanisms and malignant transformation; parasexual approaches to human genetics and chromosome mapping. *Mailing Add:* 3233 E Elida St Tucson AZ 85716. *Fax:* 520-621-7528; *E-Mail:* shimizu@ccit.arizona.edu

SHIMIZU, YUZURU, NATURAL PRODUCTS CHEMISTRY, PHARMACOGNOSY. *Current Pos:* asst prof pharmacog, 69-73, assoc prof, 73-77, PROF PHARMACOG, UNIV RI, 77-, PROF CHEM. 82- *Personal Data:* b Gifu, Japan, Jan 17, 35; m 63, Hiroko Tan; c Ken Daniel & Keike Hannah. *Educ:* Hokkaido Univ, BS, 58, MS, 60, PhD(pharm sci), 63. *Honors & Awards:* Award, Matsunaga Sci Found, Japan, 69. *Prof Exp:* Scientist, Worcester Found Exp Biol, 63-64; res assoc dept chem, Univ Ga, 64-65; instr pharm sci, Hokkaido Univ, 65-69. *Concurrent Pos:* Water resources grant, 71-75; Dept Health, Educ & Welfare grant, 74-; chmn marine natural prod sect, Gordon Res Conf, 75- *Mem:* Am Chem Soc; Am Soc Pharmacog; Pharmaceut Soc Japan; Sigma Xi. *Res:* Isolation, structural elucidation and synthesis of natural products, especially of marine origins; marine pharmacognosy. *Mailing Add:* Col Pharm Univ RI Kingston RI 02881. *Fax:* 401-874-2181; *E-Mail:* yuzurus@uriacc.uri.edu

SHIMKETS, LAWRENCE JOSEPH, MICROBIOL DEVELOPMENT, MICROBIOL ECOLOGY. *Current Pos:* from asst prof to assoc prof, 82-93, PROF, DEPT MICROBIOL, UNIV GA, 93-, HEAD DEPT, 97- *Personal Data:* b May 16, 52; m 80, Diane Schoettle; c Anthony Tyler. *Educ:* Fla State Univ, BS, 74; Univ Minn, PhD, 80. *Honors & Awards:* Bacawer Res Award, 80. *Prof Exp:* Fel, Stanford Univ, 80-82. *Concurrent Pos:* Pres young investr, NSF, 84-89. *Mem:* Am Soc Microbiol; Am Acad Microbiol; Sigma Xi. *Res:* Bacterial cell-cell interactions and the role they play in regulation of gene expression; microbial diversity, cell movement and gene transfer in aquatic environments. *Mailing Add:* Dept Microbiol Univ Ga Athens GA 30602. *Fax:* 706-542-2674; *E-Mail:* shimkets@bscr.uga.edu

SHIMM, ROBERT A, internal medicine, for more information see previous edition

SHIMONY, ABNER, THEORETICAL PHYSICS, PHILOSOPHY OF SCIENCE. *Current Pos:* assoc prof, 68-73, PROF PHYSICS & PHILOS, BOSTON UNIV, 73- *Personal Data:* b Columbus, Ohio, Mar 10, 28; m 51; c 2. *Educ:* Yale Univ, BA, 48, PhD(philos), 53; Univ Chicago, MA, 50; Princeton Univ, PhD(physics), 62. *Prof Exp:* Instr philos, Yale Univ, 52-53; from asst prof to assoc prof, Mass Inst Technol, 59-68. *Concurrent Pos:* Sr NSF fel, 66-67; fel, Am Coun Learned Soc, 67 & Guggenheim Found fel, 72-73; Luce prof cosmol, Mt Holyoke Col, 81; Nat Endowment Humanities, 91. *Mem:* Am Philos Soc; Am Phys Soc; fel Am Acad Arts & Sci. *Res:* Foundations of quantum mechanics; foundations of statistical mechanics; philosophy of physics; naturalistic epistemology; inductive logic. *Mailing Add:* Eight Dover Rd Wellesley MA 02181

SHIMOTAKE, HIROSHI, CHEMICAL ENGINEERING. *Current Pos:* DIR, ATx TELECOM SYS, 95- *Personal Data:* b Dec 6, 28; US citizen. *Educ:* Nihon Univ, Tokyo, BS, 51; Northwestern Univ, MS, 57, PhD(chem eng), 60. *Prof Exp:* Res engr, Whirlpool Res Labs, 60-63; chem engr & group leader, Argonne Nat Lab, 63-85; sr res engr, Amoco Laser Co, 85-87, mgr, 88-95. *Concurrent Pos:* Adj prof chem eng, Case Western Res Univ 85- *Mem:* Am Chem Soc; Electrochem Soc Japan; Japanese Soc Chem Engrs; Electrochem Soc. *Res:* Energy conversion and storage; high energy electrochemical cells and batteries. *Mailing Add:* PO Box 453 Hinsdale IL 60521

SHIMP, NEIL FREDERICK, ANALYTICAL CHEMISTRY. *Current Pos:* RETIRED. *Personal Data:* b Akron, Ohio, Aug 19, 27; m 49; c 2. *Educ:* Mich State Univ, BS, 50, MS, 51; Rutgers Univ, PhD, 56. *Honors & Awards:* R A Glenn Award, Am Soc Testing & Mat. *Prof Exp:* Res chemist citrus exp sta, Univ Fla, 51-52; asst prof, Rutgers Univ, 56-57; assoc chemist, Ill State Geol Surv, 57-63, chemist head analytical chem sect, 63-73, prin chemist, 73-88. *Mem:* Am Chem Soc; Soc Appl Spectros; Am Soc Test & Mat. *Res:* Geochemistry; trace elements; instrumental analysis; coal chemistry; environmental geology; spectrochemistry. *Mailing Add:* 2900 Oak Ct Spring Lake MI 49456

SHIMURA, GORO, MATHEMATICS. *Current Pos:* vis prof, 62-64, PROF MATH, PRINCETON UNIV, 64 - *Personal Data:* b Hamamatsu, Japan, Feb 23, 30; m 59; c 2. *Educ:* Univ Tokyo, BS, 52, DSc(math), 58. *Honors & Awards:* Cole Prize in Number Theory, Am Math Soc, 77. *Prof Exp:* Asst prof math, Univ Tokyo, 57-61; prof, Univ Osaka, 61-64. *Concurrent Pos:* Res mem, Nat Ctr Sci Res, Paris, France, 57-58; mem, Inst Advan Study, 58-59, 67, 70-71 & 74-75; John Simon Guggenheim fel, 70-71. *Mem:* Am Math Soc; Math Soc Japan. *Res:* Number theory; automorphic functions; algebraic geometry. *Mailing Add:* Princeton Univ Princeton NJ 08544-0001

SHIN, ERNEST EUN-HO, DENSITY MATRIX THEORY, RECIPROCITY PRINCIPLE. *Current Pos:* DIR, CHESTNUT HILL INST, 84-, CHMN & CHIEF EXEC OFFICER, CHESTNUT HILL GROUP, 89- *Personal Data:* b Chindo, Korea, Dec 31, 35; US citizen; m 63, Shin-Ai Park; c Irene, Juliet, Mariette & Michelle. *Educ:* Carneigie Inst Technol, BS, 57; Harvard Univ, Am, 60, PhD(physics), 61. *Prof Exp:* Res assoc physics, Advan Res Div, Arthur D Little, Inc, 60-62; res assoc, Nat Magnet Lab, Mass Inst Technol, 62-66; prof, Univ Miami, 66-72; dir, Nieman Inst, 72-74; chmn & chief exec officer, Yulsan Am, Inc, 74-89. *Concurrent Pos:* Vis scientist, Korea Atomic Energy Res Inst, 73-74. *Mem:* Am Physical Soc; NY Acad Sci; AAAS; Int Platform Asn. *Res:* Quantum theory of optical and electrical properties of solids; nonlocal field theory and symmetry properties of elementary particles; nonlinear optical properties of electrons. *Mailing Add:* Chestnut Hill Inst PO Box 3510 Napa CA 94558. *Fax:* 707-253-8058; *E-Mail:* eunho@aol.com

SHIN, HYUNG KYU, PHYSICAL CHEMISTRY, THEORETICAL CHEMISTRY. *Current Pos:* from asst prof to assoc prof, 65-70, chmn dept, 76-80, PROF PHYS CHEM, UNIV NEV, RENO, 70-, CHMN DEPT, 91- *Personal Data:* b Kochang, Korea, Sept 3, 33; m 63; c 3. *Educ:* Univ Utah, BS, 59, PhD(phys chem), 61. *Honors & Awards:* Award, Sigma Xi Soc, 61. *Prof Exp:* Res chemist, Nat Bur Stand, Washington, DC, 61-63; fel theoret chem, Cornell Univ. 63-65. *Concurrent Pos:* Petrol Res Fund grant, 65-67; Air Force Off Sci Res grant, 67-78; vis res prof, Univ Calif, Berkeley, 80; Petrol Res Fund grant, 81-84; univ found prof, Univ Nev, Reno, 84-87, fel, Ctr Advan Study, 84- *Mem:* Am Phys Soc; Sigma Xi; Am Chem Soc. *Res:* Theory of inelastic collisions; theory of non-equilibrium rate processes; dynamics of weakly bound complexes. *Mailing Add:* Dept Chem Univ Nev Reno NV 89557-0901

SHIN, HYUNGCHEOL, DEVICES & PROCESS ENGINEERING. *Current Pos:* researcher, 90-93, instr integrated circuit devices, 93, FEL, UNIV CALIF, BERKELEY, 94- *Personal Data:* m 90, Heejung; c Alice. *Educ:* Seoul Nat Univ, BS, 85, MS, 87; Univ Calif, Berkeley, PhD(elec eng), 93. *Prof Exp:* Teaching asst semiconductor properties, Seoul Nat Univ, 85-86, res asst, 85-87; res asst, Inter-Univ Res Ctr, 87-89. *Concurrent Pos:* Intern, Appl Mats, 92-93. *Mem:* Inst Elec & Electronics Engrs. *Res:* Characterizing oxide damage by plasma etching of polysilicon, aluminum and oxide; study on oxide and transister reliability. *Mailing Add:* Elec Eng Dept Adv Inst Sci & Technol 373-1 Kusong Dong Taejon Yusong-Gu 305-701 South Korea. *E-Mail:* hcshin@eekaist.kaist.ac.kr

SHIN, KJU HI, CHEMISTRY. *Current Pos:* RETIRED. *Personal Data:* b Pusan, Korea, Nov 11, 29; US citizen; c 3. *Educ:* Seoul Nat Univ, BS, 52; Univ Frankfurt, MS, 58, PhD(chem), 60. *Prof Exp:* Fel & res assoc, Cornell Univ, 60-62; Nat Res Coun Can fel, 62-63; staff chemist res labs, UniRoyal Co, Can, 63-66; res chemist, Ethyl Corp, 66-75, res adv, 75-94. *Mem:* Am Chem Soc; Korean Chem Soc; Korean Scientists & Engrs Am. *Res:* Organic synthesis and catalysis; antioxidants; oxidation; synthesis of fine chemicals. *Mailing Add:* 4037 Lake Sherwood Ave Baton Rouge LA 70816

SHIN, MOON L, NEUROIMMUNOLOGY. *Current Pos:* Assoc prof, 78-85, PROF, DEPT PATH, UNIV MD, BALTIMORE, 85- *Personal Data:* b Seoul, Korea, Feb 1, 38. *Educ:* Korean Univ, MD, 62. *Mem:* Am Asn Immunologists; Am Asn Pathologists. *Mailing Add:* Dept Pathol Sch Med Univ Md 105 Pine St MSTF 600E Baltimore MD 21201-1116. *Fax:* 410-706-7706

SHIN, MYUNG SOO, RADIOLOGY. *Current Pos:* from asst prof to assoc prof, 69-75, PROF RADIOL, SCH MED, UNIV ALA, BIRMINGHAM, 75- *Personal Data:* b Seoul, Korea, May 5, 30; m 60, Soon Cha; c Joseph H, Jordan T & Joel L. *Educ:* Seoul Nat Univ, MD, 56, PhD(radiol), 67. *Prof Exp:* Instr radiol, Sch Med, Seoul Nat Univ, 63-67, asst prof, 67-68. *Concurrent Pos:* Consult, Radiol Serv, Vet Admin Hosp, Birmingham, 68- *Mem:* AMA; fel Am Col Radiol; Radiol Soc NAm; Am Roentgen Ray Soc; Asn Univ Radiol; Soc Thoracic Radiol; fel Am Col Chest Physicians. *Res:* Chest imaging: computed tomography and magnetic resonance imaging; published over 150 science articles and papers. *Mailing Add:* Dept Diag Radiol Univ Ala Hosp Birmingham AL 35233. *Fax:* 205-934-1526

SHIN, SEUNG-IL, genetics, cell biology, for more information see previous edition

SHIN, SOO H, ii-vi semiconductors, infrared detectors, for more information see previous edition

SHIN, YONG AE IM, INORGANIC CHEMISTRY, MOLECULAR BIOLOGY. *Current Pos:* fel, 65-67, RES CHEMIST, GERONT RES CTR, NIH, 67- *Personal Data:* b Seoul, Korea, Aug 2, 32; m 61; c 3. *Educ:* Tift Col, BA, 56; Ohio State Univ, MSc, 58, PhD(chem), 60. *Prof Exp:* Res fel chem, Univ Ill, 61-62; res assoc chem, Ohio State Univ, 62-64. *Concurrent Pos:* Mem, Health Sci Admin, Nat Inst Aging, Nat Inst Diabetes & Digestive Dis & Kidney, Nat Inst Gen Med Sci. *Mem:* Biophys Soc; Am Soc Biol Chemists; Korean Scientists & Engrs Am; fel Am Inst Chemists. *Res:* Stereospecificity in coordination compounds; the role of metals in nucleic acids and proteins; structure and function of nucleic acids and nucleoproteins; aging; polymorphism of nucleic acids. *Mailing Add:* NIH 45 Center Dr Rm 4AU-38B Bethesda MD 20892

SHIN, YONG-MOO, NUCLEAR PHYSICS. *Current Pos:* from asst prof to assoc prof, 65-75, PROF PHYSICS & DIR ACCELERATOR LAB, UNIV SASK, 75- *Personal Data:* b Seoul, Korea, June 14, 31; m 56; c 2. *Educ:* Yonsei Univ, Korea, BS, 57; Univ Pa, MS, 60, PhD(physics), 63. *Prof Exp:* From res assoc to asst prof, Univ Tex, 63-65. *Mem:* Can Asn Physics; Can Nuclear Soc; Am Phys Soc. *Res:* Nuclear structure and reaction mechanism. *Mailing Add:* Dept Physics Univ Sask Saskatoon SK S7N 0W0 Can

SHINDALA, ADNAN, SANITARY ENGINEERING. *Current Pos:* from asst prof to assoc prof sanit eng, 67-77, PROF ENVIRON ENG, MISS STATE UNIV, 77-; PRIN, COOK COGGIN ENGRS, INC, 76- *Personal Data:* b Mosul, Iraq, July 1, 37; m 64; c 3. *Educ:* Univ Baghdad, BSc, 58; Va Polytech Inst, MSc, 61, PhD(civil eng), 64. *Prof Exp:* Asst resident engr, Govt Iraq, 59-60; asst prof civil eng, Lehigh Univ, 64-65; lectr, Univ Baghdad, 65-67. *Concurrent Pos:* Vpres, Cook Coggin Engrs, Inc; Herrin-Hess outstanding prof civil eng, 89. *Mem:* Am Soc Civil Engrs; Water Pollution Control Fedn; Am Water Works Asn; Am Water Resources Asn; Asn Environ Eng Prof. *Res:* Water resources engineering; water quality modeling; water and waste treatment. *Mailing Add:* 1106 Nottingham Rd Starkville MS 39759

SHINE, ANDREW J(OSEPH), MECHANICAL ENGINEERING. *Current Pos:* from asst prof to assoc prof, 49-58, PROF MECH ENG & HEAD DEPT, US AIR FORCE INST TECHNOL, 58- *Personal Data:* b Cass, WVa, Jan 3, 22; m 46; c 5. *Educ:* Rensselaer Polytech Inst, BME, 46, MME, 47; Ohio State Univ, PhD(mech eng), 57. *Prof Exp:* Asst, Univ Minn, 47-48; instr & asst, Rensselaer Polytech Inst, 48-49. *Mem:* Am Soc Mech Engrs; Am Soc Eng Educ. *Res:* Heat transfer; fluid flow. *Mailing Add:* 2065 SR 235 Xenia OH 45385

SHINE, ANNETTE DUDEK, CHEMICAL ENGINEERING. *Current Pos:* ASST PROF CHEM ENG, DEPT CHEM ENG, UNIV DEL, 89- *Personal Data:* b Toledo, Ohio, Jan 20, 54; m 81; c 2. *Educ:* Wash Univ, BS & AB, 76; Case Western Res Univ, MSE, 79; Mass Inst Technol, PhD(chem eng), 83. *Prof Exp:* Res scientist, Eastman Kodak Co, 82-85; asst prof chem eng, Colo Sch Mines, 86-88. *Mem:* Am Inst Chem Engrs; Am Chem Soc; Soc Women Engrs; Soc Rheology. *Res:* Relationship between structure and processing of polymeric materials, especially liquid crystalline polymers and polymer blends and composites. *Mailing Add:* 4 Karen Circle Newark DE 19713

SHINE, CARL, CORROSION, MOS-SEMICONDUCTOR PHYSICS. *Current Pos:* PVT CONSULT, 91- *Personal Data:* b Newton Center, Mass, Feb 27, 37. *Educ:* Univ Pa, BS, 59, PhD(metal), 68; Mass Inst Technol, MS, 61, Engrs, 62. *Prof Exp:* Staff engr, Thomas J Watson Labs, IBM, 68-70, E Fishkill, NY, 70-73; sr scientist, TRW Philadelphia Labs, 73-75; prin metallurgist, Fischer & Porter, Warminster, Pa, 76-79; sr scientist, P R Mallory, Burlington, Mass, 79-80; sr metallurgist, Raytheon Corp, Waltham, Mass, 80-81; prin engr, Digital Equip, Andover, Mass, 81-88, consult engr, Cupertino, Calif, 88-91. *Concurrent Pos:* Consult, Fischer & Porter Corp, Warminster, Pa, 75-76; Nat Semiconductor Corp, Santa Clara, Calif, 93-94 & Siliconix, Santa Clara, Calif, 95- *Res:* Metallurgical kinetics; thermal fatigue, creep, superplasticity in solder joints; MOS semiconductor physics; fast states, concentration profiling analysis, dielectric trapping analysis; corrosion, electromigration, dielectric relaxation; metal/plastic adhesion; surface mount technology (smt). *Mailing Add:* 11592 Bridge Park Ct Cupertino CA 95014. *Fax:* 408-252-7941

SHINE, DANIEL PHILLIP, cosmetic chemistry, for more information see previous edition

SHINE, HENRY JOSEPH, ORGANIC CHEMISTRY. *Current Pos:* from asst prof to prof chem, 54-68, chmn dept, 69-75, PAUL WHITFIELD HORN PROF CHEM, TEX TECH UNIV, 68- *Personal Data:* b London, Eng, Jan 4, 23; m 53; c 2. *Educ:* London Univ, BSc, 44, PhD(chem), 47. *Prof Exp:* Chemist, Shell Develop Co, Eng, 44-45; res fel org chem, Iowa State Univ, 48-49; res fel, Calif Inst Technol, 49-51; res chemist, US Rubber Co, 51-54. *Concurrent Pos:* Distinguished Sr US Scientist Award, Alexander von Humboldt Found, 86-87. *Mem:* AAAS; Am Chem Soc; Royal Soc Chem; Sigma Xi. *Res:* Reaction mechanisms; aromatic rearrangements; organosulfur chemistry; ion radical reactions; electron spin spectroscopy; heavy-atom kinetic isotope effects. *Mailing Add:* Dept Chem & Biochem Tex Tech Univ Lubbock TX 79409

SHINE, KENNETH I, MEDICAL ADMINISTRATION. *Current Pos:* from asst prof to prof med, Sch Med, Univ Calif, Los Angeles, 71-92, dir Coronary Care Unit, 71-75, chief, Div Cardiol, 75-79, vchmn, Dept Med, 79-81, exec chmn, 81-86, dean, Sch Med, 86-92, provost med sci, 91-92, EMER PROF MED, SCH MED, UNIV CALIF, LOS ANGELES, 93-; PRES, INST MED-NAT ACAD SCI, WASHINGTON, DC, 92-; CLIN PROF MED, GEORGETOWN UNIV, 93- *Personal Data:* b Worcester, Mass; m, Carolyn; c Rebecca & Daniel. *Educ:* Harvard Univ, MD, 61. *Hon Degrees:* DSc, Univ Mass & NY Med Col, 93, Med Col Pa, 94. *Honors & Awards:* Third Ann Harold Mazur Lectr, Cedars-Sinai Med Ctr, 89; Howard Schneiderman Distinguished Lectr, Univ Calif, Los Angeles, 92; Gennaro Tisi Mem Lectr, Univ Calif, San Diego, 93; August J Carroll Lectr, Asn Am Med Col, 93; Am Urol Lectr, Am Col Surgeons, 94; 16th Joseph Mountin Lectr, Ctr Dis Control & Prev, 95; Adam Linton Lectr, Ont Med Asn, 96. *Prof Exp:* Assoc med, Beth Israel Hosp, Boston, 61; intern, Mass Gen Hosp, 61-62, res, 62-63 & 65-66, fel cardiologist, 66-68; assoc med, Beth Israel Hosp, Boston, 61-71. *Concurrent Pos:* Surgeon, USPHS, 63-65; instr med, Harvard, 68; vis prof numerous US & foreign univs, 70-; consult, NSF & NIH, 87-88. *Mem:* Nat Acad Sci; Inst Med-Nat Acad Sci (pres, 92-); Sigma Xi; Am Fedn Clin Res; Am Heart Asn; Am Psychol Soc; Asn Am Physicians; fel Am Acad Arts & Sci; fel Am Col Cardiol; fel Am Col Physicians; Soc Med Adminr. *Res:* Metabolic events in the heart muscle; relation of behavior to heart disease and emergency medicine; author of numerous articles and scientific papers. *Mailing Add:* Inst Med 2101 Constitution Ave NW Washington DC 20418. *Fax:* 202-334-1694

SHINE, ROBERT JOHN, ORGANIC CHEMISTRY, COMPUTER SCIENCE. *Current Pos:* from asst prof to assoc prof, 71-74, PROF CHEM, RAMAPO COL, NJ, 74-, PROF COMPUT SCI, 85- *Personal Data:* b Orange, NJ, May 21, 41; m 67, Dorothy McCaffrey; c Robert Jr, Daniel & Margaret. *Educ:* Seton Hall Univ, BS, 62; Pa State Univ, PhD(org chem), 66; Stevens Inst Techonol, MSc, 85. *Prof Exp:* Teaching asst, Pa State Univ, 62; res chemist, Walter Reed Army Inst Res, 67-69; asst prof chem, Trinity Col, DC, 69-71. *Mem:* Am Chem Soc; Sigma Xi; Asn Comput Mach. *Res:* Structural determination of alkaloids; chemistry of organic sulfur and organic selenium compounds; database systems design. *Mailing Add:* Sch Theoret & Appl Sci Ramapo Col Mahwah NJ 07430-1680

SHINE, TIMOTHY D, ORGANIC CHEMISTRY. *Current Pos:* asst prof, 67-71, assoc prof, 71-77, PROF CHEM, 77-, CHAIR CHEM DEPT, CENT CONN STATE UNIV, 84- *Personal Data:* b New York, NY, June 6, 39. *Educ:* Merrimack Col, BS, 60; Univ Conn, PhD(org chem), 67. *Prof Exp:* Asst instr chem, Univ Conn, 62-66; res assoc, Univ Mich, 66-67. *Mem:* Sigma Xi; Am Chem Soc. *Res:* Acyl and alkoxy group migrations between oxygen and nitrogen in oo-aminophenols; sulfur and nitrogen in o-aminothiophenols. *Mailing Add:* Dept Chem Cent Conn State Univ 1615 Stanley St New Britain CT 06053-2439

SHINE, WILLIAM MORTON, organic chemistry, for more information see previous edition

SHINEFIELD, HENRY R, MEDICINE, PEDIATRICS. *Current Pos:* chief, 65-68, EMER CHIEF PEDIAT, KAISER FOUND HOSP, 68-; CLIN PROF, SCH MED, UNIV CALIF, SAN FRANCISCO, 68- *Personal Data:* b Paterson, NJ, Oct 11, 25; m 83, Jacqueline Walker; c Jill, Michael, Kim (Strome) & Melissa (Strome). *Educ:* Columbia Univ, AB, 44, MD, 48; Am Bd Pediat, dipl, 54 & 88. *Prof Exp:* From asst prof to assoc prof pediat, Med Col, Cornell Univ, 59-65; chief, 65-68, EMER CHIEF PEDIAT, KAISER FOUND HOSP, 68- *Concurrent Pos:* Nat Found res fel, 59-61; Lederle med fac award, 61-63; assoc clin prof, Univ Calif, San Francisco, 66-68; chief pediat, Permanente Med Group, San Francisco; mem bact & mycol study sect, Res Rev Br, NIH, 70-74; co-dir, Kaiser-Permanente Vaccine Res Ctr, 65-; co-dir, Vaccine Study Ctr, 84- *Mem:* Inst Med-Nat Acad Sci; fel Am Acad Pediat; Soc Pediat Res; Infectious Dis Soc Am; Am Pediat Soc; Am Bd Pediat. *Res:* Infectious diseases; epidemiology; medical care. *Mailing Add:* 2200 O'Farrell St San Francisco CA 94115. *Fax:* 415-202-3566

SHINEMAN, RICHARD SHUBERT, INORGANIC CHEMISTRY. *Current Pos:* PROF CHEM, STATE UNIV NY COL, OSWEGO, 62- *Personal Data:* b Albany, NY, May 21, 24. *Educ:* Cornell Univ, AB, 45; Syracuse Univ, MS, 50; Ohio State Univ, PhD(inorg chem), 57. *Prof Exp:* From instr to asst prof chem, Purdue Univ, 59-62. *Concurrent Pos:* Chmn dept chem, State Univ NY Col, Oswego, 62-67. *Mem:* AAAS; Am Chem Soc. *Res:* Inorganic nitrogen chemistry; x-ray crystallography. *Mailing Add:* 308 Washington Blvd Oswego NY 13126

SHINER, EDWARD ARNOLD, ORGANIC CHEMISTRY. *Current Pos:* RETIRED. *Personal Data:* b Chicago, Ill, Feb 18, 24; m 51; c 3. *Educ:* Northwestern Univ, BS, 47; Univ Wis, PhD(chem), 51. *Prof Exp:* Instr chem, Univ Wis-Milwaukee, 47-48; res chemist, Food Prod Div, Union Carbide Corp, 51-60, mgr food casing develop, 60-65, tech mgr, 65-69, asst dir res & develop, 69-73, dir res & develop, 73-83; market res, Viskase Corp, 83-90. *Mem:* Am Chem Soc. *Res:* Cellulose; lignin; polymer science. *Mailing Add:* 400 N Linden Ave Oak Park IL 60302

SHINER, VERNON JACK, JR, PHYSICAL ORGANIC CHEMISTRY. *Current Pos:* from instr to assoc prof chem, Ind Univ, Bloomington, 52-60, chmn dept, 62-67, dean, Col Arts & Sci, 73-78, PROF CHEM, IND UNIV, BLOOMINGTON, 60-, CHMN DEPT, 82- *Personal Data:* b Laredo, Tex, Aug 11, 25; m 46; c 3. *Educ:* Tex Western Col, BS, 47; Cornell Univ, PhD(chem), 50. *Prof Exp:* Res assoc org chem, State Agr Exp Sta, NY, 47; Fulbright scholar, London Univ, 50-51; Du Pont fel, Harvard Univ, 51-52. *Mem:* Am Chem Soc; Royal Soc Chem; Sigma Xi. *Res:* Kinetics and mechanisms of organic reactions; deuterium isotope rate effects. *Mailing Add:* Dept Chem Ind Univ Bloomington IN 47405

SHING, YUEN WAN, GROWTH FACTORS, HORMONE RECEPTORS. *Current Pos:* RES ASSOC, CHILDREN'S HOSP, BOSTON, 80- *Personal Data:* b Kunming, China, Apr 29, 45; m 73; c 2. *Educ:* Taiwan Univ, BSc, 66; Univ Kans, PhD(biochem), 74. *Prof Exp:* Res assoc growth factors, State Univ NY, Albany, 74-76; res assoc receptors, Univ Wis-Madison, 76-80; asst prof biochem, Southeastern Mass Univ, North Dartmouth, 80-81. *Concurrent Pos:* Teaching fel biochem, Harvard Univ, 82-84, asst prof surg & biochem, Med Sch, 84- *Mem:* Am Soc Biol Chemists; Am Soc Cell Biol; NY Acad Sci; AAAS. *Res:* Characterization and purification of tumor-derived angiogenic factors; biochemical and physiological properties of polypeptide growth factors, especially those derived from milk; molecular biology of hormone receptors. *Mailing Add:* Dept Surg Biol Chem Children's Hosp Harvard Med Sch 300 Longwood Ave Boston MA 02115-5737. *Fax:* 617-735-7043

SHING, YUH-HAN, thin film materials, device physics, for more information see previous edition

SHINGLETON, HUGH MAURICE, OBSTETRICS & GYNECOLOGY, ONCOLOGY. *Current Pos:* assoc prof, 69-74, asst prof, 69-81, PROF OBSTET & GYNEC, SCH MED, UNIV ALA, BIRMINGHAM, 74-, ASSOC PROF PATH, 81-, CHMN DEPT, MED CTR, 78- *Personal Data:* b Stantonsburg, NC, Oct 11, 31; c 3. *Educ:* Duke Univ, AB, 54, MD, 57; Am Bd Obstet & Gynec, dipl. *Prof Exp:* Intern, Jefferson Med Col Hosp, 57-58; asst resident obstet & gynec, NC Mem Hosp, Chapel Hill, 60-61 & Margaret Hague Maternity Hosp, Jersey City, NJ, 62; resident, NC Mem Hosp, Chapel Hill, 62-63, chief resident, 63-64; from instr to asst prof obstet & gynec, Sch Med, Univ NC, Chapel Hill, 64-69, asst prof path, 68-69. *Concurrent Pos:* Am Cancer Soc fel, Mem Hosp, Chapel Hill, NC, 62-63; Nat Cancer Inst spec fel, Col Physicians & Surgeons, Columbia Univ, 66-67. *Mem:* Am Col Obstet & Gynec; Am Col Surgeons; AMA; Soc Gynec Oncol (secy-treas, 81); Am Gynec Soc. *Res:* Gynecologic oncology; use of electron microscope and clinical research. *Mailing Add:* Dept Obstet & Gynecol Univ Ala Sch Med Old Hillman Bldg Rm 560 618 S 20th St Birmingham AL 35233-7333

SHINKAI, ICHIRO, ORGANIC & ANALYTICAL CHEMISTRY. *Current Pos:* DIR PROCESS CHEM, MERCK, SHARP & DOHME RES LABS, MERCK & CO, INC, 76- *Personal Data:* b Japan, Dec 4, 41; m 66; c 2. *Educ:* Doshisha Univ, BSc, 64, MSc, 66; Kyushu Univ, PhD(org chem), 71. *Prof Exp:* Res asst & lectr org chem, Kyushu Univ, 66-72; res assoc Dept Chem, Univ Ala, 72-76. *Mem:* Am Chem Soc; Japan Chem Soc; Int Union Pure & Appl Chem. *Res:* Synthetic organic chemistry; reaction mechanisms of heterocycles; reactive intermediate. *Mailing Add:* 1101 Prospect St Westfield NJ 07090

SHINKMAN, PAUL G, PHYSIOLOGICAL PSYCHOLOGY. *Current Pos:* from asst prof to assoc prof psychol & neurobiol, 67-77, PROF PSYCHOL & NEUROBIOL, UNIV NC, CHAPEL HILL, 77-, DIR EXP PSYCHOL PROG, 75- *Personal Data:* b New York, NY, June 18, 36; m 69. *Educ:* Harvard Univ, AB, 58; Univ Mich, AM, 62, PhD(psychol), 62. *Prof Exp:* Instr psychol, Univ Mich, 61-62, NIMH fel, Brain Res Lab, 64-66; vis asst prof psychobiol, Univ Calif, Irvine, 66-67. *Mem:* Am Psychol Asn; Psychonomic Soc; Soc Neurosci. *Res:* Central nervous system and behavior. *Mailing Add:* Dept Psychol Univ NC Chapel Hill NC 27599-3270

SHINN, DENNIS BURTON, INORGANIC CHEMISTRY. *Current Pos:* Adv develop engr, Sylvania Lighting Ctr, 68-70, engr in charge chem appln, 70-72, prog mgr high intensity discharge mat, 72-78, PROG MGR MAT ENG LAB, SYLVANIA LIGHTING CTR, 78- *Personal Data:* b Keene, NH, Sept 2, 39; m 60; c 3. *Educ:* Univ NH, BS, 61, MS, 64; Mich State Univ, PhD(chem), 68. *Mem:* Am Chem Soc; Am Crystallog Asn; Am Ceramic Soc; Sigma Xi. *Res:* Synthesis and properties of solid state inorganic materials. *Mailing Add:* 28 Colrain Rd Topsfield MA 01983-1320

SHINN, JOSEPH HANCOCK, METEOROLOGY, POLLUTION ECOLOGY. *Current Pos:* meteorologist pollutant effects, Environ Sci Div, 73-93, METEOROLOGIST AIR PATHWAY ANALYSIS, HEALTH & ECOL ASSESSMENT DIV, LAWRENCE LIVERMORE NAT LAB, 93- *Personal Data:* b Atlantic City, NJ, Jan 4, 38; m 75; c 2. *Educ:* Del Valley Col, BS, 59; Cornell Univ, MS, 62; Univ Wis-Madison, PhD(meteorol), 71. *Prof Exp:* Phys sci aide microclimate, Agr Res Serv, USDA, 59-62; proj asst meteorol, Univ Wis-Madison, 62-67; res meteorologist, US Army Electronics Command, Ft Huachuca, 67-70 & White Sands Missile Range, 70-73. *Concurrent Pos:* Chmn, US Army Electronics Command Res Bd, 71-72; adv tactical environ support study, US Army Intel Sch, 72-73; br chief automatic meteorol systs, US Army Atmospheric Sci Lab, 72-73; dep sect chief environ sci div, Lawrence Livermore Lab, 77-84, sect leader, 85- *Mem:* Sigma Xi; Am Meteorol Soc; Air & Waste Mgt Asn; Am Asn Aerosol Res. *Res:* Dynamics of the atmospheric boundary layer; inhalation exposure and suspension of toxic particles; processes of deposition of gases and particles on vegetation; forest meteorology; air pollution meteorology. *Mailing Add:* Lawrence Livermore Nat Lab L-396 PO Box 808 Livermore CA 94551-9900. *Fax:* 510-423-6785; *E-Mail:* shinn1@llnl.gov

SHINNAR, REUEL, CHEMICAL ENGINEERING. *Current Pos:* prof, 64-79, DISTINGUISHED PROF CHEM ENG, CITY COL NEW YORK, 79- *Personal Data:* b Vienna, Austria, Sept 15, 23; US citizen; m 48; c 2. *Educ:* Israel Inst Technol, BSc, 45; Columbia Univ, ScD(chem eng), 57. *Honors & Awards:* Wilhelm Mem lectr, Princeton Univ, 85; Kelly lectr, Purdue Univ, 91; Founders Award, Am Inst Chem Engrs, 92. *Prof Exp:* Chem engr indust, 45-54; assoc prof chem eng, Israel Inst Technol, 58-62; res assoc aeronaut eng, Princeton Univ, 62-64. *Concurrent Pos:* Consult chem & petrol indust, 64- *Mem:* Nat Acad Eng; AAAS; fel NY Acad Sci; fel Am Inst Chem Engrs; Am Chem Soc. *Res:* Process dynamics and control; process design and economics; industrial economics; chemical reactor design. *Mailing Add:* Dept Chem Eng City Col New York New York NY 10031

SHINNERS, CARL W, PHYSICS. *Current Pos:* assoc prof, Univ Wis, Whitewater, 65-67, chmn dept, 67-71, prof, 67-92, EMER PROF PHYSICS, UNIV WIS, WHITEWATER, 92- *Personal Data:* b Milwaukee, Wis, Aug 13, 28; m 54; c 3. *Educ:* Marquette Univ, PhB, 52; La State Univ, MS, 60, PhD(nuclear spectros), 65. *Prof Exp:* Instr physics, La State Univ, 59-63. *Concurrent Pos:* Wis State res grants, 68 & 70; NSF grants, 70 & 71. *Mem:* AAAS; Am Phys Soc; Am Asn Physics Teachers. *Res:* Beta and gamma ray spectroscopy; nuclear structures; solar energy and energy education. *Mailing Add:* 1919 N Summit Ave Unit 1E Milwaukee WI 53202-1378

SHINNERS, STANLEY MARVIN, ELECTRICAL ENGINEERING, EDUCATION. *Current Pos:* SR RES SECT HEAD, LOCKHEED MARTIN. *Personal Data:* b New York, NY, May 9, 33; m 58, Doris Pinsker; c Sharon R, Walter & Daniel L. *Educ:* City Col New York, BEE, 54; Columbia Univ, MS, 59. *Prof Exp:* Engr, Western Elec Co, 53-55; staff engr, Electronics Div, Otis Elevator Co, 55-56; proj engr, Polarad Electronics Corp, 56-57 & Consol Avionic Corp, 57-58. *Concurrent Pos:* Adj prof, Polytech Inst Brooklyn, 59-71, Cooper Union, 66-73 & 79- & NY Inst Technol, 74-92. *Mem:* Fel Inst Elec & Electronics Engrs; Am Soc Eng Educ. *Res:* Control systems and systems engineering. *Mailing Add:* 28 Sagamore Way N Jericho NY 11753

SHINNICK-GALLAGHER, PATRICIA L, NEUROPHARMACOLOGY, NEUROPHYSIOLOGY. *Current Pos:* instr, 75-76, asst prof, 76-81, ASSOC PROF PHARMACOL, UNIV TEX MED BR, GALVESTON, 81- *Personal Data:* b Chicago, Ill, July 28, 47; m 74; c 2. *Educ:* Univ Ill, BS, 70; Loyola Univ Chicago, PhD(pharmacol), 74. *Prof Exp:* Pharmacist, Nosek Apothecary, 71-73; res assoc neurophysiol, Sch Med, Loyola Univ Chicago, 74-75. *Mem:* AAAS; Am Pharmaceut Asn; Am Soc Pharmacol Exp Therapy; Sigma Xi. *Res:* Pharmacological and physiological dissection of reflex pathways in the isolated spinal cord; analysis of drug action on ganglionic and neuromuscular transmission. *Mailing Add:* Dept Pharmacol & Toxicol Univ Tex Med Br Galveston TX 77555-1031

SHINOHARA, MAKOTO, POLYMER CHEMISTRY, POLYMER SCIENCE. *Current Pos:* TECH DIR, CIBA-GEIGY CORP, 87- *Personal Data:* b Naha, Japan, Jan 30, 37; m 64, Yaeko Tamura; c Mayumi & Elly. *Educ:* Tokyo Inst Technol, BSc, 60, MSc, 62; State Univ NY Col Forestry, PhD(phys chem), 69; Syracuse Univ, PhD(phys chem), 69. *Prof Exp:* Res Found fel, State Univ NY Col Forestry, Syracuse Univ, 64-69; proj chemist, Dow Corning Corp, 69-74, sr proj chemist, 74-75; res assoc, Int Playtex, Inc, 75-78; mgr molding compound res & develop, Morton Chem Co, 78-84; tech mgr, polyset, Dynachem Corp, Morton-Thiokol Inc, 84-87. *Mem:* Am Chem Soc; Am Geog Soc; Sigma Xi; AAAS; NY Acad Sci. *Res:* Structure-mechanical, electrical and physico-chemical property relation in thermo-plastic and thermosetting polymers; polymer composites and toughening; polymer characterization; mechanisms and kinetics of polymerization, polyaddition, polycondensation and ring-opening polymerization; water soluble polymers and gels; organo-silicone polymers. *Mailing Add:* 21202 Georgetown Dr Santa Clarita CA 91350. *Fax:* 818-507-0167

SHINOZUKA, HISASHI, ONCOLOGY. *Current Pos:* PROF PATH, UNIV PITTSBURGH, 79- *Educ:* McGill Univ, Can, PhD(exp path), 63. *Mailing Add:* Dept Path Univ Pittsburgh Sch Med Pittsburgh PA 15261-0001. *Fax:* 412-648-1716

SHINOZUKA, MASANOBU, CIVIL ENGINEERING, ENGINEERING MECHANICS. *Current Pos:* SOLLENBERGER PROF CIVIL ENG, PRINCETON UNIV, 88- *Personal Data:* b Tokyo, Japan, Dec 23, 30; m 54; c 3. *Educ:* Kyoto Univ, BS, 53, MS, 55; Columbia Univ, PhD(civil eng), 60. *Honors & Awards:* Walter L Huber Civil Eng Res Prize, Am Soc Civil Engrs, 72, Am Freudenthal Medal, Nathan M Newmark Medal, 85, Theodore von Karmen Medal, 94; Moisseiff Award, 88; S C Martin Duke Award, 91. *Prof Exp:* Res asst, Columbia Univ, 59-61, from asst prof to prof, 61-77, Renwick prof civil eng, 77-88. *Concurrent Pos:* US coordr, US-Japan Joint Seminars; res analyst, USAF, 67-68; consult, Jet Propulsion Lab, 68- & Kawasaki Heavy Indust, Kobe, Japan, 71; res struct engr, Naval Civil Eng Lab, 70; consult, USAF, Flight Dynamics Lab, Wright-Patterson AFB, Ohio, US Army Mat & Mech Res Ctr, Watertown, Mass, US Navy Strategic Eng Surv Off, Bethesda, Md, US Atomic Energy Comn, US Naval Civil Eng Lab, Port Hueneme, Calif, US Nuclear Res Coun, Adv Comt Reactor Safeguards, Washington, DC; Gen Dynamics, Ft Worth Div, Tex, Northrop Corp, Aircraft Div, Hawthorne, Calif, Rockwell Int, Los Angles, Eng Decision Anal Co, Inc, Palo Alto, US Nuclear Regulatory Comn, Wash, Lawrence Livermore Lab, Livermore, Calif, Kawasaki Heavy Indust, Ltd, Kobe, Japan, Shimizu Construct Co, Tokyo, Japan; dir, Nat Ctr Earthquake Eng Res, State Univ NY, Buffalo, 90- *Mem:* Nat Acad Eng; hon mem Am Soc Civil Engrs; Am Soc Mech Engrs; Am Inst Aeronaut & Astronaut. *Res:* Structural reliability analysis; random vibration; inelasticity; structural analysis. *Mailing Add:* E210 Eng Quad Princeton NJ 08540

SHINSKEY, FRANCIS GREGWAY, PH CONTROL, DISTILLATION CONTROL. *Current Pos:* RETIRED. *Personal Data:* b North Tonawanda, NY, Oct 29, 31; m 58; c 8. *Educ:* Univ Notre Dame, BSc, 52. *Honors & Awards:* Sprange Appln Award, Instrument Soc Am, 77, Eckman Educ Award, 83, Sperry Founders Award, 88. *Prof Exp:* Process engr, E I du Pont Co, 54-55; process engr, Olin-Mathieson Chem Co, 55-57, instrument engr, 57-60; syst engr, Foxboro Co, 60-68, control systs consult, 68-72, sr systs consult, 72-83, chief consult, 83-90, res fel, 90-93. *Concurrent Pos:* Bristol fel, Foxboro Co, 82. *Mem:* Fel Instrument Soc Am. *Res:* Evaluation of feedback controller performance; design of a self-turning high-performance model-based controller. *Mailing Add:* Whiteface Rd ND Center Sandwich NH 03227

SHIONO, RYONOSUKE, CRYSTALLOGRAPHY. *Current Pos:* res assoc lectr, Univ Pittsburgh, 56-61, asst res prof, 61-65, assoc res prof crystallog, 66-69, ASSOC PROF CRYSTALLOGRAPHY, UNIV PITTSBURGH, 69- *Personal Data:* b Kobe, Japan, Nov 12, 23; m 58; c 3. *Educ:* Osaka Univ, MSc, 45, DSc(physics), 60. *Prof Exp:* Instr physics, Osaka Univ, 49-56. *Concurrent Pos:* Vis prof, Univ Sao Paulo, 69. *Mem:* Am Crystallog Asn; Royal Soc Chem; Chem Soc Japan; Phys Soc Japan. *Res:* Crystal structure analysis and application of computer in crystallography. *Mailing Add:* Dept Metall Eng Univ Pittsburgh 848 Benedum Hall Pittsburgh PA 15260-0001

SHIPBAUGH, CALVIN, PHYSICS & NANOTECHNOLOGY, POLICY ANALYSIS. *Current Pos:* ASSOC ENGR, RAND, 88- *Personal Data:* b Huntington, India, Aug 28, 58. *Educ:* Rice Univ, BA, 80; Univ Ill, MS, 82, PhD(physics), 88. *Mem:* Am Phys Soc; Int Meteoritical Soc. *Res:* Policy analysis and feasibility studies of space systems, nanotechnology and biotechnology. *Mailing Add:* 1439 Saltair Ave No 17 Los Angeles CA 90025

SHIPCHANDLER, MOHAMMED TYEBJI, MEDICINAL CHEMISTRY, ORGANIC CHEMISTRY. *Current Pos:* SR SCIENTIST, ABBOTT LABS, 80- *Personal Data:* b Surat, India, May 19, 41; m 71; c 2. *Educ:* Univ Bombay, BSc, 62, BSc, 64; Univ Minn, Minneapolis, PhD(med chem), 69. *Prof Exp:* NIH fel & res assoc med chem, Univ Kans, 68-70; NIH fel & res assoc natural prod chem, Col Pharm, Ohio State Univ, 70-72; instr, Columbus Tech Inst, Ohio, 72-73; res chemist, Com Solvents Corp, Terre Haute, Ind, 73-80. *Mem:* Am Chem Soc; Sigma Xi; Am Asn Clin Chem. *Res:* Synthesis of medicinal agents and natural products; immuno assay development. *Mailing Add:* 640 Burdick St Libertyville IL 60048

SHIPE, EMERSON RUSSELL, AGRONOMY, PLANT BREEDING. *Current Pos:* from asst prof to assoc prof, 80-89, PROF AGRON & SOILS, CLEMSON UNIV, 89- *Personal Data:* b Knoxville, Tenn, July 28, 47; m 76; c 3. *Educ:* Univ Tenn, BS, 69; Western Ky Univ, MS, 70; Va Polytech Inst & State Univ, PhD(agron), 78. *Prof Exp:* Teaching asst, Western Ky Univ, 69-70; agriculturalist, US Peace Corps, Cent Am, 73-75; teaching asst, Va Polytech Inst & State Univ, 75-78; asst prof soil & crop sci, Tex Agr Exp Sta, 78-80. *Mem:* Am Soc Agron; Crop Sci Soc Am; Sigma Xi. *Res:* Development of soybean germplasm, cultivars with improved nematode and insect resistance, higher seed yields, and adaptation to southeast soil and climatic conditions. *Mailing Add:* Dept Agron & Soils Clemson Univ Clemson SC 29632-0001

SHIPE, JAMES R, JR, BIOCHEMISTRY, DRUG TESTING. *Current Pos:* res assoc clin chem, 77-79, anal chemist path, 79-87, CLIN ASST PROF GEN MED FAC, ASSOC DIR CLIN CHEM & SCI DIR FORENSIC DRUG TESTING PROG, UNIV VA MED CTR, 87- *Personal Data:* b Louisville, Ky, Oct 14, 48. *Educ:* Randolph-Macon Col, BSc, 70; Univ Fla, MS, 72; Univ NC, PhD (biochem), 79. *Prof Exp:* Med technologist II clin chem, NC Mem Hosp, Chapel Hill, 72-77. *Mem:* Am Asn Clin Chemists; Asn Clin Scientist; Am Chem Soc; Am Inst Chemists; NY Acad Sci; Sigma Xi. *Res:* Gas chromatographic spectrometric measurements of drugs in serum and urine; analytical toxicology; applications of high resolution analytical techniques, such as tandem mass spectrometry, for the analysis of drugs and metabolites in biological fluids. *Mailing Add:* 2501 Bennington Rd Charlottesville VA 22901

SHIPE, W(ILLIAM) FRANK(LIN), FOOD SCIENCE. *Current Pos:* from asst to assoc prof dairy indust, 46-60, prof Food Sci, 61-88, EMER PROF, CORNELL UNIV, 88- *Personal Data:* b Middletown, Va, Mar 8, 20; m 48; c 2. *Educ:* Va Polytech Inst, BS, 41; Cornell Univ, PhD(dairy chem), 49. *Honors & Awards:* Kraft Teaching Award, Am Dairy Sci Asn, 82. *Prof Exp:* Instr dairy mfg, Va Polytech Inst, 45-46. *Concurrent Pos:* Res assoc, NC State Col, 56; travel fel, Cornell Univ, 62; res consult, Dept Agr & Mkt, 63; Nat Inst Res Dairying fel, Reading, Eng, 70 & 79. *Mem:* Am Chem Soc; Am Dairy Sci Asn; Int Food Technologists. *Res:* Enzymatic changes in food products; flavor and texture of foods; nutritional quality of foods. *Mailing Add:* 236 Forest Home Dr Ithaca NY 14850

SHIPKOWITZ, NATHAN L, MICROBIOLOGY. *Current Pos:* sr res microbiologist, 63-75, ASSOC RES FEL, ABBOTT LABS, 76- *Personal Data:* b Chicago, Ill, Mar 29, 25; m 56; c 4. *Educ:* Univ Ill, BS, 49, MS, 50; Mich State Univ, PhD(bact, pub health), 52. *Prof Exp:* Asst prof vet sci, Univ Mass, 52-54; asst res bacteriologist, Hooper Found, Med Ctr, Univ Calif, San Francisco, 54-58; bacteriologist & virologist, Path Dept, Good Samaritan Hosp, Portland, Ore, 59-62. *Mem:* AAAS; Am Soc Microbiol; Sigma Xi. *Res:* microbiology. *Mailing Add:* 95 Beech Ave Waukegan IL 60087

SHIPLEY, EDWARD NICHOLAS, DATABASE TECHNOLOGY, COMMUNICATION NETWORKS. *Current Pos:* distinguished mem, 81-96, MEM TECH STAFF, BELL LABS, 72-, PRIN TECH STAFF MEM, 97- *Personal Data:* b Baltimore, Md, Jan 26, 34; m 63, Joan E Troik; c Elisabeth A, Linda M & Edward N Jr. *Educ:* Johns Hopkins Univ, AB, 54, PhD(physics), 58. *Prof Exp:* From instr to asst prof physics, Northwestern Univ, 58-63; mem tech staff, Bellcomm, Inc, Washington, DC, 63-72. *Concurrent Pos:* Consult, Argonne Nat Lab, 59-63. *Mem:* Am Phys Soc; Sigma Xi. *Res:* Low energy nuclear reactions; lifetimes of excited nuclear states; hyperfragment decay modes; K meson reactions; lunar surface mechanical properties; Martian atmospheric phenomena; maintenance and operations of telephone switching systems; database administration; numbering for telecommunication services; systems planning and development; granted 2 patents. *Mailing Add:* AT&T Rm 3C-101 200 Laurel Ave Middletown NJ 07748. *Fax:* 732-957-4303; *E-Mail:* enshipley@att.com

SHIPLEY, GEORGE GRAHAM, BIOPHYSICS, BIOCHEMISTRY. *Current Pos:* from asst res prof to assoc res prof med, 71-82, from asst prof to assoc prof biochem, 73-82, PROF BIOCHEM & RES PROF MED, SCH MED, BOSTON UNIV, 82- *Personal Data:* b London, Eng, Nov 18, 37. *Educ:* Univ Nottingham, Eng, BSc, 59, PhD(phys chem), 63 & DSc, 84. *Prof Exp:* Scientist biophys, Unilever Res Lab, Eng, 63-69, sect leader, 69-71. *Mem:* AAAS; Am Chem Soc; Am Crystallog Asn; Am Heart Asn; Am Soc Biol Chemists; Biophys Soc. *Res:* Structure and function of biological lipids, cell membranes and serum lipoproteins and their relationship to pathological processes, notably atherosclerosis and hyperlipidemia. *Mailing Add:* Dept Biophys Boston Univ Sch Med 80 E Concord St Boston MA 02118-2394. *Fax:* 617-634-4041; *E-Mail:* shipley@medbiophy.bu.edu

SHIPLEY, JAMES PARISH, JR, SCIENCE POLICY, TECHNICAL MANAGEMENT. *Current Pos:* OWNER & PRES, JP SYSTS INC, 95- *Personal Data:* b Clovis, NMex, Jan 3, 45; m 62, Carolyn Hall; c Gary D, Martin E & James C. *Educ:* NMex State Univ, BS, 66; Univ NMex, MS, 69, PhD(elec eng), 73. *Prof Exp:* Staff mem electronics, Los Alamos Nat Lab, 66-73, nuclear sci & solar energy, 73-76, systs sci, 76-78, group leader safeguards systs, 78-82, prog mgr safeguards & security, low-intensity conflict, 82-87, prog mgr arms reduction treaty verification, 89-91 & environ mgt technol develop, 91-92, prog dir environ mgt, 92-95; sr adv to ambassador nonproliferation policy, Dept State, 87-89. *Mem:* Inst Elec & Electronics Engrs; AAAS; Inst Nuclear Mat Mgt; Am Soc Indust Security; Am Nuclear Soc. *Res:* Nuclear safeguards systems; systems science; statistical decision theory; science and technology policy; environmental management; arms control. *Mailing Add:* 29 La Serena Irvine CA 92715

SHIPLEY, MICHAEL THOMAS, NEUROANATOMY, NEUROPHYSIOLOGY. *Current Pos:* PROF ANAT DEPT, UNIV CINCINNATI. *Personal Data:* b Kansas City, Mo, Apr 22, 41; m 76; c 2. *Educ:* Univ Mo, Kansas City, BA, 67; Mass Inst Technol, PhD(neurosci), 72. *Prof Exp:* Fel anat, Univ Aarhus, 72-74; asst prof, Univ Lausanne, 74-78; asst prof cell biol & anat, Med Sch, Northwestern Univ, 78- *Concurrent Pos:* Prin investr, NIH grants, 82-, mem study sect, 83-89; Woodrow Wilson fel. *Mem:* Soc Neurosci; Am Asn Anatomists; AAAS; Am Chem Soc. *Res:* Neuroanatomy and physiology of sensory-lumbic interactions in cerebral cortex and neuroanatomy; development of olfactory nervous system; image analysis. *Mailing Add:* 14826 View Way Ct Glenelg MD 21737

SHIPLEY, REGINALD A, tracers for in vivo kinetics, for more information see previous edition

SHIPLEY, ROCH JOSEPH, FAILURE ANALYSIS, MECHANICAL PROPERTIES OF MATERIALS. *Current Pos:* sr consult, 90-92, mgr mat eng, 92-94, DIR MAT ENG, ENG SYST INC, 95- *Personal Data:* b Chicago Heights, Ill, June 5, 54; m 75, Debra Riechel; c Matthew, Bradley, Laurel & Jeffrey. *Educ:* Ill Inst Technol, BS, 76, PhD(metall eng), 80. *Prof Exp:* Res engr, Int Harvester, 80-82; prin engr, TRW Inc, 82-86 & Textron Inc, 86-90. *Concurrent Pos:* Indust review bd mem, USAF Res, 88-90; prof metall eng, Ill Inst Technol, 91- *Mem:* Am Soc Mats Int; Nat Soc Prof Engrs. *Res:* Interaction between process parameters employed in producing a material or manufactured product and the properties and performance of that material or product. *Mailing Add:* Eng Systs Inc 3851 Exchange Ave Aurora IL 60504. *Fax:* 630-851-4870; *E-Mail:* rj_shipley@juno.com

SHIPLEY, THORNE, PSYCHOLOGY, OPHTHALMOLOGY. *Current Pos:* RETIRED. *Personal Data:* b New York, NY, Apr 11, 27; m 71; c 2. *Educ:* Johns Hopkins Univ, BA, 49; New Sch Social Res, MA, 53; NY Univ, PhD(psychol), 55. *Prof Exp:* Instr psychol, Long Island Univ, 53-55; res, Am Optical Co, 55-58; NIH spec fel, Imp Col, Univ London, 58-59 & Fac Med, Univ Paris, 59-60; assoc prof visual sci, Med Sch & assoc prof neurophychol, Sch Arts & Sci, Univ Miami, 60-77, prof visual sci, Med Sch & prof neurophychol, Sch Arts & Sci, 77- *Concurrent Pos:* Founding ed, Vision Res, 60-78; dir, Inst Advan Study Sci & Humanities, 80- *Mem:* AAAS; Am Psychol Asn; Soc Neurosci; Soc Social Responsibility in Sci; Optical Soc Am; fel World Acad Arts & Sci. *Res:* Theoretical psychology; sensory communication; sense function in children; cognition; communication and learning disabilities; history and philosophy of science. *Mailing Add:* 3575 N Moorings Way Miami FL 33133

SHIPMAN, C(HARLES) WILLIAM, COMBUSTION, THERMODYNAMICS. *Current Pos:* CONSULT, 86- *Personal Data:* b Phillipsburg, NJ, Aug 29, 24; m 46, Louise J Hendrickson; c Nancy R, Jane L & Robert W G. *Educ:* Mass Inst Technol, SB, 48, SM, 49, ScD(chem eng), 52. *Honors & Awards:* Silver Combustion Medal, 64. *Prof Exp:* Instr chem eng, Mass Inst Technol, 49-50, asst combustion res, 50-52, res assoc, 55-58; asst prof chem eng, Univ Del, 52-55; from asst prof to prof, Worcester Polytech Inst, 58-74, dean grad studies, 71-74; asst dir, Corp Res Dept, Cabot Corp, 78-80, engr, 74-86, mgr, Carbon Black Res & Develop, 80-86. *Concurrent Pos:* Consult, Avco Corp, 58-65, United Aircraft Corp, 65-74 & Kennecott Corp, 68-74; dir, Combustion Inst, 78-90. *Mem:* Am Chem Soc; Am Inst Chem Engrs; Combustion Inst. *Res:* Thermodynamics; combustion; mass transfer; fine particles technology. *Mailing Add:* PO Box 32 Prospect Harbor ME 04669-0032. *E-Mail:* shipman@acadia.net

SHIPMAN, CHARLES, JR, VIROLOGY. *Current Pos:* asst prof microbiol, Sch Med, Univ Mich, 68-75, from asst prof to assoc prof oral biol, Sch Dent, 68-84, assoc prof microbiol, Med Sch, 75-93, prof biol & mat sci, 84-96, EMER PROF, SCH DENT, UNIV MICH, ANN ARBOR, 96- *Personal Data:* b Ventura, Calif, Nov 1, 34; m 73; c 2. *Educ:* Univ Calif, Los Angeles, AB, 56; Calif State Univ, Fresno, MA, 63; Ind Univ, PhD(microbiol), 66. *Prof Exp:* Assoc res microbiologist, Parke-Davis & Co, 66-68. *Concurrent Pos:* Consult, Coun Dent Educ, 72-73; vis assoc prof mol biol & biochem, Univ Calif, Irvine, 78; coun dent therapeut, Am Dent Asn, 83-96; co-chmn, Virol Div, Inter-Am Soc Chemother, 84-87. *Mem:* Am Soc Microbiol; Tissue Cult Asn; Am Soc Virol; Soc Gen Microbiol; Am Asn Dent Schs. *Res:* Mechanism of action of antiviral drugs on human herpesviruses and human immunodeficiency virus. *Mailing Add:* 1519 Clower Creek Dr No 254 Sarasota FL 34231. *Fax:* 941-966-4118; *E-Mail:* vaquero@agte.net

SHIPMAN, HAROLD R, sanitary engineering; deceased, see previous edition for last biography

SHIPMAN, HARRY LONGFELLOW, ASTROPHYSICS, PHYSICS. *Current Pos:* from asst prof to assoc prof, 74-81, PROF PHYSICS, UNIV DEL, 81- *Personal Data:* b Hartford, Conn, Feb 20, 48; m 70, Valerie Bergeron; c 5. *Educ:* Harvard Univ, BA, 69; Calif Inst Technol, MS, 70, PhD(astron), 71. *Prof Exp:* J W Gibbs instr astron, Yale Univ, 71-73; asst prof physics, Univ Mo, St Louis, 73-74. *Concurrent Pos:* Guest investr, Kitt Peak Nat Observ, 72-74 & var satellite progs, NASA, 74-; astronr, McDonnell Planetarium, 73-74; prin investr grants, NSF, 74-, Res Corp, 74-76, Univ Del Res Found, 75-76 & NASA, 76-79, 81, & 83-; John Simon Guggenheim Mem fel, 80-81. *Mem:* Sigma Xi; Am Astron Soc; AAAS; Am Asn Physics Teachers; Astron Soc Pac; Int Astron Union. *Res:* Analysis of stellar spectra via stellar-atmosphere calculations; white-dwarf stars and other final stages of stellar evolution; theoretical astrophysics; science educaton; use of groups and collaborative learning as large classes; conceptual change. *Mailing Add:* Dept Physics & Astron Univ Del Newark DE 19711. *Fax:* 302-831-1637; *E-Mail:* harrys@mdel.edu

SHIPMAN, JERRY, DISCRIMINANT ANALYSIS. *Current Pos:* Assoc prof & chmn, dept physics & math, 73-78, PROF & CHMN, DEPT MATH, ALA A&M UNIV, 78- *Personal Data:* b Elamville, Ala, Feb 20, 43. *Educ:* Ala A&M Univ, BS, 63; Western Wash Univ, MS, 66; Pa State Univ, PhD(math), 73. *Concurrent Pos:* Assoc mathematician, Northrop Space Labs, 63-64. *Mem:* Math Asn Am; Soc Indust & Appl Math. *Mailing Add:* Dept Math Ala A&M Univ Normal AL 35762

SHIPMAN, LESTER LYNN, INTELLIGENT SYSTEMS. *Current Pos:* res scientist, 81-85, sr specialist, 85-87, CONSULT, E I DUPONT DE NEMOURS & CO, 87- *Personal Data:* b Topeka, Kans, Mar 28, 47; m 69. *Educ:* Washburn Univ, BA & BS, 69; Univ Kans, PhD(chem), 72. *Prof Exp:* Fel chem, Cornell Univ, 72-74; appointee, Argonne Nat Lab, 74-75, res assoc chem, 75-76, asst chemist, 76-80, chemist, 80-81. *Concurrent Pos:* Consult, Norwich Pharmacal Co, 73-75. *Mem:* Am Asn Artifical Intelligence. *Res:* Ab initio molecular quantum mechanics; conformational and intermolecular potential energy functions; primary events of photosynthesis; structure-activity relationships; theoretical biophysical chemistry; molecular aspects of chemical carcinogenesis; mechanisms of energy transfer; theory of excitons in molecular aggregates; expert systems; intelligent scheduling systems. *Mailing Add:* 707 Halstead Rd Wilmington DE 19803

SHIPMAN, ROBERT DEAN, FOREST ECOLOGY, SILVICULTURE. *Current Pos:* from assoc prof to prof forest ecol, 63-90, EMER PROF FOREST ECOL, SCH FOREST RESOURCES, PA STATE UNIV, 90- *Personal Data:* b Moundsville, WVa, May 12, 21; m 46; c 2. *Educ:* Univ Mich, BSF & MF, 42; Mich State Univ, PhD(forestry), 52. *Prof Exp:* Asst forest soils, Childs-Walcott Forest, Conn, 42; munic park forester, Oglebay Park, Wheeling, WVa, 47; agr aide, US Forest Serv, 49, mem staff, 52-58; asst forest res, Mich State Univ, 50-51; assoc prof forestry, Clemson Univ, 58-63. *Concurrent Pos:* Moderator Northeast Weed Control Conf, NY, 64; mem, Soc Am Foresters Nat Task Force on Herbicides, 75-76. *Mem:* Soil Sci Soc Am; Soc Am Foresters; Ecol Soc Am; Weed Sci Soc Am; Sigma Xi. *Res:* Tree physiology and soils; silvics and herbicides. *Mailing Add:* 209 Twigs Lane State College PA 16801

SHIPMAN, ROSS LOVELACE, GEOLOGY. *Current Pos:* PETROL INVEST CONS, 87- *Personal Data:* b Jackson, Miss, Nov 20, 26; m 48; c 1. *Educ:* Univ Miss, BA, 50. *Honors & Awards:* Distinguished Serv Award, Am Asn Petrol Geol. *Prof Exp:* Geologist, Miss State Geol Surv, 49-50; jr geologist, Humble Oil & Refining Co, 50-51; dist geologist, 51-55; petrol consult, 55-67; asst exec dir, Am Geol Inst, 67-71; res prog mgr, Bur Econ Geol & Div Natural Resources & Environ, 71-75, assoc dir admin, Marine Sci Inst, 75-79, assoc vpres, Res Admin, Univ Tex, Austin, 79-85; pres & chief exec officer, Live Oak Energy, 85-87. *Concurrent Pos:* Tex Coastal & Marine Coun; Cons Intl Bound & Wtr Comn; dir, Indust Assoc Prog, Univ Tex. *Mem:* Fel Geol Soc Am; Am Asn Petrol Geol; Fel Geol Soc (London); Soc Indep Prof Earth Sci; hon mem Am Inst Prof Geologists. *Res:* Petroleum exploration and production; mining exploration; environmental geology; marine geophysics. *Mailing Add:* 1911 E Lawndale Dr San Antonio TX 78209

SHIPP, JOSEPH CALVIN, MEDICINE. *Current Pos:* PROF MED & CHMN DEPT, COL MED, UNIV NEBR MED CTR, 70- *Personal Data:* b Northport, Ala, Feb 10, 27; m 62, Marjorie Morris; c Joseph C II, Sherise, Dane & Michele. *Educ:* Univ Ala, BS, 48; Columbia Univ, MD, 52. *Honors & Awards:* Gold Medal Excellence Clin Med, Columbia Univ, Col Physicians & Surgeons. *Prof Exp:* Intern & asst resident med, Presby Hosp, New York, 52-54; Nat Res Coun res fel, Harvard Med Sch, 54-56; res fel biochem, Oxford Univ, 58-59; instr med, Harvard Med Sch, 59-60; from asst prof to assoc prof med, Med Col, Univ Fla, 60-68, prof & dir clin res ctr, 68-70, dir diabetes res & training prog, 64-70. *Concurrent Pos:* Sr asst resident, Peter Bent Brigham Hosp, 56-57; chief resident physician, 57-58, jr assoc, 59-60; sr investr, Boston Med Found, 59-60; Markle scholar, 61; res fel biochem, Univ Munich, 65-66. *Mem:* Am Diabetes Asn; Am Fedn Clin Res; Am Soc Clin Invest; Asn Am Physicians; Endocrine Soc. *Res:* Endocrinology; diabetes; acting of hormones at the cellular level. *Mailing Add:* 7463 Laguna Vista Fresno CA 93711

SHIPP, RAYMOND FRANCIS, AGRONOMY. *Current Pos:* exten agronomist, 72-91, assoc prof, 78-94, EMER PROF, AGRON EXTEN, PA STATE UNIV, 94- *Personal Data:* b Hay Springs, Nebr, June 1, 31; m 66; c 3. *Educ:* Univ Nebr, BS, 53, MS, 58; Pa State Univ, PhD(agron), 62. *Prof Exp:* Soil scientist, Pa State Dept Health, 62-66 & US Dept Interior Bur Reclamation, 66-72. *Mem:* Fel AAAS; Soil Sci Soc Am; Sigma Xi. *Res:* Use of sewage sludge by-products from municipal waste water treatment plants for the enhancement of crop production. *Mailing Add:* 288 Nimipz State College PA 16801

SHIPP, ROBERT LEWIS, ICHTHYOLOGY. *Current Pos:* from asst prof to assoc prof, 71-78, PROF BIOL, UNIV S ALA, 79- *Personal Data:* b Tallahassee, Fla, Aug 22, 42; m 64; c 3. *Educ:* Spring Hill Col, BS, 64; Fla State Univ, MS, 66, PhD(biol), 70. *Prof Exp:* Instr biol, Fla A&M Univ, 68-70. *Concurrent Pos:* Ed, Northeast Gulf Sci, 77-, Systematic Zoology, 87-90. *Mem:* Am Soc Ichthyologists & Herpetologists; Am Fisheries Soc; Soc Syst Zool. *Res:* Marine zoogeography; fish systematics and phylogeny; artificial reef development; development of Guatemalan fisheries; river ecology. *Mailing Add:* Marine Sci Univ S Ala 307 University Blvd N Mobile AL 36688-0001

SHIPPEE-RICE, RAELENE V, GERONTOLOGICAL NURSING. *Current Pos:* dir undergrad nursing prog, Univ NH, 87-92, chairperson, Dept Nursing, 92-95, assoc dean & dir, Ctr Health Prom & Res, 96, DIR GERONT INTERDISCIPLINARY PROG, UNIV NH, 87- *Educ:* Carroll Col, BSN, 64; Univ Rochester, MS, 79; Brandeis Univ, PhD(health policy & aging), 90. *Honors & Awards:* Fulbright Lectr, Russia, 87. *Mem:* Sigma Xi; Gerontol Soc Am; Am Pub Health Asn. *Res:* Experience of older adults receiving care from adult children; health care ethics; contributed articles to professional journals. *Mailing Add:* Sch Health & Human Servs Univ NH Hewitt Hall Durham NH 03824-3563. *Fax:* 603-862-3108; *E-Mail:* rvs@christa.unh.edu

SHIPPY, DAVID JAMES, ENGINEERING MECHANICS. *Current Pos:* from asst prof to assoc prof eng mech, 64-78, NSF grant, 66-67, PROF ENG MECH, UNIV KY, 78- *Personal Data:* b Oelwein, Iowa, July 26, 31; m 54; c 2. *Educ:* Iowa State Univ, BS, 53, MS, 54, PhD(theoret & appl mech), 63. *Prof Exp:* Aerophysics engr, Gen Dynamics Corp, 54-56; instr physics & eng, Graceland Col, 56-64. *Concurrent Pos:* Instr, Iowa State Univ, 60-61; Air Force Off Sci Res grant, 75-78; NSF grant, 81-84. *Mem:* Am Soc Eng Educ. *Res:* Numerical methods in solid mechanics, especially the Boundary Integral Equation Method. *Mailing Add:* 2101 Bridgeport Circle Lexington KY 40502

SHIPSEY, EDWARD JOSEPH, PHYSICAL CHEMISTRY. *Current Pos:* TEX RR COMN, 90- *Personal Data:* b New York, NY, Aug 22, 38; c 2. *Educ:* Stanford Univ, BS, 60; Ohio State Univ, PhD(phys chem), 67. *Prof Exp:* Res assoc physics, Univ Tex, Austin, 72-90. *Res:* Theory and computation of atomic and molecular collisions. *Mailing Add:* Tex RR Comn 2801 Wheless Dr Austin TX 78712

SHIRAKI, KEIZO, HUMAN PHYSIOLOGY, ENVIRONMENTAL PHYSIOLOGY. *Current Pos:* PROF RES & CHMN DEPT PHYSIOL, SCH MED, UNIV OCCUP & ENVIRON HEALTH, KITAKYUSHA, JAPAN, 78- *Educ:* Kyoto Pref Sch Med, MD, 61, PhD(physiol), 67. *Prof Exp:* Sr instr res, Dept Physiol, Kyoto Prefectural Univ Med, Japan, 67-68; asst prof res, Inst Arctic Biol, Univ Alaska, 68-69 & Dept Nutrit, Tokushima Univ Sch Med, Japan, 70-78. *Mem:* Am Physiol Soc; Am Col Sports Med; Undersea Med Soc; NY Acad Sci; Physiol Soc Japan; Japanese Soc Nutrit & Food Sci. *Res:* Environmental physiology of humans by applying humoral and neural analysis technique; adaption mechanisms of humans to extreme environments, high altitude, high pressure, hot, and cold. *Mailing Add:* Dept Physiol Sch Med Univ Occup & Environ Health 1-1 Iseigaoka Yahata-nishiku Kitakyushu 807 Japan. *Fax:* 81-93-602-9883

SHIRANE, GEN, SOLID STATE PHYSICS. *Current Pos:* physicist, 63-68, SR PHYSICIST, BROOKHAVEN NAT LAB, 68- *Personal Data:* b Nishinomiya, Japan, May 15, 24; m 50; c 2. *Educ:* Univ Tokyo, BE, 47, DSc(physics), 54. *Honors & Awards:* Buckley Prize, Am Physics Soc, 73; Warren Award, Am Crystallog Asn, 73; Humboldt Award, 85. *Prof Exp:* Res assoc physics, Tokyo Inst Technol, Japan, 48-52; res assoc, Pa State Univ, 52-55, asst prof, 55-56; assoc physicist, Brookhaven Nat Lab, 56-57; res physicist, Res Labs, Westinghouse Elec Corp, 57-58, adv physicist, 59-63. *Mem:* Nat Acad Sci; Phys Soc Japan; Am Phys Soc. *Res:* Neutron scattering; magnetism; lattice dynamics. *Mailing Add:* Dept Physics Brookhaven Nat Lab Upton NY 11973. *Fax:* 516-282-2918

SHIRAZI, MOSTAFA AYAT, FLUID DYNAMICS. *Current Pos:* res mech engr, 69-80, SR RES SCIENTIST, CORVALLIS ENVIRON RES LAB, ENVIRON PROTECTION AGENCY, 80- *Personal Data:* b Najaf, Iraq, Sept 27, 32; US citizen; m 61; c 3. *Educ:* Calif State Polytech Col, BS, 59; Univ Wash, MS, 61; Univ Ill, Urbana, PhD(mech eng), 67. *Prof Exp:* Assoc res engr, Boeing Co, Wash, 61; sr res engr, Hercules Inc, Md, 67-69. *Mem:* Am Soc Mech Engrs. *Res:* Analysis of jet diffusion for the prediction of heated plume behavior in large bodies of water; jet diffusion; ecosystems modeling and analysis. *Mailing Add:* 2025 NW Jackson Creek Dr Corvallis OR 97330

SHIREMAN, RACHEL BAKER, NUTRITION, BIOCHEMISTRY. *Current Pos:* res asst med, 78-79, asst prof, 79-84, ASSOC PROF NUTRIT, UNIV FLA, 84- *Personal Data:* b Springhill, La, Aug 3, 40; m 61; c 4. *Educ:* La State Univ, BS, 62; Iowa State Univ, MS, 66; Univ Fla, PhD(biochem), 78. *Prof Exp:* Instr biol, Univ Southwest La, 67-72. *Mem:* Soc Exp Biol & Med; Am Oil Chemists Soc; Am Soc Biol Chem; AAAS. *Res:* Relationships between the structure, composition and function of the plasma lipoproteins; low density lipoprotein. *Mailing Add:* Dept Food Sci & Human Nutrit 303 Food Sci Bldg Univ Florida Gainesville FL 32611

SHIREN, NORMAN S, QUANTUM ACOUSTICS, QUANTUM OPTICS. *Current Pos:* RETIRED. *Personal Data:* b New York, NY, Feb 7, 25; m 47; c 2. *Educ:* Tufts Univ, BS, 45; Stanford Univ, PhD(physics), 56. *Prof Exp:* Staff scientist, Hudson Lab, Columbia Univ, 51-55; staff mem, Gen Elec Res Ctr, 55-61; staff mem/mgr, T J Watson Res Ctr, IBM, 61-87, consult, 87-90. *Concurrent Pos:* Guggenheim fel, Clarendon Lab, Oxford Univ, UK, 69-70; Sci Res Coun vis fel, Lancaster Univ, UK, 82-83. *Mem:* Fel AAAS (pres, 83); fel Am Phys Soc. *Res:* Quantum acoustics, quantum optics, microwave measurements and nonlinear acoustics at microwave frequencies-primarily wave interactions; discovered backward wave phonon echoes, acoustic phase conjugation, holographic echo storage; theory of kapitza conductance; measured microwave properties of superconductors and organic conductors. *Mailing Add:* 20 Twin Ridges Rd Ossining NY 10562. *E-Mail:* 201-2245@mcimail.com

SHIRER, DONALD LEROY, COMPUTER SCIENCES, ENGINEERING PHYSICS. *Current Pos:* LAB DIR, YALE UNIV, 88- *Personal Data:* b Cleveland, Ohio, May 10, 31; m 57, Karen Kent; c Scott, Lee & Kevin. *Educ:* Case Western Res Univ, BS, 52; Ohio State Univ, MSc, 53, PhD(physics), 57. *Prof Exp:* Res assoc, Res Found, Ohio State Univ, 57; from asst prof to prof physics, Valparaiso Univ, 57-78; adj prof elec eng, Univ Ariz, Tucson, 80-81, dir, Comput-Based Instr Lab, 81-88. *Concurrent Pos:* Consult, Argonne Nat Lab, 58-65; NSF fel, Univ Ill, 71-72; assoc ed, Am J Physics, 71-76; vis prof elec eng, Univ Ariz, 78-79. *Mem:* Am Phys Soc; Am Asn Physics Teachers; Asn Develop Comput-Based Instruction Systs. *Res:* Educational uses of computers; speech and music synthesis; acoustics; computational physics. *Mailing Add:* Physics Dept Yale Univ New Haven CT 06520-8120

SHIRER, HAMPTON WHITING, PHYSIOLOGY. *Current Pos:* assoc prof physiol, Dept Comp Biochem & Physiol & Dept Elec Eng, 64-67, prof elec eng, physiol & cell biol, 67-73, PROF PHYSIOL & CELL BIOL, UNIV KANS, 73- *Personal Data:* b Newton, Mass, Aug 8, 24; m 47; c 5. *Educ:* Washburn Univ, BS, 45; Univ Kans, MD, 48. *Prof Exp:* Intern, Med Ctr, Univ Kans, 48-49, USPHS res fel, 49-51, instr surg, 53-54, from instr to asst prof physiol, 54-61; head biophys group biol sci & systs dept, Gen Motors Defense Res Labs, 61-63; asst prof physiol, Univ Mich, 63-64. *Concurrent Pos:* Lederle Med Fac Award, 56-59. *Mem:* AAAS; Biophys Soc; Am Meteorol Soc; Inst Elec & Electronics Engrs; Sigma Xi. *Res:* Bioelectricity; cardiovascular regulation; physiological instrumentation; biotelemetry. *Mailing Add:* 1940 Hillview Rd Lawrence KS 66046

SHIRES, GEORGE THOMAS, SURGERY. *Current Pos:* PROF SURG, SCH MED, UNIV NEV, LAS VEGAS, 97- *Personal Data:* b Waco, Tex, Nov 22, 25; m 48, Robbie J; c G Tom III, Donna J (Blain) & Jo E. *Educ:* Univ Tex, BS, 44, MD, 48; Am Bd Surg, cert, 56. *Honors & Awards:* Numerous named lectureships, 71-90; Distinguished Achievement Award, Am Trauma Soc, 81, Curtis P Artz Mem Award, 84; Sheen Award, 85; Harvey Stuart Allen Distinguished Serv Award, Am Burn Asn, 88. *Prof Exp:* From asst prof to prof surg & chmn dept, Southwest Med Sch, Univ Tex, Dallas, 57-74; chmn & prof, Sch Med, Univ Wash, 74-75; Lewis Atterbury Stimson prof & chmn, Dept Surg, Med Col, Cornell Univ, 75-91, Stephen & Suzanne Weiss dean & provost med affairs, 87-91; prof surg & chmn dept, Health Sci Ctr, Tex Tech Univ, 91-95, Carizara distinguished prof, 95-97. *Concurrent Pos:* Surgeon-in-chief, Parkland Mem Hosp, Dallas, 60-74, Harborview Med Ctr & Univ Hosp, Seattle, 74-75 & NY Hosp, 75-91; consult, Surgeon Gen, Nat Inst Gen Med Sci, 65- & var hosps, 74; mem coun, Am Surg Asn, 69-74 & 80-, Ad Hoc External Exam Rev Comt, Asn Am Med Cols, 80-, Adv Comt & Work Groups Health Policy Agenda, AMA, 83-; assoc ed-in-chief, Infections Surg, 81-89, sr contrib ed, 82-89; ed, Surg, Gynec & Obstet, 82-; chief surg, Univ Med Ctr, Lubbock, Tex, 91- *Mem:* Inst Med-Nat Acad Sci; Am Surg Asn (secy, 69-74, pres, 79-80); Am Col Surg (pres, 82); Soc Univ Surg; Soc Int Surg; Am Asn Surg Trauma; AMA; Am Burn Asn. *Res:* Surgical trauma; author of numerous technical publications. *Mailing Add:* Sch Med Univ Nev 2040 W Charleston Suite 304 Las Vegas NV 89102

SHIRES, THOMAS KAY, CELL BIOLOGY. *Current Pos:* from asst prof to assoc prof, 72-81, PROF PHARMACOL, COL MED, UNIV IOWA, 81- *Personal Data:* b Buffalo, NY, July 12, 35; m 61; c 3. *Educ:* Colgate Univ, BA, 57; Univ Okla, MS, 61, PhD(cell biol), 65. *Prof Exp:* Res lectr depts anat & urol, Sch Med, Univ Okla, 65-68; res fel, McArdle Cancer Res Inst, Univ Wis-Madison, 68-72. *Concurrent Pos:* Vis prof, Univ Wis-Madison, 81-82. *Mem:* Am Asn Cancer Res; NY Acad Sci; Am Soc Pharmacol & Exp Therapeut; Am Soc Cell Biol; Am Asn Pathologists; Am Ornithologists Union. *Res:* Glycation of proteins; toxicology of glucose; transcytosis of proteins. *Mailing Add:* Dept Pharmacol Col Med Univ Iowa 200 Hawkins Dr Iowa City IA 52242-1087

SHIRK, B(RIAN) THOMAS, SOLID STATE SCIENCE, ELECTRICAL ENGINEERING. *Current Pos:* PRES, HOOSIER MAGNETICS, INC, 75- *Personal Data:* b Schoeneck, Pa, Sept 20, 41; m 66; c 4. *Educ:* Pa State Univ, BS, 63, PhD(solid state sci), 68. *Prof Exp:* Res scientist, Stackpole Carbon Co, 68-72; tech dir, Lydall Magnetics Co, 72-75. *Mem:* Inst Elec & Electronics Engrs; Am Ceramic Soc. *Res:* Magnetic oxides and glasses; single crystal growth and characterization; research and development of ferrites. *Mailing Add:* Hoosier Magnetics Inc 6545 W Central Ave Toledo OH 43617

SHIRK, JAMES SILER, SPECTROSCOPY, NON-LINEAR OPTICS. *Current Pos:* SR RES CHEMIST, NAVAL RES LAB, 87- *Personal Data:* b Chambersburg, Pa, Mar 7, 40; m 72, Amy Goya; c 2. *Educ:* Col Wooster, BA, 62; Univ Calif, Berkeley, PhD(chem), 66. *Prof Exp:* Res assoc chem, Imp Col, Univ London, 66-67; Nat Acad Sci-Nat Res Coun res assoc fel spectros, Nat Bur Standards, 67-69; from asst prof to prof chem, Ill Inst Technol, 69-87. *Concurrent Pos:* Mem tech staff, Bell Labs, Murray Hill, NJ, 77-78. *Mem:* Am Chem Soc; Am Phys Soc; Sigma Xi; Optical Soc Am. *Res:* Non linear optical materials and processes; infrared and ultraviolet spectroscopy; lasers; instrumentation. *Mailing Add:* Code 5613 Naval Res Lab Washington DC 20375. *Fax:* 202-404-8114

SHIRK, PAUL DAVID, MOLECULAR GENETICS, MOLECULAR ENDOCRINOLOGY. *Current Pos:* RES PHYSIOLOGIST, AGR RES SERV, USDA, 85- *Personal Data:* b Waterloo, Iowa, June 7, 48; m 75, Lynna K Lehew; c Heather E & Bryce D. *Educ:* Univ Northern Iowa, BA, 70; Tex A&M Univ, MS, 75, PhD(zool), 78. *Prof Exp:* Res assoc, Univ Ore, 78-79, NIH fel, 79-81; asst prof, Ore State Univ, 81-84. *Mem:* Am Soc Cell Biol; Soc Develop Biol; Sigma Xi. *Res:* Hormonal control of yolk polypeptide expression and control of reproduction in stored product insect pests. *Mailing Add:* USDA Agr Res Serv 1700 SW 23rd Dr PO Box 14565 Gainesville FL 32604. *Fax:* 352-374-5781; *E-Mail:* shirk@icbr.ifas.ufl.edu

SHIRK, RICHARD JAY, BACTERIOLOGY, DATA PROCESSING. *Current Pos:* RETIRED. *Personal Data:* b Tyrone, Pa, Feb 10, 30; m 51; c 4. *Educ:* Pa State Univ, BS, 51. *Prof Exp:* Bacteriologist fermentation process develop, Heyden Chem Corp, 51-53; bacteriologist, Am Cyanamid Co, 53-55, res bacteriologist, food res group, 55-64 & back chemother group, 64-74, sr tech systs analyst, 74-83, supervising analyst, 83-92. *Mem:* Data Processing Mgt Asn; Asn Comput Machinery. *Res:* Antibiotic fermentations; food technology; antioxidants; food preservatives; food coatings; bioassays; experimental infections; chemotherapy of animal diseases; statistical analysis; computer programming; computerized biological screening systems; research and development computer applications; research administration systems. *Mailing Add:* 1215 N Cambria St Bellwood PA 16617

SHIRKEY, HARRY CAMERON, PEDIATRICS. *Current Pos:* RETIRED. *Personal Data:* b Cincinnati, Ohio, July 2, 16; m 58; c 3. *Educ:* Univ Cincinnati, BS, 39, MD, 45, DSc(pharm), 76; Am Bd Pediat, dipl, 52; Am Bd Clin Toxicol, dipl, 76. *Prof Exp:* Assoc prof pharm, Col Pharm, Univ Cincinnati, 40-41; pharmacist, Children's Hosp, 41-42; asst pharmacol, Col Med, Univ Cincinnati, 43-46 & 48-53, instr pediat, 53-57, asst clin prof, 57-60; prof pediat, Med Col Ala, 60-68; prof pediat & chmn dept & prof pharmacol, Sch Med, Univ Hawaii, 68-71; prof pediat & chmn dept, Med Ctr, Tulane Univ, 71-77. *Concurrent Pos:* Resident, Children's Hosp, Cincinnati, 48-51; assoc prof pharmacol, Col Pharm, Univ Cincinnati, 48-60; mem rev comt & chmn panel pediat, US Pharmacopeia, 52-; dir pediat, Cincinnati Gen Hosp, 53-60; chmn admis comt, Nat Formulary, 60-; med & admin dir, Children's Hosp, 60-68; dir, Jefferson County Poison Control Ctr, 60-68; mem staff, Univ Hosp, 60-68; consult, Baptist Hosp, Crippled Children's Hosp & Clin & St Vincent Hosp, 60-68; prof pharmacol, Samford Univ, 60-68; med & exec dir, Kauikeolani Children's Hosp, 68-71; dir pediat serv, Charity Hosp New Orleans, 71-77; mem adv comt drug efficacy study, Nat Res Coun-Nat Acad Sci, mem drug res bd, 71-74. *Mem:* Fel Am Acad Pediat; Am Pediat Soc; Am Soc Pharmacol & Exp Therapeut. *Mailing Add:* 1214 Paxton Ave Cincinnati OH 45208-2833

SHIRLEY, AARON, PEDIATRICS. *Current Pos:* CLIN INSTR PEDIAT, MED SCH, UNIV MISS, 67-; MED DIR, JACKSON MED HALL, 96- *Personal Data:* b Gluckstadt, Miss, Jan 3, 33; m; c 4. *Educ:* Tougaloo Col, BS, 55; McHarry Med Col, MD, 59; Univ Miss, MD, 68. *Honors & Awards:* MacArthur Fel Award, 93. *Prof Exp:* Intern, Herbert Hosp, Tenn, 59-60; gen pract, Vicksburg, 60-65. *Concurrent Pos:* Fac med, Tufts Univ Med, Mass, 68-73 & Univ Miss Med Sch, 70-; head start consult, Am Acad Pediat, 69-74; proj dir, Jackson-Hinds Comprehensive Health Ctr, 70-96; mem bd dirs, Field Found, 73-89; mem adv bd, Rural Pract Proj, Robert Wood Johnson Found, 74-78; mem, Select Panel Prom Child Health, Washington, DC, 79-81; mem coun, Inst Med-Nat Acad Sci, 88- *Mem:* Inst Med-Nat Acad Sci. *Res:* Various health services for the poor and under served population; author of several publications. *Mailing Add:* Jackson Med Mall 350 W Woodrow Wilson Blvd Suite 302-A Jackson MS 39213. *Fax:* 601-982-0489

SHIRLEY, BARBARA ANNE, REPRODUCTIVE PHYSIOLOGY, ENDOCRINOLOGY. *Current Pos:* from asst prof to assoc prof, 64-79, PROF ZOOL, UNIV TULSA, 79- *Personal Data:* b Muskogee, Okla, Oct 15, 36. *Educ:* Okla Baptist Univ, BA, 56; Univ Okla, MS, 61, PhD(zool), 64. *Prof Exp:* Asst, Univ Okla, 58-62. *Mem:* AAAS; Soc Study Reproduction; Am Physiol Soc. *Res:* Reproduction; embryo culture. *Mailing Add:* Dept Biol Sci Univ Tulsa 600 S College Tulsa OK 74104-3189. *E-Mail:* biol_bas@vax1.utulsa.edu

SHIRLEY, DAVID ARTHUR, CHEMICAL PHYSICS. *Current Pos:* lectr chem, Univ Calif, Berkeley, 59-60, from asst prof to prof, 60-92, from vchmn to chmn dept, 68-75, assoc lab dir & head, Mat & Molecular Res Div, 75-80, dir, 80-89, EMER DIR, LAWRENCE BERKELEY NAT LAB, UNIV CALIF, BERKELEY, 97- *Personal Data:* b North Conway, NH, Mar 30, 34; m 56; c 5. *Educ:* Univ Maine, BS, 55; Univ Calif, Berkeley, PhD(chem), 59. *Hon Degrees:* ScD, Univ Maine, 78; Dr Rer Nat, FU Berlin, 87. *Honors & Awards:* Ernest O Lawrence Award, USAEC, 72. *Prof Exp:* Sr vpres res & dean, Grad Sch, Pa State Univ, 92-96. *Concurrent Pos:* NSF fels, Oxford Univ, 66-67 & Free Univ Berlin, 70; assoc ed, J Chem Physics, 74-76. *Mem:* Nat Acad Sci; AAAS; Am Chem Soc; Am Phys Soc; Fedn Am Scientists; Am Acad Arts & Sci. *Res:* Electron spectroscopy of atoms, molecules and solids with emphasis on surfaces and many-electron effects. *Mailing Add:* Lawrence Berkeley Nat Lab MS-4-230 1 Cyclotron Rd Berkeley CA 94720

SHIRLEY, FRANK CONNARD, FOREST MANAGEMENT, FOREST ECONOMICS. *Current Pos:* PRES, SHIRLEY FORESTS, INC, 81-; PRES, ASPEN FOREST CONSERV SYSTS, 85- *Personal Data:* b Minneapolis, Minn, Dec 18, 33; wid; c Crawford F, Timothy C, David H & Spencer W. *Educ:* Cornell Univ, AB, 55; State Univ NY Col Forestry, Syracuse, MF, 60; Univ Mich, Ann Arbor, AM, PhD(forestry), 69. *Prof Exp:* Forester, US Forest Serv, 60-64; asst prof forest econ, Colo State Univ, 69-72; consult forest mgt policy & econ, 72-74; opers res analyst, St Regis Paper Co, 74-85. *Mem:* Fel Soc Am Foresters; Am Forestry Asn; Sigma Xi. *Res:* Forest land management in an affluent society. *Mailing Add:* 18219 S Vaughn Rd KPN Vaughn WA 98394

SHIRLEY, HERSCHEL VINCENT, JR, ANIMAL GENETICS, ANIMAL PHYSIOLOGY. *Current Pos:* RETIRED. *Personal Data:* b Alpharetta, Ga, Aug 29, 23; m 51; c 3. *Educ:* Univ Ga, BSA, 49, MSA, 51; Univ Ill, PhD(animal genetics & physiol), 55. *Prof Exp:* Assoc prof & assoc poultry geneticist, Agr Exp Sta, Univ Tenn, 55-75, prof animal physiol & poultry geneticist, 75-90. *Mem:* Poultry Sci Asn; Am Genetic Asn. *Res:* Endocrinology of reproduction and stress physiology. *Mailing Add:* 232 Essex Dr Knoxville TN 37922

SHIRLEY, RAY LOUIS, ANIMAL NUTRITION. *Current Pos:* prof, 53-82, EMER PROF ANIMAL SCI & ANIMAL NUTRITIONIST, UNIV FLA, 82- *Personal Data:* b Berkeley Co, WVa, Dec 11, 12; m 43, 78; c 5. *Educ:* WVa Univ, BS, 37, MS, 39; Mich State Univ, PhD(biochem), 49. *Honors & Awards:* Gustav Bohstedt Award, Am Soc Animal Sci, 75. *Prof Exp:* Asst agr chem, WVa Univ, 37-39; asst biochem, Mich State Univ, 39-41, asst prof, 41-42; res chemist, Hercules Powder Co, 42-47; asst prof biochem, Mich State Univ, 47-49; prof animal nutrit & biochemist, Univ Fla, 49-51; prof chem, Shepherd Col, 51-53. *Mem:* AAAS; Soc Exp Biol & Med; fel Am Soc Animal Sci; Am Inst Nutrit. *Res:* Nitrogen compounds and minerals, isotopes, enzymes, energy in diets. *Mailing Add:* Univ Fla Gainesville FL 32611

SHIRLEY, ROBERT LOUIS, ORGANIC CHEMISTRY. *Current Pos:* OWNER/PRES, TECK-TOOL SUPPLY, 86- *Personal Data:* b Fairview Village, Ohio, Jan 11, 33; m 55; c 3. *Educ:* Col Wooster, BA, 55; Ohio State Univ, PhD(org chem), 60. *Prof Exp:* Res chemist, Jefferson Chem Co, Inc, 60-63, mem staff mkt develop, 63-70; mgr mkt develop, Ott Chem Co, 70-73; sales mgr, Story Chem Corp, 73-77; tech sales rep, Polymer Chem Div Upjohn, 77-85; sr sales specialist, Dow Chem Co, 85-86. *Mem:* Soc Plastics Engrs; Soc Automotive Engrs. *Res:* Phosgene chemistry; isocyanates, specialty organic chemicals. *Mailing Add:* 725 Lyncott St North Muskegon MI 49445-2836

SHIRLEY, THOMAS CLIFTON, CRUSTACEAN BIOLOGY, BENTHIC ECOLOGY. *Current Pos:* ASSOC PROF MARINE ECOL & FISHERIES, JUNEAU CTR FISHERIES & OCEAN SCI, UNIV ALASKA, FAIRBANKS, 88-, DIR, DIV FISHERIES, 92-, PROF, INVERT BIOL, 96- *Personal Data:* b Falfurrias, Tex, Sept 17, 47; m 79, Susan McCorkle. *Educ:* Tex A&I Univ, BS, 69, MS, 74; La State Univ, PhD(zool), 82. *Prof Exp:* Instr biol & invertebrate zool, La State Univ, 78-82; res scientist, Auke Bay Labs, Nat Marine Fisheries Serv, 82; asst prof biol & fisheries, Univ Alaska, Juneau, 82-87; assoc prof biol & fisheries, Univ Alaska Southeast, 87-88. *Concurrent Pos:* Mem plan team, NPac Fisheries Mgt Coun, 87-; vis assoc prof, Marine Lab, Duke Univ, 88-89; vis scientist, Univ Sydney, 94-95. *Mem:* AAAS; Am Soc Limnol & Oceanog; Soc Integrative & Comp Biol; Ecol Soc Am; Crustacean Soc; Int Asn Meiobenthologists. *Res:* Early life history of decapod crustaceans, benthic ecology, benthic-pelagic coupling, meiofauna ecology, bioenergetics and physiology of marine invertebrates. *Mailing Add:* Juneau Ctr Fisheries & Ocean Sci Univ Alaska 11120 Glacier Hwy Juneau AK 99801. *Fax:* 907-465-6447; *E-Mail:* jftcs@acad1.alaska.edu

SHIRN, GEORGE AARON, PHYSICS. *Current Pos:* RETIRED. *Personal Data:* b Williamsport, Pa, June 30, 21; m 46, Lula B Everidge; c 2. *Educ:* Columbia Univ, BS, 46; Rensselaer Polytech Inst, MS, 50, PhD(physics), 54. *Prof Exp:* Sr scientist, Res & Develop Ctr, Sprague Elec Co, 54-87. *Concurrent Pos:* Adj prof physics, N Adams State Col, Mass, 68- *Res:* Solid state physics; semiconductors; oxides; metals; thin films. *Mailing Add:* 37 Jamieson Heights Williamstown MA 01267-2001

SHIRTS, RANDALL BRENT, INTRAMOLECULAR VIBRATIONAL & ROTATIONAL DYNAMICS, SEMICLASSICAL METHODS. *Current Pos:* ASSOC, PROF CHEM, BRIGHAM YOUNG UNIV, 91- *Personal Data:* b Mt Pleasant, Utah, Apr 28, 50; m 74, Kathryn Adelle Hanson; c Michael R, Brian H, Caitlin E, Peter B, Kristen M & Erica A. *Educ:* Brigham Young Univ, BS, 73; Harvard Univ, AM, 78, PhD(chem physics), 79. *Prof Exp:* Res assoc, Joint Inst, Lab Astrophys & Dept Chem, Univ Colo, 79-81; asst prof chem, Georgetown Univ, 81-82, Univ Utah, 82-87; sci specialist, Idaho Nat Eng Lab, 87-91. *Concurrent Pos:* Vis scientist, Los Alamos Nat Lab, 86. *Mem:* Am Chem Soc; Am Phys Soc; Sigma Xi. *Res:* Spectroscopy and dynamics of intramolecular vibrational-rotational motion; laser-molecule interactions. *Mailing Add:* Dept Chem 220 ESC Brigham Young Univ Provo UT 84602. *Fax:* 801-378-6474

SHIU, ROBERT P C, MOLECULAR BIOLOGY, BREAST CANCER. *Current Pos:* PROF ENDOCRINOL & CELL BIOL, UNIV MAN, 77- *Educ:* McGill Univ, PhD(endocrinol), 74. *Mailing Add:* Dept Pysiol Univ Man Winnipeg MB R3E 0W3 Can. *Fax:* 204-774-6695; *E-Mail:* rshiu@ccu.umanitoba.ca

SHIUE, CHYNG-YANN, ORGANIC & MEDICINAL CHEMISTRY, NEUROSCIENCES. *Current Pos:* PROF RADIOL & DIR PET CHEM, UNIV PA, 93- *Personal Data:* b Tainan, Taiwan, Dec 15, 41; m 67, Grace; c Peter & Linda. *Educ:* Taiwan Normal Univ, BSc, 65; Brown Univ, PhD(chem), 70. *Prof Exp:* Asst org chem, Inst Chem, Acad Sinica, 64-65; res asst, Brown Univ, 66-70; res assoc, Univ Ky, 70-72; res assoc biochem pharmacol, 72-74; instr biochem, Brown Univ, 74-76; chemist, Brookhaven Nat Lab, 76-89; prof radiol & pharmacol, dir Ctr Metals Imaging, Creighton Univ, 89-93. *Concurrent Pos:* Mem, Ad Hoc Tech Rev Group, Nat Cancer Inst, 87, 88 & 91, US Dept Energy, 87, 89 & 90. *Mem:* Am Chem Soc; Soc Nuclear Med; NY Acad Sci; AAAS. *Res:* Synthesis of radiopharmaceuticals and other biologically active compounds; nuclear medicine. *Mailing Add:* Hosp Univ Pa 3400 Spruce St Philadelphia PA 19104. *Fax:* 215-662-7551

SHIUE, PETER JAY-SHYONG, FINITE FIELDS & THEIR APPLICATIONS. *Current Pos:* assoc prof, 85-89, PROF, DEPT MATH SCI, UNIV NEV, LAS VEGAS, 89-, CHMN DEPT, 90- *Personal Data:* b Taiwan, July 1, 41; US citizen; m 68, Stella; c Katherine & Min-Po. *Educ:* Nat Taiwan Normal Univ, Taipei, BS, 65; Southern Ill Univ, Carbondale, MS, 69, PhD(math), 71. *Honors & Awards:* Burrick Distinguished Scholar Award. *Prof Exp:* From assoc prof to prof & chmn, Chengchi Univ, Taipei, 72-81; assoc prof, Gardner-Webb Col, NC, 82-84 & Saginaw Valley State Univ, 84-85. *Concurrent Pos:* Italian Nat Res Coun fel, Univ Rome, 70-71; vis assoc prof, Nat Taiwan Univ, Taipei, 71-72 & Southern Ill Univ, 81-82; Alexander von Humboldt fel, Univ Gottingen, Ger, 73 & Univ Cologne, Ger, 74; vis lectr, Univ Ill, Urbana, 77 & Univ SFla, 78. *Mem:* Am Math Soc; Soc Indust & Appl Math. *Res:* Coding theory for the error-free transmission of information; generation of pseudorandom numbers for simulation; shift register sequences for the implementation of linear recurring sequences and combinatorial design. *Mailing Add:* Dept Math Sci Univ Nev Las Vegas NV 89154-4001

SHIVAKUMAR, KUNIGAL NANJUNDAIAH, ENGINEERING, STRUCTURAL ANALYSIS. *Current Pos:* PROF COMPOSITE MAT & FRACTURE MECH, NC A&T STATE UNIV, 91- *Personal Data:* m 84, Netra Dodde Gowda; c Nishkala & Nirmala. *Educ:* Bangalore Univ, BE, 72; Indian Inst Sci, Bangalore, ME, 74, PhD(aerospace eng), 79. *Honors & Awards:* Nat Res Coun Res Assoc Award, Nat Acad Sci & Nat Acad Eng, 79; Group Achievement Award, NASA, 86. *Prof Exp:* Resident res assoc, Nat Res Coun, 80-81; res assoc prof, Old Dominion Univ, 82-84; sr scientist & group leader, Anal Serv & Mat Inc, 85-91. *Concurrent Pos:* Consult Aerotech Corp, 90, Anal Serv & Mat Inc, 91-93; prin investr, NASA, 93-, Fed Aviation Admin, 95-97. *Mem:* Assoc fel Am Inst Aeronaut & Astronaut; Am Soc Testing & Mat; Am Soc Mech Engrs; Am Soc Composite Mat. *Res:* Develop mechanics models and test methods to determine mechanical properties of current and future composite materials; multidisciplinary analysis models and computer programs to study response of rocket and jet engines and components. *Mailing Add:* NC A&T State Univ 1601 E Market St Greensboro NC 27411

SHIVANANDAN, KANDIAH, ASTROPHYSICS, COSMOLOGY. *Current Pos:* PHYSICIST, NAVAL RES LAB, 65- *Personal Data:* b Parit Buntar, Malaya, Aug 22, 29; US citizen; m 62; c 2. *Educ:* Univ Melbourne, BSc, 58; Univ Toronto, MA, 59; Cath Univ Am, PhD(physics), 69. *Prof Exp:* Tech asst, Weapons Res Estab, Melbourne, Australia, 50-57; radiation physicist, Australian Atomic Energy Comn, 57-58; res physicist, Mass Inst Technol, 59-64. *Concurrent Pos:* Consult mem, Fed Radiation Coun, 60-63 & Int Atomic Energy Asn, Vienna, 60-65; mem, US Nuclear Weapons Study Comt, 63-; adv mem, US Arms Control & Disarmament Agency, 66, Europ Space Res Orgn, Paris, 68, Defense Sci Bd, 88 & Sci adv bd, NAtlantic Treaty Orgn, 85. *Mem:* Am Astron Soc; fel Royal Astron Soc; Europ Phys Soc; NY Acad Sci; Indian Inst Physics. *Res:* Biological effects of radiation from nuclear weapon tests; relativistic astrophysics and experimental infrared astronomy in relation to cosmology; infrared and submillimeter astronomy. *Mailing Add:* 4711 Overbrook Rd Bethesda MD 20816

SHIVA PRASAD, BELLUR GOPALIAH, FLUID MECHANICS, HEAT TRANSFER. *Current Pos:* mech engr II, 90-91, SR ENGR, DRESSER-RAND, 91- *Personal Data:* b Mysore, India, July 7, 47; US citizen. *Educ:* Bangalore Univ, India, BE, 67, Indian Inst Sci, ME, 70, PhD(aeronaut eng) 76. *Prof Exp:* Aerodyn eng, Indian Space Res orgn, 70; postdoctoral res assoc & vis asst prof, Southern Methodist Univ, Dallas, 78-82; engr IV, United Technol Elliott, 82-84; develop engr, AVCO Lycoming Textron, 84-87; assoc prof aeronaut, Dowling Col, 87-88; res scientist, Va Polytech Inst, 88-90. *Mem:* Am Soc Mech Engrs; Soc Automotive Engrs. *Res:* Structure of turbulence in steady and unsteady separated boundary layers; effect of streamline curvature on turbulence; fluid mechanics and heat transfer in positive displacement compressors; published several papers. *Mailing Add:* 43 Fox Lane Exten Painted Post NY 14870. *Fax:* 607-937-2390; *E-Mail:* b_g_shiva_prasad@dresser-rand.com

SHIVE, DONALD WAYNE, ANALYTICAL CHEMISTRY. *Current Pos:* From asst prof to assoc prof, 69-78, PROF CHEM, MUHLENBERG COL, 78- *Personal Data:* b Hanover, Pa, June 24, 42; m 71; c 2. *Educ:* Pa State Univ, BS, 64; Mass Inst Technol, PhD(chem), 69. *Honors & Awards:* Lindback Award, 78. *Concurrent Pos:* Consult, J T Baker Chem Co, 79-, Microchagnostics Inc, 85- *Mem:* Am Chem Soc. *Res:* Electrochemistry; chromatography. *Mailing Add:* 8031 Orchard View Lane Fogelsville PA 18051

SHIVE, PETER NORTHROP, GEOPHYSICS. *Current Pos:* asst prof geol, 69-72, assoc prof geol & physics, 72-76, PROF GEOL & PHYSICS, UNIV WYO, 76- *Personal Data:* b Plainfield, NJ, July 2, 41; m 64. *Educ:* Wesleyan Univ, BA, 64; Stanford Univ, PhD(geophys), 68. *Prof Exp:* Res assoc geophys, Stanford Univ, 68-69. *Mem:* AAAS; Am Geophys Union; Soc Terrestrial Magnetism & Elec; Soc Explor Geophys. *Res:* Rock magnetism; paleomagnetism; time series analysis; exploration seismology. *Mailing Add:* Dept Geol Univ Wyo PO Box 3006 Laramie WY 82071-3006

SHIVE, ROBERT ALLEN, JR, MATHEMATICS. *Current Pos:* asst prof, 69-74, assoc prof, 74-79, PROF MATH & ASSOC DEAN, MILLSAPS COL, 79-, DIR INFO SYSTS, 81- *Personal Data:* b Dallas, Tex, Oct 27, 42; m 64; c 3. *Educ:* Southern Methodist Univ, BA, 64, MS, 66; Iowa State Univ, PhD(math), 69. *Prof Exp:* Instr math, Iowa State Univ, 67-69. *Concurrent Pos:* Consult comput; adm intern, Am Coun Educ, 78-79. *Mem:* Am Math Soc; Math Asn Am. *Res:* Integration theory; computers in education. *Mailing Add:* 22 Moss Forest Circle Jackson MS 39211

SHIVE, WILLIAM, AMINO ACIDS, CONTROL MECHANISMS. *Current Pos:* RJ WILLIAMS PROF CHEM, UNIV TEX, 45- *Educ:* Univ Tex, PhD(chem), 41. *Res:* Control mechanisms. *Mailing Add:* Dept Chem Univ Tex Austin TX 78712

SHIVELY, CARL E, BACTERIOLOGY. *Current Pos:* asst prof bact & genetics, Alfred Univ, 68-71, assoc prof, 71-77, head, div biol sci, 77-83, PROF BACT & BIOCHEM, ALFRED UNIV, 78- *Personal Data:* b Laurelton, Pa, June 8, 36; wid; c Brian, Denise (Hughes) & Gretchen. *Educ:* Bloomsburg State Col, BS, 58; Bucknell Univ, MS, 61; St Bonaventure Univ, PhD(biol), 68. *Honors & Awards:* Outstanding Scientist Award, Eastman Kodak. *Prof Exp:* Instr bact, Bucknell Univ, 61; asst prof bact & genetics, State Univ NY Col Cortland, 63-65. *Mem:* Am Soc Microbiol; Sigma Xi; Am Soc Enol & Viticulture. *Res:* Biochemistry and fermentation chemistry; production of ethanol on a continuous basis by immobilized Zymomonas mobilis s c in an immobilized cell reactor; immobilizing material, foam glass; decreasing aging time of methode champenoise sparkling wines. *Mailing Add:* 26 N Main St Alfred NY 14802-1232. *Fax:* 607-871-2342; *E-Mail:* fshively@bigvax.alfred.edu

SHIVELY, CHARLES DEAN, PHARMACEUTICAL CHEMISTRY. *Current Pos:* MGR PHARM DEVELOP, COOPER LABS, INC, 77- *Personal Data:* b Dyersburg, Tenn, Feb 4, 44; m 66; c 2. *Educ:* Purdue Univ, BS, 67, PhD(indust & phys pharm), 72. *Prof Exp:* Sr scientist pharm develop, Alcon Labs, Inc, 71-75, prod mkt mgr, 75-76, res sect head, 76-77. *Concurrent Pos:* Lectr, Calif Bd Pharm Continuing Educ, 77-; adv bd mem, Nat Eye Res Found, 77- *Mem:* Am Pharmaceut Asn; Nat Eye Res Found; Sigma Xi. *Res:* Pharmaceutical dosage form development; pharmaceutical formulation; physical pharmacy; surface chemistry. *Mailing Add:* 18816 N 94th Ave Peoria AZ 85382

SHIVELY, FRANK THOMAS, PHYSICAL & ATMOSPHERIC OPTICS. *Current Pos:* PRIN SCIENTIST, ORION INT, 82- *Personal Data:* b Cuyahoga Falls, Ohio, Oct 31, 34; m 69. *Educ:* Oberlin Col, BA, 54; Yale Univ, MS, 57, PhD(physics), 61. *Prof Exp:* Asst physicist, Physics Dept, Yale Univ, 60-61; res physicist, Ctr Nuclear Studies, France, 61-63; res assoc, Lawrence Radiation Lab, Univ Calif, 63-66; sr researcher, Inst Nuclear Physics, Univ Paris, 66-68; mem staff, Los Alamos Meson Physics Facil, Univ Calif, 69-74; staff scientist & consult, Lawrence Berkeley Lab, Univ Calif, & Univ Calif, Los Angeles, 74-77; consult & sr scientist, Sci Simulation, Inc, 78-81. *Concurrent Pos:* Adj instr, Physics Dept, Univ Calif, Berkeley, 64; vis lectr, Colo Col, 75; dir consult, C D Sci Consults, 75-78; lectr, Honors Prog, Univ NMex, 76; vis prof physics, Univ Calif, Los Angeles, 77. *Mem:* Am Phys Soc; Sigma Xi; Optical Soc Am. *Res:* Strong, weak electromagnetic and weak interactions of particles and nuclei; particle beam propagation, physical optics; atmospheric physics & remote sensing theory; simulation methodology; author or coauthor of over 50 publications. *Mailing Add:* 1094 Governor Dempsey Dr Santa Fe NM 87501

SHIVELY, JAMES NELSON, VETERINARY PATHOLOGY. *Current Pos:* RETIRED. *Personal Data:* b Moran, Kans, Feb 9, 25; m 53, Ann Webster; c 3. *Educ:* Kans State Univ, DVM, 46; Johns Hopkins Univ, MPH, 53; Univ Rochester, MS, 56; Colo State Univ, PhD, 71. *Prof Exp:* Officer in charge vet med, Army Med Lab, 46-52; res vet, Agr Res Prog, Univ Tenn, AEC, 54-55; chief vet virol, Div Vet Med, Walter Reed Army Inst Res, 56-60; vet, Res Br, Div Radiol Health, USPHS, 60-62, Radiol Health Lab, Colo, 62-68 & Path Sect, Div Biol Effects, Bur Radiol Health, Md, 68-70; assoc prof ultrastructural path, NY State Vet Col, Cornell Univ, 71-75; prof vet sci, Univ Ariz, 75-90. *Mem:* Am Vet Med Asn; Electron Micros Soc Am; Int Acad Path; Sigma Xi. *Res:* Pathology; electron microscopy. *Mailing Add:* 17591 Canitro Coafianza Sahuarita AZ 86004

SHIVELY, JESSUP MACLEAN, BIOCHEMISTRY, MICROBIOLOGY. *Current Pos:* chmn, Biochem Sect, Biol Div, Clemson Univ, 70-71, from assoc prof to prof, 70-94, head dept, 71-82, DISTINGUISHED PROF BIOCHEM, CLEMSON UNIV, 94- *Personal Data:* b Monrovia, Ind, Nov 9, 35; m, Karen L Fromm; c 2. *Educ:* Purdue Univ, BS, 57, MS, 59, PhD(microbiol), 62. *Prof Exp:* Instr microbiol, Purdue Univ, 61-62; from asst prof to assoc prof, Univ Nebr, Lincoln, 62-70. *Concurrent Pos:* NSF fel, Scripps Inst Oceanog, 65; fel, Inst Enzyme Res, Univ Wis-Madison, 68-69, Dept Physiol Chem, Med Sch, Johns Hopkins Univ, 69-70, Med Div, Oak Ridge Assoc Univs, 71, Wash State Univ, 76; guest prof, Univ Hamburg, Fed Repub Ger, 81-82, St Louis Univ, 82, Pa State Univ, 83, Exxon Res, 84, Univ Ill, 86, Idaho Nat Eng Lab, 88 & 89 & Meharry Med Col, 90. *Mem:* AAAS; Am Soc Microbiol; Brit Soc Gen Microbiol; Am Soc Biochem & Molecular Biol. *Res:* Lipids and membranes of bacteria; ribulose bisphosphate carboxylase/oxygenase, carboxysomes, sulfur oxidation, autotrophic microbes, Calvin cycle, carbon dioxide fixation. *Mailing Add:* Dept Biol Sci Clemson Univ Clemson SC 29634-1903. *Fax:* 864-656-0435; *E-Mail:* sjessup@clemson.edu

SHIVELY, JOHN ADRIAN, CLINICAL PATHOLOGY, HEMATOLOGY. *Current Pos:* clin prof, Col Med, Univ SFla, 83-88, prof, 88-93, assoc dean, 90-93, interim chmn, Dept Path, 93-95, EMER PROF PATH, COL MED, UNIV SFLA, 93- *Personal Data:* b Rossville, Ind, Oct 29, 22; m 45, Lois L Faris; c David, Ann, Theodore & Janet. *Educ:* Ind Univ, BA, 44, MD, 46. *Prof Exp:* Lab asst physiol, Ind Univ, 43-44; clin pathologist, Clin Hosp, Bluffton, Ind, 52-54; asst prof path, Sch Med, Ind Univ, 54-57; pathologist, Manatee Mem Hosp, Bradenton, Fla, 57-62; assoc prof path, Col Med, Univ Ky, 62-63; pathologist, Univ Tex M D Anderson Hosp & Tumor Inst, 63-68; prof path, Sch Med, Univ Mo, Columbia, 68-71; chmn dept, Univ Tenn, Memphis, 71-76, prof path, 71-83, vchancellor acad affairs, Ctr Health Sci, 76-83; med dir, Smith Kline Bio-Sci Labs, Tampa, 83-88. *Mem:* AAAS; Col Am Pathologists; Am Soc Clin Path; Am Col Physicians; Am Asn Blood Banks (pres, 67-68); Am Soc Hemat; Sigma Xi. *Res:* Bone marrow failure; platelet pathology; oncology; medical education. *Mailing Add:* 12901 N 30th St PO Box 11 Tampa FL 33612. *Fax:* 813-974-5536

SHIVELY, JOHN ERNEST, BIOCHEMISTRY, IMMUNOLOGY. *Current Pos:* SCIENTIST IMMUNOCHEM, BECKMAN RES INST CITY OF HOPE, 75- *Personal Data:* b Chicago, Ill, Aug 25, 46; m 67, Louise Neilsen; c Joanie & Katy. *Educ:* Univ Ill, Urbana, BS, 68, MS, 69, PhD(biochem), 75. *Mem:* Am Soc Biochem & Molecular Biol; Protein Soc; AAAS. *Res:* Microsequence studies on carcinoembryonic antigen and to antibodies; protein structural analysis; antibody engineering; chelate conjugations. *Mailing Add:* Dept Immunol Beckman Res Inst City Hope 1450 E Duarte Rd Duarte CA 91010-3000. *E-Mail:* jshively@coh.org

SHIVELY, RALPH LELAND, MATHEMATICS. *Current Pos:* prof math & chmn dept, 65-87, EMER PROF MATH, LAKE FOREST COL, 87- *Personal Data:* b Mt Morris, Ill, Nov 22, 21; m 50, Catherine Miller; c Thomas S & Philip A. *Educ:* Univ Mich, BSE, 47, MA, 48, PhD(math), 54. *Prof Exp:* From instr to asst prof math, Western Res Univ, 51-55, assoc prof, 56-61; assoc prof, Manchester Col, 55-56 & Col, 61-64; sr mathematician, Oak Ridge Nat Lab, 64-65. *Concurrent Pos:* NSF fac fel, Univ Calif, Berkeley, 60-61; vis res fel, Comput Lab, Oxford Univ, 71-72 & Univ Chicago, 83. *Mem:* Am Math Soc; Math Asn Am; Sigma Xi. *Res:* Special functions of classical analysis. *Mailing Add:* 224 Mountain View Dr Bridgewater VA 22812

SHIVER, JOHN W, EXPERIMENTAL IMMUNOLOGY, VACCINES. *Current Pos:* SR STAFF RES, MERCK RES LABS, 91- *Personal Data:* b Jacksonville, Fla, Aug 31, 57. *Educ:* Wofford Col, BS, 78; Univ Fla, PhD(chem), 85. *Prof Exp:* Postdoctoral res assoc, Purdue Univ, 85-88; sr staff scientist, NIH, 88-91, sr staff res fel, 90-91. *Mem:* Am Soc Biochem & Molecular Biol; Am Asn Immunologists. *Mailing Add:* Dept Virus & Cell Biol Res Labs WP16-306 West Point PA 19486. *Fax:* 215-652-7320

SHIVERICK, KATHLEEN THOMAS, BIOCHEMICAL PHARMACOLOGY, PHYSIOLOGY. *Current Pos:* ASST PROF PHARMACOL, UNIV FLA, 78- *Personal Data:* b Burlington, Vt, Dec 1, 43; c 1. *Educ:* Univ Vt, BS, 65, PhD(physiol), 74. *Prof Exp:* Res asst, Univ Vt, 65-68; fel endocrinol, McGill Univ, 74-76, res assoc pharmacol, 76-78. *Concurrent Pos:* Fel, Am Lung Asn, 74-76; res assoc, Roche Develop Pharm Unit, McGill Univ, 76-78. *Res:* Endocrine pharmacology. *Mailing Add:* Dept Pharmacol & Therapeut Univ Fla UHMHC Box J-267 Gainesville FL 32610-0267. *Fax:* 904-392-9696

SHIVERS, CHARLES ALEX, REPRODUCTIVE BIOLOGY, DEVELOPMENTAL BIOLOGY. *Current Pos:* from asst prof to assoc prof zool, 63-71, PROF ZOOL, UNIV TENN, KNOXVILLE, 71- *Personal Data:* b Goodlettsville, Tenn, Sept 16, 32; m 55; c 3. *Educ:* George Peabody Col, BS, 55, MA, 56; Mich State Univ, PhD(zool), 61. *Prof Exp:* Instr chem, Cumberland Univ, 56-58, res asst develop, Mich State Univ, 59-60; USPHS fel, Fla State Univ, 61-63. *Concurrent Pos:* Dir, IVF Lab, E Tenn Baptist Hosp, 84-87 & Ft Sauders Hosp, 88-89; vis prof, Cambridge Univ, Catholic Univ & Monash Univ. *Mem:* AAAS; Am Soc Zoologists. *Res:* Immunochemical studies on fertilization mechanisms. *Mailing Add:* 2112 Manor Rd Knoxville TN 37920

SHIVERS, RICHARD RAY, ZOOLOGY, CELL BIOLOGY. *Current Pos:* From asst prof to assoc prof, 67-86, PROF ZOOL, UNIV WESTERN ONT, 86- *Personal Data:* b Salina, Kans, Dec 18, 40; m 92, Sarah A Siegner; c Shaun & Stephanie. *Educ:* Univ Kans, AB, 63, MA, 65, PhD(zool), 67. *Concurrent Pos:* Helen Battle res prof zool, 97-98. *Mem:* Am Soc Cell Biol; Am Asn Anat; Can Asn Anat; Soc Neurosci; Pan-Am Asn Anat. *Res:* Electron microscopic anatomy of invertebrate nervous systems; freeze-fracture of nerve regeneration; neurosecretory portions of the crayfish optic ganglia; reptile blood-brain interface, ultrastructure and freeze-fracture of vertebrate blood-brain barrier; freeze-fracture and ultrastructure of human brain tumor vascular systems; culture of brain microvessel endothelial cells; development of endothelial cells in vitro; brain tumor angiogenesis. *Mailing Add:* Dept Zool Univ Western Ont London ON N6A 5B7 Can. *Fax:* 519-661-2014; *E-Mail:* rshivers@julian.uwo.ca

SHIZGAL, HARRY M, PALLIATIVE MEDICINE. *Current Pos:* from asst prof to assoc prof, 71-80, PROF SURG, MCGILL UNIV, 80- *Personal Data:* b Montreal, Que, June 23, 38; m 90, Wendy Fine; c Debbie, Lisa & Andrew. *Educ:* McGill Univ, BSc, 59, MD, 63, FRCPS(C). *Prof Exp:* Intern, Royal Victoria Hosp, 63-64, surg resident, 64-65 & 67-69, res fel, 65-67, asst surgeon, 71-77, assoc surgeon, 77-84, fel, Univ Calif, San Francisco, 70-71. *Concurrent Pos:* Sr surgeon & dir res inst, Royal Victoria Hosp, 84- *Mem:* Fel Am Col Surg; Soc Univ Surgeons; Am Surg Asn; Am Soc Clin Nutrit; Am Soc Parenteral & Enteral Nutrit. *Res:* Nutritional support of the hospitalized critially ill patient. *Mailing Add:* 687 Pine Ave W Montreal PQ H3A 1A1 Can. *Fax:* 514-843-1687; *E-Mail:* shizgel@rvhr1.lan.mcgill.ca

SHKAROFSKY, ISSIE PETER, PLASMA & FUSION PHYSICS, MICROWAVE ELECTRONICS. *Current Pos:* res & develop fel, 77-88, DIR FUSION TECHNOL DIV, MPB TECHNOL INC, POINTE-CLAIRE, QUE, 88- *Personal Data:* b Montreal, Que, July 4, 31; m 57, Agnes Spira; c Marvin, Sema, Lou & Aviva. *Educ:* McGill Univ, BSc, 52, MSc, 53, PhD(physics), 57. *Prof Exp:* Res & develop fel, Res & Develop Labs, RCA Ltd, Ste Anne de Bellevue, 57-76. *Mem:* Can Asn Physicists; fel Am Phys Soc; Am Geophys Union. *Res:* Plasma kinetics and waves; fusion; lasers and microwaves; propagation; turbulence; space and ionosphere; radar. *Mailing Add:* 1959 Clinton Ave Montreal PQ H3S 1L2 Can. *Fax:* 514-695-7492; *E-Mail:* u1114@k.nersc.gov

SHKLAR, GERALD, ORAL PATHOLOGY. *Current Pos:* chmn, Dept Oral Med & Oral Path, 71-93, CHARLES A BRACKETT PROF, DEPT ORAL MED & DIAG SCI, SCH DENT MED, HARVARD UNIV, 71- *Personal Data:* b Montreal, Que, Dec 2, 24; nat US; wid; c David, Michael & Ruth. *Educ:* McGill Univ, BSc, 47, DDS, 49; Tufts Univ, MS, 52; Am Bd Oral Path, dipl; Am Bd Periodont, dipl. *Hon Degrees:* MA, Harvard Univ, 71. *Honors & Awards:* Int Researcher Award, Acad Int Dent Studies. *Prof Exp:* Res assoc oral path & periodont, Sch Dent Med, Tufts Univ, 51-52, from instr to assoc prof, 52-60, assoc prof oral path & assoc res prof periodont, 60-61, prof oral path & chmn dept, 61-71. *Concurrent Pos:* Nat Res Coun Can dent res fel, 51-52; dir cancer training prog, Sch Dent Med, Tufts Univ, 52-71; prof dent hist, 60-63, lectr social dent, 63-71, lectr oral path, Forsyth Sch Dent Hygienists, 53-71, res prof periodont, 60-71; oral pathologist, Boston City Hosp, 61-88; consult, Mass Gen Hosp, Brigham & Women's Hosp & Children's Hosp Med Ctr. *Mem:* Am Dent Asn; Am Acad Oral Path; Am Acad Periodont; fel Int Col Dentists; fel Am Col Dentists; Am Asn Cancer Res. *Res:* Tumors of mouth and jaws; experimental pathology of salivary glands and periodontal tissues; pathology and physiology of bone; experimental carcinogensis; histochemistry of oral diseases; ultrastructure oral tissues; radiation biology. *Mailing Add:* 7 Chauncy Lane Cambridge MA 02138

SHKLOV, NATHAN, COMBINATORICS & FINITE MATHEMATICS. *Current Pos:* PROF MATH, UNIV WINDSOR, 67- *Personal Data:* b Winnipeg, Man, Aug 3, 18; m 51; c 1. *Educ:* Univ Man, BA, 40; Univ Toronto, MA, 49. *Prof Exp:* Spec lectr math, Univ Sask, 51-52, from instr to assoc prof, 52-67, chmn comput ctr, 62-67. *Concurrent Pos:* Consult, Defense Res Bd Can, 56-60; ed-in-chief, Can Comput Sci Asn, 66-71. *Mem:* Math Asn Am; Inst Math Statist; Statist Soc Can (pres, 72-74). *Res:* Non-associative algebras; statistical design of experiments; quadrature formulas. *Mailing Add:* 2667 St Patrick's Dr Windsor ON N9E 3G5 Can

SHKOLNIKOV, MOISEY B, FINITE ELEMENT METHOD TECHNOLOGY, STRUCTURAL MECHANICS. *Current Pos:* STAFF RES ENGR, GEN MOTORS CORP, MICH, 85- *Personal Data:* b USSR; US citizen; c 1. *Educ:* Maritime Univ, USSR, MS, 50; Automotive Univ, USSR, PhD(mech eng), 61; Supreme Certifying Comn, USSR, DSc, 74. *Prof Exp:* Sr scientist, Combat Eng Res Inst, Moscow, 61-66; head, Res Lab, NAMI, Major Res Inst USSR Automotive Indust, 66-81; sr engr, Gramman Flexible Corp, Ohio, 81-85. *Res:* Nonlinear finite element technology; simulation of complex automotive structures and occupant behavior under impact loads in collision using super computers; computer metal forming simulation, analysis crash worthiness and occupant computer simulation. *Mailing Add:* 1408 S Bates Birmingham MI 48009

SHLAFER, MARSHAL, CARDIAC ISCHEMIA, OXYGEN RADICALS. *Current Pos:* ASSOC PROF PHARMACOL & SURG, UNIV MICH MED CTR, 77- *Educ:* Med Col Ga, PhD(pharmacol), 74. *Mailing Add:* Dept Pharmacol Med Sci Bldg 1 Univ Mich Med Sch M6322 Ann Arbor MI 48109. *Fax:* 313-763-4450

SHLANTA, ALEXIS, ATMOSPHERIC PHYSICS. *Current Pos:* physicist atmospheric physics, 73-84, PROG MGR, NAVAL WEAPONS CTR, CHINA LAKE, 84- *Personal Data:* b Scranton, Pa, June 17, 37; m 65, 83; c 3. *Educ:* Univ Tex, El Paso, BS, 62, MS, 65; NMex Inst Mining & Technol, PhD(atmospheric physics), 72. *Prof Exp:* Res engr space physics & radar, NAm Aviation, Inc, 62-63; instr physics, Buena Vista Col, 66-67. *Concurrent Pos:* Fel, Nat Oceanic & Atmospheric Admin, 72-73. *Mem:* Am Meteorol Soc; Fed Mgrs Assn; fel Naval Weapons Ctr. *Res:* The determination and quantification of the effects of atmospheric conditions on the performance of tactical weapon systems; currently Phoenix Missile Program Technical Manager. *Mailing Add:* PO Box 815 Ridgecrest CA 93556-0815

SHLEIEN, BERNARD, DOSE RECONSTRUCTION, ENVIRONMENTAL EPIDEMIOLOGY. *Current Pos:* PRES, SCINTA, INC, 90- *Personal Data:* b New York, NY, Feb 5, 34; m 60; c 2. *Educ:* Univ Southern Calif, PharmD, 57; Harvard Univ, MS, 63; Am Bd Health Physics, dipl, 66; Am Bd Health Physics, cert health physicist. *Honors & Awards:* Commendation Medal, US Pub Health Sect. *Prof Exp:* Staff pharmacist, USPHS Hosp, Seattle, 57-59, anal chemist, Med Supply Depot, 59-60; asst to chief radiol intel fallout studies, Robert A Taft Sanit Eng Ctr, Bur Radiol Health, 60-62, chief dosimetry, Northeastern Radiol Health Lab, 63-70, chief environ radiation, 68-70; co-proj officer, Fed Radiation Coun-Nat Acad Sci Risk Eval, Dept Health, Educ & Welfare, 70-72, tech adv, Off Bur Dir, 72-78, asst dir sci affairs, Bur Radiol Health, Food & Drug Admin, 78-84; head, Isotopes & Radiol Health Inst Environ Health, Tel Aviv Univ, 84-86. *Concurrent Pos:* Mem Intersoc Comn Ambient Air Sampling, chmn radioactive substances, 66-72; mem temporary staff, Fed Radiation Coun-Environ Protection Agency spec studies group, 70-; pres, Nucleon Lectr Assocs; exec secy, tech steering panel, Hanford Environ Dose Reconstruct Proj, 88- *Mem:* AAAS; fel Health Physics Soc; Am Indust Hyg Asn; fel Am Pub Health Asn. *Res:* Radiation hazards; radioactive aerosols; population doses; radiation carcinogenesis, and standards setting; energy planning for radiation accidents; dose reconstruction. *Mailing Add:* 2421 Homestead Dr Silver Spring MD 20902. *Fax:* 301-593-1018

SHLESINGER, MICHAEL, NON-LINEAR DYNAMICS. *Current Pos:* Res scientist, 83-95, CHIEF SCIENTIST, OFF NAVAL RES, 95- *Personal Data:* b Brooklyn, NY, Aug 8, 48. *Educ:* State Univ NY, BS, 70; Univ Rochester, MA, 72, PhD(physics), 75. *Mem:* Fel Am Phys Soc. *Mailing Add:* Off Naval Res Code 330 800 N Quincy St Arlington VA 22217

SHLEVIN, HAROLD H, OPHTHALMOLOGY, PHARMACEUTICAL RESEARCH & DEVELOPMENT. *Current Pos:* VPRES, RES, PROD & BUS DEVELOP, CIBA-GEIGY/CIBA VISION OPHTHALMICS, DULUTH, GA, 90- *Personal Data:* b Providence, RI, Sept 15, 49; m 72, Barbara Fellner; c Annie. *Educ:* Boston Univ, BA, 71; Univ Rochester, MS, 75, PhD(physiol), 77. *Prof Exp:* Sr scientist, G D Searle & Co, Skokie, Ill, 80-82 dir, Strategy & Bus Develop, 88-89; mgr cardiac res, Pharmaceut Div, Ciba-Geigy, Summit, NJ, 83-84, dir, Sci Info Syst, 84-86, dir strategy, sci & technol, 87-90, dir strategy & bus develop, 88-89. *Concurrent Pos:* Postdoctoral, Mayo Clinic. *Mem:* Am Soc Pharmacol & Exp Therapeut; Asn Res Vision & Ophthal; Am Physiol Soc; Biophys Soc; Licensing Execs Soc; Drug Info Asn; Inst Elec & Electronics Engrs. *Res:* Ophthalmology; research & clinical development of innovative pharmaceutical products to treat acute and chronic eye diseases; major interest/specialities include: dry eye, glaucoma, inflammation/allergy, ocular pain, antivirals and autoimmune disease. *Mailing Add:* CIBA Vision Ophthalmics CIBA-Geigy 11460 Johns Creek Pkwy Duluth GA 30155. *Fax:* 770-418-3040

SHMAEFSKY, BRIAN ROBERT, SCIENCE & TECHNOLOGY PUBLIC EDUCATION, GENETICS ETHICS EDUCATION. *Current Pos:* ASST PROF & CHMN BIOL, NORTHWESTERN OKLA STATE UNIV, 88- *Personal Data:* b Brooklyn, NY, July 13, 56; m 86; c 2. *Educ:* City Univ New York, BS, 79; Southern Ill Univ, Edwardsville, MS, 81, EdD(sci educ), 87. *Prof Exp:* Chemist, Sigma Chem Co, 82-85; instr biol educ, Southern Ill Univ, Edwardsville, 85-88. *Concurrent Pos:* Vis instr, McKendree Col, Ill, 82-88, St Louis Community Col, 88; pres, Sci Ed Sect, Okla Acad Sci, 88-89 & 90-91, vpres, 89-90; contrib ed, Nat Sci Teachers Asn, 88-; consult, sci educ, sponsored by Soc Col Sci Teaching, 89-; book reviewer, J Biopharm, 90- *Mem:* Nat Sci Teachers Asn; Nat Biol Teachers Asn; Sigma Xi; Nat Asn Sci Technol & Soc. *Res:* Genetic ethics-the social attitudes and origins; conducting a study introducing simple scientific research into elementary classes in US and Canada. *Mailing Add:* Dept Math & Sci Kingwood Col 20000 Kingwood Dr Humble TX 77339-3801

SHMOYS, JERRY, ELECTROPHYSICS. *Current Pos:* from instr to asst prof elec eng, Polytech Univ, 55-60, assoc prof electrophys, 60-68, prof, 68-80, prof elec eng, 80-91, EMER PROF, POLYTECH UNIV, 91- *Personal Data:* b Warsaw, Poland, Oct 6, 23; US citizen; m 53; c 2. *Educ:* Cooper Union, BEE, 45; NY Univ, PhD(physics), 52. *Prof Exp:* Jr electronic engr, Marine Div, Bendix Aviation Corp, 45; asst proj engr, Res Labs, Sperry Gyroscope Co, 45-46; res asst, Physics Dept, NY Univ, 46-49, math res group, 49-52, res assoc, Inst Math Sci, 52-55. *Concurrent Pos:* Mem US Comn B, Int Sci Radio Union, 66-; Nat Acad Sci-Nat Res Coun sr res fel, Ames Res Ctr, NASA, 67-68. *Mem:* Sr mem Inst Elec & Electronics Engrs; Am Phys Soc. *Res:* Diffraction and propagation of electromagnetic waves; antenna theory; plasma research; linear accelerator theory. *Mailing Add:* 18 Crandon St Melville NY 11747-1253. *E-Mail:* shmoys@rama.poly.edu

SHNEIDERMAN, BEN, HUMAN-COMPUTER INTERACTION. *Current Pos:* from asst prof to assoc prof, DEPT COMPUT SCI, 76-89, HEAD, HUMAN-COMPUT INTERACTION LAB, INST ADVAN COMPUT STUDIES, UNIV MD, 83-, PROF COMPUT SCI, 89- *Personal Data:* b New York, NY, Aug 21, 47; m 73; c 2. *Educ:* City Col NY, BS, 68; State Univ NY, Stony Brook, MS, 72, PhD(comput sci), 73. *Hon Degrees:* PhD, Univ Guelph, Can, 95. *Prof Exp:* Instr data processing, State Univ NY, Farmingdale, 68-72, comput sci, Stony Brook, 72-73; asst prof, Ind Univ, 73-76. *Mem:* fel Asn Comput Mach; Inst Elec & Electronics Engrs Comput Soc. *Res:* Human factors of designing software, user interfaces, information visualization and interactive information systems; hypertex and database systems; high level problem solving and learning; impact of computers on society. *Mailing Add:* Univ Md AV Williams Bldg Rm 3175 College Park MD 20742-3255. *E-Mail:* ben@cs.umd.edu

SHNEOUR, ELIE ALEXIS, BIOCHEMISTRY, NEUROSCIENCES. *Current Pos:* PRES & CHIEF EXEC OFFICER, BIOSYST INSTS INC & DIR, BIOSYSTS RES INST, 74- *Personal Data:* b Paris, France, Dec 11, 25; nat US; m 90, Polly Marvick Henderson; c Mark Z & Alan B. *Educ:* Columbia Univ, BA, 47; Univ Calif, Berkeley, MA, 55, Univ Calif, Los Angeles, PhD(biol chem), 58. *Hon Degrees:* DSc, Bard Col, 68. *Prof Exp:* Asst dir res & develop, J A E Color Works, NY, 48-50; sr res technician, Univ Calif, Berkeley, 50-53, asst biochem, 53-55, asst, Univ Calif, Los Angeles, 55-58; Am Heart Asn res fel, Univ Calif, Berkeley, 58-62; res assoc genetics, Stanford Univ, 62-65; assoc prof molecular & genetic biol, Univ Utah, 65-69; vis res neurochemist, Div Neurosci, City of Hope Nat Med Ctr, Duarte, Calif, 69-71; dir res, Calbiochem, 71-74. *Concurrent Pos:* Consult, Melpar Inc, 64-65, Gen Elec Co, 65- & NAm Aviation, Inc, 66-70 & other maj US & Foreign Corps, 74-; exec secy biol & explor Mars study group, Nat Acad Sci, 64-65; chmn regional biosci res coun manned earth orbiting missions, Am Inst Biol Sci, 66-69; chmn sci adv prog, Am Soc Biol Chemists, 73-78, mem sci & pub policy comt, 74-76; mem sci adv coun, Cousteau Soc, Inc, 77-; mem bd dir, San Diego Biomed Inst, 81-86; chmn; Sci Adv Bd, Quadroma, Inc, 81-84; mem, Sci Adv Bd, Advan Polymer Systs Inc. *Mem:* Am Chem Soc; Int Soc Neurochem; NY Acad Sci; Am Soc Biochem & Molecular Biol; Am Soc Neurosci; Int Soc Neurochem. *Res:* Pharmacology and biochemistry of natural substances; developmental neurochemistry; information processing by biological systems; research administration; science communications; science policy. *Mailing Add:* Biosysts Res Inst 700 Front St CDM-608 San Diego CA 92101-6009. *E-Mail:* eshneour@uesd.edu

SHNIDER, BRUCE I, INTERNAL MEDICINE, ONCOLOGY. *Current Pos:* Intern, DC Gen Hosp, 48-49, from jr asst resident to chief resident, Georgetown Univ Hosp, 49-52, from instr to assoc prof med, 52-66, from asst prof to assoc prof pharmacol, 61-66, cancer coordr, 60-66, from asst dean to assoc dean, 61-79, prog dir clin cancer training, 70-75, dir, Breast Cancer Detection Demonstration Prog, 76-79, prof med, sch med, 68-85, EMER PROF, SCH MED, GEORGETOWN UNIV, 86- *Personal Data:* b Ludzk, Poland, Jan 20, 20; nat US; m 42, Doris Benjamin; c Steven D, Marc R & Reed M. *Educ:* Wilson Teachers Col, BS, 41; Georgetown Univ, MD, 48; Am Bd Internal Med, dipl, 55. *Concurrent Pos:* Dir Tumor serv & cancer chemother res prog, Georgetown Univ Med Div, DC Gen Hosp, 57-, chief vis physician, 57-59, exec officer, 59-60, coord teaching activ, 61-; prin investr, East Coop Group Solid Tumor Chemother, 57-, chmn, 61-71; dir div oncol, Dept Med, Georgetown Univ, 61-80; consult, oncol clin & vis physician, Georgetown Univ Med Ctr, Holy Cross Hosp, Wash Hosp Ctr & Mt Alto Vet Hosp; consult, Clin Ctr, NIH; vis prof oncol, Sch Med, Tel Aviv Univ, 72-73 & 89-90, Sch Med, Hebrew Univ, 79-80, 88, 91, 92 & 93, Ben Gurion Univ, Fac Health Sci, 85, Inst Oncol, Shaare Zedek Med Ctr, Jerusalem, 93-; emer consult Walter Reed Med Ctr, 76. *Mem:* Am Soc Clin Oncol; fel Col Clin Pharmacol & Chemother; Am Asn Cancer Res; fel Am Col Physicians; Am Soc Clin Pharmacol & Therapeut. *Res:* Medical oncology; clinical pharmacology; chemotherapy of cancer; controlled clinical oncology trials. *Mailing Add:* 610 Sisson St Silver Spring MD 20902

SHNIDER, RUTH WOLKOW, applied mathematics, physics; deceased, see previous edition for last biography

SHNIDER, SOL M, medicine; deceased, see previous edition for last biography

SHNITKA, THEODOR KHYAM, PATHOLOGY, CELL BIOLOGY. *Current Pos:* from instr to prof, Univ Alta, 54-87, dir, Electron Micros Unit, Dept Path, 68-87, chmn, Dept Path, Fac Med, 80-87, EMER PROF PATH, UNIV ALTA, 87- *Personal Data:* b Calgary, Alta, Nov 21, 27; m 87, Toby Garfin. *Educ:* Univ Alta, BSc, 48, MSc, 52, MD, 53; Royal Col Physicians & Surgeons Can, cert path, 58; FRCP(C), 72. *Concurrent Pos:* Jr intern, Univ Alta Hosp, 53-54, from asst resident to resident path, 54-59; fel, Sch Med, Johns Hopkins Univ, 59-60; McEachern Mem, Can Cancer Soc, 59-60. *Mem:* Electron Micros Soc Am; Histochem Soc; Am Soc Cell Biol; Am Soc Exp Path; Int Acad Path. *Res:* Experimental and molecular pathology, utilizing techniques of enzyme cytochemistry and electron microscopy; cell structure and function; diagnostic electron microscopy; neurobiology of reactive astrocytes; neurosciences. *Mailing Add:* 12010 87th Ave Edmonton AB T6G 0Y7 Can

SHOAF, CHARLES JEFFERSON, TEXTILE CHEMISTRY, INTELLECTUAL PROPERTY. *Current Pos:* res chemist, 59-63, from patent chemist to sr patent chemist, 63-74, patent agent, 74-80, patent atty, 80-87, SR COUN, LEGAL DEPT, E I DU PONT DE NEMOURS & CO, INC, 87- *Personal Data:* b Roanoke, Va, July 22, 30; m 58, Mary La Salle; c Susan & Sarah. *Educ:* Va Mil Inst, BS, 52; Purdue Univ, MS, 54, PhD(chem), 57; Del Law Sch, JD, 80. *Prof Exp:* Res chemist, E I du Pont de Nemours & Co, 57; instr chem, USAF Inst Technol, 57-59, asst prof, 59. *Mem:* Am Chem Soc; Sigma Xi; Am Intellectual Law Asn. *Res:* Synthetic textile fibers. *Mailing Add:* 1113 Independence Dr West Chester PA 19382-8042

SHOAF, MARY LA SALLE, PHYSICAL CHEMISTRY. *Current Pos:* CONSULT, TECH MGT SERV, 89- *Personal Data:* b Milwaukee, Wis, Feb 29, 32; m 58; c 2. *Educ:* Cardinal Stritch Col, BA, 53; Univ Calif, MS, 55; Purdue Univ, PhD(phys chem), 60. *Prof Exp:* Phys chemist, US Dept Air Force, 58-59; assoc prof, ECarolina Univ, 61-63; mem sci fac, Tatnall Sch, Del, 64-66; from assoc prof to prof physics, West Chester State Col, 66-75, dean grad studies, 75-77; asst dir, Princeton Plasma Physics Lab, 79-89. *Concurrent Pos:* Mem, Nuclear Safety Res Rev Comt, Nat Res Coun. *Mem:* Fel Am Inst Chemists; Am Chem Soc; fel Am Phys Soc; fel AAAS. *Res:* Ion-induced fission reactions; determination of thermodynamic data for transition ions; technical management. *Mailing Add:* 1113 Independence Dr West Chester PA 19382-8042. *Fax:* 215-793-3224

SHOAF, SUSAN E, PHARMACOLOGY. *Current Pos:* TENURE TRACK INVESTR, CLIN & BIOL RES LAB CLIN STUDIES, NAT INST ALCOHOL ABUSE & ALCOHOLISM, NIH, 85- *Personal Data:* b Kingston, NC, June 2, 59. *Educ:* Col William & Mary, BS, 81; Purdue Univ, MS, 83; Cornell Univ, PhD(pharmacol), 87. *Concurrent Pos:* Sr staff fel, Ctr Food Safety & Appl Nutrit, 87-90; Post doctoral fel, US Food & Drug Admin. *Mem:* Am Soc Clin Pharmacol & Therapeut; AAAS. *Mailing Add:* NIH Nat Inst on Alcohol Abuse & Alcoholism 10 Center Dr MSC-1256 Bethesda MD 20892-1256. *Fax:* 301-402-0445; *E-Mail:* shoaf@clinpharm.niara.nih.gov

SHOBE, L(OUIS) RAYMON, MATHEMATICS, ENGINEERING MECHANICS. *Current Pos:* assoc prof civil eng & eng mech, 47-56, prof, 57-78, EMER PROF ENG SCI & MECH, UNIV TENN, KNOXVILLE, 78- *Personal Data:* b Waverly, Kans, Apr 22, 13; m 36; c 3. *Educ:* Emporia State Univ, BS, 36; Kans State Univ, MS, 40. *Prof Exp:* Lab asst physics, Emporia State Univ, 35-36; teacher high schs, Kans, 36-38; instr math, Kans State Univ, 38-40 & Univ Kans, 40-41; instr math & mech, Gen Motors Inst, 41-46; assoc prof math, Bemidji State Teachers Col, 46-47. *Concurrent Pos:* Consult, Oak Ridge Nat Lab, 59- *Mem:* Fel Am Soc Civil Engrs; Nat Soc Prof Engrs; Am Soc Eng Educ. *Res:* Solid mechanics; stress analysis. *Mailing Add:* 1432 Tugaloo Dr Knoxville TN 37919

SHOBER, ROBERT ANTHONY, supercomputers, numerical analysis, for more information see previous edition

SHOBERT, ERLE IRWIN, II, SOLID STATE, GRAPHITE MATERIALS TRIBOLOGY. *Current Pos:* Res engr, Stackpole Corp, 39-46, eng dir, 46-54, res dir 54-72, vpres res, 72-78, CONSULT, STACKPOLE CORP, 78-; TECH ADV, CONTACT TECH, INC, 91- *Personal Data:* b DuBois, Pa, Nov 19, 13; m 39, Marjorie Sullivan; c Judie (Marsden) & Margaret (Hayes). *Educ:* Susquehanna Univ, AB, 35; Princeton Univ, MA, 39. *Hon Degrees:* DSc, Susquehanna Univ, 57. *Honors & Awards:* Holm Award, 73 & Armington Award, Inst Elec & Electronics Engrs, 86. *Concurrent Pos:* Bd dirs, Chem Corp, 62-82, chmn, 80-82; bd dirs, Am Soc Testing Mats, 64-72; mem bd dir, Susquehanna Univ, 65-, chmn, 78-86. *Mem:* Life fel Inst Elec & Electronics Engrs; fel Am Soc Testing Mats (pres, 71-72). *Res:* Solid state, friction, commutation, contacts, electrical machines, carbon and graphite materials tribology. *Mailing Add:* PO Box 343 St Marys PA 15857

SHOCH, DAVID EUGENE, ophthalmology; deceased, see previous edition for last biography

SHOCH, JOHN F, COMPUTER COMMUNICATIONS, DISTRIBUTED SYSTEMS. *Current Pos:* PARTNER, ASSET MGT CO, 85- *Personal Data:* b Evanston, Ill. *Educ:* Stanford Univ, BA, 71, MS, 77, PhD(comput sci), 79. *Prof Exp:* Mem res staff, Xerox Palo Res Ctr, 71-80, from exec asst to pres & dir, Corp Policy Comt, 80-81, vpres, Xerox Off Systs Div, 82-83, pres, 83-85. *Concurrent Pos:* Vis fac mem, Comput Sci Dept, Stanford Univ, 78; mem, Nat Conf Lawyers & Scientists, AAAS, 91-94; chmn, Conducturs Inc. *Mem:* Asn Comput Mach; Inst Elec & Electronics Engrs. *Res:* Computer communication and distributed systems; local computer networks; internetwork communication; packet radio; protocol design. *Mailing Add:* Asset Mgt Co 2275 E Bayshore Rd Palo Alto CA 94303

SHOCHET, MELVYN JAY, ELEMENTARY PARTICLE PHYSICS. *Current Pos:* Res assoc, Enrico Fermi Inst, 72-73, from instr to assoc prof, 73-85, PROF PHYSICS, UNIV CHICAGO, 85-, KERSTEN PROF PHYS SCI, 95- *Personal Data:* b Philadelphia, Pa, Oct 31, 44; m 67, Sheila Mazer; c Stephen & Tara. *Educ:* Univ Pa, BA, 66; Princeton Univ, MA & PhD(physics), 72. *Concurrent Pos:* Co-spokesman, CDF Collab, 88-95. *Mem:* Am Phys Soc; AAAS. *Res:* Experimental elementary particle physics. *Mailing Add:* Univ Chicago 5640 S Ellis Ave Chicago IL 60637. *Fax:* 773-702-1914; *E-Mail:* shochet@uccdfuchicago.edu

SHOCK, CLINTON C, AGRICULTURAL RESEARCH. *Current Pos:* ASSOC PROF & SUPT, MALHEUR EXP STA, ORE STATE UNIV, 84- *Personal Data:* b Los Angeles, Calif, June 11, 44; m 66; c 3. *Educ:* Univ Calif-Berkeley, BA, 66; Univ Calif-Davis, MS, 73, PhD(plant physiol), 82. *Prof Exp:* Asst prof, La State Univ, 82-84. *Concurrent Pos:* Proj leader revegation res, IRI Res Inst, Brazil, 73-75, actg gen mgr, 78, mgr & supt, IRI Exp Sta, 75-78; res asst & grad student, Univ Calif, Davis, 78-82; mem, Am Forage & Grassland Coun. *Mem:* Am Soc Agron; AAAS; Am Soc Plant Physiol; Crop Sci Soc Am; Soil Sci Soc Am; Soc Range Mgt; Nitrogen Fixing Tree Asn; Am Potato Asn; Nat Onion Asn; Sigma Xi. *Res:* Soil and irrigation management effects on potato production and quality; variety evaluation and management of cereals and forages for eastern Oregon; performance of soybean genotypes grown at four locations in Oregon. *Mailing Add:* Oregon State Univ 595 Onion Ave Ontario OR 97914

SHOCK, D'ARCY ADRIANCE, PHYSICAL CHEMISTRY. *Current Pos:* CONSULT SOLUTION MINING & SLURRY TRANSPORT, 78- *Personal Data:* b Fowler, Colo, June 13, 11; m 55; c 4. *Educ:* Colo Col, BS, 33; Univ Tex, MA, 46. *Prof Exp:* Chemist, Dow Chem Co, Mich, 33-36 & McGean Chem Co, 36-42; chief chemist, Int Minerals & Chem Corp, 42-44; instr chem, Univ Tex, 44-45; field correlator, Nat Gas Asn, 46-47, res scientist, 47-49; sr res chemist, Prod Res Lab, Continental Oil Co, 49-51, res group leader chem & metal sect, Prod Res Div, 51-56, mgr, Cent Res Div, 56-75, mgr, Mining Res Div, 75-78. *Concurrent Pos:* Comt Waste Isolation Pilot Plant, Nat Acad Sci, 76-90. *Mem:* Am Chem Soc; Nat Asn Corrosion Eng; Am Inst Mining, Metall & Petrol Eng; distinguished mem Soc Mining Engrs. *Res:* Corrosion of iron and steel in oil production and processing; anodic passivation; manufacture, transportation and storage of cryogenic gases; hydraulic fracturing technology; solution mining; waste disposal; solids pipelining; mining and milling of uranium and copper ores; coal mining research. *Mailing Add:* 233 Virginia Ave Ponca City OK 74601

SHOCK, ROBERT CHARLES, SOFTWARE ENGINEERING. *Current Pos:* ASSOC PROF COMPUT SCI, WRIGHT STATE UNIV, 81- *Personal Data:* b Dayton, Ohio, July 18, 40; m 64, Vicky Miller; c Jeffrey, Michael & Timothy. *Educ:* Bowling Green State Univ, BS, 62; Univ Ariz, MA, 64; Univ NC, Chapel Hill, PhD(math), 68; Wright State Univ, MS, 84. *Prof Exp:* From asst prof to assoc prof math, Southern Ill Univ, 68-78; prof math & chairperson dept, East Carolina Univ, 78-81. *Mem:* Am Math Soc. *Res:* Software engineering, large scale programming; linear programming. *Mailing Add:* Dept Comput Sci Wright State Univ Dayton OH 45435

SHOCKEY, DONALD ALBERT, MATERIALS SCIENCE. *Current Pos:* PHYSICIST, STANFORD RES INST INT, 71- *Personal Data:* b New Kensington, Pa, July 26, 41; m 68; c 1. *Educ:* Grove City Col, BS, 63; Carnegie Inst Technol, MS, 65; Carnegie-Mellon Univ, PhD(metall, mat sci), 68. *Prof Exp:* Scientist, Ernst-Mach Inst Freiburg, Ger, 68-71. *Res:* Fracture behavior of materials; fracture mechanics; response of materials to high rate loading; effects of environment, radiation, and microstructure on plasticity and fracture. *Mailing Add:* 467 Claremont Way Menlo Park CA 94025

SHOCKEY, WILLIAM LEE, DAIRY CATTLE, RUMINANT NUTRITION. *Current Pos:* DAIRY CONSULT, PURINA MILLS, INC, 91- *Personal Data:* b Frostburg, Md, Apr 7, 53; m 79, Alcinda K Trickett; c Joshua W, Amanda K & Zachery R. *Educ:* WVa Univ, AB, 75, PhD(agr biochem), 79. *Prof Exp:* res assoc, Ohio Agr Res & Develop Ctr, 79-81, res scientist, 90-91; res dairy scientist, USDA Agr Res Serv, 81-90. *Concurrent Pos:* Adj asst prof, Ohio State Univ, 82-; rep, Am Forage & Grassland Coun, Am Dairy Sci Asn, 88- *Mem:* Am Dairy Sci Asn; Am Soc Animal Sci; Am Inst Nutrit; Am Registry Prof Animal Scientists; Am Soc Agron; Am Forage & Grassland Coun. *Res:* Chemistry and microbiology of hay crop silage fermentations and related changes in fermentation; utilization of silage by lactating dairy cows; contribution of inorganic forage components to the silage fermentation. *Mailing Add:* Purina Mills Inc PO Box 606 Milford IN 46542

SHOCKLEY, DOLORES COOPER, PHARMACOLOGY. *Current Pos:* asst prof, 55-67, ASSOC PROF PHARMACOL, MEHARRY MED COL, 67- *Personal Data:* b Clarksdale, Miss, Apr 21, 30; m 57; c 4. *Educ:* La State Univ, BS, 51; Purdue Univ, MS, 53, PhD(pharmacol), 55. *Prof Exp:* Asst pharmacol, Purdue Univ, 51-53. *Concurrent Pos:* Fulbright fel, Copenhagen Univ, 55-56; vis asst prof, Albert Einstein Col Med, 59-62; Lederle fac award, 63-66. *Mem:* AAAS; Am Pharmaceut Asn. *Res:* Measurement of non-narcotic analgesics; effect of drugs on stress conditions; effect of hormones on connective tissues; nutrition effects and drug action. *Mailing Add:* 4141 W Hamilton Rd Nashville TN 37218-1834

SHOCKLEY, GILBERT R, CHEMICAL ENGINEERING. *Current Pos:* RETIRED. *Personal Data:* b Mo, Sept 20, 19; m 43, Louise McNarm; c 2. *Educ:* Univ Mo, BS, 42 & CEng, 60. *Hon Degrees:* DEng, Univ Mo, 70DE, 70. *Prof Exp:* Design chem engr, Monsanto Chem Co, 42-46; design & supvry engr, Wood Res Inst, 46-47; design chem engr, Goslin Birmingham Mfg Co, 47-49; asst mgr, Filter Div, Eimco Corp, 49-53; vpres, Metals Div, Olin Mathieson Chem Corp, 53-61; gen dir, Prod Develop Div, Reynolds Metals Co, 61-74, gen mgr opers serv, Mill Prod Div, 74-85, exec vpres, Reynolds Res Corp, 66-74. *Concurrent Pos:* Mem bd dirs, Am Nat Stand Inst, 80-85. *Mem:* NY Acad Sci; Am Chem Soc; Am Inst Chem Engrs; Am Soc Metals; Soc Automotive Engrs. *Mailing Add:* 207 Nottingham Rd Richmond VA 23221

SHOCKLEY, JAMES EDGAR, MATHEMATICS. *Current Pos:* ASSOC PROF MATH, VA POLYTECH INST & STATE UNIV, 66- *Personal Data:* b Richmond, Va, Dec 26, 31; div; c 3. *Educ:* Univ NC, AB, 57, AM, 59, PhD(math), 62. *Prof Exp:* Asst prof math, Col William & Mary, 61-64; assoc prof, Univ Wyo, 64-66. *Mem:* Am Math Soc; Math Asn Am. *Res:* Elementary number theory. *Mailing Add:* Dept Math Va Polytech Inst & State Univ Blacksburg VA 24061-0123

SHOCKLEY, MICHAEL WILLIAM, ORGANIC CHEMISTRY, SCIENCE EDUCATION. *Personal Data:* b Roanoke, Va, Jan 18, 64; m 97, Frances F Ford. *Educ:* Va Polytech Inst, BS, 86; NC State Univ, PhD(chem), 93. *Prof Exp:* Res assoc, Agr Res Serv, US Dept Agr, 93-97. *Mem:* Am Chem Soc. *Res:* Develop alternative fuels for combustion ignition engines; synthesize additives for low-temperature property improvement of soy esters. *Mailing Add:* 4503 Lauder Ave Bartonville IL 61607

SHOCKLEY, THOMAS D(EWEY), JR, ELECTRICAL ENGINEERING. *Current Pos:* AT DEPT ELEC ENG, MEMPHIS STATE UNIV. *Personal Data:* b Haynesville, La, Nov 2, 23; m 47; c 2. *Educ:* La State Univ, BS, 50, MS, 52; Ga Inst Technol, PhD(elec eng), 63. *Prof Exp:* Instr eng, La State Univ, 50-53; aerophys eng, Gen Dynamics/Ft Worth, 53-56; res engr, Ga Inst Technol, 56-58, asst prof elec eng, 58-63; assoc prof, Univ Ala, 63-64; prof, Univ Okla, 64-67; chmn dept, Memphis State Univ, 67-78; pres, SSC, Inc, 78- *Mem:* Inst Elec & Electronics Engrs; Am Soc Eng Educ; Nat Fire Protection Asn; Nat Soc Prof Engrs. *Res:* Microwave and antenna systems; computer systems. *Mailing Add:* 1526 Poplar Estates Pkwy Germantown TN 38138

SHOCKLEY, THOMAS E, BACTERIOLOGY. *Current Pos:* assoc prof, 62-67, vchmn dept, 67-71, PROF MICROBIOL, MEHARRY MED COL, 67-, CHMN DEPT, 71- *Personal Data:* b Rock Island, Tenn, Mar 15, 29; m 57; c 4. *Educ:* Fisk Univ, BA, 49; Ohio State Univ, MSc, 52, PhD, 54. *Prof Exp:* Asst, Ohio State Univ, 50-52; asst prof, Meharry Med Col, 54-59; Rockefeller Found fel, 59-60; Am Cancer scholar, 59-60. *Concurrent Pos:* Vis investr, Rockefeller Univ, 59-61. *Mem:* Am Soc Microbiol. *Res:* Microbial physiology and genetics; molecular biology; medical microbiology. *Mailing Add:* Dept Microbiol Meharry Med Col Sch Med 1005 Dr DB Todd Blvd Nashville TN 37208-3501

SHOCKMAN, GERALD DAVID, MICROBIAL BIOCHEMISTRY & PHYSIOLOGY. *Current Pos:* assoc prof, 60-66, chmn, Dept Microbiol & Immunol, 74-90, PROF MICROBIOL, SCH MED, TEMPLE UNIV, 66- *Personal Data:* b Mt Clemens, Mich, Dec 22, 25; m 49, Arlyne Taub; c Joel & Deborah. *Educ:* Cornell Univ, BS, 46; Rutgers Univ, PhD(microbiol), 50. *Hon Degrees:* Docteur honoris causa, Univ de l'Etat a Liege. *Prof Exp:* Fel, Rutgers Univ, New Brunswick, 47-50; res assoc, Univ Pa, 50-51; res fel, Inst Cancer Res, 51-60. *Concurrent Pos:* Am Cancer Soc-Brit Empire Cancer Campaign exchange fel, 54-55; NIH res career develop award, 65-70; vis scientist, Lab Enzymol, Nat Ctr Sci Res, Gif-sur-Yvette, France, 68-69; vis prof, Univ Liege, 71-72. *Mem:* Am Soc Microbiol; Am Acad Microbiol; Am Soc Biol Chemists; AAAS; Sigma Xi. *Res:* Physiology and biochemistry of the surface structures (walls, membranes); secreted polymers of bacteria; synthesis, nature, action and significance of autolysins and peptidoglycan hydrolases; mode of action of cell wall antibiotics. *Mailing Add:* Dept Microbiol & Immunol Temple Univ Sch Med 3400 N Broad St Philadelphia PA 19140. *Fax:* 215-704-7788

SHODELL, MICHAEL J, CELL BIOLOGY. *Current Pos:* PROF BIOL, LONG ISLAND UNIV, 83- *Personal Data:* b New York, NY, Mar 9, 41; m 68; c 2. *Educ:* NY State Univ Stony Brook, BS, 62; Univ Calif, Berkeley, PhD(molecular biol), 68. *Prof Exp:* Vis prof tissue cult, Ctr Invest Polytechnic, Mex, 68; Damon Runyon fel cancer res, Imp Cancer Res Fund, London, 69, Am Cancer Soc fel, 69-71, head, Dept Cell Proliferation Studies, 71-75; asst prof, 75-80, prof biol, C W Post Col, 80-83. *Concurrent Pos:* Dir, Banbury Ctr Cold Spring Harbor Lab, 82-86; contrib ed, Science, 84-86. *Res:* Regulation of growth in normal and neoplastic cells. *Mailing Add:* Dept Biol Long Island Univ C W Post Campus 720 Northern Blvd Greenvale NY 11548-1319

SHOEMAKER, CARLYLE EDWARD, INORGAINC CHEMISTRY. *Current Pos:* RETIRED. *Personal Data:* b Columbus, Ohio, Feb 19, 23; m 48; c 3. *Educ:* Ohio State Univ BChE, 43; Univ Ill, MS, 46, PhD(inorg chem), 49. *Prof Exp:* Asst smoke munitions res, Univ Ill, 44-45, asst anal rubber res, 45-46 & asst inorg chem, 46-49; res chemist atomic energy, Monsanto Chem Co, 49-54; from sr res & develop chemist to group leader inorg & chem eng develop, J T Baker Chem Co, 54-60; mem tech staff, Bell Tel Labs, Inc, 60-64; res engr, Bethlehem Steel Corp, 64-72, sr res engr, 72-77; proj mgr, Elec Power Res Inst, 78-89. *Mem:* Nat Asn Corrosion Engrs; Am Chem Soc. *Res:* Analytical and preparative inorganic chemistry; surface chemistry of metals; corrosion; metallurgy; high temperature aqueous chemistry. *Mailing Add:* 3561 Amber Dr San Jose CA 95117-2907

SHOEMAKER, CHRISTINE ANNETTE, ENVIRONMENTAL QUALITY MODELING, LARGE SCALE NUMERICAL OPTIMAL CONTROL ALGORITHMS. *Current Pos:* from asst prof to assoc prof, 72-85, chairperson, Dept Environ Eng, 85-88, PROF, SCH CIVIL & ENVIRON ENG, CORNELL UNIV, 85- *Personal Data:* b Berkeley, Calif, July 2, 44; m 67, 80; c Erica & Gregory T. *Educ:* Univ Calif, BS, 66; Univ Southern Calif, MS, 69, PhD(math), 71. *Prof Exp:* Vis asst syst ecologist entom, Univ Calif, Berkeley, 76-77. *Concurrent Pos:* Panel mem, Study Pest Control, Nat Acad Sci, 73-75; Pest Mgt, FAO-UN, 81-84 & Groundwater Contamination, 84-86; conf organizer, Conf Resource Mgt, NATO, Parma, Italy, 78 & Math Anal Environ Issues, Ithaca, NY, 87; co-chair, Int Groundwater Contamination Proj Sci Comt Probs Environ, 87-; consult, World Bank & Int Irrigation Mgt Inst; prin investr res grants, NSF, Environ Protection Agency, US Geol Surv, US Dept Agr, Ford Found & Int Bus Mach. *Mem:* Opers Res Soc Am; Entom Soc Am; Am Geophys Union; Am Soc Civil Engrs; Soc Indust & Appl Math; Inst Elec & Electronics Engrs. *Res:* Application of operations research techniques to environmental problems, especially pesticide use and water quality management; mathematical modeling of pest management, ecosystems, pollution of groundwater and sewage networks; optimization techniques and statistical analysis of environmental data; acid rain; development of numerically efficient serial and parallel algorithms for large scale nonlinear optimal control problems and the application of these algorithms to environmental problems, especially for groundwater quality and pesticide management; author and co-author journal papers. *Mailing Add:* Sch Civil & Environ Eng Cornell Univ 220 Hillister Hall Ithaca NY 14853-3501. *Fax:* 607-255-9004; *E-Mail:* christine.shoemaker@cornell.edu

SHOEMAKER, CLARA BRINK, CRYSTALLOGRAPHY. *Current Pos:* res assoc, 70-75, res assoc prof, 75-82, sr res prof, 82-84, EMER PROF CHEM, ORE STATE UNIV, 84- *Personal Data:* b Rolde, Netherlands, June 20, 21; US citizen; wid, David P Shoemaker; c Robert B. *Educ:* State Univ Leiden, Doctoraal, 46, PhD(chem), 50. *Prof Exp:* Instr inorg chem, State Univ Leiden, 46-53; res assoc, Mass Inst Technol, 53-55; res assoc biochem lab, Harvard Med Sch, 55-56 & Mass Inst Technol, 58-70. *Concurrent Pos:* Int Fedn Univ Women fel, Oxford Univ, 50-51; proj supvr chem, Boston Univ, 63-64; mem comt alloy phases, Metall Soc, 69-79, struct reports, Int Union Crystallog, 70-90; mem crystallographic data comt, Am Crystallog Asn, 75-78, Fankuchen Award Comt, 76. *Mem:* Am Crystallog Asn. *Res:* X-ray crystallography; crystal structures of metals, alloys (including alloys related to quasicrystals) and organometallic compounds. *Mailing Add:* 3453 NW Hayes Ave Corvallis OR 97330-1729. *E-Mail:* shoemakc@ccmail.orst.edu

SHOEMAKER, DALE, CANCER RESEARCH. *Current Pos:* BR CHIEF, REGULATORY AFFAIRS BR, NAT CANCER INST, NIH, 85- *Mailing Add:* NIH Nat Cancer Inst Regulatory Affairs Br 6130 Executive Blvd Rm 718 Rockville MD 20852

SHOEMAKER, DAVID POWELL, solid state chemistry, structural chemistry; deceased, see previous edition for last biography

SHOEMAKER, EDWARD MILTON, APPLIED MATHEMATICS. *Current Pos:* PROF MATH, SIMON FRASER UNIV, 65- *Personal Data:* b Wilkinsburg, Pa, Jan 5, 29; m 70; c Rhett & Garth. *Educ:* Carnegie Inst Technol, MS, 51, PhD(math), 55. *Prof Exp:* Res engr, Chance Vought Aircraft, Inc, 55-56; res mathematician, Boeing Airplane Co, 56-60; assoc prof theoret & appl mech, Univ Ill, Urbana, 60-65. *Concurrent Pos:* Consult, Sandia Labs, 62-70. *Mem:* Am Geophys Union; Int Soc Glaciol. *Res:* Glaciology; glacial geomorphology; solid mechanics. *Mailing Add:* Dept Math Simon Fraser Univ Vancouver BC V5A 1S6 Can

SHOEMAKER, EUGENE MERLE, astrogeology; deceased, see previous edition for last biography

SHOEMAKER, FRANK CRAWFORD, EXPERIMENTAL HIGH ENERGY PHYSICS. *Current Pos:* prof physics, 62-89, MEM FAC, PRINCETON UNIV, 50-, EMER PROF PHYSICS, 89- *Personal Data:* b Ogden, Utah, Mar 26, 22; m 44, Ruth Nelson; c Barbara & Mary. *Educ:* Whitman Col, AB, 43; Univ Wis, PhD(physics), 49. *Hon Degrees:* DSc, Whitman Col, 78. *Prof Exp:* Mem staff radiation lab, Mass Inst Technol, 43-45; asst, Univ Wis, 46-49; instr physics, 49-50. *Concurrent Pos:* Vis scientist, Rutherford High Energy Lab, Eng, 65-66; head main ring sect, Nat Accelerator Lab, 68-69. *Mem:* Fel Am Phys Soc; Sigma Xi. *Res:* High energy accelerator design and construction; elementary particle physics. *Mailing Add:* Dept Physics Princeton Univ PO Box 708 Princeton NJ 08544. *Fax:* 609-258-6360; *E-Mail:* shoemaker@puphep.princeton.edu

SHOEMAKER, GRADUS LAWRENCE, ORGANIC CHEMISTRY. *Current Pos:* from asst prof to assoc prof chem, 49-65, actg chmn dept, 63-64, chmn, 65-67, chmn div natural sci, 67-80, prof, 65-87, EMER PROF CHEM, UNIV LOUISVILLE, 88- *Personal Data:* b Zeeland, Mich, Jan 18, 21; m 52, Florence Wright; c Robert N & Betty L. *Educ:* Hope Col, AB, 44; Univ Ill, MS, 47, PhD(org chem), 49. *Prof Exp:* Asst org chem, Univ Ill, 46-47; res fel, Rutgers Univ, 49. *Mem:* Am Chem Soc. *Res:* Reactions of nitroparaffins; adaptation of the chemistry laboratory for handicapped students; synthesis of alkylboranes and alkylboronic acids. *Mailing Add:* Dept Chem Univ Louisville Louisville KY 40292

SHOEMAKER, JAMES DANIEL, NUTRITIONAL & GENETIC DIAGNOSIS BY GAS CHROMATOGRAPHY-MASS SPECTROMETRY. *Current Pos:* trainee, 88-91, instr, 91-92, DIR, METAB SCREENING LAB, ST LOUIS UNIV MED CTR, 89-, ASST PROF BIOCHEM, 92- *Personal Data:* b Champaign, Ill, Oct 13, 53; m 87, Mary Nielson; c Kathryn, Laura & Joanna. *Educ:* New Col, Sarasota, BA, 74; Univ Ill, Urbana-Champaign, MD & MS, 81, PhD(nutrit sci), 84. *Prof Exp:* Res asst nutrit sci, Univ Ill, Urbana, 76-83, instr med, Urbana-Champaign, 83-84, resident internal med, 84-88. *Mem:* Sigma Xi; Am Soc Clin Nutrit; Am Soc Mass Spectrometry; Soc Inherited Metab Dis; Fedn Am Socs Exp Biol; Am Soc Nutrit Sci. *Res:* Diagnosis of genetic and nutritional diseases by quantitation of intermediary metabolites by gas chromatography- mass spectrometry. *Mailing Add:* Dept Biochem St Louis Univ Med Ctr 1402 S Grand Blvd St Louis MO 63104. *Fax:* 314-577-8156; *E-Mail:* shoemajd@wpugate.slu.edu

SHOEMAKER, JOHN DANIEL, JR, CHEMISTRY. *Current Pos:* from res assoc to sr res assoc, 78-90, PRIN SCIENTIST, ERLING RIIS LAB, INT PAPER CO, 90- *Personal Data:* b Lawton, Okla, May 9, 39; m 72, Anna Robechaux; c 3. *Educ:* Univ Okla, BS, 60, MS, 62; Univ Kans, PhD(org chem), 67; La State Univ, Baton Rouge, MBA, 72. *Prof Exp:* Chemist, Esso Res Labs, Humble Oil & Ref Co, La, 66-70 & Union Camp Corp, 72-78. *Mem:* Tech Asn Pulp & Paper Indust; Am Chem Soc; Sigma Xi. *Res:* Chemistry of pulp bleaching; preparation of petroleum refining catalysts; Kraft pulping process; wood chemistry. *Mailing Add:* Box 2787 Mobile AL 36652-2787

SHOEMAKER, PAUL BECK, EXTENSION, EPIDEMIOLOGY. *Current Pos:* From asst prof to assoc prof, 70-80, PROF PLANT PATH, NC STATE UNIV, 80- *Personal Data:* b Bridgeton, NJ, Feb 26, 41; m 64; c 2. *Educ:* Rutgers Univ, BS, 63, MS, 65; Cornell Univ, PhD(plant path), 71. *Concurrent Pos:* Mem, Coun Agr Sci & Technol. *Mem:* Am Phytopath Soc; Sigma Xi. *Res:* Epidemiology and control strategies for diseases of vegetables and burley tobacco; practical control of tomato Verticillium wilt, early blight and bacterial canker and tobacco blue mold and Thielaviopsis root rot. *Mailing Add:* Turnpike Rd Horse Shoe NC 28742

SHOEMAKER, RICHARD LEE, CHEMICAL PHYSICS, QUANTUM OPTICS. *Current Pos:* from asst prof to assoc prof, 72-81, PROF OPTICAL SCI, OPTICAL SCI CTR, UNIV ARIZ, 81- *Personal Data:* b Grand Rapids, Mich, Dec 31, 44; m 68; c 3. *Educ:* Calvin Col, BS, 66; Univ Ill, PhD(phys chem), 71. *Prof Exp:* Vis scientist molecular physics, IBM Res Div, San Jose Calif, 71-72. *Concurrent Pos:* Alfred P Sloan fel, 76-80. *Mem:* Optical Soc Am; Soc Photo-Optical Inst Engrs; Inst Elec & Electronics Engrs. *Res:* Coherent optical transient effects; nonlinear spectroscopic techniques; laboratory microcomputers; multiprocessor computers. *Mailing Add:* Optical Sci Ctr Univ of Ariz Tucson AZ 85721

SHOEMAKER, RICHARD LEONARD, PHYSIOLOGY. *Current Pos:* supvr animal care, Univ Ala, Birmingham, 60-66, dir animal care dept, 64-67, assoc prof, 67-73, PROF PHYSIOL & BIOPHYS, MED CTR, UNIV ALA, BIRMINGHAM, 73- *Personal Data:* b Cullman, Ala, Sept 28, 31; c 4. *Educ:* Auburn Univ, BS, 54, MS, 59; Univ Ala, Birmingham, PhD, 67. *Prof Exp:* Asst animal nutrit, Auburn Univ, 51-54. *Concurrent Pos:* Consult meteorologist, Eastern Airlines, 59-60. *Mem:* AAAS; Am Physiol Soc; Biophys Soc. *Res:* Electrophysiology and membrane transport in regards to the mechanisms of ion transport across cell membranes; alternation of membrane potential in vascular smooth muscle cells in hypertensive animals; alterations in the mechanisms of ion transport in cystic fibrosis. *Mailing Add:* Dept Physiol Univ Ala Birmingham UAB Sta Birmingham AL 35294-0005

SHOEMAKER, RICHARD NELSON, MEDICAL EDUCATION. *Current Pos:* RETIRED. *Personal Data:* b Allentown, Pa, Nov 21, 21; m 47, Jacqueline Beever; c Susan (Poirier) & Richard N. *Educ:* Lehigh Univ, PhD(microbiol), 50. *Prof Exp:* Instr biol sci, Lehigh Univ, 47-49; dir explor res, Pfizer, Inc, 52-55, tech mgr, 55-70; coordr med educ, Greater Del Valley Regional Med Prog, 70-73; dir educ, Mercy Hosp, Scranton, Pa, 73. *Concurrent Pos:* Med educ consult, Lackawanna County Med Soc, Pa, 71-73. *Res:* Microbiological conversions; antibiotics; vitamins; steroidal chemicals. *Mailing Add:* PO Box 36 Waverly PA 18471

SHOEMAKER, RICHARD W, MATHEMATICS. *Current Pos:* RETIRED. *Personal Data:* b Toledo, Ohio, Nov 8, 18; m 45; c 4. *Educ:* Univ Toledo, BS, 40, MS, 42; Univ Chicago, cert, 43; Univ Mich, MA, 49, PhD(educ math), 54. *Prof Exp:* From asst prof to assoc prof, Univ Toledo, 46-58, chmn dept, 58-63, prof math, 58- *Mem:* Math Asn Am. *Mailing Add:* 2426 Meadowwood Dr Toledo OH 43606

SHOEMAKER, ROBERT ALAN, MYCOLOGY. *Current Pos:* RETIRED. *Personal Data:* b Toronto, Ont, July 9, 28; m 50; c 4. *Educ:* Univ Guelph, BSA, 50, MSA, 52; Cornell Univ, PhD(mycol), 55. *Prof Exp:* Asst bot, Univ Guelph, 50-52; asst plant path, Cornell Univ, 52-55; asst mycologist, Plant Res Inst, Can Dept Agr, 55-56, from assoc mycologist to sr mycologist, 56-67, head mycol sect, Biosystematics Res Inst, 67- *Concurrent Pos:* Instr specialized bot, Swiss Fed Inst Technol, 61-62. *Mem:* Mycol Soc Am; Can Bot Asn; Can Phytopath Soc Res. *Res:* Taxonomy of pyrenomycetes. *Mailing Add:* 1025 Grenon Ave Apt 1125 Ottawa ON K2B 8S5 Can

SHOEMAKER, ROBERT HAROLD, METALLURGY. *Current Pos:* CHMN & CHIEF EXEC OFFICER, KOLENE CORP. *Personal Data:* b Buffalo, NY, Sept 15, 21; c 2. *Educ:* Ohio Univ, BS, 43. *Concurrent Pos:* Mem bd dirs, Am Soc Metals, 66 & Indust Heating Equip Asn, 79; chmn, Legis Action Comt, Indust Heating Equip Asn, 78-81. *Mem:* Hon mem Am Soc Metals Int; Indust Heating Equip Asn; Am Iron & Steel Inst; Soc Automotive Engrs. *Res:* Metal conditioning salt bath technology; author of numerous technical publications. *Mailing Add:* 12890 Westwood Ave Detroit MI 48223

SHOEMAKER, VAUGHAN HURST, COMPARATIVE PHYSIOLOGY, PHYSIOLOGICAL ECOLOGY. *Current Pos:* from asst prof to assoc prof zool, 65-75, chmn, Dept Biol, 82-88, PROF ZOOL, UNIV CALIF, RIVERSIDE, 75-, ASSOC DEAN BIOL SCI, 96- *Personal Data:* b Chicago, Ill, Apr 4, 38; m 82, Mary A Baker; c Lynn M & Margaret L. *Educ:* Earlham Col, AB, 59; Univ Mich, MA, 61, PhD(zool), 64. *Prof Exp:* Instr zool, Univ Mich, 64-65. *Concurrent Pos:* NIH fel, 65; NSF res grants, 66-92; mem adv panel, Pop Biol & Physiol Ecol, 79-82. *Mem:* Fel AAAS; Am Soc Zool; Am Inst Biol Sci; Am Soc Ichthyologists & Herpetologists. *Res:* Water and electrolyte metabolism, energetics, and thermal relations in terrestrial vertebrates. *Mailing Add:* Dept Biol Univ Calif Riverside CA 92521. *Fax:* 909-787-4286; *E-Mail:* vshoe@ucrac1.ucr.edu

SHOEMAKER, WILLIAM C, SURGERY. *Current Pos:* CHMN, DEPT EMERGENCY MED, KING/DREW MED CTR, 91- *Personal Data:* b Chicago, Ill, Feb 27, 23; m 53; c 4. *Educ:* Univ Calif, AB, 44, MD, 46. *Prof Exp:* Res fel surg, Harvard Med Sch, 56-59; from asst prof to prof, Chicago Med Sch, 59-69; prof, Mt Sinai Sch Med, 69-74, chief, Div Surg Metab, 71-74; prof surg, Sch Med, Univ Calif, Los Angeles, 74- *Concurrent Pos:* Dir dept surg res, Hektoen Inst Med Res, Cook County, Ill, 59-68; mem prog-proj rev comt B, Nat Heart Inst, 68-70; mem comt shock, Nat Res Coun-Nat Acad Sci, 69-71; chief third surg serv, Cook County Hosp, Ill; Nat Heart Ins res career award; chief, Acute Care Ctr, Harbor Gen Hosp, 74-85. *Mem:* AAAS; Am Physiol Soc; Soc Exp Biol & Med. *Res:* Regional hemodynamics and metabolism; hemorrhagic shock; hepatic physiology; electrolyte metabolism. *Mailing Add:* King Drew Med Ctr 12021 S Wilmington Ave Los Angeles CA 90659

SHOEMAN, DON WALTER, PHARMACOLOGY. *Personal Data:* b Tracy, Minn, Feb 24, 41; m 67; c 1. *Educ:* Macalester Col, BA, 65; Univ Minn, Minneapolis, PhD(pharmacol), 71. *Prof Exp:* Instr pharmacol, Univ Kans Med Ctr, Kansas City, 70-74, asst prof, 74-80; asst prof & chmn, Dept Physiol & Pharmacol, New Eng Col Osteopathic Med, 80-85. *Mem:* Am Soc Pharmacol & Exp Therapeut. *Res:* Drug metabolism and clinical pharmacology. *Mailing Add:* 177 Demar Ave St Paul MN 55126

SHOENFIELD, JOSEPH ROBERT, MATHEMATICS. *Current Pos:* From instr to assoc prof, 52-65, PROF MATH, DUKE UNIV, 66- *Personal Data:* b Detroit, Mich, May 1, 27. *Educ:* Univ Mich, BS, 49, MS, 51, PhD(math), 52. *Concurrent Pos:* NSF fel, 56-57. *Mem:* Am Math Soc; Asn Symbolic Logic. *Res:* Mathematical logic. *Mailing Add:* 4114 Bartlett Dr Durham NC 27705

SHOFFNER, JAMES PRIEST, ORGANIC CHEMISTRY. *Current Pos:* ADV PROF SCI, COLUMBIA COL. *Personal Data:* b New Madrid, Mo, Jan 14, 28; m 56, Cornelia Dow; c Stuart, Karen & Andrew. *Educ:* Lincoln Univ, Mo, BS, 51; DePaul Univ, MS, 56; Univ Ill, Chicago, PhD(org Chem), 65. *Prof Exp:* Res chemist, Corn Prod Co, 55-61; res specialist, Universal Oil Prods Inc, 63-93. *Mem:* Am Chem Soc; AAAS; Nat Organ Black Chemists & Chem Engs. *Res:* Synthesis of aromatic amines; rubber vulcanization; nuclear magnetic resonance spectroscopy; imine exchange reactions; corrosion inhibitors. *Mailing Add:* 296 Parkchester Rd Elk Grove Village IL 60007

SHOFFNER, ROBERT NURMAN, POULTRY GENETICS, CYTOGENETICS. *Current Pos:* From asst to prof, 40-86, actg head dept, 65-66, EMER PROF ANIMAL SCI, UNIV MINN, ST PAUL, 86- *Personal Data:* b Junction City, Kans, Mar 2, 16; m 38, Gladys Morgan; c Robert Kirk, Jane Marie & Patti Aileen. *Educ:* Kans State Col, BS, 40; Univ Minn, MS, 42, PhD(animal genetics), 46. *Honors & Awards:* Merck Res Award, 82. *Concurrent Pos:* Vis prof, Univ Calif, 57 & Univ Tex, Houston, 69; Fulbright scholar, Univ Queensland, 62; NATO consult, Govt India, 76. *Mem:* Fel AAAS; fel Poultry Sci Asn (vpres, 64 & 65, pres, 66); Am Genetic Asn; Genetics Soc Am; World Poultry Sci Asn. *Res:* Avian genetics and cytogenetics; chromosome methodology, cytotaxonomy, quantitative genetics and molecular genetics. *Mailing Add:* Dept Animal Sci Univ Minn 1404 Gortner St Paul MN 55108

SHOGER, ROSS L, ZOOLOGY, DEVELOPMENTAL BIOLOGY. *Current Pos:* From instr to assoc prof, 59-69, chmn dept, 69-73, PROF BIOL, CARLETON COL, 69- *Personal Data:* b Aurora, Ill, Jan 14, 30; m 57; c 3. *Educ:* NCent Col, BA, 51; Purdue Univ, MS, 53; Univ Minn, PhD(zool), 59. *Concurrent Pos:* NSF sci fac fel, Waseda Univ, Japan, 68-69. *Mem:* AAAS; Soc Develop Biol; Am Soc Zool. *Res:* Experimental embryology development; node regression studies. *Mailing Add:* 201 Oak St Northfield MN 55057

SHOGREN, MERLE DENNIS, CEREAL CHEMISTRY, BIOCHEMISTRY. *Current Pos:* RES FOOD TECHNOLOGIST CEREAL CHEM, USDA, 54- *Personal Data:* b Lindsborg, Kans, Nov 20, 26; m 74; c 4. *Educ:* Bethany Col, BS, 51; Kans State Univ, MS, 54. *Mem:* Sigma Xi; Am Asn Cereal Chemists; Am Chem Soc. *Res:* Improving breadmaking qualities of United States wheat (new varieties); improving nutritional qualities of bread-wheat flour. *Mailing Add:* 2000 Bluehills Rd Manhattan KS 66502-4505

SHOHET, JUDA LEON, PLASMA SCIENCE, ELECTRICAL ENGINEERING. *Current Pos:* assoc prof, 66-71, PROF ELEC ENG, UNIV WIS-MADISON, 71- *Personal Data:* b Chicago, Ill, June 26, 37; m 69; Amy Scherz; c Aaron, Lena & William. *Educ:* Purdue Univ, BS, 58; Carnegie Melon Univ, MS, 60, PhD(elec eng), 61. *Honors & Awards:* Frederick Emmons Terman Award, Am Soc Eng Educ, 77; Merit Award, Inst Elec & Electronics Engrs, 78, Centennial Award, 84, Plasma Sci & Appln Prize, 91 & Richard F Shea Award, 92; John Yarwood Mem Medal, Brit Vacuum Coun, 93. *Prof Exp:* Asst prof elec eng, Johns Hopkins Univ, 61-66. *Concurrent Pos:* Consult, US Army Res & Develop Labs, Va, 61-63, Westinghouse Elec Corp, 63-66, 81, Trane Co, 68, Argonne Nat Lab, 68-78, Abbott Labs, 86, Oak Ridge Nat Lab, 89 & Hewlett-Packard Co, 90-96; mem staff, Ctr Nuclear Study, Saclay, France, 69-70, Los Alamos Sci Lab, 77-, McGraw Edison Co, 79-80 & Nicolet Instrument Corp, 82-; vis staff mem, Inst Fusion Studies, Univ Tex, Courant Inst NY Univ & Plasma Physics Lab, Princeton Univ. *Mem:* AAAS; fel Inst Elec & Electronics Engrs; Sigma Xi; fel Am Phys Soc; Am Vacuum Soc; Mat Res Soc; Am Soc Testing & Mat. *Res:* Fusion; quantum electronics; waves and instabilities in plasmas; mathematical models of biological systems; electromagnetic theory and microwaves; plasma processing and technology; plasma-aided manufacturing; heating, confinement and diagnostics; communications, magnetohydrodynamics; biophysics, quantum electronics, lasers. *Mailing Add:* Dept Elec & Comput Eng Univ Wi 1415 Johnson Dr Madison WI 53706. *Fax:* 608-262-1267; *E-Mail:* shohet@engr.wisc.edu

SHOKEIR, MOHAMED HASSAN KAMEL, IMMUNOLOGY. *Current Pos:* RETIRED. *Personal Data:* b Mansoura, Egypt, July 2, 38: Can citizen; m 68; c 2. *Educ:* Cairo Univ, MB & BCh, 60, DCh, 63 & 64; Univ Mich, Ann Arbor, MS, 65, PhD(human genetics), 69. *Prof Exp:* Intern med, Cairo Univ Hosps, 60-62, resident orthop surg, 62-64; Fulbright scholar & trainee human & med genetics, Univ Mich, 64-66, Fulbright res scholar, 66-69; from asst prof to assoc prof pediat & Queen Elizabeth II scientist, Univ Sask, 69-72; assoc prof & Queen Elizabeth II scientist, Univ Man, 72-75; dir, Div Med Genetics, Dept Pediat, Univ Sask, 75-96, prof pediat, 77-96, head dept, 79-96. *Concurrent Pos:* Vis prof, Univ Alta, 76, Univ Fla, 80, Wayne State Univ, 82, Univ Calgary, 84, Garyounis Univ, Banghazi, Libya, 85, Arab Med Univ, Banghazi, 85 & Univ Mich, 86. *Mem:* Am Soc Human Genetics; Am Pediat Soc; Can Soc Clin Invest; Soc Pediat Res; fel Can Col Med Geneticists. *Res:* Genetics, biochemistry and immunology of copper containing enzymes and other metallo-proteins; neurobiology, especially of Huntington's chorea, Wilson's disease and Parkinsonism; congenital malformations in man; genetic polymorphisms of proteins in man. *Mailing Add:* 108 Reil Crescent Saskatoon SK S7J 2W6 Can

SHOLANDER, MARLOW, mathematics; deceased, see previous edition for last biography

SHOLDT, LESTER LANCE, MILITARY ENTOMOLOGY, MEDICAL ENTOMOLOGY. *Current Pos:* RETIRED. *Personal Data:* b Greeley, Colo, Aug 18, 38; m 62; c 2. *Educ:* Colo State Univ, BS, 62, PhD(entom), 78; Univ Hawaii, MS, 64. *Honors & Awards:* Outstanding Med & Vet Entomologist Award, Am Registry Prof Entomologists, 90. *Prof Exp:* Res asst, Cotton Insect Lab, USDA, Ariz, 65-66; asst opers officer, Dis Vector Control Ctr, Calif, 66-67; div entomologist, 1st Marine Div, Vietnam, 68; head, Dept Entom, Prev Med Unit 2, Va, 69-72; Naval Med Res Unit 5, Ethiopia, 73-76; officer in charge, Dis Vector Ecol & Control Ctr, Fla, 78-81; head, Dis Vector Control Sect, Pre Med Div, Bur Med & Surg, 81-84; Indust Col Armed Forces, 84-85; assoc prof, Uniformed Serv Univ, 85-96. *Concurrent Pos:* Consult, Trop Dis Res Orgn, Africa, Asia, Central Am & SAm. *Mem:* Entom Soc Am; Am Mosquito Control Asn; Asn Military Surgeons US; Sigma Xi. *Res:* Epidemiology and control of human lice and louse-borne diseases; insect repellents for the protection of human subjects; malaria prevention and control; vector control in post-disaster situations. *Mailing Add:* 3460 E Marshall Gulch Tucson AZ 85718

SHOLL, HOWARD ALFRED, COMPUTER SCIENCES. *Current Pos:* from instr to assoc prof, 66-85, PROF ELEC ENG & COMPUT SCI, UNIV CONN, 85-, DIR, BOOTH RES CTR, 86- *Personal Data:* b Northampton, Mass, Oct 14, 38; m 60; Beverly Beatty; c Pamela & Lisa. *Educ:* Worcester Polytech Inst, BS, 60, MS, 63; Univ Conn, PhD(comput sci), 70. *Prof Exp:* Engr, US Army Signal Res & Develop Lab, 60-61; asst elec eng, Worcester Polytech Inst, 61-63; sr engr, Sylvania Elec Co, 63-66. *Concurrent Pos:* Leverhulme vis fel, Univ Edinburgh, 73-74; mem, Task Force Software Eng, Digital Syst Eval Comt, 75; Fulbright sr res fel, Tech Univ Munich, 82-83. *Mem:* Inst Elec & Electronics Engrs; Asn Comput Mach; Int Soc Comput & Their Applns. *Res:* Digital systems design; engineering and analysis of real time, distributed, computer systems. *Mailing Add:* Booth Res Ctr Univ Conn Box U-31 Storrs CT 06269-4031. *Fax:* 860-486-1273; *E-Mail:* hasc@brc.uconn.edu

SHOMAKER, JOHN WAYNE, GROUNDWATER FLOW MODELLING. *Current Pos:* PRES, JOHN W SHOMAKER INC, 86- *Personal Data:* b Pueblo, Colo, Apr 18, 42; m 78, Dianna J Scheffer; c 6. *Educ:* Univ NMex, BS, 63 & MS, 65; St John's Col, MA, 84; Univ Birmingham, MSc, 85. *Prof Exp:* Hydrologist, Water Res Div, US Geol Surv, 65-69; geologist, NMex Bur Mines & Mineral Resource, 69-73; consult geologist, 73-86. *Concurrent Pos:* Adj assoc prof geol, Univ NMex, 76- *Mem:* Geol Soc Am; Am Asn Petrol Geologists; Am Inst Hydrol; Am Inst Prof Geologists (secy-treas, 76); Int Asn Hydrogeologists; Asn Ground-Water Scientists & Engrs. *Res:* Ground-water flow modelling; water supply and water rights studies; ground water contamination studies. *Mailing Add:* 726 13 Tramway Vista NE Albuquerque NM 87122

SHOMAY, DAVID, ZOOLOGY. *Current Pos:* From asst to instr, 49-56, from instr to asst prof, 56-63, ASSOC PROF ZOOL, UNIV ILL, CHICAGO CIRCLE, 63- *Personal Data:* b Brooklyn, NY, Aug 31, 24. *Educ:* Long Island Univ, BS, 48; Univ Ill, MS, 49, PhD(zool), 55. *Mem:* AAAS; Soc Vert Paleont; Am Soc Zoologists. *Res:* Comparative anatomy; invertebrate zoology; structure and evolution of nervous system. *Mailing Add:* Dept Biol Sci Univ Ill 845 W Taylor St Chicago IL 60607-7060

SHOMBERT, DONALD JAMES, PHYSICAL CHEMISTRY. *Current Pos:* asst prof to assoc prof chem, 62-87, EMER PROF, DOUGLASS COL, RUTGERS UNIV, NEW BRUNSWICK, 87- *Personal Data:* b Pittsburgh, Pa, Oct 31, 28; m 55; c 4. *Educ:* Univ Pittsburgh, BS, 53, PhD(chem), 58. *Prof Exp:* Res assoc phys chem, Res Labs, Merck & Co, Inc, NJ, 58-61; mgr surface physics & chem, CBS Labs, Conn, 61-62. *Mem:* Am Chem Soc; Inst Elec & Electronic Eng. *Res:* Semiconductor materials; thin-film deposition and device technology; physical measurements and electronic instrumentation. *Mailing Add:* 199 Chaucer Dr Berkeley Heights NJ 07922

SHON, FREDERICK JOHN, NUCLEAR PHYSICS. *Current Pos:* DEP CHIEF JUDGE, TECH, ATOMIC SAFETY & LICENSING BD PANEL, US NUCLEAR REGULATORY COMN, 72- *Personal Data:* b Pleasantville, NY, July 24, 26; m 46; c 1. *Educ:* Columbia Univ, BS, 46. *Prof Exp:* Jr engr, Publicker Alcohol Co, 46-47; proj engr, Thermoid Co, 47-48; opers physicist, Mound Lab, 48-52; reactor opers supvr, Lawrence Radiation Lab, Univ Calif, 52-61, lectr nuclear eng, 56-61; chief reactor oper & supvr licensing br, Div Licensing & Regulations, US AEC, 61-63, chief reactor & criticality safety br, Div Oper Safety, 63-67, asst dir nuclear facilities, 67-72. *Concurrent Pos:* Radiation chemist, Atomics Int Div, NAm Aviation, Inc, 51-52; consult, Aerojet-Gen Nucleonics Div, Gen Tire & Rubber Co, 58- & US AEC, 59-; physicist, Lawrence Radiation Lab, Univ Calif, 62-63; mem, Int Atomic Energy Agency Safety Adv Mission to the Spanish Junta De Energia Nuclear, 71-72. *Mem:* Am Nuclear Soc. *Res:* Nuclear reactor design and operation; neutron physics; radiation detection, measurement and safety. *Mailing Add:* 4212 Flower Valley Dr Rockville MD 20853

SHONE, ROBERT L, ORGANIC CHEMISTRY, MEDICINAL CHEMISTRY. *Current Pos:* sr investr, 67-71, RES SCIENTIST, G D SEARLE & CO, 71- *Personal Data:* b Gary, Ind, July 28, 37; m 61; c 2. *Educ:* Ind Univ, BS, 59; Mich State Univ, MS, 61, PhD(org chem), 65. *Prof Exp:* Res chemist, Swift & Co, 65-66; res fel, Ill Inst Technol, 66-67. *Mem:* Am Chem Soc; The Chem Soc. *Res:* Anti-viral and antihypertensive drugs; nucleic acids; enzyme inhibitors of nucleic acid metabolites; synthesis of nucleosides, amino acids and carbohydrates; antiallergy drugs; synthesis of pyrones; synthesis of gastric and secretory prostaglendins. *Mailing Add:* 1441 E Joan Dr Palatine IL 60067-5668

SHONE, ROBERT TILDEN, PHOTOGRAMMETRY, FORESTRY. *Current Pos:* DIR ENG, IMAGE INTERPRETATION SYSTS, INC, 87- *Personal Data:* b Rochester, NY, July 22, 28; m 54; c 2. *Educ:* Syracuse Univ, BS, 49, MS, 54. *Prof Exp:* Photogram aide mapping, Army Map Serv, 52-53; sect mgr photogram prod sales, Bausch & Lomb Optical Co, 54-59; mem tech staff, Ramo-Wooldridge Div, Thompson Ramo Wooldridge, Inc, 59-61; sr staff engr, Librascope Div, Gen Precision Inc, 61-63; dept head photogram instrument res & develop, Bausch & Lomb, Inc, 63-67, tech dir, Spec Prod Div, 67-73, vpres spec prod develop, 73-81, dir res & develop, Sci Optical Prod Div, 81-85. *Mem:* Can Inst Survrs; Am Soc Photogram. *Res:* Instrument accuracy studies; mapping instrument automation; system analysis; analytical photogrammetry; photographic interpretation; instrument development management. *Mailing Add:* 56 Round Trail Dr Pittsford NY 14534

SHONICK, WILLIAM, BIOSTATISTICS, PUBLIC HEALTH. *Current Pos:* RETIRED. *Personal Data:* b Poland, Oct 3, 19; US citizen; m 41; c 1. *Educ:* City Col New York, BS, 42; George Wash Univ, MA, 48; Univ Calif, Los Angeles, PhD(biostatist), 67. *Prof Exp:* Jr acct, Wm Janis CPA, New York, 42; statistician-economist, Off Price Admin, 43; bus agent, Local 203, United Fed Workers of Am-CIO, 44-45; teacher social studies, Montgomery County Sch Syst, Md, 45-51; pvt bus, 52-55; budget & statist anal, Fedn Jewish Philanthropies, New York, 55-61; coordr biostatist, Rehab Res & Training Ctr, Sch Med, Univ Southern Calif, 68-69; from asst prof to prof pub health, Sch Pub Health, Univ Calif, Los Angeles, 69-87. *Concurrent Pos:* NIH fel biostatist, Univ Calif, Los Angeles, 68; asst prof community med, Med Sch, Univ Southern Calif, 68-69. *Mem:* Am Statist Asn; Am Pub Health Asn; Opers Res Soc Am. *Res:* Governmental policies and health services; health policy formulation and planning methods, delivery. *Mailing Add:* 1244 Beverly Green Dr Los Angeles CA 90035

SHONK, CARL ELLSWORTH, BIOCHEMISTRY. *Current Pos:* assoc prof chem, 66-84, EMER PROF, CENT MICH UNIV, 84- *Personal Data:* b Plymouth, Pa, Nov 11, 22; m 51, Martha; c Karen & Carl W. *Educ:* Bucknell Univ, BS, 48; MS, 49; Rutgers Univ, PhD(biochem, physiol), 62. *Prof Exp:* Chemist, E I du Pont de Nemours & Co, Pa, 48; biochemist, Merck & Co, Inc, 49-66. *Mem:* AAAS; Am Chem Soc; Biochem Soc. *Res:* Enzyme chemistry; cancer biochemistry; analytical biochemical methods. *Mailing Add:* 8680 S Vandecar Rd Shepherd MI 48883-9549

SHONKA, JOSEPH JOHN, SHIELDING & CONSEQUENCE ANALYSIS, INSTRUMENTATION RESEARCH. *Current Pos:* RES DIR, SHONKA RES ASSOCS, INC, 87- *Personal Data:* b Chicago, Ill, May 1, 48; m 76, Deborah Burch; c Joseph J Jr, Sara E & Amy V. *Educ:* St Procopius Col, Lisle, Ill, BS, 69; Ga Inst Technol, MS, 70, PhD(nuclear eng), 78. *Prof Exp:* Lab fel, Oak Ridge Nat Lab, 72-77; group leader health physics, Brookhaven Nat Lab, 78-85; prin scientist, Atlan-Tech, Inc, 85-87. *Concurrent Pos:* Consult contract res, Meteorol Eval Serv, 82-85; Chair, Instrumentation Sect, Am Nat Stand Inst N13, Health Physics Soc, 92- *Mem:* Health Physics Soc; Am Asn Physicists Med; Sigma Xi; Am Nuclear Soc. *Res:* Develops, validates and uses environmental transport modeling codes for licensing as well as for historic dose evaluation; application of novel instrumentation techniques to radiation monitoring; radiation shielding analyses. *Mailing Add:* 5199 Sandlewood Ct Marietta GA 30068-2875. *Fax:* 770-509-7507

SHONKWILER, RONALD WESLEY, MONTE CARLO METHODS, GLOBAL OPTIMIZATION. *Current Pos:* from asst prof to assoc prof, 70-92, PROF MATH, GA INST TECHNOL, 92- *Personal Data:* b Chicago, Ill, Feb 20, 42. *Educ:* Calif State Polytech Col, Kellogg-Voorhis, BS, 64; Univ Colo, Boulder, MS, 67, PhD(math), 70. *Prof Exp:* Aerospace engr, US Naval Ord Lab, 64-65. *Mem:* Soc Math Biol; Am Math Soc; Soc Indust & Appl Math. *Res:* Global optimization by stochastic gradient methods; simulated annealing; genetic algorithms; random restart; population dynamics. *Mailing Add:* Sch Math Ga Inst Technol Atlanta GA 30332-0160. *E-Mail:* shenk@math.gatech.edu

SHONLE, JOHN IRWIN, MUSICAL ACOUSTICS. *Current Pos:* CONSULT, 79- *Personal Data:* b Indianapolis, Ind, Oct 1, 33; m 71; c 6. *Educ:* Wesleyan Univ, BA, 55; Univ Calif, Berkeley, MA, 57, PhD(physics), 61. *Prof Exp:* From asst prof to assoc prof physics, Reed Col, 60-67; assoc prof physics & astrophys, Univ Colo, Denver, 67-73, prof physics, 73-79. *Concurrent Pos:* NSF sci fac fel, 66-67. *Mem:* AAAS; Am Asn Physics Teachers; Acoust Soc Am. *Res:* Physics teaching methods; psychoacoustics of music; environmental physics. *Mailing Add:* Two Village Brook Rd Yarmouth ME 04096

SHONS, ALAN R, SURGERY. *Current Pos:* DIR PLASTIC SURG, CASE WESTERN RESERVE UNIV, UNIV HOSPS, 85- *Mailing Add:* Dept Plastic Surg Moffitt Cancer Ctr & Res Inst 12902 Magnolia Dr Tampa FL 33612-9497. *Fax:* 216-291-5353

SHONTZ, CHARLES JACK, ANIMAL ECOLOGY, HUMAN ECOLOGY. *Current Pos:* RETIRED. *Personal Data:* b Sewickley, Pa, Jan 2, 26; m 52. *Educ:* Ind State Col, Pa, BS, 49; Univ Pittsburgh, MS, 53, PhD(zool), 62. *Prof Exp:* Teacher high sch, Pa, 49-55; Fulbright lectr sci, Kambawza Col, Burma, 55-56; teacher high sch, Pa, 56-57; asst prof biol, Clarion State Col, 57-59, from assoc prof to prof biol & physiol, 59-84, head dept, 59-62, dean acad serv, 64-84, assoc vpres acad affairs, 78-84. *Concurrent Pos:* NSF fac fel, 61-62; assoc vpres acad affairs & dean summer sessions, Univ Pa. *Mem:* Am Soc Ichthyol & Herpet; Wilderness Soc; Am Nature Study Soc. *Res:* Effects of environment on the evolution of populations of fishes, especially the family Cyprinidae. *Mailing Add:* Marianne Estates Clarion PA 16214

SHONTZ, JOHN PAUL, PLANT ECOLOGY. *Current Pos:* from asst prof to assoc prof, 74-82, chmn, 79-89, PROF BIOL, GRAND VALLEY STATE UNIV, 82- *Personal Data:* b Meadville, Pa, Oct 11, 40; m 67, Nancy Nickerson; c Jeffrey & Douglas. *Educ:* Edinboro State Col, BS, 62; Miami Univ, MA, 64; Duke Univ, PhD(bot), 67. *Prof Exp:* Teacher pub sch, Pa, 62; instr biol sci, Mt Holyoke Col, 67-68, asst prof, 68-74. *Mem:* AAAS; Bot Soc Am; Ecol Soc Am; Sigma Xi. *Res:* Ecology of desert annuals; plant species interaction; seed germination ecology. *Mailing Add:* Dept Biol Grand Valley State Univ Allendale MI 49401. *Fax:* 616-895-3506; *E-Mail:* shontzj@gvsu.edu

SHONTZ, NANCY NICKERSON, HUMAN GENETICS. *Current Pos:* adj fac, 74-85, asst prof, 85-89, ASSOC PROF BIOL, GRAND VALLEY STATE UNIV, 89- *Personal Data:* b Pittsburgh, Pa, July 9, 42; m 67; c 2. *Educ:* Smith Col, AB, 64, PhD(biol), 69; Duke Univ, MA, 66. *Prof Exp:* Instr biol, ECarolina Univ, 66-67; lectr zool, Univ Mass, 67-68; asst prof bot, Holyoke Community Col, 69-74. *Mem:* AAAS; Sigma Xi. *Res:* Electrophoresis of salamander proteins; seed germination studies; ecotypic variation; bacterial strain identification using plasmids. *Mailing Add:* Biol Dept Grand Valley State Univ Allendale MI 49401. *E-Mail:* shontzn@gvsu.edu

SHOOK, BRENDA LEE, DEVELOPMENTAL NEUROANATOMY, PRENATAL DEVELOPMENT PHYSIOLOGY. *Current Pos:* NIH res fel & vis scholar, Univ Calif, Davis, 82-85 & vis lectr, 83-84, ASSOC RES ANATOMIST, UNIV CALIF, LOS ANGELES, 85- *Personal Data:* b Newport Beach, Calif, Nov 30, 52. *Educ:* Calif State Univ, Stanislaus, BA, 75, MA, 76; Brandeis Univ, PhD(physiol psychol), 82. *Prof Exp:* Asst res anatomist, Brandeis Univ, 79-82. *Mem:* Soc Neurosci; Int Brain Res Orgn; NY Acad Sci; Am Asn Adv Sci. *Res:* Phenomena of recovery of behavioral and physiological function after early brain damage; human mental retardation which results from prenatal and early postnatal damage, by disease or trauma to the developing central nervous system; anatomy and physiology of oculomotor system in primates. *Mailing Add:* Dept Psychol Mt St Mary's Col 12001 Chalon Rd Los Angeles CA 90049-1526

SHOOK, CLIFTON ARNOLD, FLUID & FLUID PARTICLE MECHANICS. *Current Pos:* From asst prof to assoc prof, 60-71, PROF CHEM ENG, UNIV SASK, 71- *Personal Data:* b Lamont, Alta, Oct 10, 34; m 59; c 4. *Educ:* Univ Alta, BSc, 56; Univ London, PhD(chem eng), 60. *Mem:* Chem Inst Can; Can Inst Mining & Metall. *Res:* Fluid mechanics; heat transfer; mass transfer; fluid-particle systems; rheology; pipeline flow of suspensions; flow of heavy oil emulsions. *Mailing Add:* Dept Chem Eng Univ Sask Saskatoon SK S7N 0W0 Can. *Fax:* 306-966-4777; *E-Mail:* shook@sask.usasr.ca

SHOOK, THOMAS EUGENE, CHEMISTRY. *Current Pos:* Res asst biochem, US Army, Ft Detrick, Md, 52-53, chief, Biochem Br, 53-71, environ coordr, Pine Bluff Arsenal, 72-82, CHIEF, DEVELOP & TECHNOL DIV, PINE BLUFF ARSENAL, US ARMY, 71- *Personal Data:* b Pasadena, Calif, Mar 10, 28; m 58; c 3. *Educ:* Tex Tech Univ, BS, 51. *Mem:* Am Chem Soc; Am Inst Chemists; Sigma Xi; Am Statist Asn. *Res:* Physical-engineering sciences; statistics; production development; process evaluation; research management. *Mailing Add:* 1716 Alberta Dr Little Rock AR 72207-3902

SHOOK, WILLIAM BEATTIE, CERAMICS ENGINEERING. *Current Pos:* RETIRED. *Personal Data:* b Columbus, Ohio, Oct 3, 28; m 50; c 4. *Educ:* Ohio State Univ, BCerE, 53, PhD(ceramics eng), 61. *Honors & Awards:* Cramer Award, Am Ceramic Soc, 81. *Prof Exp:* Res asst ceramics res, Eng Exp Sta, Ohio State Univ, 50-53, res assoc, 53-55, supvr building res, 55-57, dir ceramics res, 57-63; vis prof, Indian Inst Technol, Kanpur, 63-65; from asst prof to prof ceramics eng & chmn dept, Ohio State Univ, 65-82. *Mem:* Fel Am Ceramic Soc; Am Soc Eng Educ; Am Ord Asn; Nat Inst Ceramic Engrs; Am Soc Nondestruct Testing. *Res:* Brittle failure mechanisms in impact testing, especially influence of elastic properties, density and geometry of test specimens on the response system; viscosity; measurement and interpretation in melting and crystallizing at non-equilibrium; nondestructive testing of ceramics. *Mailing Add:* 111 Glencoe Rd Columbus OH 43214

SHOOLERY, JAMES NELSON, PHYSICAL CHEMISTRY. *Current Pos:* dir, Appln Lab, Varian Assocs, 52-62, mkt mgr, Anal Inst Div, Calif, 62-69, sr appln chemist, 72-90, CONSULT, VARIAN ASSOCS, 90- *Personal Data:* b Worland, Wyo, June 25, 25; m 51, 71; c 3. *Educ:* Univ Calif, BS, 48; Calif Inst Technol, PhD(chem), 52. *Honors & Awards:* Sargent Award, 64; Anachem Award, 82. *Prof Exp:* Independent consult, 69-72. *Mem:* Am Chem Soc. *Res:* Microwave spectroscopy; chemical effects in nuclear magnetic resonance. *Mailing Add:* 1300 Pilarcitos Half Moon Bay CA 94019

SHOOMAN, MARTIN L, RELIABILITY AND FAULT TOLERANT DESIGN. *Current Pos:* from instr to assoc prof elec eng, 58-74, dir, Div Comput Sic, 81-84, PROF ELEC ENG & COMPUT SCI, POLYTECH INST NY, FARMINGDALE, 74- *Personal Data:* b Trenton, NJ, Feb 24, 34; m 62; c Marc, Alice (Lebowitz), Andrew & Lisa (Tischler). *Educ:* Mass Inst Technol, SB & SM, 56; Polytech Inst Brooklyn, DEE, 61. *Prof Exp:* Teaching asst elec eng, Mass Inst Technol, 55-56; mem staff, Res & Develop Group, Sperry Gyroscope Co, NY, 56-58. *Concurrent Pos:* Consult govt & indust, 59-; vis assoc prof, Mass Inst Technol, 71. *Mem:* Fel Inst Elec & Electronics Engrs. *Res:* Reliability theory and application to computer systems; reliability of electronic and mechanical systems; software engineering; fault tolerant computing. *Mailing Add:* Dept Elec Eng Polytech Univ Long Island Ctr Rte 110 Farmingdale NY 11735-3995. *Fax:* 516-755-4404; *E-Mail:* shooman@vama.poly.edu

SHOOP, C ROBERT, ECOLOGY. *Current Pos:* assoc prof zool, 69-74, PROF ZOOL, UNIV RI, 74- *Personal Data:* b Chicago, Ill, Aug 12, 35; div; c John T & Michael C. *Educ:* Southern Ill Univ, BA, 57; Tulane Univ, MS, 59, PhD(zool, bot), 63. *Honors & Awards:* Stoye Prize, Am Soc Ichthyol & Herpet, 60. *Prof Exp:* Instr zool & physiol, Wellesley Col, 62-64, asst prof biol sci, 64-69,. *Concurrent Pos:* US AEC res contract, 65-75; dir, Inst Environ Biol, 70-72; dir NIH training grant environ physiol, 70-72; collabr, Nat Park Serv, 78-; contracts, Dept Interior, 78-82 & Nat Marine Fisheries Serv, 80-81, 82-83, 87-89 & 92-93; re awards, Wellesley Col, 62-66. *Mem:* AAAS; Soc Conserv Biol; Am Soc Ichthyol & Herpet; Am Soc Mammal; Animal Behavior Soc. *Res:* Behavior and ecology of vertebrates; radiobiology; conservation biology. *Mailing Add:* Dept Biol Sci Univ RI Kingston RI 02881. *Fax:* 401-874-4256

SHOOSMITH, JOHN NORMAN, APPLIED MATHEMATICS, COMPUTER SCIENCE. *Current Pos:* aerospace technologist comput, Manned Spacecraft Ctr, Langley Res Ctr, NASA, 59-64, aerospace technologist, Gemini Prog, 64-65, head comput appl, 65-69, CHIEF SCIENTIST, ANALYSIS & COMPUT DIV, LANGLEY RES CTR, NASA. *Personal Data:* b London, Eng, Oct 9, 34; US citizen; m 66; c 3. *Educ:* Queen's Univ, Ont, BSc, 56; Col William & Mary, MS, 67; Univ Va, PhD(appl math), 73. *Prof Exp:* Comput specialist, Avro Aircraft Corp, Can, 56-59. *Concurrent Pos:* Asst prof lectr, George Washington Univ, 74-79; adj prof appl sci, Col William & Mary, 86- *Mem:* Asn Comput Mach; Am Inst Aeronaut & Astronaut; Soc Indust & Appl Math. *Res:* Numerical analysis, specifically high-order accurate numerical solutions to bondary-value problems of ordinary and partial differential equations. *Mailing Add:* 105 Cambridge Lane Williamsburg VA 23185-4925. *E-Mail:* j.n.shoosmith@Larc.nasa.gov

SHOOTER, ERIC MANVERS, BIOCHEMISTRY. *Current Pos:* assoc prof genetics, Stanford Univ, 64-68, prof genetics & biochem, 68-75, prof neurobiol & chmn dept, 75-87, PROF NEUROBIOL, STANFORD UNIV, SCH MED, 87- *Personal Data:* b Mansfield, Eng, Apr 18, 24; m 49, Elaine Staley Arnold; c Annette. *Educ:* Cambridge Univ, BA, 45, MA, 49, PhD(chem), 50; Univ London, DSc(biochem), 64; Univ Cambridge, ScD(biochem), 86. *Honors & Awards:* Wakeman Award, 88; Ralph W Gerard Prize, Soc Neurosci, 95; Javits Neurosci Invest Award, Nat Inst Neurol & Commun Disorders & Stroke, 92. *Prof Exp:* Fel chem, Univ Wis, 49-50; sr scientist biochem, Brewing Indust Res Found, Eng, 50-53; lectr, Univ Col, Univ London, 53-64. *Concurrent Pos:* USPHS int fel, Stanford Univ, 61-62. *Mem:* Foreign assoc Inst Med Nat Acad Sci; Brit Biophys Soc; Am Soc Biol Chemists; Am Soc Neurochem; Int Soc Neurochem; Soc Neurosci; Brit Biochem Soc; fel Royal Soc London; fel AAAS; Peripheral Nerve Soc; Am Col Neuropsycholpharmacol; NY Acad Sci. *Res:* Physical chemistry of proteins; structure of normal and abnormal hemoglobins; genetic control of protein synthesis, replication of DNA; molecular neurobiology; nerve growth factor; myelination and demyelinating diseases. *Mailing Add:* Dept Neurobiol-Fairchild Sch Med Stanford Univ Stanford CA 94305-5401

SHOOTER, JACK ALLEN, ACOUSTICS, COMPUTER SCIENCE. *Current Pos:* res scientist assoc V acoust, 63-88, SPECIAL RES ASSOC, APPL RES LABS, UNIV TEX, AUSTIN, 80- *Personal Data:* b Austin, Tex, June 16, 40; m 77; c 4. *Educ:* Univ Tex, Austin, BS, 63. *Mem:* Assoc mem Acoust Soc Am; Sigma Xi. *Res:* Underwater acoustics; physical acoustics; signal processing. *Mailing Add:* 11305 January Dr Austin TX 78753-2915

SHOPE, RICHARD EDWIN, JR, VIROLOGY, IMMUNOLOGY. *Current Pos:* RETIRED. *Personal Data:* b Philadelphia, Pa, Sept 4, 26; m 61; c 6. *Educ:* Williams Col, BA, 47; Univ Wis, BS, 49; Cornell Univ, DVM, 59; Univ Minn, PhD(microbiol), 64. *Prof Exp:* Asst prof, Univ Minn, St Paul, 59-70, assoc prof vet med & microbiol, 70-95. *Concurrent Pos:* NIH career develop award, 64-68. *Mem:* Am Vet Med Asn; US Animal Health Asn; Am Asn Vet Clinicians. *Res:* Enteric and respiratory viral disease of domestic animals; mammalian leukemias and other tumors; immune tolerance and autoimmune diseases of domestic animals. *Mailing Add:* 7786 Sunset Ave Lino Lake MN 55014

SHOPE, ROBERT ELLIS, VIROLOGY. *Current Pos:* from asst prof to assoc prof, 65-75, prof epidemiol, 75-95, PROF PATH, MED BR, UNIV TEX, 95- *Personal Data:* b Princeton, NJ, Feb 21, 29; m 58, Virginia Barbour; c Peter, Steven, Deborah & Bonnie. *Educ:* Cornell Univ, BA, 51, MD, 54. *Honors & Awards:* Walter Reed Medal; Richard M Taylor Award; Bailey K Ashford Medal. *Prof Exp:* Intern, Grace-New Haven Community Hosp, Conn, 54-55, asst resident internal med, 57-58; mem, Staff Virus Labs, Rockefeller Found, NY, 58-59 & Belem Virus Lab, 59-65. *Concurrent Pos:* Dir, Yale Arbovirus Res Unit, 72-95. *Mem:* Am Soc Trop Med & Hyg; Am Soc Virol; Am Epidemiol Soc; Am Acad Microbiol; Infectious Dis Soc Am; Am Col Vet Microbiol. *Res:* Arboviruses. *Mailing Add:* Dept Path Med Br Univ Tex 301 Univ Blvd Galveston TX 77555-0609. *Fax:* 409-747-2429; *E-Mail:* rshope@mspo6.med.utmb.edu

SHOPES, BOB, GENE CLONING. *Current Pos:* PRES, TERA BIOTECH, 94- *Personal Data:* b Ger, Oct 14, 58; US citizen. *Educ:* Univ Calif, Berkeley, AB, 80; Univ Ill, Urbana, PhD(biophysics), 86. *Prof Exp:* Fel, Leukemia Soc Am, Stanford Univ, 86-89; dir res, Stratacyte, 90-94. *Res:* Develop new technology to clone genes for biotechnology uses. *Mailing Add:* 3099 Science Park Rd San Diego CA 92121. *Fax:* 619-450-5947; *E-Mail:* bshopes@aol.com

SHOPP, GEORGE MILTON, JR, IMMUNOTOXICOLOGY, MARINE MAMMAL TOXICOLOGY. *Current Pos:* SCIENTIST, GENETECH. *Personal Data:* b Harrisburg, Pa, May 21, 55. *Educ:* Bucknell Univ, BS, 77; Med Col Va, PhD(toxicol), 84. *Prof Exp:* Fel, Inhalation Toxicol Res Inst, 84-86; assoc scientist, Lovelace Med Found, 86-91; scientist, Synergen, 92- *Concurrent Pos:* Clin asst prof, Col Pharm, Univ NM, 86-, adj asst prof, Dept Biol, 88-; prin investr, Nat Inst Environ Health Sci, 89-; adj res scientist, Marine Environ Res Inst, 90-; ad hoc proposal reviewer, Health Effects Inst, 90 & Nat Oceanog Atmospheric Admin, 91- *Mem:* Am Col Toxicol; Soc Toxicol; Am Asn Immunologists. *Res:* Toxic effects of environmental chemicals and drugs on immune function in laboratory animals, marine mammals and humans. *Mailing Add:* Genetech Inc 460 Point San Bruno Blvd South San Francisco CA 94080-4990

SHOPSIS, CHARLES S, IN VITRO TOXICOLOGY. *Current Pos:* ASST PROF BIOCHEM, ROCKEFELLER UNIV, 82- *Educ:* City Univ NY, PhD(biochem), 74. *Res:* Cell membrane function. *Mailing Add:* Dept Chem Adelphi Univ Garden City NY 11530

SHOR, AARON LOUIS, VETERINARY MEDICINE, ANIMAL NUTRITION. *Current Pos:* CONSULT, 90- *Personal Data:* b New York, NY, Jan 13, 24; m 60, Rosalind Darrow. *Educ:* Cornell Univ, BS, 47, DVM, 53; Univ Del, MS, 49. *Prof Exp:* Field investr animal dis, Farm & Home Div, Am Cyanamid Co, 55-57, ruminant specialist, 57, field investr, Agr Div, 57-60, mgr, Clin Develop Lab & Poultry Prog, 63-77, regist coordr, Agr Div, 77-80; mgr clin develop, Smith Kline Animal Health Prod, 80-85; mgr, Reg Affairs & Mfg Qual Assurance, 85-90. *Concurrent Pos:* Adj prof, Trenton State Col, 73-75. *Mem:* Am Vet Med Asn; Am Soc Animal Sci; Am Dairy Sci Asn; Poultry Sci Asn; Indust Vet Asn (secy, 65-70, pres, 71-72); Am Asn Avian Pathologists. *Res:* Development of drugs to prevent or treat disease or improve production efficiency of animals. *Mailing Add:* 18 Pecan St Mt Laurel NJ 08054-4513. *Fax:* 609-231-9305

SHOR, ARTHUR JOSEPH, INORGANIC CHEMISTRY, NUCLEAR ENGINEERING. *Current Pos:* CONSULT, 94- *Personal Data:* b New York, NY, June 10, 23; m 52, 89, Ellen Arkin; c 2. *Educ:* City Col New York, BChE, 43; Univ Tenn, MS, 64, PhD(chem), 67. *Prof Exp:* Assoc chem engr, Argonne Nat Lab, 46-56; res chem engr, IIT Res Inst, 56-57; mem res staff chem, Oak Ridge Nat Lab, 58-85; res engr, Weitzmann Inst, 88-94. *Mem:* Am Chem Soc; Sigma Xi. *Res:* Fused salt phase studies; effects of reactor irradiation on nuclear fuels and fertile materials; development of reverse osmosis membranes and apparatus for cleanup of waste and brackish waters; development of solar receivers; chemical heat pipe. *Mailing Add:* 193 Outer Dr Oak Ridge TN 37830

SHOR, GEORGE G, JR, MARINE GEOPHYSICS. *Current Pos:* from asst res geophysicist to res geophysicist, Univ Calif, San Diego, 53-69, prof marine geophys & sea grant prog mgr, 69-73, assoc dir, 68-90, EMER PROF GEOPHYS, SCRIPPS INST OCEANOG, UNIV CALIF, SAN DIEGO, 90- *Personal Data:* b New York, NY, June 8, 23; m 50, Betty Noble; c Alexander, Carolyn & Donald. *Educ:* Calif Inst Technol, BS, 44, MS, 48, PhD(seismol), 54. *Prof Exp:* Seismol party chief, Seismic Explor, Inc, 48-51; res asst, Calif Inst Technol, 51-53. *Mem:* AAAS; Soc Explor Geophys; fel Geol Soc Am; fel Am Geophys Union; Am Bamboo Soc (pres, 93-96). *Res:* Marine geophysics; structure, origin and properties of ocean floor; marine technology. *Mailing Add:* Scripps Inst Oceanog Univ Calif La Jolla CA 92093-0210

SHOR, STEVEN MICHAEL, CHEMICAL ENGINEERING. *Current Pos:* Sr chem engr, 70-88, DIV SCIENTIST, 3M CO, 88- *Personal Data:* b New York, NY, Apr 5, 44; m 70. *Educ:* Univ Mass, Amherst, BS, 65; Northwestern Univ, MS, 67; Iowa State Univ, PhD(chem eng), 70. *Mem:* Am Inst Chem Engrs. *Res:* Small particle technology, especially as applied to grain size distribution involved in crystallization and precipitation processes; effects of various parameters on nucleation and growth kinetics. *Mailing Add:* 9177 Edinburgh Lane St Paul MN 55125

SHORE, BRUCE WALTER, ATOMIC PHYSICS, OPTICS. *Current Pos:* PHYSICIST, LAWRENCE LIVERMORE LAB, 72- *Personal Data:* b Visalia, Calif, Feb 27, 35; m, Randi; c Tim, Hilary, Hans, Leif & Derek. *Educ:* Col Pac, BS, 56; Mass Inst Technol, PhD(nuclear chem), 60. *Honors & Awards:* Alexander von Humboldt Res Award, 97. *Prof Exp:* Res chemist, Shell Oil Co, Calif, 56; res scientist, US Naval Radiol Defense Lab, 57; instr physics, Suffolk Univ, 57-60; analyst develop planning, Anal Serv, Inc, Va, 60-62; lectr astron & res fel astrophys, Harvard Col Observ, 62-68; assoc prof physics, Kans State Univ, 68-72. *Concurrent Pos:* Sci Res Coun fel, Imp Col, Univ London, 70-71; vis scientist, Imp Col London, 83-84 & Max Planck Inst Quantum Optics, 84. *Mem:* Am Phys Soc; Int Astron Union. *Res:* Atomic structure and theoretical spectroscopy; photon physics; quantum optics; computer application. *Mailing Add:* Lawrence Livermore Nat Lab PO Box 808 Livermore CA 94550. *E-Mail:* shore2@llnl.gov

SHORE, FERDINAND JOHN, nuclear physics; deceased, see previous edition for last biography

SHORE, FRED L, AGRICULTURAL & FOREST SCIENCES. *Current Pos:* sect head, 85-87, TECH DIR & DEPT HEAD, RADIAN CORP, 87- *Personal Data:* b Bakersfield, Calif, Sept 3, 42; m 64; c 2. *Educ:* Fresno State Col, BS, 64; Ariz State Univ, Phd(chem), 71. *Prof Exp:* From asst prof to prof chem, Jackson State Univ, 70-82; supvr, Lockheed Eng & Man Serv Co, 82-85. *Mem:* Am Chem Soc. *Res:* Environmental analytical chemistry method development with GC/MS and GC specialties. *Mailing Add:* 14 Duende Rd Santa Fe NM 87505

SHORE, GORDON CHARLES, ORGANELLE BIOGENESIS, PROTEIN TARGETING. *Current Pos:* PROF BIOCHEM, MCGILL UNIV, 86- *Educ:* McGill Univ, PhD(biochem), 74. *Mailing Add:* Dept Biochem McGill Univ 3655 Drummond St Montreal PQ H3G 1Y6 Can. *Fax:* 514-398-7384

SHORE, HERBERT BARRY, THEORETICAL SOLID STATE PHYSICS, COMPUTATIONAL PHYSICS. *Current Pos:* assoc prof, 75-79, PROF PHYSICS, SAN DIEGO STATE UNIV, 79- *Personal Data:* b Brooklyn, NY, Nov 18, 39. *Educ:* Mass Inst Technol, BS, 61; Univ Calif, Berkeley, PhD(physics), 66. *Prof Exp:* Asst res physicist, Univ Calif, San Diego, 66-67; asst prof physics, 67-75. *Mem:* Am Phys Soc; AAAS. *Res:* Electron-hole liquid; theory of electron gas; impurities in semiconductors; metal-insulator transition. *Mailing Add:* Dept Physics San Diego State Univ San Diego CA 92182. *Fax:* 619-594-5485; *E-Mail:* hshore@quantum.sdsu.edu

SHORE, JAMES H, PSYCHIATRY. *Current Pos:* PROF & CHMN, DEPT PSYCHIAT, UNIV COLO HEALTH SCI CTR, 85-; SUPT, CO PSYCHIAT HOSP, 85- *Personal Data:* b Winston-Salem, NC, Apr 6, 40; m 63, Christine Lowenbach; c Lenya & Jay. *Educ:* Duke Univ, MD, 65. *Honors & Awards:* Commendation Medal, Dept Health, Educ & Welfare, 72. *Prof Exp:* Chief, Portland Area Indian Health Serv, 69-73; from assoc prof to prof psychiat, Med Sch, Univ Ore, 73-85, dir, Community Psychiat Training Prog, Health Sci Ctr, 73-75, chmn, Dept Psychiat, 75-85. *Concurrent Pos:* Chmn Ment Health Res Comt, Health Prog Systs Ctr, Indian Health Serv, Tucson, Ariz, 70-73, Coun Med Educ, Am Psychiat Asn, 91-; consult, Psychiat Educ Br, Div Manpower & Training Progs, NIMH, 74-80, Am Indian Ment Health Res & Develop Ctr, Denver, Colo, 85-; mem dirs adv bd, Ore Ment Health Div, Salem, 75 & Ore Bd Med Examiners, 78-85; Found Fund researcher psychiat, 79; dir, Am Bd Psychiat, Neurol, 87-, chair psychiat residency rev comt, 89- *Mem:* Fel Am Psychiat Asn; Am Asn Chmn Dept Psychiat; fel Am Col

Psychiatrists; Am Bd Psychiat & Neurol (pres, 94). *Res:* Psychiatric epidemiology; psychiatric education; suicidology; civil commitment; transcultural psychiatry; impaired physicians; stress disorders. *Mailing Add:* Health Sci Ctr Univ Colo 4200 E Ninth Denver CO 80262

SHORE, JOHN EDWARD, INFORMATION THEORY, SPEECH PROCESSING. *Current Pos:* PROF LECTR COMPUT SCI, GEORGE WASHINGTON UNIV, 78- *Personal Data:* b Slough, Gt Brit, Sept 2, 46; US citizen; m 69; c 1. *Educ:* Yale Univ, BS, 68; Univ Md, PhD(theoret physics), 74. *Prof Exp:* Res scientist physics & comput sci, Naval Res Lab, 68-78. *Concurrent Pos:* Res publ award, Naval Res Lab, 71, 76 & 78; adj lectr elec engr, Univ Md, 80- *Mem:* Asn Comput Mach; Inst Elec & Electronics Engrs; Am Phys Soc. *Res:* Information theory, especially the foundations and applications of maximum entropy and related techniques; software engineering; programming language design; speech processing. *Mailing Add:* 906E Capitol St NE Washington DC 20002

SHORE, JOSEPH D, ENZYMOLOGY, PHYSICAL BIOCHEMISTRY. *Current Pos:* sr staff investr dept biochem, 66-79, HEAD DIV BIOCHEM RES, HENRY FORD HOSP, 79-, DIR RES, 82- *Personal Data:* b New York, NY, Apr 2, 34; m 68; c 2. *Educ:* Cornell Univ, BS, 55; Univ Mass, MS, 57; Rutgers Univ, PhD(biochem), 63. *Prof Exp:* Muscular Dystrophy Asn fel, Nobel Med Inst, Stockholm, Sweden, 64-66. *Concurrent Pos:* Adj prof, Med Sch, Wayne State Univ; Am Heart Asn Coun Thrombosis. *Mem:* Am Chem Soc; Am Soc Biol Chem & Molecular Biol; Biophys Soc; Nat Coun Univ Res Admin. *Res:* Blood coagulation; transient kinetics and fluorescence techniques. *Mailing Add:* Biochem Res Henry Ford Health Syst One Ford Pl 5D Detroit MI 48202. *Fax:* 313-876-2380

SHORE, LAURENCE STUART, ENDOCRINOLOGY. *Current Pos:* INVESTR, DEPT HORMONE RES, KIMRON VET INST, BET DAGAN, 78- *Personal Data:* b Philadelphia, Pa, Mar 16, 44; m 67, Maxine Frank; c 4. *Educ:* Yeshiva Univ, BA, 65; Hahnemann Med Sch, MA, 69, PhD(physiol), 72. *Prof Exp:* Postdoctoral, Med Sch, Wash Univ, 72-73; instr physiol, Dept Obstet-Gynec & Physiol, Temple Univ, Philadelphia, 73-76. *Concurrent Pos:* Vis scientist, Dept Obstet-Gynec, Hosp Univ Pa, 84-85; sr, Smithsonian fel , Smithsonian Environ Res Ctr, 93-94. *Mem:* Am Physiol Soc; Israel Endocrine Soc; Soc Study Reproduction. *Res:* Hormones present in food and water and their effects on animals; hyperestrogenism and premature puberty in cattle; prolaped oviduct and salpingitis in poultry; environmental estrogens. *Mailing Add:* Dept Hormone Res Kimron Vet Inst PO Box 12 Bet Dagan 50200 Israel. *Fax:* 972-3-9681-753; *E-Mail:* shemesh@agri.huji.ac.il

SHORE, MILES FREDERICK, PSYCHIATRY. *Current Pos:* BULLARD PROF PSYCHIAT, MED SCH, HARVARD UNIV, 75- *Personal Data:* b Chicago, Ill, May 26, 29; m 53, Eleanor Gossard; c Miles P, Rebecca M (Lewin) & Susanna A (LeBoutillier). *Educ:* Univ Chicago, AB, 48; Harvard Univ, BA, 50, MD, 54; Am Bd Psychiat & Neurol, dipl, 60. *Honors & Awards:* Admn Psychiat Award, Am Psychiat Asn; Bowis Award, Am Col Psychiatrists; Noyes Award, 94. *Prof Exp:* Intern, Univ Ill Res & Educ Hosp, 55; resident psychiat, Mass Ment Health Ctr, 55-56 & Beth Israel Hosp, Boston, 59-61; instr, Harvard Med Sch, 64-65; from asst prof to prof psychiat, Sch Med, Tufts Univ, 71-75, assoc dean community affairs, 72-75, dir, Ment Health Ctr, 68-75; Bullard Prof Psychiat, Harvard Med Sch, 75- *Concurrent Pos:* Chmn bd trustees, Boston Psychoanal Soc & Inst, 70-73; dir community & ambulatory med, New Eng Med Ctr Hosp, 72-75; supt & area dir, Mass Ment Health Ctr, 75-93; sr prog consult & dir, Prog Chronically Ment Ill, Robert Wood Johnson Found, 85-92; scholar residence, John F Kennedy Sch Govt, Harvard Univ; mem bd dirs, Med Found, Boston, Mass. *Mem:* Fel Am Psychiat Asn; Group Advan Psychiat; Am Col Psychiatrists (pres, 96-97). *Res:* Community psychiatry; psychohistory; mental health policy. *Mailing Add:* 62 Meadowbrook Rd Needham MA 02192. *Fax:* 617-496-0250

SHORE, MORIS LAWRENCE, METABOLIC KINETICS, RADIOBIOLOGY. *Current Pos:* CONSULT, 85- *Personal Data:* b Russia, Dec 7, 27; US citizen; m 58; c 3. *Educ:* Southwestern Univ, Memphis, BA, 50; Univ Tenn, PhD(physiol), 54. *Prof Exp:* Staff mem, Biophys Br, USN Radiol Defense Lab, USN Med Serv corps, 54-61; asst prof physiol, Marquette Univ, Ill 61-62; chief biophys & asst officer in command, Res Br Lab, Dept Health & Human Servs, Food & Drug Admin, 62-67, chief, Physiol & Biophys Lab, 67-69, chief, Exp Studies Br, 69-70, dir, Div Biol Effects, Bur Radiol Health, 70-85. *Concurrent Pos:* Chief, Physiol Sect, Res Serv, Wood Vet Admin Ctr, 61-62. *Mem:* Radiation Res Soc; Health Physics Soc; Res Soc; NY Acad Sci. *Res:* Tracer kinetics; phospholipid metabolism; experimental atherosclerosis; reticulo-endothelial system function; effects of ionizing and nonionizing radiation; development of regulatory and voluntary health protection standards and guidelines. *Mailing Add:* 12411 Kemp Mill Rd Silver Spring MD 20902

SHORE, NOMIE ABRAHAM, PEDIATRICS, HEMATOLOGY. *Current Pos:* ASSOC HEMATOLOGIST, CHILDREN'S HOSP, LOS ANGELES, 61- *Personal Data:* b Chicago, Ill, Oct 2, 23; div; c 2. *Educ:* Univ Calif, Los Angeles, BA, 47; Univ Southern Calif, MD, 53. *Prof Exp:* Intern med, Los Angeles Co Gen Hosp, 52-53; resident pediat, Children's Hosp Los Angeles, 53-55, fel hemat, 55-56; asst clin prof pediat, Univ Calif, Los Angeles, 57-60; asst prof, Sch Med, Univ Southern Calif, 61-68, assoc prof pediat, 68- *Concurrent Pos:* Consult pediat hemat, St John's Hosp, Santa Monica, 61-; mem hon staff, Santa Monica Hosp, 61- *Mem:* AMA; Am Soc Hemat; Am Acad Pediat; Am Asn Cancer Res. *Res:* Evaluating the effects of chemotherapeutic agents in treatment of leukemia and other neoplastic diseases; erythropoietin physiology; bone marrow stem cell kinetics. *Mailing Add:* Children's Hosp Los Angeles PO Box 54700 Los Angeles CA 90054-0700

SHORE, RICHARD A, RECURSION THEORY. *Current Pos:* from asst prof to assoc prof, 74-83, PROF MATH, CORNELL UNIV, 83- *Personal Data:* b Boston, Mass, Aug 18, 46; m 69, Naomi S Spiller; c Denna & Aviva. *Educ:* Hebrew Col, BJEd, 66; Harvard Univ, AB, 68; Mass Inst Technol, PhD(math), 72. *Prof Exp:* Instr, Univ Chicago, 72-74. *Concurrent Pos:* Asst prof, Univ Ill, 77; vis assoc prof, Univ Conn, Storrs, 79 & Mass Inst Technol, 80; vis prof, Hebrew Univ, Jerusalem, 82-83; ed, J Symbolic Logic, 84-92; managing ed, Bull Symbolic Logic, 92- *Mem:* Am Math Soc; Asn Symbolic Logic; Asn Comput Mach; Spec Interest Group Automata & Computability Theory. *Res:* Computability theory: degrees of difficulty of computability, recursively enumerable sets and degrees; generalizations of recursion theory and applications and effective mathematics. *Mailing Add:* Dept Math White Hall Cornell Univ Ithaca NY 14853. *Fax:* 607-255-7149; *E-Mail:* Shore@math.cornell.edu

SHORE, ROY E, ENVIRONMENTAL EPIDEMIOLOGY, RADIATION EPIDEMIOLOGY. *Current Pos:* res scientist environ med, 69-76, from asst prof to assoc prof, 76-87, PROF ENVIRON MED, NY UNIV MED CTR, 87- *Personal Data:* b Mina, NY, Oct 30, 40; m 62, Helen J; c 6. *Educ:* Houghton Col, BA, 62; Syracuse Univ, MA, 66, PhD(psychol), 67; Columbia Univ, DPH, 82. *Prof Exp:* Fel psychol, Educ Testing Serv, Princeton, 67-69. *Concurrent Pos:* Comt on fed res on health effects of ionizing radiation, Nat Acad Sci, 80-81; adv comt health & environ res, US Dept Energy, 83-86; bd sci counr, Div Cancer Etiol, Nat Cancer Inst, 84-91, mem, Studies Thyroid Dis from Chernobyl, 90-; mem, Comt CDC Radiation Studies, Nat Acad Sci, 91-, Int Comn Radiol Protection, 93- *Mem:* Fel Am Col Epidemiol; Nat Coun Radiation & Protection; Soc Epidemiol Res; Biometric Soc. *Res:* Cancer in relation to ionizing radiation exposures, diet, occupational exposures and biomarkers. *Mailing Add:* Dept Environ Med NY Univ Med Ctr 341 E 25th St Rm 204 New York NY 10010-2598. *E-Mail:* shore@mcgcr0.med.nyu.edu

SHORE, SAMUEL DAVID, MATHEMATICS. *Current Pos:* asst prof, 65-70, ASSOC PROF MATH, UNIV NH, 70- *Personal Data:* b Lewistown, Pa, Nov 9, 37; m 64; c 2. *Educ:* Juniata Col, BS, 59; Pa State Univ, MA, 61, PhD(gen topology), 64. *Prof Exp:* Instr math, Pa State Univ, 64-65. *Mem:* Am Math Soc; Math Asn Am. *Res:* Spaces of continuous functions; compactifications and extensions; ordered spaces. *Mailing Add:* Dept Math Univ NH Kingsbury Hall Durham NH 03824-3563

SHORE, SHELDON GERALD, INORGANIC CHEMISTRY. *Current Pos:* from asst prof to assoc prof, 57-62, PROF CHEM, OHIO STATE UNIV, 65-, CHARLES H KIMBERLY PROF CHEM, 92- *Personal Data:* b Chicago, Ill, May 8, 30. *Educ:* Univ Ill, BS, 51; Univ Mich, MS, 54, PhD(chem), 57. *Honors & Awards:* Reilley Lectr Inorg Chem, Univ Notre Dame, 82; Morley Award & Medal, Cleveland Sect, Am Chem Soc, 89, Columbus Sect Award, 90; Egon Wiberg Lectr, Univ Munich, 94. *Prof Exp:* Instr chem, Univ Mich, 56-57. *Concurrent Pos:* Distinguished lectr, Ohio State Univ, 96. *Mem:* Am Chem Soc; corresp mem Bavarian Acad Sci. *Res:* Synthesis and study of transition metal and non-metal cluster systems: polynuclear metal carbonyl hydrides, metallaboranes, and boron hydrides. *Mailing Add:* Dept Chem Ohio State Univ Columbus OH 43210

SHORE, STEVEN NEIL, THEORETICAL ASTROPHYSICS. *Current Pos:* ASSOC PROF PHYSICS & CHAIR, DEPT PHYSICS & ASTRON, IND UNIV, SOUTHBEND, 93- *Personal Data:* b New York, NY, July, 16, 53; m 74, Lys A Taylor. *Educ:* State Univ NY, Stony Brook, MSc, 74; Univ Toronto, PhD(astron), 78. *Prof Exp:* Res assoc astron, Columbia Univ, 78-79, lectr, 79; assoc prof & dir, Astrophys Res Ctr, 85-89; asst prof astron, Case Western Res Univ, 79-84; operations astronr, Comput Sci Corp, Space Telescope Sci Inst, 84-85; astrophysicist, Comput Sci Corp, Goddard Space Ctr, 89-93. *Concurrent Pos:* Shapley lectr astron, Am Astron Soc, 80-; vis asst prof astron, Ohio State Univ, 81; vis prof, Ecloe Normale Superiure; vis physicist, Am Inst Physics, 92-; adj assoc prof physics, Ariz State Univ, 92-; vis prof astrophys, Univ Pisa, 93- *Mem:* Am Astron Soc; Sigma Xi; Hist Sci Soc; Int Astron Union; Brit Soc Hist Sci. *Res:* Chemical evolution of the galaxy; ultraviolet spectroscopy; history of science; star formation; astrophysical hydrodynamics; radiative transfer; novae; nucleo synthesis; binary stars. *Mailing Add:* Dept Physics & Astron Ind Univ 1700 Mishawaka Ave South Bend IN 46634-7111. *Fax:* 219-237-4538; *E-Mail:* sshore@vines.iusb.indiana.edu

SHORE, VIRGIE GUINN, BIOCHEMISTRY, PHYSIOLOGY. *Current Pos:* RETIRED. *Personal Data:* b Lavaca, Ark, Oct 20, 28; m 52. *Educ:* Univ Calif, AB, 50, PhD(biochem), 55. *Prof Exp:* Res asst physiol, Sch Med, Wash Univ, 57-58, from res instr to res asst prof, 58-61, asst prof, 61-63; biochemist, Bio-Med Div, Lawrence Livermore Lab, Univ Calif, 63-90. *Concurrent Pos:* Mem, Metab Study Sect, NIH & Exec Comt Coun on Arteriosclerosis, Am Heart Asn. *Mem:* Am Physiol Soc. *Res:* Resonance energy transfer; structure of lipoproteins and membranes. *Mailing Add:* 1446 Lillian St Livermore CA 94550

SHORE, WILLIAM SPENCER, PHYSICAL CHEMISTRY. *Current Pos:* RETIRED. *Personal Data:* m 48, Elizabeth Adams; c David, Margaret, Mary (deceased), Sarah & Catherine. *Educ:* Iowa State Univ, BS, 49; Univ Iowa, PhD(phys chem), 53. *Prof Exp:* Sr chemist, 3M Co, St Paul, Minn, 56-60; postdoctoral fel protein chem, Univ Minn, 60; asst prof phys chem, Concordia Col, 62-66; environ coordr & res chemist, Rock Island Arsenal, 68-91. *Concurrent Pos:* Pres, Quad-City Eng & Sci Coun, 94-95. *Mem:* Am Chem Soc; Sigma Xi. *Res:* Synthesis of bisNN'(trimethyl silylmethyl)pyromeliticdimide. *Mailing Add:* 1939 Pershing Ave Davenport IA 52803-2921

SHORES, DAVID ARTHUR, METALLURGICAL CHEMISTRY. *Current Pos:* assoc prof, 82-, PROF, DEPT CHEM ENG & MAT SCI, UNIV MINN. *Personal Data:* b Towanda, Pa, Jan 10, 41; m 63; c 3. *Educ:* Pa State Univ, BS, 62, MS, 64, PhD(mat sci), 67. *Prof Exp:* Fel metall, Ohio State Univ, 68-70; metallurgist, Large Steam Turbine Generator Div, 70-74, metallurgist hot corroston, Corp Res & Develop Ctr, Gen Elec Co, 74-82. *Mem:* Electrochem Soc; Am Ceramics Soc. *Res:* High temperature oxidation; thermochemistry and electrochemistry of molten salts; high temperature fuel cells. *Mailing Add:* 455 Ripley Ave St Paul MN 55117

SHORES, THOMAS STEPHEN, MATHEMATICS. *Current Pos:* Assoc prof, 68-77, dept vchmn, 76-79, PROF MATH, UNIV NEBR, LINCOLN, 77-, ACTG CHMN, 81- *Personal Data:* b Kansas City, Kans, May 28, 42; m 68. *Educ:* Univ Kans, BA, 64, MA, 65, PhD(math), 68. *Mem:* Am Math Soc; Math Asn Am. *Res:* Generalized solvable and nilpotent groups; structure theory for modules and commutative ring theory. *Mailing Add:* Dept Math Univ Nebr Lincoln NE 68588-0323

SHORR, BERNARD, RESEARCH ADMINISTRATION. *Current Pos:* RETIRED. *Personal Data:* b New York, NY, July 5, 28; m 58. *Educ:* City Col NY, BA, 50; NY Univ, MS, 51, PhD, 70. *Prof Exp:* Meteorologist, Gen Elec Co, Wash, 51-55; staff mem univ sponsored res, Mass Inst Technol, 56-58; res assoc opers res, Corp Res Div, Travelers Ins Co, 58-63, asst dir res, 63-66, assoc dir, 66-70, second vpres, 70-92. *Concurrent Pos:* Lectr, Univ Conn, 70-77. *Mem:* Sigma Xi. *Res:* Research administration; financial and economic analysis; statistics. *Mailing Add:* PO Box 1024 Avon CT 06001

SHORT, BYRON ELLIOTT, mechanical engineering, heat transfer; deceased, see previous edition for last biography

SHORT, CHARLES ROBERT, PHARMACOLOGY. *Current Pos:* PROF VET PHARMACOL & TOXICOL, SCH VET MED, LA STATE UNIV, BATON ROUGE, 75-, VET DIAG TOXICOLOGIST, 76- *Personal Data:* b Rochester, NY, Nov 7, 38; m 64; c 2. *Educ:* Ohio State Univ, DVM, 63, MS, 65; Univ Mo-Columbia, PhD, 69. *Prof Exp:* From instr to assoc prof pharmacol, Sch Med, Univ Mo-Columbia, 65-75. *Concurrent Pos:* Spec fel med educ, Univ Southern Calif, 74. *Mem:* AAAS; NY Acad Sci; Am Soc Pharmacol & Exp Therapeutics; Am Col Vet Toxicologists. *Res:* Drug disposition pharmacology in the fetus and neonate; chemical carcinogenesis. *Mailing Add:* Dept Vet Pharm/Toxicol La State Univ Sch Vet Med Baton Rouge LA 70803-0001. Fax: 504-346-3295

SHORT, DONALD RAY, JR, MATHEMATICS. *Current Pos:* From asst prof to assoc prof, 69-75, PROF MATH & DEAN, COL SCI, SAN DIEGO STATE UNIV, 75- *Personal Data:* b Camp McCoy, Wis, Sept 13, 44; m 78; c 2. *Educ:* Univ Calif, Los Angeles, BA, 65; Ore State Univ, PhD(math), 69. *Mem:* Sigma Xi; Am Math Soc; Soc Indust & Appl Math. *Res:* Algebraic topology; cohomology theory; sheaf theory; spectral sequences; branched immersions. *Mailing Add:* 1541 Shadow Knolls El Cajon CA 92020

SHORT, EVERETT C, JR, BIOCHEMISTRY. *Current Pos:* RETIRED. *Personal Data:* b Monett, Mo, Dec 27, 31; c 3. *Educ:* Kent State Univ, BS, 58; Colo State Univ, DVM, 62; Univ Minn, PhD(biochem), 68. *Prof Exp:* From instr to assoc prof, Col Vet Med, Univ Minn, St Paul, 64-73, prof biochem & assoc dean, 73-78; prof & head physiol sci, Col Vet Med, Okla State Univ, Stillwater, 80- *Mem:* Am Soc Microbiol; Am Vet Med Asn; Soc Exp Biol Med; Soc Environ Toxicol & Chem. *Res:* Effects of toxic substances on aquatic organisms; enteric diseases of baby pigs. *Mailing Add:* Rte Box 660 Perkins OK 74059

SHORT, FRANKLIN WILLARD, MEDICINAL CHEMISTRY, CLINICAL DRUG DEVELOPMENT. *Current Pos:* RETIRED. *Personal Data:* b Charleston, WVa, Feb 24, 28; m 57; c 2. *Educ:* Univ Buffalo, BA, 48; Columbia Univ, PhD(org chem), 52. *Prof Exp:* Jr chemist, Nat Aniline Div, Allied Chem Corp, 47-48; from assoc res chemist to sr res chemist, Parke, Davis & Co, 52-67, assoc lab dir orgn chem, 67-70, sect dir chem dept, 70-78, clin scientist, Clin Res Dept, Warner-Lambert-Parke-Davis Pharmaceut Res Div, 78-86; sr sci adv, Davco Mfg Corp, 86-91. *Mem:* Am Chem Soc. *Res:* Synthesis of antiparasitic, antiinflammatory, analgetic, antifungal, antibacterial pulmonary/allergy and gastrointestinal agents; clinical development of antiinflammatory and antibacterial agents; development of water purification and automotive products. *Mailing Add:* 620 Deerlake Rd Brevard NC 28712

SHORT, HENRY LAUGHTON, ECOLOGY, WILDLIFE BIOLOGY. *Current Pos:* SR SCIENTIST, REGION 5, FISH & WILDLIFE SERV, US DEPT INTERIOR, 93- *Personal Data:* b Penn Yan, NY, Apr 6, 34; m 62, Cathleen Peeke; c Jonathan & Christopher. *Educ:* Swarthmore Col, BA, 56; Johns Hopkins Univ, MS, 59; Mich State Univ, PhD(fisheries, wildlife), 62. *Prof Exp:* Res asst vert ecol, Johns Hopkins Univ, 57-58; res asst fisheries & wildlife, Mich State Univ, 59-61; asst prof & mem grad fac forest recreation & wildlife, Colo State Univ, 61-63, wildlife nutritionist, Colo Coop Wildlife Res Unit, 61-63; wildlife biologist, Southern Forest Exp Sta, Forest Serv, USDA, 64-73, wildlife biologist, Rocky Mountain Forest & Range Exp Sta, 73-77; terrestrial ecologist, Nat Ecol Res Ctr, Fish & Wildlife Serv, US Dept Interior, 77-89, ecologist, Off Sci Authority, 89-93. *Concurrent Pos:* Mem, Grad Fac Forestry, Stephen F Austin State Univ, 64-73 & Wildlife Sci, Tex A&M Univ, 69-73; cooperator, Int Biol Prog, 65. *Mem:* Ecol Soc Am; Wildlife Soc; Am Soc Mammal; Am Soc Animal Sci. *Res:* Ecology and life history of migratory bats; anatomy, digestive physiology and nutrition of deer; determination of physiology and nutrition of deer; determination of physiological requirements of wild animals; forage quality for wild animals; predicted and determined quality of wildlife habitat; assessments of impacts from habitar change on the wildlife commmunity. *Mailing Add:* US Fish & Wildlife 300 Westgate Ctr Dr Hadley MA 01035-9589

SHORT, JAMES HAROLD, PHARMACOLOGY. *Current Pos:* REV CHEMIST, FOOD & DRUG ADMIN, 84- *Personal Data:* b Leavenworth, Kans, July 9, 28; m 73, Janice Blackburn; c Paula. *Educ:* Stanford Univ, BS, 50; Univ Kans, PhD(pharmaceut chem), 54. *Prof Exp:* Res chemist med chem, Abbott Labs, 56-71; res assoc, 72, asst prof pharmacol, Univ Louisville, 73-76; supvr chem, Adria Labs, 76-84. *Mem:* Am Chem Soc. *Mailing Add:* 19117 Rhodes Way Gaithersburg MD 20879-2153

SHORT, JAMES N, POLYMER CHEMISTRY, RESEARCH ADMINISTRATION. *Current Pos:* RETIRED. *Personal Data:* b Dayton, Ohio, Nov 14, 22; m 45; c 4. *Educ:* Univ Cincinnati, BChE, 45, MS, 47, ScD, 49. *Prof Exp:* Res chemist, Warren-Teed Labs, Ohio, 49-51; res chemist, Phillips Petrol Co, 51-55, mgr, Solution Polymerization Sect, 55-59, Rubber Synthesis Br, 59-66, Rubber & Carbon Black Processes Br, 66-69, Chem Processes Br, 69-72, mgr, Plastics Develop Br, Phillips Petrol Co, 72-83. *Mem:* Am Chem Soc; Soc Plastics Eng. *Res:* Stereospecific polymerization; polyolefins; synthetic rubber engineering plastics; fibers; technical direction; polymers. *Mailing Add:* 2360 Windsor Way Bartlesville OK 74006

SHORT, JAY M, TOXICOLOGY, MICROBIOLOGY. *Current Pos:* From staff scientist to sr staff scientist res & develop, 85-89, vpres res, develop & biol opers, 89-92, VPRES RES, DEVELOP & OPERS, STRATAGENE CLONING SYSTS, 92-; PRES, STRATACYTE, INC, 90- *Personal Data:* b Mar 5, 58. *Educ:* Taylor Univ, BA, 80; Case Western Res Univ, PhD(biochem), 85. *Concurrent Pos:* Prin investr numerous grants, 85-; consult, Europ Econ Community Transgenic Toxicol Testing, 91-94; lectr, Comt Advan Sci Educ, Ctr Drug Eval & Res, Food & Drug Admin, 92. *Mem:* NY Acad Sci; AAAS; Am Soc Biochem & Molecular Biol; Am Soc Microbiol; Environ Mutagenesis Soc; Soc Toxicol; Japanese Environ Mutagen Soc. *Res:* Toxicology; author of numerous publications and granted 17 patents. *Mailing Add:* Recombinant Biocatalysis Inc 505 Coast Blvd S 4th Fl La Jolla CA 92037

SHORT, JOHN ALBERT, cell biology, histology, for more information see previous edition

SHORT, JOHN LAWSON, MEMBRANE TECHNOLOGY, DAIRY PROCESSING. *Current Pos:* mgr process technol, 85-87, DIR COM DEVELOP, KOCH MEMBRANE SYSTS, MASS, 87- *Personal Data:* b Dorking, UK, May 22, 46; m 75; c 2. *Educ:* Univ Manchester Inst Sci & Technol, BSc, 67; Univ London, MSc, 71; Univ Col, London, dipl (biochem eng), 71. *Prof Exp:* Biotechnologist, Chem Indust Basel Geigy AG, Switz, 71-75; sect head, NZ Dairy Res Inst, 75-79; sr engr, Corning Glass Works, NY, 79-80; int mkt mgr, Romicon-Rohm & Haas, Mass, 80-85. *Concurrent Pos:* Mobil Environ grant, Mobil Oil NZ Ltd, 78. *Mem:* Inst Food Technol; Am Inst Chem Engrs; Inst Chem Engrs UK. *Res:* Application of membrane separation technology (ultrafiltration, reverse osmosis, electrodialysis) to food, pharmaceutical, industrial and other process streams. *Mailing Add:* 10 Technology Dr Lowell MA 01851

SHORT, KEVIN MICHAEL, NONLINEAR DYNAMIC, CHAOTIC COMMUNICATIONS. *Current Pos:* ASST PROF MATH, UNIV NH, 94- *Personal Data:* b NY, June 23, 63. *Educ:* Imp Col Sci Technol, PhD(physics), 88- *Prof Exp:* Sr engr, Vitro Corp, 89-92; fac instr appl math, Mass Inst Technol, 92-94. *Concurrent Pos:* Consult, Vitro Corp, 92-94, Blair & Assoc, 95- *Mem:* Am Phys Soc; Math Asn Am; Soc Indust & Appl Math. *Res:* Applications of nonlinear dynamic forecasting to signal processing, primarily for noise reduction applications; unmasking chaotic communication schemes; speech enhancement and extraction of signals from seismic background noise. *Mailing Add:* Univ NH Math Dept Kingsbury Hall Durham NH 03824. E-Mail: kevin.short@unh.edu

SHORT, LESTER LE ROY, ORNITHOLOGY. *Current Pos:* RETIRED. *Personal Data:* b Port Chester, NY, May 29, 33; m 55, 78; c 2. *Educ:* Cornell Univ, BS, 55, PhD(vert zool), 59. *Prof Exp:* Asst vert zool, Cornell Univ, 54-59; instr biol, Adelphi Univ, 60-62, asst prof, 62; Chapman fel, Am Mus Natural Hist, 62-63; chief bird sect, Bird & Mammal Labs, US Fish & Wildlife Serv, 63-66; assoc cur, Am Mus Natural Hist, 66-68, lamont cur birds, 68-97, chmn ornith dept, 80-97, chmn, 80-87. *Concurrent Pos:* Hon cur NAm birds, Smithsonian Inst, 63-66; adj prof, City Univ New York, 70- *Mem:* Soc Study Evolution; Am Ornith Union; Cooper Ornith Soc; Soc Syst Zool; Royal Australasian Ornith Union. *Res:* Systematic and evolutionary zoology; speciation; hybridization; taxonomy and classification of birds; avian ethology and ecology; zoogeography; ornithology. *Mailing Add:* PO Box 1121 Nanyuki Kenya

SHORT, MICHAEL ARTHUR, X-RAY ANALYSIS, X-RAY PHYSICS. *Current Pos:* RETIRED. *Personal Data:* b London, Eng, Aug 15, 30; US citizen; m 57, Dorothy M Havard; c David, Carol, Claire & Pamela. *Educ:* Univ Bristol, Eng, BSc, 52, MSc, 57; Pa State Univ, PhD(x-ray diffraction), 61. *Prof Exp:* Scientist, Gen Elec Co, Eng, 54-57; mem tech staff, Bell Telephone Lab, NJ, 61-64; engr, Assoc Elec Indust, 64-67; staff scientist, Ford Motor Co, Dearborn, Mich, 67-80; res assoc, Occidental Res Corp, 80-85; sr staff scientist, SRS Technol, Irving, Calif, 85-93; sr engr, Hughes

Missile Systs Co, Ranch Cucamonga, Calif, 93-96. *Mem:* Am Crystallog Asn; Am Phys Soc; Am Chem Soc; Microbeam Anal Soc. *Res:* Development of improved instrumentation and analytical techniques for X-ray diffraction, X-ray fluorescence, X-ray scattering, and electron microprobe analysis. *Mailing Add:* 24832 Weyburn Dr Laguna Hills CA 92653-4310. *E-Mail:* mashort815@aol.com

SHORT, NICHOLAS MARTIN, GEOLOGY. *Current Pos:* RETIRED. *Personal Data:* b St Louis, Mo, July 18, 27; m 61, Eleanor Wilson; c Nicholas M Jr. *Educ:* St Louis Univ, BS, 51; Wash Univ, MA, 54; Mass Inst Technol, PhD(geol), 58. *Prof Exp:* Instr geol, Univ Mo, 54-55; geologist, Gulf Res & Develop Co, Pa, 57-59; geologist-physicist, Lawrence Radiation Lab, Univ Calif, 59-64; from asst prof to assoc prof geol, Univ Houston, 64-67; Nat Acad Sci res assoc, Planetology Br, NASA, 67-69, res geologist, Earth Resources Prog, 69-77, dir training, Regional Appln Prog, 77-81, res scientist, Geophys Br, Goddard Space Flight Ctr, 81-88; prof geol & geog, Bloomsburg State Univ, 88-92. *Concurrent Pos:* Lectr, Sigma Xi, 92-94. *Mem:* Fel Geol Soc Am. *Res:* Geochemistry; astrogeology; shock effects in meteorite craters and underground nuclear explosion sites; remote sensing. *Mailing Add:* Cherry Hill Bloomsburg PA 17815

SHORT, ROBERT ALLEN, ELECTRICAL ENGINEERING, COMPUTER SCIENCE. *Current Pos:* chmn dept comput sci, 72-78, PROF ELEC ENG & COMPUT SCI, ORE STATE UNIV, 66- *Personal Data:* b Dayton, Wash, Nov 7, 27; m 49; c 7. *Educ:* Ore State Univ, BS, 49, BA, 52; Stevens Inst Technol, MS, 56; Stanford Univ, PhD(elec eng), 61. *Honors & Awards:* Computer Soc Spec Awards, Inst Elec & Electronic Engrs, 76 & 79. *Prof Exp:* Mem tech staff, Bell Tel Labs, 52-56; sr res engr, Stanford Res Inst, 56-66. *Concurrent Pos:* Lectr, Santa Clara Univ, 65-66; mem gov bd, Inst Elec & Electronics Comput Soc, 70-72, 74-76, ed-in-chief, 71-75, spec tech ed, 77-78; ed, Trans on Comput, Inst Elec & Electronic Engrs, 71-75. *Mem:* AAAS; Inst Elec & Electronic Engrs; Asn Comput Mach; Am Soc Cybernetics. *Res:* Information systems, computer science, logic design, switching theory, automata, fault-tolerant computing, coding theory, teaching effectiveness. *Mailing Add:* 1815 Hawthorne Pl Corvallis OR 97330

SHORT, ROBERT BROWN, PARASITOLOGY. *Current Pos:* from asst prof to prof biol sci, 50-90, EMER PROF, FLA STATE UNIV, 90. *Personal Data:* b Changsha, China, Feb 28, 20; US citizen; m 47, Lavinia Mullinix; c 3. *Educ:* Maryville Col, BA, 41; Univ Va, MS, 45; Univ Mich, PhD(zool), 50. *Prof Exp:* Instr math, Sewanee Mil Acad, 41-43; instr math & biol, Va Episcopal Sch, 43-44. *Concurrent Pos:* Mem, Study Sect Trop Med & Parasitol, NIH, 65-69; NIH spec res fel, Tulane Univ, La, 70-71. *Mem:* Am Soc Parasitol (vpres, 77, pres, 82); Am Soc Trop Med & Hyg; AAAS; Am Micros Soc. *Res:* Biology and cytogenetics of schistosomes and other trematodes; systematics of dicyemid mesozoans. *Mailing Add:* 2407 Miranda Ave Tallahassee FL 32306

SHORT, SARAH HARVEY, SPORTS NUTRITION, NUTRITION & BIOCHEMISTRY. *Current Pos:* PROF NUTRIT, SYRACUSE UNIV, 66- *Personal Data:* b Little Falls, NY, Sept 22, 24; m 46; c 3. *Educ:* Syracuse Univ, BS, 46, PhD(nutrit), 70, EdD(instrnl technol), 75; State Univ NY, Upstate Med Ctr, MS, 66. *Prof Exp:* Researcher chem, Bristol Labs, 46-50; asst prof, State Univ NY, Upstate Med Ctr, 63-80. *Concurrent Pos:* Bd adv, Am Coun Sci & Health, 78-; Int Cong Individualized Instr, 75-76; mem bd sci counr, USDA. *Mem:* Am Dietetic Asn; Soc Nutrit Educ; Inst Food Technologists; Am Col Sports Med. *Res:* Nutrition education at university and medical school including developing and evaluating self instruction units using computer assisted instruction, audiovisual media and rate controlled speech; evaluation of trained athletes' diet using computer analysis; TV/radio nutrition communications. *Mailing Add:* 109 Cammot Lane Fayetteville NY 13066-1452

SHORT, TED H, AGRICULTURAL ENGINEERING, HORTICULTURAL ENGINEERING. *Current Pos:* from asst prof to assoc prof, 69-82, PROF AGR ENGR, OHIO AGR RES & DEVELOP CTR, 82- *Personal Data:* b Wauseon, Ohio, Mar 13, 42; m 68; c 2. *Educ:* Ohio State Univ, BS, 65, MS, PhD(agr eng), 69. *Honors & Awards:* Concept of the Year, Am Soc Agr Engrs, 77. *Prof Exp:* Res assoc, Ohio State Univ, 65-69. *Concurrent Pos:* Consult, TVA Waste Heat Prog, 75-76 & Bechtel Corp Waste Heat Study, 78; Greenhouse res exchange, Holland, 81; host, Int Greenhouse Energy Symp, 83; solar greenhouse proj, Food & Agr Org UN Develop Prog, Antalya, Turkey, 85. *Mem:* Sigma Xi; Solar Energy Soc; Int Soc Hort Sci; Am Soc Agr Engrs. *Res:* Energy conservation for greenhouses; mechanization of greenhouse growing systems; solar ponds for heating greenhouses and rural residences; hydroponic greenhouse production systems; computer climate control for greenhouses; passive solar greenhouse heating systems. *Mailing Add:* 935 Fenwick Circle Wooster OH 44691

SHORT, W(ILLIAM) LEIGH, CHEMICAL & ENVIRONMENTAL ENGINEERING. *Current Pos:* VPRES, WOODWARD CLYDE CONSULTS, WAYNE, NJ, 87- *Personal Data:* b Calgary, Alta, Jan 30, 35; c 5. *Educ:* Univ Alta, BSc, 56, MSc, 57; Univ Mich, PhD(chem eng), 62. *Prof Exp:* Proj engr, Edmonton Works, Can Industs Ltd, 57-59; res engr, Chevron Res Co, Calif, 62-67; from asst prof to prof chem eng, Univ Mass, Amherst, 67-79, assoc head dept, 69-76, head dept, 76-79; mgr, Houston Eng Div, Environ Res & Technol Inc, 79-80, vpres & dir, Environ Eng Div, 80-85; sr prog mgr, Radian Corp, Herdon, VA, 85-87. *Concurrent Pos:* Pub Health Serv res grant & Co Dir Air Pollution training grant, 69-; consult, Kenics Corp, M W Kellogg & Arthur D Little, 69-, Environ Protection Agency, 70- & Gen Acct Off, 78; mem sci adv bd, Environ Protection Agency, 76-80; mem, SBIR, RFA, Res Grants Rev Panel, 80- *Mem:* Am Inst Chem Engrs; Am Chem Soc; Air Pollution Control Asn; AAAS. *Res:* Chemical engineering applications in air and water pollution control; thermodynamics; hazardous waste treatment technologies. *Mailing Add:* 2 Johnston Dr Convent Station NJ 07961-6043

SHORT, WALLACE W(ALTER), FLUID DYNAMICS, HIGH ENERGY LASERS. *Current Pos:* VPRES, LIVE LINE LTD, 92- *Personal Data:* b Ogdensburg, NY, May 21, 30; m 58, Gail McKay; c Kevin, Brenda, Bradley & Gwyneth. *Educ:* Mo Sch Mines, BS, 51; Calif Inst Technol, MS, 53, PhD(chem & elec eng), 58. *Prof Exp:* Prod supvr, Merck & Co, Inc, 51-52; res engr, Rocketdyne Div, NAm Aviation, Inc, 53; from res scientist to staff scientist, Convair Div, Gen Dynamics Corp, 58-62; mem tech staff, Gen Res Corp, 62-74; pres, Appl Technol Assocs, 75-90. *Concurrent Pos:* Consult, Inst Defense Analysis, Washington, DC, 64-70; bd dirs, NMex Mus Nat Hist, 88- *Res:* Theoretical and experimental heat and mass transfer, especially evaporation, ablation and boundary layer flow; rocket propulsion, especially chemical and electrical devices; reentry phenomena; hypersonic wakes; radar scattering by plasmas; ballistic missile defense; high energy laser controls; development of high pressure hydraulic dredge for cleaning large diameter pewers. *Mailing Add:* 218 River Ranch Circle Bayfield CO 81122. *Fax:* 970-884-1385; *E-Mail:* wallyws@rmi.net

SHORT, WILLIAM ARTHUR, ORGANIC CHEMISTRY, BIOCHEMISTRY. *Current Pos:* RETIRED. *Personal Data:* b West Chester, Pa, Feb 18, 25; m 50, Jessie M Cox; c John W & Steven N. *Educ:* Furman Univ, BS, 50; Univ SC, MS, 52; Univ Ala, MS, 57, PhD(biochem), 61. *Prof Exp:* Res asst org chem & biochem, Southern Res Inst, 52-61; prof chem & chmn, Div Natural Sci & Math, Athens State Col, Ala, 61-77, prof chem & chmn dept, 77-91. *Mem:* Am Chem Soc; fel Am Inst Chemists. *Res:* Carbohydrate chemistry. *Mailing Add:* 2419 41st St SE Puyallup WA 98374

SHORTELL, STEPHEN M, HOSPITAL PHYSICIAN RELATIONSHIPS. *Current Pos:* A C BUEHLER DISTINGUISHED PROF, HOSP & HEALTH SERV MGT, NORTHWESTERN UNIV, 82- *Personal Data:* b New London, Wis, Nov 9, 44. *Educ:* Univ Notre Dame, BBA, 66; Univ Calif, Los Angeles, MPH, 68; Univ Chicago, MBA, 70, PhD(behav sci), 72. *Honors & Awards:* Baxter Prize Health Servs Res. *Prof Exp:* Res asst, Nat Opinion Res Ctr, 69, instr/res assoc, Ctr Health Admin Studies, 70-72, actg dir, Grad Prog Hosp Admin, Univ Chicago, 73-74; from asst prof to assoc prof, Univ Wash, 74-79, prof, Sch Pub Health & Comm Med, Dept Health Serv, 79-82. *Concurrent Pos:* Consult, Vet Admin, Robert Wood Found, Henry Keiser Found; asst prof, Health Servs Orgn, Univ Chicago, 72-74; adj asst prof, Dept Sociol, Univ Wash, 75-76, Sch Pub Health & Community Med, Dept Health Serv, doctoral prog dir, 76-78; prof sociol, Dept Sociol, Northwestern Univ, 82; prof community med, Dept Community Health & Prev Med, Sch Med, Northwestern Univ. *Mem:* Inst Med-Nat Acad Sci; Am Pub Health Asn; Am Social Asn; Acad Mgt. *Res:* A national study of the quality of care in Intensive Care Units between Jan 1988-Dec 1990; integrated health systems; clinical application of total quality management; numerous publications in various journals. *Mailing Add:* J L Kellogg Grad Sch Mgt 2001 Sheridan Rd Leverone Hall Northwestern Univ Evanston IL 60208-2007

SHORTER, DANIEL ALBERT, ENTOMOLOGY, ZOOLOGY. *Current Pos:* dir admin, 72-75, PROF BIOL, NORTHWESTERN OKLA ST UNIV, 60-72, 75- *Personal Data:* b Goltry, Okla, May 20, 27; m 46; c 4. *Educ:* Northwestern Okla State Univ, BS, 49; Okla State Univ, MS, 60, PhD(entom), 66. *Prof Exp:* Instr pub schs, Kans, 49-58. *Mem:* Am Soc Mammal; Entom Soc Am. *Res:* Syrphidae of Oklahoma; ecology of the beaver. *Mailing Add:* 610 14th St Alva OK 73717

SHORTER, ROY GERRARD, EXPERIMENTAL MEDICINE. *Current Pos:* consult physician, Sect Path, 61-66, Sect Surg Res, 66-68 & Sect Tissue & Org Transplantation, 68-71, consult physician exp med, Sect Anat Path, 71-75, PROF PATH, MAYO MED SCH 74-, PROF MED, 75- *Personal Data:* b London, Eng, Jan 11, 25; US citizen; m 48; c 2. *Educ:* Univ London, MB, BS, 48, MD, 52. *Prof Exp:* Fulbright travel award, 58-59. *Concurrent Pos:* Consult physician, Sect Med Path & Dept Med, Mayo Clin & Found, 75- *Mem:* Am Asn Path & Bact; Am Gastroenterol Asn; Soc Exp Biol & Med; Brit Asn Clin Path; Brit Soc Gastroenterol; Sigma Xi; fel Royal Col Path; fel Am Col Physicians; fel Royal Col Physicians, London. *Res:* Immunology of idiopathic inflammatory bowel disease. *Mailing Add:* Dept Anat & Pathol Mayo Med Sch 200 First St SW Rochester MN 55902-3008

SHORTESS, DAVID KEEN, GENETICS, PLANT PHYSIOLOGY. *Current Pos:* RETIRED. *Personal Data:* b Baltimore, Md, July 29, 30; m 49; c 4. *Educ:* Lycoming Col, BA, 52; Pa State Univ, MEd, 59, PhD(genetics), 66. *Prof Exp:* Teacher high sch, Pa, 55-60; asst prof biol, Bloomsburg State Col, 61-63; prof biol, NMex Inst Mining & Technol, 66-92, actg head dept, 67-68, head dept, 68-72. *Concurrent Pos:* Fulbright-Hays lectr, Univ Jordan, 77-78. *Mem:* AAAS; Am Genetic Asn; Sigma Xi. *Res:* Genetics and physiology of pollination and seed germination. *Mailing Add:* 95 Prawn Rd Port Angeles WA 98363

SHORTLE, WALTER CHARLES, PLANT PATHOLOGY. *Current Pos:* res plant pathologist, 74-90, SUPVRY RES PLANT PATHOLOGIST, NORTHEASTERN FOREST EXP STA, US FOREST SERV, 90- *Personal Data:* b Laconia, NH, Apr 26, 45; m 66, Elizabeth Stickney; c Jennifer, Amy, Abigail & Emily. *Educ:* Univ NH, BS, 68, MS, 70; NC State Univ, PhD(plant path), 74. *Honors & Awards:* Forest Insect & Dis Res Award, USDA Forest Serv, 93. *Prof Exp:* Res asst plant path, Univ NH, 68-70 & NC State Univ, 70-74. *Concurrent Pos:* Adj prof, Univ NH, 76-88 & 95, Univ Maine, 78-83 & 90. *Mem:* Am Phytopath Soc; Am Chem Soc; Int Asn Wood Anatomists. *Res:* Basic research in biochemistry and physiology of diseases which result in decay of wood in living trees and disease defense mechanisms; influence of acid deposits on forest ecosystems. *Mailing Add:* Northeastern Forest Exp Sta Box 640 Durham NH 03824. *Fax:* 603-868-7604; *E-Mail:* w.shortle/ou1=524lo6a@mhs_fswa.attmail.com

SHORTLIFFE, EDWARD HANCE, MEDICAL COMPUTER SCIENCE. *Current Pos:* resident, Med Sch, Stanford Univ, 77-79, from asst prof to assoc prof med & comput sci, 79-85, chief, Div Gen Internal Med & head, 88-95, DIR MED INFO SCH TRAINING PROG, MED SCH, STANFORD UNIV, 81-, PROF MED & COMPUT SCI, 90-, ASSOC DEAN, INFO RESOURCES & TECHNOL, 95- *Personal Data:* b Edmonton, Alta, Aug 28, 47; m 70; c 2. *Educ:* Stanford Univ, PhD(med info sci), 75, MD, 76. *Prof Exp:* Intern, Mass Gen Hosp, 76-77. *Concurrent Pos:* Co-prin investr & med liaison, Sunex-aim Comput Resource, Stanford Univ, 80-85, prin investr, 85-92, med informatics, Dept Med, 88-93, prin investr, CAMIS Comput Res, 92- *Mem:* Inst Med-Nat Acad Sci; Am Col Physicians; Am Soc Clin Invest; Am Col Med Informatics; fel Am Asn Artificial Intel. *Res:* Medical artificial intelligence; author of numerous publications. *Mailing Add:* Dept Med Med Sch Off Bldg X-215 Stanford Med Ctr Stanford CA 94305-5479. *Fax:* 650-725-7944

SHORTRIDGE, ROBERT GLENN, JR, CHEMICAL KINETICS. *Current Pos:* MEM STAFF, BELL AEROS TEXTRON, BUFFALO, 77- *Personal Data:* b Los Angeles, Calif, Aug 19, 45. *Educ:* Loyola Univ, Los Angeles, BS, 67; Univ Calif, Irvine, PhD(chem), 71. *Prof Exp:* Res chem, Pa State Univ, 71-73; res assoc, Naval Res Lab, 73-75; asst res chemist, Dept Chem & Statewide Air Pollution Res Ctr, Univ Calif, Riverside, 75-77. *Concurrent Pos:* Res chemist, Naval Weapons Support Ctr, Crane, IN, 82- *Mem:* Am Chem Soc; Sigma Xi. *Res:* Research and development of military pyrotechnics. *Mailing Add:* RR5 Box 218C Bloomfield IN 47424-9805

SHORTRIDGE, ROBERT WILLIAM, SCIENCE COMMUNICATIONS, TECHNOLOGY COMMUNICATIONS. *Current Pos:* RETIRED. *Personal Data:* b Newport News, Va, Sept 1, 18; m 47; c 4. *Educ:* Wabash Col, AB, 38; Ohio State Univ, PhD(org chem), 43. *Prof Exp:* Res chemist, Monsanto Chem Co, Ohio, 43-45; assoc chemist, Midwest Res Inst, 45-48; res chemist, Commercial Solvents Corp, 48-51; sr chemist, Midwest Res Inst, 53-57, head phys chem sect, 57-63, head org chem sect & asst dir chem div, 63-68; dir, Tech Info Ctr, Univ Mo, 68-83. *Mem:* Sigma Xi. *Res:* Scientific and technological information transfer; non-metallic materials technology. *Mailing Add:* 4409 W 78th St Prairie Village KS 66208

SHOSTAK, STANLEY, DEVELOPMENTAL BIOLOGY, EMBRYOLOGY. *Current Pos:* asst prof, 65-70, ASSOC PROF BIOL, UNIV PITTSBURGH, 70- *Personal Data:* b Brooklyn, NY, Nov 3, 38; div; c 2. *Educ:* Cornell Univ, BA, 59; Brown Univ, ScM, 61, PhD(biol), 64. *Prof Exp:* NIH fel, Western Res Univ, 64-65. *Mem:* Soc Develop Biol; Soc Integrative Comp Biol. *Res:* Author of several books on developmental biology. *Mailing Add:* Dept Biol Sci Univ Pittsburgh Pittsburgh PA 15260. *E-Mail:* sshostk@pitt.edu

SHOTLAND, EDWIN, PHYSICS. *Current Pos:* CONSULT APPL, 86- *Personal Data:* b Rulzheim, Ger, Dec 18, 08; nat US; m 46; c 1. *Educ:* Univ Munich, BS, 31, MS, 32; Univ Heidelberg, Dr phil nat, 34. *Prof Exp:* Phys engr, Kurman Electronic Co, NY, 41-42, Kompolite Co, 42 & Kurman Electronic Co, NY, 45-46; sr proj anal engr, Chance Vought Aircraft, Inc, Conn, 46-48, Tex, 48-50; sr staff mem & physicist, Johns Hopkins Univ, 50-55, res proj supvr, 55-57, prin staff mem, Appl Physics Lab, 58-86. *Mem:* Am Phys Soc. *Res:* Dynamics of aircraft, missiles and artificial satellites; aeroelasticity of airframes; information theory and communication engineering; missile guidance and radar intelligence; investigation of communication by radio millimeter waves. *Mailing Add:* 418 E Indian Spring Dr Silver Spring MD 20901

SHOTLAND, LAWRENCE M, PALEOCLIMATOLOGY, SEISMOLOGY. *Current Pos:* SR ANALYST, HUGHES STX CORP, 89- *Personal Data:* b Bridgeport, Conn, June 13, 47. *Educ:* Johns Hopkins Univ, BA, 70; Univ Houston, MS, 83; Univ Md, College Park, BS, 88. *Honors & Awards:* NASA Group Achievement Award, NASA, 93. *Prof Exp:* Explor technologist, Amoco Prod, 78-79; analyst, Geo Quest, 79-80; sr analyst, Seismograph Serv Corp, 80-81; geophysicist, Prekla Seismos, 82-83, Arco Explor, 83-85; pres, Lightning Geophysical, 86-88; sr analyst, Gen Res Corp, 88-89. *Concurrent Pos:* Bd dirs, Tourette Syndrome Asn, 85-86. *Mem:* Am Geophys Union; Soc Explor Geophysicists; Asn Comput Mach; Am Asn Petrol Geologists. *Res:* Automated data management of large earth science data sets; collection, processing and user-friendly access of data. *Mailing Add:* 418 E Indian Spring Dr Silver Spring MD 20901. *E-Mail:* Shotland@nssdca.gsfc.nasa.gov

SHOTT, LEONARD D, veterinary pathology, for more information see previous edition

SHOTTAFER, JAMES EDWARD, MATERIALS SCIENCE, WOOD TECHNOLOGY. *Current Pos:* RETIRED. *Personal Data:* b Utica, NY, Dec 13, 30; m 53; c 2. *Educ:* State Univ NY Col Forestry, Syracuse Univ, BS, 54, MS, 56; Mich State Univ, PhD(wood sci), 64. *Prof Exp:* Design group leader, Mat Design, United Aircraft Corp, 59-61; res group leader wood, Brunswick Corp, 61-62, res group leader phys, 62-64; from assoc prof to prof wood technol, Sch Forest Resources, Univ Maine, Orono, 64-91. *Concurrent Pos:* Consult, 64- *Mem:* Soc Wood Sci & Technol; Forest Prod Res Soc; Am Soc Testing & Mat. *Res:* Materials science and technology, especially on wood, adhesives, nonmetallic materials; study of adhesion timber physics, surface phenomena; materials processing technology; operations analysis; research management. *Mailing Add:* 212 Lighthouse Circle Fernandina Beach FL 32034

SHOTTS, ADOLPH CALVERAN, ORGANIC CHEMISTRY. *Current Pos:* RETIRED. *Personal Data:* b Rush Springs, Okla, Dec 28, 25; m 54; c 2. *Educ:* Cent State Col, Okla, BS, 50. *Prof Exp:* Teacher & head sci & math, High Sch, NMex, 50-52; from asst res chemist to assoc res chemist, Continental Oil Co, 52-58; res chemist, Petrol Chem, Inc, 58-60; sect supvr anal chem, Cities Serv Res & Develop Co, 60-62; tech staff asst, Columbian Carbon Co, 62-64, asst to dir, Lake Charles Chem Res Ctr, 64-67, admin mgr, Technol & Planning Div, NJ, 67-68, mgr bus serv, Cities Serv Res & Develop Co, 68-74, prod mgr, Petrochem Sales Dept, Cities Serv Oil Co, 74-76 & proj coord, Admin Div, Chem Group, Cities Serv Co, 76-86. *Concurrent Pos:* Mgr environ & safety affairs, Columbian Chem Co, 80-86; environ & safety consult, 86-93. *Mem:* Am Chem Soc. *Res:* Organic chemical research as applied to petrochemicals; hydrocarbon oxidations. *Mailing Add:* 801 W Knollwood Broken Arrow OK 74011-6435

SHOTTS, EMMETT BOOKER, JR, MEDICAL MICROBIOLOGY, VETERINARY MICROBIOLOGY. *Current Pos:* asst prof & parasitol, Col Vet Med, Univ Ga, 66-68, chief, Clin Microbiol Lab, 66-78, from asst prof to assoc prof, 69-76, MEM GRAD FAC, COL VET MED, UNIV GA, 67-, PROF MED MICROBIOL, 76-, CONSULT, MICROBIOL LAB, 78- *Personal Data:* b Jasper, Ala, Sept 23, 31; m 56, Martha Harrison; c Lisa & Georgia. *Educ:* Univ Ala, BS, 52; Med Col Ala, cert, 53; Univ Ga, MS, 58, PhD, 66. *Honors & Awards:* Distinguished Serv Award, Wildlife Dis Asn; Snieszko Award, Am Fisheries Soc; Edwards Award, Am Soc Microbiol, Feeley Award. *Prof Exp:* Asst microbiol & prev med, Sch Vet Med, Univ Ga, 56-57, res assoc path & parasitol, Southeastern Coop Deer Dis Study, 57-58; med bacteriologist & epidemic intel serv officer, Vet Pub Health Lab, Commun Dis Ctr, USPHS, 59-62, res microbiologist, Rabies Invest Lab, 62-64. *Concurrent Pos:* Consult microbiol, Southeastern Coop Wildlife Dis Study, 66-; specialist, Pub Health & Med Lab Microbiol, Am Acad Microbiol. *Mem:* Am Soc Microbiol; Wildlife Dis Asn; Am Fisheries Soc; Int Asn Aquatic Animal Med; Conf Res Workers Animal Dis; fel Am Acad Microbiol. *Res:* Leptospira, serology, culture, isolation and identification; food borne diseases; diagnostic bacteriology; fluorescent antibody applications; virus-helminth interrelationships; zoonoses; diseases of fresh and salt water fish; Aeromonas, Edwardsiella and Flexibacter. *Mailing Add:* Dept Med Microbiol Col Vet Med Univ Ga Athens GA 30602

SHOTTS, WAYNE J, NUCLEAR SCIENCE. *Current Pos:* Physicist, Lawrence Livermore Nat Lab, 74-79, group leader, Thermonuclear Design Div, 79-85, div leader nuclear chem, 85-86, div leader prompt diag, 86-88, prin dep assoc dir mil applns, 88-92, PRIN DEP ASSOC DIR DEFENSE SYSTS & NUCLEAR DESIGN, LAWRENCE LIVERMORE NAT LAB, 92-; PHYSICST, UNIV CALIF, LIVERMORE, 74- *Personal Data:* b Des Plaines, Ill, Mar 20, 45; m 67, 79, Jacquelyn F Willis; c Kenneth W & Jeffrey A. *Educ:* Univ Calif, Santa Barbara, BA, 67; Cornell Univ, PhD(physics), 73. *Honors & Awards:* Ernest Orlando Lawrence Mem Award, Dept Energy, 90. *Prof Exp:* Res physicist, E I du Pont de Nemours & Co, 73-74. *Mem:* Am Phys Soc; AAAS. *Res:* Nuclear policy; electromagnetics and plasma physics; nuclear science and nuclear design. *Mailing Add:* 2480 Merritt Pl Livermore CA 94550

SHOTWELL, ODETTE LOUISE, ORGANIC CHEMISTRY. *Current Pos:* RETIRED. *Personal Data:* b Denver, Colo, May 4, 22. *Educ:* Mont State Col, BS, 44; Univ Ill, MS, 46, PhD(org chem), 48. *Honors & Awards:* Harvey W Wiley Award, Am Oil Chem Soc, 82. *Prof Exp:* Asst inorg chem, Univ Ill, 44-48; chemist, Northern Regional Res Lab, Bur Agr & Indust Chem, USDA, 48-52, chemist, Agr Res Serv, 53-75, res leader mycotoxin anal & chem res, 75-84, res leader mycotoxin res, Northern Region Res Ctr, 85-89. *Concurrent Pos:* Consult, Bur Vet Med, FDA, 81-86 & Can Health & Welfare Dept, 83-89; mem, Comt Protection Against Trichothecene Mycotoxins, Nat Res Coun-Nat Acad Sci, 82-83; adv, Int Found Sci, Stockholm, Sweden, 83-89; collabr, Northern Ctr Agr Utilization Res, Agr Res Serv, USDA, 90- *Mem:* AAAS; Am Chem Soc; Am Oil Chem Soc; Am Asn Cereal Chemists; fel Asn Off Anal Chemists (pres-elect, 87-88). *Res:* Synthetic organic chemistry; chemistry of natural products including isolation purification and characterization; antibiotics; microbial insecticides; mycotoxins. *Mailing Add:* 835 Tenderfoot Hill Rd Colorado Springs CO 80906

SHOTWELL, THOMAS KNIGHT, STUDY OF HEALTH RELATED PRODUCTS. *Current Pos:* PRES, SHOTWELL & CARR INC, 74-; PRES, APPL BIOMED RES INT INC, 95- *Personal Data:* b Hillsboro, Tex, May 31, 34; m 55, Shirley I Plunkett; c 1. *Educ:* Tex A&M Univ, BS, 55, MEd, 58; La State Univ, PhD(agr educ), 65. *Honors & Awards:* Distinguished Serv Award, Am Soc Agr Consults, 78 & 80. *Prof Exp:* Teacher biol & gen sci, Allen Acad, 58-60; dept head biol, Allen Col, 60-65; regulatory mgr pharmaceut, Salsbury Labs, Inc, 66-71 & Zoecon Corp, 71-74. *Concurrent Pos:* Assoc ed, J Clin Res & Drug Regulatory Affairs, 87-; chmn, Animal Drug Alliance, 93-94. *Mem:* AAAS; NY Acad Sci; Am Asn Indust Vet; Inst Relig Age Sci; US Animal Health Asn. *Res:* Strategies to assure new drug, medical advice and new animal drug studies meet requirements for approval to market products; guiding research and development programs. *Mailing Add:* 3003 LBJ Freeway No 100 Dallas TX 75234. *Fax:* 972-243-3567; *E-Mail:* 73073.3001@compuserve.com

SHOTZBERGER, GREGORY STEVEN, CARDIOVASCULAR PHARMACOLOGY, TECHNOLOGY TRANSFER. *Current Pos:* mgr technol assessment, 91-93, ASSOC DIR EXTRAMURAL RES & DEVELOP, DU PONT MERCK PHARMACEUT CO, 93- *Personal Data:* b Lewistown, Pa, Jan 17, 48; m 81, Susan Thompson; c Sean, Kurt & Jill. *Educ:* Pa State Univ, BS, 69; State Univ NY, Buffalo, PhD(pharmacol), 74; Univ Del, MBA, 94. *Prof Exp:* Res pharmacologist, E I DU Pont De Nemours & Co, Inc, 73-77, sr res pharmacologist, 77-81, proj mgr, 81-83, mgr info &

technol anal, 83-88, mgr licensing technol, 88-90. *Mem:* Am Col Clin Pharmacol; NY Acad Sci; Inflammation Res Asn; Asn Univ Technol Managers; Am Soc Clin Pharmacol & Ther. *Res:* Cardiovascular and gastrointestinal pharmacology; local anesthetics; antiarrhythmic drugs; new drug development; strategic planning. *Mailing Add:* 30 Hillstream Rd Newark DE 19711. *Fax:* 302-992-3040

SHOUB, EARLE PHELPS, OCCUPATIONAL HEALTH & SAFETY, ACCIDENT PREVENTION. *Current Pos:* CONSULT, AM OPTICAL CORP, SOUTHBRIDE, MASS, 79-, OCCUP SAFETY & HEALTH, 79- & WARNER LAMBERT CO, MORRIS PLAINS, NJ, 79- *Personal Data:* b Washington, DC, July 19, 15; m 62, Elda B Robinson; c Heather M (Dills) & Casey L. *Educ:* Polytech Univ, BS, 37. *Honors & Awards:* Gold Medal, US Dept Interior, 59; William H Revoir Memorial Award, Int Soc Respiratory Protection, 93. *Prof Exp:* Chemist, Hygrade Food Prod Corp, New York City, 40-41 & Nat Bur Standards, 41-43; US Bur Mines, 43-70; reg dir, 59-62, chief, Div Accident Prev & Health, Washington, DC, 63-70; dep dir, Appalachian Lab Occup Respiratory Dis, Nat Inst Occup Safety & Health, Morgantown, WVa, 70-79, Div Safety Res, 77-79; mgr occup safety & consult indust environ, Safety Prod Div, Amer Optical, 79. *Concurrent Pos:* Prof, Col Mineral & Energy Resources, Univ WVa, 70-79, assoc clin prof, dept anesthesiol, Med Ctr, 77-82; dir, Int Soc Respiratory Protection, pres, 91-93. *Mem:* Fel Am Inst Chemists; Am Indust Hyg Asn; Am Inst Mining, Metall & Petrol Engrs; Int Soc Respiratory Protection (past pres); Am Nat Standards Inst; Am Soc Testing & Mat; Am Soc Safety Engrs; Nat Fire Protection Asn; Nat Soc Prof Engrs; Sigma Xi; Am Conf Govt Indust Hygienists. *Res:* Occupational health and safety research and development in mineral industries; improved respiratory protective devices; metallurgy-steel scrap substitute; respiratory diseases coal workers pneumoconiosis. *Mailing Add:* 5850 Meridian Rd Apt 202C Gibsonia PA 15044-9690. *Fax:* 412-443-8541

SHOUBRIDGE, ERIC ALAN, GENE EXPRESSION REGULATION, MITOCHONDRIAL GENETICS. *Current Pos:* Asst prof, 85-91, ASSOC PROF NEUROL, MONTREAL NEUROL INST, MCGILL UNIV, 91- *Personal Data:* b Toronto, Ont, Apr 2, 51; m 91, Irene Gloor; c Justin Peter Frederick. *Educ:* McGill Univ, BSc, 74, MSc 77; Univ BC, PhD(zool), 81. *Mem:* AAAS. *Res:* Molecular genetic analysis of the mitochondrial genome and its role in human neurological disease. *Mailing Add:* Montreal Neurol Inst 3801 University St Montreal PQ H3A 2B4 Can. *Fax:* 514-398-1509; *E-Mail:* eric@ericpc.mni.mcgill.ca

SHOUGH, HERBERT RICHARD, PHARMACOGNOSY, MEDICINAL CHEMISTRY. *Current Pos:* assoc prof, Univ Okla, 78-80, asst dean, 78-83, actg dean, 82, interim dean, 83-84, PROF HEALTH SCI CTR, COL PHARM, UNIV OKLA, 80-, ASSOC DEAN, 83-, INTERIM DEAN, 86- *Personal Data:* b Springfield, Ohio, Jan 7, 42; m 63, Kay Segerson; c Richard Jr, Laura K & Evan. *Educ:* Univ Tenn, Memphis, BS, 64, PhD(pharm sci), 68. *Prof Exp:* From asst prof to assoc prof pharmacog, Col Pharm, Univ Utah, 68-78. *Concurrent Pos:* Consult, Palmer Chem & Equip Co, Ga, 65-68; res comt grant, Univ Utah, 68-72; Am Cancer Soc Inst grant, 73-74; Univ Utah res comt grant, 75-; Smith-Kline Corp grant, 81-83. *Mem:* Am Asn Pharmaceut Scientists; Am Asn Cols Pharm; Acad Pharmaceut Sci; Am Pharmaceut Asn; Am Soc Pharmacog. *Res:* Ergot alkaloid chemistry and biochemistry; pharmacy education. *Mailing Add:* Health Sci Ctr Univ of Okla Col of Pharm Oklahoma City OK 73190. *Fax:* 405-271-3830; *E-Mail:* richard-shough@suokhsc.edu

SHOUKAS, ARTIN ANDREW, CARDIOVASCULAR SURGERY, CONTROL SERIES. *Current Pos:* ASSOC PROF CARDIOVASC CONTROL, SCH MED, JOHNS HOPKINS UNIV, 72- *Educ:* Case Western Reserve Univ, PhD(biomed eng), 72. *Res:* Cardiovascular system; systems analysis. *Mailing Add:* Dept Biomed Eng Sch Med Johns Hopkins Univ 720 Rutland Ave Baltimore MD 21205-2196. *Fax:* 410-955-0549

SHOUMAN, A(HMAD) R(AAFAT), MECHANICAL ENGINEERING. *Current Pos:* from assoc prof to prof, 60-87, EMER PROF MECH ENG, N MEX STATE UNIV, 87- *Personal Data:* b Egypt, Aug 8, 29; m 60, Marjorie L Bevan; c Ahmad R, Kamal F, Suzanne, Mariam & Ramsey O. *Educ:* Cairo Univ, BS, 50; Univ Iowa, MS, 54, PhD(mech eng), 56. *Prof Exp:* Instr, Cairo Univ, 50-53; asst prof mech eng, Univ Wash, 56-60. *Concurrent Pos:* Consult, Boeing Co, 59-63, ARO Inc, 64, AiResearch Mfg Co, 66, NASA, 68, Serv Technol Corp, & E I du Pont de Nemours & Co, Inc, 69-70; vis prof, Laval Univ, 66; consult Nat Acad Sci-Nat Res Coun sr fel, Marshall Space Flight Ctr, NASA, 67. *Mem:* Fel AAAS; Am Soc Mech Engrs; Am Soc Eng Educ. *Res:* Thermodynamics; compressible fluids; gas turbines and heat transfer. *Mailing Add:* 1006 Bloomdale St Las Cruces NM 88005

SHOUP, CHARLES SAMUEL, JR, PRODUCT DEVELOPMENT, TECHNOLOGICAL INNOVATION. *Current Pos:* CHMN, BD DIRS, BLASTERZ CORP, 92- *Personal Data:* b Nashville, Tenn, Dec 10, 35; m 58, Frances DiCarlo; c Mark S, Elizabeth (Kehoe) & Margaret (Meyer). *Educ:* Princeton Univ, AB, 57; Univ Tenn, MS, 61, PhD(phys chem), 62. *Prof Exp:* Chemist, Oak Ridge Nat Lab, 57, 62-67; prod specialist, Indust Prod Div, Goodyear Tire & Rubber Co, 57-58; mgr spec projs, Electronics Div, Union Carbide Corp, NY, 67-68; vpres, Bell & Howell Schs, Inc, 68-69; mgr technol planning, Cabot Corp, 69-70, dir corp res, 70-73, vpres & gen mgr, E-A-R Corp, 73-81, gen mgr, E-A-R Div, 81-87, vpres 84-87; pres, Alphaflex Industs, Inc, 87-88; pres & mem bd dirs, CemKote Corp, 88-92. *Concurrent Pos:* Mem steering comt tech physics, Am Inst Physics, 70-73; vpres & gen mgr, Nat Res Corp, 70-73; bd trustees, Indust Safety Equip Asn, 79-82; pres, Noise Control Prod & Mat Asn, 82-84; mgr, Nonprofit Div, Exec Serv Corps Indianapolis, 93-95, bd dirs, 94-, exec comt, 96-, vpres, 97- *Res:* Infrared spectroscopy; surface chemistry; molecular force fields and structure; infrared spectra of adsorbed species; irreversible thermodynamics; technology transfer; technological innovation; new venture management; hearing protection. *Mailing Add:* 13019 Andover Dr Carmel IN 46033

SHOUP, JANE REARICK, ZOOLOGY. *Current Pos:* from asst prof to assoc prof biol, 66-82, head dept, 74-82, PROF BIOL, PURDUE UNIV, CALUMET CAMPUS, 82- *Personal Data:* b Kansas City, Mo, June 19, 41; m 62; c 2. *Educ:* Univ Rochester, AB, 62; Univ Chicago, PhD(zool), 65. *Prof Exp:* Res assoc zool, Univ Chicago, 65-66. *Concurrent Pos:* Bd mem nat abortion rights action league, 75-78. *Mem:* Bot Soc Am; Am Soc Cell Biol; AAAS; Inst Soc Ethics & Life Sci; Midwest Co Biol Teachers. *Res:* Fine structural aspects of the genetic control of development. *Mailing Add:* Dept Biol Sci Purdue Univ Calumet 2233 171 St Hammond IN 46323-2051

SHOUP, ROBERT D, COLLOIDAL OR FINE PARTICLE PROCESSING. *Current Pos:* sr res chemist, 68-75, RES SUPVR, CORNING GLASS WORKS, 75- *Personal Data:* b Sinking Spring, Pa, Mar 14, 33; m 87; c 1. *Educ:* Albright Col, BS, 60; Univ Pittsburgh, PhD(inorg chem), 64. *Prof Exp:* Res chemist, W R Grace & Co, 64-68. *Mem:* Am Chem Soc; Am Ceramic Soc. *Res:* Glass, ceramics, optical fibers by sol-gel techniques; colloidal chemistry of nuclear fuels, uranium dioxide, uranium carbide and uranium nitride; silicate materials research; catalysts and support systems for environmental pollution control; boron hydride chemistry; synthetic flourohectorites by hydrothermal reactions. *Mailing Add:* 658 E Lake Rd Hammondsport NY 14840-9526. *Fax:* 607-974-3675

SHOUP, TERRY EMERSON, MECHANICAL ENGINEERING. *Current Pos:* AT DEAN COL ENG, FLA ATLANTIC UNIV. *Personal Data:* b Troy, Ohio, July 20, 44; m 66. *Educ:* Ohio State Univ, BS, 66, MS, 67, PhD(mech eng), 69. *Prof Exp:* Res asst mech eng, Ohio State Univ, 65-66, teaching asst, 67; teaching assoc, Ohio State Univ, 69; from asst prof to assoc prof, Rutgers Univ, 69-75; assoc prof mech eng, Univ Houston, 75- *Concurrent Pos:* Ed-in-chief, Mechanism & Mach Theory, 77- *Mem:* Am Soc Mech Engrs; Am Soc Eng Educ. *Res:* Mechanisms; kinematic synthesis and analysis of linkages, machine design; dynamic analysis of machines and machine control systems; computer-aided design techniques. *Mailing Add:* Dean Eng Santa Clara Univ Santa Clara CA 95053-0001

SHOVE, GENE C(LERE), AGRICULTURAL ENGINEERING. *Current Pos:* assoc prof, 58-72, PROF AGR ENG, UNIV ILL, URBANA, 72- *Personal Data:* b Havensville, Kans, Feb 18, 27; m 49; c 3. *Educ:* Kans State Univ, BS, 52, MS, 53; Iowa State Univ, PhD(agr eng, theoret & appl mech), 59. *Honors & Awards:* Paul A Funk Recognition Award, Col Agr, Univ Ill, 80. *Prof Exp:* Asst agr eng, Kans State Univ, 52-53; asst, Iowa State Univ, 53-55, 56-58, ext agr engr, 55-56. *Concurrent Pos:* Eng aid, USDA, 52-53. *Mem:* Am Soc Agr Engrs; Am soc Eng Educ. *Res:* Crop drying and storage; feed and materials handling; farm building design and use; application of solar energy to grain drying. *Mailing Add:* 508 W California Ave Urbana IL 61801

SHOVLIN, FRANCIS EDWARD, ENDODONTICS, MICROBIOLOGY. *Current Pos:* RETIRED. *Personal Data:* b Jamaica, NY, Oct 13, 29; m 57, Marjorie McGuire; c Marjorie, Linda, Joseph, Francis Jr & Cathrine. *Educ:* City Col New York, BS, 57; Seton Hall Col, DDS, 61, MS, 65. *Prof Exp:* Nat Inst Dent Res fel, Seton Hall Col, 62-65; pvt pract endodont, 65-72; chmn dept, Col Med & Dent NJ, 72-84, prof, 72-95, assoc dean res, 84-89, dir environ safety, 89-95. *Concurrent Pos:* Nat Inst Dent Res fels, 66-72 & 74-77; Omicron Kappa Upsilon, NJ Col Med & Dent, 71. *Mem:* Int Asn Dent Res; Am Soc Microbiol; Am Asn Endodontists; Am Dent Asn; NY Acad Dent; NY Acad Sci. *Res:* Microbiology of dental caries; cell wall components of cariogenic bacteria; intracellular polyphosphate storage in bacteria; phosphoprotein used by lactobacilli; species identification of lactobacillus. *Mailing Add:* 173 Paul Ct Hillsdale NJ 07642

SHOW, IVAN TRISTAN, SYSTEMS ECOLOGY, MATHEMATICAL & NUMERICAL MODELING. *Current Pos:* INDEPENDENT CONSULT, 80- *Personal Data:* b Belleville, Ill, May 12, 43. *Educ:* Univ Southern Miss, BMEd, 66, MS, 73; Tex A&M Univ, PhD(oceanog & statist), 77. *Prof Exp:* Sr oceanographer, Sci Appl Inc, 77-80, div mgr, 79-80. *Concurrent Pos:* Res assoc, Gulf Coast Res Lab, 72-, Hubbs-Sea World Res Inst, 79-90, US Environ Protection Agency, 83-90; consult, USN, 79-90, Nat Oceanic & Atmospheric Admin, 80-90, US Environ Protection Agency, 83-90. *Mem:* AAAS; Am Soc Limnol & Oceanog; Am Soc Naturalists; Biometrics Soc; NAm Soc Phlebology. *Res:* Theoretical and applied systems ecology and biostatistics; effects of natural and man-made perturbations on ecosystem structure and function; statistical epidemiology. *Mailing Add:* PO Box 34165 Juneau AK 99803

SHOWALTER, DONALD LEE, RADIOCHEMISTRY, CHEMISTRY DEMONSTRATIONS. *Current Pos:* assoc prof, 76-83, PROF CHEM, UNIV WIS-STEVENS PT, 83- *Personal Data:* b Louisville, Ky, Jan 22, 43; m 64, Charlotte A Chambers; c Deborah, Kathy & Scott. *Educ:* Eastern Ky Univ, BS, 64; Univ Ky, PhD(chem), 70. *Prof Exp:* NASA grant radiochem anal extraterrestrial samples, under Dr Roman A Schmitt, Ore State Univ, 70-71; asst prof chem, Univ Wis-Stevens Pt, 71-73; asst prof sci, Iowa Western Community Col, 73-76. *Concurrent Pos:* Consult radiation protection, Wis State Health Lab, 80-; lab demonstr, "World of Chem" videos. *Mem:* Am Chem Soc; Sigma Xi. *Res:* Neutron activation applied to geochemical analysis; radiochemical solutions to problems of chemical analysis; environ monitoring of radioactivity; development of dramatic educational chemical demonstrations. *Mailing Add:* Dept Chem Univ Wis Stevens Point WI 54881. *Fax:* 715-346-2640; *E-Mail:* dshowalt.uwsp.edu

SHOWALTER, HOWARD DANIEL HOLLIS, MEDICINAL CHEMISTRY. *Current Pos:* res scientist, Warren Lambert/Parke David Pharmaceut Res, 76-80, sr scientist, 80-83, res assoc, 83-86, sr res assoc med chem, 86-90, assoc res fel, 90-94, RES FEL, PARK DAVIS PHARMACEUT RES, 94- *Personal Data:* b Broadway, Va, Feb 22, 48; m 73, Martha Augsburger; c Hollins & Daron. *Educ:* Univ Va, BA, 70; Ohio State Univ, PhD(nat prod chem), 74. *Honors & Awards:* Excellence in Indust Chem Res Award, Am Chem Soc, 83; Warner-Lambert Distinguished Sci Award, 87. *Prof Exp:* Fel org chem, Rice Univ, 74-76. *Concurrent Pos:* Adj prof chem, Wayne State Univ, Detroit, 94- *Mem:* Am Chem Soc; Int Soc Heterocyclic Chemistry; Am Asn Cancer Res; Am Found Pharmaceut Educ. *Res:* Total synthesis of organic compounds of therapeutic significance, especially anticancer agents; new synthetic methodology; heterocyclic synthesis; Solid-phase organic synthesis. *Mailing Add:* 2800 Plymouth Rd Ann Arbor MI 48105-2430

SHOWALTER, KENNETH, CHEMICAL REACTION KINETICS, NONLINEAR CHEMICAL DYNAMICS. *Current Pos:* from asst prof to prof, 78-89, Eberly prof, 89-96, C EUGENE BENNETT CHAIR CHEM, WVA UNIV, 96- *Personal Data:* b Boulder, Colo, Apr 9, 49; m 70, Donna M Connolly; c Paul J & Julia M. *Educ:* Ft Lewis Col, BS, 71; Univ Colo, PhD(chem), 75. *Prof Exp:* Res assoc chem, Univ Ore, 75-77, vis asst prof, 77-78. *Mem:* Fel AAAS; Am Chem Soc. *Res:* Chemical waves; multiple stationary states in pumped chemical systems; oscillatory chemical reactions. *Mailing Add:* Dept Chem WVa Univ Morgantown WV 26506-6045

SHOWALTER, ROBERT KENNETH, HORTICULTURE, FOOD SCIENCE. *Current Pos:* from assoc prof to prof hort, Exp Sta, 45-81, EMER PROF, HORT & FOOD SCI, UNIV FLA, 81- *Personal Data:* b Middlebury, Ind, Feb 17, 16; m 43; c 1. *Educ:* DePauw Univ, AB, 38; Purdue Univ, MS, 40. *Prof Exp:* Asst hort, Purdue Univ, 38-43; asst chem, Allison Div, Gen Motors Corp, 43; chemist, US Rubber Co, 43-45. *Mem:* Fel AAAS; fel Am Soc Hort Sci. *Res:* Quality maintenance and evaluation of vegetables during handling, transportation and marketing; effects of mechanization of harvesting and handling on market quality of vegetables. *Mailing Add:* 4024 NW 30th Pl Gainesville FL 32606

SHOWELL, JOHN SHELDON, ORGANIC CHEMISTRY. *Current Pos:* assoc prog dir org chem, 66-68, assoc prog dir synthetic chem, 68-72, prog dir synthetic org & natural prod chem, 72-87, PROG DIR ORG SYNTHESIS, NAT SCI FOUND, 87- *Personal Data:* b Camden, NJ, Oct 29, 25; m 51, 71; c 2. *Educ:* Calif Inst Technol, BS, 46, MS, 47; Univ Minn, PhD(org chem), 51. *Prof Exp:* Fel org chem, Univ Ill, Urbana, 51-53; asst prof, Rutgers Univ, 53-55; res fel, Columbia Univ, 55-57; from res chemist to sr res chemist, Agr Res Serv, USDA, 57-66. *Mem:* Am Chem Soc; Royal Soc Chem. *Res:* Cyclopropane chemistry; monomer and polymer synthesis; lipid chemistry; organic synthesis; chemical applications of computers; x-ray crystallography. *Mailing Add:* 1200 N Cleveland St Arlington VA 22201

SHOWERS, MARY JANE C, ANATOMY. *Current Pos:* RETIRED. *Personal Data:* b Iowa City, Iowa, June 30, 20. *Educ:* Univ Chicago, BSc, 43; Univ Mich, MSc, 49, PhD(neuroanat), 57. *Honors & Awards:* Lindback Award, 70. *Prof Exp:* USPHS fel, Kresge Found, Mich, 47-58; staff nurse, Geneva Community Hosp, Ill, 41-42 & Chicago Mem Hosp, 42-44; instr sci, Sch Nursing, Christ Hosp, Ohio, 44-55, dir educ prog, 48-55; assoc prof biol, Our Lady Cincinnati Col, 58-62; asst prof anat, Col Med, Univ Ky, 62-64; from assoc prof to prof anat, Hahnemann Med Col, 64-73, head sect neuroanat, 68-73; prof anat, Philadelphia Col Osteop Med, 73-78; prof anat, Med Sch, Univ Cincinnati, 78-84, fac, 84-94. *Concurrent Pos:* Gelston fel med res, Anat Inst, Norway, 58; spec lectr, Rutgers Univ, 64-69; consult, Sch Nursing, Christ Hosp, 55-61 & Sch Nursing, Deaconess Hosp, 61-65; mem, Comp Vert Neuroanat Comt, Study Sect, NIH, 63-67; adj prof med educ & anat, Med Col, Univ Cincinnati, 84-94. *Mem:* AAAS; NY Acad Sci; Animal Behav Soc; Am Asn Neuropath; Am Asn Anat. *Res:* Additional motor areas of brain; comparative anatomy of the vertebrate nervous system. *Mailing Add:* 5138 S Ridge Dr Cincinnati OH 45224

SHOWERS, RALPH M(ORRIS), ELECTRONICS, COMMUNICATIONS. *Current Pos:* lab asst, Univ Pa, 41-43, instr elec eng, 42-43, res engr & lab supvr, 43-45, asst prof & proj supvr, 45-53, from asst prof to prof, 45-89, EMER PROF ELEC ENG, UNIV PA, 89- *Personal Data:* b Plainfield, NJ, Aug 7, 18; m 44; c 3. *Educ:* Univ Pa, BS, 39, MS, 41, PhD(eng), 50. *Honors & Awards:* Richard R Stoddart Award, Electromagnetic Compatibility Soc, Inst Elec & Electronics Engrs, 79, Charles Proteus Steinmetz Award, 82, Centennial Medal, 85 & Stand Medallion, 91; Astin-Polk Int Stand Medal, Am Nat Stand Inst, 91. *Prof Exp:* Lab asst, Farnsworth Radio & Tel Co, 39; testing engr, Gen Elec Co, Pa & NY, 40-41. *Concurrent Pos:* Chmn, SC A Measurements, Int Spec Comt Radio Interference (CISPR), 62-69, vpres, 73-79, chmn, 80-85; chmn, Am Nat Stand Comt, C63, Electromagnetic Compatibility Soc, 68-; vpres, US Nat Comt Int Electro-tech Comn, 75- *Mem:* Fel Inst Elec & Electronics Engrs; Opers Res Soc Am; Am Soc Eng Educ; Am Asn Univ Profs. *Res:* Electrical engineering; radio interference; solid-state electronics; electromagnetic compatibility between equipments and systems. *Mailing Add:* Moore Sch Elec Eng Rm 318 Univ Pa Philadelphia PA 19104. *Fax:* 215-573-2068; *E-Mail:* showers@pender.ee.upenn.edu

SHOWERS, WILLIAM BROZE, JR, INSECT ECOLOGY, BIOCLIMATOLOGY. *Current Pos:* RETIRED. *Personal Data:* b St Joseph, Mo, Nov 9, 31; m 63; c 4. *Educ:* Univ Ariz, BS, 58; La State Univ, MS, 66; Iowa State Univ, PhD(entomol), 70. *Honors & Awards:* Cert Merit, USDA, 83, 90, 91 & 92; C V Riley Achievement Award, Entom Soc Am, 94. *Prof Exp:* Entomologist, rice insects, USDA, Baton Rouge, 63-66, res corn insects, 66-70, proj leader, ecol corn insects, Agr Res Serv, Ankeny, Iowa, 70-93. *Concurrent Pos:* From asst prof to assoc prof, Iowa State Univ, Ames, 74-82, prof, Dept Entom, 82-95; Iowa Agr & Home Econ Exp Sta, 83-95; entom consult, 95- *Mem:* Am Registry Prof Entom; Entom Soc Am; Sigma Xi. *Res:* Evaluating non-chemical insect pest suppression strategies and investigating extrinsic factors that progam noctuid moths to mate and/or migrate. *Mailing Add:* 64627 E Rosewood Dr Tucson AZ 85739

SHOWS, THOMAS BYRON, HUMAN GENETICS, CELL GENETICS. *Current Pos:* Head, Biochem Genetics Sect, 75-79, assoc chief, Dept Exp Biol, 79-80, RES PROF BIOL, ROSWELL PARK CANCER INST, STATE UNIV NY, BUFFALO, 78-, DIR DEPT HUMAN GENETICS, 80- *Personal Data:* b Brookhaven, Miss, May 4, 38; m 59; c 2. *Educ:* San Diego State Univ, BA, 61; Univ Mich, MS, 63, PhD(biochem genetics) hon, 67. *Honors & Awards:* Newcomb Cleveland Prize Sci, AAAS, 86 & 87. *Concurrent Pos:* USPHS fel, Yale Univ, 67-69. *Mem:* Sigma Xi; Genetics Soc Am; Am Soc Human Genetics; Am Soc Cell Biol; fel AAAS; Am Asn Cancer Res. *Res:* Human genetics: gene mapping and control of gene expression; biochemical and somatic cell genetics. *Mailing Add:* Dept Human Genetics Roswell Park Cancer Inst Elm & Carlton Buffalo NY 14263-0001. *Fax:* 716-845-8449

SHOZDA, RAYMOND JOHN, HETEROGENOUS CATALYSIS, PROCESS DEVELOPMENT. *Current Pos:* CHEMIST, CENT RES & DEVELOP DEPT, E I DU PONT DE NEMOURS & CO, INC, 57- *Personal Data:* b Pittsburgh, Pa, Sept 5, 31; m 59; c 4. *Educ:* Carnegie-Mellon Univ, BS, 53, MS, 56, PhD(chem), 57. *Mem:* Am Carbon Soc; Sigma Xi; NAm Thermal Anal Soc; Catalysis Soc; NY Acad Sci. *Res:* Industrial chemistry; process chemistry at high pressures and temperatures; intermediates synthesis; materials of construction. *Mailing Add:* 372 Mercer Mill Rd Landenberg PA 19350

SHRADER, JOHN STANLEY, SCIENCE EDUCATION, BIOLOGY. *Current Pos:* RETIRED. *Personal Data:* b Yakima, Wash, Apr 17, 22; m 56; c 2. *Educ:* Univ Wash, BS, 47, MA, 51, EdD, 57. *Prof Exp:* Asst zool, Univ Wash, 47-48; teacher pub schs, Wash, 48-55; asst zool, Univ Wash, 55-56; teacher pub schs, Wash, 56-57; from assoc prof to prof sci educ, Cent Wash State Col, 57-63; interim prof, Univ Fla, 63-64; prof sci educ, Cent Wash Univ, 64- *Concurrent Pos:* NSF grant dir, Earth Sci Inst, 70-71. *Mem:* Nat Asn Res Sci Teaching; Asn Educ Teachers Sci; Nat Sci Teachers Asn; Northwest Sci Asn. *Res:* Instructional problems of beginning secondary science teachers in the Pacific Northwest; understanding of college chemistry by intermediate grade pupils; analysis of middle and junior high school teaching; false explanations in science. *Mailing Add:* 14812 NE 12th St Bellevue WA 98007

SHRADER, WILLIAM D, SOILS. *Current Pos:* from asst prof to prof, 52-81, EMER PROF SOILS, IOWA STATE UNIV, 81- *Personal Data:* b Bellflower, Mo, Oct 26, 12; m 35; c 3. *Educ:* Univ Mo, BS, 35, MA, 41; Iowa State Univ, PhD(soils), 53. *Prof Exp:* Soil scientist soil conserv serv, USDA, 35-37; instr soils, Univ Mo, 37-42; soil scientist, US Forest Serv, 42-45; soil correlator, US Bur Plant Indust, Soils & Agr Eng, 45-52. *Concurrent Pos:* Consult, Govt Iran, 58-59 & Thailand, 62-; prof soils, fac agron & party chief, Iowa State Mission to Uruguay, 66. *Mem:* Am Soc Agron; Soil Sci Soc Am; Soil Conserv Soc Am. *Res:* Interpretation of soil properties in terms of plant growth. *Mailing Add:* Rt 2 No 191 Hermann MO 65041-1450

SHRADER, WILLIAM WHITNEY, RADAR SYSTEMS. *Current Pos:* CONSULT, 94- *Personal Data:* b Foochow, China, Oct 17, 30; US citizen. *Educ:* Univ Mass, BS, 53; Northeastern Univ, MS, 61. *Prof Exp:* Res engr, Boeing Airplane Co, 53-56; systs engr, Raytheon Co, 56-70, consult scientist, 70-94. *Mem:* Fel Inst Elec & Electronics Engrs. *Res:* Expert in surface based radar systems particularly large phase array radars and Moving Target Indication (MTI) radars; author of numerous papers. *Mailing Add:* Shrader Assocs 144 Harvard Rd Stow MA 01775. *Fax:* 978-897-3394; *E-Mail:* shrader@prodigy.com

SHRAGER, PETER GEORGE, PHYSIOLOGY, BIOPHYSICS. *Current Pos:* asst prof, 71-76, ASSOC PROF PHYSIOL, SCH MED & DENT, UNIV ROCHESTER, 76- *Personal Data:* b Brooklyn, NY, Apr 18, 41; m 66. *Educ:* Columbia Col, AB, 62; Columbia Univ, BS, 63; Univ Calif, Berkeley, PhD(biophys), 69. *Prof Exp:* NIH fel, Med Ctr, Duke Univ, 69-71. *Mem:* Am Physiol Soc; Soc Neurosci; Soc Gen Physiol; Biophys Soc. *Res:* Biophysics and biochemistry of cell membranes; molecular basis of excitation; conduction in demyelinated nerve; neuron-neuroglia interactions. *Mailing Add:* Dept Physiol Box 642 Univ Rochester Med Ctr 601 Elwood Ave Rochester NY 14642-8642. *Fax:* 716-461-3259; *E-Mail:* pshr@uordbv

SHRAGO, EARL, BIOCHEMISTRY, MEDICINE. *Current Pos:* From instr to asst prof med, 59-67, assoc prof, 67-71, PROF NUTRIT SCI, SCH MED, UNIV WIS-MADISON, 71-, PROF HEALTH SCI MED, 77-; PROF ASSOC, ENZYME INST, 61- *Personal Data:* b Omaha, Nebr, Apr 9, 28; m 55; c 4. *Educ:* Univ Omaha, BA, 49; Univ Nebr, MD, 52. *Concurrent Pos:* USPHS fel, 59-61. *Mem:* Am Soc Biochem & Molecular Biol; Am Inst Nutrit; Am Soc Clin Nutrit. *Res:* Mechanisms of hormonal and metabolic control. *Mailing Add:* Dept Med & Nutrit Sci Univ Wis 1415 Linden Dr Madison WI 53706

SHRAKE, ANDREW, CHEMISTRY. *Current Pos:* RES CHEMIST, CTR BIOLOGICS, FOOD & DRUG ADMIN, 80- *Personal Data:* b Cleveland, Ohio, Nov 9, 41. *Educ:* Princeton Univ, BA, 64; Yale Univ, PhD(phys chem), 69. *Prof Exp:* NATO postdoctoral fel, Dept Chem, Univ Cambridge, Eng, 69-70; NIH postdoctoral fel biochem, Univ Ariz, 71-74; sr staff fel, Nat Heart, Lung & Blood Inst, NIH, 74-80. *Mem:* Am Chem Soc; Biophys Soc; Am Soc Biochem & Molecular Biol. *Mailing Add:* Ctr Biologics Food & Drug Admin 1401 Rockville Pike Suite 200N Rockville MD 20852-1448. *Fax:* 301-402-2780

SHRAUNER, BARBARA ABRAHAM, SYMMETRIES OF NONLINEAR DIFFERENTIAL EQUATIONS, PLASMA PHYSICS. *Current Pos:* from asst prof to assoc prof, 66-77, PROF ELEC ENG, WASH UNIV, 77- *Personal Data:* b Morristown, NJ, June 21, 34; m 65, James E; c Elizabeth A (Caspori) & Jay A. *Educ:* Univ Colo, BA, 56; Harvard Univ, AM, 57, PhD(physics), 62. *Prof Exp:* Researcher statist mech & plasma physics, Free Univ Brussels, 62-64; resident res assoc plasma & space physics, Ames Res Ctr, NASA, 64-65. *Concurrent Pos:* Am Asn Univ Women fel, 62-63; Air Force grant, 63-64; vis scientist, Los Alamos Sci Lab, 75-76, consult, 79 & collabr, 84; vis scientist, Lawrence Berkeley Lab, 85. *Mem:* Am Phys Soc; Am Geophys Union; Am Asn Univ Profs; Sigma Xi; Inst Elec & Electronics Engrs; Am Phys Soc. *Res:* Plasma processing of semiconductor wafers, including plasma etching and deposition in the fabrication of integrated circuits; lie and hidden symmetries used to solve nonlinear differential equations. *Mailing Add:* Washington Univ Campus Box 1127 1 Brookings Dr St Louis MO 63130. *Fax:* 314-935-7500; *E-Mail:* bas@wueei.wustl.edu

SHRAUNER, JAMES ELY, PHYSICS. *Current Pos:* from asst prof to assoc prof, 65-77, PROF PHYSICS, WASH UNIV, 77- *Personal Data:* b Dodge City, Kans, Mar 10, 33; m 65, Barbara W Abraham; c Jay A & Elizabeth A (Caspari). *Educ:* Univ Kans, BS, 56; Columbia Univ, MA, 60; Univ Chicago, PhD(physics), 63. *Prof Exp:* Res asst biophys, Radio Res Lab, Columbia Univ, 56-58 & theoret physics, Enrico Fermi Inst Nuclear Res, Univ Chicago, 60-63; res assoc physics, Inst Theoret Physics, Stanford Univ, 63-65. *Concurrent Pos:* Vis scientist, Los Alamos Sci Lab, 75-76; assoc scientist, Ames Lab, Dept of Energy, 77-85; trustee, Univs Res Asn, 79-85; vis scientist, superconducting super collider cent design group, Lawrence Berkeley Lab, Univ Calif, Berkeley, 85-86, consult, 86-89. *Mem:* Fel Am Phys Soc; Fedn Am Sci. *Res:* Theoretical physics; quantum field and elementary particle theories; Structure of the ground state of quantum chromodynamics and consequences for hadronic physics. *Mailing Add:* Dept of Physics Wash Univ, PO Box 1105 St Louis MO 63130. *Fax:* 314-935-6219; *E-Mail:* jes@howdy.wustl.edu

SHRAWDER, ELSIE JUNE, clinical biochemistry, dna probes, for more information see previous edition

SHREEVE, JEAN'NE MARIE, INORGANIC CHEMISTRY. *Current Pos:* from asst prof to assoc prof, 61-67, head dept, 73-87, PROF CHEM, 67-, ASSOC VPRES RES & DEAN COL GRAD STUDIES, UNIV IDAHO, 87- *Personal Data:* b Deer Lodge, Mont, July 2, 33. *Educ:* Univ Mont, BA, 53; Univ Minn, MS, 56; Univ Wash, PhD(inorg chem), 61. *Hon Degrees:* DSc, Univ Mont, 82. *Honors & Awards:* Garvan Medal, Am Chem Soc, 72; Fluorine Award, Am Chem Soc, 78. *Prof Exp:* Teaching asst chem, Univ Minn, 53-55; asst, Univ Wash, 57-61. *Concurrent Pos:* Fel, Cambridge Univ, 67-68; NSF fel, 67-68; hon US Ramsey fel, 67-68; Alfred P Sloan Found fel, 70-72; mem chem res eval panel, Air Force Off Sci Res, 72-76 & petrol res fund adv bd, Am Chem Soc, 75-78, bd dir, 85-; vis prof, Univ Bristol, 77; Alexander von Humboldt sr scientist award, 78; guest prof, Univ Gottingen, 78; mem adv comt chem, NSF, 78-82; mem chem div, Argonne Univ Asn Rev Comt, Argonne Nat Lab, 80-86; secy, chair-elect & chair, AAAS (sec C), 84-89, bd dir, 91- *Mem:* Fel AAAS; Am Chem Soc; Royal Soc Chem; Am Inst Chemists. *Res:* Synthesis of inorganic and organic fluorine-containing compounds. *Mailing Add:* Dept Chem Univ Idaho Moscow ID 83843. *Fax:* 208-885-6198

SHREEVE, WALTON WALLACE, MEDICINE, NUTRITION. *Current Pos:* prof med, 73-91, prof radiol, 81-91, EMER PROF MED & RADIOL, STATE UNIV NY, STONYBROOK, 91-; SR RES ASSOC, MED DEPT, BROOKHAVEN NAT LAB, UPTON, NY. *Personal Data:* b 21; m 45, Phyllis Heidenreich; c Thomas, Daniel, James & Elizabeth. *Educ:* DePauw Univ, BA, 43; Ind Univ, MD, 44; Western Res Univ, PhD(biochem), 51. *Prof Exp:* Lab instr biochem, Sch Med, Western Res Univ, 46-47, sr instr, 51-52; head, Radioisotope Lab, US Naval Hosp, Oakland, Calif, 52-54; scientist & assoc physician, Biochem Div, Med Res Ctr, Brookhaven Nat Lab, 54-64, sr scientist & attend physician, 64-73; chief nuclear med, Vet Admin Med Ctr, Northport, 73-91, dir, Sch Nuclear Med Technol, 75-91, dir, Nuclear Med Residency Prog, 76-91, dep dir, Nuclear Med, Vet Admin, Region 1, 86-91. *Concurrent Pos:* Res physician, Radioisotope Unit, Vet Admin Hosp, Cleveland, Ohio, 50-52; guest prof & NIH spec fel, Karolinska Inst, Sweden, 67; consult, Nassau Co Med Ctr, 69- & WHO, India, 71; vis staff mem, Los Alamos Sci Lab, NMex, 72; guest scientist, Inst Med, Nuclear Res Ctr, Juelich, Fed Repub Ger, 81-82. *Mem:* Am Soc Biol Chemists; Endocrine Soc; Am Diabetes Asn; Soc Nuclear Med; NY Acad Sci. *Res:* Intermediary metabolism of carbohydrates, fats and amino acids; clinical applications of radioactive and stable nuclides in diabetes, liver disease and other endocrine, metabolic or nutritional disorders; isotope tracer methodology and uses in nuclear medicine. *Mailing Add:* Med Dept Brookhaven Nat Lab Upton NY 11973. *Fax:* 516-344-5311; *E-Mail:* shreeve@bnlarm.bnl.gov

SHREFFLER, DONALD CECIL, immunogenetics; deceased, see previous edition for last biography

SHREFFLER, JACK HENRY, METEOROLOGY, AIR POLLUTION. *Current Pos:* dep dir, Atmospheric Sci Res Lab, 83-88, DIR, CHEM PROCESSES DIV, ATMOSPHERIC RES & EXPOSURE ASSESSMENT LAB, US ENVIRON PROTECTION AGENCY, 88- *Personal Data:* b Melrose Park, Ill, May 26, 44; m 70; c 2. *Educ:* Univ Wis, BS, 65, MS, 67; Ore State Univ, PhD(oceanog), 75. *Prof Exp:* Aerospace engr, Manned Spacecraft Ctr, NASA, 67-70; phys scientist, Nat Oceanic & Atmospheric Admin, 75-80, supvry phys scientist, Air Resources Lab, 80-83. *Mem:* Am Meteorol Soc; Sigma Xi. *Res:* Numerical modeling related to air pollution meteorology; statistical analysis of air pollution data. *Mailing Add:* 117 Lynwood Pl Chapel Hill NC 27514-6522

SHRENSEL, J(ULIUS), ECONOMIC & DECISION ANALYSIS, STRATEGIC PLANNING. *Current Pos:* CONSULT, 86- *Personal Data:* b Newark, NJ, Feb 6, 22; m 47, Marilyn Goldstein; c 2. *Educ:* Newark Col Eng, BS, 44; Stevens Inst Technol, MS, 49. *Prof Exp:* Engr, Baker & Co, Inc, 44-46; instr physics, Newark Col Eng, 46-51; res engr, Allied Chem & Dye Corp, 51-60, res engr, Nat Aniline Div, Allied Chem Dye Corp, 60-63, supvr fiber process eng, Fibers Div, 63-65, proj mgr Mid E, Int Div, 65-69, mgr tech econ sect, eng dept, Specialty Chem Div, 69-71, mgr Bus Analysis Sect Planning Dept Allied Chem Co, Allied Chem Corp, 71-86. *Mem:* Am Chem Soc. *Res:* Plastics extrusion; equipment design; production of synthetic fibers; decision analysis; strategic planning. *Mailing Add:* 97 Laurel Dr Springfield NJ 07081

SHREVE, DAVID CARR, MATHEMATICS. *Current Pos:* RES MATHEMATICIAN, CITIES SERV CO, 81- *Personal Data:* b Lafayette, Ind, May 25, 42. *Educ:* NC State Univ, BS, 64; Rice Univ, PhD(math), 69. *Prof Exp:* Instr, Univ Minn, Minneapolis, 68-69, asst prof, 69-72; from asst prof to assoc prof, Univ Wis, Milwaukee, 72-81. *Mem:* Am Math Soc; Math Asn Am; Soc Indust & Appl Math. *Res:* Numerical analysis and Fourier analysis. *Mailing Add:* 537 Penn St El Segundo CA 90245-3025

SHREVE, GEORGE WILCOX, PHYSICAL CHEMISTRY. *Current Pos:* RES & DEVELOP CONTRACTOR & CONSULT, 57- *Personal Data:* b Cincinnati, Ohio, Jan 11, 13; m 33, Louise Byrne; c Mimi (Osborne) & Deborah (Bundy). *Educ:* Stanford Univ, AB, 35, PhD(chem), 46. *Prof Exp:* Chemist, B Cribari & Sons, Calif, 35-36, Paraffine Co, 37 & Standard Oil Co, Calif, 37-38; res dir, Pac Can Co, Calif, 39-40; res group leader, Permanente Corp, 45; res chemist, Gen Elec Co, NY, 45-46; asst prof chem, Kenyon Col, 46-49; sr phys chemist, Stanford Res Inst, 49-53; res chemist, Monsanto Chem Co, 53-54; chief chemist, Hewlett-Packard Co, 54-57. *Concurrent Pos:* Res Corp grant. *Mem:* AAAS; Am Chem Soc; NY Acad Sci. *Res:* Colloidal properties of non-alkali soaps; chromatography; phase systems of sodium soaps; surface potentials; adsorption; electrochemical cells; alcoholic fermentation, preservation and spoilage of food; protective linings for food containers; catalysis; lignin derivatives; air pollution; solid state chemistry; materials of electronics. *Mailing Add:* 20 Berenda Way Menlo Park CA 94028

SHREVE, LOY WILLIAM, FORESTRY, HORTICULTURE. *Current Pos:* area exten horticulturist, 76-81, exten horticulturist, Dept Hort, ASST EMER PROF, EXTEN HORTICULTURIST, TEX A&M UNIV, 91- *Personal Data:* b Smoke Hole, WVa, Oct 8, 26; m 51; c 3. *Educ:* WVa Univ, BSF, 51; Kans State Univ, MS, 67,PhD(hort), 72. *Prof Exp:* Serv forester, Ky Div Forestry, 54-57, asst dist forester, 57-59, dist forester, 59-63; exten forester fire control, Dept Hort & Forestry, Kans State Univ, 64-68, exten forester tree improv, Dept State & Exten Forestry, 68-76. *Concurrent Pos:* Mem, Tree Improv Comt, Walnut Coun, 72-79, crop adv comt, Juglans, 85-; exchange scientist, Romania & Hungary, 80; consult, Forestry & Hort, 91- *Res:* Development of practical and economical methods for production of genetic duplicates of forest tree species and horticultural varieties of trees and shrubs; breeding of walnuts, pecans and poplars; plant adaptation to site; plant exploration and collection; high density orchards; dwarfing fruit and nut trees. *Mailing Add:* 741 Skylane Dr N Uvalde TX 78801-4032

SHREVE, RONALD LEE, GEOMORPHOLOGY, GLACIOLOGY. *Current Pos:* from instr to prof, 58-94, EMER PROF GEOL & GEOPHYS, UNIV CALIF, LOS ANGELES, 94- *Personal Data:* b Los Angeles, Calif, Oct 18, 30; m 62, Jean Malcolm; c Beth (Rosenberg). *Educ:* Calif Inst Technol, BS, 52, PhD(geol), 59. *Honors & Awards:* Kirk Bryan Award, Geol Soc Am, 69; Ouallinne lectr, Univ Texas, 88. *Prof Exp:* Instr geol, Calif Inst Technol, 57-58. *Concurrent Pos:* NSF fel, Swiss Fed Inst Technol, 58-59; hon res fel geol, Harvard Univ, 65-66, hon res assoc, 71-72; vis assoc prof, Univ Minn, 68; vis prof & Crosby lectr, Mass Inst Technol, 71-72; Sherman Fairchild Distinguished Scholar, Calif Inst Technol, 78-79; distinguished vis prof, Univ Wash, 85; distinguished vis scientist, Cascades Volcano Observ, 87. *Mem:* AAAS; Geol Soc Am; Am Geophys Union. *Res:* Geomorphology; glaciology; physical geology; geophysics. *Mailing Add:* Dept Earth & Space Sci Univ Calif Los Angeles CA 90095-1567

SHRI, THANEDAR, CHEMISTRY, CHEMICAL ANALYSIS. *Current Pos:* CHEM ANALYST, CHEMIR LAB INC, 91- *Personal Data:* b Belgaum, India, 1955. *Educ:* Karnataka Univ, BS, 73; Bombay Univ, MS, 77; Univ Akron, PhD(polymer chem), 82. *Prof Exp:* Sr chemist, Petrolite Corp, 85-91. *Mem:* Am Chem Soc. *Mailing Add:* Chemir Lab Inc 2672 Metro Blvd Maryland Height MO 63043

SHRIER, ADAM LOUIS, COMMERCIALIZATION OF TECHNOLOGY, TECHNOLOGY POLICY. *Current Pos:* MANAGING PARTNER, SPECIALTY TECHNOL ASSOCS, 88- *Personal Data:* b Warsaw, Poland, Mar 26, 38; US citizen; m 61, Diane Kesler; c Jonathan, Lydia, Catherine &

David. *Educ:* Columbia Univ, BS, 59; Mass Inst Technol, SM, 60; Yale Univ, DEng, 65; Fordham Univ, JD, 76. *Prof Exp:* Sr tech staff, Exxon Res & Eng Co, 63-72, environ coordr, Exxon Int Co, 72-73, div mgr, 83-86, venture mgr, Exxon Enterprises Inc, 74-81; hq consult, Exxon Corp, 81-82; mgr policy & planning, Exxon Co, Int, 83-88. *Concurrent Pos:* Vis scholar, Dept Chem Eng, Cambridge Univ, 65-66; lectr, Dept Chem Eng, Columbia Univ, 67-69; mem, Indust Adv Bd, Int Energy Agency OECD, 83-88; adv, Int Res Ctr Energy & Econ Develop, Univ Colo, 84-88, Energy & Environ Policy Ctr, Harvard Univ, 86-88, Int Energy Prog, Johns Hopkins Univ, 86-88; sr adv, Global Bus Forum, 88-; sr assoc, Cambridge Energy Res Assocs, 88-; vis lectr, Peking Univ, 95. *Mem:* Am Inst Chem Engrs; US Asn Energy Econs. *Res:* Commercialization of technology in the fields of energy supply and use; environmental conservation, and the manufacture of specialty chemicals and materials; formulation and implementation of energy, environmental, and technology policy; start up of technology-based business. *Mailing Add:* 4000 Cathedral Ave NW Apt 317-B Washington DC 20016. *Fax:* 202-965-2942

SHRIER, STEFAN, machine intelligence, numerical analysis, for more information see previous edition

SHRIGLEY, ROBERT LEROY, SCIENCE EDUCATION. *Current Pos:* assoc prof, 66-80, PROF SCI EDUC, PA STATE UNIV, 80- *Personal Data:* b Zanesville, Ohio, Apr 10, 29; m 52; c 3. *Educ:* Ohio Univ, BS, 53, ME, 54; Pa State Univ, DEd, 68. *Prof Exp:* Asst prof educ, Ohio Univ, 55-63; sci adv, Kano Teachers Col, Nigeria, 63-65. *Mem:* Nat Asn Res Sci Teaching; Sch Sci & Math Asn; Nat Sci Teachers Asn. *Res:* Attitude modification theory, preservice and in-service elementary teachers toward science. *Mailing Add:* 452 Westgate Dr State College PA 16803

SHRIME, GEORGE P, ELECTRICAL ENGINEERING. *Current Pos:* PRES, COMP U ROUTE, 90- *Personal Data:* b Fakeha, Lebanon, Nov 27, 40. *Educ:* Am Univ Beirut, BS, 62; Northwestern Univ, MS, 63, PhD(elec eng), 65. *Prof Exp:* Asst prof elec eng, Univ Hawaii, 65-66; sr engr, Tex Instruments, Inc, 65-69, br mgr, Semi-Conductor Circuits Div, 69-87; pres, EMI Inc, 88-90. *Res:* Computer control of industrial processes; semi-conductor manufacturing; automatic control; deltamodulation. *Mailing Add:* 9611 Mill Trail Dr Dallas TX 75238

SHRIMPTON, DOUGLAS MALCOLM, PLANT BIOCHEMISTRY. *Current Pos:* RETIRED. *Personal Data:* b Nuneaton Warks, Eng, Mar 29, 35; Can citizen; m 56; c 4. *Educ:* Univ BC, BA, 57, MA, 58; Univ Chicago, PhD(plant biochem), 61. *Prof Exp:* Nat Res Coun Can fel, 61-63; enzyme chemist, Can Packers Ltd, Ont, 63-65; res officer biochem, Can Forestry Serv, 65-74, res scientist, 74-92. *Mem:* Can Soc Plant Physiol. *Res:* Formation of heartwound and wound response tissues in conifers; enzyme preparations and methods of preservation. *Mailing Add:* 1345 Readings Dr Sidney BC V8L 5K7 Can

SHRINER, DAVID SYLVA, PHYTOPATHOLOGY, FOREST ECOLOGY. *Current Pos:* Res ecol, Environ Sci Div, 74-82, res group leader, 82-90, SECT HEAD, ENVIRON SCI DIV, OAK RIDGE NAT LAB, 90- *Personal Data:* b Spokane, Wash, July 20, 45; m 68, Sue Phillips; c Meagan. *Educ:* Univ Idaho, BS, 67; Pa State Univ, MS, 69; NC State Univ, PhD(plant path), 74. *Concurrent Pos:* Sr policy analyst, Environ Div, Off Sci & Technol Policy, Exec Off Pres, Washington, DC, 94-96. *Mem:* Fel AAAS; Sigma Xi. *Res:* Effects of air pollutants on terrestrial ecosystems; biogeochemical cycling of pollutants; stress physiology of plants; plant host-parasite interactions; assessment of regional-scale environmental problems; environmental policy. *Mailing Add:* Environ Sci Div Oak Ridge Nat Lab PO Box 2008 Oak Ridge TN 37831-6038

SHRINER, JOHN FRANKLIN, JR, PROTON RESONANCES, STATISTICAL PROPERTIES OF NUCLEI. *Current Pos:* ASST PROF PHYSICS, TENN TECHNOL UNIV, 85- *Personal Data:* b Montgomery, Ala, Feb 6, 57. *Educ:* Univ South, BS, 78; Duke Univ, MA, 80, PhD(physics), 83. *Prof Exp:* Res assoc, Duke Univ, 83; assoc res physicist, Yale Univ, 83-85. *Mem:* Am Phys Soc; Sigma Xi; AAAS. *Res:* Nuclear spectroscopy of unbound levels studied with proton resonances; applications to statistical theories of nuclei. *Mailing Add:* Tenn Technol Univ Box 5051 Cookeville TN 38505

SHRIVASTAVA, PRAKASH NARAYAN, RADIOLOGIC PHYSICS. *Current Pos:* PROF RADIATION ONCOL, UNIV SOUTHERN CALIF, 89-, CHIEF PHYSICIST, LOS ANGELES CAMPUS, MED CTR, 89-, PROF RADIOL, 93-, PROF BIOMED ENG, 95- *Personal Data:* b Narsingpur, India, Sept 5, 40; m 68, Uma Ravipaty; c Anil, Rashmi & Anupama. *Educ:* Univ Nagpur, BSc, 58, MSc, 61; Univ Tex, Austin, PhD(nuclear physics), 66; Univ Carnegie Mellon Pittsburgh, MPM, 92; Am Bd Radiol, cert therapeut radiol physics, 75, cert health physics, 75. *Honors & Awards:* Gupta Gold Medal, 58; Thamma Silver Medal, 61; Paranjpe Gold Medal, 61; First Robinson Mem Lectr, 84; Third Dr Padam Singh Mem Lectr, Indian Cong Radiation & Oncol, 84. *Prof Exp:* Res assoc nuclear physics, Ctr Nuclear Studies, Univ Tex, Austin, 66-68; Ont Cancer Inst fel, Princess Margaret Hosp, Toronto, Ont, 68-69; attend radiol physicist, Allegheny Gen Hosp, Pittsburgh, Pa, 69-73, dir, Div Physics, 74-89. *Concurrent Pos:* Dir, Mideast Ctr Radiol Physics, 74-86, Med Physics & Eng Res Proj, Allegheny-Singer Res Inst, 76-89, Computational Resource Group, 83-89, Nat Hyperthermia Physics Ctr & Allegheny-Singer Dosimetry Calibration Lab, 83-89; sr lectr eng, Carnegie-Mellon Univ Med, 82-89; clin prof, Dept Human Oncol, Univ Wis-Madison, 84-89. *Mem:* Am Asn Physicists in Med; Am Col Radiol; NY Acad Sci; Soc Nuclear Med; Am Soc Therapeut Radiol & Oncol; Radiation Res Soc; NAm Hyperthermia Soc. *Res:* Therapeutic and diagnostic radiologic physics; radiation measurement and 3-D dosimetry, hyperthermia for cancer therapy biological effects of heat telemedicin and radiahim oncology. *Mailing Add:* Dept Radiation Oncol LAC & USC Med Ctr Rm OPD 1P17 1200 N State St Los Angeles CA 90033. *Fax:* 213-226-5970; *E-Mail:* pshriva@hsc.usc.edu

SHRIVER, BRUCE DOUGLAS, COMPUTER SCIENCE. *Current Pos:* DIR RES, D N BROWN ASSOCS, TARRYTOWN, NY, 90- *Personal Data:* b Buffalo, NY, Oct 18, 40; m 63; c 4. *Educ:* Calif State Polytech Univ, BS, 63; W Coast Univ, MS, 68; State Univ NY Buffalo, PhD(comput sci), 71. *Prof Exp:* Res engr, Millard D Shriver Co Inc, 63-68; res asst comput sci, State Univ NY Buffalo, 68; NSF fel, 69-71; vis lectr, Aarhus Univ, 71-73; from assoc prof to prof, Univ Southwestern La, 73-84, Alfred Lamson prof comput sci, 81-84, vpres res, 89-90; dept group mgr software technol, IBM T J Watson, 84-88; dir, Pac Res Inst Info Syts, Univ Hawaii, 88-89. *Concurrent Pos:* Consult educ, IBM Corp, 74-; proj investr, NATO grant, 74-75; ed, Inst Elec & Electronic Engrs Software, 83-87, computer, 87-91. *Mem:* Asn Comput Mach; fel Inst Elec & Electronic Engrs; Am Math Asn; Soc Indust & Appl Math; Inst Elec & Electronic Engrs Computer Soc (pres-elect, 91). *Res:* Parallel architectures, programming languages, algorithms and implementation technology; multi-paradigm design and programming suites; object-oriented systems technology; artificial neural networks and architectures; dataflow languages and architectures; computer supported cooperative work. *Mailing Add:* 17 Bethea Dr Ossining NY 10562

SHRIVER, DAVID A, gastrointestinal pharmacology, for more information see previous edition

SHRIVER, DUWARD F, INORGANIC CHEMISTRY. *Current Pos:* from instr to prof, 61-87, dept chair, 92-95, MORRISON PROF CHEM, NORTHWESTERN UNIV, 87- *Personal Data:* b Glendale, Calif, Nov 20, 34; m 57; c 2. *Educ:* Univ Calif, Berkeley, BS, 58; Univ Mich, PhD(chem), 61. *Honors & Awards:* Distinguished Serv Award, Am Chem Soc, 87; L Mond Medal, Royal Soc Chem, 89; Medal, Mat Res Soc, 90. *Prof Exp:* Chemist, Univ Calif Radiation Lab, Livermore, 58. *Concurrent Pos:* Mem, Mat Res Ctr & Ipatieff Catalysis Ctr, Northwestern Univ; Alfred P Sloan Found res fel, 67-69; vis prof, Univ Tokyo, 77 & Univ Western Ontario, 79; pres, Inorg Syntheses, Inc, 81-83; Guggenheim fel, Cambridge Univ, 84; consult, Los Alamos Nat Lab, 84-91, Gen Motors, 88-91, Medtronic, 90-91, E O Systs, 93- *Mem:* AAAS; Am Chem Soc; Royal Soc Chem; Electrochem Soc; Mat Res Soc. *Res:* Synthesis and physical investigation of organometallics, metal cluster compounds, solid-state superionic conductors and mixed ionic-electronic conductors; infrared and Raman spectroscopy of inorganic systems, homogenous and heterogenous catalysis. *Mailing Add:* Dept Chem Northwestern Univ Evanston IL 60208

SHRIVER, JOHN WILLIAM, MUSCLE CONTRACTION, NUCLEAR MAGNETIC RESONANCE. *Current Pos:* ASST PROF MED BIOCHEM, SCH MED & ASST PROF CHEM, SOUTHERN ILL UNIV, 81- *Personal Data:* b Fairmont, WVa, Aug 9, 49; m 80. *Educ:* WVa Univ, BA, 71; Case Western Reserve Univ, PhD(chem), 77. *Prof Exp:* Fel biochem, Univ Alta, 77-81. *Mem:* Biophys Soc; Sigma Xi. *Res:* Energetics of conformational state changes in myosin associated with energy transduction in muscle contraction; use of nuclear magnetic resonance in biophysical problems. *Mailing Add:* Dept Med Biochem Southern Ill Univ Sch Med Carbondale IL 62901-4413. *Fax:* 618-453-6408; *E-Mail:* john.shriver@gmcchemistrysiu.edu

SHRIVER, JOYCE ELIZABETH, ANATOMY. *Current Pos:* asst prof, 68-71, asst dean student affairs, 76-81, ASSOC PROF ANAT, MT SINAI SCH MED, 71-, MEM FAC, MT SINAI GRAD SCH BIOL SCI, 71-, ASSOC DEAN STUDENT AFFAIRS, 81- *Personal Data:* b Quincy, Ill, Sept 14, 37. *Educ:* William Jewell Col, AB, 59; Univ Kans, PhD(anat), 65. *Prof Exp:* Nat Inst Neurol Dis & Stroke fel, Col Physicians & Surgeons, Columbia Univ, 64-68. *Mem:* AAAS; Am Asn Anat; Am Soc Zoologists; Int Primatol Soc; Soc Neurosci; Sigma Xi. *Res:* Comparative and experimental neurology; study of integration of sensory and motor pathways. *Mailing Add:* Dept Anat & Cell Biol Mt Sinai Sch Med Box 1007 One Gustave L Levey Pl New York NY 10029

SHRIVER, M KATHLEEN, VIROLOGY, PRODUCT DEVELOPMENT. *Current Pos:* Sr scientist, Genetic Syst Corp, 82-84, proj leader, 84-89, prog mgr, 89-91, sr prog mgr, 91-92, DIR RES & DEVELOP, GENETIC SYST CORP, 92- *Personal Data:* b July 14, 49; c Kristi & Lisa. *Educ:* Ind Univ, BS, 71; Univ Wash, PhD(biochem), 78. *Res:* Blood virus screening and diagnostic products. *Mailing Add:* Genetics Syst Corp 6565 185th Ave NE Redmond WA 98052-5039. *Fax:* 425-861-5012

SHRODE, ROBERT RAY, ANIMAL BREEDING. *Current Pos:* PROF ANIMAL SCI, UNIV TENN, KNOXVILLE, 66- *Personal Data:* b Louisville, Colo, Oct 23, 19. *Educ:* Colo State Univ, BS, 43; Iowa State Univ, MS, 45, PhD(animal breeding), 49. *Prof Exp:* From assoc prof to prof genetics, Agr & Mech Col, Tex, 48-58; geneticist, Wm H Miner Agr Res Inst, NY, 58-60; prog manager, De Kalb Agr Asn, Inc, 60-66. *Mem:* AAAS; Am Soc Animal Sci; Biometric Soc; Am Genetic Asn; Nat Asn Cols & Teachers Agr. *Res:* Quantitative genetics of beef cattle, swine, sheep and flour beetles; general biometrical genetics; computer applications; beef cattle breeding. *Mailing Add:* 1851 Springbrook Rd Alcoa TN 37701

SHRODER, JOHN FORD, JR, GEOLOGY, GEOMORPHOLOGY. *Personal Data:* b Troy, NY, July 5, 39. *Educ:* Union Col, BS, 61; Univ Mass, Amherst, MS, 63; Univ Utah, PhD(geol), 67. *Prof Exp:* Instr geol, Westminster Col, 66; lectr geol & geog, Univ Malawi, 67-69; from asst prof geol to assoc prof geog & geol, Univ Nebr, Omaha, 69-78, prof, 78-94. *Concurrent Pos:* Grants, Univ Malawi, 68-69, NSF, 70, 73-74, 79, 91, Univ Nebr, Omaha, 70-71, 80, 85, 93, Fulbright, 78, 84 & Smithsonian, 84 & 86, US AID, 88, Nat Park Serv, 89-90, Kiewit Found, 90-91, Nat Geog Soc, 91-93, NSF, 94-97. *Mem:* Fel AAAS; fel Geol Soc Am; Int Asn Quaternary Res; Sigma Xi; Am Asn Geogrs. *Res:* Mass wasting; periglacial geomorphology; glacial geomorphology; tree ring dating; forensic geomorphology. *Mailing Add:* Dept Geog & Geol Univ Nebr Omaha Omaha NE 68182. *E-Mail:* shroder@cwis.unomaha.edu

SHROFF, ARVIN PRANLAL, PHARMACEUTICAL CHEMISTRY. *Current Pos:* chemist, Food & Drug Admin, 74-75, chief Prod Surveillance Br, 75-81, dir, Div Field Sci, 81-86, actg dep dir, 86-88, dep dir, Off Regional Opers, 88-91, DEP DIR, OFF ENFORCEMENT, FOOD & DRUG ADMIN, 91- *Personal Data:* b Surat, India, July 2, 33; US citizen; m 91, Theresa; c Susan & Sarah. *Educ:* Univ Baroda, BS, 54; Duquesne Univ, MS, 58; Univ Md, PhD(pharmaceut chem), 62. *Honors & Awards:* Philip B Hoffman Award, Johnson & Johnson, 72. *Prof Exp:* Lectr, Univ Col, Md, 61-63, fel, Univ, 62-63; sr scientist & group leader analysis res, Ortho Res Found, 63-74. *Mem:* Am Chem Soc; Am Pharmaceut Asn. *Res:* Steroids, alkaloids and heterocyclics; biotransformation, bioavailability and bioequivalence; pharmaceutical analyses and stability; chromatography; spectroscopy. *Mailing Add:* 182 Kendrick Pl Gaithersburg MD 20878. *Fax:* 301-443-3496

SHROFF, RAMESH N, POLYMER PHYSICS, POLYMER RHEOLOGY. *Current Pos:* sr res scientist, Norchem, 68-77, asst mgr polymer res, 77-81, res assoc, 81-86, assoc scientist, 86-89, RES SCIENTIST, NORCHEM, 90- *Personal Data:* b Jambusar, India, Apr 27, 37; m 65, Nirmala G Vora; c Monica R & Bella S (Curtis). *Educ:* St Xavier's Col, India, BS, 59; Lehigh Univ, MS, 61, PhD(chem), 66. *Prof Exp:* Sr res physicist, Goodyear Tire & Rubber Co, Ohio, 65-68. *Mem:* Am Chem Soc; Soc Rheology; Soc Plastics Engrs. *Res:* Rheology; extrusion; screw and die design; molecular weight and distribution; long-chain branching; morphology; short-chain branching and distribution; new product development; coextrusion. *Mailing Add:* Quantum Chem 11530 Northlake Dr MSN 44 Cincinnati OH 45249-1642. *Fax:* 513-530-4266

SHRONTZ, JOHN WILLIAM, RUBBER COMPOUNDING, RUBBER & PETROLEUM NEW PRODUCT DEVELOPMENT. *Current Pos:* RETIRED. *Personal Data:* b Newark, Ohio, Mar 6, 16; m 42, 70; c 4. *Educ:* Denison Univ, Granville, Ohio, BSc, 38. *Hon Degrees:* PhD, Am Inst Chemists, 77. *Prof Exp:* Chemist qual control, Pharis Tire & Rubber Co, Newark, Ohio, 40-43, chemist res & develop, 44-48; tech rep rubber & plastics chem sales, Harwick Chem Co, Akron, Ohio, 48-60, br mgr, 60-66, asst to vpres, 66-69; asst to pres & dir pub rels, Edgington Oil Co, Long beach, Calif, 69-77. *Mem:* Emer mem Am Chem Soc; fel Am Inst Chemists; sr mem Soc Plastics Engrs; AAAS. *Res:* Synthetic rubber and guayule; rubber chemicals for specialized compounding; low temperature plasticizer esters of ethylene glycol. *Mailing Add:* 3261 Orangewood Ave Los Alamitos CA 90720

SHROPSHIRE, WALTER, JR, BIOPHYSICS, PLANT PHYSIOLOGY. *Current Pos:* DIR, OMEGA LAB, 86- *Personal Data:* b Washington, DC, Sept 4, 32; m 58, Audrey McConkey; c Janet M, Susan L & Edward A. *Educ:* George Washington Univ, BS, 54, MS, 56, PhD(plant physiol, photobiol), 58; Wesley Theol Sem, MDiv, 90. *Honors & Awards:* Spec Act Award, Smithsonian Inst, 68, Merton Award, 68. *Prof Exp:* Plant physiologist, Astrophys Observ, Smithsonian Inst, 54-57; res fel biophys, Calif Inst Technol, 57-59; physicist, Div Radiation & Organisms, Smithsonian Inst, 59-64, asst dir, Radiation Biol Lab, 64-83, asst dir, Environ Res Ctr, 83-86, acting dir, 86. *Concurrent Pos:* Prof lectr, George Washington Univ, 63-86; Smithsonian res award, 65-67; consult, Nat Acad Sci Pre & Postdoctoral Fel Award Panels, 65-71; guest prof, Univ Freiburg, 68-69; mem coun, AAAS, 67-77, mem, Comt Coun Affairs, 75-78; mem, US Nat Comt Photobiol, Nat Res Coun, 73-75; chmn, Am Sect, Int Solar Energy Soc, 75-76; guest prof, Univ Zurich, Switz, 85-86; adj prof, Wesley Theol Sem, 90- *Mem:* Fel AAAS; Am Soc Plant Physiol; Biophys Soc; Int Solar Energy Soc; Am Soc Photobiol (pres, 84-85). *Res:* Photobiology; action and transmission spectra; photomorphogenesis; seed germination; spectral distribution of solar radiation; cell physiology; phototropism and light growth responses of fungi. *Mailing Add:* Foundry U M Church 1500 16th St NW Washington DC 20036. *Fax:* 202-332-4035; *E-Mail:* wshrop@erols.com

SHRUM, JOHN W, GEOLOGY, SCIENCE EDUCATION. *Current Pos:* prof sci educ, 67-87, assoc dir, Biosci Teaching Ctr, 77-82, assoc dean educ, 84-87, EMER PROF SCI EDUC, UNIV GA, 87- *Personal Data:* b Jeannette, Pa, Apr 30, 25; m 47, Louise Raber; c Rebecca, Elizabeth & James. *Educ:* Pa State Univ, BS, 48; Bowling Green State Univ, MEd, 59; Ohio State Univ, PhD(earth sci, sci educ), 63. *Prof Exp:* Teacher pub schs, Ohio, 56-59; from instr to assoc prof geol & sci educ, Ohio State Univ, 60-68. *Concurrent Pos:* Dir teacher prep, Earth Sci Curric Proj, Colo, 64-66, Ga Sci Teacher Proj, 68-75; mem panel teacher prep, Coun Educ Geol Sci, 64-67; mem inst eval panel, NSF, 64-75; field reader, US Off Educ Res Proposals, 65-72; chmn dept sci educ, Univ Ga, 67-74. *Mem:* Nat Sci Teachers Asn; Nat Asn Res Sci Teaching; Nat Asn Geol Teachers. *Res:* Evaluation of science instruction; photomacrography; biology science education; course development in geology. *Mailing Add:* 195 Dogwood Dr Athens GA 30606

SHRYOCK, A JERRY, MATHEMATICS. *Current Pos:* Mem fac math, 55-72, chmn dept, 70-76, PROF MATH, WESTERN ILL UNIV, 72- *Personal Data:* b Canton, Ill, Apr 16, 30; m 50; c 2. *Educ:* Bradley Univ, BS, 50; Ill State Univ, MS, 55; Univ Iowa, PhD(math educ), 62. *Mem:* Math Asn Am. *Res:* Logic and its applications. *Mailing Add:* 70 Lake Michael Dr Macomb IL 61455-1328

SHRYOCK, GERALD DUANE, ORGANIC CHEMISTRY. *Current Pos:* from asst prof to assoc prof, 63-67, chmn, Div Sci & Math, 68-89, PROF CHEM, BLACK HILLS STATE COL, 67- *Personal Data:* b Sharon, Okla, Jan 24, 33; m 59; c 4. *Educ:* Northwestern State Col, BS, 56; Okla State Univ, MS, 59; Univ of the Pac, PhD(chem), 66. *Prof Exp:* Instr chem, Murray State Col, 58-59 & Imp Ethiopian Col, 59-61; instr chem, Murray State Col, 61-62. *Mem:* Am Chem Soc. *Res:* Carbohydrate chemistry. *Mailing Add:* 14418 W Morning Star Surprise AZ 85374

SHTRIKMAN, SHMUEL, PURE & APPLIED PHYSICS. *Current Pos:* Researcher, Electronics Dept, Weizmann Inst Sci, 54-64, from assoc prof to prof, 64-71, dept head, 81-82 & 86-87, SAMUEL SEBBA PROF PURE & APPL PHYSICS, ELECTRONICS DEPT, WEIZMANN INST SCI, 72- *Personal Data:* b Brisk, Poland, Oct 21, 30; Israeli citizen. *Educ:* Technion, Israel Inst Technol, BSc, 53, Diplomaed Engr, 54, DSc, 58. *Honors & Awards:* Michael Landau Prize, Mifal Hapayis Found, Israel, 75 & Select Michael Landau Prize, 92; Rothschild Prize, Yad Hanadiv Found, Israel, 84; Armando Kaminitz Prize, Weizmann Inst Sci, Israel, 85. *Concurrent Pos:* Vis prof, Physics Dept, Univ Pa, 64-65; vis res prof, Imp Col Sci & Technol, London, 71-72; adj prof, Physics Dept, Univ Calif, San Diego, 85- *Mem:* Fel Inst Elec & Electronics Engrs; Am Phys Soc; Israel Acad Sci & Humanities. *Res:* Basic research and mission oriented research and developments in pure and applied physics. *Mailing Add:* Dept Electronics Weizmann Inst Sci Rehovot 76100 Israel. *Fax:* 972-89344109

SHTURMAKOV, ALEXANDER JOSEPH, FERROUS ALLOYS, METALLOGRAPHY. *Current Pos:* TECH DIR, IROQUOIS FOUNDRY CORP, 95- *Personal Data:* b Moscow, Russia, Apr 15, 53; US citizen; m 86, Olga Nikoshkova; c Marina. *Educ:* Moscow Automotive Inst, BSME, 74, MSME, 75, PhD(metall & mat sci), 82. *Honors & Awards:* Bronze Medal Tech & Sci Achievements, Coun Ministers Russia, Moscow, 86; Inventor USSR Award, Soc Inventors USSR, Moscow, 90. *Prof Exp:* Sr res engr, Mosco Res & Develop Inst Automotive Indust, 75-80, head res, 80-85, chief res engr, 85-91; qual assurance mgr/metallurgist, ME Int, St Cloud, Minn, 92-95. *Concurrent Pos:* Mem, 5-H Comt Gray Iron Res, Am Foundrymans Soc, 96- *Mem:* Am Foundrymens Soc; Mat Info Soc; Heat Treating Soc; Am Soc Metals. *Res:* Ferrous metallurgy; alloys research and development; analysis of foundry defects; ion implantation; ferrous casting technology and surface hardening. *Mailing Add:* 2589 Chesapeake Dr Madison WI 53719-1691

SHU, FRANK H, ASTROPHYSICS. *Current Pos:* assoc prof, 73-76, chmn, Astron Dept, 84-88, PROF ASTRON, UNIV CALIF, BERKELEY, 76- *Personal Data:* b Kunming, China, June 2, 43. *Educ:* Mass Inst Technol, BS, 63; Harvard Univ, PhD(astron), 68. *Honors & Awards:* Bok Prize, Harvard Univ, 72; Warner Prize, Am Astron Soc, 77. *Prof Exp:* From asst prof to assoc prof earth & space sci, State Univ NY, Stony Brook, 68-73. *Concurrent Pos:* Alfred P Sloan Found fel, 72-74; vis scientist, Kapteyn Astron Inst, Groningen, Neth, 73; lectr, Harlow Shapley Vis Prof Prog, Am Astron Soc, 75-79, 81-84, counr, 82-85, chmn, Mem Questionnair Subcomt, 89-; mem, Brouwer Award Comt, Div Dynamical Astron, Am Astron Soc, 84-87, chmn, 86-87; mem, Class Mem Comt, Nat Acad Sci, 89, US Nat Comt, Int Astron Union, 90- *Mem:* Nat Acad Sci; Int Astron Union; Am Astron Soc (vpres, 88-92, pres, 94-); Sigma Xi. *Res:* Author of various publications. *Mailing Add:* Astronomy Dept 403 Campbell Hall Univ Calif Berkeley CA 94720-3411

SHU, LARRY STEVEN, BUILDING SCIENCE & TECHNOLOGY. *Current Pos:* mat scientist, W R Grace & Co, 71-72, sr group leader, 72-82, res sect mgr, Bldg Sci & Technol, 83-89, DIR RES, W R GRACE & CO, 89- *Personal Data:* b Kuala Lumpur, Malaysia, Mar 8, 36; US citizen; m 65; c 2. *Educ:* Taiwan Cheng Kung Univ, BS, 58; Brown Univ, MS, 61, PhD(eng), 66. *Prof Exp:* Res scientist fiber-reinforced composites, Space Sci Lab, Gen Elec Co, 65-69; sr res chemist, Celanese Res Co, Celanese Corp, 69-70. *Mem:* Am Soc Mech Engrs; Am Soc Testing & Mat; NY Acad Sci; AAAS. *Res:* Fiber-reinforced composites; materials science and engineering; building science and technology. *Mailing Add:* 272 Woodcliff Rd Newton Highlands MA 02161-2128

SHU, MARK CHONG-SHENG, BIOFLUID MECHANICS, BIOINSTRUMENTATION. *Current Pos:* SR BIOMED ENGR, MEDTRONIC, INC, 89- *Personal Data:* b Chongging, China, Sept 16, 54. *Educ:* Sichuan Inst Tech, China, BS, 78; Univ Houston, MS, 84, PhD(biomed eng), 88. *Prof Exp:* Fel, Univ Akron, 89. *Concurrent Pos:* Lectr, Sichuan Inst Technol, 78-81. *Mem:* Am Soc Mech Engrs; Biomed Eng Soc; Am Soc Artificial Internal Organs. *Res:* Cardiovascular dynamics, blood rheology, artificial internal organs, medical device design, laser doppler measurement, acoustic measurement, vibration analysis, finite element analysis, fracture mechanics and computational fluid dynamics. *Mailing Add:* 223 Amherst Aisle Irvine CA 92612. *Fax:* 612-574-2899; *E-Mail:* shum@medheart.medtronic.com

SHUB, MICHAEL I, MATHEMATICS, COMPUTER SCIENCE THEORY. *Current Pos:* RES STAFF MEM IBM, T J WATSON RES CTR, 86- *Personal Data:* b Brooklyn, NY, Aug 17, 43; m 88, Beate E Kessler; c Alexander. *Educ:* Columbia Col, AB, 64; Univ Calif, Berkeley, MA, 66, PhD(math), 67. *Prof Exp:* Lectr & asst prof math, Brandeis Univ, 67-71; from asst prof to assoc prof math, Univ Calif, Santa Cruz, 71-73; from assoc prof to prof math, Queens Col, NY, 75-86. *Concurrent Pos:* NATO fel, 69; Sloan res fel, 72. *Mem:* Am Math Soc; Soc Indust & Appl Math; fel NY Acad Sci. *Res:* Orbit structure of discrete and continuous differentiable dynamical systems; geometric theory of computational complexity. *Mailing Add:* IBM T J Watson Res Ctr 32-2 Yorktown Heights NY 10598-0218

SHUBE, EUGENE E, ELECTROMECHANICAL ACTUATION, ELECTRO MECHANICAL SYSTEMS. *Current Pos:* VPRES ENG, G E C AEROSPACE INC, UK, 71- *Personal Data:* b New York, NY, Jan 26, 27; m 48; c 3. *Educ:* City Col New York, BME, 46; Stevens Inst Technol, MS, 51. *Prof Exp:* Self-employed, Metro Cooling Systs Inc, 46-51; asst proj engr, Wright Aeronaut Div, Curtiss Wright Corp, 51-54; chief preliminary design, Stratos Div, Fairchild Stratos Corp, 54-61; chief engr, 66-71; asst to pres, Dorne & Margolin Inc, 61-76. *Concurrent Pos:* Teacher related tech subjects, NY Bd Educ, 48-51. *Mem:* Soc Automotive Engrs. *Mailing Add:* 564 Ridge Rd Elmont NY 11003

SHUBECK, PAUL PETER, ECOLOGY, ENTOMOLOGY. *Current Pos:* from asst prof to prof, 67-92, chmn dept, 76-79, EMER PROF BIOL, MONTCLAIR STATE UNIV, 92- *Personal Data:* b Elizabeth, NJ, Oct 21, 26; m 53; c 2. *Educ:* Seton Hall Univ, BS, 50; Montclair State Univ, AM, 55; Rutgers Univ, PhD(zool), 67. *Prof Exp:* Instr biol, Thomas Jefferson High Sch, 51-60; guid counsr, Battin High Sch, 61-67. *Concurrent Pos:* Vis prof entom, Rutgers Univ, 80. *Mem:* Sigma Xi; Entom Soc Am; Coleopterists Soc; Am Entom Soc. *Res:* Insect ecology and behavior; orientation of carrion beetles to carrion; phenology and flight activity of carrion beetles. *Mailing Add:* 65 Pleasantview Ave New Providence NJ 07974

SHUBERT, BRUNO OTTO, MATHEMATICS, OPERATIONS RESEARCH. *Current Pos:* asst prof, 69-73, ASSOC PROF OPERS RES, NAVAL POSTGRAD SCH, 73- *Personal Data:* b Ostrava, Czech, Apr 15, 34; m 60; c 1. *Educ:* Czech Tech Univ, MS, 60; Charles Univ, Prague, PhD(probability, statist), 65; Stanford Univ, PhD(elec eng), 68. *Prof Exp:* Res assoc appl probability, Inst Info Theory & Automation, Czech Acad Sci, 64-68; vis asst prof math, Morehouse Col, 68; vis asst prof elec eng, Univ Colo, Boulder, 68-69. *Mem:* Inst Math Statist; Am Math Soc; Math Asn Am. *Res:* Stochastic models, theory of games, statistical decisions and learning. *Mailing Add:* Dept Opers Analysis Naval Postgrad Sch Monterey CA 93943-5000

SHUBERT, L ELLIOT, PHYCOLOGY. *Current Pos:* RES ASSOC, NATURAL HIST MUS, LONDON, 94-; EDU & SCI CONSULT, 95- *Personal Data:* b St Louis, Mo, May 16, 43; m, Eileen J Cox; c Andrew, Nathan & Angela. *Educ:* Univ Mo, Kansas City, BS, 66; Univ Conn, PhD(phycol), 73. *Prof Exp:* From asst prof to prof biol, Univ NDak, 73-94. *Concurrent Pos:* Prin-invstr, Dept Interior Bur Reclamation grant, Univ NDak, 74-78; co-invstr, Proj Reclamation, 75-80; co-dir, Inst for Energy & Coal Develop for Educr, 77-81; hon vis prof, Univ Durham, Eng, 80-81; sr assoc, Off Instrnl Develop, Univ NDak, 82-83; res assoc, USDA/Agr Res Serv, Human Nutrit Res Ctr, 83-85; fac lect ser, Univ NDak, 86; vis scientist, NASA, Ames Research Ctr, 86-87; prin invstr, Kellyslough Res Proj, 93-95. *Mem:* Phycol Soc Am; Brit Phycol Soc; Int Phycol Soc; Inst Biol UK; Int Diatom Soc; Soc Int Limnol Theor et Appl. *Res:* Freshwater algae-aquatic and soil; ecology, physiology and nutrition of algae; algal bioassays; algal succession on disturbed and natural soils; soil microcosms; uptake of heay metals; ecotoxicology. *Mailing Add:* Natural Hist Mus Dept Bot Cromwell Rd London SW7 5BD England. *Fax:* 44-171-938-9260; *E-Mail:* e.shubert@nhm.ac.uk

SHUBIK, PHILIPPE, PATHOLOGY, ONCOLOGY. *Current Pos:* sr res fel, 80-90, VIS FEL, GREEN COL, OXFORD, ENG, 90- *Personal Data:* b London, Eng, Apr 28, 21; US citizen; m 64; c 3. *Educ:* Oxford Univ, BMBCh, 43, DPhil, 49, DM, 71. *Honors & Awards:* Co-recipient, Ernest W Bertner Mem Award, 78. *Prof Exp:* Demonstr path, Sir William Dunn Sch Path, Oxford Univ, 47-49; instr & biologist, Med Sch, Northwestern Univ, 49-50; cancer coordr, Chicago Med Sch, 50-53, prof oncol & dir dept, 53-68; Eppley prof oncol & path & dir, Eppley Inst, Col Med, Univ Nebr Med Ctr, 68-80. *Concurrent Pos:* Mem, Morphol Study Sect, 58-59, Cell Biol Study Sect, 58-60 & Path Study Sect, 60-62; expert adv panel, WHO, 59-; Nat Adv Cancer Coun, 62-66 & sr mem, Nat Cancer Adv Bd, 70-; pres, Toxicol Forum, Inc, Washington, DC, 74-; co-managing ed, Cancer Lett, 75-; toxicologist, Eppley Inst, Univ Nebr, dir, Eppley Inst Res Cancer. *Mem:* Am Soc Path & Bact; Am Soc Exp Path; Am Asn Cancer Res; Am Soc Prev Oncol; Soc Toxicol. *Res:* Experimental pathology; chemical carcinogenesis; environmental and industrial cancer; toxicology; tumor biology. *Mailing Add:* Green Col Univ Oxford Oxford OX2 6HG England. *Fax:* 202-789-0905; *E-Mail:* 100551.1653@compuserve.com

SHUBKIN, RONALD LEE, SYNTHETIC LUBRICANTS, CLEANING SOLVENTS. *Current Pos:* RES ADV, ALBEMARLE CORP, 96- *Personal Data:* b New York, NY, Aug 27, 40; m 67, Swee C Quek; c Catherine D & Teresa L. *Educ:* Univ NC, BS, 62; Univ Wis, PhD(inorg chem), 67; Mich State Univ, MBA, 81. *Prof Exp:* Res fel, Queen Mary Col, London, 66-67; from res chemist to sr res chemist, Ethyl Corp, 67-79, res assoc, 79-81, econ eval, 82-83, res supvr, 81-88, res mgr, 89-93, res adv, 93-96. *Concurrent Pos:* Instr, Wayne Co Community Col; assoc prof, Oakland Community Col; vis lectr, synthetics lubricants, Col Petrol & Energy Studies, Oxford, Eng, 90-96; Synthetic Lubricants & High-Performance Functional Fluids, 92; mem, Tech Task Group Synthetic Fluids, Econ Defense Adv Comt, Secy State; chmn & lectr, Advan Synthetic Lubricants Educ Course, Soc Tribologists & Lubrication Engrs, 93-96; secy, treas, vchmn & chmn Synthetic Lube Tech Comt, Nat Lubricating Grease Inst, 93-94. *Mem:* Am Chem Soc; Soc Tribologists & Lubrication Engrs; Am Soc Testing & Mat. *Res:* Synthetic lubricants; industrial chemistry; organic chemistry; processes for the manufacture of synthetic lubricants; applications development for solvent cleaners. *Mailing Add:* Albemarle Corp 8000 GSRI Ave Baton Rouge LA 70820-7497

SHUCH, H PAUL, ELECTRONIC COMMUNICATIONS, AVIATION SAFETY. *Current Pos:* EXEC DIR, SEARCH EXTRATERRESTRIAL INTEL, INC, 95- *Personal Data:* b Chicago, Ill, May 23, 46; m 96, Muriel Hykes; c Andrew & Erika. *Educ:* West Valley Col, AS, 72; San Jose State Univ, BS, 75, MA, 86; Univ Calif, Berkeley, PhD(eng), 90. *Honors & Awards:* Safety Achievement Award, Exp Aircraft Asn, 87; John T Chambers Mem Award, Cent States UHF Soc, 93; Robert Goddard Mem Award, Nat Space Club, 88. *Prof Exp:* Telecommunications systs controller, USAF, 65-69; prod eng technician, TransAction Systs, 69-71; res & develop engr, Appl Technol Div, Itek, 72-75; sr eng instr, Lockheed Missiles & Space Co, 75-77; instr microwave technol, San Jose City Col, 77-90; prof electronics, Pa Col Technol, 90-95. *Concurrent Pos:* Electronics instr, W Valley Col, 73-77; chief engr, Microcomm, 75-90; chmn, Santa Clara County Airport Comn, 82-87; avionics lectr, Aeronaut Dept, San Jose State Univ, 84-87; accident prev counr, Fed Aviation Admin, 84-; Horon Jeff grant, Univ Calif, Berkeley, 90; mil prog evaluator, Am Coun Educ, 91-; guest lectr, Air Safety Found, 92; mem adv comt, Midd Atlantic Ctr Advan Technol Educ, NSF. *Res:* First home satellite television receiver; aviation safety, especially midair collision avoidance; over 50 publications; patented anticollision radar; radioastronomy; microwave survey for signals from possible extra-terrestrial civilizations. *Mailing Add:* 21 Hoover St Williamsport PA 17701. *Fax:* 201-641-1771; *E-Mail:* n6tx@setileague.org

SHUCHAT, ALAN HOWARD, MATHEMATICAL MODELING. *Current Pos:* from asst prof to assoc prof, 74-83, assoc dean, 89-92, PROF MATH, WELLESLEY COL, 83- *Personal Data:* b Brooklyn, NY, Oct 6, 42; m 85, Alix E Ginsburg; c Mark & Vera. *Educ:* Mass Inst Technol, SB, 63; Univ Mich, Ann Arbor, MS, 65, PhD(math), 69. *Prof Exp:* Asst prof math, Univ Toledo, 69-71 & Mt Holyoke Col, 71-74. *Concurrent Pos:* Fac fel, Transp Systs Ctr, 81; reviewer, Math Revs, 72-; sci fac prof develop grant, NSF, 79-80, improv lab instrumentation grant, 89-91; vis scientist, Mass Inst Technol, 84; translr, Russ math; vis lectr, Math Asn Am. *Mem:* Am Math Soc; Math Asn Am; Opers Res Soc Am. *Res:* Mathematical models in operations research; curriculum and software development in mathematics and technology. *Mailing Add:* Dept Math Wellesley Col Wellesley MA 02181. *E-Mail:* ashuchat@wellesley.edu

SHUCK, FRANK O, CHEMICAL ENGINEERING. *Current Pos:* Asst prof, 62-77, ASSOC PROF CHEM ENG, IOWA STATE UNIV, 77- *Personal Data:* b Glasgow, Mont, Feb 19, 36; m 56; c 2. *Educ:* Carnegie Inst Technol, BS, 58, MS, 60, PhD(chem eng), 62. *Mem:* Am Inst Chem Engrs. *Res:* Diffusion in binary and multicomponent liquids and liquid metals; mass transfer in liquid systems. *Mailing Add:* 4202 Lake St Lake Charles LA 70605

SHUCK, JERRY MARK, GENERAL SURGERY, SURGICAL EDUCATION. *Current Pos:* vpres med affairs, 93-95, OLIVER H PAYNE PROF & CHMN SURG, CASE WESTERN RES UNIV, 80-; DIR SURG, UNIV HOSP CLEVELAND, 80- *Personal Data:* b Bucyrus, Ohio, Apr 23, 34; m, Linda Wayne; c Kimberly, Gail, Jay, Lynn & Steven. *Educ:* Univ Cincinnati, BS, 55, MD, 59, DSc(surg infection), 66. *Prof Exp:* Staff surgeon & clin chief, US Army Inst Surg Res, 66-68; prof surg, Univ NMex Hosp, 68-79, dir, Burn & Trauma Unit, 69-79, chief staff, 75-77. *Concurrent Pos:* Dir, Am Bd Surg, 87-95, chmn, 94-95, sr mem, 95- *Mem:* Am Asn Surg Trauma (treas, 80-83); Am Col Surgeons; Am Surg Asn; hon mem Int Cong Surg. *Res:* Surgery and administration; trauma, gastrointestinal and endocrine studies. *Mailing Add:* 11100 Euclid Ave Cleveland OH 44106

SHUCK, JOHN WINFIELD, MATHEMATICS EDUCATION. *Current Pos:* from asst prof to assoc prof math, 77-90, dept head, 83-88, PROF URSINUS COL, 90-, DEPT ADMINR, 93- *Personal Data:* b Cumberland, Md, Apr 9, 40; m 64, Dianne Cunnington; c Amy E. *Educ:* Mass Inst Technol, BS, 63; Tufts Univ, MS, 68; Northeastern Univ, PhD(math), 69. *Prof Exp:* Asst prof math, Univ Mich, 69-70 & Univ Rochester, 70-77. *Concurrent Pos:* NSF teaching fel, 68-69. *Mem:* Math Asn Am; Sigma Xi; Coun Undergrad Res; Asn Women Maths. *Res:* Algebraic number theory; non-Archimedean analysis and its applications to number theory; Diophantine equations. *Mailing Add:* Dept Math & Comput Sci Ursinus Col Collegeville PA 19426-1000. *E-Mail:* jshuck@acad.ursinus.edu

SHUCK, LOWELL ZANE, MECHANICAL ENGINEERING, PETROLEUM ENGINEERING. *Current Pos:* PRES, TECHNOL DEVELOP INC, 80- *Personal Data:* b Bluefield, WVa, Oct 23, 36; c Kirsten. *Educ:* WVa Inst Technol, BSME, 58; WVa Univ, MSME, 65, PhD (theoret & appl mech-biomech), 70. *Honors & Awards:* Mat Testing Award, Am Soc Testing & Mat, 70; Ralph James Award, Am Soc Mech Engrs, 80. *Prof Exp:* Sales engr, WVa Armature Co, 58-59; from instr to assoc prof mech eng, WVa Inst Technol, 59-69, chmn dept, 65-69; res mech engr & proj leader, Morgantown Energy Res Ctr, 70-76; prof mech eng & mech & assoc dir Eng Exp Sta, WVa Univ, 76-80. *Concurrent Pos:* Consult, Railcar Div, Food Mach Corp, WVa, 65-66; NSF faculty fel & res eng, 68-70; res mech engr,

Morgantown Energy Technol Ctr, 76-; Governor's appointee to WVa Coal & Energy Res Adv Comt, 77-81; sci adv to WVa Gov Jay Rockefeller IV, 78-81; adj prof, Col Eng, WVa Univ, 80- *Mem:* Am Soc Eng Educ; Am Soc Mech Engrs; Soc Petrol Engrs; Instrument Soc Am; Nat Soc Prof Engrs; Sigma Xi. *Res:* Vibrations; acoustics; data acquisition; metrology; biomechanics; rheology; theoretical and experimental stress analysis; design and development of transducers; instrumentation; biomechanics; petroleum, natural gas and coal in situ recovery technology research and development including theoretical, laboratory and field projects; energy extraction and conversion technology; oil and gas recovery. *Mailing Add:* 401 Highview Pl Morgantown WV 26505

SHUDDE, REX HAWKINS, NUCLEAR CHEMISTRY. *Current Pos:* RETIRED. *Personal Data:* b Santa Monica, Calif, Dec 25, 29; m 58; c 2. *Educ:* Univ Calif, Los Angeles, BS & AB, 52, Berkeley, PhD(chem), 56. *Prof Exp:* Sr res chemist, Atomics Int Div, NAm Aviation, Inc, 56-61; supvr reactor code develop, 61, supvr numerical appplns, 61-62; assoc prof, opers anal, Naval Postgrad Sch, 62-76, assoc prof opers res, 76-90. *Mem:* Opers Res Soc Am; Asn Comput Mach; Am Phys Soc. *Res:* Mathematics; electronics; operations research; mathematical programming; computer systems; numerical analysis. *Mailing Add:* 27105 Arriba Way Carmel CA 93923-9713

SHUE, ROBERT SIDNEY, POLYMER CHEMISTRY, ORGANOMETALLIC CHEMISTRY. *Current Pos:* mgr mkt develop, Phillips Eng Plastics, Phillips Chem Co, 78-80, group leader, Res Ctr, 80-82, planning & budgeting specialist, 82-84, mkt develop specialist, 84-87, SR PATENT DEVELOP CHEMIST, PHILLIPS PETROL CO, 87- *Personal Data:* b Burlington, NC, May 24, 43; m 67, Ramona Stallings; c Maria & David. *Educ:* Univ NC, Chapel Hill, AB, 64, PhD(org chem), 68. *Prof Exp:* Teaching asst org chem, Univ NC, Chapel Hill, 67-68; res chemist, Res Ctr, Phillips Petrol Co, 68-72, sr res chemist, 72-77, group leader, 77-78. *Mem:* Soc Plastic Engrs. *Res:* Homogeneous transition metal catalyzed organic reactions; reaction mechanisms; synthesis, characterization and structure-property relationships of macromolecules. *Mailing Add:* 3508 SE Oakdale Dr Bartlesville OK 74006

SHUEY, MERLIN ARTHUR, MANNED VEHICLE ENVIRONMENTAL CONTROL SYSTEMS, THERMAL CONTROL SYSTEMS. *Current Pos:* Exp engr, Hamilton Standard, Div United Technol Corp, 60-61, engr preliminary design/tech mkt, 61-64, sr engr, 64-65, asst preliminary design/engr tech mkt & group leader, 65-73 & 74-76, asst prog mgr, 73-74, sr mkt engr, Prod Line Tech Mkt, 76-78, prod mkt mgr, 78-88, prog mgr, 88-89, MGR BUS DEVELOP, HAMILTON STANDARD, DIV OF UNITED TECHNOL CORP, 89- *Personal Data:* b Pottsville, Pa, Sept 6, 36; m 60, 80, Jewel Grissom; c Dawn L, Randall J & Raymond M. *Educ:* Drexel Univ, BSME, 60; Rensselaer Polytech Univ, MSME, 65; Univ Conn, MBA, 71. *Concurrent Pos:* Mem bd, Inst Advan Studies in Life Support, 90-; mem, Emission Control Syst Comt, Soc Automative Engrs, 93-, dep chmn, 94-95. *Mem:* Am Inst Aeronaut & Astronaut. *Res:* Support of life in enclosed environment, primarily manned spacecraft; author of numerous papers and publications; support of plants in closed environment. *Mailing Add:* 11 Wood Duck Lane Tariffville CT 06081. *E-Mail:* shueyme@utc.hsd.com

SHUEY, R(ICHARD) L(YMAN), ELECTRONICS, INFORMATION SCIENCE. *Current Pos:* ADJ PROF, RENSSELAER POLYTECH INST, 87- *Personal Data:* b Chicago, Ill, May 7, 20; m 44, Frances Fortier; c Roy F & Marie F. *Educ:* Univ Mich, BS(eng physics) & BS(eng math), 42; Univ Calif, MS, 47, PhD(elec eng), 50. *Prof Exp:* Engr, Radiation Lab, Univ Calif, 46-50; res assoc res lab, 50-55, mgr info studies sect, 55-65, mgr info studies br, Res & Develop Ctr, 65-75, staff consult, Res & Develop Ctr, Gen Elec Co, 75-84. *Concurrent Pos:* Adj prof, Rensselaer Polytech Inst, 53-59. *Mem:* Inst Elec & Electronics Engrs; Asn Comput Mach; Soc Mfg Engrs; AAAS. *Res:* Information theory; communications systems; computers; distributed computer and information systems. *Mailing Add:* 2338 Rosendale Rd Schenectady NY 12309. *Fax:* 518-276-4033

SHUEY, WILLIAM CARPENTER, CEREAL CHEMISTRY. *Current Pos:* res cereal food technologist in chg hard red spring & durum wheat qual lab, Agr Res Serv, USDA, 62-77, ADJ PROF CEREAL CHEM & TECHNOL, AGR EXP STA, NDAK STATE UNIV, 77- *Personal Data:* b Emporia, Kans, July 1, 24; m 43; c 4. *Educ:* Univ Wichita, BS, 48; NDak State Univ, MS, 67, PhD(cereal technol), 70. *Honors & Awards:* Carl Wilhelm Brabender Award, Am Asn Cereal Chem, 70. *Prof Exp:* Exp miller & baker, Gen Mills, Inc, 48-51, in chg exp milling & phys dough test sect, 51-62. *Mem:* AAAS; Am Asn Cereal Chem. *Res:* Chemical composition of wheat and flour, their physical properties, finished products, influence of nutrition, temperature, disease, and other environmental factors on quality of wheat. *Mailing Add:* 5142 26th Ave S St Petersburg FL 33707

SHUFORD, RICHARD JOSEPH, ORGANIC POLYMER CHEMISTRY. *Current Pos:* RES CHEMIST POLYMERS, ORG MAT LAB, ARMY MAT & MECH RES CTR, 71- *Personal Data:* b Hobart, Okla, Dec 20, 44. *Educ:* Stetson Univ, BS, 66; Southern Ill Univ, Carbondale, PhD(org chem), 71. *Mem:* Am Chem Soc; Sigma Xi; Catalysis Soc; Am Soc Nondestructive Testing; Soc Adv Mat & Process Eng. *Res:* Piezoelectric and pyroelectric polymers; polymer morphology; nondestructive evaluation of composites; fabrication and characterization of fiber reinforced composites; develop and evaluate quality control and cure monitoring techniques for composites. *Mailing Add:* Army Res Lab attn: AMSRL-WM-MA Aberdeen Proving Ground MA 02172

SHUGARMAN, PETER MELVIN, PLANT PHYSIOLOGY, BIOCHEMISTRY. *Current Pos:* asst prof biol sci, Univ Southern Calif, 66-70, asst dean student affairs, 73-78, from asst dean to assoc dean, 78-86, assoc dean student affairs to assoc dean nat sci, 86-89, dir, interdisciplinary maj, 90-93, ASSOC PROF CELL PHYSIOL, UNIV SOUTHERN CALIF, 70- *Personal Data:* b Duluth, Minn, July 28, 27. *Educ:* Univ Calif, Los Angeles, PhD(chlorophyll biosynthesis), 66. *Prof Exp:* Lab technician leukocyte metab, Dept Med, 51-58, chlorella physiol, Dept Bot & Plant Biochem, 58-66. *Mem:* AAAS; Am Soc Plant Physiol; Am Inst Biol Sci. *Res:* Control of chlorophyll biosynthesis in Chlorella. *Mailing Add:* 5554 Harold Way No 1 Los Angeles CA 90028

SHUGARS, JONAS P, PLANT SCIENCE, SOIL SCIENCE. *Current Pos:* ASSOC PROF HORT, BEREA COL, 60- *Personal Data:* b Liberty, Ky, Feb 8, 34; m 60; c 2. *Educ:* Univ Ky, BSA, 55, MS, 57; Univ Tenn, Knoxville, PhD(agr plant & soil sci), 70. *Prof Exp:* Teacher high sch, Ky, 59-60. *Mem:* Am Soc Hort Sci. *Res:* Plant nutrition; flower physiology of plants; pollen study related to allergic reactions. *Mailing Add:* Dept Agr Berea Col 101 Chestnut St Berea KY 40404-0001

SHUGART, ALAN F, COMPUTER SCIENCES. *Current Pos:* CHMN BD, PRES & CHIEF EXEC OFFICER, SEAGATE TECHNOL, 79- *Educ:* Univ Redlands, BS. *Prof Exp:* Field engr, IBM Corp, 51-69; vpres prod develop, Memorex, 69-73; co-founder, Shugart Assocs, 73-74; pvt consult technol indust, 75-79. *Mem:* Nat Acad Eng. *Res:* Development of software tools and applications in the area of data management, including information management, network and systems management and storage management. *Mailing Add:* Seagate Technol PO Box 66360 Scotts Valley CA 95067-0360

SHUGART, CECIL G, NUCLEAR PHYSICS, POLYMER PHYSICS. *Current Pos:* PROF PHYSICS & CHMN DEPT, MEMPHIS STATE UNIV, 77- *Personal Data:* b Ennis, Tex, Oct 13, 30; m 55, Anita Brumbelow; c David N & Peter G. *Educ:* North Tex State Univ, BA, 57; Univ Tex, Austin, MA, 61, PhD(nuclear physics), 68. *Prof Exp:* Staff asst physics, Southwestern Bell Tel Co, 57-58; res scientist, Defense Res Lab, Univ Tex, Austin, 58-61; assoc engr, Develop Lab, Int Bus Mach Corp, 61-62; asst prof physics & chmn dept, Hardin-Simmons Univ, 62-65; asst prof physics, Southwestern Univ, 65-66; res assoc nuclear physics, Univ Tex, Austin, 67-68; dir, Soc Physics Students, Am Inst Physics, 68-70; assoc prof, 70-73, prof physics & head dept, Northeast La Univ, 73-77. *Concurrent Pos:* Sci fac fel, NSF, 66-67; vis scientist, Am Asn Physics Teachers, 68-70. *Mem:* Fel AAAS; Am Phys Soc; Am Asn Physics Teachers. *Res:* Nuclear and polymer physics; atmospheric electricity; magnetics; physics education. *Mailing Add:* Dept Physics Memphis State Univ Memphis TN 38152. *Fax:* 901-MSU-FAXX

SHUGART, HERMAN HENRY, JR, ECOLOGY, ZOOLOGY. *Current Pos:* ECOLOGIST, OAK RIDGE NAT LAB, 71- *Personal Data:* b El Dorado, Ark, Jan 19, 44; m 66; c 2. *Educ:* Univ Ark, BS, 66, MS, 68, PhD(zool), 71. *Concurrent Pos:* Lectureship, asst to assoc prof, Dept Bot, Univ Tenn, 71- *Mem:* Am Ornith Union; Ecol Soc Am; AAAS. *Res:* Systems analysis in ecology; theoretical ecology; synecology; niche theory, mathematical ecology, use of multivariate statistics in ecology. *Mailing Add:* Dept Envir Sci Clark Hall Univ Va Charlottesville VA 22903

SHUGART, HOWARD ALAN, PHYSICS. *Current Pos:* Teaching asst, Univ Calif, Berkeley, 53-56, assoc, 57, lectr, 57-58, from actg asst prof to assoc prof, 58-67, group leader, Lawrence Berkeley Lab, 64-79, vchmn dept physics, 68-70, 79-87, prof physics, 67-93, VCHMN DEPT, UNIV CALIF, BERKELEY, 88-, EMER PROF PHYSICS, 93- *Personal Data:* b Orange, Calif, Sept 21, 31; m 71, Elizabeth L Hanson. *Educ:* Calif Inst Technol, BS, 53; Univ Calif, MA, 55, PhD, 57. *Concurrent Pos:* Consult, Gen Dynamics/Convair, 60-61; mem comt nuclear constants, Nat Res Coun, 60-63. *Mem:* Fel Am Phys Soc; fel Nat Speleol Soc; Sigma Xi. *Res:* Atomic and molecular beams; low energy nuclear physics; atomic and nuclear properties, including lifetimes, hyperfine structure, spins and static multipole moments. *Mailing Add:* Dept Physics Univ Calif Berkeley CA 94720-7300

SHUGART, LEE RALEIGH, BIOCHEMISTRY, ENVIRONMENTAL GENOTOXICITY. *Current Pos:* NIH fel biol, 65-67, BIOCHEMIST, ENVIRON SCI, OAK RIDGE NAT LAB, 67- *Personal Data:* b Corbin, Ky, Dec 23, 31; m 52, 84; c 3. *Educ:* East Tenn State Univ, BS, 51; Univ Tenn, MS, 62, PhD(microbiol), 65. *Mem:* Soc Environ Toxicol & Chem; Am Chem Soc; Am Soc Biochem & Molecular Biol; Sigma Xi. *Res:* Biochemical measurement of damage to DNA; molecular mechanisms of environmental genotoxicity; interaction of proteins with nucleic acids; isolation and characterization of nucleic acids. *Mailing Add:* Environ Sci Div Oak Ridge Nat Lab Box 2008-6036 Oak Ridge TN 37831-6036

SHUH, DAVID KELLY, SPECTROSCOPY & SPECTROMETRY, ENVIRONMENTAL SCIENCES. *Current Pos:* STAFF SCIENTIST II, LAWRENCE BERKELEY LAB, 92- *Personal Data:* m 93. *Educ:* Univ Calif, Los Angeles, PhD(phys chem), 90. *Prof Exp:* Scholar, Univ Calif, Riverside, 92. *Mem:* Am Chem Soc; Mat Res Soc; Am Phys Soc; Am Vacuum Soc. *Res:* Surface science of semi-conductors. *Mailing Add:* Lawrence Berkeley Lab MS 70A-1150 1 Cyclotron Rd Berkeley CA 94720

SHUKLA, ATUL J, PHARMACEUTICS, CONTROLLED RELEASE TECHNOLOGY. *Current Pos:* ASST PROF PHARMACEUT, DEPT PHARMACEUT, COL PHARM, UNIV TENN, MEMPHIS, 89- *Personal Data:* b Dar-Es-Salaam, Tanzania, May 31, 57; m 82; c 2. *Educ:* Univ

Bombay, India, BS, 79; Univ Ga, MS, 82, PhD(pharmaceut), 85. *Prof Exp:* Asst prof pharaceut, Duquesne Univ, 85-89. *Concurrent Pos:* Invited speaker, Tanzania, Pharmaceut Coun, 88; Journees Galenique, Gatlefosse Corp, France, 88; prin investr grants, Gatlefosse Corp, 88-90, Edward Mendell Corp, 91- *Mem:* Am Asn Pharmaceut Scientists; Controlled Release Soc; NAm Thermal Analy Soc. *Res:* Design and formulation of controlled release drug delivery systems, such as microcapsules; biodegradable injectable drug delivery systems; oral controlled release drug delivery systems; transdermal drug delivery systems and evaluation of excipients for their use in the manufacturing of tablets. *Mailing Add:* Dept Pharmaceut Scis Col Pharmacy Univ Tenn 26 S Dunlap Rm 214 Memphis TN 38163

SHUKLA, KAMAL KANT, MUSCLE BIOCHEMISTRY. *Current Pos:* ASSOC PROG DIR, BIOPHYS PROG, NSF. *Personal Data:* b India, Jan 1, 42. *Educ:* Agra Univ, India, BS, 61; Banaras Hindu Univ, MS, 63; State Univ NY Stony Brook, PhD(physiol & biophysics), 77. *Prof Exp:* Asst prof physics, K N Govt Col, India, 63; jr sci officer radiation physics, Inst Nuclear Med, India, 64-70; med assoc, Brookhaven Nat Lab, 71-73; lectr, State Univ NY, Stony Brook, 78-79, asst prof muscle biochem, 79- *Concurrent Pos:* Sr sci officer, Inst Nuclear Med, India, 70-81. *Res:* Muscle biochemistry, in particular the mechanism of adenosine triphosphate hydrolysis by acto-myosin and its relation to contractions. *Mailing Add:* NSF 4201 Wilson Blvd Arlington VA 22230. *Fax:* 202-357-9783; *E-Mail:* kshukla@nsf.gov

SHUKLA, SHIVENDRA DUTT, MEMBRANES & RECEPTOR FUNCTIONS. *Current Pos:* assoc prof, 84-93, dir grad studies, 89-93, PROF PHARMACOL, SCH MED, UNIV MO, 93- *Personal Data:* b Mirzapur, India, Oct 11, 51; m 70, Asha; c Roshni, Sundeep & Bivek. *Educ:* Banaras Hindu Univ, India, BSc, 68, MSc, 70; Univ Liverpool, Eng, PhD(biochem), 77. *Prof Exp:* Res fel, Univ Birmingham, Eng, 76-80; res asst prof biochem, Univ Tex Health Ctr, 80-84. *Concurrent Pos:* Lectr, Banaras Hindu Univ, 71-73; prin investr, Am Heart Asn, 81-84 & NIH, 84- *Mem:* AAAS; Am Heart Asn; Am Soc Biochem & Molecular Biol; Am Soc Pharmacol & Exp Therapeut. *Res:* Biochemical and pharmacological investigations on the transmembrane signalling events in cells and its molecular regulation. *Mailing Add:* Dept Pharmacol Univ Mo Sch Med 1 Hospital Dr Columbia MO 65212-0001. *Fax:* 573-884-4558

SHUKLA, SHYAM SWAROOP, CHEMOMETRICS, SURFACTANT. *Current Pos:* asst prof & dir environ ctr, 85-90, ASSOC PROF CHEM, LAMAR UNIV, 90- *Personal Data:* m 82, Alka Mishra; c Richa & Ankit. *Educ:* Lucknow Univ, India, MSc, 72; Univ Sask, MS, 81; Clarkson Univ, PhD(anal chem), 84. *Prof Exp:* Fel, Univ Conn, 83-85. *Concurrent Pos:* Vis prof, Ecole Normale Superieure de Cachan, France, 91; Rice Univ, 91-93; consult, Houston Advan Res Ctr, Woodland, Tex, 91- *Res:* Disposal of waste by photochemical, electrochemical, biological means; measurement and abatement of pollutants; chemistry in micellar media and microemulsion; chemometrics. *Mailing Add:* Lamar Univ Dept Chem PO Box 10022 Beaumont TX 77710. *Fax:* 409-880-8007; *E-Mail:* shuklass@hal.lamar.edu

SHULDINER, PAUL W(ILLIAM), CIVIL ENGINEERING. *Current Pos:* PROF CIVIL ENG & REGIONAL PLANNING, UNIV MASS, AMHERST, 71- *Personal Data:* b New York, NY, June 19, 30; m 51; c 7. *Educ:* Univ Ill, Urbana, BSCE, 51, MSCE, 53; Univ Calif, Berkeley, DrEng(transp), 61. *Honors & Awards:* Walter L Huber Res Prize, Am Soc Civil Engrs, 66. *Prof Exp:* Instr civil eng, Ohio Northern Univ, 53-54, asst prof, 54-55; asst prof, Northwestern Univ, 60-63, assoc prof, 63-65; consult transp planning, Off Under Secy Transp, 65-66, sr transp engr, Off High Speed Ground Transp, US Dept Transp, 66-67, chief transp systs planning div, 68-69; fed exec fel, Brookings Inst, 70; dep dir nat transp planning study, Nat Acad Sci, 70-71. *Concurrent Pos:* Adv, Northeastern Ill Planning Comn, 64-65; mem Hwy Res Bd, Nat Acad Sci-Nat Res Coun. *Mem:* Am Soc Civil Engrs. *Res:* Transportation systems engineering; urban and regional planning. *Mailing Add:* Dept Civil Eng Univ Mass 214 Marston Hall Amherst MA 01003

SHULER, CHARLES F, BIOLOGY. *Current Pos:* ASST PROF DENT, UNIV SOUTHERN CALIF, 89- *Personal Data:* b Jamesville, Wis, Feb 17, 53. *Educ:* Univ Wis-Madison, BS, 75; Harvard Univ, DMD, 79; Univ Chicago, PhD(path), 84. *Prof Exp:* Asst prof dent, Ohio State Univ, 84-89. *Mem:* Am Soc Cell Biol; AAAS; Am Soc Dent Res. *Mailing Add:* Ctr Craniofacial Molecular Biol Univ Southern Calif 2250 Alcazar St CSA 103 Los Angeles CA 90033-4523. *Fax:* 213-342-2981

SHULER, CRAIG EDWARD, FOREST PRODUCTS, WOOD SCIENCE & TECHNOLOGY. *Current Pos:* ASSOC PROF WOOD SCI & TECHNOL, COLO STATE UNIV, 79- *Personal Data:* b Wichita, Kans, Aug 27, 38; m 60, Lorraine Luck; c Bren, Darn, Tor & Tiana. *Educ:* Colo State Univ, BS, 60, MS, 66, PhD(wood sci), 69. *Prof Exp:* Instr wood technol, Colo State Univ, 67-68; asst prof wood technol, Sch Forest Resources, Univ Maine, 69-75, assoc prof, 75-79. *Concurrent Pos:* Fulbright sr lectr, Moi Univ, Kenya, 90-91. *Mem:* Soc Wood Sci & Technol; Forest Prod Soc; Sigma Xi. *Res:* Timber mechanics; particle board production and use; timber physics; residue utilization. *Mailing Add:* 2413 Constitution Ft Collins CO 80526. *Fax:* 970-491-6754; *E-Mail:* craigs@picea.cvir.colostate.edu

SHULER, KURT EGON, THEORETICAL CHEMISTRY, CHEMICAL PHYSICS. *Current Pos:* chmn dept, Univ Calif, 68-70, prof, 68-92, chmn dept, 84-87, EMER PROF CHEM, UNIV CALIF, SAN DIEGO, 92- *Personal Data:* b Nuremberg, Ger, July 10, 22; nat US; m 44, Beatrice London. *Educ:* Ga Inst Technol, BS, 42; Cath Univ, PhD(theoret chem), 49. *Honors & Awards:* Gold Medal, US Dept Com, 68. *Prof Exp:* AEC fel, Appl Physics Lab, Johns Hopkins Univ, 49-51, sr staff mem, 51-55; mem sr staff, Nat Bur Stand, 55-58, consult to chief, Heat Div, 58-60, consult to dir, 60-61, sr res fel & asst dir, 63-68. *Concurrent Pos:* Consult, Advan Res Proj Agency, Dept Defense, 61-74, spec asst to vpres res, Inst Defense Analysis, 61-63; vis prof chem, Univ Calif, San Diego, 66-67; mem adv panel, Chem Sect, NSF, 73-75; Solvay Found fel, Solvay Inst, Univ Brussels, Belg, 75; consult indust. *Mem:* Fel AAAS; fel Am Inst Chemists; Am Chem Soc; fel Am Phys Soc. *Res:* Statistical mechanics; nonlinear phenomena and processes; stochastic processes. *Mailing Add:* Dept Chem 0-340 Univ Calif San Diego La Jolla CA 92093

SHULER, MICHAEL LOUIS, BIOTECHNOLOGY, BIOENGINEERING. *Current Pos:* From asst prof to prof chem eng, Cornell Univ, 74-92, actg dir, Sch Chem Eng, 86-87 & 93, SAMUEL B ECKERT PROF CHEM ENG, CORNELL UNIV, 92-, DIR, BIOENG PROG, 96- *Personal Data:* b Joliet, Ill, Jan 2, 47; m 72, Karen J Beck; c Andrew, Eric, Kristin & Katherine. *Educ:* Univ Notre Dame, BS, 69; Univ Minn, PhD(chem eng), 73. *Honors & Awards:* Colburn lectr, Univ Del, 82; Marvin Johnson Award, Am Chem Soc, 86; Food, Pharm & Bioeng Award, Am Inst Chem Eng, 89, Prof Progress Award, 91. *Concurrent Pos:* Vis scholar, Univ Wash, 80-81; ed-in-chief, Biotechnol Progress, 85-88; vis prof, Univ Wis, 88-89; bd dirs, PhytonCatalytic Inc, 90-; vpres educ, Am Inst Med Biol Eng; chair, Food, Pharm & Bioeng Div, Am Inst Chem Engrs, 94; guest prof, ETH, Zurich, 95. *Mem:* Nat Acad Eng; Am Chem Soc; Am Soc Microbiol; Am Soc Pharmacog; Am Inst Chem Engrs; fel Am Inst Med Biol Eng; Am Acad Arts & Sci. *Res:* Biochemical engineering; mathematical models of individual cells; plant cell cultures; bioreactors for genetically-modified cells; interaction of heavy metals and biofilms; bioremediation; insect cell tissue culture; pharmacodynamics; targeted drug delivery. *Mailing Add:* Sch Chem Eng Cornell Univ Ithaca NY 14853. *Fax:* 607-255-1136

SHULER, PATRICK JAMES, PETROLEUM & CHEM ENGINEERING. *Current Pos:* RES ENGR PETROL ENG, CHEVRON OIL FIELD RES CO, DIV STAND OIL CALIF, 78- *Personal Data:* b Joliet, Ill, Dec 11, 48; m 80. *Educ:* Univ Notre Dame, BS, 71; Univ Colo, MS, 74, PhD(chem eng), 78. *Mem:* Sigma Xi; Am Inst Chem Engrs; Soc Petrol Engrs. *Res:* Enhanced oil recovery by chemical flooding. *Mailing Add:* 17400 Briardale Lane Yorba Linda CA 92886

SHULER, ROBERT LEE, SURFACE CHEMISTRY. *Current Pos:* Chemist aeronaut fuels res, 54-61, res chemist biochem, 61-69, RES CHEMIST SURFACE CHEM, LAB CHEM PHYSICS, NAVAL RES LAB, 69- *Personal Data:* b West Columbia, SC, Mar 18, 26. *Educ:* Guilford Col, BS, 50; Georgetown Univ, MS, 60, PhD(chem), 69. *Mem:* Am Chem Soc; Sigma Xi. *Res:* Study of the behavior of various types of polymers spread as monomolecular films on aqueous and nonaqueous liquids. *Mailing Add:* 5840 Cameron Run Terr Alexandria VA 22303

SHULL, CHARLES MORELL, JR, PHYSICAL CHEMISTRY, ANALYTICAL CHEMISTRY. *Current Pos:* assoc prof, San Diego State Univ, 69-72, chmn dept, 74-80, prof natural sci, 72-83, ACTG ASSOC DEAN, IMPERIAL VALLEY CAMPUS, SAN DIEGO STATE UNIV, 80- *Personal Data:* b Connellsville, Pa, Apr 8, 22; m 52; c 5. *Educ:* Univ Tulsa, BS, 48; Univ Utah, MA, 50, PhD(chem), 53. *Honors & Awards:* Fulbright, Uruguay SA, 87. *Prof Exp:* Instr chem, Univ Tulsa, 48-49; chemist, Newmont Explor, Ltd, 53-56; res metallurgical eng labs, Litton Eng Labs, Inc, 56-58; asst prof chem, Colo Sch Mines, 59-64, assoc prof, 64-66; tech writer curric develop, Educ Develop Ctr, 66-69. *Concurrent Pos:* Consult curric res & writing, Ed Servs Inc, 66-67. *Mem:* Am Soc Eng Educ; Am Chem Soc; Royal Soc Chem; Am Inst Mining, Metall & Petrol Eng. *Res:* Reaction rates; formation constants and molecular structure of complex ions; curriculum development in science education. *Mailing Add:* 1188 Bowman Rd Acme WA 98220-9610

SHULL, CLIFFORD GLENWOOD, SOLID STATE PHYSICS. *Current Pos:* prof, 55-86, EMER PROF PHYSICS, MASS INST TECHNOL, 86- *Personal Data:* b Pittsburgh, Pa, Sept 23, 15; m 41, Martha-Nuel Summer; c John C, Robert D & William F. *Educ:* Carnegie Inst Technol, BS, 37; NY Univ, PhD(nuclear physics), 41. *Hon Degrees:* ScD, NY Univ, 95. *Honors & Awards:* Nobel Prize in Phys, 94; Humboldt Sr Scientist Award, 80; Frank Prize, Russ Acad Scis, 93; Buckley Prize, Am Phys Soc, 56. *Prof Exp:* Asst, NY Univ, 37-41; res physicist, Tex Col, 41-46; from prin physicist to chief physicist, Oak Ridge Nat Lab, 46-55. *Mem:* Nat Acad Sci; AAAS; fel Am Acad Arts & Sci; Am Phys Soc; Sigma Xi. *Res:* Solid state and neutron physics. *Mailing Add:* 4 Wingate Rd Lexington MA 02173

SHULL, DON LOUIS, physical chemistry, for more information see previous edition

SHULL, FRANKLIN BUCKLEY, physics; deceased, see previous edition for last biography

SHULL, HARRISON, QUANTUM CHEMISTRY, SCIENCE POLICY & EDUCATION. *Current Pos:* chancellor, 82-85, prof chem, 82-97, PROF EMER, UNIV COLO, BOULDER, 97-; PROF EMER, NAVAL POSTGRAD SCH, MONTEREY, CALIF, 97- *Personal Data:* b Princeton, NJ, Aug 17, 23; m 48, 62, Wil J Bentley; c James R, Kathy, George, Holly, Warren, Jeffrey, Stan & Sarah. *Educ:* Princeton Univ, AB, 43; Univ Calif, Berkeley, PhD(phys chem), 48. *Prof Exp:* Assoc chemist, US Naval Res Lab,

Washington, DC, 43-45; Nat Res Coun fel, Univ Chicago, 48-49; assoc scientist, Ames Lab, AEC, 49-54; asst prof phys chem, Iowa State Univ, 49-55; vpres acad affairs, provost & prof chem, Rensselaer Polytech Inst, 79-82. *Concurrent Pos:* Guggenheim Found fel, 54-55 & Sloan res fel, 56-58; asst dir res, Quantum Chem Group, Sweden, 58-59; mem, comt awards, Div Chem & Chem Technol, 59-67, chmn, 63-67, mem, comt phys chem, 63-66, mem, panel surv chem, Westheimer Comt, 64-65, chmn, Comn Human Resources, 77-81, mem, comt adv Off Naval Res chem, Nat Res Coun, 85-87; mem, adv panel chem, NSF, 64-67, chmn, 66-67, sr fel, 68-69, adv comn res, 74-76; consult, Off Sci Info Serv, 65-70; mem, chem vis comt, Brookhaven Nat Lab, 67-69, chmn, 69-70; mem, comt sci & pub policy, Nat Acad Sci, 69-72, mem coun & exec comt, 71-74, Naval Studies Bd, 73-79, 96-99; mem, adv comt, Chem Abstr Serv, 72-75; trustee, Assoc Univs, Inc, 73-74; dir, Storage Technol Corp, 83-; mem, bd trustees, Argonne Univs Asn, 70-75 & Inst Defense Analysis, 84-96; mem, exec panel, Chief Naval Opers, 84-89; provost & acad dean, Naval Postgrad Sch, Monterey Calif. *Mem:* Nat Acad Sci; fel AAAS; fel Am Phys Soc; fel Am Acad Arts & Sci (vpres, 75-79, 80-83); Am Chem Soc; foreign mem Royal Swedish Acad Sci; foreign mem Royal Uppsala Acad Arts & Sci. *Res:* Quantum chemistry; theoretical and experimental molecular spectroscopy and structure; scientific human resources; information technology. *Mailing Add:* 2 Cramden Dr Monterey CA 93940-4144

SHULL, JAMES JAY, microbiology, biochemistry; deceased, see previous edition for last biography

SHULL, PETER OTTO, JR, SUPERNOVA REMNANTS, ASTROPHYSICAL JETS. *Current Pos:* asst prof, 84-89, ASSOC PROF ASTRON, PHYSICS DEPT, OKLA STATE UNIV, 89- *Personal Data:* b Summit, NJ, July 24, 54. *Educ:* Princeton Univ, AB, 76; Rice Univ, MS, 79, PhD(astron), 81. *Prof Exp:* Res assoc, Max Planck Inst Astron, 82-83 & physics dept, Ariz State Univ, 84. *Concurrent Pos:* Vis scientist, Max Planck Inst Astron, 85, 88; Sci & Eng Res Coun vis fel, Univ Manchester, 83, 85, 88. *Mem:* Am Astron Soc; Sigma Xi. *Res:* Observational and theoretical astrophysics; structure and evolution of supernova remnants; Crab Nebula's jet; expansion of the Cygnus Loop; interactions of supernova progenitor stars with the interstellar medium. *Mailing Add:* Dept Physics Okla State Univ Stillwater OK 74078-0001

SHULLS, WELLS ALEXANDER, microbiology; deceased, see previous edition for last biography

SHULMAN, CARL, electrical engineering, optics, for more information see previous edition

SHULMAN, GEORGE, INDUSTRIAL ORGANIC CHEMISTRY. *Current Pos:* res chemist, 39-40, plant chemist, 40-51, tech dir, 51-64, VPRES, PFISTER CHEM INC, 64- *Personal Data:* b West New York, NJ, Sept 3, 14; m 43; c 4. *Educ:* City Col New York, BS, 36. *Prof Exp:* Res chemist, Insl-X co, 37-39. *Mem:* Am Chem Soc; Math Asn Am; NY Acad Sci. *Res:* Organic synthesis; dye intermediates; thickeners for liquid hydrocarbons; plastics and plasticizers; textile chemicals. *Mailing Add:* 715 Winthrop Rd Teaneck NJ 07666-2266

SHULMAN, HAROLD, MATHEMATICS. *Current Pos:* ASST PROF MATH, LEHMAN COL, 68- *Personal Data:* b Newark, NJ, Feb 12, 25; m 58; c 3. *Educ:* George Washington Univ, BS, 48; Johns Hopkins Univ, MA, 51; NY Univ, PhD(math), 58. *Prof Exp:* Tutor, Queens Col, NY, 52-54; assoc res scientist, Inst Math Sci, NY Univ, 54-60; sr analyst, Comput Usage Co, 60-62; prin comput engr, Repub Aviation Corp, 62-64; asst prof math, Hunter Col, 64-68. *Concurrent Pos:* Consult, Corps Engrs, Dept Defense, 57-59. *Mem:* Am Math Soc; Math Asn Am. *Res:* Numerical analysis; applied mathematics; statistics. *Mailing Add:* 144-43 Jewel Ave Flushing NY 11367

SHULMAN, HERBERT BYRON, COMPUTER PERFORMANCE ANALYSIS, SYSTEMS ENGINEERING. *Current Pos:* mem tech staff, 78-82, SUPVR, BELL TELEPHONE LABS, 82- *Personal Data:* b Weehawken, NJ, June 29, 47; m 73; c 2. *Educ:* Cornell Univ, AB, 68; Univ Calif, Berkeley, PhD(math), 72. *Prof Exp:* Instr math, Yale Univ, 72-74 & Univ Pa, 74-75; asst prof math, Belfer Grad Sch Sci, Yeshiva Univ, 75-78. *Concurrent Pos:* NSF grant, 72-78. *Res:* Queuing theory; traffic engineering. *Mailing Add:* 521 Marl Rd Colts Neck NJ 07722

SHULMAN, HERMAN L, CHEMICAL ENGINEERING, EDUCATIONAL ADMINISTRATION. *Current Pos:* from asst prof to prof, Clarkson Univ, 48-77, assoc dir, Div Res, 54-59, dir, 59-77, chmn dept, 59-64, dean grad sch, 64-77, vpres, 68-77, dean sch eng, 68-85, provost, 77-85, exec vpres, 85-87, EMER PROF & PROVOST, CLARKSON UNIV, 88- *Personal Data:* b New York, NY, Feb 24, 22; m 42, Florence I; c Nancy L (Weigel) & Richard A. *Educ:* City Univ New York, BChE, 42; Univ Pa, MS, 48, PhD(chem eng), 50. *Hon Degrees:* DSc, Clarkson Univ, 87. *Prof Exp:* Chem engr, Gen Motors Corp, 42-43, Barrett Div, Allied Chem & Dye Corp, 43-46; res chem engr, Publicker Industs, Inc, 46-47. *Mem:* Am Soc Eng Educ; Am Chem Soc; fel Am Inst Chem Engrs; Nat Soc Prof Engrs; Sigma Xi. *Res:* Mass transfer absorption; packed columns; ion exchange; gas-bubble columns; organic processes; flowmeters. *Mailing Add:* 464 Palm Tree Dr Bradenton FL 34210

SHULMAN, IRA ANDREW, TRANSFUSION MEDICINE. *Current Pos:* BLOOD BANK DIR & ASSOC PROF TRANSFUSION MED, UNIV SOUTHERN CALIF MED CTR, 81-, CHIEF, DIV TRANSFUSION MED, IMMUNOL & INFECTIOUS DIS DIAG, 93- *Personal Data:* b Los Angeles, Calif, Feb 26, 49; m 72; c 2. *Educ:* Univ Calif, Los Angeles, BA, 71; Univ Southern Calif, MD, 75. *Concurrent Pos:* Co-chmn, teleconf planning group, Am Soc Clin Pathol, 87-, coun transfusion med, 86-; pres, Coun Blood Bank dir, 85-; bd dir, Calif Blood Bank Soc, 88-, chmn sci prog comt, 85-88; mem, Am Bd Pathol Blood Bank Test Comt. *Mem:* Am Assoc Blook Banks; Am Soc Clin Pathol; Col Am Pathol. *Res:* Investigating the clinical significance of red blood cell alloantibodies and auto antibodies. *Mailing Add:* 1200 N State St PO Box 778 Los Angeles CA 90033

SHULMAN, JONES A(LVIN), INTERNAL MEDICINE. *Current Pos:* from asst prof to assoc prof infectious dis, Emory Univ, 70-74, coordr clin curric, 70-76, dir Div Infectious Dis, 72-84, assoc dean clin educ, 76-86, PROF MED & PREV MED & COMMUNITY HEALTH, EMORY UNIV, 74- *Personal Data:* b Baltimore, Md, Sept 5, 36; m 58; c 2. *Educ:* Univ Md, MD, 60; Am Bd Internal Med, dipl, 68. *Prof Exp:* Intern internal med, Univ Md Hosp, Baltimore, 60-61; asst resident med, Univ Wash, 61-62, R G Petersdorf fel infectious dis & med, 62-64, instr & chief resident med, Univ Wash Hosp, 66-67. *Concurrent Pos:* Chief med, Crawford Long Hosp, Emory Univ. *Mem:* Infectious Dis Soc Am. *Res:* Epidemiology of hospital infections; antibiotics, clinical pharmacology and efficacy studies. *Mailing Add:* 1440 Clifton Rd Emory Univ Rm 309 Atlanta GA 30322

SHULMAN, LAWRENCE EDWARD, INTERNAL MEDICINE, RHEUMATOLOGY. *Current Pos:* dir, Connective Tissue Div, Dept Med, 54-75, from instr to assoc prof, 53-63, ASSOC PROF MED, SCH MED, JOHNS HOPKINS UNIV, 63-; EMER DIR, NAT INST ARTHRITIS & MUSCULOSKELETAL & SKIN DIS, 94- *Personal Data:* b Boston, Mass, July 25, 19; m 59, Reni Trudinger; c Kathryn & Barbara. *Educ:* Harvard Univ, AB, 41; Yale Univ, PhD(pub health), 45, MD, 49. *Honors & Awards:* Heberden Medal Res, 76; Superior Serv Award, Pub Health Serv, 85; Gold Medal, Am Col Rheumatology, 95; Award of Merit, NASA, 96. *Prof Exp:* Res assoc, John B Pierce Found, Conn, 42-45; intern med, Johns Hopkins Hosp, 49-50, asst resident, 52-53, physician, 53. *Concurrent Pos:* Fel, Sch Med, Johns Hopkins Univ, 50-52; sr investr, Arthritis & Rheumatism Found, 57-62; dir, Div Arthritis, Musculoskeletal & Skin Dis, Nat Inst Arthritis, Diabetes & Digestive & Kidney Dis, 76-86, dir, Nat Inst Arthritis & Musculoskeletal & Skin Dis, 86-94. *Mem:* AAAS; Am Rheumatism Asn (pres, 74-75); Am Fedn Clin Res; PanAm League Against Rheumatism (pres, 82-86); Am Soc Bone & Mineral Res; Soc Invest Dermat; master Am Col Physicians. *Res:* Connective tissue disorders, including rheumatic diseases, especially collagen disorders; immunologic and epidemiologic studies; osteoporosis; discoverer; eosinophilic facilities. *Mailing Add:* NIH Bldg 31 Rm 4C-32 Bethesda MD 20892-2350

SHULMAN, MORTON, ANESTHESIOLOGY. *Current Pos:* Asst, Univ Ill, 59-61, res fel, 61-62, from instr to asst prof, 63-70, clin prof anesthesiol, 81, ASSOC PROF ANESTHESIOL, UNIV ILL COL MED, 70- *Personal Data:* b Chicago, Ill, July 7, 33; m 55, Ina Rubin; c David, Jay & Nancy. *Educ:* Univ Ill, BS, 55, MD, 58. *Concurrent Pos:* Attend anesthesiologist, Ill Masonic Med Ctr, 66-89, Shriners Hosp Crippled Children, Chicago, 78; consult, Col Vet Med, Univ Ill, 68-70; vis prof, Univ Louisville, 69, Med Col Wis, 70, Mayo Clin, 78 & Brigham Women's Hosp, Harvard Univ, 81; sr attend anesthesiologist, Rush Presby St Lukes Med Ctr, Chicago, Ill, 89; prof anesthesiol, Rush Med Col, 89. *Mem:* Am Soc Anesthesiol; Int Anesthesia Res Soc; Am Soc Regional Anesthesia; Am Acad Pain Med. *Res:* Local anesthetics and analgesics; pain control. *Mailing Add:* 1115 Thorn Tree Lane Highland Park IL 60035

SHULMAN, N RAPHAEL, clinical hematology; deceased, see previous edition for last biography

SHULMAN, ROBERT GERSON, CHEMICAL PHYSICS. *Current Pos:* STERLING PROF, DEPT MOLECULAR BIOPHYS & BIOCHEM & PROF CHEM, YALE UNIV, 79- *Personal Data:* b New York, NY, Mar 3, 24; m 85; c 3. *Educ:* Columbia Univ, AB, 43, AM, 47, PhD(chem), 49. *Honors & Awards:* Rask Oersted lectr, Copenhagen Univ, 59; Appleton lectr, Brown Univ, 65; Reilly lectr, Univ Notre Dame, 69. *Prof Exp:* AEC fel, Calif Inst Technol, 49-50; head semiconductor res, Hughes Aircraft Co, 50-53; mem tech staff, Bell Labs, Inc, 53-79. *Concurrent Pos:* Guggenheim fel, Lab Molecular Biol, Med Res Coun Eng, 61; vis prof, Ecole Normale Superieur Univ, Paris, 62; vis lectr, Princeton Univ, 71-72. *Mem:* Nat Acad Sci; Inst Med-Nat Acad Sci; Biophys Soc. *Res:* Microwave spectroscopy; semi-conductors; nuclear magnetic resonance; molecular orbital theory of transition metal complexes; radiation damage to DNA; metalloenzymes; phage genetics; paramagnetic metal ion complexes of nucleic acids; high resolution nuclear magnetic resonance of hemoglobin and tRNA NMR of metabolism in vivo. *Mailing Add:* Yale Univ Dept Molec Biophys & Biochem PO Box 3333 New Haven CT 06510. *Fax:* 203-785-6643

SHULMAN, ROBERT JAY, GASTROENTEROLOGY, PEDIATRICS. *Current Pos:* pediat fel, Baylor Col Med, 79-81, instr gastroenterol & nutrit, 81-82, asst prof, 82-90, ASSOC PROF GASTRONTEROL & NUTRIT, BAYLOR COL MED, 90- *Personal Data:* b Newark, NJ, Jan 6, 50. *Educ:* Emory Univ, BA, 72; Chicago Med Sch, MD, 76. *Prof Exp:* Pediat residency, Univ Mich, 76-79. *Concurrent Pos:* Dir nutrit support team, Tex Childrens Hosp, 82- *Mem:* Soc Pediat Res; Am Gastroent; Am Acad Pediats; Am Soc Parenteral & Enteral Nutrit; NAm Soc Pediat. *Res:* Growth and repair of the small intestine; factors involved in normal growth of the intestine; repair of the damaged or surgically shortened intestine and the effects of these on carbohydrate digestion and absorption. *Mailing Add:* Dept Pediat Baylor Col Med One Baylor Plaza Houston TX 77030. *Fax:* 713-798-7171

SHULMAN, SETH DAVID, X-RAY ASTRONOMY. *Current Pos:* PRES, BIOSCAN, INC, 80- *Personal Data:* b Lynn, Mass, Mar 11, 43; m 69; c 3. *Educ:* Harvard Univ, BA, 63; Columbia Univ, PhD(physics), 70. *Prof Exp:* Res physician, E O Hulburt Ctr Space Res, 70-81, consult x-ray astron, Naval Res Lab, 81-95. *Mem:* Am Astron Soc; Am Phys Soc; Am Chem Soc. *Res:* X-ray astronomy and studies of the interstellar medium; nuclear radiation detectors. *Mailing Add:* 5000 V St NW Washington DC 20007-1550

SHULMAN, SIDNEY, IMMUNOLOGY. *Current Pos:* asst chem, Univ Wis, 46-48, proj assoc, 49-52, assoc immunochem, Sch Med, State Univ NY, Buffalo, 52-54, asst prof, 54-58, assoc prof immunochem & biophys, 58-65, prof immunochem, 65-68, chmn dept microbiol, 68-69, PROF MICROBIOL, NEW YORK MED COL, 68-, DIR SPERM ANTIBODY LAB, 70-, RES PROF UROL, 73- *Personal Data:* b Baltimore, Md, Aug 22, 23; m 45, 68; c 6. *Educ:* George Washington Univ, BS, 44; Univ Wis, PhD(chem), 49. *Prof Exp:* Assoc, Allegany Ballistics Lab, US Army Ballistics Missile Agency, Md, 44-46. *Concurrent Pos:* Lederle med fac fel, 54-57; USPHS sr res fel, 58-62; NIH res career award, 63-68; consult immunol, Buffalo Vet Admin Hosp, 64-; Fulbright travel award, 65; Commonwealth Fund travel award, 65; vpres, Int Coord Comt Immunol Reproduction, 67-; assoc ed, Cryobiol, 69-; chmn workshop on immunoreproduction, 1st Int Cong Immunol, 71; assoc ed, Contraception, 73-; assoc ed, Int J Fertil; mem WHO task force immunol methods fertil regulation, 75-; res prof obstet & gynec, New York Col Med, 74- *Mem:* Int Soc Immunol Reproduction (vpres, 75); Am Chem Soc; assoc fel Am Col Obstet & Gynec; Am Soc Microbiol; Am Acad Allergy. *Res:* Tissue proteins; autoantibodies; cryobiology; urogenital tract antigens and enzymes; immunology of reproduction and infertility. *Mailing Add:* 134 Fort Lee Rd Leonia NJ 07605

SHULMAN, SOL, ORGANIC CHEMISTRY, POLYMER CHEMISTRY. *Current Pos:* RETIRED. *Personal Data:* b Smorgon, White Russia, Nov 6, 29; US citizen; m 53; c 4. *Educ:* Univ Wash, BS, 52; Univ Wis, MS, 54; NDak State Univ, PhD(chem), 63. *Prof Exp:* Teaching asst chem, Univ Wis, 53-54; res chemist, Archer-Daniels-Midland Co, Minn, 54-59; from instr to asst prof, NDak State Univ, 59-65; from assoc prof to prof, Moorhead State Col, 65-69, chmn dept, 66-69; head dept, Ill State Univ, 69-75, prof, 69-92. *Concurrent Pos:* Sr res assoc, Rice Univ, 75. *Mem:* Fel AAAS; Am Chem Soc; fel Am Inst Chemists. *Res:* Chemistry of lipids; derivatives of fats and oils, polyurethanes and synthesis. *Mailing Add:* 111 Eastview Dr Normal IL 61761

SHULMAN, STANFORD TAYLOR, PEDIATRICS, INFECTIOUS DISEASES. *Current Pos:* actg chmn, Dept Pediat, 81-83, PROF PEDIAT, MED SCH, NORTHWESTERN UNIV, 79-, ASSOC DEAN ACAD AFFAIRS, 91-, CHIEF INFECTIOUS DIS, CHILDRENS MEM HOSP, 79- *Personal Data:* b Kalamazoo, Mich, May 13, 42; m 64, Claire Zaner; c Deborah, Elizabeth & Edward. *Educ:* Univ Cincinnati, BS, 63; Univ Chicago, MD, 67. *Prof Exp:* Intern-resident pediat, Univ Chicago, 67-69, chief resident, 69-70; fel, Univ Fla, 70-73, asst prof, 73-75, assoc prof pediat infant dis & immunol, 75-79; fel immunol, Inst Child Health, London, Eng, 70; chief infectious dis, Children's Mem Hosp, Chicago, 79-; chmn, comt rheumatic fever & infective endocarditis, Am Heart Asn, 81-89; vis prof, Univ Minn, Yale Univ; chair, sect infectious dis, Am Acad Pediat, 95-; coun, Pediat Infectious Dis Soc, 95- *Mem:* Soc Pediat Res; Am Acad Pediat; Infectious Dis Soc Am; Am Asn Immunol; AAAS; Am Pediat Soc. *Res:* Pathogenesis of rheumatic fever; Kawasaki disease: etiology, pathogenesis and therapy; clinical immunology; streptococcal infections. *Mailing Add:* 1222 Asbury Ave Evanston IL 60202. *Fax:* 773-880-8226; *E-Mail:* sshulman@nwu.edu

SHULMAN, YECHIEL, ENGINEERING, MANAGEMENT. *Current Pos:* adj prof mech eng, 86-89, H W SWEATT CHAIR & DIR, CTR DEVELOP TECHNOL LEADERSHIP, UNIV MINN, 90-, PROF MECH ENG, 90- *Personal Data:* b Tel Aviv, Israel, Jan 28, 30; nat US; m 50, Ruth Danzig; c 3. *Educ:* Mass Inst Technol, SB(aeronaut eng), SB(bus & eng admin) & SM, 54, ScD(aeronaut & astronaut eng), 59; Univ Chicago, MBA, 73. *Prof Exp:* Res engr, Aeroelastic & Struct Res Lab, Mass Inst Technol, 54-56, asst, 57-59; asst prof mech eng, Tech Inst, Northwestern Univ, 59-62, assoc prof mech eng & astronaut, 62-67; res consult, Anocut Eng Co, 67-68, vpres advan eng, 69-72, dir electronic systs group, 70-72; vpres corp planning, Alden Press, Inc, John Blair & Co, 72-84; pres, MMT Environ, Inc, 84-86. *Concurrent Pos:* Consult, Am Mach & Foundry Co, 60-62 & Res Div, Gen Am Transp Corp, 62-67; mem res & develop comt, Nat Mach Tool Builders Asn, 68-72. *Mem:* Am Inst Aeronaut & Astronaut; Soc Mfg Engrs; Am Soc Eng Educ; Am Soc Mech Engrs; Graphic Commun Asn. *Res:* Electrochemical machining; digital control systems for process machinery; laser metrology, aerothermoelasticity; shell structures; astrodynamics and optimization; structural dynamics; flight mechanics; management of technology. *Mailing Add:* 1201 Yale Pl No 1504 Minneapolis MN 55403-1959. *Fax:* 612-624-7510; *E-Mail:* shulman@mailbox.cdtl.umn.edu

SHULT, ERNEST E, ALGEBRA, COMBINATORICS. *Current Pos:* DISTINGUISHED REGENTS PROF MATH, KANS STATE UNIV, 74- *Personal Data:* b Tonica, Ill, Sept 29, 33; m 57; c 3. *Educ:* Southern Ill Univ, BA, 58, MA, 60; Univ Ill, PhD(math), 64. *Honors & Awards:* Leo Kaplan Res Prize, Sigma Xi, 70. *Prof Exp:* Res assoc genetics yeast, Biol Res Lab, Southern Ill Univ, 54-57, chief theoretician, 58-61, instr math, 63-64, asst prof, 64-65; NSF fel, Univ Chicago, 65-66; from assoc prof to prof math, Southern Ill Univ, 66-70; prof, Univ Fla, 70-74. *Concurrent Pos:* Mem, Inst Advan Study, 68-69; Alexander von Humboldt Sr Am Scientist award. *Mem:* Sigma Xi; Am Math Soc. *Res:* Abstract algebra; finite geometry; microbial genetics, especially yeast genetics; theory of finite groups combinatorics. *Mailing Add:* Dept Math Kans State Univ Manhattan KS 66502-2602

SHULTIS, J KENNETH, RADIATION SHIELDING & PROTECTION, RADIATION TRANSPORT. *Current Pos:* PROF NUCLEAR ENG, KANS STATE UNIV, 69- *Personal Data:* b Toronto, Ont, Aug 22, 41; m 67; c 2. *Educ:* Univ Toronto, BASc, 64; Univ Mich, MSc, 65, PhD(nuclear sci & eng), 68. *Honors & Awards:* Western Elec Award, Am Soc Eng Educ, 79 & Glenn Murphy Award, 81. *Concurrent Pos:* Sci officer, Univ Groningen, Neth, 68-69; Black & Veatch distinguished prof, Kans State Univ, 78; von Humboldt res fel, Univ Karlsruhe, 80; guest prof, Univ Karlsruhe, Ger, 80-81; consult, many elec utilities & eng firms; prin investr, over 30 fed & state grants; mem, Exec Comt, RP&S Div, Am Nuclear Soc, 86-90, 95-97. *Mem:* Am Soc Eng Educ; Am Nuclear Soc. *Res:* Numerical and computer analyses; neutron transport theory; radiative transfer; combustion modeling; remote sensing; radiation shielding; reactor physics; author of over 100 publications. *Mailing Add:* Dept Mech & Nuclear Eng Ward Hall Kans State Univ Manhattan KS 66506. *E-Mail:* jks@ksu.edu

SHULTS, WILBUR DOTRY, II, ANALYTICAL CHEMISTRY. *Current Pos:* From jr chemist to assoc chemist, 51-55, from chemist to group leader, 57-67, asst div dir, 67-71, assoc div dir, 71-76, DIV DIR ANAL CHEM, OAK RIDGE NAT LAB, 76- *Personal Data:* b Atlanta, Ga, Nov 24, 29; m 50; c 3. *Educ:* Emory Univ, AB, 50, MS, 51; Ind Univ, PhD(chem), 66. *Mem:* Am Chem Soc; AAAS; Sigma Xi. *Res:* Instrumental analysis. *Mailing Add:* 1011 W Outer Dr Oak Ridge TN 37830

SHULTZ, ALLAN R, PHYSICAL CHEMISTRY, POLYMER PHYSICS. *Current Pos:* ADJ PROF, VA POLYTECH INST & STATE UNIV, BLACKSBURG, VA, 91- *Personal Data:* b Huntington, Ind, Jan 8, 26; m 49, Wylan Becker; c Londa, Kent, Erik & Ellen. *Educ:* Manchester Col, AB, 48; Cornell Univ, PhD(chem), 53. *Prof Exp:* Res assoc chem, Mass Inst Technol, 52-54; res chemist, Minn Mining & Mfg Co, 54-63; res chemist, Gen Elec Res & Develop Ctr Schenectady, 63-91. *Mem:* AAAS; Am Chem Soc; NY Acad Sci. *Res:* Polymer chemistry and physics; radiation chemistry of polymers; thermodynamics; polymer structure/property relationships. *Mailing Add:* 5020 Preston Forest Dr Blacksburg VA 24060. *E-Mail:* ashultz@vt.edu

SHULTZ, CHARLES H, VOLCANIC GEOLOGY, SCIENCE EDITING. *Current Pos:* assoc prof, 70-72, PROF GEOL, SLIPPERY ROCK UNIV, 72- *Personal Data:* b Lancaster, Pa, May 29, 36. *Educ:* Franklin & Marshall Col, BS, 58; Ohio State Univ, PhD(petrol), 62. *Prof Exp:* Geologist, Humble Oil & Refinery Co, 62-64; asst prof geol, Ohio State Univ, 64-70. *Concurrent Pos:* Ed, Geol Pa, 83- *Mem:* Fel Geol Soc Am; Am Geophys Union; AAAS; Int Asn Volcanic & Chem Earth Interiors; Sigma Xi. *Res:* Tertiary volcanic petrology; tectonics and metamorphism of the Appalachian Mountains; volcanology of Antarctica. *Mailing Add:* Dept Geol Slippery Rock Univ Slippery Rock PA 16057

SHULTZ, CLIFFORD GLEN, SCIENCE ADMINISTRATION, ANALYTICAL CHEMISTRY. *Current Pos:* PRES, NAT LABS, INC, 69- *Personal Data:* b Wichita, Kans, Sept 9, 24; m 50; c 3. *Educ:* McPherson Col, AB, 49; Univ NMex, PhD(chem), 57. *Prof Exp:* Group leader, anal res, Mich Chem Corp, 57-60; assoc prof chem, Evansville Col, Ind, 60-66. *Concurrent Pos:* Mem coun, Am Chem Soc, 63-64. *Mem:* Am Chem Soc; Am Inst Chemists; Nat Soc Prof Engrs; Water Pollution Control Fedn; Air & Waste Mgt Asn. *Res:* Destruction of hazardous chemical and biological wastes by thermal reduction with molten aluminum; recovery of valuable materials from waste products; extraction of hazardous materials from contaminated soils and sludge; five US patents. *Mailing Add:* 3210 Claremont Ave River City One Evansville IN 47712-4930

SHULTZ, DAVID A, ORGANIC CHEMISTRY. *Current Pos:* ASST PROF, DEPT CHEM, NC STATE UNIV, 92- *Educ:* Shippensburg Univ, BA, 84; Univ Tex, PhD(org chem), 89. *Prof Exp:* Postdoctoral res fel, Calif Inst Technol, 89-92. *Concurrent Pos:* NSF career award, 95- *Res:* High-spin organic molecules and materials, including charge transfer salts, molecular crystals, liquid crystals polymers, magnetoptic switches and paramagnetic-liguand transition metal complexes; mechanisms of spin-spin communication in organic-based magnetic materials; organic photochemistry. *Mailing Add:* Dept Chem NC State Univ Raleigh NC 27695-8204

SHULTZ, FRED TOWNSEND, GENETICS. *Current Pos:* Asst poultry husb, 49-52, jr res geneticist, 52-53, RES ASSOC POULTRY HUSB, UNIV CALIF, 53; DIR, BIOL FRONTIERS INST, 60- *Personal Data:* b Grinnell, Iowa, Mar 5, 23; m 61, Carolyn Covell; c Trina M, Rebecca L, Daniel K & Brian G. *Educ:* Stanford Univ, AB, 47; Univ Calif, Berkeley, PhD(genetics), 52. *Honors & Awards:* Res Prize, Am Poultry Sci Asn, 53. *Concurrent Pos:* Pres, Animal Breeding Consult, 52- *Mem:* Am Poultry Sci Asn; World Aquacult Soc; World Poultry Sci Asn. *Res:* Aquaculture; animal breeding; marine biology. *Mailing Add:* PO Box 313 Sonoma CA 95476

SHULTZ, LEILA MCREYNOLDS, PLANT SYSTEMATICS. *Current Pos:* Res taxonomist, 94-96, RES ASSOC PROF, DEPT FOREST RESOURCES, HARVARD UNIV, 92- *Personal Data:* b Bartlesville, Okla, April 20, 46; c 1. *Educ:* Univ Tulsa, BS, 69; Univ Colo, MA, 75; Claremont Grad Sch, PhD(bot), 83. *Prof Exp:* Cur, Intermountain Herbarium, Utah State Univ, 78-92, adj asst prof, Biol Dept, 86-92. *Concurrent Pos:* Ed, Flora NAm Proj, 86-; vis scholar, Harvard Univ, 88-89; vis researcher, Univ Calif, Los Angeles, 88-89; coun mem, Am Soc Plant Taxonomist; syst rep, Bot Soc. *Mem:* Am Soc Plant Taxonomist; Bot Soc Am; Int Asn Plant Taxonomists. *Res:* Systematics of Artemisia; ecology and evolutionary specializations in leaf anatomy. *Mailing Add:* Harvard Univ Herbania 22 Divinity Ave Cambridge MA 02138. *E-Mail:* shultz@oeb.harvard.edu

SHULTZ, LEONARD DONALD, CANCER, AIDS. *Current Pos:* trainee, 72-74, res assoc cancer, 74-76, assoc staff scientist, 76-79, STAFF SCIENTIST, JACKSON LAB, 80- *Personal Data:* b Boston, Mass, Apr 16, 45; m 69, Kathyn Jacobs; c David & Sarah. *Educ:* Northeastern Univ, BA, 67; Univ Mass, PhD(med microbiol), 72. *Prof Exp:* Res asst cancer, Sch Med, Tufts Univ, 67-68; teaching asst microbiol, Univ Mass, 68-70, lectr immunol, 70-71. *Concurrent Pos:* Prin investr grants, Nat Cancer Inst & Nat Inst Allergy & Infectious Dis. *Mem:* Am Soc Microbiol; Am Asn Immunologists. *Res:* Lymphoid cell differentiation and immunoregulatory mechanisms in tumorigenesis; immuno-deficiency diseases; autoimmunity; AIDS. *Mailing Add:* Jackson Lab Bar Harbor ME 04609

SHULTZ, TERRY D, NUTRITION ASSESSMENT, VITAMIN B-SIX METABOLISM. *Current Pos:* ASST PROF BIOCHEM & NUTRIT, SCH MED, LOMA LINDA UNIV, 82- *Personal Data:* b Caldwell, Idaho, July 26, 47. *Educ:* Ore State Univ, PhD(human nutrit biochem), 80. *Mem:* Am Inst Nutrit; Endocrine Soc; Sigma Xi; Am Soc Bone & Mineral Res. *Mailing Add:* Dept Food Sci & Human Nutrit Wash State Univ Pullman WA 99164-6376. *Fax:* 509-335-4815

SHULTZ, WALTER, BIOPHARMACEUTICS. *Current Pos:* Develop chemist, 60-68, group leader pharmaceut prod develop, 68-78, SR RES SCIENTIST, LEDERLE LABS DIV, AM CYANAMID CO, 78- *Personal Data:* b Philadelphia, Pa, Nov 11, 31; m 58; c 3. *Educ:* Temple Univ, BS, 53; Philadelphia Col Pharm, MS, 54, PhD(pharmaceut chem), 61. *Mem:* AAAS; Am Chem Soc; Am Pharmaceut Asn; Acad Pharmaceut Sci. *Res:* Physical pharmacy; synthesis of steroid derivatives. *Mailing Add:* 3 Merrick Dr Spring Valley NY 10977

SHUM, ANNIE WAICHING, COMPUTER SCIENCE, MATHEMATICAL MODELING. *Current Pos:* ASST PROF COMPUT SCI, DIV APPL SCI, HARVARD UNIV, 78- *Personal Data:* b US. *Educ:* Univ Calif, Berkeley, BA, 72; Harvard Univ, MSc, 73, PhD(comput sci), 76. *Prof Exp:* Res staff comput sci, IBM Corp, 77-78. *Concurrent Pos:* Consult, BGS Systs Inc, 78-; res grant div appl sci, Harvard Univ, 78-79. *Mem:* Asn Comput Mach; Sigma Xi; Inst Elec & Electronics Engrs; Math Soc. *Res:* Queueing theory; mathematical models; operating system design and performance evaluation of computer systems; efficient computational algorithms of combinatoric problems. *Mailing Add:* c/o General Electric Co PO Box 5043 Westborough MA 01581-5043

SHUM, ARCHIE CHUE, CLINICAL MICROBIOLOGY, BIOCHEMISTRY. *Current Pos:* intern, clin labs, 76-77, MICROBIOLOGIST, UNIV CALIF, LOS ANGELES, 88- *Personal Data:* b Hong Kong, Aug 13, 42; US citizen; m 73. *Educ:* Idaho State Univ, BS, 68, MS, 70; Univ Iowa, PhD(microbiol), 73. *Prof Exp:* Asst prof microbiol, Calif State Univ, Los Angeles, 73-76; clin microbiologist, St John's Hosp, 77-89. *Concurrent Pos:* Consult, Santa Paula Hosp, Santa Paula, Calif & Pleasant Valley Hosp, Camarillo, Calif, 77. *Mem:* Am Soc Microbiol; AAAS; Sigma Xi. *Res:* Antimicrobial susceptibility testing on anaerobic bacteria of clinical significance; bacteriological studies on bowhead whales; cellular immunology. *Mailing Add:* 1420 N M St Oxnard CA 93030-3358

SHUM, HENRY, OPERATIONS RESEARCH & THEORY. *Current Pos:* PRES, SHUM PARTNERS, INC, 95- *Educ:* Cornell Univ, PhD(opers res), 89. *Prof Exp:* Sr res assoc, Int Paper, 89-95. *Concurrent Pos:* Adj prof, Columbia Univ, NY, 95- *Res:* Large scale discrete optimization. *Mailing Add:* 10 Summerland Lane Briarcliff Manor NY 10510

SHUMACKER, HARRIS B, JR, SURGERY. *Current Pos:* prof & sr adv, Dept Surg, 81-88, DISTINGUISHED PROF SURG, UNIFORMED SERVS UNIV HEALTH SCI, 88- *Personal Data:* b Laurel, Miss, May 20, 08; m 33; c 2. *Educ:* Univ Tenn, Chattanooga, BS, 27; Vanderbilt Univ, MA, 28; Johns Hopkins Univ, MD, 32; Am Bd Surg, dipl, 46; Am Bd Thoracic Surg, dipl, 67. *Hon Degrees:* DSc, Ind Univ, 85. *Honors & Awards:* Roswell Park Medal, 68; Curtis Medal, 70; Distinguished Serv Medal, Am Col Surgeons, 68 & Uniformed Serv Univ, Dept of Defense. *Prof Exp:* Instr surg, Yale Univ, Sch Med, 37-38, assoc prof, 46-48; instr, Johns Hopkins Univ, 38-41, asst prof, 41-46; prof & chmn dept, 48-70, emer distinguished prof surg, Ind Univ, 78- *Concurrent Pos:* Consult, Surgeon Gen, US Army, 50-55, mem adv comt, Environ Med, 57-61; surg study sect, US Pub Health Dept, 50-56 & Therapeut Eval Comt, 69-73; vpres, Int Soc Surg, 57-59, pres, NAm Chap, 56-58; vchmn, Am Bd Surg, 59-60; chmn, surg sect, AMA, 60-61; vpres, Pan-Pac Surg Asn, 69-72; vpres, Int Surg Group, 74-75, pres, 75-76; mem adv comt, Off Naval Res, 48-53; hon fel, Societa Italiana di Chirwegia, Polish Surg Soc & Royal Col Surgeons, Eng. *Mem:* Fel Am Col Surgeons; Am Surg Asn (1st vpres, 60-61, secy, 64-68); Soc Clin Surg (pres, 60-62); Soc Univ Surg (pres, 50-51); Soc Vascular Surg (treas, 47-53, pres, 58-59); Am Heart Asn; Coun Cardiovasc Asn (vpres). *Mailing Add:* 1000 Lowry St Apt 7D Delray Beach FL 33483

SHUMAKER, JOHN BENJAMIN, JR, OPTICAL PHYSICS. *Current Pos:* RETIRED. *Personal Data:* b Ames, Iowa, Jan 17, 26; m 54; c 1. *Educ:* Iowa State Col, BS, 49; Yale Univ, PhD(chem), 52. *Prof Exp:* Analyst opers res, Opers Eval Group, Mass Inst Technol, 52-55; res physicist, Nat Bur Stand, 55-86. *Mem:* Optical Soc Am. *Res:* Plasma physics; plasma spectroscopy; spectral radiometry; physical optics. *Mailing Add:* 905 Montrose Rd Rockville MD 20852-4203

SHUMAKER, ROBERT C, BASIN ANALYSIS, REMOTE SENSING. *Current Pos:* PROF GEOL, IV VA UNIV, 72- *Personal Data:* b Fort Wayne, In, June 06, 31; m 53; c 3. *Educ:* Brown Univ, AB, 53; Cornell Univ, MS, 57 & PhD(geol), 60. *Prof Exp:* Staff mem geol, Exxon, 60-72. *Concurrent Pos:* Dir, Appalachian Petrol Geol Symp, 72- & Appalachian Basin Indust Assoc, 81-; consult major grants, DOE & Gas Res Inst. *Mem:* Fel Geol Soc Am; Sigma Xi; Am Asn Petrol Geologist. *Res:* Study of structural styles in geology; their expression and distribution in paleozoic sedimentary basins; fracture permeability in tight reservoirs such as the Devonian shale Appalachian basin. *Mailing Add:* Dept Geol & Geog WVa Univ Whitehall Morgantown WV 26506-0001

SHUMAN, BERTRAM MARVIN, GEOPHYSICS, SPACE PHYSICS. *Current Pos:* PROG MGR, MEGAPULSE, INC, 92- *Personal Data:* b Boston, Mass, May 2, 31; m 59, Henriette Koning; c Anne & Kenneth R. *Educ:* Harvard Univ, AB, 52; Boston Univ, AM, 68. *Prof Exp:* Res physicist geophys, Air Force Geophys Lab, 53-87; mem tech staff, W J Schafer Assoc, 87-88. *Mem:* Am Geophys Union. *Res:* Magnetic field measurements in space using rocket and satellite-borne sensors; active control of spacecraft charging. *Mailing Add:* 78 Hill St Lexington MA 02173

SHUMAN, CHARLES ROSS, INTERNAL MEDICINE. *Current Pos:* From instr to prof med, 49-72, clin prof, 63-66, EMER PROF MED, SCH MED, TEMPLE UNIV, 72- *Personal Data:* b Harrisburg, Pa, Sept 18, 18; m 44; c 2. *Educ:* Gettysburg Col, AB, 40; Temple Univ, MD, 43, MS, 49. *Hon Degrees:* DSc, Gettysburg Col, 73. *Concurrent Pos:* Consult, Vet Admin Hosp & Philadelphia Gen Hosp, 57-68; mem bd trustees, Am Diabetes Asn, 76-; pres, Philadelphia Co Med Soc, 77- *Mem:* Am Col Physicians; Am Diabetes Asn; Am Fedn Clin Res; AMA; Sigma Xi. *Res:* Metabolism of carbohydrate, fat and protein; oral antiabetic agents; nutrition; disease. *Mailing Add:* 1111 Delene Rd Jenkintown PA 19046

SHUMAN, CORNWELL A, PHYSICAL CHEMISTRY, CRYSTALLIZATION. *Current Pos:* RETIRED. *Personal Data:* b Charlotte, NC, 1908. *Educ:* Cornell Univ, BS, 30, PhD(chem), 35. *Prof Exp:* Assoc prof food chem, Purdue Univ, 54-57; owner & operator food anal, Shuman Chem Lab, 57-86. *Mem:* Am Chem Soc; fel Am Inst Chemists; Inst Food Technol. *Mailing Add:* 1715 Northwestern Ave West Lafayette IN 47906-2270

SHUMAN, LARRY MYERS, SOIL CHEMISTRY, SOIL FERTILITY & PLANT NUTRITION. *Current Pos:* From asst prof to assoc prof, 72-91, PROF AGRON, UNIV GA, 91- *Personal Data:* b Harrisburg, Pa, Apr 3, 44; m 70, Catherine Yost; c Rebecca & Karen. *Educ:* Pa State Univ, BS, 66, MS, 68, PhD(agron), 70. *Concurrent Pos:* Assoc ed, Soil Sci Soc Am J, 86-91; mem, Coun Agr Sci & Technol; chair, Div S-2, Soil Chem, Soil Sci Soc Am, 93-94. *Mem:* Am Soc Agron; fel Soil Sci Soc Am; Soc Environ Geochem & Health. *Res:* Influence of soil properties on the retention and release of microelements to plants; chemical forms of microelements in soil; chemistry of soil aluminum and manganese. *Mailing Add:* Ga Exp Sta Griffin GA 30223-1797. *Fax:* 770-229-3215; *E-Mail:* lshuman@gaes.griffin.peachnet.edu

SHUMAN, MARK S, ENVIRONMENTAL CHEMISTRY, ELECTROANALYTICAL CHEMISTRY. *Current Pos:* asst prof, 70-75, assoc prof, 75-80, PROF ENVIRON SCI & ENG, UNIV NC, CHAPEL HILL, 80- *Personal Data:* b Yakima, Wash, July 29, 36; m 63; c 3. *Educ:* Wash State Univ, BS, 59; Univ Wis, PhD(chem), 66. *Prof Exp:* Asst prof chem, Tex Christian Univ, 66-69 & Whitman Col, 69-70. *Mem:* Am Chem Soc. *Res:* Transport of trace inorganics in natural water systems; trace metal-organic associations in natural water; electroanalytical chemistry. *Mailing Add:* Environ Sci & Eng Univ NC Chapel Hill NC 27599-8140

SHUMATE, KENNETH MCCLELLAN, ORGANIC CHEMISTRY, SCIENCE EDUCATION. *Current Pos:* VCHMN ACAD AFFAIRS, ALAMO COMMUNITY COL DIST. *Personal Data:* b Houston, Tex, Nov 9, 36; m 66; c 2. *Educ:* Baylor Univ, BS, 58, MS, 63; Univ Tex, PhD(org chem), 66. *Prof Exp:* Res chemist, Petro-Tex Chem Corp, 66-67; from asst prof to assoc prof, San Antonio Col, 67-75, chmn dept, 73-86, prof chem, 75-, vpres acad affairs, 86- *Mem:* Am Chem Soc. *Res:* Thermal and photochemical reactions of conjugated medium ring dienes; low molecular weight polymers of butadiene. *Mailing Add:* Acad Affairs Alamo Community Col Dist 201 W Sheridan San Antonio TX 78204-1429

SHUMATE, PAUL WILLIAM, JR, FIBER OPTICS, LIGHTWAVE DEVICES. *Current Pos:* mem tech staff, Bell Labs, 69-75, supvr, 75-83, dist mgr, 83-86, div mgr, 86-91, EXEC DIR, BELL COMMUN RES, 91- *Personal Data:* b Philadelphia, Pa, July 15, 41; m 64, Randi Atkins; c Angela L. *Educ:* Col William & Mary, BS, 63; Univ Va, PhD(physics), 68. *Honors & Awards:* E H Armstrong Award, Inst Elec & Electronics Engrs, 93. *Prof Exp:* Asst prof physics, Univ Va, 68-69. *Concurrent Pos:* Ed-in-chief, Transactions on Magnetics, Inst Elec & Electronics Engrs, 74-79 & Photonics Technol Lett, 89-94; vpres publ, Lasers & Electro-Optics Soc, 94-96. *Mem:* Fel Inst Elec & Electronics Engrs; Sigma Xi; Optical Soc Am. *Res:* Researcher and lecturer in the fields of optical networks, devices and systems; current responsibilities include fiber-in-the-loop, powering, home networks and gateways, economic studies and fiber installation. *Mailing Add:* Bell Commun Res 445 South St Morristown NJ 07960-1910. *Fax:* 973-829-5886; *E-Mail:* pws@bellcore.com; p.shumate@ieee.org

SHUMATE, STARLING EVERETT, II, BIOCHEMICAL ENGINEERING. *Current Pos:* VPRES, RES & DEVELOP, ENGENICS, INC, 82- *Personal Data:* b Martinsville, Va, Aug 20, 47. *Educ:* Va Polytech Inst & State Univ, BS, 70; Univ Tenn, MS, 74, PhD(chem eng), 75. *Prof Exp:* Res engr bioeng, 74-76, leader bioeng res group, 76-81, mgr biotechnol & environ prof, Oak Ridge Nat Lab, 81-82. *Concurrent Pos:* Lectr, Dept Chem, Metall & Polymer Engr, Univ Tenn, 80- *Mem:* Am Inst Chem Engrs; Am Chem Soc; Sigma Xi. *Res:* Bioengineering; chemical engineering science, especially reaction kinetics and mass transfer; separation processes; chemical and biochemical reactor design. *Mailing Add:* 250 Lake Rd Basking Ridge NJ 07920-1098

SHUMRICK, DONALD A, OTORHINOLARYNGOLOGY. *Current Pos:* PROF OTOLARYNGOL & MAXILLOFACIAL SURG & PROF & CHMN, MED CTR, UNIV CINCINNATI, 66- *Personal Data:* b Newark, NJ, Mar 8, 25; c 9. *Educ:* Seton Hall Univ, BS, 49; Univ Minn, Minneapolis, MS, 52, MD, 57; Am Bd Otolaryngol, dipl, 64. *Prof Exp:* Teaching asst physiol, Univ Minn, Minneapolis, 52-57; intern surg, San Francisco City & Co Hosp, 57-58, resident gen surg, 58-59; resident, instr otolaryngol & NIH fel, Washington Univ, 59-63; asst prof, Univ Iowa, 63-66. *Concurrent Pos:* Consult, Study Sect, NIH, 70- *Mem:* Am Acad Otolaryngal-Head & Neck Surg; Am Acad Facial Plastic & Reconstructive Surg; Am Soc Head & Neck Surgeons; Am Acad Ophthal & Otolaryngol; Pan Am Asn Oto-Rhino-Laryngol & Broncho-Esophagol; Soc Univ Otolaryngol (secy, 70-); Am Col Surg. *Res:* Head and neck cancer; maxillofacial surgery. *Mailing Add:* Dept Otolaryngol Head & Neck Surg Univ Cincinnati Med Ctr 6507 Cincinnati OH 45267

SHUMWAY, CLARE NELSON, (JR), PEDIATRICS, HEMATOLOGY. *Current Pos:* RETIRED. *Personal Data:* b Painted Post, NY, Oct 28, 25; m 55; c 2. *Educ:* Univ Buffalo, MD, 48; Am Bd Pediat, dipl, 53, cert pediat hemat-oncol, 74. *Prof Exp:* Intern med, Buffalo Gen Hosp, 48-49; resident pediat, Buffalo Children's Hosp, 49-52; instr, Sch Med & Dent, Univ Rochester, 52-57; assoc prof, Sch Med, Univ Buffalo, 57-64; prof pediat, Med Col Va, 64-72; dir pediat, Harrisburg Polyclin Hosp, 72-77; dir health serv, Gettysburg Col, 77-91. *Concurrent Pos:* Am Cancer Soc fel, Univ Rochester, 52-53, USPHS res fel, 55-57; dir hemat, Buffalo Children's Hosp, 57-64; spec res fel, Univ Wash, 69-70. *Mem:* AAAS; Am Acad Pediat; Am Pediat Soc; NY Acad Sci; Am Soc Hemat. *Res:* The role of bacterial hemolysin in the pathogenesis of pneumococcal infections. *Mailing Add:* 20 Byers Rd Dillsburg PA 17019-9638

SHUMWAY, LEWIS KAY, PLANT GENETICS. *Current Pos:* RETIRED. *Personal Data:* b Salt Lake City, Utah, Dec 3, 34; m 58; c 7. *Educ:* Brigham Young Univ, BS, 60, MS, 62; Purdue Univ, PhD(plant genetics), 65. *Prof Exp:* Res botanist, Univ Calif, Davis, 65-66; asst res botanist, Univ Calif, Berkeley, 66-67; from asst prof to assoc prof genetics & bot, Wash State Univ, 67-77; dean, San Juan Campus, Col Eastern Utah, 77- *Mem:* AAAS. *Res:* Plant cell ultrastructure; chloroplast inheritance, development and ultrastructure; protoplasts. *Mailing Add:* Apple Lane 9-7 Blanding UT 84511. *Fax:* 435-678-2220; *E-Mail:* lkshumway@sisna.com

SHUMWAY, NORMAN EDWARD, CARDIOVASCULAR SURGERY. *Current Pos:* from asst prof to assoc prof, 59-65, PROF SURG, STANFORD UNIV HOSPS, 65-, HEAD, DIV CARDIOVASC SURG, SCH MED, 74-; FRANCES & CHARLES D FIELD PROF, STANFORD UNIV, 76- *Personal Data:* b Kalamazoo, Mich, 23. *Educ:* Vanderbilt Univ, MD, 49; Univ Minn, PhD(surg), 56; Am Bd Surg, dipl; Am Bd Thoracic Surg, dipl. *Prof Exp:* Intern, Univ Minn Hosps, 49-50, med fel surg, 50-51 & 53-54, Nat Heart Inst res fel, 54-56, Nat Heart Inst spec trainee, 56-57. *Concurrent Pos:* Mem surg staff, Stanford Univ Hosps, 58- *Mem:* AMA; Soc Univ Surgeons; Am Asn Thoracic Surg; Am Col Cardiol; Transplantation Soc; Soc Vascular Surg. *Res:* Cardiovascular and thoracic surgery. *Mailing Add:* Stanford Univ Med Ctr 300 Pasteur Dr Stanford CA 94305-5247. *Fax:* 650-725-3846

SHUMWAY, RICHARD PHIL, ANIMAL PHYSIOLOGY, ANIMAL HUSBANDRY. *Current Pos:* RETIRED. *Personal Data:* b Taylor, Ariz, Aug 21, 21; m 43; c 6. *Educ:* Utah State Univ, BS, 47, PhD, 59; Univ Minn, MS, 49. *Prof Exp:* Asst prof agr, Utah State Univ, 47-48; from asst prof to assoc prof, 49-63, prof animal sci, Brigham Young Univ, 63-87. *Concurrent Pos:* Chmn dept animal sci, Brigham Young Univ, 63-74. *Mem:* Am Soc Animal Sci. *Res:* Animal science and nutrition. *Mailing Add:* 890 S 725 W Orem UT 84058

SHUMWAY, SANDRA ELISABETH, SHELLFISH BIOLOGY. *Current Pos:* PROF, SOUTHAMPTON COL, 94- *Personal Data:* b Taunton, Mass, Mar 29, 52. *Educ:* Long Island Univ, BS, 74; Univ Col NWales, PhD(marine biol), 76. *Hon Degrees:* DSc, Univ Col NWales, 92. *Prof Exp:* Fel, Portobello Marine Lab, NZ, 78-79; res asst, State Univ NY, Stony Brook, 80-82; scientist, State Maine, 83-92 & Bigelow Lab, 92-93. *Concurrent Pos:* Adj grad fac mem, Univ Maine, Orono, 83-; adj prin investr, Bigelow Lab Ocean Sci, 84-; ed, J Shellfish Res, 87- *Mem:* Nat Shellfish Asn (pres, 91-92); Asn Women Sci; Am Malacological Union; Am Soc Zoologists; Marine Biol Asn UK; Coun Biol Ed. *Res:* Physiological ecology of marine invertebrates, primarily respiratory and osmoregulatory physiology; toxic algal blooms and their effects on shellfish. *Mailing Add:* Natural Sci Div Southampton Col LIU Southampton NY 11968. *Fax:* 516-287-8419; *E-Mail:* shumway@seaweed.liunet.edu

SHUNG, K KIRK, BIOMEDICAL ULTRASOUND, BIOINSTRUMENTATION. *Current Pos:* from asst prof to assoc prof bioeng, 79-87, actg head dept, 87-88, PROF BIOENG, PA STATE UNIV, 89- *Personal Data:* b China, June 2, 45; US citizen; m 71, Linda Shaw; c 3. *Educ:* Nat Cheng-Kung Univ, Taiwan, BSEE, 68; Univ Mo, MSEE, 70; Univ Wash, PhD(elec eng), 75. *Honors & Awards:* Early Career Achievement Award, Inst Elec & Electronics Engrs, Eng Med & Biol Soc, 85. *Prof Exp:* Res assoc, Ctr Bioeng, Univ Wash, 70-75; res fel, Providence Med Ctr, Seattle, Wash, 75-76, res engr, 76-79. *Concurrent Pos:* Prin investr, NSF, 77-81 NIH, 79-; NIH diag radiol, 85-89. *Mem:* Fel Inst Elec & Electronics Engrs; fel Am Inst Ultrasound Med; fel Acoust Soc Am. *Res:* Ultrasonic imaging and tissue characterization; diagnostic imaging; ultrasonic transducers. *Mailing Add:* 233 Halowell Bldg Pa State Univ University Park PA 16802. *Fax:* 814-863-0490; *E-Mail:* kksbio@engr.psu.edu

SHUPE, DEAN STANLEY, TECHNICAL WRITING. *Current Pos:* from instr to prof, 63-89, EMER PROF MECH ENG, UNIV CINCINNATI, 89-; PRIN, SHUPE & ASSOCS, 89- *Personal Data:* b Clarion, Iowa, July 7, 37; m 62; c 2. *Educ:* Iowa State Univ, BS, 60; Stanford Univ, MS, 61; Mass Inst Technol, ScD(mech eng), 69. *Honors & Awards:* Ralph R Teetor Award, Soc Automotive Engrs, 80. *Prof Exp:* Process engr, Procter & Gamble Co, 61-62. *Concurrent Pos:* Prin, Eng & Mgt Assocs, 77-89; exec vpres, Cincinnati Industs, Inc. *Mem:* Am Soc Mech Engrs; Am Soc Heating, Refrig & Air Conditioning Engrs. *Res:* Energy conservation and energy sciences; applied heat transfer and thermodynamics; technical writer, including textbooks and software manuals. *Mailing Add:* 10304 Gunpowder Rd Florence KY 41042

SHUPE, JAMES LEGRANDE, VETERINARY MEDICINE. *Current Pos:* prof vet med, Utah State Univ, 66-80, head, Dept Vet Sci, 73-76, prof animal dairy & vet sci, 80-90, EMER PROF ANIMAL DAIRY & VET SCI, UTAH STATE UNIV, 90- *Personal Data:* b Ogden, Utah, Nov 5, 18; m 57; c 2. *Educ:* Utah State Univ, BS, 48; Cornell Univ, DVM, 52. *Prof Exp:* From asst prof to prof vet med, Utah State Univ, 52-61; res vet animal dis & parasite res div, Agr Res Serv, USDA, 61-66. *Concurrent Pos:* Resident path, Armed Forces Inst Path, Walter Reed Med Ctr, 57-58; chmn subcomt fluorosis, Nat Res Coun. *Mem:* Am Vet Med Asn; Am Col Vet Toxicol (pres, 72); Am Acad Clin Toxicol; Pan-Am Med Asn; Int Acad Path; Sigma Xi. *Res:* Toxicology; pathology. *Mailing Add:* 296 S 250 W Box 342 Hyde Park UT 84318

SHUPE, JOHN W(ALLACE), CIVIL ENGINEERING, RENEWABLE ENERGY. *Current Pos:* RETIRED. *Personal Data:* b Liberal, Kans, Mar 30, 24; m 53, Elizabeth Mendenhall; c 4. *Educ:* Kans State Univ, BS, 48; Univ Calif, MS, 51; Purdue Univ, PhD(civil eng), 58. *Honors & Awards:* Templin Award, Am Soc Testing & Mat, 60. *Prof Exp:* Instr appl mech, Kans State Univ, 48-49, asst prof, 51-53; lectr civil eng, Univ Calif, 49-51; struct engr, Convair Div, Gen Dynamics Corp, 53-54; assoc prof appl mech, Kans State Univ, 54-65, assoc dean eng, 60-65; dean eng, Univ Hawaii, 65-80, dir, Hawaii Natural Energy Inst, 80-83; dir, Pac Site Off, US Dept Energy, 83-92. *Mem:* Am Soc Civil Engrs; Am Soc Eng Educ; Nat Soc Prof Engrs; Inst Solar Energy Soc; Geothermal Resources Coun. *Res:* Geothermal and solar energy. *Mailing Add:* 8515 Costa Verde Blvd No 1101 San Diego CA 92122

SHUR, BARRY DAVID, DEVELOPMENTAL BIOLOGY. *Current Pos:* ASST PROF ANAT, HEALTH CTR, UNIV CONN, 78- *Personal Data:* b Elizabeth, NJ, Jan 3, 50; m 71; c 1. *Educ:* Marietta Col, BS, 71; Johns Hopkins Univ, PhD(biol), 76. *Prof Exp:* Fel develop genetics, Mem Sloan-Kettering Cancer Ctr, 76-78. *Concurrent Pos:* Helen Hay Whitney Found fel, 76-78. *Mem:* Am Soc Zoologists; Am Soc Anatomists; AAAS. *Res:* Cell surface biochemistry of normal and mutant morphogenesis. *Mailing Add:* Dept Biochem & Molecular Biol Univ Tex Anderson Cancer Ctr 1515 Holcombe Blvd Box 117 Houston TX 77030-4009. *Fax:* 713-790-0329

SHUR, MICHAEL, ELECTRICAL ENGINEERING, SOLID STATE PHYSICS. *Current Pos:* JOHN MARSHALL MONEY PROF, UNIV VA, 89-; PATRICIA W & C SHELDON ROBERT PROF SOLID STATE ELECTRONICS, DEPT ELEC COMPUT & SYSTS ENG, RENSSELAER POLYTECHNIC INST. *Personal Data:* b Kamensk-Uralski, USSR, Nov 13, 42; US citizen; m 66, Paulina; c Luba & Nataska. *Educ:* Leningrad Electrotech Inst, MSEE, 65; A F Ioffe Inst Physics & Technol, PhD(physics), 67. *Hon Degrees:* DSc, A F Ioffe Inst Physics & Technol, 92. *Prof Exp:* Researcher, A F Ioffe Inst Physics & Technol, Leningrad, USSR, 65-76; res assoc, Wayne State Univ, 76-77, asst prof elec eng, 77-78; asst prof, Oakland Univ, Rochester, Mich, 78-79; from assoc prof to prof elec eng, Univ Minn, 79-89. *Concurrent Pos:* Vis res assoc, Cornell Univ, 76-80; consult, Honeywell, Xerox & Gen Elec; mem, Ctr Advan Studies, Univ Va, 89-91. *Mem:* Fel Inst Elec & Electronic Engrs; fel Am Phys Soc. *Res:* Semiconductor devices and integrated circuits; compound semiconductor devices; ballistic devices and amorphous silicon devices. *Mailing Add:* Dept Elec Comp & Syst Eng Rensselaer Polytechnic Inst Charlottesville VA 22903-2442. *Fax:* 804-924-8818

SHURBET, DESKIN HUNT, JR, SEISMOLOGY. *Current Pos:* PROF GEOL & DIR SEISMOL OBSERV, TEX TECH UNIV, 56- *Personal Data:* b Lockney, Tex, Aug 27, 25; m 53; c 3. *Educ:* Univ Tex, BS, 50, MA, 51. *Prof Exp:* Dir Bermuda-Columbia Seismograph Sta, Lamont Geol Observ, 51-56. *Mem:* Fel AAAS; Seismol Soc Am; Am Geophys Union; Soc Explor Geophys. *Res:* Earthquake seismology. *Mailing Add:* 5002 46th St Lubbock TX 79414

SHURE, DONALD JOSEPH, ECOSYSTEM PROCESSES, PLANT-HERBIVORE INTERACTIONS. *Current Pos:* from asst prof to assoc prof, 69-93, PROF BIOL, EMORY UNIV, 93- *Personal Data:* b Washington, DC, July 21, 39; m 65, Janice M Hack; c Jeff & Melissa. *Educ:* Western Md Col, BA, 61; Rutgers Univ, MS, 66, PhD(zool), 69. *Prof Exp:* Teaching asst zool, Rutgers Univ, 64-67, NSF fel ecol, 68-69. *Concurrent Pos:* Consult, Allied Gen Nuclear Serv, 70-80; dir grad studies, Dept Biol, Emory Univ, 78-81. *Mem:* Ecol Soc Am; Am Soc Mammalogists; Am Inst Biol Sci; AAAS. *Res:* Perturbation effects on ecosystem structure and function; consumer dynamics and plant-animal interactions in systems undergoing natural succession. *Mailing Add:* Dept Biol Emory Univ 1510 Clifton Rd Atlanta GA 30322. *Fax:* 404-727-2880; *E-Mail:* dshure@biology.emory.edu

SHURE, FRED C(HARLES), PHYSICS, NUCLEAR ENGINEERING. *Current Pos:* RETIRED. *Personal Data:* b New York, NY, Feb 26, 34; m 63; c 3. *Educ:* Harvard Col, AB, 55; Univ Mich, MS, 57, PhD(physics), 61. *Prof Exp:* Instr physics, Univ Mich, 59-61; assoc res physicist, Conductron Corp, 61-62; from lectr to assoc prof nuclear eng, Univ Mich, Ann Arbor, 62-80. *Concurrent Pos:* Physicist plasma physics lab, Princeton Univ, 63-64; pres, ESZ Assocs, Inc. *Mem:* Am Phys Soc; Am Nuclear Soc. *Res:* Transport theory; reactor theory; plasma physics; applied mathematics. *Mailing Add:* 1127 Brooks Ann Arbor MI 48103

SHURE, KALMAN, NUCLEAR SCIENCE. *Current Pos:* sr scientist, Bettis Atomic Power Div, Westinghouse Elec Corp, 51-54, supvry scientist, 54-65, adv scientist, 65-73, CONSULT, BETTIS ATOMIC POWER LAB, WESTINGHOUSE ELEC CORP, 73- *Personal Data:* b Brooklyn, NY, Mar 14, 25; m 51; c 2. *Educ:* Brooklyn Col, AB, 45; Mass Inst Technol, PhD(physics), 51. *Prof Exp:* Gen phys scientist, USAF Cambridge Res Ctr, 49. *Mem:* Am Phys Soc; fel Am Nuclear Soc. *Res:* Shielding, penetration of gamma rays and neutrons in materials; decay energies of radioactive isotopes. *Mailing Add:* 5612 Woodmont St Pittsburgh PA 15217

SHURMAN, MICHAEL MENDELSOHN, ASTRONOMY. *Current Pos:* from asst prof to prof physics, 55-83, assoc dean sci, 62-65, EMER PROF PHYSICS, UNIV WIS-MILWAUKEE, 83- *Personal Data:* b St Louis, Mo, Aug 4, 21. *Educ:* Univ Wis, BA, 43, MA, 46, PhD(physics), 51. *Prof Exp:* Instr physics, Exten, Univ Wis, 46-48; physicist, Los Alamos Sci Lab, 52-55. *Mem:* Am Asn Physics Teachers. *Mailing Add:* PO Box 32188 Jerusalem Israel

SHURTLEFF, DAVID B, PEDIATRICS. *Current Pos:* from instr to assoc prof, 60-71, PROF PEDIAT, SCH MED, UNIV WASH, 71- *Personal Data:* b Fall River, Mass, July 1, 30; m 52; c 3. *Educ:* Tufts Univ, MD, 55. *Honors & Awards:* Casey Holter Lectr, Hydrocepholus & Spina Befida, Int Soc Res; Gallagher Lectr, Soc Adolescent Med. *Prof Exp:* Intern pediat, Mass Gen Hosp, Boston, 55-56, asst resident, 56-57; chief resident, Children's Orthop Hosp, Seattle, Wash, 57-58. *Concurrent Pos:* Teaching fel, Harvard Med Sch, 55-57; assoc, Sch Med, Univ Wash, 57-58; sr consult, US Army, Madigan Hosp, 61-85; Nat Found March of Dimes fel, Welsh Nat Sch Med, Univ Wales, 69-70, vis prof & consult, 69-71; Ross award res, Western Soc Pediat Res. *Mem:* Am Acad Pediat; Soc Pediat Res; Am Pediat Soc. *Res:* Congenital defects; clinical study of epidemiology and cerebrospinal fluid dynamics and ecology of children with hydrocephalus and meningomyelocele. *Mailing Add:* Dept Peds Childrens Orth Hosp Ch-47 Univ Wash Sch Med Seattle WA 98195

SHURTLEFF, MALCOLM C, JR, PHYTOPATHOLOGY. *Current Pos:* assoc prof plant path, Univ Ill, Urbana, 61-65, exten plant pathologist, 61-92, prof, 65-92, EMER PROF, UNIV ILL, URBANA, 92- *Personal Data:* b Fall River, Mass, June 24, 22; m 50, Margaret E Johnson; c Robert G, Janet L & Mark S. *Educ:* Univ RI, BS, 43; Univ Minn, MS, 50, PhD(plant path), 53. *Honors & Awards:* Adventurers in Agr Sci Award Distinction, IX Int Cong Plant Protection, 79; Distinguished Serv Award, USDA, 86. *Prof Exp:* Asst, Univ Minn, 47-50; instr bot, Univ RI, 50-51, asst res prof plant path & asst exten prof plant path & entom, 51-54; asst prof plant path & exten plant pathologist, Iowa State Univ, 54-58, assoc prof bot & plant path, 58-61. *Concurrent Pos:* Chmn exten comt, Int Soc Plant Path, 78-80; chief ed, Plant Dis, 79-82; consult. *Mem:* AAAS; fel Am Phytopath Soc; Bot Soc Am. *Res:* Fungicides; turf, field crop and ornamental diseases. *Mailing Add:* 2707 Holcomb Dr Urbana IL 61801. *Fax:* 217-244-1230

SHURVELL, HERBERT FRANCIS, SPECTROCHEMISTRY. *Current Pos:* from asst prof to prof, 65-96, EMER PROF CHEM, QUEEN'S UNIV, ONT, 97- *Personal Data:* b London, Eng, Sept 3, 34; m 60, Irene A E Bullock; c Joanne, David & Andrew. *Educ:* Univ Exeter, BSc, 59; Univ BC, MSc, 62, PhD(chem), 64. *Hon Degrees:* DSc, Univ Exeter, 81. *Honors & Awards:* Bicentennial Medal, Ont, 84. *Prof Exp:* Res attache, Nat Ctr Sci Res, Fac Sci, Marseille, France, 64-65. *Concurrent Pos:* Res fel, Univ Queensland, 72-73; vis prof, Sao Paulo, Brazil, 79, Univ Queensland, 78, 81 & 87 & Queensland Univ Technol, 95; res ed, Thornton Res Ctr, Shell Res Ltd, Chester, UK, 87-88 & 96. *Mem:* Fel Chem Inst Can; Spectros Soc Can (pres, 78-79); Royal Soc Chem. *Res:* Infrared and Raman spectroscopy. *Mailing Add:* Dept Chem Queen's Univ Kingston ON K7L 3N6 Can. *Fax:* 613-545-6669; *E-Mail:* shurvell@queensu.ca

SHUSHAN, MORRIS, allergy food, wellness medicine; deceased, see previous edition for last biography

SHUSHAN, SAM, LICHENOLOGY, MYCOLOGY. *Current Pos:* From instr to assoc prof, 49-72, PROF BOT, UNIV COLO, BOULDER, 72- *Personal Data:* b Bronx, NY, July 6, 22; m 46; c 3. *Educ:* City Col New York, BS, 43; Rutgers Univ, MS, 47, PhD(bot), 49. *Mem:* AAAS; Bot Soc Am; Am Bryol & Lichenological Soc; Mycol Soc Am; Phycol Soc Am; Sigma Xi. *Res:* Developmental plant anatomy; lichen taxonomy. *Mailing Add:* 2010 Mariposa Ave Boulder CO 80302

SHUSKUS, ALEXANDER J, SOLID STATE PHYSICS. *Current Pos:* RETIRED. *Personal Data:* b Hartford, Conn, June 15, 29; m 55; c 3. *Educ:* Univ Conn, BA, 50; Univ Ala, MS, 57; Univ Conn, PhD(physics), 61. *Prof Exp:* Engr, Hart Mfg Co, 50-51; engr, Pratt & Whitney Aircraft Div, United Aircraft Corp, 53-55, physicist, Res Labs, 61-65, group leader microwave physics, 65-68, mgr microelectronics lab, 68-71, sr res consult, res ctr, United Technologies Corp, 71-91. *Mem:* Inst Elec & Electronics Engrs; Am Phys Soc. *Res:* Electron spin resonance studies; radiation effects in solids; microwave properties of solids; semiconductor physics; thin films; photovoltaics; ion implantation. *Mailing Add:* 30 Paxton Rd West Hartford CT 06107

SHUSTER, CARL NATHANIEL, JR, AQUATIC ECOLOGY, INVERTEBRATE ZOOLOGY. *Current Pos:* RETIRED. *Personal Data:* b Randolph, Vt, Nov 16, 19; m 44; c 5. *Educ:* Rutgers Univ, BSc, 42, MSc, 48; NY Univ, PhD(biol), 55. *Prof Exp:* Instr zool, Rutgers Univ, 49-54, lectr & demonstr sci, Univ Col, 53-55, lectr zool, 54-55; asst prof biol sci & dir marine labs, Univ Del, 55-63; dir Northeast Marine Health Serv Lab, USPHS, 63-69, ecologist, Bur Water Hyg, 69-71; br chief water progs, Environ Protection Agency, 71-72; asst adv environ qual, 72-74, actg adv environ qual, 74-75, ecol systs analyst, Fed Energy Regulatory Comn, 75-84. *Concurrent Pos:* Mem, US Nat Mus Smithsonian-Bredin Caribbean exped, 58; adj prof zool & oceanogr, Univ RI, 63-70; adj prof biol oceanogr, Va Inst Sch Marine Sci, Williams & Mary, 79- *Mem:* Fel AAAS; Am Soc Limnol & Oceanog; Ecol Soc Am; fel NY Acad Sci; Am Soc Zoologists. *Res:* Authority on ecology of llmulidae; estuarine ecology, especially of arthropods and mollusks; evaluation of environmental impacts on aquatic ecosystems from federal actions, particularly interrelations within river basins, electrical power systems and water use management. *Mailing Add:* 3733 N 25th St Arlington VA 22207-5011

SHUSTER, CHARLES W, GRAM NEGATIVE TOXINS, BACTERIAL INVASION MECHANISMS. *Current Pos:* ASSOC PROF, MOLECULAR BIOL & MICROBIOL, SCH MED, CASE WESTERN RESERVE UNIV, 64- *Educ:* Univ Ill, PhD(biochem), 58. *Mailing Add:* Dept Microbiol Sch Med Case Western Res 2119 Abington Rd Cleveland OH 44106-2333

SHUSTER, JOSEPH, CANCER, IMMUNOLOGY. *Current Pos:* From asst prof to assoc prof med, 68-78, assoc dir, McGill Cancer Ctr, 78-81, PROF MED, MCGILL UNIV, 78-; SCI DIR, MONTREAL GEN HOSP RES INST, 81-, DIR CLIN CHEM, 86- *Personal Data:* b Montreal, Que, Jan 29, 37; m 64; c 2. *Educ:* McGill Univ, BS, 58; Univ Alta, MD, 62; Univ Calif, PhD(immunol), 68. *Prof Exp:* From asst physician to assoc physician, Montreal Gen Hosp, 68-77, sr physician, 77-, dir, Div Clin Immunol & Allergy, 80- *Concurrent Pos:* Med Res Coun Can scholar, 68-73; clin res assoc, Nat Cancer Inst Can, 74-80; fac med, Univ Uruguay, 83; dir, Div Clin Immunol & Allergy, Montreal Childrens Hosp, 90. *Mem:* NY Acad Sci; Can Soc Immunol; Can Soc Oncol; Can Soc Clin Invest; Asn Am Immunologists; Am Soc Cancer Res; Clin Immunol Soc; Am Acad Allergy. *Res:* Identification and characterization of human tumor antigens, particularly alpha fetoprotein, carcinoembryonic antigen and tumor modified histocompatibility antigens; AIDS and hemophilia. *Mailing Add:* Clin Immunol & Allergy Mont Gen Hosp Res Inst 1650 Cedar Ave Rm A6173 Montreal PQ H3G 1A4 Can. *Fax:* 514-934-8239

SHUSTER, KENNETH ASHTON, ENVIRONMENTAL SYSTEMS & TECHNOLOGY. *Current Pos:* staff engr, 70-71, sect chief solid waste systs, 71-74, PROG MGR LAND DISPOSAL, US ENVIRON PROTECTION AGENCY, 74- *Personal Data:* b Trenton, NJ, Apr 3, 46; m 69; c 1. *Educ:* Rutgers Univ, BS & BA, 69; Xavier Univ, MBA, 72. *Honors & Awards:* Bronze Medal, US Environ Protection Agency, 77, Silver Medal, 79. *Prof Exp:* Staff engr solid waste collection, Dept HEW, USPHS, 69-70. *Concurrent Pos:* Staff comt safety standards solid waste equip, Am Nat Standards Inst, 74-77; adv staff task force solid waste, Nat Comn Prod, 72-73; chmn, Environ Protection Agency Disposal Regs Work Group, 76-79. *Mem:* Am Pub Works Asn. *Res:* Environmental and economic analyses technologies and regulations of solid waste management systems, particularly land disposal of hazardous and non-hazardous wastes, resource conservation and recovery and waste storage and collection systems. *Mailing Add:* US Environ Protection Agency 5303 W Washington DC 20460

SHUSTER, LOUIS, PHARMACOLOGY, NEUROCHEMISTRY. *Current Pos:* from asst prof to assoc prof pharmacol, Sch Med, Tufts Univ, 58-70, assoc prof biochem, 67-70, actg chmn pharmacol, 87-91, PROF BIOCHEM & PHARMACOL, SCH MED, TUFTS UNIV, 70- *Personal Data:* b Wysock, Poland, Apr 17, 29; nat US; m 59; c 2. *Educ:* Univ BC, BA, 50; Johns Hopkins Univ, PhD(biochem), 54. *Prof Exp:* Nat Res Coun Can overseas fel, Nat Inst Med Res, Eng, 54-55; vis scientist, Nat Cancer Inst, 55-58. *Mem:* Am Chem Soc; Am Soc Biol Chemists; Brit Biochem Soc; Am Soc Pharmacol & Exp Therapeut; Soc Neurosci. *Res:* Mechanisms of drug action; liver damage from drugs; addiction to narcotics and stimulants; pharmacogenetics. *Mailing Add:* Dept Pharmacol Tufts Univ Sch Med 136 Harrison Ave Boston MA 02111-1800. *Fax:* 617-956-5783

SHUSTER, ROBERT C, BIOCHEMISTRY, MOLECULAR BIOLOGY. *Current Pos:* asst prof, 68-74, ASSOC PROF BIOCHEM, EMORY UNIV, 74- *Personal Data:* b Brooklyn, NY, Dec 15, 32; m 58, Myrna Silver; c Todd & Lauren (Kazlow). *Educ:* Brooklyn Col, BA, 53; Purdue Univ, MS, 59; Albany Med Col, PhD(biochem), 63. *Prof Exp:* Res assoc biochem, Sch Med, Yale Univ, 63-66; staff fel, NIH, 66-68. *Mem:* Am Soc Biol Chemists. *Res:* Studies of the human insulin receptor gene in disorders affecting glucose homeostasis. *Mailing Add:* Dept Biochem Emory Univ Atlanta GA 30322. Fax: 404-727-2738

SHUTER, ELI RONALD, NEUROLOGY, NEUROCHEMISTRY. *Current Pos:* PRES, ST LOUIS NEUROL, INST, 76-; ASST PROF CLIN NEUROL, SCH MED, WASHINGTON UNIV, 79- *Personal Data:* b New York, NY, June 16, 35; m 58, Adrienne Bertenthal; c 4. *Educ:* Cornell Univ, AB, 56; Washington Univ, MD, 60; Am Bd Psychiat & Neurol, dipl, 71. *Prof Exp:* Intern med, NY Hosp, 60-61; asst resident neurol, Mass Gen Hosp, 61-62; resident neurol, Cleveland Metrop Gen Hosp, 64-65 & neuropath, 65-66; Nat Inst Neurol Dis & Stroke spec res fel, Washington Univ, 66-69; asst prof neurol, Sch Med, St Louis Univ, 69-75, asst clin prof, 75-79. *Concurrent Pos:* Teaching fel, Harvard Univ, 61-62; consult, Vet Admin Hosps, St Louis, 70-77; USPHS res grant, St Louis Univ, 70-75; mem active staff, Christian Hosp Northeast-Northwest, 75-; asst neurologist, Barnes Hosp, 79-; consult staff, St Anthony's Hosp, 80-, Alton Mem Hosp, 81- & Jewish Hosp, 82- & DePaul Community Health Ctr, 87- *Mem:* Asn Res Nerv & Ment Dis; Am Acad Neurol; Soc Neurosci; Am Asn Study Headache. *Res:* Biochemical changes in neuropathologic conditions; biochemical changes during development of the central nervous system; metabolism of gangliosides; hexosaminidases in the nervous system; pseudobulbar palsy; headache. *Mailing Add:* 11155 Dunn Rd St Louis MO 63136

SHUTER, WILLIAM LESLIE HAZLEWOOD, radio astronomy; deceased, see previous edition for last biography

SHUTSKE, GREGORY MICHAEL, MEDICINAL CHEMISTRY, DRUG DESIGN. *Current Pos:* Sr res chemist, Hoechst-Roussel Pharmaceut, 75-78, res assoc, 78-81, sr res assoc, 81-89, prin res scientist, 89-94, RES FEL, HOECHST-RUSSELL PHARMACEUT, 94- *Personal Data:* US citizen. *Educ:* Rose-Hulman Inst Technol, BS, 71; Ind Univ, PhD(org chem), 75. *Concurrent Pos:* Exchange scientist, Hoechst AG, Frankfurt, WGer, 80-81. *Mem:* Am Chem Soc; Int Soc Heterocyclic Chem. *Res:* Synthesis of heterocyclic compounds of medicinal interest; drugs affecting the central nervous system; determination of organic structures by nuclear magnetic resonance methods; automated parallel synthesis. *Mailing Add:* Hoechst-Marion Roussel Inc Rte 202-206 PO Box 6800 Somerville NJ 08807-0800. Fax: 908-231-4774

SHUTT, RALPH P, PHYSICS. *Current Pos:* RES SCIENTIST, BROOKHAVEN NAT LAB, UPTON, NY. *Honors & Awards:* W K H Panofsky Prize, Am Phys Soc, 93. *Mailing Add:* Brookhaven Nat Lab Upton NY 11973

SHUTZE, JOHN V, POULTRY NUTRITION. *Current Pos:* EMER PROF, UNIV GA, 85- *Personal Data:* b Hale, Colo, Apr 21, 24; m 47, Leta B Hill; c 2. *Educ:* Colo State Univ, BS, 55, MS, 57; Wash State Univ, PhD(poultry nutrit), 64. *Honors & Awards:* Pfizer Exten Poultry Sci Award, 77. *Prof Exp:* Rancher, Imperial, Nebr, 49-52; instr poultry sci, Wash State Univ, 57-63; exten poultryman, Pa State Univ, 63-65; exten poultryman & assoc poultry scientist, Colo State Univ, 65-70; head exten poultry sci dept & exten poultry scientist, 70-85. *Concurrent Pos:* Consult poultry scientist & nutritionist, 85- *Mem:* AAAS; Poultry Sci Asn; World Poultry Sci Asn. *Res:* Effect of pesticides on growth and reproduction; effect of polychlorinated biphenyls on hatchability and tissue residue; effect of calcium sources and additives on eggshell quality; effect of calorie protein ratio and energy sources on the thiamine requirement in chicks; fatty acid metabolism in laying hens. *Mailing Add:* 115 Witherspoon Rd Athens GA 30606. Fax: 706-354-6868

SHUVAL, HILLEL ISAIAH, environmental engineering, environmental health, for more information see previous edition

SHVARTZ, ESAR, SPORTS MEDICINE, HUMAN FACTORS IN EQUIPMENT DESIGN. *Current Pos:* SYST SAFETY ENGR, SYST SAFETY, ROCKWELL INT, 84- *Personal Data:* b Tel-Aviv, Israel, Aug 1, 35; US citizen; m 71; c 2. *Educ:* Univ Calif, Los Angeles, BA, 60 MS, 62; Univ SC, PhD (phys educ), 65. *Honors & Awards:* Environ Sci Award, Aerospace Med Asn, 82. *Prof Exp:* Asst prof phys educ, Washington State Univ, 65-66; asst prof, Ind State Univ, 66-67; dir, Environ Physiol Lab, Negen Inst Arid Zone Res, Beer Sheva, Israel, 67-70; sr scientist environ physiol, Heller Inst Med Res, Sheba Med Ctr, Israel, 70-76; sr res assoc, NASA-Ames Res Ctr, Moffett Field, Calif, 76-77; sr engr & scientist human factors, Douglas Aircraft Co, 78-84. *Concurrent Pos:* Res adv, Ben-Gurion Univ, Israel, 67-73; vis prof, Tel-Aviv Univ, 70-73; dir, Res in Fitness, Med Corps, Israel Defence Forces, 70-76; vis scientist, Human Sci, Capital Chamber of Mines of SAfrica, Johannesburg, 73-74. *Mem:* Am Physiol Soc; fel Am Col Sports Med; Human Factors Soc; assoc fel Aerospace Med Asn. *Res:* Crew safety in space flights; environmental physiology, mainly effects of heat, cold, altitude on man; industrial safety; physical fitness and training. *Mailing Add:* Dept Safety Rockwell Inst MC AD-60 12214 Lakewood Blvd Downey CA 90241

SHWE, HLA, HIGH ENERGY PHYSICS, NUCLEAR PHYSICS. *Current Pos:* chmn dept, 69-74, dean fac sci, 74-79, dean, Sch Arts & Sci, 79-83, PROF PHYSICS, EAST STROUDSBURG UNIV. 69- *Personal Data:* b Rangoon, Burma, May 2, 34; US citizen; m 62; c 3. *Educ:* Univ Calif, Berkeley, AB, 58, MA, 59, PhD(physics), 62. *Prof Exp:* US AEC fel, Lawrence Radiation Lab, 62; from asst prof to assoc prof physics, Ripon Col, 63-69. *Concurrent Pos:* US AEC & Assoc Cols Midwest fel, Argonne Nat Lab, 66-67; consult, Argonne Nat Lab, 68-72, Oak Ridge Nat Lab, 70-72 & Lawrence Berkeley Lab, 72-76. *Mem:* Am Asn Univ Prof; Sigma Xi; NY Acad Sci; Am Phys Soc; Am Asn Physics Teachers. *Res:* Particle physics; neutron physics, especially in the area of cross section work; heavy-ion nuclear physics; high-energy heavy ions. *Mailing Add:* 143 Back Heights Rd East Stroudsburg PA 18301

SHYAMSUNDER, ERRAMILLI, physics, biophysics, for more information see previous edition

SHYKIND, DAVID, solid state nmr, optically detected nmr, for more information see previous edition

SHYKIND, EDWIN B, MARINE GEOLOGY, SCIENCE POLICY. *Current Pos:* dir, Environ Affairs Div, 71-77, dir, Off Bux & Policy Anal, Bus Domestic Com, 71-79, sr tech adv, Off Regulatory Policy, 79-82, SCI ADV TRADE ADMIN, US DEPT COM, 82- *Personal Data:* b Los Angeles, Calif, Oct 10, 31; m 57; c 3. *Educ:* Northwestern Univ, BS, 53; Univ Chicago, SM, 55, PhD(geol), 56. *Prof Exp:* Instr geol, Wright Jr Col, 54-55; res engr, Montaine Corp, Ill, 56-57; asst prof earth sci, Northern Ill Univ, 57-62; chief earth sci br & spec asst to dir sci inform exchange, Smithsonian Inst, 62-64; assoc staff dir interagency comt oceanog, Fed Coun Sci & Technol, Exec Off of Pres, 64-67; actg exec secy, 67, exec secy interagency comt marine res educ & fac, Nat Coun Marine Resources & Eng Develop, 67-69; staff dir marine sci affairs staff, Off Oceanogr, Dept Navy, 69; sr staff mem, Nat Coun Marine Resources & Eng Develop, Exec Off of Pres, 69-71. *Mem:* AAAS; Am Asn Petrol Geol. *Res:* Sedimentation; hydrodynamics; scientific information; ocean engineering; environmental affairs. *Mailing Add:* 903 Burnt Crest Lane Silver Spring MD 20903

SHYNE, J(OHN) C(ORNELIUS), METALLURGY. *Current Pos:* from asst prof to prof mat sci, 60-86, chmn, Dept Mat Sci & Eng, 71-75, EMER PROF MAT SCI, STANFORD UNIV, 86- *Personal Data:* b Detroit, Mich, Nov 26, 25; m 47; c 5. *Educ:* Univ Mich, BS(math) & BS(metall), 51, MS, 52, PhD(metall), 58. *Prof Exp:* Res engr, Ford Motor Co, 52-59; proj dir mat res, Mueller Brass Co, 59-60. *Concurrent Pos:* Head, Metall & Mat Sect, NSF, 75-77. *Mem:* Am Soc Metals; Am Inst Mining, Metall & Petrol Engrs. *Res:* Internal friction, crystalline defects and phase transformations in metals; relation of structure to properties in metals; metallurgical failure analysis. *Mailing Add:* 4195 Dake Ave Palo Alto CA 94306

SHYSH, ALEC, bionucleonics, radiopharmacy, for more information see previous edition

SI, JENNIE, ARTIFICIAL NEURAL LEARNING THEORY, ARTIFICIAL NEURAL COMPUTING IN MODELING, CONTROL & SIGNAL PROCESSING. *Current Pos:* Asst prof, 91-96, ASSOC PROF ELEC ENG, ARIZ STATE UNIV, 96- *Personal Data:* b China, Mar 16, 63; m 88, Jun Shen. *Educ:* Tsinghua Univ, China, BS, 85, MS, 88; Univ Notre Dame, PhD(elec eng), 92. *Honors & Awards:* Motorola Excellence Award, 95. *Concurrent Pos:* Presidential fac fel, White House & NSF, 95; consult, Intel Corp, 96, Ariz Pub Serv & Intel Automation, Inc, 97. *Mem:* Inst Elec & Electronics Engrs; Asn Chinese Scientists & Engrs. *Res:* Nonlinear dynamic system analysis; artificial neural systems for function approximation and nonlinear dynamic system modeling; analyses and applications of learning algorithms, neural computing in modeling, control, and signal processing applications; semiconductor manufacturing, neuronal information processing and neuromechanical control. *Mailing Add:* Ctr Systs Sci Ariz State Univ Tempe AZ 85287-7606

SIAKOTOS, ARISTOTLE N, BIOCHEMISTRY. *Current Pos:* from asst prof to assoc prof, 68-78, PROF PATH, MED CTR, IND UNIV, INDIANAPOLIS, 78- *Personal Data:* b Dedham, Mass, July 19, 28; m 72; c 4. *Educ:* Univ Mass, BS, 52, MS, 54; Cornell Univ, PhD(entom), 58. *Prof Exp:* Res asst entom, Cornell Univ, 54-56; entomologist, Med Res Labs, US Army Chem Ctr, 58-62; biochemist, 62-68. *Concurrent Pos:* Nat Retinitis Pigmentosa sr res fel, 74-76. *Mem:* Am Chem Soc; Am Oil Chem Soc; Am Soc Neurochem; Am Soc Neurosci; Am Soc Exp Path. *Res:* Subcellular particulates of the central nervous system; drug induced changes in brain; lipid composition and metabolism in subcellular particles; retinal degeneration; biochemistry of the eye; vision; ophthalmology; biochemical pathology; atypical slow virus diseases; lipopigments; aldehyde metabolism. *Mailing Add:* Dept Pathol Ind Univ Med Sch 635 Barnhill Dr Indianapolis IN 46202-5120. Fax: 317-274-1069

SIANO, DONALD BRUCE, PHYSICAL CHEMISTRY, BIOPHYSICS. *Current Pos:* res physicist emulsion sci, Exxon Res & Eng Co, 78-86, res physicist polymer sci, 86-92, AT EXXON RES & ENG CTR, 92- *Personal Data:* b Sewickley, Pa, June 30, 42; m 72, Elizabeth Moore; c Julian. *Educ:* Kent State Univ, BS, 66; Iowa State Univ, MS, 68, PhD(biophys), 78. *Prof Exp:* Res chem mem, Columbia Univ, 76-78. *Mem:* AAAS; Am Chem Soc. *Res:* Rayleigh and dynamic light scattering; biopolymers; microemulsions; enhanced oil recovery; polymer blends; asphalt properties. *Mailing Add:* 624 Clark St Westfield NJ 07090

SIAPNO, WILLIAM DAVID, marine geology, exploration, for more information see previous edition

SIAS, FRED R, JR, PHYSIOLOGICAL CONTROL SYSTEMS, ROBOTICS. *Current Pos:* assoc prof, 76-94, EMER ADJ ASSOC PROF ELEC & COMPUT ENG, CLEMSON UNIV, 94- *Personal Data:* b Jacksonville, Fla, Aug 17, 31; m 61, Dorris Fischer; c Patricia L & Christina L. *Educ:* Univ Fla, BS, 54, MS, 59; Univ Miss, PhD(physiol & biophys), 70. *Prof Exp:* Asst prof, Sch Med, Univ Miss, 70-72; asst prof, Sch Info & Comput Sci, Ga Inst Technol, 74-76. *Concurrent Pos:* Prin investr, several res grants & contracts. *Mem:* Inst Elec & Electronic Engrs; Am Physiol Soc; Biomed Eng Soc; Am Soc Eng Educ. *Res:* Microcomputer applications in medicine; modeling physiological control systems; mobile robots for environmental restoration and waste management. *Mailing Add:* Dept Elec & Comput Eng Riggs Hall Clemson Univ Clemson SC 29634-0915. *Fax:* 864-656-5910; *E-Mail:* frsias@ces.clemson.edu

SIATKOWSKI, RONALD E, ENVIRONMENTAL CHEMISTRY, MARINE POLLUTION ABATEMENT SYSTEMS. *Current Pos:* sr engr, 95-96, PRIN ENGR, MARINE ENVIRON ENG GROUP, MAN-TECH ADVAN TECHNOL SYSTS, MD, 96- *Personal Data:* b Newark, NJ, Oct 30, 50. *Educ:* Pa State Univ, BS, 72; Temple Univ, MA, 78, PhD(biophys chem), 85. *Prof Exp:* Teaching asst, Biol Dept, Temple Univ, 76-78, teaching assoc, Chem Dept, 78-85; Naval res assoc, Nuclear Magnetic Resonance Spectroscopy Lab, 85-87, consult/res biol & Naval res lab scientist, Chem Warfare Defense, 87-88; asst prop, US Naval Acad, 88-95. *Concurrent Pos:* Res scientist, ImClone Systs Inc, New York, NY, 89, McNeil Consumer Prod Co, Ft Washington, Pa, 90, Purdue-Frederick Pharmaceut, Yonkers, NY, 91; assoc/consult, Trident Eng Assoc Inc, 95. *Mem:* Sigma Xi; fel Am Inst Chemists; NY Acad Sci; Am Chem Soc; Am Phys Soc; Int Union Pure & Appl Chem. *Res:* Molecular devices; theoretical and experimental circular dichroism spectroscopy; solid-state nuclear magnetic resonance spectroscopy; molecular modeling and computer assisted analysis; environmental chemistry, marine pollution abatement systems. *Mailing Add:* Rockville MD 20851. *Fax:* 410-320-8901; *E-Mail:* rsiatkowski@mantech.com

SIAU, JOHN FINN, wood science, chemical engineering; deceased, see previous edition for last biography

SIBAL, LOUIS RICHARD, MICROBIOLOGY. *Current Pos:* spec fel, Nat Cancer Inst, 65-66, res microbiologist, 66-71, dep assoc dir, 71-76, actg assoc dir viral oncol, 76-80, assoc dir, Div Cancer Cause & Prev, 80-82, extramural prog procedures off, 82-89, DIR, OFF LAB ANIMAL RES, NIH, 89- *Personal Data:* b Chicago, Ill, Aug 6, 27; m 64; c 2. *Educ:* Univ Ill, BS, 49; Univ Colo, MS, 54, PhD(microbiol), 57. *Prof Exp:* Assoc prof microbiol, Col Med, Univ Ill, 57-65. *Mem:* AAAS; Am Asn Cancer Res; Am Soc Microbiol; Am Asn Immunol. *Res:* Viral oncology; immunologic aspects of virus-induced cancer of animals and man. *Mailing Add:* NIH Bldg 1 Rm 252 Bethesda MD 20892

SIBBACH, WILLIAM ROBERT, EXTRUSION COATING, ADHESIVE LAMINATING. *Current Pos:* SR SCIENTIST, SMURFIT FLEXIBLE PACKAGING, 94- *Personal Data:* b Chicago, Ill, Mar 9, 27; m 50; c 2. *Educ:* Northwestern Univ, Evanston, PhD(chem & math), 55. *Prof Exp:* Chemist, Kraft Foods Co, 49-55 & Tee-Pak, Inc, 55-58; int adminr, Pillsbury Co, 58-59; tech dir & plant mgr, Champion Paper Co, 59-65; sr scientist, Chicopee Div, Johnson & Johnson, 65-68; tech dir, Ludlow Corp, 68-78; tech dir, Laminating & Coating Co, Jefferson Smurfit Corp, 78-94. *Concurrent Pos:* Chmn, Polymers, Laminations & Coatings Div, Tech Asn Pulp & Paper Indust, 83-85. *Mem:* Tech Asn Pulp & Paper Indust. *Res:* New packaging structure for food and pharmaceuticals; awarded six patents. *Mailing Add:* 4400 N Wildwood Ct Schaumburg IL 60195

SIBBALD, IAN RAMSAY, NUTRITION. *Current Pos:* RETIRED. *Personal Data:* b Eng, Sept 20, 31; nat Can; m 55; c 4. *Educ:* Univ Leeds, BSc, 53; Univ Alta, MSc, 55, PhD(animal nutrit), 57; DSc, Leeds Univ, 82. *Honors & Awards:* Borden Award, Nutrit Soc Can, 60; Tom Newman Mem Int Award, 77; Am Feed Mfgs Award, Poultry Sci Asn, 79. *Prof Exp:* Asst nutrit, Macdonald Col, McGill Univ, 57; asst prof, Ont Agr Col, 57-63; group leader, Animal Prod Res, John Labatt Ltd, 63-70, mgr food res sect, 70-72; prin res scientist, Animal Res Ctr, Agr Can, Ottawa, 72-89. *Mem:* Poultry Sci Asn; World's Poultry Sci Asn; Nutrit Soc Can. *Res:* Utilization of energy and nitrogen by monogastrics; various aspects of poultry nutrition; feeding stuff evaluation. *Mailing Add:* Box 291 South Mountain ON K0E 1W0 Can

SIBBALD, WILLIAM JOHN, CRITICAL CARE. *Current Pos:* AT PROG CTR, CRITICAL CARE TRAUMA UNIT, VICTORIA HOSP CORP, 79-; PROF MED & SURG, UNIV WESTERN ONT, 85- *Personal Data:* b London, Ont, June 28, 46; c 5. *Educ:* Univ Western Ont, MD, 70. *Res:* Technology evaluation; clinical-basis research; sepsis-multiple organ failure. *Mailing Add:* Dept Med Crit Care Trauma Unit Victoria Hosp Corp Univ W Ontario 375 South St PO Box 5375 London ON N6A 4G5 Can. *Fax:* 519-667-6698

SIBECK, DAVID G, ATMOSPHERIC SCIENCES. *Current Pos:* Res assoc, 85-87, SR PHYSICIST, APPL PHYSICS LAB, JOHNS HOPKINS UNIV, 87- *Educ:* Univ Calif, Los Angeles, PhD(atmospheric sci), 84. *Honors & Awards:* James B Macelwane Medal, Am Geophys Union, 92. *Res:* Geophysics. *Mailing Add:* Johns Hopkins Univ Appl Physics Lab, 24-E 155 Laurel MD 20723

SIBENER, STEVEN JAY, SURFACE CHEMISTRY, MOLECULAR BEAM SCATTERING. *Current Pos:* from asst prof to assoc prof, 85-89, PROF, DEPT CHEM & JAMES FRANCK INST, UNIV CHICAGO, 89- *Personal Data:* b Brooklyn, NY, Apr, 3, 54; c 2, Linda Young; c Leah & Leslie. *Educ:* Univ Rochester, BA & ScB, 75; Univ Calif, Berkeley, MS, 77, PhD(chem), 79. *Honors & Awards:* Marlow Medal, Faraday Div, Royal Soc Chem, 88. *Prof Exp:* Res fel, Bell Labs, 79-80. *Concurrent Pos:* Alfred P Sloan res fel, 83-87; fac develop award, IBM, 84-86; vis fel, Joint Inst Lab Astrophys, 92-93; chmn, Chem Phys Div, Am Phys Soc, 96-97. *Mem:* Am Phys Soc; Sigma Xi; AAAS; Am Chem Soc. *Res:* Molecular beam, laser spectroscopic, and ultra-high vacuum surface characterization techniques; gas-surface interaction potentials; chemisorption; physisorption; heterogeneous catalysis; two-dimensional phase transitions; surface structure; surface phonons; semiconductor reconstruction; epitaxial film growth; metallic oxidation; materials growth. *Mailing Add:* James Franck Inst Univ Chicago 5640 S Ellis Ave Chicago IL 60637

SIBERT, ELBERT ERNEST, computer science, mathematics, for more information see previous edition

SIBERT, JOHN RICKARD, MARINE ECOLOGY, STATISTICS. *Current Pos:* AT UNIV HAWAII. *Personal Data:* b Glendale, Calif, Dec 3, 40; Can citizen; c 1. *Educ:* Univ Pac, BA, 62; Columbia Univ, PhD(zool), 68. *Prof Exp:* Fel oceanog, Univ BC, 68-69, teaching fel bot, 69-70; res scientist marine ecol, Pac Biol Sta, 70-82; sr fisheries scientist, S Pac Comn, 84-87, coordr, Tuna & Billfish Prog, 84-87. *Mem:* AAAS; Am Soc Limnol & Oceanog. *Res:* Sources and fates of detritus in aquatic ecosystems; productivity of estuarine meiofauna; mathematical modelling of estuarine ecosystems; statistical descriptions of community structure; population dynamics; fisheries management. *Mailing Add:* 3039 Alencastre Pl Honolulu HI 96816-1909

SIBILIA, JOHN PHILIP, CHEMICAL PHYSICS. *Current Pos:* PRES, SIBILIA ASSOCS INC, 96- *Personal Data:* b Newark, NJ, Mar 12, 33; m 58, Phyllis Ann Capozzi; c John A, Robert V & Richard J. *Educ:* Rutgers Univ, BA, 53; Univ Md, PhD(chem), 58. *Prof Exp:* Res chemist, US Rubber Co, 59-61; res chemist, Allied Corp, 61-62, group leader, 62-67, res supvr, 67-77, mgr, Chem Physics Dept, 77-83, dir, Anal Sci Lab, 83-93, vpres enabling technologies, Allied Signal Inc, 94-95. *Concurrent Pos:* Lectr spectros & molecular workshop, Fairleigh Dickinson Univ, 65-66, instr polymer sci, 72-78; vchmn, Res & Develop Coun NJ, 85, chmn, 87-89; lectr, Polytechnic Inst, 91. *Mem:* Am Chem Soc; Am Soc Testing & Mat; Soc Appl Spectros. *Res:* Molecular structure of organic compounds, morphology of polymers; analysis of materials through spectroscopic; x-ray diffraction; microscopy, nuclear magnetic resonance and thermal analytical techniques; material structure-property relationships and pollution analysis; nylon films, fibers and plastics; published 53 articles; author of two books; granted 24 US patents. *Mailing Add:* 12 Balmoral Dr Livingston NJ 07039. *Fax:* 973-994-9623

SIBLEY, CAROL HOPKINS, MOLECULAR PARASITOLOGY. *Current Pos:* from asst prof to assoc prof, 76-89, PROF GENETICS, UNIV WASH, 89- *Personal Data:* b Freeport, NY, Oct 9, 43; m 66, Thomas; c David & Sarah. *Educ:* Univ Rochester, BA, 65, MS, 69; Univ Calif, San Francisco, PhD(biochem), 74. *Prof Exp:* Fel, Calif Inst Technol, 74-76. *Concurrent Pos:* Vis prof, Calif Inst Technol, 81; Fogarty Int fel, Free Univ Brussels, 84-85; assoc ed, J Immunol; vis scientist, Inst Molecular Med, Oxford, Eng, 92. *Mem:* AAAS; Asn Women Sci; Am Asn Microbiologists; Am Soc Trop Med & Hyg. *Res:* Drug resistance in malaria parisite, plasmodium falciporum and in opportunistic pathogens; cryptosporidium parvum and pneumocystis carinii. *Mailing Add:* Dept Genetics Box 357360 Univ Wash Seattle WA 98195-7360. *Fax:* 206-543-0754; *E-Mail:* sibley@genetics.washington.edu

SIBLEY, CHARLES GALD, SYSTEMATIC ZOOLOGY, ORNITHOLOGY. *Current Pos:* RETIRED. *Personal Data:* b Fresno, Calif, Aug 7, 17; m 42, Frances L Kelly; c Barbara, Dorothy & Carol. *Educ:* Univ Calif, Berkeley, AB, 40 & PhD(zool), 48. *Honors & Awards:* Brewster Mem Award, Am Ornith Union, 71; Daniel Giraud Elliot Medal, Nat Acad Sci, 88. *Prof Exp:* Instr zool, Univ Kans, 48-49; asst prof, San Jose State Col, Calif, 49-53; from assoc prof to prof zool, Cornell Univ, 53-65; from prof to emer prof biol & William R Coe prof ornith, Yale Univ, 65-86, cur birds, Peabody Mus Natural Hist, 65-86; dean's prof sci & prof biol, San Francisco State Univ, 86-92. *Concurrent Pos:* Guggenheim fel, 59-60; dir, Peabody Mus Natural Hist, Yale Univ, 70-76. *Mem:* Nat Acad Sci; Soc Syst Zool; Am Soc Naturalists; Am Ornith Union (treas, 53-62, pres, 86-88); Int Ornith Cong (pres, 86-90); AAAS. *Res:* Fossil birds; geographic variation, speciation and interspecific hybridization in wild populations of birds; biochemical and molecular techniques applied to proteins and DNA to reconstruct evolutionary history of birds and mammals; rates of genomic evolution; dating of divergence events; published 130 titles mostly pertaining to molecular evolution. *Mailing Add:* 433 Woodley Pl Santa Rosa CA 95409. *Fax:* 707-539-1026

SIBLEY, DUNCAN FAWCETT, SEDIMENTARY PETROLOGY. *Current Pos:* Asst prof, 74-80, ASSOC PROF GEOL, MICH STATE UNIV, 80- *Personal Data:* b Newton, Mass, Mar 9, 46; m 68. *Educ:* Lafayette Col, BA, 68; Rutgers Univ, MS, 71; Univ Okla, PhD(geol), 75. *Mem:* Soc Econ Paleontologists & Mineralogists. *Res:* Understanding of diagenesis in sandstone and carbonate rocks with specific interest in the origin and evolution of porosity. *Mailing Add:* Dept Geol Mich State Univ 206 Nat Sci Bldg East Lansing MI 48824

SIBLEY, LUCY ROY, TEXTILE FABRIC PSEUDOMORPHS, RADIOCARBON DATING OF TEXTILES. *Current Pos:* assoc prof, 84-85, CHMN DEPT TEXTILES & CLOTHING, OHIO STATE UNIV, 85- *Personal Data:* b Fayetteville, Ark, June 10, 34; m 56; c 3. *Educ:* Auburn Univ, BS, 56, MS, 58; Univ Mo, PhD(hist textiles), 81. *Prof Exp:* Instr textiles, La State Univ, 58-61, Univ Puget Sound, 69; lectr home economics, St Mary Col, 74-80, dir, Life Planning Ctr, 78-80; asst prof textile hist, Univ Ga, 80-84. *Concurrent Pos:* Prin investr, Am Philos Soc grant, 81-83, Ohio State Univ seed grant, 85-86; co-prin investr, Werner-Gren Found Anthrop Res, 84-86. *Mem:* Archaeol Inst Am. *Res:* Direct forms of archaeological fabric evidence, including textile fabric pseudomorphs, the application of small sample radiocarbon dating to Coptic textiles; developing of a sampling methodology for ancient textiles; ancient textile technology. *Mailing Add:* Textiles & Clothing Ohio State Univ 1787 Neil Ave Columbus OH 43210-1220

SIBLEY, WILLIAM ARTHUR, SOLID STATE PHYSICS. *Current Pos:* vpres acad affairs, 89-96, PROF PHYSICS, UNIV ALA, BIRMINGHAM & NSF, 96- *Personal Data:* b Ft Worth, Tex, Nov 22, 32; m 57; c 3. *Educ:* Univ Okla, BS, 56, MS, 58, PhD(physics), 60. *Prof Exp:* Res physicist, Nuclear Res Estab, Julich & Inst Metal Physics, Aachen Tech Univ, 60-61; res physicist, Oak Ridge Nat Lab, 61-70; chmn dept physics, Okla State Univ, 70-78, prof physics, 70-89, vpres res, 78-89. *Concurrent Pos:* Sigma Xi lectr, Okla State Univ, 84. *Mem:* Fel Am Phys Soc; Sigma Xi. *Res:* Optical and mechanical properties of both irradiated and unirradiated materials; light scattering; optical absorption and luminescence of laser materials. *Mailing Add:* NSF Arlington VA 22230. *Fax:* 703-306-0423; *E-Mail:* wsibley@nsf.gov

SIBLEY, WILLIAM AUSTIN, NEUROLOGY. *Current Pos:* dir dept neurol, 67-82, PROF, COL MED, UNIV ARIZ, 67- *Personal Data:* b Miami, Okla, Jan 25, 25; m 54, Joanne Shaw; c John, Jane, Peter & Andrew. *Educ:* Yale Univ, BS, 45, MD, 48. *Prof Exp:* Asst resident neurologist, Presby Hosp, New York, 51 & 53-55, resident neurologist, 56; asst neurol, Col Physicians & Surgeons, Columbia Univ, 55-56; from asst prof to assoc prof, Sch Med, Western Res Univ, 56-67, actg dir div, 59-61. *Concurrent Pos:* Consult neurologist, Vet Admin & Benjamin Rose Hosps, Cleveland, 58-; physician-in-chg neurol, Univ Hosps, 59-61. *Mem:* Am Neurol Asn (vpres, 79-80); fel Am Acad Neurol (vpres, 85-87); Asn Res Nerv & Ment Dis; Int Fed Multiple Sclerosis Soc (exec comt). *Res:* Multiple sclerosis: treatment, cause and triggering factors. *Mailing Add:* Dept Neurol Univ Ariz Health Sci Ctr Tucson AZ 85724

SIBOO, RUSSELL, IMMUNOLOGY, MICROBIOLOGY. *Current Pos:* RETIRED. *Personal Data:* b Trinidad, Wis, Mar 21, 30; Can citizen; m 66; c 2. *Educ:* McMaster Univ, BA, 58; Univ Toronto, MSc, 62; McGill Univ, PhD(immunol), 64. *Prof Exp:* Med Res Coun Can fel immunol, Univ Lund, 64-65; asst prof, Univ Sask, 65-67; asst prof, Univ Ottawa, 67-69; from asst prof to assoc prof, McGill Univ, 69-96. *Concurrent Pos:* Head, Diag Immunol Lab, Kuwait Univ, 83-85. *Mem:* Can Soc Immunol; Can Soc Microbiol. *Res:* Complement synthesis; complement synthesis; membrane receptors; CRP; fluorescence immunoassay; oral spirochete infection; DR-typing in multiple sclerosis and diabetes; &-chain disease. *Mailing Add:* 65 Hillside Ave Pointe Claire PQ H9S 5E4 Can

SIBUL, LEON HENRY, APPLIED MATHEMATICS, UNDERWATER ACOUSTICS. *Current Pos:* SR SCIENTIST & PROF ACOUST, STOCHASTIC PROCESSES, ADAPTIVE SYSTS, APPL RES LAB, PA STATE UNIV, UNIVERSITY PARK, 64- *Personal Data:* b Voru, Estonia, Aug 30, 32; US citizen; m 61; c 2. *Educ:* George Washington Univ, BEE, 60; NY Univ, MEE, 63; Pa State Univ, PhD(appl math & elec eng), 68. *Prof Exp:* Mem tech staff syst design, Bell Tel Labs, 60-64. *Concurrent Pos:* Consult, Nat Acad Sci, Nat Res Coun, 72-73; assoc ed, Trans Electronic & Aerospace Systs, Inst Elec & Electronic Engrs, 80- *Mem:* Soc Indust & Appl Math; Inst Elec & Electronic Engrs. *Res:* Adaptive systems and application of adaptive algorithms to array processing with applications to sonar, radar and seismic signal processing; broadband ambiguity function and signal design; system optimization theory; stochastic system theory. *Mailing Add:* Appl Res Lab PA State Univ PO Box 30 State College PA 16801

SIBULKIN, MERWIN, FLUID DYNAMICS. *Current Pos:* from assoc prof to prof, 63-91, EMER PROF ENG, BROWN UNIV, 91- *Personal Data:* b New York, NY, Aug 20, 26; m 49, Lucille Weiss; c Ira & Amy. *Educ:* NY Univ, BS, 48; Univ Md, MS, 53; Calif Inst Technol, AeroE, 56. *Prof Exp:* Aeronaut res scientist, Nat Adv Comt Aeronaut, 48-51; res engr, US Naval Ord Lab, 51-53 & Jet Propulsion Lab, Calif Inst Technol, 53-56; staff scientist, Sci Res Lab, Convair Div, Gen Dynamics Corp, 56-63. *Mem:* Am Soc Mech Engrs; Combustion Inst. *Res:* Combustion and fire research; heat transfer; viscous flow. *Mailing Add:* Div Eng Brown Univ Providence RI 02912. *Fax:* 401-863-1157; *E-Mail:* merwin__sibulkin@brown.edu

SIBUYA, YASUTAKA, MATHEMATICS. *Current Pos:* assoc prof, 63-65, PROF MATH, UNIV MINN, 65- *Personal Data:* b Maizuru, Japan, Oct 16, 30; m 62; c 4. *Educ:* Univ Tokyo, BS, 53, MS, 55; Univ Calif, Los Angeles, PhD(math), 59; Univ Tokyo, DS(math), 61. *Prof Exp:* Res assoc, Mass Inst Technol, 59-60; temp mem, Courant Inst, NY Univ, 60-61; asst prof math, Ochanomizu Univ, Tokyo, 62-63. *Concurrent Pos:* Vis prof, Math Res Ctr, Univ Wis-Madison, 72-73. *Mem:* Math Soc Japan; Am Math Soc; Soc Indust & Appl Math. *Res:* Field of analytic theory of ordinary differential equations. *Mailing Add:* Sch Math Univ Minn Minneapolis MN 55455-0488

SICA, LOUIS, UNCONVENTIONAL IMAGING, OPTICAL PHYSICS. *Current Pos:* RES PHYSICIST OPTICAL PHYSICS, NAVAL RES LAB, 67- *Personal Data:* b Miami, Fla, June 14, 35; m 78, Anna Glasow. *Educ:* Fla State Univ, BA, 58; Johns Hopkins Univ, PhD(physics), 66. *Prof Exp:* Res asst infrared spectros, Lab Astrophys & Phys Meteorol, Johns Hopkins Univ, 63-67. *Concurrent Pos:* Surveyor res topics mod optics, Off Naval Res, 75-76; consult, Bur Engraving & Printing, 82-84. *Mem:* Optical Soc Am. *Res:* Unconventional imaging optical coherence effects; nonlinear propagation; interferometry; space variant imaging, image-sharpness criteria. *Mailing Add:* 5952 Berkshire Ct Alexandria VA 22303. *Fax:* 302-767-9203

SICARD, RAYMOND E(DWARD), DEVELOPMENTAL PHYSIOLOGY. *Current Pos:* ASST PROF, DEPT SURG, UNIV MINN, 91-, ASST PROF, GRAD PROG MOLECULAR, CELLULAR, DEVELOPMENTAL BIOL & GENETICS, 96- *Personal Data:* b Lawrence, Mass, Apr 18, 48; m 92, Florinda Defelice; c Kathleen. *Educ:* Merrimack Col, AB, 69; Univ RI, MS, 72, PhD(biol sci), 75. *Prof Exp:* Jr bacteriologist anal, Mass Dept Pub Health, 69; hemat tech anal, New Eng Deaconess Hosp, 70-73; res assoc, Dept Biol, Amherst Col, 74; res fel, Shriners Burns Inst, Mass Gen Hosp & Harvard Med Sch, 75-76; asst prof, Dept Biol, Boston Col, 76-83; res assoc, Dept Biol, Amherst Col, 83-84; res proj develop asst, Dept Pediat, RI Hosp, 84-91. *Concurrent Pos:* Lectr, Div Pharm & Allied Health, Northeastern Univ, 75-76 & Dept Biol & Continuing Educ, Regis Col, 83-84; grant, RI Found, 86, NIH, 94, Minn Med Found, 96; tech consult, Dept Surg, Univ Minn, 91- & Dept Pediat, RI Hosp, 91. *Mem:* Sigma Xi; NY Acad Sci; Int Soc Develop Biologists; Soc Develop Biol; Wound Healing Soc. *Res:* Physiological (neural, endocrine, and immunological) regulation of the developmental events occurring during forelimb regeneration in amphibians; growth factors and cell interactions in mammalian wound healing and tissue regeneration. *Mailing Add:* Dept Surg Box 120 UMHC Univ Minn Sch Med Minneapolis MN 55455. *Fax:* 612-624-8909; *E-Mail:* sicar@maroon.tc.umn.edu

SICCAMA, THOMAS G, ECOLOGY. *Current Pos:* Assoc in res ecol, Yale Univ, 67-69, asst prof, 69-80, lectr forest ecol, 77-80, PROF, YALE FORESTRY SCH, 80- *Personal Data:* b Philadelphia, Pa, July 6, 36; m 62; c 1. *Educ:* Univ Vt, BS, 62, MS, 63, PhD(bot), 68. *Mem:* AAAS; Ecol Soc Am; Torrey Bot Club. *Res:* Ecosystem analysis; computer applications in ecology; heavy metals cycling in natural ecosystems. *Mailing Add:* Yale Univ PO Box 208240 New Haven CT 06520

SICH, JEFFREY JOHN, IMMUNOMODULATION, NEUTROPHIL FUNCTION. *Current Pos:* DIR ADMIS, SCH MED, WASHINGTON UNIV, 94- *Personal Data:* b Youngstown, Ohio, Oct 8, 54. *Educ:* Davidson Col, NC, BS, 77; Univ Cincinnati, MS, 81, PhD(microbiol), 83. *Prof Exp:* Asst prof biol, Denison Univ, 83-84, Univ Tampa, 84-86 & Youngstown State Univ, 86-92; res scientist, NIH, 92-94. *Concurrent Pos:* Res biologist, Nat Inst Arthritis, Diabetes, Digestive & Kidney Dis, NIH, 85; mem bd educ & training, Am Soc Microbiol, 90- *Mem:* Am Soc Microbiol; Sigma Xi. *Res:* Immunomodulation of macrophage and neutrophil function; effects of immunopotentiators; immunosuppressive effects associated with tumor growth. *Mailing Add:* Washington Univ Sch Med Div Biol & Biomed Sci 660 S Euclid Ave Box 8226 St Louis MO 63110

SICHEL, ENID KEIL, PHYSICS, MATERIALS SCIENCE ENGINEERING. *Current Pos:* CONSULT, 88- *Personal Data:* b Burlington, Vt, May 14, 46. *Educ:* Smith Col, Mass, AB, 67; Rutgers Univ, New Brunswick, PhD(physics), 71. *Prof Exp:* Vis scientist, Nat Magnet Lab, Mass Inst Technol, 70-71; res assoc, Rutgers Univ, New Brunswick, 71-73; mem tech staff, David Sarnoff Res Ctr, RCA Labs, 73-79; mem staff, GTE Advan Technol Lab, 79-85. *Concurrent Pos:* Consult electro-optics, Tufts Univ, 86; vis prof elec eng, Mass Inst Technol, 86-88 & 94-97; prog dir, NSF, 88-89; sr scientist, Hyperion Catalysis, 95- *Mem:* AAAS; Am Phys Soc; Mat Res Soc; Inst Elec & Electronic Engrs. *Res:* Thermophysical properties; transport and optical properties of thin solid films; conducting polymers; amorphous semi-conductors; carbon black-polymer composites; carbon nanotubes. *Mailing Add:* Box 236 Lincoln MA 01773

SICHEL, JOHN MARTIN, MOLECULAR ORBITAL CALCULATIONS. *Current Pos:* from asst prof to assoc prof, 72-83, PROF CHEM, UNIV MONCTON, 83- *Personal Data:* b Montreal, Que, Dec 2, 43; m 67, Joan Ilson; c Mindy, Daniel & Benjamin. *Educ:* McGill Univ, BS, 64, PhD(quantum chem), 68. *Prof Exp:* Fel theoret chem, Univ Bristol, 67-69; res assoc chem & physics, Ctr Res Atoms Molecules, Laval Univ, 69-70, asst prof physics, 70-72. *Concurrent Pos:* Vis prof, Univ Montreal, 81-82. *Mem:* Chem Inst Can; Can Asn Physicists; Fr Can Asn Advan Sci. *Res:* Molecular orbital calculations on molecules and surfaces. *Mailing Add:* Dept Chem & Biochem Univ Moncton Moncton NB E1A 3E9 Can. *E-Mail:* sichelj@umoncton.ca

SICHEL, MARTIN, AEROSPACE ENGINEERING, FLUID DYNAMICS. *Current Pos:* from asst prof to assoc prof, 61-68, PROF AEROSPACE ENG, UNIV MICH, ANN ARBOR, 68- *Personal Data:* b Stuttgart, Ger, Sept 1, 28; m 52, Ilse Anne Kohn; c 3. *Educ:* Rensselaer Polytech Inst, BME, 50, MME, 51; Princeton Univ, PhD(aerospace eng), 61. *Honors & Awards:* A K Oppenheim Award; Cybolski Medal, Polish Acad Sci. *Prof Exp:* Develop engr thermal power, Gen Elec Co, 51-54; res aide aerospace, Princeton Univ, 58-61. *Mem:* Am Phys Soc; fel Am Inst Aeronaut & Astronaut; Am Soc Eng Educ; Combustion Inst; AAAS. *Res:* Fluid dynamics; shock wave structure; boundary layer theory; flow with chemical reactions; hypersonic flow; detonations. *Mailing Add:* Dept Aerospace Eng Univ Mich Ann Arbor MI 48109-2140

SICHLER, JIRI JAN, MATHEMATICS. *Current Pos:* Nat Res Coun Can fel, 69-70, asst prof math, 70-75, PROF MATH, UNIV MAN, 75- *Personal Data:* b Prague, Czech, Dec 30, 41; m 68. *Educ:* Charles Univ Prague, MSc, 66, PhD(math), 68. *Concurrent Pos:* Nat Res Coun Can grants, 70-92. *Mem:* Am Math Soc; Can Math Soc. *Res:* Algebra; general mathematical systems; category theory. *Mailing Add:* Dept of Math Univ of Man Winnipeg MB R3T 2N2 Can

SICILIAN, JAMES MICHAEL, NUMERICAL ANALYSIS. *Current Pos:* SR SCIENTIST, FLOW SCI INC, 80-, VPRES, 92- *Personal Data:* b Bronx, NY, May 25, 47; m 89, Graciela Cainelli. *Educ:* Mass Inst Technol, BS, 69; Stanford Univ, MS, 70, PhD(nuclear eng), 73. *Prof Exp:* Res analyst, Savannah River Lab, 73-76; asst group leader, Los Alamos Sci Lab, 76-80. *Concurrent Pos:* Special fel, Nuclear Sci & Eng, AEC, 69-72. *Mem:* Sigma Xi; Am Soc Mech Engrs; Am Inst Aeronaut & Astronaut. *Res:* Application of numerical simulation methods to the analysis and solution of problems in hydrodynamics with emphasis on the development of convenient, efficient programs. *Mailing Add:* 1345 Los Pueblos St Los Alamos NM 87544-2663

SICILIANO, EDWARD RONALD, NUCLEAR SCATTERING THEORY, REACTION THEORY. *Current Pos:* PRIN SCIENTIST, WESTINGHOUSE HANFORD CO, 91- *Personal Data:* b Brooklyn, NY, Aug, 13, 48; m 75. *Educ:* Univ Conn, BA, 70; Ind Univ, MS, 73, PhD(physics), 76. *Prof Exp:* Fel, Dept Physics, Case Western Res Univ, 76-78 & Meson Physics Div, Los Alamos Nat Lab, 78-80; asst prof physics, Univ Colo, 80-83 & Univ Ga, 83-86; staff mem, Los Alamos Nat Lab, 86-91. *Concurrent Pos:* Vis staff mem, Meson Physics Div, Los Alamos Nat Lab, 80-86. *Mem:* Am Phys Soc; Am Asn Physics Teachers; Sigma Xi; Am Nuclear Soc. *Res:* Nuclear structure, scattering and reaction theories; electron, pion, proton, and kaon induced reactions; applied research and development for materials separation, resource recovery and isotope enrichment; computer modeling and visualization of complex processes. *Mailing Add:* Westinghouse Hanford Co MS HO-31 PO Box 1970 Richland WA 99352. *Fax:* 509-372-3777; *E-Mail:* w82929@pnlg.pnl.gov

SICILIANO, MICHAEL J, BIOCHEMICAL GENETICS. *Current Pos:* asst prof, 72-76, assoc prof, 76-, PROF BIOL & HEAD, DEPT GENETICS, SYST CANCER CTR, M D ANDERSON HOSP & TUMOR INST, UNIV TEX. *Personal Data:* b Brooklyn, NY, May 12, 37; m 61; c 3. *Educ:* St Peter's Col, BS, 59; Long Island Univ, MS, 62; NY Univ, PhD(biol), 70. *Prof Exp:* From instr to assoc prof biol, Long Island Univ, 61-72. *Concurrent Pos:* Fel, Dept Biol, M D Anderson Hosp & Tumor Inst, 70-72; consult, Tex Epidemiol Studies Prog, 77- *Mem:* Fel Genetics Soc Am; Am Soc Cell Biol; Am Soc Ichthyologists & Herpetologists; Environ Mutagen Soc. *Res:* Control of gene expression in normal and neoplastic cells; somatic cell, animal model and human tissue materials used to study the genetics of the control of enzyme phenotypes. *Mailing Add:* 12462 Barry Knoll Houston TX 77024

SICILIO, FRED, INORGANIC CHEMISTRY, RADIOCHEMISTRY. *Current Pos:* RETIRED. *Personal Data:* b Italy, Aug 10, 20; nat US; m 44; c 4. *Educ:* Centenary Col, BS, 51; Vanderbilt Univ, MA, 53, PhD(chem), 56. *Prof Exp:* Asst chemist, Springhill Paper Co, 49-51; asst, Vanderbilt Univ, 53-56; sr nuclear engr, Convair Div, Gen Dynamics Corp, Tex, 56-58; res assoc prof chem, assoc prof chem eng & head, Radioisotopes Lab, Ga Inst Technol, 58-61; from assoc prof to prof chem, Tex A&M Univ, 61-85, emer prof, 85. *Mem:* Am Chem Soc. *Res:* Radioisotope separations and purifications; radiation chemistry of organic substances; studies on free radicals in solution. *Mailing Add:* 100 Moss Ave College Station TX 77840

SICK, LOWELL VICTOR, organometallic chemistry, for more information see previous edition

SICK, THOMAS J, BRAIN METABOLISM, NEUROPHYSIOLOGY. *Current Pos:* ASSOC PROF NEUROL, SCH MED, UNIV MIAMI, 81- *Educ:* Tulane Univ, PhD(physiol), 79. *Mailing Add:* Dept Neurol Sch Med Univ Miami Miami FL 33101. *Fax:* 305-547-5380

SICKA, RICHARD WALTER, physical chemistry, polymer science, for more information see previous edition

SICKAFUS, EDWARD N, SOLID STATE PHYSICS. *Current Pos:* prin res scientist surface sci, Ford Sci Lab, 67-80, mgr, Electronic Mat & Devices Dept, 80-86, mgr, Miniature Sensors & Actuators Dept, 85-94, sr staff scientist, Automotive Components Div, 94-96, MGR PHYSICS DEPT, FORD SCI LAB, 96- *Personal Data:* b St Louis, Mo, Mar 7, 31; m 53, Mary S (Gist); c 2. *Educ:* Mo Sch Mines, BS, 55, MS, 56; Univ Va, PhD(physics), 60. *Prof Exp:* Vis lectr, Sweet Briar Col, 59-60; res physicist, Denver Res Inst, 60-67; actg head physics div, Univ Denver, 61-62, from asst prof to assoc prof physics, 62-67. *Mem:* Am Phys Soc; Am Vacuum Soc; Sigma Xi. *Res:* Electron spectroscopy and crystal physics related to surface physics; secondary electron cascade theory; auger electron spectroscopy; low energy electron diffraction; crystal defect state and growth; dynamic transmission analysis of x-rays and electrons; theoretical calculations of interstitial geometry; smart sensors; developer of structured invitive thinking. *Mailing Add:* 27981 Elba Dr Grosse Ile MI 48138

SICKO-GOAD, LINDA MAY, PHYCOLOGY. *Current Pos:* res assoc, 74-76, asst res scientist, 76-78, assoc res scientist, 78-84, RES SCIENTIST, GREAT LAKES RES DIV, UNIV MICH, 84-, MARINE SUPT, 86- *Personal Data:* b Highland Park, Mich, Sept 21, 48; m 74, Earl G; c Aaron M. *Educ:* Wayne State Univ, BS, 70; City Univ New York, PhD(biol), 74. *Prof Exp:* Technician elec micros, Mich Cancer Found, 69-70; adj lectr biol, Herbert H Lehman Col, City Univ New York, 70-72 & Bronx Community Col, 72, lab technician elec micros, Herbert H Lehman Col, 72-74. *Mem:* Phycol Soc Am; Electron Micros Soc Am; Am Soc Limnol & Oceanog; Int Asn Stereology. *Res:* Algal ultrastructure, lipid metabolism in phytoplankton and quantitative electron microscopy and ecological applications. *Mailing Add:* Ctr Great Lakes & Aquatic Sci Inst Sci & Technol Bldg Univ Mich Ann Arbor MI 48109-2099. *Fax:* 313-747-2748

SICOTTE, RAYMOND L, PRODUCT DESIGNER MICROWAVE. *Current Pos:* pres, 79-90, CHMN, AM MICROWAVE CORP, 90- *Personal Data:* b Waltham, Mass, Feb 21, 39; m 64, Margaret O'Neill; c Bradford, Charles & Brenda. *Educ:* Northeastern Univ, BSEE, 62; Univ Conn, MS, 64. *Prof Exp:* Staff mem, Mass Inst Technol, Lincoln Lab, 64-69; mem technol staff, Comsat Lab, 69-75; lab mgr, Fairchild Indust, 75-79. *Mem:* Sr mem Inst Elec & Electronics Engrs. *Res:* Development of microwave solid state circuits for communications and radar systems; published on wide band varactor upconverters and C-M wave impatt amplifiers; solid state microwave switch and attenuator and detector log video amplifier products. *Mailing Add:* American Microwave Corp 7311 G Grove Rd Frederick MD 21701

SICOTTE, YVON, PHYSICAL CHEMISTRY. *Current Pos:* From asst prof to assoc prof, 58-74, PROF CHEM, UNIV MONTREAL, 74- *Personal Data:* b Montreal, Que, Oct 12, 30; m 59; c 2. *Educ:* Univ Montreal, BSc, 54, MS, 56, PhD(chem), 59. *Concurrent Pos:* NATO fel, Res Ctr Macromolecules, Strasbourg, France, 59-60; guest prof phys chem, Univ Bordeaux, 66-67. *Mem:* Chem Inst Can; Fr-Can Asn Advan Sci. *Res:* Light scattering by pure liquids and solutions; molecular anisotropy and dielectric polarization at optical frequencies, correlations of molecular orientations in liquids; polymer chemistry and polymer characterization in solution. *Mailing Add:* Univ Montreal Dept Chem PO Box 6128 Sta A Montreal PQ H3C 3J7 Can

SICULAR, GEORGE M, HYDRAULICS, HYDROLOGY. *Current Pos:* RETIRED. *Personal Data:* b New York, NY, Aug 15, 21; m 48; c 2. *Educ:* Cooper Union, BS, 49; Columbia Univ, MS, 53; Stanford Univ, Engr, 71. *Prof Exp:* Lectr civil eng, City Col, 49-54; prof, San Jose State Univ, 54-90. *Concurrent Pos:* Consult, 55-; vis prof, Univ Roorkee, 63-64; Ford Found-Univ Wis adv, Univ Singapore, 67-69. *Mem:* Fel Am Soc Civil Engrs; Am Geophys Union. *Res:* Hydraulics; planning in water resources. *Mailing Add:* 387 Canon Del Sol Dr Watsonville CA 95076

SIDA, DEREK WILLIAM, applied mathematics, astronomy, for more information see previous edition

SIDBURY, JAMES BUREN, JR, PEDIATRICS. *Current Pos:* sci dir, 75-82, sr scientist, 82-86, EMER SR SCIENTIST, NAT INST CHILD HEALTH & HUMAN DEVELOP, NIH, 86- *Personal Data:* b Wilmington, NC, Jan 13, 22; m 53; c 5. *Educ:* Yale Univ, BS, 44; Columbia Univ, MD, 47. *Prof Exp:* Intern med, Roosevelt Hosp, NY, 47-48, asst resident, 48-49; intern pediat, Johns Hopkins Hosp, 49-50; asst resident, Univ Hosps Cleveland, Ohio, 50-51; asst & instr, Sch Med, Emory Univ, 51-53; from instr to asst prof, Johns Hopkins Univ, 54-61; assoc prof, Sch Med, Duke Univ, 61-68, prof & dir clin res unit, 68-75. *Concurrent Pos:* Fel, Sch Med, Johns Hopkins Univ, 54-57. *Mem:* AAAS; Soc Pediat Res; Am Pediat Soc; Am Soc Human Genetics; Am Acad Pediat. *Res:* Biochemical genetics. *Mailing Add:* NIH Bldg 10 Rm 95242 Bethesda MD 20892

SIDDALL, ERNEST, SAFETY RESEARCH, SOCIO-ECONOMIC IMPACT STUDIES. *Current Pos:* MEM, INST RISK RES, UNIV WATERLOO, ONT, 86-, ADJ PROF, DEPT SYSTS DESIGN ENG, 89- *Personal Data:* b Halifax, Eng, Dec 10, 19; Can citizen; m 45; c 3. *Educ:* Univ London, Eng, BSc, 39; Banff Sch Advan Mgt, Alta, dipl, 67. *Hon Degrees:* DEng, Univ Waterloo, Ont, 91. *Honors & Awards:* W B Lewis Medal, Can Nuclear Asn, 82. *Prof Exp:* Engr tel technol, Post Off Tel Syst, Brit, 39-49; sr scientist blast instrumentation, Ministry of Supply, Brit, 49-51; engr flight simulators, Can Aviation Electronics Ltd, 52-54; div head, nuclear plant design, Atomic Energy Can Ltd, 54-76 & 79-84. *Concurrent Pos:* Major, Royal Corps Signals, Brit Army, 40-46; assoc consult, Canatom Inc, Toronto, 77-79. *Mem:* Fel Can Acad Eng. *Res:* Fundamentals of safety in modern society; the total socio-economic impact of technology; use of computers in highly reliable systems. *Mailing Add:* PH307 1271 Walden Circle Mississauga ON L5J 4R4 Can

SIDDALL, THOMAS HENRY, III, CHEMISTRY. *Current Pos:* PROF CHEM, UNIV NEW ORLEANS, 69- *Personal Data:* b Sumter, SC, Oct 4, 22. *Educ:* Univ NC, AB, 42; Univ Chicago, MS, 48; Duke Univ, PhD(chem), 51. *Prof Exp:* Chemist, E I Du Pont De Nemours & Co, 50-54, res supvr chem, 54-63, res assoc, 63-69. *Mem:* Am Chem Soc. *Res:* Chemistry of actinide elements and fission products; role of structure in determining behavior of organic extractants toward actinides and fission products; molecular dynamics; isomerism; nuclear magnetic resonance. *Mailing Add:* 10918 Major Oak Dr Baton Rouge LA 70815

SIDDELL, DERRECK, STEELMAKING, NUCLEAR ENGINEERING. *Current Pos:* struct mat engr, Nuclear Fuel Handling, 73-78, supvr, Qual Assurance Dept, 78-80, MGR, METALS BR, GE CAN, 80- *Personal Data:* b Consett, Co Durham, Eng, Aug 11, 42; Can & Brit citizen; m 69, Ann Lee Taylor; c Tania Rebecca & Jeanne Yvonne. *Educ:* Lanchester Col Technol, Coventry Eng, Assoc Inst Metallurgists, 65; Univ Surrey, Eng, PhD(metall), 68. *Prof Exp:* Apprentice metallurgist, Consett Iron Co, 58-65; researcher, Univ Surrey, 65-68; res engr, Atlas Steels, Welland, Ont, 69-73. *Concurrent Pos:* Mem comt, Am Soc Mat, 80-84, chmn, 90-91; mem res bd, Can Welding Inst, 82-; vis prof, Univ Montreal, 86- *Mem:* Fel Inst Metals UK; Am Soc Mat. *Res:* Development of improved processes and designs to improve efficiency of electric motors from appliance size to major motors and large generators. *Mailing Add:* Eng Lab GE Can 107 Park St N Peterborough ON K9J 7B5 Can. *Fax:* 705-748-7948; *E-Mail:* siddelde@cnmtl.sch.ge.com

SIDDER, GARY BRIAN, METALLIC MINERAL DEPOSITS, IGNEOUS ROCKS. *Current Pos:* field asst, 75, GEOLOGIST, US GEOL SURV, 85- *Personal Data:* b Detroit, Mich, Nov 27, 54; m 81, Frances Steinzeig; c Aaron & Daniel. *Educ:* Colo State Univ, BS, 76; Univ Ore, MS, 81; Ore State Univ, PhD(geol), 85. *Prof Exp:* Geologist, Amarillo Oil Co, Pioneer Nuclear, Inc, 76-78, Houston Oil & Minerals Corp, 79 & Western Mining Corp Ltd, 80; teaching asst econ geol, Univ Ore, 80; teaching asst petrography, Ore State Univ, 80-84. *Mem:* Soc Econ Geologists; Geol Soc Am; Am Geophys Union. *Res:* Geology, geochemistry, petrology and origin of mineral deposits in the Guayana Shield of Venezuela and in the southeast Missouri iron province of the midcontinent of the United States. *Mailing Add:* 7832 S Clayton Way Littleton CO 80122. *Fax:* 303-236-5603; *E-Mail:* gbsidder@greenwood.cr.usgs.gov

SIDDIQEE, MUHAMMAD WAHEEDUDDIN, TRANSPORTATION SYSTEMS. *Current Pos:* INFO SYSTS SPECIALIST, LOCKHEED, 82- *Personal Data:* b Pakistan, Aug 23, 31; US citizen; m 61; c 2. *Educ:* Panjab Univ, BA, 51, BSc, 55; Univ Tenn, MS, 60; Univ Minn, PhD(control sci), 67. *Prof Exp:* Elec engr, Siemens Pakistan, 55-56 & Siemens Schuckertwerke, WGer, 56-58; sr elec engr, Siemens Pakistan, 58-59, exec engr, 60-62; res engr, 67-69, sr res engr, 69-74, staff scientist & mgr transp, Sri Int, 74-82. *Mem:* Inst Elec Engrs, Pakistan. *Res:* Advanced transportation systems; air traffic analysis; railroad analysis; urban transportation systems and electric power systems and information systems; software metrics and measurements; author of 27 technical papers. *Mailing Add:* 1733 Banff Dr Sunnyvale CA 94087

SIDDIQUE, IRTAZA H, VETERINARY MEDICINE, MICROBIOLOGY & PUBLIC HEALTH. *Current Pos:* from asst prof to assoc prof, 64-71, PROF MICROBIOL, SCH VET MED, TUSKEGEE INST, 71-, PROF PUB HEALTH, 78-, ACTG HEAD, 92- *Personal Data:* b Budaun, India, July 4, 29; m 54, Shana K Siddique; c Najeeb I & Asim I. *Educ:* Bihar Vet Col, Patna, GBVC, 50; Univ Minn, St Paul, MS, 61, PhD(vet med), 63; Univ Ala, Birmingham, MPH, 78. *Prof Exp:* Vet, Govt Uttar Pradesh, India, 50-59. *Concurrent Pos:* Proj dir, USPHS grant, 64-69, proj dir, 69-; dir, NSF grant, 65-75; dir, USDA-Coop State Res Serv grant, 74-; chmn, S-92 Tech Comt, Southern Regional Proj, 77-78; dir, USDA-CSRS grant, 83-88, 95-97, MBRS grant, 84-87; pres, World Asn Vet Educrs, 95- *Mem:* Conf Res Workers Animal Dis; Am Vet Med Asn; Am Soc Microbiol; Ny Acad Sci; Sigma Xi; World Asn Vet Educr (vpres, 91-); Am Asn Food Hyg Vet; Asn Vet Med Cols. *Res:* Listeriosis; immunofluorescent techniques and electron microscopy; cattle abortion and bacterial infections and pathogenesis. *Mailing Add:* Sch Vet Med Tuskegee Inst Tuskegee AL 36088

SIDDIQUI, ASLAM RASHEED, NUCLEAR MEDICINE. *Current Pos:* From asst prof to assoc prof, 76-84, PROF RADIOL, SCH MED, IND UNIV, 84- *Personal Data:* b British India, Dec 12, 46; US citizen; m 73; c 3. *Educ:* Chittagong Med Col, EPakistan, MD, 69. *Concurrent Pos:* Consult radiol, Vet Admin Hosp, Indianapolis & staff physician radiol, Wishard Mem Hosp, Indianapolis, 76- *Mem:* Soc Nuclear Med; AMA; Radiol Soc NAm; Am Col Physicians; AAAS. *Res:* Nuclear medicine studies in pediatric oncology; nuclear thyroidology. *Mailing Add:* Radiol Dept Hosp Children Rm 1053P Indianapolis IN 46202-5200

SIDDIQUI, IQBAL RAFAT, ORGANIC CHEMISTRY. *Current Pos:* RETIRED. *Personal Data:* b India, Jan 28, 31; m 56. *Educ:* Univ Sind, Pakistan, BSc, 48, MSc, 50; Univ Birmingham, PhD(chem), 57. *Hon Degrees:* DSc, Univ Birmingham, 69. *Prof Exp:* Lectr chem, Govt Col, Lahore, Pakistan, 51-52; Sugar Res Found fel, Univ London, 57-58; Nat Res Coun Can fel, 58-60; Harold Hibbert Mem fels, McGill Univ, 61-62; group leader struct & sensory team, Food Res Inst, Can Dept Agr, 62-93. *Mem:* Fel Royal Soc Chem; fel Chem Inst Can; Am Chem Soc. *Res:* Structural, synthetic and analytical studies of carbohydrates; carbohydrates of honey; polysaccharide of bacteria, fungi, rapeseed, alginates and tobacco; dietary fibers from Canadian vegetables. *Mailing Add:* 1153 Trent St Ottawa ON K1Z 8J5 Can

SIDDIQUI, M A Q, GENE EXPRESSION IN CARDIAC MUSCLE, CARDIOVASCULAR DISORDERS. *Current Pos:* PROF & CHMN, DEPT ANAT & CELL BIOL, HEALTH SCI CTR, STATE UNIV NY, BROOKLYN, 87- *Personal Data:* b Hyderabad, India, Feb 10, 37; US citizen; m 84, Samena; c Norain & Umair. *Educ:* Osmania Univ, BS, 57; Univ Houston, MS, 64, PhD(biol sci), 67. *Prof Exp:* Res chemist III, Univ Calif, Berkeley, 67-69; res assoc, Dept Biochem, Roche Inst Molecular Biol, 69-72, from asst mem to mem, 72-87. *Concurrent Pos:* Vis prof, Dept Biochem, Rutgers State Univ, 75-85; assoc ed, Cellular & Molecular Biol, 91-92; ed-in-chief, Cellular & Molecular Biol Res, 93- *Mem:* Am Soc Biol Chemists; Int Cell Res Orgn; Am Soc Microbiol; Int Soc Differentiation; Int Soc Heart Res; Am Soc Cell Biol; Soc Develop Biol; Am Soc Hypertension; Am Heart Asn; Int Soc Heart Res. *Res:* Molecular aspect of cardiac muscle development; early embryonic development; gene expression in normal and diseased muscles. *Mailing Add:* Dept Anat & Cell Biol State Univ NY Health Sci Ctr 450 Clarkson Ave Box 5 Brooklyn NY 11203-2012. *Fax:* 718-270-3732

SIDDIQUI, MOHAMMED MOINUDDIN, mathematical statistics, for more information see previous edition

SIDDIQUI, WAHEED HASAN, TERATOLOGY, PHARMACOKENETICS. *Current Pos:* ASSOC SCIENTIST, DOW CORNING CORP, MICH, 79- *Personal Data:* b Bijnor, India, Aug 2, 39; US citizen; m 69, Nuzhat; c Jafar & Asma. *Educ:* Agra Univ, India, BSc, 60; Sind Univ, Pakistan, MSc, 64; Carleton Univ, Ont, PhD(biol), 71; Univ Western Ont, MEng, 77. *Prof Exp:* Sr biologist, Environ Control Consult, Ltd & Natural Mus Nat Sci, Can, 72-76; res scientist toxicol, Health Protection Br, Dept Health & Welfare, Govt Can, 77-79. *Mem:* Soc Toxicol; Soc Toxicol Can; Sigma Xi; Teratology Soc. *Res:* Safety evaluation of new chemicals; long and short-term effects of chemicals in animal models; risk assessment for human exposure; metabolism and pharmacokinetics; developmental toxicology. *Mailing Add:* Dow Corning Corp Mail Co 3101 Midland MI 48686-0994

SIDDIQUI, WASIM A, PARASITOLOGY, TROPICAL MEDICINE. *Current Pos:* assoc prof, 69-73, PROF TROP MED & MICROBIOL, SCH MED, UNIV HAWAII, MANOA, 73- *Personal Data:* b India, May 10, 34; m 65; c 2. *Educ:* Aligarh Muslim Univ, India, BSc, 52, MSc, 54; Univ Calif, Berkeley, PhD(zool), 61. *Prof Exp:* Lectr zool, Aligarh Muslim Univ, 54-57; res asst, Univ Calif, Berkeley, 57-61; lectr, Aligarh Muslim Univ, 61-62; NIH res fel parasitol, Rockefeller Univ, 62-65; instr trop med, Sch Med, Stanford Univ, 65-69. *Mem:* Soc Protozool; Am Soc Parasitol; Am Soc Trop Med & Hyg; Int Soc Immunopharmacol. *Res:* Protozoa, especially parasitic protozoans; amoebiasis and malaria. *Mailing Add:* 512 Halemaumau St Honolulu HI 96821

SIDDOWAY, CHRISTINE SMITH, STRUCTURAL & METAMORPHIC GEOLOGY. *Current Pos:* Vis asst prof, 94-95, ASST PROF GEOL, COLO COL, 96- *Educ:* Carleton Col, Minn, BA, 84; Univ Ariz, MS, 89; Univ Calif, Santa Barbara, PhD(geol), 95. *Concurrent Pos:* Geologist, R/V Polar Duke, 89, scientist, R/V Polar Queen, 92-93; res asst, Inst Crustal Studies, 89-92; mem, Antarctic Res Prog Italy, Univ Siena, 95-97; Fulbright fel, Italy, 95-96. *Mem:* Am Geophys Union; Geol Soc Am; Asn Women Geologists. *Res:* Geology of Antarctica/Pacific sector; Gondwana tectonics; structural and metamorphic geology of the Colorado Front Range. *Mailing Add:* Dept Geol Colo Col 14 E Cache la Poudre Colorado Springs CO 80903. *Fax:* 719-389-6910; *E-Mail:* csiddoway@cc.colorado.edu

SIDEBOTTOM, OMAR M(ARION), mechanics, for more information see previous edition

SIDEL, VICTOR WILLIAM, COMMUNITY HEALTH, PREVENTIVE MEDICINE. *Current Pos:* prof community health, 69-74, chmn dept social med, 69-74, DISTINGUISHED UNIV PROF SOCIAL MED, MONTEFIORE MED CTR, ALBERT EINSTEIN COL MED, 74- *Personal Data:* b Trenton, NJ, July 7, 31; m 56; c 2. *Educ:* Princeton Univ, AB, 53; Harvard Med Sch, MD, 57. *Prof Exp:* From intern to jr asst resident med, Peter Bent Brigham Hosp, 57-59; clin assoc, Nat Heart Inst, 59-61; sr asst res, Peter Bent Brigham Hosp, 61-62; instr biophys, Harvard Med Sch, 62-64, assoc prev med, 64-68, asst prof med, 68-69. *Concurrent Pos:* Am Heart Asn advan res fel, 62-64; consult physician, Child Health Div, Children's Hosp Med Ctr, Boston, 63-67; Med Found, Inc res fel, 64-68; asst med & chief prev & community med units, Mass Gen Hosp, 64-69; Milbank Mem Fund fac fel, 64-71; consult, USPHS, 64-70, WHO, 69, 74 & 77 & Int J Health Serv, 71-79; vis prof community health & social med, City Col New York, 73-; vis prof, Scand Sch Pub Health, 75-88; attend physician, NCent Bronx Hosp, 76-; adj prof pub health, Cornell Univ Med Col, 87- *Mem:* Am Pub Health Asn (pres, 84-85); NY Acad Med; Asn Teachers Prev Med; Physicians Soc Responsibility (pres, 87-88); Royal Soc Health Gt Brit. *Res:* International health care comparisons; health care delivery; medical ethics; health policy. *Mailing Add:* Dept Epidemiol Pub Health Albert Einstein Col Med 1300 Morris Park Ave Bronx NY 10461-1926

SIDELL, BRUCE DAVID, COMPARATIVE PHYSIOLOGY, FISH BIOLOGY. *Current Pos:* from asst prof to assoc prof zool, 82-88, assoc dean res, Col Sci, 89-90, PROF ZOOL & COOP PROF BIOCHEM, UNIV MAINE, 88- *Personal Data:* b Manchester, NH, Mar 20, 48; m 70, Mary P Keegan; c Amy R, Jessica M & Amanda L. *Educ:* Boston Univ, AB, 70; Univ Ill, MS, 72, PhD(physiol), 75. *Prof Exp:* Asst res scientist aquatic biol, Chesapeake Bay Inst, Johns Hopkins Univ, 75-77. *Concurrent Pos:* Mem res comt Maine affil, Am Heart Asn, 82-86; ed adv, Marine Ecol Prog Ser, 83-90; assoc ed, J Exp Zool, 85-88. *Mem:* Am Soc Zoologists; Sigma Xi; Am Physiol Soc; Soc Exp Biol. *Res:* Physiological and biochemical adaptations of aquatic ectotherms; physiology of fishes. *Mailing Add:* Dept Zool Univ Maine 5751 Marray Hall Orono ME 04469-5751. *Fax:* 207-581-2537; *E-Mail:* bsidell@maine.maine.edu

SIDELL, FREDERICK R, CHEMISTRY. *Current Pos:* DIR, MED MGT CHEM CASUALTIES COURSE & SR MED OFFICER, US ARMY MED RES INST CHEM DEFENSE, 64- *Personal Data:* b Marietta, Ohio, July 27, 34. *Educ:* Marietta Col, BS, 56; NY Univ, MD, 60. *Mem:* Am Soc Pharmacol & Exp Therapeut; Am Soc Clin Pharmacol. *Mailing Add:* 14 Brooks Rd Bel Air MD 21014-3610

SIDEN, EDWARD JOEL, MOLECULAR IMMUNOLOGY, B CELL DEVELOPMENT. *Current Pos:* ASST PROF MED, MT SINAI MED SCH, NEW YORK, 87- *Personal Data:* b Miami Beach, Fla, Aug 5, 47; m 84. *Educ:* Brandeis Univ, BA, 69; Univ Calif, San Diego, PhD(biol), 75. *Prof Exp:* Teaching fel bacteriophage, Univ Calif, San Diego, 75-76 & molecular immunol, Mass Inst Technol, 76-80; asst prof immunol & med microbiol, Col Med, Univ Fla, 80-87. *Mem:* Am Soc Microbiol; Am Asn Immunologists. *Res:* Immortalizing immature hemopoietic cells using Abelson murine leukemia virus to study early stages of B cell differentiation. *Mailing Add:* 29 S Clinton Ave Hastings on Hudson NY 10706. *Fax:* 212-241-6357

SIDEROPOULOS, ARIS S, PHOTOBIOLOGY, ENVIRONMENTAL POLLUTANTS. *Current Pos:* PROF MICROBIOL, DUQUESNE UNIV, 75- *Personal Data:* b Thessaloniki, Greece, Jan 30, 37; US citizen. *Educ:* Concordia Col, Minn, BS, 60; NDak State Univ, MS, 62; Univ Kans, PhD(molecular genetics), 67. *Prof Exp:* Fel microbiol genetics, Palo Alto Res Found, 67-70; res assoc, Univ Tex, Austin, 70-71; asst prof, Med Col Pa, 71-75. *Concurrent Pos:* Chief, Microbiol Lab, Fairmont Dairy Co, Minn & instr bacteriol, NDak State Univ, 62-63. *Mem:* Am Soc Microbiol; Sigma Xi; AAAS. *Res:* Cellular repair of potentially mutagenic damage to establish and utilize an experimental method in evelation of mutagenic effects of chemicals on ultraviolet irradiated living cells. *Mailing Add:* Dept Biol Sci Duquesne Univ Pittsburgh PA 15282. *Fax:* 412-396-6332

SIDES, GARY DONALD, INSTRUMENT DEVELOPMENT, ENVIRONMENTAL MONITORING. *Current Pos:* PRES, CMS RES CORP, 86- *Personal Data:* b Tuscaloosa, Ala, Oct 5, 47; c 3. *Educ:* Univ Ala, BS, 69; Univ Fla, MS, 71, PhD(phys chem), 75. *Prof Exp:* Res scientist, Aerospace Res Labs, 71-75; res assoc prof, Wright State Univ, 75-77; sr scientist, Chem Defense Div, Southern Res Inst, head, 78-86. *Mem:* Am Soc Mass Spectrometry; Am Chem Soc. *Res:* Automated analytical instruments for the detection of nanogram levels of toxic organophosphorus and organosulfur compounds. *Mailing Add:* 2009 Sweetgum Dr Birmingham AL 35244-1612

SIDES, PAUL JOSEPH, ELECTROCHEMICAL ENGINEERING, SEMICONDUCTOR PROCESSING. *Current Pos:* From asst prof to assoc prof, 81-92, PROF CHEM ENG, CARNEGIE MELLON UNIV, 92- *Personal Data:* b Birmingham, Ala, Jan 23, 51; m 87. *Educ:* Univ Utah, BS, 73; Univ Calif, Berkeley, PhD(chem eng), 81. *Mem:* Am Inst Chem Engrs; Am Inst Mining, Metall & Petrol Engrs; Electrochem Soc. *Res:* Investigation of electrolytic gas evolution; electrochemical engineering of primary aluminum production; organometallic vapor phase epitaxy of mercury cadmium tellwride. *Mailing Add:* Dept Chem Eng Carnegie Mellon Univ 5000 Forbes Ave Pittsburgh PA 15213-3816

SIDHU, BHAG SINGH, PLANT GENETICS, PLANT SCIENCE. *Current Pos:* PROF BIOL, WINSTON-SALEM STATE UNIV, 69- *Personal Data:* b Ludhiana, India, Apr 30, 29; m 54; c 2. *Educ:* Punjab Univ, India, BSc, 51, MSc, 53; Cornell Univ, PhD(genetics, plant sci), 60. *Prof Exp:* Chmn dept bot, Govt Col, Rupar, India, 54-57; chmn dept agr & biol, Govt Col, Faridkot, India, 61-62, prin-pres, 63; Nat Res Coun Can fel, McGill Univ, 64-65; assoc prof biol, Winston-Salem State Col, 65-66; UN adv agron & biol, UNESCO, UN Develop Prog, Manila, P I, 66-68. *Concurrent Pos:* Res award, Asn Cols Agr, Philippines, 67; NSF fel, NC State Univ, 70. *Mem:* AAAS; Am Inst Biol Sci; Am Soc Agron; Crop Sci Soc Am. *Res:* Biosystematics and germ plasm screening of international field food crops materials; radiation genetics and international seed production and distribution. *Mailing Add:* 1230 Bunny Trail Winston-Salem NC 27105

SIDHU, DEEPINDER PAL, THEORETICAL PHYSICS, COMPUTER SCIENCE. *Current Pos:* PROF COMPUT SCI, UNIV MD, 88- *Personal Data:* b Chachrari, India, May 13, 44; m 69; c 4. *Educ:* Univ Kans, BE, 66; State Univ NY Stony Brook, PhD(theoret physics), 73, MS, 79. *Prof Exp:* Res assoc physics, Rutgers Univ, New Brunswick, 73-75; asst physicist, Brookhaven Nat Lab, 75-77, assoc physicist, 77-80; mem tech staff, Mitre Corp, 80-82; mgr, Secure Distrib Systs Dept, Dept Computer Sci, Iowa State Univ, 84-88. *Res:* Unified gauge theories of strong, electromagnetic and weak interactions; computer communication networks. *Mailing Add:* Dept Computer Sci Univ Md Baltimore MD 21228

SIDHU, GURMEL SINGH, GENETICS, PLANT PATHOLOGY. *Current Pos:* RES SCIENTIST & PROF, CALIF STATE UNIV, 86-; RES SCIENTIST, GERMAIN'S INC, FRESNO, 91- *Personal Data:* b Pasla, India, May 23, 44; Can citizen; m 79, Buljel K Aulakh; c Vikram S & Roop S. *Educ:* Punjab Univ, BSc, 58, MSc, 60; Univ BC, PhD(genetics), 72. *Prof Exp:* Res assoc plant genetics, Punjab Agr Univ, 62-64, lectr genetics/cytogenetics, 64-66; res assoc plant sci, Univ BC, 66-67; fel, Simon Fraser Univ, 72-76, res scientist genetics & path, 76-80; asst prof plant pathol, Univ Nebr, 80-86. *Concurrent Pos:* Vis prof, Punjab Agr Univ, 76-77; Genetics Soc Am Travel grant, 78 & 83; assoc ed, Phytopath, 82-86, Crop Sci, India, 82-86; res fel, Univ Wis, 85. *Mem:* Genetics Soc Can; Genetics Soc Am; Am Soc Phytopath; Can Phytopath Soc; Indian Soc Crop Improvement; AAAS. *Res:* Genetics of host-parasite interactions; genetics of plant disease complexes; breeding for disease resistance; fungal genetics; molecular biology of host-parasite interaction; analysis of pathotoxins. *Mailing Add:* Dept Biol Calif State-Fresno Fresno CA 93740. *Fax:* 209-233-8839

SIDI, HENRI, ORGANIC CHEMISTRY, POLYMER CHEMISTRY. *Current Pos:* group leader, Heyden Div, Garfield, 61-71, SR SCIENTIST, INTERMEDIATES DIV, TENNECO CHEM, INC, PISCATAWAY, 71- *Personal Data:* b Provadia, Bulgaria, Mar 13, 19; US citizen; m 56; c 2. *Educ:* Univ Toulouse, ChE, 41, PhD(org chem), 48. *Prof Exp:* Asst anal chem, Univ Toulouse, 46-47; sr chemist, Poudrerie Nationale, Toulouse, France, 47-48; asst dir dyestuffs, Francolor, Oissel, 48-50; fel, Rutgers Univ, 50-51; sr chemist, Heyden Chem Corp, 51-61. *Mem:* AAAS; Am Chem Soc; Chem Soc France. *Res:* Polymerization of formaldehyde; fire retardant chemicals; amino-alcohols; pesticides. *Mailing Add:* 156 Victoria Ave Paramus NJ 07652-1923

SIDIE, JAMES MICHAEL, NEUROETHOLOGY, COMPARATIVE PHYSIOLOGY. *Current Pos:* ASST PROF PHYSIOL/NEUROBIOL, STATE UNIV NY, BUFFALO, 76- *Personal Data:* b Elizabeth, NJ, May 22, 41; m 66; c 1. *Educ:* Univ Notre Dame, BS, 64, MS, 67, PhD(biol), 70. *Prof Exp:* Pub Health Serv fel, Ind Univ, 69-71; vis lectr, Princeton Univ, 71-72; res assoc, Univ Ore, 72-74, vis asst prof, 74-76. *Concurrent Pos:* NSF fel, Woods Hole, 71. *Mem:* AAAS; Am Soc Zoologists; Animal Behav Soc; Sigma Xi. *Res:* Neuroethological studies of communication in honeybees, Apis mellifera; computer assisted analyses of neural spike trains in nerve/muscle systems. *Mailing Add:* Dept Biol Urisinus Col Collegeville PA 19426

SIDKY, YOUNAN ABDEL MALIK, IMMUNOLOGY, TUMOR BIOLOGY. *Current Pos:* RETIRED. *Personal Data:* b Khartoum, Sudan, Feb 9, 28; div; c 2. *Educ:* Cairo Univ, BSc, 50, MSc, 55; Univ Marburg, PhD(zool), 56. *Prof Exp:* Demonstr zool, Cairo Univ, 50-59, lectr, 59-65; res assoc, Univ Wis-Madison, 65-69, proj res assoc, 72-76, assoc scientist, 76-87, sr scientist, 87-90, res assoc prof, 90-93; fel, Univ Alta, 69-72. *Mem:* Am Asn Immunologists; Am Asn Cancer Res; Int Soc Interferon Res. *Res:* Parathyroid glands in reptiles; effect of steroids on mouse thymus development; development of immunity in turtles; hibernation and immunity in hamsters; inhibitory effect of brown fat on the immune response; tumor and lymphocyte induced angiogenesis; effects of interferons and cytotoxic drugs on tumor growth. *Mailing Add:* 440 S Gulfview Blvd No 1201 Clearwater FL 34630-8253. *Fax:* 414-778-4411

SIDLE, ROY CARL, LANDSLIDES, CUMULATIVE EFFECTS. *Current Pos:* RES SOIL SCIENTIST & HYDROLOGIST, FORESTRY SCI LAB, FOREST SERV, USDA, 80- *Personal Data:* b Quakertown, Pa, Oct 31, 48; c 2. *Educ:* Univ Ariz, BS, 70, MS, 72; Pa State Univ, PhD(soil sci), 76. *Prof Exp:* Hydrologist, Wright Water Engrs, Inc, 72; res asst soil sci, Pa State Univ, 72-76; res soil scientist, Agr Res Serv, USDA, 76-78; asst prof watershed sci, Dept Forest Eng, Ore State Univ, 78-80. *Concurrent Pos:* Assoc ed, J Environ Qual, 90-; res fel, Japan, 91. *Mem:* Soil Sci Soc Am; Am Soc Agron; Sigma Xi; Int Soc Soil Sci; Am Geophys Union; Am Water Resources Asn; Int Asn Hydrol Sci; Japan Soc Hydrol & Water Resources. *Res:* Cumulative effects of land management practices; modeling slope stability; processes of erosion and sediment transport; role of subsurface flow on landslide initiation; natural hazards; water quality, environmental impacts of mining; subsurface hydrology; watershed management. *Mailing Add:* 518 E 600 S Logan UT 84321. *Fax:* 435-753-8625; *E-Mail:* sidle@cc.usu.edu

SIDLER, JACK D, ORGANIC CHEMISTRY. *Current Pos:* assoc prof, 67-72, PROF CHEM, MANSFIELD UNIV, 72- *Personal Data:* b Rochester, Pa, Sept 19, 39; m 58; c 3. *Educ:* Geneva Col, BS, 61; State Univ NY Buffalo, PhD(chem), 66. *Prof Exp:* Teaching asst, State Univ NY, Buffalo, 61-62; asst prof chem, Geneva Col, 65-67. *Mem:* Am Chem Soc. *Res:* Organic synthesis; organolithium chemistry; organic reaction mechanisms. *Mailing Add:* Dept Chem Mansfield Univ Mansfield PA 16933

SIDMAN, CHARLES L, IMMUNOLOGY, IMMUNOGENETICS. *Current Pos:* PROF MOLECULAR GENETICS BIOCHEM & MICROBIOL, UNIV CINCINNATI COL MED, 91- *Personal Data:* b New York, NY, June 7, 50; m 70, Amy Stapleton; c Alfred & Elanor. *Educ:* Harvard Univ, AB, 71, AM, 72, PhD(immunol), 76. *Prof Exp:* Fel, Dept Path, Harvard Med Sch, 76-78; mem, Basel Inst Immunol, 78-82; staff scientist, Jackson Lab, 82-92. *Concurrent Pos:* Coop fac, Univ Maine, 83-91; guest fac, Col of the Atlantic, 87-; consult, Maine Cytometry Res Inst, 88-91; adv & consult, Maine Ctr Innovation Biomed Technol, 89-; prin investr, Mt Desert Island Biol Lab, 92-; assoc, Pac Ctr Ethics & Appl Biol, 92- *Mem:* Am Asn Immunologists; Am Soc Biochem & Molecular Biol; AAAS; Human Genome Orgn; Am Asn Cancer Res. *Res:* Immunogenetics, including autoimmunity, immunodeficiency, immunotoxicology; carcinogenesis; genetic and environmental toxicology, ecology; genomics, mutation and evolution; ethics of scientific research. *Mailing Add:* Univ Cincinnati Col Med 3110 Med Sci Bldg ML-524 231 Bethesda Ave Cincinnati OH 45267-0524. *Fax:* 513-558-8474; *E-Mail:* sidmancl@ucbeh.san.uc.edu

SIDMAN, RICHARD LEON, NEUROPATHOLOGY, DEVELOPMENTAL GENETICS. *Current Pos:* from assoc prof to prof, 63-68, BULLARD PROF NEUROPATH, HARVARD MED SCH, 69-; CHIEF, DIV NEUROGENETICS, NEW ENG REGIONAL PRIMATE RES CTR, 91- *Personal Data:* b Boston, Mass, Sept 19, 28; m 50, 74; c 2. *Educ:* Harvard Univ, AB, 49, MD, 53. *Honors & Awards:* Stearns Mem Lectr, Albert Einstein Col Med, 58. *Prof Exp:* Intern med, Boston City Hosp, Mass, 53-54; Moseley traveling fel, Strangeways Res Lab, Cambridge Univ & Dept Human Anat, Oxford Univ, 54-55; asst resident neurol, Mass Gen Hosp, Boston, 55-56; asst, Mass Gen Hosp, 59-69. *Concurrent Pos:* Chief, Div Neurosci, Children's Hosp, Boston, 72-88. *Mem:* Nat Acad Sci; Am Asn Anat; Tissue Cult Asn (secy, 64-70); Am Asn Neuropath; Soc Neurosci; Int Soc Develop Neurosci; Histochem Soc; Am Acad Arts & Sci. *Res:*

Developmental genetics of the normal and diseased mammalian brain. *Mailing Add:* Div Neurogenetics New Eng Regional Primate Res Ctr One Pine Hill Dr Southboro MA 01772. *Fax:* 508-624-8075; *E-Mail:* rsid@wavpen.med.harvard.edu

SIDNEY, STUART JAY, MATHEMATICAL ANAYLSIS. *Current Pos:* assoc prof, 71-80, PROF, UNIV CONN, 80- *Personal Data:* b New Haven, Conn, June 8, 41; m 65; c 4. *Educ:* Yale Univ, BA, 62; Harvard Univ, MA, 63, PhD(math), 66. *Prof Exp:* Instr math, Yale Univ, 66-68, asst prof, 68-71. *Concurrent Pos:* Vis prof, Univ Grenoble, 71-72 & 78-79. *Mem:* Am Math Soc; Math Asn Am. *Res:* Analysis, especially uniform algebras and Banach spaces; geometry. *Mailing Add:* Dept Math Univ Conn Storrs CT 06269-3009

SIDOTI, DANIEL ROBERT, NUTRITION. *Current Pos:* CONSULT, FOOD PROD RES & DEVELOP. *Personal Data:* b North Bergen, NJ, Jan 17, 21; m 51, Gloria Ebaugh; c Lisa. *Educ:* Union Col, Schenectady, BA, 47; Stevens Inst Technol, MS, 59. *Prof Exp:* Qual control chemist, Robert A Johnston Co Inc, 40-42; group leader, Gen Foods Corp, 46-66; sect head, Monsanto Co, 66-69; res mgr, Anheuser-Busch Co Inc, 69-91. *Concurrent Pos:* Prod mgr, Carter-Wallace, 69; chmn, St Louis Sect, Inst Food Technol, 72-73; counr, Inst Food Technologists, 78-91. *Mem:* Inst Food Technologists; Am Asn Cereal Chemists; Soc Advan Food Serv Res. *Res:* New product and process development; functional oil applications in food products; fat and oil substitutes; high intensity sweeteners; new functional ingredients in food products; awarded six patents. *Mailing Add:* 500 Wellshire Ct Ballwin MO 63011

SIDRAN, MIRIAM, SOLID STATE PHYSICS. *Current Pos:* prof, 72-90, chmn, 83-89, EMER PROF PHYSICS, BARUCH COL, 90- *Personal Data:* b Washington, DC, May 25, 20. *Educ:* Brooklyn Col, BA, 42; Columbia Univ, MA, 49; NY Univ, PhD(physics), 56. *Honors & Awards:* NY Univ Founder's Day Award, 56. *Prof Exp:* Instr physics & chem, Brothers Col, Drew Univ, 46-47; instr physics, Adelphi Col, 47-49; asst solid state physics, NY Univ, 50-55, Nat Carbon Co fel, 55-58; sr physicist, Balco Res Labs, NJ, 55; asst prof chem & physics, Staten Island Community Col, State Univ NY, 58-59; res scientist, Grumman Aircraft Eng Corp, 59-67; prof physics & dep chmn dept, NY Inst Technol, NY Campus, 67-72. *Concurrent Pos:* NSF sci fac fel, Nat Marine Fisheries Serv, Nat Oceanic & Atmospheric Admin, 71-72. *Mem:* Assoc fel Am Inst Aeronaut & Astronaut; NY Acad Sci; Soc Women Engrs; Sigma Xi; Am Asn Physics Teachers. *Res:* Microwave spectrometry; optical spectrometry; infrared astronomy; lunar luminescence; lunar surface studies; radiation dosimetry; rotational energy levels of asymmetric molecules; remote sensing of sea surface temperature. *Mailing Add:* Baruch Col 17 Lexington Avee New York NY 10010

SIDRANSKY, HERSCHEL, PATHOLOGY. *Current Pos:* PROF PATH & CHMN DEPT, GEORGE WASHINGTON UNIV MED CTR, 77- *Personal Data:* b Pensacola, Fla, Oct 17, 25; m 52, Evelyn Lipsitz; c Ellen & David I. *Educ:* Tulane Univ, BS, 48, MD, 53, MS, 58; Am Bd Path, dipl, 58. *Prof Exp:* Intern, Charity Hosp La, New Orleans, 53-54, vis asst pathologist, 54-58; instr path, Tulane Univ, 54-58; med officer, Nat Cancer Inst, 58-61; prof path, Sch Med, Univ Pittsburgh, 61-72; prof path & chmn dept, Col Med, Univ SFla, 72-77. *Concurrent Pos:* Consult, Div Biologics, Stand Contract Comt, NIH, 66-67, mem path study sect res grants rev br, Div Res Grants, 68-72, mem nutrit study sect, 73-77; vis scientist, Weizmann Inst Sci, 67-68, Eleanor Roosevelt Int Cancer fel travel award & USPHS spec res fel, 67-68; mem bd, Am Registry Path, 79-87; adv comt, Life Sci Res Off, FASEB, 82-88; mem, Intersoc Comt Path Info, 82-83, chmn, 83- *Mem:* Soc Exp Biol & Med; Am Inst Nutrit; Sigma Xi; AAAS; Int Acad Path; Am Soc Clin Nutrit; Am Asn Cancer Res; Am Asn Path; NY Acad Sci. *Res:* Chemical pathology of nutritional deficiencies; experimental liver tumor igenesis; tryptophan metabolism. *Mailing Add:* Dept Path George Washington Univ Med Ctr 2300 Eye St NW Washington DC 20037

SIDWELL, ROBERT WILLIAM, VIROLOGY, CHEMOTHERAPY. *Current Pos:* res prof, Depts Biol & Animal, Dairy & Vet Sci, 77-87, PROF VIROL, UTAH STATE UNIV, 87-, DIR, INST ANTIVIRAL RES, 91- *Personal Data:* b Huntington Park, Calif, Mar 17, 37; m 57, Rhea Julander; c Richard D, Jeanette K, David E, Cynthia D, Michael J & Robert O. *Educ:* Brigham Young Univ, BS, 58; Univ Utah, MS, 61, PhD(microbiol), 63. *Honors & Awards:* D Wynne Thorne Res Award, Utah State Univ, 87. *Prof Exp:* Head serol & rickettsial res, Univ Utah, 58-63; head virus res, Univ Utah & Dugway Proving Grounds, 63; sr virologist, Chemother Dept, Southern Res Inst, 63-66, head virus sect, 66-69; head dept virol, ICN Pharmaceut Nucleic Acid Res Inst, 69-72, chemother div, 72-75, dir, 75-77. *Concurrent Pos:* Prin investr, NIH, 63-69, 87-, Thrasher Res Found, 79-84 & US Army Med Res & Develop Command, 85-; asst prof, Dept Microbiol, Univ Ala, Birmingham, 64-69; rev ed, J Chemother, J Antiviral Res, Antimicrobial Agts & Chemother, 69-; mem, Tech Adv Comt, Thrasher Res Fund Found, 84-89; chmn, Basic Res Subcomt, Div AIDS, NIH & mem, AIDS Liaison Subcomt; bd trustees, Inter-Am Soc Chemother, 90-; ed, Int Soc Antiviral Res News, 91- *Mem:* Am Asn Immunologists; Soc Exp Biol & Med; Am Soc Microbiol; Am Soc Virol; Inter-Am Soc Chemother (secy, 86-89, pres, 93-); Int Soc Antiviral Res; Int Soc Chemother; Nat Asn Col Teachers Agr; Sigma Xi. *Res:* Discovery and development of vidarabine; a drug used for herpesvirus infections and ribavirin; a drug approved for respiratory syncytial virus infections; basic and applied research on viral disease chemotherapy and immunotherapy. *Mailing Add:* Inst Antiviral Res Utah State Univ Logan UT 84322-5600. *Fax:* 435-750-3959

SIE, CHARLES H, ELECTRICAL ENGINEERING, MATERIAL SCIENCE. *Current Pos:* mgr component & packaging technol, 77-84, mgr, electronic design & technol, 84-92, vpres, corp eng ctr, w coast site, XEROX CORP, 92- *Personal Data:* b Shanghai, China, Sept 12, 34; US citizen; m 58; c 3. *Educ:* Manhattan Col, BS, 57; Drexel Univ, MS, 60; Iowa State Univ, PhD(elec eng), 69. *Prof Exp:* Elec engr, Radio Corp Am, NJ, 57-63; mem res staff, Watson Res Ctr, IBM Corp, NY, 66-69; mgr, Memory Device Develop, Energy Conversion Devices, Inc, 69-74; mgr, Component Lab, Burroughs Corp, 74-77. *Concurrent Pos:* Consult, World Bank. *Mem:* Inst Elec & Electronics Engrs; Am Phys Soc. *Res:* Semiconductor and ferromagnetic memory devices; amorphous chalcogenide semiconductor; electrical circuit design; component and reliability engineering; software management; technology management. *Mailing Add:* Xerox Corp 1701 S Aviation Blvd ESAE MS375 El Segundo CA 90245

SIE, EDWARD HSIEN CHOH, BIOCHEMISTRY. *Current Pos:* SR SCIENTIST, MICROBICS CORP, 85- *Personal Data:* b Shanghai, China, Jan 17, 25; US citizen; wid; c 1. *Educ:* Univ Nanking, BS, 46; Ill Inst Technol, MS, 51; Princeton Univ, PhD(biochem), 57. *Prof Exp:* Int trainee, Joseph E Seagram & Sons, Inc, Ky, 47-48; biochemist trainee, E R Squibb & Sons, Inc, NY, 51-52; jr biochemist, Ethicon Inc, 52-54; res assoc biochem, Princeton Univ, 57-59; res assoc microbial chem, Mt Sinai Hosp, New York, 59-62; sr chemist, Space Div, NAm Aviation, Inc, 62-63; res specialist, 63-66, sr tech specialist, Autonetics Div, NAm Rockwell Corp, 66-68; res supvr, Biomed Div, Gillette Res Inst, 68-70; sr scientist, 70-73, sales mgr, Eastern region US, 73-78, sr develop scientist, Carlsbad opers, Beckman Instruments Inc, 78-83; mgr, tech mkt, Carlsbad Opers, Smith, Kline, Beckman, 84-85. *Mem:* AAAS; Am Chem Soc; NY Acad Sci. *Res:* Industrial enzymology and fermentation; chemistry of bioluminescence and its application; growth and nutrition of thermophilic bacteria; keratin of hair and skin; action of keratinase; clinical enzymology and diagnostic reagents. *Mailing Add:* 15281 Notre Dame St Westminster CA 92683. *Fax:* 760-438-2980

SIEBEIN, GARY WALTER, ARCHITECTURAL ACOUSTICS, AUDITORIUM DESIGN & ANALYSIS. *Current Pos:* from asst prof to assoc prof, 80-92, PROF ARCHIT, ARCHIT TECHNOL RES CTR, UNIV FLA 93-, DIR. *Personal Data:* b New York, NY, Jan 3, 51; m 84, Rita A Wooten; c Lana, Alan, Lisa, Keely, Gary & Kara. *Educ:* Rensselaer Polytech Inst, BS, 72, BArch, 78; Univ Fla, MArch, 80. *Honors & Awards:* Educ Hon Citation, Am Inst Archit, 88 & 92; Progressive Archit Citation for Appl Res Acoustics, 89 & 94; Res Citation, Nat Coun Acoust Consults, 89. *Prof Exp:* Health facil planner, Philips Med Syts, Inc, 73-75; proj coordr, Elec Eng Servs, Norwalk, Conn, 75-77. *Concurrent Pos:* Consult, archit acoust, 82-; prin invest, NSF, 83-94; vis lectr, various univs, Registration Inst, 84-; mem, Nat Coun Acoust Consults & Inst Noise Control Engrs. *Mem:* Fel Acoust Soc Am; Soc Bldg Sci Educrs; Am Soc Heating, Refrig & Air Conditioning Engrs. *Res:* Architectural acoustical modeling; development of acoustical design criteria; analysis of auditoria and concert halls; electric lighting quality and day lighting; thermal performance evaluation of buildings. *Mailing Add:* Dept Archit Univ Fla 231 Arch PO Box 11S702 Gainesville FL 32611-5702. *Fax:* 352-371-1990

SIEBEL, M(ATHIAS) P(AUL), MECHANICAL ENGINEERING. *Current Pos:* CONSULT, 87- *Personal Data:* b Witten, Ger, Mar 6, 24; nat US; m 60, Katherine E Jente. *Educ:* Bristol Univ, BS, 49, PhD, 52. *Prof Exp:* In charge res & develop & asst works mgr, Tube Investments, Ltd, Eng, 53-57; res assoc, Columbia Univ, 58-59; gen mgr, Pressure Equip Div, Pall Corp, 59-64; vpres & mgr opers, Radiation Dynamics, Inc, NY, 64-65; dep dir, Mfg Eng Lab, NASA, 65-68, dir, Process Eng Lab, 68-74, staff scientist, Marshall Space Flight Ctr, 74-79, mgr, Michoud Assembly Facil, 79-87. *Concurrent Pos:* Assoc dean, Col Eng, Univ New Orleans, 89-92. *Mem:* Sigma Xi. *Res:* Industrial and research management; strength of materials; space sciences. *Mailing Add:* 5204 Janice Ave Kenner LA 70065

SIEBELING, RONALD JON, MICROBIOLOGY. *Current Pos:* Asst prof, 66-74, ASSOC PROF MICROBIOL, LA STATE UNIV, BATON ROUGE, 74- *Personal Data:* b Oostburg, Wis, Nov 10, 37; m 59; c 4. *Educ:* Hope Col, AB, 60; Univ Ariz, MS, 62, PhD(microbiol), 66. *Mem:* Am Soc Microbiol. *Res:* Immunobiology; immune suppression and antigenic competition. *Mailing Add:* Dept Microbiol La State Univ Baton Rouge LA 70803-0001

SIEBENS, ARTHUR ALEXANDRE, PHYSIOLOGY, REHABILITATION MEDICINE. *Current Pos:* prof rehab med & surg, 71-76, RICHARD BENNETT DARNALL PROF REHAB MED & PROF SURG, JOHNS HOPKINS UNIV, 77-, CHIEF DIV REHAB MED, UNIV & DIR REHAB MED, HOSP, 71- *Personal Data:* b Atlanta, Ga, July 13, 21; m 48; c 6. *Educ:* Oberlin Col AB, 43; Johns Hopkins Univ, MD, 47. *Prof Exp:* Asst physiol, Sch Med, Johns Hopkins Univ, 45-48; asst prof physiol & pharmacol, Long Island Col Med, State Univ NY Downstate Med Ctr, 48-52; from assoc prof physiol to prof, 54-58; prof physiol, Sch Med & dir respiratory & rehab ctr, Hosps, Univ Wis-Madison, 58-71. *Concurrent Pos:* Mem physiol study sect, USPHS, 49-64 & prog-proj comt, Nat Heart Inst, 65-69; dir dept rehab med, Good Samaritan Hosp, Baltimore, Md, 71-; consult, Vet Admin Hosp, Madison, Wis. *Mem:* AAAS; Am Physiol Soc; fel Am Acad Phys Med & Rehab; Am Cong Rehab Med. *Res:* Respiratory, cardiovascular and nervous system physiology; swallowing impairment; orthotics. *Mailing Add:* Good Samaritan Hosp 5601 Loch Raven Blvd Baltimore MD 21239-2905

SIEBENTRITT, CARL R, JR, HEALTH PHYSICS. *Current Pos:* chief, Radiol Defense Br & Chmn Interagency Subcomt Offsite Emergency Instrumentation, 79-88, RES PHYS SCIENTIST, FED EMERGENCY MGT AGENCY, 88- *Personal Data:* b Jersey City, NJ, Aug 14, 22; m 57; c

6. *Educ:* Univ Cincinnati, BSME, 47, MS, 49. *Prof Exp:* Physicist, Instrument Div, Keleket X-ray Corp, 49-51; supvr nuclear instrument develop, Cincinnati Div, Bendix Corp, 51-62; dir, Nucleonics Div, Defense Civil Preparedness Agency, Dept Defense, 62-73; staff dir, Detection & Countermeasures Div, 73-79. *Concurrent Pos:* Chmn, Interagency Task Force Instrumentation Radiol Emergencies Involving Fixed Nuclear Facil, 73-81. *Mem:* Health Physics Soc. *Res:* Instrumentation and systems for detection and measurement of radioactivity; nuclear instrumentation for radiological emergency response; radiation damage to insulators; granted 5 US patents. *Mailing Add:* Fed Emergency Mgt Agency Rte 601 Bldg 217 PO Box 129 Berryville VA 22611-0129. *Fax:* 540-542-2083; *E-Mail:* carlsieb@aol.com

SIEBER, FRITZ, CANCER RESEARCH, BLOOD PRODUCTS. *Current Pos:* assoc prof, 85-90, PROF PEDIAT, MED COL WIS, 90- *Personal Data:* b Erstfeld, Switz, Jan 28, 46; m 74, Maya F Blum; c Peter E & Alex D. *Educ:* Swiss Fed Inst Technol, PhD(biochem & cell biol), 76. *Honors & Awards:* Frederick Stohlman Mem Award, 87. *Prof Exp:* Asst prof med & oncol, Sch Med, Johns Hopkins Univ, 75-85. *Concurrent Pos:* Joint Apppointments cell biol & anat, microbiol & biophys, Med Col Wis, 86-, Med, 92- *Mem:* AAAS; Am Soc Cell Biol; Am Soc Hemat; Am Asn Cancer Res; Am Soc Photobiol; Int Soc Exp Hemat. *Res:* Autologous bone marrow transplantation, photodynamic therapy; antiviral agents. *Mailing Add:* Dept Pediat Med Col Wis 8701 Watertown Plank Rd Milwaukee WI 53226. *Fax:* 414-266-8642

SIEBER, JAMES LEO, MATHEMATICS, DISCRETE STRUCTURES. *Current Pos:* From asst prof to assoc prof, 63-67, chmn dept, 64-85, PROF MATH & COMPUT SCI, SHIPPENSBURG STATE COL, 67- *Personal Data:* b New Glasgow, NS, Nov 3, 36; US citizen. *Educ:* Shippensburg State Col, BS, 58; Pa State Univ, MA, 61, PhD(math), 63. *Concurrent Pos:* Actg dir comput ctr, Shippensburg State Col, 67-68; dir, NSF Inst, 69-71. *Mem:* Math Asn Am; Asn Comput Mach. *Res:* Abstract spaces in general topology, syntopogenous spaces, quasi-uniform spaces and quasi-proximity spaces; computer science and mathematics administration. *Mailing Add:* Dept Math & Comput Sci Shippensburg Univ Shippensburg PA 17257. *Fax:* 717-530-4009

SIEBER, SUSAN M, CANCER EITIOLOGY, TECATOLOGY. *Current Pos:* DEP DIR, DIV CANCER EPIDEMIOL & GENETICS, NAT CANCER INST, MD, 96- *Personal Data:* b Hattiesburg, Miss, May 18, 42. *Educ:* George Washington Univ, MS, 69, PhD(pharmacol), 71. *Mem:* Am Asn Cancer Res; Am Soc Pharmacol & Exp Therapeut. *Mailing Add:* Div Cancer Epidemiol & Genetics Nat Cancer Inst 6130 Executive Blvd Rm 540 Rockville MD 20852. *Fax:* 301-402-3256; *E-Mail:* siebers@epndce.nci.nih.gov

SIEBERT, ALAN ROGER, PHYSICAL CHEMISTRY, POLYMER CHEMISTRY. *Current Pos:* Sr res chemist, Res Ctr, BF Goodrich Co, 56-68, res assoc, 68-69, sect leader specialty elastomer, 69-73, proj tech mgr, Res & Develop Ctr, 73-77, prod mgr reactive liquid polymers, 77-78, sr prod mgr new prod, Chem Div, 78-80, MKT MGR & RES & DEVELOP MGR, REACTIVE LIQUID POLYMERS, CHEM GROUP, B F GOODRICH CO, 80- *Personal Data:* b Cleveland, Ohio, July 16, 30; m 54; c 3. *Educ:* Fenn Col, BChemEng, 53; Western Reserve Univ, MS, 54, PhD(chem), 57. *Mem:* Am Chem Soc; Soc Aeorspace Mat & Process Engrs. *Res:* Relation between structure and properties of polymers; emulsion and solution polymerization; polymerization and characterization of reactive liquid polymers; polymerization and characterization of rubber and plastic latexes; impact resistant; thermo setting and thermoplastic resins. *Mailing Add:* 3999 E Meadow Lane Cleveland OH 44122-4705

SIEBERT, DONALD ROBERT, SOLID STATE LASERS, OPTICS & FIBER OPTIC SENSORS. *Current Pos:* SR PROG MGR, ADVAN PROD DEVELOP, PRECISION PROD, 96- *Personal Data:* b Oak Ridge, Tenn, July 6, 46; m 68, Lynn Laitman; c Arielle J & Asher B. *Educ:* Union Col, NY, BS, 68; Columbia Univ, NY, PhD(phys chem), 73. *Prof Exp:* Asst prof chem, Drew Univ, Madison, NJ, 74-80; res chemist, Photon Chem Dept, Allied Corp, 78-79, res physicist electro-optic prod, 80-81, proj engr electro-optic prod, 81-82, proj leader sci lasers, 82-83, sr res physicist, 83-84, res assoc & prog mgr, Laser Res & Develop Dept, 84-90, prog mgr, Laser & Systs, 90-93, prog mgr, Laser & Fiber Optic Gyro Systs, 93-94, eng mgr, Electro-optics, 94-95, mg concurrent eng, 95-96. *Mem:* Soc Photo-Optical Instrumentation Engrs; Am Phys Soc; Optical Soc Am. *Res:* Design and development of scientific solid state lasers and laser systems; molecular spectroscopy; thermal lensing; applications of lasers to chemical, physical and environmental problems; design of fiber optic gyro sensors and systems. *Mailing Add:* 178 Hillcrest Ave Morris Township NJ 07960. *Fax:* 201-393-2121; *E-Mail:* donald.siebert@alliedsignal.com

SIEBERT, ELEANOR DANTZLER, PHYSICAL CHEMISTRY, SCIENCE EDUCATION. *Current Pos:* assoc prof, 74-83, PROF PHYS SCI, MT ST MARY'S COL, 83- *Personal Data:* b Birmingham, Ala, July 18, 41; m 67, Raymond A; c Cynthia & Gregory. *Educ:* Duke Univ, BA, 63; Univ Calif, Los Angeles, PhD(chem), 69. *Prof Exp:* Res chemist, Allied Chem Corp, 63-65; mem fac, Dept Chem, Univ Calif, Los Angeles, 70-71; mem fac, Dept Phys Sci, Westlake Sch, 71-73. *Concurrent Pos:* Proj dir, NSF CAUSE Prog, 76-79; staff res, Univ Calif, Los Angeles, 83-85; proj dir, NSF/CSIP Prog, 87-89; prin invest, NIH-MBRS Prog, 86-89, MARC Prog, 91- *Mem:* AAAS; Am Chem Soc; Sigma Xi; Soc Col Sci Teachers; Nat Sci Teachers Asn (pres, 91-93). *Res:* Nucleation and growth in phase separation; equation of state data; corresponding states; thermodynamic measurements; molecular potentials; individualized learning. *Mailing Add:* 3863 Marcasel Ave Los Angeles CA 90066. *Fax:* 310-954-4379; *E-Mail:* esiebert@msmc.le.edu

SIEBERT, JEROME BERNARD, AGRICULTURAL ECONOMICS. *Current Pos:* economist agr econ, 66-69, assoc dir admin, Univ Calif Coop Exten, 72-80, dir, 80-88, ECONOMIST DEPT AGR RES ECON, UNIV CALIF BERKELEY, 88- *Personal Data:* b Fresno, Calif, Dec 12, 38; m 60; c 2. *Educ:* Univ Calif, Davis, BS, 60; Univ Calif, Berkeley, PhD(agr econ), 64. *Prof Exp:* Asst undersecy admin, USDA, 69-70, exec asst admin, Consumer & Mkt Serv, 70-71, asst secy, 71-72. *Concurrent Pos:* Consult to dir, Calif Dept Food & Agr, 67-69; alt, Walnut Control Bd, USDA, 67-69, mem, Joint USDA & Nat Asn State Univ & Land Grant Cols Comt Educ & chmn, Independent Study & Exten Educ Comt, USDA Grad Sch, 71-72; dir, Tri Valley Growers Inc, 72-75; mem, Blue Ribbon Comt Agr, State Calif, Lt Gov Off, 73-74; dir, Calif Farm Bur, 80-88; chmn, Walnut Mkt Bd, 82- *Mem:* Am Agr Econ Asn; Am Econ Asn. *Res:* Agricultural marketing and policy; environmental policy. *Mailing Add:* Dept Agr Resource Econ Univ Calif 338 Giannini Hall Berkeley CA 94720-3310

SIEBERT, JOHN, organic chemistry, business administration, for more information see previous edition

SIEBERT, KARL JOSEPH, MULTIVARIATE ANALYSIS, CHEMOMETRICS. *Current Pos:* chmn, 90-95, PROF BIOCHEM, FOOD SCI & TECHNOL DEPT, CORNELL UNIV, 90- *Personal Data:* b Harrisburg, Pa, Oct 29, 45; m 70, Sui T Atienza; c Trina & Sabrina. *Educ:* Pa State Univ, BS, 67, MS, 68, PhD(biochem), 70. *Honors & Awards:* Nat Sci Found Fel, 69; Master Brew Pres Award, 86, 90. *Prof Exp:* Synthetic chemist, Appl Sci Labs, Inc, 70; res assoc, Stroh Brewery Co, 71, head res & develop sect, 71-76, mgr res & develop lab, 76-82, dir res, 82-90. *Concurrent Pos:* Mem, tech comt, Am Soc Brewing Chemists, 83-89, chmn, 86-88; bd visitors, Oakland Univ Biol Dept, Rochester, Mich, 85-89; vpres, Strohtech, 86-89; assoc dir, Cornell Inst Food Sci, 90-95, mem bd dirs, Cornell Res Found, 90-96; int consult brewing & food sci, 90-; hon prof, Moscow State Acad Food Prod, Moscow, Russia, 96. *Mem:* Am Chem Soc; Am Soc Brewing Chemists; Master Brewers Asn Am; Inst Food Technologists; Int Chemometrics Soc. *Res:* Beverage properties and processing; fermentation; process monitoring and controlling instrumentation; computer programming; laboratory automation; laboratory management; experiment design and statistical analysis; development and optimization of analytical methods, processes, and fermentation operations, using statistical experiment designs, mathematical modeling and multivariate analysis techniques; use of pattern recognition for cultivar identification, adulteration detection; extensive beverage experience. *Mailing Add:* Dept Food Sci & Technol Cornell Univ NYSAES Geneva NY 14456. *Fax:* 315-787-2397; *E-Mail:* karl_siebert@cornell.edu

SIEBERT, W(ILLIAM) M(CCONWAY), COMMUNICATIONS. *Current Pos:* asst & instr elec eng, Mass Inst Tech, 47, from asst prof to prof elec eng, 52-84, mem staff & group leader, Lincoln Lab, 53-55, FORD PROF ENG, MASS INST TECHNOL, 84- *Personal Data:* b Pittsburgh, Pa, Nov 19, 25; m 49, Anne Decker; c Thomas, Terry, Peter & Theodore. *Educ:* Mass Inst Technol, SB, 46, ScD, 52. *Honors & Awards:* Pioneer Award, Inst Elect & Electronics Engrs Aerospace & Electronic Syst Soc, 88. *Prof Exp:* Jr res engr, Res Labs, Westinghouse Elec Corp, 46-47. *Concurrent Pos:* Mem, security resources panel, Gaither Comt, 56. *Mem:* Fel Inst Elec & Electronics Engrs; Acoust Soc Am. *Res:* Statistical communication theory; radar theory; electrical communications; communications biophysics. *Mailing Add:* Dept Elec Eng & Comput Sci Mass Inst Technol Cambridge MA 02139

SIEBES, MARIA, BLOOD FLOW IN DISEASED ARTERIES, FUNCTIONAL CARDIOVASCULAR IMAGING. *Current Pos:* ASST PROF, DEPT BIOMED ENG, UNIV IOWA, IOWA CITY, 89- *Personal Data:* b Dinslaken, Ger, Feb 14, 58. *Educ:* Fachhochschule Giessen, Ger, Dipl-Ing, 81; Univ Southern Calif, MS, 84, PhD(biomed eng), 89. *Honors & Awards:* Honor for Meritorious Res, AMA, 88. *Prof Exp:* Res engr, Kerckhoff Klinik, Max Planck Inst Physiol & Clin Res, Bad Nauheim, Ger, 81-83; mem tech staff, Caltech, Biomed Image Processing Group, Jet Propulsion Lab, 83-89. *Mem:* Sigma Xi; Am Soc Mech Engrs; Inst Elec & Electronics Engrs. *Res:* Hemodynamics of coronary artery stenoses, including arterial wall mechanics; quantitative image processing of coronary angiograms to obtain functional information regarding coronary physiology; mathematical modeling of coronary blood flow. *Mailing Add:* Dept Biomed Eng Univ Iowa Iowa City IA 52242. *Fax:* 319-335-5631; *E-Mail:* siebes@hanna.eng.uiowa.edu

SIEBRAND, WILLEM, CHEMICAL PHYSICS, THEORETICAL CHEMISTRY. *Current Pos:* From asst res officer to assoc res officer, 63-72, sr res officer, 72-83, PRIN RES OFFICER THEORET CHEM, NAT RES COUN CAN, 83- *Personal Data:* b Ijsselmuiden, Neth, Aug 12, 32; wid; c Barbara & Saskia. *Educ:* Univ Amsterdam, Drs, 60, Dr(phys chem). 63. *Honors & Awards:* H M Tory Medal, Royal Soc Can. *Concurrent Pos:* Ed, Can J Chem, 85-95; corresp, Royal Dutch Soc Arts & Sci. *Mem:* Fel Royal Soc Can; Can Inst Chem. *Res:* Electronic and spectroscopic properties of molecular crystals; vibrational-electronic coupling in molecules; radiationless transitions; hydrogen tunneling. *Mailing Add:* Steacie Inst Molecular Sci Nat Res Coun Can Ottawa ON K1A 0R6 Can. *Fax:* 613-954-5242; *E-Mail:* willem.siebrand@nrc.ca

SIEBRING, BARTELD RICHARD, INORGANIC CHEMISTRY. *Current Pos:* from asst prof to prof, 53-92, EMER PROF CHEM, UNIV WIS, MILWAUKEE, 92- *Personal Data:* b George, Iowa, Sept 24, 24. *Educ:* Macalester Col, BA, 47; Univ Minn, BS, 48, MS, 49; Syracuse Univ, PhD, 53. *Prof Exp:* Instr chem, Worthington Jr Col, 48-50; prof, Jamestown Col, 53. *Concurrent Pos:* Vis prof, US Mil Acad, West Point, 81-82 & 88-90. *Mem:* Am Chem Soc. *Res:* History of chemistry; coordination compounds;

identification and description of areas of excellence in the training of scientists, especially the study of institutions and professors; modern trends and issues of chemical education; identification of personal attributes of leading personalities in the history of chemistry, with emphasis on possibly common characteristics. *Mailing Add:* 3018 E Newport Ct Milwaukee WI 53211

SIEBURTH, JOHN MCNEILL, MARINE MICOROBIOLOGY, ATMOSPHERIC CHEMISTRY & PHYSICS. *Current Pos:* RETIRED. *Personal Data:* b Calgary, Alta, Sept 1, 27; nat US; m 50; c 5. *Educ:* Univ BC, BSA, 49; Wash State Univ, MS, 51; Univ Minn, PhD(bact), 54. *Prof Exp:* Assoc prof vet sci, Va Polytech Inst & State Univ, 55-60; researcher biol oceanog, Univ RI, 60-61, prof oceanog, 66-, prof microbiol, 68-91. *Concurrent Pos:* Antarctic microbiologist, Int Geophys Yr, Arg Navy, 57-59; vis prof, Marine Biol Lab, Woods Hole, Mass, 73-74 & Norweg Inst Seaweed Res, Trondheim, 66-67. *Mem:* Am Soc Microbiol; Am Soc Limnol & Oceanog; Phycol Soc Am; Sigma Xi; AAAS; Soc Protozoologists; Brit Phycol Soc. *Res:* Physics, chemistry and microbiology of the oxic-anoxic transition zone of anoxic marine basins; microbial production and consumption of greenhouse gases in the upper ocean; role of bacteria, microalgae and protozoa in marine microbial food webs. *Mailing Add:* 408 Barbers Pond Rd West Kingston RI 02892

SIECKHAUS, JOHN FRANCIS, INDUSTRIAL CHEMISTRY. *Current Pos:* Sr chemist & group leader, 66-80, MGR, LIFE SCI RES & DEVELOP DEPT, OLIN CORP, 80- *Personal Data:* b St Louis, Mo, Sept 23, 39; m 63; c 3. *Educ:* Rockhurst Col, AB, 61; St Louis Univ, MS, 65, PhD(chem), 67. *Honors & Awards:* IR-100 Award, Indust Res Mag, 71. *Mem:* Am Chem Soc; Sigma Xi. *Res:* Biotechnology development related to agriculture, energy and chemical production. *Mailing Add:* 89 Brooklawn Dr Milford CT 06460-2806

SIECKMANN, DONNA G, CELLULAR IMMUNOLOGY, IDIOTYPIC REGULATION. *Current Pos:* MICROBIOLOGIST, INFECTIOUS DIS DEPT, NAVAL MED RES INST, 79- *Personal Data:* b Austin, Tex, Mar 26, 46; m 84. *Educ:* Univ Nebr, BS, 69; Mont State Univ, MS, 70; Univ Calif, San Diego, PhD(biol), 75. *Prof Exp:* Fel, Lab Immunol, Nat Inst Allergy & Infectious Dis, NIH, 75-78, staff fel, 78-79. *Mem:* Am Soc Microbiol; Am Asn Immunologists; NY Acad Sci; Sigma Xi; AAAS; Am Soc Trop Med & Hyg. *Res:* B lymphocyte activation by anti-immunoglobulin antibody; anti-idiotypic vaccines; regulation of immune responsiveness by anti-idiotypic antibody. *Mailing Add:* Naval Med Res Inst 8901 Wisconsin Ave Bethesda MD 20889-5607. *Fax:* 301-295-6641

SIECKMANN, EVERETT FREDERICK, THEORETICAL PHYSICS, EXPERIMENTAL SOLID STATE PHYSICS & PHYSICAL CHEMISTRY. *Current Pos:* assoc prof, 62-67, PROF PHYSICS, UNIV IDAHO, 67- *Personal Data:* b Alexandria, Nebr, Dec 31, 28; m 51, Lois Lavone Rippe; c Sharlene Katherine & Christine Elizabeth. *Educ:* Doane Col, BA, 50; Fla State Univ, MS, 52; Cornell Univ, PhD(theoret solid state physics), 60. *Prof Exp:* Asst chem, Fla State Univ, 50-52; asst prof, Univ Ky, 57-62. *Concurrent Pos:* Consult, Librascope Div, Gen Precision, Inc, Calif, 61 & Holloman AFB, USAF, NMex, 62-63; vis prof physics, Univ Calif, Berkeley, 76, Jet Propulsion Lab, 80. *Mem:* Am Asn Physics Teachers; Am Phys Soc. *Res:* Impurity states in ionic crystals; single crystals of alkaline earth oxides; electrochemistry; applied mathematics; theoretical calculations on electron hole drops in Ge; optical dispersion of crystals containing color centers; heat storage by alkaliflourides. *Mailing Add:* 509 S Polk Moscow ID 83843. *E-Mail:* everetts@uidaho.edu

SIEDBAND, MELVIN PAUL, X-RAY MACHINE DESIGN, ELECTRON INSTRUMENT DESIGN. *Current Pos:* prof, 72-91, EMER PROF MED PHYSICS, UNIV WIS, 91- *Personal Data:* b Chicago, Ill, Dec 17, 28; m 50, Dorothy Shicmover; c Marc & Eric. *Educ:* Univ Wash, BA, 52; Johns Hopkins Univ, MS, 70; Med Col Wis, PhD(med physics), 94. *Prof Exp:* Eng mgr, Westinghouse X-ray, 52-72. *Concurrent Pos:* Chair design & x-ray, Am Asn Physicists Med, 76-83. *Mem:* Int Soc Optical Eng; Inst Elec & Electronics Engrs; Am Asn Physicists Med. *Res:* Beam filtration in diagnostic radiology; design of small x-ray systems; design of specialized instruments. *Mailing Add:* 5821 Dorsett Dr Madison WI 53711. *Fax:* 608-274-4737

SIEDE, WOLFRAM, YEAST GENETICS, RADIATION BIOLOGY. *Current Pos:* instr path, ASST PROF PATH RES, UNIV TEX SOUTHWESTERN MED CTR, 94- *Personal Data:* b Darmstadt, Ger, Sept 10, 58. *Educ:* Univ Frankfurt, Ger, dipl biol, 81, PhD(microbiol), 86. *Prof Exp:* Res fel, Stanford Univ, Sch Med, 86-90. *Mem:* Genetics Soc Am; Am Soc Microbiol. *Res:* Yeast genetics; DNA repair with emphasis on regulation and interaction with cell cycle controls. *Mailing Add:* 5030 Maple Springs Blvd Dallas TX 75235. *Fax:* 214-648-4067; *E-Mail:* siede@utsw.swmed.edu

SIEDLE, ALLEN R, INORGANIC CHEMISTRY. *Current Pos:* res chemist, 77-85, SR RES SPECIALIST, SCI RES LAB, 3M CENT RES LAB, 85- *Personal Data:* b Pittsburgh, Pa. *Educ:* Ind Univ, PhD(chem), 73. *Prof Exp:* Fel chem, Nat Bur Stand, 73-75, res chemist, 75-77. *Res:* Synthetic inorganic chemistry; catalytic and surface chemistry; materials science-ceramics. *Mailing Add:* Bldg 201-2E-02 3M Ctr 3M Cent Res Lab 201-2E 3M Ct St Paul MN 55144

SIEDLER, ARTHUR JAMES, FOOD SCIENCE, NUTRITION. *Current Pos:* head, Dept Food Sci, Univ Ill, Urbana, 72-89, prof nutrit sci, 72-94, prof food sci, 89-94, EMER PROF FOOD SCI, UNIV ILL, URBANA, 94- *Personal Data:* b Milwaukee, Wis, Mar 17, 27; m 76, Doris J Northrup; c William, Sandra (Lowman), Nancy (Wilhite), Randall R & Roxanne (Butler). *Educ:* Univ Wis, BS, 51; Univ Chicago, MS, 56, PhD(biochem), 59. *Prof Exp:* Asst biochem, Am Meat Inst Found, 51-53, from asst biochemist to biochemist, 53-64, chief, Div Biochem & Nutrit, 59-64; group leader spec biol, Norwich Pharmacal Co, 64-65, chief physiol, 65-69, biochem, 69-72. *Concurrent Pos:* Instr & asst prof, Univ Chicago, 59-64. *Mem:* Coun Agr Sci & Technol; fel Inst Food Technologists; Am Chem Soc; Am Inst Nutrit; Sigma Xi. *Res:* Antimicrobial agent; biological activity napthoquinones; chemotherapeutic agents; food additives. *Mailing Add:* Dept Food Sci Univ Ill 1304 W Pennsylvania Urbana IL 61801. *Fax:* 217-333-9329

SIEDOW, JAMES N, PLANT PHYSIOLOGY. *Current Pos:* ASSOC PROF BOT, DUKE UNIV, 81- *Personal Data:* b Chicago, Ill, Sept 21, 47. *Educ:* Ind Univ, PhD(plant biochem), 72. *Mailing Add:* Dept DCMB/Bot Duke Univ PO Box 1000 Durham NC 27708-1000. *Fax:* 919-684-5412; *E-Mail:* Bitnet: djsiedw@dukems.bitnet

SIEDSCHLAG, KARL GLENN, JR, ORGANIC CHEMISTRY. *Current Pos:* RETIRED. *Personal Data:* b Akron, Ohio, Oct 28, 20; m 41; c 1. *Educ:* Western Reserve Univ, BS, 46, MS, 48, PhD(chem), 49. *Prof Exp:* Asst prof chem, Univ WVa, 49-51; res chemist, Benger Lab, E I du Pont de Nemours & Co, 51-54, res chemist, Patent Div, Textile Fibers Dept, 54-74, patent assoc, 74-79. *Mem:* Am Chem Soc; Sigma Xi. *Res:* Condensation polymer fibers; inorganic fibers. *Mailing Add:* 1936 Holmes County Rd 160 WI Winesburg OH 44690

SIEFKEN, HUGH EDWARD, EXPERIMENTAL NUCLEAR PHYSICS. *Current Pos:* from asst prof to assoc prof, 69-77, PROF PHYSICS, GREENVILLE COL, 77- *Personal Data:* b Warsaw, Ind, Apr 13, 40; m 62; c 2. *Educ:* Greenville Col, BA, 62; Univ Kans, MS, 65, PhD(physics), 68. *Prof Exp:* Res fel nuclear physics, Univ BC, 68-69. *Concurrent Pos:* Vis scientist, Nuclear Res Ctr, Univ Alta, 76-77, 86-87, McDonnell Douglas Astronaut Co, Neutral Particle Beam Integrated Exp. *Mem:* Am Phys Soc; Sigma Xi; Am Asn Physics Teachers. *Res:* low energy nuclear physics; gamma ray spectroscopy and ion bombardment of solids & gases; ion optics & in source design. *Mailing Add:* Physics Dept Greenville Col Greenville IL 62246

SIEFKEN, MARK WILLIAM, PAPER WETEND CHEMISTRY. *Current Pos:* div mgr, 81-90, nat sales mgr, 90-91, VPRES, PULP & PAPER GROUP, TEXO, 92- *Personal Data:* b Hankinson, NDak, Oct 3, 39; m 61, Sharon Y Heinzeroth; c 3. *Educ:* NDak State Univ, BS, 61; Univ Wis, Madison, PhD(org chem), 67. *Prof Exp:* Capt chem, Med Res Lab, Edgewood Arsenal, Md, 67-69; sr chemist, Cent Res Lab, 3M Co, 69-73, res scientist recreation & athletic prod, 73-74, supvr, Res & Develop Indust Mineral Prod Div, Minn, 74-77; res mgr metals, detergents, surfactants, cleaning & sanitizing compounds, Diversey Chem, 77-78; tech vpres, Diversey Corp, 78-81. *Concurrent Pos:* Fulbright grant, Tech Univ, Stuttgart, Ger. *Mem:* Am Chem Soc; Tech Asn Pulp & Paper Indust; Paper Indust Mgt Asn. *Res:* Tricyclic hydrocarbon rearrangements; polymer synthesis and development; new product research and development. *Mailing Add:* 2367 N Ridge Ave Ct N Stillwater MN 55082. *Fax:* 513-731-8113

SIEFKER, JOSEPH ROY, ANALYTICAL CHEMISTRY, INORGANIC CHEMISTRY. *Current Pos:* from asst prof to assoc prof, 62-71, PROF CHEM, IND STATE UNIV, TERRE HAUTE, 71- *Personal Data:* b Brownstown, Ind, Mar 14, 33; m 56, Joyce Taylor; c Ann & Gail. *Educ:* Wabash Col, AB, 55; Univ NDak, MS, 57; Ind Univ, PhD(chem), 60. *Prof Exp:* Res chemist, E I du Pont de Nemours & Co, 57; instr chem, St Louis Univ, 60-62. *Concurrent Pos:* Consult, Sporlan Valve Co, St Louis, 61 & OA Labs, Indianapolis, 70-; vis asst prof, Ind Univ, 62 & 64. *Mem:* Am Chem Soc; Sigma Xi. *Res:* Water pollution; coordination compounds and complex ions; spectrophotometry; polarography; non-aqueous solvents; redox titrants; electroanalytical chemistry. *Mailing Add:* 68 Heritage Dr Terre Haute IN 47803-2374. *Fax:* 812-237-2232

SIEG, ALBERT LOUIS, ORGANIC CHEMISTRY. *Current Pos:* Anal chemist, Eastman Kodak Co, 54-55, develop engr, 55-59, sr develop engr, 59-66, supvr chem testing, Paper Div, 67-69, supvr process develop, 69-71, supvr emulsion control, 71-72, corp coordr instant photog, 72-76, asst dir, 74-76, dir, Paper Serv Div, 76-78, asst mgr paper mfg, 78-80, mgr, 80-81, dir photog strategic planning, 81-84, vpres, 81, GEN MGR JAPANESE REGION, PRES & CHIEF EXEC OFFICER, EASTMAN KODAK CO, JAPAN, 84- *Personal Data:* b Chicago, Ill, Mar 25, 30; m 55; c 3. *Educ:* Univ Ill, BS, 51; Univ Rochester, PhD, 55; Harvard Grad Sch Bus, PMD, 72. *Concurrent Pos:* Lectr, Univ Rochester, 59-65, sr lectr, 65-69. *Mem:* AAAS; fel Am Inst Chemists; Am Chem Soc; Soc Photog Sci & Eng. *Res:* Synthesis of natural products; photographic chemistry; chemistry of gelatins; lithographic chemistry. *Mailing Add:* 159 Hillhurst Lane Rochester NY 14617-1938

SIEGAL, BERNARD, PHARMACEUTICAL SCIENCES. *Current Pos:* DIR RES & DEVELOP, H V SHUSTER, INC, 77- *Personal Data:* b Brooklyn, NY, Nov 11, 24; m 48; c 3. *Educ:* Yeshiva Univ, BA, 45; Rutgers Univ, PhD(pharmaceut), 68. *Prof Exp:* Chemist, Estro Chem Co, 49-53; from chemist to lab dir, Prod Div, Bristol Meyers, 53-69; dir res & develop, Toiletries Div, Gillette Co, 69-77. *Mem:* Am Chem Soc; Am Pharmaceut Asn; Acad Pharmaceut Sci; Soc Cosmetic Chem; Am Asn Textile Chemists

& Colorists. *Res:* Over-the-counter pharmacy, health aids and allied products; product research and development; safety and claim substantiation; regulatory compliance. *Mailing Add:* Shuster Labs Inc 5 Hayward St Quincy MA 02171

SIEGAL, BURTON L, PATENT AVOIDANCE, ALUMINUM EXTENSION DESIGN. *Current Pos:* PRES, CONSULT, BUDD ENG CORP, 59- *Personal Data:* b Chicago, Ill, Sept 27, 31; m 54, Rita Goran; c Norman & Larry. *Educ:* Univ Ill, BS, 53. *Honors & Awards:* Winner, Int Aluminum Extrusion Design Competition, 75. *Prof Exp:* Torpedo designer, US Naval Ord, 53-54; chief engr, Gen Aluminum Corp, 54-55; prod designer, Chicago Aerial Indust, 55-58; chief designer, Emil J Paider Co, 58-59. *Concurrent Pos:* Bd mem, Math, Eng & Sci Adv Bd, Niles TWP, 75-79; lectr, Am Soc Mech Engrs, 91; mem, President's Asn Ill. *Mem:* Soc Mech Engrs; Soc Plastic Engrs; Soc Mfg Engrs; Soc Automotive Engrs. *Res:* Expert in conception, design, engineering and placing into production of products for annual quantities from five to a million; approximately 114 patents in over 30 industries; expert witness on mechanical patents. *Mailing Add:* 8707 Skokie Blvd Skokie IL 60077-2297

SIEGAL, FREDERICK PAUL, IMMUNOLOGY, INTERNAL MEDICINE. *Current Pos:* ASSOC PROF MED & DIR, DIV CLIN IMMUNOL, MT SINAI SCH MED, NY, 78- *Personal Data:* b New York, NY, Sept 24, 39; m 66; c 2. *Educ:* Cornell Univ, AB, 61; Columbia Univ, MD, 65. *Prof Exp:* From intern to resident internal med, Mt Sinai Hosp, NY, 65-67; asst prev med officer, Walter Reed Army Med Ctr, 67-69; resident internal med, Mt Sinai Hosp, NY, 69-70, clin asst physician, 70-73; assoc immunol, Mem Sloan-Kettering Cancer Ctr, 73-79, assoc mem, 77-78, head, Lab Human Lymphocyte Differentiation, Sloan-Kettering Inst, 75-78; asst prof med, Cornell Univ Col Med, 75-78. *Concurrent Pos:* Helen Hay Whitney Found fel, Rockefeller Univ, 70-73, asst res physician, Rockefeller Univ Hosp, 70-73, vis assoc physician, 73-74; adj asst prof, Rockefeller Univ, 73-74; asst attend physician, Mem Hosp, NY, 73-78; asst prof biol, Sloan-Kettering Div, Cornell Univ, 74-78; assoc sci, Mem Sloan-Kettering Cancer Ctr, 78- *Mem:* AAAS; Am Asn Immunologists; Am Fedn Clin Res; NY Acad Sci. *Res:* Clinical immunology; immunodeficiency diseases; development of lymphoid cells; cell surfaces. *Mailing Add:* 269-11 76th Ave 430 Lakeville Rd New Hyde Park NY 11042-1124. *Fax:* 718-470-0169

SIEGAL, GENE PHILIP, TUMOR INVASION & METASTASIS, NEOPLASMS OF BONE. *Current Pos:* PROF PATH, UNIV ALA BIRMINGHAM, 90-, PROF CELL BIOL & SURG, 91- *Personal Data:* b Bronx, NY, Nov 16, 48; m 72; c 2. *Educ:* Adelphi Univ, BA, 70; Univ Louisville, MD, 74; Univ Minn, PhD(exp path), 79; Am Bd Path, dipl, 78. *Prof Exp:* Intern path, Mayo Grad Sch Med, Mayo Clinic, 74-75, resident, 75-76, res fel, 76-77, sr resident, 77-78, chief resident, dept anat path, 78-79; res assoc exp path & biochem, Lab Pathophysiol, Nat Cancer Inst, NIH, 79-81; med specialist & fel surg path, dept lab med & path, Div Surg Path, Univ Minn, Minneapolis, 81-82; from asst prof to assoc prof path, Univ NC, Chapel Hill, 82-90; assoc dir, surg path, NC Mem Hosp, Chapel Hill, 88-90. *Concurrent Pos:* Instr path, Mayo Med Sch, Rochester, Minn, 76-79; clin fel, Am Cancer Soc, 81-82, jr fac fel, 83-86; attend pathologist, Univ NC Hosp, Chapel Hill, 82-90, dir histopath labs, 84-90 & dir spec procedures lab, 88-90; mem, Lineberger Cancer Res Ctr, Univ NC, Chapel Hill, 83-90; assoc ed, Arch Path Lab Med, 89-90; sr scientist, Comp Cancer Ctr Ala, 90-, group leader, Develop Prog Breast, Ovary & Prostate Cancer, 93-; dir anat path, Univ Ala Birmingham Hosp, 90-; chmn, Osteosarcoma Path Comn, Pediat Oncol Group, 90- *Mem:* Am Soc Invest Path; US-Can Acad Path; Am Asn Cancer Res; A P Stout Soc Surg Pathologists; Metastasis Res Soc; Sigma Xi. *Res:* Experimental tumor invasion and metastasis; immunohistochemistry of solid tumors; human uterine carcinogenesis; neoplasms of bone and related conditions; micro-nutrient modulation of tumor-matrix interactions; cell-matrix interactions. *Mailing Add:* Dept Path UAB Sta Univ Ala Sch Med Birmingham AL 35294-0001. *Fax:* 205-975-7284; *E-Mail:* siegal@lh.path.uab.edu

SIEGART, WILLIAM RAYMOND, ORGANIC CHEMISTRY, ALTERNATE ENERGIES. *Current Pos:* CONSULT, 93- *Personal Data:* b Paterson, NJ, July 28, 31; m 55, Judith A Clemens; c William R, John R & Ann E. *Educ:* Gettysburg Col, BA, 53; Univ Pa, MS, 55, PhD(org chem), 57. *Prof Exp:* Asst instr chem, Univ Pa, 53-54, res assoc org chem, 54-56; chemist, Texaco Inc, 58-59, sr chemist, 59-62, res chemist, 62-67, group leader, 67-69, asst supvr petrochem res, 69-71, sr technologist, Mfg Div, Res & Technol Dept, 71-72, sr technologist prog planning & coord, 72-76, staff coordr, 76-78, sr staff coordr, Strategic Planning Dept, 78-80, sr coordr, 80-82, assoc dir, Alt Energy & Resources Dept, 82-88, sr staff consult, 88-93; vpres, Texaco Syngas, Inc, 84-93. *Mem:* Am Chem Soc; Sigma Xi; NY Acad Sci; AAAS. *Res:* Petrochemicals; products and processes; lubricant additives and products; long range research planning; coal gasification; corporate planning; alternate energy; environmental regulations and remediations. *Mailing Add:* 91 Round Hill Rd Poughkeepsie NY 12603. *E-Mail:* racg71a@prodigy.com

SIEGBAHN, KAI MANNE BORJE, PHYSICS. *Current Pos:* prof, 54-83, EMER PROF PHYSICS, UNIV UPPSALA, 83- *Personal Data:* b Lund, Sweden, Apr 20, 18. *Educ:* Univ Uppsala, PhD, 44. *Hon Degrees:* DSc, Univ Durham, 72, Univ Basel, 80, Univ Liege, 80, Upsala Col, 82, Univ Sussex, 83. *Honors & Awards:* Nobel Prize in Physics, 81; Lindblom Prize, 45; Bjorken Prize, 55 & 77; Celsius Medal, 62; Sixten Heyman Award, 71; Harrison Howe Award, 73; Maurice F Hasler Award, 75; Charles Fredrick Chandler Award, 76; Torbern Bergman Medal, 79; Fiuggi Award, 86; Humboldt Award, 86; Premio Castiglione Di Sicilia, 90. *Prof Exp:* Res assoc, Nobel Inst Physics, 42-51; prof physics, Royal Inst Technol, Stockholm, 51-54. *Mem:* Nat Acad Sci; Royal Swed Acad Sci; Papal Acad Sci; Royal Soc Arts & Sci; Japan Acad Sci; Royal Swed Acad Eng; for Nat Acad Sci; Europ Arts, Sci & Humanities; Int Union Pure & Appl Physics (pres, 81-84); Russ Acad Sci; Am Acad Arts & Sci. *Mailing Add:* Inst Physics Univ Uppsala Box 530s Uppsala 751 21 Sweden

SIEGEL, ALBERT, molecular genetics, plant virology, for more information see previous edition

SIEGEL, ALLAN, NEUROBIOLOGY, NEUROANATOMY. *Current Pos:* instr anat, NJ Sch Med, 67-69, asst prof, 69-73, assoc prof anat & neurosci, 73-77, PROF NEUROSCI, NJ MED SCH, 77- *Personal Data:* b New York, NY, June 18, 39. *Educ:* City Col New York, BS, 61; State Univ NY Buffalo, PhD(psychol), 66. *Prof Exp:* USPHS fel, Sch Med, Yale Univ, 65-67. *Concurrent Pos:* Consult neurol & res, East Orange Vet Admin Hosp, 72-; mem Neurol Sci II Study Sect, Nat Inst Neurol & Commun Dis & Stroke, 84-; vis prof, Cornell Univ Med Sch, 85. *Mem:* AAAS; Am Asn Anat; Soc Neurosci; NY Acad Sci; Int Soc Res Aggression; Int Soc Res Emotions. *Res:* Experimental psychology; anatomy and neurophysiology of limbic system; biology of aggressive behavior. *Mailing Add:* Dept Neuro Sci UMDNJ NJ Med Sch 185 S Orange Ave Newark NJ 07103

SIEGEL, ALVIN, CHEMICAL OCEANOGRAPHY. *Current Pos:* assoc prof, Southampton Col, Long Island Univ, 67-71, dir, Natural Sci Div, 80-86, acad dean, 89-96, PROF CHEM, SOUTHAMPTON COL, LONG ISLAND UNIV, 71-, DIR, MARINE SCI PROG, 73-, PROF MARINE SCI, 75- *Personal Data:* b New York, NY, Aug 29, 31; m 59; c Rebecca, David, Daniel & Deborah. *Educ:* City Col New York, BS, 53; Rutgers Univ, PhD(phys chem), 62. *Prof Exp:* Asst scientist, Woods Hole Oceanog Inst, 61-67. *Concurrent Pos:* Treas, NY State Marine Educ Asn. *Mem:* AAAS; Am Soc Limnol & Oceanog; Am Chem Soc. *Res:* Polyelectrolytes; speciation of metal ions in natural waters; organic bonding to metal ions; extraction of polar organics from sea water. *Mailing Add:* Southampton Col Long Island Univ Southampton NY 11968. *Fax:* 516-287-8419

SIEGEL, ANDREW FRANCIS, GEOMETRICAL PROBABILITY, BIOSTATISTICS. *Current Pos:* vis asst prof biostatist & vis scholar statist, Univ Wash, 82-83, assoc prof & adj prof zool, 83-89, adj prof statist, 87-89, PROF & ADJ PROF STATIST, UNIV WASH, 89- *Personal Data:* b Cambridge, Mass, Jan 6, 50. *Educ:* Boston Univ, AB, 73; Stanford Univ, MS, 75, PhD(statist), 77. *Prof Exp:* Asst prof, Univ Wis-Madison, 77-79; asst prof, Princeton Univ, 79-83. *Concurrent Pos:* Vis res assoc, Dept Paleobiol, Smithsonian Inst, 78; res fel, Dept Biostatist, Harvard Univ, 78-79; vis staff mem, Statist Group, Los Alamos Nat Lab, 79; consult, Statist Group, Bell Telephone Labs, 79-80; co-prin investr, US Army Res Off, 79-83; vis scholar, Dept Statist, Stanford Univ, 80, Univ Wash, Seattle, 81; secy & treas, Bus & Econ Statist Sect, Am Statist Asn, 89-90; vis prof, Fac & Sci Econ Et Gestion Univ Bourgogne, France, 94 & 96. *Mem:* Am Statist Asn; Inst Oper Res & Mgt Sci. *Res:* Geometric probability; statistical robustness; pattern matching; morphology; probability distributions; biological and medical applications of statistics; financial and economic application of mathematics and statistics. *Mailing Add:* Dept Math Sci Box 353200 Univ Wash Seattle WA 98195-3200. *Fax:* 206-685-9392; *E-Mail:* asiegel@u.washington.edu

SIEGEL, ARMAND, STATISTICAL MECHANICS, BIOMATHEMATICS. *Current Pos:* from instr to prof, 50-80, prof psychiat physics, 75-83, EMER PROF PHYSICS, BOSTON UNIV, 80- *Personal Data:* b New York, NY, Oct 10, 14; m 43, Mildred Marks; c Jonathan, Andrew & Jeffrey. *Educ:* NY Univ, AB, 36; Univ Pa, AM, 44; Mass Inst Technol, PhD(physics), 49. *Prof Exp:* Asst physics, Univ Pa, 42-43, instr, 43-44; instr elec commun, Radar Sch, Mass Inst Technol, 44-45, res assoc physics, 52-53; instr, Worcester Polytech Inst, 49-50. *Concurrent Pos:* Guggenheim fel, Univ Mich, 57-58. *Mem:* Am Phys Soc. *Res:* Relativistic nucleon-nucleon interactions; differential space formulation of quantum mechanics; kinetic theory; stochastic processes; mathematical theory of turbulence; electroencephalography of petit-mal epilepsy; stochastic aspects of the origin of the electroencephalogram. *Mailing Add:* 56 Marshall St Brookline MA 02146

SIEGEL, BARBARA ZENZ, ENVIRONMENTAL PUBLIC HEALTH. *Current Pos:* PROF, NMEX STATE UNIV, 96- *Personal Data:* b Detroit, Mich, July 22, 31; wid; c Stephanie, Andrea, Peter & David. *Educ:* Univ Chicago, AB, 60; Columbia Univ, MA, 63; Yale Univ, PhD(biol), 66. *Honors & Awards:* vis researcher Inst of Biophysics, PISA award, Nat Res Coun, Italy, 87-88. *Prof Exp:* Purchasing liaison, Army Chem Corp, Ft Detrick, Md, 50-52; res assoc human genetics, Sch Med, NY Univ, 62-63; res staff mem biol, Yale Univ, 66-67; from asst prof to assoc prof microbiol, Univ Hawaii, 67-75, dir biol prog, 71-75, researcher Biomed Res Ctr & assoc prof Current Res & Develop, 75-76, interim dir Res Admin & interim dean Grad Sch, 79-82, res prof Pac Biomed Res Ctr, 76-, dir, Pesticide Hazard Assessment Proj, 83-87; prof & sr researcher environ health sci, dean, Sch Pub Health & assoc dean acad affairs, Univ Hawaii, 88. *Concurrent Pos:* Mem, Boston Univ-NASA exped, Iceland & Surtsey, 70 & Nat Geog Soc-Hawaii Found & Cottrell Found expeds, Iceland & Surtsey, 72; Fulbright-Hays sr res scholar, Univ Belgrade, Marine Sta, Montenegro, Yugoslavia & Univ Heidelberg, 73-74; sr NATO fel, Nordic Volcanol Inst, Iceland, 75; res assoc, Volcani Agr Ctr, Israel; proj leader, US Antarctic Res Prog, NSF, McMurdo, Antarctic, 78-79; vis prof bot & geol, Univ BC, 82; vis prof, Weizmann Inst, Israel, 86-87; vis researcher, Inst Biophys, PISA award, Nat Res Coun, Italy, 87-88; Fulbright Hay sr res scholar, Oalu Univ, Finland, 88-89. *Mem:* Am Chem Soc; Am Asn Pub Health; Am Inst Biol Sci; Int Soc Chem Ecol; Sigma Xi. *Res:* Biochemical mechanisms in growth and development; biological oxidations, biochemical interactions in eco-systems; volcanic gas emissions on biological systems; ecology of heavy metals; impact of alternate energy sources (geothermal, wind, ocean thermal energy conversion, etc) on the environment; environmental factors effecting human health; natural and man-made disasters; physiological stress; enzyme peroxidase as stress indicator. *Mailing Add:* Health Sci NMex State Univ Las Cruces NM 88001. *E-Mail:* bsiegel@nmsu.edu

SIEGEL, BARRY ALAN, NUCLEAR MEDICINE, RADIOLOGY. *Current Pos:* assoc prof med, 80-83, from asst prof to assoc prof, 73-79, PROF RADIOL, SCH MED, WASH UNIV, 79-, PROF MED, 83-; DIR NUCLEAR MED, EDWARD MALLINCKRODT INST RADIOL, 73- *Personal Data:* b Nashville, Tenn, Dec 30, 44; m 83, Marilyn J; c Peter A & William A. *Educ:* Washington Univ, AB, 66, MD, 69. *Honors & Awards:* Comnr Spec Citation, Food & Drug Admin, 88. *Prof Exp:* Intern med, Barnes Hosp, St Louis, 69-70; resident nuclear med & radiol, Edward Mallinckrodt Inst Radiol, 70-73. *Concurrent Pos:* asst prof radiol, Sch Med, Johns Hopkins Univ, 74-76; chief, Radiol Sci Div, Armed Forces Radiobiol Res Inst, Defense Nuclear Agency, 74-76; mem radioactive pharmaceut adv comt, Food & Drug Admin, 74-77, 81-85, chmn, 82-85 & task force short-lived radionuclides appln nuclear med, 75-76; mem task force nuclear med, Energy Res & Develop Admin, 75-76; mem adv panel radiopharmaceut, US Pharmacopeia, 76-; consult ed bd, J Nuclear Med, 76-81; mem adv comt on med radioisotopes, Los Alamos Sci Lab, 76-79; assoc ed, Radiol, 80-; mem, Residency Rev Comt Nuclear Med, 84-85, Mo Low Level Radioactive Waste Adv Comt, 84-86; trustee, Am Bd Nuclear Med, 85-90; asst ed, Am J Roentgenol, 87-; chmn, US Nuclear Regulatory Comn Adv Comt Med Uses Isotopes, 90-; mem, Radiol Devices Panel, Food & Drug Admin, 92-, St Louis Co Radioactive & Hazardous Waste Oversight Comm, 92-, Radiol Safety & Protection Nuclear Med, Int Comm Radiol Protection, 93-; from assoc ed to ed-in-chief, Am Col Radiol Prof Self Eval & Continuing Educ Prog, 86- *Mem:* Fel Am Col Nuclear Physicians; fel Am Col Radiol; Radiol Soc NAm; fel Am Col Physicians; Soc Nuclear Med; AMA. *Res:* Clinical research with positron-emitting radionuclides and coincidence axial tomographic detection systems; radioisotopic evaluation of cancer; continuing education in radiology. *Mailing Add:* Edward Mallinckrodt Inst Radiol Washington Univ Sch Med 510 S Kingshighway Blvd St Louis MO 63110-1016. *Fax:* 314-362-2806; *E-Mail:* siegelb@mirlink.wustl.edu

SIEGEL, BENJAMIN VINCENT, VIROLOGY, IMMUNOLOGY. *Current Pos:* prof, 61-79, RES PROF PATH, MED SCH, ORE HEALTH SCI UNIV, PORTLAND, 79- *Personal Data:* b New York, NY, Dec 14, 13; m 43, Jane Morton; c Marilyn, Benjamin Jr & Andrew. *Educ:* Univ Ga, BS, 34; Columbia Univ, MA, 37; Stanford Univ, PhD(bact, exp path), 50; Am Bd Microbiol, dipl. *Prof Exp:* Teacher pub schs, Calif, 39-42; chmn biol & phys sci high sch, 46-48; asst bact physiol, Stanford Univ, 49-50, instr bact & exp path, 50-52, Nat Found Infantile Paralysis fel, 52-53; fel med phys & virol, Univ Calif, Berkeley, 53-54, asst res virologist, 54-56; assoc res virologist, Sch Med, San Francisco & res microbiologist, Donner Radiation Lab, Berkeley, 56-61, lectr microbiol, 59-60. *Concurrent Pos:* Hon vis prof, Univ Wis-Madison, 85. *Mem:* Fel Am Acad Microbiol; fel NY Acad Sci; Am Soc Exp Path; Int Acad Path; fel AAAS. *Res:* Tumor virology; experimental pathology; immunology. *Mailing Add:* 3900 SW Pendleton St Portland OR 97221. *Fax:* 503-494-5799

SIEGEL, BERNARD, physical chemistry, inorganic chemistry, for more information see previous edition

SIEGEL, BROCK MARTIN, ORGANIC CHEMISTRY, BIOORGANIC CHEMISTRY. *Current Pos:* RES & DEVELOP MGR, MILLIPORE CORP, 89- *Personal Data:* b Binghamton, NY, Aug 25, 47; m 78; c 3. *Educ:* Syracuse Univ, BS, 69; Univ Ill, PhD(chem), 74. *Prof Exp:* NIH fel, Columbia Univ, 74-76; asst prof chem, Univ Minn, Minneapolis, 76-80; res mgr, Henkel Corp, 80-89. *Concurrent Pos:* DuPont fac fel, Univ Minn, 76-77, NIH grant, 78-79. *Mem:* AAAS; Am Chem Soc; NY Acad Sci; Sigma Xi. *Res:* Kinetics mechanisms; synthetic and physical-organic chemistry; biomimetic enzyme catalysts; emerging technologies; oleochemical lipid specialties; aromatic substitution chemistry; nucleic acid and peptide synthesis; carbohydrate chemistry. *Mailing Add:* 2462 Hallmark Dr Belmont CA 94002-2908

SIEGEL, CAROLE ETHEL, BIOSTATISTICS. *Current Pos:* Prin res scientist math, 65-73, HEAD, EPIDEMIOL & HEALTH SERV RES LAB, NATHAN KLINE INST, 73- *Personal Data:* b US, Sept 29, 36; m 57, Bertram; c David & Sharon. *Educ:* NY Univ, BA, 57, MS, 59, PhD(math), 63. *Concurrent Pos:* Adj asst prof math, NY Univ, 65-68 & 69, res prof, Dept Psychiat, 79-; adj prof, Fairleigh Dickinson Univ, 68; dep dir, WHO Ctr Training & Res Ment Health Prog Mgt, 87-; co-prin investr, Ctr Study Issues Pub Ment Health, 93-94, prin investr, 94- *Mem:* Inst Math Statist; Asn Women Math; Asn Clin Pharmacol & Therapeut; Am Pub Health Asn. *Res:* The development and application of statistical and quantitative models for examining mental health issues covering: epidemiology, health services and economics; mathematical and statistical approaches to mental health data; epidemiology; health services research. *Mailing Add:* Statist Sci & Epidemiol Div Nathan Kline Inst Orangeburg NY 10962. *E-Mail:* siegel@rfmh.iris.org

SIEGEL, CLIFFORD M(YRON), ELECTRICAL NETWORK THEORY, COMPUTER AIDED INSTRUCTION. *Current Pos:* RETIRED. *Personal Data:* b Apple River, Ill, Apr 15, 21; m 46; c 4. *Educ:* Marquette Univ, BEE, 47; Univ NH, MSEE, 49; Univ Wis, PhD(elec eng), 51. *Prof Exp:* Engr, Wis Elec Power Co, 41-43; instr elec eng, Marquette Univ, 47; asst, Univ NH, 47-48, instr, 48-49; asst, Univ Wis, 49-51; from asst prof to prof elec eng, Univ Va, 51-90, actg chmn dept, 67-69. *Mem:* Am Soc Eng Educ; Inst Elec & Electronics Engrs. *Res:* Methods for electrical engineering education; computer-assisted instruction. *Mailing Add:* 2503 Hillwood Pl Charlottesville VA 22901

SIEGEL, DALE ALAN, MATHEMATICS SOFTWARE FOR EDUCATION. *Current Pos:* ASST PROF MATH, KINGSBOROUGH COMMUNITY COL, 93- *Personal Data:* b Brooklyn, NY, June 27, 66. *Educ:* Polytech Univ, BS, 87, MS, 89 & 91, PhD(appl statist), 91. *Mem:* Math Asn Am; Am Math Asn Two-Yr Cols. *Res:* Mathematics software for classroom use or for use as tutorials in a mathematics laboratory. *Mailing Add:* 2652 Cropsey Ave Apt 15H Brooklyn NY 11214. *E-Mail:* daskb@juno.com

SIEGEL, EDWARD, BIOPHYSICS, MEDICAL PHYSICS. *Current Pos:* ADJ PROF RADIOL, DEPT RADIOL, UNIV CALIF, SAN FRANCISCO, 88- *Personal Data:* b New York, NY, Aug 1, 19; m 44, Elsie Polonsky. *Educ:* City Col New York, BS, 41; Univ Calif, Berkeley, PhD(biophys), 66. *Prof Exp:* Physicist-in-chg optical res, Universal Camera Corp, NY, 41-44; physicist, Frankford Arsenal, US Dept Army, 45, biophysicist, Aero-Med Lab, Wright Field, 45-46; res assoc, Col Eng, Rutgers Univ, 47-48; physicist-in-chg, Med Physics Lab, Montefiore Hosp, 48-62; spec fel cellular biophys, USPHS, 62-66; assoc prof radiol physics, Sch Med, Stanford Univ, 66-70; actg dir, Nuclear Med Sect, Sch Med, Univ Mo-Columbia, 71-73, prof radiol sci & med, 70-76, prof biol sci, 75-76, dir, Nuclear Med Sect, 73-76; prof radiol & radiation sci & dir, Dept Radiol & Radiation Sci, Sch Med, Vanderbilt Univ, 76-83, prof physics, Col Arts & Sci, 79-88. *Concurrent Pos:* Consult physicist, Radioisotope Dept, Newark Beth Israel Hosp, NJ, 50-55 & Radioisotope Dept, Lebanon Hosp, NY, 53-62; guest scientist, Donner Lab, Univ Calif, 66-70; consult physicist, Palo Alto Vet Admin Hosp, 67-70; consult adv comt human uses radioactive mat, Bur Radiol Health, State of Calif, 67-70; consult physicist, USPHS Hosp, San Francisco, 68-70 & Vet Admin Hosp, Columbia, Mo, 72-76; ed, Med Physics, 79-81; radiation safety off, Vet Admin Hosp, San Francisco, 88-92. *Mem:* Endocrine Soc; Am Asn Physicists Med; Radiation Res Soc; Biophys Soc; Am Phys Soc; Soc Nuclear Med. *Res:* Applications of radioisotopes to biology and medicine; radiation physics; thyroid physiology and thyroid cancer; cell culture; radiation dosimetry; nuclear medicine; high resolution radioautography; radiation biology; biological effects of radiation and ultrasound; radiation safety. *Mailing Add:* 2 Milland Ct Mill Valley CA 94941

SIEGEL, ELI CHARLES, MICROBIAL GENETICS. *Current Pos:* from asst prof to assoc prof, 68-82, PROF BIOL, TUFTS UNIV, 82- *Personal Data:* b Newark, NJ, July 25, 38; m 86, Tess Wishengrad; c Michael. *Educ:* Rutgers Univ, BA, 60, PhD(microbiol), 66. *Prof Exp:* Fel biochem, Albert Einstein Col Med, 66-68. *Concurrent Pos:* USPHS fel, 67-68. *Mem:* AAAS; Am Soc Microbiol; Genetics Soc Am. *Res:* Mutator genes; DNA repair; bacterial genetics. *Mailing Add:* Dept Biol Tufts Univ Medford MA 02155. *Fax:* 617-627-3805; *E-Mail:* esiegel@pearl.tufts.edu

SIEGEL, ELLIOT ROBERT, COMMUNICATIONS SCIENCE, INFORMATION SCIENCE. *Current Pos:* info scientist commun, Lister Hill Nat Ctr Biomed Commun, Nat Libr Med, 76-82, spec asst opers res, off dir, 82-87, asst dir plan & eval, 87-92, ASSOC DIR HEALTHY INFO PROG DEVELOP, NAT LIBR MED, 92- *Personal Data:* b New York, NY, May 31, 42; m 67, Nancy Linn; c Erica B & Joshua L. *Educ:* Brooklyn Col, BA, 64; Mich State Univ, MA, 66, PhD(commun), 69. *Honors & Awards:* Award Merit, NIH, 88; Dir Honor Award, Nat Lib Sci, 89. *Prof Exp:* Res scientist commun, Human Sci Res, Inc, 69-70; res assoc commun & info sci, Off Commun, Am Psychol Asn, 70-72, mgr & exec ed, 72-74 & sci affairs officer, 75-76. *Concurrent Pos:* Assoc ed, Am Psychologist J, 75-76; mem adv comt med appl res, NIH, 83-, eval res rev comt, 84-90 & technol transfer comt, 89-; mem, Fed Libr & Info Ctr Comn, 85-88; secy info, comput & commun, AAAS, 85-96; mem, CENDI, 85-, High Performance Comput & Info Transfer Comt, 90- & Int Coun Sci & Tech Info, 91-95. *Mem:* AAAS; Am Soc Info Sci; Am Med Informatics Asn; Int Commun Asn. *Res:* Information transfer and knowledge utilization in the health sciences; medical informatics; information systems research, development and evaluation; scientific and technical communication processes; science policy research. *Mailing Add:* Nat Libr Med Bethesda MD 20894. *Fax:* 301-496-4450; *E-Mail:* siegel@nlm.nih.gov

SIEGEL, FRANK LEONARD, BIOCHEMISTRY. *Current Pos:* from instr to asst prof, 64-71, assoc prof pediat & physiol chem, Sch Med, 71-75, PROF PEDIAT & PHYSIOL CHEM, NEUROCHEM SECT, WAISMAN CTR, UNIV WIS-MADISON, 75- *Personal Data:* b Brooklyn, NY, Apr 15, 31; m 62; c 2. *Educ:* Reed Col, BA, 53; Univ Tex, PhD(chem), 60. *Honors & Awards:* Javits Neurosci Investr Award, 87. *Prof Exp:* Asst chem, Univ Tex, 54; Clayton Found fel biochem, 60-64. *Concurrent Pos:* Res scientist, NIMH Develop Comt. *Mem:* AAAS; Am Chem Soc; Am Soc Biol Chemists; Am Soc Neurochem; Soc Neurosci. *Res:* Protein methylation; calmodulin, glutathione S-transferases. *Mailing Add:* Waisman Ctr Univ Wis Madison WI 53705. *Fax:* 608-265-4103; *E-Mail:* siegel@waisman.wisc.edu

SIEGEL, FREDERIC RICHARD, GEOCHEMISTRY, INORGANIC GEOCHEMISTRY. *Current Pos:* assoc prof, 65-69, chmn geol dept, 76-86, PROF GEOCHEM, GEORGE WASHINGTON UNIV, 69- *Personal Data:* b Chelsea, Mass, Feb 8, 32; m 62, Felisa M Puszkin; c Gabriela D & Galia D. *Educ:* Harvard Univ, BA, 54; Univ Kans, MS, 58, PhD(geol), 61. *Prof Exp:* Prof & researcher geochem & sedimentology, Inst Miguel Lillo, Nat Univ Tucuman, 61-63; div head geochem, Kans Geol Surv, 63-65; res assoc, Univ Kans, 64-65. *Concurrent Pos:* Vis prof, Univ Buenos Aires, 63; lectr, Univ Kans, 65; res assoc, Smithsonian Inst, 67-; Fulbright scholar, Facultad de Minas, Medellin, Colombia, 70; consult, World Bank, 79, UN Develop Prog, 80, minerals indust, 82, 84 &93, US Dept State, 88-96; ed, United Nations Educ Sci Cult Orgn, volume geochem, 79; assoc ed, exploration geochem, 72-76; counr, Asn Explor Geochem, 88-95. *Mem:* Asn Explor Geochem; Geochem Soc; Soc Environ Geochem & Health; Int Asn Geochemists & Cosmochemists. *Res:* Geochemical prospecting; suspended sediment

SIEGEL, GEORGE JACOB, NEUROLOGY, NEUROBIOLOGY. *Current Pos:* assoc prof, 73-75, CHIEF NEUROL CHEM LAB MED SCH, UNIV MICH, ANN ARBOR, 73-, PROF NEUROL, 75- *Personal Data:* b Bronx, NY, Aug 6, 36; m 57; c 3. *Educ:* Yeshiva Col, BA, 57; Univ Miami, MD, 61. *Prof Exp:* Resident neurol, Mt Sinai Hosp, New York, 62-65; res assoc neurochem, Nat Inst Neurol Dis & Stroke, 65-68; from asst prof to assoc prof physiol & neurol, Mt Sinai Sch Med, 68-73. *Concurrent Pos:* Assoc attend neurologist, Mt Sinai Hosp & chmn neurosci integrated curric comt. *Mem:* Am Neurol Asn; Int Soc Neurochem; Am Asn Neuropath; Am Acad Neurol; Harvey Soc. *Res:* Biology of active transport and neural membrane development. *Mailing Add:* Dept Neurol Cell & Molec Biol Loyola Univ Stritch Sch Med Hines Vet Admin Hosp Hines IL 60141-5000. *Fax:* 708-531-7936

SIEGEL, GEORGES G, thermodynamics & material properties, for more information see previous edition

SIEGEL, HENRY, pathology; deceased, see previous edition for last biography

SIEGEL, HERBERT, INFORMATION SCIENCE, ORGANIC CHEMISTRY. *Current Pos:* RETIRED. *Personal Data:* b New York, NY, Apr 23, 25; m 56; c 2. *Educ:* Ind Univ, BS, 47; WVa Univ, PhD(org chem), 56. *Prof Exp:* Chemist, Ohio-Apex, Inc, WVa, 48-50; assoc prof chem, Waynesburg Col, 55-58; asst ed, Chem Abstr Serv, 59-61, asst dept head appl org ed, 62-63, dept head, 64-66, spec projs mgr, 66-69, mgr org ed anal dept, 69-72, asst mgr chem technol dept, 72-73, asst mgr org chem dept, 73-75; info chemist, Int Occup Safety & Health Info Ctr, 75-79, head, 80-85. *Concurrent Pos:* Res fel & lectr, Bedford Col, Univ London, 58-59. *Mem:* Am Chem Soc; Am Soc Info Sci. *Res:* Biphenyl stereochemistry; chemical information storage and retrieval; abstracting and indexing. *Mailing Add:* BP 52 F 01212 Ferney-Voltaire Cedex France

SIEGEL, HERBERT S, PHYSIOLOGY, IMMUNOLOGY. *Current Pos:* HEAD DEPT POULTRY SCI, PA STATE UNIV, 84-, MEM GRAD FAC PHYSIOL, 84- *Personal Data:* b Mt Vernon, NY, Aug 29, 26; m 48, Rhea S Spiro; c Alan, Charles & Lisa. *Educ:* Pa State Univ, BS, 50, MS, 57, PhD, 59. *Honors & Awards:* Res Award, Poultry Sci Asn, 61. *Prof Exp:* Asst poultry husb, Pa State Univ, 55-57; from asst prof to assoc prof, Va Polytech Inst & State Univ, 58-64; res physiologist, Agr Res Serv, USDA, 64-84. *Concurrent Pos:* Adj mem grad fac vet physiol & pharmacol, Univ Ga, 66-84; Fulbright-Hays res award, Neth, 80-81; ed-in-chief, Poultry Sci, 80-86; sr res fel, Agr Univ, Wageningen, Net, 91-92. *Mem:* AAAS; Am Soc Zoologists; Poultry Sci Asn; fel NY Acad Sci; Soc Exp Biol & Med. *Res:* Avian physiology; environmental physiology, stress, adrenals and the immune systems; pesticide residues. *Mailing Add:* Dept Poultry Sci Pa State Univ 206 Henning Bldg University Park PA 16802

SIEGEL, HOWARD JAY, COMPUTER ARCHITECTURE. *Current Pos:* asst prof elec eng, 76-81, res staff, LARS, 79-81, assoc prof, 81-85, PROF ELEC ENG, PURDUE UNIV, 85-, COORDR, PARALLEL PROCESSING LAB, 89- *Personal Data:* b Newark, NJ, Jan 16, 50; m 72. *Educ:* Mass Inst Technol, BS(mgt) & BS(elec eng), 72; Princeton Univ, MA, 74, MSE, 74, PhD(elec eng), 77. *Honors & Awards:* Cert Appreciation, Inst Elec & Electronic Engrs, 83, 84; Serv Award, Am Comput Mach, 86. *Prof Exp:* Researcher compiler design, Mass Inst Technol, 70, info systs, 71; researcher & teaching asst elec eng & comput sci, Princeton Univ, 72-76. *Concurrent Pos:* Consult, TRW, Huntsville, 79, Xerox Corp, Rochester, 79, Gen Motors Res Lab, Dearborn, 80, Arvin/Calspan, Advan Technol Ctr, Buffalo, 81-82, Dynamic Computer Architect Inc, Lincoln, 82, IBM Fed Systs Div, Manassas, Va, 83-87, Hewlett-Packard, Ft Collins, Colo, 84, Westinghouse Elec Corp, Baltimore, 84, KLA Instruments Corp, Santa Clara, 85, Ball Aerospace, Boulder, 85, MCC, Austin, Tex, 86, Citicorp/TTI, Santa Monica, 86, Gen Dynamics, Fort Worth, 86, NCR Corp, Minneapolis, 88, Sandia Nat Labs, Livermore, Ca, 88-89, NCR, San Diego, 90 & Cray Res Inc, Mendota Heights, Minn, 90; numerous res grants, 77-89; chmn, Computer Soc Tech Comt Computer Architect, Inst Elec & Electronic Engrs, 82; chmn, Assoc Comput Mach Spec Interest Group Computer Architect, 83-85, co-chmn Int Conf Parallel Processing, 83; res proj leader, Supercomput Res Ctr, Lanham, Md, 87-88. *Mem:* Asn Comput Mach; fel Inst Elec & Electronic Engrs; Sigma Xi. *Res:* Development of large-scale parallel and distributed multimicrocomputer systems for image and speech processing, including system hardware and software and study of parallel algorithms; design and analysis of interconnection networks for parallel machines; modeling of parallel processing systems; co-authored over 130 technical papers. *Mailing Add:* Sch Elec Eng Purdue Univ West Lafayette IN 47907

SIEGEL, IRVING, SOLID STATE PHYSICS, CHEMICAL PHYSICS. *Current Pos:* RETIRED. *Personal Data:* b Brooklyn, NY, June 15, 24; m 50, Else M Rymarzjck; c Edward M & Diana J. *Educ:* Univ Iowa, BA, 50; Ill Inst Technol, MS, 61; Univ Toledo, PhD, 70. *Prof Exp:* Physicist, Semiconductor Div, Battelle Mem Inst, 51-55, Physics Res Div, IIT Res Inst, 55-59 & Semiconductor & Mat Div, RCA, 59-60; res physicist fundamental res sect, Owens-Ill Tech Ctr, Ohio, 60-70; asst prof physics, Calif Polytech State Univ, 71-76; res physicist, Northrop Corp, 79-85. *Concurrent Pos:* Adj lectr, Univ Toledo, 61-70. *Mem:* Am Phys Soc; Inst Elec & Electronics Engrs; Magnetics Soc. *Res:* Electron paramagnetic resonance; ferromagnetic resonance; magnetic materials and magnetism; teaching. *Mailing Add:* 2071 Hope St San Luis Obispo CA 93405

SIEGEL, IRWIN MICHAEL, PHYSIOLOGY, GENETICS. *Current Pos:* From asst prof to assoc prof, 60-73, PROF RES OPHTHAL, MED CTR, NY UNIV, 73- *Personal Data:* b New York, NY, Apr 18, 30; m 56; c 1. *Educ:* City Col New York, BS, 51; Columbia Univ, MS, 54, MA, 58, PhD(vision), 60. *Mem:* AAAS; Asn Res Vision & Ophthal; Sigma Xi. *Res:* Vision physiology; ophthalmic genetics. *Mailing Add:* 380 Riverside Dr Apt 8T New York NY 10025-1822

SIEGEL, IVENS AARON, PHARMACOLOGY, ORAL BIOLOGY. *Current Pos:* PROF & CHMN PHARMACOL, UNIV ILL-URBANA, 79- *Personal Data:* b Bay Shore, NY, Jan 28, 32; m 59; c 3. *Educ:* Columbus Univ, BS, 53; Univ Kans, MS, 58; Univ Cincinnati, PhD(pharmacol), 62. *Prof Exp:* From instr to asst prof pharmacol, State Univ NY Buffalo, 62-68; from assoc prof to prof pharmacol & oral biol, Univ Wash, 68-79, chmn, Dept Oral Biol, 76-79. *Mem:* Int Asn Dent Res; Am Soc Pharmacol & Exp Therapeut. *Res:* Ion transport, transport in salivary glands; physiology and pharmacology of salivary glands; drug transport across the oral mucosa. *Mailing Add:* 190 Med Sci Bldg Univ Ill Col Med 506 S Matthews Ave Urbana IL 61801-3618. *Fax:* 217-333-8868; *E-Mail:* ivenssiegel@gmsllifeuivc.edu

SIEGEL, JACK S, CHEMICAL ENGINEERING. *Current Pos:* dir, Off Environ Policy, 77-83, dep dir coal utilization advan combustion & gasification, 83-84, DEP ASST SECY COAL TECHNOL, DEPT OF ENERGY, 84- *Personal Data:* b Long Branch, NJ, June 2, 46; m 71, Shari Diane Goodman; c Erica Robyn & Adam Michael. *Educ:* Worcester Polytech Inst, BSChmet, 68. *Prof Exp:* Chem Engr, Dept Navy, 68, 68-71; supvry chem engr, Environ Protection Agency, 71-76; asst dir environ planning & assessment, US Energy Res & Develop Admin, 76-77. *Concurrent Pos:* Fed rep, Nat Coal Asn, 86- *Mem:* Am Inst Chem Engrs. *Res:* Environmental planning and assessment; coal utilization, advanced combustion and gasification. *Mailing Add:* 8304 River Trail Lane Bethesda MD 20817-4328

SIEGEL, JAY PHILIP, CELLULAR IMMUNOLOGY, CYTOKINES. *Current Pos:* sr staff fel immunol, Div Virol, 82-86, sr investr, Ctr Biol Evol & Res, 86-88, LAB CHIEF, LAB IMMUNOL, DIV CYTOKINE BIOL, CTR BIOL EVAL & RES, FOOD & DRUG ADMIN, 88- *Personal Data:* b New York, NY, May 18, 52; m 82; c 2. *Educ:* Calif Inst Technol, BS, 73; Stanford Univ, MD, 77. *Honors & Awards:* Physician Recognition Award, AMA, 89. *Prof Exp:* Resident internal med, Univ Calif, San Francisco, 77-80; fel infectious dis, Sch Med, Stanford Univ, 80-82. *Concurrent Pos:* Fel immunol & infectious dis, Palo Alto Med Found, 80-82; surgeon, USPHS, 86-87, sr surgeon, 87-; attend physician, Div Infectious Dis, Nat Naval Med Ctr, Bethesda, 89- *Mem:* Am Asn Immunologists; fel Am Col Physicians; Am Fedn Clin Res; AAAS. *Res:* Regulation of cellular immune responses; cytotoxic responses; roles of cytokines in the activation and differentiation of cytotoxic lymphocytes. *Mailing Add:* Food & Drug Admin 1401 Rockville Pike Suite 200N Rockville MD 20852. *Fax:* 301-496-1610

SIEGEL, JEFFREY ALAN, COMPUTER ENGINEERING, SOLID STATE PHYSICS. *Current Pos:* PROJ SCIENTIST, VI ENG, 96- *Personal Data:* b Pittsburgh, Pa, May 24, 68. *Educ:* Amherst Col, BA, 90; Univ Mich, MS, 93, PhD(physics), 96. *Mem:* Sigma Xi; Am Phys Soc. *Res:* Computer programming; system integration for data acquisition and test/measurement systems. *Mailing Add:* 37800 Hills Tech Dr Farmington Hills MI 48331. *Fax:* 248-489-1904; *E-Mail:* jsiegel@vieng.com

SIEGEL, JEFFRY A, NUCLEAR MEDICINE. *Current Pos:* Asst prof nuclear med physics, 81-, DIR SECT PHYSICS RES & DEVELOP, TEMPLE UNIV HOSP, PROF RADIOL, UNDNJ ROBERT WOOD JOHNSON MED SCH, CONSULT RES ASSOC, GARDEN STATE CANCER CTR, CMMI. *Personal Data:* b New York, NY. *Educ:* Univ Cincinnati, BS, 73, MS(chem), 76, MS(radiol physics), 77; Univ Calif, Los Angeles, PhD(med physics), 81. *Mem:* Soc Nuclear Med; Asn Physicists Med; Inst Elec & Electronics Engrs. *Res:* Quantitative nuclear medicine; nuclear cardiology; image processing of digital data. *Mailing Add:* 1512 Lincoln Dr Voorhees NJ 08043

SIEGEL, JOHN H, SURGERY, PHYSIOLOGY. *Current Pos:* prof surg & dep dir, Md Inst Emergency Med Serv Systs, 82-91, WESLEY J HOWE PROF TRAUMA SURG, UNIV MD, NJ, 91-, CHMN, DEPT ANAT, CELL BIOL & INJURY SCI, NJ MED SCH, 91- *Personal Data:* b Baltimore, Md, Dec 12, 32; m 56, Carol Friedman; c Wendy, Thomas & Gillian. *Educ:* Cornell Univ, BA, 53; Johns Hopkins Univ, MD, 57; Am Bd Surg, dipl, 66. *Prof Exp:* Intern surg, Grace-New Haven Community Hosp, 57-58; Cardiovasc fel, Dept Surg, Yale Univ, 58-59 & Lab Cardiovasc Physiol, Nat Heart Inst, 59-61; dir cardiovasc physiol lab, Dept Surg, Sch Med, Univ Mich, 62-65; instr surg, Albert Einstein Col Med, 65-66, assoc, 66-67, from asst prof to assoc prof, 67-72; prof surg & biophys, State Univ NY, Buffalo, 72-82. *Concurrent Pos:* USPHS trainee acad surg, Dept Surg, Sch Med, Univ Mich, 62-65; Health Res Coun City of New York career scientist award, 66-71; prin investr, Nat Heart Inst grants, 62-65, 66-72 & Nat Inst Gen Med Sci grant, 69-71; dir renal transplantation serv & assoc dir clin res ctr-acute, Albert Einstein Col Med, 67-72; asst vis surgeon, Bronx Munic Hosp, 65-67, from assoc attend surgeon to attend surgeon, 67-72; attend, Hosp, Albert Einstein Col Med, 66-72; chief dept surg, Buffalo Gen Hosp, 72-82; attend surgeon, Univ Md Hosp; prof surg, Johns Hopkins Univ, Sch Med, 84-91. *Mem:* Am Physiol Soc; fel Am Col Surgeons; Am Asn Surg of Trauma; Am Surg Asn; Int Cardiovasc Soc; Shock Soc. *Res:* General and vascular surgery; computer science; physiologic evaluation of the critically ill; spesis and septic shock; hyporolemic oxygen debt; ARDS. *Mailing Add:* UMDNJ Med Sch Anat G 609 185 S Orange Ave Newark NJ 07103. *Fax:* 973-982-4860; *E-Mail:* siegeljh@umdnj.edu

SIEGEL, JONATHAN HOWARD, SENSORY NEUROBIOLOGY. *Current Pos:* ASSOC PROF AUDIOL, NORTHWESTERN UNIV, 81- *Personal Data:* b Chicago, Ill, Mar 2, 51; m 78; c 3. *Educ:* Univ Ark, Fayetteville, BS, 73; Washington Univ, St Louis, PhD(physiol & biophys), 78. *Prof Exp:* Res asst, Washington Univ, St Louis, 74-78, res fel, 78-81. *Mem:* Acoust Soc Am; Soc Neurosci; Asn Res Otolaryngol; Sigma Xi. *Res:* Synaptic transmission between the sensory receptor cells of the mammalian cochlea and the afferent neurons; active cochlear mechanical processes; receptor and nerve cell physiology; cell biology; Otoacoustic Emissions. *Mailing Add:* Northwestern Univ 2299 N Campus Dr Evanston IL 60208. *Fax:* 847-491-2523; *E-Mail:* j-siegel@nwu.edu

SIEGEL, LESTER AARON, PHYSICS. *Current Pos:* RETIRED. *Personal Data:* b New York, NY, Sept 25, 25. *Educ:* Mass Inst Technol, SB, 45, PhD(physics), 48. *Prof Exp:* Instr physics, Mass Inst Technol, 48-50; from res physicist to sr res physicist, Am Cyanamid Co, 50- 61, group leader, 61-69, sr res physicist, 69-86. *Mem:* Am Phys Soc; Am Chem Soc; Am Crystallog Asn. *Res:* X-ray diffraction. *Mailing Add:* 44 Strawberry Hill Ave Apt 10E Stamford CT 06902

SIEGEL, LEWIS MELVIN, BIOCHEMISTRY. *Current Pos:* res assoc, 66-68, PROF BIOCHEM, SCH MED, DUKE UNIV, 68- *Personal Data:* b Baltimore, Md, Aug 7, 41; m 60; c 3. *Educ:* Johns Hopkins Univ, BA, 61, PhD(biol), 65. *Prof Exp:* Res assoc biol, Brookhaven Nat Lab, 65. *Concurrent Pos:* Res chemist, Vet Admin Hosp, Durham, 68- *Mem:* Am Soc Biol Chemists; Am Chem Soc. *Res:* Mechanisms of electron transport in metalloflavoproteins; multi-electron reductions; sulfur and nitrogen metabolism. *Mailing Add:* Dept Biochem Duke Univ Med Ctr Durham NC 27710-0001. *Fax:* 919-684-2277

SIEGEL, MALCOLM RICHARD, PLANT PATHOLOGY, TOXICOLOGY. *Current Pos:* From asst prof to assoc prof, 66-73, prof, Ctr Toxicol, 75-95, PROF PLANT PATH, UNIV KY, 73- *Personal Data:* b New Haven, Conn, Nov 5, 32; m 62, Carolyn J Friedman; c Erik C & Mark A. *Educ:* Univ Conn, BS, 55; Univ Del, MS, 59; Univ Md, PhD(bot), 63. *Concurrent Pos:* Assoc ed, Phytopathology, 73-76; assoc ed, Pesticide Biochem & Physiol, 78-87; sabbatical, Inst Org Chem, 75; mem staff, USDA, 79; Thomas Poe Cooper distinguished res award, Ky Agr Exp Sta, 92. *Mem:* Fel Am Phytopath Soc; Sigma Xi. *Res:* Action and metabolic fate of fungicides; epidemiology, chemical and biological control of plant pathogens. *Mailing Add:* Dept Plant Path Univ Ky Lexington KY 40506

SIEGEL, MARILYN J, PEDIATRIC RADIOLOGY. *Current Pos:* resident diag radiol, Wash Univ Sch Med, 74-77, from instr to assoc prof radiol, 77-89, assoc prof pediat, 83-95, PROF RADIOL, MALLINCKRODT INST RADIOL, WASH UNIV SCH MED, 89-, PROF PEDIAT, 95- *Personal Data:* m 83, Barry A. *Educ:* Wash Univ, AB, 65; State Univ NY, Downstate, MD, 69. *Prof Exp:* Intern, Montefiore Med Ctr, NY, 69-70; resident pediat, Cardinal Glenron Mem Hosp, 70-72; fel pediat oncol, Children's Orthop Hosp, Wash, 72-73. *Concurrent Pos:* Assoc ed, Radiol, 91; mem, Sci Comt Radiation Protection in Med, Nat Coun Radiation Protection & Measurements, 93-; NIH prin investr grant pediat solid tumors, 93-; consult, Food & Drug Admin, 96-; assoc ed, Am Col Radiol, Prof Self-Eval Prog. *Mem:* Fel Am Col Radiol; Am Roentgen Ray Soc; Radiol Soc NAm; Soc Comput Body Tomography; Soc Pediat Radiol. *Res:* Imaging neuroblastoma; techniques of contrast administration in CT; color Doppler imaging of acute abdominal disease. *Mailing Add:* Mallinckrodt Inst Radiol 510 S Kingshighway Blvd St Louis MO 63110-1016. *Fax:* 314-454-2868; *E-Mail:* siegelm@mirlink.wustl.edu

SIEGEL, MARTHA J, MATHEMATICS. *Current Pos:* assoc prof, 71-77, PROF MATH, TOWSON STATE UNIV, 77- *Personal Data:* b New York, NY, Nov 5, 39; m 62; c Rachel & Norman Eli. *Educ:* Russell Sage Col, BA, 60; Univ Rochester, MA, 63, PhD(math), 69. *Prof Exp:* Asst prof, Goucher Col, 67-71. *Concurrent Pos:* Fel, Sch Hyg & Pub Health, Johns Hopkins Univ, 77-78. *Mem:* Math Asn Am; Am Math Soc; Soc Indust & Appl Math. *Res:* Birth and death processes; collegiate mathematics curriculum reform. *Mailing Add:* Dept Math Towson State Univ Towson MD 21252-7097

SIEGEL, MARVIN I, BIOCHEMISTRY. *Current Pos:* assoc dir biol res, Schering Plough Co, 82-85, dir biol res, 85-88, sr dir biol res, 88-92, VPRES BIOL RES, SCHERING PLOUGH CO, 92- *Personal Data:* b Brooklyn, NY, July 11, 46; m 87, Debra F Miller; c Deborah G & Rachel L. *Educ:* Lafayette Col, BS; Columbia Univ, MA, 67; Johns Hopkins Univ, PhD(biochem), 73. *Honors & Awards:* Am Inst Chemists Award, 67. *Prof Exp:* Res scientist, Burroughs Corp, 75-82. *Concurrent Pos:* Adj assoc prof, Dept Biochem & Nutrit, Univ NC Sch Med, Chapel Hill, 82-; adj prof, Dept Biol Sci, Rutgers Univ, 87- *Mem:* Am Soc Pharmacol & Exp Therapeut; Sigma Xi; Am Soc Biochem & Molecular Biol; Am Acad Allergy & Immunol; Am Asn Immunologists; Am Chem Soc; Am Inst Chemists. *Res:* Allergy; inflamation; immunology. *Mailing Add:* 32 Lakewood Circle San Mateo CA 94402

SIEGEL, MAURICE L, ORGANIC CHEMISTRY. *Current Pos:* CONSULT, 87- *Personal Data:* b New York, NY, Aug 7, 27; m 59. *Educ:* City Col New York, BS, 49; NY Univ, MS, 51, PhD, 58. *Prof Exp:* Dir res, Caryl Richards Co, 57-67; vpres, Faberge, Inc, 67-78, dir res, 67-87, exec vpres, 78-87. *Concurrent Pos:* Adj asst prof, NY Univ, 59-67. *Mem:* AAAS; Soc Cosmetic Chem; Am Chem Soc. *Res:* Hair technology. *Mailing Add:* 560 W 43rd St Apt 30A New York NY 10036

SIEGEL, MELVIN WALTER, SENSORS, INTELLIGENT SYSTEMS. *Current Pos:* SR RES SCIENTIST, ROBOTICS INST, CARNEGIE MELLON UNIV, 82- *Personal Data:* b New York, NY, May 26, 41; m 68; c 1. *Educ:* Cornell Univ, BA, 62; Univ Colo, MS, 67, PhD(physics), 70. *Honors & Awards:* IR-100 Awards, 78, 79 & 86. *Prof Exp:* Instr physics & math, Achimota Col, Ghana, 62-64; res assoc physics, Joint Inst Lab Astrophysics, Univ Colo, 70; sr scientist, Univ Va, 70-72, lectr, 71-72; asst prof physics, State Univ NY Buffalo, 72-74; physicist, Extranuclear Labs, Inc, 74-82, dir, res & develop, 78-82. *Mem:* AAAS; Am Phys Soc; Am Soc Mass Spectros; Am Asn Artificial Intelligence; Inst Elec & Electronics Engrs; Soc Photo Optical Instrumentation Engrs. *Res:* Ionization phenomena; mass spectrometry; intelligent sensors and their applications in artificial intelligence based systems control; ion optics; instrumentation, robotics, sensors and artificial intelligence. *Mailing Add:* Robotics Inst Carnegie Mellon Univ Pittsburgh PA 15213

SIEGEL, MICHAEL ELLIOT, NUCLEAR MEDICINE, RADIOLOGY. *Current Pos:* ASSOC PROF RADIOPHARM, SCH PHARM & ASSOC PROF RADIOL & MED, SCH MED, UNIV SOUTHERN CALIF, 76- *Personal Data:* b New York, NY, May 13, 42; m 66; c 2. *Educ:* Cornell Univ, BA, 64; Chicago Med Sch, MD, 68. *Honors & Awards:* Silver Medal, Soc Nuclear Med, 74 & 75. *Prof Exp:* NIH fel diag radiol, Temple Univ Med Ctr, 70-71; NIH fel nuclear med, Johns Hopkins Univ, 71-73, asst prof radiol & environ health, 73-76; asst clin prof radiol, George Washington Univ, 75-77. *Concurrent Pos:* Radiologist, Johns Hopkins Univ, 71-76; consult nuclear med, Ann Arundel Hosp, Annapolis, Md, 74-76; dir, Dept Nuclear Med, Orthop Hosp, Los Angeles, 76-; dir, Dept Nuclear Med & sr attend physician, Los Angeles County-Univ Southern Calif Med Ctr, 76-; dir nuclear med, Kenneth Norris Cancer Hosp & res Ctr, Los Angeles. *Mem:* Soc Nuclear Med; Am Col Nuclear Physicians; Radiol Soc NAm; Asn Univ Radiologists; Am Col Nuclear Med. *Res:* Development of new applications of radioisotopes for prognostic and diagnostic evaluation of vascular disease, both cardiac and peripheral; diagnosis and therapy of malignancies. *Mailing Add:* Los Angeles County-Univ Southern Calif Med Ctr 1200 N State St Box 693 Los Angeles CA 90033

SIEGEL, MICHAEL IAN, PHYSICAL ANTHROPOLOGY, PRIMATOLOGY. *Current Pos:* from asst prof to assoc prof phys anthrop, Univ Pittsburgh, 71-82, prof orthod, Col Dent, 75-76, assoc prof anat & cell biol, 78-80, chmn, Dept Anthrop, 92-95, PROF PHYSICS ANTHROP, UNIV PITTSBURGH, 82- *Personal Data:* b Brooklyn, NY, Nov 24, 42; m 84. *Educ:* Queens Col, NY, BA, 67; City Univ, NY, PhD(phys anthrop), 71. *Prof Exp:* Lectr phys anthrop, Hunter Col, 67-69; instr, Adelphi Univ, 69-71. *Concurrent Pos:* Vis scientist, Lab Exp Med & Surg Primates, 70-79; adj lectr prev dent, NY Univ, 70-79; sr res, Cleff Palate Ctr, 75-, NIH grants, 77, 80 & 85. *Mem:* Fel AAAS; Am Asn Anat; Am Asn Phys Anthropologists; Am Soc Mammalogists. *Res:* Experimental morphology and functional anatomy; growth and development; cleft palate models; middle ear disease; 3D computers. *Mailing Add:* Dept Anthrop Univ Pittsburgh Pittsburgh PA 15260

SIEGEL, MORRIS, PREVENTIVE MEDICINE, EPIDEMIOLOGY. *Current Pos:* from assoc prof to prof, 52-74, EMER PROF PREV MED, STATE UNIV NY, DOWNSTATE MED CTR, 74- *Personal Data:* b US, Mar 2, 04; m 33; c 2. *Educ:* City Col New York, BA, 24; NY Univ, MD, 28; Johns Hopkins Univ, MPH, 39. *Prof Exp:* Intern, Bellevue Hosp, New York, 29 & 31; resident physician, Sea View Hosp, 32-34; res assoc, New York Health Dept, 35-41; assoc, Pub Health Res Inst New York, 41-47; health officer, New York Health Dept, 47-52, chief poliomeylitis div, 49-50. *Concurrent Pos:* Vis lectr, Sch Pub Health, Harvard Univ, 59-61. *Mem:* Harvey Soc; Epidemiol Soc; NY Acad Med; Sigma Xi. *Res:* Public health, preventive medicine and epidemiology of acute and chronic diseases. *Mailing Add:* 345 E 69th St New York NY 10021-5583

SIEGEL, NORMAN JOSEPH, PEDIATRIC NEPHROLOGY, PATHOPHYSIOLOGY. *Current Pos:* Fel nephrol, Sch Med, Yale Univ, 70-72, asst prof pediat, 72-75, from asst prof to assoc prof pediat & med, 75-82, VCHMN PEDIAT, SCH MED, YALE UNIV, 76-, PROF PEDIAT & MED, 82- *Personal Data:* b Houston, Tex, Mar 8, 43; m 67, Rise Ross; c Andrew & Karen. *Educ:* Tulane Univ, BA, 64; Univ Tex, Galveston, MA & MD, 68. *Honors & Awards:* Spec Recognition Award, Soc Pediat Res, 85; Mitchell I Rubin Award, 92. *Concurrent Pos:* Chmn, Sub-Bd Pediat Nephrol, Am Bd Pediat, 85-89 & coun Pediat Nephrol & Urol, Nat Kidney Found, 87-; mem, Sci Adv Comt, Nat Kidney Found, 88-; assoc ed, Am J Kidney Dis, 90-; distinguished vis physician, Nat Kidney Found Western Tenn, 90; chmn, Coun Pediat Nephrol & Urol, Nat Kidney Found, 87-91 & Nat Bd Med Examrs Pediat Test Comt, 93- *Mem:* Am Soc Pediat Nephrol (pres, 88-89); Soc Pediat Res; Am Soc Pediat; Am Pediat Soc (secy-treas, 93-); Am Soc Clin Invest; Am Soc Nephrol. *Res:* Recovery of the kidney from injury; pathophysiology, cellular and molecular mechanisms responsible for the restoration and regeneration of renal tubular epithelium following ischemia, toxins and ureteral obstructions. *Mailing Add:* 43 Wellington Dr Orange CT 06447-3035. *Fax:* 203-785-3462

SIEGEL, PAUL BENJAMIN, GENETICS. *Current Pos:* From asst prof to prof, 57-75, UNIV DISTINGUISHED PROF ANIMAL & POULTRY SCI, VA POLYTECH INST & STATE UNIV, 75- *Personal Data:* b Hartford, Conn, Nov 19, 32; m 57, Anita O'Brien; c Amy, Alec & Audrey. *Educ:* Univ Conn, BS, 53; Kans State Univ, MS, 54, PhD(genetics), 57. *Mem:* AAAS; Animal Behav Soc; Am Genetic Asn; Poultry Sci Asn. *Res:* Genetic aspects of behavior; population genetics. *Mailing Add:* Dept Animal & Poultry Sci Va Polytech Inst & State Univ Blacksburg VA 24063-0306

SIEGEL, RICHARD C, IMMUNOCHEMISTRY, ANALYTICAL BIOCHEMISTRY. *Current Pos:* ASSOC DIR BIOPHARMACEUT RES & DEVELOP, CENTOCOR CORP, 88- *Personal Data:* b New York, NY, Jan 25, 52; m 75; c 2. *Educ:* Boston Univ, AB, 74, Tufts Univ, PhD(biochem), 80. *Prof Exp:* Postdoctoral chem & immunol, Univ Calif Los Angeles, 79-81; sr scientist res & develop, Technicon Instruments Corp, 81-83; group leader res & develop, Cytogen Corp, 83-88. *Mem:* Am Chem Soc; Fedn Am Socs Exp Biol; AAAS. *Res:* Therapeutic monoclonal antibodies; development of manufacturing methods, protein characterization and assay development. *Mailing Add:* Centocor Inc 200 Great Valley Pkwy Malvern PA 19355-1339. *Fax:* 215-651-6201

SIEGEL, RICHARD W(HITE), materials science, metal physics, for more information see previous edition

SIEGEL, ROBERT, MECHANICAL ENGINEERING, HEAT TRANSFER. *Current Pos:* res engr, 55-92, SR RES SCIENTIST, NASA, 92- *Personal Data:* b Cleveland, Ohio, July 10, 27; m 51, Elaine Jaffe; c Stephen D & Lawrence C. *Educ:* Case Inst Technol, BS, 50, MS, 51; Mass Inst Technol, ScD(mech eng), 53. *Honors & Awards:* Heat Transfer Mem Award, Am Soc Mech Engrs, 70; Thermophysics Award, Am Inst Aeronaut & Astronaut, 93. *Prof Exp:* Asst mech eng, Case Inst Technol, 50-51; fluid dynamics, Mass Inst Technol, 52-53; res engr, Gen Eng Lab, Gen Elec Co, 53-54; res engr, Knolls Atomic Power Lab, 54-55. *Concurrent Pos:* Assoc tech ed, J Heat Transfer, 73-83, J Thermophysics & Heat Transfer, 86- *Mem:* Fel Am Soc Mech Engrs; fel Am Inst Aeronaut & Astronaut. *Res:* Heat transfer theory; forced and free convection; transient heat convection; thermal radiation exchange, thermal radiation in absorbing, emitting, and scattering media, boiling and solidification. *Mailing Add:* MS5-9 NASA Lewis Res Ctr 21000 Brookpark Rd Cleveland OH 44135. *Fax:* 216-433-8864

SIEGEL, ROBERT TED, PARTICLE PHYSICS. *Current Pos:* dean grad studies, Col William & Mary, 64-67, dir, Space Radiation Effects Lab, Newport News, Va, 67-78, prof physics, 63-69, W F C FERGISON PROF PHYSICS, COL WILLIAM & MARY, 79- *Personal Data:* b Springfield, Mass, June 10, 28; m 95, Wendy P Kramer; c 5. *Educ:* Carnegie Inst Technol, BS, 48, MS, 50, DSc, 52. *Prof Exp:* Resident physicist, Carnegie Inst Technol, 52-54, from asst prof to assoc prof physics, 54-63. *Mem:* Fel Am Phys Soc; AAAS. *Res:* Elementary particle physics; weak interactions; muon physics. *Mailing Add:* Dept Physics Col William & Mary Williamsburg VA 23185. *Fax:* 757-221-3540; *E-Mail:* siegel@muon.physics.wsu.edu

SIEGEL, SAMUEL, ORGANIC CHEMISTRY. *Current Pos:* assoc prof, 51-57, chmn dept, 57-63, prof chem, 57-86, univ prof, 86-87, EMER PROF, UNIV ARK, FAYETTEVILLE, 87- *Personal Data:* b Lake Mills, Wis, Feb 15, 17; m 48, Betty Howard; c Jonathan Howard & Robert Varner. *Educ:* Univ Calif, BS, 38; Univ Calif, Los Angeles, MA, 40, PhD(chem), 42. *Prof Exp:* Res assoc, Northwestern Univ, 42-43; res assoc chem warfare agents & insect repellants, Nat Defense Res Comt Proj, Harvard Univ, 43-45; asst prof chem, Ill Inst Technol, 46-51. *Concurrent Pos:* Consult, Universal Oil Prod Co, 56-62; Am Chem Soc-Petrol Res Fund Int fac award, 63-64; vis prof, Queen's Univ, Belfast, 63-64, Res Inst Catalysis, Hokkaido, Japan, 78, Northwestern Univ, 84; sr fel, Japan Soc Promotion of Sci, 77; exchange fel, Inst Isotopes, Hungarian Acad Sci, 83. *Mem:* AAAS; Am Chem Soc; Royal Soc Chem; Catalysis Soc; NY Acad Sci. *Res:* Stereochemistry; quantitative structure-reactivity relationships; mechanism of heterogeneous and homogeneous catalytic hydrogenation. *Mailing Add:* Dept Chem & Biochem Univ Ark Fayetteville AR 72701-1202

SIEGEL, SANFORD MARVIN, environmental chemistry, biogeochemistry; deceased, see previous edition for last biography

SIEGEL, SEYMOUR, TECHNOLOGY IMPLEMENTATION, TECHNOLOGOLICAL STRATEGY. *Current Pos:* PROF TECHNOL MGT, SCH BUS & MGT, PEPPERDINE UNIV, 89- *Personal Data:* b New York, NY, Oct 19, 32; m 55, Dorothy S Goldberg; c Eric B & Marc D. *Educ:* Brooklyn Col, BS, 54; Harvard Univ, MA, 56, PhD(phys chem), 59. *Prof Exp:* Mem sr staff, Appl Physics Lab, Johns Hopkins Univ, 58-59; chem physicist, Aerojet-Gen Corp, 59-61; head chem physics dept, Mat Sci Lab, Aerospace Corp, 61-73, dir, Chem & Phys Lab, 73-80; dir explor res, Occidental Res Corp, 81-83; assoc vchancellor res progs, Univ Calif, Los Angeles, 84-89. *Mem:* Am Phys Soc; Am Chem Soc; AAAS; Am Acad Mgt. *Res:* Technology transfer; organizational management; technology management; technology implementation; technological strategy. *Mailing Add:* 11432 Bolas St Los Angeles CA 90049

SIEGEL, SHELDON, pharmaceutical chemistry, for more information see previous edition

SIEGEL, SIDNEY, PHYSICS OF SOLIDS, NUCLEAR TECHNOLOGY. *Current Pos:* CONSULT, ADVAN ENERGY SYSTS, 74- *Personal Data:* b New York, NY, Jan 10, 12; m 37, Lilyan Ferges; c Maria (Watt), Anne (Podney), Laura (Venning) & Gail (Maltun). *Educ:* Columbia Univ, AB, 32, PhD(physics), 36. *Prof Exp:* Asst physics, Columbia Univ, 33-38; res engr, Res Labs, Westinghouse Elec Corp, 38-44, sect mgr, 44-46, mgr, Physics Dept, Atomic Power Div, 49-50; chief physicist, Oak Ridge Nat Lab, 46-49; assoc dir, Atomic Res Dept, NAm Aviation, Inc, 50-55, tech dir, Atomic Int Div, 55-60, vpres, Atomic Int Div, NAm Rockwell Corp, 60-72; dep assoc dir, Oak Ridge Nat Lab, 72-74. *Concurrent Pos:* Lectr, Univ Pittsburgh, 38-40; res assoc, Calif Inst Technol, 51. *Mem:* Fel Am Nuclear Soc (vpres, 65, pres, 66); fel Am Phys Soc; Sigma Xi. *Res:* Solid state physics; ferromagnetism; radiation effects; nuclear reactor development; energy economics. *Mailing Add:* 722 Jacon Way Pacific Palisades CA 90272

SIEGEL, STANLEY, crystallography; deceased, see previous edition for last biography

SIEGEL, WILLIAM CARL, RESOURCE ECONOMICS & RESOURCE LAW, TIMBER TAXATION. *Current Pos:* CONSULT, FOREST RESOURCE ECON, 93- *Personal Data:* b Eau Claire, Wis, Sept 11, 32; m 62, Alma Troxclair; c Carlin, Sharon, Jill, Kimberly & Brian. *Educ:* Mich State Univ, BS, 54, MS, 57; Loyola Univ, La, LLB, 65, JD, 68. *Honors & Awards:* Super Serv Award, USDA, 85. *Prof Exp:* Timber mgt asst, Sam Houston Nat Forest, US Forest Serv, 58, asst economist, Southern Forest Exp Sta, 58-60, assoc economist, 60-66, economist, 66-68, prin economist, 68-77, proj leader & chief economist, 77-93. *Concurrent Pos:* Univ teaching, 75-; adj prof forestry, La State Univ. *Mem:* Soc Am Foresters; Nat Tax Asn; Am Bar Asn; Forest Prod Res Soc; Southern Econ Asn. *Res:* Forestry economics, especially forest taxation, insurance and credit with emphasis on the relationship between law and economics. *Mailing Add:* 9110 Hermitage Pl River Ridge LA 70123. *Fax:* 504-737-1074

SIEGER, JOHN S(YLVESTER), CHEMICAL ENGINEERING. *Current Pos:* RETIRED. *Personal Data:* b Pittsburgh, Pa, Oct 3, 25; m 51; c 4. *Educ:* Carnegie Inst Technol, BS, 45; Columbia Univ, MS, 47, PhD(chem eng), 50. *Prof Exp:* Res engr, Pittsburgh Coke & Chem Co, 45-47; fel, Mellon Inst, 50-56; group leader, Pittsburgh Plate Glass Co, 56-59, head surfacing res dept, 59-64, sr res assoc, Glass Res Labs, PPG Indust Inc, 64-84. *Res:* Research and development on the production and properties of flat glass. *Mailing Add:* 540 Landsdale Pl Pittsburgh PA 15228

SIEGERT, ARNOLD JOHN FREDERICK, STATISTICAL PHYSICS. *Current Pos:* RETIRED. *Personal Data:* b Dresden, Ger, Jan 1, 11; nat US; m 44; c 1. *Educ:* Univ Leipzig, PhD(theoret physics), 34. *Prof Exp:* Lorentz Funds fel, Univ Leiden, Holland, 34-36; asst physics, Stanford Univ, 36-39; physicist, Tex Co, 39-42, Nat Geophys Co, 42, Stanolind Oil & Gas Co, Okla, 42 & radiation lab, Mass Inst Technol, 42-46; assoc prof physics, Syracuse Univ, 46-47; prof physics, Northwestern Univ, Evanston, 47-79. *Concurrent Pos:* Consult, Pan-Am Petrol Corp, 42-66, Rand Corp, 50-57, Lockheed Aircraft Corp, 58-61 & Argonne Nat Lab, 65-71; Guggenheim fel, Inst Adv Study, 53-54; NSF sr fels, Inst Theoret Physics, Amsterdam, Neth, 62-63 & Weizmann Inst, Israel, 63-64; vis prof, Univ Utrecht, Neth, 71-72 & 79-80, Kramers prof, 80. *Mem:* Fel Am Phys Soc. *Res:* Theoretical physics; quantum theory; random processes; exploration geophysics; gravity and magnetic methods; statistical mechanics. *Mailing Add:* 2347 Lake Ave Wilmette IL 60091

SIEGESMUND, KENNETH A, ELECTRON MICROSCOPY, FORENSIC PATHOLOGY. *Current Pos:* DIR RES, CRYSTAL MED, 96- *Personal Data:* b Milwaukee, Wis, Nov 28, 33; m 59, Pat Dreyer; c Mark, John, Carolyn & Sandra. *Educ:* Univ Wis, BS, 55, PhD(bot), 60. *Prof Exp:* Res assoc bot, Med Col Wis, 60-62, assoc prof anat, 62-96. *Concurrent Pos:* Consult, Vet Admin Hosp, 62-78, Milwaukee Co Hosp, 62-65 & Trinity Hosp, 78-85. *Mem:* Am Asn Anat; Electron Micros Soc Am; Neuroelec Soc; Am Acad Forensic Sci; AAAS. *Res:* Ultrastructure of the nervous system; applications of electron microscopy in diagnostic pathology, diagnosis and pathogenesis of occupational lung disease; forensic sci; immunodiagnostics; author of 120 publications; granted 5 patents. *Mailing Add:* 17825 Primrose Lane Brookfield WI 53045

SIEGFRIED, CLIFFORD ANTON, AQUATIC ECOLOGY, ACIDIC DEPOSITION EFFECTS. *Current Pos:* ASSOC SCIENTIST ENVIRON BIOL, BIOL SURV, NY STATE MUS, 79-; DEP DIR RES & COLLECTIONS, NY STATE BIOL SURV, 96- *Personal Data:* b Bismarck, ND, Oct 19, 47; m 70, Dianne M Rooney; c Laurie, Amy & Adam. *Educ:* Univ Calif, BS, 69, PhD(ecol), 74. *Prof Exp:* Post grad res scientist aquatic ecol, Univ Calif, Davis, 74-79. *Concurrent Pos:* Instr, Life Sci Div, Yuba Col, 74; consult, Big Bear Munic Water Dist, 76-79; chair, NY State Biol Surv, 92-95. *Mem:* Am Soc Limnol & Oceanog; NAm Lake Mgt Soc; Int Asn Ecol; AAAS. *Res:* Population dynamics, life history, production, and community structure of plankton and benthos communities; response of lake systems to acidification and effects of nutrient enrichment; impacts of exotic species in aquatic systems. *Mailing Add:* Biol Surv NY State Mus Albany NY 12230. *E-Mail:* csiegfri@museum.nysed.gov

SIEGFRIED, JOHN BARTON, VISUAL PHYSIOLOGY, ELECTROPHYSIOLOGY. *Current Pos:* PROF PHYSIOL OPTICS, PA COL OPTOM, 73- *Personal Data:* b Philadelphia, Pa, Mar 19, 38; m 87, Dorothy Sweeney; c 7. *Educ:* Univ Rochester, BA, 60; Brown Univ, MS, 62, PhD(physiol psychol), 67. *Prof Exp:* From asst prof to assoc prof psychol,

Univ Houston, 66-73. *Concurrent Pos:* Asst prof, Dept Neural Sci, Grad Sch Biomed Sci, Univ Tex, Houston, 67-70; consult, US Army Human Eng Labs, Aberdeen Proving Ground, 67-; asst prof, Dept Ophthal, Baylor Col Med, 68-70; lectr, Dept Psychol, Univ Tex, Austin, 73; mem vision comt, Nat Acad Sci-Nat Res Coun, 73-85; adj assoc prof psychol, Lehigh Univ, 73-80; NSF res grant, 73, Nat Eye Inst, 80-88, & NIH res develop grant, 80; consult, Retina Dept, Wills Eye Hosp, Philadelphia, 76-80, Ophthal Dept, St Christopher's Hosp for Children, Philadelphia, 78-86 & Nat Inst Aging, 91-94. *Mem:* Asn Res Vision & Ophthal; Int Soc Clin Electrophysiol Vision. *Res:* Processing of information by the human visual cortex as measured by the visual evoked cortical potential; the relation between electrophysiological measures and perception; color vision; electro-diagnostic procedures. *Mailing Add:* 15 Angela Ave Mornsville PA 19067. *Fax:* 215-276-6081

SIEGFRIED, ROBERT, HISTORY OF SCIENCE, CHEMISTRY. *Current Pos:* assoc prof, 63-65, chmn dept, 64-73, PROF HIST SCI, UNIV WIS-MADISON, 65- *Personal Data:* b Columbus, Ohio, Jan 18, 21; m 46; c 4. *Educ:* Marietta Col, BA, 42; Univ Wis, PhD(chem, hist sci), 52. *Prof Exp:* Asst prof sci, Col Gen Educ, Boston Univ, 52-54; asst prof chem, Univ Ark, 54-58; from asst prof to assoc prof div gen studies, Univ Ill, 58-63. *Concurrent Pos:* NSF fel, Royal Inst London, 67-68. *Mem:* AAAS; Hist Sci Soc. *Res:* History of chemistry, and the structure of matter, 1700-1850; chemical revolution. *Mailing Add:* 2206 W Lawn Ave Madison WI 53711

SIEGFRIED, ROBERT WAYNE, II, MATERIAL PROPERTIES, ACOUSTICS. *Current Pos:* PRIN PROD MGR, GAS RES INST, CHICAGO, 94- *Personal Data:* b Elmhurst, Ill, July 1, 50; m 78, Jessie Olcott; c Robert & Richard. *Educ:* Calif Inst Technol, BS, 72; Mass Inst Technol, PhD(geophys), 77. *Prof Exp:* Sr scientist geophys, Corning Glass Works, 77-80; res geophysicist, Atlantic Richfield Co, 80-94. *Mem:* Am Geophys Union; Soc Explor Geophysicist; Soc Petrol Engrs; Soc Prof Well Log Analysts; Soc Core Analysts; Sigma Xi. *Res:* Vapor phase deposition processes; effect of microstructure on the physical properties of materials; well log interpretation; acoustic wave propagation. *Mailing Add:* 711 Millbrook Dr Downers Grove IL 60516. *Fax:* 773-399-4609; *E-Mail:* rsiegfri@gri.org

SIEGFRIED, WILLIAM, ORGANIC CHEMISTRY. *Current Pos:* CHIEF CHEMIST, J F MCCAUGHIN CO, 85- *Personal Data:* b Philadelphia, Pa, July 4, 25; m 49; c 2. *Educ:* Bucknell Univ, BS, 50. *Prof Exp:* Chemist, Ohio Apex Div, FMC Corp, 50-52; chief chemist, Kindt-Collins Co, 52-62; dir res, Freeman Mfg Co, 62-65; Munray Prod Div, Fanner Mfg, 65-68 & Victrylite Candle Co, 68-70; chief chemist & prod mgr, Freeman Mfg Co, 70-79; managing dir res & develop, Blended Waxes Inc, 79-85. *Res:* Developed high-temp sheet wax and the method of manufacturing it for use in tooling; developed instrumental color development methods to accurately color waxes for the manufacture of candles; developed waxes for use in investment casting. *Mailing Add:* 1409 Tamar Dr La Puente CA 91746

SIEGL, WALTER OTTO, ENVIRONMENTAL, ORGANIC & ANALYTICAL CHEMISTRY. *Current Pos:* res scientist, 72-95, SR TECH SPECIALIST, FORD MOTOR CO, 95- *Personal Data:* b Rochester, NY, Mar 7, 42; m 88, Dorothy; c Erica. *Educ:* Ohio Wesleyan Univ, BA, 63; Emory Univ, MS, 66; Wayne State Univ, PhD(org chem), 69. *Honors & Awards:* Arch T Colwell Award, Soc Automotive Engrs. *Prof Exp:* Fel chem, Stanford Univ, 69-72. *Mem:* Am Chem Soc; Sigma Xi; Anal Chem Soc. *Res:* Environmental analytical chemistry; gas chromatography; vehicle emissions. *Mailing Add:* 1560 Beaver St Dearborn MI 48128. *E-Mail:* wsiegl@ford.com

SIEGLAFF, CHARLES LEWIS, POLYMER CHEMISTRY, COLLOID CHEMISTRY. *Current Pos:* PRES, MYSCI, 86- *Personal Data:* b Waterloo, Iowa, Sept 30, 27; m 50; c 2. *Educ:* Univ Iowa, BS, 50, PhD(chem), 56; Univ Cincinnati, MS, 53. *Prof Exp:* Res chemist, Corn Prod Refining Co, 53 & Polymer Res Lab, Dow Chem Co, 55-60; res assoc, Diamond Shamrock Corp, 60-73, sr res assoc, 73-76, res fel, 76-84; vpres, Mitech, 84-86. *Concurrent Pos:* Chmn, Gordon Res Conf Polymers, 74-75; chmn, Soc Rheol Ann Meeting. *Mem:* Soc Rheol; Am Chem Soc; Japanese Soc Polymer Sci; Royal Soc Chem; NY Acad Sci. *Res:* Electrochemistry and transport phenomena; physical chemistry of polymer solutions; surface and polymer flow properties; colloid chemistry of latex systems; catalytic surface chemistry; rheology of polymers and dispersions. *Mailing Add:* 9768 Johnny Cake Ridge Mentor OH 44060

SIEGLER, PETER EMERY, INTERNAL MEDICINE, ALLERGY. *Current Pos:* RETIRED. *Personal Data:* b Budapest, Hungary, Feb 3, 24; m 57. *Educ:* Eotvos Lorand Univ, Budapest, MD, 51. *Prof Exp:* Instr path, Med Univ Budapest, 48-51, from instr to asst prof med, 51-56; instr, Hahnemann Med Col & Hosp, 59-61, assoc, 61-63, assoc prof, 63-68, dir clin pharmacol, 66-68, asst prof med, 68-95. *Mem:* Am Soc Pharmacol & Exp Therapeut; Am Soc Clin Pharmacol & Therapeut; Am Fedn Clin Res; Am Acad Allergy; Am Col Allergists. *Res:* Clinical pharmacology; allergy. *Mailing Add:* 228 Stacey Rd Narbeth PA 19072

SIEGLER, RICHARD E, BLOOD DISEASES, LEUKEMIA. *Current Pos:* PROF PATH, CHARLES R DREW MED SCH, UNIV CALIF, LOS ANGELES, 78- *Educ:* Univ Chicago, MD, 55. *Mailing Add:* 35 Binney St Boston MA 02115-6014

SIEGMAN, A(NTHONY) E(DWARD), LASERS, ELECTRO-OPTICS. *Current Pos:* asst, Electronics Lab, Stanford Univ, 54-56, from asst prof to assoc prof elec eng, 56-86, dir, Edward L Ginzton Lab, 78-83 & 88-89, BURTON J & ANN M MCMURTRY PROF ENG, STANFORD UNIV, 86- *Personal Data:* b Detroit, Mich, Nov 23, 31; m 56, 74; c 3. *Educ:* Harvard Univ, AB, 52; Univ Calif, Los Angeles, MS, 54; Stanford Univ, PhD(elec eng), 57. *Honors & Awards:* W R G Baker Award, Inst Elec & Electronics Engrs, 72, J J Ebers Award, 77; R W Wood Prize, Optical Soc Am, 80, Frederic Ives Medal, 87; Benjamin W Lee Mem Lectr Physics, Seoul, Korea, 81; Alexander von Humboldt Sr Scientist Award, 84; Quantum Electronics Award, Lasers & Electro-Optics Soc, Inst Elec & Electronics Engrs, 89; Schawlow Award, Laser Inst Am, 91. *Prof Exp:* Mem tech staff, Hughes Aircraft Co, 52-54. *Concurrent Pos:* Vis prof appl physics, Harvard Univ, 65; consult, GTE Sylvania, United Technol & others; chmn, Int Quantum Electronics Conf, 66, conf chmn, 68; mem, Air Force Sci Adv Bd; Guggenheim fel, Univ Zurich, 69-70; co-dir, Far Eastern Laser Sch, Korea, 83, Winter Sch Lasers & Laser Optics, Taiwan, 84. *Mem:* Nat Acad Sci; Nat Acad Eng; fel Am Phys Soc; fel Inst Elec & Electronics Engrs; fel Optical Soc Am; fel Laser Inst Am; fel AAAS; Am Asn Univ Profs; Optical Soc Am (vpres, 97); Sigma Xi. *Res:* Lasers; quantum electronics; optics; laser physics; laser devices; laser applications; methods for displaying and visualizing scientific and engineering phenomena on personal computers for classroom and student use. *Mailing Add:* Ginzton Lab Stanford Univ Stanford CA 94305-4085. *E-Mail:* siegman@ec.stanford.edu

SIEGMAN, FRED STEPHEN, BIOCHEMISTRY. *Current Pos:* corp biotechnol, 88-90, SR SALES SPECIALIST, MILLIPORE CORP, 90-; APPLNS MGR, QIAGEN, INC. *Personal Data:* b Brooklyn, NY, Apr 15, 46. *Educ:* Brooklyn Col, BS, 67; Ind Univ, Bloomington, PhD(biochem), 75. *Prof Exp:* Asst biochemist, Evansville Ctr Med Educ, 73-76; appl specialist, Millipore Corp, 76-80, ultrafiltration prod mgr, 80-84, sales specialist, 84-87; Europ oper mgr, Intellegenetics Corp, 87-88. *Concurrent Pos:* Regional sales mgr, Molecular Devices Corp, 93, OEM mgr, 94. *Mem:* Parenteral Drug Asn. *Res:* The study of nucleic acid and protein synthesis and its controls in bacteriophage T4-infected E coli; metabolism of rat liver cells in in vitro cell suspensions, specifically the effect of alcohol on metabolism. *Mailing Add:* 1234 12th St No 6 Santa Monica CA 90401

SIEGMAN, MARION JOYCE, PHARMACOLOGY, PHYSIOLOGY. *Current Pos:* from instr to assoc prof, 67-77, PROF PHYSIOL, JEFFERSON MED COL, 77- *Personal Data:* b Brooklyn, NY, Sept 7, 33. *Educ:* Tulane Univ, BA, 54; State Univ NY, PhD(pharmacol), 66. *Honors & Awards:* Burlington Northern Found Award, 85; Lindback Award, 86. *Prof Exp:* Teaching asst pharmacol, State Univ NY Downstate Med Ctr, 61-66, res assoc, 66-67. *Concurrent Pos:* NIH res grants, 68-; mem panel regulatory biol, NSF, 78-79; mem physiol study sect, NIH, 79-83. *Mem:* Biophys Soc; Am Physiol Soc; Soc Gen Physiol; Sigma Xi. *Res:* Mechanical properties of smooth muscle; regulation and energetics of contraction. *Mailing Add:* Dept Physiol Jefferson Med Col 1020 Locust St Philadelphia PA 19107-6799. *Fax:* 215-955-2073; *E-Mail:* siegmanm@jeflin.tju.med.edu

SIEGMANN, WILLIAM LEWIS, UNDERWATER ACOUSTICS. *Current Pos:* from asst prof to assoc prof, 70-83, PROF MATH SCI, RENSSELAER POLYTECH INST, 83- *Personal Data:* b Pittsburgh, Pa, Sept 14, 43; m 65, Nancy L Hall; c Lisa K, Sara E, Lora A, Katherine R, Jonathan W, Ruthann L & Andrew D. *Educ:* Mass Inst Technol, BS, 64, MS, 67, PhD(appl math), 68. *Prof Exp:* Fel & res assoc mech, Johns Hopkins Univ, 68-70. *Concurrent Pos:* Prin investr, Off Naval Res, 77-, Unisys Corp, 85-87, Inst Naval Oceanog, 87-92 & NASA, 88-91; vis mathematician, Naval Underwater Systs Ctr, 83 & 89. *Mem:* Fel Acoust Soc Am; Soc Indust & Appl Math; Am Phys Soc; Am Meteorol Soc; Am Asn Univ Prof. *Res:* Oceanic sound transmission and reception; atmospheric acoust propagation; asymptotic and numerical methods. *Mailing Add:* Dept Math Sci Rensselaer Polytech Inst Amos Eaton Bldg Rm 421 Troy NY 12180-3590. *Fax:* 518-276-4824; *E-Mail:* siegmn@evler.math.rpi.edu

SIEGMUND, OTTO HANNS, VETERINARY MEDICINE. *Current Pos:* RETIRED. *Personal Data:* b Gross Neudorf, Ger, Aug 25, 20; nat US; m 50. *Educ:* Mich State Col, DVM, 44. *Prof Exp:* Asst animal path, Univ Ill, 45-46; pharmacologist, Sterling-Winthrop Res Inst, 46-49; pathologist, Chem Corps, US Dept Army, 49-50; lectr vet therapeut, Univ Calif, 50-51; dir vet publ, animal sci res, Merck, Sharp & Dohme Res Labs, 51-83. *Mem:* Fel AAAS; Sigma Xi; Am Soc Mammal; Am Vet Med Asn; NY Acad Sci. *Res:* Veterinary pharmaceuticals and literature. *Mailing Add:* Prospect Hill Rd Royalston MA 01331

SIEGMUND, WALTER PAUL, FIBER OPTICS. *Current Pos:* CONSULT, 92- *Personal Data:* b Bremen, Germany, Aug 26, 25; US citizen; m 50, Lois M Schramm; c Paul, Lisa & Kurt. *Educ:* Univ Rochester, NY, BA, 45, PhD, 52. *Honors & Awards:* Karl Fairbanks Award, Soc Photo-Optical Instrumentation Engrs, 70; David Richardson Medal, Optical Soc Am, 77. *Prof Exp:* Assoc dir res, Am Optical Corp, Southbridge, Mass, 53-64, mgr, Fiber Optics Dept, 64-66, mgr, fiber optics res & develop, 66-84; dir fiber optics technol, Reichert Fiber Optics, Div Reichert-Jung Inc, Southbridge, Mass, 84-85, dir advan technol, 85-86; dir res & develop, Schott Fiber Optics, Inc, Southbridge, Mass, 86-92. *Concurrent Pos:* Vpres res & develop & co-owner, Taper Vision, Inc, Newton, Mass. *Mem:* Fel Soc Photo-Optical Instrumentation Engrs. *Res:* Fiber optics including manufacturing processes and products; fiber optic components for image intensifiers; borescopic inspection instruments; medical endoscopes. *Mailing Add:* 31 Cassidy Rd Box 246 Pomfret Center CT 06529. *Fax:* 860-974-2050

SIEGRIST, JACOB C, veterinary medicine, dairy husbandry, for more information see previous edition

SIEGWARTH, JAMES DAVID, SOLID STATE PHYSICS, CRYOGENICS. *Current Pos:* PHYSICIST, NAT INST STAND & TECHNOL, 67- *Personal Data:* b Chehalis, Wash, June 22, 34; m 62; c 1. *Educ:* Univ Wash, 57, PhD(physics), 66. *Prof Exp:* Reactor physicist, Atomic Energy Div, Phillips Petrol Co, 57-60; res asst physics, Univ Wash, 61-66, sr res assoc ceramic eng, 66-67. *Mem:* Am Phys Soc. *Res:* Behavior of antiferromagnetic materials as a function of temperature using the Mossauer effect; low temperature physics and engineering. *Mailing Add:* 85 S 35th St Boulder CO 80303-5524

SIEH, DAVID HENRY, CHROMATOGRAPHIC SEPARATIONS. *Current Pos:* res investr, Bristol-Myers Squibb, 81-87, sr res investr, E R Squibb & Sons, Inc, 87-88, group leader, 88-91, ASSOC DIR, BRISTOL-MYERS SQUIBB, 91- *Personal Data:* b Columbus, Nebr, Aug 21, 47; M 91, Linda L Connerley. *Educ:* Unvi Nebr-Lincoln, BA, 69, PhD(chem), 79. *Prof Exp:* Scientist, Frederick Cancer Res Facil, 78-81. *Concurrent Pos:* Mem, Anal Div, Am Chem Soc, Org Div, AAPS. *Mem:* Am Chem Soc; Am Asn Pharmaceut Scientists. *Res:* Trialkyltriazenes, including the carcinogenic and tumor inhibiting properties; develop analytical methods, emphasizing high-pressure liquid chromatography, thin-layer chromatography, GC, CZE and chiral chromatography. *Mailing Add:* Agouron Pharmaceut 11099 N Torrey Pines Rd La Jolla CA 92037

SIEH, KERRY EDWARD, EARTHQUAKE GEOLOGY. *Current Pos:* PROF GEOL, CALIF INST TECHNOL, 77- *Personal Data:* b Waterloo, Iowa, Oct 11, 50; c 3. *Educ:* Univ Calif, Riverside, AB, 72; Stanford Univ, PhD(geol), 77. *Honors & Awards:* E B Burwell Jr Mem Award, Geol Soc Am, 80; Initiatives in Res Award, Nat Acad Sci, 82. *Mem:* Am Geophys Union; Geol Soc Am; Seismol Soc Am. *Res:* Historic and prehistoric behavior of earthquake faults, in particular the San Andreas fault of California, using geomorphologic and stratigraphic methods; volcanic stratigraphy and processes. *Mailing Add:* Geol & Planetary Sci 170-25 Calif Inst Technol 1201 E Calif Pasadena CA 91125-0001. *Fax:* 626-564-0715; *E-Mail:* sieh@seismo.gps.caltech.edu

SIEHR, DONALD JOSEPH, FUNGAL PHYSIOLOGY, NATURAL PRODUCTS. *Current Pos:* from assoc prof to prof, 61-91, EMER PROF CHEM, UNIV MO, ROLLA, 91- *Personal Data:* b Milwaukee, Wis, Nov 13, 28; m 56; c 2. *Educ:* Univ Wis, PhD(biochem), 57. *Prof Exp:* Res biochemist, Abbott Labs, 57-61. *Concurrent Pos:* NIH sr fel, 68-69. *Mem:* AAAS; Am Chem Soc; Brit Biochem Soc; Mycol Soc Am; Brit Mycol Soc. *Res:* Differentiation in Basidiomycetes; plant growth substances; chemical transformations in biological systems; microbial chemistry and technology. *Mailing Add:* Dept Chem Univ Mo Rolla MO 65401. *Fax:* 573-341-6033; *E-Mail:* dsiehr@umrumb.umr.edu

SIEKERT, ROBERT GEORGE, NEUROLOGY. *Current Pos:* fel neurol, Mayo Grad Sch Med, 50 & 53-54, from instr to assoc prof, 55-73, prof, 69-91, EMER PROF NEUROL, MAYO MED SCH, MAYO CLIN, 91- *Personal Data:* b Milwaukee, Wis, July 23, 24; m 51, Mary J Evans; c Robert G Jr, John E & Friedricha. *Educ:* Northwestern Univ, BS, 45, MS, 47, MD, 48. *Honors & Awards:* Robert G Siekert Young Investr Award, Am Heart Asn. *Prof Exp:* Instr anat, Sch Med, Univ Pa, 48-49. *Concurrent Pos:* Head A sect neurol, Mayo Clin, 66-76, assoc bd govs, 73-80; mem bd trustees, Mayo Found, 74-81; ed-in-chief, Mayo Clin Proc, 82-86. *Mem:* Corresp mem Swiss Neurol Soc; AMA; fel Am Acad Neurol; Am Neurol Asn. *Res:* Cerebrovascular disease; descriptions of transient ischemic episodes and investigation of therapeutic programs. *Mailing Add:* Dept Neurol Mayo Clin W8 200 First Ave SW Rochester MN 55905

SIEKEVITZ, PHILIP, BIOCHEMISTRY. *Current Pos:* from asst prof to prof, 54-88, EMER PROF CELL BIOL, ROCKEFELLER UNIV, 88- *Personal Data:* b Philadelphia, Pa, Feb 25, 18; m 49; c 2. *Educ:* Philadelphia Col Pharm & Sci, BS, 42; Univ Calif, PhD(biochem), 49. *Hon Degrees:* DSc, Philadelphia Col Pharm & Sci, 71; PhD, Univ Stockholm, 74. *Prof Exp:* USPHS res fel biochem, Harvard Univ, 49-51; fel oncol, Univ Wis, 51-54. *Mem:* Nat Acad Sci; Am Soc Biol Chemists; Am Soc Cell Biol (pres, 66-67); Am Soc Neurosci; NY Acad Sci (pres, 76). *Res:* Protein synthesis; oxidative phosphorylation; cell biology; neurobiology. *Mailing Add:* Rockefeller Univ York Ave & 66th St New York NY 10021. *Fax:* 212-327-7974

SIELKEN, ROBERT LEWIS, JR, MATHEMATICAL STATISTICS, OPERATIONS RESEARCH. *Current Pos:* PRES, SIELKEN INC. *Personal Data:* b Little Rock, Ark, July 10, 44; m 68. *Educ:* DePauw Univ, BA, 66; Fla State Univ, MS, 68, PhD(statist), 71. *Prof Exp:* From asst prof to assoc prof statist, Tex A&M Univ, 71- *Mem:* Inst Math Statist; Am Statist Asn; Biomet Soc; Opers Res Soc Am; Math Prog Soc. *Res:* Optimization theory; risk estimation; mathematical programming; stochastic approximation methods. *Mailing Add:* 1181 Hondo Dr College Station TX 77840

SIELOFF, RONALD F, PROCESS OPTIMIZATION, PROCESS DEVELOPMENT. *Current Pos:* advan process chemist coatings, 86-88, MGR RES & DEVELOP, G E PLASTICS, 89- *Personal Data:* b Detroit, Mich. *Educ:* Wayne State Univ, BS, 76; Ga Tech, PhD(org), 81. *Honors & Awards:* Most Outstanding Sr Researcher, Am Chem Soc, 76. *Prof Exp:* Sr scientist process develop, Owens Corning Fiberglas, 82-86. *Res:* Phenolic binder development; statistical process optimization; optical coatings development; coatings application development. *Mailing Add:* 4120 Kuebler Rd Evansville IN 47720

SIEMANKOWSKI, FRANCIS THEODORE, GEOLOGY, SCIENCE EDUCATION. *Current Pos:* assoc prof phys sci, 64-71, prof, 71-79, EMER PROG GEOSCI & SCI EDUC, DEPT GEOSCI, PHYSICS & INTERDISCIPLINARY SCI, STATE UNIV NY, BUFFALO, 79- *Personal Data:* b Buffalo, NY, Nov 12, 14; m 42, Stephanie Zajaczek; c Raymond & Michael (deceased). *Educ:* State Col Teachers, BS, 39; Univ Buffalo, MEd, 50; State Univ NY, Buffalo, EdD(sci educ), 70. *Prof Exp:* Teacher pub schs, NY, 39-41 & 45-49, prin & adult educ dir, 49-51, teacher, 51-64. *Concurrent Pos:* Consult, Teacher Corps, Peace Corps Spec Prog, Afghanistan, 71-74. *Mem:* AAAS; Nat Asn Geol Teachers; Geol Soc Am; Nat Asn Res Sci Teaching; Nat Sci Teachers Asn. *Res:* Individualizing the teaching of science in geology and other physical sciences. *Mailing Add:* 50 Cayuga Creek Rd Cheektowaga NY 14227

SIEMANN, DIETMAR W, CANCER RESEARCH, MEDICAL BIOPHYSICS. *Current Pos:* Res assoc, Univ Rochester Sch Med & Dent, 77-78, sr instr, 78-79, asst prof radiation oncol, 80-85, radiation biol & biophys, 81-85, assoc prof radiation oncol, biol & biophys, 85-88, DIR, EXP THERAPEUT DIV, CANCER CTR, UNIV ROCHESTER SCH MED & DENT, 88-, ASSOC PROF & CHAIR RES, DEPT RADIATION ONCOL, 92- *Personal Data:* b Hanover, WGer, Jan 11, 50; Can citizen; m 72; c 1. *Educ:* Univ Man, BSc, 72; Univ Toronto, MSc, 75, PhD(med biophysics), 77. *Honors & Awards:* Res Award, Radiation Res Soc, 90. *Concurrent Pos:* Prin investr grants, NIH, 82-; mem, Ad Hoc Rev Comt, Nat Cancer Inst, 82-, Rev Comt, Nat Cancer Inst Can, 87-, actg mem, Radiation Sensitizer/Radiation Protector Working Group, 83-; vchmn, Radiation Ther Oncol Group Tumor Biol Comt, 87-; assoc ed, Int J Radiation Oncol Biol Physics, 83-87, bd of ed, 86-89, sr ed, Biol, 89-; assoc dir, Univ Rochester Cancer Ctr, 88-; co-chair, 7th Chem Modifiers of Cancer Treatment Conf, 91; chair, 3rd Int Workshop on Tumor Hypoxia, 90; asst dir, Exp Therapeut Div, Univ Rochester Cancer Ctr, 84-88. *Mem:* Radiation Res Soc; Am Asn Cancer Res. *Res:* Response to antitumor agents assessed in cell cultures, multicell spheroids and in solid tumors and normal tissue in the laboratory as models for clinical cancer therapy; multi-modality therapies with chemotherapeutic agents, radiation, sensitizers and protectors. *Mailing Add:* 4605 NW 56th Dr Gainesville FL 32606

SIEMANN, ROBERT HERMAN, high energy physics, for more information see previous edition

SIEMENS, ALBERT JOHN, PHARMACOLOGY. *Current Pos:* EXEC VPRES, CLIN TRIALS, INC, 92- *Personal Data:* b Winnipeg, Man, Dec 7, 43; m 65; c 2. *Educ:* Univ Man, BSc, 66, MSc, 69; Univ Toronto, PhD(pharmacol), 73. *Prof Exp:* Sr res scientist alcoholism & drug abuse, Res Inst Alcoholism, NY State Dept Ment Hyg, 73-80; asst dir, New Drug Develop, Pfizer, Inc, 80-82, assoc dir, Clin Res, 82-83; dir, Clin Trials, Family Health Int, 84-87; pres & chief exec officer, Clin Res Int, Inc, 88-92. *Concurrent Pos:* Adj asst prof biochem pharmacol, Sch Pharm, State Univ NY Buffalo, 74- *Mem:* Int Cannabis Res Soc; Res Soc Alcoholism; Drug Info Asn; Am Soc Pharmacol & Exp Therapeut; Am Soc Clin Pharmacol & Thrapeut; Am Pharmaceut Asn. *Res:* Drug metabolism; drug interactions; pharmacology of marijuana; biochemical pharmacology of drug tolerance, dependence and addiction; alcoholism. *Mailing Add:* Clin Trials Res Inc PO Box 13991 Research Triangle Park NC 27709

SIEMENS, JOHN CORNELIUS, AGRICULTURAL ENGINEERING. *Current Pos:* assoc prof, 68-76, PROF AGR ENG, UNIV ILL, URBANA, 76- *Personal Data:* b Shafter, Calif, Feb 22, 34; m 61; c 3. *Educ:* Univ Calif, BS, 57; Univ Ill, MS, 58, PhD(soil mech), 63. *Prof Exp:* Instr agr eng, Univ Ill, 58-63; asst prof, Cornell Univ, 63-68. *Mem:* Am Soc Agr Engrs. *Res:* Power and machinery area of agricultural engineering. *Mailing Add:* Dept Agr Eng Univ Ill 1304 W Pa Ave Urbana IL 61801-4726. *Fax:* 217-244-0323; *E-Mail:* jsiemens@uiuc.edu

SIEMENS, PHILIP JOHN, NUCLEAR PHYSICS. *Current Pos:* PROF PHYSICS, ORE STATE UNIV, 88- *Personal Data:* b Elgin, Ill, Nov 13, 43. *Educ:* Mass Inst Technol, BSc, 65; Cornell Univ, PhD(physics), 70. *Prof Exp:* Actg Amanuensis, Niels Bohr Inst, 70-71; NATO fel, Univ Copenhagen, 71-72, univ fel, 72-73, lectr, 74-81; prof physics, Tex A&M Univ, 80-86; distinguished prof, Univ Tenn, 86-88; distinguished scientist, Oak Ridge Nat Lab, 86-88. *Concurrent Pos:* Vis assoc prof, Univ Ill, 77; vis scientist, Lawrence Berkeley Lab, Univ Calif, 78-79. *Mem:* Fel Am Phys Soc; fel AAAS. *Res:* Theoretical nuclear, many-body, and particle physics. *Mailing Add:* Physics Dept Ore State Univ 301 Weniger Hall Corvallis OR 97331. *Fax:* 541-737-1683; *E-Mail:* siemens@physics.orst.edu

SIEMENS, RICHARD ERNEST, PHYSICAL SCIENCE ADMINISTRATOR, HYDROMETALLURY RESEARCH. *Current Pos:* RETIRED. *Personal Data:* b Coeur d'Alene, Idaho, July 7, 38; m 59, Louise I Niehaus; c Rhonda K (Burlington) & Leann M. *Educ:* Ore State Univ, BS, 60. *Prof Exp:* Fel, Nat Defense Educ Act, Ore State Univ, 60-63; res physicist, Albany Res Ctr, US Bur Mines, 61-80, sr tech monitor, Pilot Plant, 80-81; grp supvr, Albany Res Ctr, 80-84, res supvr, 84-88, acting res dir, 88, res supvr, 88-89, res dir, Reno Res Ctr, 89-94. *Mem:* Soc Mining Engrs; Sigma Xi. *Res:* Hydrometallurgical process development; superconductivity in metal alloys and compounds. *Mailing Add:* 39416 Hwy 62 Chiloquin OR 97624

SIEMER, EUGENE GLEN, agronomy, plant morphology, for more information see previous edition

SIEMERS-BLAY, CHARLES T, SEDIMENTOLOGY, OCEANOGRAPHY. *Current Pos:* PRIN OWNER, TEOK INVEST, HAWAII, 96- *Personal Data:* b Lodi, Calif, Aug 30, 44; div; c Troy J & Robert J. *Educ:* Ore State Univ, BS, 66; Ind Univ, MA, 68, PhD(geol), 71. *Honors & Awards:* A I Levorsen Award, Am Asn Petrol Geologists, 78. *Prof Exp:* Asst prof geol, Ind Univ, NW Campus, 70-71 & Univ NMex, 71-75; sr res geologist, Cities Serv Co, 75-80; prof geol, Univ Wyo, 80-82; pres, Sedimentology Inc, Boulder, Colo, 82-90, chief scientist, RPI, 88-90; chief scientist, PT Geoservs, Indonesia, 90-96. *Concurrent Pos:* Founder & pres, Alaska Res Assoc, Inc, 83-85; vis prof appl sedimentology, Wuhan Col Geol, Wuham & Beijing, People's Repub China, 88; lectr, Inst Technol Bandung, Indonesia, 89-; int consult, 90-96. *Mem:* Soc Econ Paleontologists & Mineralogists; Am Asn Petrol Geologists; Sigma Xi; Int Asn Sedimentologists. *Res:* Sedimentology; stratigraphy; sedimentary petrology; paleoecology and interpretation of depositional paleoenvironments; genesis and hydrocarbon-bearing potential of ancient depositional systems; major work north slope and peninsular areas of Alaska, Rocky Mountain basins, Gulf Coast region, Columbia, Argentina and North Sea basin; character and orign of shorelines, Kauai, Hawaii; stratigraphy, depositional systems and petroleum potential of Indonesian petroliferous basins; geologic, natural and cultural history. *Mailing Add:* PO Box 1078 Waimea HI 96796. *E-Mail:* teole@aloha.net

SIEMIATKOSKI, ALBERTA MARIE ALBRECHT, MICROBIAL PHYSIOLOGY, CANCER. *Current Pos:* assoc prof, 82-93, EMER PROF BIOL DEPT, MANHATTANVILLE COL, 93- *Personal Data:* b Reading, Pa, June 30, 30; M 96, Thomas M Siemiatkoski. *Educ:* Seton Hill Col, BA, 51; Fordham Univ, MS, 52; Rutgers Univ, PhD(microbiol), 61. *Prof Exp:* Biologist, Res Div, Am Cyanamid, 52-58; res fel, Sloan-Kettering Inst Cancer Res, 61-63, res assoc, 63-65, assoc, 65-75, assoc mem, 75-82. *Concurrent Pos:* From instr to prof microbiol, Sloan-Kettering Div, Grad Sch Med Sci, Cornell Univ, 64-82; vis scholar biochem dept, Vanderbilt Univ, 90-91. *Mem:* Am Soc Biol Chemists; AAAS; Sigma Xi; NY Acad Sci. *Res:* Interests in folic acid and vitamin A metabolism, nutrition of malignant cells. *Mailing Add:* 3065 Artemis Circle Bethlehem PA 18017

SIEMIATYCKI, JACK, PUBLIC HEALTH & EPIDEMIOLOGY, BIOSTATISTICS. *Current Pos:* from asst prof to assoc prof, 78-84, PROF EPIDEMIOL, ARMAND-FRAPPIER INST, UNIV QUE, CAN, 84- *Personal Data:* b Innsbruck, Austria, Dec 31, 46; Can citizen; m 82, Lesley Young; c Emma & Kate. *Educ:* McGill Univ, BSc, 67, MSc, 71, PhD(epidemiol), 76. *Prof Exp:* Res dir community health, Pointe St Charles Community Clin, 70-72; postdoctoral fel epidemiol, Int Agency Res Cancer, WHO, 77-78. *Concurrent Pos:* Adj prof epidemiol & biostatist, McGill Univ, 79-, Sch Occup Health, 81-; consult, Int Joint Comn, Can-US, 82-88, Int Agency Res Cancer & Can Fed Health Dept; assoc ed, Am J Epidemiol, 89-, Int J Environ Health Res, 90- *Mem:* Soc Epidemiol Res; Am Pub Health Asn; Int Epidemiol Asn; Int Soc Environ Epidemiol; Can Pub Health Asn. *Res:* Epidemiologic research on role of environmental agents in causing human cancer; causes of insulin dependent diabetes; studies to advance the methodology of epidemiology and biostatistics; abestos exposure and risk of cancer. *Mailing Add:* 106 Columbia St Westmount PQ H3Z 2C3 Can. *Fax:* 514-686-5599

SIEMS, NORMAN EDWARD, NUCLEAR SCIENCE, ASTRONOMY. *Current Pos:* from asst prof to assoc prof, 80-87, chmn dept, 84-87, PROF PHYSICS, JUNIATA COL, 87- *Personal Data:* b St Louis, Mo, Feb 28, 44; m 66; c 2. *Educ:* Rensselaer Polytechnic Inst, BS, 66; Johns Hopkins Univ, MS, 70; Cornell Univ, PhD(nuclear sci), 76. *Prof Exp:* Instr math, physics & reactor prin, US Naval Nuclear Power Sch, Bainbridge, Md, 66-70; instr, Quincy Col, 73-75, asst prof physics, 75-80, chmn dept, 77-80. *Concurrent Pos:* Instr, Malaysia, Ind Univ, 87-88; Beachley distinguished prof, Juniata Col, 94. *Mem:* Am Asn Physics Teachers; Am Nuclear Sci Teachers Asn. *Res:* Investigation of the low-lying first excited state of Silver-110. *Mailing Add:* Dept Physics Juniata Col 1700 Moore St Huntingdon PA 16652-2196. *E-Mail:* siems@juniata.edu

SIEMS, PETER LAURENCE, GEOLOGY. *Current Pos:* from asst prof to assoc prof, 65-72, PROF GEOL, UNIV IDAHO, 72- *Personal Data:* b London, Eng, Jan 26, 32; m 57; c 4. *Educ:* Univ London, BSc, 57; Colo Sch Mines, DSc(geol), 67. *Prof Exp:* Geologist, Anglo Am Corp S Africa, 57-61. *Concurrent Pos:* Vis prof, Fed Univ Bahia, Brazil, 70-71. *Mem:* Soc Econ Geol; Asn Explor Geochem; Am Inst Mining, Metall & Petrol Eng; Brit Inst Mining & Metall; Geol Soc Am. *Res:* Origin of mineral deposits; geochemical exploration for mineral deposits. *Mailing Add:* Geol Univ Idaho 375 S Line St Moscow ID 83843-4140

SIEPMANN, JOERN ILJA, CHEMISTRY. *Current Pos:* ASST PROF CHEM, UNIV MINN, 94- *Personal Data:* b Cologne, Ger, June 28, 64; m 90, Silke Schmid; c Tim Christopher. *Educ:* Cambridge Univ, PhD, 92. *Prof Exp:* Fel, Koninklijke/Shell Lab, Amsterdam, 92-93; res assoc, Univ Pa, 93-94. *Mem:* Am Inst Chem Engrs; Am Chem Soc. *Mailing Add:* Dept Chem Univ Minn 207 Pleasant St Minneapolis MN 55455

SIERAKOWSKI, ROBERT L, ENGINEERING MECHANICS, MATERIALS SCIENCE. *Current Pos:* CHMN, CIVIL ENG DEPT, OHIO STATE UNIV 83- *Personal Data:* b Vernon, Conn, Apr 11, 37; m 75; c 2. *Educ:* Brown Univ, BSc, 58; Yale Univ, MS, 60, PhD(eng mech), 64. *Prof Exp:* Sr engr mech, Sikorsky Aircraft Div, United Technol Corp, 58-60; res asst, Yale Univ, 60-63; sr res scientist, United Technol Res Labs, 63-67; prof eng sci, Univ Fla, 67-83. *Concurrent Pos:* Adj asst prof eng mech, Rensselaer Polytech Inst, 64-67; Nat Res Coun fel, 72-73. *Mem:* Am Soc Mech Engrs; Am Inst Aeronaut & Astronaut; Soc Exp Stress Anal; Soc Advan Mat & Processing Eng; Am Soc Eng Educ. *Res:* Advanced structural composites; structural vibrations; biomechanics. *Mailing Add:* 2725 Lymington Rd Columbus OH 43220

SIEREN, DAVID JOSEPH, TAXONOMIC BOTANY. *Current Pos:* From asst prof to assoc prof, 69-83, chmn dept, 73-78, DIR HERBARIUM, UNIV NC, WILMINGTON, 69-, PROF BIOL, PLANT TAXONOMY & PLANT MORPHOLOGY, 83- *Personal Data:* b Ashland, Wis, May 10, 41; m 72, Tsai-En Wu; c Jeffrey D. *Educ:* Northland Col, AB, 63; Univ Ill, Urbana, MS, 65, PhD(bot), 70. *Mem:* Nature Conserv. *Res:* Vascular plant floristics. *Mailing Add:* Dept Biol Sci Univ NC Wilmington NC 28403-3297. *Fax:* 910-962-4066; *E-Mail:* sierend@uncwil.edu

SIERK, ARNOLD JOHN, NUCLEAR PHYSICS. *Current Pos:* STAFF MEM, THEORET DIV, LOS ALAMOS NAT LAB, 77- *Personal Data:* b Batavia, NY, Nov 10, 46; m 68, Christina Hebenstreit; c Michael, Brian & Kimberly. *Educ:* Cornell Univ, BS, 68; Calif Inst Technol, PhD(nuclear physics), 73. *Prof Exp:* Fel theoret nuclear physics, Los Alamos Sci Lab, Univ Calif, 72-74; asst prof nuclear physics, Calif Inst Technol, 74-77. *Concurrent Pos:* Vis staff mem, Los Alamos Sci Lab, Univ Calif, 74-77; fel, Alfred P Sloan Found, 75-77. *Mem:* Fel Am Phys Soc; Sigma Xi. *Res:* Models of fission and heavy-ion fusion reactions; fission barriers; turbulence. *Mailing Add:* T-2 MS B243 Los Alamos Nat Lab PO Box 1663 Los Alamos NM 87545

SIERVOGEL, ROGER M, GENETIC EPIDEMIOLOGY, CARDIOVASCULAR DISEASE. *Current Pos:* res scientist human genetics, Fels Res Inst, Wright State Univ, 74-77, asst prof, 77-78, assoc prof, 79-84, PROF COMMUNITY HEALTH, SCH MED, WRIGHT STATE UNIV, 85-, DIR, DIV HUMAN BIOL, 93- *Personal Data:* b Phoenix, Ariz, Dec 17, 44; m 90, Renee Harber; c Jeffrey & Wendy. *Educ:* Ariz State Univ, BS, 67, MS, 68; Univ Ore, PhD, 71. *Honors & Awards:* Outstanding Achievement Award, Acad Med. *Prof Exp:* NIH fel human quant genetics, Sch Pub Health, Univ NC, 71-73, vis asst prof, Dept Biostatist, 73-74. *Concurrent Pos:* Prin investr grants, Nat Heart, Lung & Blood Inst, 76-77, 77-79 & 79-82, Nat Inst Child Health Human Dev, 76-94, 90- & 93-, Am Heart Asn, Miami Valley Chap, 77-78 & 78-79; mem, Epidemiol & Dis Control Study Sect, NIH, 84-88; exec comt, Human Biol Coun, 88-92; mem High Blood Pressure Res Coun & fel Epidemiol Coun, Am Heart Asn. *Mem:* Am Soc Human Genetics; Am Heart Asn; fel Human Biol Coun (secy-treas, 80-84); Soc Pediat Res; Int Genetic Epidemiol Soc. *Res:* Long term serial studies of body composition and cardiovascular disease risk factors in children and adults using Fels Longitudinal Study; genetics of multifactorial traits, major gene effects, and genetic linkage in humans, especially genetic epidemiology of traits related to hypertension, body composition and growth. *Mailing Add:* Dept Community Health Div Human Biol Wright State Univ Sch Med 1005 Xenia Ave Yellow Springs OH 45387-1698. *Fax:* 937-767-6922; *E-Mail:* rsiervog@wright.edu

SIESS, CHESTER P(AUL), STRUCTURAL ENGINEERING. *Current Pos:* spec res assoc, Univ Ill, Urbana, 41-45, from res asst prof to res assoc prof, 45-55, prof, 55-78, EMER PROF CIVIL ENG, UNIV ILL, URBANA, 78- *Personal Data:* b Alexandria, La, July 28, 16; m 41, Helen Kranson; c Judith. *Educ:* La State Univ, BS, 36; Univ Ill, MS, 39, PhD(struct eng), 48. *Honors & Awards:* Wason Medal, Am Concrete Inst, 49; Turner Medal, 64; Award, Concrete Reinforcing Steel Inst, 56; Huber Award, Am Soc Civil Engrs, 56, Howard Award, 68, Reese Award, 70. *Prof Exp:* Staff mem, State Hwy Dept, La, 36-37; asst, Univ Ill, 37-39; testing engr, Dept Subways, Chicago, 39-41; engr, NY Cent Rwy, Ill, 41. *Mem:* Nat Acad Eng; hon mem Am Soc Civil Engrs; Int Asn Bridge & Struct Engrs; hon mem Am Concrete Inst (pres, 73-74). *Res:* Reinforced and prestressed concrete. *Mailing Add:* 401 Burwash Ave Savoy IL 61874-9599

SIESSER, WILLIAM GARY, PALEONTOLOGY, STRATIGRAPHY-SEDIMENTATION. *Current Pos:* assoc prof, 79-85, chmn geol dept, 82-85, PROF GEOL, VANDERBILT UNIV, 85- *Personal Data:* b Parsons, Kans, Apr 25, 40; m 71; c 2. *Educ:* Univ Kans, BS, 62; La State Univ, MS, 67; Univ Cape Town, PhD(geol), 71. *Prof Exp:* Res officer marine geol, Univ Cape Town, 67-71, sr res officer marine geol, 71-78. *Concurrent Pos:* Vis prof, Cambridge Univ, UK, 74, Univ Melbourne, Australia, 78 & Univ Col London, UK, 85. *Mem:* Sigma Xi; Int Nannoplankton Asn; Soc Sedimentary Geol. *Res:* Biostratigraphy and paleoceanography using calcareous nannofossils. *Mailing Add:* 2009 Overhill Dr Nashville TN 37240-0001

SIEVER, LARRY JOSEPH, PSYCHIATRY. *Current Pos:* dir, Out-Patient Clin, 82-87, DIR, OUT-PATIENT PSYCHIAT DIV, BRONX VET ADMIN MED CTR, 87-; DIR, OUT-PATIENT PSYCHIAT DIV, MT SINAI SCH MED, 87-, PROF, 90- *Personal Data:* b Chicago, Ill, Sept 2, 47; m 89, Lissa Weinstein; c David W & Daniel R. *Educ:* Harvard Col, BA, 69; Stanford Med Sch, MD, 75. *Honors & Awards:* A G Bennet Award, Soc Biol Psychiat, 83. *Prof Exp:* Staff physician res, NIMH, 78-82. *Concurrent Pos:* Assoc prof, Mt Sinai Sch Med, 82-90. *Mem:* AAAS; Soc Biol Psychiat; Am Psychiat Asn; Am Col Neuropharmacol. *Res:* The investigation of neurotransmitter, hormone, and brain structural alterations in affective and personality disorders. *Mailing Add:* Dept Psychiat 116a Bronx Vet Admin Med Ctr 130 W Kingsbridge Rd Bronx NY 10468

SIEVER, RAYMOND, SEDIMENTARY PETROLOGY, GEOCHEMISTRY. *Current Pos:* NSF sr fel & res assoc, 56-57, from asst prof to prof, 57-94, chmn, Dept Geol Sci, 68-71 & 76-81, EMER PROF GEOL, HARVARD UNIV, 94- *Personal Data:* b Chicago, Ill, Sept 14, 23; m 45; c Larry J & Michael D. *Educ:* Univ Chicago, BS, 43, MS, 47, PhD(geol), 50. *Hon Degrees:* MA, Harvard Univ, 60. *Honors & Awards:* Am Asn Petrol Geologists Award, 52; Soc Sedimentary Geol Award, 59, 90 & 91. *Prof Exp:* Asst, Ill Geol Surv, 43-44, from asst geologist to geologist, 47-57. *Concurrent Pos:* Res assoc, Oceanog Inst, Woods Hole, Mass, 57-70; vis scholar, Scripps Inst Oceanog, 81-82; Guggenheim fel, 81-82; fel, Japan Soc Prom Sci, Univ Tokyo, 81. *Mem:* Fel Am Acad Arts & Sci; fel Geol Soc Am; hon mem Soc Sedimentary Geol; Geochem Soc; Am Geophys Union. *Res:* Stratigraphy and sedimentation; origin of coal; silica in sediments; cementation of sandstones; marine sediments; plate tectonics and sediment formation; evolution of atmosphere and oceans. *Mailing Add:* Hoffman Lab Harvard Univ Cambridge MA 02138. *Fax:* 617-495-8839

SIEVERS, ALBERT JOHN, III, SOLID STATE PHYSICS, OPTICS. *Current Pos:* res assoc, 62-63, from instr to prof solid state physics, 63-91, E L NICHOLS PROF PHYSICS, CORNELL UNIV, 91- *Personal Data:* b Oakland, Calif, June 28, 33; m 59, Betsy F Ross; c Karla, John, Martha & Sylvia. *Educ:* Univ Calif, Berkeley, AB, 58, PhD(physics), 62. *Honors & Awards:* Frank Iskson Prize, Am Phys Soc, 88. *Prof Exp:* Model maker microwave tubes, Varian Assocs, 51-54; res asst solid state physics, Univ Calif, Berkeley, 59-62. *Concurrent Pos:* Consult, Lockheed Res & Develop, 66-67, Los Alamos Sci Lab, 68-69 & 78-87, Nat Acad Sci, 75 & Gen Motors Corp, 78-85, mem, Mat Res Coun, Advan Res Projs Agency, 69-75; vis prof, Stanford Univ, 70, Univ Calif, Irvine, 71, Univ Canterbury, NZ, 76, Los Alamos Sci Lab, 77, Int Bus Mach, San Jose, 81, Sci Univ Tokyo, 84, Max Planck Inst, Fed Repub Ger, Stuttgart, 85, Sci Univ Tokyo, 91 & Seoul Nat Univ, 92; sr fel, NSF, 70-71; Erskine fel, Univ Canterbury, NZ, 75, 76 & 93; vis scientist, NSF, 81; Humbolt sr scientist, 85; feature ed high temperature superconductivity, J Optical Soc Am, 89; Buckley Prize comt chmn, Am Phys Soc, 93. *Mem:* Fel Am Phys Soc; fel Optical Soc Am. *Res:* Infrared spectroscopy of condensed matter in both time and frequency domain; surfaces superconductivity; semi-metals; semiconductors; lattice vibrations; far infrared spectroscopy of biological molecules; impurity modes; persistent infrared spectral hole burning interfaces; selective surfaces; high Tc superconductor small particle and composite structures, solid state infrared vibrational lasers, pure and applied infrared photonics. *Mailing Add:* 518 Clark Hall Dept Physics Cornell Univ Ithaca NY 14853. *E-Mail:* sievers@msc.cornell.edu

SIEVERS, DENNIS MORLINE, ENVIRONMENTAL ENGINEERING, AGRICULTURAL ENGINEERING. *Current Pos:* Res asst agr eng, Univ Mo, Columbia, 67-69, Environ Protection Agency fel, 69-71, asst prof, 72-79, assoc prof, 79-90, PROF AGR ENG, UNIV MO, COLUMBIA, 90- *Personal Data:* b Fremont, Nebr, June 15, 44; m 64; c 1. *Educ:* Univ Nebr, BS, 67; Univ Mo, Columbia, MS, 69, PhD(sanit eng), 71. *Mem:* Am Soc Agr Engrs; Water Environ Fedn; Sigma Xi. *Res:* Water quality; aquatic ecology; waste treatment systems. *Mailing Add:* Biol & Agr Eng Dept Univ Mo Columbia MO 65211

SIEVERS, GERALD LESTER, MATHEMATICAL STATISTICS. *Current Pos:* Assoc prof, 67-77, PROF MATH, WESTERN MICH UNIV, 77- *Personal Data:* b Winona, Minn, July 15, 40; m 67. *Educ:* St Mary's Col, Minn, BA, 62; Univ Iowa, MS & PhD(statist), 67. *Mem:* Inst Math Statist; Am Statist Asn. *Res:* Nonparametric statistics; linear models. *Mailing Add:* 425 E Melody Portage MI 49002

SIEVERS, ROBERT EUGENE, ANALYTICAL CHEMISTRY, INORGANIC CHEMISTRY. *Current Pos:* PROF CHEM & CHMN DEPT, UNIV COLO, BOULDER, 75- *Personal Data:* b Anthony, Kans, Mar 28, 35; m 61; c 2. *Educ:* Univ Tulsa, BChem, 56; Univ Ill, MS, 58, PhD(inorg chem), 60. *Honors & Awards:* Res & Develop Award, US Air Force, 62, Tech Achievement Award, 71. *Prof Exp:* Res chemist, Monsanto Chem Co, Mo, 60; res chemist, Aerospace Res Labs, Wright-Patterson AFB, 60-63, group leader anal & inorg chem, 63-69, sr scientist & dir inorg & anal chem, 69-75. *Concurrent Pos:* Vis prof, Univ Tubingen, 68-69; adj prof, Wright State Univ, 69-75. *Mem:* Am Chem Soc; Royal Soc Chem; Soc Environ Geochem & Health. *Res:* Trace analysis, environmental analytical chemistry; chromatography, highly volatile and soluble metal chelates, lanthanide Nuclear Magnetic Resonance shift reagents; inorganic stereochemistry, gas chromatography and mass spectrometry of metal chelates; fuel additives; trace analysis of anions. *Mailing Add:* Univ Colo Cires Campus Box 216 Boulder CO 80303

SIEVERS, SALLY RIEDEL, COMPUTER SCIENCES. *Current Pos:* LECTR MATH & COMPUT SCI, WELLS COL, 77- *Personal Data:* b Butte, Mont, Dec 23, 41; m 70, Anil Nerode; c Nathanael N. *Educ:* Stanford Univ, BS, 63; Cornell Univ, PhD(math), 72. *Prof Exp:* Res assoc social psychol, Cornell Univ, 68-69; instr math, Ithaca Col, 69-72; res assoc math statist, Cornell Univ, 72-74, lectr math, 72-74. *Concurrent Pos:* Statist consult, Environ Protection Agency & Energy Dept Studies, Tech Empirics Corp, 78-80. *Mem:* Inst Math Statist; Am Statist Asn; Asn Women Math. *Res:* Theory of Ranking procedures; applied statistics. *Mailing Add:* Dept Math Wells Col Aurora NY 13026. *E-Mail:* sievers@wells.edu

SIEVERT, CARL FRANK, CHEMISTRY. *Current Pos:* RETIRED. *Personal Data:* b Blue Island, Ill, Oct 25, 20; m 43; c 3. *Educ:* Capital Univ, BS, 42; Univ Ill, PhD(biochem), 47. *Prof Exp:* Asst chem, Univ Ill, 42-44 & 46-47; from asst to assoc prof, Franklin & Marshall Col, 47-57; prof & head dept, Catawba Col, 57-59; prof chem. Capital Univ, 59-86, chmn dept, 63-86. *Concurrent Pos:* At Armstrong Cork Co, Pa, 48. *Mem:* AAAS; Am Chem Soc. *Res:* Fatty acid metabolism; omega oxidation of fatty acids. *Mailing Add:* 8981 Winchester Rd NW Carroll OH 43112

SIEVERT, HERMAN WILLIAM, BIOCHEMISTRY. *Current Pos:* RETIRED. *Personal Data:* b Aurora, Ill, Sept 19, 28; m 53; c 2. *Educ:* NCent Col, Ill, BA, 50; Univ Wis, MS, 52, PhD(biochem), 58. *Prof Exp:* Biochemist, Abbott Labs, 58-70, head dept molecular biol, 70-74, mgr planning & admin, 74-77, mgr res qual assurance, 77-87, clin proj mgt, pharm prod, 87-93. *Mem:* AAAS; Am Chem Soc. *Mailing Add:* 233 E Washington Ave Lake Bluff IL 60044-2156

SIEVERT, RICHARD CARL, plant pathology; deceased, see previous edition for last biography

SIEW, ERNEST L, COMPUTER SCIENCES, ENVIRONMENTAL HEALTH. *Current Pos:* ASST PROF CHEM, STATE UNIV NY, ALBANY, 84- *Personal Data:* b Nanking, Kiangsu, Dec 26, 40; US citizen; m 58; c 2. *Educ:* Columbia Univ, BA, 60; NY Univ, PhD(chem), 69. *Prof Exp:* Instr chem, Friends Acad, Long Island, 65-66; sr scientist, GAF Corp, 69-70; res scientist, Comput Dynetec Corp, 71-72; sr scientist, NY Univ Med Ctr, 72-73; res assoc chem, Univ Ky, 73-74; asst prof chem, Trenton State Col, 74-75; asst prof chem, State Univ NY, New Paltz, 75-76; instr chem, Roc Land Community Col, 76-77; res assoc chem, Adelphi Univ, 78-83; asst prof chem, Wagner Col, 83-84. *Concurrent Pos:* Res assoc chem, Rochester Univ, 74-75; res assoc radiochemistry, Albany Med Col, 85-86; adj assoc prof chem, Hofstra Univ & Nassau Community Col, 79-; Presidential fel, Univ Ky, 73; chmn, Acad-Indust Rel Comt, Am Chem Soc, 88- *Mem:* Am Chem Soc; Sigma Xi. *Res:* Spectroscopic investigation of cataract formation; ionizing radiation such as X-rays; microwaves; drugs such as steroids; metabolic disease; aging (senile cataract); light scanning method; differential scanning calorimetry. *Mailing Add:* 16 Linden St Congers NY 10920-1804

SIEWERT, CHARLES EDWARD, NUCLEAR ENGINEERING, ASTROPHYSICS. *Current Pos:* asst prof nuclear eng, 65-69, ASSOC PROF NUCLEAR ENG, NC STATE UNIV, 69- *Personal Data:* b Richmond, Va, Oct 20, 37. *Educ:* NC State Univ, BS, 60, MS, 62; Univ NC, PhD(nuclear eng), 65. *Prof Exp:* Teaching asst physics, NC State Univ, 60-62 & Mid East Tech Univ, Ankara, 64-65. *Mem:* Am Nuclear Soc; Am Phys Soc. *Res:* Neutron transport theory and radiative transfer. *Mailing Add:* Dept Math NC State Univ PO Box 8205 Raleigh NC 27695-8205

SIEWIOREK, DANIEL PAUL, ELECTRICAL ENGINEERING, COMPUTER SCIENCE. *Current Pos:* assoc prof, 72-80, PROF ELEC ENG & COMPUT SCI, CARNEGIE-MELLON UNIV, 80- *Personal Data:* b Cleveland, Ohio, June 2, 46; m 72, Karan Walker; c Nora & Gail. *Educ:* Univ Mich, BSEE, 68; Stanford Univ, MSEE, 69, PhD(elec eng), 72. *Honors & Awards:* Frederick Emmos Terman Award, Am Soc Eng Educ,83; Eckert-Mauchly Award, Asn Comput Mach-Inst Elec & Electronics Engrs, 88. *Concurrent Pos:* Consult engr, Digital Equip Corp, 72-86; mem, Bd Dirs, Spec Interest Group Comput Archit, 75-79; consult, Naval Res Lab, 75-77, Res Triangle Inst, 78- & United Technol, 78-92; chief tech officer, Ultra Systs Div, Encore Comput Corp, 83-86; dir, Design Mfg Lab, Eng Design Res Ctr, 89- *Mem:* Fel Inst Elec & Electronics Engrs; Asn Comput Mach; Sigma Xi. *Res:* Computer architecture; multiprocessors; reliability; fault tolerant computing; design automation; mobile computers. *Mailing Add:* 1259 Bellerock St Pittsburgh PA 15217-1230. *E-Mail:* dps@a.gp.cs.cmu.edu

SIFFERMAN, THOMAS RAYMOND, FLUID MECHANICS, RHEOLOGY. *Current Pos:* RES FEL, KEL CO, 92- *Personal Data:* b Chicago, Ill, July 28, 41; m 68; c 3. *Educ:* Marquette Univ, BME, 64; Purdue Univ, MSME, 66, PhD(fluid mech), 70. *Prof Exp:* Co-op student, Allis-Chalmers, 61-64; res & teaching asst, Purdue Univ, 68-70; sr res scientist fluid flow, res & develop, Conoco, Inc, 70-82; res assoc, Dallas Res Lab, Mobil Res & Develop Corp, 82-92. *Concurrent Pos:* Vis assoc prof & consult petrol eng, Univ Tulsa, 81-82; activ leader, Explor & Prod Res, Cent Res Lab, Mobil Res & Develop Corp, Princeton, NJ, 87-88. *Mem:* Soc Petrol Engrs; Soc Rheology; Am Soc Mech Engrs; Sigma Xi. *Res:* Drilling fluids, especially thermal stability, formation damage and hole cleaning; the rheology of non-Newtonian fluids including drilling muds, fracturing fluids, and heavy and waxy crudes; 11 US patents; 25 publications. *Mailing Add:* 8225 Aero Dr San Diego CA 92123

SIFFERT, ROBERT S, ORTHOPEDIC SURGERY. *Current Pos:* prof orthop & chmn dept, 66-86, LASKER-SIFFERT DISTINGUISHED SERV PROF, MT SINAI SCH MED, 86- *Personal Data:* b NY, June 16, 18; m 41, Miriam Sand; c Joan & John. *Educ:* NY Univ, BA, 39, MD, 43. *Concurrent Pos:* Dir, Dept Orthop, Mt Sinai Hosp, 60-86 & City Hosp Elmhurst, 63-86; mem bd, Care-Medico, 72, Care, 78. *Mem:* Am Orthop Asn; Am Acad Orthop Surg; Asn Bone & Joint Surg; Am Col Surgeons; NY Acad Med. *Res:* Clinical and laboratory research in problems relating to growth, deformity and osteoporosis; community research. *Mailing Add:* 955 Fifth Ave New York NY 10021

SIFFORD, DEWEY H, ORGANIC CHEMISTRY. *Current Pos:* From asst prof to assoc prof, 61-65, actg chmn div, 68-69, prof chem, 65-83, chmn, div phys sci, 70-83, ACTG DEAN, ARK STATE UNIV, 80-, CHMN, DEPT CHEM, 83- *Personal Data:* b La Grange, Ark, Sept 9, 30; m 58; c 6. *Educ:* Ark State Univ, BS, 52; Univ Okla, PhD(org chem), 62. *Mem:* Sigma Xi; Am Chem Soc. *Res:* Terpenes; venoms. *Mailing Add:* Dept Chem Box 429 Ark State Univ State University AR 72467-0429

SIFNEOS, PETER E, MEDICINE. *Current Pos:* assoc clin prof, 68-71, from assoc prof to prof, 71-91, prof, 74-91, EMER PROF PSYCHIAT, HARVARD MED SCH, 91-; ASSOC DIR PSYCHIAT DEPT, BETH ISRAEL HOSP, 68- *Personal Data:* b Greece, Oct 22, 20; nat US; div; c 3. *Educ:* Sorbonne, cert, 40; Harvard Univ, MD, 46. *Honors & Awards:* Dikemark H Froshaug Prize, 85. *Prof Exp:* Teaching fel psychiat, Harvard Univ, 52-53, res fel ment health, 53-54, asst psychiat, 54-55, instr, 55-58, assoc, 58-64, asst prof, 64-68. *Concurrent Pos:* Asst, Mass Gen Hosp, 53-55, from asst psychiatrist to assoc psychiatrist, 55-64, psychiatrist, 64-, dir, Inpatient & Outpatient Psychiat Serv, 65-68; vis prof, Med Sch, Univ Oslo, 71-84; ed-in-chief, Psychother & Psychosom, 75-91 & Int Fedn Med Psychother, 73-88; vis prof psychiat, McGill Univ, 75-79. *Mem:* AAAS; AMA; Am Psychiat Asn; Am Psychosom Soc; Royal Soc Med. *Res:* Psychophysiological correlates of psychosomatic disorders; neurophysiological, neurochemical and psychological correlates of emotions; manipulative suicide attempts; short-term dynamic psychotherapy; teaching of psychiatry. *Mailing Add:* Beth Israel Hosp 330 Brookline Ave Boston MA 02115-5491

SIFNIADES, STYLIANOS, PHYSICAL CHEMISTRY, ORGANIC CHEMISTRY. *Current Pos:* Sr res chemist, Allied-Signal Inc, 65-67, res group leader, 67-71, res assoc, 71-76, res tech supvr, 76-80, RES FEL RES & TECHNOL, ALLIED-SIGNAL INC, 80- *Personal Data:* b Piraeus, Greece, Dec 22, 35; US citizen; div; c 2. *Educ:* Univ Athens, Dipl, 57; Univ BC, MSc, 62, PhD(chem), 65. *Mem:* Am Chem Soc. *Res:* Computer simulation of chemical processes; kinetic methods of optical resolution and asymmetric transformation; ion exchange processes; liquid membranes and extraction. *Mailing Add:* Allied-Signal Inc Box 1021R Morristown NJ 07962

SIFONTES, JOSE E, PEDIATRICS, PULMONARY. *Current Pos:* assoc prof, Tuberc Res Ctr, USPHS, 58-66; dean, Sch Med, 66-71, chmn dept, 74-77, PROF PEDIAT, SCH MED, UNIV PR, SAN JUAN, 66- *Personal Data:* b Arecibo, PR, Oct 17, 26; US citizen; m 52, Iris Sotomayor; c 7. *Educ:* Syracuse Univ, MD, 48; Am Bd Pediat, dipl, 54. *Prof Exp:* Chief pediat, A Ruiz Soler Tuberc Hosp, 52-56; med officer in chg, Tuberc Res Ctr, USPHS, 56-58. *Concurrent Pos:* Spec consult, USPHS, 58-66; consult & vis Prof, CARE proj, Honduras, 66; Nat Adv Coun, CDC 67-70; WHO consult, Med Educ, Surinam Proj, 72; mem adv comt, spec projs grant for med educ, USPHS, 70-71; mem comt, Int Child Health, Am Acad Pediat, 76-80; chmn, Sect Dis of Chest, Am Acad Pediat, 64. *Mem:* Am Thoracic Soc; Am Acad Pediat; AMA; emer mem Am Pediat Soc; AAAS. *Res:* Pediatric pulmonary diseases tuberculosis; medical education. *Mailing Add:* 1658 Lilas San Juan PR 00927

SIFRE, RAMON ALBERTO, INTERNAL MEDICINE, GASTROENTEROLOGY. *Current Pos:* asst prof, 53-57, ASSOC PROF CLIN MED, MED SCH, UNIV PR, SAN JUAN, 57- *Personal Data:* b Vega Alta, PR, May 15, 24; m 47; c 6. *Educ:* Univ Louisville, MD, 46; Univ PR, BS, 47; Am Bd Internal Med, dipl, 54 & 77; Am Bd Gastroenterol, dipl, 57, 77. *Prof Exp:* Intern, Grad Hosp, Univ Pa, 47-48, post grad student internal med, Grad Sch Med, 48-49, resident, Grad Hosp, 49-50, resident gastroenterol, 50-51; chief gastroenterol sect, Fitzsimons Army Hosp, 51-53. *Concurrent Pos:* Asst attend physician, San Juan City Hosp, 54-57, assoc attend, 57-; asst attend physician, Presby Hosp, San Juan, 54-57, consult, 57-; consult, Mimiya Hosp, 54-; attend, Doctors' Hosp, 58-; chief gastroenterol sect, Univ Hosp, 59-62. *Mem:* Fel Am Col Physicians. *Mailing Add:* Cacique 2070 Ocean Park Santurce PR 00911-1514

SIGAFOOS, ROBERT SUMNER, PLANT ECOLOGY. *Current Pos:* RETIRED. *Personal Data:* b Akron, Ohio, June 4, 20; m 74; c 3. *Educ:* Ohio State Univ, BS, 42, MSc, 43; Harvard Univ, MA, 48, PhD(biol), 51. *Prof Exp:* Assoc bot, Ohio State Univ, 42-43; botanist, Mil Geol Br, US Geol Surv, 48-57, botanist & hydrologist, Gen Hydrol Br, 57-66, res botanist, Water Resourses Div, 66-80. *Concurrent Pos:* Assoc prof lectr, George Washington Univ, 58-70, prof lectr, 70-76. *Mem:* Fel AAAS; fel Arctic Inst NAm. *Res:* Relationship of drainage basin vegetation to streamflow; effects of flooding upon flood-plain forests; tree growth in natural environments; botanical evidence of alpine glacier history; effects of high natural sulfur and carbon dioxide emissions upon wild plants. *Mailing Add:* 910 McDaniel Ct Herndon VA 20170

SIGAFUS, ROY EDWARD, AGRICULTURE. *Current Pos:* RETIRED. *Personal Data:* b Warren, Ill, Nov 15, 20; m 43; c 4. *Educ:* Univ Mass, BS, 48, MS, 49; Cornell Univ, PhD(crops), 51. *Prof Exp:* Teacher elem sch, Ill, 40-42; asst forage crops, Cornell Univ, 48-50; asst agronomist, Univ Ky, 50-52, asst prof crops, 52-53, from assoc prof to prof agron, 53-85. *Concurrent Pos:* Mem, Univ Ky-US Agency Int Develop contract team, Agr Univ Develop, Indonesia, 64-66 & Agr Res Sta Develop, Thailand, 66-69; mem comt forage crop variety eval, 69- *Res:* Forage crop variety evaluation. *Mailing Add:* 396 Bob-O-Link Dr Lexington KY 40503

SIGAI, ANDREW GARY, HIGH TEMPERATURE CHEMISTRY. *Current Pos:* STAFF SCIENTIST, GTE LABS, 80- *Personal Data:* b Baltimore, Md, Dec 3, 44; m 69; c 1. *Educ:* Rensselaer Polytech Inst, BS, 65, MS, 68, PhD(chem), 70. *Honors & Awards:* Leslie H Warner Tech Achievement Award, GTE Corp, 87. *Prof Exp:* Mem tech staff vapor phase crystal growth & characterization, RCA Labs, David Sarnoff Res Ctr, RCA Corp, 69-72; scientist photoreceptor technol, Joseph C Wilson Ctr Technol, Xerox Corp, 72-80. *Mem:* Am Chem Soc; Electrochem Soc; Am Vacuum Soc. *Res:* High temperature thermodynamics; vapor-phase crystal growth; xerography and photoreceptor technology; investigation of the evaporation properties of selenium alloys for xerographic applications; electroluminescence and lasers; III-V compound semiconductor technology; phosphor and phosphor coating research and development. *Mailing Add:* 419 E Lake Rd Penn Yan NY 14527

SIGAL, ISRAEL MICHAEL, MATHEMATICS. *Current Pos:* PROF, UNIV TORONTO, 85- *Personal Data:* b Kiev, Ukraine, Aug 31, 45; m, Brenda Lynn Tipper; c Alexander & Daniel. *Educ:* Gorky Univ, BA, 68; Tel-Aviv Univ, PhD, 76. *Honors & Awards:* Jeffrey-Williams Lectr, Can Math Soc, 92; John L Synge Award, Royal Soc Can, 93. *Prof Exp:* Fel, Swiss Inst Technol, Switz, 76-78; asst prof, Princeton Univ, 78-81; RH Revson sr scientist, Weizmann Inst, Israel, 81-85. *Concurrent Pos:* Prof, Univ Calif, Irvine, 84-90; res fel, I W Killam Found, 89-91. *Mem:* Fel Royal Soc Can. *Res:* Contributed several articles to professional and science publications. *Mailing Add:* Dept Math Univ Toronto 100 St George St Toronto ON M5S 3G3 Can

SIGAL, NOLAN H, SIGNAL TRANSDUCTION, LYMPHOKINES. *Current Pos:* VPRES BIOL, PHARMACOPEIA, INC, 94- *Personal Data:* b Rochester, Pa, Dec 3, 49; m 71; c 3. *Educ:* Princeton Univ, AB, 71; Univ Pa, PhD(immunol), 76, MD, 77. *Prof Exp:* asst prof pediat & immunol, Hosp Sick Children, Toronto, Ont Can, 80-83; exec dir immunol res, Merck, Sharp & Dohme Res Labs, 83-93. *Mem:* Am Asn Immunologists; Clin Immunol Soc. *Res:* Immunosuppression. *Mailing Add:* Dept Biol Pharmacopeia Inc 101 College Rd E Princeton NJ 08540. *Fax:* 609-987-0445

SIGAL, RICHARD FREDERICK, EXPLORATION GEOPHYSICS, THEORETICAL PHYSICS. *Current Pos:* staff res scientist, 78-92, RES ASSOC, AMOCO PROD CO, 92- *Personal Data:* b Cleveland, Ohio, Mar 19, 43; m 79, Mary G Penix; c Robert E. *Educ:* Case Inst Technol, BS, 65; Yeshiva Univ, MA, 67, PhD(physics), 71. *Prof Exp:* Adj asst prof physics, Hunter Col City Univ New York, 71-72; fel physics, Univ Alta, 72-74, res assoc, 74-75, vis asst prof physics, 75-76, res assoc, 76-77, instr, Col New Caledonia, 77-78. *Mem:* Am Phys Soc; Am Geophys Union; AAAS; Soc Exp Geophysicists. *Res:* The use of various electrical and electro-magnetic methods in geophysical exploration; estimation of rock parometers from geophysical methods for application to reservoir description. *Mailing Add:* 6617 E 65th St Tulsa OK 74133. *Fax:* 918-660-4163; *E-Mail:* rsigal@trc.amoco.com

SIGEL, BERNARD, SURGERY. *Current Pos:* PROF & DIR SURG RES, MED COL PA, 89- *Personal Data:* b Wilno, Poland, May 14, 30; US citizen; m 56; c 5. *Educ:* Univ Tex, MD, 53. *Prof Exp:* Staff mem surg, Vet Admin Hosp, Coral Gables, Fla, 59-60; from asst prof to prof surg, Med Col Pa, 60-74; prof surg & dean, Abraham Lincoln Sch Med, Col Med, Univ Ill, 74-78. *Concurrent Pos:* Mem coun thrombosis, Am Heart Asn; USPHS res career develop award, 63- *Mem:* Soc Univ Surgeons; Am Gastroenterol Asn; Am Col Surgeons; Am Asn Pathologists. *Mailing Add:* Dept Surg Med Col Pa 3300 Henry Ave Philadelphia PA 19129-1121

SIGEL, CARL WILLIAM, ORGANIC CHEMISTRY. *Current Pos:* assoc head Dept Med Biochem, 85-86, DIV DIR, PHARMACOKINETICS & DRUG METAB, BURROUGHS-WELLCOME & CO, 86- *Personal Data:* b Skokie, Ill, Apr 10, 42; m 69, Emilie Selbo; c Keith M & Carlie S. *Educ:* Univ Ill, Urbana, BS, 63; Ind Univ, Bloomington, PhD(org chem), 67. *Prof Exp:* NIH fel, Univ Wis-Madison, 67-69; NIH fel, Univ Va, 69, res assoc cancer, 69-71. *Mem:* Am Chem Soc; Am Asn Cancer Res. *Res:* Drug metabolism and pharmacokinetics, isolation, structural elucidation and synthesis of biologically active molecules. *Mailing Add:* 1116 Bramerton Ct Raleigh NC 27613. *Fax:* 919-315-8375

SIGEL, M(OLA) MICHAEL, virology, immunology; deceased, see previous edition for last biography

SIGELL, LEONARD, PHARMACOLOGY. *Current Pos:* Instr pharmacol, Univ Cincinnati, 64-66, instr clin pharmacol & exp med, 66-68, asst prof pharmacol & instr med, 68-72, assoc prof pharmacol, 72-81, DIR DRUG & POISON INFO CTR, COL MED, UNIV CINCINNATI, 72-, PROF PHARMACOL & ASSOC PROF EXP MED, 81- *Personal Data:* b Portland, Ore, Dec 28, 38. *Educ:* Ore State Univ, BS, 61; Univ Ore, PhD(pharmacol), 64. *Concurrent Pos:* Dir drug info, Cincinnati Gen Hosp, 66-72. *Mem:* Drug Info Asn; Am Asn Poison Control Ctrs. *Res:* Information science; cardiovascular and behavioral pharmacology; clinical pharmacology-drug epidemiology. *Mailing Add:* Dept Pharmacol Col Med Univ Cincinnati 231 Bethesda Ave Cincinnati OH 45267-0001

SIGGIA, ERIC DEAN, STATISTICAL MECHANICS, FLUID DYNAMICS. *Current Pos:* from asst prof to assoc prof, 77-85, PROF PHYSICS, CORNELL UNIV, 85- *Personal Data:* b Easton, Pa, Nov 24, 49. *Educ:* Harvard Univ, AB & AM, 71, PhD(physics), 72. *Prof Exp:* Asst prof physics, Univ Pa, 75-77. *Concurrent Pos:* Soc Fel jr fel, Harvard Univ, 71-75; Sloan Found grant, 81-83; Guggenheim Fel, 88-89. *Mem:* Am Phys Soc. *Res:* Theory of fluid turbulence and dynamics of phase transitions. *Mailing Add:* Dept Physics 109 Clark Hall Cornell Univ Ithaca NY 14853

SIGGIA, SIDNEY, ANALYTICAL CHEMISTRY. *Current Pos:* PROF CHEM, UNIV MASS, AMHERST, 66- *Personal Data:* b New York, NY, June 22, 20; m 44; c 2. *Educ:* Queens Col, NY, BS, 42; Polytech Inst Brooklyn, MS, 43, PhD(org chem), 44. *Honors & Awards:* Anachem Soc Award, 69; Fisher Award, Am Chem Soc, 75. *Prof Exp:* From res analyst to mgr, Anal Dept, Gen Aniline & Film Corp, Pa, 44-58; dir anal res & serv, Res Lab, Olin Mathieson Chem Corp, 58-66. *Mem:* AAAS; Sigma Xi; Am Chem Soc. *Res:* Organic and functional group analysis; analysis of mixtures, surface active agents and polymers; analytical separation; establishment of specifications; chemical kinetics; management of analytical chemical facilities. *Mailing Add:* Cortland Dr S Amherst MA 01002

SIGGINS, GEORGE ROBERT, NEUROSCIENCES, NEUROPHARMACOLOGY. *Current Pos:* PROF, SCRIPPS CLIN & RES FOUND, 84- *Personal Data:* b Miami, Okla, Dec 29, 37; m 78, Marcia D Lee; c Leah, Shannon & Graham. *Educ:* Harvard Univ, AB, 60; Boston Univ, MA, 63, PhD(biol & physiol), 67. *Honors & Awards:* A E Bennett Award, Soc Biol Psychiat, 71; A Cressy Morrison Award, NY Acad Sci, 71; Sr US Scientist Award, Alexander von Humboldt Found, 78; Bissendorf Lect Award, 88. *Prof Exp:* Fel vascular physiol, Boston Univ, 67-68; fel pharmacol, NIH-NIMH, 68-70; res scientist, Lab Neuropharmacol, St Elizabeth's Hosp, 70-72, sect chief, 72-76, actg lab chief, 75-76; assoc dir neurobiol, A V Davis Ctr, Salk Inst, 76-84. *Mem:* Am Soc Pharmacol & Exp Therapy; Soc Neurosci. *Res:* Neurophysiology; psychopharmacology; autonomic physiology; microcirculation; neuronal cytochemistry; tissue cultures. *Mailing Add:* CVN-12 Scripps Res Inst 10550 N Torrey Pines Rd La Jolla CA 92037-1092. *E-Mail:* geobob@scripps.edu

SIGGINS, JAMES ERNEST, MEDICINAL CHEMISTRY. *Current Pos:* CHEMIST, NY STATE HEALTH LABS, 79- *Personal Data:* b Salt Lake City, Utah, Oct 14, 28; m 58; c 2. *Educ:* Amherst Col, BA, 52; Univ Chicago, MS, 57, PhD(chem), 59. *Prof Exp:* Chemist, Res Ctr, Lever Bros Co, 52-54; res assoc synthetic org chem, Sterling-Winthrop Res Inst, 59-74. *Mem:* Am Chem Soc. *Res:* Heterocyclics; synthetic organic medicinals; radiopaque contrast agents. *Mailing Add:* 107 Van Dyke Pl Apt 10 Guilderland NY 12084-9699

SIGILLITO, VINCENT GEORGE, APPLIED MATHEMATICS. *Current Pos:* Assoc chemist, Appl Physics Lab, Johns Hopkins Univ, 58-62, assoc mathematician, 62-65, sr staff mathematician, 65-76, PRIN STAFF MATHEMATICIAN, APPL PHYSICS LAB, JOHNS HOPKINS UNIV, 76-, GROUP SUPVR, INFO & SCI INFIRMARY GROUP, 81- *Personal Data:* b Washington, DC, Feb 20, 37; m 58; c 2. *Educ:* Univ Md, College Park, BS, 58, MA, 62, PhD(math), 65. *Concurrent Pos:* Instr eve col grad prog, NIH, 65-68; lectr, Johns Hopkins Univ, 66-; Parsons vis prof, Dept Math Sci, Johns Hopkins Univ, 78-79. *Res:* Neural networks. *Mailing Add:* 13209 Bellvue St Silver Spring MD 20904

SIGLER, JOHN WILLIAM, ecological & environmental assessments, for more information see previous edition

SIGLER, JULIUS ALFRED, JR, SOLID STATE PHYSICS. *Current Pos:* Assoc prof, 67-71, assoc dean, 85-88, PROF PHYSICS, CHMN DEPT & DIR, GRAD SCI PROG, LYNCHBURG COL, 71- *Personal Data:* b Kissimmee, Fla, Dec 22, 40; m 65, Janet Cocke; c Jonathan, James & Jeffrey. *Educ:* Lynchburg Col, BS, 62; Univ Va, MS, 66, PhD(physics), 67. *Concurrent Pos:* Consult, Oak Ridge Assoc Univs, 73-74; vis prof physics, Ind State Univ & re-write ed, NSF Physics Technol Proj, 74-75; consult, Solar Tech Proj, NSF, 80 & Cybernet Corp, 80- *Mem:* Am Asn Physics Teachers; Soc Physics Students; Nat Rwy Hist Soc. *Res:* Theoretical calculations of relative energies of various defects in quenched face centered cubic metals; variation of mechanical density of gold wires with tensile strains; development of physics curricula and teaching strategies; general curriculum development. *Mailing Add:* Dept Physics Lynchburg Col 1501 Lakeside Dr Lynchburg VA 24501. *Fax:* 804-522-0658; *E-Mail:* sigler@acavax.lynchburg.edu

SIGLER, LAURENCE EDWARD, MATHEMATICS. *Current Pos:* from assoc prof to prof, 67-92, EMER PROF MATH, BUCKNELL UNIV, 92- *Personal Data:* b Tulsa, Okla, Aug 26, 28; m 82, Judith Szager; c 3. *Educ:* Okla State Univ, ScB, 50; Columbia Univ, AM, 54, PhD(math), 63. *Prof Exp:* Instr math, Columbia Univ, 56-59; asst prof, Hunter Col, 61-65 & Hofstra Univ, 65-67. *Mem:* Am Math Soc; Math Asn Am; Ital Math Union. *Res:* Asymptotic theory of ordinary differential equations; set theory; mathematical history. *Mailing Add:* Dept Math Bucknell Univ Lewisburg PA 17837. *E-Mail:* sigler@bucknell.edu

SIGLER, MILES HAROLD, NEPHROLOGY. *Current Pos:* assoc med, 64-69, CHIEF DEPT NEPHROL, LANKENAU HOSP, 69- *Personal Data:* b Buffalo, NY, Feb 11, 29; m 54, Elaine Aser; c Allison, Gwen & Philip. *Educ:* Univ Rochester, BA, 51; Cornell Univ, MD, 55. *Prof Exp:* Intern med, State Univ NY Syracuse, 55-56; resident, Col Med, Thomas Jefferson Univ, 56-58; NIH fel nephrol, Hosp Univ Pa, 60-62; assoc med, Jefferson Med Col Hosp, 62-64. *Concurrent Pos:* Clin prof med, Col Med, Thomas Jefferson Univ, 72- *Mem:* Am Fedn Clin Res; Am Soc Nephrol; fel Am Col Physicians; Int Soc Nephrol; Am Heart Asn; Sigma Xi. *Res:* Renal mechanisms controlling fluid and electrolyte excretion during fasting; mechanism of the sodium diuresis of fasting; mechanism of the phosphateuresis of fasting; energy metabolism in uremia; slow continuous hemodialysis. *Mailing Add:* 416 Haywood Rd Merion Station PA 19066

SIGLER, PAUL BENJAMIN, BIOCHEMISTRY. *Current Pos:* PROF MOLECULAR BIOPHYS & BIOCHEM, YALE UNIV, 89-, INVESTR, HOWARD HUGHES MED INST, 89- *Personal Data:* b Richmond, Va, Feb 19, 34; m 58, Althea J Martin; c Jennifer, Michele, Jonathan, Deborah & Rebecca. *Educ:* Princeton Univ, AB, 55; Columbia Univ, MD, 59; Cambridge Univ, PhD(biochem), 68. *Honors & Awards:* Dewitt Stetten Jr Lectr, 87; Welch Lectr, Univ Tex, 90; George Koury Mem Lectr, Univ Pa, Wistar Inst, 92; Squibb Lectr, Univ Colo, 92; Nathan Kaplan Lectr, Univ Calif, San Diego, 92; Weizmann Mem Lectr, Weizmann Inst, 95; Zuricher Vorlesung Lectr, Eidgenoessische Technische Hoshule, 95; Proctor & Gamble Lectr, Univ Ill, 96. *Prof Exp:* Intern & resident med, Col Physicians & Surgeons, Columbia Univ, 59-61; res assoc protein crystallog, Nat Inst Arthritis & Metab Dis, 61-63, mem staff, 63-64; fel, Lab Molecular Biol, Med Res Coun, Eng, 64-67, from assoc prof to prof biophys & theoret biol, Univ Chicago, 67-84, prof biochem & molecular biol, 84-88. *Concurrent Pos:* Guggenheim fel, 74-75; Katzir-Katchalsky fel, 75; resident fel, Churchill Col, Cambridge, 84-85; trustee, Assoc Univ Inc, 92-; chair, Prin Users Group, Struct Biol Ctr, Am Physics Soc, 93-; Humboldt sr scientist res award, 95. *Mem:* Nat Acad Sci; Am Chem Soc; Am Crystallog Soc; AAAS; fel Am Acad Arts & Sci; hon mem Japanese Biochem Soc. *Res:* X-ray diffraction; protein crystallography; membrane interactive proteins; genetic control; transfer ribonucleic acid; nucleic acid interactions of proteins; signal transduction. *Mailing Add:* Dept Molecular Biophys & Biochem Howard Hughes Med Inst Boyer Ctr Molecular Med Yale Univ 295 Congress Ave New Haven CT 06510. *Fax:* 203-776-3550, 432-5239

SIGLER, WILLIAM FRANKLIN, fisheries; deceased, see previous edition for last biography

SIGMAN, DAVID STEPHAN, BIOCHEMISTRY. *Current Pos:* from asst prof to assoc prof, 68-79, PROF BIOCHEM, SCH MED, UNIV CALIF, LOS ANGELES, 79- *Personal Data:* b New York, NY, June 14, 39; m 63, Marian Diamond; c Daniel & Hilary. *Educ:* Oberlin Col, AB, 60; Harvard Univ, AM, 62, PhD(chem), 65. *Prof Exp:* NIH res fel biochem, Sch Med, Harvard Univ, 65-67, instr, 67-68. *Concurrent Pos:* Alfred P Sloan fel, 72-74; Josiah May fel, 75-76; mem, Molecular Biol Inst, 77- *Mem:* Am Soc Biochemists; Am Chem Soc; Sigma Xi. *Res:* Mechanism of enzyme action chemical nuleicses; structure of nucleic acids. *Mailing Add:* Molecular Biol Inst Univ Calif Los Angeles CA 90024-1570. *Fax:* 310-206-7286

SIGMAR, DIETER JOSEPH, PLASMA PHYSICS, NUCLEAR ENGINEERING. *Current Pos:* SR SCIENTIST, FUSION ENERGY DIV, OAIC RIDGE NAT LAB, 82- *Personal Data:* b Vienna, Austria, 1935; c 3. *Educ:* Tech Univ Vienna, MS, 60, ScD(theoret physics), 65. *Prof Exp:* Asst prof theoret physics, Tech Univ, Vienna, Austria, 65-66; res staff plasma physics & thermonuclear fusion, Oak Ridge Nat Lab, Tenn, 66-70; res staff plasma physics, Res Lab Electronics, 70-72, from adj prof nuclear eng to assoc prof nuclear eng & aeronaut & astronaut, 76-84, sr res scientist, Plasma Fusion Ctr, Mass Inst Technol, 89- *Concurrent Pos:* Consult, Fusion Energy Div, Oak Ridge Nat Lab, 70-76 & Argonne Nat Lab, 74-76; vis fac mem, Los Alamos Sci Lab, 74 & 75; lectr plasma physics, Tech Univ, Vienna, 78, prof theoret physics. *Mem:* Fel Am Phys Soc; Am Nuclear Soc; Austrian Phys Soc. *Res:* Theoretical plasma physics; controlled thermonuclear fusion research; fundamental transport theory of magnetically confined fully ionized gases and its application to toroidal fusion reactors. *Mailing Add:* Plasma Fusion Ctr NW 16-243 Mass Inst Technol 167 Albany St Cambridge MA 02139

SIGMON, KERMIT NEAL, NUMERICAL ANALYSIS, PARALLEL COMPUTING. *Current Pos:* PROF MATH, UNIV FLA, 66- *Personal Data:* b Lincoln Co, NC, Apr 18, 36; m 60, Ruth Tucker; c Kristina. *Educ:* Appalachian State Univ, BS, 58; Univ NC, Chapel Hill, MEd, 59; Univ Fla, PhD(math), 66. *Prof Exp:* Teacher, Charlotte-Mecklenburg Schs, NC, 59-63. *Concurrent Pos:* Ger Res Asn study grant, Hannover Tech Univ, 72-73; consult, Oak Ridge Nat Lab, 87-89. *Mem:* Am Math Soc; Math Asn Am; Sigma Xi; Soc Indust Appl Math. *Res:* Topological algebra; algebraic topology; numerical analysis; parallel computing. *Mailing Add:* Univ Fla Gainesville FL 32611-8105. *Fax:* 904-392-8357; *E-Mail:* sigma@math.ufe.edu

SIGNELL, PETER STUART, THEORETICAL PHYSICS, SCIENCE EDUCATION. *Current Pos:* assoc prof, 64-65, PROF PHYSICS, MICH STATE UNIV, 65- *Personal Data:* b Lima, Ohio, June 29, 28; m 52; c 2. *Educ:* Antioch Col, BS, 52; Univ Rochester, MS, 54, PhD, 58. *Prof Exp:* From instr to asst prof physics, Bucknell Univ, 57-59; from asst prof to assoc prof, Pa State Univ, 59-64. *Res:* Nuclear forces; research and development for independent study instruction. *Mailing Add:* 447 Butterfield Dr East Lansing MI 48823

SIGNER, ETHAN ROYAL, PLANT MOLECULAR BIOLOGY, PHARMACEUTICAL BIOTECHNOLOGY. *Current Pos:* from asst prof to assoc prof microbiol, 66-72, prof, 72-97, EMER PROF BIOL, DEPT BIOL, MASS INST TECHNOL, 77-; EMER DIR, PRAECIS PHARMACEUT INC, 97- *Personal Data:* b Brooklyn, NY, Apr 3, 37; m 62, 79, Laura Karp; c Kira R, Rachel L & Jasper K. *Educ:* Yale Univ, BS, 58; Mass Inst Technol, PhD(biophys), 63. *Prof Exp:* NSF fel, Med Res Coun Lab Molecular Biol, Eng, 62-64; Am Cancer Soc fel, Pasteur Inst, Paris, 64-65; Jane Coffin Childs Mem Fund fel, 65-66. *Concurrent Pos:* Wellcome vis prof microbiol, Univ Calif, San Francisco, 82; vis prof genetics, Harvard Med Sch, 86-87; fel, Marion & Jasper Whiting Found, 88; vis prof biochem, Univ Paris, 92 & 93; chief exec officer & chief sci officer, Pharmaceut Peptides Inc, Mass, 93-96, vchmn, 96. *Mem:* AAAS; Am Soc Microbiol; NY Acad Sci; Int Soc Plant Molecular Biol; Genetics Soc Am; Am Soc Plant Physiologists; Int Soc Molecular Plant-Microbe Interactions. *Res:* Peptide mimics for human therapeutics; genetics, genetic engineering, genetic recombination and gene silencing in plants; gene expression, symbiotic nitrogen fixation, bacteriophage genetics and endosymbiosis in bacteria. *Mailing Add:* Dept Biol Mass Inst Technol Rm 68-625 Cambridge MA 02139-4307. *Fax:* 617-253-5072

SIGNORINO, CHARLES ANTHONY, ORGANIC CHEMISTRY, PHYSICAL CHEMISTRY. *Current Pos:* PRES, EMERSON RESOURCES, 88- *Personal Data:* b Beaverdale, Pa, July 28, 32; m 54; c 8. *Educ:* Pa State Univ, BS, 54; Univ Pa, MS, 56, PhD, 59; Westminster Theol Seminary, MAR, 78. *Prof Exp:* Asst instr chem, Univ Pa, 54-58; res chemist, Atlantic Refining

Co, 58-62; assoc prof chem, Eastern Baptist Col, 62-68; dir tech serv, Colorcon, Inc, 66-68, vpres, 68-72, mem bd dirs, 72-83. *Concurrent Pos:* Vis prof, Eastern Baptist Col, 68-69; consult, 84- *Mem:* Am Chem Soc; Am Pharmaceut Asn; Am Asn Pharmaceut Scientists. *Res:* New processes for monomer synthesis; polymerization kinetics; radiation induced polymerization; selective oxidation of hydrocarbons, especially olefins; patented lake manufacturing processes; patented special tablet coatings; specialty chemicals formulations. *Mailing Add:* 600 Markley St Suite 1 Norristown PA 19401-3704

SIGURDSSON, HARALDUR, PETROLOGY, VOLCANOLOGY. *Current Pos:* assoc prof, 74-80, PROF OCEANOG, UNIV RI, 80- *Personal Data:* b Iceland, May 31, 39; div; c 2. *Educ:* Queen's Univ, Belfast, BSc, 65; Durham Univ, Eng, PhD(geol), 70. *Prof Exp:* Res fel geol, Univ W Indes, Trinidad, 70-73. *Mem:* Am Geophys Union; Geochem Soc. *Res:* Petrology of ocean ridge basalts; volcanic geology of Iceland and the Lesser Antilles Island Arc. *Mailing Add:* Dept Oceanog Univ RI 29 Fish Rd, 107 Horn Lab Narragansett RI 02882

SIH, ANDREW, PREDATOR-PREY INTERACTIONS, EVOLUTION OF BEHAVIOR. *Current Pos:* from asst prof to assoc prof, 82-91, PROF, SCH BIOL SCI, UNIV KY, 91- *Personal Data:* b New York, NY, Mar 10, 54; m 83, Marie-Sylvie Baltus; c Lorie. *Educ:* State Univ NY, Stony Brook, BS, 74; Univ Calif, Santa Barbara, MS, 77, PhD(biol), 80. *Honors & Awards:* Murray F Buell Award, Ecol Soc Am, 80. *Prof Exp:* Postdoctoral fel, Ohio State Univ, 80-81, Mich State Univ, 81-82 & Univ Calif, Berkeley, 82. *Concurrent Pos:* Prin investr, NSF, 85-, panel mem, 91-; vis scientist, Univ Calif, Berkeley & Oxford Univ, 91; Univ res prof, Univ Ky, 96-97. *Mem:* Ecol Soc Am; Am Soc Naturalists; Soc Study Evolution; Sixma Xi; Animal Behav Soc (2nd pres elect, 97). *Res:* Evolution of behaviors, feeding, mating, predator avoidance, and life history traits that influence species interactions; mathematical modeling; focal organisms studied include amphibians, fish, aquatic insects and other freshwater invertebrates. *Mailing Add:* Sch Biol Sci Univ Ky Lexington KY 40506-0001. *Fax:* 606-257-1717; *E-Mail:* andy@ceeb.uky.edu

SIH, CHARLES JOHN, BIO-ORGANIC CHEMISTRY. *Current Pos:* from assoc prof to prof, 60-77, F B POWER PROF PHARMACEUT CHEM, UNIV WIS-MADISON, 77- *Personal Data:* b Shanghai, China; nat US; m 59. *Educ:* Carroll Col, Mont, AB, 52; Mont State Col, MS, 55; Univ Wis, PhD(bact), 58. *Honors & Awards:* Ernest Volwiler Award, 77; Roussel Prize, 80. *Prof Exp:* Sr res microbiologist, Squibb Inst Med Res, 58-60. *Concurrent Pos:* Sci adv, Eastman Kodak. *Mem:* Am Soc Microbiol; Am Soc Biol Chemists; Acad Pharmaceut Sci; Am Chem Soc. *Res:* Chemical syntheses using enzymes; enzymatic mechanism of sterol side chain degradation; suicide inhibitors; natural products chemistry; natural products chemistry. *Mailing Add:* Univ Wis Sch Pharm Madison WI 53706

SIHAG, RAM K, BIOCHEMISTRY & CELL BIOLOGY, PROTEIN SCIENCES. *Current Pos:* res assoc biochem, 85-89, instr, 89-91, ASST PROF, DEPT PSYCHIAT, HARVARD MED SCH, 91-; ASSOC BIOCHEMIST, MCLEAN HOSP, 92- *Personal Data:* b India, Jan 1, 50; m, Christine Ptak. *Educ:* P U Chandigarh, India, BS, 69; H A Univ Hisar, MS, 72; J-Nehru Univ, New Delhi, PhD(life sci), 77. *Prof Exp:* Fel, Univ Conn Health Ctr, 81-84, Pa State Univ, 84-85; asst biochemist, McLean Hosp, 85-91. *Mem:* Protein Soc; AAAS; Am Soc Cell Biol; Am Soc Biochem & Molecular Biol. *Res:* Protein phosphorylation; neuronal plasticity; biochemical basis of neurodegeneration. *Mailing Add:* Labs Molecular Neurosci McLean Hosp Harvard Med Sch 115 Mill St Belmont MA 02178-1048. *Fax:* 617-855-3299

SIIROLA, JEFFREY JOHN, CHEMICAL PROCESS SYNTHESIS, CHEMICAL TECHNOLOGY ASSESSMENT. *Current Pos:* Res engr, Eastman Chem Co, 72-74, sr res engr, 74-80, res assoc, 80-88, sr res assoc, 88-95, RES FEL, EASTMAN CHEM CO, 95- *Personal Data:* b Patuxent River, Md, July 17, 45; m 71, Sharon A Atwood; c John D & Jennifer A. *Educ:* Univ Utah, BS, 67; Univ Wis-Madison, PhD, 70. *Concurrent Pos:* Mem exec comt, Comput & Systs Technol Div, Am Inst Chem Engrs, 81-, prog chmn, 88-, trustee, Comput Aids Chem Eng Educ Corp, 83-, pres, 90-92, ed bd, Indust & Eng Chem Res, 86-89. *Mem:* Nat Acad Eng; Am Chem Soc; Am Asn Artificial Intel; fel Am Inst Chem Engrs; Am Asn Eng Educ. *Res:* Computer-aided chemical process design synthesis, analysis and optimization; symbolic programming; artificial intelligence; chemical technology assessment; chemical engineering education. *Mailing Add:* Eastman Chem Co PO Box 1972 Kingsport TN 37662-5150. *Fax:* 423-229-4558; *E-Mail:* siirola@eastman.com

SIITERI, PENTTI KASPER, biochemistry, for more information see previous edition

SIJ, JOHN WILLIAM, PLANT PHYSIOLOGY. *Current Pos:* from asst prof to assoc prof, 72-83, PROF, AGR RES & EXTEN CTR, TEX A&M UNIV, 83- *Personal Data:* b St Louis, Mo, June 21, 43; m 65, Susan Ammon; c Mark & Amanda. *Educ:* Eastern Ill Univ, BSEd, 65; Ohio State Univ, MS, 67, PhD(plant physiol), 71. *Honors & Awards:* Am Soybean Asn ICI Am Award, Soybean Researcher's Prog. *Prof Exp:* Res assoc, Evapotranspiration Lab, Kans State Univ, 71-72. *Mem:* Crop Sci Soc Am; Am Soc Agron; Sigma Xi. *Res:* Soybean physiology and management; alternate crop and cropping systems. *Mailing Add:* Tex A&M Univ Rte 7 Box 999 Beaumont TX 77713-8530. *Fax:* 409-752-5560

SIKAND, RAJINDER S, PHYSIOLOGY, MEDICINE. *Current Pos:* CO-DIR, SECT PULMONARY DIS, DEPT MED, ST RAPHAEL'S HOSP, NEW HAVEN, CT, 75- *Personal Data:* b Barnala, India. *Educ:* King Edward Med Col, Lahore, Punjab, MB, BS, 46. *Prof Exp:* Res fel physiol, Sch Med, Yale Univ, 49-52; med officer, West Middlesex Hosp, UK, 53-54; med registr, King George V Hosp, Godalming, UK, 54-56; res fel physiol, Sch Med, Univ Md, Baltimore City, 61-63; res assoc, State Univ NY Buffalo, 63-64; res assoc, Max Planck Inst Med Res, Gottingen, 64-65; assoc clin prof internal med, Sch Med, Yale Univ, 65-75. *Mem:* Am Physiol Soc; fel Am Col Physicians; fel Am Col Chest Physicians; Am Thoracic Soc; Am Fedn Clin Res. *Res:* Cardiopulmonary physiology. *Mailing Add:* Yale Univ Sch Med Pulmonary Unit Rm 589 St Raphael's Hosp 1450 Chapel St New Haven CT 06511-4440

SIKARSKIE, DAVID L(AWRENCE), ENGINEERING MECHANICS. *Current Pos:* dean, 85-90, DIR SPEC PROJS, COL ENG, MICH TECH UNIV, 90-, PROF ENG MECH, 85- *Personal Data:* b Marquette, Mich, Aug 3, 37; m 86, Martha A Banks; c David L Jr, Anya M, Paul B, Lari, Amy & James B. *Educ:* Univ Pa, BS, 59; Columbia Univ, MS, 60, ScD(eng mech), 64. *Prof Exp:* Res asst solid mech, Columbia Univ, 62-63; mem tech staff, Ingersoll Rand Res Ctr, 63-66; from asst prof to assoc prof aerospace eng, Univ Mich, Ann Arbor, 66-72, prof aerospace eng, 72-79, chmn metall, mech & mats sci, 79-84. *Concurrent Pos:* Vis lectr, Princeton Univ, 65-66. *Mem:* Am Soc Mech Engrs; Soc Eng Sci; Sigma Xi; Nat Soc Prof Engrs; Am Asn Eng Educ. *Res:* Brittle fracture; rock mechanics; elasticity; nonlinear structural mechanics; biomechanics; composite material mechanics. *Mailing Add:* Mech Eng Dept Mich Tech Univ ME-EM Bldg Houghton MI 49931. *Fax:* 906-487-2822; *E-Mail:* sikarsk@mtu.edu

SIKARSKIE, JAMES GERARD, ZOO MEDICINE, ENVIRONMENTAL TOXICOLOGY. *Current Pos:* From instr to asst prof, 75-90, ASSOC PROF VET MED, COL VET MED, MICH STATE UNIV, 90- *Personal Data:* b Manistique, Mich, Sept 13, 52; m 76, Mary J Sleder; c Matthew J, Anna T & Sarah J. *Educ:* Mich Univ, BS, 74, DVM, 75, MS, 81. *Concurrent Pos:* Adj prof, Col Agr & Natural Resources, Fisheries & Wildlife Dept, Mich State Univ, 89- *Mem:* Am Vet Med Asn; Am Asn Zoo Vets; Am Asn Wildlife Vets; Wildlife Dis Asn; Am Col Zool Med. *Res:* Toxicology using wild animals as indicators of environmental quality while monitoring the impact of agriculture and industry on wildlife, especially game and endangered species; medicine, management and nutrition of zoo and wildlife species. *Mailing Add:* A226 Vet Med Ctr East Lansing MI 48824-1314

SIKDER, SANTOSH K, IMMUNOCHEMISTRY, VIRAL IMMUNOLOGY. *Current Pos:* instr, 88-90, ASST PROF MED, CORNELL UNIV MED COL, NY, 90- *Personal Data:* b Faridpur, Bangladesh, Jan 1, 49; m 86. *Educ:* Dhaka Univ, Bangladesh, BS, 69, MS, 70; Jadapur Univ, Calcutta, India, PhD(org chem), 81. *Prof Exp:* Res & develop chemist pharmaceut labs, Universal Drug House, Calcutta, 71-74; jr res fel org chem, Jadapur Univ, Calcutta, 75-78, sr res fel, 78-81; postdoctoral res scientist microbiol, Columbia Univ, NY, 82-87. *Mem:* Am Asn Immunologists. *Res:* Regulation of human-immunodeficiency virus transcription; effect of different hormones-antihormones on the HIV-transactivation; contribution of different cellular factors and its interaction with viral genes and proteins particularly to explain the viral latency. *Mailing Add:* 528 Cumberland Ave Teaneck NJ 07666

SIKES, JAMES KLINGMAN, ANALYTICAL CHEMISTRY, PHYSIOLOGY. *Current Pos:* PRES, SCAN, INC, 75- *Personal Data:* b Henderson, Tenn, Apr 12, 24; m 50; c 2. *Educ:* Abilene Christian Col, BS, 47; Tex Technol Col, MS, 51; Tex Tech Univ, MS, 67. *Prof Exp:* Supvr lab, Paymaster Oil Mills, Anderson Clayton Co, 47-54; chief chemist res, Plains Coop Oil Mill, 54-65; partner, Plains Lab, 65-73; dept head lab, Brookside Farms Lab Asn, 73-75. *Concurrent Pos:* Mem res comt, Nat Cottonseed Prods Asn, 60-62. *Mem:* Am Oil Chemists Soc; Am Inst Chemists; AAAS; Am Soc Animal Sci; Asn Consult Chemists & Chem Engrs. *Res:* Cottonseed oil processing and refining; laboratory methodology; water quality; insecticides; herbicides; animal feeds; animal nutrition; soil and crop improvement. *Mailing Add:* Rte 2 PO Box 350-A15 Lubbock TX 79415

SIKINA, THOMAS, ANTENNA ENGINEERING. *Current Pos:* PRIN ENGR, RAYTHEON CO, 89- *Personal Data:* b Philadelphia, Pa, July 24, 50; c 1. *Educ:* Pa State Univ, BS, 72; Del Valley Col, BS, 77; Drexel Univ, MS, 85. *Prof Exp:* Antenna engr, RCA, 79-84; design specialist, ITT-Gilfillan, 84-86; chief engr, Chu Assoc Inc, 86-89. *Mem:* Inst Elec & Electronic Engrs. *Mailing Add:* Raytheon Co Boston Post Rd Wayland MA 01778

SIKIVIE, PIERRE, COSMOLOGY DARK MATTER GALACTIC HALO FORMATION, PROPERTIES OF THE AXION. *Current Pos:* from asst prof to assoc prof, 81-88, PROF PHYSICS, UNIV FLA, 88- *Personal Data:* b Sint-Truiden, Belgium, Oct 29, 49; m 80, Cynthia L Chennault; c Paul & Michael. *Educ:* Licencie en Sci, Univ Liege, Belg, 70; Yale Univ, MS, 72, PhD(physics), 75. *Honors & Awards:* Jesse W Beams Medal, Southern Sect, Am Phys Soc, 96. *Prof Exp:* Res assoc, Univ Md, 75-77, Stanford Linear Accelator Ctr, 77-79; sr fel, Europ Orgn Nuclear Res, Switz, 79-81. *Concurrent Pos:* Fel, Guggenheim Mem Found, 97- *Mem:* AAAS; fel Am Phys Soc. *Res:* Dark matter detection; galactic halo formation; properties of axion strings and domain walls; properties of wiggly strings; Casimir type forces. *Mailing Add:* Dept Phys Univ Fla 215 Williamson Hall Gainesville FL 32611

SIKLOSI, MICHAEL PETER, ORGANIC CHEMISTRY. *Current Pos:* RESEARCHER CHEM, PROCTER & GAMBLE CO, 77- *Personal Data:* b Akron, Ohio, Sept 8, 48; m 71. *Educ:* Montclair State Col, BA, 70; Purdue Univ, MS, 72, PhD(chem), 77. *Mem:* Am Chem Soc. *Res:* Peroxyacids; reactivity; decomposition mechanisms, reaction mechanisms; organometallic chemistry; reactions of allylic Grignard reagents; detergency. *Mailing Add:* 7299 Bobby Lane Cincinnati OH 45243-2003

SIKORA, JEROME PAUL, STRUCTURAL MECHANICS, PHOTOMECHANICS. *Current Pos:* PHYSICIST, D TAYLOR NAVAL SHIP RES & DEVELOP CTR, 69- *Personal Data:* b Cleveland, Ohio, Apr 9, 47; m 71; c 2. *Educ:* Univ Detroit, BS, 69. *Mem:* Sigma Xi. *Res:* Optical methods such as holography, speckle, moire and photoelasticity to measure displacements, stresses, vibrations, and contour mapping of hard structures. *Mailing Add:* 14126 Chadwick Lane Rockville MD 20853-2166

SIKOROWSKI, PETER P, INSECT VIRUSES, SEROLOGY. *Current Pos:* From asst prof to assoc prof, 68-79, PROF ENTOM & INSECT PATH, MISS STATE UNIV, 79- *Personal Data:* b Poland; US citizen; m, Betty Matchler; c Peter & Lilah. *Educ:* Utah State Univ, BS, 57; Ore State Univ, MS, 60; Wash State Univ, PhD(plant path), 64. *Concurrent Pos:* Lectr & prin investr, Miss State Univ, 68- *Mem:* Entom Soc Am; Sigma Xi; Soc Insect Path. *Res:* Insect pathology; mass reared insects and the histology, biochemistry, and host specificity of cytoplasmic polyhedrosis virus. *Mailing Add:* PO Box 9775 Mississippi State MS 39762. *Fax:* 601-325-8837; *E-Mail:* aml3@ra.msstate.edu

SIKORSKA, HANNA, MONOCLONAL ANTIBODIES, TUMOR IMMUNOLOGY. *Current Pos:* VPRES RES & DEVELOP, ROUGIER BIO-TECH LTD, MONTREAL, 85- *Personal Data:* b Warsaw, Poland, July 7, 50; Polish & Can citizen. *Educ:* Univ Warsaw, BS & MS, 73; Polish Acad Sci, PhD(immunol), 78. *Prof Exp:* PhD fel immunol, Inst Rheumatology, Warsaw, 75-78, adj, 78-81; fel immunol, Inst Arnand-Frappier, Que, 81-82; fel thyroidology, Queen's Univ, Ont, 82; fel autoimmunity, McGill Univ, Que, 82-85. *Mem:* Am Asn Immunologists; Am Soc Nuclear Med; Parenteral Drug Asn; Drug Info Asn; NY Acad Sci; Soc Nuclear Med; Am Soc Nuclear Cardiol. *Res:* Development of monoclonal antibody based radiopharmaceuticals for imaging of myocardial cell necrosis, tumors and occult infactions; monoclonal antibody conjugates for cancer therapy; anti-idiotypes as cancer vaccines; antibody delivery systems; marine toxins; pseudomonas aernginosa serotyping in cystic fibrosis. *Mailing Add:* Rougier Bio-Tech Ltd 8480 St Laurent Montreal PQ H2P 2M6 Can. *Fax:* 514-383-4493

SIKORSKA, MARIANNA, CELL & MOLECULAR BIOLOGY, NEUROBIOLOGY & BIOCHEMISTRY. *Current Pos:* res assoc animal & cell physiol, Div Biol Sci, 78-82, from asst res officer to assoc res officer, 82-92, SR RES OFFICER, APOPTOSIS RES GROUP, INST BIOL SCI, NAT RES COUN, 92- *Personal Data:* b Wilkolaz, Poland. *Educ:* Polytech Univ, Warsaw, BChemE, 72; Polish Acad Sci, PhD(biochem), 78. *Prof Exp:* Res asst neuropath, Polish Acad Sci, Warsaw, 72-78. *Concurrent Pos:* Adj prof & mem, Sch Grad Studies, Dept Biochem, Univ Ottawa. *Mem:* Can Soc Biochem Molecular & Cell Biol; Am Soc Cell Biol; Am Asn Cancer Res; NY Acad Sci; AAAS. *Res:* Molecular mechanisms of cell proliferation, differentiation and active cell death; molecular basis of gene expression-chromatin structure, chromatin loops, DNA-binding proteins, transcription factors. *Mailing Add:* Inst Biol Sci Nat Res Coun Can 1500 Montreal Rd Bldg M-54 Ottawa ON K1A 0R6 Can

SIKORSKI, JAMES ALAN, ENZYME INHIBITOR DESIGN & SYNTHESIS, PEPTIDOMIMETIC CHEMISTRY. *Current Pos:* FEL, G D SEARLE RES & DEVELOP, 94-; ADJ PROF BIOCHEM, CENTRAL METHODIST COL, 95- *Personal Data:* b Stevens Pt, Wis, Nov 9, 48; m 77, Georgina Weber; c Christine R. *Educ:* Northeast La State Col, BS, 70; Purdue Univ, MS, 76, PhD(org chem), 81. *Honors & Awards:* St Louis Award, Am Chem Soc, 94. *Prof Exp:* Res chemist II, Monsanto Agr Co, 76-78, sr res chemist, 78-82, res specialist, 82, res group leader, 82-87, sci fel, 87-91, fel, Monsanto Corp Res, 91-93. *Concurrent Pos:* Instr org chem, St Louis Community Col, Florisant Valley, 77-78. *Mem:* Am Chem Soc; AAAS; Sigma Xi; Int Soc Heterocyclic Chem. *Res:* Medicinal chemistry; peptidomimetic chemistry; organophosphorus chemistry; rational design and synthesis of mechanism-based enzyme inhibitors; molecular modeling; Plant biochemistry; heterocycle synthesis. *Mailing Add:* G D Searle Res & Develop 700 Chesterfield Pkwy N St Louis MO 63198. *E-Mail:* jasiko@ccmail.monsanto.com

SIKOV, MELVIN RICHARD, RADIATION BIOLOGY. *Current Pos:* sr res scientist, Pac Northwest Labs, 65-68, res assoc, 68-78, mgr develop toxicol, 78-81, SR STAFF SCIENTIST, PAC NORTHWEST LABS, BATTELLE MEM INST, 81- *Personal Data:* b Detroit, Mich, July 8, 28; m 52, Shirley Dressler; c Peter H, Stacy J & Thomas R. *Educ:* Wayne State Univ, BS, 51; Univ Rochester, PhD(radiation biol), 55. *Prof Exp:* Res assoc radiation biol, Univ Rochester, 52-55; asst prof radiobiol, Col Med, Wayne State Univ, 55-61, assoc prof, 61-65. *Mem:* Radiation Res Soc; Health Physics Soc; Am Asn Invest Path; Soc Toxicol; Teratol Soc; fel Am Inst Ultrasound Med. *Res:* Age and environmental factors in radionuclide metabolism; effects of radiation and chemicals on development; relationships between teratogenic and oncogenic mechanisms; multidisciplinary technologies for biomedical diagnostics. *Mailing Add:* 2105 Davison Ave Richland WA 99352-2016. *Fax:* 509-376-0302

SILAGI, SELMA, GENETICS, CANCER. *Current Pos:* from asst prof to prof, genetics, 65-87, EMER PROF OF GENETICS, MED COL, CORNELL, UNIV, 87- *Personal Data:* b Sept 5, 16; US citizen; m 36; c 2. *Educ:* Hunter Col, AB, 36; Columbia Univ, MA, 38, PhD(genetics), 61. *Prof Exp:* Teacher pub schs, NY, 38-50; lectr biol, Queens Col, 57-59; NIH fel, 59-62; res assoc biochem genetics, Rockefeller Univ, 62-65. *Concurrent Pos:* Guest investr, Rockefeller Univ & vis investr, Sloan-Kettering Inst Cancer Res, 65-66; fac res award, Am Cancer Soc, 70-75; mem, Cancer Spec Prog Adv Comt, Nat Cancer Inst, 73-75. *Mem:* AAAS; Genetics Soc Am; Am Soc Cell Biol; Harvey Soc; Tissue Cult Asn; Sigma Xi. *Res:* Cellular differentiation and gene action in mammalian cells in tissue culture; reversible suppression of malignancy by 5-bromodeoxyuridine; cancer immunology; cell hybridization and somatic cell genetics; mechanism of action of bromodeoxyuridine. *Mailing Add:* 3535 First Ave 11C San Diego CA 92103-4845

SILANDER, JOHN AUGUST, JR, PLANT ECOLOGY, EVOLUTION. *Current Pos:* asst prof, 76-83, ASSOC PROF BIOL SCI, UNIV CONN, 84- *Personal Data:* b Highland Park, Ill, Mar 1, 45; m 71; c 3. *Educ:* Pomona Col, BA, 67; Univ Mich, MA, 69; Duke Univ, PhD(bot), 76. *Prof Exp:* Instr biol, Peace Corps Prog, Ghana, 69-71. *Concurrent Pos:* Fulbright fel, Australian Nat Univ, 77-78. *Mem:* Ecol Soc Am; Soc Study Evolution; Am Soc Naturalists; Brit Ecol Soc. *Res:* Genetic, evolutionary, population and community aspects of plant ecology. *Mailing Add:* Dept Ecol Univ Conn U-42 75 N Eagleville Storrs Manfield CT 06269-0002

SILBAR, RICHARD R(OBERT), PHYSICS, MULTIMEDIA SOFTWARE FOR SCIENCE & ENGINEERING. *Current Pos:* group leader, 75-78, STAFF PHYSICIST, MEDIUM ENERGY NUCLEAR PHYSICS THEORY, LOS ALAMOS NAT LAB, 67- *Personal Data:* b Milwaukee, Wis, Jan 19, 37; m 63, Margaret Lincoln. *Educ:* Univ Mich, BS, 59, MS, 60, PhD(physics), 63. *Prof Exp:* Res assoc & instr physics, Johns Hopkins Univ, 63-65; res asst prof, Cath Univ Am, 65-67. *Concurrent Pos:* Vis scientist, Swiss Inst Nuclear Res, 73-74; vis prof, State Univ NY, 76-77, Univ Mass, 85-86; longterm acad sci exchange, Inst Nuclear Res, Moscow, USSR, 78; detaillee, Div Nuclear Physics, Dept Energy, 81-82, Div Adv Energy Proj, 91; pres, Whistlesoft, Inc. *Mem:* Fel Am Phys Soc; Am Asn Physics Teachers. *Res:* Particle and nuclear physics theory; medium energy physics; beam optics; simulation. *Mailing Add:* Los Alamos Nat Lab T-5 MS-B283 Los Alamos NM 87545. *Fax:* 505-662-7601; *E-Mail:* silbar@whistlesoft.com

SILBART, LAWRENCE K, CANCER RESEARCH. *Current Pos:* ASST PROF PATH, UNIV CONN, 91-, DIR, CTR ENVIRON HEALTH, 91- *Personal Data:* b Chicago, Ill, Jan 22, 58. *Educ:* Univ Mich, BS, 80, MS, 83, PhD(toxicol), 87. *Prof Exp:* Postdoctoral fel, Univ Mich, 87-89, res investr path, 89-91. *Mem:* Am Asn Immunologists; Am Asn Path; Soc Mucosal Immunol. *Mailing Add:* Univ Conn Ctr Environ Health 3636 Horsebarn Rd Box U-39 Storrs CT 06269-4039. *Fax:* 860-486-4375; *E-Mail:* lsilbart@anscicag.uconn.edu

SILBAUGH, STEVEN A, LUNG PHYSIOLOGY, PHARMACOLOGY. *Current Pos:* SR RES SCIENTIST, LILLY CORP CTR, 87- *Personal Data:* b Davenport, Iowa, Aug 27, 49; m 77; c 1. *Educ:* Univ NMex, PhD(biol), 80. *Mem:* Am Physiol Soc; Ind Thoracic Soc; Sigma Xi. *Res:* Pulmonary physiology and pharmacology, aerosol science, development of novel agents to treat asthma; inflammation research. *Mailing Add:* Eli Lilly & Co Lilly Corporate Ctr Indianapolis IN 46285-0001

SILBER, HERBERT BRUCE, INORGANIC CHEMISTRY. *Current Pos:* PROF CHEM, SAN JOSE STATE UNIV, 86-; DIR, NUCLEAR SCI FACIL. *Personal Data:* b New York, NY, Apr 3, 41; m 66; c 2. *Educ:* Lehigh Univ, BS, 62, MS, 64; Univ Calif, Davis, PhD(inorg chem), 67. *Prof Exp:* Swedish Govt fel & Fulbright-Hays travel grant, Royal Inst Technol, Stockholm, 67-68 & Univ Md, College Park, 68-69; asst prof chem, Univ Md, Baltimore County, 69-75; prof chem, Univ Tex, San Antonio, 75-85. *Mem:* Am Chem Soc. *Res:* Lanthanide chemistry; metal ion complexation chemistry; solvation; relaxation kinetics; ultrasonic absorption. *Mailing Add:* Chem Dept San Jose State Univ San Jose CA 95192-0101

SILBER, ROBERT, internal medicine, hematology, for more information see previous edition

SILBER, ROBERT, MATHEMATICS. *Current Pos:* asst prof math, 68-81, ASSOC PROF MATH, NC STATE UNIV, 81- *Personal Data:* b Montgomery, WVa, Nov 8, 37; m 64; c 2. *Educ:* Vanderbilt Univ, BA, 57; Univ Ala, MA, 63; Clemson Univ, PhD(math), 68. *Prof Exp:* Aerospace technologist, NASA, 58-63. *Mem:* Am Math Soc; Math Asn Am. *Res:* Optimization theory; functional analysis. *Mailing Add:* 2743 Sevier St Durham NC 27705

SILBERBERG, DONALD H, NEUROLOGY. *Current Pos:* assoc neurol, Univ Pa, 63-65, from asst prof to assoc prof neurol & ophthal, 65-71, vchmn neurol dept, 74-82, chmn, Neurol Dept, 82-94, PROF NEUROL & OPHTHAL, SCH MED, UNIV PA, 71- *Personal Data:* b Washington, DC, Mar 2, 34; m 59; c 2. *Educ:* Univ Mich, MD, 58. *Hon Degrees:* MA, Univ Pa, 71. *Prof Exp:* Resident neurol, NIH, 59-61; Fulbright fel neurol & neuro-ophthal, Nat Hosp, London, Eng, 61-62; USPHS spec fel neuro-ophthal, Sch Med, Wash Univ, 62-63. *Concurrent Pos:* Consult, Philadelphia Vet Admin Hosp, 66-82 & Childrens Hosp Philadelphia, 67- *Mem:* Am Acad Neurol; Am Neurol Asn; Am Asn Neuropath; Am Soc Neurochem; Soc Neurosci. *Res:* Pathogenesis and treatment of multiple sclerosis. *Mailing Add:* Dept Neurol Univ Pa Med Ctr Philadelphia PA 19104

SILBERBERG, I(RWIN) HAROLD, CHEMICAL ENGINEERING. *Current Pos:* ASST DIR, UNIV DIV, TEX PETROL RES COMT, UNIV TEX, AUSTIN, 60- *Personal Data:* b Austin, Tex, Feb 25, 26; m 49; c 4. *Educ:* Univ Tex, BS, 47, MS, 51, PhD(chem eng), 58. *Prof Exp:* Sr res technologist, Field Res Lab, Socony Mobil Oil Co, 57-60. *Mem:* Am Chem Soc; Am Inst Chem Engrs; Am Soc Petrol Engrs; Am Inst Chemists; Nat Soc Prof Engrs. *Res:* Volumetric and phase behavior of fluids, particularly hydrocarbons; petroleum production and reservoir engineering; thermodynamics. *Mailing Add:* Petroleum Eng Dept Univ Tex CPE 3118 Austin TX 78712-1061

SILBERBERG, REIN, COSMIC RAY PHYSICS, NUCLEAR ASTROPHYSICS. *Current Pos:* CONSULT, HIGH ENERGY ASTROPHYSICS, ROANOKE COL, 95- *Personal Data:* b Tallinn, Estonia, Jan 15, 32; US citizen; m 65, Ene-Liis Rammul; c Hugo & Ingrid. *Educ:* Univ Calif, Berkeley, AB, 55, MA, 56, PhD(physics), 60. *Honors & Awards:* Sigma Xi Award for Pure Sci. *Prof Exp:* Res asst physics, Univ Calif, 56-60; res assoc, Nat Acad Sci-Nat Res Coun, US Naval Res Lab, 60-62, res physicist, 62-90, actg chief scientist, Lab Cosmic Ray Physics, 81-83, dep br head, Gamma & Cosmic Ray, Astrophys, 84-90; consult, Univ Space Res Asn, 90-95. *Concurrent Pos:* Assoc Dir, Int Sch Cosmic Ray Astrophys, Erice, Italy, 78-86. *Mem:* Am Geophys Union; Radiation Res Soc; Am Astron Soc; Sigma Xi; Int Astron Union; fel Am Phys Soc; Asn Sci; N 70 Acad Sci. *Res:* Cosmic ray effects on microelectronics; acceleration of cosmic rays in accretion disks of ultra-massive black holes; isotopic and elementary composition of cosmic rays; solar modulation and transformation of cosmic ray composition in space; spallation and fission reactions; neutrino astronomy; radiobiological effects of heavy cosmic ray nuclei. *Mailing Add:* 7507 Hamilton Spring Rd Bethesda MD 20817-4541

SILBERBERG, RUTH, PATHOLOGY. *Current Pos:* VIS SCIENTIST, HEBREW HADASSAH UNIV, 76- *Personal Data:* b Kassel, Germany, Mar 20, 06; nat US; m 33. *Educ:* Breslau Univ, MD, 31. *Prof Exp:* Asst, Path Inst, Breslau Univ, 30-33; pathologist, Jewish Hosp, 33; vol res path, Dalhousie Univ, 34-36 & Wash Univ, 37-41; asst, NY Univ, 41-44; from instr to prof, 45-74, emer prof path, Sch Med, Wash Univ, 74-76. *Concurrent Pos:* Dean fel, NY Univ, 41-44; actg pathologist, Jewish Hosp, St Louis, 45-46; pathologist, Barnard Free Skin & Cancer Hosp, 47; sr pathologist, Hosp Div, City of St Louis, 47-59. *Mem:* Am Soc Exp Path; Soc Exp Biol & Med; Soc Develop Biol; Am Asn Path & Bact; Am Asn Cancer Res. *Res:* Experimental pathology; skeletal growth and aging; hormonal carcinogenesis; developmental potencies of the lymphocyte; pathogenesis of osteoarthrosis. *Mailing Add:* Dept Path Hebrew Univ Box 1172 Jerusalem Israel

SILBERFELD, MICHEL, PSYCHIATRY, EPIDEMIOLOGY. *Current Pos:* COORDR COMPETENCY CLINIC, 88- *Personal Data:* b Paris, France, Feb 15, 46; Can citizen; c 1. *Educ:* McGill Univ, BSc, 66, MDCM, 70; Univ Toronto, MSc, 73. *Prof Exp:* ASST PROF EPIDEMIOL & PSYCHIAT, UNIV TORONTO, 76-; staff psychiatrist, Wellesley Hosp, 78-85, Psychiatrist, Baycrest Ctr Geriat Care, 85-88. *Concurrent Pos:* Consult & res scientist psychiat & epidemiol, Addiction Res Found, 76-78; consult, Princess Margaret Hosp, 78-, mem staff, 79- *Res:* Social psychiatry. *Mailing Add:* Baycrest Ctr Geriat Care 3560 Bathurst St North York ON M6A 2E1 Can

SILBERG, STANLEY LOUIS, EPIDEMIOLOGY, INFECTIOUS DISEASES. *Current Pos:* assoc prof biostatist & epidemiol, 69-72, actg chmn, 78-84, vchmn 81-84, PROF BIOSTATIST & EPIDEMIOL, SCH PUB HEALTH, HEALTH SCI CTR, UNIV OKLA, 72- *Personal Data:* b Kansas City, Mo, Dec 27, 27; m 56, Irene Goldstein; c Craig R & Steven H. *Educ:* Univ Kans, AB, 51, MA, 52; Univ Minn, MPH, 59, PhD(epidemiol), 65. *Honors & Awards:* Sigma Xi Res Asst. *Prof Exp:* Res asst mycol, Kans State Health Dept, 52-53 & Sch Med, Univ Kans, 53-54; res fel epidemiol, Univ Minn, 57-61; asst prof, Sch Med, Univ Mo-Columbia, 61-69. *Concurrent Pos:* Mo Div Health grant, 63-65; USPHS grant, 65-; consult, USPHS Commun Dis Ctr, Ga, 66-76, US Pub Health Comn Corps, 57- *Mem:* Sigma Xi. *Res:* Infectious disease epidemiology. *Mailing Add:* 2905 NW 112th St Oklahoma City OK 73120

SILBERGELD, ELLEN K, EPIDEMIOLOGY, TOXICOLOGY. *Current Pos:* PROF EPIDEM & PREV MED, PATH & TOXICOL, UNIV MD, 91- *Personal Data:* b Washington, DC, 1945; m 69, Mark; c Sophia & Nick. *Educ:* Vassar Col, AB, 67; Johns Hopkins Univ, PhD(eng), 72. *Hon Degrees:* LLD, Col Notre Dame, 93. *Honors & Awards:* Barsky Award, Am Pub Health Asn, 92. *Prof Exp:* Fel neurosci, Johns Hopkins Sch Hyg, 72-75; staff fel neuropharm, Nat Inst Neurol & Commun Disorders & Stroke, NIH, 75-79, sect chief neurotoxicol, 79-81; chief scientist Toxicol Environ Defense Fund, 82-91. *Concurrent Pos:* Deleg, US & USSR Environ Health Exchange, 77-78; mem, US Dept Human Health Serv, 77-81; lectr continuing med, educ environ & occup med, 78-88; adv, Hyperkinesis & Diet, Nutrit Found, 75-78; bd mem toxicology, Nat Acad Sci, 83-89, US Environ Protection Agency Sci Bd, 83-90, & 94-, Sci Counr, Nat Inst Environ Health Sci, 90-93; Baldwin Scholar, Col of Notre Dame; Fulbright Scholar; MacArthur fel, 93-; consult, Who-Ilo, World Bank. *Mem:* Soc Neurosci; Int Brain Res Orgn; Am Soc Pharmacol & Exp Therapeut; Am Soc Neurochem; Soc Occup & Environ Health; Am Pub Health Asn; Soc Toxicol. *Res:* Neurotoxicology and environmental epidemiology and toxicology; adverse effects of chemicals and drugs on nervous system function; lead poisoning; developmental neurosciences. *Mailing Add:* 4640 Schenley Rd Baltimore MD 21210-2526. *E-Mail:* esilber@epin.ab.umd.edu

SILBERGELD, SAM, psychiatry, stress, for more information see previous edition

SILBERGER, ALLAN JOSEPH, MATHEMATICS. *Current Pos:* assoc prof, 75-80, PROF MATH, CLEVELAND STATE UNIV, 80- *Personal Data:* b York, Pa, Aug 24, 33; m 57; c 4. *Educ:* Univ Rochester, AB, 55; Johns Hopkins Univ, MA, 62, PhD(math), 66. *Prof Exp:* Assoc math, Appl Physics Lab, Johns Hopkins Univ, 58-64, instr, Univ, 64-66; asst prof, Bowdoin Col, 66-71; mem, Inst Advan Study, 71-73; guest prof, Math Inst, Univ Bonn, WGer, 73-74; vis assoc prof, Univ Mass, 74-75. *Mem:* Am Math Soc; Math Asn Am. *Res:* Representation theory; group theory. *Mailing Add:* Dept Math Cleveland State Univ Euclid Ave at E 24th St Cleveland OH 44115-2403

SILBERGER, DONALD MORISON, MATHEMATICS. *Current Pos:* ASSOC PROF MATH, STATE UNIV NY, NEW PALTZ, 83- *Personal Data:* b York, Pa, Feb 26, 30; m 80, Kathryn Kemp; c Frieda, Eva, Sylvia, Julia & Daniel. *Educ:* Harvard Univ, BA, 53; Univ Wash, MS, 61, PhD(math), 73. *Prof Exp:* High sch instr, Ohio, 56-58; NSF res asst, 62-63; instr math, Idaho State Univ, 63-65; assoc prof, Butler Univ, 65-67; lectr, Western Wash State Col, 67-68; from asst prof to assoc prof, Tougaloo Southern Christian Col, 68-74 & 76-77; spec asst prof math, Univ Colo, Boulder, 74-76; prof post grad math, Fed Univ Santa Catarina, Brazil, 77-82; assoc prof math, St Martin's Col, Olympia, Wash, 82-83. *Mem:* NY Acad Sci; Am Math Soc; Planetary Soc; Math Asn Am; Brazilian Soc Math. *Res:* Finite combinatorics; algebraic theory of semigroups; theory of regular finite simple hypergraphs; logic; universal terms; combinational algebra; sequence-valued functions of a sequence variable. *Mailing Add:* 44 Church St PO Box 1080 New Paltz NY 12561-1080. *E-Mail:* silbergd@npvm.newpaltz.edu

SILBERGLEIT, ALLEN, SURGERY, PHYSIOLOGY. *Current Pos:* from instr to assoc prof, 62-80, PROF SURG & PHYSIOL, SCH MED, WAYNE STATE UNIV, 80- *Personal Data:* b Springfield, Mass, Mar 8, 28; m 56, Ina Richman; c Richard, Nina & Robert. *Educ:* Univ Mass, BA, 49, MS, 51; Univ Cincinnati, MD, 55; Wayne State Univ, PhD(physiol), 65; Am Bd Surg, dipl, 61; Bd Thoracic Surg, dipl, 65. *Prof Exp:* From intern to resident surg, Univ Minn, 55-60; med officer, USAF & chief surg serv, Sheppard AFB Hosp, Tex, 60-62. *Concurrent Pos:* Mich Heart Asn res grants; resident thoracic surg & clin investr, Allen Park Vet Admin Hosp, Detroit, 62-65; surgeon, Detroit Receiving Hosp, 62-, Harper Hosp, Detroit, 87- & dir surg, St Joseph Mercy Hosp, Pontiac, 66-; gov, Am Col Surgeons, 90- *Mem:* Fel Am Col Surgeons; Soc Thoracic Surg; Am Heart Asn; Am Physiol Soc; Sigma Xi; Am Trauma Soc. *Res:* Cardiopulmonary, vascular and gastrointestinal problems; surgical physiology; research methods; application of basic science in training of surgical residents. *Mailing Add:* St Joseph Mercy Hosp 900 Woodward Ave Pontiac MI 48341-2985

SILBERGLITT, RICHARD STEPHEN, MICROWAVE PROCESSING OF MATERIALS, JOINING OF CERAMICS. *Current Pos:* VPRES MAT PROCESSING, FM TECHNOLOGIES, INC, 93- *Personal Data:* b Brooklyn, NY, Mar 9, 42; m 66; c 2. *Educ:* Stevens Inst Technol, BS, 63; Univ Pa, MS, 64, PhD(physics), 68. *Prof Exp:* Res assoc theoret solid state physics, Univ Pa, 68; lectr physics, Univ Calif, Santa Barbara, 68-69; res assoc solid state physics, Brookhaven Nat Lab, 69-71; asst prog dir theoret physics, Physics Sect, NSF, 71, asst prog dir solid state & low temperature physics, Div Mat Res, 71-72, assoc prog dir solid state physics, 72-75; mem energy study staff, Nat Acad Sci, 76-77; mem staff, DHR Inc, vpres, 84-87; sr scientist, Ques Tech, Inc, 87-90; co sr scientist, Tech Assessment & Transfer, Inc, 90-93. *Mem:* Am Phys Soc; Am Ceramic Soc; Mat Res Soc. *Res:* Materials processing using microwaves, electron beams and pulsed power; ceramic-ceramic and ceramic-metal joining; smart materials; coatings for suppression of voltage breakdown; microwave. *Mailing Add:* FM Tech Inc Patriot Sq 10529-B Braddock Rd Fairfax VA 22032. *E-Mail:* rsilberg@osf1.gmu.edu

SILBERHORN, GENE MICHAEL, MARINE BOTANY. *Current Pos:* sect head, Wetlands Res Sect, 72-80, assoc prof, 80-86, DEPT HEAD, WETLANDS ECOLOGY DEPT, VA INST MARINE SCI, 80- *Personal Data:* b Lenawee Co, Mich, Apr 30, 38; m 60; c 2. *Educ:* Eastern Mich Univ, BS, 63; WVA Univ, MS, 65; Kent State Univ, PhD(bot), 70. *Prof Exp:* Teaching asst gen bot & gen biol, WVa Univ, 63-65, NSF teaching fel, 65; asst prof ecol & Plant ecol, Radford Col, 65-67; NSF trainee gen bot, Kent State Univ, 67-70; Killian fel & instr, Univ Alta, 70-72. *Concurrent Pos:* ed, Wetlands J, Soc Wetlands Scientists, 84-87 & vpres, 88. *Mem:* Sigma Xi; Soc of Wetland Scientists. *Res:* Inventory and evaluation of tidal wetlands of Virginia; community structure of tidal freshwater marshes; monitoring of coastal habitats; reproductive life cycle of submerged aquatic vegetation. *Mailing Add:* Dept Marine Sci Col William & Mary Gloucester VA 23062

SILBERKLANG, MELVIN, TISSUE ENGINEERING, LARGE-SCALE PRODUCTION OF BIOPHARMACEUTICALS. *Current Pos:* VPRES RES & DEVELOP, ORTEC INT INC, 96- *Personal Data:* m 77, Roselyn M Wroblewski; c Lara M & Emily D. *Educ:* Columbia Univ, BA, 71; Mass Inst Technol, PhD(biochem), 77. *Prof Exp:* Fel, Dept Biochem & Biophys, Univ Calif, San Francisco, 77-80; asst res biochemist, 80-81; res fel, Merck & Co Inc Res Labs, 81-89, assoc dir, Dept Cell & Molecular Biol, 89-93; sr dir process res & develop, Enzon Inc, 93-95. *Concurrent Pos:* Consult, R-Gene Therapeut, 95, Johnson & Johnson Ortho, 96 & Cellstat Technol, 96. *Mem:* AAAS; Am Soc Cell Biol. *Res:* Expression of recombinant genes and production of corresponding proteins; scale-up of recombinant microbial and animal cell culture to produce such proteins as well as to produce viral vaccines; process research and development to produce natural and recombinant-derived proteins to pharmaceutical standards. *Mailing Add:* Ortec Int 21 Hillside Ave Englewood NJ 07631

SILBERLING, NORMAN JOHN, STRATIGRAPHY, TECTONICS. *Current Pos:* GEOLOGIST, US GEOL SURV, 75- *Personal Data:* b Oakland, Calif, Nov 28, 28; m 78; c 2. *Educ:* Stanford Univ, BS, 50, MS, 53, PhD(geol), 57. *Prof Exp:* Geologist, US Geol Surv, 50-66; from assoc prof to prof geol, Stanford Univ, 66-75. *Mem:* AAAS; Geol Soc Am; Am Geophys Union. *Res:* Pre-Tertiary stratigraphy and tectonics of western North America; paleontology and biostratigraphy of Triassic marine invertebrates. *Mailing Add:* 1235 Estes St Denver CO 80215

SILBERMAN, EDWARD, FLUID MECHANICS, WATER RESOURCES MANAGEMENT. *Current Pos:* RETIRED. *Personal Data:* b Minneapolis, Minn, Feb 8, 14; m 41, Idell Hillman; c Marilyn (Condon), Cyril J, Mark D & Sheldon I. *Educ:* Univ Minn, BCE, 35, MS, 36. *Prof Exp:* Water technician, State Planning Bd, Minn, 36; jr engr, flood control, Tenn Valley Authority, 37; jr engr construct, Minneapolis Dredging Co, 38; engr construct, US Civil Aeronaut Admin, 38-41 & 46; from res assoc to prof civil eng, Univ Minn, Minneapolis, 46-81, dir, St Anthony Falls Hydraul Lab, 63-74, emer prof civil eng, 82-88. *Concurrent Pos:* Comnr, Bassett Creek Water Mgt Comn, Hennepin Co, Minn, 72-; chmn, Water Resources Planning & Mgt Div, Am Soc Civil Engrs, 81. *Mem:* Hon mem Am Soc Civil Engrs; Soc Am Mil Engrs; fel Am Water Resources Asn (pres, 69); Int Asn Hydraul Res; AAAS. *Res:* Water resources management; model studies of hydraulic and fluid flow phenomena, supercavitating flows; boundary layers; turbulence; air-water mixtures; flow losses in closed and open conduits; underwater acoustics. *Mailing Add:* 5901 Laurel Ave Minneapolis MN 55416

SILBERMAN, ENRIQUE, MOLECULAR SPECTROSCOPY. *Current Pos:* PROF PHYSICS, FISK UNIV, 66-; DIR PHOTONIC MAT & DEVICES, NASA CTR, 92- *Personal Data:* b Buenos Aires, Arg, Dec 9, 21; m 49; c 2. *Educ:* Univ Buenos Aires, PhD(eng), 45. *Prof Exp:* Investr physics, Arg Atomic Energy Comn, 53-58, head dept, 58-63; prof, Univ Buenos Aires, 63-66. *Concurrent Pos:* Guest prof, Univ Notre Dame, 63; consult, Arg Nat Coun Sci Res, 64; vis prof, Vanderbilt Univ, 67- *Mem:* AAAS; Am Asn Physics Teachers; Am Phys Soc; Arg Physics Asn. *Res:* Infrared and Raman spectroscopy; normal coordinates analysis; inorganic ions in solid solutions; vibrational determination of crystal structures; ferroelectrics; semiconductors. *Mailing Add:* Dept Physics Fisk Univ Nashville TN 37208-3051. *Fax:* 615-329-8634; *E-Mail:* esilber@dubois.fisk.edu

SILBERMAN, MILES LOUIS, GEOCHEMISTRY. *Current Pos:* geologist, Pac Mineral Resources Br, US Geol Surv, 67-75, geologist, Alaskan Geol Br, 76-81, geologist, Marine Geol, 81-82, SR GEOLOGIST, OFF MINERAL RESOURCES, US GEOL SURV, 83- *Personal Data:* b New York, NY, Sept 25, 40; m 83, Karen Wenrich; c Daryl & Kevin. *Educ:* City Univ New York, BS, 63; Univ Rochester, MS, 67, PhD(geol), 71. *Prof Exp:* Sr geologist, Anaconda Minerals Co, 82-83. *Concurrent Pos:* Adj Prof Geol, Mackay Sch Mines, Univ Nev. *Mem:* Geochem Soc; Soc Econ Geologists. *Res:* Geochronology and geochemistry of igneous rocks and their associated ore deposits using chemical, isotopic and geol mapping techniques; exploration for precious and base metal deposits; regional and structural controls on localization of ore deposits. *Mailing Add:* 63 S Devinney St Golden CO 80401-5314. *Fax:* 303-236-5608

SILBERMAN, ROBERT G, ORGANIC CHEMISTRY, CHEMICAL EDUCATION. *Current Pos:* From asst prof to assoc prof, 65-82, PROF CHEM, STATE UNIV NY CORTLAND, 82- *Personal Data:* b New York, NY, Aug 20, 39; m 61; c 2. *Educ:* Brooklyn Col, BS, 60; Cornell Univ, MS, 63, PhD(org chem), 65. *Concurrent Pos:* Vis prof, Cornell Univ, 84 & 85, Univ Glasgow, Scotland; consult, Crown Restoration; mem chem & community implementation team, Chem Educ Div, Am Chem Soc, 88-90; consult, KSR Inc. *Mem:* Am Chem Soc; Nat Sci Teachers Asn; Sigma Xi. *Res:* Organic analysis; chemical education; laboratory programs; historic paint analysis; historic restoration of art objects. *Mailing Add:* Dept Chem State Univ NY Cortland NY 13045-0900

SILBERMAN, RONALD, CLINICAL MICROBIOLOGY, IMMUNOLOGY. *Current Pos:* Asst prof microbiol & immunol, 69-74, from asst prof to assoc prof, 71-93, PROF PATH, SCH MED, MED CTR, LA STATE UNIV, SHREVEPORT, 93- *Personal Data:* b Jackson, Mich, July 31, 32; m 55, Shirley G Novek; c Marc, David & Lisa. *Educ:* Temple Univ, BA, 58; Hahnemann Med Col, MS, 60; Univ Md, Baltimore City, PhD(microbiol), 70. *Concurrent Pos:* Chief microbiologist, Lab Serv, Vet Admin Med Ctr, Shreveport, 71-84; dir microbiol, Clin Lab, Med Ctr, La State Univ Hosp, Shreveport, 71-, asst dir, 72-; clin prof microbiol, Med Technol, La Tech Univ, Ruston, 81- *Mem:* Am Soc Microbiol; Asn Practrs in Infection Control. *Res:* Clinical microbiology; antimicrobial susceptibility; blood culture diagnostic methods. *Mailing Add:* Dept Path La State Univ Med Ctr 1501 Kings Hwy Shreveport LA 71130-3932. *Fax:* 318-674-5565

SILBERNAGEL, BERNARD GEORGE, MAGNETIC RESONANCE. *Current Pos:* mem staff, 72-81, SR RES ASSOC, EXXON RES & ENG CO, 81-, SECT HEAD, 86- *Personal Data:* b Wausau, Wis, Dec 13, 40; m 65, Susan Beitel; c Kathrine & Anne. *Educ:* Yale Univ, BS, 62; Univ Calif, San Diego, MS, 64, PhD(physics), 66. *Prof Exp:* Lectr physics, Univ Calif, Santa Barbara, 66-68, asst prof, 68-72. *Mem:* AAAS; fel Am Phys Soc; Am Chem Soc; Sigma Xi. *Res:* Magnetic resonance; solid state physics; superconductivity; magnetism; catalysis; coal science; molecular dynamics. *Mailing Add:* Exxon Res/Engr Co Clinton Township Rte 22 E Annandale NJ 08801. *Fax:* 908-730-3042; *E-Mail:* bgsil8e@erenj.com

SILBERNAGEL, MATT JOSEPH, PLANT PATHOLOGY, PLANT BREEDING. *Current Pos:* RETIRED. *Personal Data:* b Hague, NDak, May 13, 33; m 55; c 5. *Educ:* Univ Wash, BS, 57; Wash State Univ, PhD(plant path), 61. *Prof Exp:* Plant pathologist, Crops Res Div, Agr Res Serv, USDA, 61-95. *Concurrent Pos:* AID consult, Brazil, 70, India-Pakistan, 77, Cent Int de Agr Trop Workshops, 75 & 81 & AID Title XII Tanzanian-Wash State Univ, Bean Collabr Res Support Prog, 80-92. *Mem:* Am Phytopath Soc; Am Soc Hort Sci. *Res:* Breeding common beans for disease resistance, environmental stress tolerance and seed quality; study of bean-disease-environment interactions; improvement of beans for direct mechanical harvesting. *Mailing Add:* 904 Crescent Dr Grandview WA 98930

SILBERSCHATZ, ABRAHAM, OPERATING SYSTEMS, DATABASE SYSTEMS. *Current Pos:* From asst prof to assoc prof, 76-84, PROF COMPUTER SCI, UNIV TEX, AUSTIN, 84- *Personal Data:* b Haifa, Israel, May 1, 47; m 68; c 3. *Educ:* State Univ NY, Stony Brook, PhD(comput sci), 76. *Mem:* Asn Comput Mach; Inst Elec & Electronic Engrs. *Res:* Operating systems; distributed systems; database systems. *Mailing Add:* Info Sci Res Ctr MH 2T-210 Lucent Technol Bell Labs 600 Mountain Ave Murray Hill NJ 07974

SILBERSTEIN, EDWARD B, NUCLEAR MEDICINE, ONCOLOGY. *Current Pos:* from asst prof to assoc prof med, 70-78, assoc prof radiol, 72-77, ASSOC DIR NUCLEAR MED, RADIOISOTOPE LAB, UNIV CINCINNATI MED CTR, 68-, PROF RADIOL, 77-, PROF MED, 78- *Personal Data:* b Cincinnati, Ohio, Sept 3, 36; m 88, Jacqueline Merris Mack; c Scott & Lisa. *Educ:* Yale Univ, BS, 58; Harvard Univ, MD, 62; Am Bd Internal Med, cert, 69, recert, 80, cert hemat, 72, cert oncol, 81; Am Bd Nuclear Med, cert, 72. *Prof Exp:* Resident internal med, Cincinnati Gen Hosp, 63-64 & Univ Hosps of Cleveland, 66-67; trainee hemat, New Eng Med Ctr Hosps, 67-68. *Concurrent Pos:* Am Cancer Soc res grants, 72 & 74; chmn adv panel radiopharmaceut, US Pharmacopoeia, 85 & 90 & mem, stand subcomt on radiopharmaceut, 85-90; dir, Nuclear Med, Jewish Hosp, 76-95; agency for healthcare policy & res cancer pain panel, 92-94; chair, adv comt environ safety & health, Fernald, Ohio, Uranium Refinery, 86-91. *Mem:* AAAS; Am Col Physicians; Radiation Res Soc; fel Royal Soc Health; Am Soc Clin Oncol; Sigma Xi; Soc Nuclear Med; fel Am Col Nuclear Physicians. *Res:* Diagnosis of tumors with radiopharmaceuticals; treatment of bone pain from cancer with beta-omitting radicpharmaceutials. *Mailing Add:* ML 577 Univ Cincinnati Med Ctr Cincinnati OH 45267. *Fax:* 513-558-7690; *E-Mail:* silbereb@healthu.com

SILBERSTEIN, OTMAR OTTO, FOOD SCIENCE. *Current Pos:* CONSULT, 86-; VPRES TECHNOL ASSESSMENT, MONTEREY BAY FOOD GROUP. *Personal Data:* b Graz, Austria, Apr 18, 21; US citizen; m 47, Natasha Altschuller; c David & Robert. *Educ:* Mich State Univ, BS, 49, MS, 50; Cornell Univ, PhD(veg crops), 53. *Prof Exp:* Res asst, US Plant, Soil & Nutrit Lab, NY, 53-54; res chemist, Welch Grape Juice Co, 54-58; head, Dept Food Technol, Wallerstein Labs Div Baxter Labs, 58-63; dir res & develop, Gilroy Foods, Inc, 63-80; dir explor technol, McCormick & Co, Inc, 80-86. *Concurrent Pos:* Chmn educ comt, Hydroponic Soc Am. *Mem:* Am Chem Soc; Inst Food Technologists; Hydroponic Soc Am. *Res:* Food enzymology and flavor chemistry; dehydration of vegetables; biotechnology; tissue culture; hydroponics. *Mailing Add:* 841 Sixth St Gilroy CA 95020-5287

SILBERT, DAVID FREDERICK, BIOCHEMISTRY. *Current Pos:* Am Cancer Soc fel biol chem, Sch Med, 66-68, from asst prof to assoc prof, 68-77, PROF BIOL CHEM, SCH MED, WASHINGTON UNIV, 77- *Personal Data:* b Cambridge, Mass. *Educ:* Harvard Univ, AB, 58, MD, 62. *Prof Exp:* Intern & resident med, Sch Med, Washington Univ, 62-64; res assoc microbial genetics, Nat Inst Arthritis & Metab Dis, 64-66. *Concurrent Pos:* NIH res grant, 68-; res grant, Am Chem Soc, 75-; mem microbiol chem study sect, NIH, 75- *Mem:* Am Soc Biol Chem; Am Soc Microbiol; Am Chem Soc. *Res:* Biochemical genetics; membrane chemistry. *Mailing Add:* Dept Biochem & Molec Biophys Wash Univ Med Sch 4566 Scott Ave Box 8231 St Louis MO 63110-1093. *Fax:* 314-362-7183

SILBERT, JEREMIAH ELI, BIOCHEMISTRY, METABOLISM OF PROTEOGLYCANS. *Current Pos:* PROF MED, MED SCH, HARVARD UNIV, 81- *Educ:* Harvard Univ, MD, 57. *Mailing Add:* Vet Admin Med Ctr Bldg 70 200 Springs Rd Bedford MA 01730-1114. *Fax:* 781-275-3177

SILBERT, LEONARD STANTON, PHYSICAL CHEMISTRY, ORGANIC CHEMISTRY. *Current Pos:* RETIRED. *Personal Data:* b Philadelphia, Pa, Dec 16, 20. *Educ:* Philadelphia Col Pharm, BSc, 43; Univ Pittsburgh, PhD(chem), 53. *Prof Exp:* Jr prof asst, Eastern Regional Res Labs, USDA, 46-47, Nat Renderers Asn res fel, Eastern Utilization Res Br, 53-56, res chemist, Eastern Regional Res Ctr, 56-85. *Mem:* AAAS; Am Chem Soc; Am Oil Chemists Soc; Royal Soc Chem. *Res:* Synthesis of lipid compounds and their physical properties; structural determinations and applications of peroxide chemistry; organic thiocyanations; isopropenylation chemistry; free radical studies; food irradiation; carbanian. *Mailing Add:* Apt 105 Pastorius Bldg 7800 C Stenton Ave Philadelphia PA 19118-3007

SILBEY, ROBERT JAMES, PHYSICAL CHEMISTRY. *Current Pos:* from asst prof to assoc prof, 66-76, dept head chem, 90-95, PROF CHEM, MASS INST TECHNOL, 76- *Personal Data:* b Brooklyn, NY, Oct 19, 40; m 62, Susan Sorkin; c Jessica & Anna. *Educ:* Brooklyn Col, BS, 61; Univ Chicago, PhD(chem), 65. *Honors & Awards:* Alexander von Humboldt Sr Scientist Award, 89; Max Planck Award, 92. *Prof Exp:* Nat Acad Sci-Nat Res

Coun-Air Force Off Sci Res fel, Univ Wis, 65-66. *Concurrent Pos:* Res fel, Sloan Found, 68-70; Camille & Henry Dreyfus Found teacher scholar, 71-76; vis prof, Inst Theoret Physics, Univ Utrecht, 72-73 & 86; Guggenheim Found fel, 72-73. *Mem:* Fel Am Phys Soc; fel Am Acad Arts & Scis; fel AAAS; Am Chem Soc. *Res:* Quantum chemistry; theory of excited states of solids and molecules; theory of relaxation; theory of non linear optical materials. *Mailing Add:* Dept Chem Mass Inst Technol Cambridge MA 02139-4307. *E-Mail:* silbey@mit.edu

SILCOX, JOHN, INELASTIC ELECTRON SCATTERING. *Current Pos:* From asst prof to assoc prof eng physics, Cornell Univ, 61-70, actg chmn dept appl physics, 70-71, dir sch appl & eng physics, 71-74 & 79-83, PROF ENG PHYSICS, CORNELL UNIV, 70- *Personal Data:* b Saltash, Eng, May 26, 35; m 60; c 3. *Educ:* Bristol Univ, BSc, 57; Cambridge Univ, PhD(physics), 61. *Prof Exp:* Guggenheim Found fel, 67-68; mem solid state sci comt, Nat Res Coun, Nat Acad Sci, 78-82, chmn, 87-88. *Mem:* Fel Am Phys Soc; Electron Micros Soc Am(pres, 79). *Res:* Transmission electron microscopy; defects in crystals; inelastic electron scattering. *Mailing Add:* Dept Appl & Eng Physics Cornell Univ Clark Hall Ithaca NY 14853

SILCOX, WILLIAM HENRY, OFFSHORE DRILLING & OIL PRODUCTION SYSTEMS. *Current Pos:* RETIRED. *Personal Data:* b Taft, Calif, July 21, 22; m 52; c 5. *Educ:* Univ Calif, Berkeley, BS, 47. *Honors & Awards:* Offshore Distinguished Achievement Award for Individuals, 88. *Prof Exp:* Engr, Stand Oil Co, Calif, 47-51, lead mech engr, 54-62; proj engr, USAF, Wright Field, 53-54; sr offshore engr, Offshore Technol & Planning Staff, Chevron Corp, 62-67, div offshore engr, 67-78, offshore eng mgr, 75-85; consult, 85-88; vpres technol, Wellstream Corp, 88-89. *Concurrent Pos:* Consult, NSF Deep Sea Drilling Proj, 67-85; mem, Nat Petrol Coun Task Group Arctic Oil & Gas Res, 78-79, Nat Res Coun Marine Bd, 80-83 & Ad Hoc Comt Int Stand, Am Petrol Inst, 83-85. *Mem:* Nat Acad Eng; Soc Petrol Engrs. *Res:* Operation and development of offshore oil platforms; subsea drilling and production systems; arctic drilling and production systems for water depth to 6000 feet. *Mailing Add:* PO Box 4532 Incline Village NV 89450

SILEN, WILLIAM, SURGERY. *Current Pos:* Johnson & Johnson prof surg, 75, PROF SURG, HARVARD MED SCH, 66-, DIR, ADVAN CLIN SURG, 66-; EMER SURGEON-IN-CHIEF, BETH ISRAEL HOSP, BOSTON. *Personal Data:* b San Francisco, Calif, Sept 13, 27; m 47; c 3. *Educ:* Univ Calif, Berkeley, BA, 46; Univ Calif, San Francisco, MD, 49; Am Bd Surg, dipl, 58. *Hon Degrees:* MA, Harvard Univ, 66. *Prof Exp:* Intern, Univ Calif Hosp, San Francisco, 49-50, asst resident gen surg, 50; ward surgeon, Travis AFB, 50-52; asst resident gen surg, Univ Calif Hosp, San Francisco, 52-56, chief resident, 56-57; from instr to asst prof surg, Sch Med, Univ Colo, 57-60; from asst prof to assoc prof, Sch Med, Univ Calif, San Francisco, 60-66. *Concurrent Pos:* Asst chief surg, Denver Vet Admin Hosp, 57-59, chief, 59-60; asst chief, San Francisco Gen Hosp, 60-61, chief, 61-66; chmn & surgeon-in-chief, Dept Surg, Beth Israel Hosp, 66-; mem, Vet Admin Res Comt, 69-73; consult surg, Children's Hosp Med Ctr, Boston, 68-; mem, Am Bd Surg, 70-73, sr mem, 73-; ed, Yr Bk Surg, 70-84; chmn, Comt Res, Am Gastroenterol Asn, 71-73, mem gov bd, 72-75; mem, Surg B Study Sect, NIH, 72-76; chmn, Workgroup Eval Ther, Nat Comn Digestive Dis, 77-78; co-ed Surg Alert, 84, consult ed, Gastroenterol, 86-91. *Mem:* Inst Med-Nat Acad Sci; Soc Clin Surgeons; Soc Univ Surgeons; fel Am Col Surgeons; Asn Acad Surg; Am Surg Asn; AMA; Soc Exp Biol & Med; Am Fedn Clin Res; Am Gastroenterol Asn (vpres, 76, pres-elect, 77, pres, 78). *Res:* Protective mechanisms in gastric and duodenal mucosa; physiologic effects of gastrointestinal operations. *Mailing Add:* Beth Israel Hosp 330 Brookline Ave Boston MA 02215

SILER, WILLIAM MACDOWELL, BIOMATHEMATICS, THEORETICAL BIOLOGY. *Current Pos:* CONSULT, 87- *Personal Data:* b Houston, Tex, Aug 5, 20; m 74; c 3. *Educ:* Stevens Inst Technol, MS, 49; City Univ New York, PhD(biol), 72. *Honors & Awards:* Distinguished Data Processing Prof, Data Processing Mgt Asn, 84. *Prof Exp:* Proj engr, Exp Towing Tank, Stevens Inst Technol, 47-49; physicist radiol physics, Mem Sloan-Kettering Cancer Ctr, Mem Hosp, New York, 59-65; assoc prof & chmn med comput sci prog, Downstate Med Ctr, Brooklyn, 65-72; prof biomath, Univ Ala, Birmingham, 72-80, chmn dept, 72-75; dir clin comput, Caraway Med Ctr, Birmingham, Ala, 80-87. *Concurrent Pos:* Mem, Study Sect Comput & Biomath Res, NIH, 69-73; Biostatist & Epidemiol Contract Rev Comt, Nat Cancer Inst, 81-85. *Mem:* Am Asn Physicists Med; Biomed Eng Soc; Sigma Xi; Inst Elec & Electronics Engrs. *Res:* Artificial intelligence and image processing; modelling biological systems; radiological physics; computers in cardiology. *Mailing Add:* 1901 Hoke Ave Birmingham AL 35217

SILER-KHODR, THERESA M, REPRODUCTIVE ENDOCRINOLOGY. *Current Pos:* from asst prof to assoc prof, 76-86, PROF OBSTET & GYNEC, UNIV TEX, SAN ANTONIO, 86- *Personal Data:* b Pomona, Calif, June 17, 47; m 74; c 3. *Educ:* Immaculate Heart Col, BA, 68; Univ Hawaii, PhD(biochem), 71. *Prof Exp:* Teaching asst biochem, Univ Hawaii, 68-71; scientist reproductive biol, Univ Calif, San Diego, 72-74; asst prof obstet & gynec, Am Univ Beirut, 74-76. *Concurrent Pos:* Prin investr, NIH, 81-84 & 88-92, core dir, 78-92. *Mem:* Am Endocrine Soc; Soc Gynec Invest; Endocrine Soc; Sigma Xi; Soc Study Reproduction. *Res:* Endocrine and parocrine control of human pregnancy; physiology and role in pathophysiologies of pregnancy. *Mailing Add:* 7703 Floyd Curl Dr San Antonio TX 78230

SILEVITCH, MICHAEL B, ELECTROMAGNETISM. *Current Pos:* PROF ELEC & COMPUT ENG, NORTHEASTERN UNIV, 81-, DIR, CTR ELECTROMAGNETICS RES, 83- *Educ:* Northeastern Univ, BS, 65, MS, 66, PhD(elec eng), 71; Brandeis Univ, MA, 70. *Mem:* Inst Elec & Electronical Engrs; Am Geophysical Union. *Res:* Space physics, particularly in the temporal and spatial structure of the Aurora Borealis and the propagation of magnetic storms; additional research interests include the kinetics of the photographic development process, the statistical mechanics of dense plasmas, properties of solid state plasma, electron and ion beam dynamics, and high power microwave devices. *Mailing Add:* Ctr for Electromagnetics Res Northeastern Univ 235 Forsyth Bldg Boston MA 02115

SILFLOW, CAROLYN DOROTHY, CELL BIOLOGY. *Current Pos:* asst prof cell & develop biol, 82-88, assoc prof, Dept Genetics & Cell Biol, 88-93, ADJ PROF, DEPT PLANT BIOL, UNIV MINN, 89-, PROF, DEPT GENETICS & CELL BIOL, 93- *Personal Data:* b Kendrick, Idaho, Jan 8, 50; m 81, Paul Lefebvre; c Matthew. *Educ:* Pac Lutheran Univ, BS, 72; Univ Ga, PhD(bot), 77. *Prof Exp:* Fel, Dept Biol, Yale Univ, 77-81. *Concurrent Pos:* Instr physiol, MBL, Woods Hole, Mass, 83. *Mem:* Am Soc Cell Biol; Soc Develop Biol; Int Soc Plant Molecular Biol. *Res:* Molecular/genetic analysis of microtubule function in chlamydomonas and higher plants. *Mailing Add:* Dept Genetics & Cell Biol Univ Minn 1445 Gortner Ave 250 Biosci Ctr St Paul MN 55108-1095. *Fax:* 612-625-5754; *E-Mail:* carolyn@molbio.cbs.umn.edu

SILFVAST, WILLIAM THOMAS, PHYSICS. *Current Pos:* MEM TECH STAFF, BELL TEL LABS, 67- *Personal Data:* b Salt Lake City, Utah, June 7, 37; m 59; c 3. *Educ:* Univ Utah, BS(math) & BS(physics), 61, PhD(physics), 65. *Prof Exp:* Res assoc physics, Univ Utah, 65-66; NATO fel, Oxford Univ, 66-67. *Concurrent Pos:* NATO fel. *Mem:* Am Phys Soc; Optical Soc Am. *Res:* Lasers and plasma physics, with specific interest in gaseous and metal vapor lasers; recombination lasers and laser-produced plasmas. *Mailing Add:* 702 Iron Wood Ct Winter Springs FL 32708

SILHACEK, DONALD LE ROY, ENDOCRINOLOGY, INSECT DEVELOPMENT. *Current Pos:* RES CHEMIST, INSECT ATTRACTANTS LAB, AGR RES SERV, USDA, 65- *Personal Data:* b Norfolk, Nebr, Nov 9, 37; m 60; c 2. *Educ:* Univ Nebr, Lincoln, BSc, 58, MSc, 61; Univ Wis-Madison, PhD(biochem, entom), 66. *Concurrent Pos:* Instr, Armstrong State Col, 66-68; asst prof, Univ Fla, 70-80, prof, 80- *Mem:* Am Chem Soc; Am Soc Zoologists. *Res:* Endogenous mechanisms controlling developmental protein metabolism in insects; hormonal mechanisms controlling development of insects. *Mailing Add:* 4600 NW 33rd Ct Gainesville FL 32606

SILHAVY, THOMAS J, PROTEIN EXPORT. *Current Pos:* PROF MOLECULAR BIOL, PRINCETON UNIV, 84-, DIR GRAD STUDIES, MOLECULAR BIOL DEPT, 89- *Personal Data:* b Wauseon, Ohio, Jan 13, 48; m 69, Daileen Stutzman; c Marc & Ned. *Educ:* Ferris State Col, BS, 71; Harvard Univ, MA, 74, PhD(biochem), 75. *Hon Degrees:* DSc, Ferris State Col, 82. *Honors & Awards:* Advan Technol Achievement Award, Litton, 82. *Prof Exp:* Jane Coffin Childs Found fel, 75-77; Med Found Res fel, 78-79; instr microbiol & molecular genetics, Harvard Med Sch, 78-79; dir, Lab Genetics & Recombinant DNA, Nat Cancer Inst, Fredrick Cancer Ctr, Md, 79-84; instr advan bact genetics, Cold Spring Harbor Lab, 81-85. *Concurrent Pos:* Mem, Life Sci Peer Rev Comt, 85-, prog dir, Genetics Predoctoral Training Grant, NIH, 87-, co-dir, Life Sci Res Found, 89-; mem, microbial physiol & genetics study sect, NIH, 85-89, genetic basis dis study sect, NIH, 93-; mem bd trustees, Cold Spring Harbor Lab, 86-90; organizer, Bact Genetics Course, Int Ctr Genetic Eng & Biotechnol, Trieste, Italy, 90-93; div chmn, Am Soc Microbiol, 92. *Mem:* Am Soc Microbiol. *Res:* Genetic analysis in Escherichia coli; molecular mechanisms of protein export and secretion; control of gene expression by transmember signal transduction. *Mailing Add:* Dept Molecular Biol Princeton Univ 310 Lewis Thomas Lab Princeton NJ 08544. *Fax:* 609-258-6175; *E-Mail:* tsilhavy@molecular.princeton.edu

SILJAK, DRAGOSLAV (D), SYSTEMS THEORY, CONTROL ENGINEERING. *Current Pos:* from assoc prof to prof, 64-84, B & M PROF ELEC ENG, UNIV SANTA CLARA, 84- *Personal Data:* b Beograd, Yugoslavia, Sept, 10, 33; m 67; c 2. *Educ:* Univ Beograd, BSEG, 58, MSEE, 61, ScD(elec eng), 63. *Prof Exp:* Docent prof elec eng, Univ Beograd, 63-64. *Concurrent Pos:* NASA res grant, Univ Santa Clara, 65-77; NSF grant, 68-69; Dept Energy contract, 77-80; fel Japan Soc Promotion Sci; Distinguished prof, Fulbright Found. *Mem:* Fel Inst Elec & Electronics Engrs; hon mem Serbian Acad Arts & Sci. *Res:* Concepts, characterizations and methodology in studies of dimensionality, uncertainty and structure of complex dynamic systems, with applications to electric power networks, large space structures, model ecosystems and economics; population biology; space vehicles. *Mailing Add:* Dept Elec Eng Univ Santa Clara Santa Clara CA 95053. *Fax:* 408-554-5474; *E-Mail:* dsiljak@scuacc.scu.edu

SILK, JOSEPH IVOR, COSMOLOGY, PARTICLE ASTROPHYSICS. *Current Pos:* from asst prof to assoc prof, 70-78, PROF ASTRON, UNIV CALIF, BERKELEY, 78-, PROF PHYSICS, 89- *Personal Data:* b London, Eng, Dec 3, 42; m 68, Margaret W Kuhn; c Jonathan & Timothy. *Educ:* Cambridge Univ, MA, 63; Harvard Univ, PhD(astron), 68. *Prof Exp:* Res fel, Cambridge Univ, 68-69; res assoc, Princeton Univ, 69-70. *Concurrent Pos:* Alfred P Sloan Found fel, 72-74; John Simon Guggenheim Found fel, 75-76; mem, Inst Advan Study, Princeton, 75-76; Miller prof, Miller Found Basic Res, 80-81; res assoc, Inst Astrophys, Paris, 82-83; prin investr, NASA, NSF, Dept Energy & Calspace; vis fel, Army & Navy Union, 90. *Mem:* Am Astron Soc; Royal Astron Soc; Int Astron Union; fel AAAS; Am Phys Soc. *Res:*

Theoretical studies of cosmology, galaxy formation and star formation; interface of particle physics and astrophysics. *Mailing Add:* Dept Astron Univ Calif Berkeley CA 94720. *Fax:* 510-642-3411; *E-Mail:* silk@ucbast.berkeley.edu

SILK, MARGARET WENDY KUHN, QUANTITATIVE BOTANY. *Current Pos:* ASST, ASSOC & RES SCIENTIST, AGR EXP STA & ASST, ASSOC & PROF QUANT PLANT SCI, UNIV CALIF, DAVIS, 76- *Personal Data:* b Baltimore, Md, Nov 16, 46; m 68; c Timothy & Jonathan. *Educ:* Harvard Univ, BA, 68; Univ Calif, Berkeley, PhD(bot), 75. *Prof Exp:* Teaching asst, Univ Calif, Berkeley, 70-75; res fel biol, Univ Pa, 75-76. *Concurrent Pos:* Vis Professorship Women, NSF, Univ Calif, Berkeley, 86; vis res fel, Sch Biol Sci, Australian Nat Univ, Canberra, 90. *Mem:* Am Soc Plant Physiol; Bot Soc Am; Soc Develop Biol; Soc Math Biol. *Res:* Quantitative aspects of plant development, morphogenesis, physiology and plant-water-environment interactions; biomechanics. *Mailing Add:* Land Air & Water Resources Univ Calif Davis CA 95616

SILL, ALAN F, HIGH ENERGY PHYSICS. *Current Pos:* ASST PROF, DEPT PHYSICS, TEX TECH UNIV, 92- *Personal Data:* b Scotts Bluff, Nebr, Dec 6, 55. *Educ:* Lewis & Clark Col, BS, 77; Am Univ, PhD(physics), 87. *Prof Exp:* Asst prof, Dept Physics & Astron, Univ Rochester, 87-92. *Concurrent Pos:* SST nat fel, Tex Nat Lab, 90-91. *Mem:* Am Phys Soc. *Res:* High energy physics. *Mailing Add:* Dept Physics Tex Tech Univ PO Box 41051 Lubbock TX 79409

SILL, ARTHUR DEWITT, STRUCTURAL CHEMISTRY, ORGANIC CHEMISTRY. *Current Pos:* RETIRED. *Personal Data:* b Akron, Ohio, Dec 1, 21; m 47, Grace Nuzum; c Barbara I (Woods), James J & Robert T. *Educ:* Ohio State Univ, BS, 48; Univ Cincinnati, MS, 61, PhD(org chem), 64. *Prof Exp:* Prin chemist, Battelle Mem Inst, 49-55; res asst org prod res, Merrell-Nat Labs Div, Richardson-Merrell, Inc, 55-64, proj leader org res dept, 64-71, org chemist, Anal Res Dept, 71-80, sr anal chemist, Merrell Dow Res Inst, 80-86. *Res:* Identification of structure of organic substances, including impurities and metabolites, via spectroscopic methods, including mass spectrometry and nuclear magnetic resonance; organic synthesis; development of analytical methods for drug substances. *Mailing Add:* 22 Beckford Dr Greenhills OH 45218

SILL, CLAUDE WOODROW, ANALYTICAL CHEMISTRY, RADIOCHEMISTRY. *Current Pos:* RETIRED. *Personal Data:* b Layton, Utah, Oct 29, 18; m 55, Lorraine McAllister; c Steven, David & Claudia. *Educ:* Univ Utah, AB, 39, MA, 41. *Prof Exp:* Researcher, Iowa State Col, 41-42; chemist, US Bur Mines, 42-51; chief anal chem br, AEC, 51-75; chief anal chem br, Health Serv Lab, Energy Res & Develop Admin, 75-77; sr scientist, Radiol & Environ Sci Lab, Dept Energy, 77-80; sr scientist, EG&G Idaho Inc, 80-82, sci specialist, 82-87, prin scientist, 87-95. *Mem:* Sigma Xi. *Res:* Synthesis of organo-uranium compounds; analytical methods; high-resolution alpha spectrometry. *Mailing Add:* 2751 S Blvd Idaho Falls ID 83404

SILL, LARRY R, MAGNETISM, LOW TEMPERATURE SOLID STATE PHYSICS. *Current Pos:* Prof physics, Northern Ill Univ, 64-95, actg head, Physics Dept, 66-68, assoc dean, Col Lib Arts & Sci, 69-80, dir, Technol Commercialization Ctr, 86-95, EMER PROF PHYSICS, NORTHERN ILL UNIV, 95- *Personal Data:* b Fairmont, Minn, Sept 10, 37; m 59, Judith A Larson; c Jennifer & Stephen. *Educ:* Carleton Col, BA, 59; Iowa State Univ, PhD(physics), 64. *Concurrent Pos:* Vis scientist, Argonne Nat Lab, 83-84. *Mem:* Am Phys Soc; Am Asn Physics Teachers; Sigma Xi; Licensing Exec Soc; Asn Univ Technol Mgrs; Technol Transfer Soc. *Res:* Measurements of the low temperature transport and magnetic properties of rare earth compounds and alloys in bulk and in multilayered structures; methodology of technology transfer. *Mailing Add:* Dept Physics Northern Ill Univ De Kalb IL 60115-2854. *E-Mail:* lrsill@physics.niu.edu

SILL, WILLIAM ROBERT, GEOPHYSICS. *Current Pos:* PROF PHYSICS, MONTANA COL MINERAL SCI, 83- *Personal Data:* b Cleveland, Ohio, Oct 14, 37; m 63; c 2. *Educ:* Mich State Univ, BS, 60; Mass Inst Technol, MS, 63, PhD(geophys), 68. *Prof Exp:* Mem tech staff, Bellcomm Inc, Washington, DC, 67-72; assoc res prof, Univ Utah, 72-81, res prof geophys, 81-82. *Mem:* AAAS; Am Geophys Union. *Res:* Electrical properties of rocks and planetary interiors; solar wind-planetary interactions; lunar geophysics; mineral exploration. *Mailing Add:* Dept Physics & Geophys Eng Montana Col Mineral, Sci & Technol Butte MT 59701-8997

SILLA, HARRY, CHEMICAL ENGINEERING, CHEMICAL PROCESS ANALYSIS & SYNTHESIS. *Current Pos:* from asst prof to assoc prof, 70-78, PROF CHEM ENG, STEVENS INST TECHNOL, 78-, DEPT HEAD, CHEM & CHEM ENG, 90- *Personal Data:* b Jersey City, NJ, Dec 7, 29; m 57, Christiane; c Michele, Catherine & Eric. *Educ:* City Col New York, BChE, 54; Stevens Inst Technol, MS, 61, PhD(chem eng), 70. *Prof Exp:* Proj engr, Eng Ctr, Columbia Univ, 54 & 56-57; chem engr, Stevens Inst Technol, 57-59; proj leader, Aerochem Res Labs, Sybron Corp, 59-64. *Concurrent Pos:* Mem, Solid Waste Task Force, NJ Energy Inst; chmn, NJ sect, Am Inst Chem Engrs, 79. *Mem:* Am Soc Eng Educ; Am Chem Soc; Am Inst Chem Engrs; Sigma Xi. *Res:* Combustion; process engineering; waste treatment. *Mailing Add:* 26 Lucille St Edison NJ 08820-2043

SILLECK, CLARENCE FREDERICK, CHEMISTRY, PIGMENT DISPERSION. *Current Pos:* VPRES, C J OSBORN CHEM, INC, PENNSAUKEN, NJ, 69- *Personal Data:* b Brooklyn, NY, Nov 12, 09; m 34; c 1. *Educ:* Polytech Inst Brooklyn, BS, 32, MS, 36. *Hon Degrees:* DSc, Polytech Inst NY, 79. *Prof Exp:* Tech dir, C J Osborn Co, 32-68, pres, 68-69. *Concurrent Pos:* Trustee, Polytech Inst New York. *Mem:* AAAS; Am Chem Soc; fel Am Inst Chemists; NY Acad Sci; Fedn Socs Coatings Technol. *Res:* Synthetic resins and pigment dispersions for protective coatings; colloidal dispersion of carbon black in cellulose nitrate; dispersion of carbon black in alkyd resins; specialty finishes. *Mailing Add:* 186-20 Henley Rd Jamaica NY 11432

SILLIKER, JOHN HAROLD, MICROBIOLOGY. *Current Pos:* pres, 67-87, CONSULT MICROBIOLOGIST, SILLIKER LABS, 87- *Personal Data:* b Ayer's Cliff, Que, June 20, 22; nat US; m 79; c 2. *Educ:* Univ Southern Calif, AB, 47, MS, 48, PhD(bact), 50; Am Bd Med Microbiol, dipl. *Honors & Awards:* Sci Award, Am Pub Health Asn, 63; Harold Barnum Indust Award, Int Asn Milk, Food & Environ Sanitarians, 87. *Prof Exp:* USPHS fel bact, Hopkins Marine Sta, Stanford Univ, 50-51; asst prof, Sch Med, Univ Rochester, 51-52; bacteriologist, George W Gooch Labs, Ltd, Calif, 52-53; chief bacteriologist & assoc dir res, Swift & Co, Ill, 53-61; res assoc & consult, Dept Path, St James Hosp, Chicago Heights, Ill, 61-67. *Concurrent Pos:* Mem res coun, Inst Am Poultry Industs & Am Meat Inst Found, 53-61; lectr, Meat Hyg Training Ctr, USDA, 61-; mem, Comt on Salmonella Sampling & Methodology in Egg Prod, 64-; vis prof food sci, Univ Ill, 65; mem, Comt Salmonella, Nat Res Coun-Nat Acad Sci, 67-68; consult, Int Comn Microbiol Specifications for Foods, 70-74, mem, 74 & treas, 80; div lectr, Food Microbiol Div, Am Soc Microbiol, 78 & consult, 87-; mem, Subcomt Microbiol Criteria for Foods, Bat Res Coun-Nat Acad Sci, 80-84. *Mem:* Fel Am Pub Health Asn; fel Inst Food Technologists; fel Am Acad Microbiol; Soc Appl Microbiol; Royal Soc Health. *Res:* Fatty acid oxidation by bacteria; enteric and food bacteriology; microbiological methods for examination of foods, particularly Salmonella and other enteric organisms. *Mailing Add:* 900 Maple Rd Homewood IL 60430

SILLIMAN, RALPH PARKS, FISH BIOLOGY. *Current Pos:* CONSULT FISHERY BIOLOGIST, 73- *Personal Data:* b Seattle, Wash, June 26, 13; m 37; c 2. *Educ:* Univ Wash, BS, 36. *Honors & Awards:* Bronze Med, US DC, 73. *Prof Exp:* Tech asst Pac halibut res, Int Fish Comn, 36-37; aquatic biologist Pac sardine res, US Fish & Wildlife Serv, 38-45, aquatic biologist, Pac salmon res, 45-49, adminr anadromous & inland fishery res, 49-63, fish pop res, US Bur Commercial Fisheries, 64-69 & Nat Marine Fisheries Serv, 70-73. *Mem:* Am Fisheries Soc; Am Inst Fishery Res Biol (pres, 64-66); Am Inst Biol Sci; Sigma Xi. *Res:* Population dynamics; mathematical population models. *Mailing Add:* 4135 Baker NW Seattle WA 98107

SILLMAN, EMMANUEL I, PARASITOLOGY, INVERTEBRATE ZOOLOGY. *Current Pos:* RETIRED. *Personal Data:* b Philadelphia, Pa, Dec 7, 15. *Educ:* Univ Mich, PhD(zool), 54. *Prof Exp:* Lectr & asst prof zool, Ont Agr Col, 53-58; asst prof, Univ Man, 58-60; from assoc prof to prof biol, Duquesne Univ, 60-80. *Concurrent Pos:* Epidemiol of trop dis, US Army. *Mem:* AAAS; Am Soc Parasitologists; Soc Syst Zool; Am Micros Soc; Nat Ctr Sci Educ. *Res:* Life histories of digenetic trematodes and warble flies; disease and parasites of fish; biology and ecology of protozoa, flatworms and gastropods. *Mailing Add:* 4700 Fifth Ave Pittsburgh PA 15213-2942

SILLS, MATTHEW A, BIOCHEMISTRY. *Current Pos:* sr scientist, 86-87, sr res scientist, 88-89, MGR, BIOCHEM PROFILING, CIBA-GEIGY PHARMACEUT, 89- *Personal Data:* b New York, NY, May 17, 55. *Educ:* Rutgers Univ, BS, 78; Univ Pa, PhD(pharmacol), 84. *Prof Exp:* Res assoc pharmacol, NIH, 84-86. *Concurrent Pos:* Pratt fel, Nat Inst Gen Med Sci, NIH, 84-86. *Mem:* Nat Soc Neurosci; Am Chem Soc; Am Soc Pharmacol & Exp Therapeut; AAAS. *Mailing Add:* Pharmaceut Div Ciba-Geigy Corp 556 Morris Ave Summit NJ 07901-1398. *Fax:* 908-277-2084

SILSBEE, HENRY BRIGGS, physics; deceased, see previous edition for last biography

SILSBEE, PETER LIVINGSTON, SPEECH RECOGNITION, AUTOMATIC SPEECH READING. *Current Pos:* ASST PROF ELEC COMPUT & ENG, OLD DOMINION UNIV, 93- *Personal Data:* b Ithaca, NY, Sept 18, 58. *Educ:* Dartmouth Univ, AB, 87; Univ Tex, Austin, MS, 89, PhD(elec eng), 93. *Mem:* Inst Elec & Electronics Engrs; Inst Elec & Electronics Engrs Comput Soc; Inst Elec & Electronics Engrs Signal Processing Soc. *Mailing Add:* Elec & Comput Eng Old Dominion Univ Hampton Blvd Norfolk VA 23529. *E-Mail:* silsbee@ece.odu.edu

SILSBEE, ROBERT HERMAN, SOLID STATE PHYSICS, MAGNETIC RESONANCE. *Current Pos:* from instr to assoc prof, 57-65, PROF PHYSICS, CORNELL UNIV, 65- *Personal Data:* b Washington, DC, Feb 24, 29; m 50; c 3. *Educ:* Harvard Univ, AB, 50, MA, 51, PhD(physics), 56. *Prof Exp:* Mem staff, Solid State Div, Oak Ridge Nat Lab, 56-57. *Concurrent Pos:* Sloan res fel, 58-60; NSF sr fel, 65-66; Guggenheim Found fel, 73-74; ed, Solid State Communs, 71- *Mem:* Am Phys Soc; AAAS. *Res:* Solid state physics; magnetic resonance; radiation damage; optical properties; electronic and spin transport in small conducting systems. *Mailing Add:* Dept Physics Cornell Univ Clark Hall Ithaca NY 14853. *Fax:* 607-255-6428

SILVA, ARMAND JOSEPH, OCEAN & CIVIL ENGINEERING. *Current Pos:* chmn ocean eng, 84-92, PROF OCEAN & CIVIL ENG, UNIV RI, 76-, DIR, MARINE GEOMECH RES GROUP, 78. *Personal Data:* b Waterbury, Conn, June 1, 31; m 54, 68; c 3. *Educ:* Univ Conn, BSE, 54, MS, 56, PhD(civil eng), 65. *Prof Exp:* Instr civil eng, Univ Conn, 55-56; soils engr, Thompson & Lichtner Co, 56-58; from instr to prof civil eng, Worcester Polytech Inst, 58-76, head dept, 71-76. *Concurrent Pos:* Consult, 58-; pres & treas, Geotechnics, Inc, 56-67; NSF sci-fac fel, 62-63; grants & contracts, Worcester Polytech Inst, 66-67 & 71-72, NSF, 70, 79, 80-83, 87-90, 92-, Shell Develop Co, 71 & 85-, Off Naval Res, 72-82, Dept Energy, 74-87, US Geol Surv, 82-84, Bedford Inst Oceanog, 82-85 & SAIC/Corps Engrs, 90-, Naval Res Lab, 92- *Mem:* Am Soc Civil Engrs; Int Soc Soil Mech & Found Engrs; Am Geophys Union; Marine Technol Soc; Am Soc Testing Mats. *Res:* Ocean engineering; soil mechanics; geotechnical properties of ocean sediments; marine sediment processes; sediment coring technology; soil-structure interaction; marine geomechanics; creep behavior; dredge disposal; downslope processes; geoacoustic properties of seabed. *Mailing Add:* Dept Ocean Eng Univ RI Narragansett RI 02882

SILVA, JAMES ANTHONY, SOIL FERTILITY. *Current Pos:* asst prof soil sci, 64-70, assoc prof soil sci & sta statistician, 70-76, PROF SOIL SCI, COL TROP AGR, UNIV HAWAII, HONOLULU, 76- *Personal Data:* b Kilauea, Hawaii, Sept 4, 30; m 67, Lorraine Zirger; c Nancy & Malia. *Educ:* Univ Hawaii, BS, 51, MS, 59; Iowa State Univ, PhD(soil biochem), 64. *Prof Exp:* Asst-in-training sugar cane, Exp Sta, Hawaiian Sugar Planter's Asn, 51-53, asst agronomist, 53-59; asst soil biochem, Iowa State Univ, 59-64. *Concurrent Pos:* NSF fel, 64-66; sabbatical, Cornell Univ, 71-72 & Ore State Univ, 82; prin investr int proj, Benchmark Soils Proj, AID, 76-84. *Mem:* Soil Sci Soc Am; Am Soc Agron; Int Soc Soil Sci. *Res:* Nutrient availability and uptake by plants, especially nitrogen, phosphorus, silicon and zinc; soil and plant tissue testing for nutrient requirements of tropical soils and crops, especially vegetables and sugarcane; transfer of agrotechnology based on the soil family of soil taxonomy; modeling growth of sugar cane. *Mailing Add:* Dept Soil Sci Univ Hawaii Honolulu HI 96822. *Fax:* 808-956-6539; *E-Mail:* jsilva@hawaii.edu

SILVA, OMEGA LOGAN, INTERNAL MEDICINE, ENDOCRINOLOGY. *Current Pos:* adj assoc prof oncol, 77-85, PROF ONCOL, HOWARD UNIV, 85- *Personal Data:* b Dec 14, 36; US citizen; m 58, 82; c 1. *Educ:* Howard Univ, BS, 58, MD, 67; Am Bd Internal Med, dipl, 74, Am Bd Internal Med, Endocrinol & Metabolism, cert, 79. *Honors & Awards:* Merck Index Award, 57. *Prof Exp:* Chemist, NIMH, 58-63; from intern to resident internal med, Vet Admin Hosp, 67-70, res assoc endocrinol, 71-74, clin investr, 74-77; from asst prof to assoc prof med, George Washington Univ, 74-85. *Concurrent Pos:* Lucy Moten Travel fel for Study & Travel, Europe, 58; fel endocrinol, Vet Admin Hosp, Washington, DC, 70-71. *Mem:* Am Chem Soc; Am Med Women's Asn; Endocrine Soc; Am Diabetes Asn; fel Am Col Physicians. *Res:* Calcium metabolism; function of human calcitonin. *Mailing Add:* 354 N St SW Washington DC 20024-2904

SILVA, PATRICIO, NEPHROLOGY. *Current Pos:* instr, Harvard Med Sch, 72-74, asst prof, 74-79, ASSOC PROF MED, HARVARD MED SCH, 79-; CHIEF, RENAL DIV, NEW ENG DEACONESS HOSP & JOSLIN DIABETES CTR, 90- *Personal Data:* b Santiago, Chile, July 7, 39; m 64, Vjera M Bokovic; c Patricio, Jose P & Marcela. *Educ:* Cath Univ Chile, BS, 59, MD, 64. *Prof Exp:* Resident, Clin Hosp, Univ Chile, 64-67; staff physician & consult nephrol, Regional Hosp Talca, Chile, 67-69; prof nutrit, Univ Chile, 68, prof pathophysiol, Cent Univ Talca, 69; res assoc pharmacol, Dartmouth Med Sch, 69-70; fel, Yale Univ Sch Med, 70-71, res assoc, 72. *Concurrent Pos:* Fel, Nat Kidney Found, 70 & Conn Heart Asn, 71; clin asst, Boston City Hosp, 72-74; asst to assoc physician, Beth Israel Hosp, 74-88, physician, 88-; investr, Am Heart Asn, 77-82; sr staff, Joslin Diabetes Ctr & New Eng Deaconess Hosp, 90- *Mem:* Am Fedn Clin Res; Am Soc Nephrol; Am Physiol Soc; Am Soc Exp Biol & Med; AAAS; Am Soc Clin Invest. *Res:* Mechanism and regulation of the transport of salt; mechanism and prevention of acute renal failure. *Mailing Add:* New Eng Deaconess Hosp Joslin Diabetes Ctr 1 Joslin Pl Boston MA 02215. *Fax:* 617-632-7468

SILVA, PAUL CLAUDE, PHYCOLOGY. *Current Pos:* from instr to assoc prof, Univ Ill, 52-61, sr herbarium botanist, 61-67, RES BOTANIST, UNIV CALIF, BERKELEY, 67- *Personal Data:* b San Diego, Calif, Oct 31, 22. *Educ:* Univ Southern Calif, BA, 46; Stanford Univ, MA, 48; Univ Calif, PhD(bot), 51. *Honors & Awards:* Darbaker Award, Bot Soc Am, 58. *Prof Exp:* Res fel bot, Univ Calif, 51-52. *Concurrent Pos:* Guggenheim fel, 58-59; ed, Phycologia 61-69. *Mem:* Bot Soc Am; Am Soc Plant Taxonomists; Phycol Soc Am (secy, 54-57, vpres, 57, pres, 58); Int Asn Plant Taxon; Int Phycol Soc (pres, 65). *Res:* Morphology, taxonomy and ecology of marine algae. *Mailing Add:* 1516 Westview Dr Berkeley CA 94705

SILVA, PEDRO JOAO NEVES, population genetics, molecular evolution, for more information see previous edition

SILVA, RICARDO, ORGANIC CHEMISTRY. *Current Pos:* from asst prof to assoc prof, 62-70, chmn dept, 73-83 & 91-94, PROF CHEM, CALIF STATE UNIV, NORTHRIDGE, 70- *Personal Data:* b Hong Kong, Nov 20, 31; US citizen; m 63, Moira Coombes; c Marc, Frances, Vincent & James. *Educ:* Univ Sydney, BS, 53; Univ Calif, Los Angeles, PhD(chem), 61. *Prof Exp:* NIH fel, Imp Col, Univ London, 61-62. *Concurrent Pos:* NSF inst grants, 62-63 & 64-65, fel, 66-67; NIH res grant, 64-65; Calif Inst Technol Pres Fund grant, 72-73, Air Force Off Sci Res, 85. *Mem:* Am Chem Soc. *Res:* Nuclear magnetic resonance; polycyclic compounds; natural products; structure and reactivity; biogenetic origins; photochemical reactions of naturally occurring compounds; synthesis of indole alkaloids. *Mailing Add:* Dept Chem Calif State Univ Northridge CA 91330-8262. *Fax:* 818-885-2912; *E-Mail:* rsilva@huey.csun.edu

SILVA, ROBERT JOSEPH, NUCLEAR CHEMISTRY. *Current Pos:* STAFF SCIENTIST, LAWRENCE BERKELEY LAB, UNIV CALIF, 77- *Personal Data:* b Oakland, Calif, Feb 16, 27; m 50; c 3. *Educ:* Univ Ore, BS, 51; Univ Calif, Berkeley, PhD(chem), 59. *Prof Exp:* Chem engr, Kaiser Aluminum Corp, Calif, 50-51; health physicist, Radiation Lab, Univ Calif, 51-54, lab technician, 54-57, res asst, 57-59; chemist, Oak Ridge Nat Lab, 59-66; nuclear chemist, Lawrence Radiation Lab, Univ Calif, 66-68; res scientist, Spec Training Div, Oak Ridge Assoc Univs, 68-70; mem staff, Oak Ridge Nat Lab, 70-77. *Mem:* Am Phys Soc; Am Chem Soc; Sigma Xi. *Res:* Low energy nuclear reactions and scattering; nuclear spectroscopy; nuclear instruments; transuranium nuclear research; transuranium chemical research. *Mailing Add:* 111 Regent Pl Alamo CA 94507-1801

SILVEIRA, AUGUSTINE, JR, ORGANIC CHEMISTRY, CHEMICAL EDUCATION. *Current Pos:* assoc prof chem, 63-64, prof chem, 64-76, CHMN, CHEM DEPT, STATE UNIV NY COL OSWEGO, 67-, DISTINGUISHED TEACHING PROF, 76- *Personal Data:* b New Bedford, Mass, July 17, 34; m 60, Beverly A Washburn; c Linda & Karen. *Educ:* Univ Mass Dartmouth, BS, 57; Univ Mass, Amherst, PhD(chem), 62. *Hon Degrees:* ScD, Univ Mass Dartmouth, 75. *Honors & Awards:* President's Res Award, 83, Am Chem Soc, Sect Award, 88. *Prof Exp:* Teaching fel chem, Univ Mass, Amherst, 57-58, teaching assoc, 58-60, instr, 60-62; asst prof, Rutgers Univ, 62-63. *Concurrent Pos:* Dir res, NIH res grant, 62-63; State Univ NY fac res fel, 64 & 67, res grant in aid, 64-65 & 67-69; dir, NSF Undergrad Sci Equip grant, 65-67 & 77-78, partic grant org mech, NSF Conf, Vt, 66; evaluator grad progs, State Univ NY Col Oswego, 68-, Middle States Asn, 88- & Am Chem Soc Prof Training, 91-; indust consult, 70-; mem comn higher educ, Mid States Asn Cols & Sec Schs, 71-; dir, NSF res grants, 73-74, 77-78, 79-82, 85-88 & 95-97, Sloan Grant, 86, PDQWL Develop grants, 90 & 94, Inst Chem Educ, grants, 91-92 & 92-93; consult, NY State Educ Dept, 75; vis prof, Univ Calif, Irvine, 76-77, 84 & 91, Calif State Univ, Long Beach, 76-77; res corp grant, State Univ NY, 77-78, fac grant, 78-79, fac grant undergrad instr, 77-79 & 80-82; grant, Eastern Col Sci Conf, 78; mem optom bd, State NY, 80-90; State Univ NY fac exchange scholar, 81-; teaching assoc, Inst Chem Educ, 91- *Mem:* AAAS; Am Chem Soc; fel Am Inst Chemists; Sigma Xi. *Res:* Structure, synthesis and reactions involving organonitrogen and organometallic chemistry; studies in chemical education. *Mailing Add:* 88 Co Rte 24 PO Box 98 Minetto NY 13115

SILVEIRA, MILTON ANTHONY, MECHANICAL ENGINEERING, AERONAUTICAL & ASTRONAUTICAL ENGINEERING. *Current Pos:* Res intern, Dynamic Loads Div, Langley Field, NASA, 51 & studies on helicopter vibration & dynamic probs, Vibration & Flutter Br, 55-61, actg head, Loads Sect, Struct Br, Space Task Group, 61-63, from asst br chief to dep chief, Aerodyn Br, Spacecraft Res Div, 63-65, from tech mgr to prog mgr, Little Joe II Launch Vehicle, 64-65, head, Flight Performance & Dynamics Br, 65-67, asst to dir eng & develop for spec proj, 67-68, chief, Eng Analysis Off, 68-69, mgr, Space Shuttle Eng Off, 69-73, dep prog, Space Orbiter Proj, Johnson Spacecraft Ctr, 73-81, asst to dep adminr, 81-82, CHIEF ENGR, HQ, NASA, 83-; PRES, SEL. *Personal Data:* b Mattapoisett, Mass, May 4, 29; c 4. *Educ:* Univ Vt, BSME, 51; Univ Va, MSAE, 60. *Hon Degrees:* Dr, Univ Vt, 77. *Honors & Awards:* Sustained Super Performance Award, NASA, 65 & 69, Except Serv Medal, 69 & 81. *Mem:* Am Inst Aeronaut & Astronaut. *Res:* Engineering systems analysis; engineering of the space shuttle systems and directing in-house design and analysis efforts. *Mailing Add:* 7213 Evans Mill McLean VA 22101

SILVER, ALENE FREUDENHEIM, DEVELOPMENTAL BIOLOGY, DERMATOLOGY. *Current Pos:* from assoc prof to prof, 70-89, EMER PROF BIOL, RI COL, 89- *Personal Data:* b New York, NY, Oct 31, 16; div; c 3. *Educ:* Columbia Univ, BA, 38; Univ Ill, PhD(physiol), 47. *Prof Exp:* Res asst circulatory physiol, Col Med, Univ Ill, 42-46; res assoc, Michael Reese Hosp, Chicago, 46-47; res assoc wound healing, Johns Hopkins Hosp, Baltimore, 48-49; res assoc skin physiol, Brown Univ, 61-64, res assoc develop genetics, 65-70, res asst prof, 69-70. *Concurrent Pos:* USPHS biomed sci support grant, 66-68; assoc mem, Inst Life Sci, Brown Univ, 70-75; sr investr biol & med, Brown Univ, 75- *Mem:* Int Pigment Cell Soc; Sigma Xi; Am Soc Cell Biol; Am Soc Zoologists; Soc Develop Biol. *Res:* Physiology of skin; developmental genetics of hair regeneration; phenotypic modulation of hair germ melanocytes during hair cycle; development of the eye in mutant and normal mice. *Mailing Add:* 12 Blackstone Blvd Providence RI 02906

SILVER, ARNOLD HERBERT, SOLID STATE PHYSICS. *Current Pos:* MGR, SUPERCONDUCTIVE ELECTRONICS RES, 87- *Personal Data:* b Brooklyn, NY, Sept 27, 31; m 52; c 5. *Educ:* Rensselaer Polytech Inst, BS, 52, MS, 54, PhD(physics), 58. *Honors & Awards:* Inst Elec & Electronics Engrs Microwave Theory & Techniques Distinguished Microwave Lectr, 88-89. *Prof Exp:* Asst physics, Rensselaer Polytech Inst, 52-55 & Brown Univ, 55-57; res engr, Sci Lab, Ford Motor Co, 57-62, sr res scientist, 62-64, prin res scientist assoc, 64-65; staff scientist, 65-69; dir, Electronics Res Lab, Aerospace Corp, 69-80; Sr scientist, 81-84, sr staff engr, TRW, Inc, 84-87. *Mem:* AAAS; fel Am Phys Soc; Inst Elec & Electronics Engrs. *Res:* Nuclear and electron magnetic resonance; radio frequency spectroscopy; superconductivity; quantum effects in superconductors; electronic techniques and instrumentation; superconducting and cryogenic devices. *Mailing Add:* R1 2178 TRW Space & Electron Group One Space Park Redondo Beach CA 90278. *Fax:* 310-813-4873

SILVER, BARNARD STEWART, ENERGY ENGINEERING. *Current Pos:* PRES, SILVER ENTERPRISES, 71-; PRES, SILVER ENERGY SYSTS CORP, 80-; PRES & GEN MGR, SILVER CHIEF CORP, 83-; PRES, SILVER CORP, 84-86 & 93-; CHMN BD, SILVER PUBL INC, 93- *Personal Data:* b Salt Lake City, Utah, Mar 9, 33; m 63, Cherry Bushman; c Madelyn

S (Palmer), Brenda P (Call) & Cannon F. *Educ:* Mass Inst Technol, BS, 57; Stanford Univ, MS, 58; Harvard Grad Sch Bus, AMP, 76. *Honors & Awards:* Decorated Chevalier, l'Orde Nat, Repub de Cote d'Ivoire, 76. *Prof Exp:* Engr, Aircraft Nuclear Propulsion Div, Gen Elec, 57; engr sugar mach, Silver Eng Works, 59-66, mgr sales, 66-71; chief engr, Union Sugar Div, Consol Foods Co, 71-74; dir du complexe, Sodesucre, Abidjan, Cote d'Ivoire, 74-76; supt eng & maint, Moses Lake Factory, U&I, Inc, 76-79. *Concurrent Pos:* Instr eng, Big Bend Community Col, 80-81. *Mem:* Am Soc Mech Engrs; Asn Energy Engrs; Am Soc Sugar Beet Technologists; Sigma Xi; Int Soc Sugar Cane Technol. *Res:* Agronomic practices, production and utilization of Jerusalem artichokes in world climates; extraction of inulin and accompanying constituents from the Jerusalem Artichoke; aeronomic and processing practices of sugar beet and sugar cane; counter-current extraction. *Mailing Add:* 4391 S Carol Jane Dr Salt Lake City UT 84124-3601

SILVER, DAVID MARTIN, THEORETICAL CHEMISTRY. *Current Pos:* supvr chem physics res, 77-83, supvr comput physics res, 84-95, CHEMIST, APPL PHYSICS LAB, JOHNS HOPKINS UNIV, 70-, PRIN STAFF, 76-, SR SCIENTIST, 95- *Personal Data:* b Chicago, Ill, Sept 25, 41; m 63, Sylvia Doktorsky; c Deborah & Joel. *Educ:* Ill Inst Technol, BS, 62; Johns Hopkins Univ, MA, 64; Iowa State Univ, PhD(chem), 68. *Prof Exp:* NSF fel chem, Harvard Univ, 68-69; vis scientist, Europ Ctr Atomic & Molecular Calculations, Orsay, France, 70. *Concurrent Pos:* Vis prof chem, Johns Hopkins Univ, 74-75 & 84-85. *Mem:* AAAS; Am Chem Soc; Am Phys Soc; Am Geophys Union; Asn Res Vision & Ophthal; Am Inst Aeronaut & Astronaut. *Res:* Molecular physics; electron correlation and electronic structure of atoms and molecules; fluid mechanics; ophthalmology; excited state chemical reactions; mathematical analysis; electromagnetic scattering; molecular, particulate and plasma interactions with spacecraft. *Mailing Add:* Appl Physics Lab Johns Hopkins Univ Laurel MD 20723. *E-Mail:* david.silver@jhuapl.edu

SILVER, DONALD, VASCULAR SURGERY, THORACIC SURGERY. *Current Pos:* PROF SURG & CHMN DEPT, UNIV MO MED CTR, 75- *Personal Data:* b New York, NY, Oct 19, 29; m 58, Helen Harnden; c Elizabeth T (Smith), Donald M, Stephanie D & William P. *Educ:* Duke Univ, AB, 50, BS & MD, 55; Am Bd Surg, dipl, 65, Gen Vascular Surg, 83 & 93; Am Bd Thoracic Surg, dipl, 67. *Honors & Awards:* Carl Moyer lectr, Wash Univ, 93; Alton Oschner lectr, Tulane Univ, 94. *Prof Exp:* Asst prof surg, Med Ctr, Duke Univ, 64-66, from assoc prof surg & dir vascular clin to prof, 66-75. *Concurrent Pos:* Co-prin investr, NIH grant, 64-71, prin investr, 71-75 & 75-80; attend physician, Vet Admin Hosp, Durham, 65-75; consult, Watts Hosp, Durham, 65-75; consult, Harry S Truman Vet Admin Hosp, Columbia, Mo, 75; mem bd sci adv, Cancer Res Ctr, Columbia, Mo, 75; James IV Surg traveler. *Mem:* Sigma Xi; fel Am Col Surgeons; Int Cardiovasc Soc; Soc Univ Surgeons; Am Surg Asn; Soc Vascular Surg. *Res:* Thromboembolic phenomena with special emphasis on the vascular and fibrinolytic systems. *Mailing Add:* Dept Surg Univ Mo Med Ctr Columbia MO 65212. *Fax:* 573-884-4585

SILVER, EDWARD A, MATHEMATICS, MATHEMATICS EDUCATION. *Current Pos:* asst prof, 79-81, ASSOC PROF MATH, SAN DIEGO STATE UNIV, 81- *Personal Data:* b Mt Vernon, NY, Aug 20, 48; m 71; c 1. *Educ:* Iona Col, BA, 70; Columbia Univ, MA, 73, MS & EDD(math educ), 77. *Prof Exp:* asst prof math, Northern Ill Univ, 77-79. *Mem:* Math Asn Am; Am Educ Res Asn; Nat Coun Teachers Math; Cognitive Sci Soc. *Res:* Study of mathematical cognition, especially mathematical problem solving, using an eclectic approach that leans heavily on techniques drawn from artificial intelligence, cognitive psychology, and mathematics education. *Mailing Add:* 414 Manordale Rd Upper St Clair PA 15241-2122

SILVER, EDWARD ALLAN, OPERATIONS MANAGEMENT, INDUSTRIAL ENGINEERING. *Current Pos:* PROF OPERS MGT, UNIV CALGARY, 81-, CARMA CHAIR OPERS MGT, 91- *Personal Data:* b Montreal, Que, June 13, 37; m 66, Maxine J Locke; c Michelle, Norman (deceased) & Heidi. *Educ:* McGill Univ, BEng, 59; Mass Inst Technol, ScD(opers res), 63. *Honors & Awards:* Opers Res Div Award, Inst Indust Engrs, 86; Award Merit, Can Oper Res Soc, 90. *Prof Exp:* Prof staff mem, Opers Res Group, Arthur D Little, Inc, Mass, 63-67; assoc prof bus admin, Boston Univ, 67-69; from assoc prof to prof mgt sci, Univ Waterloo, 69-81. *Concurrent Pos:* Lectr, Mass Inst Technol, 65-67; consult, Arthur D Little Inc, 63-67, Bell Can, US Army Inventory Res Off, Defense Res Bd Can, Can Ctr Remote Sensing, Can Gen Tower, Am Optical, Uniroyal, Stand Oil Ind, Nova & PanCan Petrol; vis prof, Ecole Polytech Federale de Lausanne, Switz, 76-77, 90, 92-93, Stanford Univ, 86, Xian Jiatong Univ, China, 87, Inst Advan Studies, Vienna, 90; Sem & In-house workshops, many orgn. *Mem:* Can Oper Res Soc (pres, 80-81); Opers Mgt Asn; Inst Mgt Sci; Am Prod & Inventory Control Soc; fel Inst Indust Engrs; Int Soc Inventory Res (pres, 94-96). *Res:* Applications of approximate solutions to quantitative models of complex problems in operations management and industrial engineering; contributions to methodology of continuous process improvement. *Mailing Add:* Fac Mgt Univ Calgary Calgary AB T2N 1N4 Can. *Fax:* 403-282-0095; *E-Mail:* silver@mgmt.ucalgary.ca

SILVER, ELI ALFRED, OCEANOGRAPHY, GEOLOGY. *Current Pos:* from asst prof to assoc prof, 73-79, chmn dept, 75-77, PROF EARTH SCI, UNIV CALIF, SANTA CRUZ, 79-, ACTG DEAN NATURAL SCI, 94-, DIR, INST TECTONICS, 95- *Personal Data:* b Worcester, Mass, June 3, 42; m 67, 87, Martha Jordan; c Monica & Joel. *Educ:* Univ Calif, Berkeley, AB, 64; Scripps Inst Oceanog, PhD(oceanog), 69. *Prof Exp:* Res fel, Scripps Inst Oceanog, 69-70; res geologist, US Geol Surv, 70-73. *Concurrent Pos:* Chmn, Active Margins Panel, Ocean Drilling Prog, 80-82 & Western Pac Panel, 83-85; assoc ed, J Geophys Res, 85-87. *Mem:* Fel Geol Soc Am; Am Geophys Union; Soc Explor Geophysicists; Seismol Soc Am; AAAS; Europ Asn Explor Geophysicists. *Res:* Structure and evolution of subduction zones and collision zones, using marine geophysical tools, focused on Indonesia, the Caribbean, the western coast of the United States, and Papua New Guinea; chief scientist on 20 marine geophysical expeditions; numerous land expeditions. *Mailing Add:* Earth Sci Dept Univ Calif Santa Cruz CA 95064. *Fax:* 408-459-3074; *E-Mail:* silver@earthsci.ucsc.edu

SILVER, ERNEST GERARD, EXPERIMENTAL PHYSICS, NUCLEAR SAFETY. *Current Pos:* RETIRED. *Personal Data:* b Munich, Ger, Dec 26, 29; US citizen; m 54; c Carolyn. *Educ:* Boston Univ, BA, 52; Harvard Univ Grad Sch, MS, 54; Oak Ridge Sch Reactor Technol, dipl, 55; Univ Tenn, Knoxville, PhD(physics), 65. *Prof Exp:* Staff physicist reactor physics & neutron physics, Oak Ridge Nat Lab, 55-74, staff mem, Inst Energy Anal, 74-75, exec officer, 75-77, asst mgr, Breeder Reactor Proj, 77-79, asst mgr, Nuclear Stand Mgt Ctr, 79-81; asst ed, Nuclear Safety J, 81-84, ed chief, 85-95; ed chief, Nuclear Safety J, 85-95. *Mem:* Fel Am Nuclear Soc. *Res:* Energy policy; relation of energy use to national economy; neutron cross section for reactor application; time-dependent neutron diffusion. *Mailing Add:* 107 Lehigh Lane Oak Ridge TN 37830

SILVER, FRANK MORRIS, TECHNOLOGY ACQUISITIONS & POLYMER ALLOYS, PLASTICS & FIBERS. *Current Pos:* PRES, SILVER CONSULT INT, 94- *Personal Data:* b Eden, NC, Aug 30, 43; m 69; c Erika, Mandie, Jared. *Educ:* Univ NC, Chapel Hill, BS, 65; Univ Wis-Madison, PhD(org chem), 70. *Prof Exp:* Sr res chemist, Monsanto Co, 70-74, res specialist, 74-78, group leader, 78-79, sr group leader, 79-81, mgr, 81-93. *Mem:* Am Chem Soc; Soc Plastics Engrs. *Res:* Organic and polymer reaction mechanisms; solution and melt polymerization of novel polymers; organic and polymer synthesis and characterization; fiber spinning, characterization and end-use application of novel polymers; rubber-plastic blends; injection molding; thermoplastic elastomers; polymer alloys; nonwoven fabrics. *Mailing Add:* 3280 Villafane Dr Pensacola FL 32503. *Fax:* 850-433-9693

SILVER, FREDERICK HOWARD, BIOMATERIALS, MEDICAL DEVICES. *Current Pos:* assoc prof, 81-92, PROF PATH, ROBERT WOOD JOHNSON MED SCH, 92- *Personal Data:* b Passaic, NJ, Nov 26, 49. *Educ:* Northeastern Univ, BS, 72; Mass Inst Technol, SM, 75, PhD(polymer sci), 77. *Prof Exp:* Res fel path, Mass Gen Hosp, 77; adj asst prof biomed eng, Boston Univ, 78-81; asst prof path, Harvard Med Sch, 80-81. *Concurrent Pos:* Bakken prof biomed eng, Univ Minn, 92-93. *Mem:* Soc Biomat; Biomed Eng Soc. *Res:* Research on collagen structure and mechanical properties of vertebrate tissues, biomaterial and pathobiological responses to implant materials, artificial skin, tendon/ligament replacement and tissue adhesives. *Mailing Add:* Robert Wood Johnson Med Sch 675 Hoes Lane Piscataway NJ 08854. *Fax:* 732-235-4825

SILVER, GARY LEE, ANALYTICAL CHEMISTRY. *Current Pos:* STAFF MEM, LOS ALAMOS NAT LAB, 96- *Personal Data:* b Columbus, Ga, Nov, 22, 36; m 68, Marcine Robohm; c Meredith. *Educ:* Mass Inst Technol, BS, 59; Univ NC, PhD(anal chem), 63. *Prof Exp:* Sr chemist, Mound Lab, 63-80, fel, 80-95. *Mem:* Am Chem Soc. *Res:* Inorganic chemistry: lanthanides and actinides, particularly plutonium; radioactive materials and radioactive waste treatment; numerical methods; response surface modeling. *Mailing Add:* 868 Kristi Lane Los Alamos NM 87544

SILVER, GEORGE ALBERT, MEDICINE, PUBLIC HEALTH. *Current Pos:* prof, 69-84, EMER PROF PUB HEALTH, SCH MED, YALE UNIV, 84- *Personal Data:* b Philadelphia, Pa, Dec 23, 13; m 37; c 3. *Educ:* Univ Pa, BA, 34; Jefferson Med Col, MD, 38; Johns Hopkins Univ, MPH, 48. *Hon Degrees:* MA, Yale Univ, 70. *Prof Exp:* Asst demonstr bact, Jefferson Med Col, 39-42; asst prof pub health admin, Sch Hyg & Pub Health, Johns Hopkins Univ, 48-51; asst prof admin med, Col Physicians & Surgeons, Columbia Univ, 53-59; prof social med, Albert Einstein Col Med, 59-65; dep asst secy health, US Dept HEW, Washington, DC, 66-68, Health Exec Urban Coalition, Health Prog, 68-70. *Concurrent Pos:* Regional med officer, US Dept Agr Migrant Prog, 47-48; health officer, Eastern Health Dist, City Dept Health, Baltimore, Md, 48-51; chief, Dept Social Med, Montefiore Hosp, 51-65; mem tech bd, Milbank Mem Fund, 63-76; consult, WHO, 68- *Mem:* Sr mem Inst Med-Nat Acad Sci; Am Pub Health Asn; Sigma Xi; Fedn Am Scientists (secy, 80-89). *Res:* Social medicine; medical care organization and administration; health policy. *Mailing Add:* Dept Pub Health Sch Med Yale Univ 89 Trumbull New Haven CT 06510

SILVER, HERBERT GRAHAM, PHYSICAL CHEMISTRY, ELECTROCHEMISTRY. *Current Pos:* PROCESS ENG MGR, AEROFLEX LABS INC, 93- *Personal Data:* b Somerset, Eng, Sept 10, 38, US citizen; m 92, Miriam Oginski. *Educ:* Univ London, BSc & ARCS, 60, PhD(phys chem), 63; Imp Col, Univ London, dipl, 63. *Prof Exp:* NIH grant & Fulbright scholar, Harvard Univ, 63-65; mem tech staff chem, Bell Tel Labs, Inc, 65-67 & Gen Tel & Electronics Labs, Inc, 67-72, eng specialist, GTE Sylvania Inc, 72-75; chief lamp engr & mgr linear lamps, Canrad-Hanovia, Inc Div, Canrad Precision Industs Inc, 75-77; mgr, Filter Performance & Contamination Labs, Pall Corp, 78-81; sr scientist, Advan Develop, Components Div Burndy Corp, 81-83; engr, Defense Electronics Div, Unisys Corp, 83-93. *Mem:* AAAS; fel Royal Soc Chem; Sigma Xi; NY Acad Sci. *Res:* Gas discharges; materials research; electrochemistry; electroplating; development of high-efficiency gas discharge lamps for lighting, photochemical processes, medical therapeutics; filters and fluid clarification devices; adhesives and elastomers consultant; EMI/RFI elastomer gasketing consultant. *Mailing Add:* 14 Gay Dr Kings Point NY 11024

SILVER, HOWARD FINDLAY, chemical engineering; deceased, see previous edition for last biography

SILVER, HOWARD I(RA), ELECTRICAL ENGINEERING. *Current Pos:* from asst prof to assoc prof, 68-76, chmn dept, 71-76, PROF ELEC ENG, FAIRLEIGH DICKINSON UNIV, 76-, CHMN DEPT, 93- *Personal Data:* b New York, NY, June 2, 39; m 62, Ronnie Brenner; c Sharon Brody & Michael. *Educ:* City Col New York, BEE, 61; NY Univ, MEE, 64, PhD(elec eng), 68. *Prof Exp:* Eng trainee, Missile & Space Div, Gen Elec Co, 61-62; engr, Fed Labs, Int Tel & Tel Corp, 62-64; assoc engr, Sperry Gyroscope Co, 64-66; instr elec eng, NY Univ, 66-68. *Concurrent Pos:* Consult, Devenco Res Lab, 69, ATT Technol, 83-; instr & consult, Bell Tel Labs, 71-83. *Res:* Microprocessor system design; digital signal processing; logic design; application of computers to solving engineering problems. *Mailing Add:* Dept Elec Eng Fairleigh Dickinson Univ Teaneck NJ 07666

SILVER, HULBERT KEYES BELFORD, MEDICINE. *Current Pos:* MED ONCOLOGIST, CANCER CONTROL AGENCY BC, 76- *Personal Data:* b Montreal, Que, July 15, 41; m 66; c 3. *Educ:* Bishop's Univ, BSc, 62; McGill Univ, MD & CM, 66, PhD(immunol), 74. *Honors & Awards:* Medal Med, Royal Col Physicians & Surgeons Can, 75. *Prof Exp:* Asst res oncologist, Sch Med, Univ Calif, Los Angeles, 73-74; asst prof surg, 75-76; from asst prof to assoc prof, 76-84, prof med, Univ BC, 84- *Mem:* Am Asn Cancer Res; Am Soc Clin Oncol; Int Soc Interferon Res; Royal Col Physicians & Surgeons Can; Am Col Physicians. *Res:* Clinical cancer treatment with chemotherapy and biological response modifiers; immune effects of biological response modifiers; immunodiagnosis. *Mailing Add:* BC Cancer Agency 600 W 10th Ave Vancouver BC V5Z 4E6 Can

SILVER, JACK, MEDICINE. *Current Pos:* CHIEF DIV MOLECULAR MED & PROF MED, NORTH SHORE UNIV HOSP, CORNELL UNIV MED COL, 88- *Mailing Add:* Dept Med North Shore Univ Hosp Cornell Univ Res Bldg 350 Community Dr Manhasset NY 11030-3816. *Fax:* 516-562-2866

SILVER, LAWRENCE, MEDICINE. *Current Pos:* PHYSICIAN-IN-CHARGE, DEPT NUCLEAR MED, QUEENS HOSP CTR, 64- *Personal Data:* b New York, NY, Apr 15, 21; m 52; c 3. *Educ:* Queens Col, BS, 41; Univ Idaho, MS, 42; NY Univ, MD, 50. *Prof Exp:* Intern, Beth Israel Hosp, New York, 50-51; asst resident internal med, Vet Admin Hosp, Bronx, NY, 51-52; fel, Mayo Found, Univ Minn, 52-53; asst physician & vis investr hypertension, Hosp, Rockefeller Inst, 53-54; assoc scientist, Med Res Ctr, Brookhaven Nat Lab, 56-58, res assoc hypertension, 59-61; assoc med dir, Dept Clin Invest, Chas Pfizer & Co, 58-59; assoc med dir, Dept Clin Infest, Chas Pfizer & Co, 61-64. *Mem:* AAAS; Am Physiol Soc; Soc Exp Biol & Med. *Res:* Relationship of salt to hypertensive disease states; influence and mechanism of action of hormones on movement of salt and water in normals and hypertensives. *Mailing Add:* 9 Chelsea Dr Syosset NY 11791-2908

SILVER, LEE MERRILL, DEVELOPMENTAL GENETICS, MOLECULAR BIOLOGY. *Current Pos:* PROF, PRINCETON UNIV, 84- *Personal Data:* b Philadelphia, Pa, Apr 27, 52; m 74; c 2. *Educ:* Univ Pa, BA & MS, 73; Harvard Univ, PhD(biophys), 78. *Prof Exp:* Res fel genetics, Sloan Kettering Cancer Inst, 77-79, assoc, 79-80; sr staff investr, Cold Spring Harbor Lab, 80-84. *Concurrent Pos:* Fel, Pop Coun, 77-78 & NIH, 78-79; asst prof genetics, Med Sch, Cornell Univ, 79-80 & State Univ NY Stony Brook, 80-; vis asst prof genetics, Albert Einstein Col Med, 80; ed, Mammalian Arome, 89- *Mem:* Am Soc Cell Biol; AAAS; Int Soc Differentiation; Genetics Soc Am. *Res:* Molecular embryology; molecular biology of spermatogenesis; the mouse T/t complex; chromosomal proteins; cell surface proteins. *Mailing Add:* 24 Andrews Lane Princeton NJ 08540-7633

SILVER, LEON THEODORE, PETROLOGY, GEOCHEMISTRY. *Current Pos:* res geologist geochem uranium, AEC Contract Res, Div Geol Sci, 52-55, from asst prof to prof geol, 55-83, W M KECK FOUND PROF RESOURCE GEOL, CALIF INST TECHNOL, 83- *Personal Data:* b Monticello, NY, Apr 9, 25; m 47; c 2. *Educ:* Univ Colo, BS, 45; Univ NMex, MS, 48; Calif Inst Technol, PhD(geol & geochem), 55. *Honors & Awards:* Except Sci Achievement Medal, NASA, 71; Prof Excellence Award, Am Inst Prof Geologists, 72; Cert Spec Commendation, Geol Soc Am, 73. *Prof Exp:* Field asst, jr geologist & asst geologist, US Geol Surv, Mineral Deposits Br, Colo & Ariz, 47-54. *Concurrent Pos:* Guggenheim fel, 64; geologist, Astrogeol Br, US Geol Surv, 70-76; mem, Subcomn Geochronology, Int Union Geol Sci, 70-; consult, NASA, 71-; counr, Am Geol Soc, 74-76; chmn, Sci Eng & Pub Policy, Nat Acad Sci, 84-, counr, 89-92; mem, Gov Bd, Nat Res Coun, 89-92, chair, Comt Int Orgn & Progs, 90- *Mem:* Nat Acad Sci; fel Geol Soc Am (vpres, 78, pres 79); fel Mineral Soc Am; Geochem Soc; Am Geophys Union; fel AAAS; Am Acad Arts & Sci. *Res:* Igneous and metamorphic petrology; geochemistry of uranium, thorium and lead; geochronology; regional geology of southwestern United States; tectonic history of North America; mineralogy and petrology of meteorites and lunar materials. *Mailing Add:* Div Geol & Planetary Sci Calif Inst Technol Pasadena CA 91125

SILVER, MALCOLM DAVID, PATHOLOGY. *Current Pos:* chief path, 85-92, SR PATHOLOGIST TORONTO HOSP, 85-; PROF PATH, UNIV TORONTO, 85- *Personal Data:* b Adelaide, SAustralia, Apr 29, 33; m 57; c 3. *Educ:* Univ Adelaide, MB, BS, 57, MD, 72; McGill Univ, MSc, 61, PhD(path), 63; Am Bd Path, dipl, 63; FRACP, 64; FRCPC, 75. *Prof Exp:* Resident med officer, Royal Adelaide Hosp, Australia, 57-58; resident path, Royal Victoria Hosp, Montreal, 58-63; res fel exp path, John Curtin Sch Med Res, Australian Nat Univ, 63-65; from asst prof to prof, 65-79, chmn, Dept Path, Univ Toronto, 85-95. *Concurrent Pos:* Resident path, Path Inst, McGill Univ, 58-63; staff pathologist, Toronto Gen Hosp, 65-72, sr staff pathologist, 72-79; chmn, Dept Path, Univ Western Ont & chief path, Univ Hosp, London, Ont, 79-85. *Mem:* Am Soc Invest Path; Am Heart Asn; Can Asn Path; Can Cardiovasc Soc; Int Acad Path. *Res:* Cardiovascular pathology. *Mailing Add:* Dept Path Banting Inst 100 College St Rm 72 Toronto ON M5G 1L5 Can. *Fax:* 416-978-7361; *E-Mail:* md.silver@utoronto.ca

SILVER, MARC STAMM, BIO-ORGANIC CHEMISTRY. *Current Pos:* From instr to assoc prof, 58-69, PROF CHEM, AMHERST COL, 69- *Personal Data:* b Philadelphia, Pa, Jan 5, 34; m 61; c 3. *Educ:* Harvard Univ, AB, 55; Calif Inst Technol, PhD(chem, physics), 59. *Hon Degrees:* MA, Amherst Col, 69. *Concurrent Pos:* NSF fels, Northwestern Univ, 61-62 & Weizmann Inst, 66-67; vis prof, Yale Univ, 77-78; res fel, Oxford Univ, 71 & Imp Col, 81-82, 86-87. *Mem:* AAAS; Am Soc Biol Chemists; Am Chem Soc. *Res:* Organic reaction mechanisms; mechanism of enzyme action. *Mailing Add:* Dept Chem Amherst Col Amherst MA 01002-5002

SILVER, MARSHALL LAWRENCE, civil engineering, for more information see previous edition

SILVER, MARVIN, solid state physics; deceased, see previous edition for last biography

SILVER, MARY WILCOX, BIOLOGICAL OCEANOGRAPHY, MARINE ECOLOGY. *Current Pos:* from asst prof to assoc prof, 72-87, PROF MARINE SCI, UNIV CALIF, SANTA CRUZ, 87- *Personal Data:* b San Francisco, Calif, July 13, 41; c 2. *Educ:* Univ Calif, Berkeley, AB, 63; Scripps Inst Oceanog, Univ Calif, San Diego, PhD(oceanog), 71. *Prof Exp:* Lectr marine biol, Moss Landing Marine Labs, Moss Landing, Calif, 70-71; asst prof marine biol, San Francisco State Univ, 71-72. *Mem:* Am Soc Limnol & Oceanog; Am Geophys Union; Phycol Soc Am; AAAS. *Res:* Biology of planktonic tunicates; ecology of suspended particulates (marine snow); pelagic detrital food webs; deep ocean particle flux. *Mailing Add:* Dept Marine Sci Univ Calif 1156 High St Santa Cruz CA 95064-1077

SILVER, MELVIN JOEL, BIOCHEMISTRY, PHARMACOLOGY. *Current Pos:* Res biochemist, 53-57, assoc prof pharmacol, 59-72, PROF PHARMACOL, JEFFERSON MED COL, THOMAS JEFFERSON UNIV, 72-, ASSOC, CARDEZA FOUND, 57-, SR MEM, 72- *Personal Data:* b Philadelphia, Pa, June 22, 20; m 55; c 1. *Educ:* Temple Univ, AB, 41; Philadelphia Col Pharm, MSc, 43, DSc(bact), 53. *Concurrent Pos:* Wellcome Trust res fel, Royal Col Surgeons Eng, 70-71. *Mem:* Am Soc Pharmacol & Exp Therapeut; Am Chem Soc; NY Acad Sci; Int Soc Thrombosis & Haemostasis; Sigma Xi. *Res:* Role of prostaglandin synthesis, phospholipids and platelets in hemostasis. *Mailing Add:* 6640 Wissahickon Ave Philadelphia PA 19119-3724

SILVER, MEYER, QUANTUM ELECTRONICS, LASERS. *Current Pos:* RETIRED. *Personal Data:* b New York, NY, Sept 12, 26; m 47, Vivian Y Lamel; c Robin, Barbara & Bonnie. *Educ:* Brooklyn Col, BA, 49; Rensselaer Polytech Inst, MS, 57; Univ Notre Dame, PhD, 60. *Prof Exp:* Physicist, US Naval Ord Test Sta, 52-55, 60-62 & TRW Systs, Inc, Calif, 62-67; mem tech staff, Aerospace Corp, 67-70; chief, Laser Systs Sect, Martin-Marietta Corp, Fla, 70-71; div chief mil progs, Zenith Radio Res Corp, Calif, 71-72; dir advan eng, Appl Technol Div, Itek Corp, 72-75; mgr, Advan Technol Dept, Lockheed Missiles & Space Corp, 75-77; asst mgr, Optics Dept, TRW Defense, 77-80, mgr, Optical Components Dept, Space Systs Group, 80-88; sr scientist, RDA/Logicon, 88-90 & W J Schafer Assoc Inc, 90-93. *Mem:* Am Phys Soc; Sigma Xi; Res Soc Am; Optical Soc Am. *Res:* Acousto-optics-electronics; laser research; gas discharges; atomic physics; multiple photon processes; free electron lasers; high energy chemical lasers. *Mailing Add:* 148 Rutgers Pl Clifton NJ 07013-1457

SILVER, PAUL J, cardiopulmonary pharmacology, for more information see previous edition

SILVER, RICHARD N, THEORETICAL SOLID STATE PHYSICS. *Current Pos:* staff mem solid state physics, 74-79, neutron scattering, 79-86, STAFF MEM CONDENSED MATTER PHYSICS, 86- *Personal Data:* b Bridgeport, Conn, July 18, 45; m 69; c 4. *Educ:* Calif Inst Technol, BS, 66, PhD(theoret physics), 71. *Prof Exp:* Res assoc elem particle physics, Brown Univ, 71-72; res assoc solid state physics, Calif Inst Technol, 72-74. *Concurrent Pos:* IBM fel, Calif Inst Technol, 72-74. *Mem:* Am Phys Soc. *Res:* High excitation conditions in semiconductors; solid state lasers; statistical mechanics of phase transitions; neutron scattering experiments with pulsed spallation neutron sources; maximum entropy data analysis; quantum Monte Carlo. *Mailing Add:* MSB 262 Group T11 Los Alamos Nat Lab Los Alamos NM 87545

SILVER, RICHARD TOBIAS, MEDICINE. *Current Pos:* from instr to assoc prof, 58-73, PROF CLIN MED, MED COL, CORNELL UNIV, 73, CHIEF ONCOL SERV, NY HOSP-CORNELL MED CTR, 77- *Personal Data:* b New York, NY, Jan 18, 29; m 63; c 1. *Educ:* Cornell Univ, AB, 50, State Univ NY, MD, 53; Am Bd Internal Med, dipl, 62, cert med oncol, 73. *Prof Exp:* Intern med, NY Hosp-Cornell Med Ctr, 53-54, resident physician, 56-58; clin assoc, Gen Med Br, Nat Cancer Inst, 54-56. *Concurrent Pos:* Vis Fulbright lectr, res scholar & vis prof, Sch Med, Univ Bahia, 58-59; physician outpatients, NY Hosp, 58-62, from asst attend physician to assoc attend physician, 62-73, attend physician, 73-; hematologist & consult, Gracie Sq Gen Hosp, 59-; asst vis physician, 2nd Cornell Div, Bellevue Hosp, 62-68; consult leukemia & mem, Leukemia-Myeloma Task Force, NIH, 65-69, mem polycythemia study group, 67-; dir chemother serv, Div Hemat & Oncol, Cornell Med Ctr, 67-75; consult & attend hematologist, Englewood Hosp, NJ & Manhattan Eye, Ear & Throat Hosp; prin investr, Clin Chemother Prog, Cancer Control, 73-80; group vchmn, Cancer & Leukemia Group B, 76-; mem, Comt Pub Affairs, Am Soc Clin Oncol, 81. *Mem:* Am Soc Hemat; Harvey Soc; Am Fedn Clin Res; fel Am Col Physicians; Am Soc Clin Oncol. *Res:* Hematology and oncology, especially leukemia and oncology chemotherapy; over 130 publications and articles. *Mailing Add:* 1440 York Ave New York NY 10021-2577

SILVER, ROBERT, PHYSICS. *Current Pos:* assoc prof, 66-71, chmn dept, 74-82, PROF PHYSICS & ASTRON, EASTERN MICH UNIV, 71- *Personal Data:* b Detroit, Mich, Aug 3, 21; m 47; c 2. *Educ:* Wayne State Univ, BS, 48; Univ Calif, Berkeley, PhD(physics), 58. *Prof Exp:* Physicist, Lawrence Radiation Lab, Univ Calif, 51-57; sr res physicist, Gen Motors Res Labs, 57-66. *Concurrent Pos:* Instr, Wayne State Univ, 59-61 & Univ Detroit, 63-66. *Mem:* Am Phys Soc; Am Asn Physics Teachers; Soc Sigma Xi. *Res:* Low energy particle scattering; nuclear reactors and neutron moderation; thermionic conversion; traffic dynamics; electrooptics; Mossbauer effect. *Mailing Add:* 3 Buckingham Ct Ann Arbor MI 48104-4909

SILVER, SIMON DAVID, MOLECULAR BIOLOGY, MICROBIAL PHYSIOLOGY. *Current Pos:* from asst prof to assoc prof, 66-76, PROF BIOL & MICROBIOL, WASHINGTON UNIV, 76- *Personal Data:* b Detroit, Mich, June 22, 36; m 58; c 2. *Educ:* Univ Mich, BA, 57; Mass Inst Technol, PhD(biophys), 62. *Prof Exp:* NSF fel, Med Res Coun-Microbial Genetics Res Unit, Hammersmith Hosp, London, 62-64; asst res biophysicist, Virus Lab, Univ Calif, Berkeley, 64-66. *Concurrent Pos:* Vis fel, Dept Biochem, John Curtin Sch Med Res, Australian Nat Univ, 74-75 & 79-80; ed-in-chief, J Bacteriol, 78-87; mem metabolic biol panel, NSF, 80-84. *Mem:* Am Soc Microbiol; Genetics Soc Am; Biophys Soc; Am Soc Biol Chemists; Soc Gen Microbiol. *Res:* Bacterial physiology; molecular genetics. *Mailing Add:* Univ Ill-Chicago 835 S Wolcott Ave Rm 703 Chicago IL 60612-7344. *Fax:* 312-996-6415

SILVER, SYLVIA, MICROBIOLOGY, HUMAN IMMUNODEFICIENCY VIRUS EDUCATION & PREVENTION. *Current Pos:* asst prof, 78-84, ASSOC PROF PATH, SCH MED & HEALTH SCI, GEORGE WASHINGTON UNIV, 84-, DIR, CLIN LAB SCI PROG, 78-, ASSOC PROF HEALTH CARE SCI, 88-, ASSOC PROF PATH, GRAD SCH ARTS & SCI, 88-, ASSOC PROF OF MED, 95-, DIR, OFF HIV ACTIV, 95- *Personal Data:* b Chicago, Ill, Dec 11, 42; m 63, David M; c 2. *Educ:* Drake Univ, BA, 65; Cath Univ Am, MTS, 75, DA(clin microbiol), 77. *Prof Exp:* Res asst biochem & vet physiol, Iowa State Univ, 66-68; res asst surg res, Harvard Med Sch, 68-69; instr med technol, Sch Med, Univ Md, 71-73; lectr, Montgomery Col, 75-78. *Concurrent Pos:* Consult, Dept Health & Human Serv, health professions, 79-81, Lister Hill Nat Ctr Biomed, Commun Nat Libr Med, 83-85; Wear vis prof, Wichita State Univ, 84-85. *Mem:* Am Soc Microbiol; Am Pub Health Asn; Am Soc Clin Lab Sci; Asn Schs Allied Health Professions; Sigma Xi; Int Soc AIDS Educ. *Res:* Clinical microbiology; laboratory medicine; HIV prevention; natural history of human immunodeficiency virus disease; community human immunodeficiency virus education, HIV-related malignancies. *Mailing Add:* George Wash Univ Med Ctr 2300 Eye St NW Washington DC 20037. *Fax:* 202-994-5056; *E-Mail:* ssilver@gwis2.cire.gwu.edu

SILVER, WARREN SEYMOUR, BIOLOGICAL NITROGEN FIXATION, PLANT MICROBE SYMBIOSIS. *Current Pos:* prof, 70-91, EMER PROF MICROBIOL & BOT, UNIV SFLA, 91- *Personal Data:* b New York, NY, Nov 14, 24; m 50, Irene R Lee; c Gordon J, Ellen A (Coates), Karin J & Thomas C. *Educ:* Univ Md, BS, 49, MS, 50; Johns Hopkins Univ, PhD(biochem), 53. *Prof Exp:* Jr instr biol, Johns Hopkins Univ, 50-53; res scientist, Upjohn Co, 53-54; Nat Cancer Inst fel, Inst Microbiol, Rutgers Univ, 54-56; from asst prof to prof bact, Univ Fla, 56-67; prof life sci & chmn dept, Ind State Univ, 67-70. *Concurrent Pos:* Prog mgr, Competitive Res Grants Off, USDA, 79-80. *Mem:* AAAS; Am Soc Microbiol; Brit Soc Gen Microbiol; fel Am Acad Microbiol. *Res:* Bacterial nutrition; inorganic nitrogen metabolism by microorganisms; microbiol ecology; respiratory enzymes; plant-microbe symbiosis; biological nitrogen fixation. *Mailing Add:* Dept Biol Univ SFla 4202 Fowler Ave Tampa FL 33620-5150. *Fax:* 813-974-3263

SILVERA, ISAAC F, SOLID STATE PHYSICS. *Current Pos:* AT LYMAN LAB PHYSICS, HARVARD UNIV. *Personal Data:* b San Diego, Calif, Mar 25, 37; m 61; c 4. *Educ:* Univ Calif, Berkeley, AB, 59, PhD(physics), 65. *Prof Exp:* Franco-Am exchange fel, Lab Electrostatics & Physics of Metal, 65-66; mem tech staff, Sci Ctr, NAm Rockwell Corp, 66-71; prof exp physics, physics lab, Univ Amsterdam, 71- *Mem:* Am Phys Soc. *Res:* Far infrared and Raman spectroscopy of solids at low temperature; critical phenomena; light scattering in quantum solids and molecular beams; atomic hydrogen in the condensed phase; high pressure physics. *Mailing Add:* Lyman Lab Physics Harvard Univ Cambridge MA 02138. *Fax:* 617-496-5144

SILVERBERG, ALICE, ARITHMETIC ALGEBRAIC GEOMETRY. *Current Pos:* from asst prof to assoc prof, 84-96, PROF MATH, OHIO STATE UNIV, 96- *Personal Data:* b New York, NY, Oct 6, 58. *Educ:* Harvard Univ, AB, 79; Princeton Univ, MA, 81, PhD(math), 84. *Concurrent Pos:* Postdoctoral res fel, NSF, 84-87; postdoctoral & jr fac res fel, IBM, 88-89; vis scholar, Harvard Univ, 90-91; Sloan res fel, 90-92; res prof, Math Sci Res Inst, Berkeley, 92-93; mem, Centennial Fel Comt, Am Math Soc, 93-95, chair, 94-95, Meetings & Confs Comt, 95-96, Publ Comt, 96-98; ed, Trans & Memoirs of Am Math Soc, 96- *Mem:* Am Math Soc. *Res:* Arithmetic algebraic geometry and number theory; abelian varieties and Shimura varieties; fields of definition, torsion points and homomorphisms of abelian varieties and l-adic representations. *Mailing Add:* Dept Math Ohio State Univ Columbus OH 43210-1174

SILVERBERG, STEVEN GEORGE, SURGICAL PATHOLOGY. *Current Pos:* PROF PATH & DIR ANAT PATH, UNIV MD MED SYS, 96- *Personal Data:* b New York, NY, Nov 30, 38; m 68, Kiyoe Ono. *Educ:* Brooklyn Col, AB, 58; Johns Hopkins Univ, MD, 62. *Honors & Awards:* Elaine Snyder Cancer Res Award, 95. *Prof Exp:* Intern med, Bellevue Hosp, 62-63; resident path, Yale Univ-Grace New Haven Hosp, 63-65; fel path, Mem Hosp for Cancer & Allied Dis, 65-66; from asst prof to assoc prof surg path, Med Col Va, 68-72; from assoc prof to prof path, Sch Med, Univ Colo, Denver, 72-81; prof path, George Washington Univ, Med Ctr, 81-96. *Concurrent Pos:* Exec dir, Colo Regional Cancer Ctr, 76-79; ed-in-chief, Int J Gynec Path, 85-93; coun mem, Asn Dir Anat Surg Path & Int Gynec Cancer Soc, 90-96. *Mem:* Am Soc Clin Path; Int Acad Path; Int Soc Gynec Path (vpres & pres-elect, 96-); Arthur Purdy Stout Soc Surg Path (secy, 79-83); Asn Dir Anat Surg Path (vpres & pres-elect, 96-); Int Gyn Cancer Soc. *Res:* Natural history and histogenesis of neoplasms; ultrastructure in surgical pathology; gynecologic and breast pathology; epidemiologic pathology; intraoperative consultation and cytology. *Mailing Add:* Univ Md Med Syst 22 S Greene St Baltimore MD 21201. *Fax:* 410-328-0644

SILVERBORG, SAVEL BENHARD, FORESTRY. *Current Pos:* forest pathologist, 47-60, assoc prof, 60-66, prof, 66-77, EMER PROF FOREST PATH & FOREST BOT, 77- *Personal Data:* b Gardner, Mass, Jan 20, 13; m 43. *Educ:* UNiv Idaho, BS, 36; Univ Minn, PhD(forest path), 48. *Prof Exp:* Asst, Univ Minn, 40-42; prin procurement inspector, US Dept Army Air Force, Ill, 42-43. *Mem:* AAAS; Soc Am Foresters; Am Phytopath Soc; Sigma Xi. *Res:* Diseases of Hevea brasiliensis; wood decay in buildings in New York; factors affecting the growth and survival of phytophthora palmivora; estimating cull in northern hardwoods; forest plantation diseases. *Mailing Add:* 6676 Colton Rd Lafayette NY 13084

SILVERMAN, ALBERT, NUCLEAR PHYSICS APPLIED TO ARCHAEOLOGY, ARCHAEOMETRY. *Current Pos:* Res assoc physics, 50-52, from asst prof to prof, 52-90, MEM STAFF, LAB NUCLEAR STUDIES, CORNELL UNIV, 77-, EMER PROF PHYSICS, 90- *Personal Data:* b Boston, Mass, Oct 29, 19; m 41, Irene Samuels; c Lynn (Gaillard) & Martin. *Educ:* Univ Calif, PhD(physics), 50. *Concurrent Pos:* Guggenheim & Fulbright fels, 59-60 & 86-87; Cern fel, 74-75. *Mem:* Fel Am Phys Soc. *Res:* Experimental elementary particle physics; heavy quark physics. *Mailing Add:* Lab Nuclear Studies Cornell Univ Ithaca NY 14853

SILVERMAN, ALBERT JACK, PSYCHIATRY, PSYCHOPHYSIOLOGY. *Current Pos:* chmn dept, 70-81, PROF PSYCHIAT, MED CTR, UNIV MICH, ANN ARBOR, 70- *Personal Data:* b Montreal, Que, Jan 27, 25; nat US; m 47; c Barry & Marcy. *Educ:* McGill Univ, BSc, 47, MD & CM, 49; Am Bd Psychiat & Neurol, dipl, 55; Wash Psychoanal Inst, grad, 64. *Prof Exp:* Intern, Jewish Gen Hosp, Montreal, 49-50; resident psychiat, Med Ctr, Univ Colo, 50-53, instr, 53; instr, Sch Med, Duke Univ, 53-54, assoc, 54-56, from asst prof to assoc prof, 56-63; prof & chmn dept, Med Sch, Rutgers Univ, 63-70. *Concurrent Pos:* Chief, Stress-Fatigue Sect, Aeromed Lab, Wright-Patterson AFB, 56-57; attend psychiatrist, Durham Vet Admin Hosp, 57-60, consult, 60-63; consult, Watts Hosp, 59-63, Lyons Vet Admin Hosp, 63-70, Fitkin Mem Hosp & Carrier Clin, 64-70, Ann Arbor Vet Admin Hosp, 70-; & Dept of Defense, 70-; mem, Comt Biol Sci, Nat Inst Ment Health, 64-69, chmn, 68-69, mem, Res Scientist Develop Comt, 70-74, chmn, 72-74, mem, Small Grants Comt, 82-87; mem, Merit Rev Bd Behav Sci, Vet Admin, 75-78, chmn, 77-78; mem, Behav Sci Test Comt, Nat Bd Med Examrs, 78-82, chmn, 84-87, mem, Behav Sci Task Force, 83-84, Comprehensive Com, 87-94. *Mem:* Soc Biol Psychiat; Am Psychosom Soc (pres, 76-77); Am Psychiat Asn; Am Col Psychiat; Am Acad Psychoanal; Sigma Xi. *Res:* Psychosomatic medicine; psycho-endocrinology. *Mailing Add:* 19 Regent Dr Ann Arbor MI 48104-1738

SILVERMAN, ANN JUDITH, NEUROENDOCRINOLOGY. *Current Pos:* from asst prof to assoc prof, 76-85, PROF ANAT & CELL BIOL, COL PHYSICIANS & SURGEONS, COLUMBIA UNIV, 88- *Personal Data:* b Providence, RI, Nov 4, 46. *Educ:* Univ Calif, Los Angeles, BA, 67, PhD(zool), 70. *Prof Exp:* Fel, Dept Anat, Sch Med, Univ Rochester, 70-72, Dept Biol, Univ Calif, Los Angeles, 72-74; asst scientist, Wis Regional Primate Res Ctr, Univ Wis, 74-76. *Concurrent Pos:* Prin investr grant, Nat Inst Child Health & Human Develop, US PHS, 75-, co-prin investr, Nat Inst Arthritis, Metabolic & Digestive Dis, 77-; fel, Alfred P Sloan Found, 76; mem, Molecular Cell Neurobiol Panel, NSF, 81-84. *Mem:* AAAS; Soc Neurosci; Am Soc Anatomists. *Res:* Distribution and function of neurosecretory neurons related to reproductive function and stress. *Mailing Add:* Col Physicians & Surgeons Columbia Univ 360 W 168th St New York NY 10032

SILVERMAN, BENJAMIN DAVID, SOLID STATE PHYSICS, COMPUTATIONAL BIOLOGY. *Current Pos:* RES STAFF MEM, IBM CORP, 69- *Personal Data:* b New York, NY, Mar 14, 31. *Educ:* Brooklyn Col, BA, 53; Univ Rochester, MA, 55; Rutgers Univ, PhD, 59. *Prof Exp:* Prin res scientist, Raytheon Co, 59-66 & Electronics Res Ctr, NASA, 66-69. *Mem:* Fel Am Phys Soc; Am Chem Soc. *Res:* Solid state theory; dielectrics; ferroelectrics; lattice dynamics; organic solids; polymers; theoretical biology. *Mailing Add:* T J Watson Lab IBM Corp Res Ctr 30 Sawmill River Rd Hawthorne NY 10532. *Fax:* 914-784-7455; *E-Mail:* sil@watson.ibm.com

SILVERMAN, BERNARD, ELECTRICAL ENGINEERING. *Current Pos:* RETIRED. *Personal Data:* b Richmond, Va, Aug 15, 22; m 57, Hilda Wasserman; c Lisa & Elaine. *Educ:* Va Polytech Inst, BS, 42; Univ Ill, MS, 47, PhD(elec eng), 54. *Prof Exp:* Instr elec eng, Univ Ill, 47-53; engr, Gen Elec Co, 53-58; assoc prof elec eng, Syracuse Univ, 58-86. *Concurrent Pos:* Consult, NASA, 67 & IBM, 81. *Mem:* Sr mem Inst Elec & Electronics Engrs. *Res:* Nonlinear analysis; stability; communications; magnetic and dielectric devices; digital signal processing; reliability. *Mailing Add:* 205 Windsor Dr Syracuse NY 13214

SILVERMAN, CHARLOTTE, EPIDEMIOLOGY, MEDICINE. *Current Pos:* RETIRED. *Personal Data:* b New York, NY, May 21, 13. *Educ:* Brooklyn Col, BA, 33; Med Col Pa, MD, 38; Johns Hopkins Univ, MPH, 42, DrPH, 48; Am Bd Prev Med, dipl, 49. *Honors & Awards:* Award of Merit, Food & Drug Admin, 74. *Prof Exp:* Field analyst, US Children's Bur, DC, 42-43; field researcher, Tuberc Control Div, USPHS, 43-45; from asst dir to dir bur tuberc, Baltimore City Health Dept, 46-56; chief div epidemiol, State Dept Health, Md, 56-59 & Off Planning & Res, 59-62; consult, NIMH, 62-64, asst chief social psychiat sect, 65-66, chief epidemiol studies br, 66-67, chief pop studies prog, Nat Ctr Radiol Health, 68-70, dep dir biol effects, Bur Radiol Health, 71-83, assoc dir human studies, Off Sci & Technol, Ctr Devices & Radiol Health, Food & Drug Admin, 83-92. *Concurrent Pos:* Lectr prev med, Sch Med, Johns Hopkins Univ, 47-52, lectr epidemiol, Sch Hyg & Pub Health, 54-56 & 66-85, asst prof, 55-64, assoc, 85- *Mem:* Fel Am Col Prev Med; fel Am Orthopsychiat Asn; Soc Epidemiol Res; fel Am Col Epidemiol; fel Am Pub Health Asn. *Res:* Epidemiology of chronic conditions, including ionizing and nonionizing radiation; health effects; mental depression. *Mailing Add:* 4977 Battery Lane No 1001 Bethesda MD 20814-4927

SILVERMAN, DAVID J, MICROBIOLOGY, CELL BIOLOGY. *Current Pos:* asst prof, 73-81, ASSOC PROF MICROBIOL, 81-, ASSOC PROF PATH, SCH MED, UNIV MD, 87- *Personal Data:* b Summerville, SC, July 13, 43; m 66; c 2. *Educ:* Muhlenberg Col, BS, 65; Univ Tenn, Knoxville, MS, 67; WVa Univ, PhD(med microbiol), 71. *Honors & Awards:* Eastman Kodak Med Photog Award, Am Soc Clin Pathologists. *Prof Exp:* Res assoc microbiol, Dartmouth Med Sch, 71-73, instr, 73. *Concurrent Pos:* Nat Cancer Inst fel, Dartmouth Med Sch, 71-73. *Mem:* Am Soc Microbiol; Electron Micros Soc Am; Am Soc Trop Med Hyg; Am Soc Rickettsiol & Rickettsial Dis; Int Col Rickettsiologists. *Res:* Pathogenesis of rickettsial diseases; host-parasite interaction; electron microscopy. *Mailing Add:* Dept Microbiol & Immunol Univ Md Sch Med 655 W Baltimore St Baltimore MD 21201-1559

SILVERMAN, DAVID NORMAN, PHARMACOLOGY, BIOPHYSICS. *Current Pos:* from asst prof to assoc prof pharmacol & biochem, 71-80, assoc dean, acad affairs & sponsored prog, 86-90, PROF PHARMACOL & BIOCHEM, COL MED, UNIV FLA, 80- *Personal Data:* b South Bend, Ind, July 22, 42; m 66; c 2. *Educ:* Mich State Univ, BS, 64; Columbia Univ, MA, 66, PhD(phys chem), 68. *Prof Exp:* NIH fel, Cornell Univ, 69-71. *Concurrent Pos:* Fogarty fel, Umea Univ, Sweden, 78; mem adv bd, Molecular Pharmacol, 78-84. *Mem:* Am Soc Biol Chemist; Am Chem Soc; Am Soc Pharmacol & Exp Therapeut. *Res:* Stable isotopes in pharmacology and biochemistry; magnetic resonance; mass spectrometry; carbonic anhydrase. *Mailing Add:* Dept Pharmacol Univ Fla Col of Med Gainesville FL 32610-0267. *Fax:* 352-392-9696; *E-Mail:* silvrmn@nervm.neroc.ufl.edu

SILVERMAN, DENNIS JOSEPH, ELEMENTARY PARTICLE PHYSICS. *Current Pos:* from asst prof to assoc prof, 71-82, PROF PHYSICS, UNIV CALIF, IRVINE, 82- *Personal Data:* b Long Beach, Calif, Oct 7, 41; m 93, Joan Alexander; c Daniel. *Educ:* Univ Calif, Los Angeles, BA, 63; Stanford Univ, MS, 64, PhD(physics), 68. *Prof Exp:* Res assoc, Princeton Univ, 68-69, instr, 69-70; res assoc, Univ Calif, San Diego, 70-71. *Mem:* Am Phys Soc. *Res:* CP violation in new physics models; tests of quark compositions. *Mailing Add:* Dept Physics & Astron Univ Calif 4129 Physical Sciences 2 Irvine CA 92697-4575. *Fax:* 714-824-2174; *E-Mail:* djsilver@ucu.edu

SILVERMAN, EDWARD, MATHEMATICS. *Current Pos:* from assoc prof to prof, 57-88, EMER PROF MATH, PURDUE UNIV, LAFAYETTE, 88- *Personal Data:* b Minneapolis, Minn, Nov 23, 17; div; c Judith & Emily. *Educ:* Univ Calif, AB, 38, MA, 39, PhD(math), 48. *Prof Exp:* Asst math, Univ Calif, 46-48; Off Naval Res fel, Inst Adv Study, 48-49; asst prof math, Kenyon Col, 49-51 & Mich State Univ, 54-57; mem staff, Sandia Corp, 51-54. *Mem:* Am Math Soc. *Res:* Multiple integral problems in the calculus of variations; lebesge area. *Mailing Add:* 1425 N Salisbury West Lafayette IN 47906

SILVERMAN, ELLEN-MARIE, SPEECH PATHOLOGY. *Current Pos:* PRES & OWNER, TSS-THE SPEECH SOURCE, INC, 86- *Personal Data:* b Milwaukee, Wis, Oct 12, 42; div; c Catherine B. *Educ:* Univ Wis-Milwaukee, BS, 64; Univ Iowa, MA, 67, PhD(speech path), 70. *Prof Exp:* Speech clinician, Curative Workshop Milwaukee, 64-65; res assoc commun, Univ Ill, Urbana, 69-71; from asst prof to assoc prof speech path, Marquette Univ, 73-86; assoc clin prof otolaryngol, Med Col Wis, 79-83, speech pathologist, 85. *Concurrent Pos:* Nat Inst Dent Res fel, 69-71; postdoctoral fel, Univ Ill, Urbana-Champaign, 69-71; asst prof otolaryngol, Med Col Wis, 75-79. *Mem:* Am Speech & Hearing Asn; Sigma Xi. *Res:* Speech pathology, especially stuttering and counseling methods. *Mailing Add:* 5567 N Diversey Blvd Milwaukee WI 53217-5202. *E-Mail:* 755920999@aol.com

SILVERMAN, FRANKLIN HAROLD, SPEECH PATHOLOGY, APPLIED STATISTICS. *Current Pos:* assoc prof, 71-77, PROF SPEECH PATH, MARQUETTE UNIV, 77-; CLIN PROF REHABILITATION MED, MED COL WIS, 80- *Personal Data:* b Providence, RI, Aug 16, 33; m 83, Evelyn Chanda; c Catherine. *Educ:* Emerson Col, BS, 60; Northwestern Univ, MA, 61; Univ Iowa, PhD(speech path), 66. *Prof Exp:* Res assoc stuttering, Univ Iowa, 65-68; asst prof speech path, Univ Ill, Urbana-Champaign, 68-71. *Mem:* Fel Am Speech Lang Hearing Asn; Sigma Xi. *Res:* Stuttering in elementary-school children; assessment of the impacts of stuttering therapy methods; research design in speech pathology and audiology; augmentative communication strategies for the severely communicatively impaired. *Mailing Add:* Col Health Sci Marquette Univ Milwaukee WI 53201-1881. *Fax:* 414-288-3980

SILVERMAN, GARY S, ENVIRONMENTAL SCIENCE, INTERNATIONAL ENVIRONMENTAL EDUCATION. *Current Pos:* from asst prof & dir to assoc prof & dir, 86-95, GRAD FAC, BOWLING GREEN STATE UNIV, 89-, PROF & DIR, ENVIRON HEALTH PROG, 95- *Personal Data:* b Philadelphia, Pa, Dec 10, 52; m 75, Marion K Grant; c Rachel & Natalie. *Educ:* Claremont Men's Col, BA, 74; Univ Calif, Berkeley, MS, 76; Univ Calif, Los Angeles, PhD(environ sci & eng), 83. *Prof Exp:* Staff res assoc, Sanitary Res Lab, Univ Calif, Berkeley, 76-77; proj mgr & microbiologist, Metrop Water Dist Southern Calif, 77-80; prog mgr & sr environ engr, Assoc Bay Area Govts, Calif, 81-86. *Concurrent Pos:* Mem, Grad Prog Environ Mgt, Univ San Francisco & 83-86, Allied Health-Indust Hygiene Med Col Ohio, 87-; Fulbright scholar, Malaysia, 96. *Mem:* Am Water Works Asn; Nat Asn Environ Profs; Nat Environ Health Asn; Nat Environ Health Sci & Protection Accreditation Coun; NAm Asn Environ Educ; Sigma Xi. *Res:* Authored numerous publications. *Mailing Add:* Environ Health Prog/Bowling Green State Univ 102 Health Ctr Bowling Green OH 43403. *E-Mail:* silverma@bgnet.bgsu.edu

SILVERMAN, GORDON, ELECTRONICS. *Current Pos:* affil, 64-80, SR RES ASSOC ELEC ENG, ROCKEFELLER UNIV, 80- *Personal Data:* b Brooklyn, NY, Mar 4, 34; m 57; c 3. *Educ:* Columbia Col, AB, 55, BS, 56, MS, 57; Polytech Inst Brooklyn, PhD(syst sci), 72. *Prof Exp:* Sr engr, Int Tel & Tel Corp, 57-61; proj engr, Loral Electronics Corp, 61-64. *Concurrent Pos:* Mem adj fac, Fairleigh Dickinson Univ, 58- & Polytech Inst Brooklyn, 65-68. *Mem:* Inst Elec & Electronics Engrs; Sigma Xi. *Res:* Application of electronic instrumentation to the study of biological systems; analysis and simulation of human learning. *Mailing Add:* 70 Riverside Dr New York NY 10024-5714

SILVERMAN, HAROLD, BIOMINERALIZATION, SKELETAL MUSCLE FORM & FUNCTION. *Current Pos:* asst prof zool & physiol, 81-86, ASSOC PROF ZOOL & PHYSIOL, LA STATE UNIV, 86-, ASSOC DEAN, COL BASIC SCI. *Personal Data:* b Detroit, Mich, Jan 30, 50; m 81; c 2. *Educ:* Univ Mich, BS, 72; Ohio Univ, MS, 74, PhD(zool), 77. *Prof Exp:* Asst muscle physiol, Muscular Dystrophy Asn, Univ Toronto, 77-80; asst prof biol, Pan Am Univ, 80-81. *Concurrent Pos:* NSF grants, 83- *Mem:* Am Asn Anat; Am Soc Zoologist. *Res:* Cellular and physiological processes of biominerazation of calcium concretions in freshwater mussels; skeletal muscle fiber response to neural overactivity biochemically and morphologically. *Mailing Add:* Dept Zool & Physiol La State Univ Baton Rouge LA 70803

SILVERMAN, HAROLD I, PHARMACY. *Current Pos:* AT THOMPSON MED CO. *Personal Data:* b Lawrence, Mass, Apr 27, 28; m 51; c 2. *Educ:* Philadelphia Col Pharm & Sci, BSc, 51, MSc, 52, DSc, 56. *Honors & Awards:* Newcomb Award, 56; Am Cyanamid Co Lederle res awards, 62, 63; Distinguished Serv Award, Am Optom Asn, 74. *Prof Exp:* Instr pharmacog, Philadelphia Col Pharm & Sci, 52-56; asst prof pharm, Brooklyn Col Pharm & Long Island Univ, 56-59, assoc prof pharm & dir aerosol res lab, 59-64; vpres & sci dir, Knoll Pharmaceut Co, NJ, 64-68; chmn dept pharm, 68-73, prof pharm & assoc dean, Mass Col Pharm, 68-, dir Div Appl Sci, 73- *Concurrent Pos:* Sr scientist pharmaceut prod res & develop, Warner Lambert Res Inst, NJ, 58-61; lectr, New Eng Col Optom, 71- & Sch Med, Boston Univ, 71-; consult, Malmstrom Chem Corp, Warner Lambert Res Inst, J T Baker Chem Co, Gallard & Schlessinger Co, Thompson Med Co, Topps Chewing Gum, Inc, Cooper Labs, Inc, H V Shuster, Inc, Gillette Co, Corneal Sci, Inc, Arthur D Little, Inc, NJ Bd Pharm, Mass Bd Pharm, Boston Mus of Sci & R I Bd Optom; partic, US Pharmacopea, Nat Formulary Rev, 68-; mem human subjects comt, Peter Bent Brigham Hosp, Boston Univ Med Ctr, 74-; sci ed, Pharm Lett, 74-; contrib ed, Apothecary, 74-; grants from Smith, Kline & French, S B Penick, Baker Castor Oil Co & Pfeiffer Found. *Mem:* Am Pharmaceut Asn; AAAS; Am Chem Soc; Soc Pharmacists in Indust; fel Soc Cosmetic Chemists. *Res:* Pharmaceutical chemistry and drug development; drug stabilization; methods of analysis; pharmacokinetics. *Mailing Add:* 45 Crest Rd Framingham MA 01701-5606

SILVERMAN, HARVEY FOX, ELECTRICAL ENGINEERING, COMPUTER ENGINEERING. *Current Pos:* prof eng, 80-91, dir undergrad eng prog, 88-90, DEAN ENG, BROWN UNIV, 91- *Educ:* Trinity Col, BS, 63, BSE, 66; Brown Univ, ScM, 68, PhD, 71. *Prof Exp:* Res assoc, Gerber Sci Instrument Co, 64-66; researcher & mgr, T J Watson Res Ctr, IBM, 70-80. *Concurrent Pos:* Consult, Submarine Signal Div, Raytheon Co, 68; grantee, IBM, 81-85, Analog Devices, 82-87, Glak, 82, AMP, 84-85, Tektronix, 85 & US West, 88; IBM fel, 84-87, Metrabyte, 92. *Mem:* Inst Elec & Electronics Engrs; Sigma Xi. *Res:* Home designed networks of processing nodes, each of which has a high-speed reduced instruction set computer host coupled to a large, reconfigurable system, general C functions, time-varying speech analysis, talker independent connected-speech recognition algorithms and systems and non-linear optimization. *Mailing Add:* Div Eng Brown Univ Box D Providence RI 02912

SILVERMAN, HERBERT PHILIP, ELECTROCHEMISTRY, SENSORS. *Current Pos:* RES & DEVELOP CONSULT, SILVERMAN & ASSOCS, 92- *Personal Data:* b Brooklyn, NY, Sept 8, 24; m 49, Gloria Pokrass; c Sandra, Marsha & Steven. *Educ:* City Col New York, BS, 48; Stanford Univ, PhD(chem), 57. *Honors & Awards:* Ralph B Derr Mem lÖctr. *Prof Exp:* Actg instr anal chem, Stanford Univ, 55; res chemist, Kaiser Aluminum & Chem Co, 55-58; sr scientist, Lockheed Missiles & Space Co, 58-61; group leader electrochem, Magna Corp, TRW, Inc, Anaheim, 61-62, dept mgr phys chem, 62-64, div mgr res & develop, 64-65, assoc mgr chem sci, TRW Systs, 65-66, mgr biosci, 66-78; mgr electrochem res, Occidental Res Corp, 78-81, mgr prof relations, 81-83, mgr oper comt, 81-83; vpres res & develop, USI, Inc, 83-92. *Concurrent Pos:* Lectr, Univ Southern Calif; chmn, Res Inst Task Force Antioch Col; career consult, Am Chem Soc. *Mem:* Am Chem Soc; Electrochem Soc; Sigma Xi. *Res:* Electrochemical processes;

electrobiochemistry; photochemical influence on electrochemical reactions; biochemical influence on electrochemical reactions; nonaqueous electrochemistry; ion exchange membranes. *Mailing Add:* 1590 Via Corsica Laguna Beach CA 92651-1333

SILVERMAN, JACOB, PHYSICAL CHEMISTRY, SCIENCE ADMINISTRATION. *Current Pos:* RETIRED. *Personal Data:* b Brooklyn, NY, May 11, 23; m 51; c 2. *Educ:* Wayne State Univ, BSc, 43, PhD(phys chem), 49. *Prof Exp:* Lectr & res assoc chem, Univ Southern Calif, 49-51; radiol chemist, US Naval Radiol Defense Lab, 51-53; res chemist, Aerojet Gen Corp Div, Gen Tire & Rubber Co, 53-54; mgr chem & mat sci, Rocketdyne Div, NAm Rockwell, Inc, 54-75, dir energy systs, Rocketdyne Div, 75-78, dir, fossil energy systs, Energy Systs Group, Rockwell Int Corp, 78-84. *Mem:* AAAS; Am Chem Soc; Sigma Xi. *Res:* Technical management; research administration; fuel technology; physical chemistry. *Mailing Add:* 22963 Darien St Woodland Hills CA 91364

SILVERMAN, JEFFREY ALAN, CANCER RESEARCH, GROWTH REGULATION. *Current Pos:* DIR DRUG TRANSP, AV MAX, CALIF, 96-. *Educ:* Univ Pittsburgh, PhD(exp path), 84. *Prof Exp:* Res assoc, Med Sch, Dartmouth Col, 84-89; sr staff fel, NIH, 89-96. *Mailing Add:* Av Max Inc 890 Heinz Ave Berkeley CA 94710. *Fax:* 301-496-0734; *E-Mail:* jeffs@elsienci.nih.gov

SILVERMAN, JERALD, NUTRITIONAL CARCINOGENESIS, ALTERNATIVES TO USE OF LABORATORY ANIMALS. *Current Pos:* ASST VPRES, RES ANIMAL FACIL & ASSOC PROF, PATH & LAB MED & DIR, LAB ANIMAL SCI PROG, ALLEGHENY UNIV HEALTH SCI, 92- *Personal Data:* b Brooklyn, NY, Mar 23, 42; m 90, Lisa G Barber; c 2. *Educ:* Cornell Univ, BS, 64, DVM, 66; Am Col Lab Animal Med, dipl, 81; New Sch Soc Res, MPS, 85. *Prof Exp:* Staff vet, Humane Soc NY, 66-67; pvt vet pract, Brooklyn, NY, 68-69 & Pearl River, NY, 70-75; res assoc prof path, NY Med Col, 78-85; dir, Res Animal Facil, Naylor Dana Inst Dis Prev, Am Health Found, 75-85; dir, Lab Animal Ctr, Ohio State Univ, 85-92, assoc dir, Lab Animal Resources & assoc prof, Vet Prev Med, 85-92. *Concurrent Pos:* Assoc ed, Lab Animal, 79-, Lab Animal Sci, 82-86; consult, Revlon Health Care Group, Inc, 80-85, Avon Res, 82-89, Am Health Found, 85-87, Eugene Tech Int, 85-89. *Mem:* Am Vet Med Asn; Am Asn Lab Animal Sci; Am Soc Lab Animal Practitioners; Am Col Lab Animal Med; Am Asn Cancer Res; Vet Cancer Soc; Int Soc Vitamin & Nutrit Oncol; Soc Vet Med Ethics. *Res:* Nutritional aspects of cancer prevention, especially dietary fat and vitamins; diseases of laboratory animals; alternatives to animal usage. *Mailing Add:* MS 436 Univ Lab Animal Res Allegheny Univ Health Sci Broad & Vine Sts Philadelphia PA 19102. *E-Mail:* silvermanj@allegheny.edu

SILVERMAN, JOSEPH, RADIATION CHEMISTRY, POLYMER CHEMISTRY. *Current Pos:* from assoc prof to prof, 60-91, dir, Inst Phys Sci & Technol, 77-83, EMER PROF CHEM & NUCLEAR ENG, UNIV MD, COLLEGE PARK, 91- *Personal Data:* b New York, NY, Nov 5, 22; m 51, Joan Jacks; c Joshua & David. *Educ:* Brooklyn Col, BA, 44; Columbia Univ, AM, 45, PhD(chem), 51. *Honors & Awards:* Radiation Indust Award, Am Nuclear Soc, 75. *Prof Exp:* Staff phys chemist, Atomic Energy Div, H K Ferguson Co, NY, 51-52; res dir, Nuclear Labs, Walter Kidde Nuclear labs, Inc, 52-55; vpres & lab dir, Radiation Appln, Inc, 55-58; assoc prof chem, State Univ NY, 58-59. *Concurrent Pos:* Guggenheim fel, 66-67; consult, Danish Atomic Energy Comn, 67-76; guest scientist, Atomic Energy Res Estab, Denmark; vis prof, Royal Mil Col Sci, Eng; ed, Int J Appl Radiation & Isotopes, 73-78; consult, Indust Res Inst, Japan, 73-; vis distinguished prof nuclear energy, Univ Tokyo, 74; consult, Boris Kidric Nuclear Sci Inst, Yugoslavia, 74-85; consult, UN Develop Prog, 76-83; consult, Int Atomic Energy Agency, 81-; consult, Gen Pub Utilities (3 Mile Island), 83-86. *Mem:* Am Chem Soc; fel Am Nuclear Soc; fel Am Phys Soc; fel Nordic Soc Radiation Chem & Technol; Sigma Xi. *Res:* Pure and applied polymer and radiation chemistry; radiation source technology; effects of ionizing radiation on polymers and vinyl monomers; radiation processing. *Mailing Add:* Dept Mat & Nuclear Eng Univ Md College Park MD 20742-2115. *Fax:* 301-314-9467; *E-Mail:* jagman@eng.umd.edu

SILVERMAN, LEONARD, ENGINEERING. *Current Pos:* from asst prof to assoc prof, Dept Elec Eng-Systs, 68-77, chmn, 82-84, PROF, DEPT ELEC ENG-SYSTS, UNIV SOUTHERN CALIF, 77-, DEAN ENG, 84- *Educ:* Columbia Univ, BS, 62, MS, 63, PhD(elec eng), 66. *Honors & Awards:* Centennial Medal, Inst Elec & Electronics Engrs, 84. *Prof Exp:* Actg asst prof elec eng & comput sci, Univ Calif, Berkeley, 66-68. *Concurrent Pos:* Consult var aerospace & electronic co; dir bd, Tandon Co, 88- *Mem:* Nat Acad Eng; fel Inst Elec & Electronics Engrs; Soc Indust & Appl Math. *Res:* Theory and application of multivariable systems and control; author of more than 100 publications. *Mailing Add:* Sch Eng Univ Southern Calif Univ Par Los Angeles CA 90089-1450

SILVERMAN, MARK PHILIP, QUANTUM INTERFERENCE PHENOMENA, LIGHT SCATTERING. *Current Pos:* PROF PHYSICS, TRINITY COL, 82-; CONSULT PHYSICS RES, SCI & GRAD EDUC, NSF, 90- *Educ:* Harvard Univ, PhD(physics), 73. *Honors & Awards:* Royal Soc Prince & Princess of Wales Award, Royal Soc, 93. *Prof Exp:* Vis prof atomic physics, Ecole Normale Superieure Paris, 73-75. *Concurrent Pos:* Vis chief researcher, Hitachi Advan Res Lab, Tokyo, 86 & 89; vis prof electromagnetics, Helsinki Univ Technol & chem physics, Ecole Superieure de Physique et Chimie, 95. *Mem:* Am Phys Soc; Optical Soc Am; Sigma Xi. *Res:* Fundamental quantum processes, atomic structures and interactions, fourier optics and diffractive imaging, optics and electrodynamics of chiral media and light scattering from turbid media; author of 3 books. *Mailing Add:* Trinity Col Hartford CT 06106. *Fax:* 860-297-2569

SILVERMAN, MELVIN, MEDICINE. *Current Pos:* from asst prof to assoc prof med, 71-81, assoc prof physics, 75-81, PROF MED & PHYSICS, UNIV TORONTO, 81- *Personal Data:* b Montreal, Que, Jan 4, 40. *Educ:* McGill Univ, BSc, 60, MD, CM, 64, FRCP(C), 69. *Honors & Awards:* J Francis Mem Prize in Med, 64; Starr Medal, 74; William Goldie Prize, 75; Trillium Award, 90. *Prof Exp:* Assoc res scientist, Dept Med, NY Univ, 66-68; Med Res Coun Centennial fel, McGill Univ Med Clin Montreal Gen Hosp, 69-71, asst prof, Dept Med, McGill Univ, 70-71. *Concurrent Pos:* Asst physician, Montreal Gen Hosp, 70-71; staff physician nephrol, Toronto Gen Hosp, 71-84; dir, Trihosp Nephrol Serv, Toronto Gen Hosp, Mt Sinai Hosp & Women's Col Hosp, 84-90, sr staff physician, Trihosp Nephrol Serv, 90-; dir, MRC Group Membrane Biol, Dept Med, Univ Toronto, 87-, subspecialty training prog, 90-; mem sci coun, Kidney Found Can, 77-85 & 78-84, Med Res Coun Can, 84-89; numerous res grants var orgn, 72- *Mem:* Am Soc Clin Invest; Am Physiol Soc; Am Soc Nephrol; Am Biophys Soc; NY Acad Sci. *Res:* Membrane transport; renal microcirculation; renal disease mechanism. *Mailing Add:* Med Sci Bldg Rm 7207 Dept Med Univ Toronto Toronto ON M5S 1A8 Can. *Fax:* 416-971-2132

SILVERMAN, MELVIN, CONTINUING ENGINEERING EDUCATION IN MANAGEMENT, INDUSTRIAL PSYCHOLOGY. *Current Pos:* MANAGING DIR & OWNER, ATRIUM ASSOCS, 75- *Personal Data:* b Perth Amboy, NJ, Sept 11, 25; m 90, Ann Elizabeth Eggen; c Seth W, Gregg J & Brett N. *Educ:* Rutgers Univ, BSME, 49; Univ Calif, Berkeley, MSIE, 51; Baruch Col, NY, MBA, 73; New Sch Social Res, MA, 78; Union Inst, PhD(indust-social psychol), 82. *Concurrent Pos:* Simon Fell, Univ Manchester, Eng, 93; Fulbright scholar, Malaysia 97. *Mem:* Am Soc Mech Engrs; Am Soc Qual Control; Am Soc Eng Educ. *Res:* Management and operations of large hi-tech organizations, primarily concerned with managing complex projects; central area emphasizing effective training of organizational professionals. *Mailing Add:* Atrium Assocs Inc 770 Anderson Ave Suite Penthouse "C" Cliffside Park NJ 07010

SILVERMAN, MEYER DAVID, PHYSICAL INORGANIC CHEMISTRY. *Current Pos:* CONSULT, 83- *Personal Data:* b New York, NY, Jan 8, 15; m 40, Dorothy Cohen; c Roberta (Limor). *Educ:* Yale Univ, BChE, 34; George Washington Univ, MA, 42; Univ Tenn, PhD(phys chem), 50. *Prof Exp:* Sci aide, Food & Drug Admin, USDA, Washington, DC, 38, sci aide, Cotton Mkt Div, 39-41; jr chem engr, Edgewood Arsenal, Md, 41-42; res chem engr, Permutit Water Conditioning Corp, NY, 42-43; assoc chem engr, Oak Ridge Nat Lab, 43-46, chemist, 47-52, sr chemist, 52-75, res staff mem chem eng, 75-82. *Concurrent Pos:* Fel, Oak Ridge Inst Nuclear Studies; consult chem eng, waste disposal (radioactive), coal conversion & recovery of metals from eastern oil shales, 82- *Mem:* Am Chem Soc; Sigma Xi. *Res:* Chemical potentials; ion exchange; reactor chemistry; radiation-induced corrosion; aerosol physics; nuclear reactor safety; coal conversion processes and plant equipment; high temperature energy storage; mineral recovery from eastern oil shales. *Mailing Add:* 397 East Dr Oak Ridge TN 37830

SILVERMAN, MICHAEL ROBERT, MOLECULAR & MICROBIAL GENETICS. *Current Pos:* RES BIOLOGIST, AGOURON INST, LA JOLLA, 80- *Personal Data:* b Ft Collins, Colo, Oct 7, 43; m 64; c 2. *Educ:* Univ Nebr, BS, 66, MS, 68; Univ Calif, San Diego, PhD(biol), 72. *Prof Exp:* USPHS trainee tumor virol, Med Sch, Univ Colo, 73-75; asst res biologist molecular genetics, Univ Calif, San Diego, 75-80. *Mem:* Am Soc Microbiol. *Res:* Regulation of gene expression, particularly of genes which determine components of the flagellar organelle of Escherichia coli. *Mailing Add:* 9472 Poole St La Jolla CA 92037

SILVERMAN, MORRIS, BIOCHEMISTRY, BACTERIOLOGY. *Current Pos:* instr, 61-63, ASST PROF BIOCHEM, COL MED, STATE UNIV NY DOWNSTATE MED CTR, 63- *Personal Data:* b Brooklyn, NY, June 19, 26; m 55; c 2. *Educ:* NY Univ, BA, 49; Univ Mich, MS, 51; Yale Univ, PhD(biochem), 60. *Prof Exp:* USPHS fel biochem, Pub Health Res Inst New York, 59-61. *Mem:* AAAS; Am Chem Soc. *Res:* Carbohydrate metabolism; oxidative phosphorylation; oxidative enzymes; microbial metabolism. *Mailing Add:* Dept Biochem State Univ NY Health Sci Col Med 450 Clarkson Ave Brooklyn NY 11203-2012

SILVERMAN, MORRIS BERNARD, INORGANIC CHEMISTRY. *Current Pos:* ASSOC PROF CHEM, PORTLAND STATE UNIV, 59- *Personal Data:* b Roxbury, Mass, June 28, 24; m 56. *Educ:* Boston Univ, AB, 48; Univ Wash, Seattle, PhD(chem), 56. *Prof Exp:* Radiochemist, Tracerlab, Inc, 49-50; draftsman, Johnson Fare Box Co, 51; develop chemist, Armour & Co, 52-53; fel organometallics, Univ Wash, Seattle, 56-57; chemist, Chula Res Corp, Stand Oil Co Calif, 57-59. *Mem:* Am Chem Soc; Soc Cosmetic Chemists. *Mailing Add:* 7124 SW Fifth St Portland OR 97219. *E-Mail:* chem@spiritone.com

SILVERMAN, MYRON SIMEON, BACTERIOLOGY, IMMUNOLOGY. *Current Pos:* RETIRED. *Personal Data:* b New York, NY, Aug 2, 15. *Educ:* Cornell Univ, BS, 37, MS, 38; Univ Calif, PhD, 50; Am Bd Microbiol, dipl. *Prof Exp:* Lab technician, Div Lab & Res, NY State Dept Health, 39-41; asst bact, Univ Calif, 48-50; supvry bacteriologist, US Naval Radiol Defense Lab, 50-62, head, Microbiol & Immunol Br, 62-69; res microbiologist, Naval Med Res Unit 1, Calif, 69-70; assoc dean, Grad Sch, Univ NC, Chapel Hill, 79-81, prof oral biol & bact, Dent Res Ctr & Sch Med, 70-90, spec asst to dean, Grad Sch, 81-90. *Concurrent Pos:* Nat Cancer Inst res fel, Guy's Hosp, Med Sch, Univ London, 60-61; Naval Radiol Defense Lab fel, Brookhaven Nat Lab, 68-69; res assoc, Univ Calif, Berkeley, 50-59, lectr, 58-68; mem, Comn Radiation & Infection & Comn Epidemiol Surv, Armed Forces Epidemiol Bd. *Mem:* AAAS; Am Soc Microbiol; Radiation Res Soc; Soc Exp Biol & Med; Am Asn Immunol; Sigma Xi. *Res:* Induction of immune response; cellular interactions in the immune response; immunological aspects of oral disease. *Mailing Add:* 320 Ridgecrest Dr Chapel Hill NC 27514-2102

SILVERMAN, NORMAN A, CARDIOTHORACIC SURGERY, INTRAOPERATIVE MIOCARDIAL PROTECTION. *Current Pos:* PROF SURG, COL MED, UNIV ILL, 80- *Personal Data:* b Boston, Mass, Dec 19, 46. *Educ:* Boston Univ, MD, 71. *Mem:* Soc Univ Surgeons; Am Asn Thoracic Surg; Am Physiol Soc. *Res:* Adjudication of the efficacy of cardioplegia by postichemic assessment of ventricular function and energetics. *Mailing Add:* Div Cardiac & Thoracic Surg Henry Ford Hosp 2799 W Grand Blvd Detroit MI 48202-2689. *Fax:* 313-876-2687

SILVERMAN, PAUL HYMAN, PARASITOLOGY, IMMUNOLOGY. *Current Pos:* RETIRED. *Personal Data:* b Minneapolis, Minn, Oct 8, 24; m 45; c 2. *Educ:* Roosevelt Univ, BS, 49; Northwestern Univ, MS, 51; Univ Liverpool, PhD(parasitol), 55. *Hon Degrees:* DSc, Univ Liverpool, 68. *Prof Exp:* Sr sci officer, Dept Parasitol, Moredun Inst, Edinburgh, Scotland, 56-59; head, Dept Immunoparasitol, Allen & Hansburys, Ltd, Ware, Eng, 60-62; prof zool, vet path & hyg, Univ Ill, Urbana, 63-72, chmn, Dept Zool, 64-65, head, 65-69; chmn, Dept Biol, Univ NMex, 72-73, actg vpres res & grad affairs, 73-74, vpres res & grad affairs, 74-77; provost res & grad studies, State Univ NY Albany, 77-79, pres res found, 79-80; pres, Univ Maine, 80-84; fel, Biol & Med Div, Lawrence Berkeley Lab, Univ Calif, 84-86, actg head, Biol & Med Div & actg dir, 86-87, dir, Donner Lab, 84-90, dir, Biotechnol Prog, 89-90; dir, sci affairs, Beckman Instruments, Inc, 90-95. *Concurrent Pos:* Consult-examr, Comn Cols & Univs, NCent Asn; prof & head, Natural Sci Div, Temple Buell Col, 70-71; adj prof, Univ Colo, Boulder, 70-72; consult comn malaria, Armed Forces Epidemiol Bd, 71-; mem bd dirs, NCent Asn Cols & Sec Schs, 71-, vchmn, Comn on Insts Higher Educ, 72-74 & 76-, chmn, 74-76 & mem bd dirs, Inhalation Toxicol Lab, Albuquerque, NMex; chmn acad bd, US Army Command & Gen Staff Col, Ft Levenworth, Ky, 84-; assoc dir, Lawrence Berkeley Lab, 86-90. *Mem:* Am Soc Microbologists; Am Asn Immunol; Am Soc Trop Med & Hyg; Am Soc Microbiologists; Royal Soc Trop Med & Hyg; NY Acad Sic; Sigma Xi. *Res:* Nature of host-parasite of relationship, particularly on immunological phenomena; in vitro culture of parasites. *Mailing Add:* 8 Whitman Ct Irvine CA 92612. *Fax:* 714-773-6611

SILVERMAN, PHILIP MICHAEL, BIOCHEMISTRY, MOLECULAR BIOLOGY. *Current Pos:* MEM & HEAD PROG MOLECULAR & CELL BIOL, OKLA MED RES FOUND, 88- *Personal Data:* b Chicago, Ill, Oct 21, 42; div; c 2. *Educ:* Univ Ill, Urbana, BS, 64; Univ Calif, Berkeley, PhD(biochem), 68. *Prof Exp:* From asst prof to prof molecular biol, Albert Einstein Col Med,. *Concurrent Pos:* Damon Runyon Mem Fund Cancer Res fel, Albert Einstein Col Med, 69-71; estab investr, Am Heart Asn, 75-80; Irma T Hirschl career scientist, 81-85; mem adv panel genetic biol, NSF, 81-86; Marjorie Nichlos chair med res, 88- *Mem:* Am Soc Biol Chemists; Am Soc Microbiol; Am Soc Cell Biol. *Res:* Biochemistry and genetics of bacterial conjugation; synthesis and function of membrane proteins. *Mailing Add:* Dept Molecular & Cell Biol Okla Med Res Found 825 Northeast 13th St Oklahoma City OK 73104-5097. *Fax:* 405-271-3153; *E-Mail:* philip-silverman@omrf.uokhsc.edu

SILVERMAN, RICHARD BRUCE, ENZYME INHIBITION, ENZYME MECHANISMS. *Current Pos:* from asst prof to assoc prof, 76-82, PROF CHEM, BIOCHEM, MOLECULAR & CELL BIOL, NORTHWESTERN UNIV, 86- *Personal Data:* b Philadelphia, Pa, May 12, 46; m 83; c 3. *Educ:* Pa State Univ, BS, 68; Harvard Univ, MA, 72, PhD(org chem), 74. *Prof Exp:* Fel biochem, Brandeis Univ, 74-76. *Concurrent Pos:* DuPont Young Fac fel, 76; prin investr, NIH, 77-; mem adv panels, NIH, 81-85, 87-, Res Career Develop Award, 82-87; Alfred P Sloan Found fel, 81-85; consult, Proctor & Gamble, 84, Abbott Labs, 87, Monsanto/Searle, 88-90 & Dow Elanco, 93-94. *Mem:* Am Chem Soc; fel AAAS; Am Soc Biochem & Molecular Biol; fel Am Inst Chemists. *Res:* Molecular mechanism of action, rational design and synthesis of medicinal agents that act as enzyme inactivators; elucidation of enzyme mechanisms. *Mailing Add:* Dept Chem Northwestern Univ 2145 Sheridan Rd Evanston IL 60208-3113. *Fax:* 847-491-7713; *E-Mail:* agman@chem.nwu.edu

SILVERMAN, ROBERT, MATHEMATICS. *Current Pos:* from assoc prof to prof, 68-80, EMER PROF MATH, WRIGHT STATE UNIV, 84- *Personal Data:* b Cleveland, Ohio, Oct 23, 28; m 48, 71; c 4. *Educ:* Ohio State Univ, BSc, 51, MA, 54, PhD(math), 58. *Prof Exp:* Instr math, Ohio State Univ, 59; Nat Acad Sci-Nat Res Coun res assoc, Nat Bur Standards, 59-60; asst prof math, Syracuse Univ, 60-65. *Concurrent Pos:* Res assoc, Univ Western Ont, 80, 82. *Mem:* Math Asn Am; Am Math Soc; Sigma Xi. *Res:* Combinatorial analysis; algebra. *Mailing Add:* Dept Math PO Box 709 Yellow Springs OH 45387-0709

SILVERMAN, ROBERT ELIOT, endocrinology, for more information see previous edition

SILVERMAN, ROBERT HUGH, INTERFERON, AUTISENSE. *Current Pos:* STAFF & PROF, DEPT CANCER BIOL, CLEVELAND CLIN FOUND, 91- *Personal Data:* b Houston, Tex, Nov 24, 48; m 84, Jane Glickman; c Kenneth & Samuel. *Educ:* Mich State Univ, BS, 70; Iowa State Univ, PhD(molecular, cellular & develop biol), 77. *Honors & Awards:* Milstein Award, Int Soc Interferon & Cytokine Res, 93. *Prof Exp:* Fel, Roche Inst Molecular Biol, 77-79, Nat Inst Med Res, London, 79-80, Imp Cancer Res Fund, London, 80-82; from asst prof to prof path, Uniformed Servs Univ Health Sci, 82-91. *Concurrent Pos:* Eleanor Roosevelt Int Cancer res fel, Toronto, 90-91; mem, Acquired Immune Deficiency Syndrome & Related Res Study Sect, NIH, 90-91; adj prof, Dept Biochem, Case Western Res Univ. *Mem:* Int Soc Interferon & Cytokine Res; Int Acquired Immune Deficiency Syndrome Soc; Am Asn Invest Pathol; Am Soc Microbiol; Am Soc Virol. *Res:* Molecular mechanisms of interferon action; Role of unusual oligonucleotide known as 2-5A. *Mailing Add:* Dept Cancer Biol NN1-06 Cleveland Clin Found 9500 Euclid Ave Cleveland OH 44195. *Fax:* 216-445-6269; *E-Mail:* silverr@ccsmtp.ccf.org

SILVERMAN, SAM M, GEOPHYSICS, HISTORY & PHILOSOPHY OF SCIENCE. *Current Pos:* RETIRED. *Personal Data:* b New York. NY, Nov 16, 25; m 48, 66, Phyllis Rolfe; c Ann, William, Nancy, Gila & Aaron. *Educ:* City Col New York, BChE, 45; Ohio State Univ, PhD(phys chem), 52; Suffolk Univ Law Sch, JD, 82. *Prof Exp:* Res assoc phys chem, Ohio State Univ, 52-55; asst prof silicate chem, Univ Toledo, 55-57; chief, Polar Atmospheric Processes Br & dir, Geopole Observ, Air Force Cambridge Res Labs, 63-74, res physicist, 57-80; sr res physicist, Physics Dept, Boston Col, 81-97. *Concurrent Pos:* Vis res assoc, Queens Univ, Belfast, 63-64; adv bd, Inst Space & Atmospheric Studies, Univ Sask, 65-69; abstractor & reviewer psychohist, Am J Psychother, 75-77; co-chmn, Interdivi Comn Hist, Int Asn Geomagnetism & Aeronomy. *Mem:* Fel Am Phys Soc; Am Geophys Union; Sigma Xi; fel Explorers Club. *Res:* Polar cap upper atmosphere; aurora, airglow and related fields of upper atmosphere physics; law; solar-terrestrial relations. *Mailing Add:* 18 Ingleside Rd Lexington MA 02173

SILVERMAN, SOL RICHARD, AUDIOLOGY, SPEECH PRODUCTION. *Current Pos:* Instr audiol, Wash Univ, 35-45, assoc prof educ, 45-48, dir, 47-72, prof audiol, 48-81, EMER DIR, CENT INST DEAF, WASH UNIV, 72-, EMER PROF AUDIOL, 81- *Personal Data:* b New York, NY, Oct 2, 11; m 38; c 1. *Educ:* Cornell Univ, BA, 33; Wash Univ, MS, 38, PhD(psychol), 42. *Hon Degrees:* DLitt, Gallaudet Col, 61; LHD, Hebrew Union Col, 62; LLD, Emerson Col, 66; DSc, Rochester Inst Technol, 89. *Honors & Awards:* Herbert Birkett Mem Lectr, McGill Univ, 49; J McKenzie Brown Mem Lectr, Children's Hosp, Los Angeles. *Concurrent Pos:* Dir, proj hearing & deafness, Cent Inst Deaf, Off Sci Res & Develop, 42-45; consult, probs deafness, Secy War, 44-48 & audiol, US Air Force, 51-53; mem, comt conserv hearing, Am Acad Ophthal & Otolaryngol, 57-76; mem, Nat Adv Coun Voc Rehab, 62-66; co-chmn, Int Cong Educ Deaf, Washington, DC, 63; chmn, Nat Adv Comt Educ Deaf, 66-70; mem, commun dis res training comt, Nat Inst Neurol Dis & Blindness, 67-71; mem nat adv group, Nat Tech Inst Deaf, 77-, chmn, 78-82; adj res scientist audiol, Inst Advan Study Commun Processes, Univ Fla, 82- *Mem:* Am Speech & Hearing Asn (pres, 53); Alexander Graham Bell Asn Deaf (pres, 57-60); Coun Educ Deaf (pres, 60-64); fel Acoust Soc Am; hon mem Asn Res Otolaryngol. *Res:* Speech production; hearings aids; auditory tests. *Mailing Add:* 2510 NW 38th St Gainesville FL 32605-2650

SILVERMAN, SOL ROBERT, ORGANIC GEOCHEMISTRY. *Current Pos:* RETIRED. *Personal Data:* b New York, NY, Nov 5, 18; m 51; c 3. *Educ:* NY Univ, BA, 40; Univ Chicago, MS & PhD(geol), 50. *Prof Exp:* Chemist, Chem Warfare Serv, US War Dept, 42-44 & Mat Lab, US Dept Navy, 46-47; geochemist, US Geol Surv, 50-51; res assoc, Calif Res Corp, 51-63, sr res assoc, Chevron Oil Field Res Co, 63-83. *Concurrent Pos:* Lectr petrol geol, Calif State Polytech Univ, 76- *Mem:* Fel AAAS; Am Chem Soc; Geochem Soc; Am Asn Petrol Geologists. *Res:* Distribution of stable isotopes in nature; petroleum geochemistry; biogeochemistry. *Mailing Add:* 1230 Casa del Rey La Habra CA 90631

SILVERMAN, WILLIAM BERNARD, PLANT PATHOLOGY. *Current Pos:* from asst prof to prof, 59-90, EMER PROF BIOL, COL ST THOMAS, 90- *Personal Data:* b New York, NY, Mar 3, 32. *Educ:* City Col New York, BSc, 53; Univ Minn, MSc, 56, PhD(plant path, bot), 58. *Prof Exp:* Asst plant path & bot, Univ Minn, 53-58; res assoc polyacetylenes, NY Bot Garden, 58-59. *Res:* Histology-cytology; microbiology. *Mailing Add:* 1924 Walnut St St Paul MN 55113

SILVERN, LEONARD CHARLES, ENGINEERING PSYCHOLOGY, MAN-MACHINE SYSTEMS. *Current Pos:* PRES, SYSTS ENG LABS, 80- *Personal Data:* b New York, NY, May 20, 19; m 48, 69 & 85, Gwendolyn G Taylor; c Ronald. *Educ:* Long Island Univ, BS, 46; Columbia Univ, MA, 48, EdD, 52. *Prof Exp:* Training supvr & coord, US Dept Navy, 39-49; training dir, Exec Dept, State Div Safety, NY, 49-55; resident eng psychologist, Lincoln Lab, Mass Inst Technol, Rand Corp, 55-56; head tech training eval & develop, Hughes Aircraft Co, 56-58, asst head sci educ, Corp Off, 58-60, dir, Educ & Training Res Lab, Ground Systs Group, 60-62; dir, Human Performance Eng Lab & Consult Eng Psychologist to vpres tech, Norair Div, Northrop Corp, 62-64; prin scientist, Educ & Training Consult Co, 64-66, vpres behav systs, 66-68, pres, 68-97. *Concurrent Pos:* Adj prof, Grad Sch, Univ Southern Calif, 57-65; reviewer, Comput Rev, 62-92; vis prof, Univ Calif, Los Angeles, 63-72; consult, Electronic Industs Asn, 61-69, Univ Hawaii, 70-76, Hq, Air Training Command, USAF, Randolph AFB, Tex, 64-69, Centro Nacional de Productividad, Mexico City, 73-75, Ford Motor Co, 75-76, NS Dept Educ, Halifax, 75-79, Nat Training Systs, Inc, 76-81, Search, 76-, Nfld Pub Serv Comn, 78 & Legis Affairs Off, US Dept Agr, 80; dist opers officer, Los Angeles Co Sheriff's Dept, Disaster Commun Serv, 73-75 & dist commun officer, 75-76; chair, bd dirs, VOX POP, 83-93; mem adv Comt, W Sedona Commun Plan, 86-88; councilman, City of Sedona, Ariz, 88-92; treas, Sedona-Verde Valley Group, Sierra Club, 91-93. *Mem:* Sr mem Inst Elec & Electronics Engrs; Am Psychol Asn; Soc Eng Psychol; Soc Wireless Pioneers; Am Radio Relay League. *Res:* Human learning in engineering and physical science environments; computer-assisted instruction; systems engineering applied to complex social and political systems; systems engineering applied to radio communications by radio operators. *Mailing Add:* PO Box 2085 Sedona AZ 86339-2085

SILVERNAIL, WALTER LAWRENCE, INDUSTRIAL CHEMISTRY. *Current Pos:* CONSULT, SILVERNAIL TECH SERV, 74- *Personal Data:* b St Louis, Mo, Sept 8, 21; m 44, Cynthia M Shoens; c Bruce, Gordon & Laura. *Educ:* Park Col, AB, 47; Univ Mo, AM, 49, PhD(chem), 54. *Prof Exp:* From assoc prof to prof chem, Ill Col, 49-56; assoc prof, Ferris Inst, 56-57; res chemist, Lindsay Chem Div, Am Potash & Chem Corp, 57-64, mgr tech serv, Kerr-McGee Chem Corp, West Chicago Plant, 64-73. *Res:* Rare earth and thorium chemistry; ion exchange; glass polishing; chemical education. *Mailing Add:* 140 E Stimmel St Chicago IL 60185

SILVERS, J(OHN) P(HILLIP), THERMODYNAMICS. *Current Pos:* ENERGY CONSULT, 77-; COMPUT CONSULT, 87- *Personal Data:* b Chicago, Ill, Jan 23, 20; m 45; c 3. *Educ:* Purdue Univ, BS, 44, MS, 46, PhD(heat transfer, thermodyn), 51. *Prof Exp:* Asst heat transfer & vibration anal, Eng Exp Sta, Purdue Univ, 44-47, instr & admin asst to head dept thermodyn & heat transfer, 47-50; assoc scientist, Argonne Nat Lab, 50-55; soc mgr dept appl res, Res & Adv Develop Div, Avco Corp, 55-57, tech asst to vpres res, 57-60, head adv prog undersea technol, 60-65, mgr marine technol dept, 65-66, mgr prog planning, Avco Space Systs Div, 66-68, asst dir eng, Avco Systs Div, 68-71; exec dir, Mass Sci & Technol Found, 72-77. *Concurrent Pos:* Sr scientist, res staff, Mass Inst Technol, 78-81; mgr thermal systs, Res & Develop Div, Dynatech, 81-85; sr scientist, Textron Defense Systs, 85-87. *Mem:* Marine Technol Soc; Sigma Xi. *Res:* Nuclear reactor development; heat transfer; numerical analysis; marine technology; environmental science. *Mailing Add:* 327 Salem St Wilmington MA 01887

SILVERS, WILLYS KENT, GENETICS. *Current Pos:* assoc prof med genetics, 65-67, chmn genetics grad group, 80-90, PROF GENETICS, SCH MED, UNIV PA, 67-, PROF PATH, 69-, CHMN, MOLECULAR BIOL GRAD GROUP, 93- *Personal Data:* b New York, NY, Jan 12, 29; m 56, Abigail Adams; c Willys K Jr & Deborah. *Educ:* Johns Hopkins Univ, BA, 50; Univ Chicago, PhD(zool), 54. *Prof Exp:* Assoc staff scientist, Jackson Lab, Bar Harbor, 57; assoc mem, Wistar Inst, Philadelphia, 57-65. *Concurrent Pos:* USPHS fel, Brown Univ, 55-56 & Jackson Lab, Bar Harbor, Maine, 56; NIH career develop award, 64-71; mem allergy & immunol study sect, NIH, 62-66; assoc ed, J Exp Zool, 65-70 & 82-; mem primate res ctr adv comt, NIH, 68-71; sect ed, Immunogenetics & Transplantation, J Immunol, 73-77; mem comt cancer immunobiol, Nat Cancer Inst, 74-77; mem bd sci oversers, Jackson Lab, Bar Harbor, Maine, 81-89; chmn bd sci oversers, Jackson Lab, 87-89. *Mem:* AAAS; Genetics Soc Am; Am Genetic Asn (pres, 81-); Am Soc Human Genetics. *Res:* Mammalian genetics, with particular reference to the genetics of coat-color determinant and immunogenetics; biology and immunology of tissue transplantation; biology of skin. *Mailing Add:* Dept Genetics Univ Pa Sch Med Philadelphia PA 19104. *Fax:* 215-573-5892

SILVERSMITH, ERNEST FRANK, ORGANIC CHEMISTRY. *Current Pos:* PROF CHEM, MORGAN STATE UNIV, 67- *Personal Data:* b Nuernberg, Ger, Oct 3, 30; nat US; m 53, Eva Perlman; c Ann J, Ruth E, Edward M & Daniel J. *Educ:* Harvard Univ, AB, 52; Univ Wis, PhD(chem), 55. *Honors & Awards:* E Emmet Reid Awrd, Mid Atlantic Region, Am Chem Soc, 87. *Prof Exp:* Res fel chem, Calif Inst Technol, 55-56; asst prof, Mt Holyoke Col, 56-58; res chemist, E I du Pont de Nemours & Co, 58-67. *Mem:* Am Chem Soc. *Res:* Photochemistry; spectroscopy; modern organic synthesis. *Mailing Add:* Dept Chem Morgan State Univ Baltimore MD 21251. *Fax:* 410-319-3778; *E-Mail:* esilvers@jewel.morgan.edu

SILVERSTEIN, ABE, MECHANICAL ENGINEERING. *Current Pos:* RETIRED. *Personal Data:* b Terre Haute, Ind, Sept 15, 08; m 50; c 3. *Educ:* Rose Polytech Inst, BS, 29, MechEng, 34. *Hon Degrees:* ScD, Rose Polytech Inst, 59; DEng, Case Western Res Univ, 58; LHD, Yeshiva Univ, 60; DAS, Fenn Col, 64. *Prof Exp:* Aerodyn res engr, Langley Res Ctr, Nat Adv Comt Aeronaut, Va, 29-40, head full scale wind tunnel, 40-43, chief, Engine Installation Res Div, Lewis Flight Propulsion Lab, Ohio, 43-45, chief, Wind Tunnel & Flight Res Div, 45-49, chief res, 49-52, assoc dir, 52-58, dir, Off Space Flight Progs, NASA, Washington, DC, 58-61, dir, Lewis Res Ctr, 61-70; dir environ planning, Repub Steel Corp, 70-78. *Concurrent Pos:* Consult mech eng, 76- *Mem:* Nat Acad Eng; fel Am Astronaut Soc; fel Am Inst Aeronaut & Astronaut; fel Royal Aeronaut Soc; Int Acad Astronaut. *Res:* Aerodynamic and propulsion aspects of aeronautical research; propulsion and power generation aspects of space; design and construction of facilities for space research. *Mailing Add:* 21160 Seabury Ave Fairview Park OH 44126-2753

SILVERSTEIN, ARTHUR M, IMMUNOLOGY, HISTORY OF MEDICINE. *Current Pos:* assoc prof, 64-67, Odd Fellows res prof, 67-90, EMER PROF OPHTHALMIC IMMUNOL, JOHNS HOPKINS UNIV SCH MED, 91- *Personal Data:* b Aug 6, 28. *Educ:* Ohio State Univ, AB, 48, MSc, 51; Rensselaer Polytech Inst, PhD(phys chem), 54. *Hon Degrees:* DSc, Univ Granada, Spain, 86. *Honors & Awards:* Macy lectr, Harvard Univ Med Sch, 65; Ralph English Miller Mem lectr, Dartmouth Med Sch, 69; Jonas S Friedenwald Mem Award & lectr, Asn Vision Opthalmol, 73; Doyne Mem Medal & lectr, Oxford Ophthalmol Cong, 74. *Prof Exp:* Res asst, Dept Immunochem, Sloan-Kettering Inst Cancer Res, 48-49; biochemist, Dept Serol, NY State Dept Health Res Labs, 49-52, sr biochemist, 52-54; chief, Immunobiol Br, Armed Forces Inst Path, 54-64. *Concurrent Pos:* Res fel, Coun Res in Glaucoma & Allied Dis, 60; lectr, Int Cong Opthalmol, Kyoto, Japan, 78, Rome, Italy, 86, Ger Opthalmol Cong, 80; Dept Defense res & develop award, 64. *Mem:* Sigma Xi; Am Asn Immunologists; Am Soc Exp Pathol; Brit Soc Immunol; Asn Res Vision & Ophthalmol; fel AAAS. *Res:* History of immunology; ocular immunology. *Mailing Add:* Inst Hist Med Sch Med Johns Hopkins Univ 1900 E Monument St Baltimore MD 21205. *Fax:* 410-955-8020

SILVERSTEIN, CALVIN C(ARLTON), HEAT TRANSFER, ENERGY CONVERSION. *Current Pos:* PRES, CCS ASSOCS, 81- *Personal Data:* b Newark, NJ, Jan 31, 29; m 59; c 3. *Educ:* Newark Col Eng, BS, 50; Princeton Univ, MSE, 51. *Prof Exp:* Res engr, Bendix Aviation Corp Res Labs, 52-54; asst proj engr, Martin Co, 55-57; proj eng, Bell Aircraft Corp, 57; prin mech engr, Cornell Aeronaut Lab, Inc, 57-61; res specialist, Atomics Int Div, N Am Aviation, Inc, 61-62; chief analyst & sr staff analyst, Hittman Assoc, Inc, 63-65; eng consult, 65-73; mgr prog develop, Westinghouse Elec Corp, 73-81. *Mem:* Am Soc Mech Engrs. *Res:* Heat transfer; energy conversion; energy storage; power generation; heat pipe technology and applications; capillary-pumped heat transfer loops; hydrogen production and applications; fluidized beds; solar energy. *Mailing Add:* PO Box 563 Bethel Park PA 15102

SILVERSTEIN, ELLIOT MORTON, ELECTROOPTICS, INFRARED SYSTEMS. *Current Pos:* RETIRED. *Personal Data:* b Chicago, Ill, Jan 2, 28; m 57, Irma Arenz; c Marc, Julie & Frances. *Educ:* Univ Chicago, BA, 50, MS, 53, PhD(physics), 58. *Prof Exp:* Mem tech staff, Opers Anal Group, Hughes Aircraft Co, Calif, 58-61, group head, Surveyor Spacecraft Lab, 61-64, sr proj engr, Surveyor Lab, 64-65, sr staff physicist, 66-68; prin engr/scientist, Avionics Control & Info Systs Div, McDonnell Douglas Astronaut Co, Huntington Beach, 68-81; proj engr, Defense & Surveillance Opers, Aerospace Corp, Calif, 81-88, proj engr, Prog Off, Defense Support Prog, 89-93. *Concurrent Pos:* Mem, Stand Comt, Optical Soc Am, 82-85. *Mem:* AAAS; Am Phys Soc; Optical Soc Am; Sigma Xi; Inst Elec & Electronics Engrs. *Res:* Theoretical and experimental studies in infrared and optical physics and in optical and electrooptical imaging, image processing, detection, communications and radar; design and analysis of spacecraft instrumentation. *Mailing Add:* 8004 El Manor Ave Los Angeles CA 90045-1434

SILVERSTEIN, EMANUEL, BIOCHEMISTRY, GENETICS. *Current Pos:* from asst prof to assoc prof med, 64-77, PROF MED & BIOCHEM, STATE UNIV NY DOWNSTATE MED CTR, 77- *Personal Data:* b New York, NY, Feb 14, 30; m 65; c 2. *Educ:* City Col New York, BS, 50; State Univ NY Downstate Med Ctr, MD, 54; Univ Minn, PhD(biochem), 63. *Prof Exp:* Intern med, Med Sch, Univ Minn, 54-55; intern path, Sch Med, Yale Univ, 55-56; res assoc exp path, Nat Inst Arthritis & Metab Dis, 56-58; fel med, Med Sch, Univ Minn, 58-59 & fel biochem 59-63. *Concurrent Pos:* Fel molecular biol, Mass Inst Technol, 63-64; vis scientist, Weizmann Inst Sci, 71 & 81; posdoc fel, Am Cancer Soc, 59-64. *Mem:* AAAS; Am Asn Path; Am Soc Biochem & Molecular Biol; Am Soc Microbiol; Genetics Soc Am; Am Soc Human Genetics. *Res:* Enzyme mechanism and regulation; medical and molecular genetics; protein synthesis; hormone receptors; cell differentiation; porphyrins and oxidative enzymes; chemical diagnosis and therapy of disease, neurochemistry; neurochemistry; molecular mechanism of behavior and brain function. *Mailing Add:* Biochem Prog & Med State Univ NY Health Sci Ctr 450 Clarkson Ave Brooklyn NY 11203-2098. *Fax:* 718-270-4070

SILVERSTEIN, HERBERT, HEARING & BALANCE DISORDERS, OTOLOGY & NEUROTOLOGY. *Current Pos:* PRES & FOUNDER, EAR RES FOUND FLA, 79- *Personal Data:* b Philadelphia, Pa, Aug, 35; m 88; c 2. *Educ:* Dickenson Col, BSc, 57; Temple Univ, MD, 61, MSc, 63; Am Bd Otolaryngol, dipl, 67. *Honors & Awards:* Charles Burr Award, 62; Res Award, Am Acad Otolaryngol, 66. *Prof Exp:* Intern, Philadelphia Gen Hosp, 61-62; resident surg, Philadelphia Vet Hosp, 62-63; resident otolaryngol, Mass Eye & Ear Infirmary, 63-66, asst, 68-71; attend otolaryngologist, Hosp Univ Pa, 71-74; assoc prof, Univ S Fla, 74-75. *Concurrent Pos:* Asst prof otolaryngol, Univ Pa Med Sch, 71-73; asst clin prof surg, Univ Fla, Gainesville, 77; clin prof surg, Univ S Fla, 84; dir, Walker Biochem Lab, Mass Eye & Ear Infirmary, 68-71; assoc dir, Otology Res Lab, Presby Univ Pa Med Ctr, 71-72; consult, Philadelphia Vet Admin Hosp, 71-74, Childrens Hosp, 71. *Mem:* Fel Am Acad Ophthal & Otolaryngol; AMA; fel Am Col Surgeons; fel Am Laryngol, Rhinological & Otol Soc. *Res:* Author of over 120 technical publications. *Mailing Add:* 1961 Floyd St Suite A Sarasota FL 34239-2931

SILVERSTEIN, MARTIN ELLIOT, MEDICAL SCIENCE, HEALTH SCIENCES. *Current Pos:* CLIN PROF SURG DISASTER, F EDWARD HEBERT SCH MED, UNIFORMED SERVS UNIV HEALTH SCI, 85- *Personal Data:* b New York, NY, Sept 6, 22; m 62, Mabelle Cremer. *Educ:* Columbia Univ, AB, 45; NY Med Col, MD, 48. *Prof Exp:* Asst res surg, Flower & Fifth Ave Hosps, 49-50, chief res, 51-52, instr bact & surg, NY Med Col, 53-57, assoc prof surg & assoc dean, 57-63; chmn exp surg, Menorah Inst Med Educ & Res, 63-66, chmn dept exp surg & exec dir, Menorah Med Ctr, 63-66, gen dir, 66; dir grad med educ, Bronx-Lebanon Hosp Ctr, 67-69; chief surg, Grand Canyon Hosp, 69-70; pres, Health Anal Inc, 70-73; assoc prof surg & chief, Surg Trauma Sect, Col Med, Univ Ariz, 74-84, res prof surg, 84-85. *Concurrent Pos:* Asst res, Metrop Hosp, New York, 50, chief res surg, 52-53, res investr, Col Burn Study, 52-54, mem staff, Res Unit, 54-55, vis surgeon, 55-63; asst surgeon & asst vis surgeon, Flower & Fifth Ave Hosps, 53-57, vis surgeon, 57-63; Dazian Found fel, 54-55; vis surgeon, Bird S Coler Hosp & Hebrew Home for Aged; trustee, Midwest Res Inst, 64-66, mem exec comt, Bd Trustees, 65-66; pres, Claudia Gips Found, 67-; dir med systs, Resource & Mgt Systs Corp, DC; NSF vis scientist, Auburn Univ; lectr, UNIVAC Int Exec Ctr, Italy, 69-70; Gov & dep secy gen, Int Coun Comput Commun, 74-; consult, US Arms Control & Disarmament Agency, 76; vis scholar, Ctr Strategic & Int Studies, 81-82; adj prof health care sci, Sch Med, George Washington Univ, 81-; sr fel sci & technol, Ctr Strategic & Inst Studies, 83-89, clin prof family & community int med, Sch Med, 84-85. *Mem:* Am Asn Surg Trauma; Harvey Soc; NY Acad Sci; fel Am Col Nuclear Med; fel Am Col Surgeons; fel Am Col Gastroenterol; Critical Care Soc; fel Am Col Emergency Physicians; fel Am Col Nuclear Med; fel NY Acad Med. *Res:* Control of hemodynamics and neurovascular syndromes in man; physiology of body water; burns; shock; metabolism of trauma; surgical physiology; curriculum design; man-machine systems; bioinstrumentation; operations research; computer applications; shock and hemodynamics; biological sensing; processing and telecommunications; emergency medical systems; societal impact of disasters; mitigation of mass casualties; disaster planning; causes and management of natural, technological-industrial and conflict disasters; telecommunications as support in disasters. *Mailing Add:* 7041 N Corrida de Venado Tucson AZ 85718. *Fax:* 520-297-7301; *E-Mail:* msilver606@aol.com

SILVERSTEIN, MARTIN L, BOUNDARY THEORY, TIME CHANGE. *Current Pos:* PROF MATH, WASH UNIV, 77- *Personal Data:* b Philadelphia, Pa, May 22, 39. *Educ:* Princeton Univ, PhD(math), 65. *Prof Exp:* Asst prof math, Rutgers Univ, 68-70; assoc prof, Univ Southern Calif, 70-77. *Mem:* Am Math Soc; Math Asn Am. *Mailing Add:* Wash Univ Campus Box 1146 St Louis MO 63130

SILVERSTEIN, RICHARD, BIOCHEMISTRY. *Current Pos:* asst prof, 69-77, ASSOC PROF BIOCHEM, UNIV KANS MED CTR, 69- *Personal Data:* b Boston, Mass, Aug 9, 39; m 62; c 3. *Educ:* Brandeis Univ, BA, 60; Fla State Univ, PhD(chem), 65. *Prof Exp:* Staff scientist, Charles F Kettering Res Lab, 68-69. *Mem:* Am Soc Biol Chem; Am Chem Soc; NY Acad Sci; Sigma Xi. *Res:* Defense against endotoxin and tumor necrosis factor cachectin. *Mailing Add:* Dept Biochem Univ Kans Med Ctr 3900 Rainbow Blvd Kansas City KS 66160

SILVERSTEIN, ROBERT MILTON, NATURAL PRODUCTS CHEMISTRY. *Current Pos:* prof, 69-87, EMER PROF CHEM, STATE UNIV NY COL FORESTRY, SYRACUSE UNIV, 87- *Personal Data:* b Baltimore, Md, Mar 26, 16; m 43; c 1. *Educ:* Univ Pa, BS, 37; NY Univ, PhD, 49. *Honors & Awards:* Medal, Royal Swed Acad Agr, Int Soc Chem Ecol Award; Nat Award, Entomol Soc Am. *Prof Exp:* Asst, NY Univ, 46-48; sr org chemist, Stanford Res Inst, 48-64, res fel, 64-69. *Concurrent Pos:* Co-ed, J Chem Ecol, 75-85. *Mem:* Am Chem Soc; Sigma Xi; Entom Soc Am; Int Soc Chem Ecol. *Res:* Organic synthesis; mechanisms and isolation and structure elucidation of natural products; application of spectrometry to organic chemistry. *Mailing Add:* Dept Chem State Univ NY Col Forestry Syracuse NY 13210

SILVERSTEIN, SAMUEL CHARLES, CELL BIOLOGY, CELLULAR IMMUNOLOGY & PHYSIOLOGY. *Current Pos:* JOHN C DALTON PROF & CHMN, DEPT PHYSIOL & CELLULAR BIOPHYS & PROF MED, COL PHYSICIANS & SURGEONS, COLUMBIA UNIV, 83-, FOUNDER & DIR, SUMMER RES PROG FOR SEC SCH SCI TEACHERS, 89- *Personal Data:* b New York, NY, Feb 11, 37; m 67, Jo A Kleinman; c David P & Jennifer K. *Educ:* Dartmouth Col, BA, 58; Albert Einstein Col Med, MD, 63. *Honors & Awards:* Soc Leucocyte Biol Award, 84. *Prof Exp:* Intern med, Univ Col Med Ctr, Rockefeller Univ, 63-64, cell biologist, 64-67, from asst to assoc prof cellular physiol & immunol, 72-83; resident med, Mass Gen Hosp, 67-68. *Concurrent Pos:* Helen Hay Whitney fel, 64-67; established investr, Am Heart Asn, 72-77; ed, J Cell Biol, 79-88; Guggenheim fel, 94. *Mem:* Inst Med-Nat Acad Sci; Am Soc Biol Chem & Molecular Biol; Am Physiol Soc; Am Soc Clin Investigation; Infect Dis Soc Am; Am Asn Immunol; fel AAAS; Am Acad Microbiol; Fedn Am Soc Exp Biol (vpres, 93-94, pres, 94-); Am Soc Cell Biol. *Res:* Cell and molecular biology of neutrophils monocytes platelets and vascular endothelial cells and their roles in immunity; inflammation host defense against infection; atherosclerosis. *Mailing Add:* Dept Physiol Rm 11-511 Columbia Univ Col Physicians & Surgeons 630 W 168th St New York NY 10032. *Fax:* 212-305-5775; *E-Mail:* scs3@columbia.edu

SILVERSTEIN, SAUL JAY, MOLECULAR BIOLOGY, GENE EXPRESSION. *Current Pos:* From asst prof to assoc prof, 74-87, PROF MICROBIOL, COLUMBIA UNIV, 87- *Personal Data:* b Brooklyn, NY, Aug 23, 46; m 76; c 3. *Educ:* Cornell Univ, BS, 68; Univ Fla, PhD(microbiol), 71. *Honors & Awards:* Career Develop Award, NIH. *Concurrent Pos:* Fel virol, Univ Chicago, 71; fel, Damon Runyon Walter-Wincholl Cancer Fund, 78; ed, Somatic Cell Genetics, 80-; mem, Exp Virol Study Sect, 82-86; vis prof, Japanese Nat Cancer Inst, 87. *Mem:* Harvey Soc; Am Soc Microbiol; Am Soc Virol. *Res:* Gene regulation, particularly applied to eukaryotic virus-host cell interactions. *Mailing Add:* Dept Microbiol Columbia Univ Col Phys Surg 630 W 168th St New York NY 10032-3702

SILVERSTONE, ALLEN EDGAR, IMMUNOTOXICOLOGY, DEVELOPMENTAL IMMUNOLOGY. *Current Pos:* assoc prof, 85-95, PROF, MICROBIOL & IMMUNOL; HEALTH SCI CTR, STATE UNIV NY, 95- *Personal Data:* b Chicago, Ill, Sept 20, 42; m 79, Barbara Julia Kowalchuk; c David Walter. *Educ:* Reed Col, BA, 65; Mass Inst Technol, PhD(microbiol), 70. *Prof Exp:* Jane Coffin Childs Mem postdoctoral fel, 70-72; asst prof biochem, Univ Mass, Amherst, 72-73; postdoctoral fel & res assoc, Cancer Res Ctr, Mass Inst Technol, 73-77; assoc viral oncol, Mem Sloan-Kettering Cancer Ctr, 77-81, asst mem cell biol & genetics, 83-85. *Concurrent Pos:* Instr biol, Mass Inst Technol, 70 & 74; instr & teaching asst gen educ, Harvard Univ, 75-77; asst prof, Sch Med, Cornell Univ, 79-85; Leukemia Soc Am scholar, 85-90; vis scientist, Sch Med, Univ Rochester, 93. *Mem:* Am Asn Immunologists; Soc Toxicologists; AAAS; Sigma Xi. *Res:* Study the effects of dioxins, estrogens, environmental estrogens and other compounds on development of t-cells and stem cells in the immune system. *Mailing Add:* Univ Finance Sta PO Box 7156 Syracuse NY 13210. *Fax:* 315-464-7652; *E-Mail:* silversa@vax.cs.hscsyr.edu

SILVERSTONE, HARRIS JULIAN, QUANTUM CHEMISTRY. *Current Pos:* from asst prof to assoc prof, 65-71, PROF CHEM, JOHNS HOPKINS UNIV, 71- *Personal Data:* b New York, NY, Sept 18, 39; m 60; c 4. *Educ:* Harvard Univ, AB, 60; Calif Inst Technol, PhD(chem), 64. *Prof Exp:* NSF fel, Yale Univ, 64. *Concurrent Pos:* Sloan Found fel, 69. *Mem:* Am Phys Soc; Am Chem Soc. *Res:* Application of quantum mechanics to chemistry. *Mailing Add:* Dept Chem Johns Hopkins Univ Baltimore MD 21218. *Fax:* 410-516-8420; *E-Mail:* hjsilverstone@jhu.edu

SILVERT, WILLIAM LAWRENCE, MARINE ECOLOGY, MODELLING. *Current Pos:* res scientist, Marine Ecol Lab, 78-87, RES SCIENTIST, MARINE ENVIRON SCI DIV, BEDFORD INST OCEANOG, 88- *Personal Data:* b New York, NY, Dec 11, 37; Can citizen; div; c Richard & Rebecca. *Educ:* Brown Univ, ScB, 58, PhD(physics), 65. *Prof Exp:* Res assoc physics, Mich State Univ, 64-66; asst prof, Case Western Res Univ, 66-69; asst prof physics & astron, Univ Kans, 69-72; assoc prof physics, 72-75, dir, E Coast Fisheries Mgt Proj, Inst Environ Studies, Dalhousie Univ, 75-78. *Concurrent Pos:* Lectr, Univ Mich, 65-66; consult, Bendix Corp, 66; Nat Acad Sci exchange scholar, Inst Physics Probs, Moscow, 66-67. *Mem:* Can Soc Theoret Biol (secy-treas, 92-). *Res:* Theoretical marine ecology; systems analysis; resource management; bioeconomics; trophodynamics; ecosystem modeling. *Mailing Add:* 7 Horizon Ct Apt 1500 Dartmouth NS B3A 4R2 Can. *Fax:* 902-426-2256; *E-Mail:* silvert@biome.bio.ns.ca, silvert@ecology.gio.dfo.ca

SILVERTHORN, DEE UNGLAUB, INVERTEBRATE PHYSIOLOGY. *Current Pos:* lectr, Dept Zool, 86-91, SR LECTR, UNIV TEX, AUSTIN, 91- *Personal Data:* b New Orleans, La, Dec 3, 48; m 72, Andrew C. *Educ:* Tulane Univ, BS, 70; Univ SC, PhD(marine sci), 73. *Prof Exp:* Res assoc biochem, Med Univ SC, 73-74, from instr to asst prof physiol, 74-77; res scientist physiol & biophys, Med Br, Univ Tex, Galveston, 78-80. *Concurrent Pos:* Vis asst prof biol, Univ Houston, 77-78. *Mem:* Soc Comp Integrative Biol; Human Anat Physiol Soc; Am Physiol Soc; Sigma Xi. *Res:* Endocrinology and physiology of thermal acclimation and osmoregulation in crustaceans; biochemistry and physiology of osmoregulation in crustaceans. *Mailing Add:* Dept Zool Univ Tex Austin TX 78712-1064. *Fax:* 512-471-9651; *E-Mail:* silverth@vms.cc.utexas.edu

SILVER-THORN, M BARBARA, BIOMEDICAL ENGINEERING. *Current Pos:* ASST PROF BIOMED ENG, MARQUETTE UNIV, 92- *Personal Data:* b Milwaukee, Wis, May 8, 63. *Educ:* Northwestern Univ, BS, 85, PhD(biomed eng), 91; Ariz State Univ MS, 87. *Prof Exp:* Res fel biomed eng, Northwestern Univ, 91-92. *Mem:* Am Soc Biomed Eng; Am Soc Mech Engrs; Inst Elec & Electronics Engrs; Biomed Eng Soc; Sigma Xi. *Mailing Add:* Biomed Eng Dept Marquette Univ 1515 W Wisconsin Ave Milwaukee WI 53233

SILVERTON, JAMES VINCENT, PHYSICAL CHEMISTRY, CRYSTALLOGRAPHY. *Current Pos:* SCIENTIST, NIH, 70- *Personal Data:* b Seaton Delaval, Eng, May 10, 34; m 64, Enid S Willstadter; c Geoffrey & Kathy. *Educ:* Glasgow Univ, BSc, 55, PhD(chem), 63. *Prof Exp:* Res assoc chem, Cornell Univ, 58-61; sr res fel solid state physics, UK Atomic Energy Authority, Eng, 61-62; asst lectr chem, Glasgow Univ, 62-63; asst prof, Georgetown Univ, 63-70. *Concurrent Pos:* Petrol Res Fund starter grant, 63-65; prog dir, Nat Inst Dent Res training grant x-ray crystallog, 65-70. *Mem:* Am Chem Soc; Am Crystallog Asn; Royal Soc Chem; Sigma Xi. *Res:* Structures of complex inorganic and organic compounds by x-ray crystallographic techniques. *Mailing Add:* 8609 Hidden Hill Lane Potomac MD 20854-4226. *Fax:* 301-402-3404; *E-Mail:* jvs@helix.nih.gov

SILVESTER, JOHN ANDREW, PERFORMANCE MODELING, COMPUTER COMMUNICATION. *Current Pos:* dir, 86-91, PROF, DEPT ELEC ENG SYST, UNIV SOUTHERN CALIF, 79-, VICE PROVOST ACADEMIC COMPUT, 94- *Personal Data:* b Kent, Eng, Apr 26, 50; m 80, Maria Penedo; c Alexander & Karina. *Educ:* Cambridge Univ, BA, 71, MA, 75; WVa Univ, MS, 73; Univ Calif, Los Angeles, PhD(comput sci), 80. *Prof Exp:* Mem staff comput sci, Univ Calif, Los Angeles, 73-78. *Concurrent Pos:* Consult, 79-; chmn, Comsoc tech comt, comput commun, Inst Elec & Electronics Engrs. *Mem:* Inst Elec & Electronics Engrs; Asn Comput Mach. *Res:* Performance modelling of computer systems and networks, especially computer communications and multiple access techniques. *Mailing Add:* Dept Elec Eng Syst Univ Southern Calif Los Angeles CA 90089. *Fax:* 213-740-4631; *E-Mail:* silvester@usc.edu

SILVESTER, PETER PEET, electrical engineering; deceased, see previous edition for last biography

SILVESTON, PETER LEWIS, REACTOR ENGINEERING, POLLUTION CONTROL. *Current Pos:* assoc prof, 63-69, PROF CHEM ENG, UNIV WATERLOO, 69- *Personal Data:* b New York, NY, Mar 10, 31; c 3. *Educ:* Mass Inst Technol, SB, 51, SM, 53; Munich Tech Univ, Dr Ing, 56. *Prof Exp:* Chem engr, Esso Res & Eng Co, 57-59; res engr, Res Div, Am Standard Corp, 59-61; asst prof chem eng, Univ BC, 61-63. *Mem:* Am Chem Soc; Chem Inst Can; Am Inst Chem Engrs. *Res:* Reactor design; kinetics; catalysis; waste treatment. *Mailing Add:* Dept Chem Eng Univ Waterloo Waterloo ON N2L 3G1 Can

SILVESTRI, ANTHONY JOHN, PETROLEUM CHEMISTRY. *Current Pos:* Res chemist, Mobil Res & Develop Corp, 61-63, sr res chemist, 63-68, res assoc, 68-73, mgr, Anal & Spec Technol Group, 73-75, Catalysis Res Sect, Mobil Res & Develop Corp, 75-77, mgr Process Res & Develop Sect, 77-79, planning & eval, 79-80, Process Res & Tech Serv Div, 80-84, Prod Res & Tech Serv Div, 84-89, VPRES ENVIRON HEALTH & SAFETY, MOBIL RES & DEVELOP CORP, 89- *Personal Data:* b Glassboro, NJ, Mar 14, 36; m 60, Heand Johns; c Joseph & Jeffrey. *Educ:* Villanova Univ, BS, 58; Pa State Univ, PhD(chem), 61. *Mem:* Am Inst Chem Engrs; Am Chem Soc; Soc Automotive Engrs. *Res:* Heterogeneous catalysis and chemical kinetics. *Mailing Add:* 104 N Stockton Ave Wenonah NJ 08090

SILVESTRI, GEORGE J, JR, THERMODYNAMICS, POWER GENERATION CYCLE PERFORMANCE & ANALYSIS. *Current Pos:* RETIRED. *Personal Data:* b Jessup, Pa, Aug 3, 27; m 61, Betty A Huber; c Mary E (Philbrick) & Janet C (Travis). *Educ:* Drexel Univ, BS, 53, MS, 56. *Honors & Awards:* James Harry Potter Gold Medal, Am Soc Mech Engrs, 93. *Prof Exp:* Develop engr, Westinghouse Elec Corp, 53-69, fel engr, 69-72 & 74, appl engr, 72-73; proj mgr, Elec Power Res Inst, 73-74; adv engr, Westinghouse Elec Corp, 74-94. *Concurrent Pos:* Chmn educ & res comt, Power Div, Am Soc Mech Engrs, 82-85 & 90-91; bd res & technol develop,

85-91, lectr, course on steam turbines, Power Div, 89-, perf test code course on testing, 91-, res comt properties steam. *Mem:* Am Soc Mech Engrs; Am Nuclear Soc. *Res:* Advanced power generation cycles; operation procedures to enhance steam turbine performance; low pressure turbine laboratory testing; improved steam property algorithms; steam turbine performance computer program. *Mailing Add:* 1840 Cheryl Dr Winter Park FL 32792

SILVETTE, HERBERT, tobacco, for more information see previous edition

SILVIDI, ANTHONY ALFRED, BIOPHYSICS. *Current Pos:* RETIRED. *Personal Data:* b Steubenville, Ohio, Jan 17, 20; m 47, Lillian E Ferrelli; c Anita, Gina, Julius & Anthony C. *Educ:* Ohio Univ, BS, 45; Ohio State Univ, PhD(physics), 49. *Prof Exp:* Assoc prof physics & head dept, Col Steubenville, 49-51; res physicist, Cornell Aeronaut Lab, Inc, 51-52; from asst prof to physics prof, Kent State Univ, 52-83, res assoc, 52-59, coord grad progs, 68-73. *Concurrent Pos:* Res physicist, Goodyear Aircraft Corp, 52-58; prin investr, DOE, NSF, AEC grants, 60-85; consult, Biochem Dept, Children's Hosp of Akron, Ohio, 70- *Mem:* Am Phys Soc; Biophys Soc; Sigma Xi. *Res:* Nuclear magnetic resonance; biophysics; application of physical techniques for solutions of biological problems. *Mailing Add:* 311 Valley View Dr Kent OH 44240

SILVIUS, JOHN EDWARD, PLANT PHYSIOLOGY, BOTANY. *Current Pos:* MEM FAC, SCI DEPT, CEDARVILLE COL, OHIO, 80- *Personal Data:* b Dover, Ohio, May 9, 47; m 69; c 2. *Educ:* Malone Col, BA, 69; WVa Univ, PhD(plant physiol), 74. *Prof Exp:* Teacher biol, Dover Pub Schs, 69-71; vis lectr bot, Univ Ill, Champaign-Urbana, 74-75, res assoc agron, 75-76; plant physiologist, Sci & Educ Admin-Agr Res, USDA, 76-80. *Mem:* Nat Asn Biol Teachers; Am Inst Biol Sci; Bot Soc Am; Creation Res Soc. *Res:* Physiological and biochemical mechanisms which regulate the photosynthetic production, partitioning and translocation of carbon assimilates in plants; methods and techniques for teaching biology in high schools and colleges. *Mailing Add:* Cedarville Col Box 601 Biol Dept Cedarville OH 45314. *E-Mail:* silviusj@cedarville.edu

SILZARS, ARIS, electrical engineering, physics, for more information see previous edition

SIMA, ANDERS ADOLPH FREDRIK, ANATOMICAL PATHOLOGY, NEUROPATHOLOGY. *Current Pos:* PROF PATH & NEUROL, WAYNE STATE UNIV, 96- *Personal Data:* b Jonkoping, Sweden, Dec 3, 43; Can citizen. *Educ:* Univ Vienna, BS, 67; Univ Goteborg, Sweden, MD, 73; FRCP(C), 78. *Honors & Awards:* Acad Achievement Award, Chinese Acad Med, 81; Prezzo d'ora Consiglio Nat delle Ricerche, Rome, Italy, 87; William Harvey Lectr, Royal Col London, 93; Distinguished Scientist Award, Pfizer, 96. *Prof Exp:* Asst prof, Dept Path, Univ Goteborg, Sweden, 74-83; prof & head, Sect Neuropath, Univ Man, 85-90; dir, Diabetes Res Ctr, Health Sci Ctr & Univ Man, 88-90; dir, Morphometric Imaging Core, Mich Diabetes Res & Training Ctr, Univ Mich, 90-96, prof, Dept Path, 90-96. *Concurrent Pos:* From asst prof to assoc prof, Dept Path, Univ Toronto, 78-82; hon chmn, Juvenile Diabetes Found Int, 84; hon prof neurosci, Med Univ, Shanghai, China, 88; consult, NIH/Food & Drug Admin, 88-, Sigma Tau, Md, 92-; Hofmann La Roche, Basel, Switz, 92-97 & Sigma Tau, SPA, Rome, 96-; dir, Neuropath Core, Mich Alzheimer Dis Res Ctr, Univ Mich, 92-, vis prof, Dept Path, 96-; regional ed, Int J Diabetes, 92- *Mem:* Am Asn Neuropathologists; hon mem Japanese Diabetes Soc; NY Acad Sci; Peripheral Neuropath Asn Am; Am Asn Pathologists; Am Diabetes Asn; Friends Armed Forces Inst Path. *Res:* Diabetic neuropathy and senile dementias; authored more than 500 publications; published the first systemic description of diffuse Lew body disease; described the rare chromosome-17-linked dementia. *Mailing Add:* 345 Moross Pl Grosse Pointe Farms MI 48236. *Fax:* 313-577-0057; *E-Mail:* asima@med.wayne.edu

SIMAAN, MARWAN, ELECTRICAL ENGINEERING, GEOPHYSICS. *Current Pos:* from assoc prof to prof, 76-85, BELL OF PA PROF ELEC ENG, UNIV PITTSBURGH, 89-, CHMN DEPT, 91- *Personal Data:* b July 23, 46; US citizen; m 84, Rita. *Educ:* Am Univ Beirut, BEE, 68; Univ Pittsburgh, MS, 70; Univ Ill, PhD(elec eng), 72. *Prof Exp:* Vis asst prof elec eng, Univ Ill, 72-74; res engr geophys, Shell Develop Co, 74-75. *Concurrent Pos:* Tech consult, Gulf Res & Develop Co, 79-85, Alcoa, 85-; assoc ed, J Optimization Theory & Applns, 86-; prin investr, numerous govt & indust grants, 76-; co-ed, Multidimensional Systs & Signal Processing J, 89- *Mem:* Fel Inst Elec & Electronics Engrs; Am Asn Artificial Intelligence; Soc Explor Geophysicists; NY Acad Sci; Sigma Xi; Am Soc Eng Educ. *Res:* Optimization and optimal control; differential game theory; digital signal processing and geophysical applications; array signal processing and target tracking; artificial intelligence and knowledge based engineering; manufacturing systems. *Mailing Add:* Dept Elec Eng Univ Pittsburgh Pittsburgh PA 15261. *E-Mail:* simaan@ee.pitt.edu

SIMANEK, EUGEN, PHYSICS. *Current Pos:* prof, 69-94, EMER PROF PHYSICS, UNIV CALIF, RIVERSIDE, 94- *Personal Data:* b Prague, Czech, July 15, 33; m 55, 69; c 1. *Educ:* Prague Tech Univ, MEE, 56; Czech Acad Sci, Cand Sci, 63. *Prof Exp:* Res physicist, Inst Physics, Czech Acad Sci, 56-68; theoret physicist, IBM Res Lab, Switz, 68-69. *Concurrent Pos:* Vis assoc prof, Univ Calif, Los Angeles, 65-67; Energy Res & Develop Admin contract theory of superconductivity, 75; vis prof, Univ Neuchatel, Switz, 81; guest prof physics, Troisieme Cycle of French Switz, 81. *Res:* Theoretical solid state physics; quantum theory of metals; many body problem; critical phenomena; low temperature physics; superconductivity. *Mailing Add:* Dept Physics Univ Calif 900 University Ave Riverside CA 92521-0001

SIMANTEL, GERALD M, PLANT BREEDING, RESEARCH & DEVELOPMENT ADMINISTRATION. *Current Pos:* plant breeder, Res Dept, Amalgamated Sugar Co, 63-87, mgr, seed prod & develop, 87-90, sr plant breeder, 90-91, DIR RES & PLANT BREEDING, HILLESHOG MONO-HY INC, 91- *Personal Data:* b Huron, SDak, Oct 12, 34; m 55, Joan D Horning; c David, Daniel & Debra. *Educ:* Ore State Univ, BS, 59; SDak State Univ, PhD(agron), 63. *Honors & Awards:* Meritorious Serv Award, Am Soc Sugar Beet Technologists. *Mem:* Am Soc Agron; Crop Sci Soc Am; Am Soc Sugar Beet Technologists. *Res:* Development of more productive sugar beet varieties. *Mailing Add:* Hilleshog Mono-Hy Inc 11939 Sugar Mill Rd Longmont CO 80503

SIMARD, ALBERT JOSEPH, FOREST FIRE SCIENCE, SYSTEMS ANALYSIS. *Current Pos:* FIRE COORDR, CAN FOREST SERV, 92- *Personal Data:* b Hartford, Conn, July 11, 42. *Educ:* Univ Conn, BS, 63; Univ Calif, Berkeley, MSc, 68; Univ Wash, PhD(fire sci), 78. *Honors & Awards:* Forest Serv & USDA Merit Awards. *Prof Exp:* Res scientist, Forest Fire Res Inst, Can Forest Serv, 67-79; proj leader, NCent Forest Exp Sta, US Forest Serv, 79-91. *Concurrent Pos:* Adj prof, Mich State Univ, 80-91. *Mem:* Int Asn Wildland Fire. *Res:* Atmospheric relations to wildland fire; fire danger rating, fire management systems, fire weather, fire economics, fire ecology; information systems; fire severity. *Mailing Add:* 6651 Forest Rd Osgoode ON K0A 2W0 Can. *Fax:* 814-994-3384; *E-Mail:* asimard@am.ncr.forestry.ca

SIMARD, GERALD LIONEL, PHYSICAL CHEMISTRY. *Current Pos:* assoc prof, 67-77, EMER PROF CHEM ENG, UNIV MAINE, ORONO, 77- *Personal Data:* b Lewiston, Maine, May 11, 12; m 46; c 5. *Educ:* Bates Col, BS, 33; Mass Inst Technol, PhD(phys chem), 37. *Prof Exp:* Res chemist, Atlantic Refining Co, 37-38; indust fel, Battelle Mem Inst, 39, res engr, 39-43; group leader, Am Cyanamid Co, 43-53; sect leader, Schlumberger Well Surv Corp, Conn, 53-60, res mgr, 60-67. *Mem:* Am Chem Soc; Am Inst Chem Engrs; Sigma Xi. *Res:* Thermodynamics; surface chemistry; kinetics, catalysis; electrochemistry; instrumental analysis; pulp and paper technology; environmental chemistry. *Mailing Add:* LeBanon Rd Winterport ME 04496-0086

SIMARD, RENE, CELL BIOLOGY, MOLECULAR BIOLOGY. *Current Pos:* PROF PATH & DIR MONTREAL CANCER INST, UNIV MONTREAL, 75-, VPRIN ACAD, 85- *Personal Data:* b Montreal, Que, Oct 4, 35; m 69; c 3. *Educ:* Univ Montreal, BA, 56, MD, 62; Univ Paris, DSc, 68, FRCP, 76. *Prof Exp:* Resident path, Mt Sinai Sch Med, 65; asst prof path, Univ Montreal, 68-69; from asst prof to assoc prof & dir cell biol, Sch Med, Univ Sherbrooke, 69-75. *Concurrent Pos:* Med Res Coun Can fel, Inst Cancer Res, Villejuif, France, 65-68 & scholar, Univ Sherbrooke, 68-; mem grants comt anat & path, Med Res Coun Can, 70-77; mem res adv group & grants comt, Nat Cancer Inst Can, 72-77; chmn, Quebec Health Res Coun, 75-78; pres, Med Res Coun, 78-81. *Mem:* AAAS; Am Soc Cell Biol; Inst Soc Cell Biol; Fr Soc Electron Micros; Can Soc Oncol (pres, 82-83). *Res:* Regulation of nucleic acids synthesis in eukaryotic cells; herpes viruses and cancer of the cervix. *Mailing Add:* Univ Montreal CP 6128 Succ "A" Montreal PQ H3C 3J7 Can. *Fax:* 514-343-6776

SIMARD, THERESE GABRIELLE, ANATOMY. *Current Pos:* RETIRED. *Personal Data:* b St-Lambert, Que, Mar 3, 28. *Educ:* Univ Montreal, BA, 56, BSc, 62; Univ Mich, MSc, 64; Queen's Univ, Ont, PhD(anat), 66. *Honors & Awards:* Gold Medal, Int Soc Phys Med & Rehab, 72. *Prof Exp:* Prof anat, Univ Mich, 64 & Queens Univ, Ont, 65-66; asst prof anat, Univ Montreal, 66-71, assoc prof, 71-93. *Mem:* Biofeedback Res Soc; Can Asn Anat; Am Asn Anat; Can Asn Phys Med & Rehab; Int Soc Electrophysiol Kinesiology (treas, 73-77). *Res:* Electromyographic studies on the kinesiology of muscles and developmental method of studies; training of the neuromuscular action potential. *Mailing Add:* 730 Logan St Lambert PQ J4P 1K6 Can

SIMBERLOFF, DANIEL S, ECOLOGY, MATHEMATICAL BIOLOGY. *Current Pos:* From asst prof to assoc prof biol, 68-78, PROF BIOL, FLA STATE UNIV, 78- *Personal Data:* b Easton, Pa, Apr 7, 42. *Educ:* Harvard Univ, AB, 64, PhD(biol), 69. *Honors & Awards:* Mercer Award, Ecol Soc Am, 71. *Concurrent Pos:* NSF grants ecol, 69-82. *Mem:* Ecol Soc Am; Soc Study Evolution; Brit Ecol Soc; Japanese Soc Pop Ecol; Soc Syst Zool. *Res:* Biogeography; evolution. *Mailing Add:* Dept Biol Sci Fla State Univ, 600 W College Ave Tallahassee FL 32306-1096

SIMCHOWITZ, LOUIS, RHEUMATOLOGY. *Current Pos:* ASSOC PROF MED, WASHINGTON UNIV, 85- *Educ:* New York Univ, MD, 70. *Mailing Add:* Dept Med Wash Univ Sch Med 660 S Euclid Ave Box 8045 St Louis MO 63110. *Fax:* 314-454-1621

SIMCO, BILL AL, ICHTHYOLOGY. *Current Pos:* from asst prof to assoc prof, 66-77, PROF BIOL, MEMPHIS STATE UNIV, 77- *Personal Data:* b Mountainburg, Ark, July 14, 38; m 60. *Educ:* Col of Ozarks, BS, 60; Univ Kans, MA, 62, PhD(zool), 66. *Prof Exp:* Kettering intern biol, Kenyon Col, 65-66. *Mem:* AAAS; Am Fisheries Soc; Sigma Xi; World Aquaculture Soc. *Res:* Studies on reproductive and stress physiology and factors limiting production of channel catfish in ponds and raceways; culture of catfish in recirculating raceways. *Mailing Add:* Dept Biol Univ Memphis Memphis TN 38152-6080

SIME, DAVID GILBERT, ELECTRO LUMINESCENCE, INTERPLANETARY PHYSICS. *Current Pos:* HEAD RES & DEVELOP, METROMARK INC, 95- *Personal Data:* b Glasgow, Scotland, July 4, 48; m 82, Marsha LaPointe. *Educ:* Univ Edinburgh, BSc, 70; Univ Calif, San Diego, PhD(appl physics), 76. *Prof Exp:* Res asst, Univ Calif, San Diego, 70-76; res assoc, Swiss Fed Inst Technol, Zurich, 76-77; vis scientist, High Altitude Observ, Boulder, 77-78, spec proj scientist, 78-80, staff scientist I, 80-81, staff scientist II, 81-85, scientist III, 81-87; prog dir solar terrestrial res, NSF, 94-95. *Mem:* Am Geophys Union; Am Astron Soc. *Res:* Three-dimensional structure of the solar corona and the interplanetary medium; instrument development and data processing, especially as applied to the sun. *Mailing Add:* Metromark Inc 11574 Encore Circle Minnetonka MN 55343

SIME, RODNEY J, PHYSICAL CHEMISTRY. *Current Pos:* From asst prof to assoc prof, 59-67, PROF CHEM, CALIF STATE UNIV, SACRAMENTO, 67- *Personal Data:* b Madison, Wis, July 3, 31; m 67, Ruth Lewin; c 4. *Educ:* Univ Wis, BS, 55; Univ Wash, PhD(chem), 59. *Concurrent Pos:* Alexander von Humboldt fel, Univ T'Bingen, 64-66; guest prof, Swiss Fed Inst Technol, 74-75. *Mem:* Am Chem Soc; Am Phys Soc. *Res:* High temperature chemistry and vaporization processes of transition element halides; x-ray diffraction studies of crystal and molecular structure. *Mailing Add:* 609 Shangri Lane Sacramento CA 95825. *E-Mail:* rodsime@csus.edu

SIME, RUTH LEWIN, PHYSICAL CHEMISTRY. *Current Pos:* INSTR CHEM, SACRAMENTO CITY COL, 68- *Personal Data:* b New York, NY, July 2, 39; m 68; c 2. *Educ:* Barnard Col, BA, 60; Radcliffe Col, MA, 61; Harvard Univ, PhD(chem), 65. *Prof Exp:* Asst prof chem, Calif State Col, Long Beach, 64-65; Sacramento State Col, 65-67 & Hunter Col, 67-68. *Mem:* AAAS; Am Crystallog Asn. *Res:* Biographical research of physicist Lise Meitner. *Mailing Add:* Dept Math & Sci Sacramento City Col 3835 Freeport Blvd Sacramento CA 95822-1386

SIMENSTAD, CHARLES ARTHUR, MARINE ECOLOGY, FISHERIES BIOLOGY. *Current Pos:* FISHERIES BIOLOGIST, FISHERIES RES INST, UNIV WASH, 71-, COORDR, WETLAND ECOSYST TEAM, SCH FISHERIES, 90- *Personal Data:* b Yakima, Wash, Feb 22, 47. *Educ:* Univ Wash, BS, 69, MS, 71. *Mem:* AAAS; Sigma Xi; Am Inst Fisheries Res Biologists; Ecol Soc Am. *Res:* Community and trophic ecology of estuarine and nearshore marine communities; ecology of epibenthic zooplankton; food web structure and feeding ecology of marine fish assemblages; early marine life history of Pacific salmon. *Mailing Add:* Fisheries Res Inst 366 Fisheries Ctr Box 357980 Seattle WA 98195. *Fax:* 206-685-7471; *E-Mail:* csimenstad@hernet.edu

SIMEON, GEORGE JOHN, INDIGENOUS NAVIGATIONAL SYSTEMS, TRADITIONAL MEDICAL SYSTEMS. *Current Pos:* CONSULT, 91- *Personal Data:* b New York, NY, July 21, 34; m 65, Evelyn Takeuchi; c Laura, Scott & Michele (Chenie). *Educ:* Univ Hawaii, BA, 62, MPH, 77; Univ Southern Calif, PhD 68. *Prof Exp:* Fel & researcher med anthrop, Org Am States, 68-69; researcher anthrop, US Fulbright Comn, 70-71 & Macquarie Univ, 72-74; researcher med anthrop, Nat Geog Soc & Wenner-Gren Found, 74; med data analyst, Dept Health Educ & Welfare, Kaiser Found Hosps, 75; researcher med anthrop, Cross-Cult res fel, Univ Hawaii & Indonesia Schs Pub Health, 76; researcher, Nat Mus Man, 79-80; fel, Nat Inst Alcohol Abuse & Alcoholism, Brown Univ, 80-81; prof, Hirosaki Gakuin Univ, Japan, 91. *Concurrent Pos:* Vis lectr, Ohio State Univ, 79; consult, Pub Health Social Sci. *Res:* Ethnomedicine and medical anthropology in reference to the acquisition and analysis of field data with a view towards developing an ethnomedical theory; traditional terrestrial and sea navigational systems; Japanese society and culture; anthropological linguistics. *Mailing Add:* 820 S Highland St Arlington VA 22204-2418. *E-Mail:* giselle@msn.com

SIMEONE, JOHN BABTISTA, FOREST ENTOMOLOGY, CHEMICAL ECOLOGY. *Current Pos:* Asst entom, State Univ NY, 48-56, from asst prof to assoc prof, 56-64, chmn, Dept Entom, 62-77, chmn, Dept Environ & Forest Biol, 77-81, PROF FOREST ENTOM, STATE UNIV NY COL ENVIRON SCI & FORESTRY, SYRACUSE, 64- *Personal Data:* b Providence, RI, Nov 20, 19; m 45, Henrietta E McDermott. *Educ:* Univ RI, BS, 42; Yale Univ, MF, 48; Cornell Univ, PhD(entom), 60. *Honors & Awards:* L O Howard Award, Entom Soc Am. *Concurrent Pos:* Co-ed, J Chem Ecol, 75-; fel, NSF. *Mem:* AAAS; Entom Soc Am; Soc Am Foresters; Ecol Soc Am; NY Acad Sci; Sigma Xi. *Res:* Biology of insects causing deterioration of wood; chemical ecology; chemical ecology of forest insects. *Mailing Add:* State Univ NY Col Environ Sci & Forestry Syracuse NY 13210

SIMERAL, WILLIAM GOODRICH, MANAGEMENT. *Current Pos:* RETIRED. *Personal Data:* b Portland, Ore, May 22, 26; m 49; c 4. *Educ:* Franklin & Marshall Col, BS, 48; Univ Mich, MS, 50, PhD(physics), 53. *Prof Exp:* Res physicist, E I Du Pont de Nemours & Co, Inc, 53-56, res supvr, 56-57, sr res supvr, 57-64, res mgr, 64-66, asst dir res & develop, Plastics Dept, 66-68, dir Commercial Resins Div, 68-71, asst dir Cent Res Dept, 71-74, asst gen mgr, Plastics Dept, 74, vpres & gen mgr, 74-77, sr vpres, 77-81, dir, 77-87, exec vpres, 81-87. *Mem:* Am Phys Soc. *Res:* Physics of high polymers. *Mailing Add:* 800 Slash Pine Ct Naples FL 34108

SIMERL, L(INTON) E(ARL), CHEMICAL ENGINEERING. *Current Pos:* RETIRED. *Personal Data:* b Chillicothe, Ohio, Dec 2, 11; m 41, Martha Rodda; c Jane (Rodeheffer), Margery (Howell), James & Nancy (McConnel). *Educ:* Ohio State Univ, BChE, 35; Lawrence Col, MS, 37, PhD(chem eng), 39. *Prof Exp:* Develop engr, Mead Corp, Ohio, 39-41; supvr mat eng lab, Mfg Eng Dept, Marathon Corp, Wis, 46-53; chief develop sect, Res & Develop Dept, Film Div, Olin Indusrs, Inc, 53-56, dir res & develop, Film Div, Olin Mathieson Chem Corp, 56-62, dir packaging opers, Int Div, 62-65; vpres res & develop, Oxford Paper Co, 65-70; gen mgr, C H Dexter Div, Dexter Corp, Scotland, 71-73; consult, 73-95. *Concurrent Pos:* Vol consult, Int Exec Serv Corps, 73-79. *Mem:* Am Chem Soc; Tech Asn Pulp & Paper Indust; Inst Food Technol. *Res:* Cellulose and lignin chemistry; protective packaging; design and construction of chemical plants; pulp; paper; cellophane; high polymers; chemical warfare agents. *Mailing Add:* 74 Ashlar Village Wallingford CT 06492

SIMHA, ROBERT, MACROMOLECULAR SYSTEMS. *Current Pos:* PROF MACROMOLECULAR SCI, CASE WESTERN RES UNIV, 68- *Personal Data:* b Vienna, Austria, Aug 4, 12; nat US; m 41, Genevieve M Cowling. *Educ:* Univ Vienna, PhD(physics), 35. *Hon Degrees:* Dr, Tech Univ Dresden, 87. *Honors & Awards:* Cert Recognition, NASA, 88 & 89; Morrison Prize, NY Acad Sci, 48; US Dept Com Award, 48; Bingham Medal, Soc Rheol, 73; High Polymer Physics Prize, Am Phys Soc, 81. *Prof Exp:* Res assoc, Univ Vienna, 35-38; fac fel, Columbia Univ, 39-40, res assoc, Lalor Found Award, 40-41; lectr, Polytech Inst Brooklyn, 41-42; asst prof, Howard Univ, 42-45; lectr, Nat Bur Stand Grad Sch, 44-45, consult & coordr polymer res, 45-51, lectr, 47-48; prof chem eng, NY Univ, 51-59; prof chem, Univ Southern Calif, 59-67. *Concurrent Pos:* Lectr, Grad Div, Brooklyn Col, 40-42; vis prof, Univ Southern Calif, 58-59; chmn, First Winter Gordon Res Conf, 63; John F Kennedy Mem Found sr fel, Weizmann Inst, 66-67; sr vis res fel, Univ Manchester, 67-68; consult, UNIDO, India, 77-78; guest prof, Tech Univ, Dresden, 85 & 89, Tech Univ Eindhoven, 89-91 & Univ Freiburg, 91 & 93; vis res fel, Univ Stirling, 87. *Mem:* Fel AAAS; fel Am Phys Soc; Am Chem Soc; fel Am Inst Chemists; fel NY Acad Sci; Soc Rheol; Sigma Xi. *Res:* Hydrodynamics of colloidal solutions; viscosity of liquids and macromolecular solutions; physical and thermodynamic properties of polymers; polymerization and depolymerization processes, including biological macromolecules. *Mailing Add:* Dept Macromolecular Sci Case Western Res Univ Cleveland OH 44106-7202. *Fax:* 216-368-4202; *E-Mail:* rxbio@po.cwnu.edu

SIMHAN, RAJ, GLASS & CERAMIC FIBERS, ELECTRIC MELTING OF GLASS. *Current Pos:* MGR RES, GAF BLDG MAT CORP, 87- *Personal Data:* b Visakhapatnam, India, Sept 18, 33; US citizen; m 72; c 2. *Educ:* Andhra Univ, India, BS, 54; Banaras Hindu Univ, India, BS, 57, MS, 61; Sheffield Univ, UK, PhD(glass), 74. *Prof Exp:* Design engr furnace design, Karrena Fuerungshan, Ger, 62-67; glass technologist, Consumers Glass, Can, 67-69; res assoc glass, Manville Corp, 73-87. *Mem:* Am Ceramic Soc; Soc Glass Technol UK. *Res:* Surface studies of glass fiber surfaces; the sol-gel process of making ceramic fibers and coatings; effect of redox equilibrium on the fiberizing process; the electric melting of glass; glass compositions. *Mailing Add:* 1523 Crockett Hill Blvd Brentwood TN 37027

SIMIC, MICHAEL G, ANTIOXIDANTS, FREE RADICAL PROCESSES. *Current Pos:* proj leader, 80-86, GROUP LEADER BIOCHEM EFFECTS RADIATION, NAT BUR STANDARDS, 86- *Personal Data:* b N Becej, Yugoslavia, Jan 29, 32; m 68; c 1. *Educ:* Univ Belgrade, dipl, 56; Durham Univ, Eng, PhD (radiation chem), 64. *Hon Degrees:* DSc, Univ Newcastle Tyne, 84. *Prof Exp:* Res Assoc radiation biol, zool dept, Univ Tex, 70-75; res staff food chem, US Army Res & Develop, Lab, Natrick, Mass, 75-80. *Concurrent Pos:* Lectr mats sci, Univ Newcastle, Eng, 68-86; vis scientist pulse radiolysis, US Army Res & Develop Lab, Natrick, 70-86; res prof, Am Univ, 84-88. *Mem:* Am Chem Soc; Am Soc Photobiology; Biophys Soc; Radiation Res Soc; Soc Risk Anal; Oxygen Soc. *Res:* Mechanisms of electron transfer and free radical processes. *Mailing Add:* 9404 Bac Pl Gaithersburg MD 20877-3503

SIMILON, PHILIPPE LOUIS, TURBULENT TRANSPORT, WAVE PROPOGATION. *Current Pos:* MED DOCTOR, NY CITY, 94- *Personal Data:* b Liege, Belg, Oct 1, 53. *Educ:* Univ Liege, Belg, MA, 76; Princeton Univ, PhD(astrophys), 81. *Prof Exp:* Sr res assoc, Cornell Univ, 85-88; assoc prof, Yale Univ, 88-94. *Mem:* Fel Am Phys Soc. *Res:* Theoretical and numerical study of waves and turbulence in plasma, with applications to magnetic confinement fusion devices and to the solar atmosphere. *Mailing Add:* 90 Morning Side Dr Apt 4B New York NY 10027

SIMINOFF, PAUL, VIROLOGY, IMMUNOBIOLOGY. *Current Pos:* RETIRED. *Personal Data:* b Brooklyn, NY, May 8, 23; m 51; c 3. *Educ:* Mich State Col, BS, 48; Univ Ill, MS, 49, PhD, 51. *Prof Exp:* Microbiologist, S B Penick and Co, NJ, 51-54, Upjohn Co, Mich, 54-58, Bristol Labs, Inc, 58-86. *Mem:* AAAS; Am Soc Microbiol; Sigma Xi. *Res:* Fermentation of antibiotics and vitamins; application of tissue culture to virus and cancer research; immunology and cancer; interferon induction; drug research in allergic and immune complex diseases. *Mailing Add:* 705 Sycamore Terr Syracuse NY 13214

SIMINOVITCH, DAVID, PLANT PHYSIOLOGY & BIOCHEMISTRY, AGRICULTURAL CHEMISTRY. *Current Pos:* RETIRED. *Personal Data:* b Montreal, Que, May 29, 16; wid; c David J, Sara J(Bickis) & Michael J. *Educ:* McGill Univ, BS, MS & PhD(plant physiol), 39; Univ Minn, PhD, 46. *Honors & Awards:* Gold Medal, Can Soc Plant Physiologists, 72. *Prof Exp:* Herman Frasch Found res assoc & lectr, Minn, 46-50; res scientist, Dept Agr, Can, 50-81. *Concurrent Pos:* Ed, J Am Soc Plant Physiol, 40-45. *Mem:* Can Soc Plant Physiol (vpres, 74-75); Am Soc Plant Physiol; Am Soc Cryobiol; Royal Soc Can. *Res:* Freezing behavior of plant cells; properties of cells adapted to freezing; annual periodic chemical adaption of tree cells to winter and freezing; lipid liposomes undergoing freezing. *Mailing Add:* 2625 Regina St No 202 Ottawa ON K2B 5W8 Can

SIMINOVITCH, LOUIS, BIOPHYSICS, MICROBIOLOGY. *Current Pos:* Nat Cancer Inst Can fel, Connaught Med Res Lab, Univ Toronto, Ontario, 53-56, from asst prof to prof, Dept Med Biophysics, 56-85, prof, Inst Med Sci, 68-85, chmn, Dept Med Cell Biol, Fac Med, 69-72, assoc prof, Dept Pediat, 72-78, prof, Dept Med Cell Biol, 69-85, chmn, Dept Med Genetics, Fac Med, 72-79, EMER PROF, DEPT MED & MOLECULAR GENETICS, UNIV TORONTO, 85-; EMER DIR RES, SAMUEL LUNENFELD RES INST, MT SINAI HOSP, 94- *Personal Data:* b Montreal, Que, May 1, 20; wid; c Harriet Jane, Katherine Anne & Margo Ruth. *Educ:* McGill Univ, BSc, 41, PhD(chem), 44. *Hon Degrees:* Dr Mem Univ, 78, McMaster Univ, 78, Univ Montreal, 90, McGill Univ, 90, Western Univ, 90, Univ Toronto, 95. *Honors & Awards:* Louis Rapkine Mem Lectr, Inst Pasteur, Paris, 64; Major G Seelig Lectr, Washington Univ, St Louis, 66; Centennial Medal, Can, 67; Elizabeth Laird Lectr, Univ Winnipeg, 76; Queen Elizabeth II Jubilee Silver Medal, 77; Flavelle Gold Medal, Royal Soc Can, 78; G Malcolm Brown Mem Lectr, Royal Col Physicians & Surgeons Can, 78; Jack Schultz Mem Lectr, Inst Cancer Res, Pa, 78; Officer of the Order of Can, 80; Izaak Walton Killam Mem Prize, 81; Wightman Award, Gairdner Found, 81; V W Scully Mem Lectr, Hamilton, Ont, 81; Maurice Grimes Mem Lectr, Can Cancer Soc, 81, RP Taylor Award, Nat Cancer Inst, 86; Herzberg Mem Lectr, Carleton Univ, Ottawa, 85; Environ Mutagen Soc Award, 86; Distinguished Serv Award, Can Soc Clin Invest, 90. *Prof Exp:* Res phys chemist, Nat Res Coun Can, 44-47; Royal Soc Can fel biochem & microbiol, Pasteur Inst, Paris, 47-49, microbiol, Nat Ctr Sci Res, 49-53. *Concurrent Pos:* Fel, Can Royal Soc, 47-49 & Nat Cancer Inst Can, 53-55; scientist, Div Biol Res, Ont Cancer Inst, Toronto, 56-69, head, Subdiv Microbiol, Div Biol Res, 57-63, head, Div Biol Res, 63-69; ed, Virol, 60-80, Bact Revs, 69-72 & J Molecular & Cellular Biol, 80-90; mem, panel sect, Nat Cancer Inst Can, 65-69, res adv group, 69-74, chmn, 70-72, virol & richettsiology study sect, NIH, 66-68, adv comt, 78-83, grants comts, cellular biol & genetics, Nat Res Coun Can, 66-69 & cancer, growth & differentiation, Med Res Coun Can, 67-70 & genetics, 71-74, health res & develop comt, Ont Coun Health, 66-82, chmn, 74, task force res grants rev comt, Prov Ont, 70-74, task force joint res rev comt, 73-79, Prov task force health res req, 74-76, & adv comt genetic serv, 76-82, gen coun comn genetic eng, United Church Can, 74-78 & adv bd, Ont Ment Health Found, 74-78; mem, working group human experimentation, Med Res Coun Can, 76-78, exec, 77-83, task force res Can, Sci Coun Can, 76-80 & comt sci & legal process, 78-81, adv comt Duke Univ Comprehensive Cancer Ctr, 77-82, sci adv comt, Connaught Res Inst, 80-84, res comt, Ont Cancer Treatment & Res Found, 81-86, adv bd, Gairdner Found, 83-, Health Res & Develop Coun Ont, 83-86, med planning comt, 83-87, med planning comt, Arthritis Soc, 83-87 & sci adv bd, Huntington's Soc Can, 84-89; chmn, subcomt study basic biol Can, Biol Coun Can, 68-69, task force genetic serv, Prov Ont, 74-76 & ad hoc comt guidelines handling recombinant DNA molecules & certain animal viruses, Med Res Coun Can, 75-77; geneticist-in-chief, Hosp Sick Children, Toronto, 70-85; mem bd dir, Mt Sinai Inst, Mt Sinai Hosp, Toronto, 75-82, Nat Cancer Inst Can, 75-85, pres, 82-84, Can Cancer Soc, 81-84, Can Weizmann Inst Sci, 72- & Ont Cancer Treatment & Res Found, 79-93; nat corresp, comt genetic experimentation, Int Coun Sci Unions, 77-85; consult, Allelix, Inc, 82-87; mem fac res comt, Univ Toronto, 84-; mem, AIDS Study Steering Comt, Royal Soc Can, 87-88, Subcomt Task Force Coord Cancer Res, Univ Toronto, 87-89, Sci-Technol-Serv Subcomt, Sci Coun Can, Ottawa, 88-89; chmn, Subcomt Res, Royal Soc Study AIDS, 87-88, adv comt evolutionary biol, Can Inst Adv Res, 86-, external adv comt, Loeb Inst Med Res, 87-, sci adv comt, Rotman Res Inst Baycrest Ctr, 90-, sci adv comt, Montreal Cancer Inst, 90-; chmn res adv panel, Ont Cancer Treatment & Res Found, Toronto, 86-, mem exec comt of the bd, 91- *Mem:* Am Asn Cancer Res; fel Royal Soc Can; Genetics Soc Can; Can Soc Cell Biol(pres-elect, 66, pres, 67); AAAS; fel Royal Soc London; Canadians for Health Res; Genetics Soc Am; Can Inst Med. *Res:* Differentiation in haemopoietic tissues in mice; biochemical and physiological genetics of bacteriophages; tumor viruses; author of numerous publications. *Mailing Add:* 130 Carlton St Suite 805 Toronto ON M5A 4K3 Can

SIMITSES, GEORGE JOHN, ENGINEERING & STRUCTURAL MECHANICS. *Current Pos:* RETIRED. *Personal Data:* b Athens, Greece, July 31, 32; US citizen; m 60, Nena Economy; c John G, William G & Alexandra G. *Educ:* Ga Inst Technol, BS, 55, MS, 56; Stanford Univ, PhD(aeronaut & astronaut), 65. *Honors & Awards:* Sustained Res Award, Sigma Xi, 80. *Prof Exp:* Instr, Ga Inst Technol, 56-59, proj engr, Eng Exp Sta, 58-61, asst prof struct & design, 59-66, assoc prof spacecraft struct, 66-68, assoc prof eng sci & mech, 68-74, prof eng sci & mech, 74-86, prof aerospace eng, 86-89; prof & head aerospace eng & eng mech, Univ Cincinnati, 89-94, interim dean eng, 95-97. *Concurrent Pos:* Consult to numerous industs & co, 66- *Mem:* Soc Engr Sci; fel Am Inst Aeronaut & Astronaut; fel Am Soc Mech Engrs; Am Acad Mech; Sigma Xi; Struct Stability Res Coun; Hellenic Soc Theoret & Appl Mech; Soc Eng Sci; Am Soc Eng Educ; Am Soc Civil Engrs. *Res:* Stability theory; optimization of structures; dynamic stability; structural stability; mechanics of composite materials; structural similitude. *Mailing Add:* Dept Aerospace Eng & Eng Mech Univ Cincinnati Cincinnati OH 45221-0070. *Fax:* 513-556-5038; *E-Mail:* gsimitse@uceng.uc.edu

SIMIU, EMIL, STRUCTURAL ENGINEERING. *Current Pos:* FEL, NAT INST STANDS & TECHNOL, 88- *Personal Data:* b Bucharest, Romania, Apr 8, 34; US citizen; m 70, Devra Beck; c Erica & Michael P. *Educ:* Inst Civil Eng, Bucharest, Dipl Ing, 56; Polytech Inst Brooklyn, MS, 68; Princeton Univ, PhD(civil eng), 71. *Honors & Awards:* Fed Engr of Year Award, Nat Soc Prof Engrs, 84; Gold Medal US Dept Com, 89. *Prof Exp:* Design engr struct eng, Bucharest Design Inst, 56-62, Bechtel Corp, 63-65, Lev Zetlin & Assocs, 65-66 & Ammann & Whitney, Inc, 66-68; res asst civil eng, Princeton Univ, 68-71; res assoc, Nat Bur Stands, 71-73, res eng struct eng, 71-88. *Concurrent Pos:* Res prof, Dept Civil Eng, Johns Hopkins Univ. *Mem:* Am Soc Civil Engrs; Sigma Xi. *Res:* Dynamic loads on structures induced by wind, earthquake, and ocean waves; dynamic, chaotic and fluidelastic response. *Mailing Add:* Bldg & Fire Res Lab Nat Inst Stand & Technol Gaithersburg MD 20899. *Fax:* 301-869-6275; *E-Mail:* emil.simiu@nist.gov

SIMKIN, BENJAMIN, ENDOCRINOLOGY. *Current Pos:* ATTEND PHYSICIAN, CEDARS-SINAI MED CTR, 69- *Personal Data:* b Philadelphia, Pa, Apr 17, 21; m 47; c 2. *Educ:* Univ Southern Calif, AB, 41, MD, 44. *Prof Exp:* Intern, Los Angeles County Hosp, 43-44; resident med, Cedars of Lebanon Hosp, 44-46; instr, 49-66, asst clin prof, Sch Med, Univ Southern Calif, 66- *Concurrent Pos:* Beaumont res fel med, Cedars of Lebanon Hosp, 46-47; fel, Michael Reese Hosp, 47-48; res fel, May Inst, Jewish Hosp, Cincinnati, 48-49; jr attend physician, Los Angeles County Hosp, 49-65, attend physician, 65-; asst adj, Cedars of Lebanon Hosp, 52-58, assoc attend physician, 58-60, attend physician & chief endocrine clin, 61-69. *Mem:* AAAS; Soc Exp Biol & Med; Endocrine Soc; Am Diabetes Asn; AMA; Sigma Xi. *Res:* Pituitary hormones; obesity; clinical endocrinology. *Mailing Add:* 444S San Vicente Los Angeles CA 90048

SIMKIN, DONALD JULES, AEROSPACE ENGINEERING & TECHNOLOGY. *Current Pos:* ENGR, ENG DEPT, MCDONNELL DOUGLAS SPACE SYSTS, 89-, PRIN ENGR, DELTA III LAUNCH VEHICLE FIRST STAGE. *Personal Data:* b Brooklyn, NY, Sept 5, 25; m 51, Natalie von Gering; c Michael, Sharon & David. *Educ:* Univ Calif, Berkeley, BS, 45, MS, 49,. *Honors & Awards:* Shuttle Flag Award, Am Soc Mech Engrs; NASA Astronauts Personal Achievement Award. *Prof Exp:* Engr, Shell Develop Co, 49-57; sr engr, Marquardt Corp, 57-58, supvr rocket propulsion, 58-60; dept head, Astropower Lab, Douglas Aircraft Co, 60-62; supvr spacecraft propulsion, Space & Info Div, Downey, Rockwell Int Corp, 62, chief, 62-66, mgr, 66-67, sr proj engr advan systs dept, 67-69, mgr mission & opers anal, space shuttle proj, 69-82, mgr independent res & develop, orbiter div, assoc chief proj engr, 84-87, proj mgr, adv eng, Orbiter Div, 88-90. *Concurrent Pos:* Lectr, Space Technol Series, Univ Calif, Los Angeles, 58-68; lectr propulsion thermodynamics, Edward AFB, USAF, 67-68; lectr mgt, West Coast Univ, 83-84. *Mem:* Assoc fel Am Inst Aeronaut & Astronaut; Am Chem Soc; Am Inst Chem Engrs; Combustion Inst; Am Soc Mech Engrs. *Res:* Spacecraft propulsion systems; thermodynamics of propellants; combustion phenomena; chemical kinetics; fluid dynamics; unit operations of chemical engineering; spacecraft design; space mission planning and operations; analysis structural design management. *Mailing Add:* Mail Code H010-C014 McDonnell Douglas Space Systs 5301 Bolsa Ave Huntington Beach CA 92647. *Fax:* 714-896-5034

SIMKIN, SUSAN MARGUERITE, ASTRONOMY. *Current Pos:* res assoc, Mich State Univ, 74-75, asst prof astron, 76-79, assoc prof physics & astron, 79-84, PROF PHYSICS & ASTRON, MICH STATE UNIV, 84- *Personal Data:* b Detroit, Mich, July 26, 40; m 61; c 2. *Educ:* Earlham Col, BA, 62; Univ Wis, PhD(astron), 67. *Prof Exp:* Res assoc & lectr astron, Columbia Univ, 66-73; NATO fel, Kapteyn Labs, Groningen-NL, 75; sr res fel, Mt St romlo Observ, 76-80. *Concurrent Pos:* NATO fel, Kapteyn Lab, 75-76; sr res fel, Mt Stromlo Observ, 76-80, vis fel, 80-81. *Mem:* AAAS; Int Astron Union; Am Astron Soc; Sigma Xi; Am Women Sci. *Res:* Astronomical photometry; spectroscopy; structure of galaxies; radio galaxies; space telescope images. *Mailing Add:* Dept Physics & Astron Mich State Univ East Lansing MI 48824

SIMKIN, THOMAS EDWARD, VOLCANOLOGY, GEOLOGY. *Current Pos:* supvr geol, Smithsonian Oceanog Sorting Ctr & res assoc, Petrol Div, Smithsonian Inst, 67-72, CUR PETROLOGY & VOLCANOLOGY, SMITHSONIAN INST, 72- *Personal Data:* b Auburn, NY, Nov 11, 33; m 65, Sharon Russell; c Shona & Adam. *Educ:* Swarthmore Col, BS, 55; Princeton Univ, MSE, 60, PhD(geol), 65. *Prof Exp:* Indust engr, Proctor & Gamble Co, 55-56; hydrographer, US Coast & Geodetic Surv, 56-58; instr geol, State Univ NY Binghamton, 64-65; res assoc geophys sci, Univ Chicago, 65-67. *Concurrent Pos:* Secy for Americas Sci, Charles Darwin Found for Galapagos Isles, 70-90; dir, Global Volcanism Prog, Smithsonian, 84-95. *Mem:* Am Geophys Union; Int Asn Volcanology & Chem Earth's Interior. *Res:* Global volcanism and volcanology, particularly oceanic volcano evolution, calderas and contemporary volcanism; volcanology and petrology of Galapagos Islands and Scottish Tertiary Province. *Mailing Add:* Dept Mineral Sci NHB MRC-199 Smithsonian Inst Washington DC 20560. *E-Mail:* simkin@simnh.si.edu

SIMKINS, KARL LEROY, JR, ANIMAL SCIENCE. *Current Pos:* ASSOC DIR, ANIMAL SCI RES, FT DODGE ANIMAL HEALTH, 95- *Personal Data:* b Aldine, NJ, July 2, 39; m 61, Alberta Hitchner; c Sandra, David, John & Kevin. *Educ:* Rutgers Univ, BS, 61; Univ Wis, MS, 62, PhD(animal nutrit & biochem), 65. *Prof Exp:* Res asst dairy sci, Univ Wis, 61-62, res asst dairy sci & biochem, 62-65; res nutritionist, Am Cyanamid Co, 65-70, group leader, Clin Develop Lab, 70-77, mgr, animal indust develop, agr res ctr, 77-88, mgr clin develop, 88-94. *Mem:* Am Soc Animal Sci; Am Dairy Sci Asn. *Res:* Appetite and growth regulation in domestic animals; development of recombinant bovine somatotropin in ruminants; efficacy and safety of growth regulators, antibacterials, anthelmintics, coccidiostats and pesticides; evaluation of compounds which alter rumen fermentation. *Mailing Add:* 4 Wellington Dr Princeton Junction NJ 08550

SIMKOVER, HAROLD GEORGE, ENTOMOLOGY. *Current Pos:* RETIRED. *Personal Data:* b Montreal, Que, Mar 27, 23; nat US; m 47; c 2. *Educ:* McGill Univ, BSc, 47; Univ Wis, MS, 48, PhD(entom), 51. *Prof Exp:* Jr entomologist & instr, Wash State Univ, 51-53; entomologist, Shell Develop Co, 53-63, patent agt, 63-66, sr field rep, Shell Chem Co, 66-69, sr field rep, Biol Sci Res Ctr, Shell Develop Co, Dublin, Calif, 69-84, sr field rep 84-86. *Mem:* AAAS; Entom Soc Am. *Res:* Economic entomology; pesticides. *Mailing Add:* 181 Sandringham Rd Piedmont CA 94611

SIMKOVICH, GEORGE, MATERIAL SCIENCES, METALLURGY. *Current Pos:* assoc prof, 64-71, PROF METALL, PA STATE UNIV, UNIVERSITY PARK, 71- *Personal Data:* b Smithton, Pa, Apr 19, 28; m 63, Hannelore Quentin; c Boris A, Alexandra H & Natasha M. *Educ:* Pa State Univ, BS, 52, MS, 55, PhD(metall), 59. *Prof Exp:* Res asst mineral prep, Pa State Univ, 52-55, asst, 55; res assoc metall, Yale Univ, 58-60; Nat Sci Found res fel, 60-61; res fel, Max Planck Inst Phys Chem, 61-62; scientist, Fundamental Res Lab, US Steel Corp, 62-64. *Mem:* Am Inst Mining, Metall & Petrol Engrs; Am Soc Metals; Nat Asn Corrosion Engrs; Electrochem Soc. *Res:* Physical chemistry of metallurgy; physical chemistry of materials; high-temperature studies; oxidation; point defects in solids. *Mailing Add:* 841 Oak Ridge Ave State College PA 16801. *Fax:* 814-865-0016; *E-Mail:* gas@ems.psu.edu

SIMMANG, C(LIFFORD) M(AX), mechanical engineering; deceased, see previous edition for last biography

SIMMEL, EDWARD CLEMENS, BEHAVIORAL GENETICS, AVIATION PSYCHOLOGY. *Current Pos:* from asst prof to prof psychol, 65-90, dir, Behav Genetics Lab, 70-84, EMER PROF PSYCHOL, MIAMI UNIV, 90- *Personal Data:* b Berlin, Ger, Jan 30, 32; US citizen; m 83, Wendy Taylor; c 3. *Educ:* Univ Calif, Berkeley, AB, 55; Wash State Univ, PhD(exp psychol), 60. *Prof Exp:* Res trainee, Vet Admin Hosp, American Lake, Wash, 60; asst prof psychol, Western Wash Univ, 60-62 & Calif State Univ, Los Angeles, 62-65. *Concurrent Pos:* Vis prof, Univ Victoria, BC, 71; vis investr, Jackson lab, Maine, 70,73,75 & 82. *Mem:* Fel Am Psychol Soc; Behav Genetics Asn; Sigma Xi. *Res:* Recent history and theory in behavioral genetics; stress effects. *Mailing Add:* PO Box 759 Borrego Springs CA 92004. *E-Mail:* esimmel@aol.com

SIMMON, VINCENT FOWLER, microbiology, for more information see previous edition

SIMMONDS, JAMES G, APPLIED MECHANICS, SHELL THEORY. *Current Pos:* From asst prof to prof, 66-86, CHAIRED PROF APPL MATH, UNIV VA, 86- *Personal Data:* b Washington, DC, July 26, 35; m 88, Monique van den Eyde; c Robin & Katherine. *Educ:* Mass Inst Technol, BS, 58, MS, 58, PhD (math), 65. *Concurrent Pos:* Chair, Dent Appl Math, 89-94. *Mem:* Soc Nat Philosophers; Math Asn Am; fel Am Soc Mech Engrs; AAAS; fel Am Acad Mech. *Res:* Nonlinear theory of elastic shells; perturbation theory. *Mailing Add:* Dept Appl Math 2116 Morris Rd Charlottesville VA 22903-1723

SIMMONDS, RICHARD CARROLL, LABORATORY ANIMAL SCIENCE, RESEARCH ADMINISTRATION. *Current Pos:* DIR, LAB ANIMAL MED, UNIV NEV, 88-, ASST DEAN, SCH MED, 89- *Personal Data:* b Baltimore, Md, Aug 22, 40. *Educ:* Univ Ga, DVM, 64; Tex A&M Univ, MS, 70. *Honors & Awards:* Commendation Medal, US Air Force & US Army, 68; Meritorious Serv Medal, US Air Force, 74, 77; Meritorious Serv Medal, NASA, 76. *Prof Exp:* US Air Force, 64-85, res vet, Arctic Aeromed Lab, 64-67 & Arctic Med Res Lab, Alaska, 67-68; staff vet & resident, Lab Animal Med, Sch Aerospace Med, 68-70; area test dir, Lunar Quarantine Prog & staff vet, Air Force Detailee, Johnson Space Ctr, 70-73; staff vet & mgr, Joint US/USSR Biol Satellite Proj, Air Force Detailee, Ames Res Ctr, NASA, 73-76; dir, Dept Lab Animal Med, Sch Med, 76-82, dir, Instnl & Res Support, Uniformed Serv Univ Health Sci, 82-88. *Mem:* Am Vet Med Asn; Am Asn Lab Animal Sci; Am Col Lab Animal Med; AAAS; Am Soc Mammal. *Res:* Biomedical effects of altered geophysical environments; laboratory animal science and mammalian thermal regulation. *Mailing Add:* Dir Lab Animal Med Univ Nev MS-340 Reno NV 89557-0040

SIMMONDS, ROBERT T, PALEOBIOLOGY. *Personal Data:* b Hackensack, NJ, Aug 2, 32; m 57. *Educ:* Columbia Univ, BS, 54; Syracuse Univ, MS, 58; Univ Ill, PhD(geol), 61. *Prof Exp:* Instr geol, Denison Univ, 61; from assoc prof to prof earth sci, State Univ NY, Col Oneonta, 61-87. *Mem:* AAAS; Nat Asn Geol Teachers. *Res:* Paleoecology, evolution, geotectonics. *Mailing Add:* 190 E Beach Rd Nordland WA 98358

SIMMONDS, SIDNEY HERBERT, STRUCTURAL. *Current Pos:* From asst prof civil eng to prof, 57-93, EMER PROF CIVIL ENG, UNIV ALTA, 93- *Personal Data:* b Winnipeg, Man, Aug 29, 31; m 55, Elizabeth Tilson; c Douglas, Patricia & Gordon. *Educ:* Univ Alta, BSc, 54, MSc, 56; Univ Ill, PhD, 62. *Concurrent Pos:* Consult struct engr, 57-; vis prof, Univ Tex, Austin, 77, Univ SC, 78, Royal Mil Col Can, 87, Swiss Fed Inst Technol, Zurich, 92. *Mem:* Fel Am Concrete Inst; fel Am Soc Civil Engrs; Int Asn Shell Struct; fel Can Soc Civil Engrs. *Res:* Structural analysis and design. *Mailing Add:* Dept Civil Eng Univ Alta Edmonton AB T6G 2G7 Can. *Fax:* 403-492-0249; *E-Mail:* shsimmonds@civil.ualbeta.ca

SIMMONDS, SOFIA, BIOCHEMISTRY. *Current Pos:* instr physiol chem, Yale Univ, 45-46, from instr to asst prof microbiol, 46-50, from asst prof to assoc prof biochem & microbiol, 50-62, assoc prof biochem, 62-69, assoc prof, 69-75, dir undergrad studies, 73-85, prof molecular biophys & biochem, 75-88, assoc dean & dean undergrad studies, 88, lectr & dir undergrad studies, 90-91, EMER PROF, MOLECULAR BIOPHYSICS & BIOCHEM, YALE UNIV, 88- *Personal Data:* b New York, July 31, 17; m 38, Joseph S Fruton. *Educ:* Columbia Univ, BA, 38; Cornell Univ, PhD(biochem), 42. *Honors & Awards:* Garvan Medal, Am Chem Soc, 69. *Prof Exp:* Asst biochem, Med Col, Cornell Univ, 41-42, res assoc, 42-45. *Mem:* Am Soc Biol Chem; Am Chem Soc. *Res:* Amino acid metabolism; transmethylation in animals; amino acid and protein metabolism in micro-organisms. *Mailing Add:* Dept Molecular Biophys & Biochem Yale Univ PO Box 208024 333 Cedar St New Haven CT 06510-8024

SIMMONS, ALAN J(AY), ELECTRICAL ENGINEERING. *Current Pos:* CONSULT, 87- *Personal Data:* b New York, NY, Oct 14, 24; m 47, Mary Bachhuber; c David, Peter, Michael, Philip & Paul. *Educ:* Harvard Univ, BS, 45; Mass Inst Technol, MS, 48; Univ Md, PhD(elec eng), 57. *Prof Exp:* Electronic scientist, US Naval Res Lab, 48-57; head, Microwave Dept, TRG, Inc, 57-71; group leader, Lincoln Lab, Mass Inst Technol, 71-87. *Mem:* AAAS; fel Inst Elec & Electronics Engrs; Antennas Propagation Soc (pres, 86). *Res:* Microwave antennas, waveguides and components; electromagnetic theory; communication satellites. *Mailing Add:* PO Box 207 Center Sandwich NH 03227

SIMMONS, BETTYE H, NURSING. *Current Pos:* US Army, 71-, clin staff nurse, Hematol & Oncol Ward, Brooke Army Med Ctr, counr, US Army Recruiting Command, head nurse, Med Ward & Coronary Unit, 121st Evacuation Hosp, Med Intensive Care Unit, Walter Reed Army Med Ctr, dir practical nurse course, Fitzsimons Army Med Ctr, asst inspector gen, Health Servs Command, dep chief, Nursing Sci Div, Acad Health Sci, chief nurse, Bayne-Jones US Army Community Hosp, consult, Surgeon Gen Nursing Admin, chief nurse, US Army Command, CHIEF, ARMY NURSING CORPS, US ARMY, 95-, DEP COMDR, US ARMY MED DEPT CTR & SCH, 96- DEPT INSTALLATION COMDR, FT SAM HOUSTON, 96- *Personal Data:* b San Antonio, Tex; m, Charles W. *Educ:* Incarnate Word Col, BS; Univ Tex, MS. *Res:* Hematology and oncology. *Mailing Add:* US Army Med Dept Ctr & Sch & Ft Sam Houston 2250 Stanley Rd Ft Sam Houston TX 78234-6100

SIMMONS, CHARLES EDWARD, PSYCHIATRY. *Current Pos:* RETIRED. *Personal Data:* b Oklahoma City, Okla, Apr 5, 27; m 53; c 2. *Educ:* Univ Okla, BS, 50, MD, 54. *Prof Exp:* Intern, Gorgas Hosp, Ancon, Panama, CZ, 54-55; resident psychiat, Griffith Mem Hosp, Norman, Okla, 55-57; resident, Parkland Hosp, Dallas, Tex, 57-58; from instr to asst prof, Southwest Med Sch, Univ Tex, Dallas, 58-60; mem staff, Chestnut Lodge, Md, 62-63; prof psychiat, Med Sch, Univ Tex, San Antonio, 67-89. *Concurrent Pos:* NIMH teaching fel psychiat, Southwest Med Sch, Univ Tex, Dallas, 57-58; consult, Wilford Hall Air Force Hosp, San Antonio, Tex, 67- *Mem:* AMA; Am Psychiat Asn; Am Psychoanal Asn. *Res:* Psychoanalysis. *Mailing Add:* PO Box 254 Port Mansfield TX 78598

SIMMONS, DANIEL HAROLD, PULMONARY DISEASE. *Current Pos:* asst prof med, Univ Calif, Los Angeles, 53-55, from asst prof to assoc prof med & physiol, 55-65, prof physiol, 65-81, prof med, 65-89, EMER PROF MED, UNIV CALIF, LOS ANGELES, 89- *Personal Data:* b New York, NY, June 22, 19; m 42; c Anthony & Michael. *Educ:* Univ Calif, Los Angeles, BA, 41; Univ Southern Calif, MD, 48; Univ Minn, PhD(physiol), 53. *Prof Exp:* Instr math, Univ Calif, Los Angeles, 43. *Concurrent Pos:* Nat Heart Inst trainee, Univ Minn, 51-53; sect chief, Vet Admin Ctr, Los Angeles, 53-61; dir res & assoc dir div med, Mt Sinai Hosp, 61-64, dir med res inst, Cedars-Sinai Med Ctr, 64-66. *Mem:* Am Physiol Soc; Am Fedn Clin Res; fel Am Col Chest Physicians; Am Thoracic Soc; fel Am Col Physicians. *Res:* Mechanisms of clinically-related problems in respiration physiology. *Mailing Add:* Dept Med Univ Calif Med Ctr Los Angeles CA 90024. *Fax:* 310-206-8622; *E-Mail:* dsimmons@medicine.medsch.ucla.edu

SIMMONS, DANIEL L, MOLECULAR BIOLOGY. *Current Pos:* ASSOC PROF BIOCHEM, BRIGHAM YOUNG UNIV, 89- *Personal Data:* b Provo, Utah, May 14, 55; c 3. *Educ:* Brigham Young Univ, BS, 78, MS, 80; Univ Wis-Madison, PhD(oncol), 86. *Prof Exp:* Fel, Biol Labs, Harvard Univ, Cambridge, Mass, 86-89. *Concurrent Pos:* Vis prof, William Harvey Res Inst, London, 95-96. *Mem:* Sigma Xi; AAAS. *Res:* Signal transduction; immediate-early genes induced by Rous sarcoma virus; mitogen-inducible cyclooxygenase. *Mailing Add:* E280 BNSN Brigham Young Univ Provo UT 84602

SIMMONS, DARYL MICHAEL, CHEMISTRY, DRUG INVESTIGATION. *Current Pos:* SR RES SCIENTIST, STERLING WINTHROP PHARMACEUT RES DIV, 82- *Personal Data:* b Hudson, NY, May 14, 52. *Educ:* Col St Rose, BA, 79; Slippery Rock Univ, MS, 81. *Prof Exp:* Lab tech, Bender Hyg Labs, 75; prod tech, Sterling Org, 76-78; anal chemist, Stiefel Res Inst, 81-82. *Concurrent Pos:* Adj instr chem, biol & algebra, Columbia-Greene Commun Col, 82-; presenter, Am Asn Pharmaceut Scientists & Asn Off Anal Chemists, 89-; vis scientist, Pharmaceut Mfg Asn, 89-; judge, Pa Acad Sci. *Mem:* Pharmaceut Mfg Asn; Am Asn Pharmaceut Scientists. *Res:* Determination of chemical and physical properties of drugs corresponding to oral absorption and bioavailability; development of small animal models to evaluate absorption and bioavailability; development of a formulation for maximum systemic blood levels of investigation drugs; numerous publications. *Mailing Add:* 103 Develin Dr Phoenixville PA 19460-1505

SIMMONS, DAVID J, PHYSIOLOGY, ENDOCRINOLOGY. *Current Pos:* assoc prof, 86-90, PROF, UNIV TEX MED BR, GALVESTON, 90- *Personal Data:* b Jamaica Plain, Mass, Mar 10, 31; m 57; c 1. *Educ:* Boston Univ, BA, 54; Clark Univ, MA, 56; Univ Chicago, PhD(paleozool), 59. *Prof Exp:* Instr biol, Wright Jr Col, 59-60; res assoc physiol, Univ Chicago, 59-62; from asst physiologist to assoc physiologist, Radiol Physics Div, Argonne Nat Lab, 62-72; asst prof orthop surg, Sch Med, Wash Univ, 72-75, assoc prof res orthop surg, 75-86. *Concurrent Pos:* NIH fel, Univ Chicago, 60-62. *Mem:* AAAS; Am Asn Anatomists; Int Soc Chronobiol; Soc Vert Paleont; Orthop Res Soc; Am Soc Bone & Mineral Res. *Res:* Skeletal development; collagen formation; cell population dynamics. *Mailing Add:* 3 Adler Circle Galveston TX 77551-5829

SIMMONS, DAVID RAE, MATHEMATICS. *Current Pos:* full prof math & chmn Dept Math & Comput Sci, La Col, 74-88. *Personal Data:* b Oklahoma City, Okla, May 4, 40; m 61; c 3. *Educ:* Centenary Col La, BS, 62; Univ Ark, MS, 66, PhD(math), 69. *Prof Exp:* Asst prof math, Centenary Col La, 69-74, actg chmn dept, 70-72. *Mem:* Am Math Soc; Asn Comput Mach; Math Asn Am. *Res:* Category theory; universal algebra, computer studies of semigroups of relations. *Mailing Add:* Dept Math & Phys Sci La Col Pineville LA 71359-0001

SIMMONS, DICK BEDFORD, COMPUTER & INFORMATION SCIENCES. *Current Pos:* assoc prof, 71-81, PROF COMPUT SCI, TEX A&M UNIV, 81-, DIR COMPUT CTR, 72- *Personal Data:* b Houston, Tex, Dec 24, 37; m 59; c 3. *Educ:* Tex A&M Univ, BS, 59; Univ Pa, MS, 61, PhD(comput & info sci), 68. *Prof Exp:* Design engr, Radio Corp Am, 59-61; mem tech staff, Bell Tel Labs, 63-69, supvr comput lang & systs, 69-70. *Concurrent Pos:* Consult, Tex A&M Univ, 70-71 & Datamaster Div, Am Chain & Cable Co, 72-; prin investr, Unitech Oper Systs Proj, 71-72 & NASA Automated Doc Study, 72. *Mem:* Asn Comput Mach; Inst Elec & Electronics Engrs; Asn Educ Data Systs; Am Soc Eng Educ. *Res:* Automatic documentation; computer languages; programmer productivity; computer architecture. *Mailing Add:* Dept Comput Sci Tex A&M Univ 301 Harvey R Bright Bldg College Station TX 77843-3112

SIMMONS, DONALD GLICK, VETERINARY MICROBIOLOGY. *Current Pos:* DIR, DIV EDUC & RES AM VET MED ASSOC. *Personal Data:* b Waynesboro, Va, Sept 6, 38; m 84, Cheryl M Stroud; c 2. *Educ:* Bridgewater Col, BA, 62; Univ Ga, DVM, 67, MS, 69, PhD(vet microbiol), 71. *Honors & Awards:* P P Levine Award, 80. *Prof Exp:* NIH spec fel, vet med microbiol, Univ Ga, 67-71; from asst prof to prof vet med microbiol, NC State Univ, 71-80, prof microbiol, path & parasitol, 80-87; prof & head, Dept Vet Sci, Pa State Univ, 88-94, prof vet sci, 94-96. *Mem:* Sigma Xi; Am Vet Med Asn; Am Col Vet Microbiologists; Am Asn Avian Pathologists. *Res:* Veterinary medical microbiology; avian medicine; respiratory and enteric viruses of poultry; respiratory bacteria of poultry. *Mailing Add:* 10129 N River Rd Barrington Hill IL 60102. *Fax:* 847-925-1329; *E-Mail:* 104436.444@compuserve.com

SIMMONS, DWAYNE DEANGELO, DEVELOPMENTAL NEUROBIOLOGY, CHEMICAL NEUROANATOMY. *Current Pos:* ASST PROF, DEPT BIOL, UNIV CALIF, LOS ANGELES, 90- *Personal Data:* m 93, D'Nisa Hoover. *Educ:* Pepperdine Univ, BS, 80; Harvard Univ, PhD(med scis), 86. *Prof Exp:* Teaching fel, Harvard Univ, 82-85; asst prof, Pepperdine Univ, 85-90. *Concurrent Pos:* Prin investr, NSF, 87-94, NIH, 92-; fel, Alfred P Sloan Res Found, 90-92; vis scientist electron micros, House Ear Inst, 90-; mem, Brain Res Inst, 90-; res consult, Pepperdine Univ, 90- *Mem:* Asn Res Otolaryngol; Soc Neurosci; Int Soc Neuroethology; Am Sci Affil; AAAS; NY Acad Sci. *Res:* Expression and pharmacology of neuroactive substances in the developing auditory system; studies focus on both sensory and efferent neuronal populations that innervate the cochlea. *Mailing Add:* Dept Biol UCLA 405 Hilgard Ave Los Angeles CA 90024-1301. *Fax:* 310-206-3987; *E-Mail:* simmons@cognet.ucla.edu

SIMMONS, ELIZABETH H, ELECTROWEAK SYMMETRY BREAKING, PARTICLE PHENOMENOLOGY BEYOND THE STANDARD MODEL. *Current Pos:* ASST PROF PHYSICS, BOSTON UNIV, 93- *Personal Data:* b Buffalo, NY, Oct 22, 63; m 90, R Sekhar Chivukula; c Ari. *Educ:* Harvard Univ, AB, 85, AM, 87, PhD(physics), 90; Univ Cambridge, MPhil, 86. *Prof Exp:* Fel, Tex Nat Res Lab, 90-91; Harvard Univ, 90-93. *Concurrent Pos:* Mem & coun rep, Gem Collab, 91-93. *Mem:* Am Phys Soc; fel Asn Women Sci. *Res:* Standard model of high energy physics; origin of electroweak symmetry breaking; effective field theories and collider phenomenology, including exotic strong-interaction physics. *Mailing Add:* Physics Dept Boston Univ 590 Commonwealth Ave Boston MA 02215. *Fax:* 617-353-9393; *E-Mail:* simmons@bu.edu

SIMMONS, EMORY GUY, MYCOLOGY. *Current Pos:* RETIRED. *Personal Data:* b Ind, Apr 12, 20. *Educ:* Wabash Col, AB, 41; DePauw Univ, AM, 46; Univ Mich, PhD(bot), 50. *Hon Degrees:* DSc(microbiol) Kasetsant Univ, Thailand, 88. *Prof Exp:* Instr bact & bot, DePauw, 46-47; asst prof bot, Dartmouth Col, 50-53; mycologist, US Army Natick Labs, 53-58, head mycol lab, 58-74, prin investr, Develop Ctr Cult Collection of Fungi, 74-77; prof bot, 74-77, prof microbiol, Univ Mass, Amherst, 77-87. *Concurrent Pos:* Chmn adv comt fungi, Am Type Cult Collection; US rep, Expert Group on Fungus Taxon, Orgn Econ Coop & Develop; Secy Army res fel, Thailand, Indonesia, 68-69; adj prof, Univ RI, 72-74; mem exec bd, US Fedn Cult Collections, 74-76, pres, 76-78; pres & chmn bd, Second Int Mycol Cong, Inc, 75-78; mem adv comt cult collections, UN Environ Prog/UNESCO/Int Cell Res Orgn, 77- *Mem:* AAAS; Mycol Soc Am (secy-treas, 63-65, vpres, 66, pres, 68); Brit Mycol Soc; Int Asn Plant Taxonomists. *Res:* Taxonomic mycology; taxonomy of Fungi imperfecti; taxonomy and cultural characteristics of Ascomycetes. *Mailing Add:* 717 Thornwood Rd Crawfordsville IN 47933-2760

SIMMONS, ERIC LESLIE, BIOLOGY. *Current Pos:* RETIRED. *Personal Data:* b Santo Domingo, Dominican Repub, Feb 11, 17; nat US; m 43, 54, Phyllis Rye; c Nancy, Eric Jr, David & Gregory. *Educ:* Swarthmore Col, AB, 38; Ind Univ, PhD(zool), 44. *Prof Exp:* Res assoc, Metall Lab, Sch Med, Univ Chicago, 43-46, from instr to asst prof biol sci, 46-55, premed adv, 48-52, asst dean students, 52-54, from assoc prof to prof med, 55-84. *Concurrent Pos:* Prof lectr, Col Univ Chicago, 80-84, dir, Undergrad Labs, 81-84. *Mem:* Sigma Xi; assoc Am Soc Zoologists; Radiation Res Soc; Am Asn Lab Animal Sci; Int Soc Exp Hemat. *Res:* Radiobiology; effect of radiation on the hemopoietic system; cancer induction; pioneering studies on bone-marrow transplantation. *Mailing Add:* 1909 E Windsor Dr Bloomington IN 47401

SIMMONS, FRANCIS BLAIR, PHYSIOLOGY. *Current Pos:* resident physician & res assoc otolaryngol, Sch Med, Stanford Univ, 59-62, assoc prof, 65-71, chief dept,665-80, PROF OTOLARYNGOL, SCH MED, STANFORD UNIV, 71- *Personal Data:* b Los Angeles, Calif, Nov 15, 30; m 71; c 4. *Educ:* Transylvania Col, AB, 52; Univ Louisville, MD, 56. *Prof Exp:* Intern med, Madigan Army Hosp, 56-57; res physiologist, Walter Reed Army Inst Res, 58-59. *Res:* Auditory physiology and psychophysics; neurophysiology. *Mailing Add:* Stanford Univ Med Ctr 300 Pasteur Dr R 135 Stanford CA 94305

SIMMONS, GARY WAYNE, PHYSICAL CHEMISTRY, SURFACE CHEMISTRY. *Current Pos:* asst prof, 70-74, assoc prof, 74-79, PROF CHEM, LEHIGH UNIV, 79- *Personal Data:* b Parsons, WVa, June 17, 39; m 64; c 1. *Educ:* WVa Univ, BS, 61; Univ Va, PhD(chem), 67. *Honors & Awards:* Melvin Romanoff Award, Nat Asn Corrosion Engrs, 74; Henry Marion Howe Medal, Am Soc Metals, 79. *Prof Exp:* Fel physics, Ga Inst Technol, 66-67, res chemist, 67-70. *Mem:* Am Chem Soc; Sigma Xi. *Res:* Fundamental properties of the solid-gas and solid-liquid interface and application of these properties to practical problems of catalysis, corrosion, stress corrosion cracking and corrosion fatigue; low energy electron diffraction, Auger electron spectroscopy, Mossbauer spectroscopy, x-ray photoelectron spectroscopy and electron microscopy. *Mailing Add:* 1829 Alder Lane Bethlehem PA 10815-9053

SIMMONS, GEORGE ALLEN, CHEMISTRY GLASS, CERAMICS. *Current Pos:* RETIRED. *Personal Data:* b Birmingham, Ala, May 2, 26; m 51, Marilyn Boyer; c Roger, Grile & Elaine. *Educ:* Birmingham Southern Col, BS, 47; Ohio State Univ, MS, 49, PhD(chem), 52. *Prof Exp:* From asst prof to assoc prof chem, Birmingham Southern Col, 49-55; mgr res serv, Pittsburgh Plate Glass Co, 55-61, coordr melting, 61-62; spec proj chief, Owens Ill-Toledo, 62-66, tech dir new prod develop, 66-69, sr mkt mgr, 69-71; tech dir, Dominion Glass Co, Mississauga, Ont, Can, 71-76; sr vpres res & develop, Thatcher Glass Co, Elmira, NY, 76-81; tech dir, Ga Marble Co, Atlanta, 81-87. *Concurrent Pos:* Asst prof, Purdue Univ, 52-53; Du Pont fel, 52. *Mem:* Fel Am Inst Chemists; Am Chem Soc; fel Am Ceramic Soc. *Res:* Crystallized glasses; ultrafine grinding; mineral processing. *Mailing Add:* 411 Roland Rd Woodstock VA 22664-1200

SIMMONS, GEORGE FINLAY, MATHEMATICS. *Current Pos:* from assoc prof to prof, 62-90, EMER PROF MATH, COLO COL, 90- *Personal Data:* b Austin, Tex, Mar 3, 25; m 54, Hope Bridgeford; c Nancy. *Educ:* Calif Inst Technol, BS, 46; Univ Chicago, MS, 48; Yale Univ, PhD(math), 57. *Prof Exp:* Instr math, Univ Col, Univ Chicago, 47-50, Univ Maine, 50-52 & Yale Univ, 52-56; asst prof, Univ RI, 56-58 & Williams Col, 58-62. *Mem:* Math Asn Am. *Res:* Topology; abstract algebra; analysis. *Mailing Add:* Dept Math Colo Col Colorado Springs CO 80903

SIMMONS, GEORGE MATTHEW, JR, LIMNOLOGY, GROUNDWATER ECOLOGY. *Current Pos:* from asst prof to assoc prof limnol, Va Polytechnic Inst & State Univ, 71-78, assoc prof zool, 78-83, interim head, 88-89, PROF ZOOL, VA POLYTECHNIC INST & STATE UNIV, 83-, ALUMNI DISTINGUISHED PROF, 92- *Personal Data:* b Charleston, SC, Dec 25, 42; m 63; c 1. *Educ:* Appalachian State Univ, BS, 64; Va Polytech Inst & State Univ, PhD(zool), 68. *Honors & Awards:* Soil & Water Conserv Award, 92. *Prof Exp:* Asst prof biol & ecol, Va Commonwealth Univ, 68-71. *Mem:* Int Soc Theoret Appl Limnol; Am Soc Limnol & Oceanog; Explorer's Club. *Res:* Limnological studies of reservoir ecosystems; origin and role of freshwater benthic communities in antarctic lakes; productivity of tropical marine sand flats; submarine ground water discharge and nutrient flux in coastal marine environments. *Mailing Add:* Dept Biol Va Polytech Inst & State Univ PO Box 0406 Blacksburg VA 24063-0001

SIMMONS, GUSTAVUS JAMES, INFORMATION THEORY, CRYPTOGRAPHY. *Current Pos:* mgr, Math Dept, 71-87, SR RES FEL, SANDIA NAT LABS, 87- *Personal Data:* b Ansted, WVa, Oct 27, 30; m 50; c 1. *Educ:* NMex Highlands Univ, BS, 55; Univ Okla, MS, 58; Univ NMex, PhD(math), 69. *Honors & Awards:* Nuclear Weapon Excellence Award, Dept Energy, 86; Ernest Orlando Lawrence Award, 86. *Prof Exp:* Res assoc, Sandia Corp, 54-55, physicist, Nuclear Test Dept, 58-60; res scientist res staff, Lockheed Aircraft Corp, 55-56; sr group engr, Adv Electronics Div, McDonnell Aircraft Corp, 60-61; chief electronic engr, Electronic & Res Div, Fairbanks Morse & Co, 61; div supvr advan systs res, Sandia Corp, 62-70; dir res, Rolamite, 70-71. *Concurrent Pos:* Mem subcomt facil, Gov Tech Excellence Comt; ed, J Cryptology, Calif & Ars Combinatoria, Can. *Mem:* Math Asn Am. *Res:* Digital message authentication theory; nuclear weapon system, especially the control and engineered use of such systems; combinatorial mathematics and graph theory; algorithms for high speed computation; cryptography. *Mailing Add:* Box 365 Sandia Park NM 87047

SIMMONS, GUY HELD, JR, NUCLEAR MEDICINE, RADIOLOGY. *Current Pos:* PROF RADIOL, MED CTR, UNIV KY, 91- *Personal Data:* b Lafayette, Tenn, Oct 9, 36; m 59, 89, Patricia Roth; c Tracy, Scott, David, Sarah & Lydia. *Educ:* Western Ky Univ, BA, 61; Univ NC, MS, 64; Univ Cincinnati, PhD(nuclear eng), 72. *Prof Exp:* Instr physics, Western Ky Univ, 61; physicist radiation physics, USPHS, 61-72; med physicist, Vet Admin Med Ctr, Lexington, Ky, 72-93. *Concurrent Pos:* instr radiol, Med Ctr, Univ Cincinnati, 66-72; Ky Heart Asn grant, Univ Ky, 74-, Nat Cancer Inst grant, 75-; Vet Admin grant, 78; Food & Drug Admin grant, 88. *Mem:* Soc Nuclear Med; Am Asn Physicists Med; Am Col Radiol; Am Col Nuclear Physicians. *Res:* Nuclear medicine instrumentation development and evaluation; digital image processing for clinical applications. *Mailing Add:* Univ Ky Med Ctr Radiol Dept 800 Rose St Lexington KY 40536

SIMMONS, HARRY DADY, JR, MEDICINAL CHEMISTRY, ONCOLOGY. *Current Pos:* PRO ED COMMUN INC, 97- *Personal Data:* b Chicago, Ill, June 10, 38. *Educ:* Univ Ill, BS, 60; Mass Inst Technol, PhD(chem), 66, State Univ NY, MD, 77. *Prof Exp:* NIH fel inorg chem, Munich Inst Technol, 66-67; NIH fel chem, Brandeis Univ, 67-69; res chemist, Allied Chem Corp, 69-71; lab supvr, Kingsbrook Jewish Med Ctr, 71-74; med resident, Berkshire Med Ctr, 77-78, path resident, 78-80; res fel molecular biol, Albany Med Col, 80-81; res fel med eng, Polytech Inst, Troy, NY, 81-85; path resident, Mt Sinai Med Ctr, NY, 85-87; path fel, Montefiore Med Ctr, Bronx, NY, 87-91, Huntington Vet Admin Med Ctr, 91-93, Marshall Univ Med Sch, Huntington WVa, 91-93; pathologist, Timken-Mercy Med Ctr, Ohio, 93-95; scientific writer, 96-97. *Mem:* NY Acad Sci; AMA; Am Meteorol Soc; Sigma Xi; Col Am Pathologists; Am Soc Clin Pathologists. *Res:* Synthetic organometallic chemistry of mercury, chromium, iron, group IV A metals; biomedical engineering; anatomic pathology; educational programs for personal computer use; flow cytometry and image cytometry of neoplasms cytopathology. *Mailing Add:* 3515 Fairmount Blvd Cleveland Heights OH 44118-4322

SIMMONS, HOWARD ENSIGN, JR, organic chemistry; deceased, see previous edition for last biography

SIMMONS, JAMES, GEOGRAPHY. *Current Pos:* PROF GEOGRAPHY, UNIV TORONTO. *Mailing Add:* Dept Geog Univ Toronto 100 St George St Toronto ON M5S 1A1 Can

SIMMONS, JAMES E, EXPERIMENTAL NUCLEAR PHYSICS. *Current Pos:* PHYSICIST, LOS ALAMOS NAT LAB, UNIV CALIF, 57- *Personal Data:* b Chicago, Ill, Sept 16, 25; m 48; c 2. *Educ:* Univ Calif, BS, 49, MA, 54, PhD(physics), 57; Univ Paris, dipl, 52. *Concurrent Pos:* Vis scientist, Cen-Saclay Synchrotron, France, 80. *Mem:* Fel Am Phys Soc. *Res:* Low energy nuclear physics with neutron beams; medium energy experiments on spin dependence of nuclear forces; development of cryogenic instrumentation for nuclear physics; measurement of medium energy atomic beam properties by optical imaging methods. *Mailing Add:* 125 E-L Gancho Los Alamos NM 87544

SIMMONS, JAMES EDWIN, child psychiatry, for more information see previous edition

SIMMONS, JAMES QUIMBY, III, PSYCHIATRY. *Current Pos:* chief inpatient child psychiat, 62-68, assoc clin prof psychiat & assoc prog dir ment retardation, 68-72, PROF PSYCHIAT IN RESIDENCE & CHIEF MENT RETARDATION & CHILD PSYCHOL, NEUROPSYCHIAT INST, CTR FOR HEALTH SCI, UNIV CALIF, LOS ANGELES, 82- *Personal Data:* b Philadelphia, Pa, Apr 16, 25; m 54; c 4. *Educ:* Rutgers Univ, BS, 48; Bowman Gray Sch Med, Wake Forest Univ, MD, 52. *Honors & Awards:* Distinguished Serv Medal; Army & Defense Superior Serv Medal, US Dept Defense. *Prof Exp:* Intern, Walter Reed Army Med Ctr, 52-53. *Concurrent Pos:* Asst prof in residence psychiat, Neuropsychiat Inst, Ctr for Health Sci, Univ Calif, Los Angeles, 64-68; attend psychiatrist, Vet Admin Ctr, Los Angeles, 65-85. *Mem:* AAAS; fel Am Psychiat Asn; fel Am Acad Child & Adolescent Psychol; fel Am Col Psychol; Am Orthopsychiat Asn; Sigma Xi. *Res:* Behavior modification in schizophrenic and retarded children utilizing reinforcement principles; language in autistic and developmentally disabled children. *Mailing Add:* 760 Westwood Plaza Los Angeles CA 90024-8300

SIMMONS, JAMES WOOD, MOLECULAR SPECTROSCOPY, SCIENCE EDUCATION. *Current Pos:* RETIRED. *Personal Data:* b Chase City, Va, Sept 20, 16; m 41; c Ruth Worley; c Kibbie, Terry & Jeffrey. *Educ:* Hampden-Sydney Col, BS, 37; Va Polytech Inst, MS, 39; Duke Univ, PhD(physics), 48. *Prof Exp:* Instr physics, Va Polytech Inst, 39-41, asst prof, 46; from asst prof to assoc prof, Emory Univ, 48-59, chmn dept, 58-63, prof physics, 59-83. *Concurrent Pos:* Consult, Eng Exp Sta, Ga Inst Technol, 65-75. *Mem:* Am Phys Soc; Am Asn Physics Teachers. *Res:* Determination of molecular and nuclear properties by microwave spectroscopy; electronics instrumentation. *Mailing Add:* 2127 Spring Creek Rd Decatur GA 30033

SIMMONS, JEAN ELIZABETH MARGARET, ORGANIC CHEMISTRY, BIOCHEMISTRY. *Current Pos:* RETIRED. *Personal Data:* b Cleveland, Ohio, Jan 20, 14; m 35; c 3. *Educ:* Western Reserve Univ, BA, 33; Univ Chicago, PhD(org chem), 38. *Honors & Awards:* Citation, Surgeon Gen US, 45; Award, Lindback Found, 64. *Prof Exp:* From instr to prof chem & chmn dept, Barat Col, 38-58; prof chem, Upsala Col, 59-84, chmn dept, 65-71 & 76-81, chmn div nat sci, 66-69, emer prof chem, 84-95, asst to pres, 69-73 & 78-95. *Concurrent Pos:* Instr, Univ Chicago, 38-41; coordr basic sci, Sch Nursing, Evangelical Hosp, 43-47; chmn comt study sci div of Upsala Col, Lutheran Church Am grant, 65-68; pres & trustee, Va Gildersleeve Int Fund Univ Women, Inc; delegate Int Fed Univ Women, Germany, 68, Japan, 74, Scotland, 77; pres, Grad Women in Sci, 70-71; Fedn Orgns Prof Women, 74-75; consult fund raising, Higher Educ, 72-; vis fel, Hist of Sci, Princeton Univ, 77; dir, officer & mem comt, NJ Educ Comput Ctr, 69-72; Int Fed deleg to UN conf, Austria, 79, Kenya, 81. *Mem:* Fel AAAS; Am Chem Soc; Am Asn Univ Women; Int Alliance Women; fel Sigma Xi; Int Fedn Univ Women. *Res:* Biuret reactions of polypeptides; respiratory pigments; protein chemistry; history of women in science. *Mailing Add:* 40 Balsam Lane Princeton NJ 08540-5327

SIMMONS, JENNINGS (JAY), AEROSPACE ENGINEERING. *Current Pos:* DIR SPACE LAB PROG, MCDONNELL DOUGLAS AEROSPACE. *Educ:* Tenn Tech Inst, BSME, 56. *Honors & Awards:* Space Syst Award, Am Inst Aeronaut & Astronaut, 94. *Mailing Add:* McDonnell Douglas Aerospace Mail Stop 33 EZ 689 Discovery Dr Huntsville AL 35806

SIMMONS, JOE DENTON, physical chemistry, molecular spectroscopy; deceased, see previous edition for last biography

SIMMONS, JOHN ARTHUR, THEORETICAL MECHANICS, MATERIALS SCIENCE. *Current Pos:* RES MATHEMATICIAN, NAT BUR STANDARDS, 62- *Personal Data:* b Santa Monica, Calif, Jan 25, 32; m 97, Catherine Wilson; c David, Sean, Angus & Halina. *Educ:* Univ Calif, Berkeley, BA, 53, MA, 56, PhD(appl math), 62. *Prof Exp:* Res mathematician, Inst Eng Res, Univ Calif, Berkeley, 57-60, mathematician, Lawrence Radiation Lab, 60-61; fel, Miller Inst Basic Res Sci, 61-62. *Concurrent Pos:* Com sci & te chnol fel, Staff of Congressman J W Symington, 72-73. *Mem:* Am Soch Mech Engrs; Am Phys Soc; Soc Indust & Appl Math; Am Inst Mech Eng; Am Soc Testing & Mat. *Res:* Dislocation theory; elastodynamics; plastic flow and fracture; acoustic emission and ultrasonics; residual and internal stresses; phase transformation kinetics. *Mailing Add:* Nat Inst Standards & Technol A153 Mat Bldg Gaithersburg MD 20899. *Fax:* 301-990-6287

SIMMONS, JOHN ROBERT, BIOCHEMISTRY, GENETICS. *Current Pos:* RETIRED. *Personal Data:* b Cokeville, Wyo, May 28, 28; m 52; c 4. *Educ:* Utah State Univ, BS, 55, MS, 56; Calif Inst Technol, PhD(biochem), 59. *Prof Exp:* USPHS fel biochem, Sch Med, Stanford Univ, 59-61; from asst prof to prof zool, Utah State Univ, 61-74, prof biol, 74-93. *Res:* Proteins and nucleic acids in genetic function; genetic studies of plant tissues in vitro. *Mailing Add:* 1672 E 1140 N Logan UT 84341

SIMMONS, JOSEPH HABIB, SOLID STATE PHYSICS. *Current Pos:* PROF, DEPT MAT SCI, UNIV FLA, 84- *Personal Data:* b Marrakech, Morocco, Feb 19, 41; US citizen; m 62; c 2. *Educ:* Univ Md, College Park, BS, 62; John Carroll Univ, MS, 66; Cath Univ Am, PhD(physics), 69. *Honors & Awards:* Super Accomplishment Award, Nat Bur Stand, 71. *Prof Exp:* Res physicist, Lewis Res Ctr, NASA, 62-66; sr scientist solid state physics, Inorg Mat Div, Nat Bur Stand, 66-74; adj assoc prof physics, Cath Univ Am, 74-84. *Concurrent Pos:* Consult, Inorg Mat Div, Nat Bur Stand, 74- *Mem:* Am Ceramic Soc; Am Phys Soc. *Res:* Phase transitions in glasses; thermodynamics and kinetics of liquid state; relaxation processes; optical fiber transmission lines. *Mailing Add:* Mat Sci & Eng Dept Univ Fla Gainesville FL 32611

SIMMONS, LEE GUYTON, JR, ZOOLOGY. *Current Pos:* DIR, HENRY DOORLY ZOO, OMAHA. *Personal Data:* b Tucson, Ariz, Feb 20, 38; m 59, Marie Annette Geim; c Lee Guyton, Heather & Heidi. *Educ:* Okla State Univ, DVM. *Prof Exp:* Resident vet, Columbus Zoo, 63-66. *Concurrent Pos:* Res consult, Vet Admin Hosp; assoc instr, Univ Nebr Med Ctr; assoc clin prof, Creighton Univ Sch Dent. *Mem:* Fel Am Vet Med Asn; Am Asn Zool Vet (pres); Am Asn Zool Parks. *Res:* Contributed several articles to professional journals. *Mailing Add:* Henry Doorly Zoo Dir Off 3701 S Tenth St Omaha NE 68107-2299

SIMMONS, LEONARD MICAJAH, JR, THEORETICAL PHYSICS. *Current Pos:* MANAGING DIR, SANTA FE CTR EMERGENCY STRATEGIES, 96- *Personal Data:* b Hattiesburg, Miss, Nov 23, 37; m 59; c 3. *Educ:* Rice Univ, BA, 59; La State Univ, Baton Rouge, MS, 61; Cornell Univ, PhD(theoret phys), 65. *Prof Exp:* Res assoc physics, Univ Minn, 65-67 & Univ Wis-Madison, 67-69; asst prof, Univ Tex, Austin, 69-71; vis asst prof, Univ NH, 71-73; asst theoret div leader, Los Alamos Nat Lab, 74-76 & 83-86, assoc theoret div leader, 76-81 & 86-87, dep assoc dir physics & math, 81-83, staff mem, 73-96. *Concurrent Pos:* NSF fel, 61; trustee, Aspen Ctr Physics, 76-82, treas, 79-82 & pres, 85-88; co-ed, Los Alamos Series Basic & Appl Sci, Univ Calif Press, 78-; vis prof physics, Washington Univ, 80-81; vpres, Santa Fe Inst, 86-88, exec vpres, 88-, trustee & sci bd, 90-, vpres res acad affairs, 96; vis prof physics, Univ Ariz, 87-88; consult, Ariz Super Conducting Super Collider Proj, 87, Ariz Ctr Study Complex Syst, 87. *Mem:* AAAS; Am Phys Soc; NY Acad Sci; Int Asn Math & Physics. *Res:* Novel methods in field theory and for solution of nonlinear equations; coherent states; mathematical physics, properties of special functions; theory of elementary particles. *Mailing Add:* Santa Fe Ctr Emergency Stratgies 23 Chusco Rd Santa Fe NM 87505. *E-Mail:* mikesahtafe_strategy.com

SIMMONS, MARVIN GENE, GEOPHYSICS, APPLICATION OF GEOPHYSICS TO ENVIRONMENTAL PROBLEMS. *Current Pos:* prof, 65-89, EMER PROF GEOPHYS, MASS INST TECHNOL, 89-; PRIN GEOPHYSICIST, HAGER-RICHTER GEOSCI, INC, SALEM, NH, 89- *Personal Data:* b Dallas, Tex, May 15, 29; div; c Jon E, Debra L, Sandra K & Pamela J. *Educ:* Tex A&M Univ, BS, 49; Southern Methodist Univ, MS, 58; Harvard Univ, PhD(geophys), 62. *Honors & Awards:* Except Sci Achievement Medal, NASA, 71. *Prof Exp:* Petrol engr, Humble Oil & Refining Co, 49-51; partner, Simmons Gravel Co, 53-62; asst prof geol, Southern Methodist Univ, 62-65. *Concurrent Pos:* Mem var adv groups, NASA, 65-72, chief scientist, Manned Spacecraft Ctr, 69-71; mem, Comt C18 & D18, Am Soc Testing & Mat. *Mem:* Fel Am Geophys Union; Soc Explor Geophys; fel Geol Soc Am; Seismol Soc Am. *Res:* Thermal measurements of earth, moon and planets; physical properties of rocks at high pressures and temperatures; application of geophysical techniques to geological problems. *Mailing Add:* 180 N Policy St Salem NH 03079

SIMMONS, NORMAN STANLEY, BIOLOGY, MEDICAL SCIENCES. *Current Pos:* EMER PROF HEALTH SCI, UNIV CALIF, LOS ANGELES, 50- *Personal Data:* b New York, NY, May 28, 15; c 2. *Educ:* City Univ New York, BS, 39; Harvard Univ, DMD, 39; Univ Rochester, PhD(exp path), 50. *Concurrent Pos:* Fel & vis scientist, Harvard Univ; Career Res Award, NIH,

65-78. *Mem:* Biochem Soc; Biophys Soc; Inst Animal Dis Res. *Res:* Isolation and characterization of biological macromolecules; first isolation of pure and undegraded DNA; tobacco Mosai Virus first discovery of conformation dependent optically active electronic transitions in proteins and polypeptides; calcification of dental enamel, protein and apetile crystals. *Mailing Add:* Health Sci Univ Calif Los Angeles 886 Hilgard Ave Los Angeles CA 90024-3136

SIMMONS, PAUL C, METALLURGY, MATERIALS ENGINEERING. *Current Pos:* CONSULT, 91- *Personal Data:* b Jerome, Ariz, July 14, 32; m 52; c 3. *Educ:* Univ Ariz, BS, 54, MS, 61, PhD(metall), 67. *Hon Degrees:* Prof Eng, Univ Ariz, 70. *Prof Exp:* Metallurgist, Guided Missile Mfg Div, Hughes Aircraft Co, 54-59, supvr metall eng, 59-63, process engr, 63-65, group head mat & processes, Missile Systs Div, 66-67 & Res & Develop Div, 67-68, sr tech staff asst mat & processes & prod effectiveness, 68-71, sect head prod anal & develop, 71-74, sr & chief scientist, asst labs mgr & prog mgr, Missile Develop Div, 74-91. *Res:* High strength wire; precipitation hardening; fracture dynamics; short arc lamp technology; rocket motor and pressure vessel design; missile finish systems; long term storage of missiles; guidance unit technology; management principles; standardization; producibility. *Mailing Add:* 6465 N San Ignacio Dr Tucson AZ 85704

SIMMONS, RALPH OLIVER, DYNAMICS & DEFECTS IN QUANTUM SOLIDS & FLUIDS. *Current Pos:* Asst, Univ Ill, Urbana-Champaign, 54-55, res assoc, 57-59, from asst prof to assoc prof, 59-65, head physics dept, 70-86, PROF PHYSICS, UNIV ILL, URBANA-CHAMPAIGN, 65- *Personal Data:* b Kensington, Kans, Feb 19, 28; m 52; Janet Lull; c Katherine A, Bradley A, Jill C & Joy D. *Educ:* Univ Kans, BA, 50; Oxford Univ, BA, 53, MA, 57; Univ Ill, PhD(physics), 57. *Honors & Awards:* Sr US Scientist Award, Alexander Von Humboldt Found, 92. *Concurrent Pos:* NSF sr fel, Ctr Study Nuclear Energy, Mol, Belg, 65; mem, Int Adv Bd, J of Physics C: Solid State Physics, 70-76; chmn, Div Solid State Physics, Am Phys Soc, 76-77, Off Phys Sci, Nat Res Coun, Nat Acad Sci, 78-81; mem assembly math & phys sci & Geophys Res Bd, Nat Res Coun, Nat Acad Sci, 78-81; consult, Argonne Nat Lab, 78-85; trustee, Argonne Univs Asn, 79-82; coun mem, Am Phys Soc, 88-; coun mem & chmn physics sect, AAAS, 85-86; vis scientist, L'Ecole Nonuale Supéneure, Paris, France, 85; chmn, adv comt Physics Today, Am Inst Physics, 88-89; Rhodes Scholar, 50-52. *Mem:* Fel AAAS; fel Am Phys Soc; Am Crystallog Asn; Am Asn Physics Teachers; Sigma Xi; Europ Phys Soc. *Res:* Lattice defects in solid helium, metals, semiconductors and ionic crystals; irradiation damage of solids; thermal, elastic and defect properties of noble gas crystals and other molecular solids; structure and dynamics of solids and fluids by neutron and x-ray scattering. *Mailing Add:* Dept Physics Univ Ill 1110 W Green St Urbana IL 61801. *Fax:* 217-333-9819; *E-Mail:* ros@uiuc.edu

SIMMONS, RICHARD LAWRENCE, SURGERY, IMMUNOLOGY. *Current Pos:* assoc vpres clin affairs, Med Ctr, 89-95, GEORGE V FOSTER PROF SURG & CHMN, DEPT SURG, UNIV PITTSBURGH, 87-, ASSOC DEAN CLIN AFFAIRS, SCH MED, 89-, PROF MOLECULAR GENETICS & BIOCHEM, 92-, DISTINGUISHED SERV PROF SURG, 94-, MED DIR, 96- *Personal Data:* b Boston, Mass, Feb 23, 34; wid; c Janine & Nicole. *Educ:* Harvard Univ, AB, 55; Boston Univ, MD, 59; Am Bd Surg, dipl, 67. *Honors & Awards:* Found Award, Am Asn Obstet & Gynec, 62; 32nd Ann Alfred A Stauss Lectr, Univ Wash, 81; Sommer Mem lectr, Sommer Mem Found, 86; Edgar J Ploth Lectr, Singleton Surg Soc, 89; George H A Clowes Lectr, Harvard Med Sch, 90; Folse/Birtch Lectr Gen Surg, Southern Ill Univ, 92; Loyal Davis Lectr, Northwestern Univ Med Sch, 94; Culpeper Lectr, Univ Minn, 94; Mellon Lectr, Univ Pittsburgh Med Sch, 95; 2nd Helen & John Schilling Lectr, Univ Wash, 96; Harry Delozier Memorial Lectr, Ohio State Univ, 96. *Prof Exp:* Asst surg, Columbia Univ, 63-64, instr, 64-68; from asst prof to prof surg & microbiol, Univ Minn, Minneapolis, 72-87. *Concurrent Pos:* NIH fel, Columbia Univ, 60-61, Am Cancer Soc clin fel, 63-64; Markle Found scholar acad med, 69-75; consult, Vet Admin Hosp, Minneapolis, 71-87; chief surg, consult, staff & mem, Univ Pittsburgh, 87-; Alexander E Pearce vis prof, Allegheny Univ Health Sci, Pa, 97. *Mem:* Inst Med-Nat Acad Sci; Soc Univ Surgeons (pres, 77-78); AAAS; Transplantation Soc; Surg Infection Soc (pres, 88); AAAS; Am Asn Immunologists; Am Col Surgeons; Am Med Asn; Am Soc Microbiol; Am Surg Asn; Cell Transplant Soc; Am Soc Transplant Surgeons (pres, 80-81); Surg Infection Soc (pres, 88). *Res:* Transplantation biology; immunology of cancer; immunoregulatory roles of nitric oxide in inflammation and transplantation. *Mailing Add:* Dept Surg Univ Pittsburgh Med Ctr 497 Scaife Hall Pittsburgh PA 15261-0001

SIMMONS, RICHARD PAUL, MATERIALS SCIENCE ENGINEERING. *Current Pos:* vpres mfg, Allegheny Ludlum Steel, 68-71, pres, 72-75, pres metals group, 76-80, pres & chief exec officer, 80-86, chmn & chief exec officer, 86-90, CHMN, ALLEGHENY LUDLUM CORP, 90- *Personal Data:* b Bridgeport, Conn, May 3, 31; m 59; c 2. *Educ:* Mass Inst Technol, BS, 53. *Hon Degrees:* DCom, Robert Morris Col, 87; LLD, Washington & Jefferson Col, 91. *Honors & Awards:* Ben Fairless Medal, Asn Inst Mech Engrs & Prof Engrs. *Prof Exp:* Metallurgist, Allegheny Ludlum Steel Corp, 53-57; mgr processing, Titanium Metals Corp, 57-59; mgr qual control, Latrobe Steel Co, 59-62; asst gen mgr, Repub Steel Corp, 62-68. *Mem:* Fel Am Soc Metals Int; Am Inst Mech Engrs & Prof Engrs. *Res:* Metallurgy; processing and quality control of steel. *Mailing Add:* Allegheny Teledyne 1000 Six PGG Pl Pittsburgh PA 15222

SIMMONS, ROBERT ARTHUR, ENGINEERING. *Current Pos:* CONSULT, SIMMONS CONSULTING LTD, LETHBRIDGE, CAN. *Concurrent Pos:* Fel, Agr Inst Can, 92. *Mailing Add:* Simmons Consult Ltd 1010-29 St A S Lethbridge AB T1K 2X7 Can

SIMMONS, THOMAS CARL, ORGANIC CHEMISTRY. *Current Pos:* RETIRED. *Personal Data:* b Williamsport, Pa, Nov 14, 20; m 52, Dolores Van Gorder. *Educ:* Pa State Univ, BS, 45, MS, 50, PhD(biochem), 52. *Prof Exp:* Asst biochem, Pa State Col, 45-52; org res chemist, US Army Chem Systs Lab, 52-68, chief, Org Chem Sect, 68-88. *Mem:* AAAS; Am Chem Soc; Sigma Xi; Am Defense Preparedness Asn; NY Acad Sci. *Res:* Physiological, fluorine, natural product and medicinal chemistry; chemistry of organo-phosphorus compounds and chemical warfare agents. *Mailing Add:* 2706 Bynum Hills Circle Bel Air MD 21015

SIMMONS, WILLIAM BRUCE, JR, MINERALOGY, PETROLOGY. *Current Pos:* from instr to asst prof, 72-75, assoc prof, 75-79, PROF EARTH SCI, UNIV NEW ORLEANS, 79- *Personal Data:* b Bay City, Tex, Nov 5, 43; m 66; c 2. *Educ:* Duke Univ, BS, 66; Univ Ga, MS, 68; Univ Mich, Ann Arbor, PhD(mineral), 72. *Prof Exp:* Field geologist, Owens Ill Glass Co, 68. *Mem:* AAAS; Mineral Soc Am; Geol Soc Am; Sigma Xi. *Res:* Mineralogy, petrology and geochemistry of pegmatite systems; mineralogy and petrology. *Mailing Add:* Dept Geol & Geophys Univ New Orleans New Orleans LA 70148-0001

SIMMONS, WILLIAM FREDERICK, engineering, mechanics, for more information see previous edition

SIMMONS, WILLIAM HOWARD, PROTEIN-PEPTIDE CHEMISTRY. *Current Pos:* from asst prof to assoc prof, 81-94, PROF BIOCHEM, MED CTR, LOYOLA UNIV, CHICAGO, 94- *Personal Data:* b Mansfield, Ohio, May 15, 47. *Educ:* Wittenburg Univ, BA, 69; Bowling Green State Univ, MS, 73; Univ Ill, PhD(physiol), 79. *Prof Exp:* Teaching asst chem, Bowling Green State Univ, 71-75; res asst physiol chem, Ohio State Univ, 75-76; teaching asst physiol, Med Ctr, Univ Ill, 76-79, res assoc, 79-81. *Concurrent Pos:* Lectr, Univ Ill Schs Dent & Pharm, 80-81; prin investr res grants, NIH, 81-87 & 91-94, Am Heart Asn, 87-90. *Mem:* Am Soc Biol Chemists; Soc Neurosci; Am Chem Soc; AAAS; Protein Soc. *Res:* Mechanism of metabolism of vasoactive peptides; mechanism of metabolism of peptide neurotransmitters in the brain; purification of skin proteases. *Mailing Add:* Dept Molecular & Cellular Biochem Loyola Univ Chicago Stritch Sch Med 2160 S First Ave Maywood IL 60153. *Fax:* 708-216-8523; *E-Mail:* wsimmon@wpo.it.luc.edu

SIMMS, JOHN ALVIN, ORGANIC POLYMER CHEMISTRY. *Current Pos:* Sr res fel, 55-94, DU PONT FEL, CENT SCI & ENG, E I DU PONT DE NEMOURS & CO INC, 94- *Personal Data:* b Cleveland, Ohio, Apr 2, 31; m 55, Imogene E Brown; c Stephen & Barbara. *Educ:* NGa Col, BS, 51; Purdue Univ, MS, 53, PhD(org chem), 56. *Mem:* Am Chem Soc; Sigma Xi. *Res:* Synthesis of monomers a polymers; free radical polymerization; adhesives; elastoplastic film formers with superior photooxidative stability; isocyanate functional oligomers; group transfer polymerization; pigment dispersants. *Mailing Add:* Du Pont Exp Sta Bldg 328/109 Wilmington DE 19880-0328. *Fax:* 302-695-7742

SIMMS, JOHN JAY, GEOLOGY, PHYSICAL SCIENCE. *Current Pos:* ASST PROF GEOL & PHYS SCI, NORTHEASTERN STATE UNIV, 85- *Personal Data:* b Kansas City, Mo, July 2, 45; m 72, Dorothy Fay Slimmer; c Alexander Ray & James Andrew. *Educ:* Emporia State Univ, BS, 67; Univ Kans, MS, 75. *Prof Exp:* Educr, Shawnee Mission, High Sch Dist, 67-69, Lamar High Sch, 73-74; instr geol, SWMo State Univ, 75-80; area resource geologist, Dept Interior, 79-80 & 82-85; prof geol, Cent Wyo Col, 80-82. *Concurrent Pos:* Consult, Simms Consult, 85- *Mem:* Nat Asn Earth Sci Teachers; Nat Earth Sci Teachers Asn. *Res:* Compile field trip information for Southwestern United States; geology of Eastern Oklahoma. *Mailing Add:* Dept Physics & Earth Sci Northeastern State Univ 600 N Grand Ave Tahlequah OK 74464. *E-Mail:* simmsj@cherokee.nsuok.edu

SIMMS, NATHAN FRANK, JR, PURE MATHEMATICS. *Current Pos:* AT DEPT MATH & COMPUT SCI, NC STATE UNIV. *Personal Data:* b Winston-Salem, NC, Oct 20, 32; m 59; c 3. *Educ:* NC Cent Univ, BS, 54, MS, 59; Lehigh Univ, PhD(math), 70. *Prof Exp:* Instr math, Fla A&M Univ, 59-60 & NC Cent Univ, 60-62; from asst prof to assoc prof math, Winston-Salem Univ, 64-72, prof, 72- *Concurrent Pos:* Consult, Regional Educ Lab Carolinas & Va, 70-72, Math Asn Am Minority Insts, 72-73 & Metric Educ Prog Winston-Salem/Forsyth Schs, 74-; NSF res grant, 73; dir, Div of Lib Arts & Sci. *Mem:* Math Asn Am; Sigma Xi; Am Math Soc. *Res:* Category theory and homological algebra; frobenius categories and spectral sequences. *Mailing Add:* 209 Windhover Dr Chapel Hill NC 27514

SIMMS, PAUL C, NUCLEAR PHYSICS. *Current Pos:* assoc prof, 64-73, PROF PHYSICS, PURDUE UNIV, LAFAYETTE, 73- *Personal Data:* b Jackson, Tenn, Nov 10, 32; m 59; c 2. *Educ:* NGa Col, BS, 53; Purdue Univ, PhD(physics), 58. *Prof Exp:* Res assoc physics, Columbia Univ, 59-60, asst prof, 60-64. *Mem:* Am Phys Soc. *Res:* Nuclear structure. *Mailing Add:* Physics Purdue Univ Lafayette IN 47907-1968. *Fax:* 765-494-0706

SIMNAD, MASSOUD T, MATERIALS SCIENCE. *Current Pos:* CONSULT, 82- *Personal Data:* b Teheran, Iran, Mar 11, 20; nat US; m 54, Lenora Brown; c Virginia & Jeffrey. *Educ:* Univ London, BS, 41; Cambridge Univ, PhD(phys chem), 45. *Honors & Awards:* Cert of Merit, Am Nuclear Soc, 65; Outstanding Achievement Award, Mats Sci Div, Am Nuclear Soc, 93. *Prof Exp:* Res assoc, Imp Col, Univ London, 41-42 & Cambridge Univ, 45-48; Am Electrochem Soc Weston fel, Carnegie Inst Technol, 48, mem staff, Metals Res Lab, 49-56; head chem & metall II div, Gen Atomic Div, Gen Dynamics Corp, Calif, 56-60, asst chmn metall dept, 60-69; sr res adv,

Gen Atomic Co, Inc, 69-73, sr tech adv, 73-81. *Concurrent Pos:* Vis prof, Mass Inst Technol, 62-63; vis lectr nuclear energy, Univ Calif, San Diego, 78-, adj prof, 82-; mem, Ctr Energy & Combustion Res, 82- *Mem:* Nat Acad Eng; Am Inst Aeronaut & Astronaut; fel Am Soc Metals; fel AAAS; fel Am Nuclear Soc; Electrochem Soc. *Res:* Nuclear reactor materials and fuels research and development; materials science and technology; energy conversion and utilization. *Mailing Add:* PO Box 1806 Rancho Santa Fe CA 92067. *Fax:* 619-534-5698; *E-Mail:* msimnad@ames.ucsd.edu

SIMNICK, JAMES J, PETROLEUM REFINING TECHNOLOGY, TECHNICAL SERVICE & QUALITY ASSURANCE. *Current Pos:* Staff res engr, Amoco Oil Co, 85-91, supvr process res, 91-93, sr res engr tech serv, 93-95, SUPVR QUAL ASSURANCE/TECH SERV, AMOCO PETROL PROD, 95. *Personal Data:* b Blue Island, Ill, Jan 19, 52; m 79, Suzanne E Horrall; c 3. *Educ:* Purdue Univ, BS, 74, PhD(chem eng), 79. *Mem:* Am Inst Chem Engrs; Soc Automotive Engrs; Am Chem Soc; Am Soc Testing & Mat. *Res:* Quality assurance and technical service; quality fuel products. *Mailing Add:* Amoco Res Ctr J-8 Naperville IL 60563-8460

SIMON, ALBERT, PLASMA PHYSICS, CONTROLLED FUSION. *Current Pos:* chmn dept mech & eng, 77-84, PROF MECH & ENG, UNIV ROCHESTER, 66-, PROF PHYSICS, 67- *Personal Data:* b New York, NY, Dec 27, 24; m 72, Rita Sautman; c Richard, Janet & David. *Educ:* City Col New York, BS, 47; Univ Rochester, PhD(physics), 50. *Prof Exp:* Physicist, Oak Ridge Nat Lab, 50-55, assoc dir neutron physics div, 55-61; head plasma physics div, Gen Atomic Div, Gen Dynamics Corp, 61-66. *Concurrent Pos:* Chmn, Div Plasma Physics, Physics Soc, 63-64; Guggenheim fel, 64-65; mem, Inst Advan Study, 74-75; sr vis fel, UK Sci Res Coun, Oxford Univ, 75; chmn, Nuclear Eng Div, Am Soc Eng Educ, 85-86. *Mem:* Fel Physics Soc; Am Soc Mech Engrs; AAAS; Am Soc Eng Educ. *Res:* Controlled thermonuclear reactor research. *Mailing Add:* Dept Mech Eng Univ Rochester Rochester NY 14627. *Fax:* 716-256-2509; *E-Mail:* simo@me.rochester.edu

SIMON, ALLAN LESTER, RADIOLOGY. *Current Pos:* CLIN PROF RADIOL, UNIV CALIF, SAN DIEGO, 75- *Personal Data:* b Boston, Mass, Mar 18, 34; m 55; c 3. *Educ:* Boston Univ, AB, 55; Tufts Univ, MD, 59. *Hon Degrees:* MA, Yale Univ, 73. *Prof Exp:* Intern med, Univ Md, 59-60; resident radiol, Beth Israel Hosp, Boston, 60-63; instr radiol, Yale-New Haven Med Ctr, 65-66; sr surgeon, NIH, 66-68; assoc prof radiol, Johns Hopkins Univ, 68-69; assoc prof, Univ Calif, San Diego, 69-72; prof diag radiol, Sch Med, Yale Univ, 72-75. *Concurrent Pos:* Nat Cancer Inst trainee radiol, 61-62; USPHS res fel cardiovasc radiol, Yale-New Haven Med Ctr, 63-65; consult, Nat Heart & Lung Inst & Clin Ctr, NIH, 68- *Mem:* Am Heart Asn; Am Col Radiol. *Res:* Diagnostic methods in cardiovascular disease; electronic processing of radiographic images. *Mailing Add:* Radiol Dept Alvarado Hosp Med Ctr 6655 Alvarado Rd San Diego CA 92120

SIMON, BARRY MARTIN, MATHEMATICAL PHYSICS. *Current Pos:* prof math & theoret physics, 81-84, IBM PROF MATH & THEORET PHYSICS, CALIF INST TECHNOL, 84- *Personal Data:* b Brooklyn, NY, Apr 16, 46; m 71; c 5. *Educ:* Harvard Univ, BA, 66; Princeton Univ, PhD(physics), 70. *Prof Exp:* Instr math, Princeton Univ, 69-70, from asst prof to assoc prof math & physics, 70-76, prof, 76-81. *Concurrent Pos:* Sloan fel, Princeton Univ, 71-73; assoc ed, J Operator Theory, 78-, J Math Physics & J Statist Physics, 79-81 & Commun Math Physics, 81-; Sherman B Fairchild distinguished vis scholar, Calif Inst Technol, 80-81. *Mem:* Am Math Soc; Am Phys Soc; Austrian Acad Sci. *Res:* Applications of rigorous mathematics to theoretical physics, especially to quantum physics; atomic and molecular physics; nonrelativistic quantum mechanics; quantum field theory; statistical mechanics. *Mailing Add:* Dept Math & Theoret Physics Mail Code 253-37 Calif Inst Technol Pasadena CA 91125. *Fax:* 626-585-1728; *E-Mail:* bsimon@caltech.edu

SIMON, CARL PAUL, MATHEMATICAL ECONOMICS, APPLIED DYNAMICAL SYSTEMS. *Current Pos:* asst prof, 72-78, assoc prof math & econ, 78-88, PROF MATH & ECON, UNIV MICH, 88- *Personal Data:* b Chicago, Ill, Feb 7, 45; c 2. *Educ:* Univ Chicago, BS, 66; Northwestern Univ, MS, 67, PhD(math), 70. *Honors & Awards:* Howard M Temin Award, J AIDS, 95. *Prof Exp:* Instr math, Univ Calif, Berkeley, 70-72. *Concurrent Pos:* Vis asst prof math, Northwestern Univ, 75; assoc prof math & econ, Univ NC, 78-80. *Mem:* Am Math Soc; Soc Indust & Appl Math; Economet Soc; Sigma Xi; Soc Math Biol. *Res:* Stability of dynamical systems; index of fixed points and singularities; mathematical economics; mathematical epidemiology. *Mailing Add:* Dept Math Univ Mich Ann Arbor MI 48109

SIMON, CAROL A, BEHAVIORAL ECOLOGY OF REPTILES. *Current Pos:* PROF, DEPT BIOL, CITY COL NY, 76-; RES ASSOC, AM MUS NATURAL HIST. *Personal Data:* b Johnstown, Pa, Apr 18, 47; m 76, Howard Topoff; c Andrea Simon-Topoff. *Educ:* Univ Calif, Riverside, AB, 69, PhD(biol), 73; Mich State Univ, MS, 70. *Prof Exp:* Postdoctoral fel, Am Mus Natural Hist, 73-75; asst prof, Ramapo Col NJ, 75-76. *Concurrent Pos:* Lectr discovery tours, Am Mus Natural Hist, 88- *Mem:* Am Asn Univ Women; Am Women Sci; Soc Study Amphibians & Reptiles; Animal Behav Soc; Herpetologists' League; Am Soc Ichthyologist & Herpetologists. *Res:* Behavioral ecology of reptiles, especially lizards, focusing on issues of territoriality, habitat usage, chemical communication, foraging and homing behavior. *Mailing Add:* Dept Biol City Col NY Convent Ave at 138th St New York NY 10031. *Fax:* 212-650-8585; *E-Mail:* casimon48@aol.com

SIMON, CHRISTINE MAE, MOLECULAR SYSTEMATICS. *Current Pos:* RES ASSOC, ZOOL DEPT, UNIV HAWAII, 80-, ASSOC ENTOMOLOGIST, BERNICE P BISHOP MUS, 81- *Personal Data:* b Memphis, Tenn, Oct 14, 49. *Educ:* Univ Fla, BS, 71, MS, 74; State Univ NY, Stony Brook, PhD(ecol & evolution), 79. *Prof Exp:* Res assoc evolutionary syst, Univ Chicago, 78-79; NSF res fel, Dept Biol, Washington Univ, 84-85; from asst prof gen sci to assoc prof, Univ Hawaii, 85-90, grad fac zool, 85-90. *Concurrent Pos:* T Roosevelt Mem Fund grant, 76-77; vis researcher biochem, Univ Calif, Berkeley, 88, Dept Zool, Univ NH, 92, biol sci, Victoria Univ, 92; Fulbright fel, New Zealand, 95-98; Fulbright fel, New Zealand, 95-98. *Mem:* Assoc mem Sigma Xi; Soc Syst Biol; Soc Molecular Biol & Evolution; Int Soc Molecular Evolution; Soc Study Evolution; AAAS; Asn Trop Biol. *Res:* Patterns of evolution; processes of evolution; numerical systematics; systematics theory; character evolution; geographic variation and its relation to speciation; conservation genetics; Hawaiian terrestrial and cave invertebrates; periodical cicadas; family cicadidae; New Zealand cicadas; green lacewings; collembola; author of numerous publications. *Mailing Add:* Ecol & Evolutionary Biol U-43 Univ Conn Storrs CT 06269-3043. *Fax:* 860-486-6364

SIMON, DOROTHY MARTIN, PHYSICAL CHEMISTRY. *Current Pos:* RETIRED. *Personal Data:* b Harwood, Mo, Sept 18, 19; m 46. *Educ:* Southwest Mo State Col, AB, 40; Univ Ill, PhD(chem), 45. *Hon Degrees:* DSc, Worcester Polytech Inst, 71; DE, Lehigh Univ, 78. *Honors & Awards:* Rockefeller Pub Serv Award, 53; Achievement Award, Soc Women Engrs, 56. *Prof Exp:* Asst chem, Univ Ill, 41-45; res chemist, E I du Pont de Nemours & Co, NY, 45-46; chemist, Clinton Lab, Tenn, 47; assoc chemist, Argonne Nat Lab, 48-49; aeronaut res scientist, Lewis Lab, Nat Adv Comt Aeronaut, 49-53, asst chief chem br, 54-55; Rockefeller fel, Cambridge Univ, 53-54; group leader combustion, Magnolia Petrol Co, Tex, 55-56; prin scientist & tech asst to pres res & advan develop div, Avco Corp, 56-62, dir corp res, 62-64, vpres, Defense & Indust Prod Group, 64-68, corp vpres & dir res, 68-85. *Concurrent Pos:* Fel, Univ Ill, 45; Marie Curie lectr, Pa State Univ, 62; dir, Econ Systs Corp, 66-72; mem comt sponsored res, Mass Inst Technol, 72-; Harvard Bd of Overseers Comt for Appl Res & NASA Space Systs & Technol Adv Comt, 78-; trustee, Worcester Polytech Inst, 73-; dir, Crown Zellerbach Corp & Conn Nat Bank, 78-; dir, Warner Lambert Co, 80 & The Charles Stark Draper Lab, 81; trustee, NEastern Univ, 80-; mem, Nat Mats Adv Bd, Nat Res Coun/Nat Acad Sci, 81; mem, Pres Comt, Nat Medal Sci, 78-81; Chmn bd, Guggenheim Medal Award, 79-82. *Mem:* AAAS; Am Chem Soc; fel Am Inst Aeronaut & Astronaut; Combustion Int; fel Am Inst Chemists. *Res:* Combustion; aerothermo chemistry; research management and strategic planning. *Mailing Add:* 1001 Fearrington Post Pittsboro NC 27312-8514

SIMON, EDWARD, SOLID STATE SCIENCE. *Current Pos:* RETIRED. *Personal Data:* b Bradley Beach, NJ, Sept 24, 27; m 50, Dorothy R Koeing; c Martin David, Sherry Ann, Sandra Lee, Keith Michael & Jonathan Mark. *Educ:* Rutgers Univ, BS, 50; Purdue Univ, MS, 52, PhD(physics), 55. *Prof Exp:* Res engr, Transitron, Inc, 54-58; vpres & founder, Solid State Prod, Inc, Unitrode Corp, 58-67, vpres, Unitrode Corp, 67-90. *Concurrent Pos:* Dir, Mass Microelectronics Ctr, 82-87, chmn bd, 87-89, emer chmn, 89- *Mem:* AAAS; Am Phys Soc; Electrochem Soc; Inst Elec & Electronics Engrs. *Res:* Semiconductor devices, design, research and development. *Mailing Add:* 72 Winding Pond Dr Londonderry NH 03053

SIMON, EDWARD HARVEY, VIROLOGY. *Current Pos:* from asst prof to assoc prof, 60-70, PROF BIOL, PURDUE UNIV, LAFAYETTE, 70- *Personal Data:* b Elizabeth, NJ, June 25, 34; m 56, Cyrelle Ovsiew; c Shira, Rashj, Hillel & Ronit. *Educ:* Rutgers Univ, BS, 56; Calif Inst Technol, PhD(biol), 60. *Prof Exp:* USPHS fel genetics, Carnegie Inst, 59-60. *Concurrent Pos:* NSF sr res fel, Weizmann Inst, 66; vis prof, Hebrew Univ, Israel, 73 & Weizmann Inst, 79, 85 & 91. *Mem:* AAAS; Am Soc Microbiol; Am Soc Virol; Am Asn Univ Professors; Int Soc Interferon Res. *Res:* Genetics of animal viruses; mode of action of interferon; isolation of interferon response mutants of cells and viruses. *Mailing Add:* Dept Biol Sci Purdue Univ Lafayette IN 47907. *Fax:* 765-494-0876; *E-Mail:* esimon@bilbo.bio.purdue.edu

SIMON, ELLEN MCMURTRIE, PROTOZOOLOGY, CRYOBIOLOGY. *Current Pos:* res scientist genetics & develop, 77-86, ECOL, ETHNOL & EVOLUTION, UNIV ILL, URBANA, 87- *Personal Data:* b Norristown, Pa, Mar 29, 19; wid; c Darien. *Educ:* Ursinus Col, AB, 40; Univ Wis, MS, 52, PhD, 55. *Prof Exp:* Res assoc bact, Univ Wis, 55-58; res assoc zool, 63-64, asst prof, 64-76. *Concurrent Pos:* Vis asst prof microbiol, Univ Ill, 75 & 76, vis assoc prof, 77, 78, 79 & 85-86; mem exec bd, US Fedn for Cult Collections, 76-85; org lect, wet lab workshops, cyropreservation, 79, 80, 84, 88. *Mem:* Am Soc Microbiol; Soc Protozoologists. *Res:* Genetics; variants of Salmonella and Brucella; preservation of protozoa in liquid nitrogen; genetics molecular biology and aging of ciliated protozoa. *Mailing Add:* Dept Ecol Ethnol & Evolution Univ Ill 515 Morrill Hall 505 S Goodwin Urbana IL 61801. *Fax:* 217-244-1648

SIMON, ERIC, CHEMICAL ENGINEERING, CHEMISTRY. *Current Pos:* OWNER, E S CONSULT ENG CO, 74- *Personal Data:* b Egelsbach, Ger, Jan 8, 20; US citizen; m 51; c 3. *Educ:* City Col NY, BChE, 45. *Prof Exp:* Prof supvr, Harmon Color Works, 46-48; group leader res, Sun Chem Corp, 48-53; tech dir chem prod, Pigmentos y Oxidos, 54-74. *Concurrent Pos:* Lectr, Cent Patronal de Nuevo Leon, 70-74. *Mem:* Asn Consult Chemists & Engrs; AAAS; Am Chem Soc; Inst Chem Eng Mex. *Res:* Development of appropriate technology for developing countries. *Mailing Add:* 6374 Creekbend Houston TX 77096-5661. *Fax:* 713-988-8936

SIMON, ERIC JACOB, NEUROCHEMISTRY, PHARMACOLOGY. *Current Pos:* from asst prof to prof exp med, 59-80, PROF PSYCHIAT & PHARMACOL, MED SCH, NY UNIV, 80- *Personal Data:* b Wiesbaden, Ger, June 2, 24; US citizen; m 47, Irene Ronis; c Martin, Faye & Lawrence. *Educ:* Case Inst Technol, BS, 44; Univ Chicago, MS, 47, PhD(org chem), 51. *Hon Degrees:* Dr, Univ Paris, 82. *Honors & Awards:* Res Pacesetter Award, Nat Inst on Drug Abuse, 79; Louis & Bert Freedman Found Award, NY Acad Sci, 80; Nathan B Eddy Mem Prize, Comt on Probs Drug Dependence, 83. *Prof Exp:* Res assoc muscular dystrophy, Med Col, Cornell Univ, 53-59. *Concurrent Pos:* Nat Found Infantile Paralysis fel biochem, Col Physicians & Surgeons, Columbia Univ, 51-53; lectr chem, City Col of New York, 53-59; chmn, Sect Biochem, NY Acad Sci, 84-86; gov-at-large, 86-89; mem, biomed review comt, Nat Inst Drug Abuse, 76-80, chairperson, 79-80; chmn, Int Narcotic Res Conf, 80-84; mem, Nat Adv Coun Drug Abuse, 88-92; gov-at-large, NY Acad Sci, 86-88. *Mem:* Fel AAAS; Am Chem Soc; Am Soc Pharmacol & Exp Therapeut; Am Soc Neurochem; Am Soc Biol Chem; fel NY Acad Sci. *Res:* Study of opiate receptors and endogenous opioid peptides; metabolism of vitamin E; neurochemical studies in nerve cells in culture; receptor isolation and characterization; endogenous opioids. *Mailing Add:* Dept Psychiat 550 First Ave NY Univ Med Ctr New York NY 10016. *Fax:* 212-263-5591; *E-Mail:* simonej@is2.nyu.edu

SIMON, FREDERICK OTTO, GEOCHEMISTRY, ANALYTICAL CHEMISTRY. *Current Pos:* Chemist, 61-73, proj leader, 73-75, supvr chemist anal chem & geochem, 75-79, RES CHEMIST, US GEOL SURV, 79- *Personal Data:* b New York, NY, Dec 11, 39. *Educ:* Am Univ, BS, 61, MS, 63; Univ Md, PhD(chem), 72. *Concurrent Pos:* Ed, Geochem Int J, Am Geol Inst, 72-76. *Mem:* Am Chem Soc; Geochem Soc; Geol Soc Am. *Res:* Inorganic geochemistry of coal; coal quality; application of analytical, inorganic and physical chemistry to problems in earth science; analysis of rarer elements in geologic materials. *Mailing Add:* 11813 Stuart Mill Rd Oakton VA 22124-1227

SIMON, FREDERICK TYLER, PHYSICAL CHEMISTRY, COLOR SCIENCE. *Current Pos:* J E SIRRINE PROF TEXTILE SCI, CLEMSON UNIV, 68- *Personal Data:* b Pittsburgh, Pa, May 9, 17; m 46; c 2. *Educ:* Morris Harvey Col, BS, 55; Marshall Univ, MS, 57. *Prof Exp:* Res specialist, Union Carbide Corp, 54-68. *Concurrent Pos:* Consult, Burlington Industs, Inc, 70-, Cherokee Finishing Corp, 70-, Sandoz Wander Inc, 71- & Diano Corp, 74-; deleg, Comt Colorimetry, Int Comn Illum, 71; chairholder, Color Mkt Group; mem, The Colour Group, Gt Brit. *Mem:* Am Chem Soc; Am Asn Textile Chem & Colorists; Intersoc Color Coun; Optical Soc Am; Sigma Xi. *Res:* Color science, including dyeing and coloration chemistry of dyes and pigments; polymer morphology, including microscopy, x-ray diffraction, crystallization kinetics, neutron scattering and general textile processing and fiber manufacture; computer color matching and industrial color tolerancess as well as fluorescent colorants. *Mailing Add:* PO Box 391 Clemso SC 29631-0391

SIMON, GARY ALBERT, STATISTICS, APPLIED STATISTICS. *Current Pos:* ASSOC PROF, DEPT APPL MATH & STATIST, STATE UNIV NY, STONY BROOK, 75- *Personal Data:* b Wilkes-Barre, Pa, Apr 24, 45. *Educ:* Carnegie-Mellon Univ, BS, 66; Stanford Univ, PhD(statist), 72. *Prof Exp:* Asst prof statist, Princeton Univ, 71-75. *Mem:* Am Statist Asn. *Res:* Analysis of categorical data and nonparametric statistics. *Mailing Add:* Dept Statist & Oper Res NY Univ Mgt Ctr 44 W 4th St Rm 853 New York NY 10003-6607

SIMON, GEORGE WARREN, SOLAR PHYSICS, MAGNETOCONVECTION. *Current Pos:* SR SCIENTIST, AIR FORCE PHILLIPS LAB, 83- *Personal Data:* b Frankfurt, Ger, Apr 22, 34; US citizen; m 58, Patricia Ann Young; c David, Karen & Susan. *Educ:* Grinnell Col, AB, 55; Calif Inst Technol, MS, 61, PhD(physics), 63; Univ Utah, MBA, 76. *Hon Degrees:* DSc, Grinnell Col, 83. *Prof Exp:* Jr scientist, Atomic Power Div, Westinghouse Elec Corp, 55-56, assoc scientist, 58; mem tech staff radiation effects, Hughes Res Labs, 58-61 & Space Technol Labs, 61-63; dir comput lab, Nat Solar Observ, 69-76, dep dir observ, 75-76; chief solar res br, Air Force Geophys Lab, 76-83; space shuttle astronaut, 78-88; res astrophysicist, Nat Solar Observ, 63- *Concurrent Pos:* Physicist, Max Planck Inst Physics & Astrophys, 65-66 & 77; consult, NASA, 67-; vis assoc, Harvard Col Observ, 69-70; vis scientist, Univ Cambridge, UK, 76, 82, 86, 88, 89, 90, 92, 93, 94 & 95, Kiepenheuer Inst Solar Physics, 93, 94 & 96, Astron Inst Canary Islands, 93 & 94; adj prof, Univ Calif Los Angeles, Univ Colo, Univ Ariz, 70- *Mem:* Am Astron Soc; Am Phys Soc; Int Astron Union; Am Geophys Union; fel Royal Astron Soc. *Res:* Magnetic and velocity fields and other inhomogeneities in the solar atmosphere; observations and kinematical modeling of solar magnetoconvection; nuclear reactor physics; radiation effects in semiconductors; space physics. *Mailing Add:* 2821 Plaza Verde Santa Fe NM 87505. *Fax:* 505-434-7029; *E-Mail:* simon@sunspot.noao.edu

SIMON, GEZA, CARDIOVASCULAR DISEASES, INTERNAL MEDICINE. *Current Pos:* asst prof, 76-82, assoc prof, 82-94, PROF MED, UNIV MINN, MINNEAPOLIS, 94- *Personal Data:* b Budapest, Hungary, Mar 6, 41; US citizen; m 65, Jane H Classen; c 2. *Educ:* NY Univ, BA, 64; State Univ NY Downstate Med Ctr, MD, 68; Mich State Univ, PhD(physiol), 74; Am Bd Internal Med, dipl, 73. *Prof Exp:* From intern to resident med, NY Univ-Bellevue Hosp, 68-70; med officer, US Army, 70-72; fel physiol & clin instr med, Mich State Univ, 72-74; NIH res fel med, Univ Mich Med Ctr, 74-75, res scientist, 75-76. *Mem:* Fel Am Heart Asn; Int Soc Hypertension; Inter-Am Soc Hypertension; Am Soc Hypertension. *Res:* Experimental hypertension with emphasis on the slow pressor action of angiotensin II and its potentiation by high sodium diet. *Mailing Add:* Vet Admin Med Ctr 111J2 One Veterans Dr Minneapolis MN 55417. *Fax:* 612-725-2093

SIMON, HAROLD J, MEDICINE. *Current Pos:* asst dean, 66-69, assoc dean educ & student affairs, 69-78, PROF MED & COMMUNITY MED, SCH MED, UNIV CALIF, SAN DIEGO, 66-, DIR INT PROGS, 87-, CHIEF, DIV INT HEATED & CROSS CULT MED, 87- *Personal Data:* b Karlsruhe, Ger, Jan 22, 28; US citizen; m 73, Ruth M Covell; c Leslie, Lynne & David. *Educ:* Harvard Med Sch, MD, 53; Rockefeller Inst, PhD(microbiol), 59. *Prof Exp:* Intern med, NY Hosp-Cornell Med Ctr, 53-54, asst resident, 54-56; asst prof med, Sch Med, Stanford Univ, 59-66. *Concurrent Pos:* Arthritis Found fel, 59-61; USPHS grant, 59-78 & career develop award, 62-65; asst, Med Col, Cornell Univ, 54-56; asst physician, Hosp, Rockefeller Inst, 56-59; physician outpatients, NY Hosp-Cornell Med Ctr, 56-59; mem study sect commun dis, USPHS, 66-71; panelist & chmn sect III, Pac Intersci Cong, Japan, 66; convener, Panel Coccal Infections, Int Cong Chemother, Austria, 67; mem comt manned probs space flight, Nat Acad Sci, 68-; vis sr scholar, Div Int Health, Inst Med, Nat Acad Sci, 78-79; vis prof, Technion-Israel Inst Technol, Univ Capetown, SAfrica, Univ Colgne, Ger & Fiji Sch Med. *Mem:* Fel AAAS; Infectious Dis Soc Am; Am Col Physicians; Am Soc Clin Pharmacol & Therapeut; Am Fedn Clin Res; Sigma Xi. *Res:* Studies in host-parasite interactions; clinical pharmacology of antimicrobial agents; prevention of hospital-acquired infections; international medicine and epidemiology; medical education; student affairs; international health policy. *Mailing Add:* Dept Family & Prev Med Univ Calif San Diego La Jolla CA 92093-0622

SIMON, HENRY JOHN, SOLID STATE PHYSICS. *Current Pos:* asst prof, 72-81, PROF PHYSICS, UNIV TOLEDO, 81- *Personal Data:* b London, Eng, May 4, 39; US citizen; m 60; c 4. *Educ:* Tufts Univ, BSEE, 60; Harvard Univ, MA, 65, PhD(appl physics), 69. *Prof Exp:* Sr res scientist, United Aircraft Res Lab, East Hartford, 69-70; asst prof physics, Worcester Polytech Inst, 70-72. *Concurrent Pos:* Vis prof physics, Univ Pa, 78-79; vis prof elec eng, Univ Md, 86-87. *Mem:* Am Phys Soc. *Res:* Interaction of intense light with matter; nonlinear optics; harmonic generation of light; surface plasmons. *Mailing Add:* Dept Physics & Astron Univ Toledo 2801 W Bancroft Toledo OH 43606

SIMON, HERBERT A, SIMULATION OF HUMAN THINKING. *Current Pos:* UNIV PROF COMPUT SCI & PSYCHOL, CARNEGIE-MELLON UNIV, 66- *Personal Data:* Milwaukee, Wis, June 15, 16; m 37, Dorothea Pye; c Katherine, Peter & Barbara. *Educ:* Univ Chicago, BA, 36, PhD(polit sci), 43. *Hon Degrees:* Honorary degrees from many Am & Europ univs. *Honors & Awards:* Nobel Prize Econ, 78; Mosher Award, 74; Turing Award, Asn Comput Mach, 75; James Madison Award, 84; Nat Medal of Sci, 86; John von Neuman Theory Award, Inst Mgt Sci, 88; Dwight Waldo Award, 95. *Prof Exp:* Res asst, Int City Mgr Asn, 36-39; res dir pub admin, Univ Calif, Berkeley, 39-42; from asst prof to prof polit sci, Ill Inst Technol, 42-49; prof admin, Carnegie Inst Technol, 49-67. *Concurrent Pos:* Consult, Cowles Comns, 46-60 & Rand Corp, 68-70; vis lectr var univs, 59-; chmn, Social Sci Res Coun, 61-65 & Nat Res Coun, 68-70; mem coun, Nat Acad Sci, 78-81 & 83-86. *Mem:* Asn Comput Mach; fel Am Psychol Asn; fel Asn Am Artificial Intel; fel Am Acad Arts & Sci; fel AAAS; fel Am Econ Asn; fel Am Sociol Soc; fel Econometric Soc; fel Int Acad Mat; hon fel Brit Psychol Soc; fel Am Pspychol Soc. *Res:* Computer simulation of human cognitive processes including problem solving, scientific discovery, learning, imagery; representation and testing of simulation models. *Mailing Add:* Dept Psychol Carnegie Mellon Univ Pittsburgh PA 15213-3890

SIMON, HORST D, algorithms, for more information see previous edition

SIMON, JACK AARON, COAL GEOLOGY. *Current Pos:* RETIRED. *Personal Data:* b Champaign, Ill, June 17, 19. *Educ:* Univ Ill, BA, 41, MS, 46. *Hon Degrees:* DSc, Northwestern Univ, 81. *Honors & Awards:* Gilbert H Cady Award, Geol Soc Am, 75; Percy W Nicholls Award, Am Inst Mining, Metall & Petrol Engrs, 81; Gordon M Wood, Jr Mem Award, Am Asn Petrol Geologists, 91. *Prof Exp:* Tech & res asst, Ill State Geol Surv, 37-42, from asst geologist to geologist, 45-67, prin geologist, 67-73, chief, 73-81, prin scientist, 81-83. *Concurrent Pos:* From assoc prof to prof metall & mining, Univ Ill, 67-77, 80-85, adj prof geol, 79-86. *Mem:* AAAS; Geol Soc Am; Soc Econ Geologists; Am Asn Petrol Geol; Am Inst Mining, Metall & Petrol Engrs; Am Inst Prof Geologists (vpres, 73). *Res:* Coal resources; coal mining geology; Pennsylvanian stratigraphy. *Mailing Add:* 101 W Windsor Rd Urbana IL 61802-6697

SIMON, JEROME BARNET, GASTROENTEROLOGY. *Current Pos:* from lectr to assoc prof, 69-88, PROF GASTROENTEROL, DEPT MED, QUEENS UNIV, 88-, ATTEND STAFF, HOTEL DIEU HOSP, 92- *Personal Data:* b Regina, Sask, Aug 21, 39; m 91, Cindy Boyer; c Nancy & David. *Educ:* Queens Univ, Can, MD, 62; Royal Col Physicians & Surgeons, FRCP(C), 67; Am Bd Internal Med, dipl, 69; Am Col Gastroenterol, FACG, 83; Am Col Physicians, FACP, 86. *Prof Exp:* House officer med, Montreal Gen Hosp, McGill Univ, 62-65, training resident gastroenterol, 65-66; fel, Liver Study Unit, Yale Univ, 66-69. *Concurrent Pos:* Attend staff, Kingston Gen Hosp, Ont, 69-, head, Div Gastroenterol, 75-89; consult staff, Hotel Dieu Hosp, 69-92; vis prof, Univ Alta, 72, Univ Toronto, 73, 77, 79 & 81, Dalhousie Univ, 75, Univ Conn & Mem Univ, 76, Univ Calgary, 77, McMaster Univ, 78, Wayne State Univ, 85, Univ Alta, 89, Univ Manitoba, 92, Univ Calgary, 95; mem, Med Adv Bd, Can Liver Found, 72-75, vchmn & mem, Bd Dirs, 88-90; mem, Prog Grants Comt, Med Res Coun Can, 75-76, Clin Invest Comt, 77-79; mem res comts, Can Asn Gastroenterol, 76-81, mem, Educ Comt, 85-87; mem, Admis Comt, Am Asn Study Liver Dis, 78-80; fel & bursaries comt, Can Cancer Soc, Ont Div, 79-86, chmn, 82-84; postgrad course comt, Am Col Gastroenterol, 83-84; examr, Int Med, Royal Col Physicians & Surgeons, 85; mem, Gov Bd, Can Asn Study Liver, 85-89, vpres, 87-88 & pres, 88-89; counr, Can Soc Clin Invest, 86-89, secy-treas, 90-93;

mem, Bd Dirs, Ont Med Asn, 90-94. *Mem:* Am Asn Study Liver Dis; Am Gastroenterol Asn; Am Col Physicians; Can Med Asn; Am Col Gastroenterol; Royal Col Physicians & Surgeons. *Res:* Lipid metabolism in liver disease; clinical research gastroenterology and liver diseases. *Mailing Add:* Dept Med Hotel Dieu Hosp Kingston ON K7L 5G2 Can. *Fax:* 613-544-3114; *E-Mail:* simonj@post.queensu.ca

SIMON, JIMMY L, MEDICINE. *Current Pos:* prof pediat & chmn dept, 74-96, EMER PROF PEDIAT & EMER CHMN DEPT, BOWMAN GRAY SCH MED, 96- *Personal Data:* b San Francisco, Calif, Dec 27, 30; m 53, Marilyn Wachter; c 2. *Educ:* Univ Calif, Berkeley, AB, 52; Univ Calif, San Francisco, MD, 55. *Prof Exp:* Intern, Hosp, Univ Calif, 55-56; asst resident pediat, Grace-New Haven Hosp, 56-57; sr resident, Children's Hosp, Boston, Mass, 57-58; from instr to asst prof, Sch Med, Univ Okla, 60-64; dir, Kern County Gen Hosp, Bakersfield, Calif, 65-66; from assoc prof to prof pediat, Univ Tex Med Br Galveston & dep chmn dept, 66-74. *Mem:* Am Pediat Soc; Am Acad Pediat; Ambulatory Pediat Asn; Am Bd Pediat. *Res:* Clinical pediatrics; ambulatory medical care. *Mailing Add:* Dept Pediat Bowman Gray Sch Med Winston-Salem NC 27157

SIMON, JOHN DOUGLAS, PHYSICAL CHEMISTRY, CHEMICAL DYNAMICS. *Current Pos:* Res assoc, Los Angeles, 83-85, from asst prof to assoc prof, 85-90, PROF CHEM, UNIV CALIF, SAN DIEGO, 90- *Personal Data:* b Cincinnati, Ohio, Feb, 11, 57; m 91, Diane Szaflarski. *Educ:* Williams Col, BA, 79; Harvard Univ, MA, 81, PhD(chem), 83. *Honors & Awards:* Fresenius Nat Award in Chem. *Concurrent Pos:* Prin young investr, NSF; Alfred P Sloan fel. *Mem:* Am Chem Soc; Am Phys Soc; AAAS. *Res:* Application of picosecond and subpicosecond spectroscopic techniques to chemical problems. *Mailing Add:* Dept Chem 0341 Univ Calif San Diego La Jolla CA 92093-0341. *E-Mail:* jds@chem.ucsd.edu

SIMON, JOSEPH LESLIE, ZOOLOGY. *Current Pos:* From instr to assoc prof, 63-78, PROF ZOOL, UNIV S FLA, 78 - *Personal Data:* b Everett, Mass, Mar 16, 37. *Educ:* Tufts Univ, BS, 58; Univ NH, MS, 60, PhD(zool), 63. *Concurrent Pos:* Fel, Systs Ecol Prog, Marine Biol Lab, Woods Hole, Mass, 65-67; Fulbright fel, Taiwan, 90-91. *Mem:* AAAS; Am Soc Zool. *Res:* Systematics of and reproduction and development of Polychaetous Annelids; ecology of marine benthic communities. *Mailing Add:* Dept Biol Univ SFla 4202 Fowler Ave Tampa FL 33620. *E-Mail:* simon@chump.cas.usf.edu

SIMON, JOSEPH MATTHEW, ANALYTICAL CHEMISTRY. *Current Pos:* Asst prof, Point Park Col, 69-74, assoc prof, 74--81, chmn dept natural sci & technol, 74-86, PROF CHEM, POINT PARK COL, 81-, PRES, 86- *Personal Data:* b Reading, Pa, July 14, 41; m 67. *Educ:* Albright Col, BS, 63; Univ Pittsburgh, PhD(chem), 69. *Mem:* AAAS; Am Chem Soc. *Res:* Medium effects and nonaqueous solutions; electrochemistry; polarography. *Mailing Add:* 114 Yorkshire Dr Pittsburgh PA 15208-2641

SIMON, LEE WILL, ASTRONOMY. *Current Pos:* FOUNDER, STROKE ASSOCS MARIN, COL MARIN, KENTFIELD, CA, 84- *Personal Data:* b Evanston, Ill, Feb 18, 40; m 66, Mary Jo Welsh; c John, Daniel & Stephen. *Educ:* Northwestern Univ, Evanston, BA, 62, MS, 64, PhD(astron), 72. *Prof Exp:* Staff astronomer & prog suprv, Adler Planetarium, 69-76; planetarium dir, Morrison Planetarium, Calif Acad Sci, Golden Gate Park, San Francisco, 77-84. *Mem:* Am Astron Soc; Sigma Xi; Astron Soc Pac; Planetary Soc. *Res:* Stellar spectroscopy. *Mailing Add:* 245 San Marin Dr Novato CA 94945-1220

SIMON, MARK ROBERT, ANATOMY, PHYSICAL ANTHROPOLOGY. *Current Pos:* Asst prof, 77-83, ASSOC PROF VET ANAT, UNIV ILL SCH VET MED, 83- *Personal Data:* b New York, NY, July 26, 41; m 78. *Educ:* Hunter Col, City Univ NY, BA, 66, PhD(anthrop), 74. *Mem:* Am Asn Vet Anatomists; Sigma Xi. *Res:* Experimental morphology; gross anatomy; craniofacial morphogenesis; mechanical and hormonal factors in cartilage growth. *Mailing Add:* Dept Vet Biosci Univ Ill 2001 S Lincoln Ave Urbana IL 61801-6178

SIMON, MARTHA NICHOLS, BIOCHEMISTRY, MOLECULAR & STRUCTURAL BIOLOGY. *Current Pos:* sr res assoc biol, Brookheaven Nat Lab, 72-75, asst biologist, 75-77, assoc biologist, 77-84, BIOL ASSOC, BROOKHEAVEN NAT LAB, 85- *Personal Data:* b New York, NY, Dec 31, 40; m 81, Alan H Rosenberg; c Daniel W. *Educ:* Radcliffe, Col, AB, 62; Cornell Univ, PhD(chem), 68. *Prof Exp:* Res fel chem, Calif Inst Technol, 67-69; res assoc biochem, State Univ NY, Stony Brook, 69-72. *Concurrent Pos:* Spec fel, NIH, 71-72, co-investr, 75-77, investr, 77- *Mem:* AAAS; Biophys Soc; Micros Soc Am. *Res:* Coordinator of users/collaborators for scanning transmission electron microscope facility; structural studies of biological molecules. *Mailing Add:* 145 Main St Setauket NY 11733

SIMON, MARVIN KENNETH, ELECTRICAL ENGINEERING. *Current Pos:* mem tech staff commun, 68-80, SR RES ENGR, JET PROPULSION LAB, 80- *Personal Data:* b New York, NY, Sept 10, 39; m 66; c 2. *Educ:* City Col New York, BEE, 60; Princeton Univ, MSEE, 61; NY Univ, PhD(elec eng), 66. *Honors & Awards:* Bicentennial Paper Award, Inst Medal, Elec & Electronics Engrs, 84, Vehicular Tech Paper Award, 90; Exception Serv Medal, NASA, 79, Exception Eng Achievement Medal, 95, Group Achievement Awards, 81, 86. *Prof Exp:* Mem tech staff commun, Bell Tel Labs, 61-63; instr elec eng, NY Univ, 63-66; mem tech staff commun, Bell Tel Labs, 66-68. *Concurrent Pos:* Instr elec eng, West Coast Univ, 69; consult, LinCom Corp, 73-76 & Axiomatix Corp, 76-; ed Communications, Inst Elec & Electronics Engrs, 74-76, chmn commun theory workshop, 75, chmn commun theory comt, 77-, fel grade, 78; vis prop elec eng, Calif Inst Technol, 89-96. *Mem:* Sigma Xi; fel Inst Elec & Electronics Engrs; fel Inst Advan Eng. *Res:* Digital communications as applied to space and satellite communication systems; modulation theory; synchronization techniques; trellis-coding; spread spectrum communications. *Mailing Add:* Jet Propulsion Lab 4800 Oak Grove Dr Mail Stop 238-343 Pasadena CA 91109

SIMON, MELVIN, BIOLOGY. *Current Pos:* PROF, DIV BIOL, CALIF INST TECHNOL, PASADENA, 82-, CHMN, DIV BIOL, 95- *Personal Data:* b New York, NY, Feb 8, 37; m; c 3. *Educ:* City Col NY, BS, 59; Brandeis Univ, PhD(biochem), 63. *Honors & Awards:* Carter-Wallace Lectr, Princeton Univ, 88; Selman A Waksman Award Microbiol, Nat Acad Sci, 91. *Prof Exp:* Postdoctoral fel, Princeton Univ, NJ, 64-65; from asst prof to prof, Dept Biol, Univ Calif, San Diego, La Jolla, 65-82. *Concurrent Pos:* Postdoctoral fel, USPHS, 63-64; John Simon Guggenheim mem fel, 78; Anne P & Benjamin F Biaggini prof biol sci, 87. *Mem:* Nat Acad Sci; Am Acad Arts & Sci. *Res:* Author of various publications. *Mailing Add:* Div Biol Calif Inst Technol Pasadena CA 91125. *Fax:* 626-796-7600

SIMON, MICHAEL RICHARD, IMMUNOLOGY, INTERNAL MEDICINE. *Current Pos:* asst prof, 77-90, ASSOC PROF INTERNAL MED, SCH MED, WAYNE STATE UNIV, 90-, ASSOC PROF PEDIATS, 92- *Personal Data:* b New York, Oct 12, 43; m 70; c 2. *Educ:* State Univ NY, Binghamton, BA, 65; NY Univ, MD, 69; Stanford Univ, MA, 73; Am Bd Internal Med, dipl, 75; Am Bd Allergy & Immunol, dipl, 77, 91; Am Bd Med Lab Immunol, dipl, 85. *Honors & Awards:* Educom Medal, 95. *Prof Exp:* Intern internal med, Kings County Hosp-Downstate Med Ctr, Brooklyn, 69-70; gen med officer, Indian Hosp, USPHS, San Carlos, Ariz, 70-72; resident internal med, Affil Intern-Resident Phys Prog, Wayne State Univ, 73-75; fel allergy & immunol, Med Ctr, Univ Mich, 75-77. *Concurrent Pos:* Allergy Found Am fel clin allergy & immunol res, 76-77; co-chief, Allergy-Immunol Sect, Vet Admin Med Ctr, Detroit, 77-; training prog dir, Allergy Immunol, Detroit Med Ctr, 91- *Mem:* Fel Am Col Physicians; fel Am Acad Allergy Asthma & Immunol; Am Fedn Clin Res; Soc Exp Biol Med; fel Royal Col Physicians & Surgeons Can. *Res:* Immunology of infectious and granulomatous diseases; immunopharmacology; anaphylaxis; sarcoidosis. *Mailing Add:* Allergy & Immunol Sect 111F Vet Admin Med Ctr 4646 John R St Detroit MI 48201. *Fax:* 313-576-1122; *E-Mail:* simon.michael_r@allen-park.va.gov

SIMON, MICHAL, ASTRONOMY. *Current Pos:* from asst prof to assoc prof, 69-74, from chmn dept earth & space sci, 80-83, PROF ASTRON, STATE UNIV NY STONY BROOK, 74- *Personal Data:* b Prague, Czech, Sept 28, 40; US citizen; c 1. *Educ:* Harvard Univ, AB, 62; Cornell Univ, PhD(astrophys), 67. *Prof Exp:* Res fel astron, Calif Inst Technol, 67-69. *Mem:* AAAS; Am Astron Soc; Int Astron Union. *Res:* Infrared astronomy; star formation. *Mailing Add:* Dept of Earth & Space Sci State Univ of New York Stony Brook NY 11794

SIMON, MYRON SYDNEY, ORGANIC & PHOTOGRAPHIC CHEMISTRY, CHEMISTRY OF DYES. *Current Pos:* FOUNDER & PRES, IMAGE-INATION ASSOCS, 88- *Personal Data:* b Burlington, Vt, Sept 23, 26; m 50, Rose Reguera; c Laurel (Bobrowich), Amy (Berg) & Ethan. *Educ:* Harvard Univ, AB, 46, AM, 48, PhD(chem), 49. *Prof Exp:* Res chemist, Polaroid Corp, 49-55, group leader, 55-59, from asst mgr to mgr, Org Chem Res Dept, 59-73, asst dir, Org Chem Res Div, 74-80, assoc dir, 81-88, res fel, 85-88. *Mem:* Am Chem Soc. *Res:* Photographic materials; monomers; organic synthesis; diffusion transfer color photographic research; chemistry of dyes. *Mailing Add:* 20 Somerset Rd West Newton MA 02165-2722

SIMON, NANCY JANE, LOW TEMPERATURE PHYSICS. *Current Pos:* CONSULT, 95- *Personal Data:* b Pittsburgh, Pa, June 1, 39. *Educ:* Univ Chicago, BS, 60; Radcliffe Col, AM, 61; Harvard Univ, PhD(physics), 68; Univ Colo, BA, 81. *Prof Exp:* Physicist, Mat Sci & Eng Lab, Nat Inst Stand & Technol, 68-95. *Mem:* Sigma Xi. *Res:* Mossbauer effect; Kapitza conductance; low temperature physics and engineering; cryogenic information retrieval; properties of structural and insulating materials at cryogenic temperatures; superconducting magnets for fusion energy systems; radiation damage. *Mailing Add:* 770 31st St Boulder CO 80303. *Fax:* 303-494-0134

SIMON, NORMAN M, NEPHROLOGY, HYPERTENSION. *Current Pos:* From instr to assoc prof, 63-82, PROF MED, NORTHWESTERN UNIV, 82- *Personal Data:* b Chicago, Ill, Mar 30, 29; m 57, Harriet Devorkin; c Judith, Daniel & Amy. *Educ:* Harvard Univ, BA, 50; Yale Univ, MS, 51; Northwestern Univ, MD, 55; Am Bd Internal Med, dipl, 63; Sub-Comt Nephrology, dipl, 76. *Concurrent Pos:* Nat Heart Inst res fel, Michael Reese Hosp, 56-57; fel med, Med Sch, Northwestern Univ, 61-63; assoc chief med, Passavant Mem Hosp, Chicago, 72-73; sr attend physician, Evanston Hosp, 79-, head, Div Nephrology, 88- *Mem:* AAAS; Int Soc Nephrology; Cent Soc Clin Res; fel Am Col Physicians; Am Soc Nephrology. *Res:* Renal hypertension; natural history of renal diseases; metabolism of uremia; chronic dialysis and renal transplantation. *Mailing Add:* Evanston Hosp 2650 Ridge Ave Evanston IL 60201-1718

SIMON, NORMAN ROBERT, ASTROPHYSICS. *Current Pos:* asst prof, 70-74, assoc prof, 74-79, PROF PHYSICS & ASTRON, UNIV NEBR, 79- *Personal Data:* b New York, NY. *Educ:* Syracuse Univ, BA, 59; City Col New York, MS, 64; Yeshiva Univ, PhD(physics), 68. *Prof Exp:* Fel astrophys, Nat Acad Sci-Nat Res Coun, 68-70. *Mem:* Am Astron Soc; Int Astron Union. *Res:* Stellar interiors; pulsations of stars; stellar evolution; cepheid variable stars. *Mailing Add:* Univ Nebr 116 Brace Lab PO Box 880111 Lincoln NE 68588-0111

SIMON, PHILIPP WILLIAM, PLANT BREEDING, HORTICULTURE. *Current Pos:* from asst prof to assoc prof, 80-85, PROF, DEPT HORT, UNIV WIS, 85-; RES PLANT GENETICIST, USDA AGR RES SERV, 78- *Personal Data:* b Sturgeon Bay, Wis, Mar 19, 50; m 73, Sandra L Larson; c 2. *Educ:* Carroll Col, BS, 72; Univ Wis, MS, 75, PhD(genetics), 77. *Honors & Awards:* Nat Food Processors Award, 81, 84. *Mem:* AAAS; Genetics Soc Am; Am Soc Hort Sci; Bot Soc Am; Am Genetics Asn. *Res:* Genetics and breeding of carrot, onion, garlic and cucumber; biochemical genetics and improvement of nutritional quality and culinary guality; gene mapping in carrot, onion, cucumber. *Mailing Add:* USDA ARS Dept Hort Univ Wis 1575 Linden Dr Madison WI 53706. *Fax:* 608-262-4743; *E-Mail:* simon@calshp.cals.wisc.edu

SIMON, RALPH EMANUEL, PHYSICS. *Current Pos:* EXEC VPRES & CHIEF OPER OFFICER, LYTEL INC, SOMERVILLE, NJ, 87- *Personal Data:* b Passaic, NJ, Oct 20, 30; m 52; c 3. *Educ:* Princeton Univ, BA, 52; Cornell Univ, PhD, 59. *Prof Exp:* Asst, Cornell Univ, 52-57; mem tech staff, Labs, RCA Corp, 59-68, dir, Conversion Devices Lab, David Sarnoff Res Ctr, 68-69, mgr advan technol, Electrooptics Oper, RCA Electronic Components, 69-70, mgr, Electrooptics Oper, 70-76, vpres, Electro-Optics Devices Div, RCA Electronics Components, 76- *Mem:* Am Phys Soc; fel Inst Elec & Electronics Engrs. *Res:* Solid state physics. *Mailing Add:* 11857 Woodhill Ct Cupertino CA 95014-5149

SIMON, RICHARD L, MICRO-CLIMATOLOGY, FORENSIC METEOROLOGY. *Current Pos:* METEOROL CONSULT, 83- *Personal Data:* b Oakland, Calif, Dec 1, 50; m 85, Kathy Burwell; c Emylena & Kyra. *Educ:* Univ Calif, Berkeley, BS, 73; San Jose State Univ, MS, 76. *Prof Exp:* Res asst, Ames Res Ctr, NASA, 74-75; meteorologist, Nat Environ Satellite Serv, Nat Oceanic & Atmospheric Admin, 76 & Pac Gas & Elect Co, 80-82; res assoc, San Jose State Univ, 77-78; meteorologist & pres, Global Weather Consults, Inc, 77-80; sr meteorologist, Am Energy Projs, Inc, 82-83. *Concurrent Pos:* Lectr, San Jose State Univ, 76 & 86 & San Jose Metrop Adult Educ Prog, 77-78. *Mem:* Am Meteorol Soc; Am Wind Energy Asn. *Res:* Wind energy meteorology; practical methodologies for the siting of wind turbines and assessment of their potential energy production. *Mailing Add:* 80 Alta Vista Ave Mill Valley CA 94941. *Fax:* 415-381-2248; *E-Mail:* 104505.14@compuserve.com

SIMON, RICHARD MACY, BIOMETRIC RESEARCH. *Current Pos:* comput scientist, Div Comput Res & Technol, NIH, 69-71, head, Biostatist Info Systs Unit, Med Oncol, 71-75, head, Biostatist & Data Mgt Sect, Clin Oncol Prog, 76-78, CHIEF, BIOMET RES BR, CANCER THER EVAL PROG, DIV CANCER TREAT, NAT CANCER INST, NIH, BETHESDA, MD, 78- *Personal Data:* b St Louis, Mo, July 27, 43. *Educ:* Wash Univ, St Louis, BS, 65, PhD, 69. *Prof Exp:* Consult statist, Gen Elec Ctr Advan Studies, Santa Barbara, Calif, 67-69, Rand Corp, Santa Monica, Calif, 68-69. *Concurrent Pos:* Adv, Am Diabetes Asn; mem, Task Force Endpoints, AIDS studies, NIH, Proj Controlled Therapeut Trials, Int Union Control Cancer, 87-; mem, Bd Dirs, Soc Clin Trails, 86-; vis prof internal med, Univ Va, 89-90; reviewer, Am J Epidemiol, Can J Statist, J Chronic Dis, J Am Statist Asn, J Nat Cancer Inst. *Mem:* Fel Am Statist Asn; Am Asn Cancer Res; Am Soc Clin Oncol; Asn Comput Mach; Biomet Soc; Soc Clin Trials. *Mailing Add:* 5516 Cedar Pkwy Chevy Chase MD 20815

SIMON, ROBERT DAVID, MICROBIOLOGY, ECOLOGY. *Current Pos:* DEPT BIOL, STATE UNIV NY COL GENESEO, 82- *Personal Data:* b Chicago, Ill, June 14, 45; m 67; c 3. *Educ:* Univ Chicago, BS, 67; Mich State Univ, PhD(bot), 71. *Prof Exp:* Assoc prof biol, Univ Rochester, 71-82. *Mem:* Am Soc Microbiol. *Res:* Microbiology, ecology and biochemistry of the cyanabacteria. *Mailing Add:* Dept Biol State Univ NY Col 1 College Cir Geneseo NY 14454-1401

SIMON, ROBERT H, chemical engineering, for more information see previous edition

SIMON, ROBERT H(ERBERT) M(ELVIN), MATERIALS SCIENCE ENGINEERING, POLYMER ENGINEERING. *Current Pos:* PVT CONSULT, 91- *Personal Data:* b New York, NY, Nov 11, 24; m 50, Sheila Levy; c Burton, Stewart, Diana & Alice. *Educ:* Univ Del, BChE, 48; Yale Univ, DEng(chem eng), 57. *Prof Exp:* Develop engr, Gen Elec Co, 48-52; sr engr, Monsanto Co, 56-66, specialist process technol, 66-68, group supvr, 68-74, sr technol specialist, 74-80, Monsanto fel, 80-91. *Concurrent Pos:* Adj lectr chem eng, Yale Univ, 84-85. *Mem:* Am Inst Chem Engrs; Am Chem Soc. *Res:* Polymer process development polymer foams; polymer fabrication techniques; high pressure reactions; polymer devolatilization; polymerization reactor design. *Mailing Add:* 23 Caravelle Dr Longmeadow MA 01106. *E-Mail:* bobhms@aol.com

SIMON, ROBERT MICHAEL, ORGANOSILICON & ORGANOLITHIUM CHEMISTRY. *Current Pos:* sci fel, comt energy & natural resources, 93-97, SCI & TECH ADV, OFF SEN JEFF BINGAMAN, US SENATE, WASH, DC, 97- *Personal Data:* b Philadelphia, Pa, Jan 12, 56; m 81, Karen Barcant; c Stephen, Cathryn, Gregory & Anne-Marie Wanla. *Educ:* Ursinus Col, BS, 77; Mass Inst Technol, PhD(inorg chem), 82. *Prof Exp:* Mellon Found sci policy fel, Nat Acad Sci, 82-83, staff officer, 83-85, sr staff officer, 85-88, staff dir, bd chem sci & technol, Nat Res Coun, 88-89; prin dep dir, Off Energy Res, US Dept Energy, 91-93. *Mem:* Am Chem Soc; Am Inst Chem Engrs; Sigma Xi; AAAS; Mat Res Soc; Am Nuclear Soc. *Res:* Science and technology policy related to the health of fundamental science, defense issues, energy issues, environmental regulation, and economic competitiveness; science administration. *Mailing Add:* 6116 Quebec Pl College Park MD 20740. *Fax:* 202-224-2852; *E-Mail:* bob_simon@bingaman.senate.gov

SIMON, SANFORD RALPH, PATHOLOGY. *Current Pos:* from asst prof to assoc prof, 69-87, PROF BIOCHEM & PATH, STATE UNIV NY STONY BROOK, 87- *Personal Data:* b New York, NY, Nov 6, 42; m 64; c 2. *Educ:* Columbia Univ, AB, 63; Rockefeller Univ, PhD(biochem), 67. *Prof Exp:* Guest investr biochem, Rockefeller Univ, 67-69. *Concurrent Pos:* Nat Heart, Lung & Blood Inst grant & Am Heart Asn grant-in-aid, 70-; Alfred P Sloan Found res fel, 72; Nat Heart, Lung & Blood Inst career develop award, 75-80. *Mem:* Am Soc Biochem & Molecular Biol. *Res:* Structure-function relationships of normal and modified hemoglobins and metalloproteins; role of protein conformation in mechanisms of enzyme action; applications of physical biochemistry in protein research; design and characterization of protease inhibitors; interactions of inflammatory cells with extracellular matrix. *Mailing Add:* Dept Path State Univ NY Stony Brook NY 11794-1869. *Fax:* 516-444-7507

SIMON, SELWYN, microbiology, for more information see previous edition

SIMON, SHERIDAN ALAN, astrophysics, writing; deceased, see previous edition for last biography

SIMON, SIDNEY ARTHUR, PHYSICAL BIOLOGY. *Current Pos:* fel physiol, Duke Univ, 73-74, assoc anesthesiol, 74-80, asst prof physiol, 74-80, anesthesiol, 80-88, ASSOC PROF PHYSIOL, 80-, ASSOC PROF ANESTHESIOL & PROF NEUROBIOL, DUKE UNIV, 88- *Personal Data:* b New York, NY, Feb 16, 43; div. *Educ:* Ind Inst Technol, BS, 65; Ariz State Univ, MS, 68; Northwestern Univ, PhD(mat sci), 73. *Prof Exp:* Fel biol, Northwestern Univ, 73. *Mem:* Biophys Soc; Soc Gen Physiologists; Soc Neurosci. *Mailing Add:* 2203 Stuart Dr Durham NC 27707

SIMON, SOLOMON HENRY, INFORMATION KNOWLEDGE DISCOVERY, ELECTRONIC COMMERCE. *Current Pos:* SR MANAGING CONSULT, LOCKHEED MARTIN, 97- *Personal Data:* b Charleston, SC, Jan 2, 55. *Educ:* Clemson Univ, BS, 77; Tex A&M Univ, MS, 83, PhD(info technol), 85. *Honors & Awards:* Welch Award, 80; Gold Quill Award, 80, Int Asn Bus Communicators, 96. *Prof Exp:* Asst prof chem, Tex A&M Univ, 77-82, asst prof calculus, 83-85; sr res scientist, Chem Abstr Serv, 85-88; mgr, Loral, 88-97. *Mem:* Am Chem Soc; Am Asn Artificial Intel. *Res:* Organization, management and discovery as it applies to global databases such as the internet and world wide web. *Mailing Add:* 3712 Pimlico Dr Arlington TX 76017-2422

SIMON, TERRENCE WILLIAM, MECHANICAL ENGINEERING. *Current Pos:* ASST PROF THERMOSCI, MECH ENG DEPT, UNIV MINN, 80- *Personal Data:* b Cottonwood, Idaho, Aug 16, 46; m 71; c 1. *Educ:* Wash State Univ, BS, 68; Univ Calif, Berkeley, MS, 71; Stanford Univ, PhD(mech eng), 80. *Prof Exp:* Engr, Nuclear Energy Div, Gen Elec Co, 68-74, Stearns Roger, Inc, 74-76. *Concurrent Pos:* Consult, Stanford Linear Accelerator Ctr, 77-78, Hewlett-Packard Inc, 78-80, Control Data Corp, 83. *Mem:* Am Soc Mech Engrs. *Res:* Experimental and analytical studies in the fundamentals of heat transfer and fluid mechanics. *Mailing Add:* Dept Mech Eng Univ Minn 111 Church St SE Minneapolis MN 55455

SIMON, WILBUR, CHEMISTRY. *Current Pos:* OWNER & DIR, SIMON RES LAB, 64- *Personal Data:* b Geneva, Ill, July 5, 17; m 57; c 2. *Educ:* Univ Ill, BS, 39; Univ Iowa, MS, 40, PhD(anal chem), 51. *Prof Exp:* Chem engr, Tenn Copper Co, 40-44; assoc chemist, Metall Lab, Univ Chicago, 44-45; jr res chemist, Carbide & Carbon Chem Corp, 45-49; head analyst & stand br, US Naval Radiol Defense Lab, 51-53; res chemist, Princeton Radiation Chem Lab Inc, 53-55 & Morton Chem Co Ill, 55-61; assoc res coordr, Universal Oil Prod Co, 61-64. *Mem:* AAAS; Am Chem Soc. *Res:* Analytical development; application of nuclear magnetic resonance to organic chemistry; nuclear magnetic resonance spectroscopy; disposal of solid and liquid wastes; removal of contaminants from sewage; environmental problems; overflow and backup of sewers; corrosion; metal cleaning; adhesives. *Mailing Add:* 816 Murray Ave Elgin IL 60123-3408

SIMON, WILLIAM, PHYSICS, BIOMATHEMATICS. *Current Pos:* assoc prof, 68-77, prof biomath, Rochester Sch Med & Dent, 77-82, PROF BIOPHYS, UNIV ROCHESTER, 82-, PROF MED INFORMATICS, 88- *Personal Data:* b Pittsburgh, Pa, May 27, 29. *Educ:* Carnegie Inst Technol, BS, 50; Harvard Univ, MA, 52, PhD(appl physics), 58. *Prof Exp:* Instrument sect head elec eng, Spencer Kennedy Lab, Boston, Mass, 53-57; sr systs engr, Nat Radio Co, Malden, 57-59; chief physicist, Image Instruments, Inc, Newton, 59-60; mem staff comput, Lincoln Lab, Mass Inst Technol, 61-64; res assoc, Dept Physiol, Harvard Med Sch, 64-68; consult physicist, Comstock & Westcott, Cambridge, Mass. *Concurrent Pos:* Vis assoc prof elec eng, Mass Inst Technol, 74-75. *Mailing Add:* Dept Biochem & Biophys Univ Rochester Med Ctr Rochester NY 14642. *Fax:* 716-275-6007

SIMONDS, JOHN ORMSBEE, ECOLOGY. *Current Pos:* partner, 70-82, EMER PARTNER, ENVIRON PLANNING & DESIGN PARTNERSHIP, 83-; CONSULT, COMPREHENSIVE LAND PLANNING, 83- *Personal Data:* b Jamestown, NDak, Mar 11, 13; m 43, Marjorie Todd; c John T, Taye A, Polly J & Leslie B. *Educ:* Mich State Univ, BS, 35; Harvard Univ, MLA, 39. *Hon Degrees:* DSc, Mich State Univ, 68. *Honors & Awards:* Am Soc Landscape Architects Medal, Am Soc Landscape Architects, 73. *Prof Exp:* Partner, Simonds & Simonds, Landscape Architects, 39-52, Collins, Simonds & Simonds, Landscape Architects, 52-70; fac, Dept Archit, Carnegie-Mellon Univ, 55-67. *Concurrent Pos:* US consult, InterAm Housing & Planning Ctr, Bogota, 60 & 61; vis critic, Archit & Planning, Yale

Univ, 61 & 62; lectr, 40 Univs in US & abroad, 61-; consult, Chicago Cent Area Comt, 62 & Land & Nature Trust, Lexington, Ky, 87-92; adv, US Bur Pub Roads, Dept Transp, 65-68; chmn, Urban Open Space Panel, White House Conf, 65; founding pres, Am Soc Landscape Architects Found, 66-68; mem, President's Task Force Environ, 68-70 & Fla Gov's Task Force Resources & Environ, 68-71; hon corresp, Royal Town Planning Inst, Gt Brit. *Mem:* Am Soc Landscape Architects (vpres, 61-63, pres, 63-65); Royal Town Planning Inst; assoc mem Nat Acad Design. *Res:* Author and/or editor of 5 books and many articles and technical reports in field of environmental science, landscape architecture, community and regional planning, urban design, riverfront development, parks, recreation and growth management. *Mailing Add:* 17 Penhurst Rd Pittsburgh PA 15202

SIMONE, JOSEPH VINCENT, HEMATOLOGY, PEDIATRICS. *Current Pos:* assoc dir clin res, 78-83, DIR CLIN RES, ST JUDE CHILDREN'S RES HOSP, 83- *Personal Data:* b Chicago, Ill, Sept 19, 35; m 60; c 3. *Educ:* Loyola Univ, Chicago, MD, 60; Am Bd Internal Med & Am Bd Pediat, dipl, 67; Am Bd Pediat Hemat-Oncol, cert, 74. *Honors & Awards:* Richard & Hinda Rosenthal Award, 79. *Prof Exp:* Instr pediat, Col Med, Univ Ill, 66-67; from asst prof to assoc prof pediat, Univ Tenn Health Sci Ctr, 67-77; chief hemat & oncol, St Jude Children's Hosp, 73-77; prof pediat, Stanford Univ, 77-78. *Concurrent Pos:* Trainee pediat hemat, Col Med, Univ Ill, 63-66; chief hemat, St Jude Children's Hosp, 69-73. *Mem:* Fel Am Col Physicians; Am Soc Hemat; Soc Pediat Res; Am Asn Cancer Res; Am Pediat Soc; Am Soc Clin Oncol. *Res:* Cancer therapy. *Mailing Add:* 332 N Lauderdale St Memphis TN 38105-2729

SIMONE, LEO DANIEL, PLANT MORPHOLOGY, BRYOLOGY. *Current Pos:* PROF BIOL, STATE UNIV NY POTSDAM, 66- *Personal Data:* b New York, NY, Oct 6, 35; m 75, Karin E Stephan; c Michelle J & Brigitte D. *Educ:* Manhattan Col, BS, 57; Columbia Univ, MA, 59, PhD(bot), 67. *Prof Exp:* Teaching asst bot, Columbia Univ, 60-64, preceptor, 64-66. *Mem:* AAAS; Am Soc Plant Physiol; Am Inst Biol Sci; Bot Soc Am; Am Soc Cell Biol; Mycol Soc Am. *Res:* Apogamy and apospory in the Hepaticae; experimental plant morphology and aseptic culture of liverworts; spermatogenesis in leafy hepatics; mineralization in plants. *Mailing Add:* Dept of Biol State Univ NY Col Potsdam Potsdam NY 13676-2294. Fax: 315-267-3170; E-Mail: simoneld@potsdam.edu

SIMONELLI, ANTHONY PETER, DRUG DELIVERY SYSTEMS, CHEMICAL KINETICS & SOLID STATE CHEMISTRY. *Current Pos:* PROF PHARMACEUT & DIR PHD PROG INDUST PHARM & PHARMACEUT, COL PHARM LONG ISLAND UNIV, 93- *Personal Data:* b Bridgeport, Conn, June 28, 24; m 56, Joan LaStoria; c David, Gloria & Peter. *Educ:* Univ Conn, BA & BS, 55; Univ Wis, MS, 58, PhD(pharm), 60. *Honors & Awards:* Ebert Prize, 67 & 69. *Prof Exp:* From asst prof to assoc prof pharm, Med Col Va, 60-64; from asst prof to assoc prof, Univ Mich, Ann Arbor, 64-72; prof pharmaceut & chmn sect, Univ Conn, 72-89, emer prof, 89-93. *Concurrent Pos:* Consult, Eli Lilly Labs, 69, Pfizer Labs, 73-83, Northeastern Univ, 75, Ortho Labs, 78, Ives Labs, 79-84, SK&F Labs, 81-82, Bristol Myers, 83, Lederle Labs, 84, Sando Labs, 85, Merck Labs, 87, Warner Lambert Labs, 88, Oramed Labs, 89, 92-93 & Cambridge Neurosci, 93; chmn, Parmaceut Sect, Am Pharmaceut Asn Acad Parmaceut Sci, 69, Pharmaceut sci, AAAS, 83 & Pharmaceut Sect, Am Asn Cols Pharm, 85; vis prof, Univ Wis, 74, Univ Minn, 76 & Univ Assiut, Egypt, 83 & Univ Monsurh, Egypt, 88; mem, Sci Bd, Menley James Labs, 82-85. *Mem:* Fel AAAS; Am Chem Soc; fel Am Pharmaceut Asn Acad Pharmaceut Sci; Am Asn Cols Pharm; fel Am Asn Pharaceut Scientists. *Res:* Drug degradation and stabilization; amorphous-polymorphic drugs; solution drug interactions; transport phenomena; rheology; drug solubility and dissolution rates; biodegradable polymers as drug delivery systems; thermal analysis; drug formulations; solid state transformation kinetics; interfacial phenomena; reactions in polyphasic systems. *Mailing Add:* Col Pharm Long Island Univ 75 Dekalb At Univ Plaza Brooklyn NY 11201. Fax: 718-780-4586

SIMONEN, THOMAS CHARLES, PLASMA PHYSICS. *Current Pos:* DIR, DII-D PROG, GEN ATOMICS, 88- *Personal Data:* b Munising, Mich, Aug 25, 38; m 64, Candace McDonnell; c Kathrina & Brenda. *Educ:* Mich Technol Univ, BS, 60; Stanford Univ, MS, 64, PhD(elec eng), 66. *Prof Exp:* Mem tech staff elec eng, Hughes Aircraft Co, 60-62; res asst plasma physics, Garching, Ger, 67-68; res assoc plasma physics, Plasma Physics Lab, Princeton Univ, 68-70; exp physics prog leader, Lawrence Livermore Nat Lab, 70-88. *Mem:* Fel Am Phys Soc; AAAS. *Res:* Plasma confinement of magnetic fusion plasmas. *Mailing Add:* Gen Atomics 13-255 PO Box 85608 San Diego CA 92138

SIMONI, ROBERT DARIO, BIOCHEMISTRY. *Current Pos:* from asst prof to assoc prof, 71-81, PROF BIOL SCI, STANFORD UNIV, 81- *Personal Data:* b San Jose, Calif, Aug 18, 39; m 61; c 3. *Educ:* San Jose State Col, BA, 62; Univ Calif, Davis, PhD(biochem), 66. *Prof Exp:* Fel biochem, Johns Hopkins Univ, 66-70. *Mem:* AAAS; Am Soc Biol Chemists. *Res:* Structure and function of biological membranes; mechanisms of solute transport; regulation of cholesterol metabolism. *Mailing Add:* Dept Biol Sci Stanford Univ Stanford CA 94305-5020. Fax: 650-725-5807; E-Mail: fa.rds@forsythe.stanford.edu

SIMONIS, GEORGE JEROME, MILLIMETER WAVE MATERIALS, INFRARED LASERS. *Current Pos:* RES PHYSICIST LASER RES, HARRY DIAMOND LABS, DEPT ARMY, 72- *Personal Data:* b Wisconsin Rapids, Wis, Nov 9, 46; m 68, Toni Bullai. *Educ:* Univ Wis-Platteville, BS, 68; Kans State Univ, PhD(physics), 73. *Mem:* Am Phys Soc; Optical Soc Am; Inst Elec & Electronics Engrs; Int Soc Optical Eng. *Res:* Infrared lasers; nonlinear optical interactions; diode lasers; near-millimeter waves; integrated optics; vertical cavity lasers. *Mailing Add:* 15230 Baughman Dr Silver Spring MD 20906

SIMONIS, JOHN CHARLES, FLUID STRUCTURAL INTERACTION, REVERSE ENGINEERING OF PARTS FOR COMMERCIAL & MILITARY SYSTEMS. *Current Pos:* PRIN ENGR, SOUTHWEST RES INST, 80- *Personal Data:* b Marion, Ohio, July 24, 40; m 63, Millicent Mills; c Charles, William & Theresa. *Educ:* Case Inst Technol, BS, 62; Ga Inst Technol, MS, 64, PhD(eng mech), 68. *Prof Exp:* Teaching asst eng mech, Ga Inst Technol, 63-67; prin engr, Babock & Wilcox, 67-80; instr math, San Antonio Community Col, 83-87. *Concurrent Pos:* Adj prof mech engr, Univ Tex, San Antonio, 87- *Mem:* fel Am Soc Mech Engrs. *Res:* Evaluate the effects of vibrating forces on structures, buildings and machines; developed unique technique to reverse engineer mechanical components in commercial or military systems. *Mailing Add:* 5118 Timber Trace St San Antonio TX 78250. Fax: 210-522-5122

SIMONOFF, ROBERT, ORGANIC CHEMISTRY. *Current Pos:* RETIRED. *Personal Data:* b Baltimore, Md, Feb 27, 20; m 43; c 2. *Educ:* Univ Md, BS, 40, MS, 42, PhD(chem), 45. *Prof Exp:* Asst biochem, Sch Dent, Univ Md, 41-45, fel pharmacol, Sch Med, 49-50; org chemist, Gen Elec Co, 45-49; res chemist, Nat Aniline Div, Allied Chem & Dye Corp, 50-51; chief chemist, William H Rorer, Inc, 51-54; sr res chemist, L Sonneborn Sons, Inc, 54-60, asst supt, Sulfonate Dept, Sonneborn Chem & Refining Corp, 60, supt, 60-65; dir sulfonate res, Sonneborn Div, Witco Chem Co, Inc, Pa, 65-68, tech dir, Sonneborn Div, 68-80, sr div scientist, Sonneborn Div, Witco Chem Corp, 80-89. *Mem:* Am Chem Soc; fel Am Inst Chemists; Am Soc Testing & Mat. *Res:* Petroleum sulfonates; hydrogenations; synthetic medicinals; mineral oil; petrolatum. *Mailing Add:* 13-3 Tamaron Dr Waldwick NJ 07463-1160

SIMONS, BARBARA BLUESTEIN, DETERMINISTIC SCHEDULING THEORY, GRAPH THEORETIC ALGORITHMS & TECHNOLOGY POLICY. *Current Pos:* Res staff mem, 80-92, RESEARCHER & SR PROGRAMMER, IBM, SANTA TERESA LAB, 92-, BUS & RES STRATEGIST, 96- *Personal Data:* b Boston, Mass, Jan 26, 41; div; c 3. *Educ:* Univ Calif, Berkeley, PhD(comput sci), 81. *Honors & Awards:* Norbert Wiener Award, Prof & Social Responsibility Comput, 92. *Concurrent Pos:* Vis fac, Univ Calif, Santa Cruz, 84; mem, Grad Fel Eval Panel Comput Sci, Nat Res Coun, 85-87 & Res Initiation Awards Panel, NSF, 89; ed, Fault Tolerant Distributed Comput, Springer-Verlag Lect Notes Comput Sci, 90; chair, US Pub Policy Comt, Asn Comput Mach, 93. *Mem:* Fel Asn Comput Mach (secy, 90-92); fel AAAS. *Res:* Algorithms and graph theory, with an emphasis on scheduling and on optimization problems arising from parallelizing compilers; fault tolerant distributed computing; compiler optimization. *Mailing Add:* 770 Homer Ave Palo Alto CA 94301. Fax: 408-256-2069; E-Mail: simons@acm.org

SIMONS, DANIEL J, MICROBIOLOGY, INVERTEBRATE PHYSIOLOGY. *Current Pos:* from instr to assoc prof, 69-80, PROF ZOOL, MONTGOMERY COL, 80-, CHMN, DEPT BIOL, 80- *Personal Data:* b Rochester, NY, Jan 17, 40; m 67. *Educ:* Univ Rochester, AB, 61, MS, 63, PhD(biol), 68. *Prof Exp:* Res assoc biol, Univ Rochester, 68; sr res microbiologist, Biospherics, Inc, 68-69. *Mem:* AAAS; Am Soc Microbiol; Am Soc Zool. *Res:* Innovative learning experiences in teaching zoological sciences. *Mailing Add:* Dept Biol Montgomery Col Rockville MD 20850-1101

SIMONS, DARYL B, HYDRAULIC ENGINEERING. *Current Pos:* pres & prin engr, Simons, Li & Assocs Inc, 81-84, PRIN ENGR, SIMONS & ASSOC INC, 84- *Personal Data:* b Payson, Utah, Feb 12, 28; m 44. *Educ:* Utah State Univ, BS, 47, MS, 48; Colo State Univ, PhD(civil eng), 57. *Honors & Awards:* J C Stevens Award, Am Soc Civil Engrs, 60, Croes Award, 64, co-recipient Karl Emil Hilgard Hydraul Prize, 79, Hunter Rouse Award, 91. *Prof Exp:* Design engr, McGraw Constructors & Engrs, 48; prof civil eng, Univ Wyo, 49-57; proj chief fluid mech res, US Geol Surv, 57-63; sect chief eng, Colo State Univ, 63-65, assoc dean res, 65-77, prof civil eng, 63-83. *Concurrent Pos:* Consult, Int Boundary Water Comn, US Bur Pub Rds & Corps Engrs. *Mem:* Am Soc Civil Engrs; Int Asn Hydraul Res; Am Geophys Union; Int Comn Irrig & Drainage; Sigma Xi. *Res:* Hydrology, hydraulics, flood control, river geomorphology, sediment transport; mathematical modeling, expert systems, water quality; environmental analysis, navigation, routing pollutants litigation; author of over 425 papers, co-author of 5 text books. *Mailing Add:* Simons & Assoc Inc 3538 John F Kennedy Pkwy 1 Ft Collins CO 80525-2615. Fax: 970-223-9958

SIMONS, DAVID STUART, SECONDARY ION MASS SPECTROMETRY, SEMICONDUCTOR MATERIALS CHARACTERIZATION. *Current Pos:* res physicist, 79-94, LEADER, ANALYTICAL MICROS GROUP, NAT INST STAND & TECHNOL, 94- *Personal Data:* b Columbus, Ohio, July 29, 45; m 76, Rachel Cropsey; c Daniel & Julia. *Educ:* Carnegie-Mellon Univ, BS, 67; Univ Ill, MS, 70, PhD(physics), 73. *Honors & Awards:* Bronze Medal, US Dept Com, 84, Silver Medal, 94. *Prof Exp:* Res assoc mass spectrometry, Univ Ill, 73-76; lead chemist, Knolls Atomic Power Lab, 76-79. *Concurrent Pos:* Comt E42, Am Soc Testing & Mat. *Mem:* Am Soc Mass Spectrometry; Microbeam Anal Soc (secy, 93-95); Am Vacuum Soc; Am Soc Testing & Mat. *Res:* Applications of secondary ion mass spectrometry and laser microprobe mass spectrometry to chemical and isotopic analysis of advanced materials and particles; depth-profiling of dopant elements and impurities in semiconductor materials. *Mailing Add:* Bldg 222 Rm A113 Nat Inst Stand & Technol Gaithersburg MD 20899-0001. E-Mail: david.simons@nist.gov

SIMONS, EDWARD LOUIS, ENVIRONMENTAL CHEMISTRY. *Current Pos:* RETIRED. *Personal Data:* b New York, NY, May 9, 21; m 43; c 2. *Educ:* City Col New York, BS, 41; NY Univ, MS, 43, PhD(phys chem), 45. *Honors & Awards:* Award, Nat Asn Corrosion Engrs, 56. *Prof Exp:* Asst chemist, NY Univ, 41-44; asst group leader, Kellex Corp, NJ, 44-45; res scientist, Carbide & Carbon Chem Corp, NY, 45-46; from instr to asst prof chem, Rutgers Univ, 46-51; res assoc, Gen Elec Res & Develop Ctr, 51-68, mgr fuel cells prog, 68-69, inorg chemist, 69-71, mgr, Environ Info Ctr, 71-73, mgr Environ Protection Oper, 73-82. *Concurrent Pos:* Environ consult, 85- *Mem:* Am Chem Soc. *Res:* Fuel cells; corrosion; phase equilibria; thermogravimetry. *Mailing Add:* 354 S Manning Blvd Albany NY 12208-1733

SIMONS, ELIZABETH REIMAN, BIOPHYSICAL CHEMISTRY. *Current Pos:* assoc prof biochem, 72-78, PROF BIOCHEM, SCH MED, BOSTON UNIV, 78- *Personal Data:* b Vienna, Austria, Sept 1, 29; nat US; m 51, Harold L; c 2. *Educ:* Cooper Union, BChE, 50; Yale Univ, MS, 51, PhD(phys chem), 54. *Prof Exp:* Asst, Biophys Div, Dept Physics, Yale Univ, 50-53; res chemist, Tech Opers, Inc, 53-54; instr chem, Wellesley Col, 54-57; from res asst to res assoc path, Children's Cancer Res Found, 57-63; res assoc biol chem, Harvard Med Sch, 63-65, lectr, 65-72. *Concurrent Pos:* Tutor, Harvard Univ, 71-94. *Mem:* Am Soc Biol Chemists; Am Chem Soc; Biophys Soc; Am Soc Hemat; Am Heart Asn; Soc Cell Biol. *Res:* Protein structure; hemostasis and platelet interactions; cell membrane biophysics; neutrophil biochemistry; neurosciences. *Mailing Add:* 117 Chestnut St West Newton MA 02165. *Fax:* 617-638-5339; *E-Mail:* simons@med-biochm.bu.edu

SIMONS, ELWYN L, VERTEBRATE PALEONTOLOGY, PRIMATOLOGY. *Current Pos:* prof anthrop & anat, 77-82, DIR, PRIMATE CTR, DUKE UNIV, 77-, JAMES B DUKE PROF BIOL ANTHROP & ANAT, 82- *Personal Data:* b Lawrence, Kans, July 14, 30; m 72, Friderum Ankel; c Cornelia, Verne & David. *Educ:* Rice Univ, BS, 53; Princeton Univ, MA, 55, PhD, 56; Univ Col, Oxford, DPhil, 59; Yale Univ, MA, 67. *Honors & Awards:* Anadale Mem Medal, Asiatic Soc Calcutta, 73; Alexander von Humboldt Sr Scientist Award, WGer, 75 & 76. *Prof Exp:* Lectr, Dept Geol, Princeton Univ, 59; asst prof zool, Univ Pa, 59-61; appointment fac head, Div Vert Paleont, Yale Peabody Mus, 60-77; prof paleont, Dept Geol & Geophys, Yale Univ, 67. *Concurrent Pos:* Gen George Marshall scholar, Oxford Univ, 56-59, Boise Fund fel, 58-59; res assoc, Am Mus Natural Hist, 59-76; vis assoc prof geol & cur vert paleont, Yale Univ, 60-61; R C Hunt Mem fel anthrop, Viking Found, 65; mem, Grad Res Panel, NSF, 90- *Mem:* Nat Acad Sci; Am Soc Zool; Am Asn Phys Anthrop; Brit Soc Study Human Biol; Am Soc Primatology; Int Primatological Soc; Soc Vert Paleont; Soc Study Evolution; Sigma Xi; AAAS. *Res:* Primatology; primate and human paleontology, early mammalian evolution and anatomy, particularly Pantodonta and related subungulates; primate husbandry and behavioral evolution of prosimians; fossil prosimians; paleocene of North America and Europe; earliest apes and monkeys of Africa; late Tertiary Old World apes, including human origins; author of various publications. *Mailing Add:* Duke Primate Ctr 3705 Erwin Rd Durham NC 27705. *Fax:* 919-490-5394

SIMONS, FRANK, GEOLOGY. *Current Pos:* RETIRED. *Personal Data:* b Detroit, Mich, Nov 14, 17. *Educ:* Univ Calif, Los Angeles, BA, 40; Stanford Univ, PhD(geol), 51. *Prof Exp:* Res geologist, US Geol Surv, 41-88, consult res geologist, 88-89. *Mem:* Geol Soc Am; Soc Eng Geologists; AAAS. *Mailing Add:* 9005 W Second Ave Lakewood CO 80226

SIMONS, GALE GENE, NUCLEAR ENGINEERING. *Current Pos:* PROF NUCLEAR ENG, KANS STATE UNIV, MANHATTAN, 77-, PROF ELEC & COMPUT ENG, COL ENG, 88- *Personal Data:* b Kingman, Kans, Sept 25, 39; m 66, Barbara I Rinkel; c Curtis D. *Educ:* Kans State Univ, BS, 62, MS, 64, PhD, 68. *Prof Exp:* Engr, Argonne Nat Lab, Idaho Falls, 68-77, mgr fast source reactor & head exp support group, 72-77. *Concurrent Pos:* Numerous grants from fed agencies, 79-; consult pvt & fed agencies, 83-; presidential lectr, Kans State Univ, 83-, career counr, 84- & bd dirs, Res Found, 88-; comt mem, Gov's Energy Policy Comt, Kans, 92- *Mem:* AAAS; Inst Elec & Electronics Engrs; Am Nuclear Soc; Health Physics Soc; Am Soc Eng Educ. *Res:* Radiation dosimetry. *Mailing Add:* Durland Hall Rm 261 Kans State Univ Manhattan KS 66506-5103

SIMONS, GENE R, MANAGEMENT ENGINEERING. *Current Pos:* instr, 66-69, asst prof, 69-70, curriculum chmn mgt eng, 71-77, ASSOC PROF MGT ENG, RENSSELAER POLYTECH INST, 70-, DIR INDUST & MGT ENG, 77- *Personal Data:* b Staten Island, NY, July 19, 36; m 61; c 4. *Educ:* Rensselaer Polytech Inst, BS, 57, PhD(mgt sci), 69; Stevens Inst Technol, MS, 61. *Prof Exp:* Planning engr indust eng, Western Elec Co, 57-61; mem staff indust eng, Am Cyanamid Co, 61-62; asst prof indust eng, New Haven Col, 62-64, chmn, 64-66. *Concurrent Pos:* Curric chmn mgt eng, Rensselaer Polytech Inst, 71-77; Pres, Gene Simons, Inc, 80-; vpres, Workshops, Menands, NY, 81-83. *Mem:* Inst Indust Engrs (vpres, 82-83); Proj Mgt Inst; Am Soc Eng Educ; Sigma Xi. *Res:* Management systems; maintenance planning and control. *Mailing Add:* Dept Decision Sci Rensellaer Polytech Main Campus 110 Eighth St Rm 7019 CII Troy NY 12180-3520

SIMONS, HAROLD LEE, PHYSICAL CHEMISTRY. *Current Pos:* RETIRED. *Personal Data:* b New York, NY, Aug 25, 26; m 51, Elizabeth Reiman; c 2. *Educ:* Princeton Univ, AB, 49; Yale Univ, MS, 51, PhD(chem), 53. *Prof Exp:* Res chemist, Kendall Co, 53-70, group leader, 70-74, sr res assoc, 75-94. *Concurrent Pos:* Lectr, Div Continuing Educ, Boston Univ, 62-65. *Mem:* Am Chem Soc; Soc Rheology; Am Phys Soc. *Res:* Characterization of polymers; physical properties of polymers. *Mailing Add:* 117 Chestnut St West Newton MA 02165

SIMONS, JOHN NORTON, ENTOMOLOGY. *Current Pos:* PRES JMS FLOWER FARMS, INC, 77- *Personal Data:* b Lennox, SDak, Aug 13, 26; m 48; c 4. *Educ:* Univ Calif, PhD(entom), 53. *Prof Exp:* Asst virologist, Everglades Exp Sta, Univ Fla, 53-59; sr entomologist, Stanford Res Inst, 59-70; sr scientist, Ciba-Geigy Corp, 70-77. *Concurrent Pos:* Vis prof entom, Univ Calif, Berkeley, 74-75. *Mem:* Entom Soc Am; Am Phytopath Soc. *Res:* Insect transmission of plant virus diseases; plant virus disease control. *Mailing Add:* 1105 25th Ave Vero Beach FL 32960

SIMONS, KAI LENNART, CELL BIOLOGY. *Current Pos:* GROUP LEADER, EUROP MOLECULAR BIOL LAB, 75-, PROG COORDR, 82-; HON PROF, UNIV HEIDELBERG, 84- *Personal Data:* b Helsinki, Finland, May 24, 38. *Educ:* Univ Helsinki, MD, 64. *Honors & Awards:* Fed Europ Biochem Socs Prize, 75; Jahre Prize, 91. *Prof Exp:* Postdoctoral fel, Rockefeller Univ, 65-67; researcher, Univ Helsinki, 67-75, prof, 76. *Concurrent Pos:* Ed, Current Opinion Cell Biol. *Mem:* Foreign assoc Nat Acad Sci; Europ Molecular Biol Orgn. *Mailing Add:* Europ Molecular Biol Lab 069012 Heidelberg Germany

SIMONS, MAYRANT, JR, ELECTRICAL ENGINEERING. *Current Pos:* SR ENGR, SEMICONDUCTOR RES CTR, RES TRIANGLE INST, 66- *Personal Data:* b Charleston, SC, Aug 10, 36; m 59; c 3. *Educ:* Clemson Univ, BS, 58; Duke Univ, MS, 64, PhD(elec eng), 68. *Prof Exp:* Mem tech staff eng, Bell Tel Labs, NC, 61-66. *Res:* Investigation of nuclear radiation effects on semiconductor materials, devices and circuits; semiconductors. *Mailing Add:* Res Triangle Inst Box 12194 Research Triangle Park NC 27709

SIMONS, ROBERT W, CONTROL GENE EXPRESSION, MOBILE GENETIC ELEMENTS. *Current Pos:* asst prof, 85-90, ASSOC PROF GENETICS, UNIV CALIF, LOS ANGELES, 90- *Personal Data:* b Rockford, Ill, Jan 28, 45; m 74, Elizabeth L Crum; c Sarah C & Rebecca A. *Educ:* Univ Ill, Urbana, BS, 72; Univ Calif, Irvine, PhD(molecular biol), 80. *Prof Exp:* Teaching asst genetics & biochem, Univ Calif, Irvine, 77-80; lectr genetics, Harvard Univ, 80-85. *Concurrent Pos:* Damon Runyon Walter Winchel fel, Harvard Univ, 80-82, Leukemia Soc spec fel, 83-85; mem, Molecular Biol Inst, 85-; Am Cancer Soc fac researcher, Univ Calif, Los Angeles, 86-89. *Mem:* Genetics Soc Am; AAAS; Am Soc Microbiol; Sigma Xi. *Res:* Molecular genetics of the control of gene expression with emphasis on mobile genetic elements and the determinants of RNA function, stability and translation. *Mailing Add:* Dept Microbiol & Molecular Genetics Univ Calif 405 Hilgard Ave Los Angeles CA 90024-1301. *Fax:* 310-206-5231

SIMONS, ROGER ALAN, COMPUTER ALGORITHMS. *Current Pos:* PROF MATH & COMPUT SCI, RI COL, 81- *Personal Data:* b Detroit, Mich, May 11, 43; m 74, Patricia Uchill; c Ben Calica & Elissa. *Educ:* Univ Calif, Los Angeles, AB, 64; Univ Calif, Berkeley, MA, 66, PhD(math), 72; Brown Univ, Providence, ScM, 83. *Prof Exp:* From instr to assoc prof math, Univ Wis-Green Bay, 70-81. *Concurrent Pos:* From vis asst prof to vis prof, 75-88, vis lectr, Univ Hawaii, 77, 85, 95 & 97; consult, Appln Prog, US Fish & Wildlife Agency, 77, Woodbury Comput Assocs, Paramus, NJ, 83-84, Subcomt Children & Families, RI State Legis, 86. *Mem:* Asn Comput Mach; Asn Symbolic Logic; Am Math Soc; Sigma Xi; Inst Elec & Electronics Engrs Comput Soc. *Res:* Parallel and sequential algorithms, complexity theory; boolean algebra and mathematical logic; applying mathematics to philosophical problems; theoretical aspects of computer design. *Mailing Add:* Dept Math & CS RI Col Providence RI 02908. *E-Mail:* rsimons@ric.edu

SIMONS, ROY KENNETH, HORTICULTURE, ABSCISSION. *Current Pos:* instr pomol, 51-53, from asst prof to prof hort, 53-87, EMER PROF HORT, UNIV ILL, URBANA, 87- *Personal Data:* b Kincheloe, WVa, Dec 26, 20; m 53, Frances Jensen; c 2. *Educ:* Univ WVa, BS & MS, 47; Mich State Univ, PhD, 51. *Honors & Awards:* Stark Award, Am Soc Hort Sci, 67, Promotion Incentive Award, 77 & 78; Wilder Silver Medal, Am Pomol Soc, Dedicated Serv Award, Shepard Award; Res & Serv Award, Int Dwarf Fruit & Tree Asn. *Prof Exp:* Pomologist, Univ Del, 47-48; asst, Mich State Univ, 48-51. *Concurrent Pos:* Ed, Fruit Varieties J, Am Pomol Soc, 72-84; secy, Rontotoik Res Found, 77-87. *Mem:* Fel AAAS; Fel Am Soc Hort Sci; Int Soc Hort Sci; Int Dwarf Fruit Tree Asn; Am Pomol Soc. *Res:* Nutrition of deciduous fruit trees; soil moisture conservation to maintain optimum production of quality fruit; morphological and anatomical development of deciduous fruits; orchard cultural management practices in relation to dwarfing rootstocks; growth and development of fruit; scanning electron microscopy on malus and pranus plant development. *Mailing Add:* 1517 Alma Dr Champaign IL 61820

SIMONS, SAMUEL STONEY, JR, MOLECULAR ENDOCRINOLOGY, STEROID HORMONES. *Current Pos:* staff fel, 75-78, sr staff fel, 78-80, RES CHEMIST ENDOCRINOL, NAT INST, DIABETES & DIGESTIVE & KIDNEY DIS, NIH, 80-, CHIEF, STEROID HORMONES SECT, 85- *Personal Data:* b Philadelphia, Pa, Sept 13, 45; m 70; c 2. *Educ:* Princeton Univ, AB, 67; Harvard Univ, MA, 69, PhD(chem), 72. *Prof Exp:* Fel molecular biol, Univ Calif, San Francisco, 72-75. *Mem:* Am Chem Soc; Am Soc Biochem & Molecular Biol. *Res:* Mechanism of action of steroid hormones; steroid-receptor interactions; affinity labelling of steroid receptors; steroid control of gene transcription; glucocorticoid and antiglucocorticoid steroids. *Mailing Add:* Nat Inst Diabetes & Digestive & Kidney Dis NIH Bldg 8 Rm B2A-07 Bethesda MD 20892. *Fax:* 301-402-3572; *E-Mail:* steroids@helix.nih.gov

SIMONS, SANFORD L(AWRENCE), METALLURGY. *Current Pos:* dir med eng, 66-72, CONSULT MED ENGR, SCH MED, UNIV COLO, 72-; PRES, SIENCO, INC, 72- *Personal Data:* b New York, NY, Apr 10, 22; m 47; c 5. *Educ:* Univ Mo, BS, 44. *Prof Exp:* Res engr, Battelle Mem Inst, 44; jr scientist, Manhattan Dist Proj, Los Alamos Sci Lab, 44-46; consult engr, Alldredge & Simons Labs, 46-48; asst, US Army Rocket Prog, Denver, 48-50; consult engr, 50-53; design engr, Heckethorn Mfg Co, 53-55; chief develop engr, Metron Instrument Co, 56-57; consult engr, 57-66. *Mem:* Am Soc Metals; Am Soc Testing & Mat; Nat Soc Prof Engrs; Am Inst Mining, Metall & Petrol Engrs. *Res:* Metallurgy of copper-manganese systems and plutonium; development of rocketborne spectrographs; automatic perfusion apparatus; surgical prosthetics; medical and bio-engineering. *Mailing Add:* SIENCO 9188 S Turkey Creek Rd Morrison CO 80465

SIMONS, STEPHEN, MATHEMATICS. *Current Pos:* from asst prof to assoc prof, 65-73, chmn dept math, 75-77, 88-89, PROF MATH, UNIV CALIF, SANTA BARBARA, 73- *Personal Data:* b London, Eng, Aug 11. 38; m 63; c Mark. *Educ:* Cambridge Univ, BA, 59, PhD(math), 62. *Prof Exp:* Instr math, Univ BC, 62-63; res fel math, Peterhouse, Cambridge Univ, 63-64; asst prof, Univ BC, 64-65. *Concurrent Pos:* NSF res grant, 65-76; mem bd dir, Calif Educ Comput Consortium, 74-75; mem bd trustees, Math Sci Res Inst, 88-94. *Mem:* Am Math Soc; Inst Opers Res & Mgt Sci. *Res:* Functional analysis, linear and non-linear. *Mailing Add:* Dept Math Univ Calif Santa Barbara CA 93106-3080

SIMONS, WILLIAM HADDOCK, MATHEMATICS. *Current Pos:* RETIRED. *Personal Data:* b Vancouver, BC, Dec 2, 14; m 44; c 4. *Educ:* Univ BC, BA, 35, MA, 37; Univ Calif, PhD(math), 47. *Prof Exp:* From asst prof to assoc prof math, Univ BC, 46-70; prof math, Ore State Univ, 70-82. *Concurrent Pos:* Lectr, Khaki Col Can, Eng; meteorologist, Can Meteorol Serv. *Mem:* Am Math Soc; Math Asn Am; Can Math Cong; London Math Soc. *Res:* Fourier coefficients of modular functions. *Mailing Add:* 3295 SW Chintimini St Corvallis OR 97333

SIMONS, WILLIAM HARRIS, MATHEMATICS. *Current Pos:* Asst prof, 69-74, assoc prof, 74-79, PROF MATH, WVA UNIV, 79- *Personal Data:* b Norwich, Conn, Apr 14, 38. *Educ:* Carnegie-Mellon Univ, BS, 61, MS, 65, PhD(math), 69. *Concurrent Pos:* Consult, US Bur Mines, 66-75 & US Dept Energy, 76-80. *Mem:* Soc Indust & Appl Math; Math Asn Am; Sigma Xi. *Res:* Disconjugacy of ordinary differential equations; magnetohydrodynamic generators and power plants; magnetic and electrostatic filtration; hydrogasification of coal to pipeline gas; biomechanics. *Mailing Add:* Dept Math WVa Univ PO Box 6310 Morgantown WV 26506

SIMONSEN, DAVID RAYMOND, PHYSICAL CHEMISTRY. *Current Pos:* RETIRED. *Personal Data:* b Clay Co, Nebr, July 29, 16; m 47, Lillie Fuller; c Karen (Ward), Kathleen (Wallace),David Jr, John & Laurie (Cuddington). *Educ:* Dana Col, BA, 38; Univ Nebr, MA, 43, PhD(chem), 44. *Prof Exp:* Prin & instr high schs, Nebr, 38-41; teaching asst, Univ Nebr, 41-44; res chemist, Eastman Kodak Co, 44-52, asst suprv, 52-64, suprv, 64-81. *Concurrent Pos:* Chmn int comt, Contamination Control Soc, 76-78. *Mem:* Am Chem Soc; Instrument Soc Am; fel Inst Environ Sci; Sigma Xi. *Res:* Contamination control; instrumental gas analysis. *Mailing Add:* 106 White Oak Lane Greenwood SC 29646-9226

SIMONSEN, DONALD HOWARD, BIOCHEMISTRY. *Current Pos:* from asst prof to assoc prof chem, Calif State Univ, Long Beach, 56-63, chmn, Dept Phys Sci & Math, 60-61, chmn, Dept Chem, 61-64, prof chem, 63-80, assoc dean instr, 66-67, acad vpres, 67-69, actg pres, 69-70, EMER PROF CHEM, 80- *Personal Data:* b Portland, Ore, June 12, 21; m 47; c 4. *Educ:* Reed Col, BA, 43; Ore State Col, MA, 45; Ind Univ, PhD(chem), 51. *Prof Exp:* Res assoc zool, Ind Univ, 47-50, fel, 51-52; res scientist virol, Upjohn Co, 52-56. *Mem:* AAAS; Am Chem Soc; fel Am Inst Chem; Brit Biochem Soc; NY Acad Sci. *Res:* Growth factors for guinea pigs; tissue metabolism; salt and nitrogen metabolism in surgical patients; methods of blood volume determination; human plasma and plasma substitutes in treatment of clinical hypoproteinemia; biochemical genetics of Paramecia; microrespiration techniques; chemotherapy of virus disease. *Mailing Add:* 6350 El Paseo Ct Long Beach CA 90815

SIMONSEN, STANLEY HAROLD, CHEMISTRY. *Current Pos:* asst chem, 49-53, assoc prof, 53-63, assoc dir, Anal Chem Res Lab, 51-52, PROF CHEM, UNIV TEX, AUSTIN, 63- *Personal Data:* b Missoula, Mont, Aug 25, 18; m 43; c 4. *Educ:* Iowa State Teachers Col, AB, 40; Univ Ill, MS, 47, PhD(chem), 49. *Prof Exp:* Anal chemist, Vanadium Corp Am, 40-44; asst analytical chem, Univ Ill, 46-49. *Concurrent Pos:* Instr, Pa State Col, 43-44. *Mem:* Am Chem Soc. *Res:* Structural investigations with x-rays; x-ray diffraction; instrumental analytical methods; investigation of metallo-organic compounds useful in analytical chemistry. *Mailing Add:* 1800 E 38 1/2 St Austin TX 78722

SIMONSON, JOHN C, GEOLOGY. *Current Pos:* HYDRO-GEOLOGIST, ENVIRON RESOURCE MGT INC, 87- *Personal Data:* b Washington, DC, Nov 16, 60. *Educ:* Col William & Mary, BS, 82; Univ Tenn, MS, 85. *Prof Exp:* Explor geologist, Amoco Prod Co, 85-87. *Concurrent Pos:* Res fel, Oak Ridge Nat Lab, 85-87. *Mem:* Geol Soc Am. *Mailing Add:* 2124 S Hicks St Philadelphia PA 19145

SIMONSON, LLOYD GRANT, MICROBIOLOGY, IMMUNOBIOLOGY. *Current Pos:* Investr, 68-88, CHIEF SCIENTIST, NAVAL DENT RES INST, 88-; ADJ PROF, DENT SCH, NORTHWESTERN UNIV, 90- *Personal Data:* b San Jose, Calif, Dec 1, 43; m 68, Katherine Peck. *Educ:* Western Ill Univ, BA, 66; Ill State Univ, MS, 68, PhD(microbiol), 74; Roosevelt Univ, MBA, 84. *Honors & Awards:* Outstanding Young Investr Award, Am Acad Dent Res, 79. *Concurrent Pos:* Consult, Chicago Med Sch, 77-80; prog chmn, microbiol-immunol group Int Asn Dent Res-Am Asn Dent Res, Chicago Sect, 84-87, treas, 86-87, vpres, 87-88, pres, 88-89; grant reviewer, Med Res Coun, Can, NIH, Oral Biol & Med Study Sect. *Mem:* Am Soc Microbiol; Int Asn Dent Res; Am Asn Dent Res; Sigma Xi. *Res:* Monoclonal antibodies; enzyme-linked immunoassay; affinity chromatography; development of immunodiagnostics; hybridoma technique; dental caries therapeutics; enzymology and molecular biology; cell mediated immunity and cancer; immobilized enzymes and intermolecular conjugation; bacterial adherence to surfaces and adherence-inhibition; surveys for microbial enzymes and fermentation; fluorescence immunoassay; diagnostics; prognostics. *Mailing Add:* Naval Dent Res Inst 2701 Sheridan Rd Bldg 1-H NTC Great Lakes IL 60088-5259. *E-Mail:* drg1lgs@grl10.med.navy.mil

SIMONYI, CHARLES, COMPUTER SOFTWARE. *Current Pos:* mgr, 81-91, CHIEF ARCHITECT, MICROSOFT RES CORP, 91- *Personal Data:* b Budapest, Hungary. *Educ:* Univ Calif, Berkeley, BS, 72; Stanford Univ, PhD(comput sci), 76. *Prof Exp:* Developer, Xerox Palo Alto Res Ctr, 72-80. *Mem:* Nat Acad Eng. *Res:* New approaches in programming technology; program representation where new abstraction mechanisms can be introduced without invalidating legacy code. *Mailing Add:* Microsoft Res Corp 1 Microsoft Way Redmond WA 98052-6399

SIMOPOULOS, ARTEMIS PANAGEOTIS, PEDIATRICS, ENDOCRINOLOGY. *Current Pos:* dir, 89-90, PRES, CTR GENETICS, NUTRIT & HEALTH, INC, 90- *Personal Data:* b Kampos-Avias, Greece, Apr 3, 33; US citizen; m 57, Alan Lee Pinkerson; c 3. *Educ:* Barnard Col, Columbia Univ, BA, 52; Boston Univ, MD, 56; Am Bd Pediat, dipl, 64. *Honors & Awards:* Presidential Award, Columbia-Presby Med Ctr, 93. *Prof Exp:* Spec lectr pediat, Sch Med, Ewha Woman's Univ, Seoul, Korea, 58-59; NIH fel hemat, 60-61; asst prof, Sch Med, George Washington Univ, 62-67; staff pediatrician, Nat Heart & Lung Inst, 68-71; prof assoc, Div Med Sci, Nat Acad Sci-Nat Res Coun, 71-74, actg exec secy, 74-75, exec secy, 75-76; co-chmn & exec secy, Joint Subcomt, Human Nutrit Res, Off Sci & Technol Policy, Exec Off of the President, 79-83; chief develop biol & nutrit br, Nat Inst Child Health & Human Develop, 77, vchmn & exec secy nutrit coord comt, Off of Dir, 77-78; chmn nutrit coord comt & spec asst for coordr nutrit res, Off of Dir, NIH, 78-86; dir, Div Nutrit Sci, Int Life Sci Inst Res Found, 87-88. *Concurrent Pos:* Mem acad staff pediat, Children's Hosp of DC, 62-67; mem assoc staff, Nursery Serv, 67-71; dir nurseries, George Washington Univ Hosp, 65-67; co-chmn perinatal comt, Working Party Biol Aspects Prev Ment Retardation for DC, 67-68; clin asst prof pediat, Sch Med, George Washington Univ, 67-71; mem bd, Capitol Head Start, Inc, Washington, DC, 68-70; consult, Endocrinol Br, Nat Heart & Lung Inst, 71-78; liaison, Div Med Sci, Nat Acad Sci-Nat Res Coun to Am Acad Pediat Comt Drugs, 71-76; mem res adv comt, Maternity Ctr Assoc, New York, 72-; exec dir bd, Maternal, Child & Family Health Res, 74-76; adv & mem, US deleg, Ad Hoc Comt Food & Nutrit Policy, UN Food & Agr Orgn, 78, mem, US deleg, Meeting on Infant & Young Child Feeding, WHO-UNICEF, 79, tech adv, US Govt Deleg, Meeting on the 3rd Draft Int Code Mkt Breast Milk Substitutes, WHO, 80; contrib ed, Nutrit Rev, 79-86; consult ed, Nutrit Res, 83-, Ann Internal Med, 84- & J AMA, 85-; mem, Expert Comt Nutrit, Int Life Sci Inst, 84-88; ed, World Rev Nutrit & Dietetics, 89- *Mem:* Fel Am Acad Pediat; Soc Pediat Res; Endocrine Soc; Am Pediat Soc; Am Inst Nutrit; Am Asn World Health (asst treas & vpres, 81-90); NAm Soc Study Obesity; fel Am Col Nutrit; Int Soc Study Fatty Acids and Lipids. *Res:* Genetics of endocrine diseases and growth problems in children; clinical nutrition; body weight, health, longevity and nutrition; body weight standards; omega-3 fatty acids; genetic variation and nutrition; nutrition and fitness; antioxidant vitamins. *Mailing Add:* 4330 Klingle St NW Washington DC 20016. *Fax:* 202-462-5241

SIMOVICI, DAN, DATABASES, SEMANTIC MODELS. *Current Pos:* assoc prof, 82-84, PROF COMPUT SCI, UNIV MASS, 85- *Personal Data:* b Iassy, Romania, Feb 15, 43; US citizen; m 65; c Alex. *Educ:* Polytech Inst Iassy, Romania, MS, 65; Univ Iassy, MS, 70; Univ Bucharest, PhD(math), 74. *Prof Exp:* From asst prof to assoc prof comput sci, Univ Iassy, 71-80; assoc prof comput sci, Univ Miami, 81-82. *Concurrent Pos:* Chmn tech comt mult-valved logic, Comput Soc; managing ed, Multiple-Valued Logic. *Mem:* Am Math Soc; Asn Comput Mach; Comput Soc Inst Elec & Electronics Engrs. *Res:* Database systems, semantic database models; theoretical computer science and related areas; formal languages; automata theory; switching theory; boolean algebras. *Mailing Add:* Dept Math & Comput Sci Univ Mass Boston MA 02125. *E-Mail:* dsim@cs.umb.edu

SIMPKINS, JAMES W, PHARMACODYNAMICS. *Current Pos:* assoc chmn, Dept Pharmacodynamics, Univ Fla, 84-86, chmn, 86-88, asst dean res & grad studies, Col Pharm, 88-89, assoc dean, 89-91, from asst prof to assoc prof, 77-86, PROF, DEPT PHARMACODYNAMICS, UNIV FLA, 86- *Personal Data:* b Port Clinton, Ohio, Sept 22, 48; c 3. *Educ:* Univ Toledo, BS, 71, MS, 74; Mich State Univ, PhD(physiol), 77. *Prof Exp:* Teaching asst, Dept Biol, Univ Toledo, 71-74; technician, Dept Physiol, Med Col Ohio, Toledo, 72-74; instr, Sci Dept, Lansing Community Col, Mich, 75-77; res asst, Dept Physiol, Mich State Univ, 74-77. *Mem:* Endocrine Soc; Am Physiol Soc; Sigma Xi; AAAS; Soc Neurosci; Gerontol Soc Am; Am Asn Pharmaceut Scientists; Am Asn Col Pharm. *Res:* Mechanism of hypothalmic control on anterior pituitary function with particular interest in the role of catechol- and indolemines in the secretion of pituitary hormones during development, aging and the feedback of steroids and peptide hormones; pharmacology of opiate agonists and antagonists; pharmacology of brain-specific drug delivery system; numerous technical publications. *Mailing Add:* Dept Pharmacodynamics Col Pharm Univ Fla Box J-487 JHMEC Gainesville FL 32610-0001

SIMPKINS, PETER G, FLUID MECHANICS, AERONAUTICS. *Current Pos:* mem tech staff, Anal Mech Dept, AT&T Bell Labs, 68-71 & Ocean Physics Res Dept, 71-74, mem tech staff, Mat Res Labs, Bell Labs, 74-83, DISTINGUISHED TECH STAFF, PHYS SCI & ENG RES, AT&T BELL LABS, 83- *Personal Data:* b London, Eng, Nov 28, 34; m 59; c 3. *Educ:* Univ London, Dipl technol, 58, PhD(aeronaut), 64; Calif Inst Technol, MSc, 60. *Prof Exp:* Apprentice engr, Handley Page Co, Ltd, 53-57, mem res staff aerodyn, 57-58; res asst aeronaut, Imp Col, Univ London, 60-65; sr consult scientist, Avco Res & Develop Labs, 65-68. *Concurrent Pos:* Sr res fel, Southampton Univ, Eng, 73-74; consult, Eng Mech Div, NSF, 75-; mem, Space Lab 3 rev bd, NASA, 78-79, Mat Processing in Space Panel, 80-81; adj prof chem eng, Lehigh Univ, 90- *Mem:* Am Inst Physics; Am Phys Soc; fel Am Soc Mech Engr. *Res:* Fluid mechanics, convection, gas dynamics, heat transfer, fracture mechanics and wave propagation in solids. *Mailing Add:* 1A-121 AT&T Bell Labs 600 Mountain Ave Murray Hill NJ 07974

SIMPLICIO, JON, BIOCHEMISTRY, INORGANIC CHEMISTRY. *Current Pos:* MEM STAFF, CELANESE CORP, 82- *Personal Data:* b Bronx, NY, Sept 18, 42; m 69. *Educ:* State Univ NY, Stony Brook, BS, 64; State Univ NY Buffalo, PhD(chem), 69. *Prof Exp:* Res assoc biochem, Cornell Univ, 68-69; asst prof chem, Univ Miami, 70-77; mem staff, Allied Chem Corp, 77-82. *Mem:* Am Chem Soc. *Res:* Fast reaction mechanisms and kinetics of enzymes; kinetics of metalloporphyrins with nucelophiles and their interactions with micelles. *Mailing Add:* 12 Stonelea Dr Princeton Junction NJ 08550

SIMPSON, ANTONY MICHAEL, SOLID STATE PHYSICS, ULTRASONICS. *Current Pos:* from asst prof to assoc prof, 68-89, chair, Physics Dept, 89-95, PROF PHYSICS, DALHOUSIE UNIV, 89- *Personal Data:* b Leamington, Eng, May 8, 41; m 69, C Lynne Brodie; c Miles A K & Alison M. *Educ:* Cambridge Univ, BA, 63; Dalhousie Univ, MSc, 65, PhD(physics), 69. *Concurrent Pos:* Fel, Cambridge Univ, 71-72; vis sci, Univ BC, 83-84; vis fel, Victoria Univ, Wellington, NS. *Mem:* Am Phys Soc; Can Asn Physicists; Can Acousts Asn. *Res:* Transport properties, ultrasonics and thermal expansion in solids. *Mailing Add:* Dept Physics Dalhousie Univ Halifax NS B3H 3J5 Can. *Fax:* 902-494-5191; *E-Mail:* antony.simpson@dal.ca

SIMPSON, BERYL BRINTNALL, SYSTEMATICS. *Current Pos:* chmn dept, 90-96, PROF BOT, UNIV TEX, AUSTIN, 78-, C L LUNDELL CHAIR SYST BOT, 95- *Personal Data:* b Dallas, Tex, Apr 28, 42; div; c Jonathan & Meghan. *Educ:* Radcliffe Col, BA, 64; Harvard Univ, MA & PhD(biol), 67. *Honors & Awards:* Greenman Award, 70; Cooley Award, 71. *Prof Exp:* Res botanist, Arnold Arboretum, Harvard Univ, 68, res fel bot, Gray Herbarium, 68-69, res assoc, 69-71; assoc cur dept bot, US Mus Natural Hist, Smithsonian Inst, 72-78. *Mem:* Soc Study Evolution (pres, 86); Bot Soc Am (pres, 92); Am Soc Plant Taxon (pres, 94); fel AAAS; Am Acad Arts & Sci. *Res:* Speciation problems of Andean plant genera; systematics of Andean genera; reproductive systems of angiosperms; pollination biology; legome systematics. *Mailing Add:* Dept Bot Univ Tex Austin TX 78713. *Fax:* 512-471-3878

SIMPSON, BILLY DOYLE, ORGANIC CHEMISTRY. *Current Pos:* Res chemist, Phillips Petrol Co, 57-66, adhesives develop & sales consult, 66-75, adhesive develop & lab coordr, 75-77, mkt segment mgr molded & extruded goods, 77-80, TECH SERV & DEVELOP MGR, PHILLIPS PETROL CO, 80- *Personal Data:* b Holdenville, Okla, Mar 12, 29; m 57; c 2. *Educ:* Okla State Univ, BS, 51, MS, 53; Univ Kans, PhD(org chem), 57. *Mem:* Am Chem Soc; Soc Petrol Engrs. *Res:* Nitrogen-containing compounds; petrochemicals; adhesives. *Mailing Add:* 1630 Candlelight Lane Houston Houston TX 77018

SIMPSON, CLAY E, JR, MINORITY HEALTH. *Current Pos:* DEP ASST SECY MINORITY HEALTH, DEPT HEALTH & HUMAN SERVS, USPHS, 95- *Personal Data:* b Owensboro, Ky, Apr 3, 32; m 58, Jessie Johnson. *Educ:* Univ Ky, BA, MA; Univ Okla, PhD. *Hon Degrees:* LHD, New Eng Col Optom, Scholl Col Pediat Med, Meharry Med Col; DSc, Tuskegee Univ, LLD, Miles Col, cert, Harvard Univ. *Concurrent Pos:* Mgr, Health Careers Opportunity Prog & Ctr Excellence Prog; instr, Benedict Col, Miss Valley State Univ, Delta State Univ & Towson State Univ; adj prof, Tufts Med Sch; dep dir, Tufts Delta Health Ctr, Miss. *Res:* Improving health status and access to services for America's racial and ethnic minority populations. *Mailing Add:* Off Minority Health Off Pub Health & Sci Rockwall II Bldg Suite 1000 10th Fl 5515 Security Lane Rockville MD 20857

SIMPSON, DALE R, PETROLOGY, MINERALOGY. *Current Pos:* From asst prof to prof geol, 60-95, EMER PROF GEOL, LEHIGH UNIV, 95- *Personal Data:* b Wilmar, Calif, Dec 29, 30; m 58; c 2. *Educ:* Pa State Univ, BS, 56; Calif Inst Technol, MS, 58, PhD(geol), 60. *Mem:* Mineral Soc Am; fel Geol Soc Am. *Res:* Synthesis, stability and chemical variants of phosphate minerals; petrology of granitic pegmatites; energy storage using latent heat; effect of saline waters on igneous rocks. *Mailing Add:* Dept Earth & Environ Sci Lehigh Univ Bethlehem PA 18015

SIMPSON, DAVID ALEXANDER, PHYSICAL ORGANIC CHEMISTRY. *Current Pos:* SR RES CHEMIST, ORG & PHYS ORG CHEM, HERCULES, INC, 74- *Personal Data:* b Englewood, NJ, Mar 2, 43. *Educ:* Allegheny Col, BS, 65; Univ Ill, MS, 68, PhD(org chem), 69. *Prof Exp:* Res chemist, 69-74. *Mem:* Am Chem Soc; Inter-Am Photochem Soc; Sigma Xi. *Res:* Photochemistry; photopolymerization; photooxidation; photo crosslinking and photodegradation of polymers; laser induced chemical and photochemical reactions. *Mailing Add:* 1121 Flint Hill Rd Arundel Wilmington DE 19808-1911

SIMPSON, DAVID GORDON, INTERNAL MEDICINE. *Current Pos:* RETIRED. *Personal Data:* b Belfast, Northern Ireland, Jan 24, 20; US citizen; m 56; c 4. *Educ:* Queen's Univ, Belfast, MB, BCh & BAO, 42, MD, 50. *Prof Exp:* Sr registr med, Northern Ireland Hosps Authority, 49-52; from resident to chief resident chest serv, Bellevue Hosp, Columbia Univ Div, New York, 52-56, instr med, Col Physicians & Surgeons, Columbia Univ, 56-64; assoc prof med & head div pulmonary dis, Sch Med, Univ Md, Baltimore, 64-76, assoc prof internal med, 76-84. *Concurrent Pos:* Consult, Vet Admin Hosp, Baltimore, 64-, Keswick Home, 64-, Md Gen Hosp, 64-, Mercy Hosp, 64- & Montebello State Hosp, 64- *Mem:* Am Thoracic Soc. *Res:* Pulmonary tuberculosis and other respiratory diseases. *Mailing Add:* 641 W University Pkwy Baltimore MD 21210

SIMPSON, DAVID PATTEN, CELL & ORGAN GROWTH. *Current Pos:* DIR, MADRONA RES INST, 90- *Personal Data:* b Eugene, Ore, Mar 20, 30; m 56, Marcia Stoke; c 4. *Educ:* Harvard Univ, AB, 52; McGill Univ, MD, 57. *Prof Exp:* Intern, Grace-New Haven Community Hosp, 57-58; resident med, Scripps Clin & Res Found, 58-60; vis scholar, Col Physicians & Surgeons, Columbia Univ, 60-65; from asst prof to assoc prof med, Univ Wash, 65-74; prof med & dir nephrol prog, Univ Wis Ctr Health Sci, 74-89. *Concurrent Pos:* USPHS res fel, 60-62; NY Heart Asn sr res fel, 62-65; chief nephrology, USPHS Hosp, 70-74. *Res:* Regulation of cell division and growth in regenerating liver and kidney; regulation of organ growth. *Mailing Add:* Rte 2 Box 1080 Lopez WA 98261. *E-Mail:* dpsmri@rockisland.com

SIMPSON, EUGENE SIDNEY, hydrology; deceased, see previous edition for last biography

SIMPSON, EVAN RUTHERFORD, REPRODUCTIVE ENDOCRINOLOGY. *Current Pos:* PROF OBSTET & GYNECOL & BIOCHEM, SOUTHWESTERN MED SCH, UNIV TEX, 82- *Educ:* Univ Edinburgh, Scotland, PhD(biochem), 67. *Res:* Regulation of steroid hormone biosynthesis. *Mailing Add:* Green Ctr Southwestern Med Sch Univ Tex 5323 Harry Hines Blvd Dallas TX 75235-9051. *Fax:* 214-688-8683

SIMPSON, EVERETT COY, ZOOLOGY, ENDOCRINOLOGY. *Current Pos:* assoc prof, 61-64, assoc dir dept, 71, PROF BIOL, E CAROLINA UNIV, 64- *Personal Data:* b Maysville, NC, Feb 13, 25; m 51; c 4. *Educ:* Okla State Univ, BS, 50; Univ Ky, MS, 52, PhD(genetics), 60. *Prof Exp:* Res asst animal sci, Univ Ky, 51-52 & genetics, 55-60; asst prof biol, Memphis State Univ, 60-61. *Concurrent Pos:* Res grants, 63-65 & 66-68; NSF Inserv Inst Awards, 65-67; dir three inserv insts, 66, 67 & 68. *Mem:* AAAS; Am Genetic Asn. *Res:* Endocrinology, especially the physiology of reproduction. *Mailing Add:* 1700 Treemont Dr Greenville NC 27858

SIMPSON, FRANK, RESERVOIR GEOLOGY. *Current Pos:* assoc prof, 74-80, PROF GEOL, UNIV WINDSOR, 80- *Personal Data:* b Gatley, Eng, Dec 4, 41; Can & UK citizen; m 68, Barbara Marszal; c Moira T & Sean A. *Educ:* Univ Edinburgh, BSc, 65; Jagiellonian Univ, Krakow, Dr Nat Sci(geol), 68. *Honors & Awards:* Ludwik Zejszner Sci Award, Geol Soc Poland, 70. *Prof Exp:* Res geol, Sask Dept Mineral Resources, 69-74. *Concurrent Pos:* Chmn dept, Univ Windsor, 82-88; hon prof geol, Univ St Andrews, Scotland, 83; pres, Dept Geol, Coun Univ, Ont, 84-85. *Mem:* Can Soc Petrol Geologists; Geol Soc Poland; Soc Econ Paleontologists & Mineralogists; Asn Geoscientists Int Develop. *Res:* Sedimentology of siliciclastic deposits; Cretaceous stratigraphy; petroleum geology; solution-generated collapse features; environmental management; geology of east and central Africa; integration of water-resource management, soil conservation and agroforestry. *Mailing Add:* Dept Earth Sci Univ Windsor 401 Sunset Ave Windsor ON N9B 3P4 Can. *Fax:* 519-973-7081; *E-Mail:* franks@server.uwindsor.ca

SIMPSON, FREDERICK JAMES, BACTERIOLOGY, SCIENCE ADMINISTRATION. *Current Pos:* RETIRED. *Personal Data:* b Regina, Sask, June 8, 22; m 44; c 5. *Educ:* Univ Alta, BSc, 44, MSc, 46; Univ Wis, PhD(bact), 52. *Honors & Awards:* Queen's Silver Anniversary Medal. *Prof Exp:* Jr res officer div appl biol, Nat Res Coun, Can, 46-48, asst res officer bact, Prairie Regional Lab, 52-57, from assoc res officer to sr res officer, 58-70, head physiol & biochem of bacteria, 58-70, asst dir, Atlantic Regional Lab, 70-73, dir Atlantic Regional Lab, 73-84. *Concurrent Pos:* Chmn, Atlantic Coun Provinces Coun Sci, 81-84. *Mem:* Aquaculture Asn Can; Can Soc Microbiol. *Res:* Metabolism of sugars; enzymic degradation of hemicelluloses and aromatic compounds; marine phycology. *Mailing Add:* 95 Empire St Apt 11 Bridgewater NS B4V 2L5 Can

SIMPSON, G(ERALD DUANE), SPECTROSCOPY-HOLOGRAPHY, CLINICAL-FORENSIC CHEMISTRY. *Current Pos:* RETIRED. *Personal Data:* b Calif, 1943; m 69, Lisa R Goodlaw. *Educ:* Univ Calif, Santa Barbara, AB, 66, PhD(phys chem), 70. *Prof Exp:* Postdoctoral fel, Inst Molecular Biophys, Fla State Univ, 70-73; mem tech staff, Sci Ctr, Rockwell Int, 73-75,

Rocketdyne Div, 75-81; instr chem, Calif Lutheran Univ, 83-84. *Concurrent Pos:* Prin investr, Rocketdyne Div, Rockwell Int, 77-78, actg mgr laser physics & diag, 78-79; vis investr cardiology res, Cedars-Sinai Med, 88-89. *Mem:* AAAS; Nat Asn Criminal Defense Lawyers. *Res:* Luminescence spectra/lifetimes of organic molecules; non-exponential decay; photochemistry; condensed-phase high pressure spectroscopy; S-T transition in iodine; proton tunneling in DNA base pairs; electrochemistry/optical displays; gas-phase organic dye lasers; holography; heterodyne laser interferometry; excimer laser angioplasty of coronary arteries; magnitude of error in breath alcohol analysis; science and the law, especially involving scientific evidence. *Mailing Add:* PO Box 1551 Thousand Oaks CA 91358

SIMPSON, GEDDES WILSON, ECONOMIC ENTOMOLOGY. *Current Pos:* asst entomologist, Maine Exp Sta, Univ Maine, 31-44, chg roguing serv, 38-46, chg Fla test plot, 39-59, assoc entomologist, 44-52, entomologist, 52-74, prof entom & chmn dept, Univ, 54-74, EMER PROF ENTOM, UNIV MAINE, ORONO, 74- *Personal Data:* b Scranton, Pa, Aug 15, 08; m 33, Florine Moore; c Mary, Frank, Blanche & Geddes Jr. *Educ:* Bucknell Univ, AB, 29; Cornell Univ, AM, 31, PhD(econ entom), 35. *Prof Exp:* Asst entom, State Univ NY Col Agr, Cornell Univ, 30-31. *Concurrent Pos:* Ed-in-chief, Am Potato J, 75-88; asst to dir, Maine Agr Exp Sta, 76-88. *Mem:* Fel AAAS; Entom Soc Am; Potato Asn Am; Acadian Entom Soc. *Res:* Insect transmission of plant virus diseases; biology and control of aphids affecting potatoes. *Mailing Add:* 235 Fairground Rd Lewisburg PA 17837-1289

SIMPSON, HOWARD DOUGLAS, CATALYSIS, HYDROTREATING. *Current Pos:* CONSULT, HALDORTOPSOE, 95- *Personal Data:* b Carrizozo, NMex, May 30, 37; m 67, Dianne Kennedy; c Stephen. *Educ:* Univ NMex, BS, 59; Univ Tex, Austin, MS, 65, PhD(chem eng), 69. *Prof Exp:* Res engr, Unocal Corp, 71-76, sr res engr, 76-81, res assoc, 81-85, sr res assoc, 85-89, staff consult, 89-95. *Mem:* Catalysis Soc; Am Chem Soc; Am Crystallog Asn; Sigma Xi. *Res:* New and improved hydrotreating catalysts for the petroleum industry. *Mailing Add:* 3772 Hamilton St Irvine CA 92614-6631

SIMPSON, HOWARD EDWIN, GEOLOGY. *Current Pos:* CONSULT GEOL & QUAL ASSURANCE ENG, 81- *Personal Data:* b Grand Forks, NDak, June 27, 17; m 43; c 4. *Educ:* Univ NDak, BA, 40; Univ Ill, MS, 42; Yale Univ, PhD(geol), 53. *Prof Exp:* Geologist, Eng Geol Br, US Geol Surv, 47-60, geologist, Regional Geol Br, 60-66, geologist, Eng Geol Br, 66-77, geologist, Spec Proj Br, 77-81. *Mem:* Asn Eng Geol; Am Inst Prof Geologists; Geol Soc Am. *Res:* Application of geology to problems of urban development; geomorphology; Pleistocene geology. *Mailing Add:* 2020 Washington Ave Golden CO 80401-2361

SIMPSON, IAN ALEXANDER, DIABETES RESEARCH. *Current Pos:* vis assoc, Cellular Metabolism & Obesity Sect, Nat Inst Arthritis, Diabetes & Digestive & Kidney Dis, NIH, 79-82, vis scientist, 82-85, VIS SCIENTIST & ASSOC CHIEF, EXP DIABETES METABOLISM & NUTRIT SECT, NIH, 85- *Personal Data:* b East Grinstead, Gt Brit, Mar 27, 48; m 77; c 2. *Educ:* Hull Univ, BSc, 71; Univ Col, London, PhD(biochem), 75. *Prof Exp:* Grad fel, Univ Col, London, 71-74; res assoc, Muscular Dystrophy Group, Gt Brit, Guys Hosp Med Sch, London, 74-77; res assoc, Physiologisch-Chemisches Inst, Univ Wuerzburg, WGer, 77-79. *Concurrent Pos:* Res grants, Muscular Dystrophy Group Gt Brit, Guy's Hosp Med Sch, 74-77, Deutsche Forschungsgemeinschaft, Univ Wuerzburg, 77-79 & Am Diabetes Asn, NIH, 87-88 & 88-89. *Mem:* Am Diabetes Asn; Am Soc Biochem & Molecular Biol; Endocrine Soc. *Res:* Diabetes; biology; biochemistry. *Mailing Add:* EDMNS DB DIDDK Bldg 10 Rm 5N102 NIH Bethesda MD 20892-0001. *Fax:* 301-402-0432

SIMPSON, JAMES EDWARD, GRAPH THEORY, COMBINATORICS. *Current Pos:* RETIRED. *Personal Data:* b Chicago, Ill, July 6, 31; div; c 3. *Educ:* Loyola Univ, Ill, BSEd, 53, MA, 56; Yale Univ, PhD(math), 61. *Prof Exp:* From instr to assoc prof math, Marquette Univ, 55-66; assoc prof math, Univ Ky, 66-93. *Concurrent Pos:* NSF res grants, 63-66; vis Fulbright prof, Arya-Mehr Univ Technol, 68-70. *Mem:* Am Math Soc; Math Asn Am. *Res:* Functional analysis; spectral analysis of operators; graph theory; combinatorics; database management. *Mailing Add:* 1863 NW Estaview Dr Corvallis OR 97330-1052

SIMPSON, JAMES HENRY, PHYSICS. *Current Pos:* CONSULT, 90- *Personal Data:* b Haledon, NJ, Oct 13, 29; m 61; c 3. *Educ:* Rutgers Univ, BS, 51, PhD(physics), 58. *Prof Exp:* Asst prof physics, Univ Del, 57-58; prin scientist, Singer Co, 58-80, mgr appl physics dept, Kearfott Div, 80-90. *Concurrent Pos:* adj prof, Fordham Univ, 70- *Mem:* Am Phys Soc; Inst Elec & Electronic Eng; Sigma Xi. *Res:* Magnetic resonance; atomic physics; ring laser gyroscopes; optically-pumped, magnetic-resonance gyroscopes. *Mailing Add:* 112 Lily Pond Lane Katonah NY 10536

SIMPSON, JAMES R(USSELL), CIVIL ENGINEERING. *Current Pos:* RETIRED. *Personal Data:* b Passaic, NJ, Mar 22, 11; m 35, 73; c 2. *Educ:* Va Polytech Inst, BS, 34, MS, 42; Environ Engrs Intersoc, dipl, 56. *Prof Exp:* Indust hyg engr, USPHS, 35-36, sanit engr, 44-47; sanit engr, State Dept Health, Va, 36-37, pub health engr, 38-42; sanit engr, Fed Housing Admin, 43-44 & 47-56, chief, Sanit Eng Sect & Spec Asst Tech Studies Prog, 56-59, chief, Standards & Studies Sect, 59-64, dep dir, Archit Standards Div, 64-67, dir, Off Advan Bldg Technol, Dept Housing & Urban Develop, 67-70; housing indust consult, 70-95. *Mem:* Inst Elec & Electronics Engrs. *Res:* Building research. *Mailing Add:* 7721 Weber Ct Annandale VA 22003

SIMPSON, JAMES URBAN, UNSATURATED POLYESTER POLYMERS FOR COMMERCIAL USE, SATURATED & UNSATURATED POLYMERS FOR PROTECTIVE COATINGS. *Current Pos:* VPRES, PLEXMAR RESINS INC, 90- *Personal Data:* b Springfield, Mo, Dec 11, 29; m 53, Patricia L Conger. *Educ:* Cent Mo State Univ, BS, 51. *Prof Exp:* Chemist, Cook Paint & Varnish Co, 53-56; prod mgr, Reichhold Chem Inc, 56-91, plant mgr, 61-68; chief chemist, Denton Vacuum Corp, 69-72; sr chemist, Immont Corp, 72-74; tech supvr, Stepan Corp, 74-79; tech mgr resins, O'Brien Corp, 79-86; tech dir, Reliance Universal Inc, 86-89. *Concurrent Pos:* Sergeant maj chem warfare & defense, biol defense, nuclear weapons employ & defense. *Mem:* Fel Am Inst Chemists; Am Chem Soc; Soc Plastics Engrs; Fedn Soc Coatings Technol. *Res:* Reclamation of polyethyleneterephthalate plastic scrap for use as raw material for production of unsaturated polyester and alkyd resins; granted 3 US patents. *Mailing Add:* 9711 El Chaco St Baytown TX 77521. *Fax:* 713-678-4959

SIMPSON, JOANNE, METEOROLOGY. *Current Pos:* head, Severe Storms Br, 79-88, CHIEF SCIENTIST, METEOROL & EARTH SCI DIRECTORATE & SR FEL, GODDARD SPACE FLIGHT CTR, NASA, 88- *Personal Data:* b Boston, Mass, Mar 23, 23; m 48, 65; c 3. *Educ:* Univ Chicago, PhD, 49. *Hon Degrees:* DSc, State Univ NY, Albany, 91. *Honors & Awards:* Meisinger Award, Am Meteorol Soc, 62, Rossby Res Medal, 83; Silver Medal, Dept Com, 67, Gold Medal, 72; Vincent J Schaefer Award, Weather Modification Asn, 79; Except Sci Achievement Medal, NASA, 82. *Prof Exp:* Instr meteorol, NY Univ, 43-44; instr, Univ Chicago, 44-45; instr physics & meteorol, Ill Inst Technol, 46-49, asst prof, 49-51; meteorologist, Woods Hole Oceanog Inst, 51-60; prof meteorol, Univ Calif, Los Angeles, 60-65; head, Exp Br Atmospheric Physics & Chem Lab, Environ Sci Serv Admin, Nat Oceanic & Atmospheric Admin, 65-71, dir, Exp Meteorol Lab, 71-74; prof environ sci & mem, Ctr Advan Studies, Univ Va, 74-76, W W Corcoran prof, 76-81. *Concurrent Pos:* Hon lectr, Imp Col, Univ London & Guggenheim fel, 54-55; chief scientist, Simpson Weather Assocs, 74-79; counr, Am Meteorol Soc, 75-77 & 79-81; comnr, Sci Technol Activities, 82-87; proj scientist, Trop Rainfall Measuring Mission, Goddard Space Flight Ctr, NASA, 86-, sci dir, 92. *Mem:* Nat Acad Eng; fel Am Meteorol Soc. *Res:* Convection in atmosphere; cumulus clouds; tropical meteorology; weather modification; satellite meteorology. *Mailing Add:* Code 912 Earth Sci Directorate Severe Storms Br Goddard Space Flight Ctr MC 912 Greenbelt MD 20771

SIMPSON, JOE LEIGH, PRENATAL GENETIC DIAGNOSIS & ETIOLOGY OF BIRTH DEFECTS, DISORDERS OF HUMAN SEX DIFFERENTIATION. *Current Pos:* ERNST W BERTNER CHMN & PROF, DEPT OBSTET & GYNEC, BAYLOR COL MED, 94-, PROF MOLECULAR & HUMAN GENETICS. *Personal Data:* b Birmingham, Ala, Apr 9, 43; m 78, Sandra Carson; c Scott & Reid. *Educ:* Duke Univ, MD, 78. *Honors & Awards:* Pres Achievement Award, Soc Gynec Invest, 86; deWatteville Lectr, Int Fedn Gynec & Obstet, 91. *Prof Exp:* Chief obstet serv & head, Sect Human Genetics, Brooke Army Med Ctr, 73-75, from assoc prof to prof, Dept Obstet & Gynec, 75-80; fac prof & chmn, Univ Tenn, Memphis, 86-94. *Mem:* Inst Med-Nat Acad Sci; Am Col Obstet & Gynec; Soc Gynec Invest; Am Soc Human Genetics; Am Soc Reproductive Med (pres, 93-94); Am Col Med Genetics. *Res:* Elucidates causes of birth defects, particularly cytogenetic in origin; develops and assesses accuracy of prenatal diagnostic procedures. *Mailing Add:* Baylor Col Med Dept Obstet & Gynec 6550 Fannin Suite 701 Houston TX 77030. *Fax:* 713-798-8410; *E-Mail:* jsimpson@bmc.tmc.edu

SIMPSON, JOHN ALEXANDER, PHYSICS. *Current Pos:* sci group leader, Manhattan Dist Proj, Metall Lab, Univ Chicago, 43-46, from instr to prof, 45-68, Edward L Ryerson distinguished serv prof, 68-74, Arthur H Compton distinguished serv prof physics, Univ Chicago & Enrico Fermi Inst Nuclear Studies, 74-87, dir, Inst, 73-87, EMER ARTHUR H COMPTON DISTINGUISHED SERV PROF PHYSICS, UNIV CHICAGO & ENRICO FERMI INST NUCLEAR STUDIES, 87- *Personal Data:* b Portland, Ore, Nov 3, 16; m 46; c 2. *Educ:* Reed Col, AB, 40; NY Univ, MS, 42, PhD(physics), 43. *Prof Exp:* Asst physics, NY Univ, 40-42, res assoc, Off Sci Res & Develop proj, 42-43. *Concurrent Pos:* Sci consult, Argonne Nat Lab, 46-54; chmn, Comt Biophys, Univ Chicago, 51-52; mem, Spec Int Comt, Int Geophys Yr, 54-60 & US Nat Comt & Tech Panel Cosmic Rays, 55-58; mem, Space Sci Bd, Nat Acad Sci, 58-66, consult, 66-; estab lab astrophys & space res in Enrico Fermi Inst, Univ Chicago, 64; pres, Int Comn Cosmic Radiation, 64-67; fel, Ctr Policy Study, 66-; mem, Astron Missions Bd, NASA. *Mem:* Nat Acad Sci; fel Am Phys Soc; fel Am Geophys Union; Am Astron Soc; Int Acad Astronaut. *Res:* Cosmic radiation origin; galactic, solar and magnetospheric acceleration of particles; experiments on nuclear composition, spectra, time variations of radiation with neutron monitors, satellite and space probes; interplanetary and solar magnetic fields reduced from particle propagation. *Mailing Add:* Enrico Fermi Inst Nuclear Studies Dept Physics Univ Chicago Chicago IL 60637. *Fax:* 773-702-6645; *E-Mail:* simpson@odysseus.uchicago.edu

SIMPSON, JOHN AROL, PHYSICS, SCIENCE ADMINISTRATION. *Current Pos:* RETIRED. *Personal Data:* b Toronto, Ont, Mar 30, 23; nat US; m 48; c 1. *Educ:* Lehigh Univ, BS, 46, MS, 48, PhD(physics), 53. *Honors & Awards:* Doc Silver Medal & Gold Medal; Allen V Austin Measurement Sci Award; Am Machinist Award. *Prof Exp:* Physicist, Nat Bur Stands, 48-62, chief, Electron Physics Sect, 62-69, dep chief, Optical Physics Div, 69-75, chief, Mech Div, 75-78, dir CTR Mfg Eng, 81-91, dir, Mfg Eng Lab, Nat Inst Stands & Technol, 91-93. *Concurrent Pos:* Asst, Lehigh Univ, 51-52. *Mem:* Nat Acad Eng; Am Phys Soc. *Res:* Metrology; optics. *Mailing Add:* 312 Riley St Falls Church VA 22046

SIMPSON, JOHN BARCLAY, BEHAVIORAL NEUROSCIENCE. *Current Pos:* from asst prof to assoc prof, Univ Wash, 75-82, dir, Physiol & Psychol Prog, 85-90, assoc dean res, Col Arts & Sci, 91-94, PROF PSYCHOL, UNIV WASH, 82-, DEAN, COL ARTS & SCI, 95- *Personal Data:* b Oakland, Calif, June 8, 47; m 67, Diane C; c 2. *Educ:* Univ Calif, Santa Barbara, BA, 69; Northwestern Univ, MA, 72, PhD(neurobiol & behav), 73. *Prof Exp:* Instr, Col Gen Studies, Univ Pa, 74-75. *Concurrent Pos:* Fel, Inst Neurol Sci, Univ Pa, 73-75; vis assoc prof physiol, Univ Calif, San Francisco, 76-80; vis prof, Howard Florey Inst Exp Physiol & Med, Univ Melbourne, Australia, 83. *Mem:* AAAS; Soc Neurosci; Soc Study Ingestive Behavior. *Res:* Neural involvement in body fluid regulation; neural control of ingestive behaviors. *Mailing Add:* Col Arts & Sci Univ Wash Box 353765 Seattle WA 98195. *Fax:* 206-543-5462

SIMPSON, JOHN ERNEST, ORGANIC CHEMISTRY, ENOLOGY. *Current Pos:* assoc prof, 68-80, PROF CHEM, CALIF STATE POLYTECH UNIV, POMONA, 80- *Personal Data:* b Toledo, Ohio, Feb 10, 42; m 66; c 1. *Educ:* Univ NMex, BS, 63, MS, 66, PhD(chem), 68. *Prof Exp:* Asst prof chem, Pomona Col, 67-68. *Mem:* Am Chem Soc; AAAS; Sigma Xi; Am Soc Enologists. *Res:* Organic synthesis-crown ethers; bridged aromatics; C-13 labeled compounds; phenolics, isolation and identification in grapes and wines; nuclear magnetic resonance spectroscopy. *Mailing Add:* 226 E Cucamonga Claremont CA 91711-5015

SIMPSON, JOHN HAMILTON, THEORETICAL SOLID STATE PHYSICS, SOLID STATE ELECTRONICS. *Current Pos:* CONSULT PHOTOVOLTAICS, 81- *Personal Data:* b Montreal, Que, May 28, 15; m 53; c 2. *Educ:* McGill Univ, BEng, 37; Bristol Univ, PhD(theoret physics), 50. *Prof Exp:* Test engr, Can Gen Elec Co, 37-38; res officer, Radio & Elec Eng Div, Nat Res Coun Can, 38-46, sr res officer, 48-61, prin res officer, Physics Div, 61-76, energy consult, 77-81. *Concurrent Pos:* Lectr, Univ Ottawa & Carleton Univ; pres, Cosim Solar Res Ltd. *Mem:* Am Phys Soc; Can Asn Physicists; Inst Elec & Electronics Engrs. *Res:* Theory of optical-electrical properties of defects in ionic crystals; theory of semiconducting devices; theory of cooperative effects in dielectrics; direct current transmission line theory. *Mailing Add:* 2184 Braeside Ave Ottawa ON K1H 7J5 Can

SIMPSON, JOHN JOSEPH, BETA-SPECTROSCOPY & NEUTRINO MASS & MIXING MEASUREMENTS, SOLAR NEUTRINO MEASUREMENTS. *Current Pos:* From asst prof to assoc prof, 67-80, PROF PHYSICS, UNIV GUELPH, 80- *Personal Data:* b North Bay, Ont, May 26, 39; m 68, Marianne Van der Veen; c James & Sarah. *Educ:* Univ Toronto, BASc, 61, MA, 62; Oxford Univ, DPhil(physics), 66. *Honors & Awards:* Rutherford Mem Medal Physics, Royal Soc Can, 85. *Concurrent Pos:* Sci assoc, Niels Bohr Inst, Copenhagen, 75-76, Europ Organ Nuclear Res, Geneva, 82-83. *Mem:* Fel Royal Soc Can; Can Asn Physicists. *Res:* Measurement of beta-spectra to limit and determine neutrino masses and mixings; solar neutrino detection using heavy-water. *Mailing Add:* Dept Physics Univ Guelph Guelph ON N1G 2W1 Can. *Fax:* 519-836-9967

SIMPSON, JOHN W(ISTAR), ELECTRICAL ENGINEERING & NUCLEAR ENERGY. *Current Pos:* supv engr circuit breaker design, Westinghouse Elec Corp, 48-49, asst eng mgr, Bettis Atomic Power Lab, 48-52, asst div mgr, 52-54, mgr, Pressurized Water Reactor Proj, 54-55, div mgr, 55-58, vpres & gen mgr, 58-59, vpres & gen mgr, Atomic Power Div, 59-62, vpres eng & res, 62-63, vpres & gen mgr, Elec Utility Group, 63-69, PRES POWER SYSTS, WESTINGHOUSE ELEC CORP, 69- *Personal Data:* b Glenn Springs, SC, Sept 25, 14; m 48, Esther Slattery; c John W Jr, Carter B, Patricia A & Barbara J. *Educ:* US Naval Acad, BS, 37; Univ Pittsburgh, MS, 41. *Hon Degrees:* DSc, Seton Hill Col, 68 & Wofford Col, 72. *Honors & Awards:* Edison Medal, 71; G Westinghouse Medal, Am Soc Mech Engrs, 75; Gold Medal Advan Res, Am Soc Metals; Walter Zinn Medal, Am Nuclear Soc. *Prof Exp:* Res engr, Westinghouse Elec Corp, 38-39, mgr, Navy & Marine Switchbd Sect, 39-46; mgr nuclear eng, Power Pile Div, Oak Ridge Nat Lab, 46-48. *Concurrent Pos:* Consult, USN, 45; mem US deleg, Int Conf Peaceful Uses Atomic Energy, 55 & 58. *Mem:* Nat Acad Eng; fel Inst Elec & Electronics Engrs; fel Am Soc Mech Engrs; fel Am Nuclear Soc. *Res:* Design of nuclear reactors; author of one publication. *Mailing Add:* 36 E Beach Lagoon Dr Hilton Head SC 29928. *Fax:* 803-671-2523; *E-Mail:* jws@hangray.com

SIMPSON, JOHN WAYNE, BIOCHEMISTRY. *Current Pos:* RETIRED. *Personal Data:* b Henryetta, Okla, Aug 17, 35; m 66. *Educ:* Phillips Univ, BA, 57; Rice Univ, MA, 59, PhD(biochem), 65. *Prof Exp:* Asst mem biochem, Univ Tex Dent Sci Inst, Houston, 67-71, assoc prof biochem, 71-89. *Concurrent Pos:* Fel, Rice Univ, 65-67. *Mem:* AAAS; Am Physiol Soc; Int Asn Dent Res. *Res:* Comparative aspects of free amino acid distribution; pathways of glucose degradation in invertebrates; intermediary metabolism in oral tissues. *Mailing Add:* 9106 Petersham Dr Houston TX 77031-2722

SIMPSON, KENNETH L, FOOD SCIENCE. *Current Pos:* RETIRED. *Personal Data:* b Los Angeles, Calif, June 24, 31; m 57; c 3. *Educ:* Univ Calif, Davis, BS, 54, MS, 60, PhD(agr chem), 63. *Honors & Awards:* Emil Racovitza Sci Medallion, Govt Romania, 76. *Prof Exp:* NSF fel biochem, Unv Col, Wales, 63-64; from asst prof to assoc prof agr chem, Univ RI, 64-69, assoc prof food & resource chem, 69-72, prof food sci & technol, 72. *Concurrent Pos:* NSF res grants, sea grant; NIH grants; Sci Res Coun vis fel, Univ Liverpool, 71-72. *Mem:* Am Chem Soc; Inst Food Technol; World Maricultures Soc. *Res:* Chemistry and biochemistry of carotenoids in microorganism plants and animals; fish nutrition; utilization of fish processing waste; provitamin A analysis in fruit and vegetables; aquaculture of artemia-brine shrimp. *Mailing Add:* 73 North Rd Peace Dale RI 02883

SIMPSON, LARRY P, CELL BIOLOGY, PROTOZOOLOGY. *Current Pos:* Asst prof zool, 67-74, assoc prof cell biol, 74-75, PROF CELL BIOL, UNIV CALIF, LOS ANGELES, 75- *Personal Data:* b Philadelphia, Pa, Oct 31, 40; m 68. *Educ:* Princeton Univ, AB, 62; Rockefeller Univ, PhD(cell biol), 67. *Honors & Awards:* Hutner Award, Soc Protogeol, 80. *Concurrent Pos:* NATO fel sci, Univ Brussels, 67-68; Molecular Biol Inst. *Mem:* Soc Protozool; Am Soc Cell Biol; Molecular Biol Inst. *Res:* Cell biology of parasitic protozoa, especially mitochondrial biogenesis. *Mailing Add:* Dept Biol Univ Calif 405 Hilgard Ave Los Angeles CA 90024-1301

SIMPSON, LEONARD, INVERTEBRATE ZOOLOGY. *Current Pos:* asst prof, 68-72, ASSOC PROF BIOL, PORTLAND STATE UNIV, 72- *Personal Data:* b Hale Center, Tex, Apr 25, 32; m 64. *Educ:* Univ Calif, Berkeley, AB, 55, MA, 62, PhD(zool), 68. *Prof Exp:* Instr biol, Diablo Valley Col, 61-66. *Mem:* AAAS; Am Soc Zool; Sigma Xi; Western Soc Naturalists. *Res:* Neurosecretion and neuroendocrinology of Mollusca; reproductive endocrinology of invertebrates. *Mailing Add:* 4570 NW Columbia Ave Portland OR 97229-2052

SIMPSON, LEONARD ANGUS, MATERIALS SCIENCE, FRACTURE MECHANICS. *Current Pos:* Res officer, 68-83, mgr, Mat & Mech Br, 83-91, DIR, REACTOR SAFETY DIV, ATOMIC ENERGY CAN LTD, PINAWA, 91- *Personal Data:* b Vancouver, BC, Aug 1, 39; m 67; c 3. *Educ:* Univ BC, BSc, 61, MSc, 63; Univ Wales, PhD(metall), 68. *Prof Exp:* Metallurgist, Res Lab, Gen Elec Co, NY, 63-64. *Concurrent Pos:* Vis scientist, Mat Res Lab, Brown Univ, 78-80; mem OECD/NEA Principle Working Group 3. *Mem:* Am Soc Testing & Mat. *Res:* Fracture mechanics of metals and nonmetals elastic-plastic fracture criteria; hydrogen embrittlement. *Mailing Add:* Whiteshell Lab AECL Res Pinawa MB R0E 1L0 Can

SIMPSON, MARGARET, INVERTEBRATE ZOOLOGY. *Current Pos:* assoc prof, 73-80, PROF BIOL, SWEET BRIAR COL, 80- *Personal Data:* b Hong Kong, Jan 19, 35; US citizen. *Educ:* Immaculate Heart Col, BA, 56; Cath Univ, MS, 59, PhD(zool), 61. *Prof Exp:* Technician sch med, Univ Southern Calif, 56-57; USPHS fel, 62-63; assoc prof biol, St Francis Col, Maine, 63-67; asst prof, Adelphi Univ, 67-73. *Concurrent Pos:* Danforth assoc, 78-83. *Mem:* Sigma Xi; Am Inst Biol Sci; Marine Biol Asn UK; Am Soc Zoologists. *Res:* Biology of polychaetes, specifically family Glyceridae, especially histology, embryology and venom glands. *Mailing Add:* Dept Biol Sweet Briar Col Box F Sweet Briar VA 24595-1056

SIMPSON, MARION EMMA, PLANT PHYSIOLOGY, BOTANY. *Current Pos:* Clerk, 44-46, sci aid, 46-58, plant pathologist, 58-60, res plant pathologist, Plant Indust Sta, Cotton Div, 60-77, mem staff, 77-88, CONSULT, BELTSVILLE AGR RES CTR, USDA, 88- *Personal Data:* b Odenton, Md, Feb 3, 27. *Educ:* Univ Md, BS, 52, MS, 59, PhD(plant physiol), 62. *Mem:* Am Soc Plant Physiologists; Am Phytopath Soc; Mycol Soc Am; Soc Indust Microbiol. *Res:* Field deterioration of cotton fiber and physiology of organisms involved; cellulase production by fungi and characterization of this enzyme. *Mailing Add:* 1546 Meyers Sta Rd Odenton MD 21113

SIMPSON, MELVIN VERNON, BIOCHEMISTRY. *Current Pos:* chmn dept biochem, 66-75, AM CANCER SOC PROF BIOCHEM, STATE UNIV NY STONY BROOK, 76- *Personal Data:* b New York, NY, July 5, 21; m 76; c 3. *Educ:* City Col New York, BS, 42; Univ Calif, PhD(biochem), 49. *Honors & Awards:* Res Award, Union Carbide Co, 69 & 70. *Prof Exp:* Physicist, Philadelphia Navy Yard, 42-44; physicist, US Naval Ord Lab, 44-45; instr physiol med sch, Tufts Col, 49-51; from asst prof to assoc prof biochem sch med, Yale Univ, 52-62; Am Cancer Soc prof, Dartmouth Med Sch, 62-66. *Concurrent Pos:* USPHS fel, Wash Univ, 51-52; mem fel review panel, NIH, 66-70; mem adv comt nucleic acids & protein synthesis, Am Cancer Soc, 70-75; mem merit rev bd basic sci, US Vet Admin. *Mem:* Am Soc Biol Chemists; Am Chem Soc; Am Soc Cell Biol; Biophys Soc. *Res:* Protein biosynthesis; ribosomes; mitochondria; DNA biosynthesis. *Mailing Add:* Dept Biochem & Cell Biol State Univ NY Stony Brook NY 11794-5215

SIMPSON, MURRAY, ELECTRONIC WARFARE SYSTEMS, ANTENNAS. *Current Pos:* CONSULT, SIMPSON ASSOC, 86- *Personal Data:* b New York, NY, July 27, 21; m 47, Ethel Gladstein; c Anne (Everet), David, Mindy & Jonathan. *Educ:* City Col New York, BEE, 42; Polytech Univ NY, MEE, 52. *Honors & Awards:* Silver Medal, Electronic Warfare Soc, 81; Special Award, Inst Elec & Electronics Engrs. *Prof Exp:* Engr, Int Tel & Tel Co, 42-44; engr, US Naval Res Lab, 44-46; sr engr, Raytheon Co, 46-48; proj engr, Fairchild Guided Missiles Co, 48-50; vpres & tech dir, Maxson Electronics Co, 50-62; pres, Sedco Systs Inc, 63-86. *Mem:* Fel Inst Elec & Electronics Engrs; Air Force Asn. *Res:* Microwave electronic systems; development of advanced radar and electronic warfare systems; phased array antenna systems. *Mailing Add:* 466 Susan Ct West Hempstead NY 11552

SIMPSON, OCLERIS C, AGRICULTURAL RESEARCH. *Personal Data:* b Normangee, Tex, Sept 10, 39; c 1. *Educ:* Prairie View A&M Univ, BS, 60; Iowa State, MS, 62; Univ Nebr, PhD(animal sci), 65. *Prof Exp:* Assoc prof, Ft Valley State Col, Ga, 65-69; res instr, Med Col Ga, 70-71; res assoc, Meharry Med Col, Nashville, Tenn, 72-74; res coordr, Ft Valley State Col, Ga, 74-78; res dir, Prairie View A&M Univ, 78-83, asst dir planning & eval, 83; dean res & exten, Res Dir & Exten Adminr, Langston Univ, 83-97. *Concurrent Pos:* Mem US Invest Team China, 82, Joint Coun Food & Agr Sci, 1890 Land-Grant Col & Univs, 85-88, Int Sci & Educ Coun Tech Assistance Subcomt. *Res:* Animal science; biochemical studies on the metabolites of Vitamin A, C and TIBC; nutrition; numerous technical publications. *Mailing Add:* 2974 Hwy 105 Guthrie OK 73044

SIMPSON, RAE GOODELL, SCIENCE & THE MEDIA. *Current Pos:* PARENT EDUCR, 86- *Personal Data:* b Cambridge, Mass, May 16, 44; m 65; c 3. *Educ:* Pomona Col, AB, 67; Stanford Univ, MA, 71, PhD(commun), 75. *Prof Exp:* Res assoc oral hist prog, Mass Inst Technol, 75-77, asst prof, 71-81, assoc prof sci writing, 81-86. *Mem:* Fel AAAS; Nat Asn Sci Writers; Soc Social Studies Sci; Coun Advan Sci Writing. *Res:* Relationship between science and the media; public understanding of science; science policy issues. *Mailing Add:* Mass Inst Technol Rm 4-144 77 Massachusetts Ave Cambridge MA 02139

SIMPSON, RICHARD ALLAN, RADAR ASTRONOMY. *Current Pos:* Res assoc, 73-76, SR RES ASSOC RADAR ASTRON, STANFORD UNIV, 76- *Personal Data:* b Portsmouth, NH, June 25, 45; m 91, Ann M Reisenauer. *Educ:* Mass Inst Technol, BS, 67; Stanford Univ, MS, 69, PhD(elec eng), 73. *Concurrent Pos:* Vis res assoc, Arecibo Observ, 75-76 & 78. *Mem:* Am Astron Soc; Am Geophys Union; Inst Elec & Electronics Engrs; AAAS; Union Radio Scientifique Internationale. *Res:* Theoretical and experimental research on scattering of radio waves by planetary surfaces; inference of geophysical properties of surfaces from scattered waves. *Mailing Add:* 3326 Kipling St Palo Alto CA 94306-3012. *E-Mail:* rsimpson@magellan.stanford.edu

SIMPSON, RICHARD S, ELECTRICAL ENGINEERING. *Current Pos:* RETIRED. *Personal Data:* b Pensacola, Fla, Sept 25, 35; m 59; c 3. *Educ:* Univ Fla, BSEE, 57, MSE, 58, PhD(elec eng), 61. *Prof Exp:* Res assoc elec eng, Univ Fla, 58-61; from asst prof to prof, Univ Ala, 61-69; prof elec eng, Univ Houston, 69-; scientist, Texaco USA, Houston Res Ctr. *Mem:* Sr mem Inst Elec & Electronics Engrs; Am Soc Eng Educ. *Res:* Communication and telemetry systems; detection theory; video compression. *Mailing Add:* 1627 Milford Houston TX 77006

SIMPSON, ROBERT BLAKE, MOLECULAR BIOLOGY. *Current Pos:* DIR PROJ PLANNING, INSIGHT VISION, 91- *Personal Data:* US citizen; c 1. *Educ:* Univ Ill, Urbana, BS,69; Harvard Univ, Cambridge, MA, 72, PhD(biophysics), 79. *Prof Exp:* Sr fel, Dept Microbiol, Univ Wash, Seattle, 79-81; res scientist & group leader, Molecular Biol Group, Plant Cell Res Inst, Atlantic Richfield Co, Dublin, Calif, 81-91. *Mem:* Am Soc Microbiol; Plant Molecular Biol Asn; AAAS; Am Soc Plant Physiologists. *Res:* The mechanism of Ti-plasmid DNA transfer from Agrobacterium to plant cells; the introduction of useful genes into plants; regulation of gene expression in plants and resistance of plants to pathogens. *Mailing Add:* 226 Montego Dr Danville CA 94526-4815

SIMPSON, ROBERT GENE, entomology; deceased, see previous edition for last biography

SIMPSON, ROBERT JOHN, ANIMAL PHYSIOLOGY, ENDOCRINOLOGY. *Current Pos:* RETIRED. *Personal Data:* b Newburgh, NY, Feb 2, 27; m 52; c 4. *Educ:* Houghton Col, BA, 50; Univ Ill, MS, 60, PhD(physiol), 63. *Prof Exp:* Biologist, Lederle Labs, Am Cyanamid Co, 52-58; teaching asst & physiol, Univ Ill, 58-62; asst prof biol & human & cell physiol, Muskingum Col, 62-65; asst prof human & animal physiol, Univ Northern Iowa, 65-68, assoc prof human & animal physiol & endocrinol, 68-92. *Mem:* AAAS; Sigma Xi; Am Soc Zoologists; NY Acad Sci. *Res:* Mechanisms in calcification of epiphyseal cartilage; vitamin D actions; factors in calciphylaxis; calcium metabolism and hormones; effects of estrogen and progesterone on cartilage calcification; mineral metabolism interrelations; normal and pathological calcium deposition; lipoprotein metabolism. *Mailing Add:* 128 Angie Dr Cedar Falls IA 50613

SIMPSON, ROBERT LEE, LIMNOLOGY, FRESHWATER WETLAND ECOLOGY. *Current Pos:* DEAN, SCH SCI & MATH, WILLIAM PATERSON COL. *Personal Data:* b San Francisco, Calif, Apr 3, 42; m 70; c 1. *Educ:* Fresno State Col, BA, 65, MA, 67; Cornell Univ, PhD(limnol), 71. *Prof Exp:* Teaching asst zool, Fresno State Col, 65-67; res asst limnol, Cornell Univ, 67-70; from asst prof to assoc prof, 70-79, chmn dept, 72-80, prof biol, Rider Col, 79-95. *Concurrent Pos:* Grants, Off Water Res & Technol 75-78, 79-82, Environ Protection Agency, 76-77 & 78-81. *Mem:* Am Soc Limnol & Oceanog; Ecol Soc Am; Brit Ecol Soc; Estuarine Res Fedn; Am Inst Biol Sci. *Res:* Ecology of freshwater tidal and non-tidal wetlands including analysis of production, decomposition and nutrient cycling processes; impact of sewage and non-point source pollutants on freshwater wetlands. *Mailing Add:* Univ Mich 4901 Evergreen Rd Dearborn MI 48128-1491

SIMPSON, ROBERT TODD, BIOCHEMISTRY. *Current Pos:* CAPT, USPHS, 77- *Personal Data:* b Chicago, Ill, June 28, 38; m 63; c 4. *Educ:* Swarthmore Col, BA, 59; Harvard Univ, MD, 63, PhD(biol chem), 69. *Honors & Awards:* USPHS Commendation, 82. *Prof Exp:* Intern med, Peter Bent Brigham Hosp, Boston, 63-64; teaching asst biol chem, Harvard Med Sch, 65-69; sr surgeon, 69-77, CHIEF SECT DEVELOP BIOCHEM, LAB NUTRIT & ENDOCRINOL, NAT INST ARTHRITIS, METAB & DIGESTIVE DIS, NIH, 73-, CHIEF, LAB CELL & DEVELOP BIOL, 80- *Mem:* Am Soc Biol Chem; Am Soc Develop Biol. *Res:* Chromatin structure; histone-DNA interactions; chemical basis for gene regulation in eucaryotic cells. *Mailing Add:* Pa State Univ 308 Althouse Lab University Park PA 16802. *Fax:* 301-496-5239

SIMPSON, ROBERT WAYNE, VIROLOGY. *Current Pos:* from assoc prof to prof, 68-93, EMER PROF VIROL, WAKSMAN INST, RUTGERS UNIV, PISCATAWAY, 93-; CONSULT & TECH WRITER, 93- *Personal Data:* b Providence, RI, Dec 28, 28; m 54, Glenna Reddish; c Sandra, Wendy, Peter & Geoffry. *Educ:* Univ RI, BS, 51; Brown Univ, MS, 56; Rutgers Univ, PhD(virol), 58. *Honors & Awards:* Minnie Rosen Award, Sch Med, Ross Univ, 84. *Prof Exp:* Asst virol, Inst Microbiol, Rutgers Univ, 55-58; mem res staff, Dept Virol, Pub Health Res Inst New York, Inc, 58-68. *Concurrent Pos:* Res asst prof path, Sch Med, NY Univ, 66-70; instr microbiol, Hunter Col, City Univ New York, 68; mem virol study sect, NIH, USPHS, 72-76, clin sci study sect, 79-80 & 83; mem Triage Rev, NIH, 82, NJ State Comn Cancer Res, 83-, trustee, Biomed Res Fund, New Life Found, 85- *Mem:* AAAS; Sigma Xi; Am Soc Microbiol; Brit Soc Gen Microbiol; Am Soc Virol. *Res:* Arthritis-associated parvoviruses; antiviral agents. *Mailing Add:* Waksman Inst Rutgers Univ PO Box 759 Piscataway NJ 08855-0759. *Fax:* 908-369-7802

SIMPSON, ROGER LYNDON, FLUID MECHANICS, HEAT TRANSFER. *Current Pos:* PROF AEROSPACE & OCEAN ENG, VA POLYTECH INST, 83- *Personal Data:* b Roanoke, Va, Oct 25, 42; m 64; c 2. *Educ:* Univ Va, BME, 64; Stanford Univ, MSME, 65, PhD(mech eng), 68. *Prof Exp:* Develop engr, Atomic Power Equip Dept, Gen Elec Co, Calif, 68; from asst prof to assoc prof thermal & fluid sci, Southern Methodist Univ, 69-70, from assoc prof to prof civil & mech eng, 74-83. *Concurrent Pos:* Vis scientist, Max-Planck Inst fur Stroemungsforschung, W Ger, 75-76, NASA-Ames, 90, Univ Erlangen, Ger, 90. *Mem:* Fel Am Inst Aeronaut & Astronaut; fel Am Soc Mech Engrs; Sigma Xi. *Res:* Turbulent shear flows; structure of turbulent flows; laser anemometry; unsteady and separated flows; mass transfer; boundary layer control. *Mailing Add:* Dept Aerospace & Oceanog Eng Va Polytech Inst Blacksburg VA 24061

SIMPSON, RUSSELL BRUCE, VETERINARY MICROBIOLOGY. *Current Pos:* instr & asst prof vet microbiol, 69-76, assoc prof vet microbiol & parasitol, PROF, COL VET MED, TEX A&M UNIV. *Personal Data:* b Jersey City, NJ, Feb 15, 42; m 66; c 2. *Educ:* Tex A&M Univ, BS, 65, DVM, 66, MS, 74; Am Col Vet Microbiologists, dipl, 75. *Prof Exp:* Lab officer microbiol, Vet Div, Walter Reed Army Inst Res, 66-68 & USN Prev Med Univ, DaNang, 68-69. *Mem:* Am Asn Equine Practr; Am Asn Vet Lab Diagnosticians; Asn Am Vet Med Cols; Am Vet Med Asn. *Mailing Add:* Dept Vet Pathobiol Tex A&M Univ College Station TX 77843

SIMPSON, S(TEPHEN) H(ARBERT), JR, electrical engineering, communications; deceased, see previous edition for last biography

SIMPSON, SIDNEY BURGESS, JR, DEVELOPMENTAL BIOLOGY, NEUROBIOLOGY. *Current Pos:* prof & head, Dept Biol Sci, 85-95, DEAN, COL LIB ARTS & SCI, UNIV ILL, CHICAGO, 95- *Personal Data:* b Russellville, Ark, Oct 8, 35; m 63; c 1. *Educ:* Ark Polytech Col, BS, 57; Tulane Univ, MS, 62, PhD(zool), 63. *Honors & Awards:* Marcus Singer Medal, 86. *Prof Exp:* NIH fel, Case Western Res Univ, 64, sr instr anat, Sch Med, 64-65, asst prof, 65-71; from assoc prof to prof biol sci, Dept Biochem & Molecular Biol, Northwest Univ, 71-85. *Concurrent Pos:* NIH career develop award, 66- *Mem:* AAAS; Soc Develop Biol; Soc Cell Biol; Soc Neurosci. *Res:* Vertebrate and invertebrate regeneration. *Mailing Add:* Off Dean Col Lib Arts & Sci M/C 228 Univ Ill 601 S Morgan St Chicago IL 60607-7104. *Fax:* 312-413-2511; *E-Mail:* sid@uic.edu

SIMPSON, STEPHEN G, MATHEMATICS, MATHEMATICAL LOGIC. *Current Pos:* asst prof, 75-77, assoc prof, 77-80, PROF MATH, PA STATE UNIV, 81- *Personal Data:* b Allentown, Pa, Sept 8, 45; m 73; c 2. *Educ:* Lehigh Univ, BA & MS, 66; Mass Inst Technol, PhD(math), 71. *Prof Exp:* Gibbs instr, Yale Univ, 71-72; lectr, Univ Calif, Berkeley, 72-74; res fel, Oxford Univ, 74-75. *Concurrent Pos:* NSF res grants, 71-74 & 75-; res fel, Sci Res Coun, UK, 74-75; res fel Alfred P Sloan Found, 80-82 & Deutsche Forschungsgemeinschaft, West Germany, 83-84; vis assoc prof, Univ Chicago, 78 & Univ Conn, 79-80; vis prof, Univ Paris, 81 & Univ Munich, 83-84. *Mem:* Am Math Soc; Asn for Symbolic Logic. *Res:* Foundation of mathematics; mathematical logic; combinatorics. *Mailing Add:* Dept Math Pa State Univ University Park PA 16802-6401

SIMPSON, THOMAS A, MINING, GEOLOGY. *Current Pos:* RETIRED. *Personal Data:* b Adams, Mass, Oct 23, 25; m 54; c 2. *Educ:* Univ Mo-Rolla, BS, 51, EMines, 65; Univ Ala, MS, 59. *Prof Exp:* Geologist, US Geol Surv, 54-61; chief geologist, Econ Geol Div, Geol Surv Ala, 61-65, asst state geologist, planning sect, 65-75; actg head dept, Univ Ala, 78-79, assoc prof mineral eng, 75-86, res assoc, Mineral Resources Inst, 76-86, emer adj assoc prof mineral eng, 86-90. *Concurrent Pos:* Res assoc, Mus Natural Hist, Univ Ala, 63-86, lectr univ, 65-75; mining geologist, Surinam, 64 & Venezuela, 67. *Mem:* Am Inst Mining, Metall & Petrol Engrs; fel Geol Soc Am; Am Eng Geologists; Am Inst Prof Geologists; Am Asn Petrol Geol. *Res:* Economic geology; mining hydrology and hydrogeologic investigations; mine blasting studies; Southeast iron ore studies. *Mailing Add:* 1108 Greystone Northport AL 35476-2684

SIMPSON, TRACY L, BIOSILICIFICATION, SPONGE BIOLOGY. *Current Pos:* assoc prof, 67-76, PROF BIOL, UNIV HARTFORD, 76- *Personal Data:* b New York, NY, July 12, 37. *Educ:* Brown Univ, AB, 59; Yale Univ, PhD(biol), 65. *Prof Exp:* From instr to asst prof, Tufts Univ, 64-67. *Concurrent Pos:* Asst proj dir, Undergrad Equip Grant, NSF, 65-67 & prin investr res grant, 65-68, 68-70 & 71-73; vis assoc prof, Dartmouth Col, 74, Health Ctr, Univ Conn & Res Found grant, 74-76; prin investr, Int Silicon Symposium, 77-78; exchange scientist, US-France Sci Prog & res prof, Univ Claude Bernard, Lyon, 82-85. *Mem:* AAAS; Am Soc Zool; Am Micros Soc; NY Acad Sci; Sigma Xi; Micros Soc Am. *Res:* Cell biology of sponges; biology of silicon and silicification. *Mailing Add:* Dept Biol Univ Hartford West Hartford CT 06117

SIMPSON, WILBURN DWAIN, TELECOMMUNICATIONS, NUCLEAR PHYSICS. *Current Pos:* VPRES TECHNOL, SABER EQUIP CORP, 89- *Personal Data:* b Long Grove, Okla, Oct 4, 37; m 67, Ann M Coratello; c Ketam M & Rebecca E. *Educ:* Univ Miss, BS, 59, MS, 61; Rice Univ, MA, 63, PhD(nuclear physics), 65. *Prof Exp:* Res assoc nuclear physics, Rice Univ, 65-67; asst physicist, Brookhaven Nat Lab, 67-69; vpres syst develop, Periphonics Corp, 69-80; vpres technol, Alta Technol Inc, 80-85; pres, Ayentka Consult Corp, 80-81; pres, W D Simpson Technol, Inc, 85-89. *Concurrent Pos:* Author, New Tech in Software Proj Mgt, 87. *Mem:* AAAS; Am Phys Soc; NY Acad Sci; Inst Elec & Electronics Engrs; Asn Comput Mach. *Res:* Three-body systems in nuclear physics; intermediate energy nuclear physics; nuclear structure; nucleon-nucleon and nucleon-nucleus interactions; meson-nucleon interactions; computer controlled audio response; communication processors; electronic funds transfer terminals; computer controlled networks; automated fare collection; telecommunication devices; magnetic encoding; vapor collection in fuel dispensing systems; vapor pump design; electronic control of self-service fueling systems. *Mailing Add:* 124 Catalpa Rd Wilton CT 06897. *Fax:* 203-337-1470; *E-Mail:* wdsimp@aol.com

SIMPSON, WILLIAM ALBERT, FRACTALS, HISTORY OF MATHEMATICS. *Current Pos:* asst prof, Off Institutional Res, 73-85, PROF MATH, LYMAN BRIGGS SCH, MICH STATE UNIV, 85- *Personal Data:* b Pittsburgh, Pa, Oct 29, 34; m 58, Janice Dutcher; c Brent Meriwether. *Educ:* US Naval Acad, BS, 58; Univ Mich, MS, 64; Mich State Univ, PhD(math), 71. *Prof Exp:* Res asst, Inst Sci Technol, 65-66, asst prof math, Univ Mich, 71-73. *Concurrent Pos:* Adj math instr, Univ Maryland, 61-63; adj asst prof, dept math, 73-74, adj assoc prof, mgt dept, 81-82, adj assoc prof, Dept Educ Admin, Mich State Univ, 82-85; Fulbright sr scholar, Univ Bath, England, 84. *Mem:* Math Asn Am; Asn Inst Res; AAAS. *Res:* Higher education, policy analysis, statistic studies, computer models; teaching the standard calculus to undergraduates. *Mailing Add:* 1410 Sherwood East Lansing MI 48823. *Fax:* 517-432-2758; *E-Mail:* simpsonw@pilot.msu.edu

SIMPSON, WILLIAM HENRY, SOLID STATE CHEMISTRY, PHOTOGRAPHIC CHEMISTRY. *Current Pos:* RES ASSOC, EASTMAN KODAK CO, 91- *Personal Data:* b Woodbury, NJ, Mar 24, 42; m 69, Carolyn E Hoffman; c William H Jr & Thomas E. *Educ:* Col William & Mary, BS, 63; Univ Pa, PhD(phys chem), 67. *Prof Exp:* Fel org solid state, Franklin Inst Res Labs, Pa, 68-70, res chemist, 71-77; scientist, Polaroid Corp, 77-86, sr res scientist, 86-89; res fel, Mead Imaging, 89-91. *Mem:* Am Chem Soc; Soc Imaging Sci & Technol. *Res:* Photochemistry; radiation chemistry of organic materials; photographic science; silver halide photographic emulsions; microencapsulation; dye diffusion thermal transfer; laser thermal transfer. *Mailing Add:* 32 Whittlers Ridge Pittsford NY 14534-4527. *Fax:* 716-588-9402; *E-Mail:* wsimpson@kodak.com

SIMPSON, WILLIAM ROY, plant pathology; deceased, see previous edition for last biography

SIMPSON, WILLIAM STEWART, PSYCHIATRY, HOSPITAL ADMINISTRATION. *Current Pos:* RETIRED. *Personal Data:* b Edmonton, Alta, Apr 11, 24; US citizen; m 50, Eleanor E Whitbread; c David R, Ian S, James W & Bert E. *Educ:* Univ Alta, Edmonton, BS, 44, MD, 48. *Honors & Awards:* Silver Key Award, Nat Coun Alcoholism, 75. *Prof Exp:* Sect chief psychiat, C F Menninger Mem Hosp, 59-66; assoc dir psychiat, Menninger Sch Psychiat, Menninger Found, 66-68, dir, Field Serv Fund Raising, 72-74; dir psychiat residency training & chief, Psychiat Serv, Topeka Vet Admin Hosp, 74-77; sr psychiatrist & psychoanalyst, Menninger Found, 77-84, assoc dir, Med Serv, Adult Outpatient Dept, 84-88, dir, Ctr Sexual Health, 86-92. *Concurrent Pos:* Mem fac, Menninger Sch Psychiat, 53-, mem exec comt & mgt comt, 54-77; clin dir psychiat & hosp admin, Topeka State Hosp, 54-59 & 68-72; first pres, Topeka Alcoholism Info Ctr, 63-67; assoc ed, Bull Menninger Clin, 64-70; mem bd dirs, Nat Coun Alcoholism, 68-77, vpres, 70-73, pres, 73-75; mem, Kans Citizens Adv Alcoholism, 73-77; lectr sex ther, Chinese Med Asn, Taipei, Taiwan, 85, Dept Psychol, Univ Warsaw, Poland, 87, Dept Psychiat, Tokai Univ Med Sch, Japan, 85. *Mem:* Fel Am Psychiat Asn; Am Psychoanal Asn; Am Asn Sex Educr, Counr & Therapists; Soc Sci Study Sex; Int Psychoanal Asn; Soc Sex Ther & Res. *Res:* Relationship between sex therapy and psychoanalysis; sexual dysfunctions in women with anorexia and bulimia nervosa. *Mailing Add:* 834 Buchanan Topeka KS 66606

SIMPSON, WILLIAM TRACY, CHEMISTRY. *Current Pos:* prof, 65-77, chmn dept, 72-75, EMER PROF CHEM, UNIV ORE, 77- *Personal Data:* b Berkeley, Calif, Dec 7, 20; m 44, 61, Carmen Tschudi; c Elizabeth, Jane, Carlos, Marjorie & John. *Educ:* Univ Calif, AB, 43, PhD(chem), 48. *Honors & Awards:* Calif Sect Award, Am Chem Soc. *Prof Exp:* Asst chem, Univ Calif, 46-48; instr, Univ Wash, 48-49, from asst prof to prof, 49-64. *Concurrent Pos:* Vis lectr, Univ Calif; vis prof, Fla State Univ; chmn, Gordon Conf Theoret Chem, 66; Fulbright vis prof, Lima, Peru, 71; assoc, Neurosci Res Prog, 63-65; assoc ed, J Chem Physics, 66-69. *Res:* Theoretical and experimental study of molecular electronic spectra; vacuum ultraviolet spectroscopy; electronic spectra of thin films and molecular crystals; theory of the index of refraction. *Mailing Add:* 1760 Royal Way San Luis Obispo CA 93405

SIMPSON-HERREN, LINDA, CHEMOTHERAPY, EXPERIMENTAL THERAPEUTICS. *Current Pos:* assoc physicist, Southern Res Inst, 48-57, res physicist, 57-69, sr physicist, 69-71, sect head cell & tissue kinetics, 71-94, PRIN SCIENTIST, SOUTHERN RES INST, 95- *Personal Data:* b Birmingham, Ala, July 7, 27; m 63, Thomas C; c 1. *Educ:* Univ Ala, BS, 48. *Prof Exp:* Instr physics, Univ Ala, 48. *Mem:* Am Asn Cancer Res; Cell Kinetics Soc (vpres, 77-78, pres, 78-79); AAAS; Sigma Xi; Health Physics Soc; Int Cell Cycle Soc. *Res:* Cell and tumor kinetics of experimental tumor systems to optimize scheduling of chemotherapy alone or in combination with surgery; radiation and drug effects; tumor and host heterogeneity; drug distribution; autoradiography. *Mailing Add:* Southern Res Inst PO Box 55305 Birmingham AL 35255-5305. *Fax:* 205-581-2877; *E-Mail:* herren@srj

SIMRALL, HARRY C(HARLES) F(LEMING), ELECTRICAL & MECHANICAL ENGINEERING. *Current Pos:* assoc prof elec eng, 45-47, prof elec eng & head dept, 47-57, dean col eng, 57-78, EMER DEAN COL ENG & EMER PROF ELEC ENG, MISS STATE UNIV, 78- *Personal Data:* b Memphis, Tenn, Oct 16, 12; m 36, Mary Virginia Miller. *Educ:* Miss State Univ, BS, 34 & 35; Univ Ill, MS, 39. *Prof Exp:* Instr elec eng, Miss State Univ, 34-35, instr drawing, 35-37, from instr to assoc prof elec eng, 37-44; engr, Cent Sta Eng, Indust Eng Dept, Westinghouse Elec Corp, 44-45. *Mem:* Fel Inst Elec & Electronics Engrs; Am Soc Eng Educ; Nat Soc Prof Engrs (vpres, 62-64, pres elect, 69-70, pres, 70-71). *Res:* Electric power. *Mailing Add:* 107 White Dr W Starkville MS 39759-2634

SIMRING, MARVIN, PERIODONTOLOGY, NUTRITION. *Current Pos:* VIS LECTR PERIODONT, NY UNIV, 79- *Personal Data:* b Brooklyn, NY, June 16, 22; m 49; c 4. *Educ:* Brooklyn Col, BA, 42; NY Univ Col Dent, DDS, 44; Am Bd Periodont, dipl, 55. *Honors & Awards:* Isadore Hirschfeld Award, NE Soc Periodontists, 75; Otto Loos Medal, Univ Frankfurt, WGer, 80; Meritorious Award Distinguished Serv, Am Acad Oral Med, 82. *Prof Exp:* Captain, US Army, Dent Corps, 44-47; clin prof & dir periodont, NY Univ Col Dent, 47-79; assoc prof, Univ Fla, 79-82. *Concurrent Pos:* Pvt pract dent, 47-55, periodont, 55-79 & 83-88; dir & attend dentist, Dept Periodont, Jewish Hosp, Brooklyn, 53-79; consult, US First Army Hosp, New York, 62-69, Brooklyn Vet Hosp, 70-79, US Vet Hosp, Gainesville, Fla, 79-82; pres, NE Soc Periodontists, 68-70 & NY Univ Br, Res Soc Am, 69-70; attend dentist, Shands Teaching Hosp, Fla, 79-82. *Mem:* Am Dent Asn; Am Acad Periodontol; fel Am Acad Oral Med; fel Am Col Dent; Am Asn Dent Res; fel Int Col Dent. *Res:* Relating periodontal health and disease to occlusion, splinting, appliances, nutrition, tooth movement, pulpal status, and root canal therapy; erosive lesions of teeth (abfractions). *Mailing Add:* 2501 NW 21st Ave Gainesville FL 32605

SIMS, ASA C, JR, PLANT PATHOLOGY. *Current Pos:* prof, Southern Univ, New Orleans, 68-70, chmn, Dept Biol, 68-69, chmn, Div Sci, 69-70, DEAN ACAD AFFAIRS, SOUTHERN UNIV, NEW ORLEANS, 70- *Personal Data:* b Asheville, NC, Sept 30, 19; m 43; c 2. *Educ:* Hampton Inst, BS, 40; Ohio State Univ, MS, 54, PhD, 56; Harvard Univ, dipl educ mgt, 73. *Prof Exp:* Instr hort, Fla Agr & Mech Col, 48-49; asst prof, SC State Col, 49-52; asst bot, Ohio State Univ, 53-56; from assoc prof to prof biol, Southern Univ, Baton Rouge, 56-68. *Concurrent Pos:* Sci fac fel, Univ Minn, 65-66. *Mem:* Am Phytopath Soc; Bot Soc Am. *Res:* Fungus physiology; nature of disease; radioisotopes. *Mailing Add:* 13617 Explorers Ave New Orleans LA 70126

SIMS, BENJAMIN TURNER, mathematics; deceased, see previous edition for last biography

SIMS, CHESTER THOMAS, metallurgical engineering; deceased, see previous edition for last biography

SIMS, ETHAN ALLEN HITCHCOCK, MEDICINE, BIOCHEMISTRY. *Current Pos:* from asst prof to prof, 50-85, EMER PROF MED, COL MED, UNIV VT, 85- *Personal Data:* b Newport, RI, Apr 22, 16; m 39; c 3. *Educ:* Harvard Univ, BS, 38; Columbia Univ, MD, 42. *Hon Degrees:* ScD, Univ Vt, 90. *Honors & Awards:* Herman Award, Am Soc Clin Nutrit, 87. *Prof Exp:* House officer, New Haven Hosp, Conn, 42-44; instr med, Sch Med, Yale Univ, 47-50. *Concurrent Pos:* Brown res fel, New Haven Hosp, Conn, 46-47; Commonwealth fel, Sch Med, Case Western Reserve Univ, 64-65; assoc attend physician, Mary Fletcher & DeGoesbriand Mem Hosps, 50-64; dir metab unit, Dept Med, Univ Vt, 57-73; attend physician, Med Ctr, Hosp of Vt, 64-; vis prof med, Div Endocrinol, Sch Med, Tufts Univ, 74-75. *Mem:* Fel Am Col Physicians; Am Fedn Clin Res; Endocrine Soc; Am Diabetes Asn; Am Soc Clin Nutrit; Sigma Xi. *Res:* Metabolic diseases; diabetes and obesity; software systems. *Mailing Add:* 3314 Wake Robin Dr Shelburne VT 05482. *Fax:* 802-656-8031

SIMS, JAMES JOSEPH, BIOLOGICALLY ACTIVE NATURAL PRODUCTS. *Current Pos:* lectr chem, Univ Calif, 64-65, asst chemist, 65-70, assoc prof, 70-74, dept chmn, 92-96, PROF PLANT PATH & CHEM, UNIV CALIF, RIVERSIDE, 74- *Personal Data:* b Woodland, Calif, June 13, 37; div; c 2. *Educ:* Ariz State Univ, BS, 59; Univ Calif, Los Angeles, PhD(org chem), 63. *Prof Exp:* NSF fel, Swiss Fed Inst Technol, 63-64. *Mem:* Am Chem Soc; Royal Soc Chem; Am Phytopathol Soc. *Res:* The chemistry of natural products; isolation; structure proof; synthesis. *Mailing Add:* Dept Plant Path Univ Calif Riverside CA 92521. *Fax:* 909-787-4294; *E-Mail:* james.sims@ucr.edu

SIMS, JAMES R(EDDING), CIVIL ENGINEERING. *Current Pos:* Instr civil eng, Rice Univ, 42-44 & 46-47, from asst prof to assoc prof, 47-58, chmn dept, 58-63, prof civil eng, 58-87, mgr campus bus affairs, 63-69, vpres, 69-70, dir campus bus, 70-74, Herman & George R Brown chair civil eng, 74-87, 74-87, EMER HERMAN & GEORGE R BROWN PROF CIVIL ENG, RICE UNIV,87- *Personal Data:* b Macon, Ga, July 2, 18; m 46, Marjorie Brittain; c 3. *Educ:* Rice Inst, BS, 41; Univ Ill, MS, 50, PhD(eng), 56. *Concurrent Pos:* Consult, Humble Oil & Refining Co, Exxon, 53-62. *Mem:* Fel Am Soc Civil Engrs (vpres, 70-71, pres, 81-82). *Res:* Structural materials, particularly steel and concrete; structures in open sea subject to storm loading; protective construction subject to blast loading. *Mailing Add:* 5111 Westerdale St Rice Univ PO Box 1892 Fulshear TX 77441-4208

SIMS, JOHN DAVID, SEDIMENTOLOGY, QUATERNARY GEOLOGY. *Current Pos:* geologist, 67-82, sr res geologist, 82-93, DEP CHIEF FOR EXTERNAL RES, US GEOL SURV, 93- *Personal Data:* b Decatur, Ill, Dec 7, 39; c 2. *Educ:* Univ Ill, BS, 63; Univ Cincinnati, MS, 64; Northwestern Univ, PhD(geol), 67. *Honors & Awards:* Meritorious Award, Am Planning Asn, 80 & 81. *Prof Exp:* Res asst, Ill Geol Surv, 60-63. *Concurrent Pos:* Consult, Yugoslavia Post Earthquake Study, NSF, 79, People's Repub China, Earthquake Hazards, 87. *Mem:* Int Asn Sedimentologists; Soc Econ Paleont & Mineral; Am Geophys Union; Sigma Xi; Geol Soc Am; Am Quaternary Asn. *Res:* Late Cenozoic stratigraphic and sedimentologic studies of lacustrine sediments; earthquake-induced deformation of soft sediments; pleistocene paleolimnology and paleoclimatology; detailed geologic studies in and near the San Andreas fault zone. *Mailing Add:* US Geol Surv 12201 Sunrise Valley Dr MS 905 Reston VA 20192

SIMS, JOHN LEONIDAS, AGRONOMY. *Current Pos:* RETIRED. *Personal Data:* b Sedalia, Ky, May 4, 30; m 51; c 4. *Educ:* Univ Ky, BS, 55, MS, 56; Iowa State Univ, PhD(soil microbiol), 60. *Prof Exp:* Asst soils, Univ Ky, 55-56 & Iowa State Univ, 56-60; asst prof agron, Univ Ark, 60-66; from asst prof to prof agron, Univ Ky, 66-95. *Concurrent Pos:* Vis assoc prof agron, La State Univ, 73-74. *Mem:* Am Soc Agron; Soil Sci Soc Am. *Res:* Soil plant relationships in the mineral nutrition of tobacco; microbial processes in soil as related to soil fertility and nitrogen fertilization of tobacco. *Mailing Add:* Dept Agron Agr Sci Ctr Univ Ky N Bldg Off N122 Lexington KY 40546-0091

SIMS, JOHN LEROY, INTERNAL MEDICINE, GASTROENTEROLOGY. *Current Pos:* from instr to assoc prof, 46-56, PROF MED, MED SCH, UNIV WIS-MADISON, 56-, COORDR, OUTREACH POSTGRAD MED EDUC, 83- *Personal Data:* b Houston, Tex, Sept 21, 12; m 42, Anne Schuroh; c John E, Elizabeth A & Thomas L. *Educ:* Rice Inst, BA, 33; Univ Tex, MD, 37. *Prof Exp:* From intern to resident med, Wis Gen Hosp, 37-42. *Concurrent Pos:* Mem staff, Wis Gen Hosp, 42- *Mem:* AAAS; fel AMA; Am Soc Internal Med; Am Fedn Clin Res; fel Am Col Physicians; Cent Soc Clin Res. *Res:* Internal medicine; hepatic disease. *Mailing Add:* H6/516 Univ Hosp Univ Wis Med Sch Madison WI 53792

SIMS, LESLIE BERL, PHYSICAL CHEMISTRY. *Current Pos:* asst prof, 67-70, assoc prof, 70-76, PROF CHEM, UNIV ARK, FAYETTEVILLE, 76-, CHMN DEPT, 79- *Personal Data:* b Royalton, Ill, Mar 21, 37; m 58; c 3. *Educ:* Southern Ill Univ, BA, 58; Univ Ill, MS, 61, PhD(chem), 67. *Prof Exp:* Asst prof chem, Mich State Univ, 64-67. *Mem:* Am Chem Soc; Sigma Xi. *Res:* Chemical kinetics; kinetic isotope effects; gas phase unimolecular reactions; theoretical kinetics; reaction dynamics; molecular vibrations. *Mailing Add:* 404 Linder Rd E Iowa City IA 52240-9112

SIMS, PAUL KIBLER, GEOLOGY. *Current Pos:* GEOLOGIST, US GEOL SURV, 73- *Personal Data:* b Newton, Ill, Sept 8, 18; m 40, Dolores Thomes; c Thomas C & Charlotte Ann. *Educ:* Univ Ill, AB, 40, MS, 42; Princeton Univ, PhD(geol), 50. *Honors & Awards:* Thayer Lindsley Distinguished lectr, Soc Econ Geologists, 84-85; Ralph W Marsden Medal Award, 89; Goldich Medal, Inst Lake Superior Geol, 85; Distinguished Serv Award, Dept Interior, 91. *Prof Exp:* Asst, Univ Ill, 40-42; spec asst geologist, State Geol Surv, Ill, 42-43; geologist, US Geol Surv, 43-44 & 46-61; dir, Minn Geol Surv, 61-73. *Concurrent Pos:* Asst, Princeton Univ, 46-47; pres, Econ Geol Publ Co, 79-96; co-ed, 75th Anniversary Vol, Econ Geol, 81. *Mem:* Geol Soc Am; Soc Econ Geol; Soc Econ Geol (pres, 75-76). *Res:* Early crustal evolution in Lake Superior and Midcontinent region; geology and magnetite iron ore deposits in New Jersey; geology and ore deposits of the Front Range, Colorado; precambrian geology and ore deposits of Minnesota, Wisconsin, Michigan and Southeastern Wyoming. *Mailing Add:* US Geol Surv Denver Fed Ctr Box 25046 MS 905 Denver CO 80225

SIMS, PETER JAY, IMMUNOCHEMISTRY, MEMBRANE BIOPHYSICS. *Current Pos:* ASSOC PROF MED, HEALTH SCI CTR, OKLA UNIV, 85- *Educ:* Duke Univ, MD, 80, PhD(physiol & pharmacol), 80. *Concurrent Pos:* Assoc mem, Okla Med Res Found, 85-; sci dir, Okla Blood Inst, 85- *Res:* Physical biochemistry. *Mailing Add:* Blood Res Inst Blood Ctr SE Wisconsin PO Box 2178 Milwaukee WI 53201-2178. *Fax:* 414-937-6284

SIMS, PHILLIP LEON, RANGE SCIENCE. *Current Pos:* RES LEADER, US SOUTHERN GREAT PLAINS FIELD STA, SCI & EDUC ADMIN-AGR RES, USDA, 77- *Personal Data:* b Mountain View, Okla, Apr 7, 40; m 62; c 2. *Educ:* Okla State Univ, BS, 62, MS, 64; Utah State Univ, PhD(range sci), 67. *Prof Exp:* From asst prof to assoc prof range sci, Colo State Univ, 67-77. *Mem:* Soc Range Mgt; Am Soc Animal Sci; Brit Ecol Soc. *Res:* Range animal nutrition, management and improvements; dynamics of primary producer; grazing systems; secondary productivity of range ecosystems. *Mailing Add:* 2712 Oak Hollow Rd Woodward OK 73801

SIMS, REX J, ORGANIC CHEMISTRY. *Current Pos:* RETIRED. *Personal Data:* b Racine, Wis, July 1, 22; m 45; c 2. *Educ:* Wabash Col, AB, 44; Northwestern Univ, PhD(org chem), 49. *Honors & Awards:* Indust Achievement Award, Inst Food Technologists, 70. *Prof Exp:* Asst, Nat Defense Res Comt, Northwestern Univ, 43-45; res chemist, Swift & Co, Ill, 49-61; res scientist, Gen Foods Corp, 61-80, prin scientist, Tech Ctr, 80-88. *Mem:* Am Chem Soc; Am Oil Chemists Soc. *Res:* Fats and oils; kojic acid and pyrones; fat oxidation; emulsification. *Mailing Add:* 51 Guion St Pleasantville NY 10570

SIMS, ROBERT ALAN, INSTRUMENTATION, COMPUTER SCIENCE. *Current Pos:* asst prof instrumentation, 69-80, ASSOC PROF ELECTRONICS & INSTRUMENTATION, GRAD INST TECHNOL, UNIV ARK, LITTLE ROCK, 80- *Personal Data:* b Colorado Springs, Colo, Nov 1, 36; m 59; c 1. *Educ:* Colo Sch Mines, Engr, 58, MS, 61; Univ Okla, PhD(chem eng), 68. *Prof Exp:* Asst prof eng, Wright State Univ, 68-69. *Mem:* Instrument Soc Am; Sigma Xi. *Res:* Process control; computer simulation; instrumental applications of microcomputers and microcontrollers. *Mailing Add:* Univ Ark Etas 575 2801 S University Ave Little Rock AR 72204-1099

SIMS, SAMUEL JOHN, ECONOMIC GEOLOGY. *Current Pos:* CONSULT GEOLOGIST, 85- *Personal Data:* b Los Angeles, Calif, Feb 20, 34; m 61; c 2. *Educ:* Calif Inst Technol, BS, 55; Univ Tex, MA, 57; Stanford Univ, PhD(geol), 60. *Prof Exp:* Geologist, Soc des Mines de Fer de Mekambo, 60-62 Companhia Minas de Jangada, 62-64; geologist, Dept Geol, Bethlehem Steel Corp, 64-78, sr geologist, 78-82, admnr, 82-85. *Mem:* Geol Soc Am; Soc Econ Geol; Am Inst Mining, Metall & Petrol Eng. *Res:* Geological exploration for economic mineral deposits. *Mailing Add:* 768 Redfern Lane Bethlehem PA 18017. *E-Mail:* 5768@aol.com

SIMS, WILLIAM LYNN, VEGETABLE CROPS. *Current Pos:* RETIRED. *Personal Data:* b Hazen, Ark, May 30, 24; m 51, Jewel Sanner; c William L, John M & Julie B. *Educ:* Univ Wis, BS, 48, MS, 49, PhD, 54. *Honors & Awards:* Carl Bittner Ext Award, 72; Hort Hon Award, Asn Portuguese Hort, 79. *Prof Exp:* From asst prof to assoc prof hort, Tex Col Arts & Industs, 52-57; assoc agriculturist, Univ Calif, Davis, 57-63, agriculturist, 63-88. *Concurrent Pos:* Fulbright res scholar, NZ-US Educ Found, 74-75; assoc dir, Agr Develop Systs, Univ Calif/Egypt, US Agency Int Develop, 81-82; Int Exec Serv Corps, Dominican Republic & Morocco, 87 & 88. *Mem:* Fel Am Soc Hort Sci; fel AAAS. *Res:* Agricultural extension; variety evaluation and growth regulations. *Mailing Add:* 823 Linden Lane Davis CA 95616. *Fax:* 530-752-9659

SIMSKE, STEVEN JOHN, DISEASE ISOMORPHISMS-ANIMAL MODELS FOR HUMAN DISEASES, BONE IMPLANTS FOR BONY INGROWTH. *Current Pos:* RES ASSOC, BIOSERVE SPACE TECHNOL, 90-, FAC INSTR, REGIS UNIV, 92- *Personal Data:* b San Diego, Calif, July 28, 64; m, Teresa Gritmon. *Educ:* Marquette Univ, BS, 86; Rensselaer Polytech Inst, MS, 87; Univ Colo, PhD(elec eng), 90. *Prof Exp:* Instr, Weber State, 86; res asst, Rensselaer Polytech Inst, 86-87 & Univ Colo, 88-90. *Concurrent Pos:* Fac, Dept Elec Eng, Univ Colo, 90-; consult, Omnitech, 92- *Mem:* Inst Elec & Electronics Engrs; Soc Biomat. *Res:* Space flight and ground-based research on osteopenia and other bone disorders; investigation of biocompatibility of porous bone implants and immune system disorders. *Mailing Add:* Univ Colo Box 425 Boulder CO 80309-0425. *Fax:* 303-492-8883; *E-Mail:* simske@spot.colorado.edu

SIMSON, JO ANNE V, ELECTRON MICROSCOPY, CYTOCHEMISTRY. *Current Pos:* asst prof path, 70-75, from asst prof to prof anat, 75-96, EMER PROF ANAT, MED UNIV SC, 96- *Personal Data:* b Chicago, Ill, Nov 19, 36; div; c Maria, Elisabeth (Smith) & Briana (Smith). *Educ:* Kalamazoo Col, BA, 59; Univ Mich, MS, 61; State Univ NY, PhD(anat), 69. *Prof Exp:* Instr anat, State Univ NY Upstate Med Ctr, 67-68; Nat Cancer Inst fel cell biol, Fels Res Inst, Sch Med, Temple Univ, 68-70. *Concurrent Pos:* Ed bd, Anat Rec, 75-85; Fogarty Int Fel, 87-88. *Mem:* Am Asn Cell Biol; Am Asn Anat; Histochem Soc (secy, 79-83, coun, 85-89). *Res:* Light and electron microscopic morphology and cytochemistry, especially of secretory processes; cellular ion localization and transport; membrane alterations during both exocytosis and endocytosis; cell membrane traffic. *Mailing Add:* Dept Anat Med Univ SC 171 Ashley Ave Charleston SC 29425. *Fax:* 803-792-0664; *E-Mail:* joanne__simson@smtpqw.musc.edu

SIMUNEK, JIRI, NUMERIC MODELING, SOLUTE TRANSPORT. *Current Pos:* SOIL SCIENTIST & RES ASSOC, UNIV CALIF, 90- *Personal Data:* b Teplice, Czech, Oct 24, 59; m 87, Alena Taxova; c Katerina S. *Educ:* Czech Tech Univ Prague, MSc, 84; Czech Acad Sci, PhD(solute transport), 93. *Prof Exp:* Res assoc, Res Inst Soil Protection, 84-90. *Mem:* Am Geophys Union. *Res:* Multicomponent solute transport in variably saturated porous media; numerical modeling; carbon dioxide transport; kinetic and equilibrium reaction. *Mailing Add:* 450 W Big Springs Rd Riverside CA 92507. *Fax:* 909-369-4818

SINAI, JOHN JOSEPH, PHYSICS. *Current Pos:* asst prof, 64-68, dir comput ctr, 66-70, assoc dean arts & sci, 70-74, actg chmn Dept Physics, 74-75, chmn dept, 75-78, assoc prof, 68-79, PROF PHYSICS, UNIV LOUISVILLE, 79- *Personal Data:* b Whiting, Ind, Oct 27, 30; m 57; c 5. *Educ:* Miami Univ, BA, 53; Univ Ill, MS, 55; Purdue Univ, PhD(physics), 63. *Prof Exp:* Res assoc physics, Univ Chicago, 63-64. *Mem:* Am Phys Soc; Sigma Xi. *Res:* Vibrational spectra of disordered solids. *Mailing Add:* 60 Eastover Ct Louisville KY 40206

SINAI, YAKOV G, THEORETICAL MATHEMATICS. *Current Pos:* SR RESEARCHER, LANDAU INST THEORET PHYSICS, ACAD SCI, MOSCOW, 71-; PROF, DEPT MATH, PRINCETON UNIV, 93- *Personal Data:* b Moscow, Sept 21, 35. *Educ:* Moscow State Univ, BS, 57, PhD(math), 60, Dr, 63. *Hon Degrees:* Dr, Warsaw Univ, 93. *Honors & Awards:* Loeb lectr, Harvard Univ, 78; Boltzman Gold Medal, 86; Heineman Prize, 89; S Lefshetz lectr, Mex, 90; Markov Prize, 90; Paul Adrian Maurice Dirac Medal, Int Ctr Theoret Physics, 92; Wolf Prize Math, 97. *Prof Exp:* Sci researcher, Lab Probabilistic & Statist Methods, Moscow State Univ, 60-71, prof math, 71-93. *Concurrent Pos:* Distinguished lectr, Tunis Univ, 89. *Mem:* Foreign hon mem Am Acad Arts & Sci; Russian Acad Sci; foreign mem Hungarian Acad Sci. *Res:* Probabilistic and statistical methods. *Mailing Add:* Dept Math Princeton Univ Fine Hall Washington Rd Princeton NJ 08544-1000

SINANOGLU, OKTAY, THEORETICAL CHEMISTRY. *Current Pos:* RETIRED. *Personal Data:* b Bari, Italy, Feb 25, 35; Turkish citizen; m 63; c 2. *Educ:* Univ Calif, Berkeley, BS, 56, PhD(theoret chem), 59; Mass Inst Technol, MS, 57. *Honors & Awards:* Turkish Sci Medal, 66; Alexander von Humboldt Award, 73. *Prof Exp:* Chemist, Lawrence Radiation Lab, Univ Calif, Berkeley, 59-60; from asst prof to prof chem, Yale Univ, 60-97, prof molecular biophys, 65-97. *Concurrent Pos:* Sloan fel, 61-64; vis prof, Middle East Tech Univ, Ankara, Turkey, 62-64, consult prof, 64-; consult, Rocket Oxidizers Res Prog, Adv Res Projs Agency, 64 & Turkish Sci & Tech Res Coun, 73-; ed of biol & phys scientists, NIH, 64; mem, Parr Subcomt on Theoret Chem of Westheimer Comt, Nat Acad Sci, 64-65; co-chmn elect, Gordon Res Conf physics & chem of biopolymers, 66; mem subpanel on atomic, molecular physics, Inst Defense Anal, 66; mem chem rev comt & consult, Argonne Univ Asn for Argonne Nat Lab; consult prof, Bogazici Univ, Turkey, 73- *Mem:* Am Inst Chem Engrs; Inst Am Chemists; Am Chem Soc; Am Phys Soc; Am Acad Arts & Sci. *Res:* Theoretical chemistry; quantum chemistry; theory of intermolecular forces; theory of solvent effects of biopolymer structure; biochemical reaction networks; many-electron theory of atoms and molecules. *Mailing Add:* 1693 SW Boatswain Pl Palm City FL 34990

SINCLAIR, A RICHARD, hydraulic fracturing, well stimulation, for more information see previous edition

SINCLAIR, ALASTAIR JAMES, EARTH SCIENCES, MINERAL DEPOSITS. *Current Pos:* from asst prof to assoc prof, 64-74, dept head, 85-90, PROF GEOL, UNIV BC, 74-, DIR GEOL ENG, 93-; PRES, SINCLAIR CONSULT, LTD, VANCOUVER, 80- *Personal Data:* b Hamilton, Ont, Aug 1, 35; m 64, Elizabeth Mary Sylvia Hill; c Alison (Trevena) & Fiona (Tamsin). *Educ:* Univ Toronto, BASc, 57, MASc, 58; Univ BC, PhD(geol), 64. *Honors & Awards:* Distinguished Serv Award, Mineral Deposits Div, Geol Asn Can, 90. *Prof Exp:* Asst prof geol, Univ Wash, 62-64. *Concurrent Pos:* Consult, numerous mining co, 64-, Placer Dome Ltd, 78-91 & UN Seatrad Ctr, Malaysia, 83-85; exchange scientist, France, 72-73 & Brazil, 81, 82 & 87; hon mem, Sci Tech Comn Geochem, Geol Soc Brazil, 82; Killam sr fel, 90-91. *Mem:* Can Inst Mining, Metall & Petrol; Asn Explor Geochemists; Soc Econ Geol; Geol Asn Can. *Res:* Origin of mineral deposits; isotope geology related to mineral deposits; zoning applied to mineral exploration; geostatistics; mineral exploration data analysis. *Mailing Add:* Dept Earth & Ocean Sci Univ BC Vancouver BC V6T 1Z4 Can. *Fax:* 604-822-6088; *E-Mail:* asinclai@earth.eos.ubc.ca

SINCLAIR, ANNETTE, MATHEMATICS. *Current Pos:* RETIRED. *Personal Data:* b Hale, Mo, Aug 14, 16. *Educ:* Cent Mo State Col, BS, 40; Univ Ill, AM, 45, PhD(math), 49. *Prof Exp:* Teacher pub schs, Mo, 34-42; actuarial clerk, Gen Am Life Ins Co, 42-44; asst, Univ Ill, 44-49; instr, Univ Tenn, 49-52; from asst prof to assoc prof math, Southern Ill Univ, 52-57; assoc prof math, Purdue Univ, West Lafayette, 57-86. *Concurrent Pos:* Vis assoc prof, Univ Okla, 66-68. *Mem:* Am Math Soc; Math Asn Am; Sigma Xi. *Res:* Theory of approximation by analytic functions. *Mailing Add:* 1857 Restful Dr Bradenton FL 34207

SINCLAIR, CHARLES KENT, EXPERIMENTAL HIGH ENERGY PHYSICS, APPLIED PHYSICS & ACCELERATOR PHYSICS. *Current Pos:* SR SCIENTIST, CEBAF, 87- *Personal Data:* b Watertown, NY, Aug 9, 38; m 83, Mary F Paine. *Educ:* Rensselaer Polytech Inst, BS, 60; Cornell Univ, PhD(Physics), 67. *Prof Exp:* Res assoc physics, Tufts Univ, 66-68, asst prof, 68-69; staff physicist, Stanford Linear Accelerator Ctr, 69-87. *Concurrent Pos:* Adj prof, Col William & Mary. *Mem:* Fel Am Phys Soc; Sigma Xi; Am Vacuum Soc. *Res:* Research with polarized high energy electrons and gamma rays; photocathode studies; electron polarimetry; accelerator research and development. *Mailing Add:* Jefferson Lab 12000 Jefferson Ave Newport News VA 23606. *Fax:* 757-269-5024; *E-Mail:* sinclair@cebaf.gov

SINCLAIR, D G, ACADEMIC ADMINISTRATION. *Current Pos:* from asst prof to assoc prof, Queen's Univ, Ont, 66-72, prof physiol, 72, dean, Fac Arts & Sci, 74-84, vprin, 84-88, dean fac med & vprin health sci, 88-96, CHAIR, HEALTH SERV RESTRUCTURING COMT, QUEENS UNIV, ONT, 96- *Personal Data:* b Rochester, NY, Nov 2, 33; Can citizen; m 58; c 1. *Educ:* Univ Toronto, DVM, 58, MSA, 60; Queen's Univ, PhD(physiol), 63. *Prof Exp:* USPHS fel, Columbia Univ, 62-63; fel physiol & Meres sr scholar med res, St John's Col, Cambridge Univ, 63-65. *Concurrent Pos:* Markle Scholar acad med, 66-71; dir, Med Res Coun, Ottawa, 83-84. *Mem:* Can Physiol Soc. *Res:* Gastrointestinal physiology. *Mailing Add:* Health Serv Restructuring Comm 56 Wellesley St W 12th Floor Toronto ON M5S 2S3 Can

SINCLAIR, DOUGLAS C, OPTICAL ENGINEERING. *Current Pos:* PRES, SINCLAIR OPTICS, NY, 80- *Personal Data:* b Cambridge, Mass, July 13, 38; m 60; c 2. *Educ:* Mass Inst Technol, BS, 60; Univ Rochester, PhD(optics), 63. *Honors & Awards:* Adolph Lomb Medal, Optical Soc Am, 68. *Prof Exp:* Asst prof optics, Univ Rochester, 65-67; tech dir, Spectra-Physics, Calif, 67-69; from assoc prof to prof optics, Univ Rochester, 69-80. *Concurrent Pos:* Lectr, Stanford Univ, 69; consult, Nat Acad Sci, 70; ed, Optical Eng, 72; ed, J Optical Soc Am, 76-78. *Mem:* AAAS; Optical Soc Am. *Res:* Design of optical systems; development of software for optical design. *Mailing Add:* 6780 Palmyra Rd Fairport NY 14450-3342

SINCLAIR, GLENN BRUCE, SOLID MECHANICS. *Current Pos:* from asst prof to assoc prof, 77-82, head dept, 86-92, PROF MECH ENG, CARNEGIE-MELLON UNIV, 82- *Personal Data:* b Auckland, NZ, Mar 7, 46; c 4. *Educ:* Univ Auckland, BSc, 67, BE, 69; Calif Inst Technol, PhD(appl mech), 72. *Prof Exp:* Res scientist, Dept Sci & Indust Res, Appl Math Div, Wellington, 68-69; J Willard Gibbs instr appl sci & eng, Yale Univ, 72-74; lectr appl mech, Univ Auckland, 74-77. *Concurrent Pos:* Instr, Auckland Tech Inst, 64-66, 69, & 75-77; prof, Pratt & Whitney Aircraft Corp, Conn, 78, Fla, 79; vis prof, Dept Eng, Cambridge Univ, 81. *Mem:* Am Acad Mech. *Res:* Modelling and analysis of engineering problems in solid and structural mechanics particularly as related to fatigue and fracture mechanics and contact problems; development of both analytical and numerical methods for such problems. *Mailing Add:* Dept Mech Eng Carnegie-Mellon Univ Pittsburgh PA 15213

SINCLAIR, HENRY BEALL, ORGANIC CHEMISTRY. *Current Pos:* RETIRED. *Personal Data:* b St Louis, Mo, Jan 11, 30; m 55; c 2. *Educ:* Univ Calif, Berkeley, BS, 52; Mass Inst Technol, PhD(org chem), 59. *Prof Exp:* Res chemist, Mallinckrodt Chem Works, 52-54 & Procter & Gamble Co, 58-63; res chemist, Northern Regional Res Lab, USDA, 63-69, prin chemist, 69-78, res chemist, 78-90. *Mem:* Am Chem Soc; AAAS. *Res:* Amino acids; heterocyclics; opium alkaloids; carbohydrates and their derivatives. *Mailing Add:* 1019 W Teton Dr Peoria IL 61614-1945

SINCLAIR, J CAMERON, NEUROPHYSIOLOGY & BIOMEDICAL ENGINEERING, MATH & SCIENCE EDUCATION. *Current Pos:* RETIRED. *Personal Data:* b Butte, Mont, Dec 19, 18; m 45, Una Winstead; c Marti, Mary & Michael. *Educ:* Univ Calif, Berkeley, AB, 48; Univ Calif, Los Angeles, MA, 56; Iowa State Univ, PhD(physiol), 66. *Prof Exp:* Res asst biochem, White Mem Hosp, Los Angeles, 48-52; res asst surg, Univ Calif, Los Angeles, 54-56 & anat, 56-57; res assoc physiol, Univ Calif, San Francisco, 60-61; assoc prof biol, Gordon Col, 62-63; assoc prof, Buena Vista Col, 67-70; res scientist, Div Neuro-Pharmacol, NJ Neuropsychiat Inst, 70-72, educ consult elem math, 73-88. *Concurrent Pos:* Res fel physiol, Univ Minn, 66-67; assoc prof psychol, Rider Col, 70-73; consult, Lift Inc; life mem, Woman's pace. *Mem:* AAAS. *Res:* Instrumentation for cardiovascular physiology; neurophysiology of behavior and sensory integration; neurophysiological bases of mental health; diagnosis of mental illness; teaching math to children as a language is taught via computers. *Mailing Add:* 320 Genesee St Trenton NJ 08611-1912. *E-Mail:* camsinc@aol.com

SINCLAIR, JAMES BURTON, PLANT PATHOLOGY. *Current Pos:* RETIRED. *Personal Data:* b Chicago, Ill, Dec 21, 27. *Educ:* Lawrence Univ, BS, 51; Univ Wis-Madison, PhD(plant path), 55. *Honors & Awards:* Paul A Funk Award, 85; Soybean Res Recognition Award, ICI Americas/Am Soybean Asn, 83; Award of Distinguished Serv, US Dept Agr, 88; Res Award, Am Soybean Asn, 89; Distinguished Serv Award, N Cent Div, Am Phytopath Soc, 91. *Prof Exp:* Res asst plant path, Univ Wis-Madison, 51-55, res assoc, 55-56; from asst prof to prof, La State Univ, Baton Rouge, 56-68, asst to chancellor, 66-68; prof plant path, Univ Ill, Urbana, 68-96. *Concurrent Pos:* Grants, Olin Mathieson Chem Corp, 60-66; partic, Adv Virol Sem, Univ Md, 63; secy, Cotton Dis Coun, 63-64; chmn, 65-66; Allied Chem Co, 64; partic conf seed & soil treatment, Am Phytopath Soc, 65-67, chmn, 67, partic conf plant dis control & diag, 67; La State Univ Found res grants, 65-67, grad sch for travel grant, 68; US Rubber Co, 66-68; E I Du Pont de Nemours & Co Inc, 66-68; Diamond Alkali Co, 66; Conf Control Soil Fungi, Ariz, 68; Am Phytopath Soc for travel grant, 68; Agency Int Develop develop grant, 68-73; Int Cong Plant Path, London, 68, Minneapolis, 73 & Munich, 78; Indian Sci Cong, Kharapur, 70; Int Cong Plant Protection, Paris, 70; Sem Plant Protection Trop Food Crops, Ibadan, 71; travel grant, Ford Found, 71; campus coordr, Ill-Tehran Res Unit, 73-78; develop progs, Pakistan & Zambia, 80-90; dir, Nat Soybean Res Lab, 92-96. *Mem:* AAAS; fel Am Phytopath Soc; Am Inst Biol Sci; hon mem Am Soc Agron; fel Nat Acad Sci India. *Res:* Cotton seedling disease control and tolerance to fungicides; cytology and ultrastructure of Rhizoctonia; pathogenicity of Geotrichum; citrus fruit rots and viral diseases; seed and soil-borne diseases and microorganisms of soybean; soybean seed quality; biological control of plant diseases. *Mailing Add:* Dept Plant Path Univ Ill 1102 S Goodwin Ave Urbana IL 61801-4709. *Fax:* 217-244-1706; *E-Mail:* jsinclai@staff.uiuc.edu

SINCLAIR, JAMES DOUGLAS, RELIABILITY OF ELECTRONICS, ANALYTICAL CHEMISTRY. *Current Pos:* HEAD MAT RELIABILITY & ELECTROCHEM RES, AT&T BELL LABS, 85- *Personal Data:* b Evanston, Ill, Nov 23, 45; m 67; c 3. *Educ:* Purdue Univ, BS, 67; Univ Wis, PhD(inorg chem), 72. *Concurrent Pos:* Supvr, Contamination Res Group, 72-85. *Mem:* Am Chem Soc; Inst Elec & Electronic Engrs; Electrochem Soc; Nat Asn Corrosion Engrs; Am Asn Aerosol Res. *Res:* Materials reliability of electronic devices; contamination research and control; interaction of corrosive particles and corrosive gases with electronic equipment; analytical techniques for measuring ionic contaminants on surfaces; clean room manufacturing technology; electrochemical corrosion processes. *Mailing Add:* 11 Mount Vernon Ave Summit NJ 07901

SINCLAIR, JAMES LEWIS, BIODEGRADATION OF PESTICIDES IN THE SUBSURFACE & GROUND WATER, MICROBIAL POPULATIONS OF THE SUBSURFACE. *Current Pos:* RES MICROBIOLOGIST, MANTECH ENVIRON RES SERVS CORP, 88- *Personal Data:* b Salina, Kans, Aug 12, 49; m 79, Martha Walker; c Michael & Anne. *Educ:* Colo State Univ, BS, 71, PhD(microbial ecol), 80. *Prof Exp:* Postdoctoral assoc, Dept Agron, Cornell Univ, 80-84, res assoc, Dept Microbiol, 84-88. *Mem:* Am Soc Microbiol; Soc Protozoologists. *Res:* Studies of biodegradation of pesticides in the subsurface and subsurface microbial ecology focusing on protozoa. *Mailing Add:* ManTech Environ Res Servs Corp Robert S Kerr Environ Res Lab PO Box 1198 Ada OK 74821

SINCLAIR, JOHN G, PHARMACOLOGY, PAIN. *Current Pos:* PROF PHARMACOL, SCH PHARMACEUT, UNIV BC, 80- *Personal Data:* b Saskatoon, Sask, Sept 4, 40; m; c Todd, Leah & Shauna. *Educ:* Purdue Univ, PhD(neuropharmacol), 68. *Mem:* Int Asn Study Pain; Am Soc Pharmacol Therapeut; Neurosci Soc; Pharmacol Soc Can. *Res:* Neurophysiol and pharmacology of pain in animals. *Mailing Add:* Div Pharmacol Fac Pharmaceut Sci Univ BC 2329 West Mall Vancouver BC V6T 1W5 Can. *Fax:* 604-822-3035; *E-Mail:* jsinc@unixg.ubc.ca

SINCLAIR, KENNETH F(RANCIS), ENGINEERING PHYSICS. *Current Pos:* RETIRED. *Personal Data:* b Kentfield, Calif, Jan 26, 25; m 53; c 6. *Educ:* Univ Calif, BS, 50. *Prof Exp:* Jr investr, Lab Instrumentation Prog, US Naval Radiol Defense Labs, 50-54, investr, 54-56, head, Radiac Eng Prog, 56-58, head, Radiation Instrumentation Br, 58-67; res scientist, Hq, NASA, Moffett Field, 67-72; pres, Xetex, Inc, Mountain View, 72-90. *Mem:* Sr mem Inst Elec & Electronics Engrs; Health Physics Soc; Am Soc Nondestructive Testing. *Res:* Remote sensing; systems analysis; nuclear instrumentation; nondestructive testing; data handling and processing; radiation detectors. *Mailing Add:* 19615 Saratoga Los Gatos Rd Saratoga CA 95070

SINCLAIR, MICHAEL MACKAY, FISHERIES MANAGEMENT, POPULATION BIOLOGY. *Current Pos:* DIR, BIOL SCI BR, SCOTIA-FUNDY REGION DEPT FISHERIES & OCEAN, BEDFORD INST OCEANOG, 88- *Personal Data:* b New Glasgow, NS, June 20, 44; m 70; c 1. *Educ:* Queen's Univ, Can, Bsc, 67; Southampton Univ, UK, MSc, 69; Univ Calif, San Diego, PhD(oceanog), 77. *Prof Exp:* Prof oceanog, Univ Que, Rimouski, 73-77, dir, MSc Oceanog Prog, 76-77; res scientist fisheries mgt, Bedford Inst Oceanog, 78-82, head, Pop Dynamics Sect, Marine Fish Div, 81-82; chief, Invert & Marine Plants Div, Halifax Lab, 82-88,. *Concurrent Pos:* Vis researcher, Sta Zoologique, Ville Franche-sur-Mer, 78. *Res:* Phytoplankton temporal and spatial distributions in relation to physical processes; population biology of marine animals. *Mailing Add:* Bedford Inst Oceanog PO Box 1006 Dartmouth NS B2Y 4A2 Can

SINCLAIR, NICHOLAS RODERICK, IMMUNOLOGY. *Current Pos:* asst prof, Univ Western Ont, 67-73, assoc prof microbiol & immunol, 73-77, assoc prof med, 77-80, actg chmn, Dept Bact & Immunol, 74-76, asst dean res, Fac Med, 78-80, PROF MICROBIOL & IMMUNOL, UNIV WESTERN ONT, 79-, PROF MED, 80-, CHMN, DEPT MICROBIOL & IMMUNOL, 81- *Personal Data:* b Bradford-on-Avon, Eng, Apr 20, 36; Can citizen; m 61, 76, Rose Magliano; c Roderick, Geoffry, Matthew, Emily, James & Nicole. *Educ:* Dalhousie Univ, BSc, 57, MD, 62, PhD(biochem), 65. *Prof Exp:* Vis scientist immunol, Chester Beatty Res Inst, Eng, 65-67. *Concurrent Pos:* Med Res Coun Can fel, 64-67 & scholar, 67-72; assoc dir, Transplant Monitoring Lab, dept nephrol, Univ Hosp, 73-80. *Mem:* Can Soc Immunol (vpres, 81-); Am Asn Immunologists. *Res:* Immunobiology; autoimmunity. *Mailing Add:* Dept Microbiol & Immunol Univ Western Ont London ON N6A 5C1 Can. *Fax:* 519-661-3499

SINCLAIR, NORVAL A, MICROBIOLOGY. *Current Pos:* from asst prof to assoc prof microbiol, 68-82, ASSOC HEAD MICROBIOL & IMMUNOL, UNIV ARIZ, 82- *Personal Data:* b Sturgis, SDak, Sept 1, 35; m 58; c 3. *Educ:* SDak State Univ, BS, 57, MS, 59; Wash State Univ, PhD(bact), 64. *Prof Exp:* Bacteriologist, Minn State Health Dept, 57-58; from instr to asst prof microbiol, Colo State Univ, 64-67; USPHS trainee, Hopkins Marine Sta, 67-68. *Mem:* AAAS; Am Soc Microbiol. *Res:* Psychrophilic microbes; microbial physiology, growth and ecology; microbiology of groundwater. *Mailing Add:* Dept Microbiol Univ Ariz Tucson AZ 85721-0001

SINCLAIR, PETER C, ATMOSPHERIC PHYSICS. *Current Pos:* asst prof, 65-68, ASSOC PROF ATMOSPHERIC SCI, COLO STATE UNIV, 69- *Personal Data:* b Seattle, Wash, Feb 17, 29; m 60; c 4. *Educ:* Univ Wash, BS, 52; Univ Calif, Los Angeles, MS, 58; Univ Ariz, PhD(atmospheric physics), 66. *Prof Exp:* Res asst meteorol, Univ Wash, 48-52, Univ Calif, Los Angeles, 57-60 & Univ Ariz, 60-65. *Concurrent Pos:* Mem bd dir, Waverly West Soaring Ranch, 68- *Mem:* AAAS; Am Meteorol Soc; Am Geophys Union. *Res:* Severe storms; atmospheric convection; airborne atmospheric instrumentation; weather modification. *Mailing Add:* Dept of Atmospheric Sci Colo State Univ Ft Collins CO 80523-1371

SINCLAIR, PETER ROBERT, PORPHYRIN BIO-SYNTHESIS. *Current Pos:* RES ASSOC PROF BIOCHEM, DARTMOUTH MED SCH, 77-; RES BIOLOGIST, VET ADMIN, WHITE RIVER JUNCTION, VT, 77- *Personal Data:* b Sydney, Australia, Jan 17, 42; m 71. *Educ:* Univ Sydney, MS, 66; Univ Ky, PhD(biochem), 70. *Mem:* Am Soc Biochem & Molecular Biol. *Res:* Regulation of heme and cytochrome P450 especially in hepatocyte cultures. *Mailing Add:* Vet Res Serv White River Junction VT 05009-0001. *Fax:* 802-296-6308; *E-Mail:* psinc@dartmouth.edu

SINCLAIR, RICHARD GLENN, II, POLYMER CHEMISTRY. *Current Pos:* sr res chemist, 66-68, ASSOC SECT MGR, ORG & POLYMER CHEM SECT, BATTELLE MEM INST, 78- *Personal Data:* b Parsons, Kans, Mar 10, 33; m 55; c 3. *Educ:* Univ Mo, Kansas City, BS, 60, PhD(polymer sci), 67. *Prof Exp:* Analyst, E I du Pont de Nemours & Co, 58-61; chemist, Chemagro Corp, 61-63. *Mem:* Am Chem Soc. *Res:* Discovery and development of novel high polymer systems; poly (lactic acid) controlled-release systems. *Mailing Add:* 985 Kenway Ct Columbus OH 43220

SINCLAIR, ROBERT, MATERIALS SCIENCE, ELECTRON MICROSCOPY. *Current Pos:* from asst prof to assoc prof, 77-84, PROF MAT SCI, STANFORD UNIV, 84- *Personal Data:* b Liverpool, Eng, Feb 15, 47; c 2. *Educ:* Cambridge Univ, BA, 68, PhD(mat sci), 72. *Honors & Awards:* Robert Lansing Hardy Gold Medal, Am Inst Mining, Metall & Petrol Engrs, 76; Eli Franklin Burton Award, Electron Micros Soc Am, 77; Marcus E Grossman Award, Am Soc Metals, 82. *Prof Exp:* Res assoc, Univ Newcastle, Tyne, 71-73; res engr, Univ Calif, Berkeley, 73-76. *Concurrent Pos:* Res consult, Xerox Corp, 78-80, Raychem Corp, 84-88, Matsushita Elec, 87- & Kobe Develop Corp, 90-; Alfred P Sloan Found fel, 79. *Mem:* Am Inst Mining, Metall & Petrol Engrs; Electron Micros Soc Am; Mat Res Soc. *Res:* Solid state phase transformations; high-resolution transmission electron microscopy; microstructure property relationships of materials; semiconductor interfaces. *Mailing Add:* Dept Mat Sci & Eng Stanford Univ Stanford CA 94305-2205

SINCLAIR, ROLF MALCOLM, PHYSICS, ARCHAEOASTRONOMY. *Current Pos:* PROG DIR, PHYSICS DIV, NSF, 69- *Personal Data:* b New York, NY, Aug 15, 29; m 60, 91, Allyn Miner; c Elizabeth & Andrew. *Educ:* Calif Inst Technol, BS, 49; Rice Inst, MA, 51, PhD(exp physics), 54. *Prof Exp:* Res physicist, Westinghouse Res Labs, 53-56; res assoc nuclear physics, Physics Inst, Univ Hamburg, 56-57; res asst, Univ Paris, 57-58; mem res staff, Plasma Physics Lab, Princeton Univ, 58-69. *Concurrent Pos:* Res assoc, UK Atomic Energy Auth, 65-66, Culham Lab, Eng; secy, Physics Sect, AAAS, 72; mem, Solstice Proj, 78-91; NSF rep, US Solar Eclipse Exped, India, 80 & Amundsen-Scott South Pole Sta, 95 & 96; vis distinguished prof, NMex State Univ, 85; vis prof, Northern Arizona Univ, 86; vis scientist, Los Alamos Nat Lab, 88-89, consult, 90- *Mem:* Fel AAAS; fel Am Phys Soc; Sigma Xi; Soc Am Archaeol. *Res:* Atomic, plasma and nuclear physics; controlled thermonuclear power; administration of science; archaeoastronomy of US southwest and Meso America. *Mailing Add:* Physics Div NSF 4201 Wilson Blvd Arlington VA 22230. *Fax:* 703-306-0566; *E-Mail:* rsinclai@nsf.gov

SINCLAIR, RONALD, cell biology, biochemistry, for more information see previous edition

SINCLAIR, THOMAS RUSSELL, AGRONOMY, PLANT PHYSIOLOGY. *Current Pos:* plant physiologist, Microclimate Proj, Sci & Educ Admin-Agr Res, 74-79, PLANT PHYSIOLOGIST, ENVIRON PHYSIOL UNIT, AGR RES SERV, USDA, 80- *Personal Data:* b Indianapolis, Ind, Aug 4, 44; m 67; c 3. *Educ:* Purdue Univ, Lafayette, BS, 66, MS, 68; Cornell Univ, PhD(field crop sci), 71. *Prof Exp:* Mem staff, Nat Sci Found Int Biol Prog, Duke Univ, 71-74. *Concurrent Pos:* Vis scientist, State Agr Univ, Wageningen, Neth, 73-74; mem staff, Dept Agron, Cornell Univ, 74-79; adj prof, Dept Agron & Fruit Crops, Univ Fla, 80- *Mem:* Am Soc Agron; Crop Sci Soc Am; Am Soc Plant Physiol. *Res:* Experimental and computer simulation research on crop productivity, especially soybean, by improving carbon dioxide assimilation rates, nitrogen fixation rates, seed growth characteristics, use of vegetative stands. *Mailing Add:* Dept Agron & Physiol Univ Fla PO Box 110965 Gainesville FL 32611-0965

SINCLAIR, WARREN KEITH, BIOPHYSICS. *Current Pos:* pres, 77-91 EMER PRES, NAT COUN RADIATION PROTECTION & MEASUREMENTS, 91-; EMER PROF RADIOBIOL, UNIV CHICAGO, 85- *Personal Data:* b Dunedin, NZ, Mar 9, 24; nat US; m 48, Joy Edwards; c Bruce W & Roslyn E (Mann). *Educ:* Univ NZ, BSc, 44, MSc, 45; Univ London, PhD(physics), 50. *Honors & Awards:* Curie lectr, 79; Failla lectr, Radiation Res Soc, 87; Coolidge Award, Am Asn Physicists Med, 86; Taylor lectr, Nat Coun Radiation Protection & Measurements, 93. *Prof Exp:* Physicist, Dept Sci & Indust Res, NZ Govt, 44-45; lectr radiol physics, Univ Otago & radiol physicist, Dunedin Pub Hosp, 45-47; teacher & lectr, Univ London & physicist, Royal Cancer Hosp, 47-54; prof physics, Univ Tex & chief physicist, MD Anderson Hosp & Tumor Inst, 54-60; sr biophysicist, Div Biol & Med, Argonne Nat Lab, 60-83, dir, 70-74, assoc lab dir, 74-81; prof radiobiol, Univ Chicago, 64-85. *Concurrent Pos:* Consult, Humble Oil & Refining Co & Univ Tex MD Anderson Hosp & Tumor Inst; mem, US Nat Comt Pure & Appl Biophys & chmn, US Nat Comt Med Physics, 64-70; mem, Int Comn Radiation Units, 69-85; mem, Int Comn Radiation Protection, 77-; US alt deleg, UN Sci Comn on the Effects of Atomic Radiation, 77-; chmn, Bd Radiation Effects Res, Nat Acad Sci; secy gen, Vth Int Cong Radiation Res, 74. *Mem:* Radiation Res Soc (pres, 78-79); Soc Nuclear Med; Asn Physicists in Med (pres, 60-61); Radiol Soc NAm; Brit Inst Radiol; Biophys Soc; Soc Risk Analysis; Health Physics Soc. *Res:* Radiation protection and radiological physics; radiation response in synchronized cell cultures; quantitative aspects of radiobiology; radiation risk estimation in humans. *Mailing Add:* Nat Coun on Radiation Prot Meas 7910 Woodmont Ave Ste 800 Bethesda MD 20814-3045

SINCLAIR, WAYNE A, FOREST PATHOLOGY. *Current Pos:* From asst prof to assoc prof, 62-75, PROF PLANT PATH, CORNELL UNIV, 75- *Personal Data:* b Medford, Mass, Dec 15, 36; m 58; c 3. *Educ:* Univ NH, BS, 58; Cornell Univ, PhD(plant path), 62. *Concurrent Pos:* Vis forest pathologist, Weyerhaeuser Co, Wash, 70. *Mem:* Am Phytopath Soc; Int Soc Arboricult. *Res:* Forest pathology; mycoplasmal diseases of trees. *Mailing Add:* Dept Plant Path 334 Plant Sci Bldg Cornell Univ Ithaca NY 14853-4203

SINCLAIR, WILLIAM ROBERT, physical inorganic chemistry, for more information see previous edition

SINCOVEC, RICHARD FRANK, COMPUTER SCIENCES, SOFTWARE SYSTEMS. *Current Pos:* HEAD MATH SCI, OAK RIDGE NAT LAB, 91- *Personal Data:* b Pueblo, Colo, July 14, 42; c 2. *Educ:* Univ Colo, Boulder, BS, 64; Iowa State Univ, MS, 67, PhD(appl math), 68. *Prof Exp:* Instr math, Iowa State Univ, 64-68, jr mathematician, Ames Lab, 66-68; sr res mathematician, Exxon Prod Res Co, 68-70; asst prof comput sci & math, Kans State Univ, 70-74, from assoc prof to prof comput sci, 74-77; mgr numerical anal, Boeing Comput Serv Co, 77-80; prof & chmn comput sci, Univ Colo, 80-86; Ames Res Ctr, NASA, 86-91. *Concurrent Pos:* Am Chem Soc Petrol Res Fund fel, 71-74; consult, Lawrence Livermore Lab, 71-88. *Mem:* Soc Indust & Appl Math; Asn Comput Mach. *Res:* Software engineering with Ada mathematical software components in Ada; Galerkin, finite element and collocation methods for solving ordinary and partial differential equations; numerical linear algebra; parallel computing. *Mailing Add:* Dept Math & Comput Sci Oak Ridge Nat Lab PO Box 2008 Oak Ridge TN 37831-6359

SINDELAR, ROBERT D, MEDICINAL CHEMISTRY, MOLECULAR MODELING. *Current Pos:* asst prof med chem, Univ Miss, 83-89, res asst prof, 85-89, assoc prof med chem & res assoc prof, 89-93, CHAIR, ASSOC PROF, 93-96, CHAIR, PROF MED CHEM & RES PROF, RES INST PHARMACEUT SCI, UNIV MISS, 96- *Personal Data:* b Chicago, Ill, Dec 3, 52; m 76, Arlene M Wiese; c Emily, Robert & Melissa. *Educ:* Millikin Univ, BA, 74; Univ Iowa, MS, 75, PhD(med chem & natural prod), 80. *Prof Exp:* Fel chem, Univ BC, 80-81; fel chem, State Univ NY, Buffalo, 81-83. *Concurrent Pos:* Prin investr, Am Heart Asn, 85-90, First Chem Corp, 87-88, T-Cell Scis, 87-; comt mem, Nat Rho Chi Grad Scholar Comt, 88-93, Div Med Chem, Am Chem Soc, 85-91, Comt Chem Abstracts, 96, Comt Chem Nomenclature, 96; dir, Molecular Modeling Lab, Univ Miss Sch Pharm, 86-; vis res scientist, Ctr Molecular Design, Wash Univ, St Louis, Mo, 90; prin investr for numerous grants, 84-95. *Mem:* Am Chem Soc; Am Asn Col Pharm; Int Soc Heterocyclic Chem; Molecular Graphics Soc; Sigma Xi. *Res:* Complex biologically-active natural products serve as topographical models for drug design, molecular modeling, synthesis and pharmacological evaluation are utilized to study natural products with immunomodulatory, cardiovascular and antiviral activity; contributed numerous articles to professional journals; granted 5 patents. *Mailing Add:* Dept Med Chem Univ Miss Sch Pharm University MS 38677. *Fax:* 601-232-5638; *E-Mail:* mcrds@cotton.vislab.olemiss.edu

SINDEN, JAMES WHAPLES, plant pathology; deceased, see previous edition for last biography

SINDERMANN, CARL JAMES, MARINE BIOLOGY, PARASITOLOGY. *Current Pos:* MARINE BIOLOGIST, NAT OCEANIC & ATMOSPHERIC ADMIN, OXFORD LAB, NAT MARINE FISHERIES SERV, 85- *Personal Data:* b North Adams, Mass, Aug 28, 22; m 43, Joan Provencher; c Nancy, Jeanne, James, Dana & Carl. *Educ:* Univ Mass, BS, 49; Harvard Univ, AM, 51, PhD(biol), 53. *Hon Degrees:* DSc, Monmouth Univ, 89. *Honors & Awards:* Silver Medal, US Dept Com. *Prof Exp:* Teaching fel biol, Harvard Univ, 50; parasitologist, Biol Surv, State Dept Conserv, Mass, 50; instr biol, Brandeis Univ, 51-53, asst prof, 53-56; res biologist, Bur Commercial Fisheries, US Fish & Wildlife Serv, 54-59, chief Atlantic herring invests, 59-62, prog coordr, Atlantic herring progs, 62-63, dir biol lab, Md, 63-68, dir, Trop Atlantic Biol Lab, Fla, 68-71; dir, Middle Atlantic Coastal Fisheries Ctr, Nat Marine Fisheries Serv, Nat Oceanic & Atmospheric Admin, 71-76; dir, Sandy Hook Marine Lab, 76-85. *Concurrent Pos:* Asst, Harvard Med Sch, 52; marine biologist, State Dept Sea & Shore Fisheries, Maine, 52-54; vis lectr, Georgetown Univ, 66-68; adj prof, Div Fisheries Sci, Rosenstiel Sch Marine & Atmospheric Sci, Univ Miami, 69-72; adj prof biol, Lehigh Univ, 73-; adj prof vet microbiol, NY State Vet Col, Cornell Univ, 75-; vis prof, Ont Vet Col, Guelph, 78-79; sci ed, Fishery Bull, US Dept Com, 80-83; vis prof, Univ Miami, 85-88, adj prof, 88- *Mem:* Soc Invert Path; Nat Shellfisheries Asn; World Aquacult Soc. *Res:* Parasites and diseases of marine organisms; immune responses of marine invertebrates; marine pollution, ecology; coastal pollution. *Mailing Add:* NOAA Oxford Lab Nat Marine Fisheries Serv Oxford MD 21654. *Fax:* 410-226-5925; *E-Mail:* csindermann@hatteras.bea.nmfs.gov

SINE, ROBERT C, operator theory, markov; deceased, see previous edition for last biography

SINENSKY, MICHAEL, BIOCHEMISTRY. *Current Pos:* prof, 80-85, ADJOINT PROF, BIOCHEM, BIOPHYS & GENETICS & PATH, UNIV COLO HEALTH SCI CTR, 85- *Personal Data:* b New York, NY, July, 2, 45; c 2. *Educ:* Columbia Col, NY, BS, 66; Harvard Univ, PhD(biochem & molecular biol), 72. *Prof Exp:* Jr fel biochem, Soc Fels, Harvard Univ, 72-74; asst prof chem, Univ Pa, 74-75; sr fel, Eleanor Roosevelt Inst Cancer Res, 75- *Mem:* Am Soc Biol Chemists. *Res:* Mechanism of regulation of cholesterol biosynthesis. *Mailing Add:* Dept Biochem E Tenn State Univ Col Med PO Box 70581 Johnson City TN 37614-0581. *Fax:* 303-333-8423

SINES, GEORGE, JR, METALLURGY, CERAMICS. *Current Pos:* assoc prof eng, 56-62, PROF MAT, UNIV CALIF, LOS ANGELES, 62- *Personal Data:* b Salem, Ohio, July 12, 23; m 56; c Laura & Steven. *Educ:* Ohio State Univ, BME, 43; Univ Calif, Los Angeles, MS, 49, PhD(metall), 53. *Honors & Awards:* Templin Award, Am Soc Testing & Mat, 78. *Prof Exp:* Design & test engr, Krouse Testing Mach Co, Ohio, 43-44; asst instr physics, San Diego State Col, 46-47; lectr & asst engr, Univ Calif, Los Angeles, 47-53; asst prof metall, Inst Study Metals, Univ Chicago, 53-56. *Concurrent Pos:* Fulbright res prof, Tokyo Inst Technol, 58-59; consult, Japanese Atomic Energy Res Inst, 58-59 & Douglas Aircraft Co, Inc, 59-71; NSF sr fel, Ctr Nuclear Studies, Mol, Belg, 65-66; assoc ed, J Eng Mat & Technol, 73-85. *Mem:* Am Soc Testing & Mat; Am Soc Metals; Am Ceramic Soc; Am Soc Mech Engrs. *Res:* Fracture of solids; interactions between crystal defects; diffusion in solids; mechanical properties of ceramics. *Mailing Add:* Dept Mat Sch Eng Univ Calif Los Angeles CA 90095

SINEX, FRANCIS MAROTT, BIOCHEMISTRY. *Current Pos:* chmn dept, 57-77, PROF BIOCHEM, SCH MED, BOSTON UNIV, 57-, HEAD SECT BIOMED GERONT, 78- *Personal Data:* b Indianapolis, Ind, Jan 11, 23; c 2. *Educ:* DePauw Univ, AB, 44; Ind Univ, MA, 45; Harvard Univ, PhD, 51. *Prof Exp:* Jr biochemist, Brookhaven Nat Labs, 50-51, biochemist & exec officer, Biochem Div, 51-57. *Mem:* Geront Soc (pres, 69-70); Am Soc Biol Chem; Alzheimer's Dis & Related Dis Asn. *Mailing Add:* Dept Biochem Sch Med Boston Univ 80 E Concord St Boston MA 02118

SINFELT, JOHN HENRY, CATALYSIS. *Current Pos:* RETIRED. *Personal Data:* b Munson, Pa, Feb 18, 31; m 56, Muriel J Vadersen; c Klaus H. *Educ:* Pa State Univ, BS, 51; Univ Ill, MS, 53, PhD(chem eng), 54. *Hon Degrees:* DSc, Univ Ill, 81. *Honors & Awards:* Emmett Award, Catalysis Soc, 73; Lacey Lectr, Calif Inst Technol, 73; Reilly Lectr, Notre Dame Univ, 74; Petrol Chem Award, Am Chem Soc, 76, Murphree Award Indust & Eng Chem, 86; Dickson Prize Sci, Carnegie-Mellon Univ, 77; Am Phys Soc Int Prize for New Mat, 78; Nat Medal Sci, 79; Gault Lectr, Coun Europ Res Group Catalysis, 80; Welch Lectr, Conf Chem Res, Robert A Welch Found, 81; Chem Pioneer Award, Am Inst Chemists, 81, Gold Medal, 84; Perkin Medal, Soc Chem Indust, 84. *Prof Exp:* Chem engr, Exxon Res & Eng Co, 54-57, group leader, 57-62, res assoc, 62-68, sr res assoc, 68-72, sci adv, 72-79, sr sci adv, 79-96. *Concurrent Pos:* Vis prof, Univ Minn, 69. *Mem:* Nat Acad Sci; Nat Acad Eng; Am Chem Soc; Catalysis Soc; Am Acad Arts & Sci. *Res:* Heterogeneous catalysis; surface science; petroleum chemistry. *Mailing Add:* Corp Res Sci Lab Exxon Res & Eng Co Clinton Twp Rte 22E Annandale NJ 08801. *Fax:* 908-730-3042

SING, CHARLES F, HUMAN GENETICS, STATISTICS. *Current Pos:* Assoc prof, 72-76, PROF HUMAN GENETICS, MED SCH, UNIV MICH, ANN ARBOR, 76- *Personal Data:* b Joliet, Ill, July 6, 36. *Educ:* Iowa State Univ, BS, 60; Kans State Univ, MS, 63; NC State Univ, PhD(statist genetics), 66. *Mem:* Am Soc Human Genetics; Biometrics Soc; Genetics Soc; Sigma Xi. *Res:* Genetics of common diseases. *Mailing Add:* Dept Human Genetics Univ Mich PO Box 0618 Ann Arbor MI 48109

SINGAL, DHARAM PARKASH, HUMAN HISTOCOMPATABILITY ANTIGENS. *Current Pos:* lectr path, 70-72, from asst prof to assoc prof, 72-78, SPEC PROF, LAB MED & DIR, HISTOCOMPATABILITY LAB, MED CTR, MCMASTER UNIV, 70- *Personal Data:* b Sonepat, India, May 5, 34; Can citizen; m 64, Vijay Jain; c Shaila & Rita. *Educ:* Univ Delhi, India, BSc, 52, MSc, 57; Wash State Univ, PhD(genetics), 68. *Honors & Awards:* Distinguished Scientist Award, UN Develop Prog, 92. *Prof Exp:* Asst fel immunol, Univ Calif, Los Angeles, 67-69. *Concurrent Pos:* Consult, Can Red Cross Nat Lab, 77-84. *Mem:* Am Asn Immunologists; Int Transplantation Soc; Am Soc Histocompatibility & Immunogenetics; Can Soc Immunol. *Res:* Polymorphism; complexibility and characterization of human histocompatibility (HLA) antigens by serological, cellular and molecular techniques; the role of HLA antigens in disease and clinical transplantation; mechanism of enhanced allograft survival by blood transfusion; transplantation immunology. *Mailing Add:* Dept Path McMaster Univ 1200 Main St W Hamilton ON L8N 3Z5 Can. *Fax:* 905-522-6750

SINGAL, PAWAN KUMAR, CELL BIOLOGY, PHYSIOLOGY. *Current Pos:* PROF CARDIOVASC PHYSIOL, DEPT PHYSIOL, UNIV MAN, 77- *Personal Data:* b Oct 2, 46; m, Roop; c Rohit & Mona. *Educ:* Univ Alberta, Edmonton, Can, PhD(physiol), 74. *Concurrent Pos:* Staff scientist, St Bonniface Gen Hosp. *Mem:* Am Physiol Soc; Int Soc Heart Found; Am Heart Asn; Canadian Physiol Soc. *Res:* Oxygen radical injury in the heart; author of 5 books and proceedings as well as 115 papers published. *Mailing Add:* Dept Psysiol Univ Manitoba St Bonniface Gen Hosp Res Ctr R 3022 Winnipeg MB R3H 2A6 Can. *Fax:* 204-233-6723

SINGARAM, BAKTHAN, ORGANOBORANE CHEMISTRY, CHIRAL SYNTHESIS VIA ORGANOBORANES. *Current Pos:* ASST PROF ORG CHEM, UNIV CALIF, SANTA CRUZ, 89- *Personal Data:* b Andrha Pradesh, India, May 20, 50; m 77, Saraswathi Enatarajan; c Surendra. *Educ:* Madras Univ, India, BSc, 69, MSc, 71, PhD(org chem), 77. *Prof Exp:* Res assoc, Purdue Univ, 77-80, Univ Col Swansea, Wales, UK, 80-82; asst res sci, Purdue Univ, 82-87, assoc res sci, 87-89. *Concurrent Pos:* Consult, Wallace Labs, Cranbury, NJ, 83- *Mem:* Am Chem Soc. *Res:* Organic chemistry; exploratory synthetic organic chemistry; asymmetric synthesis; development of synthetic methods and organometallic reagents for the synthesis of optically active organic compounds of biological and medicinal significance. *Mailing Add:* Dept Chem & Biochem Univ Calif Santa Cruz CA 95064-9980. *Fax:* 408-459-2935; *E-Mail:* singaram@secs.ucsc.edu

SINGER, ALAN G, VERTEBRATE PHEROMONES. *Current Pos:* ASSOC MEM, MONEL CHEM SENSES CTR, 89- *Personal Data:* b Berkeley, Calif, Sept 28, 40; m 63; c 3. *Educ:* Univ Calif, Berkeley, AB, 65; State Univ NY, PhD(chem), 74. *Prof Exp:* res asst, Kaiser Found Res Inst, 68-69; res assoc, Rockefeller Univ, 73-76, asst prof org chem, 76-87; assoc prof biochem, NY Osteop Med, 87-89. *Concurrent Pos:* Asst prof chem, Kingsborough Community Col, 74-75. *Mem:* AAAS; NY Acad Sci; Sigma Xi; Am Chem Soc; Asn Chemoreception Sci. *Res:* Chemical identification of pheromones regulating hormone levels, reproductive behavior, and fertility in mammals; characterization and cloning of an aphrodisiac protein pheromone detected in the vomeronasal organ. *Mailing Add:* Monel Chem Senses Ctr 3500 Market St Philadelphia PA 19104. *Fax:* 215-898-2084

SINGER, ALFRED, IMMUNOLOGY. *Current Pos:* SR INVESTR IMMUNOL, NAT CANCER INST, 78- *Personal Data:* b Berlin, Germany, Dec 10, 46. *Educ:* Columbia Univ, MD, 72. *Mailing Add:* Nat Cancer Inst NIH Bldg 10 Rm 4B-17 Bethesda MD 20892-1360. *Fax:* 301-496-0887

SINGER, ARTHUR CHESTER, biostatistics, for more information see previous edition

SINGER, B, MOLECULAR BIOLOGY, BIOCHEMISTRY. *Current Pos:* from res assoc molecular biol to res biochemist, 46-79, res prof, 79-85, PRIN INVESTR MOLECULAR BIOL, UNIV CALIF, BERKELEY, 69-, FAC SCIENTIST, DONNER LAB, 75-, EMER PROF BIOCHEM, 85- *Personal Data:* b San Francisco, Calif; m, H Fraenkel-Conrat. *Educ:* Univ Calif, Berkeley, BS, PhD. *Prof Exp:* Jr chemist, Shell Develop Co, 42-43; jr chemist biochem, Western Regional Res Lab, USDA, 43-46. *Concurrent Pos:* Assoc ed, Cancer Res, 80-92, Ed, Carcinogenesis, Ed Bd, Chem, Res Toxic 90-; vis prof, Univ Queensland, Australia, 82, vis prof, Polish Acad Sci, Warsaw, 86; mem, chem pathol study sect, NIH, 81-86, mem, Sci Adv Bd, Nat Ctr Toxicol Res, Fed Drug Admin, 82-85; mem, Bd Sci Counr, Nat Inst Environ Health Sci, NIH, 91- *Mem:* Am Assoc Cancer Res. *Res:* Relationship of nucleic acid structure to function; effect of modification by mutagens and/or carcinogens on biological activity of nucleic acids and mammalian cells; mechanism of repair of DNA damage; fidelity of replication over modified bases in DNA; in vitro and in vivo, modified base-containing oligonucleotide synthesis, characterization and molecular modelling structural studies of enzyme-substrete recognition. *Mailing Add:* Donner Lab Univ Calif Berkeley CA 94720

SINGER, BARRY M, DEVICE PHYSICS, SUB-SYSTEMS RESEARCH. *Current Pos:* sr prog leader component & device res, Philips Labs, 69-79, group dir, 79-82, group dir component & device res, 82-84, dir physics & mat res sector, 84-91, sr vpres, Philips Lighting, 91-94, DEP DIR, PHILIPS LABS, 84-, VPRES & CHIEF SCIENTIST, 94- *Personal Data:* b New York, NY, Feb 15, 40; m 64; c 2. *Educ:* Univ Colo, Boulder, BS, 61; NY Univ, MS, 64; Polytech Inst NY, PhD(electrophysics), 68. *Prof Exp:* Sr engr, Raytheon Co, 60-63, sect engr, 63-65, sect head, 65-69. *Concurrent Pos:* Consult, Vita Corp. *Mem:* Inst Elec & Electronics Engrs; Sigma Xi. *Mailing Add:* Philips Res 345 Scarborough Rd Briarcliff Manor NY 10510

SINGER, BURTON HERBERT, STATISTICS. *Current Pos:* PROF DEMOG PUB AFFAIRS, PRINCETON UNIV, 93- *Personal Data:* b Chicago, Ill, June 12, 38; m 71; c 1. *Educ:* Case Inst Technol, BS, 59, MS, 61; Stanford Univ, PhD(statist), 67. *Honors & Awards:* Mindel Sheps Award, Pop Asn Am, 94. *Prof Exp:* From asst prof to prof math statist, Columbia Univ, 67-84; prof epidemiol, econs & statist, Yale Univ, 83-94. *Concurrent Pos:* Statist consult, Rand Corp, & Union Carbide Corp, 71-, US AEC, 72-75; res assoc statist, Princeton Univ, 72-73. *Mem:* Nat Acad Sci; Am Statist Asn; Psychomet Soc; AAAS. *Res:* Discrimination and identification of mathematical models in the social sciences; designs for observational studies; inverse problems. *Mailing Add:* Off Pop Res Princeton Univ 21 Prospect Ave Princeton NJ 08544. *Fax:* 609-258-1039

SINGER, DON B, DEVELOPMENTAL PATHOLOGY. *Current Pos:* PROF PATH, BROWN UNIV MED PROG, 75-; CHIEF PATH, WOMEN & INFANTS HOSP, PROVIDENCE, RI, 75- *Personal Data:* b Woodward, Okla, May 18, 34; m 58; c 3. *Educ:* Baylor Col Med, Houston, Tex, MD, 59. *Hon Degrees:* MA, Brown Univ, 76. *Prof Exp:* Pathologist, Baylor Col Med & Tex Children's Hosp, Houston, 63-75. *Mem:* Soc Pediat Path (treas, 85-); Int Acad Path; Am Asn Pathologists; Col Am Pathologists; Am Soc Clin Pathologists. *Res:* Clinical-pathologic relationships in fetal and neonatal diseases, particularly infectious diseases of neonates. *Mailing Add:* Dept Path Women & Infants Hosp 101 Dudley St Providence RI 02905-2499. *Fax:* 401-444-5151

SINGER, DONALD ALLEN, APPLIED STATISTICS, MINERAL ECONOMICS. *Current Pos:* GEOLOGIST, BR RESOURCE ANALYST, US GEOL SURV, 73- *Personal Data:* b Ukiah, Calif, 43; c 2. *Educ:* San Francisco State Univ, BA, 66; Pa State Univ, MS, 68, PhD(mineral & petrol), 71. *Honors & Awards:* Meritorious Serv Award, US Dept Interior. *Prof Exp:* Syst analyst, Kennecott Copper Corp, 71-72, sr comput programmer, 72-73. *Mem:* Sigma Xi; Am Statist Asn; Int Asn Math Geol; Soc Econ Geologists; Soc Resource Geol. *Res:* Operational mineral resource classification; predicting the occurrence of mineral resources; modeling the search for mineral resources; mineral resource predictions for large regions. *Mailing Add:* US Geol Surv Mail Stop 984 345 Middlefield Rd Menlo Park CA 94025. *Fax:* 650-329-5490; *E-Mail:* singer@mojave.wr.usgs.gov

SINGER, DONALD H, CARDIOLOGY. *Current Pos:* assoc prof, 68-77, PROF MED & PHARMACOL, NORTHWESTERN UNIV MED SCH, 77-, DIR REINGOLD ECG CTR, 68-, CHESTER C & DEBORAH M COOLEY PROF CARDIOL, 89-, MEM FEINBERG CARDIOL RES INST, 89- *Personal Data:* b New York, NY, Sept 27, 29; m 58; c 3. *Educ:* Cornell Univ, AB, 48; Stanford Univ, MA, 50; Northwestern Univ, MD, 54; Am Bd Internal Med, dipl, 63. *Prof Exp:* Intern, Michael Reese Hosp, Chicago, 54-55, fel, Cardiovasc Dis, Nat Heart Inst trainee, Cardiovasc Inst, 55-57; asst resident med, Beth Israel Hosp, Boston, Mass, 57-58; fel cardiol, Sch Med, Georgetown Univ, 60-61, chief med res & instr med, 61-62; res assoc, Col Physicians & Surgeons, Columbia Univ, 62-63, asst prof pharmacol, 63-68. *Concurrent Pos:* Fel, John Polachek Found Med Res, 63-66; estab investr, AMA, 67-72; mem res comt, Chicago Heart Asn, 68-75; attend physician, Passavant Mem Hosp, 69-73, Northwestern Mem Hosp, 73-; vis scientist, Univ Chicago, 78-79; dir cardiol clin, Northwestern Med Fac Found, 86-87; fel coun, circ Am Heart Asn, 78- *Mem:* Fel Am Col Physicians; Am Asn Univ Prof; Cardiac Muscle Soc; Am Physiol Soc; Electrophysiol Soc; AMA; Am Fed Clin Res; Am Soc Pharmacol & Exp Therapeut. *Res:* Cellular electrophysiology and electropharmacology (cellular mechanisms of cardiac arrhythmias and anti-arrhythmic agents, standard microelectrode, whole cell voltage clamp and patch clamp studies on human cardiac tissue/cells); autonomic regulation of heart rate/rhythm (normal and diseased hearts) using heart rate variability and power spectral analysis. *Mailing Add:* Dept Med & Cardiol Univ Ill 2769 Sheridan Rd Evanston IL 60201. *Fax:* 312-503-3891

SINGER, ELIZABETH H, INFORMATION SCIENCE. *Current Pos:* DIR, OFF HEALTH RES REPORTS, NAT INST DIABETES & DIGESTIVE & KIDNEY DIS, NIH, 79- *Personal Data:* b Los Angeles, Calif. *Educ:* La State Univ, BA, 69; Am Univ, MS, 80. *Prof Exp:* Writer/ed, Corp Engrs, New Orleans, 69-76 & Health Resources Admin, Nat Ctr Health Servs Res, 76; pub info officer, Nat Comn Protection Human Subj of Biomed & Behav Res, 77-78; pub info specialist, Nat Inst Arthritis Diabetes & Digestive & Kidney Dis, 78. *Concurrent Pos:* Pub info specialist, Corp Engrs, New Orleans, 72-76; actg info officer, Nat Inst Arthritis & Musculoskeletal & Skin Dis, NIH, 86-87. *Mailing Add:* Nat Inst Diabetes & Digestive & Kidney Dis NIH 31 Center Dr Bldg 31 Rm 9404 Bethesda MD 20892. *Fax:* 301-496-7422; *E-Mail:* inquires@hq.niddk.nih.gov

SINGER, EUGEN, CHEMICAL ENGINEERING, INSTRUMENTATION. *Current Pos:* RETIRED. *Personal Data:* b Levoca, Czech, Apr 1, 26; Can citizen; m 53; c 1. *Educ:* Prague Tech Univ, Dipl eng, 52, PhD(anal chem), 63. *Prof Exp:* Asst prof anal chem, Prague Tech Univ, 52-53; chief gas treatment div, Res Inst Inorganic Chem, Czech, 53-68; supvr monitoring & instrumentation develop, Ministry Environ Ont, 68-89. *Concurrent Pos:* consult, Dept Chem, Univ York. *Res:* Monitoring of ambient air pollutants, instrumentation development, acquisition, reduction and interpretation. *Mailing Add:* 43 Thorncliffe Park Dr No 1520 Toronto ON M4H 1J4 Can

SINGER, GEORGE, ACAROLOGY. *Current Pos:* RETIRED. *Personal Data:* b Belgrade, Yugoslavia, Apr 23, 37; US citizen; m 60; c 2. *Educ:* City Col New York, BSc, 59; Univ Kans, MS, 62; Ore State Univ, PhD(entom), 65. *Prof Exp:* Asst prof zool, Univ Mont, 65-68; fel entom, McGill Univ, 69-71; proj assoc entom, Univ Wis-Madison, 71-75. *Res:* Biochemistry of chemoreception and repellency; sensory physiology; host parasite relationships; ecology and bionomics; systematics and evolution; pest control. *Mailing Add:* 4913 Goldfinch Dr Madison WI 53714

SINGER, HOWARD JOSEPH, SPACE PHYSICS, MAGNETOSPHERIC PHYSICS. *Current Pos:* res assoc, 80-81, ASST RES PROF, DEPT ASTRON, BOSTON UNIV, 82- *Personal Data:* b Annapolis, Md, Mar 2, 44; m 73; c 2. *Educ:* Univ Md, BS, 67; Boston Univ, MA, 72; Univ Calif, Los Angeles, MS, 75, PhD(geophysics & space physics), 80. *Prof Exp:* Instr astron, Wellesley Col, 69-70; mathematician, Fed Systs Div, IBM, 70-72; staff res assoc, Inst Geophysics & Planetary Physics, Univ Calif, Los Angeles, 72-74, res assoc, 74-80. *Concurrent Pos:* Dep sta sci leader, S Pole Sta Antarctica, Inst Geophysics & Planetary Physics, Univ Calif, Los Angeles, 72-73. *Mem:* Am Geophys Union; AAAS; Am Asn Physics Teachers; Sigma Xi. *Res:* Analysis of hydromagnetic waves in the earth's magnetosphere; solar wind interaction with the magnetosphere; management and analysis of digital data. *Mailing Add:* NOAA R/E/SE 325 Broadway St Boulder CO 80303-3328

SINGER, IRA, MEDICAL EDUCATION. *Current Pos:* RETIRED. *Personal Data:* b New York City, NY, May 28, 23. *Educ:* Johns Hopkins Univ, AB, 47; Univ Chicago, MS, 49, PhD, 53; Am Bd Microbiol, dipl, 63. *Prof Exp:* Asst, Dept Bact & Parasitol, Univ Chicago, 49-53; res assoc, Rockefeller Inst Med Res, 54-56, assoc, 56-59; assoc prof microbiol, Dept Microbiol & Trop Med, Georgetown Univ, 59-63, prof microbiol, 63-65; assoc dir sci prog, Dept Postgrad Prog, AMA, 65-66, asst dir, Dept Undergrad Eval & Standards, 75-93, dir, Dept Med Sch Serv, 79-93. *Concurrent Pos:* Prof & actg chmn, Dept Microbiol, Georgetown Univ, 64-65. *Mem:* AAAS; Am Soc Parasitologists; Am Soc Trop Med & Hyg; Am Soc Exp Path; Am Soc Microbiol; NY Acad Sci; Soc Exp Biol & Med; Soc Protozollogists; AMA; World Med Asn. *Mailing Add:* 1300 N LaSalle Blvd Chicago IL 60610

SINGER, IRWIN, WATER METABOLISM RESEARCH, HOSPITAL ADMINISTRATION EMPLOYMENT. *Current Pos:* PROF MED, NORTHWESTERN UNIV MED SCH, 86- *Personal Data:* b Brooklyn, NY. *Educ:* Cornell Univ, BA, 58; Albert Einstein Col, MD, 62. *Hon Degrees:* MA, Univ Pa, 73. *Prof Exp:* Intern & resident internal med, Bronx Munic Hosp Ctr, Albert Einstein Col Med, 62-64, sr resident internal med, 66-67; res assoc neurophysiol, Nat Inst Ment Health, NIH, 64-66; instr & fel med, Mass Gen Hosp, Harvard Med Sch, 67-69, asst prof med, 69-70; from asst prof to prof med, Sch Med, Univ Pa, 70-86; assoc dean vet affairs, 86-89, assoc dean acad affairs, Vet Admin Lakeside Med Ctr, 89- *Concurrent Pos:* Investr, Marine Biol Lab, Woods Hole, Mass, 64-66, investr, 72-73; asst med, Mass Gen Hosp, Boston, Mass, 69-70; estab investr, Am Heart Asn, 69-74; chief, Renal-Electrolyte Sect, Tech Serv, Philadelphia Vet Admin Med Ctr, 70-78, asst chief, Med Serv, 72-76 & chief, 77-82; staff physician, Hosp Univ Pa, 70-86, dir, Cont Ambulatory Peritoneal Dialysis Prog, Renal-Electrolyte Sect, 84-86; mem, Gov Adv Comt, Am Col Physicians, 76-86; vchmn, Dept Med, Sch Med, Univ Pa, 78-82, dir, Clin Res Prog, Renal-Electrolyte Sect, Dept Med, 83-86; vis prof med, Med Col Pa, 79-86; pres, John Morgan Soc, 80-81; chief staff, Vet Admin Lakeside Med Ctr, Chicago, 86- *Mem:* Soc Gen Physiologists; Am Physiol Soc; Am Soc Nephrol; Int Soc Nephrology; Am

Soc Clin Invest; Cent Soc Clin Res; fel Am Col Physicians; fel NY Acad Sci. *Res:* Salt and water metabolism, particularly the latter, mostly writing; clinical nephrology (acid-base, electrolytes, salt and water) and some health services research. *Mailing Add:* Va Admin Lakeside Med Ctr 333 E Huron St Chicago IL 60611-3004

SINGER, IRWIN I, CELL BIOLOGY, VIROLOGY. *Current Pos:* sr res fel, 82-85, SR INVESTR, MERCK SHARP & DOHME RES LABS, 85- *Personal Data:* b New York, NY, Dec 20, 43; m 67; c 2. *Educ:* City Col New York, BS, 65; NY Univ, MS, 67, PhD(biol), 70. *Prof Exp:* Instr biol, Mercy Col, 69-70; asst prof, St Louis Univ, 70-71; assoc investr electron micros, Inst Med Res, Bennington, 71-82. *Mem:* Electron Micros Soc Am; Am Soc Cell Biol. *Res:* Ultrastructure and cytochemistry in regenerating Cnidaria; electron microscopy and pathobiology of the Parvoviruses; interactions between fibronectin, fibronectin receptors and the cytoskeleton at the cell attachment surface in vitro and during wound healing and rheumatoid arthritis in vivo; analysis of HMG-CoA reductase in hepatocytes and enterocytes treated with inhibitors of cholestrol synthesis; roles of laminin receptors and basement membranes in leukocytes during inflammation; intracellular localization of interleukin - 1B. *Mailing Add:* Merck Res Labs PO Box 2000 Rahway NJ 07065-0900. *Fax:* 732-594-3111

SINGER, ISADORE MANUAL, PURE MATHEMATICS. *Current Pos:* John D MacArthur prof math, 83-87, INST PROF, MASS INST TECHNOL, 87- *Personal Data:* b Detroit, Mich, May 3, 24; m 44; c 3. *Educ:* Univ Mich, BS, 44; Univ Chicago, MS, 48, PhD(math), 50. *Hon Degrees:* DSc, Tulane Univ, 81; Univ Chicago, 93; LLD, Univ Mich, 89 & Univ Ill Chicago, 90. *Honors & Awards:* Nat Medal Sci, 85; Bocher Prize, Am Math Soc, 69; Eugene Wigner Medal, 88; Pub Serv Award, Am Math Soc, 93. *Prof Exp:* Moore instr math, Mass Inst Technol, 50-52; asst prof, Univ Calif, Los Angeles, 52-54; vis asst prof, Columbia Univ, 54-55; vis mem, Inst Advan Study, Princeton Univ, 56; prof, Mass Inst Technol, 56-70, Norbert Wiener prof, 70-79; vis prof, Univ Calif, Berkeley, 77-79, prof, 79-83, Miller prof, 82-83. *Concurrent Pos:* Sloan fel, 59-62; Guggenheim fel, 68-69, 75-76; chmn, Comt Sci & Pub Policy, Nat Acad Sci, 73-78, counr & mem, Comn Math & Phys Sci, 78-81; White House Sci Coun, 82-88; chair, Geom & Physics, Found France, 87-88; chmn, Coop Appl Sci Comt, Nat Res Coun, 92. *Mem:* Nat Acad Sci; Am Acad Arts & Sci; Am Math Soc (vpres, 70-72); Am Phys Soc; Am Philos Soc. *Res:* Differential geometry; commutative Banach algebras; global analysis; author of various publications. *Mailing Add:* Bldg 387 Math Dept Mass Inst Technol Cambridge MA 02139. *E-Mail:* ims@math.mit.edu

SINGER, JACK W, CELL BIOLOGY. *Current Pos:* RES CHMN, CELL THERAPEUT INC, 92- *Personal Data:* b New York, NY, Nov 09, 42; m 84; c 1. *Educ:* Columbia Col, AB, 64; State Univ NY, MD, 68. *Prof Exp:* Intern & resident med, Univ Chicago Hosp, 68-70; chief, Hemat Lab Div, Nat Ctr Dis Control, 70-72; fel hemat oncol, Univ Wash, 72-75; from asst prof to prof med & oncol, Univ Wash, 75-92. *Concurrent Pos:* Chief med oncol, Vet Admin Med Ctr, 75-; mem, Fred Hutchinson Cancer Res Ctr. *Mem:* AAAS; Am Fedn Clin Res; Am Soc Hemat; Int Soc Exp Hemat; Am Soc Clin Oncol; Am Soc Clin Invest. *Res:* Control of cell proliferation in normal and leukemia hemopoiesis; cytokine regulation; human leukemia. *Mailing Add:* Cell Therapeut Inc 201 Elliott Ave West Suite 400 Seattle WA 98119

SINGER, JEROME RALPH, BIOENGINEERING & BIOPHYSICS, MAGNETIC RESONANCE IMAGING. *Current Pos:* assoc prof elec eng, 57-77, PROF ENG SCI, UNIV CALIF, BERKELEY, 77- *Personal Data:* b Cleveland, Ohio, Oct 16, 21; m 56; c 2. *Educ:* Univ Ill, BS, 51; Northwestern Univ, MS, 53; Univ Conn, PhD(physics), 55. *Prof Exp:* Engr, Van de Graaff Proj, Northwestern Univ, 51-53; instr physics, Univ Conn, 53-55; physicist, Solid State Div, US Naval Ord Lab, 55-56; chief staff physicist, Nat Sci Labs, Inc, Washington, DC, 56-57. *Concurrent Pos:* Vis lectr, Catholic Univ, 55-56 & George Washington Univ, 56-57; proj engr, Sperry Corp, 54; sci consult, Missile Systs Div, Lockheed Aircraft Corp, 57-; Telemeter Magnetics, Inc, 57-58; Aeroneutronics, Inc div, Ford Motor Co, 58- *Mem:* AAAS; Am Phys Soc; Optical Soc Am; sr mem Inst Elec & Electronics Engrs; Brit Inst Physics. *Res:* Electronics; magnetic phenomena; quantum mechanical amplifiers; magnetic resonance; blood studies; flow and magnetic properties of blood; rheological properties of body fluids. *Mailing Add:* Electronic Res Labs Univ Calif 477 Cory Hall Berkeley CA 94720

SINGER, JOSHUA J, MEMBRANE BIOPHYSICS, SMOOTH MUSCLE. *Current Pos:* Assoc prof, 74-86, PROF PHYSIOL, UNIV MASS MED SCH, 86- *Personal Data:* b Hartford, Conn, Feb 15, 42. *Educ:* Mass Inst Technol, SB, SM, EE(elec eng), 66; Harvard Univ, PhD(med sci physiol), 70. *Mem:* Biophys Soc; Soc Neurosci; Soc Gen Physiologist; Am Physiol Soc; Inst Elec & Electronics Engrs; Am Heart Asn. *Res:* Voltage, chemical, and mechanical control of ion channels in dissociated smooth muscle cells and other cell types; relationship of membrane electrical events to cellular biochemical and physiological processes. *Mailing Add:* Dept Physiol Univ Mass Med Sch 55 Lake Ave N Worcester MA 01655

SINGER, KAY HIEMSTRA, LYMPHOID & EPITHELIAL INTERACTION, T-CELL MATURATION. *Current Pos:* RES ASST PROF MED & MICROBIOL-IMMUNOL, DUKE UNIV, 79- *Educ:* Duke Univ, PhD(immunol), 77. *Res:* Immunology. *Mailing Add:* Duke Univ Box 90924 Durham NC 27708-0924

SINGER, LAWRENCE ALAN, ORGANIC CHEMISTRY. *Current Pos:* assoc prof, 67-71, PROF CHEM, UNIV SOUTHERN CALIF, 73- *Personal Data:* b Chicago, Ill, June 7, 36; m 67; c 2. *Educ:* Northwestern Univ, BA, 58; Univ Calif, Los Angeles, PhD(org chem), 62. *Prof Exp:* Fel, Harvard Univ, 62-64; asst prof chem, Univ Chicago, 64-67. *Concurrent Pos:* A P Sloan fel, 70-72. *Mem:* Am Chem Soc; Royal Soc Chem; Sigma Xi. *Res:* Organic photochemistry; laser spectroscopic studies; organic free radicals; photoinduced electron transfer reactions. *Mailing Add:* Dept Chem Univ Southern Calif Los Angeles CA 90089-0744. *E-Mail:* lsinger@mizar.usc.edu

SINGER, LEONARD SIDNEY, CARBON & GRAPHITE, CARBON FIBERS. *Current Pos:* INDEPENDENT CONSULT, 85- *Personal Data:* b Middletown, Pa, Oct 9, 23; m 48, Lenore Wexler; c Ruth & Meredith. *Educ:* Pa State Col, BS, 43; Univ Chicago, PhD(phys chem), 50. *Honors & Awards:* Charles E Pettinos Award, Am Carbon Soc, 77, George D Graffin Lectureship, 83. *Prof Exp:* Chem engr, Celanese Corp Am, 43-44; Du Pont fel chem, Cornell Univ, 50-51; phys chemist, US Naval Res Lab, 51-55; phys chemist, Union Carbide Corp, 55-75, corp res fel, Res Lab, Carbon Prod Div, 75-85. *Mem:* Am Chem Soc; Am Carbon Soc; Int Electron Paramagnetic Resonance Soc. *Res:* Magnetism; magnetic resonance; free radicals; carbon and graphite; carbon fibers; composites; materials science. *Mailing Add:* 525 Race St Berea OH 44017-2220

SINGER, MARCUS, anatomy; deceased, see previous edition for last biography

SINGER, MAXINE FRANK, BIOCHEMISTRY. *Current Pos:* USPHS fel, NIH, 57, biochemist, Nat Inst Arthritis & Metab Dis, 58-74, head sect nucleic acid enzymol, 74-79, chief, Lab Biochem, 79-87, EMER SCIENTIST, NAT CANCER INST, NIH, 88-; PRES, CARNEGIE INST WASH, WASHINGTON, DC, 88- *Personal Data:* b New York, NY, Feb 15, 31; m 52, Daniel; c Amy, Ellen, David & Stephanie. *Educ:* Swarthmore Col, AB, 52; Yale Univ, PhD, 57. *Hon Degrees:* Numerous hon degrees, 77-93. *Honors & Awards:* Superior Serv Award, HEW, 75; NIH Dirs Award, 77; G Burroughs Mider lectr, NIH, 77; Nat Medal Sci, 92. *Concurrent Pos:* Guest scientist, Weizmann Inst Sci, 71-72; bd of trustees, Wesleyan Univ, Conn, 72-75, dir, Whitehead Inst Biomed Res, 86-94; fel, Yale Corp, Yale Univ, 75-90; Dreyfus distinguished scholar, Swarthmore Col, 82; John Simon Guggenheim mem fel, 87; mem, Human Genome Orgn & Comt Sci, Eng & Pub Policy, Nat Acad Sci, 89-92 & Int Adv Bd Chulabborn Res Inst, Bangkok, 90; mem, Smithsonian Coun, 91-93. *Mem:* Nat Acad Sci; Inst Med-Nat Acad Sci; Am Soc Biol Chem; Am Philos Soc; fel Am Acad Arts & Sci; AAAS. *Res:* Nucleic acid chemistry and metabolism; biochemistry of animal viruses; genome organization; transposable elements in the human genome. *Mailing Add:* 5410 39th St NW Washington DC 20015-2902

SINGER, MICHAEL, ALGEBRA, DIFFERENTIAL EQUATIONS. *Current Pos:* PROF MATH, NC STATE UNIV, 85- *Personal Data:* b New York, NY, Feb 25, 50. *Educ:* Univ Calif, Berkeley, PhD(math), 74. *Mem:* Am Math Soc; Math Asn Am. *Mailing Add:* Dept Math NC State Univ Box 8205 Raleigh NC 27695-8205

SINGER, PAUL A, CLINICAL RESEARCH. *Current Pos:* ASSOC MEM, DEPT CLIN RES, WHITTIER INST DIABETES & ENDOCRINOL, LA JOLLA, 90- *Personal Data:* b July 18, 49; m. *Educ:* Univ Calif, Berkeley, BA, 71; Glasgow Univ, Scotland, PhD(biochem/immunol), 78. *Prof Exp:* Res asst, Dept Microbiol & Immunol, Los Angeles Med Sch, Univ Calif, 72-74; postdoctoral fel, Dept Immunogenetics, Max-Planck Inst Biol, 78-80; asst mem, Dept Immunol, Scripps Clin & Res Found, La Jolla, 83-89; consult, 89-90. *Concurrent Pos:* Calif Lupus res award, 88, NIH res grant, 89. *Mem:* AAAS; Am Asn Immunologists; Brit Soc Immunol. *Res:* T cell receptor genes in autoimmune diabetes; molecular analyses of T cell receptor repertoire expression in murine models of SLE. *Mailing Add:* 14004 Mango Dr 2670 Del Mar Heights Rd Suite 219 Del Mar CA 92014. *Fax:* 619-755-6537

SINGER, PHILIP C, WATER QUALITY ENGINEERING, DRINKING WATER TREATMENT. *Current Pos:* assoc prof, 73-78, PROF ENVIRON SCI & ENG, UNIV NC, 78-, DIR WATER RESOURCES ENG PROG, 79- *Personal Data:* b Brooklyn, NY, Sept 6, 42; m 65, Ellen Becker; c Naomi, Elizabeth, Robert & Jennifer. *Educ:* Cooper Union, BCE, 63; Northwestern Univ, MS, 65; Harvard Univ, SM, 65, PhD, 69. *Honors & Awards:* Freese lectr, Am Soc Civil Engrs, 93; A P Black Res Award, Am Water Works Asn, 95. *Prof Exp:* Asst prof civil eng, Univ Notre Dame, 69-73. *Concurrent Pos:* Guest prof, Swiss Fed Inst Water Res & Water Pollution Control, Dubendorf, Switz, 79; assoc ed, Environ Sci & Technol, J Am Chem Soc, 83-90; mem ed bd, Ozone Sci & Eng, J Int Ozone Asn, 86-; vis prof, Stanford Univ, 89-90; dipl, Am Acad Environ Engrs. *Mem:* Nat Acad Eng; Am Chem Soc; Am Water Works Asn; Water Environ Fedn; Asn Environ Eng Prof; Int Ozone Asn; Am Soc Civil Engrs; Am Acad Envrion Engrs. *Res:* Control of disinfection by-products in drinking water; ozonation for water and wastewater treatment; chemical and physical processes for water quality management; aquatic chemistry; metal-organic interactions; coagulation of natural organic material. *Mailing Add:* Dept Environ Sci Eng Univ NC Pub Health Chapel Hill NC 27599-7400

SINGER, RICHARD ALAN, TELECOMMUNICATIONS SOFTWARE ENGINEERING. *Current Pos:* mem tech staff, 80-85, DISTINGUISHED MEM TECH STAFF, AT&T BELL LABS, 85- *Personal Data:* b New York, NY, May 21, 45; m 71, Tina Spar; c Bryan. *Educ:* Mass Inst Technol, BS, 67, PhD(physics), 72. *Prof Exp:* Fel, Argonne Nat Lab, 72-75, from asst physicist to assoc physicist, 75-80. *Mem:* Am Phys Soc; Sigma Xi. *Res:* Software engineering of telecommunications switching systems with emphasis on performance analysis. *Mailing Add:* 474 Cassin Rd Naperville IL 60565-3317

SINGER, ROBERT MARK, cell biology, anatomy, for more information see previous edition

SINGER, ROLF, mycology, for more information see previous edition

SINGER, RONALD, ANATOMY, PHYSICAL ANTHROPOLOGY. *Current Pos:* PROF ANAT & ANTHROP, UNIV CHICAGO, 62-, R R BENSLEY PROF BIOL & MED SCI, 73- *Personal Data:* b Cape Town, SAfrica, Aug 12, 24; m 50, Shirley B Gersohn; c Hazel L, Eric G, Sonia E & Charles M. *Educ:* Univ Cape Town, MB, ChB, 47, DSc(anat), 62. *Honors & Awards:* Cornwall & York Prize, 50. *Prof Exp:* Lectr anat, Univ Cape Town, 49-51, sr lectr, 51-60, assoc prof, 60-62. *Concurrent Pos:* Rotary Found & Johns Hopkins Univ fels, 51-52; vis prof, Univ Ill, 59-60, Robert J Terry lectr, 64; mem sci group pop genetics primitive pop, WHO, 62; consult, Nat Found, 65-; subcomt phys anthrop, Int Anat Nomenclature Comt, 71- *Mem:* Fel AAAS; fel Royal Soc SAfrica; SAfrican Asn Adv Sci (vpres, 58-62); SAfrican Archaeol Soc (pres, 61-62); Int Quaternary Asn; Am Asn Phys Anthropol; Sigma Xi (pres, 68-69, 81-83). *Res:* Gross anatomy; paleoanthropology; genetics of African indigenous populations. *Mailing Add:* Dept Anat Univ Chicago 1027 E 57th St Chicago IL 60637-1839. *Fax:* 773-702-0037; *E-Mail:* dlhawkin@midway.uchicago.edu

SINGER, S(IEGFRIED) FRED, GEOPHYSICS. *Current Pos:* RETIRED. *Personal Data:* b Vienna, Austria, Sept 27, 24; nat US. *Educ:* Ohio State Univ, BEE, 43; Princeton Univ, AM, 44, PhD(physics), 48. *Hon Degrees:* DSc, Ohio State Univ, 70. *Honors & Awards:* President's Commendation Award, 58; 1st Astronaut Medal, Brit Interplanetary Soc, 62. *Prof Exp:* Instr physics, Princeton Univ, 43-44; mem staff electronic comput design, Naval Ord Lab, Md, 45-46; physicist, Appl Physics Lab, Johns Hopkins Univ, 46-50; sci liaison officer, Off Naval Attache, US Embassy, London, 50-53; from assoc prof to prof physics, Univ Md, 53-62; dir, Nat Weather Satellite Ctr, US Dept Com, 62-64; prof atmospheric sci & dean sch environ & planetary sci, Univ Miami, 64-67; dep asst secy sci progs, US Dept Interior, 67-70; dep asst adminr, Environ Protection Agency, 70-71; prof environ sci & mem, Energy Policy Studies Ctr, Univ Va, 71-87; chief scientist, US Dept Transp, Washington, DC, 87-90; pres, Sci & Environ Comt, Fairfax, Va. *Concurrent Pos:* Mem, Comn IV, Int Sci Radio Union, 54-; tech panels, rockets & cosmis rays, US Nat Comt, Int Geophys Year, 57-58; head sci eval group & sci consult, Select Comt Astronaut & Space Explor, US House Rep, 58; dir, Ctr Atmospheric & Space Physics, Univ Md, 59-62; chmn subcomt basic res, Comt Sci & Technol, US Chamber Com, 60-62 & mem environ pollution adv bd, 66-67; vis researcher, Jet Propulsion Lab, Calif Inst Technol, 61-62; mem spacecraft oceanog adv group, Naval Oceanog Off, 66-67; chmn adv comt environ effects supersonic transport, Dept Transp, 71; fed exec fel, Brookings Inst, 71; consult, Inst Defense Analysis, AEC & major industs; vchmn, Nat Adv Comt Oceans & Atmosphere, 81-87; vchmn, Nat Adv Comt Oceans & Atmosphere, 81-87. *Mem:* Fel AAAS; fel Am Phys Soc; fel Am Inst Aeronaut & Astronaut; fel Brit Interplanetary Soc; fel Am Astronaut Soc. *Res:* Upper atmosphere, ionospheric currents, theory of magnetic storms, radiation belts; origin of meteorites, moon, solar system; environmental effects of pollution, especially on global climate; remote sensing, from earth satellites; pollution control techniques and economics; water and energy resources; effects of population growth. *Mailing Add:* 9812 Doulton Ct Fairfax VA 22032

SINGER, S(EYMOUR) J(ONATHAN), BIOLOGY. *Current Pos:* prof, 61-95, EMER PROF BIOL, UNIV CALIF, SAN DIEGO, 61- *Personal Data:* b New York, NY, May 23, 24; m 47; c 3. *Educ:* Columbia Univ, AB, 43, AM, 45; Polytech Inst Brooklyn, PhD(chem), 47, MA, 60. *Prof Exp:* Abbott fel, Calif Inst Technol, 47-48, USPHS fel, 48-50, sr res fel, 50-51; from asst prof to prof phys chem, Yale Univ, 51-61. *Concurrent Pos:* Guggenheim fel, 59-60; mem adv panel molecular biol, NSF, 60-63; mem, Allergy & Immunol Study Sect, USPHS, 63-64; emer prof, Am Cancer Soc, 76- *Mem:* Nat Acad Sci; Am Acad Arts & Sci; Am Soc Cell Biol; Am Soc Biol Chemists. *Res:* Molecular biology; physical chemistry of proteins; immunochemistry; membrane biology; chemical cytology. *Mailing Add:* 9500 Gillman Dr Univ Calif San Diego La Jolla CA 92037. *Fax:* 619-534-0053; *E-Mail:* ssinger@ucsd.edu

SINGER, SAMUEL, MICROBIOLOGY. *Current Pos:* assoc prof, 70-75, PROF BIOL SCI, WESTERN ILL UNIV, 75- *Personal Data:* b New York, NY, June 22, 27; m 57, Nee Sheps; c Mitchell H, Elissa F & Jonathan E. *Educ:* City Col New York, BS, 50; Univ Ky, MS, 52; NY Univ, PhD(protozool, physiol), 58. *Prof Exp:* Res microbiologist, Div Chemother, Burroughs Wellcome & Co, 52-62; sr res microbiologist, Dept Microbiol, Bioferm Div, Int Mineral & Chem Corp, Calif, 62-68; microbiologist, Brown & Williamson Tobacco Corp, Ky, 68-70. *Mem:* AAAS; Am Soc Microbiol; Soc Invert Path; Brit Soc Gen Microbiol; Sigma Xi; Soc Indust Microbiol. *Res:* Microbiol insecticides; fermentation of insecticidal bacillus; microbial nutrition; bacterial ecology; bacterial biocontrol of agricultural, public health,vectors and environmental pest such as insects mosquitos, lepidoptera, molluses schistosmal snails, zebra mussels. *Mailing Add:* Dept Biol Sci Western Ill Univ 900 W Adams St Macomb IL 61455-1328. *Fax:* 309-298-2270; *E-Mail:* s-singer@wiu.edu

SINGER, SANFORD SANDY, BIOCHEMISTRY. *Current Pos:* from asst prof to assoc prof, 72-84, PROF CHEM, UNIV DAYTON, 84- *Personal Data:* b Brooklyn, NY, Sept 14, 40; m 71; c 2. *Educ:* Brooklyn Col, BS, 62; Univ Mich, Ann Arbor, MS, 64, PhD(biochem), 67. *Prof Exp:* Fel, Albert Einstein Col Med, 67 & 68; fel, Fels Res Inst, Med Sch, Temple Univ, 68-72. *Concurrent Pos:* Am Cancer Soc fel, Albert Einstein Col Med, 67-69. *Mem:* Sigma Xi; Am Soc Biochem & Molecular Biol; Endocrine Soc. *Res:* Studies of mechanism of action of adrenal glucocorticosteroids; studies of mechanism of carcinogenesis. *Mailing Add:* Dept Chem Univ Dayton 111 Wohleben Hall Dayton OH 45469. *Fax:* 937-229-2635

SINGER, SHERWIN, STATISTICAL MECHANICS. *Current Pos:* ASSOC PROF CHEM, OHIO STATE UNIV, 87- *Personal Data:* b Chicago, Ill, Mar 20, 54; m 85; c 2. *Educ:* Univ Chicago, BA, 76, PhD(chem), 84. *Prof Exp:* Fel, Univ Pa, 84-86, AT&T Bell Labs, 86-87. *Mem:* Am Phys Soc; Am Chem Soc. *Res:* Statistical mechanics of clusters and condensed phases; complex fluids and self-organization; quantum processes in condensed phases. *Mailing Add:* Dept Chem Ohio State Univ Columbus OH 43210. *Fax:* 614-292-1685; *E-Mail:* singer@mps.ohio.state.edu

SINGER, STANLEY, CHEMISTRY, PHYSICS. *Current Pos:* DIR, ATHENEX RES ASSOC, 65- *Personal Data:* b North Adams, Mass, Oct 2, 25. *Educ:* Univ Calif, Los Angeles, BS, 46, PhD(chem), 50. *Prof Exp:* Res assoc chem, Univ Calif, Los Angeles, 50-51; chemist, US Naval Ord Test Sta, 51-52, res assoc, 53, head properties sect, 54-55, liquid propellants & combustion br, 55-58; head phys & inorg chem, Hughes Tool Co, 58-59; head propulsion physics dept & assoc head chem dept, Rocket Power, 59-64; dir physics, Dynamic Sci Corp, 64-65. *Concurrent Pos:* Engr in residence, Eng Socs Comn Energy, 81-83; pres, Int Comt Ball Lightning. *Mem:* AAAS; Am Chem Soc; Sigma Xi; Am Inst Aeronaut & Astronaut; Combustion Inst. *Res:* Synthesis; polymers; combustion; rocket propellants; ion sources; arc-plasma chemistry; refractory metals; ion-molecule reactions; electric space propulsion; plasma-magnetic field interaction; fine particles; atmospheric electricity; lightning; atmospheric particles; superconductivity; synthetic fuels; environmental health hazards. *Mailing Add:* 381 S Meridith Ave Pasadena CA 91106-3576

SINGER, SUSAN RUNDELL, PLANT DEVELOPMENT, FLOWERING. *Current Pos:* asst prof, 86-91, ASSOC PROF BIOL, CARLETON COL, 92- *Personal Data:* b Schenectady, NY, July 1, 59; m 81, Gary; c Jessica, Peter & Emma. *Educ:* Rensselaer Polytech Inst, BS, 81, MS, 82, PhD(biol), 85. *Prof Exp:* Fel, Rensselaer Polytech Inst, 85. *Concurrent Pos:* Fel, Rensselaer Polytech Inst, 85. *Mem:* Soc Develop Biol; Bot Soc Am; Am Soc Plant Physiol; Int Soc Plant Molecular Biol; Int Working Group on Flowering. *Res:* Developmental regulation of early events leading to flowering; tissue culture with genetic and molecular approaches are utilized. *Mailing Add:* Dept Biol Carlton Col 1 N College St Northfield MN 55057-4001. *Fax:* 507-663-4384; *E-Mail:* ssinger@carleton.edu

SINGER, THOMAS PETER, BIOCHEMISTRY. *Current Pos:* prof biochem, 65-68, prof biochem & biophys, 68-70, ADJ PROF BIOCHEM & BIOPHYS, SCH MED, UNIV CALIF, SAN FRANCISCO, 70-, HEAD MOLECULAR BIOL DIV, VET ADMIN HOSP, 66- *Personal Data:* b Budapest, Hungary, July 10, 20; nat US; m 62; c 2. *Educ:* Univ Chicago, SB, 41, SM, 43, PhD(biochem), 44. *Prof Exp:* Asst med, Off Sci Res & Develop & Comt Med Res Projs, Chicago, 42-44, res assoc, Manhattan Proj, 44-46; asst prof agr biochem, Univ Minn, 46-47; asst prof, Sch Med, Western Reserve Univ, 47-51; mem, Inst Enzyme Res, Univ Wis, 52-54; chief div enzyme res, Edsel B Ford Inst Med Res, Henry Ford Hosp, Detroit, Mich, 54-65. *Concurrent Pos:* Guggenheim fel, Univ Paris & Cambridge Univ, 51-52 & 59; Orgn Am States fel, 71; Fulbright fel, 72; estab investr, Am Heart Asn, 54-59. *Mem:* Am Soc Biol Chemists; Am Chem Soc. *Res:* Flavin and flavoenzyme structure; enzyme regulation; mechanism of action and regulation of enzymes of the respiratory chain, nonheme iron-sulfur roles in oxidizing enzymes; mitochondrial biogenesis. *Mailing Add:* Dept Biochem Biophys & Biopharmaceut Sci VA Med Ctr 151-S Bldg 12 4150 Clement St San Francisco CA 94121-1598. *Fax:* 415-750-6959

SINGER, WILLIAM MERRILL, HOMOTOPY THEORY, HOMOLOGICAL ALGEBRA. *Current Pos:* assoc prof, 74-82, chmn, Dept Math, 84-87, PROF MATH, FORDHAM UNIV, 82- *Personal Data:* b New York, NY, Feb 26, 42; m 92, Eileen Angell. *Educ:* Cornell Univ, BA, 63; Princeton Univ, MA, 65, PhD(math), 67. *Prof Exp:* Instr math, Mass Inst Technol, 67-69; asst prof, Boston Col, 69-74. *Concurrent Pos:* NSF res grant, Boston Col, 71-72; NSF res grants, 73-74, 75-76, 76-77, 81-83, 83-85 & 85-87. *Mem:* Am Math Soc. *Res:* Algebraic topology; Steenrod algebra; Hopf algebras; homological algebra and its applications to homotopy theory; semi-simplicial methods; Adams spectral sequences; homotopy groups of spheres. *Mailing Add:* Dept Math Fordham Univ 441 E Fordham Rd Bronx NY 10458. *E-Mail:* singer@murray.fordham.edu

SINGEWALD, MARTIN LOUIS, INTERNAL MEDICINE. *Current Pos:* From asst prof to assoc prof, 55-74, EMER ASSOC PROF MED, SCH MED, JOHNS HOPKINS UNIV, 74- *Personal Data:* b Baltimore, Md, May 10, 09; m 33; c 3. *Educ:* Johns Hopkins Univ, BE, 30, MD, 38. *Concurrent Pos:* Mem, Coun Arteriosclerosis, Am Heart Asn. *Mem:* Am Soc Internal Med; AMA; fel Am Col Physicians; Am Clin & Climat Asn. *Res:* Coronary artery diseases. *Mailing Add:* 36 Langham Rd Providence RI 02906-3548

SINGH, AJAIB, PHYSICAL ORGANIC CHEMISTRY, POLYMER CHEMISTRY. *Current Pos:* sr group leader, 78-82, TECH MGR POLYURETHANES, UNIROYAL CHEM CO, UNIROYAL INC, 82- *Personal Data:* b Dholan Hithar, Pakistan, Jan 14, 35; m 64. *Educ:* Punjab Univ, India, BSc, 54, Hons, 56, MSc, 58; Univ Calif, Davis, PhD(phys org chem), 61. *Prof Exp:* Res fel chem, Harvard Univ, 61-62; res chemist, Am Cyanamid Co, 62-68, sr res chemist, Org Chem Div, 68-77, prin res chemist, Chem Res Div, 77-78. *Concurrent Pos:* Vis res fel, Queen Mary Col, Univ London, 68-69. *Mem:* Am Chem Soc. *Res:* Polymer structure properties, degradation kinetics and mechanisms; specialty, polyurethane elastomers. *Mailing Add:* 58 Autumn Ridge Rd Huntington CT 06484-3631

SINGH, AJIT, POLYMER CHEMISTRY, PULP CHEMISTRY. *Current Pos:* asst res officer, Atomic Energy Can Ltd, 66-68, assoc res officer, 69-81, sr res officer, 81-87, SR SCIENTIST, WHITESHELL LABS, ATOMIC ENERGY CAN LTD, 88- *Personal Data:* b Indore, India, Oct 31, 32; m 55, Harwant Wadhna. *Educ:* Agra Univ, BSc, 50, MSc, 52; Univ Alta, PhD(radiation chem), 64. *Prof Exp:* Lectr chem, Holkar Col, Indore, 56-59; teaching asst, Univ Alta, 59-63; res assoc, Chem Div, Argonne Nat Lab, 63-65. *Concurrent Pos:* Guest ed, Int J Radiation Physics & Chem, 75, Photochem & Photobiol, 78; ed, Radiation Physics & Chem, 76-; co-ed, Radiation Processing & Polymers, 92. *Mem:* Fel Chem Inst Can; Tech Asn Pulp & Paper Indust; Am Chem Soc; Am Soc Photobiol; Can Pulp Paper Asn. *Res:* Mechanisms of reactions in radiation chemistry, radiation biology, photochemistry and photobiology; physical and chemical properties of transient molecular species by the pulse radiolysis and flash photolysis techniques; industrial applications of radiation; role of free radicals in pulping; pulp bleaching; polymerization and polymer cross-linking. *Mailing Add:* Radiation Appln Res Atomic Energy Can Ltd Pinawa MB R0E 1L0 Can. *E-Mail:* singha@aecl.ca

SINGH, AMARJIT, MICROWAVE ELECTRON DEVICES & PLASMAS, SEMICONDUCTOR DEVICES. *Current Pos:* VIS SCIENTIST ELECTRON TUBES, UNIV MD, COL PARK, 87- *Personal Data:* b Ramdas, India, Nov 19, 24; m 53, Surinder Judge; c Harinder, Narinder & Arrind. *Educ:* Punjab Univ, BSc, 44, MSc, 45; Harvard Univ, MEngSc, 47, PhD(electron physics), 49. *Hon Degrees:* DSc, Punjabi Univ, 75. *Prof Exp:* Lectr electronics, Univ Delhi, India, 49-53; sci officer microwave tubes, Nat Phys Lab, New Delhi, India, 53-57; asst dep dir electron tubes, Cent Electronics Eng Res Inst, India, 57-62; res engr microwave tubes, Univ Mich, Ann Arbor, 62-63; res engr semiconductor devices, Bell Tel Labs, Murray Hill, NJ, 63; dir electron tubes & electronics, Cent Electronics Eng Res Inst, India, 63-84; nat proj coordr semiconductor & power electronics, UN Develop Prog, 84-87. *Concurrent Pos:* Mem electronics comt, Govt India, 63-68, chmn Working Group Consumer Electronics & Instrumentation, 68-75, mem Univ Grants Comn, 75-78, mem Sci & Eng Res Coun, 78-82, chmn Res & Develop Comt, 78-84, mem gov body, Coun Sci & Indust Res, 74-76 & 80-82; vis scientist, Stanford Linear Accelerator Ctr, Palo Alto, 82, Plasma Fusion Lab, Mass Inst Technol, 86. *Mem:* Fel Inst Elec & Electronic Engrs; fel Inst Electronic & Telecommun Engrs; fel Indian Acad Sci. *Res:* Microwave electronics and microwave tubes; tuning of interdigital magnetrons, wide ranges obtained; depressed collectors for large-orbit gyrotrons, new scheme proposed and verified; depressed collectors for small-orbit gyrotrons of cavity as well as quasi-optical type; microwave plasmas: surface waves on plasma columns, launching efficiency studied; microwave semiconductors: millimeter wave source using surface plasmons. *Mailing Add:* 1201 T Energy Res Bldg Univ Md College Park MD 20742-3511. *Fax:* 301-314-9437; *E-Mail:* singh@glue.umd.edu

SINGH, AMARJIT, CONSTRUCTION ENGINEERING MANAGEMENT. *Current Pos:* ASST PROF, UNIV HAWAII, 93- *Educ:* Indian Inst Technol, Delhi, BTech, 76; Tex A&M Univ, ME, 87; Purdue Univ, PhD(civil eng), 90. *Prof Exp:* Construct mgr, Gammon India Ltd, Bombay, 76-79; resident engr, Sami Badr Architect, Kuwait, 80-82; estimating engr, Al-Hamra Construct Co, Kuwait, 82-84; planning engr, M A Kharafi Construct Co, Kuwait, 84-86; construct consult, Found Co Can, 90-91; asst prof construct eng mgt, NDak State Univ, 91-93. *Mem:* Am Soc Civil Engrs; Am Asn Cost Engrs. *Res:* Computer integrated construction; cost schedule control systems; conflict management; advance the practice of construction engineering management. *Mailing Add:* Dept Civil Eng Univ Hawaii 2540 Dole St Honolulu HI 96822-2333

SINGH, AMREEK, HISTOLOGY, ULTRASTRUCTURAL PATHOLOGY. *Current Pos:* PROF HISTOL, ATLANTIC VET COL, CHARLOTTETOWN, PEI, CAN, 85- *Personal Data:* b Etah, Uttar Pradesh, India, Apr 13, 35; Can citizen; m 77, Davinder; c Ameet. *Educ:* Agra Univ, India, BVSc & AH, 55; Univ Guelph, Can, MS, 68 & PhD(morphol), 71. *Prof Exp:* Instr path, Vet Col, Agra Univ, Mathura, India, 56-58, lectr; asst prof histol & embryol, Col Vet Med Pant Nagar, India, 61-65; asst med histol, Sch Med, Geneva Univ, Switz, 71-74; from asst prof to assoc prof histol, Ont Vet Col, Guelph, Can, 74-85. *Concurrent Pos:* Vis fel, Commonwealth Sci & Indust Res Orgn, Australia, 78; Brit coun fel, Christie Hosp, Eng, 82; referee, Can J Comp Med; consult, Nat Dept Health, Can, 77-85 & 89- *Mem:* AAAS; Am Asn Anatomists; Swiss Soc Cell & Molecular Biol; Soc Toxicol Can; World Asn Vet Anatomists. *Res:* Histology of normal and experimentally altered organ and tissues of animals; electron microscopy of liver, kidney and thyroid gland of animals exposed to known environmental pollutants in laboratory conditions; electron microscopical analysis of liver from the rats fed various polychlorinated bipheryl congeners. *Mailing Add:* Dept Anat & Physiol Atlantic Vet Col 550 University Ave Charlottetown PE C1A 4P3 Can. *E-Mail:* singh@upel.ca

SINGH, BALDEV, PHARMACEUTICAL CHEMISTRY, GENERAL CHEMISTRY. *Current Pos:* from assoc chemist to res chemist, 67-80, res fel, 80-90, FEL, STERLING RES GROUP, 90- *Personal Data:* b Takhtupura, Punjab, India, Jan 9, 39; US citizen; m 67; c 2. *Educ:* D M Col Moga, Punjab, India, BSc, 59; Banaras Hindu Univ, India, MSc, 62; State Univ NY, PhD(med chem), 67. *Prof Exp:* Lab instr chem, D M Col Moga, Punjab, India, 59-60; lectr chem, S D Col Barnala, Punjab, India, 62-63. *Mem:* Am Chem Soc. *Res:* Design and synthesis of organic compounds of biological interest with major emphasis on heterocyclic chemistry; fifty United States patents and published about 40 papers relating to chemotherapy and pulmonary and cardiovascular pharmacology. *Mailing Add:* NY Comed Inc Res & Develop Wayne PA 19087-8630

SINGH, BALWANT, MICROBIOLOGY, EPIDEMIOLOGY. *Current Pos:* CONSULT, HEALTH RES INT, SCI TECH INT, 86- *Personal Data:* b Hasanpur, India, Jan 21, 34; US citizen; m 72, Joyce A Brengarth; c Tejpal, Prem & Davinder. *Educ:* Aligarh Muslim Univ, India, BSc, 53; Agra Univ, BVSc & AH, 57; Univ Mo, MS, 62; Univ Pittsburgh, PhD(microbiol), 65. *Prof Exp:* Vet officer, Uttar Pradesh State Animal Husb Dept, 57-61; res assoc epidemiol & microbiol, Univ Pittsburgh, 66-70, asst res prof, 70-76, res assoc prof epidemiol & microbiol, Grad Sch Pub Health, 76-86. *Concurrent Pos:* Adj prof biol sci, Fla Atlantic Univ, 81; chmn, Sci-Tech Corp. *Mem:* Am Soc Microbiol; Am Pub Health Asn; Int Epidemiol Asn; Soc Epidemiol Res; Am Venereal Dis Asn; Sigma Xi; Int Health Soc; fel Nat Acad Vet Sci India. *Res:* Venereal diseases; public health microbiology; uterine cancer; reproductive health; food sciences; veterinary medicine. *Mailing Add:* 5409 Guarino Rd Pittsburgh PA 15217

SINGH, BHAGIRATH, MOLECULAR IMMUNOLOGY, PEPTIDE SYNTHESIS & DIABETES. *Current Pos:* PROF & CHAIR, DEPT MICROBIOL & IMMUNOL, UNIV WESTERN ONT, 92- *Personal Data:* b Jaipur, India, Feb 8, 46; m 68, Rajkumari Yadav; c Gargi, Vivek, Somya. *Educ:* Rajasthan Univ, BSc, 63, MSc, 65; Agra Univ, PhD(med chem), 69. *Honors & Awards:* Gold Medal Chem, Rajasthan Univ. *Prof Exp:* Jr res fel chem, Cent Drug Res Inst, 66-69, sr res fel, 69-70; res fel org chem, Liverpool Univ, 70-73; res fel immunol, Univ Alta, 73-77, from asst prof to prof immunol, 77-93, actg chmn immunol, 88-89. *Concurrent Pos:* Prin investr, Med Res Coun Group Immunoregulation, 82-87; Heritage Scholar, Alta Heritage Found Med Res, 85-89, Heritage scientist, 89-93; co-dir, Immunol Group, Robarts Res Inst, Univ Western Ont, 92- & Int Prog, Med Res Coun/ Juv Diabetes Found, 96- *Mem:* Am Asn Immunologists; Can Soc Immunol; NY Acad Sci; Am Diabetes Asn; AAAS; Am Peptide Soc; Can Diabetes Asn; Juv Diabetes Found Int. *Res:* Molecular immunology of proteins and synthetic peptides antigens; immunodomint sites on auto antigens; diabetes and autoimmunity; activation and antigen receptors on T lymphocytes; molecular biology of immune recognition; monoclonal antibodies; immuneotherapy of autoimmunity; diabetes. *Mailing Add:* Dept Microbiol & Immunol Univ Western Ont London ON N6A 5C1 Can

SINGH, BHARAT, plant physiology, food science; deceased, see previous edition for last biography

SINGH, CHANCHAL, APPLIED MATHEMATICS. *Current Pos:* Asst prof math, State Univ NY, Potsdam, 66-69, asst prof math, St Lawrence Univ, Canton, NY, 72-76, assoc prof, 76-82, CUMMINGS PROF MATH, ST LAWRENCE UNIV, CANTON, NY, 82- *Personal Data:* b Singapore, Apr 4, 34; m 66; c 3. *Educ:* Punjab Univ, India, BA, 57; Univ Mich, Ann Arbor, MA, 65; Fla State Univ, MSc, 70, PhD(statistics), 72. *Honors & Awards:* Fulbright lectr, Univ Delhi, India, 88. *Concurrent Pos:* Chmn, Dept Math, St Lawrence Univ, Canton, NY; assoc ed, J Info Optimization Sci. *Mem:* Indian Genetics Soc; fel Am Dermatoglyphics Asn; Sigma Xi; Oper Res Soc Am; Int Math Prog Soc; Oper Res Soc India. *Res:* Optimization theory; duality theory and optimality conditions; finger prints as applied to genetics and physical anthropology; recreational mathematics; mathematical modeling. *Mailing Add:* Dept Math St Lawrence Univ Canton NY 13617. *Fax:* 315-379-5804

SINGH, DAULAT, SOIL CHEMISTRY, ANALYTICAL CHEMISTRY. *Current Pos:* CHEMIST, ENVIRON LAB DIV, MICH DEPT AGR, 69- *Personal Data:* b Dihwa, India, July 27, 39; m 54; c 3. *Educ:* Agra Univ, BSc, 57, MSc, 59; Univ Guelph, MSc, 65; Mich State Univ, PhD(soil chem), 69. *Prof Exp:* Res asst soil chem, Nat Sugar Inst, Kanpur, India, 60-63; res asst soil phosphorous, MacDonald Col, McGill Univ, 66. *Mem:* Am Soc Agron; Int Soc Soil Sci; Indian Soil Sci Soc; Asn Off Anal Chem. *Res:* Mechanisms of soil-fertilizer interaction; soil phosphorous reaction products. *Mailing Add:* 2089 Ashland Okemos MI 48864

SINGH, DILBAGH, PLANT PATHOLOGY. *Current Pos:* chmn, Div Natural Sci, 77-80 & 83-89, PROF BIOL, BLACKBURN COL, 67-, CHMN, BIOL DEPT, 89- *Personal Data:* b Partabpura, India, Oct 15, 34; m 54; c 3. *Educ:* Govt Col, Ludhiana, India, BSc, 56; Panjab Univ, India, BSc, 59, MSc, 61; Univ Wis, Madison, PhD(plant path), 68. *Prof Exp:* Lectr biol, Sikh Nat Col, India, 61-62; res asst plant path, Univ Wis, 62-67. *Concurrent Pos:* Vis scientist, Univ Mass, 74-76. *Mem:* Bot Soc Am; Am Inst Biol Sci; Mycol Soc Am; Nat Geog Soc; Am Mus Natural Hist; Nat Asn Biol Teachers. *Res:* Vascular diseases of plants; effects of pathogenesis on the nitrogenous and carbohydrate contents of the xylem sap; seasonal variation in the xylem sap components; effects of water stress on growth and metabolism of wilt inducing fungi; effects of water stress on the flowering behavior of various ornamental plants, Begonia, Impatiens and Cloeus. *Mailing Add:* Natural Sci Blackburn Col 700 Col Ave Carlinville IL 62626-1454

SINGH, GAJENDRA, agricultural engineering, for more information see previous edition

SINGH, GURDIAL, POLYMER CHEMISTRY. *Current Pos:* RETIRED. *Personal Data:* b Punjab, India, Aug 15, 34; m 60, Nirmal Kang; c Vindy, Guri & Raj. *Educ:* Panjab Univ, India, BSc, 57, MSc, 59; Univ Cincinnati, PhD(chem), 64. *Prof Exp:* Demonstrator chem, Panjab Univ, India, 58, 59, jr fel, 59-60; teaching asst, Univ Cincinnati, 60-61, fel, 63-64; res assoc, Mass Inst Technol, 64-65; from res chemist to sr res chemist, E I DuPont De Nemours & Co, 65-72, res assoc, 79-89, sr res assoc, Textile Fibers Dept, Exp Sta, 79-93. *Mem:* Am Chem Soc. *Res:* Synthetic polymer chemistry; organophosphorus chemistry; organic chemistry; organometallic chemistry. *Mailing Add:* 1829 Graves Rd Hockessin DE 19707

SINGH, GURMUKH, PULMONARY PATHOLOGY. *Current Pos:* CHIEF LAB SERV, VET ADMIN MED CTR. *Personal Data:* b Dhoodt-Kalan, India, Mar 12, 50. *Educ:* Univ Poona, MD, 71; Univ Pittsburgh, PhD(path), 78. *Mem:* Int Acad Path; Am Asn Pathologists. *Mailing Add:* Dept Path Vet Admin Med Ctr University Dr C #646 Pittsburgh PA 15240-0055. *Fax:* 412-692-3497

SINGH, HAKAM, POLYMER CHEMISTRY, SURFACE CHEMISTRY. *Current Pos:* SR RES FEL & CONSULT, COURTAULDS AEROSPACE INC, 93- *Personal Data:* b Bagh, WPakistan, Feb 11, 28; m 50; c 4. *Educ:* Univ Delhi, BSc, 52, MSc, 54, PhD(chem), 59. *Prof Exp:* Lectr chem, Univ Delhi, 57-60; res assoc & lectr, Univ Southern Calif, 60-62; lectr, Univ Delhi, 62-63; reader, Punjabi Univ, 63-65; asst prof, IIT, New Delhi, 65-68; vis assoc prof, Univ Southern Calif, 68; res supvr, Prod Res & Chem Corp, 68-81, mgr, Polymer Labs, 81-87, vpres polymer res, 87-89, sr div vpres polymer res & corp res & develop, 89-93. *Concurrent Pos:* Nat fel polymer technol, Intra Sci Res Found, 70- *Mem:* NY Acad Sci; AAAS; Am Chem Soc. *Res:* Structural chemistry of clay minerals; electrochemistry of nerve impulse initiation; interactions of surfactants with metal ions; electrochemistry of crevice corrosion; design and development of protective coatings; development of high performing elastomers and their processing; synthesis of high temperature polysulfide polymers; development of cyanosiloxane sealants for aerospace applications; polythioether polymers, hybrid polymers, modified silicone polymers, perfluoroether polymers. *Mailing Add:* 2820 Empire Ave Burbank CA 91504

SINGH, HANWANT B, TROPOSPHERIC CHEMISTRY, GLOBAL CHANGE. *Current Pos:* GROUP LEADER & RES SCIENTIST, NASA AMES RES CTR, 87- *Personal Data:* b New Delhi, India, Dec 7, 46; US citizen; m 76, Raman H Sethi; c Keshav M & Meena K. *Educ:* Indian Inst Technol, Delhi, BTech, 68; Univ Pittsburgh, MS, 70, PhD(chem eng), 72. *Honors & Awards:* Frank Chambers Award, Air & Waste Mgt Asn, 89. *Prof Exp:* Res assoc, Rutgers Univ, 72-74; sr engr, Stanford Res Inst, 75-80, dir Atmospheric Chem Prog, 80-87. *Concurrent Pos:* Mem, Dist Adv Coun Bay Area Air Qual Mgt, 87-; exec ed, J Atmospheric Environ, 89-; assoc ed, J Geophys Res, 92-; consult to numerous insts. *Mem:* Am Geophys Union; Air & Waste Mgt Asn. *Res:* Study of the changing composition, chemistry and climate of the atmosphere; published 106 scientific papers. *Mailing Add:* 681 Arastradero Rd Palo Alto CA 94306. *Fax:* 650-604-3625; *E-Mail:* hanwant__singh@gmgate.arc.nasa.gov

SINGH, HARBHAJAN, CHEMISTRY, BIOCHEMISTRY. *Current Pos:* from res specialist to sr res specialist, Monsanto Agr Prod Co, 77-81, res group leader, 81-83, sr res group leader, Dept Environ Sci, 83-91, TEAM LEADER ENVIRON SCI, MONSANTO AGR PROD CO, 92- *Personal Data:* b Delhi, India, July 12, 41; m 71, Rama; c Arjun & Supriya. *Educ:* Univ Delhi, BS, 61, MS, 63, PhD(chem), 66; Southern Ill Univ, MBA, 83. *Prof Exp:* Asst prof exp med, Sch Med, NY Univ, 66-77, adj assoc prof biochem, Sch Dent, 75-77. *Concurrent Pos:* Sr res fel natural prod, Coun Sci & Inndust Res India, Univ Delhi, 66-67; Med Res Coun Can fel, Univ Western Ont, 67-68; Hormel Inst fel, Univ Minn, 69; res biochemist, Lipid Metab Lab, Vet Admin Hosp, New York, 69-; adj asst prof biochem, Sch Dent, NY Univ, 72-74. *Mem:* Am Chem Soc; Int Soc Study Xenobiotics. *Res:* Chemistry and metabolism of myelin; bacterial lipid metabolism; spingolipids; chemistry of natural products; development of analytical methods; lipid metabolism; metabolic and environmental fate studies on pesticides; synthesis of labeled pesticides. *Mailing Add:* 12545 Royal Manor Dr St Louis MO 63141

SINGH, HARPAL P, TOXICOLOGY, REPRODUCTIVE TOXICOLOGY. *Current Pos:* assoc prof & coordr allied health, 74-80, PROF BIOL & COORDR MED TECHNOL, SAVANNAH STATE UNIV, 80-; DIR, MARC HONORS UNDERGRAD RES TRAINING PROG, ASSOC DIR BIOMED RES & SPONSORED PROGS. *Personal Data:* b India, Aug 16, 41; US citizen; m 70, Harbhajan; c Reema, Arvin & Amit. *Educ:* Panjab Univ, India, BS, 60, MS, 62; Univ Tenn, Knoxville, PhD(conc radiation biol), 70, MPH, 74. *Prof Exp:* Res asst zool, Punjab Agr Univ, Ludhiana, India, 62-64; asst prof biol, Bennett Col, Greensboro, NC, 69-70; assoc prof biol, Knox Col, Knoxville, 70-74. *Concurrent Pos:* NIH grants, 77-97; dir, MARC Prog, NIH, 84-96; dir, Extramural Assocs Res Develop Prog, 94-97. *Mem:* Nat Sci Teachers Asn; Am Soc Allied Health Prof; AAAS; Environ Mutagen Soc; Reproductive Toxicol Soc. *Res:* molecular toxicology of hemolytic anemia; chemical-induced hemolytic anemia; reproductive and developmnetal toxicology; nutiagenesis; chemical drug sensitivity of germ-cells; developmental toxicology of brine shrimp; image and morphometric analysis. *Mailing Add:* Savannah State Univ PO Box 20425 Savannah GA 31404

SINGH, HARWANT, FOOD IRRADIATION, BIOLOGICAL SYSTEMS. *Current Pos:* CONSULT, AHA ENTERPRISES, 92- *Personal Data:* b Amritsar, India, Nov 20, 34; m 55, Wadhwa. *Educ:* Agra Univ, BSc, 55; Vikram Univ, India, MSc, 59; Univ Alta, PhD(biochem), 62. *Prof Exp:* NIH res fel biochem, Univ Alta, 62-63; res assoc, Med Sch, Northwestern Univ, 63-65; asst res officer, Whiteshell Labs, Atomic Energy Can Ltd, 66-68, assoc res officer, 68-81, sr res officer, 81-87, sr scientist, 88-92. *Concurrent Pos:* Adj prof, Univ Man, 90-92; attached staff, Atomic Energy Can Ltd Res, 92- *Mem:* Chem Inst Can. *Res:* Structure of oligonucleotides and nucleic acids; mechanisms involved in protein synthesis; ribosome interactions; photo and radiation chemistry of ribosomes and their constituents; roles of free radicals in photo; radiation biology; food irradiation; industrial applications of radiation. *Mailing Add:* AHA Enterprises Box 273 Pinawa MB R0E 1L0 Can. *Fax:* 204-753-8802

SINGH, INDER JIT, ANATOMY, DENTISTRY. *Current Pos:* asst res scientist, Inst Dent Res, NY Univ, 69-71, assoc res scientist, 71-78, from asst prof to assoc prof, 72-79, assoc chmn, Dept Anat, 78-84, PROF ANAT, COL DENT & GRAD SCH ARTS & SCI, NY UNIV, 79- *Personal Data:* b India, Apr 28, 39. *Educ:* Panjab Univ, India, BDS, 59; Univ Ore, PhD(anat), 69; Columbia Univ, DDS, 84. *Prof Exp:* House surgeon, Govt Dent Col & Hosp, India, 59-60; asst pedodont, Dent Sch, Univ Ore, 61-65; res assoc med psychol, Med Sch, 68-69. *Concurrent Pos:* Fel, Guggenheim Dent Clin, New York, 60-61; NIH spec res fel, Lab Cellular Res, Inst Dent Res, 71 & 72; adj asst prof, Fordham Univ, 70-71; assoc prof, City Univ New York, 71- *Mem:* AAAS; Am Asn Anat; fel Geront Soc; NY Acad Sci; Int Asn Dent Res; Am Dent Asn; Acad Gen Dent; Sigma Xi. *Res:* Mammalian growth and development; experimental teratology; skeletal biology. *Mailing Add:* NY Univ Dent Ctr 345 E 24th St New York NY 10010

SINGH, INDERJIT, NEUROCHEMISTRY, NEUROBIOLOGY. *Current Pos:* res fel, 76-77, instr, 77-78, ASST PROF NEUROL, JOHNS HOPKINS SCH MED, 78- *Personal Data:* b Langrian, India, July 13, 43; US citizen; m 80. *Educ:* Panjab Univ, India, BSc, 65, MSc, 67; Iowa State Univ, PhD(biochem), 74. *Prof Exp:* Res fel neurochem, Mass Gen Hosp, 75-76. *Mem:* Am Soc Neurochem; Int Soc Neurochem; Am Soc Biol Chem. *Res:* Molecular mechanisms of the development of oligodendrocytes, myelinogenesis and the status of myelin in neuropathological disorders. *Mailing Add:* Dept Pediat & Cell Biol Med Univ SC 171 Ashley Ave Charleston SC 29464

SINGH, IQBAL, ORTHOPEDIC SURGERY, IMMUNOLOGY & INTERNAL MEDICINE. *Current Pos:* AT HARRIMAN JONES MED CLIN. *Personal Data:* b Muzafaagarh, India, Feb 23, 26; nat US. *Educ:* Panjab Univ, FSc, 42, MD, 49. *Prof Exp:* Instr physiol, Mission Med Col, India, 51; asst instr orthop, Univ Pa, 55-57; clin asst, Univ Calif, Los Angeles, 59-61; asst clin prof, Univ Calif, Irvine, 66-69; assoc prof orthop & chmn div, Dept Surg, Med Col Ohio, 69-76, assoc prof, 76-80, prof surg, 80- *Mem:* AMA; AAAS; Asn Clin Scientists; Can Orthop Asn; Am Asn Surg Trauma; Sigma Xi. *Res:* Cell mediated and humoral immunity; blocking factor; surgical extirpation supplemented with immunotherapy; horizontal and vertical transmission of immunity in patients; an animal model for human osteosarcoma. *Mailing Add:* 1437 Park Ave South Plainfield NJ 07080

SINGH, JAG JEET, OPTICS, ATOMIC & MOLECULAR PHYSICS. *Current Pos:* staff scientist aerospace sci, 64-80, CHIEF SCIENTIST, INSTRUMENT RES DIV, LANGLEY RES CTR, NASA, 80-, DISTINGUISHED RES SCIENTIST, 91- *Personal Data:* b Rohtak, India, May 20, 26; c Surendar K. *Educ:* Panjab Univ, BS, MS, 48; Liverpool Univ, PhD(nuclear physics), 56. *Honors & Awards:* Appolo Achievement Award, NASA, 69, Technol Utilization Awards, 77, 82, 86, 87, 92 & 93; US Civil Serv Outstanding Performance Award, NASA, 86, 90 & 93, Sci Medal, 90. *Prof Exp:* Lectr physics, Panjab Educ Serv, India, 50-53; res fel nuclear physics, Univ Liverpool, 56-57; prof physics, Panjab Govt Col, 57-58; USAEC res fel nuclear physics, Univ Kans, 58-59; asst prof physics, Mem Univ Nfld, 59-60; assoc prof, WVa State Col, 60-62 & Col William & Mary, 62-64. *Concurrent Pos:* Adv Gov Va, William & Mary Repr, Govs Adv Coun, Va Assoc Res Ctr, 62-63; lectr-consult, Langley Res Ctr, NASA, 62-64; adj prof physics & geophys sci, Old Dominion Univ & consult physicist, Col William & Mary, 74-; consult, Med Res Serv, Vet Admin Ctr, Hampton, 76-83. *Mem:* Fel Brit Inst Physics; fel AAAS; fel Am Inst Aeronaut & Astronaut; fel Am Phys Soc. *Res:* Materials science, environmental and optical physics relevant to NASA mission; Mossbauer spectroscopy and positron annihilation spectroscopy of structural alloys and molecular solids. *Mailing Add:* PO Box 325 Yorktown VA 23690

SINGH, JAGBIR, SURVIVAL ANALYSIS. *Current Pos:* assoc prof, 74-78, PROF STATIST, TEMPLE UNIV, 78- *Personal Data:* b Baraut, India, Jan 2, 40; m 68. *Educ:* Aligarh Muslim Univ, India, MS, 60; Fla State Univ, PhD(statist), 67. *Prof Exp:* Asst prof statist, J V Col, Baraut, India, 60-62; asst prof math, Ohio State Univ, 67-74. *Concurrent Pos:* Sr prof, Indian Agr Res Sci Inst, New Delhi, 77-78. *Mem:* Inst Math Statist; Am Statist Asn; Biomet Soc; Int Statist Inst. *Res:* Paired comparison model building; estimation; applied probability; sampling. *Mailing Add:* Dept Statist Temple Univ Philadelphia PA 19122. *E-Mail:* jagbir@surfer.sbm.temple.edu

SINGH, JAI PRAKASH, PROTEINS & PEPTIDES IN DIAGNOSTICS, ANALYTICAL CHEMISTRY. *Current Pos:* staff scientist, Life Technol, Inc, Gaithersburg, MD, ORGANIC CHEM, LOS RIOS COMMUNITY COL DIST, SACRAMENTO, CA, 96- *Personal Data:* b Bhawapar, Gorakhpur, Uttar Pradesh, Jan 8, 50; m 85, Singh. *Educ:* Agra Univ, India, BSc, 74, MSc, 76; Laurentian Univ, Sudbury, Can, MSc, 81; Univ BC, PhD(org chem), 87. *Prof Exp:* Res fel, Nat Coun Sci & Indust Res, India, 76-77; fel, Univ Calif, Davis, 87-90; scientist III, 90-93, sr scientist I, Microscan Div, Baxter Diag Inc, 93- *Mem:* Am Chem Soc. *Res:* Synthesis of peptides and substrates (amino acids, carbohydrates) involved in diagnosis of infectious bacteria; analytical methods development using high-performance liquid chromatography and capillary electrophoresis for carbohydrates, ions, organic ions, antimicrobics and amino acids; synthesis of nucleotides using chemical & enzymatic methods; HPLC and CE methods development for the separation of nucleotides & oligonucleotids, DNA, RNA, plasmids etc. *Mailing Add:* 204 Spurlock Ct Roseville CA 95661. *Fax:* 916-372-2081; *E-Mail:* jsingh@lifetech.com

SINGH, JARNAIL, TERATOLOGY, TOXICOLOGY. *Current Pos:* Assoc prof biol, 69-82, chmn, Div Math & Sci, 70-73, assoc dir Math Sci Inst, 83-85, PROF BIOL, STILLMAN COL, TUSCALOOSA, ALA, 82- *Personal Data:* b Amritsar, Punjab, India, Oct 26, 41; US citizen; m 68; c 2. *Educ:* Panjab Univ, BS, 61; Punjab Agr Univ, MS, 64; Kans State Univ, PhD(cytogenetics), 68. *Concurrent Pos:* Prin investr, MBRS prog, Stillman Col, 73-, fac res & grant helper, 84-; Nat Res Serv fel, Univ Ala, 83-85; extramural assoc, NIH, 85. *Mem:* Behav Teratology Soc; Teratology Soc; Nat Minority Health Affairs Asn. *Res:* Teratological effects of air pollution gases; toxicological effect of air pollution gases during prenatal and postnatal development; teratogenicity of mycotoxins under protein deprived conditions. *Mailing Add:* Dept Math & Sci Stillman Col PO Drawer 1430 Tuscaloosa AL 35403-1430

SINGH, JASWANT, PLANT PATHOLOGY. *Current Pos:* assoc prof, 68-69, head dept, 77-82, PROF BIOL, MISS VALLEY STATE UNIV, 69-, HEAD DEPT, 83- *Personal Data:* b Gunna Ur, W Punjab, Sept 29, 37; m 69; c 1. *Educ:* Khalsa Col, India, BSc, 58; Panjab Univ, India, MSc, 60; Univ Ill, Urbana, PhD(plant path), 66. *Prof Exp:* Demonstr chem, Khalsa Col, India, 58-61; res assoc & asst prof bot & plant path, Sci Res Inst, Ore State Univ, 66-68. *Mem:* AAAS. *Res:* Reproductive physiology; physiology and biochemistry of fungi; waste water treatment efficiencies. *Mailing Add:* 21005 Barclay El Toro CA 92630

SINGH, KANHAYA LAL, ANALYSIS, FUNCTIONAL ANALYSIS. *Current Pos:* ASST PROF CALCULUS & DIFFERENTIAL EQUATIONS, UNIV MINN, DULUTH, 81- *Personal Data:* b Varanasi, India, Feb 15, 44; m 65; c 2. *Educ:* Agra Univ, BSc, 62; Mem Univ, MA, 69; Tex A&M Univ, PhD(math), 80. *Prof Exp:* Fel, Lakehead Univ, 80-81. *Mem:* Am Math Soc; Math Asn Am. *Res:* Nonlinear functional analysis, fixed point theory, and approximation theory. *Mailing Add:* 5739 Danville Dr Fayetteville NC 28311

SINGH, KAPIL M, PRODUCT DEVELOPMENT, APPLIED PHYSICS IN END-USE OF PAPER. *Current Pos:* Res assoc, 90-93, sr res assoc, 93-96, RES SCIENTIST, INT PAPER, 97- *Personal Data:* b India, Nov 11, 60. *Educ:* Indian Inst Technol, BTech, 83; State Univ NY, MS, 85, PhD(paper sci), 90. *Concurrent Pos:* Mem, Steering Comt Paper Physics Res, Envelope State Paper Res Inst, 94- *Mem:* Tech Asn Pulp & Paper Indust; Envelope Mfrs Asn. *Res:* Developing paper properties for new end-uses of envelope paper, forms paper and other converted paper grades. *Mailing Add:* Int Paper 1446 E Lake Rd Erie PA 16533

SINGH, LAL PRATAP S, THEORITICAL PHYSICS. *Current Pos:* Mem fac, 83-85, PROF, DEPT PHYSICS, CENT MICH UNIV, 85- *Personal Data:* b India, Jan 7, 49. *Educ:* India Univ, BS, 66, MS, 68; Univ Rochester, PhD(physics), 74. *Mem:* Am Phys Soc; Inst Elec & Electronics Engrs. *Mailing Add:* Dept Comput Sci Cent Mich Univ Mt Pleasant MI 48859

SINGH, LAXMAN, AGRICULTURAL & FOOD CHEMISTRY, ANALYTICAL CHEMISTRY. *Current Pos:* MGR RES & DEVELOP, VITAMINS, INC, CHICAGO, 73- *Personal Data:* b Meerut, India, Sept 23, 44; US citizen; m 66, Indra; c Anjena & Rajiv. *Educ:* Agra Univ, India, BS, 64; Indian Agr Res Inst, MS, 66; Miss State Univ, PhD(soil chem), 70. *Prof Exp:* Chief chemist, Runyon Testing Labs, Chicago, 70-73. *Mem:* Am Chem Soc. *Res:* Vitamins and vitamin D products; vegetable oil processing; molecular distillation; supercritical fluid extractions; liquid chromatography. *Mailing Add:* Vitamins Inc 809 W 58th St Chicago IL 60621-2219

SINGH, MADAN GOPAL, DECISION TECHNOLOGIES, SYSTEMS ENGINEERING. *Current Pos:* prof control eng, 79-87, head dept, 81-83 & 85-87, PROF INFO ENG, UNIV MANCHESTER INST SCI & TECHNOL, 87- *Personal Data:* b Batala, India, Mar 17, 46; Brit & French citizen; m 79; c 2. *Educ:* Univ Exeter, UK, BSc Hons, 69; Univ Cambridge, PhD(eng), 73; French State, Docteur es Sci, 78. *Hon Degrees:* MSc, Univ Manchester, 82. *Honors & Awards:* Rank Zerox lectr, 87; Outstanding Contrib Award, Inst Elec & Electronics Engrs, 91, Norbert Wiener Award, 93. *Prof Exp:* Fel, St John's Col, Cambridge, 74-77; assoc prof eng, Univ Toulouse, 76-78; researcher, CNRS, France, 78-79. *Concurrent Pos:* Co-ed-in-chief, J Large Scale Syts, 80-88 & J Info & Decision Technol, 88-; ed-in-chief, Encycl Systs & Control, 81-91; vchmn systs eng, Int Fedn Automatic Control, 81-84; hon prof, Beijing Univ Aeronaut, 88. *Mem:* Fel Inst Elec & Electronics Engrs; fel Inst Elec Engrs. *Res:* Decision technologies for managerial decision making; complex systems theory. *Mailing Add:* Univ Manchester Inst Sci & Technol PO Box 88 Manchester M60 1QD England

SINGH, MADHO, GENETICS, BIOMETRICS. *Current Pos:* from asst prof to assoc prof, 69-87, PROF BIOL, STATE UNIV NY COL, ONEONTA, 88- *Personal Data:* b Mandha, India, Apr 25, 36; m, Keshar Kanwar; c Indira, Vidhyotma, Vijaya, Jyotsana & Krishna K. *Educ:* Univ Rajasthan, BScAg, 54; Agra Univ, MScAg, 56; Univ Minn, PhD, 65. *Prof Exp:* Lectr animal genetics, SKN Col, Jobner, India, 56-60; res asst genetics, Univ Minn, 61-65; res assoc biol, Univ Chicago, 65-66; reader animal sci & head dept, Univ Udaipur, India, 66-68; res scientist zool, Univ Tex Austin, 68-69. *Concurrent Pos:* Vis prof genetics, Sch Med, Univ Hawaii, 74-75; vis fel, Cornell Univ, 76; res awards, State Univ NY Res Found. *Mem:* NY Acad Sci; Genetics Soc Am; Biomet Soc; Soc Study Evolution; Am Soc Human Genetics; Sigma Xi. *Res:* Human genetics; biometrics; evolutionary biology; selection studies in mice; application of computers in genetic research; theoretical studies in population genetics. *Mailing Add:* Dept Biol State Univ NY Col Oneonta NY 13820-9318

SINGH, MAHENDRA PAL, STRUCTURAL ANALYSIS & DESIGN. *Current Pos:* assoc prof, 77-82, PROF ENG MECH, VA POLYTECH INST & STATE UNIV, 82- *Personal Data:* b India, Sept 20, 41; m 65; c 3. *Educ:* Univ Roorkee, BE, 62, ME, 66; Univ Ill, PhD(civil eng), 72. *Prof Exp:* Asst engr civil eng, Western Railway, India, 63-68; sr engr struct design, Sargent & Lundy, Chicago, 72-76, supvr, 76-77. *Concurrent Pos:* Consult, Sargent & Lundy, Chicago, 77-79, Woodward Clyde Consult, 79-80 & Stevenson & Assoc, Cleveland, 81-; engr, Lawrence Livermore Nat Lab, 79-80; prog dir, NSF, Washington, DC, 92-94. *Mem:* Am Soc Civil Engrs; Earthquake Eng Res Inst; Indian Soc Earthquake Technol. *Res:* Structural engineering; structural reliability; soil dynamics; structural dynamics; earthquake and wind engineering. *Mailing Add:* 219 Norris Hall Virginia Tech Univ Blacksburg VA 24061-4572

SINGH, MANOHAR, APPLIED MATHEMATICS, CONTINUUM MECHANICS. *Current Pos:* chmn dept, 78-81, PROF MATH, SIMON FRASER UNIV, 67- *Personal Data:* b Punjab, India, Apr 13, 30; m 56; c 3. *Educ:* Panjab Univ, India, BA, 50, MA, 53; Brown Univ, MSc, 63, PhD(appl math), 65. *Prof Exp:* Lectr math, Govt Col, Panjab Univ, 53-61; asst prof, NC State Univ, 65-67. *Concurrent Pos:* Vis prof, Panjab Univ, 69-70. *Mem:* Can Math Cong; Can Appl Math Soc. *Mailing Add:* Dept Math & Statist Simon Fraser Univ Burnaby BC V5A 1S6 Can

SINGH, MANSA C, ENGINEERING MECHANICS, STRUCTURAL ENGINEERING. *Current Pos:* ASSOC PROF MECH ENG, UNIV CALGARY, 68- *Personal Data:* b Lyallpur, India, Oct 10, 28; m 63; c 3. *Educ:* Panjab Univ, India, BSc, 52; Univ Minn, MS, 56, PhD(struct & appl mech), 62. *Prof Exp:* Asst engr, Bhakra Dam Designs Directorate, 52-55; asst prof civil eng, Univ Kans, 61-63 & Punjab Eng Col, 63-64; asst prof eng mech, SDak State Univ, 64-68. *Mem:* AAAS; Am Soc Civil Engrs; Am Soc Eng Educ. *Res:* Viscoelastic behavior of surfaces of revolution under combined mechanical and thermal loads; thermoelastoplastic bending and stability of beam columns; application of group theory to problems of vibrations and wave propagation; impact of nonlinear viscoplastic and viscous rods; problem of notation in vector mechanics. *Mailing Add:* Mech Eng Dept Univ Calgary Calgary AB T2N 1N4 Can

SINGH, MOHINDAR, BIOTECHNOLOGY, MEDICAL SCIENCES. *Current Pos:* SR SCIENTIST, BOEHRINGER MANNHEIM CORP, 93- *Personal Data:* m, Surinder K; c Jatinder Jeet K, Kanwaljit & Jasjeet. *Educ:* Danjab Univ, India, BSc, 63; Vikram Univ, India, MS, 66. *Prof Exp:* Sr pilot plant res & develop engr, Hoffman La Roche, 71-80; sr res & develop coordr, Alza Corp, 80-82; sr res assoc, Lawrence Berkeley Lab, 82-88; sr scientist, EA Eng, 88-91, Marks Bros, 91-92; sr engr, Appl Immune Sci, 92-93. *Mem:* Am Chem Soc; Soc Nuclear Med; Int Asn Radio Pharmacol. *Res:* Nuclear medicine development and diagnostics pharmaceuticals; petroleum contamination and other enviromental issues; published several articles. *Mailing Add:* 2380 Bisso Lane Concord CA 94523

SINGH, MOHINDER, develop over the counter drug products for lips, skin, cold sores & fever blisters, for more information see previous edition

SINGH, MRITYUNJAY, CERAMIC COMPOSITES, HIGH TEMPERATURE MATERIALS. *Current Pos:* SR RES ENGR, LEWIS RES CTR, NASA, 94- *Personal Data:* b Khujjhi, India, Mar 2, 57; US citizen; m 74, Gita; c Kumar, Madhvi, Pallavi & Abhishek. *Educ:* Gorakhpur Univ, India, BS, 77, MS, 80; Banaras Hindu Univ, PhD(metall eng), 83. *Honors & Awards:* Jacquet-Lucas Award, Am Soc Metals Int/Int Metallographic Soc, 93; R&D 100 Award, 95. *Prof Exp:* Proj scientist, Banaras Hindu Univ, India, 83-86; res assoc, La State Univ, 86-87; sr researcher, Rensselaer Polytech Inst, 87-91; sr assoc, Nat Res Coun, 91-93; prin researcher, Case Western Res Univ, 93-94. *Mem:* Mat Res Soc; Am Ceramic Soc; fel Am Soc Metals Int; Minerals, Metals & Mat Soc. *Res:* Processing, fabrication and characterization of advance high temperature structural ceramics and fiber reinoreced composites; composite materials. *Mailing Add:* Lewis Res Ctr NASA MS 106-5 Cleveland OH 44135. *Fax:* 216-433-5544

SINGH, NARSINGH B, CRYSTAL GROWTH OF OPTOELECTRONIC MATERIALS, DEVELOPMENT OF MATERIALS FOR NOVEL ELECTRO-OPTICAL DEVICES. *Current Pos:* sr engr, Westinghouse Sci & Tech Ctr, 84-86, fel engr, 86-89, adv engr, 86-91, adv engr, 91-92, PROG MGR, WESTINGHOUSE STC, 91- *Personal Data:* m 71, Kusum; c Manisha, Manish & Mamata. *Educ:* Gorakhpur Univ, India, BSc, 69, MSc, 71, PhD(eutetic solidification), 78. *Prof Exp:* Lectr chem, T D Postgrad, Gorakhpur, 71-79; res scientist, Rensselaer Polytech Inst, 79-84. *Concurrent Pos:* Assoc ed, J Progress in Crystal Growth Characterization. *Mem:* Fel Am Soc Metals Int; Mining, Mineral & Mat Soc; Am Inst Aeronaut & Astronaut; Sigma Xi; Am Asn Crystal Growers. *Res:* Materials developed for nonlinear optical, acousto-optical and x-ray and gamma-ray detector applications; single crystals grown by physical vapor transport, solution growth and Bridgman crystal growth method. *Mailing Add:* 2401 Willow Dr Export PA 15632. *Fax:* 412-256-1331

SINGH, PARAM INDAR, CARDIO-VASCULAR DEVICES. *Current Pos:* prin staff scientist & vpres, 82-86, exec vpres, 86-90, CONSULT, ABIOMED, 90- *Personal Data:* b Ferozepore, India, Nov 27, 46; US citizen; m 69; c 2. *Educ:* Univ Colo, BS, 68, MS, 70, PhD(aerospace eng sci), 74. *Prof Exp:* sr scientist, Avco Everrett Res Lab, 74-76, prin res scientist aerophysics, 76-82. *Concurrent Pos:* Prin investr, Permanent Cardiac Assistance Systs. *Mem:* AAAS; Am Heart Asn; Int Soc Artifical Internal Organs. *Res:* Applied physics; development of medical devices for cardio-vascular systems; biological fluid mechanics; laser effects and propagation; prosthetic calcification. *Mailing Add:* 28 Slocum Rd Lexington MA 02173-5622

SINGH, PRITHE PAUL, NUCLEAR PHYSICS. *Current Pos:* RETIRED. *Personal Data:* b Havialian, India, Sept 10, 30; m 59; c 2. *Educ:* Univ Agra, BSc, 51, MSc, 53; Univ BC, PhD(nuclear physics), 60. *Prof Exp:* Lectr physics, D C Jain Col, India, 53-54; res asst nuclear physics, Dept Atomic Energy, Govt of India, 54-55; Nat Res Coun Can fel, Atomic Energy Can, Ltd, 59-62; res assoc nuclear physics, Argonne Nat Lab, 62-64; from asst prof to emer prof physics, Ind Univ, Bloomington, 64-92. *Concurrent Pos:* Fac assoc, Argonne Nat Lab, 66-72; consult, US Naval Res Lab, 69-70; assoc dir res, Ind Univ Cyclotron Facil, 78-79, co-dir, 79-86. *Mem:* Fel Am Phys Soc; Sigma Xi. *Res:* Nuclear spectroscopy with neutrons and charged particles; inverse photodisintegration studies; nuclear reaction mechanism for alpha particle interaction with nuclei; statistical properties of nuclear cross sections; pion production; medium energy nuclear physics; heavy ion reactions; producer of radio series A Moment of Science. *Mailing Add:* 4937 E Ridgewood Dr Bloomington IN 47401

SINGH, PRITHIPAL, ORGANIC CHEMISTRY. *Current Pos:* res chemist, 70-73, group leader, 73-74, sect mgr chem, 74-77, asst dir, 77-81, VPRES, SYVA CORP, 81- *Personal Data:* b Amritsar, India, Apr 6, 39; m 63; c 2. *Educ:* Khalsa Col, India, BS, 59; Banaras Hindu Univ, MS, 61; Toronto Univ, PhD(org chem), 67. *Prof Exp:* Teacher chem, Khalsa Col, Delhi Univ, 61-68 & Banaras Hindu Univ, 68-69. *Concurrent Pos:* Fel, Southampton Univ & Brit Coun travel grant, 69-70. *Mem:* Am Chem Soc; fel The Chem Soc; Am Asn Clin Chem; Interam Soc Photochemists; Am Asn Photochem & Photobiol. *Res:* Synthetic, structural organic chemistry; immunochemistry; photochemistry. *Mailing Add:* Chemtrak 929 E Arques Ave Sunnyvale CA 94086-4521

SINGH, RABINDAR NATH, AGRONOMY, SOILS. *Current Pos:* res assoc soil chem & fertil, WVA Univ 66-69, res assoc clay mineral, 69-71, asst prof soil fertil & clay mineral, 71-75, a assoc prof, 75-78 PROF AGRON & AGRONOMIST, WVA UNIV, 78- *Personal Data:* b Ludhiana, India, Apr 10, 31; m 57; c 3. *Educ:* Panjab Univ, India, BSc, 55; Univ Tenn, MS, 59; Va Polytech Inst & State Univ, PhD(agron), 65. *Prof Exp:* Res asst soil fertil, Va Polytech Inst & State Univ, 63-65, fel & res assoc, 65-66. *Concurrent Pos:* Mem, Nat Task Force Sewage Sludge Crop Land, Coun Agr Sci & Technol, Environ Protection Agency. *Mem:* Am Soc Agron; Am Soc Soil Sci; Int Soc Soil Sci; Am Chem Soc. *Res:* Chemistry of soil phosphorus and micronutrients and their availability to crops; disposal of sewage sludge on agricultural land and mine soils; chemistry and mineralogy of coal overburden material; reclamation of strip mined land with industrial waste such as fly ash, balloon ash, kiln dust etc. *Mailing Add:* Plant Sci WVa Univ Box 6108 Morgantown WV 26506-0001

SINGH, RAGHBIR, AGRONOMY, PLANT PHYSIOLOGY. *Current Pos:* PROF BIOL, BENEDICT COL, 67-, CHMN DIV SCI & MATH, 68- *Personal Data:* b Punjab, India, Nov 1, 31; US citizen; m 66; c 1. *Educ:* Panjab Univ, India, BSc, 52, MSc, 55; Univ Minn, PhD(agron), 64. *Prof Exp:* Res asst plant physiol, Ministry of Agr, India, 55-59; res fel, Univ Minn, 64-65; from asst prof to assoc prof biol, Chadron State Col, 65-67. *Concurrent Pos:* NSF res grant, 66, undergrad equip, 67-69. *Res:* Nutrition, physiology and biochemistry of crop plants. *Mailing Add:* 1708 Pinewood Dr Columbia SC 29205-3247

SINGH, RAJENDRA, ACOUSTICS, VIBRATIONS. *Current Pos:* from asst prof to assoc prof, Mech Eng Dept, 79-87, DIR, FLUID POWER LAB, OHIO STATE UNIV, 82-, PROF, MECH ENG DEPT, 87-, DIR, ACOUST & DYNAMICS LAB, 91- *Personal Data:* b Feb 13, 1950; nat US; m 79; c 2. *Educ:* Birla Inst Technol & Sci, India, BS Hons, 71; Univ Roorkee, India, MS, 73; Purdue Univ, PhD(mech eng), 75. *Honors & Awards:* Award Excellence Teaching, Inst Noise Control Eng, 89; Westinghouse Award, Am Soc Eng Educ, 93. *Prof Exp:* Grad inst res, Ray W Herrick Lab, Purdue Univ, 73-75, teaching asst, Mech Eng Dept, 74-75; adj lectr, Indust Eng & Opers Res Dept, 77-79; acoust dynamics engr, Carlyle Compressor Co, 75-77, sr acoust dynamics engr, 77-79. *Concurrent Pos:* Mem, Computer Appln Tech Comt, Am Soc Heating, Refrig & Air Conditioning Engrs, chmn, subcomt on standards, 78-79, Comt Numerical Methods, Am Soc Mech Engrs, 83-, task group Impedance Tube Standards, 82-86; consult, over 25 orgns, 80-; grants & contracts, var corp & orgn, 80-93; key prof, Fluid Power Educ Found, 83-; bd gov, Nat Conf Fluid Power, 83-; gen chmn, NOISE-CON Conf, 85; vis prof, Univ Calif, Berkeley, 87-88; chmn tech comt, Noise Control Methods, Inst Noise Control Eng, 90-; prin investr, OBR Invest Fund Proj, 96- *Mem:* Fel Acoust Soc Am; Am Acad Mech; Am Soc Heating, Refrig & Air Conditioning Engrs; fel Am Soc Mech Engrs; Am Soc Eng Educ; Inst Noise Control Eng. *Res:* Acoustics, noise and vibration control; nonlinear dynamics; fluid power; digital signal processing; author of one book, one patent and over 150 articles in archival journals and international conferences. *Mailing Add:* Dept Mech Eng Ohio State Univ 206 W 18th Ave Columbus OH 43210-1107. *E-Mail:* singh.3@osu.edu

SINGH, RAJINDER, MATHEMATICAL STATISTICS. *Current Pos:* from asst prof to assoc prof, 66-75, PROF MATH, UNIV SASK, 75- *Personal Data:* b Adamke Cheema, WPakistan, Apr 1, 31; m 61; c 2. *Educ:* Panjab Univ, India, MA, 52; Univ Ill, Urbana, PhD(statist), 60. *Prof Exp:* Lectr statist, Panjab Univ, India, 52-56 & 60-62, reader, 62-64; asst prof math, Univ Ill, Urbana, 64-66. *Res:* Estimation problems in statistics. *Mailing Add:* Dept Math & Statist 142 McLean Hall Univ Sask 106 Wiggins Rd Saskatoon SK S7N 5E6 Can

SINGH, RAJIV K, ENGINEERING. *Current Pos:* ASSOC PROF ENG & DIR, ENG RES CTR, UNIV FLA. *Honors & Awards:* Robert Lansing Hardy Gold Medal, Mineral Metals & Mat Soc, 95. *Mailing Add:* Eng Res Ctr Univ Fla Gainesville FL 32611

SINGH, RAMA SHANKAR, SOLID STATE PHYSICS. *Current Pos:* SR PROF STAFF, MARTIN MARIETTA CO, 84- *Personal Data:* b Varanasi, India, Sept 27, 38. *Educ:* Banaras Hindu Univ, India, BSc, 59, MSc, 61; Univ RI, PhD(elec eng), 71. *Prof Exp:* Resident res asst solid state physics, US Army Munition Command & Nat Res Coun/Nat Acad Sci, 71-72; from asst prof to assoc prof physics, Univ PR, Mayaguez, 72-78; staff mem, Lincoln Lab, Mass Inst Technol, Lexington, 78-80; sr process engr, Gen Elec Co, 80-84. *Concurrent Pos:* Scientist I, PR Nuclear Ctr, Mayaguez, 72-78. *Mem:* Soc Photo-Optical Instrumentation Engrs; Am Phys Soc; sr mem Inst Elec & Electronics Engrs; Electrochem Soc. *Res:* Optical properties of materials from ultraviolet to far infrared; lattice dynamics and phase transition; Raman and Brillouin scattering; semiconductor memory devices; very-large-scale integrated circuits fabrication; radiation; hardening processing, testing and risk assessment of very-large-scale integration devices in radiation environments. *Mailing Add:* 444 Saratoga Ave Apt 13H Santa Clara CA 95050

SINGH, RAMA SHANKAR, POPULATION GENETICS, EVOLUTIONARY THEORY. *Current Pos:* from asst prof to assoc prof, 75-85, PROF BIOL, MCMASTER UNIV, 86- *Personal Data:* b Azamgarh, India, Mar 2, 45; m 76, Rekha; c Karun & Anuj. *Educ:* Agra Univ, India, BSc, 65; Kanpur Univ, India, MSc, 67; Univ Calif, Davis, PhD(genetics), 72. *Prof Exp:* Lectr bot, Govt Agr Col Kanpur, 67-68; Ford Found fel biol, Univ Chicago, 72-73; res assoc, Harvard Univ, 73-75. *Mem:* AAAS; Genetics Soc Am; Genetics Soc Can; Soc Study Evolution; Soc Am Naturalists; Am Soc Human Genetics. *Res:* Genetic variation and its role in adaptation and species formation; the role of sex in speciation; history of biology and philosophy. *Mailing Add:* Dept Biol McMaster Univ Hamilton ON L8S 4K1 Can. *Fax:* 905-522-6066; *E-Mail:* singh@mcmaster.ca

SINGH, RAMAN J, INVERTEBRATE PALEONTOLOGY, TREPOSTOME BRYOZOANS. *Current Pos:* from asst prof to prof, 71-95, EMER PROF GEOL, NORTHERN KY UNIV, 95- *Personal Data:* b Nabha, Panjab, India, Apr 16, 40; US citizen; m 69, Sharon. *Educ:* Panjab Univ, BSc, 59, MSc, 61; Univ Cincinnati, MS, 66, PhD(geol), 71. *Prof Exp:* Asst geologist, Panjab Govt, Chandigarh, 61-62; asst prof geol, Univ Tenn, Chattanooga, 69-71. *Concurrent Pos:* Trustee, Behringer-Crawford Mus, Covington, Ky, 80-84. *Mem:* Paleont Res Inst; Nat Asn Geol Teachers. *Res:* Ultrastructure of trepostome bryozoans; teaching earth science. *Mailing Add:* Dept Physics & Geology Northern Ky Univ Highland Heights KY 41099

SINGH, RAMESHWAR, HYDRAULICS, FLUID MECHANICS. *Current Pos:* assoc prof, 67-77, PROF CIVIL ENG, SAN JOSE STATE UNIV, 77- *Personal Data:* b Bihar, India, July 2, 37; m 54; c 4. *Educ:* Auburn Univ, BCE, 62, MS, 63; Stanford Univ, PhD(civil eng), 65. *Prof Exp:* Sectional officer design & construct, Irrig Dept, Govt Bihar, India, 56-60; asst prof civil eng, Univ BC, 65-67. *Concurrent Pos:* Consult, Fraser River Flood Res, Can, 65-67 & Jennings, McDermitt & Heis Consult Firm, Calif, 68-70, Santa Clara Valley Water Dist, 70-90. *Mem:* Fel Am Soc Civil Engrs; Am Geophys Union; Soil Conserv Soc Am; Nat Soc Prof Engrs. *Res:* Hydraulics; hydrology; fluid mechanics with application of applied mathematics and computers. *Mailing Add:* Dept Civil Eng & Appl Mech San Jose State Univ One Washington Sq San Jose CA 95192-0001

SINGH, RIPU DAMAN, PHYSICAL ANTHROPOLOGY, PRIMATOLOGY. *Current Pos:* from asst prof to assoc prof, 70-73, prof, 83-93, EMER PROF ANTHROP, UNIV WINDSOR, 94- *Personal Data:* b Patmau, India; m 80, Joan M Bruno. *Educ:* Univ Lucknow, BA, 51, MA, 53; Univ Ore, MA, 69, PhD(anthrop), 71. *Honors & Awards:* Birbal Sahni Award, 76. *Prof Exp:* Asst prof anthrop, Univ Lucknow, 56-60; asst anthropologist, Anthrop Surv India, Govt India, 60-66; instr anthrop, Univ Ore, 66-70. *Concurrent Pos:* Assoc anthrop. *Mem:* Am Asn Phys Anthrop; Can Asn Phys Anthrop; Ethnog & Folk Cult Soc India; Int Dermatoglyphic Asn; Am Dermatoglyphic Asn; fel Human Biol Coun. *Res:* Human population variations; dermatoglyphic variations and genetic patterns in caste populations of India and Canada; primate behavior and comparative primatology; human evolution. *Mailing Add:* Dept Sociol & Anthrop Univ Windsor Windsor ON N9B 3P4 Can. *Fax:* 519-971-3621

SINGH, RODERICK PATAUDI, ANATOMY. *Current Pos:* from lectr to asst prof, 67-72, ASSOC PROF ANAT, UNIV WESTERN ONT, 72- *Personal Data:* b Georgetown, Guyana, Feb 26, 35; Can citizen; m 61; c 3. *Educ:* Univ Western Ont, BA, 61, MSc, 63, PhD(anat), 66. *Honors & Awards:* Award, Soc Obstet & Gynec Can, 68. *Prof Exp:* Instr anat, Med Sch, Wayne State Univ, 66-67. *Concurrent Pos:* Cytogeneticist, Dept Path, Univ Hosp, London, Ont, 70-; consult, Depts Pediat & Obstet & Gynec, St Joseph's Hosp, London, Ont. *Mem:* Am Asn Anat; Can Asn Anat; Am Asn Phys Anthrop; Soc Study Human Biol. *Res:* Cytogenetics of human abortuses; embryology and morphology of the human ovary; mutagenesis. *Mailing Add:* Dept Anat Univ Western Ont Richmond St N London ON N6A 5C1 Can

SINGH, RUDRA PRASAD, VIROLOGY. *Current Pos:* res scientist plant virol, 68-78, sr res scientist, 78-91, PRIN RES SCIENTIST, AGR CAN RES STA, 92- *Personal Data:* b Sariya, India, Sept 1, 40; Can citizen; m 56; c 3. *Educ:* Agra Univ, India, BScAg, 59, MScAg, 61; NDak State Univ, Fargo, PhD(plant path), 66. *Prof Exp:* Sr res asst plant virol, Dept Agr, Uttar Pradesh, India, 61-62; fel, Nat Res Coun Can, 66-67. *Concurrent Pos:* Vis scientist, Nat Res Coun Can, 73-75; head, Potato Pest Mgt Sect, 85-90. *Mem:* Am Phytopath Soc; Potato Asn Am; Can Phytopath Soc; Indian Potato Asn; Europ Asn Potato Res. *Res:* Development of detection procedure for potato spindle tuber viroid; development of serological methods for the detection of potato viruses; development of cDNA probes for potato virus detection in tubers; virus indicator plants; sequencing and cloning of potato viruses and viroids; development of the transgenic plants. *Mailing Add:* Agrifood Can Res Sta PO Box 20280 Fredericton NB E3B 4Z7 Can

SINGH, SANKATHA PRASAD, APPROXIMATION THEORY, FIXED POINT THEORY. *Current Pos:* assoc prof, 67-72, PROF MATH, MEM UNIV NFLD, 72- *Personal Data:* b Varanasi, India, Jan 27, 37; m 59, Suman; c Sudha & Manoj. *Educ:* Agra Univ, BSc, 57; Benaras Hindu Univ, MSc, 59, PhD(math), 64. *Prof Exp:* Lectr math, Benaras Hindu Univ, 59-63; lectr, Univ Ill, 63-64; asst prof, Wayne State Univ, 64-65 & Univ Windsor, 65-67. *Concurrent Pos:* Nat Res Coun grant, 65- & NATO res grants, 80; ed, Indian J Math; proj leader, Int Res Group, NATO, 80-82; dir, NATO Adv Study Inst, 82-83, 84-85, 90-91 & 93-94. *Mem:* Am Math Soc; Can Math Soc; fel Nat Acad Sci India; Indian Math Soc; fel Inst Math & Applns. *Res:* Transform calculus; approximation theory; fixed point theory (nonlinear functional analysis). *Mailing Add:* Dept Math Mem Univ Nfld St John's NF A1C 5S7 Can. *Fax:* 709-737-3010; *E-Mail:* Spsingh@kean.ucs.mun.ca

SINGH, SANT PARKASH, ENDOCRINOLOGY, NUTRITION. *Current Pos:* assoc prof, 74-78, dir, Div Endocrinol & Metab, 74-85, PROF & CHIEF ENDOCRINOL METAB, CHICAGO MED SCH, 74-; ASSOC CHIEF OF STAFF & CHIEF ENDOCRINE-METAB SECT, VET ADMIN HOSP, NORTH CHICAGO, 73- *Personal Data:* b Anokh Singh Wala, India, Oct 2, 36; m 68, Satinder M; c Kiran. *Educ:* Panjab Univ, India, MBBS, 59; McGill Univ, MSc, 70; Am Bd Internal Med, dipl, 68; Am Bd Nuclear Med, dipl, 76; Am Bd Endocrinol & Metab, dipl, 77. *Prof Exp:* Intern med, Kingston Gen Hosp, Ont, 60-61; resident, Bergen Pines County Hosp, Paramus, NJ, 61-63; resident endocrinol, Philadelphia Gen Hosp, 63-64; resident med, Bergen Pines Co Hosp, Paramus, NJ, 64-65; assoc endocrinologist, Brooklyn-Cumberland Med Ctr, 70-72; dir endocrinol sect, 72-73; asst prof med, State Univ NY Downstate Med Ctr, 71-73; assoc prof clin med, Northwestern Univ, Chicago, 73-74. *Concurrent Pos:* Fel, State Univ NY Downstate Med Ctr, 65-66; Med Res Coun Can fel, McGill Univ Clin Royal Victoria Hosp, Montreal, 66-70. *Mem:* Fel Am Col Physicians; Endocrine Soc; Am Diabetes Asn; Am Fedn Clin Res; AMA. *Res:* Diabetes, growth, thyroid pathophysiology; carbohydrate metabolism. *Mailing Add:* Chicago Med Sch North Chicago IL 60064. *Fax:* 847-578-3818

SINGH, SHIVA PUJAN, IMMUNOLOGY, MICROBIOLOGY. *Current Pos:* from asst prof to assoc prof, 76-86, coordr biomed res, 84-86, PROF BIOL & DIR SCI RES, ALA STATE UNIV, 86- *Personal Data:* b Gonda, India, July 15, 47; US citizen; m 73; c 3. *Educ:* Pant Univ Agr & Technol, India, BSc, 69, MSc, 71; Auburn Univ, PhD(microbiol), 76. *Prof Exp:* Res assoc, Tuskegee Univ, 76. *Concurrent Pos:* Fac fel, Argonne Nat Lab, 79; trainee, Auburn Univ, 80, 81 & 82; trainee & extramural assoc, NIH, 83; prog dir & prin investr, Minority Biomed Res Support Prog, 84-; prog dir, Minority Access to Res Careers Prog, 85-; orgnr & dir, Nat Workshop on Use of Monoclonal Antibodies, 87; consult, NIH, 87-; mem, Nat Minority Health Affairs Asn, 87- *Mem:* Indian Microbiologists Asn Am (pres, 87-88); Am Soc Microbiol. *Res:* Outer membrane proteins of gram-negative bacteria; preparation and use of monoclonal antibodies for detection and identification of microorganisms. *Mailing Add:* 6636 Hollis Dr Montgomery AL 36117

SINGH, SHOBHA, LASERS, SOLID STATE PHYSICS. *Current Pos:* prin scientist, 90-94, RES FEL & DIR OPTOELECTRONICS RES, POLAROID CORP, 95- *Personal Data:* b Delhi, India, July 15, 28; m 46, Kamlesh; c Kuldip, Devender, Devbala, Satish & Sushil. *Educ:* Univ Delhi, BSc, 49, MSc, 51; Johns Hopkins Univ, PhD(physics), 57. *Prof Exp:* Res asst physics, Nat Phys Lab, India, 51-53; asst prof, Wilson Col, 57-59; res officer, Atomic Energy Estab, India, 59-61; Nat Res Coun Can, 61-64; distinguished mem tech staff physics, Bell Tel Labs, 64-89. *Concurrent Pos:* Fel, Johns Hopkins Univ, 57-59; Nat Res Coun Can fel, 61-63. *Mem:* Fel Am Phys Soc; fel Optical Soc Am; Sigma Xi; sr mem Inst Elec & Electronics Engrs. *Res:* Spectra of solids, Raman spectra, laser induced non-linear phenomena in solids, electrochromics, three five compound semiconductors; displays; solid state lasers; optical storage. *Mailing Add:* Polaroid Corp 730 Main Cambridge MA 02139. *Fax:* 781-386-9884; *E-Mail:* singhs@polaroid.com

SINGH, SHYAM N, FUNDAMENTAL & APPLIED COMBUSTION RESEARCH, EMISSION CONTROL & HEAT TRANSFER EQUIPMENT DESIGN. *Current Pos:* mgr res eng, 87-88, res & develop, 88-89, MGR, NEW PROD DEVELOP, COMBUSTION DIV, ECLIPSE INC, 89- *Personal Data:* b Ballia, India, Jan 1, 52; m 75; c 3. *Educ:* Banares Hindu Univ, India, BTech, 75; Pa State Univ, MS, 82. *Honors & Awards:* Ralph James Award, Am Soc Mech Eng, 91. *Prof Exp:* Combustion develop engr, Midland Ross Corp, 79-81; res & develop engr, Agua-Chem Div, Cleaver-Brooks, 81-83, proj mgr prod heat recovery, Energy Systs Div, 83-85; dir res & eng, WB Combustion Inc, 85-87. *Concurrent Pos:* Lectr, Dept Mech Eng, Univ Wis-Milwaukee, 87-; consult, Fredefort Malt Corp, 86-; prin investr, Ceramic Radiant Tube Tech, Gas Res Inst, 86- & combination of oil & gas fired burner, 87-, gas fired infrared technol, low emission burner. *Mem:* Combustion Inst; Am Soc Mech Eng. *Res:* Combustion, heat transfer and pollution control areas; high temperature ceramic materials for conducting advanced combustion research to improve industrial burner use; solid fuel combustion. *Mailing Add:* 2113 Silverthorn Dr Rockford IL 61107

SINGH, SUKHJIT, TOPOLOGY. *Current Pos:* PROF MATH, SOUTHWEST TEX STATE UNIV, 85- *Personal Data:* b Ramidi, India, July 21, 41; US citizen; m. *Educ:* Ariz State Univ, BA, 69; Pa State Univ, MA, 70, PhD(math), 73. *Prof Exp:* Asst, 70-73, Pa State Univ, 70-73, from asst prof to assoc prof math, 73-84. *Mem:* Am Math Soc. *Res:* Decomposition spaces, shape theory and manifolds. *Mailing Add:* SW Tex State Univ Dept Math San Marcos TX 78666-4615. *E-Mail:* ss04@academia.swt.edu

SINGH, SUMAN PRIYADARSHI NARAIN, FOSSIL ENERGY PROCESSES. *Current Pos:* from develop staff mem I to develop staff mem II coal processing, Oak Ridge Nat Lab, 76-81, task leader environ control technol, 81-82, prog mgr environ control tech, 82-86, PROG MGR, WASTE MGMT TECHNOL CTR, OAK RIDGE NAT LAB, 86- *Personal Data:* b Ludhiana, India, June 23, 41; US citizen; m 75; c 1. *Educ:* Indian Inst Technol, Bombay, BTech, 64; Okla State Univ, MS, 67, PhD (chem eng), 73. *Prof Exp:* Process design engr natural gas liquids processing, Phillips Petrol Co, 66-69; engr petrol res, Exxon Res & Develop Labs, 74-75. *Concurrent Pos:* NSF fel, Okla State Univ, 76; mem, Control Technol Task Group, Nat Acid Precipitation Assessment Prog. *Mem:* Am Inst Chem Engrs; Sigma Xi. *Res:* Development and assessment of environmental control processes, fossil energy liquefaction, gasification and beneficiation processes and petroleum technology. *Mailing Add:* 600 Fernwood Rd Knoxville TN 37923-2210

SINGH, SURENDRA PAL, QUANTUM & NONLINEAR OPTICS, LASERS. *Current Pos:* From asst prof to assoc prof, 82-92, PROF PHYSICS, UNIV ARK, 92- *Personal Data:* b Mawana, India, June 24, 53; m 82, Reeta Vyas; c Savith C. *Educ:* Banaras Hindu Univ, Varanasi, BS, 73, MS, 75; Univ Rochester, PhD(physics), 82. *Concurrent Pos:* Coun Sci & Indust Res jr res fel, Banaros Hindu Univ, Varanasi, 75-76; Rhush Rhees fel, Univ Rochester, 76-79; vis fel, Joint Inst Lab Astrophys, Univ Colo, Boulder, 89-90. *Mem:* Am Phys Soc; Optical Soc Am; India Phys Asn. *Res:* Coherence and fluctuations in light-matter interactions; more than 50 research articles in professional journals and books. *Mailing Add:* Dept Physics Univ Ark Fayetteville Fayetteville AR 72701. *E-Mail:* ssingh@comp.uark.edu

SINGH, SURINDER SHAH, clay mineralogy, soil chemistry, for more information see previous edition

SINGH, SURJIT, PHYSICAL CHEMISTRY, ENVIRONMENTAL SAFETY. *Current Pos:* assoc prof, 67-80, PROF CHEM, STATE UNIV NY BUFFALO, 80- *Personal Data:* b Roorkee, India, Oct 9, 31; m 64; c 7. *Educ:* Khalsa Col, Amritsar, India, BSc, 52; Panjab Univ, India, MSc, 55; St Louis Univ, PhD(chem), 63. *Prof Exp:* Instr chem, Hindu Col, Amritsar, 52-53; asst prof, Khalsa Col, India, 55-56 & Govt Col, Gurdaspur, 56-59; asst, St Louis Univ, 59-63; from asst prof to assoc prof, Waynesburg Col, 63-67. *Concurrent Pos:* Res assoc, Centre Neurochimie, Strasbourg, 78; pres & consult, Eagle Res Corp, Scipar, Inc. *Mem:* Am Chem Soc; Am Inst Chem Eng. *Res:* Hazardous waste management and resource recovery; nucleation phenomena; atmospheric chemistry; charge transfer spectra; fire safety of construction materials (thermodynamics and material properties); photochromism. *Mailing Add:* Chem Buffalo State Col 1300 Elmwood Ave Buffalo NY 14222-1004

SINGH, SURJIT, STATISTICAL MECHANICS, CHEMICAL REACTION THEORY. *Current Pos:* SCIENTIST, SUBPICOSECOND & QUANTUM RADIATION LAB, 87- *Personal Data:* b Lahore, Pakistan, Dec 5, 47; m 77, Harmesh Singh; c Jaideep & Rajdeep. *Educ:* Panjab Univ, India, BSc, 66, MSc, 68; Univ Pittsburgh, PhD(physics), 75. *Prof Exp:* Res fel physics, Tata Inst Fundamental Res, India, 75-76; lectr, Northeastern Hill Univ, India, 76-83; res asst prof, Univ Waterloo, Can, 83-87. *Concurrent Pos:* Res fel, Tata Inst Fundamental Res, India, 82-83; vis prof physics, Tex Technol Univ, 97. *Mem:* Am Phys Soc. *Res:* Finite-size systems, chemical reaction theory and anomalous properties of water; author of two books. *Mailing Add:* SPQR Lab Tex Tech Univ Lubbock TX 79409. *Fax:* 806-742-3590; *E-Mail:* dussh@ttacs.ttu.edu

SINGH, TEJA, FOREST HYDROLOGY, BIOMETRICS-BIOSTATISTICS. *Current Pos:* RES SCIENTIST & BIOMETRICIAN, NORTHERN FORESTRY CTR, CAN FORESTRY SERV, AGR CAN, 79-; PRES, CAN RESOURCES DEVELOP & MGT LTD, 80- *Personal Data:* b June 18, 28; Can citizen; c 2. *Educ:* E Punjab Univ, India, BA, 49; Utah State Univ, Logan, MSc, 63. *Hon Degrees:* Doctorate, World Univ, 86. *Prof Exp:* Forestry training, Dehra Dun, India, 49-51; oper forestry, Himachal Pradesh & Punjab, India, 51-59; res asst, Utah State Univ, 60-62, Eastern Rockies Forest Conserv Bd, 63; tutor, Utah State Univ, 64; res officer, Can Dept Forestry, Calgary, 65-66; res scientist, Can Dept Environ & Fisheries, 67-77; res expert, UN Develop Porg, 77-79. *Concurrent Pos:* Chief tech adv multidisciplinary hydrol res, Food & Agr Orgn Watershed Mgt & Coord Proj, Iran, 77-79; consult environ impact, Food & Agr Orgn & UNESCO, Rome, 80; Can ed, Nat Woodlands, 87-90; chmn, Alta Climat Asn, 89-90. *Mem:* Sigma Xi; Can Wildlife Fedn; Am Geophys Union; Soc Range Mgt; Can Inst Forestry; Soc Am Foresters; Ecol Soc Am; Soil Conserv Soc Am; Soc Int Develop; NZ Hydrol Soc. *Res:* Forestry ecosystem modeling; climatology; environmental quality, ecology, global warming, biometrics, computer simulation; energy from biomass; hydrologic research prairie provinces of Alberta, Saskatchewan & Manitoba; risk analysis; author of over 120 publications. *Mailing Add:* N Forest Res Ctr Can Forrestry Sevr Edmonton AB T6H 3S5 Can

SINGH, TOOLSEE J, ALZHEIMERS DISEASE, BIOLOGY OF AGING. *Current Pos:* RES SCIENTIST, INST BASIC RES, 91- *Personal Data:* b Berbice, Guyana, Jan 7, 48; Can citizen. *Educ:* Univ Man, BSc, 74; PhD(biochem), 79. *Prof Exp:* Teaching & res asst, Univ Man, 74-79; vis fel, Nat Cancer Inst & Nat Inst Child Health & Human Develop, NIH, 79-82, vis assoc, 82-85; res assoc, Dept Med Biochem, Univ Calgary, 85-86; asst prof, Dept Biol, Univ Waterloo, 86-91. *Concurrent Pos:* vis fel, NIH, 79-82; prin investr, Natural Sci & Eng Res Coun Can, 86-91; univ res fel, Natural Sci & Eng Res Can, 86-91. *Mem:* Am Soc Biochem & Molecular Biol; NY Acad Sci; AAAS; Can Biochem Soc; Soc Neurosci. *Res:* Etiology and pathogenesis of Alzheimer's disease; role of hyperphosphorylation of paired helical filaments in the survival of neurons. *Mailing Add:* Inst Basic Res 1050 Forest Hill Rd Staten Island NY 10314-6330. *Fax:* 718-494-1080

SINGH, TRILOCHAN (HARDEEP), MECHANICAL ENGINEERING. *Current Pos:* asst prof, 70-76, NSF res initiation grant, 72-74, ASSOC PROF MECH ENG SCI, WAYNE STATE UNIV, 76- *Personal Data:* b Vehari, Pakistan, Dec 31, 37; m 64; c 2. *Educ:* Punjab Eng Col, BSc, 61; Univ Calif, Berkeley, MS, 66, PhD(mech eng), 70. *Prof Exp:* Asst engr, Oil & Natural Gas Comn, Dehradum, India, 60-64; lectr mech eng, Thapar Col Eng, Patiala, 64-65; res asst, Univ Calif, Berkeley, 65-70. *Mem:* Soc Automotive Engrs; Combustion Inst; Air Pollution Control Asn. *Res:* Basic combustion studies; pollutant species formation; eliminations and control in different types of combustion systems. *Mailing Add:* Dept Mech Eng Wayne State Univ 2100 W Engineering Detroit MI 48202-4095

SINGH, VIJAY P, MATHEMATICAL MODELING, SYSTEM ANALYSIS. *Current Pos:* PROF CIVIL ENG & COORDR, WATER RESOURCES PROG, LA STATE UNIV, 81- *Personal Data:* b Agra, UP, India, July 15, 46; m 76; c 2. *Educ:* UP Agr Univ, BS, 67; Univ Guelph, MS, 70; Colo State Univ, PhD(civil eng), 74. *Prof Exp:* Engr irrig, Rockefeller Found, 67-68; res asst hydrol, Univ Guelph, 68-70; res asst, Colo State Univ, 70-74, res assoc, 74; asst hydrol, NMex Inst Mining & Technol, 74-77; assoc res prof civil eng, George Washington Univ, 77-78; assoc prof civil eng, Miss State Univ, 78-81. *Concurrent Pos:* Vis scientist, Coun Sci & Indust Res, Govt India, 80-81; vis acad, Univ Wollongong, Australia, 82; sr res engr, US Army Engr Waterways Exp Sta, 82-85; ed, Indian Asn Hydrologists, India, 81-, Hydroelec Energy, China, 86-, Stochastic Hydrol & Hydraul, Agr Water Mgt, Irrig Sci, Natural Hazards & Water Mgt; dir, La Water Resources Res Inst, 83-85; consult, US Govt Agencies, Int Orgn, Pvt Co & Univs, 86-; sr res engr, US Army Engr Waterways Exp Sta, 87-88; vis prof, Lab Hydrol, Vrije Univ Brussel, Belg, 88, Inst Hydraul & Hydraul Struct, Univ Basilicata, Italy, 90 & 94 Inst Hydraul & Energy, Inst Soil & Water Mgt, Swiss Fed Inst Technol, 90, 92, 94 & 95; res grants, NSF, US Geol Surv, US Dept Army, US Dept Agr, UN Educ, Sci, & Cultural Orgn & US Agency Int Develop. *Mem:* Am Geophys Union; fel Am Soc Civil Engrs; Int Asn Hydraul Res; fel Inst Engrs India; fel Indian Asn Hydrologists; fel Am Water Res Asn; Sigma Xi; Int Asn Hydrol Sci. *Res:* Continuum mechanics; control theoretic and stochastic modeling of hydrologic processes, with particular regard to stream flow, sediment yield, irrigation, flood, frequency analysis, entropy theory, free boundary problems, and system applications; author of more than 408 research papers and 26 books. *Mailing Add:* Dept Civil & Environ Eng La State Univ Baton Rouge LA 70803-6405. *Fax:* 504-388-5990, 388-8652; *E-Mail:* cesing@unix1.sncc.lsu.edu

SINGH, VIJAY PAL, ELECTROLUMINSCENT DISPLAY, SOLAR CELLS. *Current Pos:* assoc prof, 83-90, PROF, ELEC ENG DEPT, UNIV TEX, EL PASO, 90-, SCHELLENGER CHAIR ELEC RES, 93-, PROF MAT SCI & ENG, PROF ENVIRON SCI & ENG. *Personal Data:* b New Delhi, India, July 25, 47; US citizen; m 72, Carolyn Schmitz; c Vincent & Gordon. *Educ:* Indian Inst Technol, Delhi, BTech, 68; Univ Minn, MS, 70, PhD(elec eng), 74. *Prof Exp:* Res asst prof, Inst Energy Conversion, Univ Del, 74-76; res engr, Photon Power Inc, El Paso, Tex, 76-80, sect head device res, 80-81, mgr mat & device res, 81-83. *Concurrent Pos:* Secy, El Paso sect Inst Elec & Electronics Engrs, 84-87; consult, Battelle, 86-91; Prin investr, NSF Grant, 89-92 & 93- *Mem:* Inst Elec & Electronics Engrs; Soc Info Display; Electrochem Soc; Am Soc Eng Educr. *Res:* Design, analysis and electro-optical characterization of electroluminescent displays; development of thin-film CdTe solar cells for terrestrial and space applications; high speed electron devices for supercomputers. *Mailing Add:* Elec Eng Dept Univ Tex El Paso TX 79968. *E-Mail:* vsingh@mail.utep.edu

SINGH, VIJENDRA KUMAR, NEUROIMMUNOLOGY. *Current Pos:* DIR, PSYCHOIMMUNOL LAB & ASSOC RES SCIENTIST, UNIV MICH, ANN ARBOR, 93- *Personal Data:* b Moradabad, India, Aug 15, 47; m 74, Kimlan. *Educ:* Lucknow Univ, India, BSc, 64, MSc, 66; Univ BC, PhD(biochem), 72. *Prof Exp:* Res asst biochem, Coun Sci & Indust Res, India, 66-68; fel, Univ BC, 72-74, res assoc neurosci, 74-78, asst prof, Dept Path, 79-85; mem staff, Children's Hosp, 78-81, dir res, Div Immunol, 81-85; asst prof basic & clin immunol, Med Univ SC, Charleston, 85-88; assoc res prof, Dept Biol, Utah State Univ, Logan, 88-93. *Mem:* AAAS; Int Soc Immunopharmacol; Am Asn Immunologists; Int Soc Neuroimmunol. *Res:* Structural-functional relationships between immune system and nervous system; immunologic mechanisms in neuropsychiatric disorders, especially Alzheimer's dementia and autism; neuropeptide modulation of immune response. *Mailing Add:* Neuroimmunol Lab Brain Immunol Res Serv Univ Mich Med Ctr 1643 Westherstone Dr Ann Arbor MI 48109-0656. *Fax:* 313-764-6837; *E-Mail:* vijendra.singh@med.umich.edu

SINGH, VISHWA NATH, NUTRITION, BIOCHEMISTRY. *Current Pos:* CLIN RES SCIENTIST, HOFFMANN LA ROCHE, INC, 80- *Personal Data:* b July 6, 36; m; c 2. *Educ:* Univ Delhi, India, PhD(biochem), 62. *Res:* Nutrition requirements of special population groups; diabetes; roles of vitamins in health and disease; carbohydrate and lipid metabolism. *Mailing Add:* Human Nutrit Res Hoffman La Roche Inc 45 Eisenhower Dr Paramus NJ 07652-1429. *Fax:* 973-235-6847

SINGHA, SUMAN, PLANT TISSUE CULTURE, WOODY PLANT PHYSIOLOGY. *Current Pos:* PROF & HEAD, DEPT PLANT SCI, UNIV CONN, 90- *Personal Data:* b Simla, India, Jan 12, 48; US citizen. *Educ:* Punjab Agr Univ, BS, 68, MS, 70; Cornell Univ, PhD(pomol), 77. *Prof Exp:* From asst prof to prof, WVa Univ, 77-90. *Mem:* Am Soc Hort Sci; Tissue Cult Asn; Am Pomol Soc; Nat Asn Cols & Teachers Agr; Sigma Xi. *Res:* Tissue culture with emphasis on micropropagation and influence of culture medium; production and physiology of fruit trees with emphasis on instrumental analysis of color. *Mailing Add:* Univ Conn Acad Progs CANR U-90 1376 Storrs Rd Storrs CT 06269-4090. *Fax:* 860-486-0682; *E-Mail:* ssingha@canr1.cag.uconn.edu

SINGHAL, AVINASH CHANDRA, SEISMIC ENGINEERING, STRUCTURAL ENGINEERING. *Current Pos:* assoc prof, 77-84, dir, Cent Bldg Res Inst, 92-93, PROF CIVIL ENG & DIR, EARTHQUAKE RES LAB, ARIZ STATE UNIV, 84- *Personal Data:* b Aligarh, India, Nov 4, 41; m 67, Uma Sharma; c Neil R, Anita & Ritu. *Educ:* St Andrews Univ, BSc, 59 & 60; Mass Inst Technol, SM, 61, CE, 62, ScD(civil eng), 64. *Honors & Awards:* First Prize, Int Asn Shell Struct, 61; Henry Adams Medal, Inst Struct Eng, London, 71. *Prof Exp:* Prof civil eng, Laval Univ, Que, 65-69; asst prog mgr, TRW, 69-71; mgr systs eng, Gen Elec, 71-72 & Engrs India Ltd, 72-74; proj engr consult eng, Weidlinger Assoc, 74-77. *Concurrent Pos:* Chmn, Eng Mech Sub Task Comn, Am Soc Civil Eng, 68-70; fel, Am Soc Civil Eng Comts, 69-73 & Tech Coun Lifeline Earthquake Eng, 78-; chmn subcomt, Am Soc Mech Eng, 82-86, 88 & 89; vis prof, Melbourne Univ, Australia, 84; res fel, Kobe Univ, Japan, 90. *Mem:* Am Soc Civil Engrs; Earthquake Engr Res Inst. *Res:* Earthquake engineering; soil engineering; blast and vibrations; pipelines; author of 236 publications including six books. *Mailing Add:* 2258 W Monterey Ave Mesa AZ 85202-7330. *Fax:* 602-897-0167; *E-Mail:* avi.singhal@asu.edu

SINGHAL, JAYA ASTHANA, MIXED INTEGER PROGRAMMING, MATHEMATICAL PROGRAMMING. *Current Pos:* from asst prof to assoc prof, 83-93, PROF OPER RES, UNIV BALTIMORE, 93- *Personal Data:* m 75, Kalyan. *Educ:* Marathwada Univ, BSc, 72, MSc, 74; Univ Ariz, PhD(bus admin), 82. *Prof Exp:* Res fel nuclear physics, Marathwada Univ. *Mem:* Math Prog Soc; Oper Res Soc Am; Decision Scis Inst. *Res:* Algorithms and software for large scale linear and integer programming models; development and implementation of operations research models for applications in business and engineering. *Mailing Add:* 11317 Ridermark Row Columbia MD 21044

SINGHAL, KISHORE, APPLICATION OF STATISTICAL METHODS TO ENGINEERING PROBLEMS. *Current Pos:* TECH MGR, BELL LABS, LUCENT TECHNOL, 85- *Personal Data:* b Allahabad, India, Dec 28, 44; US citizen; m 73, Kumud Agrawal; c Monica & Nina. *Educ:* India Inst Technol, BTech, 66; Columbia Univ, MS, 67, PhD(elec eng), 70. *Prof Exp:* Postdoctoral fel elec eng, Univ Waterloo, 70-71, lectr, 72, from asst prof to assoc prof, 73-83, assoc chmn system design, 77-83, prof systs design, 83-85. *Concurrent Pos:* Consult, Bell Northern Res, Ottawa, 71-84; mem tech staff, Bell Labs, Murray Hill, 84. *Mem:* Fel Inst Elec & Electronics Engrs; Soc Indust & Appl Math; Am Statist Asn. *Res:* Methods for formulation and solution of equations describing electronic and other physical systems including optimization and statistical design; publications in circuit analysis and design for graduate students. *Mailing Add:* 1247 Cedar Crest Blvd Allentown PA 18103. *E-Mail:* kishore.singhal@lucent.com

SINGHAL, RADHEY LAL, PHARMACOLOGY. *Current Pos:* PROF LAB EXP ONCOL, IND UNIV SCH MED, INDIANAPOLIS, 92- *Personal Data:* b Gulaothi, India, July 12, 40; m 61; c 3. *Educ:* Univ Lucknow, BSc, 57, MSc, 59, PhD(pharmacol), 61. *Prof Exp:* Res assoc pharmacol, Ind Univ, 62-64, instr, 64-65; from asst prof to prof, Univ Ottawa, 66-92, chmn, 74-92. *Concurrent Pos:* Med Res Coun Can scholar, Univ Ottawa, 67-72. *Mem:* Endocrine Soc; Int Soc Neurochem; Soc Toxicol; Am Soc Pharmacol & Exp Therapeut; Am Soc Biol Chem; Am Chemother & Biochem. *Res:* Endocrine and biochemical pharmacology; neuroendocrinological approaches to the study of brain function; environmental toxicology; cancer chemotherapy and biochemistry; author of 386 publications and editor of six books. *Mailing Add:* New Drug Discovery Res Ranbaxy Res Lab A-2 Phase 1 Okhla Industrial Area New Delhi 110020 India

SINGHAL, RAM P, BIOCHEMISTRY, ANALYTICAL CHEMISTRY. *Current Pos:* from asst prof to assoc prof, 74-86, PROF BIOCHEM, WICHITA STATE UNIV, 86- *Personal Data:* b New Delhi, India, Aug 12, 39; US citizen; m 68; c Vivek & Nikhyl. *Educ:* Univ Lucknow, BS, 58, MS, 60; Univ Sci & Technol, France, Dipl, 64, PhD(biochem), 67. *Honors & Awards:* Cancer Res Award, Am Cancer Soc, 75, Acad Res Enhancement Award, 85. *Prof Exp:* Instr biochem, All-India Inst Med Sci, 60-62; researcher, Cancer Res Inst, Univ Lille, 62-67; scientist, Coun Sci & Indust Res, India, 67-68; USPHS fel, Wayne State Univ, 68-69; Univ Tenn-Oak Ridge Nat Lab fel, Oak Ridge Nat Lab, 70-71, res scientist, 72-74; vis scientist, Scripps Res Found, 74. *Concurrent Pos:* Nat Ctr Sci Res researcher, Univ Sci & Technol, Univ Lille, 64-67; NSF exchange 64-67; NIH expert scientist, 82-83, WHO scientist, 86-87. *Mem:* AAAS; Am Chem Soc; Am Soc Biol Chemists & Molecular Biologists. *Res:* Novel methods in molecular biology; high-performance liquid chromatography, methods development, capillary electrophoresis; reaction to anticancer agent dirhodium tetraacetate with nucleic acids; significance of minor, modified components of RNAs and DNAs; chemical probe of DNA conformation; biotechnology; chemical probe of the nucleic acid structure-function relation; noval antiviral drug; reaction mechanism of boronate complexing; high-performance liquid chromatography; affinity chromatography. *Mailing Add:* Dept Chem Wichita State Univ 1845 N Fairmount St Wichita KS 67260-0051. *Fax:* 316-689-3431; *E-Mail:* singhal@cs.tswu.edu

SINGHAL, SHARWAN KUMAR, IMMUNOLOGY. *Current Pos:* assoc prof, 70-79, PROF IMMUNOL, UNIV WESTERN ONT, 80- *Personal Data:* b Oct 8, 39; Can citizen; m 64; c 2. *Educ:* McGill Univ, PhD(immunol), 68. *Prof Exp:* Med Res Coun Can fel tumor biol, Karolinska Inst, Sweden, 68-70. *Mem:* Am Asn Immunol; Can Soc Immunol; Scand Soc Immunol. *Res:* Regulation of the immune response at the cellular level. *Mailing Add:* Dept Microbiol & Immunol Dental Sci Bldg Univ Western Ont London ON N6A 5C1 Can

SINGHAL, SUBHASH CHANDRA, ADVANCED MATERIALS, ADVANCED POWER GENERATION SYSTEMS. *Current Pos:* sr & fel eng, 71-81, mgr high temperature mat, 81-84, MGR FUEL CELL TECH, WESTINGHOUSE ELEC CORP, 84- *Personal Data:* b Meerut City, India, June 26, 45; US citizen; m 69, Neelima; c Ronak & Reena. *Educ:* Agra Univ, BS, 63; Indian Inst Sci, BEng, 65; Univ Pa, PhD(mat sci & eng), 69; Univ Pittsburgh, MBA, 77. *Honors & Awards:* Outstanding Achievement Award, Electrochem Soc, 84. *Prof Exp:* Scientist & mgr, Chromalloy Am Corp, 69-71. *Concurrent Pos:* Prin lectr, Advan Study Inst Nitrogen Ceramics, NATO, 76; dir, Advan Study Inst Surface Eng, NATO, 83. *Mem:* Fel Electrochem Soc; fel Am Soc Metals Int; fel Am Ceramic Soc; Metall Soc. *Res:* Advanced metallic, ceramic and composite materials; advanced energy conversion systems; solid oxide fuel cells; materials chemistry; oxidation, corrosion and protective coatings; research management. *Mailing Add:* 1310 Beulah Rd Pittsburgh PA 15235-5098. *Fax:* 412-256-1233; *E-Mail:* wx-singhasc@westinghouse.com

SINGHVI, SAMPAT MANAKCHAND, BIOPHARMACEUTICS, PHARMACOKINETICS. *Current Pos:* res investr, E R Squibb & Sons Inc, 74-78, sr res investr, 78-79, res group leader drug metab, 79-88, assoc dir, 88-94, DIR, WORLDWIDE REGULATORY AFFAIRS, BRISTOL-MYERS SQUIBB, 95- *Personal Data:* b Jodhpur, India, Oct 14, 47; m 71, Usha Mutha; c Nikhil & Nilima. *Educ:* BITS Pilani, Rajasthan, India, BPharm, 67; Philadelphia Col Pharm & Sci, MS, 70; State Univ NY, Buffalo, PhD(pharmaceut), 74; Rider Col, MBA, 79. *Prof Exp:* Res sci, Wyeth Labs, Am Home Prod, 69 & 70; teaching asst chem, Philadelphia Col Pharm & Sci, 69-70; res asst pharmaceut, State Univ NY, Buffalo, 70-73. *Mem:* Am Soc Pharmacol & Exp Therapeut; Am Pharm Asn; Am Asn Pharmaceut Scientists; Int Soc Study Xenobiotics; Regulatory Affairs Prof Soc; Drug Info Asn. *Res:* Drug metabolism in animals; bioavailability and pharmacokinetics of various new drugs in animals and man. *Mailing Add:* Bristol-Myers Squibb PO Box 4000 Princeton NJ 08543-4000. *Fax:* 609-252-6396

SINGISER, ROBERT EUGENE, RESEARCH ADMINISTRATION, PHARMACEUTICS. *Current Pos:* res pharmacist, 58-64, dept mgr, Pharmaceut Prod Res, 64-66, dir pharmaceut res & develop, 66-68, sci dir, Pharmaceut Prod Div, 68-70, vpres sci affairs, Pharmaceut Prod Div, 70-86, DIR NEW TECHNOL, PHARMACEUT PROD DIV, ABBOTT LABS, 86- *Personal Data:* b Mechanicsburg, Pa, Aug 7, 30; m 54; c 2. *Educ:* Temple Univ, BS, 52; Univ Fla, MS, 56; Univ Conn, PhD(pharm), 59. *Prof Exp:* Pharmaceut chemist, Merck & Co, Inc, 52-55. *Mem:* Fel Am Found Pharmaceut Educ; Am Pharmaceut Asn; Am Soc Hosp Pharmacists; Int Pharmaceut Fedn; Am Asn Pharmaceut Scientists. *Res:* Ultrasonic emulsification; thermo-stable ointment bases; air-suspension tablet coating techniques; non-sterile, human pharmaceutical dosage forms; biopharmaceutics. *Mailing Add:* 326 S Hickory Haven Dr Gurnee IL 60031

SINGLER, ROBERT EDWARD, ORGANIC CHEMISTRY, POLYMER CHEMISTRY. *Current Pos:* GROUP LEADER, POLYMER CHEM GROUP, POLYMER RES BR, US ARMY RES LAB, 85-, RES CHEMIST, POLYMER RES, 70- *Personal Data:* b Chicago, Ill, Mar 21, 41; m 70; c 3. *Educ:* Loyola Univ, BS, 63; Southern Ill Univ, MA, 65; Univ Calif, Los Angeles, PhD(chem), 70. *Concurrent Pos:* Army res fel, Macromolecular Inst, Freiburg, Ger, 79-80. *Mem:* Am Chem Soc; Mat Res Soc. *Res:* Synthesis, characterization and development of cyclic phosphazenes and polyphosphazenes; fire resistant materials; rubber technology; thermal analysis of elastomeric materials. *Mailing Add:* 53 Selwyn Rd Belmont MA 02178-3557. *Fax:* 617-923-5154, 923-5046; *E-Mail:* rsingle@watertown_emhl.army.mil

SINGLETARY, JOHN BOON, NUCLEAR PHYSICS. *Current Pos:* LAB SCIENTIST, HUGHES AIRCRAFT CO, 71- *Personal Data:* b Houston, Tex, May 6, 28; m 55. *Educ:* Agr & Mech Col Tex, BS, 49, MS, 51; Northwestern Univ, PhD, 58. *Prof Exp:* Mem staff, Los Alamos Sci Lab, 57-59; res scientist, Lockheed Aircraft Co, 59-70; dept mgr, Braddock, Dunn & McDonald, 70-71. *Mem:* Am Phys Soc; Sigma Xi. *Res:* Neutron and low energy nuclear physics; environmental effects on spacecraft materials; radiation effects on electronic components; electromagnetic pulse environment and effects on components and systems. *Mailing Add:* 22316 Barbacoa Dr Santa Clarita CA 91350

SINGLETARY, LILLIAN DARLINGTON, NUCLEAR PHYSICS. *Current Pos:* SECT HEAD ADV TECHNOL, VULNERABILITY & HARDNESS LAB, TRW SYSTS GROUP, 71- *Personal Data:* b Chicago, Ill. *Educ:* Northwestern Univ, BS, PhD(exp neutron & charged particle physics), 62. *Prof Exp:* Res scientist, Lockheed Res Lab, 62-69; EMP sect head, Lockheed Missiles & Space Co, 69-70; dept mgr, EMP & Appl Nuclear Technol Dept, Braddock, Dunn & McDonald, Inc, NMex, 70-71. *Concurrent Pos:* Consult, Los Alamos Sci Lab, 69-71. *Mem:* Inst Elec & Electronic Engrs; Am Phys Soc; Sigma Xi. *Res:* Analytical and test programs investigating electromagnetic pulse generated by nuclear weapon and system generated electromagnetic pulse generated by nuclear weapon photons incident on systems. *Mailing Add:* 32759 Seagate Dr No Unit 106 Rancho Palos Verdes CA 90274-5818

SINGLETARY, ROBERT LOMBARD, MARINE ECOLOGY, INVERTEBRATE ZOOLOGY. *Current Pos:* PROF BIOL, UNIV BRIDGEPORT, 70. *Personal Data:* b Atlanta, Ga, Mar 21, 41; m 64, Virginia Lloyd; c James & David. *Educ:* Univ NC, AB, 63; Univ RI, MS, 67; Univ Miami, PhD(marine biol), 70. *Mem:* Estuarine Res Fedn; Sigma Xi. *Res:* Biology of Echinoderms; benthic and intertidal ecology. *Mailing Add:* Dept Biol Univ Bridgeport Bridgeport CT 06601

SINGLETARY, THOMAS ALEXANDER, ELECTRONICS, TECHNOLOGY. *Current Pos:* Assoc prof, 60-77, INSTR ELECTRONICS TECHNOL, GA SOUTHERN COL, 77-, EMER PROF. *Personal Data:* b Cairo, Ga, Sept 17, 37; m 65; c 1. *Educ:* Ga Southern Col, BS, 59; Stout Univ, MS, 60; Univ Mo-Columbia, EdD(indust educ), 68. *Concurrent Pos:* Systs consult, Statesboro Telephone Inc, 60-; TV consult, Westinghouse Elec Corp, 62-65; tech instr, Rockwell Mfg Co, 64-; reviewing consult, Delmar Publs, 72- *Mem:* Am Indust Arts Asn. *Res:* Electrofinishing technology as applied to metals; photographic media as applied to education. *Mailing Add:* Pitt Moore Rd Statesboro GA 30458

SINGLETON, ALAN HERBERT, CHEMICAL ENGINEERING. *Current Pos:* PRES, ENERGY INT CORP, 85- *Personal Data:* b Punxsutawney, Pa, Nov 28, 36; m 58, Nancy Walton; c Alan, David, Kimberly & Jennifer. *Educ:* Univ Md, College Park, BS, 58; Lehigh Univ, MS, 62, PhD(chem eng), 68. *Prof Exp:* Res engr, US Naval Propellant Plant, 58-59; mgr explor eng, Air Prod & Chem, Inc, 59-68; section mgr, Res Dept, Bethlehem Steel Corp, 68-77; prog mgr, UCG Opers, 77-81, dept mgr synthetic fuels develop, Gulf Oil Corp Res, 81-85. *Concurrent Pos:* mem, Tex Energy & Natural Resources Adv Coun, 81-83; mem, vis comt, WVa Univ, 82-; mem, Adv Bd Pittsburgh Coal Conference, 81- *Mem:* Am Inst Chem Eng; Am Chem Soc; Sigma Xi. *Res:* Synthetic fuels process development; underground coal gasification process development and operations; Fischer Tropsch catalyst and process development; catalysis; cryogenic refrigeration, liquefaction, and containment system development; synthesis gas conversion processes. *Mailing Add:* 1265 Woodland Rd Baden PA 15005-2533

SINGLETON, BERT, ANALYTICAL CHEMISTRY, ORGANIC CHEMISTRY. *Current Pos:* RETIRED. *Personal Data:* b New York, NY, July 13, 28; m 56, Diane Danziger; c Judith & Ruth. *Educ:* Cornell Univ, BChE, 50. *Prof Exp:* Res asst org fluorine chem, Cornell Univ, 51-53; process develop chemist, Merck Sharp & Dohme Res Labs, 55- 57, foreign projs chemist, 57-59, sr develop chemist, 59-65, sect head, Process Controls Res, 65-69, mgr process controls, 69-80, assoc dir anal res, 80-90. *Mem:* AAAS; Am Chem Soc; Sigma Xi. *Res:* Analytical methods; gas and liquid chromatography; ultraviolet and infrared spectrophotometry; microanalysis; automatic chemical and process control instrumentation; pharmaceuticals; steroids and vitamins; synthetic organic chemistry. *Mailing Add:* 443 Beechwood Pl Westfield NJ 07090-3201

SINGLETON, CHLOE JOI, MACROMOLECULAR SCIENCE. *Current Pos:* MKT RES MGR, WESTVACO CORP, 90- *Personal Data:* b Cleveland, Ohio, Dec 4, 43; m 84. *Educ:* Case Inst Technol, BS, 67; Case Western Res Univ, MSE, 74, PhD(macromolecular sci), 75; Baldwin-Wallace Col, MBA, 81. *Prof Exp:* Physicist x-ray diffraction, B F Goodrich Tech Ctr, 67-69, res physicist, 69-70, physicist res & develop electron micros, 74-78, sr physicist thermal anal polymers, Res & Develop Ctr, 78-79, sr res & develop physicist/appns engr thermoplastic polyurethanes, 78-84; dir technol & mkt planning, Sherwin-Williams Co, 84-85, dir prof develop, 85-88; mkt res & commun mgr, Desoto Inc, 88-89, bus develop mgr, anal serv, 89-90. *Mem:* Am Chem Soc; Am Phys Soc; Soc Plastics Engrs; Soc Competitor Intel Prof. *Res:* Morphological characterization of plastic and rubber materials, using the tools of thermal analysis; electron microscopy and x-ray diffraction; applications engineering of thermoplastic polyurethanes; paints and coatings technology; market and business research. *Mailing Add:* 522 Brown Sugar Retreat Mt Pleasant SC 29464-2754

SINGLETON, DAVID MICHAEL, FREE RADICAL CHEMISTRY, CATALYSIS. *Current Pos:* chemist, Petrol Chem Dept, Shell Develop Co, Calif, 67-72, Hydroprocessing Dept, 72-74, sr res chemist, Chem Res & Appl Dept, 77-96, SR RES CHEMIST, SHELL DEVELOP CO, 74-, CHEM DEVELOP DEPT, 96- *Personal Data:* b Poole, Eng, Nov 3, 39; m 62, Elizabeth Sloan; c 2. *Educ:* Univ London, BSc, 60; McMaster Univ, PhD(org chem), 65. *Prof Exp:* Res assoc reductive reactions chromous ion, Case Western Reserve Univ, 65-67. *Concurrent Pos:* Shell exchange scientist, Shell Res & Develop Co, Amsterdam, 75-76; adj prof, Univ Houston, 83-91. *Mem:* Am Chem Soc; Chem Inst Can; fel Royal Soc Chem; Southwest Catalysis Soc. *Res:* Free radical reactions; organic redox reactions by metal complexes; organometallic chemistry; catalysis of organic reactions by metal complexes; hydrocarbon chemistry; heterogeneous catalysis. *Mailing Add:* Westhollow Tech Ctr Box 1380 Shell Chem Co Houston TX 77251-1380. *Fax:* 281-544-8687; *E-Mail:* davesingleton@shellus.com

SINGLETON, DONALD LEE, PHYSICAL CHEMISTRY. *Current Pos:* fel, 72-74, RES OFFICER, NAT RES COUN CAN, 74- *Personal Data:* b Lyons, Kans, Mar 26, 44; m 66; c 2. *Educ:* Univ Calif, Davis, BS, 66; Northwestern Univ, MS, 70, PhD(phys chem), 71. *Prof Exp:* Vis scientist atmospheric chem, Nat Ctr Atmospheric Res, 70-72. *Mem:* Am Chem Soc; Can Inst Chem. *Res:* Kinetics and mechanisms of atomic and free radical reactions; atmospheric chemistry; laser processing. *Mailing Add:* Inst Chem Process Nat Res Coun Ottawa ON K1A 0R6 Can

SINGLETON, EDGAR BRYSON, MOLECULAR PHYSICS. *Current Pos:* RETIRED. *Personal Data:* b Warren, Ohio, June 17, 26; m 53; c 3. *Educ:* Ohio Univ, BS, 49, MS, 51; Ohio State Univ, PhD(physics), 58. *Prof Exp:* Instr & res assoc chem, Ohio State Univ, 58-59; from asst prof to prof, Bowling Green State Univ, 59-95. *Mem:* Optical Soc Am; Am Asn Physics Teachers; Sigma Xi. *Res:* Molecular physics and infrared spectroscopy in absorption and emission of radiation. *Mailing Add:* 4251 Appomattox Dr Sylvania OH 43560-4107

SINGLETON, GEORGE TERRELL, OTOLARYNGOLOGY, PEDIATRIC OTOLARYNGOLOGY. *Current Pos:* assoc prof surg & head, Div Otolaryngol, Univ Fla, 61-68, chief otolaryngol, 68-75, asst dean clin affairs, 70-77, PROF SURG & OTOLARYNGOL, UNIV FLA, 68-, PROF PEDIAT, 78- *Personal Data:* b Wichita Falls, Tex, Dec 16, 27; m 52, Jacqueline Green; c 3. *Educ:* Midwestern Univ, BA & BS, 49; Baylor Univ, MD, 54; Am Bd Otolaryngol, dipl, 59. *Honors & Awards:* Am Acad Ophthal & Otolaryngol Award, 60; Harris P Mosher Mem Award, Am Laryngol, Rhinol & Otolaryngol Soc. *Prof Exp:* Intern, Henry Ford Hosp, 54-55, asst resident, 55-57, sr resident, 57-58; MedServ Corp, US Army, 58-60. *Concurrent Pos:* NIH spec fel otolaryngol, Univ Chicago, 60-61; mem communicative dis res training comt, Nat Inst Neurol Dis & Stroke, 69-73; chief of staff, Shands Teaching Hosp & Clins, 72-76, actg hosp dir, 75-77; mem, Grad Coun Div Sponsored Res, Univ Fla, 78-, Univ Senate, 86-89. *Mem:* Am Acad Ophthal & Otolaryngol; Am Laryngol, Rhinol & Otol Soc; Soc Univ Otolaryngol; Am Otol Soc; Sigma Xi; Asn Res Otolaryngol. *Res:* Adjuvant therapy of juvenile laryngeal papillomatosis; autoimmune factors in sensorineural hearing loss and vestibular dysfunction. *Mailing Add:* Dept Otolaryngol Box 100264 JHMHC Univ Fla Gainesville FL 32610-0264. *Fax:* 904-392-6781

SINGLETON, HENRY E, INDUSTRIAL & MANUFACTURING ENGINEERING. *Current Pos:* chief exec & chmn bd, 60-87, chmn, 87-91, CHMN, EXEC COMT BD DIRS, ALLEGHENY TELEDYNE CORP, 91- *Personal Data:* b Haslet, Tex, Nov 27, 16. *Educ:* Mass Inst Technol, SB & SM, 40, ScD, 50. *Prof Exp:* Vpres, Litton Industs, 54-60. *Mem:* Nat Acad Eng. *Mailing Add:* Allegheny Teledyne Corp 2049 Century Park E Los Angeles CA 90067

SINGLETON, JACK HOWARD, PHYSICAL CHEMISTRY. *Current Pos:* CONSULT, 86- *Personal Data:* b Rawtenstall, Eng, Sept 27, 26; m 54; c Margaret & Kathleen. *Educ:* Univ London, BSc, 47, dipl & PhD, 50. *Prof Exp:* Asst phys chem, Aberdeen Univ, 49-52; res assoc, Univ Wash, 52-55; engr, Res Labs, Westinghouse Elec Corp, 55-86. *Mem:* Am Chem Soc; hon mem Am Vacuum Soc (pres,86). *Res:* Physical and chemi-sorption; catalysis on metals; ultrahigh vacuum. *Mailing Add:* 1184 St Vincent Dr Monroeville PA 15146

SINGLETON, JOHN BYRNE, ENGINEERING. *Current Pos:* RETIRED. *Personal Data:* b Troy, NY, May 16, 30; m 52, Marie; c Ben, Paul, David, John Jr, Christopher & Patricia. *Educ:* Col of the Holy Cross, BS, 52; Univ RI, MS, 54. *Honors & Awards:* Centennial Medal, Inst Elec & Electronics Engrs. *Prof Exp:* Mem tech staff, Bell Tel Labs, 54-60, head, Integrated Circuits Dept, 60-70, Data & Digital Dept, 71-76, Digital Systs Dept, 77-84 & D-Channel Banks Dept, 84-; prog mgr, Raynet Corp, 88-93. *Mem:* Sr mem Inst Elec & Electronics Engrs. *Res:* Design and development of digital and fiber optic transmission lines and terminals. *Mailing Add:* Boxford MA 01921

SINGLETON, RICHARD COLLOM, MATHEMATICAL STATISTICS, INFORMATION SCIENCE. *Current Pos:* CONSULT, SINGLETON CONSULT, 96- *Personal Data:* b Schenectady, NY, Feb 21, 28; m 50; c Pamela, Peter, Nancy, Gordon, Lisa & Martin. *Educ:* Mass Inst Technol, BS & MS, 50; Stanford Univ, MBA, 52, MS, 59, PhD(math statist), 60. *Prof Exp:* Economist, Stanford Res Inst, 52-54, res engr, 54-56, systs analyst, 56-59, res math statistician, 59-63, sr res math statistician, Dept Math, 63-72, staff scientist, Dept Math Statist, Info, Serv & Systs Div, 72-96. *Concurrent Pos:* Assoc ed, Info Sci, 68- *Mem:* Inst Math Statist; Opers Res Soc Am; sr mem Inst Elec & Electronics Engrs. *Res:* Design of experiments in the physical and biological sciences; time series analysis; statistical inference; theory of error-correcting codes; economics; litigation support statistical analysis. *Mailing Add:* Singleton Consult 2130 Rocky Ridge Rd Morgan Hill CA 95037. *Fax:* 650-859-3154; *E-Mail:* singleton@sri.com

SINGLETON, RIVERS, JR, MICROBIOL PHYSIOLOGY, SCIENCE & SOCIETY INTERACTION. *Current Pos:* res asst prof microbiol, 74-88, res scientist, Sch Life & Health Sci, 88-89, ASSOC PROF, SCH LIFE & HEALTH SCI & DEPT ENGLISH, UNIV DEL, 89-, DIR, CTR SCI & CULT, 89- *Personal Data:* b New Orleans, La, Sept 2, 39; m 63, Patricia S; c David R, Melissa G & Eric C. *Educ:* Trinity Univ, BS, 61; Mich State Univ, MS, 63; Univ Kans, PhD(biochem), 69. *Prof Exp:* Dir clin chem, Chem Div, First US Army Med Lab, 63-65; fel biochem, Case Western Res Univ, 69-72; Nat Res Coun fel biochem microbiol, Ames Res Ctr, NASA, 72-74. *Concurrent Pos:* Fel, NIH, 66-69; fel, Am Cancer Soc, 70-72; res assoc, Nat Acad Sci, 72-74; cong sci fel, Am Soc Microbiol, 88-89; vis assoc prof, Dept Biochem, Case Western Res Univ, 96-97. *Mem:* Sigma Xi; Am Soc Microbiol; Asn Integrative Studies; AAAS; Int Soc Hist, Philos & Social Studies Biol. *Res:* The evolutionary aspects and chemical mechanisms whereby microorganisms adapt to and grow under extreme environmental conditions; interdisciplinary studies on science and society interaction; history of biochemistry. *Mailing Add:* Dept Biol Univ Del Newark DE 19716. *Fax:* 302-831-2281; *E-Mail:* oneton@udel.edu

SINGLETON, TOMMY CLARK, ORGANIC CHEMISTRY. *Current Pos:* RETIRED. *Personal Data:* b Lufkin, Tex, Oct 5, 28; m 58; c 3. *Educ:* Stephen F Austin State Col, BS, 49; Rice Univ, PhD(chem), 54. *Prof Exp:* Chemist, Naval Stores Sta, USDA, 55-56; sr process chemist, Res Dept, Monsanto Co, 56-69, process specialist, Process Technol Dept, 69-75, sr process specialist, 75-91. *Mem:* Am Chem Soc. *Res:* Carbonylation chemistry; plant process problems; syntheses of vinyl monomers. *Mailing Add:* 22 Skyland Pl The Woodlands TX 77381-4054

SINGLETON, VERNON LEROY, NATURAL PRODUCTS CHEMISTRY, ENOLOGY. *Current Pos:* asst enologist, Univ Calif, Davis, 58-63, assoc enologist, 63-66, assoc chemist, 66-69, lectr, 59-69, prof enol & chemist, 69-91, EMER PROF ENOL, AGR EXP STA, UNIV CALIF, DAVIS, 91- *Personal Data:* b Mill City, Ore, June 28, 23; m 47, Kathryn L Brattain; c Steven L, Stanley L & Sue L. *Educ:* Purdue Univ, BSA, 47, MS, 49, PhD(agr biochem), 51. *Hon Degrees:* DSc, Univ Stellenbosch, 83. *Honors & Awards:* Andre Simon Lit Prize, 65; Biennial Wine Res Award, Soc Med Friends Wine, 77; Merit Award, Am Soc Enol & Viticult, 92; Award of Merit, Am Wine Soc, 93. *Prof Exp:* Grad asst biochem, Purdue Univ, 47-49; res chemist, Lederle Labs, Am Cyanamid Co, 51-54; assoc biochemist, Pineapple Res Inst, Univ Hawaii, 54-58, biochemist, 58. *Concurrent Pos:* Assoc prof, Univ Hawaii, 56-58; consult, Pineapple Res Inst, 59; abstr ed, Am Soc Enol, 59-73; sr res fel, Inst Denology & Viticulture, Univ Stellenbosch, SAfrica, 68-69; vis scientist Long Ashton Res Sta, Univ Bristol, UK, 75-76; vis prof, Univ Stellenbosch, 82, Lincoln Univ, NZ, 89. *Mem:* Am Chem Soc; fel Am Inst Chem; Am Soc Enol & Viticult (treas, 69-73, pres, 75-76); Inst Food Technologists; Phytochem Soc NAm; Sigma Xi; AAAS. *Res:* Chemistry of natural products, especially flavonoids, phenolic acids, tannins, mold products, and wines; food storage reactions; sensory analysis; biochemistry of fruits; chromatography; oxidation-enzymic and nonenzymic. *Mailing Add:* Dept Viticult & Enology Univ Calif Davis CA 95616-8749. *Fax:* 530-752-0382

SINGLETON, WAYNE LOUIS, ANIMAL SCIENCE, REPRODUCTIVE PHYSIOLOGY. *Current Pos:* Asst prof, 70-76, ASSOC PROF ANIMAL SCI, COOP EXTEN SERV, PURDUE UNIV, LAFAYETTE, 76- *Personal Data:* b Oaktown, Ind, Feb 2, 44; m 69. *Educ:* Purdue Univ, Lafayette, BS, 66; SDak State Univ, MS, 68, PhD(animal sci), 70. *Mem:* Soc Study Reproduction; Sigma Xi. *Res:* Swine and beef cattle artificial insemination; reproductive efficiency of beef cattle and swine. *Mailing Add:* Dept Animal Sci Purdue Univ West Lafayette IN 47907-1968

SINGLEY, GEORGE, ENGINEERING MECHANICS. *Current Pos:* DEP DIR DEFENSE RES & ENG, US DEPT DEFENSE, 95- *Personal Data:* b Mar 29, 45. *Educ:* Univ Del, BEA, 68; Col William & Mary, MBA, 71; Old Dominion Univ, ME, 77. *Mailing Add:* US Dept Defense 3080 Defense Pentagon Washington DC 20301

SINGLEY, JOHN EDWARD, WATER CHEMISTRY, POTABLE WATER TREATMENT. *Current Pos:* from assoc prof to prof, 67-90, EMER PROF WATER CHEM, UNIV FLA, 90- *Personal Data:* b Wildwood, NJ, July 31, 24; m 50, Virginia Hyland Ragsdale Warner; c Elizabeth, Ann, Margaret & Patricia. *Educ:* Ga Inst Technol, BS, 50, MS, 52; Univ Fla, PhD(water chem), 66. *Honors & Awards:* Ambassador's Award, Am Water Works Asn, 73, Res Award, 85; Fuller Award, 76; Donald Boyd Award, Asn Metrop Water Agencies, 92; Wolman Award of Excellence, 85. *Prof Exp:* Asst chem, Ga Inst Technol, 49-50; phys chemist, US Army Ord Rocket Res Ctr, Redstone Arsenal, Ala, 50-51; chemist & group leader, Res & Develop Dept, Tenn Corp, 51-58, supvr tech serv, 58-65; from instr to assoc prof, Ga State Col, 54-67. *Concurrent Pos:* Consult, Panel on Pub Water Supplies, Nat Acad Sci, 71-72 & President's Coun on Environ Qual, 74; sr staff consult, Environ Sci & Eng, Inc, Gainesville, 77-82, sr vpres res & develop, 82-84; vpres, James M Montgomery Consult Engrs, 84-90, Montgomery Watson, 91-96 & Metcalf & Eddy, 96-. *Mem:* Hon mem Am Water Works Asn (pres, 91-92); fel Am Inst Chem; Inter-Am Asn Sanit Eng; Sigma Xi; fel Inst Water & Environ Mgt UK. *Res:* Coagulation mechanisms; corrosion in potable water systems; color, iron and manganese in water supplies; water treatment processes. *Mailing Add:* 1719 NW 23 Blvd PHE Gainesville FL 32605. *Fax:* 352-372-2592; *E-Mail:* h20doceds@aol.com

SINGLEY, MARK E(LDRIDGE), AGRICULTURAL ENGINEERING, BIOLOGICAL ENGINEERING. *Current Pos:* From instr to prof, 47-82, prof II, 82-87, EMER PROF AGR ENG, RUTGERS UNIV, 87-; VPRES RES & DEVELOP, BEDMINSTER BIOCONVERSION CORP. *Personal Data:* b Delano, Pa, Jan 25, 21; m 42, Janet Twichell; c Donald H, Frances M, Jeremy M & Paul V. *Educ:* Pa State Univ, BS, 42; Rutgers Univ, MS, 49. *Honors & Awards:* Massey-Ferguson Medal, Am Soc Agr Engrs, 87. *Concurrent Pos:* Pres, Agr Mus, State NJ, 85-89, trustee, 89-92. *Mem:* Fel AAAS; fel Am Soc Agr Engrs; Sigma Xi. *Res:* Deep bed drying, pneumatic handling and characteristics of fibrous and granular farm crops; resource management; land use planning; composting of soild waste. *Mailing Add:* Rd 3 335 Amwell Rd Belle Mead NJ 08502-1203

SINGPURWALLA, NOZER DARABSHA, RELIABILITY, STATISTICS. *Current Pos:* PROF OPERS RES, PROF STATIST & DIR, INST RELIABILITY & RISK ANALYSIS, GEORGE WASHINGTON UNIV, 69- *Personal Data:* b Hubli, India, Apr 8, 39; m 69, Norah Jackson; c Rachel & Darius. *Educ:* B V B Col Eng & Tech, India, BS, 59; Rutgers Univ, MS, 64; NY Univ, PhD, 68. *Honors & Awards:* Wilks Award for Contributions to Reliability & Life Testing Methodologies. *Concurrent Pos:* Vis prof statist, Stanford Univ, 78-79. *Mem:* Int Asn Statist Phys Sci; fel Am Statist Asn; fel Inst Math Statist; Int Statist Inst; fel AAAS. *Res:* Applications of statistics to reliability theory; development of statistical methodology. *Mailing Add:* Dept Opers Res Straughton Hall George Washington Univ 702 22nd St Washington DC 20052

SINHA, AKHOURI ACHYUTANAND, CELL & MOLECULAR BIOLOGY, PROSTATE BIOLOGY. *Current Pos:* PROF GENETICS & CELL BIOL, UNIV MINN, ST PAUL, 81-; RES SCIENTIST, RES SERV, VET AFFAIRS MED CTR, 96- *Personal Data:* b Churamanpur, Bihar, India, Dec 17, 33; US citizen; m 79, Dorothy K Pamer. *Educ:* Univ Allahabad, BS,

54; Patna Univ, MS, 56; Univ Mo, Columbia, PhD(zool), 65. *Prof Exp:* Lectr zool, Ranchi Univ, India, 56-61; fel anat, Univ Wis, 65; asst prof biol, Wis State Univ, Wis Claire, 65-67; sr scientist, Univ Minn, Minneapolis, 67-69, assoc prof zool & vet anat, 69-76, assoc prof genetics & cell biol, 76-81; res physiologist, Res Serv, Vet Affairs Med Ctr, 69-96. *Mem:* Am Asn Can Res; Am Asn Anat; Soc Study Reproduction; Am Soc Cell Biol; Indian Sci Cong Asn; Int Soc Differentiation; Soc Basic Urol Res. *Res:* Reproductive physiology; prostate biology and cancer of prostate including differentiation and regulation; tissue culture; immunocytochemistry; endocrinology; molecular biology. *Mailing Add:* Bldg 70, Res Serv 151 Vet Affairs Med Ctr One Veterans Dr Minneapolis MN 55417. *Fax:* 612-725-2093; *E-Mail:* sinha001@maroon.tc.umn.edu

SINHA, AKHOURI SURESH CHANDRA, ELECTRICAL ENGINEERING. *Current Pos:* assoc prof, 77-80, PROF ELEC ENG & CHMN DIV ENG, IND UNIV-PURDUE UNIV, 80- *Personal Data:* b Churamanpur, India, Mar 14, 38; m 68. *Educ:* Bihar Univ, BS, 57; Banaras Hindu Univ, BS, 61; Univ Mo-Columbia, MS, 66, PhD(elec eng), 69. *Prof Exp:* Asst prof elec eng, Ind Inst Technol, 69-77. *Res:* Control systems; stability theory; optimal control theory. *Mailing Add:* Dept Elec Eng Ind Univ-Purdue Univ 723 W Michigan St SL 160 Indianapolis IN 46202-5132

SINHA, AKHUARY KRISHNA, GEOLOGY. *Current Pos:* asst prof, 71-76, ASSOC PROF GEOL, VA POLYTECH INST & STATE UNIV, 76- *Personal Data:* b Churamanpur, India, Jan 5, 41; m 70. *Educ:* Sci Col, Patna, BSc, 60; Patna Univ, MSc, 62; Univ Calif, Santa Barbara, PhD(geol), 69. *Honors & Awards:* Cottrell Award, Res Corp, USA, 72. *Prof Exp:* Lectr geol, Patna Univ, 63-65; Carnegie Inst fel, Dept Terrestrial Magnetism, Washington, DC, 69-71. *Concurrent Pos:* NSF res grant, Va Polytech Inst & State Univ, 71- *Mem:* AAAS; Am Geophys Union; Geochem Soc; Geol Soc Am. *Res:* Common lead and strontium systematics, geochronology; trace element geochemistry; isotope geology; regional tectonics. *Mailing Add:* Geol Sci Va Polytech Inst & State Univ PO Box 0420 Blacksburg VA 24063-0001

SINHA, ARABINDA KUMAR, PHYSIOLOGY, NEUROBIOLOGY. *Current Pos:* asst prof, 72-78, ASSOC PROF PHYSIOL, ROBERT WOOD JOHNSON MED SCH, UNIV MED & DENT NJ, 78- *Personal Data:* b Kasiadanga, India, Mar 1, 33; m 62; c 1. *Educ:* Calcutta Univ, BSc, 56, MSc, 61; Univ Calif, San Francisco, PhD(physiol), 69. *Prof Exp:* Demonstr & lectr physiol, Presidency Col, Calcutta, 61-62; actg asst prof, Univ Calif, Berkeley, 68; assoc, Univ Calif, San Francisco, 68-69. *Concurrent Pos:* Mem grad fac, Rutgers Univ, 72- *Mem:* Am Physiol Soc; Soc Neurosci. *Res:* Cerebra circulation. *Mailing Add:* Robert Wood Johnson Med Sch Dept Physiol & Biophys Univ Med & Dent NJ 675 Hoes Lane Piscataway NJ 08854-5635. *Fax:* 732-235-5038; *E-Mail:* sinha@rwja.umdnj.edu

SINHA, ASRU KUMAR, HORMONAL REGULATION, THROMBOTIC DISORDERS. *Current Pos:* ASST PROF, THROMBOSIS CTR, TEMPLE UNIV, 78- *Personal Data:* b Tamluk, India, Aug 10, 43; m 69; c 1. *Educ:* City Col Calcutta, BSC, 61; Univ Col Sci, Calcutta, MSC, 63; Calcutta Univ, DSc, 70. *Prof Exp:* Res assoc microbiol, Miami Univ, Oxford, Ohio, 69-72, Med Ctr, Kans Univ, 72-74; res investr med, Univ Pa, 74-78. *Mem:* Am Soc Cell Biol; AAAS; Am Soc Biol Chem. *Res:* Hormonal control of cellular behaviors, particularly by prostaglandins through cyclic nucleotides dependent and independent pathways and the hormonal memories. *Mailing Add:* Dept Biotechnol Jadavpur Univ Calcutta 700032 India

SINHA, ATISH PRASAD, CASE-BASED REASONING, EXPERT SYSTEMS. *Current Pos:* asst prof, 91-97, ASSOC PROF MGT INFO SYSTS, UNIV DAYTON, 97- *Personal Data:* b Calcutta, India, Apr 4, 58; m 87, Nandini Mookerjee; c Ishan. *Educ:* Univ Calcutta, BSc, 80, BTech, 83, MTech, 86; Univ Pittsburgh, PhD(bus), 93. *Mem:* Am Asn Artificial Intel; Asn Comput Mach; Inst Opers Res & Mgt Sci. *Res:* Case-based reasoning, expert systems, object-oriented systems and human factors in software engineering. *Mailing Add:* 1245 Spring Ash Dr Centerville OH 45458

SINHA, BIDHU BHUSHAN PRASAD, BIOPHYSICS, HISTORY & PHILOSOPHY OF SCIENCE. *Current Pos:* DIR & PRES, INST SCI & MATH, 79- *Personal Data:* b Mallehpur, India; Can citizen. *Educ:* Patna Univ, India, MSc, 61; Mem Univ Nfld, MSc, 67; Univ Mass, PhD(nuclear physics), 71. *Prof Exp:* Lectr physics, Patna Univ, 62-64; instr physics & sci, Eastport Cent Sch, Nfld, 66-68; lectr & instr physics, Univ Guelph, Ont, 72-73; dir, Inst Sci & Math, 74-75; prof physics & sci, Fanshawe Col Appl Arts & Technol, Ont, 78-79. *Concurrent Pos:* Lectr tech physics, PATNA Inst Technol, India, 61-64; teaching fel, Physics Dept, Mem Univ Nfld, 64-66; dir sports, Eastport Sch, Nfld, 66-68; fel physics, Univ Toronto, 71-72; vis prof, World Open Univ, Calif & SD, 74-; vis student adminr, Grad Bus Sch, York Univ, 75-77. *Mem:* Am Phys Soc. *Res:* X-rays; molecular physics; nuclear accelerator physics; pioneering theoretical works in faster-than-light relativity; fundamental particles; parapsychophysics; pioneering quantum-relativity theory of life physics & species; faster-than-light physics--100% certainty-relation & cosmic-evolutionary-cycle of nothing-to-things-to-nothing as 4-dimensions-mix & break/up; relativity-theory based clean and cold real (4-D, D equals dimension) - nuclear energy as coupling of space (3-D) and time (1-D) - holes energy of (3/2)m C2-process (m equals any mass) (c equals light-velocity constant) (mistakeable in/name as cold fusion of 1989-public-news); proposed (1993-94) Hope of Panacea (universal medicine) for mankind from faster-than-light relativity (1974-75) based life species theory of 1983-84. *Mailing Add:* PO Box 892 Sta B London ON N6A 4Z3 Can

SINHA, BIKASH KUMAR, SONIC & ULTRASONIC TECHNIQUES IN GEOPHYSICAL PROSPECTING, WAVE PROPAGATION IN QUARTZ PRESSURE SENSORS. *Current Pos:* mem prof staff, Schlumberger-Doll Res, 79-81, prog leader, 81-86, tech adv, Schlumberger KK, Japan, 86-89, scientist, 89-95, SR RES SCIENTIST, SCHLUMBERGER-DOLL RES, 96- *Personal Data:* b Patna, Bihar, India, Dec 14, 47; US citizen; m 76, Asha; c Monica & Seema Anita. *Educ:* St Xavier's Col, India, BSc, 65; Indian Inst Technol, Kharagpur, India, 68; Univ Toronto, Can, MASc, 70; Rensselaer Polytech Inst, PhD(mech), 73. *Prof Exp:* Postdoctoral fel, Elec Eng Dept, McGill Univ, Montreal, 73-74; vis asst prof mech eng & sr res assoc, Rensselaer Polytech Inst, 74-79. *Concurrent Pos:* Assoc ed, Inst Elec & Electronics Engrs Trans Ultrasonics, Ferroelectrics & Frequency Control, 94- *Mem:* Soc Explor Geophysicists; fel Inst Elec & Electronics Engrs. *Res:* Wave propagation in elastic continua in the presence of prestress and temperature gradients; applications of elastic wave propagation in the determination of lithology, porosity and residual stresses in subsurface geological formations. *Mailing Add:* 39 Topledge Rd West Redding CT 06896-1807. *Fax:* 203-438-3819; *E-Mail:* sinha@ridgefield.sdr.slb.com

SINHA, BIRANDRA KUMAR, MEDICINAL CHEMISTRY, BIOPHYSICS. *Current Pos:* SR INVESTR, NAT CANCER INST, 82- *Personal Data:* b Gaya, India, Jan 10, 45; US citizen; m 70. *Educ:* Ohio State Univ, PhD(med chem), 72. *Prof Exp:* Fel biochem, Ohio State Univ, 72-73; NIH fel molecular pharmacol, 74-75; sr investr med chem, Microbiol Assocs, 75-77; sr staff fel biophysics, Nat Inst Environ Health Sci, 77-82. *Mem:* Sigma Xi; Am Asn Cancer Res; Am Soc Pharmacol & Exp Therapeutics. *Res:* Pharmacology of antitumor agents; mechanism of drug resistance; free radicals in toxicity. *Mailing Add:* Lab Chem Pharmacol NIH Bldg 10 6N119 Bethesda MD 20892-0001

SINHA, DIPEN N, NONDESTRUCTING EVALUATION USING ULTRASOUND, SENSORS & DEVICES FOR BIOMEDICAL APPLICATIONS. *Current Pos:* fel physics, Los Alamos Nat Lab, 80-83, staff physicist, 86-90, proj leader, 91-95, TEAM LEADER, LOS ALAMOS NAT LAB, 95- *Personal Data:* b Mosaboni Mines, India, Mar 9, 51; US citizen; m 75, Barbara A Rehor; c Naveen. *Educ:* St Xavier's Col, BSc, 70; Indian Inst Technol, MSc, 72, DIIT, 73; Portland State Univ, PhD(physics), 80. *Honors & Awards:* R&D 100 Award, 90 & 95; Popular Sci 100 Award, 92. *Prof Exp:* Staff mem, Rockwell Int, 83-86. *Concurrent Pos:* Prin investr, Electronics Res Group, Los Alamos Nat Lab, 87-90, proj leader, 90-, chief tech adv, 91- *Mem:* Am Phys Soc; Sigma Xi. *Res:* Development of a new nondestructive evaluation technique called acoustic resonance spectroscopy; vibrational characteristics of complex objects; physical characterization of fluids in sealed containers using ultrasound; development of ultrasonic interferometry for noninvasive fluid characterization and identification. *Mailing Add:* Los Alamos Nat Lab MS D429 PO Box 1663 Los Alamos NM 87545. *Fax:* 505-665-4292; *E-Mail:* sinha@lanl.gov

SINHA, HELEN LUELLA, QUALITY ASSURANCE, NURSING DOCUMENTATION & CANCER NURSING RESEARCH. *Current Pos:* RES NURSE, UNIV MAN, 95- *Personal Data:* b Man, Can, July 29, 36; m 63, Ranendra Nath; c Mala & Jay. *Educ:* Univ Man, BN, 79 & MA, 83. *Prof Exp:* Instr eye, ear, nose, throat nursing, St Boniface Gen Hosp, 63-64; staff nurse, Palliative Care Unit, Munic Hosp, 81; res assoc qual assurance, Univ Man, 83-85; spec proj qual assurance doc, St Boniface Gen Hosp, 85-91, utilization analyst, 91-94. *Concurrent Pos:* Res award, Man Nursing Res Inst, Univ Man, 91. *Mem:* Can Asn Qual Assurance Prof; NAm Nursing Diag Asn; Can Nurses Asn; Sigma Xi. *Res:* Project to develop, evaluate and implement a new documentation system for nursing and a project to update and expand to all areas of nursing, the quality monitoring system in use in hospital; utilization management. *Mailing Add:* St Boniface Gen Hosp 409 Tache Ave Winnipeg MB R2H 2A6 Can

SINHA, INDRANAND, MATHEMATICS. *Current Pos:* assoc prof, 68-71, PROF MATH, MICH STATE UNIV, 71- *Personal Data:* b Bihar, India, July 3, 31; m 52; c 3. *Educ:* Benares Hindu Univ, BSc, 51, MSc, 53; Univ Wis, PhD(algebra), 62. *Prof Exp:* Lectr math, Univ Bihar, 53-63; asst prof, Mich State Univ, 63-65; assoc prof, Indian Inst Technol, Kanpur, 65-68. *Res:* Linear algebra, Grour-rings, linear groups. *Mailing Add:* 1010 Blanchette Dr East Lansing MI 48823

SINHA, KUMARES C, TRANSPORTATION ENGINEERING, URBAN SYSTEMS ENGINEERING. *Current Pos:* assoc prof, 74-78, assoc dir, Ctr Pub Policy & Pub Admin, 78-80, PROF CIVIL ENG & HEAD TRANSP ENG, PURDUE UNIV, 78- *Personal Data:* b Calcutta, India, July 12, 42; m 67; c 5. *Educ:* Jadavpur Univ, India, BCE, 61; Calcutta Univ, DTRP, 64; Univ Conn, MS, 66, PhD(civil eng), 68. *Honors & Awards:* Fred Burggraf Award, Nat Acad Sci, 72; Frank M Masters Award, Am Soc Civil Eng, 86. *Prof Exp:* Jr lectr civil eng, Jadavpur Univ, India, 61-62; asst engr, Govt W Bengal, India, 62-64; res asst civil eng, Univ Conn, 64-68; asst prof civil eng, 68-72, assoc prof & dir urban transp prog, Marquette Univ, 72-74. *Concurrent Pos:* Systs eng consult, Southeast Wis Regional Planning Comn, 69-72; mem, Nat Transp Res Bd. *Mem:* Am Pub Works Asn; Am Soc Eng Educ; Am Planning Asn; Am Inst Cert Planners; Am Road & Transp Builders Asn; fel Am Soc Civil Eng; fel Inst Transp Eng. *Res:* Transportation systems analysis; urban and regional planning and policy analysis; author or co-author of 200 technical publications. *Mailing Add:* Purdue Univ Sch Civil Eng West Lafayette IN 47907

SINHA, MAHENDRA KUMAR, SURFACE PHYSICS. *Current Pos:* from asst prof to assoc prof, NDak State Univ, 66-74, prof, 74-, actg chmn dept, 77-78, EMER PROF PHYSICS, N DAK STATE UNIV. *Personal Data:* b Kanpur, India, July 8, 31; m 57; c 2. *Educ:* Agra Univ, BSc, 49, MSc, 52; Pa State Univ, PhD(physics), 61. *Prof Exp:* Lectr physics, Christ Church Col, Kanpur, India, 52-57; res assoc, Pa State Univ, 61-62; sci officer, Atomic Energy Estab, Bombay, India, 62-64; fel, Radio & Elec Eng Div, Nat Res Coun Can, 64-66. *Concurrent Pos:* Guest scientist, Max Planck Inst Plasma Phys, Ger, 75-76. *Mem:* Am Phys Soc. *Res:* Field ion and field ion microscopy; sputtering of solids by medium energy gas ions; high voltage breakdown in vacuum and insulators; entrapment and surface damage of solid due to kiloelectron volt gas ions. *Mailing Add:* Dept Physics NDak State Univ Univ Station Fargo ND 58105

SINHA, NARESH KUMAR, ELECTRICAL ENGINEERING. *Current Pos:* assoc prof, 65-71, chmn dept elec & comput eng, 82-88, PROF ELEC ENG, MCMASTER UNIV, 71-, DIR INSTRNL COMPUT, FAC ENG, 88- *Personal Data:* b Gaya, India, July 25, 27; m 51; c 3. *Educ:* Benares Hindu Univ, BSc, 48; Manchester Univ, PhD(elec eng), 55. *Prof Exp:* From asst prof to assoc prof elec eng, Bihar Inst Technol, India, 50-61; asst res scientist, NY Univ, 61; assoc prof elec eng, Univ Tenn, 61-65. *Concurrent Pos:* Res contract, NASA, Ala, 64-65, Dept Commun, Ottawa, 73-76 & 77-78; Nat Res Coun Can res grant, 66-. *Mem:* Sr mem Inst Elec & Electronics Engrs; Eng Inst Can; fel Inst Elec Engrs; Can Soc Elec Eng. *Res:* Optimum nonlinear filtering of random signals embedded in noise; adaptive and learning control systems; optimal control theory; sensitivity of systems to variations in parameters; application of microcomputer to process control. *Mailing Add:* Dept Elec Eng & Comput McMaster Univ 1280 Main St W Hamilton ON L8S 4L7 Can

SINHA, NAVIN KUMAR, MOLECULAR BIOLOGY. *Current Pos:* asst prof, 76-82, ASSOC PROF MICROBIOL, RUTGERS UNIV, 82- *Personal Data:* b Patna, India, Oct 14, 45; m 71; c 2. *Educ:* Patna Univ, BSc, 62, MSc, 64; Univ Minn, PhD(genetics), 72. *Prof Exp:* Res assoc biol, Mass Inst Technol, 72-73; fel biochem, Princeton Univ, 73-76. *Concurrent Pos:* NIH fel, Nat Cancer Inst, 74-76; prin investr, Nat Inst Gen Med Sci, 77-; vis scientist, Max-Planck Inst, Cologne, WGer, 84-85; Alexander von Humboldt fel, 84-85. *Mem:* Am Soc Microbiol; Genetics Soc Am. *Res:* Mechanism of DNA replication; DNA protein interaction; molecular mechanisms of mutation. *Mailing Add:* 10 Cambridge Lane Somerset NJ 08873

SINHA, OM PRAKASH, theoretical solid state physics, for more information see previous edition

SINHA, RAMESH CHANDRA, PLANT PATHOLOGY. *Current Pos:* res scientist, 65-76, PRIN RES SCIENTIST PLANT VIROL & MYCOPLASMA, AGR CAN, OTTAWA, 76- *Personal Data:* b Bareilly, India, Feb 10, 34; Can citizen; m 57; c 2. *Educ:* Agr Univ, India, BSc, 53; Lucknow Univ, India, MSc, 56; London Univ, Eng, PhD(plant virol), 60, DSc(plant virol & mycoplasma), 74. *Prof Exp:* Exp officer plant virol, Rothamsted Exp Sta, Eng, 59-60; res assoc plant virol, Univ Ill, Urbana, 60-65. *Mem:* Can Phytopath Soc; Am Phytopath Soc; Indian Phytopath Soc; Int Orgn Mycoplasmologists; fel Royal Soc Can. *Res:* Developed serological methods for rapid diagnosis of diseases in plants caused by non-helical, non-culturable mycoplasmas. *Mailing Add:* Eastern Cereal & Oil Res Ctr Ottawa ON K1A 0C6 Can. *Fax:* 613-992-7909

SINHA, RANENDRA NATH, INSECT ECOLOGY, ACAROLOGY. *Current Pos:* RETIRED. *Personal Data:* b Calcutta, India, Jan 25, 30; Can citizen; m 63; c 2. *Educ:* Univ Calcutta, BSc, 50; Univ Kans, PhD(entom, zool), 56. *Honors & Awards:* Gold Medal Award, Entom Soc Can, 85. *Prof Exp:* Instr biol, St Xavier's Col, India, 51-52; res assoc zool, McGill Univ, 56-57; res scientist, Res Sta, Can Dept Agr, 57-69, sr res scientist, 70-76, prin res scientist, 76-93. *Concurrent Pos:* Nat Res Coun Can fel, 56-57; hon prof fac grad studies, Univ Man, 61-; hon lectr entom, Kyoto Univ, 66-67. *Mem:* Entom Soc Am. *Res:* Ecology of stored grain and its products; ecosystem analysis by multivariate statistics; stored-product entomology and acarology; insect resistance to cereal varieties; arthropod-fungus interrelations. *Mailing Add:* 582 Queenston St Winnipeg MB R3N 0X3 Can

SINHA, SHOME NATH, SYNTHESIS & PROCESSING OF MATERIALS BY DESIGN, MICROSTRUCTURE-PROPERTY-PROCESSING RELATIONSHIPS. *Current Pos:* MEM STAFF, ANL, 96- *Personal Data:* b Dhanbad, India, Sept 15, 52. *Educ:* BIT, Sindri, India, BScEngg, 73; Indian Inst Technol, Bombay, India, MScEngg, 77; Univ Utah, Salt Lake City, PhD(metall), 84. *Prof Exp:* Process metallurgist, Alloy Steels Plant, HSL, India, 74-79; postdoctoral appointee, Argonne Nat Lab, Ill, 85-88; asst prof metall mat processing majors, Univ Ill, Chicago, 88-96. *Concurrent Pos:* Adj asst prof, Univ Ill, Chicago, 86-87; fac assoc, Argonne Nat Lab, 89- *Mem:* Mat Res Soc; Am Ceramic Soc; Am Soc Metals. *Res:* Material processing of high temperature superconductors; high performance ceramic; metal composites; innovative synthesis; mechanical alloying; nanometer range particles; inductive plasma scintering; modeling and development of process by design. *Mailing Add:* 220 N Lombard Ave Oak Park IL 60302

SINHA, SNEHESH KUMAR, APPLIED STATISTICS. *Current Pos:* from asst prof to assoc prof, 61-72, PROF STATIST, UNIV MAN, 72- *Personal Data:* b Banaras, India; Can citizen; m 56; c 2. *Educ:* Patna Univ, BA, 46, MA, 49 & 54; Univ London, MSc, 59, PhD(statist), 72; Univ Chicago, AM, 68. *Prof Exp:* Lectr math, Jamshedpur Coop Col, Univ Bihar, 53-57; asst prof math & statist, St Mary's Univ, NS, 59-61. *Mem:* Fel Royal Statist Soc; Int Statist Inst. *Res:* Life testing and reliability estimation; bayesian inference; properties of associated distributions in the presence of an outlier observation. *Mailing Add:* Dept Statist Univ Man Winnipeg MB R3T 2N2 Can

SINHA, SUDHIR K, DNA TESTING-DETERMINE PATERNITY & FOR FORENSIC PURPOSES. *Current Pos:* PRES & LAB DIR, GENTEST LABS INC, 90- *Personal Data:* b Dec 18, 43. *Educ:* Ranchi Univ, Ranchi, India, BS, 64, MS, 66; Indian Inst Technol, Kanpur, India, PhD(chem), 73. *Prof Exp:* Res asst, Indian Inst Technol, 70-73; lectr chem, Bihar Univ, 73-77; res assoc fel, Dept Biochem, Univ Miami, 77-80, from res asst prof to res assoc prof, Med Sch, 80-84; dir biochem, IMREG, 84-90. *Concurrent Pos:* Adj assoc prof biochem, Med Ctr, Tulane Univ, 84- *Mem:* Am Soc Biochem & Molecular Biol; NY Acad Sci; Am Chem Soc; Am Asn Blood Banks; Am Acad Forensic Scientists; Int AIDS Soc. *Res:* Protein structure DNA analysis. *Mailing Add:* Relia Gene Technol Inc 5525 Mounes St Suite 101 New Orleans LA 70123

SINHA, SUNIL K, SOLID STATE PHYSICS. *Current Pos:* SR RES ASSOC & HEAD, CONDENSED MATTER GROUP, EXXON RES ENG CO, 83- *Personal Data:* b Calcutta, India, Sept 13, 39; m 62, Lonny Olsen; c Arjun & Ranjan. *Educ:* Cambridge Univ, BA, 60, PhD(physics), 64. *Honors & Awards:* Doe-Bes Mat Sci Award, 82. *Prof Exp:* Vis scientist, Atomic Energy Estab, Trombay, India, 64-65; assoc, Iowa State Univ, 65-66, from asst prof to prof physics, 66-75; sr scientist, Argonne Nat Lab, 75-83. *Concurrent Pos:* Vis fel, Japanese Soc Prom Sci, 77; adj prof physics, Northwestern Univ & Northern Ill Univ, 80-83 & Johns Hopkins Univ, 89-; Guggenheim fel, 82; act group head, x-ray scattering, Brookhaven Nat Lab, 89-90. *Mem:* Am Phys Soc; Mat Res Soc; fel Am Phys Soc; Am Crystallog Asn. *Res:* Experimental investigation of magnetic structures and dynamics of magnetic system by neutron scattering; neutron and x-ray studies of fractal structure and dynamics, porous media; colloidal crystals, polymer conformations and phase transitions; synchrotron x-ray studies of surfaces, interfaces, thin films and surface phase transitions; high-temperature superconductivity. *Mailing Add:* 14 Stevens St Bernardsville NJ 07924. *Fax:* 908-730-3042; *E-Mail:* sksinha@erenj.com

SINHA, VINOD T(ARKESHWAR), CHEMICAL ENGINEERING. *Current Pos:* ASSOC RES FEL, CYTEC INDUST, 93- *Personal Data:* b Patna, India, June 10, 41; m 66, Teresa L Meyer; c Leela & Steven. *Educ:* Bombay Univ, BChemEng, 64; Univ Alta, MSc, 64; Univ Calif, Davis, PhD(chem eng), 67. *Prof Exp:* Res chem engr, Am Cyanamid Co, 67-74, sr res chem engr, 74-82, proj leader, 77-80, prin res chem engr, 83-89, assoc res fel, 90-93. *Mem:* Am Inst Chem Engrs; Am Chem Soc. *Res:* Fluid mechanics and hydrodynamic stability; heat and mass transfer; impact thermoplastics; extrusion, three phase fluidization, cost estimating; polymerization. *Mailing Add:* 1937 W Main St PO Box 60 Stamford CT 06904-0060. *E-Mail:* vinod_sinha@st.cytec.com

SINHA, YAGYA NAND, ENDOCRINOLOGY. *Current Pos:* asst mem II, Scripps Clin & Res Found, 69-81, radiation safety officer, 82-87, SR MEM & DIR ANIMAL RES, WHITTIER INST DIABETES & ENDOCRINOL, SCRIPPS MEM HOSP, 82- *Personal Data:* b Muzaffarpur, Bihar, India, Oct 21, 36; m 58, Savitri; c Manjula, Anita, Suman & Arun. *Educ:* Bihar Univ, GBVC, 57; Mich State Univ, MS, 64, PhD(physiol), 67. *Prof Exp:* Vet asst surgeon, Bihar Govt, India, 57-59; res asst, Livestock Res Sta, Patna, India, 59-61; grad asst, Mich State Univ, 62-67; res assoc, Cornell Univ, 67-69. *Concurrent Pos:* Res grants, Nat Inst Health. *Mem:* AAAS; Soc Exp Biol & Med; Endocrine Soc. *Res:* Endocrinology of prolactin and growth hormone. *Mailing Add:* 8385 Arles Rd San Diego CA 92126

SINIBALDI, RALPH MICHAEL, heat shock gene expression, developmental genetics, for more information see previous edition

SINIFF, DONALD BLAIR, ECOLOGY, BIOMETRY. *Current Pos:* res fel, 64-67, assoc prof, 67-75, DIR, ITASCA BIOL PROG, PROF ECOL, DEPT ECOL-BEHAV BIOL, UNIV MINN, MINNEAPOLIS, 75- *Personal Data:* b Bexley, Ohio, July 7, 35; m 59; c 3. *Educ:* Mich State Univ, BS, 57, MS, 58; Univ Minn, PhD(entom, fish & wildlife), 67. *Prof Exp:* Biometrician, Alaska Dept Fish & Game, 60-64. *Concurrent Pos:* Prin investr, NSF Off Polar Prog grant, 67-; comnr, Marine Mammal Comn, 75-81. *Mem:* Wildlife Soc; Soc Conserv Biol; Marine Mammal Soc; Am Soc Mammalogists. *Res:* Vertebrate ecology; statistical and computer applications in field studies; population dynamics large mammals, specializing in marine mammals. *Mailing Add:* Dept Ecol & Behav Biol 100 Ecol Bldg Univ Minn St Paul MN 55108. *Fax:* 612-624-6777

SINK, DAVID SCOTT, industrial engineering, for more information see previous edition

SINK, DONALD WOODFIN, INORGANIC CHEMISTRY. *Current Pos:* from asst prof to assoc prof, Appalachian State Univ, 68-72, prof chem & sec educ, 73-75, asst dean, 75-86, assoc dean, 86-90, actg dean, 90-91, PROF CHEM, APPALACHIAN STATE UNIV, 72-, DEAN, COL ARTS & SCI, 91- *Personal Data:* b Salisbury, NC, Nov 10, 37; m 60, Gwendolyn Sloan; c Donna, Daryl & Tamberlyn. *Educ:* Catawba Col, AB, 59; Univ SC, PhD(inorg chem), 65. *Prof Exp:* Instr chem, Appalachian State Teachers Col, 60-61; asst prof, Lenior-Rhyne Col, 65-67, Northern Mich Univ, 67-68. *Mem:* Am Chem Soc; Sigma Xi; Nat Teachers Asn. *Res:* Synthesis and study of cis-trans square planar isomers of palladium and platinum complexes; far infrared spectra of square planar complexes of palladium and platinum. *Mailing Add:* 210 Hillcrest Circle Boone NC 28607-3829. *E-Mail:* sinkdw@conrad.appstate.edu

SINK, JOHN DAVIS, BIOCHEMISTRY, BIOPHYSICS. *Current Pos:* PRES & MANAGING PARTNER, SINK, PADDEN & ASSOC, 92- *Personal Data:* b Homer City, Pa, Dec 19, 34; m 89, Sharon Fernando; c Kara J, Karl J & Lisa M. *Educ:* Pa State Univ, BS, 56, MS, 60, PhD(biochem, animal sci), 62; Univ Pittsburgh, EdD, 86. *Honors & Awards:* Darbaker Prize, Pa Acad Sci, 67. *Prof Exp:* Admin officer, Pa Dept Agr, 62; asst prof animal sci, Pa State Univ, 62-66, assoc prof meat sci, 66-72, prof, 72-80; prof & chmn animal & vet sci, WVa Univ, 80-85; chief exec officer, Pa State Univ, 85-92. *Concurrent Pos:* NSF fel, 64-65; consult, Pa Dept Agr, 62-79; joint staff officer, USDA, 79-80. *Mem:* AAAS; Am Meat Sci Asn (pres, 74-75); Am Chem Soc; Biophys Soc; Am Soc Animal Sci; Am Asn Higher Ed; Soc Res Adminr; Am Asn Univ Adminr; Inst Food Technologists. *Res:* Lipid and steroid biochemistry; muscle biophysics and physiology; higher education; public policy. *Mailing Add:* 2726 Phillips Dr Marietta GA 30064

SINK, KENNETH C, JR, CELL GENETICS. *Current Pos:* From asst prof to assoc prof, 63-75, PROF, MICH STATE UNIV, 75- *Personal Data:* b Altoona, Pa, Oct 7, 37. *Educ:* Pa State Univ, BS, 59, MS, 61, PhD(genetics, plant breeding), 63. *Mem:* Am Soc Hort Sci; Am Genetic Asn. *Res:* Cell and protoplast culture and fusion. *Mailing Add:* Dept Hort Mich State Univ 288 Plant Sci Bldg East Lansing MI 48824-1325

SINKE, CARL, MATHEMATICS. *Current Pos:* Asst prof, 56-64, chmn dept, 64-74, PROF MATH, CALVIN COL, 64- *Personal Data:* b Moline, Mich, Oct 15, 28; m 56; c 4. *Educ:* Calvin Col, AB, 49; Purdue Univ, MS, 51, PhD(math), 54. *Concurrent Pos:* Consult, Hq, Ord Weapons Command, Ill, 56-57 & Off Ord Res, NC, 57-58. *Mem:* Am Math Soc; Math Asn Am. *Res:* Analysis; asymptotic series; operations research; optimization problems. *Mailing Add:* 4511 36th St SE Grand Rapids MI 49512-1946

SINKFORD, JEANNE C, DENTISTRY, PHYSIOLOGY. *Current Pos:* spec asst, 91-93, ASST EXEC DIR, DIV WOMEN & MINORITY AFFAIRS, AM ASN DENT SCHS, 92- *Personal Data:* b Washington, DC, Jan 30, 33; m 51; c 3. *Educ:* Howard Univ, BS, 53, DDS, 58; Northwestern Univ, MS, 62, PhD(physiol), 63. *Hon Degrees:* DSc, Georgetown Univ, 78, Univ Med & Dent NJ, 92. *Prof Exp:* Res asst psychol, US Dept Health, Educ & Welfare, 53; instr dent, Col Dent, Howard Univ, 58-60; clin instr, Dent Sch, Northwestern Univ, 63-64; assoc prof & head, Dept Prosthodont, Howard Univ, 64-68, assoc dean, 67-74, prof, 68-92, dean, Col Dent, 75-92, prof, Dept Physiol, Grad Sch Arts & Sci, 76-92. *Concurrent Pos:* Consult prosthodont, Freedmen's Hosp, Washington, DC, 64, res & prosthodont, Vet Admin Hosp, 65 & US Army grants, 65-; attend staff, Freedmen's Hosp, Howard Univ Hosp, 64-, Children's Hosp Nat Med Ctr, 75- & DC Gen Hosp, 75-; USPHS gen res & training grant, 65-; mem numerous adv comts, govt agencies & nat socs, 65- *Mem:* Inst Med-Nat Acad Sci; Am Dent Asn; Int Asn Dent Res; fel Am Col Dent; Int Col Dent; Am Prosthodontic Soc; Sigma Xi; NY Acad Sci; Am Soc Geriat Dent; Am Inst Oral Biol. *Res:* Endogenous anti-inflammatory substances; chemical healing agent; cyanoacrylates; gingival retraction agents; hereditary dental defects; oral endocrine effects; neuromuscular problems and temporomandibular joint. *Mailing Add:* Am Asn Dent Schs 1625 Massachusetts Ave NW Washington DC 20036

SINKO, JOHN, CHEMICAL RESEARCH, INORGANIC CHEMISTRY. *Current Pos:* CHEM RES SCIENTIST, WAYNE PIGMENT CORP, 84- *Personal Data:* b Romania, 1940. *Educ:* Babes-Bolyai Univ, BS, 62; Univ Bucharest, MS, 74; Veszprem Univ, Hungary, PhD(inorg chem), 90. *Prof Exp:* Sr res scientist, Inst Mining & Metall, Hungary, 64-83. *Mem:* Fel Am Chem Soc; fel Am Inst Chemists. *Mailing Add:* Wayne Pigment Corp 306 N Milwaukee St Milwaukee WI 53202-5832

SINKOVICS, JOSEPH G, INFECTIOUS DISEASES & MEDICAL ONCOLOGY, HEMATOLOGY. *Current Pos:* dir, Cancer Inst, 83-96, DIR CANCER RES & DEVELOP, ST JOSEPH'S HOSP, TAMPA, FLA, 96-; PROF MED, DEPT MED & MED MICROBIOL, MED COL, UNIV SFLA, 83- *Personal Data:* b Budapest, Hungary, June 17, 24; nat US; div; c Geza & Eszter. *Educ:* Peter Pazmany Univ, Budapest, MD, 48; Am Bd Med Microbiol, dipl, 62; Am Bd Internal Med, dipl, 65, recert, 80, cert infectious dis, 72, cert med oncol, 77. *Honors & Awards:* Purdue Frederick Award, Am Col Obstet & Gynec, 71; Grace Faullace Award, Leo Goodwin Inst, 80. *Prof Exp:* Adj prof virol, Eotvos Lorant Univ, Budapest, 49-53; sr investr, State Inst Pub Health, Hungary, 54-56; intern & resident internal med, Cook Co Hosp, Chicago, 58-62; from asst prof to prof oncolhemat, M D Anderson Hosp, Univ Tex, Houston, 59-80; prof virol, Baylor Col Med, Tex, 80-89. *Concurrent Pos:* Rockefeller fel, Inst Microbiol, Rutgers Univ, 57; Am Cancer Soc fel, Univ Tex M D Anderson Hosp & Tumor Inst, 59, consult adj prof oncol, 80-; specialist in lab diag, Univ Budapest, 54; prin investr, USPHS res grants & Nat Cancer Inst grants & contracts, NIH, 62-78; vis prof virol, Baylor Col Med, Tex, 83-89; consult oncol, Bay Pines Vet Admin Hosp, St Petersburg, Fla, 83-90; mem, Nat Adv Coun Allergy Infectious Dis, NIH, Bethesda, 84-88. *Mem:* AMA; Am Asn Cancer Res; Am Soc Microbiol; Am Soc Clin Oncol; Infectious Dis Soc Am; Worldwide Hungarian Med Acad; Int Asn Comp Res; Hungarian Sci Acad. *Res:* Virology; tumor immunology; immunotherapy of human tumors; cytotoxic lymphocytes; viral oncolysates; chemoimmunotherapy of sarcomas; established tissue cultures of human tumors; chemotherapy of human tumors; infectious diseases; septicemias in cancer patients; oncology; hematology. *Mailing Add:* Cancer Inst PO Box 4227 St Joseph's Hosp 3001 W Dr Martin Luther King Jr Blvd Tampa FL 33677-4227. *Fax:* 813-874-7218

SINKS, LUCIUS FREDERICK, BIOPHYSICS, PEDIATRICS. *Current Pos:* CHIEF, CANCER CTR BR, DIV CANCER PREV & CONTROL, NAT CANCER INST. *Personal Data:* b Newburyport, Mass, Mar 14, 31; m 56, 85; c 4. *Educ:* Yale Univ, BS, 53; Jefferson Med Col, MD, 57; Ohio State Univ, MMSc, 63. *Prof Exp:* Assoc cancer res pediatrician, Roswell Park Mem Inst, 66-67, chief cancer res pediatrician, 67-76; prof pediat, Georgetown Univ, 76-81, chief, Div Pediat & Adolescent Oncol/Hemat, Vincent T Lombardi Cancer Res Ctr, 76-81; prof pediat, Tufts Univ, 81-87. *Concurrent Pos:* Nat Cancer Inst spec fel, Cambridge, Eng, 64-66; Nat Cancer Inst grant, Roswell Park Mem Inst, 66-74; Nat Cancer Inst Advan Clin Oncol Training Prog grant, 68-78; from asst res prof to assoc res prof pediat, State Univ NY, Buffalo, 66-69, res prof pediat, 69-; chief, Div Pediat & Adolescent Oncol & Hemat, New Eng Med Ctr Hosps, 81- *Mem:* Am Asn Cancer Res; Soc Pediat Res; Am Soc Clin Oncol. *Res:* Pediatric oncology; cell biology. *Mailing Add:* Middlesex Hosp Cancer Ctr 28 Crescent St Middletown CT 06457

SINKULA, ANTHONY ARTHUR, PHARMACEUTICAL & MEDICINAL CHEMISTRY. *Current Pos:* Res assoc pharm, Upjohn Co, 63-68, sr res scientist, 68-76, res head, 76-78, mgr, Res Prog Planning, 78-83, dir, Pharm Res & Drug Del Syst Res, 83-88, dir, Pharmaceut Res Lab, 88-90, DIR, RES PLANNING, UPJOHN CO, 90- *Personal Data:* b Laona, Wis, Jan 2, 38; m 63; c 2. *Educ:* Univ Wis, BS, 59; Ohio State Univ, MS, 61, PhD(med chem), 63; Western Mich Univ, MBA, 66. *Honors & Awards:* W E Upjohn Award. *Concurrent Pos:* Fel, NIMH, 60-63. *Mem:* Am Pharmaceut Asn; Acad Pharmaceut Sci; Am Asn Pharmaceut Scientists. *Res:* Chemical modification of drugs; drug formulation research; pro-drug chemistry research; research administration. *Mailing Add:* 2607 Pine Ridge Rd Kalamazoo MI 49008

SINNER, DONALD H, regulations & compliance, product and process development, for more information see previous edition

SINNETT, CARL E(ARL), PROCESS DESIGN & ECONOMIC EVALUATION, PETROLEUM REFINING & SYNTHETIC FUELS DEVELOPMENT. *Current Pos:* RETIRED. *Personal Data:* b Wilkinsburg, Pa, Aug 26, 22; m 48, Helen McNair; c William, Nancy & Mary. *Educ:* Carnegie Inst Technol, BS, 46, MS, 47. *Prof Exp:* Asst tech man, B F Goodrich Co, Ohio, 46; proj engr, Econ & Comput Sci Div, Gulf Res & Develop Co, 51-68, sr proj engr, Corp Res & Chem Div, Gulf Sci & Technol Co, 68-78, sr proj engr, Chem & Minerals Div, Gulf Res & Develop Co, 78-83; chem engr, Stand Oil Co, Ind, 47-51. *Mem:* Am Inst Chem Engrs. *Res:* Design of equipment for and economic evaluation of processes to refine and upgrade petroleum, oil shale, tar sands, and coal to marketable transportation fuels, combustion fuels, and chemical products. *Mailing Add:* 43 Crystal Dr Oakmont PA 15139

SINNHUBER, RUSSELL OTTO, FOOD SCIENCE, TOXICOLOGY. *Current Pos:* RETIRED. *Personal Data:* b Detroit, Mich, Apr 28, 17; m 42, Dorthy A Collins; c John R, Carol A (Lehman) & Gary F. *Educ:* Mich State Univ, BS, 39; Ore State Univ, MS, 41. *Honors & Awards:* Conserv Serv Award, US Dept Interior, 66. *Prof Exp:* From asst prof to assoc prof, Ore State Univ, 43-63, prof food sci & technol, 63-82. *Concurrent Pos:* Mem Agr Res Inst agr bd subcomt fish nutrit, Nat Acad Sci-Nat Res Coun. *Mem:* Fel AAAS; Am Inst Nutrit; Am Oil Chem Soc; Inst Food Technol; Am Chem Soc; Am Asn Cancer Res. *Res:* Lipid chemistry and autoxidation; irradiation of seafoods; fish and shellfish nutrition; fatty acid metabolism; carcinogenesis; mycotoxins. *Mailing Add:* 5852 S Bay Rd Toledo OR 97391-9752

SINNIS, JAMES CONSTANTINE, PLASMA PHYSICS. *Current Pos:* RES STAFF, PLASMA PHYSICS LAB, PRINCETON UNIV, 63- *Personal Data:* b Dover, NJ, May 31, 35; m 57; c 3. *Educ:* Stevens Inst Technol, ME, 57, MS, 59, PhD(physics), 63. *Mem:* Am Phys Soc; AAAS. *Res:* Plasma physics research with special interest in development of fusion power via the magnetic confinement approach. *Mailing Add:* Plasma Physics Lab James Forrestal Campus Princeton Univ PO Box 451 Princeton NJ 08543

SINNOTT, GEORGE, MOLECULAR PHYSICS. *Current Pos:* cong liaison officer, 75-78, assoc dir tech eval, 78-90, DIR INT & ACAD AFFAIRS, NAT INST STAND & TECHNOL, 90- *Personal Data:* b St Louis, Mo, Mar 13, 32; m 57; Arlene Kozlowski; c Kevin, Eileen & Megan. *Educ:* Univ Chicago, AB, 53, MS, 57; Washington Univ, PhD(physics), 64. *Prof Exp:* Physicist, Argonne Nat Lab, 56-58, Lockheed-Palo Alto Labs, Calif, 64-68 & Joint Inst Lab Astrophys, Univ Colo, Boulder, 68-71; chief, Fire Physics & Dynamics Prog, Nat Bur Stand, 72-74; sci policy asst to Congressman Charles Mosher & Timothy Wirth, 74-75. *Mem:* Am Phys Soc; Sigma Xi. *Mailing Add:* 16732 Frontenac Terr Derwood MD 20855. *Fax:* 301-975-3530; *E-Mail:* gsinnott@nist.gov

SINNOTT, M(AURICE) J(OSEPH), METALLURGICAL ENGINEERING. *Current Pos:* RETIRED. *Personal Data:* b Detroit, Mich, Jan 19, 16; m 44; c 5. *Educ:* Univ Mich, BS, 38, MS, 41, ScD(metall eng), 46. *Prof Exp:* Plant metallurgist, Great Lakes Steel Corp, 38-40; res assoc, Eng Res Inst, Univ Mich, 40-43; sr develop engr, Goodyear Aircraft Corp, 43; instr chem & metall eng, Univ Mich, Ann Arbor, 44-46, from asst prof to assoc prof, 46-54, prof chem & metall eng, 54-84, assoc dean eng, 73-82. *Mem:* Am Soc Metals; Am Inst Mining, Metall & Petrol Engrs; Brit Inst Metal; Sigma Xi. *Res:* Metal physics; grain boundary phenomena; x-ray analysis; nucleation; growth. *Mailing Add:* 2115 Woodside Rd Ann Arbor MI 48104-4514

SINNOTT, SUSAN BUTHAINA, SURFACE & INTERFACE SCIENCE, COMPUTATIONAL MATERIALS SCIENCE & ENGINEERING. *Current Pos:* ASST PROF MAT ENG, UNIV KY, 95- *Personal Data:* b Manhattan, Kans, Aug 14, 66. *Educ:* Univ Tex, Austin, BS, 87; Iowa State Univ, PhD(phys chem), 93. *Prof Exp:* Nat Res Coun postdoctoral assoc, Naval Res Lab, Dept Defense, 93-95. *Concurrent Pos:* Fac res partic, Oak Ridge Nat Lab, US Dept Energy, 96. *Mem:* Minerals Metals & Mat Soc; Am Ceramic Soc; Mat Res Soc; Am Vacuum Soc; Am Phys Soc; Am Chem Soc. *Res:* Design and study of new composite materials; computational nanometer scale materials engineering; investigation of affect of material defects on material properties; study of thin film growth. *Mailing Add:* Univ Ky 177 Anderson Hall Lexington KY 40506-0046. *Fax:* 606-323-1929; *E-Mail:* sinnott@engr.uky.edu

SINOR, LYLE TOLBOT, BLOOD BANKING. *Current Pos:* ASST DIR RES, COMMUNITY BLOOD CTR OF GREATER KANSAS CITY, MO, 83-, DIR SCI COMPUT & AUTOMATION, 85- *Personal Data:* b Columbus, Ga, May 24, 57; m 79; c 2. *Educ:* Univ Kans, BS, 80, PhD(immunohemat), 83. *Concurrent Pos:* Consult, Immucor, Inc, 85- *Mem:* Am Asn Pathologists; assoc Am Soc Clin Pathologists; Am Asn Blood Banks; AAAS; NY Acad Sci; Int Soc Blood Transfusion. *Res:* Development of new clinical test procedures; study and characterization of blood group antigens. *Mailing Add:* Immucor Inc 3130 Gateway Dr Norcross GA 30091-5625

SINOTTE, LOUIS PAUL, PHARMACEUTICAL CHEMISTRY, ORGANIC CHEMISTRY. *Current Pos:* Tech asst to dir qual control, 54-55, mgr pharmaceut control, 55-61, DIR QUAL CONTROL, MERCK SHARP & DOHME DIV, MERCK & CO, INC, 61- *Personal Data:* b Haverhill, Mass, June 12, 27; m 55; c 5. *Educ:* Mass Col Pharm, BS, 50; Purdue Univ, MS, 52, PhD(pharmaceut chem), 54. *Concurrent Pos:* Mem trustee adv comt, Rutgers Col Pharm. *Mem:* Am Chem Soc; Soc Cosmetic Chemists; Am Soc Qual Control; Am Pharmaceut Asn; Pharmaceut Mfrs Asn. *Res:* Pharmaceutical and medicinal research; quality control; manufacturing pharmacy. *Mailing Add:* Pharm Qual Reg Serv PO Box 1203 North Wales PA 19454-0203

SINSHEIMER, JANET SUZANNE, MOLECULAR EVOLUTION, STATISTICAL GENETICS. *Current Pos:* ASST PROF, DEPT BIOMATH, UNIV CALIF, LOS ANGELES, 94- *Personal Data:* b Glenridge, NJ, Aug 28, 57. *Educ:* Brown Univ, ScB, 79; Brandeis Univ, MA, 84; Univ Calif, Los Angeles, MS, 88, PhD(biomath), 94. *Prof Exp:* Scientist, Roche Diagnostic Systs, Hoffmann-La Roche, 82-87. *Concurrent Pos:* Sr Statist geneticist, Wellcome Trust Ctr Human Genetics, 96-97. *Mem:* Sigma Xi; Am Women Math; Am Statist Asn. *Res:* Bayesian inference of evolutionary relationships using molecular sequence data; Bayesian diagnostics for model discrimination/assessment in phylogenetic reconstruction; designing studies for linkage analysis of quantitative traits. *Mailing Add:* Dept Biomath Univ Calif Med Sch Los Angeles CA 90095. *E-Mail:* janet@sunlab.ph.ucla.edu

SINSHEIMER, JOSEPH EUGENE, MEDICINAL CHEMISTRY, XENOBIOTIC METABOLISM. *Current Pos:* assoc prof, 60-68, prof med & pharmaceut chem, Col Pharm, 68-93, Prof Toxicol, Sch Pub Health, 80-93, EMER PROF MED CHEM & TOXICOL, UNIV MICH, ANN ARBOR, 93- *Personal Data:* b New York, NY, Dec 30, 22; m 54; c 3. *Educ:* Univ Mich, BS, 48, MS, 50, PhD(pharmaceut chem), 53. *Hon Degrees:* Dr, Univ Ghent, Belgium, 74. *Prof Exp:* Assoc technologist org chem, Gen Foods Corp, 53-57, proj leader, 57; from asst prof to assoc prof pharmaceut chem, Univ RI, 57-60. *Concurrent Pos:* Consult, Labs Criminal Invest, Univ RI, 58-60; Am Found Pharmaceut Educ Pfeiffer Mem res fel, St Mary's Med Sch, London, 72; mem comt rev, US Pharmacopeia, 75-; fel, Belgium Nat Found Sci Res, Univ Ghent, 78-79. *Mem:* Am Chem Soc; fel Am Asn Pharmaceut Sci; Am Asn Univ Professors; Environ Mutagen Soc; Soc Toxicol. *Res:* Analytical medicinal chemistry; drug metabolism; natural product and flavor chemistry; toxicology of aliphatic epoxides; genotoxicity of benzidine analogs. *Mailing Add:* Col Pharm Univ Mich Ann Arbor MI 48109-1065

SINSHEIMER, ROBERT LOUIS, BIOCHEMISTRY, BIOPHYSICS. *Current Pos:* prof, 88-90, EMER PROF BIOL, UNIV CALIF, SANTA BARBARA, 90- *Personal Data:* b Washington, DC, Feb 5, 20; m, Karen Keeton; c Lois (Wickstrom), Kathy (Vandagriff) & Roger. *Educ:* Mass Inst Technol, SB, 41, SM, 42, PhD(biophys), 48. *Hon Degrees:* DSc, St Olaf Col, 74, Northwestern Univ, 76. *Honors & Awards:* Beijerinck Virol Medal, Royal Neth Acad Sci & Lett, 69. *Prof Exp:* Res assoc biol, Mass Inst Technol, 48-49; from assoc prof to prof biophys, Iowa State Col, 49-57; prof biophys, Calif Inst Technol, 57-77, chmn div biol, 68-77; chancellor, Univ Calif, Santa Cruz, 77-87. *Concurrent Pos:* Chmn ed bd, Proc Nat Acad Sci, 72-80; mem bd sci adv, Jane Coffin Childs Fund Med Res, 73-82. *Mem:* Nat Acad Sci; Inst Med-Nat Acad Sci; Am Acad Arts & Sci; Am Soc Biol Chem; Biophys Soc (pres, 70-71). *Res:* Physical and chemical properties of nucleic acids; replication of nucleic acids; bacterial viruses; molecular biology. *Mailing Add:* Dept Biol Sci Univ Calif Santa Barbara CA 93106. *Fax:* 805-893-4724; *E-Mail:* sinsheimer@lifesci.ucsb.edu

SINSKEY, ANTHONY J, FOOD SCIENCE, MICROBIOLOGY. *Current Pos:* from asst prof to assoc prof microbiol, 67-77, PROF APPL MICROBIOL, MASS INST TECHNOL, 77- *Personal Data:* b Highland, Ill, Apr 1, 40; m 69. *Educ:* Univ Ill, BSc, 62; Mass Inst Technol, ScD(food sci), 66. *Honors & Awards:* Samuel Cate Prescott Award, 75. *Prof Exp:* Fel, Sch Pub Health, Harvard Univ, 66-67. *Mem:* Fel Am Acad Microbiol; Am Chem Soc; Inst Food Technol; Brit Soc Appl Bact; Am Soc Microbiol. *Res:* Applied microbiology; single cell protein; recovery and characterization of microorganisms; genetics of industrial microorganism; mommolion cell culture. *Mailing Add:* Dept Biol Mass Inst Technol 77 Massachusetts Ave Cambridge MA 02139-4307

SINSKI, JAMES THOMAS, MEDICAL MYCOLOGY. *Current Pos:* assoc prof, 66-92, EMER PROF MED MYCOL, UNIV ARIZ, 92- *Personal Data:* b Milwaukee, Wis, June 23, 27. *Educ:* Marquette Univ, BS, 50, MS, 52; Purdue Univ, PhD(mycol), 55; Am Bd Med Microbiol, dipl, 69. *Prof Exp:* Instr biol, Spring Hill Col, 55-57; head chem anal lab sugar ref, Am Sugar Refinery, New Orleans, 57-58; chief mycol sect, Fort Detrick, Frederick, Md, 60-66. *Concurrent Pos:* US HEW trainee med mycol, Tulane Univ, 58-60; fac, Sino-Am Advan Workshop Med Mycol, Nanjing, China, 85. *Mem:* Am Soc Microbiol; Med Mycol Soc of the Americas; Int Soc Human & Animal Mycol; fel Am Acad Microbiol. *Res:* Coccidioidomycosis; dermatomycosis. *Mailing Add:* Univ Ariz Bldg 90 Tucson AZ 85721. *Fax:* 520-621-6366; *E-Mail:* sinskij@ccit.arizona.edu

SINTON, JOHN MAYNARD, GEOLOGY, PETROLOGY. *Current Pos:* asst prof, 77-81, ASSOC PROF GEOL, UNIV HAWAII, 81- *Personal Data:* b Bozeman, Mont, Apr 12, 46; div; c 2. *Educ:* Univ Calif, Santa Barbara, AB, 69; Univ Ore, MS, 71; Univ Otago, NZ, PhD(geol), 76. *Prof Exp:* Teaching fel geol, Univ Otago, NZ, 71-75; fel mineral sci, Smithsonian Inst, 76-77. *Mem:* Am Geophys Union. *Res:* Ophiolites; the oceanic crust; Hawaiian volcanic and plutonic rocks. *Mailing Add:* Geol & Geophysics Univ Hawaii Manoa Honolulu HI 96822-2270

SINTON, STEVEN WILLIAMS, SOLID STATE PHYSICS. *Current Pos:* SR RES CHEMIST, EXXON PROD RES CO, 81- *Educ:* Univ Colo, Boulder, BS, 76; Univ Calif, Berkeley, PhD(chem), 81. *Mem:* Am Chem Soc. *Res:* Solid and liquid state nuclear magnetic resonance spectroscopy; multiphoton processes. *Mailing Add:* 21 Somerset Palo Alto CA 94301-3059

SINTON, WILLIAM MERZ, ASTRONOMY. *Current Pos:* CONSULT, 90- *Personal Data:* b Baltimore, Md, Apr 11, 25; m 60; c 3. *Educ:* Johns Hopkins Univ, AB, 49, PhD(physics), 53. *Honors & Awards:* Lomb Medal, Optical Soc Am, 54. *Prof Exp:* Asst, Johns Hopkins Univ, 49-53, res staff, 53-54; res assoc, Harvard Univ, 54-56; astrophysicist, Smithsonian Inst, 56-57; astronr, Lowell Observ, Ariz, 57-66; prof astron, Univ Hawaii, 65-90, mem, Inst Astron, 67-90. *Mem:* Optical Soc Am; Am Astron Soc; Int Astron Union; AAAS. *Res:* Infrared spectroscopy; temperatures of planets; infrared spectra of planets and stars; volcanism on Io. *Mailing Add:* 850 E David Dr Flagstaff AZ 86001-4731

SION, EDWARD MICHAEL, STELLAR STRUCTURE & EVOLUTION, STELLAR SPECTROSCOPY. *Current Pos:* asst prof astron, 75-83, assoc prof, 83-88, PROF ASTRON & ASTROPHYS, VILLANOVA UNIV, 88- *Personal Data:* b Wichita, Kans, Jan 18, 46; m 68; c 2. *Educ:* Univ Kans, BA, 68, MA, 69; Univ Pa, PhD(astrophys), 75. *Prof Exp:* Teaching asst, Ohio State Univ, 68-69; res asst, Univ Pa, 69-70, teaching fel, 71-75. *Concurrent Pos:* Prin investr, NSF, 78-, NASA, 80-; vis assoc prof physics, Ariz State Univ, 83-85; res assoc astrophys, Ctr Nat Res Sci, Toulouse, France, 90-91; vis scientist astrophys, Hubble Space Telescope Sci Inst, Baltimore, 91- *Mem:* Int Astron Union; Am Astron Soc; fel Royal Astron Soc; Sigma Xi; AAAS. *Res:* Late stages of stellar evolution, white dwarfs, cataclysmic variable stars, symbiotic stars. *Mailing Add:* Dept Astron & Astrophys 800 Lancaster Ave Villanova PA 19085

SION, MAURICE, MATHEMATICS. *Current Pos:* from asst prof to prof, 60-89, head dept, 84-86, EMER PROF MATH, UNIV BC, 89- *Personal Data:* b Skopje, Yugoslavia, Oct 17, 28; Can citizen; m 57, Emilie Chisholm; c 3. *Educ:* NY Univ, BA, 47, MS, 48; Univ Calif, PhD(math), 51. *Prof Exp:* Asst, Inst Math & Mech, NY Univ, 47-48; asst math, Univ Calif, Berkeley, 48-51, lectr, 50-51; mathematician, Nat Bur Stand, 51-52; mem, Inst Advan Study, 55-57. *Concurrent Pos:* Instr, Univ Calif, Berkeley, 52-53, asst prof, 57-60; mem, Inst Advan Study, 62; Can Coun fel, Univ Florence & Univ Pisa, 70-71; vis prof, Univ of Strasbourg, France, 74-76, Univ Paris Six, France, 86-87. *Mem:* Am Math Soc. *Res:* Measure theory. *Mailing Add:* Dept Math Univ BC Vancouver BC V6T 1Z2 Can

SIOPES, THOMAS DAVID, AVIAN PHYSIOLOGY & BIOCHEMISTRY. *Current Pos:* From asst prof to assoc prof, 78-89, PROF POULTRY SCI, NC STATE UNIV, 89- *Personal Data:* b Bremerton, Wash, July 9, 39; m 62; c 2. *Educ:* Calif State Univ, Sacramento, BA, 64; Univ Calif, Davis, MS, 72, PhD(physiol), 78. *Mem:* Poultry Sci Asn; Worlds Poultry Sci Asn; AAAS. *Res:* Environmental and reproductive physiology of birds; photo-periodism, biological rhythms and thermoregulation. *Mailing Add:* Dept Poultry Sci NC State Univ Box 7608 Raleigh NC 27695-0001

SIOUI, RICHARD HENRY, CHEMICAL ENGINEERING. *Current Pos:* Sr res engr, Grinding Wheel Div, Norton Co, 68-71, res supvr, 71-78, tech mgr, 78-81, res mgr, 81-83, dir res, Diamond Prod Div, 83-87, DIR TECHNOL, SUPERABRASIVES DIV, NORTON CO, 87. *Personal Data:* b Brooklyn, NY, Sept 25, 37; m 62, Mary Ann Kapinos; c Kathleen, Thomas, Daniel, Rebecca, Linda & Michelle. *Educ:* Northeastern Univ, BS, 64; Univ Mass, Amherst, MS, 67, PhD(chem eng), 68; Sch Indust Mgt, Worcester Polytech Inst, dipl, 76; Dartmouth Col, Tuck Exec Prog dipl, 86. *Concurrent Pos:* Mem, Stands, Safety & Health Comt, Diamond Wheel Mfg Inst. *Mem:* Am Inst Chem Engrs; Am Indian Sci & Eng Soc. *Res:* Development of new products which utilize the superabrasives--diamond and cubic boron nitride--for the grinding of hard materials much as ceramics and tool steels and processes for the manufacture of such products. *Mailing Add:* 22 Streeter Rd Hubbardston MA 01452. *E-Mail:* tsi8i@aol.com

SIPE, DAVID MICHAEL, FLOW CYTOMETRY, FLUORESCENCE. *Current Pos:* ASST PROF CHEM, WESTMINSTER COL, 96- *Personal Data:* b Yokosuka, Japan, Apr 29, 59; US citizen; m 88, Sara Ellen Yant; c Victor Scott. *Educ:* Stanford Univ, BS, 81; Carnegie Mellon Univ, PhD(biol sci & biochem), 90. *Prof Exp:* Immunochemist, Becton-Dickinson Immunocytometry Systs, 81-84; res asst biochem, Dept Biol Sci, Carnegie Mellon Univ, 84-90; postdoctoral fel biochem, Dept Path, Univ Utah, 90-92. *Concurrent Pos:* adj instr, biol & chem, Salt Lake Community Col, 93-, coordr, Biol Lab, 95- *Mem:* Sigma Xi. *Res:* Physiology and biochemistry of iron metabolism in yeast and mammalian cells; receptor-mediated endocytosis; flow cytometry; fluorescence. *Mailing Add:* 1134 S Denver St Salt Lake City UT 84111

SIPE, HARRY CRAIG, SCIENCE EDUCATION. *Current Pos:* prof, 67-82, EMER PROF TECH EDUC, STATE UNIV NY, ALBANY, 82- *Personal Data:* b Flushing, Ohio, Nov 22, 17; m 46, 70. *Educ:* Bethany Col, WVa, AB, 37; Univ Va, MA, 38; Peabody Col, PhD(sci educ), 52. *Prof Exp:* Teacher high sch, Va, 38-41; develop chemist, O'Sullivan Rubber Co, 41-42; instr physics, Bethany Col, WVa, 43-44; master, Woodberry Forest Sch, 44-46; asst prof, Mars Hill Col, 46-47; from asst prof to prof, Florence State Col, 47-54; phys scientist, Indian Springs Sch, 54-57; prof physics & sci ed, George Peabody Col, 57-67. *Concurrent Pos:* Vis prof, Ohio State Univ, 66-67. *Mem:* AAAS; Am Chem Soc; Nat Asn Res Sci Teaching (pres, 66); Nat Sci Teachers Asn; Am Asn Physics Teachers. *Res:* Theory of science education; cognitive development; teacher education. *Mailing Add:* 40 Autumn Dr No 255 Slingerlands NY 12159

SIPE, HERBERT JAMES, JR, PHYSICAL CHEMISTRY. *Current Pos:* From asst prof to prof, 68-92, chmn dept, 76-82, SPALDING PROF CHEM, HAMPDEN SYDNEY COL, 93- *Personal Data:* b Lewistown, Pa, Aug 17, 40. *Educ:* Juniata Col, BS, 62; Univ Wis-Madison, PhD(chem), 69. *Concurrent Pos:* NSF-Undergrad Res Partic grants, 72, 73, 77 & 78; NSF-ISEP grants, 73 & 78; vis prof, Univ Ala, 80-81; NSF-RUI grant, 84; NSF grant, 85, 87, 92; sabbatical leave, Nat Inst Environ Health Sci, 87-88 & 96. *Mem:* AAAS; Am Chem Soc; Sigma Xi; Am Asn Univ Professors; Int Electron Paramagnetic Resonance Soc; Oxygen Soc. *Res:* Electron paramagnetic resonance spectroscopy of organo-metallic compounds and free radical metabolites of xenobiotic compounds; endor spectroscopy. *Mailing Add:* Dept Chem Hampden-Sydney Col Hampden-Sydney VA 23943. *Fax:* 804-223-6374; *E-Mail:* herbs@tiger.hsc.edu

SIPE, JEAN DOW, ACUTE PHASE RESPONSE PROTEINS, AMYLOIDOSIS. *Current Pos:* assoc prof biochem & med, 80-92, PROF BIOCHEM, BOSTON UNIV, 92- *Personal Data:* b Decorah, Iowa, Oct 24, 41; m 66, Richard D; c Peter B & Byron L. *Educ:* Iowa State Univ, BS, 63; Univ Wash, MS, 66; Univ Md, PhD(chem), 71. *Prof Exp:* Staff scientist, Electro-Nucleonics Labs, 71-73; staff fel, Nat Inst Arthritis, Metab & Digestive Dis, 73-79; health scientist adminr, Nat Cancer Inst, 79-80. *Concurrent Pos:* Ad hoc mem, NIH, Study Sections, 89, 91 & 94; assoc ed, Amyloid, 93- *Mem:* Am Soc Biochem & Molecular Biol; Am Asn Immunol; AAAS; Am Chem Soc; Am Col Rheumatology. *Res:* Acute phase response proteins; amyloidosis; injury specific apolipoprotein family serum amyloid A; acute and chronic inflammation. *Mailing Add:* Dept Biochem Bldg K Rm 121 Boston Univ Boston MA 02118. *Fax:* 617-638-5339; *E-Mail:* jsipemed-biochem.bu.edu

SIPE, JERRY EUGENE, BIOCHEMISTRY, MICROBIOLOGY. *Current Pos:* assoc prof biol, 74-87, PROF BIOL & CHEM ANDERSON UNIV, 88- *Personal Data:* b Hickory, NC, Sept 19, 42; m 63; c 3. *Educ:* Lenoir-Rhyne Col, BS, 64; Wake Forest Univ, PhD(biochem), 69 Univ Evansville, AAS, 88. *Prof Exp:* From instr biochem to asst prof, Bowman Gray Sch Med, Wake Forest Univ, 71-74. *Concurrent Pos:* Dir teaching labs, Bowman Gray Sch Med, Wake Forest Univ, 69-74; Fulbright lectr fel biochem, Univ Nairobi, 81-83. *Mem:* AAAS; Am Soc Microbiol. *Res:* Nucleic acid methylation, especially ribosomal RNA methylation; methylation contributions to the growing cell. *Mailing Add:* Dept Biol Chem Anderson Univ Anderson IN 46011

SIPE, JOHN EDWARD, THEORETICAL PHYSICS, OPTICS. *Current Pos:* from asst prof to prof, 84-88, PROF PHYSICS, UNIV TORONTO, 88- *Personal Data:* b Detroit, Mich, Aug 15, 48; Can citizen; m 90, Margaret Grisdale. *Educ:* Brown Univ, ScB, 70; Univ Waterloo, MS, 71; Univ Toronto, PhD(physics), 75. *Prof Exp:* Asst prof, Old Dominion Univ, 80-81; Univ Toronto, 81-84. *Concurrent Pos:* Consult, Ciena Corp & Lucent Technologies; proj leader, Ont Laser & Lightwave Res Ctr, 87- *Mem:* Fel Optical Soc Am; Am Phys Soc; Can Asn Physicists. *Res:* Linear and nonlinear optical properties of semiconductors; nonlinear dynamics of systems of interest in telecommunications; effects of quantum coherence and the emergence of classical behavior. *Mailing Add:* Dept Physics Univ Toronto Toronto ON M5S 1A7 Can

SIPERSTEIN, MARVIN DAVID, BIOCHEMISTRY, INTERNAL MEDICINE. *Current Pos:* CHIEF METAB SECT, VET ADMIN HOSP, 73-; PROF MED, UNIV CALIF, SAN FRANCISCO, 73- *Personal Data:* b Minneapolis, Minn, Sept 21, 25; m 52; c 3. *Educ:* Univ Minn, BS, 46, MB, 47, MD, 48; Univ Calif, PhD(physiol), 53. *Honors & Awards:* Marchman Award, 59; Lilly Award, Am Diabetes Asn, 59. *Prof Exp:* From asst prof to prof internal med, Univ Tex Health Sci Ctr Dallas, 64-73. *Concurrent Pos:* NIH res career award, 61-73. *Mem:* AAAS; Am Soc Biol Chem; Am Soc Clin Invest; Soc Exp Biol & Med; Asn Am Physicians (pres, 79-80). *Res:* Control of isoprene synthesis in normal and cancer cells; diabetes. *Mailing Add:* Vet Admin Med Ctr 111-F 4150 Clement St San Francisco CA 94121-1598. *Fax:* 415-750-6927

SIPES, BRENT STEVEN, NEMATOLOGY. *Current Pos:* Jr researcher, 91-92, ASST PROF PLANT PATH, UNIV HAWAII, MANOA, 93- *Personal Data:* b Indianapolis, Ind, Oct 26, 60; m 94, SukMei Ho. *Educ:* Purdue Univ, BS, 83; NC State Univ, MS, 87, PhD(plant path), 90. *Concurrent Pos:* Lectr plant path, Univ Hawaii, Manoa, 91. *Mem:* Soc Nematologists; Am Phytopath Soc; Soc Study Evolution; Orgn Trop Nematologist; Afro-Asian Soc Nematologist. *Res:* Nematode control in tropical cropping systems; elucidating the population genetics of plant-parasitic nematodes. *Mailing Add:* Dept Plant Path Univ Hawaii 3190 Maile Way Honolulu HI 96822. *Fax:* 808-956-2832; *E-Mail:* sipes@hawaii.edu

SIPES, IVAN GLENN, PHARMACOLOGY, TOXICOLOGY. *Current Pos:* from asst prof to assoc prof, 73-82, PROF & HEAD PHARMACOL & TOXICOL, COL PHARM, UNIV ARIZ, 82-, PROF & HEAD PHARMACOL, COL MED, 93-, DIR CTR TOXICOL, 94- *Personal Data:* b Tarentum, Pa, July 26, 42. *Educ:* Univ Cincinnati, BS, 65; Univ Pittsburgh, PhD(pharmacol), 69. *Prof Exp:* Staff fel pharmacol, Nat Heart, Lung & Blood Inst, 69-71; sr staff fel, 71-73. *Concurrent Pos:* Spec lectr, George Washington Univ, 71-73; assoc ed, Life Sci J, 73-; fel, Off Naval Res, 77-, Nat Inst Environ Health Sci, 77-79 & 78-83, Nat Cancer Inst, 77-80 & Int Union Pharmacol, Toxicol Sect; ed, Toxicol & Appl Pharmacol, 85-93, NAS/NRC Comt Toxicol & Bd Environ Studies & Toxicol; Burroughs Wellcome toxicol scholar award, 85-93. *Mem:* Soc Toxicol (pres, 93-94); Am Soc Pharmacol & Exp Therapeut; Am Asn Cancer Res; Am Asn Study Liver Dis; AAAS. *Res:* Role of biotransformation in drug or xenobiotic induced liver injury; organohalogen induced chemical carcinogenesis; pharmacokinetics of xenobiotics; disposition of polychlorinated biphenyls; halothane induced hepatitis. *Mailing Add:* Dept Pharmacol & Toxicol Univ Ariz Col Pharm PO Box 210207 Tucson AZ 85721-0207. *Fax:* 510-626-2466; *E-Mail:* sipes@tonic.pharm.arizona.edu

SIPKIN, STUART A, GEOPHYSICS, SEISMOLOGY. *Current Pos:* GEOPHYSICIST, CENT REG GEOL TEAM, US GEOL SURV, 79- *Personal Data:* b Washington, DC, Aug 23, 49. *Educ:* Calif Inst Technol, BS, 71; Princeton Univ, MA, 75, Univ Calif, PhD(earth sci), 79. *Mem:* Seismol Soc Am; Am Geophys Union. *Mailing Add:* US Geol Surv Fed Ctr MS 967 Box 25046 Denver CO 80225. *Fax:* 303-273-8450; *E-Mail:* sipkin@gldfs.cr.usgs.gov

SIPOS, FRANK, PEPTIDE CHEMISTRY. *Current Pos:* sr res investr, Squibb Inst Med Res, 70-81, CHEM PROCESS TECHNICIAN, E R SQUIBB, 81- *Personal Data:* b Lucenec, Czech, July 13, 26; div; c 2. *Educ:* Charles Univ, Prague, Dr nat, 51; Czech Acad Sci, PhD(org chem), 56. *Honors & Awards:* Czech State Prize, 63. *Prof Exp:* Teaching asst pharmaceut chem, Charles Univ, 48-51; scientist, Inst Org Chem & Biochem, Czech Acad Sci, 51-65; sr res chemist, Norwich Pharmacal Co, 66-70. *Mem:* Am Chem Soc. *Res:* Reaction mechanism; stereochemistry; synthesis of polypeptides. *Mailing Add:* 2325 Tamalpais Ave El Cerrito CA 94530-1511

SIPOS, TIBOR, BIOCHEMISTRY, MICROBIOLOGY. *Current Pos:* PRES & VPRES RES & DEVELOP, DIGESTIVE CARE, INC, 90- *Personal Data:* b Budapest, Hungary, May 13, 35; US citizen; m 59, Elizabet J Bramwell; c Tibor Jr, Miklos & Gabor. *Educ:* Lebanon Valley Col, BS, 64; Lehigh Univ, PhD(biochem), 68. *Honors & Awards:* Philip B Hofmann Res Scientist Award, 78; Johnson, Medal, 82. *Prof Exp:* Sr res scientist enzymol, Wallerstein Co, Baxter Labs, 68-69; sr res scientist enzymol, 69-74, res assoc, Johnson & Johnson Res, 74-77, sr res assoc, 77-78, asst mgr, 78-79, mgr consumer prod care res, 80-87, dir res, Johnson & Johnson Dental Care, Co, 87-90. *Concurrent Pos:* Adj asst prof med, Col Med & Dent, NJ Med Sch, 74-; NIH/SBIR consult, 88-; adj prof chem, Lehigh Univ, 90- *Mem:* AAAS; Am Chem Soc; Am Soc Microbiol; Int Asn Dent Res. *Res:* Application of enzymes in the health care field; development of advanced therapeutic modalites for cystic fibrosis and cholestotic liver diseases; prevention of dental caries, gingivitis and periodontitis; development of a targeted drug delivery systems. *Mailing Add:* 75 Bissell Rd Lebanon NJ 08833-9331. *Fax:* 215-861-8247

SIPOSS, GEORGE G, BIOMEDICAL ENGINEERING. *Current Pos:* PRES, UNIVERSAL CONSULT DEVELOPMENTS, 89- *Personal Data:* b Hungary, Apr 18, 31; m 57, Glenna; c 4. *Educ:* Can Inst Sci & Technol, dipl advan mech eng, 59; Pepperdine Univ, MBA, 76. *Honors & Awards:* IR-100 Award, 80. *Prof Exp:* Pres, Delta Med Industs, 75-83; pres & chief exec officer, Am Onni Med Inc, 85-91. *Concurrent Pos:* Consult & lectr, var co, univs & insts, 71- *Mem:* Nat Asn Prof Engrs. *Res:* Open heart surgery disposable valves, filters, oxygenators; ambulatory insulin pumps. *Mailing Add:* 2855 Velasco Lane Costa Mesa CA 92626

SIPPEL, THEODORE OTTO, ANATOMY. *Current Pos:* from asst prof to assoc prof, 59-69, PROF ANAT, SCH MED, UNIV MICH, ANN ARBOR, 69- *Personal Data:* b West Englewood, NJ, Aug 19, 27; m 52; c 2. *Educ:* Univ Rochester, AB, 48; Yale Univ, PhD(zool), 52. *Prof Exp:* From instr to asst prof biol, Johns Hopkins Univ, 52-57; sr instr anat, Sch Med, Western Reserve Univ, 57-59. *Concurrent Pos:* Nat Eye Inst sr fel anat, Univ Dundee, 71-72; res assoc, Kresge Eye Inst, Mich, 64-65. *Mem:* Asn Res Vision & Ophthal; Am Asn Anat; Histochem Soc. *Res:* Metabolism of the lens; histochemistry. *Mailing Add:* Dept Anat 4643 Med Sci 2 Univ Mich Med Sch 1301 Catherine Rd Ann Arbor MI 48109-0600

SIPRESS, JACK M, LIGHTWAVE COMMUNICATIONS, UNDERSEA COMMUNICATIONS. *Current Pos:* mem tech staff, AT&T Bell Labs, NJ, 58-61, supvr, Digital Transmission Studies Group, 61-69, head, T2 Digital Line Dept, 69-72, T4M Digital Line Dept, 72-76, Satellite Transmission Dept, 76-79, Lightwave Syst Develop Dept, 78-79, dir, Transmission Technol Lab, 80, vpres devel & mfg submarine systs, 89-92, CHIEF TECH OFFICER & SR VPRES RES & DEVELOP, SUBMARINE SYSTS, AT&T BELL LABS, 92- *Personal Data:* b Brooklyn, NY, Apr 9, 35; m 56, Sydelle; c Alan & Joel. *Educ:* Polytech Inst Brooklyn, BEE, 56, MEE, 57, DrEE, 61. *Honors & Awards:* Edwin Howard Armstrong Achievement Award, Inst Elec & Electronics Engrs Commun Soc, 88, Int Commun Award, 91; Simon Remo Medal, Inst Elec & Electronics Engrs, 94. *Prof Exp:* sr res asst & teaching fel, Microwave Res Inst & Elec Eng Dept, Polytech Inst Brooklyn, 56-58. *Mem:* Fel Inst Elec & Electronics Engrs. *Res:* Light wave and undersea communications; fifteen technical papers/talks related to design of active RC networks, digital transmission and underseas communications. *Mailing Add:* AT&T Submarine Syst 101 Crawfords Corner Rd Holmdel NJ 07733-3030. *Fax:* 732-949-3833; *E-Mail:* jsipress@attmail.com

SIPSON, ROGER FREDRICK, PHYSICS. *Current Pos:* From asst prof to assoc prof, 68-97, PROF PHYSICS, MOORHEAD STATE UNIV, 97- *Personal Data:* b Buffalo, NY, Oct 7, 40; m 67. *Educ:* Union Col, NY, BS, 62; Syracuse Univ, PhD(physics), 68. *Mem:* Am Asn Physics Teachers. *Res:* Quantum theory of fields; mathematical physics. *Mailing Add:* 2503 Rivershore Dr Moorhead MN 56560

SIQUIG, RICHARD ANTHONY, UNDERWATER ACOUSTICS. *Current Pos:* SR TECH ASSOC, OCEAN DATA SYSTS, INC, 80- *Personal Data:* b Gilroy, Calif, Feb 2, 42; m 74. *Educ:* Calif Inst Technol, BS, 66; Univ Colo, MS, 71, PhD(astrophys), 74. *Prof Exp:* Vis asst prof astron, Ohio State Univ, 74-75; vis asst prof, Univ Wis-Madison, 75-76; res assoc, Hamburg Observ, 76-77; vis scientist, Nat Ctr Atmospheric Res, 78-79; res assoc, Univ Colo, 79. *Mem:* Am Geophys Union. *Res:* Stability of stellar models during their evolution; solar variability and climate; planetary atmosphere cooling rates. *Mailing Add:* 54 Middle Canyon Rd Carmel Valley CA 93924

SIRAGANIAN, REUBEN PAUL, IMMUNOLOGY. *Current Pos:* HEAD SECT CLIN IMMUNOL, LAB IMMUNOL, NAT INST DENT RES, NIH, 73- *Personal Data:* b Aleppo, Syria, Feb 7, 40; US citizen; m 70, Patricia Cimperman; c Lisa M & Jennifer L. *Educ:* Am Univ Beirut, BS, 59; State Univ NY Downstate Med Ctr, MD, 62; Johns Hopkins Univ, PhD(immunol), 68. *Prof Exp:* Assoc mem immunol, Pub Health Res Inst New York, 68-73. *Concurrent Pos:* Res career develop award, NIH, 70-73, mem immunobiol study sect, 74-78, mem, Allergy & Clin Immunol Comt, Nat Inst Allergy & Infectious Dis, 79-83; asst prof med, NY Univ, 71-73. *Mem:* Am Asn Immunol; Am Acad Allergy; AAAS; Am Soc Clin Invest. *Res:* Inflammation; immediate hypersensitivity reactions. *Mailing Add:* Lab Immunol Nat Inst Dent Res NIH Bldg 10 Rm 1N106 Bethesda MD 20892-0001. *Fax:* 301-480-8328; *E-Mail:* rs53x@nih.gov

SIRAGUSA, GREGORY ROSS, FOOD SAFETY, RAPID METHODOLOGY FOR FOOD BORNE INFECTIOUS DISEASE. *Current Pos:* MICROBIOLOGIST, USDA-AGR RES SERV, 90- *Personal Data:* b New Orleans, La, Jan 15, 60; m 82; c 1. *Educ:* La State Univ, BS, 82, MS 85; Univ Ark, PhD(food microbiol), 89. *Concurrent Pos:* Adj asst prof, Univ Ark, 92- *Mem:* Am Soc Microbiol; Soc Indust Microbiol; Sigma Xi; Inst Food Technologists; Int Asn Milk, Food, Environ Sanitarians. *Res:* Microbial food safety; develop methods to conduct real time assays; isolate and characterize antimicrobial proteins for potential food use; produce and characterize monoclonal antibodies for foodborne infectious disease detection. *Mailing Add:* 3100 Outrigger Dr Hastings NE 68901-2547. *Fax:* 402-762-4149; *E-Mail:* siragusa@marcvm.marc.usda.gov

SIRBASKU, DAVID ANDREW, BIOCHEMISTRY, CELL BIOLOGY. *Current Pos:* from asst prof to assoc prof, 72-86, PROF BIOCHEM, UNIV TEX MED SCH, HOUSTON, 86- *Personal Data:* b St Paul, Minn, Nov 25, 41; m 64, Donna Jenkins; c Sarah & Rachel. *Educ:* Col St Thomas, BA, 63; Univ Ill, PhD(biochem), 67. *Prof Exp:* NIH fel, Mass Inst Technol, 67-70; NIH spec fel, Univ Calif, San Diego, 70-72. *Concurrent Pos:* Grant reviewer, NIH, Am Chem Soc, NSF, NATO US Army Res & Develop Prog, Am Cancer Soc; recipient, fac res award, Am Cancer Soc, 80-85. *Mem:* Am Soc Cell Biol; Endocrine Soc; Am Chem Soc; AAAS; Am Tissue Cult Asn; Am Asn Cancer Res. *Res:* Hormonal control of cell growth; growth promoting serum factors. *Mailing Add:* Dept Biochem & Molecular Biol Univ Tex Med Sch 6431 Fannin St Houston TX 77030-1504. *Fax:* 713-794-4150

SIRCAR, ANIL KUMER, POLYMER CHEMISTRY. *Current Pos:* polymer res scientist, Ctr Basic & Appl Polymer Res, 85-93, CONSULT, UNIV DAYTON, 93- *Personal Data:* b Calcutta, India, Jan 1, 28; m 52; c Polly, Nahash & Tapash. *Educ:* Univ Dacca, BS, 48, MS, 49; Univ Calcutta, DPhil(polymer chem), 55. *Prof Exp:* Chemist, Sindri Fertilizers & Chem Ltd, India, 51-52; res asst polymer chem, Indian Asn Cultivation Sci, 52-57; NSF fel emulsion polymerization, Univ Minn, 58; res officer rubber chem, Indian Asn Cultivation Sci, 58-59; sr sci officer, Indian Rubber Mfrs Res Asn, 60; sect mgr rubber lab, Nat Rubber Mfrs Ltd, 60-65; Nat Acad Sci res assoc cotton fiber, Southern Regional Res Lab, USDA, 65-67; res chemist, 67-81, J Huber Corp, sr scientist, 81-83; anal scientist, Engelhardt Corp, 83-84. *Concurrent Pos:* Mem bd examrs, Univ Calcutta, 62-65 & Indian Inst Technol, Kharagpur, India, 75. *Mem:* Fel NAm Thermal Anal Soc; Am Chem Soc; Soc Plastics Engrs; SAMPE; Inst Confederation Thermal Anal. *Res:* Physical chemistry of polymers; rubber reinforcement, processing and compounding; thermal and thermomechanical analysis; cotton fiber; polyelectrolytes; polymer blends; material science; vibration clamping. *Mailing Add:* Res Inst Univ Dayton 300 College Park Dayton OH 45469-0131. *Fax:* 937-229-3433; *E-Mail:* strca@udri.udayton.edu

SIRCAR, ILA, synthetic organic chemistry, medicinal research, for more information see previous edition

SIRCAR, JAGADISH CHANDRA, organic chemistry, medicinal chemistry, for more information see previous edition

SIREK, ANNA, PHYSIOLOGY, SURGERY. *Current Pos:* Res assoc, Banting R Best Dept Med Res, Univ Toronto, 54-60, lectr, 60-63, from asst prof to prof, 63-86, dir, Dept Teaching Labs, 75-86, EMER PROF PHYSIOL, 86- *Personal Data:* b Velke Senkvice, Slovak, Jan 12, 21; Can citizen; m 46, Otakar; c Ann, Jan, Peter & Terese. *Educ:* Univ Bratislava, MD, 46; Univ Toronto, MA, 55, PhD, 60. *Honors & Awards:* Hoechst Centennial Medal, Frankfurt, Ger, 66. *Concurrent Pos:* Vis fel surg, Kronprinsessan Lovissas Barnsjukhus, Stockholm, Sweden, 47-50; fel, Hosp Sick Children, Toronto, Ont, 50-54; asst dir, Dept Teaching Labs, Univ Toronto, 69-75; vis prof, Dept Physiol, Sackler Sch Med, Univ Tel-Aviv, 78. *Mem:* Can Fedn Biol Socs; Int Diabetes Fedn; Can Endocrine Soc; Can Diabetic Asn; Soc Exp Biol & Med. *Res:* Metabolic studies in animals deprived of endocrines by experimental surgery and the response of diabetic and Houssay animals to insulin and growth hormone. *Mailing Add:* Dept Physiol Med Sci Bldg Univ Toronto Toronto ON M5S 1A1 Can

SIREK, OTAKAR VICTOR, PHYSIOLOGY, ENDOCRINOLOGY. *Current Pos:* Res assoc, Banting & Best Dept Med Res, 50-57, from asst prof to prof, 57-87, EMER PROF PHYSIOL, FAC MED, UNIV TORONTO, 87- *Personal Data:* b Bratislava, Slovak, Dec 1, 21; Can citizen; m 46, Anna Janek; c Ann, Jan, Peter & Terese. *Educ:* Univ Bratislava, MD, 46; Univ Toronto, MA, 51, PhD(physiol), 54. *Honors & Awards:* Hoechst Centennial Medal, Frankfurt, Ger, 66; C H Best Prize, Can Workshops Diabetes, 75. *Concurrent Pos:* Vis fel biochem, Wenner Gren Inst, 47-50; asst biochemist, Hosp Sick Children, Toronto, 55-57; vis scientist, La Rabida Inst, Univ Chicago, 62-63; vis prof, Univ Calif, Los Angeles, 67 & Univ Tel-Aviv, 78. *Mem:* Am Diabetes Asn; Am Physiol Soc; Endocrine Soc; Int Diabetes Fedn; Can Fedn Biol Soc. *Res:* Diabetes mellitus in humans and experimental animals; effect of hormones on vascular connective tissue. *Mailing Add:* Dept Physiol Med Sci Bldg Univ Toronto Toronto ON M5S 1A8 Can

SIRI, WILLIAM E, BIOPHYSICS, ENERGY & ENVIRONMENT. *Current Pos:* RETIRED. *Personal Data:* b Philadelphia, Pa, Jan 2, 19; m 49, Margaret J Brandenburg; c Margaret L & Ann K. *Educ:* Univ Chicago, BSc, 42. *Honors & Awards:* Hubbard Medal, Nat Geog Soc, 63; Sol Feinstone Environ Award, 77. *Prof Exp:* Res engr, Baldwin-Lima-Hamilton Corp, 43; physicist, Manhattan Proj, Lawrence Berkeley Lab, Univ Calif, 43-45, prin investr biophys & res, 45-74, mgr, Energy Anal Prog, 74-81, emer sr scientist, 81. *Concurrent Pos:* Lectr, Univ Calif Summer Inst, 62-72; vis scientist, Nat Cancer Inst, 70; exec vpres, Am Mt Everest Exped; consult energy & environ, 82-; gov gen, Mountain Med Inst, 88- *Mem:* Am Phys Soc; Biophys Soc; Am Asn Physicists Med; Sigma Xi. *Res:* Nuclear radiations and isotopic tracers; energy systems analyses. *Mailing Add:* 1015 Leneve Pl El Cerrito CA 94530-2751

SIRIANNI, JOYCE E, PHYSICAL & DENTAL ANTHROPOLOGY. *Current Pos:* From asst prof to prof, 72-92, DISTINGUISHED PROF PHYS ANTHROP, STATE UNIV NY, BUFFALO, 92-, VPROVOST GRAD EDUC & DEAN GRAD SCH, 92- *Personal Data:* b Niagara Falls, NY, Apr 27, 42. *Educ:* State Univ NY Buffalo, BA, 65, MA, 67; Univ Wash, PhD(phys anthrop), 74. *Mem:* Am Asn Phys Anthropologists; Int Primatol Soc; Am Asn Anatomists; AAAS; Am Asn Dental Res; Am Soc Primatologists; Can Asn Phys Anthropologists. *Res:* Study of normal craniofacial growth and development in old world monkeys; study of the normal range of dental variability seen in old world monkeys. *Mailing Add:* Dept Anthrop State Univ NY 365 MFAC Elliott Complex Buffalo NY 14261. *E-Mail:* apyjoyce@ubvms.bitnet

SIRICA, ALPHONSE EUGENE, LIVER CARCINOGENESIS, LIVER CELL CULTURE. *Current Pos:* assoc prof, 84-90, PROF, DEPT PATH, MED COL VA, 90-, CHAIR, DIV EXP PATH, 92- *Personal Data:* b Waterbury, Conn, Jan 16, 44; m, Annette M Murray; c Gabrielle T & Nicholas S. *Educ:* St Michaels Col, BA, 65; Fordham Univ, MS, 68; Univ Conn Health Ctr, PhD(biomed sci), 76. *Prof Exp:* Res assoc cancer chemother, Microbiol Assocs Cancer Chemother Res Lab, 69-71; fel trainee chem carcinogenesis, McArdle Lab Cancer Res, 76-79; asst prof anat & hepatic path, Med Sch, Univ Wis, 79-84. *Concurrent Pos:* Prin investr, NIH Grant, 81-83, 81-84, 84-87, 88-89, 88-90, 91-; mem, Sci Adv Comt Carcinogenesis & Nutrit, Am Cancer Soc, 89-92; ed, Pathobiol Neoplasia, 89; organizer & dir, symp & workshop pathobiol of neoplasia, 89 & 93; mem, metab path study sect, NIH, 91- *Mem:* Am Asn Cancer Res; Am Soc Cell Biol; Tissue Cul Asn; AAAS; NY Acad Sci; Am Soc Investigative Path; Asn Clin Scientists; Am Asn Study Liver Dis; Soc Exp Biol & Med. *Res:* Pathobiology of hepatocarcinogenesis and cholangiocarcinogenesis; pathology of intrahepatic biliary epithelium; bile ductular cell culture; regulation of biliary cell differentiation; growth neoplastic transformation of biliary cells in vivo and in culture. *Mailing Add:* Dept Path Med Col Va Va Commonwealth Univ PO Box 980297 Richmond VA 23298-0297. *Fax:* 804-786-9749

SIRIGNANO, WILLIAM ALFONSO, COMBUSTION. *Current Pos:* DEAN & PROF MECH ENG, SCH ENG, UNIV CALIF, IRVINE, 85- *Personal Data:* b Bronx, NY, Apr 14, 38; m 77, Lynn Haisfield; c Jacqueline, Monica & Justin. *Educ:* Rensselaer Polytech Inst, BAEng, 59; Princeton Univ, MA, 62, PhD(aeronaut aerospace & mech sci), 64. *Honors & Awards:*

Pendray Aerospace Lit Award, Am Inst Aeronaut & Astronaut, 91; Propellants & Combustion Award, 92; Freeman Scholar Fluids Eng Award, Am Soc Mech Engrs, 92; Oppenheim Award, Inst Dynamics Explosions & Reactive Systs, 93. *Prof Exp:* Mem res staff, Guggenheim Labs, Princeton Univ, 64-67, asst prof mech & aero eng, from assoc prof, to prof, 69; Ladd prof & head mech eng, Carnegie-Mellon Univ, 79-84. *Concurrent Pos:* Consult, indust & govt, 66-; lectr & consult, aeronaut res & develop, NATO Adv Group, 67, 75 & 80; chmn, Nat & Int Tech Conferences, Acad Adv Coun, Indust Res Inst, 85-88 & Combustion Sci Microgravity Disciplinary Working Group, 87-90; mem, Space Sci Applications Adv Comt, NASA, 85-90 & Comt Microgravity Res, Space Studies Bd, Nat Res Coun, 90-; assoc ed, Combustion Sci & Technol, 69-70; tech ed, J Heat Transfer, 85-92; United Aircraft Res fel, 73-74; treas int orgn & chmn, Eastern Sect, Combustion Inst. *Mem:* Fel Am Inst Aeronaut & Astronaut; Soc Indust & Appl Math; fel Am Soc Mech Engrs; Soc Automotive Engrs; fel AAAS; Combustion Inst. *Res:* Theoretical, computational and some experimental studies of turbulent reacting flows, spray combustion, fuel-droplet heating and vaporization, ignition, combustion instability, and fire safety; contributed articles to national and international professional journals, also research monographs. *Mailing Add:* Univ Calif 3202 Engr Gateway Bldg Irvine CA 92717

SIRIWARDANE, UPALI, BORON CHEMISTRY, ORGANOMETALLIC CHEMISTRY. *Current Pos:* asst prof, 89-93, ASST PROF CHEM, LA TECH UNIV, 93- *Personal Data:* b Columbo, Sri Lanka, Mar 16, 50; m 78, Nilanthi; c Mevan. *Educ:* Univ Sri Lanka, BSc, 76; Concordia Univ, Can, MSc, 81; Ohio State Univ, Columbus, PhD(chem), 85. *Prof Exp:* Asst analyst, Govt Analyst's Dept, Columbo, Sri Lanka, 76-77; res officer minerals technol, Ceylon Inst Sci & Indust Res, 77-79; res assoc organometallic chem, Southern Methodist Univ, 86-87, staff crystallogr, 87-89. *Mem:* Am Chem Soc; Sigma Xi. *Res:* Synthesis and characterization of air-sensitive organometallic compounds using vacuum line and inert atmosphere techniques; structure determination using x-ray crystallography and multi-nuclear nuclear magnetic resonance spectroscopy; computations and graphics using personal computers; glass blowing. *Mailing Add:* PO Box 3159 Ruston LA 71272. *Fax:* 318-257-4912; *E-Mail:* upali@latech.edu

SIRKEN, MONROE GILBERT, MATHEMATICAL STATISTICS, APPLIED STATISTICS. *Current Pos:* dir, Div Health Records Statist, Nat Ctr Health Statist, 63-67, dir, Off Statist Methods, 67-73, chief math statistician & statist adv, 73-76, assoc dir math statist, 76-80, assoc dir Res & Methodology, 80-97, SR RES SCIENTIST, NAT CTR HEALTH STATIST, 97- *Personal Data:* b New York, NY, Jan 11, 21; m 54; c 2. *Educ:* Univ Calif, Los Angeles, BA, 46, MA, 47; Univ Wash, PhD(sociol & math statist), 50. *Honors & Awards:* Roger Harriot Award for Innovations in Federal Statist. *Prof Exp:* Soc Sci Res Coun fel, Univ Calif, Berkeley, 50-51; math statistician & soc sci analyst, US Bur Census, 51-53; actuary, Nat Off Vital Statist, 53-55, chief, Actuarial Anal & Surv Methods Br, Vital Statist Div, 55-63. *Concurrent Pos:* Lectr, Dept Prev Med, Sch Med, Univ Wash, 50; ed collabr, Am Statist Asn, 60-72; adj prof, Sch Pub Health, Univ NC, 68-70, mem fac, 68-; vis prof, Sch Pub Health, Univ Calif, Berkeley, 71; adv consult, Nat Inst Neurol & Communicative Disorders & Stroke, 75- *Mem:* AAAS; fel Am Statist Asn; Int Statist Inst; Pop Asn Am; Am Pub Health Asn. *Res:* Investigation of errors of measurement in population data systems and designs of efficient sample surveys; Survey sampling, cognition and survey research. *Mailing Add:* Nat Ctr Health Statist 6525 Belcrest Rd Rm 915 Hyattsville MD 20782. *E-Mail:* mgs2@ncho9a.em.cec.gov

SIRKIN, ALAN N, CONSTRUCTION RELATED ACTIVITIES. *Current Pos:* PRIN ENGR, ALAN SIRKIN CONSULT ENGRS, 69- *Personal Data:* b Newark, NJ, June 3, 44; m 73; c 1. *Educ:* Univ Miami, BS, 67; Ga Inst Technol, MS, 69. *Concurrent Pos:* Pres construct, Sirkin Bldg Corp; partner real estate, Sirkin Enterprises; mem, Subsurface Drainage Task Force & Environ Qual Control Bd; reviewer, Urban Planning J. *Mem:* Am Soc Civil Engrs; Nat Asn Homebuilders. *Mailing Add:* One Lincoln Rd Bldg Suite 217 Miami Beach FL 33139

SIRKIN, LESLIE A, GEOLOGY, PALYNOLOGY. *Current Pos:* CONSULT GEOL, 68- *Personal Data:* b Dover, Del, Sept 18, 33; m 59; c 3. *Educ:* Hamilton Col, BA, 54; Cornell Univ, MS, 57; NY Univ, PhD(geol), 65. *Prof Exp:* From asst prof to prof earth sci, Adelphi Univ, 62-96, chmn dept, 67-75, 83-87 & 90-93. *Mem:* AAAS; fel Geol Soc Am; Am Asn Stratig Palynologists; Int Asn Quaternary Res. *Res:* Mesozoic, Cenozoic stratigraphy; environmental geology. *Mailing Add:* Dept Earth Sci Adelphi Univ Garden City NY 11530-4299

SIRLIN, ALBERTO, THEORETICAL PARTICLE PHYSICS. *Current Pos:* from asst to assoc prof, 59-68, PROF PHYSICS, NEW YORK UNIV, 68- *Personal Data:* b Buenos Aires, Arg, Nov 25, 30; m 63, Sonia; c Claude Bernard & Diana Karina. *Educ:* Univ Buenos Aires, Dr(phys & math sci), 53; Cornell Univ, PhD(physics), 58. *Prof Exp:* Res assoc physics, Columbia Univ, 57-59. *Concurrent Pos:* NSF res grant, 70-; Guggenheim Found fel, 83; adj prof physics, Rockefeller Univ, 85-91. *Mem:* Am Phys Soc. *Res:* Theoretical particle physics; weak and electromagnetic interactions; unified gauge theories; precision electroweak physics. *Mailing Add:* Dept Physics NY Univ 4 Washington Pl New York NY 10003

SIRLIN, JULIO LEO, REPRODUCTIVE BIOLOGY, NEUROSCIENCES. *Current Pos:* assoc prof, 67-73, PROF, DEPT ANAT, MED COL, CORNELL UNIV, 73- *Personal Data:* b Buenos Aires, Argentina, Dec 18, 26; m 68; c 2. *Educ:* Univ Buenos Aires, BSc, 50, DSc, 54. *Prof Exp:* Res fel genetics, Dept Biol, Univ Chile, 51-52; res assoc, Dept Animal Genetics, Univ Endinburgh, 53-59, mem staff, 60-61. *Mem:* Int Cell Res Orgn. *Res:* Fertilizing capacity of human spermatozoa: functional and structural correlates. *Mailing Add:* Dept Anat Cornell Univ Med Campus 1300 York Ave New York NY 10021-4805

SIROIS, DAVID LEON, PLANT PHYSIOLOGY. *Current Pos:* RETIRED. *Personal Data:* b Skowhegan, Maine, Oct 15, 33; m 67; c 3. *Educ:* Univ Maine, BS, 61, MS, 63; Iowa State Univ, PhD(plant physiol), 67. *Prof Exp:* From asst prof to prof plant physiologist, Boyce Thompson Inst Plant Res, 67-90. *Mem:* Plant Growth Regulator Soc Am; Weed Sci Soc Am; Sigma Xi. *Res:* Effects of exogenous chemical compounds on plant growth including herbicides and plant growth regulators with particular interest in chemicals with potential for enhancing crop yields. *Mailing Add:* 3 Highgate NE Ithaca NY 14850

SIROIS, PIERRE, IMMUNOPHARMACOLOGY. *Current Pos:* asst prof, 78-83, assoc prof, 83-87, PROF PHARMACOL, UNIV SHERBROOKE, 87- *Personal Data:* b Que, Can, Dec 12, 45; m 73; c Caroline R. *Educ:* Univ Laval, Que, BA, 67; Univ Sherbrooke, BSc, 71, MSc, 72, PhD(pharmacol), 75. *Prof Exp:* Fel, Royal Col Surgeons, Eng, 75-77 & Hosp Sick Children, Toronto, 77-78. *Concurrent Pos:* Instr, Regionale L'estrie, Sherbrooke, 69-71 & Col Sherbrooke, 72-74; fel, Imp Col Sci & Technol, 76-77; scientist award, Med Res Coun, 87-92. *Mem:* Brit Pharmacol Soc; Can Soc Clin Invest; Can Soc Immunologists; Fr-Can Asn Advan Sci; Am Soc Pharmacol Exp Therapeut; Pharmacol Soc Can. *Res:* Non-respiratory functions of lungs; mediators of hypersensitivity; leukotrienes; asthma, endothelin, inflammation, lung cells; infrared-rated pilot. *Mailing Add:* Dept Pharmacol Fac Med Univ Sherbrooke Sherbrooke PQ J1H 5N4 Can. *Fax:* 819-564-5400; *E-Mail:* p.sirois@courrier.usherb.ca

SIROTA, JONAS H, experimental biology; deceased, see previous edition for last biography

SIROTNAK, FRANCIS MICHAEL, MOLECULAR PHARMACOLOGY, GENETICS. *Current Pos:* from asst prof to assoc prof, 63-76, PROF PHARMACOL, SLOAN-KETTERING DIV, MED COL, CORNELL UNIV, 76-; MEM, SLOAN KETTERING INST CANCER RES, 75- *Personal Data:* b Throop, Pa, Aug 10, 31. *Educ:* Univ Scranton, BS, 52; Univ NH, MS, 53; Univ Md, PhD(microbiol), 56. *Prof Exp:* Asst microbiol, Agr Exp Sta, Univ NH, 51-52; asst, Univ Md, 52-54; bacteriologist, US Army Chem Corps, 56-57. *Concurrent Pos:* Nat Cancer Inst career develop award, 66; res assoc, Mem Sloan Kettering Inst Cancer Res, 57-59, assoc, 59-66, assoc mem, 66-75, sect head, 67-74, lab head, 74-; instr, Fairleigh-Dickinson Univ, 58-59; asst prof, Long Island Univ, 61- *Mem:* Am Soc Microbiol; Am Asn Cancer Res; NY Acad Sci; AAAS; Am Asn Pharmacol & Exp Therapeut. *Res:* Chemotherapy and drug resistance; biochemical genetics; biochemical control mechanisms; genetics of neoplastic transformation; molecular pharmacology of anticancer agents. *Mailing Add:* Mem Sloan-Kettering Cancer Ctr 1275 York Ave New York NY 10021-6094. *Fax:* 212-794-4342

SIROVICH, LAWRENCE, APPLIED MATHEMATICS. *Current Pos:* from asst prof to assoc prof, 63-67, PROF APPL MATH, BROWN UNIV, 67- *Personal Data:* b Brooklyn, NY, Mar 1, 33; m 60; c 2. *Educ:* Johns Hopkins Univ, AB, 56, PhD, 60; Brown Univ, MA, 65. *Prof Exp:* Res scientist appl math, Courant Inst Math Sci, NY Univ, 62-63. *Concurrent Pos:* Fulbright fel, Free Univ Brussels, 61-62; prof, Inst Henri Poincare, Univ Paris, 68-69; vis prof, Rockefeller Univ, 71-72, adj prof, 72-; Guggenheim fel, 78-79; ed, Appl Math Sci, Quart Appl Math & Bull Sci Math; assoc managing ed, Soc Indust & Appl Math J. *Mem:* AAAS; Am Phys Soc; Am Math Soc. *Res:* Applied mathematics; kinetic theory of gases; fluid dynamics; biophysics; asymptotic analysis. *Mailing Add:* 37 Riverside Dr New York NY 10023. *Fax:* 401-863-2722

SIRRIDGE, MARJORIE SPURRIER, HEMATOLOGY, LABORATORY MEDICINE. *Current Pos:* DOCENT & PROF INTERNAL MED & HEMAT, SCH MED, UNIV MO, KANSAS CITY, 71-, ASST DEAN CURRIC, 85- *Personal Data:* b Kingman, Kans, Oct 6, 21; m 44; c 4. *Educ:* Kans State Univ, BS, 42; Univ Kans, MD, 44. *Prof Exp:* Pvt pract hemat, 55-71. *Concurrent Pos:* Consult, Providence-St Margaret's Health Ctr, 60-, Children's Mercy Hosp, 83- *Mem:* Am Soc Hemat; AMA. *Res:* Antithrombin III; platelet function studies; monitoring heparin therapy; hypercoagulability; lupus anticoagulant. *Mailing Add:* Sch Med Univ Mo 2411 Holmes St Kansas City MO 64108-2741

SIRTORI, CARLO, PHYSICS. *Current Pos:* RES SCIENTIST, AT&T BELL LABS. *Honors & Awards:* New Comb Cleveland Prize, AAAS, 93 & 94. *Mailing Add:* AT&T Bell Labs 600 Mountain Ave New Providence NJ 07974-2008

SIRY, JOSEPH WILLIAM, MATHEMATICS, PHYSICS. *Current Pos:* head theory & anal br, Vanguard Div, 58-59, head theory & planning staff, Beltsville Space Ctr, 59, CHIEF THEORY & ANAL STAFF & DIR TRACKING & DATA SYSTS DIRECTORATE, GODDARD SPACE FLIGHT CTR, NASA, 59- *Personal Data:* b New York, NY, Aug 7, 20; m 44; c 2. *Educ:* Rutgers Univ, BS, 41; Univ Md, MA, 47, PhD(math), 53. *Prof Exp:* Mem, Actuarial Div, Metrop Life Ins Co, 40-42; physicist, Naval Res Lab, 46-58, actg head theoret anal sect, Rocket-Sonde Res Br, 49-51, head, 51-53, lectr, 53, consult, 53-56, head theory & anal br, Proj Vanguard, 56-58, chmn, Vanguard Working Group on Orbits, 56-59. *Concurrent Pos:* Lectr grad math, Univ Md, 53-55; exec secy, Upper Atmosphere Rocket Res Panel, Spec Comt, Int Geophys Year, 54 & rep, US Nat Comt Spec Comt Meeting, Moscow, 58; lectr space technol, Univ Calif, 58; vis lectr, Univ Tex, 58; mem, Equatorial Range Comt, NASA, 59; vis lectr, NY Univ, 60; Am Geophys Union deleg, Gen Assembly Int Union Geodesy & Geophys, Helsinki, 60; mem comt high atmosphere, Int Asn Geomagnetism & Aeronomy. *Mem:* Am Math Soc; Am Astron Soc. *Res:* Chromatic polynomials; topology; compressible fluids; ionosphere; cosmic rays; orbit determination; flight mechanics; astrodynamics; upper atmosphere densities; space research, science and technology. *Mailing Add:* 4438 42 St NW Washington DC 20016-2104

SIS, RAYMOND FRANCIS, VETERINARY ANATOMY, AQUATIC ANIMAL MEDICINE. *Current Pos:* assoc prof, 66-68, head dept, 68-83, PROF VET ANAT, TEX A&M UNIV, 68- *Personal Data:* b Munden, Kans, July 22, 31; m 53, Janice Murphy; c Susan, Valerie, Mark, Michael & Amy. *Educ:* Kans State Univ, BS, 53, DVM & BS, 57; Iowa State Univ, MS, 62, PhD(vet anat), 65. *Prof Exp:* Asst vet clins, Iowa State Univ, 61-62, instr vet anat, 62-64, asst prof vet clin sci, 64-66. *Concurrent Pos:* Bd dir, Int Asn Aquatic Animal Med, 85-87 & 91-94. *Mem:* Am Vet Med Asn; Int Asn Aquatic Animal Med; Am Asn Vet Anat; World Asn Vet Anat. *Res:* Surgical anatomy; radiographic anatomy of the cat; feline anatomy and physiology; histology of marine fish and marine mammals. *Mailing Add:* Dept Vet Anat & Publ Health Tex A&M Univ College Station TX 77843. *Fax:* 409-847-8981

SISCOE, GEORGE L, space physics, for more information see previous edition

SISCOVICK, DAVID STUART, PREVENTIVE CARDIOLOGY, CLINICAL EPIDEMIOLOGY. *Current Pos:* ASSOC PROF MED & EPIDEMIOL, HARBORVIEW MED CTR, 88-; CO-DIR, CARDIOVASC HEALTH RES UNIT, UNIV WASH, 91- *Personal Data:* b Baltimore, Md, Feb 19, 51; m 75; c 3. *Educ:* Univ Pa, Philadelphia, BA, 71; Univ Md, MD, 76; Univ Wash, Seattle, MPH, 81. *Prof Exp:* Intern internal med, Univ Wash, Seattle, 76-77, resident internal med, 77-79, resident prev med & actg instr med, 79-81; clin asst prof epidemiol, Dept Epidemiol, Sch Pub Health & asst prof med, Dept Med, Sch Med, Univ NC, 81-88, res assoc, Health Serv Res Ctr, 82-88, educ health professions, Sch Med, 85-88. *Concurrent Pos:* Fels, US Teaching Sem Epidemiol & Prev Cardiovasc Dis, Am Heart Asn-Nat Heart, Lung & Blood Inst, 78 & Stud Work Shop Epidemiol Methods, Soc Epidemiol Res, Nat Cancer Inst; teaching & res scholar, Am Col Physicians, 84-87; assoc ed, J Gen Internal Med, 85-; prev cardiol award, Nat Heart, Lung & Blood Inst, 86-90; reviewer, J Chronic Dis, Annals Internal Med & Health Serv Res; consult, Ctr Dis Control, Behav Epidemiol & Eval, Army Phys Fitness Res Inst, World Health Orgn, Community Health, Vet Admin Health Serv Res; assoc fel, Coun Epidemiol, Am Heart Asn, 86. *Mem:* Am Heart Asn; Soc Prev Cardiol; Am Fedn Clin Res; Soc Res & Educ Primary Internal Med; Am Col Physicians. *Res:* Cardiovascular epidemiology and preventive cardiology health services; physical activity, lipids, alcohol, hypertension, coronary heart disease and sudden cardiac death. *Mailing Add:* 5781 S Eddy St Seattle WA 98118-3070

SISENWINE, SAMUEL FRED, DRUG METABOLISM, ORGANIC CHEMISTRY. *Current Pos:* Sr chemist, Wyeth Ayerst Res, 66-71, group leader, Metab Chem Sect, 71-78, corp radiation health safety officer, 71-85, mgr, Drug Diposition Sect, 78-85, assoc dir, 85-87, dir, drug metab div, 87-97, CHIEF SCIENTIST, WYETH AYERST RES, 97- *Personal Data:* b Philadelphia, Pa, Dec 30, 40; m 62, Phyllis; c 3. *Educ:* Philadelphia Col Pharm, BSc, 62; Univ Pa, PhD(chem), 66. *Mem:* Am Soc Pharmacol & Exp Therapeut; Int Soc Study Xenobiohes. *Res:* Absorption, distribution, excretion and biotransformation; pharmacokinetics, species differences in drug metabolism. *Mailing Add:* Drug Metab Div Wyeth Ayerst Res CN 8000 Princeton NJ 08543-8000. *Fax:* 732-274-0334

SISKA, PETER EMIL, PHYSICAL CHEMISTRY, CHEMICAL PHYSICS. *Current Pos:* from asst prof to assoc prof, 71-91, PROF CHEM, UNIV PITTSBURGH, 91- *Personal Data:* b Evergreen Park, Ill, Apr 11, 43; m 67; c 2. *Educ:* DePaul Univ, BS, 65; Harvard Univ, AM, 66, PhD(chem), 70. *Prof Exp:* Res assoc chem, James Franck Inst, Univ Chicago, 70-71. *Concurrent Pos:* Alfred P Sloan Found res fel, 75. *Mem:* Am Chem Soc; Am Phys Soc. *Res:* Molecular dynamics of chemical reactions and energy transfer; intermolecular forces; crossed molecular beam studies; model calculations of collision dynamics and electronic structure. *Mailing Add:* Dept Chem Univ Pittsburgh Pittsburgh PA 15260. *E-Mail:* pes@vms.cis.pitt.edu

SISKEN, JESSE ERNEST, CELL BIOLOGY. *Current Pos:* assoc prof, 67-75, PROF MICROBIOL & IMMUNOL, COL MED, UNIV KY, 75- *Personal Data:* b Bridgeport, Conn, Dec 7, 30; m 54; c 3. *Educ:* Syracuse Univ, AB, 52; Univ Conn, MS, 54; Columbia Univ, PhD(bot, cytochem), 57. *Prof Exp:* Asst bot, Univ Conn, 53-54; res asst bot & cytochem, Columbia Univ, 54-55; res assoc, City of Hope Med Ctr, 57-60, assoc res scientist, 60-66, scientist, 66-67. *Mem:* Am Soc Cell Biol; Int Cell Cycle Soc (pres, 84-86); Soc Anal Cytol; NY Acad Sci; Am Asn Advan Sci; Sigma Xi; Cell Kinetics Soc. *Res:* Nucleic acid and protein synthesis in the mitotic cycle; population kinetics of proliferating cells; regulation of cell metabolism related to cell division; role of calcium in regulation of proliferation and cell division and cell metabolism. *Mailing Add:* Dept Microbiol & Immunol Univ Ky Med Ctr Lexington KY 40536-0048

SISKIN, MICHAEL, ORGANIC CHEMISTRY, AQUEOUS CHEMISTRY. *Current Pos:* RESEARCHER CHEM, EXXON RES & ENG CORP, 69- *Personal Data:* b Brooklyn, NY, June 30, 43. *Educ:* City Univ NY, BS, 65; Univ Pa, PhD(org chem), 68. *Prof Exp:* Fel phys & org chem, Harvard Univ, 68-69. *Mem:* Am Chem Soc; AAAS. *Res:* Aqueous chemistry; coal shale structure and activity. *Mailing Add:* Exxon Res & Eng Corp Products Res Div PO Box 51 Linden NJ 07036

SISKIN, MILTON, ORAL MEDICINE, ENDODONTICS. *Current Pos:* RETIRED. *Personal Data:* b Cleveland, Tenn, May 14, 21; m 48. *Educ:* Univ Tenn, BA, 42, DDS, 45; Am Acad Oral Med, dipl; Am Bd Endodontics, dipl, 63. *Honors & Awards:* Hinman Medallion, 66. *Prof Exp:* From intern to resident, Walter G Zoller Mem Dent Clin, Billings Hosp, Univ Chicago, 46-47; from instr to assoc prof oral med & surg, Col Dent, Univ Tenn, Memphis, 47-64, chief div oral med & surg & head dept oral med, 55-58, prof oral med & surg, 64-86, lectr, Grad Sch Orthod & Dept Gen Anat & Embryol, 54-86. *Concurrent Pos:* Consult various orgns & hosps, 51-; Am Dent Asn del, Int Dent Cong, 62; asst ed, J Dent Med, 63; ed, Biol Human Dent Pulp, 73; ed endodontics sect, Clin Dent, 75 & Oral Surg, Oral Med & Oral Path, 75-; dir, Registry Periapical Lesions, Am Asn Endodontists, 65-66 & Am Col Stomatologic Surgeons; mem rev bd, Am Asn Endodontists & Nat Med AV Ctr; mem bd, Am Bd Endodontics, 63-69 & 71-73; mem exec comt, Am Cancer Soc, 71-72, bd dirs, 71-72; mem exec comt, Am Inst Oral Sci, 66-; mem, Coun Fed Dent Serv, Am Dent Asn, 71-; Am Dent Europe lectr, 62; lectr, Can Govt & Can Asn Endodontists, 70, Brit Dent Soc, 72, Royal Col Denmark, 74 & Int Dent Congress, 74. *Mem:* AAAS; fel Am Col Dent; fel Am Acad Oral Path; fel Am Asn Endodont; Am Acad Oral Med. *Res:* Oral diagnosis; pathology. *Mailing Add:* 5180 Park Ave Memphis TN 38119

SISKIND, GREGORY WILLIAM, IMMUNOLOGY. *Current Pos:* assoc prof, 69-76, head, Div Allergy & Immunol, 69-92, PROF MED, MED SCH, CORNELL UNIV, 76-, ASSOC DEAN RES & SPONSORED PROGS, 85- *Personal Data:* b New York, NY, Mar 3, 34. *Educ:* Cornell Univ, BA, 55; NY Univ, MD, 59. *Prof Exp:* From instr to asst prof med, Med Ctr, NY Univ, 65-69. *Concurrent Pos:* Res fel microbiol, Sch Med, Wash Univ, 61-62; fel biol, Harvard Univ, 62-64; fel med, Med Ctr, NY Univ, 64-65. *Mem:* AAAS; Am Asn Immunol; Am Acad Allergy & Immunol; Am Soc Clin Invest; Am Asn Phys. *Res:* Runting syndrome; immunologic tolerance; heterogeneity of antibody binding affinity and changes in antibody affinity during immunization; antigenic competition; idiopathic thrombocytopenic purpura; ontogeny of B-lymphocyte function; regulation of the immune response by auto-anti-idiotype antibody; IqD. *Mailing Add:* Off Res & Spousound Prog Cornell Univ Med Col 1300 York Ave New York NY 10021-4896. *Fax:* 212-746-8745; *E-Mail:* gsiskind@mail.med.cornel.edu

SISLER, CHARLES CARLETON, CHEMICAL ENGINEERING. *Current Pos:* Eng supvr, Monsanto Co, 53-64, eng mgr, 64-69, res mgr chem intermediates, 69-78, res mgr spec chem, 78-81, MGR PROCESS DEVELOP NUTRIT CHEM, MONSANTO CO, 81- *Personal Data:* b Oklahoma City, Okla, Jan 13, 22; m 57; c 3. *Educ:* Mich State Univ, BS, 59, MS, 54. *Mem:* Am Inst Chem Engrs; Am Chem Soc; Sci Res Soc Am. *Res:* Food and feed chemicals. *Mailing Add:* 762 Oak Valley Dr St Louis MO 63131-3933

SISLER, EDWARD C, PLANT PHYSIOLOGY. *Current Pos:* from asst prof to assoc prof, 61-85, PROF BIOCHEM, NC STATE UNIV, 85- *Personal Data:* b Friendsville, Md, Jan 25, 30. *Educ:* Univ Md, BS, 54, MS, 55; NC State Univ, PhD, 58. *Prof Exp:* Res assoc, Brookhaven Nat Lab, 58-59; biochemist, Smithsonian Inst, 59-61. *Concurrent Pos:* Vis prof, Univ Calif, Davis, 82, Hebrew Univ Jerusalem, Rehouot, Israel, 83-84. *Res:* Role of boron in plants; electron transport; citric acid and glyoxylate cycles in the purple sulfur bacteria; nucleotide phosphates levels as affected by visible radiation; alkaloid metabolism; ethylene action in plants. *Mailing Add:* Biochem NC State Univ Box 7622 Raleigh NC 27695-0001

SISLER, GEORGE C, PSYCHIATRY. *Current Pos:* lectr, Univ Man, 52-54, head dept, 54-75, prof psychiat, 54-89, PSYCHIATRIST, HEALTH SCI CTR, UNIV MAN, 75-, SR SCHOLAR, FAC MED, 89- *Personal Data:* b Winnipeg, Man, Dec 28, 23; m 48; c 2. *Educ:* Univ Man, MD, 46; FRCP(C), 55. *Prof Exp:* Resident, Winnipeg Psychopath Hosp, 47-49 & Norton Mem Infirmary, 50-51; resident neurol, Louisville Gen Hosp, 51-52. *Concurrent Pos:* Clin instr, Univ Louisville, 50-52; clin dir, Winnipeg Psychopath Hosp, 52-54; chief psychiatrist, Winnipeg Gen Hosp, 54-75; psychiatrist, St Boniface Gen Hosp, 54-90; Sandoz traveling prof, 64. *Mem:* Fel Am Psychiat Asn; Can Psychiat Asn. *Res:* Psychopathology of organic brain damage; teaching and learning process in psychiatry. *Mailing Add:* 771 Bannatyne Ave Rm 202 Winnipeg MB R3E 3N4 Can

SISLER, HARRY HALL, CHLORAMINATION REACTIONS, HIGH ENERGY FUELS. *Current Pos:* prof & chmn, 56-68, dean arts & sci, 68-70, exec vpres, 70-73, dean, Grad Sch, 73-79, DISTINGUISHED SERV PROF CHEM, UNIV FLA, 79- *Personal Data:* b Ironton, Ohio, Mar 13, 17; m 78, Hannelore Lina Wass; c Elizabeth Ann, David Franklin, Raymond Keith & Susan Carol. *Educ:* Ohio State Univ, BSc, 36; Univ Ill, MSc, 37, PhD(chem), 39. *Hon Degrees:* DSc, Adam Mickewiec Univ, Poznan, Poland, 77. *Honors & Awards:* James Flack Norris Award, Am Chem Soc, 79. *Prof Exp:* Instr chem, Chicago City Col, 39-41; from instr to assoc prof chem, Univ Kans, 41-46; from asst prof to prof, Ohio State Univ, 46-56. *Concurrent Pos:* Chem consult, W R Grace & Co, 51-75, Koppers Co, 56-59, Batelle Mem Inst, 64-67, Tenn Valley Authority, 67, Martin Marietta, 74-77, Naval Ordinance Lab, Indian Head, Md, 74-77 & Mats Technol, Inc, 82-83; NSF lectr various univs, 55-80; mem chem adv panel, NSF, 59-62 & Oak Ridge Nat Lab, 62-66; Sloan vis prof chem, Harvard Univ, 62-63. *Mem:* Am Chem Soc. *Res:* Inorganic nitrogen and phosphorus chemistry; molecular addition compounds; hydrazine, chloramine and triazanium; salt chemistry. *Mailing Add:* Dept Chem Univ Fla Gainesville FL 32611

SISLER, HUGH DELANE, PLANT PATHOLOGY. *Current Pos:* Asst, Univ Md, 53-55, from asst prof to prof, 55-89, chmn, Dept Bot, 73-77, EMER PROF PLANT PATH, UNIV MD, COLLEGE PARK, 90- *Personal Data:* b Friendsville, Md, Nov 4, 22; m 50, Patricia H Smith; c Barbara, Roger & Nancy. *Educ:* Univ Md, BS, 49, MS, 51, PhD(bot), 53. *Honors & Awards:* Pour le Merite Medal, 92. *Concurrent Pos:* Ed, Phytopath, Am Phytopath Soc, 60-63; mem fel rev panel, NIH, 61-; NIH spec fel, State Univ Utrecht, Neth, 66- *Mem:* AAAS; fel Am Phytopath Soc; AAAS; Pesticide Sci Soc Japan; Sigma Xi. *Res:* Fungicidal action; fungus physiology; viruses. *Mailing Add:* 10004 Emack Rd Beltsville MD 20705

SISSENWINE, MICHAEL P, BIOLOGICAL OCEANOGRAPHY, FISHERIES BIOLOGY. *Current Pos:* SR SCIENTIST, NAT MARINE FISHERIES SERV, NOAA, 91- *Personal Data:* b Washington, DC, Feb 16, 47. *Educ:* Univ Mass, BS, 69; Univ RI, PhD(oceanog), 75. *Prof Exp:* Res assoc oceanog, Univ RI, 73-75; opers res analyst & chief, Fisheries Systs Invest, Northeast Fisheries Ctr, Nat Marine Fisheries Serv, 75-91, dep chief, Resource Assessment Div, 80-91, chief, Fisheries Ecol Div, 85-91. *Concurrent Pos:* Consult, US Environ Protection Agency, 76-; US mem Demersal Fish Comt, Int Coun Explor Sea, Copenhagen, 77- *Mem:* Am Fisheries Soc; Int Estuarine Res Fedn. *Res:* Fish population dynamics; fisheries management systems; trophic interrelationships in marine ecosystems; biological systems models and simulations. *Mailing Add:* Nat Marine Fisheries Serv NOAA 166 Water St Woods Hole MA 02543-0197

SISSOM, LEIGHTON E(STEN), MECHANICAL ENGINEERING, ACCIDENT RECONSTRUCTION. *Current Pos:* PRES, SISSOM & ASSOCS, INC, 78- *Personal Data:* b Manchester, Tenn, Aug 26, 34; m 53, Evelyn Lee; c Terry & Denny. *Educ:* Mid Tenn State Col, BS, 56; Tenn Polytech Inst, BSME, 62; Ga Inst Technol, MSME, 64, PhD(mech eng), 65. *Honors & Awards:* Marlowe Award, Am Soc Eng Educ, 88,; Scrievner Award, Am Soc Safety Engrs, 89; Gold Vector Award, Pan-Am Fedn Eng Soc, 94. *Prof Exp:* Draftsman, Westinghouse Elec Corp, 53-57; mech designer, ARO, Inc, 57-58; instr eng sci, Tenn Polytech Inst, 58-61 & mech eng, 61-62; prof mech eng & chmn dept, Tenn Tech Univ, 65-79, dean eng, 79-88, prof mech eng, 88-89. *Concurrent Pos:* Eng consult industs, ins co, law firms & govt agencies, 64-; secy-treas, vpres & pres, Tenn Tech Eng Develop Found, Inc, 70-; evaluator, Southern Asn Cols & Schs; chmn, Eng Deans Coun, 84-87; bd dir, Accreditation Bd Eng & Technol, 80-86, Am Soc Eng Educ, 84-87. *Mem:* Fel Am Soc Mech Engrs; fel Am Soc Eng Educ (pres, 91-92); Soc Automotive Engrs; Nat Soc Prof Engrs; fel Nat Acad Forensic Engrs. *Res:* Fluid handling; energy utilization; products liability; accident reconstruction; product liability; author or coauthor of over 100 publications, including 4 books. *Mailing Add:* Sissom & Assocs Inc 1151 Shipley Church Rd Cookeville TN 38501-7730. *Fax:* 615-526-9123; *E-Mail:* les8220@tntech.edu

SISSOM, STANLEY LEWIS, INVERTEBRATE ZOOLOGY, AQUATIC ECOLOGY. *Current Pos:* asst prof, 67-70, assoc prof, 70-77, PROF BIOL, SOUTHWEST TEX STATE UNIV, 77- *Personal Data:* b Italy, Tex, June 19, 32; m 60; c 2. *Educ:* NTex State Univ, BS, 54, MS, 59; Tex A&M Univ, PhD(zool), 67. *Prof Exp:* Instr biol, NTex State Univ, 59-61, Lamar State Col, 61-63 & Tex A&M Univ, 65-67. *Mem:* Am Micros Soc; Crustacan Soc; Am Soc Zoologists. *Res:* Taxonomy and ecology of phyllopod crustaceans; ecology of temporary ponds; limnology. *Mailing Add:* Dept Biol SW Tex State Univ San Marcos TX 78666-4602

SISSON, DONALD VICTOR, APPLIED STATISTICS. *Current Pos:* from assoc prof toprof, appl statist & comput sci, 66-87, asst dean, Col Sci, 71-82 & 87-88, asst dean sci, 76-87, head, Appl Statist Dept, 82-87, PROF STATIST & EXP STA STATIST, UTAH STATE UNIV, 76- *Personal Data:* b East Chain, Minn, Apr 18, 34; m 60, Dorothy Jean Dewey; c 4. *Educ:* Gustavus Adolphus Col, BS, 56; Iowa State Univ, MS, 58, PhD(entom & statist), 62. *Prof Exp:* Asst prof appl statist, Utah State Univ, 59-60 & 62-65, assoc prof, 65-66; biol statistician, Abbott Labs, Ill, 66. *Concurrent Pos:* Vis assoc prof statist, NC State Univ, 75-76; statist consult, Nepal, 87. *Mem:* Biomet Soc. *Res:* Biological statistics; design and analysis of experiments. *Mailing Add:* Agr Exp Sta UMC 4810 Utah State Univ Logan UT 84322

SISSON, GEORGE ALLEN, OTOLARYNGOLOGY. *Current Pos:* prof, 68-89, EMER PROF OTOLARYNGOL-HEAD & NECK SURG & CHMN DEPT, SCH MED, NORTHWESTERN UNIV, CHICAGO, 92-; PROF DEPT OTOLARYNGOL & BRACHOESOPHAGOLOGY, RUSH MED COL, 93- *Personal Data:* b Minneapolis, Minn, May 11, 20; m 44; c 3. *Educ:* Syracuse Univ, AB, 42, MD, 45; Am Bd Otolaryngol, Cert. *Honors & Awards:* Francis Lederer Mem Lectr, 71; Fitzhugh Mem lectr, 82; John Conley Spec lectr, 86; James Harrill Mem lectr, 87; John Hopkins Broyles Mem lectr, 88; Joseph Ogura Mem lectr, 88; Frederick Turnbull Mem lectr, 91; Hayes Martin Mem Lectr, 92. *Prof Exp:* Clin instr otolaryngol, State Univ NY Upstate Med Ctr, 51-54, from clin instr to clin asst prof surg, 51-68, from clin asst prof to clin prof otolaryngol, 55-68. *Concurrent Pos:* Fel, Head & Neck Serv, Manhattan Eye, Ear & Throat Hosp, NY, 52-53; mem exec comt, Bd Dirs & Exam, Am Bd Otolaryngol; mem adv coun, Head & Neck Cancer Cadre, Nat Inst Neurol Dis & Stroke. *Mem:* Am Cancer Soc; Am Laryngol, Rhinol & Otol Soc; AMA; Am Col Surg; Am Acad Otolaryngol-Head & Neck Surg. *Res:* Cancer of the head and neck. *Mailing Add:* 303 E Chicago Ave Chicago IL 60611-3008

SISSON, GEORGE MAYNARD, PHYSIOLOGY, PHARMACOLOGY. *Current Pos:* RETIRED. *Personal Data:* b Boston, Mass, Feb 3, 22; div; c Barbara C, Brenda H & Richard L. *Educ:* Tufts Col, BS, 43; Univ Rochester, PhD(physiol), 52. *Prof Exp:* Asst, Univ Rochester, 48-49; jr physiologist, Brookhaven Nat Lab, 52; Nat Res Coun fel, Columbia Univ, 52-54; group leader pharmacol res, Am Cyanamid Co, 54-59; asst dir dept pharmacol, US Vitamin & Pharmaceut Corp, 59-61; dir pharmaceut prod info, Mead Johnson Res Ctr, 61-66, dir sci info & regulatory affairs, 66-77, dir drug regulatory affairs, 77-87; consult, Adria Labs, Dublin, Ohio, 88-90. *Mem:* AAAS; Drug Info Asn; NY Acad Sci; Am Thoracic Soc; Am Fedn Clin Res. *Res:* Regulatory activities; pharmacodynamics; clinical pharmacology; toxicology; chronic obstructive lung disease; normal and pathological renal function; peripheral and cerebral vascular disease. *Mailing Add:* 4800 Ridge Knoll Dr Evansville IN 47710

SISSON, HARRIET E, pharmacy; deceased, see previous edition for last biography

SISSON, JOSEPH A, PATHOLOGY. *Current Pos:* RETIRED. *Personal Data:* b San Diego, Calif, Oct 24, 30; m 59; c 2. *Educ:* San Diego Col, BA, 55; Wash Univ, MD, 60. *Prof Exp:* Res asst biochem, Scripps Clin, La Jolla, Calif, 55-56; intern path, Yale Univ New Haven Med Ctr, Conn, 60-61; resident, Albany Med Ctr, NY, 61-64; from instr to asst prof, Albany Med Col, 63-67; asst prof path, Creighton Univ, 68-69, chmn dept, 68-73, prof, 69-80; prof path, Eastern Va Med Sch, 80-83. *Concurrent Pos:* Fel, Albany New Med Col, 61-63; res grant, 65-67; asst attend pathologist, Albany Med Ctr Hosp, 65-67; attend pathologist, Vet Admin Hosp, Albany, NY, 66-67; dir path, Creighton Mem St Joseph's Hosp, 68-72; consult radiologist, US Vet Admin Hosp, Omaha, 68- *Mem:* Am Asn Path & Bact; Am Soc Exp Path. *Res:* Amino acid and lipid metabolism in pregnancy; biochemical aspects of atherosclerosis and thrombosis. *Mailing Add:* PO Box 1189 Casper IL 82682

SISSON, RAY L, ELECTRICAL ENGINEERING. *Current Pos:* RETIRED. *Personal Data:* b Pueblo, Colo, Apr 24, 34; m 52, Dixie L McConnell; c Mark L, Bryan K & Tammy S. *Educ:* Univ Colo, BSEE, 60; Colo State Univ, MS, 66; Univ Northern Colo, EdD(voc educ), 73. *Honors & Awards:* James H McGraw Award, Am Soc Eng Educ, 90. *Prof Exp:* Asst res engr, Univ Colo Exp Sta, 60; asst engr, Parker & Assoc, Consult Engrs, 61-62; prof eng, Univ Southern Colo, 60-63, head dept, 63-69, head electronics & instrumentation, 68-73, dir elec area instr, 68-73, dean appl sci & eng technol, 73-96. *Concurrent Pos:* Consult, Exec Sys Prob Oriental Lang, 79; chmn, Eng Technol Leadership Inst, 84-87; consult, NMex Highlands Univ, 85-90, Mooreheat State Univ, State Univ NY, Alfred & Farmingdale, 85; prog evaluate, Tech Adv Comt Accreditation Bd Eng Technol, Inst Elec & Electronics Engrs; chmn eng technol coun, Am Soc Eng Educ, 86-88, bd dirs, 86-88; chmn, Eng Spectrum Task Force, Am Soc Eng Educ, 88; vchmn tech accredited comm, Accred Bd Eng & Tech, 93- *Mem:* Am Soc Eng Educ; Inst Elec & Electronics Engrs. *Res:* Electrical networks; computer science; feedback control; antenna studies research. *Mailing Add:* 403 Starlite Dr Pueblo CO 81005

SISTEK, VLADIMIR, ANATOMY, SURGERY. *Current Pos:* asst prof anat, 69-73, ASSOC PROF ANAT, UNIV OTTAWA, 73- *Personal Data:* b Prague, Czech, Sept 22, 31; m 54; c 3. *Educ:* Charles Univ, Prague, MD, 56, PhD(surg), 67. *Prof Exp:* Resident surg, Regional Hosp, Most, Czech, 56-59; mem staff, Charles Univ, Prague, 59-63, asst prof surg, 63-68. *Mem:* Can Asn Anat; Can Fedn Biol Socs. *Res:* Surgical anatomy; gastroenterology; medical education. *Mailing Add:* Dept Anat Fac Med Univ Ottawa 451 Smyth Rd Ottawa ON K1H 8M5 Can

SISTERSON, JANET M, NUCLEAR & MEDICAL PHYSICS. *Current Pos:* res fel, 73-79, RES ASSOC PHYSICS, CYCLOTRON LAB, HARVARD UNIV, 73- *Personal Data:* b Edinburgh, Scotland, July 7, 40; m 65; c 2. *Educ:* Univ Durham, UK, BSc, 61; Univ London, UK, DIC & PhD(physics), 65; CAS, Radcliffe Col, 89. *Prof Exp:* Basic grade physicist, London Hosp, 64-66; sr physicist, Chelsea Hosp Women, London, 66-68; res fel physics, Cambridge Electronic Accelerator, 68-73. *Mem:* Am Phys Soc; Am Asn Physicist Med; Meteoritical Soc; Am Women Sci. *Res:* Medical applications of proton beams; isotope cosmochemistry. *Mailing Add:* Harvard Univ 44 Oxford St Cambridge MA 02138. *E-Mail:* sisterson@huhepl.harvard.edu

SISTO, FERNANDO, AEROELASTICITY, TURBOMACHINERY. *Current Pos:* from assoc prof to prof, Stevens Inst Technol, 58-79, head dept, 66-79, dean, Grad Sch 93-94, GEORGE M BOND PROF MECH ENG, STEVENS INST TECHNOL, 79-, EMER GEORGE M BOND PROF, 96- *Personal Data:* b Spain, Aug 2, 24; US citizen; m 46, Grace Wexler; c Jane (Long), Ellen & Todd. *Educ:* US Naval Acad, BS, 46; Mass Inst Technol, ScD, 52. *Hon Degrees:* MEng, Stevens Inst Technol, 62. *Honors & Awards:* Maury prize in physics, 45. *Prof Exp:* Chief propulsion div, Res Div, Curtiss-Wright Corp, 52-58. *Concurrent Pos:* Consult, Curtiss-Wright Corp, NJ, 58-60, Gen Elec Co, Ohio, 59-63, Gen Motors, Ind, 66-70, United Technol Corp, Conn, 73-79 & Westinghouse Corp, Philadelphia, 80-84; UNESCO-United Nations Develop Prog consult, Nat Aeronaut Lab, Bangalore, India, 78; lectr, Academia Sinica, China, 81; chair, Int Symp Airbreathing Engines, Bangalore, 81 & Beijing, China, 85, Int Gas Turbine Conf, London, 82; rep, NSF workshop powerplant dynamics, Nat Aeronaut Lab, Bangalore, India, 88. *Mem:* Assoc fel Am Inst Aeronaut & Astronaut; fel Am Soc Mech Engrs; Sigma Xi. *Res:* Aeroelasticity of turbomachines; turbomachinery theory; aerodynamics, unsteady flow; flight propulsion; applied mechanics; energy conversion; fluid dynamics; author of several publications. *Mailing Add:* Dept Mech Eng Stevens Inst Technol Castle Point Hoboken NJ 07030-5991. *Fax:* 201-216-8315

SISTRUNK, WILLIAM ALLEN, FOOD TECHNOLOGY, BACTERIOLOGY. *Current Pos:* RETIRED. *Personal Data:* b Mitchell, La, June 29, 19; m 45; c 5. *Educ:* Southwestern La Inst, BS, 47; Ore State Col, MS, 49, PhD, 59. *Prof Exp:* Mkt specialist, USDA, 49-52; assoc horticulturist, Univ Ark, Fayetteville, 62-68, prof food sci, 68-88. *Mem:* Am Soc Hort Sci; Inst Food Technol. *Res:* Biochemistry; new horticultural varieties; plant nutrition effects on processing quality; objective tests for measuring quality of fruits and vegetables. *Mailing Add:* 1307 Success St Carthage TX 75633

SIT, WILLIAM YU, ALGEBRA. *Current Pos:* Lectr, 71-72, instr, 72-73, asst prof, 73-80, ASSOC PROF MATH, CITY COL CITY UNIV NEW YORK, 80- *Personal Data:* b Hong Kong, Feb 18, 44; m 70. *Educ:* Univ Hong Kong, BA, 67; Columbia Univ, MA, 69, PhD(math), 72; City Col City Univ NY, MS, 78. *Mem:* Math Asn Am; Am Math Soc. *Res:* Differential algebra; invariants of differential dimension polynomials. *Mailing Add:* 5901 Liebig Ave Bronx NY 10471-1609

SITAR, DANIEL SAMUEL, CLINICAL PHARMACOLOGY, PHARMACOLOGY. *Current Pos:* from asst prof to assoc prof, 78-87, PROF MED & PHARMACOL, FAC MED, UNIV MAN, 87- *Personal Data:* b Thunder Bay, Ont, May 1, 44; m 68; c 2. *Educ:* Univ Man, BSc, 66, MSc, 68, PhD(pharmacol), 72. *Prof Exp:* Teaching fel pharmacol, Fac Med, Univ Man, 68-71; assoc fel, Univ Minn Sch Med, 71-73; lectr, Fac Med, McGill Univ, 73-75; asst prof med, 74-78, asst prof pharmacol, 75-78; res asst, Div Clin Pharmacol, Montreal Gen Hosp Res Inst, 73-78. *Concurrent Pos:* Monat Scholar, McGill Univ, 75-78; sci staff, Health Sci Ctr, Univ Man & Deer Lodge Ctr, Winnipeg, 78-; Rh Inst grant, 80; res grant, Man Heart Found, 83-; Rosenstadt prof, Univ Toronto, 89-90. *Mem:* Am Soc Pharmacol & Exp Therapeut; Can Soc Clin Invest; Soc Toxicol Can; Pharmacol Soc Can; Am Soc Clin Pharmacol & Therapeut; fel Gerontol Soc Am; Can Soc Clin Pharmacol. *Res:* Effects of development and disease on drug disposition and effect in man. *Mailing Add:* Dept Pharmacol & Therapeut Univ Man Winnipeg MB R3E 0W3 Can. *Fax:* 204-783-6915; *E-Mail:* sitar@cc.umanitoba.ca

SITARAMAN, YEGNASESHAN, ANALYSIS APPROXIMATION. *Current Pos:* PROF, MATH, KY WESLEYAN COL, 88- *Personal Data:* b India, Oct 26, 36. *Educ:* Banaras Univ, MA, 50; Univ Kerala, PhD(math), 67. *Prof Exp:* Chmn, Math Dept & prof, math, Univ Kerala, 75-83; vis prof, Univ Toledo, 83-84; vis prof, math, Univ Louisville, 84-88. *Mem:* Am Math Soc; Math Asn Am; India Math Soc; Math Sci India. *Mailing Add:* 703 Scherm Rd Owensboro KY 42301

SITARZ, ANNELIESE LOTTE, PEDIATRIC HEMATOLOGY, PEDIATRIC ONCOLOGY. *Current Pos:* asst pediatrician, Col Physicians & Surgeons, Columbia Univ, 57-62, instr, 62-64, assoc, 64-68, asst prof, 68-74, assoc prof clin pediat, 74-83, PROF CLIN PEDIAT, COL PHYSICIANS & SURGEONS & CANCER RES CTR, COLUMBIA UNIV, 83-, ATTEND PEDIATRICIAN, BABIES HOSP, CTR WOMEN & CHILDREN, 83- *Personal Data:* b Medellin, Columbia, Aug 31, 28; US citizen. *Educ:* Bryn Mawr Col, BA, 50; Columbia Univ, MD, 54. *Concurrent Pos:* Vis fel, Babies Hosp, Ctr Women & Children, NY, 57-59; fel, Pediat Hemat, NIH, Nat Cancer Inst, 57-61; advan clin fel, Am Cancer Soc, 62-65; consult, Overlook Hosp, Summit, NJ, 75- *Mem:* Fel Am Acad Pediat; Am Soc Hemat; Am Soc Clin Oncol; Am Asn Cancer Res; Int Soc Hemat; NY Acad Sci. *Res:* Cancer in children; efficacy of chemotherapy in pediatric solid tumors. *Mailing Add:* Babies & Children's Hosp Harkness Pavilion 180 Ft Washington Ave New York NY 10032. *Fax:* 212-305-5848

SITES, JACK WALTER, JR, FISH & WILDLIFE SCIENCES. *Current Pos:* asst prof biol, zool & genetics, 82-86, assoc prof zool, Dept Zool, 86-92, PROF ZOOL, CUR HERPET, BRIGHAM UNIV, 92- *Personal Data:* b Clarksville, Tenn, Aug 6, 51; m 73; c 1. *Educ:* Austin Peay State Univ, BS, 73, MS, 75; Tex A&M Univ, PhD(vertebrate zool), 80. *Prof Exp:* Asst prof biol, zool & genetics, Dept Biol, Tex A&M Univ, 80-82. *Concurrent Pos:* Res zoologist, The Nature Conservancy, 75-76; Sloan Sr fel Molecular Evolution, 92. *Mem:* AAAS; Soc Study Evolution; Soc Syst Biol; Soc Conservation Biol; Am Soc Icthyologists & Herpetologists; Herpetologists League. *Res:* Mechanisms of chromosomal evolution and speciation, rates of speciation; genetic structure of natural populations of vertebrates; conservation genetics; evolutionary biology; systematics. *Mailing Add:* Brigham Young Univ 151 Widb Provo UT 84602-1049

SITES, JAMES RUSSELL, SOLID STATE ELECTRONICS, LOW TEMPERATURE PHYSICS. *Current Pos:* from instr to asst prof, 71-77, ASSOC PROF PHYSICS, COLO STATE UNIV, 77- *Personal Data:* b Manhattan, Kans, Nov 18, 43; m 64; c 3. *Educ:* Duke Univ, BS, 65; Cornell Univ, MS, 68, PhD(physics), 69. *Prof Exp:* Programmer, Union Carbide Corp, 62-64; NSF fel, 65-69; fel physics, Los Alamos Sci Lab, 69-71. *Mem:* Am Vacuum Soc; Am Phys Soc. *Res:* Investigation of electronic properties of compound semiconductor surfaces and interfaces; studies of thermal transport mechanisms in solid helium three; development of heterojunction solar cells. *Mailing Add:* 1707 Norwood Lane Ft Collins CO 80525

SITKOVSKY, MICHAIL V, IMMUNOPHARMACOLOGY, MOLECULAR IMMUNOLOGY. *Current Pos:* SR INVESTR & HEAD, BIOCHEM & IMMUNOPHARMACOL UNIT, LAB IMMUNOL, NAT INST ALLERGY & INFECTIOUS DIS, NIH, 84- *Personal Data:* b Pervomalsk, USSR, Sept 12, 47; US citizen; m 80. *Educ:* Moscow State Univ, MSc, 70, PhD(biophys physiol), 73. *Prof Exp:* Res assoc biochem, Ctr Cancer Res, Mass Inst Technol, 81-83, res scientist, 83-84. *Concurrent Pos:* Assoc ed, J Immunol Am Asn Immunologists, 91-93. *Mem:* Am Asn Immunologists. *Res:* Key proteins, enzymes, and messengers involved in the triggering and effector functions of cytotoxic T-lymphocytes; cytotoxicity and exocytosis; immunomodulating agents. *Mailing Add:* Lab Immunol Bldg 10 Rm 11N-311 Nat Inst Allergy & Infectious Dis-NIH Bethesda MD 20892-0001. *Fax:* 301-496-0222; *E-Mail:* sit@dioniaidpcniaid.nih.edu

SITRIN, MICHAEL DAVID, GASTROENTEROLOGY, NUTRITION. *Current Pos:* from asst prof to assoc prof, 80-92, PROF MED, UNIV CHICAGO, 92- *Personal Data:* b Detroit, Mich, June 18, 48. *Educ:* Harvard Univ, MD, 74. *Res:* Vitamin D; calcium medabsorption. *Mailing Add:* Dept Med Univ Chicago 5841 S Maryland Ave Chicago IL 60637-1463

SITRIN, ROBERT DAVID, BIOCHEMISTRY, ANALYTICAL CHEMISTRY. *Current Pos:* dir biochem process res & develop, Merck Sharp & Dohme Res Labs, 87-92, sr dir bioprocess res & develop, 93-96, EXEC DIR BIOPROCESS BIOANALYTICAL RES, MERCK RES LABS, 96- *Personal Data:* b Utica, NY, July 24, 45; m 81; c 4. *Educ:* Mass Inst Technol, BS, 67; Harvard Univ, MS, 68, PhD(chem), 72. *Prof Exp:* Fel chem, Woodard Res Inst, Switz, 72-73; assoc sr investr chem, Smith Kline & French Labs, 73-77, sr investr chem, 77-84, asst dir, protein biochem, 84-87. *Mem:* Am Chem Soc; AAAS; Soc Induct Microbiol. *Res:* Amino glycoside antibiotics; natural product isolations; structure determination; natural products chemistry; high performance liquid chromatography; analytical biochemistry; instrumental analysis; laboratory automation antibiotic fermentation screen development; process development biopharmaceuticals; protein purification; process development; vaccine development and characterization. *Mailing Add:* Merck Res Labs WP16-100 West Point PA 19486

SITTEL, CHESTER NACHAND, PROJECT MANAGEMENT. *Current Pos:* Res chem engr, Eastman Kodak Co, 69-72, sr res chem engr, 72-79, res assoc, 79, develop assoc, 79-81, res assoc, 81-88, SR RES ASSOC & SR DEVELOP ASSOC, EASTMAN CHEM DIV, EASTMAN KODAK CO, 88- *Personal Data:* b Nashville, Tenn, Sept 2, 41; m 63, Carol A Hunt; c Holly A (Pichiarella) & Matthew C. *Educ:* Vanderbilt Univ, BE, 63, MS, 66, PhD(chem eng), 69. *Mem:* Am Inst Chem Engrs; Sigma Xi. *Res:* Development and implementation of process designs from laboratory-scale to commercialization. *Mailing Add:* 220 Brookfield Dr Kingsport TN 37663. *E-Mail:* crsittel@eastman.com

SITTEL, KARL, APPLIED PHYSICS. *Current Pos:* RETIRED. *Personal Data:* b Frankfurt am Main, Ger, Oct 10, 16; nat US; wid; c Frederick K. *Educ:* Goethe Univ, Ger, PhD(physics), 42. *Prof Exp:* Asst, Max Planck Inst Biophys, Ger, 39-40; chief, Radiosonde Lab, Aerological Instruments, Marine Observ, 41-45; res & develop physicist, Aeromed Equip Lab, Naval Air Exp Sta, 47-50; sr staff physicist, Labs Res & Develop, Franklin Inst, 50-59; sr systs engr, Radio Corp Am, 59-63, leader systs physics, 63-67; consult, Environ Sci Lab, Valley Forge Space Tech Ctr, Gen Elec Co, 67-73, staff engr res & develop, 73-81. *Concurrent Pos:* Res assoc, Max Plank Inst Biophys, Ger, 46-47; consult, Jefferson Med Col, 53-56; grantee, Woehler Found; mem, Coun Basic Sci, Am Heart Asn; consult, 68-85. *Mem:* Am Phys Soc; Sigma Xi. *Res:* Radiosonde development; viscoelasticity; advanced systems; biomedical technology; nuclear effects engineering. *Mailing Add:* 1801 Morris Rd Apt B-112 Blue Bell PA 19422

SITTIG, DEAN FORREST, medical informatics, expert systems, for more information see previous edition

SITTLER, EDWARD CHARLES, JR, astrophysics, for more information see previous edition

SITZ, THOMAS O, BIOCHEMISTRY. *Current Pos:* ASSOC PROF BIOCHEM, VA TECH, 82- *Personal Data:* b Newport, RI, Dec 9, 44; m 64; c 1. *Educ:* Va Polytech Inst, BS, 67, PhD(biochem), 71. *Prof Exp:* Fel pharmacol, Baylor Col Med, 71-73, instr, 73-74, res assoc cell biol, 74-75; from asst prof to assoc prof chem, Old Dominion Univ, 75-82. *Mem:* Am Chem Soc; Am Soc Microbiol; AAAS. *Res:* Secondary structure and methylation of 5.8S rRNA. *Mailing Add:* Dept Biochem Va Polytech State Univ Blacksburg VA 24061-0308

SIU, CHI-HUNG, CELL & MOLECULAR BIOLOGY, NEUROSCIENCES. *Current Pos:* from asst prof to assoc prof, 76-90, PROF, BANTING & BEST DEPT, MED RES, UNIV TORONTO, CAN, 90- *Personal Data:* b Hong Kong, July 29, 47; m 76, Dorcas Lu; c Joshua, Joanne & Joyce. *Educ:* Int Christian Univ, Tokyo, BA, 69; Univ Chicago, PhD, 74. *Prof Exp:* Fel sci res, Scripps Clin & Res Found, 74-76. *Concurrent Pos:* Med Res Coun scholar, 78-83; vis prof, Hokkaido Univ, Japan, 95, Tsinghau Univ, China, 96. *Mem:* Am Soc Cell Biol; Can Biochem Soc; AAAS; Soc Neurosci. *Res:* Role of cell adhesion molecules in neuronal cell differentiation, metastasis and dictyostelium development. *Mailing Add:* C H Best Inst Univ Toronto Toronto ON M5G 1L6 Can. *Fax:* 416-978-8528; *E-Mail:* chi.hung.siu@utoronto.ca

SIU, TSUNPUI OSWALD, CANCER PREVENTION & ETIOLOGY, MANAGEMENT SCIENCE. *Current Pos:* PRIN LECTR, DIV COM, CITY UNIV HONG KONG, 90-, ASSOC HEAD, 96- *Personal Data:* b Hong Kong, Dec 26, 45; m 78, Diane T Ming; c Charisse D, Justin J, Gillian J & Samuel J. *Educ:* Univ Calif, Los Angeles, BS, 69; Yale Univ, MS, 73; Harvard Univ, MS, 75, DSc(biostatist), 78. *Prof Exp:* Teaching fel biophysics, Yale Univ, 70-73, res asst theoret studies atomic struct, 70-73; analyst epidemiol data mgt, Sch Pub Health, Harvard Univ, 73-74, sr analyst, 74-76; asst prof community health & epidemiol, Queen's Univ, Ont, 76-81; assoc prof community health, Univ Calgary, 81-90. *Concurrent Pos:* Lab instr biostatist, Sch Pub Health, Harvard Univ, 74-76; Nat Health Sci scholar, Health & Welfare Can, 78-81; sr scientist epidemiol, Alta Cancer Hosp Bd, 81-; expert lectr, World Bank Workshops Epidemiol Methods, China, 85; hon lectr community med, Univ Hong Kong, 85-86; consult, Hong Kong Sports, 90-; hon vis lectr, Community & Family Med, Chinese Univ Hong Kong, 92-; hon prof, Hawaii Pac Univ, 93- *Mem:* Am Col Epidemiol. *Res:* Cancer prevention with micro-nutrients; intelligent microcomputer systems in medicine; breast milk banking; epidemiology of Crohn's disease; epidemiology of cancer; folic acid on fragile x-syndrome; clinical trials; quality evaluation and management; sports science; education administration. *Mailing Add:* Div Com City Univ Hong Kong 83 Tat Chee Kowloon Tong Hong Kong People's Republic of China. *Fax:* 27887925; *E-Mail:* cmtosiu@cityu.edu.hk

SIU, YUM-TONG, PURE MATHEMATICS. *Current Pos:* PROF MATH, HARVARD UNIV, 82- *Personal Data:* b Canton, China, May 6, 43; m 67; c 2. *Educ:* Univ Hong Kong, BA, 63; Univ Minn, MA, 64; Princeton Univ, PhD(math), 66; Yale Univ, MA, 70; Harvard Univ, MA, 82. *Prof Exp:* Asst prof math, Purdue Univ, 66-67 & Univ Notre Dame, 67-70; from assoc prof to prof math, Yale Univ, 70-78; prof math, Stanford Univ, 78-82. *Concurrent Pos:* Sloan fel, 71-73; Guggenheim fel, 86-87. *Mem:* AAAS; Am Math Soc. *Res:* Cohomology groups of coherent analytic sheaves on complex analytic spaces; extension of coherent analytic sheaves. *Mailing Add:* Dept Math Harvard Univ Cambridge MA 02138-2901

SIURU, WILLIAM D, JR, AUTOMOTIVE JOURNALISM, AEROSPACE JOURNALISM. *Current Pos:* CONSULT FREELANCE PROF JOUR, 95- *Personal Data:* b Detroit, Mich, Jan 29, 38; c 2. *Educ:* Wayne State Univ, BSME, 60; Airforce Inst Technol, MSAE, 64; Ariz State Univ, PhD(mech eng), 75. *Prof Exp:* Chief, Launch Systs Br, Foreign Technol Div, 65-71, Technol Br, Air Force Rocket Propulsion Lab, 74-76; asst prof mech eng, US Mil Head, 76-79; comdr, Frank J Seilor Res Labs, 79-83; dir flight systs eng, Aeronaut Systs Div, 83-84; sr res assoc, Univ Colo, Colorado Springs, 86-; vpres eng, Space & Aeronaut Sci Inc, 88-95. *Mem:* Soc Automotive Engrs; Am Inst Aeronaut & Astronaut; Soc Body Engrs. *Res:* Aircraft fire control systems; intelligent vehicle/highway systems; author of automotive and aviation technology. *Mailing Add:* 4050 Dolphin Circle Colorado Springs CO 80918

SIUTA, GERALD JOSEPH, ORGANIC CHEMISTRY, MEDICINAL CHEMISTRY. *Current Pos:* Res organic chemist, Med Res Div, 74-81, MGR, NEW PROD LICENSING, MED GROUP, LEDERLE LABS, AM CYANAMID CO, 81- *Personal Data:* b Yonkers, NY, Apr 6, 47; m 69; c 1. *Educ:* Lehman Col, BA, 69; Fordham Univ, PhD(org chem), 74. *Concurrent Pos:* Lectr chem, Ladycliff Col, 76- *Mem:* Am Chem Soc; Sigma Xi; NY Acad Sci. *Res:* Synthetic organic chemistry; prostaglandins; complement inhibitors; antidiabetic agents; anti-atherosclerotic agents. *Mailing Add:* 14 Georgetown Oval New York NY 10965

SIVAK, ANDREW, BIOCHEMISTRY, CELL BIOLOGY. *Personal Data:* b New Brunswick, NJ, May 31, 31; m 58; c 2. *Educ:* Rutgers Univ, BS, 52, MS, 57, PhD(microbiol), 60. *Prof Exp:* USPHS fel, Univ Vienna, 60-61; biochemist Arthur D Little, Inc, 61-63; res dir, Bio-Dynamics, Inc, 63-64; res assoc, Med Ctr, NY Univ, 64-68, from asst prof to assoc prof environ med, 68-74; sr staff mem cell biol, Arthur D Little, Inc, 75-77, sect mgr, 75-87, vpres life sci, 77-89; pres, Health Effects Inst, 89-92. *Concurrent Pos:* Vis lectr, Harvard Sch Pub Health, 86- *Mem:* AAAS; Am Asn Cancer Res; Environ Mutagen Soc; Am Soc Cell Biol; Am Col Toxicol; Soc Toxicol. *Res:* Environmental toxicology; mechanisms of carcinogenesis and mutagenesis; cell membranes and control of cell division. *Mailing Add:* PO Box 2128 St Augustine FL 32085. *Fax:* 617-773-0277

SIVAK, JACOB GERSHON, COMPARATIVE PHYSIOLOGY, PHYSIOLOGICAL OPTICS. *Current Pos:* From asst prof to assoc prof, 72-79, PROF OPTOM & BIOL, UNIV WATERLOO, 79-, DIR, SCH OPTOM, 84- *Personal Data:* b Montreal, Que, June 22, 44; m 67; c 3. *Educ:* Univ Montreal, LScO, 67; Ind Univ, MS, 70; Cornell Univ, PhD(physiol), 72, Pa Col Optometry, OD, 81. *Honors & Awards:* Fry Award, Am Optom Found, 84. *Concurrent Pos:* Res assoc, Mote Marine Lab, Fla; fel, Am Acad Optom, 71-; Lady Davis vis prof, Technion-Israel Inst Technol, 78-79 & I Taylor chmn biol, 82. *Mem:* Am Acad Optom; Asn Res Vision & Ophthal. *Res:* Comparative anatomy and physiology of the eye with emphasis on refractive state and accomodative mechanisms; operations of the eye and refraction; optics of the crystalline lens and cataractogenesis. *Mailing Add:* Lab Comp Optom Univ Waterloo Sch Optom Waterloo ON N2L 3G1 Can

SIVASUBRAMANIAN, PAKKIRISAMY, DEVELOPMENTAL BIOLOGY. *Current Pos:* from asst prof to assoc prof, 75-83, PROF DEVELOP BIOL, UNIV NB, CAN, 83- *Personal Data:* b Andimadam, India, Aug 28, 39; m 67, Meena; c 3. *Educ:* Annamalai Univ, India, BSc, 61; Univ Ill, MS, 71, PhD(physiol), 73. *Prof Exp:* Sci officer entom, Bhabha Atomic Res Ctr, India, 63-69; res fel insect develop, Biol Labs, Harvard Univ, 73-74. *Mem:* Soc Develop Biol; Am Soc Zoologists; Entom Soc Am. *Res:* Developmental neurobiology of insects; investigation of neuronal specificity and the mechanisms of establishment of neural networks in flies during metamorphosis by following the development of nerves in transplanted imaginal discs; insect neurochemistry. *Mailing Add:* Dept Biol Univ NB Fredericton NB E3B 6E1 Can

SIVAZLIAN, BOGHOS D, OPERATIONS RESEARCH. *Current Pos:* from asst prof to assoc prof, 66-72, PROF INDUST & SYSTS ENG, UNIV FLA, 72- *Personal Data:* b Cairo, Egypt, Feb 11, 36; US citizen; m 63; c 2. *Educ:* Cairo Univ, BSc, 59; Case Western Reserve Univ, MS, 62, PhD(opers res), 66. *Prof Exp:* Sr mgt sci assoc opers res, B F Goodrich Co, 62-65. *Concurrent Pos:* Consult, M&M Candies, Hackettstown, 61; consult scientist, Ft Belvoir, US Army, 68-69; White Sands Missile Range, 70-76 & Eglin AFB, 82-89; Nat Acad Sci exchange scholar, Poland, 73-74, Fulbright scholar to USSR, 80; res partic, Inst Energy Anal, Oak Ridge Assoc Univs, 77-78. *Mem:* Opers Res Soc Am. *Res:* Inventory and replacement theory; operations research; analysis of military systems; applied stochastic processes. *Mailing Add:* Dept Indust & Systs Eng Univ Fla 303 Weil Hall Gainesville FL 32611-2002

SIVCO, DEBORAH L, MOLECULAR BEAM EPITAXY, III-V CRYSTAL GROWTH. *Current Pos:* MEM TECH STAFF, BELL LABS LUCENT TECHNOL, 81- *Personal Data:* b Somerville, NJ, Dec 21, 57; m 81, Gregory C; c Scott G, Michelle E, Carolyn S & David C. *Educ:* Rutgers Univ, BA, 80; Stevens Inst Technol, MS, 88. *Honors & Awards:* Electronics Lett Premium, Inst Elec Engr UK, 95. *Prof Exp:* Lab technician, Laser Diode Labs, 80-81. *Concurrent Pos:* Newcomb Cleveland prize, AAAS, 94-95. *Res:* Molecular beam epitaxial crystal growth of III-V semiconductor materials for optoelectronics and photonics. *Mailing Add:* Bell Labs Lucent Technol Rm 1C-404 600 Mountain Ave Murray Hill NJ 07974-0636. *Fax:* 908-582-2043

SIVERS, DENNIS WAYNE, HIGH ENERGY PHYSICS. *Current Pos:* DIR, PORTLAND PHYSICS INST, 91- *Personal Data:* b Greeley, Colo, Jan 20, 44; m, E Anne Cruyder; c Derek & Heidi. *Educ:* Mass Inst Technol, BS, 66; Univ Calif, Berkeley, PhD(physics), 70. *Prof Exp:* Res assoc theoret physics, Argonne Nat Lab, 71-73, asst physicist, 76-77, physicist, 78-91; res assoc theoret physics, Stanford Linear Accelerator, 73-75; vis scientist, Rutherford Lab, 75-76. *Mem:* Fel Am Phys Soc. *Res:* Theory and phenomenology of high energy physics. *Mailing Add:* Portland Physics Inst 4730 SW Macadam Rm 101 Portland OR 97201. *Fax:* 503-223-2750

SIVIER, KENNETH R(OBERT), AEROSPACE ENGINEERING. *Current Pos:* assoc prof, 67-93, EMER ASSOC PROF AERONAUT & ASTRONAUT ENG, UNIV ILL, URBANA, 93- *Personal Data:* b Standish, Mich, Dec 10, 28; m 52; c 6. *Educ:* Univ Mich, BSE(aeronaut eng) & BS(eng math), 51, PhD(aerospace eng), 67; Princeton Univ, MSE, 55. *Prof Exp:* Eng trainee, Naval Ord Lab, Aro, Inc, Tenn, 51-52; aeronaut eng, Aro, Inc, 52-53; res asst, Gas Dynamics Lab, Princeton Univ, 53-55; engr, McDonnell Aircraft Corp, 55-59, sr group engr, 59-62; res engr, Univ Mich, 62-67. *Mem:* Am Inst Aeronaut & Astronaut. *Res:* Aerodynamic testing techniques and facilities; aerodynamic and aircraft design; aircraft flight mechanics; wind power; combustion of gases. *Mailing Add:* Dept Aeornaut & Astronaut Univ Ill 306 Talbot Lab 104 S Wright St Urbana IL 61801

SIVINSKI, JACEK STEFAN, FOOD IRRADIATION & POSTHARVEST TECHNOLOGY, WATER TREATMENT & PURIFICATION. *Current Pos:* DIR RADIATION TECHNOL PROGS, CH2M HILL, NMEX, 81- *Personal Data:* b Ashton, Nebr, June 23, 26; m 87, Krystyna W Plachecka; c 5. *Educ:* Iowa State Univ, BS, 57. *Honors & Awards:* Hon Award for Eng Excellence, Am Consult Engrs Coun, 83. *Prof Exp:* Sect supvr, Facil Eng Div, Sandia Lab, 57-64, mem adv systs res staff, 64-66, mgr, Planetary Quarantine Dept, 66-74, mgr, Appl Biol & Isotope Utilization Dept, Sandia Labs, 74-81. *Concurrent Pos:* Mem, Planetary Quarantine Adv Panel, NASA, 72-; mem, Comt Technol Transfer Develop Countries, Int Atomic Energy Agency; mem task force food irradiation, Coun Agr Sci & Technol, mem joint food irradiation technol & econ, UN Food & Agr Orgn/Int Atomic Energy Agency, mem Int Consult Group Food Irradiation; chmn, Food Irradiation Comt, Am Stand Testing & Mat, Food Irradiation Task Group, Agr Res Inst. *Mem:* Europ Soc Nuclear Methods Agr; Am Nuclear Soc; Inst Food Technol; Eng Found; Water Qual Asn. *Res:* Systems analysis for low level aircraft penetration; desalination, particularly brackish waters; systems analysis for re-entry vehicle systems, lunar and planetary quarantine, space environments; radiation biology; radiation treatment of agricultural commodities; beneficial uses of nuclear byproducts; linear accelerator process development; isotope and linear accelerator facility and process technologies; water treatment technology. *Mailing Add:* 12800 Comanche NE No 26 Albuquerque NM 87111. *Fax:* 505-296-1491; *E-Mail:* 73172.3423@compuserve.com

SIVINSKI, JOHN A, PHYSICS. *Current Pos:* PROG MGR, HUGHES DANBURY OPTICAL SYSTS, 72- *Personal Data:* b San Cloud, Minn, Nov 22, 38; m 62; c 3. *Educ:* St Johns Univ, BS, 60; Vanderbilt Univ, MS, 64, PhD(physics), 65. *Prof Exp:* Proj mgr, Gen Electric Space Div, 65-72. *Mem:* Am Phys Soc. *Mailing Add:* 5 Parker Hill Brookfield CT 06804. *Fax:* 203-797-5114

SIVINSKI, JOHN MICHAEL, SEXUAL BEHAVIOR OF FLIES & OTHER INSECTS, BIOLOGICAL CONTROL OF TEPHRITID FRUIT FLIES. *Current Pos:* Res assoc, 82-85, RES ENTOMOLOGIST, INSECT ATTRACTANTS, USDA-AGR RES SERV, 85- *Personal Data:* b Omaha, Nebr, Nov 3, 48; c Jennifer & Robert. *Educ:* Univ NMex, BS, 73, MS, 77; Univ Fla, PhD(entomol), 82. *Concurrent Pos:* Assoc ed Fla Entomologist, 87-88; adj asst prof, Univ Fla, 87- *Mem:* AAAS; Entom Soc Am. *Res:* Behavior of tephritid fruit flies and their natural enemies; control programs using sterile males and augmented parasite releases; exploration for biocontrol agents. *Mailing Add:* 3621 NW 28th Terr Gainesville FL 32605. *Fax:* 352-374-5781

SIVJEE, GULAMABAS GULAMHUSEN, AERONOMY. *Current Pos:* RES SCIENTIST, EMBRY RIDDLE AERON UNIV. *Personal Data:* b Zanzibar, Tanzania, Mar 11, 38; US citizen; m 59; c 3. *Educ:* Univ London, BSc, 63; Johns Hopkins Univ, PhD(physics), 70. *Prof Exp:* Asst lectr physics, Makerere Col, Univ London, 63-65; res scientist physics, Stand Tel & Cables, Div Int Tel & Tel, 65-66; sr system analyst physics, Bendix Field Eng Corp, 70; fel physics, Johns Hopkins Univ, 71 & Space & Atmospheric Studies, Univ Sask, 71-72; asst prof, Univ Alaska, 72-76, assoc prof geophys, Geophys Inst, 76- *Concurrent Pos:* Convener, Comt Airborne Studies Airglow, Auroral & Magnetospheric Physics, aboard NASA's Convair 990 Jet Aircraft, 73- *Mem:* Am Geophys Union. *Res:* Energy, flux and pitch angle distribution of magnetospheric particles and their interactions with atmospheric constituents; UV spectroscopy of Venus and Jupiter; minor constituents, including gaseous pollutants in terrestrial atmosphere. *Mailing Add:* Math & Sci Embry Riddle Aeron Univ 600 S Clyde Morris Daytona Beach FL 32114-3766

SIX, ERICH WALTHER, BIOPHYSICS. *Current Pos:* from asst prof to assoc prof, 60-73, PROF MICROBIAL GENETICS, UNIV IOWA, 73- *Personal Data:* b Frankfurt, Ger, Sept 22, 26; m 57; c 1. *Educ:* Univ Frankfurt, Dr phil nat, 54. *Prof Exp:* Res fel radiobiol, Max Planck Inst Marine Biol, Ger, 54-56; res fel microbial genetics, Calif Inst Technol, 56-57; res assoc, Univ Southern Calif, 57, Max Planck Inst Biol, Ger, 58-59 & Univ Rochester, 59-60. *Mem:* Am Soc Microbiol; Genetics Soc Am. *Res:* Microbial genetics; virology; molecular biology. *Mailing Add:* Dept of Microbiol Univ of Iowa Iowa City IA 52242

SIX, HOWARD R, VACCINE DEVELOPMENT, IMMUNOCHEMISTRY. *Current Pos:* VPRES RES & DEVELOP, CONNAUGHT LABS, INC, 89- *Personal Data:* b Princeton, WVa, Jan 5, 42; m 64, Bobbye J Young; c Kimberly G (Holcomb) & Robert H. *Educ:* David Lipscomb Col, BA, 63; Vanderbilt Univ, PhD(microbiol), 72. *Prof Exp:* Post doctorate pharmacol, Wash Univ, 72-74; post doctorate molecular biol, Vanderbilt Univ, 74-75; from asst prof to assoc prof microbiol, Baylor Col Med, 75-88. *Concurrent Pos:* Adj prof, Univ Tex Med Sch, Houston, 76-79, adj assoc prof, 79-81; assoc ed, J Med Virol, 88- *Mem:* Inst Med-Nat Acad Sci; Infectious Dis Soc Am; Fedn Socs Exp Biol & Med; Am Soc Microbiol; Am Asn Immunol. *Res:* Development of vaccines for use in humans for the prevention of infectious diseases; definition of the pathogenic mechanisms producing disease during infection with microbial agents. *Mailing Add:* Connaught Labs Rte 611 PO Box 187 Swiftwater PA 18370-0187

SIX, NORMAN FRANK, JR, PHYSICS. *Current Pos:* asst dir, Space Sci Lab, 88-89, asst assoc dir sci, 89-, CHIEF PHYSICS & ASTRON, MARSHALL SPACE LAB CTR, NASA. *Personal Data:* b Tampa, Fla, July 24, 35; m 54; c 4. *Educ:* Univ Fla, BS, 57, PhD(physics), 63; Univ Calif, Los Angeles, MS, 59. *Prof Exp:* Mem tech staff-physicist, Hughes Aircraft Co, Calif, 57-59; res asst astrophys, Univ Fla, 59-63; mgr, Geo-Astrophys Lab, Sci Res Labs, Brown Eng Co, Ala, 63-66; prof physics, Western Ky Univ, 66-74, prof physics & astron, 74-83, head dept, 66-83; asst to dir, Arecibo Observ, Cornell Univ, 83-86; vis scientist, Univ Space Res Asn, 86-88. *Concurrent Pos:* Res assoc, Univ Fla, 64-66; consult, Brown Eng Co, Ala, 66- *Mem:* Am Astron Soc; Am Geophys Union. *Res:* Analytical and experimental studies in planetary radio emissions; lunar and solar physics; electromagnetic wave propagation; space environment; radio astronomy experiments from earth satellites and from the moon. *Mailing Add:* 1220 Kingsway Rd SE Huntsville AL 35802

SIZE, WILLIAM BACHTRUP, GEOLOGY. *Current Pos:* asst prof, 73-78, ASSOC PROF GEOL, EMORY UNIV, 78-, DIR, GEOSCIENCES PROG, 89- *Personal Data:* b Chicago, Ill, June 8, 43; m 68; c 3. *Educ:* Northern Ill Univ, BS, 65, MS, 67; Univ Ill, Urbana, PhD(geol), 71. *Prof Exp:* Asst prof geol, Eastern Ill Univ, 70-71; geologist, Hawaii Inst Geophys, 71-72. *Concurrent Pos:* Vis asst prof geol, Univ Hawaii, 71-72; corresp, Geodynamics Proj, Nat Acad Sci, 73-; Int Geol Correlation Prog, 77-; sr Fulbright res award, Norway, 87; vis geologist, NZ Geol Surv, 90. *Mem:* Sigma Xi; Geol Soc Am; Am Geophys Union; Int Asn Math Geol. *Res:* Petrogenetic history of igneous rock textures; mechanics of igneous intrusions; origin of alkaline rocks; computer applications in petrology; anatexis and origin of migmatites; geostatistics. *Mailing Add:* Geosci Prog Emory Univ 1577 Clifton Rd NE Atlanta GA 30322. *Fax:* 404-727-6492; *E-Mail:* wsize@emory.edu

SIZEMORE, DOUGLAS REECE, SOFTWARE SYSTEMS, STATISTICAL COMPUTING. *Current Pos:* assoc prof psychol, 74-82, assoc prof, 82-87, PROF COMPUT SCI, COVENANT COL, 87- *Personal Data:* b Detroit, Mich, Nov 2, 47; m 70; c 1. *Educ:* Taylor Univ, BA, 69; Conservative Baptist Theol Sem, MA, 72; Univ Northern Colo, PhD(appl statist), 74. *Prof Exp:* Res fel, Univ Northern Colo, 73-74. *Concurrent Pos:* Consult, Chattem Inc, 77-, Tenn Valley Authority, 83- *Mem:* Asn Comput Mach; Am Statist Asn; AAAS; Data Processing Mgt Asn. *Res:* Regression methodology; software systems performance and measurement (software engineering); computer science education. *Mailing Add:* 402 Ft Trace Lookout Mountain GA 30750

SIZEMORE, ROBERT CARLEN, CELLULAR IMMUNOLOGY, IMMUNOREGULATION. *Current Pos:* DIR IMMUNOL, IMREG, INC, 84- *Personal Data:* b Lexington, Ky, Sept 30, 51; m 90, Katherine Killelea; c Katherine P & Robert C. *Educ:* Univ Ky, BS, 73, MS, 75; Univ Louisville, PhD(microbiol & immunol), 82. *Prof Exp:* Postdoctoral res assoc, Univ Miss Med Ctr, 82-84. *Concurrent Pos:* Adj asst prof, Tulane Univ Sch Med, 85- *Mem:* Am Asn Immunologists; Int Soc Develop & Comp Immunol; AAAS; Fedn Am Scientists; Int AIDS Soc; Am Soc Trop Med & Hyg. *Res:* Immunotherapeutics for acquired immune deficiency syndrome and other immune diseases; cellular immunology; immunoregulation; comparative immunology; immunoparasitology; immunomodulators; neuropeptides as links between the neuroendocrine and immune systems. *Mailing Add:* Dept Microbiol & Immunol Tulane Univ Sch Med 1430 Tulane Ave New Orleans LA 70112. *Fax:* 504-523-6201

SIZEMORE, RONALD KELLY, MARINE MICROBIOLOGY. *Current Pos:* assoc prof, 81-89, PROF BIOL & CHAIR, UNIV NC, WILMINGTON, 89- *Personal Data:* b Farmville, Va, Feb 27, 47; m 84; c 2. *Educ:* Wake Forest Univ, BS, 69; Univ SC, MS, 71; Univ Md, PhD(microbiol), 75. *Prof Exp:* Asst prof, Univ Houston, 75-81. *Concurrent Pos:* Vis res scientist, Galveston Lab, Nat Marine Fisheries Serv, 75-81. *Mem:* Sigma Xi; Am Soc Microbiol; AAAS. *Res:* Ecology, taxonomy and molecular biology of marine bacteria with emphasis on the members of the genus Vibrio. *Mailing Add:* Dept Biol Univ NC 601 S College Rd Wilmington NC 28403-3297

SIZER, IRWIN WHITING, BIOCHEMISTRY. *Current Pos:* from instr to prof, Mass Inst Technol, 35-75, exec officer, 54-55, from actg head dept to head dept, 55-67, dean grad sch, 67-75, EMER PROF BIOCHEM, MASS INST TECHNOL, 75- *Personal Data:* b Bridgewater, Mass, Apr 4, 10; m 35; c 1. *Educ:* Brown Univ, AB, 31; Rutgers Univ, PhD(physiol & biochem), 35. *Hon Degrees:* ScD, Brown Univ, 71. *Honors & Awards:* Irwin Sizer Award, Mass Inst Technol, 75. *Prof Exp:* Lab asst physiol, Rutgers Univ, 31-35. *Concurrent Pos:* Mem comt physiol training, NIH, 48-64, chmn, 65, chmn comt gen res support, 65-69 & nat adv coun health res facilities, 70-72; consult, Johnson & Johnson Co, 49-77; trustee, Rutgers Univ, 62-71, mem bd gov, 68-71; mem, Corp Lesley Col, 62-88; trustee, Boston Mus Sci, 63-75; mem adv comt, Inst Microbiol, 63-68; consult probs Latin Am, Ford Found, 65-67; dir, Boston Fed Savings Bank, Lexington, 67; consult, Neurosci Res Prog, 67-75; trustee, Boston Biomed Res Inst, 68-; mem adv comt grad educ, Mass State Bd Higher Educ, 68-75; consult resource develop, Mass Inst Technol, 75-85; pres, Whitaker Health Sci Fund, Inc, 74-93; trustee, Theobald Smith Res Inst, 85- *Mem:* Am Chem Soc; fel Am Inst Chem; Am Soc Biol Chem; fel Am Acad Arts & Sci. *Res:* Chemical stimulation of animals; spectroscopy of biological materials; enzyme kinetics; action of oxidases on proteins; x-ray photography of insects; intermediary metabolism of sulfur; enzymes of oxidation and transamination; enzymology & molecular biology. *Mailing Add:* 52 Dartmouth Ct Bedford MA 01730

SIZER, WALTER SCOTT, LINEAR ALGEBRA. *Current Pos:* asst prof, 80-85, assoc prof, 85-90, PROF MATH, MOORHEAD STATE UNIV, 90- *Personal Data:* b Providence, RI, Aug 15, 47; m 77, Judy Kerr. *Educ:* Dartmouth Col, AB, 69; Univ Mass, MA, 72; Univ London, PhD(math), 76. *Prof Exp:* Vis lectr math, Univ Mass, Amherst, 76-77; vis asst prof, Southern Ill Univ, 77-80. *Concurrent Pos:* Vis lectr math, Mara Community Col, Kuantan, Malaysia, 86-87; Fulbright prof, Univ Cape Coast, Ghana, 91-92. *Mem:* Am Math Soc; Math Asn Am; Asn Women Math. *Res:* Similarity of matrices; representations of semigroup actions. *Mailing Add:* Dept Math Moorhead State Univ Moorhead MN 56563

SJOBERG, SIGURD A, ENGINEERING. *Current Pos:* RETIRED. *Mem:* Nat Acad Eng. *Mailing Add:* 203 Pine Shadows Dr Seabrook TX 77586

SJOBLAD, ROY DAVID, MICROBIOLOGY, BIOCHEMISTRY. *Current Pos:* ASST PROF MICROBIOL, UNIV MD, 78- *Personal Data:* b Worcester, Mass, Nov 22, 47; m 69; c 2. *Educ:* Gordon Col, BS, 69; Univ Mass, MS, 71; Pa State Univ, PhD(agron), 76. *Prof Exp:* Res fel appl biol, Harvard Univ, 76-78. *Concurrent Pos:* Rockefeller Found fel, Harvard Univ, 76-77. *Mem:* Sigma Xi; Am Soc Microbiol; NY Acad Sci. *Res:* Microbial ecology; chemoreception in microorganisms; transformation of pesticides by microorganisms; fungal and algal enzymes. *Mailing Add:* 5806 Maryhurst Dr Hyattsville MD 20782

SJODIN, RAYMOND ANDREW, BIOPHYSICS. *Current Pos:* assoc prof, 60-66, PROF BIOPHYS, UNIV MD, BALTIMORE, 66-, INTERIM CHMN BIOPHYS, 88- *Personal Data:* b Salt Lake City, Utah, Oct 10, 27; m 54; c 2. *Educ:* Calif Inst Technol, BS, 51; Univ Calif, PhD(physiol), 55. *Prof Exp:* Asst physiol, Univ Calif, 51-55; res assoc biophys, Purdue Univ, 55-58; NIH fel, Univ Col, London, 58-59; res assoc physiol, Univ Uppsala, Sweden, 59-60. *Mem:* Fel AAAS; Soc Gen Physiol; Am Physiol Soc; Biophys Soc. *Res:* Physical chemistry of membranes, nerve excitation and conduction of nerve impulses; ion fluxes across cell membranes in relation to electrical events and transport problems; cell electrofusion. *Mailing Add:* Dept Biophysics Univ Md Sch Med Baltimore MD 21201-1596

SJOERDSMA, ALBERT, EXPERIMENTAL MEDICINE, CLINICAL PHARMACOLOGY. *Current Pos:* CONSULT MED SCI, 94- *Personal Data:* b Lansing, Ill, Aug 31, 24; m 50, Fern E MacAllister; c Leslie, Ann, Al Jr & Britt. *Educ:* Univ Chicago, BS, 45, PhD(pharmacol), 48, MD, 49; Am Bd Internal Med, dipl, 58. *Honors & Awards:* Theobold Smith Award, AAAS, 58; Harry Gold Award, Am Soc Pharmacol & Exp Therapeut, 77, Exp Therapeut Award, 90; Oscar B Hunter Award, Am Soc Clin Pharmacol & Therapeut, 81. *Prof Exp:* Intern, Univ Hosp, Univ Mich, 49-50; resident, Cardiovasc Dept, Michael Reese Hosp, 51; resident med, USPHS Hosp, 51-53; clin investr, Nat Heart Inst, 53-58, chief exp therapeut br, 58-71; vpres & dir, Merrell Int Res Ctr, France, 71-76, sr vpres & dir, Merrell Nat Labs, Cincinnati & France, 76-78, vpres pharmaceut res & develop, Richardson-Merrell Inc, 78-81; vpres Pharmaceut Res, Dow Chem Co, 81-83; pres, Merrell Dow Res Inst, 83-89, emer pres, 89-94. *Concurrent Pos:* Nat Heart Inst res fel, Univ Chicago, 50-51; NIH fel, Malmo, Sweden, 59-60; spec lectr, George Washington Univ, 59-71; mem coun high blood pressure res, Am Heart Asn; hon chmn, Second World Conf, Clin Pharmacol & Therapeutics, 83. *Mem:* AAAS; Am Soc Pharmacol & Exp Therapeut; Am Soc Clin Invest; Asn Am Physicians; Am Soc Clin Pharmacol & Therapeut; Am Chem Soc; Am Col Neuropsychopharmacol; Am Fedn Clin Res; AMA; Am Med Asn. *Res:* Metabolism of biogenic amines; collagen metabolism; drug discovery. *Mailing Add:* 263 N Dogwood Trail Kitty Hawk NC 27949

SJOGREN, JON ARNE, COMBINATORICS & FINITE MATHEMATICS. *Current Pos:* PROG MGR, MATH & INFO SCI, AIR FORCE OFF SCI RES, 89- *Personal Data:* b Karlstad, Wermland, Sweden, Oct 23, 51; US citizen. *Educ:* Ore State Univ, BS, 70; Univ Calif, Berkeley, PhD(math), 75; Duke Univ, MSEE, 86. *Prof Exp:* Mem tech staff, AT&T Bell Labs, 69-70; mathematician, Inst Hautes Etudes Sci, 75-76; res assoc math, Max-Planck Inst, Bonn, Ger, 76-78; lectr math, Fac Sci, Kuwait Univ, 78-80; instr, Ore State Univ, 80-81; asst prof math, Univ Portland, 81-84; eng consult, Res Triangle Inst, NC, 85-86; computer engr, Langley Res Ctr, NASA, 86-89. *Mem:* Sr mem Inst Elec & Electronics Engrs; Am Math Soc; Soc Indust &

Appl Math. *Res:* Combinatorial group theory and topology; enumerative combinatorics; matrix theory; applied functional analysis; signal processing; stochastic theory. *Mailing Add:* Air Force Off Sci Res NM 110 Duncan Ave Suite B115 Bolling AFB Washington DC 20332-0001

SJOGREN, ROBERT ERIK, MICROBIOLOGY, BIOCHEMISTRY. *Current Pos:* ASSOC PROF MICROBIOL & BIOCHEM, UNIV VT, 67- *Personal Data:* b Schenectady, NY, June 13, 31; m 72. *Educ:* Cornell Univ, BS, 53; Univ Cincinnati, MS, 60, PhD(microbiol), 67. *Prof Exp:* Asst clin chemist, Ellis Hosp Lab, NY, 55-58; res assoc microbiol, Sterling Winthrop Res Inst, 60-64. *Concurrent Pos:* Hatch Act grant, Vt Agr Exp Sta, 68- *Mem:* Am Soc Microbiol; Sigma Xi. *Res:* Fungal metabolism; physical-chemical properties of protein; microbial ecology. *Mailing Add:* Dept Microbiol Given Bldg Univ Vt Col Med Burlington VT 05405-0001

SJOGREN, ROBERT W, JR, GASTROENTEROLOGY, HEPATOLOGY. *Current Pos:* STAFF GASTROENTEROLOGIST, FAIRFAX HOSP, FAIRFAX, VA, 94-, KAISER PERMANENTE MED CTR, FALLS CHURCH, VA, 94-, HOLY CROSS HOSP, SILVER SPRING, MD, 94-, GEORGETOWN UNIV HOSP, 94-; ASSOC PROF MED, DEPT MED, GEORGETOWN UNIV, 94-; STAFF GASTROENTEROLIGIST WASHINGTON HOSP CTR, 97- *Personal Data:* b Charlottesville, Va, Aug 19, 45; m 80; c 1. *Educ:* Davidson Col, NC, BS, 67; Med Col Va, MD, 71. *Prof Exp:* Chief practice, Dept Med, Meddac, Ft McPherson, Ga, 75-76; chief teaching & practice, Dept Gastroenterol, Eisenhower Hosp, Ft Gordon, Ga, 78-80; staff physician practice, Dept Gastroenterol, Walter Reed Army Med Ctr, Wash, DC, 80-94, asst chief res, Dept Gastroenterol, Inst Med, 80-93, chief, Dept Clin Physiol, 93-94. *Concurrent Pos:* Asst prof med teaching, Dept Med, Uniformed Serv Univ Health Sci, Bethesda, Md, 81- & Dept Med, Sch Med, Georgetown Univ, 95- *Mem:* Fel Am Col Physicians; fel Am Col Gastroenterol; Am Soc Gastrointestinal Endoscopy; Am Motility Soc. *Res:* In vivo gastrointestinal motility in enteric infection and inflammation; human and animal studies; computer signal analysis; drug therapy. *Mailing Add:* Kaiser Permanente Med Ctr Gastroenterol Serv 201 N Washington St Falls Church VA 22046. *Fax:* 703-536-1400

SJOLANDER, JOHN ROGERS, organic chemistry; deceased, see previous edition for last biography

SJOLUND, RICHARD DAVID, PLANT CELL BIOLOGY. *Current Pos:* ASSOC PROF BOT, UNIV IOWA, 73- *Personal Data:* b Iron River, Mich, Dec 9, 39. *Educ:* Univ Wis-Milwaukee, BS, 63; Univ Calif, Davis, PhD(bot), 68. *Prof Exp:* Botanist, Ames Res Ctr, NASA, 63-64. *Concurrent Pos:* DAA fel, Ger, USA-USSR Res Exchange, Leningrad. *Mem:* Bot Soc Am; Am Soc Plant Physiol; Am Phytopathol Soc; AAAS; Am Soc Cell Biol. *Res:* Development of phloem sieve elements in plant tissue cultures; cell structures; protein synthesis; membrane transport; developing techniques for the isolation of phloem cells from tissue cultures; their use in forming phloem-specific monoclonal antibodies; identifying phloem-specific gene expressions. *Mailing Add:* Dept Biol Sci Rm 222 Chem Bldg Univ Univ Iowa Iowa City IA 52242. *Fax:* 319-335-3620; *E-Mail:* r-sjolund@uiowa.edu

SJOSTRAND, FRITIOF S, NEUROPHYSIOLOGY. *Current Pos:* vis prof, 59-60, prof, 60-83, EMER PROF ZOOL, UNIV CALIF, LOS ANGELES, 83- *Personal Data:* b Stockholm, Sweden, Nov 5, 12; m 41, 55, 68, Birgitta Pettersson; c Rutger, Johan & Peter. *Educ:* Karolinska Inst, Sweden, MD, 41, PhD, 45. *Hon Degrees:* PhD(biol), Univ Siena, Italy, 74 & NEastern Hill Univ, Shillong, India, 89. *Honors & Awards:* Swed Med Asn Award, 59; Anders Retzius Gold Medal, 67; Paul Ehrlich & Ludwig Darmstaedter Prize, 71; Distinguished Scientist Award, Electron Micros Soc Am, 92. *Prof Exp:* Asst prof anat, Karolinska Inst, Sweden, 45; Swedish Med Res Coun fel biol, Mass Inst Technol, 47-48; assoc prof anat, Karolinska Inst, Sweden, 49-60. *Concurrent Pos:* Mem & founder exec comt, Int Fedn Electron Micros Socs, 54-62 & Int Brain Res Orgn; ed & founder, J Ultrastruct Res, 57-89; prof & head, Dept Histol, Karolinska Inst, Sweden, 60-62, NSF spec fel, 65-66; sr consult, Vet Admin Radioisotope Serv, 61, 65 & 66. *Mem:* Fel Am Acad Arts & Sci; hon mem Soc Electron Micros Japan; hon mem Scand Electron Micros Soc; hon mem Electron Micros Soc Am. *Res:* Ultrastructure of cells as related to function; molecular structure and functional significance of cellular membranes; neuronal circuitry of the retina; neurophysiology of vision. *Mailing Add:* 1345 Casiano Rd Los Angeles CA 90049

SKADRON, GEORGE, PHYSICS, ASTROPHYSICS. *Current Pos:* PROF & CHMN, PHYSICS DEPT, ILL STATE UNIV, 86- *Personal Data:* b Vienna, Austria, July 1, 36; US citizen; m 65; c 1. *Educ:* Purdue Univ, BS, 57; Univ Rochester, MA, 60, PhD(physics), 65. *Prof Exp:* Res assoc physics, Univ Md, 65-67; Nat Acad Sci-Nat Res Coun res assoc, Res Labs, Environ Sci Serv Admin, 67-69; from asst prof to assoc prof, 69-75, prof physics, Drake Univ, 75-86. *Concurrent Pos:* Vis scientist, Max-Planck Inst Aeronomy, WGer, 75-76 & Max-Planck Inst Physics & Astrophys, 83. *Mem:* Am Phys Soc; Am Geophys Union; Union Concerned Scientists. *Res:* Cosmic radiation; plasma astrophysics; ionospheric physics; charged particle acceleration by shock waves in space. *Mailing Add:* Dept Physics Ill State Univ Normal IL 61761

SKADRON, PETER, SOLID STATE PHYSICS. *Current Pos:* asst prof, 67-71, assoc prof, 71-80, PROF PHYSICS, BUTLER UNIV, 80- *Personal Data:* b Vienna, Austria, Jan 19, 34; US citizen; m 63; c 1. *Educ:* Purdue Univ, BS, 54, MS, 57, PhD(physics), 65. *Prof Exp:* Res physicist, Res & Develop Lab, Sprague Elec Co, 64-67. *Mem:* AAAS; Am Phys Soc. *Res:* Electrical transport properties in metals and semiconductors. *Mailing Add:* 6445 Park Central Dr W Indianapolis IN 46260

SKAFF, MICHAEL SAMUEL, MATHEMATICS. *Current Pos:* PROF MATH, UNIV DETROIT, 68-, PRES, MICRO SCI, 84- *Personal Data:* b Boston, Mass, June 21, 36; m 64; c 3. *Educ:* Univ Mich, BS, 58; Univ Ill, MS, 60; Univ Calif, Los Angeles, PhD(math), 68. *Prof Exp:* Comput engr, Douglas Aircraft Co, 62-63; sr staff mathematician, Hughes Aircraft Co, 63-68. *Concurrent Pos:* Adj prof, Lincoln Inst Land Policy, Harvard Univ, 68- & Int Asn Assessing Officers. *Mem:* Am Math Soc; Math Asn Am; Int Asn Assessing Officers. *Res:* Vector valued Orlicz spaces; computer simulation and modeling; calculus of variation and optimization; computer assisted mass appraisal systems and computerized governmental software. *Mailing Add:* 585 Saddle Lane Grosse Pointe MI 48236-2728

SKAGGS, LESTER S, PHYSICS. *Current Pos:* from asst prof to assoc prof, 48-56, prof med physics, 56-79, EMER PROF MED PHYSICS, UNIV CHICAGO, 79- *Personal Data:* b Trenton, Mo, Nov 21, 11; m 39, Ruth Coffnedu; c Margaret L, John B & Mary (Anderson). *Educ:* Univ Mo, AB, 33, AM, 34; Univ Chicago, PhD(physics), 39. *Prof Exp:* Asst math, Univ Mo, 35; asst physics, Univ Chicago, 37-41; physicist, Michael Reese Hosp, 40-41, Carnegie Inst Technol, 41-43, Univ Mich, 43-44 & Univ Calif, 44-45, Michael Reese Hosp, 45-48. *Concurrent Pos:* Physicist, Michael Reese Hosp, 45-49; sr scientist, King Faisal Specialist Hosp & Res Ctr, Riyadh, Saudi Arabia, 79-84. *Mem:* Fel Am Phys Soc; fel AAAS; fel Am Col Radiol; Am Asn Physicists Med; Radiol Soc NAm; fel Royal Soc Med. *Res:* High energy sources of radiation for therapy; dosimetry; neutron therapy. *Mailing Add:* 359 Osage St Park Forest IL 60466

SKAGGS, RICHARD WAYNE, AGRICULTURAL DRAINAGE, WETLAND HYDROLOGY. *Current Pos:* from asst prof to prof, 70-84, DISTINGUISHED UNIV PROF & WILLIAM NEAL REYNOLDS PROF, BIOL & AGR ENG DEPT, NC STATE UNIV, 84- *Personal Data:* b Grayson, Ky, Aug 20, 42; m 62, Judy A Kuhn; c Rebecca & Steven. *Educ:* Univ Ky, BS, 64, MS, 66; Purdue Univ, PhD(agr eng), 70. *Honors & Awards:* Super Serv Award, USDA, 86 & 90; Hancor Soil & Water Eng Award, Am Soc Agr Engrs, 86, John Deere Gold Medal Award, 93; Alexander Quarles Holladay Medal for Excellence, NC State Univ, 94. *Prof Exp:* Res asst, Agr Eng Dept, Univ Ky, 62-64, grad res asst, 64-66; grad instr, Agr Eng Dept, Purdue Univ, 66-70. *Concurrent Pos:* Vchmn, Unsaturated Flow Comt, Am Soc Agr Engrs, 69-72, chmn, 72-75, mem, Benefits Agr Drainage Comt, 77-, vchmn, Drainage Res Comt, 77-79, chmn, 79-82, chmn & vchmn, Drainage Group, 83-87, mem, Res Comt, 84-86, Monograph Comt, 85-90, assoc ed, Trans Am Soc Agr Engrs, 85-87; mem, Tech Comt Subsurface Water, Am Geophys Union, 75-79; adv, Res Comt, Irrigation & Drainage Div, Am Soc Civil Engrs, 79-85; young researcher award, Am Soc Agr Engrs, 81; consult var terms, 81-90; vis prof, Ohio State Univ, Columbus, 86. *Mem:* Nat Acad Eng; fel Am Soc Agr Engrs; Am Geophys Union; Soil Conserv Soc Am; Sigma Xi. *Res:* Agricultural drainage and water table management; developed the computer simulation mode, DRAINMOD, used internationally to design and evaluate water management systems for production, water quality, and salinity control; author of various publications. *Mailing Add:* Dept Biol & Agr Eng NC State Univ PO Box 7625 Raleigh NC 27695-7625. *Fax:* 919-515-7760; *E-Mail:* Wayne_skaggs@ncsu.edu

SKAGGS, ROBERT L, METALLURGICAL ENGINEERING. *Current Pos:* assoc prof eng, 69-72, chmn dept, 72-77, PROF ENG, UNIV NEV, LAS VEGAS, 72- *Personal Data:* b St Louis, Mo, Apr 2, 32; m 61; c 3. *Educ:* Mo Sch Mines, BS, 55; Iowa State Univ, MS, 58, PhD(metall), 67. *Prof Exp:* Develop engr, Pigments Dept, E I du Pont de Nemours & Co, 55-56; mat engr, Standard Oil Co, Calif, 58-61; sr mat engr, Aeronaut Div, Honeywell Corp, 62-64; asst prof metall eng, Univ Ky, 67-69. *Mem:* Am Soc Metals; Am Soc Eng Educ. *Res:* Metal joining; plastic deformation of alloys; corrosion. *Mailing Add:* Dept Mech Eng Univ Nev 4505 S Maryland Pkwy Las Vegas NV 89154-4027

SKALA, JAMES HERBERT, ANALYTICAL BIOCHEMISTRY, NUTRITION. *Current Pos:* RETIRED. *Personal Data:* b Oak Park, Ill, July 27, 29; m 49, Virginia L Braun. *Educ:* Beloit Col, BS, 50; Univ Minn, MS, 57, PhD(poultry sci), 61. *Prof Exp:* Food chemist tech serv div, Am Can Co, 50-53; biochemist, Peru Surv, Interdept Comt Nutrit Nat Defense, 59; asst prof poultry prod technol, Univ Wis-Madison, 60-69; chief anal biochem br, Chem Div, US Army Med Res & Nutrit Lab, Denver, 69-74; chief, Anal Biochem Sect, Letterman Army Inst Res, 74-76, chief, Biochem Div, Dept Nutrit, 76-81; res chemist, Western Human Nutrit Res Ctr, Agr Res Serv, USDA, 81-89. *Concurrent Pos:* Nutritionist, Uruguay Surv, Interdept Comt Nutrit Nat Defense, 62. *Mem:* Inst Food Technologists; Am Asn Clin Chem; Am Inst Nutrit; Am Chem Soc. *Res:* Analytical biochemistry; clinical chemistry; human nutrition; especially biochemistry and dietary survey techniques; food chemistry; poultry meat and egg products. *Mailing Add:* PO Box 868 Winchester OR 97495-0868

SKALA, JOSEF PETR, CANCER RESEARCH, DEVELOPMENTAL MEDICINE. *Current Pos:* sr lectr, Univ BC, 73-74, from asst prof to assoc prof, 74-84, assoc obstet & gynec & assoc physiol, 78, PROF PEDIAT, UNIV BC, 84-, PRIN INVESTR, RES CTR, 85- *Personal Data:* b Prague Czech, Aug 15, 41; Can citizen; c Peter & Martin. *Educ:* Charles Univ Prague, MD, 64; Univ BC, PhD(physiol), 73; FRCP(C), 77. *Honors & Awards:* Med Res Coun Scholar, 75-80. *Prof Exp:* Resident pediat, As-Cheb Gen Hosp, Czech, 64-66; asst prof exp physiol, Charles Univ Prague, 66-68; vis scientist biochem, Univ Stockholm, Sweden, 68-69; fel, pediat, obstet & gynec, Univ BC, 69-72 & metabolism, Hammersmith Hosp, London, UK, 72-73. *Concurrent Pos:* Vis prof, Charles Univ, 96. *Mem:* Am Soc Biochem & Molecular Biol; Biochem Soc; Can Soc Biochem & Molecular Biol; Soc Pediat Res; Can Med Asn; Czech Soc Arts & Scis. *Res:* Molecular mechanisms of hormonal regulation; thermogenesis of brown adipose tissue; hormonal regulation in ontogenic development and cancer; bone marrow transplantation; oncology. *Mailing Add:* Res Ctr Univ BC 950 W 28th Ave Vancouver BC V5Z 4H4 Can. *Fax:* 604-875-2496; *E-Mail:* skalaj@unixg.ubc.ca

SKALAK, RICHARD, BIOENGINEERING, FLUID MECHANICS. *Current Pos:* dir, Inst Mech & Mat, 92-96, PROF BIOENG, UNIV CALIF, SAN DIEGO, 88-, DIR, INST MECH & MAT, 92- *Personal Data:* b New York, NY, Feb 5, 23; m 53, Anna L Allison; c Steven L, Thomas C, Martha J & Barbara A. *Educ:* Columbia Univ, BS, 43, CE, 46, PhD(civil eng), 54. *Hon Degrees:* MD Univ Gothenburg, Sweden, 89. *Honors & Awards:* Alza Medal, Biomed Engr Soc, 83; Lissner Award, Am Soc Mech Engrs, 85, Melville Medal, 90; von Karman Medal, Am Soc Civil Engrs, 87; Poiseville Medal, Int Soc Biorheology, 89; Medal of Merit, Czech Acad Sci, 90; Frederick Birnberg Award, Sch Dent & Oral Surg, Columbia Univ, 93. *Prof Exp:* Instr struct anal & design, Columbia Univ, 46-54, from asst prof to prof fluid mech, 54-88, dir, inst bioeng, 85-88. *Concurrent Pos:* NSF fel, Cambridge Univ, 60-61; sr res fel, Gothenburg Univ, 67-68; mem, Bd Dir, Inst Appl Biotechnol, Gothenburg, Sweden, 76- *Mem:* Nat Acad Eng; fel Am Soc Mech Engrs; fel Am Acad Mech; fel Am Soc Civil Engrs; fel NY Acad Med; Biomed Eng Soc; fel Soc Eng Sci; fel Am Inst Med & Biol Eng. *Res:* Surface waves, vibration and shock wave phenomena in liquids; fluid mechanics of biological systems; mechanics of blood flow. *Mailing Add:* Dept Bioeng Univ Calif San Diego La Jolla CA 92093-0412. *Fax:* 619-534-5722; *E-Mail:* vskalak@bioeng.ucsd.edu

SKALKA, ANNA MARIE, MOLECULAR BIOLOGY, VIROLOGY. *Current Pos:* asst mem, Dept Cell Biol, 69-71, assoc mem, 71-76, mem, 76-80, HEAD, LAB MOLECULAR & BIOCHEM GENETICS, ROCHE INST MOLECULAR BIOL, 80- *Personal Data:* b New York, NY, July 2, 38; m 60; c 2. *Educ:* Adelphi Univ, AB, 59; NY Univ, PhD(microbiol), 64. *Prof Exp:* Am Cancer Soc fel molecular biol, Carnegie Inst Genetics Res Unit, 64-66, fel, 66-69. *Concurrent Pos:* Vis prof, Dept Molecular Biol, Albert Einstein Col Med, 73- & Rockefeller Univ, 75. *Mem:* AAAS; Am Soc Microbiol; Am Soc Biol Chem; Sigma Xi; Asn Women Sci. *Res:* Structure and function of DNA; host and viral functions in the synthesis of viral DNA and RNA; phage DNA as a vehicle for the amplification and study of eukaryotic genes; molecular biology of avian retroviruses. *Mailing Add:* Fox Chase Cancer Ctr 7701 Burholme Ave Philadelphia PA 19111-2412. *Fax:* 215-728-2778

SKALKA, HAROLD WALTER, OPHTHALMOLOGY. *Current Pos:* from asst prof to prof ophthal, Univ Ala, Birmingham, 73-81, actg chmn, Combined Prog Ophthal, 74-76, ASSOC PROF, DEPT MED, UNIV ALA, BRIMINGHAM, 80-, PROF & CHMN, COMBINED PROG OPHTHAL, 81- *Personal Data:* b New York City, NY, Aug 22, 41; m 65, Barbara J Herbert; c Jennifer, Gretchen & Kirsten. *Educ:* Cornell Univ, AB, 62; New York Univ, MD, 66. *Prof Exp:* Intern, Greenwich Hosp, Conn, 66-67; resident ophthal, Bellevue Hosp, Univ Hosp, Manhattan Vet Admin Hosp, 67-70; consult ophtal, St Judes Hosp, Montgomery, Ala, 71-73. *Concurrent Pos:* chief ophthal, USAF Regional Hosp, Maxwell AFB, Montgomery, 71-73; ophthalmologist, Lowndes Co Bd, Health Community Health Proj, 72. *Mem:* Am Col Surgeons; Am Acad Ophthal; Am Inst Ultrasound Med; Int Soc Clin Electrophysiol; Am Asn Univ Profs; Asn Res Vision & Ophthal; Ultrasound Soc. *Res:* Metabolic cataracts, ocular drug effects; ophthalmic ultrasonography; visual electrophysiology and psychophysics. *Mailing Add:* Eye Found Hosp Univ Ala 700 18th St S Suite 300 Birmingham AL 35233-1859. *Fax:* 205-325-8654

SKALKO, RICHARD G(ALLANT), DEVELOPMENTAL TOXICOLOGY, REPRODUCTIVE TOXICOLOGY. *Current Pos:* PROF ANAT & CELL BIOL & CHAIR DEPT, ETENN STATE UNIV COL MED, 77- *Personal Data:* b Providence, RI, Apr 10, 36; div; c Patricia L, Margaret A & Christine M. *Educ:* Providence Col, AB, 57; St Johns Univ, NY, MS, 59; Univ Fla, PhD(anat), 63. *Prof Exp:* From instr to asst prof anat, Cornell Univ Med Col, 63-67; from asst prof to assoc prof, La State Univ Med Ctr, New Orleans, 67-70; from assoc prof to prof anat & toxicol, Albany Med Ctr, 70-77. *Concurrent Pos:* Dir embryol, NY Dept Health Birth Defects, Inst, 70-77; vis prof, Inst Toxicol & Develop Pharmacol, Berlin, 78; mem, Toxicol Study Sect, NIH, 84-89 & Human Embryol Study Sect, 90-94. *Mem:* Soc Toxicol; Teratology Soc; Am Asn Anatomists; Am Soc Cell Biol; Europ Teratology Soc; Soc Develop Biol. *Res:* Embryology; toxicology; anatomy; cytology; developmental toxicology; reproductive toxicology. *Mailing Add:* Dept Anat & Cell Biol ETenn State Univ PO Box 70582 Johnson City TN 37614-0582. *Fax:* 423-461-7040; *E-Mail:* skalko@etsu-tn.edu

SKALNIK, J(OHN) G(ORDON), ELECTRICAL ENGINEERING. *Current Pos:* chmn dept, 68-71, dean, Col Eng, 71-76, PROF ELEC ENG, UNIV CALIF, SANTA BARBARA, 65- *Personal Data:* b Medford, Okla, May 30, 23; m 47; c 2. *Educ:* Okla Agr & Mech Col, BS, 44; Yale Univ, ME, 46, DEng, 55. *Prof Exp:* Instr elec eng, Yale Univ, 44-49, from asst prof to assoc prof, 49-65. *Mem:* Sr mem Inst Elec & Electronics Engrs. *Res:* Splitanode magnetrons; signal-to-noise ratio study; solid-state devices and circuits. *Mailing Add:* 567 Ronda Dr Santa Barbara CA 93111-1521

SKALNY, JAN PETER, SILICATE CHEMISTRY. *Current Pos:* CONSULT, 91- *Personal Data:* b Bratislava, Czech, Mar 19, 35; div; c 2. *Educ:* Univ Chem Tech, Prague, Eng Chem, 58; Acad Mining & Metall, Cracow, PhD(silicate chem), 65. *Prof Exp:* Technologist, Pragocement, Prague, 58-60; asst prof bldg mat, Slovak Tech Univ, Bratislava, 60-66; vis res worker cement chem, Cement & Concrete Asn Res Sta, Slough, Eng, 67; res fel cement & surface chem, Clarkson Col, 68-69; group leader, Tech Ctr, Am Cement Corp, 69-71; mgr prod develop, Pac Southwest Region, 71-72; res scientist, Martin Marietta Labs, 72-73, sr res scientist, 73-74, head, Cement Dept, 74-78, assoc dir, 78-85; dir, Construct Mat Res, Res Div, W R Grace & Co, 85-91. *Concurrent Pos:* Mem, Panel Waste Solidification, Comt Radioactive Waste Disposal, 76-77; Comt Status of US Cement & Concrete Res & Develop, 77-78, chmn, Comt Concrete Durability, Nat Acad Sci, 85-86. *Mem:* Fel Am Ceramic Soc (vpres, 86); Int Union Testing & Res Labs Mat & Structure; Am Soc Testing & Mat; Nat Acad Sci. *Res:* Building materials; cement production and hydration; admixture chemistry; research administration. *Mailing Add:* 11910 Thurloe Dr Lutherville MD 21093

SKALSKI, STANISLAUS, SOLID STATE PHYSICS. *Current Pos:* Asst prof, 64-72, chmn dept, 72-78, ASSOC PROF PHYSICS, FORDHAM UNIV, 72- *Personal Data:* b Englewood, NJ, Feb 1, 34. *Educ:* Polytech Inst Brooklyn, BS, 58; Rutgers Univ, MS, 60, PhD(physics), 64. *Mem:* Am Phys Soc. *Res:* Ferromagnetism and superconductivity. *Mailing Add:* 9 Donnybrook Dr Demarest NJ 07627-1006

SKAMENE, EMIL, CLINICAL IMMUNOLOGY. *Current Pos:* PROF MED, MCGILL UNIV, 84- *Personal Data:* b Aug 27, 41. *Educ:* Charles Univ, Prague, MD, 64; Czech Acad Sci, PhD(immunol), 68; FRCP(C), 73, FACP, 74. *Honors & Awards:* Gold Medal, Royal Col Physicians & Surgeons, 80; Alexandre-Besredka Award, French-Ger Found Soc Immunol, 89; Cinader Award, Can Soc Immunol, 91. *Prof Exp:* Postdoctoral res fel, Harvard Med Sch, 68-70; postdoctoral clin fel, McGill Univ, 70-74; res assoc, 74-84, sr scientist, Montreal Gen Hosp Res Inst, 85- *Concurrent Pos:* Assoc dir, Div Clin Immunol & Allergy, Montreal Gen Hosp, 84-, sr physician, 87-; prof, McGill's Ctr Studies in Aging, 86-, McGill Ctr Human Genetics, 87- & McGill Inst Parasitol, 89-; dir, McGill Ctr Study Host Resistance, 88-; mem sci prog comt, Royal Col Physicians & Surgeons, Can, 89-91, res comt, 91-92, strategic plan task force, Can Inst Acad Med, 89-90; gov, Am Col Physicians, 91- *Res:* Application of genetics to the study of macrophage responses to infection; genetic control of susceptibility to tuberculosis and leprosy in human populations; genetic basis for human disease; innovations for health care. *Mailing Add:* Montreal Gen Hosp 1650 Cedar Ave Montreal PQ H3G 1A4 Can. *Fax:* 514-933-7146

SKANAVIS, CONSTANTINA, MICROBIOLOGY. *Current Pos:* instr, Dept Microbiol, 84-85, ASSOC PROF, DEPT HEALTH & NUTRIT SCI, CALIF STATE UNIV, LOS ANGELES, 88- *Educ:* Calif State Univ, BS, 80, MS, 82; Univ Calif, Los Angeles, PhD, 88. *Prof Exp:* Health educr, Dow Chem, Greece, 82-83; res asst, Vet Admin Hosp, 83-84; asst prof, Los Angeles Col Chiropractic, 85-88. *Concurrent Pos:* Grantee, Calif State Univ, Los Angeles, 93, 94 & 95; Papageorgiou Found, 95; Sr Fulbright Prog, 95 & Can Studies Fac Enrichment, 95-96. *Mailing Add:* Dept Health & Nutrit Sci Calif State Univ Los Angeles CA 90032

SKANDALAKIS, JOHN ELIAS, SURGICAL ANATOMY & TECHNIQUE. *Current Pos:* PROF ANAT, SCH MED, EMORY UNIV, 63-, CHRIS CARLOS PROF SURG ANAT & TECHNIQUE, 77-, DIR CTR SURG ANAT & TECHNIQUE, 84- *Personal Data:* b Molai, Sparta, Greece, Jan 20, 20; nat US; m 50; c 3. *Educ:* Nat Univ, Athens, MD, 46; Emory Univ, MS, 50, PhD, 62. *Hon Degrees:* LLD, Woodrow Wilson Col Law, 87. *Honors & Awards:* Reader Award, Am J Gastroenterol, 65. *Prof Exp:* Dir surg training prog, 57-72, chmn dept postgrad educ, 73-77, sr attend surgeon, Piedmont Hosp, 77- *Concurrent Pos:* Mem Bd Regents, Univ Syst Ga, regent at large, 81-, chmn, 83-84; pvt pract; distinguished prof, Emory Univ, 80. *Mem:* AMA; fel Am Col Surg; Greek Surg Soc; Am Asn Anat; Am Asn Clin Anatomists; Soc Int Chir. *Res:* General and clinical surgery; surgical embryology; surgical anatomy and technique. *Mailing Add:* Ctr Surg Emory Univ Sch Med 1462 Clifton Rd Suite 307 Atlanta GA 30322

SKAPERDAS, GEORGE T(HEODORE), FUEL TECHNOLOGY & PETROLEUM ENGINEERING. *Current Pos:* RETIRED. *Personal Data:* b New York, NY, Jan 25, 14; m 45, Hope Strezou; c Theodore G & Peter G. *Educ:* McGill Univ, BEng, 36; Mass Inst Technol, SM, 38, ScD(chem eng), 41. *Prof Exp:* Lab chemist, British-Am Oil Co, Can, 36; test engr, Aluminum Co Can, Ltd, Que, 38; asst, Mass Inst Technol, 38-40; chem & process engr, M W Kellogg Co, New York, 40-51, assoc dir chem eng, 51-67, mgr develop, 67-73, mgr process eng, Pullman Kellogg, 73-74, dir coal develop, 74-75, sr consult, 75-79, pres, G T Skaperdas, P C, 80-93. *Concurrent Pos:* Adj prof, NY Univ, 47-53; consult engr, 79-93. *Mem:* Am Chem Soc; fel Am Inst Chem Engrs. *Res:* Gas absorption; heat transfer; corrosion; process development engineering; oxychlorination; coal gasification; hydrogen recovery; synthetic chemicals; air separation; economic evaluation; silicon manufacture. *Mailing Add:* 14 Wychview Dr Westfield NJ 07090-1821

SKARDA, R VENCIL, JR, MATHEMATICS. *Current Pos:* Asst prof, 65-71, ASSOC PROF MATH, BRIGHAM YOUNG UNIV, 71- *Personal Data:* b Los Angeles, Calif, May 22, 40; m 71; c 7. *Educ:* Pomona Col, BA, 61; Calif Inst Technol, MS, 64, PhD(math), 66. *Mem:* Math Asn Am; Am Math Soc; London Math Soc. *Res:* Analytic number theory; functional analysis and functional iterations; combinatorics; inequalities in l-1-space; control theory. *Mailing Add:* Dept Math Brigham Young Univ TMCB 318 Provo UT 84602

SKARLOS, LEONIDAS, CHEMISTRY, MATHEMATICS. *Current Pos:* Sr chemist, Texaco Inc, 69-74, res chemist, Richmond Res Labs, 74-79, PROJ CHEMIST, PORT ARTHUR RES LABS, TEXACO INC, 79- *Personal Data:* b Manchester, NH, Apr 11, 41; m 70. *Educ:* Univ Vt, BA, 64; Univ NH, MS, 66; Boston Col, PhD(chem), 69. *Res:* Developing methods of determining pollution resulting from coal gasification. *Mailing Add:* 9475 Glen Meadow Lane Beaumont TX 77706

SKARSGARD, HARVEY MILTON, PHYSICS. *Current Pos:* from asst prof to assoc prof, 58-69, PROF PHYSICS, UNIV SASK, 69- *Personal Data:* b Viscount, Sask, Feb 27, 29; m 59; c 3. *Educ:* Univ Sask, MSc, 50; McGill Univ, PhD(physics), 55. *Prof Exp:* Seismic interpreter, Explor Dept, Imp Oil, Ltd, 51-53; Nat Res Coun fel nuclear physics, Atomic Energy Res Estab, Eng, 56-57; Nat Res Coun fel plasma physics, European Orgn Nuclear Res, Switz, 57-58. *Mem:* Am Phys Soc; Can Asn Physicists; Can Asn Univ Teachers. *Res:* Plasma physics; beam-plasma interactions; current-generated wave instabilities in toroidal geometry; turbulent heating. *Mailing Add:* 1515 Shannon Crescent Saskatoon SK S7H 2T6 Can

SKARSGARD, LLOYD DONALD, RADIATION BIOLOGY, BIOPHYSICS. *Current Pos:* head, Biophysics Dept, BC Cancer Found, 72-78, head, Med Biophys Univ, 78-92, res dir, 81-87, HEAD, DEPT MED BIOPHYS, BC CANCER FOUND, 92- *Personal Data:* b Viscount, Sask, Aug 16, 33; m 60, Margaret Ready; c Erik, Paul, Peter & Kirsten. *Educ:* Univ Sask, BE, 55, MSc, 56; Univ Toronto, PhD(radiation physics), 60. *Prof Exp:* Res assoc biophys, Yale Univ, 60-62, asst prof, 62-67; assoc prof physics, McMaster Univ, 67-72. *Concurrent Pos:* Consult physicist, Hartford Hosp, Conn, 61-67; head, Batho Biomed Facil, Tri-Univ Meson Facil, Univ BC, & hon prof physics & path, 72- *Mem:* AAAS; Radiation Res Soc; Biophys Soc; Can Biophys Soc; cellular response to low radiation doses; cellular response to bioreductive drugs. *Res:* X-ray and gamma-ray spectra; radiobiology of pi-mesons and heavy ions; radiation damage and repair; radiosensitization of hypoxic cells. *Mailing Add:* Med Biophys BC Cancer Res Ctr 601 West Tenth Ave Vancouver BC V5Z 1L3 Can

SKARSTEDT, MARK T(EOFIL), biochemistry, research administration, for more information see previous edition

SKARULIS, JOHN ANTHONY, PHYSICAL CHEMISTRY. *Current Pos:* from instr to assoc prof, 45-54, PROF CHEM, ST JOHN'S UNIV, NY, 54- *Personal Data:* b New Haven, Conn, Feb 18, 17; m 42; c 2. *Educ:* St John's Univ, NY, BS, 37, MS, 39; NY Univ, PhD(chem), 49. *Prof Exp:* Asst res chemist, Gen Chem Co, 40-42, res chemist, 44-45, supvr & explosive chemist, Gen Chem Defense Corp, 42-44. *Mem:* Am Chem Soc. *Res:* Phase rule studies; inorganic fluorine compounds. *Mailing Add:* 1 Harris Ct Bellmore NY 11710-3524

SKATRUD, THOMAS JOSEPH, BIOENGINEERING. *Current Pos:* DIR OPERS UNIVERSAL BIOVENTURES, UNIVERSAL FOODS CORP, MILWAUKEE, WIS, 88-; DIR OPERS, FLAVOR INGREDIENTS, INT FLAVORS & FRAGRANCES, INC. *Personal Data:* b Manitowoc, Wis, Feb 27, 53. *Educ:* Univ Wis, Madison, BS, 75, PhD(biochem), 79. *Prof Exp:* Dir biochem, Bio-Tech Resources, Inc, 79-80, vpres, 80-86; sr res mgr, Anheuser Busch Co, St Louis, 86-88. *Mem:* Am Chem Soc. *Mailing Add:* Int Flavors & Fragrances Inc N92W 14224 Anthony Ave Menomonee Falls WI 53051. *Fax:* 414-253-5641

SKAU, KENNETH ANTHONY, PHARMACOLOGY. *Current Pos:* asst prof, 83-89, ASSOC PROF PHARMACOL, UNIV CINCINNATI, 89- *Personal Data:* b Chicago, Ill, Apr 18, 47; m 72, Kathleen Canty; c Michael B & Colleen T. *Educ:* Ohio State Univ, BS, 70, PhD(pharm), 77. *Prof Exp:* Trainee pharmacol, May Grad Sch Med, 77-80, instr, 79-80; res asst prof pharmacol, Col Pharm, Univ Utah, 80-82. *Mem:* Soc Neurosci; AAAS; NY Acad Sci. *Res:* Pharmacology, biochemistry and neurobiology of acetylcholinesterase molecular forms and pathological conditions related to aberrations of these forms; mechanisms of muscle and nerve diseases; diabetic neuropathy. *Mailing Add:* Col Pharm Univ Cincinnati Cincinnati OH 45267. *E-Mail:* ken.skau@uc.edu

SKAUEN, DONALD M, PHARMACY, SONOPHORESIS. *Current Pos:* from asst prof to prof, 48-79, EMER PROF PHARM, UNIV CONN, 79- *Personal Data:* b Newton, Mass, May 14, 16; m 42, Rachel M Burns; c Deborah & Bruce. *Educ:* Mass Col Pharm, BS, 38, MS, 42; Purdue Univ, PhD(pharm), 49. *Prof Exp:* Asst, Mass Col Pharm, 38-40; chief pharmacist, Children's Med Ctr, Boston, 40-46; asst, Purdue Univ, 46-48. *Concurrent Pos:* Res assoc, Marine Res Labs, Univ Conn, 59-64. *Mem:* Am Soc Hosp Pharmacists; Am Pharmaceut Asn; Acad Pharmaceut Sci; AAAS; Sigma Xi. *Res:* Ultrasound and radioisotopes in pharmacy research; pharmaceutical research and development; radio ecology. *Mailing Add:* 16 Storrs Heights Rd Storrs CT 06268

SKAVARIL, RUSSELL VINCENT, GENETICS. *Current Pos:* Assoc prof, 64-77, PROF GENETICS, STATIST & COMPUT APPLN, OHIO STATE UNIV, 77- *Personal Data:* b Omaha, Nebr, Dec 6, 36; m 60; c 4. *Educ:* Univ Omaha, BA, 58; Creighton Univ, MT, 59; Ohio State Univ, MSc, 60, PhD(zool), 64. *Mem:* Am Genetic Asn; Biomet Soc. *Res:* Use of computers in biology. *Mailing Add:* 222 E Torrence Rd Columbus OH 43224

SKAVDAHL, R(ICHARD) E(ARL), NUCLEAR ENGINEERING. *Current Pos:* RETIRED. *Personal Data:* b Detroit, Mich, Nov 24, 34; m 59, Patricia A Wolfe; c Kristen, Karen & Eric. *Educ:* Mass Inst Technol, SB, 56, ScD(nuclear eng), 62; Univ Mich, MSE, 57. *Prof Exp:* Res engr, Am Metal Prod Co, Mich, 58-60; sr engr, Gen Elec Co, Wash, 62-64; mgr fuel element design & eval, 64-65; mgr fuel element design & eval, Pac Northwest Labs, Battelle Mem Inst, 65-66; proj engr, Fast Ceramic Reactor Develop Prog, Gen Elec Co, 66-69; proj engr demonstration plant develop, 69-70, mgr develop & test progs, 70-73, mgr, Clinch River Proj, 73-78, mgr, Boiling Water Reactor 4 Proj, 78-79, mgr, Boiling Water Reactor 4 & 5 Proj, 79-81, mgr, Nuclear Serv Mkt & Prod Planning, 83, mgr, Piping Improv Prog, 83-84, mgr, Waste Mgt Serv Oper, 84-85, serv gen mgr, Eng Serv, 85-92, eng gen mgr, 92-94. *Mem:* Am Nuclear Soc; Sigma Xi. *Res:* Nuclear power reactor design, development and project management. *Mailing Add:* 6680 Leyland Park Dr San Jose CA 95120

SKAVENSKI, ALEXANDER ANTHONY, PSYCHOPHYSIOLOGY, NEUROPHYSIOLOGY. *Current Pos:* from asst prof to assoc prof, 72-80, PROF PSYCHOL, NORTHEASTERN UNIV, 80- *Personal Data:* b East Liverpool, Ohio, Jan 27, 43; m 67, Nina J Ludwig; c Matt & Stephanie. *Educ:* Univ Md, BS, 65, PhD(psychol), 70. *Prof Exp:* Fel biomed eng, Johns Hopkins Univ, 70-72. *Concurrent Pos:* Vis scholar, Univ Calif, Berkeley, 78-79, Dept Psychol, Harvard Univ, 92-93; vis sr scientist, Eye Res Inst Retina Found, Boston. *Mem:* AAAS; Asn Res Vision & Ophthal; Soc Neurosci; Sigma Xi. *Res:* Eye movement control and the consequence of eye movement on vision and visual space perception. *Mailing Add:* Dept Psychol 125 NI Bldg Northeastern Univ 360 Huntington Ave Boston MA 02115. *Fax:* 617-373-8714; *E-Mail:* skavenski@neu.edu

SKEAN, JAMES DAN, MICROBIOLOGY. *Current Pos:* asst prof, 66-70, assoc prof, 70-80, PROF BIOL, WESTERN KY UNIV, 80- *Personal Data:* b Kenova, WVa, Feb 19, 32; m 55; c 4. *Educ:* Berea Col, BS, 56; Univ Tenn, MS, 59, PhD(microbiol), 66. *Prof Exp:* Res asst dairying, Univ Tenn, 56-66. *Mem:* AAAS; Am Soc Microbiol. *Res:* Influence of psychophilic bacteria on quality of milk and dairy products; use of autogenous vaccines in control of staphylococcal bovine mastitis. *Mailing Add:* Dept Biol Albion Col Albion MI 49224

SKEATH, J EDWARD, mathematics; deceased, see previous edition for last biography

SKEEL, ROBERT DAVID, NUMERICAL ANALYSIS, SCIENTIFIC COMPUTING. *Current Pos:* From asst prof to assoc prof, 74-86, PROF COMPUT SCI, UNIV ILL, 86- *Personal Data:* b Calgary, Alta, Can, Dec 17, 47. *Educ:* Univ Alta, BSc, 69, PhD(comput sci), 74; Univ Toronto, MSc, 70. *Concurrent Pos:* Vis res asst prof comput sci, Univ Ill, 73-74; res assoc, Univ Manchester, 80-81. *Mem:* Asn Comput Mach; Soc Indust & Appl Math. *Res:* Numerical methods for differential equations; computational molecular biophysics. *Mailing Add:* Dept Comput Sci Univ Ill 1304 W Springfield Ave Urbana IL 61801-2987

SKEELES, JOHN KIRKPATRICK, VETERINARY MEDICINE, MICROBIOLOGY. *Current Pos:* PROF POULTRY DIS, UNIV ARK, 78- *Personal Data:* b Alexandria, La, June 27, 45; m 67; c 4. *Educ:* Okla State Univ, BS, 67, DVM, 69; Univ Ga, MS, 77, PhD(microbiol), 78, Am Col Vet Microbiologists, dipl. *Prof Exp:* Vet, US Army, 69-75; vet med resident microbiol, Univ Ga, 75-78. *Mem:* Am Vet Med Asn; Am Asn Avian Pathologists; Sigma Xi; Am Col Vet Microbiologists. *Res:* Microbial diseases of poultry. *Mailing Add:* Poultry Sci B114 Animal Sci Univ of Ark Fayetteville AR 72701-1202

SKEEN, JAMES NORMAN, FOREST ECOLOGY, TERRESTRIAL COMMUNITY ECOLOGY. *Current Pos:* PRIN, JAMES N SKEEN CONSULTING SERV, 93- *Personal Data:* b Knoxville, Tenn, Feb 23, 42; m 66, Marianne Jefferson. *Educ:* Maryville Col, Tenn, BS, 64; Univ Ga, MS, 66, PhD(bot ecol), 69. *Prof Exp:* Asst prof biol, Mercer Univ, Atlanta, 69-70, actg chmn dept, 70-71; ecologist, Fernbank Sci Ctr, Atlanta, Ga, 72-85; assoc dir, Fernbank Mus Natural Hist, 85-93. *Concurrent Pos:* Consult, Environ Sci Div, Oak Ridge Nat Lab, 76-77; adj assoc prof, Dept Biol, Emory Univ, 78-95; sci adv bd, Marshall Forest (Nature Conserv), 80-90. *Mem:* Wilderness Med Soc; Torrey Bot Club. *Res:* Community analysis and system maturity; regeneration dynamics; micrometeorology; selection and evaluation of biomass fuel species. *Mailing Add:* 553 N Superior Ave Decatur GA 30033. *Fax:* 404-633-1486; *E-Mail:* jnscon@cris.com

SKEEN, LESLIE CARLISLE, NEUROANATOMY, COMPARATIVE NEUROLOGY. *Current Pos:* ASST PROF NEUROSCI & PSYCHOL, UNIV DEL, 77- *Personal Data:* b Dearborn, Mich, Feb 28, 42; m 63; c 3. *Educ:* Fla State Univ, PhD(psychobiol), 72. *Prof Exp:* Fel anat, Duke Univ Med Ctr, 73-76, asst prof med res, 76-77. *Concurrent Pos:* Prin investr, Brain Res Lab, Univ Del, 77- *Mem:* AAAS; Am Asn Anatomists; Soc Neurosci; Sigma Xi. *Res:* Evolutionary, developmental, and structural aspects of the vertebrate olfactory system, and its contributions to complex behavioral patterns. *Mailing Add:* Dept Psychol Univ Del Newark DE 19717-0001

SKEES, HUGH BENEDICT, APPLIED CHEMISTRY, INTELLECTUAL PROPERTY ADMINISTRATION. *Current Pos:* RETIRED. *Personal Data:* b Elizabethtown, Ky, Sept 6, 27; m 56; c 7. *Educ:* St Louis Univ, BS, 54, MS, 63. *Prof Exp:* Chemist, Petrolite Corp, 56-62; proj engr explor res, Stand Register Co, 62-64, supvr, 64-67; tech dir, Wallace Bus Forms Inc, 67-70; appl res mgr, Stand Register Co, 70-80, printing prod res mgr, 80-95, tech dir res, 85-87, tech dir advan graphic arts, 87-89, tech dir intellectual property, 89-95. *Concurrent Pos:* Consult, 95- *Mem:* AAAS; Am Chem Soc. *Res:* Petroleum waxes and derivatives; application of waxes in packaging, polishes and carbon paper; business forms technology; printing; carbon paper; adhesives; coating technology; chemical and instrumental analysis; physical testing; instrument design; test development; carbonless paper and imaging technology; document security systems; electronic printing and imaging technology; administration of intellectual property program. *Mailing Add:* Standard Regist Co LTB PO Box 1167 Dayton OH 45401-1167

SKEGGS, LEONARD TUCKER, JR, BIOCHEMISTRY. *Current Pos:* RETIRED. *Personal Data:* b Fremont, Ohio, June 9, 18; m 41, Jean Hossel; c 3. *Educ:* Youngstown Univ, AB, 40; Western Reserve Univ, MS, 42, PhD(biochem), 48; Am Bd Clin Chem, dipl. *Hon Degrees:* DSc, Youngstown Univ, 60; LHD, Baldwin-Wallace Col, 80. *Honors & Awards:* Flemming Award, 57; Van Slyke Medal, 63; Am Chem Soc Award, 66; Ames Award, 66; Middleton Award, 68; Stouffer Award, 68; Bendetti-Pichler Award Microchem, 71; John Scott Award, 72; Cleveland Award Artificial Organs, 78; Edward Longstreth Medal, Fraklin Inst, 80. *Prof Exp:* Chief, Biochem Sect & Hypertension Res Lab, Vet Admin Hosp, Cleveland, 47-68, dir, Hypertension Res Lab, 68-83, med investr hypertension, 76-82; res fel clin biochem, Case Western Reserve Univ, 48-49, from instr to sr instr biochem, 50-52, from asst prof to assoc prof, 52-69, prof, 69-83, emer prof, biochem, 83- *Mem:* Am Chem Soc; Am Soc Biol Chem; fel Am Asn Clin Chem; fel NY Acad Sci; Sigma Xi. *Res:* Hypertension; automatic chemical analysis; multiple automatic analysis. *Mailing Add:* 10212 Blair Lane Kirtland OH 44094-9514

SKEHAN, JAMES WILLIAM, REGIONAL GEOLOGY, TECTONICS. *Current Pos:* Asst prof geophys, Boston Col, 56-61, from asst dir to assoc dir, Weston Observ, 56-72, dir, 73-93, chmn, Dept Geol, 58-68, from assoc prof to prof geophys & geol, 62-93, chmn, Dept Geol & Geophys, 68-70, dir, Environ Ctr, 70-72, actg dean, Col Arts & Sci, 72-73, EMER PROF GEOPHYS & GEOL, BOSTON COL, 93- *Personal Data:* b Houlton, Maine, Apr 25, 23. *Educ:* Boston Col, AB, 46, AM, 47; Weston Col, PhL, 47, STB, 54, STL, 55; Harvard Univ, AM, 51, PhD(geol), 53. *Hon Degrees:* DHumL, St Joseph's Col, 78; DSc, Univ Maine, Presque Isle, 89. *Honors & Awards:* Neil Miner Award, Nat Asn Geol Teachers. *Concurrent Pos:* Chmn, Eng Geol Div, Geol Soc Am, 75; dir & proj mgr, Narragansett Basin Coal Proj, 76-; vpres, Int Div, Geol Soc Am, 93- *Mem:* AAAS; Geol Soc Am; Nat Asn Geol Teachers (pres, 71-72); Am Geophys Union; Geol Soc London; Asn Eng Geols. *Res:* Global tectonics and plate tectonics, origin and evolution of the earth's crust with special reference to origin of mountains and terranes in the circum-atlantic region; origin and evolution of metamorphic coal basins. *Mailing Add:* Weston Observ 381 Concord Rd Weston MA 02193

SKEIST, IRVING, POLYMER CHEMISTRY. *Current Pos:* RETIRED. *Personal Data:* b Worcester, Mass, Apr 9, 15; m 39; c 4. *Educ:* Worcester Polytech Inst, BS, 35; Polytech Inst Brooklyn, MS, 43, PhD(polymer chem), 49. *Prof Exp:* Res chemist, Celanese Corp Am, 37-51; tech dir, Newark Paraffine Paper Co, 51-53 & Am Molding Powder, 53; mkt specialist, Gering Prod Inc, 53-54; consult & pres, Skeist Labs Inc, 54-81. *Mem:* Am Chem Soc; Soc Plastics Indust; Soc Plastics Engrs; Com Develop Asn; Chem Mkt Res Asn; Sigma Xi. *Res:* Epoxy resins; polymers; plastics; adhesives; coatings; fibers. *Mailing Add:* 32 Laurel Ave Summit NJ 07901

SKELCEY, JAMES STANLEY, CERAMICS ENGINEERING. *Current Pos:* RETIRED. *Personal Data:* b Saginaw, Mich, Sept 26, 33; m 55; c 3. *Educ:* Univ Detroit, BS, 56; Mich State Univ, PhD(chem), 61. *Prof Exp:* Proj leader, Dow Chem Co, 61-72, res specialist, Inorg Res & Semiplants, 72-79, res leader ceramics & advan mat res, 79-93. *Mem:* Am Chem Soc; Sigma Xi. *Res:* Brine chemicals; inorganic fluids and polymers; flame retardant fillers; high temperature chemistry; ceramics. *Mailing Add:* 2807 Schade West Dr Midland MI 48640-2237

SKELL, PHILIP S, ORGANIC CHEMISTRY. *Current Pos:* from asst prof to prof, 52-74, Evan Pugh prof, 74-84, EMER EVAN PUGH PROF CHEM, PA STATE UNIV, 84- *Personal Data:* b New York, NY, Dec 30, 18; m 48, Dorthy M; c 4. *Educ:* City Col, BS, 38; Columbia Univ, MA, 41; Duke Univ, PhD(chem), 42. *Hon Degrees:* LLD, Lewis Col, 65. *Prof Exp:* Instr chem, City Col, 38-39; asst, North Regional Res Lab, USDA, Ill, 42-43; res assoc antibiotics, Univ Ill, 43-46; instr chem, Univ Chicago, 46-47; asst prof, Univ Portland, 47-52. *Concurrent Pos:* Committeeman, Nat Res Coun; NSF Sr Scientist Award, 61; Guggenheim fel, 68; Alexander von Humboldt Found sr scientist award, 74-75. *Mem:* Nat Acad Sci; Am Chem Soc. *Res:* Free radicals; carbenes; methylenes; carbonium ions; nonmetal atomic chemistry; ground and excited states; transition metal atomic chemistry. *Mailing Add:* Davey Lab Pa State Univ 220 Whitmore Lab University Park PA 16802. *Fax:* 814-238-0290; *E-Mail:* tvk@psu.edu

SKELLAND, ANTHONY HAROLD PETER, CHEMICAL ENGINEERING. *Current Pos:* PROF CHEM ENG, GA INST TECHNOL, 79- *Personal Data:* b Birmingham, Eng, Feb 21, 28. *Educ:* Univ Birmingham, Eng, BSc, 48, PhD(chem eng), 52. *Prof Exp:* Postdoctoral, Univ Birmingham, Eng, 52-54; factory dept mgr, Procter & Gamble, Eng, 54-56, res & develop chem engr, 56-59; asst prof chem eng, Ill Inst Technol, 59-62; assoc prof, Univ Notre Dame, 62-66, prof, 66-69; Ashland prof, Univ Ky, 69-79. *Concurrent Pos:* Vis prof chem eng, Fed Univ Rio de Janeiro, 78-79. *Mem:* Fel Am Inst Chem Engrs; Royal Soc Chem; Am Inst Chem Eng; fel Inst Petrol. *Res:* Mass transfer, extraction, droplet phenomena, non-Newtonian flow and heat transfer; mixing and scaleup. *Mailing Add:* Sch Chem Eng Ga Inst Technol Atlanta GA 30332-0100. *Fax:* 404-894-2866

SKELLEY, DEAN SUTHERLAND, ENDOCRINOLOGY, CLINICAL CHEMISTRY. *Current Pos:* TECH DIR, LAB CORP, INC, SAN ANTONIO, TEX, 89- *Personal Data:* b Melrose, Mass, Mar 27, 38; m 66, Eleanor Bachofen; c Caroline, Rachel, Jonathan & Susanna. *Educ:* Bates Col, BS, 60; Ohio State Univ, MS, 65, PhD(physiol), 68. *Prof Exp:* Dir, Steroid Lab, Col Vet Med, Ohio State Univ, 68-70; asst prof obstet & gynec & assoc dir, Reproduction Res Lab, Baylor Col Med, 70-77; clin biochemist, Dept Path, Mem Hosp Syst, Houston, 77-83; dir opers, Severance Ref Lab, San Antonio, Tex, 83-84; vpres sci affairs, Cone Biotech Inc, Seguin, Tex, 85-86; vpres med prod develop, Biosysts Develop Co, San Antonio, Tex, 86-88. *Concurrent Pos:* Consult biol diag prod, AMF, Inc, 73-85; consult, Ctr Dis Control, 74-76; consult radioimmunoassay, Dept Path, Mem Hosp Syst, Houston, 74-; exec ed, Ligand Rev, 79-82; pres, Tech & Prof Serv, Inc, 79- *Mem:* Coun Biol Ed; Am Asn Clin Chem; Am Med Writers Asn. *Res:* Radioimmunoassay of steroids, polypeptide hormones and pharmacological agents; competitive protein binding and radioreceptor assays; ligand assays; regulatory affairs; product development; chemiluminescent assays; clinical laboratory operations. *Mailing Add:* PO Box 160879 San Antonio TX 78280

SKELLEY, GEORGE CALVIN, JR, ANIMAL SCIENCE, FOOD SCIENCE. *Current Pos:* from asst prof to assoc prof, 62-72, prof animal sci, 72-95, PROF & CHAIR, ANIMAL DAIRY & VET SCI, CLEMSON UNIV, 95- *Personal Data:* b Boise City, Okla, Jan 28, 37; m 58, Aletha Brown; c Mary (Tripp) & Martha (Blanton). *Educ:* Panhandle Agr & Mech Col, BS, 58; Univ Ky, MS, 60, PhD(meats), 63. *Honors & Awards:* Frank Burtner Award; Am Meat Sci Asn, Teaching Award. *Prof Exp:* Res asst meats, Univ Ky, 58-62. *Mem:* Am Meat Sci Asn; Sigma Xi; Am Soc Animal Sci; Inst Food Technol; Int Meat Sci Asn. *Res:* Evaluation of and effect of nutrition on beef and pork carcasses; studies on meat tenderness; reduced fat in processed meats. *Mailing Add:* Dept Animal Dairy & Vet Sci Clemson Univ Clemson SC 29634-0361. *Fax:* 864-656-3131

SKELLY, DAVID W, THIN FILM, VACUUM DEPOSITION. *Current Pos:* PHYS CHEMIST, GEN ELEC RES & DEVELOP LAB, 65- *Personal Data:* b Buffalo, NY, Dec 9, 38; m 62; c 4. *Educ:* Canisius Col, BS, 60; Univ Notre Dame, PhD(phys chem), 65. *Honors & Awards:* Gen Elec Dushman Award. *Concurrent Pos:* Fel, Univ Notre Dame, 65; lectr, training courses in sputter deposition, vacuum technol; consult, thin film process develop & equipment deposition. *Mem:* Am Vacuum Soc. *Res:* Metallizations for semiconductor devices; thin film deposition processes; sensor technology; liquid crystal display technology; electroluminescent displays; radiation effects in condensed matter; environmental coatings for high temperature applications. *Mailing Add:* 8 Hollywood Dr Burnt Hills NY 12027

SKELLY, JEROME PHILIP, SR, BIOCHEMISTRY, BIOPHARMACEUTICS. *Current Pos:* chief, Pharmacokinetics & Biopharmaceut Br, Food & Drug Admin, 75-79, dep dir, 79-83, dir, Div Biopharmaceut, 83-89, DEP DIR, OFF RES, CTR DRUG EVAL & RES, FOOD & DRUG ADMIN, 88-, ASSOC DIR, OFF GENERIC DRUGS, 90- *Personal Data:* b Vermillion Twp, Ill, Dec 15, 32; m 57; c 3. *Educ:* Wayne State Univ, BS, 64, MS, 66, PhD(chem), 69. *Prof Exp:* Res asst connective tissue res, Wayne State Univ, 63-68; chemist, Bur Med, Food & Drug Admin, 68-72, dir, Div Clin Res, Bur Drugs, 72-74, chmn bioavailability comt, 73-77; scholar, Sch Pharm, Univ Calif, 74-75. *Concurrent Pos:* Sr exec serv & chmn, Pharmacokinetics, Pharmacodynamics & Drug Metab Sect, Am Asn Pharmaceut Scientists. *Mem:* Sigma Xi; Am Soc Clin Pharmacol & Therapeut; fel Am Asn Pharmaceut Scientists; Am Chem Soc; fel Am Col Clin Pharmacol; Controlled Release Soc. *Res:* Drug bioavailability, absorption, disposition, metabolism, elimination; drug dosage regimen; analysis of drug in physiological fluids; physical pharmacy; dosage form processing; development of in vitro systems to correlate and predict in vivo drug bioavailability and activity; dermato pharmacokinetics; controlled release drugs and specialized drug delivery systems. *Mailing Add:* 78 Harborside Rd Quincy MA 02171

SKELLY, MICHAEL FRANCIS, PHARMACOLOGY, BIOCHEMISTRY. *Current Pos:* develop anal chemist, 89-91, ASSOC DIR TECH OPERS, ANAL SERV DIV, HILL TOP BIOLABS INC, CINCINNATI, 91- *Personal Data:* b Washington, DC, Sept 22, 50; m 72, Ann Joyce; c Katherine. *Educ:* Univ Va, Charlottesville, BA, 72; George Washington Univ, PhD(pharmacol), 81. *Prof Exp:* Lab technician, dept clin path, Univ Va, 70-72, lab specialist, dept pharmacol, 72-73; postdoctoral fel toxicol, dept environ health, Univ Cincinnati, 80-83, sr fel geriat, 83-85; cell biologist, Environ Health Res & Testing, Inc, Cincinnati, 86-88; Staff scientist, Biol Res Faculty & Facility Inc, 88-90. *Mem:* Am Acad Clin Toxicol; Biomet Soc; fel Am Acad Vet Comp Toxicol; Am Asn Pharmaceut Scientists; Int Asn Therapeut Drug Monitoring & Clin Toxicol. *Res:* Pharmacokinetics; analytical biochemistry. *Mailing Add:* 1051 Timber Trail Cincinnati OH 45224-1617. *E-Mail:* usr13069@tso.uc.edu

SKELLY, NORMAN EDWARD, ANALYTICAL CHEMISTRY, PHYSICAL CHEMISTRY. *Current Pos:* RETIRED. *Personal Data:* b Minneapolis, Minn, Nov 27, 28; m 53; c 6. *Educ:* Col St Thomas, BS, 51; Univ Iowa, MS, 53, PhD, 55. *Prof Exp:* Assoc scientist, Dow Chem Co, 55-90. *Mem:* Am Chem Soc; Sigma Xi. *Res:* Liquid chromatography. *Mailing Add:* 2007 Sharon Ct Midland MI 48642

SKELTON, BOBBY JOE, horticulture, plant physiology, for more information see previous edition

SKELTON, EARL FRANKLIN, SOLID STATE PHYSICS. *Current Pos:* Nat Acad Sci-Nat Res Coun res assoc solid state physics, Solid State Div, 67-68, res physicist, 68-76, HEAD, PHASE TRANSFORMATION SECT, US NAVAL RES LAB, 76- *Personal Data:* b Hackensack, NJ, Apr 8, 40; m 87, T Francesca Fried; c Diana L Faujour & Isaac P. *Educ:* Fairleigh Dickinson Univ, BS, 62; Rensselaer Polytech Inst, PhD(physics), 67. *Honors & Awards:* Yuri Gargaran Satellite Commun Medal, USSR, 79; Thomas Edison Chapter Sigma Xi Res Award-Pure Science, 95; 5 pub awards, Nat Res Lab. *Concurrent Pos:* Lectr, Prince George's Community Col, 68-74; assoc prof lectr, George Washington Univ, 74-79, prof lectr, 79-; lectr, Univ Md, 75-; liaison scientist, Off Naval Res, Tokyo, 78; vis scholar, Stanford Univ, 80-81;

mem, Exec Comt, Stanford Synchrotron Radiation Lab Users' Orgn, 84-86, Nat Synchrotron Light Source, Users Exec Comt, 89-93. *Mem:* Fel Am Phys Soc; Am Crystallog Asn; Am Asn Physics Teachers; Sigma Xi; Am Asn Univ Professors. *Res:* Theoretical and experimental investigation of response of materials to conditions of extreme pressure and temperature; high transition temperature superconductors; selected III-V and II-VI compounds; phase transformation toughening mechanisms in ceramics; conventional x-ray scattering techniques and synchrotron produced radiation for very rapid in situ measurements; phase transformation kinetics and ultra-high temperature studies; Over 280 publications author or co-author. *Mailing Add:* US Naval Res Lab Code 6683 4555 Overlook Ave SE Washington DC 20375-5000. *Fax:* 202-767-4868; *E-Mail:* skelton@anvil.nrl.navy.mil

SKELTON, JOHN EDWARD, COMPUTER SCIENCE. *Current Pos:* PROF & DIR COMPUT SERVS, ORE STATE UNIV, CORVALLIS, 85- *Personal Data:* b Amarillo, Tex, May 10, 34; m 59, Katherine Dow; c Laura A, Jeanette K & Jeffrey E. *Educ:* Univ Denver, BA, 56, MA, 62, PhD, 71. *Prof Exp:* Mathematician, US Naval Ord Lab, Corona, Calif, 56-59; asst prof, Univ Denver, 67-74; dir, Comput Ctr, Univ Minn, Duluth, 74-85. *Concurrent Pos:* Fac adv, Univ Minn, 80-82. *Mem:* Asn Comput Mach; Asn Spec Interest Group Univ Comput; Sigma Xi. *Res:* Computer science; computing machinery. *Mailing Add:* 4140 NW Dale Dr Corvallis OR 97330

SKELTON, MARILYN MAE, FOOD SCIENCE, BIOCHEMISTRY. *Current Pos:* DEAN INSTR, NAT AM UNIV, COLO, 93- *Personal Data:* b Coffeyville, Kans, May 3, 36; m 58; c 3. *Educ:* Kans State Univ, BS, 57, MS, 58; Univ Wyo, PhD(biochem), 70. *Prof Exp:* Instr res foods & nutrit, Dept Foods & Nutrit, Kans State Univ, 59-62; asst prof foods & nutrit, Div Home Econ, Univ Wyo, 62-69; teacher sci & math, Army Educ Ctr, US Army, Ger, 71-72, educ counsr couns & admin, 72-74; asst prof foods & nutrit, Kans State Univ, 75-77; assoc prof hotel & restaurant mgt & acad coordr, Weekend Col, Univ Denver, 78-93. *Mem:* Inst Food Technologists; Int Food Serv Exec Asn. *Res:* Relationship of chemical composition and histology to meat tenderness; alkaline degradation of pectin; relationship of chemical and physical properties of fruits and vegetables to palatability; sensory evaluation of food service products. *Mailing Add:* 18121 E Berry Dr Aurora CO 80015

SKELTON, ROBERT EUGENE, ELECTRICAL ENGINEERING, AERONAUTICAL & ASTRONAUTICAL ENGINEERING. *Current Pos:* from asst prof to assoc prof, PROF AERONAUT & ASTRONAUT, PURDUE UNIV, 82- *Personal Data:* b Elberton, Ga, March 21, 38; m 71; c 4. *Educ:* Clemson, Univ BS, 63; Univ Alabama, MS, 70; UNiv Calif, Los Angeles, PhD(mech), 76. *Prof Exp:* Engr Lockheed Missiles & Space Co, Huntsville, Ala, 63-65; engr consult, Sperry Rand Corp, Huntsville, Ala, 65-75. *Concurrent Pos:* Mem, Aeronaut & Space Engr Bd, Nat Res Coun, 83-88; prin investr, numerous res grants Nat Aeronaut & Space Admin, Air Force Off Sci Res, Nat Sci Found, 76-; vis prof, Australian Nat Univ, 84-85 & 87; fel Japan Soc Prom Sci, 86; Nat Res Coun ad hoc comt on Nat Aeronaut & Space Admin-Univ Relationships in Aero & Space Eng, 84-85; chmn, Automatic Control Soc, Int Elec & Elec Engr, Huntsville, Ala, 69. *Mem:* Sigma Xi; Inst Elec & Electron Engrs; assoc fel, Am Inst Aeronaut & Astronaut. *Res:* Dynamics & control of space vehicles. *Mailing Add:* 2601 Nottingham Pl West Lafayette IN 47906-5024

SKELTON, THOMAS EUGENE, ENTOMOLOGY. *Current Pos:* Asst entomologist, 56-60, from asst prof to assoc prof entom, 69-76, PROF ENTOM, CLEMSON UNIV, 76- *Personal Data:* b Six Mile, SC, Dec 15, 30; m 53; c 3. *Educ:* Clemson Univ, BS, 53, MS, 56; Univ Ga, PhD(entom), 69. *Honors & Awards:* Distinguished Achievement Award, Entom Soc Am, 79. *Concurrent Pos:* Actg head, Dept Entom, Clemson Univ, 87-88. *Mem:* Entom Soc Am; Sigma Xi. *Res:* Economic entomology; insects affecting apples, peaches and vegetables. *Mailing Add:* Dept Entom Clemson Univ Clemson SC 29631

SKETCH, MICHAEL HUGH, CARDIOLOGY. *Current Pos:* from asst prof to assoc prof, Creighton Univ, Omaha, 68-77, assoc dir, Div Cardiol, 71-72, co-dir, 72-78, DIR, CARDIAC LABS, CREIGHTON UNIV, OMAHA, 69-, PROF MED, 77-, DIR DIV CARDIOL, 78- *Personal Data:* b Paris, June 25, 31; m 56, Nancy A Wilcox; c Michael H, Peter G, Sarah A, James C & Martin H. *Educ:* Creighton Univ, BS, 59, MD, 63. *Prof Exp:* Intern, Creighton Mem, St Joseph Hosp, Omaha, 63-64; resident fel cardiol, 64-68. *Mem:* Fel Am Col Cardiol; Am Heart Asn; Am Col Chest Physicians; Am Col Physicians. *Res:* Cardiology; medicine. *Mailing Add:* Cardiac Ctr 3006 Webster St Omaha NE 68131-2044

SKEWIS, JOHN DAVID, PHYSICAL CHEMISTRY. *Current Pos:* res chemist, Res Ctr, US Rubber Co, NJ, 60-68, sr res scientist, 68-72, mgr polymer physics res, 72-78, MGR CORP TIRE RES, RES CTR, UNIROYAL, INC, 78- *Personal Data:* b Lancaster, Pa, Dec 18, 32; m 57; c 3. *Educ:* Pa State Univ, BA, 54; Lehigh Univ, MS, 57, PhD(chem), 59. *Prof Exp:* Asst chem, Lehigh Univ, 54-56; fel, Univ Southern Calif, 59-60. *Mem:* Am Chem Soc. *Res:* Surface and colloid chemistry. *Mailing Add:* Apple Lane Roxbury CT 06783

SKIBINSKY, MORRIS, MOMENT SPACES, ADEQUATE SUBFIELDS. *Current Pos:* prof, 68-94, EMER PROF STATIST, UNIV MASS, AMHERST, 94- *Personal Data:* b New York, NY, Aug 3, 25; m 51; c Clifford. *Educ:* City Col, BS, 48; Univ NC, MA, 51, PhD(math statist), 54. *Prof Exp:* Asst prof math & statist, Purdue Univ, 54-55; vis asst prof math statist, Mich State Univ, 56; from asst prof to assoc prof math & statist, Purdue Univ, 57-62; vis assoc prof statist, Univ Minn, Minneapolis, 62-63; mathematician, Brookhaven Nat Lab, 63-68. *Concurrent Pos:* Vis scholar, Univ Calif, 61-62; vis prof statist, Fla State Univ, 81-82. *Mem:* Math Asn Am; Inst Math Statist. *Res:* Probability; decision theory; theory of moment spaces; introduced (1967) and developed the concepts of "adequate subfields" and "canonical" (or "normalized") moments; current work on moment spaces for distributions on simplices. *Mailing Add:* Dept Math & Statist Univ Mass Amherst MA 01003. *E-Mail:* morris@math.umass.edu

SKIBNIEWSKI, MIROSLAW JAN, CONSTRUCTION AUTOMATION & TECHNOLOGY TRANSFER, ENGINEERING & MANAGEMENT. *Current Pos:* from asst prof to assoc prof, 86-95, PROF CONSTRUCT ENG, PURDUE UNIV, 95- *Personal Data:* b Warsaw, Poland, Sept 14, 57; US citizen; m 90, Hanna Dudzin; c Maria. *Educ:* Warsaw Tech Univ, MCE, 81; Carnegie Mellon Univ, MS, 83, PhD(civil eng), 86. *Prof Exp:* Staff engr, Pittsburgh Testing Lab, 81-82; res asst construct eng, Carnegie Mellon Univ, 82-86. *Concurrent Pos:* NSF presidential young investr award, 87-92, prin investr, 87-; control group mem, Task Force Construct Robotics, Am Soc Civil; co-prin investr, Construct Indust Inst; comt appointee, Int Coun Bldg Res, Studies & Doc, 89-; lectr, Commonwealth Sci & Indust Res Orgn, Australia, 90; vis prof, Slovak Tech Univ, 90, CSIRO Australia & Inst Mechanized Construct, Poland, 92-93; dir, Int Asn Automation & Robotics Construct, 90-; co-chair, Comt Int Coun Tall Bldg, 91- *Mem:* Am Soc Civil Engrs. *Res:* Technology transfer in the construction industry, with particular emphasis on construction automation, including application of robotics and expert systems in this domain; author of one book on robotics in civil engineering, six book chapters and approximately 100 technical papers in research journals and conference proceedings on construction engineering and management. *Mailing Add:* Div Construct Eng & Mgt Purdue Univ Civil Eng Bldg 1245 West Lafayette IN 47907-1294. *Fax:* 765-494-0644; *E-Mail:* mirek@ecn.purdue.edu

SKIDMORE, DUANE R(ICHARD), chemical engineering, physical chemistry; deceased, see previous edition for last biography

SKIDMORE, EDWARD LYMAN, WIND EROSION MODELING, SOIL & WATER CONSERVATION & AGRICULTURE CLIMATOLOGY. *Current Pos:* RES SOIL SCIENTIST, WIND EROSION LAB, AGR RES SERV, USDA, 63-; PROF AGRON, KANS STATE UNIV, 75- *Personal Data:* b Delta, Utah, Jan 21, 33; m 53, Velma Williams; c Alan, Andrew, Cary, James, Thomas & Joanne. *Educ:* Utah State Univ, BS, 58; Okla State Univ, PhD(soil sci), 63. *Concurrent Pos:* Assoc prof, Kans State Univ, 70-75; Consult, US Agency Int Develop, 83; dir, Col on Soil Physics, Int Ctr Theoret Physics, Trieste, Italy, 83, 85, 87, 89 & 93; assoc ed, Sci Soc Am J, 84-85; mem, bd dir, Am Soc Agron & Sci Soc Am, 84-87. *Mem:* AAAS; fel Am Soc Agron; fel Soil Sci Soc Am; fel Soil & Water Conserv Soc; Int Soil Tillage Res Orgn; World Asn Soil & Water Conserv. *Res:* Soil plant water relations; soil physics; wind erosion; agricultural micrometeorology; develop submodels to predict surface soil wetness; soil aggregate status; stochastic weather simulator. *Mailing Add:* Agron 2004 Throckmorton Hall Kans State Univ Manhattan KS 66506. *Fax:* 785-532-6528; *E-Mail:* skidmore@weru.ksu.edu

SKIDMORE, WESLEY DEAN, BIOCHEMISTRY, ENVIRONMENTAL SCIENCE. *Current Pos:* RETIRED. *Personal Data:* b Pocatello, Idaho, Jan 18, 31; m 87, Yvonne Marcelle; c Wesley R, Shauna, Laura (Shepherd-Larson), Brett D & Mark A. *Educ:* Univ Utah, BS, 53; George Washington Univ, MS, 58; Univ Calif, San Francisco, PhD(biochem), 65. *Prof Exp:* Prin investr radiobiol, Armed Forces Radiobiol Res Inst, 65-69, proj dir, 70-74; chemist, CVM, Food & Drug Admin, 74-93. *Concurrent Pos:* Consult environ sci. *Mem:* Am Chem Soc; Soc Environ Toxicol & Chem. *Res:* Animal drugs. *Mailing Add:* 10721 Game Preserve Rd Gaithersburg MD 20879-3105

SKIENS, WILLIAM EUGENE, LOW DIELECTRIC POLYMER INSULATORS, PERMSELECTIVE SYNTHETIC MEMBRANES. *Current Pos:* CHIEF SCIENTIST, PRECISION INTERCONNECT INC, 89- *Personal Data:* b Burns, Ore, Feb 21, 28; m 55, Vesta L Franz; c Rebecca E, Beverly S & Michael W. *Educ:* Ore State Univ, BS, 51; Univ Wash, PhD(phys & inorg chem), 57. *Prof Exp:* Chemist, Dow Chem Co, Pittsburg, Calif, 51-53, res chemist, Walnut Creek, Calif, 57-73; res chemist, E I Dupont de Nemours, 55; sr res scientist, Battelle Mem Inst, 73-84; mgr optical disc develop, Optical Data Inc, 84-89. *Concurrent Pos:* Consult, WHO, 76-75; Battelle Mem Inst, 85-, PI Med, 91- *Mem:* Am Chem Soc; Soc Plastic Engrs; Soc Advan Mat & Process Eng; Am Soc Testing & Mat. *Res:* Development of permselection synthetic, polymeric membranes for desalination, venaldialysis and blood oxygenators (fine hollow fibers); controlled (sustained) release of drugs and bioactive chemicals from polymer matrices; erasable optical data storage discs; biocompatible electrical interconnect systems for neural sensors. *Mailing Add:* 31179 SW Country View Lane Wilsonville OR 97070-7479. *Fax:* 503-620-7131

SKIEST, EUGENE NORMAN, FOOD CHEMISTRY. *Current Pos:* group leader, Borden Chem Co, 66-69, develop mgr, 69-77, dir develop & applns, 76-78, assoc dir qual assurance & compliance, Borden Inc, 78-79, dir, 79-81, corp tech dir chem, 81-84, corp tech dir, 84-88, corp dir res, develop & technol, 89-91, CORP VPRES SCI & TECHNOL, BORDEN INC, 92- *Personal Data:* b Worcester, Mass, Feb 2, 35; m 57, 74, Carol Tata; c Jody, Daniel & Nancy. *Educ:* Mass Col Pharm, BS, 56; Univ Mich, MS, 58, PhD, 61. *Prof Exp:* Res chemist, Foster Grant Co, 61-62; sr res chemist, Thompson Chem Co, 62-64; pres, C&S Polymers, 65-66. *Concurrent Pos:* Mem, Vinyl Toxicol Subcomt, Soc Plastics Industs, 78-82, Vinyl Acetate Task Force, 80-82; chmn tech comt, Formaldehyde Inst, 79-84, bd dirs, 81; co-rep, Indust Res Inst, 83-; coun mem, Nat Food Process, 93- *Mem:* Am Chem Soc; Soc Plastics Engrs; Formaldehyde Inst; Chem Mfrs Asn; Soc Plastic Industs. *Res:* Food science and technology; Chemistry; Plastics. *Mailing Add:* 7330 Eaton Ct University Park FL 34201

SKIFF, FREDERICK NORMAN, PLASMA WAVES, PLASMA DIAGNOSTICS. *Current Pos:* ASST PROF, DEPT PHYSICS, UNIV MD, COLLEGE PARK, 89- *Personal Data:* b Albany, NY, Jan 22, 57; m 81; c 3. *Educ:* Cornell Univ, BS, 79; Princeton Univ, MA, 81, PhD(physics), 85. *Prof Exp:* Res physicist, Ecole Polytech Fed Lausanne, Switz, 85-89. *Concurrent Pos:* NSF presidential young investr, 90; Alfred P Sloan fel, 90-92. *Mem:* Am Phys Soc. *Res:* Plasma waves: excitation, propagation, absorption; both theory and experimental study of linear and non-linear plasma wave phenomena; chaos and non-liner dynamics in plasma physics; plasma diagnostics by laser induced fluorescence and by electromagnetic wave transmission. *Mailing Add:* Lab Plasma Res Univ Md College Park MD 20742

SKIFF, PETER DUANE, HISTORY & PHILOSOPHY OF SCIENCE. *Current Pos:* from asst prof to assoc prof, 65-75, PROF PHYSICS, BARD COL, 75- *Personal Data:* b Pittsburgh, Pa, Dec 16, 38; m 65. *Educ:* Univ Calif, Berkeley, AB, 59; Univ Houston, MS, 61; La State Univ, PhD(physics), 66. *Prof Exp:* Instr, La State Univ, 63-65. *Concurrent Pos:* Vis instr, Marist Col, 67-68; adj fac, Norwich Univ, 84-85. *Mem:* Am Phys Soc; Am Asn Physics Teachers; History Sci Soc; Archaeol Inst Am; Philos Sci Asn. *Res:* Foundations of quantum theory; quantum statistical mechanics; archaeometry; history of science; philosophy of science; quantum field theory. *Mailing Add:* Bard Col Annandale on Hudson NY 12504-5000

SKILES, JAMES J(EAN), ELECTRICAL ENGINEERING, ELECTRIC POWER SYSTEMS. *Current Pos:* instr elec eng, Univ Wis-Madison, 51-54, from asst prof to assoc prof, 54-62, assoc chmn dept, 63-67, chmn dept, 67-72, dir, Univ-Indust Res Prog, 72-75, dir, Energy Res Ctr, 75-89, Wis Elec Utilities res found prof energy eng, 75-89, prof, 62-89, EMER PROF ELEC ENG, UNIV WIS-MADISON, 89- *Personal Data:* b St Louis, Mo, Oct 16, 28; m 48, Deloris McKenney; c Steven, Randall & Jeffrey. *Educ:* Wash Univ, BSEE, 48; Univ Mo-Rolla, MSEE, 51; Univ Wis, PhD, 54. *Prof Exp:* Engr, Union Elec Co, Mo, 48-49; instr elec eng, Univ Mo-Rolla, 49-51. *Concurrent Pos:* Consult, Allis-Chalmers Mfg Co, 56-62, Space Technol Labs, Inc, 60-63 & Astronaut Corp Am, Wis, 66-69; consult for numerous co. *Mem:* Am Soc Eng Educ; Inst Elec & Electronics Engrs. *Res:* Computer applications; power systems analysis; energy conservation and systems; real-time computer applications. *Mailing Add:* 8099 Coray Lane Verona WI 53593-9073

SKILLING, DARROLL DEAN, PLANT PATHOLOGY, FORESTRY. *Current Pos:* Res forester, Lake States Forest Exp Sta, 54-61, RES PLANT PATHOLOGIST, NCENT FOREST EXP STA, US FOREST SERV, 61-, PROJ LEADER, FOREST DIS PROJ, 86- *Personal Data:* b Carson City, Mich, June 18, 31; m 51, Marie Harper; c Ann, James & Stephen. *Educ:* Univ Mich, BS, 53, MFor, 54; Univ Minn, PhD(plant path), 68. *Concurrent Pos:* Prof, Dept Plant Path, Univ Minn, 83- *Mem:* Am Phytopath Soc; Int Soc Plant Pathologists. *Res:* Epidemiology of conifer tree diseases; fungicide screening and control of foliage tree diseases; Scleroderris canker, Lophodermium needlecast, brown spot disease and Cylindrocladium root rot; development of disease resistance in forest trees using tissue culture and somaclonal variation; epidemiology of conifer tree diseases; fungicide screening and control of conifer foliage pathogens scleroderris canker. *Mailing Add:* NCent Forest Exp Sta US Forest Serv Folwell Ave St Paul MN 55108. *Fax:* 612-649-5285

SKILLING, JOHN BOWER, STRUCTURAL ENGINEERING. *Current Pos:* CHMN, STRUCT & CIVIL ENG, SKILLING WARD MAGNUSSON BARKSHIRE INC, 82- *Personal Data:* b Los Angeles, Calif, Oct 8, 21; m 43, Mary Jane Stender; c Susan, Bill & Ann. *Educ:* Univ Wash, BS, 47. *Prof Exp:* Design engr, W H Witt Co, 47-54; sr partner struct & civil eng, Skilling, Helle, Christiansen, Robertson, 54-82. *Concurrent Pos:* Mem adv comt, Am Inst Steel Construct, 67-68; mem bldg res adv bd, Nat Acad Eng, 65-; mem seismic design comt, Nat Acad Eng & Nat Res Coun; Nat Res Coun Bldg Res Adv Bd. *Mem:* Nat Acad Eng; fel Am Soc Civil Engrs; Int Asn Bridge & Struct Eng; Int Asn Shell Struct; Am Concrete Inst; Am Inst Steel Construct. *Mailing Add:* 1301 Fifth Ave Seattle WA 98101-2341

SKILLMAN, ROBERT ALLEN, FISHERIES MANAGEMENT, POPULATION ECOLOGY. *Current Pos:* FISHERY BIOLOGIST, NAT MARINE FISHERIES SERV, HONOLULU LAB, 69-79 & 81- *Personal Data:* b Peoria, Ill, Aug 21, 41; m 85, Gail J Woodhouse. *Educ:* Bradley Univ, BA, 63; Iowa State Univ, MS, 65; Univ Calif, Davis, PhD(zool), 69. *Honors & Awards:* Bronze Medal Award, US Dept Com. *Prof Exp:* Tuna specialist, UN Food & Agr Rogn, 79-80. *Mem:* Am Fisheries Soc; Ecol Soc Am. *Res:* Quantitative analysis of the population dynamics of marine fishes, including but not limited to production model analysis and the estimation of population parameters for growth, mortality, and recruitment. *Mailing Add:* Nat Marine Fisheries Serv Lab 2570 Dole St Honolulu HI 96822-2396. *Fax:* 808-943-1290; *E-Mail:* rskillma@honlab.nmfs.hawaii.edu

SKILLMAN, THOMAS G, MEDICINE. *Current Pos:* prof, 67-82, Kurtz Prof Endocrinol, 74-82, EMER PROF MED, OHIO STATE UNIV, 82- *Personal Data:* b Cincinnati, Ohio, Jan 7, 25; m 47; c 2. *Educ:* Baldwin-Wallace Col, BS, 46; Univ Cincinnati, MD, 49. *Prof Exp:* Instr med, Univ Cincinnati, 54-57; asst prof, Ohio State Univ, 57-61; from assoc prof to prof, Creighton Univ, 61-67. *Mem:* Am Diabetes Asn; Am Fedn Clin Res. *Res:* Clinical diabetes. *Mailing Add:* 1206 40th St Cape Coral FL 33904

SKILLMAN, WILLIAM A, ELECTRICAL ENGINEERING. *Current Pos:* CONSULT, 93- *Personal Data:* b Lakehurst, NJ, Jan 22, 28; m 48, Anne Carender; c Thomas R, Gregory A & Karen L. *Educ:* Lehigh Univ, BS, 52; Univ Rochester, MS, 54. *Honors & Awards:* Pioneer Award, Aeropsace & Electonic Syst Soc, 94. *Prof Exp:* Consult engr, Westinghouse Corp, 54-93. *Concurrent Pos:* Mem, Radar Syst Panel, Aeropsace & Electronic Syst Soc. *Mem:* Fel Inst Elec & Electronics Engrs; Aerospace & Electronic Syst Soc. *Mailing Add:* 605 Forest View Rd Linthicum Heights MD 21090-2819. *E-Mail:* wskillman@aol.com

SKINNER, BRIAN JOHN, GEOCHEMISTRY, ECONOMIC GEOLOGY. *Current Pos:* prof geol, 66-72, chmn dept geol & geophys, 67-72, EUGENE HIGGINS PROF, YALE UNIV, 72- *Personal Data:* b Wallaroo, SAustralia, Dec 15, 28; nat US; m 54; c 3. *Educ:* Univ Adelaide, BSc, 50; Harvard Univ, AM, 52, PhD, 55. *Honors & Awards:* McKinstry Mem lectr, Harvard Univ, 78; DuToit Mem lectr, SAfrica, 79; Medal, Soc Econ Geologists, 81. *Prof Exp:* Lectr crystallog, Univ Adelaide, 55-58; res geologist, US Geol Surv, 58-62, chief, Br Exp Geochem & Mineral, 62-66. *Concurrent Pos:* Ed, Econ Geol, 70-; chmn comt mineral resources & the environ, Nat Acad Sci-Nat Res Coun, 73-75; chmn bd, Earth Sci & Resources, 88-90. *Mem:* Fel Mineral Soc Am; Geochem Soc (pres, 73); Soc Econ Geologists; Geol Soc Am (pres, 85); Geol Asn Can; Geol Soc Australia. *Res:* Phase equilibria in systems containing sulfur; geochemistry of ore deposits. *Mailing Add:* Dept Geol & Geophys Yale Univ PO Box 208109 New Haven CT 06520-8109

SKINNER, CHARLES GORDON, ORGANIC CHEMISTRY, BIOCHEMISTRY. *Current Pos:* chmn dept, 69-74, PROF CHEM, NTEX STATE UNIV, 64-, CHMN DEPT BASIC HEALTH SCI, 79- *Personal Data:* b Dallas, Tex, Apr 23, 23; m 44; c 2. *Educ:* NTex State Univ, BS, 44, MS, 47; Univ Tex, PhD(org chem), 53. *Honors & Awards:* Daugherty Award, Am Chem Soc, 78. *Prof Exp:* Res chemist, Celanese Corp Am, 49-50; Lilly fel, Univ Tex, 53-54; res scientist, Clayton Found Biochem Inst, 55-64; asst dean basic sci, Tex Col Osteop Med, 75-79, prof biochem, 72-83. *Concurrent Pos:* Consult eng, AID, Dallas. *Mem:* Am Chem Soc; Am Soc Biol Chem; Sigma Xi; Am Inst Chem. *Res:* Synthesis and biological activity of metabolite antagonists; vitamins; purine and pyrimidines; antitumor agents. *Mailing Add:* Dept Chem Box 5006 Univ N Tex Denton TX 76203-0006

SKINNER, DALE DEAN, UNDERWATER ACOUSTICS, ELECTRICAL ENGINEERING. *Current Pos:* CONSULT ULTRASONICS & SONAR, 94- *Personal Data:* b Payette, Idaho, July 23, 31; m 56, Gail Truninger; c Donald, Richard, Robert & Barbara. *Educ:* Univ Idaho, BSEE, 53. *Prof Exp:* Jr engr, Westinghouse Elec Corp, 53-54, intermediate res engr, Res Labs, 54-61, res engr, 61-63, fel engr, 63-69, mgr ultrasonic technol, Underwater Acoust, 69-73, fel engr, Ocean Res & Eng Ctr, 74-94. *Res:* Underwater sound scattering; sonar system and transducer designs; use of ultrasonics for medical diagnostics and nondestructive testing. *Mailing Add:* 297 Riverdale Rd Severna Park MD 21146

SKINNER, DAVID BERNT, SURGERY. *Current Pos:* PROF SURG, MED COL, CORNELL UNIV, 87-; PRES, CHIEF EXEC OFFICER & ATTEND PHYSICIAN, NY HOSP, 87-, VCHMN & CHIEF EXEC OFFICER, NY & PRESBY HOSPS, 96- *Personal Data:* b Joliet, Ill, Apr 28, 35; m 56; c 4. *Educ:* Univ Rochester, BA, 58; Yale Univ, MD, 59; Am Bd Surg, cert, 66; Am Bd Thoracic Surg, cert, 66; FRCPS(E), 87. *Hon Degrees:* ScD, Univ Rochester, 80. *Honors & Awards:* J Murray Beardsly Lectr, Brown Univ, 86; First Francis D Moore Lectr, Harvard Univ, 86; William Seybold Lectr, Univ Tex, 86; Edward Hallaran Benett Lectr, Univ Dublin, 86; D Hayes Agnew Centennial Lectr, Univ Pa, 87; Arnold Seligman Lectr, Mt Sinai Hosp, 87; First Joseph Bulkley Lectr, Little Co Mary Hosp, 87; Charles B Huggins Sci Lectr, Univ Acadia, 88; Dallas B Phemister Lectr, Univ Chicago, 88; Rosario P San Filippo Lectr, Lutheran Med Ctr, 88; McGraw Lectr, Detroit Surg Asn, 89; Karl Klassen Lectr, Ohio State Univ, 89. *Prof Exp:* Intern, Mass Gen Hosp, Boston, 59-60, asst resident, 60-64, resident, 65; clin asst prof surg, Univ Tex Med Sch, San Antonio, 66-68; from asst prof to prof, Johns Hopkins Univ, 68-72; Dallas B Phemister Prof Surg & Chmn Dept, Pritzker Sch Med, Univ Chicago, 72-87. *Concurrent Pos:* Am Cancer Soc fel, Harvard Med Sch, 65, teaching fel, 65; NIH res grants, Johns Hopkins Univ, 68-72, Markle Scholar, 69-74; NIH res grant, Univ Chicago, 72-; sr registr, Frenchay Hosp, Britol, Eng, 63-64; asst chief exp surg, USAF Sch Aerospace Med, San Antonio, 66-68; consult surg, Robert B Green Hosp, San Antonio, 66-68, Loch Raven Vet Admin Hosp, 68-72, Good Samaritan Hosp, 68-72, USPHS Hosp, Baltimore, 69-72 & US Naval Med Ctr, Bethesda, 70-72; asst & assoc ed, J Surg Res, 68-72, ed, 72-82 & Current Topics Surg Res, 69-71, assoc ed, Dis Esophagus, 86-; mem, Pres Biomed Res Panel, 75-76; vis physician, Rockefeller Univ Hosp, 89- *Mem:* Inst Med-Nat Acad Sci; Soc Univ Surgeons (pres, 79); Soc Surg Chmn (pres, 80-82); Am Asn Thoracic Surg; Soc Vascular Surg; Am Surg Asn; AMA. *Res:* Esophageal and upper gastrointestinal physiology and disorders; pulmonary disorders; cardiovascular physiology and artificial circulation; author of numerous technical publications. *Mailing Add:* NY Hosp 525 E 68th St New York NY 10021

SKINNER, DOROTHY M, MOLECULAR BIOLOGY. *Current Pos:* SR SCIENTIST, OAK RIDGE NAT LAB, 68- *Personal Data:* b Newton, Mass, May 22, 30; m 65. *Educ:* Tufts Univ, BS, 52; Harvard Univ, PhD(biol), 58. *Prof Exp:* Asst dir admis, Jackson Col, Tufts Univ, 52-54; fel biochem, Yale Univ & Brandeis Univ, 58-62; asst prof physiol & biophys, Med Ctr, NY Univ, 62-66; fel, Oak Ridge Inst Nuclear Studies, 66-68. *Concurrent Pos:* Prof, Oak Ridge Grad Sch Biomed Sci, Univ Tenn, 68-83; mem molecular biol study sect, NIH, 72-76; assoc ed, Growth, 79-88; instr marine biol lab, Wood Hole, Mass, 71; adj prof biophys, E Tenn State Univ, 83-; vis prof women, NSF, 83, 85, mem selection comt panel, physiol processes, 86-89; chair elect, AAAS, chair, retiring chair, sect G, 83-86; governing bd, Crustacean Soc, 87- *Mem:* Soc Gen Physiol (treas, 73-75); fel AAAS; Am Soc Cell Biol; Am Soc Biol Chem; Soc Develop Biol; Sigma Xi; Crustacean Soc. *Res:* Macromolecular changes associated with growth and development in Crustacea; satellite DNAs, structure and functions. *Mailing Add:* Biol Div Oak Ridge Nat Lab PO Box 2009 Oak Ridge TN 37831-8080. *Fax:* 423-574-1274

SKINNER, G(EORGE) M(ACGILLIVRAY), ENGINEERING PHYSICS. *Current Pos:* RETIRED. *Personal Data:* b Buffalo, NY, Aug 26, 09; m 38; c 1. *Educ:* Univ Mich, BS, 33, MS, 34. *Prof Exp:* Res engr, Linde Air Prod Co, Union Carbide & Carbon Corp, 34-40, group leader, 40-48, sect head, 48-56, res supvr, Linde Div, Union Carbide Corp, 56-62, head, Develop Lab Div, 62-69, mgr admin, Linde Div Lab, Tarrytown Tech Ctr, Union Carbide Corp, 69-79. *Mem:* Am Welding Soc; Inst Elec & Electronics Engrs. *Res:* High temperature technique; high frequency dielectrics; metallurgy; method of oxyacetylene cutting; welding arc and gaseous conduction; fluid dynamics; magnetohydrodynamics; high intensity, high pressure arc research. *Mailing Add:* 464 Retama Way Dr San Antonio TX 78240-1533

SKINNER, G(EORGE) WILLIAM, ANTHROPOLOGY. *Current Pos:* PROF ANTHROP, UNIV CALIF, DAVIS, 90- *Personal Data:* b Oakland, Calif, Feb 14, 25; m 51, 80, Susan Mann; c Geoffrey C, James L, Mark W, Jeremy B & Allison J. *Educ:* Cornell Univ, BA, 47, PhD(cult anthrop), 54. *Prof Exp:* Field dir, SE Asia Prog & Cornell Res Ctr, Cornell Univ, 51-55, from assoc prof to prof anthrop, 60-65; res assoc, Indonesia, 56-58; asst prof sociol, Columbia Univ, 58-60; sr specialist in residence, East-West Ctr, Honolulu, 65-66; prof anthrop, Stanford Univ, 66-89, Barbara Kimball Browning prof humanities & sci, 87-89. *Concurrent Pos:* Mem, Subcomt Res, Chinese Soc Sci Res Coun, 61-70, chmn, 63-70; assoc dir, Cornell China Prog, 61-63; dir, London-Cornell Proj Social Res, 62-65; mem, Int Comt Chinese Studies, China Soc Sci Res Coun-Am Acad Learned Socs, 63-64, Joint Comt Chinese Studies, 81-83; mem, Comt Scholarly Commun with Peoples Repub China, Nat Acad Sci, 66-70, Soc Sci & Humanities Panel, 82-83; dir, Prog EAsian Local Systs, 69-71; Guggenheim fel, 69; fel, Ctr Advan Study Behav Sci, 69-70; NIMH spec fel, 70; vis prof, Univ Pa, 77, Duke Univ, 78, Keio Univ, 85 & 88, Univ Calif, San Diego, 86. *Mem:* Nat Acad Sci; AAAS; Am Anthrop Asn; Am Sociol Asn; Asn Asian Studies (pres, 83-84); Soc Cult Anthrop; Int Union Sci Study Pop; Soc Sci Hist Asn; Am Ethnol Soc; Pop Asn Am; Soc Econ Anthrop; Sigma Xi. *Res:* Chinese society in Thailand. *Mailing Add:* Dept Anthrop Univ Calif Davis CA 95616. *Fax:* 350-752-8885; *E-Mail:* gwskinner@ucdavis.edu

SKINNER, GEORGE T, ATMOSPHERE DYNAMICS, COMPUTER HARDWARE SYSTEMS. *Current Pos:* TEACHING & CONSULT, 89- *Personal Data:* b Dundee, Scotland, July 22, 23; US citizen; m 88, Julia K Shank; c 2. *Educ:* St Andrews Univ, BS, 48; Calif Inst Technol, MS, 49, AE, 51, PhD(aeronaut), 55. *Prof Exp:* Asst res officer aerodyn, Nat Res Coun Can, 51; res engr, Calspan Corp, 58-63, prin aeronaut engr, 63-88. *Concurrent Pos:* Pres, G T Skinner, Inc, Tullahoma, Tenn. *Mem:* Am Phys Soc; Sigma Xi. *Res:* Atmospheric boundary layer flows; molecular beam research using shock tubes as gas source; radiation from collisionally excited molecules; contained airflow in automobile tires; space systems testing technology. *Mailing Add:* 108 Oak Park Dr Tullahoma TN 37388-4621

SKINNER, GORDON BANNATYNE, KINETICS, HIGH TEMPERATURE CHEMISTRY. *Current Pos:* from assoc prof to prof, 64-86, EMER PROF CHEM, WRIGHT STATE UNIV, 86- *Personal Data:* b Winnipeg, Man, Jan 7, 26; nat US; m 52, Marjorie Wilkinson; c Jane, Ellen & Laura. *Educ:* Univ Man, BSc, 47, MSc, 49; Ohio State Univ, PhD(phys chem), 51. *Prof Exp:* Chemist, Monsanto Co, 51-64. *Mem:* Am Chem Soc; AAAS. *Res:* Thermodynamic studies of zirconium and titanium; kinetics of gas reactions at high temperatures; application of kinetics to problems in combustion and detonation; computer simulation of complex systems. *Mailing Add:* 15410 NW Satellite Dr Banks OR 97106-9700

SKINNER, H CATHERINE W, MINERALOGY, BIOINORGANIC CHEMISTRY. *Current Pos:* res assoc molecular biophys & geol, sr res assoc & lectr surg, 72-75, assoc prof biochem in surg, 78-82, RES AFFIL GEOL & GEOPHYS & LECTR ORTHOP SURG, YALE UNIV, 82- *Personal Data:* b Brooklyn, NY, Jan 25, 31; m 54, Brian J; c Adrienne W (Scott), Stephanie W (Timmons) & Thalassa W. *Educ:* Mt Holyoke Col, BA, 52; Radcliffe Col, MA, 54; Univ Adelaide, PhD(mineral), 59. *Prof Exp:* Mineralogist crystallog, Harvard Med Sch, 54-55; mineralogist, Nat Inst Arthritis & Metab Dis, 61-65 & Nat Inst Dent Res, 65-66. *Concurrent Pos:* Mem insts & spec progs comt, Nat Inst Dent Res, 71-75; mem publ comt, Yale Univ Press 74-76; Agassiz vis lectr biol, Harvard Univ, 76-77; assoc ed, Am Mineral, 77-83 & counr, Mineral Soc Am, 78-81; co-chmn panel geochem of fibrous materials related to health risks, Nat Acad Sci, 79-; master, Jonathan Edwards Col, 77-82; pres, Conn Acad Arts & Sci, 85-; vis prof, Dept Biol, Cornell Univ, 80-83, Dept Geol, Univ Adelaide, SAustralia, 91-92. *Mem:* Fel Mineral Soc Am; Am Crystallog Asn; Am Asn Crystal Growth; Am Asn Dent Res; Int Soc Dent Res; fel Geol Soc Am; Mineral Asn Can; Am Soc Bone & Mineral Res; fel AAAS. *Res:* Phase equilibria studies of calcium phosphates; crystal chemistry of the mineral portion of calcified tissues; teeth, bone and invertebrate hard tissues; mineral metabolism; sedimentary carbonate deposits; geochemistry; fibrous inorganic materials, asbestos materials and health; health effects of mineral materials and mineral materials in living species; over 50 publications and 2 books. *Mailing Add:* Yale Univ Dept Geol & Geophys PO Box 208109 New Haven CT 06520-8109. *Fax:* 203-432-9819; *E-Mail:* skinnerhcw@climat.decnet.yale.edu

SKINNER, HUBERT CLAYTON, GEOLOGY. *Current Pos:* from asst prof to assoc prof, 54-62, PROF GEOL, TULANE UNIV, 62- *Personal Data:* b Tulsa, Okla, Oct 3, 29; m 58; c 3. *Educ:* Univ Okla, BS, 51, MS, 53, PhD(geol), 54. *Prof Exp:* Mus technician, Univ Okla, 51-52, asst geol, 52-53, instr, 53-54. *Concurrent Pos:* Supvr paleo lab, La Div, Texaco, 54-57; ed, Tulane Studies Geol & Paleont, 62- *Mem:* Paleont Soc; Geol Soc Am; Am Asn Petrol Geologists; Brit Palaeont Asn. *Res:* Paleontology; stratigraphy; Cretaceous and Tertiary micropaleontology, paleoecology and stratigraphy of the Gulf Coast; history of geology. *Mailing Add:* 3737 Napoleon Ave New Orleans LA 70125

SKINNER, JAMES ERNEST, neurosciences, for more information see previous edition

SKINNER, JAMES LAURISTON, STATISTICAL MECHANICS. *Current Pos:* JOSEPH O HIRSCHFELDER PROF CHEM, UNIV WIS, 90-, DIR THEORET CHEM INST, 90- *Personal Data:* b Ithaca, NY, Aug 17, 53; m 86, Wendy Moore; c Colin A & Duncan G. *Educ:* Univ Calif, Santa Cruz, BA, 75; Harvard Univ, MA, 77, PhD(chem physics), 79. *Honors & Awards:* Presidential Young Investr Award, NSF, 84. *Prof Exp:* NSF fel, Stanford Univ, 80-81; from asst prof to prof chem, Columbia Univ, 81-90. *Concurrent Pos:* Sloan fel, 84; Dreyfus teacher-scholar, 84; vis scientist, Inst Theoret Physics, Univ Calif, Santa Barbara, 87; vis prof physics, Univ Grenoble, 87 & Univ Bordeaux, 95; Guggenheim fel, 93; Humboldt Found sr scientist, 93. *Mem:* Am Phys Soc; Am Chem Soc; AAAS. *Res:* Spectroscopy and relaxation; statistical mechanics; chemical reactions; theoretical chemistry. *Mailing Add:* Dept Chem Univ Wis Madison WI 53706. *Fax:* 608-262-9918; *E-Mail:* skinner@chem.wisc.edu

SKINNER, JAMES STANFORD, PHYSIOLOGY. *Current Pos:* DIR HERITAGE STUDY, 94- *Personal Data:* b Lucedale, Miss, Sept 22, 36; m 63, 77; c 2. *Educ:* Univ Ill, Urbana, BS, 58, MS, 60, PhD(phys educ & physiol), 63. *Honors & Awards:* Citation Award, Am Col Sports Med, 86. *Prof Exp:* Assoc physiol, Sch Med, George Washington Univ, 64, asst prof lectr, 64-65; res assoc cardiol, Sch Med, Univ Wash, Seattle, 65-66; asst prof, Lab Human Performance Res, Pa State Univ, University Park, 66-70; res assoc, Med Clin, Univ Freiburg, Ger, 70-71; assoc prof phys educ, Univ Montreal & res assoc, Inst Cardiol, 71-77; prof phys educ, Univ Western Ont, 77-82; prof phys educ exercise sci, Ariz State Univ, 82-94. *Concurrent Pos:* Dir, Exercise & Sport Res Inst, Ariz State Univ, 83- *Mem:* Fel Am Col Sports Med (pres-elect, 78-79, pres, 79-80); Can Asn Sports Sci (secy, 76-78); Am Asn Health Phys Educ & Recreation; fel Am Heart Asn; Am Acad Phys Educ (secy-treas, 90-92). *Res:* Physiology of exercise, especially pertaining to cardiovascular system; effects of increased physical activity on the course and severity of cardiovascular disorders; exercise, training and genetics. *Mailing Add:* Nat Inst Fitness & Sports 250 Univ Blvd Indianapolis IN 46202

SKINNER, JOHN PAUL, electromagnetic field theory, low observables, for more information see previous edition

SKINNER, JOSEPH L, CHEMICAL ENGINEERING. *Current Pos:* Res engr, Continental Oil Co, 62-64, sr res engr, 64-66, res group leader, 66-72, STAFF ENGR, CHEM RES, CONTINENTAL OIL CO, 72- *Personal Data:* b Bartlesville, Okla, Dec 2, 31; m 54; c 2. *Educ:* Okla Baptist Univ, AB, 53; Univ Okla, BS, 56, MS, 58, PhD(chem eng), 62. *Res:* Aluminum alkyl chemistry; chemical reactor design; high pressure equipment; chemical kinetics; crystallization; sulfation-sulfonation reaction; process development studies; research in production of alcohols and olefins. *Mailing Add:* 1712 Dover Ponca City OK 74604

SKINNER, KATHLEEN MARY, CELL BIOLOGY, ANIMAL BEHAVIOR. *Current Pos:* asst prof biol, 80-83, ASSOC PROF BIOL, RUSSELL SAGE COL, TROY, NY, 83- *Personal Data:* b Amsterdam, NY, May 29, 48. *Educ:* State Univ NY, Albany, BS, 70, PhD(biophysics), 76; Col St Rose, MS, 72. *Prof Exp:* Res assoc fel biophys cell biol, State Univ NY, Albany, 76-79; res assoc fel toxicol, Albany Med Col, 79-80. *Concurrent Pos:* Res assoc, State Univ NY, Albany, 80, 81 & 82. *Mem:* Biophys Soc; Am Soc Cell Biol; AAAS. *Res:* Control of the mobility of cellular flagella. *Mailing Add:* Biol Dept Russel Sage Col Main Campus 65 N First St Troy NY 12180-1538

SKINNER, LINDSAY A, APPLIED MATHEMATICS. *Current Pos:* ASSOC PROF MATH, UNIV WIS-MILWAUKEE, 69- *Personal Data:* b Chicago, Ill, Mar 28, 38; m 62; c 3. *Educ:* Northwestern Univ, BS, 60, PhD, 63. *Prof Exp:* Mem res staff, Int Bus Mach Corp, Calif, 63-64; asst prof math, Purdue Univ, Lafayette, 64-69. *Mem:* Soc Indust & Appl Math. *Res:* Perturbation theory and asymptotic expansions. *Mailing Add:* Dept Math Sci Univ Wis Milwaukee WI 53201-0413

SKINNER, LOREN COURTLAND, II, PHYSICS, METALLURGY. *Current Pos:* mgr, Solid State Technol Ctr, 78-86, DIR RES, NAT SEMICONDUCTOR CORP, SANTA CLARA, 86- *Personal Data:* b Borger, Tex, Aug 16, 40; m 65; c 3. *Educ:* Mass Inst Technol, SB, 62, SM, 64, PhD(metall), 65. *Prof Exp:* Res assoc metall, Mass Inst Technol, 65-66; physicist, Integrated Circuits Ctr, Motorola, Inc, 66-70; dept mgr res & develop, Microprod Div, Am Micro-Systs Inc, 70-72, M O S Mgr, Data Gen Semiconductor Div, 72-76; mem tech staff, Advan Microdevices, Inc, 76-78. *Mem:* Am Inst Mining, Metall & Petrol Engrs; Am Phys Soc; Am Vacuum Soc; Electrochem Soc. *Res:* Metal oxide semiconductor integrated circuit processing; electronic materials research, including device behavior, thin film deposition and patterning; circuit application development. *Mailing Add:* 310 Donohoe St East Palo Alto CA 94303-1813

SKINNER, MARGARET SHEPPARD, PATHOLOGY. *Current Pos:* PATHOLOGIST, PALM BEACH PATHOLOGY, 89- *Personal Data:* b Jamaica, NY, May 8, 38; m 69; c 2. *Educ:* Emory Univ, MD, 62. *Prof Exp:* From instr to assoc prof path, Sch Med, Tulane Univ, 65-73; pathologist, Cedars of Lebanon Hosp, Miami, 73-89. *Concurrent Pos:* NIH fel path, Tulane Univ, 65-68; asst vis pathologist, Charity Hosp, New Orleans, 65-68; vis pathologist, 68-73; consult staff, Lallie Kemp Charity Hosp, 72-73; clin assoc prof path, Univ Miami, 77- *Mem:* Am Asn Pathologists; Am Soc Microbiol; AMA; Col Am Pathologists. *Res:* Experimental cell pathology; surgical pathology. *Mailing Add:* 33 Grand Bay Circle Juno Beach FL 33406

SKINNER, MICHAEL P, POLYMER CHEMISTRY. *Current Pos:* LARGE AREA PROCESSING MANUFACTURING ENG MGR, MICRO MODULE SYSTS, 97- *Personal Data:* b Jan 16, 58; m, Patrici Nerio. *Educ:* Univ Mich, BS(chem) & BS(biol), 80; Polytech Univ, MS, 85, PhD(polymer chem), 93. *Prof Exp:* Sr assoc, Int Bus Mach Corp, 81-85, staff engr, 85-89, develop mgr, 89-90 & adv engr, 90-93; proj engr, Dow Chem, 93-96. *Mem:* AAAS; Am Chem Soc; Soc Plastics Engrs; Int Soc Hybrid Microelectronics; Int Soc Optical Eng. *Res:* Converting 6 inch process line to 16 by 16 inch process. *Mailing Add:* Micro Module Systs 10500 Ridgeview Ct Suite A Cupertino CA 95014-0736. *Fax:* 408-864-5950; *E-Mail:* mskinner@mms.com

SKINNER, NATHAN LESTON, INTERMETALLIC & COMPOUND SEMICONDUCTOR MATERIALS SYNTHESIS-PURIFICATION-CRYSTAL GROWTH, COMMERCIAL PRODUCT DEVELOPMENT. *Current Pos:* TECH DIR, ADVAN DETECTORS INC, 91- *Personal Data:* b Longview, Wash, Jan 11, 37; m 59, 81, Susan Kay Brunkhorst; c Shannon Elizabeth, Niles Bentley & Kelci Nicole. *Prof Exp:* Lab technician prod develop, Long-Bell Lumber Co, 55, plastics res & develop, Narmco Inc, 56-59, intermetallic semiconductors, Crys-Tech, 60-61; res asst mat res & develop, Hughes Semiconductor, 59-60; res engr, Diffusion Lab, Western Semiconductor, 62-65; engr, Diffusion Lab Semco Inc, 65-67; sr res asst, Highes Res Ctr, 67-70; engr Santa Barbara Res Ctr, 70-76; scientist II, EG&G Energy Measurements, 76-91. *Concurrent Pos:* Res dir, Zog Indust Inc, 70-, Sweetwater Co, 78-, Practichem Co, 88-, Sumus Co, 89- & Bent Nickel Co, 91-; sci educr/founder, Reacts, 72-; nat planning comt consult, USDA, 91. *Mem:* Am Chem Soc. *Res:* Pioneered synthesis, purification and single crystal growth of gallium antimonide, indium antimonide, gallium arsenide, indium arsenide, indium gallium antimonide and mercuric iodide; research and development VCGs, experiment and flight equipment; ground control science lead for VCGS on Spacelab III; several publications on mercuric iodide; granted 2 US patents. *Mailing Add:* 1561 Meadow Circle Carpinteria CA 93013

SKINNER, NEWMAN SHELDON, JR, medicine, physiology, for more information see previous edition

SKINNER, RICHARD EMERY, ENGINEERING PHYSICS, MATHEMATICS. *Current Pos:* pres, Skinner Industs, Inc, 69-70, INDEPENDENT CONSULT, PRES & CHIEF ENGR, R E SKINNER & ASSOCS INC, 70- *Personal Data:* b Anderson, Ind, Feb 15, 34; m 54, Dorothy A Leavit; c Eugene R & James J. *Educ:* Reed Col, BA, 55; Calif Inst Technol, MS, 57. *Prof Exp:* Physicist, Atomics Int Div, NAm Aviation, Inc, 55 & 56-59, consult, 55-56; physicist, Radio Corp Am, 59-64; supvry physicist, Electromagnetic Res Inc, 64-65; tech dir, Manst Corp, 66-68; vpres & gen mgr, Parzen Res Div, Ovitron, 68-69. *Mem:* Am Phys Soc; Am Nuclear Soc; Nat Soc Prof Engrs. *Res:* Electronics; electrical, mechanical and structural engineering; land surveying and communications; plasma physics; nuclear reactor dynamics theory; computer science. *Mailing Add:* R E Skinner & Assocs Inc 1731 SE 55th Ave Portland OR 97215. *Fax:* 503-232-6903; *E-Mail:* 72160.403@compuserve.com

SKINNER, ROBERT DOWELL, NEUROPHYSIOLOGY. *Current Pos:* Instr, 70-71, from asst prof to assoc prof, 71-89, PROF ANAT, COL MED, UNIV ARK MED SCI, LITTLE ROCK, 89- *Personal Data:* b Waxahachie, Tex, Nov 23, 42; m 66, Raynell McLean; c James, Christopher, Andrew & Stephen. *Educ:* Univ Tex, Arlington, BS, 65; Univ Tex Southwestern Med Sch, Dallas, PhD(biophys), 69. *Concurrent Pos:* NIH fel, Harvard Med Sch, 69-70. *Mem:* Am Asn Anat; Soc Neurosci; Int Brain Res Orgn. *Res:* Locomotor systems; spinal cord physiology; brain stem physiology; human and animal mid-latency auditory evoked potentials. *Mailing Add:* Dept Anat Slot 510 Univ Ark Med Sci Little Rock AR 72205. *Fax:* 501-686-6382; *E-Mail:* rskinner@comdean2.uams.edu

SKINNER, ROBERT EARLE, JR, CIVIL ENGINEERING, TRANSPORTATION RESEARCH & POLICY. *Current Pos:* sr staff officer, 83-86, dir, Studies & Info Serv, 86-94, EXEC DIR, TRANSP RES BD, 94- *Personal Data:* b Washington, DC, Aug 10, 46; m, Dianne Lynette Sands; c Martha & Jeffrey. *Educ:* Univ Va, BSCE, 69; Mass Inst Technol, MSCE, 71. *Prof Exp:* Sr assoc, PRC Voorhees, McLean, Va, 71-83, vpres, 79-83. *Concurrent Pos:* Mem, Intersectional Transp Serv, Am Coord Coun, Washington, 94- *Mem:* Am Soc Civil Engrs; Int Soc Asphalt Pavements. *Res:* Research management; dissemination of research findings to encourage innovation in transportation; transportation policy; contributed articles to professional journals. *Mailing Add:* Transp Res Bd 2101 Constitution Ave NW Washington DC 20418

SKINNER, ROBERT L, ELECTRICAL ENGINEERING. *Current Pos:* AT PRE ENGR TECHNOL. *Personal Data:* b Salt Lake City, Utah, Nov 6, 30; m 53; c 4. *Educ:* Univ Utah, BS, 54, MS, 55. *Prof Exp:* Res dir, Ensco, Inc, 54-68; pres, Entec Inc, 68- *Concurrent Pos:* Instr, Univ Utah, 55-56. *Mem:* Inst Elec & Electronics Engrs. *Res:* Specialized systems and instrumentation used in medical research. *Mailing Add:* 8456 S 1430 E Sandy UT 84091

SKINNER, WALTER SWART, earth science, for more information see previous edition

SKINNER, WILLIAM ROBERT, PETROLOGY, STRUCTURAL GEOLOGY. *Current Pos:* asst prof, 66-71, ASSOC PROF GEOL, OBERLIN COL, 71-, CHMN DEPT, 74- *Personal Data:* b Tampa, Fla, Jan 1, 30; m 57; c 4. *Educ:* Univ Tex, BS, 53; Columbia Univ, PhD(geol), 66. *Prof Exp:* Inspector construct, Pittsburgh Testing Lab, 57-59. *Mem:* Geol Soc Am. *Res:* Structure and petrogenesis of Precambrian metamorphic terranes; petrology and geochemistry of Alpine-type and stratiform igneous complexes. *Mailing Add:* Dept of Geol Oberlin Col Oberlin OH 44074

SKINNIDER, LEO F, PATHOLOGY, HEMATOLOGY. *Current Pos:* Assoc prof, 69-73, PROF PATH, UNIV SASK, SASKATOON, 73- *Personal Data:* b Paisley, Scotland, Oct 2, 29; Can citizen; c 8. *Educ:* Univ Glasgow, MB, ChB, 51; FRCP(C), 68. *Concurrent Pos:* Consult, Can Tumor Reference Ctr, 72-; Nat Cancer Inst Can grant, 74-; deleg, Col Am Pathologists, 70-78. *Mem:* Am Soc Clin Pathologists; Can Asn Pathologists; Col Am Pathologists; Can Soc Hematol; Can Health Res. *Res:* Ultrastructure and agar-culture characteristics of cells of lymphomas and leukemias; effect of retinol and its analogies on the proliferation of lymphoid cells. *Mailing Add:* Univ Sask Col Med Saskatoon SK S7N 5E5 Can

SKIPP, BETTY ANN, GEOLOGIC MAPPING, MICROPALEONTOLOGY. *Current Pos:* Geologist, 52-64, RES GEOLOGIST, US GEOL SURV, 65- *Personal Data:* b Chicago, Ill, May 7, 28; m 51; c 2. *Educ:* Northwestern Univ, BA, 49; Univ Colo, MS, 56, PhD(struct geol), 85. *Mem:* Fel Geol Soc Am; Am Asn Petrol Geologists; Soc Econ Paleontologists & Geologists; Paleont Res Inst. *Res:* Structure and stratigraphy of Proterozoic through Tertiary rocks of south-central Idaho and adjacent Montana using geologic mapping and geophysical surveys; the biostratigraphy of Carboniferous smaller calcareous foraminifera worldwide; Mississippian smaller calcareous foraminifers and algae. *Mailing Add:* 2035 Grape Ave Boulder CO 80304-2337

SKIRVIN, ROBERT MICHAEL, PLANT BREEDING, PLANT PHYSIOLOGY. *Current Pos:* asst prof hort, 76-81, assoc prof, 81-88, PROF HORT & FORESTRY, UNIV ILL, 88- *Personal Data:* b Burlington, Wash, Oct 27, 47; m 73, Mary M Van Horn; c Timothy Michael & Daniel Charles. *Educ:* Southern Ill Univ, BS, 69, MS, 71; Purdue Univ, PhD(hort), 75. *Prof Exp:* Lab & field asst, Fruit Res Sta, 68-69; res asst grape physiol, Southern Ill Univ, 69-71; David Ross fel hort, Purdue Univ, 71-73, res asst, 73-74, from instr to asst prof, 74-76. *Concurrent Pos:* Vis prof, plant breeding, DISR, Lincoln, NZ, 85-86 & plant biotechnol, Burnley Gardens, Inst Plant Sci, Victoria, Australia, 91-92. *Mem:* Am Soc Hort Sci; Am Pomol Soc; Int Asn Plant Tissue Cult; Sigma Xi. *Res:* Development of methods to utilize tissue culture techniques for the improvement of asexually propagated crops; breeding and genetic studies of small fruits with a particular interest in thornless blackberries. *Mailing Add:* Dept Hort 258 Plant & Animal Biotechnol Lab Univ Ill 1201 Gregory Dr Urbana IL 61801. *Fax:* 217-333-4777; *E-Mail:* skirvin@uiuc.edu

SKJEGSTAD, KENNETH, BOTANY. *Current Pos:* RETIRED. *Personal Data:* b Henning, Minn, Oct 18, 31. *Educ:* Moorhead State Col, BS, 53; Univ Calif, Los Angeles, PhD(bot), 60. *Prof Exp:* Assoc biol, Univ Calif, 58-60; from instr to assoc prof bot, Univ Minn, Minneapolis, 60-66; assoc prof to prof biol, Moorhead State Univ, 66-94. *Mem:* AAAS; Bot Soc Am; Am Soc Plant Physiol. *Res:* Physiology of plant growth and development; plant genetics. *Mailing Add:* Dept Biol Moorhead State Univ Moorhead MN 56563

SKJOLD, ARTHUR CHRISTOPHER, BIOCHEMISTRY, MICROBIAL GENETICS. *Current Pos:* PRAGMATICS, 92- *Personal Data:* b Minneapolis, Minn, Dec 20, 43; m 72; c 1. *Educ:* Macalester Col, BA, 66; Kans State Univ, PhD(biochem), 70. *Prof Exp:* Res assoc microbiol genetics, Albert Einstein Med Ctr, 70-73; asst dir res immunodiag, Kallestad Labs Inc, 73-77; sr res scientist, Urine Chem Lab, Miles Lab, 77-85, sr staff scientist, Dry Reagent Chem Lab, Ames Div, 85-92. *Mem:* Am Asn Clin Chem. *Res:* Nucleic acids; microbial genetics; regulation of RNA and protein synthesis; immunochemistry; protein purification; urinalysis; regulation of bacterial growth. *Mailing Add:* 1602 Victoria Dr Elkhart IN 46514

SKJONSBY, HAROLD SAMUEL, HISTOLOGY, ANATOMY. *Current Pos:* From asst prof to assoc prof, 64-74, PROF, 74-, ANAT SCI & CHMN DEPT, UNIV TEX DENT BR HOUSTON, 84- *Personal Data:* b Sisseton, SDak, July 6, 37; m 61; c 3. *Educ:* Concordia Col, BA, 59; Univ NDak, MS, 62, PhD(anat), 64. *Mem:* Int Asn Dent Res; Am Asn Dent Schs. *Res:* Histochemistry of tooth development; structure of bone and connective tissue. *Mailing Add:* 406 Sul Ross St Houston TX 77006

SKLANSKY, J(ACK), ELECTRICAL ENGINEERING, COMPUTER SCIENCE. *Current Pos:* assoc prof elec eng, 66-69, chmn dept, 78-80, PROF ELEC ENG, INFO & COMUT SCI & RADIOL SCI, UNIV CALIF, IRVINE, 69- *Personal Data:* b Brooklyn, NY, Nov 15, 28; m 57; c 3. *Educ:* City Col New York, BEE, 50; Purdue Univ, MSEE, 52; Columbia Univ, DSc(eng), 55. *Honors & Awards:* Fourth Ann Award, Pattern Recognition Soc. *Prof Exp:* Res engr, Electronics Res Labs, Columbia Univ, 54-55 & RCA Labs, NJ, 55-65; head systs res sect, Nat Cash Register Co, Ohio, 65-66. *Concurrent Pos:* Res grants, Nat Inst Gen Med Sci, NSF & Army Res Off. *Mem:* Asn Comput Mach; fel Inst Elec & Electronics Engrs; Comput Soc. *Res:* Automatic pattern classifiers; image processing by computer; medical imaging; biomedical engineering; digital system theory. *Mailing Add:* 43 Cambria Newport Beach CA 92625

SKLAR, LARRY A, BIOPHYSICS, IMMUNOLOGY. *Current Pos:* ASSOC MEM, SCRIPPS CLIN & RES FOUND, 79- *Educ:* Stanford Univ, PhD(phys chem), 76. *Mailing Add:* Dept Cytometry Univ NMex Sch Med 900 Camino de Salud NE Rm 331 Albuquerque NM 87131-5636. *Fax:* 505-277-6677

SKLAR, STANLEY, PHARMACEUTICS. *Current Pos:* res pharmacist, Radnor, 67-72, unit supvr, 72-73, unit supvr, Pilot Plant, 73-80, QUAL ASSURANCE MGR, WYETH LABS, WEST CHESTER, 80- *Personal Data:* b Bronx, NY, July 12, 37; m 63; c 2. *Educ:* Philadelphia Col Pharm & Sci, BS, 59; Purdue Univ, Lafayette, MS, 61; Univ Conn, PhD(pharm), 65. *Prof Exp:* Res pharmacist, Bristol Labs, 65-67. *Concurrent Pos:* Secy, Parenteral Drug Asn, 80-81. *Mem:* Am Pharmaceut Asn; Acad Pharmaceut Sci; Am Chem Soc. *Res:* Quality assurance and quality control functions, including parenteral dosage forms, fermentation production and a fine chemical facility. *Mailing Add:* Four Selwyn Dr Broomall PA 19008

SKLAREW, DEBORAH S, ORGANIC GEOCHEMISTRY, ANALYTICAL CHEMISTRY. *Current Pos:* SR RES SCIENTIST, BATTELLE PAC NORTHWEST LABS, 78- *Personal Data:* b New York, NY, Apr 6, 50; m 77; c 1. *Educ:* City Col NY, BS, 70; Univ Calif, Berkeley, MS, 72; Univ Ariz, PhD(geosci), 78. *Mem:* Geochem Soc; Am Chem Soc. *Res:* Kerogen analysis in Precambrian and recent sedimentary rocks; characterization of fossil fuel effluents; sulfur and nitrogen gas analysis in oil shale retorts; organomercury analysis; PCB sorption studies. *Mailing Add:* 544 Franklin Richland WA 99352-1815

SKLAREW, ROBERT J, CYTOKINETICS, MICROSCOPIC-IMAGING. *Current Pos:* prof med & anat, 88-89, PROF MED CELL BIOL & MED, NY MED COL, VALHALLA, 89- *Personal Data:* b New York, NY, Nov 25, 41; m 70, Toby Willner; c David M & Gary R. *Educ:* Cornell Univ, Ithaca, NY, BA, 63; New York Univ, MS, 65, PhD(biol), 70. *Honors & Awards:* Shannon Award, Nat Cancer Inst, 91. *Prof Exp:* Asst res scientist, Dept Med, Goldwater Mem Hosp, New York Univ Med Ctr, 65-70, assoc res sci, 70-71, res sci, 71-73, sr res sci, 73-79, res asst prof, Dept Pathol, 79-86, dir, Cytokinetics & Imaging Lab, 80-88. *Concurrent Pos:* Res assoc, Dept Pathol, Lenox Hill Hosp, NY, 81-86; adj asst prof clin dermatol, New York Med Col, 85-86. *Mem:* Cell Kinetics Soc (secy, 83-86, pres, 87-88)); AAAS; Tissue Cult Asn; Int Cell Cycle Soc; Am Soc Cell Biol; Soc Anal Cytol. *Res:* Cell cycle kinetics of heteroploid subpopulations in solid tumors determined by microscopic imaging of autoradiographic labeling and DNA distribution patterns; perturbation of cytokinetics by hormones and cytotoxins in relation to the sensitivity spectrum of subpopulations as a basis for optimization of therapy. *Mailing Add:* Cancer Res Inst 100 Grasslands Rd Elmsford NY 10523. *Fax:* 914-347-2804

SKOBE, ZIEDOMIS, CELL BIOLOGY. *Current Pos:* DEPT HEAD ELECTRON MICROS, FORSYTH DENT CTR, 72- *Personal Data:* b Riga, Latvia, Apr 29, 41; US citizen; c 4. *Educ:* Boston Univ, BA, 63, PhD(biol), 72; Clark Univ, MA, 67. *Concurrent Pos:* Lectr, Boston Univ, 75- *Mem:* Am Asn Dent Res; Int Asn Dent Res; Am Soc Cell Biol. *Res:* Structure of tooth enamel and the ultrastructure of the cells involved in amelogenesis in several mammals using both scanning and transmission electron microscopy. *Mailing Add:* Forsyth Dent Ctr 140 Fenway Boston MA 02115

SKOCHDOPOLE, RICHARD E, POLYMER BLENDS, PLASTIC FOAMS. *Current Pos:* CONSULT, SKOCHDOPOLE CONSULT, 89- *Personal Data:* b Ravenna, Nebr, Dec 11, 27; m 53, Nancy McClenahan; c Jill, Todd, James & Mark. *Educ:* Univ Nebr, BSc, 49; Iowa State Univ, PhD(phys chem), 54. *Prof Exp:* Fel, Ames Lab, AEC, 54-55; res chemist, Phys Res Lab, Dow Chem Co, 56-63, sr res chemist, 63-64, assoc scientist, 64-68, dir converted plastics lab, 68, res mgr designed plastics res, 68-70, res mgr foam prod res, 70-73, assoc scientist foam prods res, 73-76, assoc scientist chem prod lab, 76-83, assoc develop scientist, Eng Plastics Tech Serv & Develop, 83-89. *Mem:* Am Chem Soc; Sigma Xi; Soc Plastics Engrs. *Res:* Preparation and characterization of cellular plastics, particularly thermal properties; physical chemistry of polymers and polymer solutions; preparation and characterization of polymers; polymer blends. *Mailing Add:* 2525 Lambros Midland MI 48642

SKOCPOL, WILLIAM JOHN, HIGH TEMPERATURE SUPERCONDUCTING THIN FILMS, NANOMETER-SCALE DEVICES. *Current Pos:* PROF PHYSICS, BOSTON UNIV, 87- *Personal Data:* m 67, Theda Barron; c Michael A. *Educ:* Mich State Univ, BA, 68; Harvard Univ, MA, 71, PhD(physics), 74. *Prof Exp:* From asst prof to assoc prof physics, Harvard Univ, 74-81; mem tech staff, AT&T Bell Labs, 81-87, distinguished mem tech staff, 87. *Mem:* Fel Am Phys Soc; Inst Elec & Electronics Engrs; Mat Res Soc; AAAS. *Res:* Properties and applications of thin films of high-temperature superconductors; gallium nobelium and aluminum nobelium field effect transistors; nanofabrication and quantum physics of submicron silicon metal-oxide-semiconductor field-effect transistor devices. *Mailing Add:* Dept Physics Boston Univ 590 Commonwealth Ave Boston MA 02215. *Fax:* 617-353-9393; *E-Mail:* skocpol@buphy.bu.edu

SKOFRONICK, JAMES GUST, CHEMICAL & SURFACE PHYSICS, EPITAXIAL GROWTH. *Current Pos:* from asst prof to assoc prof, 64-74, interim dir, Ctr Mat Res & Technol, 91-94, PROF PHYSICS, FLA STATE UNIV, 74- *Personal Data:* b Merrill, Wis, Oct 11, 31; m 59, Dorothy Nilles; c Gregory, Gail, Gary & Gretchen. *Educ:* Univ Wis, BS, 59, MS, 61, PhD(nuclear physics), 64. *Prof Exp:* Res asst physics, Univ Wis, 59-64. *Concurrent Pos:* Mem vis staff, Max Planck Inst Fluid Dynamics, 79-96. *Mem:* Am Phys Soc; Europ Phys Soc; Sigma Xi. *Res:* Physics of surfaces; dynamics and structure of crystalline surfaces; high-resolution helium scattering experiments; epitaxial growth; surface phase transitions; formation of self-assembling film surfaces. *Mailing Add:* Dept Physics Fla State Univ Tallahassee FL 32306. *Fax:* 850-644-6504; *E-Mail:* skofronick@phy.fsu.edu

SKOG, JUDITH ELLEN, PALEOBOTANY, EVOLUTION & RELATIONSHIPS OF PTERIDOPHYTES. *Current Pos:* PROF BIOL, GEORGE MASON UNIV, 72- *Personal Data:* b Beverly, Mass, Apr 14, 44; m 68, Laurence E; c Jeremy O. *Educ:* Tufts Univ, BS, 66; Univ Conn, MS, 68; Cornell Univ, PhD(bot-paleobot), 72. *Concurrent Pos:* Res assoc, Smithsonian Inst, 73-; vis scientist, US Geol Survey, 80-; vis res assoc, Manchester Univ, Eng, 84; vis prof, Univ Fla, 91. *Mem:* Am Fern Soc (vpres, pres, 86-89); Bot Soc Am; Paleont Asn; Int Orgn for Paleobot; Int Asn Plant Taxonomists; Brit Pteridological Soc. *Res:* Focus on the evolution and relationships of the lower vascular plants, especially ferns, and many fossil ferns of the cretaceous time period; fossils from the eastern and central United States and their relationships to modern groups of ferns. *Mailing Add:* Biol Dept George Mason Univ Fairfax VA 22030-4444

SKOG, LAURENCE EDGAR, PLANT TAXONOMY. *Current Pos:* asst ed, Flora NAm Prog, Smithsonian Inst, 72-73, assoc cur bot, 73-86, chmn bot, 87-92, CUR BOT, SMITHSONIAN INST, 86- *Personal Data:* b Duluth, Minn, Apr 9, 43; m 68, Judith E Troop; c Jeremy O. *Educ:* Univ Minn, BA, 65; Univ Conn, MS, 68; Cornell Univ, PhD(bot), 72. *Prof Exp:* Teaching asst bot, Univ Conn, 65-68; fel, Royal Bot Garden, Edinburgh, 68-69; res asst bot, Cornell Univ, 68-72. *Concurrent Pos:* Adj prof biol, George Mason Univ, 80-91; res fel, Manchester Mus, Univ Manchester, Eng, 84; bd dirs, Int Asn Plant Taxon, 87-; bd dirs, Int Orgn Plant Info, 90-93; comn mem, Orgn Flora Neotropica, 90-, bd mem, 92-96; mem coun, Am Inst Biol Sci, 91-; hon prof, Open Lab, Chinese Acad Sci, Bejing, China. *Mem:* Bot Soc Am; Am Soc Plant Taxonomists; Int Asn Plant Taxon; Asn Trop Biol (secy-treas, 81-85); Orgn Flora Neotropica; Am Inst Biol Sci; Sigma Xi. *Res:* Taxonomy and floristics of neotropical Gesneriaceae, Coriariaceae; pollination biology; Flora of the Guianas; Flora of China. *Mailing Add:* Dept Bot NHB-166 Nat Mus Natural Hist Smithsonian Inst Washington DC 20560-0001. *Fax:* 202-786-2563; *E-Mail:* skog.larry@nmnh.si.edu

SKOGERBOE, GAYLORD VINCENT, AGRICULTURAL ENGINEERING, CIVIL ENGINEERING. *Current Pos:* PROF AGR & IRRIGATION ENG, UTAH STATE UNIV, 84- *Personal Data:* b Cresco, Iowa, Apr 1, 35; m 58; c 2. *Educ:* Univ Utah, BS, 58, MS, 59. *Prof Exp:* Hydraulic engr, Utah Water & Power Bd, 60-63; res proj engr hydraulics, Utah Water Res Lab, Utah State Univ, 63-68; prof irrigation & drainage, Colo State Univ, 68-84. *Mem:* Am Soc Agr Engrs; Am Soc Civil Engrs; Int Soc Ecol Modelling; Int Water Resources Asn. *Res:* Interdisciplinary research involving physical and social scientists on topics related to agricultural development and environmental problems of irrigated agriculture. *Mailing Add:* 627 S 200 W Logan UT 84321

SKOGERBOE, RODNEY K, ANALYTICAL CHEMISTRY. *Current Pos:* RETIRED. *Personal Data:* b Blue Earth, Minn, June 25, 31; m 58; c 4. *Educ:* Mankato State Col, BA, 58; Mont State Univ, PhD(chem), 63. *Prof Exp:* Jr chemist, Ames Lab, US AEC, 58-60; asst prof chem, SDak Sch Mines & Technol, 63-64; res mgr, Cornell Univ, 64-69; from asst prof to assoc prof chem, Colo State Univ, 69-73, prof chem & atmospheric sci, 73-80, chmn Dept Chem, 80-91. *Mem:* Am Chem Soc; Soc Appl Spectros (pres, 72). *Res:* Spectrochemical and radiochemical methods of trace analysis; application of statistics to chemical problems. *Mailing Add:* 16889 N County Rd 25E Loveland CO 80538

SKOGERSON, LAWRENCE EUGENE, BIOCHEMISTRY. *Current Pos:* ASSOC PROF BIOCHEM, MED COL WIS, 77- *Personal Data:* b Ft Collins, Colo, Aug 19, 42; m 69; c 3. *Educ:* Grinnell Col, AB, 64; Univ Pittsburgh, PhD(biochem), 68. *Prof Exp:* Asst prof biochem, Col Physicians & Surgeons, Columbia Univ, 70-77. *Concurrent Pos:* Am Cancer Soc fel, NIH, Bethesda, 68-70; USPHS res grant, Columbia Univ, 71-78, Am Cancer Soc fac res award, 72-77. *Mem:* Am Soc Biol Chemists; Harvey Soc. *Res:* Regulation of RNA and protein synthesis. *Mailing Add:* Gist Brocades Food Ingred Inc 85 Main St East Brunswick NJ 08816. *Fax:* 732-251-6658

SKOGLEY, CONRAD RICHARD, AGRONOMY, TURFGRASS MANAGEMENT. *Current Pos:* assoc prof agron, 60-70, prof plant & soil sci, 70-90, EMER PROF PLANT & SOIL SCI, UNIV RI, 90- *Personal Data:* b Deer Lodge, Mont, Nov 9, 24; m 48; c 3. *Educ:* Univ RI, BS, 50, MS, 52; Rutgers Univ, PhD, 57. *Prof Exp:* Asst agronomist, Univ RI, 51-53; asst & res assoc, Rutgers Univ, 53-56, exten assoc, 56-57, asst exten specialist, 57-59, assoc exten specialist, 59-60. *Mem:* Am Soc Agron; Crop Sci Soc Am; Int Turfgrass Soc. *Res:* Turfgrass management; establishment and maintenance of fine turf grasses; turfgrass breeding. *Mailing Add:* 10 Liberty Rd Exeter RI 02822

SKOGLEY, EARL O, SOIL FERTILITY, PLANT NUTRITION. *Current Pos:* from asst prof to assoc prof, 63-71, PROF SOIL FERTIL, MONT STATE UNIV, 71- *Personal Data:* b Mott, NDak, Mar 18, 33; m 55; c 3. *Educ:* NDak State Univ, BS, 55, MS, 57; NC State Univ, PhD(soil fertility), 62. *Prof Exp:* Instr soils, NC State Univ, 57-62; res assoc soil fertil, Cornell Univ, 62-63. *Concurrent Pos:* Res adv, USAID, Brazil, 67 & 68 & on contract with IRI Res Inst, Inc, NY; consult/team mem develop transmission environ report proposed twin 500 Kv power lines Mont, 77-78. *Mem:* Fel AAAS; Soil Sci Soc Am; Am Soc Agron; Int Soil Sci Soc. *Res:* Development of synthetic growth media for plant nutrition studies; investigation of plant nutrient relations in soils and plants; development of new soil test based on phytoavailability of nutrients. *Mailing Add:* 3535 Stucky Rd Bozeman MT 59715-9034

SKOGLUND, WINTHROP CHARLES, POULTRY HUSBANDRY. *Current Pos:* RETIRED. *Personal Data:* b Lynn, Mass, Dec 7, 16; m 41; c 1. *Educ:* Univ NH, BS, 38; Pa State Col, MS, 40, PhD, 58. *Prof Exp:* Asst, Pa State Col, 38-40; instr poultry indust & asst res poultryman, Univ Del, 40-42, exten poultry specialist, 42-46, from asst prof to assoc prof poultry indust, 46-50, dir agr short course, 49-50; prof poultry husb & chmn dept, Univ NH, 50-81. *Mem:* Sigma Xi. *Res:* Nutrition; breeding; hatching; egg production. *Mailing Add:* 30 Bagdad Rd Durham NH 03824

SKOK, JOHN, plant physiology; deceased, see previous edition for last biography

SKOK, RICHARD ARNOLD, FOREST ECONOMICS. *Current Pos:* from instr to assoc prof, Univ Minn, 59-65, asst dir, Col Forestry, 67-71, assoc dean, 71-74, dean, 74-93, PROF FOREST ECON, UNIV MINN, ST PAUL, 65-, EMER DEAN, COL FORESTRY, 93- *Personal Data:* b St Paul, Minn, June 19, 28; c 2. *Educ:* Univ Minn, BS, 50, MF, 54, PhD, 60. *Prof Exp:* Asst prof forest econ, Sch Forestry, Mont State Univ, 58-59. *Concurrent Pos:* Mem, Exec Bd, Joint Coun Food & Agr Sci; mem, Int Forestry Res Orgn, 86-90. *Mem:* Fel Soc Am Foresters. *Res:* Forest resource development-economics and policy. *Mailing Add:* 115 Green Hall Univ Minn St Paul MN 55108

SKOLD, LAURENCE NELSON, agronomy, for more information see previous edition

SKOLMEN, ROGER GODFREY, TREE PHYSIOLOGY, FOREST PRODUCTS. *Current Pos:* RETIRED. *Personal Data:* b San Francisco, Calif, Dec 30, 29. *Educ:* Univ Calif, BS, 57, MS, 58; Univ Hawaii, PhD, 77. *Prof Exp:* Asst chem, Shell Develop Co, 55; res asst forestry, Univ Calif, 56-59; soil scientist, Pac Southwest Forest Exp Sta, US Forest Serv, 59-60, wood scientist, Hawaii Res Ctr, 61-72, res forester, Inst Pac Islands Forestry, 72-86. *Concurrent Pos:* Consult, Trop Forestry & Woods. *Mem:* Forest Prod Res Soc; Soc Am Foresters; Plant Tissue Cult Asn. *Res:* Tissue culture propagation of trees; genetic tree improvement; eucalyptus biomass production; utilization of Hawaii-grown woods; tree, log, and wood quality; durability; preservation; seasoning; sawmilling; marketing; silviculture. *Mailing Add:* 403 Koko Isle Circle Honolulu HI 96825

SKOLNICK, HERBERT, GEOLOGY. *Current Pos:* RETIRED. *Personal Data:* b Brooklyn, NY, Jan 15, 19; m 48, Marilyn Kassel; c Tamara. *Educ:* Brooklyn Col, BS, 47; Univ Okla, MS, 49; Univ Iowa, PhD(geol), 52. *Prof Exp:* Sedimentologist, Gulf Res & Develop Co, 52-53, supvr geol lab, Western Gulf Oil Co, 53-56, div stratigrapher, 56-60, chief stratigrapher & paleontologist, Spanish Gulf Oil Co, 60-64, supvr stratig lab, Nigerian Gulf Oil Co, 64-67; supvr Stratig Lab, Houston Tech Serv Ctr, Gulf Res & Develop Co, 67-71, res assoc, 71-73, supvr Geol Sect, 73-77, sr res assoc, 77-80, adminr explor res function, 80-82. *Concurrent Pos:* Consult, environ groups concerned with air & water quality & hazardous waste & municipal dumps. *Mem:* Geol Soc Am; Am Asn Petrol Geologists; Soc Econ Paleontologists and Mineralogists; Sigma Xi. *Res:* Petrology, petrography and diagenesis of sedimentary rocks; evolution of subsurface fluid systems; plate tectonics; oceanography; geochemistry; stratigraphy and sedimentology; integration of listed disciplines as a tool for hydrocarbon exploration. *Mailing Add:* 109 S Ridge Dr Monroeville PA 15146

SKOLNICK, JEFFREY, POLYMER DYNAMICS, BIOPHYSICS. *Current Pos:* FULL MEM, RES INST SCRIPPS CLIN, 89- *Personal Data:* b Brooklyn, NY, June 27, 53. *Educ:* Wash Univ, BA, 75; Yale Univ, MPhil, 77, PhD(chem), 78. *Honors & Awards:* Wolfgang Prize, Yale Univ; Sowven Prize, Washington Univ. *Prof Exp:* Asst prof chem, La State Univ, 79-82; from asst prof to prof, Wash Univ, 82-89. *Concurrent Pos:* Vis prof, Wash Univ, 81; fel, Alfred P Sloan Found. *Mem:* Am Chem Soc; Am Phys Soc; Sigma Xi; NY Acad Sci; AAAS; Biophys Soc. *Res:* Statistical mechanics of polymer solutions, glasses and melts with an emphasis on local main chain dynamics; stress strain behavior of polymer glasses; theory of protein structure, folding kinetics and protein dynamics. *Mailing Add:* Dept Molec Biol MB-1 Scripps Res Inst 10666 N Torrey Pines Rd La Jolla CA 92037

SKOLNICK, MALCOLM HARRIS, PATENTS, INTELLECTUAL PROPERTY TECHNOLOGY TRANSFER. *Current Pos:* prof & chmn, Dept Biomed Commun, Health Sci Ctr, 71-83, dir, Neurophysiol Res Ctr, 84-91, dir technol mgt, 91-96, PROF BIOPHYS & BIOMED SCI, HEALTH SCI CTR, UNIV TEX, 71-, PROF TECHNOL & HEALTH LAW, SCH PUB HEALTH, 96- *Personal Data:* b Salt Lake City, Utah, Aug 11, 35; m 59, Lois M Ray; c Michael, David, Sara & Jonathan. *Educ:* Univ Utah, BS, 56; Cornell Univ, MS, 59, PhD(theoret physics), 63; Univ Houston, JD, 86. *Prof Exp:* Staff scientist elem sci study, Educ Develop Ctr, Mass, 62-63; mem, Sch Math, Inst Advan Study, Princeton Univ, 63-64; instr physics, Mass Inst Technol, 64-65; staff scientist elem sci study & dir, Peace Corps Training & Support Serv, Educ Develop Ctr, Mass, 65-67; assoc prof physics, Health Sci Ctr, State Univ NY, Stony Brook, 67-70, dir health sci commun, 68-71, assoc prof path, 70-71. *Concurrent Pos:* Consult, Educ Develop Ctr, Mass, Comn Col Physics, US Peace Corps, NSF & Nat Sci Teachers Asn; chmn, Health Care Technol Study Sect, Nat Ctr Health Serv Res, 74-78; dir, Biodyn Inc, S W Asn, Biotechnol COS & Tex Tech Transfer Asn; pres, Tex Empowerment Network, bd dir, Drug Policy Forum, Tex. *Mem:* Soc Neurosci; Sigma Xi; Soc Accident Reconstructionists; Am Bar Asn. *Res:* Electrostimulation effects on neuromodulation; simulation and modeling in biophysical systems; product liability; health care technology assessment. *Mailing Add:* Sch Public Health PO Box 20186 Houston TX 77225. *Fax:* 713-794-1601

SKOLNICK, MARK HENRY, GENETICS, POPULATION GENETICS. *Current Pos:* asst res prof, 74-76, ASST PROF DEPT MED BIOPHYSICS & COMPUT, UNIV UTAH, 76-, ADJ ASST PROF DEPT BIOL, 78- *Personal Data:* b Temple, Tex, Jan 28, 46; m 70; c 2. *Educ:* Univ Calif, Berkeley, BA, 68; Stanford Univ, PhD(genetics), 75. *Prof Exp:* Res asst prof dept biol, 74-77. *Concurrent Pos:* NIH res grant, 74-81, 76-80, 77-80 & 79-; Pub Health grant, 76-81; mem Int Union Sci Study of Pop, 76-; dir, Div Health, Utah State Dept Soc Serv, 77-; mem epidemiol comn, Nat Cancer Inst, NIH, 78- *Mem:* Am Soc Human Genetics. *Res:* Genetic epidemiological studies of Mormon genealogies; historical and genetic demography; computerized genealogical data bases, human chromosome mapping, relationship of HLA to disease; preventive medicine and screening for genetic diseases. *Mailing Add:* Dept Med Biophys Univ Utah Sch Med 50 N Medical Dr Salt Lake City UT 84132-0001

SKOLNICK, PHIL, PHARMACOLOGY. *Current Pos:* sr investr & pharmacologist, 78-83, chief neurobiol, 83-87, CHIEF, LAB NEUROSCI, NIH, 87-; RES PROF PSYCHIAT, UNIFORMED SERV UNIV HEALTH SCI, 89- *Personal Data:* b New York, NY, Feb 26, 47; m 85, Nancy Ostrowski; c Michael N & Stephen D. *Educ:* Long Island Univ, BSc, 68; George Washington Univ, PhD(pharmacol), 72. *Hon Degrees:* DSc, Long Island Univ, 93, Univ Wis, 95- *Honors & Awards:* A E Bennett Award, 80; Mathilde Solowey Award, 83; Anna Monika Prize, 95. *Prof Exp:* Staff fel, NIH, 72-75, sr staff fel pharmacol, 75-77; pharmacologist, Nat Inst Alcohol Abuse, Alcoholism, Alcohol, Drug Abuse & Ment Health Admin, 77-78. *Concurrent Pos:* Wellcome prof basic med sci, 87 & 92; sr exec serv, Dept Health & Human Serv, 89-; adj prof anesthesiol, Johns Hopkins Univ, 94- *Mem:* Am Soc Pharmacol & Exp Therapeut; Int Soc Neurochem; Soc Biol Psychiat; Am Col Neuropsychopharmacol; Am Soc Neuroscience. *Res:* Neuropharmacology; neuroendocrinology; neurochemical correlates of behavior; neuroimmunology. *Mailing Add:* Lab Neurosci NIH Bldg 8 Rm 111 Bethesda MD 20892. *E-Mail:* dpoga@helix.nih.gov

SKOLNIK, HERMAN, organic chemistry, information science, for more information see previous edition

SKOLNIK, MERRILL I, RADAR, ELECTRONIC ENGINEERING SYSTEMS. *Current Pos:* supt, 65-96, CONSULT, RADAR DIV, US NAVAL RES LAB, 96- *Personal Data:* b Baltimore, Md, Nov 6, 27; m 50, Judith Magid; c 4. *Educ:* Johns Hopkins Univ, BE, 47, MSE, 49, DrEng, 51. *Honors & Awards:* Heinrich Hertz Premium, Brit Inst Electronic & Radio Engrs, 65; Harry Diamond Award, Inst Elect & Electronics Engrs, 83, Centennial Medal, 84; Distinguished Civilian Serv Award, USN, 82. *Prof Exp:* Res asst elec eng, Johns Hopkins Univ, 47-50, res assoc, Radiation Lab, 50-53; eng specialist, Sylvania Elec Prod Co, 54; staff mem, Lincoln Lab, Mass Inst Technol, 54-59; res mgr, Electronic Commun Inc, 59-64; staff mem, Inst Defense Anal, 64-65. *Concurrent Pos:* Lectr, eve div, Northeastern Univ, 56-59, & Continuing Eng Educ, George Washington Univ, 73-93; adj prof, Drexel Inst Technol, 60-66 & eve div, Johns Hopkins Univ, 70-; vis prof, Johns Hopkins Univ, 73-74; ed, Proc Inst Elec & Electronics Engrs, 86-89; distinguished vis scientist, Jet Propulsion Lab, 90-92. *Mem:* Nat Acad Eng; Fel Inst Elec & Electronics Engrs. *Res:* Radar; antennas; electronic systems; electronic warfare; electric arc discharges. *Mailing Add:* Code 5007 US Naval Res Lab Washington DC 20375. *Fax:* 202-767-3658

SKOLNIKOFF, EUGENE B, SCIENCE TECHNOLOGY & INTERNATIONAL AFFAIRS, SCIENCE & INTERNATIONAL ORGANIZATIONS. *Current Pos:* chmn, Polit Sci Dept, 70-74, dir, Ctr Int Studies, 72-87, PROF POLIT SCI, MASS INST TECHNOL, 65- *Personal Data:* b Philadelphia, Pa, Aug 29, 28; m 57, Winifred S Weinstein; c David, Matthew & Jessica. *Educ:* Mass Inst Technol, SB & SM, 50, PhD(polit sci), 65; Oxford Univ, BA, 52, MA, 55. *Honors & Awards:* Comdr Cross Decoration, Fed Repub Ger; Order of the Rising Sun, Golden Rays, Neck Ribbon, Japan. *Prof Exp:* Res asst elec eng, Uppsala Univ, Sweden, 50; indust liaison admin, Mass Inst Technol, 52-55; pvt & proj engr, US Army Security Agency, 55-57; systs analyst, Inst Defense Anal, 57-58; White House staff, Off Spec Asst to Pres, 58-63. *Concurrent Pos:* Consult, Sloan Found, Ford Found, Carnegie Corp, Resources for the Future, Agency Int Develop, Off Technol Assessment, Orgn Econ Coop & Develop, White House Off Sci & Tech Policy, 63-73; adj prof, Fletcher Sch Law & Diplomacy, Tufts Univ, Medford, Mass, 65-72; founder & pres, Sci & Pub Policy Studies Group, 68-73; vis res scholar, Carnegie Endowment Int Peace, 69-70; counr, Class III, AAAS, 73-77; sr consult, White House Off Sci & Technol, 77-81; Montague Burton vis prof, Univ Edinburgh, 77; bd trustees, UN Res Inst Social Develop, 79-85; chmn bd, Ger Marshall Fund US, 80-86; mem, Adv Comt, Nat Low Level Nuclear Waste, 80-87 & Adv Comt Sci & Technol, Dept State, 87-; chmn, Sci Policy Group, Nat Acad Sci, 82-84; mem, Comt Sci Eng & Pub Policy, AAAS, 84-89; vis fel, Balliol Col, Univ Oxford, 89. *Mem:* Fel Am Acad Arts & Sci; fel AAAS; Foreign Aid Soc; Am Polit Sci Asn; Sigma Xi; Coun Foreign Rels; Overseas Develop Coun. *Res:* Interaction of science, technology and public policy, with special emphasis on international scene and affairs, including national and comparative science policy. *Mailing Add:* Mass Inst Technol E51-263A Cambridge MA 02139

SKOMAL, EDWARD N, RADIO SYSTEMS & MAN-MADE NOISE, ELECTROMAGNETIC SCATTERING. *Current Pos:* RETIRED. *Personal Data:* b Kansas City, Mo, Apr 15, 26; m 51, Elizabeth Birkbeck; c Susan B, Catherine A & Margaret E. *Educ:* Rice Univ, BA, 47, MA, 49. *Honors & Awards:* Cert of Achievement, Electromagnetic Compatibility Soc, 71; Richar S Stoddart Award, 80. *Prof Exp:* Physicist, Socony-Mobil Field Res Lab, 49-51; supvry physicist, Nat Bur Stand, 51-56; adv develop engr, Sylvania Elec Microwave Physics Lab, 56-59; chief appl engr, Solid State Electronics Div, Motorola, Inc, 59-63; sr develop engr & physicist, Aerospace Corp, El Segundo, 63-67; staff scientist, 67-80, sr eng specialist, off chief engr, 80-84, dir Commun Dept, 84-86. *Concurrent Pos:* Mem, Presidential Joint Tech Adv Comt Electromagnetic Compatibility, 65-74; mem Comn, E, 72-; chmn, Tech Comt Electromagnetic Environ, Inst Elec & Electronics Engrs, 78-86, Electromagnetic Compatability Soc Stand Comt, 80-86, assoc ed, Trans Electromagnetic Compatibility, 83-86, chmn, Tech Adv Comt, 83-84, Stand coordr definitions; mem, US Nat Comt, Int Union Radio Sci, 84- *Mem:* Am Phys Soc; hon mem & fel Inst Elec & Electronics Engrs; Sigma Xi; Union Radio Scientists; Inst Elec & Electronics Engrs Electromagnetic Compatibility Soc. *Res:* Electromagnetism; microwave physics and interaction with solids; radio wave propagation; electromagnetic interference processes; stochastic progresses; radio scattering; guided wave propagation; cryogenics; automatic vehicle locating systems; man-made radio noise theory and measurement. *Mailing Add:* 1831 Valle Vista Dr Redlands CA 92373

SKONER, PETER RAYMOND, SCIENCE & MATHEMATICS EDUCATION. *Current Pos:* ASST PROF PHYS SCI, ST FRANCIS COL, 84-, CHMN PHYSICS DEPT, 87- *Personal Data:* b Johnstown, Pa, July 22, 57; m 80; c 3. *Educ:* Pa State Univ, BS, 79; Ind Univ Pa, MBA, 84; St Francis Col, MEd, 85. *Prof Exp:* Mining engr, Bethlehem Mines Corp, 79-82. *Concurrent Pos:* Res fel, NASA & Am Soc Eng Educ, 85. *Mem:* Am Soc Eng Educ; Nat Sci Teachers Am; Nat Coun Teachers Math. *Res:* Science and mathematics education; study of retention of pre-engineering college students; use of computers in teaching statistics. *Mailing Add:* Physics Dept St Francis Col Loretto PA 15940-0600

SKOOG, DOUGLAS ARVID, CHEMISTRY. *Current Pos:* from asst prof to prof, 47-76, assoc exec head dept chem, 61-76, EMER PROF CHEM, STANFORD UNIV, 76- *Personal Data:* b Willmar, Minn, May 4, 18; m 42, Judith Bone; c James A & Jon D. *Educ:* Ore State Col, BS, 40; Univ Ill, PhD(anal chem), 43. *Prof Exp:* Res chemist, Calif Res Corp, Standard Oil Co Calif, 43-47. *Mem:* Am Chem Soc; AAAS; Sigma Xi. *Res:* Instrumental analysis; spectrophotometry; organic reagents; complex ions. *Mailing Add:* Dept Chem Stanford Univ Stanford CA 94305. *Fax:* 650-725-0259; *E-Mail:* fb.das@stanford.edu

SKOOG, FOLKE, BIOCHEMISTRY. *Current Pos:* from assoc prof to prof, 47-49, EMER PROF BOT, UNIV WIS-MADISON, 79- *Personal Data:* b Fjaras, Sweden, July 15, 08; nat US; m 47, Birgit A L Bergner; c Karin B (Shephard). *Educ:* Calif Inst Technol, BS, 32, PhD(biol), 36. *Hon Degrees:* DPhil, Univ Lund, 56; DSc, Univ Ill, 80 & Univ Pisa, Italy, 91; DAgr, Swed Univ Agr, 91. *Honors & Awards:* Hales Prize, 54, Barnes Life Mem Award, Am Soc Plant Physiol, 70; Nat Medal Sci, 91; Distinguished Life Achievement Award, World Cong Cult, 92. *Prof Exp:* Teaching asst, Calif Inst Technol, 34-36; Nat Res Coun fel bot, Univ Calif, 36-37; instr & res assoc, Harvard Univ, 37-41; assoc prof bot, Johns Hopkins Univ, 41-44; biochemist, Off Qm Gen, Washington, DC, 43-44; tech rep, US Army Europ Theater Opers, Eng, Scand, Ger, France & Austria, 45-46. *Concurrent Pos:* Vis physiologist, Exp Sta, Pineapple Res Inst, Univ, Hawaii, 38; assoc physiologist, NIH, 43; lectr, Washington Univ, 46; vpres, Physiol Sect, Int Bot Cong, Paris, 54, Edinburgh, 64, Leningrad, 75; mem, Study Sect Genetics & Morphol, NIH, 56-60, Study Sect Cell Biol, 61-64; mem, Panel Regulatory Biol, NSF, 56-60; mem, Surv Comn Sci & Technol Educ, Brazil, Nat Acad Sci, 60; mem, Adv Panel Appl Math, Phys Sci, Biol & Eng, NSF, 79-81; mem, Adv Comt, USSR & E Europe, Nat Acad Sci, 80-84. *Mem:* Nat Acad Sci; hon mem Int Plant Growth Subst Asn (vpres, 76-79, pres, 79-82); foreign mem Swed Nat Acad Sci; Dutch Acad Naturalists; Am Acad Arts & Sci; foreign mem Acad Reg Sci Upsaliensis; Am Soc Plant Physiologists (vpres, 52-53, pres, 57-58); Am Soc Gen Physiologists (pres, 56-57); Soc Develop Biologists (pres, 70-71); Bot Soc Am; foreign mem Russ Soc Plant Physiologists. *Res:* Plant growth and development; cytokinins; plant tissue culture. *Mailing Add:* 2820 Marshall Ct Madison WI 53705-2270

SKOOG, IVAN HOOGLUND, ORGANIC CHEMISTRY. *Current Pos:* CHEMIST, MINN MINING & MFG CO, 54- *Personal Data:* b Kewanee, Ill, July 26, 28; m 55. *Educ:* Univ Ill, BS, 50; Northwestern Univ, MS, 52, PhD, 55. *Mem:* Am Chem Soc; Soc Photog Sci & Eng. *Res:* Organic synthesis; photography. *Mailing Add:* 8573 Hidden Bay Trail N Lake Elmo MN 55042-9526

SKOOG, WILLIAM ARTHUR, MEDICAL ONCOLOGY. *Current Pos:* lectr, Univ Calif, Los Angeles, 61, co-dir, Health Sci Clin Res Ctr, 65-67, dir, Health Sci Clin Res Ctr, 67-72, assoc prof, 62-73, ASSOC CLIN PROF MED, SCH MED, UNIV CALIF, LOS ANGELES, 73- *Personal Data:* b Culver City, Calif, Apr 10, 25; m 49; c 4. *Educ:* Stanford Univ, AB, 46, MD, 49; Am Bd Internal Med, dipl, 57. *Prof Exp:* Intern med, Univ Hosp, Stanford Univ, 48-49, asst resident, 49-50; asst resident med, NY Hosp-Cornell Med Ctr & asst in med col, 50-51; sr resident, Wadsworth Vet Admin Hosp, Los Angeles, Calif, 51; jr res physician, Atomic Energy Proj, Univ Calif, Los Angeles, 54-55; from instr to asst prof med, Sch Med, 55-59, jr res physician, 55-56, asst res physician & co-dir, Metab Res Unit, Ctr Health Sci, 56-59; asst clin prof med & assoc res physician oncol, Sch Med & assoc staff, Med Ctr, Univ Calif, San Francisco, 59-61. *Concurrent Pos:* Clin assoc hemat, Vet Admin Ctr, Los Angeles, 56-59; clin instr, Sch Med, Stanford Univ, 59-61; mem staff, Palo Alto-Stanford Hosp Ctr, 59-61; attend specialist, Wadsworth Vet Admin Hosp, Los Angeles, 62-68; vis physician, Harbor Gen Hosp, Torrance, 62-65, attend physician, 65-77; consult, Clin Lab, Univ Calif, Los Angeles Hosp, 63-68; mem affil consult staff, St John's Hosp, Santa Monica, 64-71, courtesy staff, 71-72; active staff, St Bernardine Hosp, San Bernardino, 72-; active staff, San Bernardino Community Hosp, 72-; consult staff, Redlands Community Hosp, 72-; chief, Oncol Sect, San Bernardino Co Med Ctr, 72-76. *Mem:* AMA; fel Am Col Physicians; Am Soc Clin Oncol; Am Fedn Clin Res; Western Soc Clin Res. *Res:* Hematology; hematologic malignancies, especially multiple myeloma; cancer chemotherapy. *Mailing Add:* 1119 Kimberly Pl Redlands CA 92373

SKOP, RICHARD ALLEN, APPLIED MECHANICS. *Current Pos:* chmn, marine physics, 86-90, PROF MARINE PHYSICS, UNIV MIAMI, 90- *Personal Data:* b Baltimore, Md, Mar 12, 43; m 64; c 3. *Educ:* Wash Univ, St Louis, BA, 64; Univ Rochester, PhD(appl mech), 68. *Prof Exp:* Res engr appl mech, US Naval Res Lab, 67-71, head fluid mech sect, 71-78, head appl mech br, 78-86. *Mem:* Am Soc Mech Engrs; Marine Technol Soc; Sigma Xi. *Res:* Fluid and structure interaction problems; wake dynamics; computational fluid dynamics. *Mailing Add:* Univ Miami 1252 Memorial Dr Coral Gables FL 33146

SKOPIK, STEVEN D, PHYSIOLOGY. *Current Pos:* asst prof, 67-71, assoc chairperson, Dept Biol Sci, 73-76, ASSOC PROF BIOL, UNIV DEL, 71-, COORDR PHYSIOL SECT, 76- *Personal Data:* b Detroit, Mich, Dec 9, 40; m 60; c 3. *Educ:* Defiance Col, BS, 62; Princeton Univ, MA, 64, PhD, 66. *Prof Exp:* From instr to lectr biol, Princeton Univ, 65-67. *Mem:* AAAS; Entom Soc Am. *Res:* Role of biological clocks in the development of insects; role of clock systems in insect photoperiodism. *Mailing Add:* Biol Univ Del Newark DE 19717-0001

SKOPP, JOSEPH MICHAEL, SOIL PHYSICS. *Current Pos:* ASSOC PROF SOIL PHYSICS, UNIV NEBR, 80- *Personal Data:* b Long Beach, Calif, Nov 24, 49; m 77; c 3. *Educ:* Univ Calif, Davis, BS, 71; Univ Ariz, MS, 75; Univ Wis, PhD(soils), 80. *Mem:* Soil Sci Soc Am; Am Geophys Union; AAAS. *Res:* Measurement and description of solute (plant nutrients, pollutants or microorganisms) movement in soils; physical processes, particularly oxygen and nutrient transport, limiting microbial activity in soil. *Mailing Add:* Dept Agron Unvi Nebr Lincoln NE 68583-0915. *E-Mail:* jskopp@unlinfo.unl.edu

SKORCZ, JOSEPH ANTHONY, industrial organic chemistry, for more information see previous edition

SKORINKO, GEORGE, PHYSICS. *Current Pos:* RETIRED. *Personal Data:* b Palmerton, Pa, Sept 25, 30; m 60; c 2. *Educ:* Lehigh Univ, BS, 52; Boston Univ, MA, 53; Pa State Univ, PhD(physics), 60. *Prof Exp:* Physicist, Westinghouse Res Lab, 60-62; from assoc prof to prof physics, Brooklyn Col, 74-91. *Mem:* Optical Soc Am. *Res:* Infrared spectroscopy of molecules; extreme ultraviolet spectroscopy; solid state physics. *Mailing Add:* 251 W Fourth Ave Roselle NJ 07203

SKORYNA, STANLEY C, GASTROENTEROLOGY, EXPERIMENTAL SURGERY. *Current Pos:* Lectr, 55-59, asst prof, 59-62, DIR, GASTROINTESTINAL RES LAB, MCGILL UNIV, 59-, ASSOC PROF SURG, 62-, DIR, RIDEAU INST, 69- *Personal Data:* b Warsaw, Poland, Sept 4, 20; Can citizen; m 70; c Christopher, Elizabeth & Richard. *Educ:* Univ Vienna, MD, 43, PhD(biol), 62; McGill Univ, MSc, 50. *Honors & Awards:* Gold Medal Surg, Royal Col Physicians & Surgeons, Can, 57. *Concurrent Pos:* Res fel cancer, McGill Univ, 47-49; res fel, Nat Cancer Inst Can, 49-51, sr res fel, 51-54; dir, Can Med Exped to Easter Island, 64-65; deleg, Biol Coun Can, 67; assoc prof biol, Univ de Montreal, 85- *Mem:* Am San Cancer Res; Am Gastroenterol Asn; Am Col Surgeons; Nutrit Soc Can; Am Physiol Soc; Can Physiol Soc. *Res:* Experimental carcinogenesis; pathophysiology of peptic ulcer; intestinal absorption of the metal ions, strontium and calcium; mucolytic action of amides; growth curve studies on Coelenterata; alcoholism; environmental conservation research. *Mailing Add:* Gastrointestinal Res Lab-McGill 740 Ave Dr Penfield Montreal ON H3A 1A4 Can. *Fax:* 514-398-824

SKOSEY, JOHN LYLE, MEDICINE, PHYSIOLOGY. *Current Pos:* ACAD DIR INTERNAL MED, CHIEF ACAD OFF, MACNEAL HOSP, 94, CLIN PROF MED & ASST DEAN, MACNEAL HOSP PROG, UNIV CHICAGO, 96- *Personal Data:* b Gillespie, Ill, Jan 19, 36; m 60, Consuelo Lira; c Laura A (LaLonde), John L & Peter J. *Educ:* Univ Southern Ill, BA, 57; Univ Chicago, MD, 61, PhD(physiol), 64. *Prof Exp:* Intern, Univ Chicago Hosp, 61-62; jr asst resident med, Univ Chicago, 62-63; clin assoc, Endocrinol Br, Nat Cancer Inst, 63-65; sr asst resident med, Univ Chicago, 65-66, resident, 66-67, instr, 67-69, from asst prof to assoc prof, 69-78; assoc prof, Univ Ill, 78-82, prof, Dept Med, 82-94. *Concurrent Pos:* USPHS trainee physiol, Univ Chicago, 62-63, USPHS clin trainee, 65-67; Arthritis Found fel, 68-71. *Mem:* Am Fedn Clin Res; Am Physiol Soc; Am Col Rheumatology; Sigma Xi; Am Col Physicians. *Res:* Cell physiology and pathophysiology of inflammation; clinical studies in rheumatic diseases. *Mailing Add:* Dept Med Educ MacNeal Hosp 3249 S Oak Park Berwyn IL 60402. *Fax:* 708-795-3341; *E-Mail:* jskosey@macneal.com

SKOTNICKI, JERAULD S, MEDICINAL CHEMISTRY, HETEROCYCLIC CHEMISTRY. *Current Pos:* sr chemist, Wyeth Labs, 82-86, res scientist, 86-88, PRIN SCIENTIST, WYETH-AYERST RES, 88- *Personal Data:* b Niagara Falls, NY, Jan 28, 51; m 74. *Educ:* Col of the Holy

Cross, AB, 73; Dartmouth Col, MA, 75; Princeton Univ, PhD(chem), 81. *Prof Exp:* Chemist, Lederle Labs, 74-77; res chemist, Du Pont, 81-82. *Concurrent Pos:* Adj fac, Villanova Univ, 85-88 & 91- *Mem:* Am Chem Soc; AAAS; Inflammation Res Asn. *Res:* Design and synthesis of biologically important molecules including rapamycin analogs, interleuken-1 inhibitors, prostaglandins, folic acid analogs and beta-lactam antibiotics; introduction and development of new synthetic methodologies. *Mailing Add:* Wyeth-Ayerst Res B222 Rm 3190 Lederle Labs Pearl River NY 10965-1299

SKOU, JENS CHRISTIAN, BIOPHYSICS. *Current Pos:* RETIRED. *Personal Data:* b Lemvig, Denmark, Oct 8, 18; m 47, Ellen-Margrethe Nielsen; c Hanne & Karen. *Educ:* Univ Copenhagen, MD, 44, DrMed, 54. *Hon Degrees:* DrMedSci, Univ Copenhagen, 86. *Honors & Awards:* Nobel Prize in Chem, 97; Leo Prize, 54; Novo Prize, 58; Consul Carlsen Prize, 73; A Retzius Gold Medal, Swiss Med Asn, 77; E K Fernstrom Big Nordic Prize, 85; Prakash Datta Medal, Fedn Europ Biochem Socs. *Prof Exp:* Clin trainee, Hosp Hjorring & Orthop Clin, Aarhus, 44-47; from asst prof to prof biochem, Inst Biophys, Univ Aarhus, 54-88, chmn dept, 63-73. *Mem:* Foreign assoc Nat Acad Sci; Danish Royal Acad Sci; Europ Molecular Biol Orgn; hon mem Japanese Biochem Soc; hon mem Am Physiol Soc. *Res:* Mechanism of action of local anesthetics; transmembrane transport of niacin and potassium; author of over 90 papers and reviews. *Mailing Add:* Inst Biophys Ole Worms Alle Bygning 185 Aarhus 8000C Denmark

SKOUG, DAVID L, MATHEMATICAL ANALYSIS. *Current Pos:* From asst prof to assoc prof, 66-75, chmn dept, 75-83, PROF MATH, UNIV NEBR, LINCOLN, 76- *Personal Data:* b Rice Lake, Wis, Dec 31, 37; m 61, Muriel Peterson; c Ruth & Kathryn. *Educ:* Wis State Univ, River Falls, BA, 60; Univ Minn, PhD(math), 66. *Honors & Awards:* Cert Meritorious Serv, Math Asn Am, 94. *Mem:* Am Math Soc; Math Asn Am; Korean Math Soc. *Res:* Mathematical research in the areas of integration in function space, Wiener space and integrals, Feynman integrals. *Mailing Add:* Math Dept 932 Oldfather Hall Univ Nebr Lincoln NE 68588-0323. *E-Mail:* dskoug@math.unl.edu

SKOULTCHI, ARTHUR, CELL BIOLOGY. *Current Pos:* PROF CELL BIOL, ALBERT EINSTEIN COL MED, 73- *Personal Data:* b New York, NY, Aug 8, 40; m 65; c 2. *Educ:* Princeton Univ, AB, 62; Yale Univ, MS, 65, PhD(molecular biophys & biochem), 69. *Honors & Awards:* Fac res award, Am Cancer Soc, 74. *Prof Exp:* Fel biochem, Yale Univ, 69-70, spec fel, 72-73; fel biol, Mass Inst Technol, 70-72. *Mem:* Sigma Xi; Am Soc Cell Biol. *Res:* Mechanisms for controlling gene expression during differentiation of mammalian cells; somatic cell genetics of differentiation; messenger RNA biosynthesis in animal cells. *Mailing Add:* Dept Cell Biol Albert Einstein Col Med 1300 Morris Park Ave Bronx NY 10461-1926

SKOULTCHI, MARTIN MILTON, ORGANIC CHEMISTRY, POLYMER CHEMISTRY. *Current Pos:* SR RES ASSOC, NAT STARCH & CHEM CORP, 60- *Personal Data:* b New York, NY, Oct 27, 33; m 93, Frieda Chudnowsky; c Barry, Alan & Gail. *Educ:* NY Univ, BA, 54, MS, 57, PhD(org chem), 60. *Prof Exp:* Assoc chemist organometallic chem, Res Div, Col Eng, NY Univ, 55-60. *Mem:* AAAS; Am Chem Soc; Soc Photog Sci & Eng; NY Acad Sci. *Res:* Synthesis of speciality monomers and polymers; chemical reactions of and on polymers; photochemistry. *Mailing Add:* 6 Lilac Lane Somerset NJ 08873-2808

SKOUTAKIS, VASILIOS A, TOXICOLOGY. *Current Pos:* From asst prof to assoc prof, 74-83, dir, 77-83, PROF & DIR, DRUGS-CLIN PHARMACOL & TOXICOL, UNIV TENN, MEMPHIS, 83- *Personal Data:* b Skoura-Spartis, Greece, Sept 24, 43; US citizen; m 68. *Educ:* Univ NC, Charlotte, BS, 70, Chapel Hill, BS, 72; Univ Tenn Memphis, Dr Pharm, 74. *Concurrent Pos:* Pres, Clin Toxicol Consult, Inc, 79-; ed & publ, J Clin Toxicol Counsult, 79-; dir, Drug & Toxicol Info Ctr. *Mem:* Am Col Clin Pharm (treas, 83-86); Am Col Clin Pharmacol; Am Soc Hosp Phamacists; Am Asn Col Pharm. *Res:* Clinical drug research trials; developmental therapeutics; pharmcotherapeutics. *Mailing Add:* 7271 Deep Valley Dr Memphis TN 38138

SKOV, CHARLES E, SOLID STATE PHYSICS. *Current Pos:* From assoc prof to prof, 63-94, EMER PROF PHYSICS, MONMOUTH COL, ILL, 94- *Personal Data:* b Kearney, Nebr, June 29, 33; m 54; c 3. *Educ:* Nebr State Col, Kearney, BA, 54; Univ Nebr, PhD(physics), 63. *Mem:* Am Phys Soc; Am Optical Soc; Am Asn Physics Teachers; Sigma Xi. *Res:* Electrical and optical properties of insulating crystals. *Mailing Add:* 827 N Second St Monmouth IL 61462

SKOVE, MALCOLM JOHN, SOLID STATE PHYSICS. *Current Pos:* from asst prof to assoc prof, 61-68, PROF PHYSICS, CLEMSON UNIV, 68- *Personal Data:* b Cleveland, Ohio, Mar 3, 31; m 56, Janet Crawford; c Anthony & Benjamin. *Educ:* Clemson Univ, BS, 56; Univ Va, PhD(physics), 60. *Prof Exp:* Asst prof physics, Ill State Univ, 60-61 & Univ PR, 61. *Concurrent Pos:* Fulbright lectr, Haile Selassie Univ, 66-67; vis prof, Swiss Fed Inst Technol, 74-75; prog dir, NSF, 87-88. *Mem:* Am Phys Soc. *Res:* Effect of elastic strain on electrical properties of metals. *Mailing Add:* 1032 Old Central Rd Central SC 29630

SKOVLIN, JON MATTHEW, RANGE SCIENCE, WILDLIFE BIOLOGY. *Current Pos:* CONSULT, 85- *Personal Data:* b Colfax, Wash, Oct 31, 30; m 52; c 4. *Educ:* Ore State Univ, BS, 52; Univ Idaho, MS, 59. *Prof Exp:* Range scientist, Res Br, US Forest Serv, Ore, 56-68; ecologist, UN Food & Agr Orgn, Nairobi, Kenya, 68-71; res biologist wildlife habitat res, Range & Wildlife Habitat Lab, 71-76, range scientist/proj leader, USDA Forest Serv, Ore, 76-81; range & animal scientist, Winrock Int, Kenya, 82-85. *Concurrent Pos:* Consult, EAfrica natural resources & environ, 77, 78 & 80; prin investr, EAfrica rangeland invest, Kenya; cert rangeland consult, Soc Range Mgt; cert wildlife biologist, Wildlife Soc. *Mem:* Soc Range Mgt; Soc Am Foresters; EAfrican Wildlife Soc; Wildlife Soc; Int Soc Trop Foresters; Grassland Soc, Southern Africa. *Res:* Investigations of levels, seasons and systems of livestock grazing and interactions on related resources throughout semi-arid zones of western North America and arid zones of East Africa; over 50 scientific publications. *Mailing Add:* 702 Rose Cove OR 97824

SKOVRONEK, HERBERT SAMUEL, ORGANIC CHEMISTRY, ENVIRONMENTAL ENGINEERING. *Current Pos:* SR ENVIRON SCIENTIST, SCI APPLICATIONS INT CORP, 88- *Personal Data:* b Brooklyn, NY, Apr 19, 36; div; c Eric & Alex. *Educ:* Brooklyn Col, BS, 56; Pa State Univ, PhD(carbenes), 61. *Honors & Awards:* Gold Medal Award, Am Electroplaters Soc, 78. *Prof Exp:* From chemist to sr chemist, Texaco, Inc, 61-62; res chemist, Rayonier, Inc, 62-67; res chemist, J P Stevens & Co, Inc, 67, group leader, 67-71; res chemist, Indust Waste Technol Br, US Environ Protection Agency, 71-74, tech adv to dir, Indust Waste Treatment Res Lab, 74-75, tech adv to dir, Indust Environ Res Lab, 75-78; mgr environ control, Semet-Solvay Div, Allied Chem Corp, 78-79, environ specialist, 79-82; adj prof, NJ Inst Technol, 82- *Concurrent Pos:* Environ consult, Environ Serv, 82- *Mem:* Water Pollution Control Fedn; Am Chem Soc. *Res:* Pollution abatement, waste minimization technology for metal finishing, pharmaceuticals, paints and chemicals manufacturing; environmental impacts of industrial energy conservation practices; innovative use of canine olfaction in toxic pollutant detection; management and control of industrial, hazardous and waterborne wastes; hazard communication. *Mailing Add:* 88 Moraine Rd Morris Plains NJ 07950

SKOW, LOREN CURTIS, GENETICS, BIOCHEMISTRY. *Current Pos:* AT DEPT VET ANAT, COL VET MED, TEX A&M UNIV. *Personal Data:* b Gainesville, Tex, Sept 4, 46; m 74. *Educ:* Abilene Christian Col, BSEd, 69, MS, 71; Tex A&M Univ, PhD(fisheries sci), 76. *Prof Exp:* Res assoc mammalian genetics, Oak Ridge Nat Lab, 78-79, staff scientist mammalian mutagenesis, 79-81; sr staff fel genetics, Nat Inst Environ Health Sci, 81- *Concurrent Pos:* NIH fel, Jackson Lab, 76-78; cystic fibrosis consult, NIH, 78- *Mem:* Genetics Soc Am; AAAS. *Res:* Comparative vertebrate genetics; gene mapping; organization of genes controlling rodent salivary secretions; genetics of rodent lens crystallins. *Mailing Add:* 2734 San Felipe Dr College Station TX 77845

SKOWRONSKI, RAYMUND PAUL, ADVANCED MATERIALS, COMPOSITES & COATINGS. *Current Pos:* MAT SCIENTIST, ROCKWELL INT/BOEING NAM, 75- *Personal Data:* b Detroit, Mich, Feb 7, 48; m 70, Joann Mantz. *Educ:* Univ Mich, BS, 69; Tex A&M Univ, PhD(chem), 75. *Prof Exp:* Teaching asst chem, Tex A&M Univ, 69-70, instr, 70-72. *Mem:* Am Chem Soc; Sigma Xi (pres, 83-84); Am Ceramic Soc; Am Soc Metals Int. *Res:* Materials science; coatings; carbon-carbon composites, ceramic-matrix composites; emissivity; emissivity coatings; spacecraft armor; atomic oxygen; narrow-band reflectors, heat pipes, survivability, radiation shielding; silicon nitride; granted 3 US patents. *Mailing Add:* Boeing NAm 6633 Canoga Ave Canoga Park CA 91303. *Fax:* 818-586-9875; *E-Mail:* raymund.p.skowronski@boeing.com

SKRABEK, EMANUEL ANDREW, ENERGY CONVERSION, MATERIALS SCIENCE ENGINEERING. *Current Pos:* sr staff engr, Fairchild Space & Defense, 80-95, SR SCIENTIST, ORBITAL SCI CORP, 95- *Personal Data:* b Baltimore, Md, Mar 3, 34; m 72, Geraldine Bonsall; c Lisa & Alison. *Educ:* Univ Md, BS, 56; Univ Wis, MS, 58; Univ Pittsburgh, PhD(phys chem), 62. *Prof Exp:* Sr res scientist energy conversion, Martin-Marietta Corp, 62-69; sr scientist heat pipe mat, Dynatherm Corp, 69-72; mgr res thermoelec, Teledyne Energy Systs, 72-78, chief chemist, 78-80. *Mem:* Am Chem Soc; AAAS; Am Soc Testing & Mat; Sigma Xi. *Res:* Safety analysis and testing of nuclear powered interplanetary spacecraft; design, analysis and testing of direct energy conversion devices; heat pipe design and materials compatibility; high temperature thermal insulations. *Mailing Add:* 1510 Cranwell Rd Lutherville MD 21093-5836. *Fax:* 301-353-8619; *E-Mail:* skrabek@osesystems.com

SKRABLE, KENNETH WILLIAM, PHYSICS, RADIOLOGICAL HEALTH. *Current Pos:* PROF RADIOLOGICAL SCI, UNIV LOWELL, 74- *Personal Data:* b Teaneck, NJ, Oct 10, 35; m 57; c 2. *Educ:* Moravian Col, BS, 58; Vanderbilt Univ, MS, 63; Rutgers Univ, PhD(environ sci), 70. *Prof Exp:* Health physics supvr, Indust Reactor Lab, Inc, 59-63; radiation safety officer & lectr radiation sci, Rutgers Univ, 63-68; prof & chmn, Radiological Sci Dept, Lowell Technol Inst, 68-74. *Concurrent Pos:* Chmn, New Eng Consortium on Environ Protection, 71-72; consult, Yankee Atomic Elec Co, 75-76, US Nuclear Regulatory Comn, 80- *Mem:* Health Physics Soc; Am Nuclear Soc; Sigma Xi. *Res:* Air pollution, aerosols; naturally occurring and man-made radioactive aerosols; measurement and control of air pollutants and radioactivity; internal and external radiation dosimetry. *Mailing Add:* Dept Physics Univ Mass One University Ave Lowell MA 01854

SKRAMSTAD, HAROLD KENNETH, PHYSICS. *Current Pos:* prof indust eng & sci dir comput ctr, 67-74, EMER PROF MGT SCI & EMER ADJ PROF MATH, UNIV MIAMI, 74- *Personal Data:* b Tacoma, Wash, July 26, 08; m 40; c 4. *Educ:* Univ Puget Sound, BS, 30; Univ Wash, Seattle, PhD(physics), 35. *Honors & Awards:* Reed Award, Am Inst Aeronaut & Astronaut, 47. *Prof Exp:* Teacher high sch, Wash, 30-31; physicist, Nat Bur

Stand, 35-46, chief, Guided Missiles Sect, 46-50, asst chief, Missile Develop Div, 50-53; chief, Missile Systs Div, US Naval Ord Lab, 53-54; asst chief systs, Data Processing Systs Div, Nat Bur Stand, 54-61; assoc tech dir, US Naval Ord Lab, 61-67. *Concurrent Pos:* Life mem, Simulation Coun; adj prof, Fla Inst Technol, 76-84. *Mem:* Assoc fel Am Inst Aeronaut & Astronaut; life sr mem Inst Elec & Electronics Engrs. *Res:* Primary ionization of gases; wind tunnel turbulence; boundary layer flow; development of guided missiles; aerodynamics; computers; simulators; automatic control. *Mailing Add:* 8045 S A1A Hwy Melbourne Beach FL 32951

SKRDLA, WILLIS HOWARD, AGRONOMY & HORTICULTURE, PLANT BREEDING & PHYTOPATHOLOGY. *Current Pos:* prof agron, 57-83, agronomist res leader & coordr, NCent Regional Plant Sta, USDA, 57-83, EMER PROF AGRON, UNIV IOWA STATE UNIV, 83- *Personal Data:* b DeWitt, Nebr, Feb 22, 20; m 42, Betty J Spalding; c Ronald K, Robert A & Kay E (Thompson). *Educ:* Univ Nebr, BSc, 41; Purdue Univ, PhD(agron), 49. *Honors & Awards:* King Charles Award, Govt Czech; Govt India Spec Award for Leadership, New Delhi, India, 96. *Prof Exp:* Asst, Purdue Univ, 46-49; assoc prof agron, Va Agr Exp Sta, Va Polytech Inst, 49-53; agronomist airport turfing, USAF, 53-57. *Concurrent Pos:* Consult constructions, Gene Bank, Foreign Agr Orgn, Bulgaria, 80; leader, Genetic Resources Unit, Int Ctr Res Semi-Arid Tropics, Hyderabad, India, 84-86; leader design team, Indo-US Proj, Plant Genetic Resources, New Delhi, 86. *Mem:* Fel AAAS; Sigma Xi; Soc Econ Bot; Am Soc Agron. *Res:* Plant introduction; seed increase, distribution, evaluation and permanent storage of world collections of agronomic and horticultural crops; coordinate regional program in 13 states; field crop, forage and turf investigations; participate in and provide leadership for selected international plant germplasm activities; distribution of seed and plants of genetic resources having great genetic diversity for use in improving/developing food and feed crops and other agriculture utilization. *Mailing Add:* 2136 Duff Ave Ames IA 50010-4915

SKRINAR, GARY STEPHEN, EXERCISE PHYSIOLOGY. *Current Pos:* PROF HEALTH SCI, BOSTON UNIV, 78- *Personal Data:* b Teaneck, NJ, Aug 28, 42; c 3. *Educ:* Oklahoma City Univ, BA, 64; Univ Ill, MS, 65; Univ Pittsburgh, PhD(exercise phys motor learning), 78. *Prof Exp:* Instr phys educ, Midland Mich Pub Schs, 65-68, Oklahoma City Univ, 68-70 & Ore Sta Univ, 70-71; asst prof, Brookdale Community Col, 71-74. *Concurrent Pos:* Exercise tech, exercise leader, Univ Pittsburgh Cardiac Rehab Prog, 74-78; exercise prog dir, Am Col Sports Med, 78; assoc ed, Med & Sci in Sports Exercise. *Mem:* Fel Am Col Sports Med. *Res:* Exercise physiology; cardiac rehabilitation; acquisition and maintenance of physical fitness; exercise training effects on mental illness. *Mailing Add:* Dept Health Sci 635 Commonwealth Ave Boston MA 02215

SKRINDE, ROLF T, CIVIL & ENVIRONMENTAL ENGINEERING. *Current Pos:* FAC, CIVIL ENG DEPT, SEATTLE UNIV, 84- *Personal Data:* b Stanwood, Wash, Sept 1, 28; m 58; c 3. *Educ:* Wash State Univ, SB & CE, 51; Mass Inst Technol, SM, 52, SanE, 56, PhD(sanit eng), 59. *Prof Exp:* Sanit eng adv, Ministry Health, Saudi Arabia & Thailand, 53-55; asst sanit eng, Mass Inst Technol, 55-58; asst prof civil eng, Wash State Univ, 58-60, assoc prof, 60-61; assoc prof, Wash Univ, 61-64, chmn dept civil eng, 64-65; dir res, SEATO Grad Sch Eng, Bangkok, 65-67; prof civil eng, Univ Mass, Amherst, 67-69; prof & chmn dept civil eng, Univ Iowa, 69-77; mem staff, Olympic Assocs Co, 77-84. *Mem:* Am Soc Civil Eng; Water Pollution Control Fedn; Am Water Works Asn; Nat Soc Prof Engrs. *Res:* Corrosion control in potable water systems; stream pollution; waste water treatment; determination of public health effects of agricultural use on return irrigation waters; pesticide residues; reverse osmosis water treatment; metal plating waste treatment. *Mailing Add:* 16327 Inglewood Place NE Bothell WA 98011

SKRIVAN, J(OSEPH) F(RANCIS), CHEMICAL ENGINEERING. *Current Pos:* Res engr, Am Cyanamid Co, 58-63, sr res engr, 64-66, group leader eng res, 66-72, res mgr, 72-75, tech dir, 75-78, mgr mfg catalyst dept, 78-81, res dir, 81-86, DIR, ENG & OPERS, AM CYANAMID CO, 86- *Personal Data:* b Baltimore, Md, Oct 25, 31; m 54; c 6. *Educ:* Johns Hopkins Univ, BE, 53, MS, 56, DEng, 58. *Mem:* Am Inst Chem Engrs; Sigma Xi. *Res:* Kinetics; heat transfer; high temperature processing and plasma technology; process development; auto exhaust catalysts. *Mailing Add:* 154 Berrian Rd Stamford CT 06905

SKROCH, WALTER ARTHUR, WEED SCIENCE. *Current Pos:* From assoc prof to prof, 68-95, EMER PROF HORT SCI, NC STATE UNIV, 95- *Personal Data:* b Arcadia, Wis, July 1, 37; m 63; c 2. *Educ:* Wis State Univ, River Falls, BS, 59; Univ Wis-Madison, MS, 61, PhD(hort), 65. *Mem:* Am Pomol Soc; fel Weed Sci Soc Am; Am Soc Hort Sci. *Res:* Herbicide activity, tree fruits, ornamental, Christmas trees, landscape and broadrange fumigation as preplant treatment of horticultural crops. *Mailing Add:* Dept Hort Sci NC State Univ Box 7609 Raleigh NC 27695-7609

SKROMME, LAWRENCE H, FARM MACHINERY DESIGN, AGRICULTURAL MECHANIZATION IN DEVELOPING COUNTRIES. *Current Pos:* CONSULT, AGR ENGR, 79- *Personal Data:* b Roland, Iowa, Aug 26, 13; m 39, Margaret E Gleason; c Cherlyn S (Granrose), Inga J (Hill) & Karen A (Sequino). *Educ:* Iowa State Univ, BSc, 37. *Honors & Awards:* John Deere Gold Medal, Am Soc Agr Engrs; Outstanding Eng Achievement Award, Iowa State Univ; Medal Merit Agricole, France. *Prof Exp:* From draftsman to design engr, Goodyear Tire & Rubber Co, 37-41; from proj engr to asst chief engr, Harry Ferguson, Inc, 41-51; chief engr, Sperry New Holland, Sperry Rand Corp, 51-61, vpres eng, 61-79. *Concurrent Pos:* Mem, Farm Resources & Facil Res Adv Comt, USDA, 65; mem, Int Rels Comt & Nat Medal of Sci Comt, Engrs Joint Coun; mem, Gov Comt Preserv Agr Land; vpres, Farm & Home Found, Lancaster Co, Pa; mem div eng, Nat Res Coun; power & mach rep, Int Comn Agr Eng; vpres, bd mem & pres, Agr Mach Sect, Comn Int Genie Rurale, 73-; consult agr eng, 79-; mem & secy, Lancaster Co Agr Land Preserv Bd, 77- *Mem:* Nat Acad Eng; fel Am Soc Agr Engrs (vpres, 52-55, pres, 59-60); Am Soc Eng Educ; Nat Soc Prof Engrs; Soc Automotive Engrs; NY Acad Sci. *Res:* Development of efficient farm machines to reduce labor and improve productivity; appropriate agricultural mechanization of developing countries. *Mailing Add:* 2144 Landis Valley Rd Lancaster PA 17601

SKRYPA, MICHAEL JOHN, COMMERCIALIZATION OF RESEARCH DISCOVERIES. *Current Pos:* Res chemist, Solvay Process Div, Allied Chem Corp, 53-61, assoc res supvr, 61-62, res supvr, 62-63, mgr appl res, 63-67, mgr new polymer applns develop, Plastics Div, 67-72, res consult, Corp Res Ctr, 72-76, mgr com develop, Venture Mgt Div, 76-79, mgr mkt develop, New Ventures Group, Allied Corp, 79-83, consult, 83-86, MANAGING ASSOC, MISKCO ASSOC, 86- *Personal Data:* b Woonsocket, RI, Sept 26, 27; m 53, Aldona Chekas; c John, Edward & Catherine. *Educ:* Brown Univ, BSc, 50; Clark Univ, PhD(org chem), 54. *Mem:* Soc Plastics Eng; Com Develop Asn; Am Chem Soc; Am Soc Metals. *Res:* Organic syntheses; polymerizations; physical chemistry of polymers; physical chemistry of metals; development of applications for chemicals, polymers and metals; direction and management of research organizations. *Mailing Add:* Three Village Rd Florham Park NJ 07932

SKRZYPEK, JOSEF, computational neuroscience, computer vision; deceased, see previous edition for last biography

SKUBIC, PATRICK LOUIS, ELEMENTARY PARTICLE PHYSICS. *Current Pos:* asst prof, 81-93, PROF PHYSICS & ASTRON, UNIV OKLA, 93- *Personal Data:* b Eveleth, Minn, Sept 9, 47. *Educ:* SDak State Univ, BS, 69; Univ Mich, MS, 70, PhD(physics), 77. *Prof Exp:* Fel, Rutgers Univ, 77-80. *Mem:* Am Phys Soc; Sigma Xi. *Res:* Experimental elementary particle physics; precise measurement of neutral hyperon polarization and magnetic moments in high energy neutral hyperon beams; evidence for production of particles containing heavy quarks in electron-positron collisions. *Mailing Add:* 4809 Stonehenge Lane Norman OK 73071-0931

SKUCAS, JOVITAS, RADIOLOGY. *Current Pos:* from asst prof to assoc prof, 73-81, PROF RADIOL, UNIV ROCHESTER, 82- *Personal Data:* b Klaipeda, Lithuania, Sept 21, 36; US citizen; m 65, Gail; c 3. *Educ:* Newark Col Eng, BS, 58, MS, 64; Hahnemann Med Col, MD, 68. *Prof Exp:* Intern med, St Vincent's Hosp, New York, 68-69, resident radiol, 69-72; instr, Univ Ind, 72-73. *Concurrent Pos:* Vis radiologist, Isaac Gordon Ctr Digestive Dis, Genesee Hosp, NY, 75- *Mem:* Radiol Soc NAm; Inst Elec & Electronics Engrs; Asn Univ Radiologists; Roentgen Ray Soc; Am Gastroenterol Asn; AAAS. *Res:* Application of engineering to radiological science; gastro-intestinal radiology. *Mailing Add:* Univ Rochester Med Ctr Rochester NY 14642

SKUDRZYK, FRANK J, ROCK MECHANICS, EXPLOSIVES AND BLASTING. *Current Pos:* head dept mining & geol eng, 83-84, PROF MINING ENG, UNIV ALASKA, FAIRBANKS, 82- *Personal Data:* b Cieszyn, Poland, Jan 19, 43; m 85. *Educ:* Univ Mining & Metall, BS, 68, MS, 68, PhD(rock mech), 73. *Hon Degrees:* Dir Mines, Sec Level, Ministry Coal Mining, Poland, 75. *Prof Exp:* From asst prof to assoc prof mining eng, Univ Mining & Metall, 68-79; sr researcher rock mech, Univ Miss, Rolla, 79-82. *Concurrent Pos:* Prin investr var proj, Univ Alaska, Fairbanks, 82- *Mem:* Soc Exp Mech; Am Soc Testing & Mech; Soc Mining Eng; Soc Explosive Eng; Marine Technol Soc. *Res:* Experimental and theoretical rock mechanics with applications to design and stability of mining and civil structures in rock and frozen ground; rock fragmentation methods; design of lab and insitu testing equipment. *Mailing Add:* 4611 Dartmouth Rd Fairbanks AK 99709

SKUJINS, JANIS, SOIL BIOCHEMISTRY, SOIL ECOLOGY. *Current Pos:* from assoc prof to prof, 69-89, EMER PROF BIOL & SOIL SCI, UTAH STATE UNIV, 89- *Personal Data:* b Latvia, Apr 13, 26; US citizen; div; c Andrejs & Juris. *Educ:* Univ Calif, Berkeley, BA, 57, PhD(agr chem), 63. *Prof Exp:* Fel soil microbiol, Cornell Univ, 62-64; res biochemist, Univ Calif, Berkeley, 64-69. *Concurrent Pos:* NSF, US Environ Protection Agency, USDA, study grants, soil microbiol, US Int Biol Prog; chmn, Int Symp Environ Biogeochem Inc, 73-91; consult, SAMDENE proj, Egypt, 74-79; teacher & researcher, Helsinki Univ, 77-78, Finland Agr Univ, 77-78, Saltillo Univ, Mex, 78, Swedish Univ Agr Sci, Uppsala, 84 & Agr Univ, Riga Latvi, 91; mem, Int Comt Microbial Ecol, 78-89; assoc ed, Geomicrobiol J, 78-; ed, Arid Soil Res & Rehab, 85-; mem US Environ Protection Agency Rev Panel, 86; mem US Environ Protection Agency working group on Methods for Assessing Environmental Impacts of Microbial Prods, 87-88; mem, US Dept Energy Rev Panel, 83; mem, Latvian Acad Sci, 90-; res grant, Latvian Sci Coun, 95. *Mem:* Am Chem Soc; Am Soc Microbiol; Soil Sci Soc Am; AAAS; Int Soil Sci Soc; Am Soc Agron. *Res:* Ecology of arid lands; nitrogen fixation and cycling; soil enzymology; microbial ecology; enzymatic and microbial activities in adverse environmental conditions; ecology of forest soils. *Mailing Add:* Dept Biol Utah State Univ Logan UT 84322-5305. *Fax:* 435-797-1575; *E-Mail:* skujins@cc.usu.edu

SKULAN, THOMAS WILLIAM, PHARMACOLOGY, PHYSIOLOGY. *Current Pos:* RETIRED. *Personal Data:* b Milwaukee, Wis, Feb 12, 32; m 52; c 3. *Educ:* Univ Wis-Madison, BS, 58, PhD(pharmacol), 62. *Prof Exp:* NIH fel, Univ Fla, 62-63; group leader diuretics, Sterling-Winthrop Res Inst, 66-81, head cardiovasc sect, 69-81. *Res:* Renal pharmacology, hypertension. *Mailing Add:* Steele Bottom Rd Warsaw KY 41095

SKULTETY, FRANCIS MILES, MEDICINE. *Current Pos:* interim dean, Col Med, Univ Nebr, Omaha, 78-79, Shakleford prof neurosurg & neuroanat, 66-87, assoc dean clin affairs, 74-78 & 79-82, prof & chmn dept neurosurg, 75-87, EMER PROF SURG & NEUROSURG, COL MED, UNIV NEBR, 87- *Personal Data:* b Rochester, NY, June 6, 22; m 51, Constance Schmitt; c 3. *Educ:* Univ Rochester, BS, 44, MD, 46; Univ Iowa, PhD(anat), 58; Am Bd Neurol Surg, dipl, 54. *Prof Exp:* Intern, Worcester City Hosp, Mass, 46-47; asst resident neurol, Cushing Vet Admin Hosp, 49-50; sr resident neurosurg, Univ Iowa Hosps, 51-52, instr surg, 52-53, assoc, 53-54, from asst prof to prof, 54-66. *Concurrent Pos:* Fel neurosurg, Lahey Clin, 50-51; clin traineeship Nat Inst Neurol Dis & Stroke, Dept Physiol, Oxford Univ, 57-58. *Mem:* AMA; Am Asn Neurol Surg; fel Am Col Surg; Am Neurol Asn; Soc Neurosci. *Res:* Neuroanatomy; neurophysiology; neural regulation of intake. *Mailing Add:* 840 Crestridge Rd Omaha NE 68154

SKUMANICH, ANDREW P, SOLAR PHYSICS. *Current Pos:* MEM SR STAFF, HIGH ALTITUDE OBSERV, NAT CTR ATMOSPHERIC RES, 61- *Personal Data:* b Wilkes-Barre, Pa, Oct 5, 29; m 55, Mary Berdy; c Andrew, Marina & Monna. *Educ:* Pa State Univ, BS, 51; Princeton Univ, PhD(astrophys), 54. *Prof Exp:* Staff mem, Los Alamos Sci Lab, Univ Calif, 54-60; asst prof & res assoc physics & astron, Univ Rochester, 60-61. *Concurrent Pos:* Consult, Los Alamos Sci Lab, 61-73, NASA, 74-84; lectr, Univ Colo, 61-69, adj prof, 69-84; vis scientist, Lab Stellar & Planetary Physics, 73-74; adj prof, Univ Firenze, Italy, 93; res assoc, Obs de Paris, 96. *Mem:* Am Phys Soc; Am Astron Soc; Int Astron Union. *Res:* Spectropolarimetry; visible, ultraviolet and x-ray spectroscopy; radiative processes; atomic and electronic collision phenomena; solar, atmospheric and chromospheric physics. *Mailing Add:* High Altitude Observ PO Box 3000 Boulder CO 80307. *E-Mail:* sku@hao.ucar.edu

SKUP, DANIEL, INTERFERON GENE EXPRESSION, PROTEASE INHIBITORS IN METASTATIC TUMOR CELLS. *Current Pos:* PROF, UNIV MONTREAL, 93- *Personal Data:* b Chicago, Ill, Apr 1, 51; Can citizen; m 72; c 2. *Educ:* Moscow State Univ, BSc, 73, MSc, 74; McGill Univ, Montreal, PhD(biochem), 80. *Prof Exp:* Postdoctoral researcher, Inst Curie, Orsay, France, 80-82; from asst prof to assoc prof, Montreal Cancer Inst, 82-88, sci dir, 87-88, assoc prof & dir, 88-93. *Concurrent Pos:* Consult, New Eng Nuclear, 79; Med Res Coun vis prof, Fac Med, Univ Ottawa, 83 & Mem Univ, St-Johns, 91; panel mem, Cell Biol & Metastasis Panel, Nat Cancer Inst Can, 84-87, Molecular Biol Comt, Med Res Coun Can, 87-89, Cancer Comt, Med Res Coun Can, Fels Panel, Nat Cancer Inst Can, 89- & Que Govt Mission Biotechnol Israel, 91. *Mem:* Am Soc Microbiologists; Int Soc Interferon Res. *Res:* Regulation of gene expression during cell differentiation and during tumor progression and metastasis; role of interferon as a modulator of mammalian development; role of protease inhibitors in metastatic tumor cells as a tool for molecular basis of tumor invasion. *Mailing Add:* 3432 Ave de l'Hotel de V Montreal PQ H2X 3B4 Can

SKUPSKY, STANLEY, LASER SCIENCE. *Current Pos:* GROUP LEADER, THEORY & COMPUT LAB LASER ENERGETICS, UNIV ROCHESTER. *Honors & Awards:* Excellence in Plasma Physics Res Award, Am Phys Soc, 93. *Mailing Add:* Lab Laser Energetics Univ Rochester Rochester NY 14627

SKUTCHES, CHARLES L, NUTRITIONAL BIOCHEMISTRY. *Current Pos:* assoc investr, 87, sr scientist, 89, DIR SCI ADMINR, LANKENAU MED RES CTR, 91- *Personal Data:* b Northampton, Pa, Nov 3, 41; m 67, Jeanette M Yenser; c Christopher & Laura. *Educ:* Catawba Col, AB, 63; NC State Univ, MS, 66, PhD(nutrit biochem), 73. *Prof Exp:* Biochemist, Smith, Kline & French Lab, 66-69; res assoc, Tex A & M Univ, 73-75; asst investr, Lamkenau Hosp, 75-81. *Concurrent Pos:* Mem, Animal Care & Use Comt, Lankenau Med Res Ctr, 79-83, chmn, 83-; consult, Renal Care Adv Panel, Abbott Labs, Ill, 85-86; adj assoc prof, Dept Med, Sch Med, Temple Univ, 89-93. *Mem:* Sigma Xi; Am Diabetes Asn; AAAS; Am Soc Biochem & Molecular Biol; Am Asn Lab Animal Sci. *Res:* Author of numerous publications; production/utilization of major energy yielding substrates in disease; effects of acetone, acetol, 1,2 propanediol production on insulin response in diabetes; glucose and acetate metabolism in chronic renal failure. *Mailing Add:* Lankenau Med Res Ctr 100 Lancaster Ave W Wynnewood PA 19096-3425

SKUTNIK, BOLESH JOSEPH, PHYSICAL CHEMISTRY, MATERIALS SCIENCE. *Personal Data:* b Passaic, NJ, Aug 19, 41; m 67, 97, Anita Marie Bacon; c Pam, Janeen & Todd. *Educ:* Seton Hall Univ, BS, 62; Yale Univ, MS, 64, PhD(theoret phys chem), 67; Univ Conn, JD, 95. *Prof Exp:* Res assoc phys chem, Brandeis Univ, 67-69; sr res scientist, Firestone Radiation Res Div, Firestone Tire & Rubber Co, 69-73; asst prof chem, Fairfield Univ, 73-79; res scientist, Ensign-Bickford Industs, Inc, 79-81, new prod mgr, 81-87, chief scientist, Ensign-Bickford Optics Co, 87-91 & Ensign-Bickford Coatings Co, 90-91. *Concurrent Pos:* Lectr, Brandeis Univ, 68-69; abstractor, Chem Abstr Serv, 69-85; consult, Acad Press, Inc, 74-76, J Wiley & Sons, 79 & Darworth Corp, 82; adj prof, Univ Hartford, 90. *Mem:* Am Chem Soc; Am Ceramics Soc; Optical Soc Am; Mat Res Soc; Soc Photo-Optical Instrumentation Engrs; Soc Plastics Engrs. *Res:* Effects of radiation on matter, theoretical and applied; characterization and physical properties of irradiated polymers; electronic structure of atoms and molecules; inter- and intra-molecular energy transfer; theoretical atomic structure and spectroscopy; photochemistry; radiation chemistry; polymer science; specialty coatings; quantum chemistry; interaction of matter and energy; polymer processing; photo initiation of polymerization; specialty coatings for optics; solventless coatings; polymeric composites for conductivity; electron & UV radiation processing of materials; reinforced polymers; flush photolysis & kenetic studies of organic and bio-organic systems; water soluble vehicles for pigments and wood preservatives. *Mailing Add:* PO Box 602 New Britain CT 06050. *E-Mail:* boleshskutnik@compuserve.com

SKY-PECK, HOWARD H, BIOCHEMISTRY. *Current Pos:* from instr to assoc prof, Col Med, 55-67, from assoc prof to prof, Grad Sch, 58-90, EMER PROF BIOCHEM, GRAD SCH, UNIV ILL. *Personal Data:* b London, Eng, July 24, 23; nat US; m 52; c 3. *Educ:* Univ Southern Calif, BS, 49, PhD, 56. *Hon Degrees:* MD, Royal Soc Med, Eng, 57. *Prof Exp:* Lab instr biochem, Univ Southern Calif, 50-52; res assoc, Presby Hosp, Chicago, 55. *Concurrent Pos:* Asst attend biochemist, Presby-St Lukes Hosp, 58-62, sr attend biochemist, 62-, dir, Clin Chem Lab, 67-75; mem biochem comt, Nat Cancer Chemother Serv Ctr, NIH, 60; actg chmn dept, Rush Med Col, 70-71, prof biochem & chmn dept, 71-80. *Mem:* AAAS; Am Chem Soc; Am Cancer Soc; Am Asn Clin Chem; Am Asn Cancer Res; Nat Acad Clin Biochem; Sigma Xi. *Res:* Amino acid metabolism in mouse brains; biochemical comparison between normal and neoplastic human cancer tissues and use of biochemical techniques in evaluation of chemotherapeutic agents in cancer. *Mailing Add:* 187 Olmsted Rd Riverside IL 60546

SKYPEK, DORA HELEN, mathematics education, mathematics; deceased, see previous edition for last biography

SLABY, FRANK J, ANATOMY. *Current Pos:* ASSOC PROF ANAT, GEORGE WASHINGTON UNIV MED CTR, 81- *Mailing Add:* Dept Anat George Washington Univ Med Sch 2300 I St NW Washington DC 20037-2337

SLABY, HAROLD THEODORE, NONASSOCIATIVE ALGEBRA, PROJECTIVE PLANES. *Current Pos:* From instr to assoc prof, 53-89, EMER ASSOC PROF MATH, WAYNE STATE UNIV, 89- *Personal Data:* b Traverse City, Mich, Oct 11, 20; m 51, Myrtle Keryluk; c Robert T. *Educ:* Wayne State Univ, AB, 46, MA, 48; Univ Wis, PhD(math), 53. *Concurrent Pos:* Mem consult bur, Math Asn Am, 68-83. *Mem:* Am Math Soc; Math Asn Am; Sigma Xi. *Res:* Central milpotency of commutative moufang loops. *Mailing Add:* 2691 Burnham Rd Royal Oak MI 48073

SLABYJ, BOHDAN M, FOOD SCIENCE. *Current Pos:* fel, Albert Einstein Med Ctr, 69-72, from asst prof to assoc prof, 72-85, PROF FOOD SCI, UNIV MAINE, 85- *Personal Data:* b Chernivci, Ukraine, Dec 3, 31; US citizen; m 63, Irene Fedoriw; c Natalko, Stefania & Nicholas. *Educ:* Univ Alta, BSc, 58, MSc, 60; Univ Wash, PhD(food sci), 68. *Prof Exp:* Instr bact, Univ Alta, 60-62; asst microbiologist, Univ Wash, 62-67; asst prof microbiol, Duquesne Univ, 67-69. *Mem:* Am Soc Microbiol; Inst Food Technol; Soc Appl Bacteriol; Int Asn Milk Food & Environ Sanitarians. *Res:* Seafood processing, quality, and safety. *Mailing Add:* 43 Robinhood Dr Brewer ME 04412. *Fax:* 207-581-1636; *E-Mail:* rfst701@maine.maine.edu

SLACK, DERALD ALLEN, PHYTOPATHOLOGY, NEMATOLOGY. *Current Pos:* from asst prof to assoc prof, 52-60, PROF PLANT PATH, UNIV ARK, FAYETTEVILLE, 60-, HEAD DEPT, 64- *Personal Data:* b Cedar City, Utah, Dec 22, 24; m 45; c 2. *Educ:* Utah State Agr Col, BS, 48, MS, 49; Univ Wis, PhD, 53. *Honors & Awards:* Outstanding Plant Pathologist, Am Phytopath Soc. *Prof Exp:* Asst res & collabr, USDA, Utah State Agr Col, 46-47, asst, 47-49; asst, Univ Wis, 49-52. *Concurrent Pos:* Mem & secy, Ark State Plant Bd, 64- *Mem:* Am Phytopath Soc (secy, 78-80); Soc Nematol; Int Soc Plant Path. *Res:* Fruit diseases; plant parasitic nematodes. *Mailing Add:* 1535 Hefley St Fayetteville AR 72703

SLACK, GLEN ALFRED, SOLID STATE PHYSICS. *Current Pos:* AT RENSSELAER POLYTECH INST, 93- *Personal Data:* b Rochester, NY, Sept 29, 28; m 51, Nancy Gottmann; c Margaret, David & Jonathan. *Educ:* Rensselaer Polytech Inst, BS, 50; Cornell Univ, PhD, 56. *Prof Exp:* Physicist, Gen Elec Res & Develop Ctr, 56-93. *Concurrent Pos:* Guggenheim fel, Oxford Univ, 66; Coolidge fel, Yale Univ, 88. *Mem:* Fel Am Phys Soc; Sigma Xi; Am Ceramic Soc. *Res:* Thermal properties and heat transport in solids; preparation and chemistry of crystals; properties of semiconductors; ultrasonic phonon propagation in solids; thermoelectrics; optical properties of solids. *Mailing Add:* Dept Physics Rensselaer Polytech Inst Troy NY 12180

SLACK, JIM MARSHALL, physiology, for more information see previous edition

SLACK, JOHN MADISON, MEDICAL BACTERIOLOGY. *Current Pos:* prof, 46-77, EMER PROF MICROBIOL, MED CTR, W VA UNIV, 77- *Personal Data:* b Polson, Mont, Mar 9, 14; m 69, Gearlean M Swentzel; c John Harvey. *Educ:* Univ Minn, AB, 36, MS, 37, PhD(bact), 40; Am Bd Microbiol, dipl, 62. *Prof Exp:* Asst bact, Univ Minn, 38-40; instr path & bact, Col Med, Univ Nebr, 40-42; bacteriologist, US Army Chem Warfare Labs, Ft Detrick, Md, 46. *Mem:* AAAS; Am Soc Microbiol; fel Am Pub Health Asn. *Res:* Identification and classification of Actinomyces; fluorescent antibody techniques; nocardin; food poisoning. *Mailing Add:* Univ Village 12401 N 22nd St Apt B-209 Tampa FL 33612

SLACK, KEITH VOLLMER, STREAM LIMNOLOGY, BIOLOGICAL WATER QUALITY. *Current Pos:* RES LIMNOLOGIST, US GEOL SURV, 60- *Personal Data:* b Louisville, Ky, May 20, 24; m 62; c 4. *Educ:* Univ Ky, BS, 49, MS, 50; Ind Univ, PhD(zool), 54. *Prof Exp:* Asst zool, Univ Ky, 49-50, State Lake & Stream Surv, Ind Univ, 50-52 & Ind Univ, 52-53; oceanogr, US Navy Oceanog, 53-60. *Concurrent Pos:* Lectr limnol & aquatic ecol, Univ Ariz, Tucson, 65-71 & Geol Surv Nat Training Ctr, Denver; res adv ecol, Water Resources Div, US Geol Surv, 74-76 & 78-; mem, Interagency Working Group Biol & Microbiol Methods, 75-84. *Mem:* Am Inst Biol Sci;

Ecol Soc Am; Am Soc Limnol & Oceanog; Int Asn Theoret & Appl Limnol; NAm Benthological Soc. *Res:* Interrelations between aquatic organisms and their environment; stream limnology; controls on benthic invertebrate community; distribution and abundance; aquatic biological methods. *Mailing Add:* 805 Gailen Ave Palo Alto CA 94303-4534

SLACK, LEWIS, nuclear physics, science education for general public, for more information see previous edition

SLACK, LYLE HOWARD, CERAMICS. *Current Pos:* SR RES CHEMIST, E I DU PONT DE NEMOURS & CO, INC, NY, 80- *Personal Data:* b Wellsville, NY, Jan 6, 37; m 54; c 4. *Educ:* Alfred Univ, BS, 58, PhD(ceramic sci), 65. *Prof Exp:* Res engr, Hommel Co, Pa, 58-60 & Lexington Labs, Mass, 60-61; mem tech staff thin film electronics, Bell Tel Labs, 65-67; asst prof ceramic eng, Va Polytech Inst & State Univ, 67-71, assoc prof, 71-80. *Concurrent Pos:* Consult, Naval Res Labs, 69-81. *Mem:* Fel Am Ceramic Soc; Nat Inst Ceramic Engrs; Am Soc Eng Educ; Electrochem Soc; Int Soc Hybrid Microelectronics. *Res:* Structure and electric properties of semiconducting glasses; structure and electronic conduction in oxide thin films; solar photovoltaic materials; solar thermal coatings; thick film resistors; thick film dielectrics. *Mailing Add:* 3203 Kammerer Dr Wilmington DE 19803

SLACK, NANCY G, PLANT ECOLOGY. *Current Pos:* from asst prof to assoc prof biol, 71-81, chmn dept, 78-84, PROF BIOL, RUSSELL SAGE COL, TROY, NY, 81- *Personal Data:* b New York, NY, Aug 12, 30; m 51; c 3. *Educ:* Cornell Univ, BS, 52, MS, 54; State Univ NY, Albany, PhD(ecol), 71. *Honors & Awards:* Donald Richards Fund Award, NY Bot Garden, 74, Diamond Award, 75. *Prof Exp:* Demonstr bot & evolution, Bot Sch, Oxford Univ, Eng, 66-67; lectr bot, State Univ NY, Albany, 69. *Concurrent Pos:* Consult, Environ Impact Studies, Environ-One Corp, 73-, Environ Assessment Study, Dunn Geosci, 74-, Environ Impact Studies, Environmed Inc, 75-; trustee & ecol consult land acquisition, The Nature Conserv, 73-, mem bd trustees, 89-; consult col sci progs, NY State Educ Dept, 75-76, 78, 82 & 83-90; Am Asn Univ Professors fel, 79-80; NSF travel award, 81; vis fel, Rensselaer Polytech Inst, 85; vis res scholar, Yale Univ, 90-91. *Mem:* Ecol Soc Am; Am Bryol & Lichenol Soc; Int Bryol Asn; AAAS; Sigma Xi; Hist Sci Soc. *Res:* Community ecology of bryophytes and vascular plants including Sphagnum bog ecology; species diversity and community structure in bryophytes; ecology of epiphytic bryophytes in North America; island biogeography and vegetation changes on islands due to human disturbance; bryophytes in relation to ecological niche theory; history of botany and ecology in US; biology of rare and endangered plant species. *Mailing Add:* Dept Biol Russell Sage Col Main Campus, 65 N First St Troy NY 12180-1538

SLACK, NELSON HOSKING, BIOSTATISTICS. *Current Pos:* assoc cancer res scientist biostatist, 64-77, dep dir clin trials, Nat Prostatic Cancer Proj, 77-84, MEM STAFF, BIOMATHEMATICS DEPT, ROSWELL PARK MEM INST, 84- *Personal Data:* b Burlington, Vt, Feb 7, 35; m 60; c 3. *Educ:* Univ Vt, BS, 57; Rutgers Univ, MS, 63, PhD(reproductive phys & statist), 64. *Prof Exp:* Res asst dairy sci, Rutgers Univ, 63-64. *Concurrent Pos:* Res prof, Niagara Univ; asst res prof, State Univ NY Buffalo. *Mem:* AAAS; Am Statist Asn; Sigma Xi. *Res:* Cancer research. *Mailing Add:* RR 9 Waterville VT 05492

SLACK, STEVEN ALLEN, PLANT PATHOLOGY, PLANT VIROLOGY. *Current Pos:* PROF PLANT PATH, CORNELL UNIV, 88- *Personal Data:* b Logan, Utah, May 6, 47; m 70; c 2. *Educ:* Univ Ark, BSA, 69, MS, 71; Univ Calif, Davis, PhD(plant path), 74. *Prof Exp:* From asst prof to prof plant path, Univ Wis-Madison, 75-88. *Mem:* Am Phytopath Soc; Potato Asn Am; AAAS. *Res:* Characterization and serology of plant viruses, epidemiology and control of plant virus and bacterial diseases, and potato diseases. *Mailing Add:* Dept Plant Path 334 Plant Sci Bldg Cornell Univ Ithaca NY 14853-0001

SLACK, STEVEN M, BIOMATERIALS. *Current Pos:* fel, 90-91, asst prof res, 91-93, ASST PROF BIOMED ENG, MEMPHIS STATE UNIV, 93- *Personal Data:* b Albuquerque, NMex, Nov 27, 61. *Educ:* Carnegie-Mellon Inst, BS, 83; Univ Wash, PhD(chem eng), 89. *Prof Exp:* Vis prof chem eng, Univ Calif, Davis, 89-90. *Mem:* Soc Biomat; Int Soc Thrombosis & Hemat; Am Soc Hemat. *Mailing Add:* Dept Biomed Eng Univ Memphis Memphis TN 38152

SLACK, WARNER VINCENT, COMPUTER SCIENCE, PATIENT-COMPUTER DIALOGUE. *Current Pos:* CO-PRES, CTR CLIN COMPUT, 86- *Personal Data:* b East Orange, NJ, June 10, 33; m 56; c 3. *Educ:* Princeton Univ, AB, 55; Columbia Univ, MD, 59. *Prof Exp:* Intern med, Univ Wis Hosps, 59-60, resident, 60-61, instr, Univ, 65-66, from asst prof to assoc prof med & comput sci, 66-70; asst prof, 70-73, assoc prof med, Harvard Med Sch, 73-, assoc prof psychiat, 90- *Concurrent Pos:* Alumni Res Found fel, Univ Wis Hosps, 61 & 64-65; NIH spec res fel, 65-66; lectr, Univ Philippines, 63-64; co-dir, Div Comput Med, Beth Israel Hosp & Brigham & Women's Hosp, 80- *Res:* Application of computer techniques to clinical medicine, specifically the use of computers to interview and counsel patients regarding their medical problems and to help patients to make their own medical decisions; computers in psychiatry and psychotherapy; hospital-wide clinical computing systems. *Mailing Add:* Ctr Clin Comput Harvard Med Sch 350 Longwood Ave GL-1 Boston MA 02115. *Fax:* 617-667-1002

SLADE, ARTHUR LAIRD, POLYMER CHEMISTRY, COMPUTER SCIENCE. *Current Pos:* Res chemist, Marshall Res & Develop Lab, E I Du Pont de Nemours & Co, 64-69, staff chemist, 69, res supvr, 69-72, sr financial analyst, 72-73, distrib mgr, 73-75, prin consult corp planning, 75-78, mgr planning & financial commun, 78-80, pub affairs mgr chem & pigments, 80-81, pub affairs mgr, textile fibers, 81-83, group mgr pub affairs, 83-85, planning dir external affairs, 85-93, DIR EXTERNAL AFFAIRS, PLANS & OPERS, E I DU PONT DE NEMOURS & CO, 93- *Personal Data:* b Aiken, SC, Oct 21, 37; m 78, M Trudy Pavlik; c David M & Julian L. *Educ:* Duke Univ, AB, 59; Univ NC, PhD(phys chem), 64. *Mem:* Sigma Xi; Am Chem Soc. *Res:* Electrolyte solutions; electrochemistry; polymer coatings; automotive specialty products; man made textile fibers; science communications; technical management. *Mailing Add:* E I Du Pont de Nemours & Co 9516 106 Orchard Ave Moylan PA 19065-4118

SLADE, BERNARD NEWTON, ELECTRICAL ENGINEERING, ELECTRONICS ENGINEERING. *Current Pos:* SR VPRES, YIELDUP INT, LOS ALTOS, CALIF, 93- *Personal Data:* b Sioux City, Iowa, Dec 21, 23; m 46, Margot Friedleih; c Steven & Eric. *Educ:* Univ Wis, BS, 48; Stevens Inst Technol, MS, 54. *Prof Exp:* Advan develop engr, Tube Div, Radio Corp Am, NJ, 48-53, mgr advan develop, 53-55, res engr labs, 55-56; mgr semiconductor develop, IBM Corp, Hopewell, NY, 56-60, mgr components prod opers, 60-65, corp dir advan mfg tech, 65-66, corp dir mfg planning & controls, 66-69, corp dir mfg eng & technol, 69-81, adv, Mfg Technol, 81-84; consult, Arthur D Little, Inc, Cambridge, Mass, 84-86; sr mgr consult, United Res Co, Morristown, NJ, 86-93. *Concurrent Pos:* Adj instr, Pace Univ, 77-79; guest lectr, Harvard Grad Sch Bus, 84, Stanford Grad Sch Bus, 85, Cornell, Chicago Univ, Pa State Univ & Univ Pa, Wharton; founder, vpres & bd dirs, Yieldup Int, Mountain View, Calif, 93-; mem bd dirs, V3 Semiconductor, Toronto, Ont, Can. *Mem:* Sr mem Inst Elec & Electronics Engrs; Sigma Xi. *Res:* Development and design of solid state components, including transistors, diodes and other semiconductor devices; manufacturing productivity with emphasis on high technology; management of product cycle; author of 2 books. *Mailing Add:* 12 Merry Hill Rd Poughkeepsie NY 12603. *E-Mail:* 120263.2704@compuserve.com

SLADE, EDWARD COLIN, NATIONALLY RECOGNIZED AUTHORITY ON VALVES, FLUID FLOW COMPUTER APPLICATIONS. *Current Pos:* CONSULT, 86- *Personal Data:* b Stockport, Eng, Mar 24, 35; US citizen; m 62; c 2. *Educ:* Stockport Col, Eng, BSME, 55. *Honors & Awards:* Silver Medalist, Geneva, Switz, 80. *Prof Exp:* Design engr, Standard Steel, 57-60, James M Montgomery, 60-61, Carnation Co, 61-66, Stone & Webster, 66-67 & Donald R Warren, 67-68; sr design engr, Stearns Roger Corp, 68-69 & 72-76; sr engr & qual assurance engr, Holmes & Narver, 69-71; staff engr, Bechtel, 72; sr design engr, Dravo Corp, 76-77; engr fluid systs, Martin Marietta Energy Systs, Dept Energy, US Oak Ridge Nat Lab, 77-86; pres, Containment, Oak Ridge, Tenn, 86- *Concurrent Pos:* Peer reviewer nuclear valves, Oak Ridge Nat Lab, 77-; secy & mem, Bd Human Resources, Oak Ridge, Tenn. *Mem:* Int Platform Asn. *Res:* Designed and built a valve that could have avoided the catastrophe of Three Mile Island; work and writing are directed at the complexities of flow and materials in this area; one US patent. *Mailing Add:* 203 Tusculum Dr Oak Ridge TN 37830

SLADE, H CLYDE, INTERNAL MEDICINE, PSYCHIATRY. *Current Pos:* Assoc prof health care & epidemiol, Univ BC, 68-71, hon assoc prof psychiat, 68-84, assoc prof primary health care & dir div, 71-77, EMER PROF PSYCHIAT, UNIV BC, 84- *Personal Data:* b Millestown, Nfld, July 2, 18; m 44; c 4. *Educ:* Dalhousie Univ, MD & CM, 49; FRCPS(C), 49. *Concurrent Pos:* Assoc med, The Vancouver Hosp, 50- *Mem:* Can Med Asn; Can Psychiat Asn. *Res:* Psychosomatic medicine; rheumatology. *Mailing Add:* 3070 W 44th Ave Vancouver BC V6N 3K6 Can

SLADE, JOEL S, HETEROCYCLIC CHEMISTRY, ASYMMETRIC SYNTHESIS. *Current Pos:* sr res chemist med chem, 80-85, PROCESS RES CHEMIST, CIBA-GEIGY CORP, 85- *Personal Data:* b Brooklyn, NY, Jan 1, 47; m 78. *Educ:* Lowell Tech Inst, BS, 68, MS, 74; Colo State Univ, PhD(chem), 79. *Prof Exp:* Fel org chem res, Univ Pa, 79-80. *Mem:* Am Chem Soc. *Res:* Preparation of biologically interesting molecules which have the potential to become new therapeutic agents. *Mailing Add:* 14 Theresa Dr Flanders NJ 07836

SLADE, LARRY MALCOM, HORSE HUSBANDRY, NUTRITION. *Current Pos:* ASSOC PROF ANIMAL SCI, UTAH STATE UNIV, 78- *Personal Data:* b Durango, Colo, Feb 20, 36; m 62; c 5. *Educ:* Brigham Young Univ, BS, 62; Va Polytech Inst, MS, 65; Univ Calif, Davis, PhD(animal nutrit), 71. *Prof Exp:* Teacher high sch, Calif, 65-66; asst prof animal sci, Calif State Polytech Col, 70-72; assoc prof animal sci, Colo State Univ, 71-78. *Concurrent Pos:* Subcomt Horse Nutrit, Nat Res Coun; consult. *Mem:* Am Soc Animal Sci; Equine Nutrit & Physiol Soc; Asn Equine Sports Med; Int Conf Equine Exercise Physiol. *Res:* Nutrient requirements of horses; conformation and performance of horses. *Mailing Add:* Dept Animal Sci Utah State Univ Logan UT 84322-0001. *Fax:* 501-750-2118

SLADE, MARTIN ALPHONSE, III, CELESTIAL MECHANICS, RADIO ASTRONOMY. *Current Pos:* RESEARCHER, EARTH & LUNAR PHYSICS APPLN GROUP, JET PROPULSION LAB, CALIF INST TECHNOL, 71- *Personal Data:* b Dunedin, Fla. *Educ:* Mass Inst Technol, SB, 64, SM, 67, PhD(planetary sci), 71. *Concurrent Pos:* Mem, Lunar Sci Rev Panel, Lunar Sci Inst, Houston, 75- *Mem:* Am Astron Soc; Am Geophys Union. *Res:* Rotational dynamics of the moon; very long baseline interferometry; analysis of lunar laser ranging data; testing gravitational theories; radar astronomy. *Mailing Add:* 1320 E Cordova St Pasadena CA 91107

SLADE, NORMAN ANDREW, POPULATION ECOLOGY. *Current Pos:* from asst prof to assoc prof, 72-81, PROF SYST & ECOL, UNIV KANS, 81- *Personal Data:* b Wichita, Kans, Oct 14, 43; m 64, Sherry L Irons; c Davis A, Richard C & Shauna L. *Educ:* Kans State Univ, BS, 65; Utah State Univ, MS, 69, PhD(ecol), 72. *Prof Exp:* Res assoc statist ecol, San Diego State Univ, 71-72. *Concurrent Pos:* Vis scientist pop ecol, Unit Behav Syst, NIMH, 76. *Mem:* Ecol Soc Am; Am Soc Mammalogists; Biometric Soc; AAAS; Am Soc Naturalists. *Res:* Mammalian population dynamics, computer simulation models of ecological systems; biostatistics. *Mailing Add:* Mus Natural Hist Dept Syst & Ecol Univ Kans Lawrence KS 66045-2454. *Fax:* 785-864-5335; *E-Mail:* n-slade@ukans.edu

SLADE, PAUL GRAHAM, CIRCUIT BREAKER DEVELOPMENT, SURFACE SCIENCE. *Current Pos:* MGR, VACUUM INTERRUPTER TECH, CUTLER-HAMMER, 93- *Personal Data:* b Blackpool, Eng, Dec, 1941; US citizen; m 65; c 2. *Educ:* Univ Wales, BS, 63, PhD (physics), 66; Univ Pittsburgh, MBA, 73. *Honors & Awards:* Ragnar Holm Sci Achievement Award, 85. *Prof Exp:* Sr engr, Westinghouse Sci & Technol Ctr, 66-72, mgr, Power Interruption Res, 72-75, Power Interruption & Plasma Systs, 75-83 & Plasma & Nuclear Sci, 83-90, dir int technol develop, 90-93. *Concurrent Pos:* Mem, organizing comt, Holm Conf, Inst Elec & Electronics Engrs, 77-, ad com trans ed, Components Hybrids & Mfg Soc, 87-95; pres & vpres bd dirs, Pittsburgh CLO Assocs, 92-93. *Mem:* Fel Inst Elec & Electronics Engrs; Inst Physics. *Res:* Science of electric contacts for power application; arcs and their interaction with electric contacts; contactor, molded case breaker, vacuum interruption and SF interruption phenomena; strategic planning. *Mailing Add:* Cutler-Hammer 200 Westinghouse Circle Horseheads NY 14845. *Fax:* 607-796-3364

SLADE, PHILIP EARL, JR, POLYMER CHEMISTRY, FIBER LUBRICATION. *Current Pos:* PRES, GULF RES SERV, 92- *Personal Data:* b Hattiesburg, Miss, Sept 2, 29; m 65, Nancy R Burris; c Kenneth, Cynthia, Susan & Kara. *Educ:* Miss Southern Col, BA, 51; Tulane Univ, MS, 53, PhD(chem), 55. *Prof Exp:* Res chemist, Chemstrand Corp, Ala, 55; assoc chem, George Washington Univ, 56-57; assoc prof, Miss Southern Col, 57-60; sr res chemist, Chemstrand Res Ctr, Inc, 60-67; group supvr, Nylon Tech Ctr, Monsanto Textiles Co, 67-74, supvr, 74-91. *Mem:* Am Chem Soc; Fiber Soc. *Res:* Polymer characterization; polymer solution properties; thermal analysis; fiber characterization; fiber finish analysis; fiber finish formulation. *Mailing Add:* 4190 Aiken Rd Pensacola FL 32503-3404

SLADEK, CELIA DAVIS, MEDICAL NEUROENDOCRINOLOGY. *Current Pos:* PROF PHYSIOL, UNIV HEALTH SCI/CHICAGO MED SCH, 92- *Personal Data:* b Denver, Colo, Mar 25, 44; m 70, John R Jr; c Jonathan, Stefan & Jessica. *Educ:* Hastings Col, BA, 66; Northwestern Univ, Chicago, MS, 69, PhD(physiol), 70. *Prof Exp:* Asst prof physiol, Univ Ill Med Ctr, 70-73; res associate prof neuroendocrinol, Univ Rochester Med Sch, 74-76, from asst prof to assoc prof neurol & anat, 76-88, prof neurol & neurobiol, 88-92. *Concurrent Pos:* Am Cancer Soc grant, Univ Ill Med Ctr, 71-72; Am Diabetes Asn grant, 74-75; Nat Inst Arthritis, Metab & Digestive Dis grant, 77-91; NIH res develop career award, 77-82 & Nat Heart Lung Blood Inst, 82-89; NSF equipment grant, 80, Nat Inst Neurol Dis & Stroke, 91-99, Nat Inst Aging, 95-; mem, Neurol Sci Study Sect, NIH, 97- *Mem:* Soc Neurosci; Am Asn Anatomists; NY Acad Sci; Endocrine Soc; Am Physiol Soc. *Res:* Regulation of vasopressin and oxytocin secretion and gene expression; clinical abnormalities associated with inappropriate vasopressin secretion; hypertension; development and aging of the neurohypophyseal system; trophic regulation of mesencepholic dopamanine neurons. *Mailing Add:* Dept Physiol Univ Health Sci/Chicago Med Sch North Chicago IL 60064

SLADEK, JOHN RICHARD, JR, NEUROSCIENCE, AGING & DEVELOPMENT. *Current Pos:* PROF & CHMN, DEPT NEUROSCI, FINCH UNIV HEALTH SCI, CHICAGO MED SCH, 91- *Personal Data:* b Chicago, Ill, Feb 6, 43; m 70; c 3. *Educ:* Carthage Col, BA, 65; Northwestern Univ, MS, 68; Univ Health Sci, PhD(anat), 71. *Prof Exp:* From asst prof to assoc prof, Anat Univ Rochester, 73-82, assoc prof, Ctr Brain Res, 79-82, prof & chair neurobiol-anat, Sch Med, Univ Rochester, 82-91, Kilian & Caroline Schmitt prof, 87. *Concurrent Pos:* Consult, Nat Inst Aging, Nat Inst Neurol & Commun Dis & Stroke & NSF, 80; mem, Biol Neurosci Study Sect, NIMH, 80-84, Neurol B2 Study Sect, NIH, 85-89; d-in-chief, Exp Neurol, 88- *Mem:* Am Asn Anatomists; Histochem Soc; NY Acad Sci; Soc Neurosci. *Res:* Neuron interactions of aminergic and peptidergic neurons during development, aging and following transplantation; neuroendocrinology of the hypothalamo-neurohypophyseal system of vasopressin and oxytocin neurons; Parkinson's disease. *Mailing Add:* Dept Neurosci Finch Univ Health Sci Chicago Med Sch 3333 Green Bay Rd North Chicago IL 60064

SLADEK, NORMAN ELMER, PHARMACOLOGY, CANCER CHEMOTHERAPY. *Current Pos:* from asst prof to assoc prof, 68-79, PROF PHARMACOL, MED SCH, UNIV MINN, MINNEAPOLIS, 79- *Personal Data:* b Montgomery, Minn, Aug 20, 39; m 64, Joyce L Poole; c Theresa L, Rebecca L & Melissa A. *Educ:* Univ Minn, Minneapolis, BS, 62, PhD(pharmacol), 66. *Prof Exp:* NIH fel, Univ Wis-Madison, 66-68. *Concurrent Pos:* NIH res career develop award, 72-77. *Mem:* AAAS; Am Asn Cancer Res; Am Soc Pharmacol & Exp Therapeut. *Res:* Cancer chemotherapy; drug interactions; drug metabolism; carcinogenesis; immunopharmacology; chemoprevention toxicology. *Mailing Add:* Dept Pharmacol 3-249 Millard Hall Univ Minn Minneapolis MN 55455-0347. *Fax:* 612-625-8408; *E-Mail:* slade001@maroon.tc.umn.edu

SLADEK, RONALD JOHN, SOLID STATE PHYSICS. *Current Pos:* RETIRED. *Personal Data:* b Chicago, Ill, Sept 19, 26; m 53; c 6. *Educ:* Univ Chicago, PhD(physics), 54. *Prof Exp:* Res physicist, Westinghouse Elec Corp, 53-61; from assoc prof to prof physics, Purdue Univ, 61-91, actg head dept, 69-71, assoc dean sci, 74-87. *Mem:* Fel Am Phys Soc; Sigma Xi. *Res:* Ultrasonic and electrical properties of solids, especially crystalline solids exhibiting a phase transition and superionic glasses; effects of low temperatures, stress, and magnetic fields thereon. *Mailing Add:* 963 Ridgeview Dr Reno NV 89511

SLAGA, THOMAS JOSEPH, BIOCHEMICAL PHARMACOLOGY. *Current Pos:* AT DEPT BIOCHEM, SCI PARK-RES DIV, UNIV TEX SYST CANCER CTR. *Personal Data:* b Smithfield, Ohio, Dec 15, 41; m 66; c 2. *Educ:* Col Steubenville, BA, 64; Univ Ark, PhD(physiol biophys), 69. *Prof Exp:* Fel, McArdle Lab Cancer Res, Univ Wis-Madison, 68-71; res investr chem carcinogenesis, Pac Northwest Res Ctr, 71-73; asst mem, Fred Hutchinson Cancer Res Ctr, 73-76; staff mem, E Tenn Cancer Res Ctr, 76-78; sr staff mem cancer & toxicol, biol div, Oak Ridge Nat Lab, 76- *Concurrent Pos:* Asst prof pharmacol, Sch Med, Univ Wash, 74-76. *Mem:* Am Asn Cancer Res; Am Soc Invest Dermatol; Sigma Xi. *Res:* Mechanism of chemical carcinogenesis in both in vivo and in vitro; in particular, the early molecular events after the application of chemical carcinogens and tumor promoters, mechanism of action of the antitumor agents of the skin. *Mailing Add:* Dept Biochem Sci Park Res Div Univ Tex Syst Cancer Ctr PO Box 389 Smithville TX 78957-0389. *Fax:* 512-237-2522

SLAGEL, DONALD E, BIOCHEMISTRY, NEUROBIOLOGY. *Current Pos:* ASSOC PROF SURG, UNIV KY, 64- *Personal Data:* b Louisville, Ky, Sept 30, 30; m 57; c 3. *Educ:* Univ Ky, BS, 54; Univ Wis, MS, 56, PhD(biochem, phys chem), 61. *Concurrent Pos:* NIH fel neuropath, Univ Wis, 61-63 & neurobiol, Gothenburg Univ, 63-64. *Mem:* Am Chem Soc; Int Soc Neurochem; Am Asn Neuropath; Am Soc Neurochem; Sigma Xi; AAAS. *Res:* Chemistry and ultrastructure of the nervous system; use of athymic mouse-human tumor xenograft in experimental studies, including combined modality treatment studies; study of the athymic mouse-human brain tumor xenogroft genome for sequences related to cell transformation. *Mailing Add:* 4468 Leestown Rd Lexington KY 40511

SLAGEL, ROBERT CLAYTON, ORGANIC CHEMISTRY. *Current Pos:* tech dir, Union Camp Corp, 79-88, mgr mkt & com develop, 88-89, bus mgr inks & coasteing group, Chem Prod Div, 89-92, GEN MGR EUROPE, UNION CHEM LTD, 92- *Personal Data:* b Sabetha, Kans, Jan 4, 37; m 61, Barbara Schoening; c David & Deborah (Kruchten). *Educ:* Western Mich Univ, BS, 58; Univ Ill, PhD(sesquiterpenoids), 62. *Prof Exp:* Res chemist, Archer Daniels Midland Co, 62-64, sr res chemist, 64-67; group leader basic res, ADM Chem Div, Ashland Oil & Refining Co, 67-68; group leader polymer synthesis, Calgon Corp, Subsid Merck & Co Inc, 68-69, sect leader specialty chem res, 69-71, mgr polymer res, 71-77, asst dir res & develop, 77-78, dir specialty chem res, 78-79. *Mem:* Am Chem Soc; Tech Asn Pulp & Paper Indust. *Res:* Monomers and polymers, chiefly polyelectrolytes; organonitrogen chemistry; ozonization of organic compounds; carbenes, chiefly halocarbenes; rosin based resins; fatty acid derivatives; tall oil distillation. *Mailing Add:* 3 Marsh Haven Lane Savannah GA 31411

SLAGER, URSULA TRAUGOTT, PATHOLOGY. *Current Pos:* RETIRED. *Personal Data:* b Frankfurt, Germany, Sept 15, 25; nat US; m 49, Donald. *Educ:* Wellesley Col, BA, 48; Univ Md, MD, 52; Am Bd Path, dipl, 58. *Prof Exp:* Instr path, Sch Med, Univ Md, 54-55, assoc, 56-57; pathologist, Los Alamos Med Ctr, 57-59 & Res Dept, Martin Co, 59-60; assoc clin prof path, Univ Southern Calif, 61-67, assoc prof, 67-90; pathologist, Rancho Los Amigos Med Ctr, 68-88. *Concurrent Pos:* Hitchcock fel neuropath, Univ Md, 53-55; assoc pathologist, Orange County Gen Hosp, 61-65, actg dir path serv, 65-67; mem staff, Univ Southern Calif Med Ctr, 67-89. *Mem:* AMA; Am Col Path; Int Acad Path; Am Soc Clin Path; Am Soc Neuropath. *Res:* Neuropathology; radiation damage. *Mailing Add:* 2800 Sunset Rd Bishop CA 93514

SLAGG, NORMAN, PHYSICAL CHEMISTRY, CHEMICAL KINETICS. *Current Pos:* HEAD FAST REACTION SECT, EXPLOSIVE LAB, PICATINNY ARSENAL, 67- *Personal Data:* b New York, NY, Jan 8, 31; m 57; c 2. *Educ:* Brooklyn Col, BS, 52; Polytech Inst Brooklyn, PhD(chem), 60. *Prof Exp:* Res chemist, Reaction Motors Div, Thiokol Chem Corp, 60-62; sr res engr, Lamp Div, Westinghouse Elec Corp, 62-67; instr phys chem, Fairleigh Dickinson Univ, 65-67; lectr, Rutgers Univ, 67-75. *Mem:* Am Chem Soc; Am Phys Soc; Sigma Xi. *Res:* Kinetics; mechanism of chemical reactions; photochemistry; reactions of molten salts with glasses and ceramics; shock tube techniques; time resolved spectroscopy; explosive phenomena. *Mailing Add:* 22 Marlton Dr Wayne NJ 07470-5331

SLAGLE, JAMES R, computer science, mathematics; deceased, see previous edition for last biography

SLAGLE, WAYNE GREY, PARASITOLOGY. *Current Pos:* asst prof 70-77, ASSOC PROF BIOL, STEPHEN F AUSTIN STATE UNIV, 77- *Personal Data:* b Monkstown, Tex, Nov 23, 34; m 57. *Educ:* Tex A&M Univ, BS, 63, MS, 66, PhD(zool), 70. *Prof Exp:* Asst biol, Tex A&M Univ, 63-66, instr, 66-70. *Mem:* Am Soc Parasitol. *Res:* Biological control of helminth parasites which cause human disease. *Mailing Add:* 2910 Dogwood Dr Nacogdoches TX 75961

SLAKEY, LINDA LOUISE, BIOCHEMISTRY. *Current Pos:* from asst prof to prof biochem, 73-91, head biochem, 85-91, DEAN, COL NATURAL SCI & MATH, UNIV MASS, 93- *Personal Data:* b Oakland, Calif, Jan 2, 39. *Educ:* Siena Heights Col, BS, 62; Univ Mich, PhD(biochem), 67. *Prof Exp:* Instr chem, St Dominic's Col, 67-69; fel biochem, Univ Wis, 70-73. *Mem:* Tissue Culture Asn; Am Soc Biol Chemists; Am Soc Cell Biol. *Res:* lipid structure and metabolism; interaction of vascular endothelium with blood components; regulation of plasma membrane protein turnover; purinoceptors, extracellular nueleotide metabolism. *Mailing Add:* Col Natural Sci & Math Univ Mass Amherst MA 01003-7110. *Fax:* 413-545-9784

SLAMA, FRANCIS J, CHEMISTRY. *Current Pos:* VPRES TECHNOL, FINISHES UNLIMITED INC, 93- *Personal Data:* b St Louis, Mo, Apr 17, 39; m 63, Patricia Powers; c Mary, Karen, Rebecca & Cristin. *Educ:* St Louis Univ, AB, 62, PhD(chem), 69. *Prof Exp:* Chemist, Commercial Div, Calgon Corp, 62-66; res chemist, Amoco Chem Corp, 69-75, res supvr, 75-84, res assoc, 85-92. *Concurrent Pos:* Instr, Col of DuPage, 70-73; instr, Waybonsee Community Col, 74-93. *Mem:* Am Chem Soc; Fedn Socs Coatings Technol. *Res:* Plastics; polymer structure and properties; motor oil and fuel additives - coatings. *Mailing Add:* 3 Caymen Ct Montgomery IL 60538

SLAMECKA, VLADIMIR, INFORMATION SCIENCE, COMPUTER SCIENCE. *Current Pos:* clin prof, 80-88, EMER PROF MED, EMORY UNIV, 88-; PROF INFO & COMPUT SCI, GA INST TECHNOL, 64- *Personal Data:* b Brno, Czech, May 8, 28; US citizen; m 62, Elba Seoane; c John & Al. *Educ:* Columbia Univ, MS, 58, DLS, 62. *Hon Degrees:* DSc, Bruo Tech univ, 94. *Honors & Awards:* Systs Res Found Award, 86. *Prof Exp:* Chemist, Brookvale Brewery, 52-54; assoc ed, Mid-Europ Press, Inc, 56-57; head chem libr, Columbia Univ, 58-60, proj investr sci orgn, 60-62; mgr info systs design, Documentation, Inc, Md, 62-64. *Concurrent Pos:* NSF grant, Sci Orgn Eastern Europe, 60-62; Fulbright prof, 63-64; consult, NSF, 65- & NIH, 70-; vchmn comt, Int Sci & Technol Prog, Nat Acad Sci, 74-76; chmn, US Nat Comt FID, 74-78; vchmn US Nat Comt, UNESCO/Gen Info Prog, 78-81; USAID grant, Nat Info Syst Egypt, 80-86; consult, Nat Acad Sci, Nat Info Systs Thailand & Indonesia, 89-93, Interu Bank Develop, Nat Info Syst, Costa Rica, 92-94. *Mem:* Fel AAAS; Am Soc Info Sci; Asn Comput Mach; Sigma Xi; NY Acad Sci. *Res:* Information science; national and international information systems. *Mailing Add:* Col Comput Ga Inst Technol Atlanta GA 30332. *Fax:* 404-894-5984; *E-Mail:* vs@cc.gatech.edu

SLANSKY, CYRIL M, CHEMISTRY. *Current Pos:* NUCLEAR CONSULT, 78- *Personal Data:* b Albuquerque, NMex, July 8, 13; m 39; c 3. *Educ:* Col of Idaho, BS, 36; Univ Calif, PhD(chem), 40. *Prof Exp:* Asst chem, Univ Calif, 37-39; res chemist, Dow Chem Co, Mich, 40-44 & Calif, 44-47; chemist, Hanford Works, Gen Elec Co, 47-52; chief, Works Lab, Am Cyanamid Co, 52-53; chem develop, Atomic Energy Div, Phillips Petrol Co, 53, sect head, 53-60, mgr, Chem Develop Br, 60-62, mem staff nuclear & chem tech, 62-66; mem staff nuclear & chem tech, 66-71; sr tech adv, Allied Chem Corp, 71-78, nuclear consult, Chem Progs, 78. *Concurrent Pos:* Mem radioactive waste mgt, Int Atomic Energy Agency, 69-71. *Mem:* AAAS; Am Chem Soc; Am Nuclear Soc; Am Inst Chem Eng. *Res:* Chemistry and technology of inorganic compounds and compounds from calcined dolomite; electrolytic production of magnesium; separations processes; nuclear fuel cycle; radioactive waste disposal; applications of nuclear heat. *Mailing Add:* 2815 Holly Pl Idaho Falls ID 83402-4631

SLANSKY, RICHARD CYRIL, THEORETICAL HIGH ENERGY PHYSICS. *Current Pos:* mem staff, 74-89, DIV DIR, LOS ALAMOS NAT LAB, 89- *Personal Data:* b Oakland, Calif, Apr 3, 40; m 63, 77; c 2. *Educ:* Harvard Univ, BA, 62; Univ Calif, Berkeley, PhD(physics), 67. *Prof Exp:* Res fel physics, Calif Inst Technol, 67-69; from instr to asst prof, Yale Univ, 69-74. *Concurrent Pos:* Adj prof, Univ Calif, Irvine, 85-95. *Mem:* Fel Am Phys Soc; fel AAAS. *Res:* Elementary particle physics. *Mailing Add:* PO Box 804 Tesuque NM 87574. *E-Mail:* vcs@lanl.gov

SLAPIKOFF, SAUL ABRAHAM, BIOCHEMISTRY. *Current Pos:* asst prof, 66-72, ASSOC PROF BIOL, TUFTS UNIV, 72- *Personal Data:* b Bronx, NY, Nov 5, 31; m 75; c 2. *Educ:* Brooklyn Col, BA, 52; Tufts Univ, PhD(biochem), 64. *Prof Exp:* USPHS fel biochem, Sch Med, Stanford Univ, 64-66. *Concurrent Pos:* NRS fel genetic toxicol, 76-77; vis scientist, Mass Inst Technol, 77-78; vis prof , Environ Health Sect, Boston Univ Sch Pub Health, 85. *Mem:* AAAS; Am Chem Soc; Am Pub Health Asn; Sigma Xi; Soc Environ Toxicol & Chem. *Res:* Environmental toxicology. *Mailing Add:* Dept Biol Tufts Univ Medford MA 02155

SLATE, FLOYD OWEN, APPLIED CHEMISTRY, CONCRETE. *Current Pos:* prof eng mat, concrete, low-cost housing, 49-87, EMER PROF ENG MAT, CORNELL UNIV, 87-; CONSULT, 87- *Personal Data:* b Carroll Co, Ind, July 26, 20; m 39, Margaret Magley; c Sally, Sandra & Rex. *Educ:* Purdue Univ, BS, 41, MS, 42, PhD(anal chem), 44. *Honors & Awards:* Wason Medal, Am Concrete Inst, 57, 65, 74 & 84; Anderson Award, Am Concrete Inst, 83. *Prof Exp:* Chemist, Purdue Univ, 41-44, chemist & asst prof hwy eng, 46-49; lab supvr, Manhattan Dist Proj, Columbia Univ, 44; asst chief chemist, Garfield Div, Houdaille-Hershey, Ill, 44-46. *Concurrent Pos:* Adv, Int Coop Admin, Pakistan, 56; vpres res & develop & mem bd, Geotech & Resources, Inc, White Plains, NY, 59-63; consult, Pure Waters Prog, 69-75, & many others, 49-; prin investr, NSF, 59-87; sr fel low-cost housing, E-W Ctr, Univ Hawaii, 76; vis prof, Univ NSW, Australia, 81, Univ Witwatersrand, 83. *Mem:* Am Chem Soc; Am Soc Test & Mat; fel & hon mem Am Concrete Inst; Am Inst Chem; Am Soc Civil Eng. *Res:* Low cost housing; concrete; engineering materials; soils; chemistry applied to engineering problems. *Mailing Add:* Sch Civil Eng Cornell Univ Ithaca NY 14853

SLATER, C STEWART, CHEMICAL ENGINEERING, MEMBRANE TECHNOLOGY. *Current Pos:* PROF & CHAIR CHEM ENG, ROWAN UNIV, 83- *Personal Data:* b Feb 24, 57; US citizen. *Educ:* Rutgers Univ, BS, 79, MS, 82, MPh, 83, PhD(chem eng), 83. *Honors & Awards:* Ralph R Teetor Award, 86; New Eng Educr Award, Am Soc Eng Educ, 87; John Fluke Award, 92; George Westinghouse Award, 96. *Prof Exp:* Process develop engr, Proctor & Gamble Co, Cincinnati, Ohio, 79-81; teaching asst, Dept Chem & Biochem Eng, Rutgers Univ, 81-83. *Concurrent Pos:* Consult, 86- *Mem:* Am Inst Chem Engrs; Sigma Xi; Am Chem Soc; NAm Membrane Soc; Am Soc Eng Educ. *Res:* Membrane process research, modeling and computer simulation; biochemical engineering purification processes; application of engineering processes to industrial and hazardous watewater renovation and reuse systems; separation processes; research and development in pervaporation, reverse osmosis, ultrafiltration, and gas permeation. *Mailing Add:* Dept Chem Eng Rowan Univ Glassboro NJ 08028. *Fax:* 609-256-4950; *E-Mail:* slater@rowan.edu

SLATER, CARL DAVID, ORGANIC CHEMISTRY. *Current Pos:* DEAN, COL ARTS & SCI, WASHBURN UNIV, 90- *Personal Data:* b Moundsville, WVa, Oct 26, 33; m 65, Glenda Richmond; c Keith W & Derek C. *Educ:* WVa Univ, BS, 55; Ohio State Univ, PhD(org chem), 60. *Prof Exp:* Res assoc org chem, Mass Inst Technol, 60-61; proj chemist, Chem Div, Union Carbide Corp, 61-62; from asst prof to assoc prof org chem, NDak State Univ, 62-67; assoc prof org chem, Memphis State Univ, 67-80; prof & chmn dept phys sci, Northern Ky Univ, 80-87, prof, dept chem, 87-90. *Mem:* Am Chem Soc. *Res:* Nuclear magnetic resonance shift correlations. *Mailing Add:* Dept Chem Mich State Univ East Lansing MI 48824. *E-Mail:* zzslat@acc.wuacc.edu

SLATER, DONALD CARLIN, LASER SYSTEM ENGINEERING. *Current Pos:* MGR, ROCKETDYNE, 85- *Personal Data:* b Pensacola, Fla, July 27, 45; m 75, Kathleen; c 1. *Educ:* Stanford Univ, BS, 67; Mass Inst Technol, PhD(physics), 71. *Prof Exp:* Res assoc physics, Stanford Univ, 71-74 & Univ Va, 74-76; res scientist, KMS Fusion, Inc, 76-78, mgr, 79-85. *Mem:* Am Phys Soc. *Res:* High energy laser system design; system engineering. *Mailing Add:* Rocketdyne 6633 Canoga Ave PO Box 7922 Canoga Park CA 91303. *E-Mail:* donald.c.slater@boeing.com

SLATER, EVE ELIZABETH, CARDIOLOGY, ENDOCRINOLOGY. *Current Pos:* EXEC DIR BIOCHEM & MOLECULAR BIOL, MERCK SHARP DOHME RES LABS, 83- *Personal Data:* b W Orange, NJ, May 16, 45; m 81; c 2. *Educ:* Vassar Col, AB, 67; Col Physicians & Surgeons, Columbia Univ, MD, 71. *Prof Exp:* Intern & resident med, Mass Gen Hosp, Boston, 71-73, fel cardiol, 73-75; chief resident med, 76; asst prof, Sch Med, Harvard Univ, 79-83; assoc prof med, Col Physicians & Surgeons, Columbia Univ, 83- *Concurrent Pos:* Estab investr, Am Heart Asn, 80 & mem, Coun High Blood Pressure; consult med, Mass Gen Hosp, Boston, 83- *Mem:* Fel Am Col Cardiol; Chilean Soc Cardiol; Am Soc Biol Chemists; Endocrine Soc; Am Heart Asn. *Res:* Biochemistry of the renin-angiotensin system; mechanism of insulin resistance. *Mailing Add:* 19 Kenilworth Ave Short Hills NJ 07078-1606

SLATER, GARY W, THEORY OF GEL ELECTROPHORESIS OF DNA, THEORY OF POLYMER DYNAMICS. *Current Pos:* assoc prof, 90-96, PROF PHYSICS, UNIV OTTAWA, 96- *Personal Data:* b Ste-Clothilde-de-Horton, Que, Jan 30, 57; m 78, Louise Campagna; c Valerie & Pascale. *Educ:* Univ Sherbrooke, BSc, 78, MSc, 80, PhD(physics), 84. *Prof Exp:* Mem res staff, Xerox Res Ctr Can, 84-90. *Concurrent Pos:* Mem, Grant Selection Comt Condensed Matter Physics, Nat Sci & Eng Res Coun Can, 93-96. *Mem:* Am Phys Soc; Am Chem Soc; Electrophoresis Soc; Can Asn Physicists; Chem Inst Can. *Res:* Theoretical and computer simulation studies of the dynamics of polymers in gels and porous media with application to the separation of nucleic acids and proteins; development of new DNA sequencing methods for the human genome project; statistical mechanics; computer modelling. *Mailing Add:* Dept Physics Univ Ottawa Ottawa ON K1N 6N5 Can. *Fax:* 613-562-5190; *E-Mail:* gary@physics.uottawa.ca

SLATER, GEORGE P, GAS CHROMATOGRAPHY. *Current Pos:* RETIRED. *Personal Data:* b Findochty, Scotland, Mar 11, 30; m 56; c 2. *Educ:* Aberdeen Univ, BSc, 54; Univ Sask, MSc, 57; Queen's Univ, Belfast, PhD(chem), 61. *Prof Exp:* Anal chemist, Swift Canadian Co, 54-55; res asst chem, Univ Sask, 57-58; chemist, Polymer Corp, Can, 58; Nat Res Coun Can fel chem, Univ Sask, 61-62; sr res officer, Nat Res Coun Can, 62- *Mem:* Chem Inst Can. *Res:* Water pollution; analysis of pulp mill effluent; gas chromatography-mass spectroscopy; volatile plant products affecting insect behavior; taste and odor problems in water supplies; biosynthesis of plant lipids. *Mailing Add:* 211 Egbert Ave Saskatoon SK S7N 1X2 Can

SLATER, GRANT GAY, NUTRITION, MEDICAL RESEARCH. *Current Pos:* CONSULT, 82- *Personal Data:* b Rochester, NY, Jan 6, 18; m 48, Roslyn B Alfin; c Robert & Joanne (Catani). *Educ:* Univ Miami, BS, 40, Univ Southern Calif, MS, 50, PhD(biochem), 54. *Prof Exp:* Lab dir, Chem Warefare Lab, Alaska, 43-44; biochemist, Res Inst, Cedars Lebanon Hosp, Los Angeles, 54-55; res physiol chemist, Univ Calif, Los Angeles, 55-58; res specialist, State Dept Ment Hyg, 58-61; biochemist, Vet Admin Ctr, 61-68; res biochemist, Gateways Hosp, 68-72; researcher I, Div Environ & Nutrit Sci, Sch Pub Health & Dept Psychiat, Med Sch, Univ Calif, 72-82. *Concurrent Pos:* Vis instr, Univ Southern Calif, 55-57, vis asst prof, 58-59; mem fac, Dept Psychiat, Univ Calif, Los Angeles, 58-88 & Brain Res Inst, 61-68; study grants, Anti-trypsin in Lung Dis from Air Pollution, Div Lung Dis, NIH, 74-75. *Mem:* Emer mem Am Chem Soc; emer mem Am Inst Chem; emer mem Am Physiol Soc; emer mem Endocrine Soc; emer mem Soc Neurosci; emer mem Electrophoresis Soc; emer mem Am Oil Chemists; Sigma Xi. *Res:*

Basic methodological research on plasma proteins and studies on the relationship of plasma proteins in humans to lung and brain disease; nutritional studies relating dietary and plasma cholesterol in humans; design of medical equipment. *Mailing Add:* 986 Somera Rd Los Angeles CA 90077-2624

SLATER, JAMES ALEXANDER, ENTOMOLOGY, SYSTEMATICS. *Current Pos:* RETIRED. *Personal Data:* b Belvidere, Ill, Jan 10, 20; m 43, Elizabeth Thackston; c James Alexander II, Jacqueline Rae (Neil-Boss), Samuel Thackston & Lydia Ann (Grzywa). *Educ:* Univ Ill, BA, 42, MS, 47; Iowa State Col, PhD(entom), 50. *Honors & Awards:* Harriet Merrifield Forbes Award, Asn Gravestone Studies, 82; L D Howard Award, Entom Soc Am, 85, Thomas Say Award, 96, Founders Mem Aw ard, 96. *Prof Exp:* From instr to prof entom, Univ Conn, 50-88, head dept zool, entom & biochem, 64-67, head systs & evolutionary biol sect, 70-80. *Concurrent Pos:* Comnr, Conn Geol & Natural Hist Surv & state ornithologist, 63-72; panelist, Sci Div, NSF, 63-66; res assoc, Nat Insect Col Pretoria, SAfrica, 67-68, Am Mus Natural Hist, 76- *Mem:* Entom Soc Am; Soc Syst Zool (pres, 81-83); Royal Entom Soc; SAfrican Entom Soc; Asn Gravestone Studies (vpres, 88-95). *Res:* Systematics and bionomics of Hemiptera, Lygaeidae and Miridae. *Mailing Add:* Dept Ecol Evolutionary Biol Life Sci U-43 Storrs CT 06268

SLATER, JAMES LOUIS, INORGANIC CHEMISTRY. *Current Pos:* asst prof inorg chem, 74-77, ASST PROF CHEM, COL STEUBENVILLE, 77- *Personal Data:* b Grand Rapids, Mich, Dec 2, 44; c 2. *Educ:* Mich State Univ, BS, 67; Fla State Univ, PhD(inorg chem), 71. *Prof Exp:* Fel inorg chem, Ames Lab, US AEC, Iowa State Univ, 71-73; instr inorg chem, Univ Va, 73-74. *Mem:* Am Chem Soc. *Res:* Chemical studies of the metal carbonyls. *Mailing Add:* Dept Chem Franciscan Univ Steubenville OH 43952

SLATER, JAMES MUNRO, RADIOTHERAPY. *Current Pos:* Instr radiother, 67-68, asst clin prof radiol radiother, 68-70, from asst prof to assoc prof, 70-74, PROF RADIOL RADIOTHER, SCH MED, LOMA LINDA UNIV, 75- *Personal Data:* b Salt Lake City, Utah, Jan 7, 29; m 48; c 5. *Educ:* Univ Utah & Utah State, BS, 54; Sch Med, Loma Linda Univ, MD, 63. *Honors & Awards:* Physician's Recognition Award, AMA, 69, 72 & 75. *Concurrent Pos:* Fel, White Mem Med Ctr, 67-68 & Univ Tex, M D Anderson Hosp & Tumor Inst, 68-69; dir radiation oncol, Sch Med, Loma Linda Univ, 70-, dir nuclear med, 75-; interim chmn dept radiol sci, 78-; mem prof educ comt, Am Cancer Soc, 75-76, chmn, 76-77, vpres, 78-79. *Mem:* Am Soc Therapeut Radiologists; Am Soc Clin Oncol; AAAS; Am Cancer Soc; Am Radium Soc. *Res:* Cancer immunology, emphasizing the effect of ionizing radiation on the human immune system; computerized dosimetry for radiation therapy planning; treatment of malignant disease using ionizing irradiation. *Mailing Add:* Dept Radiation Sci 11234 Anderson St Rm MC B121 Loma Linda CA 92354

SLATER, KEITH, TEXTILES. *Current Pos:* from asst prof to assoc prof, 65-75, PROF TEXTILES, UNIV GUELPH, 75-, ACAD DIR, PARIS SEMESTER, 90- *Personal Data:* b Oldham, Eng, Dec 20, 35; m 59, Rosalind Hampson; c Diane L, Hilary D & Keirsten F. *Educ:* Univ Leeds, BSc, 56, MSc, 58, PhD(textiles), 65. *Prof Exp:* Asst master, Leeds Cent High Sch, Eng, 60-65. *Concurrent Pos:* Nat Res Coun grant, Univ Guelph, 66-, Defence Res Bd grant, 68-; consult, Wool Bur Can, 69-70, Hart Chem Ltd, 69-71, Harding Carpets Ltd, 70-78, Johnson & Johnson, 80-82 & ISKA, 84-85; vis fel, Gonville & Caius Col, Cambridge, UK, 83-84; vis prof, Eng Dept, Cambridge Univ, UK, 83-84; vis fel, Clare Hall, Cambridge, UK, 90-91; life mem, Can Auth Asn, 93-, pres, Waterloo-Wellington Br, 94-97. *Mem:* Fel Textile Inst (vpres, 74-78); Textile Fedn Can (pres, 79-81). *Res:* Yarn irregularity; yarn hairiness; acoustic properties of textiles; comfort of textiles; textile drying behavior; progressive deterioration of textiles; design of surgical operating theater gowns; design of clothing for severe climates; social consequences of technological abuse. *Mailing Add:* Sch Eng Univ Guelph Guelph ON N1G 2W1 Can. *Fax:* 519-836-0227; *E-Mail:* slaterk@net.2.eos.uoguelph.ca

SLATER, PETER JOHN, MATHEMATICS, OPERATIONS RESEARCH. *Current Pos:* ASSOC PROF MATH, UNIV ALA, 81- *Personal Data:* b Mt Vernon, NY, Sept 30, 46; m 70. *Educ:* Iona Col, BS, 68; Univ Iowa, MS, 72, PhD(math), 73. *Prof Exp:* Asst prof math, Cleveland State Univ, 74; res assoc, Nat Bur Stand, 74-75; mathematician, Sandia Labs, 75-81. *Mem:* Am Math Soc; Opers Res Soc Am. *Res:* The field of graph theory with particular emphasis on problems of N-connectivity, geodesics and facility location; network modelling of facilities. *Mailing Add:* 801 Cornelia Dr SE Huntsville AL 35802

SLATER, RICHARD CRAIG, PHYSICAL CHEMISTRY. *Current Pos:* RES SCIENTIST, AVCO EVERETT RES LAB, 76- *Personal Data:* b Jersey City, NJ, Nov 16, 46; m 73; c 1. *Educ:* Stevens Inst Technol, BS, 68; Columbia Univ, PhD(chem), 73. *Prof Exp:* Fel chem, Dept Chem, Columbia Univ, 73-76. *Mem:* Am Chem Soc; Am Phys Soc; Sigma Xi. *Res:* Laser applications in chemistry; chemical kinetics; vibrational energy transfer. *Mailing Add:* 37 Wyman St Waban MA 02168-1516

SLATER, SCHUYLER G, ORGANIC CHEMISTRY, NATURAL PRODUCTS CHEMISTRY. *Current Pos:* PROF CHEM, SALEM STATE COL, 56-, CHMN DEPT, 80- *Personal Data:* b New Haven, Conn, Feb 22, 23. *Educ:* Univ Conn, BS, 44, MS, 47; Boston Univ, EdD(sci educ), 65. *Prof Exp:* Instr chem, Univ Conn, 46-49; instr sci, Boston Univ, 50-54 & Cent Conn State Col, 54-55; assoc prof, Univ Maine, 54-56. *Concurrent Pos:* Observer, Brit Open Univ, 71-72. *Mem:* Am Chem Soc. *Res:* Curriculum development. *Mailing Add:* PO Box 689 Charlestown RI 02813-0689

SLATER, WILLIAM E, EXPERIMENTAL HIGH ENERGY PHYSICS. *Current Pos:* Fel, 60-62, from asst prof to assoc prof, 62-73, PROF PHYSICS, UNIV CALIF, LOS ANGELES, 73- *Personal Data:* b Springfield, Ohio, July 16, 31; m 58. *Mem:* Am Phys Soc. *Res:* Track chamber and counter experiments. *Mailing Add:* Dept Physics & Astron Univ Calif Knudsen Hall 405 Hilgard Ave Los Angeles CA 90095

SLATES, HARRY LOVELL, ORGANIC CHEMISTRY. *Current Pos:* RETIRED. *Personal Data:* b Canton, Ohio, Feb 7, 23; m 51; c 1. *Educ:* Mt Union Col, BSc, 44; Ohio State Univ, MSc, 48. *Prof Exp:* Chemist qual control, Goodyear Tire & Rubber Co, 45; asst chem, Ohio State Univ, 47-48; sr res chemist, Merck & Co, Inc, 48-89. *Mem:* AAAS; Am Chem Soc; Am Inst Chem; Royal Soc Chem; Swiss Chem Soc. *Res:* Steroid sapogenins; organic synthesis and structure determination. *Mailing Add:* 601 S Chestnut St Westfield NJ 07090

SLATKIN, DANIEL NATHAN, PATHOLOGY. *Current Pos:* GUEST SCIENTIST, MED DEPT, BROOKHAVEN NAT LAB, 97- *Personal Data:* b Montreal, Que, Aug 5, 34; US citizen. *Educ:* McGill Univ, BSc, 55, MD, 59. *Prof Exp:* Intern, Mt Sinai Hosp, New York, 59-60; res assoc med, Brookhaven Nat Lab, 60-61; resident path, Montefiore Hosp, New York, 61-63 & neuropath, 63-64; resident pediat path, Presby Hosp, New York, 64-65; registr morbid anat, Hammersmith Hosp, London, Eng, 65-66; Anna Fuller Found fel biochem, Inst Sci Res Cancer, Villejuif, France, 66-67; assoc pathologist, McKellar Gen Hosp, Ft William, Ont, 68-69; from instr to asst prof path, State Univ NY, Stony Brook, 69-83; cons path, Vet Admin Hosp, Northport, NY, 72-89; pathologist & scientist, Brookhaven Nat Lab, 72-96. *Concurrent Pos:* Consult, Inst Path, Univ Bern, Switz, 96-; res independent consult radiation risk, 96- *Res:* Experimental neutron-captive therapy; experimental microbeam radiation therapy. *Mailing Add:* 2415 Long Creek Dr Southold NY 11971-5313. *E-Mail:* dslatkin@bnl.gov

SLATKIN, MONTGOMERY (WILSON), EVOLUTIONARY BIOLOGY. *Current Pos:* assoc prof zool, 77-85, PROF INTEGRATIVE BIOL, UNIV WASH, 85- *Personal Data:* b Toronto, Ont, June 29, 45; US citizen. *Educ:* Mass Inst Technol, SB, 66; Harvard Univ, PhD(appl math), 70. *Prof Exp:* Res assoc biol, Univ Chicago, 70-71; asst prof theoret biol, biophys & biol, 71-76, assoc prof, 76-77. *Concurrent Pos:* Vis staff mem, Los Alamos Sci Labs, 70- *Res:* Mathematical population genetics and population ecology. *Mailing Add:* Dept Integrated Biol Univ Calif Berkeley CA 94720-3140

SLATON, JACK H(AMILTON), design electronic & underwater acoustic systems, for more information see previous edition

SLATOPOLSKY, EDUARDO, VITAMIN D METABOLISM, RENAL OSTEODYSTROPHY. *Current Pos:* Postdoctoral renal, USPHS, Renal Div, Dept Int Med, Wash Univ Sch Med, 63-65, instr med nephrol, 65-67, from asst prof to assoc prof med, Dept Nephrol, 67-75, dir, Chromalloy Am Kidney Ctr, 67-, CO-DIR RENAL DIV, WASH UNIV SCH MED, 72-, PROF MED, NEPHROL DEPT, 75-, JOSEPH FRIEDMAN PROF RENAL DIS MED, 91- *Personal Data:* b Buenos Aires, Arg, Dec 12, 34; US citizen; m 59; c 3. *Educ:* Nat Col Nicolas Avellaneda, BS, 52; Univ Buenos Aires, Arg, MD, 59. *Honors & Awards:* Frederick C Bartter Award, 91. *Concurrent Pos:* Adv mem, regional med prog, renal prog, 70-75; chmn, Transplantation Comt, Barne Hosp, 75-, fel comt, Kidney Found Eastern Mo & Metro-East, 78; adv comt mem, Artificial Kidney-Chronic Uremia Prog, NIH, 78-90; rep, Latin-Am Nephrol, 83-88; mem, Study Sect Gen Med, NIH, 84-88. *Mem:* Am Fedn Clin Res; Int Soc Nephrol; Am Soc Nephrol; AAAS; Sigma Xi; Endocrine Soc. *Res:* Pathogenesis and treatment of secondary hyperparathyroidism and bone disease in renal failure; studies are conducted at both levels: clinical, on patients maintained on chronic dialysis and on animals with experimentally induced renal failure; effects of calcitriol on PTH MRNA and the extra-renal production of calcitriol by macrophages are studies in great detail; vitro studies in primary culture of bovine parathyroid cells are used to understand the mechanisms that control the secretion of PTH. *Mailing Add:* Wash Univ Barnes Hosp St Louis MO 63110. *Fax:* 314-362-7875

SLATTERY, CHARLES WILBUR, PHYSICAL CHEMISTRY. *Current Pos:* from asst prof to assoc prof, 70-78, PROF BIOCHEM, SCH MED, LOMA LINDA UNIV, 78-, PROF PEDIAT, 80-, DEPT CHMN, 83- *Personal Data:* b LaJunta, Colo, Nov 18, 37; m 58, Arline S Reile; c Scott & Coleen. *Educ:* Union Col, Nebr, BA, 59; Univ Nebr, MS, 61, PhD(phys chem), 65. *Prof Exp:* From asst prof to assoc prof chem, Atlantic Union Col, 63-69; res assoc, Mass Inst Technol, 69-70. *Concurrent Pos:* Prin investr, NIH Grants, 78-81 & 86-89. *Mem:* Sigma Xi; Am Soc Biochem & Molecular Biol; AAAS; Am Chem Soc; Am Heart Asn; Protein Soc. *Res:* Ultracentrifuge theory with computer application to the problem of sedimentation in multicomponent systems; physical chemistry of macromolecules, principally on the structure and interactions of the bovine and human caseins; enzyme complexes in blood coagulation. *Mailing Add:* Dept Biochem Loma Linda Univ Sch Med Loma Linda CA 92350. *Fax:* 909-824-4887; *E-Mail:* CSlattery@ccmail.llu.edu

SLATTERY, JOHN C, CHEMICAL ENGINEERING. *Current Pos:* From asst prof to assoc prof, 59-67, PROF CHEM ENG, NORTHWESTERN UNIV, EVANSTON, 67- *Personal Data:* b St Louis, Mo, July 20, 32; m 56; c 5. *Educ:* Washington Univ, St Louis, BS, 54; Univ Wis, MS, 55, PhD(chem eng), 59. *Mem:* Am Inst Chem Engrs; Soc Rheol; Am Chem Soc; Soc Natural Philos. *Res:* Interfacial phenomena; multiphase flows; fluid mechanics; continuum mechanics. *Mailing Add:* Dept Chem Eng Tex A&M Univ MS 3122 College Station TX 77843-3122

SLATTERY, LOUIS R, SURGERY. *Current Pos:* PROF CLIN SURG, MED CTR, NY UNIV, 50- *Personal Data:* b Ft Leavenworth, Kans, Oct 16, 08; m 44; c 2. *Educ:* Columbia Univ, AB, 29, MD, 33; Am Bd Surg, dipl, 40. *Concurrent Pos:* Consult, Inst Rehab & Phys Med, 48- & St Francis Hosp, Port Jervis, 50-; vis surgeon, Bellevue Univ & Doctors Hosps, 50-; consult surgeon, Lenox Hill Hosp, 68 & Vet Admin Hosp, 68. *Mem:* AMA; Am Col Surg. *Mailing Add:* 536 First Ave New York NY 10016-6402

SLATTERY, PAUL FRANCIS, EXPERIMENTAL HIGH ENERGY PHYSICS. *Current Pos:* Atomic Energy Comn fel, 67-69, from asst prof to assoc prof, 69-78, PROF PHYSICS, UNIV ROCHESTER, 78-, CHAIR, DEPT PHYSICS & ASTRON, 86- *Personal Data:* b Hartford, Conn, July 21, 40; m 64, Jean Breitenbach; c Ryan L. *Educ:* Univ Notre Dame, BS, 62; Yale Univ, MS, 63, PhD(physics), 67. *Honors & Awards:* Leigh Page Mem Prize, 63. *Concurrent Pos:* Sci spokesperson, Fermilab Exp E706, 81-; regional rep, Fermilab Bd Overseers, 89-; Guggenheim Mem Found fel, 92-93. *Mem:* Fel Am Phys Soc. *Res:* Experimental high energy physics; study of hadron induced reactions via electronic techniques. *Mailing Add:* Dept Physics & Astron Univ Rochester Rochester NY 14627. *Fax:* 716-275-8527; *E-Mail:* slattery@urhep.pas.rochester.edu

SLAUGH, LYNN H, CHEMISTRY. *Current Pos:* STAFF, SHELL DEVELOP CO, HOUSTON. *Personal Data:* b Apr 9, 31. *Educ:* Brigham Young Univ, BS, 52; Univ Wash, Seattle, PhD, 56. *Honors & Awards:* Indust Chem Award, Am Chem Soc, 95. *Res:* Granted 132 patents; inventor of two industrial processes; contributed to professional journals. *Mailing Add:* Shell Chem Co PO Box 1380 Houston TX 77251-1380

SLAUGHTER, CHARLES D, SYSTEMS DESIGN & SYSTEMS SCIENCE. *Current Pos:* AT UNIFORTH SYSTS. *Personal Data:* B Kansas City, Kans, Jan 23, 36; m 75; c 3. *Educ:* Northern Ariz Univ, BS, 58. *Prof Exp:* Res asst astron, Kitt Peak Nat Observ, 59-65, res assoc, 65-66, sr res assoc, 67-75; sr sci programmer astron, NOAO, 76-80, chief programmer, 81-84; software systs engr, Photometrics, 85-86, mgr systs eng, 87-89, mgr div eng, 90. *Concurrent Pos:* Pres, Uniforth Systs Inc, 84-91. *Mem:* Inst Elec & Electronic Engrs. *Res:* Imaging software for scientific CCD camera control systems, real-time process control and instrumentation control software. *Mailing Add:* Uniforth Systs Inc 2626 N Grannen Rd Tucson AZ 85745

SLAUGHTER, CHARLES WESLEY, FOREST HYDROLOGY. *Current Pos:* Res hydrologist, US Army Cold Regions Res & Eng Lab, 68-76, PRIN WATERSHED SCIENTIST, INST NORTHERN FORESTRY, US FOREST SERV, 76- *Personal Data:* b Baker, Ore, Oct 28, 41; m 62; c 3. *Educ:* Wash State Univ, BS, 62; Colo State Univ, PhD(watershed mgt), 68. *Concurrent Pos:* Adj assoc prof, Univ Alaska, 69-76 & adj prof water resources, 76-; chmn, Res Coord Subcomt, Inter-Agency Tech Comt, Alaska, 69-; chmn, Arctic Directorate, US-MAB, 81-89; Fulbright res fel, Iceland, 85. *Mem:* Soc Am Foresters; Soil Conserv Soc Am; Am Geophys Union; Am Water Resources Asn. *Res:* Wildland and snow hydrology; watershed management; permafrost hydrology; sustainable development and conservation. *Mailing Add:* 869 Landon Lane Fairbanks AK 99712

SLAUGHTER, FRANK GILL, JR, MATHEMATICS. *Current Pos:* Asst prof, 66-70, ASSOC PROF MATH & STATIST, UNIV PITTSBURGH, 71- *Personal Data:* b Jacksonville, Fla, May 15, 40; m 59; c 2. *Educ:* Harvard Univ, BA, 61; Duke Univ, PhD(math), 66. *Mem:* Am Math Soc; Math Asn Am. *Res:* General topology; generalizations of metric spaces. *Mailing Add:* 608 Dorseyville Rd Pittsburgh PA 15238

SLAUGHTER, GERALD M, WELDING & INSPECTION, CORROSION. *Current Pos:* CONSULT, 93- *Personal Data:* b Ilion, NY, June 8, 28; m 53; c 2. *Educ:* Rensselaer Polytech Inst, BS, 49, MS, 51. *Honors & Awards:* Wasserman Award, Am Welding Soc, 78, McKay-Helm Award & Adams Lectr, 79. *Prof Exp:* Res fel mat, Rensselaer Polytech Inst, 49-51; develop eng mat, Oak Ridge Nat Lab, Union Carbide, 51-63, group leader, 63-76, sect mgr mat, Oak Ridge Nat Lab, Martin Marietta, 76-93. *Concurrent Pos:* Chmn, Brazing & Soldering Comn, Am Welding Soc, 74-77, joint comt, Am Soc Testing Mat, Am Soc Mech Eng & Mat Properties Coun, 81-86; tech div bd, Am Soc Metals Int, 81, 84; bd trustees, Am Soc Metals Int, 84-87, Fedn Mat Soc, 87- *Mem:* Fel Am Soc Mat Int; fel Am Soc Nondestructive Testing; fel Am Welding Soc; Fedn Mat Sci; Am Soc Testing Mat. *Res:* Energy producing and energy conserving concepts; clean fossil fuel; fusion; solar and advanced heat engines; nondestructive testing; metal processing; corrosion. *Mailing Add:* 123 Mason Lane Oak Ridge TN 37830

SLAUGHTER, JOHN BROOKS, COMPUTER SCIENCES. *Current Pos:* PRES, OCCIDENTAL COL, 88- *Personal Data:* b Topeka, Kans, Mar 16, 34; m 56; c 2. *Educ:* Kans State Univ, BS, 56; Univ Calif, Los Angeles, MS, 61; Univ Calif, San Diego, PhD(eng sci), 71. *Hon Degrees:* Numerous from US Univs, 81-92. *Honors & Awards:* Louis Clark Vanaxem Lectr, Princeton Univ, 83; David Dodds Henry Lectr, Univ Ill, 85; Croft Lectr, Univ Mo, Columbia, 85. *Prof Exp:* Engr simulation, Convair Div, Gen Dynamics Corp, 56-60; phys sci admin info systs, Naval Electronics Lab Ctr, 60-75; dir, Appl Physics Lab, Univ Wash, 75-77; asst dir, NSF, 77-79, dir, 80-82; acad vpres & provost, Wash State Univ, 79-80; chancellor, Univ Md, College Park, 82-88. *Concurrent Pos:* Instr eng, Calif Western Univ, 61-63 & UCLA, 63; lectr, San Diego State Univ, 64-66; fel, Naval Electronics Lab Ctr, 69; ed, J Comput & Elec Eng Pergamon Press, 72-; elected bd dirs, Am Cancer Soc, 74; chair, Minority Comt, Inst Elec & Electronics Engrs, 76-80, Gov Task Force Teen Pregnancy, Md, 84-85, Prince George's Co Pub Schs Adv Coun, 85-86 & Pres Comn, Nat Col Athletics Asn, 86-88; mem, Nat Medal Sci Bd, 79-81, Nat Sci Bd, 80-83, Bd Dirs Md State Chamber Com, 83-88, Prince George's Chamber Com, 84-88 & Prince George's Co Econ Develop Corp, 84-88. *Mem:* Nat Acad Eng; fel AAAS; fel Inst Elec & Electronics Engrs; fel Am Acad Arts & Sci. *Res:* Development of computer algorithms for system optimization and discrete signal processing with emphasis on application to ocean and environmental system problems; author of 15 publications. *Mailing Add:* Occidental Col Pres Off 1600 Campus Rd Los Angeles CA 90041

SLAUGHTER, JOHN SIM, PSYCHOPHYSIOLOGY, EXPERIMENTAL PSYCHOLOGY. *Current Pos:* asst prof, 71-76, ASSOC PROF PSYCHOL, STATE UNIV NY COL, FREDONIA, 76- *Personal Data:* b Muskagee, Okla, Aug 2, 43; m 73, Margo Fitzgerald; c Jamie & Carly. *Educ:* Lynchburg Col, BA, 67; Univ Denver, MA, 70, PhD(exp psychol), 71. *Prof Exp:* Instr psychol, Lynchburg Col, 67-68; res asst, Univ Denver, 68-71; instr, Fitzsimmons Army Hosp, 69-70. *Concurrent Pos:* Res grants, State Univ NY, 72-74. *Mem:* Am Psychol Asn; Soc Psychophysiol Res. *Res:* Role of peripheral autonomic responses in determining emotional development; computer applications for improving classsroom teachig including simulations, data collection and data analysis. *Mailing Add:* Dept Psychol State Univ NY Col Fredonia Fredonia NY 14063-1198

SLAUGHTER, LYNNARD J, COMPARATIVE PATHOLOGY. *Current Pos:* ASSOC PROF PATH, HOWARD UNIV, 81- *Personal Data:* b Pittsburgh, Pa, Apr 28, 38. *Educ:* Tuskegee Univ, DVM, 65. *Mailing Add:* Dept Path Col Howard Univ Col Med 520 W St NW Washington DC 20001-2337

SLAUGHTER, MAYNARD, CRYSTALLOGRAPHY. *Current Pos:* PROF GEOCHEM, COLO SCH MINES, 69- *Personal Data:* b Athens, Ohio, Jan 13, 34; m 53; c 5. *Educ:* Ohio Univ, BS, 55; Univ Mo-Columbia, AM, 57; Univ Pittsburgh, PhD, 62. *Prof Exp:* Chem mineralogist, Gulf Res & Develop Co, 57-60; from asst prof to prof geochem, Univ Mo-Columbia, 60-69. *Concurrent Pos:* Chief scientist, Crystal Res Lab, Golden, Colo. *Mem:* Fel Mineral Soc Am; Am Crystallog Asn; Geol Soc Am; Clay Mineral Soc. *Res:* Crystalline structure of minerals; clay mineralogy; methods of rock analysis; theoretical mineralogy. *Mailing Add:* 303 Lookout View Ct Golden CO 80401

SLAUGHTER, MILTON DEAN, THEORETICAL ELEMENTARY PARTICLE PHYSICS. *Current Pos:* CHMN & PROF PHYSICS, UNIV NEW ORLEANS, 89- *Personal Data:* b New Orleans, La, June 9, 44; m 67; c 3. *Educ:* Univ New Orleans, BS, 71, PhD(physics), 74. *Prof Exp:* Postdoctoral particle physics, Univ Md, College Park, 74-76; postdoctoral particle physics, Los Alamos Nat Lab, 76-77, staff mem detonation theory, 77-81, asst div leader, Theory Div, 81-87, staff mem particle physics, 87-89. *Concurrent Pos:* Vis assoc prof physics, Univ Md, College Park, 84-85; tech exec officer, Nat Soc Black Physicists, 84-90. *Mem:* Am Phys Soc. *Res:* Development of the algebraic approach to hadrons and glueballs; vector meson to pseudoscalar radiative and pionic transitions and mass splittings; theoretical description of the radiative decays of baryons, mesons and glueballs. *Mailing Add:* 2208 Loen C Simon Dr New Orleans LA 70122

SLAUNWHITE, WILSON ROY, JR, BIOCHEMISTRY. *Current Pos:* RETIRED. *Personal Data:* b Waltham, Mass, Sept 25, 19; m 42; c 4. *Educ:* Mass Inst Technol, BS & MS, 42, PhD(org chem), 48. *Prof Exp:* Res assoc, Radiation Lab, Mass Inst Technol, 42-45 & Naval Res Lab, 45-46; res fel med, Mass Gen Hosp, 48-52; Damon Runyon fel, Med Sch, Univ Utah, 52-53; sr cancer res scientist, Roswell Park Mem Inst, 53-55, assoc scientist cancer res, 55-60, prin cancer res scientist, 60-67; res dir, Med Found Buffalo, 67-69; dir endocrine labs, Childrens Hosp, 69-73; assoc res prof pediat, State Univ NY Buffalo, 70-84, prof biochem, 70-89, adj assoc prof med technol, 85-89. *Concurrent Pos:* From asst res prof to assoc res prof biochem, State Univ NY Buffalo, 56-63, res prof, Roswell Park Grad Div, 63-70, chmn dept, 63-67; consult, Med Found Buffalo, 58-67; ed, Steroids, 64- & J Clin Endocrinol & Metab, Endocrine Soc, 68-70; consult, Roswell Park Mem Inst, 70-89. *Mem:* Endocrine Soc; Am Soc Biol Chem. *Res:* Steroid and thyroid endocrinology; glycoprotein structure. *Mailing Add:* 27243 N 71st Pl Cave Creek AZ 85331-6937

SLAUTTERBACK, DAVID BUELL, CELL BIOLOGY. *Current Pos:* from asst prof to assoc prof, 59-67, chmn dept, 67-83, PROF ANAT, MED SCH, UNIV WIS-MADISON, 67- *Personal Data:* b Indianapolis, Ind, July 15, 26; m 52, Marilyn Clarke; c Sarah, Catherine, Dan & Peter. *Educ:* Univ Mich, BS, 48, MS, 49; Cornell Univ, PhD(anat), 52. *Prof Exp:* Instr anat, Med Sch, NY Univ, 54-55; instr, Med Col, Cornell Univ, 55-59. *Concurrent Pos:* Am Cancer Soc res fel, Med Sch, NY Univ, 52-54; Nat Cancer Inst fel, 54-55. *Mem:* AAAS; Am Soc Cell Biol; Am Asn Anatomists. *Res:* Integral and peripheral membrane proteins; smooth endoplasmic reticulum; immunocytochemistry of muscle proteins. *Mailing Add:* Dept Anat Univ Wis 1300 University Ave Madison WI 53706-1532. *Fax:* 608-262-7306; *E-Mail:* dbslautt@macc.wisc.edu

SLAVEN, ROBERT WALTER, ORGANIC CHEMISTRY, ANALYTICAL CHEMISTRY. *Current Pos:* sr chemist, 84-95, MGR ANAL CHEM/D+C DIV, CIBA GEIGY, 85- *Personal Data:* b Salem, Mass, Mar 8, 48; m 69; c 2. *Educ:* Univ Lowell, BSc, 69; Univ Wis, PhD(org chem), 74. *Prof Exp:* Fel, Northeastern Univ, 74-76; res chemist org chem, Lorillard Res Ctr, 76-84. *Mem:* Am Chem Soc; Sigma Xi. *Res:* Nuclear magnetic resonance; structure elucidation. *Mailing Add:* 16018 Malvern Hill Ave Baton Rouge LA 70817

SLAVIK, MILAN, CLINICAL PHARMACOLOGY. *Current Pos:* PROF MED, DIV CLIN ONCOL, UNIV KANS MED CTR & MED ONCOL SECT, VET ADMIN MED CTR, 83- *Personal Data:* b Kosice, Czech, May 18, 30; m; c 1. *Educ:* Charles Univ, Prague, MD, 60; Czech Acad Sci, PhD(pharmacol), 69; Bd Internal Med, cert internal med, 63. *Prof Exp:* Instr Clin Internal Dis, Charles Univ, Prague, 59-60; intern & resident, Dept Internal Med, Inst Nat Health, Melnik, 60-63, internist, 63-66; asst prof, Charles Univ, 67-69; clin pharmacologist, Inst Pharmacol, Czech Acad Sci, 68-69; spec asst to chief, Cancer Ther Eval Br, Nat Cancer Inst, NIH, 71-73, from actg chief to chief, 73-76; vis asst prof, Georgetown Univ, 76-77, asst prof, 77-78; prof med & pharmacol, Univ NMex, 78-83. *Concurrent Pos:* Chief, Invest Drug Br, Cancer Ther Eval Prog, DCT, Nat Cancer Inst, 74-76; consult physician, Med Oncol Br, NCI & Vet Admin, 73-75; consult fac mem, Inst Clin Toxicol, 73-; mem, chemother subcomt, NCI, 75-79, Ref Panel Am Hosp Formulary Serv, Am Soc Hosp Planning, 75-83, US Japan Coop Res Prog, 76-82, adv comt amino acid analog & depleting enzymes, NCI, 78-82, assoc mem, Southwest Oncol Group, 78-80, mem, 80-, Clin Res Ctr adv comt & chief clin pharmacol & exp therapeut, Cancer Res & Treatment Ctr, Univ NMex, 78-83, hemat & oncol vertical comt, 79-83; adj prof obstet & gynecol, Jefferson Med Col, Thomas Jefferson Univ, 79; consult physician, Vet Admin Med Ctr, 81-83; courtesy prof pharmaceut chem, Col Pharm, Univ Kans & staff physician, Med Serv, Vet Admin Med Ctr, 83-; mem res & develop comt, Vet Admin Med Ctr, 84-85, 89-, cancer res fel rev comt, Ladies Auxillary Vet Foreign War US, 85- *Mem:* Am Asn Cancer Res; Am Soc Clin Oncol; Am Soc Pharmacol & Exp Therapeut; Am Fedn Clin Res; Am Soc Clin Toxicol; Int Asn Study Lung Cancer; Czech Med Soc; Czech Soc Arts & Sci; Int Soc Chronobiol; Sigma Xi. *Res:* Clinical pharmacology and therapeutics; medical oncology; skin and connective tissue diseases. *Mailing Add:* Vet Admin Hosp 5500 E Kellogg Wichita KS 67218-1698

SLAVIK, NELSON SIGMAN, BIOLOGICAL SAFETY, OCCUPATIONAL HEALTH & SAFETY. *Current Pos:* PRES, ENVIRON HEALTH MGT SYSTS INC, 85- *Personal Data:* b St Louis, Mo, Feb 28, 48; m 70. *Educ:* Kalamazoo Col, BA, 70; Univ Ill, Urbana, MS, 72, PhD(microbiol), 75. *Prof Exp:* Res assoc plant tissue cult, Univ Ill, Urbana, 75-77, biol safety officer, 77-85, asst prof, Occup Health & Safety, 81-85. *Concurrent Pos:* Asst dir, Div Environ Health & Safety, Univ Ill, Urbana, 78-81. *Mem:* Sigma Xi. *Mailing Add:* 2617 Korn St Niles MI 49120-9325

SLAVIN, ANDREI NICKOLAY, MAGNETISM, NONLINEAR DYNAMICS. *Current Pos:* asst prof, 91-94, ASSOC PROF PHYSICS, OAKLAND UNIV, 94- *Personal Data:* b St Petersburg, Russia, Aug 19, 51; m 83, Olga Afanassieva; c Jana & Dimitry. *Educ:* St Petersburg Tech Univ, Russia, MS, 74, PhD(physics), 77. *Prof Exp:* From asst prof to assoc prof physics, St Petersburg Marine Tech Univ, Russia, 77-90; sr vis fel, Univ Western Ont, London, 90-91. *Concurrent Pos:* Vis scientist, Univ Helsinki, Finland, 85-86; vis prof, Wolverhampton Univ, Eng, 89, Inst Solid State Electronics, Rome 92, St Petersburg Elec Eng Univ, 93 & Tech Univ Darmstadt, Ger, 95-96. *Mem:* Am Phys Soc; Am Asn Univ Profs. *Res:* Spin wave solitons in magnetic films; spin wave instabilities; magnetic excitations in finite-size magnetic samples, multilayers and superlattices; Brillouin light scattering from magnetic excitations; microwave magnetics. *Mailing Add:* Physics Dept Oakland Univ Rochester MI 48309. *Fax:* 248-370-3408; *E-Mail:* slavin@vela.acs.oakland.edu

SLAVIN, BERNARD GEOFFREY, ANATOMY & ULTRASTRUCTURE, IMMUNOCYTOCHEMISTRY & MOLECULAR BIOLOGY. *Current Pos:* asst prof, 69-74, ASSOC PROF ANAT, UNIV SOUTHERN CALIF, 74- *Personal Data:* b San Francisco, Calif, Oct 18, 36; m 60; c 3. *Educ:* Univ Calif, Berkeley, BA, 59; Univ Calif, San Francisco, MA, 62, PhD(anat), 67. *Prof Exp:* Teaching fel anat, Univ Calif, 64-65, res asst, 65-66, lectr, 66-67; NIH fel, Yale Univ, 67-69. *Concurrent Pos:* NIH res grant, 75-78; vis prof, Hebrew Univ, 78-79; vis scientist, Cedars-Sinai Med Ctr, 90-91. *Mem:* AAAS; Am Asn Anatomists. *Res:* Hormonal influence on adipose tissue in vitro; histochemistry and electron microscopy of adipose cells; innervation of adipose tissue; immunocytochemistry of the endocrine pancreas with age. *Mailing Add:* Dept Anat Univ Southern Calif Sch Med Los Angeles CA 90033. *Fax:* 314-577-8459

SLAVIN, JOANNE LOUISE, DIETARY FIBER, SPORTS NUTRITION. *Current Pos:* PROF NUTRIT, DEPT FOOD SCI & NUTRIT, UNIV MINN, 81- *Personal Data:* b Harvard, Ill, Apr 2, 52; m 79; c 3. *Educ:* Univ Wis-Madison, BS, 74, RD, 78, MS, 78, PhD(nutrit), 81. *Mem:* Am Dietetic Asn; Inst Food Technologists; Soc Nutrit Educ; Am Inst Nutrit. *Res:* Human nutrition; dietary fiber; nutrient bioavailability; sports nutrition; carbohydrate metabolism; diet and cancer. *Mailing Add:* Dept Food Sci & Nutrit Univ Minn 1334 Eckles Ave St Paul MN 55108. *Fax:* 612-625-5272; *E-Mail:* jslavin@chel.che.umn.edu

SLAVIN, OVID, DENTISTRY, BIOLOGY. *Current Pos:* RETIRED. *Personal Data:* b Romania, Dec 20, 21; US citizen; m 45. *Educ:* Washington Univ, AB, 42, DDS, 45. *Prof Exp:* Intern, Guggenheim Dent Clin, NY, 45-46; instr pedodont, Sch Dent & Oral Surg, Columbia Univ, 52-58; asst prof, Seton Hall Col Med & Dent, 58-62, asst dir prototype prog handicapped children, 61-62; prof biomed eng, NY Inst Technol, 64-65, prof life sci & chmn dept, 65-67, dean admin, Brookdale Hosp Ctr, Long Island Ctr, 64-66; chief dentist, Brookdale Hosp Ctr, Brooklyn, NY, 67-71, asst dir, Comprehensive Child Care Prog, 68-71; regional dent consult, Maternal & Child Health Serv, Health Serv & Ment Health Admin, Dept Health, Educ & Welfare, Philadelphia, 71-77; assoc prof, Sch Dent, Temple Univ, 77-87. *Concurrent Pos:* Chief pedodont sect, Long Island Jewish Hosp, NY, 53-55; chief pedodont serv, Jewish Chronic Dis Hosp, NY, 53-62. *Mem:* Am Asn Pub Health Dentists; Am Acad Pedodont; Am Dent Asn; Am Soc Dent Children. *Res:* Dentistry for handicapped children; biomedical engineering, particularly its application to clinical procedures; pedodontics. *Mailing Add:* 6 Bourne Hay Rd Sandwich MA 02563

SLAVIN, RAYMOND GRANAM, INTERNAL MEDICINE, ALLERGY. *Current Pos:* from asst prof to assoc prof, 65-73, PROF INTERNAL MED, SCH MED, ST LOUIS UNIV, 73- *Personal Data:* b Cleveland, Ohio, June 29, 30; m 53; c 4. *Educ:* Univ Mich, AB, 52; St Louis Univ, MD, 56; Northwestern Univ, Chicago, MS, 63. *Honors & Awards:* John M Sheldon Lectr, 90. *Prof Exp:* Resident internal med, Sch Med, St Louis Univ, 59-61; asst clinical internal med, Northwestern Univ, 64-65. *Concurrent Pos:* NIH Immunol Sci Study Sect grant, 85-89; bd chmn, Asthma & Allergy Found Am. *Mem:* Fel Am Acad Allergy & Immunol (past pres); fel Am Col Physicians; Am Asn Immunologists. *Res:* Immunology, clinical allergy; allergic bronchopulmonary aspergillosis and other pulmonary hypersensitivity syndromes; delayed hypersensitivity-clinical states in which delayed hypersensitivity is suppressed; sinusitis and asthma. *Mailing Add:* Dept Int Med St Louis Univ Sch Med 1402 S Grand Blvd St Louis MO 63104-1078. *Fax:* 314-577-8459

SLAVIN, ROBERT EDWARD, PSYCHOLOGY. *Current Pos:* PRIN RES SCIENTIST, JOHNS HOPKINS UNIV, 75- *Personal Data:* b Bethesda, Md, Sept 17, 50; m 73, Nancy Abigail Madden; c Jacob, Benjamin & Rebecca. *Educ:* Reed Col, BA, 72; Johns Hopkins Univ, PhD, 75. *Honors & Awards:* Raymond Cattell Award, Am Educ Res Asn, 86, Palmer O Johnson Award, 88. *Prof Exp:* Teacher, Beaverton Pub Schs, Ore, 72-73. *Mem:* Am Educ Res Asn; Int Asn Study Coop Educ (pres, 88-90). *Res:* Author of 15 books in field. *Mailing Add:* 805 Stevenson Lane Baltimore MD 21286-7915

SLAVKIN, HAROLD CHARLES, DEVELOPMENTAL BIOLOGY, CELL BIOLOGY. *Personal Data:* b Chicago, Ill, Mar 20, 38. *Educ:* Univ Southern Calif, BA, 63, DDS, 65. *Prof Exp:* Fel, Dept Anat, Sch Med, Univ Calif, Los Angeles, 65-66; fel, Dept Biochem, Univ Southern Calif, 66-68, asst prof, Sch Dent, 68-70, fac gerontol, Gerontol Inst, 69-70, assoc prof, 71-73, prof biochem & nutrit, Sch Dent, 74-95. *Concurrent Pos:* Consult, NIH, 67-, NSF, 73-75, Med Res Coun, Australia, Can, & Gt Brit, 72-, Bd Sci Dirs, Nat Inst Dent Res, NIH, 76-80, Human Biol Ser, US News & World Report, 81-85 & Oral Biol & Med Study Sect, NIH, 81-85; res career develop award, US Pub Health Serv, 68-72; prin investr, Southern Calif State Dent Asn grants, 69-70, NIH, Prog Proj grants, 69-, Intercellular Commun grants, 72-80, Training grants, 69-85 & NIH grants, 81-84; vis scientist, Intramural Prog, Nat Inst Dent Res, NIH, 75-76; co-ed, J Craniogacial Genetics & Develop Biol, 80-, co-managing ed, Differentiation, 80-81. *Mem:* Inst Med-Nat Acad Sci; Am Soc Cell Biol; Int Asn Dent Res; Int Soc Develop Biol; NY Acad Sci; AAAS. *Res:* Epithelial-mesenchymal interactions during vertebrate epidermal organ development; induction of epithelial-specific gene products such as enamel proteins during tooth morphogenesis; immunogenetic studies of drug-induced craniofacial malformations in murine and human embryogenesis. *Mailing Add:* Nat Inst Dent Res 31 Center Dr Bldg 31C Rm 2C39 Bethesda MD 20892

SLAWSKY, ZAKA I, PHYSICS. *Current Pos:* PROF PHYSICS, UNIV MD, 88- *Personal Data:* b Chevy Chase, Md, Apr 2, 10. *Educ:* R P Inst, BS, 33; Calif Inst Technol, MS, 35; Univ Mich, PhD(physics), 38. *Mem:* Nat Acad Sci; Am Phys Soc. *Mailing Add:* 4701 Willard Ave Apt 318 Chevy Chase MD 20815

SLAWSON, PETER (ROBERT), AIR POLLUTION, MECHANICAL ENGINEERING. *Current Pos:* Res assoc air pollution, 67-69, from asst prof to assoc prof, 69-80, PROF MECH ENG, UNIV WATERLOO, 80- *Personal Data:* b Toronto, Ont, July 10, 39; m 62; c 3. *Educ:* Univ Waterloo, BASc, 64, MASc, 66, PhD(mech eng), 67. *Concurrent Pos:* Pres, Envirodyne Ltd, 74- *Res:* Diffusion; atmospheric dynamics as applied to the dispersal of air pollutants. *Mailing Add:* Dept Mech Eng Univ Waterloo Waterloo ON N2L 3G1 Can

SLAYDEN, SUZANNE WEEMS, ORGANIC CHEMISTRY. *Current Pos:* ASST PROF CHEM, GEORGE MASON UNIV, 76- *Personal Data:* b Heidelberg, Ger, Aug 11, 48; US citizen. *Educ:* Univ Tenn, BS, 70, PhD(org chem), 76. *Mem:* Am Chem Soc. *Res:* Mechanisms of organoborate rearrangements. *Mailing Add:* Chem Dept MSN 3E2 George Mason Univ Fairfax VA 22030

SLAYMAKER, FRANK HARRIS, ELECTRICAL ENGINEERING. *Current Pos:* RETIRED. *Personal Data:* b Lincoln, Nebr, April 22, 14; m 49; c 4. *Educ:* Univ Nebr, BS, 41, MS, 46. *Prof Exp:* Prof elec engr, The Stomberg Carlson Co, 41-50, sr elec engr, sound equipment, 50-51, chief engr, 51-56, mgr appl physics Lab, 56-61; assoc dir, Stromberg-Carson Div, Gen Dynamics Corp, 61-62, exec asst vpres engr & res, 62-63; dir ASW prog, Elec Div, 63-65, res specialist, 65-70, scientist, Tropel Inc, 70-75; sr engr, Univ Rochester, 75-77, res assoc, Ctr Visual Sci, 77-79; scientist, Tropel Div, Coherent Radiation Inc, 79-85. *Mem:* Fel Inst Elec & Electronic Engrs; fel Acoustics Soc Am. *Res:* Research and development in fields of speech analysis-synthesis, transducer development, musical tone analysis-synthesis; optical interferometers, optical transfer functions. *Mailing Add:* 134 Glen Haven Rd Rochester NY 14609-2057

SLAYMAKER, HERBERT OLAV, MOUNTAIN ENVIRONMENTS. *Current Pos:* from asst prof to assoc prof, 68-81, head geog, 82-91, PROF GEOG, UNIV BC, 81-, ASSOC VPRES RES, 91- *Personal Data:* b Swansea, Wales, Jan 31, 39; Can citizen; m 67, Margaret Rapson; c Karen, Paul, Sarah & Heidi. *Educ:* Cambridge Univ, BA, 61, PhD(geomorphol), 68; Harvard Univ, AM, 63. *Prof Exp:* Asst lectr geog, Univ Col, Wales, Aberystwyth, 64-66, lectr, 66-68. *Concurrent Pos:* Vis lectr, Dept Geog, Cambridge Univ, 66-68; vis prof, Dept Geog, Southern Ill Univ, 73; coordr interdisciplinary hydrol, Univ BC, 75-, pres fac asn, 78-79 & mem bd gov, 84-87; chmn, Int Geog Union Comn, 80-84; sr Killam, res fel, 87-88. *Mem:* Can Asn Geogrs; Can Quaternary Asn; Am Geophys Union; Int Asn Geomorphol (treas, 89-93, vpres, 93-). *Res:* Hydrology and geomorphology of drainage basins; sediment and solute budgets of British Columbia's mountain regions; natural rates of erosion and land use impacts. *Mailing Add:* 3988 SW Marine Dr Vancouver BC V6N 4A3 Can. Fax: 604-822-6150; E-Mail: olavslaymaker@mtsg.ubc.ca

SLAYMAN, CAROLYN WALCH, GENETICS. *Current Pos:* asst prof microbiol & physiol, Yale Univ, 67-70, assoc prof, 70-72, assoc prof human genetics & physiol, 72-77, chmn, dept Genetics, 84-95, PROF GENETICS & PHYSIOL, SCH MED, YALE UNIV, 77-, STERLING PROF, 91-, DEP DEAN ACAD & SCI AFFAIRS, 95- *Personal Data:* b Portland, Maine, Mar 11, 37; m 59; c 2. *Educ:* Swarthmore Col, BA, 58; Rockefeller Univ, PhD(biochem genetics), 63. *Hon Degrees:* DSc, Bowdoin Col, 85. *Prof Exp:* Instr biol, Western Res Univ, 64-65, asst prof, 65-67. *Concurrent Pos:* NSF fel, Cambridge Univ, 63-64; consult, Adv Panel Genetic Biol, NSF, 74-77; assoc ed, Genetics, 77-82; mem bd overseers, Bowdoin Col, 77-89, bd trustees, 89-; chmn, Genetic Basis Dis Rev Comt, NIH, 83-85; mem, Nat Adv Gen Med Sci Coun, NIH, 89-93, sci review bd, Howard Hughes Med Inst. *Mem:* Inst Med-Nat Acad Sci. *Res:* Genetic control of membrane transport. *Mailing Add:* Dept Genetics Sch Med Yale Univ New Haven CT 06520

SLAYMAN, CLIFFORD L, PHYSIOLOGY. *Current Pos:* from asst prof to assoc prof, 67-83, PROF PHYSIOL, SCH, MED, YALE UNIV, 83- *Personal Data:* b Mt Vernon, Ohio, July 7, 36; m 59, Carolyn Walch; c Andrew L & Rachel W. *Educ:* Kenyon Col, AB, 58; Rockefeller Univ, PhD(physiol), 63. *Hon Degrees:* DSc, Kenyon Col, 91. *Prof Exp:* NSF fel physiol, Cambridge Univ, 63-64; asst prof, Sch Med, Western Res Univ, 64-67. *Concurrent Pos:* NIH res grants, 65, 68, 73, 78, 81 & 86-91, res career develop award, 69; NSF res grant, 79-82; Dept Energy res grant, 85- *Mem:* Am Physiol Soc; Soc Gen Physiologists; Am Soc Plant Physiologists; Am Soc Cell Biol; US Biophys Soc; NY Acad Scis. *Res:* Membrane biophysics; transport, energy-coupling, and electrogenesis in microorganisms; physics of biological channels. *Mailing Add:* Dept Cellular & Molecular Physiol Yale Univ Sch Med New Haven CT 06510. Fax: 203-785-5535; E-Mail: clifford__slayman@gm.yale.edu

SLEATOR, DANIEL DOMINIC, NATURAL LANGUAGE PROCESSING. *Current Pos:* PROF, COMPUT SCI DEPT, CARNEGIE MELLON UNIV, PA, 85- *Personal Data:* b St Louis, Mo, Dec 10, 53. *Educ:* Univ Ill, BS, 76, Stanford Univ, PhD(comput), 81. *Prof Exp:* Researcher, Bell Labs, NJ, 81-85. *Mailing Add:* Sch Comput Sci Carnegie Mellon Univ 5000 Forbes Ave Wean Hall Pittsburgh PA 15213

SLEATOR, TYCHO, PHYSICS. *Current Pos:* ASST PROF, PHYSICS DEPT, NY UNIV. *Mailing Add:* Dept Physics NY Univ 70 Washington Sq S New York NY 10012-1019

SLEATOR, WILLIAM WARNER, JR, BIOPHYSICS, PHYSIOLOGY. *Current Pos:* head dept physiol & biophys, 69-76, PROF PHYSIOL & BIOPHYSICS, UNIV ILL, URBANA, 69- *Personal Data:* b Ann Arbor, Mich, Apr 5, 17; m 40; c 4. *Educ:* Univ Mich, AB, 38, MS, 39, PhD(physics), 46. *Prof Exp:* Physicist, Ballistic Res Lab, Aberdeen Proving Ground, Md, 42-45; res assoc physics, Univ Minn, 46-49; from asst prof biophys to assoc prof physiol, Sch Med, Wash Univ, St Louis, 49-64, prof physiol & biophys, 64-69, actg chmn dept, 66-68. *Concurrent Pos:* Mem, Physiol Study Sect, NIH, 76-80. *Mem:* Fel Am Phys Soc; Am Physiol Soc; Biophys Soc (secy, 62-67); Sigma Xi. *Res:* Scattering of elementary particles and light nuclei; light scattering and absorption by living muscle and muscle proteins; fundamental cellular processes in heart, skeletal and smooth muscle; ionic conductance changes during cardiac action potential; mechanism of contraction process and of coupling between excitation and contraction; ion flux measurements will tracers and ion-selective electrodes. *Mailing Add:* Dept Physiol & Biophysics Univ Ill 524 Burrill Hall 407 S Goodwin Ave Urbana IL 61801-3704

SLECHTA, ROBERT FRANK, REPRODUCTIVE PHYSIOLOGY. *Current Pos:* from asst prof to assoc prof, 58-65, assoc dean, Grad Sch, 67-79, PROF BIOL, BOSTON UNIV, 65- *Personal Data:* b New York, NY, June 4, 28; m 53; c 1. *Educ:* Clark Univ, AB, 49, MA, 51; Boston Univ, PhD(biol), 55. *Prof Exp:* Asst physiol, Worcester Found Exp Biol, 52-53; res assoc & instr, Tufts Univ, 55-58. *Mem:* AAAS; Soc Study Reproduction. *Res:* Reproductive and microcirculatory physiology. *Mailing Add:* 101 Wilson Rd Bedford MA 01730

SLEDD, WILLIAM T, MATHEMATICS. *Current Pos:* from asst prof to assoc prof, 61-69, PROF MATH, MICH STATE UNIV, 69- *Personal Data:* b Murray, Ky, Aug 25, 35; div; c Luanne (Leavitt) & Jane (Watkins). *Educ:* Murray State Col, BA, 56; Univ Ky, MA, 59, PhD(math), 61. *Prof Exp:* Asst math, Univ Ky, 56-60. *Mem:* Math Asn Am; Am Math Soc. *Res:* Summability theory; Fourier analysis. *Mailing Add:* Dept Math Mich State Univ East Lansing MI 48824-0001. Fax: 517-432-1562; E-Mail: sledd@math.msm.edu

SLEDGE, CLEMENT BLOUNT, ORTHOPEDICS. *Current Pos:* RETIRED. *Personal Data:* b Ada, Okla, Nov 1, 30; m 57, Georgia Kurrus; c Margaret, John, Matthew & Claire. *Educ:* Yale Univ, MD, 55; Am Bd Orthop Surg, dipl. *Hon Degrees:* MA, Harvard Univ, 70; ScD, Univ South, 87. *Prof Exp:* Intern, Barnes Hosp, Louis, 55-56; fel orthop path, Armed Forces, Inst Path, 63; vis scientist, Strangeways Res Lab, Cambridge Univ Eng, 63-66; resident orthop surg, Harvard Univ, 60-63, from asst prof to prof & chmn dept, 63-96. *Concurrent Pos:* Fel, Med Found Boston, 63-66; prin investr, NIH, 67-; Gebbie res fel, 68; chmn, Dept Orthop Surg, Brigham & Women's Hosp. *Mem:* Inst Med-Nat Acad Sci; Am Acad Orthop Surgeons (pres, 85-86); Orthop Res (pres, 78-80); Am Rheumatism Asn; Hip Soc (pres, 85). *Res:* Orthopedics; rheumatism; medicine. *Mailing Add:* Brigham & Women's Hosp 75 Francis St Boston MA 02115-6195

SLEDGE, EUGENE BONDURANT, BIOLOGY. *Current Pos:* chmn dept, 70-72, PROF BIOL, UNIV MONTEVALLO, 70- *Personal Data:* b Mobile, Ala, Nov 4, 23; m 52; c 2. *Educ:* Auburn Univ, BS, 49, MS, 55; Univ Fla, PhD(biol), 60. *Prof Exp:* Res asst, Auburn Univ, 53-55; asst, Univ Fla, 56-59; nematologist, Div Plant Indust, Fla State Dept Agr, 59-62; asst prof biol, Ala Col, 62-70. *Mem:* Am Ornith Union; Wilson Ornith Soc. *Res:* Ornithology, particularly avian myology. *Mailing Add:* 200 Cardinal Crest Dr Montevallo AL 35115

SLEE, FREDERICK WATFORD, NUCLEAR PHYSICS. *Current Pos:* ASSOC PROF PHYSICS, UNIV PUGET SOUND, 66-, CHMN, 80- *Personal Data:* b Spokane, Wash, Mar 16, 37. *Educ:* Univ Wash, BS, 59, MS, 60, PhD(physics), 66. *Mem:* Am Phys Soc; AAAS. *Res:* Electronic instrumentation applied to physics, geophysics and biophysics. *Mailing Add:* 8610 41st Ave SW Seattle WA 98136

SLEEMAN, CANDACE KIM, MATHEMATICAL MODELLING, SCIENTIFIC COMPUTING. *Current Pos:* RESEARCHER, DEPT MATH & COMPUT SCI, DREXEL UNIV, 87- *Personal Data:* b North Adams, Mass, Mar 7, 61. *Educ:* Univ Vt, BS, 83; Monmouth Univ, MS, 85; Drexel Univ, PhD(math), 94. *Prof Exp:* Programmer analyst, Defense Systs Div, Comput Sci Corp, 84-86. *Concurrent Pos:* Sr engr, Pacer Systs, Inc, 86-90; comput engr, US Dept Navy, Naval Air Warfare Ctr, 90-95; numerical methods programmer & analyst, Gorca Systs, Inc, 95-97; consult, Pocono Data Power, Inc, 97- *Mem:* Inst Opers Res & Mgt Sci. *Res:* Epidemiological modelling of HIV-AIDS using Philadelphia and New Jersey public health data; partnership models in HIV-AIDS and other infectious diseases; stochastic and embedded deterministic models; Monte Carlo simulation experiments. *Mailing Add:* 282 Hurffville Grenloch Rd Sewell NJ 08080. E-Mail: 104765.2117@compuserve.com

SLEEMAN, RICHARD ALEXANDER, CHEMISTRY. *Current Pos:* PROF CHEM, NORTH ADAMS STATE COL, 60-, MEM FAC DEPT EDUC, 76- *Personal Data:* b Bennington, Vt, Sept 15, 26; m 50. *Educ:* Fordham Univ, BS, 49; NY Univ, MA, 51, EdD(phys sci), 55. *Prof Exp:* Instr phys sci, Vt State Teachers Col, Castleton, 49-54 & NY Univ, 54-55; asst prof chem, Kent State Univ, 56-60. *Mem:* AAAS; Nat Asn Res Sci Teaching. *Res:* Physics; quantum mechanics and black body radiation. *Mailing Add:* Educ N Adams State Col 375 Church St North Adams MA 01247-4127

SLEEP, NORMAN H, GEOLOGY, GEOPHYSICS. *Current Pos:* PROF, DEPT GEOL & GEOPHYS, STANFORD UNIV, 79- *Personal Data:* b Kalamazoo, Mich, Feb 14, 45. *Educ:* Mich State Univ, BS, 67; Mass Inst Technol, MS, 69, PhD(geol), 73. *Prof Exp:* Asst prof, dept geol, Northwestern Univ, 73-79. *Mem:* Geol Soc Am. *Mailing Add:* Geophys Stanford Univ Mitchell Bldg Stanford CA 94305-9991

SLEEPER, DAVID ALLANBROOK, BIOLOGY, ENTOMOLOGY. *Current Pos:* RETIRED. *Personal Data:* b Exeter, NH, Feb 1, 22; m 49; c 1. *Educ:* Univ NH, BS, 43; Cornell Univ, PhD(entom), 63. *Prof Exp:* Entomologist, Alaska Insect Proj, USDA, 48 & Arctic Health Res Ctr, USPHS, 49-54; instr biol, Cornell Univ, 61-63; asst prof, Elmira Col, 63-65; asst prof, 65-71, assoc prof, 71-81, prof biol, Hobart & William Smith Cols, 81-87. *Mem:* Ecol Soc Am; Soc Syst Zool; Animal Behav Soc. *Res:* Ecology, taxonomy, and physiology of biting diptera, especially blackflies of the family Simuliidae. *Mailing Add:* 156 Westview Lane Ithaca NY 14850-1744

SLEEPER, ELBERT LAUNEE, ENTOMOLOGY. *Current Pos:* from asst prof to assoc prof, 57-66, PROF ENTOM, CALIF STATE UNIV, LONG BEACH, 66- *Personal Data:* b Newton, Iowa, July 27, 27; m 49, 72, 77; c 4. *Educ:* Ohio State Univ, BS, 50, MS, 51, PhD(entom), 56. *Prof Exp:* Asst, Ohio Biol Surv, Ohio State Univ, 53-56. *Concurrent Pos:* Collabr, US Nat Park Serv, 57-80; consult lab nuclear med & radiation biol, Univ Calif, Los Angeles, 70-80. *Mem:* Ecol Soc Am; Am Entom Soc; Am Forestry Soc; Entom Soc Am. *Res:* Systematics of the Curculionoidea excluding the Scolytidae; dynamics of desert insect populations; systematics, zoogeography and ecological distribution of Curculionoidea of the new world. *Mailing Add:* Dept Biol Calif State Univ LB 1250 Bellflower Blvd Long Beach CA 90840

SLEETER, THOMAS DAVID, aquaculture, environmental resource assessment, for more information see previous edition

SLEETH, BAILEY, plant pathology; deceased, see previous edition for last biography

SLEETH, RHULE BAILEY, FOOD TECHNOLOGY, ANIMAL NUTRITION. *Current Pos:* RETIRED. *Personal Data:* b Linn, WVa, Feb 6, 29; m 53, Wanda Vaudelinde; c Mark & Jeffrey. *Educ:* WVa Univ, BS, 51; Univ Fla, MS, 53; Univ Mo, PhD(meat & food technol), 59. *Honors & Awards:* Signal Serv Award, Am Meat Sci, 71, Special Recognition Award,

81, R C Pollock Award, 84, Sxten Indust Serv Award, 91. *Prof Exp:* Instr meat technol, Univ Mo, 55-59; food technologist, Armour & Co, 59-63, sect head fresh meat develop, 63-64, asst mgr, Food Res Div, 64-68, asst dir, Food Res Div, 68-78, dir, Food Res & Develop, 78-80, vpres, Food Res & Develop, 81-90, vpres, sci affairs, 90-94. *Concurrent Pos:* Mem prog comt, Meat Indust Res Conf, 65-66, chmn, 67; chmn, Reciprocal Meat Conf, 68; contact, Europ Meeting Meat Res Workers. *Mem:* Fel Inst Food Technologists; Am Soc Animal Sci; Am Meat Sci Asn (pres, 73-74); Soc Advan Food Serv Res. *Res:* Sausage and cured meat development; sterile and refrigerated canned meats; food service research; food chemistry; dairy, poultry and food oils; packaging research. *Mailing Add:* 8047 N Ironwood Dr Paradise Valley AZ 85253. *Fax:* 602-368-0222

SLEEZER, PAUL DAVID, ANALYTICAL CHEMISTRY. *Current Pos:* sr develop chemist, Bristol Labs, 66-72, DEPT HEAD ORG SYNTHESIS LABS, INDUST DIV, BRISTOL-MYERS CO, 72- *Personal Data:* b Chicago, Ill, Jan 26, 36; m 63. *Educ:* Univ Rochester, BS, 58; Univ Calif, Los Angeles, PhD(chem), 63. *Prof Exp:* Sr res chemist, Solvay Process Div, Allied Chem Corp, NY, 63-66. *Mem:* Am Chem Soc. *Res:* Exploratory organic research; synthesis and process development; process analysis and control; organic reaction mechanisms; physical-organic; organometallics. *Mailing Add:* 122 Downing Rd Dewitt NY 13214

SLEICHER, CHARLES A, CHEMICAL ENGINEERING. *Current Pos:* from assoc prof to prof chem eng, 60-91, chmn dept, 77-89, EMER PROF, UNIV WASH, 91- *Personal Data:* b Albany, NY, Aug 15, 24; m 53, Janis Jorgenson; c Jeffrey M & Gretchen G. *Educ:* Brown Univ, ScB, 46; Mass Inst Technol, MS, 49; Univ Mich, PhD(chem eng), 55. *Prof Exp:* Res engr, Shell Develop Co, 55-59; NSF fel, Cambridge Univ, 59-60. *Concurrent Pos:* Grants, Am Chem Soc, 60-64, NSF, 61- & Chevron Res Found, 64-67; consult, Westinghouse-Hanford Co, 73-85; vis prof, Univ Guadalajara, 91-92. *Mem:* Fel AAAS; Am Chem Soc; fel Am Inst Chem Engrs. *Res:* Turbulent diffusion, heat transfer; heat transfer with variable fluid properties; dispersion of toxins in the environment; aerosol deposition in the lung. *Mailing Add:* Dept Chem Eng BF-10 Univ Wash Seattle WA 98195. *Fax:* 206-527-9170; *E-Mail:* sleicher@cheme.washington.edu

SLEIGHT, ARTHUR WILLIAM, SOLID STATE CHEMISTRY. *Current Pos:* MILTON HARRIS PROF MAT SCI, ORE STATE UNIV, 89-, DIR, CTR ADVAN MAT RES, 95- *Personal Data:* b Ballston Spa, NY, Apr 1, 39; m 63, Betty Hilberg; c Jeffrey W, Jeanette A & Jason A. *Educ:* Hamilton Col, BA, 60; Univ Conn, PhD(inorg chem), 63. *Honors & Awards:* Welch Found Lectr, 88; Gold Medal, Nat Asn Sci, Technol & Soc, 94; Mat Chem Award, Am Chem Soc, 97. *Prof Exp:* Fel crystallog, Univ Stockholm, 63-64; res chemist solid state chem, E I du Pont de Nemours & Co, 64-79, res suprv, 79-81, res mgr, 81-85, res leader, 85-89. *Concurrent Pos:* Assoc ed, Mat Res Bull, 76-94, Inorg Chem Rev, 79-; adj prof, Univ Del, 78-89; mem panel, Sci Challenges Arising from Technol Needs, 78; chmn, Solid State Chem Subdiv, Am Chem Soc, 81; mem, Major Mat Facil Comt, Nat Acad Sci, 84; mem, Comt Interdisciplinary Aspects Crystallog, Nat Res Coun, 86-; mem, Panel High-Temperature Superconductivity, Nat Acad Sci, 87-; vis prof, Univ Rennes, France, 88, Univ Calif, Santa Barbara, 89, Univ Bordeaux, 95; mem, Nat Comn Superconductivity, 88-90; consult, Exxon, 91-92, Catalytica, 92-, DuPont, 90-93, Superconductor Technol, Inc, 90-, Monsanto, 94-; ed, Mat Res Bull, 94- *Mem:* Am Chem Soc; Mats Res Soc. *Res:* Solid state chemistry, structure-property relationships for inorganic solids, especially oxides, superconductivity, ionic conductivity, defects; crystal growth; crystallography; structural chemistry; heterogeneous catalysis; electrical, magnetic and optical properties, thermal expansion. *Mailing Add:* Dept Chem Ore State Univ Corvallis OR 97331-4003. *Fax:* 541-737-4407; *E-Mail:* sleighta@ccmail.orst.edu

SLEIGHT, STUART DUANE, VETERINARY PATHOLOGY. *Current Pos:* from asst prof to assoc prof, 61-68, PROF PATH, MICH STATE UNIV, 68- *Personal Data:* b Lansing, Mich, Oct 19, 27; m 50; c 4. *Educ:* Mich State Univ, DVM, 51, MS, 59, PhD(vet path), 61. *Prof Exp:* Vet, Columbus Vet Hosp, Wis, 51-58. *Mem:* Am Col Vet Path; Conf Res Workers Animal Dis; Am Vet Med Asn; NY Acad Sci; Soc Toxicol. *Res:* Studies emphasize assessment of the toxic & carcinogenic effects of exposure to important environmental chemicals, including N-nitrosamines & polyhalogenated aromatic hydrocarbons. *Mailing Add:* 522 E Fee Hall Dept Path Mich State Univ East Lansing MI 48824

SLEIGHT, THOMAS PERRY, SYSTEMS ENGINEERING, PROGRAM MANAGEMENT. *Current Pos:* advan systs design suprv, Johns Hopkins Univ, 77-83, dir's asst, comput & info systs, 83-89, cruise missiles systs engr, 89-90, PRIN STAFF, APPL PHYSICS LAB, JOHNS HOPKINS UNIV, 69-, PROG MGR, 90- *Personal Data:* b Glens Falls, NY, May 15, 43; m 66; c 4. *Educ:* Ohio Univ, BS(chem) & BS(math), 65; State Univ NY Buffalo, PhD(chem), 69. *Prof Exp:* Sci Res Coun fel, Univ Leicester, 68-69. *Concurrent Pos:* Lectr, Johns Hopkins Univ, 75- *Mem:* Am Chem Soc; Int Elec & Electronic Engrs Comput Soc. *Res:* Advanced systems; software engineering; systems engineering. *Mailing Add:* Appl Physics Lab John Hopkins Univ John Hopkins Rd Laurel MD 20723-6099

SLEIN, MILTON WILBUR, biochemistry; deceased, see previous edition for last biography

SLEISENGER, MARVIN HERBERT, MEDICINE, GASTROENTEROLOGY. *Current Pos:* PROF MED & VCHMN DEPT, MED CTR, UNIV CALIF, SAN FRANCISCO, 68-; DISTINGUISHED PHYSICIAN, DEPT VET AFFAIRS, SAN FRANCISCO, CALIF, 93- *Personal Data:* b Pittsburgh, Pa, June 3, 24; m 48, Lenore R Cohen; c Thomas P. *Educ:* Harvard Med Sch, MD, 47; Am Bd Internal Med, dipl, 54. *Hon Degrees:* DSC, Univ Nice, France, 75. *Honors & Awards:* Friedenwald Medal, Am Gastroenterol Asn. *Prof Exp:* Intern med, Beth Israel Hosp, Boston, Mass, 47-48, chief resident, 49-50; intern, Beth Israel Hosp, Newark, NJ, 48-49; resident gastroenterol, Hosp Univ Pa, 50-51; instr med, Med Col, Cornell Univ, 52-53, from asst prof to assoc prof clin med, 54-65, prof med, 65-68. *Concurrent Pos:* Fel gastroenterol, Hosp Univ Pa, 50-51; fel med, Med Col, Cornell Univ, 51-52; assoc, Harvard Med Sch, 49-50; instr, Sch Med, Tufts Univ, 49-50; asst physician, out-patient clin, New York Hosp, 51-54, physician, 54-56, chief gastrointestinal clin, 54-68, from asst attend physician to attend physician, 56-68; consult, Rockefeller Inst Hosp, New York & aerospace prog, USAF, 64-; chief med serv, Ft Miley Vet Admin Hosp, San Francisco, Calif, 68- *Mem:* Am Soc Clin Invest; Harvey Soc; Am Gastroenterol Asn; Am Fedn Clin Res; Asn Am Physicians; master Am Col Physicians. *Res:* Intestinal absorption; esophageal motility; fractionation of gastric juice mucoproteins; experimental ulcerative colitis; measurement of enzymes. *Mailing Add:* Dept Vet Affairs Med Ctr 4150 Clement St San Francisco CA 94121

SLEMMONS, DAVID BURTON, GEOLOGY, GEOPHYSICS. *Current Pos:* From asst prof to assoc prof, Univ Nev, 51-63, dir seismog sta, 52-64, chmn dept geol & geog, 66-70, prof geol & geophys, 63-89, dir ctr neotectonic studies, 85-89, EMER PROF GEOL & GEOPHYS, UNIV NEV, 89- *Personal Data:* b Alameda, Calif, Dec 31, 22; m 46, Ruth Evans; c David R & Mary Anne. *Educ:* Univ Calif, BS, 47, PhD(geol), 53. *Honors & Awards:* G K Gilbert Award, Carnegie Inst. *Concurrent Pos:* Prog dir geophys, Earth Sci Div, NSF, 70-71; del, 2nd & 3rd US-Japan Conf Earthquake Prediction; dir, Seismog Soc Am; mem, Earthquake Eng Res Inst. *Mem:* Geol Soc Am; Seismol Soc Am; Soc Econ Geol; Am Inst Mining, Metall & Petrol Eng; Asn Eng Geol. *Res:* Geology, geomorphology, neotectonics, seismology and volcanology; petrography; universal stage determination of plagioclase; surface faulting; seismicity, faulting mechanics, earthquake hazards, seismic risk for engineering structures, seismic potential of faults; seismic safety of dams and nuclear reactors. *Mailing Add:* PO Box 81050 Las Vegas NV 89180. *Fax:* 702-363-5555; *E-Mail:* bslemmons@aol.com

SLEMON, GORDON R(ICHARD), ELECTRICAL ENGINEERING. *Current Pos:* prof, Univ Toronto, 55-90, head dept, 66-76, dean, fac appl sci & eng, 79-86, EMER PROF ELEC ENG, UNIV TORONTO, 90- *Personal Data:* b Bowmanville, Ont, Aug 15, 24; m 49, Margaret Matheson; c Sally, Stephen, Mark & Jane. *Educ:* Univ Toronto, BASc, 46, MASc, 48; Univ London, DIC & PhD(eng), 52, DSc, 68. *Hon Degrees:* DEng, Mem Univ Nfld, 94. *Honors & Awards:* Western Elec Award, Am Soc Eng Educ, 65; Centennial Medal, Can, 67; Gold Medal, Yugoslav Union Elec Power Indust & Yugoslav Union Nikola Tesla Socs; Ross Medal, 78 & 83; Centennial Medal, Inst Elec & Electronics Engrs, 84; Nikola Tesla Award, Inst Elec & Electronics Engrs, 90; Order of Can, 95. *Prof Exp:* Lectr, Imp Col, Univ London, 49-53; asst prof elec eng, NS Tech Col, 53-55. *Concurrent Pos:* Pres, Elec Eng Consociates, 76-79; chmn bd, Innovation Found, 80-93 & Microelectronics Develop Ctr, 83-87; dir, Inverpower Controls, Ltd, 80-, Mett Net Inc, 94- *Mem:* Am Soc Eng Educ; hon fel Inst Elec & Electronics Engrs; fel Inst Elec Engrs UK; fel Eng Inst Can; Can Soc Elec Eng; fel Can Acad Engrs. *Res:* Power systems; electric propulsion; rotating machines; magnetics. *Mailing Add:* Dept Elec Eng Univ Toronto Toronto ON M5S 3G4 Can. *Fax:* 416-971-2325; *E-Mail:* slemon@ecf.utoronto.ca

SLEPECKY, RALPH ANDREW, MICROBIOLOGY. *Current Pos:* assoc prof microbiol, 63-68, adminr biol res labs, 64-70, PROF MICROBIOL, SYRACUSE UNIV, 68- *Personal Data:* b Nanticoke, Pa, Oct 8, 24; m 67; c 2. *Educ:* Franklin & Marshall Col, BS, 48; Pa State Univ, MS, 50; Univ Md, PhD(bact), 53. *Prof Exp:* Asst bact, Pa State Univ, 48-50 & Univ Md, 50-53; asst prof biol, Franklin & Marshall Col, 53-56; res scientist, Univ Tex, 56-58; asst prof biol, Northwestern Univ, 58-63. *Concurrent Pos:* Instr, Montgomery Jr Col, 52; bacteriologist, Stand Brands, Inc, 52; Found Microbiol lectr, 71-72; vis scientist, NIH, 76-77. *Mem:* AAAS; Am Soc Microbiol; Am Chem Soc. *Res:* Morphogenesis differentiation and heat resistance of bacterial spores. *Mailing Add:* 100 Dorset Rd Syracuse NY 13210-3048

SLEPER, DAVID ALLEN, PLANT BREEDING, GENETICS. *Current Pos:* from asst prof to assoc prof, 74-84, PROF AGRON, UNIV MO, 84- *Personal Data:* b Buffalo Ctr, Iowa, Aug 25, 45; m 65, Elaine M; c Daniel E & Kimberly S. *Educ:* Iowa State Univ, BS, 67, MS, 69; Univ Wis, PhD(plant breeding, genetics), 73. *Honors & Awards:* Merit Cert Am Forage & Grassland Coun, 82. *Prof Exp:* Asst prof agron, Univ Fla, 73-74. *Mem:* Fel Crop Sci Soc Am; Am Forage & Grass Coun; Sigma Xi; fel Am Soc Agron. *Res:* Investigations on the breeding and genetics of Festuca arundinacea and soybean. *Mailing Add:* Dept Agron Rm 210 Waters Hall Univ Mo Columbia MO 65211

SLEPETYS, RICHARD ALGIMANTAS, physical chemistry, pigment technology, for more information see previous edition

SLEPIAN, DAVID, MATHEMATICS, ELECTRICAL ENGINEERING. *Current Pos:* RETIRED. *Personal Data:* b Pittsburgh, Pa, June 30, 23; m 50, Janice Berek; c Steven L, Don J & Anne M. *Educ:* Harvard Univ, PhD(physics), 49. *Honors & Awards:* Von Neumann lectr, Soc Indust & Appl Math, 82; Alexander Graham Bell Medal, Inst Elec & Electronics Engrs, 81. *Prof Exp:* Parker fel, Harvard Univ, 49-50; res mathematician, Bell Tel Labs

Inc, 50-82; prof elec eng, Univ Hawaii, 70-80. Concurrent Pos: Vis Mackay prof, Univ Calif, Berkeley, 58-59, regent's lectr, 77. Mem: Nat Acad Sci; Nat Acad Eng; AAAS; Inst Elec & Electronics Engrs; AAAS. Res: Communication theory; applied mathematics. Mailing Add: 212 Summit Ave Summit NJ 07901

SLEPIAN, PAUL, MATHEMATICS. Current Pos: PROF MATH, HOWARD UNIV, 70- Personal Data: b Boston, Mass, Mar 26, 23; c Laura & Jean. Educ: Mass Inst Technol, SB, 50; Brown Univ, PhD(math), 56. Prof Exp: Instr math, Brown Univ, 54-56; mathematician, Ramo-Wooldridge Corp, Calif, 56 & Hughes Aircraft Co, 56-60; assoc prof math, Univ Ariz, 60-62; from assoc prof to prof, Rensselaer Polytech Inst, 62-69; chmn dept, Bucknell Univ, 69-70. Concurrent Pos: Lectr, Univ Southern Calif, 56-60; vis staff mem, Los Alamos Sci Lab, Los Alamos, NMex, 76, 78 & 79; instr, Lorton Prison Col Prog, Lorton, Va, 78-89. Mem: Am Math Soc; Soc Indust & Appl Math; Math Asn Am. Res: Surface area; applications of mathematics to circuit theory; general topology. Mailing Add: 1331 W 40th St Baltimore MD 21211

SLESNICK, IRWIN LEONARD, SCIENCE EDUCATION, CURRICULUM DEVELOPMENT. Current Pos: assoc prof, Western Wash Univ, 63-66, coordr sci educ, 71-73, coordr sci educ, 80-85, dir sci educ, 90-96, PROF BIOL, WESTERN WASH UNIV, 66- Personal Data: b Canton, Ohio, Aug 5, 26; m 47, 85, Carole Ketchum; c Trina (Padoll), Twila, Daniel, Tanya & Natasha. Educ: Bowling Green State Univ, BA & BS, 49; Univ Mich, MS, 53; Ohio State Univ, PhD, 62. Prof Exp: Instr high sch, Ohio, 49-55; instr unified sci, Ohio State Univ, 56-63. Concurrent Pos: Consult, AID, India, 66-67; sci educ adv, 67-70; consult, UNESCO, 71-; consult, Biol Sci Curric Study, Scott, Foresman & Co, 72-76, ed adv, 77- Mem: Nat Sci Teachers Asn; AAAS. Res: Population education; curriculum development in interdisciplinary studies. Mailing Add: Dept Biol Western Wash Univ Bellingham WA 98225-9160. Fax: 360-733-4321; E-Mail: sles1@aol.con

SLESNICK, WILLIAM ELLIS, MATHEMATICS. Current Pos: from asst prof to assoc prof, Dartmouth Col, 62-71, vis instr, 58-59, asst dir educ uses, Kiewit Comput Ctr, 66-69, PROF MATH, DARTMOUTH COL, 71- Personal Data: b Oklahoma City, Okla, Feb 24, 25. Educ: US Naval Acad, BS, 45; Univ Okla, BA, 48; Oxford Univ, BA, 50, MA, 54; Harvard Univ, AM, 52. Hon Degrees: AM, Dartmouth Col, 72. Prof Exp: Teacher, St Paul's Sch, NH, 52-62. Concurrent Pos: Mem, advan placement exam comt math, Col Entrance Exam Bd, 67-71; Nat Humanities Fac, 72-; Rhodes Scholar, 48. Mem: Nat Coun Teachers of Math; Math Asn Am. Mailing Add: 19 S Park St Hanover NH 03755. Fax: 603-646-1312

SLESSOR, KEITH NORMAN, INSECT SEMIOCHEMICALS. Current Pos: from asst to assoc prof, 66-82, PROF ORG BIOCHEM, SIMON FRASER UNIV, 82- Personal Data: b Comox, BC, Nov 4, 38; m 60, Marie E Goldack; c Michael D, Graham H & Karen M. Educ: Univ BC, BSc, 60, PhD(org chem), 64. Prof Exp: Nat Res Coun Can fels, Royal Free Hosp Med Sch, Univ London, 64-65 & Inst Org Chem, Univ Stockholm, 65-66. Concurrent Pos: Nat Res Coun Can sr fel, Can Forest Serv, Sault Ste Marie, Can, 79-80; res prof, Simon Fraser Univ, 93. Mem: Am Chem Soc; Entom Soc Am. Res: Pheromone determination, structure and synthesis; the isolation, identification, synthesis and application of insect semiochemicals; forest lepidopteran pests - such as defoliators, cone and seed pests, wood boring beetles - responsible for the destruction of commercial timber, and social insects, particularly the honey bee and fire ant. Mailing Add: Dept Chem Simon Fraser Univ Burnaby BC V5A 1S6 Can. Fax: 604-291-3765; E-Mail: sless@bohr.chem.sfu.ca

SLETTEBAK, ARNE, ASTROPHYSICS. Current Pos: from instr to prof, Ohio State Univ, 49-94, dir, Perkins Observ, 59-78, chmn dept, 62-78, EMER PROF ASTRON, OHIO STATE UNIV, 94- Personal Data: b Danzig, Aug 8, 25; nat US; m 49, Constance Pixler; c Marcia D & John A. Educ: Univ Chicago, SB, 45, PhD(astron), 49. Prof Exp: Asst, Yerkes Observ, Univ Chicago, 45-49. Concurrent Pos: Fulbright res fel, Hamburg Observ, Ger, 55-56; mem bd dirs, Asn Univs for Res Astron, 61-79, chmn sci comt, 70-73, steering comt earth sci curric proj, 65-68; comt astron, Nat Res Coun; adv, Off Naval Res, 63-66; coun mem, Am Astron Soc, 64-67; mem, Adv Panel Astron, NSF, 68-71; Fulbright lectr & guest prof, Univ Vienna Observ, Austria, 74-75, 81 & 91; chmn, Working Group B-emission line Stars, Int Astron Union, 82-85; vis prof, Univ Louis Pasteur, Strasbourg Observ, 91. Mem: Am Astron Soc; Int Astron Union (pres, 79-82); fel Japan Soc Prom Sci; Sigma Xi. Res: Stellar rotation; spectroscopic investigations of normal and peculiar stars, especially B-emissionline stars. Mailing Add: Dept Astron Ohio State Univ 174 W 18 Ave Columbus OH 43210. Fax: 614-292-2928; E-Mail: slettebak@ohstpy.mps.ohio.state.edu

SLETTER, LLOYD E, BIOLOGICAL MONITORING, OCCUPATIONAL CHEMICALS. Current Pos: res chemist, 71-76, chief, Biophys Particulate Measurements Support Sect, 76-84, CHIEF APPL BIOMED BR, NAT INST OCCUP SAFETY & HEALTH, 84- Personal Data: b Cincinnati, Ohio, Mar 7, 40. Educ: Case Inst Technol, BS, 62; Univ Cincinnati, MA, 66, PhD(chem), 71. Mem: Am Chem Soc; Sigma Xi. Res: Development of biological monitoring methods for measuring worker uptake of occupational chemicals. Mailing Add: Nat Inst Occup Safety & Health 4676 Columbia Pkwy Cincinnati OH 45226. Fax: 513-533-8494

SLEVIN, JOHN THOMAS, NEUROLOGY. Current Pos: asst prof neurol, Univ Ky Med Ctr, 81-86, asst prof pharmacol, 82-86, assoc prof, 86-93, PROF NEUROL & PHARMACOL, UNIV KY MED CTR, 93- Personal Data: b Parkersburg, WVa, Dec 15, 48; M 71, Barbara Nyere; c Rob & Amie. Educ: Johns Hopkins Univ, BA, 70; WVa Univ, MD, 75. Honors & Awards: Klingman lectr neurol, Univ Va, 83. Prof Exp: Intern med, WVa Univ, 75-76; resident neurol, Univ Va, 76-79; fel neuropharmacol, Johns Hopkins Univ, 79-81. Concurrent Pos: Trainee neurol, Nat Inst Neurol Dis & Stroke, 77-78, fel, 79-81, teacher-investr develop award, 82-87; staff neurologist Vet Admin Med Ctr, 81-; examr, Am Board Psychiat & Neurol, Inc, 88- Mem: Fel Am Acad Neurol; Am Neurol Asn; Am Soc Pharmacol & Exp Therapeut; Soc Neurosci; Int soc Neurochem. Res: Role of phosphatases and kinases in neuronal signaling, plasticity and epilepsy; clinical investigation of movement disorders; biochemistry of neurodegenerative disease. Mailing Add: Dept Neurol Univ Ky Lexington KY 40536-0084. Fax: 606-323-5943; E-Mail: jsievin@pop.uky.edu

SLEZAK, FRANK BIER, ORGANIC CHEMISTRY, POLYMER CHEMISTRY. Current Pos: assoc prof, 69-74, chmn dept biol & chem, 71-77, PROF CHEM, MERCER CO COMMUNITY COL, 74- Personal Data: b Manhasset, NY, Nov, 19, 28; m 51, Barbara Castricum; c James F & Carolyn J. Educ: Antioch Col, BS, 51; Okla State Univ, MS, 53, PhD(org chem), 55. Prof Exp: Org res chemist, Diamond Alkali Co, 54-59, group leader condensation polymers, 59-63; group leader chem res & develop, Union Camp Corp, NJ, 63-69. Mem: AAAS; Am Chem Soc; Sigma Xi. Res: Synthetic organic chemistry related to biological activity; heterocyclics; condensation polymerization. Mailing Add: 9 Pine Knoll Dr Lawrenceville NJ 08648-3142. Fax: 609-890-6338; E-Mail: slezak@mccc.edu

SLEZAK, JANE ANN, BIOMEDICAL ENGINEERING. Current Pos: CHMN, CHEM DEPT, FULTON MONTGOMERY COMMUNITY COL. Personal Data: b Amsterdam, NY. Educ: State Univ NY, Albany, BS, MS; Rensselaer Polytech Inst, PhD(chem). Prof Exp: Res assoc chem, Univ Pittsburgh & Syracuse Univ; lectr chem, State Univ NY; assoc prof chem, Schenectady Community Col; res assoc biomed eng, Rensselaer Polytech Inst, 79- Concurrent Pos: Fel, AEC, NSF, Gen Elec, & NIH. Mem: Am Phys Soc; Sigma Xi; Am Chem Soc. Res: Materials properties of biological and calcified tissue using spectroscopy, magnetic resonance and physical chemistry; analyses of composite behavior and methods of failure of biological specimens. Mailing Add: 191 Church St Amsterdam NY 12010-3934

SLICHTER, CHARLES PENCE, SOLID STATE & CHEMICAL PHYSICS, SURFACE SCIENCE. Current Pos: From instr to assoc prof, 49-54, PROF PHYSICS, UNIV ILL, URBANA-CHAMPAIGN, 55-, CTR ADVAN STUDY, 68-, PROF CHEM, 86- Personal Data: b Ithaca, NY, Jan 21, 24; m 80, Anne Fitzgerald; c Summer P, William A, Jacob H, Ann T, Daniel H & David P. Educ: Harvard Univ, AB, 45, AM, 47, PhD(physics), 49. Hon Degrees: DSc, Univ Waterloo, 93; LLD, Harvard Univ, 96. Honors & Awards: Morris Loeb Lectr, Harvard Univ, 61; Langmuir Prize, Am Phys Soc, 69, Buckley Prize, 96; Int Soc Magnetic Resonance Prize, 86; Award for Sustained Outstanding Res in Solid State Physics, Div Mat Sci, US Dept Energy, 84 & 92, Award for Outstanding Sci Accomplishments in Solid State Physics, 93; Comstock Prize, Nat Acad Sci, 93. Concurrent Pos: Res Assoc, Underwater Explosives Res Lab, Woods Hole Oceanog Inst, 43-46; mem, Sci Adv Comt, Off of the Pres, 65-69, Comt Nat Medal Sci, 69-74, Comt Sci Technol, 76; Harvard Corp, 70-95; dir, Polaroid Corp, 75-97; mem corp former trustee, Woods Hole Oceanog Inst. Mem: Nat Acad Sci; fel AAAS; Am Acad Arts & Sci; Am Philos Soc; fel Am Phys Soc. Res: Electron and nuclear magnetic resonance in solids. Mailing Add: 61 Chestnut Ct Champaign IL 61821-7121

SLIDER, H C (SLIP), PETROLEUM ENGINEERING. Current Pos: RETIRED. Personal Data: b Paden City, WVa, June 26, 24; m 46, Virginia Moore; c Jeff & Terry. Educ: Ohio State Univ, BEM & MS, 49. Prof Exp: Exploitation engr, Shell Oil Co, 49-50, reservoir engr, 51-52, div reservoir engr, 53-56; prof, Ohio State Univ, 56-83, emer prof petrol eng, 83-90. Concurrent Pos: Consult, Shell Oil Co, 56, Humble Oil Co, 57 & 65, Esso Prod Res, Jersey Prod Res & Carter Prod Res Co, 58-65, Ins Co Am, 62-63 & 65-66, Texaco Inc, 66-, Schlumberger, 69 & 72, Petroleos del Peru, 70-71, Off Technol Assessment, US Cong, 76, Japan Petrol Develop Co, 77, Caltex, Indonesia, 79, Aramco, Saudi Arabia, Texaco, Angola & Nigeria, & Texaco Prod Serv, Eng, 80, Occidental of Peru, 83, Union Tex Petrol, Sun Oil & TRINMAR, Trinidad, 84, US Bur Land Mgt, 85, PT Indrillco Sakti, Indonesia, 88, China Nat Petrol, Peoples Republic China, 90, PT Loka Datamus Induh, Indonesia, 90, Ohio Oil & Gas Asn, 89, Quakerstate, 89-92-; vis prof, Univ Indust de Santander, Colombia, 77 & Tech Univ Clausthal, Ger, 78; distinguished lectr, Soc Petroleum Eng, 78-79. Mem: Am Inst Mining, Metall & Petrol Engrs; Am Inst Chem Engrs; Am Soc Eng Educ; Am Arbit Asn. Res: Petroleum production reservoir engineering. Mailing Add: 2013 Willow Glen Lane Columbus OH 43229. Fax: 614-292-3769

SLIEMERS, FRANCIS ANTHONY, JR, POLYMER CHEMISTRY, PLASMA POLYMERIZATION. Current Pos: RETIRED. Personal Data: b Lima, Ohio, June 28, 29; m 52; c 8. Educ: Univ Notre Dame, BS, 51; Ohio State Univ, MSc, 54. Prof Exp: Res assoc chem, Ohio State Univ, 54-56; prin chemist, Battelle Mem Inst, 56-62, sr res chemist, 62-71 & 73-79, assoc chief, 71-73, assoc sect mgr, 79-82, proj mgr, 82-87. Concurrent Pos: Consult, FAS, 87- Mem: Am Chem Soc. Res: Physical characterization of polymers; plasma polymerization. Mailing Add: 1514 Bolingbrook Dr Columbus OH 43228-9589

SLIEPCEVICH, CEDOMIR M, CHEMICAL ENGINEERING. *Current Pos:* RETIRED. *Personal Data:* b Anaconda, Mont, Oct 4, 20; m 55. *Educ:* Univ Mich, BS, 41, MS, 42, PhD(chem eng), 48. *Honors & Awards:* McGraw Award, Am Soc Eng Educ, 58, Westinghouse Award, 64; Int Ipatieff Award, Am Chem Soc, 59; Sigma Xi lectr, 62; Peter C Reilly lectr, Notre Dame, 72; Donald L Katz lectr, Univ Mich, 76; Walker Award, Am Inst Chem Engrs, 78; Gas Indust Res Award, Sprague Schlumberger-AGA Operating Sect, 86. *Prof Exp:* Asst, Univ Mich, 41-46, from instr to assoc prof chem & metall eng, 46-55; prof chem eng, Univ Okla, 55-63, chmn, Sch Chem Eng, 55-59, assoc dean, Col Eng, 56-63, chmn, Sch Gen Eng, 58-63, res prof eng, 63-91, emer prof eng, 91-92. *Concurrent Pos:* Consult, 43-; sr chem engr, Monsanto Chem Co, 52-53; dir res & eng, Constock Liquid Methane Corp, NY, 55-60; mem adv panel to engr sec, NSF & numerous comts, 61-64; dir, Constock-Pritchard Corp, 61-63, Autoclave Engrs, Inc, 61-, Repub Geothermal, Inc, 74-75 & E-C Corp, 66-78; mem, adv comt to US Coast Guard on Transp of Hazardous Mat, Nat Acad Sci, 64-76; dir, Engr Col Res Coun, Am Soc Engr Educ, 65-68; OK rep, Southern Interstate Nuclear Bd, 65-68; pres, Univ Engrs, Inc, 65-78 & Univ Technologiists, Inc, 77-; mem-at-large, Div Chem & Chem Technol, Nat Acad Sci-Nat Res Coun, 66-69; mem, Liquid Natural Gas Task Force Nat Gas Surv, Fed Power Comn, 72-73; mem, adv panel on energy, US Off Sci & Technol, 72-73; mem, comt processing & utilization of fossil fuels & chmn, coal liquefaction ad hoc comt, Nat Res Coun, 75-77, mem hydrogen panel, comt advan energy storage systs, 77-79, mem, comt demilitarizing chem munitions & agents, 83-84, mem, Nat Transp Bd Pipelines, Land Use & Pub Safety, 87-88. *Mem:* Nat Acad Eng; fel AAAS; Am Chem Soc; Am Soc Eng Educ; fel Am Inst Chem Engrs. *Res:* High pressure equipment design; chemical reaction kinetics; process control and system identification; energy scattering; cryogenics; thermodynamics; flame dynamics; liquefaction; ocean transport and storage of natural gas; fundamental behavior of flames and combustion; desalination. *Mailing Add:* Rte 1 Box 41-B1 Washington OK 73093

SLIFE, CHARLES W, EXTRACELLULAR MATRIX, STRUCTURE AND FUNCTION OF SKIN. *Current Pos:* group leader, Dept Biochem, 89-91, MGR, PHYSIOL, GILLETTE RES INST, GILLETTE CO, 91- *Personal Data:* b Urbana, Ill, Dec 10, 49; m 71, Kristen; c Leah, Carrie & Amy. *Educ:* Univ Ill, BS, 73; Univ Wis, PhD(biochem), 78. *Prof Exp:* Res fel biochem, Johns Hopkins Univ, 78-82; from asst prof to assoc prof, Sch Med, Emory Univ, 82-89. *Concurrent Pos:* Prin investr, NIH, 83-89. *Mem:* Am Soc Biochem & Molecular Biol; Am Soc Cell Biol; AAAS; Soc Invest Dermat; Soc Cosmetic Chemists. *Res:* The structure and function of skin and hair and the effects of personal care products on skin and hair properties. *Mailing Add:* Gillette Res Inst 401 Professional Dr Gaithersburg MD 20879-3400

SLIFE, FRED WARREN, AGRONOMY. *Current Pos:* From instr to prof agron, 47-77, PROF CROP PROD, UNIV ILL, URBANA, 77- *Personal Data:* b Milford, Ill, Nov 6, 23; m 47; c 4. *Educ:* Univ Ill, BS, 47, MS, 48, PhD, 52. *Mem:* Am Soc Agron; Weed Sci Soc Am. *Res:* Weed control, especially penetration and translocation; metabolism of herbicides in plants. *Mailing Add:* 2025 Burlison Dr Urbana IL 61801

SLIFKIN, LAWRENCE, SOLID STATE PHYSICS, PHOTOGRAPHIC SCIENCE. *Current Pos:* from asst prof to prof physics, Univ NC, Chapel Hill, 55-91, Bowman Gray prof undergrad teaching, 79-82, alumni distinguished prof, 83-91, EMER PROF, UNIV NC, CHAPEL HILL, 91- *Personal Data:* b Bluefield, WVa, Sept 29, 25; m 48, Miriam Kresses; c Anne, Rebecca, Merle & Naomi. *Educ:* NY Univ, BA, 47; Princeton Univ, PhD(phys chem), 50. *Honors & Awards:* Jesse Beams Award, Am Phys Soc, 77. *Prof Exp:* Res assoc physics, Univ Ill, 50-52, res asst prof, 52-54; asst prof, Univ Minn, 54-55. *Concurrent Pos:* NSF sr fel, Clarendon Lab, Oxford Univ, 62-63; liason scientist, US Off Naval Res, London, Eng, 69-70; foreign collabr, Ctr Nuclear Studies, Saclay, France, 75-76; res fel, Tel Aviv Univ, 91. *Mem:* Fel Am Phys Soc; Am Asn Physics Teachers; fel Soc Photog Scientists & Engrs. *Res:* Diffusion in solids; defects in ionic crystals; the photographic process. *Mailing Add:* Dept Physics & Astron Univ NC Chapel Hill NC 27599-3255. *Fax:* 919-962-0480

SLIFKIN, MALCOLM, MEDICAL MICROBIOLOGY, VIROLOGY. *Current Pos:* microbiologist, 65-71, HEAD SECT MICROBIOL, DEPT LAB MED, ALLEGHENY GEN HOSP, 71-; PROF, PATH & LAB MED, MED COL PA, ALLEGHENY CAMPUS, 90-, PROF MICROBIOL & IMMUNOL, 91- *Personal Data:* b Newark, NJ, Nov 9, 33; m 66, Janet Saperstein; c Joshua & Robert. *Educ:* Furman Univ, BS, 55; Univ NC, MSPH, 56, MS, 59; Rutgers Univ, PhD(serol), 62; Am Bd Med Microbiol, dipl, 69. *Honors & Awards:* Sci Award on Biol Sci, Electron Micros Soc Am, 77. *Prof Exp:* Instr parasitol, Sch Med, Yale Univ, 6264; clin asst prof path, Sch Med, Univ Pittsburgh, 75-90. *Concurrent Pos:* Fel microbiol, Sch Med, Yale Univ, 62-64; adj asst prof, Pa State Univ, 65-71, adj assoc prof, 71- *Mem:* Am Soc Microbiol; fel Am Acad Microbiol; NY Acad Sci; Sigma Xi. *Res:* Oncogenic simian adenoviruses; tissue culture of chemically induced liver cancer and preneoplastic liver; microcolony varients of Staphylococcus aureus; rapid niacin tests for Mycobacterium tuberculosis; applied clinical microbiology; choriogonadotropin-like antigens in bacteria and cancer cells; rapid identification of bacteria; rapid detection of bacteria from clinical specimens; development of new parasitological staining methods; diagnostic use of lectins in microbiology; parasitology, mycology and immunology. *Mailing Add:* Microbiol Sect Dept Lab Med Allegheny Gen Hosp Pittsburgh PA 15212. *Fax:* 412-359-3598

SLIGAR, STEPHEN GARY, BIOCHEMISTRY. *Current Pos:* LYCAN PROF DEPT CHEM & BIOCHEM, UNIV ILL, URBANA, 82- *Personal Data:* b Inglewood, Calif, Mar 19, 48; m 87; c 2. *Educ:* Drexel Univ, BS, 70; Univ Ill, Urbana, MS, 71, PhD(physics, biochem), 75. *Prof Exp:* Physicist, Naval Air Propulsion Test Ctr, Aeronaut Eng Lab, Philadelphia, 66-69; res student physics, Drexel Univ, 68-70; resident, Cent States Univ Honors Prog, Argonne Nat Lab, 70, guest assoc molecular biol, Div Biol & Med Res, 71-73; res asst, Univ Ill, Urbana, 72-75, res assoc biochem, 75-77; asst prof, dept molecular biophys & biochem, Yale Univ, 77-82. *Concurrent Pos:* Fulbright Res Scholar, Paris, France, 89-90. *Mem:* Biophys Soc; Am Soc Biol Chemists; Am Chem Soc; Am Phys Soc; AAAS. *Res:* Physical biochemistry, mechanisms of energy transfer and oxygenation reactions; thermodynamics of regulation and control in biological catalysis; kinetic and equilibrium description of multi-protein systems and complexes; biochemical pharmacology; genetic engineering; protein structure-function. *Mailing Add:* Sch Chem Sci Univ Ill 600 S Mathews Ave Urbana IL 61801

SLIGER, WILBURN ANDREW, FISH BIOLOGY, FRESH WATER BIOLOGY. *Current Pos:* from instr to assoc prof, 66-84, chmn dept, 85, PROF BIOL, UNIV TENN, MARTIN, 84- *Personal Data:* b Oklahoma City, Okla, Jan 21, 40; m 58; c 3. *Educ:* Cent State Univ, Okla, BS, 64; Okla State Univ, Stillwater, MS, 67, PhD(zool), 75. *Concurrent Pos:* Vis prof biol, Murray State Univ, Ky, 76-77; pres, Tenn Acad Sci, 94. *Mem:* Am Fisheries Soc; Sigma Xi (secy, 75-79). *Res:* Effects of water pollutants on the physiology of fish. *Mailing Add:* Dept Biol Univ Tenn Martin TN 38238

SLIKER, ALAN, WOOD TECHNOLOGY. *Current Pos:* RETIRED. *Personal Data:* b Cleveland, Ohio, June 7, 27; m 56; c 3. *Educ:* Duke Univ, BS, 51, MF, 52; NY Col Forestry, Syracuse Univ, PhD, 58. *Prof Exp:* Packaging engr, US Forest Prod Lab, Wis, 52-53; from instr to assoc prof forest prod, Mich State Univ, 55-74, prof forestry, 74-91. *Mem:* Forest Prod Soc; Sigma Xi; Soc Wood Sci & Technol. *Res:* Mechanical properties of wood, particularly those properties concerned with structural use of wood. *Mailing Add:* 4330 Hulett Rd Okemos MI 48864-2434

SLIKER, TODD RICHARD, SOLID STATE PHYSICS. *Personal Data:* b Rochester, NY, Feb 9, 36; m 63; c 2. *Educ:* Univ Wis, BS, 55; Cornell Univ, PhD(physics), 62; Harvard Univ, MBA, 70; Univ Denver, JD, 82. *Prof Exp:* Res assoc physics, Cornell Univ, 62; sr staff physicist, Electronic Res Div, Clevite Corp, 62-65, head, Appl Physics Sect, 65-68; asst to pres, Granville-Phillips Co, 70; vpres & gen mgr, McDowell Electronics, Inc, 70-71; pres, CA Compton Inc, 71-77; chief acct, C & S Inc, 77-80, vpres finance, 80-82. *Concurrent Pos:* Real estate mgr, 72- *Res:* Nuclear magnetic and electron paramagnetic resonance of solids; photolysis of silver chloride; linear electro-optic effects and devices; low frequency piezoelectric tuning fork filters; high frequency resonators and acoustic delay lines. *Mailing Add:* 12500 Oxford Rd PO Box 715 Niwot CO 80544-0715

SLIKKER, WILLIAM, JR, DEVELOPMENTAL TOXICOLOGY, METABOLISM. *Current Pos:* CHIEF PHARMACODYNAMICS, NAT CTR TOXICOL RES, 78- *Educ:* Univ Calif, Davis, PhD(pharmacol & toxicol), 78. *Res:* Neurotoxicology. *Mailing Add:* Div Neuro Toxicol Nat Ctr Toxicol Res Jefferson AR 72079-9502. *Fax:* 870-543-7136

SLILATY, STEVE N, BIOCHEMISTRY, MOLECULAR BIOLOGY. *Current Pos:* SCI DIR & CHIEF EXEC OFFICER, GENOMICS ONE CORP, 95- *Personal Data:* b Feb 11, 52; US citizen; m 89, Suzanne Lebel; c Catherine-Elise. *Educ:* Cornell Univ, BS, 76; Univ Ariz, PhD(cell & develop biol), 83. *Prof Exp:* Res assoc, Univ Ariz, 83-87; coun scientist, Protein Eng, Enzyme Mechanisms & Molecular Biol, Nat Res Coun, Montreal, 87-91; founder, pres & chief, exec officer, Quantum Biotechnol Inc, Montreal, 91-95. *Concurrent Pos:* Fel cancer biol, Med Ctr, Univ Ariz, 84-86; adj prof, Dept Virol, Univ Que. *Mem:* AAAS. *Res:* Determination of the chemical events at the level of bond rearrangement responsible for cleavage and, therefore, inactivation of the repressor protein LexA; gene transfer; high level expression systems (E. coli, human); protein enzyme engineering, proteases mechanism/cloning; gene isolation /cloning/synthesis; enzyme rate enhancement. *Mailing Add:* Genomics One 270 Samson Blvd Ste 105 Laval PQ H7X 2Y9 Can

SLINEY, DAVID H, MEDICAL PHYSICS. *Current Pos:* Chief, Laser Br, US Army Environ Hyg Agency, 65-95, MGR, LASER/OPTICAL RADIATION PROG, US ARMY CTR HEALTH PROM & PREV MED, ABERDEEN PROVING GROUND, MD, 95- *Personal Data:* b Washington, DC, Feb 21, 41; div; c Sean, David & Stephen. *Educ:* Va Polytech Inst, BS, 63; Emory Univ, MS, 65; Univ London, PhD, 91. *Concurrent Pos:* Consult, WHO, 65-, UNESCO, 85-; mem Army-Indust Comt Laser Safety, 67; consult laser hazards, NASA, 67-; US Coast & Geod Surv, 68-; mem comt laser safety, Am Nat Stand Inst, 68-; ed, Health Physics J, 76-87; Hayes-Fulbright fel, Yugoslavia, 76; US chief deleg, Comt TC76, Lasers of Int Electrotech Comm, 77-85; mem, Nat Acad Sci/Nat Res Coun Panel, Health Aspects Video Viewing, 80-82, Food & Drug Admin Tech Electronic Prod Radiation Safety Comt, 81-84 & Int Non-Ionizing Radiation Comt, 80-91, Int Comn Non-Ionizing Radiation Protection, 90-, Nat Comn Radiation & Measurements, 92-; chmn, Comt Phys Agents, Am Conf Govt Indust Hygienists; consult, Laser Technol UN Educ & Sci Cult, 86-92; pres, Laser Inst Am, 97. *Mem:* Optical Soc Am; Health Physics Soc; Am Conf Govt Indust Hygienists; Sigma Xi; Asn Res Vision & Ophthal; Am Soc Laser Med & Surg; Soc Photo-optical Instrumentation Engrs. *Res:* Criteria for laser hazard analysis; standards for laser exposure; optical radiation hazards; non-ionizing radiation; medical application lasers. *Mailing Add:* US Army Ctr Health Prom & Prev Med Aberdeen Proving Ground MD 21010-5422. *Fax:* 410-877-1646; *E-Mail:* dsliney@aeha1.apgea.army.mil

SLINGERLAND, RUDY LYNN, GEOLOGY, SEDIMENTOLOGY. *Current Pos:* From asst prof to assoc prof, 83-88, PROF GEOL, PA STATE UNIV, 89- *Personal Data:* b Troy, Pa, Apr 7, 47; m 84, Ellen Wecker; c 2. *Educ:* Dickinson Col, BS, 69; Pa State Univ, MS, 73, PhD(geol), 77. *Concurrent Pos:* Consult sedimentary basin anal. *Mem:* Geol Soc Am; Am Geophys Union; Sigma Xi; Soc Econ Paleontologists & Mineralogists; Int Asn Sedimentologists. *Res:* Sedimentology; coastal geology; fluvial geomorphology; tectonic geomorphology; paleoceanography. *Mailing Add:* 204A Deike Bldg University Park PA 16802. *Fax:* 814-865-3191; *E-Mail:* sling@geosc.psu.edu

SLINKARD, ALFRED EUGENE, PULSE CROPS. *Current Pos:* White chair, 90-93, SR RES SCIENTIST, UNIV SASK, 72- *Personal Data:* b Rockford, Wash, Apr 5, 31; m 51, Marie R Pierce; c William, Peggy, Donald, Roberta & Mary. *Educ:* Wash State Univ, BS, 52, MS, 54; Univ Minn, PhD(plant genetics), 57. *Honors & Awards:* Agron Merit Award, W Coop Fertilizers, 88. *Prof Exp:* Asst prof agron & asst agronomist, Univ Idaho, 57-66, assoc prof agron & assoc agronomist, 66-72. *Concurrent Pos:* Ed, Can J Plant Sci, 83-85; consult, numerous foreign countries; fel, Indian Soc Genetics & Plant Breeding, 89. *Mem:* Fel AAAS; Crop Sci Soc Am; Fel Am Soc Agron; Fel Agr Inst Can; Genetics Soc Can; Can Soc Agron; Sigma Xi; hon mem Can Seed Growers Asn, 91. *Res:* Genetics and breeding of pea and lentil; establishment of lentil as a commercial crop in Western Canada, including development of a package of agronomic practices and the registration of ten cultivars, Laird, Eston, Rose, CDC Richlea, CDC Gold, CDC Royale, ZT4, CDC Rodwing, CDC Matador and Indianhead; registered pea cultivars Bellevue, CDC Winfield, PC12-89-335 forage pea and P41G-9. *Mailing Add:* Dept Crop Sci Univ Sask 51 Campus Dr Saskatoon SK S7N 5A8 Can. *Fax:* 306-966-5015

SLINKARD, WILLIAM EARL, INORGANIC CHEMISTRY. *Current Pos:* STAFF CHEMIST, HOECHST CELANESE CHEM CO, 69- *Personal Data:* b Omaha, Nebr, May 14, 43; m 65; c 2. *Educ:* Trinity Univ, Tex, BS, 65; Ohio State Univ, PhD(inorg chem), 69; Corpus Christi State Univ, Tex, BS, 86. *Mem:* Am Chem Soc; Catalysis Soc. *Res:* catalytic vapor phase oxidation of hydrocarbons, methanol synthesis, steam reforming of natural gas, methanol homologation reactions and fuel applications of methanol. *Mailing Add:* Tech Ctr Hoechst Celanese Chem Group Box 9077 Corpus Christi TX 78469-9077

SLIVA, PHILIP OSCAR, SOLID STATE PHYSICS. *Current Pos:* Assoc scientist, Solid State Res Br, Xerox Corp, 67-68, scientist, Exp Physics Br, 68-73, sr scientist, Explor Photoconductor Physics Area, 73-76, mgr, Photoconductor Characterization area, 76-90, VPRES SUPPLIES DEVELOP & MFG, XEROX CORP, 90- *Personal Data:* b Yonkers, NY, Apr 22, 38; m 61; c 2. *Educ:* Clarkson Col Technol, BS, 60; Purdue Univ, PhD(solid state physics), 67. *Mem:* Am Phys Soc. *Res:* Acoustoelectric effects in III-IV semiconductors; solid state switching and memory devices in amorphous and polycrystalline materials; charge generation and transport in photoconductors. *Mailing Add:* 2400 Turk Hill Rd Victor NY 14564

SLIVINSKY, CHARLES R, ELECTRICAL ENGINEERING, COMPUTER SCIENCE. *Current Pos:* From asst prof to assoc prof, 68-77, PROF ELEC ENG, UNIV MO, COLUMBIA, 77- *Personal Data:* b St Clair, Pa, May 20, 41; m 63; c 2. *Educ:* Princeton Univ, BSE, 63; Univ Ariz, MS, 66, PhD(elec eng), 69. *Concurrent Pos:* NSF sci equip grant, 69-71, res initiation grant, 71-72, solid state power control stability anal grant, 72-74, res equip grant, 77-79; consult, Air Force Flight Dynamics Lab, 75-; US Air Force Off Sci Res grant, 76-79; NSF res Eqpt grants, 80, sci res grant, 81, Power Systs Res grants, 82-90. *Mem:* AAAS; Inst Elec & Electronics Engrs; Am Soc Eng Educ; Sigma Xi. *Res:* Automatic control; computer control and signal processing; electrical power systems. *Mailing Add:* 108 E Ridgeley Rd Columbia MO 65203-3530

SLIVINSKY, SANDRA HARRIET, HIGH TEMPERATURE TECHNOLOGY, LASER PROCESSING. *Current Pos:* prin investr, Astronaut Lab/Univ Dayton, 90-91, RES PHYS SCIENTIST, PHILLIPS LAB, EDWARDS AFB, 91- *Personal Data:* b New York, NY; c Barry K. *Educ:* Alfred Univ, BA, 62; Pa State Univ, MS(physics), 66; Univ Calif, Davis-Livermore, MS(appl sci), 73; Stanford Univ, PhD(mat sci), 83. *Prof Exp:* Res assoc, Dikewood Corp, 66-68; physicist, Lawrence Livermore Lab, 68-73; sr res engr, Lockheed Missiles & Space Co, 73-76; sr engr, Gen Elec Co, 76-85, mat specialist, Watkins Johnson, 85-86; sr scientist, United Technol-CSD, 86-90. *Mem:* Am Physics Soc; Soc Women Engrs; Inst Elec & Electronics Engrs; Am Ceramic Soc; Sigma Xi; Soc Advan Mat & Process Eng. *Res:* Development of a laser processing methods for skiving plastics over metal substrates; nitrogen-nitride equilibria in molten tin alloys, particularly for uranium and thorium metals using a modified sieverts apparatus. *Mailing Add:* PO Box 9302 Albuquerque NM 87119

SLIWKOWSKI, MARY BURKE, EFFECT OF CULTURE CONDITIONS ON STRUCTURE OF PROTEIN PHARMACEUTICALS, ANALYSIS OF RECOMBINANT PROTEINS. *Current Pos:* SR SCIENTIST, GENENTECH INC, 85- *Personal Data:* b Rochester, NY, May 5, 54; m 76, Mark; c Daniel B & Emily J. *Educ:* Univ Del, BS, 76; NC State Univ, PhD(biochem), 82. *Prof Exp:* From staff fel to sr staff fel, NIH, Nat Inst Arth, Diabetes, Digestive & Kidney Dis, 82-85. *Mem:* Am Soc Biochem & Molecular Biol; Am Chem Soc; AAAS; Asn Women Sci. *Res:* Identification and characterization of protein post-translational modifications which give rise to product structural heterogeneity; investigation of effects of culture conditions on product heterogeneity and development of methods of control which can be incorporated into cell culture production processes; identification of factors influencing recombinant protein biosynthesis and secretion. *Mailing Add:* Genentech Inc Cell Cult Res & Develop Dept MS32 460 Pt San Bruno Blvd South San Francisco CA 94080-4990

SLOAN, ALAN DAVID, APPLIED MATHEMATICS. *Current Pos:* from instr to asst prof, 72-77, ASSOC PROF MATH, GA INST TECHNOL, 77- *Personal Data:* b New York, NY, July 5, 45; m 69. *Educ:* Mass Inst Technol, BS, 67; Cornell Univ, PhD(math), 71. *Prof Exp:* Fel, Carnegie-Mellon Univ, 71-72; vis asst prof physics, Princeton Univ, 74-75. *Mem:* Am Math Soc; Soc Indust & Appl Math; Math Asn Am; Sigma Xi. *Res:* Applications of functional analysis and nonstandard analysis to mathematical physics especially to the area of quantum theory. *Mailing Add:* 1266 Holly Lane NE Atlanta GA 30329

SLOAN, FRANK A, HEALTH POLICY. *Current Pos:* J ALEXANDRIA MCMAHON PROF HEALTH POLICY & MGT & PROF ECON, DUKE UNIV, 93- *Personal Data:* b Greensboro, NC, Aug 15, 42; m; c 2. *Educ:* Oberlin Col, AB, 64; Harvard Univ, PhD(econ), 69. *Prof Exp:* Res assoc, Dept Econ, Rand Corp, 68-71; asst prof, Dept Econ, Col Bus Admin, Univ Fla, 71-73, asst prof, Dept Community Health & Family Med, 72-73, res assoc, Health Systs Div, 72-76, assoc prof, Dept Econ, Community Health & Family Med, 73-76; prof econ, Vanderbilt Univ, 76-84, sr res fel & dir, Health Policy Ctr, Inst Pub Policy, 76-93, Centennial prof econ, 84-93, chmn, Dept Econ & Bus Admin, 86-89. *Concurrent Pos:* Mem, Nat Adv Allergy & Infectious Dis Coun, HEW, 71-74, Adv Comt Cost & Financing Grad Med Educ, Nat Acad Sci, 77, Health Resources Admin Nursing Res & Educ Adv Comt, 77-78, Nat Coun Health Care Technol, Dept Health & Human Servs, 79-81, Coun Res & Develop, Am Hosp Asn, 82-84 & Study Sect, Health Serv Res Rev, 85-89; prin investr, HEW, 72-78, Nat Ctr Health Serv Res, 75-90, Social Security Admin, 75-77, Health Care Financing Admin, Dept Health & Human Servs, 78- & Robert Wood Johnson Found, 85-89; consult, numerous govt agencies & indust, 83-91; res assoc, Nat Bur Econ Res, Inc, 88; res economist, Rand Corp. *Mem:* Inst Med-Nat Acad Sci; Am Econ Asn. *Res:* Health care law and economics; author of numerous technical publications; alcohol use prevention long-term care; medical malpractice; cost effective analysis of medical technologies; hospitals, health care financing and health manpower. *Mailing Add:* Ctr Health Policy Duke Univ 125 Old Chemistry Bldg Box 90253 Durham NC 27708. *Fax:* 919-684-6246

SLOAN, GILBERT JACOB, PHYSICAL ORGANIC CHEMISTRY. *Current Pos:* RES ASSOC, NORQUAY TECHNOL INC, 96- *Personal Data:* b Elizabeth, NJ, July 25, 28; m 57, Sonia Schorr; c Victor S & Jonathan L. *Educ:* Mich Col Mining & Technol, BS, 48; Univ Mich, PhD(chem), 54. *Prof Exp:* Res chemist, E I DuPont de Nemours & Co Inc, 53-73, supvr, 73-80, res mgr cent res & develop dept, 80-85, sr res fel, polymer prod dept, 85-89, sr res fel, DuPont Fibers, 89-95. *Concurrent Pos:* Assoc ed, J Crystal Growth, 67-84. *Mem:* Am Chem Soc; Sigma Xi. *Res:* Stable free radicals; purification of organic compounds; crystal growth. *Mailing Add:* 25 Indian Field Rd Wilmington DE 19810. *Fax:* 610-874-3575

SLOAN, HERBERT, THORACIC SURGERY. *Current Pos:* RETIRED. *Personal Data:* b Clarksburg, WVa, Oct 10, 14; m 43; c 5. *Educ:* Washington & Lee Univ, AB, 36; Johns Hopkins Univ, MD, 40. *Prof Exp:* Assoc prof, Univ Mich, Ann Arbor, 53-62, prof surg, 62, head sect thoracic surg, 70-86. *Concurrent Pos:* Assoc ed, Ann Thoracic Surg, 64-69, ed, 69-84; mem, Am Bd Thoracic Surg, 66-71, vchmn, 71-72, chmn credentials comt, 69-, vchmn nominating comt, 71-72, secy, 73-86; mem, Residency Rev Comt Thoracic Surg, 72-73; mem, Adv Group Cardiac Surg, Vet Admin, 71-81; mem, Surg Study Group, Inter-Soc Comn Heart Dis Resources, 71-72, Cardiac Surg Rev Panel, 73-; liaison mem, Am Bd Thoracic Surg to Inter-Soc Comn Heart Dis Resources, 73; mem, Adv Comt, Second Henry Ford Hosp Int Symp Cardiac Surg, 73-75, assoc ed, Proc Symp, 75; prog chmn, Adv Comt Thoracic Surg, Am Col Surgeons, 75-78. *Mem:* Am Surg Asn; Am Col Surgeons; Am Heart Asn; Soc Thoracic Surgeons (vpres, 73-74, pres, 74-75); Am Asn Thoracic Surg (vpres, 78-79); Sigma Xi. *Res:* Cardiac surgery. *Mailing Add:* 471 Barton N Dr Ann Arbor MI 48105-1017

SLOAN, JEWELL W, NEUROSCIENCES, BIOCHEMISTRY. *Current Pos:* asst res prof, 89-90, interim dir res, 93-96, ASST RES PROF, ANESTHESIOL DEPT, COL MED, UNIV KY, 90-, DIR BASIC RES, 96- *Personal Data:* b Bumpus Mills, Ky, Aug 11, 23; m 47, William E; c Lisa (Levin) & Walker E. *Prof Exp:* Chemist & supvry res chemist, Addiction Res Ctr, NIMH, 50-77. *Mem:* Am Soc Pharmacol & Exp Therapeut; Sigma Xi; Soc Neurosci; NY Acad Sci. *Res:* Study of the abuse potential of the narcotic analgesics plus nicotine; study of the sedative hypnotics; determine which sites in the brain become dependent on benzodiazepenes and how one site differs from the other relative to sex and drug of dependence. *Mailing Add:* MDRF No 3 Rm 244 Univ Ky Limestone & Kentucky Clinic Dr Lexington KY 40536-0216. *Fax:* 606-323-1924; *E-Mail:* sjewell@pop.uky.edu

SLOAN, LISA CIRBUS, EARTH SCIENCE. *Current Pos:* res scientist & lectr, 92-95, ASST PROF, EARTH SCI DEPT, UNIV CALIF, SANTA CRUZ, 95- *Educ:* Allegheny Col, BS, 82; Kent State Univ, MS, 86; Pa State Univ, PhD(geosci), 90. *Prof Exp:* Postdoctoral res fel & instr, Dept Geol Sci & Atmospheric, Oceanic & Space Sci Dept, Univ Mich, 90-92. *Mem:* Am Geophys Union; Geol Soc Am; Soc Sedimentary Geol. *Mailing Add:* Earth Sci Dept Univ Calif Santa Cruz CA 95064. *Fax:* 408-459-3074

SLOAN, MARTHA ANN, COMPUTER NETWORKS, QUALITY. *Current Pos:* PROF ELEC ENG, MICH TECHNOL UNIV, 69- *Personal Data:* wid; c Elizabeth D (DeArmond) & Graham F. *Educ:* Stanford Univ, BS, 61, MS, 63, PhD(elec eng), 73. *Hon Degrees:* LLD, Concordia Univ, 93. *Honors & Awards:* Frederick Emmons Terman Award, Am Soc Eng Educ, 78; Centrennial Medal, Inst Elec & Electronics Engrs, 84; Richard E Merwin Award, 91. *Prof Exp:* Res engr, Lockheed Missiles & Space Co, 61-63; teacher math & sci, Franfort Int Sch, 65-67. *Mem:* Fel Inst Elec & Electronics Engrs; fel Asn Comput Mach; AAAS; Am Soc Eng Educ; Soc Women Engrs. *Res:* Computer engineering. *Mailing Add:* Dept Elec Eng Mich Technol Univ 1400 Townsend Dr Houghton MI 49931. *Fax:* 906-487-2949

SLOAN, MARTIN FRANK, INDUSTRIAL ORGANIC CHEMISTRY. *Current Pos:* Res chemist, Hercules Inc, 60-69, res supvr, 69-74, supvr mkt develop, 74-76, develop mgr, 76-80, res assoc, 80-87, mgr patent coord, 88-94, SR PATENT AGENT, HERCULES INC, 94- *Personal Data:* b St Louis, Mo, Oct 9, 34; m 60; c 2. *Educ:* Wash Univ, BA, 56; Univ Wis, PhD, 60. *Mem:* Am Chem Soc. *Mailing Add:* 2203 Pennington Dr Wilmington DE 19810-2506

SLOAN, MICHAEL ALLAN, CEREBROVASCULAR DISEASES-NEUROLOGY, NEUROSONOLOGY. *Current Pos:* asst prof, 88-93, ASSOC PROF NEUROL, SCH MED, UNIV MD, 93- *Personal Data:* b Detroit, Mich, July 26, 54; m 83, Janet Mahmarian; c Jessica & Brittany. *Educ:* Univ Mich, BS, 76; Wayne State Univ, MD, 80. *Prof Exp:* Fel cerebrovasc dis, Univ Va, 87-88. *Concurrent Pos:* Fel, Am Heart Asn Stroke Coun, 88- *Mem:* AMA; Am Col Physicians; Am Acad Neurol; Am Heart Asn; Am Soc Neuroimaging; Int Cerebral Hemodynamics Soc. *Res:* Investigation into putative risk factors for stroke, clinical trials of novel therapeutic regimens for ischemic and hemorrhagic stroke and non-invasive evaluation of the cerebral circulation. *Mailing Add:* Dept Neurol Univ Md 22 S Greene St Baltimore MD 21201-1544. *Fax:* 410-328-0697

SLOAN, NORMAN GRADY, engineering, for more information see previous edition

SLOAN, ROBERT DYE, MEDICINE. *Current Pos:* RETIRED. *Personal Data:* b Clarksburg, WVa, Feb 17, 18; m 46; c 2. *Educ:* Washington & Lee Univ, AB, 39; Johns Hopkins Univ, MD, 43. *Prof Exp:* From instr to assoc prof radiol, Johns Hopkins Univ, 48-55; prof radiol & chmn dept, Med Ctr, Univ Miss, 55-82. *Concurrent Pos:* Consult, Vet Admin Hosp, 55- *Mem:* Am Roentgen Ray Soc; Radiol Soc NAm. *Res:* Diagnostic radiology; intestinal obstruction. *Mailing Add:* PO Box 1225 Raton NM 87740-1225

SLOAN, ROBERT EVAN, STRATIGRAPHY, PALEONTOLOGY. *Current Pos:* Asst prof, 53-63, assoc prof, 64-71, PROF GEOL, UNIV MINN, MINNEAPOLIS, 71- *Personal Data:* b Champaign, Ill, July 17, 29; m 53; c 2. *Educ:* Univ Chicago, PhB, 48, SB, 50, SM, 52, PhD(geol), 53. *Mem:* Soc Econ Paleont & Mineral; Soc Vert Paleont; Soc Study Evolution; Geol Soc Am; Soc Syst Zool. *Res:* Mesozoic and Paleocene mammals; Multituberculata; terrestrial vertebrate paleoecology; Cretaceous and Paleocene stratigraphy of western North America. *Mailing Add:* Geol Univ Minn 106 Pillsbury Dr SE Minneapolis MN 55455-0219

SLOAN, ROBERT W, MATHEMATICS. *Current Pos:* chmn dept, 65-76, PROF MATH, ALFRED UNIV, 65- *Personal Data:* b Rankin, Ill, July 18, 24; m 49; c 2. *Educ:* US Naval Acad, BS, 46; Univ Ill, MS, 51, PhD(math), 55. *Prof Exp:* Asst prof math, Univ NH, 55-56; asst prof, Carleton Col, 56-59; prof, State Univ NY Col Oswego, 59-65. *Mem:* Math Asn Am. *Res:* Analysis and numerical analysis. *Mailing Add:* Dept of Math Alfred Univ Alfred NY 14802

SLOAN, TOD BURNS, NEUROANESTHESIA, NEUROLOGICAL MONITORING. *Current Pos:* PROF, UNIV TEX HEALTH SCI CTR, 89- *Personal Data:* b Washington, DC, Dec 21, 48; m 72, Celia Kaye; c Heather & Gwendolin. *Educ:* Calif State Polytech Univ, BSEE, 72, BS, 72; Northwestern Univ, PhD(biochem), 78, MD, 79. *Prof Exp:* Asst prof anesthesia, Northwestern Univ, 82-86, assoc prof, anesthesia & neurol, 86-89. *Mem:* Inst Elec & Electronics Engrs; Am Soc Anesthesiologists; fel Am Inst Chem; Am Soc Anesthetists; Soc Neurosurg Anesthesia & Critical Care. *Res:* Electrophysiology of central nervous system during surgery and during anesthesia. *Mailing Add:* 28573 Dapper Dan Fair Oaks Ranch TX 78015. *Fax:* 210-567-6135; *E-Mail:* sloan@uthscsa.edu

SLOAN, WILLIAM COOPER, biology, for more information see previous edition

SLOANE, BONNIE FIEDOREK, PROTEASES & INHIBITORS, CANCER BIOLOGY. *Current Pos:* from asst prof to assoc prof, 80-89, PROF PHARMACOL, WAYNE STATE UNIV SCH MED, 89-, CHAIR PHARMACOL, 95- *Personal Data:* b Pittsburgh, Pa, Aug 12, 44; m 87, Douglas Yingst. *Educ:* Duke Univ, BS, 66, MA, 68; Rutgers Univ, PhD(physiol), 76. *Prof Exp:* Nat Res Serv Awards, fel, Univ Pa, 76-79, asst prof physiol, 79; asst prof physiol, Mich State, 79-80. *Concurrent Pos:* Adj scientist, Mich Cancer Found, 84-94, vis scientist, 93; mem, Path B Study Sect, NIH, 87-91 & 92-94; asst dir, Tumor Biol Prog, Comprehensive Cancer Ctr, Metro Detroit, 90-97; dep assoc dir clin res, Karmanos Cancer Inst, 95-97, dir Tumor/Stromal Interactions Prof, 97- *Mem:* Am Physiol Soc; Am Soc Cell Biol; Am Asn Cancer Res; AAAS; Metastasis Res Soc. *Res:* Lysosomal proteases, particularly cysteine proteases and their inhibitors in tumor progression, invasion and metastasis. *Mailing Add:* Dept Pharmacol Wayne State Univ Sch Med Detroit MI 48201. *Fax:* 313-577-6739; *E-Mail:* bsloane@med.wayne.edu

SLOANE, CHRISTINE SCHEID, atmospheric chemistry & physics, for more information see previous edition

SLOANE, HOWARD J, SPECTROCHEMISTRY. *Current Pos:* PRES, SAVANT, SLOANE AV ANALYSIS & TRAINING, 77- *Personal Data:* b New York, NY, May 9, 31; m 57, Valerie Sloane; c Perri & Hal. *Educ:* Trinity Col, BS, 53; Wesleyan Univ, MA, 55. *Prof Exp:* Infrared spectroscopist, Dow Chem Co, 55-60; chief chemist, Beckman Instruments, Inc, 60-67; dir appln res, Cary Instruments Div, Varian Assocs, 67-72; sr scientist, Beckman Instruments, Inc, 72-74, mgr appln res, Sci Instruments Div, 74-77. *Concurrent Pos:* Lectr, Raman Inst & Workshop, Univ Md, 68-72 & absorption spectros, Ariz State Univ, 60-, Am Chem Soc, 83-, Finnigan MAT Inst, 79-86. *Mem:* Am Chem Soc; Soc Appl Spectros; Coblentz Soc (treas, 72-83); NY Acad Sci. *Res:* Instrumentation and applications of spectroscopy, especially vibrational and atomic. *Mailing Add:* Savant Sloane AV Anal Training PO Box 3670 Fullerton CA 92634-3670

SLOANE, NATHAN HOWARD, BIOCHEMISTRY. *Current Pos:* ADJ PROF, UNIV MEMPHIS, 88- *Personal Data:* b Boston, Mass, Sept 15, 17; m 46, 85, Carmen Morgan; c Donald, Wendi & Gary. *Educ:* Mass Col Pharm, BS, 39; Mass Inst Technol, MPH, 43; Harvard Univ, PhD, 50. *Prof Exp:* Chemist, Lederle Labs, Am Cyanamid Co, 43-45, group leader biochem, 51-56; biochemist, Ciba Pharmaceut Prod, Inc, 49-51, Nat Drug Co, Vick Chem Co, 56-58; biochemist & sr fel, Mellon Inst, 58-64; prof biochem, Col Med, Univ Tenn, Memphis, 64-86; vis prof, Sch Pub Health, Harvard Univ, 86-87 & Christian Brothers Col, 86-88. *Concurrent Pos:* Pres, Antitumor Res Prods, Inc. *Mem:* Am Chem Soc; Am Soc Biochem & Molecular Biol. *Res:* Anti-carcogenic proteins in urine and plasma; chemical carcinogenesis; study immune modulators; protein structure; peptide synthesis. *Mailing Add:* 1842 Brookside Dr Memphis TN 38138-2547

SLOANE, NEIL JAMES ALEXANDER, MATHEMATICS, ELECTRICAL ENGINEERING. *Current Pos:* PRIN MEM TECH STAFF, AT&T RES LABS, 96- *Personal Data:* b Beaumaris, Wales, Oct 10, 39. *Educ:* Univ Melbourne, BEE, 59, BA, 60; Cornell Univ, MS, 64, PhD(elec eng), 67. *Honors & Awards:* Chauvenet Prize, Math Asn Am, 79. *Prof Exp:* Asst prof elec eng, Cornell Univ, 67-69; mem tech staff, Math Dept, Bell Tel Labs, 69-96. *Mem:* Am Math Soc; Math Asn Am; fel Inst Elec & Electronics Engrs; Am Statist Asn. *Res:* Coding theory; communication theory; combinatorial mathematics, graph theory. *Mailing Add:* AT&T Res Labs 600 Mountain Ave Rm 2C-376 Murray Hill NJ 07974

SLOANE, ROBERT BRUCE, psychiatry, for more information see previous edition

SLOANE, THOMPSON MILTON, COMBUSTION CHEMISTRY. *Current Pos:* from assoc sr res chemist to sr res chemist, 73-82, asst dept head, 84-87, PRIN RES SCIENTIST, PHYS CHEM DEPT, GEN MOTORS CORP, 87- *Personal Data:* b Baltimore, Md, Aug 30, 45; m 69, Christine Scheid; c Luke N & Derek W. *Educ:* Univ Ariz, BS, 67; Mass Inst Technol, PhD(phys chem), 72. *Prof Exp:* Chemist, Lawrence Berkeley Lab, Univ Calif, 72-73. *Concurrent Pos:* Tech group leader, Battelle Pac NW Lab, 92-94. *Mem:* Am Chem Soc; Sigma Xi; Combustion Inst. *Res:* Combustion chemistry. *Mailing Add:* Phys Chem Dept NAO Res & Develop Ctr Gen Motors Tech Ctr Warren MI 48090-9055

SLOAT, BARBARA FURIN, YEAST CELL MORPHOGENESIS, GENDER & SCIENCE. *Current Pos:* LECTR BIOL, RESIDENTIAL COL, UNIV MICH, 86- *Personal Data:* b Jan 20, 42; m 68, J Barry Sloat; c John Andrew & Eric Daniel. *Educ:* Univ Mich, BS, 63, MS, 66, PhD(zool), 68. *Concurrent Pos:* Dir, Women Sci Prog, Univ Mich, 80-84, assoc dir, honors prog, 86-87; lectr, Residential Col, 84- *Mem:* Am Soc Cell Biol; NY Acad Sci; AAAS; Sigma Xi; Am Women Sci (pres elect, 90). *Res:* Cellular morphogenesis in yeast; liposomal hydrolase characterization and activity in developing brain and liver of rat; factors that influence girls and women to choose and remain in scientific majors and careers. *Mailing Add:* Univ Mich 240 Indian River Pl Ann Arbor MI 48104. *Fax:* 313-761-8778; *E-Mail:* bsloat@umich.edu

SLOAT, CHARLES ALLEN, CHEMISTRY. *Current Pos:* from asst prof to prof, 27-68, EMER PROF CHEM, GETTYSBURG COL, 68- *Personal Data:* b Cashtown, Pa, Dec 12, 98; m 46, Marion Biggs. *Educ:* Gettysburg Col, BS, 23; Haverford Col, AM, 24; Princeton Univ, PhD(chem), 30. *Prof Exp:* Teaching asst chem, Haverford Col, 23-24 & Princeton Univ, 24-27. *Concurrent Pos:* Capt, Chem Warfare Serv, US Army, 42-45, major, 45-46. *Mem:* AAAS; Am Chem Soc; Am Soc Metals. *Res:* Crystals; phenomena due to forces at crystal faces as studied by mutual orientation; adsorption of solutes by crystals in relation to compatability of space lattice. *Mailing Add:* 29 W Broadway Gettysburg PA 17325-1202

SLOBIN, LAWRENCE I, IMMUNOLOGY. *Current Pos:* assoc prof, 77-83, PROF BIOCHEM, SCH MED, UNIV MISS, 83- *Personal Data:* b New York, NY, June 20, 38; m 64; c 1. *Educ:* Queens Col, City Univ New York, BS, 59; Univ Calif, Berkeley, PhD(biochem), 64. *Prof Exp:* USPHS Teaching fel, Weizmann Inst Sci, 64-65; USPHS teaching fel, Univ Calif, San Diego, 65-66, Ann Cancer Soc fel biochem, 66-67; asst prof microbiol, Cornell Univ, 67-73; sr res assoc biochem, State Univ Leiden, Neth, 74-77. *Mem:* Am Soc Biol Chemists; AAAS; Am Soc Microbiol; Am Soc Cell Biol. *Res:* Regulation of protein synthesis in mammaliam cells; structure and function of protein synthesis factors. *Mailing Add:* Dept Biochem Sch Med Univ Miss 2500 N State St Jackson MS 39216-4505. *Fax:* 601-984-1501

SLOBODA, ADOLPH EDWARD, CELL PHYSIOLOGY, PHARMACOLOGY. *Current Pos:* Biologist, 52-56, biostatistician, 57, res biologist, 58-65, SR RES BIOLOGIST & GROUP LEADER INFLAMMATION & IMMUNOSUPPRESSION, LEDERLE LABS, AM CYANAMID CO, 66- *Personal Data:* b New York, NY, Jan 17, 28; m 54; c 4. *Educ:* Champlain Col, AB, 52; NY Univ, MS, 57, PhD(cytophysiol), 61. *Mem:* Am Soc Pharmacol & Exp Therapeut; NY Acad Sci. *Res:* Drug effects on various aspects of inflammation and the immune system; relationship of immunosuppression and cancer. *Mailing Add:* 323 Buena Vista Rd New York NY 10956

SLOBODA, ROGER D, BIOLOGY, BIOCHEMISTRY. *Current Pos:* from asst prof to prof biol, 77-92, IRA ALLEN EASTMAN PROF, DARTMOUTH COL, 92- *Personal Data:* b Troy, NY, May 18, 48; m 70, Carol Joly; c Aaron & Lara. *Educ:* State Univ NY, BS, 70; Rensselaer Polytech Inst, PhD(develop biol), 74. *Prof Exp:* Fel biol, Yale Univ, 74-77. *Concurrent Pos:* Instr, Physiol Course, Marine Biol Lab, 81-83 & 93-96, bd trustees, 90-93; investr, Palmer Sta, Antarctica, 85. *Mem:* Am Soc Cell Biol; AAAS; Sigma Xi; Soc Develop Biol. *Res:* Biochemistry of assembly and function of microtubules and associated proteins with specific interests in their roles in cell division and intracellular particle motility. *Mailing Add:* Dept Biol Sci Dartmouth Col Hanover NH 03755. *Fax:* 603-646-1347; *E-Mail:* rds@dartmouth.edu

SLOBODCHIKOFF, CONSTANTINE NICHOLAS, BEHAVIORAL ECOLOGY. *Current Pos:* From asst prof to assoc prof, 71-82, PROF BIOL, NORTHERN ARIZ UNIV, 82- *Personal Data:* b Shanghai, China, Apr 23, 44; US citizen; m 71; c 2. *Educ:* Univ Calif, Berkeley, BS, 66, PhD, 71. *Concurrent Pos:* Fulbrigt fel, Kenya, 83; vis prof, Kenyatta Univ, 83. *Mem:* Ecol Soc Am; Soc Study Evolution; AAAS; Animal Behavior Soc. *Res:* Ecological, genetic, and behavioral factors contributing to the development and maintenance of social systems; communication in animal systems; development of animal "language" systems. *Mailing Add:* Dept Biol Sci Northern Ariz Univ Flagstaff AZ 86011

SLOBODKIN, LAWRENCE BASIL, ECOLOGY. *Current Pos:* chmn prog ecol & evolution, 69-74, PROF BIOL, STATE UNIV NY STONY BROOK, 68- *Personal Data:* b New York, NY, June 22, 28; m 52, Tamara Jonas; c Nathan, David & Naomi. *Educ:* Bethany Col, WVa, BS, 47; Yale Univ, PhD(zool), 51. *Honors & Awards:* Russel Award, 61. *Prof Exp:* Chief invests, US Fish & Wildlife Serv, 51-52, fisheries res biologist, 52-53; vis investr, Univ Mich, Ann Arbor, 53-54, instr zool, 53-57, from asst prof to prof, 57-68. *Concurrent Pos:* Guggenheim fel, 61, 74, fel, Woodrow Wilson Inst, 90; vis prof, Tel Aviv Univ, 65-66, Tsukua Univ, Japan, 89; distinguished vis scientist, Smithsonian Inst, 74-75. *Mem:* Soc Gen Syst Res (pres, 67); Am Acad Arts & Sci; Am Soc Nat (pres, 85); Ecol Soc Am. *Res:* Theoretical and experimental population ecology; evolutionary strategy; ecological planning and decision making with reference to environmental management; biology of hydra; theory of simplicity; hydrobiology. *Mailing Add:* Dept Ecol & Evolution SUNY at Stonybrook, 1100 Nicholls Rd Stony Brook NY 11794-0001. *E-Mail:* bzil@sbbiovm

SLOBODRIAN, RODOLFO JOSE, PHYSICS. *Current Pos:* chmn dept, 85-88, PROF PHYSICS, LAVAL UNIV, 68- *Personal Data:* b Buenos Aires, Arg, Jan 1, 30; m 59, Maria L Libatto; c Sergio R, Jose D & Maria L. *Educ:* Univ Buenos Aires, Bachelor, 48, LicSc, 53, DSc (physics), 55. *Prof Exp:* Investr nuclear physics, Arg Nat AEC, 53-63; prof physics, Nat Univ La Plata, 58-63; physicist, Lawrence Radiation Lab, Univ Calif, 63-68. *Concurrent Pos:* Asst to chair theoret physics, Univ Buenos Aires, 54-55, head lab spec physics, 57-58; Arg Nat AEC study mission, Radiation Lab, Univ Calif, 55-57. *Mem:* Am Phys Soc; NY Acad Sci; Can Asn Physicists; AAAS; Am Inst Aeronaut & Astronaut. *Res:* Nuclear reactions; nucleon-nucleon interactions, final state interactions, polarization phenomena, multibody channels and nucleon transfer reactions; space physics. *Mailing Add:* Dept Physics Laval Univ Quebec PQ G1K 7P4 Can. *Fax:* 418-656-2040; *E-Mail:* 36130008@vmi.ulaval.ca

SLOCOMBE, DONALD SCOTT, ECOSYSTEM HEALTH & INTEGRITY, ECOSYSTEM MODELLING & MANAGEMENT. *Current Pos:* asst prof geog & dir, Cold Regions Res Ctr, 89-94, ASSOC PROF, WILFRID LAURIER UNIV, 94- *Personal Data:* b Halifax, NS, Apr 15, 61; m 93, Anna C Waldvogel. *Educ:* Univ Waterloo, BIS, 83, PhD(resource & environ planning), 90; Univ BC, MS, 86. *Prof Exp:* Systs ecologist, Environ & Social Systs Analysts, 85-86. *Concurrent Pos:* Contract consult, Westwater Res Ctr, Univ BC, 84, Can Parks Serv, 88-90, Environ Can, 92-94; Prin investr, Soc Sci & Humanities Res Coun Can, 90- *Mem:* Can Asn Geogrs; Int Soc Ecol Modelling; Soil & Water Conserv Soc. *Res:* Interconnected sustainability of ecological systems and human economic and social systems; defining and assessing ecosystem health and integrity, mechanisms for ecosystem management and computer and other tools for fostering sustainable resource use and ecosystem management. *Mailing Add:* Dept Geog & Environ Studies Wilfrid Laurier Univ Waterloo ON N2L 3C5 Can. *E-Mail:* sslocomb@mach1.wlu.ca

SLOCOMBE, JOSEPH OWEN DOUGLAS, PARASITOLOGY, VETERINARY MEDICINE. *Current Pos:* from asst prof to assoc prof, 69-76, PROF PARASITOL, ONT VET COL, UNIV GUELPH, 76- *Personal Data:* b Port-of-Spain, Trinidad, July 27, 31; Can citizen; m 63; c 3. *Educ:* Univ West Indies, dipl, 55; Univ Toronto, DVM, 61; Cornell Univ, PhD(parasitol), 69. *Prof Exp:* Asst to plant pathologist, Cent Exp Sta, Govt Trinidad & Tobago, 55-56, vet, Tobago, 61-65; asst parasitol, NY State Vet Col, Cornell Univ, 65-69. *Concurrent Pos:* Ont Racing Comn grant, Univ Guelph, 70-78; Nat Res Coun Can grant, 71-89; res grants, Ont Ministry Agr & Food, 74-78, E P Taylor res fund, 76-78, Can Vet res fund, 77-79 & Can Dept Agr, 78-79. *Mem:* Am Soc Parasitol; Am Asn Vet Parasitologists; Am Asn Equine Practrs; Am Heartworm Soc; Am Soc Parasitol; Am Vet Med Asn; Can Asn Advan Vet Parasitol; Can Vet Med Asn; Conf Res Workers Animal Dis; World Asn Advan Vet Parasitol. *Res:* Strongyles in horses; heartworm in dogs; Bovine parasitism; surveillance for parasitisms in domestic animals. *Mailing Add:* Dept Path Biol Univ Guelph Guelph ON N1G 2W1 Can

SLOCOMBE, ROBERT JACKSON, ORGANIC POLYMER CHEMISTRY. *Current Pos:* RETIRED. *Personal Data:* b Peabody, Kans, May 22, 17; div; c 2. *Educ:* Univ Kans, AB, 39, MA, 41, PhD(org chem), 43; Univ Mo, St Louis, AB, 86. *Prof Exp:* Asst instr chem, Univ Kans, 40-43; res chemist, Monsanto Co, 43-45, res group leader, Ala, 45-50, Ohio, 50-61, Mo, 61-69, sr res specialist, 69-79. *Concurrent Pos:* Consult, 79- *Mem:* AAAS; Am Chem Soc; Am Inst Chem Eng. *Res:* Preparation and production of isocyanates; reactions of phosgene; synthesis and stabilization of high polymers; multicomponent copolymerization; protein fractionation; reactive copolymers; epoxy matrix resins in composites; electrostatic printing inks; photopolymers; cellular plastics; bio-medical polymer systems; light activated printing inks. *Mailing Add:* 8600 Delmar Blvd Apt 7A St Louis MO 63124

SLOCUM, DONALD HILLMAN, TRADITIONAL MEDICINE, PHYTOLOGY. *Current Pos:* PRES, DONER-VIKING CO, 85- *Personal Data:* b Flushing, NY, Jan 6, 30; m 85, Barbara M Ruane; c Richard A, Mark E & Carol L (Basteris). *Educ:* Davis & Elkins Col, BS, 51; Univ Vt, MSc, 56; Ohio State Univ, PhD(biochem-biophys), 58; Rider Col, MBA, 72. *Hon Degrees:* DSc, Norton Col, 73; LLD, Williams Col, 75. *Prof Exp:* Chemist technician, Charles Pfizer & Co, 53-54; fel, AEC, 55-56; Kettering Found fel, Ohio State Univ, 56-58; res scientist, Procter & Gamble Co, 58-60; mgr, E I DuPont de Nemours & Co, Inc, 60-68; dir new bus, Nat Lead Co, 68-71, Hoffmann La Roche, 71-74, dir financial planning, Hoffman La Roche, 71-74; vpres, Curtiss Wright Corp, 74-78; sr vpres, Masonited Corp, 78-85. *Res:* Egg white substitute; corian solid surface; woodruf roofing; vyrak siding; polymer chemistry in building products; water treatment; traditional medicine and vitamin therapy. *Mailing Add:* Doner-Viking Co 61 Chimney Ridge Convent Station NJ 07961. *Fax:* 973-644-0411

SLOCUM, DONALD WARREN, MATERIALS CHEMISTRY, MACROCYCLES. *Current Pos:* head, Dept Chem, 90-95, PROF CHEM, WESTERN KY UNIV, BOWLING GREEN, 95- *Personal Data:* b Rochester, NY; m 90, Laurel A Hopper; c Warren D & Matthew G. *Educ:* Univ Rochester, BA & BS; NY Univ, PhD(chem), 63. *Prof Exp:* From assoc prof to prof chem, Southern Ill Univ, 69-81, adj prof, 81-84; sr scientist, Gulf Res & Develop Co, Pittsburgh, 79-82; prog dir, Chem Div, NSF, Washington, DC, 84-85; prog leader, Div Educ Progs, Argonne Nat Lab, 85-90. *Concurrent Pos:* Vis prof, Dept Chem, Univ Ill, 70, Dept Inorg Chem, Univ Bristol, UK, 72 & 73 & Dept Chem, Univ Cincinnati, 76; vis consult, Hooker Res Labs, Grand Island, NY, 75; vis scientist, Pittsburgh Energy Res Ctr, US Energy Res & Develop Admin, 77; fac res partic, Chem Eng Div, Argonne Nat Lab, 78 & 79; vis lectr, Carnegie-Mellon Univ & Univ Pittsburgh, 83-84. *Mem:* Am Chem Soc; Chem Soc Gt Brit; Catalysis Soc; Org Reactions Catalysis Soc; coun undergrad res. *Res:* Organic, organometallic and inorganic synthesis and mechanism; stereochemistry; heterocyclic chemistry; homogeneous and heterogeneous catalysis; synthetic fuels, fine chemicals, polymers; chelating and encapsulating agents; chemistry of coal; supercritical media; separation and spectrascopic techniques; zeolites; macrocycles; organolithium chemistry; pharmaceutical chemistry. *Mailing Add:* Dept Chem Western Ky Univ Bowling Green KY 42101. *Fax:* 502-745-6471

SLOCUM, HARRY KIM, CELL BIOLOGY. *Current Pos:* cancer res scientist I, Roswell Park Mem Inst, 76-77, scientist II pharmacol, 77- 92, scientist III, Molecular Pharmacol & Cancer Therapeut, 92-97, SCIENTIST IV, EXP THERAPEUT & PATH, ROSEWELL PARK MEM INST, 97- *Personal Data:* b Buffalo, NY, June 8, 47; m 74; c 3. *Educ:* State Univ NY, Buffalo, BA, 69, PhD(biochem), 74. *Prof Exp:* Res assoc immunol, Scripps Clin & Res Found, 74-76. *Mem:* Tissue Cult Asn; Am Asn Cancer Res; Am Soc Clin Oncol; Int Soc Anal Cytol. *Res:* Characterization of cells comprising human solid tumors, including determinants of drug action, cellular interactions and heterogeneity in drug response. *Mailing Add:* Grace Cancer Drug Ctr Roswell Park Cancer Inst Buffalo NY 14263. *E-Mail:* slocum@sc3103.med.buffalo.edu

SLOCUM, RICHARD WILLIAM, ENGINEERING. *Current Pos:* DIR RES & DEVELOP, AIR LOGISTICS CORP, 72- *Personal Data:* b Bryn Mawr, Pa, May 16, 34; c 5. *Educ:* Mass Inst Technol, BS, 55, PhD(nuclear physics), 59. *Prof Exp:* Scientist, Raytheon Co, 58-61; sect head, Aerospace Corp, 61-69; spec asst to dir, Advan Res Proj Agency, US Govt, 69-71. *Concurrent Pos:* Instr, Calif State Univ, Long Beach, 62-64, Marymount Col, 62-65, Univ Calif, Los Angeles, 63, Univ Southern Calif, 63-64. *Mem:* Soc Naval Architects & Engrs; Inst Elec & Electronics Engrs; Am Phys Soc; Arctic Inst NAm. *Res:* Arctic operations; ships and platforms; undersea vehicles and systems; air cushion vehicles; meteorological and surveillance satellites and systems. *Mailing Add:* 2138 Kinneloa Canyon Rd Pasadena CA 91107

SLOCUM, ROBERT DALE, BIOCHEMISTRY & MOLECULAR BIOLOGY PLANT STRESS, AMINO ACID METABOLISM. *Current Pos:* asst prof, 92-96, ASSOC PROF BIOL SCI, GOUCHER COL, 96- *Personal Data:* b Columbus, GA, Aug 24, 52; m 80, Cynthia L Williamson; c Brian & Christine. *Educ:* Univ Maine, BA, 74; Ohio State Univ, MS, 77, Univ Tex, Austin, PhD(bot), 81. *Prof Exp:* Fel, Yale Univ, 82-85; asst prof biol, Williams Col, 85-92. *Concurrent Pos:* Prin investr, NASA, 87-92, Res Corp, 88-90, NSF, 88-; vis prof, Boyce Thompson Inst, Cornell Univ, 89. *Mem:* AAAS; Am Soc Plant Physiologists; Int Soc Plant Molecular Biol; Sigma Xi. *Res:* Investigating biochemistry and molecular biology of plant stress responses focusing on proline and arginine biosynthetic pathways; regulation of the pyrimidine pathway. *Mailing Add:* Dept Biol Sci Goucher Col 1021 Dulaney Valley Rd Baltimore MD 21204-2794. *Fax:* 410-337-6508

SLOCUM, ROBERT EARLE, PHYSICS. *Current Pos:* CHMN, POLATOMIC INC, RICHARDSON, TEX, 82- *Personal Data:* b El Reno, Okla, Nov 28, 38; m 67, Linda L Collum; c Paul. *Educ:* Univ Okla, BS, 60, MEP, 63; Univ Tex, Austin, PhD(physics), 69. *Prof Exp:* Res engr, Tex Instruments Inc, 60-63; res engr, Boeing Co, 63-64; mem tech staff atomic physics, Equip Res & Develop Lab, Tex Instruments Inc, 66-73, mgr, Advan Magnetics Progs, 74-82. *Mem:* AAAS; Am Phys Soc; Optical Soc Am. *Res:* Optical pumping with application to magnetometers for space and geophysical applications; thin film polarizers; polarized optical systems. *Mailing Add:* 307 Arborcrest Richardson TX 75080. *E-Mail:* polatomr@mindspring.com

SLOCUM, ROBERT RICHARD, SOLID STATE PHYSICS, RADIOLOGICAL PHYSICS. *Current Pos:* ASSOC PROF PHYSICS, CENT MICH UNIV, 69- *Personal Data:* b Traverse City, Mich, June 21, 31; m 60; c 2. *Educ:* Berea Col, AB, 52; Mich State Univ, MS, 56; Col William & Mary, PhD(physics), 69. *Prof Exp:* Instr physics, Colgate Univ, 56-57, 58-59; res physicist, Airborne Instruments Labs, NY, 59-60; from asst prof to assoc prof physics, Old Dom Col, 60-69. *Concurrent Pos:* NSF sci fac fel, 66-67. *Mem:* Am Asn Physics Teachers; Am Phys Soc. *Res:* Semiconductor devices; nuclear magnetic resonance in metals. *Mailing Add:* Dept Physics 211 Dow Cent Mich Univ Mt Pleasant MI 48859

SLODKI, MOREY ELI, BIOCHEMISTRY. *Current Pos:* LEAD SCIENTIST MICROBIOL PROPERTIES RES, NORTHERN REGIONAL RES CTR, AGR RES SERV, USDA, 55- *Personal Data:* b Chicago, Ill, June 16, 28; m 67; c 2. *Educ:* Univ Ill, BS, 48; Univ Iowa, PhD, 55. *Mem:* Am Chem Soc; Am Soc Microbiol; Soc Indust Microbiol. *Res:* Microbial enzymes; biological nitrogen fixation; exocellular microbial polysaccharides. *Mailing Add:* 1110 W Pembrook Peoria IL 61614-4143

SLOGER, CHARLES, PLANT PHYSIOLOGY. *Current Pos:* PLANT PHYSIOLOGIST, NITROGEN FIXATION & SOYBEAN GENETICS LAB, PLANT SCI INST, BELTSVILLE AGR RES CTR, USDA, 68- *Personal Data:* b Albany, NY, Dec 22, 38; m 67; c 2. *Educ:* State Univ NY Albany, BS, 61, MS, 63; Univ Fla, PhD(bot), 68. *Mem:* Am Soc Plant Physiol; Am Soc Microbiol. *Res:* Physiology of symbiotic nitrogen fixation; mineral nutrition. *Mailing Add:* 4007 Stoconga Dr Beltsville MD 20705

SLOMA, LEONARD VINCENT, ENGINEERING PHYSICS. *Current Pos:* scientist, Borg-Warner Corp, 56-57, sect mgr, 57-59, assoc dir & head physics & electronics dept, 59-84, SR TECH COUN, RES CTR, BORG-WARNER CORP, 84- *Personal Data:* b Chicago, Ill, June 28, 20; m 46; c 2. *Educ:* Northwestern Univ, BS, 42, PhD, 51; Mass Inst Technol, SM, 48. *Prof Exp:* Consult, Arthur D Little, Inc, 46-48; instr mech eng, Northwestern Univ, 48-51; res engr, Autonetics Div, NAm Aviation, Inc, 51-53, supvr systs anal, 53-55, staff specialist, 55-56. *Mem:* Sigma Xi; Soc Photo-optical Instrumentation Engrs. *Res:* Applied and fluid mechanics; heat transfer; refrigeration; air conditioning; acoustics; electronics; solid state circuitry; solid state physics; electrochemical physics; servo controls; systems analysis. *Mailing Add:* 6221 N Kirkwood Ave Chicago IL 60646-5025

SLOMIANY, AMALIA, DIGESTIVE DISEASE. *Current Pos:* PROF MED, NY MED COL, 81- *Educ:* NY Med Col, PhD(biochem), 73. *Res:* Glycoconjugates; glycoprotein and glycolipids. *Mailing Add:* Res Ctr UMDNJ 110 Bergen St Newark NJ 07103-2400. *Fax:* 973-982-3689

SLOMP, GEORGE, PHYSICAL CHEMISTRY. *Current Pos:* RETIRED. *Personal Data:* b Grand Rapids, Mich, Feb 15, 22; m 51; c 4. *Educ:* Calvin Col, AB, 42; Ohio State Univ, PhD(chem), 49. *Prof Exp:* Lab asst chem, Calvin Col, 41-42; asst inorg chem, Ohio State Univ, 42-43, org chem, 46-49; asst org synthesis, Am Petrol Inst, 43-44; res chemist, Am Oil Co, Tex, 44-46; sr scientist, Upjohn Co, 49-90. *Res:* Synthesis and reactions of steroidal hormones and natural products; reaction mechanisms; ozonolysis; catalytic hydrogenation; Grignard reactions; nuclear magnetic resonance spectroscopy; molecular structure determination; computer programming. *Mailing Add:* 4029 Lakeside Dr Kalamazoo MI 49008

SLONCZEWSKI, JOAN LYN, BACTERIAL PHYSIOLOGY. *Current Pos:* ASST PROF BIOL, KENYON COL, 84- *Personal Data:* b Hyde Park, NY, Aug 14, 56; m, Michael Barich; c Daniel & Matthew. *Educ:* Bryn Maur Col, AB; Yale Univ, PhD(molecular biophys-biochem), 82. *Honors & Awards:* Young Investr Award, Am Soc Microbiol, 87. *Prof Exp:* Fel NIH Grant, Univ Pa, 82-84. *Concurrent Pos:* Vis asst prof molecular biol, Princeton, 90-91. *Mem:* Am Soc Microbiol; Am Soc Cell Biol; AAAS. *Res:* Bacterial pH regulation and gene expression. *Mailing Add:* Dept Biol Kenyon Col Gambier OH 43022. *E-Mail:* slonczewski@kenyon.edu

SLONCZEWSKI, JOHN CASIMIR, SOLID STATE PHYSICS. *Current Pos:* RES STAFF MEM, WATSON RES CTR, IBM CORP, 55- *Personal Data:* b New York, NY, July 26, 29; m 55; c 3. *Educ:* Worcester Polytech Inst, BS, 50; Rutgers Univ, PhD(physics), 55. *Mem:* Fel Am Phys Soc. *Res:* Theories of ferromagnetism; magnetic domain phenomena; structural phase transitions and electron-lattice interactions. *Mailing Add:* 161 Allison Rd Katonah NY 10536. *Fax:* 914-945-4506

SLONECKER, CHARLES EDWARD, ANATOMY. *Current Pos:* from asst prof to assoc prof anat, 68-76, head dept, 81-92, PROF ANAT, UNIV BC, 76-, DIR, CEREMONIES & UNIV RELATIONS, 90- *Personal Data:* b Gig Harbor, Wash, Nov 30, 38; m 61, Jan Hunter; c 3. *Educ:* Univ Wash, DDS, 65, PhD(biol struct), 67. *Honors & Awards:* Centennial Gold Medal, Am Asn Anatomists, 87. *Prof Exp:* Sci asst path, Int Path, Univ Bern, 67-68. *Concurrent Pos:* Nat Inst Allergy & Infectious Dis fels, Univ Wash, 65-67; Swiss Nat Fund grant, 67-69; BC Med Res Found grant, 68-69; Med Res Coun grant, 70-75; res grants, G&F Heighway Fund, 75- & Muscular Dystrophy Can, 78-80. *Mem:* Am Asn Anatomists; Can Asn Anatomists; Am Col Dentists. *Res:* Lymphocytic tissue morphology and physiology; cellular immunology; radiobiology; hematology and radioautography. *Mailing Add:* Dept Anat Fac Med Univ BC Vancouver BC V6T 1Z2 Can. *Fax:* 604-822-9060; *E-Mail:* charles.slonecker@ubc.ca

SLONIM, ARNOLD ROBERT, BIOTECHNOLOGY, SCIENCE ADMINISTRATION. *Current Pos:* CONSULT & PRES, ARSLO ASSOCS, COLUMBUS, OHIO, 87- *Personal Data:* b Springfield, Mass, Feb 15, 26; m 51, 84, Alice Benis; c Charles B, Susan H & Elyse G. *Educ:* Tufts Col, BS, 47; Boston Univ, AM, 48; Johns Hopkins Univ, PhD(biol), 53. *Prof Exp:* Res asst nutrit, Sterling-Winthrop Res Inst, 48-49; res asst, NIH grantee pharmacol, Sch Med, George Washington Univ, 49-50; res asst & jr instr biol, Johns Hopkins Univ, 50-53; res assoc chemother, Children's Cancer Res Found, Harvard Med Sch, 53-54; head chem lab, Lynn Hosp, Mass, 55-56; res scientist (chief appl ecol, supvry res biologist, physiologist, biochemist, phys sci admin, mgr biotechnol), Aerospace Med Res Lab, Wright-Patterson AFB, Ohio, 56-86. *Concurrent Pos:* Lectr, Mass Sch Physiother, 55-56, Antioch Univ, 84-85; mem, Int Bioastronaut Comt, Int Astronaut Fedn, 67-70 & 84-; mem, comt biol handbooks, Fedn Am Socs Exp Biol, 67-71; mem, environ carcinogens prog, Int Agency Res Cancer/WHO, 81-; legal expert, Environ Pollution, Denver, Co, 89-90. *Mem:* Sigma Xi; NY Acad Sci; Aerospace Med Asn; Am Soc Biochem & Molecular Biol; Am Physiol Soc; Int Acad Aviation & Space Med. *Res:* Aerospace physiology and biochemistry; life support system requirements; environmental pollution (esp potable water standards, aquatic toxicity); biomechanical/biodynamic stress (esp acceleration, vibration); biotechnology and environmental health consultant. *Mailing Add:* 630 Cranfield Pl Columbus OH 43213-3407

SLONIM, JACOB, NAMING IN DISTRIBUTED SYSTEMS, LANGUAGES FOR DISTRIBUTED SYSTEMS. *Current Pos:* HEAD RES, IBM CAN CTR ADVAN SCI, 89-, ARCHITECT, DATABASES, 89-; PROF DISTRIB DATA BASE MGT SOFTWARE, UNIV WATERLOO, 91- *Personal Data:* b Israel, June 25, 45; Can citizen; m 66; c David, John & Karen. *Educ:* Univ Western Ont, BS, 72, MS, 73; Univ Kans State, PhD(comput sci), 78. *Honors & Awards:* Kaplan Award, Pres Israel for Contribution to Israel Computer Indust, 80. *Prof Exp:* Asst prof, distrib data base mgt software, Kans State Univ, 77-78; researcher distrib data base mgt software, NDX Corp, 79-82, Geac Comput, 82-88; prof, distrib data base mgt software, Univ Western Ont, 86-89. *Concurrent Pos:* Asst prof, Kans State Univ, 78-79; exec vpres, Res & Develop Dept, NDX Corp, 79-82; software dir, Res & Develop Dept, Geac Computers Coun, 82-88; prof, Univ Western Ont, 86-89; head res, IBM, Can, 90; adj prof, Univ Waterloo, 91; adj prof, Univ Western Ont; mem, IBM Acad Technol. *Mem:* Asn Comput Mach; sr mem Inst Elec & Electronics Engrs. *Res:* Creating a complete application level architecture and a set of tools for building reliable distributed systems; multidatabase, software engineering. *Mailing Add:* IBM Canada Lab 895 Don Mills Rd North York ON M3C 1W3 Can

SLOOP, CHARLES HENRY, PHYSIOLOGY, MICROCIRCULATION. *Current Pos:* ASSOC PROF PHYSIOL, LA STATE UNIV MED CTR, 76- *Educ:* Wake Forest Univ, PhD(physiol), 73. *Res:* Lipoproteins. *Mailing Add:* Dept Physiol La State Univ Med Ctr 1542 Tulane Ave New Orleans LA 70112-2865. *Fax:* 504-568-3942

SLOOPE, BILLY WARREN, PHYSICS, THIN FILMS. *Current Pos:* RETIRED. *Personal Data:* b Clifton Forge, Va, Jan 4, 24; m 51; c 2. *Educ:* Univ Richmond, BS, 49; Univ Va, MS, 51, PhD(physics), 53. *Prof Exp:* Asst prof physics, Clemson Col, 53-55; from asst prof to assoc prof, Univ Richmond, 55-61, adj assoc prof, 61-68; head dept physics,Va Commonwealth Univ, 68-79, prof, 68-88. *Concurrent Pos:* Sr res physicist, Va Inst Sci Res, 56-68, head, Physics Div, 61-68; Horsley Res Award, Va Acad Sci, 61. *Mem:* Am Vacuum Soc; Am Asn Physics Teachers. *Res:* Epitaxial thin films and their properties. *Mailing Add:* 8718 Avalon Dr Richmond VA 23229

SLOSS, JAMES M, PARTIAL DIFFERENTIAL EQUATIONS, NUMERICAL ANALYSIS. *Current Pos:* Actg asst prof, 61-62, from asst prof to assoc prof, 63-73, PROF MATH, UNIV CALIF, SANTA BARBARA, 74- *Personal Data:* b Birmingham, Ala, Feb 14, 31. *Educ:* Pamona Col, BA, 53; Univ Calif, Berkeley, PhD(math), 62. *Mem:* Am Math Soc; Soc Indust & Appl Math. *Mailing Add:* Dept Math Univ Calif Santa Barbara CA 93106-0001

SLOSS, PETER WILLIAM, GEOLOGY, OCEANOGRAPHY. *Current Pos:* phys scientist oceanog, 73-78, GEOLOGIST, NAT OCEANIC & ATMOSPHERIC ADMIN, NAT GEOPHYS DATA CTR, 78-, CHIEF DATA SYSTEMS & PROD, MARINE GEOL & GEOPHYS DIV, 81- *Personal Data:* b Butte, Mont, May 11, 42; m 66; c 3. *Educ:* Northwestern Univ, BS, 64; Univ Chicago, MS, 66; Rice Univ, PhD(geol), 72. *Prof Exp:* Sr res technician meteorol, Univ Chicago, 67-68; assoc researcher, Inst Storm Res, Houston, 68-69; vis asst prof geol, Mich State Univ, 72-73. *Mem:* Am Meteorol Soc; Am Geophys Union; Sigma Xi. *Res:* Interdisciplinary studies spanning geology, meteorology and oceanography; management of data from such studies; tsunamis; computer graphics. *Mailing Add:* 1111 Westview Dr Boulder CO 80303-1428

SLOSSER, JEFFREY ERIC, INSECT ECOLOGY, COTTON INSECTS. *Current Pos:* from asst prof to assoc prof, 75-86, PROF ENTOM, TEX A&M UNIV, 86- *Personal Data:* b Winslow, Ariz, Dec 1, 43; m 68, H Christine Ellis; c Tracy S & Tamara J. *Educ:* Ariz State Univ, BS, 66; Univ Ariz, MS, 68, PhD(entom), 71. *Honors & Awards:* Recognition Award, Entiom Soc Am, 94. *Prof Exp:* Res assoc entom, Univ Ariz, 68-70 & Univ Ark, 72-75. *Concurrent Pos:* Ed, Southwestern Entomologist, 86-90; pres elect, Southwestern Entom Soc, 91, pres, 92. *Mem:* Entom Soc Am; Sigma Xi. *Res:* Integrated control and population dynamics of cotton and rangeland insect pests in the rolling plains of Texas. *Mailing Add:* Tex Agr Exp Sta PO Box 1658 Vernon TX 76385

SLOSSON, JAMES E, HYDROLOGY AND WATER RESOURCES. *Current Pos:* CONSULT ENG GEOLOGIST, 60- *Personal Data:* b Van Nuys, Calif, Apr 12, 23; m 47; c 2. *Educ:* Univ Southern Calif, BA, 49, MS, 50, PhD(geol), 58. *Honors & Awards:* Ichard Jahns distinguished lectr, GSA, 89. *Prof Exp:* Prof geol, Los Angeles Valley Col, 50-73 & 75-84. *Concurrent Pos:* Geologist, US Geol Surv, 49-50; res geologist, Gulf Oil Corp, 52-56; NSF grant mineralogy & geol, Univ Ill, 57; consult eng geologist for various projs, 58-73; chief eng geol, Slosson & Assoc, 60-73 & 75-; mem, Eng Geologists Qual Bd, City of Los Angeles, 61-76, County of Los Angeles, 66-68 & 81-, chmn, Eng Geol Rev & Appeals Bd, 72; mem, Gov Earthquake Coun, 73-74, Am Asn State Geologists, 73-75 & Nat Acad Sci panel on mudslides, 74; state geologist, Calif Div Mines & Geol, 73-75; comnr, Seismic Safety Comn, 75-78; lectr, Environ Mgt Inst, Sch Pub Admin, Univ Southern Calif, 74-; mem, Adv Comt for Socioecon & Polit Consequences of Earthquake Prediction, Univ Colo, NSF Study, 75-76; mem, Bd Registration Geologists & Geophys, 78-85; mem, Calif Earthquake Prediction Eval Coun, 75-; guest lectr, Harvard Univ Grad Sch, Calif State Northridge, Occidental Col, Univ Nev & Univ Calif, Los Angeles, Berkeley, Irvine & Davis; mem Nat Res Coun Comt Ground Failure Hazards, 86-; chair, FEMA/Colo Pub Safety Comt, Landslide Hazard Mitigation Proj, 86-; coord, ASCR/Off Emergency Serv, Disaster Preparedness Comt, 83- *Mem:* Am Asn Petrol Geol; fel Earthquake Eng Res Inst; Am Soc Civil Eng; Asn Eng Geol; fel Geol Soc Am; Sigma Xi; Am Geophys Union; Seismol Soc Am. *Res:* Engineering geology; seismic research; authored over 120 papers on geol practices. *Mailing Add:* 15373 Valley Vista Blvd Sherman Oaks CA 91403-3810

SLOTA, PETER JOHN, JR, chemistry, for more information see previous edition

SLOTKIN, THEODORE ALAN, PHARMACOLOGY. *Current Pos:* NIMH trainee biochem, Duke Univ; 70-71, from asst prof to assoc prof, 71-79, PROF PHARMACOL, DUKE UNIV, 79-, PROF PSYCHIAT, 84-, PROF NEUROBIOL, 91. *Personal Data:* b Brooklyn, NY, Feb 17, 47; m 67, Linda Yarowenko; c Alexander P, Matthew C & Joanna S. *Educ:* Brooklyn Col, BS, 67; Univ Rochester, PhD(pharmacol), 70. *Honors & Awards:* John Jacob Abel Award, 82; Alton Ochsner Award Relating Smoking & Health, 92. *Mem:* Am Soc Pharmacol & Exp Therapeut; Soc Neurosci. *Res:* Neuropharmacology; neurochemistry; developmental neurobiology; drug abuse. *Mailing Add:* Dept Pharmacol Duke Univ Med Ctr Durham NC 27710-0001. *Fax:* 919-684-8197; *E-Mail:* slotk001@dukemc.bitner

SLOTNICK, HERBERT, CHEMICAL ENGINEERING, PHYSICAL CHEMISTRY. *Current Pos:* PROF CHEM, CENT CONN STATE COL, 67- *Personal Data:* b Malden, Mass, Oct 6, 28; m 53; c 2. *Educ:* Northeastern Univ, BS, 51; Worcester Polytech Inst, MS, 53; Mass Inst Technol, SM, 55; Univ Conn, PhD(eng), 64. *Prof Exp:* Proj chemist, Pratt & Whitney Aircraft, United Aircraft Corp, 54-67. *Concurrent Pos:* Res partic, NSF Acad Year Exten, Cent Conn State Col, 70-72. *Mem:* Am Chem Soc; Am Inst Chem Engrs; Sigma Xi. *Res:* Active nitrogen reactions; air-water pollution; materials; high vacuum, inert gas, liquid metal technology; materials related to biomedical science. *Mailing Add:* 134 Hyde Rd West Hartford CT 06117-1620

SLOTNICK, VICTOR BERNARD, MICROBIOLOGY, MEDICINE. *Current Pos:* ASSOC DIR, ZENECA PHARMACEUT, 83- *Personal Data:* b Chicago, Ill, Oct 27, 31; m, Beth Zevin; c Laura, Michael, Nina, Michael, Jeffrey & Brian. *Educ:* Roosevelt Univ, BS, 53; Univ Chicago, MS, 55; Hahnemann Med Col, PhD(microbiol), 60; Jefferson Med Col, MD, 65; Am Bd Family Pract, dipl, 77. *Prof Exp:* Assoc microbiol, Univ Chicago, 54; res assoc, Virus Lab, Ill State Dept Pub Health, 54-55; assoc microbiol, Hahnemann Med Col, 57-60; sr virologist, Merck Inst, 60-61; intern, Albert Einstein Med Ctr, 65-66; from asst dir to dir clin res, McNeil Labs Inc, McNeil Pharmaceut, 66-81, clin res fel, 81-83. *Concurrent Pos:* NIH res fel, Jefferson Med Col, 64-65, clin instr, Dept Family Med, 75- *Mem:* Am Soc Microbiol; AMA; NY Acad Sci; Am Col Neuropsychopharmacol; Am Acad Family Pract. *Res:* Virology; immunology; antiviral chemotherapy; cytology; biochemistry; experimental teratology; psychopharmacology; antibacterial chemotherapy; pharmacology. *Mailing Add:* 312 Melrose Ave Merion Station PA 19066

SLOTSKY, MYRON NORTON, INDUSTRIAL PHARMACY. *Current Pos:* RETIRED. *Personal Data:* b Portland, Maine, Apr 30, 35; m 62; c 2. *Educ:* Mass Col Pharm, BS, 57, MS, 59, PhD(pharm), 67. *Prof Exp:* Chemist, Res Dept, Gillette Safety Razor Co, 59-62, sr cosmetic chemist, Toiletries Develop Sect, 62-64, chem & biol sect, 64; sr pharmaceut chemist, Colgate-Palmolive Co, 66-68; dir prod develop, Marion Labs Inc, 68-75, spec develop proj analyst, 75-80, mgr pilot opers, 80-86, mgr clin supplies, 86-96. *Mem:* Am Chem Soc. *Res:* Tablet and capsule formulation, suspension and solution technology; emulsion and aerosol technology; problems related to stabilization, preservation and production scale-up of cosmetics and pharmaceuticals; dandruff; acne; processes development; all areas of clinical manufacturing and packaging. *Mailing Add:* 8337 W 120th St Overland Park MO 66213-1219

SLOTTA, LARRY STEWART, civil engineering, hydraulics, for more information see previous edition

SLOTTER, RICHARD ARDEN, INORGANIC CHEMISTRY. *Current Pos:* DEAN ACAD AFFAIRS, BLUFFTON COL, 86- *Personal Data:* b Souderton, Pa, Mar 3, 32; m 54; c 3. *Educ:* Bluffton Col, BS, 54; Univ Mich, MS, 57, PhD(chem), 60. *Prof Exp:* From asst prof to assoc prof chem, Bluffton Col, 58-64; from assoc prof to prof, Robert Col, Istanbul, 64-71, chmn dept, 66-71; vis assoc prof, Bucknell Univ, 71-72; asst chmn dept chem, Northwestern Univ, Evanston, 72-86, lectr, 72-86. *Mem:* AAAS; Am Chem Soc; Sigma Xi. *Res:* Polarography; coordination complexes; electrochemical kinetics. *Mailing Add:* 175 Sunset Dr Bluffton OH 45817-1113

SLOTTERBECK-BAKER, OBERTA ANN, symbolic algebra, parallel computing, for more information see previous edition

SLOVACEK, RUDOLF EDWARD, BIOCHEMISTRY, BIOENERGETICS. *Current Pos:* res assoc, Ciba Corning Diagnostics Corp, 86-87, mgr, Phys Measurement Systs, 88-89, SR STAFF SCIENTIST, CHIRON DIAGNOSTICS CORP, 90- *Personal Data:* b Bloomington, Ind, Jan 4, 48; m 93, Patricia Paquin; c Joel, Greg & Caitlyn. *Educ:* Univ Rochester, BA, 70, MS, 72, PhD(biol), 75. *Prof Exp:* Res assoc marine biol, Nat Res Coun, 75-76; res assoc, Brookhaven Nat Lab, 76-78, asst biophysicist biol, 78-80; sr scientist biol, Corning Glass Works, 80-86. *Mem:* AAAS; NY Acad Sci; Int Soc Optical Eng. *Res:* Physical and chemical studies of energy conversion process and its regulatory mechanisms in photosynthesis; application of fiber optics and optical techniques to immunodiagnostic and clinical chemistry measurements in medicine. *Mailing Add:* Chiron Diagnostics 63 North St Medfield MA 02052. *E-Mail:* rudolf.slovacek@chirondiag.com

SLOVIN, SUSAN FAITH, CELL-MEDIATED IMMUNOLOGY, IMMUNOTHERAPY. *Current Pos:* FEL, DEPT MED, MEM SLOAN-KETTERING CANCER CTR, NY, 90- *Personal Data:* b Feb 5, 53; m 90. *Educ:* Columbia Univ, MA, 76, MPhil, 77, PhD(pathobiol), 78; Jefferson Med Col, MD, 90. *Prof Exp:* Res asst prof med & microbiol, Sch Med, Thomas Jefferson Univ, 84-90. *Concurrent Pos:* Adj asst prof microbiol & immunol, NY Med Col, Valhalla. *Mem:* Sigma Xi; Am Asn Immunologists; NY Acad Sci; Am Asn Cancer Res; Soc Biol Ther. *Res:* Tumor immunology. *Mailing Add:* Sloan-Kettering Cancer Ctr 1275 York Ave New York NY 10021

SLOVITER, HENRY ALLAN, PHYSIOLOGICAL CHEMISTRY. *Current Pos:* asst prof physiol chem & res asst prof surg, Univ Pa, 52-57, res assoc prof neurosurg, 57-66, res prof, 66-75, prof biochem, 66-75, PROF SURG RES & PROF BIOCHEM & BIOPHYSICS, SCH MED, UNIV PA, 75- *Personal Data:* b Philadelphia, Pa, June 16, 14; m, Dolores Korman; c Vikki. *Educ:* Temple Univ, AB, 35, AM, 36; Univ Pa, PhD(org chem), 42, MD, 49. *Honors & Awards:* Glycerine Res Award, 54. *Prof Exp:* Chemist, US Navy Yard, Philadelphia, 36-45; chemist, Harrison Dept Surg Res, Sch Med, Univ Pa, 45-49, intern, Hosp, 49-50; res fel, Nat Inst Med Res, London, 50-52. *Concurrent Pos:* Vis scientist, Univ Tokyo, 63; US-USSR health exchange scientist, Sechenov Inst Physiol, Moscow, 65, Inst Biol & Med Chem Moscow, 71; US-India exchange scientist, Christian Med Col, Vellore, India, 67; proj officer award to Inst for Biol Res, Fogarty Int Ctr, NIH, Belgrade, Yugoslavia, 72-75, fel, Med Res Coun Exp Haemat Unit, St Mary's Hosp Med Sch, London, 78; vis scientist, Tokyo Metrop Inst Med Sci, 84; vis scientist & lectr, Shanghai Inst Org Chem, 94. *Mem:* AAAS; Am Physiol Soc; Am Soc Biol Chem; Int Soc Neurochem; Int Soc Blood Transfusion; hon mem Belgian Soc Anesthesiol. *Res:* Brain metabolism; erythrocyte lipids and metabolism; erythrocyte substitutes; magnetic resonance imaging. *Mailing Add:* Sch Med Univ Pa Philadelphia PA 19104

SLOVITER, ROBERT SETH, ELECTROPHYSIOLOGY, NEUROANATOMY. *Current Pos:* DIR, NEUROL RES CTR, HELEN HAYES HOSP, 86; ASSOC PROF PHARMACOL & NEUROL, COL PHYSICIANS & SURGEONS, COLUMBIA UNIV, 88- *Personal Data:* b Nov 29, 50; m; c 2. *Educ:* Penn State Univ, PhD(pharmacol), 78. *Mailing Add:* Neurol Res Ctr Helen Hayes Hosp NY State Dept Health West Haverstraw NY 10993. *Fax:* 914-947-3856

SLOWEY, JACK WILLIAM, aeronomy; deceased, see previous edition for last biography

SLOWIK, JOHN HENRY, SOLID STATE PHYSICS. *Current Pos:* assoc scientist, 73-74, SCIENTIST SOLID STATE PHYSICS, XEROX CORP, 75- *Personal Data:* b Hastings, Nebr, Sept 12, 45; m 72; c 2. *Educ:* Manhattan Col, BS, 67; Univ Ill, MS, 71, PhD(solid state physics), 73. *Prof Exp:* Nuclear physics, Johns Hopkins Univ, 67; asst physics, Univ Ill, 68-73. *Mem:* Am Inst Physics; Sigma Xi; Am Phys Soc. *Res:* Extreme-ultraviolet spectroscopy; charge transport in disordered solids; interfacial charge transport; transient electronics. *Mailing Add:* 35 Coach Dr Webster NY 14526

SLOWINSKI, EMIL J, JR, PHYSICAL CHEMISTRY. *Current Pos:* RETIRED. *Personal Data:* b Newark, NJ, Oct 12, 22; m 51; c 5. *Educ:* Mass State Col, BS, 46; Mass Inst Technol, PhD(phys chem), 49. *Prof Exp:* Instr chem, Swarthmore Col, 49-52; from instr to assoc prof, Univ Conn, 53-64; prof chem, Macalester Col, 64-88. *Concurrent Pos:* Indust fel, Monsanto Chem Co, 53-54; NSF fel, 60-61; Nat Acad Sci exchange prof, 68-69. *Mem:* Am Chem Soc. *Res:* Mathematical preparation for general chemistry; qualitative analysis and the properties of ions in aqueous solution; chemical principles; chemical principles in the laboratory. *Mailing Add:* 806 Bachelor Ave St Paul MN 55118

SLOYAN, MARY STEPHANIE, MATHEMATICS. *Current Pos:* from asst prof to assoc prof math, 52-59, pres, 68-74, PROF MATH, GEORGIAN COURT COL, 59- *Personal Data:* b New York, NY, Apr 18, 18. *Educ:* Georgian Court Col, AB, 45; Cath Univ, MA, 49, PhD(math), 52. *Prof Exp:* Teacher, Cathedral High Sch, 45-48. *Concurrent Pos:* Vis lectr math, Cath Univ Am, 60-82; bd gov, Math Asn Am, 88-91, Comt Sect, 88-94. *Mem:* Am Math Soc; Math Asn Am; Sigma Xi; Asn Women Maths; Nat Coun Teachers Maths. *Res:* Metric geometry; application of complex variables to geometry. *Mailing Add:* Dept Math Georgian Court Col Lakewood NJ 08701

SLOYER, CLIFFORD W, JR, TOPOLOGY. *Current Pos:* from asst prof to assoc prof, 64-74, asst chmn dept, 69-78, PROF MATH, UNIV DEL, 74- *Personal Data:* b Easton, Pa, Apr 30, 34; m 62, Barbara Bartos; c Gregory, Christopher, Jonathan & Elena. *Educ:* Lehigh Univ, BA, 56, MS, 58, PhD(math), 64. *Prof Exp:* Instr math, Lehigh Univ, 58-64. *Concurrent Pos:* Vis prof, Grad Lib Studies Prog, Wesleyan Univ, Middleton, Conn, 64-84; vis lectr pub schs, Pa, 65-66 & Del, 66-97. *Mem:* Math Asn Am; Nat Coun Teachers Math; Sch Sci & Math Assoc. *Res:* Several complex variables; continuation of meromorphic functions on complex analytic manifolds; secondary programs for gifted students. *Mailing Add:* Dept Math Univ Del Newark DE 19716

SLUDER, EARL RAY, FORESTRY, GENETICS. *Current Pos:* res forester timber mgt, 57-66, RES FORESTER TREE IMPROV, SOUTHEASTERN FOREST EXP STA, USDA FOREST SERV, 66- *Personal Data:* b Newland, NC, Nov 9, 30; m 57; c 3. *Educ:* NC State Univ, BS, 56, MS, 60, PhD(forestry, genetics), 70. *Prof Exp:* Forester, Container Corp Am, 56-57. *Mem:* Soc Am Foresters. *Res:* Genetic improvement of the southern yellow pines; tree breeding southern pines. *Mailing Add:* 742 Forest Lake Dr N Macon GA 31210

SLUDER, GREENFIELD, CELL BIOLOGY. *Current Pos:* SR STAFF SCIENTIST, WORCESTER FOUND EXP BIOL, 81- *Educ:* Univ Pa, PhD(biol), 76. *Res:* Biophysical analysis of spinal assembly; analysis of centrosome formation & reproduction. *Mailing Add:* Cell Biol Group Worcester Found Biomed Res 222 Maple Ave Shrewsbury MA 01545. *Fax:* 508-842-3915

SLUSARCHYK, WILLIAM ALLEN, ORGANIC CHEMISTRY, PHARMACEUTICAL CHEMISTRY. *Current Pos:* Res investr, sr res investr, PRIN SCIENTIST, BRISTOL MYERS SQUIBB PHARM RES INST, PRINCETON, 65- *Personal Data:* b Port Jefferson, NY, June 6, 40; m 68; c Theodore. *Educ:* Brown Univ, BS, 61; Pa State Univ, PhD(org chem), 65. *Honors & Awards:* Thomas Alva Edison Patent Award, 92. *Mem:* Am Chem Soc; NY Acad Sci; Am Soc Microbiol; Int Soc Antiviral Res. *Res:* Cardiovascular agents, antivirals semi-synthetic antibiotics, monobactams, penicillins and cephalosporins; isolation, synthesis and structural elucidation of antibiotics. *Mailing Add:* 19 Richmond Dr Skillman NJ 08558

SLUSARCZUK, GEORGE MARCELIUS JAREMIAS, ORGANIC CHEMISTRY, ENVIRONMENTAL ANALYSIS. *Current Pos:* SR RES ASSOC, CORP RES CTR, INT PAPER CORP, 76- *Personal Data:* b Stanyslaviv, Ukraine, Jan 14, 32; US citizen; m 64, Aurelia M Sereda; c Borys I. *Educ:* Wayne State Univ, BS, 60, MS, 62; Univ Pa, PhD(org chem), 67. *Prof Exp:* Chemist, Res & Develop Ctr, Gen Elec Corp, 62-64; mem staff res & develop, 67-76; spectroscopist, Univ Pa, 65-67. *Mem:* Am Chem Soc; Am Indust Hyg Asn; Shevchenko Sci Soc. *Res:* Environmental organic trace pollutants; pollutants of the working place; trace elemental analysis. *Mailing Add:* 53 Bayberry Dr Monroe NY 10950

SLUSAREK, LIDIA, ANALYTICAL CHEMISTRY. *Current Pos:* group leader, Indust Lab Div, 79-80, sect supvr, 80-88, UNIT DIR, ANAL LABS, EASTMAN KODAK, 88-, WORLDWIDE CORP COORDR, CORE MEASUREMENT TECHNOL, 90- *Personal Data:* b Poland; US citizen; m; c 1. *Educ:* Polytech Inst, Poland, MS, 69; Columbia Univ, PhD(chem), 78. *Prof Exp:* Res asst med chem, Albert Einstein Col Med, 69-71; res investr anal chem, Squibb Inst Med Res, 76-78; sect head mat control, E R Squibb & Sons, 78-79. *Res:* Development assays for drugs and impurities in formulations, bulk materials and body fluids; electrochemical analysis; chemical and physical analysis of photographic components; in-process measurements. *Mailing Add:* 270 Panorama Trail Rochester NY 14625

SLUSHER, RICHART ELLIOTT, PHYSICS. *Current Pos:* MEM TECH STAFF, BELL TEL LABS, 65- *Personal Data:* b Higginsville, Mo, May 20, 38; m 61; c 3. *Educ:* Univ Mo-Rolla, BS, 60; Univ Calif, Berkeley, PhD(physics), 66. *Honors & Awards:* Einstein Prize for Laser Sci, 89. *Mem:* Fel Am Phys Soc; fel Optical Soc Am. *Res:* Laser scattering from plasmas, solids and liquids; nonlinear optics of resonant coherent pulses; nuclear double resonance; astrophysics; quantum optics. *Mailing Add:* AT&T Bell Labs Rm 1D-227 600 Mountain Ave Murray Hill NJ 07974

SLUSKY, SUSAN E G, SOLID STATE PHYSICS, APPLIED PHYSICS. *Current Pos:* MEM TECH STAFF PHYSICS, BELL LABS, 78- *Personal Data:* b New York, NY, Dec 6, 49; m 71; c 3. *Educ:* Brown Univ, AB, 71; Univ Pa, MS, 72; Princeton Univ, PhD(physics), 78. *Mem:* Am Phys Soc. *Res:* Magnetic materials; superconducting electronics; III-V semiconductors; telecommunications network traffic engineering; systems engineering. *Mailing Add:* AT&T Bell Labs RM 2F270 480 Red Hill Rd Middletown NJ 07748

SLUSS, ROBERT REGINALD, ENTOMOLOGY, ECOLOGY. *Current Pos:* PROF BIOL, EVERGREEN STATE COL, 70- *Personal Data:* b Louisville, Ohio, July 18, 28; m 71; c 1. *Educ:* Colo Col, BS, 53; Colo State Univ, MS, 55; Univ Calif, Berkeley, PhD(entom), 66. *Prof Exp:* Microbiologist, Pink Bollworm Res Ctr, USDA, 55-59; res assoc entom, Gill Tract, Univ Calif, 59-66; from asst to assoc biol, San Jose State Col, 66-69; assoc prof, State Univ NY Col Old Westbury, 69-70. *Mem:* Ecol Soc Am. *Res:* Insect pathology; insect population ecology; insect physiology; natural history. *Mailing Add:* 1391 Skyline Terr NW Olympia WA 98502

SLUSSER, M(ARION) L(ILES), CHEMICAL ENGINEERING. *Current Pos:* PRES, PROD DIAGNOSTICS, INC, 82- *Personal Data:* b Memphis, Tenn, May 9, 19; m 46; c Wiliam C, James Michael, John S & David Andrew. *Educ:* Univ Okla, BS, 48; Univ Colo, MS, 49. *Prof Exp:* Res engr, Field Res Lab, Mobil Res & Develop Corp, 49-55, sr res engr, 55-67, engr assoc, 67-82. *Concurrent Pos:* Consult, 82-84. *Mem:* Sigma Xi; Soc Petrol Engrs. *Res:* Well completion and oil production problems; oil well stimulation; thermal recovery methods for recovery of oil from oil shale by in-place methods; oil well stimulation by fracturing and acidizing. *Mailing Add:* 3804 Glenbrook Arlington TX 76015

SLUTSKY, ARTHUR, ADULT RESPIRATORY DISTRESS SYNDROME, MECHANISMS OF LUNG INJURY. *Current Pos:* assoc prof med, 84-88, PROF MED, SURG & BIOMED ENG, UNIV TORONTO, 88- *Personal Data:* b Toronto, Ont, Dec 31, 48; m 71, Myra; c 2. *Educ:* Univ Toronto, BASc, 70, MASc, 72; McMaster Univ, MD, 76. *Prof Exp:* From instr to asst prof med, Harvard Univ, 80-84. *Concurrent Pos:* Mem, Adv Comt & Anesthesia Devices, Food & Drug Admin, 83-88, consult, Adv Comt Respiratory & Anesthesia Devices, 88-95; scientist A, Med Res Coun Can, 85-90; counr, Can Soc Clin Invest, 86-90; mem, Steering Comt Crit Care Med, Am Col Chest Physicians, 87-89. *Mem:* Am Col Chest Physicians; Am Physiol Soc; AAAS; Am Soc Clin Invest; Am Thoracic Soc. *Res:* Biology and pathophysiology of acute lung injury; genetics of asthma. *Mailing Add:* 600 University Ave Suite 656A Toronto ON M5G 1X5 Can

SLUTSKY, HERBERT L, EPIDEMIOLOGY. *Current Pos:* assoc prof, 59-67, PROF GEOG, ROOSEVELT UNIV, 67-, HEAD DEPT, 59- *Personal Data:* b Chicago, Ill, Nov 6, 25; m 55; c 2. *Educ:* Univ Ill, BS, 50, MS, 51, PhD(geog, physiol), 59. *Prof Exp:* Vis lectr geog, Univ Ill, 58. *Mem:* Am Geog Soc; Asn Am Geog; Int Soc Biometeorol; Am Pub Health Asn. *Res:* Physiology; geographical distribution of disease; ecological studies of protein, malnutrition and kwashiorkor; pediatric lead poisoning; tuberculosis; salmenella. *Mailing Add:* Dept Geog Roosevelt Univ 430 S Michigan Ave Chicago IL 60605

SLUTSKY, LEON JUDAH, PHYSICAL CHEMISTRY. *Current Pos:* asst prof, 61-69, PROF CHEM, UNIV WASH, 69- *Personal Data:* b New York, NY, Oct 9, 32. *Educ:* Cornell Univ, BA, 53; Mass Inst Technol, PhD, 57. *Prof Exp:* Instr chem, Univ Tex, 57-59, asst prof, 59-61. *Mem:* Am Phys Soc. *Res:* Lattice dynamics; mechanical properties of solids; surface chemistry. *Mailing Add:* Univ Was 3900 Seventh Ave NE Univ Wash Seattle WA 98195-0001

SLUTZ, RALPH JEFFERY, NUMERICAL METHODS. *Current Pos:* GUEST RESEARCHER, NAT OCEANIC & ATMOSPHERIC ADMIN, 90- *Personal Data:* b Cleveland, Ohio, May 18, 17; m 46; c 4. *Educ:* Mass Inst Technol, BS & MS, 39; Princeton Univ, PhD(theoret physics), 46. *Honors & Awards:* Gold Medal, Dept Commerce, 52. *Prof Exp:* Asst, Mass Inst Technol, 37-38; asst, Princeton Univ, 39-42, instr, 41-42; tech aide, Nat Defense Res Comt, 42-45; comput design engr, Inst Adv Study, 46-48; physicist, Nat Bur Standards, 48-49, asst chief, Electronic Comput Sect, 49-53, consult comput & math, 53-54, asst chief, Cent Radio Propagatiop Lab, 54, chief radio, Propagation Physics Div, 54-60; guest worker magnetosphere res, Max-Planck Inst Physics & Astrophys, 60-61; sr scientist & consult, Upper Atmosphere & Space Physics Div, Nat Bur Stand, 61-65; sr scientist, Space Disturbances Lab, Environ Sci Serv Admin, Nat Oceanic & Atmospheric Admin, 65-69, actg dir, Space Environ Lab, 69-70, chief numerical anal & comput techniques group, 70-73, sr scientist, Environ Res Labs, 73-80; sr res assoc, Univ Colo Coop Inst Res Environ Sci, 80-90. *Concurrent Pos:* Mem, US nat comt, Int Sci Radio Union, 56-59; consult, President's Sci Adv Comt, 64-67; mem study group IV, US preparatory comt, Int Radio Consult Comt; vis lectr, Univ Col, 70-72, adj prof elec eng, 72- *Mem:* Am Phys Soc; Inst Elec & Electronics Engrs; Am Geophys Union; Int Asn Geomag & Aeronomy; AAAS. *Res:* Climate analysis; numerical forecasting; computer techniques. *Mailing Add:* 745 Mapleton Ave Boulder CO 80304

SLUTZKY, GALE DAVID, MATERIALS HANDLING, ROBOTICS. *Current Pos:* CTR MGR MAT HANDLING PACKAGING, CTR AUTOMATED PACKAGING & MAT HANDLING, IAMS, 90- *Personal Data:* b Omaha, Nebr, Mar 13, 52; m 72, 83; c 2. *Educ:* Univ Wyo, BA, 76; Univ Tenn, MA, 81. *Prof Exp:* Res asst image processing elec eng, Univ Tenn, 76-83; asst dir, 83-87, assoc dir robotics, Cincinnati Ctr Robotics Res, Univ Cincinnati, 87- *Concurrent Pos:* Consult, Nichols Res Corp, 83-, anthropology, Univ Cincinnati, 86. *Mem:* Soc Mfg Engrs; Inst Indust Engrs; Am Soc Mech Engrs; Sigma Xi. *Res:* Pragmatic solutions of day-to-day problems encountered in packaging and materials handling; order picking; automated palletizing; load forming; simulation; warehousing; environmental packaging; robotics; machine vision applications. *Mailing Add:* 3308 N 36th St St Joseph MO 64506

SLY, RIDGE MICHAEL, PEDIATRIC ALLERGY & IMMUNOLOGY. *Current Pos:* PROF PEDIAT, SCH MED & HEALTH SCI, GEORGE WASHINGTON UNIV & DIR ALLERGY & IMMUNOL, CHILDREN'S NAT MED CTR, 78- *Personal Data:* b Seattle, Wash, Nov 3, 33; m 57, Ann T Jennings; c Teresa A & Cynthia M. *Educ:* Kenyon Col, AB, 56; Washington Univ, MD, 60; Am Bd Pediat, dipl, 65, cert allergy, 67; Am Bd Allergy & Immunol, cert 72, recert, 77 & 87. *Honors & Awards:* Peshkin Mem Award, Asn Care Asthma, 83. *Prof Exp:* NIH fel pediat allergy & immunol, Med Sch, Univ Calif, Los Angeles, 65-67; from asst prof to prof pediat, La State Univ Sch Med, New Orleans, 67-78. *Concurrent Pos:* Vis physician, Charity Hosp, New Orleans, 67-78; assoc ed, Annals Allergy, 89, ed, 90- *Mem:* Am Acad Allergy; Am Acad Pediat; distinguished fel Am Col Allergy & Immunol; Am Thoracic Soc; Asn for the Care of Asthma (pres, 80-81). *Res:* Pulmonary physiology and pharmacology of asthma; exercise induced asthma; mortality from asthma. *Mailing Add:* Children's Nat Med Ctr 111 Michigan Ave NW Washington DC 20010-2970

SLY, WILLIAM GLENN, PHYSICAL CHEMISTRY. *Current Pos:* from asst prof to assoc prof, 58-66, PROF CHEM, HARVEY MUDD COL, 66- *Personal Data:* b Arcara, Calif, June 15, 22. *Educ:* San Diego State Col, BS, 51; Calif Inst Technol, PhD(chem), 55. *Prof Exp:* NSF fel, Calif Inst Technol, 55-56, Hale fel, 56-57; fel, Mass Inst Technol, 57-58. *Concurrent Pos:* Res assoc, Calif Inst Technol, 59-61, sr res fel, 61-62; NSF sr fel, Swiss Fed Inst Technol, 65-66; guest prof, Ore State Univ, Corvallis, 72-73; vis scholar, Univ Calif, San Diego, 80. *Mem:* Am Chem Soc; Am Crystallog Asn; Inst Elec & Electronics Eng; Am Inst Physics. *Res:* Molecular structure; x-ray crystallography; application of high speed computers to structural analysis; metal complexes; organic molecules. *Mailing Add:* Dept Chem Harvey Mudd Col Claremont CA 91711

SLY, WILLIAM S, BIOCHEMISTRY, GENETICS. *Current Pos:* PROF BIOCHEM & CHMN , E A DOISY DEPT BIOCHEM & PROF PEDIAT, SCH MED, ST LOUIS UNIV, 84- *Personal Data:* b East St Louis, Ill, Oct 19, 32; m 60; c 7. *Educ:* St Louis Univ, MD, 57. *Honors & Awards:* Merit Award, NIH, 88; Passaro Found Award, 91. *Prof Exp:* Intern & asst resident, Ward Med Barnes Hosp, St Louis, Mo, 57-59; clin assoc, Nat Heart Inst, NIH, Bethesda, Md, 59-63; res biochemist, 59-63; dir, Div Med Genetics, Dept Med & Pediat, Sch Med, Wash Univ, 64-84, from asst prof to prof med, 64-78, from asst prof to prof pediat, 67-78, prof pediat, med & genetics, 78-84. *Concurrent Pos:* Vis physician, Nat Heart Inst, Bethesda, Md, 61-63 & Pediat Genetics Clin, Univ Wis-Madison, 63-64; Am Cancer Soc fel, Lab Enzymol, Nat Ctr Sci Res, Gif-sur-Yvette, France, 63 & Dept Biochem & Genetics, Univ Wis, 63-64; attend physician, St Louis County Hosp, Mo, 64-84; asst physician, Barnes Hosp, St Louis, Mo, 64-84 & St Louis Children's Hosp, Mo, 67-84; consult genetics, Homer G Philips Hosp, St Louis, Mo, 69-81; mem, Steering Comt, Human Cell Biol Prog, 71-73 & Comt Genetic Coun, Am Soc Human Genetics, 72-76; Genetics Study Sect, Div Res Grants, NIH, 71-75; traveling fel award, Royal Soc Med, 73; sabbatical, Genetics Lab, Dept Biochem, Oxford Univ, Eng, 73-74, & Dept Biochem, Stanford Univ, Calif, 81-82; active staff, Cardinal Glennon Children's Hosp, St Louis, Mo, 84-; mem, Med Adv Bd, Howard Hughes Med Inst, 89- *Mem:* Nat Acad Sci; Soc Pediat Res; Am Soc Human Genetics; Am Soc Clin Invest; Am Chem Soc; AMA; Sigma Xi; AAAS; Genetics Soc Am; Am Soc Microbiol. *Res:* Biochemical regulation; enveloped viruses as membrane probes in human diseases; lysosomal enzyme replacement in storage diseases; somatic cell genetics. *Mailing Add:* E A Doisy Dept Biochem St Louis Univ Sch Med 1402 S Grand Blvd St Louis MO 63104. *Fax:* 315-577-1183; *E-Mail:* slyws@wpogate.siu.edu

SLYE, JOHN MARSHALL, PURE MATHEMATICS. *Current Pos:* ASSOC PROF MATH, UNIV HOUSTON, 69- *Personal Data:* b Boulder, Colo, Nov 27, 23. *Educ:* Calif Inst Technol, BS, 45; Univ Tex, PhD(pure math), 53. *Prof Exp:* Technician physics cyclotron oper, Los Alamos Sci Lab, Calif, 46-48; instr pure math, Univ Tex, 50-53; from instr to assoc prof math, Univ Minn, Minneapolis, 53-69. *Mem:* AAAS; Am Math Soc; Am Phys Soc. *Res:* Two dimensional spaces; point set theory. *Mailing Add:* Dept Math Univ Houston Houston TX 77204-0001

SLYSH, ROMAN STEPHAN, polymer analysis, for more information see previous edition

SLYTER, ARTHUR LOWELL, REPRODUCTIVE PHYSIOLOGY, ANIMAL SCIENCE. *Current Pos:* PROF ANIMAL SCI & LIVESTOCK RES, SDAK STATE UNIV, 70- *Personal Data:* b Havre, Mont, Oct 23, 41; m 64; c 2. *Educ:* Kans State Univ, BS, 64, PhD(reproductive physiol), 69; Univ Nebr, Lincoln, MS, 66. *Mem:* Am Soc Animal Sci; Soc Study Reproduction. *Res:* Reproductive physiology and efficiency in sheep. *Mailing Add:* Dept Animal Sci SDak State Univ Brookings SD 57007

SLYTER, LEONARD L, MICROBIOLOGY, NUTRITION. *Current Pos:* res chemist animal sci, Res Div, USDA, 64-72, nutrit microbiol lab, Nutrit Inst, Agr Res Serv, 72-75, res chemist feed energy conserve lab, Animal Phys Genetics Inst, 75-78, RES MICROBIOL, RUMINAL NUTRIT LAB, ANIMAL SCI INST, AGR RES SERV, USDA, 79- *Personal Data:* b Fontana, Kans, Nov 13, 33; m 48; c 2. *Educ:* Kans State Univ, BS, 55; Univ Mo, MS, 49; NC State Univ, PhD(animal nutrit), 63. *Prof Exp:* Res assoc bacteriol, Univ Ill, 62-64. *Mem:* Am Soc Microbiol; Am Soc Animal Sci. *Res:* Nutritional requirements, ecology and biochemical processes of microorganisms, particularly those involving ruminal bacteria and protozoa, pure and mixed cultures and continuous culture techniques. *Mailing Add:* 117 Periwinkle Ct Greenbelt MD 20770

SLYWKA, GERALD WILLIAM ALEXANDER, ANALYTICAL CHEMISTRY, TOXICOLOGY. *Current Pos:* assoc prof, 75-84, PROF MED CHEM, SCH PHARM, FERRIS STATE COL, 84- *Personal Data:* b Hafford, Sask, Apr 23, 39; m 65; c 4. *Educ:* Univ Sask, BSP, 61, MSc, 63; Univ Alta, PhD(pharmaceut chem), 69; Univ Tenn, BS, 76; Cent Mich Univ, MA, 78. *Prof Exp:* Res chemist, Food & Drug Directorate, Ottawa, Ont, 63-64; lectr pharm, Univ Sask, 64-65; toxicologist, Crime Detection Lab, Royal Can Mounted Police, Regina, Sask, 69-71; head toxicol sect, Vancouver, BC, 71-72; asst prof med chem & head anal sect, Col Pharm, Univ Tenn Ctr Health Sci, Memphis, 72-75. *Mem:* Int Asn Forensic Toxicologists; Am Chem Soc; Am Asn Poison Control Ctrs. *Res:* Bioavailability; instrumentation; drug metabolism; drug abuse. *Mailing Add:* Col Pharmacol Ferris State Univ 901 S State St Big Rapids MI 49307-2251

SMAGORINSKY, JOSEPH, DYNAMIC METEOROLOGY. *Current Pos:* head numerical weather prediction unit, Nat Weather Serv, Nat Oceanic & Atmospheric admin, 53-54, chief comput sect, Joint Numerical Weather Prediction Unit, 54-55, chief gen circulation res lab, 55-63, dir geophys fluid dynamics lab & dep dir meteorol res, 64-65, actg dir inst atmospheric sci, 65-66, dir geophys fluid dynamics lab, 65-83, CONSULT, NAT OCEANIC & ATMOSPHERIC ADMIN, 83- *Personal Data:* b New York, NY, Jan 29, 24; m 48, Margaret Knoepfel; c Anne, Peter, Teresa, Julia & Fredrick. *Educ:* NY Univ, BS, 47, MS, 48, PhD(meteorol), 53. *Hon Degrees:* DSc, Univ Munich, 72. *Honors & Awards:* Gold Medal, US Dept Com, 66; Environ Sci Serv Admin Award, 70; Meisinger Award, Am Meteorol Soc, 67, Carl-Gustaf Rossby Res Medal, 72, Cleveland Abbe Award, 80, Charles Franklin Brooks Award, 91; Buys Ballot Medal, Royal Neth Acad Arts & Sci, 73; Int Meteorol Orgn Prize, World Meteorol Orgn, 74; Symons Mem Award, Royal Meteorol Soc, 81. *Prof Exp:* Asst & instr meteorol, NY Univ, 46-48; res meteorologist, US Weather Bur, 48-50, Inst Adv Study, 50-53. *Concurrent Pos:* Mem comt atmospheric sci, panel weather & climate modification, Nat Acad Sci, 63, interdept comt panel comput tech, 64, panel on pollution, Presidential Sci Adv Comt, 65; vis prof, Princeton Univ, 83-; officer, Int Joint Organ Comt Global Atmospheric Res Prog, 68-80, chmn, Int Joint Sci Comt World Climate Res Prog, 80-81; vchmn, US Comt Global Atmospheric Res Prog, Nat Acad Sci, 67-73 & 80-87, officer, 74-77, mem, Climate Bd, 77-87, chmn, Climate Res Comt, 81-87; Brittingham vis prof, Univ Wis, 86. *Mem:* Hon mem Am Meteorol Soc (pres, 86); hon mem Royal Meteorol Soc; fel Am Acad Arts & Sci; Sigma Xi. *Res:* Geophysical fluid dynamics and thermodynamics; geophysical applications of high speed computers; atmospheric general circulation and theory of climate; atmospheric predictability. *Mailing Add:* 21 Duffield Pl Princeton NJ 08540-2605

SMAIL, JAMES RICHARD, embryology, marine biology; deceased, see previous edition for last biography

SMALE, STEPHEN, MATHEMATICS. *Current Pos:* assoc prof, 60-61, PROF MATH, DEPT MATH, UNIV CALIF, BERKELEY, 64- *Personal Data:* b Flint, Mich, July 15, 30; m 54; c 2. *Educ:* Univ Mich, BS, 52, MS, 53, PhD(math), 56. *Hon Degrees:* DSc, Univ Warwick, Eng, 74; Queens Univ, 87. *Honors & Awards:* Veblen Prize for Geom, Am Math Soc, 65; Fields Medal, Int Math Union, 66; Chauvenet Prize, Math Asn Am, 88; Von Neumann Award, Soc Indust & Appl Math, 89; Nat Medal of Sci, 96. *Prof Exp:* Instr math, Univ Chicago, 56-58; mem, Inst Advan Study, 58-60; prof, Columbia Univ, 61-64. *Concurrent Pos:* Alfred P Sloan res fel, 60-62; res prof, Miller Inst Basic Res Sci, Berkeley, 67-68, 79-80 & 90; colloquium lectr, Am Math Soc, 72; fac res lectr, Univ Calif, Berkeley, 83. *Mem:* Nat Acad Sci; Am Acad Arts & Sci; Int Union Math; Am Math Soc; fel Econometric Soc. *Res:* Differential topology; global analysis. *Mailing Add:* Dept Math Univ Calif Berkeley CA 94720

SMALL, ARNOLD MCCOLLUM, JR, PSYCHOACOUSTICS. *Current Pos:* from asst prof to assoc prof, 58-64, dir, Div Phys Ed, 86-90, PROF SPEECH PATH, AUDIOL & PSYCHOL, UNIV IOWA, 64-, CHAIR, 93- *Personal Data:* b Springfield, Mo, Sept 16, 29; m 88, Gerri Kahn; c Janet, Laurence, Rebecca, Tara & Brian. *Educ:* San Diego State Univ, BA, 51; Univ Wis, MS, 53, PhD(psychol), 54. *Prof Exp:* Res assoc, Mass Inst Technol, 51; asst psychol, Univ Wis-Madison, 51-54; asst prof & dir, Bioelec Lab, Lehigh Univ, 54-58. *Concurrent Pos:* NIH fel, 54 & res grants, 56-58 & 68-73; NSF res grants, 54-56, 60-66 & 77-80; Off Naval Res res grant, 54-58; assoc ed, J Speech & Hearing Res, 58-64 & J Acoust Soc Am 70-77; consult, Vet Admin, 63-, Radio Corp Am, 66 & Cent Inst Deaf, 78-; vis scholar, Stanford Univ, 76-77, Univ Sydney, Australia, 89. *Mem:* Fel AAAS; fel Am Speech & Hearing Asn; fel Acoust Soc Am; sr mem Inst Elec & Electronics Engrs; Psychonomic Soc. *Res:* Psycho-acoustics and physiological acoustics; psychological and physiological aspects of sensory processes; audition; computer science. *Mailing Add:* Dept Speech Path & Audiol Univ Iowa 127 WJSHC Iowa City IA 52242. *E-Mail:* arnold-small@uiowa.edu

SMALL, DONALD BRIDGHAM, MATHEMATICS. *Current Pos:* PROF MATH, US MIL ACAD, 93- *Personal Data:* b Philadelphia, Pa, May 25, 35; m 60; c James, Janet & Robert. *Educ:* Middlebury Col, BA, 57; Univ Kans, MA, 59; Univ Conn, PhD(math), 68. *Honors & Awards:* Cert Meritorious Serv, Math Asn Am. *Prof Exp:* Instr math, Univ Conn, 60-67; asst prof, Eastern Conn State Col, 67-68; asst prof, Colby Col, 68-74, chmn div nat sci, 76-80, assoc prof math, 74-93. *Concurrent Pos:* Dir, Maine High Sch Lect Prog; chmn, Northeastern Sect, Math Asn Am, 77-79, Calculus Articulation Panel, 82-86, gov, 82-85 & 88-91; vis prof, Harvey Mudd Col, 85-86, Claremont McKenna Col, 86, Pomona Col, 87 & US Mil Acad, 91-93; proj dir, Comput Algebra Syst & Calculus Reform Workshops, NSF, 89- *Mem:* Am Math Soc; Math Asn Am. *Res:* Graph theory; curriculum development (computer algebra systems in calculus). *Mailing Add:* Dept Math Sci US Mil Acad West Point NY 10996. *Fax:* 914-938-2409; *E-Mail:* ad5712@usma2.usma.edu

SMALL, DONALD MACFARLAND, LIPID & FAT PHYSICAL CHEMISTRY, STRUCTURAL BIOLOGY OF LIPOPROTEINS & ATHEROSCLEROSIS. *Current Pos:* CHMN, DEPT BIOPHYS, BOSTON UNIV SCH MED, 72-, PROF BIOPHYS, MED & BIOCHEM, 73- *Personal Data:* b Sept 15, 31; m 57, 86, Kathryn Ross; c Geoffrey, Philip & Samuel. *Educ:* Occidental Col, BA, 54; Oxford Univ, BA & MA, 58; Univ Calif, Los Angeles, MD, 60. *Honors & Awards:* Ann Distinguished Achievement Award, Am Gastroenterol Asn, 72; Eppinger Prize, Fourth Int Cong Liver Dis, Basel, Switz, 76; George Lyman Duff Mem Lectr, Coun Atherosclerosis, Am Heart Asn, 86. *Concurrent Pos:* Mem grad fac med scis, Boston Univ Med Ctr, 69-; ed, J Lipid Res 79-83, Advances Lipid Res, 89-, Current Opinion Struct Biol (Lipids), 92; chmn, Coun Arteriosclerosis, Am Heart Asn, 89- *Mem:* Am Heart Asn; Am Asn Physicians; Am Soc Biol Chemists; Biophys Soc; Am Soc Clin Invest; Am Oil Chemists Soc. *Res:* Physical chemistry and structure of lipids and proteins, particularly as they apply to biology (membranes, lipoproteins, fats, oils) and pathology (atherosclerosis, lipoproteinemia, gallstones, membrane disorders). *Mailing Add:* Boston Univ Sch Med Dept Biophysics 700 Albany St W-308 Boston MA 02118-2394

SMALL, ERNEST, BIOSYSTEMATICS. *Current Pos:* RES BIOLOGIST, ECONOMIC PLANT SECT, CAN DEPT AGR, 69- *Personal Data:* b Ottawa, Ont, Mar 10, 40. *Educ:* Carleton Univ, BA, 63, BSc, 65, MSc, 66; Univ Calif, Los Angeles, PhD, 69. *Honors & Awards:* G M Cooley Award, Am Soc Plant Taxon, 74. *Mem:* Am Soc Plant Taxon; Int Asn Plant Taxon; Linnean Soc London; Can Bot Asn. *Res:* Systematics of cultivated plants. *Mailing Add:* Agri Food CLBRR Cent Exp Farm Ottawa ON K1A 0C6 Can

SMALL, ERWIN, VETERINARY MEDICINE. *Current Pos:* from instr to assoc prof, Univ Ill, Urbana, 58-67, head small animal med, Col Vet Med, 70-80, interim dept chair, 87-88, PROF VET CLIN MED, UNIV ILL, URBANA, 67-, ASSOC DEAN, ALUMNI & PUB AFFAIRS, 78-, DIR VET MED TEACHING HOSP, 88- *Personal Data:* b Boston, Mass, Nov 28, 24. *Educ:* Univ Ill, BS, 55, DVM, 57, MS, 65. *Honors & Awards:* AAHA Award, 83. *Prof Exp:* Intern, Angell Mem Hosp, Boston, Mass, 57-58. *Concurrent Pos:* Fel, Nat Heart Inst, 65 & Morris Animal Found, 67-68. *Mem:* NY Acad Sci; Sigma Xi; Am Col Vet Dermat (pres, 79-82); Am Acad Vet Allergy (pres, 86-88); Nat Acad Pract Vet Med. *Res:* Serodiagnostic and immunologic approaches to the study of hemotrophic parasites. *Mailing Add:* Col Vet Med Univ Ill 2001 S Lincoln Ave Urbana IL 61801

SMALL, EUGENE BEACH, PROTISTOLOGY, MICROBIAL ECOLOGY. *Current Pos:* ASSOC PROF ZOOL, UNIV MD, COLLEGE PARK, 70- *Personal Data:* b Reed City, Mich, Jan 7, 31; m 65; c 4. *Educ:* Wayne State Univ, BS, 53, MS, 56; Univ Calif, Los Angeles, PhD(zool), 64. *Prof Exp:* Asst prof zool, Univ Ill, 64-70. *Mem:* Soc Protozoologists (treas, 62-64); Am Micros Soc; AAAS; Soc Evolutionary Protistologists; Sigma Xi. *Res:* Protistan organisms: their morphology, morphogenesis, ecology, and evolutionary history; development of electron microscopical techniques applicable to the study of unicellular organisms; systematics of the phylum ciliophora. *Mailing Add:* Dept Zool Univ Md College Park MD 20742-0001

SMALL, GARY D, BIOCHEMISTRY. *Current Pos:* from asst prof to assoc prof, 67-76, PROF BIOCHEM, UNIV SDAK, 76- *Personal Data:* b Atkinson, Nebr, Oct 17, 37; m 64; c 2. *Educ:* Nebr State Col, BS, 59; Western Reserve Univ, PhD(biochem), 65. *Prof Exp:* Nat Cancer Inst fel Dept Biochem, Univ Wash, 65-67. *Concurrent Pos:* Vis biochemist, Nat Cancer Inst fel, Brookhaven Nat Lab, 74-75. *Mem:* AAAS; Sigma Xi; Am Soc Biol Chemists; Am Soc Photobiol. *Res:* Enzymology of nucleases; effects of ultraviolet radiation on nucleic acids; biological repair of nucleic acid damage. *Mailing Add:* Dept Biochem & Molec Biol Univ SDak Sch Med 414 E Clark St Vermillion SD 57069-2390. *Fax:* 605-677-5124; *E-Mail:* gsmall@charlie.usd.edu

SMALL, GERALD J, PHYSICAL CHEMISTRY. *Current Pos:* PROF, DEPT CHEM, IOWA STATE UNIV, 70- *Personal Data:* b Vancouver, BC, Jan 18, 41. *Educ:* Univ BC, BS, 63; Univ Pa, PhD(phys chem), 67. *Mem:* Fel Am Phys Soc; Am Chem Soc. *Res:* Physical chemistry. *Mailing Add:* Dept Chem Iowa State Univ Ames IA 50011-0061

SMALL, HAMISH, PHYSICAL CHEMISTRY, ANALYTICAL CHEMISTRY. *Current Pos:* CONSULT, 83- *Personal Data:* b Antrim, Northern Ireland, Oct 5, 29; US citizen; m 54, Beryl M Burley; c Deborah & Claire. *Educ:* Queen's Univ, Belfast, BSc, 49, MSc, 52. *Honors & Awards:* Appl Anal Chem Award, Soc Anal Chemists Pittsburgh, 77; Albert F Sperry Medal, Instrument Soc Am, 78; A O Beckman Award, Instrument Soc Am, 83; Herbert H Dow Gold Medal, 83; Stephen Dal Nogare Chromatography Award, 84; Chromatography Award, Am Chem Soc, 91. *Prof Exp:* Chemist phys chem, Atomic Energy Res Estab, Eng, 49-55; chemist, Dow Chem Co, 55-62, sr res chemist, 62-63, assoc scientist, 63-74, res scientist phys chem, 74-83. *Mem:* Am Chem Soc. *Res:* Separation science; liquid chromatography; hydrodynamic chromatography; ion chromatography. *Mailing Add:* 4176 Oxford Dr Leland MI 49654-9701. *Fax:* 616-256-2691

SMALL, HENRY GILBERT, CITATION ANALYSIS & BIBLIOMETRICS, INFORMATION SCIENCE. *Current Pos:* sr res scientist, 72-77, dir contract res, 77-80, DIR CORP RES, INST SCI INFO, 80- *Personal Data:* b Chicago, Ill, June 17, 41; m 71; c 1. *Educ:* Univ Ill, BA, 63; Univ Wis, MA, 66, PhD(hist sci & chem), 71. *Honors & Awards:* Derek Price Medal, 87. *Prof Exp:* Res assoc, Ctr Hist & Philos Physics, Am Inst Physics, 69-70, actg dir, 71-72. *Concurrent Pos:* Sr fel, dept hist & sociol sci, Univ Pa, 74-79; coun mem, Soc Social Studies Sci, 79-81; mem sci & arts comt, Franklin Inst, 85- *Mem:* Am Soc Info Sci; Soc Social Study Sci; Hist Sci Soc; fel AAAS. *Res:* Bibliometrics and especially citation and co-citation analysis, to study the structure and development of science; application of statistical methods, clustering and scaling to bibliometric data for mapping scientific fields; constructing science indicators and information retrieval. *Mailing Add:* 105 Rolling Rd Bala Cynwyd PA 19004. *E-Mail:* hsmall@isinet.com

SMALL, IVER FRANCIS, PSYCHIATRY. *Current Pos:* ASST SUPT PSYCHIAT, LARUE D CARTER MEM HOSP, 65- *Personal Data:* b Sask, Can, Sept 19, 23; US citizen; m 54; c 4. *Educ:* Univ Sask, BA, 51; Univ Man, MD, 54; Univ Mich, MS, 60. *Prof Exp:* Asst prof psychiat, Med Sch & dir inserv psychiat, Hosp, Univ Ore, 60-62; dir inpatient serv psychiat, Malcolm Bliss Ment Health Ctr, 62-65; assoc prof, 65-69, prof psychiat, Sch Med, Ind Univ, Indianapolis, 69- *Concurrent Pos:* Asst prof psychiat, Sch Med, Washington Univ, 62-65; vis physician, Unit I, St Louis City Hosp, 6265. *Mem:* AMA; Soc Biol Psychiat (secy-treas, 70-); Am Psychiat Asn; Sigma Xi. *Res:* Work in clinical psychiatry; follow-up studies; the convulsive therapies; and the neuropsychology of mental illness. *Mailing Add:* 1315 W Tenth St Indianapolis IN 46202-2802

SMALL, JAMES GRAYDON, quantum optics, medical ultrasound, for more information see previous edition

SMALL, JOYCE G, PSYCHIATRY, ELECTROENCEPMALOGRAPHY. *Current Pos:* assoc prof, 65-69, PROF PSYCHIAT, SCH MED, IND UNIV, INDIANAPOLIS, 69-; DIR RES, LARUE D CARTER MEM HOSP, 65- *Personal Data:* b Edmonton, Alta, June 12, 31; US citizen; m 54; c 4. *Educ:* Univ Sask, BA, 51; Univ Man, MD, 56; Univ Mich, MS, 59; Am Bd Psychiat & Neurol, dipl, 61. *Honors & Awards:* Clin Res Award, Am Acad Clin Psychiat, 88; Merit Award, NIMH, 90; Exemplary Psychiatrist Award, Nat Alliance Ment Ill, 92. *Prof Exp:* Intern, Winnipeg Gen Hosp, Man, 5556; resident psychiat, Ypsilanti State Hosp, Mich, 56-59; instr, Neuropsychiat Inst, Univ Mich, 59-60; from instr to asst prof, Sch Med, Univ Ore, 60-62; clin dir, Malcolm Bliss Ment Health Ctr, 62-65; asst prof psychiat, Sch Med, Washington Univ, 62-65. *Concurrent Pos:* Teaching fel biochem, Univ Man, 55-56; res assoc neurol & psychiat consult, Crippled Children's Div, Med Sch, Univ Ore, 60-62; vis physician, St Louis City Hosps, 62-65; attend staff, Vet Admin Hosp, Indianapolis, 65-69, Univ Hosp Indianapolis, 74- & Wisford Mem Hosp, 79-; assoc mem, Inst Psychiat Res, 74-; Joyce L & Iver Small prof psychiat res, Ind Univ Sch Med, 96- *Mem:* AAAS; fel Am Psychiat Asn; NY Acad Sci; Am Electroencephalog Soc; Soc Biol Psychiat; Am Psychiat Electrophysiol Asn. *Res:* Clinical psychiatry; electroencephalography; neurophysiology; psychopharmacology; improving the treatment of severe mental illness through drug and somatic therapies; clinical and qualitative electroencephalography studies. *Mailing Add:* Larue D Carter Mem Hosp 2601 Cold Spring Rd Indianapolis IN 46222. *Fax:* 317-684-9943

SMALL, JUDY ANN, NEUROGENETICS, DEVELOPMENTAL NEUROBIOLOGY. *Current Pos:* guest researcher, 86-87, sr staff fel, 90-92, HEALTH SCIENTIST ADMINR, NIH, 92- *Personal Data:* b Massena, NY, Feb 2, 59. *Educ:* Sien Col, BS, 80; Johns Hopkins Univ, PhD(biol), 86. *Prof Exp:* Res fel, Johns Hopkins Med Inst, 87-89. *Mem:* AAAS; Soc Neurosci. *Res:* Transgenic mouse model of neurodegenerative disease using JC virus and visna sequences; myelin protein expression in cultured cells; molecular biology and genetics, and training in neurochemistry and development neurosciences. *Mailing Add:* NIH Rm 8c-04 7550 Wisconsin Ave Bethesda MD 20892

SMALL, KENT W, OPHTHALMOLOGY, VITREO-RETINAL SURGERY. *Current Pos:* ASSOC PROF, JULES STEIN EYE INST, UNIV CALIF, LOS ANGELES, 94-, DIR, MACULA CTR, RETINA RES CTR, 94- *Personal Data:* b New Orleans, La, Oct 19, 56; m 83, Frances Culler; c 2. *Educ:* Tulane Univ, MD(med), 81; Duke Univ, MD(surg & ophthal), 87, MD(molecular genetics), 90. *Prof Exp:* Asst prof, Med Univ SC, 91; assoc prof, Univ Fla, 92-94. *Concurrent Pos:* Jacob Javits fel, NIH, 90. *Mem:* Macula Soc; Retina Soc; Am Soc Human Genetics; AMA; AAAS; Asn Res Vision & Ophthal. *Res:* Gene mapping and cloning of ocular disease causing genes. *Mailing Add:* Univ Calif 200 Stein Plaza Los Angeles CA 90095

SMALL, LANCE W, NONCOMMUTATIVE RING THEORY. *Current Pos:* assoc prof, 70-74, PROF MATH, UNIV CALIF SAN DIEGO, 74- *Personal Data:* b New York, NY, Apr 16, 41; m 65; c 2. *Educ:* Univ Chicago, BS & MS, 62 & PhD(math), 65. *Prof Exp:* Asst prof math, Univ Calif Berkeley, 65-69; assoc prof math, Univ Southern Calif, 69-70. *Concurrent Pos:* Sr vis fel, Univ Leeds, Eng, 67-68, 72-73 & 84, hon vis fel, 78-; fel, Inst Advan

Studies, Jerusalem, Israel, 77-78; mem coun, Am Math Soc, 83-87, assoc secy, 88- *Mem:* Am Math Soc. *Res:* Noncommutative rings, particularly rings with polynomial identity and noetherian rings. *Mailing Add:* Dept Math Univ Calif San Diego 0112 9500 Gilman Dr La Jolla CA 92093-0112. *E-Mail:* lwsmall@ucsd.edu

SMALL, LAVERNE DOREYN, MEDICINAL CHEMISTRY. *Current Pos:* assoc prof pharmaceut chem, 48-54, prof & chmn pharm & pharmaceut chem, 54-73, prof med chem & pharmacog, 73-80, prof, 80-83, EMER PROF BIOMED CHEM, COL PHARM, UNIV NEBR, 83- *Personal Data:* b Black Earth, Wis, Dec 22, 16; m 38; c 2. *Educ:* Univ Minn, BS, 38, MS, 43, PhD(pharmaceut chem), 45. *Prof Exp:* Pharmacist, Walgreen Drug Co, Minn, 38-40; pharmacist, Johnson Co, Minn, 40-42; res chemist, Sterling-Winthrop Res Inst, 45-48. *Mem:* Am Chem Soc; Am Pharmaceut Asn; Sigma Xi. *Res:* Synthesis and testing of compounds related to quinidine as cardiac antiarrhythmic agents; synthesis and testing of compounds related to allicin as antibacterial and antifungal agents. *Mailing Add:* 128 N 13th St Apt 705 Lincoln NE 68508-1501

SMALL, LAWRENCE FREDERICK, BIOLOGICAL OCEANOGRAPHY. *Current Pos:* from asst prof to assoc prof, Ore State Univ, 61-72, assoc dean, Col Oceanog, 84-93, PROF BIOL OCEANOG, ORE STATE UNIV, 72-, DEAN, COL OCEANIC & ATMOSPHERIC SCI, 93- *Personal Data:* b St Louis, Mo, Feb 16, 34; m 63, Janice Hammersley; c Karen, Stephen & Suzanne. *Educ:* Univ Mo, AB, 55; Iowa State Univ, MS, 59, PhD(zool), 61. *Prof Exp:* Instr limnol, Iowa State Univ, 60-61. *Concurrent Pos:* NSF fels, 61-64 & 70-72, res grant, 73-90; AEC fel, 63-66; USPHS training grant, 63-67, fel, 64-67; EPA res grant, 77-79, DOE grant, 81-91, Off Naval Res grant, 87-89; Int AEA spec serv res award, Monaco, 70-71, 77-78, 88 & 90; Nat Acad Sci res grant, Yugoslavia, 72; res grant, Sea Grant, Nat Oceanic & Atmospheric Asn, 72 & 85-86; res contract, US Army Corps of Engrs, 74, NASA, 83. *Mem:* AAAS; Am Soc Limnol & Oceanog; Sigma Xi; Oceanog Soc. *Res:* Phytoplankton and zooplankton ecology and physiology; energy and material transfer in lower marine trophic levels. *Mailing Add:* 3510 NW Elmwood Dr Corvallis OR 97330. *Fax:* 541-737-2064

SMALL, PARKER ADAMS, JR, IMMUNOLOGY, MEDICINE. *Current Pos:* chmn dept, 66-76, PROF IMMUNOL & MED MICROBIOL, COL MED, UNIV FLA, 66-, PROF PEDIATRICS, 79- *Personal Data:* b Cincinnati, Ohio, July 5, 32; m 56; c 3. *Educ:* Univ Cincinnati, MD, 57; Tufts Univ, BS, 86. *Prof Exp:* Intern med, Univ Pa Hosp, Philadelphia, 57-58; res assoc immunol, USPHS, 58-60, surgeon, NIMH, 61-64, sr surgeon, Sect Phys Chem, 64-66. *Concurrent Pos:* USPHS res fel, 55 & spec fel, 60; res fel, Wright-Fleming Inst Microbiol, St Mary's Hosp Med Sch, 60-61; vis prof immunol, Univ Lausanne, 72, Univ Lagos, Nigeria, 82 & Al Hada Hosp, Saudi Arabia, 83; vis scholar, Asn Am Med Cols, 73; consult, Med Scientist Training Comt, Nat Inst Gen Med Sci & WHO; mem, bd dir, Biol Sci Curriculum Studies, 84-90, exec comt, 87-90; secy-treas, City of Oakland, Md, 64-65, mayor, 65-66; chmn, Citizens Pub Sch, Gainesville, Fla, 69-70; ed, Sec Innunol Systs, 71, Patient Oriented Prob Solving Syst Immunol, 82 & Pharmacol, 85; consult ed, ed bd, Microbios & Cytobios. *Mem:* AAAS; Fedn Am Scientists; Am Asn Immunologists; Sigma Xi; Physicians for Soc Responsibility; Am Soc Med; Am Med Asn. *Res:* Host defense against influenza; medical education. *Mailing Add:* Dept Pathol Univ Fla Col Med Box 100275 Gainesville FL 32610-0275. *Fax:* 904-392-3133

SMALL, ROBERT JAMES, ORGANIC CHEMISTRY, PHOTOCHEMISTRY. *Current Pos:* RES ASSOC, FIRST CHEM CORP, 90-; SR RES ASSOC, EKC TECHNOL INC. *Personal Data:* b Philadelphia, Pa, Nov 23, 38; m 63, Helga Hoalgand; c 2. *Educ:* Norwich Univ, BS, 61; Tex Tech Univ, MS, 64; Univ Ariz, PhD(org chem), 71. *Prof Exp:* Fel org chem, Univ Ky, 72-73; res chemist, Celanese Chem Co, 73-74; sr res chemist, Ashland Chem Co, 74-80; proj leader, Ciba-Geigy Corp, 80-85; res dir, Wesley Industs, 86-90. *Concurrent Pos:* Lectr freshmen chem, Univ SAla. *Mem:* Am Chem Soc; Royal Soc Chemists; Am Inst Chemists; Sigma Xi; Electroclin Soc. *Res:* Heterogenous and homogeneous catalytic oxidation of olefins and heterogenous oxidative dehydrogenation of aliphatic systems; process development of reductive methylation of amines and hydrazine derivatives; photochemistry of oximes; paper dyes; hydroxamethylation. *Mailing Add:* 11418 Rampart Dr Dublin CA 94568. *Fax:* 510-784-9181; *E-Mail:* bsmall@ekctech.com

SMALL, S(AUL) MOUCHLY, psychiatry, for more information see previous edition

SMALL, TIMOTHY MICHAEL, RESEARCH ADMINISTRATION, TECHNICAL MANAGEMENT. *Current Pos:* RETIRED. *Personal Data:* b Muncie, Ind, Sept 29, 40; m 75, Sandra Adams; c 4. *Educ:* Ind Univ, BS, 63, MS, 64, PhD(physics), 68. *Prof Exp:* Actg mgr proj eng, Gen Elec Mgt & Tech Serv Dept, Miss Test Facil, NASA, 70-71; Actg mgr proj eng, Gen Elec Mgt & Tech Serv Dept, Miss Test Facil, NASA, 70-71; US Army, 68-95, res physicist, US Army Nuclear Effects Lab, 68-70, res physicist, 71-78, develop proj officer, 78-81, tech asst, Mobility Equip Res & Develop Command, 81-83, tech base adminr, US Army Mat Command, 83-86, dep dir res & anal, 86-92, chief, Chem Div, US Army INSCOM, Nat Ground Intel Ctr, 92-95. *Mem:* Am Phys Soc; AAAS; Sigma Xi. *Mailing Add:* 600 Poplar Spring Rd Scottsville VA 24590-9502. *E-Mail:* timsmall@worldnet.attt.net

SMALL, WILLIAM ANDREW, MATHEMATICS. *Current Pos:* chmn dept, 62-78, prof math, 62-85, EMER PROF, STATE UNIV NY COL GENESEO, 85- *Personal Data:* b Cobleskill, NY, Oct 16, 14; m 39; c 1. *Educ:* US Naval Acad, BS, 36; Univ Rochester, AB, 50, AM, 52, PhD(math), 58. *Prof Exp:* Instr math, DeVeaux Sch, NY, 45-48; instr Univ Rochester, 51-55; asst prof, Alfred Univ, 55-56; asst prof, Grinnell Col, 56-58, assoc prof & chmn dept, 58-60; prof, Tenn Polytech Inst, 60-62. *Concurrent Pos:* Fulbright-Hays lectr, Univ Aleppo, 64-65; assoc ed, Philosophia Mathematica. *Mem:* Math Asn Am. *Res:* Mathematical theory of probability; philosophy and history of mathematics; mathematical statistics. *Mailing Add:* PO Box 367 Geneseo NY 14454-0367

SMALLEY, ALFRED EVANS, ECOLOGY, ORNITHOLOGY. *Current Pos:* from instr to assoc prof, 59-75, PROF BIOL, TULANE UNIV LA, 75- *Personal Data:* b Chester, Pa, Feb 29, 28; c 2. *Educ:* Pa State Univ, BS, 50, MS, 52; Univ Ga, PhD(zool), 59. *Prof Exp:* Instr biol, Univ Ky, 58-59. *Mem:* Soc Syst Zool; Am Ornith Union; Crustacean Soc. *Res:* Ecology of aquatic ecosystems; marine invertebrate zoology; taxonomy of freshwater decapod crustacea. *Mailing Add:* 88 Egret St New Orleans LA 70124

SMALLEY, ANTHONY JAMES, PLANT & MACHINERY DYNAMICS. *Current Pos:* staff engr, 80-82, INST ENGR, SOUTHWEST RES INST, 82- *Personal Data:* b York, Eng, Nov 17, 41; US citizen; m 65, Anna; c Nicholas & Nathan. *Educ:* Univ Nottingham, UK, BSc, 63, PhD(mech eng), 66. *Honors & Awards:* Gas Turbine Award, Am Soc Mech Engrs, 82; John P Davis Award, Int Gas Turbine Inst, 90. *Prof Exp:* Supvr comput appln, Mech Technol, Inc, 68-72, mgr mach dynamics, 72-80. *Mem:* Fel Am Soc Mech Engrs; Am Concrete Inst. *Res:* Computational methods for fluid film bearings - gas and liquid; vibration control techniques including damping and balancing for rotating machinery; monitoring and diagnostic techniques for gas turbines and for reciprocating compressors. *Mailing Add:* Southwest Res Inst PO Drawer 28510 6220 Culebra Rd San Antonio TX 78228-0510. *Fax:* 210-681-9661; *E-Mail:* asmalley@swri.edu

SMALLEY, ARNOLD WINFRED, ORGANIC CHEMISTRY. *Current Pos:* ASSOC PROF CHEM, SOUTHERN UNIV, BATON ROUGE, 65- *Personal Data:* b Shreveport, La, Aug 2, 33; m 66. *Educ:* Wiley Col, BS, 59; Univ Kans, MS, 62; Univ Mass, PhD(org chem), 65. *Mem:* Am Chem Soc. *Res:* Stabilities of metallocenyl substituted cations; electrophilic substitution reactions of metallocenes; quaternary phosphonium hydroxide decompositions; organic pollutants in municipal water supplies. *Mailing Add:* 6877 Vineyard Dr Baton Rouge LA 70812

SMALLEY, EUGENE BYRON, PLANT PATHOLOGY, MYCOLOGY. *Current Pos:* asst prof plant path & forestry, Univ Wis-Madison, 57-64, assoc prof plant path, 64-69, actg chmn, 80-89, assoc chmn, Dept Plant Path, 90-92, PROF PLANT PATH, UNIV WIS-MADISON, 69- *Personal Data:* b Los Angeles, Calif, July 11, 26; m 78, Joan A Potter; c Daniel, Lisa, Sara, Anthony, Andrew & Andrew. *Educ:* Univ Calif, Los Angeles, BS, 49, Univ Calif, MS, 53, PhD(plant path), 57. *Prof Exp:* Asst plant path, Univ Calif, 53-56. *Mem:* Am Phytopath Soc; AAAS; Am Mycol Soc; Am Orchid Soc. *Res:* Forest pathology; vascular wilts of woody plants; diseases of garlic; mycotoxins; dutch elm disease; insect borne pathogens of trees; ophiostomatales-oregenes of virulence. *Mailing Add:* Dept Plant Path 284 Russell Lab Univ Wis-Madison 1630 Linden Dr Madison WI 53706-1520. *E-Mail:* ebs@plantpath.wisc.edu

SMALLEY, GLENDON WILLIAM, FOREST SOILS, SILVICULTURE. *Current Pos:* Forester, Sam Houston Nat Forest, Southern Region, USDA Forest Serv, 53-55, forester & asst dist ranger, Ouachita Nat Forest, 55-56, res forester, Southern Forest Exp Sta, Birmingham Res Ctr, 56-63, Silvicult Lab, 63-74, RES SOIL SCIENTIST SILVICULT LAB, SOUTHERN FOREST EXP STA, USDA FOREST SERV, SEWANEE, TENN, 74- *Personal Data:* b Bridgeton, NJ, Jan 23, 28; m 54; c 2. *Educ:* Mich State Univ, BS, 52, MS, 56; Univ Tenn, PhD, 75. *Mem:* Soc Am Foresters; Soil Sci Soc Am; Am Soc Agron; Ecol Soc Am. *Res:* Detailed planning, conducting, supervising and evaluating fundamental and applied research in forest soils for Cumberland Plateau and Highland Rim regions of Tennessee and Alabama. *Mailing Add:* Glenmary Farm 102 Rabbit Run Sewanee TN 37375-2753

SMALLEY, HARRY EDWIN, veterinary toxicology; deceased, see previous edition for last biography

SMALLEY, KATHERINE N, ANIMAL PHYSIOLOGY, ENDOCRINOLOGY. *Current Pos:* From asst prof to assoc prof, 66-82, PROF BIOL, EMPORIA STATE UNIV, 82- *Personal Data:* b Chicago, Ill, Oct 24, 35; m 59; c 2. *Educ:* Rockford Col, BA, 56; Univ Iowa, MS, 60, PhD(zool), 63. *Prof Exp:* Instr zool, Univ Iowa, 63-64. *Concurrent Pos:* Prin investr res grant, 64, 66, assoc prin investr res grant, NIH, 66-72; vis assoc prof, Univ Mich, 82. *Mem:* AAAS; Am Soc Zoologists; Sigma Xi. *Res:* Endocrinology of reproduction in amphibians, with emphasis on androgens and estrogens in females. *Mailing Add:* Dept Biol Sci Emporia State Univ 1200 Commercial St Emporia KS 66801-5057

SMALLEY, LARRY L, GENERAL RELATIVITY, GRAVITATION. *Current Pos:* from asst prof to assoc prof, 67-80, chmn dept, 73-85, PROF PHYSICS, UNIV ALA, HUNTSVILLE, 80- *Personal Data:* b Grand Island, Nebr, Aug 7, 37; m 57, Katherine; c 3. *Educ:* Univ Nebr, BS, 59, MS, 64, PhD, 67; Univ Ala, Huntsville, BA, 87. *Prof Exp:* Instr physics, US Naval Nuclear Power Sch, Conn, 61-62. *Concurrent Pos:* Asst reactor engr, Hallam Nuclear

Power Fac, Nebr, 65; res physicist, Phys Sci Lab, Army Missile Command, Redstone Arsenel, 68; Nat Acad Sci/Nat Res Coun sr fel, NASA, 74-75; Humboldt fel, Univ Colgne, 76-77, 80 & 93; space scientist, Space Sci Lab, Marshall Space Flight Ctr, 79-89; consult, Teledyne Brown Eng, Huntsville, Ala, 89-94; mem, Strategic Defense Comn, Huntsville, Ala, 90; prof invitee, Univ Paris VI, 93; assoc dir, Grav-Electromagnetic, 96. *Mem:* Am Phys Soc; Sigma Xi. *Res:* Theoretical physics, especially gravitational physics and discrete spacetime; fluid dynamics; impact machines. *Mailing Add:* Dept Physics Univ Ala Huntsville AL 35899. *Fax:* 205-890-6873; *E-Mail:* smalley@pluto.cs.uah.edu

SMALLEY, RALPH RAY, ORNAMENTAL HORTICULTURE, AGRONOMY. *Current Pos:* RETIRED. *Personal Data:* b Starkey, NY, Aug 26, 19; m 46; c 3. *Educ:* Cornell Univ, BS, 50, MS, 51; Univ FLa, PhD(soil fertil & hort corn), 61. *Prof Exp:* Asst prof soils & crops, State Univ NY Agr & Tech Col Farmingdale, 51-58; res asst turfgrass, Univ Fla, 58-61, turf technologist, 61-62; prof soils, field crops & turfgrass, State Univ NY Agr & Tech Col Cobleskill, 62-83. *Concurrent Pos:* Vis prof turfgrass, Cornell Univ, 73-74; Teacher fel, Nat Asn Cols & Teachers Agr, 82; consult soils & ornamental hort, 83- *Mem:* Am Soc Agron; Coun Agr Sci & Technol; fel Nat Asn Cols & Teachers Agr; Sigma Xi. *Res:* Effect of amendments on the physical and chemical properties of soil; turfgrass production and management; fine Bermudagrass response to physical soil amendments; turfgrass tillering; turfgrass irrigation. *Mailing Add:* 4 Cleveland Ave Cobleskill NY 12043

SMALLEY, RICHARD ERRETT, CHEMICAL PHYSICS. *Current Pos:* from asst prof to prof, 76-81, GENE & NORMAN HACKERMAN PROF CHEM, RICE UNIV, 82-, PROF PHYSICS, 90-; DIR, RICE CTR NANOSCALE SCI & TECHNOL, 96- *Personal Data:* b Akron, Ohio, June 6, 43; m 68, 80; c Chad. *Educ:* Univ Mich, BS, 65; Princeton Univ, MA, 71, PhD(chem), 73. *Hon Degrees:* Dr, Univ Liege, Belg, 91; DSc, Univ Chicago, 95. *Honors & Awards:* Nobel Prize in Chem, 96; Irving Langmuir Prize Chem Physics, 91; Int Prize New Mats, Am Phys Soc, 92; Ernest O Lawrence Mem Award, 92; Auburn-GM Kosolapoff Award, Auburn Sect, Am Chem Soc, 92, Southwest Regional Award, 92, William H Nichols Medal, NY Sect, 93, Harrison Howe Award, Rochester Sect, 94, Madison Marshall Award, NAla Sect, 95; Hewlett Packard Europhysics Prize, Europ Physics Soc, 94. *Prof Exp:* Res chemist, Shell Chem Co, 65-69; grad res asst, Dept Chem, Princeton Univ, 69-73; res assoc chem, Univ Chicago, 73-76. *Concurrent Pos:* Harold W Dodds fel, Princeton Univ, 73 & Alfred P Sloan fel, 78-80; mem, Steering Comt, Rice Quantum Inst, 79-, chmn, Inst, 86-96; mem vis comt, Brookhaven Nat Lab, 83-84, Comt Atomic, Molecular & Optical Sci, Nat Res Coun, 88-91; chmn, Gordon Conf Metal & Semiconductor Clusters, 87. *Mem:* Nat Acad Sci; fel Am Phys Soc; Am Chem Soc; Mat Res Soc; Sigma Xi; AAAS; Am Inst Physics; Am Acad Arts & Sci. *Res:* Spectroscopic study of the unperturbed gas-phase structure and elementary chemical and photophysical processes of polyatomic molecules, radicals, and ions, including simple clusters of these with each other and with atoms; cluster structure and surface chemistry. *Mailing Add:* CNST MS100 Rice Univ 6100 Main St Houston TX 77005-1892

SMALLEY, ROBERT GORDON, GEOLOGY, GEOCHEMISTRY. *Current Pos:* geologist, Stand Oil Co, Calif, 48-49, res geologist, La Habra Lab, Calif Res Corp, 49-59, sr res geologist, 59-66, SR RES ASSOC GEOCHEM, CHEVRON RES CO, 66- *Personal Data:* b Chicago, Ill, June 1, 21; m 46; c 2. *Educ:* Univ Chicago, SB, 42, MS, 43, PhD, 48. *Prof Exp:* Geologist, US Geol Surv, 43-44. *Mem:* Geol Soc Am; Geochem Soc; Soc Appl Spectros. *Res:* Geochemistry of sediments and sedimentary rocks, carbonates and natural waters; petrology; igneous and metamorphic rocks; economic and petroleum geology. *Mailing Add:* PO Box 180 Lake Arrowhead CA 92352-0180

SMALLWOOD, CHARLES, JR, sanitary engineering; deceased, see previous edition for last biography

SMALLWOOD, JAMES EDGAR, RADIOGRAPHIC ANATOMY, XERORADIOGRAPHY. *Current Pos:* prof, 81-89, DISTINGUISHED PROF VET ANAT, NC STATE UNIV, 89- *Personal Data:* b Dallas, Tex, Oct 26, 45; m 67, 90, Kay Williams; c Sheri & Rene. *Educ:* Tex A&M Univ, DVM, 69, MS, 72. *Prof Exp:* From instr to assoc prof vet anat, Tex A&M Univ, 69-81. *Mem:* Am Vet Med Asn; Am Asn Vet Anatomists; World Asn Vet Anatomists. *Res:* Radiographic anatomy of domestic mammals and birds; skeletal development in the horse using xeroradiography. *Mailing Add:* APR Dept NC State Univ Col Vet Med 4700 Hillsborough Raleigh NC 27606. *Fax:* 919-829-4465; *E-Mail:* ed__smallwood@ncsu.edu

SMALLWOOD, RICHARD DALE, OPERATIONS RESEARCH, SYSTEMS ANALYSIS. *Current Pos:* RETIRED. *Personal Data:* b Portsmouth, Ohio, Oct 9, 35; m 59; c 3. *Educ:* Mass Inst Technol, SB, 57, SM, 58, ScD(elec eng), 62. *Prof Exp:* Lectr opers res, Mass Inst Technol, 62-64; asst prof eng-econ systs, Stanford Univ, 64-67, assoc prof, 67-73; res scientist anal res, Xerox Palo Alto Res Ctr, 73-79; pres, Appl Decision Anal, Inc, 79-84. *Concurrent Pos:* Consult prof, Dept Eng-Econ Systs, Stanford Univ, 73-; consult var govt & indust orgn. *Mem:* Inst Mgt Sci; Opers Res Soc Am; Inst Elec & Electronics Engrs. *Res:* Decision analysis; market analysis systems; modeling; man-machine systems; analysis of health care systems. *Mailing Add:* Appl Decision Analysis Inc 2710 Sand Hill Rd Menlo Park CA 94025

SMARANDACHE, FLORENTIN, numerical functions in number theory, proposed problems of mathematics for college, for more information see previous edition

SMARDON, RICHARD CLAY, ENVIRONMENTAL PLANNING, COASTAL ZONE PLANNING. *Current Pos:* assoc, Grad Prog Environ Sci, State Univ NY, 80-82, sr res assoc, Col Environ Sci & Forestry, 82-89, dir Inst Environ Policy & Planning, 86-95, PROF, FAC ENVIRON STUDIES, STATE UNIV NY, SYRACUSE, 93-, CHAIR, FAC ENVIRON STUDIES, 96- *Personal Data:* b Burlington, Vt, May 13, 48; m 72, Anne M Graveline; c Regina E & Andrea M. *Educ:* Univ Mass, Amherst, BS, 70, MLA, 73; Univ Calif, Berkeley, PhD(environ planning), 82. *Prof Exp:* Assoc planner, Exec Off Environ Affairs, 73-75; environ impact assessment specialist, USDA Exten Serv, Ore State Univ, 75-76; landscape architect, Pac Forest & Range Exp Sta, 77; res landscape architect, Dept Landscape Archit, Univ Calif, Berkeley, 77-79. *Concurrent Pos:* Adj asst prof, Dept Forestry & Wildlife Mgt, Univ Mass, 74-75; environ planner, US Geol Surv, Syracuse, NY, 80-82; consult, Ecology Compliance Ltd, Syracuse, NY, 81-; co-dir, Great Lakes Res Comm, 86-. mem, Great Lakes Adv Coun, NY; co-owner & vpres, Integrated Site, Inc, Syracuse, NY, 90-; dir, Randolph G Pack Environ Inst, 96- *Mem:* AAAS; Int Asn Impact Assessment; Landscape Res Group; Coastal Soc. *Res:* Landscape perception and visual resource management, integrated environmental planning for developing countries, coastal zone planning; water resource and wetland policy; numerous articles published in various journals. *Mailing Add:* Randolf G Pack Environ Inst & Fac Environ Studies Col Environ Sci & Forestry Syracuse NY 13210. *Fax:* 315-470-6915; *E-Mail:* rsmardon@mailbox.syr.edu

SMARDZEWSKI, RICHARD ROMAN, ANALYTICAL CHEMISTRY. *Current Pos:* CHIEF SCIENTIST, US ARMY CHEM RES DEVELOP & ENG CTR, ABERDEEN PROVING GROUND, 79- *Personal Data:* b Nanticoke, Pa, July 4, 42. *Educ:* King's Col, Pa, BS, 64; Iowa State Univ, Ames, PhD(inorg chem), 69. *Prof Exp:* Sci Res Coun fel inorg chem, Univ Leicester, Eng, 69-70; NSF fel phys chem, Univ Va, Charlottesville, 71-72; Nat Res Coun res assoc, 72-74, res chemist inorg chem, 74-79. *Concurrent Pos:* Adv, Nat Res Coun, Washington, DC. *Mem:* Am Chem Soc; Am Inst Chemists; Sigma Xi; Am Vacuum Soc. *Res:* Analytical chemistry. *Mailing Add:* 813 Maxwell Pl Bel Air MD 21014-3293

SMARR, LARRY LEE, BLACK HOLES, RADIO JETS. *Current Pos:* from asst prof to assoc prof, 79-85, PROF ASTROPHYS, DEPT ASTRON & PHYSICS & DIR, NAT CTR SUPERCOMPUT APPLNS, UNIV ILL, 85- *Personal Data:* b Columbia, Mo, Oct 16, 48; m 73; c 2. *Educ:* Univ Mo, BA & MS, 70; Stanford Univ, MS, 72; Univ Tex, Austin, PhD(physics), 75. *Honors & Awards:* Harlow Shapley Lectr, Am Astron Soc, 81-84. *Prof Exp:* Lectr astrophys, Dept Astrophys Sci, Princeton Univ, 74-75, res assoc, Observ, 75-76; jr fel physics, Dept Physics & Astron, Harvard Soc Fellows, 76-79. *Concurrent Pos:* Physicist, B Div, Lawrence Livermore Nat Lab, 76-79, consult, 76-; vis fel, Cambridge Univ, 78; assoc ed, J Comput Physic, 77-80; res affil, Dept Physics, Yale Univ, 78-79; assoc ed, J Comput Physics, 77-80; consult, Smithsonian Astrophys Observ, 79-81, Los Alamos Nat Lab, 83-; Alfred P Sloan res fel, 80-84; mem, Subcomt Computational Theoret Res, NSF, 81; co-dir, Ill Alliance Prev Nuclear War, 81-84; Max Planck Inst fel, 82-83; mem, Comn Phys Sci Math & Resources, Nat Res Coun, 87-; mem, Govt Univ Indust Res Roundtable, Nat Acad Sci, 87- *Mem:* Nat Acad Eng; Am Astron Soc; Int Soc Gen Relativity & Gravitation; AAAS; Am Phys Soc. *Res:* Relativistic astrophysics; radio galaxies; numerical relativity; numerical hydrodynamics. *Mailing Add:* Nat Ctr Supercomput Applns-Univ Ill 152 Comput Applns 605 E Springfield Ave Champaign IL 61820-5577

SMART, BRUCE EDMUND, PHYSICAL ORGANIC CHEMISTRY. *Current Pos:* Staff scientist, 70-76, res supvr, 77-81, RES MGR, E I DU PONT DE NEMOURS & CO, INC, 82- *Personal Data:* b Philadelphia, Pa, Oct 9, 45; m 69. *Educ:* Univ Mo-Kansas City, BS(chem) & BS(math), 67; Univ Calif, Berkeley, PhD(chem), 70. *Mem:* Am Chem Soc; Sigma Xi; AAAS. *Res:* Organofluorine chemistry; small ring systems; carbonium ion chemistry; molecular rearrangements; thermochemistry; polymer chemistry. *Mailing Add:* 22 Beethoven Dr Wilmington DE 19807-1923

SMART, G N RUSSELL, ORGANIC CHEMISTRY. *Current Pos:* from asst prof to prof, Muhlenberg Col, 47-78, head dept, 62-78, sr prof, 78-87, EMER PROF CHEM, MUHLENBERG COL, 87- *Personal Data:* b Montreal, Que, May 28, 21; m 46; c 3. *Educ:* McGill Univ, BSc, 42, PhD(org chem), 45. *Honors & Awards:* Lindback Distinguished Teaching Award, 61. *Prof Exp:* Nat Res Coun Can fel, Univ Toronto, 45-46, res fel, Iowa State Univ, 46-47. *Concurrent Pos:* Indust consult; exec dir, Tuition Exchange, Inc, 72- *Mem:* Sigma Xi; Am Asn Univ Prof; Am Chem Soc. *Res:* Stereochemistry; conformational analysis; organometallic and organosilicon chemistry; explosives. *Mailing Add:* 2219 Gordon St Allentown PA 18104-4313

SMART, GROVER CLEVELAND, JR, AGRICULTURE, NEMATOLOGY. *Current Pos:* from asst prof to assoc prof, Univ Fla, 64-73, asst chmn, 76-79, actg chmn, 79-80, asst chmn, Dept Entomol & Nematol, 80-81, PROF NEMATOL, INST FOOD & AGR SCI, UNIV FLA, 73-, GRAD COORDR, 97- *Personal Data:* b Stuart, Va, Nov 6, 29; m 57, Patricia Fowler; c Jeffrey H & Gregory S. *Educ:* Univ Va, BA, 52, MA, 57; Univ Wis, PhD(plant path), 60. *Honors & Awards:* Unit Award Distinguished Serv, USDA. *Prof Exp:* Asst biol, Univ Va, 56-57; res asst plant path, Univ Wis, 57-60; asst prof plant path & physiol, Tidewater Res Sta, Va, Agr Exp Sta, Va Polytech Inst, 60-64. *Concurrent Pos:* Co-ed, Nematology News Lett, 66-68, ed-in-chief, J Nematology, 72-74; chmn, Honors & Awards comt, Soc Nematologists, 80-82, Archives comt, 83-88. *Mem:* Soc Nematologists; Sigma Xi; Soc Europ Nematol; Orgn Nematol Trop Am. *Res:* Control of insects using entomogenous nematodes; morphology of nematodes. *Mailing Add:* Dept Entomol & Nematol Univ Fla Inst Food & Agr Sci Gainesville FL 32611-0620. *Fax:* 352-392-0190; *E-Mail:* gcs@gnv.ifas.ufl.edu

SMART, JAMES BLAIR, PHYSICAL INORGANIC CHEMISTRY, CLINICAL CHEMISTRY. *Current Pos:* RES SCIENTIST, UNIV MICH MED SCH, 85- *Personal Data:* b Des Moines, Iowa, Oct 6, 36; m 63; c 3. *Educ:* Carroll Col (Mont), BA, 59; Univ Detroit, MS, 62; Wayne State Univ, PhD(inorg chem), 66. *Prof Exp:* Res assoc, Mich State Univ, 66-67; asst prof chem, Xavier Univ, 67-74; dir mfg, Nuclear Diag, Inc, 74-78, dir tech opers, 78-81, dir prod develop, 81-85. *Concurrent Pos:* Res Corp grant, 68-70. *Mem:* Am Chem Soc; Royal Soc Chem; Am Soc Qual Control; Soc Appl Spectros; Am Asn Clin Chemists. *Res:* Spectroscopic investigations of the effects on chemical and physical properties of through-space interactions between pi-systems and sigma-bonded organometallic compounds; applications of magnetic resonance spectroscopy; radioimmunoassay. *Mailing Add:* 4834 Whitman Circle Ann Arbor MI 48103-9774

SMART, JAMES SAMUEL, PHYSICS. *Current Pos:* RETIRED. *Personal Data:* b New Bloomfield, Mo, Aug 31, 19; m 42. *Educ:* Westminster Col, Mo, AB, 39; La State Univ, MS, 41; Univ Minn, PhD(physics), 48. *Prof Exp:* Instr aviation cadet eng, US Army Air Force, 41-43; physicist, Bur Ships, US Dept Navy, 43-46; asst physics, Univ Minn, 46-48; physicist, US Naval Ord Lab, 48-55; sci liaison officer, US Off Naval Res, Eng, 55-57, Wash, DC, 58-60; vis physicist, Brookhaven Nat Lab, 57-58; mem sr staff, Res Ctr, Int Business Mach Corp, 60-80. *Concurrent Pos:* Consult, US Off Naval Res, 58; mem, Nat Res Coun, 63-66; secy, Int Cong Magnetism, 67. *Mem:* Am Phys Soc; Am Asn Physics Teachers; Brit Inst Physics; Am Geophys Union. *Res:* Origin of chemical elements; magnetism; solid state physics; hydrology. *Mailing Add:* 71 Mt Airy Rd Croton-on-Hudson NY 10520

SMART, JOHN RODERICK, NUMBER THEORY. *Current Pos:* From asst prof to assoc prof, 62-71, PROF MATH, UNIV WIS-MADISON, 71- *Personal Data:* b Laramie, Wyo, Sept 16, 34; m 59; c 5. *Educ:* San Jose State Col, AB, 56; Mich State Univ, MS, 58, PhD(math), 61. *Concurrent Pos:* NSF fel, Courant Inst Math Sci, NY Univ, 61-62 & Glasgow Univ, 65-66. *Mem:* Am Math Soc; Math Asn Am. *Res:* Analytic number theory; automorphic and modular functions; discontinuous groups. *Mailing Add:* Dept Math Univ Wis 213 Van Vleck 480 Lincoln Dr Madison WI 53706-1388

SMART, LEWIS ISAAC, ANIMAL NUTRITION. *Current Pos:* asst prof, 69-71, assoc prof, 71-77, PROF ANIMAL SCI, LA STATE UNIV, BATON ROUGE, 77- *Personal Data:* b Nowata, Okla, Apr 1, 36; m 56; c 2. *Educ:* Okla State Univ, BS, 60; Univ Ill, Urbana, MS, 62; Kans State Univ, PhD, 70. *Prof Exp:* Asst, Univ Ill, Urbana, 60-62; asst prof, Southern State Col Ark, 62-67; mem staff, Kans State Univ, 67-69. *Mem:* Am Soc Animal Sci. *Res:* Beef cattle nutrition and basic nutrition as related to animals. *Mailing Add:* 500 Chris St Natchitoches LA 71457-6312

SMART, WESLEY MITCHELL, HIGH ENERGY PHYSICS, BUBBLE CHAMBERS & COLLIDING BEAM DETECTORS. *Current Pos:* PHYSICIST BUBBLE CHAMBERS & COLLIDING BEAM DETECTORS/HIGH ENERGY PHYSICS, FERMI NAT ACCELERATOR LAB, 71- *Personal Data:* b San Francisco, Calif, Dec 12, 38; div; c Karen A, Tifanie A & Mathew P. *Educ:* Univ Calif, Berkeley, BA, 61, MA, 65, PhD(high energy physics), 67. *Prof Exp:* Technician bubble chambers/high energy physics, Lawrence Berkeley Lab, Univ Calif, 56-67; physicist bubble chambers/high energy physics, Stanford Linear Accelerator Ctr, Stanford Univ, 67-71. *Mem:* Am Phys Soc. *Res:* Design, construction, and operation of the Fermi Lab bubble chamber and high energy physics experiments using bubble chambers; alignment of a large particle detector for colliding beams. *Mailing Add:* Fermi Nat Accelerator Lab PO Box 500 Batavia IL 60510. *Fax:* 630-840-4343; *E-Mail:* smart@fnal.gov

SMART, WILLIAM DONALD, ORGANIC CHEMISTRY. *Current Pos:* RETIRED. *Personal Data:* b Waukegan, Ill, Jan 26, 27; m 53; c 5. *Educ:* Northwestern Univ, BS, 51; Univ Ill, MS, 53; Univ Chicago, MBA, 64. *Prof Exp:* Chemist, Abbott Labs, North Chicago, 53-60, group leader chem develop, 60-63, sect head, 63-64, mgr, 64-67, dir chem mfg, 67-69, vpres hosp equip mfg, 69-72, vpres, Mkt Hosp Prod Div, Abbott Labs, 72-75, vpres & gen mgr, Agr & Vet Prod Div, 75-76, exec vpres, Ross Labs Div, 76-80, pres, Ross Labs Div & vpres, Abbott Labs, 80-87. *Mem:* Am Chem Soc. *Mailing Add:* 3901 W Madura Rd Gulf Breeze FL 32561-3561

SMAT, ROBERT JOSEPH, ORGANIC CHEMISTRY. *Current Pos:* Res chemist, Chem, Dyes & Pigments Dept, Org Chem Div, Jackson Lab, E I Dupont de Nemours & Co, Inc, 66-72, patent chemist, 72-78; sr patent chemist, Elastomer Chem Dept, 78-80, patents consult, Polymer Prod Dept, 80-89, patent assoc, 89-91, SR ASSOC INTELLECTUAL PROPERTY, ELECTRONICS DEPT, E I DUPONT DE NEMOURS & CO, INC, 91- *Personal Data:* b Chicago, Ill, June 24, 38; div; c Susan & David. *Educ:* St Joseph's Col, Ind, BS, 60; Iowa State Univ, MS, 62; Ill Inst Technol, PhD(org chem), 66. *Mem:* Am Chem Soc; Chem Soc; Sigma Xi. *Res:* Synthesis and stereochemistry of small ring heterocyclic compounds; textile dyes and polymer finishes; thermoplastic film-forming polymers; polyester, polyimide and fluoropolymer films. *Mailing Add:* 317 Pleasant Knoll Ct Newark DE 19711

SMATHERS, GARRETT ARTHUR, PLANT ECOLOGY, SCIENCE ADMINISTRATION. *Current Pos:* RETIRED. *Personal Data:* b Canton, NC, Mar 15, 26; m 56, Patricia Hipps; c Eric & Mark. *Educ:* Univ NC, Asheville, dipl, 50; Furman Univ, BS, 52; Western Carolina Univ, MA, 55; Univ Hawaii, PhD(plant ecol), 72. *Prof Exp:* Chemist, Taylor Colquitt Co, 52-53, Am Enka Corp, 54-55; high sch teacher sci, Waynesville, NC, 53-54, 55-59, actg prin, 55-59; supvry park naturalist & res, Nat Park Serv, 59-66; res asst plant ecol, Univ Hawaii, 66-67; res biologist, Hawaii Volcanoes Nat Park, Nat Park Serv Coop Park Studies Unit, W Carolina Univ, 67-70, instr, Mather & Albright Training Ctrs, 70-71; regional chief scientist, Univ Wash, Pac Northwest Region, 70-73, chief scientist, Res Sci Admin, Nat Park Serv Sci Ctr, 73-77, adj prof biol, 80-83, sr res scientist, 77-83. *Concurrent Pos:* Mem, Adv Coun, Dept Forestry, Miss State Univ, 74-; prof B-1 coordr, Mem Org Preserves US-USSR Bilateral Agreement, Nat Park Serv, 75-; mem, NC Forestry Coun, 80, NC environ mgt comn, 83; adj prof, Univ NC, Asheville, 83-; mem, NC Environ Mgt Comn, 85-89. *Mem:* Am Ecol Soc; Am Inst Biol Sci. *Res:* Study of the invasion, succession and recovery of vegetation on volcanic substrates; preparation of ecological atlases of present and proposed national parks; phytogeography of southern Appalachians; watershed drinking water supply, western North Carolina; environmental management and planning; environmental sciences; hydrology and water resources. *Mailing Add:* Six Brairknoll Ct Asheville NC 28803

SMATHERS, JAMES BURTON, MEDICAL PHYSICS, RADIATION SAFETY. *Current Pos:* PROF RADIATION ONCOL, DEPT RADIATION ONCOL, UNIV CALIF, LOS ANGELES, 80- *Personal Data:* b Prairie du Chieu, Wis, Aug 26, 35; m 57, Sylvia Rath; c Kristine K, Kathryn A, James S & Ernest K. *Educ:* NC State Col, BNE, 57, MS, 59; Univ Md, PhD(nuclear eng), 67. *Prof Exp:* Res engr, Atomics Int, 59; sect chief, Walter Reed Army Inst Res, 61-67; prof nuclear eng, Tex A&M Univ, 67-80, prof bioeng, 76-80. *Concurrent Pos:* Consult, Nat Cancer Inst, 82- *Mem:* Am Asn Physicists Med; Am Nuclear Soc; Health Physics Soc; Am Col Med Physics; Am Col Radiol; Am Soc Therapeut Radiation Oncol. *Res:* Applications of radiation to medicine and biology. *Mailing Add:* 18229 Minnehaha St Northridge CA 91326-3427. *Fax:* 310-794-9795; *E-Mail:* smathers@radonc.ucla.edu

SMATRESK, NEAL JOSEPH, RESPIRATION PHYSIOLOGY, SENSORY PHYSIOLOGY. *Current Pos:* from asst prof to assoc prof, 82-93, PROF BIOL, UNIV TEX, ARLINGTON, 93-, ACTG CHAIR BIOL, 93- *Personal Data:* b Worcester, Mass, July 9, 51; m 78, Deborah; c Erik & Kristen. *Educ:* Gettysburg Col, BA, 73; State Univ NY, Buffalo, MA, 78; Univ Tex, Austin, PhD(zool), 80. *Prof Exp:* Trainee physiol, Univ Pa, 80-82. *Mem:* Am Physiol Soc; Am Soc Zool; Soc Neurosci; AAAS; Sigma Xi. *Res:* Control and coordination of respiration and heart rate in lower vertebrates; oxygen sensitive chemoreceptors; neural control of ventilation in fish and bimodal breathers. *Mailing Add:* Dept Biol Univ Tex-Arlington Box 19498 Arlington TX 76019-9498. *Fax:* 817-273-2855; *E-Mail:* sma@Galbert.uta.edu

SMAY, TERRY A, ELECTRICAL ENGINEERING. *Current Pos:* assoc prof, 70-76, PROF ELEC ENG, IOWA STATE UNIV, 76- *Personal Data:* b Oakland, Iowa, Aug 30, 35; m 54; c 3. *Educ:* Iowa State Univ, BS, 57, MS, 59, PhD(elec eng), 62. *Prof Exp:* Elec engr, Remington Rand Univac Div, Sperry Rand Corp, 57-58; from instr to asst prof elec eng, Iowa State Univ, 58-62; sr res scientist, Res Div, Control Data Corp, 62-65, supvr govt systs div, 65-66, dept mgr thin film memory develop, 66-70. *Concurrent Pos:* Lectr, Univ Minn, 62-64. *Mem:* Inst Elec & Electronics Engrs. *Res:* Magnetic film memory development; high speed memory components. *Mailing Add:* Dept Elec Eng Iowa State Univ Ames IA 50011

SMAYDA, THEODORE JOHN, BIOLOGICAL OCEANOGRAPHY. *Current Pos:* Asst biol oceanogr, Grad Sch Oceanog, Univ RI, 59-61, asst prof biol oceanog, 61-66, assoc prof oceanog, 66-70, PROF OCEANOG, GRAD SCH OCEANOG, UNIV RI, 70- *Personal Data:* b Peckville, Pa, Aug 28, 31; div; c Thomas J & Susan R. *Educ:* Tufts Univ, BS, 53; Univ RI, MS, 55; Univ Oslo, Dr Philos, 67. *Concurrent Pos:* Mem working panel phytoplankton methods, comt oceanog, Nat Acad Sci, 65-69; adv comt algae, Smithsonian Oceanog Sorting Ctr, 71-74; mem SCOR Working Group 33, phytoplankton; mem working group phytoplankton ecol, Int Coun Explor Sea, 94- *Mem:* Fel AAAS; Am Soc Limnol & Oceanog; Phycol Soc Am; Int Phycol Soc; Marine Biol Asn; Plankton Soc Japan; Norweg Nat Acad Sci. *Res:* Ecology and physiology of marine phytoplankton; estuarine and coastal ecology; red tides, noxious blooms. *Mailing Add:* Oceanog Univ RI 15 S Ferry Rd Narragansett RI 02881-1197. *Fax:* 401-792-6682; *E-Mail:* tsmayda@gsosun1.gso.uri.edu

SMEAL, PAUL LESTER, ORNAMENTAL HORTICULTURE, NURSERY PRODUCTION. *Current Pos:* from asst prof to prof, 60-92, EMER PROF HORT, VA POLYTECH INST & STATE UNIV, 92- *Personal Data:* b Clearfield, Pa, June 11, 32; m 54; c 3. *Educ:* Pa State Univ, BS, 54; Univ Md, MS, 58, PhD(hort), 61. *Honors & Awards:* Carl S Bittner Exten Award, Am Soc Hort Sci, 84, Distinguished Achievement Award Nursery Crops, 91; Distinguished Serv Award, Nat Asn Co Agr Agents, 87; Nursery Exten Award, Am Asn Nurserymen, 90. *Prof Exp:* Res asst hort, Univ Md, 59-60. *Concurrent Pos:* Instr, Flower Show Sch, Nat Coun State Garden Clubs; secy-treas, Southern Region, Am Soc Hort Sci. *Mem:* Fel Am Soc Hort Sci; Int Plant Propagators Soc. *Res:* Ornamentals; plant propagation; nursery management; production of nursery stock, greenhouse flowers and bedding plants produced by nurserymen and flower growers; work with county extension personnel, nurserymen and professional grounds management personnel. *Mailing Add:* Dept Hort Va Polytech Inst & State Univ Blacksburg VA 24061-0327

SMEBY, ROBERT RUDOLPH, BIOCHEMISTRY. *Current Pos:* biochemist, 59-87, EMER STAFF, CLEVELAND CLIN FOUND, 87- *Personal Data:* b Chicago, Ill, Dec 24, 26; m 50, Patricia Dowling; c Eric, Patrick, Alec & Darrick. *Educ:* Univ Ill, BS, 50; Univ Wis, MS, 52, PhD(biochem), 54. *Prof Exp:* Biochemist, R J Reynolds Tobacco Co, 54-56; biochemist, Miles-Ames Res Lab, Miles Labs, Inc, 56-59. *Concurrent Pos:*

Adj prof, John Carroll Univ, 65-70 & Cleveland State Univ, 70-88; pres, bd trustees, Scientists Ctr Animal Welfare, 91. *Mem:* Fel AAAS; Am Chem Soc; Am Physiol Soc; fel Am Heart Asn; fel Am Inst Chemists. *Res:* Synthesis of peptides; isolation of substances from natural products with biological activity. *Mailing Add:* Res Inst Cleveland Clin Found 9500 Euclid Ave Cleveland OH 44195-0002

SMECK, NEIL EDWARD, AGRONOMY. *Current Pos:* ASSOC PROF AGRON, OHIO STATE UNIV-OHIO AGR RES & DEVELOP CTR, 71- *Personal Data:* b Lancaster, Ohio, July 9, 41; m 65; c 3. *Educ:* Ohio State Univ, BS, 63, MS, 66; Univ Ill, PhD(agron), 70. *Prof Exp:* Soil scientist soil surv, Soil Conserv Serv, 63-66; asst prof agron, NDak State Univ, 69-71. *Mem:* Am Soc Agron; Soil Sci Soc Am; Soil Conserv Soc Am. *Res:* Soil genesis, morphology, and classification; sediment chemistry and mineralogy; weathering strip mine spoils. *Mailing Add:* Dept Agron Ohio State Univ 2021 Coffey Rd Columbus OH 43210-1044

SMEDFJELD, JOHN B, AEROELASTICITY, STRUCTURAL DYNAMICS. *Current Pos:* Res engr, Grumman Aerospace Corp, 55-57, dynamic anal engr, 57-63, adv develop group leader dynamics, 63-65, aeroelasticity methods group leader, 65-72, head, Dynamic Struct Methods Group, 72-77, TECH SPECIALIST STRUCT MECH, GRUMMAN AIRCRAFT SYST DIV, BETHPAGE, 77- *Personal Data:* b Oslo, Norway, Apr 18, 35; US citizen; m 58; c 2. *Educ:* Pratt Inst, BME, 55, MS, 59. *Mem:* Am Inst Aeronaut & Astronaut. *Res:* Gust response analysis; flutter analysis; unsteady aerodynamics; applied leads; structural optimization. *Mailing Add:* 9 Darrell St East Northport NY 11731

SMEDLEY, WILLIAM MICHAEL, ORGANIC CHEMISTRY, CHEMISTRY OF EXPLOSIVES. *Current Pos:* Instr chem & physics, 40-47, from asst prof to assoc prof chem, 48-59, prof, 60-97, EMER PROF CHEM, US NAVAL ACAD, 87- *Personal Data:* b Chicago, Ill, Aug 2, 16; m 43, Margaret Thurston; c Jane Elizabeth. *Educ:* Northwestern Univ, BS, 38, MS, 40. *Concurrent Pos:* Asst prof, Univ Md, 56-58, NSF fac fel, 64-65; dir res & vpres, Appl Sci & Chem Corp, Md & Am Chem Co; dir & vpres, Everett Factories, Mass. *Mem:* Nat Asn Scholars; Am Chem Soc. *Res:* Chlorination dioxanes; 2, 5-diphenyl dioxane, 2, 5-dichlorodioxane and derivatives; heterocyclics; derivatives of quinoline-quinone; chemistry of explosives. *Mailing Add:* Chem Dept US Naval Acad 572 Holloway Rd Annapolis MD 21402-5026. Fax: 410-293-2218

SMEDSKJAER, LARS CHRISTIAN, EXPERIMENTAL PHYSICS, METALLURGY. *Current Pos:* PHYSICIST METALL, ARGONNE NAT LAB, 74- *Personal Data:* b Copenhagen, Denmark, Oct 3, 44; m 75. *Educ:* Tech Univ Denmark, Cand Polyt, 69, PhD(exp physics), 72. *Prof Exp:* Amanvensis physics, Tech Univ Denmark, 72-74, assoc prof, 74. *Mem:* Danish Soc Engrs. *Res:* Metal physics; positron physics. *Mailing Add:* 2726 63rd St Woodbridge IL 60517

SMEINS, FRED E, PLANT ECOLOGY. *Current Pos:* from asst prof to assoc prof, 69-80, PROF RANGE SCI, TEX A&M UNIV, 80- *Personal Data:* b Luverne, Minn, Feb 14, 41; m 60; c 2. *Educ:* Augustana Col, SDak, 63; Univ Sask, MA, 65, PhD(plant ecol), 67. *Prof Exp:* Asst prof biol, Univ NDak, 67-69. *Res:* Ecology of wetland and grassland vegetation. *Mailing Add:* Dept Range Ecol & Mgt Tex A&M Univ College Station TX 77843-0100

SMELLIE, ROBERT HENDERSON, JR, PHYSICAL CHEMISTRY. *Current Pos:* from instr to prof, 48-64, chmn dept, 63-71, SCOVILL PROF CHEM, TRINITY COL, CONN, 64- *Personal Data:* b Glasgow, Scotland, June 2, 20; US citizen; m 45; c 3. *Educ:* Trinity Col, Conn, BS, 42, MS, 44; Columbia Univ, PhD(phys chem), 51. *Prof Exp:* Instr chem, Trinity Col, Conn, 43-44; anal foreman & supvr, Tenn Eastman Corp, 44-46; asst chem, Columbia Univ, 47-48. *Mem:* Am Chem Soc. *Res:* Kinetics of nitrile reactions; analytical chemistry of uranium; chemistry and electrokinetics of sulfur sols; flocculation of suspensions; combustion chemistry. *Mailing Add:* 69 Montclair Dr West Hartford CT 06107-2447

SMELTZER, RICHARD HOMER, PLANT MORPHOGENESIS. *Current Pos:* res assoc plant morphogenesis, 75-, MGR BIOTECH, INT PAPER CO. *Personal Data:* b Sapulpa, Okla, Aug 14, 40; m 63; c 3. *Educ:* Okla State Univ, BS, 62; Stephen F Austin State Univ, MF, 70; Lawrence Univ, MS, 72, PhD(paper chem), 75. *Prof Exp:* Inspector lumber, Southern Pine Inspection Bur, 62-65; asst qual control supt, Temple Indust, Inc, 65-68. *Mem:* Int Plant Propagation Soc; Int Asn Plant Tissue Cult. *Res:* Asexual propagation of trees through tissue culture and related biochemistry; evaluation of vegetative propagules. *Mailing Add:* Int Paper Co 719 Southland Rd Bainbridge GA 31717

SMELTZER, WALTER WILLIAM, METALLURGY, MATERIALS SCIENCE. *Current Pos:* from asst prof to prof, 59-91, EMER PROF METALL, MCMASTER UNIV, 91- *Personal Data:* b Moose Jaw, Sask, Dec 4, 24; m 60, Grace Connor. *Educ:* Queen's Univ, Ont, BSc, 48; Univ Toronto, PhD(phys chem), 53. *Hon Degrees:* Dr, Univ Dijon, 81. *Honors & Awards:* Centennial Medal for Serv to the Nation, Govt Can, 68,; Albert Saveur Achievement Award, Am Soc Metals, 86; Fourth Can Metal Chem Award, 92. *Prof Exp:* Res chemist, Nat Res Coun Can, 48-50; res chem engr, Aluminum Co, Ltd, 53-55; res metall engr, Metals Res Lab, Carnegie Inst Technol, 56-59. *Concurrent Pos:* Sr fel, Brit Res Coun, 76 & NATO, 79-80. *Mem:* Nat Asn Corrosion Engrs; Electrochem Soc; fel Am Soc Metals; fel Royal Soc Can. *Res:* Adsorption and oxidation kinetics of metals; thermodynamic properties of solids; lattice defect structures of solid metal oxides and their influence on mass and thermal transport properties. *Mailing Add:* 332 Newbold Ct Burlington ON L7R 2Y6 Can

SMERAGE, GLEN H, SYSTEMS ENGINEERING. *Current Pos:* ASSOC PROF AGR ENG, UNIV FLA, 76- *Personal Data:* b Topsfield, Mass, May 3, 37; m 60; c 2. *Educ:* Worcester Polytech Inst, BS, 59; San Jose State Col, MS, 63; Stanford Univ, PhD(elec eng), 67. *Prof Exp:* Res asst & test engr, Instrumentation Labs, Mass Inst Technol, 59-60; jr engr, Western Develop Labs, Philco Corp, 60-61; engr, Electronic Defense Labs, Sylvania Electronics Systs, 62-67; asst prof elec eng, Utah State Univ, 67-76. *Mem:* Inst Elec & Electronics Engrs. *Res:* Modeling and analysis of systems; current emphasis on human social systems and their interaction with the physical and biological environment. *Mailing Add:* 2104 NW 15 Ave Gainesville FL 32605-5216

SMERDON, ERNEST THOMAS, CIVIL & AGRICULTURAL ENGINEERING. *Current Pos:* DEAN, COL ENG & MINES, UNIV ARIZ, TUCSON, 88- *Personal Data:* b Ritchey, Mo, Jan 19, 30; m 51; c 3. *Educ:* Univ Mo, BS, 51, MS, 56, PhD(agr eng), 59. *Prof Exp:* Res engr, Univ Mo, 56-57, instr civil eng, 57-58, instr agr eng, 58-59; from assoc prof to prof, Tex A&M Univ, 59-68, prof civil eng & dir, Water Res Inst, 64-68; prof agr eng & chmn dept, Univ Fla, 68-74, asst dean res, 74-76; vchancellor acad affairs, Univ Tex Syst, Univ Tex, Austin, 76-82, prof civil eng & dir, Ctr Res Water Resources, 82-87. *Concurrent Pos:* Inst Int Educ & Ohio State Univ consult, Punjab Agr Univ, India, 65; consult govt of SVietnam, Guyana & El Salvador, 71, Bahamas, Peru & Brazil, 76 & USAID, Pakistan, 81; chmn, Univ Coun Water Resources, 72-74. *Mem:* Nat Acad Eng; Am Soc Agr Engrs; Am Soc Civil Engrs; Am Geophys Union; Am Asn Higher Educ; fel AAAS. *Res:* Water resources development and irrigation; energy use and conservation; research administration. *Mailing Add:* Civil Eng Bldg 72 Rm 100 Univ Ariz Tucson AZ 85721

SMERDON, MICHAEL JOHN, MOLECULAR BIOLOGY. *Current Pos:* ASSOC PROF BIOCHEM & BIOPHYS, WASH STATE UNIV, 84-, ASSOC IN GENETICS & CELL BIOL, 80- *Educ:* Ore State Univ, PhD(biochem & biophysics), 76. *Res:* Repair of DNA damage by carcinogens; structure and function of DNA in human cells. *Mailing Add:* Biochem & Biophysics Dept Wash State Univ Pullman WA 99164-4660. Fax: 509-335-9688; E-Mail: wmerdon@wsuvmi

SMERIGLIO, ALFRED JOHN, BIOLOGY, COMPARATIVE ANATOMY. *Current Pos:* from asst prof to assoc prof, 67-70, PROF BIOL, NASSAU COMMUNITY COL, 75-, CHMN DEPT ALLIED HEALTH SCI, 70- *Personal Data:* b Port Chester, NY, May 17, 37; m 65. *Educ:* NY Univ, BS, 59, MA, 60, EdD(biol), 64. *Prof Exp:* From instr to asst prof biol, NY Univ, 59-66; asst prof chem, Jersey City State Col, 66-67. *Concurrent Pos:* Asst res scientist biophys res lab, NY Univ, 65- *Mem:* AAAS; Nat Sci Teachers Asn. *Res:* Mammalian biology; physiological patterns of behavior in the Albino rat; piezoelectric properties of mineralized tissue. *Mailing Add:* Dept Allied Health Sci Nassau Community Col 1 Education Dr Garden City NY 11530-6793

SMETANA, ALES, ENTOMOLOGY, ZOOGEOGRAPHY. *Current Pos:* RES SCIENTIST, RES BR, AGR & AGRIFOOD, CAN, 71- *Personal Data:* b Hradec Kralove, Czech, Apr 4, 31; m 57, Zdena Mala; c Dan, Thomas & David. *Educ:* Charles Univ, Prague, MD, 56; Czech Acad Sci, CSc, 60. *Prof Exp:* Res scientist, Inst Parasitol, Czech Acad Sci, 56-70; res scientist, Nat Mus, Prague, 70-71. *Concurrent Pos:* Nat Res Coun Can fel, Entom Res Inst, Ottawa, 67-69. *Mem:* Entom Soc Can; Entom Soc Am. *Res:* Systematics of the insect order Coleoptera, especially aquatic Coleoptera and the family Staphylinidae; zoogeography, particularly the holarctic distribution of Coleoptera. *Mailing Add:* Agr & Agrifood Can Res Br CEF KW Neatby Bldg 960 Carling Ave Ottawa ON K1A 0C6 Can. Fax: 613-996-1823; E-Mail: smetanaa@ncccot2.agr.ca

SMETANA, FREDERICK OTTO, MECHANICAL ENGINEERING, AEROSPACE ENGINEERING. *Current Pos:* from assoc prof to prof 62-94, EMER PROF MECH ENG, NC STATE UNIV, 94- *Personal Data:* b Philadelphia, Pa, Nov 29, 28; m 52, Adelaide V Sigmon; c Daniel, Martha, Andrew & Paul. *Educ:* NC State Col, BME, 50, MSME, 53; Univ Southern Calif, PhD(eng), 61. *Honors & Awards:* Cert Merit, NASA, 73 & 78. *Prof Exp:* Vpres, Philcord Corp, NC, 50-51; flight test analyst, Douglas Aircraft Co, Calif, 51-52; teaching asst mech eng, NC State Col, 52-53; res scientist, Eng Ctr, Univ Southern Calif, 55-62. *Concurrent Pos:* Asst dir, NC Sci & Technol Res Ctr, 66-84; past consult, Pneumafil Corp, Litton Systs, Inc, Corning Glass Works, Waste King Corp & Servomechanisms, Inc; consult, US Army Armament Res & Develop Command, 76-79, US Army Res Off, 84-85. *Mem:* Am Inst Aeronaut & Astronaut. *Res:* Vehicle design; air data instrumentation; dynamic response flight testing; flight data systems identification; Rankine cycle solar electric power generation. *Mailing Add:* Dept Mech & Aerospace Eng NC State Univ Raleigh NC 27695-7910. E-Mail: smetana@eos.nesu.edu

SMETHIE, WILLIAM MASSIE, JR, CHEMICAL & PHYSICAL OCEANOGRAPHY. *Current Pos:* post doctoral scientist, Lamont-Doherty Geol Observ, 79-80, assoc res scientist, 80-87, res scientist, 87-90, SR RES SCIENTIST, LAMONT-DOHERTY GEOL OBSERV, 90- *Personal Data:* b Rocky Mount, NC, Mar 29, 45; m 69, Mary K Potter; c David & Sarah. *Educ:* Wofford Col, BS, 67; San Jose State Univ, MA, 73; Univ Wash, PhD(oceanog), 79. *Prof Exp:* Sr oceanographer, Univ Wash, 78-79. *Mem:* Am Geophys Union; AAAS; Oceanog Soc. *Res:* Investigation of mixing, circulation, and water mass formation in the ocean and other marine systems from the distribution of naturally occurring and man-made substances. *Mailing Add:* Lamont-Doherty Earth Observ Palisades NY 10964

SMIALEK, JAMES L, HIGH TEMPERATURE OXIDATION, AEROSPACE MATERIALS. *Current Pos:* res scientist, 68-92, SR RES SCIENTIST, LEWIS RES CTR, NASA, 92- *Personal Data:* b Cleveland, Ohio, Sept 13, 46; m 72, Constance M Habermann; c Craig, David, Laurel & Amy. *Educ:* Case Inst Technol, BS, 68, MS, 71; Case Western Res Univ, PhD(mat sci), 81. *Concurrent Pos:* Assoc ed, Advan Ceramic Mat, 86-88; contributing ed, J Am Ceramic Soc, 88-97; mem, Int Adv Bd, Oxidation of Metals, 88-97; chmn, Gordon Conf High Temp Corrosion, 93. *Mem:* Fel Am Ceramic Soc; fel Am Soc Metals; Am Inst Mech Engrs; Am Soc Mat. *Res:* Oxidation mechanisms of coatings and superalloys; oxidation mechanisms of nickel, iron, titanium and niobium aluminides; microstructure of protective aluminum oxide scales; adhesion mechanisms of protective aluminum oxide scales; oxidation and corrosion of structural ceramics; granted 4 patents. *Mailing Add:* NASA 106-1 21000 Brookpark Rd Cleveland OH 44135. *E-Mail:* james.l.smialek@lerc.nasa.gov

SMIBERT, ROBERT MERRALL, II, MICROBIOLOGY. *Current Pos:* RETIRED. *Personal Data:* b New Haven, Conn, Dec 9, 30; m 61; c 2. *Educ:* Univ Conn, BA, 52; Univ Md, MS, 57, PhD(microbiol), 59. *Prof Exp:* Instr microbiol, Sch Med, Temple Univ, 59-60; assoc prof vet sci, Va Polytech Inst & State Univ, 60-65, prof microbiol, 68-78, prof bact, Anaerobe Lab, 78-80, prof microbiol, Dept Anaerobic Microbiol, 80-93. *Mem:* AAAS; Am Soc Microbiol; Soc Gen Microbiol; Am Venereal Dis Asn. *Res:* Microbial physiology and nutrition; taxonomy of bacteria; Mycoplasma; vibrios; campylobacter; leptospirosis; Treponemas; Borrelias. *Mailing Add:* 1201 Glen Cove Lane Blacksburg VA 24060

SMICIKLAS, KENNETH DONALD, NITROGEN USE, WHOLE PLANT PHYSIOLOGIST. *Current Pos:* ASSOC PROF PLANT SCI, ILL STATE UNIV, 91- *Personal Data:* b Oak Lawn, Ill, June 18, 62; m 89, Ruth Sinn; c Christopher. *Educ:* Univ Ill, Urbana, BS, 84; Iowa State Univ, MS 87; Univ Ill, Urbana, PhD(plant physiol), 91. *Prof Exp:* Teaching asst, Iowa State Univ, 84-87; res asst, Univ Ill, Urbana, 87-91. *Mem:* Am Soc Agron; Crop Sci Soc Am; Am Soc Plant Physiologists; Sigma X; Nat Asn Cols & Teachers Am. *Res:* Programs for maize with emphasis on nitrogen management techniques that protect the environment. *Mailing Add:* 5020 Agriculture Ill State Univ Normal IL 61790-5020. *E-Mail:* ksmicikl@ilstu.edu

SMID, JOHANNES, PHYSICAL CHEMISTRY, POLYMER CHEMISTRY. *Current Pos:* Res assoc polymer chem, 59-63, from asst prof to assoc prof, 63-70, PROF POLYMER CHEM, COL ENVIRON SCI & FORESTRY, STATE UNIV NY, 70- *Personal Data:* b Amsterdam, Netherlands, Jan 18, 31; m 56, Elizabeth Schippers; c Derk, Frank, Janneke & Hans. *Educ:* Free Univ, Amsterdam, BSc, 52, MSc, 54; State Univ NY, PhD(phys chem), 57. *Concurrent Pos:* Vis prof, Univ Nijmegen, 69-70, Louis Pasteur Univ, Strasbourg, 77-78, Univ Twente, Neth, 85-86. *Mem:* AAAS; Am Chem Soc. *Res:* Solvent-solute interactions; ion pair structures; ion-binding to macromolecules; polymer electrolytes; hydrogels; radiopaque polymers. *Mailing Add:* Dept Chem Col Environ Sci & Forestry State Univ NY Syracuse NY 13210-2786. *Fax:* 315-470-6856

SMID, ROBERT JOHN, CERAMICS ENGINEERING. *Current Pos:* Sr engr, 68-74, prin engr, 74-80, ADV SCIENTIST, BETTIS ATOMIC POWER LAB, WESTINGHOUSE ELEC CORP, 80- *Personal Data:* b US. *Educ:* Univ Ill, BS, 62, MS, 65, PhD(ceramics eng), 68. *Mem:* Am Ceramic Soc. *Res:* Advanced naval nuclear fuel systems. *Mailing Add:* 1713 Ridge Rd Library PA 15129

SMIDT, FRED AUGUST, JR, RESEARCH ADMINISTRATION, MATERIALS SCIENCE. *Current Pos:* spec prog coordr, Mat Sci & Components Directorate, Naval Res Lab, 80-82, sect head, Reactor Mat Br, Metall Div, 78-82, staff specialist, Off Secy Defense (DDR&E), 89-90, HEAD, SURFACE MODIFICATION BR, NAVAL RES LAB, 82- *Personal Data:* b Sioux City, Iowa, July 19, 32; m 56; c 3. *Educ:* Univ Nebr, BSc, 54; Iowa State Univ, PhD(phys chem), 62. *Honors & Awards:* Dudley Medal, Am Soc Testing & Mat, 79. *Prof Exp:* Sr engr, Hanford Lab, Gen Elec Co, 62-65; sr res scientist, Pac Northwest Labs, Battelle Mem Inst, 65-69; res metallurgist, Reactor Mat Br, Metall Div, Naval Res Lab, 69-71, sect head, 71-77; prog monitor, Reactor Res & Technol Div, US Dept Energy, 77-78. *Mem:* Fel Am Soc Mat; Am Inst Mining, Metall & Petrol Engrs; Sigma Xi; Mat Res Soc. *Res:* Ion implantation for materials processing; irradiation damage to metals; electron microscopy; fast breeder and controlled thermonuclear reactor materials; ion beam assisted deposition of thin films; coatings for spacecraft; wear resistant coatings; pulsed laser deposition of thin films. *Mailing Add:* 6412 Charnwood St Springfield VA 22152

SMIKA, DARRYL EUGENE, SOIL CHEMISTRY. *Current Pos:* RETIRED. *Personal Data:* b Hill City, Kans, July 1, 33; m 56, 87, Jennifer Apfel; c Rejeana, Thayne, Lavona & Tava. *Educ:* Kans State Univ, BS & MS, 56, PhD(soil chem), 69. *Honors & Awards:* Cert Merit, USDA, 82 & 83. *Prof Exp:* Soil conservationist, Soil Conserv Serv, USDA, Kans, 56-57, soil scientist, Soil & Water Conserv Res Div, Agr Res Serv NDak, 57-61, res soil scientist, Exp Sta, Nebr, 61-73, res soil scientist, Cent Great Plains Res Sta, Soil & Water Conserv Res Div, Agr Res Serv, 73-88. *Mem:* Fel Am Inst Chemists; fel Soil Conserv Soc Am; Am Soc Agron; Soil Sci Soc Am; Can Soil Sci Soc. *Res:* Soil moisture and fertility under dryland conditions with present emphasis on cropping systems with no tillage. *Mailing Add:* 9901 N Country Rd 17 Ft Collins CO 80524

SMIL, VACLAV, BIOGEOCHEMICAL CYCLES. *Current Pos:* From asst prof to assoc prof, 72-80, PROF GEOG, UNIV MAN, 80- *Personal Data:* b Pilsen, Czech Repub, Dec 1, 43; Can Citizen; m 67, Eva Fidler; c David. *Educ:* Carolinum Univ, RNDr, 65; Penn State Univ, PhD(earth & mineral sci), 72. *Mem:* AAAS; NY Acad Sci. *Res:* Interdisciplinary studies of environment, energy, economy, food and population with special focus on biogeochemical cycles and on China & Japan. *Mailing Add:* 99 Normand Park Dr Winnipeg MB R2N 3C6 Can. *Fax:* 204-275-8281

SMILEN, LOWELL I, ELECTRICAL ENGINEERING. *Current Pos:* tech consult, 90-94, ELECTRONIC INSTR, ITT TECH INST, 94- *Personal Data:* b New York, NY, Apr 18, 31; m 63; c 2. *Educ:* Cooper Union, BSEE, 52; Univ Calif, Los Angeles, MS, 56; Polytech Univ NY, PhD(elec eng), 62. *Honors & Awards:* Hughes Coop Fel, 52; Jack Chase Northcon Award, 90. *Prof Exp:* Res engr, Hughes Aircraft Co, Calif, 52-56; sr res assoc, Polytech Inst Brooklyn, 56-62, asst prof electrophys, 62-64; res sect head, Sperry Gyroscope Co, 64-67; asst chief engr res, Loral Electronic Systs, Bronx, 67-70; leader advan microwave technol, Missile & Surface Radar Div, RCA Corp, NJ, 70-72; vpres eng, Laser Link Corp, 72-74; vpres eng, Almac/Stroum Electronics Corp, Div KDM Electronics Corp, 74-85, vpres eng, Almac Corp, Div Lex Electronics, 85-90. *Concurrent Pos:* Adj prof, Polytech Inst Brooklyn; mem, Eng Sci Dept, Hofstra Univ, 65; bd mem, Northcon Electronic Conv. *Mem:* Sr mem Inst Elec & Electronics Engrs; Asn Comput Mach; Am Electronics Asn. *Res:* Network theory and synthesis; microwave components and systems; antenna feed systems; solid state phased array antennas and radars; applied information theory and coding; applications of microprocessors and microcomputers; microcomputer systems design. *Mailing Add:* 15807 NE 90th Way Redmond WA 98052

SMILEY, HARRY M, PHYSICAL CHEMISTRY. *Current Pos:* assoc prof, 67-70, PROF CHEM & CHMN DEPT, EASTERN KY UNIV, 70- *Personal Data:* b Cynthiana, Ky, Oct 6, 33; m 56; c 3. *Educ:* Eastern Ky State Col, BS, 55; Univ Ky, MS, 57, PhD(chem), 60. *Prof Exp:* Asst chem, Univ Ky, 55-60; res chemist, Union Carbide Corp, 60-67. *Mem:* Am Chem Soc. *Res:* Physical and thermodynamic properties of non-ideal solutions, especially activity coefficients and heats of mixing. *Mailing Add:* 2083 Greentree Dr Richmond KY 40475-9625

SMILEY, JAMES DONALD, IMMUNOLOGY, MEDICINE. *Current Pos:* from instr to assoc prof, Univ Tex Health Sci Ctr, 60-70, PROF MED, UNIV TEX SOUTHWESTERN MED CTR, DALLAS, 70- *Personal Data:* b Lubbock, Tex, Dec 6, 30; m 57; c 5. *Educ:* Tex Tech Col, BS, 52; Johns Hopkins Univ, MD, 56. *Prof Exp:* Intern & resident med, Columbia-Presby Hosp, 56-58; res assoc biochem, Nat Inst Arthritis & Metab Dis, 58-60. *Concurrent Pos:* USPHS spec res fel, 60-63; USPHS career develop award, 68-73; sr investr, Arthritis Found, 63-68, Russell Cecil fel, 68; mem, Rheumatol Comt, Am Bd Internal Med, 70-73; assoc ed, J Clin Invest, 72-77. *Mem:* Am Rheumatism Asn; Am Soc Clin Invest; Am Asn Immunologists; Nat Soc Clin Rheumatologists; Am Chem Soc. *Res:* Connective tissue biochemistry; clinical immunology related to research in rheumatoid arthritis. *Mailing Add:* Dept Internal Med Univ Tex Southwestern Med Ctr 8200 Walnut Hill Lane Dallas TX 75231. *Fax:* 214-345-2576

SMILEY, JAMES RICHARD, MOLECULAR BIOLOGY. *Current Pos:* asst prof path, 79-90, PROF, MCMASTER UNIV, 89-, COORDR, CANCER RES GROUP, 90- *Personal Data:* b Montreal, Que, June 22, 51; c 1. *Educ:* McGill Univ, BSc, 72; McMaster Univ, PhD(biol), 77. *Prof Exp:* Fel biol, Yale Univ, 77-78, fel virol, 78-79. *Res:* Control of the expression of herpes simplex viral genes; mechanism of viral DNA replication. *Mailing Add:* Dept Path McMaster Univ Fac Med 1200 Main St W Hamilton ON L8N 3Z5 Can. *Fax:* 905-546-9940

SMILEY, JAMES WATSON, PHYSIOLOGY. *Current Pos:* assoc prof, 71-77, chmn dept, 78-92, PROF BIOL, COL CHARLESTON, 77- *Personal Data:* b Charleston, WVa, Feb 17, 40; m 61, Elizabeth Russell; c James W IV & Elizabeth P. *Educ:* Univ SC, BS, 62, MS, 65, PhD, 68. *Prof Exp:* Instr biol, Univ SC, 65-68; asst prof, Northeast La Univ, 68-71. *Mem:* AAAS; Am Soc Zoologists; Sigma Xi. *Res:* Comparative biology of renin-angiotensin system; comparative biology of nitric oxide. *Mailing Add:* Dept Biol Col Charleston Charleston SC 29424. *Fax:* 803-953-5453

SMILEY, JONES HAZELWOOD, AGRONOMY, PLANT PATHOLOGY. *Current Pos:* asst prof agron, 63-68, assoc prof, 68-72, prof agron & plant path, 72-80, EXT PROF, DEPT AGRON, UNIV KY, 80- *Personal Data:* b Casey Co, Ky, Apr 23, 33; m 53; c 1. *Educ:* Univ Ky, BS, 59, MS, 60; Univ Wis-Madison, PhD(genetics), 63. *Prof Exp:* Res asst plant path, Univ Ky, 58-60; res asst genetics, Univ Wis-Madison, 60-63. *Mem:* Am Soc Agron. *Res:* Tobacco breeding, management and diseases. *Mailing Add:* 1640 Linstead Dr Lexington KY 40504

SMILEY, RICHARD WAYNE, SOIL BORNE PLANT PATHOGENS, DISEASE CONTROL. *Current Pos:* PROF PLANT PATH, ORE STATE UNIV, 85- *Personal Data:* b Paso Robles, Calif, Aug 17, 43; m 67, Marilyn L Wenning; c Shawn E. *Educ:* Calif State Polytech Univ, BS, 65; Wash State Univ, MS, 69, PhD(plant path), 72. *Prof Exp:* Soil scientist fertil res, Agr Res Serv, USDA, 66-69; res asst root dis, Dept Plant Path, Wash State Univ, 69-72; NATO fel, Commonwealth Sci & Indust Res Orgn, Soils Div, Adelaide, SAustralia, 72, vis res scientist soil microbiol, 73; from asst prof to assoc prof plant path, Cornell Univ, 73-85. *Concurrent Pos:* Vis scientist, Victoria Dept Agr, Melbourne, Australia, 81-82; supt, Columbia Basin Agr Res Ctr, 85-; ed-in-chief, Am Phytopath Soc Press, 87-91. *Mem:* Fel Am

Phytopath Soc; Am Soc Agron; Int Soc Plant Path; Int Turfgrass Soc. *Res:* Disease control investigations on cereal grains and turfgrasses, with emphasis on cultural or integrated chemical-biological control strategies for diseases caused by soilborne plant pathogens. *Mailing Add:* Columbia Basin Agr Res Ctr PO Box 370 Pendleton OR 97801. *Fax:* 541-278-4188; *E-Mail:* smileyr@ccmail.orst.edu

SMILEY, ROBERT ARTHUR, ORGANIC CHEMISTRY. *Current Pos:* From res chemist to sr res chemist, Explosives Dept, 54-69, tech asst, 69-70, mgr polymer intermediates dept, 70-74, res assoc, 74-81, RES FEL, PETROCHEM DEPT, E I DU PONT DE NEMOURS & CO, INC, 81- *Personal Data:* b Cleveland, Ohio, Mar 14, 25; m 49; c 10. *Educ:* Case Inst Technol, BS, 50; Purdue Univ, PhD(org chem), 54. *Mem:* Am Chem Soc; Catalysis Soc. *Res:* Preparation and reactions of aliphatic nitro compounds; reactions of nitric acid and nitrogen oxides with organic compounds; heterogeneous catalysis; preparation and reactions of nitriles. *Mailing Add:* 1103 Norbee Dr Wilmington DE 19803-4123

SMILEY, TERAH LEROY, geochronology; deceased, see previous edition for last biography

SMILEY, VERN NEWTON, ATMOSPHERIC PHYSICS. *Current Pos:* TECH STAFF, NAVAL OCEAN SYSTS CTR, 90- *Personal Data:* b Goshen, Ind, Sept 7, 30; m 56. *Educ:* Univ Wis, BS, 55, MS, 56; Univ Colo, PhD(physics), 59. *Prof Exp:* Sr engr, Gen Dynamics/Convair, 59-61; resident res assoc, US Navy Electronics Lab Ctr, 61-62, res physicist, 62-71; prof physics, Univ Nev, Reno, 71-80, res prof atmospheric optics, Desert Res Inst, 71-80; sect head, energy measurement group, EG&G, Inc, 80-86; prog mgr, Off Naval Res, Pasadena, 86-88, San Diego, 88-90. *Concurrent Pos:* Consult, Gen Dynamics/Convair, 61-63; US Navy res fel & vis scientist, York, Eng, 66-67; lectr, Appl Physics & Info Sci Dept, Univ Calif, San Diego, 71; liaison scientist, Off Naval Res, London, 77-79. *Mem:* Optical Soc Am; Sigma Xi. *Res:* Multi-layer thin films; infrared radiometers; gas phase lasers; scanning active interferometers; laser amplifiers; thin film lasers; air pollution; atmospheric remote sensing with optical instrumentation; solar energy research; electro-optics and fiber optics research and development; high power lasers; adaptive optics. *Mailing Add:* 14134 Korrey Dr San Diego CA 92129

SMILLIE, LAWRENCE BRUCE, BIOCHEMISTRY. *Current Pos:* assoc prof, 58-67, PROF BIOCHEM, UNIV ALTA, 67- *Personal Data:* b Galt, Ont, July 5, 28; m 56; c 4. *Educ:* McMaster Univ, BSc, 50; Univ Toronto, MA, 52, PhD(biochem), 55. *Prof Exp:* Asst prof biochem, Univ Alta, 55-57; Nat Acad Sci-Nat Res Coun Donner fel med res, Univ Wash, 57-58; vis scientist, Lab Molecular Biol, Cambridge Univ, 63-64, Ludwig Inst Cancer Res, MRC Ctr, 84-85; vis scientist, Dept Biochem, Univ Birmingham, 71-72. *Mem:* Can Biochem Soc; Am Soc Biol Chemists; Brit Biochem Soc; fel Royal Soc Can. *Res:* Chemistry and functional role of the proteins of muscle and contractile systems; molecular cloning; DNA sequencing and oligonucleotide directed mutagenesis. *Mailing Add:* Dept Biochem Univ Alta Edmonton AB T6G 2H7 Can. *Fax:* 403-492-0095

SMILOWITZ, BERNARD, applied physics, electrical engineering; deceased, see previous edition for last biography

SMILOWITZ, HENRY MARTIN, NEUROBIOLOGY, CELL BIOLOGY. *Current Pos:* asst prof, 76-82, ASSOC PROF PHARMACOL, HEALTH CTR, UNIV CONN, 82- *Personal Data:* b Brooklyn, NY, Sept 25, 46; c 3. *Educ:* Reed Col, AB, 68; Mass Inst Technol, PhD(biochem), 72. *Prof Exp:* Fel microbiol, Med Sch, Tufts Univ, 72-73, neurobiol, Harvard Med Sch, 73-76. *Mem:* Am Soc Cell Biol; Soc Neurosci; NY Acad Sci; Int Soc Neurosci; AAAS; Am Soc Pharmacol & Exp Therapeut. *Res:* Regulation and development of neuromuscular junction function post-synaptic mechanisms; acetylcholine receptor and esterase; development, intracellular transport and localization; phosphorylation; role of calcium in cellular regulation; studies on voltage sensitive calcium channel of skeletal and cardiac muscle. *Mailing Add:* Dept Pharmacol Univ Conn Sch Med 263 Farmington Ave Farmington CT 06030-0001

SMILOWITZ, ZANE, ENTOMOLOGY. *Current Pos:* PROF ENTOM, PA STATE UNIV, 67- *Personal Data:* b New York, NY, Sept 13, 33; m 59, Ann Kossog; c Ellen, Brian & Nancy. *Educ:* Univ Ga, BS, 61; Cornell Univ, MS, 65, PhD(entom), 67. *Prof Exp:* Entomologist, Trubeck Labs, 61; teaching & res asst, Cornell Univ, 61-67. *Mem:* AAAS; Entom Soc Am; Can Entom Soc; Sigma Xi; Potato Asn Am. *Res:* Research and development of integrated pest management systems for potato pests; insecticide resistance management; precision agriculture; insect mapping; be protein crystal growth in microgravel. *Mailing Add:* Dept Entom Pa State Univ 501 Agr Sci & Indust Bldg University Park PA 16802-3508. *Fax:* 814-865-3048; *E-Mail:* zane_smilowitz@agcs.cas.psu.edu

SMIT, CHRISTIAN JACOBUS BESTER, FOOD SCIENCE, AGRICULTURAL CHEMISTRY. *Current Pos:* RETIRED. *Personal Data:* b Piet Retief, SAfrica, Jan 10, 27; m 52, 68, Wanda A Storath; c 4. *Educ:* Univ Pretoria, BS, 47, HED, 48; Univ Calif, Berkeley, PhD, 53. *Prof Exp:* Asst prof officer, Agr Res Inst, Univ Pretoria, 48-49; prof officer, Fruit & Food Technol Res Inst, SAfrica, 53-58, first prof officer & chief food technol sect, 58-60; prof food sci & head dept, Stellenbosch, 60-63; res food scientist, Sunkist Growers Inc, 63-68; head dept & chmn div, Univ Ga, 73-80, actg dean, Col Agr, 80-81, prof food sci, 68-93, assoc dean & dir resident instr, Col Agr, 81-93. *Concurrent Pos:* Consult, Nat Nutrit Res Inst, SAfrica, 60-63. *Mem:* Inst Food Technol; hon mem SAfrican Asn Food Sci & Technol. *Res:* Fruit and vegetable chemistry and processing; occurrence, manufacture and use of pectic substances. *Mailing Add:* 1120 Eaglebluff Ct Greensboro GA 30642

SMIT, DAVID ERNST, SEDIMENTARY GEOLOGY, STRATIGRAPHY. *Current Pos:* RESOURCES INC, 79-; CONSULT GEOLOGIST, 82- *Personal Data:* b Beloit, Wis, Sept 1, 42; m 67; c 3. *Educ:* Augustana Col, AB, 64; Univ Iowa, MS, 67, PhD(geol), 71. *Prof Exp:* Teaching asst geol, Univ Iowa, 65-67, res asst, 67-70; from instr to asst prof, Univ Wis, Stevens Point, 70-74; asst prof geol, Wichita State Univ, 74-78, res assoc, 78-80; sr geologist, Energy Res Group, 80-82. *Concurrent Pos:* Res assoc, Univ Iowa, 71; pres, Quad Resources Inc, 79-; co-dir, NURE Prog, Wichita State Univ, 79-80; consult geologist, 82- *Mem:* Geol Soc Am; Soc Econ Paleontologists & Mineralogists; Int Asn Sedimentologists; Int Geol Cong. *Res:* Depositional environments and diagenesis of shallow marine-platform sedimentary rocks; comparative sedimentology of recent limestones and the equivalent ancient rocks; location and mode of occurence of uranium in sedimentary rocks. *Mailing Add:* 221 Timber Ridge Ct Edmond OK 73034

SMIT, JAN, SOLID STATE PHYSICS. *Current Pos:* prof solid state magnetism, 63-74, PROF MAT SCI, UNIV SOUTHERN CALIF, 74- *Personal Data:* b Midwoud, Neth, Aug 30, 21; m 48; c 2. *Educ:* Delft Univ Technol, Ingenieur, 48; State Univ Leiden, PhD(physics), 56. *Prof Exp:* Engr, Philips, Endhoven, Neth, 41-45, physicist, 48-63. *Concurrent Pos:* Consult, Ampex Corp, 64- *Mem:* Am Phys Soc. *Mailing Add:* 3855 Pirate Dr Rancho Palos Verdes CA 90275

SMITH, A(LBERT) LEE, PHYSICAL CHEMISTRY, THERMODYNAMICS & MATERIAL PROPERTIES. *Current Pos:* supvr, Spectros Lab, Dow Corning Corp, 51-69, mgr, Anal Dept, 69-80, scientist, 80-89, EMER SCIENTIST, DOW CORNING CORP, 89- *Personal Data:* b Omaha, Nebr, Apr 11, 24; m 48, Frances Anders; c Suzanne, Joyce, Lynn, Louise, Sandra & Sharon. *Educ:* Iowa State Univ, BS, 46; Ohio State Univ, PhD(phys chem), 50. *Honors & Awards:* Williams-Wright Award, Indust Molecular Spectros, 87; Local Sect Award, Am Chem Soc, 88. *Prof Exp:* Res assoc, Res Found, Ohio State Univ, 50-51. *Mem:* Am Chem Soc; Soc Appl Spectros; Sigma Xi. *Res:* Infrared spectra of organosilicon compounds; analytical chemistry of silicones; evaluation of physical and thermodynamic data. *Mailing Add:* 400 Rollcrest Ct Midland MI 48640

SMITH, A(POLLO) M(ILTON) O(LIN), AERONAUTICAL ENGINEERING. *Current Pos:* RETIRED. *Personal Data:* b Columbia, Mo, July 2, 11; m 43, Elisabeth C Krost; c Tore A, Gerard N & Kathleen R. *Educ:* Calif Inst Technol, BS, 36, MS, 37, MS, 38. *Hon Degrees:* DSc, Univ Colo, 75. *Honors & Awards:* Goddard Award, Am Inst Aeronaut & Astronaut, 54; co-winner Casey Baldwin Award, Can Aeronaut & Space Inst, 71; Wright Bros lectr, Am Inst Aeronaut & Astronaut, 74; Fluids Eng Award, Am Soc Mech Engrs, 85. *Prof Exp:* Aerodynamicist, Douglas Aircraft Co, 38-42; chief engr rocket propulsion, Aerojet Eng Corp, 42-44; asst chief aerodynamicist, Douglas Aircraft Co, Long Beach, McDonnell Douglas Corp, 44-48, supvr design res, 48-54, supvr aerodyn res, 54-69, chief aerodyn eng res, 69-75; consult, 75-85; prof, Calif State Univ, Long Beach, 85-86. *Concurrent Pos:* Mem, US Naval Tech Mission, Europe, 45; mem subcomt internal flow, Nat Adv Comt Aeronaut, 48-51; lectr, Univ Calif, Los Angeles, 54-58; Am ed, J Comput Methods Appl Mech & Eng, 72-77; consult, McDonnell Douglas Corp, 75-85, Dynamics Technol, Inc, 77-85 & Bolt, Beranek & Newman, 78-82; adj prof, Univ Calif, Los Angeles, 75-80; lectr, Peking Inst Aeronaut & Astronaut, 79; mem, Aeronaut Adv Comn, NASA, 80-83. *Mem:* Nat Acad Eng; hon fel Am Inst Aeronaut & Astronaut; Am Soc Mech Engrs; Am Phys Soc. *Res:* Aerodynamic and applied mechanics, especially boundary layer and heat transfer theory; inviscid flow theory; introduction of the en method of predicting transition; development of the panel method for analysing flow about arbitrary shapes. *Mailing Add:* 2245 Ashbourne Dr San Marino CA 91108

SMITH, A MASON, MICROBIOLOGY, IMMUNOLOGY. *Current Pos:* ASSOC PROF MICROBIOL & IMMUNOL, SCH MED, E CAROLINA UNIV, 74- *Educ:* NC State Univ, PhD(immunol), 70. *Mailing Add:* Dept Microbiol & Immunol Sch Med E Carolina Univ Greenville NC 27834-2882. *Fax:* 919-816-3104

SMITH, AARON, CLINICAL PSYCHOLOGY, HEALTH SERVICE RESEARCH. *Current Pos:* RES ASSOC PROF, SCH MED, UNIV NEV, 75-; DIR RES, VET ADMIN MED CTR, RENO, NEV, 75-; EXEC DIR, SIERRA BIOMED RES CORP, 89- *Personal Data:* b Boston, Mass, Nov 3, 30; m 72, D Sharon Casey; c Naomi E, Jeffrey O, David G & Andrew H. *Educ:* Brown Univ, AB, 52; Univ Ill, PhD(clin psychol), 58. *Prof Exp:* Res psychologist, Philadelphia State Hosp, 58-62; dir res, Haverford State Hosp, 62-73, asst hosp dir, 73-75. *Concurrent Pos:* Co-dir, Northeast Psychol Clin, 59-75. *Mem:* Am Psychol Asn; Geront Soc Am; Asn Health Serv Res. *Res:* Developing techniques for assessing the outcome of various health treatment programs and predicting these outcomes from patient variables. *Mailing Add:* Vet Admin Med Ctr 151 1000 Locust St Reno NV 89520

SMITH, ABIGAIL LEVAN, VIRAL IMMUNOLOGY, VIRAL PATHOGENESIS. *Current Pos:* From asst prof to assoc prof, 79-92, PROF COMP MED & EPIDEMIOL, YALE UNIV SCH MED, 92- *Personal Data:* b Newark, NJ, Oct 1, 50. *Educ:* Brown Univ, AB, 72; Yale Univ, MPh, 74, PhD(epidemiol), 78. *Honors & Awards:* Res Award, Am Asn Lab Animal Sci, 91. *Concurrent Pos:* Ed, Lab Animal Sci, 92- *Mem:* Am Soc Virol; Am Asn

Immunologists. *Res:* Naturally occurring virus infections of laboratory animals, including their influence on immunologic research; immunomodulation during Lyme borreliosis; co-factors during Pneumocystis carinii activation and exacerbation. *Mailing Add:* Dept Comp Med & Epidemiol Yale Univ Sch Med PO Box 208016 New Haven CT 06520-8016. *Fax:* 203-737-2699, 785-7499

SMITH, AL LAWRENCE, ENGINEERING. *Current Pos:* patent examr, 59-73, supvr patent examr mach tool technol, 74-77, DIR, PATENT EXAM GROUP, US PATENT & TRADEMARK OFF, 78- *Educ:* Pa State Univ, BS; George Washington Univ, JD. *Prof Exp:* Mfg process engr, Ford Motor Co. *Mailing Add:* US Patent & Trademark Off Washington DC 20231

SMITH, ALAN B, NUCLEAR PHYSICS. *Current Pos:* Assoc physicist, Argonne Nat Lab, 53-58, head, Appl Nuclear Physics Sect, Appl Physics Div, 58-61, SR PHYSICIST, APPL NUCLEAR PHYSICS SECT, APPL PHYSICS DIV, ARGONNE NAT LAB, 61- *Personal Data:* b Chicago, Ill, Dec 19, 24; m 43; c 1. *Educ:* Beloit Col, BA, 49; Ind Univ, MS, 50, PhD(nuclear physics), 53. *Mem:* Fel Am Phys Soc. *Res:* Neutron and fission physics. *Mailing Add:* Argonne Nat Lab D207 4A 115 Argonne IL 60439

SMITH, ALAN BRADFORD, MAGNETIC DATA STORAGE, MAGNETIC MEASUREMENTS. *Current Pos:* CONSULT ENGR, DIGITAL EQUIP CORP, 83- *Personal Data:* b Karuizawa, Japan, July 28, 32; US citizen; m 57, Marjorie Beebe; c Bradford A & John B. *Educ:* Swarthmore Col, BS, 53; Rensselaer Polytech Inst, MEE, 54; Harvard Univ, MA, 60, PhD(appl physics), 66. *Prof Exp:* Engr, Sprague Elec Co, 53-59; res asst appl physics, Harvard Univ, 61-65; mem res staff, Sperry Rand Res Ctr, 65-83. *Concurrent Pos:* Coordr, courses in Bubble Domain Memory Technol, Univ Calif, Los Angeles, 75, 77, 79-80; ed-in-chief, Trans on Magnetics, Inst Elec & Electronics Engrs, 79-81. *Mem:* Sr mem Inst Elec & Electronics Engrs; Magnetics Soc (pres, 85-86). *Res:* Thin-film magnetic recording heads; magneto-optics and magnetic measurements; magnetic bubble domain memory devices; ferromagnetic resonance; magnetoacoustic interactions in solids. *Mailing Add:* Quantum Corp 333 South St Shrewsbury MA 01545. *E-Mail:* asmith@tfh.enet.dec.com

SMITH, ALAN JAY, PERFORMANCE ANALYSIS. *Current Pos:* From asst prof to assoc prof, 74-86, PROF COMPUT SCI, UNIV CALIF, BERKELEY, 86- *Personal Data:* b New York, NY, Apr 10, 49. *Educ:* Mass Inst Technol, BS, 71; Stanford Univ, MS, 73, PhD(comput sci), 74. *Concurrent Pos:* Vchmn, Elec Eng & Comput Sci Dept, Univ Calif, Berkeley, 82-84; mem, Comput Measurement Group. *Mem:* Asn Comput Mach; Sigma Xi; Inst Elec & Electronics Engrs; Soc Indust & Appl Math. *Res:* Computer system performance; operating systems. *Mailing Add:* Dept Elec Eng Univ Calif Berkeley CA 94720-1776

SMITH, ALAN JERRARD, PHARMACOLOGY. *Current Pos:* CONSULT, PHARMACEUT QUAL & TECHNOL, 90- *Personal Data:* b London, Eng, May 8, 29; m 58; c 2. *Educ:* Univ London, BSc, 50, PhD(chem), 56. *Prof Exp:* Asst, Univ Col, Exeter, Eng, 53-54; res chemist, Admiralty Mat Lab, Eng, 54-57; group leader res, Rohm and Haas Co, 57-63, regulatory liaison, 63-64; asst mgr anal develop, Ayerst Labs Inc, 64-70, mgr qual control tech serv, 70-78, mgr, 78-79, asst dir, Corp Qual Assurance, 79-85; dir qual affairs, Whitehall Lab, 85-90. *Concurrent Pos:* Mem, Comt Quality Systs, Am Soc Testing & Mat, 78-80. *Mem:* Am Soc Qual Control; Am Chem Soc. *Res:* Pharmaceutical quality assurance and control; stability of pharmaceuticals; analytical methods for pharmaceuticals; ion exchange; redox polymers; chemistry of transition metals. *Mailing Add:* 21 Bedlow Ave Newport RI 02840-1403. *E-Mail:* ajajs@wsii.com

SMITH, ALAN LEWIS, VOLCANOLOGY, CARIBBEAN GEOLOGY. *Current Pos:* from asst prof to assoc prof, 69-80, DIR, GEOL DEPT, UNIV PR, 79-, PROF GEOL, 80- *Personal Data:* b Bridgend, Gt Brit, Sept 4, 41; US citizen; m 71, Mariella Pirieyro; c Gwyneth & Bethan. *Educ:* Univ London, BSc, 63; Univ Calif, Berkeley, PhD(geol), 69. *Prof Exp:* Lectr, Univ Nev, 68-69, Chico State Col, 69. *Concurrent Pos:* Mem, Sci Monitoring Team, Montserrat Volcano Observ, 95- *Mem:* Geol Soc Am; Am Geophys Union; Int Asn Volcanology & Chem Earths Interior. *Res:* Active volcanoes of the Lesser Antilles; volcanic stratigraphy, petrology and mineralogy of volcanic rocks and volcanic hazard assessment. *Mailing Add:* Box 5232 Col Sta Mayaguez PR 00681. *Fax:* 787-265-3845; *E-Mail:* al_smith@rumac.upr.clu.edu

SMITH, ALAN LYLE, PLANT ECOLOGY, WETLANDS MITIGATION. *Current Pos:* PRES, GLOBAL ENVIRON INC, 91- *Personal Data:* b Bartley, Nebr, June 27, 41; m 61; c 2. *Educ:* Kearney State Col, BS, 64; Univ Nebr, MS, 68; Tex A&M Univ, PhD(ecol), 71. *Prof Exp:* Instr chem, Cozad High Sch, Nebr, 64-65; range scientist veg control, Tex Trans Inst, 72; plant ecologist, Dames & Moore, 72-80; pres, ALS Consults, Inc, Houston, 81-90; mgr eviron serv, Gulf Coast Region, Maxim Engrs, Inc, 90-91. *Concurrent Pos:* Proj ecologist, Prep Environ Report, Seadock Inc, 73-74; ecol consult, Environ Report LOOP Inc, 73-75; proj mgr, Site Selection Petrochem Facil Int Consortium, 74 & Seagrass Transplant Prog, Lower Laguna Madre, Tex, 84. *Mem:* Nat Asn Environ Prof. *Res:* Impact of crude oil on coastal marshes and problems associated with establishing vegetation on problem soils, especially related to strip mining reclamation; wetland mitigation; transplanting seagrasses. *Mailing Add:* 5418 Arncliffe Houston TX 77088

SMITH, ALAN REID, BOTANY, SYSTEMATICS. *Current Pos:* Asst res, 69-77, assoc res, 77-83, RES BOTANIST, UNIV CALIF, BERKELEY, 83- *Personal Data:* b Sacramento, Calif, July 14, 43; m 66, Joan E Scott; c Leslie & Dana. *Educ:* Kans State Univ, BS, 65; Iowa State Univ, PhD(bot), 69. *Concurrent Pos:* Ed, Pteridologia, 78-84, Am Fern J, 85-89. *Mem:* Am Soc Plant Taxon; Am Fern Soc (vpres, 90-91, pres, 92-93); Brit Pteridological Soc; Int Asn Plant Taxon. *Res:* Taxonomy of ferns; Thelypteris; pteridophytes of Mexico, Venezuela & Bolivia. *Mailing Add:* 1001 Valley Life Sci Bldg No 2465 Univ Herbarium Univ Calif Berkeley CA 94720-2465

SMITH, ALBERT A, JR, ELECTRICAL MAGNETIC. *Current Pos:* SR ENGR, IBM CORP, 64- *Personal Data:* b Yonkers, NY, Dec 2, 35. *Educ:* Milwaukee Sch Eng, BSEE, 61, NY Univ, MSEE, 64. *Prof Exp:* Staff engr, W Tech Div, Adler, 61-64. *Concurrent Pos:* Chmn tech comt electromagnetic environ, Inst Elec & Electronics Engrs, 81. *Mem:* Inst Elec & Electronics Engrs. *Mailing Add:* Symmetrics 11 Steamside Terr Woodstock NY 12498

SMITH, ALBERT CARL, PATHOBIOLOGY, PATHOLOGY. *Current Pos:* DIR, BAY CO PUB HEALTH UNIT, 92- *Personal Data:* b Los Angeles, Calif, Sept 13, 34; m 67, Deborah J Townsend; c Shana & Chelsea. *Educ:* Univ Calif, Los Angeles, BA, 56; Univ Calif, Irvine, PhD(biol sci), 67; Univ Hawaii, MD, 75, Am Bd Path, cert path, 79. *Prof Exp:* Asst to sr scientists, Univ Hawaii, 59; res scientist, Calif Dept Fish & Game, 61-63, 65-66 & 70-71; lab technician, Allergan Pharmaceut, 63; lab technician, Orange Co Gen Hosp, 64; lab technician, Univ Calif, Irvine, 64-65; res asst organismic biol, 66, res assoc & instr pop & environ biol, 66-67; from asst prof to assoc prof biol, Univ Hawaii, Hilo, 67-73; mem grad fac zool, Honolulu, 68-77; mem staff, Oceanic Inst, Hawaii, 77-79; dir, Med Labs Hawaii, Inc, 79-80; asst prof path, Col Med & Vet Med, Univ Fla, Gainesville, 80-85; chief clin lab, Vet Admin Med Ctr, Bay Pines, Fla, 80-85, chief clin path, dir, Path Spec Studies & chief, Chem Sect, Clin Lab, 85-91; med dir, Trenton Med Ctr, 91-92. *Concurrent Pos:* Res assoc, Dept Pop & Environ & Pop Environ Biol, Univ Calif, Irvine, 67-; res grants, Bur Nat Marine Fisheries Serv, US Dept Comm, 68-69; res grant Univ Hawaii, 68-72, sea grant, 71-73; consult dir, Genetics Lab, Calif State Fisheries Lab, Long Beach, 69-; prog dir path, Aquatic Sci, Inc, Fla, 69-70, consult, 70-; grant Am Found Oceanog, 69-77, 77 & 78; Marine Biol Consults Inc, Calif, 70-; Calif Dept Fish & Game, 70-71; chief consult, Hawaii BioMarine, 70-; res assoc & consult, Oceanic Inst, 71-; sr sci staff consult pathobiol, Pan Pac Inst Ocean Sci, 73-; grants, US Energy Res & Develop Admin, 71-72, NIH, 72-73, NSF, 72-74 & Puerto Rico Undersea Lab, 73, USAID, 76- Rockefeller Found, 78-79 & Engelhard Found, 79-80; res fel path, Univ Hawaii, 75-76; clin path residency, St Francis Hosp, Honolulu, 77-78 & Queens Med Ctr, 78-79; marine affairs coordr, State Hawaii, 78; consult, Astromarine, Kuai, Hawaii, Hawaiian Elec Comp, Honolulu, State Univ Syst Fla, 81, Sea Grant, 80, clin path, Sunland Ctr, Gainesville, Fla, Med-Marine Res, 83-87, Elks, 88, Exxon, 89; res fac, Univ Fla, 81-85. *Mem:* AAAS; Soc Invert Path; NY Acad Sci; hon mem Am Longevity Soc; hon mem Int Soc Aquatic Med; Col Am Pathologists; Int Soc Develop & Comp Immunologists. *Res:* Evolution; experimental taxonomy; electrophoretic technique; diving and deep sea biology; pathobiology; proteins of the eye lens; immunobiology and serology; chemical phylogenetics; marine biomedicine; psychobiology, comparative hematology. *Mailing Add:* PO Box 12153 Panama City FL 32401

SMITH, ALBERT CHARLES, BOTANY, EVOLUTION OF FLOWERING PLANTS. *Current Pos:* RETIRED. *Personal Data:* b Springfield, Mass, Apr 5, 06; m 35, 66; c 2. *Educ:* Columbia Univ, AB, 26, PhD(bot), 33. *Honors & Awards:* Robert Allerton Award, Nat Trop Bot Garden, 79; Asa Gray Award, Am Soc Plant Taxonomists, 92. *Prof Exp:* From asst cur to assoc cur, NY Bot Garden, 28-40; cur herbarium, Arnold Arboretum, Harvard Univ, 40-48, ed j, 41-48, cur div phanerogams, Dept Bot, Smithsonian Inst, 48-56; prog dir syst biol, NSF, 56-58; dir, Mus Natural Hist, US Nat Mus, 58-62, asst secy, Smithsonian Inst, 62-63; dir res & prof bot, Univ Hawaii, 63-65, Wilder prof, 65-70; Torrey prof bot, Univ Mass, Amherst, 70-76; ed consult, Pac Trop Bot Garden, 77-91. *Concurrent Pos:* Mem bot expeds, Colombia, Peru, Brazil, Fiji, Brit Guiana & W Indies, 26-69; fel, Bishop Mus, Yale Univ, 33-34; Guggenheim fel, 46-47; ed, Brittonia, 35-40, J Arnold Arboretum, 41-48, Sargentia, 42-48 & Allertonia, 77-88. *Mem:* Nat Acad Sci; fel Am Acad Arts & Sci; Am Soc Plant Taxonomists (pres, 55); Asn Trop Biol (pres, 67-68); Int Asn Plant Taxon (vpres, 59-64). *Res:* Taxonomy and phytogeography of flowering plants, especially of tropical America and Southwest Pacific. *Mailing Add:* Dept Bot Univ Hawaii Honolulu HI 96822

SMITH, ALBERT ERNEST, JR, PLANT PHYSIOLOGY. *Current Pos:* Assoc prof, 69-80, PROF AGRON, UNIV GA, 80- *Personal Data:* b Ransom, Kans, Dec 4, 38; m 60; c 2. *Educ:* Ft Hays Kans State Col, BSc, 64; Tex A&M Univ, PhD(range sci), 69. *Honors & Awards:* Gamma Sigma Delta Distinguished Jr Fac Award, 78; Trans Am Soc Ag Eng Outstanding Paper Award, 79. *Mem:* Am Soc Plant Physiol; Am Soc Agron; Weed Sci Soc Am; Am Soc Range Mgt. *Res:* Plant physiology and biochemistry of the modes of actions of herbicides; teaching agronomy 834, advanced chemical weed control. *Mailing Add:* Dept Crop & Soil Exp Sta Griffin GA 30223

SMITH, ALBERT ERNEST, physics, for more information see previous edition

SMITH, ALBERT GOODIN, PATHOLOGY. *Current Pos:* prof path & head dept, 70-96, EMER PROF, SCH MED, LA STATE UNIV, SHREVEPORT PATH, 96- *Personal Data:* b Charleston, Mo, Aug 26, 24; m 53, Harriet Gurley; c Susan & Alan. *Educ:* Washington Univ, MD, 47. *Prof Exp:* Intern, St Luke's Hosp, St Louis, 47-48; asst resident & resident path, Hosp, Univ Ark, 48-50; vol asst surg path, Col Physicians & Surgeons, Columbia Univ,

50; asst resident, resident & instr path, Sch Med, Duke Univ, 50-51, assoc, 52-55, from asst prof to assoc prof, 55-66; prof path & dep chmn dept, Col Med, Univ Tenn & dir labs, City Memphis Hosps, 66-70. *Concurrent Pos:* Chief path serv, Confederate Mem Med Ctr, Shreveport, 71-96. *Mem:* AAAS; Am Soc Clin Path; Am Soc Exp Path; AMA; Clin Asn Path. *Res:* Surgical pathology; tissue culture. *Mailing Add:* PO Box 4159 Centenary Shreveport LA 71134-0159

SMITH, ALBERT MATTHEWS, ANIMAL NUTRITION. *Current Pos:* from asst prof to assoc prof, 57-64, chmn dept animal sci, 63-79, PROF ANIMAL NUTRIT, UNIV VT, 64-, ANIMAL NUTRITIONIST, 61-, ASSOC DEAN, COL AGR & ASSOC DIR, VT STATE AGR EXP STA, 75- *Personal Data:* b Bangor, Maine, Dec 25, 27; m 50; c 2. *Educ:* Univ Maine, BS, 52; Cornell Univ, MS, 54, PhD(animal nutrit), 56. *Prof Exp:* From instr to asst prof animal husb, Cornell Univ, 55-57. *Concurrent Pos:* Consult, Rep Korea, AID, 73. *Mem:* Am Dairy Sci Asn; Am Soc Animal Sci; Sigma Xi; fel AAAS. *Res:* Dairy cattle nutrition; forage evaluation, especially role of forages in summer and winter feeding regimes; mineral metabolism. *Mailing Add:* 1807 Spear St South Burlington VT 05403-7906

SMITH, ALDEN ERNEST, SCIENCE EDUCATION, AQUATIC BIOLOGY. *Current Pos:* RETIRED. *Personal Data:* b Lockport, NY, Apr 25, 23. *Educ:* Univ Colo, Boulder, BA, 50; Univ Buffalo, EdM, 60; Syracuse Univ, MS, 64; State Univ NY Buffalo, EdD(sci educ), 71. *Prof Exp:* Lab asst bot, Brookhaven Nat Lab, 54-56; teacher jr high sch, Lockport Bd Educ, NY, 56-59, high sch, 59-65; from assoc prof to prof biol, State Univ NY Col Buffalo, 65-88. *Mem:* AAAS; Am Inst Biol Sci; Nat Asn Biol Teachers; Nat Sci Teachers Asn. *Res:* Methods of teaching biology at the college level; aquatic plants; biology of organisms in fresh water environments; wild and cultivated poisonous plants. *Mailing Add:* 7047 Old English Rd Lockport NY 14094

SMITH, ALEXANDER GOUDY, ASTROPHYSICS, PHOTOGRAPHIC RESEARCH. *Current Pos:* from asst prof to prof physics, Univ Fla, 48-56, asst dean grad sch, 61-69, chmn dept astron, 62-71, actg dean grad sch, 71-73, distinguished alumni assoc prof, 81-83, PROF ASTRON & PHYSICS, UNIV FLA, 56-, DISTINGUISHED SERV PROF ASTRON, 82- *Personal Data:* b Clarksburg, WVa, Aug 12, 19; m 42; c 2. *Educ:* Mass Inst Technol, SB, 43; Duke Univ, PhD(physics), 49. *Honors & Awards:* Medal, Fla Acad Sci, 65. *Prof Exp:* Mem staff Radiation Lab, Mass Inst Technol, 42-46; instr & asst Duke Univ, 46-48. *Concurrent Pos:* Consult, US Air Force, 54-65; mem bd dirs, Assoc Univ for Res in Astron, 60-63, consult, 64-69; mem users' comt, Nat Radio Astron Observ, 66-78, vis comt, 68-71; mem comt astron, Nat Res Coun, 66-69, chmn, 68-69; adv panel astron, NSF, 69-72; ed, Am Astron Soc Photo Bull, 75-87; trustee SE Univ Res Asn, 82-. *Mem:* Fel AAAS; fel Am Phys Soc; fel Optical Soc Am; Am Astron Soc; Int Astron Union; Soc Photog Scientists & Engrs; fel Royal Micros Soc. *Res:* Magnetron design; microwave molecular spectroscopy; atmospheric optics; hypersensitization of photographic materials for research in astrophysics; planetary radio astronomy; optical and radio variations of quasars. *Mailing Add:* Dept Astron Univ Fla Gainesville FL 32611. *Fax:* 904-392-5089

SMITH, ALICE LORRAINE, CYTOPATHOLOGY. *Current Pos:* assoc prof, 62-76, PROF PATH, SOUTHWESTERN MED SCI CTR, UNIV TEX, DALLAS, 76-; PARKLAND MEM HOSP, 62- *Personal Data:* b Trinity, Tex. *Educ:* Univ Tex, BA, 40, MD, 46; Am Bd Path, dipl, 51, dipl cytopath, 89. *Honors & Awards:* Commissioner's Spec Citation, Food & Drug Admin. *Prof Exp:* Asst prof path, Southwestern Med Sch, Univ Tex, 50-54; asst pathologist, Univ Hosp, Baylor Univ, 54-55; from asst prof to assoc prof, Col Med, 55-57, prof, Res Inst & assoc prof, Col Dent, 57-61; dir, Div Diag Cytol & Sch Cytotechnol, Parkland Mem Hosp, 62-92. *Concurrent Pos:* Pathologist, Wadley Res Inst & Blood Bank, 57-61; clin assoc, Univ Tex Health Sci Ctr, Dallas, 58-62. *Mem:* Fel Am Col Physicians; fel Am Soc Clin Path; fel Am Col Path; AMA. *Res:* Lung cancer. *Mailing Add:* Dept Path 9072 Southwestern Med Ctr Univ Tex 5323 Harry Hines Blvd Dallas TX 75235. *Fax:* 214-648-4070; *E-Mail:* smith.alice@pathology.swmed.edu

SMITH, ALLAN EDWARD, PERSISTENCE OF HERBICIDES IN SOILS, BREAKDOWN OF HERBICIDES IN SOIL ISOLATING METABOLITES. *Current Pos:* RETIRED. *Personal Data:* b Hull, Eng, June 2, 37; US citizen; m 70, Diane Secoy. *Educ:* Univ Liverpool, BSc, 59, PhD(org chem), 63, DSc, 82. *Prof Exp:* Fel radiol sci, Johns Hopkins Hosp, 63-65; res scientist, Agr Div, Imp Chem Industs, 65-67; res scientist, Agr Can, 67-97. *Concurrent Pos:* Adj prof, Biol Dept, Univ Regina, 92- *Mem:* Europ Weed Res Soc; fel Chem Inst Can; Am Chem Soc; Weed Sci Soc Am. *Res:* Persistence of herbicides under laboratory and field conditions to understand environmental factors affecting their fate; improved analytical methodology for their extraction and analysis in soils has been developed; history of part control substances through the ages has been studied. *Mailing Add:* 3823 Bow Bay Regina SK S4S 7E1 Can. *Fax:* 306-780-7453

SMITH, ALLAN LASLETT, PHYSICAL CHEMISTRY. *Current Pos:* assoc prof, 75-82, PROF CHEM, DREXEL UNIV, 83- *Personal Data:* b Newark, NJ, June 21, 38; m 60, Charity Fletcher; c 2. *Educ:* Harvard Univ, BA, 60; Mass Inst Technol, PhD(phys chem), 65. *Honors & Awards:* Lindback Award Excellence in Teaching. *Prof Exp:* Nat Acad Sci-Nat Res Coun fel, Nat Bur Stand, 65-66; from asst prof to assoc prof chem, Yale Univ, 66-74; head, Dept Math, Daycroft Sch, Greenwich, Conn, 75. *Concurrent Pos:* Alfred P Sloan Found fel, 70; NATO sr fel, Phys Chem Lab, Oxford Univ, 71. *Mem:* Am Phys Soc; Am Chem Soc; AAAS; Soc Appl Spectros. *Res:* Thermodynamics and spectroscopy of fullerenes; chemistry curriculum reform; computers in chemical education. *Mailing Add:* Dept Chem Drexel Univ Philadelphia PA 19104

SMITH, ALLEN ANDERSON, DEVELOPMENTAL BIOLOGY, HISTOCHEMISTRY. *Current Pos:* ASSOC PROF ANAT, BARRY UNIV, SCH PODIATRIC MED, 89- *Personal Data:* b Boston, Mass; m 74; c 2. *Educ:* Brown Univ, AB, 61; Univ Ore, PhD(anat), 69. *Prof Exp:* Instr anat, Hahnemann Med Col, 69-70; instr zool, Tel Aviv Univ, 70-71; res asst, Temple Univ, 71-74; from asst prof to assoc prof biol, Widener Univ, 78-89. *Concurrent Pos:* Vis scientist, Dept Org Chem, Weizmann Inst, 81. *Mem:* Am Chem Soc; Soc Develop Biol; Histochem Soc. *Res:* Sweat glands; epithelio-mesenchymal interactions; pharmacology of rotaxanes. *Mailing Add:* Sch Grad Med Sci Barry Univ 11300 NE Second Ave Miami Shores FL 33161

SMITH, ALLIE MAITLAND, HEAT TRANSFER, OPTICS. *Current Pos:* PROF MECH ENG & DEAN, SCH ENG, UNIV MISS, 79- *Personal Data:* b Lumberton, NC, June 9, 34; m 57, Sarah L Whitlock; c Sara L (Taylor), Hollis D & Meredith L (Vaughan). *Educ:* NC State Univ, BSME, 56, MS, 61, PhD, 66. *Honors & Awards:* Space Shuttle Flag Plaque Award, Hermann Oberth Award & Thermophysics Award, Am Inst Aeronaut & Astronaut. *Prof Exp:* Assoc engr, Martin Co, 56-57; develop engr, Western Elec Co, 57-58; instr eng, NC State Col, 58-60; mem tech staff, Bell Tel Labs, 60-62; res engr, Res Triangle Inst, 62-66; supvr res, Aro, Inc, 66-79. *Concurrent Pos:* Asst prof mech eng, Exten Div, NC State Col, 61-62; part-time assoc prof aerospace eng, Space Inst, Univ Tenn, 67-79; chmn, Thermophysics Tech Comt, Am Inst Aeronaut & Astronaut, 75-77, 10th Thermophysics Conf, 75, Terrestrial Energy Systs Comt, 77-81, 17th Aerospace Sci Meetings, 79; assoc ed, Am Inst Aeronaut & Astronaut J, J Thermophysics & Heat Transfers; ed, Radiative Transfer & Thermal Control, Thermophysics of Spacecraft & Outer Planet Entry Probes. *Mem:* Fel Am Inst Aeronaut & Astronaut; fel Am Soc Mech Engrs; Am Soc Eng Educ; Nat Soc Prof Engrs. *Res:* Radiative characteristics of surfaces and solidified gases; effects of space environment on thermal control materials; space simulation; radiation gas dynamics; solid state diffusion; fundamentals and applications of radiation heat transfer; fluid mechanics; cryogenics; vacuum; developments in theoretical and applied mechanics and radiation heat transfer. *Mailing Add:* Sch Eng Univ Miss University MS 38677. *Fax:* 601-232-1287; *E-Mail:* enas@olemiss.edu

SMITH, ALTON HUTCHISON, topology, for more information see previous edition

SMITH, ALVIN WINFRED, MARINE VIROLOGY. *Current Pos:* res veterinarian, 80-81, dir res, 81-86, PROF, COL VET MED, ORE STATE UNIV, 86- *Personal Data:* b Kooskia, Idaho, Sept 25, 33; m 58; c 4. *Educ:* Wash State Univ, BA, 55, DVM, 57; Tex A&M Univ, MS, 67; Univ Calif, Berkeley, PhD(comp path), 75. *Prof Exp:* Chief, Res Animal Br, Sch Aerospace Med, 67-69, Res Animal Div, Naval Biosci Lab, 69-78, virol, Naval Ocean Syst Ctr, 78-80. *Concurrent Pos:* Chief, Marine Mammal Res Div, Naval Biosci Lab, 74-78, Virol Sect, San Diego Zoo, 78-80. *Mem:* Am Vet Med Asn; Am Col Lab Animal Med; Int Asn Aquatic Animal Med. *Res:* Mechanisms of transmission and survival of infectious disease agents in nature. *Mailing Add:* Col Vet Med Ore State Univ Magruder Hall Rm 105 Corvallis OR 97331

SMITH, AMOS BRITTAIN, III, TOTAL SYNTHESIS OF ARCHITECTURALLY NOVEL NATURAL & NON-NATURAL PRODUCTS, SYNTHETIC METHODOLOGY. *Current Pos:* from asst prof to prof, Dept Chem, Univ Pa, 73-90, from asst mem to assoc mem, Monell Chem Senses Ctr, 73-81, chmn, Dept Chem, 88-96, MEM, MONELL CHEM SENSES CTR, UNIV PA, 81-, RHODES-THOMPSON PROF CHEM, 90- *Personal Data:* b Lewisburg, Pa, Aug 26, 44; m 68, Janet L Duyckinck; c Kathryn (Schuyler) & Amos Matthew MacMillan. *Educ:* Bucknell Univ, BS & MS, 66; Rockefeller Univ, PhD(org chem), 72. *Hon Degrees:* MA, Univ Pa, 78. *Honors & Awards:* Kitasato Inst Microbial Chem Medal, Kitasato Inst, 90; Honor Scroll Award, Am Inst Chemists, 91; Arthur C Cope Award, Am Chem Soc, 91, Award for Creative Work in Synthetic Org Chem, 97; Alexander von Humboldt Res Award Sr US Scientists, Alexander von Humboldt Found, 92; Ernest Guenther Award, 93. *Prof Exp:* Res assoc, Rockefeller Univ, 72-73. *Concurrent Pos:* Camille & Henry Dreyfus teacher-scholar award, Dreyfus Found, 78-83; chmn, Gordon Res Conf, 80; vis assoc prof, Dept Chem, Columbia Univ, 80; vis prof chem, Dept Org & Theoret Chem, Cambridge Univ, 82; mem, Comn Sci & Arts, Franklin Inst, 85-; vis dir, Kitasato Inst, 90-; mem bd dirs, Org Reactions, 95- *Mem:* AAAS; Swiss Chem Soc; Am Chem Soc; Royal Soc Chem; Japanese Chem Soc. *Res:* Total synthesis of architecturally novel natural and non-natural products, synthetic methodology and reaction mechanisms; design and synthesis of renin and human immunodeficiency virus protease inhibitors; development of new reactions and the study of their mechanism; synthesis and structural analysis of novel discotic liquid crystals and new fullerene derivatives; bio organic chemistry. *Mailing Add:* Dept Chem Univ Pa Philadelphia PA 19104-6323

SMITH, ANDERSON DODD, GERONTOLOGY, EXPERIMENTAL PSYCHOLOGY. *Current Pos:* From asst prof to prof psychol, 70-84, dir, 85-95, ASSOC DEAN, COL SCI, GA INST TECHNOL, 95- *Personal Data:* b Richmond, Va, May 3, 44; m 66, Glenna Bevell; c Nancy (Taylor) & Leigh-Ellen. *Educ:* Washington & Lee Univ, BA, 66; Univ Va, MA, 69, PhD(exp psychol), 70. *Honors & Awards:* Monie Ferst Res Award, 84. *Concurrent Pos:* NIH res grant, Nat Inst Aging, 72-, NIMH grant, 81; ed psychol sci, J Gerontol, 81-84; affil scientist, Yerkes Regional Primate Ctr, 81-90; adj prof, Ga State Univ, 84-93, Univ Ga, 89-94; mem, Nat Adv Coun Aging, USPHS, 91-96. *Mem:* Sigma Xi; fel Am Psychol Asn; Psychonomic Soc; fel Gerontol Soc; fel Am Psychol Soc. *Res:* Experimental psychology of human memory; age-related differences in encoding, storage and retrieval processes. *Mailing Add:* Sch Psychol Ga Inst Technol Atlanta GA 30332. *E-Mail:* anderson.smith@psych.gatech.edu

SMITH, ANDREW DONOVAN, SUPERCONDUCTIVITY. *Current Pos:* SR SCIENTIST, TRW, 84- *Personal Data:* b Aug 23, 53. *Educ:* Univ Md, BS, 73; Harvard Univ, SM, 76, PhD(physics), 80. *Mem:* Am Phys Soc; Inst Elec & Electronics Engrs. *Mailing Add:* One Space Park Bldg D1-1039 Redondo Beach CA 90278. *E-Mail:* andy.smith@trw.com

SMITH, ANDREW GEORGE, MICROBIOLOGY, MEDICAL MYCOLOGY. *Current Pos:* from assoc prof to prof path, Sch Med, Univ Md, 72-83, dir, Microbiol Lab Hosp, 72-83, res prof med technol, 83-85, assoc prof med dermatol, 77-85, ADJ PROF, DEPT MED RES & TECHNOL, MED SCH, UNIV MD, 85- *Personal Data:* b Williamsport, Pa, July 11, 18; m 45; c 2. *Educ:* Pa State Univ, BS, 40; Univ Pa, MS, 47, PhD, 50; Am Bd Med Microbiol, dipl, 71, 83. *Honors & Awards:* Lederle Med Fac Award, 55; Barnett L Cohem Award, Am Soc Microbiol, 76. *Prof Exp:* From asst prof to assoc prof microbiol, Sch Med, Univ Md, 50-66; dir bact prod div, BBL Div, BioQuest, Md, 66-69; from assoc prof to prof microbiol, Sch Med, Univ Vt, 69-72. *Concurrent Pos:* Consult, Vet Admin Hosp, Baltimore, 62-69 & 73-84. *Mem:* Fel Am Acad Microbiol; Am Soc Microbiol; Med Mycol Soc Ams. *Res:* Bacterial cytology; applied and clinical microbiology; medical mycology. *Mailing Add:* 4025 Font Hill Dr Ellicott City MD 21042

SMITH, ANDREW THOMAS, BEHAVIORAL ECOLOGY, POPULATION BIOLOGY. *Current Pos:* asst prof, 78-83, ASSOC PROF ZOOL, ARIZ STATE UNIV, 83- *Personal Data:* b Glendale, Calif, Mar 14, 46; c 2. *Educ:* Univ Calif, Berkeley, AB, 68; Univ Calif, Los Angeles, PhD(biol), 73. *Prof Exp:* Lectr zool, Univ Alta, 73-74; asst prof biol, Univ Miami, 74-78. *Concurrent Pos:* Hon consult, Int Union Conserv Nature, 78-; prin investr, Nat Geog Soc, 84-85, Nat Acad Sci, 85; prin investr, NSF, 90-92. *Mem:* AAAS; Am Soc Mammalogists; Ecol Soc Am; Soc Study of Evolution; Soc Conserv Biol; Animal Behav Soc. *Res:* Conservation ecology; population biology; dispersal; biogeography; mammalogy; reproductive strategies; behavioral ecology. *Mailing Add:* Dept Zool Ariz State Univ Box 871501 Tempe AZ 85287-1501

SMITH, ANN, HEMEIRON METABOLISM, RECEPTOR TRANSPORT. *Current Pos:* Asst prof, 83-86, ASSOC PROF BIOCHEM, MED CTR, LA STATE UNIV, 86- *Personal Data:* b London, Eng, June 3, 46. *Educ:* Univ London, PhD(biochem), 74. *Mem:* Am Soc Biol Chemists; Biochem Soc Eng; Sigma Xi; AAAS. *Res:* Structure and function of hemopexin; liver cell functions; prothyrin phototherapy. *Mailing Add:* Univ Mo Sch Biol Sci 5100 Rockhill Rd Kansas City MO 64110. *Fax:* 816-235-5158

SMITH, ANTHONY JAMES, electrochemistry; deceased, see previous edition for last biography

SMITH, ARCHIBALD WILLIAM, LASERS. *Current Pos:* ADV ENGR, STORAGE TECHNOL CORP, 81- *Personal Data:* b Edmonton, Alta, Jan 6, 30; m 53; c 3. *Educ:* Univ Alta, BSc, 52, MSc, 53; Univ Toronto, PhD(physics), 55. *Prof Exp:* Staff mem, Defense Res Bd, Can, 56-61; staff mem, Thomas J Watson Res Ctr, IBM Corp, 62-76, sr adv engr, 77-80; with Discovision, 80-81. *Mem:* Sr mem Inst Elec & Electronics Engrs. *Res:* Laser and semiconductor physics. *Mailing Add:* Storage Technol Corp 2270 S 88 St Louisville CO 80028-6100

SMITH, ARTHUR CLARKE, SOLID STATE PHYSICS. *Current Pos:* from asst prof to assoc prof, 59-68, PROF ELEC ENG, MASS INST TECHNOL, 68- *Personal Data:* b Bartlesville, Okla, Sept 23, 29; m 55; c 3. *Educ:* Univ Kans, BS, 51; Harvard Univ, MA, 54, PhD(appl physics), 58. *Prof Exp:* Res fel & instr appl physics, Harvard Univ, 58-59. *Mem:* Am Asn Physics Teachers; Am Phys Soc. *Mailing Add:* 131 Worthen Rd Lexington MA 02173-7026

SMITH, ARTHUR GERALD, ELECTROCHEMISTRY, ACCELERATED CORROSION. *Current Pos:* res scientist, 58-68, sr res scientist, 68-76, PRIN RES SCIENTIST ASSOC, FORD MOTOR CO, 76- *Personal Data:* b Newton, Kans, Jan 12, 29; m 49; c 1. *Educ:* Phillips Univ, AB, 50; Iowa State Univ, MS, 53. *Prof Exp:* Chemist, Standard Oil Co, 53-58. *Mem:* Am Chem Soc. *Res:* Paint adhesion failure mechanism studies; development of novel paints and paint application techniques; corrosion studies of single and multimetal systems; development of accelerated corrosion tests. *Mailing Add:* 3404 Washington Midland MI 48642-3767

SMITH, ARTHUR HAMILTON, PHYSIOLOGY. *Current Pos:* lectr poultry husb, 50-51, asst prof, 51-55, assoc prof & assoc physiologist, Agr Exp Sta, Univ Calif, Davis, 55-62, prof poultry husb & physiologist, 62-64, prof physiol & physiologist, 64-86, EMER PROF PHYSIOL & EMER PHYSIOLOGIST, AGR EXP STA, UNIV CALIF, DAVIS, 86- *Personal Data:* b Santa Barbara, Calif, Mar 28, 16; m 39; c 2. *Educ:* Univ Calif, AB, 38, PhD(comp physiol), 48. *Prof Exp:* Asst animal husb, Univ Calif, Davis, 37-41 & 46-47, sr biochemist, 48; physiologist, Radiation Lab, Univ Calif, Berkeley, 48; NRC-AEC fel med sci, 48-50. *Concurrent Pos:* Mem Comn Gravitational Physiol, Int Union Physiol Sci, 73; secy-treas, Galileo Found, 87- *Mem:* Aerospace Med Soc; Soc Exp Biol & Med; Am Phys Soc; Biophys Soc; Undersea Med Soc; Hist Sci Soc. *Res:* Environmental physiology; gravitational physiology. *Mailing Add:* Univ Calif Davis CA 95616-8519. *Fax:* 530-752-5831

SMITH, ARTHUR JOHN STEWART, EXPERIMENTAL HIGH ENERGY PHYSICS. *Current Pos:* from instr to prof, Princeton Univ, 67-92, assoc chmn, 80-83, CHMN, DEPT PHYSICS & PROF PHYSICS, PRINCETON UNIV, 92- *Personal Data:* b Victoria, BC, June 28, 38; m 66; c 2. *Educ:* Univ BC, BA, 59, MSc, 61; Princeton Univ, PhD(physics), 66. *Prof Exp:* Volkswagen Found fel physics, Deutsches Elektronen-Synchrotron, Hamburg, WGer, 66-67. *Concurrent Pos:* Vis scientist, Brookhaven Nat Lab & Fern Lab, SSC Lab; vis scientist, Fern Lab & SSC Lab; tech bd, BABAR Collab, Stanford, Linear Accelerator Ctr. *Mem:* Fel Am Phys Soc. *Res:* Experimental high energy particle physics; electromagnetic and weak interactions. *Mailing Add:* Joseph Henry Labs Princeton Univ Princeton NJ 08544

SMITH, ARTHUR R, ECONOMIC GEOLOGY. *Current Pos:* SR RES GEOLOGIST, MINERAL EXPLOR & DEVELOP DEPT, UTAH INT INC, SAN FRANCISCO, 70- *Personal Data:* b Pittsburgh, Pa, Feb 9, 31; m 53; c 3. *Educ:* Pa State Univ, BS, 52; Univ Calif, Berkeley, MS, 58, MBA, 70. *Prof Exp:* Explor geologist, Phelps Dodge Corp, 58-63; geologist, Calif Div Mines & Geol, 63-70. *Mem:* Am Inst Mining, Metall & Petrol Eng. *Res:* Regional geology; mineral economic studies; geochemical exploration methods. *Mailing Add:* Dept Earth Sci 508 Schumacher Sci Ctr Bldg 2 West Chester Univ West Chester PA 19383-0002

SMITH, B(LANCHARD) D(RAKE), JR, ELECTRICAL ENGINEERING. *Current Pos:* CONSULT & CHIEF SCIENTIST, ST RES, 89- *Personal Data:* b New Orleans, La, Aug 22, 25; m 45; c 5. *Educ:* Ga Inst Technol, BS, 45; Mass Inst Technol, MS, 48. *Honors & Awards:* Thompson Award, Inst Elec & Electronic Engrs, 55. *Prof Exp:* Asst elec eng, Mass Inst Technol, 46-48; from engr to mgr transp systs ctr, Melpar, Inc, Westinghouse Air Brake Co, 48-68; vpres & tech dir, Appl Systs Technol, Inc, 68-78; consult, 78-80; chief scientist, Melpar Div, E-Systs, 80-89. *Mem:* Inst Elec & Electronic Engrs; Sigma Xi. *Res:* Electronic systems. *Mailing Add:* 2509 Ryegate Lane Alexandria VA 22308-2338

SMITH, BARBARA D, CONNECTIVE TISSUE, GENE EXPRESSION. *Current Pos:* RES CHEMIST, VET ADMIN MED CTR, BOSTON, MASS, 76- *Personal Data:* b Boston, Mass, Mar 17, 43; c 3. *Educ:* Boston Univ, PhD(biochem), 70. *Prof Exp:* From asst prof to assoc prof, 76-91, prof biochem, Sch Med, Boston Univ, 91- *Concurrent Pos:* Res, prin investr, 76- *Mem:* Am Soc Cell Biol; Am Soc Biochem & Molecular Biol. *Mailing Add:* Dept Biochem Boston Univ Med Sch 80 E Concord St Boston MA 02118-2394. *Fax:* 617-638-5339

SMITH, BENNETT HOLLY, LIFE HISTORY, DENTAL ANTHROPOLOGY. *Current Pos:* ASSOC RES SCIENTIST, MUS ANTHROP, UNIV MICH, 83- *Personal Data:* b Detroit, Mich, Mar 12, 52; m 82, Philip D Gingerich. *Educ:* Univ Tex, Austin, BA, 75; Univ Mich, MA, 76, PhD(anthrop), 83. *Concurrent Pos:* Vis asst prof anthrop, Ariz State Univ, 84-85; prin investr, NSF, 84-93. *Mem:* Am Anthrop Asn; Am Asn Phys Anthropologists; Dental Anthrop Asn; Human Biol Coun; Soc Study Evolution. *Res:* Evolution of growth and aging in humans and other primates; my research asks what determines life history in living species and how the lives of extinct species might be reconstructed from the fossil record. *Mailing Add:* Mus Anthrop Rm 4009 Univ Mich Ann Arbor MI 48109-1079

SMITH, BERNARD, PHYSICS, OPERATIONS RESEARCH. *Current Pos:* RETIRED. *Personal Data:* b New York, NY, Aug 11, 27. *Educ:* City Col New York, BS, 48; Columbia Univ, AM, 51, PhD(physics), 54. *Prof Exp:* Lectr elec eng & physics, City Col New York, 48-54; mem tech staff, Bel, Tel Labs, Inc, 54-59; staff consult, Gen Tel & Electronics Labs, Inc, 59-61, mgr, 61-63, sr scientist & mgr, 63-70; chief scientist, Marcom Inc, 70-71, vpres & chief scientist, 71-84; dir telecomm, City NY Off Telecomm, 84-88. *Mem:* Asn Comput Mach; Am Phys Soc; sr mem Inst Elec & Electronics Engrs; Soc Indust & Appl Math; Inst Elec & Electronics Engrs Commun Soc; Inst Elec & Electronics Engrs Computer Soc. *Res:* Cryophysics; telecommunication systems; statistical communication theory; operations research; computer science. *Mailing Add:* 98-05 63 Rd Rego Park NY 11374

SMITH, BERTRAM BRYAN, JR, SCIENCE POLICY. *Current Pos:* Gen phys scientist, Foreign Sci Technol Ctr, 70-79, GEN PHYS SCIENTIST, OFF OF DEP CHIEF OF STAFF FOR INTELL, DEPT ARMY, 79- *Personal Data:* b Fort Jackson, SC, Sept 20, 42; m 72. *Educ:* Univ Ala, BS, 64; Purdue Univ, PhD(chem), 70. *Mem:* Am Chem Soc; Am Phys Soc; AAAS. *Res:* Liquid theory; scattering theory. *Mailing Add:* 9543 Hunt Square Ct Springfield VA 22153-1343

SMITH, BETTY F, TEXTILE CHEMISTRY. *Current Pos:* prof & head dept, Dept Textiles & Consumer Econ, 70-91, PROF DEPT MAT & NUCLEAR ENG, UNIV MD, 91- *Personal Data:* b Magnolia, Ark, June 29, 30. *Educ:* Univ Ark, BS, 51; Univ Tenn, MS, 57; Univ Minn, PhD(textile), 60, PhD(biochem), 65. *Prof Exp:* Home agent home econ, Ark Agr Exten Serv, 51-56; assoc prof textiles, Cornell Univ, 65-70, chmn, Dept Textiles & Clothing, 68-69. *Mem:* Am Chem Soc; Am Asn Textile Chemists & Colorists; fel Textile Inst. *Res:* Flammability of polyester cotton blends and flammability test methods; performance properties of textile materials; chemical finishing of textiles. *Mailing Add:* 9216 St Andrews Pl College Park MD 20742

SMITH, BILL ROSS, SOIL SCIENCE. *Current Pos:* from asst prof to assoc prof, 73-88, PROF AGRON & SOILS, CLEMSON UNIV, 88- *Personal Data:* b Stamford, Tex, Sept 22, 41. *Educ:* Tex Tech Univ, BS, 64; Univ Ariz, MS, 66; NC State Univ, PhD(soil sci), 70. *Prof Exp:* Soil scientist, Soil Conserv Serv, USDA, 63 & Wake County Health Dept, NC, 70-73. *Mem:* Am Soc Agron; Soil Sci Soc Am; Soil & Water Conserv Soc. *Res:* Soil genesis and classification; evaluation of soils for different kinds of land use; soil mineralogy. *Mailing Add:* Agron Clemson Univ Clemson SC 29632-0001

SMITH, BOB L(EE), CIVIL ENGINEERING, HIGHWAY SAFETY. *Current Pos:* From instr to prof, 47-91, EMER PROF CIVIL ENG, KANS STATE UNIV, 91- *Personal Data:* b Topeka, Kans, Jan 26, 26; m 47, Jean Ewing; c Jan & William L. *Educ:* Kans State Univ, BS, 48, MS, 53; Purdue Univ, PhD, 64. *Honors & Awards:* Edmond Friedman Prof Recognition Award, Am Soc Civil Engrs, 90. *Concurrent Pos:* Mem low volume roads, oper effects of geometrics & Geometric Design comts, Transp Res Bd, Nat Acad Sci-Nat Res Coun, geometric design comt & edu comt, Hwy Div, Am Soc Civil Engrs. *Mem:* Fel Am Soc Civil Engrs; Sigma Xi; Inst Transp Engrs. *Res:* Highway esthetics, scenic byways; economic analysis as related to transportation systems; traffic engineering; geometric design of highways; highway safety design; accident reconstruction. *Mailing Add:* 737 Midland Ave Manhattan KS 66502. *Fax:* 785-532-7717

SMITH, BRADFORD ADELBERT, ASTRONOMY. *Current Pos:* RETIRED. *Personal Data:* b Cambridge, Mass, Sept 22, 31; m 54; c 4. *Educ:* Northeastern Univ, BS, 54. *Prof Exp:* Res engr, Williamson Develop Co, 54-55; assoc astronr, Res Ctr, NMex State Univ, 57-64; dir observ, 64-69, dir, Planetary Progs, 69-74; assoc prof, Lunar & Planetary Lab & senior astron, Steward Observ, Univ Ariz, 74-88. *Mem:* Am Astron Soc; Int Astron Union. *Res:* Planetary and lunar astronomy; image aberration electromechanical optical servo systems. *Mailing Add:* 82-6012 Puuhonua Rd Captain Cook HI 96704-8226

SMITH, BRADLEY EDGERTON, ANESTHESIOLOGY. *Current Pos:* prof anesthesiol & chmn dept, 69-93, DIR STUDY CTR ANESTHETIC TOXICITY, VANDERBILT UNIV, 93- *Personal Data:* b Cedar-Vale, Kans, Jan 4, 33; m 53, Gretchen Basore; c Bradley G & Jone L. *Educ:* Tulsa Univ, BSc, 54; Okla Univ, MD, 57. *Prof Exp:* Res fel obstet anesthesiol, Columbia Univ, 60-61; instr anesthesiol, Yale Univ, 62-63; assoc prof, Univ Miami, 63-69. *Concurrent Pos:* Consult, FDA, 68-74 & 75-76, mem adv coun anesthetic & respiratory drugs, 70-72; assoc examr, Nat Bd Respiratory Ther, 69- & Am Bd Anesthesiologists, 77-; consult, Vet Admin, 69-; mem comt anesthetic toxicity, Nat Res Coun-Nat Acad Sci, 72-74; fac Sen, Vanderbilt Univ, 72-76. *Mem:* Am Col Chest Physicians; Asn Univ Anesthetists; Am Soc Anesthesiologists; hon assoc fel Am Col Obstet & Gynec; Soc Obstet Anesthesia & Perinatology (pres, 70-71); Soc Comput Critical Care, Pulmonary Med & Anesthesiol; Teratology Soc. *Res:* Obstetric anesthesia; anesthetic toxicity; developmental pharmacology and teratology; perinatal physiology; resuscitation of the newborn. *Mailing Add:* Dept Anesthesiol Vanderbilt Univ Sch Med T-4216 MCN Nashville TN 37232-2125. *Fax:* 615-343-2041

SMITH, BRADLEY RICHARD, scientific computer-aided visualization, for more information see previous edition

SMITH, BRIAN RICHARD, HEMATOLOGY, BONE MARROW TRANSPLANTATION. *Current Pos:* assoc prof, 89-93, assoc prof med tenure, 93-96, PROF, MED SCH, YALE UNIV, 96- *Personal Data:* b Glen Cove, NY, May 7, 52; m; Keiren Donovan. *Educ:* Princeton Univ, AB, 72; Harvard Univ, MD, 76. *Hon Degrees:* MS, Yale Univ, 87. *Prof Exp:* Asst prof med, Med Sch, Harvard Univ, 85-89. *Concurrent Pos:* Stohlman scholar, Leukemia Soc Am; scholar, Nat Blood Found. *Mem:* Am Asn Immunol; Am Soc Hemat; fel Am Col Physicians; Sigma Xi; Am Soc Cell Biol. *Res:* Platelet-leukocyte structural and functional interactions; immunology of bone marrow transplantation. *Mailing Add:* Yale Med Sch 333 Cedar St PO Box 208035 New Haven CT 06520-8035

SMITH, BRIAN THOMAS, NUMERICAL ANALYSIS, NUMERICAL SOFTWARE. *Current Pos:* PROF, DEPT COMPUT SCI, FARRIS ENG CTR, UNIV NMEX, 89- *Personal Data:* b Toronto, Ont, Apr 20, 42; m 65; c 2. *Educ:* Univ Toronto, BS, 65, MS, 67, PhD(comput sci), 69. *Prof Exp:* Res asst appl math, Swiss Fed Inst Technol, 69; asst scientist comput sci, Argonne Nat Lab, 70-75, scientist, 76-89. *Concurrent Pos:* Mem numerical software work group 2.5, Int Fedn Info Processing; mem, Fortran Standards Comt, Am Nat Standards Inst; consult, Numerical Algorithms Group, Inc; mem, Lang Working Group, Dept Energy. *Mem:* Soc Indust & Appl Math; Asn Comput Mach. *Res:* Numerical software; computational aspects related to study of nonassociative algebras; automated reasoning; proving claims about programs; Fortran standardization. *Mailing Add:* Dept Comput Sci Farris Eng Ctr Univ NMex Albuquerque NM 87131-0001

SMITH, BRUCE BARTON, PLANT MORPHOLOGY. *Current Pos:* asst prof, 71-74, assoc prof, 74-81, PROF BIOL, YORK COL PA, 81-, CHMN DEPT, 81- *Personal Data:* b Poplar Bluff, Mo, Sept 28, 41; m 63; c 2. *Educ:* Ark State Univ, BS, 63; Univ Miss, MS, 66; Univ SC, PhD(biol), 71. *Prof Exp:* Instr biol, Parsons Col, 66-67; asst prof, Atlantic Christian Col, 67-68; instr, Univ SC, 69-71. *Concurrent Pos:* Sigma Xi res grant-in-aid, York Col Pa, 71- *Mem:* Bot Soc Am; Am Inst Biol Sci. *Res:* Angiosperm embryology and its use in phylogenetic studies of flowering plants. *Mailing Add:* Dept Biol York Col Pa PO Box 15199 York PA 17405-7199

SMITH, BRUCE H, MEDICINE, PATHOLOGY. *Current Pos:* PROF PATH, SCH MED, GEORGE WASHINGTON UNIV, 71- *Personal Data:* b New York, NY, Feb 16, 19; m 43; c 4. *Educ:* Syracuse Univ, AB, 40, MD, 43. *Honors & Awards:* Sir Henry Wellcome Award, 67; Hiroshima Medal, Hiroshima Univ, Japan, 67. *Prof Exp:* Med Corps, USN, 43-71, resident path, US Naval Hosp, Brooklyn, NY, 45-47; resident, Long Island Col Hosp, 47-49, dir labs, US Naval Hosp, Mare Island, Calif, 50-55, Philadelphia, 55-63, dep dir, Armed Forces Inst Path, 63-67, dir, 67-71. *Concurrent Pos:* Fel path, Harvard Univ, 49-50; vis prof, Sch Med, Temple Univ, 57-64; clin prof, Georgetown Univ, 67-71, George Washington Univ, 71-97. *Mem:* Fel Am Col Physicians; Int Acad Path; AAAS; Am Asn Pathologists; Col Am Pathol. *Res:* Pathology; urologic pathology; forensic pathology; gastro enterologic pathology. *Mailing Add:* 10531 Sweetbriar Pkwy Silver Spring MD 20903

SMITH, BRUCE M, BIOMEDICAL ENGINEERING, ELECTRICAL ENGINEERING. *Current Pos:* Biomed engr, 73-90, CHIEF, RES SERV BR, DIV INTRAMURAL RES PROGS, NIMH, 90- *Personal Data:* b Washinton, DC, Sept 22, 43. *Educ:* Va Polytech Inst & State Univ, BSEE, 65, MSEE, 67; Univ Va, PhD(biomed eng), 73. *Mem:* Inst Elec & Electronics Engrs. *Mailing Add:* NIMH 36 Convent Dr MS 4060 Bethesda MD 20892

SMITH, BRUCE NEPHI, PLANT PHYSIOLOGY. *Current Pos:* assoc prof, bot, Brigham Young Univ, 74-79, chmn bot & range sci, 76-79, dean, Col Biol & Agr, 82-88, PROF BOT, BRIGHAM YOUNG UNIV, 79- *Personal Data:* b Logan, Utah, Apr 3, 34; m 59, Ruth O Aamodt; c Rebecca, Trudy, Alan, Marilee, Edward & Samuel. *Educ:* Univ Utah, BS, 59, MS, 62; Univ Wash, PhD(bot), 64. *Prof Exp:* Asst bot, Univ Utah, 58-60; asst, Univ Wash, 60-62, actg instr, 62-63, asst, 63-64; res fel plant physiol, Univ Calif, Los Angeles, 64-65; res fel geochem, Calif Inst Technol, 65-68; asst prof bot, Univ Tex, Austin, 68-74. *Concurrent Pos:* Guest prof, Tech Univ Munich, 89; orgn, Econ Coop & Develop fel, 89; Indo-Am fel, Coun Int Exchange Scholars, India, 92. *Mem:* Ecol Soc Am; Am Soc Plant Physiol; Bot Soc Am; Japanese Soc Plant Physiologists; Am Asn Univ Prof; Sigma Xi. *Res:* Carbon, hydrogen, oxygen and nitrogen ratios followed by fractionation of natural abundance ratios of the stable isotopes; microcolorimitry; trace metals in plants; plant metabolism and growth. *Mailing Add:* Dept Bot & Range Sci Brigham Young Univ Provo UT 84602. *Fax:* 801-378-7499; *E-Mail:* bruce_smith@byu.edu

SMITH, BRYCE EVERTON, ECOLOGY. *Current Pos:* chmn dept biol sci, 70-76, assoc prof biol, 70-76, PROF BIOL, LAKE SUPERIOR STATE UNIV, 76- *Personal Data:* b Lotumbe, Zaire, Oct 21, 30; US citizen; m 52; c 3. *Educ:* Univ Mich, BSF, 52, AM, 57; Univ Wis, PhD(bot), 65. *Prof Exp:* Forester, Bowaters Southern Paper Corp, 54-55; teacher, High Schs, 57-60; asst prof biol sci, Western Ill Univ, 65-67; assoc prof biol, Eastern Conn State Col, 67-70. *Mem:* AAAS; Am Inst Biol Sci; Ecol Soc Am; Sigma Xi. *Res:* Interrelationships of higher plants in forest communities. *Mailing Add:* 6379 Scenic Dr Sault Ste Marie MI 49783

SMITH, BUFORD DON, CHEMICAL ENGINEERING. *Current Pos:* PROF CHEM ENG & DIR THERMODYN RES LAB, WASH UNIV, 65- *Personal Data:* b Omega, Okla, Feb 18, 25; m 47; c 2. *Educ:* Okla State Univ, BS, 50, MS, 51; Univ Mich, PhD(chem eng), 54. *Prof Exp:* Chem engr, Humble Oil & Refining Co, 54-58; assoc prof chem eng, Purdue Univ, 58-65. *Concurrent Pos:* Consult, Allison Div, Gen Motors Corp, 63, Sun Oil Co, 65 & Monsanto Co & Am Oil Co, 66. *Mem:* Am Inst Chem Engrs; Am Chem Soc. *Res:* Design of vapor-liquid separation processes; thermodynamics of liquid mixtures. *Mailing Add:* HC 1 Box 61 Presque Isle WI 54557-9714

SMITH, BURTON JORDAN, COMPUTER ARCHITECTURE. *Current Pos:* CHMN & CHIEF SCIENTIST, TERA COMPUT CO, 88- *Personal Data:* b Chapel Hill, NC, Mar 21, 41; m 66, Dorothy Duncan; c Katherine & Julia. *Educ:* Univ NMex, BSEE, 67; Mass Inst Technol, MSEE, 68, EE, 69, ScD(elec eng), 72. *Honors & Awards:* Eckert-Mauchly Award, Inst Elec & Electronics Engrs-Asn Comput Mach, 91. *Prof Exp:* Teaching asst elec eng, Mass Inst Technol, 67-70, instr, 70-72; from asst prof to assoc prof elec eng, Univ Colo, Denver, 72-79; vpres, Res & Develop, Denelcor, 79-85; fel, Supercomput Res Ctr, 85-88. *Concurrent Pos:* Consult, Hendrix Electronics, Inc, 67-72 & Denelcor, Inc, 74-79; dir, Sci Electronics Corp, 68-70. *Mem:* Fel Inst Elec & Electronics Engrs; fel Asn Comput Mach. *Res:* Architecture of general-purpose parallel computers. *Mailing Add:* Tera Comput Co 2815 Eastlake Ave E Seattle WA 98102

SMITH, BYRON COLMAN, COMPARATIVE ANATOMY. *Current Pos:* RETIRED. *Personal Data:* b Crawfordsville, Ind, Apr 14, 24; m 71. *Educ:* Ind State Univ, BS, 48; DePauw Univ, MA, 52; Univ Ga, PhD(zool), 58. *Prof Exp:* Asst prof zool, Univ SC, 58-64; assoc prof biol, Univ Southern Miss, 64-71, prof, 71-93. *Mem:* AAAS. *Res:* Acarology; ecology of the desert spider mite; Tetranychus desertorium banks on cotton; micro-fauna population of soils in the Sand Hill region of South Carolina and areas of the Piedmont and Coastal Plains. *Mailing Add:* 107 Mandalay Dr Hattiesburg MS 39402

SMITH, C O, CIVIL ENGINEERING, HYDRAULIC ENGINEERING. *Current Pos:* CONSULT HYDRAULIC ENGR & PROF CIVIL ENG, UNIV SASK. *Honors & Awards:* T C Keefer Medal, Can Soc Civil Eng, 91. *Mem:* Can Soc Eng. *Res:* Contributed to over 70 professional journals. *Mailing Add:* Dept Civil Eng Univ Sask Saskatoon SK S7N 5A9 Can

SMITH, C(HARLES) WILLIAM, ENGINEERING MECHANICS. *Current Pos:* From instr to prof, 47-81, alumni distinguished prof, 81-92, EMER PROF ENG SCI & MECH, VA POLYTECH INST & STATE UNIV, 92- *Personal Data:* b Va, Jan 1, 26; m 50, Doris Burton; c David & Terry. *Educ:* VaPolytech Inst, BS, 46, MS, 49. *Honors & Awards:* M M Frocht Award, Soc Exp Stress Analysis, 83; Except Sci Achievement Award, NASA, 86; W M Murray Medal, Sco Exp Mech, 93. *Concurrent Pos:* Instr, Exten, Univ Va, 57-58; lectr grad eng training progs, Western Elec Co & Gen Elec Co, 63-64; consult, Brunswick Corp, 65, Masonite Corp, 70, Polysci Corp, 71, US Army Missile Command, 71-72 & Kollmorgen Corp, 72-74; proj dir, NASA grants, 71-75; prin investr, NSF, 73-86, proj dir, 73-; proj dir, Delft Univ Technol, 75-76, Flight Dynamics Lab, US Air Force, 75-77, 86- & Oak Ridge Nat Lab, 75- 78, Phillips Lab, 83-; ed, Fracture Mech, 78; bd ed, Theoret & Appl Fracture Mechs, 82-; guest ed, J Optics & Lasers, 89-90. *Mem:* Int Asn Struct Mech in Reactor Technol; fel Soc Exp Stress Anal; Am Soc Testing & Mat; Am Soc Mech Engrs; Soc Eng Sci; fel Am Acad Mech. *Res:* Theoretical and experimental continuum solid mechanics, especially fracture mechanics and experimental stress analysis. *Mailing Add:* 107 College St Christiansburg VA 24073. *Fax:* 540-231-4574

SMITH, CALVIN ALBERT, BOTANY. *Current Pos:* From asst prof to assoc prof, 63-75, PROF BIOL, BALDWIN-WALLACE COL, 75- *Personal Data:* b Troy, NH, Mar 11, 35; m 57; c 2. *Educ:* Wheaton Col, Ill, BS, 57; Miami Univ, MA, 60; Rutgers Univ, PhD(bot), 63. *Mem:* Bot Soc Am; Am Inst Biol Sci. *Res:* Shoot apices in the family Moraceae. *Mailing Add:* Dept Biol Baldwin-Wallace Col 275 Eastland Rd Berea OH 44017-2005

SMITH, CAREY DANIEL, UNDERSEA WARFARE TECHNOLOGY. *Current Pos:* CONSULT, UNDERSEA WARFARE TECHNOL MGT, 87- *Personal Data:* b Kenedy, Tex, July 10, 32; m 54, Fan B Walker; c Daniel C, Bryan O, Ernest P & Sara E. *Educ:* Univ Tex, Austin, BA & BS, 59. *Honors & Awards:* Legion of Hon, Pres of France, 81. *Prof Exp:* Res physicist, Appl Res Labs, Univ Tex, Austin, 59-64; supvry engr, Sonar Signal Processing Sect Head, Bur Ships, Dept Navy, 64-66, supvry physicist & tech dir, Sonar Technol Br, Naval Ships Systs Command, 66-69, supvry physicist & dir, 69-74, supvry physicist & dir, Sonar Technol Off, Naval Sea Systs Command, 74-79 & Undersea Warfare Tech Off, 79-87. *Concurrent Pos:* Sonar foreign liaison officer, Naval Ship-Sea Systs Command, 66-79; ASW foreign liaison officer, Naval Sea Systs Command, 79-87, dir, Combat Systs Technol Off, 79-81; sr navy tech adv, Undersea Warfare Systs Div, Am Defense Preparedness Asn, 80-87; chmn, Sonar Panel, Tech Coop Prog, Dept Defense, 83-87. *Mem:* Fel Acoust Soc Am. *Res:* Design, field test three color display that significantly increased the dynamic range of high resolution sonars; instigate ocean environmental acoustics; measurements, modeling and low self-noise towed hydrophone arrays. *Mailing Add:* 1638 Dineen Dr McLean VA 22101. *Fax:* 703-356-3065

SMITH, CARL CLINTON, DRUG METABOLISM, PRIMATES AS ANIMAL MODELS. *Current Pos:* EMER PROF ENVIRON HEALTH, COL MED, UNIV CINCINNATI, 51- *Personal Data:* b Lima, Ohio, July 12, 14; c 3. *Educ:* DePauw Univ, AB, 36; Univ Cincinnati, MS, 37, PhD(biochem), 40. *Concurrent Pos:* Consult, toxicol. *Mem:* Soc Toxicol; Am Soc Pharmacol Exp Therapeut; Am Chem Soc; Am Col Toxicol; fel AAAS. *Res:* Toxicology; drug metabolism. *Mailing Add:* 2707 Eden Ave Cincinnati OH 45219-2201

SMITH, CARL HOFLAND, MAGNETIC MATERIALS, AMORPHOUS ALLOYS. *Current Pos:* DIR, SENSOR RES, NONVOLATILE ELECTRONICS INC, 94- *Personal Data:* b Minneapolis, Minn, June 6, 42; m 66, Margaret Heinsohn; c Benjamin & Katrina. *Educ:* Hamilton Col, AB, 64; Univ Minn, MA, 69 & PhD(physics), 71. *Prof Exp:* Vis asst prof physics, Macalester Col, St Paul, Minn, 69-71; entrepreneur, Portstar Industs, Nyack, NY, 71-72; chief scientist, Auto Res Corp, subsid of Bijur Lubricating Co, Oakland, NJ, 72-79; sr develop assoc, Metglas Prods, Allied-Signal Res & Technol, Morristown, NJ, 79-83, sr res assoc, Corp Res, 83-85, supvr magnetic alloys res, 85-94. *Concurrent Pos:* Adj prof, Ramapo Col NJ, 94- *Mem:* Sigma Xi; Am Phys Soc; sr mem Inst Elec & Electronics Engrs. *Res:* Measurement and study of magnetic properties of rapidly quenched ferromagnetic amorphous alloys and their application to high-frequency and pulse-power systems. *Mailing Add:* Nonvolatile Electronics Inc Eden Prairie MN 55344. *Fax:* 973-455-3008; *E-Mail:* csmith@research.allied.com

SMITH, CARL HUGH, PERINATAL RESEARCH, CLINICAL CHEMISTRY. *Current Pos:* From instr to asst prof path, 65-72, from asst prof to assoc prof pediat & path, 72-82, PROF PEDIAT & PATH, WASH UNIV SCH MED, 82-, DIR CLIN LABS, 88- *Personal Data:* b New York, NY, Nov 18, 34; m 69; c 2. *Educ:* Swarthmore Col, BA, 55; Yale Univ, MD, 59. *Honors & Awards:* Borden Res Award, 59. *Concurrent Pos:* Mem, Human Embryol & Develop Study Sect, NIH, 77-79. *Mem:* Perinatal Res Soc; Soc Pediat Res; Am Physiol Soc; Soc Gynecol Invest; Am Asn Clin Chemists. *Res:* Transfer of amino acids, calcium and glucose by placenta, structure and function of its plasma membranes. *Mailing Add:* Dept Pediat Wash Univ Sch Med 400 S Kings Hwy St Louis MO 63110-1014. *Fax:* 314-367-3765

SMITH, CARL WALTER, PHYSICS. *Current Pos:* RETIRED. *Personal Data:* b Salem, Mass, Dec 15, 37; m 61. *Educ:* Earlham Col, BA, 60; Brown Univ, ScM, 63, PhD(physics), 66. *Prof Exp:* Physicist, Sandia Labs, 76- 96. *Mem:* Am Geophys Union. *Res:* Mechanical wave propagation. *Mailing Add:* 3304 Calle De Daniel NW Sandia Nat Labs Box 5800 Albuquerque NM 87104

SMITH, CARL WALTER, JR, nuclear medicine, endocrinology, for more information see previous edition

SMITH, CAROLYN JEAN, CHEMISTRY. *Current Pos:* assoc prof chem, 83-90, PROF CHEM & PHYSICS, DEL CO COMMUNITY COL, 91- *Personal Data:* b Fitzgerald, Ga; m 75, James F Weiher. *Educ:* Mercer Univ, AB, 59; Emory Univ, PhD(org chem), 62. *Prof Exp:* Teaching asst chem, Emory Univ, 59-60; res chemist, E I du Pont de Nemours & Co, Inc, 62-71; asst prof, Lincoln Univ, 72-73; instr chem, Del Tech & Community Col, 73-75; lectr, Wilmington Col, 75-76; assoc prof, Cheyney State Col, 76-82. *Concurrent Pos:* Instr, Oxford Col, Emory Univ, 62; vis assoc prof, Lincoln Univ, 77; contrib ed, World Bk Encycl, 83- *Mem:* Am Chem Soc; Am Asn Univ Professors. *Mailing Add:* Del Cou Community Col 901 S Media Line Rd Media PA 19063-1094

SMITH, CARROLL N, medical entomology; deceased, see previous edition for last biography

SMITH, CARROLL WARD, BIOCHEMISTRY, ENVIRONMENTAL HEALTH. *Current Pos:* asst prof chem, Harding Univ, 68-74, res assoc physiol exercise, 68-80, assoc prof, 74-81, PROF CHEM, HARDING UNIV, 81- *Personal Data:* b Abilene, Tex, Dec 24, 27; m 55, Lorene Rose; c Walter R, John S, Charles D & Rosemary R. *Educ:* Univ Okla, BS, 58, MS, 59, PhD(environ health), 68. *Prof Exp:* Res chemist, Samuel Roberts Noble Found, Okla, 59-64; res biochemist, Civil Aeromed Res Inst, Fed Aviation Agency, Oklahoma City, 64-65. *Mem:* Am Chem Soc; Nat Speleol Soc. *Mailing Add:* Dept Phys Sci Harding Univ Box 682 900 E Center Searcy AR 72149-0001

SMITH, CASSANDRA LYNN, GENOMICS, CHROMOSOME STRUCTURE. *Current Pos:* DEP DIR, CTR ADVAN BIOTECHNOL, BOSTON UNIV, 92-, PROF BIOMED ENG, ENG COL, PROF BIOL, COL ARTS & SCI & PROF PHARMACOL & EXP THERAPEUT, COL MED. *Personal Data:* b New York, NY, May 25, 47. *Educ:* WVa Univ, BA, 67, MS, 70; Tex A&M Univ, PhD(genetics), 74. *Prof Exp:* Fel, Dept Genetics, Pub Health Res Inst of City of NY, Inc, 74-78; res assoc, Chem Dept, Columbia Univ, 78-81, assoc res scientist, Dept Genetics & Develop, 81-87, asst prof, Dept Microbiol & Dept Psychiat, 87-89; sr scientist, Human Genome Ctr, Lawrence Berkeley Lab, 89-91, sr scientist, Div Chem Biodynamics, 90-92; assoc prof in residence, Dept Molecular & Cell Biol, Univ Calif, Berkeley, 88-92. *Concurrent Pos:* Consult, Pharmacia-Lkb, Sweden, 84-89, FMC Corp, 86-89, Promega, 90 & Bolhringer-Mannheim Gmbh Ger, 90-; managing ed, Int J Human Genome, 89-; exec ed, Gene Anali Tech & Applications, 89- *Mem:* Am Soc Microbiol; Genetics Soc Am; Am Soc Biochem & Molecular Biol; AAAS; Int Human Genome Orgn; Harvey Soc. *Res:* Developing techniques that allow molecular characterization of whole chromosomes; structure and function of chromosomes in both prokaryotes and eukaryotes. *Mailing Add:* 36 Cummington St Boston MA 02215. *Fax:* 617-353-8507; *E-Mail:* cls@darwin.bu.edu

SMITH, CATHERINE AGNES, OTOLOGY, ANATOMY. *Current Pos:* prof, 69-79, EMER PROF OTOLARYNGOL, ORE HEALTH SCI UNIV, 79- *Personal Data:* b St Louis, Mo, Jan 5, 14. *Educ:* Wash Univ, PhD(anat), 51. *Honors & Awards:* Award Merit, Am Otol Soc, 75; Shambaugh Prize in Otology, 77; Award Merit, Asn Res Otologists, 81. *Prof Exp:* Asst otolaryngol, Med Sch, Wash Univ, 48-54, res assoc clin otolaryngol, 54-59, from res asst prof to res prof otolaryngol, 58-69. *Concurrent Pos:* Inst, Wash Univ, 53-54; res assoc, Cent Inst Deaf, 54-62, res collabr, 62-69. *Mem:* Am Asn Anatomists; Am Otol Soc; Am Soc Cell Biol; Col Otorhinolaryngol Amicitiae Sacrum. *Res:* Ultrastructure and histology of the ear; neurophysiology of the inner ear. *Mailing Add:* 16200 S Pac Hwy No 34 Lake Oswego OR 97034

SMITH, CECIL RANDOLPH, JR, NATURAL PRODUCTS CHEMISTRY, LIPID CHEMISTRY. *Current Pos:* RETIRED. *Personal Data:* b Denver, Colo, May 31, 24; m 54, Donna Sublette; c Stanley, David & Carolyn. *Educ:* Univ Colo, BA, 46, MS, 48; Wayne State Univ, PhD(org chem), 55. *Honors & Awards:* Alton E Bailey Award, Am Oil Chemists Soc, 84. *Prof Exp:* Asst chem, Univ Colo, 46-47; org chemist, US Bur Mines, Wyo, 47-51, Julius Hyman & Co, Colo, 51-52 & Northern Regional Res Lab, USDA, 56-62; asst prof chem, Western Mich Univ, 62-63; org chemist, Northern Regional Res Ctr, 63-85, res leader, USDA, 73-85; vis scientist, Inst Chem Natural Substances, Nat Ctr Sci Res, Gif-sur-Yvette, France, 85; asst dir, Cancer Res Inst, Ariz State Univ, 86-88; collabr, Western Cotton Res Ctr, USDA, 88-92. *Concurrent Pos:* Res fel, Nat Heart Inst, Glasgow, 55-56. *Mem:* Am Chem Soc; Am Oil Chem Soc; Sigma Xi; Am Soc Pharmacognosy. *Res:* Shale oil; alkaloids; fatty acids; natural products; medicinal chemistry; detection, isolation and characterization of biologically active natural products, especially those useful for control of cancer and insect pests. *Mailing Add:* 514 E Colgate Dr Tempe AZ 85283-1906

SMITH, CEDRIC MARTIN, ADDICTION MEDICINE, NEUROPHARMACOLOGY. *Current Pos:* chmn dept, 66-73, PROF PHARMACOL & TOXICOL, SCH MED & DENT, STATE UNIV NY, BUFFALO, 66- *Personal Data:* b Stillwater, Okla, Feb 1, 27; c 3. *Educ:* Okla State Univ, BS, 49; Univ Ill, BS, 50, MS & MD, 53. *Prof Exp:* Asst pharmacol, Col Med, Univ Ill, 55-58; intern, Philadelphia Gen Hosp, 53-54; from instr to prof pharmacol, Col Med, Univ Ill, 54-66, actg head dept, 65-66. *Concurrent Pos:* USPHS spec fel, Univ Gottingen, 61-62; staff scientist, Inst Defense Analysis, 64-65; mem, grants rev study sect pharmacol, NIH, 65-68; founding dir, NY State Res Inst Alcoholism, 70-79, sr assoc res scientist, 79-; mem med staff, Erie County Med Ctr, 76-; preceptor, Family Pract Ctr, 78-83; mem, Adv Comt Drug Abuse, NY State Dept Health & Div Substance Abuse, 79-; spec lectr, Japan Soc Neuropsychopharmacol, 85; mem, Res Rev Comt Nat Inst Drug Abuse, 85-88; vis prof, Univ Ky Col Med; cert, Am Soc

Addiction Med; mem, Adv Comt Drug Medication Information, US Pharmacopeia. *Mem:* AAAS; Am Soc Pharmacol & Exp Therapeut; Am Soc Clin Pharmacol & Therapeut; Am Soc Addiction Med; Int Brain Res Orgn; Am Col Clin Pharmacol; AMA; Col Int Neuropsychopharmacol; Sigma Xi; Res Soc Alcoholism; Asn Chemoreception Sci. *Res:* Addiction medicine; neuropharmacology of muscle sensory receptors; psychotropic drugs; non-medical drug use; alcohol and intoxication; drug-alcohol interactions; medical education. *Mailing Add:* Dept Pharmacol & Toxicol Univ NY 102 Farber Hall Buffalo NY 14214-3000. *Fax:* 716-829-2801

SMITH, CHARLES ALLEN, MOLECULAR BIOLOGY. *Current Pos:* Fel, 72-75, SR RES ASSOC BIOPHYS, STANFORD UNIV, 75- *Personal Data:* b Lexington, Ky, Aug 4, 44; m 75, Ann D Burrell; c 2. *Educ:* Mass Inst Technol, SB, 66; Calif Inst Technol, PhD(biophys), 71. *Res:* Mechanisms for replication, repair, and function of eukaryotic DNA; organization of DNA in chromosomes. *Mailing Add:* Dept Biol Stanford Univ Stanford CA 94305-5020. *Fax:* 650-725-1848; *E-Mail:* casmith@forsythe.stanford.edu

SMITH, CHARLES ALOYSIUS, ANALYTICAL CHEMISTRY. *Current Pos:* CHEMIST, MCDONNELL-DOUGLAS CORP, HUNTINGTON BEACH, CA, 80- *Personal Data:* b Minneapolis, Minn, Aug 18, 39; m 70; c 1. *Educ:* Col St Thomas, BS, 61; Kans State Univ, PhD(chem), 66. *Prof Exp:* Chemist, McDonnell-Douglas Corp, Santa Monica, 65-75; chemist, Dept Entom, Univ Calif, Riverside, 75-78; mgr qual assurance methods, McGaw Labs, Irvine, Ca, 78-80. *Mem:* Am Chem Soc. *Res:* Analytical chemical methods development and applications. *Mailing Add:* 17669 San Vicente Fountain Valley CA 92708-1699

SMITH, CHARLES BRUCE, NEUROPHARMACOLOGY, NEUROCHEMISTRY. *Current Pos:* dir neural & behav sci prog, 81-87, PROF PHARMACOL, SCH MED, UNIV MICH, 76- *Personal Data:* b Dec 23, 36. *Educ:* Harvard Univ, MD, 65, PhD(pharmacol), 66. *Mem:* Am Soc Pharmacol & Exp Therapeut; Am Col Neuropsycholpharmacol. *Res:* Neuroreceptors. *Mailing Add:* Dept Pharmacol Univ Mich Sch Med A317 Med Sci Res Bldg III Ann Arbor MI 48109-0632. *Fax:* 313-763-4450

SMITH, CHARLES E, PSYCHIATRY. *Current Pos:* RETIRED. *Personal Data:* b Omaha, Nebr, Nov 16, 17; m 41; c Timothea A (Zimmerman) & Jonathan C. *Educ:* George Washington Univ, AB, 39, MD, 41. *Prof Exp:* Intern, USPHS Hosp, Baltimore, Md, 41-42; staff psychiatrist, Vet Admin Hosp, Northport, NY, 45-49; chief med officer, Fed Correction Inst, Ky, 49-50; resident psychiatrist, USPHS Hosp, Staten Island, NY, 50-51; chief psychiat serv, Med Ctr Fed Prisoners, Mo, 51-55; asst med dir, Fed Bur Prisons, 56-62, med dir, 62-66; chief serv, West Side Div, St Elizabeth's Hosp, DC, 66-67; dir, Ment Health Serv, NC Dept Corrections, 74-82, consult psychiatrist, Dorothea Dix Hosp, Raleigh, NC, 83-86; consult psychiatrist, Pediat Neurol Clin, Univ NC Hosps, 86-96. *Concurrent Pos:* Mem, Bd Dirs, Washington DC Area Coun Alcoholism, 61-67; mem, Prof Coun, Nat Coun Crime & Delinquency, 65-70; consult, NC Dept Corrections, 67-82; from assoc prof to emer prof psychiat, Sch Med, Univ NC, Chapel Hill, 67-96. *Mem:* Fel Am Psychiat Asn; fel Am Orthopsychiat Asn. *Res:* Legal aspects of psychiatry; correctional treatment of the mentally ill offender. *Mailing Add:* 1812 S Lakeshore Dr Chapel Hill NC 27514

SMITH, CHARLES EDWARD, ELECTRICAL ENGINEERING. *Current Pos:* assoc prof, 68-76, CHMN DEPT, UNIV MISS, 75-, PROF ELEC ENG, 77- *Personal Data:* b Clayton, Ala, June 8, 34; m 60, Evelyn J; c Charles E Jr, Steven Alan & Gary Lynn. *Educ:* Auburn Univ, BEE, 59, MS, 63, PhD(elec eng), 68. *Prof Exp:* Res engr, Auburn Res Found, 59-68. *Concurrent Pos:* Actg chmn, Dept Comput & Info Sci, Univ Miss, 85-87, assoc dean grad studies, Sch Eng, 89-92. *Mem:* Inst Elec & Electronics Engrs; Am Soc Eng Educ; Sigma Xi. *Res:* Antennas; microwave circuits; communication systems; microwave measurements; computer-aided design. *Mailing Add:* Dept Elec Eng Univ Miss University MS 38677. *Fax:* 601-232-7231; *E-Mail:* eedept@olemiss.edu

SMITH, CHARLES EDWARD, JR, LIMNOLOGY, PHYCOLOGY. *Current Pos:* from asst prof to assoc prof biol, Ball State Univ, 63-71, admin asst, 67-68, assoc dir, 68-69 to dir off res, 68-83, PROF BIOL, BALL STATE UNIV, 71- *Personal Data:* b Sharpsburg, Ky, Oct 26, 27; m 49. *Educ:* Eastern Ky Univ, BS, 54; Univ Ky, MS, 56; Univ Louisville, PhD(biol), 63. *Prof Exp:* Mat testing engr, Dept Hwy, Frankfort, Ky, 49-50, off engr, 50-51; asst zool, Univ Ky, 54-56; teacher, High Sch, Ky, 56-61; res asst algal physiol, Potamological Inst, Univ Louisville, 61-63. *Mem:* AAAS; Am Soc Limnol & Oceanog; Am Phycol Soc; Int Asn Theoret & Appl Limnol. *Res:* Physiology and ecology of phytoplankton, especially members of the cyanophyta; algal physiology; tissue culture propagation of orchids; use of computers in the teaching of biology. *Mailing Add:* 1005 N Bittersweet Lane Muncie IN 47304-3254

SMITH, CHARLES EUGENE, NEUROBIOLOGY. *Current Pos:* ASSOC PROF BIOMATH, DEPT STATIST, NC STATE UNIV, 89- *Personal Data:* b Atlanta, Ga, June 22, 50; m 75; c 1. *Educ:* Mass Inst Technol, BS, 72; Univ Chicago, MS, 73, PhD(biophysics), 79. *Prof Exp:* Fel, Med Univ SC, 79-80, asst prof biomet, 80-89. *Concurrent Pos:* Co-dir, Cardiomet Scientist Training Prog, 81-82. *Mem:* Acoust Soc Am; Inst Elec & Electronics Engrs; Biomet Soc; Am Statist Asn. *Res:* Applied stochastic processes. *Mailing Add:* Dept Statist NC State Univ Box 8203 Raleigh NC 27695-8203

SMITH, CHARLES FRANCIS, JR, RADIOCHEMISTRY, ENVIRONMENTAL CHEMISTRY. *Current Pos:* Chemist, Lawrence Livermore Nat Lab, Univ Calif, 65-93, proj leader, 74-93, prog leader, 91-93, LAB ASSOC, LAWRENCE LIVERMORE NAT LAB, UNIV CALIF, 93-; PVT CONSULT, 93- *Personal Data:* b Casper, Wyo, Aug 8, 36; m 60, Ann Abbott; c Karen Ann, Sheryl Diane & Steven Charles. *Educ:* Purdue Univ, BS, 58, MS, 61; Univ Calif, Berkeley, PhD(nuclear chem), 65. *Concurrent Pos:* Staff mem anal geochem, Nat Uranium Resources Eval Prog; consult, containment underground nuclear explosions, Defense Nuclear Agency, 88-94, chmn, chem & radiochem adv team, 88-94. *Res:* Radiochemistry and chemistry of gaseous products and fission product gases; analytical geochemistry; neutron activation analyses. *Mailing Add:* Lawrence Livermore Nat Lab L-231 Box 808 Livermore CA 94551. *Fax:* 510-422-3160; *E-Mail:* csmith@llnl.gov

SMITH, CHARLES G, CANCER RESEARCH, DRUG DISCOVERY. *Current Pos:* CONSULT, 86- *Personal Data:* b Chicago, Ill,. Oct 26, 27; m 50, Angeline Formella; c C Giles Jr, Kevin B, J Paul & Tracy L. *Educ:* Ill Inst Technol, BS, 50; Purdue Univ, MS, 52; Univ Wis, PhD(biochem), 54. *Prof Exp:* Mgr biochem, Upjohn Co, 54-67; vpres res & develop & pres Squibb Inst, ER Squibb & Sons, 67-75; vpres res & develop, Revlon Health Care Group, 75-86. *Mem:* Am Chem Soc; Fedn Soc Biol Chem; Am Asn Cancer Res; AAAS. *Res:* New drug discovery and development; cancer, cardiovascular disease, anihypertensive agents, hypersensitivity diseases. *Mailing Add:* PO Box 9814 Rancho Santa Fe CA 92067-4814

SMITH, CHARLES HADDON, GEOLOGY, SCIENCE ADMINISTRATION. *Current Pos:* PRES, CHARLES H SMITH CONSULT, 82- *Personal Data:* b Dartmouth, NS, Sept 3, 26; m 49, Mary G Saint; c Charles D, Richard D, Alan M & Timothy M. *Educ:* Dalhousie Univ, BSc, 46, MSc, 48; Yale Univ, MS, 51, PhD(geol), 52. *Prof Exp:* Instr eng, Dalhousie Univ, 46-48; geologist, Cerro de Pasco Copper Corp, Peru, 49; geologist, Geol Surv Can, 51-64, chief, Petrol Sci Div, 64-67 & Crustal Geol Div, 67-68; sci adv, Sci Coun Can, 68-70; dir planning, Can Dept Energy, Mines & Resources, 70-71, asst dep minister sci & technol, 72-75, sr asst dep minister, 75-82. *Concurrent Pos:* Dep secy gen, Int Upper Mantle Comt, chmn, Can Upper Mantle Comm; Sci Adv, Can Commn for UNESCO; exec dir, Can Nat Comm for World Energy Conf; pres, Can Geosci Coun; distinguished lectr award, Soc Econ Geologists, 65; gov, Can Inst Radiation Safety, 83-86; dir, 14th World Energy Cong, Montreal, 89; hon mem, Energy Coun Can, 91; coordr, 150th Anniversary, Geol Surv Can, 92. *Mem:* Can Inst Mining & Metall (vpres); Mineral Soc Am; Soc Econ Geol (vpres, 68-70); Geol Asn Can; fel Royal Soc Can (foreign secy, 86-90). *Res:* Petrology and economic geology; study of ultrabasic rocks; history of geoscience research. *Mailing Add:* 2056 Thistle Crescent Ottawa ON K1H 5P5 Can. *Fax:* 613-733-9344

SMITH, CHARLES HOOPER, chemistry, for more information see previous edition

SMITH, CHARLES IRVEL, MEDICINAL CHEMISTRY. *Current Pos:* RETIRED. *Personal Data:* b Baltimore, Md, Aug 22, 23; m 50, Millicent L; c Millicent L (Yamin). *Educ:* Univ Md, BS, 44, PhD(pharm chem), 50. *Prof Exp:* From sr res asst to instr physiol chem, Johns Hopkins Univ, 50-52; sr res scientist, Squibb Inst Med Res, 52-60; from assoc prof to prof med chem, Col Pharm, Univ RI, 60-89, chmn dept, 75-82. *Mem:* Sigma Xi. *Res:* Drug assay; radiopharmaceuticals; drug metabolism; drug design and synthesis; medicinal chemistry on enzyme inhibitors, antispasmodics, anticonvulsants, narcotic agents, antagonists, and antimalarials. *Mailing Add:* 20 Nichols Rd Kingston RI 02881-1804

SMITH, CHARLES ISAAC, GEOLOGY. *Current Pos:* PROF GEOL, UNIV TEX, ARLINGTON, 77-, CHMN DEPT, 77- *Personal Data:* b Hearne, Tex, Feb 9, 31. *Educ:* Baylor Univ, BS, 52; La State Univ, MS, 55; Univ Mich, PhD, 66. *Prof Exp:* Geologist, Shell Develop Co, 55-65; from asst prof to assoc prof, 65-72, prof geol & mineral, Univ Mich, Ann Arbor, 72-77, chmn dept, 71-77. *Mem:* Geol Soc Am; Am Asn Petrol Geol. *Res:* Stratigraphy; sedimentation. *Mailing Add:* Elec Eng Univ Tex PO Box 19016 Arlington TX 76019-0001

SMITH, CHARLES JAMES, NEUROPSYCHOLOGY. *Current Pos:* ASSOC PROF PSYCHOL, STATE UNIV NY, BUFFALO, 61- *Personal Data:* b Buffalo, NY, Sept 29, 25. *Educ:* Univ Buffalo, BA, 48; McGill Univ, MA, 51, PhD, 54. *Prof Exp:* Instr psychol, Univ Mich, 53-61. *Concurrent Pos:* Vis res fel physiol, John Curtin Sch Med Res, Australian Nat Univ, 67-68. *Mem:* Soc Neurosci; Int Brain Res Orgn; Sigma Xi. *Res:* Brain function; psychophysiology of vision. *Mailing Add:* Dept Psychol State Univ NY Buffalo NY 14260. *Fax:* 716-645-3801

SMITH, CHARLES LEA, CHEMISTRY. *Current Pos:* RETIRED. *Personal Data:* b Alto, Tex, Mar 8, 18; m 46, Nan M Miller; c Charles M & John M. *Educ:* Stephen F Austin State Col, BA, 38. *Prof Exp:* Teacher, High Sch, 38-41; chemist, Trojan Powder Co, Pa, 42-44 & Stand Oil Co, NJ, 44-46; mat engr, Naval Air Exp Sta, Pa, 46-47; res engr, Battelle Mem Inst, 47-50, prin chemist, Battelle Develop Corp, 50-57; mgr proj develop, Southern Res Inst, 57-60; res adminr, Wyeth Labs, Inc, 60-87. *Mem:* Am Chem Soc. *Res:* Alkyd resins; lacquers; drying oils; polyhydric alcohols; preservation and protection of materials; rubber and rubber-like materials; leather. *Mailing Add:* 536 Weadley Rd Strafford PA 19087-5424

SMITH, CHARLES O(LIVER), METALLURGY, PRODUCT DESIGN. *Current Pos:* RETIRED. *Personal Data:* b Clinton, Mass, May 28, 20; m 51, Mary J Boyle; c Mary J, Charles M, John P, Susan M (Gutowski), Peter G, Robert A & Katherine M. *Educ:* Worcester Polytech Inst, BS, 41; Mass Inst Technol, MS, 47, ScD, 51. *Honors & Awards:* Machine Design Award, Am Soc Mech Engrs, 93, Triodyne Safety Award, 92. *Prof Exp:* Engr, Blake Mfg Co, 40-43; instr mech eng, Worcester Polytech Inst, 41-43; instr metall, Mass Inst Technol, 46-47, from instr mech eng to asst prof, 47-51; res engr, Mech Testing Div, Res Labs, Aluminum Co Am, 51-54; eng consult, E I du Pont de Nemours & Co, 55; lectr reactor mat, Oak Ridge Nat Lab, 55-65; prof eng, Univ Detroit, 65-76, chmn dept, 65-68; prof eng, Univ Nebr, 76-81 & Rose-Hulman Inst Technol, 81-86. *Mem:* Am Soc Metals; fel Am Soc Eng Educ; Metall Soc; fel Am Soc Mech Engrs. *Res:* Materials and their application with special reference to design; author of over 200 publications in engineering and 4 books. *Mailing Add:* 1717 Homewood Blvd Apt 156 Delray Beach FL 33445

SMITH, CHARLES R, MATHEMATICS. *Current Pos:* asst prof, 66-69, ASSOC PROF MATH, NORTHEAST LA UNIV, 69- *Personal Data:* b Campti, La, Sept 11, 36; m 59; c 2. *Educ:* Northwestern State Univ, BS, 57; Okla State Univ, MS, 64, EdD(math), 66. *Prof Exp:* Teacher, La, 59-63. *Concurrent Pos:* NSF sci faculty fel, Univ Wash, 70-71. *Mem:* Math Asn Am. *Res:* Convexity; combinatorial geometry; functional analysis. *Mailing Add:* Dept Math 1901-D Woodhaven Dr Monroe LA 71201

SMITH, CHARLES RAY, theoretical physics, for more information see previous edition

SMITH, CHARLES SYDNEY, JR, physics; deceased, see previous edition for last biography

SMITH, CHARLES WELSTEAD, PHYSIOLOGY. *Current Pos:* from assoc prof to prof, 64-88, EMER PROF PHYSIOL, COL MED, OHIO STATE UNIV, 88- *Personal Data:* b Asheville, NC, Aug 21, 27; m 50; c 4. *Educ:* Wheaton Col, BS, 48; Univ Mich, MS, 49, MS, 53, PhD(physiol), 55. *Prof Exp:* Instr physiol, Sch Med, Univ Mich, 55-56; from instr to assoc prof, NJ Col Med & Dent, 56-64. *Mem:* Am Physiol Soc. *Res:* Respiration; oxygen toxicity; blood gases; cardiac output; pulmonary blood flow; coronary blood flow. *Mailing Add:* PO Box 390 Yachats OR 97498-0390

SMITH, CHARLES WILLIAM, JR, LOW TEMPERATURE PHYSICS. *Current Pos:* From asst prof to assoc prof, 68-80, COOP ASSOC PROF ENG, UNIV MAINE, ORONO, 77-, PROF PHYSICS, 80-, DEPT CHMN, 86- *Personal Data:* b Greensburg, Pa, May 13, 40; m 64; c 2. *Educ:* Allegheny Col, BS, 62; Ohio Univ, PhD(physics), 68. *Mem:* Sigma Xi; Am Phys Soc; Am Asn Physics Teachers. *Res:* Low temperature condensed matter physics; superconductivity; liquid helium. *Mailing Add:* Dept Physics & Astron Univ Maine 5709 Bennett Hall Orono ME 04469-5709

SMITH, CHARLOTTE DAMRON, BIOCHEMISTRY. *Current Pos:* RETIRED. *Personal Data:* b Columbus, Ohio, Nov 13, 19; m 57. *Educ:* Wellesley Col, BA, 40; Rutgers Univ, MS, 42; George Washington Univ, PhD(biochem), 51. *Prof Exp:* Asst chem, Rutgers Univ, 40-42; res chemist, E I du Pont de Nemours & Co, 42-44; asst biochem, George Washington Univ, 47-51; res fel, Nat Cancer Inst, 51-54; res assoc environ med, Sch Hyg, Johns Hopkins Univ, 53-55; assoc sci info exchange, Smithsonian Inst, 55-81. *Mem:* Sigma Xi. *Res:* Metabolism of ascorbic acid in the guinea pig and of carcinogen 2-acetylamino fluorene in the rat; mode of action of chromium compounds in causing human lung cancer. *Mailing Add:* 1812 Riverside Dr Apt 22 Columbus OH 43212

SMITH, CHESTER MARTIN, JR, COMPUTER SCIENCE. *Current Pos:* Res asst comput sci, 61-62, ASST PROF COMPUT SCI, PA STATE UNIV, 63- *Personal Data:* b Randolph, Vt, Sept 8, 35; m 58; c 2. *Educ:* Univ Vt, BA, 57; Pa State Univ, MS, 59, PhD(mineral), 64. *Concurrent Pos:* Chmn, Share Inc, 67-69, mgr, 69-70, dir, 70-71, secy, 71-72; chmn, Fortran Data Base Comt, Conf Data Systs Lang, 74-79. *Mem:* Asn Comput Mach. *Res:* Programming languages; compiler construction; information retrieval; data base management and standards; historical place name data bases; micro-computers. *Mailing Add:* Dept Comput Sci Pa State Univ 215 B Comput Bldg University Park PA 16802-6103

SMITH, CHRISTINE H, FOOD & DRUG INTERACTION. *Current Pos:* PROF FOOD FOOD SCI, NUTRIT & DIETETICS, CALIF STATE UNIV, NORTHRIDGE. *Educ:* Univ Calif, MS, 69; Univ Southern Calif, PhD(pharmacol), 79. *Mem:* Am Soc Nutrit Sci; Inst Food Technologists; Am Dietetic Asn. *Mailing Add:* 9315 Wystone Ave Northridge CA 91324-2834. *Fax:* 818-886-2446; *E-Mail:* christine.smith@csun.edu

SMITH, CHRISTOPHER CARLISLE, EVOLUTIONARY ECOLOGY. *Current Pos:* assoc prof, 70-81, PROF BIOL, KANS STATE UNIV, 81- *Personal Data:* b Boston, Mass, June 18, 38; m 60, Aron Stalheim; c Heather, Andrea & Jamison. *Educ:* Univ Colo, BA, 60; Univ Wash, MA, 63, PhD(ecol), 65. *Prof Exp:* Asst prof biol, Fisk Univ, 65-67; res assoc ecol, Smithsonian Trop Res Inst, 67-68; asst prof zool, Univ Mo-Columbia, 68-70. *Mem:* AAAS; Ecol Soc Am; Soc Study Evolution; Am Soc Naturalists. *Res:* Relationship between mammalian social organization and ecology; relationship between animals and the fruiting pattern in forest trees; ecology of wind pollination. *Mailing Add:* Div Biol Ackert Hall Kans State Univ Manhattan KS 66506-4901. *Fax:* 785-532-6653; *E-Mail:* cccsmith@lter-konza.ksu.edu

SMITH, CLAIBOURNE DAVIS, ORGANIC CHEMISTRY. *Current Pos:* res chemist, Cent Res Dept, 64-71, tech prog mgr, Fabrics & Finishes Dept, 71-73, sales mgr, 73-74, TECH MGR, INDUST PROD DIV, FABRIC & FINISHES DEPT, E I DU PONT DE NEMOURS & CO, INC, 74- *Personal Data:* b Memphis, Tenn, Jan 6, 38; m 59; c 2. *Educ:* Univ Denver, BS, 59, MS, 61; Univ Ore, PhD(org chem), 64. *Prof Exp:* Res asst org chem, Denver Res Inst, Univ Denver, 59-61. *Mem:* Am Chem Soc. *Res:* Organic synthesis of polynitrafluoro aromatics; polymeric binders and thermal stable organic polymers; non-benzoid aromatic hydrocarbons and strained small ring compounds. *Mailing Add:* 901 Barnstable Ct RD 2 Hockessin DE 19707-9611

SMITH, CLAIRE LEROY, MICROBIOLOGY. *Current Pos:* RETIRED. *Personal Data:* b Atlantic, Iowa, May 1, 23; m 53; c 4. *Educ:* Univ Omaha, BS, 53; Univ Iowa, MS, 55. *Prof Exp:* Bacteriologist, Grain Processing Corp, 55-88. *Mem:* Soc Indust Microbiol; Am Soc Microbiol. *Res:* Industrial fermentations; brewing; vitamins; amino acids; antibiotics; enzymes. *Mailing Add:* 115 Lord Ave Muscatine IA 52761

SMITH, CLARENCE LAVETT, ZOOLOGY, ICHTHYOLOGY. *Current Pos:* chmn, 75-82, cur, 62-93, EMER CUR, DEPT ICHTHYOL, AM MUS NATURAL HIST, 93- *Personal Data:* b Hamburg, NY, Dec 19, 27; m 54, Marjorie Maple; c Robert L & Laura A (Bales). *Educ:* Cornell Univ, BS, 49; Tulane Univ, MS, 51; Univ Mich, PhD, 59. *Prof Exp:* Assoc prof, Col Guam, 60-61, Univ Hawaii, 61-62. *Concurrent Pos:* Vis prof, Univ Okla, 69, Ohio State Univ, 59, 63 & 71 & Univ Mich, 76, 78 & 80; scientist, Aquanaut Proj, Tektite II, 70; adj prof, City Col New York, 70- & Rutgers Univ, 82- *Mem:* Ecol Soc Am; Am Soc Ichthyol & Herpet; Am Fisheries Soc; Am Soc Limnol & Oceanog. *Res:* Ichthyology; taxonomy, ecology, morphology and distribution of recent fishes; ecology of coral reef fishes and their larvae; freshwater fishes of New York State; ecology and evolution of fishes. *Mailing Add:* Am Mus Natural Hist Central Park W at 79th New York NY 10024

SMITH, CLAY TAYLOR, GEOLOGY. *Current Pos:* asst prof eng, NMex Inst Mining & Technol, 47, from asst prof to assoc prof geol, 47-56, prof, 56-87, head dept, 52-66, dean student & admis, 67-68, EMER PROF GEOL, NMEX INST MINING & TECHNOL, 87- *Personal Data:* b Omaha, Nebr, June 30, 17; m 40, Sarah G Austin; c Dean A & Stanley D. *Educ:* Calif Inst Technol, BS, 38, MS, 40, PhD(geo), 43. *Prof Exp:* Recorder, US Geol Surv, 38, 39, jr geologist, 40-42; geol field engr, Consol Mining & Smelting Co Can, 43; asst geologist, Union Mines Develop Corp, NY, 43-46; field geologist, US Vanadium Corp, 46-47. *Concurrent Pos:* Consult raw mat resource eval, 50-; expert witness court cases involving raw mat resources, 71-; dir alumni rels & ann giving, Nmex Inst Mining & Technol, 83-87. *Mem:* Fel AAAS; fel Soc Econ Geol; fel Geol Soc Am; Nat Asn Geol Teachers; Am Inst Prof Geologists; Sigma Xi. *Res:* Secondary earth science education; raw material resources of New Mexico; low angle faulting along the Rio Grande rift; geology of chromite deposits; origin of sedimentary type uranium ores; geology of ferroalloy elements. *Mailing Add:* 1205 Vista Dr NW Socorro NM 87801. *Fax:* 505-835-6436

SMITH, CLIFFORD JAMES, ANIMAL PHYSIOLOGY. *Current Pos:* from asst prof to prof, 65-93, chmn dept, 70-75, 91-93, EMER PROF BIOL, UNIV TOLEDO, 93- *Personal Data:* b Brooklyn, NY, Oct 30, 38; m 59; c 4. *Educ:* Cornell Univ, BS, 60; Univ Md, PhD(physiol, biochem), 64. *Prof Exp:* Res asst physiol, Univ Md, 60-64; NIH fel anat, Univ Vt, 64-65. *Concurrent Pos:* HRF consult, 90- *Mem:* Sigma Xi. *Res:* Special computer programs; research data control. *Mailing Add:* Dept Biol Univ Toledo Col Arts & Sci 2801 Bancroft Toledo OH 43606. *E-Mail:* csmith@uoft02.utoledo.edu

SMITH, CLOYD VIRGIL, JR, SOLID MECHANICS. *Current Pos:* ASSOC PROF AEROSPACE ENG, GA INST TECHNOL, 64- *Personal Data:* b Seminole, Okla, Dec 2, 36; m 60; c 3. *Educ:* Ga Inst Technol, BCE, 58; Stanford Univ, MSCE, 59; Mass Inst Technol, ScD(civil eng), 62. *Prof Exp:* Res engr, Jet Propulsion Lab, Calif Inst Technol, 63-64. *Mem:* Am Inst Aeronaut & Astronaut. *Res:* Elastic stability; matrix methods of structural analysis; nonlinear elasticity; structural dynamics. *Mailing Add:* 2949 Green Oaks Circle NE Atlanta GA 30345

SMITH, CLYDE F, ENTOMOLOGY. *Current Pos:* from asst entomologist to res prof entom, 39-50, head dept, 50-64, prof, 64-78, EMER PROF ENTOM, NC STATE UNIV, 78- *Personal Data:* b Riverdale, Idaho, Aug 10, 13; m 36, Crystle Keller; c Clara B (Thorup), Carolynn (Sanda) & Clyde L. *Educ:* Utah State Agr Col, BS, 35, MS, 37; Ohio State Univ, PhD(entom), 39. *Prof Exp:* Asst entom, Utah State Agr Col, 34-36 & 37; asst, Ohio State Univ, 36-38, asst, Exten, 38 & 39. *Concurrent Pos:* chmn, NC Struct Pest Control Comn, 55-67. *Mem:* AAAS; Entom Soc Am; Soc Syst Zool. *Res:* Biology; entomology, ecology and control of fruit insects; taxonomy of Aphididae (Homoptera) and Aphidiinae (Hymenoptera). *Mailing Add:* 2716 Rosedale Ave Raleigh NC 27607-7112

SMITH, CLYDE KONRAD, VETERINARY MICROBIOLOGY. *Current Pos:* RETIRED. *Personal Data:* b Sturgeon Bay, Wis, Dec 9, 25; m 47, Mary E Canfield; c Owen S, Kevin K, Todd B & Barth J. *Educ:* Mich State Univ, BS, 47, DVM, 51, MS, 53; Univ Notre Dame, PhD, 66; Am Col Vet Microbiologists, dipl. *Prof Exp:* Instr bact, Mich State Univ, 51, asst prof, 56-66; from assoc prof to prof vet sci, Ohio Agr Res & Develop Ctr, 66-86. *Mem:* AAAS; Am Soc Microbiol; Am Vet Med Asn; Am Asn Bovine Practr; Conf Res Workers Animal Dis. *Res:* Ruminant nutrition and physiology and germfree ruminants; respiratory and enteric diseases of sheep, feeder calves and dairy calves. *Mailing Add:* 3743 Bayshore Dr Sturgeon Bay WI 54235

SMITH, COLIN MCPHERSON, PSYCHIATRY, GERIATRIC MEDICINE. *Current Pos:* CLIN PROF PSYCHIAT, UNIV SASK, 71-; PVT PRACT PSYCHIAT, 87- *Personal Data:* b Edinburgh, Scotland, Mar 14, 27; Can citizen; m 62, Eva M Stephens; c Joy, Colin J, John G & Gillian. *Educ:* Univ Glasgow, MB, ChB, 49, MD, 59; DPM & RCP(I), 53; FRCP(C), 56; Univ Sask, MD, 62; FRCPsychiat, 72. *Honors & Awards:* Ment Health Res Award, Can Ment Health Asn, 62. *Prof Exp:* Res asst psychol, Univ London, 58-59. *Concurrent Pos:* Examr psychiat, Royal Col Physicians & Surgeons Can, 65-78, consult, 87-; mem, Alcohol Comn Sask, 68-80; psychiat, Regina Gen Hosp, 74-, Wascana Hosp, 77-, Plains Health Ctr, 78- & Pasqua Hosp, 78-; consult, Royal Univ Hosp, 75- & Staff Plains Health Ctr, 81-; mem, Lt Gov's Rev Bd, Sask, 79- *Mem:* Can Psychiat Asn (pres, 74-75); fel Am Geriat Soc; fel Am Psychiat Asn; Can Asn Geront (treas, 83-87); fel Am Psychiat Asn. *Res:* Geriatric psychiatry; social psychiatry, alcoholism; gerontology; research design; author over 100 scientific articles and books. *Mailing Add:* 4437 Castle Rd Regina SK S4S 4W4 Can. *Fax:* 306-586-8926; *E-Mail:* dr.colin.smith@sk.sympatico.ca

SMITH, COLLEEN MARY, BIOCHEMISTRY. *Current Pos:* Instr, 72-74, ASST PROF BIOCHEM, SCH MED, TEMPLE UNIV, 74- *Personal Data:* b Minneapolis, Minn, Oct 4, 43. *Educ:* Univ Minn, BA, 63; Univ Utah, PhD(biochem), 69. *Concurrent Pos:* NIH fel, Johnson Res Found, Univ Pa, 70-72. *Mem:* AAAS; Am Chem Soc; Biophys Soc; Fedn Am Soc Exp Biol. *Res:* Metabolic regulation; co-factor biosynthesis; enzymology. *Mailing Add:* Dept Biochem Sch Med Temple Univ 3420 N Broad St Philadelphia PA 19140-5104

SMITH, CONSTANCE META, AGRICULTURAL FUNGICIDES. *Current Pos:* RES BIOLOGIST, E I DU PONT DE NEMOURS, 79- *Personal Data:* b Kingston NY, Dec 31, 49. *Educ:* Vassar Col, BA, 71; Northwestern Univ, MS, 73; Cornell Univ, PhD(plant path), 79. *Concurrent Pos:* Mem, Fungicide Resistance Action Comt. *Mem:* Am Phytopath Soc. *Res:* Discovery and development of agricultural fungicides. *Mailing Add:* 1004 N Broom St Wilmington DE 19806

SMITH, CORNELIA MARSCHALL, morphology, for more information see previous edition

SMITH, CRAIG LA SALLE, ORGANIC CHEMISTRY, MARINE SCIENCE. *Current Pos:* ASSOC MARINE SCIENTIST, VA INST MARINE SCI, 70-; ASST PROF MARINE SCI, COL WILLIAM & MARY, 70-; ASST PROF MARINE SCI, UNIV VA, 70- *Personal Data:* b Miami Beach, Fla, Mar 29, 43; m 67. *Educ:* Johns Hopkins Univ, BA, 64; Univ Fla, PhD(chem), 68. *Prof Exp:* Fel, Ga Inst Technol, 67-70. *Mem:* Am Chem Soc. *Res:* Heterocyclic organic chemistry; carbanion chemistry; mass spectroscopy; oil pollution; organic geochemistry. *Mailing Add:* HC One Gloucester Point VA 23062

SMITH, CURTIS ALAN, PHYSIOLOGY. *Current Pos:* FEL PHYSIOL, DEPT PREV MED, UNIV WIS-MADISON, 78- *Personal Data:* b Long Beach, Calif, Sept 8, 48. *Educ:* Calif State Col, Fullerton, BA, 70; Univ Calif, San Francisco, PhD(physiol), 78. *Mem:* Assoc Am Physiol Soc. *Res:* Control of breathing. *Mailing Add:* Dept Prev Med Univ Wis 504 N Walnut St Madison WI 53705-2368. *Fax:* 608-263-2820

SMITH, CURTIS GRIFFIN, PHYSIOLOGY. *Current Pos:* from instr to assoc prof physiol, 55-69, PROF PHYSIOL, MT HOLYOKE COL, 69- *Personal Data:* b Milwaukee, Wis, Nov 14, 23; m 47; c 3. *Educ:* Univ Chicago, AB, 47, PhD, 54. *Prof Exp:* Instr biophys, Sch Med, Univ Calif, Los Angeles, 54-55. *Concurrent Pos:* Vis prof, Univ EAnglia, 69-70. *Mem:* Am Soc Biol Chem; Am Chem Soc; Brit Soc Gen Microbiol; Sigma Xi; Soc Neurosci. *Res:* Biochemical genetics; molecular biophysics; biochemistry and physiology of neurotransmitters; neurophysiology. *Mailing Add:* Dept Biol Sci Mt Holyoke Col South Hadley MA 01075

SMITH, CURTIS PAGE, ORGANIC CHEMISTRY, MEDICAL APPLICATION OF THERMOPLASTIC POLYURETHANE. *Current Pos:* DIR RES & DEVELOP, NEW ENG URETHANE, INC, 94- *Personal Data:* b Long Prairie, Minn, Dec 25, 38; m 60, Karen Korzuck; c Richard N & David C. *Educ:* Univ Mich, BSCh, 61; State Univ NY, PhD(chem), 67. *Prof Exp:* Fel chem, State Univ NY Stony Brook, 66-68; sr res chemist, Olin Res Ctr, 68-69, res assoc, 89-94; staff scientist, D S Gilmore Res Lab, Upjohn Co, Dow Chem USA, 69-85, Upjohn Chem Div, 85-89. *Mem:* Am Chem Soc; Sigma Xi. *Res:* Organo phosphorus chemistry; mechanism of organic reactions; biomedical applications of polyurethanes. *Mailing Add:* 254 Northrolling Acres Rd Cheshire CT 06410-2150. *Fax:* 203-239-1192

SMITH, CURTIS R, AUDIOLOGY. *Current Pos:* ASSOC PROF SPEECH COMMUN, AUBURN UNIV & DIR SPEECH & HEARING CLIN, 69- *Personal Data:* b Mineola, Tex, Nov 12, 36; m 58; c 3. *Educ:* Univ Southern Miss, BS, 60, MS, 61, PhD(audiol), 65. *Prof Exp:* Chief audiol, Brooke Gen Hosp, Ft Sam Houston, Tex, 65-66; dir grad training audiol, Our Lady of the Lake Col, 66-69. *Concurrent Pos:* Chief clin audiologist, Harry Jersig Speech & Hearing Ctr, 66-69. *Mem:* Am Speech & Hearing Asn. *Res:* Hearing mechanism and vestibular system. *Mailing Add:* 395 Cary Dr Auburn AL 36830

SMITH, CURTIS WILLIAM, ORGANIC CHEMISTRY. *Current Pos:* RETIRED. *Personal Data:* b Omaha, Ill, Jan 14, 18; m 42; c 5. *Educ:* Southern Ill Univ, BEd, 40; Univ Ill, PhD(org chem), 43. *Prof Exp:* Chemist, Res & Develop, Shell Develop Co, 43-52, mem staff mgt, 52-65, mgr, Ind Chem Div, Shell Chem Co, 65-71, asst to pres, Shell Develop Co, 71-77, sr consult, Chem Indust Regulations, Shell Oil Co, 77-83. *Mem:* Sigma Xi; Am Chem Soc. *Res:* Develop synthesis of tryptophan using quaternary ammonium akylation; penicillin; chemistry of acrolein. *Mailing Add:* 163 Stoney Creek Houston TX 77024-6239

SMITH, CYRIL BEVERLEY, PLANT NUTRITION. *Current Pos:* From instr to assoc prof, 47-65, PROF PLANT NUTRIT, PA STATE UNIV, UNIVERSITY PARK, 65- *Personal Data:* b Winnipeg, Man, Feb 21, 21; m 52. *Educ:* Univ Man, BSA, 42, MSc, 45; Pa State Univ, PhD(hort), 50. *Mem:* Am Soc Hort Sci; Am Soc Plant Physiol; Am Chem Soc; Sigma Xi. *Res:* Use of plant analysis in studying nutritional status of plants. *Mailing Add:* 232 Belle Ave Boalsburg PA 16827

SMITH, D EDWARDS, MAHARISHI AYUR-VED. *Current Pos:* asst prof, 85-92, ASSOC PROF PHYSIOL, MAHARISHI INT UNIV, 92- *Personal Data:* b Baltimore, Md, Aug 1, 38; m 88; Janet P Krag; c Todd D, Sarah P & Ann M. *Educ:* Va Mil Inst, BA, 60; Johns Hopkins Univ, Sch Med, MD, 64. *Prof Exp:* NIH res trainee, Rheumatology Dis Group, Univ Calif, San Francisco, 67-68; chief rheumatology, USAR Letterman Army Hosp, 68-70; asst prof med, Eastern Va, Med Sch 77-85. *Concurrent Pos:* Clin instr med, Univ Calif, San Francisco, 68-70; consult rheumatology, Ft Miley Vet Admin Hosp, 69-70, San Francisco Gen Hosp, 69-70, Kacoughlin Vet Admin Hosp, Va, 76-82; rheumatology priv pract, 70-85; consult, NIH Off Alternative Med Nutrit & Lifestyles Study Sect, 93-; dir, Maharishi Vedic Univ, 93- *Mem:* Fel Am Col Physicians; Venereal Dis Asn; Am Asn Gyorvedic Physicians. *Res:* Experimental pharmacology to infectious disease and rheumatology; alternative medical research using Maharishi Ayur-Ved, specifically in the areas of anti-cancer effects of topically applied sesame oil and the reduction of cardiovascular risk factors. *Mailing Add:* 1115 E Cooke Rd Albuquerque NM 87112

SMITH, DALE, AGRONOMY, PLANT PHYSIOLOGY. *Current Pos:* From asst prof to prof, 46-77, EMER PROF AGRON, UNIV WIS-MADISON, 77- *Personal Data:* b Fairmont, Nebr, Apr 13, 15; m 40, Marian J Brainard; c Warren & Sharon. *Educ:* Univ Nebr, BSc, 38; Univ Wis, MSc, 40, PhD(agron, plant physiol), 47. *Honors & Awards:* Crop Sci Award, Am Soc Agron, 63; Merit Cert, Am Forage & Grassland Coun, 65, Medallion Award, 75, Distinguished Grasslander, 82. *Concurrent Pos:* NATO fel, Eng, 64; Haight travel award, Asia, Australia & NZ, 70; mem, Acad Guest, Swiss Inst Technol, Zurich, 79; adj prof plant sci, Univ Ariz, Tucson, 79-82; hon mem, NAm Alfalfa Improv Conf, 88. *Mem:* Fel AAAS; fel Am Soc Agron; fel Crop Sci Soc Am. *Res:* Forage management; chemical composition; growth responses, cold hardiness and food reserves in forage plants. *Mailing Add:* PO Box 1400 Sun City AZ 85372-1400

SMITH, DALE METZ, SYSTEMATIC BOTANY. *Current Pos:* assoc prof, 64-71, prof, 71-88, EMER PROF BOT, UNIV CALIF, SANTA BARBARA, 88- *Personal Data:* b Portland, Ind, Dec 23, 28; m 50, Ruth W; c Teresa (Prather) & Gayle (Seymour). *Educ:* Ind Univ, BS, 50, PhD(bot), 57; Purdue Univ, MS, 52. *Honors & Awards:* Cooley Award, Am Soc Plant Taxon, 63. *Prof Exp:* Instr bot, Univ Ariz, 52-53; from instr to assoc prof, Univ Ky, 55-61; assoc prof, Univ Ill, 61-64. *Concurrent Pos:* Chmn dept biol sci, Univ Calif, Santa Barbara, 79-81. *Mem:* AAAS; Bot Soc Am; Am Soc Plant Taxon; Am Fern Soc; fel Linnean Soc London. *Res:* Biosystematics of Phlox; cytotaxonomy and chemotaxonomy. *Mailing Add:* PO Box 106 Deputy IN 47230-0106

SMITH, DALLAS GLEN, JR, ENGINEERING MECHANICS. *Current Pos:* asst prof eng sci, Tenn Technol Univ, 70-74, assoc prof, 74-79, prof eng sci & mech, 79-82, PROF CIVIL ENG, TENN TECHNOL UNIV, 82- *Personal Data:* b Gainesboro, Tenn, June 25, 40; m 61; c 3. *Educ:* Tenn Polytech Inst, BS, 63; Tenn Technol Univ, MS, 66; Va Polytech Inst, PhD(eng mech), 69. *Prof Exp:* Bridge design engr, Bridge Div, Tenn Dept Hwy, 63-65; asst prof eng mech, Va Polytech Inst, 69-70. *Concurrent Pos:* Consult, US Army Missile Command, Redstone Arsenal, 71-79. *Mem:* Am Soc Testing & Mat; Soc Exp Stress Analysis; Am Soc Eng Educ. *Res:* Brittle fracture mechanics; fiber-reinforced composite materials; experimental mechanics. *Mailing Add:* Box 5015 Tenn Technol Univ Cookeville TN 38505

SMITH, DANIEL JAMES, IMMUNOLOGY, ORAL BIOLOGY. *Current Pos:* from clin instr to asst clin prof, 76-87, ASSOC CLIN PROF, HARVARD SCH DENT MED, HARVARD UNIV, 87-; SR MEM STAFF, FORSYTH DENT CTR, 84- *Personal Data:* b Rochester, NY, June 17, 44; m 67; c 3. *Educ:* Houghton Col, BS, 66; NY Med Col, PhD(immunol), 72. *Prof Exp:* Staff assoc, Forsyth Dent Ctr, 72-74, asst mem staff immunol, 74-76, assoc mem staff, 79-84; clin instr, 76-79, asst clin prof, 79-87, assoc clin prof, Harvard Sch Dent Med, Harvard Univ, 87- *Mem:* Am Asn Immunologists; Int Asn Dent Res. *Res:* Nature and function of secretory immune system; role of immunity in diseases of oral cavity, oral microbiology, and ontogeny of the secretory immune system. *Mailing Add:* Dept Immunol Forsyth Dental Ctr 140 Fenway Boston MA 02115

SMITH, DANIEL JOHN, BIOCHEMISTRY, ORGANIC CHEMISTRY. *Current Pos:* ASST PROF BIOCHEM, UNIV AKRON, 77- *Personal Data:* b Horicon, Wis, Apr 19, 46. *Educ:* Wis State Univ, BS, 68; Univ Calif, Berkeley, PhD(org chem), 74. *Prof Exp:* Fel biochem, Univ Calif, Los

Angeles, 74-76; vis scientist, Syva Res Inst, 76-77. *Mem:* Am Chem Soc; Control Release Soc. *Res:* Mechanism of photophosphorylation and oxidative phosphorylation; mechanism of control release organotin compounds as molluscicides. *Mailing Add:* Dept Chem Univ Akron Akron OH 44325-3601. *Fax:* 330-972-6934

SMITH, DANIEL MONTAGUE, PHYSICS. *Current Pos:* ENG MGR, MOTOROLA SEMICONDUCTOR PROD SECTOR, 79- *Personal Data:* b Gainesville, Tex, Oct 17, 32; m 53, Mary Beth Seale; c Gregory, Timothy & Christopher. *Educ:* NTex State Col, BA, 52, MS, 53; Univ Tex, PhD(physics), 59. *Prof Exp:* Lab asst, NTex State Col, 50-52; asst, Univ Tex, 55-58, scientist, 57-58; physicist, Oak Ridge Nat Lab, 58-61; mem tech staff, Tex Instruments Inc, Tex, 61-75; mgr device technol, Nitron Div, McDonnell Douglas, 75-77; eng mgr, Nat Semiconductor Corp, 77-79. *Mem:* Am Phys Soc; Inst Elec & Electronics Engrs. *Res:* Medium energy experimental nuclear physics; semiconductor device design and development. *Mailing Add:* 10301 Parkfield Austin TX 78758. *E-Mail:* dan__smith-rldh80@email.sps.mot.com

SMITH, DANIEL WALTER, WATER TREATMENT, WASTEWATER TREATMENT & SOLID WASTE DISPOSAL. *Current Pos:* assoc prof, 78-80, chair, 90-94, PROF ENVIRON ENG, DEPT CIVIL & ENVIRON ENG, UNIV ALTA, 80- *Personal Data:* b Santa Monica, Calif, June 6, 44; m 65, 86, Sophia Zeschuk; c David J. *Educ:* Calif State Univ, Sacramento, BS, 67; San Jose State Univ, MS, 68; Univ Kans, PhD(environ health eng), 70. *Honors & Awards:* Award of Merit, Soc Tech Commun, 87; Keefer Medal, Can Soc Civil Eng, 88, Albert E Berry Medal, 89; E F Rice Mem lectr, Am Soc Civil Engrs, 89, Can-Am Amity Civil Eng Award, 89; Izaak Walton Killam Ann Prof, Univ Alta, 93; Prof Award of Merit, Asn Prof Eng Geog & Geophys of NW Territories, 93. *Prof Exp:* Sr asst sanit eng, USPHS, Arctic Health Res Ctr, Fairbanks, 70-72; asst prof environ qual & water resources eng, Univ Alaska, Fairbanks, 72-75; head, Northern Technol Ctr, Environ Protection Serv, Can, 75-77; sr environ engr, R&M Consults, Anchorage, 77-78. *Concurrent Pos:* Consult var firms, 78-; prin investr numerous res projs, Univ Alta; mem, Nat Sci & Eng Res Coun Can, 92-95. *Mem:* Fel Can Soc Civil Eng (sr vpres, 86-87, pres, 87-88); fel Am Soc Civil Engrs; Water Environ Fedn; Am Water Works Asn; Int Ozone Asn; Am Acad Environ Engrs; Int Asn Water Qual; Am Acad Environ Eng; Asn Environ Eng Prof. *Res:* Ozone water and wastewater treatment; water treatment and distribution system corrosion studies; advanced wastewater treatment studies; solid waste management; low-temperature, dilute wastewater treatment; river water quality and indicator organism modelling; pulp mill wastewater treatment; author of over 200 publications and granted 3 patents. *Mailing Add:* 172 Roy St Edmonton AB T6R 2A8 Can. *Fax:* 403-492-0249; *E-Mail:* dwsmith@civil.ualberta.ca

SMITH, DARRELL WAYNE, MATERIALS SCIENCE, PHYSICAL METALLURGY. *Current Pos:* from asst prof to assoc prof, 70-81, PROF METALL ENG, MICH TECHNOL UNIV, 81- *Personal Data:* b Long Beach, Calif, July 31, 37; wid; c 3. *Educ:* Mich Technol Univ, BS, 59; Case Western Res Univ, MS, 65, PhD(phys metall), 69. *Prof Exp:* Metallurgist, Babcock & Wilcox Co, 59-62 & Gen Elec Co, 62-68; res assoc, Case Western Res Univ, 68-69; res metallurgist, Gen Elec Co, 69-70. *Concurrent Pos:* Mem, bd dirs, Am Powder Mettal Inst, 92-96; mem, bd trustees, Am Soc Metals, 95- *Mem:* Am Soc Metals; Am Powder Metall Inst; Am Soc Testing Mat. *Res:* Physical properties of consolidated powders; powder metallurgy. *Mailing Add:* Dept Metall Eng Mich Technol Univ Houghton MI 49931

SMITH, DARRYL LYLE, SOLID STATE PHYSICS. *Current Pos:* STAFF MEM, LOS ALAMOS NAT LAB, 83- *Personal Data:* b Minneapolis, Minn, July 30, 46. *Educ:* St Mary's Col, Minn, BA, 68; Univ Ill, MS, 71, PhD(physics), 74. *Prof Exp:* Instr appl physics, Calif Inst Technol, 74-83. *Mem:* Am Phys Soc; Sigma Xi. *Res:* Optical properties of solids. *Mailing Add:* PO Box 1663 T11/0429 Los Alamos Nat Lab Los Alamos NM 87545

SMITH, DARWIN WALDRON, PHYSICAL CHEMISTRY. *Current Pos:* assoc prof, 68-, PROF CHEM, UNIV GA. *Personal Data:* b Los Angeles, Calif, Mar 25, 31; m 52; c 3. *Educ:* Univ Calif, Los Angeles, BS, 53; Calif Inst Technol, PhD(chem), 59. *Prof Exp:* NSF fel chem, Math Inst, Oxford Univ, 59; from asst prof to assoc prof chem, Univ Fla, 60-68. *Mem:* Am Phys Soc; Am Chem Soc. *Res:* Quantum chemistry; theory of molecular structure. *Mailing Add:* Dept Chem Univ Ga Athens GA 30602. *Fax:* 706-938-5945

SMITH, DAVID, physical chemistry, for more information see previous edition

SMITH, DAVID ALEXANDER, NUMERICAL ANALYSIS, MATHEMATICS EDUCATION. *Current Pos:* asst prof math, Duke Univ, 62-68, dir grad studies, 68-71, dir undergrad studies, 82-84, ASSOC PROF MATH, DUKE UNIV, 68- *Personal Data:* b New York, NY, Jan 6, 38; m 58, Dorothy Ross; c David II, Charles, Scott & Cynthia. *Educ:* Trinity Col, Conn, BS, 58; Yale Univ, PhD(math), 63. *Concurrent Pos:* Vis assoc prof, Case Western Res Univ, 75-76 & Pa State Univ, 93-94; assoc ed, Math Mag, 81-85 & Col Math J, 86-89; vis prof, Benedict Col, 84-86; United Negro Col Fund scholar-at-large, 84-85; co-dir, Proj CALC, 89- *Mem:* Soc Indust & Appl Math; AAAS; Am Math Soc; Math Asn Am; Nat Coun Teachers Math. *Res:* Abstract algebra; arithmetic functions; algorithmic algebra; combinatorial theory; numerical analysis; uses of computers in mathematics; application in social and biological sciences. *Mailing Add:* Dept Math Duke Univ Durham NC 27708-0320. *Fax:* 919-660-2821; *E-Mail:* das@math.duke.edu

SMITH, DAVID ALLEN, MOLECULAR BIOLOGY, RADIOBIOLOGY, TOXICOLOGY. *Current Pos:* molecular biologist, Off Health & Environ Res, 77-88, actg dep dir, 79-88, DIR, HEALTH EFFECTS RES DIV, DEPT ENERGY, 88- *Personal Data:* b Osceola, Nebr, Feb 25, 33; div; c Leslie, Danelle & Deonne. *Educ:* Dana Col, BA, 59; Univ Southern Calif, PhD(biochem), 64. *Prof Exp:* Biochemist, Biomed Res Group, Los Alamos Sci Lab, Univ Calif, 64-77. *Concurrent Pos:* Exec dir, Health & Environ Res Adv Comt, Dept Energy, 83-88. *Mem:* AAAS; Am Chem Soc; Am Soc Biochem & Molecular Biol; Environ Mutagenesis Soc. *Res:* Molecular biology; molecular genetics; environmental mutagenesis; physical properties of nucleic acids and nucleic acid enzymology; biotechnology; DNA repair; radiobiology; humangenome. *Mailing Add:* 21142 Greenbrier Rd Boonsboro MD 21713. *Fax:* 301-903-8521

SMITH, DAVID CLEMENT, IV, PHYSICAL OCEANOGRAPHY, OCEAN NUMERICAL MODELS. *Current Pos:* OCEANOG, POLAR SCI CTR, APPL PHYSICS LAB, UNIV WASH, 90- *Personal Data:* b Midland, Tex, Apr 26, 51. *Educ:* Univ Houston, BS, 73; Tex A&M Univ, MS, 75, PhD(oceanog), 80. *Prof Exp:* Assoc, Mesoscale Air Sea Interaction Group, Fla State Univ, 80-81; asst res scientist, Dept Oceanog, Tex A&M Univ, 83-85; adj res prof, Naval Postgrad Sch, 81-83, asst prof, Dept Oceanog, 85-90. *Mem:* Am Meteorol Soc; Am Geophys Union. *Res:* Physical oceanographic research in ocean mesoscale dynamics through the use of regional ocean numerical models. *Mailing Add:* Univ Tex Austin Ctr Space Res 3925 W Braker Lane Suite 200 Austin TX 78759-5321

SMITH, DAVID EDMUND, SATELLITE GEODESY, CELESTIAL MECHANICS. *Current Pos:* staff scientist geophys, NASA Goddard Space Flight Ctr, 69-71, head, Geodynamics Br, 71-87, assoc chief, 88-90, CHIEF, LAB TERRESTRIAL PHYSICS, NASA GODDARD SPACE FLIGHT CTR, 90- *Personal Data:* b Brentford, Eng, Nov 3, 34; m 61; c 4. *Educ:* Univ Durham, Eng, BSc, 58, MS, 62; Univ London, PhD(satellite geod), 66. *Honors & Awards:* Except Sci Achievement Medal, NASA, 74; John C Lindsay Mem Award, Goddard Space Flight Ctr, 78. *Prof Exp:* Sci officer math, Radio & Space Res Sta, 58-68; sr scientist geod, EG&G, Wolf Res & Develop Corp, 68-69. *Concurrent Pos:* Mem working group 1 satellite geod & geodynamics, Comt Space Res, 67-; mem comn satellite geod, Joint Comt Space Res & Int Union Geod & Geophys, 71-; mem study group fundamental geod constants, Int Asn Geod, 74-87, mem study group ref systs geod & geodynamics, 76-, mem study group on parameters of common relevance to astron, geodesy & geodynamics, 87-; mem working group measurement earth rotation, Int Astron Union, 78-; proj scientist, Crustal Dynamics Proj, NASA, 80-, prin investr radar altimeter, mem radio sci team, NASA Mars Observer Mission; proj scientist, Lageos Satellite, 76-80. *Mem:* Royal Astron Soc; fel Am Geophys Union (pres, geodesy sect, 88-). *Res:* Determination of shape and size of earth, its tectonics, gravity field, internal structure, rotations and tides; motion of artificial satellites and their perturbation. *Mailing Add:* Lab Terrestrial Physics Code 920 NASA Goddard Space Flight Ctr Greenbelt MD 20771

SMITH, DAVID ENGLISH, NEUROPATHOLOGY, EDUCATIONAL EVALUATION. *Current Pos:* PROF PATH, MED BR, UNIV TEX, GALVESTON, 86- *Personal Data:* b San Francisco, Calif, June 9, 20; m 48, Margaret Bronson; c Ann S (Elbert), David B & Mary M. *Educ:* Cent Col, Mo, AB, 41; Washington Univ, MD, 44; Am Bd Path, dipl, 50. *Prof Exp:* Intern & resident path, Barnes Hosp, St Louis, Mo, 44-46; from instr to assoc prof path, Sch Med, Washington Univ, 48-55, asst head dept, 53-54; prof, Sch Med, Univ Va, 55-73, chmn dept, 58-73, dir cancer ctr, 72-73; prof path, Northwestern Univ, Evanston, 74-75; prof path, Univ Pa, Philadelphia, 76-80; prof path & assoc dean, Tulane Univ, 80-85. *Concurrent Pos:* Mem, Exec Comt, Nat Bd Med Examrs, 70-80, vpres & dir undergrad div, 75-80, secy, 77-80; trustee, Am Bd Path, 66-73; assoc dir, Am Bd Med Specialists, 74-75. *Mem:* Am Soc Clin Path; Am Asn Pathologists & Bacteriologists; AMA; Am Acad Neurol; Int Acad Path (pres, 64-65); Am Asn Neuropath. *Res:* Neuropathology; quantitative histochemistry; evaluation of medical education. *Mailing Add:* 59 Colony Park Circle Galveston TX 77551-1737. *Fax:* 409-772-5315; *E-Mail:* descolpkga@aol.com

SMITH, DAVID FLETCHER, COMMERCIAL DIAGNOSTIC ASSAYS, BIOTECHNOLOGY. *Current Pos:* BIOCHEMIST, UNIV GA, ATHENS, 89- *Personal Data:* b Sewickley, Pa, Jan 30, 46; m 67, Nancy D Braun; c Pamela D & Kristen M. *Educ:* Tex Lutheran Col, BS, 67; Univ Tex, Houston, MS, 69, PhD(biochem), 72. *Prof Exp:* Postdoctoral fel biochem, Dept Chem, Fla State Univ, Tallahassee, 72-73; res assoc membrane biol, Am Red Cross Blood Res Lab, Bethesda, Md, 73-76; sr staff fel biochem, Lab Biochem Pharm, Nat Inst Arthritis, Diabetes & Digestive & Kidney Dis, NIH, 77-80; from asst prof to assoc prof, Va Polytech Inst & State Univ, 80-89. *Concurrent Pos:* Vis prof, Biochem Inst, Univ Freiburg, Ger, 75-76; prin investr, NIH, 82-, NSF, 84- & NIH small bus innovative res grant award, 89-90; mem, Pathobiochem Study Sect, NIH, 89-; adj prof, Univ Ga, Athens, 89- & Sealite Sci, Inc, Atlanta, Ga, 91-; vpres & dir, ELA Technol, Inc, Athens, 99- *Mem:* Am Soc Biochem & Molecular Biol; Soc Complex Carbohydrates; Am Asn Clin Chem; Int Soc Bioluminescence & Chemiluminescence. *Res:* Structure and function of oligosaccharides on cell surface glyco conjugates, glycolipids and glycoproteins; methods to exploit recombinant bioluminescent proteins as reagents for diagnostic assays and nucleic acid detection/quantification. *Mailing Add:* Dept Biochem Univ Ga Athens GA 30602. *Fax:* 770-729-8735; *E-Mail:* dsmith@sealite.com

SMITH, DAVID HIBBARD, ORGANIC CHEMISTRY. *Current Pos:* From asst prof to assoc prof, 70-83, PROF CHEM, DOANE COL, 83-, CHMN, NAT SCI DIV, 79- *Personal Data:* b Springfield, Mo, July 29, 41; m 66; c 2. *Educ:* Univ Notre Dame, BS, 63; Univ Mo-Columbia, PhD(org chem), 71.

Concurrent Pos: Mem, Environ Control Coun, State Nebr, 74-79; res assoc, Univ Va, 82-83; vis prof, Univ Nebr, Lincoln, 87 & 88. *Mem:* Am Chem Soc. *Res:* Nitrosamines; azirdines; allelopathic chemicals. *Mailing Add:* 1175 Driftwood Dr Crete NE 68333-1726

SMITH, DAVID HUSTON, CHEMISTRY. *Current Pos:* CHEMIST, OAK RIDGE NAT LAB, UNION CARBIDE NUCLEAR CO, 62- *Personal Data:* b Seattle, Wash, July 14, 37; m 58; c 2. *Educ:* Whitman Col, BA, 59; Cornell Univ, MS, 62; Univ Tenn, Knoxville, PhD(analytical chem), 70. *Res:* Applications of mass spectrometry to safeguards; mass spectrometric research and development; design and development of computer programs for mass spectrometric data. *Mailing Add:* 104 Wilderness Lane Oak Ridge TN 37830

SMITH, DAVID I, MOLECULAR GENETICS OF LUNG & RENAL CANCER, PHYSICAL MAP OF CHROMOSOME THREE. *Current Pos:* asst prof, 85-90, ASSOC PROF, DEPT INTERNAL MED, WAYNE STATE UNIV, 90- *Personal Data:* b Cooperstown, NY, May 22, 54; m 81; c 3. *Educ:* Univ Wis-Madison, BS, 74, PhD(biochem), 78. *Prof Exp:* Postdoctoral researcher molecular biol, Albert Einstein Col Med, 78-80; sr res scientist, Enzo Biochem, NY, 80-81; postdoctoral fel biol chem, Univ Calif, Irvine, 81-85. *Concurrent Pos:* Mem Mammalian Genetics Study Sect, NIH, 90-; Basil O'Connor starter res grant, March of Dimes Birth Defects Found, 88. *Mem:* AAAS; Am Soc Human Genetics. *Res:* Constructing a precise physical map for human chromosome 3 to facilitate the isolation of chromosome 3 genes associated with specific diseases including small cell lung cancer, renal cell carcinoma and Von Hippel Lindau disease. *Mailing Add:* 3136 Scott Hall Wayne State Univ 540 E Canfield Detroit MI 48201

SMITH, DAVID JOHN, HIGH RESOLUTION ELECTRON MICROSCOPY, STRUCTURE OF MATERIALS. *Current Pos:* assoc prof, 84-87, PROF, CTR SOLID STATE SCI & DEPT PHYSICS, ARIZ STATE UNIV, 87-, DIR, NAT FACIL HIGH RESOLUTION ELECTRON MICROS, 91- *Personal Data:* b Melbourne, Australia, Oct 10, 48; div, Gwen Bland; c Heather & Marion. *Educ:* Univ Melbourne, BSc, 70, PhD(physics), 78, DSc, 88. *Honors & Awards:* Charles Vernon Boys Prize, Inst Physics, UK, 85. *Prof Exp:* Staff demonstr, Sch Physics, Univ Melbourne, 75, vis scientist, 84; res asst, Cavendish Lab, Cambridge Univ, 76-80, sr res asst & actg dir, High Resolution Electron Microscope, 78-80, sr res asst & dir, 80-84. *Mem:* Royal Micros Soc; fel Inst Physics UK; Electron Micros Soc Am; Mat Res Soc. *Res:* High resolution electron microscopy, instrumentation and applications; characterization of surfaces of metals, oxides and semiconductors; the atomic structure of small and extended defects in solids. *Mailing Add:* Ctr Solid State Sci Ariz State Univ Tempe AZ 85287. *Fax:* 602-965-9004; *E-Mail:* david.smith@asu.edu

SMITH, DAVID JOSEPH, PHARMACOLOGY. *Current Pos:* from asst prof to assoc prof, WVa Univ, 71-81, dir, anesthesiol res lab, 74-96, prof aneshtesiol & pharmacol, 81-96, PROF PHARMACOL & ANESTHESIOL, WVA UNIV, 96- *Personal Data:* b Parkersburg, WVa, Dec 17, 43; m 64; c 2. *Educ:* Bethany Col, BS, 65; WVa Univ, PhD(pharmacol), 69. *Prof Exp:* Fel, Univ Iowa, 69-71. *Concurrent Pos:* Field ed, Analgesia & Drugs Abuse, J Pharmacol Exp Ther, 96- *Mem:* Am Soc Pharmacol & Exp Therapeut; Am Soc Anesthesiologists; AAAS; Sigma Xi; Soc Neurosci; Int Asn Study Pain. *Res:* Neuropharmacological research of drug action on neurochemical processes of neurotransmitter metabolism; metabolic changes in transmitter metabolism are correlated with alterations in central nervous system function, particularly nociceptive behavior. *Mailing Add:* WVa Univ Health Sci Ctr Morgantown WV 26506-0001. *Fax:* 304-293-6854; *E-Mail:* dsmith5@wvu.edu

SMITH, DAVID LEE, chromatography, mass spectrometry, for more information see previous edition

SMITH, DAVID MARTYN, SILVICULTURE, FOREST ECOLOGY. *Current Pos:* Instr silvicult, Yale Univ, 46-47 & 48-51, from asst prof to prof, 51-67, asst dean sch, 53-58, Morris K Jesup prof, 67-90, EMER PROF SILVICULT, SCH FORESTRY & ENVIRON STUDIES, YALE UNIV, 90- *Personal Data:* b Bryan, Tex, Mar 10, 21; m 51, Catherine Van Aken; c Ellen & Nancy. *Educ:* Univ RI, BS, 41; Yale Univ, MF, 46, PhD, 50. *Hon Degrees:* DSc, Bates Col, 86, Univ RI, 93. *Honors & Awards:* Distinguished Serv Award, New Eng Soc Am Foresters, 69 & 93; Distinguished Serv Award, Am Forestry Asn, 90. *Concurrent Pos:* Vis prof, Univ Munich, 81; hon mem, Acad Forest Sci, Mex. *Mem:* Ecol Soc Am; fel Soc Am Foresters; Sigma Xi; Int Soc Trop Foresters. *Res:* Silviculture; regeneration and manipulation of forest vegetation, especially stratified mixtures. *Mailing Add:* Sch Forestry & Environ Studies Yale Univ New Haven CT 06520

SMITH, DAVID PHILIP, MAGNETIC RECORDING, TRIBOLOGY. *Current Pos:* DEPT ELEC ENG, UNIV MINN. *Personal Data:* b Minneapolis, Minn, July 21, 35; m 52; c 4. *Educ:* Univ Minn, BS, 62, MS, 66, PhD(elec eng), 72. *Honors & Awards:* Wayne B Nottingham Prize, Ann Phys Electronics Conf, 71. *Prof Exp:* Physicist, Cent Res Labs, 62-66, res physicist, 66-69, sr res physicist, 70-71, res specialist, Cent Res Labs, 71-72, supvr, 72-74, mgr, 74; mkt mgr anal syst, 3M Co, St Paul, Minn, 74-79; sr res specialist, 3M Data Cartridge Lab, 79-88; div scientist, 3M Data Storage Prod, 88- *Concurrent Pos:* Mem, Res Comt Tribology, Am Soc Mech Engrs, 89- *Mem:* Am Soc Mech Engrs. *Res:* Tribology of magnetic recording devices; surface science; solid state physics; ion surface interactions. *Mailing Add:* 1850 River Ridge Rd Hudson WI 54016

SMITH, DAVID R(ICHARD), ELECTRICAL ENGINEERING. *Current Pos:* assoc prof elec sci, 66-71, PROF COMPUT SCI, STATE UNIV NY STONY BROOK, 72- *Personal Data:* b London, Eng, July 29, 36; m 61; c 3. *Educ:* Univ London, BS, 57; Univ Wis, PhD(elec eng), 61. *Prof Exp:* Res fel, Nat Phys Lab, Teddington, Eng, 61-63; asst prof bioeng, Case Inst Technol, 63-66. *Mem:* Inst Elec & Electronics Engrs. *Res:* Computer architecture and digital systems design. *Mailing Add:* Dept Comput Sci State Univ NY Stony Brook NY 11794

SMITH, DAVID REEDER, SOLID STATE PHYSICS. *Current Pos:* RES PHYSICIST, US DEPT COM, NAT INST STAND & TECHNOL, BOULDER CO, 87- *Personal Data:* b Murray, Utah, Nov 1, 38; m 63; c 3. *Educ:* Univ Utah, BS, 63; Purdue Univ, West Lafayette, MS, 66, PhD(physics), 69. *Prof Exp:* From asst prof to assoc prof physics, SDak Sch Mines & Technol, 69-87. *Mem:* AAAS; Sigma Xi; Am Asn Physics Teachers; Am Soc Testing Mat. *Res:* Low temperature solid state physics; cryogenics; heat transfer; microelectronics. *Mailing Add:* 1013 Alsace Way Lafayette CO 80026. *Fax:* 303-497-5030; *E-Mail:* drsmith@boulder.nist.gov

SMITH, DAVID ROLLINS, ENTOMOLOGY, SYSTEMATICS OF SAWFLIES. *Current Pos:* RES ENTOMOLOGIST, SYST ENTOM LAB, AGR RES SERV, USDA, 65- *Personal Data:* b Rockford, Ill, July 27, 37; m 67, Jung L Hwang; c Paul & Deborah. *Educ:* Ore State Univ, BA, 60, PhD(entom), 67. *Concurrent Pos:* Ed, Proc Entom Soc Wash, 80-83 & 96-, pres, Entom Soc Wash, 91. *Mem:* Entom Soc Am; Soc Syst Zool; Am Entom Soc; Japanese Entom Soc; Brazilian Entom Soc. *Res:* Systematics of sawflies, ants and some parasitic Hymenoptera; primarily fauna of the Western Hemisphere. *Mailing Add:* Syst Entom Lab c/o US Nat Mus Washington DC 20560. *E-Mail:* dsmith@sel.barc.usda.gov

SMITH, DAVID S, PEDIATRICS. *Current Pos:* PROF PEDIAT, SCH MED, TEMPLE UNIV, 68-; ASST ED, J PEDIAT, 72- *Personal Data:* b Ipswich, Mass, June 29, 21; m 47; c David Jr, Virginia & Donald. *Educ:* Dartmouth Col, AB, 42; Univ Pa, MD, 44; Am Bd Pediat, dipl, 50. *Honors & Awards:* Arthur Dannenberg MD lectr, Albert Einstein Med Ctr, 79. *Concurrent Pos:* Consult, Nazareth Hosp, Philadelphia, 66-; prin investr, Clin Res Ctr, 76-; dir, Inpatient Serv, St Christopher's Hosp Children, 66-76, actg chmn, Dept Pediat, 76-83, dep chmn, 83-92; vis professorships, Guadalajara, Univ PR & Univ S Ill. *Mem:* Am Acad Pediat; AMA; Am Pediat Soc. *Res:* Infectious disease. *Mailing Add:* 4012 Primrose Rd Philadelphia PA 19114-2915

SMITH, DAVID SPENCER, CELL BIOLOGY. *Current Pos:* Hope prof zool & entom, 80-95, VIS PROF, OXFORD UNIV, ENG, 95-; PROF, FLA INT UNIV, MIAMI, 95- *Personal Data:* b London, Eng, Apr 10, 34; m 64. *Educ:* Cambridge Univ, BA, 55, MA & PhD(zool), 58. *Prof Exp:* Fel cell biol, Rockefeller Univ, 58-59, res assoc, 59-61; res fel zool, Cambridge Univ, 61-63; asst prof biol, Univ Va, 63-66; assoc prof med, anat & biol, Univ Miami, 66-70, prof med & pharmacol, 70-80. *Concurrent Pos:* USPHS fel, 59; NSF res grant, 63-66; external dir res, Int Ctr Insect Physiol & Ecol, 70, dir res, Nairobi, Kenya; NIH res grants, 71- *Mem:* Am Soc Cell Biol; Royal Micron Soc London. *Res:* Electron microscopic studies on vertebrate and invertebrate animal tissues, especially muscle fibers and central and peripheral nervous systems; studies on structure and function of cellular membranes. *Mailing Add:* 3000 Seminole St Miami FL 33133

SMITH, DAVID VARLEY, NEUROSCIENCE, PSYCHOLOGY. *Current Pos:* OTOLARYNGOL & MAXILLOFACIAL SURGEON, UNIV CINN, COL MED, 85- *Personal Data:* b Memphis, Tenn, Apr 21, 43; m 65; c 3. *Educ:* Univ Tenn, BS, 65, MA, 67; Univ Pittsburgh, PhD(psychobiol), 69. *Prof Exp:* Res assoc, Rockefeller UniY, 69-71; asst prof, 71-75, assoc prof, 75-80, prof psychol, Univ Wyo, 80-; assoc prof psychol, Hunter Col, City Univ New York, 70-71; Nat Inst Neurol Commun Dis & Stroke res career develop award, 76-82; asst prog dir, NSF, 77-78. *Mem:* AAAS; Soc Neurosci; Asn Chemoreceptive Sci. *Res:* Gustatory physiology and behavior; taste quality coding; neurophysiology. *Mailing Add:* Otolaryngol & Maxillofacial Surg Univ Cinn Col Med 231 Bethesda Ave Cincinnati OH 45267-0001

SMITH, DAVID WALDO EDWARD, PATHOLOGY, MOLECULAR BIOLOGY. *Current Pos:* PROF PATH, MED SCH, 69-, PROF, BUEHLER CTR AGING, NORTHWESTERN UNIV, CHICAGO, 88- *Personal Data:* b Fargo, NDak, Apr 3, 34; m 60, Diane W. *Educ:* Swarthmore Col, BA, 56; Yale Univ, MD, 60. *Prof Exp:* From intern to asst resident, Yale-New Haven Med Ctr, 60-62; res assoc, Molecular Biol Lab, Nat Inst Arthritis & Metab Dis, 62-64, investr, Lab Exp Path, 64-67; assoc prof path & microbiol, Ind Univ, Bloomington, 67-69. *Concurrent Pos:* Res fel, Yale-New Haven Med Ctr, 60-62; res career develop award, Nat Inst Gen Med Sci, 68-69; mem, Path Chem Study, NIH, 75-79, sabbatical leave, 86-87. *Mem:* AAAS; Am Asn Pathologist; Am Soc Biol Chemists; Geront Soc Am. *Res:* Longevity; aging; transfer RNA; genetic control of protein synthesis; hemoglobin synthesis; gerontology. *Mailing Add:* Dept Path Ctr Aging Northwestern Univ Med Sch 303 E Chicago Ave Chicago IL 60611-3008

SMITH, DAVID WARREN, ANALYTICAL CHEMISTRY. *Current Pos:* MGR, CHEM SERV, ETHYL PETROL ADDITIVES INC, 79- *Personal Data:* b Garden Prairie, Ill, Jan 28, 39; m 62; c 3. *Educ:* Northern Ill Univ, BS, 61; Iowa State Univ, PhD(analytical chem), 68. *Prof Exp:* Teacher, High Sch, Ill, 61-63; sr chemist, Mallinckrodt, Inc, 68-70, sr res assoc, 70-73, group leader, 73-78, mgr res & develop, 78-79. *Mem:* Am Chem Soc; Soc Tribiologist & Lubrication Engrs; Soc Automotive Engrs. *Res:* Analytical chemistry of alkaloids; analytical chromatography; process research and development of natural products. *Mailing Add:* Daniel & Henry 2350 Market St Suite 400 1530 S Second St St Louis MO 63103

SMITH, DAVID WILLIAM, FORESTRY. *Current Pos:* asst prof forestry, 72-78, assoc prof forest soils & silvicult & chmn forest biol sect, 78-85, PROF SILVICULT & FOREST SOILS & ASST DIR, SCH FORESTRY & WILDLIFE RESOURCES, VA POLYTECH INST & STATE UNIV, 85- *Personal Data:* b Wisconsin Rapids, Wis, June 16, 38; m 77; c 2. *Educ:* Iowa State Univ, BS, 60, MS, 68, PhD(forest biol), 70. *Prof Exp:* Exten forester, Iowa State Univ & Coop Exten Serv, Iowa, 66-67; asst prof forest technol & chmn, Glenville State Col, 70-72. *Mem:* Soil Sci Soc Am; Soc Am Foresters. *Res:* Nutrient cycling in forest systems, specifically the effects of silvicultural practices on site productivity through changes in soil physical and chemical properties; hardwood regeneration. *Mailing Add:* Forestry Va Polytech Inst & Sta Univ PO Box 0324 Blacksburg VA 24063-0001

SMITH, DAVID WILLIAM, PLANT ECOLOGY. *Current Pos:* RETIRED. *Personal Data:* b Edson, Alta, Jan 18, 33; m 56; c 3. *Educ:* Univ Alta, BSc, 56, MSc, 59; Univ Toronto, PhD(ecol), 67. *Prof Exp:* Res officer host, Res Br, Can Dept Agr, 58-67; asst prof geol, Univ Guelph, 67-72, asst prof, 72-77, assoc prof bot, 77-91. *Concurrent Pos:* Grants, Ont Dept Lands & Forests, Univ Guelph, 70-73 & Nat Res Coun Can, 71-80; Indian & Northern Affairs contract, 77-82. *Mem:* Can Bot Asn; Ecol Soc Am. *Res:* Vegetation dynamics and productivity of natural systems. *Mailing Add:* RR 5 Rockwood ON N0B 2K0 Can

SMITH, DAVID WILLIAM, MICROBIAL ECOLOGY, PHYSIOLOGICAL ECOLOGY. *Current Pos:* asst prof, 75-81, ASSOC PROF MICROBIOL, UNIV DEL, 81- *Personal Data:* b Dayton, Ohio, March 17, 48; m 69; c 2. *Educ:* Univ Calif, San Diego, BA, 69; Ind Univ, MA, 71; Univ Wis, PhD(bacteriol), 72. *Prof Exp:* Fel, Dept Bacteriol, Univ Calif, Los Angeles, 73-74. *Concurrent Pos:* Prin investr res grants, Sea Grant Off, Nat Oceanic & Atmospheric Admin, 77- *Mem:* Am Soc Microbiol; AAAS; Fedn Am Scientists; Soc Gen Microbiol. *Res:* Sulfur and nitrogen cycle activities in salt marsh sediments as related to physical and chemical factors. *Mailing Add:* Dept Micro Biol Univ Del Newark DE 19717-0001

SMITH, DAVID YOUNG, SOLID STATE PHYSICS, OPTICAL PHYSICS. *Current Pos:* PROF PHYSICS, UNIV VT, 86-, CHMN DEPT, 86- *Personal Data:* b Schenectady, NY, July 24, 34; m 63; c 2. *Educ:* Rensselaer Polytech Inst, BS, 56; Univ Rochester, PhD(physics), 62. *Prof Exp:* Res assoc, Univ Ill, 62-63, res asst prof, 63-66; NSF fel, Physics Inst, Univ Stuttgart, 66-67; physicist, Solid State Sci Div, Argonne Nat Lab, 67-85, asst div dir, 74-79. *Concurrent Pos:* Vis assoc prof, Mich State Univ, 71-72; Ger Acad Exchange Serv res fel, Physics Inst, Univ Stuttgart, 75-76; guest prof, Physics Inst, Univ Stuttgart & Max Planck Inst, Stuttgart, 79-80. *Mem:* Am Phys Soc; Sigma Xi. *Res:* Theoretical solid state physics especially the electronic states and optical properties of pure crystals and of defects; x-ray optics. *Mailing Add:* Cook Physical Sci Bldg Univ Vt Burlington VT 05405-0001

SMITH, DEAN FRANCIS, PLASMA PHYSICS. *Current Pos:* SR ASSOC, BERKELEY RES ASSOCS, 81- *Personal Data:* b Los Angeles, Calif, July 25, 42; m 67; c 2. *Educ:* Mass Inst Technol, BS, 64; Stanford Univ, MS, 66, PhD(astrophys), 69. *Prof Exp:* Vis scientist, High Altitude Observ, Nat Ctr Atmospheric Res, 70-72, scientist, 72-78; sr res assoc, dept astro-geophys, Univ Colo, 78-81. *Concurrent Pos:* US-USSR, Cultural Exchange fel, Sternberg Astron Inst, Moscow, 69-70; lectr, Univ Colo, 71-83; Nat Res Coun sr assoc, Nat Oceanic Atmospheric Admin Lab, 90-91, guest worker, 91- *Mem:* Int Astron Union; Am Phys Soc; Am Astron Soc; Astron Soc Australia; Int Union Radio Sci; Int Asn Geomagnetism & Aeronomy. *Res:* Plasma astrophysics; theory of solar radio bursts; theory of flares and particle acceleration on the sun; theory of reconnection; theory of pulsar and planetary magnetospheres. *Mailing Add:* Berkeley Res Assocs 290 Green Rock Dr Boulder CO 80302

SMITH, DEAN HARLEY, VETERINARY MEDICINE, CLINICAL PATHOLOGY. *Current Pos:* RETIRED. *Personal Data:* b Dayton, Wash, May 4, 22; m 45; c 2. *Educ:* Wash State Univ, BS, 44, DVM, 49; Ore State Univ, MS, 59. *Prof Exp:* Vet, Button Vet Hosp, Tacoma, Wash, 49-50 & Dayton, 50-52 & 54-56; res asst, Ore State Univ, 56-59, from asst prof to prof vet med, 59-76; supvr fed-state progs, Ore Dept Agr, 76-85. *Concurrent Pos:* Fulbright lectr, Col Vet Med, Cairo Univ, 65-66. *Mem:* Am Vet Med Asn; US Livestock Sanit Asn; Am Pub Health Asn. *Res:* Animal disease diagnosis with special emphasis on sheep and cattle. *Mailing Add:* PO Box 237 Dayton WA 99328

SMITH, DEAN ORREN, NEUROPHYSIOLOGY. *Current Pos:* from asst prof to assoc prof, 76-83, PROF PHYSIOL, UNIV WIS-MADISON, 83-, ASSOC DEAN GRAD SCH, 84- *Personal Data:* b Colorado Springs, Colo, May 28, 44; m 65; Julie L Rosenheimer; c Curtis D & Corey B. *Educ:* Harvard Univ, BA, 67; Stanford Univ, AM, 69, PhD(biol sci), 71. *Prof Exp:* Fel physiol, Univ Gotenborg, 71-72; fel, Tech Univ Munchen, 72-74, scholar, 74-75; actg asst prof biol, Univ Calif, Los Angeles, 75-76. *Concurrent Pos:* Helen Hay Whitney Found fels, Univ Gotenborg, 71-72 & Tech Univ Munchen, 72-74; A P Sloan res fel, Univ Wis-Madison, 78-80, res career develop award, 79-83, Romnes fel, 83-, mem aging rev comt, 85- *Mem:* Soc Neurosci; Am Physiol Soc; fel Geront Soc Am. *Res:* Integration in the nervous system at the level of the axon and the synapse; changes in synaptic mechanisms during aging. *Mailing Add:* Grad Educ Univ Hawaii 244 Dole St Honolulu HI 96822. *Fax:* 608-262-2327; *E-Mail:* deano@macc.wisc.edu

SMITH, DEANE KINGSLEY, JR, MINERALOGY, CRYSTALLOGRAPHY. *Current Pos:* from assoc prof to prof, 68-96, EMER PROF MINERAL, PA STATE UNIV, UNIV PARK, 96- *Personal Data:* b Berkeley, Calif, Nov 8, 30; m 53, Patricia A Lawrence; c Paula L (Sexton), Jeanette D (Metcalf), Kingsley L, Dana E & Sharon R. *Educ:* Calif Inst Technol, BS, 52; Univ Minn, PhD(geol), 56. *Honors & Awards:* Charles S Barrett Award. *Prof Exp:* Instr field geol, Univ Minn, 56; Portland Cement Asn fel, Nat Bur Stand, 56-60; chemist, Lawrence Livermore Lab, Univ Calif, 60-68. *Concurrent Pos:* Owner & operator, Gem Dugout, 72-; chmn, Joint Comt Powder Diffraction Stand, Int Ctr Diffraction Data, 78-82 & 86-90. *Mem:* Fel Geol Soc Am; fel Mineral Soc Am; Am Crystallog Asn (secy, 76-78); Mineral Asn Can; Mineral Soc Gt Brit; fel Int Ctr Diffraction Data. *Res:* Defects in crystals and crystal structures of inorganics and minerals; uranium mineralogy; applications of powder x-ray diffractometry. *Mailing Add:* Dept Geosci Pa State Univ 307 Deike Bldg University Park PA 16802. *Fax:* 814-238-4069; *E-Mail:* smith@vax1.mrl.psu.edu

SMITH, DELMONT K, ORGANIC CHEMISTRY, NONWOVEN TEXTILES. *Current Pos:* CONSULT, 85- *Personal Data:* b Pocatello, Idaho, June 9, 27; m 94, Loretta Maynes; c Linda, Constance, Dennis, Shawna & David. *Educ:* Utah State Univ, BS, 49, MS, 55; Purdue Univ, PhD(org chem), 54. *Prof Exp:* Res chemist, Rayonier, Inc, 54-56, sect supvr, 56-59, asst res mgr, 59, div mgr, 59-61; res supvr, Chicopee Mfg Co, 61-66, div woven prod res, 66-70, dir technol planning, 70-84. *Concurrent Pos:* Consult ed, Int Nonwovens J; ed & publ, Nonwovens Patent News. *Mem:* Am Chem Soc; Tech Asn Pulp & Paper Indust; Am Asn Textile Chemists & Colorists; Int Nonwovens & Disposables Asn; Am Filtration & Separation Soc. *Res:* Organic halogen compounds; high polymers; cellulose and cellulose derivatives; textile technology; nonwoven technology. *Mailing Add:* 3112 E Hampton Ave Mesa AZ 85204. *Fax:* 602-924-6966; *E-Mail:* nonwoven@aol.com

SMITH, DENISE MYRTLE, PROTEIN CHEMISTRY & FUNCTIONALITY, MEAT SCIENCE. *Current Pos:* Asst prof, 85-90, ASSOC PROF FOOD SCI, FOOD SCI & HUMAN NUTRIT, MICH STATE UNIV, 90- *Personal Data:* b Chester, Pa, Sept 15, 55; m 79, Jeffry D Culbertson; c Greg S & Doug S. *Educ:* Va Polytech Inst & State Univ, BS, 77; Ore State Univ, MS, 79; Wash State Univ, PhD(food sci), 84. *Honors & Awards:* Continental Grain Poultry Prod Res Award, Poultry Sci Asn, 93. *Concurrent Pos:* Assoc ed, Poultry Sci, Poultry Sci Asn, 89- *Mem:* Inst Food Technologists; Am Meat Sci Asn; Poultry Sci Asn. *Res:* Meat, milk and egg protein chemistry, functionality and rheology; improved technologies for the processing of meat and egg products; development of ELISAs as indicators of processing adequacy. *Mailing Add:* 106A Trout Fshn Bldg Mich State Univ East Lansing MI 48824-1224

SMITH, DENNIS CLIFFORD, BIOMATERIALS. *Personal Data:* b Lincoln, Eng, Mar 24, 28; m 55, Eileen Tierney; c 6. *Educ:* Univ London, BSc, 50, MSc, 53, DSc, 79; Univ Manchester, PhD(chem), 57. *Hon Degrees:* DSc, Univ London, 79, McGill Univ, 93. *Honors & Awards:* Wilmer Souder Award, Int Asn Dent Res, 76; Clemson Award, Soc Biomat, 76; Nakabayashi Mem Award, Pierre Fouchard Soc, Japan, 82; Hellenback Mem Prize, 90; MEDEC Award Med Achievement, 93. *Prof Exp:* Asst lectr dent mat, Univ Manchester, 52-69, reader, 69; prof biomat & dir ctr, Univ Toronto, 69-75. *Concurrent Pos:* Vis assoc prof, Northwestern Univ, 60-61. *Mem:* Int Asn Dent Res; Soc Biomat; Can Soc Biomat; Adhesion Soc; hon fel Int Col Dentists; fel Royal Soc Can; fel Royal Soc Chem. *Res:* Polymer chemistry; tissue reaction to materials; physical properties of materials. *Mailing Add:* Fac Dent Univ Toronto 124 Edward St Toronto ON M5G 1G6 Can. *Fax:* 416-421-6470

SMITH, DENNIS MATTHEW, PULMONARY PATHOBIOLOGY, BIOLOGY EDUCATION. *Current Pos:* Asst prof 80-86, chmn, 88-90, ASSOC PROF BIOL SCI, WELLESLEY COL, 86- *Personal Data:* b Chicago, Ill, Mar 18, 52; m 80; c 1. *Educ:* Loyola Univ Chicago, BS, 74, PhD(anat), 79. *Concurrent Pos:* Consult, var indust firms, 89- *Mem:* Am Soc Cell Biol; Am Asn Anatomists; Sigma Xi; AAAS. *Res:* Pathobiology of the mammalian distal lung, especially electron microscopy; injurious effects of chronic beta-adrenergic blockade on the distal lung; culture of lung cells and their interactions. *Mailing Add:* Dept Biol Sci Wellesley Col 106 Central St Wellesley MA 02181-8203. *Fax:* 781-283-3642

SMITH, DENNISON A, NEUROSCIENCES. *Current Pos:* From asst prof to assoc prof psychol, 69-87, chmn psychobiol prog, 76-87, CHMN PSYCHOL DEPT, OBERLIN COL, 78-, PROF PSYCHOL & NEUROSCI, 87- *Personal Data:* b Newton, Mass, June 19, 43; m 69. *Educ:* Colgate Univ, AB, 65; Univ Mass, MS, 67, PhD(psychol), 70. *Concurrent Pos:* Chmn, Neurosci Prog, Oberlin Col, 88- *Mem:* AAAS; Soc Neurosci; Sigma Xi. *Res:* Neuropharmacology. *Mailing Add:* Neurosci Prog Sperry Hall Oberlin Col 130 W Lorain Oberlin OH 44074-1024

SMITH, DIANE ELIZABETH, NEUROANATOMY, IMMUNOCYTOCHEMISTRY. *Current Pos:* assoc prof, 75-80, PROF ANAT, LA STATE UNIV SCH MED, 80- *Personal Data:* b New York, NY, Nov 15, 37. *Educ:* Bucknell Univ, BS, 59; Am Univ, MS, 65; Univ Pa, PhD(anat), 68. *Prof Exp:* Res biologist, Clin Neuropath Sect, Surg Neurol Br, Nat Inst Neurol Dis & Blindness, 62-65; from asst prof anat to assoc prof, Daniel Baugh Inst Anat, Jefferson Med Col, Thomas Jefferson Univ, 69-75. *Concurrent Pos:* NIH res fel anat, Harvard Med Sch, 68-69; mem sci progs & adv comn, NIH & Nat Inst Neurol & Communicative Dis & Stroke, 84-86; mem, Educ Affairs Comt, Am Asn Anatomists, 85-88; vis prof neurobiol, Cornell Univ Med Col, 85. *Mem:* AAAS; Sigma Xi; Am Asn Anatomists; Int

Soc for Dev Neurosci; Soc Neurosci; Res Soc Alcoholism. *Res:* Localization of immunocytochemically labeled neurotransmitters and neuromodulators in neurological mutant mice; alteration in neuronal circuitry as a result of genetic compromise. *Mailing Add:* Dept Anat La State Univ Med 1901 Perdido St New Orleans LA 70112

SMITH, DON WILEY, AGRONOMY, PLANT PHYSIOLOGY. *Current Pos:* ASSOC PROF BIOL, UNIV NTEX, 67- *Personal Data:* b Weinert, Tex, Nov 11, 36; m 58, Nelia M King; c Douglas W, Gregory K, Brian K & Amy L. *Educ:* Tex Tech Col, BS, 58; Univ Wis, MS, 60, PhD(agron), 63. *Prof Exp:* Res assoc agron, Univ Wis, 62-63; asst prof bot, Colo State Univ, 65-67. *Concurrent Pos:* Consult bot, pesticide safety & wildflower cult. *Mem:* Am Soc Plant Physiol; Weed Sci Soc Am; Bot Soc Am; Sigma Xi. *Res:* Mechanism of action of boron; effects of microwaves on plant cells; physiology of wildflower; estrogens in plants. *Mailing Add:* Dept Biol Sci Univ NTex Box 305220 Denton TX 76203-5220. *Fax:* 817-565-3821; *E-Mail:* dsmith@po7.cas.unt.edu

SMITH, DONALD ALAN, VERTEBRATE ZOOLOGY. *Current Pos:* Lectr, 57-58, from asst prof to assoc prof biol, 58-95, CUR, MUS ZOOL, CARLETON UNIV, 73- *Personal Data:* b Toronto, Ont, Aug 29, 30; Can citizen; m 53, Lorraine Smith; c Peter, Carol, Suzanne, Janet & Paul. *Educ:* Univ Toronto, BA, 52, MA, 53, PhD(exp biol), 57. *Concurrent Pos:* Vis prof, Makerere Univ, Uganda, 66-67; asst to ed, Can Field-Naturalist, 72-81. *Mem:* Am Soc Mammal; Can Soc Zool; Soc Preserv Nat Hist Collections. *Res:* Ecology, distribution, taxonomy, conservation, behavior and environmental physiology of vertebrates, especially rodents, bats and insectivores; reproductive biology; ectoparasites of mammals, especially fleas. *Mailing Add:* Dept Biol Carleton Univ 1125 Colonel By Dr Ottawa ON K1S 5B6 Can. *Fax:* 613-520-4497

SMITH, DONALD ARTHUR, POLYMER CHEMISTRY. *Current Pos:* RETIRED. *Personal Data:* b Can, Feb 2, 26; nat US; m 49; c 4. *Educ:* Univ BC, BA, 48; Univ Toronto, PhD(chem), 51. *Prof Exp:* Res assoc, Kodak Park Works, Eastman Kodak Co, 51-77; sr lab head, 68-77, asst dir, Chem Div, Res Labs, 77-84. *Mem:* Am Chem Soc. *Res:* Sterochemistry; high polymers; synthesis of hydrophilic monomers and polymers. *Mailing Add:* 65 Pinegrove Ave Rochester NY 14617

SMITH, DONALD ARTHUR, COMBUSTION SYSTEMS RESEARCH & DEVELOPMENT, PREDICTIVE MAINTENANCE. *Current Pos:* DIR RES & DEVELOP, HARTFORD STEAM BOILER INSPECTION & INS CO, 84- *Personal Data:* b Hartford, Conn, Apr 9, 45; m 67, Marianne Taverna; c Adam. *Educ:* Univ Hartford, BSME, 68. *Prof Exp:* Mfg combustion res, Combustion Eng, 68-84. *Concurrent Pos:* Treas, Am Flame Res Comt, 84- *Res:* Fluid modeling, low emissions firing systems, air quality control systems, bulk solids storage and transport, atomizer design, artificial intelligence, relational database design, condition based maintenance for machinery and predictive maintenance. *Mailing Add:* PO Box 95 Haddam CT 06438

SMITH, DONALD EUGENE, REPRODUCTIVE PHYSIOLOGY, ENDOCRINOLOGY. *Current Pos:* assoc prof, 67-72, dir grad prog zool, 87-93, PROF ZOOL, NC STATE UNIV, 72- *Personal Data:* b Tunkhannock, Pa, Jan 26, 34; m 58, Lillian Lathouse; c Craig, Cynthia & Cheryl. *Educ:* Bloomsburg State Col, BScEd, 55; Ohio State Univ, MSc, 58, PhD(physiol, zool), 62. *Prof Exp:* Pub sch teacher, Pa, 55-56; asst zool, Ohio State Univ, 56-59, instr, 59-60; from instr to asst prof, Ohio Wesleyan Univ, 60-66. *Concurrent Pos:* NSF res partic, Univ Ill, 65, vis asst prof, 66-67; vis scientist, NIH, 75; vis prof, Duke Univ Med Ctr, 81. *Mem:* AAAS; Am Soc Zool; Sigma Xi; Soc Study Reproduction. *Res:* Mechanisms of hormone action; effects of estrogen and progesterone on uterine glucose metabolism; effects of metals on uterine steroid hormone receptors. *Mailing Add:* Dept Zool Box 7617 NC State Univ Raleigh NC 27695. *Fax:* 919-515-5327

SMITH, DONALD EUGENE, physical chemistry, materials science, for more information see previous edition

SMITH, DONALD FOSS, PHYSICAL CHEMISTRY. *Current Pos:* RETIRED. *Personal Data:* b Athens, Tenn, Feb 14, 13; m 40; c 2. *Educ:* Univ Chattanooga, BS, 34; Univ Tenn, MS, 36; Univ Va, PhD(chem), 39. *Prof Exp:* Asst prof chem, Judson Col, 39-40 & The Citadel, 40-43; assoc explosives chemist, US Bur Mines, 43-44; asst prof chem, Pa Col Women, 44-45; from asst prof to assoc prof, Univ Vt, 45-51; from assoc prof to prof chem, Univ Ala, Tuscaloosa, 51-83, chmn dept, 81-83. *Mem:* Am Chem Soc; Am Inst Chem. *Res:* Heat capacity determinations at high temperatures; solubility determinations; cryoscopic determinations in fused salt systems; conductance in fused salts; heat capacities at low temperatures. *Mailing Add:* 25 Ridgeland Tuscaloosa AL 35406

SMITH, DONALD FREDERICK, VETERINARY SURGERY. *Current Pos:* DEAN VET EDUC, COL VET MED, CORNELL UNIV, 90- *Personal Data:* b Picton, Ont, Nov 25, 49; m 74; c 3. *Educ:* Univ Guelph, DVM, 74; Am Col Vet Surgeons, dipl. *Prof Exp:* Intern vet med, Univ Pa, 74-75, resident vet surg, 75-77; assoc prof surg, Univ Wis, Madison, 83-86; asst prof large animal surg, Col Vet Med, NY State, 77-82, prof & chmn, Dept Clin Sci, 87-90. *Mem:* Comp Gastroenterol Soc. *Res:* Surgery of the bovine gastrointestinal tract; metabolic alkalosis. *Mailing Add:* Dept Vet Med Col Vet Med Cornell Univ Ithaca NY 14853-6401

SMITH, DONALD LARNED, NUCLEAR PHYSICS. *Current Pos:* Asst physicist, 69-73, PHYSICIST, APPL PHYSICS DIV, ARGONNE NAT LAB, 73- *Personal Data:* b White Plains, NY, June 8, 40; m 67; c 1. *Educ:* Ga Inst Technol, BS, 62; Mass Inst Technol, PhD(physics), 67. *Mem:* Am Phys Soc; Am Nuclear Soc. *Res:* Nuclear measurement techniques; gamma-ray spectroscopy and associated correlations; radiation interaction with matter; neutron cross sections and neutron scattering phenomena. *Mailing Add:* 13484 S Redberry Circle Plainfield IL 60544. *Fax:* 630-252-4007

SMITH, DONALD RAY, MATHEMATICS. *Current Pos:* asst prof, 66-71, assoc prof, 71-80, PROF MATH, UNIV CALIF, SAN DIEGO, 80- *Personal Data:* b Seminole, Okla, Jan 23, 39; m 64; c 2. *Educ:* Auburn Univ, BS, 61; Stanford Univ, PhD(math), 65. *Prof Exp:* Vis mem, Courant Inst Math Sci, NY Univ, 65-66. *Concurrent Pos:* NSF res grant, 67-69. *Mem:* Am Math Soc; Soc Indust & Appl Math. *Res:* Ordinary and partial differential equations. *Mailing Add:* 2026 Balboa Ave Del Mar CA 92014

SMITH, DONALD REED, PHYSICAL CHEMISTRY. *Current Pos:* PRES, BARRIE SCI & MGT CONSULT, 93- *Personal Data:* b Hamilton, Ont, Sept 3, 36; m 60, Audrey; c Mark, Sharon & Donald. *Educ:* McMaster Univ, BSc, 58; Univ Leeds, PhD(radiation chem), 61. *Prof Exp:* Demonstr phys chem, Univ Leeds, 58-61; from asst res off to assoc res off, Chalk River Nuclear Lab, Atomic Energy Can Ltd, 61-70, head, Phys Chem Br, 69-82, sr res off, 70-82; dir nuclear reactor & prof chem, McMaster Univ, 82-87; pres, Nuclear Activation Serv Ltd, 84-87; technol develop mgr, Space Sta Prog, Can Space Agency, 88-90, dir strategic develop, 91-93. *Concurrent Pos:* Emmanuel Col vis fel, Univ Cambridge, Eng, 75-76. *Mem:* Fel Chem Inst Can. *Res:* Electron spin resonance and laser magnetic resonance spectroscopy; radiation chemistry; isotope separation. *Mailing Add:* 16 Glenmorris Dr Dundas ON L9H 1S4 Can

SMITH, DONALD ROSS, polymer chemistry, organic chemistry, for more information see previous edition

SMITH, DONALD STANLEY, MECHANICAL ENGINEERING. *Current Pos:* RETIRED. *Personal Data:* b New Westminster, BC, Dec 23, 26; US citizen; m 48; c 1. *Educ:* Univ Calif, Berkeley, BS, 50, MS, 66, PhD(mech eng), 69. *Prof Exp:* Engr, Procter & Gamble Co, 50-54; mgt consult, McKinsey & Co, 54-58; asst vpres eng, Hallamore Electronics Co, 58-59; independent consult, 59-60; asst vpres eng, Aircraft Div, Hughes Tool Co, 60-64; res engr, Univ Calif, 64-69; from assoc prof to prof, Calif State Univ, Chico, 69-88, chmn, Dept Mech Eng, 72-88. *Mem:* Combustion Inst. *Res:* Engine generated air pollution. *Mailing Add:* 2 Canterbury Circle Chico CA 95926

SMITH, DONALD W(ANAMAKER), ENVIRONMENTAL ENGINEERING. *Current Pos:* RETIRED. *Personal Data:* b Bethlehem, Pa, Aug 30, 23; m 46, Mary Morse; c C Dana & Daniel S M. *Educ:* US Naval Acad, BS, 45. *Prof Exp:* Engr chem, E I DuPont de Nemours & Co, Inc, 47-56, tech supt, 56-59, staff mem, Develop Dept, 61-76, admin asst, Off Environ Affairs, 76-86. *Concurrent Pos:* Consult, 86- *Mem:* Am Inst Chem Engrs. *Res:* Corporate environmental management. *Mailing Add:* Coffee Run Apts C4I 614 Loveville Rd Hockessin DE 19707-1609

SMITH, DONN LEROY, CLINICAL PHARMACOLOGY. *Current Pos:* dir, Med Ctr & dean, Col Med, 69-76, prof, 76-85, EMER PROF PHARMACOL & THERAPEUT & DEAN, UNIV S FLA, 85- *Personal Data:* b Denver, Colo, Nov 1, 15; m 37; c 2. *Educ:* Univ Denver, AB, 39, MS, 41; Univ Colo, PhD(physiol, pharmacol), 48, MD, 58. *Prof Exp:* Asst prof physiol, Univ Denver, 48-50; from asst prof to assoc prof pharmacol, Med Sch, Univ Colo, 50-60, assoc dean, 60-63; dean, Sch Med & prof physiol, Univ Louisville, 63-69. *Mem:* AAAS; AMA; Am Soc Pharmacol & Exp Therapeut; Soc Exp Biol & Med; fel Am Col Clin Pharmacol. *Res:* Analgesia; traumatic shock; experimental hypertension. *Mailing Add:* 5212 E 127th Ave Tampa FL 33617-1436

SMITH, DORIAN GLEN WHITNEY, GEOLOGY, MINERALOGY. *Current Pos:* from asst prof to assoc prof geol, 66-74, PROF GEOL & CUR MINERALS & METEORITES, UNIV ALTA, 74- *Personal Data:* b London, Eng, Oct 11, 34; m 59; c 3. *Educ:* Univ London, BSc, 59; Univ Alta, MSc, 60; Cambridge Univ, PhD(petrol), 63; Oxford Univ, MA, 64. *Prof Exp:* Demonstr mineral, Oxford Univ, 63-66. *Concurrent Pos:* Nuffield Found Travel Award mineral & petrol, Cambridge Univ, 71; counr, Int Mineral Asn, 82-; consult, UN, 82-84. *Mem:* Fel Geol Soc London; Mineral Soc London; Mineral Asn Can (pres, 78-79); Mineral Soc Am; Geochem Soc; Geol Asn Can. *Res:* High temperature thermal metamorphism; electron microprobe applications in mineralogy and petrology; study of bonding in minerals by soft x-ray spectroscopy; energy dispersive electron microprobe analysis; clay mineralogy; meteorites; mineral data base management. *Mailing Add:* Dept Geol Univ Alta Edmonton AB T6G 2M7 Can

SMITH, DOUGLAS, GEOLOGY. *Current Pos:* from asst prof to assoc prof, 71-82, PROF GEOL, UNIV TEX, AUSTIN, 82- *Personal Data:* b St Joseph, Mo, 1940; m 66. *Educ:* Calif Inst Technol, BS, 62, PhD(geol), 69; Harvard Univ, Am, 63. *Prof Exp:* Fel, Geophys Lab, Carnegie Inst, Washington, 68-71. *Mem:* Mineral Soc Am; Geol Soc Am; Am Geophys Union. *Res:* Igneous and metamorphic petrology; experimental studies of phase equilibria; physical conditions and chemistry of rock-forming processes. *Mailing Add:* Dept Geol Univ Tex Austin TX 78712

SMITH, DOUGLAS ALAN, MOLECULAR MODELING. *Current Pos:* PRES & CHIEF EXEC OFFICER, DAS GROUP, INC. *Personal Data:* b Hempstead, NY, Jan 16, 59; c 2. *Educ:* Univ Scranton, BS, 79; Carnegie-Mellon Univ, MS, 84, PhD(chem), 85. *Prof Exp:* Res asst prof org chem, Dept Chem, Univ SC, 85-87; asst prof, Dept Chem, Univ Toledo, 87-, mem, Ctr Drug Design & Develop, 88- *Concurrent Pos:* Consult, Afton Chem, Inc, 84-88, Chomerics, Inc, subsid W R Grace, Inc, 90-91, MacMillan, Sobanski & Todd, 90; instr org chem, Dept Chem, Univ SC, 86; postdoctoral fel Nat Res Serv Award, NIH, 87; vis scientist, Mat Lab, Polymer Br, Wright-Patterson AFB, 89-91; mem steering comt, High Temperature Polymer & Molecular Modeling Focus Group, Ohio Aerospace Inst, 90- *Mem:* Am Chem Soc; Sigma Xi. *Res:* Synthetic, physical and computational organic chemistry; synthetic and computational studies of pericyclic reactions; remote asymmetric induction; nitrenium ions and nonlinear optical properties of organic molecules. *Mailing Add:* DAS Group Inc 1732 Liter Dr 2nd Floor Johnstown PA 15905

SMITH, DOUGLAS CALVIN, PSYCHOBIOLOGY, NEUROPHYSIOLOGY. *Current Pos:* asst prof psychobiol, 79-83, ASSOC PROF, SCH MED, SOUTHERN ILL UNIV, 81-, ASSOC PROF PSYCHOBIOL, 83- *Personal Data:* b Kokomo, Ind, Aug 5, 49; m, Mila Moring; c Gabriel & Jason. *Educ:* Tex A&M Univ, BS, 71, MS, 73; Kans State Univ, PhD(psychol), 77. *Honors & Awards:* NRSA Award, NIH, 77-79. *Prof Exp:* Fel physiol & psychol, Univ Ill, 77-79. *Concurrent Pos:* Lectr, Med Sch, Univ Ill, 77-79; prin investr, Visual Suppression NSF grant, 80-82, Properties of Thermal Protein Microsphere, 93-95. *Mem:* Soc Neurosci; Asn Res Vision & Opthal. *Res:* Electrophysiological and behavioral investigation of the effects of abnormalities in the development of the visual system of mammals with binocular vision, as well as the neural basis of memory; epilepsy-cessation of focal seizures. *Mailing Add:* Dept Psychol Southern Ill Univ Carbondale IL 62901

SMITH, DOUGLAS D, MATHEMATICAL SCIENCES. *Current Pos:* CHMN, MATH SCI, UNIV NC, 83- *Educ:* Pa State Univ, PhD(math), 71. *Mem:* Am Math Soc; Math Asn Am. *Mailing Add:* Dept Math Sci Univ NC Wilmington NC 28403-3297

SMITH, DOUGLAS LEE, GEOLOGY. *Current Pos:* From asst prof to assoc prof, 72-80, PROF GEOL, UNIV FLA, 80- *Personal Data:* b St Louis, Mo, Sept 22, 43; m 65; c 2. *Educ:* Univ Ill, BS, 65; Univ Minn, PhD(geophys), 72. *Mem:* Am Geophys Union; Soc Explor Geophysicists; Geol Soc Am. *Res:* Geothermal conditions and their implications for energy resources; tectonic conditions; nature of earth's crust. *Mailing Add:* Dept Geol Univ Fla Gainesville FL 32611

SMITH, DOUGLAS LEE, x-ray crystallography, for more information see previous edition

SMITH, DOUGLAS WEMP, MOLECULAR BIOLOGY, GENETICS. *Current Pos:* from asst prof to assoc prof, 69-82, PROF BIOL, UNIV CALIF, SAN DIEGO, 83- *Personal Data:* b Los Angeles, Calif, July 13, 38; m 75; c 3. *Educ:* Stanford Univ, BS, 60, PhD(biophys), 67; Univ Ill, Urbana, MS, 62. *Prof Exp:* NIH fel, Max Planck Inst Virus Res, Tübingen, Ger, 67-69. *Concurrent Pos:* Acad res grant, Univ Calif, 70-71, Cancer Res Coord Comt grants, 70-72, 74-75, 78-79 & 81-82; Am Cancer Soc grants, 70-75; NIH grants, 76-81 & 82-86 & 86-89. *Mem:* AAAS; Biophys Soc; Am Soc Biochem Molecular Biol; NY Acad Sci; Am Soc Microbiol; Protein Soc. *Res:* Biochemistry; microbiology; recombinant DNA research; DNA replication and repair in prokaryotes; structure and function of bacterial origins; atomic physics; optical pumping and hyperfine structure; use of computers in molecular biology. *Mailing Add:* Dept Biol B-022 Univ Calif San Diego La Jolla CA 92093-0322. *E-Mail:* dsmith@ucsd.edu

SMITH, DUDLEY TEMPLETON, WEED SCIENCE, RESEARCH MANAGEMENT & ADMINISTRATION. *Current Pos:* Asst prof crop sci, 68-72, assoc prof, 72-73, asst dir, 73-79, ASSOC DIR, TEX AGR EXP STA, TEX A&M UNIV, 79- *Personal Data:* b Washington, DC, June 8, 40; m 65; c 2. *Educ:* Univ Md, College Park, BS, 63, MS, 65; Mich State Univ, PhD(crop sci), 68; Univ Houston, MBA, 82. *Concurrent Pos:* Chmn & bd dirs USAID Sorghum/Millet Consortium & Peanut CRSP. *Mem:* Am Soc Agron. *Res:* Herbicide behavior, residues and movement in soil and water; weed control in crops; growth, phenology and competition of perennial and annual weeds; international agricultural research; planning and management of in state and federal activities. *Mailing Add:* Dept Soil & Crop Scis Heep Ctr Tex A&M Univ College Station TX 77843-2474

SMITH, DURWARD A, FOOD SCIENCE, ENGINEERING. *Current Pos:* ASSOC PROF, UNIV NEBR, 90- *Personal Data:* b Raymond, Wash, Jan 4, 47. *Educ:* Univ Wash, BA, 70; Univ Idaho, BS, 72; La State Univ, MS, 73, PhD(food sci), 76; Jones Law Inst, JD, 84. *Prof Exp:* From asst prof to assoc prof food sci, Dept Hort, Auburn Univ, 83-90. *Concurrent Pos:* Atty, 85-; consult regulatory compliance food indust. *Mem:* Inst Food Technologists; Am Hort Soc. *Res:* Food engineering and science; high temperature, short time processing and its effect on product quality; nutritive value, biological and cellular integrity; improved efficiency peeling, shelling and skinning systems. *Mailing Add:* 10600 NW 27th St Lincoln NE 68524-8919

SMITH, DWIGHT GLENN, POPULATION ECOLOGY. *Current Pos:* From asst prof to assoc prof, 70-81, PROF BIOL, SOUTHERN CONN STATE UNIV, 82- *Personal Data:* b Binghampton, NY, Apr 15, 43; m 68; c 2. *Educ:* Elizabethtown Col, BS, 66; Brigham Young Univ, MS, 68, PhD(zool), 71. *Concurrent Pos:* Ecol consult, Environ Pop Educ Asn, 74-; mem sci staff referee Condor, Cooper Ornith Soc, 75- *Mem:* Am Ornithologists Union; Cooper Ornith Soc. *Res:* Investigations of vertebrate predator and prey relationships with emphasis on mathematical models of habitat partitioning; habitat evaluation. *Mailing Add:* Dept Biol Southern Conn State Univ 501 Crescent St New Haven CT 06515-1355

SMITH, DWIGHT MORRELL, PHYSICAL CHEMISTRY, ANALYTICAL CHEMISTRY. *Current Pos:* chmn, Dept Chem, Univ Denver, 72-83, acad vchancellor, 83, chancellor, 84-89, PROF CHEM, UNIV DENVER, 72- *Personal Data:* b Hudson, NY, Oct 10, 31; m 55, 91, Elfi Brodersen; c K Elizabeth (McCarthy), Susan A (Hall) & Jonathan A. *Educ:* Cent Col, Iowa, BA, 53; Pa State Univ, PhD(chem), 57. *Hon Degrees:* ScD, Central Col, 86; DLitt, Univ Denver, 90. *Honors & Awards:* Colo Sect Award, Am Chem Soc, 86. *Prof Exp:* Instr chem, Calif Inst Technol, 57-59; sr chemist, Texaco, Inc, 59-61; asst prof chem, Wesleyan Univ, 61-66; from assoc prof to prof, Hope Col, 66-72. *Concurrent Pos:* NSF fac fel, Scripps Inst Oceanog, 71-72; pres, Hawaii Loa Col, 90-92. *Mem:* Catalysis Soc; Am Chem Soc; AAAS; Soc Appl Spectros. *Res:* Catalysis; infrared spectroscopy; kinetics; electrochemistry; surface chemistry; structure and reactivity of black carbon; atmospheric chemistry and physics. *Mailing Add:* Dept Chem/Biochem Univ Denver Denver CO 80208. *Fax:* 303-871-2932

SMITH, DWIGHT RAYMOND, FISH & WILDLIFE SCIENCES. *Current Pos:* RETIRED. *Personal Data:* b Sanders, Idaho, July 28, 21; m 44; c 2. *Educ:* Univ Idaho, BS, 49, MS, 51; Utah State Univ, PhD(ecol), 71. *Prof Exp:* Res biologist, Idaho Fish & Game Dept, 50-52, area big game mgr, 53-56; range scientist, US Forest Serv, 56-61, wildlife res biologist, 62-65; from asst prof to prof wildlife biol, Colo State Univ, 65-83, emer prof, 84-89. *Mem:* Sigma Xi. *Res:* Large terrestrial ungulates and relationships to habitat; inventory procedures and ecological concepts related to wildlife planning; environmental law as a tool of natural resources management. *Mailing Add:* 1916 Harmony Dr Ft Collins CO 80525-3442

SMITH, EARL W, THEORETICAL PHYSICS. *Current Pos:* CONSULT, BALL AEROSPACE, 83- *Personal Data:* b Chicago, Ill, Oct 14, 40. *Educ:* Univ Fla, BS, 62, PhD(physics), 66. *Prof Exp:* Proj leader, Nat Bur Standards, Boulder, Colo, 67-83. *Mem:* Am Phys Soc; Soc Photo-Optical Instrumentation Engrs. *Mailing Add:* Ball Aerospace PO Box 1062 Boulder CO 80306

SMITH, EDDIE CAROL, BIOCHEMISTRY. *Current Pos:* from asst prof to prof biochem, Univ Okla, 65-80, assoc dean, Grad Col, 81-89 & 91-93, actg vprovost res admin, 89-91, actg grad dean, 90-91, DAVID ROSS BOYD PROF CHEM, UNIV OKLA, 80-, GRAD DEAN, 93-, VPRES RES, 93- *Personal Data:* b Lexington, KY, Apr 13, 37; m 61; c 1. *Educ:* Univ Ky, BS, 59; Iowa State Univ, PhD(biochem), 63. *Prof Exp:* Asst biochem, Iowa State Univ, 59-63, NIH res assoc, 63-64; scholar, Univ Calif, Los Angeles, 64-65. *Concurrent Pos:* Am Cancer Soc grant, 66-67; NSF res grant, 69-74. *Mem:* Am Chem Soc; Am Soc Biol Chemists. *Res:* Enzymic studies of alcoholic animals; regulation of metabolism; metabolic role of plant peroxidases. *Mailing Add:* Grad Col Univ Okla Norman OK 73019-5708. *Fax:* 405-325-5346; *E-Mail:* ecsmith@ou.edu

SMITH, EDGAR FITZHUGH, animal husbandry; deceased, see previous edition for last biography

SMITH, EDITH LUCILE, BIOCHEMISTRY, MICROBIOLOGY. *Current Pos:* from assoc prof to prof, 58-78, EMER PROF BIOCHEM, DARTMOUTH MED SCH, 78- *Personal Data:* b Jackson, Miss, Sept 9, 13. *Educ:* Tulane Univ, BS, 35, MS, 37; Univ Rochester, PhD(biochem), 50. *Hon Degrees:* DSc, Tulane Univ, 84. *Prof Exp:* Lab asst chem, Newcomb Col, Tulane Univ, 35-36, from lab asst to assoc instr biochem, Tulane Univ, 36-47; asst prof biophys, Univ Pa, 55-58. *Concurrent Pos:* Fel biophys, Univ Pa, 50-54; Brit & Am Cancer Socs exchange fel, Cambridge Univ, 54-55. *Mem:* AAAS; Am Soc Biol Chemists; Am Soc Microbiol; Am Chem Soc. *Res:* Oxidative enzymes, particularly cytochrome pigments; respiratory chain systems of mammalian tissues and microorganisms; oxidative enzyme systems of photosynthetic bacteria. *Mailing Add:* 80 Lyme Rd Hanover NH 03755

SMITH, EDWARD, ANALYTICAL CHEMISTRY. *Current Pos:* CONSULT, EDWARD SMITH & ASSOCS, 92- & LACHAN CONSULT SERVS, 93- *Personal Data:* b Liberty, NY, Aug 26, 34; m 65, Eileen Ann Wishner; c Michael D, Bruce A & Lawrence S. *Educ:* Long Island Univ, BSPharm, 55; Univ Mich, MS, 58, PhD(pharmaceut chem), 62. *Prof Exp:* Anal chemist, US Food & Drug Admin, 62-65, res chemist, Div Pharmaceut Chem, Bur Sci, 65-70, sr res chemist, Div Drug Chem, Bur Drugs, 70-85, sr res chemist, Biopharmaceut Res Br,85-92. *Mem:* Am Pharmaceut Asn; Am Chem Soc; Acad Pharmaceut Sci; fel Asn Off Analytical Chem; fel Am Asn Pharmaceut Scientists; Sigma Xi. *Res:* Analysis of pharmaceuticals and their active constitutents and possible degradation products using chromatographic techniques; electrometric methods and nuclear chemical techniques; structure proof using spectrophotometric techniques; analysis of drugs in biological fluid samples; sepn stereoismers (chiral sepns). *Mailing Add:* 14203 Castaway Dr Rockville MD 20853. *Fax:* 301-460-6765

SMITH, EDWARD E, PSYCHOLOGY. *Current Pos:* PROF, DEP PSYCHOL, UNIV MICH, 86-, DIR SCI & COGNITIVE NEUROSCI PROG, 94-, ARTHUR W MELTON PROF PSYCHOL, 96- *Personal Data:* b Brooklyn, NY, Apr 23, 40. *Educ:* Booklyn Col, BA, 61; Univ Mich, PhD(exp psychol), 66. *Prof Exp:* Res assoc, St Elizabeth's Hosp, NIMH, 66-68; asst prof, Dept Psychol, Univ Wis-Madison, 68-70; from asst prof to prof, Dept Psychol, Stanford Univ, 70-80; sr scientist, Bolt Beranek & Newman Inc, Mass, 79-85, prin scientist, 85-86; adj prof, Dept Psychol, Mass Inst Technol, 83-86. *Concurrent Pos:* Grantee, USPHS, 68-88, Off Naval Res, 80-85 & 91-99, NSF, 87-90 & 94-97, Am Res Inst, 87-90, McDonnel-Pew, 91; vis assoc prof, Rockefeller Univ, 76-77; vis scholar, Harvard Univ, 79-82; ed, Cognitive Sci, 81-85; del, Fedn Behav Psychol & Cognitive Sci, 82-84; chair, Cognitive Sci Soc, 87; fac assoc, Res Ctr Group Dynamics, Univ Mich, 88-; Guggenheim fel, 92-93; mem, Comn Behav Soc Sci & Educ, Nat Acad Sci, 96. *Mem:* Nat Acad Sci; fel Am Psychol Soc; Cognitive Neurosci Soc; Cognitive Sci Soc; Soc Exp Psychologists; Am Acad Arts & Sci. *Res:* Concepts and categorization; induction and reasoning; organizational and retrieval processes in memory and comprehension; neuropsychology of memory, categorization and reasoning; contributed numerous articles to professional publications. *Mailing Add:* Dept Psychol Univ Mich 525 E University Ann Arbor MI 48109

SMITH, EDWARD HOLMAN, ECONOMIC ENTOMOLOGY. *Current Pos:* RETIRED. *Personal Data:* b Abbeville, SC, Sept 2, 15; m 47; c 4. *Educ:* Clemson Univ, BS, 38; Cornell Univ, MS, 40, PhD, 47. *Prof Exp:* Asst prof entom, Exp Sta, State Univ NY Col Agr, Cornell Univ, 47-50, from assoc prof to prof, 55-64; head dept, NC State Univ, 64-67; prof entom & dir coop exten, Cornell Univ, 67-72, chmn, Dept Entom, 72-81. *Mem:* Entom Soc Am; AAAS; Sigma Xi. *Res:* Fruit insects; insect biology and control; mode of ovicidal action. *Mailing Add:* 444 Crawfields Dr Ashville NC 28803-3280

SMITH, EDWARD J(OSEPH), ELECTRICAL ENGINEERING. *Current Pos:* res assoc, Polytech Inst Brooklyn, 50-53, res assoc prof, 53-57, assoc prof, 57-59, dir, Comput Ctr, 59-63, head, Dept Elec Eng, 67-71 & Dept Elec Eng & Comput Sci, 78-81, prof, 59-86, EMER PROF ELEC ENG, POLYTECH INST BROOKLYN, 86- *Personal Data:* b New York, NY, Dec 12, 20; m 54; c 2. *Educ:* Cooper Union, BEE, 45: Polytech Inst Brooklyn, MEE, 48, PhD(elec eng), 51. *Prof Exp:* Res engr, Remington Rand Co, Conn, 45-47; instr elec eng, NY Univ, 47-48. *Concurrent Pos:* Vis prof, Eindhoven Technol Univ, 63-64. *Mem:* Asn Comput Mach; Inst Elec & Electronics Engrs; Am Soc Eng Educ; NY Acad Sci; AAAS. *Res:* Computers; logic design; computer architecture; switching and automata theory; nonlinear magnetics. *Mailing Add:* 614 Third St Brooklyn NY 11215-3004

SMITH, EDWARD JOHN, PHYSICS, SPACE MAGNETISM. *Current Pos:* MEM TECH STAFF, JET PROPULSION LAB, 61- *Personal Data:* b Dravosburg, Pa, Sept 21, 27; m 53; c 4. *Educ:* Univ Calif, Los Angeles, BA, 51, MS, 52, PhD(physics), 60. *Honors & Awards:* Medal Exceptional Sci Achievement, NASA. *Prof Exp:* Res geophysicist, Inst Geophys, Univ Calif, Los Angeles, 55-59; mem tech staff, Space Tech Labs, 59-61. *Mem:* AAAS; Sigma Xi; Int Sci Radio Union; Am Geophys Union; Am Astron Soc. *Res:* Planetary magnetism; space physics; interplanetary physics; wave-particle interactions in plasmas; propagation of electromagnetic waves; solar-terrestrial relations. *Mailing Add:* 2536 Boulder Rd Altadena CA 91001

SMITH, EDWARD LEE, PLANT GENETICS, FIELD CROPS. *Current Pos:* assoc prof, 66-71, PROF AGRON, OKLA STATE UNIV, 71- *Personal Data:* b Apache, Okla, June 6, 32; m 58; c 2. *Educ:* Okla State Univ, BS, 54, MS, 59; Univ Minn, PhD(plant genetics), 62. *Prof Exp:* Instr agron, Okla State Univ, 57-58; asst prof, Univ Tenn, 62-63; asst prof, Okla State Univ-Ethiopian Contract, 63-65; asst prof, Univ Ill, 65-66. *Mem:* AAAS; Crop Sci Soc Am; Am Soc Agron; Genetics Soc Am. *Res:* Wheat breeding and genetics; milling and baking quality in wheat; disease and insect resistance in small grains; heterosis, cytoplasmic male sterility and fertility restoration in wheat. *Mailing Add:* Dept of Agron Okla State Univ Stillwater OK 74078-0001

SMITH, EDWARD M(ANSON), AGRICULTURAL ENGINEERING. *Current Pos:* RETIRED. *Personal Data:* b Sharpsburg, Ga, Feb 16, 25; m 46; c 4. *Educ:* Univ Ga, BS, 49; Kans State Univ, MS, 50. *Prof Exp:* Asst prof, Southwest Tex State Col, 50-52; assoc prof agr eng & assoc agr engr, USDA & Okla State Univ, 52-57; assoc prof agr eng & assoc agr engr, Exp Sta, Univ Ky, 57-90. *Mem:* Am Soc Agr Engrs. *Res:* Farm machinery. *Mailing Add:* 3509 Willowood Rd Lexington KY 40517

SMITH, EDWARD RUSSELL, NUTRITION. *Current Pos:* asst prof, 75-80, ASSOC PROF OBSTET & GYNEC, UNIV TEX MED BR GALVESTON, 80- *Personal Data:* b Knoxville, Tenn, May 18, 44; m 69, 95, Beverly Braden; c 5. *Educ:* Univ Louisville, AB, 66, PhD(biochem), 71. *Prof Exp:* Instr biochem, obstet & gynec, Col Med, Univ Nebr, Omaha, 71, res asst prof, 71-75. *Mem:* AAAS; Am Chem Soc; Sigma Xi; Geront Soc; Soc Study Reproduction; fel Am Inst Chemists; Endocrine Soc. *Res:* Cause of reproductive senescence; regulation of protein synthesis and degradation; hormone action upon target tissues. *Mailing Add:* Obstet/Gynec 1062 Univ Tex Galveston TX 77550. *E-Mail:* edward.smith@utmb.edu

SMITH, EDWARD S, METALLURGICAL ENGINEERING. *Current Pos:* SR MAT ENGR, PRATT & WHITNEY, 80- *Personal Data:* b New York, NY, Dec 4, 24. *Educ:* Va Tech Inst, BS, 48; Univ Pittsburgh, MS, 67. *Mem:* Fel Am Soc Metals; Am Soc Mfg Engrs; Am Inst Mining, Metall & Petrol Engrs. *Mailing Add:* 3181 Medinah Circle Lake Worth FL 33467

SMITH, EDWIN BURNELL, PLANT TAXONOMY, BIOSYSTEMATICS. *Current Pos:* from asst prof to assoc prof, 66-76, chmn, Dept Bot & Bact, 78-81, PROF BOT, UNIV ARK, FAYETTEVILLE, 76- *Personal Data:* b Wellington, Kans, Dec 1, 36; m 58; c 3. *Educ:* Univ Kans, BS, 61, MA, 63, PhD(bot), 65. *Prof Exp:* Asst prof bot, Rutgers Univ, 65-66; vis cytologist, Brookhaven Nat Lab, 66. *Concurrent Pos:* Consult, Brookhaven Nat Lab, 66. *Mem:* Bot Soc Am; Am Soc Plant Taxon; Int Asn Plant Taxon. *Res:* Flora of Arkansas; biosystematics of flowering plants, especially Compositae; taxonomy of Coreopsis and Coreocarpus. *Mailing Add:* Dept Biol Sci Univ Ark SCEN 632 Fayetteville AR 72701-1202

SMITH, EDWIN LEE, PHYSIOLOGY. *Current Pos:* PROF PHYSIOL, UNIV TEX DENT BR HOUSTON, 47- *Personal Data:* b Shelton, Nebr, Aug 12, 07; m 33; c 2. *Educ:* Univ Nebr, BS, 35, MS, 38; Univ Chicago, PhD(physiol), 41. *Prof Exp:* Instr physiol, Col Med, Univ Ill, 41-43; asst prof, Med Col Va, 43-47. *Mem:* AAAS; Am Physiol Soc; Soc Exp Biol & Med; Int Asn Dent Res; Sigma Xi. *Res:* Bioassay; pharmacology and physiology of circulation; renal physiology; maximum capacity of the vascular system; experimental renal hypertension; digitalis assay; barbiturates. *Mailing Add:* Dept Physiol Univ Tex Health Sci Ctr 4322 Briarbend Dr Houston TX 77035-5002

SMITH, EDWIN MARK, MEDICINE. *Current Pos:* RETIRED. *Personal Data:* b Grand Rapids, Mich, Apr 10, 27; m 40; c 2. *Educ:* Univ Mich, BS, 50, MD, 53. *Prof Exp:* Intern, Univ Hosp, Univ Mich, Ann Arbor, 53-54, resident phys med & rehab, 54-57, res assoc, Univ, 57-59, from asst prof to prof phys med & rehab, Sch Med, 59-78; pvt practice, Flint, Mich, 78-92. *Mem:* AMA; Asn Electromyog & Electrodiag; Cong Rehab Med; Am Acad Phys Med & Rehab. *Res:* Physical medicine and rehabilitation; mechanics of deformity formation in rheumatoid arthritis; design and development of orthetic devices. *Mailing Add:* 1815 Arbordale Rd Ann Arbor MI 48103

SMITH, EILEEN PATRICIA, PHYSICAL ORGANIC CHEMISTRY. *Current Pos:* asst prof, 68-72, ASSOC PROF CHEM, TRENTON STATE COL, 72- *Personal Data:* b Trenton, NJ, Mar 20, 41. *Educ:* Univ Pa, BSChem, 62, PhD(org chem), 67. *Prof Exp:* Instr chem, Mercer County Community Col, 67-68. *Mem:* Sigma Xi; NY Acad Sci; Am Chem Soc; Am Inst Chemists. *Res:* Mass spectral studies; organic laboratory experiments; liquid crystal studies. *Mailing Add:* 625 Paxson Ave Trenton NJ 08619-1138

SMITH, ELBERT GEORGE, CHEMISTRY. *Current Pos:* from assoc prof to prof, 58-78, EMER PROF CHEM, MILLS COL, 78- *Personal Data:* b Eugene, Ore, July 18, 13. *Educ:* Ore State Col, BA, 36; Iowa State Col, PhD(physiol & nutrit chem), 43. *Prof Exp:* From asst to instr chem, Iowa State Col, 36-43; asst prof, Hamline Univ, 43-46 & Univ Denver, 46-47; from asst prof to assoc prof, Univ Hawaii, 47-58. *Concurrent Pos:* Staff mem surv chem notation systs, Nat Res Coun, 61-64, mem comt mod methods handling chem info, 64-70. *Mem:* Fel AAAS; Chem Notation Asn (pres, 72); Am Chem Soc. *Res:* Nutritional biochemistry; chemical structure information retrieval; Wiswesser notation. *Mailing Add:* 6360 Melville Dr Oakland CA 94611

SMITH, ELIZABETH KNAPP, CLINICAL BIOCHEMISTRY, PEDIATRIC ENDOCRINOLOGY. *Current Pos:* RETIRED. *Personal Data:* b Coraopolis, Pa, Dec 15, 17; m 51. *Educ:* Fla State Col Women, BS, 38; Univ Mich, MS, 39; Univ Iowa, PhD(biochem), 43. *Prof Exp:* Asst pediat, Univ Iowa, 39-43, res assoc, 44-47, res asst prof, 47-50; asst, Rackham Arthritis Res Unit, Univ Mich, 43-44; from asst prof to assoc prof obstet & gynec, Sch Med, Univ Wash, 50-58, res assoc prof pediat, 58-83, res assoc prof, Lab Med, 71-83, emer prof, 83- *Concurrent Pos:* Clin chemist, Children's Hosp Med Ctr, 58-83. *Mem:* AAAS; Am Chem Soc; Endocrine Soc; Am Asn Clin Chem; Lawson Wilkins Pediat Endocrine Soc. *Res:* Endocrine and metabolic disorders in children; metabolism of adrenocortical hormones in infancy and childhood. *Mailing Add:* Dept Lab Children's Hosp Med Ctr 4800 Sand Pt Way NE Seattle WA 98105

SMITH, ELIZABETH MELVA, STEROID CHEMISTRY, SYNTHETIC ORGANIC CHEMISTRY. *Current Pos:* CONSULT, 89- *Personal Data:* b Regina, Sask, Nov 4, 43. *Educ:* Univ Sask, Saskatoon, BSP, 65, PhD(pharmaceut chem), 69. *Prof Exp:* Fel chem, La State Univ, New Orleans, 69-70 & Wayne State Univ, Detroit, 70; res assoc, Dept Chem, Univ Ala, 70-72; fel, Schering Corp, 73, sr scientist, 74-77, from prin scientist chem to sr prin scientist chem, 77-89. *Concurrent Pos:* Med Res Coun Can fel, 69 & 70. *Mem:* Am Chem Soc. *Res:* Steroid synthesis; synthesis and chemistry of heterocyclic compounds; amino acid chemistry. *Mailing Add:* Schering Plough Res Inst 2015 Galloping Hill Rd Kenilworth NJ 07033-0539

SMITH, ELLEN OLIVER, BOVINE HEART-MUSCLE ISOFORM, PURIFICATION & CHARACTERIZATION OF CARBOHYDRASES. *Current Pos:* PROF MICROBIOL & GENETICS, DEPT BIOL, MADONNA UNIV, 83-, DEAN COL SCI & MATH, 91- *Personal Data:* b Nashville, Tenn, June 3, 45; m 71, John R. *Educ:* La State Univ, BS, 67, PhD(microbiol), 72. *Prof Exp:* Lab technician, Dept Microbiol, Lutheran Gen Hosp, 67; res assoc, Dept Dermat, Univ Mich Med Sch, 72-74, sr res assoc, Dept Oral Path, 74-77; vis lectr microbiol, Dept Biol, Eastern Mich Univ, 77-81. *Mem:* AAAS; Asn Women Sci; Nat Sci Teacher Asn; Soc Col Sci Teaching; Am Asn Univ Women. *Res:* Structure and function of gene for bovine heart/muscle isoform of cytochrome and oxidase subunit via; purification and characterization of carbohydrases from Alcaligenes faecalis; growth regulation of eukaryotic cells. *Mailing Add:* Madonna Univ 36600 Schoolcraft Rd Livonia MI 48150-1176

SMITH, ELMER F, III, PUBLICATIONS MANAGEMENT. *Current Pos:* CHIEF, EASTERN PUBL GROUP, US GEOL SURV, 97- *Personal Data:* b Wilmington, Del, Nov 1, 40. *Educ:* St Lawrence Univ, BA, 62. *Mem:* Asn Earth Sci Ed (vpres, 90, pres, 91). *Mailing Add:* US Geol Surv 903 Nat Ctr Reston VA 20192. *Fax:* 703-648-6148; *E-Mail:* efsmith@usgs.gov

SMITH, ELMER ROBERT, CHEMICAL ENGINEERING, BIOPHYSICS. *Current Pos:* RETIRED. *Personal Data:* b Adams, Wis, Nov 14, 23; m 57; c 2. *Educ:* Univ Wis, BS, 44. *Prof Exp:* Asst biophys, Univ Calif, 51-54 & Sloan-Kettering Inst, 54-56; instr, Med Col, Cornell Univ, 56; sr scientist, Bettis Atomic Power Lab, Westinghouse Elec Corp, 57-61; supvr radiochem, Hazleton Nuclear Sci Corp, 61-64; mgr chem & tech servs, Environ Systs Div, Nus Corp, 64-72, staff consult, 72-73, prin engr, 73-75, consult engr, 75-78, exec engr, 78-82. *Mem:* AAAS; Am Chem Soc; Sigma Xi. *Res:* Industry; air pollution; nuclear reactor safeguards and siting; radiochemistry; analytical methods in chemistry and radiochemistry; meteorology; reactor chemistry; environmental monitoring; low and high level radioactive solid waste disposal; environmental impact assessment; project management; pollution control; risk assessment. *Mailing Add:* 11206 Healy St Silver Spring MD 20902-3220

SMITH, ELSKE VAN PANHUYS, astronomy, environmental studies, for more information see previous edition

SMITH, ELTON S, NUCLEAR PHYSICS. *Current Pos:* RES SCIENTIST, JEFFERSON LAB, 87- *Personal Data:* b Bolivia, SAm, Jan 25, 55. *Educ:* Vanderbilt Univ, BS, 76; Univ Wis, PhD(physics), 83. *Mem:* Am Phys Soc. *Mailing Add:* 206 Pageland Dr Yorktown VA 23693

SMITH, EMIL L, BIOCHEMISTRY, BIOPHYSICS. *Current Pos:* prof biol chem & chmn dept, 63-79, EMER PROF, SCH MED, UNIV CALIF, LOS ANGELES, 79- *Personal Data:* b New York, NY, July 5, 11; m 34, Esther Press; c Joseph D & Jeffrey B. *Educ:* Columbia Univ, BS, 31, PhD(biophys), 37. *Honors & Awards:* Annual Lectr & Medalist, Ciba Found, 68; Margaret J Hastings Distinguished Lectr, Res Inst Scripps Clinic, 80; Abraham White Mem Lectr, 82; Stein-Moore Award, Protein Soc, 87. *Prof Exp:* Asst zool, Columbia Univ, 31-34, asst biophys, 34-36, instr, 36-38; res assoc, Rockefeller Inst, 40-42; biophysicist, Biol Lab, E R Squibb & Sons, 42-46; assoc res prof biochem & physiol, Col Med, Univ Utah, 46-47, from assoc prof to prof biochem & from assoc res prof to res prof med, 47-63. *Concurrent Pos:* Guggenheim fel, Cambridge Univ, 38-40; hon fel, Yale Univ, 40; mem, Panel Comt Growth, Nat Res Coun, 49-53; mem, Sect Arthritis & Metab, USPHS, 49-50, biochem, 50-54, Adv Comt Biochem, US Off Naval Res, 57-60, US Nat Comt Biochem, 58-62, chmn, 59-62; mem, Comt Int Orgn & Prog, Nat Acad Sci, 62-72, chmn, 64-68; mem, Bd Trustees, Calif Found Biochem Res, 64-, Adv Coun, Life Ins Med Res Fund, 66-70 & Sci Adv Panel, Ciba Found, 67-79; vis prof, Col France, 68; mem, vis comt, Dept Biol Chem, Harvard Med Sch, 68-71; mem, Comt Scholarly Commun with People's Repub China, 70-76, chmn, 72-75; mem, Bd Int Sci Exchange, Nat Res Coun-Nat Acad Sci, 73-77 & Comn Int Relations, 78-82; prog biomat & biotech, UNESCO, 79-87; exec coun, Protein Soc, 86-93. *Mem:* Nat Acad Sci; Am Chem Soc; Am Acad Art & Sci; Am Philos Soc; Am Soc Biochem & Molecular Biol; foreign mem Acad Sci USSR. *Res:* Chemistry of proteins; milk proteins; amino acids; proteolytic enzymes; peptides; enzymology; histones; cytochromes; dehydrogenases; biochemical evolution. *Mailing Add:* Dept Biol Chem Univ Calif Sch Med Los Angeles CA 90095-1737. *Fax:* 310-206-5272

SMITH, EMIL RICHARD, PHARMACOLOGY, TOXICOLOGY. *Current Pos:* PROF PHARMACOL, UNIV MASS MED SCH, WORCESTER, 75- *Personal Data:* b Bridgewater, Mass, July 25, 31; m 56, Alice J Pike; c 5. *Educ:* Northeastern Univ, BS, 54; Tufts Univ, MS, 56, PhD(pharmacol), 58. *Prof Exp:* Assoc res pharmacologist, Sterling-Winthrop Res Inst, 60-62; res pharmacologist, Mason Res Inst, Worcester, Mass, 62-67; sect head, gen pharmacol & toxicol, Res Labs, Astra Pharmaceut Prod, Inc, 67-72; sect head, chem carcinogenesis, Mason Res Inst, 72-75. *Concurrent Pos:* USPHS res fel pharmacol, Sch Med, Univ Buffalo, 58-60; lectr, Albany Med Col, 61-62, res pharmacologist, St Vincent Hosp, 63-; asst prof, Sch Med, Tufts Univ, 69-73; lectr pharmacol, Sch Med, Univ Mass, 74-75. *Mem:* Am Soc Pharmacol & Exp Therapeut; Soc Toxicol. *Res:* Cardiovascular and autonomic pharmacology; toxicology; pharmacokinetics; drug discovery and development. *Mailing Add:* Dept Pharmacol & Molecular Toxicol Univ Mass Med Sch Worcester MA 01655-0126. *Fax:* 508-856-5080

SMITH, EMMA BREEDLOVE, MATHEMATICS EDUCATION, COMPUTER ASSISTED INSTRUCTION. *Current Pos:* instr, 58-70, PROF MATH, VA STATE UNIV, 75- *Personal Data:* b Whitmell, Va, Dec 24, 31; m 55; c Sonya & James Jr. *Educ:* Va State Univ, BS, 54, MS, 55; Ind Univ, PhD(math educ), 73. *Prof Exp:* Instr math, SC State Col, 55-58, Florissant Valley Community Col, 74-75. *Concurrent Pos:* Instr, NSF Inst Math & Sci Teachers, 58-70, dir tests, Va Conf Math & Sci Teachers, 60-70; asst instr, Math Dept, Univ Pa, 61-62, Ind Univ, 71-72; supvr student teachers, Ind Univ Sch Educ, 72-73; dir math lab, Univ Middle Sch, 72-73. *Mem:* Math Asn Am; Nat Tech Asn; AAAS; Nat Coun Teachers Math. *Res:* Mathematics; mathematics education; computer assisted instruction; factors influencing achievement and attitudes toward mathematics; women and minorities overcoming barriers to success in mathematics and science. *Mailing Add:* Math Dept Va State Univ Box 9068 Petersburg VA 23806

SMITH, ERIC MORGAN, NEUROIMMUNOLOGY, PSYCHONEUROIMMUNOLOGY. *Current Pos:* Postdoctoral fel virol & immunol, Univ Tex Med Br, 79-81, from asst prof to assoc prof microbiol, 82-90, assoc prof psychiat, 86-90, PROF PSYCHIAT & MICROBIOL, UNIV TEX MED BR, 90- *Personal Data:* b Lafayette, Ind, Feb 13, 53; m 79, Janice Kelly; c David K. *Educ:* Syracuse Univ, BS, 75; Baylor Col, PhD(virol), 80. *Concurrent Pos:* Grass mem traveling scientist, 90; co-ed, Advan Neuroimmunol, 91-; session chmn, Gordon Res Conf, 92; mem, Ment Health & Acquired Immunodeficiency Syndrome Rev Group, NIMH, 92-95. *Mem:* Am Asn Immunologists; Soc Neurosci; Am Soc Microbiol; Sigma Xi; AAAS; Int Soc Neuroimmunomodulation. *Res:* Characterizing the production and action of neuropeptides in the immune system. *Mailing Add:* Dept Psychiat D28 Univ Tex Med Br Galveston TX 77555-0431. *Fax:* 409-772-3511

SMITH, ERNEST KETCHAM, RADIO PHYSICS, TELECOMMUNICATIONS. *Current Pos:* ADJ PROF, UNIV COLO, BOULDER, 87- *Personal Data:* b Peking, China, May 31, 22; US citizen; m 50, Mary L Standish; c Priscilla (Varland), Nancy & Cynthia (Jackson). *Educ:* Swarthmore Col, BA, 44; Cornell Univ, MS, 51, PhD(radio wave propagation), 56. *Prof Exp:* Asst radio engr, Mutual Broadcasting Syst, 46-47, chief plans & allocations div, 47-49; res asst, Cornell Univ, 50-51 & 52-54; proj leader, Nat Bur Stand, 51-52; proj leader, Nat Bur Stand, 54-57, asst chief, Ionosphere Res Sect, Boulder Labs, 57, chief sect, 57-60, chief, Ionosphere Res & Propagation Div, 60-62, Upper Atmosphere & Space Physics Div, 62-65 & Aeronomy Div, 65; dir, Aeronomy Lab, Inst Telecommun Sci & Aeronomy, Environ Sci Serv Admin, 65-67, actg dir, Inst Telecommun Sci, 67-68, actg dir, Off Univ Rels, Res Labs, 68-70; assoc dir, Inst Telecommun Sci, 70-72, consult to dir, Inst Telecommun Sci, Off Telecommun, US Dept Com, 72-76; mem tech staff, Calif Inst Technol, Jet Propulsion Lab, 76-87; prof adj, Univ Colo, Boulder, 87-98. *Concurrent Pos:* Int vchmn, Study Group Six, Int Telecommun Union, Consultative Comt Int Radio, Dept Stat, 59-70, chmn, US Study Group Six, US Nat Comt, 70-76; vis prof, Colo State Univ, 63; affil prof, 64-69; assoc, Harvard Col Observ, 66-75; adj prof, Univ Colo, Boulder, 69-78; mem-at-large, US Nat Comt, Int Union Radio Sci, mem, Comn C, E, F & G. *Mem:* Emer fel AAAS; emer fel Inst Elec & Electronics Engrs; Sigma Xi; Int Union Radio Sci; Am Geophys Union. *Res:* Sporadic-E region of the ionosphere; radio scattering from the ionospheric F-region; radio refractive index of the nonionized atmosphere; very high frequency propagation via the ionosphere; natural noise; earthspace propagation. *Mailing Add:* 5159 Idylwild Trail Boulder CO 80301-3618. *Fax:* 303-492-2758; *E-Mail:* smithek@boulder.colorado.edu

SMITH, ERNEST LEE, JR, operations research, for more information see previous edition

SMITH, EUCLID O'NEAL, EVOLUTIONARY THEORY, EVOLUTION OF BEHAVIOR. *Current Pos:* ASSOC PROF ANTHROP, EMORY UNIV, 83-; ASSOC SCIENTIST, YERKES REGIONAL PRIMATE RES CTR, 93- *Personal Data:* b Jackson, Miss, May 27, 47; m, Cynthia A Gelb. *Educ:* Miss State Univ, BA, 69; Univ Ga, MA, 72; Ohio State Univ, PhD(anthrop), 77. *Prof Exp:* Asst prof anthrop, Emory Univ, 76-83; asst res prof, 77-84, assoc res prof, Yerkes Regional Primate Res Ctr, 84- *Mem:* Am Asn Phys Anthropologists; Am Soc Primatologists; Animal Behav Soc; Int Primatol Soc; Human Behav & Evolution Soc; Int Soc Behav Ecol. *Res:* Primate social behavior; behavioral ecology; developmental sociobiology; evolution of behavior; human sociobiology; evolutionary theory; evolutionary medicine. *Mailing Add:* Dept Anthrop Emory Univ Atlanta GA 30322. *Fax:* 404-727-3839; *E-Mail:* antns@anthro.emory.edu

SMITH, EUGENE I(RWIN), IGNEOUS PETROLOGY, STRUCTURAL GEOLOGY. *Current Pos:* assoc prof, 80-88, PROF GEOL, UNIV NEV, LAS VEGAS, 88- *Personal Data:* b Buffalo, NY, Mar 4, 44; m 73, Diane Pyper. *Educ:* Wayne State Univ, BS, 65; Univ NMex, MS, 68, PhD(geol), 70. *Prof Exp:* Geologist, US Geol Surv, Ctr Astrogeol, 66-68; res assoc geol, Univ NMex, 70-72; asst prof, Univ Wis-Parkside, 72-76, assoc prof geol, 76-80. *Concurrent Pos:* Vis assoc prof geol, Univ Nev, Las Vegas, 78-79. *Mem:* Geol Soc Am; Am Geophys Union; AAAS. *Res:* Geological, petrographic and geochemical study of volcanic rocks formed during regional extension. *Mailing Add:* Dept Geosci Univ Nev Las Vegas NV 89154-4010. *Fax:* 702-895-4064; *E-Mail:* eismith@redrock.neveda.edu

SMITH, EUGENE JOSEPH, BIOCHEMISTRY. *Current Pos:* RES CHEMIST, INST GENETICS & PHYSIOL, SCI & EDUC ADMIN-AGR RES, USDA, 69- *Personal Data:* b New York, NY, Jan 26, 29; m 56; c 3. *Educ:* Queens Col, NY, BS, 51; Univ Conn, MS, 55; Duke Univ, PhD(biochem), 59. *Prof Exp:* Arthritis & Rheumatism Found fel, 59-61; asst prof biochem, Schs Med & Dent, Georgetown Univ, 61-68; res chemist, Food & Drug Admin, 68-69. *Concurrent Pos:* Consult, Walter Reed Armed Forces Inst Dent Res, 63-67. *Mem:* AAAS; Am Soc Biochemists. *Res:* Microbial metabolism and polysaccharides; nucleotides and amino-sugars; nucleic acid metabolism; avian tumor-virus research. *Mailing Add:* USDA Avian Dis & Oncol East Lansing MI 48823-5338. *Fax:* 517-337-6776

SMITH, F(REDERICK) DOW(SWELL), optics, for more information see previous edition

SMITH, FELIX TEISSEIRE, ATOMIC PHYSICS. *Current Pos:* PHYSICIST, SRI INT, 56-, DIR MOLECULAR PHYSICS LAB, 74- *Personal Data:* b San Francisco, Calif, Aug 19, 20. *Educ:* Williams Col, Mass, BA, 42; Harvard Univ, LLB, 49, MS, 53, PhD(chem), 56. *Concurrent Pos:* Mem comt atomic & molecular physics, Nat Acad Sci-Nat Res Coun, 71;

chmn comt atomic & molecular physics, Nat Acad Sci, 73-75; chmn, Int Conf Physics Electronic & Atomic Collisions, 75-77. *Mem:* Fel Am Phys Soc; Am Chem Soc; Brit Inst Physics. *Res:* Quantum and semiclassical collision theory of electrons, atoms, ions and small molecules; differential scattering and collision spectroscopy; three-body processes. *Mailing Add:* 1030 Palo Alto Ave Palo Alto CA 94301-2224

SMITH, FLOYD W, soil fertility, soil chemistry; deceased, see previous edition for last biography

SMITH, FRANCIS MARION, NUCLEAR CHEMISTRY. *Current Pos:* RETIRED. *Personal Data:* b Columbus, Kans, Nov 16, 23; m 45, Dorothy Green; c Michael, Jerri & Russell. *Educ:* Kans State Univ, BS, 44, MS, 48. *Prof Exp:* Instr chem, Kans State Univ, 45-49; chemist anal res & asphalt rheology, Stand Oil Co, Ind, 49-56; chemist emission spectros, Hanford Labs, Gen Elec Co, 56-65; res scientist, Battelle-Northwest Labs, 65-70; advan scientist, Westinghouse Hanford Co, 70-80, sr engr, 80-86, prin engr, 86-89. *Res:* Emission spectroscopy; radiometallurgy; nuclear safeguards; calorimetry; hazardous materials shipping. *Mailing Add:* 9013 Franklin Rd Pasco WA 99301

SMITH, FRANCIS XAVIER, ORGANIC CHEMISTRY. *Current Pos:* ASSOC PROF CHEM, KINGS COL, 74- *Personal Data:* b Chelsea, Mass, Aug 28, 45; m 71; c 3. *Educ:* Lowell Technol Inst, BS, 67, MS, 69; Tufts Univ, PhD(chem), 72. *Prof Exp:* Postdoctoral assoc org chem, Univ Va, 72-74. *Concurrent Pos:* Consult analytical chem. *Mem:* Am Chem Soc; Sigma Xi; Am Inst Chemists. *Res:* Synthesis of organic compounds; chemistry of nitrogen heterocycles; analytical methods. *Mailing Add:* Chem Kings Col 133 N River St Wilkes-Barre PA 18711-0801

SMITH, FRANK A, MATHEMATICS. *Current Pos:* assoc prof, 69-84, PROF MATH, KENT STATE UNIV, 84- *Personal Data:* b New York, NY, Jan 19, 37; m 65. *Educ:* Brooklyn Col, BA, 58; Purdue Univ, MS, 60, PhD(math), 65. *Prof Exp:* Asst prof math, Ohio State Univ, 64-66 & Univ Fla, 66-67; lectr, Univ Leicester, 67-68; fel, Carnegie-Mellon Univ, 68-69. *Concurrent Pos:* Vis prof, Pitzer Col, 80-81. *Mem:* NY Acad Sci; Am Math Soc; Math Asn Am. *Res:* Structure of ordered semigroups and semirings and extensions of such orders; embeddings of subspaces of topological spaces with certain extension properties. *Mailing Add:* Dept Math Kent State Univ Kent OH 44242-0001

SMITH, FRANK ACKROYD, physiological chemistry; deceased, see previous edition for last biography

SMITH, FRANK E, ONCOLOGY, CHEMOTHERAPY. *Current Pos:* resident med, Baylor Col Med, 61-64, instr pharmacol & med, 66-69, asst prof, 69-76, ASSOC, PROF PHARMACOL & MED, BAYLOR COL MED, 76- *Personal Data:* b Edmonton, Alta, Aug 5, 36; m 63; c 2. *Educ:* Univ Alta, MD, 60. *Prof Exp:* Intern, Edmonton Gen Hosp, Alta, 60-61. *Concurrent Pos:* Fel cancer chemother, Baylor Col Med, 64-66; attend physician & consult chemother, Vet Admin Hosp; asst, Ben Taub Hosp; assoc physician, Methodist Hosp. *Mem:* Am Col Clin Pharmacol & Chemother; Am Soc Clin Oncol; Am Col Physicians. *Res:* Internal medicine; clinical oncology and pharmacology; cancer chemotherapy. *Mailing Add:* 3626 Airport Blvd Houston TX 77051

SMITH, FRANK HOUSTON, PHYSIOLOGICAL EFFECTS OF GOSSYPOL ON ANIMALS. *Current Pos:* asst nutrit, Dept Animal Sci, 28-46, from assoc prof to prof, Dept Animal Sci, 46-73, EMER PROF ANIMAL SCI, NC STATE UNIV, 73- *Personal Data:* b Cornelius, NC, May 18, 03; m 34, Lois Ellington; c Frank H Jr & David R. *Educ:* Davidson Col, BS, 26; NC State Univ, MS, 31. *Prof Exp:* Chemist, NC Dept Agr, 27. *Mem:* Emer mem Am Chem Soc; emer mem Am Oil Chemists Soc; Am Inst Nutrit. *Res:* Toxic principle of cotton seeds; developed analytical methods for gossypol in plants and animals and preparation of puregossypol; biosynthesis of C^{14}-labeled gossypol; metabolism of C^{14}-labeled gossypol by the rat. *Mailing Add:* 2506 Stafford Ave Raleigh NC 27607

SMITH, FRANK ROYLANCE, PHYSICAL CHEMISTRY, ELECTROCHEMISTRY. *Current Pos:* from asst prof to assoc prof chem, 65-74, PROF CHEM, MEM UNIV NFLD, 74- *Personal Data:* b London, Eng, Mar 20, 32; m 61; c 2. *Educ:* Univ London, BSc, 56, PhD(chem), 64. *Prof Exp:* Sr chemist, Mullard Res Labs, 60-64; fel, La State Univ, 64-65. *Concurrent Pos:* Consult, Bell Northern Res Ltd, Ottawa, 77-79 & Instrumar, St John's, Nfld, 80, Canpolar, 87-88; vis, Phys Chem Dept, Univ Cambridge, 74-75. *Mem:* The Chem Soc; Chem Inst Can; Can Asn Physicists. *Res:* Electrochemical kinetics of electrolytic hydrogen evolution; redox reactions; solar photoelectrolysis of water with semiconductor electrodes; lead-acid batteries; metal deposition; diffusion of hydrogen isotopes through metals; catalysis and electrocatalysis. *Mailing Add:* Dept Chem Mem Univ Nfld St John's NF A1B 3X7 Can

SMITH, FRED GEORGE, JR, PEDIATRICS, NEPHROLOGY. *Current Pos:* VPRES, AM BD PEDIAT, 89- *Personal Data:* b Calif, Jan 1, 28; m 51, Lurene C Roman; c Randy, Richard & Cynthia. *Educ:* Univ Calif, Los Angeles, BS, 51, MD, 55. *Honors & Awards:* Formon-Peterson Founders Award, Midwest Soc for Pediat Res, 95. *Prof Exp:* Intern pediat, Ctr Health Sci, Univ Calif, Los Angeles, 55-56; resident, Univ Minn Hosps, 56-57; chief resident, Ctr Health Sci, Univ Calif, Los Angeles, 57-58, from asst prof to prof, Sch Med, 60-73; prof pediat, Col Med, Univ Iowa, 73-89, chmn dept, 73-86. *Concurrent Pos:* USPHS fel, St Mary's Hosp Med Sch, London, Eng, 68-69. *Mem:* Soc Pediat Res; Am Soc Pediat Nephrology; Am Pediat Soc. *Res:* Developmental and fetal renal physiology. *Mailing Add:* Am Bd Pediat 111 Silver Cedar Ct Chapel Hill NC 27514-1512

SMITH, FRED R, JR, COMPUTER SCIENCE, TEACHING FACULTY COMPUTER USE. *Current Pos:* INSTR, PHYSICS, COASTAL CAROLINA COMMUNITY COL, 74- *Personal Data:* b Pittsburgh, PA, March 23, 40; m 68; c Deborah, Fred, William & Kathryn. *Educ:* Duquesne Univ, BS, 62; WVa Univ, PhD(physics), 73. *Prof Exp:* Physicist GS-7, Nat Bur Stand, 62-64; res asst, Univ Md, 66-67; teaching asst, WVa Univ, 67-72. *Concurrent Pos:* Lab asst, Waynesburg Col, 69-71. *Mem:* Am Phys Soc; Math Asn Am. *Mailing Add:* 521 University Dr Jacksonville NC 28546

SMITH, FREDERICK ADAIR, JR, THEORETICAL MECHANICS, APPLIED MECHANICS. *Current Pos:* RETIRED. *Personal Data:* b Trinity, Tex, Dec 8, 21; m 49, Katherine Egerton; c Katherine (Ward) & Carolyn (Graves). *Educ:* US Mil Acad, BS, 44; Johns Hopkins Univ, MS, 49; George Washington Univ, MBA, 63; Univ Ill, PhD(theoret & appl mech), 68. *Hon Degrees:* LHD, Mt St Mary Col, 83. *Prof Exp:* Asst prof physics, US Mil Acad, US Army, 49-52, instr, Army Command & Gen Staff Col, 55-58, gen staff officer, 59-62, infantry comdr, Seventh Army, Europe, 63-65, prof mech, US Mil Acad, 65-74, head dept, 69-74, dean acad bd, US Mil Acad, 74-85, trustee, Asn Grad, 75-86. *Concurrent Pos:* Trustee, Asn Grad, US Mil Acad. *Mem:* Am Acad Mech. *Res:* Elasticity; materials science. *Mailing Add:* 606 Balfour Dr San Antonio TX 78239

SMITH, FREDERICK ALBERT, physical chemistry, organic chemistry; deceased, see previous edition for last biography

SMITH, FREDERICK EDWARD, THEORETICAL ECOLOGY, LANDSCAPE ECOLOGY. *Current Pos:* RETIRED. *Personal Data:* b Springfield, Mass, July 23, 20; m 45; c 3. *Educ:* Univ Mass, BS, 41; Yale Univ, PhD(zool), 50. *Prof Exp:* From instr to prof zool, Univ Mich, 50-66, prof natural resources, 66-69; prof advan environ studies in resources & ecol, Grad Sch Design, Harvard Univ, 69-82, chmn, Landscape Archit, 81-82. *Concurrent Pos:* Mem, Nat Sci Bd, 68-74. *Mem:* Ecol Soc Am (pres, 73-74). *Res:* Form of population growth and population interactions; community studies; ecosystem science; landscape ecology; computer modeling. *Mailing Add:* 122 Gardiner Rd Woods Hole MA 02543

SMITH, FREDERICK GEORGE, BIOCHEMISTRY. *Current Pos:* assoc prof bot, 48-56, head dept bot & plant path, 64-79, PROF BOT & BIOCHEM, IOWA STATE UNIV, 56- *Personal Data:* b Oak Park, Ill, Aug 16, 17; m 43; c 1. *Educ:* Univ Chicago, BS, 39; Univ Wis, MS, 41, PhD(biochem), 43. *Prof Exp:* Asst biochem & plant path, Univ Wis, 39-43, res assoc, 43-44; asst prof chem, State Univ NY Col Agr, Cornell Univ, 44-47; res assoc biochem, Univ Rochester, 47-48. *Mem:* AAAS; Am Soc Biol Chemists; Am Soc Plant Physiol; Sigma Xi. *Res:* Fungus physiology; biochemistry of plant disease resistance; respiratory enzymes. *Mailing Add:* 2216 State Ave Ames IA 50014-8346

SMITH, FREDERICK PAUL, FORENSIC DRUG TESTING, CRIMINALISTICS. *Current Pos:* asst prof, 79-82, ASSOC PROF FORENSIC SCI, UNIV ALA, BIRMINGHAM, 82- *Personal Data:* b Pittsburgh, Pa, June 14, 51; m 82, Deborah Brown; c Madeline C & Charles P. *Educ:* Antioch Col, BA, 74; Univ Pittsburgh, MS, 76, PhD(analytical chem), 78. *Prof Exp:* Res asst, Western Psychiat Inst & Clin, Univ Pittsburgh, 74-75; criminalist I, Pittsburgh & Allegheny County Crime Lab, 75-76; res scientist, Off Chief Med Examr City New York, 79. *Concurrent Pos:* Sci dir, AccuTox Anal Labs Inc, 89-92; sr appointment res fac, US Naval Res Lab, Am Soc Eng Educ, 89 & 93; Fulbright res scholar, Univ Strathclyde, Glasgow, Scotland, 90. *Mem:* Am Acad Forensic Sci; Am Chem Soc; Forensic Sci Soc. *Res:* Detection of drugs in hair and its application to legal questions; fire-related phenomena and their legal applications. *Mailing Add:* Criminal Justice Univ Ala 1717 Seventh Ave S Birmingham AL 35294-0001. *Fax:* 205-934-2067

SMITH, FREDERICK T(UCKER), SYSTEMS ENGINEERING, SOFTWARE ENGINEERING. *Current Pos:* RETIRED. *Personal Data:* b Waltham, Mass, Nov 24, 20; m 49; c 1. *Educ:* Tufts Univ, BS, 43; Mass Inst Technol, MS, 48; Univ Calif, Los Angeles, PhD, 65. *Prof Exp:* Flight test engr, Instrumentation Lab, Mass Inst Technol, 48-51; systs engr, NAm Aviation, Inc, 51-54; res engr, Rand Corp, 54-65; sr staff engr, Systs Eng, Singer-Librascope, 65-91. *Res:* Anti-submarine warfare systems; computer science; applied mathematics. *Mailing Add:* 4830 Nomad Dr Woodland Hills CA 91364

SMITH, FREDERICK W(ILSON), CHEMICAL ENGINEERING. *Current Pos:* RETIRED. *Personal Data:* b Lansdowne, Pa, Mar 15, 17; m 42; c 4. *Educ:* Univ Mich, BSE, 38, MSE, 39. *Prof Exp:* Chem engr, E I du Pont de Nemours & Co, Del & WVa, 39-44; from head sect to supvr, Chem Eng Dept, BASF Wyandotte Corp, 44-58, mgr chem eng res & semicommercial chem, 58-62, res staff consult, Res Div, 62-79. *Mem:* Am Chem Soc; Am Inst Chem Engrs. *Res:* Organic and inorganic synthesis; polyethylene; synthetic detergents; sodium carboxymethylcellulose; pilot plant research and semicommercial chemicals production supervision; research project and economic evaluations. *Mailing Add:* 7814 Park Ave Allen Park MI 48101-1714

SMITH, FREDERICK WILLIAM, EXPERIMENTAL SOLID STATE PHYSICS. *Current Pos:* asst prof, 70-77, assoc prof, 77-81, PROF PHYSICS, CITY COL NY, 81- *Personal Data:* b Albany, NY, Aug 2, 42; m 65; c 2. *Educ:* Lehigh Univ, BA, 64; Brown Univ, PhD(physics), 69. *Prof Exp:* Res fel, Rutgers Univ, New Brunswick, 68-70. *Concurrent Pos:* Alexander von Humboldt fel, Max-Planck Inst, 77-78. *Mem:* Am Phys Soc; Mat Res Soc. *Res:* Surface reactions on semiconductors; epitaxial growth of thin films; amorphous semiconductor films. *Mailing Add:* Dept Physics City Col NY Convent Ave and 138 St New York NY 10031

SMITH, FREDERICK WILLIAMS, SURGERY. *Current Pos:* RETIRED. *Personal Data:* b Mooresville, Ala, Sept 6, 22; m 46; c 2. *Educ:* Vanderbilt Univ, BA, 42, MD, 44; Am Bd Surg, dipl. *Prof Exp:* Intern surg, Duke Univ Hosp, 44-45; from jr resident to sr chief resident, Jefferson Hillman Hosp, 47-50; pathologist, Jefferson Hillman Hosp, 47-52; from instr to assoc prof surg, Med Col, Univ Ala, Birmingham, 64-73; mem clin fac, Univ Ala, Huntsville, 73-81, assoc prof surg, Sch Primary Med Care, 81-89. *Concurrent Pos:* Consult, Tuberc Sanitorium, Flint, Ala, 50-52; chief surg, Huntsville Hosp, 62-63, Crestwood Hosp, 66. *Mem:* Fel Am Col Surgeons. *Mailing Add:* 2500 Vista Dr Huntsville AL 35803-1328

SMITH, FREDERICK WILLIS, MECHANICAL ENGINEERING. *Current Pos:* MGR, SEMICONDUCTOR PROD DIV, MOTOROLA INC, 77- *Personal Data:* b Seattle, Wash, Apr 28, 38; m 60; c 2. *Educ:* Univ Wash, BS, 61, MS, 63, PhD(mech eng), 66. *Prof Exp:* From asst prof to assoc prof mech eng, Colo State Univ, 65-77. *Concurrent Pos:* Consult fracture mech. *Mem:* Am Soc Mech Engrs. *Res:* Fracture mechanics; elasticity; snow mechanics. *Mailing Add:* 1216 Parkwood Dr Ft Collins CO 80525-1931

SMITH, G(EORGE) V, METALLURGY. *Current Pos:* CONSULT ENGR, 70- *Personal Data:* b Clarksburg, WVa, Apr 7, 16; m 49; c 1. *Educ:* Carnegie Inst Technol, BS, 37, ScD(metall), 41. *Honors & Awards:* Award, Am Soc Testing & Mat; G Hall Taylor Medal, Am Soc Mech Engrs. *Prof Exp:* Asst metall, Metals Res Lab, Carnegie Inst Technol, 37-39; metallurgist, Res Lab, US Steel Corp, 41-55; Francis Norwood Bard prof metall eng, Cornell Univ, 55-70. *Concurrent Pos:* Adj prof, Polytech Inst Brooklyn, 48-55; asst dir, Sch Chem & Metall Eng, Cornell Univ, 57-62; consult, US Steel Corp, Socony Mobil Oil Co, Babcock & Wilcox Co, Gulf Gen Atomic & Metal Properties Coun, Atomic Energy Comn. *Mem:* Am Soc Metals; fel Am Soc Testing & Mat; Am Inst Mining, Metall & Petrol Engrs; Am Soc Mech Engrs. *Res:* Plastic deformation of metals; elevated temperature properties. *Mailing Add:* 104 Berkshire Rd Ithaca NY 14850

SMITH, GAIL PRESTON, APPLIED PHYSICS. *Current Pos:* RETIRED. *Personal Data:* b Unionville, Pa, Jan 25, 15; m 37, Martha Cameron; c Daniel P & Marian (Rings). *Educ:* Geneva Col, BS, 34; Syracuse Univ, MA, 36; Univ Mich, PhD(physics), 41. *Prof Exp:* Instr physics, Battle Creek Col, 36; instr math & physics, Geneva Col, 36-37; asst physics, Univ Mich, 37-41; res physicist, Corning Glass Works, 41-50, sr res assoc, 50-80, mgr gen prod develop, 61-66, mgr int res, 66-70, dir tech staff serv, 70-78, dir int res, 78-80; consult, 80-95. *Mem:* Fel AAAS; fel Brit Inst Physics; fel Am Ceramic Soc; fel Soc Glass Technol; Am Phys Soc; Europ Phys Soc. *Res:* Beta-ray spectroscopy; density and expansivity of glasses; dielectric properties of glasses and glass electronic components; optical properties and applications of glasses and coatings; structural application of glasses and glass-ceramics. *Mailing Add:* 205 E First St Corning NY 14830

SMITH, GALE EUGENE, PHOTOGRAPHIC CHEMISTRY, GRAPHIC ARTS. *Current Pos:* RETIRED. *Personal Data:* b Van Wert, Ohio, Feb 11, 33. *Educ:* Bowling Green State Univ, BA, 55; Mich State Univ, PhD, 63. *Prof Exp:* Res asst phys chem, Mich State Univ, 60-63; res chemist, Res Labs, Eastman Kodak Co, 63-91. *Mem:* Am Chem Soc; Soc Photog Sci & Eng; Tech Asn Graphic Arts. *Res:* Offset lithography; electrochemistry of photographic developers; reaction mechanisms in photographic systems. *Mailing Add:* 299 Seneca Park Ave Rochester NY 14617

SMITH, GARDNER WATKINS, SURGERY. *Current Pos:* prof surg, 70-96, EMER CHMN SECT SURG SCI, MED CTR, JOHNS HOPKINS UNIV, 96-, EMER PROF SURG, SCH MED, 96- *Personal Data:* b Boston, Mass, July 2, 31; m 58, Susan E Whiteford; c Elizabeth W (Whitehead), Tremain S (Culbertson) & George V II. *Educ:* Princeton Univ, AB, 69; Harvard Med Sch, MD, 56; Am Bd Surg, dipl, 64; Am Bd Thoracic Surg, dipl, 65. *Prof Exp:* Fel surg, Sch Med, Johns Hopkins Univ, 57-58; from instr to assoc prof surg, Sch Med, Univ Va, 63-70. *Concurrent Pos:* Consult, Vet Admin Hosps, Salem, Va, 68-70 & Baltimore, 71- & Greater Baltimore Med Ctr, 71-; prof surg, Sch Med, Univ Md, Baltimore City, 70-96; surgeon-in-chief, Baltimore City Hosps, 70-78; dep dir, Dept Surg, Johns Hopkins Hosp, 78-85. *Mem:* Am Col Surgeons; Am Surg Asn; Soc Univ Surgeons; Soc Vascular Surg; Soc Surg Alimentary Tract. *Res:* Physiology of portal hypertension; clinical research in gastrointestinal and vascular surgery. *Mailing Add:* Johns Hopkins Bayview 4940 Eastern Ave Baltimore MD 21224-2780. *Fax:* 410-550-1274

SMITH, GARMOND STANLEY, ANIMAL NUTRITION, TOXICOLOGY. *Current Pos:* prof animal nutrit, metab & toxicol, 68-94, EMER PROF METAB & TOXICOL, NMEX STATE UNIV, 94- *Personal Data:* b Wayne, WVa, July 9, 32; m 53, Eileen Hagedorn; c Stephen, Kristina, Amy, David, Susan & Elizabeth. *Educ:* WVa Univ, BS, 53, MS, 57, PhD(agr biochem), 59. *Prof Exp:* Asst agr biochem, WVa Univ, 57-59; res assoc animal sci, Univ Ill, 59-60, asst prof, 60-65; instr biol, sci & relig, Lincoln Christian Col, 63-65. *Concurrent Pos:* Invited res reports, Ger, 79, Austria & SAfrica, 81, Japan, 83, 88 & Can, 84; consult, SAfrica, Int Atomic Energy Agency & Food & Agr Orgn, Vienna, 81; vis prof toxicol, Univ Kansas Med Ctr, 82; vis prof food sci, Kyoto Univ, Japan, 88; mem, chem substances TLV Comt, Am Conf Govt Indust Hygienists. *Mem:* Fel AAAS; Am Inst Nutrit; Am Soc Animal Sci; Am Inst Biol Sci; Soc Toxicol. *Res:* Nonprotein nitrogen, ruminants; metabolic changes in starvation and refeeding; vitamin A nutrition; nitrate toxicity; potassium-40 as an index of lean body mass; silica in animal metabolism; recycling of nutrients in agricultural and municipal wastes; improving animal tolerances of toxicants in forage and feeds; xenobiotics metabolism. *Mailing Add:* Dept Animal Sci NMex State Univ Las Cruces NM 88003. *Fax:* 505-646-5441

SMITH, GARRY AUSTIN, PLANT GENETICS. *Current Pos:* supvr res geneticist, sci & educ admin, Crops Res Lab, 69-88, RES LEADER, USDA AGR RES SERV, USDA N CROPS SCI LAB, 88- *Personal Data:* b Alta, Can, Sept 25, 40; m 63; c 2. *Educ:* NMex State Univ, BS, 64, MS, 66; Ore State Univ, PhD(genetics), 68. *Prof Exp:* Res asst, NMex State Univ, 64-66, Ore State Univ, 66-68; res geneticist, USDA Agr Res Serv, Canal Pt, Fla, 68-69. *Concurrent Pos:* Acad fac affil, Colo State Univ, 69-88, grad fac, 70; assoc ed, Crop Sci, Crops Sci Soc Am, 77-80; adj prof, NDak State Univ. *Mem:* Am Genetic Asn; fel Am Soc Agron; Am Soc Sugar Beet Technologists; fel Crop Sci Soc Am. *Res:* Quantitative plant genetics; inheritance of disease resistance. *Mailing Add:* US Dept Agr Agr Res Serv N Crop Sci Lab Univ Sta Box 5677 Fargo ND 58105-5677

SMITH, GARY CHESTER, MEAT SCIENCE, FOOD SCIENCE & TECHNOLOGY. *Current Pos:* UNIV DISTINGUISHED PROF & HOLDER MONFORT ENDOWED CHAIR, COLO STATE UNIV, 90- *Personal Data:* b Ft Cobb, Okla, Oct 25, 38; m 65, Kay Camp; c Todd, Toni, Leaneta, Stephanie, Kriste & Leland. *Educ:* Calif State Univ, Fresno, BS, 60; Wash State Univ, MS, 62; Tex A&M Univ, PhD(meat sci), 68. *Honors & Awards:* Distinguished Res Award, Am Soc Animal Sci, 74; Distinguished Res Award, Nat Livestock Mkt Asn, 79; Distinguished Res Award, Am Meat Sci Asn, 82; Signal Serv Award, Am Meat Sci Asn, 91. *Prof Exp:* Mgt trainee, Armour & Co, Wash, 62; instr animal sci, Wash State Univ, 62-65; from asst prof to prof meat sci, Tex A&M Univ, 68-82, head, Dept Animal Sci, 82-90. *Concurrent Pos:* Mem, Comts Off Technol Assessment, Nat Res Coun-Nat Acad Sci & USDA. *Mem:* Am Soc Animal Sci; Am Meat Sci Asn (pres, 76-77); Inst Food Technologists; Am Dairy Sci Asn; Coun Agr Sci & Technol; Int Asn Milk, Environ & Food Sanitarians; Sigma Xi; Nat Asn Col & Teachers Agr. *Res:* Meat packaging; chemical, physical and histological muscle properties as related to palatability; quantitative and qualitative evaluation of beef, pork, lamb and goat carcasses; growth and development of meat animals; microbiological and chemical safety of red meat; animal science. *Mailing Add:* 1102 Seton Ft Collins CO 80525-1828. *Fax:* 970-491-0278

SMITH, GARY EUGENE, POLYMER CHEMISTRY. *Current Pos:* DIR TECHNOL, NEWPORT ADHESIVES & COMPOSITES, 87- *Personal Data:* b Louisville, Ky, Oct 27, 32; m 55, Anna F Siria; c Sherryl & Sandra. *Educ:* Univ Ky, BS, 55. *Prof Exp:* Sr chemist, Shell Chem Co, 55-60; tech dir, Mangolia Plastics, Inc, 60-68; prod mgr, Ciba Prod Co, 68-70; dir res & develop, Chem Dynamics, Inc, 70-76; lab dir, Resinoid Eng, Inc, 76-81; prod mgr, Wilson Sporting Goods, 81-87. *Concurrent Pos:* Chemist, Army Chem Ctr, US Army, 56-58. *Mem:* Soc Plastics Engrs. *Res:* Epoxy resin formulations and curing agents; reinforced polymer products. *Mailing Add:* 24751 Crown Royale Laguna Niguel CA 92677. *Fax:* 714-253-5692

SMITH, GARY JOSEPH, METAGENESIS, CHEMICAL CARCINOGENESIS. *Current Pos:* ASST PROF, UNIV NC, 81- *Educ:* NC State Univ, PhD(genetics), 75. *Mailing Add:* Dept Path Univ NC Sch Med Chapel Hill NC 27599-7525. *Fax:* 919-966-6718

SMITH, GARY KEITH, CELL BIOLOGY, CHEMOTHERAPY INDUCED APOPTOSIS & ANTIFOLATES. *Current Pos:* SR BIOCHEMIST, DEPT MOLECULAR BIOCHEM, GLAXO WELLCOME, 81- *Personal Data:* b Easton, Pa, Aug 31, 52; m 81, Jane E Gretsch; c Abigail K. *Educ:* Lebanon Valley Col, BS, 74; Lehigh Univ, MS, 77, PhD(chem), 78. *Prof Exp:* Fel, Pa State Univ, 78-81. *Concurrent Pos:* NIH fel, Pa State Univ, 79. *Mem:* Am Soc Biochem & Molecular Biol; Am Chem SOc; Am Asn Cancer Res; AAAS. *Res:* Biochemistry of pterins and folates and their relevance to cancer chemotherapy; mechanics of cell death induced by toxins and drugs; enzyme-antibody conjugates in therapy. *Mailing Add:* Glaxol Wellcome 5 Moore Dr Research Triangle Park NC 27709. *Fax:* 919-483-4320; *E-Mail:* gary_smith@glaxo.com

SMITH, GARY LEE, VIROLOGY. *Current Pos:* RES SCIENTIST, ELI LILLY & CO, 87- *Personal Data:* b Rock Springs, Wyo, May 27, 47; m 67; c 1. *Educ:* Univ Wyo, BS, 69; Kans State Univ, PhD(microbiol), 72. *Prof Exp:* Fel oncol, Leukemia Soc Am, Univ Wis, 73-74; asst prof, Univ Nebr, 74-77, assoc prof microbiol, 77-87. *Mem:* Am Soc Cell Biol; Sigma Xi; Am Soc Microbiol; AAAS. *Res:* Control of cellular proliferation by growth factors; endocrinology of cellular growth and development. *Mailing Add:* Lilly Res Labs Div Eli Lilly & Co Indianapolis IN 46285-3313

SMITH, GARY LEROY, NUCLEAR PHYSICS, SYSTEMS ANALYSIS. *Current Pos:* from dep asst dir to asst dir, Res Explor Develop, Johns Hopkins Univ, 88-90, asst dir, Res & Progs, 90-91, assoc dir, 91-92, DIR, APPL PHYS LAB, JOHNS HOPKINS UNIV, 92- *Personal Data:* b Mitchell, SDak, Nov 30, 35; m 59, Claire Valine; c Kelly, Cassie, Kyle & Robert. *Educ:* Univ Calif, Davis, BS, 63, MA, 65, PhD(physics), 69. *Prof Exp:* Nat Res Coun Res assoc, US Naval Res Lab, 69-70; sr staff physicist, Johns Hopkins Univ, appl physics lab, 70-75, asst group supvr, 75-76, asst acoustics prog mgr, 75-77, acoustics prog mgr, 77-79, asst dept supv, 79-84, sec prog mgr, fleet ballistic missle submarine, 81-88, assoc dept supv, 84-88. *Mem:* Am Phys Soc; AAAS; Sigma Xi; Am Defense Preparedness Asn; Am Soc Naval Engrs. *Res:* Resonance-neutron capture gamma-ray spectroscopy on rare-earth nuclei; underwater acoustics. *Mailing Add:* Johns Hopkins Appl Physics Lab Johns Hopkins Rd Laurel MD 20723-6099. *E-Mail:* gary.smith@jhuapl.edu

SMITH, GARY RICHARD, theoretical & computational plasma physics, for more information see previous edition

SMITH, GASTON, MATHEMATICS. *Current Pos:* PROF & CHMN DEPT MATH, WILLIAM CAREY COL, 67- *Personal Data:* b Poplarville, Miss, Apr 7, 27; m 50; c 2. *Educ:* Univ Southern Miss, BS, 49; Univ Ala, MA, 55 & 57, PhD(math), 63. *Prof Exp:* Instr high sch, Miss, 51-52; instr math, Sunflower Jr Col, 52-56; asst prof, Univ Southern Miss, 57-60; instr, Univ Ala, 60-63; prof, Univ Southern Miss, 63-67. *Mem:* Am Math Soc; Math Asn Am; Can Math Cong. *Res:* Summability. *Mailing Add:* 2206 S 28th Ave Ext Hattiesburg MS 39402

SMITH, GENE E, MECHANICAL ENGINEERING. *Current Pos:* From asst prof to assoc prof, 63-78, PROF MECH ENG, UNIV MICH, ANN ARBOR, 78- *Personal Data:* b Fulton Co, Ohio, June 6, 36; m 58; c 5. *Educ:* Univ Mich, BSME, 59, MSME, 60, PhD(mech eng), 63. *Concurrent Pos:* Develop engr, Gen Motors Corp, 65-67. *Mem:* Soc Automotive Engrs; Am Inst Chem Engrs; Am Soc Eng Educ; Am Soc Mech Engrs. *Res:* Thermodynamics; heat transfer; phase equilibrium at low temperatures; direct energy conversion. *Mailing Add:* Dept Mech Eng Univ Mich 2351 Herbert Ave Ann Arbor MI 48109-1189

SMITH, GEOFFREY W, GLACIAL GEOMORPHOLOGY, ENVIRONMENTAL GEOMORPHOLOGY. *Current Pos:* from asst prof to assoc prof, Ohio Univ, 69-82, dept chair, 74-80, dir environ studies, 84-91, PROF, DEPT GEOL, OHIO UNIV, 82- *Personal Data:* b Boston, Mass, Sept 29, 39; m 65, Marie Sullo; c Jennifer & Deborah. *Educ:* Tufts Univ, BS, 61; Univ Maine, MS, 64; Ohio State Univ, PhD(geol), 69. *Prof Exp:* Instr geol, Colby Col, 68-69. *Concurrent Pos:* Geologist, Maine Geol Surv, 74-93. *Mem:* Am Quaternary Asn. *Res:* Deglaciation and glacial marine sedimentation of coastal Maine; geology of the Boston Bay Group; glacial geologic controls of radon in Ohio; slope stability studies in the Appalachian Plateaus; pleistocene and recent glacial history of Mount Olympus, Greece. *Mailing Add:* Dept Geol Sci Ohio Univ Athens OH 45701

SMITH, GEORGE BYRON, PHYSICAL CHEMISTRY. *Current Pos:* Sr chemist, 59-67, SECT LEADER, ANALYTICAL & PHYS RES DEPT, MERCK, SHARP & DOHME RES LABS, 67- *Personal Data:* b Pittsburgh, Pa, Apr 18, 33; m 55; c 6. *Educ:* Univ Pittsburgh, BS, 54, PhD(phys chem), 59. *Res:* Physical analytical chemistry; chemical kinetics. *Mailing Add:* Millwright Dr Hilton Head SC 29926-1256

SMITH, GEORGE C, PHYSICS, COMPUTERS. *Current Pos:* RETIRED. *Personal Data:* b West Unity, Ohio, May 23, 35. *Educ:* Cornell Univ, AB, 57, MS, 62, PhD(eng physics), 65; Univ NMex, JD(law), 73. *Prof Exp:* Physicist solid state, Sandia Labs, 66-70; sr scientist comput, Opers Res Inc, 75-76; physicist systs, Lawrence Livermore Nat Lab, 77-91. *Concurrent Pos:* Mem, Telluride Asn, 55-56; foreign scientist, Alexander von Humboldt Found, Ger, 65-66; consult, Opers Res Inc, 76-77; Arms Control fel, Stanford Univ, 84-85. *Mem:* Am Phys Soc; Inst Elec & Electronics Engrs; Am Inst Aeronaut & Astronaut; Sigma Xi; Int Soc Optical Eng. *Res:* Systems optimization; computer modeling; strategic studies; foreign technologies; advanced energy concepts; aerospace; weapons. *Mailing Add:* 9199 Firecrest Lane San Ramon CA 94583

SMITH, GEORGE C(UNNINGHAM), CHEMICAL ENGINEERING, ENVIRONMENTAL SCIENCE. *Current Pos:* CONSULT, WASTE WATER TREATMENT & SOLID WASTE MGT, 84- *Personal Data:* b Pittsburgh, Pa, Feb 16, 26; m 53, Margaret Cary; c Sarah, Alice & Amy. *Educ:* Univ Pittsburgh, BSChE, 48, MS, 50; Carnegie Inst Technol, PhD(chem eng), 56. *Prof Exp:* Process engr, Gen Elec Co, 50-52; res engr, E I du Pont de Nemours & Co, 56-60; sr res engr, Jones & Laughling Steel Corp, 60-63, res assoc process metall, 63-69, staff engr, 69-70, tech coordr environ control, 70-84. *Mem:* Am Inst Chem Engrs; Am Chem Soc; Am Inst Mining, Metall & Petrol Engrs; Air Pollution Control Asn. *Res:* Waste water treatment and air cleaning in iron and steel industry; solid waste and toxic materials management; steelmaking processes, especially fluid mechanics of basic oxygen processes; fluid mechanics. *Mailing Add:* 866 Foxland Dr Pittsburgh PA 15243

SMITH, GEORGE DAVID, X-RAY CRYSTALLOGRAPHY, PHYSICAL CHEMISTRY. *Current Pos:* ASST RES PROF, ROSWELL PARK DIV, GRAD SCH STATE UNIV NY, BUFFALO, 82-; CANCER SCIENTIST, ROSWELL PARK CANCER INST. *Personal Data:* b Youngstown, Ohio, Aug 24, 41; m, P Lynne Howell; c 3. *Educ:* Westminster Col, Pa, BS, 63; Ohio Univ, PhD(chem), 68. *Prof Exp:* Res assoc, Mont State Univ, 68-74; sr res scientist, Med Found Buffalo, 82. *Mem:* Protein Soc; Am Crystallog Asn; AAAS. *Res:* X-ray crystal structures of ionophores, antibiotics, and polypeptides; correlation of structure to function; protein crystallography; crystallographic studies of human insulin. *Mailing Add:* Hauptman-Woodward Med Res Inst 73 High St Buffalo NY 14203-1196

SMITH, GEORGE ELWOOD, SOLID STATE ELECTRONICS. *Current Pos:* RETIRED. *Personal Data:* b White Plains, NY, May 10, 30; wid; c 3. *Educ:* Univ Pa, BS, 55; Univ Chicago, MS, 56, PhD(physics), 59. *Honors & Awards:* Ballantine Medal, Franklin Inst, 73; Liebmann Award, Inst Elec & Electronics Engrs, 74. *Prof Exp:* Mem staff, Bell Labs, 59-64, head, Mos Device Dept, 64-86. *Mem:* Nat Acad Eng; fel Inst Elec & Electronics Engrs; fel Am Phys Soc. *Res:* Band structure of semimetals; thermoelectric effects; electronic transport phenomena; optical properties of semiconductors; optoelectronic devices; electrical conduction in metal oxides; semiconductor devices; charge coupled devices; integrated circuits. *Mailing Add:* 221 Teaneck Rd Barnegat NJ 08005-0787

SMITH, GEORGE FOSTER, MICROELECTRONICS, LASERS. *Current Pos:* pres, 93-94, MEM BD DIRS, CALTECH ASSOCS, 90- *Personal Data:* b Franklin, Ind, May 9, 22; m 50, Jean Farnsworth; c David, Craig & Sharon. *Educ:* Calif Inst Technol, BS, 44, MS, 48, PhD(physics), 52. *Honors & Awards:* Frederick Philips Award, Inst Elec & Electronics Engrs, 88. *Prof Exp:* Grad asst, Calif Inst Technol, 47-50, res assoc, 48-50; res physicist, Hughes Aircraft Co, 52-57, dept mgr, 57-62, assoc dir, 62-69, vpres, 65-81, dir res labs, 69-87, sr vpres, 81-87. *Concurrent Pos:* Res engr, Eng Res Assocs, 46-48; adj assoc prof, Univ Southern Calif, 60-62; consult, Army Sci Adv Panel, 75-78; mem policy bd, Hughes Aircraft Co, 65-87. *Mem:* AAAS; fel Am Phys Soc; fel Inst Elec & Electronics Engrs; Sigma Xi (chap pres, 57-58). *Res:* Research management; electron devices; lasers; microelectronics; displays; physical electronics. *Mailing Add:* 6423 Riggs Pl Los Angeles CA 90045

SMITH, GEORGE IRVING, QUATERNARY GEOLOGY. *Current Pos:* geologist, US Geol Surv, 52-66, chief light metals & indust minerals br, 66-69, geologist, 69-78, coordr climate prog, 78-81, geologist, 81-94, Pecora fel, 94-96, EMER GEOLOGIST, US GEOL SURV, 96- *Personal Data:* b Waterville, Maine, May 20, 27; m 74, Terako Kuwada; c 5. *Educ:* Colby Col, AB, 49; Calif Inst Technol, MS, 51, PhD(geol), 56. *Honors & Awards:* Meritorious Serv Award, Dept Int, 83. *Prof Exp:* Mem staff geol, Occidental Col, 51-52. *Concurrent Pos:* Fulbright scholar grant, Australia, 81. *Mem:* Geol Soc Am; Sigma Xi; Am Quaternary Asn. *Res:* Structure and stratigraphy of Mojave Desert area; Quaternary deposits and climates; evaporite deposits; volcanic petrology. *Mailing Add:* US Geol Surv 345 Middlefield Rd Menlo Park CA 94025

SMITH, GEORGE LEONARD, JR, INDUSTRIAL ENGINEERING. *Current Pos:* prof & chmn indust eng, 68-96, EMER PROF INDUST ENG, OHIO STATE UNIV, 96- *Personal Data:* b State College, Pa, Sept 6, 35; m; c 2. *Educ:* Pa State Univ, BS, 57; Lehigh Univ, MS, 58 & 67; Okla State Univ, PhD(indust eng), 69. *Prof Exp:* Grad asst indust eng, Lehigh Univ, 57-58; instr, Prod Tech, Pa State Univ, York Campus, 58-59 & indust eng, Lehigh Univ, 59-67; grad res asst, Okla State Univ, 67-68. *Concurrent Pos:* Labor arbitrator, Fed Mediation & Conciliation Serv, 70-; dir, Ergonomics Div, Am Inst Indust Engrs, 76-78; consult, Amalgamated Meat Cutters & Butcher Workmen, 78-; ed, Human Factors, 80- *Mem:* Fel Inst Indust Eng; fel Human Factors Soc; Am Soc Eng Educ. *Res:* Person and machine systems analysis and design; human performance; design methods with particular emphasis on design of work and workspaces. *Mailing Add:* Dept Indust Welding & Systs Eng 210 Baker System Ohio State Univ Columbus OH 43210-1271

SMITH, GEORGE PEDRO, PHYSICAL CHEMISTRY. *Current Pos:* RETIRED. *Personal Data:* b Norfolk, Va, Oct 26, 23; m 45; c 3. *Educ:* Univ Va, BS, 44, PhD(chem), 50. *Honors & Awards:* Max Bredig Award, Electro Chem Soc, 89. *Prof Exp:* Group leader, Oak Ridge Nat Lab, 50-88. *Concurrent Pos:* Lectr, Univ Tenn, Knoxville, 52-63, prof, 64-78, adj prof, 81-; prof, Tech Univ Denmark, 72-73; ed, Advan in Molten Salt Chem, 71-76; lectr, Norwegian Inst Technol, 78. *Res:* Molten salt chemistry; applied spectroscopy and photochemistry. *Mailing Add:* 7925 Chesterfield Dr Knoxville TN 37909-2916

SMITH, GEORGE THOMAS, pathology, for more information see previous edition

SMITH, GEORGE WOLFRAM, LIQUID CRYSTALS, CHEMICAL PHYSICS. *Current Pos:* sr res physicist, Gen Motors Res & Develop Ctr, 59-76, dept res scientist, 76-81, sr staff res scientist, 81-87, PRIN RES SCIENTIST, GEN MOTORS RES & DEVELOP CTR, 87- *Personal Data:* b Des Plaines, Ill, Sept 19, 32; m 56, Mary L Sackett; c Dean W & Grant S. *Educ:* Knox Col, BA, 54; Rice Univ, MA, 56, PhD(physics), 58. *Honors & Awards:* Cambell Award, 80; McCuen Award, 85. *Prof Exp:* Welch Found fel physics, Rice Univ, 58-59. *Concurrent Pos:* Instr, Lawrence Inst Technol, 63-65; lectr, Cranbrook Inst Sci, 63-87; coun, Gordon Res Conf, 78; co-ed, Particulate Carbon, Formation During Combustion, 81; sci adv comt, Cranbrook Inst Sci, 89-; chmn, Comt Applns Physics, Am Phys Soc, 91, Pake Prize Comt, 93-94. *Mem:* Fel Am Phys Soc; Sigma Xi. *Res:* Low temperature physics; nuclear magnetic resonance; molecular motions in solid state; internal friction; liquid crystals, calorimetry; thermomagnetic gas torque; physics of carbon; phase transformations; metal matrix composites; 90 publications and 12 patents. *Mailing Add:* Dept Physics & Phys Chem Gen Motors Res & Develop Ctr 30500 Mound Rd Warren MI 48090-9055. *Fax:* 810-986-3091; *E-Mail:* george_w._smith@notes.gmr.com

SMITH, GERALD A, EXPERIMENTAL HIGH ENERGY PHYSICS, ANTIMATTER. *Current Pos:* prof & head dept, 83-88, PROF PHYSICS & DIR, LAB ELEM PARTICLES SCI, PA STATE UNIV, 88- *Personal Data:* b Akron, Ohio, Jan 8, 36; m 58, Vonine Klepinger; c Jennifer K & Terrilla A.

1026 / SMITH

Educ: Miami Univ, BA, 57; Yale Univ, MS, 58, PhD(physics), 61. *Prof Exp:* Physicist, Lawrence Radiation Lab, Univ Calif, Berkeley, 61-67, from lectr to asst prof, 63-67; prof physics, Mich State Univ, 67-82. *Concurrent Pos:* Consult, Argonne Nat Lab, 68-72, Argonne Univs Asn, 71-73 & NSF, 73-76; mem & chmn, Fermilab User's Orgn, 71-74; prin investr, NSF, 71-; mem, Bd Trustees, Argonne Univs Asn, 76-78; assoc lab dir high energy physics, Argonne Nat Lab, 78; mem & chmn, High Energy Discussion Group Exec Comt, Brookhaven Nat Lab, 81-85; mem, EPAC, Stanford Linear Accelerator Ctr, 82-84; mem, PSCC Comt, Europ Orgn Nuclear Res, 84; mem, Mat Res Lab Adv Comt, Pa State Univ, 84-88; consult, Rand Corp, 87-88, Los Alamos Nat Lab, 91- & Phillips Lab, Kirtland AFB, 91-; prin investr, USAF Off Sci Res grants, 87-96, Jet Propulsion Lab contract, 88-, Dept Energy grant, 90-92, Tex Nat Res Lab Comn, 90-93, Rocketdyne Corp, 93- & Marshall Space Flight Ctr, 97- *Mem:* Fel Am Phys Soc; AAAS; Sigma Xi. *Res:* High energy particle physics; electronic detectors; analysis; properties of hadronic states of matter; applications to medicine; space propulsion; antimatter synthesis and experiments. *Mailing Add:* 303 Osmond Lab Pa State Univ University Park PA 16802. *Fax:* 814-863-3297; *E-Mail:* jaz@psuleps

SMITH, GERALD DUANE, CRUSTAL DOSIMETRY. *Current Pos:* PROF CHEM/PHYSICS, HUNTINGTON COL, 67-, VPRES & DEAN, 82- *Personal Data:* b Cass City, Mich, Aug 31, 42; m 67, Nancy L Myers; c Michael L. *Educ:* Huntington Col, BS, 64; Purdue Univ, PhD(health physics), 72. *Prof Exp:* AEC fel trainee, Battelle Northwest Labs, 64-65; instr chem, Owosso Col, 65-67. *Concurrent Pos:* Consult, Ind Radiation Emergency Response Team, 74-82. *Mem:* Am Chem Soc; Sigma Xi; Am Asn Physics Teachers. *Res:* Radiation dosimetry; crystal growth; reaction kinetics. *Mailing Add:* Dept Physics Huntington Col Huntington IN 46750-1299. *E-Mail:* gsmith@huntcol.edu

SMITH, GERALD FLOYD, BLOOD COAGULATION, PHARMACEUTICAL RESEARCH. *Current Pos:* Eli Lilly sr res fel, Eli Lilly Res Clin, 71-72, SR SCIENTIST, ELI LILLY RES LABS, 73- *Personal Data:* b Louisville, Ky, Jan 4, 42; m 65; c 2. *Educ:* Univ Louisville, BS, 63, MS, 65, PhD(chem), 68; Indiana Univ, JD, 86. *Prof Exp:* NIH training grant molecular path, Sch Med, Univ Louisville, 68-71. *Mem:* Sigma Xi; AAAS; Am Chem Soc; Am Heart Asn; Int Soc Thrombosis & Haemostasis. *Res:* Fibrinogen-fibrin chemistry; blood coagulation-thrombosis; inflammation; protease-inhibitors; warfarin; heparin; therapeutic agents; vitamin K; metastasis; fibrinolysis, thrombolytics, plasminogen activators. *Mailing Add:* 825 Queenswood Ct Indianapolis IN 46217

SMITH, GERALD FRANCIS, APPLIED MATHEMATICS, MECHANICS. *Current Pos:* prof, 65-80, DIR, CTR APPLN MATH, LEHIGH UNIV, 80- *Personal Data:* b Buffalo, NY, Oct 17, 28; m 56. *Educ:* Univ Buffalo, BS, 52; Brown Univ, PhD(appl math), 56. *Prof Exp:* Res assoc appl math, Brown Univ, 56; mathematician, Calif Res Crop Div, Stand Oil Co Calif, 56-58; asst prof mech, Lehigh Univ, 58-60; asst prof eng & appl sci, Yale Univ, 60-64; assoc prof math, Univ Wis, Milwaukee, 64-65. *Concurrent Pos:* NSF study grants, 61-64 & 66-68. *Mem:* Am Math Soc. *Res:* Theory of invariants and continuum mechanics. *Mailing Add:* 2120 Sycamore St Bethlehem PA 18017

SMITH, GERALD LYNN, electrical engineering, mathematics, for more information see previous edition

SMITH, GERALD RALPH, MOLECULAR BIOLOGY. *Current Pos:* assoc mem, 82-85, MEM, FRED HUTCHINSON CANCER RES CTR, 85- *Personal Data:* b Vandalia, Ill, Feb 19, 44; m 81, Vicki Halper. *Educ:* Cornell Univ, BS, 66; Mass Inst Technol, PhD(biol), 70. *Prof Exp:* Fel, Dept Biochem, Univ Calif, Berkeley, 70-72 & Dept Molecular Biol, Univ Geneva, 72-75; from asst prof to assoc prof molecular biol, Univ Ore, 75-82. *Concurrent Pos:* Helen Hay Whitney Found fel, 70-73; NIH career develop award, 80-85. *Mem:* Am Soc Microbiol; Genetics Soc Am. *Res:* Molecular mechanisms of genetic recombination. *Mailing Add:* Fred Hutchinson Cancer Ctr 1100 Fairview Ave N PO Box 19024 MS A1-162 Seattle WA 98109. *Fax:* 206-667-6497; *E-Mail:* gsmith@fred.fhcrc.org

SMITH, GERALD RAY, ZOOLOGY. *Current Pos:* Asst prof zool & geol, Univ, 69-72, assoc cur, Mus Paleont, 69-72, assoc prof, Univ, 72-81, dir, Mus Paleont, 74-81, PROF ZOOL & GEOL, UNIV MICH, ANN ARBOR, 81-, CUR FISHES, MUS ZOOL, 69-, CUR LOWER VERT MUS PALEONT, 72- *Personal Data:* b Los Angeles, Calif, Mar 20, 35; m 55; c 3. *Educ:* Univ Utah, BS, 57, MS, 59; Univ Mich, PhD(zool), 65. *Mem:* AAAS; Soc Study Evolution; Soc Syst Zool; Am Soc Ichthyologists & Herpetologists (pres, 91); Soc Vertebrate Paleont. *Res:* Evolution of North American freshwater fishes. *Mailing Add:* Mus Zool Univ Mich Ann Arbor MI 48109

SMITH, GERALD RAY, LEGUME BREEDING, FORAGE MANAGEMENT. *Current Pos:* from asst prof to assoc prof, 81-92, PROF, TEX A&M UNIV, 92- *Personal Data:* b Prattville, Ala, May 12, 52; m 77. *Educ:* Auburn Univ, BS, 75, MS, 77; Miss State Univ, PhD(agron), 81. *Honors & Awards:* Merit Cert, Am Forage & Grassland Coun. *Prof Exp:* Plant breeder, Northrup King Co, 77-78. *Mem:* Am Soc Agron; Crop Sci Soc Am. *Res:* Plant genetic control of legumes-rhizobia dinitrogen fixation; improvement of forage legumes through breeding and selection for increased dinitrogen fixation; pest resistance and improved reseeding. *Mailing Add:* Tex Agr Exp Sta PO Box E Overton TX 75684

SMITH, GERALD WAVERN, ENGINEERING ECONOMICS, INDUSTRIAL ENGINEERING. *Current Pos:* From instr to assoc prof, Iowa State Univ, 56-67, Alcoa prof, 68-71, prof indust eng, 67-88, EMER PROF, IOWA STATE UNIV, 88- *Personal Data:* b Des Moines, Iowa, Dec 1, 29; m 58, Phyllis Seydel; c Brian. *Educ:* Iowa State Univ, BS, 52, MS, 58, PhD(eng), 61. *Honors & Awards:* Wellington Award, Eng Econ, 86. *Mem:* Am Inst Indust Engrs; Am Soc Eng Educ. *Res:* Engineering economy; engineering valuation; management of capital expenditures by public and private organizations; capital expenditures by public and private organizations; capital expenditure decisions for public utilities. *Mailing Add:* 2808 Arbor St Ames IA 50011

SMITH, GERARD PETER, NUTRITION. *Current Pos:* from asst prof to assoc prof, 68-73, PROF PSYCHIAT, MED COL, CORNELL UNIV, 73- *Personal Data:* b Philadelphia, Pa, Mar 24, 35; m 62; c 4. *Educ:* St Joseph's Univ, Pa, BS, 56; Univ Pa, MD, 60. *Honors & Awards:* Curt Richter Lecture, 76; Leon Lectr, 90. *Prof Exp:* Assoc physiol, Sch Med, Univ Pa, 64-65, asst prof, 65-68. *Concurrent Pos:* Head, Div Behav Sci, Cornell Univ, 69-; dir, Edward W Bourne Behav Res Lab, 69-, Eating Disorders Inst, NY, 84-88; NIMH career scientist award. *Mem:* Am Physiol Soc; Endocrine Soc; Soc Neurosci; Asn Res Nerv & Ment Dis; Soc Biol Psychiat; Soc Study Ingestive Behav. *Res:* Behavioral neuroscience of eating and its disorders. *Mailing Add:* NY Hosp Cornell Med Ctr 21 Bloomingdale Rd White Plains NY 10605-1596

SMITH, GERARD VINTON, PHYSICAL ORGANIC CHEMISTRY. *Current Pos:* assoc prof, 66-73, dir, Molecular Sci Prog, 78-96, PROF CHEM, SOUTHERN ILL UNIV, 73- *Personal Data:* b Delano, Calif, Oct 14, 31; m 56, Jolynn Fenn; c Kenneth, Craig & Elise. *Educ:* Col Pac, BA, 53, MS, 56; Univ Ark, PhD(phys org chem), 59. *Hon Degrees:* Dr, Jozsef Attila Univ, Szeged, Hungary, 96. *Honors & Awards:* Paul N Rylander Award, Org Reactions Catalysis Soc, 95. *Prof Exp:* Res assoc, Northwestern Univ, 59-60; instr chem, 60-61; asst prof, Ill Inst Technol, 61-66. *Concurrent Pos:* Chmn, Gordon Res Conf, 78; chmn, Org Reactions Catalysis Soc, 78-80, bd, 89-94; consult, Pfizer, PPG Indust, Lederle Lab, Diversified Indust, Nat Iranian Oil Co, Earthline Corp, Dow Chem, Uniroyal Chem Co, Inst Gas Technol, Teltech, Catalyst Consult Inc; chmn, Am Chem Soc, 89, treas, 92-96; bd, Ill State Acad Sci, 91-93. *Mem:* AAAS; Am Chem Soc; Catalysis Soc (treas, 76-89); Org Reactions Catalysis Soc; Int Cong Catalysis. *Res:* Mechanisms of heterogeneous catalysis; hydrogenation and exchange; oxidation; stereochemistry; asymmetric induction; hydrodesulfurization; substituent effects; nuclear magnetic resonance; mass spectrometry; gas-liquid chromatography; coal conversion processes. *Mailing Add:* Dept Chem Southern Ill Univ Carbondale IL 62901-4409. *Fax:* 618-453-6408; *E-Mail:* gvs@mols.siu.edu

SMITH, GILBERT EDWIN, GEOLOGY. *Current Pos:* geologist & head coal sect, 78-80, ASSOC DIR, INST MINING & MINERALS RES, UNIV KY, 78- *Personal Data:* b Nelsonville, Ohio, Oct 26, 22; m 51. *Educ:* Ohio Univ, BS, 50; WVa Univ, MS, 51. *Prof Exp:* Geologist, Ohio Div Geol Surv, 51-53, coal geologist, 53-56; geologist, Aluminum Co Am, 56-61; consult, 61-63; coal geologist, Ky Geol Surv, 63-66, geologist & head coal sect, 66-78. *Mem:* Am Inst Mining Metall & Petrol Engrs; Fel Geol Soc Am; Am Asn Stratig Palynologists; Mine Inspectors Inst Am. *Res:* Coal geology; mapping; resources; Pennsylvanian stratigraphy; reclamation; mining geology. *Mailing Add:* 1710 Blue Licks Rd Lexington KY 40504-2217

SMITH, GILBERT HOWLETT, CELL BIOLOGY, MOLECULAR BIOLOGY. *Current Pos:* SR INVESTR ONCOGENETICS, LAB TUMOR IMMUNOL & BIOL, NAT CANCER INST, 85- *Personal Data:* b Cornwall, NY, July 25, 38; m 61; c 5. *Educ:* Hartwick Col, AB, 59; Brown Univ, ScM, 63, PhD(biol), 65. *Prof Exp:* Staff fel, 65-67, head, Ultrastruct Res Sect, 67-70, sr staff scientist, Lab Biol, 70-75, sr staff scientist cancer res, lab molecularbiol, Nat Cancer Inst, NIH, 76-85. *Mem:* Am Asn Cancer Res; Am Soc Cell Biol; Am Soc Microbiol; Sigma Xi. *Res:* Genetic, molecular and cellular mechanisms by which mammary epithelial cells functionally differentiate and the relationship of these mechanisms to malignant transformation of mammary cells by various carcinogenic stimuli; identification and characterization of mammary specific epithelial stem cells. *Mailing Add:* Lab Tumor Immunol Nat Cancer Inst NIH Bldg 10 Rm 8BO7 Bethesda MD 20892-1750. *Fax:* 301-402-0711

SMITH, GLENN EDWARD, PLANT PATHOLOGY. *Current Pos:* RETIRED. *Personal Data:* b Charleston, WVa, Mar 26, 23; m 54; c 4. *Educ:* Morris Harvey Col, BS, 52; Ohio State Univ, MS, 54, PhD(bot & plant path), 60. *Prof Exp:* Asst prof bot & plant path, Ohio State Univ, 57-67; prof biol, Univ Charleston, 67-95. *Mem:* Am Phytopath Soc; Soc Nematol. *Res:* Phytonematology. *Mailing Add:* 1806 Rosewood Rd Charleston WV 25314

SMITH, GLENN S, DRILLING EXPLORATION. *Current Pos:* PRES, SMITH ENERGY CORP, 81- *Personal Data:* b Huron, SDak, Aug 4, 52. *Educ:* Colo State Univ, BS, 74; Ga Inst Technol, MSEE, 75. *Prof Exp:* Sr develop engr, Schlumberger Well Serv, Tex, 75-81. *Mem:* Inst Elec & Electronics Engrs. *Mailing Add:* Smith Energy Corp PO Box 5172 Greeley CO 80631

SMITH, GLENN SANBORN, PLANT BREEDING. *Current Pos:* assoc dean sch agr & assoc dir exp sta, NDak State Univ, 47-51, prof, 47-78, chief div plant indust, Exp Sta, 51-54, dean grad sch, 54-73, fac lectr, 65, EMER PROF AGRON, NDAK STATE UNIV, 78- *Personal Data:* b Antler, NDak, Dec 21, 07; m, Doris E Abel; c Nancy, Ronald & Robert. *Educ:* NDak Agr

Col, BS, 29; Kans State Univ, MS, 31; Univ Minn, PhD(plant breeding, genetics), 47. *Hon Degrees:* DSc, NDak State Univ, 90. *Prof Exp:* Jr agronomist, Bur Plant Indust, USDA, 29-35, asst agronomist, 35-42, from assoc agronomist to agronomist, Bur Plant Indust, Soils & Agr Eng, 42-47. *Concurrent Pos:* Consult wheat breeding, Ministry Agr, Repub Uruguay, 77-78 & agron curriculum, Fac Agr, Univ Repub, Uruguay, 79; Agron Deleg, China, 83. *Mem:* Sigma Xi; Crop Sci Soc Am; fel Am Soc Agron. *Res:* Durum, hard red spring wheat, and oat breeding and genetics; pathology and quality problems. *Mailing Add:* 3140 Tenth St N Fargo ND 58102-1336

SMITH, GLORIA RICHARDSON, NURSING. *Current Pos:* VPRES PROGS, W K KELLOGG FOUND, 91- *Personal Data:* b Chicago, Ill, Sept 29, 34. *Educ:* Wayne State Univ, BS, 55; Univ Mich, MPH, 59; Univ Okla, MA, 77; Union Exp Cols & Univs, PhD, 79. *Hon Degrees:* DSc, Univ Cincinnati, 92. *Honors & Awards:* Phillips Medal Pub Sci, Col Osteop Med, Ohio State Univ, 96. *Prof Exp:* Pub health nurse, Detroit Vis Nurse Asn, 55-56, sr pub health nurse, 57-58, asst dist off supvr, 59-63; asst prof nursing, Tuskegee Inst Sch Nursing, 63-66, Albany State Col, Ga, 66-68; consult nurse home health care, Okla State Dept Health, 68-70, dist nurse supvr, 68-70, medicare nurse consult, 70-71; asst prof, Col Nursing, Univ Okla, 71-73, assoc prof & interim dean, 73-75, prof & dean, 75-83; state health dir, Mich Dept Pub Health, 83-88; prof & dean, Col Nursing, Wayne State Univ, 88-91. *Concurrent Pos:* Consult, Vet Admin Hosp, 75-77, HEW, 77-78; dir, Nat League Nursing, 79-; mem, Study Comt Health Care for Homeless, Inst Med-Nat Acad Sci, 87-88; chair, Mich Task Force Nursing Issues, 89-90. *Mem:* Inst Med-Nat Acad Sci; Nat League Nursing; Am Nurses Asn; Am Asn Cols Nursing; Am Asn Higher Educ; Am Acad Nursing; Am Pub Health Asn. *Res:* Contributed articles on healthcare and nursing to professional publications. *Mailing Add:* W K Kellogg Found 1 Michigan Ave E Battle Creek MI 49017-4005

SMITH, GORDON MEADE, physical chemistry, for more information see previous edition

SMITH, GRAHAM MONRO, PHYSICAL PROPERTIES MEASUREMENTS. *Current Pos:* SR INVESTR ANALYTICAL CHEM, MERCK RES LABS, 92- *Personal Data:* b Bayshore, NY, Nov 11, 47; m 71; c 2. *Educ:* Adelphi Univ, BA, 69; Univ Buffalo, PhD(chem), 74. *Prof Exp:* Fel theoret chem, Princeton Univ, 74-75; fel theoret chem, Univ Calif, Santa Cruz, 75-76; sr investr theoret chem, Merck Sharp & Dohme Res Labs, 76-92. *Mem:* Am Chem Soc; AAAS; NY Acad Sci; Am Crystallog Asn. *Res:* Directing research in analytical chemistry in the medicinal chemistry department; developing new assays to solve problems in the department. *Mailing Add:* Merck Res Labs WP42-3 West Point PA 19486. *Fax:* 215-652-6913; *E-Mail:* graham_smith@merck.com

SMITH, GRAHAME J C, INSECT ECOLOGY. *Current Pos:* DIR, CTR MGT SCI & TECHNOL, BABSON COL, BABSON PARK, MASS, 92- *Personal Data:* b Kapuda, SAustralia, Feb 16, 42. *Educ:* Univ Adelaide, BS, 62; Cornell Univ, MS, 65, PhD(insect ecol), 67. *Prof Exp:* From instr to asst prof ecol, Brown Univ, 67-72; assoc prof ecol, Boston Univ, 72-76, asst dean, Col Lib Arts, 75-76; acquisitions ed, G K Hall & Co, Mass Inst Technol Press, 76-82; pres, Custom Reports Inc, 82-87; vpres, Decision Resources, Inc, 87-92. *Mem:* Ecol Soc Am. *Res:* Behavior of insect parasitoids on different host species and factors which affect this behavior, particularly interactions with other individuals of the same parasitoid species. *Mailing Add:* PO Box 106 Lincoln MA 01773-0106. *Fax:* 781-239-6465

SMITH, GRANT GILL, ORGANIC CHEMISTRY, MASS SPECTROMETRY. *Current Pos:* RETIRED. *Personal Data:* b Fielding, Utah, Sept 25, 21; m 46, Phyllis Cook; c Meredith L (Ashton), Kathleen S (Phinney), Geoffrey G, Randall C, Vivienne S (Lewis) & Roger T. *Educ:* Univ Utah, BA, 43; Univ Minn, PhD(org chem), 49. *Honors & Awards:* Utah Award, Am Chem Soc, 77. *Prof Exp:* Asst chem, Univ Minn, 43-44, 46-48, actg instr, 48-49; from instr to assoc prof, Wash State Univ, 49-61; from assoc prof to prof chem, Utah State Univ, 63-90, fac honors lectr, 67. *Concurrent Pos:* Researcher, Univ London, 57-58; NIH sr fel, Stanford Univ, 69-70; res fel, Res Sch Chem, Australian Nat Univ, 82-83, Fundamentals Matter Inst Atomic & Molecular Physics. *Mem:* AAAS; Am Chem Soc; Royal Soc Chem; Int Soc for Study Origin Life; Am Soc Mass Spectros. *Res:* Physical organic chemistry; mechanisms of gas phase reactions, proximity effects in organic reactions; organic mass spectroscopy; organic geochemistry; chemometrics; biotechnology. *Mailing Add:* 805 River Heights Blue Logan UT 84321

SMITH, GRANT WARREN, II, ETHNOPHARMACOLOGY, CHEMICAL SAFETY. *Current Pos:* vpres acad affairs, 84-86, PRES & PROF CHEM, SOUTHEASTERN LA UNIV, 86-, HONORS PROF ARTS & SCI, 95- *Personal Data:* b Kansas City, Mo, Jan 21, 41; m 62, Constance M Krambeer; c Grant W III. *Educ:* Grinnell Col, BA, 62; Cornell Univ, PhD(chem), 66. *Prof Exp:* Asst chem, Grinnell Col, 62; teaching asst, Cornell Univ, 62-63, asst prof, 66-68; head dept chem & chem eng, Univ Alaska, Fairbanks, 68-73, actg head dept gen sci, 72-73, assoc prof chem, 68-77, prof 77-78; dean, Sch Sci & Technol & prof phys sci, Univ Houston, Clear Lake, 78-84. *Concurrent Pos:* DuPont fel, Cornell Univ, 67; vis prof, Cornell Univ, 73-74; Am Coun Educ fel, Acad Admin Internship Prog, 73-74; pres, Statewide Assembly, Univ Alaska Syst, 76-77; chartered chemist, Royal Soc Chem, 92. *Mem:* AAAS; Am Chem Soc; Am Asn Higher Educ; Sigma Xi; Soc Econ Bot; Am Asn Univ Adminr; Am Soc Pharmacog; fel Royal Soc Chem. *Res:* Organic photochemistry of unsaturated molecules and arctic water pollutants; ethnopharmacology and chemistry of arctic natural products. *Mailing Add:* Southeastern La Univ 942 University Sta Hammond LA 70402. *Fax:* 504-549-3595; *E-Mail:* gwsmith@selu.edu

SMITH, HADLEY J(AMES), ENGINEERING MECHANICS. *Current Pos:* res engr, Res Inst, Univ Mich, Ann Arbor, 52-55, from instr to assoc prof, 55-62, prof, 62-85, EMER PROF ENG MECH, UNIV MICH, ANN ARBOR, 85- *Personal Data:* b Detroit, Mich, May 5, 18; m 52; c 6. *Educ:* Univ Mich, BS, 40, PhD(eng mech), 57. *Prof Exp:* Jr engr, Res Lab, Detroit Edison Co, 40-41; prod engr, Com Res Labs, Inc, 46-51. *Concurrent Pos:* Fac res fel, Rackham Sch Grad Studies, 58; NSF fel, Harvard Univ, 59; guest scientist, Los Alamos Sci Lab, 74. *Mem:* Am Phys Soc; Am Soc Mech Engrs. *Res:* Mathematical physics; hydraulics; hydrodynamics; thermodynamics; kinetic theory; statistical mechanics; heat and mass transfer. *Mailing Add:* 2001 Hall Ave Ann Arbor MI 48104

SMITH, HAL LESLIE, DYNAMICAL SYSTEMS & APPLICATIONS TO BIOLOGY. *Current Pos:* from asst prof to assoc prof, 79-87, PROF, ARIZ STATE UNIV, 87- *Personal Data:* b Cedar Rapids, Iowa, Mar 18, 47; m 70, Kathryn Silagy; c Erin. *Educ:* Univ Iowa, BA, 69, PhD(math), 76. *Prof Exp:* Instr math, Univ Utah, 76-79. *Concurrent Pos:* Vis res scientist, Lefchetz Ctr Dynamical Systs, Brown Univ, 85-86, Ctr Dynamical Systs & Nonlinear Studies, Ga Inst Tech, 92-93. *Mem:* Am Math Soc; Soc Indust & Appl Math; AAAS; Soc Math Biol. *Res:* Differential equations; biomathematics. *Mailing Add:* Dept Math Ariz State Univ Tempe AZ 85287-1804. *E-Mail:* halsmith@math.la.asu.edu

SMITH, HAMILTON OTHANEL, MICROBIAL GENETICS. *Current Pos:* from asst prof to assoc prof microbiol, 67-73, prof, 73-81, PROF MOLECULAR BIOL & GENETICS, SCH MED, JOHNS HOPKINS UNIV, 81- *Personal Data:* b New York, NY, Aug 23, 31; m 57; c 5. *Educ:* Univ Calif, Berkeley, AB, 52; Johns Hopkins Univ, MD, 56. *Honors & Awards:* Nobel Prize Med, 78. *Prof Exp:* Intern, Barnes Hosp, St Louis, 56-57; res, Henry Ford Hosp, Detroit, 59-62; USPHS res fel microbial genetics, Univ Mich, 62-64, res assoc, 64-67. *Concurrent Pos:* Guggenheim fel, 75-76; ed, Gene, 76- *Mem:* Nat Acad Sci; Am Soc Microbiol; Am Soc Biol Chemists; AAAS; fel Am Acad Arts & Sci. *Res:* Genetic recombination; biochemistry of DNA recombination and DNA methylation and restriction. *Mailing Add:* Dept Molecular Biol & Genetics Sch Med Johns Hopkins Univ Baltimore MD 21205. *Fax:* 410-550-6718; *E-Mail:* hamsmith@qmail.bs.jhu.edu

SMITH, HARDING EUGENE, OBSERVATIONAL COSMOLOGY, ACTIVE GALAXIES & QUASARS. *Current Pos:* Asst res physicist, 74-78, from asst prof to assoc prof, 78-86, PROF PHYSICS, UNIV CALIF, SAN DIEGO, 86- *Personal Data:* b San Jose, Calif, May 10, 47; m 89, Carol J Lonsdale. *Educ:* Calif Inst Technol, BS, 69; Univ Calif, Berkeley, MA, 72, PhD(astron), 74. *Concurrent Pos:* Consult, Cosmos Telecourse, Univ Calif, San Diego Sci Teacher Insts & other sci educ; chair, Keck Telescope Sci Steering Comt, 84-86; Morrison fel, Lick Observ, Univ Calif, Santa Cruz, 88; vis scholar, Inst Astron, Cambridge, 89; vis assoc physics, Calif Inst Technol, 89- *Mem:* Am Astron Soc; Int Astron Union; Astron Soc Pac; AAAS. *Res:* Chemical and physical evolution of galaxies; physics of active galactic nuclei; luminous infrared galaxies. *Mailing Add:* Ctr Astrophys Univ Calif San Diego La Jolla CA 92093-0424. *Fax:* 619-534-7051; *E-Mail:* hsmith@ucsd.edu

SMITH, HARLAN MILLARD, PHYSICAL CHEMISTRY. *Current Pos:* RETIRED. *Personal Data:* b Iowa City, Iowa, Sept 2, 21; m 54; c 3. *Educ:* Carroll Col, BA, 42; Univ Chicago, PhD(phys chem), 49. *Prof Exp:* From res chemist to head, fertilizer res sect, Exxon Res & Eng Co, Exxon Chem Co, 49-65, proj develop adv, 65-79, sr res assoc, 79-85. *Concurrent Pos:* Consult, 85-87. *Mem:* Am Chem Soc. *Res:* Raman spectra of aqueous sulfuric acid solutions; lubricating oil additives; industrial lubricants; fertilizers; pesticides. *Mailing Add:* 66 Cray Terr Fanwood NJ 07023-1507

SMITH, HAROLD CARTER, BIOCHEMISTRY. *Current Pos:* asst prof, 70-82, EMER LECTR, SURG & BIOCHEM, SCH MED, UNIV NC, CHAPEL HILL, 82- *Personal Data:* b Statesboro, Ga, Aug 13, 20; m 49; c 2. *Educ:* Ga Southern Col, BS, 60; Univ NC, PhD(biochem), 64. *Prof Exp:* Dir labs, Evans County Heart Res Proj, Claxton, Ga, 59-60; res fel, McArdle Lab Cancer Res, Sch Med, Univ Wis, 64-67; dir biochem sect, Surg Biol Lab & asst prof biochem, Sch Med, Univ NC, Chapel Hill, 67-69; chemist, Res Dept, R J Reynolds Tobacco Co, 69-70. *Mem:* AAAS; Am Chem Soc; NY Acad Sci. *Res:* Chemical carcinogenesis; enzymes and steroids in breast and thyroid cancer; iodoamino acids; biochemistry of wound healing. *Mailing Add:* 744 Tinkerbell Rd Chapel Hill NC 27514-2607

SMITH, HAROLD GLENN, LATTICE DYNAMICS, SUPERCONDUCTIVITY. *Current Pos:* PHYSICIST, OAK RIDGE NAT LAB, 57- *Personal Data:* b Lafayette, La, July 3, 27; m 50; c 3. *Educ:* Univ Southwestern La, BS, 49; Tulane Univ, MS, 51; Iowa State Univ, PhD(physics), 57. *Prof Exp:* Jr res assoc physics, Iowa State Univ, 51-54, asst, 54-57. *Concurrent Pos:* Guest scientist, AERE, Harwell Eng, 61-62, Laue-Langeuin Inst, Genoble, France, 74-75. *Mem:* Fel Am Phys Soc; Sigma Xi; Am Crystallog Asn. *Res:* Neutron diffraction; x-ray crystallography; atomic, molecular, and solid state physics; martensitic transformations. *Mailing Add:* 103 Walton Lane Oak Ridge TN 37830

SMITH, HAROLD HILL, genetics; deceased, see previous edition for last biography

SMITH, HAROLD LINWOOD, PHYSICAL PHARMACY, BIOPHARMACEUTICS & PHARMACOKINETICS. *Current Pos:* asst prof, 68-76, ASSOC PROF PHARM, MED COL VA, VA COMMONWEALTH UNIV, 76- *Personal Data:* b Richmond, Va, Dec 7, 27;

m 49; c 2. *Educ:* Med Col Va, BS, 56, PhD(pharm chem), 62. *Honors & Awards:* Lunsford Richardson Pharm Award, Merrell-Nat Labs, Richardson-Merrell Inc, 60. *Prof Exp:* Lederle fel, Univ Mich, 61-63; chemist, Lederle Labs, Am Cyanamid, 63-64, proj leader, 64-68, group leader, 68. *Concurrent Pos:* Dir opers, Bioclid Inc, 89- *Mem:* Am Pharmaceut Asn; Acad Pharmaceut Sci. *Res:* Rheology of pharmaceutical and biological systems; protein binding; solution theory; solid dissolution rate studies; pharmaceutic dosage form studies. *Mailing Add:* Dept Pharm Va Commonwealth Univ All Health PO Box 233 Richmond VA 23202-0233

SMITH, HAROLD PALMER, NUCLEAR ENGINEERING. *Current Pos:* ASST SECY ATOMIC ENERGY, US DEPT DEFENSE, 93- *Personal Data:* b Nov 30, 35. *Educ:* Mass Inst Technol, PhD(nuclear eng), 60. *Mailing Add:* US Dept Defense Atomic Energy 3050 Defense Pentagon Washington DC 20301

SMITH, HAROLD W(OOD), ELECTRICAL ENGINEERING. *Current Pos:* Asst prof, 46-58, PROF ELEC ENG, UNIV TEX, AUSTIN, 58-, DIR GEOMAGNETICS LAB, 66- *Personal Data:* b Brookfield, Mo, Feb 8, 23; m 42; c 1. *Educ:* Univ Tex, BS, 44, MS, 49, PhD(elec eng), 54. *Mem:* Inst Elec & Electronics Engrs; Am Geophys Union. *Res:* Geomagnetics; electrical geoscience; information science. *Mailing Add:* Dept Elec Eng Univ Tex Austin TX 78712

SMITH, HAROLD WILLIAM, CONTROL ENGINEERING. *Current Pos:* Assoc prof, 66-69, PROF ELEC ENG, UNIV TORONTO, 69- *Personal Data:* b Toronto, Ont, Aug 15, 28; m 50; c 2. *Educ:* Univ Toronto, BASc, 50; Mass Inst Technol, ScD(instrumentation), 61. *Concurrent Pos:* Mem assoc comt automatic control, Nat Res Coun Can, 64-, chmn, 70-; consult, Falconbridge Nickel Mines Ltd, 67-; mem reactor control comt, Atomic Energy Control Bd Can, 72- *Res:* Modeling and control of industrial processes; multivariable systems; metallurgical applications. *Mailing Add:* 1248 St David St Victoria BC B8S 4Y9 Can

SMITH, HARRY ANDREW, ORGANIC CHEMISTRY, POLYMER CHEMISTRY. *Current Pos:* Chemist, Polymer Res Lab, Dow Chem Co, 60-62, res chemist, 62-66, Sci Proj Lab, 66-68, sr res chemist, Chem Lab, 68-71 & Org Chem Prod Res Lab, 71-74, res specialist II, Org Chem Res Lab, 74-76, res assoc, Designed Polymers & Chem Lab, 76-84, res assoc, Saran & Convented Prod, 84-87, RES ASSOC CONSUMER PROD LAB, DOW CHEM CO, 87- *Personal Data:* b Grand Rapids, Mich, Aug 29, 33; m 56; c 3. *Educ:* Univ Mich, BS, 55, MS, 57, PhD(org chem), 60. *Concurrent Pos:* Fel, NSF, 56 & 57. *Mem:* AAAS; Am Chem Soc; Sigma Xi; Soc Cosmetic Chemists; Cosmetic Toiletry & Fragrance Asn. *Res:* Condensation and ring opening polymerization, including preparation and characterization of phenylene sulfide polymers, carbonyl polymers, carbonyl-epoxide copolymers, phenolic resins, solvents and solvency; formulated consumer products. *Mailing Add:* 4608 James Dr Midland MI 48642

SMITH, HARRY FRANCIS, RING THEORY. *Current Pos:* lectr, 88-91, SR LECTR, UNIV NEW ENG, ARMIDALE, NSW, AUSTRALIA, 88- *Personal Data:* b Sioux City, Iowa, Mar 29, 41; m 65, 86, M Lucita Robin; c Nancy M, Jennifer, Michaela, Harry, Francis, Lucien & Ida L. *Educ:* Univ Calif, Berkeley, BA, 67; Univ Iowa, MS, 69, PhD(math), 72. *Prof Exp:* Asst prof math, Univ Iowa, 72-73; asst prof math, Madison Col, 73-77; from asst prof to prof, Iowa State Univ, 77-87. *Concurrent Pos:* Nat Acad Sci exchange scientist, Steklov Inst Math-Acad Sci USSR & Moscow State Pedag Inst, 82-83; Fulbright lectr, Univ Philippines & Ateneo Univ, Manila, 85-86; vis sr lectr, Univ Papua New Guinea, 87. *Mem:* Am Math Soc; Australian Math Soc. *Res:* Nonassociative algebra, alternative rings and their generalizations. *Mailing Add:* Dept Math Univ New Eng Armidale NSW 2351 Australia

SMITH, HARRY JOHN, VETERINARY PARASITOLOGY, MEDICAL ENTOMOLOGY. *Current Pos:* RETIRED. *Personal Data:* b Arundel, Quebec, Sept 3, 27; wid; c 2. *Educ:* McGill Univ, BSc, 54; Ont Vet Col, DVM, 58; Univ Toronto, MVSc, 60. *Prof Exp:* Res officer parasitol, Agr Can, 58-62, vet, 62-65, res scientist, 65-90. *Concurrent Pos:* Hon lectr, Mt Allison Univ, 72-77; vis prof, AVC, 91. *Mem:* Am Asn Vet Parasitologist; World Asn Advan Vet Parasitol; Wildlife Dis Asn; Can Asn Advan Vet Parisitol. *Res:* Epidemiology and ecology of livestock gastrointestinal helminths with special emphasis on parasitic gastroenteritis; ecology and diagnosis of trichinosis. *Mailing Add:* 9 Weldon St PO Box 184 Sackville NB E0A 3C0 Can

SMITH, HARRY LOGAN, JR, MICROBIOLOGY. *Current Pos:* Asst, 53-57, from instr to assoc prof, 57-74, PROF MICROBIOL, JEFFERSON MED COL, 74- *Personal Data:* b Philadelphia, Pa, June 4, 30; m 53; c 5. *Educ:* Temple Univ, AB, 52; Jefferson Med Col, MS, 54, PhD, 57. *Concurrent Pos:* NIH res career develop award, 62-66; consult cholera, WHO, 66. *Mem:* Am Soc Microbiol. *Res:* Vibrios; cholera. *Mailing Add:* Jefferson Med Col 1025 Walnut St Philadelphia PA 19107-5001

SMITH, HARVEY ALVIN, REPRESENTATION THEORY, SYSTEMS ANALYSIS. *Current Pos:* chmn dept, 77-82, PROF MATH, ARIZ STATE UNIV, 82- *Personal Data:* b Easton, Pa, Jan 30, 32; m 55, Ruth Kolb; c Deirdre L, Kirsten N & Brinton A. *Educ:* Lehigh Univ, BS, 52; Univ Pa, MS, 55, AM, 58, PhD(math), 64. *Honors & Awards:* Exec Off of President Meritorious Serv Award. *Prof Exp:* Physicist, Opers Res Div, Fire Control Instrument Group, Frankford Arsenal, 52-54; engr, Radio Corp Am, 54-57; sr systs analyst, Remington Rand Univac Div, Sperry Rand Corp, 57-58; mem tech staff, Auerbach Electronics Corp, 58-59; instr math, Drexel Inst, 59-60, asst prof, 60-64; NSF sci fel, Univ Pa, 64-65; mem, Tech Staff Weapons Systs Eval Group, Inst Defense Anal, DC, 65-66; from assoc prof to prof math, Oakland Univ, 66-77. *Concurrent Pos:* Consult, Ford Found proj measurement of delinquency, Dept Sociol, Univ Pa, 63-64, US Army Security Agency, 67-68 & Inst Defense Anal, 67-69; consult, Exec Off Pres, 68-73, dep chief systs eval, Off Emergency Preparedness; consult, US Arms Control & Disarmament Agency, 73-79 & Los Alamos Nat Lab, 80-91. *Mem:* Am Math Soc; Soc Indust & Appl Math; Sigma Xi. *Res:* Functional analysis; applied mathematics; systems analysis; operations research; representations of locally compact groups; strategic policy studies; twisted group algebras; integral operators. *Mailing Add:* Dept Math Ariz State Univ Tempe AZ 85287. *Fax:* 602-968-7780; *E-Mail:* hsmith@math.la.asu.edu

SMITH, HASTINGS ALEXANDER, JR, NUCLEAR PHYSICS. *Current Pos:* STAFF SCIENTIST, LOS ALAMOS NAT LAB, UNIV CALIF, 78- *Personal Data:* b Lexington, Ky, Apr 20, 43; m 65; c 2. *Educ:* Purdue Univ, BS, 65, MS, 67, PhD(nuclear physics), 70. *Prof Exp:* Appointee nuclear physics, Los Alamos Sci Lab, Univ Calif, 70-72; from asst prof to assoc prof physics, Ind Univ, 72-78. *Mem:* Am Phys Soc; AAAS; Am Asn Physics Teachers. *Res:* Intermediate and low-energy nuclear physics; gamma-ray and beta-ray spectroscopy; nuclear reactions; nuclei far from stability; non-destructive assay of special nuclear materials. *Mailing Add:* 760 Los Pueblos Los Alamos NM 87544

SMITH, HAYWOOD CLARK, JR, DYNAMICAL ASTRONOMY, STATISTICAL ASTRONOMY. *Current Pos:* ASSOC PROF ASTRON, UNIV FLA, 79- *Personal Data:* b Raleigh, NC, Oct 11, 45; m 69, Sylvia Mullis; c 2. *Educ:* Univ NC, Chapel Hill, AB, 67; Univ Va, MA, 69, PhD(astron), 72. *Prof Exp:* Vis asst prof, Univ SFla, 72-78, asst prof, 78-79. *Concurrent Pos:* Exec comt, Div Dynamical Astron, Am Astron Soc, 79-81, 84-86. *Mem:* Int Astron Union; Am Statist Asn. *Res:* Dynamical evolution of clusters of stars and galaxies; statistical astronomy. *Mailing Add:* Dept Astron Univ Fla PO Box 112055 Gainesville FL 32611-2055. *Fax:* 904-392-5089; *E-Mail:* hsmith@astro.ufl.edu

SMITH, HELENE SHEILA, MOLECULAR BIOLOGY. *Current Pos:* ASST DIR, PERALTA CANCER RES INST, 80- *Personal Data:* b Philadelphia, Pa, Feb 13, 41; m 62; c 1. *Educ:* Univ Pa, BS, 62, PhD(microbiol), 67. *Prof Exp:* Asst res virol, Univ Calif, Berkeley, 71-75, assoc res prof, 75-77; staff researcher biol, Donner Lab, Lawrence Berkeley Lab, 77-82. *Concurrent Pos:* Mem, Grad Group Genetics, Univ Calif, Berkeley, 79-82, Cell Biol Panel, NSF, 80-84; adj assoc prof, Univ Calif, San Francisco, 84- *Mem:* Am Asn Cancer Res; Am Asn Cell Biol; Tissue Cult Asn; Soc Anal Cytol. *Res:* Biology of human mammary epithelial cells in culture, and the use of these cells to study radiation induced survival and carcinogenesis, chemotherapeutic drug sensitivity, and tumor heterogeneity. *Mailing Add:* Geraldine Bruch Cancer Res Ctr 2330 Clay St San Francisco CA 94115-1932

SMITH, HENRY I, ELECTRICAL ENGINEERING. *Current Pos:* Engr, Lincoln Lab, 68-80, mgr, 77-80, PROF ELEC ENG, MASS INST TECHNOL, 80- *Personal Data:* b May 26, 57. *Educ:* Holy Cross Col, BS; Boston Col, PhD, 66. *Honors & Awards:* Cledo Brunetti Award, 95. *Concurrent Pos:* Vis scientist, Univ Col, London, 72, Thompson CSF, Paris, 74, Norweg Inst Technol, Trondheim, Norway, 76, Nippon Tel & Tel Corp, Atsugi, Japan, 90 & Univ Glasgow, 90; Adj prof, Submicron Struct Lab, Mass Inst Technol, 77-80. *Mem:* Nat Acad Eng; Am Phys Soc; Am Vacuum Soc; Mat Res Soc; Sigma Xi; fel Inst Elec & Electronics Engrs. *Res:* Submicron structures; nanofabrication; methods for preparing semiconductor-on-insulator films; electronic devices; quantum effects in sub-100 nm structures. *Mailing Add:* Mass Inst Technol 77 Massachusetts Ave Rm 39-427 Cambridge MA 02139

SMITH, HERBERT L, INORGANIC CHEMISTRY. *Current Pos:* RETIRED. *Personal Data:* b Mayport, Pa, June 28, 29; m 52; c 4. *Educ:* Univ Pittsburgh, BSEd, 53, MLitt, 57, PhD(inorg chem), 65. *Prof Exp:* Jr fel glass sci, Mellon Inst, 54-65; prof chem, Slippery Rock State Col, 65-91, chmn dept, 71-79. *Mem:* Am Chem Soc; Sigma Xi. *Res:* Effects of irradiation on glasses and crystals; effects of electrolytes on the circular dichroism of coordination compounds. *Mailing Add:* 518 Mercer Rd Slippery Rock PA 16057

SMITH, HOBART MUIR, VERTEBRATE ZOOLOGY. *Current Pos:* chmn dept environ, pop & organismic biol, 70-74 & 78-79, prof, 68-83, EMER PROF ENVIRON, POP & ORGANISMIC BIOL, UNIV COLO, BOULDER, 83- *Personal Data:* b Stanwood, Iowa, Sept 26, 12; wid; c Bruce D & Sally F (Nadvornik). *Educ:* Kans State Col, BS, 32; Univ Kans, AM, 33, PhD(zool), 36. *Prof Exp:* Nat Res Coun fel biol, Univ Mich, 36-37; asst, Chicago Acad Sci, 37-38 & Chicago Mus Natural Hist, 38; Bacon traveling scholar, Smithsonian Inst, 38-41; instr zool, Univ Rochester, 41-45; asst prof comp anat, Univ Kans, 45-46; assoc prof, Agr & Mech Col, Tex, 46-47; from asst prof to prof comp anat & herpet, Univ Ill, Urbana, 47-68. *Mem:* Am Soc Ichthyologists & Herpetologists (vpres, 37); Soc Study Amphibians & Reptiles; Soc Syst Zool (pres, 65); Herpetologists League (pres, 47-59). *Res:* Herpetology; principles of taxonomy; zoogeography; comparative anatomy. *Mailing Add:* Dept Environ Pop & Org Biol Univ Colo Boulder CO 80309-0334

SMITH, HOMER ALVIN, JR, ORGANOMETALLIC CHEMISTRY, ORGANIC NOMENCLATURE. *Current Pos:* chmn dept, 85-91, PROF CHEM, MILLIKIN UNIV, 85- *Personal Data:* b Houston, Tex, Feb 23, 32; m 59, Martha A Abendroth; c Melinda A & Matthew B. *Educ:* Rice Univ, BA, 53; Okla State Univ, PhD(chem), 61. *Prof Exp:* Asst prof chem, Tarkio Col, 61-64; from assoc prof to prof chem, Hampden-Sydney Col, 64-85, chmn dept, 66-68, 74-76 & 80-81. *Concurrent Pos:* NSF sci fac fel, Duke Univ, 68-69 & Ind Univ, 76-78; assoc mem comn, Nomenclature Org Chem. *Mem:* Am Chem Soc; Royal Soc Chem; Int Union Pure & Appl Chem. *Res:* Syntheses involving organometallic intermediates and strong base systems; synthesis of potential medicinals. *Mailing Add:* Dept Chem Millikin Univ Decatur IL 62522. *Fax:* 217-424-3993

SMITH, HORACE VERNON, JR, ACCELERATOR PHYSICS. *Current Pos:* STAFF MEM, LOS ALAMOS NAT LAB, 78- *Personal Data:* b Rockford, Ill, July 23, 42; m 64; c 1. *Educ:* Univ Tex, Austin, BES, 64; Univ Ill, Urbana, MS, 65; Univ Wis-Madison, PhD(physics), 71. *Prof Exp:* Res asst prof physics, Prairie View Agr & Mech Col, 70-71; res assoc, 71-74, asst scientist nuclear eng & physics, Univ Wis-Madison, 74-78. *Concurrent Pos:* Consult. *Mem:* Am Phys Soc; Inst Elec & Electronics Engrs. *Res:* Ion source development. *Mailing Add:* Los Alamos Nat Lab AOT-2 MS-H838 PO Box 1663 Los Alamos NM 87545. *E-Mail:* hvsmith@lanl.gov

SMITH, HOWARD E, ORGANIC CHEMISTRY. *Current Pos:* from asst prof to prof, 59-93, EMER PROF CHEM, VANDERBILT UNIV, 93- *Personal Data:* b San Francisco, Calif, Aug 1, 25; m 60, Louise Meier; c David C, Marie-Louise & Erika B. *Educ:* Univ Calif, BS, 51; Stanford Univ, MS, 54, PhD(chem), 57. *Prof Exp:* Asst res chemist, Calif Res Corp, Stand Oil Co, Calif, 51-52; res assoc, Stanford Univ, 56; USPHS fel, Wayne State Univ, 56-58; fel, Swiss Fed Inst Technol, Zurich, 58-59. *Mem:* Fel AAAS; Am Chem Soc; The Chem Soc. *Res:* Natural products; stereochemistry. *Mailing Add:* Dept Chem Vanderbilt Univ Nashville TN 37235. *Fax:* 615-322-4936

SMITH, HOWARD EDWIN, mechanical engineering, aerospace engineering; deceased, see previous edition for last biography

SMITH, HOWARD JOHN TREWEEK, LOW TEMPERATURE PHYSICS. *Current Pos:* from asst prof to assoc prof, 64-85, PROF PHYSICS, UNIV WATERLOO, 85- *Personal Data:* b Hornchurch, Eng, June 21, 37; m 63; c 2. *Educ:* Univ London, BSc, 58, PhD(physics), 61. *Prof Exp:* Res physicist, Petrocarbon Develop Ltd, Eng, 61-64; res physicist, Ferranti Electronics Ltd, Ont, 64. *Res:* Superconductivity tunneling; low temperature heat engines; chaos. *Mailing Add:* Dept Physics Univ Waterloo 200 Univ Ave Waterloo ON N2L 3G1 Can

SMITH, HOWARD LEROY, ORGANIC CHEMISTRY. *Current Pos:* Org chemist, Jackson Lab, 51-55, div head, 55-59, asst lab dir, 59-60, res dir, 60-65, asst gen supt process dept, Chambers Works, 65-66, supt miscellaneous intermediates area, 66-67, asst gen supt dyes & chem dept, 67-68, asst works mgr, 68-70, works mgr, 70-71, dir mfg serv, Org Chem Dept, 71-75, dir mfg, 75-76, DIR, EQUIP & MAGNETIC PROD, PHOTO PROD DEPT, E I DU PONT DE NEMOURS & CO, INC, 76- *Personal Data:* b Eldorado, Kans, Nov 12, 24; m 47; c 5. *Educ:* Univ Calif, BS, 48; Mass Inst Technol, PhD, 51. *Mem:* Am Chem Soc. *Res:* Dyes and textile chemicals; fluorocarbon chemistry; petroleum chemicals. *Mailing Add:* 302 Glen Rd Landenberg PA 19350-9100

SMITH, HOWARD WESLEY, AEROSPACE ENGINEERING. *Current Pos:* EMER PROF AEROSPACE STRUCT, UNIV KANS, 70- *Personal Data:* b New York, NY, Nov 24, 29. *Educ:* Wichita State Univ, BS, 51, MS, 58; Okla State Univ, PhD(aerospace eng), 68. *Honors & Awards:* Tasker Howard Bliss Medal, Soc Am Mil Engrs, 74; Space Shuttle Plaque, Am Inst Aeronaut & Astronaut, 84. *Prof Exp:* Jr engr, Boeing Co, Kans, 50-51, stress analyst, 52-55, struct engr, 56-58, group supvr, 59-63, struct res mgr, 65-68, mem hq staff, Seattle, Wash, 69-70. *Concurrent Pos:* Geront fel, Univ Kans, 80. *Mem:* Am Inst Aeronaut & Astronaut; Soc Exp Stress Anal; Am Soc Eng Educ; Soc Am Mil Engrs; Soc Advan Mat & Process Eng. *Res:* Aircraft loads; stresses; materials; composites; crashworthiness; cost models; optimization; teaching methods; biomechanics of bone. *Mailing Add:* 1612 Crescent Rd Lawrence KS 66044

SMITH, HUBERT COULSON, AIRCRAFT DESIGN, AIRCRAFT FLIGHT MECHANICS. *Current Pos:* res asst, 65-67, ASST PROF AEROSPACE ENG, PA STATE UNIV, 68-, DIR, UNDER GRAD STUDIES, 86- *Personal Data:* Dillsburg, Pa, June 20, 30. *Educ:* Gettysburg Col, BA, 52; Pa State Univ, BS, 59, MS, 67; Univ Va, PhD(syst eng), 78. *Honors & Awards:* Teetor Outstanding Educr Award, Soc Automotive Engrs, 83; Hon Accident Prev Counr, Fed Aviation Admin, 83; Eng Educ Centennial Cert, Am Soc Eng Educ, 93; Piper Gen Aviation Award, Am Inst Aeronaut & Astronaut, 96. *Prof Exp:* Aerospace engr, Middletown Air Mat Area, USAF, 59-65. *Concurrent Pos:* Vis prof aerospace eng, Embry-Riddle Aeronaut Univ, 83-84 & 91-92; mem, Transp Res Bd, Nat Res Coun, 86- *Mem:* Assoc fel Am Inst Aeronaut & Astronaut; Am Soc Eng Educ; Soc Automotive Engrs. *Res:* Aircraft aerodynamics and flight mechanics, flight testing methods, aviation safety analysis, aircraft operations; authored books and articles. *Mailing Add:* 233 Hammond Bldg University Park PA 16802. *Fax:* 814-865-7092

SMITH, HUGO DUNLAP, pediatrics; deceased, see previous edition for last biography

SMITH, IAN CORMACK PALMER, MEDICAL PHYSICS. *Current Pos:* res officer, 67-87, DIR GEN, NAT RES COUN CAN, 87- *Personal Data:* b Winnipeg, Man, Sept 23, 39; m 65; c 4. *Educ:* Univ Manitoba, BSc, 61, MSc, 62; Cambridge Univ, PhD(theoret chem), 65. *Hon Degrees:* FilDr, Stockholm, 86; DSc, Winnipeg, 90. *Honors & Awards:* Merck, Sharp & Dohme Award, Chem Inst Can, Labatt Award; Ayerst Award, Can Biochem Soc; Barringer Award, Can Spectros Soc, Herzberg Award; Organon Teknika Award, Can Soc Clin Chem. *Prof Exp:* NATO fel, Stanford Univ, 65-66; mem res staff, Bell Tel Labs, 66-67. *Concurrent Pos:* Consult, Bell Tel Labs, 68-70, CPC Int, 75-85 & Smith Kline & French, 79-82; adj prof chem, Carleton Univ, 73-90; adj prof biophys, Univ Ill, Chicago, 75-80; adj prof chem & biochem, Univ Ottawa, 77-; allied scientist, Ottawa Civic Hosp, 85-, Ottawa Gen Hosp, 87- & Ont Cancer Found, 88- *Mem:* AAAS; fel Chem Inst Can; Am Chem Soc; Biophys Soc; Can Biochem Soc; fel Royal Soc Can. *Res:* Nuclear magnetic resonance, imaging and spectroscopy; optical spectroscopy; infrared spectroscopy application of these techniques to problems in molecular biology and medicine, especially biological membranes and cancer. *Mailing Add:* Inst Biodiagnostics Natl Res Council Can 435 Ellice Ave Winnipeg MB R3B 1Y6 Can

SMITH, IAN MACLEAN, INFECTIOUS DISEASES, GERIATRIC INTERNAL MEDICINE. *Current Pos:* PROF INTERNAL MED, COL MED, UNIV IOWA, 78- *Personal Data:* b Glasgow, Scotland, May 21, 22; nat US; m 48; c 5. *Educ:* Glasgow Univ, MB, ChB, 44, MD, 57; FRCPG, 49; FRCPath, 76. *Prof Exp:* House physician internal med, Stobhill Hosp, Scotland, 44-45; clin asst, Royal infirmary, 47; registr path, Post-grad Med Sch, London, 47-48, house physician internal med, 48; tutor med path, Royal Hosp & Univ Sheffield, 48-49; fel internal med, Johns Hopkins Hosp, 49-51; asst resident, Wash Univ & Barnes Hosp, 51-53; asst prof, Rockefeller Inst & asst physician, Hosp, 53-55; chief infectious dis lab, Univ Hosps, Univ Iowa, 55-74, from asst prof to prof internal med, Col Med, 55-76; prof & chmn dept, Col Med, East Tenn State Univ, 76-78. *Concurrent Pos:* Consult, Iowa State Dept Health, 58-76. *Mem:* Am Geriatric Soc. *Res:* Epidemiology and treatment of infectious diseases; epidemiology of elderly patients in acute care hospital. *Mailing Add:* 1013 Tower Ct Iowa City IA 52246

SMITH, IEUAN TREVOR, CHEMISTRY. *Current Pos:* FREELANCE SCI & MED WRITER & ED, 87- *Personal Data:* b Bromley, Eng, Jan 11, 33; m 58; c 3. *Educ:* Univ London, BSc, 54, MSc, 60. *Prof Exp:* Res chemist, Cray Valley Prod Ltd, Eng, 57-61; sr res officer, Paint Res Sta, 61-64; tech mgr, Epoxlite Ltd, 64-66; sr res chemist, Toni Co, 66-67, res supvr, 67-69, res supvr, 69-77, prin res assoc, 78-80, group leader, Gillette Res Inst, Gillette Co, 80-87. *Res:* Properties and structure of polymers; polyelectrolyte behavior; surface and colloid chemistry; infrared spectroscopy, especially of surface species and proteins; keratin fibers, structure and properties; health, fitness, science and technology writing. *Mailing Add:* 11203 Lund Pl Kensington MD 20895

SMITH, ISAAC LITTON, ANALYTICAL CHEMISTRY. *Current Pos:* ANALYTICAL CHEMIST, ETHYL CORP, 74- *Personal Data:* b Russellville, Ala. *Educ:* Florence State Univ, Ala, 61; Univ Ala, PhD(analyt chem), 74. *Prof Exp:* Chemist, Reynolds Metals Co, 68-70. *Concurrent Pos:* Mem res comt, Water Pollution Control Fedn, 74. *Mem:* Am Chem Soc; Water Pollution Control Fedn; Sigma Xi. *Res:* Analytical methods development; investigation of plant production problems; development and design of continuous monitor instrumentation. *Mailing Add:* Res & Develop Ctr Ethyl Corp PO Box 2158 Richmond VA 23218-2158

SMITH, ISSAR, MOLECULAR BIOLOGY. *Current Pos:* RES PROF, SCH MED, NY UNIV, 79- *Personal Data:* b New York, NY, Dec 4, 33; m 55; c 2. *Educ:* City Col New York, BA, 55; Columbia Univ, MA, 57, PhD(biol), 61. *Prof Exp:* Fel, Sloan-Kettering Inst Cancer Res, 61-62; fel microbiol, Sch Med, NY Univ, 62-63; fel molecular biol, Albert Einstein Col Med, 63-64, res asst prof path, 64-67; assoc microbiol, 67-74, assoc mem, 74-79, mem, Pub Health Res Inst City New York, 79- *Concurrent Pos:* USPHS fel, 61-62, trainee, 62-63; Am Cancer Soc fel, 63-64, res grant, 65-; NIH career develop award, 71-, res grant, 72- *Mem:* AAAS; Am Soc Microbiol. *Res:* Genetics and physiology of ribosomes; evolutionary interrelationships between bacteria; nucleic acids; prokaryote differentiation and regulation. *Mailing Add:* 343 E 30th St New York NY 10016

SMITH, J C, STRUCTURAL ENGINEERING. *Current Pos:* Teaching asst, 55-56 & 58-60, from instr to asst prof, 60-74, ASSOC PROF CIVIL ENG, NC STATE UNIV, 74- *Personal Data:* b Hudson, NC, Apr 19, 33; m 55, Lois O Herman; c Jonathan & Olivia. *Educ:* NC State Univ, BCE, 55, MS, 60; Purdue Univ, PhD(civil eng), 66. *Honors & Awards:* outstanding Civil Engr Award, NC Sect, Am Soc Civil Eng, 91. *Mem:* Fel Am Soc Civil Engrs. *Res:* Structural analysis and design. *Mailing Add:* Dept of Civil Eng NC State Univ Box 7908 Raleigh NC 27695-7908

SMITH, J DUNGAN, PHYSICAL OCEANOGRAPHY, GEOLOGICAL OCEANOGRAPHY. *Current Pos:* HYDROLOGIST, US GEOL SURVEY, 91- *Personal Data:* b Attleboro, Mass, May 24, 39; m 59; c 3. *Educ:* Brown Univ, BA, 62, MS, 63; Univ Chicago, PhD(geophys), 68. *Prof Exp:* From actg asst prof to assoc prof, Dept Oceanog & Geophys Prog, Univ Wash, 67-77, prof & adj prof geol sci, 77-91, chmn, Geophys Prog, 80-85. *Mem:* AAAS; Am Geophys Union; Sigma Xi; Int Asn Hydraul Res. *Res:* Coastal oceanography; mechanics of turbulent boundary layers; erosion and sediment transport; fluvial geomorphology; geophysical fluid mechanics. *Mailing Add:* US Geol Surv 3215 Marine St Boulder CO 80303

SMITH, J RICHARD, NUCLEAR PHYSICS. *Current Pos:* RETIRED. *Personal Data:* b Utah, July 18, 24. *Educ:* Brigham Young Univ, BA, 49; Rice Univ, MA, 51, PhD(physics), 53. *Prof Exp:* Consult, IAEA South Korea, 85-88; sci specialist, EG&G, Idaho, 88-91. *Mem:* Am Phys Soc; Am Nuclear Soc. *Res:* Measurement of neutron multiplication. *Mailing Add:* 854 Claire View Lane Idaho Falls ID 83402

SMITH, JACK, ELECTROMAGNETICS, ATMOSPHERIC SENSING. *Current Pos:* assoc prof, 64-73, dean, Col Eng, 76-82, PROF ELEC ENG, UNIV TEX, EL PASO, 73-, SCHELLENGER PROF ELEC ENG, 82- *Personal Data:* b Morristown, NJ, Nov 28, 27; m 54; c 3. *Educ:* Univ Ariz, BS, 52, MS, 58, PhD(elec eng), 64. *Prof Exp:* Test engr, Gen Elec Co, 52-53, engr, 53-56; instr elec eng, Univ Ariz, 57-64, asst prof, 64, res assoc, Appl Res Lab, 57-64. *Concurrent Pos:* NSF sci fac fel, 61-62; consult, Atmospheric Sci Lab, US Army, 71- *Mem:* Inst Elec & Electronics Engrs; Am Geophys Union; Am Soc Eng Educ. *Res:* Atmospheric effects on high frequency electromagnetic wave propagation; lightning; upper atmosphere and ionospheric ionization characteristics and variations. *Mailing Add:* Dept Elec & Comput Eng Univ Tex El Paso TX 79968

SMITH, JACK C, BIOSTATISTICS. *Current Pos:* CHIEF, STATIST & COMPUT RESOURCES BR, DIV REPRODUCTIVE HEALTH, CTR DIS CONTROL, 66- *Personal Data:* b Tex, Mar 25, 41. *Educ:* Howard Payne Univ, BA, 63; Tulane Univ, MS, 65. *Prof Exp:* Statistician, La State Health Dept, 65-66. *Mailing Add:* Div Reproductive Health CDC MS K21 Atlanta GA 30333. *Fax:* 770-488-5967

SMITH, JACK HOWARD, THEORETICAL PHYSICS. *Current Pos:* RETIRED. *Personal Data:* b Middletown, NY, Nov 8, 21; m 49; c 3. *Educ:* Cornell Univ, AB, 43, PhD(theoret physics), 51. *Prof Exp:* Asst, Cornell Univ, 43-44; jr scientist, Theoret Div, Los Alamos Sci Lab, 44-46; asst, Cornell Univ, 46-49; mem staff, Theoret Div, Los Alamos Sci Lab, 49-51; res assoc theoret physics, Knolls Atomic Power Lab, Gen Elec Co, 51-63; prof, State Univ NY, Albany, 63-96. *Mem:* AAAS; Am Asn Physics Teachers; Acoust Soc Am; Am Phys Soc. *Res:* Electromagnetic scattering; nuclear scattering of high energy electrons; neutron diffusion; reactor physics; reactor shielding; musical acoustics. *Mailing Add:* 1030 Atateka Rd Schenectady NY 12309. *E-Mail:* jh546@cdc.albany.edu

SMITH, JACK LOUIS, BIOCHEMISTRY, NUTRITION. *Current Pos:* SWANSON ASSOC PROF BIOCHEM, 74- *Personal Data:* b Huntington, WVa, July 15, 34; m 61; c 2. *Educ:* Univ Cincinnati, BS, 56, PhD(biochem), 62. *Prof Exp:* NIH trainee animal nutrit, Univ Ill, 61-63; Muscular Dystrophy Asn Am fel, Stanford Res Inst, 64; from asst prof to assoc prof biochem, Sch Med, Tulane Univ, 65-74, from asst prof to assoc prof biochem-nutrit, Sch Pub Health & Trop Med, 68-74, adj prof biochem, Sch Pub Health & Trop Med, 74-79. *Concurrent Pos:* Prin investr biochem, Touro Res Inst, 69-74. *Mem:* AAAS; Am Chem Soc; Am Inst Nutrit; Am Soc Clin Nutrit; Am Bd Nutrit; Am Dietetic Asn. *Res:* Nutritional biochemistry; nutritional assessment. *Mailing Add:* Col Human Resources Univ Del 238 Alison Hall Newark DE 19716-0001. *Fax:* 302-831-4186

SMITH, JACK R(EGINALD), ELECTRICAL ENGINEERING. *Current Pos:* from asst prof to assoc prof, 64-70, PROF ELEC ENG, UNIV FLA, 70- *Personal Data:* b Carrington, NDak, June 16, 35; m 59; c 3. *Educ:* Univ Southern Calif, BS, 58, MS, 60, PhD(elec eng), 64. *Prof Exp:* Mem tech staff, Hughes Aircraft Co, 58-59; res engr, Jet Propulsion Lab, 61; res assoc elec eng, Univ Southern Calif, 74-76. *Mem:* Inst Elec & Electronics Engrs; Int Fedn Med Electronics & Biol Eng. *Res:* Biomedical engineering. *Mailing Add:* Dept Elec Eng Univ Fla 13 13th St at University Ave Gainesville FL 32611

SMITH, JACKSON BRUCE, INTERNAL MEDICINE, IMMUNOLOGY. *Current Pos:* assoc prof, 81-85, PROF MED & MICROBIOL, JEFFERSON MED COL, 85- *Personal Data:* b Mt Holly, NJ, Mar 2, 38; m 63; c 2. *Educ:* Wake Forest Col, BS, 60, MD, 65. *Prof Exp:* Clin res fel, Inst Cancer Res, 67-69; fel, Univ Col, London, Eng, 72-74; clin assoc med, Univ Pa, 75-78; res physician, Inst Cancer Res, 74-81. *Concurrent Pos:* Clin assoc med, Pa Hosp, 76-81; Am Cancer Soc, grant, 78-80; adj asst prof med, Univ Pa Sch Med, 78-81; grant, NIH, 81-85 & 89-92. *Mem:* AAAS; Am Col Physicians; Am Fedn Clin Res; Am Asn Immunologists; Am Asn Cancer Res. *Res:* Immune system regulatory mechanisms in normal individuals and in patients and laboratory animals with lymphoproliferative and autoimmune disorders; immunological mechanisms of repeated pregnancy loss; maternal-fetal immunology. *Mailing Add:* Jefferson Med Col 1015 Walnut St Suite 613 Philadelphia PA 19107

SMITH, JAMES ALAN, REMOTE SENSING, SCENE RADIATION MODELING. *Current Pos:* head, Biospheric Sci Br, 85-90, assoc chief, Sci Info Systs Ctr, 90, STAFF SCIENTIST, LAB TERRESTRIAL PHYSICS, NASA GSFC, 90- *Personal Data:* b Detroit, Mich, Nov 19, 42; m 65; c 2. *Educ:* Univ Mich, BS, 63, MS, 65, PhD(physics), 70; Johns Hopkins Univ, MS, 92. *Prof Exp:* Res asst, Willow Run Labs, Univ Mich, 64-66, from res asst to assoc, Dept Physics, 66-70; asst prof remote sensing, Dept Earth Resources, Colo State Univ, 70-74, assoc prof, 74-78, prof remote sensing & comput appl, Dept Forestry, 78-85. *Concurrent Pos:* Assoc dir, Comput Ctr, Colo State Univ, 74-76; consult, numerous Fed Agencies & Indust; prin investr, NASA, Army Res Off, US Forest Serv, US Geol Surv, Corp Engrs, & US Fish & Wildlife Serv; assoc ed, Inst Elec & Electronics Engrs, Trans Geosci & Rem Sens, 83-91, ed, 91-95; mem, US Nat Comt, Union Radio Sci Int. *Mem:* Fel Inst Elec & Electronic Engrs; Geosci & Remote Sensing Soc; Am Geophys Union; Soc Photo-Optical Instrumentation Engrs; AAAS; Inst Elec & Electronics Engrs Comput Soc. *Res:* Modeling of optical reflective and thermal radiation patterns from earth surface features and the application of such models to remote sensing; large scale ecosystem analysis and modeling; information systems. *Mailing Add:* 11808 Bright Passage Columbia MD 21044-4139. *Fax:* 301-286-1757

SMITH, JAMES ALLBEE, ANALYTICAL CHEMISTRY. *Current Pos:* MGR, TECH TESTING LABS, 81- *Personal Data:* b Detroit, Mich, Oct 20, 37; m 58; c 2. *Educ:* Univ Mich, Ann Arbor, BS, 59; Ohio State Univ, PhD(org chem), 64. *Prof Exp:* Res chemist, Res & Develop Dept, Union Carbide Corp, 64-67, proj scientist catalysis, 67-68; res assoc coordr chem, Case Western Reserve Univ, 68-70; sr res chemist, Eng Develop Ctr, C E Lummus Co, 70-73; chemist, WVa Dept Agr, 73-78, asst dir, 78-81. *Mem:* Am Chem Soc; Asn Off Anal Chemists. *Res:* Development of methodology for residue analysis. *Mailing Add:* 1207 Larchwood Rd Charleston WV 25314-1232

SMITH, JAMES CECIL, PHYSIOLOGY, BIOCHEMISTRY. *Current Pos:* res leader, 77-93, RES CHEMIST PHY, NUTRIT LAB, USDA, 93- *Personal Data:* b Little Orleans, Md, Jan 17, 34; m 61, Kay Plummer; c James III, Michelle & Deborah. *Educ:* Univ Md, BS, 56, MS, 59, PhD(animal nutrit), 64. *Honors & Awards:* Klaus Schwarz Award, 82. *Prof Exp:* Health serv officer, NIH, 59-61; biol chemist, Univ Calif, Los Angeles, 64-65; res physiologist, Vet Admin Hosp, Long Beach, Calif, 65-66; res biochemist, Vet Admin Hosp, Washington, DC, 66-77, chief, Trace Element Res Lab, 71-77. *Mem:* Am Inst Nutrit; Am Soc Clin Nutrit. *Res:* Trace element metabolism such as zinc and copper; vitamin trace mineral interactions; carotenoid interactions; tissue culture; phy/to/nutrient research. *Mailing Add:* Human Nutrit Res Ctr Phy to Nutrient Lab US Dept Agr Rm 206 Bldg 307 BARC-E Beltsville MD 20705. *Fax:* 301-504-9062; *E-Mail:* smith@307.bhnrc.usda.gov

SMITH, JAMES CLARENCE, JR, MATHEMATICS. *Current Pos:* asst prof, 67-71, ASSOC PROF MATH, VA POLYTECH INST & STATE UNIV, 71- *Personal Data:* b Martinsville, Va, Aug 16, 39; m 62; c 2. *Educ:* Davidson Col, BS, 61; Col William & Mary, MS, 64; Duke Univ, PhD(math), 67. *Prof Exp:* Aerospace technologist, Langley Res Ctr, NASA, 61-67. *Concurrent Pos:* Consult, Langley Res Ctr, NASA, 68 & 69. *Mem:* Am Math Soc; Math Asn Am. *Res:* Topology; dimension theory. *Mailing Add:* Dept Math Va Polytech Inst & State Univ Blacksburg VA 24061. *Fax:* 540-231-5960; *E-Mail:* smithj@math.vt.edu

SMITH, JAMES DAVID BLACKHALL, POLYMER CHEMISTRY. *Current Pos:* mgr instalation systs, Res & Develop Ctr, 68-82, Polymer & Composite Res Dept, 82-87, CONSULT SCIENTIST, MATS TECHNOL DIV, WESTINGHOUSE ELEC CORP, 87- *Personal Data:* b Peterhead, Scotland, Apr 25, 40; m 80, Paula; c Alison & Bryan. *Educ:* Aberdeen Univ, BSc, 62, PhD(polymer chem), 65. *Prof Exp:* NSF res grant, Polymer Res Ctr, State Univ NY, 65-66; sr chemist, Laporte Industs Ltd, Luton, Eng, 67-68. *Mem:* Am Chem Soc; Royal Soc Chem; Inst Elec & Electronics Engrs. *Res:* Polymerization kinetics; electroinitiated polymerization reactions; polyester and epoxy resin technology; flame retardants; insulation and dielectric properties of polymers. *Mailing Add:* Insulation Dept Westinghouse Elec Corp Res & Develop Ctr Churchill Boro Pittsburgh PA 15235. *Fax:* 412-256-1222; *E-Mail:* wx_smithjd@westinghouse.com

SMITH, JAMES DOUGLAS, DEVELOPMENTAL GENETICS, REGULATION OF SEED DEVELOPMENT. *Current Pos:* from asst prof to assoc prof, Tex A&M Univ, 59-70, chmn fac, 62-80, prof genetics, 70-97, EMER PROF GENETICS, TEX A&M UNIV, 97- *Personal Data:* b Paullina, Iowa, Dec 14, 27; m 55; c 2. *Educ:* Iowa State Univ, BS, 50, MS, 56, PhD(genetics), 60. *Prof Exp:* Plant breeder, United-Hagie Hybrids, Inc, 53, consult, 53-59. *Mem:* Am Genetics Asn; Genetics Soc Can; Genetics Soc Am; Bot Soc Am; Am Soc Plant Physiol. *Res:* Genetic, metabolic and environmental regulation of seed development; genetic dissection of the biosynthesis and functions of abscisic acid and gibberellins in developing seed of Zea mays; metabolic effects resulting from modulation of water, temperature, phytohormones, carbohydrates and amino acids on seed grown in vitro. *Mailing Add:* 1126 Terrace Dr Bryan TX 77802

SMITH, JAMES DOYLE, ORGANIC CHEMISTRY. *Current Pos:* RETIRED. *Personal Data:* b Charlottesville, Va, Jan 27, 21; m 44, Nancy Page; c Elizabeth & Stephen. *Educ:* Univ Va, BS, 42, MS, 44, PhD(chem), 46. *Prof Exp:* Assoc, Med Col Va, Va Commonwealth Univ, 46-48, asst prof chem, 48-51, assoc prof, 51-62, actg chmn, 61, prof, 62-81, chmn dept, 62-74, actg chmn, Dept Pharmaceut Chem, 76-77. *Mem:* AAAS; Am Chem Soc; Am Pharmaceut Asn. *Res:* Synthetic organic and medicinal chemistry; amino acids; antimalarials; anti-tumor agents; anticytotoxic agents, compounds that bind at the sigma sites. *Mailing Add:* Sch Pharm Med Col Va Va Commonwealth Univ PO Box 980540 Richmond VA 23298-0540

SMITH, JAMES EARL, MECHANICAL & AEROSPACE ENGINEERING. *Current Pos:* instr, Dept Aerospace Eng, WVa Univ, 76-78, adj asst prof, Dept Gen Eng, 78-84, asst res prof, Col Eng, 84-85, ASST RES PROF, DEPT MECH & AEROSPACE ENG, WVA UNIV, 85- *Personal Data:* b May 28, 49; c 3. *Educ:* WVa Univ, BSAE, 72, MSAE, 74, PhD, 84. *Prof Exp:* Staff engr, Morgantown Energy Res Ctr, Dept of Energy, 74-76. *Mem:* Sigma Xi; Am Inst Aeronaut & Astronaut; Am Soc Mech Engrs; Soc Automotive Engrs; Am Soc Eng Educ. *Res:* New concept of movement to engine design. *Mailing Add:* PO Box 6101 Morgantown WV 26506

SMITH, JAMES EDWARD, JR, TECHNOLOGY TRANSFER. *Current Pos:* Res sanitary engr, Advan Waste Treatment Lab, 68-71, sanitary engr, 71-76, head municipal technol transfer staff, 76-77, ENVIRON ENGR, CTR ENVIRON INFO, US ENVIRON PROTECTION AGENCY, 77- *Personal Data:* b Cincinnati, Ohio, Dec 5, 41; m 69; c 4. *Educ:* Univ Cincinnati, BS, 63, MS, 66; Wash Univ, DSc, 69. *Concurrent Pos:* Consult, sludge treatment & disposal for indust residues, Arg govt, 81 & 85; consult, Environ Hazards & Food Protection Unit, Environ Health Div, WHO, Switz, 84-85. *Mem:* Am Soc Civil Engrs; Water Pollution Control Fedn; Int Asn Water Pollution Res. *Res:* Land application of sludge; sludge dewatering; drinking water treatment; definition of the effects and control of non-ionizing radiation; 60 publications. *Mailing Add:* 5821 Marlborough Dr Cincinnati OH 45230-3513

SMITH, JAMES ELDON, microbiology, for more information see previous edition

SMITH, JAMES F, MATHEMATICAL ANALYSIS. *Current Pos:* From instr to assoc prof, 64-74, PROF MATH, LE MOYNE COL, NY, 74- *Personal Data:* b Syracuse, NY, Apr 26, 30. *Educ:* Bellarmine Col, NY, AB, 54; Cath Univ Am, MS, 57, PhD(math), 59; Woodstock Col, Md, STL. *Mem:* Am Math Soc; Math Asn Am. *Res:* Banach algebras; Hilbert space; structure and spectral theory. *Mailing Add:* Jesuit Residence Le Moyne Col Syracuse NY 13214

SMITH, JAMES G(ILBERT), ELECTRICAL ENGINEERING. *Current Pos:* asst prof, Sch Technol, Southern Ill Univ, 66-69, assoc prof, 69-72, chmn, Dept Elec Sci & Systs Eng, 71-80, prof, 72-93, EMER PROF ELEC ENG, COL ENG & TECHNOL, SOUTHERN ILL UNIV, 93- *Personal Data:* b Benton, Ill, May 1, 30; m 55, Barbara Smothers; c Julie. *Educ:* Univ Mo, BSEE, 57, MSEE, 59, PhD(eng physics), 67. *Prof Exp:* Instr elec eng, Sch Mines, Univ Mo, Rolla, 57-59 & 61-66, asst prof, 59-61. *Concurrent Pos:* Fac Fel, NSF, 62-63. *Res:* Electromagnetics and antennas, lightning and electrical properties of materials; electrophoresis and electroosmosis, physical and chemical properties of coal, and supercapaciters. *Mailing Add:* Dept Elec Eng Southern Ill Univ Carbondale IL 62901-6603. *Fax:* 618-453-7972

SMITH, JAMES HAMMOND, NUCLEAR PHYSICS. *Current Pos:* instr physics, Univ Ill, Urbana, 51, from asst prof to prof, 53-92, assoc head dept, 72-80, EMER PROF PHYSICS, UNIV ILL, URBANA, 92- *Personal Data:* b Colorado Springs, Colo, Feb 2, 25; m 50, 55, E Jean Walker; c 4. *Educ:* Stanford Univ, AB, 45; Harvard Univ, AM, 47, PhD(physics), 52. *Prof Exp:* Jr lab technician, Oak Ridge Nat Lab, 50-51. *Concurrent Pos:* Guggenheim fel, 66. *Mem:* Fel Am Phys Soc. *Res:* Photonuclear reactions; K meson decays; high energy nuclear reactions. *Mailing Add:* Dept Physics Loomis Lab Univ Ill 1110 W Green St Urbana IL 61801

SMITH, JAMES HART, environmental chemistry, for more information see previous edition

SMITH, JAMES JOHN, PHYSIOLOGY, CIRCULATORY PHYSIOLOGY. *Current Pos:* chmn dept, 52-78, PROF PHYSIOL, MED COL WIS, 52-; PROF MED, 78-; DIR, HUMAN PERFORMANCE LAB, ZABLOCKI VET ADMIN CTR, MILWAUKEE, WIS, 82- *Personal Data:* b St Paul, Minn, Jan 28, 14; div; c Philip, Lucy, Paul & Gregory. *Educ:* St Louis Univ, BS, 35, MD, 37; Northwestern Univ, MS, 40, PhD(physiol), 46. *Honors & Awards:* Legion Merit, USAF. *Prof Exp:* Intern, St Paul Ramsey Med Ctr, St Paul, Minn, 37-38; asst path, Cook Co Hosp, Chicago, Ill, 38-39; assoc prof physiol & dean, Sch Med, Loyola Univ Chicago, 46-50; chief, Med Educ Div, Cent Off, US Vet Admin, DC, 50-52. *Concurrent Pos:* Fulbright res prof, Heidelberg, 59-60; fel, Cardiovasc Sect, Am Physiol Soc, 64; nat bd consults to surgeon gen, USAF, 52-54. *Mem:* Soc Exp Biol & Med; Am Physiol Soc; Sigma Xi; Am Heart Asn; Geront Soc Am. *Res:* Cardiovascular physiology, particularly effect of aging and circulatory disease on autonomic response of circulatory system to non-exercise and exercise stress; cardiovascular evaluation; peripheral circulation; circulatory control, aging, stress response. *Mailing Add:* Dept Physiol Med Col Wis Milwaukee WI 53226. *Fax:* 414-266-8705

SMITH, JAMES L, MATHEMATICS, GEOMETRY. *Current Pos:* assoc prof, Muskingum Col, 63-75, chmn dept, 65-71 & 76-82, prof, 75-93, EMER PROF MATH, MUSKINGUM COL, 93- *Personal Data:* b Lackawanna, NY, Aug 5, 29; m 54, Anne Wilson; c Catherine, David, Douglas & Stephan. *Educ:* Univ Louisville, BA, 51; Univ Pittsburgh, MS, 55; Okla State Univ, EdD(found in geom), 63. *Prof Exp:* Asst math, Univ Pittsburgh, 54-56; instr, Westminster Col, Pa, 56-61; asst, Okla State Univ, 61-63. *Concurrent Pos:* Vis lectr, NSF Summer Insts, Southwestern State Col, Okla, 63 & Northeast Mo State Col, 64, dir & instr, Teacher Oriented Insts, 65-66; NSF sci fac fel, Wash State Univ, 67-68; vis assoc prof, Univ NH, 71-72; assoc dir, NSF Pre-Col Teacher Develop Proj, 77-78, dir, NSF CAUSE Comput Lit Proj, 77-81; Fulbright prof math, Univ Malawi, Africa, 79-80; vis prof, Ohio State Univ, 87-88. *Mem:* Math Asn Am; Am Math Soc; Nat Coun Teachers Math. *Res:* Function approach to geometry; technology applications to geometry. *Mailing Add:* Dept Math & Comput Sci Muskingum Col New Concord OH 43762. *Fax:* 740-826-8404; *E-Mail:* jasmith@muskingum.edu

SMITH, JAMES LAWRENCE, MAGNETISM, SUPERCONDUCTIVITY. *Current Pos:* Staff mem physics, 73-82, fel, Los Alamos, 82-86, dir, Ctr Mat Sci, 86-87, FEL, LOS ALAMOS NAT LAB, UNIV CALIF, 87-, CHIEF SCIENTIST, SUPERCONDUCTIVITY TECHNOL CTR, 88- *Personal Data:* b Detroit, Mich, Sept 3, 43; m 65, Carol A Adam; c David A & William L. *Educ:* Wayne State Univ, BS, 65; Brown Univ, PhD(physics), 74. *Honors & Awards:* E O Lawrence Award, 86; Int Prize for New Mat, Am Phys Soc, 90. *Concurrent Pos:* NAm ed, Philosophical Mag, 90-95, ed, Philos Mag B, 95-; adj prof, Fla State Univ, 91- *Mem:* Fel Am Phys Soc; AAAS; Mat Res Soc; Am Crystallog Soc; Am Soc Metals Int; Minerals Metals & Mats Soc. *Res:* Study of electronic behavior of actinides; occurence of superconductivity and magnetism in transition metals; high temperature superconductivity. *Mailing Add:* MS K763 Los Alamos Nat Lab PO Box 1663 Los Alamos NM 87545. *Fax:* 505-665-8601; *E-Mail:* jlsmith@lanl.gov

SMITH, JAMES LEE, MICROBIOLOGY. *Current Pos:* RES MICROBIOLOGIST, EASTERN MKT & NUTRIT RES DIV, USDA, 63- *Personal Data:* b Clinton Co, Ind, Dec 23, 28. *Educ:* Ind Univ, AB, 52, MA, 54, PhD(bact), 62. *Prof Exp:* Med bacteriologist, US Army, Ft Detrick, Md, 54-59; USPHS fel microbiol, Univ Chicago, 61-63. *Mem:* AAAS; Am Soc Microbiol; Am Chem Soc; Brit Soc Gen Microbiol. *Res:* Bacterial physiology and nutrition. *Mailing Add:* 507 Oak St North Wales PA 19454-3020

SMITH, JAMES LEE, BIOLOGY. *Current Pos:* asst prof, 69-74, ASSOC PROF BIOL, CENT MO STATE UNIV, 74- *Personal Data:* b Thayer, Kans, Feb 27, 35; m 68; c 2. *Educ:* San Francisco State Col, BA, 58; Univ Calif, Berkeley, PhD(bot), 63. *Prof Exp:* Asst prof biol, Chico State Col, 63-64 & Univ Colo, Boulder, 64-69. *Mem:* AAAS; Bot Soc Am; Am Bryol & Lichenological Soc; Sigma Xi. *Res:* Phytoplankton ecology. *Mailing Add:* Dept of Biol Cent Mo State Univ Warrensburg MO 64093

SMITH, JAMES LEE, EROSION, IRRIGATION & MACHINE DEVELOPMENT. *Current Pos:* head prof, 81-91, dir, Int Teach Asst, 91-93, PROF CIVIL ENG, UNIV WYO, LARAMIE, 91- *Personal Data:* b Peoria, Ill, Feb 16, 37; m 87; c 4. *Educ:* Univ Ill, BS, 61, MS, 64; Univ Minn, PhD(agr eng), 71. *Prof Exp:* Proj engr, Air Force Weapons Lab, Kirkland AFB, 63-64; instr, Univ Utah, Salt Lake City, 64-67; proj engr, Int Harvester Co, Hinsdale, 67-69; NSF trainee, Univ Minn, St Paul, 69-71; from assoc prof to prof, Colo State Univ, Ft Collins, 71-81. *Concurrent Pos:* Lectr, Ill Inst Technol, 67-69; Fulbright lectr & vis prof, Univ Nairobi, Kenya, 87-88. *Mem:* Am Soc Agr Engrs; Soc Range Mgmt; Am Soc Surface Mining & Reclamation. *Res:* Erosion, irrigation and machine development; problems relating to soil and water conservation, erosion control; constructed wetlands. *Mailing Add:* Civil Eng Dept Univ Wyo Laramie PO Box 3295 Laramie WY 82071

SMITH, JAMES LEWIS, ANALYTICAL CHEMISTRY. *Current Pos:* asst prof, 81-86, ASSOC PROF CHEM, NMEX INST MINING & TECHNOL, 86- *Personal Data:* b Tacoma, Wash, Feb 19, 49; m 84, Jimmie C Oxley. *Educ:* Univ Puget Sound, BSc, 71, MSc, 74; Univ BC, PhD(chem), 80. *Prof Exp:* Sr anal chemist, Seattle Trace Organics Monitoring Lab, 80-81; res chemist analytical chem, Nat Oceanic & Atmospheric Admin, 81. *Concurrent Pos:* Res collabr, Environ Sci Res Group, Los Alamos Nat Lab, 86; res scientist, NMex Petrol Recovery Res Ctr, 87-92. *Mem:* Am Chem Soc; Sigma Xi. *Res:* Analytical chemistry method development as applied to environmental and petroleum chemistry; applications of nuclear magnetic resonance to study nucleic acids and fluid flow. *Mailing Add:* Chem Dept 51 Lower College Rd Pastore Hall Kingston RI 02881

SMITH, JAMES PAYNE, JR, PLANT TAXONOMY, AGROSTOLOGY. *Current Pos:* Chmn biol sci, 78-83, PROF BOT, HUMBOLDT STATE UNIV, 78-, DEAN, COL NATURAL RESOURCES & SCI, 84- *Personal Data:* b Oklahoma City, Okla, Apr 13, 41. *Educ:* Tulsa Univ, BA & BS, 63; Iowa State Univ, PhD(bot), 68. *Mem:* Am Soc Plant Taxon; Bot Soc Am; Soc Econ Bot; Int Asn Plant Taxonomists. *Res:* Taxonomy of flowering plants; flowering plants of northern California; grasses of the US, especially California. *Mailing Add:* Off Dean Col Natural Resources & Sci Humboldt State Univ Arcata CA 95521

SMITH, JAMES R, CELL BIOLOGY. *Current Pos:* assoc prof, 83-87, PROF CELL GENETICS, DIV MOLECULAR VIROL, BAYLOR COL MED, 87- *Personal Data:* b Springfield, Mo, Apr 28, 41; m 75; c 2. *Educ:* Univ Mo, BS, 63; Univ Ariz, BS, 66; Yale Univ, MPh, 68, PhD(molecular biophys), 70. *Prof Exp:* Teaching asst, Biophys Lab, Yale Univ, 68-69; res assoc microbiol, Stanford Univ, 70-72; res physiologist, Vet Admin Hosp, Martinez, Calif, 72-75; assoc scientist, 75-80, sr scientist, Walton Jones Cell Sci Ctr, 80-83. *Concurrent Pos:* Vis asst res physiologist, Univ Calif, Berkeley, 72-75; adj prof, Dept Biol Sci, State Univ NY, Plattsburgh & Biol Dept, North Country Community Col, NY, Saranac Lake; adj assoc prof, Dept Molecular Pharmacol, Univ RI, Kingston & Dept Med Microbiol, Univ Vt, Burlington; adj affil assoc prof life sci, Worcester Polytech Inst, Mass; co-dir, Roy M & Phyllis Gough Huffington Ctr Aging, 86-; mem, Nat Adv Coun Aging, NIH, founder & dir, AGIS Pharmaceut, Inc, 93- *Mem:* Tissue Cult Asn; Am Soc Cell Biol; fel Gerontol Soc Am; AAAS. *Res:* Cellular aging; control of cell proliferation. *Mailing Add:* Div Molecular Virol Baylor Col Med 1 Baylor Plaza Houston TX 77030-3411. *Fax:* 713-798-4161

SMITH, JAMES REAVES, ALGEBRA. *Current Pos:* Asst prof, 68-72, assoc prof, 72-78, PROF MATH, APPALACHIAN STATE UNIV, 78- *Personal Data:* b Columbia, SC, June 6, 42; m 64; c 2. *Educ:* Univ SC, BS, 63, PhD(math), 68. *Mem:* Am Math Soc; Math Asn Am; Nat Coun Teachers Math. *Res:* Study of regular modules, those whose submodules are all pure; also projective simple modules. *Mailing Add:* Dept Math Sci Appalachian State Univ Boone NC 28608-0001

SMITH, JAMES ROSS, QUALITY CONTROL, OPERATIONS RESEARCH. *Current Pos:* asst prof, 71-74, ASSOC PROF INDUST ENG, TENN TECHNOL UNIV, 74- *Personal Data:* b Kingsport, Tenn, Nov 15, 43; m 63; c 2. *Educ:* Va Polytech Inst & State Univ, BS, 65, MS, 67, PhD(indust eng & opers res), 71. *Prof Exp:* Indust engr, Holston Defense Corp, 66-69; grad asst indust eng, Va Polytech Inst & State Univ, 69-71. *Mem:* Am Inst Indust Engrs; Am Soc Qual Control. *Res:* Applied statistics and applied operations research. *Mailing Add:* Dept Indust Eng Tenn Technol Univ Cookville TN 38505-0001

SMITH, JAMES S(TERRETT), metallurgy, chemistry; deceased, see previous edition for last biography

SMITH, JAMES STANLEY, ENVIRONMENTAL ANALYTICAL CHEMISTRY. *Current Pos:* PRES, FOUNDER & CHEMIST, TRILLIUM, INC, 87- *Personal Data:* b Ithaca, NY, Apr 7, 39; m 76, Janis M Fiore; c James S Jr, Douglas S, Matthew S, Laura L, Montree J, Timothy O & Toby B. *Educ:* Williams Col, AB, 60; Iowa State Univ, PhD(org chem), 64. *Prof Exp:* Fel org chem, Univ Ill, 64-65; asst prof, Eastern Mich Univ, 66-68; fel mass spectros, Cornell Univ, 68-69; supvr anal chem, Allied Corp, 69-81; dir anal lab, Roy F Weston, Inc, 81-85; chemist, Walter B Satterthwaite & Assoc, 85-87. *Concurrent Pos:* Vis lectr org chem, Univ Ill, 65-66. *Mem:* Am Soc Testing Mat; Am Soc Mass Spectrometry; Am Chem Soc; Am Acad Forensic Sci; Nat Water Well Asn; Am Inst Chemists; Int Asn Off Anal Chemists. *Res:* Analysis of drinking water, waste water, air, hazardous chemical waste, volatile organic chemicals in soil; development of methodologies to determine environmental pollutants. *Mailing Add:* 28 Grace's Dr Coatesville PA 19320-1206. *Fax:* 610-383-7907; *E-Mail:* jsmith@trilliuminc.com

SMITH, JAMES THOMAS, MATHEMATICS. *Current Pos:* assoc prof, 69-77, PROF MATH, SAN FRANCISCO STATE UNIV, 77- *Personal Data:* b Springfield, Ohio, Nov 8, 39; m 63, Helen M Patteson; c Jedediah. *Educ:* Harvard Univ, BA, 61; San Francisco State Col, MA, 64; Stanford Univ, MS, 67; Univ Sask, PhD(math), 70. *Prof Exp:* Mathematician, US Naval Radiol Defense Lab, 62-67; instr math, San Francisco State Col, 66-67 & Univ Sask, Regina Campus, 68. *Concurrent Pos:* Chmn dept, San Francisco State Univ 75-82; software engr, Blaise Comput Inc, 84-85; lectr, State Univ NY, Subang Jaya, 88-89. *Mem:* Ger Math Asn; Math Asn Am; Am Math Soc. *Res:* Foundations of geometry; object oriented scientific application software. *Mailing Add:* Dept Math San Francisco State Univ 1600 Holloway Ave San Francisco CA 94132. *E-Mail:* smith@math.sfsu.edu

SMITH, JAMES W(ILMER), CHEMICAL ENGINEERING. *Current Pos:* from asst prof to prof, Univ Toronto, 62-70, assoc chmn chem eng, 75-81, dir, Occup Health & Safety, 80-85, PROF CHEM ENG, UNIV TORONTO, 70-, CHMN, 85-; CHMN CHEM ENG, RES CONSULTS LTD, 85- *Personal Data:* b Kamloops, BC, June 13, 31; m 58; c 3. *Educ:* Univ BC, BASc, 54, MASc, 55; PhD(chem); Univ London, PhD(chem eng), 60, CIH, 81. *Prof Exp:* Process engr, Du Pont Can, Ont, 55-57; fel chem eng, Univ BC, 61-62. *Concurrent Pos:* Pres, Res Consults Ltd, 75-85. *Mem:* Chem Inst Can; Can Soc Chem Eng; Air Pollution Control Asn; Am Indust Hygiene Asn; Brit Occup Hyg Asn; Am Conf Govt Indust Hygienists. *Res:* Mass transfer, fluid flow and chemical reaction; properties of particulate systems; industrial hygiene. *Mailing Add:* Dept Chem Eng Univ Toronto Toronto ON M5S 3E5 Can

SMITH, JAMES WARREN, CLINICAL PATHOLOGY, PARASITOLOGY. *Current Pos:* PROF PATH, IND UNIV MED CTR, INDIANAPOLIS, 70- *Personal Data:* b Logan, Utah, July 5, 34; m 58; c 2. *Educ:* Univ Iowa, BA, 56, MD, 59. *Prof Exp:* Resident path, Univ Iowa Hosp, 60-65; pathologist, US Naval Hosp, Chelsea, Mass, 65-67; asst prof, Med Col, Univ Vt, 67-70. *Mem:* Am Soc Clin Path; Col Am Path; Am Soc Microbiol; AMA; Infectious Dis Soc Am; Am Soc Trop Med & Hyg. *Res:* Pneumocystis carinii; clinical microbiology. *Mailing Add:* Dept Pathol & Lab Med Ind Univ 635 Barnhill Dr Rm 128-A Indianapolis IN 46202-5120

SMITH, JAMES WILLIE, JR, ENTOMOLOGY. *Current Pos:* asst prof, 70-74, ASSOC PROF ENTOM, TEX A&M UNIV, 74- *Personal Data:* b Jackson, Miss, Mar 17, 44; m 69. *Educ:* Miss State Univ, BS, 66; Univ Calif, Riverside, PhD(entom), 70. *Prof Exp:* Res asst entom, Univ Calif, Riverside, 66-69. *Mem:* AAAS; Entom Soc Am. *Res:* Insect pest management of field crops; population ecology; resistant plant varieties; biological control. *Mailing Add:* Dept Entom Tex A&M Univ College Station TX 77843-0100

SMITH, JAMES WINFRED, ENTOMOLOGY, ECOLOGY. *Current Pos:* HEAD, DELTA RES & EXTEN CTR, 94- *Personal Data:* b Greenwood, Miss, Jan 27, 43; m 66; c 3. *Educ:* Miss State Univ, BS, 65; La State Univ, MS, 67, PhD(entom), 70. *Prof Exp:* Asst prof biol, Motlow State Community Col, 70-71; res entomologist & res leader, Bioenviron Insect Lab, Agr Res Serv, USDA, 71-94, res leader, Boll Weevil Res Unit, 87-94. *Concurrent Pos:* Assoc, Dept Entom, Miss State Univ, 74-; Delta Coun res award, 85-86. *Mem:* Entomol Soc Am; Acarological Soc Am; Sigma Xi. *Res:* Field research on the ecology, population dynamics, and control of insect pests by bioenvironmental methods. *Mailing Add:* Delta Res & Exten Ctr PO Box 197 Stoneville MS 38776

SMITH, JAN D, ANESTHESIOLOGY, INTERNAL MEDICINE. *Current Pos:* PROF ANESTHESIOL & INTERNAL MED, UNIV PITTSBURGH, 87- *Personal Data:* b Pretoria, SAfrica, Feb 6, 39; m 62; c 3. *Educ:* Univ Pretoria, MB ChB, 62; Royal Col Physicians UK, MRCP, 73; Am Bd Anesthesiol, dipl, 69; Am Bd Internal Med, dipl, 80, Am Bd Internal Med (pulmonary disorder), dipl, 82. *Prof Exp:* Resident anesthesiol, Sch Med, Harvard Univ, Peter Bent Brigham Hosp, 64-66; fel, Sch Med, Univ Pittsburgh, 66-69, resident, 71; resident int med, Groote Schuur Hosp, Univ Cape Town, 70-71; asst prof int med, Sch Med, Univ Iowa, 74-76; from asst prof to assoc prof anesthesiol & internal med, Health Sci Ctr, Univ Tex, 76-83, distinguished prof, 83; prof anesthesiol & internal med, Univ Neb, 83-85; prof anesthesiol, NE Ohio Col Med, 85-87. *Mem:* Am Fedn Clin Res; Am Col Chest Physicians; Am Col Physicians; Am Bd Anesthesiol; Am Thoracic Soc; Soc Critical Care Med; AM A; Int Anesthesiol Soc. *Res:* Pathogenesis of Shock Lung; carbon dioxide physiology; the arhepatic state-hepatopectmorary syndrome. *Mailing Add:* 200 Lothrop St Rm C-224 Pittsburgh PA 15213

SMITH, JANICE GORZYNSKI, SYNTHETIC ORGANIC CHEMISTRY, SYNTHETIC METHODOLOGY, USING UNSATURATED ORGANOSITANTS. *Current Pos:* from asst prof to assoc prof, 79-92, PROF CHEM MOUNT HOLYOKE COL, 92-, CHAIR, DEPT CHEM, 93- *Personal Data:* b Schenectady, NY, Apr 28, 51; m 74, Daniel C; c Erin, Megan (deceased), Jenna, Matthew & Zachary. *Educ:* Cornell Univ, AB, 73; Harvard Univ, Am, 75, PhD(chem), 78. *Prof Exp:* Nat Needs postdoctoral fel, NSF, 78. *Concurrent Pos:* Vis prof, Brown Univ, 85-86 & Univ Hawaii, 92. *Mem:* Am Chem Soc; AAAS; Sigma Xi. *Res:* Development of new synthetic methodology, organosilicon chemistry, approaches to the synthesis of natural products. *Mailing Add:* Dept Chem Mount Holyoke Col South Hadley MA 01075. *Fax:* 413-538-2327; *E-Mail:* jgsmith@mtholyoke.edu

SMITH, JAY HAMILTON, SOIL MICROBIOLOGY. *Current Pos:* RETIRED. *Personal Data:* b Rexburg, Idaho, June 5, 27; m 49; c 5. *Educ:* Brigham Young Univ, BS, 51; Utah State Univ, MS, 53; Cornell Univ, PhD(soil microbiol), 55. *Prof Exp:* Soil microbiologist, Soil & Water Conserv Res Div, US Dept Agr, SC, 55-58, soil scientist, Soils Lab, Agr Res Serv, Md, 58-64, soil scientist, Snake River Conserv Res Ctr, Agr Res Serv, USDA, 64-87. *Concurrent Pos:* Soil scientist, Clemson Col, 55-58; prof, Utah State Univ, 64- & Univ Idaho, 68- *Mem:* Int Humic Substances Soc; Soil Sci Soc Am; Sigma Xi; Am Soc Agron. *Res:* Instrumentation of soil organic matter and nitrogen; chemistry of soil nitrogen; microbiology of irrigation water and drainage; land disposal of food processing wastes. *Mailing Add:* 3787 N 3575 E Kimberly ID 83341-5090

SMITH, JEAN BLAIR, analytical & biochemistry, protein science, for more information see previous edition

SMITH, JEAN E, animal ecology, for more information see previous edition

SMITH, JEFFREY DREW, PLANT PATHOLOGY, MYCOLOGY OF TURF GRASSES. *Current Pos:* res scientist, 85-89, VIS PROF, DEPT HORT SCI, UNIV SASK, 89- *Personal Data:* b Wearhead, Durham, Eng, Aug 2, 22; m 50, Audree Hub; c Andrew & Stephen. *Educ:* Univ Durham, BSc, 46, MSc, 57. *Honors & Awards:* Dr & Mrs Bailey Award, Can Phytopath Soc, 90. *Prof Exp:* Demonstr agr bot, King's Col, Univ Durham, 46-48; jr lectr plant path, 48-51; res plant pathologist, Sports Turf Res Inst, Eng, 51-58; exten plant pathologist, NScotland Col Agr, Aberdeen, 58-60; prin sci officer, Res Div, NZ Dept Agr, 60-64; res scientist, Res Br, Can Dept Agr, 65-84. *Concurrent Pos:* NZ Dept Agr overseas res grant, Rothamsted Exp Sta, Eng, 62; vis scientist, Ore State Univ, 70 & Norweg Plant Protection Inst, 74-75; res scientist, Can Int Develop Agency, Kenya, 81-82. *Mem:* Can Phytopath Soc; Brit Inst Biol; Brit Mycol Soc. *Res:* Epidemiology and control of diseases of forage, range and turf grasses; psychophilic fungi and mycotoxicology. *Mailing Add:* 306 Egbert Ave Saskatoon SK S7N 1X1 Can. *Fax:* 306-966-8106

SMITH, JEROME ALLAN, TECHNICAL MANAGEMENT, AERONAUTICAL ENGINEERING. *Current Pos:* VPRES, COM SYST GROUP, LOCKHEED MARTIN CORP, 96- *Personal Data:* b Lansing, Mich, Apr 17, 40; m 62, Ruth A Schlotter; c Kirsten & Sarah. *Educ:* Univ Mich, BSE, 62, Calif Inst Technol, MS, 63, PhD, 67. *Prof Exp:* From asst prof to prof aerospace & mech sci, Princeton Univ, 67-79; tech dir, Off Naval Res, 79-83; pres, Indust Technol Inst, 83-87; vpres, Missile Syst, Martin Marietta, 89-92 & Info Syst, 92-96. *Concurrent Pos:* Mem, Lab Adv Bd Surface Weapons, USN, 73-78, chmn, 75-78, consult, McDonnell Douglas Res Labs, 74-79; mem, Mfg Studies Bd, NSF, 84-88. *Mem:* Am Phys Soc; AAAS; Sigma Xi. *Res:* Experimental investigation of high speed flow-shock tubes and hypersonic wind tunnels; fingerprint identification technology. *Mailing Add:* 6028 Lexington Park Orlando FL 32819-4434

SMITH, JEROME H, INFECTIOUS & TROPICAL DISEASES, PARASITOLOGY. *Current Pos:* PROF PATH, UNIV TEX MED BR, GALVESTON, 76-84, 90- *Personal Data:* b Omaha, Nebr, Oct 9, 36; m 61, Marilyn K Stauber; c Nathaniel H, Kathryn H (Felts) & Andrew K. *Educ:* Univ Nebr, BS, 61, MS, 62, MD, 63; Harvard Sch Pub Health, MSc, 69. *Prof Exp:* Prof path & lab med, Tex A&M Univ, 84-89. *Mem:* Am Soc Parasitologists; Am Soc Clin Path; Am Soc Trop Med & Hyg; Am Soc Microbiol; US-Can Acad Path. *Res:* Schistosomiasis; sarcocystosis; infectious diseases; anthrax pathology. *Mailing Add:* 2706 Wilmington Dr Dickinson TX 77539-4664. *Fax:* 409-772-9350; *E-Mail:* js@path.utmb.edu

SMITH, JEROME PAUL, ANALYTICAL CHEMISTRY, OCCUPATIONAL HEALTH. *Current Pos:* AEROSOL RES SPECIALIST, NAT INST OCCUP SAFETY & HEALTH, 78- *Personal Data:* b Ft Wayne, Ind, Apr 18, 46. *Educ:* Col St Thomas, BA, 69; Univ Colo, PhD(analytical chem), 73. *Prof Exp:* Asst res chemist, Univ Calif, Riverside, 73-77. *Res:* Analytical chemistry applied to the measurement of contaminants in the workplace; health assessment for contaminants in the workplace. *Mailing Add:* MCRB NIOSH MS R-7 4676 Columbia Pkwy Cincinnati OH 45226-1922

SMITH, JERRY HOWARD, ORGANIC CHEMISTRY, BIO-ORGANIC CHEMISTRY. *Current Pos:* SR RES CHEMIST, ZENECA, 93- *Personal Data:* b Mobile, Ala, Jan 28, 44. *Educ:* Auburn Univ, BS, 66; Emory Univ, PhD(org chem), 70. *Prof Exp:* Fel, Univ Chicago, 70-72, NIH fel, 71-72; asst prof chem, Marquette Univ, 72-76; res chemist, ICI Americas, 77-93. *Mem:* Am Chem Soc. *Res:* Organic chemistry. *Mailing Add:* Zeneca PO Box 152 Mt Pleasant TN 38474

SMITH, JERRY MORGAN, PHARMACOLOGY, TOXICOLOGY. *Current Pos:* RES ANALYST, UNIV DEL, 90- *Personal Data:* b Winchester, Va, Mar 13, 34; m 57; c 2. *Educ:* The Citadel, BS, 56; Med Col SC, MS, 59; Univ Kans, PhD(pharmacol), 64. *Prof Exp:* Fel pharmacol, Emory Univ, 63-65; NIH fel, 64-65; res pharmacologist, Lederle Labs, Am Cyanamid Co, 65-69; sect head toxicol, Wellcome Res Labs, Burroughs Wellcome & Co, 69-70; dir toxicity, Biodynamics, Inc, 70-73; dir toxicol, Rohm & Haas Co, 73-90. *Res:* Renal and biochemical pharmacology; teratology; toxicology, especially pharmaceutical, pesticide, food and chemical. *Mailing Add:* 12560 Coopers Lane Worton MD 21678

SMITH, JERRY WARREN, VIROLOGY, IMMUNOLOGY. *Current Pos:* dir res & develop, 82-86, vpres, 86-92, EXEC VPRES SCI & TECHNOL, DIFCO LABS, INC, 92- *Personal Data:* b Welch, WVa, Oct 8, 42; m 67, Deborah Main; c Brian & Graham. *Educ:* Marshall Univ, BS, 64; Ohio Univ, MS, 66; Univ Iowa, PhD(microbiol), 70; Harvard Bus Sch, PMD Exec Educ, 92. *Prof Exp:* NIH fel, Baylor Col Med, 70-72; asst prof microbiol, Med Ctr, La State Univ, New Orleans, 72-77, assoc prof, 77-82, prof, 82. *Concurrent Pos:* Adj prof, Univ Mich, 83-, Wayne State Univ, 93- *Mem:* Am Soc Microbiol; Am Asn Immunologists. *Res:* Immunological interactions between viruses and hosts; relationship between herpes viruses and human cancers; rapid and automated microbiological diagnostic methods. *Mailing Add:* Technol Develop Difco Labs 2540 E Delhi Rd Ann Arbor MI 48108

SMITH, JESSE GRAHAM, JR, dermatology, gerontology, for more information see previous edition

SMITH, JOE K, MATHEMATICS. *Current Pos:* assoc prof, 71-75, PROF MATH, NORTHERN KY UNIV, 75- *Personal Data:* b Burlington, Ky, Feb 5, 30; m 85, Edith. *Educ:* Eastern Ky State Col, BS, 52; Fla State Univ, MS, 57, EdD(math ed), 67. *Prof Exp:* Instr math, Cent Fla Jr Col, 58-60; instr, Miami Dade Jr Col, 60-63, assoc prof, 64-65; teacher high sch, Fla, 65-66; asst prof, Western Ky Univ, 66-69, assoc prof, 69-71. *Mem:* Math Asn Am; Am Meteorol Soc; Nat Coun Teachers Math. *Res:* Mathematics education. *Mailing Add:* 214 Buckingham Dr Florence KY 41042-9736

SMITH, JOE M(AUK), CHEMICAL ENGINEERING. *Current Pos:* PROF CHEM ENG & CHMN DEPT, UNIV CALIF, DAVIS, 61- *Personal Data:* b Sterling, Colo, Feb 14, 16; m 43; c 2. *Educ:* Calif Inst Technol, BS, 37; Mass Inst Technol, ScD(chem eng), 43. *Honors & Awards:* William H Walker Award, Am Inst Chem Engrs, 60, R H Wilhelm Award, 77, W K Lewis Award, 83. *Prof Exp:* Design engr, Tex Co, NY, 37-38; res engr, Stand Oil Co, Calif, 38-41; asst, Nat Defense Res Comt, Mass Inst Technol, 42-43, instr chem eng, 43; asst prof, Univ Md, 43-44; proj engr, Publicker Com Alcohol Co, Pa, 44-45; from asst prof to prof chem eng, Purdue Univ, 45-57, asst dir, Eng Exp Sta, 54-57; dean, Col Technol, Univ NH, 57; prof & chmn dept, Northwestern Univ, 57-60, Walter P Murphy disttnguished prof, 59-61. *Concurrent Pos:* Res Corp grant, 46-48; Guggenheim fel & Fulbright res scholar, Delft Univ Technol, 53-54; Ford Found scholar, Argentina, 61; hon prof, Univ Buenos Aires, 63-; Fulbright awards, Arg, 43-66, Spain, 65 & Brazil, 90; lectr chem eng, Am Soc Eng Educ, 70. *Mem:* Nat Acad Eng; Am Chem Soc; Am Inst Chem Engrs. *Res:* Interaction of physical and chemical processes in heterogeneous reactions; heat transfer combined with chemical reaction; applied chemical kinetics and reactor design. *Mailing Add:* Dept Eng Univ Calif Davis CA 95616

SMITH, JOE NELSON, JR, SURFACE PHYSICS, SOLID STATE PHYSICS. *Current Pos:* STAFF SCIENTIST, GEN ATOMICS, 88- *Personal Data:* b Washington, DC, June 24, 32; m 52; c 3. *Educ:* Calif Inst Technol, BS, 58, MS, 59; Nat Univ Leiden, PhD, 70. *Prof Exp:* Staff mem atomic physics, Gen Atomic Div, Gen Dynamics Corp, 59-69; vis scientist, FOM Inst Atomic & Molecular Physics, Neth, 69-70; sr staff physicist, Gulf Radiation Technol Div, Gulf Energy & Environ Systs Co, 70-72; sr staff physicist, IRT Corp, 72-74; staff surface physicist, Gen Atomic Co, 74-83; Staff scientist, Ga Technol, Inc, 83-88. *Mem:* Am Phys Soc; Am Vacuum Soc; Am Nuclear Soc. *Res:* Experimental research in particle-surface interactions including momentum and energy transfer, chemical reaction and catalysis, surface ionization; sputtering, radiation damage in surface region of solids, secondary ion mass spectrometry,auger electron spectroscopy, thin film phenomena and high voltage vacuum breakdown; thermionic energy conversion. *Mailing Add:* 4688 Sun Valley Rd Del Mar CA 92014

SMITH, JOHN, ELEMENTARY PARTICLE PHYSICS. *Current Pos:* res assoc, 67-69, asst prof, 69-74, assoc prof, 74-78, PROF PHYSICS, INST THEORET PHYSICS, STATE UNIV NY STONY BROOK, 78- *Personal Data:* b Selkirk, Scotland, May 4, 38; m 64; c 1. *Educ:* Univ Edinburgh, BS, 60, MS, 61, PhD, 63. *Prof Exp:* Joint Inst Nuclear Res, Dubna, Russia, 63; NATO res fel, Niels Bohr Inst, Copenhagen, Denmark, 64-65; Rothman res fel, Univ Adelaide, 66-67. *Mem:* Am Inst Physics. *Res:* Elementary particle physics. *Mailing Add:* Inst Theoret Phys State Univ NY Stony Brook Stony Brook NY 11794. *Fax:* 516-632-7954

SMITH, JOHN, FOOD SCIENCE, FLAVOR TECHNOLOGY. *Current Pos:* FOOD SCIENTIST, QUAKER OATS CO, 80- *Personal Data:* b Gary, Ind, 1952. *Educ:* Wabash Col, BA, 74; Purdue Univ, MS, 77, PhD(food sci), 80. *Mem:* Am Chem Soc; fel Am Inst Chemists. *Mailing Add:* Quaker Oats Co 617 Main St Barrington IL 60010

SMITH, JOHN B, COMPUTER SCIENCE. *Current Pos:* assoc prof, 84-85, PROF COMPUT SCI, UNIV NC, 95- *Educ:* Univ of South, BA, 62; Univ SC, MA, 64; Univ NC, PhD, 70. *Prof Exp:* From asst prof to assoc prof Eng, Pa State Univ, 70-83. *Concurrent Pos:* Res consult, Comput Ctr, Pa State Univ, 70-77; consult, Citicorp, IBM, Data Gen, SAS, Glaxo, Monsanto, RTI, Microelectronics Ctr NC, US Gen Acct Off, Getty Trust, Ctr Creative Leadership, Duke Univ, NC State Univ, Ariz State Univ, Univ Pa, Columbia Univ, Princeton Univ, City Univ NY, Brown Univ, Buckwell Univ, Univ Chicago, Rutgers Univ, Amherst Col & Newberry Libr; fel, NSF, 93-96, IBM, 95-96; IBM fel, 95-96. *Mem:* Asn Comput Mach; Inst Elec & Electronics Engrs Comput Soc; Sigma Xi. *Res:* Natural language analysis; published numerous articles for professional journals. *Mailing Add:* Dept Comput Sci Univ NC Chapel Hill NC 27599-3175

SMITH, JOHN BRYAN, HEMATOLOGY, THROMBOSIS. *Current Pos:* PROF PHARMACOL, TEMPLE UNIV MED SCH, 82-, CHMN, DEPT PHARMACOL, 86- *Personal Data:* b June 17, 42; Brit citizen; m 67, Angela; c Timothy & Susanne. *Educ:* London Univ, PhD(biochem), 71. *Prof Exp:* Prof pharmacol, Thomas Jefferson Univ, 71-82. *Concurrent Pos:* Mem, Prog Comt, Am Soc Pharmacol & Exp Therapeut, 87-93; vpres, Mid-Atlantic Pharmacol Asn, 89-91, pres, 91-93. *Mem:* AAAS; Am Soc Pharmacol & Exp Therapeut; Sigma Xi. *Res:* Involvement of blood platelets in hemostasis and thrombosis. *Mailing Add:* Dept Pharmacol Temple Univ Med Sch Philadelphia PA 19140

SMITH, JOHN COLE, entomology; deceased, see previous edition for last biography

SMITH, JOHN EDGAR, NUTRITIONAL BIOCHEMISTRY, VITAMINS. *Current Pos:* MEM FAC NUTRIT DEPT, COL HEALTH & HUMAN DEVELOP, PA STATE UNIV, 80- *Personal Data:* b West Alexander, Pa, June 14, 39. *Educ:* WLiberty State Col, BS, 61; WVa Univ, MS, 65; Univ Nebr, Lincoln, PhD(nutrit), 70. *Prof Exp:* Teacher high sch, Ohio, 61-62; trainee med, Columbia Univ, 69-72, res assoc, 72-80. *Mem:* Am Chem Soc; Am Soc Cell Biol; Am Soc Nutrit Sci. *Res:* Fat-soluble vitamin transport in blood. *Mailing Add:* Pa State Univ S-128 Henderson Bldg University Park PA 16802-6504. *Fax:* 814-863-6103; *E-Mail:* jes12@psu.edu

SMITH, JOHN F(RANCIS), PHASE EQUILIBRIA & MICROSTRUCTURE, ULTRASONICS & NONDESTRUCTIVE EVALUATION. *Current Pos:* Chemist & metallurgist, 53-66, from assoc prof to prof, Iowa State Univ, 54-88, chmn dept, 66-70, div chief, Inst Atomic Res, 66-70, sr metallurgist & sect chief, Ames Lab, Dept Energy, 70-88, EMER PROF MAT SCI & ENG, IOWA STATE UNIV, 88-; CONSULT, J F SMITH CONSULT SERV, 88- *Personal Data:* b Kansas City, Kans, May 9, 23; m 47, Evelyn A Ross; c Mark F & Letitia A (Harder). *Educ:* Univ Mo, Kansas City, BA, 48; Iowa State Univ, PhD(phys chem), 53. *Concurrent Pos:* Mem, World Metall Cong, Chicago, 57; consult, Tex Instruments, 58-63, Argonne Nat Lab, 64-70, Pioneer Instruments, 68, Iowa Hwy Comn, 69-70, Los Alamos Nat Lab, 82-84, Nat Bur Stand, 88-91 & Sandia Nat Lab, 90-91. *Mem:* Fel Am Inst Chemists; fel Am Soc Metals Int; Am Crystallog Asn; Metall Soc; Am Inst Mining, Metall & Petrol Engrs. *Res:* Crystal structures and thermodynamics of alloys and intermetallic compounds; relationships between energetics, crystal structures, and physical properties; nondestructive evaluation. *Mailing Add:* 2919 S Riverside Ames IA 50010. *E-Mail:* jfsmith@iastate.edu

SMITH, JOHN HENRY, STATISTICS. *Current Pos:* prof statist, 47-73, EMER PROF STATIST, AM UNIV, 73- *Personal Data:* b Gilman, Iowa, July 18, 04; m 36, Agnes Davison. *Educ:* Iowa State Teachers Col, BA, 35; Univ Chicago, MBA, 39, PhD(bus), 41. *Prof Exp:* Instr statist, Univ Chicago, 40-42; statistician, US Bur Labor Statist, 42-47. *Mem:* Fel Am Statist Asn. *Mailing Add:* 235 22nd St SE Apt 121 Owatonna MN 55060

SMITH, JOHN HENRY, MECHANICAL PROPERTIES, FRACTURE MECHANICS. *Current Pos:* metallurgist, 74-86, DEP CHIEF, METALL DIV, NAT BUR STANDARDS, 86- *Personal Data:* b Rome, NY, July 3, 37. *Educ:* Lafayette Col, AB & BS, 58; Univ Mo, MS, 59; Mass Inst Technol, ScD(metall), 64. *Prof Exp:* Aerospace scientist, NASA Lewis Res Ctr, 64-66; metallurgist, Res Ctr, US Steel Corp, 66-74. *Concurrent Pos:* Res assoc, dept metall, Mass Inst Technol, 66; Dept Commerce Sci & Technol fel, 80-81. *Mem:* Am Soc Testing & Mat; Am Soc Metals; Am Inst Mining, Metall & Petrol Engrs; Am Welding Soc; Am Soc Mech Engrs; Int Inst Welding. *Res:* Mechanical properties of materials; non-destructive testing; structural integrity; physical metallurgy; welding; pressure vessels and piping materials; structural analysis and fracture mechanics. *Mailing Add:* 8174 Inverness Ridge Rd Potomac MD 20854

SMITH, JOHN HOWARD, MATHEMATICS. *Current Pos:* from asst prof to assoc prof, 67-82, PROF MATH, BOSTON COL, 82- *Personal Data:* b Ithaca, NY, Jan 21, 37. *Educ:* Cornell Univ, AB, 58; Mass Inst Technol, PhD(math), 63. *Prof Exp:* Instr math, Univ Mich, 63-65, asst prof, 65-66; vis lectr, Mass Inst Technol, 66-67. *Mem:* Am Math Soc; Math Asn Am. *Res:* Algebraic number theory; linear algebra; combinatorics. *Mailing Add:* Dept Math Boston Col Chestnut Hill MA 02167-3806

SMITH, JOHN LESLIE, JR, medicine, dermatopathology; deceased, see previous edition for last biography

SMITH, JOHN M, ECONOMIC GEOLOGY, CLAY MINERALOGY. *Current Pos:* RETIRED. *Personal Data:* b Indianapolis, Ind, May 20, 22; m 48; c 3. *Educ:* Ind Univ, BS, 52, MA, 54. *Prof Exp:* Geologist, Ind Geol Surv, 54-57; geologist, Ga Kaolin Co Inc, 57-67, chief geologist & dir, 67-84. *Concurrent Pos:* Mem, State Bd Regist Prof Geologists, Ga, 75-81. *Mem:* Fel Geol Soc Am; Clay Minerals Soc; Am Inst Mining, Metall & Petrol Engrs. *Res:* Evaluation of United States and foreign nonmetallic mineral deposits; direction of exploration and development of nonmetallics; research and development of clay minerals, especially kaolinite. *Mailing Add:* 121 Covington Pl Macon GA 31210-4444

SMITH, JOHN M, ENVIRONMENTAL CONSERVATION, USE OF BIOMASS AS AN ENERGY SOURCE. *Current Pos:* PROF MICROBIOL, BETHEL COL, 80-, CHMN, DIV NATURAL SCI, 88- *Personal Data:* b Elmira, NY, Mar 25, 31; m 55, Joan Hiles; c Jonathan, Joanna, Jan, Jennifer & Julie. *Educ:* Asbury Col, BA, 54; Ohio State Univ, MSC, 63, PhD(microbiol), 70. *Prof Exp:* Prof microbiol & biochem, Asbury Col, 70-78; researcher, Univ Ky, 78-79; prof chem & math, Midway Col, 79-80. *Concurrent Pos:* Vis prof, Notre Dame, 90-92. *Mem:* Am Soc Microbiol; AAAS. *Mailing Add:* Bethel Col Mishawaka IN 46545

SMITH, JOHN MELVIN, mathematics education; deceased, see previous edition for last biography

SMITH, JOHN ROBERT, THEORETICAL SOLID STATE PHYSICS. *Current Pos:* sr res physicist & head, Surface & Interface Physics Group, 72-80, sr staff scientist & head, Solid State Physics Group, 80-86, PRIN RES SCIENTIST, GEN MOTORS, 86- *Personal Data:* b Salt Lake City, Utah, Oct 1, 40; m 62; c 2. *Educ:* Toledo Univ, BS, 62; Ohio State Univ, PhD(physics), 68. *Honors & Awards:* David J Adler Award, Am Phys Soc, 91. *Prof Exp:* Aerospace engr surface physics, Lewis Res Ctr, NASA, 65-68, fel solid state theory, Univ Calif, San Diego, 70-72. *Concurrent Pos:* Air Force Off Sci Res & Nat Res Coun fel, Univ Calif, 70-72; adj prof, physics dept, Univ Mich, 83- *Mem:* Am Vacuum Soc; Sigma Xi; fel Am Phys Soc. *Res:* Theory of solid surfaces, electronic properties, magnetic properties and chemisorption; adhesion, ceramic-metal interfaces; defects and universal features of bonding in solids. *Mailing Add:* Physics Dept GM NAO R&D Ctr 30500 Mound Rd 1-6 Warren MI 48090

SMITH, JOHN ROBERT, PHARMACOLOGY. *Current Pos:* ASSOC PROF, DEPT PHYSIOL & PHARMACOL, SCH DENT, ORE HEALTH SCI UNIV; ASST PROF & SR RESEARCHER COMP PHARMACOL MARINE SCI CTR, ORE STATE UNIV, 79- *Personal Data:* b Los Angeles, Calif, Apr 17, 48; c 2. *Educ:* Loyola Univ, Calif, BS, 70; Ore State Univ, MS, 74, PhD(pharmacol), 76. *Prof Exp:* Fel pharmacol, Sch Med, Univ Wash, 75-77; asst prof, Sch Dent Med, Southern Ill Univ, 77-79. *Mem:* Am Soc Pharmacol & Exp Therapeut; Int Asn Dent Res; PANWAT. *Res:* Comparative neuropharmacology and toxicology. *Mailing Add:* Dept Biol Struct & Funet Dent Sch Ore Health Sci Univ 611 SW Campus Dr Portland OR 97201-3097. Fax: 503-494-4666

SMITH, JOHN STEPHEN, EDUCATION, MANAGEMENT OF BASIC & CLINICAL RESEARCH. *Current Pos:* asst to vpres Health Affairs, 74-78, asst vpres, 78-88, dep dir Int Prog, 80-90, ASSOC VPRES HEALTH AFFAIRS, UNIV ALA, BIRMINGHAM MED CTR, 88- *Personal Data:* b Wheeling, WVa, Aug 16, 38; m 63, Bernice Eichenlaub; c Karl B, Ann K & Suzanne L. *Educ:* Wheeling Jesuit Col, BS, 60; Duquesne Univ, 65; Univ Pittsburgh, PhD, 71. *Prof Exp:* Instr biochem, Univ Pittsburgh, 62-69, mgr budget syst, 69-72; asst dean & asst to chancellor, La State Univ, Med Ctr, New Orleans, 72-74. *Concurrent Pos:* Bd dirs, Red Mt Mus Soc, Birmingham, 82; mem, Comt Foreign Rels, Soc Col & Univ Planning. *Mem:* Asn Am Med Cols; Asn Instnl Res. *Res:* Education; health affairs; biochemistry; resource administration: design and implementation of management systems for effective/efficient use of space in support of specialized (P-3, BMP) research and related cost efficiencies. *Mailing Add:* 212 Shades Crest Rd Birmingham AL 35226. Fax: 205-975-7677; *E-Mail:* ssmith@vpha.vpha.uab.edu

SMITH, JOHN THURMOND, BIOCHEMISTRY. *Current Pos:* res assoc biochem, 56-58, from instr to prof, 58-90, EMER PROF NUTRIT, UNIV TENN, KNOXVILLE, 90- *Personal Data:* b Mo, May 29, 25; wid. *Educ:* Culver-Stockton Col, BA, 51; Univ Mo, MS, 53, PhD(agr chem), 55. *Prof Exp:* Asst agr chem, Univ Mo, 52-55, res assoc biochem, 55. *Mem:* Am Inst Nutrit; Am Chem Soc. *Res:* Chemistry of sulfur compounds and sulphatases; dietary sulfur and xenobiotic metabolism; enzyme chemistry; food phosphates; importance of inorganic sulfate, enzymes, metabolic obesity. *Mailing Add:* 4524 Silverhill Dr Knoxville TN 37921-2423

SMITH, JOHN W(ARREN), ENVIRONMENTAL ENGINEERING, CIVIL ENGINEERING. *Current Pos:* from asst prof to assoc prof environ eng, 70-75, actg dir, Ctr Alluvial Valley Studies, 77-79, PROF CIVIL ENG, MEMPHIS STATE UNIV, 75- *Personal Data:* b De Soto, Mo, Nov 18, 43; m 64; c 3. *Educ:* Mo Sch Mines & Metall, BS, 65; Univ Mo-Rolla, MS, 67, PhD(civil eng), 68. *Prof Exp:* Instr civil eng & res asst environ eng, Univ Mo-Rolla, 65-68; proj engr, Esso Res & Eng Co, 68-70. *Concurrent Pos:* Mem bd consults, Ryckman, Edgerly, Tomlinson & Assocs, 71-72; actg dep city engr, City of Memphis, 73-74. *Mem:* Water Pollution Control Fedn; Am Water Works Asn. *Res:* Industrial and municipal waste treatment; water resources; biological wastewater treatment using fixed film reactors, hazardous waste analysis and management, water reuse; kinetics of fixed film reactors and low energy treatment systems. *Mailing Add:* Dept Civil Eng Univ Memphis Box 526-570 Memphis TN 38152-6570

SMITH, JOHN WOLFGANG, mathematics, for more information see previous edition

SMITH, JONATHAN JEREMY BERKELEY, SENSORY PHYSIOLOGY. *Current Pos:* From asst prof to assoc prof, 65-82, vdean arts & sci, 83-88, PROF ZOOL, UNIV TORONTO, 82- *Personal Data:* b Leicester, Eng, Dec 26, 40; m 67, 81; c 2. *Educ:* Cambridge Univ, BA, 62, PhD(zool), 65, MA, 66. *Mem:* Brit Soc Exp Biol; Can Soc Zool; Asn Chemoreception Scis. *Res:* Sensory physiology; chemoreception and feeding in insects, particularly blood-feeders; hearing mechanisms in lower vertebrates. *Mailing Add:* Dept Zool Univ Toronto Toronto ON M5S 3G5 Can

SMITH, JOSEF RILEY, PULMONARY PHYSIOLOGY. *Current Pos:* PVT PRACT INTERNAL MED, 87- *Personal Data:* b Council Bluffs, Iowa, Oct 1, 26; m 73; c 7. *Educ:* Northwestern Univ, MB, 50, MD, 51; Marquette Univ, MSc, 64; Am Bd Internal Med, cert, 57. *Prof Exp:* Instr, Dept Med, Univ Miss, Jackson, 56-59; asst prof, Dept Med, Marquette Univ, Milwaukee, 59-63; from assoc prof to prof internal med, Univ Mich, Ann Arbor, 63-72; prof, Col Med, Northeast Ohio Univ, 77-79. *Concurrent Pos:* Nat Tuberc Asn fel, Univ Miss Med Sch, 57-59; Vet Admin clin investr cardiol, Vet Admin Hosp, Wood, Wis, 59-62; NIH fel biomed eng, Drexel Inst Technol & Marquette Univ, 62-63; counr, Dept Internal Med, Univ Mich Med Sch, 69-72; mem, Ad Hoc Comt Biomed Eng, Am Col Physicians, 69-71; controller, Mahoning Co Tuberc Clin, 73-79; med dir respiratory ther, St Joseph Hosp, Tucson, Ariz, 86-91. *Mem:* Fel Am Col Physicians; fel Sigma Xi; Am Thoracic Soc. *Res:* Pulmonary physiology with particular interest in gas transfer. *Mailing Add:* 2224 N Craycroft Rd Tucson AZ 85712

SMITH, JOSEPH COLLINS, ENGINEERING, ASTRONOMY. *Current Pos:* VPRES, AM PRIDE, INC, 85- *Personal Data:* b Knoxville, Tenn, Oct 26, 28; m 53; c 1. *Educ:* US Naval Acad, BS, 53; George Washington Univ, MA, 64. *Prof Exp:* Mem staff opers of Comdr Submarines Pac, 64-66; commanding officer submarines, USS Odax (55-484), 66-68; mem staff opers & plans submarines of Chief Naval Opers, 68-71; asst chief staff opers of Comdr Antisubmarine Warfare Forces, US Sixth Fleet, 71-74; prof & head dept naval sci, Iowa State Univ, 74-76; supt-in-chg time & navig, US Naval Observ, 76-79; consult, 79-82; dir, Space Studies & spec asst to pres, Nat Defense Univ, 82-85. *Concurrent Pos:* Mem bd, Coast Guard Adv Bd, 76-; mem found, Nat Defense Univ; consult, 85- *Mem:* Naval Inst; Inst Navig. *Res:* Astrometric instrumentation; timing; fundamental positioning; global navigational equipment; systems improvements; radio interferometry; Strategic Defense Initiative; satellite systems. *Mailing Add:* 2711 Churchcreek Lane Poplar Pt Edgewater MD 21037

SMITH, JOSEPH D, COMPUTATIONAL FLUID DYNAMICS COMBUSTION. *Current Pos:* vis prof & consult, 88-89, PROJ LEADER, DOW CHEM CO, 90- *Personal Data:* b Salt lake City, Utah, Jan 30, 57; m 78, Eileen R Sanford; c Nathan, Adam, Kimberlie, Zachary & Amanda. *Educ:* Brigham Young Univ, BS, 83, MS, 84, PhD(chem eng), 90. *Prof Exp:* Assoc Western Univs fel, Los Alamos Nat Lab, 85-86; asst prof, Tenn Technol Univ, 88-90; res assoc, Advan Combustion Eng Res Ctr, 89-90. *Concurrent Pos:* Consult, Synco Energy, 86-89, Nuturn Corp, 88-89, Pioneer Air Systs, 89-90 & Southern Co Serv, 90-91. *Mem:* Sigma Xi; Am Inst Chem Engrs; Am Soc Eng Educ. *Res:* Development and application of computational fluid dynamics to industrial opportunities with a focus on combustion related phenomena; expert system development and sensitivity analysis application for chemical processes, evaluation/minimization of hazardous waste for chemical plants. *Mailing Add:* 3121 Lawndale Midland MI 48642. *E-Mail:* jdsmith@dow.com

SMITH, JOSEPH DONALD, BIOCHEMISTRY. *Current Pos:* assoc prof, 82-89, PROF CHEM, UNIV MASS, DARTMOUTH, 89-, CHAIRPERSON, CHEM DEPT, 90- *Personal Data:* b New Brunswick, NJ, Sept 18, 43. *Educ:* Columbia Univ, AB, 65; Univ Chicago, PhD(biochem), 69. *Prof Exp:* Fel molecular biol, Albert Einstein Col Med, 70-74; res scientist neurosci, NY State Psychiat Inst, 74-75; asst prof chem, Miami Univ, 75-82. *Concurrent Pos:* Asst prof biochem, Sch Med, Wright State Univ, 75-77. *Mem:* Am Chem Soc; AAAS; Am Soc Microbiol; NY Acad Sci; Am Soc Biochem & Molecular Biol; Protein Soc. *Mailing Add:* Dept Chem Univ Mass Dartmouth North Dartmouth MA 02747. *E-Mail:* dsmith@umassd.edu

SMITH, JOSEPH EMMITT, CLINICAL PATHOLOGY, PHYSIOLOGY. *Current Pos:* head, Dept Path, 87-92, head, Dept Path & Microbiol, 92-95, PROF PATH, COL VET MED, KANS STATE UNIV, 69- *Personal Data:* b Big Spring, Tex, Jan 24, 38; m 60, Leola; c 2. *Educ:* Tex A&M Univ, BS, 59, DVM, 61; Univ Calif, Davis, PhD(comp path), 64. *Prof Exp:* Lab asst vet anat, Tex A&M Univ, 58-59, NSF res trainee reproduction physiol, 59-61; USPHS trainee metab & hemat dis, Univ Calif, Davis, 61-64; assoc res scientist, City of Hope Med Ctr, Duarte, Calif, 64-66; from asst prof to assoc prof path, Okla State Univ, 66-69. *Concurrent Pos:* USPHS res grant, 65-; career develop awardee, NIH. *Mem:* Am Vet Med Asn; Am Asn Clin Chemists; Am Soc Vet Clin Path; Soc Exp Biol & Med; Am Col Vet Path; Am Asn Hemat; Am Soc Hematol. *Res:* Inherited metabolic errors of animals which serve as models of human disorders, particularly those of erythrocyte metabolism; clinical enzymology; iron metabolism; veterinary transfusion medicine; acute phase reactants; comparative hematology. *Mailing Add:* Col Vet Med Dept Diag Med/Pathobiol Kans State Univ Manhattan KS 66502. *Fax:* 785-532-4039; *E-Mail:* smithj@vet.ksu.edu

SMITH, JOSEPH HAROLD, physical chemistry, inorganic chemistry, for more information see previous edition

SMITH, JOSEPH JAMES, CREATIVITY, INNOVATION. *Current Pos:* RETIRED. *Personal Data:* b New York, NY, Apr 6, 21; m 46; c 7. *Educ:* Fordham Univ BS, 43. *Hon Degrees:* DS, WVa State Col, 75; DS, Marshall Univ, 76. *Honors & Awards:* Medal, Am Inst Chemists, 43. *Prof Exp:* Res chemist, Bakelite Co Div, Union Carbide & Carbon Corp, 43-51, proj leader, 51-53, group leader, 53-56, sect head, Union Carbide Plastics Co, 56-64, asst dir, 64-66, tech mgr polyolefins & asst dir res & develop, Chem Div, 66-67, dir, Chem & Plastics Div, 67-82; consult, creativity, innovation, Res & Develop Orgn, J J Smith Consult, 82-87. *Mem:* Am Chem Soc. *Res:* Surface chemistry; corrosion and protective coatings; infrared and ultraviolet spectrophotometry; chemistry of organic high polymers; catalysis; organometallic compounds; polyolefins; electron irradiation; program management of research and development organizations; creativity and innovation. *Mailing Add:* 905 Charlotte Pl Charleston WV 25314

SMITH, JOSEPH JAY, obstetrics & gynecology; deceased, see previous edition for last biography

SMITH, JOSEPH LECONTE, JR, MECHANICAL & CRYOGENIC ENGINEERING. *Current Pos:* Res asst, 55-56, from instr to assoc prof, 56-69, PROF MECH ENG, MASS INST TECHNOL, 69-, PROF-IN-CHG CRYOGENIC ENG LAB, 64- *Personal Data:* b Macon, Ga, Sept 4, 29; m 53; c 3. *Educ:* Ga Inst Technol, BME, 52, MS, 53; Mass Inst Technol, DSc(mech eng), 59. *Concurrent Pos:* Consult, Los Alamos Sci Lab, 58-66, Cambridge Electron Accelerator, Harvard Univ, 59-65, Arthur D Little, Inc, 69-71 & Westinghouse Res Lab, 70- *Mem:* Nat Acad Eng; Am Soc Mech Engrs; Inst Elec & Electronics Engrs; Sigma Xi. *Res:* Thermodynamics; heat transfer; fluid mechanics. *Mailing Add:* Dept Mech Eng Bldg 41-206 Mass Inst Technol Cambridge MA 02139

SMITH, JOSEPH PATRICK, ENVIRONMENTAL SCIENCE. *Current Pos:* sr res chemist, Long Range Res Div, 81-86, res specialist, Reservoir Div, 86-90, SR RES SPECIALIST, PROD OPERS DIV, EXXON PROD RES CO, 90- *Personal Data:* b Lackawanna, NY, July 9, 51; m 79, Jean B Ruggles; c Eileen. *Educ:* Univ Rochester, BS, 72; Univ Calif, Berkeley, PhD(phys chem), 78. *Prof Exp:* NSF Nat Needs Res fel, Dept Biochem, Univ Wis-Madison, 78-79; fel, Chem Div, Argonne Nat Lab, 79-81. *Mem:* Am Chem Soc; Soc Petrol Eng. *Res:* Environmental science: modeling of offshore and coastal discharges. *Mailing Add:* Exxon Prod Res Co PO Box 2189 Houston TX 77252-2189

SMITH, JOSEPH VICTOR, MINERALOGY. *Current Pos:* prof mineral & crystallog, 60-76, LOUIS BLOCK PROF PHYS SCI, UNIV CHICAGO, 76- *Personal Data:* b Eng, July 30, 28; nat US; m 51; c 2. *Educ:* Cambridge Univ, BA, 48, MA & PhD(physics), 51. *Honors & Awards:* Mineral Soc Am Award, 61; Murchison Medal, 80; Roebling Medal, 81. *Prof Exp:* Fel crystallog, Geophys Lab, Carnegie Inst, 51-54; demonstr mineral & petrol, Cambridge Univ, 54-56; from asst prof to assoc prof mineral, Pa State Univ, 56-60; exec dir, Consortium Advan Radiation Sources, 89-93. *Concurrent Pos:* Consult, Linde Div, Union Carbide Corp, 56-87, UOP 88-; ed, X-ray Powder Data File, Am Soc Testing & Mat, 58-68; coordr sci prog, Consortium Advan Radiation Sources, 89-92. *Mem:* Nat Acad Sci; fel Geol Soc Am; fel Royal Soc; fel Am Geophys Union; fel Am Acad Arts & Sci; fel Mineral Soc Am (pres, 72-73); hon fel Mineral Soc Great Britain; fel Meteoritical Soc; fel AAAS. *Res:* Mineralogy applied to petrology, geochemistry and industrial chemistry. *Mailing Add:* Dept Geophys Sci Univ Chicago Chicago IL 60637

SMITH, JOSEPHINE REIST, MEDICAL MICROBIOLOGY. *Current Pos:* INSTR MICROBIOL, DEPT BIOL, MONTGOMERY COUNTY COMMUNITY COL, 75- *Personal Data:* b Altoona, Pa, Nov 26, 29; m 51; c 3. *Educ:* Pa State Univ, BS, 52; Temple Univ, MS, 71, PhD(pharm chem), 76. *Prof Exp:* Technician immunol, Protein Found, Dept Phys Chem, Harvard Univ, 53-54; res asst, Dept Biol, Haverford Col, 64-69. *Mem:* Am Soc Microbiol; Sigma Xi; AAAS. *Res:* Application of pharmacokinetics to the study of immune responses. *Mailing Add:* 12 Forest Rd Wayne PA 19087

SMITH, JUDITH TERRY, PALEONTOLOGY. *Current Pos:* curatorial asst, 68-69, RES ASSOC PALEONT, DEPT GEOL, STANFORD UNIV, 69-, FUND RAISER, EARTH SCI. *Personal Data:* b New York, NY, Mar 4, 40; m 69; c 3. *Educ:* Barnard Col, Columbia Univ, AB, 62; Stanford Univ, MS, 64, PhD(geol), 68. *Prof Exp:* Geologist, US Geol Surv, 70 & 72- *Concurrent Pos:* Res assoc, US Geol Surv, 72-73. *Mem:* Geol Soc Am; Paleont Soc; Paleont Res Inst. *Res:* Cenozoic molluscan paleontology; biostratigraphy and paleoecology, especially zonation and distribution problems involving pectinids; Tethyan and related faunas. *Mailing Add:* 1527 Byron St Palo Alto CA 94301

SMITH, JULIAN CLEVELAND, CHEMICAL ENGINEERING. *Current Pos:* from asst prof to prof, 46-86, assoc dir, 73-75, dir, 75-83, EMER PROF CHEM ENG, CORNELL UNIV, 86- *Personal Data:* b Westmount, Que, Mar 10, 19; US citizen; m 46; Joan Elsen; c Robert E, Diane L (Brook) & Brian R. *Educ:* Cornell Univ, BChem, 41, ChemE, 42. *Honors & Awards:* Julian C Smith Lectr Chem Eng, Cornell Univ, 88- *Prof Exp:* Engr chem eng, E I du Pont de Nemours & Co, 42-46. *Concurrent Pos:* Prof engr, NY State Educ Dept, 57-; consult, E I du Pont de Nemours & Co, 55-89, US Army Corps Engrs, 57-65, Atlantic Richfield Hanford Co, 71-77, Rockwell Int Co, 77-87, Westinghouse Hanford Co, 87-88, Am Cyanamid, 89-93. *Mem:* Fel Am Inst Chem Engrs; Am Chem Soc. *Res:* Mixing of liquids and pastes; flow of granular solids; centrifugal separation. *Mailing Add:* 711 The Parkway Ithaca NY 14850-1546. *E-Mail:* jcs29@cornell.edu

SMITH, KAREN ANN, ANALYTICAL CHEMISTRY. *Current Pos:* SR RES SCIENTIST, UNIV NMEX, 95- *Personal Data:* b Idaho Falls, Idaho, Aug 30, 58; m 89; c 4. *Educ:* Pa State Univ, BS, 78; Univ Ill, PhD(phys chem), 84. *Prof Exp:* res chemist, Res & Develop Div, Colgate-Palmolive Co, 84-90; nuclear magnetic resonance spectroscopist, Iowa State Univ, 91-95. *Mem:* Am Chem Soc; Am Inst Chemists; NY Acad Sci; AAAS. *Res:* Solid-state and solution nuclear magnetic resonance. *Mailing Add:* Dept Chem Clark Hall Univ NMex Albuquerque NM 87131

SMITH, KATHLEEN, PSYCHIATRY. *Current Pos:* RETIRED. *Personal Data:* b Fayetteville, Ark, Oct 9, 22. *Educ:* Univ Ark, BS, 44; Wash Univ, MD, 49; Am Bd Psychiat & Neurol, dipl, 56. *Prof Exp:* Intern, St Louis City Hosp, 49-50; resident psychiat, Barnes & McMillan Hosps, 50-52 & Malcolm Bliss Psychiat Hosp, 52-53; from instr to assoc prof, Sch Med, Washington Univ, 53-72, prof psychiat, 72- *Concurrent Pos:* USPHS fel, 52-53; physician, Malcolm Bliss Ment Health Ctr, 53-, dir inpatient serv, 57-60, dir training, 60-64, med supt, 64-84; vis physician, St Louis City Hosp, 56-, consult, Nurses Infirmary, 55-57. *Mem:* AMA; Am Psychiat Asn. *Res:* Odor of schizophrenic sweat; gas chromatography; multihospital studies of tranquilizers and antidepressants. *Mailing Add:* APA Rte 1 Box 312 Du Quoin IL 62832-9731

SMITH, KEITH DAVIS, ENDOCRINOLOGY, INTERNAL MEDICINE. *Current Pos:* from assoc prof to prof reproductive med, 71-83, CLIN PROF INTERNAL MED, UNIV TEX MED SCH, HOUSTON, 83- *Personal Data:* b Portsmouth, Ohio, Dec 14, 30; m 58, Connie Beahan; c Karen (Dodd), Brian & Valerie (Yake). *Educ:* Pa State Univ, BS, 52; Sch Med, Univ Pittsburgh, MD, 59. *Prof Exp:* Chief div endocrinol, Mercy Hosp, Pittsburgh, 64-67; asst prof med, Sch Med, Temple Univ, 68-71. *Concurrent Pos:* USPHS fel, Albert Einstein Med Ctr, Philadelphia, 62-64, assoc mem div endocrinol, 68-71; clin instr med, Sch Med, Univ Pittsburgh, 65-67; prin investr contract endocrine changes vasectomized men, NIH, 72-79, co-investr prog proj multidisciplinary approach control male reproduction, 74-83; co-investr grant develop contraceptive agents human male, Ford Found, 74-78; vpres, Tex Inst Reproductive Med & Endocrinol, 83-, Tex Hormone Assay Lab, 83- *Mem:* Am Soc Reproductive Med; Am Asn Clin Endocrinologists; Endocrine Soc; Am Soc Andrology; Am Col Endocrinol. *Res:* Ovarian and testicular function; control by the pituitary and hypothalamus; effects of various physical, emotional and chemical stimuli on the hypothalmo-pituitary-gonadal axis. *Mailing Add:* Tex Inst Reprod Med & Endo 7400 Fannin St Suite 850 Houston TX 77054. *Fax:* 713-796-2343

SMITH, KEITH JAMES, animal nutrition, for more information see previous edition

SMITH, KELLY L, CONTROLLED RELEASE. *Current Pos:* dir, Controlled Release Div, 78-91, SECY, BEND RES INC, 87-, SR FEL, 91- *Personal Data:* b Eugene, Ore, Mar 10, 51; m 74. *Educ:* Stanford Univ, BS & MS, 74. *Prof Exp:* Chem engr, Alza Corp, 74-78. *Concurrent Pos:* Mem bd dirs, Bend Res Inc, 81-; dir, Consep Membranes Inc, 84-92, secy, 87-; mem bd gov, Controlled Release Soc, 87-90, treas, 92- *Mem:* Am Chem Soc; Am Inst Chem Engrs; Controlled Release Soc. *Res:* Controlled release theory; development of controlled release technologies and products in pharmaceuticals, animal health and agricultural fields. *Mailing Add:* Bend Res Inc 64550 Res Rd Bend OR 97701

SMITH, KENDALL A, T-CELLS. *Current Pos:* From asst prof to assoc prof, 74-82, PROF MED, DARTMOUTH MED SCH, 82- *Personal Data:* b Akron, Ohio, Feb 28, 42. *Educ:* Ohio State Univ, MD, 68. *Mem:* Am Soc Clin Invest; Am Asn Immunologists; Am Soc Hemat; Am Soc Clin Oncol; Am Fedn Cancer Res. *Mailing Add:* Div Allergy & Immunol NY Hosp Cornell Univ Med Ctr 525 E 68th St Box 41 New York NY 10021. *Fax:* 212-747-8167

SMITH, KENDALL O, MICROBIOLOGY, VIROLOGY. *Current Pos:* RETIRED. *Personal Data:* b Wilson, NC, Sept 5, 28; m 49; c 1. *Educ:* George Washington Univ, BA, 51; Univ NC, MS, 57, PhD(microbiol), 59. *Prof Exp:* Fel biophys, Univ NC, 59-60; from instr to assoc prof virol, Col Med, Baylor Univ, 60-65; res microbiologist, Div Biol Stand, NIH, 65-69; prof microbiol, Med Sch, Univ Tex, San Antonio, 69-92. *Concurrent Pos:* Res fel, NIH, Baylor Univ, 61-62, res career develop award, 63. *Mem:* Am Soc Microbiol; Am Asn Immunol. *Res:* Correlation of physical and biological properties of viruses; viruses associated with chronic, degenerative diseases of man; chemotherapy of herpes infections; detection of viral antigens and antibodies by enzyme linked immunosorbent assay; reliable medical diagnostic technology for developing countries. *Mailing Add:* 102 Fabra St Boerne TX 78006-1656

SMITH, KENDRIC CHARLES, PHOTOBIOLOGY, RADIATION BIOLOGY. *Current Pos:* prof radiol, 73-88, prof radiation oncol, 88-91, EMER PROF, SCH MED, STANFORD UNIV, 92- *Personal Data:* b Oakwood, Ill, Oct 13, 26; m 55, Marion Edmonds; c Nancy & Martha. *Educ:* Stanford Univ, BS, 47; Univ Calif, PhD(biochem), 52. *Honors & Awards:* Finsen Medal in Photobiol, 84. *Prof Exp:* Res asst radiol, Med Sch, Univ Calif, 54-56; res assoc, 56-62, from asst prof to assoc prof, 62-73. *Concurrent Pos:* USPHS fel, Univ Calif, 52-54; USPHS career develop award, Stanford Univ, 66-71; mem, Comt Photobiol, Nat Acad Sci-Nat Res Coun, 64-74, chmn, 70-74; exec ed, Photochem & Photobiol, 66-72 & Photochem Photobiol Rev, 76-83; mem, US Nat Comt, Int Union Biol Sci, 67-73 & secy, 71-73; mem, Radiation Bio-effects & epidemiol Adv Comt, Food & Drug Admin, 74-75. *Mem:* Am Inst Biol Sci(v pres, 81-82, pres, 82-83, past pres, 83-84); Am Soc Biol Chemists; Am Soc Microbiol; Brit Photobiol Soc; Am Soc Photobiol (pres, 72-74); Radiation Res Soc. *Res:* Photochemical and radiation chemical reactions of nucleic acids; genetic control and biochemical mechanisms for repair of radiation damage; the molecular mechanisms of mutagenesis. *Mailing Add:* 927 Mears Ct Stanford CA 94305-1041

SMITH, KENNAN TAYLOR, MATHEMATICS. *Current Pos:* PROF MATH, ORE STATE UNIV, 68- *Personal Data:* b Green Bay, Wis, July 17, 26; m 48; c 2. *Educ:* Bowling Green State Univ, BA, 47; Harvard Univ, MA, 48; Univ Wis, PhD(math), 51. *Prof Exp:* Asst prof math, Univ Kans, 52-59; from assoc prof to prof, Univ Wis-Madison, 59-68. *Concurrent Pos:* Fulbright scholar, France, 51-52. *Mem:* Am Math Soc. *Res:* Linear topological spaces; Hilbert spaces. *Mailing Add:* 1411 NW Vista Pl Corvallis OR 97330

SMITH, KENNETH A, MECHANICAL ENGINEERING. *Current Pos:* from asst prof to assoc prof chem eng, Mass Inst Technol, 61-71, actg head, Dept Chem Eng, 76-77, Joseph R Mares prof chem eng, 78-81, assoc provost, 80-91, vpres res, 81-91, PROF CHEM ENG, MASS INST TECHNOL, 71-, EDWIN R GILLILAND PROF, 89- *Personal Data:* b Winthrop, Mass, Nov 28, 36; m 61, Ambia M Olsson; c Kirsten H, Edward E, Andrew I B & Thurston G. *Educ:* Mass Inst Technol, SB, 58, SM, 59, ScD(chem eng), 62. *Honors & Awards:* Prof Progress Award, Am Inst Chem Engrs, 81. *Prof Exp:* Dir, Whitaker Col Health Sci & Technol, 89-91. *Concurrent Pos:* Consult for major int petrol & chem co; postdoctoral fel, Cavendish Lab, Univ Cambridge, 64-65; Churchill fel, Cambridge, Eng, 93. *Mem:* Nat Acad Eng; Am Chem Soc; Am Inst Chem Engrs; AAAS; Sigma Xi. *Res:* Fluid mechanics; heat and mass transfer; desalination; liquified natural gas; biomedical engineering; author of 98 publications. *Mailing Add:* Dept Chem Eng Bldg 66-540 Mass Inst Technol Cambridge MA 02139. *Fax:* 617-253-2701; *E-Mail:* kas@eagle.mit.edu

SMITH, KENNETH CARLESS, MAN-MACHINE INTERFACE, SPECIAL PURPOSE PROCESSORS. *Current Pos:* assoc prof, 65-70, chmn dept, 76-81, PROF ELEC ENG & COMPUT SCI, DEPT ELEC & COMPUT ENG, UNIV TORONTO, 70-, PROF INFO SCI, FAC LIBR SCI, 81-, PROF MECH ENG, 88- *Personal Data:* b Toronto, Ont, May 8, 32; m 83, Laura Fujino; c Kevin A & K David. *Educ:* Univ Toronto, BASc, 54, MASc, 56, PhD(physics), 60. *Prof Exp:* Transmission engr tel, Can Nat Tel, 54-55; res engr digital electronics, Univ Toronto, 56-58, asst prof electronics, 60-61; res asst prof comput design, Dept Elec Eng, Univ Ill, 61-64, assoc prof, 64-65. *Concurrent Pos:* Res engr, Comput Ctr, Univ Toronto, 60-61; chief engr & prin investr, Digital Comput Lab, Univ Ill, 61-65, eng consult, Training Res Lab, 62-64, consult, Pattern Processor Proj, 65-70; dir & co-founder, Elec Eng Consociates, Ltd, 68-87, pres, 74-76; founding mem, Comput Systs Res Inst, Univ Toronto, 68-; dir, several small US & Can co, 68-; vpres, Owl Instruments, Ltd, Med Instrument Mfg, 70-80; assoc, Inst Biomed Eng, Univ Toronto, 74-; mem exec comt, awards chmn, Inst Elec & Electronics Engrs, Solid State Circuits Conf, 75-; chmn pub coun, Can Soc Elec Eng, 83-90; mem bd dir, Can Soc Prof Eng, 85-; chmn, Mult Valued Tech Comt, Inst Elec & Electronics Engrs Comput Soc, 93-94; vis prof, Hong Kong Univ Sci & Technol. *Mem:* Fel Inst Elec & Electronics Engrs; Can Soc Elec Eng; Can Soc Prof Engrs (pres, 88-91). *Res:* Linear and digital circuits and systems including multiple-valued logic, parallel and other special-purpose processors, the man-machine interface instrumentation and input and output systems with application in manufacturing, education, medicine and computer music. *Mailing Add:* Dept Elec & Comput Eng Univ Toronto 10 King's College Rd Toronto ON M5S 1A4 Can. *E-Mail:* tfujino@esri.toronto.edu

SMITH, KENNETH EDWARD, ANALYTICAL CHEMISTRY, SPECTROSCOPY. *Current Pos:* VPRES CONFORMITY ASSESSMENT, 92- *Personal Data:* b Milwaukee, Wis, Dec 29, 43; m 66; c 2. *Educ:* Univ Wis-Milwaukee, BS, 66; Univ Iowa, PhD(analytical chem), 71. *Prof Exp:* NSF fel, Kans State Univ, 70-72; asst prof chem, Eastern Ill Univ, 72-73; assoc chemist, Wildlife Res Sect, Ill Natural Hist Surv, 73-80; mgr anal chem, Inst Gas Technol, 80-83; mgr anal chem, Swift Adhesives, 83-92, mgr aqueous adhesives, 87-90; sr dir lab serv, NSF Int, Ann Arbor, Mich, 90-92. *Concurrent Pos:* Instr, Kans State Univ. *Mem:* Am Chem Soc; Soc Appl Spectros; Am Soc Testing & Mat. *Res:* Analytical atomic spectroscopy; non-flame absorption systems; low-pressure plasmas in spectroscopy; temperature effects in plasmas; environmental metal analysis as contaminants. *Mailing Add:* 1020 Imperial A Pt Las Vegas NV 89104

SMITH, KENNETH JUDSON, JR, PHYSICAL CHEMISTRY, POLYMER PHYSICS. *Current Pos:* RETIRED. *Personal Data:* b Raleigh, NC, Sept 4, 30; m 54; c 2. *Educ:* ECarolina Col, AB, 57; Duke Univ, MA, 59, PhD(phys chem), 62. *Prof Exp:* From res chemist to sr res chemist, Chemstrand Res Ctr, Inc, 61-68; from asst prof to prof chem, Col Environ Sci & Forestry, State Univ NY, 68-84, asst dir, Polymer Res Ctr, 71-82, chmn dept, 72-84. *Concurrent Pos:* Dir, Org Mat Sci Prog, Col Environ Sci & Forestry, State Univ NY, 71-74. *Mem:* AAAS. *Res:* Mechanical behavior of polymers; rubber elasticity; statistical mechanics of rubber networks at large deformations; stress induced crystallization in polymer networks; elastic behavior of composite and interpenetrating networks; thermoelastic behavior of polyelectrolyte networks. *Mailing Add:* 108 Scottholm Blvd Syracuse NY 13224

SMITH, KENNETH LARRY, DAIRY SCIENCE, MASTITIS. *Current Pos:* Res assoc dairy sci, 64-70, from asst prof to assoc prof, 70-84, PROF DAIRY SCI, OHIO AGR RES & DEVELOP CTR, OHIO STATE UNIV, 84- *Personal Data:* b Minerva, Ohio, Apr 30, 41; m 78; c 2. *Educ:* NMex State Univ, BS, 64; Ohio State Univ, MS, 66, PhD(dairy sci), 70. *Honors & Awards:* West Agro Award, Am Dairy Sci Asn, 84. *Concurrent Pos:* Vis scientist, Commonwealth Sci & Indust Res Orgn, Armindale Australia, 81. *Mem:* Am Dairy Sci Asn; Nat Mastitis Coun. *Res:* Specific and nonspecific resistance to infection of the bovine mammary gland; diagnosis, therapy and control of bovine mash. *Mailing Add:* Dept Dairy Sci Ohio Agr Res & Develop Ctr 1680 Madison Ave Wooster OH 44691

SMITH, KENNETH LAWRENCE, JR, DEEP-SEA ECOLOGY. *Current Pos:* RES BIOLOGIST, UNIV CALIF-SCRIPPS INST OCEANOG, 76- *Personal Data:* b East Orange, NJ, July 16, 43. *Educ:* Southern Ill Univ, BS, 65; Univ Del, MS, 67; Univ Ga, PhD(zool), 71. *Prof Exp:* Asst scientist, Woods Hole Oceanographic Inst, 71-76. *Concurrent Pos:* Lectr, Univ Calif, San Diego, 78- *Mem:* fel AAAS; Am Soc Limnol & Oceanog; Geol Soc Am; Oceanog Soc. *Res:* Ecological studies of deep sea communities and carbon cycling in the deep ocean; development of instrumentation to measure biological and chemical processes in the deep ocean. *Mailing Add:* Marine Biol Res Div Scripps Inst Oceanog La Jolla CA 92093-0202. *Fax:* 619-534-7313; *E-Mail:* ksmith@ucsd.edu

SMITH, KENNETH RUPERT, JR, NEUROSURGERY. *Current Pos:* from asst prof to assoc prof, 66-71, PROF NEUROSURG, SCH MED, ST LOUIS UNIV, 71-, CHMN SECT, 68- *Personal Data:* b St Louis, Mo, Sept 23, 32; m 56, Marjorie Sandin; c 7. *Educ:* Wash Univ, MD, 57. *Prof Exp:* Trainee anat, Wash Univ, 59-60 & 62, instr neurosurg, 63-66, instr anat, 64-66. *Concurrent Pos:* Nat Inst Neurol Dis & Blindness spec fel, Wash Univ, 64-65 & Oxford Univ, 65-66. *Mem:* AAAS; AMA; Cong Neurol Surg (vpres, 75); Am Asn Anatomists; Am Asn Neurol Surg; Soc Neurol Surg. *Res:* Electron microscopy of the nervous system; neurophysiology of sensory receptors; clinical evaluation of cerebral circulation. *Mailing Add:* Dept Surg 3635 Vista & Grand St Louis MO 63110-0250. *Fax:* 573-771-1945

SMITH, KENNETH THOMAS, TRACE MINERAL METABOLISM, CALCIUM METABOLISM. *Current Pos:* sect head, nutrit res, 85-89, ASSOC DIR, FOOD & BEVERAGE TECHNOL, MIAMI VALLEY LABS, PROCTER & GAMBLE CO, 89- *Personal Data:* b Jan 4, 49; m 70; c 3. *Educ:* St Francis Col, BS, 70; Fordham Univ, MS, 76, Rutgers Univ, PhD(nutrit), 79. *Mem:* Sigma Xi; Inst Food Technologists; Am Inst Nutrit; Fel Am Col Nutrit; Am Soc Clin Nutrit. *Res:* Res into the bioavailability and metabolism of calcium and trace minerals. *Mailing Add:* Food Bev & Cosmet Technol Procter & Gamble Co PO Box 398707 Cincinnati OH 45239-8707. *Fax:* 513-627-1940

SMITH, KENT ASHTON, SCIENTIFIC & TECHNICAL INFORMATION. *Current Pos:* admin officer, Div Res Facil & Resources, NIH, 65-67, asst exec officer, 67-68, exec officer, 68-71, asst dir admin, Nat Libr Med, 71-78, DEP DIR, NIH, 78- *Personal Data:* b Boston, Mass, Sept 3, 38; m 91, Mary Margaret Gaffney; c Holly L (Smith-Volz) & Kent W. *Educ:* Hobart Col, BA, 60, Cornell Univ, MBA, 62. *Honors & Awards:* President's Award, Med Libr Asn, 97; Miles Conrad Lectr, Nat Fed Abstracting & Info Sci, 98. *Prof Exp:* Mgt analyst, Off Secy, HEW, 62-65. *Concurrent Pos:* Vpres, US Nat Comt UNESCO-Gen Info Prog, 83-85. *Mem:* Am Soc Info Serv; Med Libr Asn; AAAS; Int Coun Sci & Tech Info, Paris (treas, 86-88, pres-elect, 89, pres, 90-94); Nat Fedn Abstracting & Info Sci (treas, 86-88, pres-elect, 89, pres, 90). *Res:* Contributed several articles to professional journals. *Mailing Add:* 17903 Gainford Pl Olney MD 20832. *Fax:* 301-480-3271; *E-Mail:* smith@lhc.nlm.nih.gov

SMITH, KENT FARRELL, INTEGRATED CIRCUITS. *Current Pos:* scientist, Res Inst, 72-78, ASSOC PROF COMPUT SCI, UNIV UTAH, 78-, ACTG CHMN DEPT, 85- *Personal Data:* b Fish Haven, Idaho, June 26, 35; m 57; c 5. *Educ:* Utah State Univ, BS, 57, MS, 58; Univ Utah, PhD(elec eng), 82. *Prof Exp:* Res engr, Stanford Res Inst, 59-61; electronic specialist, Phillips Petrol Co, 61-66; tech dir, Res & Develop Ctr, Gen Instrument, 66-72. *Concurrent Pos:* VPres, LSI Testing, 67-72; consult, Gen Instrument Corp, 72- *Res:* Design methodology for the implementation of very large scale integrated circuits, using path programmable logic. *Mailing Add:* Dept Comput Sci Univ Utah 3190 MEB Salt Lake City UT 84112-1180

SMITH, KEVIN MALCOLM, ORGANIC CHEMISTRY, BIOLOGICAL CHEMISTRY. *Current Pos:* chmn, 90-94, PROF CHEM, UNIV CALIF, DAVIS, 77-, ASSOC VCHANCELLOR RES, 95- *Personal Data:* b Birmingham, Eng, Mar 15, 42; div; c Kimberley & Juliette. *Educ:* Univ Liverpool, Eng, BSc, 64, PhD(chem), 67, DSc, 77; FRIC, 77. *Honors & Awards:* Leverhulme Prize, Soc Chem Indust, Eng, 64; Parke-Davis Prize, Parke-Davis & Co, 67; Corday-Morgan Medal & Prize, Chem Soc, 78; Potts Medal, Univ Liverpool, 88. *Prof Exp:* Fel chem, Harvard Univ, 67-69; lectr, Univ Liverpool, Eng, 69-77. *Concurrent Pos:* Fulbright travel grant, 67-69; org chem consult, Palmer Res Labs, 74-77; consult & sci adv bd, Aquanautics Corp, 85-90; sci adv bd, Quadralogic Technol, 89-92; fel, Japan Soc Prom Sci, 92. *Mem:* Am Chem Soc; Royal Soc Chem; Sigma Xi. *Res:* Chemistry, biochemistry and spectroscopy of porphyrins, chlorophylls, bile pigments and their diverse metal complexes. *Mailing Add:* Dept Chem Univ Calif Davis CA 95616. *Fax:* 530-752-8995; *E-Mail:* smith@chem.ucdavis.edu

SMITH, KIMBERLY GRAY, VERTEBRATE ECOLOGY, COMMUNITY ECOLOGY. *Current Pos:* vis asst prof, Univ Ark, 81-85, asst prof, 85-87, assoc prof, 87-92, PROF ZOOL, UNIV ARK, 92- *Personal Data:* b Manchester, Conn, July 19, 48; m 72, Peggy Jones; c Mallory E. *Educ:* Tufts Univ, BS, 71; Univ Ark, MS, 75; Utah State Univ, PhD(biol & ecol) 82. *Prof Exp:* Res assoc ecol, Manomet Bird Observ, 77-80; res asst ecol, Utah State Univ, 78-80; res ecologist, Bodega Marine Lab, Univ Calif, Berkeley, 80-81. *Mem:* Fel AAAS; fel Am Ornithologists Union; Cooper Ornith Soc; Ecol Soc Am; Wildlife Soc; Wilson Ornith Soc; Sigma Xi. *Res:* Vertebrate ecology; habitat selection; community structure; reproductive ecology; role of food supplies. *Mailing Add:* Dept Biol Sci Univ Ark SE632 Fayetteville AR 72701. *Fax:* 501-575-4010; *E-Mail:* ksmith@mercury.uark.edu

SMITH, KIRBY CAMPBELL, MATHEMATICS. *Current Pos:* ASSOC PROF MATH, TEX A&M UNIV, 75- *Personal Data:* b Dallas, Tex, Feb 7, 40. *Educ:* Southern Methodist Univ, BA, 62; Univ Wis, MS, 64, PhD(algebra), 69. *Prof Exp:* Asst prof math, Univ Miss, 68-70; asst prof math, Univ Okla, 70-75. *Mem:* Math Asn Am; Am Math Soc. *Res:* Noncommutative ring theory. *Mailing Add:* Dept Math Tex A&M Univ College Station TX 77843-3368

SMITH, KIRK ROBERT, ENERGY, ENVIRONMENTAL SCIENCE. *Current Pos:* PROF ENVIRON HEALTH SCI, SCH PUB HEALTH, UNIV CALIF, 95-, ASSOC DIR INT PROG, CTR OCCUP & ENVIRON HEALTH. *Personal Data:* b Berkeley, Calif, Jan 19, 47; m 77; c 1. *Educ:* Univ Calif, Berkeley, MPH, 72, PhD(environ health sci), 77. *Honors & Awards:* Graves Lectr, Yale Univ, 88. *Prof Exp:* Res staff sci educ, Lawrence Hall Sci, 69; founder & leader energy prog, Resource Systs Inst, East-West Ctr, 78-85, coordr environ risk, 86-95. *Concurrent Pos:* Res asst, Radio Astron Lab, Univ Calif, Berkeley, 69-; expert & lectr, US Cult & Sci Exchange Prog, 71-74; NIH fel, 74-77; seismic risk consult, State Calif, 73-74; researcher energy & resources prog, Univ Calif, Berkeley, 74-75; consult nuclear fuel cycle study, Am Phys Soc, 76; tech adv bd, Pres Interagency Review Group Nuclear Waste, 78-; affil & adj prof, Geog Dept & adj prof occup & environ health, Univ Hawaii; head, Collab Ctr Study Environ Risk & Develop, WHO; sr fel, Prog Environ, East-West Ctr, Honolulu. *Mem:* Nat Acad Sci; Fedn Am Scientists; Air & Waste Mgt Asn; AAAS; Int Soc Exposure Anal; Am Chem Soc; Soc Risk Anal; Int Soc Indoor Air Qual & Climat. *Res:* Relationships among environmental quality, health, resource use, development, and policy in the Asia-Pacific Region; evaluation of and control strategies for traditional and modern environmental hazards, particularly health-damaging and climate-warming air pollution from fuel use in developing countries; environmental issues in rural and urban economic development; development and application of risk assessment techniques to energy and chemical production/use in developing countries. *Mailing Add:* Sch Pub Health Univ Calif 140 Warren Hall Berkeley CA 94720-7360

SMITH, L(EROY) H(ARRINGTON), JR, MECHANICAL ENGINEERING. *Current Pos:* Compressor aerodynamicist gas turbines, Flight Propulsion Div, Gen Elec Aircraft Engines, 54-61, supvr turbomach develop, 61-67, mgr, Compressor Aerodyn Develop Unit, 67-69, mgr compressor & fan design tech opers, 69-71, mgr adv fan & compressor aerodyn, 71-74, mgr adv turbomach aerodyn, 75-80, mgr turbomach aero technol, 81-92, CONSULT TECHNOLOGIST TURBOMACH AERODYNAMICS, GEN ELEC AIRCRAFT ENGINES, 92- *Personal Data:* b Baltimore, Md, Nov 3, 28; m 51, Barbara Williams; c Glenn, Bruce & Cynthia. *Educ:* Johns Hopkins Univ, BE, 49, MS, 51, DEng, 54. *Honors & Awards:* Gas Turbine Award, Am Soc Mech Engrs, 81 & 87, R Tom Sawyer Award, 87, Aircraft Engine Award, 93; Charles P Stienmetz Award, Gen Elec Co, 87. *Mem:* Nat Acad Eng; fel Am Soc Mech Engrs. *Res:* Fluid mechanics; turbomachinery. *Mailing Add:* Gen Elec Aircraft Engines Mail Drop X211 Cincinnati OH 45215-6301

SMITH, LARRY, COLLOID CHEMISTRY, MANAGEMENT OF TECHNOLOGY APPLICATION. *Current Pos:* DIR RES ADMIN, SOUTHERN METHODIST UNIV, 88- *Personal Data:* b Hughes Springs, Tex, June 26, 44; m 66; c 2. *Educ:* NTex State Univ, BA, 68, PhD(phys chem, org chem), 70; Southern Methodist Univ, MBA, 87. *Prof Exp:* Res chemist, Corp Res, Am Hoechst Corp, 71-72; res chemist, 73-82, mgr, Adv Recovery Processes, Sun Oil Co, 82-86. *Concurrent Pos:* Res assoc, Univ Tex, Dallas, 72-73. *Mem:* Am Chem Soc; Soc Petrol Engrs; Soc Res Admin. *Res:* Surfactant, polymer and caustic flooding as methods of enhancing oil recovery; project management and the process of technology transfer from research and development lab to field pilots and to field-wide application; management of technology transfer. *Mailing Add:* 604 Stardust Lane Richardson TX 75080-5119

SMITH, LARRY, MATHEMATICS. *Current Pos:* INSTR MATH, CALIF STATE UNIV, LONG BEACH & CHAPMAN COL, 77- *Personal Data:* b New York, NY, May 13, 42; m 64. *Educ:* Brooklyn Col, BS, 62; Yale Univ, PhD(math), 66. *Prof Exp:* Actg instr math, Yale Univ, 65-66; instr, Princeton Univ, 66-68, asst prof, 68-69; assoc prof math, Univ Va, 69-77. *Concurrent Pos:* Air Force Off Sci Res fel math, Inst Advan Sci Study, France, 68-69. *Mem:* Am Math Soc. *Res:* Algebraic topology. *Mailing Add:* 19622 Canberra Lane Huntington Beach CA 92646-3750

SMITH, LARRY DEAN, ENZYMOLOGY, CELL CULTURE. *Current Pos:* DIR, H L SNYDER MEM RES FOUND, 73- *Personal Data:* b Tonkawa, Okla, Apr 1, 39; m 61; c 3. *Educ:* Okla State Univ, BS, 62, PhD(biochem), 67. *Prof Exp:* Assoc chemist, S R Noble Found, 67-71; assoc prof chem, Southwestern Col, 71-88. *Concurrent Pos:* Trainee endocrinol, Univ Calif, Riverside, 86-87. *Mem:* Am Asn Cancer Res; Am Asn Clin Chem; Am Chem Soc; Sigma Xi; AAAS. *Res:* Mechanism of neoplastic transformation as well as from neoplasia to metastasis; clinical assay procedures for detection of malignancy. *Mailing Add:* Snyder Res Found 1407 Wheat Rd Winfield KS 67156-4705

SMITH, LAURA BROOKS, MATHEMATICS EDUCATION. *Current Pos:* instr math, 84-88, ASST PROF MATH, NC CENT UNIV, 94- *Personal Data:* b Jamesville, NC, Oct 18, 44; m 65; John N; c Marchia & Marjorie. *Educ:* NC Cent Univ, BS, 65, MS, 83; NC State Univ, PhD(math educ), 93. *Prof Exp:* Asst prog mgr, Southeastern Educ Improvement Lab, 90-91; asst supvr QTEP, St Augustine's Col, 92-93. *Concurrent Pos:* Vis instr, NC Cent Univ, 77-80 & 84-87; adj instr, Univ Tampa, 83-84. *Mem:* Math Asn Am; Nat Coun Teachers Math. *Res:* Ways to increase the participation of underrepresented groups in advanced mathematics courses and in mathematics-related careers. *Mailing Add:* 1215 Little Creek Rd Durham NC 27713

SMITH, LAURA LEE WEISBRODT, food chemistry; deceased, see previous edition for last biography

SMITH, LAWRENCE HUBERT, PLANT PHYSIOLOGY. *Current Pos:* RETIRED. *Personal Data:* b Jackson, Mich, Apr 2, 30; m 50; c 5. *Educ:* Mich State Univ, PhD(crops), 59. *Prof Exp:* Instr pub schs, Mich, 55-57; asst, Mich State Univ, 57-59; from asst prof to assoc prof, Univ Minn, St Paul, 59-68, prof agron & plant genetics, 68. *Mem:* Am Soc Agron; Am Soc Plant Physiol. *Res:* Physiological genetics; crop physiology. *Mailing Add:* 10460 170th St Hugo MN 55038

SMITH, LAWTON HARCOURT, RADIOBIOLOGY. *Current Pos:* RETIRED. *Personal Data:* b Poughkeepsie, NY, Nov 15, 24; m 46; c 1. *Educ:* Univ Conn, BA, 50; Syracuse Univ, MS, 53, PhD(zool), 54. *Prof Exp:* Biologist, Oak Ridge Nat Lab, 54-90. *Concurrent Pos:* NSF sr fel, Neth, 60. *Mem:* Radiation Res Soc; Am Physiol Soc; Soc Exp Biol & Med. *Res:* Radiation injury, protection and recovery in mammals. *Mailing Add:* 77 Dolphin St Destin FL 32541

SMITH, LEHI TINGEN, MATHEMATICS. *Current Pos:* RETIRED. *Personal Data:* b Oakley, Idaho, Nov 29, 27; m 56; c 4. *Educ:* Ariz State Univ, BS, 48, MA, 55; Stanford Univ, EdD, 59. *Prof Exp:* Teacher high schs, Ariz, 53-54 & 55-57; asst math, Brigham Young Univ, 54; from asst to assoc prof, Ariz State Univ, 59-70, prof math, 70- *Mem:* Math Asn Am; Nat Coun Teachers Math. *Res:* Cultural influence on mathematical perceptions; design and appraisal of improved curricula for preparation of prospective mathematics teachers. *Mailing Add:* 514 E Broadmor Dr Tempe AZ 85282

SMITH, LELAND LEROY, ORGANIC CHEMISTRY, STEROIDS BIOCHEMISTRY. *Current Pos:* assoc prof biochem, 64-68, PROF BIOCHEM, UNIV TEX MED BR GALVESTON, 68- *Personal Data:* b Bradenton, Fla, May 14, 26; m 53; c 4. *Educ:* Univ Tex, BA, 46, MA, 48, PhD(chem), 50. *Prof Exp:* Res assoc chem, Columbia Univ, 50-51; res chemist, Southwest Found Res & Educ, 52-54; group leader, Lederle Labs, Inc, Am Cyanamid Co, 54-60 & Wyeth Labs, Inc, 60-64. *Concurrent Pos:* Vis scientist, Worcester Found Exp Biol, 51-52 & Oak Ridge Inst Nuclear Studies, 53. *Mem:* Am Chem Soc; Am Soc Biol Chemists; Oxygen Soc. *Res:* Steroid chemistry and biochemistry; steroid analysis, synthesis and biosynthesis; microbiological transformations of steroids; natural products chemistry; oxygen biochemistry. *Mailing Add:* 1 Rob Roy Rd Austin TX 78746-3137

SMITH, LEO ANTHONY, INDUSTRIAL ENGINEERING. *Current Pos:* From asst prof to assoc prof, 69-94, EMER PROF INDUST ENG, AUBURN UNIV, 94- *Personal Data:* b Waycross, Ga, May 22, 40; m 62; c 3. *Educ:* Ga Inst Technol, BS, 62, MS, 64; Purdue Univ, PhD(indust eng), 69. *Mem:* Am Inst Indust Engrs; Human Factors Soc; Ergonomics Soc; Am Indust Hyg Asn. *Res:* Evaluation of physiological and psychological aspects of human performance in man-machine systems; design of man-machine systems. *Mailing Add:* 320 Deer Run Rd Auburn AL 36832

SMITH, LESLIE E, PHYSICAL CHEMISTRY. *Current Pos:* CHIEF, POLYMERS DIV, NAT INST STANDARDS & TECHNOL, 82- *Personal Data:* b New York, NY, Jan 6, 41; m 63; c 2. *Educ:* Case Inst Technol, BSc, 62; Cath Univ Am, PhD(chem), 70. *Prof Exp:* Phys chemist, Polymers Div, Nat Bur Standards, 64-66 & 69-74, chief polymer stability & standards, 74-82. *Concurrent Pos:* Ed, Polymer Commun, 84- *Mem:* AAAS; Am Chem Soc. *Res:* Interfacial phenomena; optical properties of surfaces; ellipsometry; adsorption of polymers; polymer decomposition; diffusion and transport through polymers. *Mailing Add:* Polymers Div Nat Inst Standards & Technol Bldg 224 Rm A309 Washington DC 20899. *Fax:* 301-869-3239; *E-Mail:* smith@micf.nist.gov

SMITH, LEVERETT RALPH, SCIENCE EDUCATION. *Current Pos:* CHEM FAC MEM, CONTRA COSTA COL, 94- *Personal Data:* b Oakland, Calif, Feb 24, 49; m 78, Gretchen Peterson. *Educ:* Univ Calif, Santa Cruz, BA, 70; Cornell Univ, MS, 74, PhD(chem), 76. *Prof Exp:* Teacher chem & math, Techiman Sec Sch, Ghana, 70-72; fel chem, Dept Entomol, Cornell Univ, 76-77; assoc fel chem, Col Environ Sci & Forestry, State Univ NY, 77-78; asst prof chem, Oberlin Col, 78-81; chem ed, Acad Press, 81-83; environ lab mgr, Kennedy/Jenks/Chilton Consults, 83-91; chem fac mem, Merrit Col, 91-94. *Mem:* Am Chem Soc; Sigma Xi. *Res:* Exploratory organic chemistry; chemical ecology; environmental science; analytical chemistry. *Mailing Add:* 622 Clayton Ave El Cerrito CA 94530

SMITH, LEVERING, ordnance; deceased, see previous edition for last biography

SMITH, LEWIS DENNIS, EMBRYOLOGY, BIOLOGY. *Current Pos:* dean, Sch Biol Sci, 87-90, PROF, DEPT DEVELOP & CELL BIOL, UNIV CALIF, IRVINE, 87-, EXEC VCHANCELLOR, 90- *Personal Data:* b Muncie, Ind, Jan 18, 38; m 61; c 2. *Educ:* Indiana Univ, BA, 59, PhD(expl biol), 63. *Prof Exp:* Prof biol, Purdue Univ, 73-87, from assoc head to head, Dept Biol Sci, 79-87. *Concurrent Pos:* Asst embryologist, Argonne Nat Lab, 64-67, assoc biologist, 67-69; assoc prof, Purdue Univ, 69-73; res career develop award, Indiana Univ, 70-75; mem, NIH, 71-75; instr embryol, Woods Hole Marine Biol Lab, 72, 73, 74 & 88-89; mem, NASA, Space Biol Peer Rev Panel, Am Inst Biol Sci, 80-85 & Comt Space Biol & Med, Space Studies Bd, 84-, chmn, 86-; Guggenheim fel, 87; mem, bd sci counselors, 89- *Mem:* Soc Develop Biol; Int Soc Develop Biol; AAAS; Am Soc Biochem & Molecular Biol. *Res:* Regulation of protein synthesis during cogenesis and oocyte maturation with emphasis on recruitment of MRNA for translation; steroid interactions with the amphibian oocyte in the induction of oocyte maturation with emphasis on the mechanism(s) involved in cell cycle regulation; role of cytoplasmic germ plasm in leading to the formation, migration, and differentiation of primordial germ cells. *Mailing Add:* 509 Admin Univ Calif Irvine CA 92697. *Fax:* 714-725-2513; *E-Mail:* ldsmith@orioncf.uci.edu

SMITH, LEWIS OLIVER, JR, ORGANIC CHEMISTRY. *Current Pos:* RETIRED. *Personal Data:* b Eckley, Colo, Nov 20, 22; m 47, 68, Dorothy L Paulsen; c Creig & Darrell. *Educ:* Grove City Col, BS, 44; Univ Rochester, PhD(org chem), 47. *Prof Exp:* Asst chem, Univ Rochester, 44-46; head dept, Polytech Inst PR, 47-48; instr, Wilson Col, 48-50, asst prof, 50-52; from asst prof to prof chem, Valparaiso Univ, 52-88, chmn dept, 59-61 & 63-65. *Mem:* Am Chem Soc; Sigma Xi. *Res:* Yield studies in organic chemical reactions; molecular analogies; synthesis and comparison of properties; matrix catalysis. *Mailing Add:* 2702 Maplewood Ave Valparaiso IN 46383-2219

SMITH, LEWIS WILBERT, RUMINANT NUTRITION, FORAGE BIOCHEMISTRY. *Current Pos:* dairy scientist, Dairy Cattle Res Br, 65-72, res animal scientist, Agr Environ Qual Inst, 73-75, lab chief, Feed Energy Conserv Lab, Animal Physiol & Genetics Inst, 75-79, dir Animal Sci Inst, 79-88, NAT PROG LEADER ANIMAL NUTRIT, AGR RES SERV, USDA, BELTSVILLE, MD, 88- *Personal Data:* b York, Pa, Jan 13, 37; m 63; c 2. *Educ:* Univ Md, BS, 59, MS, 61, PhD(animal sci), 68. *Prof Exp:* health serv officer, radiochem, Comn Corps, Pub Health Serv, RA Taft Sanit Eng Ctr, Ohio, 62-64. *Concurrent Pos:* Mem, Animal Waste Mgt Comt, 70-73, chmn, 72-73, Regulatory Agency Comt, 76-, mem, Subcomt Environ Qual, 78-81, Prog Comt Animal Waste Mgt, Am Soc Animal Sci, 82-83; Grad asst animal nutrit, Dept Animal Sci, Univ Md, 58-59. *Mem:* Am Dairy Sci Asn; Am Soc Animal Sci; Am Registry Prof Animal Scientist. *Res:* Ruminant nutrition and biochemistry; the improvement of production efficiency, quality of animal products and profitability; analytical chemistry; biochemistry of forages; digestive kinetics of structural carbohydrates in forages. *Mailing Add:* 406 Neale Ct Silver Spring MD 20901

SMITH, LLOYD, PHYSICS OF BEAMS. *Current Pos:* RETIRED. *Personal Data:* b Chicago, Ill, Feb, 28, 22. *Educ:* Univ Ill, BS, 39, MS, 42; Ohio State Univ, PhD(physics), 46. *Prof Exp:* Res scientist, Lawrence Radiation Lab, Univ Calif, 48-91. *Mem:* Fel Am Phys Soc. *Res:* Physics of beams. *Mailing Add:* 1510 Olympus Ave Berkeley CA 94708

SMITH, LLOYD HENRY, SYSTEMS ENGINEERING, SYSTEMS DYNAMICS & THINKING. *Current Pos:* CONSULT, SYST SOLUTIONS, 97- *Personal Data:* b Seattle, Wash, May 1, 42; m 66, Beatrice M Forshay; c Roger H & Hilliary M. *Educ:* Calif State Polytech Univ, Pomona, BS, 64; Univ Calif, Los Angeles, MS, 68; Naval Postgrad Sch, PhD(eng), 74. *Prof Exp:* Engr, Naval Weapons Ctr, US Navy, 64-80, head, Technol Progs Off, 80-83, head, Conventional Weapons Div, 83-87, tech dir, Naval Strike Warfare Ctr, 87-91, proj dir, Weapons Div, Naval Air Warfare Ctr, 91-97. *Concurrent Pos:* Mem, Chief Naval Opers Exec Panel, 88; lectr, Chapman Col, 89-90; chmn, Survivability Tech Comt, Am Inst Aeronaut & Astronaut, 89. *Mem:* Assoc fel Am Inst Aeronaut & Astronaut. *Res:* Major innovation in acquisition reform and teaming with industry. *Mailing Add:* PO Box 1446 Ridgecrest CA 93556. *E-Mail:* lloyd@ndti.net

SMITH, LLOYD HOLLINGWORTH, JR, MEDICINE. *Current Pos:* chmn dept, 64-85, PROF MED, SCH MED, UNIV CALIF, SAN FRANCISCO, 64-, ASSOC DEAN, 85- *Personal Data:* b Easley, SC, Mar 27, 24; m 54, Margaret Avery; c Virginia (Broudy), Charlotte (Saxby), Christopher, Elizabeth (Wahl), Rebecca (Coffman) & Jeffrey. *Educ:* Washington & Lee Univ, AB, 44; Harvard Med Sch, MD, 48; Am Bd Internal Med, dipl, 59. *Honors & Awards:* Kober Medal, Asn Am Physicians. *Prof Exp:* Intern & asst resident med, Mass Gen Hosp, 48-50; chief med resident, 56, chief endocrine & metab unit, 58-63; vis investr, Oxford Univ, 63-64. *Concurrent Pos:* Harvard Soc Fels fel biochem, Harvard Univ & Pub Health Res Inst New York, Inc, 52-54; USPHS res fel, Karolinska Inst, Sweden, 54-55; res fel biochem, Huntington Labs, 57-58; counr, Nat Heart Inst; mem, President's Sci Adv Comt, 70-74; mem, Bd Overseers, Harvard Univ, 74-80. *Mem:* Inst Med-Nat Acad Sci; Am Soc Clin Invest; Endocrine Soc; Am Fedn Clin Res; Am Soc Biol Chemists; Asn Am Physicians. *Res:* Medical research, particularly areas of inherited metabolic diseases. *Mailing Add:* San Francisco Med Ctr Sch Med Univ Calif San Francisco CA 94143

SMITH, LLOYD MICHAEL, AUTOMATED DNA ANALYSIS, DNA-BASED DIAGNOSTICS FLUORESCENCE & NUCLEIC ACID CHEMISTRY. *Current Pos:* asst prof, Univ Wis-Madison, 87-92, assoc prof chem, 92-95, H I Romnes fac fel, 94-99, PROF CHEM, UNIV WIS-MADISON, 95- *Personal Data:* b Berkeley, Calif, Oct 3, 54. *Educ:* Univ Calif, Berkeley, AB, 76; Stanford Univ, PhD(biophys), 81. *Honors & Awards:* Asn Biomolecular Resource Facil Award, 97. *Prof Exp:* Res asst chem, Univ Calif, Berkeley, 75-77; res fel, Stanford Univ, lectr, 81-82; res fel biol, Calif Inst Technol, 82-85, sr res fel, 85-87. *Concurrent Pos:* Consult, Appl Biosysts Inc, 83-92, Pharmacia, Inc, 92-95; Eli Lilly anal chem award, 89-91; NSF presidential young investr award, 89-94; res scholar lectr, Drew Univ, NJ, 91; mem, Human Genome Coord Comt, Dept Energy, 91-; mem, Nat Adv Coun Human Genome Res, NIH, 92-96, Genome Study Sect, 96-; co-founder & consult bd dir, Third Wave Technol, Inc 93-; consult, bd dirs, Visible Genetics, Inc, 95- *Mem:* Am Chem Soc; AAAS; Sigma Xi; Am Soc Mass Spectrometry. *Res:* Development of novel DNA sequencing and detection technologies. *Mailing Add:* 1101 University Ave Dept Chem Madison WI 53706-1396. *E-Mail:* smith@chem.wisc.edu

SMITH, LLOYD MUIR, FOOD CHEMISTRY. *Current Pos:* RETIRED. *Personal Data:* b Calgary, Alta, Feb 20, 17; nat US; m 48; c 2. *Educ:* Univ Alta, BSc, 43, MSc, 49; Univ Calif, PhD(agr chem), 53. *Honors & Awards:* Award of Merit, Am Oil Chem Soc, 83. *Prof Exp:* Instr dairy indust, Univ Alta, 46-49, lectr, 49-50; asst dairy indust, Univ Calif, Davis, 50-52; asst prof dairying, Univ Alta, 52-54; from asst prof dairy indust to prof food sci & technol, Univ Calif, Davis, 54-87, chemist, 67-87, emer prof food sci & technol, 87- *Concurrent Pos:* Sr Fulbright res scholar, Dept Sci & Indust Res, NZ, 61-62; vis prof, Dept Food Sci, Rutgers Univ, 75-76; Fulbright lectr, Dept Foods & Exp Nutrit, Univ Sao Paulo, Sao Paulo, Brazil, 86. *Mem:* Am Oil Chem Soc; Am Dairy Sci Asn; Nutrition Today Soc; Inst Food Technologists. *Res:* Chemistry of fats and other lipids; composition, structure and deterioration of lipids in foods; technology of edible fats, oils and emulsions; chemistry of milk. *Mailing Add:* Dept Food Sci & Technol 110 FS & TB Univ Calif Davis CA 95616

SMITH, LORRAINE CATHERINE, SCIENTIFIC EDITING, TOXICOLOGICAL DATA EVALUATION. *Current Pos:* sci evaluator, Health Can, 86-92, head, Agr Chem Sect, Toxicol Eval Div, Health Protection Br, 92-95, head, Toxicol Food Sect, Health Eval Div, Pest Mgt Regulatory Agency, 95-97, HEAD, HERBICIDE TOXICOL EVAL SECT, HEALTHCAN, 97- *Personal Data:* b Toronto, Ont, May 8, 31; m 53, Donald Alan; c Peter D, Carol L (Tallman), Suzanne C (Gagnon), Janet D (Findlay) & Paul N. *Educ:* Univ Toronto, BA, 53, MA, 54; Univ Ottawa, PhD(biol), 63. *Prof Exp:* Res asst physiol, Univ Toronto, 54-55; defence res sci officer, Defence Res Med Labs, Defence Res Bd Can, 55-57; res assoc physiol biol, Univ Ottawa, 63-65; res assoc zool biol, Carleton Univ, 70-75, sessional lectr, 73, res fel, 75-77; asst ed, Can J Fisheries & Aquatic Sci, Dept Fisheries & Oceans, Can, 76-86. *Concurrent Pos:* Ed, Canadian Field-Naturalist, 72-81; contractor, Nat Mus Natural Sci, Can, 75-77; mem, Working Group Biosphere Res, Can/Man & Biosphere Proj, UNESCO, 82-89. *Mem:* Can Soc Zoologists (secy, 85-); Soc Toxicol Can; Coun Biol Ed. *Res:* Evaluation, analysis and management of toxicological scientific data; physiology and ecology of small mammals, especially population dynamics and reproductive biology; scientific editing and communications; general natural history. *Mailing Add:* 2144 Huntley Rd RR 3 Stittsville ON K2S 1B8 Can. *Fax:* 613-736-3505; *E-Mail:* lsmith@pmra.hwc.ca

SMITH, LOUIS C, BIOCHEMISTRY. *Current Pos:* asst prof, Baylor Col Med, 66-74, assoc prof biochem, 74-77, assoc prof med, biochem & cell biol, 77-79, PROF MED, BIOCHEM & CELL BIOL, BAYLOR COL MED, 79- *Personal Data:* b Hobbs, NMex, Nov 24, 37; m 92, Laurel A Buckwalter; c Sherilyn, Loree (LaChance) & Karyn. *Educ:* Abilene Christian Col, BS, 59; Univ Tex, Austin, PhD(biochem), 63. *Prof Exp:* Res assoc biochem, Mass Inst Technol, 63-66, instr, 64-66. *Concurrent Pos:* NIH fel, Mass Inst Technol, 63-65; estab investr, Am Heart Asn, 72-77; mem study sect, Nat Heart, Lung & Blood Inst, NIH, 75-87. *Mem:* AAAS; Am Chem Soc; Am Soc Cell Biol; NY Acad Sci; Soc Anal Cytol; Inst Elec & Electronics Engrs; Int Atherosclerosis Soc; Am Soc Biochem & Molecular Biol. *Res:* Lipoprotein metabolism; digital fluorescence imaging microscopy, gene therapy. *Mailing Add:* Dept Med Baylor Col Med Alkek A601 Houston TX 77030-2797. *Fax:* 713-798-7400

SMITH, LOUIS CHARLES, PHYSICAL ORGANIC CHEMISTRY. *Current Pos:* RETIRED. *Personal Data:* b Rochester, NY, Sept 16, 18; m 41, Mildred Powell; c Allyson S (Schafer) & Louis C III. *Educ:* Univ Rochester, BS, 40; Columbia Univ, PhD(chem), 44. *Prof Exp:* Instr chem, Univ Vt, 43-44; sr res assoc, Nat Defense Res Comt, Carnegie Inst Technol, 44-45; res chemist, Gen Elec Co, 45-46; sect chief, US Naval Ord Lab, 46-49; group leader, Los Alamos Sci Lab, 49-74, assoc group leader 74-79. *Concurrent Pos:* Consult, 86- *Mem:* Am Chem Soc; Am Phys Soc; Sigma Xi. *Res:* Development of military high explosives; properties of military explosives and propellants. *Mailing Add:* 27 Alleghenny Irvine CA 92620. *E-Mail:* LouCSmith@prodigy.com

SMITH, LOUIS DE SPAIN, microbiology; deceased, see previous edition for last biography

SMITH, LOUIS LIVINGSTON, SURGERY. *Current Pos:* from instr to prof surg, Loma Linda Univ, 56-92, dir, Surg Res Lab, 59-90, Chief, 71-90, EMER CHIEF, PERIPHERAL VASCULAR SURG SERV, MED CTR, LOMA LINA UNIV, 90- *Personal Data:* b College Place, Wash, May 19, 25; c 1. *Educ:* Walla Walla Col, BA, 48; Loma Linda Univ, MD, 48. *Prof Exp:* From intern to sr resident, Los Angeles Co Gen Hosp, 48-57. *Concurrent Pos:* NIH res fel, Peter Bent Brigham Hosp & Harvard Univ, 57-59; Harvey Cushing res fel, 58-59. *Mem:* AMA; fel Am Col Surgeons; Am Surg Asn; Int Cardiovasc Soc; Int Soc Surg; Soc Vasc Surg. *Res:* Surgical metabolism; shock; surgical trauma. *Mailing Add:* 1680 Smiley Heights Dr Redlands CA 92373-6533

SMITH, LOWELL R, ORGANIC CHEMISTRY. *Current Pos:* sr res chemist, Monsanto Co, 60-63, sr res specialist org chem, 63-75, sci fel, 76-90, SR SCI FEL, MONSANTO CO, 90- *Personal Data:* b Minneapolis, Minn, Nov 21, 33; m 60; c 2. *Educ:* Univ Minn, BA, 55, PhD(org chem), 60. *Prof Exp:* Chemist, Russell-Miller Milling Co, 55-56. *Mem:* Am Chem Soc. *Res:* Indole, organophosphorus and heterocyclic chemistry; chemistry of oxalyl chloride; reaction mechanisms; chemical processing; amino acids; isocyanates. *Mailing Add:* Monsanto Co T-408 800 N Lindbergh Blvd St Louis MO 63166

SMITH, LOWELL SCOTT, MEDICAL DIAGNOSTIC IMAGING, SOLID STATE PHYSICS. *Current Pos:* PHYSICIST, GEN ELEC CORP RES & DEVELOP, 76- *Personal Data:* b Akron, Ohio, July 20, 50. *Educ:* Univ Rochester, BS, 72; Univ Pa, PhD(physics), 76. *Mem:* Am Phys Soc; Inst Elec & Electronics Engrs. *Res:* Medical ultrasonic imaging; transducer design-nuclear magnetic resonance imaging and spectroscopy; physical acoustics. *Mailing Add:* Gen Elec Corp Res & Develop Div PO Box 8 Schenectady NY 12301. *E-Mail:* smithls@crd.ge.com

SMITH, LUCIAN ANDERSON, medicine; deceased, see previous edition for last biography

SMITH, LUTHER MICHAEL, ENGINEERING DEVELOPMENT, COCHLEAR IMPLANT DESIGN. *Current Pos:* PROG DIR, SINAI SAMARITAN MED CTR, 89- *Personal Data:* b Clayton, Ga, Jan 6, 48; m 68; c 2. *Educ:* Univ Colo, BS, 74; Colo State Univ, MS, 79. *Prof Exp:* Comn officer, US Publ Health Serv Corps, 74-75; sr electronic specialist, Colo State Univ, 76-77, res asst, 78-79; design engr, Varian/Diasonics Ultrasound, 79-84; proj engr, Symbion Inc, 84-89. *Concurrent Pos:* Consult, 88- *Mem:* Am Soc Artificial Internal Organs. *Res:* Totally implantable mechanical artificial heart and ventricular assistant device; design and patient testing of neural stimulation devices and patient test equipment for stimulation of the cochlea of deaf patients; cochlear implant hearing prosthesis design; author of various publications. *Mailing Add:* Sinai Samaritan Med Ctr 945 N 12th St Rm W-419 Milwaukee WI 53201-0342

SMITH, LUTHER W, PHYSICS, MATHEMATICS. *Current Pos:* RETIRED. *Personal Data:* b Greenfield, Mass, Apr 26, 32. *Educ:* Univ Mass, BA, 53; Univ Kans, MS, 56. *Prof Exp:* Res physicist, Res Ctr, 58-82; optical engr, AO Instrument Group, Warner-Lambert, 82-; optical mgr, Am Optical. *Mem:* Optical Soc Am. *Res:* Diffraction theory of image formation; phase microscopy; surface guided waves. *Mailing Add:* 31 South St Troy NH 03465

SMITH, LYLE W, PHYSICS. *Current Pos:* RETIRED. *Personal Data:* b Normal, Ill, Feb 20, 20; m 42; c 2. *Educ:* Univ Ill, BS, 42, MS, 43, PhD(physics), 48. *Prof Exp:* Asst physics, Univ Ill, 43-44 & 46-47, asst chem, 44-46, assoc physics, 47-48; physicist, Brookhaven Nat Lab, 48-61, sr physicist, 61-87. *Mem:* AAAS; fel Am Phys Soc; NY Acad Sci; Sigma Xi. *Res:* High energy particle accelerators; high energy elementary particle physics. *Mailing Add:* 112 Arlington Ave Port Jefferson NY 11777

SMITH, LYNWOOD S, FISH PHYSIOLOGY. *Current Pos:* from asst prof to prof, 65-92, assoc dir instr, Sch Fisheries, 86-91, EMER PROF FISHERIES, COL FISHERIES, UNIV WASH, 93- *Personal Data:* b Snohomish, Wash, Nov 15, 28; m 51, Betty A Mars; c 3. *Educ:* Univ Wash, BS, 52, MS, 55, PhD(zool), 62. *Prof Exp:* Teacher high sch, Wash, 52-53; instr biol & zool, Olympic Col, 55-60; asst prof zool, Univ Victoria, 62-65. *Res:* Osmoregulation and blood circulation, effects of pollutants, general environmental physiology and functional anatomy in teleost fish; effects of stress and exercise on salmonids particularly during smolting; digestion physiology in fish; physiological effects of oil on fish. *Mailing Add:* 17323 Clover Rd Bothell WA 98012-9141

SMITH, M SUSAN, neuroendocrinology, reproductive physiology, for more information see previous edition

SMITH, MALCOLM (KINMONTH), PHYSICS, INSTRUMENTATION. *Current Pos:* assoc prof to prof, 66-85, EMER PROF PHYSICS & APPL PHYSICS, UNIV MASS, LOWELL, 85- *Personal Data:* b Morristown, NJ, Dec 19, 19; m 60, Yvonne Soucie; c 3. *Educ:* Haverford Col, BS, 41; Columbia Univ, MA, 54. *Prof Exp:* Teacher, Gow Sch, NY, 48-52 & Putney Sch, Vt, 52-56; engr, Woods Hole Oceanog Inst, 56-58; ed, Phys Sci Study Comt, 58-60; exec officer physics, Sci Teaching Ctr, Mass Inst Technol, 60-66. *Concurrent Pos:* Consult, Educ Develop Ctr, Newton, Mass, 57-68, Inst Serv Educ, DC, 67-69 & Tech Educ Res Ctr, Cambridge, Mass, 70-80. *Mem:* Inst Elec & Electronics Engrs; Am Asn Physics Teachers. *Res:* Author of physics textbooks. *Mailing Add:* 1035 Scott Dr Apt 239 Prescott AZ 86301

SMITH, MALCOLM CRAWFORD, JR, FOOD SYSTEMS, NUTRITION. *Current Pos:* SR STAFF SCIENTIST, OCEANEERING SPACE SYSTS, 93- *Personal Data:* b Kingsville, Tex, Jan 2, 36; m 61; c 2. *Educ:* Tex A&M Univ, DVM, 59; Purdue Univ, MS, 65. *Prof Exp:* Base vet, USAF, Holloman AFB, NMex, 59-62; chief vet serv, Sidi Slimane Air Base, Morocco, 62-63, Toul Rosieres Air Base, France, 63-65. *Concurrent Pos:* Chief, Food & Nutrit Br, Johnson Space Ctr, NASA; food systs consult, 83- *Mem:* Asn Military Surg US; Inst Food Technol. *Res:* Food technology; nutrition; aerospace life support systems; public health; marine biology. *Mailing Add:* 3410 Miramar Dr La Porte TX 77571

SMITH, MANIS JAMES, JR, CARDIOVASCULAR ENDOCRINOLOGY. *Current Pos:* Fel, 75-77, ASST PROF, DEPT PHYSIOL & BIOPHYS, UNIV MISS MED CTR, 77- *Personal Data:* b Memphis, Tenn, Sept 26, 40; div. *Educ:* Memphis State Univ, BS, 62; Palmer Col Chiropractic, DC, 65; La State Univ Med Ctr, PhD(physiol), 74. *Concurrent Pos:* Prin investr, Miss Heart Asn, 78-85. *Mem:* AAAS. *Res:* Control of adrenal steroidogenesis; radioimmunoassay development. *Mailing Add:* Four Jennifer Ct Madison MS 39110

SMITH, MARCIA SUE, SCIENCE POLICY, SPACE POLICY. *Current Pos:* specialist, Aerospace Policy, 86-91, Sci & Technol Policy, 91-96, SPECIALIST, AEROSPACE & TELECOMMUN POLICY, CONG RES SERV, 96- *Personal Data:* b Greenfield, Mass, Feb 22, 51. *Educ:* Syracuse Univ, BA, 72. *Prof Exp:* Corresp & admin asst space, Am Inst Aeronaut & Astronaut, 73-75; analyst aerospace & energy technol, Sci Policy Res Div, Cong Res Serv, Libr Cong, 75-80, specialist, aerospace & energy systs, 80-85; exec dir, Nat Comn Space, 85-86. *Concurrent Pos:* Distinguished lectr, Am Inst Aeronaut & Astronaut, 83-88; chmn, US Task Force Int Space Yr, Int Astron Fedn, 90-92; co-chair, Comt Space Activ & Soc, Int Acad Astronaut, 93-; consult to mem & comts Cong, space progs; trustee, Int Acad Astronaut; bd dirs, Int Inst Space Law, 96- *Mem:* Fel Am Inst Aeronaut & Astronaut; fel Brit Interplanetary Soc; Sigma Xi; NY Acad Sci; Am Astronaut Soc (pres, 85-86); Int Inst Space Law; emer mem Women in Aerospace (pres, 87). *Res:* Policy analysis for congress on military and civilian space activities (foreign and domestic) and telecommunications issues. *Mailing Add:* 6015 N Ninth St Arlington VA 22205-1403

SMITH, MARIAN JOSE, BIOCHEMISTRY. *Current Pos:* from instr to assoc prof, 48-69, chmn, Chem Dept, 76-79 & 82-87, PROF CHEM, COL ST ELIZABETH, 69- *Personal Data:* b Hoboken, NJ, Oct 24, 15. *Educ:* Col St Elizabeth, AB, 36; Fordham Univ, MS, 54, PhD(biochem), 60. *Honors & Awards:* E Emmet Reid Award, Mid Atlantic Region, Am Chem Soc, 81. *Prof Exp:* Chemist, Reed & Carnrick, 37-45; teacher parochial schs, 45-47. *Concurrent Pos:* AEC equip grant, 61-62; NSF travel grant, Int Symp, Goettingen, Ger, 61; Ciba Corp res grant, Univ Glasgow, 62; USPHS grant, 65-66; NSF res partic grant, 68; NSF grant for sci educ workshops, 80 & 81 & NJ State, 87-90. *Mem:* Am Chem Soc; fel Am Inst Chemists. *Res:* Activity of enzymes related to nucleic acid metabolism in tumor-bearing rats; biochemistry aging. *Mailing Add:* Col St Elizabeth 2 Convent Rd Morristown NJ 07961-6989

SMITH, MARIAN W, METHODS TEACHING MATHEMATICS, INCORPORATING HISTORY MATHEMATICS IN TEACHING. *Current Pos:* ASSOC PROF MATH EDUC, FLA A&M UNIV, 91- *Personal Data:* b Cuthbert, Ga, Jan 17, 42; div; c Bryon F. *Educ:* Fort Valley State Col, BS, 64; Univ Ga, MEd, 71; Ga State Univ, PhD(math educ), 89. *Prof Exp:* Staff mem math, Griffin-Spalding Sch Syst, 64-77 & Fort Valley State Col, 78-91. *Concurrent Pos:* Consult implementing stand, Fla A&M Univ. *Mem:* Math Asn Am; Nat Coun Teachers Math; Nat Asn Am. *Res:* Analyze data to determine if new approach experimented with preservice teachers is a determining factor in change of attitude for their likeness of mathematics. *Mailing Add:* 1301 Smoke Rise Lane Tallahassee FL 32311. *Fax:* 850-561-2211

SMITH, MARION EDMONDS, BIOCHEMISTRY, NEUROSCIENCE & IMMUNOLOGY. *Current Pos:* res assoc med, Sch Med, Stanford Univ, 56-63, instr, 63-71, sr scientist med, 71-74, PROF NEUROL, SCH MED, STANFORD UNIV, 83-; RES BIOCHEMIST, VET ADMIN HOSP, PALO ALTO, 62- *Personal Data:* b Susanville, Calif, July 13, 26; m 55, Kendric C; c Nancy (Vincent) & Martha (Silverman). *Educ:* Univ Calif, BA, 52, MA, 54, PhD(biochem), 56. *Honors & Awards:* Javits Investr Award, 88. *Prof Exp:* Asst, Univ Calif, 53-56. *Concurrent Pos:* Prin Investr, NIH, 62-97, bd sci coun, 73-77, Neurol Disorder Prog Proj Rev Comt, NINCDS, 80-84; Nat Mult Sclerosis Fundamental Sci Adv Bd, 81-86 & 94-96; neurobiol merit rev, Vet Admin, 83-86. *Mem:* Am Soc Neurochem; Int Soc Neurochem; Am Soc Neurochem (secy, 81-87, pres, 91-93); Soc Neurosci; Am Soc Biol Chemists. *Res:* Lipid and protein metabolism in nervous system; biochemistry of demyelinating diseases; myelin metabolism and function; astrocyte activation; myelin phagocytosis immunology. *Mailing Add:* Dept Neurol 127A Vet Admin Hosp 3801 Miranda Ave Palo Alto CA 94304. *Fax:* 650-858-3999; *E-Mail:* mesmith@leland.stanford.edu

SMITH, MARION L(EROY), MECHANICAL ENGINEERING. *Current Pos:* From instr to assoc prof, 47-58, prof mech eng & assoc dean, Col Eng, 58-84, EMER ASSOC DEAN, OHIO STATE UNIV, 84- *Personal Data:* b Sharon, Pa, June 3, 23; m 44; c 3. *Educ:* La State Univ, BS, 44; Ohio State Univ, MS, 48. *Concurrent Pos:* Mem staff year-in-indust prog, Eng Dept, E I du Pont de Nemours & Co, 56-57; mem, State Bd Regist Prof Engrs & Surveyors, 75-84, chmn, 81-84; mem, Uniform Exam Comt, Nat Coun Eng Examrs, 76, chmn, 81-83. *Mem:* fel Am Soc Mech Engrs; fel Am Soc Eng Educ; Soc Automotive Eng; Nat Soc Prof Engrs; Nat Coun Eng Examrs. *Res:* Fundamentals of fuels and combustion; mechanism of oxidation of hydrocarbons, particularly pre-combustion reactions; dual fuel diesel engines; characteristics of miniature engine generator sets; methods of heat dissipation from aircraft compartments; gas turbines. *Mailing Add:* 4135 Rowanne Ct Columbus OH 43214

SMITH, MARK ALAN, MASS SPECTROMETRY, LOW TEMPERATURE KINETICS. *Current Pos:* from asst prof to assoc prof, 85-94, PROF CHEM, UNIV ARIZ, 94- *Personal Data:* b Jan 10, 56; m 78, Margaret E Helfrich; c Nicole L, Maxwell T & Emeline E. *Educ:* Univ Ore, BS, 76; Mass Inst Technol, SM, 78; Univ Colo, PhD (chem), 82. *Prof Exp:* Fel, Univ Toronto, 82-85. *Concurrent Pos:* Res award, Am Soc Mass Spectrometry, 88; Humboldt res fel, Alexander von Humboldt Stiftung, 92. *Mem:* Am Phys Soc; Am Chem Soc. *Res:* Very low temperature kinetics of ion-molecule and radical-molecule reactions of interstellar and atmospheric interest; investigation of relaxation phenomena in supersonic gas flows by experimental and theoretic means. *Mailing Add:* Dept Chem Univ Ariz Tucson AZ 85721. *Fax:* 520-621-8407; *E-Mail:* msmith@u.arizona.edu

SMITH, MARK ANDREW, MATHEMATICS, FUNCTIONAL ANALYSIS. *Current Pos:* from asst prof to assoc prof, 77-84, PROF MATH, MIAMI UNIV, 84- *Personal Data:* b East Brady, Pa, Nov 24, 47; m 69; c 2. *Educ:* Indiana Univ Pa, BS, 69; Univ Ill, Urbana, MS, 70, PhD(math), 75. *Prof Exp:* Asst prof, Lake Forest Col, 75-77. *Mem:* Am Math Soc; Sigma Xi. *Res:* Geometry of Banach spaces. *Mailing Add:* Dept Math & Statist Miami Univ Oxford OH 45056-1641

SMITH, MARK ANTHONY, POST TRANSLATIONAL PROTEIN MODIFICATIONS, PROEOLYTIC PROCESSING. *Current Pos:* res assoc, 92-93, instr neuropath, 94-95, ASST PROF DEPT NEUROPATH, CASE WESTERN RES UNIV, 95- *Personal Data:* b Leicester, Eng, Aug 15, 65. *Educ:* Univ Durham, Eng, BSc, 86; Univ Nottingham, Eng, PhD(biochem), 90. *Prof Exp:* Biochemist, Sandoz Res Inst, Vienna, Austria, 90, Karl Landsteiner res fel, 91-92. *Concurrent Pos:* Karl Landsteiner res fel, 91-92; Am Philos Soc fel, 95-97; vol scientist, McKinley Mus, 95- *Mem:* Biochem Soc; Am Asn Neuropath; Int Soc Neurochem; Histochem Soc; AAAS. *Res:* Biochemical characterization of post translational modification and proteolytic generation/fragmentation of proteins involved in neurodegenerative disease (eg, Alzheimer disease, Parkinson disease and Amyotrophic Lateral Sclerosis). *Mailing Add:* Inst Path Dept Neuropath Case Western Res Univ 2085 Adelbert Rd Cleveland OH 44106. *Fax:* 216-368-8964; *E-Mail:* mas21@po.cwru.edu

SMITH, MARK K, ENGINEERING ADMINISTRATION. *Current Pos:* CONSULT, 73- *Personal Data:* b New York, NY, Feb 14, 28. *Educ:* Mass Inst Technol, BS, 51, PhD, 54. *Prof Exp:* Vpres, Geophys Serv, Inc, 62-67, pres, 67-69; vpres, Tex Instruments, 69-73. *Mem:* Nat Acad Eng. *Mailing Add:* PO Box 189 Main St Norwich VT 05055

SMITH, MARK STEPHEN, EMERGENCY MEDICINE. *Current Pos:* Asst prof & actg chmn, 84-85, assoc prof, 85-89, PROF EMERGENCY MED, GEORGE WASHINGTON UNIV MED CTR, 89-, CHMN, 85- *Personal Data:* US citizen. *Educ:* Swarthmore Col, BA, 68; Stanford Univ, MS, 71; Yale Univ, MD, 77. *Concurrent Pos:* Dir, Ronald Reagan Inst Emergency Med. *Mem:* Am Col Emergency Physicians; Soc Acad Emergency Med; Am Col Physician Execs; Math Asn Am; Sigma Xi; AMA. *Res:* Clinical decision making in emergency medicine; emergency medicine informetrics; cardiovascular emergencies. *Mailing Add:* 9005 Jones Mill Rd Chevy Chase MD 20815-5616. *Fax:* 202-994-3924

SMITH, MARTHA KATHLEEN, MATHEMATICS. *Current Pos:* from asst prof to assoc prof, 73-85, PROF MATH, UNIV TEX, AUSTIN, 85- *Personal Data:* b Detroit, Mich, Mar 14, 44. *Educ:* Univ Mich, Ann Arbor, BA, 65; Univ Chicago, MS, 67, PhD(math), 70. *Prof Exp:* G C Evans instr math, Rice Univ, 70-72; asst prof math, Wash Univ, 72-73. *Mem:* Am Math Soc; Math Asn Am; Asn Women Math. *Res:* Ring theory. *Mailing Add:* Dept Math Univ Tex Austin TX 78712-1082

SMITH, MARTIN BRISTOW, physical chemistry; deceased, see previous edition for last biography

SMITH, MARTYN THOMAS, CARCINOGENESIS, RISK ASSESSMENT. *Current Pos:* asst prof toxicol, 82-87, ASSOC PROF TOXICOL, UNIV CALIF, BERKELEY, 87- *Personal Data:* b Lincoln, UK, Aug 17, 55; m 79; c 2. *Educ:* Queen Elizabeth Col, Univ London, BS, 77; Med Col St Bartholomews Hosp, PhD (biochem), 80. *Prof Exp:* Asst forensic med, Karolinska Inst, 80-81; teaching fel, Toxicol Pharmacol, Sch Pharmacy, Univ London, 81-82. *Concurrent Pos:* Assoc dir, Health Effects Component, UC Toxic Substances Prog, 85-; prin invest, toxicol, Health Risk Assoc, Superfund Prog Proj, NIEHS, 87-; staff scientist, Lawrence Berkeley Lab, 87- *Mem:* Genetic & Environ Toxicol Asn; Am Asn Cancer Res; Am Asn Adv Sci; Soc Toxicol; Soc Free Radical Res. *Res:* Mechanisms by which toxic chemicals damage cells and alter the genetic material to produce disease, such as cancer; specific chemicals of interest are benzene, bipyridyl herbicides, MPTP and quinones. *Mailing Add:* Sch Pub Health Univ Calif Berkeley CA 94720-0001

SMITH, MARVIN ARTELL, NUCLEIC ACIDS, PLANT MOLECULAR BIOLOGY. *Current Pos:* from asst prof to assoc prof, 66-74, PROF CHEM & BIOCHEM, BRIGHAM YOUNG UNIV, PROVO, UTAH, 74- *Personal Data:* b Ogden, Utah, Apr 8, 36; m 60; c 8. *Educ:* Utah State Univ, BS, 60; Univ Wis-Madison, MS, 62, PhD(biochem), 64. *Prof Exp:* Res fel, Med Ctr, NY Univ, 64-66. *Concurrent Pos:* Fel, Warf Res, Univ Wis, 60-62, NIH, 62-64, & 64-66, spec fel, 72-73; vis scientist chem & biochem, Union Carbide, NY, 64, Univ Calif, Davis, 72-73, plant genetics, Weizmann Inst, Israel, 80; Donald F Jones res fel, 72-73; vis prof chem & biochem, Kuwait Univ, 78-80. *Mem:* Am Soc Biol Chemists; Int Soc Plant Molecular Biol; AAAS; Sigma Xi. *Res:* Developmental biochemistry and gene expression, particularly in higher plants; coordination of nuclear and organelle genetic and enzymic systems. *Mailing Add:* Dept Chem & Biochem Brigham Young Univ Provo UT 84602-1001. *Fax:* 801-378-5474

SMITH, MARY ANN HARVEY, NUTRITION, MENTAL RETARDATION. *Current Pos:* PROF NUTRIT, CHILD DEVELOP CTR, UNIV TENN MED UNITS, MEMPHIS, 77-, PROF & DIR, DIV CLIN NUTRIT, 86-, PROF & COORDR, CLIN NUTRIT PROG, MEMPHIS STATE UNIV, 86- *Personal Data:* b Camden, Ark, Jan 29, 40; m 71. *Educ:* Henderson State Col, BSE, 60; Univ Tenn, MS, 62, PhD(food sci, nutrit), 65. *Prof Exp:* Instr food sci, Univ Ala, 61-62; therapeut dietitian, Ft Sanders Hosp, 64-65; asst prof foods & nutrit, Mid Tenn State Univ, 65-67; from asst prof to assoc prof nutrit, Child Develop Ctr, Univ Tenn Med Units, Memphis, 67-77, assoc dir, 84-87, chief dept, 67-82. *Concurrent Pos:* Adj prof nutrit, Col Home Econ, Univ Tenn, 67-87, Sch Home Econ, Univ Ark, 70-87 & Dept Home Econ, Col Educ, Univ Miss, 79-87. *Mem:* Am Dietetic Asn; Soc Nutrit Educ; Am Asn Ment Deficiency; Nutrit Today Soc. *Res:* Nutrition as related to mental retardation, including nutritional status of the retarded, feeding techniques and management of inborn errors of metabolism; imprintation of national dietary guidelines; day care-nutrition guidelines for children with special needs. *Mailing Add:* Home Econ Dept Memphis State Univ 4006 Manning Hall Memphis TN 38152

SMITH, MAURICE JOHN VERNON, urology, for more information see previous edition

SMITH, MAURICE VERNON, APICULTURE. *Current Pos:* RETIRED. *Personal Data:* b Toronto, Ont, June 4, 20; m 48, Catherine Hales; c Catherine, Judith, Brock & Derek. *Educ:* Univ Toronto, BSA, 42, MSA, 54; Cornell Univ, PhD, 57. *Prof Exp:* From asst to assoc prof environ biol, Univ Guelph, 49-83. *Mem:* Sigma Xi. *Res:* Honeybee behavior and pollination; bee breeding; insect photography. *Mailing Add:* 3 Young St Guelph ON N1G 1M1 Can

SMITH, MAYNARD E, ANALYTICAL CHEMISTRY. *Current Pos:* RETIRED. *Personal Data:* b Boston, Mass, Nov 29, 16; m 41, Frances Mahoney; c Teresa & Patricia. *Educ:* Mass Inst Technol, PhD(chem), 49. *Prof Exp:* Asst chem, Mass Inst Technol, 41-49; anal chemist, Los Alamos Nat Lab, 49-72, sect leader, 72-81. *Mem:* Am Chem Soc; Am Inst Chemists. *Res:* Gases in metals; mass spectrometry; gas chromatography. *Mailing Add:* 75 Mesa Verde Dr Los Alamos NM 87544

SMITH, MELVIN I, MECHANICAL & CHEMICAL ENGINEERING. *Current Pos:* RETIRED. *Personal Data:* b New York, NY, July 21, 24; m 46; c 4. *Educ:* City Col New York, BChE, 44; Columbia Univ, MS, 47, EngScD, 55. *Prof Exp:* Res technologist, Res Dept, Socony Mobil Oil Co, Inc, 47-58, supv technologist, 58-72, mgr lubricants, Tech Serv Dept, Mobil Oil Corp, 72-84. *Mem:* Am Soc Lubrication Engrs; Am Soc Mech Engrs. *Res:* Application problems and formulation of lubricating, hydraulic and metal processing fluids. *Mailing Add:* 75 Mallard Dr Avon CT 06001

SMITH, MEREDITH FORD, international nutrition, community nutrition, for more information see previous edition

SMITH, MICHAEL, BIOCHEMISTRY, BIOTECHNOLOGY. *Current Pos:* assoc prof, Univ BC, 66-70, dir, Biotechnol Lab, 87-96, sci leader, Potein Eng Networks Ctrs Excellence, 90-94, interim dir, Biomed Res Ctr, 91-92, PROF BIOCHEM, UNIV BC, 70-, UNIV KILLAM PROF, 93-, PETER WALL DISTINGUISHED PROF BIOTECHNOL, 94- *Personal Data:* b Blackpool, Eng, Apr 26, 32; Can citizen; m 60; c 3. *Educ:* Univ Man, BSc, 53, PhD(chem), 56. *Hon Degrees:* Various from US & foreign univs, 88-96. *Honors & Awards:* Nobel Prize Chem, 93; Boehringer Mannheim Prize, Can Biochem Soc, 81; Gairdner Found Int Award, 86; Award Excellence, Genetics Soc Can, 88; G Malcolm Brown Award, Can Fed Biol Soc, 89; Drummond Lectr, Univ Calgary, 89, Darwin Lect, 89; Flavelle Medal, Royal Soc Can, 92; Golden Plate Award, Am Acad Achievement, 94; Medal Honour, Can Med Asn, 94; Henry Friesen Award, Royal Col Physicians & Surgs Can, 94; Jack Bell Philanthropic Award, 94; R M Taylor Medal & Award, Can Cancer Soc, 95. *Prof Exp:* Fel, BC Res Coun, 56-60; res assoc, Inst Enzyme Res, Univ Wis, 60-61; head chem sect, Vancouver Lab, Fisheries Res Bd Can, 61-66. *Concurrent Pos:* Med res assoc, Med Res Coun Can, 66-79, career investr, 79; prog comt & chmn, Molecular Biol Prog Subcomt, Int Cong Biochem, 67-79; consult, Zymo Genetics Inc, Seattle, 82-88; adv comt res, Nat Cancer Inst Can, 89-95, EJLB Found, Can, 94-; adv coun sci & technol, Govt Can, 96- *Mem:* Foreign assoc Nat Acad Sci; fel Royal Soc Chem; Sigma Xi; hon mem Can Soc Chem Invest; fel Royal Soc Can; Can Biochem Soc; fel Chem Inst Can; Genetics Soc Am; AAAS; Am Soc Biol Chemists; Genetics Soc Can; Europ Acad Arts & Sci; hon fel Royal Col Physicians. *Res:* Nucleic acid and nucleotide chemistry and biochemistry using in-vitro mutagenesis to study gene expression. *Mailing Add:* Biotechnol Lab Univ BC Rm 237 Westbrook Bldg 6174 Univ Blvd Vancouver BC V6T 1Z3 Can

SMITH, MICHAEL ALEXIS, PETROLEUM GEOLOGY, GEOCHEMISTRY. *Current Pos:* CHIEF GEOLOGIST, GEO-STRAT INC, 92-; MINERALS MGT SERV, US DEPT INTERIOR, 94- *Personal Data:* b Boston, Mass, Nov 08, 44; m 71, Nancy Wilson; c Christine. *Educ:* Univ Mich, BS, 66; Univ Kans, MS, 69; Univ Tex, PhD(geol), 75. *Honors &*

Awards: Lederle Award, Am Pharm Asn, 76; Sidney Riegelman Res Achievement Award Pharmaceut, 94. *Prof Exp:* Marine geologist, US Geol Surv, 66-68, petrol geologist & geochemist, 75-81; res geochemist, Getty Oil Co, 81-83, supvr basin eval & struct geol, 83-84; res assoc, Texaco Inc, 84-92. *Concurrent Pos:* Mem, IGCP Proj 219, 86-91; adj prof, Dept Geol, Emory Univ, Atlanta, 88-89; geophysicist, Minerals Mgt Serv, New Orleans, 94- *Mem:* Fel Geol Soc Am; Am Asn Petrol Geologists; Am Geophys Union; Am Asn Stragtig Palynologists; Soc Org Petrol. *Res:* Geological and depositional facies controls on worldwide petroleum occurrence; international basin geology; organic petrology and regional source-rock geochemistry; biostratigraphy, paleogeography and paleoecology; thermal maturity analysis. *Mailing Add:* US Dept Interior Mineral Mgt Serv 1201 Elmwood Park Blvd New Orleans LA 70123. Fax: 281-579-2154

SMITH, MICHAEL CLAUDE, INDUSTRIAL & MANUFACTURING ENGINEERING. *Current Pos:* ASST VPRES/SR SCIENTIST, SCI APPLN INT CORP, 83- *Personal Data:* b Winston-Salem, NC, May 31, 49; m 70; c 4. *Educ:* Univ Tenn, Knoxville, BSIE, 71, MSIE, 74; Univ Mo, Columbia, PhD(indust eng), 77. *Prof Exp:* Indust engr, Buckeye Cellulose Corp, 71-72, St Mary's Med Ctr, Knoxville, Tenn, 72-74; asst prof, Ore State Univ, 77-79; asst prof indust eng, Univ Mo, Columbia, 79-82. *Concurrent Pos:* Consult, Pharm Serv, Vet Admin, 78-, Univ Mo Hosp & Clin, 79-82; prin investr, Directorate Mgt Sci, Air Force Logistic Command, 81-82. *Mem:* Sr mem Am Inst Indust Eng; Operations Res Soc Am. *Res:* Concurrent engineering in design and manufacturing; organizational assessment and strategic planning; information systems planning. *Mailing Add:* Sci Appln Int Corp MS 1-7-6 1710 Goodridge Dr McLean VA 22102. Fax: 703-893-2187; *E-Mail:* miksmith@mcl.saic.com

SMITH, MICHAEL HOWARD, ECOLOGY, EVOLUTION. *Current Pos:* DIR SAVANNAH RIVER ECOLOGY LAB, 73-; assoc prof, 70-77, PROF ZOOL, UNIV GA, 77- *Personal Data:* b San Pedro, Calif, Aug 30, 38; m 58; c 2. *Educ:* San Diego State Col, AB, 60, MA, 62; Univ Fla, PhD(zool), 66. *Prof Exp:* Res assoc zool, Inst Ecol, Univ Ga, 66-67, asst prof, 67-71; assoc prof, Univ Tex, 70-71. *Concurrent Pos:* NSF res grant, 66-68; AEC Comn grants, 67-; dir, Savannah River Ecol Lab, Aiken, SC, 73- *Mem:* Am Soc Mammal; Soc Study Evolution; Ecol Soc Am; Am Soc Ichthyologists & Herpetologists; Am Soc Naturalists; Soc Syst Zool; Wildlife Soc; Am Fisheries Soc; Soc Pop Ecol. *Res:* Behavior; various biological aspects of vertebrates as they relate to the study of speciation and population ecology. *Mailing Add:* Savannah River Ecol Lab Drawer E Aiken SC 29801

SMITH, MICHAEL JAMES, ENVIRONMENTAL CHEMISTRY, HAZARDOUS & NUCLEAR WASTE DISPOSAL & TREATMENT. *Current Pos:* VPRES ENVIRON & ENG SERVS, RADIAN CORP, OAK RIDGE, TENN, 91- *Personal Data:* b East St Louis, Ill, Feb 18, 45; m 67; c 2. *Educ:* Southern Ill Univ, BA, 67; Univ Mo, Columbia, MA, 69, PhD(environ chem), 72; Stanford Univ, MBA, 89. *Honors & Awards:* Am Bicentennial Comn, 75. *Prof Exp:* From asst prof to assoc prof anal & environ chem, Wright State Univ, 72-77, assoc dir to dir, Brehm Lab, 74-77; mgr, Chem Sci Lab, Rockwell Hanford Opers, 77-79, mgr engineered barriers proj, 79-80, mgr, Eng Dept, 80-84, prin mgr res, 84-86; dir, Western Eng Div, Albuquerque, IT Corp, 86-89, vpres anal serv, Knoxville, Tenn, 90-91. *Concurrent Pos:* Consult, Monsanto Res Corp, Am Nuclear Soc; Nat Mgt NSF & Inst Environ Educ, 74; mem proposal rev panel, NSF Off Exp Prog, 74-77; consult, Miami Conservancy Dist, 75-76; consult, Atlantic Richfield Hanford Co, 76-77; mem nuclear safety rev group, Dept Energy, 89- *Mem:* Am Chem Soc; AAAS. *Res:* Environmental engineering (air, water and hazardous waste systems) including hazardous chemical and nuclear waste disposal; coal acid mine drainage treatment; heavy metal contamination studies, pesticides analyses, air toxics and water and hazardous waste treatment; RI/FS and remediation projects; environmental chemistry. *Mailing Add:* 12220 Ansley Ct Knoxville TN 37922-1524

SMITH, MICHAEL JAMES, HUMAN FACTORS ENGINEERING, ERGONOMICS. *Current Pos:* PROF TEACHING & RES, DEPT INDUST ENG, UNIV WIS, 84- *Personal Data:* b Madison, Wis, May 12, 45; m 68; c 2. *Educ:* Univ Wis-Madison, BA, 68, MA, 70, PhD(indust psychol), 73. *Honors & Awards:* Super Serv Award, US Pub Health Serv, 80. *Prof Exp:* Res analyst, Wis Dept Indust & Labor, 71-74; res psychologist, Nat Inst Occup Safety & Health, 74-84. *Concurrent Pos:* Mem, World Health Orgn Panel on Psychosocial Hazards, 82-84, Am Psychol Asn Panel on Job Design & Stress, 90, Canadian Adv Panel on Cumulative Trauma Disorders, 91-94; Sci adv, Workplace Health Fund, 88-94; ed, Int J Human-Computer Interaction, 89-; bd mem, Int Comn on Human Aspects of Comput, 90- *Mem:* Human Factors Soc; Asn Comput Math; Am Soc Testing & Mat; Inst Industr Engrs; Am Psychol Asn. *Res:* Relationship between the design of work and human responses to that design; ergonomics; job stress; organizational structure; safety and health exposures. *Mailing Add:* Dept Indust Eng Univ Wis 1513 University Ave Madison WI 53706. *E-Mail:* mjsmith@engr.wisc.edu

SMITH, MICHAEL JOSEPH, DEVELOPMENTAL & MOLECULAR BIOLOGY. *Current Pos:* from asst prof to assoc prof, 76-87, PROF BIOL, SIMON FRASER UNIV, 87- *Personal Data:* b Bay City, Mich, Jan 20, 39; m 78; c 2. *Educ:* St Mary's Col, Calif, BS, 63; Univ BC, PhD(zool), 69. *Prof Exp:* Asst prof zool, Univ Nebr, Lincoln, 69-71; res fel biol, Calif Inst Technol, 71-73, sr res fel, 73-76. *Concurrent Pos:* Spec res fel, USPHS, Calif Inst Technol, 71-73; res grant, Nat Res Coun Can, Simon Fraser Univ, 77-88 & Brit Columbia Health Care Res Found grant, 78-82. *Mem:* Can Soc Cell Biologist; Soc Develop Biol. *Res:* Molecular biology of eukaryote development; phylogeny and evolution of genomic and mitochondrial DNA sequence. *Mailing Add:* Biochem Lab BC Fac Med No 237 6174 University Blvd Vancouver BC V6T 1Z3 Can

SMITH, MICHAEL KAVANAGH, PROGRAM VERIFICATION, FORMAL SEMANTICS OF PROGRAMMING LANGUAGES. *Current Pos:* vpres, Computational Logic Inc, 83-85, pres, 85-87, exec vpres, 87-95, FOUNDER & DIR, COMPUTATIONAL LOGIC INC, 83-, PRES, 95- *Personal Data:* b San Francisco, Calif, May 20, 49; m 76; c 2. *Educ:* Princeton Univ, BSE, 71; Univ Tex, PhD(computer sci), 81. *Prof Exp:* Res assoc, Univ Tex, 82-85. *Mem:* Asn Comput Mach; Inst Elec & Electronics Engrs; AAAS. *Res:* Formal semantics of programming languages, program verification, and mechanical theorem proving, especially as applied to the Ada programming lanaguage. *Mailing Add:* Computational Logic Inc 1717 W Sixth Suite 290 Austin TX 78703. *E-Mail:* mksmith@cli.com

SMITH, MICHAEL LEW, ENDOCRINOLOGY, HUMAN PHYSIOLOGY. *Current Pos:* PROF, DEPT SOCIAL WORK, SW TEX STATE UNIV, 86- *Personal Data:* b Ashland, Kans. *Educ:* Emporia Kans State Univ, BA, 70; Purdue Univ, PhD(chem), 74. *Prof Exp:* Biochemist, Madigan Army Med Ctr, 75-77, chief, Res Lab, 77-80; asst chief, Dept Clin Res, William Beaumont Army Med Ctr, 80-86. *Mem:* Endocrine Soc; Am Asn Clin Chemists. *Res:* Functions of prolactin in male mammals. *Mailing Add:* Dept Social Work SW Tex State Univ Col Univ Dr San Marcos TX 78666-4616

SMITH, MICHAEL R, BACTERIAL PHYSIOLOGY, METHANOGENESIS. *Current Pos:* RES MICROBIOLOGIST, WESTERN REGIONAL RES CTR, AGR RES SERV, USDA, 80- *Personal Data:* b Portland, Ore, June 15, 45. *Educ:* Calif State Univ, Long Beach, BS, 67; Univ Calif, Los Angeles, PhD(microbiol), 76. *Prof Exp:* Fel microbiol, Dept Microbiol, Univ Calif, Los Angeles, 70-76, postdoctoral scholar microbiol, Sch Pub Health, 76-79, res assoc, 79-80. *Mem:* Am Soc Microbiol; AAAS; Sigma Xi. *Res:* Bacterial methanogenesis; bacterial spore germination; agricultural research; methane production; anaerobic microbiology. *Mailing Add:* 1415 Ashwood Dr Martinez CA 94553

SMITH, MILTON LOUIS, INDUSTRIAL ENGINEERING. *Current Pos:* Asst, 65-68, assoc prof, 68-78, PROF INDUST ENG, TEX TECH UNIV, 78- *Personal Data:* b Childress, Tex, May 30, 39; m 66; c 2. *Educ:* Tex Tech Univ, BS, 61, MS, 66, PhD(indust eng), 68. *Mem:* Am Inst Indust Engrs; Opers Res Soc Am. *Res:* Job sequencing; hail damage to solar collectors/reflectors; risk and lacerative hazard from fractured glass; modeling of flexible manufacturing systems. *Mailing Add:* Dept Indust Eng Tex Tech Univ Lubbock TX 79409-3061

SMITH, MILTON REYNOLDS, BIOCHEMISTRY, PHYSIOLOGY. *Current Pos:* CHEMIST, NAT WILDLIFE HEALTH RES CTR, 85- *Personal Data:* b Chicago, Ill, Mar 15, 34; m 76, Gretchen Tidd; c Dirk M. *Educ:* Knox Col, BA, 56; Univ Ariz, MS, 58, PhD(biochem), 63. *Prof Exp:* Res assoc biochem, Univ Ariz, 58-63; sr biochemist, Eli Lilly & Co, 63-80; tech dir, Hepar Industs, 80-83. *Concurrent Pos:* Instr, Ind Cent Col, 67-71; career consult, Knox Col, 72. *Mem:* AAAS; Am Chem Soc; Am Inst Chemists; NY Acad Sci; Asn Off Anal Chemists Int; Int Union Pure & Appl Chem. *Res:* Isolation research in the fields of lipids, proteins and enzymes; protein chemistry and endocrinology; analytical toxicology. *Mailing Add:* 7010 Parkshore Ct Middleton WI 53562-3702

SMITH, MORRIS WADE, HORTICULTURE, PLANT PHYSIOLOGY. *Current Pos:* res horticulturist, Sci & Educ Admin-Agr Res, Coastal Plain Exp Sta, 78-84, RES HORTICULTURIST, SCI & EDUC ADMIN-AGR RES, USDA, 84- *Personal Data:* b Baytown, Tex, Aug 1, 38; m 62; c 2. *Educ:* Tex Technol Univ, BS, 64; Tex A&M Univ, MS, 72, PhD(hort), 77. *Prof Exp:* Technician II, Dept Hort, Tex A&M Univ, 65-78. *Mem:* Am Soc Hort Sci. *Res:* Nutrition concerning container-grown ornamental plants; irrigation; herbicide and plant growth regulator research. *Mailing Add:* 2423 Michael Dr Tifton GA 31794

SMITH, NAT E, MEDICINE. *Current Pos:* STAFF PHYSICIAN, VET ADMIN MED CTR, 89- *Personal Data:* b Bartow, Fla, Nov 29, 22; m 53; c 7. *Educ:* Erskine Col, AB, 43; Med Col Ga, MD, 49. *Prof Exp:* Intern, Gorgas Hosp, Ancon, CZ, 49-50; med resident, DC Gen Hosp & George Washington Univ, Hosp, 52-54; staff physician, Vet Admin, 55-57; from instr to prof med, Col Med, Univ Ill, 57-75, assoc dean, 62-75; dean sch med, Mercer Univ, 74-76; assoc dean & prof med, Bowman Gray Sch Med, Wake Forest Univ, 76-89. *Mem:* Am Rheumatism Asn. *Res:* Rheumatic diseases; methods and evaluation of medical education. *Mailing Add:* 2900 Country Club Rd Winston-Salem NC 27104

SMITH, NATHAN ELBERT, ANIMAL SCIENCE. *Current Pos:* ASST PROF ANIMAL SCI, UNIV CALIF, DAVIS, 74- *Personal Data:* b Avon, NY, Apr 30, 36; m 58; c 2. *Educ:* Cornell Univ, BS, 67; Univ Calif, Davis, PhD(nutrit), 70. *Prof Exp:* Res nutritionist, Univ Calif, Davis, 70-71; asst prof animal sci, Cornell Univ, 71-74. *Mem:* Am Dairy Sci Asn; Am Soc Animal Sci. *Res:* Animal nutrition with emphasis on dairy nutrition, animal metabolism, mathematical and computer modeling of animal metabolism and animal production systems. *Mailing Add:* Purina Mills Inc PO Box 66812 St Louis MO 63166-6812. Fax: 314-768-4433

SMITH, NATHAN JAMES, PEDIATRICS. *Current Pos:* prof pediat, 65-89, EMER PROF PEDIAT, SCH MED, UNIV WASH, 89- *Personal Data:* b Cuba City, Wis, Oct 12, 21; m 46; c 3. *Educ:* Univ Wis, BA, 43, MD, 45. *Prof Exp:* Fulbright scholar, Univ Paris, 50; instr pediat, Sch Med, Temple Univ, 51-53; from asst prof to assoc prof, Univ Calif, Los Angeles, 54-56; prof &

chmn dept, Sch Med, Univ Wis, 57-65. *Concurrent Pos:* Mem, Hemat Training Grant Comt, NIH, 60-; spec asst nutrit progs to Secy Health, Educ & Welfare, 70-71; pediatrician-in-chief, King Co Hosp, 65-89. *Mem:* Am Soc Hemat; Soc Pediat Res; Am Pediat Soc; Soc Exp Biol & Med; Am Acad Pediat. *Res:* Nutrition as applied to pediatrics; sports and nutrition; sports and children. *Mailing Add:* Univ Wash Sports Med Box 354060 Seattle WA 98195-4060

SMITH, NATHAN LEWIS, III, ENZYMOLOGY, IMMUNOCHEMISTRY. *Current Pos:* CONSULT, 77- *Personal Data:* b Baltimore, Md, May 12, 43; m 65; c 2. *Educ:* Univ Miami, BS, 66; Univ Calif, Irvine, PhD(biol), 72. *Prof Exp:* Jr specialist biochem, Univ Calif, Irvine, 71-72; asst res biologist, 72-74; group leader diag, Nelson Res & Develop Co, 73-74; staff immunologist, Cordis Corp, 75-77. *Mem:* Am Chem Soc. *Res:* Design and development of clinical diagnostic test procedures especially enzyme tagged immunoassays. *Mailing Add:* 192 Lacy St North Andover MA 01845

SMITH, NATHAN MCKAY, ZOOLOGY. *Current Pos:* RETIRED. *Personal Data:* b Wendell, Idaho, Apr 22, 35; m 53; c 5. *Educ:* Eastern Ore Col, BS, 61; Ore State Univ, MS, 64; Brigham Young Univ, MLS, 69, PhD(zool), 72. *Prof Exp:* Teacher, The Dalles, Ore, 61-63 & La Grande, 65-66; prof libr info sci, Brigham Young Univ, 70-97. *Mem:* Soc Study Amphibians & Reptiles. *Res:* Reptilian taxonomy, comparative anatomy and natural history. *Mailing Add:* Brigham Young Univ 5042 Harold B Lee Libr Provo UT 84602-1035

SMITH, NED ALLAN, COASTAL BIOLOGY. *Current Pos:* ASST DIR, SCRIPPS AQUARIUM, 95- *Personal Data:* b Philadelphia, Pa, Feb 21, 40; m 63; c 2. *Educ:* Juniata Col, BS, 62; Univ Pittsburgh, MS, 65, PhD(biol), 67. *Prof Exp:* USPHS fel, Tufts Univ, Medford, 67-69; asst prof zool, Univ NC, Chapel Hill, 69-75; educ & exhibs consult, NC Off Marine Affairs, 75, dir, NC Aquarium Pine Knoll Shores, 75-89, dir, NC Aquariums, 89-95. *Mem:* AAAS; Am Asn Zool Parks & Aquariums. *Res:* Neurophysiological control of spontaneously active invertebrate muscle. *Mailing Add:* 9500 Gilman Dr La Jolla CA 92093-0207

SMITH, NED PHILIP, PHYSICAL OCEANOGRAPHY. *Current Pos:* assoc res scientist, 77-82, sr res scientist, Ft Pierce, Fla, 82-90, SR SCI, HARBOR BR OCEANOG INST, 90- *Personal Data:* b Beaver Dam, Wis, Dec 3, 42. *Educ:* Univ Wis-Madison, BS, 65, MS, 67, PhD(limnol & oceanog), 72. *Prof Exp:* Asst prof phys oceanog, Univ Tex, Austin, 72-77. *Mem:* Am Meteorol Soc; Oceanog Soc; Am Geophys Union. *Res:* Descriptive physical oceanography, including continental shelf circulation and intracoastal tides; heat budget of estuaries. *Mailing Add:* Harbor Br Oceanog Inst 5600 US 1 N Ft Pierce FL 34946

SMITH, NELSON S(TUART), JR, ELECTRICAL ENGINEERING. *Current Pos:* From instr to assoc prof, 56-70, PROF ELEC ENG, WVA UNIV, 70- *Personal Data:* b Weirton, WVa, Aug 9, 29; m 51; c 3. *Educ:* WVa Univ, BSEE, 56, MSEE, 58; Univ Pittsburgh, DSc(electrets), 62. *Concurrent Pos:* NSF res grant, 63-66; elec engr, Morgantown Energy Technol Ctr, 65- *Mem:* Am Soc Eng Educ; Inst Elec & Electronics Engrs. *Res:* Dielectric absorption currents; electrets; electrogasdynamics; solid state gas sensors. *Mailing Add:* Dept Elec Eng WVa Univ Morgantown WV 26506-6101

SMITH, NEVILLE VINCENT, SURFACE SCIENCE. *Current Pos:* MEM STAFF, BELL LABS, 69- *Personal Data:* b Leeds, Eng, Apr 21, 42; m 70; c 2. *Educ:* Queens' Col, Cambridge Univ, BA, 63, MA & PhD(physics), 67. *Honors & Awards:* Davisson-Germer Prize, Am Phys Soc, 91. *Prof Exp:* Res assoc physics, Stanford Univ, 66-69. *Concurrent Pos:* Res head, Condensed State Physics Dept, Bell Labs, 78-81. *Mem:* Fel Am Phys Soc. *Res:* Optical properties and band structures of solids; photoemission and electronic structure of solids and surfaces; synchrotron radiation spectroscopies; inverse photoemission; spin-polarized electron spectroscopy. *Mailing Add:* Lawrence Berkeley Lab 1 Cyclotron Rd Berkeley CA 94720. *Fax:* 908-582-2783

SMITH, NORMAN B, DEXTROSE CRYSTALLIZATION, FLUE GAS DESULFURIZATION. *Current Pos:* CHIEF CHEM ENGR & CHIEF EXEC OFFICER, BIOTEK ASSOC INT, 87- *Personal Data:* b Springfield, Ill, May 27, 27; m 51, Marilyn Augspurger; c Peter B, Debbie J, Suzanne L & Holly A. *Educ:* Univ Ill, BS, 51, BS, 52. *Prof Exp:* Asst supt fermentation, Pabst Brewing Co, Peoria, Ill, 52-55; mgr fermentation, Grain Processing Corp, Muscatine, Iowa, 55-59, res engr, 59-66; chief chem engr, Stanley Consults Inc, 66-87. *Mem:* Am Chem Soc; Nat Soc Prof Engrs; Am Stand Testing Methods; Soc Indust Microbiologists. *Res:* Enzyme purification/utilization for starch hydrolysis; awarded US and foreign patents in field of dextrose crystallization and production of corn starch/ethyl alcohol; author on subjects of flue gas desulfurization, fuel alcohol production, energy conservation, quality control procedures. *Mailing Add:* 1110 Robin Rd Muscatine IA 52761. *Fax:* 319-263-7201; *E-Mail:* nsbiotek@muscanet.com

SMITH, NORMAN CUTLER, PHOTOGEOLOGY, SCIENTIFIC EDITING & WRITING. *Current Pos:* VPRES, OIL MINING CORP, 87- *Personal Data:* b Paterson, NJ, Mar 18, 15; m 42, Dorothy P Barnes; c Roxanne L (German) & Lee C. *Educ:* Washington & Lee Univ, AB, 37. *Prof Exp:* Field geologist, Stand Oil Co, Venezuela, 38-40; teaching fel, Harvard Univ Grad Sch Geol, 40-42; geologist, Humble Oil & Refining Co, 46-49; independent consult geologist, 72-79; mgr data anal & reporting, Law Eng Testing Co, 79-82; dir, 88-93, coordr res prog, sr acad int learning, NC Ctr Creative Retirement, Univ NC, Asheville, 93. *Concurrent Pos:* Consult geologist, 46-; founder, pres & chmn bd, Coun Sci Socs, Dallas-Ft Worth, 57-60; exec dir, Am Asn Petrol Geologists, 62-72; mem, Nat Comt Geol, 63-72; bd dirs, Tulsa Found, 74-78, Tulsa Sci Ctr, 76-78; fac & pres bd, Geol Col Srs, Univ NC, Asheville, 88-93, dir, 88-93, coordr res prog, Sr Acad Int Learning, NC Ctr Creative Retirement, 93; adult educ, Brevard Col & Blue Ridge Col, 88-89. *Mem:* Fel Geol Soc Am; fel AAAS; emer mem Am Asn Petrol Geologists. *Res:* Articles and chapters in books on exploration geology; more than 150 proprietary reports, photogeological reconnaissance, petroleum exploration for more than 50 oil companies and engineering firms; numerous scientific and technical publications. *Mailing Add:* 105 Windward Dr Asheville NC 28803-9555

SMITH, NORMAN DWIGHT, SEDIMENTOLOGY. *Current Pos:* From asst prof to assoc prof, 67-78, dept head, 88-93, PROF GEOL, UNIV ILL, CHICAGO, 78- *Personal Data:* b Natural Bridge, NY, Jan 26, 41; m 67; c 2. *Educ:* St Lawrence Univ, BS, 62; Brown Univ, MS, 64, PhD(geol), 67. *Concurrent Pos:* Vis assoc prof geol, Univ Alta, 74-75; consult geologist, Anglo-Am Corp, SAfrica, 78-80 & Coun Sci & Indust Res, SAfrica, 82; Fulbright fel, 82; ed, J Sedimentary Petrol, 83-88; fel, Coun Sci & Indust Res, SAfrica, 89. *Mem:* Soc Econ Paleontologists & Mineralogists; Geol Soc Am; Int Asn Sedimentologists; Nat Asn Geol Teachers; Am Asn Petrol Geologists. *Res:* Fluvial sedimentology; stratigraphy and sedimentology of clastic rocks; limnology and lacustrine sedimentology; origin of placers; glacimarine sedimentation. *Mailing Add:* Dept Geol Sci Univ Ill Chicago Chicago IL 60607

SMITH, NORMAN OBED, PHYSICAL CHEMISTRY. *Current Pos:* from assoc prof to prof, 50-84, chmn dept, 74-78, EMER PROF CHEM, FORDHAM UNIV, 84- *Personal Data:* b Winnipeg, Man, Jan 23, 14; nat US; m 44; c 3. *Educ:* Univ Man, BSc, 35, MSc, 36; NY Univ, PhD(phys chem), 39. *Prof Exp:* Asst chem, Univ Man, 39-40, lectr, 40-46, from asst prof to assoc prof, 46-50. *Concurrent Pos:* Res assoc, Air Force contract, 50-51. *Mem:* Sr mem Am Chem Soc; fel Chem Inst Can. *Res:* Heterogeneous equilibria; hydrates; solid solutions; clathrates; solubility of gases; author or co-author of more than 50 publications. *Mailing Add:* Dept Chem Fordham Univ Bronx NY 10458

SMITH, NORMAN SHERRILL, WILDLIFE ECOLOGY. *Current Pos:* RETIRED. *Personal Data:* b Roseburg, Ore, May 22, 32; m 57; c 2. *Educ:* Ore State Univ, BSc, 58; Univ Mont, MSc, 62; Wash State Univ, PhD(zool), 69. *Prof Exp:* Lab technician II, Hopland Field Sta, Univ Calif, Davis, 60-62; res biologist, EAfrica Agr Forest Res Orgn, Kenya, 62-64; asst unit leader wildlife res, Ariz Coop Wildlife Res Univ, Univ Ariz, 68-92. *Concurrent Pos:* Fulbright Sr res scholar, 62-63; Rockefeller Res grant, 63-64. *Mem:* Wildlife Soc; Am Soc Mammal. *Res:* Ecology of big game animals; reproduction physiology of wild mammals; metabolism and water requirements of game mammals. *Mailing Add:* 214 Biol Sci Bldg E Univ Ariz Tucson AZ 85721-0001

SMITH, NORMAN TY, ANESTHESIOLOGY & PHARMACOLOGY, BIOLOGICAL ENGINEERING. *Current Pos:* assoc prof, Univ Calif, San Diego, 72-74, vchmn dept, 72-77, prof, Dept Anesthesia, 74-94, EMER PROF, UNIV CALIF, SAN DIEGO, 94- *Personal Data:* b Ft Madison, Iowa, May 5, 32; m 58, Penelope Cave; c Saskia. *Educ:* Harvard Med Sch, MD, 57; Am Bd Anesthesiol, dipl, 63. *Honors & Awards:* Detur Award, 53. *Prof Exp:* Intern pediat, Children's Med Ctr, Boston, Mass, 57-58; resident anesthesia, Mass Gen Hosp, 58-60; from instr to asst prof, Sch Med, Stanford Univ, 62-72. *Concurrent Pos:* NIH career develop award, 66-71; actg chief anesthesia, Vet Admin Hosp, Palo Alto, 62-64; vis scientist, Univ Wash, 67; vis prof, Inst Med Physics, Utrecht, Holland, 70-71; chief anesthesia, Vet Admin Hosp, San Diego, 72-77; dir anesthesia res, Univ Calif & US Naval Hosps, 75-77; ed, J Clin Monitoring, 84-; pres, Soc Technol in Anesthesia, 88-93. *Mem:* fel Am Col Anesthesiol; Am Heart Asn; Am Soc Pharmacol & Exp Therapeut; Biomed Eng Soc Inst Elec & Electronics Engrs. *Res:* Cardiovascular pharmacology and physiology; bioengineering; control systems theory; control systems; analog and digital computation; on-line data processing; multiple drug interaction; mathematical modeling (physiologic and pharmacologic) simulation. *Mailing Add:* Dept Anesthesia Univ Calif San Diego VA Med Ctr San Diego CA 92161. *E-Mail:* tsmith@ucd.edu

SMITH, OLIN DAIL, PLANT BREEDING. *Current Pos:* asst prof agron, 70-75, assoc prof, 75-82, PROF SOIL & CROP SCI, TEX A&M UNIV, 82- *Personal Data:* b Tonkawa, Okla, Dec 15, 31; m 51, Thelma Fairless; c Brenda, Brent & Beth. *Educ:* Okla State Univ, BS, 54, MS, 61; Univ Minn, PhD(agron), 69. *Prof Exp:* Supt, Wheatland Conserv, Exp Sta, Okla State Univ, 57-58, univ instr agron 58-62, asst secy-mgr, Okla Crop Improv Asn, 62-65; res fel, Univ Minn, 65-70. *Mem:* Am Soc Agron; Crop Sci Soc Am; fel Am Peanut Res & Educ Soc (pres, 72-73). *Res:* Plant breeding and genetics; inheritance by Arachis Hypogaea; peanut variety improvement; breeding peanuts for disease and insect resistance. *Mailing Add:* Dept Soil & Crop Sci Tex A&M Univ College Station TX 77843-0100

SMITH, OMAR EWING, JR, ECONOMIC ENTOMOLOGY, MEDICAL ENTOMOLOGY. *Current Pos:* from asst prof to assoc prof, 61-77, PROF BIOL, MEMPHIS STATE UNIV, 77- *Personal Data:* b Memphis, Tenn, Oct 21, 31; m 55; c 3. *Educ:* Memphis State Univ, BS, 54; Iowa State Univ, MS, 58, PhD, 61. *Prof Exp:* Instr entom, Iowa State Univ, 60-61. *Concurrent Pos:* Univ grant, 65-67. *Mem:* Entom Soc Am. *Res:* Mosquito and arthropod research; agricultural pests and insecticides; taxonomy of insects; extension entomology and related fields. *Mailing Add:* Dept Biol Memphis Univ 3706 Alumni St Memphis TN 38152-0001

SMITH, ORA KINGSLEY, physiology, medicine, for more information see previous edition

SMITH, ORRIN ERNEST, HORTICULTURE, PLANT PHYSIOLOGY. *Current Pos:* RETIRED. *Personal Data:* b Albany, Ore, Nov 20, 35; m 56; c 2. *Educ:* Ore State Univ, BS, 57; Univ Calif, Davis, PhD(plant physiol), 62. *Prof Exp:* Res plant physiologist, Cotton Br, Crops Res Div, Agr Res Serv, USDA, 62-66; asst plant physiologist, Univ Calif, Riverside, 66-70, assoc prof plant physiol, assoc plant physiologist & vchmn, Dept Plant Sci, 70-75; chmn, Dept Hort, Wash State Univ, 75-80; Assoc dean & dir resident instr, Ore State Univ, 80-83, assoc dean & dir extension serv, 83-96. *Concurrent Pos:* Fulbright sr res scholarship, 72; review ed, Am Soc Hort Sci, 74-78. *Mem:* Fel Am Soc Hort Sci (vpres, 82-83); Am Soc Plant Physiol. *Res:* Hormonal regulation of plant growth and development; physiology of dormancy and germination; seed vigor. *Mailing Add:* USDA 14th & Independence Ave Rm 3449 S Mail Stop 2225 Washington DC 20250-2225

SMITH, ORVILLE AUVERNE, NEUROPHYSIOLOGY. *Current Pos:* from instr to asst prof anat & physiol, 58-59, from asst prof to assoc prof physiol & biophys, 62-67, from asst dir to assoc dir ctr, 62-71, DIR REGIONAL PRIMATE RES CTR, SCH MED, UNIV WASH, 71-, PROF PHYSIOL & BIOPHYS, 67- *Personal Data:* b Nogales, Ariz, June 16, 27; m 53; c 2. *Educ:* Univ Ariz, BA, 49; Mich State Univ, MA, 50, PhD, 53. *Prof Exp:* Instr psychol, Mich State Univ, 51-54; fel neuroanat, Univ Pa, 54-56; fel neurophysiol, Sch Med, Univ Wash, 56-58. *Mem:* Am Physiol Soc; Am Asn Anatomists; Am Soc Primatologists (pres, 77-80); Pavlovian Soc NAm (pres, 78-79). *Res:* Physiological basis of behavior; cardiovascular control; neuroanatomy. *Mailing Add:* Dept Physiol & Biophys Univ Washington Health Ctr Box 357330 Seattle WA 98195

SMITH, OTTO J(OSEPH) M(ITCHELL), LARGE MOTORS, SOLAR ENERGY. *Current Pos:* from lectr to prof, 47-88, EMER PROF CONTROL & LARGE SYSTS, UNIV CALIF, BERKELEY, 88- *Personal Data:* b Urbana, Ill, Aug 6, 17; m 41, Phyllis Sterling; c Candace B, Otto J A, Sterling M & Stanford D. *Educ:* Okla State Univ, BS, 38; Stanford Univ, PhD(elec eng), 41. *Prof Exp:* Instr power & high voltage, Tufts Col, 41-43; asst prof commun, Univ Denver, 43-44; res engr, Electronics Dept, Westinghouse Elec Corp, Pa, 44-45; chief elec engr, Summit Corp, 45-47. *Concurrent Pos:* Vis prof, Inst Tech Aeronaut, Brazil, 54-56; Guggenheim fel, Polytech Univ, Darmstadt, Ger, 60; vis lectr, Kiev Inst Electrotechnol, Polytech Mus & Inst Electromech, USSR, 60; deleg, Cong Int Fedn Automatic Control, Moscow, 60; vis sr res fel, Monash Univ, Australia, 66-67; vis lectr, Fed Sch Eng, Itajuba, Brazil, 71, prof, 74; mem rev comt, Solar Thermal Test Facil, Users Asn, 77-78; NSF appointee, Acad Econ Studies & Inst Power Designs, Romania, 73; vis prof, Tech Univ Eindhoven, Neth, 74. *Mem:* Fel AAAS; fel Inst Elec & Electronics Engrs; Am Soc Eng Educ; Am Wind Energy Asn; Int Solar Energy Soc. *Res:* Electronics; feedback systems; servomechanisms; statistical and nonlinear synthesis; economic analogs; cybernetics; optimal economic planning; programs for optimizing the use of government resources for maximum economic growth; solar-thermal-electric power system design; wind-electric systems; high-efficiency motors. *Mailing Add:* 612 Euclid Ave Berkeley CA 94708-1332

SMITH, P(AUL) DENNIS, ENVIRONMENTAL MUTAGENESIS, MOLECULAR GENETICS. *Current Pos:* from chmn biol sci, 88-94, PROF BIOL SCI, WAYNE STATE UNIV, 94- *Personal Data:* b Baltimore, Md, Nov 14, 42; c 2. *Educ:* Loyola Col, BS, 64; Univ NC, PhD(zool), 68. *Prof Exp:* Fel genetics, Univ Conn, 68-70; from asst prof to assoc prof genetics, dept biol, Emory Univ, 70-84; prof biol & chmn dept, Southern Methodist Univ, 84-88. *Concurrent Pos:* NIH res grant, 71-, res career develop award, Gen Med Sci, 74-79. *Mem:* Environ Mutagen Soc; AAAS; Genetics Soc Am; Am Soc Microbiol. *Res:* DNA repair and mutagenesis in Drosophila. *Mailing Add:* Dept Biol Sci Wayne State Univ Detroit MI 48020

SMITH, P SCOTT, PHYSICS. *Current Pos:* from assoc prof to prof, 53-90, EMER PROF PHYSICS, EASTERN ILL UNIV, 90- *Personal Data:* b Richmond, Va, Dec 22, 22. *Educ:* Cornell Univ, PhD, 51. *Prof Exp:* Asst physics, US Naval Res Lab, 43-45 & Cornell Univ, 46-50; asst prof, Kans State Col, 51-53. *Mem:* Am Phys Soc; Am Asn Physics Teachers. *Res:* Nuclear, space and radiological physics; quantification of nuclear shell structure; rocketry and celestial mechanics; nuclear weapons. *Mailing Add:* Rte 4 Box 222 Charleston IL 61920

SMITH, PATRICIA ANNE, DEVELOPMENTAL GENETICS. *Current Pos:* asst prof, 68-71, assoc prof, 71-79, PROF GENETICS, NORTHEASTERN ILL UNIV, 79- *Personal Data:* b Rockwood, Tenn, Sept 1, 35. *Educ:* Carson-Newman Col, BS, 58; Northwestern Univ, MS, 65, PhD(genetics), 66. *Prof Exp:* Res asst genetics, Oak Ridge Nat Lab, 57-59; teacher jr high sch, Tenn, 59-61; res asst biochem, NMex Highlands Univ, 61; res assoc develop genetics, Northwestern Univ, 66-68. *Concurrent Pos:* Lectr eve div, Northwestern Univ, 65-72, NIH fel, 66-67. *Mem:* AAAS; Genetics Soc Am; Am Soc Zoologists. *Res:* Control of cell division and differentiation in the ovaries of Drosophila melanogaster; genetic control of synaptonemal complex formation. *Mailing Add:* Dept Biol NE Ill Univ, 5500 N St Louis Ave Chicago IL 60625-4625

SMITH, PATRICIA LEE, STATISTICS. *Current Pos:* assoc res mathematician, 85-, RES MATHEMATICIAN, SHELL DEVELOP CO. *Personal Data:* b Houston, Tex, Sept 16, 46. *Educ:* Southwestern Univ, BA, 68; Purdue Univ, MS, 70; Tex A&M Univ, PhD(statist), 75. *Prof Exp:* Instr math, Purdue Univ, 70-72; asst prof statist, Tex A&M Univ, 76-80 & Old Dominion Univ, 80-82; site mgr comput opers, Comput Dynamics, Inc, 82-85. *Mem:* Am Statist Asn. *Res:* Linear models with emphasis on applications of splines to design of experiments, regression and time series. *Mailing Add:* Shell Chem Co PO Box 100 Deer Park TX 77536

SMITH, PAUL AIKEN, PHYSICS, ASTRONOMY. *Current Pos:* PROF PHYSICS, COE COL, CEDAR RAPIDS, IOWA, 64- *Personal Data:* b Bucaramanga, Colombia, Jan 12, 34; US citizen; m 58, L Margaret McCluggage; c Valerie & Amy (Dorff). *Educ:* Park Col, AB, 56; Wash Univ, AM, 59; Tufts Univ, PhD(physics), 64. *Res:* Elementary particle physics; astronomy; computers; seeking to clarify the roots of the perpetual "crisis" in science education within the exclusive emphases within the scientific paradigm. *Mailing Add:* 1024 Maplewood Dr NE Cedar Rapids IA 52402. *E-Mail:* psmith@charliek.coe.edu

SMITH, PAUL CLAY, veterinary virology, veterinary pathology, for more information see previous edition

SMITH, PAUL E, JR, ELECTRICAL ENGINEERING. *Current Pos:* RETIRED. *Personal Data:* b Elizabeth, NJ, May 16, 23; m 47; c 3. *Educ:* Rensselaer Polytech Inst, BEE, 47; Mass Inst Technol, EE, 53. *Prof Exp:* Instr elec eng, Mass Inst Technol, 50-53, asst prof, 53-57; eng, Conval Corp, 57-58; chief engr, Feedback Controls, Inc, Mass, 58-68; sr eng specialist, GTE Sylvania Electronics Systs-East Div, 68-71; sr engr, Ikor, Inc, Burlington, 71-77; New Ikor Inc, Omniwave Electronics Corp, Gloucester, 77-80; Engr, Wincom Corp, 80-92. *Mem:* Inst Elec & Electronics Engrs. *Res:* Process control; servomechanics. *Mailing Add:* 189 Whitcomb Ave Littleton MA 01460-1418

SMITH, PAUL EDWARD, ECOLOGY, FISH BIOLOGY. *Current Pos:* RES BIOLOGIST & GROUP LEADER, LA JOLLA LAB, SOUTHWEST FISHERY SCI CTR, NAT MARINE FISHERIES SERV, 63- *Personal Data:* b Emmetsburg, Iowa, May 24, 33; m 57, Loretta Middleton; c Scott M, Stuart N, Marcia L, Ryan L & A Corinne. *Educ:* Northern Iowa Univ, BA, 56; Univ Iowa, PhD(zool), 62. *Honors & Awards:* Gold Medal, Dept Com, 90. *Prof Exp:* Sverdrup fel plankton behav, Scripps Inst, Univ Calif, 62-63. *Concurrent Pos:* Adj prof oceanog, Scripps Inst Oceanog, Univ Calif. *Mem:* Ecol Soc Am; Am Soc Limnol & Oceanog. *Res:* Zooplankton ecology and fish larva biology in marine environments, especially as influenced by temporal and spatial variations in small scale distribution; development of field and statistical methods for economical and concise descriptions of small scale distribution. *Mailing Add:* Southwest Fishery Sci Ctr PO Box 271 La Jolla CA 92037-0271. *Fax:* 619-546-7003; *E-Mail:* paulsmit@ucsd.edu

SMITH, PAUL FRANCIS, microbiology; deceased, see previous edition for last biography

SMITH, PAUL FREDERICK, PHYSIOLOGY, HORTICULTURE. *Current Pos:* asst physiologist, agr res serv, USDA, 43-47, assoc physiologist, 48-49, physiologist, 50-55, sr physiologist, 56-58, prin physiologist, 59-71, head physiologist, 71-75, AGR RES SERV, USDA, WORLD CITRUS CONSULT, 75- *Personal Data:* b Copeland, Kans, Dec 17, 16; m 40, Marjorie Haselwood; c Gary & Carol. *Educ:* Univ Okla, BS, 38, MS, 40; Univ Calif, PhD(physiol), 44. *Honors & Awards:* Presidential Gold Medal, Fla State Hort Soc. *Prof Exp:* Asst bot, Univ Okla, 38-39; asst plant physiol, Univ Calif, 40-42. *Concurrent Pos:* Agr consult. *Mem:* Bot Soc Am; fel Am Soc Hort Sci; Am Inst Biol Scientists; Am Soc Plant Physiol. *Res:* Pollen tube growth; bud dormancy and inhibition; vegetative propagation; mineral nutrition of citrus; citrus culture. *Mailing Add:* 2695 Ashville St Orlando FL 32818

SMITH, PAUL HOWARD, bacteriology, for more information see previous edition

SMITH, PAUL JOHN, STATISTICS, MATHEMATICS. *Current Pos:* asst prof, 71-76, ASSOC PROF MATH, UNIV MD, 76- *Personal Data:* b Philadelphia, Pa, Jan 6, 43; m 70. *Educ:* Drexel Univ, BS, 65; Case Western Res Univ, MS, 67, PhD(math), 69. *Prof Exp:* Asst prof math, Wayne State Univ, 69, Ind Univ, 69-71. *Concurrent Pos:* Statist consult, US Selective Serv Syst, 73, Sci Educ Systs, Inc, 73-74, US Consumer Prod Safety Comn, 76-77, Nat Inst Mental Health, 77-80, Nat Cancer Inst, 85-86. *Mem:* Inst Math Statist; Am Statist Asn; Am Soc Qual Control. *Res:* Nonparametric, robust and multivariate statistical inference. *Mailing Add:* Dept Math Univ Md College Park MD 20742-0001

SMITH, PAUL L, JURASSIC BIOCHRONOLOGY. *Current Pos:* From asst prof to assoc prof, 81-93, PROF GEOL, UNIV BC, 93- *Personal Data:* b London, Eng, Oct 12, 50; m 72, Kate Gordanier; c Gavin. *Educ:* Univ London, BSc, 72; Portland State Univ, MS, 76; McMaster Univ, PhD(geol), 81. *Concurrent Pos:* Mem, Jurassic subcommission, Int Union Geol Sci. *Mem:* Paleontol Asn; fel Geol Asn Can; Paleontol Res Inst; Paleontol Soc. *Res:* Stratigraphy biochronology and basin analysis of the Jurassic of western North America. *Mailing Add:* Dept Earth & Ocean Sci Univ BC 6339 Stores Rd Vancouver BC V6T 1Z4 Can. *Fax:* 604-822-6088; *E-Mail:* paul.l.smith@mtsg.ubc.ca

SMITH, PAUL LETTON, JR, ATMOSPHERIC PHYSICS, ELECTRICAL ENGINEERING. *Current Pos:* res engr & assoc prof meteorol, Inst Atmospheric Sci, 66-68, assoc prof meteorol & elec eng, 68-73, head eng group, 68-75, res prof meteorol & elec eng, 73-96, sr scientist & head, Data Acquisition & Anal Group, 76-81, dir, 81-96, EMER PROF, INST ATMOSPHERIC SCI, SDAK SCH MINES & TECHNOL, 96- *Personal Data:* b Columbia, Mo, Dec 16, 32; m 54, Mary B Noel; c Patrick, Melody, Timothy, Christopher & Anne. *Educ:* Carnegie Inst Technol, BS, 55, MS, 57, PhD(elec eng), 60. *Honors & Awards:* Ed Award, Am Meteorol Soc, 92;

Thunderbird Award, Weather Modification Asn, 95. *Prof Exp:* From instr to asst prof elec eng, Carnegie Inst Technol, 55-63; sr engr, Midwest Res Inst, 63-66. *Concurrent Pos:* NSF fel meteorol, McGill Univ, 64, vis prof, 69-70; chief scientist, US Air Force Air Weather Serv, Hq, 74-75; actg dir, Inst Atmospheric Sci, 76-77; vis scientist, Alta Res Coun, 84-85; Fulbright lectr, Univ Helsinki, 86. *Mem:* Am Meteorol Soc; Inst Elec & Electronics Engrs; Sigma Xi; Weather Modification Asn. *Res:* Radar meteorology; cloud and precipitation physics; weather modification; remote sensing; meteorological instrumentation; electrostatic precipitation; propagation and scattering of electromagnetic and acoustic waves in the atmosphere. *Mailing Add:* Inst Atmospheric Sci SDak Sch of Mines & Technol Rapid City SD 57701-3995. *Fax:* 605-394-6061

SMITH, PAUL VERGON, JR, CHEMISTRY. *Current Pos:* RETIRED. *Personal Data:* b Lima, Ohio, Apr 25, 21; m 45; c 4. *Educ:* Miami Univ, AB, 42; Univ Ill, MS, 43, PhD(org chem), 45. *Honors & Awards:* President's Award, Am Asn Petrol Geologists, 55. *Prof Exp:* Instr, Miami Univ, 42; asst, Univ Ill, 42-43; from asst to res chemist, Off Rubber Reserve, 43-46; res chemist & group leader, Esso Res & Eng Co, 46-54, sci liaison, Esso Res Ltd, Eng, 55-57, asst dir, Chem Res Div, NJ, 57-60, Cent Basic Res Lab, 60-66, Res Dept, Esso Petrol Co Ltd, Eng, 66-67, dir Chem Dept, Esso Res SA, Belg, 67-71, head educ & sci rels, Esso Res & Eng Co, 71-73, mgr educ & sci rels, 73-78, pub affairs, 78-81, mgr educ & prof soc rels, Pub Affairs, Exxon Res & Eng Co, 81-86. *Concurrent Pos:* Mem adv bd, Petrol Res Fund, 65-66, CACHE, Inc, 80-86; dir, Am Chem Soc, 78-86, chmn bd, 84-86; bd dirs & treas, Jr Eng Tech Soc, Inc, 80-89; bd dirs, Centcom, Ltd, 84-86. *Mem:* AAAS; Am Soc Eng Educ (dir, 78-86, vpres, 80-86); Am Inst Chem Eng; Am Chem Soc; NY Acad Sci. *Res:* Synthetic rubber; detergents; physical separation of organic compounds; oil additives and synthetic lubricants; geochemistry; origin of petroleum; oxo process; plasticizers; polypropylene. *Mailing Add:* 713 Pineside Lane Naples FL 33963-8523

SMITH, PERCY LEIGHTON, CHEMISTRY. *Current Pos:* RETIRED. *Personal Data:* b Dunbar, WVa, July 23, 19; m 39, Frances Ellis; c Francis Leighton & Sally Lynne. *Educ:* Morris Harvey Col, BSc, 50. *Prof Exp:* Lab asst, Union Carbide Corp, 39-47, res chemist, 47-66, group leader, 66-74, assoc dir res & develop, 74-79. *Mem:* Am Chem Soc. *Res:* Analytical and organophosphorus chemistry; epoxy and polyester resins; polyurethanes. *Mailing Add:* 1508 Myers Ave Dunbar WV 25064-2931

SMITH, PERRIN GARY, CHEMICAL ENGINEERING. *Current Pos:* RETIRED. *Personal Data:* b Bowie, Tex, Sept 3, 12; m 37, Charlotte Epple; c Randolph G. *Educ:* Austin Col, BS, 34; Northwestern Univ, PhD(org chem), 38. *Prof Exp:* Abbott Labs fel, Northwestern Univ, 38-40; chemist res dept, Sharples Chem Inc, Mich, 40-44, chemist develop dept, Pa, 44-54, asst to pres, 54-56; asst to gen mgr, Indust Div, Pennwalt Corp, Philadelphia, 56-65, proj evaluator, Eng Dept, King of Prussia, 65-77. *Mem:* Am Chem Soc. *Res:* Amines; rubber chemicals; pharmaceutical intermediates; sulfur chemicals; process development. *Mailing Add:* 352 Black Horse Rd Chester Springs PA 19425

SMITH, PETER, CHEMICAL DYNAMICS, POLYMER CHEMISTRY. *Current Pos:* from asst prof to, 59-95, EMER PROF CHEM, DUKE UNIV, 95- *Personal Data:* b Sale, Eng, Sept 7, 24; m 51, Hilary J Roe; c Helen A, Eric P, Richard H & Gillian C (Murrell). *Educ:* Cambridge Univ, BA, 46, MA, 49, PhD(phys chem), 53. *Prof Exp:* Jr sci officer, Chem Dept, Royal Aircraft Estab, Eng, 43-46; demonstr phys & inorg chem, Univ Leeds, 50-51; Fulbright res fel, Harvard Univ, 51-53; asst prof chem, Purdue Univ, 54-59. *Mem:* Am Chem Soc; Am Phys Soc; Royal Soc Chem. *Res:* Application of electron paramagnetic resonance spectroscopy to kinetic and structural problems; chemical kinetics, especially solution processes; biophysical chemistry. *Mailing Add:* Dept Chem Paul M Gross Chem Lab Duke Univ Box 90346 Durham NC 27708-0346

SMITH, PETER A(LAN) S(OMERVAIL), HETEROCYCLIC CHEMISTRY. *Current Pos:* from instr to prof chem, 45-90, EMER PROF, UNIV MICH, ANN ARBOR, 90- *Personal Data:* b Erskine Hill, Eng, Apr 16, 20; nat US; m 52, Mary C Walsh; c Kent A K & Leslie C. *Educ:* Univ Calif, BSc, 41; Univ Mich, PhD(inorg chem), 44. *Prof Exp:* Res assoc chem, 44-45. *Concurrent Pos:* Fulbright res scholar, Univ Auckland, 51; mem, Am Chem Soc Adv Comt, Chem Corps, US Army, 55-60, mem, Sch & Training Comt, Chem Corps Adv Coun, 58-64; consult, Parke, Davis/Warner-Lambert Co, 57-; chmn, Comt Nomenclature, Div Chem & Chem Technol, Nat Acad Sci-Nat Res Coun, 60-68; mem, Comt Nomenclature, Pub Affairs Coun, 60-68; guest res prof, Inst Org Chem, Stuttgart Tech Univ, 61-62; bk rev ed, J Am Chem Soc, 70-91; Comn Nomenclature of Org Chem, Int Union Pure & Appl Chem, 84-94; chmn, 88-94, Am Chem Soc, chmn, 90-94. *Mem:* Am Chem Soc. *Res:* Heterocyclic chemistry; carbenes and nitrenes; organic nitrogen compounds; azides; hydrazines; hydroxylamines; coal asphaltenes. *Mailing Add:* Dept Chem Univ Mich Ann Arbor MI 48109. *E-Mail:* passmith@umich.edu

SMITH, PETER BLAISE, CELL DIFFERENTIATION, MEMBRANE BIOCHEMISTRY. *Current Pos:* ASSOC PROF BIOCHEM, BOWMAN GRAY SCH MED, WAKE FOREST UNIV, 76- *Educ:* Univ Tenn, PhD(microbiol), 73. *Mailing Add:* Dept Biochem Bowman Gray Sch Med Wake Forest Univ Med Ctr Blvd Winston Salem NC 27157-1016

SMITH, PETER DAVID, MATHEMATICS, COMPUTER SCIENCE. *Current Pos:* assoc prof, 69-88, PROF MATH & COMPUT SCI, ST MARY'S COL, IND, 88- *Personal Data:* b Providence, RI, Oct 25, 38; m 80, Ellyn Stecker; c Paul, Mark & Joy. *Educ:* Col Holy Cross, AB, 60; Naval Postgrad Sch, MS, 64; Univ Wis, PhD(math), 68; Mich State Univ, MS, 75. *Prof Exp:* Instr math & comput sci, US Naval Postgrad Sch, 62-64, Xavier Univ La, 68-69. *Mem:* Asn Comput Mach; Asn Small Comput Users in Educ; Math Asn Am; Soc Ind & Appl Math. *Mailing Add:* St Mary's Col Notre Dame IN 46556. *E-Mail:* psmith@saintmarys.edu

SMITH, PETER JOHN SHAND, NON-INVASIVE MEASUREMENT OF TRANS-MEMBRANE ION FLUX. *Current Pos:* DIR, BIOCURRENTS RES CTR, ASSOC SCIENTIST, MARINE BIOL LAB. *Personal Data:* b Glasgow, Scotland, June 14, 54; US citizen. *Educ:* Univ Aberdeen, Scotland, BS, 76, PhD(zool), 79; Univ Cambridge, Eng, MA, 91. *Prof Exp:* Hisher sci officer, Unit Insect Physiol & Biochem, Univ Cambridge, Eng, 87-90, sr sci officer, Lab Molecular Signalling, 90-91. *Mem:* Soc Exp Biol; Int Biol. *Res:* Steady-state ion fluxes associated with cellular and tissue ion homeostasis and growth regeneration; develop novel techniques for the measurement of such ion movements. *Mailing Add:* Biocurrents Res Ctr Marine Biol Lab Woods Hole MA 02543. *Fax:* 508-540-6902; *E-Mail:* psmith@mbl.edu

SMITH, PETER LLOYD, ATOMIC & MOLECULAR SPECTROSCOPY, ULTRAVIOLET INSTRUMENTATION. *Current Pos:* res fel, 73-75, RES ASSOC PHYSICS, CTR ASTROPHYS, HARVARD COL OBSERV, 75- *Personal Data:* b Victoria, BC, Apr 28, 44; m 91, Donna J Coletti; c Alexandra C & Colin W. *Educ:* Univ BC, BS, 65; Calif Inst Technol, PhD(physics), 72. *Prof Exp:* Res fel physics, Calif Inst Technol, 72; asst prof, Harvey Mudd Col, 72-73. *Mem:* Am Phys Soc; Optical Soc Am; Am Astron Soc; Int Astron Union; Am Geophys Union. *Res:* Visible and ultraviolet spectroscopy of atoms, ions and molecules; astrophysical applications include interstellar clouds, the sun, comets and plasmas; atmospheric chemistry; transitions probabilities; photon and electron cross sections for allowed and forbidden transitions; ultraviolet spectroscopic instrumentation for astronomy. *Mailing Add:* MS-50 Harvard Smithsonian CFA 60 Garden St Cambridge MA 02138. *Fax:* 617-495-7455; *E-Mail:* plsmith@cfa.harvard.edu

SMITH, PETER WILLIAM E, physics, electrical engineering, for more information see previous edition

SMITH, PHILIP EDWARD, PARASITOLOGY. *Current Pos:* RETIRED. *Personal Data:* b Johnson Co, Ill, Dec 25, 16; m 42, Vivian Sweibel; c Diane M (Hainsworth), Nancy R (Friot), Ellen J (Hempling) & Sally J (Ruhl). *Educ:* Southern Ill Univ, BEd, 40; Univ Ill, MS, 42; Johns Hopkins Univ, ScD(parasitol), 49. *Prof Exp:* Mus technician, Southern Ill Univ, 36-39, asst zool, 39-40; asst zool, Univ Ill, 40-42; asst parasitol, Sch Hyg & Pub Health, Johns Hopkins Univ, 47-49; asst prof zool, Okla Agr & Mech Col, 49-52; from asst prof to prof prev med & pub health, Univ Okla Health Sci Ctr, 52-70, assoc dean grad col med, Med Ctr, 56-70, assoc dean student affairs, Sch Med, 60-70, prof parasitol, Sch Health, 70-72, dean, Sch Health Related Professions, 70-72, dean, Col Allied Health Professions, 72-73, actg dean, Col Health & Allied Health Professions, 73-74, dean, Col Health, 74-81, dean, Col Allied Health, 81-82, regents emer prof & emer dean, 82-96. *Mem:* Am Soc Parasitol; Am Soc Trop Med & Hyg; Micros Soc Am. *Res:* Morphology, life history and host-parasite relations of nematodes. *Mailing Add:* 241 NW 32nd St Oklahoma City OK 73118-8610

SMITH, PHILIP LEES, SLEEP DISORDERS. *Current Pos:* from instr to asst prof med, 77-85, INSTR ANESTHESIOL, JOHNS HOPKINS UNIV, 77-, ASSOC PROF MED, 85- *Personal Data:* b Atlanta, Ga, Mar 3, 45; m 81; c 2. *Educ:* Harvard Univ, BA, 67; Tulane Univ Med Sch, MD, 72. *Prof Exp:* Res asst, Thorndike Mem Lab, Harvard Univ, 67-68. *Concurrent Pos:* Dir, ICU, Francis Scott Key Med Ctr, 77-85, dir med ctr, 81-; dir, Johns Hopkins Sleep Disorders Ctr, 81- *Mem:* Am Col Chest Physicians; Am Thoracic Soc; Am Heart Asn; Asn Psychol Study Sleep; Geront Soc Am; Clin Sleep Society. *Mailing Add:* Johns Hopkins Asthma/Al Ctr 5501 Hopkins Bayview Circle Baltimore MD 21224

SMITH, PHILIP MEEK, GEOPHYSICS. *Current Pos:* CONSULT & WRITING, MCGEARY & SMITH, 94- *Personal Data:* b Springfield, Ohio, May 18, 32. *Educ:* Ohio State Univ, BS, 54, MA, 55. *Hon Degrees:* NC State Univ, DSc, 86. *Prof Exp:* Mem staff, US Nat Comt Int Geophys Yr, Nat Acad Sci, 57-58; prog dir, NSF, 58-63, dir opers, US Antarctic Res Prog, 64-69, dep head, Div Polar Progs, 70-73, exec asst to dir & sci adv to pres, 74-76; chief, Gen Sci Br, Off Mgt & Budget, Exec Off Pres, 73-74, assoc dir, Off Sci & Technol Policy, 76-81; spec asst to chmn, Nat Sci Bd, 81; exec officer, Nat Res Coun-Nat Acad Sci, 81-94. *Concurrent Pos:* Pres, Cave Res Found, 57-63; exec secy, Pres's Comt Nat Medal Sci, 74-76; chmn tech panels, Fed Coord Coun Sci & Eng & Technol, 76-80; corp mem, Woods Hole Oceanog Inst, 83-89. *Mem:* AAAS; Antarctican Soc. *Res:* Antarctic exploration and geophysics. *Mailing Add:* McGeary & Smith 464 M St SW Washington DC 20024

SMITH, PHILIP WESLEY, SPLINES & APPROXIMATION THEORY, NUMERICAL ANALYSIS. *Current Pos:* VPRES, WINDWARD TECHNOL, 93- *Personal Data:* b Gainesville, Fla, Nov 28, 46; m 69; c 2. *Educ:* Univ Va, BA, 68; Purdue Univ, MS, 70, PhD(math), 72. *Prof Exp:* From asst prof to assoc prof math, Tex A&M Univ, 72-78; vis res prof math, Univ Alta, 78-79; vis scientist, TJ Watson IBM Res Ctr, 79-80; prof math, Old Dom Univ, 80-85; mgr math software design, Int Math & Statist Libr, 85-93. *Concurrent Pos:* Co-prin investr, Army Res Off, 74-82; consult, White Sands Missile Range, 75-76 & Gen Motors Res, 84-85. *Mem:* Soc Indust & Appl Math; Am Math Soc. *Res:* Numerical analysis applied to problems in approximation theory; shape preserving approximations and nonlinear eigenvalue problems. *Mailing Add:* Windward Technol Inc 14311 Kellywood Houston TX 77079

SMITH, PHILLIP DOYLE, CELLULAR IMMUNOLOGY, GASTROENTEROLOGY. *Current Pos:* guest investr parasite immunol, 80-82, SR STAFF RES FEL CELL IMMUNOL, NIH, 82- *Personal Data:* b Berkeley, Calif, Apr 16, 46. *Educ:* Univ Calif, Berkeley, BA, 68; Univ Rochester, MD, 73. *Prof Exp:* Res fel cell biol, Cancer Res Inst, Univ Vienna, 71-72; intern & resident internal med, Vanderbilt, 73-76; res fel gastroenterol, Univ Colo, 76-79. *Mem:* Am Asn Immunologists; Am Fedn Clin Res; Am Gastroenterol Asn; Am Col Physicians; Am Soc Trop Med. *Res:* Cellular immune responses to gastrointestinal infections. *Mailing Add:* Univ Ala Birmingham UAB Sta 703 S 19th St Birmingham AL 35294

SMITH, PHILLIP J, SYNOPTIC METEOROLOGY, ATMOSPHERIC ENERGETICS. *Current Pos:* from asst prof to assoc prof, 67-81, PROF METEOROL, PURDUE UNIV, WEST LAFAYETTE, 81- *Personal Data:* b Muncie, Ind, Oct 2, 38; m 60, Linda A Whitney; c Amy, Andrew & Allyson. *Educ:* Ball State Univ, BS, 60; Univ Wis, MS, 64, PhD(meteorol), 67. *Prof Exp:* Res asst meteorol, Univ Wis, 63-67. *Concurrent Pos:* Prin investr, NSF & NASA grants, 69-95; sr fel, Nat Ctr Atmospheric Res, 72-73, assoc dept head, 88-85. *Mem:* Fel Am Meteorol Soc; Am Geophys Union; Sigma Xi; fel Royal Meteorolog Soc. *Res:* Energetics & dynamics of synoptic scale systems; development of extratropical cyclones. *Mailing Add:* Dept Earth & Atmospheric Sci Purdue Univ 1397 Civil Bldg West Lafayette IN 47907-1397. *Fax:* 765-496-1210; *E-Mail:* smith@meteor.atms.purdue.edu

SMITH, PIERRE FRANK, pharmacy, medicinal chemistry; deceased, see previous edition for last biography

SMITH, QUENTON TERRILL, oral biochemistry, oral biology; deceased, see previous edition for last biography

SMITH, R JAY, zoology, for more information see previous edition

SMITH, R LOWELL, ACCELERATED LIFE TESTING, PIEZOELECTRIC OSCILLATOR APPLICATIONS. *Current Pos:* SR SCIENTIST, TEX RES INST, AUSTIN, 77- *Personal Data:* b Toledo, Ohio, June 24, 40; m 63, Judith Williams; c Jennifer & Paul. *Educ:* Univ Toledo, BS, 62; Case Western Res Univ, PhD(physics), 70. *Prof Exp:* Res fel, Case Western Res Univ, 70-71; staff scientist, Ultrascan Co, 71-72; sr res assoc, Horizons Res Inc, 72-77. *Mem:* Acoust Soc Am; Inst Elec & Electronics Engrs; Am Soc Nondestructive Testing. *Res:* Electrographics; electroacoustics; viscoelasticity; experimental design; reliability analysis; nondestructive testing; mathematical modeling; impedance spectroscopy; statistical inference; regression analysis; computer controlled data acquisition; instrumentation development; project management; technical writing. *Mailing Add:* 1749 Linbrook Dr San Diego CA 92111. *Fax:* 512-263-3530; *E-Mail:* ntiac@access.texas.gov

SMITH, RALPH CARLISLE, education administration, history; deceased, see previous edition for last biography

SMITH, RALPH E(DWARD), AGRICULTURAL ENGINEERING. *Current Pos:* RETIRED. *Personal Data:* b Porterdale, Ga, May 6, 23; m 48; c Susan, Ellen & Edward. *Educ:* Univ Ga, BS, 48, MS, 61; Okla State Univ, PhD(agr eng), 66. *Prof Exp:* Instr agr, Polk County Bd Educ, Ga, 48-54; instr physics & agr eng, Abraham Baldwin Agr Col, 54-56; from instr to assoc prof agr eng, Univ Ga, 56-89. *Concurrent Pos:* Vis prof, Okla State Univ, 65-66. *Mem:* Am Soc Agr Engrs; Am Soc Eng Educ; Am Soc Heating, Refrig & Air-Conditioning Engrs; Sigma Xi. *Res:* Environmental control engineering for livestock; farm electrification engineering; process engineering for agricultural engineering; processes of transient conduction heat transfer. *Mailing Add:* Col Agr Eng Ctr Univ Ga Athens GA 30602. *Fax:* 706-542-8806

SMITH, RALPH E, VIROLOGY, ONCOLOGY. *Current Pos:* prof vet virol & head, dept microbiol, 83-87, interim vpres res, 89-90, ASSOC VPRES RES & PROF MICROBIOL, COLO STATE UNIV, FT COLLINS, 87- *Personal Data:* b Yuma, Colo, May 10, 40; m 88; c 1. *Educ:* Colo State Univ, BS, 61; Univ Colo, Denver, PhD(microbiol), 68. *Prof Exp:* Teaching fel, dept microbiol & immunol, Duke Univ Med Ctr, Durham, NC, 68-70, from asst prof to prof viral oncol, 70-82. *Concurrent Pos:* Prin investr, Nat Cancer Inst grant, NIH, 70-; consult, Bellco Glass, Vineland, NJ, 76-80, Procter & Gamble Co, 82-87 & Schering Plough Corp, Bloomfield, NJ, 87-; Eleanor Roosevelt fel, Wellcome Res Found, Beckenham, Kent, Eng, 78-79. *Mem:* Am Soc Microbiol; NY Acad Sci; Am Asn Immunologists; Am Soc Virol; Am Soc Clin Path; Am Asn Avian Pathologists. *Res:* Biology of avian retroviruses; characterization of avian osteopetrosis and associated diseases; description of widespread disease in chicken's body caused by RAV-7 avian retrovirus; cell and tissue culture techniques; molecular cloning of avian retroviruses; characterization of lung tumors caused by an avian retrovirus. *Mailing Add:* Dept Microbiol Colo State Univ Ft Collins CO 80523-0001. *Fax:* 970-491-5541; *E-Mail:* resmith@vines.colostate.edu

SMITH, RALPH EMERSON, GROUNDWATER GEOLOGY. *Current Pos:* RETIRED. *Personal Data:* b Beckley, WVa, Jan 13, 16; wid; c 2. *Educ:* Tex Christian Univ, AB, 37, MS, 39. *Prof Exp:* Asst, Tex Christian Univ, 37-39 & Univ Okla, 39-42; assoc prof geol & geog, Drury Col, 46-47; geologist, Geol Div, Fuels Br, US Geol Surv, 47-48, geologist, Water Res Div, Ground Water Br, 49-75, geologist, Pub Lands Hydrol Prog, 64-75; consult, 75-83. *Concurrent Pos:* Supvr water well drilling, Indonesia, 80. *Res:* Water supply for stock and camp sites; relation of geology, weather and vegetation to water on public domains in the western mountain states; area studies; evaluate the possibility for additional ground water. *Mailing Add:* 7100 W 13th Ave No 323 Lakewood CO 80215-5284

SMITH, RALPH G, INDUSTRIAL HYGIENE, ANALYTICAL CHEMISTRY. *Current Pos:* PROF ENVIRON & INDUST HEALTH, SCH PUB HEALTH, UNIV MICH, ANN ARBOR, 70- *Personal Data:* b St John, NB, Jan 11, 20; nat; m 42; c 6. *Educ:* Wayne State Univ, BS, 42, MS, 49, PhD(chem), 53. *Prof Exp:* Assoc indust hygienist & chief chemist, Bur Indust Hyg, Detroit Dept Health, Mich, 46-55; assoc prof indust med & hyg, Sch Med, Wayne State Univ, 55-63, prof occup & environ health, 63-70. *Mem:* AAAS; Am Conf Govt Indust Hygienists; Am Indust Hyg Asn; Air Pollution Control Asn; Am Chem Soc. *Res:* Chemistry and toxicology; air analysis; analysis of biological samples for toxic substances; analytical chemistry of beryllium, ozone, mercury and lead; toxicity of air pollutants; mercury and chlorine. *Mailing Add:* 24711 Tudor Lane Franklin MI 48025-1668

SMITH, RALPH J(UDSON), ELECTRICAL ENGINEERING. *Current Pos:* instr, 42-45, prof, 58-81, EMER PROF ELEC ENG, STANFORD UNIV, 81- *Personal Data:* b Herman, Nebr, June 5, 16; m 38; c 4. *Educ:* Univ Calif, BS, 38, MS, 40, EE, 42; Stanford Univ, PhD(elec eng), 45. *Prof Exp:* Jr engr, Stand Oil Co, Calif, 38-40; instr eng, San Jose State Col, 40-42, head dept, 45-52, chmn div eng, math & aeronaut, 52-57; adv electronics, Repub of Philippines, 57-58. *Concurrent Pos:* Consult, State Dept Educ, Calif, 60. *Mem:* Fel Am Soc Eng Educ; fel Inst Elec & Electronics Engrs. *Res:* Author of three books. *Mailing Add:* Stanford Univ 848 Pine Hill Rd Stanford CA 94305

SMITH, RAOUL NORMAND, NATURAL LANGUAGE PROCESSING, KNOWLEDGE REPRESENTATION & EXPERT SYSTEMS. *Current Pos:* PROF COMPUT SCI, NORTHEASTERN UNIV, 83- *Personal Data:* b West Warwick, RI, May 15, 38; m 66, Mary Hand; c Stephen & Timothy. *Educ:* Brown Univ, AB, 63, AM, 64, PhD(computational ling), 68. *Prof Exp:* From instr to asst prof ling, Northwestern Univ, 67-73, assoc prof computational & math ling, 73-81; prin mem tech staff, comput sci lab, Gen Tel & Electronics Labs, Inc, 81-83; dir, Grad Sch, Col Comp Sci, Northeastern Univ, 83-84, dir res, 84-85. *Concurrent Pos:* Orin investr, Am Coun Learned Socs Grant, 74, Am Philos Soc Grant, 74, Nat Endowment Humanities Res Grants, 75 & 76-77 & Dig Equip Corp Grant, 85; vis prof, Univ Maine, Orono, 78, & Jilin Univ Technol, Changchun, People's Repub China, 85; mem, Nat Acad Sci, Comn Microcomputers Develop Countries, 86; chmn bd, Cognitive Computers, Inc, 85-87; consult to various orgns. *Mem:* Asn Comput Mach; Am Asn Artificial Intel; Asn Computational Ling; Inst Elec & Electronics Engrs Comput Soc; Sigma Xi. *Res:* Natural language interfaces and expert systems; affective computing. *Mailing Add:* Col Comput Sci Northeastern Univ Boston MA 02115. *Fax:* 617-373-5121; *E-Mail:* rnsmith@ccs.neu.edu

SMITH, RAPHAEL FORD, MEDICINE, CARDIOLOGY. *Current Pos:* from asst prof to assoc prof, 69-82, PROF MED, SCH MED, VANDERBILT UNIV, 74-, SCH ENG, 76- CHIEF, CARDIOL SECT, NASHVILLE VET ADMIN HOSP, 75- *Personal Data:* b Wilson, NC, Jan 22, 33; m 58; c 4. *Educ:* Vanderbilt Univ, BA, 55; Harvard Med Sch, MD, 60; FACP, 68; FACC, 69. *Honors & Awards:* Skylab Achievement Award, NASA, 74. *Prof Exp:* Intern asst resident, Mass Gen Hosp, 60-62, resident, 65-66; res asst aviation med, US Naval Sch Aviation Med, 62-65; chief, Cardiol Br, Naval Aerospace Med Inst, 66-69. *Concurrent Pos:* Consult, US Naval Hosp, 67-69 & NIH, Specialized Ctrs Res, 74-77. *Mem:* Am Heart Asn; Southern Soc Clin Invest. *Res:* Cardiac electrophysiology; aerospace medical research. *Mailing Add:* 1310 24th Ave S Nashville TN 37212-2637

SMITH, RAY FRED, ENTOMOLOGY. *Current Pos:* field & lab asst entom, Univ Calif, Berkeley, 40-45, assoc, Exp Sta, 45-46, from instr & jr entomologist to prof 7 entomologist, 46-83, exec dir, consortium Int Corp Protection, 79-85, EMER PROF ENTOM, UNIV CALIF, BERKELEY, 83- *Personal Data:* b Los Angeles, Calif, Jan 20, 19; m 40; c 3. *Educ:* Univ Calif, BS, 40, MS, 41, PhD(entom), 46. *Hon Degrees:* DAgrSc, Landbouwhogesch, Wageningen, 76. *Honors & Awards:* C W Woodworth Award, 71; Hon Award, Consortium Integrated Pest Mgt, 85. *Prof Exp:* Field entomologist, Balfour-Guthrie Investment Co, 40. *Concurrent Pos:* Guggenheim fel, 50; consult, Food & Agr Orgn, UN. *Mem:* Nat Acad Sci; fel & hon mem Entom Soc Am (pres, 76); fel Entom Soc Can; fel AAAS; fel Am Acad Arts & Sci. *Mailing Add:* 3092 Hedaro Ct Lafayette CA 94549

SMITH, RAYMOND CALVIN, PHYSICAL OCEANOGRAPHY. *Current Pos:* AT DEPT OF GEOG, UNIV CALIF, SANTA BARBARA. *Personal Data:* b Glendale, Calif, Nov 17, 34; m 56; c 2. *Educ:* Mass Inst Technol, SB, 56; Stanford Univ, PhD(physics), 61. *Prof Exp:* Res fel, Cambridge Electron Accelerator, Harvard Univ, 61-63; res oceanogr, Univ Calif, San Diego, 63-86. *Mem:* AAAS; Optical Soc Am; Am Geophys Union; Am Soc Limnol & Oceanog. *Res:* Environmental optics; primary productivity; remote sensing; ecology of southern ocean. *Mailing Add:* Dept of Geog Univ Calif Santa Barbara CA 93106

SMITH, RAYMOND JAMES, CIVIL ENGINEERING, GEOLOGY. *Current Pos:* CONSULT CIVIL ENGR & GEOLOGIST, 71- *Personal Data:* b Manchester, NH, July 16, 24. *Educ:* Calif Inst Technol, BS, 45, MS, 48; Princeton Univ, MA, 50, PhD, 51. *Prof Exp:* Investr for Princeton, Caribbean, 48-54; asst prof, La State Univ, 54-57; res engr & geologist, NY Explor Co, 57-61; civil engr-geologist, US Naval Civil Eng Lab, Calif, 61-68; prof oceanog, Naval Postgrad Sch, 68-71. *Mem:* Geol Soc Am; Am Soc Civil Engrs; Soc Econ Geologists; Am Geophys Union. *Res:* Application of geology to civil engineering. *Mailing Add:* 791 Via Ondulando Ventura CA 93003

SMITH, RAYMOND V(IRGIL), MECHANICAL ENGINEERING, REHABILITATION ENGINEERING. *Current Pos:* CONSULT, 84- *Personal Data:* b Esbon, Kans, Nov 17, 19; m 48; c 5. *Educ:* Univ Colo, BS, 48, MS, 51; Univ Utah, MS, 57; Oxford Univ, DPhil, 68. *Honors & Awards:* NBS Distinguished Auth, NASA Tech Utilization. *Prof Exp:* Design engr, Boeing Airplane Co, 41-44 & 48; instr mech eng, Colo Sch Mines, 49-52; res engr, Sandia Corp, 52-53; asst prof mech eng, NMex State Univ, 53-54; assoc prof, Univ Utah, 54-57 & Colo State Univ, 57-61; mech engr, Cryogenic Eng Lab, Nat Bur Stand, 58-71; prof mech eng, Wichita State Univ, 71-84; Cerebral Palsy Res Found, Kans, 83-97. *Concurrent Pos:* UK Atomic Energy Res Estab, 66-67, 78 & 81; Indian Inst Sci Bangalore, 81, 82 & 84. *Mem:* Am Soc Mech Engrs; Am Soc Eng Educ; India Inst Sci. *Res:* Fuel combustion mechanism; two-phase flow cryogenic studies of heat transfer, thermodynamics and fluid mechanics; technology assessement; rehabilitation engineering. *Mailing Add:* 5 Crestview Lakes Wichita KS 67220

SMITH, REGINALD BRIAN, RESPIRATORY CARE, ANESTHESIOLOGY. *Current Pos:* PROF ANESTHESIOL, CHMN DEPT & DIR ANESTHESIOL RESIDENCY, UNIV TEX HEALTH SCI CTR, SAN ANTONIO, 78-, CHIEF ANESTHESIOLOGIST, TEACHING HOSP, 78- *Personal Data:* b Warrington, Eng, Feb 7, 31; US citizen; m 63; c 2. *Educ:* Univ London, BS & MB, 56. *Prof Exp:* Clin instr, Univ Pittsburgh, 65-69, from asst prof to prof anesthesiol, 69-78. *Concurrent Pos:* Dir, anesthesiol dept, Eye & Ear Hosp, Pittsburgh, 71-76 & Hyperbaric Med, Univ Hosp; vchmn anesthesiol dept, Univ Pittsburgh, 73-77, actg chmn, 77-78; ed, Int Ophthal Clin, 73 & Int Anesthesiol Clin, 83; anesthesiologist-in-chief, Presby Univ Hosp, Pittsburgh, 76-78. *Mem:* Royal Col Surgeons Eng; fel Am Col Anesthesiol; fel Am Col Chest Physicians; fel Am Col Physicians; Am Soc Anesthesiol; fel Am Col Hyperbaric Med, 96. *Res:* Effects of anesthetic agents in the eye (intraocular pressure, oculocardiac reflex, drug interaction); anesthetic techniques used on endoscopy; techniques of artificial ventilation (high frequency ventilation, transtracheal ventilation, apneic ventilation); hyperbaric oxygen and diabetes. *Mailing Add:* Dept Anesthesiol Univ Tex Health Sci Ctr 7703 Floyd Curl Dr San Antonio TX 78284

SMITH, REID GARFIELD, KNOWLEDGE-BASED SYSTEM DESIGN, MACHINE LEARNING. *Current Pos:* PROG LEADER, SCHLUMBERGER-DOLL RES CTR, 81- *Personal Data:* b Toronto, Ont, Oct 4, 46; m 81; c 3. *Educ:* Carleton Univ, BEng, 68, MEng, 69; Stanford Univ, PhD(elec eng), 79. *Prof Exp:* Defense sci officer, Defense Res Estab Atlantic, 69-81. *Concurrent Pos:* Lectr comput sci, Dalhousie Univ, 81. *Mem:* Asn Comput Mach; Inst Elec & Electronics Engrs; Am Asn Artificial Intel; Can Soc Comput Studies Intel; AAAS. *Res:* Knowledge-based system design, concentrating on knowledge acquisition via interactive machine learning and construction of KBS substrates for representation of domain knowledge, control and user interfaces. *Mailing Add:* Schlumberger Cambridge Res High Cross Madingley Rd Cambridge CB3 0EL England

SMITH, REX L, PLANT MOLECULAR GENETICS, PLANT BREEDING. *Current Pos:* From asst prof to assoc prof, 67-78, PROF AGRON, UNIV FLA, 78- *Personal Data:* b Beaver, Utah, June 7, 29; c 4. *Educ:* Utah State Univ, BS, 63; Iowa State Univ, PhD(plant breeding & genetics), 67. *Mem:* AAAS; Am Soc Agron; Int Soc Plant Molecular Biol; Am Genetic Asn. *Res:* Molecular genetics; genetics and plant breeding. *Mailing Add:* Dept Agron Univ Fla Plant Sci Lab Gainesville FL 32611

SMITH, RICHARD A, FAMILY MEDICINE. *Current Pos:* ADJ PROF FAMILY PRACT & COMMUNITY HEALTH & DIR, MEDEX GROUP, JOHN A BURNS SCH MED, UNIV HAWAII, 72- *Personal Data:* b Norwalk, Conn, Oct 13, 32. *Educ:* Howard Univ, BS, 53, MD, 57; Columbia Univ, MPH, 60; Am Bd Prev Med, dipl, 67. *Honors & Awards:* William A Jump Award, HEW, 68; Gerard B Lambert Award, 71; Rockefeller Pub Serv Award, 81. *Prof Exp:* Intern, USPHS Hosp, Seattle, 57-58; resident, Los Angeles City Health Dept, 58-59; epidemiologist, Wash State Health Dept, 60-61; sr Peace Corps physician, Lagos, Nigeria, 61-63; asst prof, Dept Prev Med, Howard Univ, 63-68; assoc prof & dir, Medex Prog, Sch Pub Health & Community Med, Univ Wash, 68-72. *Concurrent Pos:* Africa regional med officer, Med Prog Div, Peace Corps, 63-64, dep dir, 64-65; exec mgt trainee, Off Surgeon Gen, 65-66, spec asst dir, Off Int Health, 66, chief, Off Planning, 67, dep dir, Off Int Health, 67-68; clin asst prof, Dept Community & Int Health, Sch Med, Georgetown Univ, 67-68; adv, US deleg WHO, 67 & 70, mem, Int Task Force World Health Manpower, 70, consult, 77-; mem, Nat Adv Allied Health Prof Coun, NIH, 71 & bd dirs, Am Inst Res, 81- *Mem:* Inst Med-Nat Acad Sci; Am Pub Health Asn; Am Soc Trop Med & Hyg; fel Am Col Prev Med. *Res:* Family practice and community health care; author of 25 technical publications. *Mailing Add:* Medex Group Univ Hawaii 666 Prospect St No 610 Honolulu HI 96813

SMITH, RICHARD ALAN, BIOCHEMISTRY, ENZYMOLOGY. *Current Pos:* from asst prof to assoc prof, 69-89, chmn dept, 84-92, PROF CHEM, STATE UNIV COL ARTS & SCI, 89- *Personal Data:* b Moscow, Idaho, Aug 6, 40; m 67, Elizabeth Musil; c Mary K & Michael A. *Educ:* Whitman Col, BA, 62; Univ Minn, St Paul, PhD(biochem), 67. *Prof Exp:* Res assoc biochem, Univ Hawaii, 67-69. *Concurrent Pos:* Vis prof, Univ Rochester, 83-84. *Mem:* AAAS; Am Chem Soc; Am Soc Biochem & Molecular Biol. *Res:* Structure-function relationships in enzymes; amine oxidases; phosphatases. *Mailing Add:* Dept Chem State Univ Col Arts & Sci Geneseo NY 14454. *Fax:* 716-245-5288; *E-Mail:* smithr@uno.cc.geneseo.edu

SMITH, RICHARD ALAN, NEUROLOGY, MEDICAL ADMINISTRATION. *Current Pos:* DIR, CTR NEUROLOGIC STUDY, 79-; MEM SR STAFF, SCRIPPS MEMORIAL HOSP, LA JOLLA, CALIF, 82- *Educ:* Univ Miami, MD, 65. *Honors & Awards:* Henry Newman Award, 68. *Prof Exp:* Intern med, Jackson Mem Hosp, Miami, 65-66; resident neurol, Stanford Univ Hosp, 66-69; head, Neurol Bd, Navy Neuropsychiat Res Unit, San Diego, 69-71; mem assoc staff microbiol, Scripps Clin & Res Found, Calif, 72-79, mem assoc staff neurol, 72-82. *Concurrent Pos:* Founder, Neurosci Network Affiliated Res Ctrs. *Mem:* AAAS; Am Acad Neurol. *Res:* Patents in methodologies of enhancing the systematic delivery of dextromethorphan for the treatment of neurological disorders; reducing emotional lability in neurologically impaired patients; use of cytochrome oxidase inhibitor to increase the cough-suppressing activity of dextromethorphan; granted four US patents. *Mailing Add:* Ctr Neurol Study 9850 Genesee Ave Suite 120 La Jolla CA 92037

SMITH, RICHARD ANDREW, hematology, anatomy, for more information see previous edition

SMITH, RICHARD AVERY, earth sciences & science education, for more information see previous edition

SMITH, RICHARD BARRIE, FOREST PATHOLOGY, FOREST ECOLOGY. *Current Pos:* RETIRED. *Personal Data:* b Vernon, BC, Apr 18, 34; m 59; c 2. *Educ:* Univ BC, BSF, 57, PhD(forest ecol), 63; Yale Univ, MF, 58. *Prof Exp:* Res officer forest path, Can Dept Agr, 59-63; res officer, Forestry Can, Pac Forestry Ctr Can, 63-65, res scientist II environ forestry & forest path, 65-85, res scientist III environ forestry, 85-92. *Concurrent Pos:* Int Joint Comn, 71. *Mem:* Can Inst Forestry; Can Phytopath Soc; Int Mountain Soc; Can Soc Soil Sci; Soil & Water Conserv Soc Am. *Res:* Edaphotopes of forest ecosystems; impact and biology of dwarf mistletoes on western North American conifers; environmental impact of forest management practices; forest productivity and natural revegetation on landslides. *Mailing Add:* Gen Delivery 7797 16th St Grand Forks BC V0H 1H0 Can

SMITH, RICHARD CARPER, OPTICS. *Current Pos:* from asst prof to assoc prof, 68-88, PROF PHYSICS, UNIV WFLA, 88- *Personal Data:* b Jacksonville, Fla, May 9, 38; m 66; c 2. *Educ:* Davidson Col, BS, 60; Lehigh Univ, MS, 62, PhD(physics), 66. *Prof Exp:* Res physicist, Nat Security Agency, 67-68. *Mem:* Am Asn Physics Teachers. *Res:* Use of coherent optical processing systems for image storage and enhancement. *Mailing Add:* Dept Physics Univ WFla Pensacola FL 32504

SMITH, RICHARD CHANDLER, FOREST ECONOMICS. *Current Pos:* prof, 47-82, EMER PROF FORESTRY, UNIV MO-COLUMBIA, 82- *Personal Data:* b St Paul, Minn, Sept 10, 13; m 44, Mary Maldoon; c Chandler. *Educ:* Univ Minn, BS, 37; Duke Univ, MF, 47, DF, 50. *Honors & Awards:* Forest Conserv Award, Mo Conserv Fedn, 71. *Prof Exp:* Field asst & jr forester, Forest Serv, USDA, 33-39; forester, Am Creosoting Co, 40-42. *Concurrent Pos:* Res forester, Forest Serv, USDA, 62-63. *Mem:* Fel Soc Am Foresters. *Res:* Forest economics and management; economics of timber production and multiple-use forestry. *Mailing Add:* Sch Natural Resources Univ Mo Columbia MO 65211

SMITH, RICHARD CLARK, PLANT PHYSIOLOGY. *Current Pos:* from asst prof to assoc prof, 64-77, PROF BOT, UNIV FLA, 77- *Personal Data:* b Salem, Ind, Apr 17, 27; m 57; c 1. *Educ:* Vanderbilt Univ, AB, 49; Duke Univ, AM, 52, PhD(bot), 57. *Prof Exp:* Instr bot, Univ Tenn, 56-58 & Miami Univ, 58-59; from instr to asst prof, Rutgers Univ, 59-62; plant physiologist, Univ Calif, Davis, 62-64. *Concurrent Pos:* Consult, Univ Ill, 72. *Mem:* AAAS; Bot Soc Am; Am Soc Plant Physiol; Scand Soc Plant Physiol. *Res:* Absorption and translocation of mineral ions in plants; metabolic activities of roots; plant growth. *Mailing Add:* 4830 NW 13th Ave Gainesville FL 32605-4583

SMITH, RICHARD DALE, MASS SPECTROMETRY, CAPILLARY ELECTROPHORESIS. *Current Pos:* Res scientist, Battelle, Pac Lab, 76-78, sr res scientist, 78-83, staff scientist, 83-88, SR STAFF SCIENTIST, BATTELLE, PAC LAB, 88- *Personal Data:* b Lawrence, Mass, July 1, 49; m 85, Elaine Chapman; c Jeffrey. *Educ:* Lowell Technol Inst, BS, 71; Univ Utah, PhD(physical chem), 75. *Concurrent Pos:* Dir, FTICR Mass Spectrometry Resource. *Mem:* Am Chem Soc; AAAS; Am Soc Mass Spectrometry. *Res:* Development of advanced separation and mass spectrometric methods for use in biological and health-effects research. *Mailing Add:* Pac Northwest Nat Lab PO Box 999 Richland WA 99352. *E-Mail:* rd_smith@pnl.gov

SMITH, RICHARD ELBRIDGE, GEOLOGY, GEOCHEMISTRY. *Current Pos:* CHIEF GEOLOGIST, OFF STRATEGIC PETROL RESERVE, DEPT ENERGY, 75- *Personal Data:* b Keene, NH, May 30, 32; m 63; c 2. *Educ:* Univ NH, BA, 59; Univ Ill, Urbana, MS, 60; Pa State Univ, PhD(petrol), 66. *Prof Exp:* Res oceanogr, Ocean Sci Dept, US Naval Oceanog Off, 66-70, actg head, Marine Chem Br, Res & Develop Dept, 70-75. *Mem:* Geol Soc Am; Soc Econ Paleontologists & Mineralogists. *Res:* Geochemistry trace metals of coastal marine sediments; crude oil storage in salt domes. *Mailing Add:* 7829 Willowbrook Rd Fairfax Station VA 22039-2109

SMITH, RICHARD FREDERICK, ORGANIC CHEMISTRY. *Current Pos:* chmn dept chem, 65-68, prof 65-74, DISTINGUISHED TEACHING PROF, STATE UNIV NY COL GENESEO, 74- *Personal Data:* b Lockport, NY, Jan 31, 29; m 51; c 3. *Educ:* Allegheny Col, BS, 50; Univ Rochester, PhD(chem), 54. *Prof Exp:* Res chemist, Monsanto Chem Co, 53-55; res assoc, Sterling-Winthrop Res Inst, 55-57; from assoc prof to prof chem, State Univ NY Albany, 57-65. *Concurrent Pos:* NSF fac fel, Univ Calif, Los Angeles, 62-63; vis prof, Dartmouth Col, 81, 83 & 87 Wesleyan, 85-86. *Mem:* Am Chem Soc; Royal Soc Chem. *Res:* Heterocycles; amine-imides; organic hydrazine derivatives. *Mailing Add:* 20 Oak Geneseo NY 14454-1306

SMITH, RICHARD G(RANT), APPLIED PHYSICS, ELECTRICAL ENGINEERING. *Current Pos:* RETIRED. *Personal Data:* b Flint, Mich, Jan 19, 37; m 65, Carol Treanor; c Joseph, Judith & Heather. *Educ:* Stanford Univ, BS, 58, MS, 59, PhD(elec eng, appl physics), 63. *Honors & Awards:* Centennial Award, Inst Elec & Electronics Engrs. *Prof Exp:* Mem tech staff, Bell Tel Labs, 63-68, supvr, 68-82, dept head, 82-87, dir, AT&T Bell Labs, 87-93. *Concurrent Pos:* Chmn, Conf Laser & Electro-optical Systs, 80-; pres, Inst Elec & Electronic Engrs Lasers & Electro-optics Soc, 81. *Mem:* Fel Inst Elec & Electronics Engrs; fel Optical Soc Am. *Res:* Quantum theory of nonlinear effects; nonlinear optics; lasers; optical fiber communications. *Mailing Add:* 3111 Aspen Lane Center Valley PA 18034

SMITH, RICHARD HARDING, immunochemistry, receptor biochemistry, for more information see previous edition

SMITH, RICHARD HARRISON, FOREST ENTOMOLOGY. *Current Pos:* RETIRED. *Personal Data:* b Ellenville, NY, Nov 28, 20; m 46, Mary Casey; c Carolyn & Bruce. *Educ:* State Univ NY, BS, 42, MS, 47; Univ Calif, PhD(entom), 61. *Prof Exp:* Forest entomologist, Bur Entom & Plant Quarantine, Forest Serv, USDA, 46-52, forest entomologist, 53-89. *Mem:* Entom Soc Am; Am Inst Biol Scientists. *Res:* Biology and control of Lyctus and Dendroctonus terebrans; resistance of pines to bark beetles and the pine reproduction weevil; variation, distribution and genetics of monoterpenes of pine xylem resin; forest insect research; direct control of bark beetles; residual insecticides for bark beetles. *Mailing Add:* 3910 LeRoy Way Lafayette CA 94549

SMITH, RICHARD JAMES, SOLID STATE PHYSICS, SURFACE PHYSICS. *Current Pos:* MEM FAC PHYS DEPT, MONT STATE UNIV, 80- *Personal Data:* b Lansing, Mich, Jan 31, 47; m 70; c 4. *Educ:* St Mary's Col, Minn, BA, 69; Iowa State Univ, PhD(solid state physics), 75. *Prof Exp:* Res assoc physics, Mont State Univ, 75-77; asst scientist, Brookhaven Nat Lab, 77-80. *Concurrent Pos:* Sabbatical leave, FOM Inst, Amsterdam, Neth, 87-88. *Mem:* Am Phys Soc; Am Vacuum Soc; Mat Res Soc; Am Asn Physics Teachers. *Res:* Electronic and structural studies of surfaces of condensed matter; ion-solid interactions. *Mailing Add:* Phys Dept Mont State Univ 259 EPS Bldg Bozeman MT 59717. *Fax:* 406-994-4452; *E-Mail:* uphrs@msu.oscs.montana.edu

SMITH, RICHARD JAY, CRANIOFACIAL BIOLOGY, HOMINOID EVOLUTION. *Current Pos:* prof & chmn, Dept Orthod, 84-91, prof biomed sci, 87-91, PROF ANTHROP, WASHINGTON UNIV 91-, CHMN, DEPT ANTHROP, 93- *Personal Data:* b Brooklyn, NY, Aug 10, 48; m 70, Linda S Harris; c Jason, Owen & Hilary. *Educ:* Brooklyn Col, BA, 69; Tufts Univ, MS & DMD, 73; Yale Univ, PhD(anthrop), 80. *Prof Exp:* Resident orthod, Health Ctr, Univ Conn, 73-76, asst clin prof, 76-79; from asst prof to assoc prof orthod, Dent Sch, Univ Md, 79-84. *Concurrent Pos:* Dir, Postgrad Prog, Dept Orthod, Dent Sch, Univ Md, 80-84; vis assoc prof, Dept Cell Biol, Med Sch, Johns Hopkins Univ, 81-84; ed-in-chief, J Baltimore Col Dent Surg, 81-84; assoc dean, 87, adj prof anthrop, 85-91, dean, Sch Dent Med, Wash Univ, 89-91. *Mem:* Am Asn Orthodontists; Am Asn Phys Anthropologists; Am Dent Asn; Soc Study Evolution; Int Primatological Soc. *Res:* Functional morphology of craniofacial variation in mammals, particularly primates; biomechanical modeling correlates; paleontology; allometry; comparative methods. *Mailing Add:* Dept Anthrop Campus Box 1114 Washington Univ St Louis MO 63130

SMITH, RICHARD LLOYD, ASTROPHYSICS. *Current Pos:* STAFF MEM, ANALYTICAL SCI CORP, 85- *Personal Data:* b Binghamton, NY, Oct 15, 45; m 68; c 1. *Educ:* Rensselaer Polytech Inst, BS, 67; Mass Inst Technol, PhD(physics), 71. *Prof Exp:* Res fel physics, Calif Inst Technol, 71-72; asst prof physics, Rensselaer Polytech Inst, 72-77; staff mem, Syst Sci Div, Comput Sci Corp, 77-85. *Mem:* Am Astron Soc; Sigma Xi; Am Astronaut Soc. *Res:* Orbit determination. *Mailing Add:* 505 Burnt Mill Ave Silver Spring MD 20901

SMITH, RICHARD M, SCIENCE ADMINISTRATION. *Current Pos:* Field engr, Fed Commun Comn, Los Angeles, 63, engr-in-charge, Philadelphia, chief, Invest Br, Washington DC, chief, Field Opers Bur, 81, CHIEF OFF ENG & TECHNOL, FED COMMUN COMN. *Personal Data:* m, Patti Hawkins; c Douglas. *Educ:* Tenn Technol Univ, BS. *Mailing Add:* Off Eng & Technol Fed Commun Comn 2000 M St NW Suite 480 Washington DC 20554

SMITH, RICHARD MERRILL, PHYSIOLOGY. *Current Pos:* from asst prof to assoc prof, 71-87, PROF PHYSIOL, SCH MED, UNIV HAWAII, 87- *Personal Data:* b South Bend, Ind, Nov 3, 42; m 64; c 2. *Educ:* Ind Univ, Bloomington, AB, 64, PhD(physiol), 69. *Prof Exp:* Rockefeller Found vis prof physiol, Mahidol Univ, Thailand, 69-71. *Concurrent Pos:* NIH pulmonary fac training award, 77-82. *Res:* Lung defense mechanisms in O2 toxicity. *Mailing Add:* Dept Physiol Univ Hawaii Burns Sch Med 1960 East-West Rd Honolulu HI 96822-2319

SMITH, RICHARD NEILSON, physical chemistry, electrochemistry, for more information see previous edition

SMITH, RICHARD PAUL, SUPERCONDUCTING MAGNET TECHNOLOGY, EXPERIMENTAL HIGH ENERGY PHYSICS. *Current Pos:* MEM, E740, E771 COLLABORATIONS, 87- *Personal Data:* b Omaha, Nebr, Jan 31, 43; m 63, Ann Semin; c Paul, David & Caitlyn. *Educ:* Univ Nebr, BS, 65; Syracuse Univ, MS, 67, PhD(physics), 72. *Prof Exp:* Researcher physics, 72-79, group leader & prin investr superconducting magnets, Argonne Nat Lab, 79-83; head, dept cryogen, Fermi Nat Acclerator Lab, 83-86. *Concurrent Pos:* Consult superconducting magnets. *Mem:* Am Phys Soc; Sigma Xi. *Res:* High energy particle physics, weak interactions; computer controlled film scanning; superconducting magnet design. *Mailing Add:* Fermi Nat Accelerator Lab MS 357 PO Box 500 Batavia IL 60510. *Fax:* 630-840-8886; *E-Mail:* rpsmith@fnal.gov

SMITH, RICHARD PEARSON, PHYSICAL CHEMISTRY. *Current Pos:* RETIRED. *Personal Data:* b Garland, Utah, Mar 4, 26. *Educ:* Univ Utah, BA, 48, PhD(phys chem), 51. *Prof Exp:* Jr fel, Harvard Univ, 51-53; from asst prof to assoc prof chem, Univ Utah, 53-61; mem staff, Exxon Res & Eng Co, 61-82. *Res:* Electronic structure of molecules; polarizabilities; dipole moments; substituent effects on rates and equilibria; polymer structure and property relationships; computer applications in chemistry. *Mailing Add:* 958 Willow Grove Rd Westfield NJ 07090

SMITH, RICHARD S, JR, plant pathology, for more information see previous edition

SMITH, RICHARD SCOTT, immunology, immunochemistry, for more information see previous edition

SMITH, RICHARD THOMAS, PEDIATRICS, PATHOLOGY. *Current Pos:* prof pediat & head dept, Col Med & chief pediat, Hosp & Clin, 58-67, vpres advan, 84-88, PROF PATH & CHMN DEPT, COL MED, UNIV FLA, 67-, C A STETSON PROF EXP MED, 81- *Personal Data:* b Oklahoma City, Okla, Apr 15, 24; m 46; c 5. *Educ:* Univ Tex, BA, 44; Tulane Univ, MD, 50; Am Bd Pediat, dipl; Am Bd Allergy & Immunol, dipl. *Prof Exp:* Intern pediat, Univ Minn Hosps, 50-51, resident, Med Sch, 51-52, asst prof pediat, 55-56; assoc prof, Southwestern Med Sch, Univ Tex, 57-58. *Concurrent Pos:* Nat Res Coun fel med sci, Med Sch, Univ Minn, 52-53, Helen Hay Whitney Found res fel rheumatic fever & allied dis, 53-55; sr investr, Arthritis & Rheumatism Found, 55-58. *Mem:* AAAS; Am Pediat Soc; Soc Pediat Res; Soc Exp Biol & Med; Am Soc Path. *Res:* General and clinical immunology; tumor immunobiology. *Mailing Add:* Dept Path Univ Fla Col Med JHMHC Box 100275 Gainesville FL 32610-0275. *Fax:* 904-392-6288

SMITH, RICHARD THOMAS, nondestructive evaluation, ocean engineering, for more information see previous edition

SMITH, ROBERT ALAN, BORON CHEMISTRY, BORON IN GLASS. *Current Pos:* sr res chemist boron chem, 70-90, SR SCIENTIST, US BORAX INC, SUBSID RIO TINTO ZINC, LTD, 90- *Personal Data:* b Glendale, Calif, Oct 30, 39; m 61, Eleanor Shemld; c Brian P & D Courtney. *Educ:* Univ Calif, Los Angeles, BS, 62; State Univ NY Buffalo, PhD(org chem), 68. *Prof Exp:* Sr res chemist petrochem, Atlantic Richfield Co, 68-69; fel, Calif Inst Technol, 69-70. *Mem:* Am Chem Soc; Sigma Xi; Am Ceramic Soc; Mat Res Soc. *Res:* Inorganic and organic borate chemistry. *Mailing Add:* 21260 Trial Ridge Yorba Linda CA 92886-7806. *Fax:* 805-287-6014; *E-Mail:* boraxlab@ix.netcom.com

SMITH, ROBERT BAER, geophysics, geology, for more information see previous edition

SMITH, ROBERT C, BIOCHEMISTRY. *Current Pos:* from asst prof to assoc prof, 61-68, alumni assoc prof, 68-69, ALUMNI PROF ANIMAL SCI, AUBURN UNIV, 69- *Personal Data:* b Chicago, Ill, Sept 15, 32; m 57, Katherine Kopacz; c Robert, Laura & Jean. *Educ:* Elmhurst Col, BS, 54; Univ Ill, MS, 58, PhD(biochem), 60. *Prof Exp:* USPHS res fel, 59-61. *Mem:* NY Acad Sci; Am Soc Biol Chemists; Oxygen Soc. *Res:* Nucleic acids; nucleotides; uric acid; 3-ribosyluric acid; antioxidants. *Mailing Add:* Dept Animal & Dairy Sci Auburn Univ Auburn AL 36849-5415. *Fax:* 334-844-1519; *E-Mail:* rsmith@acesag.auburn.edu

SMITH, ROBERT CLINTON, THEORETICAL PHYSICS. *Current Pos:* Lectr, Univ Ottawa, 58-60, asst prof, 60-66, secy, Fac Sci & Eng, 78-86, chmn dept physics, 86-91, ASSOC PROF PHYSICS, UNIV OTTAWA, 66- *Personal Data:* b St Thomas, Ont, Mar 11, 32; m 55; c 2. *Educ:* Univ Western Ont, BSc, 54; McGill Univ, MSc, 56, PhD(theoret physics), 60. *Mem:* Am Asn Physics Teachers; Can Asn Physicists; Can Asn Univ Teachers. *Mailing Add:* 185 S Illinois Ave Univ Ottawa Ottawa ON K1H 6W5 Can

SMITH, ROBERT EARL, AERONOMY. *Current Pos:* SR COMPUT SCIENTIST, COMPUT SCI CORP, 96- *Personal Data:* b Indianapolis, Ind, Sept 13, 23; m 47, 88, Lyla L Lewellen; c Stephanie L (Higginbotham), Robert M, Cynthia A & Kelly A. *Educ:* Fla State Univ, BS, 59, MS, 60; Univ Mich, MS, 69, PhD(atmospheric sci), 74. *Prof Exp:* USAF, 43-63; dep chief, Atmospheric Sci Div, George C Marshall Space Flight Ctr 63-86; sr res engr,

Comput Sci Corp, 87-89; chief, Space Sci & Appln Div, FWG Assoc, Inc, 89-92; prin scientist, Physitron Inc, 92-96. *Mem:* Am Meteorol Soc; Am Inst Aeronaut & Astronaut. *Res:* Temperature and dynamic structure of the upper atmosphere from 6300 angstrom units; atomic oxygen airglow emissions; natural space environment for the Space Station; natural environment for the National Aerospace Plane. *Mailing Add:* 125 Westbury Dr Huntsville AL 35802

SMITH, ROBERT EDWARD, PEDOLOGY. *Current Pos:* RETIRED. *Personal Data:* b Winnipeg, Man, Oct 4, 29; m 56; c 4. *Educ:* Univ Man, BA, 52, 55. *Prof Exp:* Pedologist, Man Dept Agr, 56-63; pedologist, Land Resource Res Inst, Can Dept Agr, 63-68, head, Pedology Sect, 68-94, mem staff, Man Soul Surv Unit, 73-94; head soil surv, Univ Man, Winnipeg. *Concurrent Pos:* Adj prof soil sci, Univ Man, 74-94. *Mem:* Agr Inst Can; Can Soc Soil Sci; Int Soc Soil Sci. *Res:* Soil characterization, genesis and classification. *Mailing Add:* Two Bittersweet Bay Winnipeg MB R2J 2E6 Can

SMITH, ROBERT ELIJAH, COMPUTER SCIENCE, STATISTICS. *Current Pos:* RETIRED. *Personal Data:* b Pittsburgh, Pa, Aug 14, 11; m 38, Helene S; c Robert, James, William & Karen. *Educ:* State Univ Iowa, BA, 34; Univ Pittsburgh, PhD(statist, educ), 51. *Prof Exp:* Teacher, Iowa, Pa & NJ, 34-44; prof math & head dept, Duquesne Univ, 44-57; comput analyst, Univac Div, Sperry Rand Corp, Minn, 57-58; prin consult, Control Data Corp, Minneapolis, 58-80. *Mem:* Am Math Soc. *Res:* Computer programming projects; author programming books. *Mailing Add:* 6912 Creston Rd Edina MN 55435

SMITH, ROBERT ELPHIN, physiology, biomedical engineering, for more information see previous edition

SMITH, ROBERT EMERY, ENGINEERING PHYSICS. *Current Pos:* RES SCIENTIST, UCAR CARBON CO, 89- *Personal Data:* b Jacksonville, Fla, Feb 2, 42; m 63; c 2. *Educ:* Duke Univ, BS, 63; Washington Univ, MA, 65, PhD(physics), 69. *Prof Exp:* Res scientist, Carbon Prod Div, Union Carbide Corp, 69-89. *Res:* Mathematical models of industrial products and processes, principally by finite element analysis; stress and heat transfer models; physical properties of graphite. *Mailing Add:* 20270 Applewood Lane Strongsville OH 44136

SMITH, ROBERT EUGENE, ION CHROMATOGRAPHY, NUCLEAR MAGNETIC RESONANCE SPECTROSCOPY. *Current Pos:* STAFF MEM, MIDWEST RES INST, 96- *Personal Data:* b Kansas City, Mo, Aug, 26, 51; div; c Alexander H. *Educ:* Univ Mo, Kansas City, BS, 73, MS, 78, PhD(chem), 79. *Prof Exp:* Res asst, Sinclair Comp Med Res Farm, 78-79; res asst, ETH-Zurich, Switz, 79-80; staff engr, Allied Signal, Inc, Kansas City Plant, anal sci lab, 80-96. *Concurrent Pos:* Adj assoc prof, Univ Mo, Kansas City, 85- *Mem:* AAAS. *Res:* Ion and liquid chromatography methods development with environmental and biochemical applications; production and use of plastic models of biopolymers and anatomical parts to teach science to children and to blind and deaf-blind people. *Mailing Add:* Midwest Res Inst 425 Volker Blvd Kansas City MO 64141. *Fax:* 816-997-7078

SMITH, ROBERT EWING, NUTRITION. *Current Pos:* VPRES RES & DEVELOP, SWIFT CO, 79- *Personal Data:* b Montreal, Que, Sept 20, 34; m 59; c 4. *Educ:* McGill Univ, BSc, 55, MSc, 57; Univ Ill, PhD(animal sci), 63. *Prof Exp:* Res scientist, Animal Res Inst, Can Dept Agr, 57-60 & 63-67; mgr poultry res, Quaker Oats Co, 67-69, mgr nutrit res, 69-73, dir qual assurance, 73-77, vpres foods res & develop, 77-79. *Concurrent Pos:* Indust liaison, Food & Nutrit Bd, Am Acad Pediat; panel chmn nutrit comt, Am Corn Millers Fedn. *Mem:* Poultry Sci Asn; Am Inst Nutrit; Nutrit Soc Can; Am Acad Pediat; Soc Nutrit Educ. *Res:* Nutritional quality of human and pet foods; proteins and amino acid requirements and interrelationships. *Mailing Add:* Res Nabisco Foods Group 57 Twinbrooks Tr Chester NJ 07930. *Fax:* 973-503-0921

SMITH, ROBERT FRANCIS, BEHAVIOR-ETHOLOGY, BIOELECTROMAGNETICS. *Current Pos:* CO-PRIN INVESTR, BEHAV RADIOL LABS, KANS CITY VET ADMIN MED CTR, 78- *Personal Data:* b Independence, Mo, May 4, 43; m 76, Sue Quanty; c Justin & Natalie. *Educ:* Univ Mo, BA, 73, MA, 76; Univ Kans, PhD(exp psychol), 84. *Prof Exp:* Res assoc, Dept Otorhinolaryngology, Kans Univ Med Ctr, 73-78. *Concurrent Pos:* Chmn subcomt, ANSI Working Group on Biorhythms, 83-; consult, West Assocs, Rosemead, Calif, 84-85, Midwest Res Inst, 85- *Mem:* Bioelectromagnetics Soc. *Res:* Experimental study of effects of low-frequency (DC-100 Hz) electromagnetic fields on mammals; evaluation of electromagnetic effects on learning, locomotor activity, agonistic behavior, body temperature (telemetry), metabolism, development, and brain function. *Mailing Add:* 9351 E 60th Terr Raytown MO 64133. *Fax:* 816-861-1110

SMITH, ROBERT GORDON, NATURAL SYSTEMS FOR WASTEWATER TREATMENT, HAZARDOUS WASTE TREATMENT. *Current Pos:* DEVELOP ENGR & LECTR ENVIRON ENG, DEPT CIVIL ENG, UNIV CALIF, DAVIS, 78- *Personal Data:* b Reno, Nev, May 11, 47; m 70, Toni Robustellini; c Lindsay. *Educ:* Stanford Univ, BS, 69, MS, 70; Univ Calif Davis, PhD(environ eng), 80. *Prof Exp:* Proj engr, Metcalf & Eddy Inc, 70-75. *Concurrent Pos:* Consult, Environ Engrs, 75-; res engr, Tech Univ, Hamburg, Ger, 84-85; vpres, Western Environ Sci & Technol, 87-; mem, Natural Treatment Systs Task Force, Water Environ Fedn, 89-90. *Mem:* Water Environ Fedn. *Res:* Natural systems for wastewater treatment including land treatment systems and wetlands; biological treatment of liquid hazardous wastes; remediation of contaminated soil and ground water. *Mailing Add:* 2312 Lassen Pl Davis CA 95616. *Fax:* 530-752-7872

SMITH, ROBERT JAMES, ARTHRITIC DISEASES. *Current Pos:* from res scientist to sr res scientist, 78-88, SR SCIENTIST, ARTHRITIC DIS, UPJOHN CO, 88- *Personal Data:* b Brooklyn, NY, May 30, 44; m 70; c 1. *Educ:* St John's Univ, BS, 66; Univ Md, MS, 70, PhD(physiol), 71. *Prof Exp:* Instr physiol, Univ Md, 71-72; fel pharmacol, NIH, Sch Med, Tulane Univ, 72-74; sr scientist arthritic dis, Schering Corp, 74-78. *Concurrent Pos:* Field ed, CRC Press, 80-; bd mem, Inflammation Res Asn. *Mem:* Am Soc Pharmacol & Exp Therapeut; Am Asn Immunologists; Am Rheumatism Asn; Am Soc Hemat; NY Acad Sci; AAAS. *Res:* Hypersensitivity disease; discovery and development of therapeutic agents for treatment of arthritic disease; cellular components of inflammatory joint disease. *Mailing Add:* Dept Cell Biol & Inflam Res Upjohn Co 301 Henrietta St Kalamazoo MI 49001-0199. *Fax:* 616-384-9324

SMITH, ROBERT JOHNSON, ORGANIC CHEMISTRY. *Current Pos:* RETIRED. *Personal Data:* b Blodgett, Mo, July 23, 16; m 48; c 3. *Educ:* Southeast Mo State Col, BS, 36; Univ Iowa, PhD(chem), 50. *Prof Exp:* Instr high schs, Mo, 36-42; from asst prof to prof chem, Southeast Mo State Col, 46-55; asst, Univ Iowa, 49-50; assoc prof, Eastern Ill Univ, 55-60, prof chem, 60-84. *Mem:* Am Chem Soc. *Res:* Mechanism and rate of addition of bromine to olefins in carbon tetrachloride solution; preparation and reactions of mercurials derived from olefins. *Mailing Add:* 1814 McKinley Ave Charleston IL 61920-3646

SMITH, ROBERT KINGSTON, inorganic chemistry, for more information see previous edition

SMITH, ROBERT L, NEUROSCIENCE, AUDITORY NEUROPHYSIOLOGY. *Current Pos:* instr elec eng, 70-74, from asst prof to assoc prof sensory res, 74-85, PROF NEUROSCI, SYRACUSE UNIV, 85-, DIR, INST SENSORY RES, 93- *Personal Data:* b New York, NY, Mar 29, 41; m 68, Carolee; c Jana, Shayna & Marni. *Educ:* City Col New York, BEE, 62; New York Univ, MSEE, 66; Syracuse Univ, PhD(neurosci), 73. *Prof Exp:* Develop engr, Wheeler Lab, Great Neck, NY, 62-64; lectr elec eng, City Col New York, 64-66. *Concurrent Pos:* Fel res career develop, NIH, Syracuse Univ, 79-84; assoc ed, J Acoust Soc Am, 86-89. *Mem:* Fel Acoust Soc Am; Sigma Xi; Asn Res Otolaryngol; Soc Neurosci. *Res:* Neurophysiology and neural coding in the auditory nervous system; single unit recording from the cochlea, auditory nerve and cochlear nuclei; mathematical modeling of the results and systems analysis of the auditory system; biological engineering. *Mailing Add:* Dept Bioeng & Neurosci Syracuse Univ 417 Link Hall Syracuse NY 13244. *E-Mail:* bob_smith@isr.syr.edu

SMITH, ROBERT LAWRENCE, ORGANIC CHEMISTRY, MEDICINAL CHEMISTRY. *Current Pos:* sr res chemist, 67-74, res fel, 74-75, asst dir, 75-77, assoc dir, 77-79, dir, 79-84, SR DIR, MERCK SHARP & DOHME RES LABS, 84- *Personal Data:* b Albemarle, NC, Aug 29, 39; m 62; c 2. *Educ:* Univ NC, BS, 61; Univ Maine, MS, 63, PhD(org chem), 65. *Prof Exp:* NIH res fel org chem, Univ NC, 65-67. *Mem:* AAAS; Am Chem Soc; Asn Res Vision & Ophthal. *Res:* General organic synthesis; synthesis of medicinals; development of orally active HMG-CoA reductase inhibitors and topically effective carbonic anhydrase inhibitors. *Mailing Add:* 1355 Pickwick Lane Lansdale PA 19446

SMITH, ROBERT LEE, civil engineering; deceased, see previous edition for last biography

SMITH, ROBERT LELAND, VOLCANOLOGY, RARE METAL GEOCHEMISTRY. *Current Pos:* From jr geologist to prin geologist, US Geol Surv, 43-60, chief, Field Geochem & Petrol Br, 60-66, res geologist, 66-82, sr res geologist, 82-93, EMER SCIENTIST, US GEOL SURV, 93- *Personal Data:* b Sacramento, Calif, June 30, 20; m 52, Barbara R Mooers; c W Leland, R Michael & R David. *Educ:* Univ Nev, BS, 42. *Hon Degrees:* DSc, Univ Lancaster, UK, 89. *Honors & Awards:* Distinguished Serv Medal, US Dept Interior, 83; First Thorarinsson Medal, Int Asn Volcanology & Chem Earth's Interior, 87. *Concurrent Pos:* Mem, Earth Sci Div, Nat Res Coun, 62-65; mem, US-Japan Sci Coop Volcano Res, 63-65; mem preliminary exam team, First Lunar Samples, Apollo 11 & 12, NASA, 69. *Mem:* Sr fel Geol Soc Am; fel Mineral Soc Am; Geochem Soc; Am Ornithologists Union; fel AAAS; hon fel Geol Soc UK, 96. *Res:* Mineralogy; petrology; geochemistry; pyroclastic rocks; volcanic glasses; rhyolitic volcanism; volcano tectonics, calderas and eruption cycles; geology of the Valles Mountains of New Mexico; geothermal resources; rare metals in igneous rocks; volcano hazards; bolivian tin belt. *Mailing Add:* 11064 Fair Oaks Blvd Fair Oaks CA 95628-5944. *Fax:* 916-965-6270; *E-Mail:* rblsmith@mojave.wr.usgs.gov

SMITH, ROBERT LEO, wildlife management, ecology, for more information see previous edition

SMITH, ROBERT LEONARD, INDUSTRIAL HYGIENE CHEMISTRY, ENVIRONMENTAL HEALTH. *Current Pos:* DIR CORP TOXICOL, REGULATORY & ENVIRON AFFAIRS, ALBEMARLE CORP, 96- *Personal Data:* b New Orleans, La, Jan 19, 44; m 66; c 1. *Educ:* La State Univ, New Orleans, BS, 65, PhD(chem), 70. *Prof Exp:* Res chemist, Res & Develop Lab, Ethyl Corp, 70-77, environ chemist, 77-79, supvr, Toxicol & Indust Hygiene Lab, 79-83, Corp Regulatory Affairs, 83-86, mgr corp toxicol, 87-88, dir corp toxicol & regulatory affairs, 88-96. *Mem:* Am Chem Soc. *Res:* Absorption spectroscopy; photochemistry. *Mailing Add:* Albemarle Corp 451 Florida Blvd Baton Rouge LA 70815. *Fax:* 504-388-7046

SMITH, ROBERT LEWIS, BIOCHEMISTRY. *Current Pos:* asst prof biochem, 68-71, ASSOC PROF BIOCHEM, LA STATE UNIV, SHREVEPORT, 71- *Personal Data:* b Ranger, Tex, June 22, 38; m 60; c 4. *Educ:* Abilene Christian Col, BS, 61; Univ Tenn, Memphis, MS, 62, PhD(biochem), 66. *Prof Exp:* Vis lectr chem, Queens Col, NC, 65-66; res assoc protein chem & enzym, Biol Dept, Brookhaven Nat Lab, 66-68. *Concurrent Pos:* Res chemist, Vet Admin Hosp, Shreveport, La, 69-77. *Mem:* Sigma Xi; Am Chem Soc. *Res:* Protein chemistry; plasma proteins; blood coagulation; membrane transport of amino acids and peptides. *Mailing Add:* Dept Biochem Sch Med La State Univ Box 33932 Shreveport LA 71130-3932

SMITH, ROBERT LLOYD, PHYSICAL OCEANOGRAPHY. *Current Pos:* From instr to assoc prof, 62-75, PROF PHYS OCEANOG, ORE STATE UNIV, 75- *Personal Data:* b Chicago, Ill, Dec 10, 35; m 86, Adriana Huyer; c Suzanne (Banyas), Sean & Colin. *Educ:* Reed Col, BA, 57; Univ Ore, MA, 59; Ore State Univ, PhD(oceanog), 64. *Concurrent Pos:* NATO fel, Nat Inst Oceanog, Eng, 65-66; sci officer, Off Naval Res, 69-71; vis prof, Inst Meerekunde, Univ Kiel, Ger, 79; vis scientist, Commonwealth Sci & Indust Res Orgn Marine Lab, Hobart, Australia, 88; mem, outer continental shelf adv comt, Minerals Mgt Serv, Dept Interior, 86-94; ed, Progress in Oceanog, 85- *Mem:* Fel AAAS; Am Geophys Union; Oceanog Soc; Am Meteorol Soc. *Res:* General physical oceanography, currents, upwelling, coastal oceanography. *Mailing Add:* Col Oceanic & Atmospheric Sci Ore State Univ Corvallis OR 97331-5503. *Fax:* 541-737-2064; *E-Mail:* rsmith@oce.orst.edu

SMITH, ROBERT LLOYD, BEHAVIOR-ETHOLOGY, ENTOMOLOGY. *Current Pos:* asst prof, 77-83, ASSOC PROF, DEPT ENTOM, UNIV ARIZ, 83- *Personal Data:* b Spirit Lake, Iowa, July 25, 41; div; c 1. *Educ:* NMex State Univ, BS, 68, MS,71; Ariz State Univ, PhD(zool),75. *Prof Exp:* Entomologist, USDA, Agr Res Serv, Western Cotton Res Lab, 75-77. *Mem:* AAAS; Am Inst Biol Sci; Am Soc Naturalists; Animal Behav Soc; Entomol Soc Am. *Res:* Insect behavior; evolutionary biology; aquatic entomology; urban entomology; reproductive biology. *Mailing Add:* Dept Entomol Univ Ariz Tucson AZ 85721-0001

SMITH, ROBERT OWENS, EXPERIMENTAL SOLID STATE PHYSICS, ENVIRONMENTAL PHYSICS. *Current Pos:* chmn dept, 74-84, PROF PHYSICS, MONMOUTH COL, 69- *Personal Data:* b Elizabethton, Tenn, May 13, 37; m 61; c 2. *Educ:* Univ Colo, BS, 62; Rutgers Univ, MS, 64, PhD(physics), 69. *Prof Exp:* Mem tech staff explor develop, Bell Labs, 62-64; res fel solid state physics, Rutgers Univ, 64-69. *Mem:* Am Phys Soc; Am Asn Physics Teachers. *Res:* Solar energy conversion. *Mailing Add:* 72 Meyers Mill Rd Colts Neck NJ 07722

SMITH, ROBERT PAUL, MATHEMATICS, STATISTICS. *Current Pos:* ASST PROF MATH, ARK STATE UNIV, 69- *Personal Data:* b St Lucas, Iowa, Sept 9, 42; m 69; c 2. *Educ:* Loras Col, BS, 64; Univ Ariz, MA, 66, PhD(math), 71. *Mem:* Inst Math Statist. *Res:* Statistical inference and hypothesis testing for continuous time parameter stochastic processes. *Mailing Add:* Dept Math Box 70 State Univ Ark State University AR 72467

SMITH, ROBERT SEFTON, COMPUTER-AIDED INSTRUCTION IN MATHEMATICS. *Current Pos:* asst prof math, 69-77, ASSOC PROF MATH & STATIST, MIAMI UNIV, 77- *Personal Data:* b Baltimore, Md, Aug 16, 41; m; c 3. *Educ:* Morgan State Col, BS, 63; Pa State Univ, MA, 67, PhD(math), 69. *Mem:* Math Asn Am. *Res:* Computer-aided instruction in mathematics; lattice theory. *Mailing Add:* Dept Math & Statist Miami Univ Oxford OH 45056-1641

SMITH, ROBERT W, atomic physics, for more information see previous edition

SMITH, ROBERT WILLIAM, MICROBIOLOGY, BIOCHEMISTRY. *Current Pos:* Fel, Purdue Univ, West Lafayette, 64-65, res assoc, 65-67, asst prof microbiol, 67-74, EXEC OFFICER, DEPT BIOL SCI, PURDUE UNIV, WEST LAFAYETTE, 74- *Personal Data:* b Ft Worth, Tex, Apr 14, 39; m 58; c 2. *Educ:* NTex State Univ, BA, 60; Okla State Univ, PhD(microbiol), 65. *Mem:* Am Soc Microbiol. *Res:* Microbial physiology; structure genetics; protein chemistry; nature of self-associating protein systems; thermophily. *Mailing Add:* Dept Biol Sci West Lafayette IN 47907

SMITH, ROBERT WILLIAM, ECOLOGY, STATISTICS. *Current Pos:* CONSULTS DATA ANALYSIS, SOUTHERN CALIF EDISON, SCI APPL, INC, WOODWARD-CLYDE CONSULTS, INC, HARBORS ENVIRON PROJ, INST MARINE & COASTAL STUDIES, UNIV SOUTHERN CALIF, LA CO SANITATION DIST, 77- & LOCKHEED AIRCRAFT SERV, MARINE BIOL CONSULTS, 78-; PRES, ECOANALYSIS INC. *Personal Data:* b Chelsea, Mass, Mar 21, 43; m 68; c 2. *Educ:* Univ Calif, Berkeley, BA, 65; Univ Wash, BS, 69; Univ Southern Calif, PhD(biol), 76. *Prof Exp:* Instr ecol, Univ Southern Calif, 76-77. *Mem:* AAAS; Am Soc Naturalists; Ecol Soc Am; Am Statist Asn. *Res:* Development of analytical techniques for ecological-survey data; development of computer software for data analysis. *Mailing Add:* 221 E Matilija Suite A Ojai CA 93023

SMITH, ROBERTA HAWKINS, PLANT PHYSIOLOGY, PLANT SCIENCE. *Current Pos:* from asst prof to assoc prof plant sci, 74-83, PROF SOIL & CROP SCI, TEX A&M UNIV, 83-, EUGENE BUTLER PROF AGR BIOTECHNOL, 86- *Personal Data:* b Tulare, Calif, May 3, 45; m 69; c James W & Cristine L. *Educ:* Univ Calif, Riverside, BA, 67, MS, 68, PhD(plant sci & physiol), 70. *Prof Exp:* Asst prof biol, Sam Houston State Univ, 73-74. *Concurrent Pos:* Nat corresp, Int Asn Plant Tissue Cult, 82-86; chmn, Plant Div, Tissue Cult Asn, mem exec bd; chmn, fac plant physiol, Tex A&M Univ, 87-89, C-7, Crop Sci, 91; gov bd, Int Crops Res Inst for the Semi-Arid Tropics, 89-92. *Mem:* Am Soc Plant Physiol; Am Soc Plant Physiol; Int Asn Plant Tissue Cult; Tissue Cult Asn; Crop Sci Soc Am. *Res:* Plant morphology; plant tissue culture; crop improvement. *Mailing Add:* Dept Soil & Crop Sci Tex A&M Univ College Station TX 77843-0100. *Fax:* 409-862-4301

SMITH, ROBERTS ANGUS, BIOCHEMISTRY. *Current Pos:* from asst prof to prof, 58-87, EMER PROF CHEM, UNIV CALIF, LOS ANGELES, 87- *Personal Data:* b Vancouver, BC, Dec 22, 28; nat US; m 53; c 4. *Educ:* Univ BC, BSA, 52, MSc, 53; Univ Ill, PhD(biochem), 57. *Prof Exp:* Instr chem, Univ Ill, 57-58. *Concurrent Pos:* Dir, ICN Pharmaceut Inc, 61-; Guggenheim fel, Cambridge Univ, 63; pres, VIRATEK Inc, 80- *Mem:* Am Chem Soc; Am Soc Biol Chemists. *Res:* Biological phosphoryl transfer reactions; chromosomal protein modification; antiviral and anticancer agents. *Mailing Add:* 221 17th St Santa Monica CA 90402-2221

SMITH, RODERICK MACDOWELL, FISHERIES. *Current Pos:* PHYS SCI PROG COORDR, EXETER HIGH SCH, 84- *Personal Data:* b Boston, Mass, Mar 15, 44; m 66; c 3. *Educ:* Earlham Col, BA, 65; Univ Mass, MS, 69, PhD(fisheries), 72. *Prof Exp:* Consult, Mass Div Fisheries & Game, 71; prof marine sci, Stockton State Col, 71-74; asst prof zool, Univ NH, 74-81, adj asst prof zool, 81-84. *Concurrent Pos:* Mem, Acad Adv Coun Study Comn, 73; consult biologist, Wetlands Inst, Lehigh Univ, 73-74. *Mem:* Am Fisheries Soc. *Res:* The reestablishing of anadromous fish runs in New England coastal plain rivers, including Pacific salmon introductions; biocide effects on larval marine fishes. *Mailing Add:* Exeter Area High Sch Linden St Exeter NH 03833

SMITH, RODGER CHAPMAN, INORGANIC CHEMISTRY. *Current Pos:* CONSULT, CHEM MKTG & TECHNOL, 83- *Personal Data:* b South Hadley, Mass, July 18, 15; m 40; c 3. *Educ:* Univ Mass, BS, 38. *Prof Exp:* Asst head fertilizer res, Eastern States Farmers' Exchange Inc, 46-54, head fertilizer res, 55-62; mgr agr technol serv, Southwest Potash Corp, NY, 62-66, mgr mkt develop, 66-71; dir mkt develop, Amax Chem Corp, 71-83. *Mem:* Am Chem Soc; Am Soc Hort Sci; Am Inst Chemists; Am Soc Agron. *Res:* Administration of market development for potash, phosphate rock and heavy chemicals in the United States and other countries; coordination with industry and governmental agencies; processes for mixed fertilizer granulation; global consulting on marketing and technology investigations for government and industries. *Mailing Add:* 1206 W Camino Del Pato Green Valley AZ 85614-4838

SMITH, ROGER ALAN, theoretical physics, for more information see previous edition

SMITH, ROGER BRUCE, TOXICOLOGY. *Current Pos:* Res scientist, McNeil Pharmaceut, Johnson & Johnson, 77-79, prin scientist, 77-87, sr scientist, 79-82, res fel, 87-91, res mgr, 91-96, SR RES FEL, R W JOHNSON PHARMACEUT RES INST, JOHNSON & JOHNSON, 97- *Personal Data:* b New Bethlehem, Pa, Sept 12, 47; m 67, Kathleen Storey; c Tracey, Jedediah & Abigail. *Educ:* Philadelphia Col Pharm & Sci, BS, 70, MS, 73, PhD(pharmacol), 79; Am Bd Toxicol, dipl. *Concurrent Pos:* Adj assoc prof, Phil Col Pharm & Sci, 86. *Mem:* Soc Toxicol; Sigma Xi; Am Col Toxicol. *Res:* Assessing appropriateness of existing animal models for toxicity studies and establishing reliable new predictive models where routine systems have failed; preclinical toxicity assessment of pharmaceuticals. *Mailing Add:* Drug Safety Evaluation R W Johnson Pharmaceut Res Inst Mckean Rd Spring House PA 19477

SMITH, ROGER DEAN, PATHOLOGY, VIROLOGY. *Current Pos:* prof path & dir dept, 72-90, EMER PROF PATH, UNIV CINCINNATI, 90- *Personal Data:* b New York, NY, Oct 6, 32; m 57; c 4. *Educ:* Cornell Univ, AB, 54; NY Med Col, MD, 58. *Prof Exp:* Resident surg, Detroit Receiving Hosp, Mich, 59-60; instr path, Col Med, Univ Ill, Chicago, 62-66, from asst prof to assoc prof, 66-72, asst dean col med, 70-72. *Concurrent Pos:* USPHS grant, 62-65; Nat Cancer Inst spec fel, 65-66; resident, Presby-St Luke's Hosp, Chicago, 62-66, consult; co-investr, Ill Div, Am Cancer Soc grant, 65-66; asst attend pathologist, Res & Educ Hosp, 66-; consult, Vet Admin Hosp, Chicago, 62-66; prin investr, NIH grants, 67-72 & 76-79; Assoc Path Chair, Col Am Pathologists. *Mem:* Int Acad Path; Am Asn Path; Soc Exp Biol & Med; Am Soc Nephrology; Am Soc Clin Path. *Res:* Virus pathology and virus-cell relationships; renal and virus pathology; experimental renal disease; persistent virus infections and possible relation to glomerulonephritis. *Mailing Add:* Dept Path Univ Cincinnati Col Med 231 Bethesda Ave Cincinnati OH 45267-0529. *Fax:* 513-558-2289

SMITH, ROGER ELTON, CIVIL ENGINEERING, HYDROLOGY. *Current Pos:* RES HYDRAULIC ENGR, AGR ENG RES CTR. *Personal Data:* b Stillwater, Okla, Apr 16, 41. *Educ:* Tex Tech Univ, BSc, 63; Stanford Univ, MSc, 64; Colo State Univ, PhD(civil eng), 70. *Prof Exp:* Design engr, Metcalf & Eddy Engrs, Calif, 64-65; engr, Peace Corps, Pakistan, 65-67; res hydraul engr, Southwest Watershed Res Ctr, Agr Res Serv, USDA, 70-76, res hydraulic engr fed res, Sci Educ Admin, 76- *Mem:* Am Soc Civil Engrs; Am Geophys Union. *Res:* Soil infiltration from rainfall; watershed response in relation to physical features; stochastic rainfall models; hydraulics of alluvial streams, including measuring techniques and unsteady flow phenomena. *Mailing Add:* Agr Eng Res Ctr Foothills Campus Colo State Univ Fort Collins CO 80523

SMITH, ROGER FRANCIS COOPER, ZOOLOGY, ECOLOGY. *Current Pos:* asst prof, 73-79, ASSOC PROF, DEPT ZOOL, BRANDON UNIV, 79- *Personal Data:* b Kapunda, South Australia, Mar 6, 40; m 73. *Educ:* Univ Adelaide, BSc, 62; Australian Nat Univ, MSc, 66; Univ Alta, PhD(zool), 73. *Prof Exp:* Exp officer, Commonwealth Sci & Insust Res Orgn, Div Wildlife Res, 63-64; res asst physiol, Dept Zool, Australian Nat Univ, 66, res assoc, Dept Zool, Univ Alta, 72-73. *Mem:* Brit Ecol Soc; Australian & NZ AAS; Wildlife Soc; Can Soc Zoologists; Am Mammal Soc. *Mailing Add:* Dept Zool Brandon Univ Box 270 Brandon MB R7A 6A9 Can

SMITH, ROGER M, RESEARCH ADMINISTRATION. *Current Pos:* CONSULT, 83- *Personal Data:* b Winnipeg, Man, Sept 12, 18; m 47, Margaret; c Bruce, Murray, Patricia & Theresa. *Educ:* Univ Man, BSc, 40. *Honors & Awards:* Distinguished Serv Award, Inst Nuclear Mat Mgt. *Prof Exp:* Sr supvr reactor opers, Chalk River Nuclear Labs, Atomic Energy Can Ltd, 46-52, supt prod planning & control, 53-58; dir divl safeguards, Int Atomic Energy Agency, 58-60; mgr admin div, Whiteshell Nuclear Res Estab, 60-82; dir, safeguard develop, Atomic Energy Can Ltd, 76-83. *Concurrent Pos:* Chmn, ShamattawA Transmission Lime Task Force, 87-, Pukatawagan Natural Resources Co-mgt Task Force, 89- *Mem:* Can Asn Physicists; Inst Nuclear Mat Mgt. *Res:* Technical administration and planning; development of safeguard techniques. *Mailing Add:* 7 McWilliams Pl Pinawa MB R0E 1L0 Can

SMITH, ROGER POWELL, TOXICOLOGY. *Current Pos:* From instr to assoc prof, 60-73, chmn dept, 76-87, PROF PHARMACOL & TOXICOL, DARTMOUTH MED SCH, 76-, IRENE HEINZ GIVEN PROF, 93- *Personal Data:* b Hokuchin, Korea, July 16, 32; US citizen; m 56, Rena J Pointer; c Sam F, Joan B (Poitras) & Ben H. *Educ:* Purdue Univ, BS, 53, MS, 55, PhD(pharmaceut chem), 57. *Hon Degrees:* MA, Dartmouth Col, 75. *Concurrent Pos:* Consult, Vet Admin Ctr, White River Junction, Vt, 65-91; assoc staff mem, Mary Hitchcock Mem Hosp, 68-96; mem toxicol study sect, NIH, 68-72; USPHS career develop award, 66-71; assoc ed, Toxicol & Appl Pharmacol, 72-78; mem pharmacol toxicol prog comt, Nat Inst Gen Med Sci, 72-79; mem comt med & biol effects environ pollutants, Div Med Sci, Nat Res Coun, 75-77; adj prof, Vt Law Sch 81-87, Dartmouth Col, 84-; mem, Enivon Health Sci Rev Comt, 85-87; mem, Toxicol Info Prog Comt, Nat Res Coun, 86-88. *Mem:* Fel AAAS; fel Acad Toxicol Sci; Soc Toxicol; Am Soc Pharmacol & Exp Therapeut; Sigma Xi. *Res:* Experimental toxicology; red cell metabolism; nitric oxide vasodilator drugs; abnormal blood pigments. *Mailing Add:* Dept Pharmacol & Toxicol Dartmouth Med Sch 7650 Remsen Rm 519 Hanover NH 03755-3835. *Fax:* 603-650-1129; *E-Mail:* roger.p.smith@dartmouth.edu

SMITH, ROLF C, JR, INNOVATION, CREATIVE PROBLEMSOLVING TECHNIQUES. *Current Pos:* PRES, OFF STRATEGIC INNOVATION, 87-; DIR, EXXON'S INNOVATION NETWORK, HOUSTON, 87- *Educ:* Tex A&M Univ, BA, MS. *Prof Exp:* Commun electronics officer & dir, Off Innovation, USAF, 63-87. *Concurrent Pos:* Adj lectr, Ctr Creative Leadership, Greensboro, NC; adj prof, Univ Houston; headmaster, Sch Innovators, 89-; consult, Ford, DuPont, Union Carbide, E-Systs, Waste Mgt Corp & Small Bus Admin; intel officer, NATO, Ger. *Res:* Creative problem solving techniques; quality and continuous improvement facilitation; artificial intelligence. *Mailing Add:* 10682 Binhorn Rd Houston TX 77024

SMITH, RONALD E, PHYSICS. *Current Pos:* assoc prof, 66-70, head dept, 77-89, PROF PHYSICS, NE LA UNIV, 70-, DEAN, COL PURE & APPL SCI, 89- *Personal Data:* b Beeville, Tex, Mar 30, 36; m 57, Lenita Holland; c 3. *Educ:* Tex A&M Univ, BS, 58, MS, 59, PhD(physics), 68. *Prof Exp:* Instr physics, Tex A&M Univ, 60-66. *Mem:* Am Phys Soc; Am Asn Physics Teachers. *Res:* Nuclear magnetic resonance; electron spin resonance; solid state. *Mailing Add:* Physics Dept NE La Univ Monroe LA 71209. *Fax:* 318-342-1755

SMITH, RONALD GENE, ORGANIC CHEMISTRY, ANALYTICAL PHARMACOLOGY. *Current Pos:* SR RES SPECIALIST, MONSANTO AGR CO, 83- *Personal Data:* b Woodland, Wash, Jan 24, 44; m 70; c 2. *Educ:* Whitworth Col, BS, 66; Purdue Univ, PhD(org chem), 72. *Prof Exp:* Res assoc org chem, Ore Grad Ctr, 72-74, instr, 74-77; from asst prof to prof org chem, Univ Tex M D Anderson Hosp & Tumor Inst, Houston, 77-83. *Concurrent Pos:* Asst prof, Grad Sch Biomed Sci, Univ Tex Health Sci Ctr, 78-80, fac mem, 80- *Mem:* Am Asn Cancer Res; Am Chem Soc; Am Soc Mass Spectrometry. *Res:* Application of mass spectrometry to the pharmacology of antitumor agents; identification of drug metabolites; pharmacokinetics; mechanism of drug action. *Mailing Add:* Monsanto Agr Co S3C 800 N Lindbergh Blvd St Louis MO 63167

SMITH, RONALD JAMES, ATOMIC & MOLECULAR PHYSICS. *Current Pos:* GEN MGR, INTEL CORP, 77- *Personal Data:* b Allentown, Pa, July 22, 50. *Educ:* Gettysburg Col, BS, 72; Univ Minn, MS, 75, PhD, 76. *Mem:* Am Phys Soc. *Mailing Add:* 7182 Cedar Oaks Dr Roseville CA 95661

SMITH, RONALD W, PHYSICAL CHEMISTRY, CHEMICAL ENGINEERING. *Current Pos:* VPRES & GEN MGR, CHEM PROD DIV, AMETEK INC, 93- *Personal Data:* b June 15, 36; m 60, Eleanor J; c Ronald B, Stephen H & Susan K (Snavely). *Educ:* Pa State Univ, BS, 58; Univ Del, PhD, 65. *Prof Exp:* Res chemist, Hercules, Inc, 64-69, tech develop rep, 69-70, develop supvr, 70-72, tech mgr, 72-75; asst gen mgr, Haveg Industs, Inc, 75-80; prod mgr, Hercules Inc, 81-93. *Mem:* Am Chem Soc; Am Inst Chem Engrs; Sigma Xi. *Res:* Surface chemistry; environmental science, pollution control. *Mailing Add:* 708 Walnut Hill Rd Hockessin DE 19707-9609

SMITH, ROSE MARIE, MATHEMATICS. *Current Pos:* RETIRED. *Personal Data:* b Beaumont, Tex, Mar 3, 34; m 55; c 3. *Educ:* Lamar Univ, BS, 55; Tex Woman's Univ, MA, 68; Okla State Univ, EdD, 75. *Prof Exp:* Teacher math & music, Grapevine Pub Schs, Grapevine, Tex, 55-66; prof math, Tex Woman's Univ, 66-96, chmn, Dept Math, Comput Sci & Physics, 86-96. *Mem:* Nat Coun Teachers Math; Math Asn Am. *Res:* Mathematical education. *Mailing Add:* 1602 Broadway St Galveston TX 77550-4909

SMITH, ROSS W, MINERAL ENGINEERING, SURFACE CHEMISTRY. *Current Pos:* assoc prof metall, 68-69, PROF METALL & CHMN DEPT CHEM & METALL ENG, UNIV NEV, RENO, 69- *Personal Data:* b Turlock, Calif, Dec 11, 27; m 55; c 3. *Educ:* Univ Nev, BS, 50; Mass Inst Technol, SM, 55; Stanford Univ, PhD(mineral eng), 69. *Prof Exp:* Jr mining engr, Consol Coppermines Corp, Nev, 50; res asst metall, Mass Inst Technol, 53-55; assoc mfg process engr, Portland Cement Asn, 55-57; proj engr, Res Found, Colo Sch Mines, 58-60; assoc prof metall, SDak Sch Mines & Technol, 60-66; actg instr mineral eng, Stanford Univ, 66-68. *Concurrent Pos:* Dept Health, Educ & Welfare grant, 64-66. *Mem:* Am Inst Mining, Metall & Petrol Engrs; Am Chem Soc; Am Inst Chem Engrs; Sigma Xi. *Res:* Comminution; pipeline flow of liquid-solid slurries; flotation; surface chemistry. *Mailing Add:* Dept Chem & Metall Eng Univ Nev Reno NV 89557

SMITH, ROY E, SCIENCE EDUCATION, PHYSICS. *Current Pos:* RETIRED. *Personal Data:* b Chippewa Falls, Wis, Apr 28, 26; m 47; c 3. *Educ:* Wis State Univ-Eau Claire, BS, 50; Univ Wis, MS, 57; Ohio State Univ, PhD(sci educ), 66. *Prof Exp:* Jr high sch teacher, Ill, 50-51; pub sch teacher, Wis, 51-56; from asst prof to prof physics, Univ Wis-Platteville, 57-94, head dept, 66-94. *Concurrent Pos:* Consult, Wis Mold & Tool Co, 57-63. *Mem:* Am Asn Physics Teachers; Nat Sci Teachers Asn. *Res:* Use of unit operators and dimensional methods as a vehicle for teaching fundamental quantitative physical science. *Mailing Add:* 1608 County B Platteville WI 53818

SMITH, ROY JEFFERSON, JR, WEED SCIENCE. *Current Pos:* SUPVRY RES AGRONOMIST WEED SCI, AGR RES SERV, USDA, 55- *Personal Data:* b Covington, La, Nov 25, 29; m 52; c 2. *Educ:* Miss State Univ, BS, 51, MS, 52; Univ Ill, PhD(weed sci), 55. *Honors & Awards:* Super Serv Award, USDA, 67; Outstanding Researcher Award, Weed Sci Soc Am, 82. *Concurrent Pos:* Mem grad staff, Univ Ark, 55-; adv, Rockefeller Found, Int Rice Res Inst, Philippines, 64; adv, Inst Tech Interchange, East-West Ctr, 67-69; coop scientist, US Dept Army, 68-70; coop scientist for pest mgt proj in Pakistan & for biol control weeds with Univ Ark, 73-88. *Mem:* Fel Weed Sci Soc Am; Int Weed Sci Soc; Sigma Xi; Am Soc Agron. *Res:* Biology and interference of weeds in agronomic crops; integrated weed management systems for rice; biological control of weeds with plant pathogens; rice germplasm tolerance to herbicides; alleopathy of rice germplasm. *Mailing Add:* 1507 Strait Pl Stuttgart AR 72160-5719

SMITH, ROY MARTIN, DENTISTRY, ORAL PATHOLOGY. *Current Pos:* asst prof oral med & surg, Col Dent, Univ Tenn, Memphis, 58-62, assoc prof oral diag & chmn dept, 62-64, assoc prof path, 63-73, prof oral diag, Col Dent, 64-92, asst dean acad affairs, 83-92, EMER PROF ORAL DIAG, UNIV TENN, MEMPHIS, 92- *Personal Data:* b Alamo, Tenn, Oct 21, 27; m 48; c 2. *Educ:* Univ Tenn, DDS, 51, MS, 63. *Prof Exp:* Pvt pract, 58-58. *Concurrent Pos:* Consult, Vet Admin Hosp, Memphis, Tenn, Methodist Hosp, Memphis, Tenn. *Mem:* Am Dent Asn; Am Acad Oral Path; Am Col Dent; Am Asn Dent Schs. *Res:* Transplantation of intraoral tissues; oral carcinogenesis; pharmacologic effects of eugenol. *Mailing Add:* 6473 Heather Dr Memphis TN 38119

SMITH, RUFUS ALBERT, JR, HORTICULTURE. *Current Pos:* from assoc prof to prof, 73-97, EMER PROF HORT, UNIV TENN, MARTIN, 97- *Personal Data:* b Shreveport, La, Jan 29, 32; m 60, Elsie Gordon; c Gordon L & Kathy J. *Educ:* La State Univ, BS, 56, MS, 58; Wash State Univ, PhD(hort), 67. *Prof Exp:* Instr hort, Western Ill Univ, 61-63; asst prof, Ore State Univ, 67-73. *Mem:* Am Soc Hort Sci; Am Hort Soc. *Mailing Add:* 311 Hillside Rd Martin TN 38238

SMITH, RUSSELL AUBREY, MECHANICAL ENGINEERING, MOTOR VEHICLE SAFETY. *Current Pos:* FAC MECH ENGR, US NAVAL ACAD, 82- *Personal Data:* b Little Rock, Ark, June 8, 36; m 60; c 3. *Educ:* Rice Univ, BA & BSME, 58; Cath Univ Am, MME, 64, PhD(mech eng), 69. *Prof Exp:* Mem fac, Mech Eng Dept, Cath Univ Am, 66-76, chmn dept, 73-76; mem, Accident Invest Div, Nat Hwy Safety Admin, 76-82. *Concurrent Pos:* Consult, Forensic Technol Int. *Mem:* Am Soc Mech Engrs; Am Soc Eng Educ; Soc Automotive Engrs. *Res:* Engineering mechanics; vehicle collision mechanics. *Mailing Add:* Dept Mech Eng US Naval Acad Annapolis MD 21402

SMITH, RUSSELL D, CERAMICS ENGINEERING. *Personal Data:* b Mexico, Mo, Feb 7, 50; m 72, Rita Hunn; c Annette & Timothy. *Educ:* Univ Mo, Rolla, BS, 72 & MS, 73. *Prof Exp:* Res engr, Dow Chem, 73-77; prod develop mgr, Standard Oil Eng Mat, 77-84, tech mgr, 84-88; gen mgr, Carborundum, 89-96. *Mem:* Am Ceramic Soc; Nat Inst Ceramic Engrs; Int Soc Hybrid Microelectronics. *Res:* Insulation; filtration; reinforcement; electronic ceramics; ceramic packaging; application of quality principles; granted 8 US patents. *Mailing Add:* 107 Timberlink Grand Island NY 14072. *Fax:* 716-278-2090

SMITH, RUSSELL LAMAR, PHOTOSYNTHESIS, NITROGEN-FIXATION. *Current Pos:* ASST PROF BIOCHEM, DEPT CHEM, UNIV TEX, ARLINGTON, 90- *Personal Data:* b Oconee, SC, Jan 25, 59. *Educ:* Clemson Univ, BS, 80; Univ Tex, MA, 84, PhD(biol sci), 86. *Prof Exp:* Vis scientist, Ctr Nuclear Studies, Grenoble, France, 86-87; postdoctoral, Biotechnol Inst, Penn State Univ, 87-89; postdoctoral, Memphis State Univ, 89-90. *Mem:* AAAS; Am Soc Microbiol; Am Chem Soc; Am Soc Plant Physiologists; Sigma Xi. *Res:* Enzymology and molecular biology of photosynthetic prokaryotes; inorganic nitrogen utilization in cyanobacteria. *Mailing Add:* Chem Univ Tex Arlington PO Box 19065 Arlington TX 76019-0001

SMITH, SAM CORRY, NUTRITION. *Current Pos:* CONSULT, 88- *Personal Data:* b Enid, Okla, July 3, 22; m 45, Dorothy J Bank; c Linda, Nancy & Sue. *Educ:* Univ Okla, BS, 47, MS, 48; Univ Wis, PhD(biochem), 51. *Prof Exp:* Spec instr chem, Univ Okla, 47-48, from asst prof biochem to assoc prof, Sch Med, 51-55; secy, Williams-Waterman Fund, Res Corp, NY, 55-67, assoc dir grants, 57-65, dir, 65-68, chmn, Williams-Waterman Prog Comt & chmn adv comt grants, 67-75, vpres grants, 68-75; exec dir, M J Murdock Charitable Trust, 75-88. *Concurrent Pos:* Pub trustee, Nutrit Found, 76-84 & Int Life Sci Inst-Nutrit Found, 84-87; dir, Clark Col Found, 93- *Mem:* Fel AAAS; Am Chem Soc; Sigma Xi. *Res:* Human nutrition; amino acid and vitamin metabolism; international nutrition. *Mailing Add:* 5204 DuBois Dr Vancouver WA 98661-6617

SMITH, SAMUEL, POLYMER CHEMISTRY. *Current Pos:* RETIRED. *Personal Data:* b Bronx, NY, Sept 13, 27; m 51, Marian Johnson; c Bruce, Richard, Donald, Linda & Kenneth. *Educ:* City Col New York, BS, 48; Univ Mich, MS, 49. *Honors & Awards:* Henry Millson Award, Am Asn Textile Chemists & Colorists, 80; Am Chem Soc Award for Creative Invention, 88. *Prof Exp:* Chemist, Inst Paper Chem, 49-51; sr chemist, Cent Res, Minn Mining & Mfg Co, 51-57, sr chemist, Chem Div, 57-61, supvr polymer res, 61-67, res assoc, 67-75, corp scientist, Cent Res Labs, 75-83, corp scientist, Spec Film Lab, 83-91, corp scientist, Indust & Consumer Sector Res Lab, 91-92. *Mem:* Am Chem Soc. *Res:* Ring-opening polymerization; elastomeric resins; surface chemistry relating to adhesion and desorption processes; fluorochemical polymers and textile finishes. *Mailing Add:* 13274 Huntington Terr Apple Valley MN 55124

SMITH, SAMUEL COOPER, BIOCHEMISTRY. *Current Pos:* From asst prof to assoc prof, 61-74, PROF ANIMAL SCI & BIOCHEM, UNIV NH, 74- *Personal Data:* b Lock Haven, Pa, Sept 21, 34; m 55; c 2. *Educ:* Pa State Univ, BS, 55, MS, 59, PhD(biochem), 62. *Mem:* AAAS; Am Chem Soc; Am Oil Chem Soc; Sigma Xi. *Res:* Lipid biochemistry in tissue culture systems. *Mailing Add:* Dept Animal Sci 13 Kendall Hall Univ of NH Durham NH 03824-3590

SMITH, SAMUEL H, PLANT PATHOLOGY, PLANT VIROLOGY. *Current Pos:* assoc prof, Fruit Res Lab, 69-71 & Buckhout Lab, 71-74, head dept, 76-81, PROF PLANT PATH, BUCKOUT LAB, PA STATE UNIV, UNIVERSITY PARK, 74-, HEAD DEPT, 76-, DEAN, COL AGR & DIR PA AGR EXP STA & PA COOP EXTEN SERV, 81- *Personal Data:* b Salinas, Calif, Feb 4, 40; m 60; c 2. *Educ:* Univ Calif, Berkeley, BS, 61, PhD(plant path), 64. *Prof Exp:* NATO fel plant path, Glasshouse Crops Res Inst, Eng, 64-65; asst prof, Univ Calif, Berkeley, 65-69. *Mem:* Am Phytopath Soc; Brit Asn Appl Biol. *Mailing Add:* Pres Off Wash State Univ French Admin Rm 422 Pullman WA 99164-0001

SMITH, SAMUEL JOSEPH, SOIL CHEMISTRY, WATER CHEMISTRY. *Current Pos:* RETIRED. *Personal Data:* b Montgomery, Ala, July 19, 39. *Educ:* Auburn Univ, BS, 61; Iowa State Univ, PhD(soil chem), 67. *Honors & Awards:* Super Serv Award, USDA, 81, Distinguished Serv Award, 84. *Prof Exp:* Res assoc, Iowa State Univ, 67-69; soil scientist res, Agr Res Serv, USDA, 69-94. *Mem:* Am Soc Agron; Soil Sci Soc Am; Am Inst Chemists. *Res:* Behavior and fate of agricultural chemicals in the environment. *Mailing Add:* PO Box 467 Caddo OK 74729

SMITH, SELWYN MICHAEL, FORENSIC PSYCHIATRY. *Current Pos:* PVT PRACT, 86- *Personal Data:* b Sydney, Australia, Aug 12, 42; Can citizen; m 68, May Tsang; c Benjamin M & Michelle A. *Educ:* Sydney Univ, MB & BS, 66; London Univ, DPM, 69; Univ Birmingham, Eng, MD, 74; FRCP(C), 76; Am Bd Psychiat & Neurol, dipl, 78; Am Bd Forensic Psychiat, dipl, 80. *Honors & Awards:* Cloake Medal, 73; Bronze Medal, Royal Col Psychiatrists, 74. *Prof Exp:* House physician & surgeon, Sydney Hosp, 67; registrar psychiat, All Saints Hosp, Birmingham, Eng, 68-70; hon res fel psychiat, United Birmingham Hosp, 70-72, hon sr registrar, 71-75; dir forensic psychiat, Royal Ottawa Hosp, 75-80; prof psychiat, Univ Ottawa, 80-86. *Concurrent Pos:* Consult psychiat, Ottawa Gen Hosp & Brockville Hosp, 76-96; vis prof, dept psychol, Carleton Univ, 77-; chmn, forensic serv comt, Region Ottawa-Carleton & Eastern Ont, 77-; mem, fed & prov subcomt environ health, Task Force Acceptable Lead Level Blood, Health & Welfare, Can, 77-, secure serv adv comt adolescent serv, Ont Ministry Community & Social Serv, 80-, sci prog comt, Second World Cong Prison Health Care, Fed Govt Can, 83-; psychiatrist-in-chief, Royal Ottawa Hosp, 78-86; intern, Acad Law & Ment Health; consult psychiatrist, Comm Care Syst Inc, Wellesly, Mass; Consult psychiatrist, St John J Gen Hosp, Sydney Anitoke. *Mem:* Fel Royal Col Psychiatrists; Am Acad Psychiat & Law; Am Col Psychiatrists; Can Psychiat Asn; fel Am Psychiat Asn. *Res:* Child abuse; forensic and legal issues; general psychiatric issues. *Mailing Add:* 13 Grantham St Burwood Australia 2136

SMITH, SHARON LOUISE, ZOOPLANKTON ECOLOGY. *Current Pos:* from asst oceanogr to oceanogr, Brookhaven Nat Lab, 78-85, dep div head, 90-91, div head, 91-93, OCEANOGR WITH TENURE, BROOKHAVEN NAT LAB, 85-; PROF, UNIV MIAMI, 93- *Personal Data:* b Denver, Colo, June 14, 45. *Educ:* Colo Col, BA, 67; Univ Auckland, NZ, MSc, 69; Duke Univ, PhD(zool), 75. *Hon Degrees:* DSc, Colo Col, 89, Long Island Univ, 93. *Prof Exp:* Biologist, Raytheon Corp, 69-71; fel, Dalhousie Univ, 75-78. *Concurrent Pos:* Adj asst prof, Univ Wash, 80-85, State Univ NY, Stony Brook, 79-; ed bd, Am Soc Limnol & Oceanog; assoc prog mgr, NSF, 88-89, mem Rev & Oversight Comt; mem, Steering Comt, Global Ocean Flux Study, Global Ecosyst Dynamics, Artic Syst Sci, chair, Indian Ocean Study, US-JGOFS; mem, Ocean Studies Bd, Nat Res Coun, 94-96; adv comt, Geosci, NSF, 94-99; adv, Arctic Res Comn, 95-98. *Mem:* Oceanogr Soc; Am Soc Limnol & Oceanog; Am Geophys Union. *Res:* Ecology of zooplankton, herbivorous crustaceans; food chain dynamics, biogeochemical cycling in productive areas of oceans; secondary production; life history strategies; animal/plant interactions. *Mailing Add:* Univ Miami RSMAS 4600 Rickenbacker Causeway Miami FL 33149-1098. *Fax:* 305-361-4600

SMITH, SHARRON WILLIAMS, BIOCHEMISTRY. *Current Pos:* from asst prof to prof, 75-93, CHMN DEPT, HOOD COL, 82-86, 95-, WHITAKER PROF CHEM, 93- *Personal Data:* b Ashland, Ky, Apr 3, 41; m 64, William; c Dyan & Kevin. *Educ:* Transylvania Col, BA, 63; Univ Ky, PhD(biochem), 74. *Prof Exp:* Chemist, Charles Pfizer Pharmaceut Co, 63 & Procter & Gamble, 63-64; teacher sci, Lexington Pub Schs, Ky, 64-67; chemist biol membranes, Lab Cell Biol, Nat Heart & Lung Inst, 74-75. *Concurrent Pos:* Actg dean, Hood Grad Sch, 89-90. *Mem:* AAAS; Am Chem Soc. *Res:* Pedagogical methods in chemical education. *Mailing Add:* Dept Chem Hood Col Frederick MD 21701. *Fax:* 301-694-7653; *E-Mail:* ssmith@nimue.hood.edu

SMITH, SHELBY DEAN, MATHEMATICS. *Current Pos:* from asst prof to prof, 56-87, EMER PROF MATH SCI, BALL STATE UNIV, 87- *Personal Data:* b Macomb, Ill, Nov 25, 23; m 45, Barbara Tingley; c David E & Carol D. *Educ:* Western Ill Univ, BS & MS, 50; Univ Ill, PhD, 66. *Prof Exp:* High sch teacher, Ill, 50-56. *Res:* Mathematics education. *Mailing Add:* 2009 Winthrop Rd Muncie IN 47304

SMITH, SHELDON MAGILL, OPTICAL PHYSICS. *Current Pos:* res scientist solar physics, NASA, 63-72, res scientist planetary atmosphere, 74-80, res scientist space sci, Astrophy Br, 80-89, ASSOC, AMES RES CTR, NASA, 94- *Personal Data:* b St Paul, Minn, Apr 19, 31; div; c 3. *Educ:* Univ Calif, Berkeley, BS, 53, Davis, MA, 62. *Prof Exp:* Sr staff scientist, Sterling Software, 90-93. *Concurrent Pos:* Prin investr, airborn eclipse exped NASA, 63, 65, 66, 70 & 75; mem tech comt, Int Comn Illum, 85, Am Soc Testing & Mat, 89-90. *Mem:* Optical Soc Am; Am Astron Soc; Int Soc Optical Eng; AAAS. *Res:* Radial-gradient filter technique for photography of the solar corona applied to telescopes on aircraft platforms; neutral-sheet theory of the magnetic field configuration of solar streamers; infrared reflectance of the Venus clouds; reflectance of IR-black coatings and BRDF measurement; reflecting layer model of the far-infrared reflectance of coatings; scattering by very rough surfaces. *Mailing Add:* NASA Ames Res Ctr MS 244-10 Moffett Field CA 94035-1000

SMITH, SIDNEY R, JR, IMMUNOLOGY, BIOCHEMISTRY. *Current Pos:* sr res scientist, 68-71, head sect immunol, 71-83, ASSOC DIR, ALLERGY & INFLAMMATION, SCHERING CORP, 83- *Personal Data:* b New Orleans, La, Oct 5, 35; m; c 4. *Educ:* Univ Conn, BA, 57; Howard Univ, MS, 59, PhD, 63. *Prof Exp:* Fel endocrinol, Univ Wis, 63-64; asst prof biol, Morehouse Col, 64-66; NIH fel biochem, Univ Conn, 66-68. *Concurrent Pos:* Adj assoc prof, Fairleigh Dickinson Univ, 74-83. *Mem:* AAAS; Am Asn Immunol; Am Inst Chem; NY Acad Sci; Int Soc Immunopharmacol. *Res:* Embryology; endocrinology; immunology. *Mailing Add:* Schering Plough 2015 Galloping Hill Rd Kenilworth NJ 07003-0539

SMITH, SIDNEY RUVEN, PHYSICAL CHEMISTRY. *Current Pos:* from asst prof to assoc prof, 60-74, PROF CHEM, UNIV CONN, 74- *Personal Data:* b Hamilton, Ont, Aug 25, 20; m 53; c 6. *Educ:* McMaster Univ, BSc, 42, MSc, 43; Ohio State Univ, PhD(phys chem), 52. *Prof Exp:* Jr res chemist, Nat Res Coun Can, 43-46; phys chemist, US Naval Ord Test Sta, Calif, 52-60. *Mem:* Am Chem Soc; Am Phys Soc. *Res:* Mass spectrometry; kinetics; stable isotopes. *Mailing Add:* 31 Lynwood Dr Storrs Mansfield CT 06268

SMITH, SIDNEY TAYLOR, ELECTRON TUBES. *Current Pos:* head, Electron Tubes Br, 56-74, ELECTRONIC CONSULT, NAVAL RES LAB, 74- *Personal Data:* b Montezuma, Ga, May 27, 18; m 49; c 1. *Educ:* Ga Inst Technol, BS, 39; Yale Univ, DEng, 42. *Prof Exp:* Electronic scientist, Naval Res Lab, 42-51, Hughes Res Labs, 51-56. *Concurrent Pos:* Mem adv group electron tube, Dept Defense, 50-74. *Mem:* Fel Inst Elec & Electronics Engrs; Am Phys Soc. *Res:* Published 20 technical papers on electron tubes. *Mailing Add:* 4514 Bee St Alexandria VA 22310

SMITH, SPENCER B, OPERATIONS RESEARCH. *Current Pos:* assoc prof, Stuart Sch Bus Admin, Ill Inst Technol, 66-71, actg chmn dept indust eng, 70-71, prof & chmn dept indust eng, 71-77, PROF MGT SCI, STUART SCH BUS ADMIN, ILL INST TECHNOL, 77- *Personal Data:* b Ottawa, Ont, Jan 31, 27; m 54, Mildred E Spidell. *Educ:* McGill Univ, BE, 49; Columbia Univ, MS, 50, EngScD(indust eng), 58. *Prof Exp:* Instr indust eng, Columbia Univ, 50-58; admin engr, Mergenthaler Linotype Co, 53-58; mgr opers res, Semiconductor Div, Raytheon Co, 58-61 & Montgomery Ward & Co, 61-66. *Concurrent Pos:* Consult, UN, 57, Chicago Mercantile Exchange, 74 & Inst Gas Technol, 76; Harris Trust & Savings Bank res grant, 68-70; Ill Law Enforcement Comn res grant, 72-73; res grant, Am Prod & Inventory Control Soc, 80; res grant, US Army Corps Engrs, 81. *Mem:* Am Inst Indust Engrs; Am Statist Asn; Am Soc Mech Engrs; Opers Res Soc Am; Inst Mgt Sci; Am Prod & Inventory Control Soc; Soc Mfg Engrs. *Res:* Mathematical programming; inventory theory; forecasting; production planning; simulation; information systems; law enforcement; planning of energy production and distribution systems; philanthropy. *Mailing Add:* Stuart Sch Bus Admin Ill Inst Technol 565 W Adams Chicago IL 60661

SMITH, SPURGEON EUGENE, TOPOLOGY. *Current Pos:* RETIRED. *Personal Data:* b San Marcos, Tex, July 17, 25; m 48; c 2. *Educ:* Southwest Tex State Col, BS, 46. *Prof Exp:* Res mathematician, Defense Res Lab, Tex, 51-57; vpres & dir res, Textran Corp, 57-62; prin scientist & dir, Tracor Inc, 62-69, vpres & dir advan res sci & systs group, 69-89. *Concurrent Pos:* consult, cove theory. *Mem:* Am Math Soc; Acoust Soc Am. *Res:* Functions of a complex variable; probability; decision theory; complex group decision maps; data compaction. *Mailing Add:* PO Box 651 Elgin TX 78621-0651

SMITH, STAMFORD DENNIS, ENTOMOLOGY, HYDROBIOLOGY. *Current Pos:* asst prof, 68-72, assoc prof, 72-80, PROF BIOL, CENT WASH UNIV, 80- *Personal Data:* b San Jose, Calif, Feb 27, 39; m 63; c 2. *Educ:* San Jose State Col, BA, 61; Univ Idaho, MS, 64, PhD(entom), 67. *Prof Exp:* Asst prof biol, Kans State Col Pittsburg, 66-68. *Mem:* Entom Soc Am; Soc Syst Zool. *Res:* Ecology and systematics of Trichoptera; biology of aquatic insects. *Mailing Add:* Dept Biol Sci Cent Wash Univ 400 E Eighth Ave Ellensburg WA 98926-7500

SMITH, STANFORD LEE, ORGANIC CHEMISTRY. *Current Pos:* from asst prof to assoc prof chem, 62-84, PROF CHEM & RADIOL, UNIV KY, 84-, DIR, NMR SPECTROS CTR, 87- *Personal Data:* b Detroit, Mich, June 3, 35; m 58, 77, 83, Elizabeth M Church; c Michael L & Sharon L. *Educ:* Albion Col, BA, 57; Iowa State Univ, PhD(org chem), 61. *Prof Exp:* Res assoc & instr chem, Iowa State Univ, 61-62. *Concurrent Pos:* UN consult, Cent Testing Lab, Pakistan, 75; fac consult, Varian Workshops, 81-82 & 84; dir instrumentation, magnetic Resonance Imaging & Spectros Ctr, Univ Ky, 85-90. *Mem:* AAAS; Am Chem Soc; Am Asn Univ Professors; Soc Magnetic Resonance Med; Int Soc Magnetic Resonance; Am Asn Physicist Med. *Res:* High resolution nuclear magnetic resonance spectroscopy; biochemical structure studies; molecular structure and associations; magnetic resonance imaging. *Mailing Add:* Dept Chem Univ Ky 500 S Limestone Lexington KY 40506-0001

SMITH, STANLEY GALEN, SYSTEMATIC BOTANY, AQUATIC ECOLOGY. *Current Pos:* assoc prof, 65-76, PROF BIOL, UNIV WIS-WHITEWATER, 76- *Personal Data:* b Laramie, Wyo, Mar 25, 26; m 50; c 3. *Educ:* Univ Calif, Berkeley, BA, 49, MS, 51, PhD(bot), 61. *Prof Exp:* Asst prof bot, Iowa State Univ, 60-65. *Concurrent Pos:* Univ res grants, 66-68, Wis Dept Natural Resources, 67-68 & US Off Water Resources, 68-69. *Mem:* Ecol Soc Am; Asn Aquatic Vascular Plant Biologists; Sigma Xi; Soc Wetland Scientists. *Res:* Scirpus lacustris complex and Typha biosystematics, ecology, floras, wetland vegetation ecology rivers, lakes, marshes, ferns, conservation, especially freshwater wetlands. *Mailing Add:* Dept Biol Univ Wis 800 W Main Whitewater WI 53190

SMITH, STANLEY GLEN, ORGANIC CHEMISTRY. *Current Pos:* From instr to assoc prof, 60-73, PROF CHEM, UNIV ILL, URBANA, 73- *Personal Data:* b Glendale, Calif, June 20, 31; m 65. *Educ:* Univ Calif, Berkeley, BS, 53; Univ Calif, Los Angeles, PhD(chem), 59. *Concurrent Pos:* Sloan fel, 64-66. *Mem:* Am Chem Soc. *Res:* Physical organic chemistry; reaction kinetics; computer-based teaching. *Mailing Add:* 254 Roger Adam Lab 1209 California Urbana IL 61801-3731

SMITH, STEPHEN ALLEN, INVENTORY MANAGEMENT, PRICING & MARKET FORECASTING. *Current Pos:* PROF DECISION SCI, SANTA CLARA UNIV, 82- *Personal Data:* b Marietta, Ohio, Sept 7, 42; m 75. *Educ:* Univ Cincinnati, BS, 65; Stevens Inst Technol, MS, 67; Stanford Univ, PhD(eng econ), 72. *Prof Exp:* Mem tech staff opers res, Bell Tel Labs, 65-68; res scientist opers res, Xerox Palo Alto Res Ctr, 72-82. *Concurrent Pos:* Assoc ed, Opers Res J, 84-; vis prof indust eng, Univ Calif, Berkeley, 89. *Mem:* Inst Mgt Sci; Opers Res Soc. *Res:* Pricing and market forecasting for new products in retailing and the electric power industry; combination of pricing and inventory management decisions. *Mailing Add:* Santa Clara Univ Dept Decision Sci Kenna Hall 219 Santa Clara CA 95053. *E-Mail:* ssmith@scu.bitnet

SMITH, STEPHEN D, ANATOMY, EMBRYOLOGY. *Current Pos:* from instr to assoc prof, 65-88, PROF ANAT, UNIV KY, 89- *Personal Data:* b Philadelphia, Pa, Jan 15, 39; m 73; c 3. *Educ:* Wesleyan Univ, AB, 61; Tulane Univ, PhD(anat), 65. *Prof Exp:* Instr anat & ophthal, Tulane Univ, 64-65. *Mem:* AAAS; Am Asn Anatomists; Soc Develop Biol; Am Soc Zoologists; NY Acad Sci; Int Soc Bioelec; Bioelectrochem Soc; Bioelec Rep Growth Soc. *Res:* Control of regeneration and differentiation-growth-limiting mechanisms; effects of physical stress and magnetic-electrical fields development. *Mailing Add:* Dept Anat & Neurobiol Col Med & Dent Univ Ky 800 Rose St Lexington KY 40536-0084

SMITH, STEPHEN D, GROUP THEORY, REPRESENTATION THEORY. *Current Pos:* Res instr, 73-75, from asst prof to assoc prof, 75-84, PROF MATH, UNIV ILL, 84- *Personal Data:* b Houston, Tex, June 11, 48. *Educ:* Mass Inst Technol, BS, 70; Oxford Univ, PhD(math), 73. *Mem:* Am Math Soc. *Res:* Classification of finite simple groups, work groups & geometrics. *Mailing Add:* Univ Ill 851 S Morgan MC 249 Univ Ill 851 S Morgan St Chicago IL 60607-7045

SMITH, STEPHEN JUDSON, LASER SPECTROSCOPY. *Current Pos:* RETIRED. *Personal Data:* b Fairfield, Iowa, June 14, 24; m 51, Joyce W Rickman; c 5. *Educ:* Kalamazoo Col, BA, 49; Harvard Univ, MA, 50, PhD(physics), 54. *Prof Exp:* Asst physics, Harvard Univ, 53-54; physicist, Nat Bur Standards, 54-86. *Concurrent Pos:* Fel, Joint Inst Lab Astrophys, Univ Colo, Boulder, 62-, lectr, Univ, 62-66, adj prof, 66-; Dept of Com sci & technol fel, 75-76; NSF prog dir, 75-76, 89-90; Alexander von Humboldt Found sr US scientist award, Univ Munich, 78-79; assoc ed, Phys Rev A, 92- *Mem:* AAAS; Am Phys Soc; Optical Soc Am. *Res:* Multi-photon ionization including angular distributions; effects of laser field fluctuations on nonlinear absorption by atoms. *Mailing Add:* Joint Inst for Lab Astrophys Univ Colo Boulder CO 80309-0440

SMITH, STEPHEN MICHAEL, MACROPHYTE ECOPHYSIOLOGY. *Current Pos:* POSTDOCTORAL STUDENT, FLA INT UNIV, 97- *Personal Data:* b Madison, Wis, Dec 1, 66; m 95, Karen Hendriksen. *Educ:* Univ Miami, PhD(marine biol & fisheries), 97. *Prof Exp:* Sr biologist, Trop Res & Educ Ctr, Univ Fla, 95-97. *Mem:* Int Soc Mangrove Ecosysts; Soc Wetland Scientists; Ecol Soc Am. *Res:* Effects of natural and anthropogenic stresses on macrophyte growth and development. *Mailing Add:* 1990 Brickell Ave No 1 Miami FL 33129. *E-Mail:* ssmith2403@aol.com

SMITH, STEPHEN ROGER, PHYSICS. *Current Pos:* sr staff scientist, 79-80, dir res & eng, 80-84, div dir res, Fisher Controls, 84-85, GEN MGR, EMR PHOTOELECTRIC, PRINCETON, NJ, 85- *Personal Data:* b Fayette, Ala, Nov 21, 39; m 66; c 2. *Educ:* Mass Inst Technol, SB, 62, PhD(physics), 69. *Prof Exp:* Instr physics, Princeton Univ, 69-72; from asst prof physics to assoc prof, 72-79. *Mem:* Am Phys Soc; Am Asn Physics Teachers. *Res:* Quantum optics; photodetectors. *Mailing Add:* 16 Greene Dr RR 8 Lawrenceville NJ 08648

SMITH, STEVEN ELLSWORTH, PLANT REPRODUCTIVE BIOLOGY. *Current Pos:* asst prof, 84-89, ASSOC PROF, UNIV ARIZ, 89- *Personal Data:* b Lincoln, Nebr, Aug 20, 57; m 88, Margaret Livingston. *Educ:* Univ Calif, Davis, BS, 79; Cornell Univ, MS, 82, PhD(plant breeding), 84. *Prof Exp:* Res assoc, Univ Wis, 84. *Concurrent Pos:* Assoc ed, Crop Sci, Am Soc Agron, 90-93; chmn, Alfalfa Crop Adv Comt, Nat Plant Germplasma Syst, 91-; coun mem, Am Genetics Asn, 93. *Mem:* Am Soc Agron; Soc Range Mgt; Bot Am; Am Genetics Asn. *Res:* Genetic improvement of alfalfa, especially in long-season desert environments; organelle inheritance in plants; improvement of rangeland plants. *Mailing Add:* Plant Sci Univ Ariz 1600 E University Blvd Tucson AZ 85721-0001. *Fax:* 520-621-7186; *E-Mail:* azalfalf@ccit.arizona.edu

SMITH, STEVEN ESLIE, fault tolerant computer systems engineering, process safety controls engineering, for more information see previous edition

SMITH, STEVEN JOEL, pharmacology, biochemistry, for more information see previous edition

SMITH, STEVEN PATRICK DECLAND, AEROSPACE ENGINEERING, NUCLEAR PHYSICS. *Current Pos:* RES CHIEF AEROSPACE ENGR, US ARMY MISSILE RES & DEVELOP COMMAND, 67-, TECH INTEGRATION DIR. *Personal Data:* b Tampa, Fla, July 12, 39; m 63; c 2. *Educ:* Univ Fla, BSME, 62, MSE, 63, PhD(nuclear sci), 67. *Mailing Add:* 827 Tannahill Dr S E Huntsville AL 35802

SMITH, STEVEN SIDNEY, CELL BIOLOGY, TUMOR BIOLOGY. *Current Pos:* from asst res scientist to assoc res scientist, 82-94, RES SCIENTIST, CITY HOPE NAT MED CTR, 95-, DIR, DEPT CELL & TUMOR BIOL, 90- *Personal Data:* b Idaho Falls, Idaho, Feb 11, 46; m 74, Nancy L Turner. *Educ:* Univ Idaho, BS, 68; Univ Calif, Los Angeles, PhD(molecular biol), 74. *Prof Exp:* Lectr molecular biol, Univ Bern, Switz, 74-77; res assoc cell biol, Scripps Clin & Res Found, 78-81. *Concurrent Pos:* Consult, Molecular Biosyst Inc, 81-84; prin investr, Inst Gen Med Sci, NIH & Coun Tobacco Res USA, Inc, 83-93, March of Dimes, 88-91 & Smokeless Tobacco Res Coun, 92-; Welcome vis prof basic med sci, Okla State Univ, 95-96. *Mem:* Am Crystallog Asn; Am Asn Cancer Res; Am Soc Cell Biol; Am Chem Soc. *Res:* Maintenance of differentiated state; macromolecular assembly; unusual DNA; structures chromosome damage and carcinogenesis. *Mailing Add:* Dept Cell & Tumor Biol City Hope Nat Med Ctr 1500 E Duarte Rd Duarte CA 91010-0269. *Fax:* 626-301-8972; *E-Mail:* ssmith@coh.org

SMITH, STEWART EDWARD, COAL SCIENCE, CHEMICAL KINETICS. *Current Pos:* ADV ENGR, WESTINGHOUSE, 86- *Personal Data:* b Baltimore, Md, Oct 5, 37; c Nicole & Stewart. *Educ:* Howard Univ, Wash, BS, 60; Ohio State Univ, PhD(chem), 69. *Prof Exp:* Teaching asst & phys chem, Ohio State Univ, 64-69; chemist, Sun Oil Co, 69-71; chemist, E I du Pont de Nemours & Co, 63-64 & 72-74 tech serv rep, 74-78; chemist, Exxon Res & Eng Co, 78-81, group head, 81-82, coordr, 82-84, chemist, 84-86. *Mem:* Am Chem Soc; AAAS; Sigma Xi; Nat Asn Corrosion Engrs. *Res:* Gas-phase hydrocarbon oxidation kinetics; heterogeneous catalysis; polymer chemistry; coal science including coal characterization, liquefaction and combustion; surfactants; water chemistry. *Mailing Add:* 125 Amberwood Ct Bethel Park PA 15102-2252

SMITH, STEWART W, SEISMOLOGY. *Current Pos:* chmn geophys prog, 70-80, PROF GEOPHYS, UNIV WASH, 70- *Personal Data:* b Minneapolis, Minn, Sept 15, 32; m 56, Nancy L Wright; c Carol L, David S & Peter S. *Educ:* Mass Inst Technol, SB, 54; Calif Inst Technol, MS, 58, PhD(geophys), 61. *Prof Exp:* Seismologist, Shell Oil Co, 54-57; from asst prof to assoc prof geophys, Calif Inst Technol, 61-70; pres, Inc Res Insts Seismol, Washington, DC, 85-89. *Concurrent Pos:* Consult, Pac Gas & Elec Co, Diablo Canyon Nuclear Power Sta, 67-80, Southern Calif Edison Co, San Onofre Nuclear Generating Sta, 70-81, Underground Test Monitoring Technol Panel, US Dept Energy, 92-94; chmn, Workshop Seismic Verification Nuclear Test Limitation Treaties, US Cong Off Technol Assessment, 87-88, US Nat Comt, Int Asn Seismol & Physics Earths Interior, 88-92, Comt Seismol Nat Res Coun, 89-92, Comt for Joint US/USSR Seismic Prog, Inc Res Insts Seismol, 91-93; comt Interim Oversight, Dept Energy Weapons Complex, Nat Res Coun, 88-90. *Mem:* Am Geophys Union (pres, 85-87); Seismol Soc Am. *Res:* Seismology; free oscillations of the earth; elastic strain accumulation in the earth's crust; earthquake risk assessment; nonlinear dynamics and chaos applied to earthquake faulting; nuclear test ban treaty monitoring. *Mailing Add:* Geophys Prog Box 351650 Univ Wash Seattle WA 98195-1650. *E-Mail:* stew@geophys.washington.edu

SMITH, STUART, BIOCHEMISTRY, ENZYMOLOGY. *Current Pos:* from assoc res biochemist to res biochemist, 67-83, SR RES SCIENTIST, CHILDREN'S HOSP MED CTR, OAKLAND, 83- *Personal Data:* b Durham, Eng, Oct 12, 40; div; c Karen L. *Educ:* Univ Birmingham, BSc, 62, Eng, PhD(biochem), 65, DSc, 80. *Prof Exp:* Fel, Dept Biochem, Univ Birmingham, UK, 65-66, Hadassah Med Sch, Jerusalem, 66-67. *Concurrent Pos:* Estab investr, Am Heart Asn, 73-78; vis scholar, Dept Biochem, Univ Cambridge, UK, 76-77; mem, NIH Physiol Chem Study Sect, 81-84. *Mem:* Biochem Soc; AAAS; Am Soc Exp Biologists; fel Inst Biol UK. *Res:* Interested primarily in the structure, mechanism of action and regulation of enzymes involved in de novo lipogenesis. *Mailing Add:* Children's Hosp Oakland Res Inst 747 52nd St Oakland CA 94609

SMITH, STUART D, OCEANOGRAPHY, ATMOSPHERIC CHEMISTRY & PHYSICS. *Current Pos:* Sci officer oceanog, 62-66, RES SCIENTIST OCEANOG, ATLANTIC OCEANOG LAB, BEDFORD INST, 66- *Personal Data:* b Montreal, Que, Jan 9, 41; m 63, Gloria J Paull; c Tracy, Michael & Jennifer. *Educ:* McGill Univ, BEng, 62; Univ BC, PhD(oceanog & physics), 66. *Concurrent Pos:* Res assoc, Dept Oceanog, Dalhousie Univ, 92- *Mem:* Can Meteorol & Oceanog Soc (pres, 85-86 & 87-88); Am Geophys Union; Am Meteorol Soc. *Res:* Wind stress; heat flux; evaporation; evaporation, wind stress and boundary-layer turbulence over the open ocean and over drifting sea ice; surface wave generation; dynamics of iceberg drift; carbon dioxide exchange at sea surface; air-sea intraction. *Mailing Add:* Ocean Circulation Sect Bedford Inst Oceanog PO Box 1006 Dartmouth NS B2Y 4A2 Can. *Fax:* 902-426-7827; *E-Mail:* stu_smith@bionet.bio.dfo.ca@ pmdf, stu_smith@am.dfo.ca

SMITH, SUSAN MAY, ECOLOGY, ANIMAL BEHAVIOR. *Current Pos:* ASST PROF BIOL, MT HOLYOKE COL, 79- *Personal Data:* b Winnipeg, Man, Jan 14, 42. *Educ:* Univ BC, BSc, 63, MSc, 65; Univ Wash, PhD(zool), 69. *Prof Exp:* Asst prof biol, Wellesley Col, 69-73; mem fac, Dept Biol, Univ Costa Rica, 73-77; asst prof biol, Adelphi Univ, 77-79. *Mem:* AAAS; Asn Study Animal Behav; Cooper Ornith Soc; Wilson Ornith Soc; Sigma Xi. *Res:* Territoriality, social dominance and population regulation; animal communication; behavior of predators and the reactions of their prey; interspecific competition and niche overlap. *Mailing Add:* Dept Biol Sci Mt Holyoke Col South Hadley MA 01075

SMITH, SUSAN T, BIOCHEMISTRY, CLINICAL CHEMISTRY. *Current Pos:* CHAIRPERSON, DEPT CLIN LAB SCI, SCH ALLIED HEALTH SCI, ECAROLINA UNIV, 72- *Personal Data:* b Detroit, Mich, Nov 22, 37; m 64; c 2. *Educ:* Univ Mich, BS, 59; Duke Univ, PhD(biochem), 67. *Prof Exp:* Asst prof chem, ECarolina Univ, 67-69; teaching supvr, Med Lab Asst Prog, Beaufort Co Tech Inst, 69-71. *Concurrent Pos:* Site visitor, Nat Accrediting Agency Clin Lab Sci, 80-; pres, NC Soc Med Technol, 81-82. *Mem:* Am Soc Clin Lab Sci. *Res:* Biochemistry. *Mailing Add:* Sch Allied Health Sci ECarolina Univ Greenville NC 27858-4353. *Fax:* 919-757-4470

SMITH, TERENCE E, PETROLOGY, GEOCHEMISTRY. *Current Pos:* from asst prof to assoc prof, 69-76, PROF GEOL, UNIV WINDSOR, 76- *Personal Data:* b Penarth, UK, Mar 11, 36; m 62; c 2. *Educ:* Univ Wales, BSc, 59, PhD(geol), 63. *Prof Exp:* Sci off, Geol Surv Gt Brit, 62-65; lectr geol, Sunderland Tech Col, Eng, 65-67 & Univ WI, 67-69. *Res:* Metamorphic petrology and structural geology of the Scottish Highlands; clastic sedimentation and structure in British Lower Paleozoic and West Indian Tertiary sediments; petrology and geochemistry of Nova Scotia granitic batholith; coast complex of British Columbia, Pennsula Rouges batholith of Southern California and Tertiary volcanoes in Jamaica. *Mailing Add:* Geol Univ Windsor 401 Sunset Ave Windsor ON N9B 3P4 Can

SMITH, TERRY DOUGLAS, MEDICINAL CHEMISTRY. *Current Pos:* DIR, RES & DEVELOP, DIATECH INC, 92- *Personal Data:* b Bethel Springs, Tenn, Nov 20, 42. *Educ:* Univ Tenn, Memphis, BS, 64; Univ Mich, MS, 65, PhD(med chem), 68. *Prof Exp:* Res investr radiopharmaceut, E R Squibb & Sons, Inc, NJ, 69-70; asst prof pharmaceut, radiol & nuclear med, Col Pharm, Univ Tenn, Memphis, 70-72; assoc chemist, Brookhaven Nat Lab, 73-75; sr radio pharm chemist, Mallinckrodt, Inc, 75-80; dir, Res & Develop Nuclear Div, Syncor Int Corp, 80-83, dir, Biomed Group, 83-85; dir res, Berlex Labs Inc, 90-92. *Res:* Design and preparation of radiolabeled compounds for diagnosis of selected pathological conditions by external body scanning techniques. *Mailing Add:* 6 McIntosh Lane Bedford NH 03110

SMITH, TERRY EDWARD, POLYMER CHEMISTRY. *Current Pos:* res specialist, 72-76, group leader, 76-84, SECT MGR, GAF CHEMICALS CORP, 85- *Personal Data:* b Evansville, Ind, Aug 23, 40; m 62; c 3. *Educ:* David Lipscomb Col, BA, 62; Ga Inst Technol, PhD(phys chem), 67. *Prof Exp:* Res chemist, Am Cyanamid, Co, 67-72. *Mem:* Am Chem Soc. *Res:* Polymer solutions and blends; light scattering; polymer characterization; polymer synthesis. *Mailing Add:* 1615 The Lane Murray KY 42071-2293

SMITH, THEODORE BEATON, METEOROLOGY. *Current Pos:* RETIRED. *Personal Data:* b Columbus, Ohio, Feb 14, 18; m 47. *Educ:* Ohio State Univ, BA, 38; Calif Inst Technol, MS, 40 & 42, PhD(meteorol), 49. *Prof Exp:* Instr meteorol, Calif Inst Technol, 42-44 & 47-48; res meteorologist, Am Inst Aerologic Res, 48-55; res meteorologist, Meteorol Res, Inc, 55-70, vpres res, 70-78, pres, 78-87. *Mem:* AAAS; fel Am Meteorol Soc. *Res:* Cloud physics; turbulent diffusion. *Mailing Add:* 1491 Linda Vista Ave Pasadena CA 91103

SMITH, THEODORE CRAIG, ANESTHESIOLOGY, PHARMACOLOGY. *Current Pos:* CHIEF ANESTHESIOL, E A HINES JR VET AFFAIRS HOSP, HINES, ILL, 87- *Personal Data:* b Mansfield, Ohio, Sept 18, 30; m 52, 80; c 4. *Educ:* Ohio Wesleyan Univ, BA, 52; Univ Wis, MS, 60; Univ Cincinnati, MD, 56; Univ Pa, BBA, 78. *Prof Exp:* Intern & resident, Univ Wis, Hosps, 56-60; from asst prof to assoc prof anesthesia, Univ Pa, 62-72, prof, 72-82; mem fac, Dept Anesthesiol & pharmacol, 80-87, prof anesthesiol, Stritch Sch Med, Loyola Univ Chicago, 87- *Concurrent Pos:* Chief anesthesiol, Vet Admin Hosp, Philadelphia, 78-80. *Mem:* Am Physiol Soc; Asn Univ Anesthetists; Am Soc Anesthesiol. *Res:* Respiratory physiology and pharmacology and their applications to anesthesiology. *Mailing Add:* 350 Fairbank Rd Riverside IL 60546-2248

SMITH, THEODORE G, CHEMICAL ENGINEERING. *Current Pos:* from asst prof to assoc prof, 63-68, PROF CHEM ENG, UNIV MD, COLLEGE PARK, 71- *Personal Data:* b Baltimore, Md, Aug 12, 34; m 65; c 2. *Educ:* Johns Hopkins Univ, BEngSci, 56, MS, 58; Washington Univ, DSc(chem eng), 60. *Prof Exp:* Chem engr, Res Div, E I Du Pont de Nemours & Co, Del, 60-62, WVa, 62-63. *Mem:* AAAS; Am Inst Chem Engrs; Am Chem Soc. *Res:* Polymer plastics; fractionation, crystallization and solubility; diffusion through polymers; large scale chromatography; control of chemical processes; rheology; reactor design; kinetics. *Mailing Add:* Dept Chem Eng Univ Md College Park MD 20742-2111

SMITH, THEODORE ISAAC JOGUES, AQUACULTURE, FISHERIES REHABILITATION. *Current Pos:* SR MARINE SCIENTIST AQUACULT, SC WILDLIFE & MARINE RESOURCES DEPT, 73- *Personal Data:* b Brooklyn, NY, Jan 13, 45. *Educ:* Cornell Univ, BS, 66; C W Post Col, MS, 68; Univ Miami, PhD(marine sci), 73. *Mem:* World Aquacult Soc; Southeastern Estuarine Res Soc; Gulf & Caribbean Fisheries Inst; Am Fisheries Soc. *Res:* Determination of biological requirements for commercially important species; development of applicable techniques for use in mariculture; technical and advisory services for mariculture and related industries. *Mailing Add:* 33 Anderson Ave Charleston SC 29412

SMITH, THOMAS CALDWELL, PHYSIOLOGY, BIOPHYSICS. *Current Pos:* from asst prof to assoc prof, 69-83, PROF PHYSIOL, UNIV TEX HEALTH CTR, 83- *Personal Data:* b Charleston, WVa, Feb 20, 41; m 65, Nancy LaPrade; c Laura & Shannon. *Educ:* Univ Richmond, BS, 63, MS, 65; Med Col Va, PhD(physiol), 69. *Prof Exp:* Instr physiol, Med Col Va, 68-69. *Mem:* Human Anat & Physiol Soc; Soc Gen Physiol; Am Aging Asn. *Res:* Active ion transport in epithelium and biomembranes; hormonal and neural regulatory systems in aging. *Mailing Add:* Dept Physiol Univ Tex Health Sci Ctr 7703 Floyd Curl Dr San Antonio TX 78284. *Fax:* 210-567-4410; *E-Mail:* smitht@uthscsa.edu

SMITH, THOMAS DAVID, PHYSICAL CHEMISTRY. *Current Pos:* RETIRED. *Personal Data:* b Eng, Nov 25, 23; m 47, Beryl Havre; c Mitchell C, Claire M & Scobie P. *Educ:* Univ London, BSc, 44, PhD(chem), 47. *Prof Exp:* Chemist, C A Parsons & Co, Ltd, Eng, 39-44; res assoc, Brit Coke Res Asn, 44-47; res assoc, Univ Southern Calif, 48-49; res chemist, Union Oil Co, Calif, 49-50; res fel, Cambridge Univ, 50-51; res supvr, E I du Pont de Nemours & Co, Inc, 51-57, res mgr, 57-64, lab dir, 64-65, asst plant mgr, 65-66, lab dir, 66-68, asst dir res & develop, 68-72, dir res, Imaging Systs Dept, 72-86. *Mem:* Am Chem Soc; Soc Photog Sci & Eng; Royal Photog Soc Gt Brit. *Res:* Physical and colloid chemistry, especially in photographic systems; electronic imaging systems. *Mailing Add:* RR 1 Box 1330 Greensboro VT 05841-9713. *E-Mail:* 71541.363@compuserve.com

SMITH, THOMAS ELIJAH, BIOCHEMISTRY. *Current Pos:* PROF & CHMN, DEPT BIOCHEM, COL MED, HOWARD UNIV, 80- *Personal Data:* b North Augusta, SC, Apr 11, 33; m 53; c 2. *Educ:* Benedict Col, BS, 53; George Washington Univ, MS, 59, PhD(biochem), 62. *Prof Exp:* Chemist, Lab Exp Med & Clin Therapeut, Nat Heart Inst, 53-54, biochemist, Lab Clin Biochem, 56-62; NIH fel enzyme mech, Wash Univ, 62-63; sr biochemist, Biol & Med Div, Melpar, Inc, 63-65; sr biochemist, Lawrence Livermore Lab, Univ Calif, 65-74; assoc prof biochem, Univ Tex Health Sci Ctr Dallas, 74-80. *Concurrent Pos:* Dir, Biomed Div Summer Teaching & Res Inst, Lawrence Livermore Lab, Univ Calif, Livermore, Calif, 72-74; consult, E I DuPont Co, Wilmington, Del, 72-74; asst dean, Grad Sch Biomed Sci, Univ Tex Health Sci Ctr, Dallas, 74-76; mem, test comt, Nat Bd Med Examiners, 87-91 & bd sci counselors, Nat Heart Lung & Blood Inst, NIH, 88-92. *Mem:* AAAS; Am Chem Soc; Am Soc Biol Chemists; Sigma Xi. *Res:* Enzyme mechanisms. *Mailing Add:* Dept Biochem & Molecular Biol Howard Univ Col Med 520 W St NW Washington DC 20059-0001

SMITH, THOMAS GRAVES, JR, NEUROPHYSIOLOGY, IMAGE PROCESSING. *Current Pos:* res med officer physiol, 64-68, CHIEF SECT SENSORY PHYSIOL, LAB NEUROPHYSIOL, NAT INST NEUROL COMMUN & NEUROL DIS & STROKE, 68- *Personal Data:* b Winnsboro, SC, Mar 22, 31; m 56, Joann Hornsmith. *Educ:* Emory Univ, BA, 53; Oxford Univ, BA & MA, 56; Columbia Univ, MD, 60. *Prof Exp:* Intern, Bronx Munic Hosp, New York, 60-61; vis res assoc biol, Mass Inst Technol, 64-66. *Concurrent Pos:* Vis prof, John Cortin Sch Med, Australian Nat Univ, Canberra, 90. *Mem:* AAAS; Am Physiol Soc; Soc Neurophysiol. *Res:* Neurophysiology and biophysics of excitable membranes and of synaptic transmission between nerve cells; video microscopy and image processing. *Mailing Add:* Nat Inst Neurol Dis & Stroke NIH Bldg 36 Rm 2C02 Bethesda MD 20892-0001. *Fax:* 301-402-1565; *E-Mail:* tgs@helix.nih.gov

SMITH, THOMAS HENRY, ORGANIC CHEMISTRY. *Current Pos:* SR RES SCIENTIST, CLONTECH LABS, 92- *Personal Data:* b Lackawanna, NY, Aug 14, 47; m 77, Linda Mak; c Katherine & Matthew. *Educ:* Niagara Univ, BS, 69; Ariz State Univ, PhD(org chem), 74. *Prof Exp:* Res asst org chem, Ariz State Univ, 69-74; fel, Stanford Res Inst, 74-75; org chemist, SRI Int, 75-87; mgr chem process develop, Am Bionetics, 87-89, dir, Synthesis Reagents, 89-91. *Mem:* AAAS; Am Chem Soc. *Res:* Synthetic organic chemistry; synthesis of biologically active compounds; drug design; nucleic acid synthesis reagents. *Mailing Add:* 2041 Greenwood Dr San Carlos CA 94070. *Fax:* 650-858-1239; *E-Mail:* toms@clontech.com

SMITH, THOMAS JAY, OCCUPATIONAL HEALTH & SAFETY, HUMAN FACTORS. *Current Pos:* SUPVR HUMAN FACTORS RES, US BUR MINES, 87- *Personal Data:* b Rochester, NY, May 9, 40; m 62, Mary J Clemens; c Steven & Michael. *Educ:* Univ Wis-Madison, BA, 62, PhD(physiol), 77; Univ Calif, San Diego, MSc, 66. *Prof Exp:* Programmer syst, Planning Res Corp, San Diego, Calif, 66-67 & Comput Ctr, Univ Wis-Madison, 67-69; teaching asst physiol, Univ Wis-Madison, 69-75, teaching fel toxicol, 77-79; vis instr kinesiology, Simon Fraser Univ, 75-76, asst adj prof, 80-87. *Concurrent Pos:* Vis prof physiol, Dept Biol, Beloit Col, 79; consult, 80-; adj prof, Univ Minn, 90- *Mem:* Am Physiol Soc; Human Factors Soc; AAAS; Sigma Xi. *Res:* Human health and performance effects of exposure to occupational-environmental hazards; behavioral cybernetic analysis of motor performance, growth and development, and safety and hazard management; ergonomic-human factors evaluation of occupational health and safety problems. *Mailing Add:* Dept Kinesiol Univ Minn Cooke Hall 1900 University Ave SE Minneapolis MN 55455. *Fax:* 612-725-4526; *E-Mail:* smithtj@tcrca.usbm.gov

SMITH, THOMAS JEFFERSON, GEOPHYSICS, MATHEMATICS. *Current Pos:* RETIRED. *Personal Data:* b Atlanta, Ga, June 12, 30; m 57; c 2. *Educ:* Emory Univ, BA, 51; Univ Wis, MS, 57, PhD(math), 61. *Prof Exp:* Asst prof math, Kalamazoo Col, 61-62; mem staff geophys, Carnegie Inst Wash, assoc prof, 70-74; prof math, Kalamazoo Col, 74-94. *Mem:* Am Math Soc. *Res:* Minkowskian and Finsler geometries; convex sets; numerical methods. *Mailing Add:* 10462 N 44th St Augusta MI 49102

SMITH, THOMAS LOWELL, MICROCIRCULATION, HEMODYNAMICS. *Current Pos:* ASST PROF PHYSIOL, BOWMAN GRAY SCH MED, WAKE FOREST UNIV, 82- *Educ:* Wake Forest Univ, PhD(cardiovasc physiol), 79. *Mailing Add:* Dept Orthop Surg Bowman Gray Sch Med Wake Forest Univ Med Ctr Blvd Winston Salem NC 27157-1070. *Fax:* 919-716-7310

SMITH, THOMAS STEVENSON, SOLID STATE PHYSICS. *Current Pos:* pres, Lawrence Univ, 69-79. *Personal Data:* b Hubbard, Ohio, Feb 8, 21; m 44; c 3. *Educ:* Kenyon Col, AB, 47; Ohio State Univ, PhD(physics), 52. *Hon Degrees:* LHD, Kenyon Col, 70, Cardinal Stritch Col, 80; DSc, Ripon Col, 71; LLD, Lawrence Univ, 80. *Prof Exp:* Instr physics, Kenyon Col, 46-47; asst, Ohio State Univ, 47-51, res fel, 51-52; from asst prof to prof, Ohio Univ, 52-69, asst to pres, 61-62, vpres acad affairs, 62-67, provost, 67-69. *Concurrent Pos:* Chmn, Great Lakes Dist Selection Rhodes Scholar; educ consult-examr, Comn Cols & Univs, NCent Asn Cols & Sec Schs. *Mem:* Am Phys Soc; AAAS; Sigma Xi; Am Asn Physics Teachers. *Res:* Cryogenics; superconductivity; nuclear magnetic resonance; x-ray powder diffraction; vapor pressures at high temperature. *Mailing Add:* N4775 28th Court Pine River WI 54965

SMITH, THOMAS W, MEDICINE. *Current Pos:* CHIEF CARDIO-VASC DIV, BRIGHAM & WOMEN'S HOSP, 74- *Personal Data:* b Akron Ohio, Mar 29, 36; m 58; c 3. *Educ:* Harvard Univ, AB, 58, MD, 65. *Prof Exp:* From asst prof to assoc prof, Sch Med, Harvard Univ, 71-79, prof, 79- *Mem:* Am Heart Asn; Am Col Cardiol; Am Soc Clin Invest; Am Fed Clin Res; Am Physiol Soc; Am Soc Pharmacol & Exp Therapeut; Asn Am Physicians. *Res:* Mechanism of action digitalis; mechanism of inotropic agents. *Mailing Add:* Dept Med Cardiovasc Div Brigham & Women's Hosp 75 Francis St Boston MA 02115-6195

SMITH, THOMAS WOODS, ORGANIC POLYMER CHEMISTRY. *Current Pos:* assoc scientist, Xerox Corp, 73-75, scientist, 75-78, mgr polymer sci, 79-83, mgr chem mat, 83-85, mgr macromolecular org & surface chem, 85-86, RES FEL, CORP RES & TECHNOL, XEROX CORP, 86- *Personal Data:* b Portsmouth, Ohio, Dec 16, 43; m 68, Mary E Johns; c Natalie, Katherine & William. *Educ:* John Carroll Univ, BS, 69; Univ Mich, PhD(org chem), 73. *Prof Exp:* Chemist, Lubrizol Corp, 63-70. *Concurrent Pos:* Consult, Environ Res Inst Mich, 72-73. *Mem:* Am Chem Soc; Soc Imaging Sci & Technol. *Res:* Synthesis, reactivity and physical chemical studies of functional polymer systems; studies of device applications, electronic and dielectric properties of photoactive polymers, block copolymers aand polymer composites. *Mailing Add:* Xerox Corp 22 Hidden Meadow Penfield NY 14526-1652. *E-Mail:* twsmith@wb.xerox.com

SMITH, THOR LOWE, POLYMER PHYSICS & PHYSICAL CHEMISTRY. *Current Pos:* RETIRED. *Personal Data:* b Zion, Ill, June 11, 20; m 49; c 2. *Educ:* Wheaton Col, BS, 42; Ill Inst Technol, MS, 44; Univ Wis, PhD(chem), 48. *Honors & Awards:* Whitby Mem lectr, Univ Akron, 74; Bingham Medal, Soc Rheol, 78; Centennial scholars lectr, Case Western Res Univ, 80; Res Award, Soc Plastics Engrs, 83. *Prof Exp:* Res chemist, Hercules Co, 48-54; sr res engr, Jet Propulsion Lab, Calif Inst Technol, 54-56, chief, Solid Propellant Chem Sect, 56-59; chmn, Propulsion Dept, Stanford Res Inst, 59-61, dir, Propulsion Sci Div, 61-64, sci fel, 64-68; prof chem, Tex A&M Univ, 68-69; res staff mem, IBM Res Div, 69-91. *Concurrent Pos:* Mem, Eval Panel Nat Res Coun, Nat Bur Stand, 74-77; mem bd trustees, Gordon Res Conf, 78-84, chmn, 81-82; mem, Nat Mat Adv Bd Comts, 71-72 & 78-80. *Mem:* Nat Acad Eng; Soc Rheol (pres, 67-69); Am Chem Soc. *Res:* Mechanical and other physical properties of polymer systems; deformation and fracture of polymeric materials; rheology of dispersions and polymers; rejuvenation and physical aging of polymeric glasses; polymer engineering. *Mailing Add:* PO Box 1664 Los Altos CA 94023-1664

SMITH, TIM DENIS, BIOLOGY, STATISTICS. *Current Pos:* FISHERIES BIOLOGIST, NORTHEAST FISHERIES CTR, 85- *Personal Data:* b Eugene, Ore, Dec 30, 46; m 67; c 1. *Educ:* Pac Lutheran Univ, BA, 69; Univ Wash, PhD(biomath), 73. *Prof Exp:* Res assoc oceanog, Univ Wash, 72-73; fisheries biologist, Nat Marine Fisheries Serv, 73-75; asst prof zool, Univ Hawaii, 75-78; fisheries biologist, Southwest Fisheries Ctr, 78-85. *Concurrent Pos:* Mem sci comt, Int Whaling Comn, 74-; mem, Comt Sci Adv, US Marine Mammal Comn, 76-79, 89-; mem, Sci & Statist Comt, Western Pac Regional Fisheries Mgt Coun, 77-78. *Mem:* Soc Marine Mammalogy; Resource Modeling Asn. *Res:* Applied and theoretical population biology, especially of large mammals; management of living resources; dynamics of populations of fishes and large mammals, especially marine mammals; natural resource utilization; history of marine science. *Mailing Add:* Northeast Fisheries Ctr 166 Water St Woods Hole MA 02543

SMITH, TIMOTHY ANDRE, DENTAL STRESS. *Current Pos:* assoc prof psychol, 69-73, dir, Learning Resources, Col Educ & Dent, 73-75, prof community dent, 76-87, PROF ORAL HEALTH SCI, UNIV KY COL DENT, 87-, PROF BEHAV SCI, UNIV COL MED, 95- *Personal Data:* b LaCrosse, Wis, Jan 9, 37; m 64, Namida Ramanauskas; c Linda, Mark, Maura, Alicia & Aleks. *Educ:* Marquette Univ, BS, 58; Univ NC, MA, 61, PhD(psychol), 63. *Prof Exp:* Instr psychol, Fla State Univ, 62-63. *Concurrent Pos:* Consult, Chattanooga State Tech Col, 75, Mass Inst Technol, 76, Univ Minn, 77, Sci Res Assoc, 77, Univ Wash, 79, Dept Educ, State Alaska, 80-83 & 85; fel, Harvard Sch Med, 76; vis prof, Univ Wash, 83-84, Royal Dent Col, Aarhus, Denmark, 90-91; affil prof, Dept Dent Pub Health Sci, Univ Wash, Seattle. *Mem:* Am Psychol Asn; Am Educ Res Asn; Am Asn Dent Sch; Int Asn Dent Res; Am Asn Pub Health Dent. *Res:* Improving the measurement of dental stress through physiological and self-report methods; reduction of dental stress through behavioral methods. *Mailing Add:* Dept Behav Sci Med Col Univ Ky Lexington KY 40536-0084. *Fax:* 606-257-7708; *E-Mail:* tasmitoi@pop.uky.edu

SMITH, TODD IVERSEN, PHYSICS & USES OF FREE ELECTRON LASERS, ELECTRON LINEAR ACCELERATORS. *Current Pos:* from res physicist to sr res physicist, 74-89, RES PROF PHYSICS, HANSEN EXP PHYSICS LAB, STANFORD UNIV, 89- *Personal Data:* b Mobile, Ala, June 11, 40; m 70, Cecelia Scott; c Kevin & Alex. *Educ:* Cornell Univ, BA, 61; Rice Univ, MA, 63, PhD(physics), 65. *Prof Exp:* Res assoc physics, Stanford Univ, 65-68; asst prof physics & elec eng, Univ Southern Calif, 68-74. *Mem:* AAAS; Am Phys Soc; Inst Elec & Electronics Engrs; Sigma Xi. *Res:* Physics and uses of free electron lasers; superconducting microwave cavities; superconducting electron linear accelerators; intense, low emittance electron beams. *Mailing Add:* W W Hansen Exp Physics Lab Stanford Univ Stanford CA 94305-4085. *Fax:* 650-725-8311; *E-Mail:* tismith@leland.stanford.edu

SMITH, TOWNSEND JACKSON, agronomy; deceased, see previous edition for last biography

SMITH, TRUDY ENZER, PHYSICAL CHEMISTRY. *Current Pos:* from asst prof to assoc prof, 62-77, PROF CHEM, CONN COL, 77- *Personal Data:* b Eger, Czech, May 23, 24; nat US; m 53; c 6. *Educ:* Greensboro Col, AB, 44; Ohio State Univ, PhD(chem), 57. *Prof Exp:* Asst, Ohio State Univ, 45-50; res chemist, Aerojet Gen Corp, Gen Tire & Rubber Co, Calif, 51-53; phys chemist, US Naval Ord Test Sta, 53-60; instr chem, Univ Conn, 60-62. *Mem:* Am Chem Soc; Sigma Xi. *Res:* Chemical kinetics; mass spectrometry. *Mailing Add:* 31 Lynwood Rd Conn Col Storrs Mansfield CT 06268-2029

SMITH, VANN ELLIOTT, MARINE BIOLOGY. *Current Pos:* VPRES, ENVIRON SURVEY DIV, ASCI CORP, 89- *Personal Data:* b Pensacola, Fla, June 28, 40; m 69; c 2. *Educ:* Fla State Univ, BS, 62, MS, 64; Scripps Inst Oceanog, PhD(marine biol), 68. *Prof Exp:* Coordr Lake & Marine Res, Cranbrook Inst, 71-85; proj mgr, Oceanog Servs, Raytheon Serv Co, 85-89. *Concurrent Pos:* Edison scholar, Cranbrook Inst Sci, 71-72. *Mem:* Sigma Xi; Int Asn Great Lakes Res. *Res:* Contaminants in Great Lakes waters and wildlife; comparative marine biochemistry; heavy metals and pesticides in lake ecosystems; remote sensing of lakes, lake watersheds and coral reef systems. *Mailing Add:* 2004 W Spinningwheel Bloomfield Hills MI 48304

SMITH, VELMA MERRILINE, ALGEBRA. *Current Pos:* From asst prof to assoc prof, 72-81, PROF MATH, CALIF STATE POLYTECH UNIV, 81-, CHMN DEPT, 82- *Personal Data:* b San Bernardino, Calif, Mar 11, 40; m 61. *Educ:* Calif State Col, San Bernardino, BA, 67; Univ Calif, Riverside, MA, 69, PhD(math), 72. *Mem:* Am Math Soc; Math Asn Am. *Res:* Commutative algebra, especially ideal and ring theory; teacher education. *Mailing Add:* Dept Math Calif State Polytech Univ 3801 W Temple Ave Pomona CA 91768-4033

SMITH, VERNON L, COMMUNICATIONS SCIENCE. *Current Pos:* PROF, UNIV ARIZ, 75-; RES DIR, ECON SCI LAB, 86- *Personal Data:* b Jan 1, 27. *Educ:* Calif Inst Technol, BSEE, 49; Univ Kans, MA, 52; Harvard Univ, PhD(econ), 55. *Honors & Awards:* Mackintosh Lectr, Queens Univ, 84-85; Annual Undergraduate Lectr Polit Econ, Washington Univ, St Louis, 87. *Prof Exp:* Instr econ, Univ Kans, 51-52; economist, Harvard Econ Res Proj, 54-55; mem, Mgt Sci Res Group, Purdue Univ, 55-56, from asst prof to prof, 55-67; prof, Brown Univ, 67-68 & Univ Mass, 68-75. *Concurrent Pos:* Res consult, Rand Corp, 57-59; fac res fel, Ford Found, 58-59; Cowles Found vis fel, Yale Univ, 71; fel, Ctr Advan Study Behav Sci, 71-73; Fairchild distinguished scholar, Calif Inst Technol, 73-74; vis prof, Univ Southern Calif & Calif Inst Technol, 74-75; assoc ed, J Econ Behav & Orgn, 85-; distinguished vis prof, McMaster Univ, 88; CS First Boston fel & consult, Univ Victoria, NZ, 91; vis distinguished lectr, Western Mich Univ, 92 grantee, NSF, 62-, Bsrhart Found, 82-83, Fed Trade Comn, 83-84, Ariz Corp Comn, 84, Sloan Found, 86-87, Fed Energy Reg Comn, 87, Energy Info Admin, 87, Chicago Mercantile Exchange, 87-89, Inst Quantitative Res Finance, 92; consult & lectr, Prospect Elec, Paramata, NSW, Australia, 93. *Mem:* Nat Acad Sci; Southern Econ Asn (vpres, 85-86); Econ Sci Asn (vpres, 87-89); fel Econometric Soc; Western Econ Asn (vpres, 88-89, pres elect, 89-90, pres, 90-91); fel AAAS; fel Am Acad Arts & Sci; fel Am Econ Soc. *Res:* Contributed over 150 professional publications. *Mailing Add:* Dept Econ Univ Ariz 1130 E Helen PO Box 210108 Tucson AZ 85721-0108

SMITH, VICTOR HERBERT, HOSPITAL ADMINISTRATION, ENVIRONMENTAL HEALTH. *Current Pos:* MGR, KENNEWICK PRIMARY CLINIC, 82- *Personal Data:* b Lewistown, Mont, Aug 1, 25; m 50; c 5. *Educ:* Mont State Col, BS, 50; Ore State Col, PhD(chem), 55. *Prof Exp:* Biol scientist, Hanford Atomic Prod Oper, Gen Elec Co, 54-65; sr res scientist, Pac Northwest Labs, Battelle Mem Inst, 65-81. *Concurrent Pos:* AEC fel radiation chem & biophys, Univ Minn, 59-61; mem SC-37, Nat Comt Radiation Protection, 73- *Mem:* AAAS; Am Chem Soc; Radiation Res Soc; Health Physics Soc; Soc Exp Biol & Med. *Res:* Heterocyclics; radiation induced reactions and effects on organics and biological systems; radiation protection; removal of radioactive emitters; chelation therapy; effects and treatment of incorporated radionuclides, toxic metals, organometallics and combined insults. *Mailing Add:* 1007 W 27th Kennewick WA 99337-4308

SMITH, VICTORIA LYNN, PHYTOPATHOLOGY. *Current Pos:* ASST SCIENTIST, CONN AGR EXP STA, 90- *Personal Data:* b Dayton, Ohio, July 29, 59. *Educ:* Ohio Northern Univ, BS, 81; Ohio State Univ, MS, 83; NC State Univ, PhD(plant path & soil sci), 87. *Prof Exp:* Fel res assoc, Cornell Univ, 87-89; res plant pathologist, Beltsville Agr Res Ctr, USDA, 89-90. *Mem:* Am Phytopath Soc; Can Phytopath Soc; Sigma Xi. *Res:* Biological control of phytophthora cinnamomi on woody ornamental plants; biology and control of dogwood anthralnose. *Mailing Add:* Dept Plant Path & Ecol Conn Agr Exp Sta 123 Huntington St New Haven CT 06504

SMITH, VINCENT C, FLORICULTURE, MARKETING. *Current Pos:* asst prof floricult, 48-55, head dept, 56-75, prof ornamental hort, 56-80, EMER PROF, STATE UNIV NY AGR & TECH COL, 80- *Personal Data:* b Albany, NY, Nov 4, 14; m 40; c 4. *Educ:* Cornell Univ, BS, 37; NY Univ, MS, 47. *Prof Exp:* Teacher, Rockland County Voc Educ & Exten Bd, 40-47. *Mem:* Am Soc Hort Sci. *Res:* Problems involved in marketing floral and ornamental horticulture crops. *Mailing Add:* 468 Cleveland Ave Hornell NY 14843

SMITH, VIVIANNE C(AMERON), PSYCHOPHYSICS. *Current Pos:* From instr to assoc prof, 68-79, PROF OPHTHAL, UNIV CHICAGO, 79- *Personal Data:* b Woodford, Eng, July 7, 38; US citizen; m 65, Joel Pokorny; c Charles W & Julia E. *Educ:* Columbia Univ, BS, 62, MA, 64, PhD(psychol), 67. *Honors & Awards:* Tillyer Medal, Optical Soc Am, 90; Godlove Award, Int Soc Color Coun, 95; Verriest Medal, Int Res Group Colorvision Deficiencies, 95. *Mem:* Int Res Group Color Vision Deficiencies; fel Optical Soc Am; Asn Res Vision & Ophthal. *Res:* Mechanism of color vision in humans; theories of color vision; spatial and temporal factors in vision. *Mailing Add:* Visual Sci Ctr Univ Chicago 939 E 57th St Chicago IL 60637

SMITH, W JOHN, ANIMAL BEHAVIOR, CONSERVATION BIOLOGY. *Current Pos:* Asst prof zool, 63-68, assoc prof, 68-76, PROF BIOL & PSYCHOL, UNIV PA, 76-, MEM, INST NEUROL SCI, 67- *Personal Data:* b Toronto, Ont, Dec 20, 34; m 87, Anne Marie Palita; c 1. *Educ:* Carleton Univ, Can, BSc, 57; Univ Mich, MS, 58; Harvard Univ, PhD(biol), 61. *Concurrent Pos:* Res assoc, Mus Comp Zool, Harvard Univ, 61-64; consult, Penrose Res Lab, Philadelphia Zool Soc, 65-; res assoc, Smithsonian Trop Res Inst, 66-; res assoc, Acad Natural Sci, Pa, 67-; fac assoc, Annenberg Sch Commun, Univ Pa. *Mem:* Am Ornithologists Union; Animal Behavior Soc; Soc Conservation Biol. *Res:* Animal communication and social behavior; ecology; systematics; evolutionary theory; conservation biology. *Mailing Add:* Leidy Labs Univ Pa Philadelphia PA 19104-6018. *Fax:* 215-898-8780; *E-Mail:* wjsmith@sas.upenn.edu

SMITH, W NOVIS, JR, THERMOPLASTIC-THERMOSET RESIN CHEMISTRY, COMPOSITES. *Current Pos:* PRES, R K CARBON FIBERS INC, 83-; AM HYPERFORM, 82- *Personal Data:* b Chicago, Ill, May 21, 37; m, Anna Varjas. *Educ:* Mass Inst Technol, BS, 59; Univ Calif, Berkeley, PhD(org chem), 63. *Prof Exp:* Res chemist, Org Chem Dept, E I du Pont de Nemours & Co Inc, 62-64; res assoc chem, Foote Mineral Co, 64-71, mgr chem res, 72-74; asst to dir, Eastern Res Ctr, Stauffer Chem Co, 74-76; asst dir corp res, Air Prod, 76-77, asst dir contract res, 77-79; mgr develop progs, Reentry Systs Div, Gen Elec Co, 80-82. *Mem:* Am Chem Soc; Soc Plastics Indust; Am Inst Chem Engr; Am Ceramic Soc; Soc Advan Mat & Process Eng; Am Inst Aeronaut & Astronaut; Soc Plastic Engrs; AAAS. *Res:* Catalysis, inorganic and organic lithium chemistry; organometallic chemistry; extractive metallurgy, catalysts, polymers, anionic polymerization; polyolefin catalysts; composites; armor; textiles; coatings; 61 US patents, 4 books, and 12 technical publications; carbon fibers. *Mailing Add:* 412 S Perth Philadelphia PA 19147-1322. *Fax:* 215-922-1211

SMITH, W(ILLIAM) P(AYNE), ELECTRICAL ENGINEERING. *Current Pos:* prof elec eng, 50-80, chmn, dept elec eng, Sch Eng & Archit, 55-56, dean, 65-80, EMER DEAN, UNIV KANS, 80- *Personal Data:* b Superior, Wis, Jan 5, 15; m 42; c 3. *Educ:* Univ Minn, BEE, 36, MS, 37; Univ Tex, PhD, 50. *Prof Exp:* Engr, Commonwealth Edison Co, Ill, 37-39; asst prof, Chicago Tech Col, 39-41; dean, Sampson Col, 46-50. *Concurrent Pos:* Lectr, Univ Tex, 48-50. *Mem:* Am Soc Eng Educ; Inst Elec & Electronics Engrs. *Mailing Add:* Univ Kans Lawrence KS 66045

SMITH, WADE KILGORE, HEMATOLOGY, IMMUNOLOGY. *Current Pos:* asst prof, 75-80, ASSOC PROF MED, MED COL VA, 75- *Personal Data:* b Paterson, NJ, Sept 7, 37; m 63; c 2. *Educ:* Oberlin Col, AB, 59; Sch Med, Johns Hopkins Univ, MD, 63. *Prof Exp:* Intern, Mt Sinai Hosp, New York, 63-64; resident, 64-68, chief res, 68-69, fel hematol, 69; res asst immunol, Med Ctr, Duke Univ, 70-71, instr, 71-72, assoc med & immunol, 72-74; chief, hemat-oncol sect, Vet Admin Med Ctr, Richmond, 81-89. *Concurrent Pos:* Instr med, Mt Sinai Sch Med, 68-69; Nat Cancer Inst Spec fel, Med Ctr, Duke Univ, 70-72; mem, Med Col Va/Va Commonwealth Univ Cancer Ctr, 76-; curric coord, Sch Med, Med Col Va, 82-87, chmn, Inst Animal Care & Use Comt, 86-89; dir, Hunter Holmes McGuire Vet Admin Med Ctr Comprehensive Cancer Ctr. *Mem:* Am Soc Histocompatibility & Immunogenetics; Am Soc Hematol; Am Soc Microbiol; Int Soc Hematol; NY Acad Sci. *Res:* Leukocyte antigens and immune destruction of leukocytes; humoral factors suppressing immune responses in tumor bearing or normal graft bearing hosts; clinical cancer chemotherapy trials. *Mailing Add:* 1403 Wilmington Ave Richmond VA 23227. *Fax:* 804-675-5447; *E-Mail:* wksmith@gems.vcu.edu

SMITH, WALDO E(DWARD), hydraulic engineering, geophysics; deceased, see previous edition for last biography

SMITH, WALKER O, JR, BIOLOGICAL OCEANOGRAPHY, PHYCOLOGY. *Current Pos:* from asst prof to assoc prof, 76-86, PROF BOT, UNIV TENN, 86- *Personal Data:* b Buffalo, NY, Nov 21, 50; c 1. *Educ:* Univ Rochester, BS, 72; Duke Univ, PhD(bot), 76. *Prof Exp:* Res asst oceanog, Duke Univ, 72-76. *Mem:* AAAS; Phycol Soc Am; Am Soc Limnol & Oceanog; Am Geophys Union. *Res:* Flux of carbon and nitrogen in polar systems. *Mailing Add:* Bot Univ Tenn 1345 Circle Park Knoxville TN 37996-0001

SMITH, WALLACE BRITTON, APPLIED PHYSICS. *Current Pos:* PRES, SOUTHERN RES TECHNOL, INC, 88- *Personal Data:* b Parrish, Ala, Jan 21, 41; m 60; c 2. *Educ:* Jacksonville State Univ, BS, 67; Auburn Univ, MS, 69, PhD(physics), 72. *Prof Exp:* Asst prof physics, Appalachian State Univ, 72-73, res physicist, 73-74; head physics sect, Southern Res Inst, 74-77, head physics div, 77-84, assoc dir, 84-88. *Mem:* Inst Elec & Electronics Engrs; Sigma Xi; Am Asn Aerosol Res; Adv Pollution Control Asn; Ges Aerosolforschung. *Res:* Electrical breakdown in insulators and semiconductors; particle sizing techniques and instruments; physics of the electrostatic precipitation; fabric filtration processes. *Mailing Add:* 100 Cherokee Trussville AL 35173-0114

SMITH, WALTER LAWS, MATHEMATICAL STATISTICS. *Current Pos:* from asst prof to assoc prof, 53-62, PROF STATIST, UNIV NC, CHAPEL HILL, 62- *Personal Data:* b London, Eng, Nov 12, 26; m 50; c 2. *Educ:* Cambridge Univ, BA, 47, MA, 50, PhD(math statist), 53. *Prof Exp:* Statistician, Med Sch, Cambridge Univ, 53-54, lectr math, 56-58. *Mem:* Am Math Soc; fel Am Statist Asn; fel Inst Math Statist; fel Royal Statist Soc; Int Statist Inst. *Res:* Probability theory; operations research. *Mailing Add:* Dept Statist 322 Phillips Hall Campus Box 3260 Univ NC Chapel Hill NC 27599-3260

SMITH, WALTER LEE, PHYSICS. *Current Pos:* dir, 83-92, VPRES MKT, THERMA-WAVE INC, FREMONT, CALIF, 92- *Personal Data:* b Siler City, NC, Nov 12, 48; m 72. *Educ:* NC State Univ, BS, 71; Harvard Univ, PhD(appl physics), 76. *Prof Exp:* physicist optical & mat physics, Lawrence Livermore Lab, 76-83. *Mem:* Am Inst Physics; Am Phys Soc; Mat Res Soc; Electrochem Soc. *Res:* Nonlinear optics; laser physics; ultraviolet materials properties; absolute measurement techniques; laser-induced breakdown physics; semiconductor fabrication, thermal wave physics. *Mailing Add:* ThermaWave 1250 Reliance Way Fremont CA 94539

SMITH, WALTER THOMAS, JR, ORGANIC CHEMISTRY. *Current Pos:* assoc prof, 53-56, prof, 56-92, EMER PROF ORG CHEM, UNIV KY, 92- *Personal Data:* b Havana, Ill, Feb 28, 22; m 45; c 2. *Educ:* Univ Ill, BS, 43; Ind Univ, PhD(org chem), 46. *Prof Exp:* Fels fund fel, Univ Chicago, 46-47; from instr to asst prof org chem, Univ Iowa, 47-53. *Concurrent Pos:* Chemist, Mallinckrodt Chem Works, St Louis, 43 & 44; Fulbright lectr & dept head, Univ Libya, Tripoli, 62-63; Fulbright lectr, Am Univ Beirut, 64-65; vis prof, Univ Maine, 80-86; consult-legal expert, var orgn. *Mem:* Fel AAAS; fel Am Inst Chemists; Am Chem Soc. *Res:* Organic analysis; medicinal chemistry of anticancer compounds and interferon inducers; graft polymers as synthetic nucleotides; detoxification of chemical weapons; enzyme activity in mixed solvents. *Mailing Add:* Dept Chem Univ Ky Lexington KY 40506. *E-Mail:* wtsmith@ukcc.uky.edu

SMITH, WALTON RAMSAY, wood science & technology, wood physics, for more information see previous edition

SMITH, WARREN DREW, BIOMEDICAL SIGNAL PROCESSING, BIOMEDICAL MODELING & SIMULATION. *Current Pos:* From asst prof to assoc prof, 73-82, PROF BIOMED ENG, ELEC & ELECTRONIC ENG, CALIF STATE UNIV, SACRAMENTO, 82- *Personal Data:* b Tampa, Fla, Dec 22, 42; m 71, Judy Cummings. *Educ:* Princeton Univ, BS, 64; Univ NMex, MS, 68; Univ Okla, PhD(elec eng), 71. *Concurrent Pos:* Consult, Food & Drug Sect, Calif Health Dept, 75-76, Sutter Community Hosps, 76-77 & Lawrence Livermore Lab, 78-79; proj dir, Found Calif State Univ, 75-77, Sutter Hosps Med Res Found, 76-78 & Nat Inst Gen Med Sci, 86-88. *Mem:* Inst Elec & Electronics Engrs; Inst Elec & Electronics Engrs Eng Med & Biol Soc; Am Soc Eng Educ; Biomed Eng Soc; Asn Advan Med Instrumentation. *Res:* Developing anesthesia monitor that processes human brain waves to display the level of anesthesia of a patient during surgery; author of numerous technical publications. *Mailing Add:* Sch Eng & Comput Sci Calif State Univ 6000 J St Sacramento CA 95819. *Fax:* 916-278-5949; *E-Mail:* smithwd@ecs.csus.edu

SMITH, WARREN HARVEY, PHYSICAL CHEMISTRY. *Current Pos:* MGR, NUCLEAR TECHNOL, MOUND LAB, EG&G INC, 85- *Personal Data:* b Brooklyn, NY, Oct 6, 35; m 60; c 3. *Educ:* City Col NY, BS, 58; Syracuse Univ, PhD(phys chem, kinetics), 64. *Prof Exp:* Sr res chemist, Monsanto Res Corp, Miamisburg, 64-67; group leader plutonium chem, 67-69, plutonium fuels develop mgr, 69-71, isotope separation mgr, 71-73, applied physics mgr, Mound Lab, 73-85. *Mem:* AAAS; Am Chem Soc; Am Inst Chemists; Sigma Xi. *Res:* Gas phase kinetics; physical-inorganic chemistry of the actinide elements; use of plutonium-238 as a fuel for heat sources. *Mailing Add:* 5413 Coppermill Pl Dayton OH 45429-2016

SMITH, WARREN LAVERNE, PHYSICS, ELECTRICAL ENGINEERING. *Current Pos:* RETIRED. *Personal Data:* b Wayne, Nebr, July 6, 24; m 48; c 5. *Educ:* Univ Wis, BSEE, 45. *Honors & Awards:* CB Sawyer Mem Award. *Prof Exp:* Staff mem, 54-62, supvr eng, Bell Tel Labs, Ins, 62-87. *Concurrent Pos:* Tech adv to TC-49, IEC, 73- *Mem:* Fel Inst Elec & Electronics Engrs; AAAS. *Res:* Development and design of precision frequency standards, quartz crystal units and monolithic crystal filters. *Mailing Add:* 3046 Meadowbrook Circle N Allentown PA 18103

SMITH, WAYNE EARL, mathematics; deceased, see previous edition for last biography

SMITH, WAYNE H, FORESTRY. *Current Pos:* from asst prof to assoc prof forestry, Univ Fla, 64-78, asst dir res, 70-78, prof forest resources & conserv & dir, Environ & Natural Sci Progs, 78-84, PROF FORESTRY & DIR, BIOMASS ENERGY SYSTS, UNIV FLA, 80-, DIR, ENERGY EXTEN SERV, 90- *Personal Data:* b Marianna, Fla, Aug 10, 38; m 62. *Educ:* Univ Fla, BSA, 60; Miss State Univ, MS, 62, PhD(soils), 65. *Prof Exp:* Asst soils, Miss State Univ, 63-64. *Concurrent Pos:* Fac develop leave, Coop State Res Serv, USDA, Washington, DC, 73-74; dir, Fed Agency Liaison, Washington, DC, 85. *Mem:* Soc Am Foresters; Am Soc Agron; AAAS; Sigma Xi; Soil Sci Soc Am. *Res:* Nutritional problems of forest trees, particularly nitrogen metabolism and forest soil-plant relationships; environmental effects of forest practices, biomass energy production; bioenergy conversions; energy conservation. *Mailing Add:* 710 NE First St Gainesville FL 32601

SMITH, WAYNE HOWARD, ELECTROCHEMISTRY. *Current Pos:* STAFF MEM, LOS ALAMOS NAT LAB, 83- *Personal Data:* b Pittsburgh, Pa, July 18, 46; m 65; c 3. *Educ:* Univ Pittsburgh, BS, 71; Univ Tex, Austin, PhD(chem), 74. *Prof Exp:* Fel, Calif Inst Technol, 74-76; asst prof chem, Tex Tech Univ, 76-83. *Concurrent Pos:* Consult, Monogram Indust, 75-76, Westvaco, 79- & Mikro Environ Lab, 80- *Mem:* Am Chem Soc; Electrochem Soc. *Res:* Electroorganic synthesis; homogeneous transition metal catalysis via electrochemically generated organometallic; kinetics and mechanisms of reactions initiated electrochemically. *Mailing Add:* 28 Timber Ridge Los Alamos NM 87544

SMITH, WAYNE LEE, INORGANIC CHEMISTRY, PHYSICAL CHEMISTRY. *Current Pos:* from asst prof to assoc prof, 67-83, chmn dept, 82-89, PROF CHEM, COLBY COL, 83- *Personal Data:* b Oneonta, NY, Jan 29, 36; m 59; c 3. *Educ:* Hartwick Col, BA, 57; Pa State Univ, PhD(chem), 63. *Hon Degrees:* MA, Colby Col, 83. *Prof Exp:* Res assoc chem, Univ Mich, 63-64; res chemist, Allied Chem Corp, 64-66; asst prof chem, Carnegie-Mellon Univ, 66-67. *Concurrent Pos:* Vis prof, Univ Mich, Ann Arbor, 74-75, Dartmouth Col, 81-82 & Univ NC, Chapel Hill, 89-90. *Mem:* Am Chem Soc; Royal Soc Chem. *Res:* Coordination compounds of the nontransition metal elements; organometallics; heteroborane chemistry; chemical education. *Mailing Add:* Dept Chem Colby Col Waterville ME 04901. *Fax:* 207-872-3555; *E-Mail:* wlsmith@colby.edu

SMITH, WENDELL VANDERVORT, PHYSICAL CHEMISTRY. *Current Pos:* RETIRED. *Personal Data:* b Caldwell, Idaho, Apr 16, 12; m 38; c 3. *Educ:* Col Idaho, BS, 33; Univ Calif, PhD(phys chem), 37. *Prof Exp:* Res chemist, Gen Labs, US Rubber Co, 37-59 & Res Ctr, 59-72; res chemist corp res & develop, Oxford Mgt & Res Ctr, Uniroyal Inc, 72-77. *Mem:* Am Chem Soc. *Res:* Ionic entropies; new rubber products; theory of emulsion polymerization; physical properties of rubbers; radiation chemistry of polymers. *Mailing Add:* 3 Nettleton Ave Newton CT 06470-2016

SMITH, WENDY ANNE, CELLULAR ENDOCRINOLOGY, DEVELOPMENTAL BIOLOGY. *Current Pos:* asst prof, 85-91, ASSOC PROF, DEPT BIOL, NORTHEASTERN UNIV, BOSTON, 91- *Personal Data:* b Pittsburgh, Pa, July 12, 54; m 87, Stephen Soltoff; c Benjamin & Alexander. *Educ:* New Col, Sarasota, Fla, BA, 75; Duke Univ, PhD(zool), 81. *Prof Exp:* Teaching fel, Dept Zool, Duke Univ, 77-81; NRSA res fel, Dept Pharmacol, Duke Univ, 81-83 & Dept Biol, Univ NC, Chapel Hill, 83-85. *Concurrent Pos:* Prin investr, NIH, Dept Biol, Northeastern Univ, Boston, 86-94, USDA, Dept Biol, Northeastern Univ, Boston, 94- *Mem:* Am Soc Zoologists; Sigma Xi; Soc Neurosci. *Res:* Regulation of endocrine cell function in insects and of insect molting and metamorphosis; cellular mechanisms of action of the cerebral molt-stimulating peptide; prothoracicotropic hormone. *Mailing Add:* Dept Biol Northeastern Univ 414 Mugar Hall Boston MA 02115. *Fax:* 617-373-3724; *E-Mail:* w.smith@nunet.neu.edu

SMITH, WESLEY R, FLUID ACOUSTICS, GENERAL PHYSICS. *Current Pos:* from asst prof to prof, 58-95, EMER PRQF PHYSICS, LEHIGH UNIV, 95- *Personal Data:* b Allentown, Pa, Nov 5, 28; m 55; c 6. *Educ:* Lehigh Univ, BS, 50, MS, 51; Princeton Univ, PhD(physics), 57. *Prof Exp:* Instr, Princeton Univ, 56-58. *Mem:* AAAS; Am Phys Soc; Sigma Xi. *Res:* Application of shock tubes to measurements of chemical and physical properties of gases, liquids and solids; studies of acoustic waves in solids. *Mailing Add:* Dept Physics Bldg 16 Lehigh Univ 16 Memorial Dr E Bethlehem PA 18015. *E-Mail:* wrsi@lehigh.edu

SMITH, WILLARD NEWELL, cell physiology, for more information see previous edition

SMITH, WILLIAM ADAMS, JR, QUALITY ENGINEERING & ASSURANCE, INTEGRATED INFORMATION SYSTEM DEVELOPMENT. *Current Pos:* prof & head, Dept Indust Eng, 73-82, dir, productivity res & extension prog, 75-84, PROF INDUST ENG & COORDR, ADVAN PROG DEVELOP INDUST EXTEN, NC STATE UNIV, 84- *Personal Data:* b Parkersburg, WVa, July 13, 29; m 87, Yvonne Anderson; c Julia C, Sara L, C Jane, WA III & Patricia A. *Educ:* Naval Acad, BS, 51; Lehigh Univ, MS, 57; NY Univ, DEngSc, 66. *Honors & Awards:* Excellence Award, Comput & Info Systs Div, Inst Indust Engrs. *Prof Exp:* Instr indust eng, Lehigh Univ, 55-57, dir, Comput Lab, 57-67, prof indust eng, 67-73. *Concurrent Pos:* Alcoa Prof, Lehigh Univ, 68-69; Ford Found residency eng, Am Soc Eng Educ, Smith Kline Corp, 69-70; consult, IBM, Air Prod, du Pont, Western Elec Co, Corning, Gen Elec & Northern Telecom; dir, Productivity Res & Exten Prog, 78-82; chmn, Asn Coop Eng, 79-80, Pub Affairs Coun, Am Asn Eng Socs, 83-85 & Nat Productivity Network, 84-85; advan automation engr, Northern Telecom Integrated Network Systs, 84-86; pres, NC Qual Leadership Found, 89-92, chmn, 92-95, pres, 95- *Mem:* Fel Am Inst Indust Engrs (pres, 75-76); Sigma Xi; Inst Opers Res & Mat Sci; Am Soc Qual Control; fel World Acad Productivity Sci. *Res:* Management systems engineering; source data automation; productivity and quality measurement; process improvement; technology management; organizational transformation. *Mailing Add:* NC State Univ PO Box 7906 Raleigh NC 27695-7906. *Fax:* 919-515-5281

SMITH, WILLIAM ALLEN, MATHEMATICS, NUMERICAL ANALYSIS. *Current Pos:* ASSOC PROF MATH, GA STATE UNIV, 70- *Personal Data:* b Ashland, Ky, June 26, 40; m 66, Klara Moser; c Vicky S & Wendy D. *Educ:* Mass Inst Technol, BS, 62, PhD(math), 66. *Prof Exp:* Asst prof math, Univ SC, 66-70. *Mem:* Math Asn Am. *Res:* difference equations; numerical analysis. *Mailing Add:* Dept Math & Comp Sci Ga State Univ Atlanta GA 30303-3083. *Fax:* 404-651-2246; *E-Mail:* wsmith@cs.gsu.edu

SMITH, WILLIAM BOYCE, MATHEMATICAL STATISTICS. *Current Pos:* from asst prof to assoc prof, Tex A&M Univ, 66-73, asst dean col sci, 72-77, head dept, 77-86, assoc dean col sci, 84-85, PROF STATIST, TEX A&M UNIV, 73-, EXEC ASSOC DEAN SCI, 94- *Personal Data:* b Port Arthur, Tex, Sept 7, 38; m 63, Patricia Rutherford; c Leah (Tiner), Scott A & Angela R. *Educ:* Lamar Univ, BS, 59; Tex A&M Univ, MS, 60, PhD(statist), 67. *Honors & Awards:* Hartley Award, 82; Owen Award, 92. *Prof Exp:* Asst prof math, Lamar State Col, 62-64. *Concurrent Pos:* Vis prof, Southern Methodist Univ, 70, Nat Agr Exp Sta, Argentina, 77 & 87; vis scholar, Japanese Soc for Prom Sci, 80 & 86; invited prof, Ecole Nat Telecommun, Paris France, 87; ed-in-chief, Communs Statist, 91- *Mem:* Biomet Soc; fel Am Statist Asn; Math Asn Am; Int Statist Inst. *Res:* Statistical estimation theory with incomplete observation vectors; legal statistics methods; multivariate analysis. *Mailing Add:* 1040 Rose Circle College Station TX 77840

SMITH, WILLIAM BRIDGES, COMPUTER SCIENCE, ELECTRICAL ENGINEERING. *Current Pos:* PRES & CHIEF EXEC OFFICER, TELCO SYSTS, 94- *Personal Data:* b Washington, DC, Feb 13, 44; m 65; c 2. *Educ:* Univ Md, BS, 62; Princeton Univ, MS, 63; Univ Pa, PhD(elec eng), 67. *Prof Exp:* Mem tech staff prog design, AT&T Bell Labs, 62-67 supvr No 4 electronic switching syst design, 67-70, dept head toll network studies, 70-74, dir opers systs dev, 74-78, exec dir, No 5 Electronic Switching Syst Div, 79-82, exec dir opers Technol Div, 86-90, exec dir, Commun Serv Network Div, 91; chief info & technol officer, US W Technol, 91-94. *Concurrent Pos:* Instr, Ill Inst Technol Grad Sch, 68-70; bd of overseers, Armor Col Eng, Ill Inst Technol, 80-82; Gov Thompson's Technol Task Force, 81; vpres & gen tech dir, ITT, Europe, 82-86. *Mem:* Sr mem Inst Elec & Electronics Engrs. *Res:* Management of large software and hardware systems development; telecommunications networks. *Mailing Add:* Telco Syst 63 Nahatan St Norwood MA 02062

SMITH, WILLIAM BURTON, SYNTHETIC ORGANIC & NATURAL PRODUCT CHEMISTRY. *Current Pos:* chmn dept, 61-81, PROF CHEM, TEX CHRISTIAN UNIV, 61- *Personal Data:* b Muncie, Ind, Dec 13, 27; m 53; c Mark W, Frederick D & Mary F. *Educ:* Kalamazoo Col, BA, 49; Brown Univ, PhD(chem), 54. *Honors & Awards:* W T Doherty Award, Am Chem Soc, 90. *Prof Exp:* Res assoc chem, Fla State Univ, 53-54 & Univ Chicago, 54-55; from asst prof to assoc prof, Ohio Univ, 55-61. *Concurrent Pos:* Partic fel, Oak Ridge Assoc Univs, 55-; Welch vis scientist, Tex Christian Univ, 60-61; vis prof, Univ Sussex, UK, 81. *Mem:* Am Chem Soc; Sigma Xi; fel Royal Soc Chem. *Res:* Physical organic chemistry of carbonium ions and free radicals; nuclear magnetic resonance; synthesis of biomimetic molecules; theoretical organic chemistry. *Mailing Add:* Dept Chem Tex Christian Univ Ft Worth TX 76129. *Fax:* 817-921-7110; *E-Mail:* wbsmith@gamma.is.tcu.edu

SMITH, WILLIAM CONRAD, PHYSICS, INSTRUMENTATION. *Current Pos:* supvr, Electronic Design & Support Sect, Lockheed Eng & Sci Co, 83-85, staff engr, 85-86, staff meteorologist, 86-90, GROUP LEADER, ADVAN TECHNOL, LOCKHEED ENG & SCI CO, 90- *Personal Data:* b Cisco, Tex, May 20, 37; m 59, Mila Wilson; c Bret W & Tanya K. *Educ:* NTex State Univ, BS, 60, MS, 62; Iowa State Univ, PhD(physics), 71. *Prof Exp:* Instr physics & math, Decatur Baptist Col, 61-62; asst prof physics, Howard Payne Univ, 62-64 & Mankato State Col, 70-73; from asst prof to assoc prof physics, Tex Womans Univ, 73-83. *Concurrent Pos:* Sci adv, locl pub schs, 91-93. *Mem:* Am Asn Physicists in Med; Am Phys Soc; Am Asn Physics Teachers; Instrument Soc Am; Sigma Xi. *Res:* Hyperfine fields in magnetic metallic compounds; nuclear magnetic resonance; effect of magnetic fields on axon signals; design of microprocessor-based instruments; electrostatic discharge measurement; non-destructive evaluation; sensor development; granted US patent. *Mailing Add:* 705 Sundown Ct Las Cruces NM 88011-4677

SMITH, WILLIAM EDMOND, PULP CHEMISTRY, PAPER CHEMISTRY. *Current Pos:* VPRES & TECH DIR, EZE PROD INC, 85- *Personal Data:* b Wilmington, NC, Nov 16, 39; m 67; c 4. *Educ:* NC State Univ, MS, 65, PhD(wood & paper sci), 69; Univ SC, MBA, 73. *Prof Exp:* Res forest prod technologist, US Forest Prod Lab, 64-69; sr res chemist, Res Lab, 69-72, dir tech serv, Paper Div, Sonoco Prod Co, 72-85. *Mem:* Tech Asn Pulp & Paper Indust; Soc Wood Sci & Technol. *Res:* Product development; stress analysis of structures produced from paper and plastics; basic failure criteria of materials; process control; secondary fiber containment dispersion, paper machine press section optimization. *Mailing Add:* ECC Int 603 Hightech Ct Greer SC 99650

SMITH, WILLIAM EDWARD, INDUSTRIAL CHEMICAL ENGINEERING. *Current Pos:* assoc prof, DIR CHEM RES, POLAROID CORP, 88- *Personal Data:* b Philadelphia, Pa, May 30, 38; m 63; c 2. *Educ:* La Salle Col, BS, 65; Purdue Univ, Lafayette, PhD(chem), 69. *Prof Exp:* NIH fel, Mass Inst Technol, 69-70; res chemist, Gen Elec Res & Develop Corp, 70-74, mgr, Catalytic Processes Unit, 74-79, mgr, Chem Eng Br, 79-83, mgr, Inorg Mat Lab, 83-85, mgr, Phys Chem Lab, 86-88. *Mem:* Am Chem Soc; Catalysis Soc. *Res:* Materials and process research and development; homogeneous and heterogeneous catalysis; monomer synthesis. *Mailing Add:* 4 Canal Park Apt 212 Cambridge MA 02141

SMITH, WILLIAM FORTUNE, MATERIALS SCIENCE, PHYSICAL METALLURGY. *Current Pos:* assoc prof, 68-71, PROF ENG, FLA TECHNOL UNIV, 71- *Personal Data:* b Vancouver, BC, Oct 11, 31; US citizen; m 58; c 3. *Educ:* Univ BC, BA, 52; Purdue Univ, MS, 55; Mass Inst Technol, ScD(phys metall), 68. *Prof Exp:* Res engr, Metall Res Labs, Reynolds Metals Co, Va, 57-62; res engr, Metall Res Labs, Kaiser Aluminum Co, Washington, 65-67. *Mem:* Am Soc Metals; Am Inst Mining, Metall & Petrol Engrs. *Res:* Precipitation reactions in the solid state; physical metallurgy of aluminum alloys; stress corrosion cracking. *Mailing Add:* Dept Metall Univ Cent Fla PO Box 25000 Orlando FL 32816

SMITH, WILLIAM GRADY, BIOCHEMISTRY. *Current Pos:* Asst prof biochem & path, 64-66, from asst prof to assoc prof biochem, 66-77, PROF BIOCHEM, SCH MED, UNIV ARK, LITTLE ROCK, 77- *Personal Data:* b Dover, Ark, Mar 29, 37; m 59; c 3. *Educ:* Univ Ark, BS, 59, MS, 60; Okla State Univ, PhD(biochem), 64. *Concurrent Pos:* Fel biochem, Univ Minn, 63-64; res grants, NSF, 65-75 & NIH, 67-70; Lederle med fac award, 68-71. *Mem:* Am Soc Biol Chem. *Res:* Amino acid metabolism; metabolic control. *Mailing Add:* 2607 Quebec Dr Little Rock AR 72204

SMITH, WILLIAM H, ANIMAL SCIENCE. *Current Pos:* RESIDENT DIR RES, TEX A&M UNIV, 76- *Personal Data:* b Kingston, Okla, Jan 25, 29; m 54; c 2. *Educ:* Okla State Univ, BS, 56; Purdue Univ, MS, 57, PhD(animal nutrit), 59. *Prof Exp:* Prof animal nutrit & mgt, Purdue Univ, West Lafayette, 59-76. *Concurrent Pos:* Sabbatical, Univ Calif, Davis, 66. *Mem:* Am Soc Animal Sci; Sigma Xi; Am Soc Agron. *Res:* Nutrient requirements of beef cows; value of cornstalks; methods of preventing grass tetany; value of liquid supplements; total digestible nutrients for heifers; value of forage quality. *Mailing Add:* 3305 Ridgemont St Irving TX 75062

SMITH, WILLIAM HULSE, PLANT PATHOLOGY. *Current Pos:* from asst prof to assoc prof, 66-78, from asst dean to actg dean, Sch Forestry & Environ Studies, 71-83, PROF FOREST BIOL, YALE UNIV, 79- *Personal Data:* b Trenton, NJ, May 9, 39; m 63, 83, Deborah; c Scott, Philip & Tyler. *Educ:* Rutgers Univ, BS, 61, PhD(plant path), 65; Yale Univ, MF, 63. *Prof Exp:* Asst prof forestry, Rutgers Univ, 64-66. *Mem:* AAAS; Am Phytopath Soc; Ecol Soc Am; Soc Am Foresters; Sigma Xi. *Res:* Chemistry and biology of the rhizosphere; influence of gaseous and particulate air contaminants on woody plant health. *Mailing Add:* Sch Forestry & Environ Studies Yale Univ PO Box 208240 New Haven CT 06520. *Fax:* 203-432-3929

SMITH, WILLIAM KIRBY, BIOPHYSICAL ECOLOGY, ENVIRONMENTAL PHYSIOLOGY. *Current Pos:* From asst prof to assoc prof, 77-86, PROF, DEPT BOT, UNIV WYO, 87- *Personal Data:* b Greensboro, NC, Mar 6, 49; m 80, Ann Marie; c 2. *Educ:* San Diego State Col, BS, 67, MS, 71; Univ Calif, Los Angeles, PhD, 77. *Honors & Awards:* Burlington Northern Fac Award, 90. *Mem:* Am Soc Plant Physiologists; Ecol Soc Am; AAAS; Am Inst Biol Sci; Bot Soc Am. *Res:* Biophysical and physiological ecology; plant and animal adaptations in harsh or unusual environments; photosynthesis, water relations and growth physiology. *Mailing Add:* Dept Bot Univ Wyo PO Box 3165 Laramie WY 82071-3165. *Fax:* 307-766-2851; *E-Mail:* uksmith@uwyo.edu

SMITH, WILLIAM LEE, exploration geology, remote sensing, for more information see previous edition

SMITH, WILLIAM LEE, BIOCHEMISTRY. *Current Pos:* asst prof, 75-79, PROF BIOCHEM, MICH STATE UNIV, 79- *Personal Data:* b Tulsa, Okla, Oct 28, 45; m 68; c 3. *Educ:* Univ Colo, Boulder, BA, 67; Univ Mich, Ann Arbor, PhD(biol chem), 71. *Prof Exp:* NIH fel biochem, Univ Calif, Berkeley, 71-74; sr scientist biochem, Mead Johnson & Co, Bristol-Myers Co, 74-75. *Concurrent Pos:* Estab investr, Am Heart Asn; adj prof physiol, Mich State Univ, 84- *Mem:* AAAS; Am Soc Biol Chemists. *Res:* Regulation of prostaglandin metabolism; mechanism of prostaglandin action; prostaglandins; kidney. *Mailing Add:* Dept Biochem Mich State Univ Rm 510 East Lansing MI 48824-1020. *Fax:* 517-353-9334; *E-Mail:* smith@clvaxi.msu.edu

SMITH, WILLIAM LEO, METEOROLOGY. *Current Pos:* DIR, CIMSS, UNIV WIS-MADISON, 84- *Personal Data:* b Detroit, Mich, May 13, 42; m 62, Marcia J Simmerer; c William Jr, Jeanne, Steven, Julie, Joanna, Jonathon, Sarah & Kiara. *Educ:* St Louis Univ, BS, 63; Univ Wis, MS, 64, PhD, 66. *Prof Exp:* Chief br radiation, Nat Oceanic & Atmospheric Admin/Nat Environ Satellite, Data & Info Serv, US Dept Com, 66-73, dir develop lab, 73-84. *Concurrent Pos:* Secy, Int Radiation Comn, 89- *Mem:* Fel Am Meteorol Soc. *Res:* Applied meteorology; development of first algorithms for operational processing of satellite sounding data, high special resolution inferometer sounder, infrared temperature profile radiometer, earth radiation budget radiometer and high infrared radiation sounder. *Mailing Add:* Dept Atmosphere & Oceanic Scis Univ Wis 1225 W Dayton St Madison WI 53706-1695

SMITH, WILLIAM MAYO, ENVIRONMENTAL SCIENCES. *Current Pos:* RETIRED. *Personal Data:* b Fredericksburg, Va, Nov 30, 17; m 40, Patricia Johnstone; c Patricia, Carol, Lynn & Susan. *Educ:* Va Mil Inst, BS, 38; Univ Ala, MS, 41; Univ Md, PhD(org chem & biochem), 46. *Prof Exp:* Cellulose chemist, Sylvania Indust Corp, Va, 38-43; sr res chemist, Firestone Tire & Rubber Co, 47-54, group leader, Defense Res Div, 54-56; asst dir res & develop, Escambia Chem Corp, Conn, 56-58, vpres & dir res, 58-67; vpres, Air Reduction Co, Inc, NY, 67-69; tech dir polymers & plastics, Air Prod & Chem, Inc, 69-71, group res & develop coordr, Chem Group, 71-79, dir sci affairs, 79-81. *Concurrent Pos:* Consult, Chem, Plastics, Polymers, Environ Health & Safety, Cancer & Environ, 81- *Mem:* Am Chem Soc; Chem Soc London; NY Acad Sci; Chem Indust Inst Toxicol; Indust Res Inst. *Res:* Plastics; polymerizations; petrochemicals; organic reactions; chemical carcinogens and toxic substances; industrial research management; health and safety. *Mailing Add:* 19 Painted Bunting Amelia Island FL 32034

SMITH, WILLIAM OGG, MEDICINE. *Current Pos:* chief resident & clin asst med, Univ Okla, 55-56, from instr to assoc prof, 56-66, vchmn dept med, 67-75, PROF MED, MED SCH, UNIV OKLA, 66- *Personal Data:* b Shawnee, Okla, July 17, 25; m 48; c 3. *Educ:* Harvard Med Sch, MD, 49. *Prof Exp:* Intern, Univ Chicago, 49-50; resident med, Vet Admin Hosps, Boston, 52-54 & Oklahoma City, 54-55. *Concurrent Pos:* Asst dir radioisotope serv, Vet Admin Hosp, Oklahoma City, 56-60, from assoc chief to chief med serv, 60-71. *Mem:* Fel Am Col Physicians; Soc Exp Biol & Med; Am Soc Nephrol. *Res:* Renal and electrolyte physiology; magnesium metabolism. *Mailing Add:* 921 NE 13th St Oklahoma City OK 73104-5028

SMITH, WILLIAM OWEN, PHOTOBIOLOGY. *Current Pos:* PLANT PHYSIOLOGIST, RADIATION BIOL LAB, SMITHSONIAN INST, 75- *Personal Data:* b Louisville, Ky, Sept 2, 41; m 64; c 2. *Educ:* Univ Ky, BS, 67, PhD(plant physiol), 75. *Mem:* Am Soc Plant Physiologists; Am Soc Photobiol. *Res:* Molecular aspects of plant photomorphogenesis; biochemistry of phytochrome. *Mailing Add:* 2817 Rhoderick Rd Frederick MD 21701

SMITH, WILLIAM R, STRUCTURAL DYNAMICS, MATHEMATICS. *Current Pos:* SR ENGR SCIENTIST, MCDONNELL DOUGLAS AIRCRAFT CORP, 88- *Personal Data:* b Lyman, Okla, June 26, 25. *Educ:* Bethany Nazarene Col, BA, 48; Wichita State Univ, MA, 50; Univ Calif, Los Angeles, PhD(biophys), 67. *Honors & Awards:* Cert Recognition Award, NASA, 82. *Prof Exp:* Engr, Beech Aircraft Corp, 51-53; sr group engr, McDonnell Aircraft Corp, 53-60; asst prof math & physics, Pasadena Col, 60-62; sr engr, Lockheed Aircraft Corp, 62-63; sr engr-scientist, McDonnell Douglas Aircraft Corp, 66-71; teacher math, Glendale Col, Calif, 72; asst prof math & physics, Mount St Mary's Col, 72-73; tech staff, Rockwell Int Corp, 73-86; CDI Corp, 86-88. *Mem:* AAAS; Sigma Xi; NY Acad Sci; Am Inst Aeronaut & Astronaut. *Res:* Mathematical analysis of the electrical activity of the brain; mathematical modeling; time series analysis; engineering dynamics; digital signal processing; image processing. *Mailing Add:* McDonnell Douglas Aircraft Corp PO Box 516 Mc 064 1461 St Louis MO 63166

SMITH, WILLIAM ROBERT, NUCLEAR PHYSICS. *Current Pos:* LAND DEVELOPER, 83- *Personal Data:* b San Antonio, Tex, Jan 11, 35; m 63. *Educ:* Univ Tex, BS, 57, BA, 58, PhD(physics), 63. *Prof Exp:* Res assoc nuclear physics, Nuclear Physics Lab, Univ Tex, 63 & Neutron Physics Div, Oak Ridge Nat Lab, 63-65; sr res officer, Nuclear Physics Lab, Oxford Univ, 65-66; res assoc nuclear physics, Nuclear Physics Lab, Univ Southern Calif, 66; assoc prof physics, Trinity Univ, Tex, 67-83. *Concurrent Pos:* Ed low energy nuclear physics, Comput Physics Commun, 68- *Mem:* Am Phys Soc. *Res:* Low energy nuclear reaction theory. *Mailing Add:* 563 E Craig St San Antonio TX 78212

SMITH, WILLIAM RUSSELL, MICROBIOLOGY. *Current Pos:* From asst prof to prof, 46-73, REGENTS PROF BIOL, LAMAR UNIV, 73- *Personal Data:* b Denton, Tex, Jan 13, 17; m 39; c 2. *Educ:* NTex State Univ, BS, 37, MS, 38; Univ Tex, PhD(bact), 55. *Concurrent Pos:* Res scientist, Univ Tex, 51-53. *Mem:* Am Soc Microbiol; Sigma Xi; NY Acad Sci. *Res:* Chemical and heat activation of bacterial spores; bacteriology of foods; medical bacteriology; general, food and medical microbiology. *Mailing Add:* 4785 Dellwood Lane Beaumont TX 77706-3517

SMITH, WILLIAM S, ORTHOPEDIC SURGERY. *Current Pos:* RETIRED. *Personal Data:* b Greenwich, Conn, July 29, 18; c 4. *Educ:* Univ Mich, AB, 40, MD, 43; Am Bd Orthop Surg, dipl, 53. *Prof Exp:* Instr orthop surg, Univ Mich, 50; from instr to prof, Ohio State Univ, 52-63; prof orthop surg, Univ Mich, Ann Arbor, 63- *Concurrent Pos:* Res grants, Easter Seal Found, 56-59, Orthop Res & Educ Found, 60 & NIH, 61-63. *Mem:* Fel Am Acad Orthop Surg; Orthop Res Soc; Clin Orthop Soc; Am Orthop Asn; Am Asn Surg Trauma. *Res:* Congenital dislocation of the hip. *Mailing Add:* Univ Hosp 1500 E Medical Ctr Dr Ann Arbor MI 48109-0328

SMITH, WILLIAM WALKER, MATHEMATICS. *Current Pos:* From asst prof to assoc prof, 65-79, chmn dept, 76-81, PROF MATH, UNIV NC, CHAPEL HILL, 79- *Personal Data:* b Duncan, Okla, Sept 26, 40; div; c 3. *Educ:* Southeastern State Col, BS, 61; La State Univ, MS, 63, PhD(math), 65. *Mem:* Math Asn Am; Am Math Soc; Nat Coun Teachers Math. *Res:* Algebra; commutative ring and ideal theory; mathematics education. *Mailing Add:* Dept Math Univ NC Chapel Hill NC 27599-3250. *Fax:* 919-962-2568; *E-Mail:* wwsmith@math.unc.edu

SMITH, WILLIS DEAN, SOLID STATE PHYSICS. *Current Pos:* mgr strategic planning, Boeing Aerospace Co, 84-88, dir planning, 88-94, VPRES STRATEGY DEVELOP & PLANNING, BOEING DEFENSE & SPACE GROUP, 94- *Personal Data:* b Ipava, Ill, Aug 5, 42; m 66. *Educ:* Bradley Univ, BS, 64; Washington Univ, MA, 66, PhD(physics), 70. *Prof Exp:* Tech staff mem physics, Sandia Labs, NMex, 70-75; sci staff mem, Comt Sci & Technol, US House Rep, 75-77; prof staff mem, Comt on Energy & Natural Resources, US Senate, 77-; dep staff dir, Comt Armed Servs, US Senate, 83-84. *Concurrent Pos:* Energy consult, Comt Interior & Insular Affairs, US Sen, 74-75; Inst Elec & Electronics Engrs cong sci fel, 74-75. *Mem:* AAAS; sr mem Inst Elec & Electronics Engrs. *Res:* Ultrasonics; electron-phonon interactions; surface waves; ferroelectric ceramics; information processing and display; photoconductors; electrooptics and photovoltaic materials and devices; solar energy. *Mailing Add:* VPres Strategy Develop & Planning Boeing Defense & Space Group MS 80-PC PO Box 3999 Seattle WA 98124-2499

SMITH, WINFIELD SCOTT, OPTICS. *Current Pos:* AT CONTRAVES-GOERZ CORP, PITTSBURGH, 79- *Personal Data:* b Detroit, Mich, Nov 1, 41; m 63. *Educ:* Oakland Univ, BA, 63; Univ Ariz, MS, 67, PhD(physics), 70. *Prof Exp:* Asst prof physics, Univ Nev, Reno, 70-71; res assoc, Univ Ariz, 70 & 71, prog mgr, Optical Sci Ctr, 72-79. *Mem:* Optical Soc Am; Sigma Xi. *Res:* Atmospheric optics; optical testing and fabrication. *Mailing Add:* Contraves Brashear Systs Bldg 3 615 Esplanade Dr Pittsburgh PA 15238-2883

SMITH, WINTHROP WARE, EXPERIMENTAL ATOMIC PHYSICS. *Current Pos:* assoc prof, 69-75, PROF PHYSICS, UNIV CONN, 75- *Personal Data:* b New York, NY, Aug 4, 36; m 65; c 1. *Educ:* Amherst Col, BA, 58; Mass Inst Technol, PhD(physics), 63. *Prof Exp:* Nat Acad Sci-Nat Res Coun res assoc physics, Nat Bur Standards, 63-65; instr, Columbia Univ, 65-66, asst prof, 66-69. *Concurrent Pos:* Mem, Joint Inst Lab Astrophys, Boulder, Colo, 63-65, vis fel, 75-76; lectr physics, Univ Colo, 64-65; res partic, Oak Ridge Nat Lab, 69- *Mem:* AAAS; fel Am Phys Soc. *Res:* Beam-foil spectroscopy; low energy nuclear physics; atomic physics and collisions; atomic hyperfine structure and lifetimes of excited states; laser spectroscopy. *Mailing Add:* Dept Physics U-46 2152 Hillsdale Rd Univ Conn Storrs CT 06269. *Fax:* 860-486-3346

SMITH, WIRT WILSEY, medicine; deceased, see previous edition for last biography

SMITHBERG, MORRIS, EMBRYOLOGY, NEUROANATOMY. *Current Pos:* from asst prof to assoc prof, 60-69, actg head dept, 77, PROF ANAT, UNIV MINN, MINNEAPOLIS, 69- *Personal Data:* b Brooklyn, NY, Aug 28, 24; m 54; c 3. *Educ:* Univ Rochester, PhD(zool), 53. *Prof Exp:* Asst biol, Univ Rochester, 48-52; fel, Jackson Mem Lab, 52-57; asst prof anat, Univ Fla, 57-60. *Mem:* Am Asn Anat. *Res:* Development in frogs; pregnancy in prepubertal mice; teratology in mice and fish. *Mailing Add:* 10531 S Cedar Lake Rd #420 Minnetonka MN 55305-3326

SMITHER, ROBERT KARL, MATERIAL SCIENCE, X-RAY OPTICS SYNCHROTRON RADIATION. *Current Pos:* physicist, 56-93, SR PHYSICIST, ARGONNE NAT LAB, 93- *Personal Data:* b Buffalo, NY, July 18, 29; m 55; c 3. *Educ:* Univ Buffalo, BA, 51; Yale Univ, MS, 52, PhD(physics), 56. *Prof Exp:* Instr physics, Yale Univ, 55-56. *Mem:* Am Phys Soc; AAAS; Sigma Xi; Am Archaeol Soc; Am Astrophys Soc; Am Math Soc. *Res:* Structure of new materials using Synchrotron radiation; development of x-ray and gamma-ray optics; gamma ray telescopes for astrophysics experiment; crystal diffraction optics. *Mailing Add:* 537 N Washington St Hinsdale IL 60521

SMITHERMAN, RENFORD ONEAL, FISH BIOLOGY, FISH PATHOLOGY. *Current Pos:* coordr fisheries res, 67-72, chief party, AID Auburn Univ, Repub Panama Aquacult Proj, 72-73, assoc prof fisheries & allied aquacult, 72-77, PROF AQUACULT, AUBURN UNIV, 77- *Personal Data:* b Randolph, Ala, Aug 26, 37; m 59; c Shelley & Susan. *Educ:* Auburn Univ, BS, 59, PhD(fisheries), 64; NC State Col, MS, 61. *Honors & Awards:* Nat Achievement Excellence Awards, Catfish Farmers Am, 84, 85, 92. *Prof Exp:* Asst fish cult, Auburn Univ, 61-64; leader, La Coop Fishery Unit, US Bur Sportfish & Wildlife, 64-67. *Concurrent Pos:* Dir, Off Aquacult, USDA, Washington, DC. *Mem:* World Aquacult Soc; Catfish Farmers of Am; Am Fisheries Soc; Int Asn Genetics Aquacult. *Res:* Fish genetics, hybridization, pathology and ecology; biological weed control with fishes; crawfish ecology; polyculture of fishes; aquaculture. *Mailing Add:* 324 Chelvacla Rd Auburn AL 36830. *Fax:* 334-844-9208

SMITH-EVERNDEN, ROBERTA KATHERINE, MICROPALEONTOLOGY, SOIL CONSERVATION. *Current Pos:* lectr & res assoc, 75-89, CONSULT GEOL, UNIV CALIF, SANTA CRUZ, 75- *Personal Data:* b Los Angeles, Calif. *Educ:* Univ Alaska, BA, 57; Univ Calif, Berkeley, MA, 60; Univ BC, PhD(geol), 66. *Prof Exp:* Geologist, Smithsonian Inst, 65-73; asst prof lectr, George Washington Univ, 67-68; asst prof, Howard Univ, 68-70. *Concurrent Pos:* Mem, tech adv comt, Calif Bd Forestry. *Mem:* Soc Econ Paleont & Mineralogists; Soc Woman Geogrs; Sigma Xi; Asn Eng Geologists; AAAS; NAm Micropaleont Soc; Asn Women Geoscientists. *Res:* Ecology and paleoecology of living and fossil benthonic and planktonic foraminifera; Tertiary biostratigraphy; environmental geology; mass wasting and soil loss. *Mailing Add:* PO Box 174 Davenport CA 95017

SMITH-GILL, SANDRA JOYCE, DEVELOPMENTAL BIOLOGY, ENDOCRINOLOGY. *Current Pos:* microbiologist, 87-94, SR INVESTR, NAT CANCER INST, 94- *Personal Data:* b Chicago, Ill, Jan 8, 44; m 67. *Educ:* Univ Mich, BS, 65, MS, 66, PhD(zool), 71. *Prof Exp:* Asst prof biol, Swarthmore Col, 71-74 & George Washington Univ, 74-76; vis asst prof, 76-77, assoc prof zool, Univ Md, 77-87. *Concurrent Pos:* Microbiologist, Nat Cancer Inst, 80-87. *Mem:* Int Soc Develop Biol; Soc Develop Biol; Int Pigment Cell Soc; Am Soc Zoologists; Tissue Cult Asn. *Res:* Protein-protein interactions; genetic and structural basis of antibody recognition of protein antigens; antigenic structure of the mycoprotein. *Mailing Add:* Lab-Genetics NCI Bldg 37 Rm 2B10 Bethesda MD 20892

SMITHIES, OLIVER, PATHOLOGY, MOLECULAR GENETICS. *Current Pos:* EXCELLENCE PROF PATH, UNIV NC, CHAPEL HILL, 88- *Personal Data:* b Halifax, Eng, July 23, 25; US citizen. *Educ:* Oxford Univ, Eng, PhD(biochem), 51. *Hon Degrees:* DSc, Univ Chicago, 91. *Honors &*

Awards: William Allen Mem Award, Am Soc Human Genetics, 64; Karl Landsteiner Mem Award, Am Asn Blood Banks, 84; Gairdner Found Int Award, 90 & 93. *Prof Exp:* Fel phys chem, Univ Wis-Madison, 51-53; res asst & assoc, Connaught Med Res Lab, Toronto, Can, 53-60; from asst prof to prof genetics & med genetics, Univ Wis-Madison, 60-63, Leon J Cole prof, 71-80, Hilldale prof, 80-88. *Concurrent Pos:* Markle scholar, 61; mem, Nat Adv Med Sci Coun, NIH, 85. *Mem:* Nat Acad Sci; Am Acad Arts & Sci; Genetics Soc Am (vpres, 74, pres, 75); fel AAAS. *Res:* Targetted modification of specific genes in living animals; author of various publications. *Mailing Add:* Dept Path Univ NC CB No 7525 Chapel Hill NC 27599-7525

SMITH-SOMERVILLE, HARRIETT ELIZABETH, CELL BIOLOGY, ULTRASTRUCTURE. *Current Pos:* from asst prof to assoc prof, 76-86, PROF BIOL SCI, DEPT BIOL SCI, UNIV ALA, 86- *Personal Data:* b Guntersville, Ala, Jan 5, 44; m 82. *Educ:* Univ Ala, BS, 66; Univ Tex, Austin, PhD(biol sci), 70. *Prof Exp:* Fel biophys, Univ Chicago, 70-72, res assoc physiol, 73-76. *Concurrent Pos:* Teaching assoc biol, Dept Biol, Univ SFla, 73; vis asst prof, Dept Biol Sci, Univ Ill, 75-76. *Mem:* Am Soc Cell Biol; Soc Protozoologists; Am Micros Soc; AAAS; Sigma Xi. *Res:* Oral apparatus structure, food vacuole formation and membrane recycling in Tetrahymena vorax; cell motility; microtubules; microfilaments; microfilament-membrane interactions; differentiation in Tetrahymena vorax. *Mailing Add:* Dept Biol Sci Univ Ala Box 870344 Tuscaloosa AL 34587-0344

SMITHSON, GEORGE RAYMOND, JR, ENVIRONMENTAL SCIENCE, RESEARCH ADMINISTRATION. *Current Pos:* RETIRED. *Personal Data:* b New Vienna, Ohio, Mar 2, 26; m 50; c Vicki Rae (Arthur), Holly Jean (Smith) & Bonnie Lou. *Educ:* Wilmington Col, BS, 49; Miami Univ, MS, 50. *Prof Exp:* Asst chem, Miami Univ, 49-50; prof phys sci, Rio Grande Col, 50-52; prin chemist extractive metall div, Batelle-Columbus Labs, Batelle Mem Inst, 52-60, proj leader, 60-61, sr scientist, 61-65, assoc chief minerals & metall waste technol div, 68-70, chief waste control & process technol div, 70-71, asst mgr environ systs & processes dept, 71-74, mgr environ technol prog off, Environ Energy Res Dept, 74-80, mgr environ progs off, Chem Dept, 80-85. *Concurrent Pos:* Vpres & prog dir, Metcalf & Eddy Ohio, Inc, 85-87; vpres, Lawhon Assocs, 86-88; environ consult, 86- *Mem:* Fel AAAS; emer fel Am Inst Chem; Sigma Xi. *Res:* Waste management and control; process technology; fluidized-bed technology; thermodynamics of extractive metallurgical systems; electrowinning; electrodialysis; sorption technology. *Mailing Add:* 3068 Kingston Ave Grove City OH 43123

SMITHSON, SCOTT BUSBY, GEOPHYSICS, PETROLOGY. *Current Pos:* from asst prof to prof geophys, 64-77, PROF GEOL, UNIV WYO, 77- *Personal Data:* b Oak Park, Ill, Oct 28, 30; m 53; c 2. *Educ:* Univ Okla, BS, 54; Univ Wyo, MA, 59; Univ Oslo, DSc(petrol geophys), 63. *Prof Exp:* Asst seismologist, Shell Oil Co, 54-57; analyst, Geotech Corp, 57-58; Royal Norweg Coun Sci & Indust Res fel, 63-64. *Mem:* Geol Soc Am; Soc Explor Geophys; Am Geophys Union; Mineral Soc Am; Norweg Geol Soc. *Res:* Solid earth geophysics and petrology; structure and composition of the continental crust of the earth. *Mailing Add:* Dept Geol Univ Wyo PO Box 3006 Laramie WY 82071-3006

SMITH-SONNEBORN, JOAN, MOLECULAR BIOLOGY. *Current Pos:* ASSOC PROF ZOOL, UNIV WYO, 71- *Personal Data:* b Albany, NY, Nov 5, 35; div; c 2. *Educ:* Bryn Mawr Col, BA, 57; Ind Univ, PhD(zool, biochem), 62. *Prof Exp:* Fel biochem, Brandeis Univ, 61-62; fel virol & microbiol, Univ Calif, Berkeley, 62-64; res assoc zool, Univ Wis-Madison, 64-71. *Mem:* Am Soc Cell Biol; fel Gerontol Soc Am; NY Acad Sci; AAAS. *Res:* Extranuclear DNA of organelles; mutagenesis and repair; cellular aging; interaction of cell components and external environment on the determination of modulation of gene expression during development and aging as well as genotoxicology; the Paramecium system of cellular aging will be used with the new biotechnology available to try to alter the aging process; transformation of these cells with DNA coding for DNA repair genes will be explored and the effect of introduced genes on normal life span determined. *Mailing Add:* Dept Zool Univ Wyo Box 3166 Laramie WY 82071-3166

SMITH-THOMAS, BARBARA, operating system security, software engineering, for more information see previous edition

SMITHWICK, ELIZABETH MARY, PEDIATRICS, IMMUNOLOGY. *Current Pos:* PROF PEDIAT, UNIV CALIF, DAVIS, 82- *Personal Data:* b Casco, Wis, Jan 20, 28. *Educ:* Univ Wis, BS, 48, MD, 55; Am Bd Allergy & Immunol, dipl, 77. *Prof Exp:* Intern, Kings Co Hosp, NY, 55-56 & Bellevue Hosp, 56-57; resident pediat, Metrop Hosp & Babies Hosp, 57-58; sr house officer, Queen Charlotte's Hosp, London, Eng, 59-60; from instr to assoc prof, State Univ NY Downstate Med Ctr, 60-73; assoc mem & assoc prof, Sloan-Kettering Inst Cancer Res, Cornell Univ, 73-82. *Concurrent Pos:* USPHS grant, Southwestern Med Sch, Univ Tex Dallas, 63-64. *Mem:* AAAS; Soc Pediat Res; Am Acad Pediat; Am Rheumatism Asn. *Res:* Immune deficiency diseases; neutrophil and monocyte function; rheumatology. *Mailing Add:* Dept Pediat, Univ Calif Davis 436 Hartnell Pl Sacramento CA 98825

SMITS, FRIEDOLF M, PHYSICS. *Current Pos:* RETIRED. *Personal Data:* b Stuttgart, Ger, Nov 10, 24; US citizen; m 55; c 3. *Educ:* Univ Freiburg, PhD(physics), 50. *Prof Exp:* Res assoc physics, Univ Freiburg, 50-54; mem tech staff device develop, Bell Tel Labs, 54-62; mgr dept radiation physics, Sandia Corp, 62-65; dept head, Device Develop, Bell Tel Labs, 65-68, dir, Semi-Conductor Device Lab, 68-71, Mos Tech & Memory Lab, 71-75, Integrated Circuit Support Lab, 75-86. *Mem:* Fel Inst Elec & Electronics Engrs. *Res:* Geological age determinations; physics of semiconductor devices; physics of radiation damage in semiconductors; ultrasonic and optical memories. *Mailing Add:* 2079 Greenwood Rd Allentown PA 18103

SMITS, HELEN LIDA, COMMUNITY MEDICINE. *Current Pos:* PRES & MED DIR, HEALTH RIGHT INC, 96- *Personal Data:* b Long Beach, Calif, Dec 3, 36; m 76, Roger LeCompte; c Theodore. *Educ:* Swarthmore Col, BA, 58; Yale Univ, MA, 61, MD, 67. *Prof Exp:* Intern & asst resident, Hosp Univ Pa, 67-68; fel, Beth Israel Hosp, Boston, 69-70; chief resident, Hosp Univ Pa, 70-71; chief med clin, Univ Pa, 71-75; assoc adminr patient care servs, Univ Pa Hosp, 75-77; vpres med affairs community health plan, Georgetown Univ, 77; dir, Health Stand & Qual Bur, Health Care Financing Admin, Dept Health & Human Servs, Washington, 77-80; sr res assoc, Urban Inst, Washington, 80-81; assoc prof, Med Sch, Yale Univ, 81-85; assoc vpres health affairs, Univ Conn Health Ctr, Farmington, 85-87, prof community med, Sch Med, 85-93; hosp dir, John Dempsey Hosp, Farmington, 87-93; dep adminr, Health Care Financing Admin, Washington, 93-96. *Concurrent Pos:* Fel, Royal Soc Med Found, London, 73; comnr, Joint Comt Accreditation Hosps, Chicago, 89-93, chair, 91-92. *Mem:* Inst Med-Nat Acad Sci; master Am Col Physicians. *Mailing Add:* 81 Main St Ivoryton CT 06442-1032

SMITS, TALIVALDIS I(VARS), DETECTION & ESTIMATION THEORY, UNDERWATER ACOUSTICS. *Current Pos:* mem tech staff, 77-82, sect head, 82-85, STAFF ENG, TRW, 85- *Personal Data:* b Riga, Latvia, Sept 18, 36; US citizen; m 67. *Educ:* Univ Minn, BS, 58, MSEE, 62, PhD(elec eng), 66. *Prof Exp:* Res asst elec eng, Univ Minn, 58-62, res assoc, 66-67, asst prof, 66-68; assoc prof, Cath Univ Am, 68-78. *Concurrent Pos:* Assoc ed, J Acoust Soc Am, 74-86; consult, Anal Adv Group, McLean, Va, 73-75, Undersea Res Corp, Falls Church, Va, 75-76 & Planning Systs Inc, 76; lectr elec eng, Cath Univ Am, 78- *Mem:* Acoust Soc Am; Inst Elec & Electronics Engrs; Am Sci Affil. *Res:* Random signal processing; passive and active sonar-radar detection and estimation; statistical communication theory; pattern recognition; statistical methods in system analysis; non-Gaussian random processes. *Mailing Add:* 2811 Crest Ave Hyattsville MD 20785

SMITTLE, BURRELL JOE, IRRADIATION & RADIOISOTOPE RESEARCH. *Current Pos:* MGR, FLA LINEAR ACCELERATOR IRRADIATION FACIL, 89- *Personal Data:* b Paola, Kans, July 13, 34; m 55, Patsy Butler; c Sharon & Stephen. *Educ:* Univ Ark, BS, 55, MS, 56; Rutgers Univ, PhD(entom), 64. *Prof Exp:* Med entomologist, US Army, 56-59; med entomologist, Insects Affecting Man & Animal Res Lab, Agr Res Serv, USDA, 59-89. *Concurrent Pos:* Courtesy prof entom, Univ Fla, 65- *Mem:* Entom Soc Am; Am Soc Testing & Mat. *Res:* Irradiation of agricultural commodities; linear accelerator irradiation research. *Mailing Add:* 1621 NW 71st St Gainesville FL 32605. *Fax:* 352-955-3041

SMITTLE, DOYLE ALLEN, OLERICULTURE, PLANT PHYSIOLOGY. *Current Pos:* from asst prof to assoc prof, 73-81, PROF HORT, UNIV GA, 81- *Personal Data:* b Bradley, Ark, Feb 27, 39; m 57; c 2. *Educ:* Univ Ark, BS, 61, MS, 65; Univ Md, PhD(hort), 69. *Prof Exp:* Res asst hort, Univ Ark, 61-66; asst prof, Wash State Univ, 68-73. *Mem:* Sigma Xi; Am Soc Hort Sci. *Res:* Soil-plant-water relations and post-harvest handling of cucurbits, onions and edible legumes. *Mailing Add:* 2207 Rutland Rd Tifton GA 31794

SMITTLE, RICHARD BAIRD, MICROBIAL FOOD ECOLOGY. *Current Pos:* vpres opers, 90-91, EXEC VPRES & INFO SER ED, SILLIKER LABS GROUP INC, 91-, VPRES LAB OPERS. *Personal Data:* b New Martinsville, WVa, Mar 5, 43; m 67; c 2. *Educ:* WVa Univ, AB, 67, MS, 68; NC State Univ, PhD(food sci), 73. *Prof Exp:* Microbiologist, US Food & Drug Admin, 68-70; chief microbiologist, CPC Int, Best Foods, 73-77; dir, Silliker Labs NJ, 77-88 & Silliker Labs Pa, 88-91. *Concurrent Pos:* Adj prof, Kean Col NJ, 74-75 & NY Univ, 85-87; comt mem, Adv Bd Mil Personnel Supplies, Nat Res Coun, 81-83. *Mem:* Inst Food Technologists; Am Soc Microbiol; Int Asn Milk Food & Environ Sanitarians; Soc Appl Bact. *Res:* Storage and survival of lactic streptococci and lactobacilli to starvation and frozen conditions; growth and survival in high acid and high osmotic foods and environments of bacteria, yeasts and molds. *Mailing Add:* 10611 Lexington Lane Frankfort IL 60423

SMOAKE, JAMES ALVIN, PHYSIOLOGY, BIOCHEMISTRY. *Current Pos:* MEM FAC BIOL, NMEX INST MINING & TECHNOL, 73- *Personal Data:* b Langdale, Ala, Oct 5, 42. *Educ:* Jacksonville State Univ, BS, 65; Univ Tenn, Knoxville, MS, 66, PhD(zool), 69. *Prof Exp:* Nat Cancer Inst spec cancer res trainee biochem, St Jude Children's Res Hosp, 72-73. *Concurrent Pos:* Sabbatical leave, Endocrine & Metab Sect, Vet Admin Med Ctr, Memphis, 79-80. *Mem:* AAAS; Sigma Xi. *Res:* Action of insulin on liver cells. *Mailing Add:* Dept Biol NMex Inst Mining & Technol Socorro NM 87801-4796

SMOCK, DALE OWEN, ELECTRICAL ENGINEERING. *Current Pos:* instr eng, 45-49, from asst prof to assoc prof, 49-56, actg head, Eng Dept, 72-77, prof, 56-80, chmn, Eng Dept, 77-80, EMER PROF ELEC ENG, GROVE CITY COL. *Personal Data:* b Cochranton, Pa, Feb 13, 15; m 42. *Educ:* Grove City Col, BS, 42; Carnegie-Mellon Univ, BS, 48; Purdue Univ, MS, 62. *Prof Exp:* Instr pre-radar, US Naval Training Sch, Grove City Col, 42-45; jr engr, Westinghouse Elec Corp, Md, 45. *Mem:* Am Soc Eng Educ; Inst Elec & Electronics Engrs. *Res:* Electronics; electromagnetic theory; transmission circuits; electrical measurements; linear systems. *Mailing Add:* Dept Elec Eng Grove City Col Grove City PA 16127

SMOKE, WILLIAM HENRY, MATHEMATICS. *Current Pos:* Asst prof, 65-74, ASSOC PROF MATH, UNIV CALIF, IRVINE, 74- *Personal Data:* b Battle Creek, Mich, Nov 7, 28; m 65. *Educ:* Univ Mich, BA, 58, MA, 60; Univ Calif, Berkeley, PhD(math), 65. *Mem:* Am Math Soc. *Res:* Algebra. *Mailing Add:* 611 Allview Pl Laguna Beach CA 92651

SMOKER, WILLIAM ALEXANDER, fisheries, forestry; deceased, see previous edition for last biography

SMOKER, WILLIAM WILLIAMS, FISH & WILDLIFE SCI. *Current Pos:* PROF SCH FISHERIES & OCEAN SCI, UNIV ALASKA, FAIRBANKS, 78- *Personal Data:* b Washington, DC, Sept 6, 45; m 75, Janet E Van Dusen; c Rhys J & Alice E. *Educ:* Carleton Col, BA, 67; Ore State Univ, MS, 70, PhD(fisheries), 82. *Concurrent Pos:* Assoc dir, Alaska Sea Grant Col, 82-83; vis assoc prof, Fac Fisheries, Univ Hokkaido, Hakodate, 88-89. *Mem:* Am Fisheries Soc; Am Inst Fisheries Res Biologists; Int Asn Genetics in Aquacult. *Res:* Genetics of Pacific salmon, particularly as applied to fish culture; technology of the culture of Pacific salmon. *Mailing Add:* Juneau Ctr Fisheries & Ocean Sci 11120 Glacier Hwy Juneau AK 99801. *E-Mail:* ffwws@acad1.alaska.edu

SMOKOVITIS, ATHANASSIOS A, ANIMAL PHYSIOLOGY. *Current Pos:* lectr physiol teaching, 70-73, PROF & HEAD, DEPT PHYSIOL, FAC VET MED, ARISTOTELIAN UNIV, THESSALONIKI, GREECE, 81- *Personal Data:* b Thessaloniki, Greece, June 2, 35; m 65, Despina Andreadis. *Educ:* Aristotelian Univ, dipl vet med, 57, dipl biol, 66, PhD(physiol), 68. *Prof Exp:* Vis investr res, Inst Med Res, Mitchell Found, Washington, DC, 73-75; res assoc, Sch Med, Ind Univ, 75-76; vis investr & adv res, Gaubius Inst, Health Res Orgn, Holland, 76-77; vis investr & lectr res, Dept Physiol, Med Sch, Vienna, Austria, 77-81. *Concurrent Pos:* Hon prof physiol, Univ Vienna, Austria, 79. *Mem:* Am Physiol Soc; Am Heart Asn. *Res:* Physiology of fibrinolysis; author of various publications. *Mailing Add:* Dept Physiol Univ Thessaloniki Vet Sch Thessaloniki 54635 Greece

SMOL, JOHN PAUL, PALEOLIMNOLOGY. *Current Pos:* fel, Nat Sci & Eng Res Coun, 82-83, ASST PROF BIOL, QUEEN'S UNIV KINGSTON, 84- *Personal Data:* b Montreal, Que, Oct 10, 55. *Educ:* McGill Univ, BSc, 77; Brock Univ, MSc, 79; Queen's Univ, PhD(paleolimnol), 82. *Prof Exp:* Vis scientist paleolimnol, Nat Sci & Eng Res Coun, Geol Surv Can, 83-84. *Mem:* Am Soc Limnol & Oceanog; Int Asn Theoret & Appl Limnol; Freshwater Biol Asn; Int Phycol Asn; Am Phycol Asn; Soc Can Limnologists. *Res:* Limnology and paleoecology of lakes; lake acidification; entrophication; high Arctic lakes; alpine lakes. *Mailing Add:* Dept Biol Queen's Univ Kingston ON K7L 3N6 Can

SMOLANDER, MARTTI JUHANI, exercise physiology, work physiology, for more information see previous edition

SMOLARSKI, DENNIS CHESTER, COMPUTATIONAL MATHEMATICS, ITERATIVE SOLUTIONS OF LINEAR SYSTEMS. *Current Pos:* Instr math, 75-76, asst prof math & comput sci, 82-88, ASSOC PROF MATH & COMPUT SCI, SANTA CLARA UNIV, 88- *Personal Data:* b Harvey, Ill, Sept 2, 47. *Educ:* Santa Clara Univ, BS, 69; Univ Calif, Santa Barbara, MA, 75; Jesuit Sch Theol, Berkeley, MDiv, 79; Univ Ill, Urbana-Champaign, PhD(comput sci), 82. *Mem:* Math Asn Am; Am Math Soc; Asn Comput Mach; Sigma Xi; Comput Profs Social Responsibility. *Res:* Examine various iterative methods suitable for solving large, sparse linear algebraic systems. *Mailing Add:* Dept Math Santa Clara Univ Santa Clara CA 95053-0001. *E-Mail:* dsmolarski@scuacc.scu.edu

SMOLENSKY, MICHAEL HALE, MEDICAL CHRONOBIOLOGY, ENVIRONMENTAL PHYSIOLOGY. *Current Pos:* From asst prof to assoc prof, 70-87, PROF ENVIRON PHYSIOL, DIV PULMONARY MED, GRAD SCH BIOMED SCI, DEPT PHARMACEUT, UNIV TEX HEALTH SCI CTR, HOUSTON, 87- *Personal Data:* b Chicago, Ill, May 10, 42; m 80; c 3. *Educ:* Univ Ill, Urbana-Champaign, BS, 64, MS, 66, PhD(physiol), 71. *Concurrent Pos:* Res assoc, Tex Allergy Res Found, 71- & McGovern Allergy Clin, Houston, 71-; co-ed, Chronobiol Int, 84-, Ann Rev Chronopharmacol; secy-treas, organizing comt, Int Conf Chronopharmacol, 84- *Mem:* AAAS; Int Soc Study Chronobiol; Soc Menstrual Cycle Res; NY Acad Sci. *Res:* Shift work, occupational health; chronopharmacology, chronotoxicology; chronobiology; public health; allergic asthma; investigation of human biological rhythmic phenomena relative to the diagnosis and treatment (chronopharmacology) of humans, especially heart, allergic asthma and cancer disease, as well as their cause or exacerbation due to environmental factors. *Mailing Add:* 14610 Cedar Point Dr Houston TX 77070

SMOLIAR, STEPHEN WILLIAM, information science, for more information see previous edition

SMOLIGA, JOHN ANDREW, CHEMICAL MICROSCOPY, OPTICAL CRYSTALLOGRAPHY. *Current Pos:* SR SCIENTIST, BOEHRINGER INGELHEIM PHARMACEUT INC, 96- *Personal Data:* b Perth Amboy, NJ, Aug 25, 55; m 80, Anne G Grener. *Educ:* Kean Col NJ, BA, 77; Western Conn State Univ, MA, 85, McCrone Res Inst, PhD(chem micros), 93. *Prof Exp:* Geosci technician, Kean Col NJ, 77-80; sr mineral technician, Newmont Mining Corp, 80-87; res microscopist, Cytec Industs, 87-96. *Concurrent Pos:* Mineralogist, RP Cargille Labs, Inc, 79-80; adj fac geol, Western Conn State Univ, 82-89; geol & mat consult, John A Smoliga Consult, 83- *Mem:* Am Chem Soc; Geol Soc Am. *Res:* Chemical microscopy; optical crystallography; materials characterization; ultramicroanalysis; polymorphism; geological and mineralogical analysis; soil sciences; microstructural analysis of friction materials, polymer microscopy, pharmaceutical microscopy, mineral deposits and ore genesis. *Mailing Add:* 9 Chickadee Lane Brookfield CT 06804. *Fax:* 203-778-7374; *E-Mail:* jsmoliga@bi-pharm.com

SMOLIK, JAMES DARRELL, PLANT NEMATOLOGY. *Current Pos:* asst plant path, 67-69, from res asst to res assoc, 70-75, ASST PROF PLANT NEMATOL, SDAK STATE UNIV, 75- *Personal Data:* b Rapid City, SDak, Mar 28, 42. *Educ:* SDak State Univ, BS, 65, MS, 69, PhD(plant path), 73. *Prof Exp:* Foreman pest control, M L Warne Chem & Equip Co, 66. *Mem:* Sigma Xi; Soc Nematologists. *Res:* Effect of nematodes on productivity of row, field and legume crops; nematode ecology studies in native range. *Mailing Add:* 1206 Fifth St Brookings SD 57006

SMOLIN, LEE, QUANTIZATION OF THE GRAVITATIONAL FIELD, QUANTUM DESCRIPTION OF SPACE & TIME. *Current Pos:* ASSOC PROF PHYSICS, SYRACUSE UNIV, 88- *Personal Data:* b New York, NY, June 6, 55. *Educ:* Hampshire Col, BA, 75; Harvard Col, MA, 78, PhD(physic), 79. *Prof Exp:* Postdoctoral, Inst Theoret Physics, Univ Calif, Santa Barbara, 80-81; mem, Inst Advan Study, 81-83; postdoctoral, Envico Frumi Inst, Univ Chicago, 83-84; asst prof, physics, Yale Univ 84-88. *Concurrent Pos:* Vis scientist, Inst Theoret Physics. *Res:* Reconciling quantum mechanics with general relativity; elementary particle theory and the problem of the self-organization of biological systems. *Mailing Add:* Dept Physics Pa State Univ 320 Osmond Lab University Park PA 16802

SMOLINSKY, GERALD, WAFER CLEANING, DIELECTRIC FILMS. *Current Pos:* MEM TECH STAFF, BELL LABS, 59-; AT&T ASSIGNEE/SEMATECH, 92- *Personal Data:* b Philadelphia, Pa, Feb 25, 33; m 79, Marilyn Olsen; c Tanya & Paul. *Educ:* Drexel Inst, BS, 55; Univ Calif, Berkeley, PhD(org chem), 58. *Prof Exp:* Fel, Columbia Univ, 58-59. *Res:* Wet and dry cleaning of silicon wafers; plasma-deposited phtoresist; top-surace-imaged photoresists. *Mailing Add:* Sematech 2706 Montopolis Dr Austin TX 78741-6499. *Fax:* 512-356-3618; *E-Mail:* jerry_smolinsky@sematech.org

SMOLLER, JOEL A, MATHEMATICS. *Current Pos:* PROF, UNIV MICH, ANN ARBOR, 70- *Personal Data:* b New York, NY, Jan 2, 39; m 60; c 3. *Educ:* Brooklyn Col, BS, 57; Ohio Univ, MS, 58; Purdue Univ, PhD(math), 63. *Prof Exp:* Instr math, Univ Mich, 63-64; vis mem, Courant Inst Math Sci, NY Univ, 64-65; from asst prof to assoc prof, Univ Mich, Ann Arbor, 65-69; vis mem, Courant Inst Math Sci, NY Univ, 69-70. *Concurrent Pos:* Vis prof, Math Res Ctr, 72-73; fel Guggenheim, 80; vis prof, Ecole Norwale Supericure, Paris, 85, Harvard Univ, 88-89. *Mem:* Am Math Soc. *Res:* Partial differential equations; geometry. *Mailing Add:* Dept Math Univ Mich Ann Arbor MI 48109-1003

SMOLLER, SYLVIA WASSERTHEIL, BIOSTATISTICS, EPIDEMIOLOGY. *Current Pos:* PROF, EPIDEMIOL & SOCIAL MED, ALBERT EINSTEIN COL MED, 69-, HEAD DIV EPIDEMIOL & BIOSTATIST, 85- *Personal Data:* b Poland, Feb 24, 32; US citizen; m 71; c 2. *Educ:* Syracuse Univ, BS, 53, MA, 55; NY Univ, PhD(statist), 69. *Prof Exp:* Engr human factors, IBM, 58-61; statistician ment health, Astor Home Children, 62-64; asst prof math, State Univ NY Col New Paltz, 64-69. *Concurrent Pos:* Consult, Int Proj, Asn Vol Sterilization, 72-; fel coun epidemiol, Am Heart Asn, 76. *Mem:* Am Pub Health Asn; Soc Epidemiol Res; Am Statist Asn; fel NY Acad Sci; fel Am Col Epidemiol; Soc Clin Trials; Am Heart Asn. *Res:* Epidemiological studies of hypertension, cardiovascular disease, cancer and clinical traits; computer applications. *Mailing Add:* Dept Epidemiol & Social Med Albert Einstein Col Med 1300 Morris Park Ave Bronx NY 10461

SMOLUCHOWSKI, ROMAN, solid state physics, astrophysics; deceased, see previous edition for last biography

SMOOK, MALCOLM ANDREW, ORGANIC CHEMISTRY. *Current Pos:* CONSULT, 85- *Personal Data:* b Seattle, Wash, Aug 22, 24; m 45, Mary L Nominee; c Frances L (Fenton) & Valerie D. *Educ:* Univ Calif, BS, 45; Ohio State Univ, PhD(chem), 49. *Prof Exp:* Chemist, E I du Pont de Nemours & Co, Inc, 49-52, res supvr, 52-53, div head, 53-58, from asst lab dir to lab dir, 58-63, asst dir res & develop div, Elastomers Dept, 63-68, asst dir res & develop div, Plastics Dept, 68-76, gen lab dir, Plastics Prod & Resins Dept, 76-80, mgr patents & regulatory affairs, Polymer Prod Dept, 80-85. *Concurrent Pos:* Mem res & technol adv comt, Materials & Structures, NASA, 75-78. *Mem:* Am Chem Soc; Sigma Xi; Soc Rheol. *Res:* Organic fluorine chemistry; polymer and rubber chemistry. *Mailing Add:* 59 Rockford Rd Wilmington DE 19806

SMOOKE, MITCHELL D, NUMERICAL ANALYSIS, COMPUTATIONAL COMBUSTION. *Current Pos:* from asst prof to assoc prof, 84-93, PROF MECH ENG, YALE UNIV, 93-, STRATHCOND PROF ENG, 96- *Personal Data:* b Hartford, Conn, Aug 10, 51; m 77; c 1. *Educ:* Rensselaer Polytech Inst, BS, 73; Harvard Univ, MS, 74, PhD(appl math), 78; Univ Calif, Berkeley, MBA, 83. *Hon Degrees:* MA, Yale Univ, 94. *Honors & Awards:* Silver Medal, Combustion Inst. *Prof Exp:* Staff scientist, Sandia Nat Labs, 78-84. *Concurrent Pos:* Vis prof, Cath Univ, Holland, 85, Ecole Centrale, France, 88; dir undergrad studies mech eng, Yale Univ, 85-; consult, Gen Motors, 87-, United Technol, 87-, Gen Elec, 89-; mem, Comt Propellant Res, Army Res Off, 88. *Mem:* Soc Indust & Appl Math; Asn Comput Mach; Combustion Inst; Am Inst Aeronaut & Astronaut. *Res:* Development and application of adaptive numerical algorithms for problems in combustion. *Mailing Add:* Dept Mech Eng Yale Univ New Haven CT 06520

SMOOT, CHARLES RICHARD, RESEARCH ADMINISTRATION. *Current Pos:* RETIRED. *Personal Data:* b Marmet, WVa, Nov 15, 28; m 51, Irene J Thomas; c C Thomas, Douglas A, Patricia L, Carlene R, Gregory P & Angela. *Educ:* Charleston Univ, BS, 51; Purdue Univ, PhD(phys chem), 55. *Prof Exp:* Chemist, FMC Co, 47-51; chemist, EI Du Pont de Nemours & Co Inc, 55-59, from res supvr to sr res supvr, 59-72, lab supt, 72-82, res mgr, 82-90, technol mgr, 90-93; res & tech dir, ICI Acrylics, Inc, 93-95. *Concurrent Pos:* Asst prof, WVa Univ Br, Parkersburg, 61-63. *Mem:* Am Chem Soc; Sigma Xi. *Res:* Applied research on polymers; research administration. *Mailing Add:* 810 Gen Cornwallis Dr West Chester PA 19382

SMOOT, GEORGE FITZGERALD, III, ASTROPHYSICS, COSMIC RAY PHYSICS. *Current Pos:* RES PHYSICIST, UNIV CALIF, BERKELEY, 71-, RES PHYSICIST, LAWRENCE BERKELEY LAB, 74- *Personal Data:* b Yukon, Fla, Feb 20, 45. *Educ:* Mass Inst Technol, BS(math) & BS(physics), 66, PhD(physics), 70. *Prof Exp:* Res physicist, Mass Inst Technol, 70. *Mem:* Am Phys Soc; Am Astron Soc; Sigma Xi; Int Astron Union. *Res:* Measurements of cosmic background radiation as a cosmological probe of the early universe; satellite and balloon-borne superconducting magnetic spectrometer experiments on the charged cosmic rays; remote sensing using microwave radiometers. *Mailing Add:* One Cyclontron Rd MS 50-205 Berkeley CA 94720

SMOOT, LEON DOUGLAS, CHEMICAL ENGINEERING. *Current Pos:* assoc prof, Brigham Yound Univ, 67-70, chmn dept, 70-77, dean eng & techol, 77-95, PROF CHEM ENG, BRIGHAM YOUNG UNIV, 70-, DIR, ADVAN COMBUSTION ENG RES CTR, 86- *Personal Data:* b Provo, Utah, July 26, 34; m 53; c Analee (Folster), LaCinda (Lewis), Michelle (Hyde) & Melinda Lee. *Educ:* Brigham Young Univ, BS & BEngS, 57; Univ Wash, MS, 59, PhD(chem eng), 60. *Prof Exp:* Lab asst chem, Brigham Young Univ, 54-55, instr math, 55-56 res asst chem eng, 56-57; consult engr heat transfer, 58-59; asst prof, Brigham Young Univ, 60-63; sr tech specialist res & develop, Lockheed Propulsion Co, 63-67; sr tech specialist res & develop, Lockheed Propulsion Co, 63-67. *Concurrent Pos:* Asst chem eng, Univ Wash, 57-60; indust partic, US-UK-Can Tech Coop Prog, 64-72; vis asst prof, Calif Inst Technol, 66-67; chmn ad hoc hybrid combustion comt, Int Agency Chem Rocket Propulsion Group, 66; consult, many companies and agencies in the US & Europe, 70- *Mem:* Am Inst Chem Engrs; Sigma Xi; Am Soc Eng Educ; Int Combustion Inst. *Res:* Combustion; energy; fossil fuels. *Mailing Add:* Advan Combustion Eng Res Ctr 265A CTB Brigham Young Univ Provo UT 84602. *E-Mail:* lds@byu.edu

SMOSNA, RICHARD ALLAN, STRATIGRAPHY. *Current Pos:* PROF GEOL & GEOG, WVA UNIV, 78- *Personal Data:* b Chicago, Ill, Nov 3, 45; m 67; c 2. *Educ:* Mich State Univ, BS, 67; Univ Ill, MS, 70, PhD(geol), 73. *Honors & Awards:* Levorsen Award, Am Asn Petrol Geologist, 74; Distinguished Tech Commun Award, Soc Tech Commun, 75. *Prof Exp:* Instr geol, Hanover Col, 71-72; petrol geologist, WVa Geol Surv, 72-78. *Concurrent Pos:* Adj asst prof, WVa Univ, 74- *Res:* Determination of paleoenvironments, paleoecology, stratigraphy and petroleum potential of Silurian-aged carbonate rocks of central Appalachians. *Mailing Add:* 101 Birch Lane Morgantown WV 26505

SMOTHERS, JAMES LLEWELLYN, ANIMAL PHYSIOLOGY, ENDOCRINOLOGY. *Current Pos:* from asst prof to assoc prof, 62-71, PROF BIOL, UNIV LOUISVILLE, 71- *Personal Data:* b Jackson, Tenn, Aug 30, 30; m 64. *Educ:* Lambuth Col, BS, 52; Univ Tenn, MS, 53, PhD(zool), 61. *Prof Exp:* Nat Heart Found fel marine biol, Inst Marine Sci, Univ Miami, 61-62. *Mem:* Am Soc Zoologists; Sigma Xi; AAAS; Int Oceanog Found. *Res:* Effects of dietary and hormonal factors on mitochondrial structure and function, mechanisms of actions of hormones; comparative physiology of respiratory enzyme activities and respiration of animals and tissues. *Mailing Add:* 903 Riverside Dr Louisville KY 40207

SMOTHERS, WILLIAM JOSEPH, ENGINEERING. *Current Pos:* RETIRED. *Personal Data:* b Poplar Bluff, Mo, Mar 17, 19; m 43; c 2. *Educ:* Univ Mo, BS, 40, MS, 42, PhD(ceramic eng), 44. *Honors & Awards:* Toledo Glass & Ceramic Award, Am Ceramic Soc, 75. *Prof Exp:* Chem analyst, Mo Portland Cement Co, 39; lab asst physics, Mo Sch Mines, 40-42; engr, Mo Exp Sta, Rolla, 42-44; res engr, Bowes Elec Ceramic Corp, 44-50; assoc prof, Inst Sci & Technol, Univ Ark, 50-53; dir ceramic res, Ohio Brass Co, 54-63; sect mgr refractories, Homer Res Labs, Bethlehem Steel Corp, 63-82. *Mem:* Fel AAAS; fel Am Ceramic Soc (vpres, 64-65, pres, 71-72); Am Chem Soc. *Res:* Refractories research; differential thermal analysis; solid state; ceramic materials. *Mailing Add:* 2700 Woodside Rd Bethlehem PA 18017-3607

SMOUSE, PETER EDGAR, GENETICS, BIOSTATISTICS. *Current Pos:* PROF II MARINE & COASTAL SCI, RUTGERS UNIV, 89-, ASSOC DIR, CTR THEORET APPL GENETICS, 89-, ASSOC DEAN, GRAD SCH, 93- *Personal Data:* b Long Beach, Calif, Apr 17, 42; m 62, Linda Stevens. *Educ:* Univ Calif, Berkeley, BS, 65; NC State Univ, PhD(genetics), 70. *Prof Exp:* From asst prof to assoc prof human genetics, Univ Mich, Ann Arbor, 72-83, prof biol sci, 85-89. *Concurrent Pos:* Mem, Comt Quant Genetics & Common Dis, Nat Inst Gen Med Sci, NIH, 78, Study Sect Mammalian Genetics, 81; mem, Rev Panel, Pop Biol & Physiol Ecol, NSF, 80-82; vis prof demog & pop genetics, Univ Tex, 84; ed bd, Int J Quant Anthrop, 88-91; mem, Ad Hoc Comn Endangered Amphibians, Nat Res Coun, 90; assoc ed, J Heredity, 90-92; mem, Human Genome Diversity Proj, Develop Eng-Second Workshop, NIH/NSF; mem coun, Am Genetics Asn, 94- *Mem:* Int Soc Genetics; Soc Study Evolution; Genetics Soc Am; Am Soc Human Genetics; Am Soc Naturalists; Am Asn Phys Anthrop; Am Genetics Asn. *Res:* Research in population theory, spanning the fields of genetics, ecology, demography, epidemiology, anthropology and systematics. *Mailing Add:* Dept Marine Sci 063454260niv New Brunswick NJ 08903

SMOUSE, THOMAS HADLEY, food science & technology, agricultural & food chemistry; deceased, see previous edition for last biography

SMUCKER, ARTHUR ALLAN, BIOCHEMISTRY, COMPUTER-INSTRUMENT INTERFACING. *Current Pos:* RETIRED. *Personal Data:* b Dhamtari, India, Nov 27, 23; US citizen; m 48; c 6. *Educ:* Goshen Col, BA, 49; Univ Ill, MS, 51, PhD(chem), 54. *Prof Exp:* From asst to instr chem, Univ Ill, 49-53; from instr to assoc prof, 54-74, dir comput serv, 84-88, prof chem, Godshen Col, 74- *Concurrent Pos:* Consult, Miles Labs, Inc, 59-61; fels, Nat Inst Arthrities & Metab Dis, Univ Calif, Berkeley, 63-64 & Univ Iowa, 72-73. *Mem:* Am Chem Soc; Am Sci Affil. *Res:* Enzyme purification, kinetics and structure. *Mailing Add:* 414 River Vista Dr Goshen IN 46526-4913

SMUCKER, SILAS JONATHAN, SOIL CONSERVATION. *Current Pos:* RETIRED. *Personal Data:* b Goshen, Ind, Dec 31, 04; m 35; c 2. *Educ:* Goshen Col, AB, 30; Purdue Univ, MS, 32. *Prof Exp:* Asst plant pathologist, Div Forest Path, USDA, 34-44, soil conservationist, Soil Conserv Serv, 45-62; agriculturist, AID, 62-69; consult agr serv, 70- *Mem:* Am Phytopath Soc; Soil Conserv Soc Am. *Res:* Elm tree diseases; wood decay fungi and wood preservatives; soil and water conservation; wildlife biology; tropical agriculture. *Mailing Add:* 1801 Greencroft Blvd Goshen IN 46526

SMUDSKI, JAMES W, PHARMACOLOGY, DENTISTRY. *Current Pos:* RETIRED. *Personal Data:* b Greensburg, Pa, Oct 31, 25; m 49; c 3. *Educ:* Univ Pittsburgh, BS, 50, DDS, 52, Univ Calif, San Francisco, MS, 61, PhD(pharmacol), 65. *Prof Exp:* Pvt pract dent, 52-58; asst prof pharmacol, 63-64, assoc prof & head dept, 64-67, dir div grad & post grad educ, 70-73, prof pharmacol & physiol & head dept, Sch Dent, Univ Pittsburgh, 67-76; dean Sch Dent, Univ Detroit, 76-82; dean dent med, Univ Pittsburgh, 83-88. *Concurrent Pos:* Nat Inst Dent Res res-teacher trainee, 58-62 & career develop award, 62-64; consult, Oakland Vet Admin Hosp, Pittsburgh, Pa, 64-76; consult, Nat Bd Dent Exam, 65-75. *Mem:* Am Dent Asn; Am Inst Oral Biol; Int Asn Dent Res. *Res:* Pharmacology of agents affecting the central, autonomic and peripheral nervous systems. *Mailing Add:* 257 Tech Rd Pittsburgh PA 15205

SMUK, JOHN MICHAEL, CHEMICAL ENGINEERING. *Current Pos:* SR RES ENGR, POTLATCH CORP, 69-, MGR PROCESS ENG, 81- *Personal Data:* b Biwabik, Minn, Aug 16, 32; m 56; c 3. *Educ:* Univ Wis, MS, 56, PhD(chem eng), 60. *Prof Exp:* Res engr, Forest Prod Lab, USDA, 60-64, proj leader, 64-66; consult engr waste treat, Ruble-Miller Assocs, 66-69, dir res & develop. *Concurrent Pos:* Consult, UN, 63; vpres, Ramsgate, 69-77. *Mem:* Am Chem Soc; Am Inst Chem Engrs; Tech Asn Pulp & Paper Indust; Instrument Soc Am. *Res:* Furfural plant and process design; acid decomposition of simple sugars; kinetic studies; chemistry of wood; process control; secondary fiber process design; oxygen bleaching; computer applications; pulp and paper plant design. *Mailing Add:* 321 E Faribault Duluth MN 55803-1840

SMULDERS, ANTHONY PETER, PHYSIOLOGY. *Current Pos:* from asst prof to assoc prof, 70-81, assoc dean sci & eng, 72-94, PROF BIOL, LOYOLA MARYMOUNT UNIV, 81-, DIR, HEALTH PROFESSIONS INFO PROG, 94- *Personal Data:* b Oss, Neth, July 6, 42. *Educ:* Loyola Univ, Los Angeles, BS, 66; Univ Calif, Los Angeles, PhD(physiol), 70. *Concurrent Pos:* Res physiologist, Univ Calif, Los Angeles, 70-; comnr, Los Angeles Co Narcotics & Dangerous Drugs Comn, 73- *Mem:* AAAS; Sigma Xi; Biophys Soc; Nat Asn Adv Health Prof. *Res:* Transport phenomena, the movement of ions and non-electrolytes across biological and artificial membranes; improvemnt of university science teaching; drug abuse and prevention. *Mailing Add:* Col Sci & Eng Loyola Marymount Univ Los Angeles CA 90045. *Fax:* 310-338-7339; *E-mail:* asmulder@lmumail.lmu.edu

SMULLIN, LOUIS DIJOUR, ELECTRICAL ENGINEERING. *Current Pos:* head tube lab, Res Lab Electronics, Mass Inst Technol, 48-50, div head, Lincoln Lab, 50-55, from assoc prof to prof, 55-74, chmn dept, 66-74, Dugald Caleb Jackson Prof elec eng, 74-86, EMER PROF & SR LECTR ELEC ENG, MASS INST TECHNOL, 86- *Personal Data:* b Detroit, Mich, Feb 5, 16; m 39; c 4. *Educ:* Univ Mich, BSE, 36; Mass Inst Technol, SM, 39. *Prof Exp:* Draftsman, Swift Elec Welder Co, Mich, 36; engr, Ohio Brass Co, 36-38, Farnsworth TV Corp, 39-40 & Scintilla Magneto Div, Bendix Aviation Corp, 40-51; sect head radiation lab, Mass Inst Technol, 41-46; head microwave tube lab, Fed Telecommun Labs Div, Int Tel & Tel Corp, NJ, 46-48. *Concurrent Pos:* Mem steering comt, Kanpur Indo-Am Prog, 61-65; vis prof, Indian Inst Technol, Kanpur, 65-66; NSF Working Group Sci & Eng Instr, India; mem comt telecommun, Nat Acad Eng; bd govs, Israel Inst Technol. *Mem:* Nat Acad Eng; Am Phys Soc; fel Inst Elec & Electronics Engrs; fel Am Acad Arts & Sci. *Res:* Plasma physics; technology assessment. *Mailing Add:* Dept Elec Eng Mass Inst Technol 38-294 Cambridge MA 02139

SMULOW, JEROME B, ORAL PATHOLOGY, PERIODONTOLOGY. *Current Pos:* From instr to assoc prof, 60-68, PROF PERIODONT, SCH DENT MED, TUFTS UNIV, 69- *Personal Data:* b New York, NY, July 29, 30; m 68; c 1. *Educ:* NY Univ, AB, 51, DDS, 55; Tufts Univ, MS, 61, cert, 64. *Concurrent Pos:* Fulbright-Hays fel, Iran, 72-73. *Mem:* AAAS; Tissue Cult Asn; Am Dent Asn; Int Asn Dent Res. *Res:* Histopathology; tissue cultures. *Mailing Add:* 673 Boylston St Brookline MA 02146

SMULSON, MARK ELLIOTT, BIOCHEMISTRY. *Current Pos:* from asst prof to assoc prof, 67-78, PROF BIOCHEM, GEORGETOWN UNIV, SCH MED & DENT, 78- *Personal Data:* b Baltimore, Md, Mar 25, 36; m 66; c 2. *Educ:* Washington & Lee Univ, AB, 58; Cornell Univ, MNS, 61, PhD(biochem), 71. *Prof Exp:* Fel biochem, Albert Einstein Med Ctr, 64-65; USPHS fel, Nat Cancer Inst, 65-67. *Mem:* Am Asn Cancer Res; Am Soc Biol Chemists. *Res:* Molecular biology; poly adenosine diphosphoribose polymerase in control of DNA replication and in nucleosomal structure of chromatin; carcinogens interaction with nucleosomes. *Mailing Add:* Dept Biochem Georgetown Univ Sch Med 3900 Reservoir Rd NW Washington DC 20007-2195. *Fax:* 202-687-7186

SMULYAN, HAROLD, INTERNAL MEDICINE, CARDIOLOGY. *Current Pos:* from instr to assoc prof, 59-72, PROF MED, STATE UNIV NY UPSTATE MED CTR, 71- *Personal Data:* b Philadelphia, Pa, Jan 2, 29; m 52, Ruth Finkelstein; c Susan R, Lisa & Betsy. *Educ:* Univ Pa, AB, 49; Univ Buffalo, MD, 53. *Prof Exp:* Chief cardiol, State Univ NY Health Sci Ctr, Syracuse, 82-96. *Concurrent Pos:* chief cardiol, Vet Admin Med Ctr Hosp, Syracuse, 78-82; pres elect, New York Cardiological Soc. *Mem:* Am Fedn Clin Res; NY Acad Sci; Am Heart Asn; Am Col Cardiol. *Res:* Hypertension; circulatory control; exercise physiology; arterial distensibility. *Mailing Add:* Dept Med 750 E Adams St State Univ NY Health Sci Ctr Syracuse NY 13210

SMURA, BRONISLAW BERNARD, CHEMICAL ENGINEERING. *Current Pos:* ADV, PRESSURE VESSEL SERV, 89- *Personal Data:* b Solvay, NY, Aug 9, 30; m 52; c 3. *Educ:* Syracuse Univ, BChE, 52, MChE, 54, PhD(chem eng), 68. *Prof Exp:* Res engr, Indust Chem Div, Allied Chem Corp, 57-79; mgr process eng, Linden Chem & Plastics Corp, 80-89. *Mem:* Am Inst Chem Engrs. *Res:* Industrial inorganic chemicals with recent major emphasis on electrolytic production of chlorine and caustic soda. *Mailing Add:* 4051 S St Marcellus NY 13108

SMUTNY, EDGAR JOSEF, ORGANIC CHEMISTRY. *Current Pos:* res chemist, 55-68, res supvr, 68-72, SR STAFF CHEMIST, SHELL DEVELOP CO, 72- *Personal Data:* b New York, NY, Apr 20, 28. *Educ:* Univ Colo, BA, 48; Univ Minn, PhD(chem), 53. *Prof Exp:* Mem staff, Allied Chem & Dye Corp, 48-49; asst org chem, Univ Minn, 50-52; res fel, Calif Inst Technol, 53-55. *Mem:* Am Chem Soc; The Chem Soc. *Res:* Small ring compounds; strain energy; photochemistry; free radical chemistry; heterocyclic chemistry; organometallic chemistry; sulfur compounds; homogeneous palladium catalysis; heterogeneous catalysis; fuels and lubricant research. *Mailing Add:* 2306 Windsor Houston TX 77006-1725

SMUTS, MARY ELIZABETH, DEVELOPMENTAL BIOLOGY. *Current Pos:* REGIONAL TOXICOLOGIST, REGION I, US ENVIRON PROTECTION AGENCY, 83- *Personal Data:* b Waterbury, Conn, Mar 15, 48; m 72. *Educ:* Albertus Magnus Col, BA, 70; Temple Univ, PhD(develop biol), 75; Harvard Sch Pub Health, MS, 84. *Prof Exp:* Res fel, Lab Develop Biol & Anomalies, Nat Inst Dent Res, NIH, 74-76; asst prof develop biol, Cath Univ Am, 76-78; asst prof biol, Wheaton Col, 78-83. *Mem:* Soc Develop Biol; Am Soc Cell Biol; Am Soc Zoologist; Soc Risk Anal. *Res:* Cranio-facial development. *Mailing Add:* US Environ Protection Agency JFK Fed Bldg Boston MA 02203-0001

SMUTZ, MORTON, CHEMICAL ENGINEERING. *Current Pos:* RETIRED. *Personal Data:* b Twin Falls, Idaho, Jan 10, 18; m 45, 70. *Educ:* Kans State Col, BS, 40, MS, 41; Univ Wis, PhD(chem eng), 50. *Prof Exp:* Chem engr, Monsanto Chem Co, 41; asst prof chem eng, Bucknell Univ, 49-51; assoc prof, Iowa State Univ, 51-55, prof & head dept, 55-61; asst dir, Ames Lab, US Atomic Energy Comn, 55-64, dep dir, 64-69; chmn, Coastal & Oceanog Eng Dept, Col Eng, Univ Fla, 75-78, assoc dean eng res & prof chem eng, 69-79; sr prof engr, Nat Oceanic & Atmospheric Admin, 79-85. *Concurrent Pos:* Dir, Div Marine Sci, Instrument Soc Am, 82-84. *Mem:* Am Chem Soc; Am Soc Eng Educ; Am Inst Chem Engrs; Coastal Soc (secy, 77). *Res:* Laser raman spectroscopy, optical fibers. *Mailing Add:* 5901 Montrose Rd N-1302 Rockville MD 20852-4753

SMYERS, WILLIAM HAYS, parapol-a styrene-isobutylene copolymer; deceased, see previous edition for last biography

SMYLIE, DOUGLAS EDWIN, GEOPHYSICS. *Current Pos:* PROF EARTH SCI, YORK UNIV, 72- *Personal Data:* b New Liskeard, Ont, June 22, 36; wid; c 4. *Educ:* Queen's Univ, Ont, BSc, 58; Univ Toronto, MA, 59, PhD(physics), 63. *Prof Exp:* Fel geophys, Univ Toronto, 64; asst prof, Univ Western Ont, 64-68; from asst prof to assoc prof, Univ BC, 68-72. *Concurrent Pos:* Nat Res Coun Can operating grant, 65- *Mem:* Am Geophys Union; fel Royal Astron Soc. *Res:* Rotation of the earth; Chandler wobble; main magnetic field; elasticity theory of dislocations; dynamics of the earth's core. *Mailing Add:* Dept Earth Sci York Univ 4700 Keele St North York ON M3J 1P3 Can

SMYLIE, ROBERT EDWIN, MECHANICAL ENGINEERING. *Current Pos:* RETIRED. *Personal Data:* b Lincoln Co, Miss, Dec 25, 29; c 3. *Educ:* Miss State Univ, BSc, 52, MSc, 56; Mass Inst Technol, MSc, 67. *Honors & Awards:* Except Serv Medal, NASA, 69; Victor Prather Award, 71. *Prof Exp:* Indust engr, Ethyl Corp, Tex, 52-54; instr mech eng, Miss State Univ, 54-56; lead engr, Skybolt Missile Syst Thermo-Conditioning Systs, Douglas Aircraft Co, Calif, 56-62; chief, Apollo Support Off, Crew Systs Div, Manned Spacecraft Ctr, Goddard Space Flight Ctr, 62-66, asst chief div, 67-68, actg chief, 68-70, chief, Crew Systs Div, 70-76, dep dir, 76-87. *Concurrent Pos:* Mem US deleg engaged in discussions with USSR to establish common docking systems for spacecraft of the two countries. *Mem:* Am Inst Aeronaut & Astronaut. *Res:* Analyses, design and development in specific advanced system areas such as space suits, extravehicular activity support hardware and environmental and thermal control subsystems. *Mailing Add:* 11919 Winstead Lane Reston VA 20194

SMYRL, WILLIAM HIRAM, PHYSICAL CHEMISTRY, ELECTROCHEMISTRY. *Current Pos:* MEM TECH STAFF, SANDIA LABS, 72- *Personal Data:* b Brownfield, Tex, Dec 12, 38; m 64; c 2. *Educ:* Tex Tech, BS, 61; Univ Calif, Berkeley, PhD(chem), 66. *Prof Exp:* Asst prof pharmaceut chem, Univ Calif, San Francisco, 66-68; mem tech staff, Boeing Sci Res Labs, 68-72. *Mem:* Electrochem Soc; Sigma Xi. *Res:* Molten salts; corrosion science; modeling of corrosion and electrochemical processes; photoelectrochemistry; digital measurement of Faradaic impedance of electrochemical and corrosion reactions. *Mailing Add:* 2637 13th Terr NW New Brighton MN 55112-6360

SMYTH, DONALD MORGAN, SOLID STATE CHEMISTRY. *Current Pos:* assoc prof metall, mat eng & chem, Lehigh Univ, 71-73, prof, 73-88, dir, Mat Res Ctr, 71-92, PAUL B REINHOLD PROF, MAT SCI, ENG & CHEM, LEHIGH UNIV, 86- *Personal Data:* b Bangor, Maine, Mar 20, 30; m 51, Elisabeth Luce; c Carolyn & Joanne. *Educ:* Univ Maine, BS, 51; Mass Inst Technol, PhD(inorg chem), 54. *Honors & Awards:* Battery Div Res Award, Electrochem Soc, 60; Edward C Henry Award, Am Ceramic Soc, 87, Kraner Award, 90; Sosman Mem Lectr, 96. *Prof Exp:* Sr engr, Sprague Elec Co, 54-61, head solid state res, 61-71. *Mem:* Nat Acad Eng; Electrochem Soc; Am Inst Chem; Am Ceramic Soc; fel Mat Res Soc; Am Chem Soc. *Res:* Defect chemistry of complex metal oxides; effect of composition, impurities and nonstoichiometry on properties of insulating, semiconducting and superconducting oxides. *Mailing Add:* Mat Res Ctr Lehigh Univ 5 E Packer Ave Bethlehem PA 18015. *Fax:* 610-758-4244; *E-Mail:* dms4@lehigh.edu

SMYTH, JAY RUSSELL, CERAMICS SCIENCE, MATERIALS SCIENCE. *Current Pos:* SR ENG SUPVR, GARRETT AUXILIARY POWER DIV, ALLIED SIGNAL, 85- *Personal Data:* b Trenton, NJ, Apr 24, 39; m; c 5. *Educ:* Rutgers Univ, BS, 61, MS, 63; Pa State Univ, PhD(ceramics sci), 74. *Prof Exp:* Develop engr, Western Elec, Inc, 63-66; supvr prod eng, Mitronic, Inc, 66-68; eng mgr, Nat Berylia Corp, 68-71; from asst prof to assoc prof, Iowa State Univ, 74-81; sr mat engr, Garrett Turbine Engine Co, 81-85. *Mem:* Fel Am Ceramic Soc; Nat Inst Ceramic Engrs; Nat Asn Parliamentarian; Am Soc Metals; Am Inst Parliamentarians. *Res:* Mechanics properties of materials including fracture and deformation; advanced turbine engines; ceramics for turbine engine applications. *Mailing Add:* 223 E Garfield St Tempe AZ 85281

SMYTH, JOHN BRIDGES, ELECTROMAGNETICS, ACOUSTICS. *Current Pos:* PRES & TECH DIR, SMYTH RES ASSOCS, 55- *Personal Data:* b Pembroke, Ga, June 8, 14; m 38; c 4. *Educ:* Univ Ga, BS, 34, MS, 37; Brown Univ, PhD(physics), 42. *Prof Exp:* Teacher high sch, Ga, 34-35; asst physics, Univ Ga, 35-37; physicist, Tenn Eastman Corp, 37-38; asst physics, Brown Univ, 38-42; from assoc physicist to physicist, US Navy Electronics Lab, 42-55. *Concurrent Pos:* Mem int comn II, Int Sci Radio Union. *Mem:* Fel AAAS; Am Phys Soc; Acoust Soc Am; fel Inst Elec & Electronics Eng. *Res:* Galvanomagnetic effects; electromagnetics; atmospheric physics; thermal physics. *Mailing Add:* 3555 Aero Ct San Diego CA 92123

SMYTH, JOSEPH RICHARD, GEOLOGY, MINERALOGY. *Current Pos:* PROF GEOL, UNIV COLO, BOULDER, 84- *Personal Data:* b Louisville, Ky, Oct 10, 44; m 81, Tamsin C McCormick. *Educ:* Va Polytech Inst, BS, 66; Univ Chicago, SM, 68, PhD(mineral), 70. *Prof Exp:* Res fel geol, Harvard Univ, 70-72; vis fel, Lunar Sci Inst, 72-74; res scientist, 74-76; mem staff, Los Alamos Sci Lab, 76-84. *Concurrent Pos:* Vis sr lectr, Univ Cape Town, 75. *Mem:* Mineral Soc Am; Mineral Soc Japan; Am Geophys Union; Meteoritical Soc; Geol Soc Am. *Res:* Crystal chemistry of rock-forming silicates; igneous petrology; radioactive waste isolation. *Mailing Add:* Dept Geol Univ Colo Box 250 Boulder CO 80309-0250. *E-Mail:* joesmyth@vaxf.colorado.edu

SMYTH, MICHAEL P(AUL), ELECTRICAL ENGINEERING, SYSTEMS ANALYSIS. *Current Pos:* assoc prof, 67-71, dir eng, 71-74, PROF, WIDENER UNIV, 71- *Personal Data:* b Albany, NY, Oct 2, 34; m 77, Pamela Phillips; c Sarah. *Educ:* Syracuse Univ, BS, 57, MS, 59; Univ Pa, PhD(elec eng), 63. *Honors & Awards:* Ralph R Tetor Award, Soc Automative Engrs, 74. *Prof Exp:* Elec engr, Gen Elec Co, 57; res asst, Radar Display, Syracuse Univ, 57-59; from instr to asst prof elec eng, Univ Pa, 59-67. *Concurrent Pos:* Ed consult, Bell Tel Co, Pa, 61-; mem, Franklin Inst, 62-; consult, Gen Elec Co, 65-67 & Philadelphia Elec Co, 74. *Mem:* Inst Elec & Electronics Engrs; Am Soc Eng Educ; Soc Automative Engrs. *Res:* Methods of systems analysis; industrial educational methods. *Mailing Add:* Sch Eng Widener Univ Chester PA 19013

SMYTH, NICHOLAS PATRICK DILLON, THORACIC & CARDIOVASCULAR SURGERY. *Current Pos:* RETIRED. *Personal Data:* b Dublin, Ireland, Apr 1, 24; nat US; m 55, Elizabeth; c 5. *Educ:* Nat Univ Ireland, BSc, 46, MSc, 48, MB, BCh, 49; Univ Mich, MS, 54. *Honors & Awards:* Pioneer in Cardiac Pacing & Elechrophysiol, NAm Soc Pacing & Electrophysiol, 92. *Prof Exp:* From instr to assoc prof, Sch Med, George Washington Univ, 58-68, assoc clin prof, 68-83, clin prof surg, 83-; dir surg res, Washington Hosp Ctr, 68-, consult, 70- *Concurrent Pos:* Chief surg, St Elizabeth's Hosp, 60-63, consult, 63-; consult, DC Gen Hosp, 60- & NIH, 70-;

chmn dept surg, Washington Hosp Ctr, 63-68; consult thoracic surg, NIH & Walter Reed Army Med Ctr & Vet Admin Hosp. *Mem:* Am Heart Asn; Am Col Surgeons; Am Asn Thoracic Surg; Am Col Chest Physicians; Am Fedn Clin Res. *Res:* Thoracic and cardiovascular surgery; granted six patents. *Mailing Add:* 4041 Gulfshore Blvd N No 809 Naples FL 34103. *Fax:* 941-263-7805

SMYTH, THOMAS, JR, INSECT PHYSIOLOGY. *Current Pos:* from asst prof to prof, 55-91, EMER PROF ENTOM, PA STATE UNIV, 91- *Personal Data:* b Binghamton, NY, May 12, 27. *Educ:* Princeton Univ, AB, 47; Johns Hopkins Univ, PhD(biol), 52. *Prof Exp:* Res assoc & instr biol, Tufts Univ, 52-55. *Mem:* AAAS. *Res:* Neuromuscular and sensory physiology of arthropods; spider venom neurotoxins. *Mailing Add:* Dept Entom Pa State Univ University Park PA 16802

SMYTHE, CHEVES MCCORD, MEDICINE. *Current Pos:* dean, 70-75, PROF MED, UNIV TEX MED SCH, HOUSTON, 76- *Personal Data:* b Charleston, SC, May 25, 24; m 49; c 6. *Educ:* Harvard Univ, MD, 47. *Prof Exp:* From asst prof to assoc prof, Med Col SC, 57-66, dean sch med, 62-64; dir, Asn Am Med Cols, 66-70. *Concurrent Pos:* Teaching fels med, Harvard Univ, 48-49 & 54-55; teaching fel, Columbia Univ, 50-52, Am Col Physicians & Life Ins Med Res Fund fels, 51-52; Markle fel med, 55-60; dir gen commissioning & opers & prof med, Aga Khan Hosp & Med Col, Karachi, Pakistan, 82, prof med & dean fac Health Sci, 82-85. *Mem:* AMA; Am Fedn Clin Res; Am Col Physicians. *Res:* medical education. *Mailing Add:* 219 Stony Creek Dr Houston TX 77024

SMYTHE, RICHARD VINCENT, ENTOMOLOGY. *Current Pos:* RETIRED. *Personal Data:* b Philadelphia, Pa, June 27, 39; m 62, Mary Souce; c Kathleen (Ramage) & Laura (Champlin). *Educ:* Col Wooster, BA, 61; Univ Wis-Madison, MS, 63, PhD(entom), 66. *Prof Exp:* Entomologist, Southern Forest, Exp Sta, 66-69, proj leader entom, 69-74, staff entomologist, Forest Serv, USDA, 74-76, staff asst dep chief res, 76-77; asst dir continuing res, USDA, 77-82, dept dir, N Cent Forest Esp Sta, Forest Serv, USDA, 82-87. *Concurrent Pos:* Consult, Nat Pest Control Asn, 71-76. *Mem:* AAAS; Entom Soc Am; Sigma Xi; Soc Am Foresters. *Res:* Feeding behavior, physiology and ecology of wood products insects, chiefly subterranean termites. *Mailing Add:* 7910 Oak Hollow Lane Fairfax Station VA 22039. *Fax:* 202-265-1530

SMYTHE, ROBERT C, CIRCUIT THEORY, CRYSTAL FILTERS & RESONATORS. *Current Pos:* FROM VPRES TO SR VPRES, PIEZO TECHNOL, 65-, DIR, 70- *Personal Data:* b Orlando, Fla. *Educ:* Rice Univ, BA, 52, BS, 53; Univ Fla, MS, 57. *Honors & Awards:* W G Cady Award, Inst Elec & Electronics Engrs, 91. *Prof Exp:* Asst vpres, Syst, Inc, 62-65; dir, Sawtek, Inc, 79-87. *Mem:* Fel Inst Elec & Electronics Engrs. *Res:* Linear and nonlinear theory of piezoelectric resonators and filters especially monolithic filters; precision resonator measurement. *Mailing Add:* Piezo Technol Inc PO Box 547859 Orlando FL 32854. *Fax:* 407-293-2979; *E-Mail:* res@piezotech.com

SMYTHE, ROBERT T, STOCHASTIC PROCESSES, BIOSTATISTICS. *Current Pos:* PROF & CHAIR, DEPT STATIST, GEORGE WASHINGTON UNIV, 81- *Personal Data:* b Pittsburgh, Pa, June 23, 41; m 85, Patricia Page; c Dana & Kathy. *Educ:* Oberlin Col, AB, 63; Oxford Univ, BA, 65; Stanford Univ, PhD(math), 69. *Prof Exp:* Asst prof math, Univ Wash, 69-76; from asst prof to assoc prof, Univ Ore, 76-79; sci policy consult, Comt Sci & Technol, US House Rep, 79-81. *Concurrent Pos:* Sci res prog adv, Off Sci Res, USAF, 82-83; vis prof biostatist, Harvard Univ, 85, Univ Wash, 86; consult, Bd Math Sci, Nat Res Coun, 86-88; vis scholar, Australian Nat Univ, 93-94. *Mem:* Fel Inst Math Statist; fel Am Statist Asn; Int Statist Inst; AAAS; Biometric Soc. *Res:* Stochastic processes in biostatistics and in probabilistic analysis of algorithms; problems in bioassay for carcinogens. *Mailing Add:* Dept Statist George Wahington Univ 2035 H St NW Washington DC 20052

SMYTHE, WILLIAM RODMAN, PHYSICS. *Current Pos:* res assoc physics, Univ Colo, Boulder, 57-58, from asst prof to assoc prof, 58-67, chmn nuclear physics lab, 67-69, 81-83, 90-92, PROF PHYSICS, UNIV COLO, BOULDER, 67- *Personal Data:* b Calif, Jan 6, 30; m 54; c 4. *Educ:* Calif Inst Technol, BS, 51, MS, 52, PhD(physics), 57. *Prof Exp:* Engr, Microwave Lab, Gen Elec Co, 56-57. *Mem:* Am Phys Soc. *Res:* Nuclear physics and particle accelerators. *Mailing Add:* 2106 Knollwood Dr Boulder CO 80302-4706

SNADER, KENNETH MEANS, CHROMATOGRAPHIC TECHNIQUES. *Current Pos:* CHEMIST, NATURAL PROD BR, NAT CANCER INST, 87- *Personal Data:* b Harrisburg, Pa, Apr 6, 38; m 60; c 3. *Educ:* Philadelphia Col Pharm & Sci, BSc, 60; Mass Inst Technol, PhD(org chem), 68. *Prof Exp:* Sr investr med chem, Smith, Kline & French Labs, 68-80, asst dir, 80-84; head, Dept Chem, Sea Pharm, Inc, 84-87. *Concurrent Pos:* Lectr, Philadelphia Col Pharm, & Sci, 75-81. *Mem:* Am Chem Soc; AAAS; Am Soc Microbiol. *Res:* Natural products isolation and structure determination; marine natural products; microbial metabolites, antibiotics and mycotoxins; synthetic medicinal chemistry; anti-inflammatory oxygen heterocycles; immunological RNA; nuclear magnetic resonance and mass spectroscopy interpretations; high performance liquid chromatography. *Mailing Add:* Pharmaceut Res Branch Nat Cancer Inst Fairview 6130 Exec Blvd Ste 818 Rockville MD 20852. *Fax:* 301-846-6178; *E-Mail:* snader@dtpvx2.ncifcrf.gov

SNAPE, WILLIAM J, GASTROINTESTINAL PHYSIOLOGY. *Current Pos:* RETIRED. *Personal Data:* b Camden, NJ, July 18, 12; m 42, Barbara Fleischman; c William J Jr. *Educ:* Univ Penn, AM, 35; Thomas Jefferson Univ, MD, 40. *Mailing Add:* 5801 Crestridge Rd Palos Verdes Peninsula CA 90275-4961

SNAPE, WILLIAM J, JR, GASTROENTEROLOGY. *Current Pos:* PROF MED, SCH MED, UNIV CALIF, LOS ANGELES, 82- *Personal Data:* b Camden, NJ, Aug 24, 43; m; c 2. *Educ:* Jefferson Med Col, Philadelphia, Pa, MD, 69. *Mem:* Am Soc Clin Invest; Am Physiol Soc; Biophys Soc; Am Fedn Clin Res. *Res:* Smooth muscle physiology. *Mailing Add:* Univ Calif Los Angeles Med Ctr Bldg N-21 1124 W Carson St Torrance CA 90502-2052

SNAPER, ALVIN ALLYN, RESEARCH ADMINISTRATION. *Current Pos:* PRES, NEO-DYNE RES CORP, 82- *Personal Data:* b Hudson Co, NJ, Sept 9, 27; m 49; c 3. *Educ:* McGill Univ, BS, 49. *Prof Exp:* Sr chemist, Bakelite Div, Union Carbide Corp, 50-52; chief chemist, McGraw Colorgraph Co, 52-55; vpres, Marcal Electro-Sonics Co, 55-61 & Houston Fearless Corp, 61-63; consult, Marquardt Corp, 63-64; dir res, Fed Res & Develop Corp, 64-66; consult, Aerospace Corp, 66-70; vpres, Advan Patent Technol, Inc, 69-80; pres, Nicoa Corp, 81-82. *Concurrent Pos:* Consult, US Libr Cong, 67- & USAF Missile Command, 68-; corp staff consult, Telecommun Industs Inc, 72-, Multi-Arc Vacuum Systs, Inc, 82- & Am Methyl Corp, 82-87. *Mem:* Sr mem AAAS; sr mem Am Ord Asn; sr mem Soc Photo-Optical Instrument Eng; sr mem Instrument Soc Am. *Res:* Basic research in ultrasonics for environmental waste treatment and biological effects on bacteria and virus; inter-disciplinary technology. *Mailing Add:* 2800 Cameo Circle Las Vegas NV 89107

SNAPP, THOMAS CARTER, JR, ORGANIC CHEMISTRY, ANALYTICAL CHEMISTRY. *Current Pos:* Develop assoc, 74-78, dept head, 70-81, CHEMIST, TEX EASTMAN CO, 63-, ASST DIV HEAD, 81- *Personal Data:* b Suffolk, Va, Aug 23, 38; m 60; c 1. *Educ:* ETenn State Col, BS, 59; Univ Miss, PhD(org & anal chem), 64. *Mem:* Catalysis Soc; Am Chem Soc. *Res:* Cyclodehydrogenation reactions; organic syntheses by heterogenious catalytic vapor phase reactions; surface catalysis; epoxidation and organic peracid chemistry; chemistry of lactones. *Mailing Add:* 112 Periwinkle Pl Kingsport TN 37660

SNAPPER, ERNST, PHILOSOPHY OF MATHEMATICS. *Current Pos:* prof, 63-71, B P CHENEY PROF MATH, DARTMOUTH COL, 71- *Personal Data:* b Groningen, Neth, Dec 2, 13; nat US; m 41, Ethel Klein; c John W & James R. *Educ:* Princeton Univ, MA, 39, PhD(math), 41. *Hon Degrees:* MA, Dartmouth Col, 63. *Honors & Awards:* Carl B Allendoerfer Award, Math Asn Am, 80. *Prof Exp:* Instr math, Princeton Univ, 41-45; from asst prof to prof, Univ Southern Calif, 45-55; Andrew Jackson Buckingham prof, Miami Univ, 55-58; prof, Ind Univ, 58-63. *Concurrent Pos:* Vis assoc prof, Princeton Univ, 49-50, vis prof, 54-55; NSF fel, Harvard Univ, 53-54. *Mem:* AAAS; Am Math Soc; Math Asn Am. *Res:* Algebra; geometry; combinatorial theory; philosophy of mathematics. *Mailing Add:* Dept Math Dartmouth Col Hanover NH 03755

SNAPPER, JAMES ROBERT, PULMONARY MEDICINE, CRITICAL CARE MEDICINE. *Current Pos:* from asst prof to assoc prof, 79-91, PROF MED, VANDERBILT UNIV, 91- *Personal Data:* b Los Angeles, Calif, May 23, 48; m 72, Joyce B Tenney; c Emily K & Hannah S. *Educ:* Princeton Univ, AB, 70; Dartmouth Med Sch, BMS, 72, Harvard Med Sch, MD, 74. *Prof Exp:* Intern, Mass Gen Hosp, 74-75, resident, 75-76, clin fel internal med, 76-79; res fel, Peter Bent Brigham/Harvard Sch Pub Health, 76-79, resident, 78-79. *Concurrent Pos:* Sr investr, Pulmonary Res, Ctr Lung Res, Vanderbilt Univ, 86- *Mem:* Am Physiol Soc; Am Thoracic Soc; Am Col Chest Physicians; Am Fedn Clin Res; Am Col Physicians. *Res:* Role of mediators and the pathophysiologic mechanisms responsible for acute lung injury and altered airway responsiveness. *Mailing Add:* Dept Med T 1219 Med Ctr N Vanderbilt Univ Sch Med Nashville TN 37232-2650

SNARE, LEROY EARL, AERONAUTICS, ASTRONAUTICS. *Current Pos:* PHYSICS INSTR, IVY TECH STATE COL, 91- *Personal Data:* b Garden City, Mo, Nov 6, 31; m 60, Mary L Seabright; c Jon, Sarah & Judy. *Educ:* Univ Mo-Kansas City, BA, 53, MS, 59; Mass Inst Technol, MS, 62. *Prof Exp:* Gen res physicist, Systs Anal Div, Naval Avionics Ctr, 59-62, chief, Dynamic Anal & Simulation Br, 62-72, res physicist, 72-76, dir, Systs Anal Div, 76-80, dep dir, Appl Res Dept, 80-84, dep dir, Eng Dept, 84-86, res coordr for avionics, 86-91. *Mem:* Sr mem Inst Elec & Electronics Engrs; Am Asn Physics Teachers. *Res:* Alignment of inertial navigation systems; design, development and testing of alignment and filtering programs for airborne computers; auxiliary equipment for aligning inertial navigation systems aboard ships; analysis and conceptual design of air-to-surface missile systems and electronic intelligence systems. *Mailing Add:* Ivy Tech State Col Gen Educ Support Serv Div One W 26th St Indianapolis IN 46206-1763. *Fax:* 317-921-4586; *E-Mail:* lsnare@ivy.tec.in.us

SNARR, JOHN FREDERIC, PHYSIOLOGY. *Current Pos:* Asst prof, 67-73, assoc dean student affairs, 75-90, ASSOC PROF PHYSIOL, MED SCH, NORTHWESTERN UNIV, 73-, ASSOC DEAN STUDENT PROGS, 90- *Personal Data:* b Cincinnati, Ohio, Jan 3, 39; m 60; c 2. *Educ:* Univ Cincinnati, EE, 61; Drexel Inst, MS, 62; Northwestern Univ, PhD(physiol), 67. *Res:* Quantification of nutrient supply system operation and regulation. *Mailing Add:* Assoc Dean Student Progs Med Sch Northwestern Univ Chicago IL 60611

SNAVELY, BENJAMIN BRENEMAN, QUANTUM ELECTRONICS, SOLID STATE PHYSICS. *Current Pos:* PROG DIR, DIV ASTRON SCI, NSF, 91- *Personal Data:* b Lancaster, Pa, Jan 6, 36; m 61, Sabine von Dem Knesebeck; c Judith & Eric. *Educ:* Swarthmore Col, BS, 57; Princeton Univ, MSE, 59; Cornell Univ, PhD(eng physics), 62. *Prof Exp:* Sr res physicist, Eastman Kodak Co, 62-65, res assoc solid state physics, Res Labs, 65-69, head, Solid State & Molecular Physics Lab, 69-73; assoc div leader, Laser Div, Lawrence Livermore Lab, 73-75; asst dir, Physics Div, Eastman Kodak Co, 75-81, tech asst to dir res, Res Lab, 81-83, asst dir, Image Rec Div, 83-85, asst gen mgr, advan technol prod, Fed Systs Div, 85-91. *Concurrent Pos:* Vis prof, Phys-Chem Inst, Univ Marburg, 68-69; assoc prof, Inst Optics, Univ Rochester. *Mem:* Am Phys Soc; fel Optical Soc Am; Inst Elec & Electronics Engrs; Am Astron Soc. *Res:* Photoconductivity in silver halides and II-VI compounds; electronic and optical properties of thin films; electroluminescence; organic dye lasers; tunable lasers; laser induced photochemistry; electro-optical imaging systems. *Mailing Add:* 27 Countryside Rd Fairport NY 14450. *Fax:* 703-306-0525; *E-Mail:* bsnavely@usf.gov

SNAVELY, CLOYD A(RTEN), CHEMICAL & METALLURGICAL ENGINEERING. *Current Pos:* PRES, TECHNOVATION ENTERPRISES, INC, 80- *Personal Data:* b Massillon, Ohio, May 8, 17; m 41; c 3. *Educ:* Columbia Univ, BA, 39, BS, 40, MS, 41; Ohio State Univ, PhD(metall eng), 47. *Prof Exp:* Metall observer, Repub Steel Corp, Ohio, 40; res engr, Battelle Mem Inst, 47-49, asst div chief, 49-54, asst mgr, Chem Eng Dept, 54-60; gen mgr, Sifco Metachem, Steel Improv & Forge Co, 60-61; tech adv, Battelle Mem Inst, 61-63, tech admin, Battelle Develop Corp, 63-66, mgr develop dept, 66-69; pres, Technovation Mgt, Inc & Develop Eng, Inc, 69-70; tech consult, Nat Stand Co, 70-72, res projs mgr, 72-80. *Mem:* Am Soc Metals; Electrochem Soc. *Res:* Metallurgical processes, materials technology; industrial waste treatment; invention development; patents; coal gasification and liquefaction; chemical use of atomic hydrogen. *Mailing Add:* 3342 Henderson Rd Columbus OH 43220

SNAVELY, DEANNE LYNN, PHYSICAL CHEMISTRY. *Current Pos:* ASST PROF PHYS CHEM, BOWLING GREEN STATE UNIV, 85- *Personal Data:* b Columbus, Ohio, Nov 16, 51; m 82; c 1. *Educ:* Ohio State Univ, BS, 77; Yale Univ, PhD(phys chem), 83. *Prof Exp:* Res scholar, Stanford Univ, 83-85; assoc res scientist, Yale Univ, 85. *Mem:* Am Phys Soc. *Res:* Infrared absorption spectroscopy of supersonic jets of polyatomic molecules, vibrational and rotational analysis; photoacoustic absorbtion spectroscopy of highly excited vibrational states in gas phase molecules; kinetic studies of reactions initiated by laser pumping of highly excited vibrational states in gas phase molecules; vibrational spectroscopy of molecules; photoinitiated reaction kinetics. *Mailing Add:* Chem Bowling Green State Univ 1001 E Wooster St Bowling Green OH 43403-0001

SNAVELY, EARL SAMUEL, JR, PHYSICAL CHEMISTRY. *Current Pos:* RETIRED. *Personal Data:* b Brackettville, Tex, Apr 10, 27; m 53, Anne Johnston; c 1. *Educ:* Agr & Mech Col, Tex, BS, 47; Univ Tex, MA, 50, PhD, 58. *Prof Exp:* Chemist, Oyster Mortality Proj, Res Found, Agr & Mech Col, Tex, 47-48; chemist, Southern Alkali Corp, 50-51; res scientist, Defense Res Lab, Univ Tex, 51-58; chemist, Oak Ridge Nat Lab, 58-60; dir chem res, Tracor, Inc, 60-66; sr res chemist, Mobil Oil Corp, Tex, 66-68, res assoc, Field Res Lab, 68-80, eng consult, Mobil Oil Res & Develop Corp, 80-87. *Concurrent Pos:* Ed, Corrosion Div, J Electrochem Soc. *Mem:* Sigma Xi. *Res:* Electrochemistry; corrosion; surface chemistry; environmental science. *Mailing Add:* 2610 Oak Cliff Lane Arlington TX 76012

SNAVELY, PARKE DETWEILER, JR, GEOLOGY. *Current Pos:* From jr geologist to supvry geologist, US Geol Surv, 42-53, supvr, Pac Region, 53-59, res geologist, 59-60, chief, Pac Coast Br, 60-66, chief, Off Marine Geol & Hydrol, 66-69, asst chief geologist, 69-71, SR RES GEOLOGIST, OFF MARINE GEOL, US GEOL SURV, 71- *Personal Data:* b Yakima, Wash, Apr 7, 19; m 42; c 3. *Educ:* Univ Calif, Los Angeles, BA, 41, MA, 51. *Concurrent Pos:* Chmn marine geol panel, US-Japan Coop Prog Natural Resources, 70-; res assoc, Univ Calif, Santa Barbara, 69-76. *Mem:* Fel Geol Soc Am; Am Asn Petrol Geologists. *Res:* Tertiary geology and mineral resource potential of western Oregon and Washington and adjacent continental shelf; relation of plate tectonics to structural, stratigraphic, and igneous history of Pacific coast states. *Mailing Add:* 1210 Larnel Pl Los Altos CA 94024

SNAZELLE, THEODORE EDWARD, MICROBIOLOGY. *Current Pos:* prof biol, 80-96, PROF & CHAIR, MISS COL, CLINTON, 96- *Personal Data:* b Richmond, Ind, Aug 30, 41; m 61; c 2. *Educ:* Belmont Col, BS, 65; Purdue Univ, MS, 68, PhD(plant path), 70. *Prof Exp:* Instr biol, Rocky Valley Col, Rockford, Ill, 70-72; asst prof biol, Univ Tenn, Nashville, 72-74, assoc prof, 74-79, coordr, 75-79, prof, 79; prof biol, Tenn State Univ, 79-80. *Concurrent Pos:* Vis researcher, Gulf Coast Res Lab, Ocean Springs, Miss, 75. *Mem:* Am Soc Microbiol; Sigma Xi. *Res:* Pigment production in Bacillus cereus; Narcissus diseases and pests. *Mailing Add:* Dept Biol Sci Box 4045 Miss Col Clinton MS 39058. *Fax:* 601-925-3804; *E-Mail:* snazelle@mc.edu

SNEAD, CLARENCE LEWIS, JR, SOLID STATE PHYSICS. *Current Pos:* from asst physicist to assoc physicist, Brookhaven Nat Labs, 67-71, ed, Sect A, Phys Rev & Res Collabr, 71-74, assoc physicist, 74-80, physicist, Mat Sci Dept, 80-84, PHYSICIST, DEPT NUCLEAR ENERGY, BROOKHAVEN NAT LAB, 84-, DIV HEAD, NEUTRAL BEAM DIV, 89- *Personal Data:* b Richmond, Va, Sept 25, 36; m 60; c 3. *Educ:* Univ Richmond, BS, 59; Univ NC, PhD(physics), 65. *Prof Exp:* Res assoc physics, Univ NC, 65; res assoc mat sci, Northwestern Univ, 65-67. *Concurrent Pos:* Consult ed, Phys Rev, 74-90. *Mem:* Am Phys Soc; Am Inst Mech Engrs; Metall Soc. *Res:* Radiation effects, especially in type II superconductors and metals; positron annihilation studies in defects in metals; internal-friction studies of defects; high-energy proton irradiation effects. *Mailing Add:* Dept Nuclear Eng Brookhaven Nat Lab Bldg 830 Upton NY 11973-5000

SNEAD, LARRY L, INTERNATIONAL FISHERIES RELATIONS. *Current Pos:* DIR MARINE CONSERV, OFF MARINE CONSERV, DEPT STATE, 82- *Personal Data:* b Salina, Kans, July 21, 38; m, Joan Elizabeth Schwalm; c 3. *Educ:* Morgan State Univ, BS, 63. *Prof Exp:* Dir, Int Affairs, US Nat Marine Fishery Serv, US Dept Com, 62-63, chief, Int Negotiations Div, 75-76; sr foreign affairs officer, Atlantic Fisheries, US State Dept, 76-78. *Mailing Add:* Bur Oceans & Int Environ & Sci Affairs US Dept State Washington DC 20520. *Fax:* 202-736-7350

SNEAD, O CARTER, III, CHILD NEUROLOGY. *Current Pos:* AT NEUROL DIV, HOSP SICK CHILDREN, TORONTO, CAN. *Personal Data:* b Princeton, WVa, Oct 24, 43. *Educ:* Univ WVa, MD, 70. *Prof Exp:* prof pediat neurophysiol, Sch Med, Univ Ala, Birmingham, 84-; Neurol Div, Children's Hosp, Los Angeles. *Mailing Add:* Neurol Div Hosp for Sick Children 555 University Ave Toronto ON M5G 1X8 Can

SNEADE, BARBARA HERBERT, ANALYTICAL CHEMISTRY. *Current Pos:* TECH DIR, HF SCI, INC, 80- *Personal Data:* b Altoona, Pa, Nov 15, 47; m 69; c 2. *Educ:* Bridgewater Col, BA, 65; Nova Univ, MBA, 85. *Prof Exp:* Res assoc, Am Tobacco Co, 69-71; lab dir, Lee County Sheriff's Dept, 73-77; teacher math & sci, Lee County Schools, 71-73 & 77-80. *Mem:* Am Chem Soc; Am Asn Clin Chem; Am Soc Qual Control. *Res:* Turbidity; characterization of zero and development of permanent standards. *Mailing Add:* 2020 Pinebark Lane Clayton NC 27520-8805

SNECK, HENRY JAMES, (JR), MECHANICAL ENGINEERING. *Current Pos:* from instr to assoc prof, 53-76, PROF MECH ENG, RENSSELAER POLYTECH INST, 76- *Personal Data:* b Schenectady, NY, Nov 9, 26; m 52; c 3. *Educ:* Rensselaer Polytech Inst, BME, 51, PhD(mech eng), 63; Yale Univ, MEng, 52. *Prof Exp:* Jr engr, Eastman Kodak Co, 51; test engr, Gen Elec Co, 52-53. *Concurrent Pos:* Consult, Corp Res & Develop Ctr, Gen Elec Co, 53- *Mem:* AAAS; Am Soc Mech Engrs; Sigma Xi. *Res:* Bearings, seals, lubrication, atmospheric thermal pollution. *Mailing Add:* 21 Bolivar Ave Troy NY 12180

SNECKENBERGER, JOHN EDWARD, MANUFACTURING ENGINEERING. *Current Pos:* From asst prof to assoc prof, 70-81, PROF MECH ENG, WVA UNIV, 81- *Personal Data:* b Hagerstown, Md, Aug 17, 37; m 68, Mary Hansbrough; c Deborah, Julie & Sharon. *Educ:* WVa Univ, BS, 64, MS, 66, PhD(eng), 69. *Concurrent Pos:* Eng, IBM, 83; consult, DuPont, 84-89. *Mem:* Am Soc Mech Engrs; Am Soc Eng Educ; Soc Mfg Engrs. *Res:* Engineering systems design, automation and control; concurrent engineering. *Mailing Add:* 521 Woodhaven Dr Morgantown WV 26505-3309

SNEDAKER, SAMUEL CURRY, ECOLOGY. *Current Pos:* prof biol & living resources, Univ Miami, 75-82, prof marine affairs, 82-86, prof biol & living resources, 86-89, PROF MARINE BIOL & FISHERIES, UNIV MIAMI, 89- *Personal Data:* b Long Beach, Calif, May 22, 38; m 68; c 4. *Educ:* Univ Fla, BSA & BSF, 61, MS, 63, PhD(ecol), 70. *Prof Exp:* Res assoc ecol, 68-69, asst prof, 70-73, asst prof ecol & environ eng sci, Resource Mgt Systs Prog, 73-74, asst prof aquatic sci, Univ Fla, 71-74, asst prof ecol, Inst Food & Agr Sci, 74-75. *Concurrent Pos:* Res fel, East-West Ctr, Honolulu, Hawaii. *Mem:* AAAS; Am Inst Biol Sci; Asn Trop Biol; Ecol Soc Am. *Res:* Structure and function of tropical lowland and coastal ecosystems with respect to their relationship to man. *Mailing Add:* 7549 SW 58th Ave Miami FL 33143

SNEDDEN, WALTER, experimental medicine, mass spectrometry, for more information see previous edition

SNEDDON, LEIGH, VULNERABILITY OF SPREAD SPECTRUM COMMUNICATIONS, OBJECT ORIENTED SOFTWARE. *Current Pos:* tech staff, 89-91, PROJ MGR, TASC, 91- *Personal Data:* b New South Wales, Australia. *Educ:* Univ Sydney, BSc, 74; Univ S Wales, MSc, 75; Oxford Univ, PhD(physics), 78. *Prof Exp:* Res assoc, Oxford Univ, 78-79, & Princeton Univ, 79-82; asst prof physics, Brandeis Univ, 82-89. *Concurrent Pos:* Consult, Bell Labs, 81-82; vis scientist, Philip Morris Inc, 84-85; vis scientist, Inst Laue Langevin, France, 86-87. *Mem:* Am Phys Soc. *Res:* Vulnerability of spread spectrum communications; non-linear electronic materials; collective phenomena; scientific applications of computers; solid state physics. *Mailing Add:* 197 Eighth St Apt 623 Charlestown MA 02129. *Fax:* 781-942-7100; *E-Mail:* lsneddon@tasc.com

SNEDECOR, JAMES GEORGE, PHYSIOLOGY. *Current Pos:* from asst prof to assoc prof, 48-57, PROF PHYSIOL, UNIV MASS, AMHERST, 57- *Personal Data:* b Ames, Iowa, June 9, 17; m 44; c 2. *Educ:* Iowa State Univ, BS, 39; Univ Minn, PhD(zool), 47. *Prof Exp:* Asst prof zool, La State Univ, 47-48. *Concurrent Pos:* NIH sr res fel, 55-56. *Mem:* Endocrine Soc; Am Soc Zoologists; Am Physiol Soc. *Res:* Carbohydrate metabolism; avian thyroid physiology. *Mailing Add:* 49 Fairfield Amherst MA 01002

SNEDEGAR, WILLIAM H, NUCLEAR PHYSICS. *Current Pos:* RETIRED. *Personal Data:* b Ward, WVa, Aug 31, 26; m 48, Barbara W Dent; c Robert W & Thomas D. *Educ:* WVa Univ, AB, 48, MS, 49; Univ Ky, PhD(physics), 58. *Prof Exp:* Physicist, Nat Bur Stand, 49-52; instr physics, Wis Col, Superior, 52-53; asst prof, Univ Ky Aid Prog to Univ Indonesia, 57-61; assoc prof physics, Eastern Ky State Col, 61-63; prof & chmn dept, Parsons Col, 63-67; prof physics & chmn dept, Clarion Univ Pa, 67-88. *Mem:* Am Asn Physics Teachers. *Mailing Add:* 1057 E Main St Clarion PA 16214

SNEDEKER, ROBERT A(UDLEY), CHEMICAL ENGINEERING. *Current Pos:* SR VPRES RES & DEVELOP, ARNOX CORP, 87- *Personal Data:* b New York, NY, Aug 3, 28; m 52, Patricia Honeker; c 3. *Educ:* Mass Inst Technol, SB, 50, SM, 51; Princeton Univ, PhD, 56. *Prof Exp:* Engr, Photo Prod Dept, E I du Pont de Nemours & Co, 55-58, res supvr, 58-67; tech dir, Scott Paper Co, 67-70; vpres mfg, Merrimac Paper Co, 70-83. *Mem:* Am Chem Soc; Am Inst Chem Engrs; Sigma Xi; TAPPI; Paper Indust Mgt Asn. *Res:* Polymer fabrication; photopolymerization; coating and drying; papermaking techniques; pollution control; fire retardants. *Mailing Add:* Seven Mashie Way North Reading MA 01864-3423

SNEE, RONALD D, STATISTICS, ORGANIZATIONAL IMPROVEMENT. *Current Pos:* VPRES, OPER RES, NYNEX, 96- *Personal Data:* b Washington, Pa, Dec 11, 41; m 89, Marjorie C Case; c Jennifer E & Victoria K. *Educ:* Washinton & Jefferson Col, BA, 63; Rutgers Univ, MS, 65, PhD(statist), 67. *Honors & Awards:* Brumbaugh Award, 71, Shewell Prize, 72, Wilcoxon Prize, 72, 75 & 81, Youden Prize, 74 & 77, Ellis R Ott Award, 80, Am Soc Qual Control Shewhart Medal, 85, William G Hunter Award, 90. *Prof Exp:* Asst prof statist, Rutgers Univ, 66-68; from statistician to sr statistician, Du Pont Co, 68-75, consult, 75-76, consult supvr statistician, 76-87, qual syst mgr, Dept Eng, 87-91; vpres consult, Joiner Assocs, 92-96. *Concurrent Pos:* Statist fac, Univ Del, 70-75, 84 & 88-96. *Mem:* Fel Am Statist Asn; fel Am Soc Qual Control; Biometrics Soc; fel AAAS; Am Acad Mgt. *Res:* Design and analysis of experiments; data analysis; graphical methods; mixture experiments; model building; statistical thinking; scientific problem solving, quality management, and technology; management systems; process improvement; organizational improvement. *Mailing Add:* 140 N Broadway Unit D2 Irvington NY 10533. *Fax:* 212-395-5287

SNEIDER, ROBERT MORTON, PETROLEUM DEVELOPMENT & EXPLORATION. *Current Pos:* PRES, ROBERT M SNEIDER EXPLOR INC, 81-; PARTNER PETROTECH, 82- *Personal Data:* b Asbury Park, NJ, Mar 2, 29; m 56, Ramona Mexer; c Linda, Timothy & John. *Educ:* Rutgers Univ, BS, 51; Univ Wis, PhD(geol), 62. *Honors & Awards:* Distinguished Serv Award, Am Asn Petrol Geologists, 91. *Prof Exp:* Res geologist, Shell Develop Co, 57-65, res assoc, 65-66, from staff prod geologist to sr staff prod geologist, 66-71, res sect leader geol eng, 71-74; pres, Sneider & Meckel Assocs, Inc, 74-81; partner, Richardson, Sangree & Sneider, 86-92. *Concurrent Pos:* Distinguished lectr, Soc Petrol Engrs, 77-78, Am Asn Petrol Geol, 88-89 & 95. *Mem:* AAAS; Am Geol Inst; hon mem Am Asn Petrol Geologists; Soc Econ Paleontologists & Mineralogists; Soc Prof Well Logging; NY Acad Sci. *Res:* Exploration and reservoir geology and petrophysics of petroleum reservoirs in the Gulf Coast, California, Canadian Rocky Mountains, Alaska, Australia, Southeast Asia. *Mailing Add:* Robert M Sneider Explor, Inc 11767 Katy Fwy Suite 300 Houston TX 77079

SNEIDER, THOMAS W, BIOCHEMISTRY, MOLECULAR BIOLOGY. *Current Pos:* assoc prof, 75-81, assoc chmn biochem, 91-95, PROF BIOCHEM, COLO STATE UNIV, 81-, ASSOC DEAN INSTR & RES, COL NATURAL SCI, 96- *Personal Data:* b Fremont, Ohio, Apr 19, 38; m 65, Judith M Werderitsch; c Matthew N, Stephen G & Kristen J. *Educ:* Univ Detroit, BSc, 61; Marquette Univ, MSc, 63, PhD(physiol), 65. *Prof Exp:* Instr oncol, Univ Wis-Madison, 67-69; from asst prof to assoc prof pharmacol, Baylor Col Med, 69-75. *Concurrent Pos:* NSF fel biochem & oncol, McArdle Lab, Univ Wis-Madison, 65-67; NIH res career develop award, 73-78; chmn, Grad Fac, Cellular & Molecular Biol, Colo State Univ, 78-80; NIH Fogarty Ctr sr int fel, Inst Molecularbiol II, Univ Zurich, 82-83; mem, Nat Res Coun Life Sci Review Panel, 82-85, Nat Sci Found Biochem, Biophys & Molec Biol Review Panel, 84-87. *Mem:* Am Soc Biol Chemists. *Res:* Chemical carcinogenesis; mechanisms and functions of eukaryotic DNA modifications; control of cellular differentiation. *Mailing Add:* Dean's Off Col Natural Scis Colo State Univ Ft Collins CO 80523-1801. *Fax:* 970-491-6639

SNELGROVE, JAMES LEWIS, REACTOR PHYSICS, REACTOR FUEL DEVELOPMENT & TESTING. *Current Pos:* PHYSICIST, ARGONNE NAT LAB, 68- *Personal Data:* b Cookeville, Tenn, Jan 9, 42; m 65, Alice Medley; c Anne C & Sarah M. *Educ:* Tenn Polytech Inst, BS, 64; Mich State Univ, MS, 66, PhD(physics), 68. *Honors & Awards:* IR-100 Award, 85. *Mem:* Am Phys Soc; Am Nuclear Soc; Sigma Xi. *Res:* Development and use of fuels for research and test reactors, including design of reactor cores and testing of new high-density fuels; development of targets for molybdenum-99 production. *Mailing Add:* Technol Develop Div Argonne Nat Lab 9700 S Cass Ave Argonne IL 60439. *Fax:* 630-252-5161; *E-Mail:* jimsnelgrove@anl.gov

SNELL, A(BSALOM) W(EST), AGRICULTURAL ENGINEERING. *Current Pos:* RETIRED. *Personal Data:* b Parler, SC, Apr 29, 24; m 51, Sarah L Oliver; c Rodney M, Nancy K, Carla S (Russell) & Janet E (Snell-Kelly). *Educ:* Clemson Univ, BS, 49; Iowa State Univ, MS, 52; NC State Univ, PhD(agr eng), 64. *Prof Exp:* Asst prof agr eng, Clemson Univ, 49-51; instr & res fel, Iowa State Univ, 51-52; from asst prof to prof & head dept, Clemson Univ, 52-75, chmn directorate, Water Resources Res Inst, 64-75, assoc dir, SC Agr Exp Sta, 75-88. *Mem:* Am Soc Agr Engrs; Sigma Xi. *Res:* Water resources engineering; irrigation; drainage; water movement in soils; agricultural research; administration. *Mailing Add:* 116 Lewis Rd Clemson SC 29631

SNELL, ESMOND EMERSON, BIOCHEMISTRY. *Current Pos:* prof & chmn, Dept Microbiol, 76-80, Ashbel Smith prof, 80-90, EMER ASHBELL SMITH PROF MICROBIOL & CHEM, UNIV TEX, AUSTIN, 90- *Personal Data:* b Salt Lake City, Utah, Sept 22, 14; m 41, Mary Terrill; c Esmond E Jr (deceased), Richard T, Allan G & Margaret A. *Educ:* Brigham Young Univ, BA, 35; Univ Wis, MA, 36, PhD(biochem), 38. *Hon Degrees:* DSc, Univ Wis, 82. *Honors & Awards:* Lilly Award, Am Soc Bacteriologists, 45; Mead Johnson Award, Am Inst Nutrit, 46 & Osborne Mendel Award, 51; Kenneth A Spencer Award, Am Chem Soc, 74; William C Rose Award, Am Soc Biol Chemists, 85. *Prof Exp:* Res assoc chem, Univ Tex, 39-41, from asst prof to prof, 41-56; from assoc prof to prof biochem, Univ Wis, 45-51; prof, Univ Calif, Berkeley, 56-76. *Concurrent Pos:* Guggenheim fel, 54, 62 & 70; ed, Ann Rev Biochem, Ann Rev Inc, 69-83, pres, 72-76. *Mem:* Nat Acad Sci; AAAS; Am Soc Microbiol; Am Soc Biol Chem (pres, 61-62); Am Chem Soc; fel Am Inst Nutrit. *Res:* Metabolism and mechanism of action of vitamin B6; vitamin metabolism and transport; pyruvoyl enzymes; pyridoxal phosphate enzymes. *Mailing Add:* 5001 Greystone Dr Austin TX 87831. *E-Mail:* esnell@aol.com

SNELL, FRED MANGET, BIOPHYSICS. *Current Pos:* RETIRED. *Personal Data:* b Soochow, China, Nov 11, 21; m 46; c 3. *Educ:* Maryville Col, Tenn, AB, 42; Harvard Univ, MD, 45; Mass Inst Technol, PhD(biochem), 52. *Prof Exp:* Intern pediat, Children's Hosp, 45-46, from jr asst resident to asst resident, 48-49; res assoc biol, Mass Inst Technol, 52-54; assoc biochem, Harvard Med Sch, 54-57, asst prof, 57-59; prof biophys & chmn dept, State Univ NY, Buffalo, 59-70, dean grad sch, 67-69, master, Col A, 68-71, prof biophys sci, Sch Med, State Univ NY Buffalo, 70- *Concurrent Pos:* Nat Found Infantile Paralysis fel, Mass Inst Technol, 52-54; Nat Found Infantile Paralysis fel, Children's Med Ctr, 52-54; Palmer sr fel, Harvard Med Sch, 54-57; US Navy rep & mem atomic bomb casualty comn, Comt Atomic Casualties, Nat Res Coun; mem biophys sci training comt, Nat Inst Gen Med Sci, 62-66, chmn, 65-66; mem biophys panel, President's NIH Study Comt, 64; mem interdisciplinary panel, Comn Undergrad Educ Biol Sci, 65, chmn biomath subpanel, 66-68; consult, Comn Undergrad Progs in Math, 65-68; mem adv comt on NIH training progs, Nat Acad Sci-Nat Res Coun; ed, Biophys J, 66-69; vis prof, atmospheric sci, Ore State Univ, Corvallis, 77-78. *Mem:* AAAS; Biophys Soc (pres, 71). *Res:* Membrane processes; global thermodynamics; instructional computer simulations. *Mailing Add:* 9355 Sisson Hwy Eden NY 14057

SNELL, GEORGE DAVIS, genetics, tissue transplantation; deceased, see previous edition for last biography

SNELL, JAMES LAURIE, PROBABILITY. *Current Pos:* from asst prof to assoc prof, 54-62, PROF MATH, DARTMOUTH COL, 62- *Personal Data:* b Wheaton, Ill, Jan 15, 25; m 52; c 2. *Educ:* Univ Ill, BS, 47, MA, 48, PhD(math), 51. *Prof Exp:* Fine instr, Princeton Univ, 51-54. *Mem:* Am Math Soc; Math Asn Am. *Res:* Probability theory. *Mailing Add:* Dept Math Dartmouth Col 6188 Bradley Hall Hanover NH 03755-3551

SNELL, JOHN B, PLASTICS CHEMISTRY. *Current Pos:* Sr chemist, Tape Div, 3M Co, 64-68, res supvr, 68-71, res specialist, Indust Spec Div, 71-84, SR TECH SERV SPECIALIST, SCOTCHLITE GLASS BUBBLE PRODS, 3M CO, 84- *Personal Data:* b Waterbury, Conn, May 10, 36; m 66; c 3. *Educ:* Univ Wis, BSChE, 59; Inst Paper Chem, PhD(phys chem), 64. *Res:* Epoxy resins and curing agents for reinforced plastics and advanced composites; polymers for vibration dampening; surface treatments for glass bubbles. *Mailing Add:* 8241 Deer Pond Ct N Lake Elmo MN 55042

SNELL, JUNIUS FIELDING, biochemistry; deceased, see previous edition for last biography

SNELL, RICHARD SAXON, ANATOMY. *Current Pos:* PROF ANAT & CHMN DEPT, MED SCH, GEORGE WASHINGTON UNIV, 72- *Personal Data:* b Richmond, Eng, May 3, 25; m 49, Maureen Cashin; c Georgina Sara, Nicola Ann, Melanie Jane, Richard Robin & Charles Edward. *Educ:* Univ London, MB, 49, PhD(med), 55, MD, 61. *Prof Exp:* House surgeon, King's Col Hosp, London, 49-53, jr lectr anat, King's Col, London, 49-53, lectr anat & hist, 53-59; lectr anat, Univ Durham, 59-63; from asst prof to assoc prof, Yale Univ, 63-67; prof & chmn dept, NJ Col Med & Dent, 67-69; prof, Univ Ariz, 70-72. *Concurrent Pos:* Med Res Coun Grantee, 59; NIH grantee, 63-65; vis prof, Yale Univ, 69 & Harvard Univ, 70-71, 80 & 86. *Mem:* Am Asn Anatomists; Anat Soc Gt Brit & Ireland. *Res:* Pigmentation of mammalian skin and its control; light and electron microscopic appearances of the skin; histochemistry of cholinesterase in the peripheral and central parts of the nervous system; author of 6 publications. *Mailing Add:* 518 Boston Post Rd Madison CT 06443

SNELL, ROBERT ISAAC, mathematics, for more information see previous edition

SNELL, ROBERT L, ORGANIC CHEMISTRY. *Current Pos:* from asst prof to assoc prof, 59-66, PROF CHEM, E TENN STATE UNIV, 66- *Personal Data:* b El Dorado Springs, Mo, Jan 28, 25; m 55; c 2. *Educ:* Drury Col, BS, 48; Mo Sch Mines, MS, 52; Tex Tech Col, PhD(chem), 59. *Prof Exp:* Chemist, Dowell, Inc, 54-55. *Concurrent Pos:* Adj prof pharmacol, Quillen-Dishner Col Med. *Mem:* Am Chem Soc; Sigma Xi. *Mailing Add:* Rte 8 Johnson City TN 37601-9456

SNELL, ROBERT ROSS, CIVIL ENGINEERING. *Current Pos:* from instr to assoc prof, 57-67, head dept, 72-92, PROF CIVIL ENG, KANS STATE UNIV, 68- *Personal Data:* b St John, Kans, Apr 17, 32; m 52; c 2. *Educ:* Kans State Univ, BS, 54, MS, 60; Purdue Univ, Lafayette, PhD(civil eng struct), 63. *Prof Exp:* Civil engr, Kans State Hwy Comn, 54-55; Ford Found resident, Rust Eng Co, Pa, 67-68. *Mem:* Am Soc Eng Educ; Am Soc Civil Engrs; Nat Soc Prof Engrs. *Res:* Structural analysis and design; systems optimization; structural modeling. *Mailing Add:* 1908 Indiana Lane Manhattan KS 66502

SNELL, RONALD LEE, RADIO ASTRONOMY. *Current Pos:* Res assoc, 79-84, from asst prof to assoc prof, 84-92, PROF PHYSICS & ASTRON, UNIV MASS, 92- *Personal Data:* b Salina, Kans, May 15, 51; m 78. *Educ:* Univ Kans, BA, 73; Univ Tex, Austin, MA, 75, PhD(astron), 79. *Mem:* Am Astron Soc; Int Astron Union. *Res:* Study the structure and dynamics of interstellar clouds and the processes by which stars form through radio frequency observations of the radiation emitted by atoms and molecules in space. *Mailing Add:* GRC Tower B Five Col Radio Astron Observ Univ Mass Amherst MA 01003. *E-Mail:* snell@fcraol.phast.umass.edu

SNELL, TERRY WAYNE, POPULATION BIOLOGY, AQUATIC TOXICOLOGY. *Current Pos:* ASSOC PROF BIOL, GA INST TECHNOL, 91- *Personal Data:* b Dec 23, 48; m 83, Sandra M Malafronte; c Sara J. *Educ:* Fla Southern Col, BS, 70; Univ SFla, MS, 73, PhD(pop biol), 77. *Prof Exp:* Asst prof, Wright State Univ, 78-79; From asst prof to assoc prof, Univ Tampa, 79-91. *Mem:* Am Soc Limnol & Oceanog; AAAS; Soc Environ Toxicol & Chem; World Asn Copepodologists. *Res:* Evolution of reproductive isolation in zoo plankton populations; biochemical responses of aquatic animals to pollution induced stress. *Mailing Add:* Sch Biol Ga Inst Technol Atlanta GA 30332-0230. *E-Mail:* terry.snell@biology.gatech.edu

SNELL, WILLIAM J, SIGNAL TRANSDUCTION, FERTILIZATION. *Current Pos:* PROF CELL BIOL & NEUROSCI, SOUTHWESTERN MED CTR, UNIV TEX, DALLAS, 77- *Personal Data:* b LaSalle, Ill, Oct 11, 46; m 68; c 2. *Educ:* Univ Ill, BS, 68; Yale Univ, PhD(cell & develop biol), 75. *Concurrent Pos:* Prin investr, NIH & NSF grants. *Mem:* Am Soc Cell Biol; Sigma Xi; AAAS. *Res:* Cell-cell interactions during fertilization in chlamydomonas; signal transduction induced by cell contact; activation of adenylyl cyclose by a novel mechanism. *Mailing Add:* Dept Cell Biol & Neurosci Univ Tex Southwestern Med Ctr 5323 Harry Hines Blvd Dallas TX 75235-9039. *Fax:* 214-648-8694; *E-Mail:* snell03@utsw.swmed.edu

SNELLING, CHRISTOPHER, ELECTRICAL ENGINEERING, MATHEMATICS. *Current Pos:* scientist, 72-76, tech specialist/proj mgr I, 76-80, MEM RES STAFF, XEROX CORP, 81- *Personal Data:* b Hartford, Conn, Nov 8, 35; m 59; c 1. *Educ:* Union Col, NY, BEE, 57; Univ Rochester, MS, 64. *Prof Exp:* Assoc physicist, Haloid Corp, 57-60, physicist, Haloid-Xerox, 60-62, sr physicist, Xerox Corp, 62-65, scientist, 65-68; proj engr, Hamco Mach & Electronics Corp, 68-72. *Mem:* Inst Elec & Electronics Engrs; Soc Photographic Scientists & Engrs; Sigma Xi. *Res:* Measurement and analysis of xerographic photoreceptors; xerographic process studies; electrostatics; photoconductivity; radiometry; direct current instrumentation; development of Czochralski silicon crystal growing furnaces for semiconductor production. *Mailing Add:* 5 High Meadow Dr Penfield NY 14526

SNELLINGS, WILLIAM MORAN, TOXICOLOGY, INHALATION TOXICOLOGY. *Current Pos:* DIR, IND CHEM DIV, UNION CARBIDE CHEM & PLASTICS, INC, 89- *Personal Data:* b Norfolk, Va, May 7, 47; m 70; c 3. *Educ:* Va Polytech Inst, BS, 69; Univ Mich, PhD(toxicol), 76. *Prof Exp:* Sr technician, Hazelton Labs, 69-71; toxicologist, Carnegie-Mellon Inst Res, 76-80; mgr inhalation toxicol, Bushy Run Res Ctr, 80-81, from asst dir to assoc dir, 81-89. *Concurrent Pos:* Prin investr, Ethylene Oxide Toxicity Prog Worldwide Consortium Ethylene Oxide Toxicity Producers, 76-81. *Mem:* Soc Toxicol; Soc Toxicol Inhalation Specialty Sect. *Res:* Toxicity evaluation of various industrial chemicals; assessment of the oncogenic, developmental, reproductive and general toxic effects of test chemicals; design and development of inhalation chambers, vapor generators, aerosol generators, and atmospheric sampling systems. *Mailing Add:* 23 Trails End Lane Ridgefield CT 06877

SNELLMAN, LEONARD W, METEOROLOGY. *Current Pos:* RETIRED. *Personal Data:* b Lansford, Pa, June 27, 20; m 48; c 4. *Educ:* Kenyon Col, AB, 43. *Honors & Awards:* Silver Medal, Dept of Com, 69; Gold Medal, 78; Spec Award for Voyager Flight Support AMS, 87. *Prof Exp:* Forecaster, US Weather Bur, 46-51; civilian consult meteorol, US Air Force-Hq Air Weather Serv, 53-65; chief, Sci Serv Div, WRN RGN Nat Weather Serv, Oceanic & Atmospheric Admin, 65-82. *Concurrent Pos:* Lectr, Univ Utah, 66-68, adj asst prof, 68-; NCR comt assignments, Acad Sci, 87- *Mem:* Fel Am Meteorol Soc. *Res:* Synoptic and satellite meteorology especially weather forecasting. *Mailing Add:* 4278 S 2700 E Salt Lake City UT 84124

SNELSIRE, ROBERT W, ELECTRICAL ENGINEERING. *Current Pos:* ASSOC PROF ELEC ENG, CLEMSON UNIV, 67- *Personal Data:* b Pittsburgh, Pa, May 8, 33; m 57; c 3. *Educ:* Bethany Col, BA, 56; Carnegie Inst Technol, BS, 56, MS, 58, PhD(elec eng), 64. *Prof Exp:* Instr elec eng, Carnegie Inst Technol, 58-63; sr engr, Westinghouse Defense Ctr, 63-64; asst prof elec eng, State Univ NY Buffalo, 64-67. *Concurrent Pos:* Consult, Bell Aerosysts Co, 66-67 & Wachovia Bank & Trust Co, 66- *Mem:* Inst Elec & Electronics Engrs; Am Soc Eng Educ. *Res:* Computer science; simulation of human behavior. *Mailing Add:* Dept Elec Eng Clemson Univ Clemson SC 29634

SNELSON, ALAN, PHYSICAL CHEMISTRY, THERMODYNAMICS. *Current Pos:* SR CHEMIST, IIT RES INST, 62- *Personal Data:* b Manchester, Eng, Oct 17, 34; m 77; c 1. *Educ:* Univ Manchester, Eng, BSc, 57, MSc, 58, PhD(chem), 60. *Prof Exp:* Fel chem, Univ Calif, Berkeley, 60-62. *Concurrent Pos:* Lectr, Ill Inst Technol, 67- *Mem:* Am Chem Soc. *Res:* Thermochemistry; spectroscopy; kinetics; cryogenics atmospheric chemistry. *Mailing Add:* 935 W Argyle St Chicago IL 60640

SNELSON, FRANKLIN F, JR, ICHTHYOLOGY. *Current Pos:* From asst prof to assoc prof, chmn biol sci, 81-88, PROF BIOL, UNIV CENT FLA, 81- *Personal Data:* b Richmond, Va, June 13, 43; c 3. *Educ:* NC State Univ, BS, 65; Cornell Univ, PhD(vert zool), 70. *Concurrent Pos:* NASA grant, 72-79; US Fish Wildlife grant, 80-81; assoc ed, American Midland Naturalist, 82- *Mem:* Am Soc Ichthyologists & Herpetologists; Am Inst Biol Sci; Ecol Soc Am; Soc Syst Zool; Am Soc Zool. *Res:* Systematics and ecology of fishes; biology of sharks and stingrays; reproductive ecology of livebearing fishes; ecology of coastal marine fishes in Florida; systematics of minnows. *Mailing Add:* Dept Biol Univ Central Fla PO Box 25000 Orlando FL 32816-0001

SNETSINGER, DAVID CLARENCE, POULTRY NUTRITION. *Current Pos:* RETIRED. *Personal Data:* b Barrington, Ill, Apr 22, 30; c Penny, Tom, Carol & Sue. *Educ:* Univ Ill, BS, 52, MS, 57, PhD(poultry nutrit), 59. *Prof Exp:* Asst poultry, Univ Ill, 55-59; from asst prof to assoc prof poultry sci, Univ Minn, St Paul, 59-68; mgr, Com Layer Res Div, Ralston Purina Co, 68-70, mgr, Com Egg & Breeder Res Div, 70-72, mgr, Gen Poultry Res Div, 72-76, dir, Poultry Res & Mkt Dept, 76-85, dir, Poultry Bus Group, 85-87, vpres res, 87-90, sr adv, Purina Mills, 91-93; mgr, Com Layer Res Div, Ralston Purina Co, 68-70, mgr, com egg & breeder res div, 70-72, mgr, Gen Poultry Res Div, 72-76, dir, Poultry res & Mkt Dept, 76-85, dir, poultry bus group, 85-87, vpres res, 87-90, sr adv, Purina Mills, 91-93. *Mem:* Fel Poultry Sci Asn; Am Inst Nutrit; World Poultry Sci Asn; Animal Sci Asn. *Res:* Amino acid and mineral nutrition and metabolism; holds 3 patents in poultry nutrition and feeding equipment. *Mailing Add:* 420 Algonquin Pl St Louis MO 63119-3642

SNETSINGER, KENNETH GEORGE, GEOCHEMISTRY, MINERALOGY. *Current Pos:* Nat Acad Sci-Nat Res Coun resident res assoc, 66-69, RES SCIENTIST, NASA AMES RES CTR, 69- *Personal Data:* b San Francisco, Calif, Feb 21, 39; m 78. *Educ:* Stanford Univ, BS, 61, MS, 62, PhD(mineral), 66. *Mem:* Mineral Soc Am; Mineral Soc Can; NY Acad Sci. *Res:* Mineralogy and geochemistry of meteorites, lunar samples, platinum metals; composition and mineralogy of atmospheric aerosols. *Mailing Add:* 668 Bancroft St Santa Clara CA 95051-5656

SNETSINGER, ROBERT J, ECOMONIC ENTOMOLOGY, ARACHNOLOGY. *Current Pos:* from asst prof to assoc prof entom, 60-71, PROF ENTOM, PA STATE UNIV, UNIVERSITY PARK, 71- *Personal Data:* b Diamond Lake, Ill, Mar 6, 28; m 60; c 2. *Educ:* Univ Ill, Urbana, BS, 52, MS, 53, PhD(entom), 60. *Prof Exp:* Asst econ entom, Ill Nat Hist Surv, 55-60. *Concurrent Pos:* Ed, Int Mushroom Cong, 62, Entom Soc Pa, 64-77 & Pa Pest Control Quart, 67-75; vis prof, Univ PR, 83-84. *Mem:* Entom Soc Am; Entom Soc Can; Arachnids Soc Am. *Res:* Biology and control of animal pests of mushrooms; structural pest control and urban ecology; biology and control of arachnids; history of pest control; mushroom culture. *Mailing Add:* Dept Entom 501 Agr Sci Pa State Univ University Park PA 16802-3508

SNIDER, ALBERT MONROE, JR, POLYMERS, ANALYTICAL CHEMISTRY. *Current Pos:* MGR, CHEM & NONMETALS LAB, GEN ELEC CO, 81- *Personal Data:* b Hoffman, NC; m 66; c 2. *Educ:* Univ NC, Chapel Hill, BA, 59, MEd, 62; Appalachian State Univ, MA, 69; Univ Pittsburgh, PhD(chem), 74. *Prof Exp:* Teaching asst chem, Appalachian State Univ, 67-69; chemist, Mellon Inst, 70; instr, Community Col Allegheny County, 75; res asst, Dept Chem, Sch Eng, Univ Pittsburgh, 69-74, res assoc polymer sci, 75-76; lab dir, K Tator Assocs, 76-77; group leader, Spectros Lab, Carnegie-Mellon Inst Res, 78-79; group leader polymer characterization, Merck & Co, 79-81. *Mem:* Am Chem Soc; Soc Appl Spectros; Coblentz Soc; Sigma Xi. *Res:* Molecular spectroscopy and polymer science particularly utilizing infrared, raman, nuclear magnetic resonance, photoelectron, and mass spectroscopies, x-ray diffraction and electron microscopy. *Mailing Add:* 602 Orchard Hill Dr Pittsburgh PA 15238-2518

SNIDER, ARTHUR DAVID, MATHEMATICS. *Current Pos:* asst prof, 70-77, ASSOC PROF MATH, UNIV S FLA, 77- *Personal Data:* b Richmond, Va, Oct 7, 40. *Educ:* Mass Inst Technol, BS, 62; Boston Univ, MA, 66; NY Univ, PhD(math), 71. *Prof Exp:* Analyst, Instrumentation Lab, Mass Inst Technol, 62-66. *Concurrent Pos:* Math consult, Honeywell Aerospace Corp, 74. *Mem:* Soc Indust & Appl Math; Am Math Soc; Math Asn Am. *Res:* Applied mathematics; numerical analysis; differential equations; plasmas. *Mailing Add:* Col Eng Univ SFla Tampa FL 33620-6450

SNIDER, BARRY B, NATURAL PRODUCTS SYNTHESIS. *Current Pos:* assoc prof, 81-85, PROF CHEM, BRANDEIS UNIV, 85- *Personal Data:* b Chicago, Ill, Jan 13, 50; m 75; c 1. *Educ:* Univ Mich, BS, 70; Harvard Univ, PhD(chem), 73. *Prof Exp:* Fel chem, Columbia Univ, 73-75; asst prof, Princeton Univ, 75-81. *Concurrent Pos:* Alfred P Sloan Found fel, 79; Dreyfus Teacher Scholar, 82-87. *Mem:* Am Chem Soc; Royal Soc Chem. *Res:* Synthetic methods development; Ene reactions; Lewis acid catalysis; alkene carbofunctionalization; intramolecular cycloadditions and cyclizations; total synthesis of natural products. *Mailing Add:* Dept Chem Brandeis Univ Waltham MA 02254-9110

SNIDER, BILL CARL F, STATISTICS. *Current Pos:* Res assoc prev ment health, Child Welfare Res Sta, Univ Iowa, 56-65, res assoc comput ctr, 62-65, asst prof statist, Col Educ & Comput Ctr, 65-69, from assoc prof to prof educ, 69-91, statist consult, Comput Ctr, 74-91, EMER PROF EDUC, PSYCHOL, MEASUREMENT & STATIST, UNIV IOWA, 91- *Personal Data:* b Cedar Rapids, Iowa, July 11, 20; m 54; c 1. *Educ:* Univ Wichita, BA, 42, MA, 51; Univ Iowa, PhD, 55. *Mem:* Am Educ Res Asn. *Res:* Mental health; statistics and preventive mental health. *Mailing Add:* 300 Melrose Ct Iowa City IA 52246

SNIDER, DALE REYNOLDS, ELECTROMAGNETISM, HIGH ENERGY PHYSICS. *Current Pos:* asst prof, 70-77, ASSOC PROF PHYSICS, UNIV WIS-MILWAUKEE, 77- *Personal Data:* b Cincinnati, Ohio, Mar 21, 38; m 61; c 2. *Educ:* Ohio State Univ, BS & MS, 61; Univ Calif, San Diego, PhD(physics), 68. *Prof Exp:* Instr nuclear eng, US Navy Nuclear Power Sch, Calif, 61-65; theoret physicist, Lawrence Radiation Lab, Univ Calif, Berkeley, 68-70. *Concurrent Pos:* Vis prof physics, Univ Ill, Urbana, 74-75. *Mem:* Am Phys Soc. *Res:* Theoretical high energy physics; strong interaction theory; electromagnetic devices; nonlinear dynamic; surface studies; metallic clusters; superconductivity. *Mailing Add:* 4254 N Ardmore Ave Milwaukee WI 53211

SNIDER, DIXIE EDWARD, JR, MEDICINE. *Current Pos:* ASSOC DIR SCI, CTRS DIS CONTROL & PREVENTION, 94- *Personal Data:* b Frankfort, Ky, Jan 16, 43; m 66, Fran Fenwich; c Richard & Ann. *Educ:* Western Ky State Col, BS, 65; Univ Louisville, MD, 69; Emory Univ, MPH, 84. *Honors & Awards:* Pres Award, Lung Asn. *Prof Exp:* Intern internal med, Barnes Hosp, 69-70, resident, 70-71; resident, Vanderbilt Univ, 71-72; fel allergy & clin immunol, Wash Univ, 72-73; med officer tuberc, USPHS, 73-74; chief, Res & Develop Br, Tuberculosis Control Div, Nat Ctr Prev Servs, 74-85, dir, Div Tuberculosis Elimination, 85-92, assoc dir sci, 92-94. *Concurrent Pos:* Fel allergy & clin immunol, Wash Univ, 75-76; bd dirs, Am Col Epidemiol; clinician, Infectious Dis Serv, Vet Admin Med Ctr; chair, Health Info Systs Bd, USPHS. *Mem:* Am Thoracic Soc; Am Col Epidemiol; Am Col Physicians; Infectious Dis Soc Am; Soc Med Decision Making. *Res:* Tuberculin skin testing; mycobacterial drug resistance; preventive therapy of tuberculosis; treatment of tuberculosis; prostaglandins and asthma; lymphocyte cyclic nucleotide metabolism. *Mailing Add:* USPHS Ctr Dis Control 1600 Clifton Rd Mail Stop D-50 Atlanta GA 30333. *Fax:* 404-639-7341; *E-Mail:* des1@cdc.gov

SNIDER, GORDON LLOYD, PULMONARY DISEASES. *Current Pos:* chief pulmonary dis sect, Boston Vet Admin Hosp, 68-87, CHIEF MED SERV, BOSTON VA MED CTR, 86- *Personal Data:* b Toronto, Ont, Apr 11, 22; US citizen; m 45; c 3. *Educ:* Univ Toronto, MD, 44; Am Bd Internal Med, dipl, 53; Am Bd Pulmonary Dis, dipl, 58. *Honors & Awards:* Simon Rodbard Mem Lectr, Am Col Chest Physicians, 85; Alton Ochsner Award, 90; Parker B Francis Lectr, 91. *Prof Exp:* Intern, Toronto Gen Hosp, 44-45; resident med, Bronx Hosp, New York, 46-47, resident path, Mass Mem Hosp, Boston, 47-48; fel med, Lahey Clinic, Boston, 48-49; resident pulmonary med, Trudeau Sanitarium, NY, 49-50; asst dir, Chest Dept, Michael Reese Hosp, 50-61; chief div thoracic med, Mt Sinai Hosp, 61-66, actg chmn dept med, 65-66; chief pulmonary dis sect, Wood Vet Admin Hosp, 66-68; prof med, Sch Med & head respiratory sect, Univ Hosp, Boston Univ, 68-76. *Concurrent Pos:* Attend physician, Winfield Hosp, Ill, 52-61; consult physician & dir pulmonary function lab, Munic Tuberc Sanitarium, Chicago, 52-68; med consult, Social Security Admin, 58-66; from asst prof to prof med, Chicago Med Sch, 58-66, actg chmn dept, 65-66; consult, West Side Vet Admin Hosp, Chicago, 64-66; prof, Sch Med, Marquette Univ, 66-68; attend physician, Milwaukee Co Gen Hosp & medconsult, Mt Sinai Hosp, Milwaukee, 65-66; mem respiratory dis comt, Tuberc Inst Chicago & Cook Co; mem med adv bds, Suburban Cook Co Tuberc Sanitarium Dis & Asthma & Allergy Res Found, Greater Chicago; mem med adv comt, Chicago Chap, Cystic Fibrosis Res Found; consult comt, Div Sanatoria & Tuberc Control, Mass Dept Pub Health; mem pulmonary dis adv comt, Nat Heart, Lung & Blood Inst, 80-84; pulmonary dis adv coun, Vet Admin, 79-81, pres Vet Pulmonary Physicians Asn, 80-81; mem adv coun, Spec Ctr Res Chronic Obstructive Lung Dis, Harvard Sch Pub Health, 80-84; chmn, Fed Lung Prog Comt, Am Thoracic Soc, 85-; Int adv, Aspen Lung Conf, 85-90; chmn, NIH Safety & Data Monitoring Bd, 89-; Maurice B Strauss prof med, Boston Univ & Tufts Univ Sch Med, 86- *Mem:* Fel Am Col Chest Physicians; fel Am Col Physicians; Am Fedn Clin Res; Am Thoracic Soc. *Res:* Clinical pulmonary disease and physiology; experimental pulmonary diseases. *Mailing Add:* 150 S Huntington Ave Boston MA 02130-4820

SNIDER, JERRY ALLEN, BRYOLOGY, CYTOLOGY. *Current Pos:* from asst prof to assoc prof, 74-89, HERBARIUM CUR, DEPT BIOL SCI, UNIV CINCINNATI, 74-, PROF BIOL SCI, 90- *Personal Data:* b Danville, Ill, Feb 17, 37; m 67; c 2. *Educ:* Southern Ill Univ, BA, 67; Univ NC, Chapel Hill, MA, 70; Duke Univ, PhD(bot), 73. *Prof Exp:* Asst prof biol, Baylor Univ, 73-74. *Mem:* Am Bryol & Lichenological Soc; British Bryol Soc; Int Asn Plant Taxon; Int Asn Bryol; Norweg Bryol Soc. *Res:* Cytology and taxonomy of bryophytes; morphological development in bryophytes. *Mailing Add:* Dept Biol Sci Univ Cincinnati 2600 Clifton Ave Cincinnati OH 45220-2872. *Fax:* 513-556-5299; *E-Mail:* cinc@uc.beh.san.uc.edu

SNIDER, JOHN WILLIAM, PHYSICS. *Current Pos:* from asst prof to prof physics, 53-92, EMER PROF, MIAMI UNIV, 92- *Personal Data:* b Middleport, Ohio, Sept 13, 24; m 49, Geneva Palmer; c John A. *Educ:* Miami Univ, AB, 49, MA, 51; Ohio State Univ, PhD, 57. *Honors & Awards:* Educom NCRIPTAL Higher Educ Software Award, 90. *Prof Exp:* Res assoc, Ohio State Univ, 57-59. *Concurrent Pos:* Sr res physicist, Mound Lab, Monsanto Chem Co, 58-69; consult, Ohio River Div, Army Corps Engrs, 63-65. *Res:* Low temperature physics, especially superconductivity and thermal transpiration; calorimetry; educational software. *Mailing Add:* Dept of Physics Miami Univ Oxford OH 45056

SNIDER, JOSEPH LYONS, ATOMIC PHYSICS, ASTROPHYSICS. *Current Pos:* assoc prof, 69-75, PROF PHYSICS, OBERLIN COL, 75- *Personal Data:* b Boston, Mass, June 10, 34. *Educ:* Amherst Col, BA, 56; Princeton Univ, PhD(physics), 61. *Prof Exp:* Instr & res fel physics, Harvard Univ, 61-64, asst prof, 64-69. *Mem:* Am Phys Soc; Am Astron Soc; Am Asn Physics Teachers; Am Asn Univ Profs. *Res:* Solar physics; atomic physics; relativity and gravitation. *Mailing Add:* Dept Physics Oberlin Col Oberlin OH 44074

SNIDER, NEIL STANLEY, THEORETICAL CHEMISTRY. *Current Pos:* asst prof, 66-72, ASSOC PROF CHEM, QUEEN'S UNIV, ONT, 72- *Personal Data:* b Schenectady, NY, May 25, 38. *Educ:* Purdue Univ, BSc, 59; Princeton Univ, MA, 61, PhD(chem), 64. *Prof Exp:* NSF fel, 64-65; res assoc chem, Cornell Univ, 65 & Yale Univ, 65-66. *Mem:* Am Chem Soc; Can Asn Physicists; Chem Inst Can. *Res:* Theory of rates of homogeneous gas phase reactions; statistical mechanics of classical fluids. *Mailing Add:* Dept Chem Queen's Univ Kingston ON K7L 3N6 Can

SNIDER, PHILIP JOSEPH, GENETICS. *Current Pos:* dir univ honors prog, 65-70, ASSOC PROF BIOL, UNIV HOUSTON, 63- *Personal Data:* b Richmond, VA, Apr 5, 29; m 52; c 2. *Educ:* Richmond Univ, BS, 52; Harvard Univ, AM, 55, PhD, 57. *Prof Exp:* Res assoc biol div, Genetics Sect, Oak Ridge Nat Lab, 58-59; asst prof bot, Univ Calif, Berkeley, 59-63. *Concurrent Pos:* Consult mem, Biol Sci Curriculum Studies, 64-70. *Mem:* AAAS. *Res:* Microbial and molecular genetics, especially regulatory genetics of reproductive processes. *Mailing Add:* Dept Biol Univ Houston Houston TX 77204-0001

SNIDER, RAY MICHAEL, PEPTIDE RECEPTOR PHARMACOLOGY, DRUG DISCOVERY. *Current Pos:* SR RES SCIENTIST PHARMACOL, PFIZER CENT RES, 88- *Personal Data:* b Los Angeles, Calif, Dec 28, 48; m 82; c 2. *Educ:* Calif State Univ, Northridge, BA, 74; Ohio State Univ, PhD(pharmacol), 82. *Honors & Awards:* Individual Nat Res Serv Award, NIMH, 82. *Prof Exp:* Grad res assoc pharmacol, Ohio State Univ, 76-81; postdoctoral fel, Mayo Clinic & Found, 82-83; res investr neurochem, Univ Mich, 83-86; sr scientist immunol, T-Cell Sci, 86-88. *Mem:* AAAS; Am Soc Pharmacol & Exp Therapeut. *Res:* Discovery and pharmacological characterization of novel prototype molecules interactions with receptors; drug discovery; peptide and cytokine receptors; cholinergic and biogenic amine receptors; second messenger pharmacology. *Mailing Add:* New Lead Disc Berlex Biosci 15049 San Pablo Ave Richmond CA 94804-0099. *Fax:* 860-441-5302

SNIDER, ROBERT FOLINSBEE, THEORETICAL CHEMISTRY, ATOMIC & MOLECULAR PHYSICS. *Current Pos:* from instr to prof, 58-96, EMER PROF CHEM, UNIV BC, 96- *Personal Data:* b Calgary, Alta, Nov 22, 31; div; c 4. *Educ:* Univ Alta, BSc, 53; Univ Wis, PhD (theoret chem), 58; FRSC; FCIC. *Prof Exp:* Fel appl chem, Nat Res Coun Can, 58. *Mem:* Can Asn Physicists; Am Inst Phys; Chem Inst Can. *Res:* Statistical mechanics; transport properties of gases; collisions of non-spherical molecules. *Mailing Add:* Dept Chem 2036 Main Mall Vancouver BC V6T 1Z1 Can. *E-Mail:* snider@theory.chem.ubc.ca

SNIDER, SCOTT CHRISTIAN, POLYIMIDE FOAM, RIGID & SEMI RIGID FOAM. *Current Pos:* sr chemist, 94-96, MGR RES & DEVELOP, IMI TECH-CORP, 96- *Personal Data:* b Eau Claire, Wis, July 13, 52; m 74; c 4. *Educ:* Univ Wis-Eau Claire, BS, 74; Univ Ariz, PhD(org chem), 78. *Prof Exp:* Res asst, Univ Nebr Med Ctr, 78-79; res fel, Creighton Univ, 80; sr res chemist, Jim Walter Res Corp, 80-85, res assoc, 85-90; res assoc, Schuller Int Corp, 90-94. *Concurrent Pos:* Instr, Gen Chem Lab, St Petersburg Jr Col, 80-81; consult, foam chem, 94. *Mem:* Am Chem Soc. *Res:* Development of solimide polyimide foams; marine, aircraft and aerospace insulation. *Mailing Add:* Imi-Tech Corp PO Box 247 Galena KS 66739-0247. *E-Mail:* scott.snider@inspecusa.com

SNIDER, THEODORE EUGENE, ORGANIC CHEMISTRY. *Current Pos:* from instr to assoc prof, 68-78, PROF CHEM, CAMERON UNIV, 78-, DEPT CHAIR, 89- *Personal Data:* b Pittsburg, Kans, Apr 22, 43; m 68, Linda Lewis; c Holly A & Timothy A. *Educ:* Pittsburg State Univ, BS, 65, MS, 67; Okla State Univ, PhD(org chem), 72. *Prof Exp:* Instr chem, Eastern Okla State Col, 67-68. *Mem:* Am Chem Soc; Sigma Xi. *Res:* Synthesis of folic acid inhibitors and the calculation and significance of group electronegativity. *Mailing Add:* Phys Sci Dept Cameron State Col 2800 Gore Blvd Lawton OK 73505. *Fax:* 580-591-8011; *E-Mail:* teds@cameron.edu

SNIECKUS, VICTOR A, ORGANIC CHEMISTRY. *Current Pos:* from asst prof to assoc prof, 66-79, fel, 66-67, PROF CHEM, UNIV WATERLOO, 79- *Personal Data:* b Kaunas, Lithuania, Aug 1, 37; Can citizen; m 66; c 2. *Educ:* Univ Alta, BSc, 59; Univ Calif, Berkeley, MS, 61; Univ Ore, PhD(chem), 65; FCIC, 78. *Prof Exp:* Nat Res Coun Can fel chem, 65-66. *Concurrent Pos:* H C Orsted Found Fel, Univ Copenhagen, Denmark, 73; vis prof, Univ Geneva, Switzerland, 76-77; Can-Japan exchange fel, 81; France-Can exchange fel, 85. *Mem:* Am Chem Soc; Chem Inst Can; Int Soc Heterocyclic Chem. *Mailing Add:* Dept Chem Univ Waterloo Waterloo ON N2L 3G1 Can

SNIPES, CHARLES ANDREW, PHYSIOLOGY, PHARMACOLOGY. *Current Pos:* PHARMACOLOGIST, CTR DRUG EVAL & RES, FOOD & DRUG ADMIN, 91-; ADJ PROF ANAT & CELL BIOL, UNIFORMED SERV UNIV HEALTH SCI, 94- *Personal Data:* b Tampa, Fla, Nov 1, 36. *Educ:* Western Carolina Univ, AB, 57; Duke Univ, PhD(physiol, pharmacol), 67. *Prof Exp:* From instr to asst prof pediat, Johns Hopkins Univ, 62-68, asst dir res training prog pediat endocrinol, 62-68; from asst prof to assoc prof physiol, Sch Med, Hahnemann Univ, 68-92. *Mem:* Endocrine Soc; Am Physiol Soc; Lawson Wilkins Pediat Endocrine Soc; Am Soc Zoologists. *Res:* Neuroendocrinology; metabolism of steroid hormones; growth hormone and insulin on amino acid accumulation; control of development; validation of computer software. *Mailing Add:* Fed Drug Admin CDFR HFD-345 7520 Standish Pl Rockville MD 20855. *E-Mail:* snipesc@fdacd.bitnet

SNIPES, DAVID STRANGE, GEOLOGY. *Current Pos:* from assoc prof to prof, 68-93, EMER PROF GEOL, CLEMSON UNIV, 93- *Personal Data:* b Hartsville, SC, Apr 16, 28; m 53; c 4. *Educ:* Wake Forest Col, BS, 50; Univ NC, PhD(geol), 65. *Prof Exp:* Geologist, Calif Co, 56-59; assoc prof geol, Furman Univ, 63-68. *Concurrent Pos:* Consult var co & pvt individuals. *Res:* Hydrogeology of SC and GA coastal plain sediments; fault zones and dolerite dikes; x-ray analysis of minerals. *Mailing Add:* Dept Geol Clemson Univ Clemson SC 29634-0001

SNIPES, MORRIS BURTON, INHALATION TOXICOLOGY. *Current Pos:* ASSOC SCIENTIST, INHALATION TOXICOL RES INST, 71- *Personal Data:* b Clovis, NMex, Oct 29, 40; m 58, Leona G Swieter; c Janelle L (Peck), Wade A (Peck), Morris B Jr, Eric R, Benjamin L & Laura L. *Educ:* Univ NMex, BS, 67, MS, 68; Cornell Univ, PhD(phys biol), 71. *Mem:* Sigma Xi; Radiation Res Soc; Health Physics Soc; Soc Toxicol; Am Thoracic Soc; Int Soc Aerosols Med. *Res:* Biological responses to inhaled materials. *Mailing Add:* 782 Hwy 66 E Tijeras NM 87059. *Fax:* 505-845-1198

SNIPES, WALLACE CLAYTON, PHARMACOLOGY. *Current Pos:* VPRES RES & DEVELOP, ZETACHRON INC, 84- *Personal Data:* b Graham, NC, Oct 11, 37; m 60; c 3. *Educ:* Wake Forest Col, BS, 60; Duke Univ, PhD(phsics), 64. *Prof Exp:* From asst prof to prof biophys, Pa State Univ, University Park, 72-88. *Concurrent Pos:* Vis prof, Univ Calif, Berkeley, 69 & Univ Calif, Santa Cruz, 74-75. *Mem:* Am Phys Soc; Am Asn Pharmaceut Scientists; Biophys Soc. *Res:* Drug delivery systems. *Mailing Add:* 186 Deepwood Dr Pine Grove Mills PA 16868

SNIPP, ROBERT LEO, PHYSICAL CHEMISTRY. *Current Pos:* Asst prof, 64-71, chmn dept, 74-77, ASSOC PROF CHEM, CREIGHTON UNIV, 71- *Personal Data:* b Omaha, Nebr, Aug 13, 36; m 63; c 2. *Educ:* Creighton Univ, BS, 58, MS, 60; Univ Iowa, PhD(phys chem), 65. *Mem:* Am Chem Soc. *Res:* Physical chemistry of macromolecules, particularly polyelectrolytes in solution. *Mailing Add:* Dept Chem Creighton Univ Omaha NE 68178-0002

SNIR, MARC, PARALLEL COMPUTING & ARCHITECTURE. *Current Pos:* RES STAFF MEM, T J WATSON RES CTR, IBM, 86-, SR MGR, RES DIV, 90- *Personal Data:* b Courbevois, France, Oct 10, 48; US citizen. *Educ:* Hebrew Univ, BSc, 72, PhD(math), 79. *Prof Exp:* Asst prof comput sci, NY Univ, 80-82; sr lectr, Hebrew Univ, 82-86. *Mem:* Fel Inst Elec & Electronics Engrs; Asn Comput Mach. *Res:* Architecture, system software and application software for scalable parallel processing. *Mailing Add:* T J Watson Res Ctr IBM PO Box 218 Yorktown Heights NY 10598. *E-Mail:* snir@watson.ibm.com

SNITGEN, DONALD ALBERT, BIOLOGY, SCIENCE EDUCATION. *Current Pos:* from instr to assoc prof, 66-79, PROF BIOL, NORTHERN MICH UNIV, 79- *Personal Data:* b St Johns, Mich, Feb 25, 36; m 59; c 3. *Educ:* Cent Mich Univ, BS, 60; Mich State Univ, MS, 64, PhD(sci educ), 71. *Prof Exp:* Teacher high sch, Mich, 62-66. *Res:* Distribution of stream bottom fauna, especially insects; preservice elementary school teachers' attitudes toward biological science; development of audio-tutorial program for non-majors in biological science; feasibility study to develop a regional environmental education center in Upper Peninsula of Michigan. *Mailing Add:* Dept Biol Northern Mich Univ 1401 Presque Isle Ave Marquette MI 49855-5301

SNITZER, ELIAS, OPTICS. *Current Pos:* full prof II, 89-97, EMER PROF CERAMIC SCI & ENG, RUTGERS UNIV, 97- *Personal Data:* b Lynn, Mass, Feb 27, 25; m 50; c 5. *Educ:* Tufts Univ, BS, 45; Univ Chicago, MS, 50, PhD(physics), 53. *Honors & Awards:* George W Morey Award, Am Ceramic Soc, 71; Quantum Electronics Award, Inst Elec & Electronics Engrs, 79; Charles Hard Townes Award, Optical Soc Am, 91, John Tyndall Award, 94. *Prof Exp:* Res physicist, Minneapolis-Honeywell Regulator Co, 54-56; assoc prof electronics eng, Lowell Tech Inst, 56-58; res assoc, Mass Inst Technol, 59; res physicist, Am Optical Corp, 59-68, dir basic res, 68-75 & corp res, 75-77; mgr, tech planning, United Technol Corp Res Ctr, 77-79, mgr, Appl Physics Lab, 79-84; dir, Fiber & Integrated Optics Group, Polaroid Corp, 84-88. *Concurrent Pos:* Prof emer, Rutgers Univ, 97- *Mem:* Nat Acad Eng; Am Phys Soc; Optical Soc Am; Am Ceramic Soc; Inst Elec & Electronics Engrs. *Res:* Physical optics; glass technology; solid state physics; materials and instrument research in optics; fiber optics, glass lasers, optical amplifiers. *Mailing Add:* 8 Smoke Tree Close Piscataway NJ 08854-5109

SNIVELY, LESLIE O, MAGNETIC INTERACTIONS. *Current Pos:* PRES, INTERLINK TECH, 82- *Personal Data:* b Laramie, Wyo, Mar 11, 53; m 75. *Educ:* Colo State Univ, BS, 75; Mont State Univ, MS, 77, PhD(physics), 81. *Prof Exp:* Res assoc, Mont State Univ, 81-82. *Mem:* Am Phys Soc. *Res:* Experimental and theoretical investigation of superexchange interaction in magnetically lower-dimensional metal-halide compounds using magnetic susceptibility and magnetization measurement. *Mailing Add:* One Heather Lane Amherst NH 03031

SNOBLE, JOSEPH JERRY, PHYSICS, SCIENCE EDUCATION. *Current Pos:* PROF PHYSICS, CENT MO STATE UNIV, 67- *Personal Data:* b Center Point, Iowa, Feb 11, 31; m 55; c 2. *Educ:* Iowa State Teachers Col, BA, 57, MA, 61; State Univ Iowa, PhD(sci educ) 67. *Prof Exp:* Teacher sci, Kingsley Pub Sch, 57-59; instr, State Univ Iowa, 61-67. *Mem:* Nat Sci Teachers Asn; Nat Sci & Math Asn; Am Asn Physics Teachers; Sigma Xi. *Res:* Teacher education in science, especially elementary, secondary and collegiate teaching procedures and methods; meaningful demonstration and laboratory activities and experiments. *Mailing Add:* 15 SE 215th Rd Warrensburg MO 64093

SNODDY, EDWARD L, MEDICAL ENTOMOLOGY, ECOLOGY. *Current Pos:* MED ENTOMOLOGIST, WATER QUALITY & ECOL BR, TENN VALLEY AUTHORITY, ALA, 76- *Personal Data:* b Kelso, Tenn, Mar 6, 33; m 52; c 2. *Educ:* Mid Tenn State Univ, BS, 62; Auburn Univ, PhD(med entom), 66. *Prof Exp:* NDEA fel med entom, Auburn Univ, 62-65; prof med entom, Coastal Plain Exp Sta, Univ Ga, 65-76. *Concurrent Pos:* Consult, USAF Hosp, Robins AFB, Warner Robins, Ga, 69-76; mem, Sci Adv Panel, WHO, 74-; secy-treas, Ga Mosquito Control Asn, 75-; Ga dir, Mid-Atlantic Mosquito Control Asn, 75-; consult, Armed Forces Pest Mgt Bd, Dept Defense, 76-; mem, Fed Interagency Comt, Forest Integrated Pest Mgt, 81- *Mem:* Entom Soc Am; Ecol Soc Am; Am Mosquito Control Asn. *Res:* Ecology and taxonomy of medically important arthropods; attractants and repellents for insects of medical importance, particularly Simuliidae, Tabanidae, Ceratopogonidae and Ixodidae. *Mailing Add:* 255 Lake View Dr Muscle Shoals AL 35661

SNODGRASS, REX JACKSON, ALTERNATIVE ENERGY, INFORMATION SCIENCE. *Current Pos:* with environ sci info ctr, Nat Oceanic & Atomosperic Admin, 80- 83, spec asst, Headquarters Nat Environ Satellite Data & Info Serv, Washington, 83-84, dep dir, Nat Climate Data Ctr, Asheville, NC, 84-89, CHIEF, SYSTS DEVELOP, NAT CLIMATE DATA CTR, NAT OCEANIC & ATMOSPHERIC ADMIN, 89- *Personal Data:* b St Louis, Mo, Feb 24, 34; m 70, Denise Deleeuw; c Ryan & Heather. *Educ:* Harvard Univ, AB, 56; Univ Md, MS, 60, PhD(physics), 63. *Prof Exp:* Physicist, Harry Diamond Labs, 53-59; physicist, Nat Bur Stand, 60-66; fel, Inst Mat Sci & mem fac physics, Univ Conn, 66-72, mgr tech serv, New Eng Res Appl Ctr, 72-80. *Concurrent Pos:* Nat Bur Stand training fel, Univ Paris, 63-64. *Mem:* Am Phys Soc; AAAS; Am Soc Info Sci; Am Meteorol Soc. *Res:* Information management; energy related problems, especially solar energy research; energy conservation efficiencies; information management of large data bases of weather information using advanced automated systems. *Mailing Add:* PO Box 236 Weaverville NC 28787. *Fax:* 704-271-4134; *E-Mail:* rsnodgra@ncdc.noaa.gov

SNOEYENBOS, GLENN HOWARD, VETERINARY MEDICINE. *Current Pos:* PROF VET MED, UNIV MASS, AMHERST, 47- *Personal Data:* b Glenwood City, Wis, Sept 16, 22; m 49; c 3. *Educ:* Mich State Col, DVM, 45. *Prof Exp:* Sta vet, Univ Minn, 45-46. *Concurrent Pos:* Grants, USPHS, 65-68, Fats & Proteins Res Found, 66-69 & USDA, 66-71. *Mem:* Am Vet Med Asn; Am Asn Avian Path (secy treas, 61-70); Poultry Sci Asn; Conf Res Workers Animal Dis. *Res:* Infectious diseases of poultry; methods of preventing salmonellosis as a public health problem. *Mailing Add:* 42 Hill Rd Amherst MA 01002

SNOEYINK, VERNON LEROY, ENVIRONMENTAL ENGINEERING. *Current Pos:* from asst prof to assoc prof sanit eng, Dept Civil Eng, 69-77, IVAN RACHEFF PROF ENVIRON ENG, DEPT CIVIL ENG, UNIV ILL, 77- *Personal Data:* b Kent Co, Mich, Oct 10, 40; m 64, Virginia Stenk; c Todd & Craig. *Educ:* Univ Mich, BS, 64, MS, 66, PhD(water resources eng), 68. *Prof Exp:* Engr, Metcalf & Eddy Engrs, 68-69. *Mem:* Am Soc Civil Engrs; Am Water Works Asn; Int Asn Water Qual; Asn Environ Eng Prof; Int Water Supply Asn. *Res:* Water purification using adsorption processes; water chemistry; drinking water purification. *Mailing Add:* Dept Civil Eng Univ Ill 205 N Mathews St Urbana IL 61801-2374

SNOKE, ARTHUR WILMOT, GEOLOGY, STRUCTURAL GEOLOGY. *Current Pos:* PROF, UNIV WYO, 84- *Personal Data:* b Baltimore, Md, Oct 5, 45; m 66, Judith A Gill; c Cynthia L & Alison C. *Educ:* Franklin & Marshall Col, AB, 67; Stanford Univ, PhD(geol), 72. *Prof Exp:* Nat Res Coun assoc, US Geol Surv, 71-73; from asst prof to assoc prof geol, Univ SC, 74-84. *Concurrent Pos:* Lectr, Humboldt State Univ, 74. *Mem:* Fel Geol Soc Am; Am Geophys Union; Rocky Mountain Asn Geologists. *Res:* Structural geology and tectonics of orogenic belts; petrogenesis of mylonitic rocks; structural analysis of polyphase-deformed terranes, northeastern Nevada, Wyoming foreland, Tobago West Indies, and southern Alpine basement (northern Italy). *Mailing Add:* Dept Geol & Geophys Univ Wyo PO Box 3006 Laramie WY 82071-3006

SNOKE, J ARTHUR, SEISMOLOGY. *Current Pos:* from asst prof to assoc prof, 77-87, PROF GEOPHYSICS, VA POLYTECH INST & STATE UNIV, BLACKSBURG, 87- *Personal Data:* b Rochester, NY, Mar 3, 40; m 64; c 2. *Educ:* Stanford Univ, BS, 63; Yale Univ, MS, 64, PhD(physics), 69. *Prof Exp:* Asst prof physics, Mid East Tech Univ, Turkey, 69-72; res fel seismol, Dept Terrestrial Magnetism, Carnegie Inst, Washington, DC, 72-77. *Mem:* Am Geophys Union; Seismol Soc Am; AAAS. *Res:* Subducting plates: structure and dynamics; earthquake source: models and barameter estimates; seismicity patterns: temporal and spatial. *Mailing Add:* 2811 Mt Vernon Lane Blacksburg VA 24060-8121

SNOKE, ROY EUGENE, ENZYMOLOGY. *Current Pos:* sr res chemist, 72-79, res assoc, 79-88, RES ASST, EASTMAN KODAK CO, 88- *Personal Data:* b Shippensburg, Pa, Aug 6, 43; m 67, Sherry L Steele; c Stacie L & Stephanie E. *Educ:* Shippensburg State Col, BS, 65; Univ NDak, MS, 67, PhD(biochem), 70. *Prof Exp:* NIH fel, Inst Enzyme Res, Univ Wis-Madison, 70-72, asst prof biochem, 72. *Concurrent Pos:* Technol leader, Biochem Group, Clin Diag Res Lab, Eastman Kodak Co. *Mem:* Am Soc Microbiol; Am Chem Soc; Am Asn Clin Chem. *Res:* Regulation of gluconeogenesis; enzyme mechanisms and adaptations involved in biological control, specifically phosphoenolpyruvate carboxykinase; microbial enzyme isolation and characterization; use of enzymes for biotransformation; design of enzyme analytical systems; clinical diagnostic analysis systems. *Mailing Add:* 1085 Marigold Dr Webster NY 14580-8727

SNOOK, JAMES RONALD, geology, for more information see previous edition

SNOOK, THEODORE, HISTOLOGY, EMBRYOLOGY. *Current Pos:* chmn dept, 67-72, from assoc prof to prof, 53-77, EMER PROF ANAT, SCH MED, UNIV NDAK, 77- *Personal Data:* b Titusville, NJ, Apr 14, 07; m 33; c 1. *Educ:* Rutgers Univ, BSc, 29, MSc, 30; Cornell Univ, PhD(histol), 33. *Prof Exp:* Asst zool, Rutgers Univ, 29-30; instr histol & embryol, Cornell Univ, 30-34; from instr histol & embryol to asst prof anat, Col Med, Syracuse Univ, 34-46; asst prof, Tulane Univ, 46-49; assoc prof, Sch Med, Univ Pittsburgh, 49-53. *Mem:* AAAS; Am Asn Anatomists; Biol Photog Asn; Microcirc Soc; Sigma Xi. *Res:* Development of pharyngeal tonsil; spleen vascular connections and lymphatics; comparative mammalian spleen morphology. *Mailing Add:* 343 Sheridan Rd Racine WI 53403

SNOPE, ANDREW JOHN, GENETICS, CYTOGENETICS. *Current Pos:* from asst prof to assoc prof biol, Essex Community Col, 70-77, chmn, Div Sci & Math, 82-88, assoc dean Instr, 88-90, PROF BIOL, ESSEX COMMUNITY COL, 77-, DEAN INSTR, 90- *Personal Data:* b Paterson, NJ, Jan 19, 39; m 57; c 3. *Educ:* Del Valley Col, BS, 60; Rutgers Univ, MS, 62; Ind Univ, PhD, 66. *Prof Exp:* Asst prof biol, Univ Md, Baltimore, 66-70. *Res:* Chromosome structure and behavior; human cytogenetics; instructional methods in college biology teaching. *Mailing Add:* Essex Community Col 7201 Rossville Blvd Baltimore MD 21237-3855

SNOVER, JAMES EDWARD, MATHEMATICS. *Current Pos:* asst prof, 54-71, ASSOC PROF MATH, FLA STATE UNIV, 71- *Personal Data:* b Troy, NY, Nov 23, 20; m 42; c 4. *Educ:* State Univ NY, BA, 41; Syracuse Univ, MA, 50, PhD, 55. *Prof Exp:* Asst prof math, Assoc Cols Upper NY, 46-49. *Mem:* Am Math Soc; Math Asn Am. *Res:* Analysis. *Mailing Add:* 1704 Myrick Rd Tallahassee FL 32303-4334

SNOVER, KURT ALBERT, PHYSICS. *Current Pos:* SR RES ASSOC NUCLEAR PHYSICS, UNIV WASH, 72-, RES ASST PROF PHYSICS, 77- *Personal Data:* b Albany, NY, Apr 26, 43; m 64; c 1. *Educ:* Fla State Univ, BS, 64; Stanford Univ, MS, 68, PhD(physics), 69. *Prof Exp:* Res assoc nuclear physics, State Univ NY Stony Brook, 69-71, asst prof physics, 71-72. *Mem:* Am Phys Soc. *Res:* Low energy nuclear physics. *Mailing Add:* 6818 54th Ave NE Seattle WA 98115. *Fax:* 206-543-9285

SNOW, ADOLPH ISAAC, CHEMISTRY. *Current Pos:* RETIRED. *Personal Data:* b Providence, RI, Oct 8, 21; m 44, Carolyn A Barnes; c Allen M & Barbara A. *Educ:* Brown Univ, ScB, 43; Iowa State Col, PhD(chem), 50. *Prof Exp:* From asst to res assoc, Inst Atomic Res, Iowa State Col, 43-50; instr, Inst Study Metals, Univ Chicago, 50-52; head, Phys Chem Sect, Sinclair Res, Inc, 52-56, dir, Radiation Lab, 56-59, Radiation Div, 59-66 & Radiation & Instrumentation Div, 66-69; mgr phys res, Atlantic Richfield Co, 69-72, mgr phys & environ res, 72-78, sr consult, 78-82, sr res adv, 82-85. *Concurrent Pos:* Consult air & water qual control, Alyeska Pipeline Serv Co, 72-85; consult, A I Snow, 85- *Mem:* Am Chem Soc; Am Soc Metals; Am Crystallog Asn; Sigma Xi; AAAS. *Res:* X-ray crystallography; uranium and thorium alloy phase diagrams; metallurgy of thorium and alloys; neutron diffraction; bonding in solids; physical properties of catalysts; radiation and tracer chemistry; petroleum processing and instrumentation; environment; fate of oil in water; air and water pollution. *Mailing Add:* 731 Dunbar PO Box 487 Beecher IL 60401

SNOW, BEATRICE LEE, MAMMALIAN GENETICS, MICROCOMPUTERS. *Current Pos:* From instr to assoc prof biol, 65-74, actg chmn dept, 72-73, chmn dept biol, 73-78, COORD MED TECHNOL PROG, SUFFOLK UNIV, 68-, PROF BIOL, 74- *Personal Data:* b Boston, Mass, June 9, 41. *Educ:* Suffolk Univ, AB, 62; Univ NH, MS, 64, PhD(zool), 71. *Concurrent Pos:* Allied health adv, Brookline Pub Schs, 68-70; dir, Marine Sci Prog, NH Col & Univ Coun, 75-76; coordr, Biol-Comput Prog, Suffolk Univ, 81- *Mem:* Am Soc Human Genetics; Am Genetic Asn; Am Inst Biol Sci; Am Soc Med Technol; Am Soc Zool. *Res:* Alkaline phosphatase activity and siren mutation expressivity in the mouse. *Mailing Add:* Dept Biol Suffolk Univ 8 Ashburton Pl Boston MA 02108-2701

SNOW, CLYDE COLLINS, PHYSICAL ANTHROPOLOGY, FORENSIC ANTHROPOLOGY. *Current Pos:* FORENSIC ANTHROP CONSULT, 79- *Personal Data:* b Ft Worth, Tex, Jan 7, 28; m 55; c 5. *Educ:* Eastern NMex Univ, BS, 50; Tex Tech Col, MS, 55; Univ Ariz, PhD, 67; Am Bd Forensic Anthrop, dipl. *Prof Exp:* Res asst anat, Med Col SC, 60-61; res anthropologist, 61-65; chief, Appl Biol Sect, Civil Aeromed Inst, Fed Aviation Agency, 65-69, chief phys anthrop res, 69-79. *Concurrent Pos:* From adj instr to adj asst prof anthrop, Univ Okla, 62-80, adj prof, 80-, res assoc, Sch Med, 64-; trustee, Forensic Sci Found, 73-79; forensic anthrop consult, Okla State Med Examr, 78- & Med Examr, Cook County, Ill, 79-; consult, select comt assassinations, US House Rep, 78-79; pres, Forensic Sci Educ, Inc, 82-86. *Mem:* Am Acad Forensic Sci (vpres, 78-79); Am Anthrop Asn; Am Asn Phys Anthrop; Soc Study Human Biol; Am Soc Forensic Odontol; Sigma Xi. *Res:* Forensic anthropology; study of human skeletal remains to establish personal identification and cause of death. *Mailing Add:* 2230 Blue Creek Pky Norman OK 73071-3921

SNOW, DAVID BAKER, MATERIALS SCIENCE. *Current Pos:* SUPV, TEM & LIGHT MICROS, UNITED TECHNOL RES CTR, 77- *Personal Data:* b Albuquerque, NMex, Nov 15, 41; m 70; c 2. *Educ:* Mass Inst Technol, BS, 63, ScD(metall), 71. *Prof Exp:* Res metallurgist, Refractory Metals Prod Dept, Gen Elec Co, 70-77. *Mem:* Am Soc Metals; Metall Soc; Electron Microscopy Soc Am; Sigma Xi; Mat Res Soc. *Res:* Physical metallurgy of rapidly-solidified metals and alloys; development of advanced titanium-based alloys; recovery and recrystallization; applications of electron microscopy to materials science. *Mailing Add:* United Technol Res Ctr 411 Silver Lane MS 129-22 East Hartford CT 06108-1096

SNOW, DONALD L(OESCH), ENVIRONMENTAL HEALTH ENGINEERING. *Current Pos:* RETIRED. *Personal Data:* b Cleveland, Ohio, Apr 10, 17; m 48; c 3. *Educ:* Case Western Reserve Univ, BS, 39; Univ Wis, MS, 41; Environ Engrs Intersoc, dipl. *Honors & Awards:* Hemispheric Award, Inter-Am Asn Sanit Engrs, 54. *Prof Exp:* Sanit engr, Pan-Am Sanit Bur, USPHS, 43-48, sr sanit engr, 48-51, chief, Res Facilities Planning Br, 51-54, chief, Sanit Eng Br, 54-60, lab design documentation proj, NIH, 61-62, ed radiol health data, 62-64, chief, Radiation Surveillance Ctr, Bur Radiol Health, 64-67 & Stand & Intel Br, 68-69, dir, Off Criteria & Stand, 69-71; dir, Nat Ctr Toxicol Res Prog Off, Univ Ark, 71-79. *Concurrent Pos:* Ed, J Inter-Am Asn Sanit Eng, 46-48; pres, Fed Conf Sanit Engrs, 64; sanit eng dir, USPHS, 43-52. *Mem:* Am Soc Civil Engrs; Am Acad Environ Engrs; fel Am Pub Health Asn; Inter-Am Asn Sanit Eng (secy, 46-48); AAAS; Sigma Xi. *Res:* Medical research facilities planning; environmental health engineering; radiological health data program management; radiation standards; environmental standards. *Mailing Add:* 14300 Chenal Pkway No 7017 Little Rock AR 72211

SNOW, DONALD RAY, MATHEMATICS, COMPUTERS IN MATHEMATICS. *Current Pos:* assoc prof, 69-74, PROF MATH, BRIGHAM YOUNG UNIV, 74- *Personal Data:* b Los Angeles, Calif, Mar 19, 31; m 58, Diane Manwaring; c Donald R Jr, Linda (Westorer), Judy (Spencer), Kathleen (Gill), Jennifer (Jackson) & James R. *Educ:* Univ Utah, BSME & BA, 59; Stanford Univ, MSME, 60, MS, 62, PhD(math), 65. *Honors & Awards:* Hamilton Watch Award. *Prof Exp:* Res asst comput ctr, Stanford Univ, 61-62; res engr res labs, Lockheed Missiles & Space Co, 62-64; res assoc math, Univ Minn, Minneapolis, 64-66; asst prof, Univ Colo, Boulder, 66-69. *Concurrent Pos:* Vis prof, Fulbright-Hayes sr lectureship to Peru, 74 & vis res prof, Dept Appl Math, Univ Waterloo, Ontario, 76-77; chmn bd dir, Rocky Mountain Math Consortium, 77-78; lectr, Math Asn Am, 78-; Atomic Energy Comn fel, Stanford Univ; mem bd dirs, Utah Coun Comput in Educ, 82-85; vis res prof, Imp Col, Univ London, 90; chmn, Intermountain Sect Math Asn Am, 94-96. *Mem:* Am Math Soc; Math Asn Am; Soc Indust & Appl Math; Nat Coun Teachers Math; Am Math Asn; Sigma Xi. *Res:* Calculus of variations; functional equations; combinatorics; partial and ordinary differential and integral equations and inequalities; history of math; computers in math instruction and research; numerical analysis. *Mailing Add:* Dept Math Brigham Young Univ Provo UT 84602

SNOW, DOUGLAS OSCAR, MATHEMATICS. *Current Pos:* from asst prof to assoc prof, 47-56, PROF MATH, ACADIA UNIV, 56- *Personal Data:* b Port Maitland, NS, Nov 27, 17; m 51. *Educ:* Acadia Univ, BSc, 43, MA, 46; Brown Univ, MSc, 52; Queen's Univ, Can, PhD(math), 56. *Prof Exp:* Asst prof math, Mt Allison Univ, 46-47. *Mem:* Am Math Soc; Math Asn Am; Can Math Cong. *Res:* Analysis; integration in abstract spaces. *Mailing Add:* PO Box 583 Wolfville NS B0P 1X0 Can

SNOW, EDWARD HUNTER, SOLID STATE PHYSICS. *Current Pos:* VPRES & DIR OPERS, EG&G RETICON CORP, 71- *Personal Data:* b St George, Utah, June 26, 36; m 56; c 3. *Educ:* Univ Utah, BA, 58, PhD(physics), 63. *Honors & Awards:* Cert of Merit, Franklin Inst, 75. *Prof Exp:* Mem tech staff, Physics Dept Res & Develop Lab, Semiconductor Div, Fairchild Camera & Instrument Corp, 63-68, mgr, Physics Dept, 68-71. *Concurrent Pos:* Lectr, Univ Santa Clara. *Mem:* Fel Inst Elec & Electronics Engrs; Am Phys Soc. *Res:* Optoelectronics; electrical properties of insulators and semiconductors; semiconductor device physics; properties of interfaces between metals; insulators. *Mailing Add:* 24871 Olive Tree Lane Los Altos CA 94024

SNOW, ELEANOUR ANNE, MINERAL KINETICS. *Current Pos:* ASST PROF MINERAL, UNIV ARIZ, 87-; DEPT GEOL, UNIV SFLA. *Personal Data:* b Portland, Ore, Apr 4, 60; m 89. *Educ:* Pomona Col, BA, 82; Brown Univ, ScM, 84, PhD (geol), 87. *Mem:* Am Geophys Union; Geol Soc Am; Mineral Soc Am; Sigma Xi. *Res:* Effect of deformation on the mechanisms and kinetics of mineral reactions. *Mailing Add:* Geol Sca 203 Univ SFla 4202 Fowler Ave Tampa FL 33620-9951

SNOW, GEORGE ABRAHAM, PHYSICS. *Current Pos:* from assoc prof to prof physics, 58-92, actg chmn, Dept Physics & Astron, 70-71, EMER PROF & SR RES SCIENTIST, UNIV MD, COL PARK, 92- *Personal Data:* b New York, NY, Aug 24, 26; m 48, Lila Alpert; c Zachary, Andrew & Sara. *Educ:* City Col, BS, 45; Princeton Univ, MS, 47, PhD(physics), 49. *Prof Exp:* Jr physicist, Brookhaven Nat Lab, 48-51, assoc physicist, 51-55; physicist, US Naval Res Lab, 55-58. *Concurrent Pos:* Mem, Inst Advan Study, 52-53; vis lectr, Univ Wis, 55; NSF sr fel, Europ Orgn Nuclear Res, Geneva, 61-62, sci assoc, 80; John S Guggenheim fel & Fulbright res scholar, Univ Rome, 65-66; vis prof, Univ Paris, 72-73 & Tohoku Univ, 79; consult, Argonne Nat Lab, Fermilab, Brookhaven Nat Lab & Prentice Hall Publ Co; mem bd trustees, Univ Res Asn, 73-78, vchmn, 74, chmn sci comt, 75-77; vchmn div particles & fields, Am Phys Soc, 75, chmn, 76; gen res fel, Univ Md, 86; vis scientist, Univ Bologna, 86. *Mem:* Fel AAAS; fel Am Phys Soc; Fedn Am Sci. *Res:* Experimental and theoretical high energy physics; neutrino interactions; e-plus e-minus and muon interactions; experimental test of Pauli principle. *Mailing Add:* Dept Physics & Astron Univ Md College Park MD 20742. *Fax:* 301-699-9195; *E-Mail:* snow@umdhep.umd.edu

SNOW, GEORGE EDWARD, ZOOLOGY. *Current Pos:* asst prof, 77-84, ASSOC PROF BIOL SCI, MT ST MARYS COL, 84- *Personal Data:* b Denver, Colo, Aug 6, 45; m 83, Elizabeth K Perryman. *Educ:* Rockhurst Col, Kansas City, MO, BA, 67; Univ Colo, Boulder, MA, 74, PhD(biol), 77. *Prof Exp:* Instr biol sci, Community Col Denver, 72-77. *Concurrent Pos:* Proj dir, Local Course Improv Grant, NSF, 79-82, Undergrad Curric & Course

Develop Grant, 91-; Danforth assoc, Danforth Asn, 81; lectr, Calif Polytech State Univ, 85-89; instr, Cuesta Col, 86-89, Allan Hancock Col, 87-89; adj prof, Calif Polytech State Univ. *Mem:* AAAS; Am Soc Zoologists; Sigma Xi; Nat Asn Biol Teachers. *Res:* Control mechanisms of thermoregulation in reptiles in response to toxins. *Mailing Add:* Mt St Marys Col 12001 Chalon Rd Los Angeles CA 90049-1526. *Fax:* 310-476-9296

SNOW, JAMES BYRON, JR, OTOLARYNGOLOGY. *Current Pos:* DIR, NAT INST DEAFNESS & OTHER COMMUN DISORDERS, NIH, 90- *Personal Data:* b Oklahoma City, Okla, Mar 12, 32; m 54, Sallie Ricker; c James B III, John Andrew & Sallie (Snow Sharer). *Educ:* Univ Okla, BS, 53; Harvard Univ, MD, 56. *Hon Degrees:* MA, Univ Pa, 73. *Honors & Awards:* Presidential Citation, Am Otolaryngol Soc; Distinguished Achievement Award, Decfress Res Found. *Prof Exp:* Asst prof otorhinolaryngol, Med Ctr, Univ Okla, 62-64, prof & head dept, 64-72; prof otorhinolaryngol & chmn dept, Sch Med, Univ Pa, 72-90. *Mem:* Am Acad Otolaryngol Head & Neck Surg; Am Col Surgeons; Soc Univ Otolaryngol; Am Otolaryngol Soc; fel Am Laryngol Asn; Sigma Xi; Triological Soc; fel Japan Broncho-Esophagological Soc. *Res:* Clinical disorders of smell and taste. *Mailing Add:* NIH NIDCD Bldg 31 Rm 3C02 9000 Rockville Pike Bethesda MD 20892. *E-Mail:* snow_james@nih.gov

SNOW, JEAN ANTHONY, MYCOLOGY, AEROBIOLOGY. *Current Pos:* CONSULT, MOUNTAIN MEADOW ORCHARD, BRUSH VALLEY, PA, 89-, TREE WORKS, STATE COL PA, 93- *Personal Data:* b Richmond, Ind, Apr 18, 32; m 62, 76, Elinor R Moberly; c Melinda M & Diana J. *Educ:* DePauw Univ, AB, 54; Pa State Univ, PhD(plant path, genetics), 64. *Prof Exp:* Asst prof plant path, Univ Mass, 63-67; chief plant pathologist, Standard Fruit Co, 67-70; res assoc, Ctr Air Environ Studies, Pa State Univ, University Park, 70-77. *Concurrent Pos:* Consult, Municipal Tree Restoration Prog, Eastern States, Penn State Univ, 88-92. *Mem:* Int Soc Plant Path; Int Asn Aerobiol; Sigma Xi. *Res:* Epidemiology and biometeorology of fungal diseases of plants; aerobiology, especially occurrence and dispersal of fungus air spora and aeroallergens. *Mailing Add:* 720E W Beaver Ave State College PA 16801-3920

SNOW, JOEL A, UNIVERSITY & NATIONAL LABORATORY MANAGEMENT, TECHNOLOGY TRANSFER. *Current Pos:* DIR, INST PHYS RES & TECHNOL, IOWA STATE UNIV, 93- *Personal Data:* b Brockton, Mass, Apr 1, 37; m, Barbara Kashion; c Jon, Nicholas, James & Alex. *Educ:* Univ NC, BS, 58; Wash Univ, MS, 63, PhD(physics), 67. *Honors & Awards:* William S Jump Found Award, 73; Arthur S Flemming Award, 74. *Prof Exp:* Fel, NSF, 67, prog dir theoret physics, 68-71, head, Off Interdisciplinary Res, 70-71, dep asst dir sci & technol, Res Appln, 71-74, dir, Off Planning & Resources Mgt, 74-76, dir, Div Policy Res & Anal, 76; sr policy analyst, Off Sci & Technol Policy, Exec Off Pres, 76-77; assoc dir res policy, US Dept Energy, 77-81, dir sci & technol affairs, 81-88; assoc vpres res, Argonne Nat Lab & Univ Chicago, 88-93. *Concurrent Pos:* Instr physics & electronics, USN Nuclear Power Sch, 58-61; res assoc, Dept Physics & fel, Ctr Advan Study, Univ Ill, 67-68. *Mem:* Fel AAAS; fel Am Phys Soc; Sigma Xi; World Future Soc; Am Chem Soc; Am Nuclear Soc. *Res:* Statistical mechanics, superconductivity, transport and field theory; technology assessment; science policy; environment and energy problems; technology transfer; university-industry relationships. *Mailing Add:* 2237 Ironwood Ct Ames IA 50014. *Fax:* 515-294-2761; *E-Mail:* jasnow@iastate.edu

SNOW, JOHN ELBRIDGE, ORGANIC CHEMISTRY, FLEXIBLE PACKAGING. *Current Pos:* CONSULT, TELTECH FLEXIBLE PACKAGING, 80- *Personal Data:* b Marion, Ohio, June 4, 15; m 41; c 3. *Educ:* Oberlin Col, AB, 38; Cornell Univ, MS, 40, PhD(org chem), 42. *Prof Exp:* Group leader org synthesis res dept, Heyden Chem Corp, 42-56; mgr chem & plastics res, Res Div, Curtiss-Wright Corp, 56-61; res dir, Rap-in-Wax Co, 61-65; mgr process & prod develop, Packages Co Div, Champion Papers Co Div, US Plywood Champion Papers Co, 65-70, dir appl res, Champion Packages Co, Div Champion Int, 70-80. *Concurrent Pos:* Lectr, Dept Food Sci, Univ Minn, 70-81, vis prof, 72. *Mem:* Am Chem Soc; Packaging Inst. *Res:* Organic chemicals; pentaerythritols; resins and plastics; flexible packaging materials; films; extrusion coating and laminating; adhesives; paper technology; adhesion; coextrusion coating; surface chemistry. *Mailing Add:* 4750 Dona Lane Minneapolis MN 55422

SNOW, JOHN THOMAS, ORGANIC CHEMISTRY. *Current Pos:* res scientist, 75-76, MGR BIOCHEM, MKT DEPT, CALBIOCHEM, LA JOLLA, CALIF, 77- *Personal Data:* b St Petersburg, Fla, Dec 29, 43; m 66. *Educ:* Earlham Col, AB, 65; Middlebury Col, MS, 67; Univ Calif, Davis, PhD(chem), 70. *Prof Exp:* Res assoc chem, Univ Calif, Davis, 70-71; chief chemist, US Sugar Corp, 71-74; Nat Res Coun assoc, USDA, Western Regional Res Lab, Berkeley, Calif, 74-75. *Mem:* Am Chem Soc; Sigma Xi; Int Food Technologists. *Res:* Mechanistic and synthetic organic chemistry. *Mailing Add:* PO Box 31 Del Mar CA 92014

SNOW, JOHN THOMAS, meso-meteorology, geophysical fluid dynamics, for more information see previous edition

SNOW, JOHNNIE PARK, PLANT PATHOLOGY. *Current Pos:* from asst prof to assoc prof, 72-76, PROF PLANT PATH, LA STATE UNIV, BATON ROUGE, 81-, DEPT HEAD, 92- *Personal Data:* b Abilene, Tex, July 12, 42; m 68; c 2. *Educ:* McMurry Col, BA, 65; Univ Ark, MS, 67; Tex A&M Univ, PhD(plant path), 70. *Prof Exp:* Fel plant path, NC State Univ, 70-72. *Mem:* Sigma Xi; Am Phytopath Soc. *Res:* Basic and applied research on soybean diseases. *Mailing Add:* Dept of Plant Path La State Univ Baton Rouge LA 70803

SNOW, JONATHAN EDWARD, ISOTOPE GEOCHEMISTRY, OCEANIC PETROLOGY. *Current Pos:* SCIENTIST, MAX-PLANCK INST CHEM, 94- *Personal Data:* m 90, Laura Feld; c Samuel. *Educ:* Ind Univ, BA(econs) & BA(geol), 83; Univ Rochester, MSc, 86; Mass Inst Technol, PhD(oceanog), 93. *Prof Exp:* Postdoctoral researcher, Int Coun Sci Unions, Nancy, France, 93-94. *Mem:* Am Geophys Union; Nat Asn Geol Teachers; Europ Union Geosci. *Res:* Physics and chemistry of the evolution of the mantle as evidenced by isotopic and trace element systematics of mantle rocks. *Mailing Add:* Max Planck Inst Chem & Geochem Postfach 3060 55020 Mainz Germany. *E-Mail:* jesnow@geobar.mpcn-mainz.mpg.de

SNOW, JOSEPH WILLIAM, WIND & SOLAR ENERGY. *Current Pos:* RETIRED. *Personal Data:* b Scarborough, Maine, Apr 3, 39. *Educ:* Boston Col, BS, 61; Univ Utah, BS, 64; Univ Wis, Madison, MS, 75; Univ Va, PhD(environ sci), 81. *Prof Exp:* Weather officer, Air Weather Serv, USAF, 62-67; proj mgr, EG&G Inc, 68-69; supvr meteorologist, Panama Canal Co, Balboa, 70-71; res assoc, Dept Environ Sci, Univ Va, 80-81; asst prof meteorol, Lyndon State Col, 81-; res scientist, Hanscon AFB, 81-94. *Mem:* Am Meteorol Soc; Am Geophys Union; Am Inst Aeronaut & Astronaut. *Res:* Analytical explanation of area climates and the modifications effected by man; coastal wind power and wind shear within the atmospheric boundary layer. *Mailing Add:* 146 Pine Point Rd Scarborough ME 04074

SNOW, LLOYD DALE, PROTEIN CHEMISTRY, ENZYME KINETICS. *Current Pos:* from asst prof to assoc prof, 79-89, PROF BIOCHEM, LA TECH UNIV, 89- *Personal Data:* b Lake City, Ark, Dec 3, 47; m 78, Marcella J Moore; c Amanda C & Lloyd J. *Educ:* Ark State Univ, BS, 69, MS, 72; Okla State Univ, PhD, 76. *Prof Exp:* Sci teacher, Bay Brown Pub High Sch, Bay, Ark, 69-71; res assist, Biochem Dept, Okla State Univ, 72-76; fel, Cell Biol Dept, Baylor Col Med, 76-79. *Concurrent Pos:* Mem, Undergrad Res Comt, Am Heart Asn, La, 80-, chair, 83-87 & 93-; chair, Chem Sect, La Acad Sci, 86-93, dir, Phys Sci Div, 93-95; summer faculty fel, NASA Johnson Space Ctr, Houston, Tex, 94 & 95; fel, La Tech Univ Quest Qual, 95. *Mem:* Am Chem Soc; Sigma Xi. *Res:* Isolation and characterization of plasma membrane enzymes; kinetic studies of the mechanisms of 5'-nucleotidase and alkaline phosphatase. *Mailing Add:* Biochem Lab La Tech Univ Ruston LA 71272. *Fax:* 318-251-2823; *E-Mail:* snowchem@vm.cc.latech.edu

SNOW, LOUDELL FROMME, MEDICAL ANTHROPOLOGY. *Current Pos:* Mem fac, Col Human Med & asst prof anthrop, 71-73 & community med, 74-78, ASSOC PROF ANTHROP, MICH STATE UNIV, 78- *Personal Data:* b Kansas City, Mo, July 17, 33; m 60; c 1. *Educ:* Univ Colo, BA, 59; Univ Ariz, MA, 70, PhD(anthrop), 71. *Mem:* AAAS; Am Anthrop Asn; Soc Med Anthrop; Sigma Xi; Am Folklore Soc. *Res:* Folk medical systems; folk practitioners as psychotherapists; witchcraft beliefs; behavioral science in the medical school curriculum; spirit possession and trance states; impact of cultural background on beliefs and attitudes concerning female reproductive cycle. *Mailing Add:* Dept Anthrop Mich State Univ 354 Baker Hall East Lansing MI 48824-1118

SNOW, MICHAEL DENNIS, PHYTOPATHOLOGY, MICROBIAL ECOLOGY. *Current Pos:* From asst prof to assoc prof biol, 70-84, chmn dept phys & life sci, 77-80, PROF BIOL, UNIV PORTLAND, 85- *Personal Data:* b Sacramento, Calif, Nov 9, 42; m 66; c 2. *Educ:* Sacramento State Col, BA, 65; Wash State Univ, PhD(phytopath), 74. *Honors & Awards:* Nat Tech Achievement Award Ecol, US Environ Protection Agency, 86. *Concurrent Pos:* NSF fac develop fel, 81; res assoc, Corvallis Environ Res Lab, 81-82; vis scientist, US Environ Protection Agency, 91. *Mem:* Am Soc Plant Physiologists; AAAS; Sigma Xi. *Res:* Stress physiology of crop plants. *Mailing Add:* Univ Portland 5000 N Williamette Blvd Portland OR 97203

SNOW, MIKEL HENRY, MUSCLE REGENERATION, MUSCLE PLASTICITY. *Current Pos:* asst prof, 75-79, ASSOC PROF ANAT, UNIV SOUTHERN CALIF, 79- *Personal Data:* b Three Rivers, Mich, Sept 18, 44. *Educ:* Olivet Col, BA, 66; Univ Mich, PhD(anat), 71. *Prof Exp:* Instr anat, Sch Med, Univ Miami, 71-72, asst prof, 72-75. *Concurrent Pos:* Vis prof, Sch Med, Univ Miami, 80; ed, Anat Rec, 81- *Mem:* Am Asn Anatomists; Develop Biol. *Res:* The role of satellite cells in muscle regeneration and denervation; muscle adaptation to chronic and acute exercise in mammals. *Mailing Add:* Dept Anat Univ Southern Calif 1333 San Pablo St Los Angeles CA 90033

SNOW, MILTON LEONARD, PHYSICAL CHEMISTRY. *Current Pos:* RETIRED. *Personal Data:* b Providence, RI, Feb 16, 30; m 58, Rita Mueller; c Daniel E, Jeffrey L, Samuel D & Stanley H. *Educ:* Brown Univ, ScB, 51; Princeton Univ, MA, 53, PhD(phys chem), 56. *Prof Exp:* Chemist, Davison Chem Co, WR Grace Co, 56-59; sr chemist, Appl Physics Lab, Johns Hopkins Univ, 59-93, proj supvr, 76. *Mem:* Sigma Xi. *Res:* Heterogeneous catalysis; gas phase reaction kinetics; supersonic ramjet performance analysis and prediction; hypersonic ramjet design; air pollution analysis; chemical anti-submarine warfare. *Mailing Add:* 11304 Palatine Dr Potomac MD 20854-1445

SNOW, NICHOLAS HARRER, CHEMICAL SEPARATIONS. *Current Pos:* ASST PROF CHEM, SETON HALL UNIV, 94- *Personal Data:* b St Louis, Mo, May 13, 65; m 92, Angela Stokes. *Educ:* Univ Va, BS, 87; Va Tech, PhD(chem), 92. *Prof Exp:* Analytical chemist, Dept Path, Univ Va, 92-93, lectr, 93-94. *Concurrent Pos:* Univ teaching fel, Seton Hall Univ, 96-97; consult, Johnson & Johnson, 96- *Mem:* Am Chem Soc. *Res:* Chemical separations; gas and liquid chromatography; sampling for trace analysis in separation methods; solid phase microextraction, gas chromatography/mass spectrometry, supercritical fluid extraction, capillary electrophoresis; theoretical modeling of separation methods. *Mailing Add:* Dept Chem Seton Hall Univ South Orange NJ 07079. *E-Mail:* snowrich@shu.edu

SNOW, PHILIP ANTHONY, hydrology, mineralogy, for more information see previous edition

SNOW, RICHARD HUNTLEY, CHEMICAL ENGINEERING. *Current Pos:* RETIRED. *Personal Data:* b Worcester, Mass, Apr 26, 28; m 52, Rosemary Mixon; c Anita (Orlikoff), Luther & Sarah. *Educ:* Harvard Univ, AB, 50; Va Polytech Inst, MS, 52; Ill Inst Technol, PhD(chem eng), 56. *Prof Exp:* Res fel chem eng, 52-56, res engr, 56-63, sr engr, 63-73, mgr chem eng res, 77-83, dir, Nat Inst Petrol & Energy Res, 83-85, eng adv, Iit Res Inst, 73-; interim dir, Ctr Hazardous Waste Mgt, 87-88. *Mem:* AAAS; fel Am Inst Chem Engrs; Am Chem Soc; Soc Mining Engrs; Am Inst Mining, Metall & Petrol Engrs; Acad Hazardous Waste Mgt. *Res:* Chemical process development; chemical kinetics; thermodynamics; process simulation; hazardous waste control and minimization; particle processing. *Mailing Add:* 5000 S Cornell Ave Apt 18C Chicago IL 60615. Fax: 773-324-8645

SNOW, RICHARD L, PHYSICAL CHEMISTRY. *Current Pos:* From asst prof to assoc prof, 57-66, PROF CHEM, BRIGHAM YOUNG UNIV, 66- *Personal Data:* b Salt Lake City, Utah, Jan 27, 30; m 53; c 5. *Educ:* Univ Utah, BS, 53, PhD(phys chem), 57. *Concurrent Pos:* NSF sci fac fel, Brown Univ, 63-64; Oak Ridge Assoc Univs fel, Savannah River Lab, E I du Pont de Nemours & Co, Inc, 71-72; fac fel, Battelle Northwest Norcus, 83. *Mem:* Sigma Xi; Am Chem Soc. *Res:* Quantum chemistry; theory of liquids. *Mailing Add:* Dept Chem Brigham Young Univ Provo UT 84601

SNOW, SIDNEY RICHARD, genetics; deceased, see previous edition for last biography

SNOW, THEODORE PECK, ASTRONOMY, ASTROPHYSICS. *Current Pos:* asst prof physics & astrophys, Ctr Astrophys & Space Astron, 77-80, fel, Lab Atmospheric & Space Physics, 77-85, assoc prof astrophys, 80-87, dir, 86-96, PROF ASTROPHYS, CTR ASTROPHYS & SPACE ASTRON, 87- *Personal Data:* b Seattle, Wash, Jan 30, 47; m 69, Constance McLoughlin; c McGregor A, Tyler M & Reilly A. *Educ:* Yale Univ, BA, 69; Univ Wash, MS, 70, PhD(astron), 73. *Prof Exp:* Res assoc astrophys sci, Princeton Univ Observ, 73-76, mem res staff, 76-77. *Concurrent Pos:* Mem, many NASA & Am Astron Soc adv panels & comts. *Mem:* Int Astron Union; Am Astron Soc; Sigma Xi; Royal Astronaut Soc. *Res:* Visible wave length, infrared and ultraviolet space-borne spectroscopy of hot stars, stellar winds and interstellar gas and dust. *Mailing Add:* PO Box 43 Louisville CO 80027. Fax: 303-492-7178; E-Mail: tsnow@casa.colorado.edu

SNOW, THOMAS RUSSELL, CARDIOVASCULAR PHYSIOLOGY. *Personal Data:* b Danville, Va, Mar 29, 44. *Educ:* Carnegie-Mellon Univ, BS, 65; Duke Univ, PhD(physics), 71. *Prof Exp:* Instr biomed eng, Baylor Col Med, 71-73; res assoc physics, Duke Univ, 69-71, NIH fel physiol, 73-75, asst prof, 78-82, asst mem, 83-90, assoc prof, 84-90; assoc prof, Dept Surg, Univ SFla, 91-96. *Mem:* Biophys Soc; Int Soc Heart Res; Am Physiol Soc. *Res:* Determination of the relevant factors controlling bio-energetics of the mammalian myocardium. *Mailing Add:* 17310 Sherman Rd Lutz FL 33549. Fax: 813-974-2669

SNOW, WILLIAM MICHAEL, NEUTRON PHYSICS, WEAK INTERACTIONS. *Current Pos:* ASST PROF PHYSICS, IND UNIV, 93- *Personal Data:* b Springfield, Ill, July 30, 60; m 91, April K Sievert. *Educ:* Univ Ill, BS(physics) & BS(math), 82; Harvard Univ, MS, 85, PhD(physics), 90. *Prof Exp:* Res assoc, Argonne Nat Lab, 86-90; Nat Res Coun res assoc, Nat Inst Stand & Technol, 90-93. *Mem:* Am Phys Soc; Am Asn Physics Teachers. *Res:* Neutron scattering; weak interactions of low energy neutrons; development of neutron polarizers; absolute neutron flux measurement. *Mailing Add:* Ind Univ Bloomington IN 47405. E-Mail: snow@iucf.indiana.edu

SNOW, WILLIAM ROSEBROOK, ATOMIC PHYSICS, MOLECULAR PHYSICS. *Current Pos:* TECH DIR, STRATAGLASS, 94- *Personal Data:* b New York, NY, Jan 6, 30; m 51; c 2. *Educ:* Stanford Univ, BS, 52; Univ Wash, MS, 65, PhD(physics), 66. *Prof Exp:* Rotational trainee reactor physics, Hanford Atomic Prod Oper, Gen Elec Corp, 52-54; physicist, Precision Technol, Inc, Calif, 54-58; staff assoc afterglows & atomic beams, Gen Atomic, 58-62; mem res staff satellite mass spectrometry, Aerospace Corp, 66-68; asst prof physics, Univ Mo-Rolla, 68-73, assoc prof, 73-78; mem staff, Pac Western Syst Inc, 78-81, dir res & develop, 81-94. *Mem:* Am Phys Soc; Electrochem Soc; Am Vacuum Soc; Sigma Xi. *Res:* Ion-neutral reactions in plasmas and afterglows; negative ion charge transfer; ionosphere reactions; mass spectrometry; molecular scattering; plasma enhanced chemical vapor deposition. *Mailing Add:* Strataglass 958 San Leandro Suite 100 Mountain View CA 94043

SNOW, WOLFE, MATHEMATICS. *Current Pos:* From instr to asst prof, 64-83, ASSOC PROF MATH, BROOKLYN COL, 84- *Personal Data:* b New York, NY, May 17, 38; m 60, Ida E Galinsky; c Martin, Israel & Gail (Bohensky). *Educ:* Brooklyn Col, BS, 59; NY Univ, MS, 61, PhD(math), 64. *Mem:* Soc Actuaries; Math Asn Am. *Res:* Stability for differential-difference equations. *Mailing Add:* Dept Math Brooklyn Col 2900 Bedford Ave Brooklyn NY 11210-2889

SNOWDEN, DONALD PHILIP, SOLID STATE PHYSICS, ELECTROMAGNETIC EFFECTS. *Current Pos:* SR SCIENTIST, HI-Z TECHNOL, INC, 96- *Personal Data:* b Los Angeles, Calif, Sept 9, 31. *Educ:* Calif Inst Technol, BS, 53; Univ Calif, Berkeley, MA, 55, PhD(physics), 59. *Prof Exp:* Staff mem, Gen Atomic Div, Gen Dynamics Corp, 59-67; staff mem, Gulf Gen Atomic, 67-73; prin physicist, IRT corp, 73-82; sr scientist, Mission Res Corp, 82-94. *Mem:* Am Phys Soc; Sigma Xi. *Res:* Application of high current superconductors; semiconductor and device radiation effects; physical and electrical surface characterization; vacuum vapor deposition; photovoltaic solar cells; fiber optics communications; electromagnetic pulse (EMP) experiments; high power microwaves; thermoelectric materials. *Mailing Add:* 6656 Glidden St San Diego CA 92111-6954

SNOWDEN, JESSE O, CLAY MINERALOGY, COASTAL GEOLOGY. *Current Pos:* prof geosci & dean, Col Sci & Technol, Southeast Mo State Univ, 90-96. *Personal Data:* b McComb, Miss, Oct 19, 37; m 75, Peggy Bernard; c Michael K, Katherine E & Margaret J. *Educ:* Millsaps Col, BS, 59; Univ Mo, MA, 61, PhD(geol), 66. *Prof Exp:* Instr geol, Millsaps Col, 62-63, assoc prof, 66-69; asst prof, Miss State Univ, 64-66; from asst prof to prof, Univ New Orleans, 69-85, chmn, 85-90. *Concurrent Pos:* Vis asst prof, Univ Mo, Columbia, 65-66; vis assoc prof, Univ Miss, 67, Gulf Coast Res Lab, 68-74 & Univ Mich, 79. *Mem:* Am Asn Petrol Geologists; Clay Mineral Soc; Geol Soc Am; Soc Sedimentary Geol; AAAS. *Res:* Research in evolution of the emergent Mississippi Delta and the barrier islands of Mississippi-Alabama. *Mailing Add:* Univ Ark 2801 S Univ Little Rock AR 72209. Fax: 573-651-2223

SNOWDON, CHARLES THOMAS, ANIMAL BEHAVIOR, PHYSIOLOGICAL PSYCHOLOGY. *Current Pos:* asst prof psychol, 69-74, assoc prof, 74-79, JOHN T EMLEN PROF PSYCHOL & ZOOL, UNIV WIS-MADISON, 79- *Personal Data:* b Pittsburgh, Pa, Aug 8, 41. *Educ:* Oberlin Col, BA, 63; Univ Pa, MA, 64, PhD(psychol), 68. *Prof Exp:* Fel, Inst Neurol Sci, Univ Pa, 68-69. *Concurrent Pos:* Affil scientist, Wis Regional Primate Res Ctr, 72; fac fel, NSF, 75-76; res scientist develop award, NIMH, 77-; ed, Animal Behaviour, 85-88, J Comparative Psychol, 95-; John T Emlen prof, Univ Wis. *Mem:* Fel Animal Behav Soc (pres-elect, pres, 88-92); Am Soc Zool; Am Soc Primatologists; Int Primatological Soc; fel Am Psychol Asn; fel Soc Conserv Biologists. *Res:* Communication and social behavior; evolution of language; social development and parental care; reproductive physiology and communication of reproductive status; captive breeding of endangered primates; field studies of endangered primates. *Mailing Add:* Dept Psychol Univ Wis-Madison 1202 W Johnson St Madison WI 53706-1696. Fax: 608-262-4029

SNOWDOWNE, KENNETH WILLIAM, CALCIUM BIOLOGY. *Current Pos:* adj asst prof, 86-96, ASST PROF, DEPT ORTHOD, SCH DENT, UNIV PAC, 96- *Personal Data:* b Homestead, Pa, June 2, 47; m 68. *Educ:* Clarion State Col, BS, 70; Univ Pittsburgh, PhD(pharmacol), 77. *Prof Exp:* NIH fel, Mayo Found, 77-80; res assoc, Univ Pittsburgh, 80-82, res asst prof, 82-85. *Mem:* Biophys Soc; AAAS; Am Physiol Soc. *Res:* Cellular calcium homeostasis; role of calcium in control of cellular processes such as contraction, secretion, mitotic division and motility. *Mailing Add:* Dept Orthod Sch Dent Univ Pac 2155 Webster St San Francisco CA 94115

SNOWMAN, ALFRED, NON FERROUS METALS, PACKAGING MATERIAL. *Current Pos:* MGR, MARGOLIN CONSULTS, 89- *Personal Data:* b London, Eng, Jul 11, 36; US Citizen; m 61; c 2. *Educ:* London Univ, BSc, 58; Farleigh Dickinson Univ, MBA, 73. *Prof Exp:* Res eng, Philco Corp, 58-60; mgr, Accurate Specialties Hackensack, 60-64; tech consult, Assoc Metals, 64-67; tech dir, Potters Indust, 79-83; tech mgr, Semi Alloys Inc, 83-89. *Mem:* Am Inst Mining Metall Petrol Engrs; Am Soc Metals; Wire Asn; Am Standard Testing Mat; Wire Asn. *Res:* High purity precious metal; alloys used in soldering of semiconductor component. *Mailing Add:* 121 Huguenot Ave Englewood NJ 07631

SNUDDEN, BIRDELL HARRY, BACTERIOLOGY, FOOD SCIENCE. *Current Pos:* from asst prof to prof, 66-96, EMER PROF BIOL, UNIV WIS-EAU CLAIRE, 96- *Personal Data:* b Elkhorn, Wis, Nov 20, 35; wid; c Sarah & Geoffrey. *Educ:* Univ Wis, BS, 57, MS, 61, PhD(bact, food sci), 64. *Prof Exp:* Fel food sci, Mich State Univ, 64-66. *Mem:* Am Soc Microbiol; Int Asn Milk, Food & Environ Sanitarians. *Res:* Aquatic microbiology; food and water borne diseases. *Mailing Add:* 4645 S Lowes Creek Eau Claire WI 54702-4004. Fax: 715-836-2380

SNUSTAD, DONALD PETER, GENETICS. *Current Pos:* From asst prof to assoc prof genetics, 65-74, PROF GENETICS & CELL BIOL, UNIV MINN, ST PAUL, 74- *Personal Data:* b Bemidji, Minn, Apr 6, 40; m 64; c 1. *Educ:* Univ Minn, BS, 62; Univ Calif, Davis, MS, 63, PhD(genetics), 65. *Mem:* Genetics Soc Am; Am Genetic Asn; Am Soc Microbiol; Am Inst Biol Sci. *Res:* Plant molecular genetics; virus-host cell interactions. *Mailing Add:* Univ Minn 250 Biol Sci Ctr St Paul MN 55108

SNYDER, ALLAN WHITNACK, VISION. *Current Pos:* FOUND HEAD, OPTICAL SCI CTR & CHAIR, OPTICAL PHYSICS & VIS RES, INST ADVAN STUDIES, AUSTRALIAN NAT UNIV, 78-, DIR, CTR FOR THE MIND. *Personal Data:* b Pa, Nov, 23, 40; US & Australian citizen. *Educ:* Pa State Univ, BS; Mass Inst Technol, SM; Harvard Univ, MS; Univ Col London, PhD; Univ London, DSc. *Honors & Awards:* Edgeworth David Medal, Soc NSW, 74; Silver Medal, Royal Soc Victoria, 74; Thomas Rankin Lyle Medal, Australian Acad Sci, 85; Fel, Royal Soc London, 90; Sutherland Mem Medal, Australian Acad Tech Sci, 91; Massey Prize, 96; Australia Prize,

97. *Prof Exp:* Commun engr study ice cap Northern Greenland, Peter Kiewett & Sons, 60-61; res asst, Ionospheric Res Lab, Pa State Univ, 61-63; sr res scientist, Sylvania Appl Res Lab, Boston Mass, 63-67, Res Lab, 63-67; consult, Optical Commun Studies, Gen Tel & Tel Co, 67-68, Brit Telecommun, 68-70, Stand Telecommun Lab, 69-70, Advan Tech Lab, Telcom Australia, 72, French Ctr Nat d'Etudes Telecommun, 76, Mindmakers, 87; sr res fel, Dept Opthal & Visual Sci & Appl Physics Dept, Yale Univ Med Sch, 69-71. *Concurrent Pos:* NSF fel biophys, 70, John Simon Guggenheim fel, 77, Royal Soc guest res fel, Cambridge Univ, 87; Vis prof, Tech Univ Darmstadt, Ger, 74, Dept Opthal & Visual Sci, Yale Univ Sch Med, 77-78, Shanghai Univ Sci & Technol, 81, Univ Calif, Berkeley, 83; Marconi Int Fel Comt, 77; mem, Optic Subcomt, Australian Acad Sci, 82, Frederic White Comt, 87, Select Comt, Frederic White Prize, 88. *Mem:* fel Optical Soc Am; fel Nat Vision Res Inst; Int Electromagnetics Acad; fel Australian Acad Technol Sci; fel Australian Acad Sci; Sigma Xi; fel Royal Soc London. *Res:* Pioneered the key conceptional methods that today form the backbone of guided wave optics; manipulating and directing light with light itself; visual ecology in its relation to understand the fundamental strategies of visual information processing; granted 3 patents; author of 3 books and 238 publications. *Mailing Add:* Optical Sci Ctr Rs Phys SE Australian Nat Univ Canberra ACT 0200 Australia. *Fax:* 61-6-249-5184; *E-Mail:* a.snyder@anu.edu.au

SNYDER, ANDREW KAGEY, MATHEMATICS. *Current Pos:* asst prof, 67-69, ASSOC PROF MATH, LEHIGH UNIV, 69- *Personal Data:* b Philadelphia, Pa, May 19, 37; m 59; c 2. *Educ:* Swarthmore Col, BA, 59; Univ Colo, MA, 61; Lehigh Univ, PhD(math), 65. *Prof Exp:* Instr math, Lehigh Univ, 64-65 & Mass Inst Technol, 65-67. *Mem:* Am Math Soc; Math Asn Am; Sigma Xi. *Res:* Functional analysis; sequence spaces; summability. *Mailing Add:* Dept Math Lehigh Univ Christmas-Saucon No 14 Bethlehem PA 18015

SNYDER, ANN C, SKELETAL MUSCLE, ENDOCRINE PHYSIOLOGY. *Current Pos:* ASST PROF HUMAN KINTICS, UNIV WIS-MILWAUKEE, 86- *Personal Data:* b Lansing, Mich, July 16, 51. *Educ:* Purdue Univ, PhD(exercise physiol), 82. *Prof Exp:* Asst prof med phys cduc, Ball State Univ, 82-86. *Res:* Exercise physiology. *Mailing Add:* Human Kinetics Dept Univ Wis-Milwaukee Milwaukee WI 53201. *Fax:* 414-229-4666

SNYDER, ANN KNABB, MEDICAL RESEARCH, ENDOCRINOLOGY & METABOLISM. *Current Pos:* RES ASST PROF, DEPT MED, CHICAGO MED SCH, NORTH CHICAGO, ILL, 81-; RES PHYSIOL, 88- *Personal Data:* b West Reading, Pa, Aug 1, 44; m 65; c 1. *Educ:* Pa State Univ, BS, 65; Univ Ill, MS, 68, PhD(physiol), 71. *Prof Exp:* Med technologist, Pediat Immunol Lab, Duke Univ Med Ctr, 70-71, Dept Immunol, Rush-Presby-St Lukes Med Ctr, 71-73; med technologist endocrinol, Med Res Prog, Vet Admin Med Ctr, North Chicago, 74-83. *Mem:* Sigma Xi; AAAS. *Res:* Influence of ethanol on carbohydrate metabolism in mammals, especially in respect to its interaction with the effects of thyroxine and insulin. *Mailing Add:* 505 E North Ave Lake Bluff IL 60044-2141

SNYDER, ARNOLD LEE, JR, SPACE PHYSICS, AURORAL & IONOSPHERIC PHYSICS. *Current Pos:* scientist, 89-96, CONSULT, MITRE CORP, 96- *Personal Data:* b Washington, DC, Oct 12, 37; m 63, Patricia D Ward; c Heinrick J, Sonya D & Ross N. *Educ:* George Washington Univ, BCE, 60; Univ Colo, MS, 66; Univ Alaska, PhD(geophysics), 72. *Honors & Awards:* Prog Mgr Value Eng Award, Dept Defense, 84. *Prof Exp:* Weather officer, Detachment 15, 1st Weather Wing, US Air Force, 61-62, weather officer, NY Air Defense Sector, 62-65, solar forecaster, Space Environ Support Ctr, 66-69, sect chief, Global Weather Cent, 72-76, br chief, Geophysics Lab, 76-80, test dir, 80-81, prog dir, Electronic Systs Div, US Air Force, 81-87; tech dir & adj prof, Univ Lowell, 87-89. *Concurrent Pos:* Lectr, Western New Eng Col, 78-79. *Mem:* Am Geophys Union; Am Meteorol Soc; Sigma Xi. *Res:* Space forecasting techniques. *Mailing Add:* RR 2 Box 135 Orrington ME 04474. *Fax:* 781-377-3550; *E-Mail:* palsnyder@aol.com

SNYDER, BENJAMIN WILLARD, ENDOCRINOLOGY. *Current Pos:* ASST PROF DEPT BIOL, FRAMINGHAM STATE COL, MASS. *Personal Data:* b Albion, Mich, July 5, 39; m 65, Diane; c Hans. *Educ:* Albion Col, BA, 62; Univ Mich, MS, 67, PhD(zool), 70. *Prof Exp:* Fel reproductive biol, Sch Hyg & Pub Health, Johns Hopkins Univ, 70-71 & Harvard Med Sch, 72-73; assoc prof biol, Swarthmore Col, 73-80; sr res biol, Sterling-Winthrop Res Inst, 80-89; assoc prof, Vassar Col, 89-91; dir, TSI/Exemplar Corp, 91-95. *Mem:* Sigma Xi; AAAS; Endocrine Soc; Soc Study Reproduction. *Res:* Reproductive biology; endocrine disruptors. *Mailing Add:* 52 Hancock Hill Dr Worcester MA 01609. *E-Mail:* bsnyder@frc.mass.edu

SNYDER, CARL HENRY, ORGANIC CHEMISTRY. *Current Pos:* from asst prof to assoc prof, 61-74, PROF CHEM, UNIV MIAMI, 74- *Personal Data:* b Pittsburgh, Pa, Sept 18, 31; m 53; c 2. *Educ:* Univ Pittsburgh, BS, 53; Ohio State Univ, PhD(org chem), 58. *Prof Exp:* Res chemist, Eastman Kodak Co, 58-59; res asst chem, Purdue Univ, 59-61. *Mem:* Am Chem Soc; Sigma Xi. *Res:* Reactions in dipolar, aprotic solvents; stereochemistry of carbonyl reductions; biomolecular eliminations; organoborane chemistry. *Mailing Add:* 6890 SW 78 Terr South Miami FL 33143-4439

SNYDER, CHARLES THEODORE, HYDROLOGY. *Current Pos:* INDEPENDENT RES, 86- *Personal Data:* b Powell, Wyo, July 19, 12; m 73; c 2. *Educ:* Univ Ariz, BSc, 48. *Prof Exp:* Geologist/Hydrologist, US Geol Survey, 46, 48-75; vis scientist, Carter County Museum, Ekalaka, Mont, 83-84; res assoc, Calif Acad Sci, 85-86. *Mem:* AAAS; Arctic Inst NAm; Soc Vert Paleontologists. *Res:* Hydrology and climatology of Ice Age and modern lakes in western United States; stream environmental studies; high altitude, cold weather or arid zone field operations safety and survival; sand dune morphology. *Mailing Add:* 552-17 Bean Creek Rd Scotts Valley CA 95066

SNYDER, CHARLES THOMAS, FLIGHT DYNAMICS & CONTROL, AERODYNAMICS. *Current Pos:* DIR, NAT ROTORCRAFT TECHNOL CTR, 95- *Personal Data:* b Belle Plaine, Kans, July 2, 38; m 60; c 4. *Educ:* Univ Wichita, BS, 62; Stanford Univ, MS, 69, Engr, 76. *Prof Exp:* Aerospace eng flight dynamics, Flight & Systs Simulation Br, Ames Res Ctr, NASA, 62-65, proj engr, 65-70, group leader, 70-74, chief, Flight Systs Res Div, 74-80, dir aeronaut & flight systs, 80-85, dir aerospace systs, Ames Res Ctr, 85-94. *Concurrent Pos:* Dryden mem fel, Nat Space Club, 72; mem, NASA Adv Subcomt Aviation Safety & Oper Systs, 75-77 & Adv Subcomt Avionics & Controls, 77-80; assoc dir, Stanford/Ames Joint Inst Aeronaut & Acoust, 77-80; bd dirs, Am Helicopter Soc, 83-85, chmn, 94-95. *Mem:* Fel Am Inst Aeronaut & Astronaut; fel Am Helicopter Soc (pres, 93-94). *Res:* Flight mechanics; stability and control; handling qualities; guidance and navigation; avionics systems; aerodynamics; aircraft operating problems; simulation technology; rotorcraft technology. *Mailing Add:* NASA-Ames Res Ctr Mail Stop 207-1 Moffett Field CA 94035-1000. *Fax:* 650-604-2003; *E-Mail:* ctsnyder@mail.arc.nasa.gov

SNYDER, CLIFFORD CHARLES, PLASTIC SURGERY. *Current Pos:* EMER PROF SURG & ASSOC DEAN, SCH MED, UNIV UTAH, 67-, SURG ENDOWED PROF, 90- *Personal Data:* b Ft Worth, Tex, Feb 16, 16; m 39; c 1. *Educ:* Univ Tenn, BS, 40, MD, 44; Am Bd Surg, dipl; Am Bd Plastic Surg, dipl. *Prof Exp:* Asst prof surg, Sch Med, Univ Tex, 52-54; from asst prof to assoc prof, Sch Med, Univ Miami, 54-67. *Concurrent Pos:* Attend physician, Jackson Mem, Doctor's & Cedars of Lebanon Hosps; consult, Vet Admin Hosp, 54-67 & Nat Surg Consult, 69-; chief staff, Variety Children's Hosp, 58-67; mem, Am Bd Plastic Surg, 63-87; abstr ed, J Plastic & Reconstruct Surg, 67-73, co-ed, 73-; mem, Vet Admin Nat Adv Comt, 74- *Mem:* Am Soc Plastic & Reconstruct Surg (asst secy, 59-60, vpres, 66-67); Am Soc Surg of Hand; Am Asn Plastic Surg (pres, 74); Am Col Surgeons; hon mem Am Col Vet Surgeons. *Res:* Plastic and reconstructive surgery; transplantation of organs; snake bite; regeneration of nerves; wound healing. *Mailing Add:* 875 Donner Way Apt 1405 Salt Lake City UT 84108-2142

SNYDER, CONWAY WILSON, PHYSICS. *Current Pos:* RETIRED. *Personal Data:* b Kirksville, Mo, Jan 24, 18; m 43, Marjorie Frisius; c Donald, Sheryl (Savina) & Sylvia (Woods). *Educ:* Univ Redlands, AB, 39; Univ Iowa, MS, 41; Calif Inst Technol, PhD(physics), 48. *Hon Degrees:* DSc, Univ Redlands, 68. *Honors & Awards:* Medal for Except Sci Achievement, NASA, 68, 70, 73 & 77. *Prof Exp:* Jr physicist, US Naval Ord Lab, Washington, DC, 41-42; mem staff, Navy Rocket Proj, OEMsr-418, Calif Inst Technol, 42-45; mem staff, Off Naval Res, Washington, DC, 48-49; with Fairchild Engine & Airplane Corp Nuclear Engine Propulsion Aircraft Proj, Ky, 49-51; Oak Ridge Nat Lab, 51-54; asst prof physics, Fla State Univ, 54-56; sr res engr, Jet Propulsion Lab, Calif Inst Technol, 56-59, scientist specialist, 59-63, staff scientist, 63-69, Viking orbiter scientist, 69-77, Viking proj scientist, 77-80, asst proj mgr sci, Infrared Astron Satellite Proj, 81-84. *Mem:* Am Phys Soc; Sigma Xi. *Mailing Add:* 21206 Seep Willow Way Canyon Country CA 91351-2334. *Fax:* 805-259-7986; *E-Mail:* cwsnyder@juno.com

SNYDER, DANA PAUL, MAMMALIAN ECOLOGY. *Current Pos:* from instr to assoc prof, 55-85, EMER PROF ZOOL, UNIV MASS, AMHERST, 85- *Personal Data:* b Winnipeg, Man, Apr 29, 22; nat US; m 52, Mary E Sumner; c Mark, Amy, Tod & Ellen. *Educ:* Univ Ill, BS, 47, MS, 48; Univ Mich, PhD(zool), 51. *Prof Exp:* Res mammalogist, Carnegie Mus, 51-55; instr biol, Pa Col Women, 52-53; vis lectr biol, Smith Col, 56. *Concurrent Pos:* Prin investr, biol eastern chipmunk, 65-75. *Mem:* Am Soc Mammal; Ecol Soc Am; Soc Syst Zool; Wildlife Soc; Am Inst Biol Sci; Am Ornith Union. *Res:* Systematics and ecology of mammals, especially Tamias striatus; geographic variation; population biology. *Mailing Add:* Dept Biol Univ Mass Amherst MA 01003

SNYDER, DANIEL RAPHAEL, NEUROPSYCHOLOGY, PRIMATOLOGY. *Current Pos:* PRES, SNYDER ASSOC, PC, 91- *Personal Data:* b Detroit, Mich, July 5, 40; m 61; c 2. *Educ:* Wayne State Univ, BS, 62; Univ Mich, Ann Arbor, MS, 64, PhD(physiol psychol), 70. *Prof Exp:* Res assoc psychiat, Yale Univ, 69-70, NIMH Biol Sci Training Prog fel biol psychiat, 70-71, asst prof, Lab Animal Sci, 71-73 & comp med & anthrop, 73-76, assoc prof comp med & anthrop, Sch Med, 76-82, head, Neurobehav & Primate Res Fac, 74-82; pres, founder & chief exec officer, DRS Infusion Systs Inc, 82-91. *Concurrent Pos:* Consult, Am Asn Accreditation Lab Animal Care, 74-; sci adv, Inst Biol Sci, Univ Islamabad, Pakistan, 75-; vet neurologist, Comp Med Referral Clin, Sch Med, Yale Univ, 76- *Mem:* Soc Neurosci; Psychonomic Soc; Int Primatol Soc; AAAS; Animal Behav Soc. *Res:* Neural mechanisms of social and emotional behavior; biomedical primatology and primate behavior; neuropsychology; behavioral and neurotoxicology affective behavior; behavioral toxicology. *Mailing Add:* 47 Griffing Pond Rd Branford CT 06405

SNYDER, DAVID HILTON, VERTEBRATE BIOLOGY, ETHOLOGY. *Current Pos:* from instr to assoc prof, 62-77, PROF BIOL, AUSTIN PEAY STATE UNIV, 77- *Personal Data:* b Giles Co, Va, June 24, 38; m 54; c 5. *Educ:* Univ Mo-Columbia, BA, 58, MA, 62; Univ Notre Dame, PhD(biol), 71. *Prof Exp:* Teacher, Berkeley Pub Schs, Mo, 58-59. *Mem:* Am Soc Ichthyologists & Herpetologists; Soc Study Amphibians & Reptiles; Am Soc Zoologists; Ecol Soc Am; Am Soc Mammal; Sigma Xi. *Res:* Reproductive behavior of amphibians; taxonomy of American amphibians and reptiles. *Mailing Add:* Dept Biol Austin Peay State Univ Clarksville TN 37044-0001

SNYDER, DEXTER DEAN, PHYSICAL CHEMISTRY, ELECTROCHEMISTRY. *Current Pos:* sr assoc res chem, Gen Motors Res Labs, 72-75, sr res chemist, 75-80, staff res scientist, 80-82, sr staff res scientist, 82-93, PRIN STAFF SCIENTIST, GEN MOTORS RES LABS, 93- *Personal Data:* b Toledo, Ohio, Feb 6, 42; m 68, Elizabeth Hughes; c Matthew, Britton & Lara. *Educ:* Wabash Col, AB, 64; Mass Inst Technol, PhD(phys chem), 68. *Prof Exp:* Prof staff phys chem, Arthur D Little, Inc, 68-71; mem staff, Bendix Res Labs, 71-72. *Mem:* Am Chem Soc; Electrochem Soc; Sigma Xi. *Res:* Electrochemical power sources, alloy electrodeposition, corrosion science, wear resistant surface treatments; sensors. *Mailing Add:* Gen Motors Res & Develop Ctr Phys Chem Dept Gen Motors Corp Warren MI 48090-9055. *Fax:* 810-986-2244; *E-Mail:* dsnyder@cmsa.gmr.com

SNYDER, DONALD BENJAMIN, ORNITHOLOGY. *Current Pos:* RETIRED. *Personal Data:* b North Manchester, Ind, Oct 6, 35; m 65, Wilma F Simpson; c Douglas & Jonn. *Educ:* Manchester Col, BS, 57; Ohio State Univ, MS, 59, PhD(zool), 63. *Prof Exp:* Asst prof biol, Cent Wesleyan Col, 63-64 & Geneva Col, 64-69; prof biol, Edinboro Univ Pa, 69-96. *Mem:* Wildlife Soc; Asn Field Ornithologists. *Res:* Animal behavior; wildlife ecology. *Mailing Add:* 13190 Cambridge Rd Edinboro PA 16412-2837

SNYDER, DONALD LEE, electrochemistry, corrosion, for more information see previous edition

SNYDER, EVAN SAMUEL, PHYSICS. *Current Pos:* From instr to assoc prof, 46-69, PROF PHYSICS & DEPT CHMN, URSINUS COL, 69- *Personal Data:* b Lehighton, Pa, Aug 24, 23; m 48; c 3. *Educ:* Ursinus Col, BS, 44; Univ Pa, MS, 51, PhD(physics), 57. *Concurrent Pos:* Vis prof, NSF Inst, NMex State Univ, 59, 64-69; res partic, Oak Ridge Nat Lab, 60, 62; NSF sci fac fel, Princeton Univ, 68-69. *Mem:* Am Phys Soc; Am Asn Physics Teachers. *Mailing Add:* 80 Linfield Rd Trappe Collegeville PA 19426

SNYDER, FRANKLIN F, SURFACE WATER RUNOFF & FLOOD FORECASTING. *Current Pos:* RETIRED. *Personal Data:* b Holgate, Ohio, Nov 11, 10; m 38, Mary E Bruton; c Marilyn (Lutz), Carol (Garnett) & Gregory L. *Educ:* Ohio State Univ, BCE, 32, CE, 42. *Honors & Awards:* Croes Medal, Am Soc Civil Engrs, 40. *Prof Exp:* Surv foreman, Ohio Div Forestry, Rockbridge, Ohio, 33-34; jr hydraul engr, US Geol Surv, Washington, DC, 34-35 & Tenn Valley Authority, Knoxville, 35-37; hydraul engr, Pa Dept Forests & Waters, 37-40; assoc hydraul engr, US Weather Bur, Pittsburgh, Pa, 40 & Washington, DC, 40-42; supvry hydraul engr & asst chief, Hydrol & Hydraul Br, Corps Engrs, Washington, DC, 42-66; partner, Nunn, Snyder & Assocs, 72-78. *Concurrent Pos:* Consult var co, 56-89. *Mem:* Nat Acad Eng; fel Am Soc Civil Engrs; Sigma Xi; Am Geophys Union; Am Meteorol Soc. *Res:* Author of various publications. *Mailing Add:* 1516 Laburnum St McLean VA 22101. *Fax:* 703-536-9678

SNYDER, FRED CALVIN, AGRICULTURE. *Current Pos:* RETIRED. *Personal Data:* b Valley View, Pa, Apr 9, 16; wid. *Educ:* Pa State Univ, BS, 39, MS, 47, PhD(agr ed), 55. *Prof Exp:* Teacher pub schs, Pa, 39-41, 46-47; actg dir short courses, Pa State Univ, 56-58, dir short courses & chmn corresp agr & home econ, 58-79. *Mem:* AAAS. *Res:* Relationship of supervised farming programs and individual projects of vocational agricultural students to subsequent establishment in agricultural vocations. *Mailing Add:* 3048 SE Morningside Blvd Port St Lucie FL 34952

SNYDER, FRED LEONARD, BIOCHEMISTRY. *Current Pos:* From res scientist to chief scientist, Oak Ridge Assoc Univs, 58-75, from asst chmn to assoc chmn, 75-88, vchmn, Med & Health Sci Div, 88-92, assoc dir, Med Sci Div, Oak Ridge Inst Sci & Educ, 92-95, CORP DISTINGUISHED SCIENTIST, OAK RIDGE ASSOC UNIVS, 88-, PROF MED CHEM, UNIV NC, CHAPEL HILL, 66- *Personal Data:* b New Ulm, Minn, Nov 22, 31; m 55, 78, Joy D; c Vicki, David & Jon. *Educ:* St Cloud State Col, BS, 53; Univ NDak, MS, 55, PhD(biochem), 58. *Hon Degrees:* DSc, Univ NDak, 83. *Concurrent Pos:* Prof biochem, Med Units, Univ Tenn, Memphis, 64-86; prof med chem, Univ NC, Chapel Hill, 66-; assoc ed, Cancer Res, 71-78; ed, Handbook of Lipid Res, 87-; adj prof, Univ Tenn-Oak Ridge Grad Sch Biomed Sci, 72-; vis lectr, Cardiovasc Res Inst, Univ Calif, San Francisco, 79; exec ed, Archives Biochem & Biophys, 87; vis prof, Grad Sch & Univ Ctr, City Univ New York, 89 & 93; distinguished lectr neurosci, Sch Med, La State Univ Med Ctr, New Orleans, 93. *Mem:* Soc Exp Biol & Med; Am Soc Biochem & Molecular Biol; Am Asn Cancer Res; Sigma Xi. *Res:* Metabolism and chemistry of lipids; cancer and pulmonary disorders; membranes; bioactive phospholipids; separation techniques; author of over 360 publications. *Mailing Add:* Med Sci Div Oak Ridge Assoc Univs PO Box 117 Oak Ridge TN 37831. *Fax:* 423-482-6217; *E-Mail:* fsnyder@compuserve.com

SNYDER, FREEMAN WOODROW, PLANT PHYSIOLOGY. *Current Pos:* RETIRED. *Personal Data:* b Philadelphia, Pa, Dec 6, 17; m 38, Elizabeth Fink; c Robert G & Barbara N. *Educ:* Univ Idaho, BS, 38; Cornell Univ, PhD(plant physiol), 50. *Prof Exp:* Eng aide, Soil Conserv Serv, USDA, 42-43, agr engr, 46-47; asst bot, Cornell Univ, 48-50; asst agronomist, Univ Ark, 50-53; plant physiologist, Sugar Beet Invests, Plant Sci Res Div, Agr Res Serv, USDA, 53-64, res plant physiologist, 64-68, plant physiologist, North Cent Region, 68-75, plant physiologist, Northeastern Region, 75-78, mem staff, Sci & Educ Admin, 78-83. *Concurrent Pos:* Adj assoc prof, Crop & Soil Sci, Mich State Univ, 70-75; actg lab chief, Light & Plant Growth Lab, Beltsville Agr Res Ctr, 81; coordr, Photosynthesis Prog, Org Econ Coop & Develop, 80-83. *Mem:* AAAS; Bot Soc Am; Am Soc Plant Physiol; Soc Sugar Beet Technol; Am Soc Agron. *Res:* Role of environmental and genetic factors in growth, development and yield of crop plants. *Mailing Add:* 1615 N Fifth Ave Perkasie PA 18944-2208

SNYDER, GARY JAMES, high-spin molecules, photoacoustic calorimetry, for more information see previous edition

SNYDER, GARY WAYNE, BOTANY-PHYTOPATHOLOGY. *Current Pos:* UNIT MGR SCI & TECHNOL, SAIC, 93- *Personal Data:* b Blue Creek, WVa, May 26, 54; m 75; c 2. *Educ:* Glenville State Col, BS, 76; Miami Univ, Oxford, Ohio, MS, 79, PhD(bot), 84. *Prof Exp:* Instr bot, Miami Univ, Hamilton, 81-82; asst prof biol, Glenville State Col, 82-90; coordr, Nat Environ Act Prog, Uranium Enrichment Plant, Martin Marietta Energy Syst, 90-93. *Res:* Comparison of phenological events in forest stands and relating event to successional patterns; testing and utilization of pesticides and fungicides in orchards. *Mailing Add:* 92 Copperfield Dr Chillicothe OH 45601-8610

SNYDER, GEORGE HEFT, AGRONOMY, SOIL CHEMISTRY. *Current Pos:* from asst prof to assoc prof, 67-79, PROF SOILS, EVERGLADES RES & EDUC CTR, UNIV FLA, 79- *Personal Data:* b Evanston, Ill, July 19, 39; m 69, Caridad F Sanjorjo; c Raymond & Richard. *Educ:* Ohio State Univ, BS, 62, MS, 64, PhD(agron), 67. *Prof Exp:* Asst instr agron, Ohio State Univ, 63-64. *Mem:* Am Soc Agron; Int Turfgrass Soc; Sigma Xi. *Res:* Soil chemistry; nutrient uptake by plants; wetland agriculture; nutrient and pesticide leaching and transformations. *Mailing Add:* Univ Fla Everglades-REC PO Box 8003 Belle Glade FL 33430-8003. *Fax:* 561-996-0339; *E-Mail:* ghs@gnu.ifas.ufl.edu

SNYDER, GEORGE RICHARD, marine & freshwater fish ecology, for more information see previous edition

SNYDER, GLENN J(ACOB), MECHANICAL ENGINEERING. *Current Pos:* RETIRED. *Personal Data:* b Akron, Ohio, Aug 1, 23; m 51; c 4. *Educ:* Ohio Univ, BSME, 49. *Honors & Awards:* Centennial Medallion, Am Soc Mech Engrs, 80. *Prof Exp:* Tool designer, Gun Mount Div, Firestone Tire & Rubber Co, 42-43; engr, Ohio Boxboard Co, 49-51; sr engr, Aerospace Div, Goodyear Tire & Rubber Co, 51-55; sr engr, Nuclear Power Div, Babcock & Wilcock Co, 55-60, supvr reactor vessel, internals control rod drives, 60-77, mgr & prin engr, Nuclear Power Generation Div, 77-84; vpres eng, SM/MS Inc, 84-97. *Concurrent Pos:* Prof adj fac, Cent Va Community Col, 84-86. *Mem:* Nat Soc Prof Engrs; Am Soc Mech Engrs; Soc Mfg Engrs; Am Nuclear Soc. *Res:* Author of several technical papers, holds patents. *Mailing Add:* 3300 Woodridge Pl Lynchburg VA 24503

SNYDER, GRACE, PHYSICAL CHEMISTRY. *Current Pos:* From asst prof to assoc prof, 78-81, PROF CHEM, QUEENSBOROUGH COMMUNITY COL, 81- *Personal Data:* b Kananes, Lithuania, June 20, 38. *Educ:* Hunter Col, BA, 63, MA, 65; City Univ New York, PhD(chem), 74. *Concurrent Pos:* Res grants, City Univ New York, 91-92 & 93-94. *Mem:* Fel Am Inst Chemists; Am Chem Soc; AAAS; NY Acad Sci; Am Women Sci; Int Soc Quantum Biol & Pharmacol. *Mailing Add:* Chem Queensborough Community Col 22205 56th Ave Flushing NY 11364-1432

SNYDER, GREGORY KIRK, COMPARATIVE PHYSIOLOGY. *Current Pos:* PROF BIOL, UNIV COLO, BOULDER, 75- *Personal Data:* b Chicago, Ill, Sept 27, 39; m 75; c 2. *Educ:* Humboldt State, BS, 63; Calif State Univ, San Diego, MS, 65; Univ Calif, Los Angeles, PhD(zool), 70. *Prof Exp:* Postdoctoral fel physiol, Univ Fla, Gainesville, 70-72; asst prof biol, Univ Calif, Riverside, 72-75. *Mem:* Am Physiol Soc; Am Soc Zoologists; Fedn Am Socs Exp Biol. *Res:* Comparative physiology of cardiorespiratory function; adaptations to unique environment, especially high altitudes and diving; developmental regulation of the microvascular supply to tissues. *Mailing Add:* Dept EPO Biol Univ Colo Campus Box 334 Boulder CO 80309-0334. *Fax:* 303-492-8699; *E-Mail:* snyderg@cubldg.colorado.edu

SNYDER, HAROLD JACK, PATENT NUCLEAR FIELD, PATENT SPACE DEFENSE. *Current Pos:* DIR, SNYDER TECH LAB, 61- *Personal Data:* wid; c Susan (Nichols), Lynda (Dominick), Harold J Jr, Beverly (Hymel) & Casey B. *Educ:* Univ Pittsburgh, BS, 48, MS, 52, PhD(metall eng), 61. *Prof Exp:* Jr engr, Nat Adv Comn Aeronaut, NASA, 48; asst plant engr, Div Colonial Steel, Teledyne, 49; fel, Mellon Inst Indust Res, 49-52 & 57-60; sr engr, Westinghouse Elec Corp, 52-57 & 64-71; dir res, Scoite Co, 60-61; mgr, Dept Metall Eng, Gulf South Res Inst, 71-75. *Concurrent Pos:* Lectr, Am Soc Metals, 53, 73, 74, 80 & 83, Am Soc Chem Engrs, 69, Am Welding Soc, 72, 73 & 80, Am Soc Mech Engrs, 75, Occup Safety & Health Admin, 80; instr metall eng, Univ Pittsburgh, 57; inspector, Interstate Com Comn, 71; instr mat sci, Univ New Orleans, 72-74; instr welding eng, Am Welding Soc, New Orleans, 72; consult, Tech Compression Serv, 76-. *Mem:* Fel Am Soc Metal Int; Am Welding Soc; Nat Soc Prof Engrs; Assoc Smithsonian Inst; Nat Trust Hist Preserv. *Res:* Developed alloys for nuclear reactor control rods; solid propellant rocket motor cases and electrodes for water analysis; developed forming operations for one piece 4.2 mortar shells, solid propellant rocket motor cases and armor plate; integral bosses for pressure weasels. *Mailing Add:* 833 Jewel St New Orleans LA 70124

SNYDER, HAROLD LEE, POLYMER BLENDS, PHASE TRANSITIONS & FIBER SCIENCE. *Current Pos:* Staff scientist, 80-84, res supvr & mgr, 84-89, bus mgr specialty elastomers, 89-90, bus mgr, Engr Polymers, 91-92, TECH DIR LYCRA, E I DU PONT DE NEMOURS & CO INC, 92- *Personal Data:* b Denver, Colo, Dec 30, 52; m 77; c 2. *Educ:* Lewis & Clark Col, BS, 75; Univ Calif, Santa Barbara, PhD(phys chem), 80. *Concurrent Pos:* Lectr, Morgan State Univ, 81-82. *Res:* Dynamical aspects of chemilumenescent reactions in crossed molecular beams; dynamical aspects of phase transitions in polymer blends; structure and property relations on polymers. *Mailing Add:* 1068 Country Club Rd West Chester PA 19382

SNYDER, HARRY E, food science, biochemistry, for more information see previous edition

SNYDER, HARRY RAYMOND, JR, ORGANIC CHEMISTRY, MEDICINAL CHEMISTRY. *Current Pos:* RETIRED. *Personal Data:* b Lawrence, Mass, Jan 19, 24; m 49; c 2. *Educ:* Brown Univ, ScB, 49; Boston Univ, MA, 52, PhD(org chem), 58. *Prof Exp:* Res chemist, R J Reynolds Tobacco Co, 54-56; sr res chemist, Morton-Norwich Prod, Inc, 56-61, unit leader org chem, 61-73, sci assoc, Norwich-Eaton Pharmaceut Div, 73-83; mgr lab serv & safety, Chem Dept, Cornell Univ, Ithaca, NY, 84-90. *Concurrent Pos:* Counr, Norwich Sect, Am Chem Soc, 71-87; vis lectr org chem, Vassar Col, NY, 84- *Mem:* Am Chem Soc. *Res:* Synthesis of nitrofurans and other heterocycles for possible medicinal uses. *Mailing Add:* PO Box 371 Norwich NY 13815-0371

SNYDER, HERBERT HOWARD, APPLIED MATHEMATICS, MATHEMATICAL PHYSICS. *Current Pos:* from assoc prof to prof, 66-89, EMER PROF MATH, SOUTHERN ILL UNIV, CARBONDALE, 89- *Personal Data:* b Ravenswood, WVa, Feb 26, 27; m 66; c 1. *Educ:* Marietta Col, AB, 49; Lehigh Univ, MA, 51, PhD(math), 65; Univ SAfrica, PhD(appl math), 71. *Prof Exp:* Instr math, Lehigh Univ, 49-53; develop engr, ITT Fed Labs Div, Int Tel & Tel Corp, 53-63; instr math, Newark Col Eng, 63-64; instr math, Lehigh Univ, 64-65; asst prof, Drexel Inst, 65-66. *Concurrent Pos:* Vis assoc prof, Univ Ariz, 71-72; ed-in-chief, Handbuch der Electrotechnic; trustee, Ind Technol Univ. *Mem:* Am Math Soc; Ger Math Asn. *Res:* Function-theory on linear algebras; partial differential equations; electromagnetic theory; guided wave propagation and non-linear electron-wave interactions. *Mailing Add:* PO Box 1494 Tappahannock VA 22560

SNYDER, HOWARD ARTHUR, FLUIDS, ORYOGENIA. *Current Pos:* assoc prof, 68-89, PROF AEROSPACE ENG SCI, UNIV COLO, BOULDER, 89- *Personal Data:* b Lehighton, Pa, Mar 7, 30; m 75, Kaye Bache. *Educ:* Rensselaer Polytech Inst, BS, 52; Univ Chicago, SM, 56, PhD(physics), 61. *Prof Exp:* Asst prof physics, Brown Univ, 61-67, assoc prof, 68. *Concurrent Pos:* Prin investr, NSF, 62-78, USAF, 64-66, US Dept Energy, 90-93; consult, Storage Technol Corp, 80-93, Ball Aerospace Technol Corp, 84- *Mem:* Am Phys Soc. *Res:* Hydrodynamics and acoustics of liquid helium; laboratory modeling experiments of the atmosphere and the oceans; stability of fluid flow; low gravity fluid management; low temperature refrigerators. *Mailing Add:* Aerospace Box 429 Univ Colo Boulder CO 80309. *Fax:* 303-492-7881

SNYDER, J EDWARD, JR, OCEANOGRAPHY. *Current Pos:* RETIRED. *Personal Data:* b Grand Fork, NDak, Oct 23, 24. *Educ:* Naval Acad, BS, 44; Mass Inst Technol, MS, 55. *Prof Exp:* Oceanogr, US Navy. *Mem:* Nat Acad Eng. *Mailing Add:* 1224 Perry William Dr McLean VA 22101

SNYDER, JACK AUSTIN, BIOCHEMISTRY. *Current Pos:* RETIRED. *Personal Data:* b Lansing, Mich, Oct 21, 27; m 49; c 2. *Educ:* Mich State Univ, BS, 49; Univ Wis, MS, 51, PhD(biochem), 53. *Prof Exp:* From res scientist to res assoc, E I du Pont de Nemours & Co, Inc, 58-66, res suprv, 66-71, res assoc, 71-73, tech serv mgr, Pharmaceut Div, Biochem Dept, 73-81, consult pharmaceut res, 81- *Mem:* Am Chem Soc. *Res:* Synthesis; structure in relation to activity; process development; drug candidate evaluation. *Mailing Add:* 614 Loveville Rd BSC Hockessin DE 19707-1605

SNYDER, JOHN CRAYTON, MICROBIOLOGY, POPULATION POLICY. *Current Pos:* CONSULT, 82- *Personal Data:* b Salt Lake City, Utah, May 24, 10 005 WH; m 42, Virginia Ferry; c 3. *Educ:* Stanford Univ, AB, 31; Harvard Univ, MD, 35; dipl, Am Bd Prev Med, 49. *Hon Degrees:* LLD, Harvard Univ, 64. *Honors & Awards:* Order of the Nile, Egypt, 44. *Prof Exp:* Fel surg, Mass Gen Hosp, 36-37; Soc Fels jr fel, Harvard Univ, 39-40; mem staff, Int Health Div, Rockefeller Found, 40-46; USA Typhus Comn, 42-46, Lt Col US Army Med Corps, 42-45; prof pub health bact, Harvard Univ, 46-50 & microbiol, 50-61, dean fac, 54-71, Henry Pickering Walcott prof, 61-71, prof pop & pub health & med dir, Ctr Pop Studies, Sch Pub Health, 71-76; chief, Div Pop Policy, Pathfinder Fund, 78; lectr, Mass Inst Technol & assoc dir, Int Pop Initiatives, 79-82. *Concurrent Pos:* Chmn expert comt, Trachoma, World Health Org, 61; consult, Univ Assocs for Int Health, 74-83 & Med Pub Interest, 76-80; mem, bd dirs, Theobald Smith Res Inst, 85-91 & Emerson Hosp, 80-85. *Mem:* Am Pub Health Asn; Am Soc Trop Med & Hyg; Am Epidemiol Soc; Asn Am Physicians; Am Acad Arts & Sci; fel AAAS. *Res:* Typhus fever and other rickettsial diseases; chemotherapy and immunology; trachoma and related diseases of the eye; human fertility control and population problems. *Mailing Add:* 59 Sunset Hill Marlborough NH 03455

SNYDER, JOHN L, PHYSICAL GEOLOGY. *Current Pos:* RETIRED. *Personal Data:* b Lansing, Mich, June 23, 30; m 76, Elizabeth Lahey. *Educ:* Mich State Univ, BS, 51; Dartmouth Univ, AM, 53; Northwestern Univ, PhD(geol), 57. *Prof Exp:* Instr geol, Univ Tex, 57, asst prof, 57-62; dir educ, Am Geol Inst, 62-69; assoc prog dir, Undergrad Educ Div, NSF, 69-72, prog mgr, Div Higher Educ in Sci, 72-78, prof dir, Local Course Improv Prog, 78-82, dir, Volcanology & Mantle Geochem Prog, 82-89, dir, Petrol & Geochem Prog, 89-96. *Concurrent Pos:* Mem steering comt, Geo-Study & mem steering comt & adv bd, Earth Sci Curriculum Proj; vis prof, Dept Geol, Univ Mo, Columbia, 79, Ariz State Univ, Tempe, 92-93. *Mem:* Geol Soc Am; AAAS; Nat Asn Geol Teachers; Am Geophys Union. *Res:* Igneous petrology; science education; vocanology. *Mailing Add:* 5161 N 38th St Arlington VA 22207. *Fax:* 703-306-0382; *E-Mail:* jsnyder@nsf.gov

SNYDER, JOHN WILLIAM, PHYSICAL OPTICS, SPECTROSCOPY. *Current Pos:* Mem fac, 68-78, chmn Dept Physics, 77-83, PROF PHYSICS, SOUTHERN CONN STATE COL, 81- *Personal Data:* b Oakhill, WVa, May 12, 40. *Educ:* Ohio State Univ, BS, 63, MS, 64, PhD(physics), 68. *Mem:* Am Asn Physics Teachers; Am Optical Soc. *Res:* Fourier transform spectroscopy; microprocessors. *Mailing Add:* Dept Physics Southern Conn State Col 501 Crescent St New Haven CT 06515-1330

SNYDER, JOSEPH QUINCY, CHEMISTRY. *Current Pos:* RETIRED. *Personal Data:* b Joplin, Mo, Aug 7, 20; m 42; c 4. *Educ:* Univ Okla, BS, 42, MS, 51, PhD(chem, chem eng), 54. *Prof Exp:* Org chemist & asst dir res, Samuel Roberts Noble Found, Okla, 48-51; instr chem, Univ Okla, 51-52 & 53-54, instr chem eng, 54-55; dir res, DanCu Chem Co, 55-56; sr res chemist, Monsanto Co, 56-64, sr res group leader, 64-70, sr res specialist, 71-85. *Mem:* Am Chem Soc. *Res:* Free radical copolymerizations; hydrocarbon reactions; catalytic conversions of olefins. *Mailing Add:* 1151 Tompkins St Charles MO 63301-2618

SNYDER, JUDITH ARMSTRONG, CELL BIOLOGY. *Current Pos:* from asst prof to assoc prof biol sci, 78-89, dean, 89-93, PROF BIOL SCI, UNIV DENVER, 89- *Personal Data:* b Washington, DC, Nov 11, 46; m 72. *Educ:* Univ Calif, Berkeley, AB, 68, PhD(bot), 73. *Honors & Awards:* Barton L Weller Professorship. *Prof Exp:* Res asst bot, Univ Calif, Berkeley, 72; res assoc cell biol, Univ Colo, Boulder, 73-78. *Concurrent Pos:* Res assoc, NIH fel, 75-78. *Mem:* AAAS; Am Soc Cell Biol. *Res:* Isolation and characterization of the intact mitotic apparatus from mammalian tissue culture cells and investigation of factors controlling mitotic spindle assembly and chromosome movement. *Mailing Add:* Dept Biol Sci Univ Denver Denver CO 80208-0001. *Fax:* 303-871-4000

SNYDER, LAWRENCE CLEMENT, CHEMICAL PHYSICS. *Current Pos:* PROF & CHMN DEPT CHEM, STATE UNIV NY, ALBANY, 80-82 & 84- *Personal Data:* b Ridley Park, Pa, Apr 16, 32; m 58, 89, Lynn, Mayer; c Lenore, Evan, Leland & Justin. *Educ:* Univ Calif, Berkeley, BS, 53; Carnegie Inst Technol, MS, 54, PhD(chem), 59. *Prof Exp:* Mem tech staff, Bell Labs, 59-80 & 82-84. *Concurrent Pos:* Lectr chem, Columbia Univ, 65-67; lectureship in chem, Robert A Welch Found, 71. *Mem:* Fel AAAS; Am Chem Soc; fel Am Phys Soc; fel Am Inst Chem. *Res:* Electronic structure of molecules; structure and thermochemistry of silicon hydrides; silicon crystal surface reconstruction; chemistry and physics of defects in semiconductors. *Mailing Add:* Chem Dept State Univ NY Albany NY 12222. *Fax:* 518-442-3462; *E-Mail:* lcs64@cn3vax.albany.edu

SNYDER, LEWIS EMIL, ASTROPHYSICS, MOLECULAR PHYSICS. *Current Pos:* PROF ASTRON, UNIV ILL, 75- *Personal Data:* b Ft Wayne, Ind, Nov 26, 39; m 62; c Herman E & Catherine J. *Educ:* Ind State Univ, BS, 61; Southern Ill Univ, MA, 64; Mich State Univ, PhD(physics), 67. *Prof Exp:* Res assoc astrophys, Nat Radio Astron Observ, 67-69; from asst prof to assoc prof astron, Univ Va, 69-75. *Concurrent Pos:* Mem, Ctr Advan Studies, Univ Va, 69-75; mem, Radio & Radar Astron Comn, Int Sci Radio Union, 69-; mem, Radio Astron Subcomt, Comt Radio Frequencies, Nat Res Coun, 71-74; vis fel, Joint Inst Lab Astrophys, Boulder, Colo, 73-74; Alexander von Humboldt Found sr US scientist award, 83-84. *Mem:* Sigma Xi; Am Phys Soc; Am Astron Soc; Int Astron Union; AAAS; Astron Soc Pac. *Res:* Spectral line radio astronomy and chemical composition of the interstellar medium, comets and evolved stars. *Mailing Add:* 103 Astron Bldg Univ Ill 1002 W Green St Urbana IL 61801

SNYDER, LLOYD ROBERT, ANALYTICAL CHEMISTRY. *Current Pos:* VPRES RES, LC RESOURCES INC. *Personal Data:* b Sacramento, Calif, July 30, 31; m 52; c 4. *Educ:* Univ Calif, BS, 52, PhD, 54. *Honors & Awards:* Petrol Chem Award, Am Chem Soc, 70, Chromatography Award, 84; Dal Nogare Award, 76; Palmer Award, 85; Martin Award, 89; Nat Chromatography Award, NE Chromatography Disc Group, 91; Chem Award, Am Chem Soc, 93. *Prof Exp:* Res chemist, Shell Oil Co, 54-56 & Technicolor Corp, 56-57; from sr res chemist to sr res assoc, Union Oil Co Calif, 57-71; dir separations res, Technicon Corp, 71-72, vpres clin chem, 72-82. *Mem:* Am Chem Soc. *Res:* Preparative separations; high speed liquid chromatography; adsorption and adsorption chromatography; analytical separations; computer simulation. *Mailing Add:* 26 Silverwood Ct Orinda CA 94563-2908

SNYDER, LOREN RUSSELL, MOLECULAR BIOLOGY. *Current Pos:* from asst prof to assoc prof, 70-79, actg chair, 87-88, PROF MICROBIOL, MICH STATE UNIV, 79- *Personal Data:* b Milwaukee, Wis, June 19, 41; m 86, Wendy Champness; c Abby & Naomi. *Educ:* Univ Minn, Duluth, BA, 63; Univ Chicago, PhD(biophys), 68. *Prof Exp:* Jane Coffin Childs Mem Fund Med Res fel, Int Lab Genetics & Biophys, Naples, 68-69; fac sci, Univ Paris, 69-70. *Concurrent Pos:* NIH res grants, 74-77, 80-83 & 83-86; NSF res grants, 78-80, 80-83 & 86-89; vis prof, Harvard Univ, 84-85 & Univ Tel Aviv, 94. *Mem:* Am Soc Microbiol. *Res:* Molecular basis for control of gene expression in bacteria. *Mailing Add:* Dept Microbiol Mich State Univ East Lansing MI 48824

SNYDER, LOUIS MICHAEL, HEMATOLOGY. *Current Pos:* DIR DIV HEMAT, ST VINCENT HOSP, 68-; PROF INTERNAL MED & PEDIAT, MED SCH, UNIV MASS, 79- *Personal Data:* b Boston, Mass, May 10, 35; m 58; c 3. *Educ:* Brown Univ, AB, 57; Chicago Med Sch, MD, 62; Am Bd Internal Med, Hematol Bd, dipl. *Prof Exp:* NIH grant hemat, Mass Gen Hosp, 65-66. *Concurrent Pos:* Mem med adv bd, New Eng Hemophilia Asn, 72-; chmn med adv bd, Cent Mass, Leukemia Soc Am, 73-78. *Mem:* Am Fedn Clin Res; Am Soc Hemat; fel Am Col Physicians; NY Acad Sci. *Res:* Red cell metabolism; red cell membrane structure and function. *Mailing Add:* 25 Winthrop St Worcester MA 01604-4543

SNYDER, MELVIN H(ENRY), JR, THERMODYNAMICS. *Current Pos:* RETIRED. *Personal Data:* b Pittsburgh, Pa, Sept 22, 21; m 46, 59; c 6. *Educ:* Carnegie Inst Technol, BS, 46; Wichita State Univ, MS, 50; Okla State Univ, PhD, 67. *Prof Exp:* From instr to prof aeronaut eng, Wichita State Univ, 46-92, head dept, 51-58, asst dean, 58-67, chair dept, 77-92. *Concurrent Pos:* Consult, 51-; vis prof, Von Karman Inst Fluid Dynamics, Belg, 70-71. *Mem:* Am Inst Aeronaut & Astronaut. *Res:* Drag of bodies in sheared-flow fields; lift, drag and pitching moment of delta wings; use of power to aerothermodynamics. *Mailing Add:* 7034 Farmview Wichita KS 67206. *Fax:* 813-855-2309

SNYDER, MERRILL J, CLINICAL MICROBIOLOGY. *Current Pos:* instr bact & med, Sch Med, Univ Md, 49-53, asst prof med in clin bact, 53-57, from asst prof to assoc prof microbiol, 55-65, assoc dir div infectious dis, 57-74, from assoc prof to prof med clin microbiol, 59-83, res prof med, 83-86, EMER PROF MED, SCH MED, UNIV MD, BALTIMORE CITY, 86- *Personal Data:* b McKeesport, Pa, May 25, 19; m 42, Muriel Goodwin; c Sammie, Terry & Susan. *Educ:* Univ Pittsburgh, BS, 40; Univ Md, MS, 50, PhD(bact), 53; Am Bd Med Microbiol, dipl. *Prof Exp:* Clin chemist, McKeesport Hosp, Pa, 38-41; med bacteriologist, Dept Virus & Rickettsial Dis, US Army Med Ctr, DC, 45-49. *Concurrent Pos:* Head diag microbiol & serol, Univ Md Hosp, 59-71, hosp epidemiologist, 73-77. *Mem:* Am Soc Microbiol; Infectious Dis Soc Am; AAAS. *Res:* Infectious diseases. *Mailing Add:* Dept Med Univ Md Sch Med Baltimore MD 21201. *E-Mail:* msnyder@umalnet.ab.umd.edu

SNYDER, MITCHELL, STATISTICS. *Current Pos:* sci dir, Comput Ctr, 69-83, ADJ ASSOC PROF MATH, BAR-ILAN UNIV, ISRAEL, 68- *Personal Data:* b Philadelphia, Pa, Nov 4, 38; m 63, Rebecca Brill; c 5. *Educ:* Yeshiva Univ, BA & BHL, 60; NY Univ, MS, 62; Univ Chicago, PhD(statist), 66. *Prof Exp:* Consult, Biol Sci Comput Ctr, Univ Chicago, 62-65; mem tech staff, Bell Tel Labs, 65-68. *Concurrent Pos:* Lectr, Roosevelt Univ, 64-65; corp statistician, Tadiran Info Syst. *Mem:* Inst Math Statist; Am Statist Asn; Asn Comput Mach; Israel Statist Asn; Info Processing Asn Israel; Am Soc Qual Control; Israel Soc Qual Assurance. *Res:* Multivariate analysis; industrial statistics; computer applications in data analysis. *Mailing Add:* Dept Math Bar-Ilan Univ Ramat Gan 52100 Israel

SNYDER, NATHAN W(ILLIAM), ENERGY CONVERSION, HEAT & MASS TRANSFER. *Current Pos:* chief scientist, 72-78, mgr, Technol Dept, 81-92, TECH DIR, RALPH M PARSONS CO, 78-80, 92- *Personal Data:* b Montreal, Que, Apr 21, 18; nat US; m 44, Rosalie Shaw; c Christine E & Lorraine D. *Educ:* Univ Calif, Berkeley, BS, 41, MS, 44, PhD(mech eng, math), 47. *Honors & Awards:* Skylab Achievement Award, NASA, 74; George Washington Award & Engr of Year, Inst Advan Eng, 77. *Prof Exp:* Instr & res scientist, Univ Calif, Berkeley, 42-47, asst prof mech eng, 47-53, assoc prof process eng & chmn, Dept Nuclear Eng, 53-57, prof nuclear eng & chmn dept, 57-58; sr staff scientist in space technol, chmn, Space Power & Energy Conversion Panel & adv, Propulsion Panel, Inst Defense Anal, 58-61; vpres res & eng, Royal Res Corp, 61-62; chief scientist, Kaiser Aerospace & Electronics Corp, 62-64; Neely prof nuclear eng, Ga Inst Technol, 64-66, Neely prof aerospace eng, 66-68; asst sr vpres res & eng, NAm Rockwell Corp, 68-71; pres, N W Snyder Assocs, 71-72; adj prof, Energy & Kinetics, Univ Calif, Los Angeles, 73-74. *Concurrent Pos:* Consult various govt agencies and pvt industs, 44-; mem, Adv Comt Nuclear Systs Space, NASA, 59-61, Biotechnol & Human Res Adv Comt, 69-71 & Life Sci Comt, 71-74; energy conversion adv to Air Force, 62-70, mem, Air Force Sci Adv Bd, 67-70; mem space technol panel, President's Sci Adv Comt, 64-67; mem, Adv Comt Isotopes & Radiation Develop, Atomic Energy Comn, 66-67; mem, Environ Impacts Panel, Am Inst Biol Sci, 74-78; chmn, Transp Comt, Calif Intersoc Legis Adv Comn, 77-80; chmn tech comt, Dept Energy Strategic Petrol Reserve Prog, 78-81. *Mem:* Am Phys Soc; Am Inst Aeronaut & Astronaut; Am Nuclear Soc; Acoust Soc Am; Am Inst Chem Engrs. *Res:* Energy conversion; physics of fluids and heat; mass transfer; space technology; nuclear power; space power; acoustics; physics of boiling, originated thin film or microfilm theory of boiling; sea water desalination; nuclear propulsion; environmental control and life support; solid waste conversion to energy and resource recovery; interbasin transfer of water from Alaska to the United States, Canada and Mexico; alternative technologies for toxic waste disposal. *Mailing Add:* PO Box 2965 Carmel CA 93921

SNYDER, PATRICIA ANN, VACUUM ULTRAVIOLET SPECTROSCOPY. *Current Pos:* from asst prof to assoc prof, 75-83, PROF CHEM, FLA ATLANTIC UNIV, 83-; PROF CHEM, GRAD FAC, UNIV FLA, 83- *Personal Data:* b Batavia, NY, Sept 24, 40; c 1. *Educ:* Syracuse Univ, BS, 62; Univ Calif, San Diego, PhD(chem), 70. *Prof Exp:* Teaching asst chem, Syracuse Univ, 61-62; chemist, Allied Chem, 61-62 & E I Du Pont de Nemours & Co, 62-64; res asst chem, Univ Calif, San Diego, 64-70; res assoc, Ore State Univ, 70-73, instr, 73-74; asst prof, Baylor Univ, 74-75. *Concurrent Pos:* From asst prof to assoc prof chem, grad fac, Univ Fla, 77-83, vis prof, 79; vis scientist, Brookhaven Nat Lab, 80, 82 & 83, consult, 85. *Mem:* Am Chem Soc; Sigma Xi. *Res:* Vacuum ultraviolet natural circular dichroism; magnetic circular dichroism; absorption spectroscopy with synchrotron radiation; electronic and geometric structure of molecules. *Mailing Add:* Dept Chem Fla Atlantic Univ Boca Raton FL 33431. *E-Mail:* snyder@acc.fau.edu

SNYDER, R L, engineering; deceased, see previous edition for last biography

SNYDER, RICHARD GERALD, INJURY BIOMECHANICS & HUMAN IMPACT, BIOLOGICAL & FORENSIC ANTHROPOLOGY. *Current Pos:* EMER PROF ANTHROP, UNIV MICH, ANN ARBOR, 85-; EMER RES SCIENTIST, HWY SAFETY RES INST, N HIGHLANDS, CALIF, 89- *Personal Data:* b Northampton, Mass, Feb 14, 28; m 49; c 6. *Educ:* Univ Ariz, BA, 56, MA, 57, PhD(phys anthrop), 59; Am Bd Forensic Anthropology, dipl. *Honors & Awards:* Nat Safety Coun Metrop Life Award, 70; Arch T Colwell Merit Award, Soc Automotive Engrs, 73; Harry G Moselsy Award, Aerospace Med Asn, 75, John Paul Stapp Award, 94; T Dale Stewart Award, Am Acad Forensic Sci, 92. *Prof Exp:* Asst anthrop, Univ Ariz, 57-59, from assoc res engr to res phys anthropologist, Appl Res Lab, 59-60; chief phys anthrop, Civil Aeromed Res Inst, Fed Aviation Agency, 60-66; mgr, Biomech Dept, Automotive Safety Res Off, Ford Motor Co, Mich, 66; assoc prof anthrop, Mich State Univ, 66-68; from assoc prof to prof anthrop, Univ Mich, Ann Arbor, 68-85, head, Biomed Dept & res scientist, Hwy Safety Res Inst, Inst Sci & Technol, 69-84, dir, NASA Ctr Excellence Man-Syst Res, Transp Inst, 84-85. *Concurrent Pos:* Mem staff, Ariz Transp & Traffic Inst, 59-60; assoc prof syst eng, Univ Ariz, 60; adj assoc prof, Univ Okla, 61-66; res assoc, Univ Chicago, 63-66; consult, USAF, US Navy, NASA, US Dept Transp, Southwest Res Inst, US Army, Dept Health, Educ & Welfare & Am Inst Biol Scientists; mem biodynamics comt aerospace med panel, Adv Group Aeronaut Res & Develop-NATO, 63-, planning comt, Int Meeting on Impact, Portugal, 71, adv comt, Stapp Car Crash Conf, 69- & adv panel grad prog systs safety eng, NC State Univ, 69-; mem fac, Bioeng Prog, Univ Mich, Ann Arbor, 70; mem, Comt Hearing, Bioacoust & Biomech, Nat Acad Sci-Nat Res Coun, 70-72, Trauma Res Comt, 84-85; pres, Biodynamics Int, 86-, George Snively Res Found, 93-; dir, NMex Res Inst, alamagordo, 96- *Mem:* Fel AAAS; fel Am Anthrop Asn; Aerospace Indust Life Sci Asn (vpres, 74); fel Aerospace Med Asn; fel Am Acad Forensic Sci; assoc fel Am Inst Aeronaut & Astronaut; Soc Automotive Engrs. *Res:* Human biology; aviation and automotive medicine; biomedical sciences; human tolerances to impact trauma; occupant restraint systems; dental morphology; forensic medicine. *Mailing Add:* 3720 N Silver Dr Tucson AZ 85749. *Fax:* 520-760-0794

SNYDER, ROBERT, BIOCHEMICAL PHARMACOLOGY. *Current Pos:* PROF TOXICOL & DIR JOINT GRAD PROG TOXICOL, COL PHARM, 81-, PROF PHARMACOL & CHEM RES TOXICOL, & CHMN DEPT PHARMACOL & TOXICOL, RUTGERS UNIV, 82-; DIR, HEALTH EFFECTS ASSESSMENT DIV, NJ INST TECHNOL, 84- *Personal Data:* b Brooklyn, NY, Jan 17, 35; m 57; c 2. *Educ:* Queens Col, NY, BS, 57; State Univ NY, PhD(biochem), 61. *Prof Exp:* Trainee pharmacol, Col Med, Univ Ill, 61-63; prof, Jefferson Med Col, Pa, 63-81. *Concurrent Pos:* Vis prof toxicol, Univ Tubingen, Germany, 71-72; adj prof, Thomas Jefferson Univ, Pa, 81- & Univ Med & Dent NJ, 82- *Mem:* Am Col Toxicol; Am Asn Univ Prof; Am Soc Pharmacol & Exp Therapeut; Soc Toxicol; Int Soc Biochem Pharmacol. *Res:* Metabolic conversion of xenobiotics to reactive metabolites which are ultimately responsible for toxicological or carcinogenic processes; the mechanism(s) by which benzene produces bone marrow damage leading to aplastic anemia or leukemia; enzymes which metabolize benzene; characterization of the metabolites of benzene which result in the formation of adducts to DNA; target cells for benzene in bone marrow; mechanism of neurotoxicity of monochloroacetic acid; strategies for investigation of the toxicology of complex mixtures such as those found in leachates from chemical waste dumps. *Mailing Add:* Dept Pharmacol & Toxicol EOHSI Busch Campus 681 Frelinghuysen Rd Piscataway NJ 08855-1179. *Fax:* 732-932-5767

SNYDER, ROBERT, POLYMER CHEMISTRY, RUBBER & TIRE RESEARCH. *Current Pos:* RESEARCHER CHEM RES, TIRE TECHNOL INC, 90- *Personal Data:* b Mont, Oct, 1918. *Educ:* Univ Mich, BS, 40; Univ Chicago, PhD(chem), 48. *Prof Exp:* Dir car technol & rubber res, Uniroyal Goodrich Tire Co, 45-90. *Mem:* NY Acad Sci; Am Chem Soc. *Mailing Add:* Tire Technol Inc 51 Willison Grosse Pointe MI 48236-7564

SNYDER, ROBERT DOUGLAS, ENGINEERING MECHANICS, APPLIED MATHEMATICS. *Current Pos:* chmn, Dept Eng Sci, Mech & Mat, 75-76, DEAN ENG, UNIV NC, CHARLOTTE, 76- *Personal Data:* b Lancaster, Pa, Apr 15, 34; m 55; c 3. *Educ:* Ind Inst Technol, BSME, 55; Clemson Univ, MSME, 59; WVa Univ, PhD(theoret & appl mech), 65. *Prof Exp:* Servo engr, Bell Aircraft Corp, 55; instr mech eng, Ind Inst Technol, 55-57; from instr to asst prof mech, Clemson Univ, 57-60; from instr to prof, WVa Univ, 62-75. *Mem:* Nat Soc Prof Engrs; Am Soc Mech Engrs; Sigma Xi. *Res:* Continuum mechanics. *Mailing Add:* Col Eng Univ NC Charlotte NC 28223

SNYDER, ROBERT GENE, VIBRATIONAL SPECTROSCOPY & STRUCTURE OF CHAIN MOLECULES, PHASE TRANSITIONS IN MOLECULAR SOLIDS. *Current Pos:* RES FEL, DEPT CHEM, UNIV CALIF, BERKELEY, 77- *Personal Data:* b Boise, Idaho, July 4, 29; m 53, Kay Newhouse; c 4. *Educ:* Ore State Univ, BA, 51, MA, 53, PhD(chem), 55. *Honors & Awards:* Cobentz Soc Award, 65. *Prof Exp:* Fel vibrational spectros, Univ Minn, 55-56; chemist, Shell Develop Co, 56-63; res fel, Polytech Inst Indust Chem, Milan, Italy, 63-64; chemist, Shell Develop Co, 64-72; res chemist, Western Regional Res Lab, 72-75; res scientist, Midland Macromolecular Inst, 75-77. *Mem:* Am Phys Soc; Am Chem Soc; Soc Appl Spectros; Biophys Soc. *Res:* Development of relations between the vibrational, spectra, structure and phase behavior of chain molecules, polymers and biopolymers. *Mailing Add:* Dept Chem Univ Calif Berkeley CA 94720-1460. *Fax:* 510-642-8369

SNYDER, ROBERT L(EON), MATERIALS SCIENCE, ENGINEERING. *Current Pos:* assoc prof mat, 67-70, PROF MECH ENG, ROCHESTER INST TECHNOL, 70- *Personal Data:* b Albion, NY, Sept 3, 34; m 60; c 2. *Educ:* Rochester Inst Technol, BS, 56; Iowa State Univ, PhD(metall), 60. *Prof Exp:* Res engr, Metall, Res & Eng Ctr, Ford Motor Co, 60-65; res scientist, Res Div, Am Standard, Inc, 65-67. *Mem:* Am Soc Metals; Am Soc Eng Educ; Am Soc Mech Engrs; Nat Soc Prof Engrs. *Mailing Add:* Dept Mech Eng Rochester Inst Technol 76 Lomb Mem Dr Rochester NY 14623-5604

SNYDER, ROBERT LEROY, COMPARATIVE PATHOLOGY, VERTEBRATE ECOLOGY. *Current Pos:* asst instr path, Univ Pa, 61-62, assoc comp path, 62-66, asst prof, 66-70, dir, Penrose Res Lab, Zool Soc Philadelphia, 69-89, ASSOC PROF PATH, DIV GRAD MED, UNIV PA, 70- *Personal Data:* b Ellwood City, Pa, Apr 24, 26; m 49, Patricia Daugherty; c David, James, Mark & Matthew. *Educ:* Pa State Univ, BS, 50, MS, 52; Johns Hopkins Univ, ScD(hyg), 60. *Prof Exp:* Res aide wildlife ecol, US Fish & Wildlife Serv, 50-52; biologist, Pa State Game Comn, 52-56; res asst vert ecol, Johns Hopkins Univ, 56-59; from res assoc to assoc dir, Penrose Res Lab, Zool Soc Philadelphia, 59-69. *Concurrent Pos:* Adj prof, Beaver Col, 89- *Res:* Comparative pathology, viral hepatitis and population ecology; study of chronic viral diseases and their role in the development of cancer; woodchuck hepatitis virus and similar agents of importance in cancer research. *Mailing Add:* 305 Hampton Rd King of Prussia PA 19406

SNYDER, ROBERT LYMAN, HIGH TEMPERATURE SUPERCONDUCTIVITY, X-RAY CRYSTALLOGRAPHY. *Current Pos:* from asst prof to prof, 70-96, dir, Inst Ceramic Super-conductivity, 87-96, EMER PROF ALFRED UNIV, 96-; PROF & CHAIR, DEPT MAT SCI & ENG, OHIO STATE UNIV, 96- *Personal Data:* b Plattsburg, NY, June 5, 41; m 63, Sheila Nolan; c Robert N & Kristina M. *Educ:* Marist Col, BS, 63; Fordham Univ, PhD(phys chem), 68. *Prof Exp:* Res asst & guest assoc, Brookhaven Nat Lab, NY, 66-68. *Concurrent Pos:* NIH fel, Crystallog Lab, Univ Pittsburgh, Pa, 68; Nat Res Coun fel, Electronics Res Ctr, NASA, Cambridge, Mass, 69; vis scientist, Lawrence Livermore Lab, Livermore, Calif, 77 & 78 & US Nat Bur Stand, Gaithersburg, Md, 80 & 81; vis prof, Siemens Cent Res Lab, Munich, Ger, 83 & 91; chmn tech comt, Int Centre Diffraction Data JCPDS, 86-90; chmn, Appl Crystallog Div, Am Crystallog Asn, 89-91; mem, US Nat Comt for Crystallog, Nat Acad Sci, 91-94; Prof Invite, Univ Rennes, France, 95; chmn bd dirs, Inter Ctr Diffraction Data, 96- *Mem:* Am Crystallog Asn; fel Am Ceramic Soc; Joint Comt Powder Diffraction Stand; Mat Res Soc; Nat Inst Ceramic Eng; Am Soc Metals. *Res:* Establishing structure-property relationships in technologically important materials; broad range of analytical techniques with a particular emphasis on x-ray, neutron and electron diffraction and thermal analysis; development of advanced manufacturing techniques. *Mailing Add:* Dept Mat Sci Eng Mid State Univ 177 Watts Hall Columbus OH 43210-1179. *Fax:* 614-292-4668; *E-Mail:* snyder.s55@csu.edu

SNYDER, RUTH EVELYN, MEDICINE, RADIOLOGY. *Current Pos:* attend roentgenologist & sr staff, 77-81, CONSULT, MEM SLOAN-KETTERING CTR, 81- *Personal Data:* b Canadian, Tex, May 21, 11; m 42; c 3. *Educ:* Park Col, BA, 32; Univ Tex, MD, 36; Am Bd Radiol, cert, 43. *Prof Exp:* Intern, NY Infirmary, Women & Child, 36-37; fel, Strang Clinic, 37-38; clin fel radiation ther, Mem Hosp, 39-42; asst radiologist, NY Hosp, 42-45; asst roentgenologist, Mem Hosp, 42-45; assoc roentgenologist & radiation ther, Hosp Spec Surg, 44-47; roentgenologist, Strang Clinic, Mem Hosp, 48-51; asst roentgenologist, 51-52; assoc roentgenologist, Mem Hosp, 52-77; consult radiol, NY Infirmary, 54- *Concurrent Pos:* Instr radiol, Cornell Univ Med Col, 52-61, clin instr, 61-63, clin asst prof, 64- *Mem:* AMA; Am Women's Med Asn; Radiol Soc NAm; Soc Surg Oncol; Asn Women Sci; Am Col Radiol. *Res:* Mammography. *Mailing Add:* 222 E 68th St New York NY 10021-6001

SNYDER, SOLOMON H, NEUROPHARMACOLOGY. *Current Pos:* from asst prof pharmacol to prof psychiat & pharmacol, 66-77, DISTINGUISHED SERV PROF PSYCHIAT & PHARMACOL, MED SCH, JOHNS HOPKINS UNIV, 77-, DIR DEPT NEUROSCI, 80- *Personal Data:* b Washington, DC, Dec 26, 38; m 62, Elaine Borko; c Judith R & Deborah L. *Educ:* Georgetown Univ, MD, 62. *Hon Degrees:* DSc, Northwestern Univ, 81, Georgetown Univ, 86 & Ben-Gurlon Univ, 90. *Honors & Awards:* John Jacob Abel Award, Am Soc Pharmacol & Exp Therapeut, 70, Goodman & Gilman Award, 80; A E Bennett Award, Soc Biol Psychiat, 70; Hofheimer Prize, Am Psychiat Asn, 72 & Spec Presidential Commendation, 85, Distinguished Serv Award, 89; Gaddum Prize, Brit Pharmacol Soc, 74; Francis O Schmitt Award, 74; Daniel Efron Award, Am Col Neuropsychopharmacol, 74; Salmon Award, 78; Lasker Prize, 78; Harvey Lectr, 78; Wolf Prize Med, Israel, 83; George Cotzias Award, Am Acad Neurol, 85; Sci Achievement Award, AMA, 85; J Allyn Taylor Prize, 90; Bower Award, Franklin Inst, 91; Baxter Award, Am Asn Med Col, 95. *Prof Exp:* Intern med, Kaiser Found Hosp, 62-63; res assoc pharmacol, NIMH, 63-65. *Concurrent Pos:* Asst resident psychiat, Johns Hopkins Hosp, 65-68. *Mem:* Nat Acad Sci; fel Inst Med-Nat Acad Sci; Am Col Neuropsychopharmacol; Am Soc Pharmacol & Exp Therapeut; assoc Neurosci Res Prog; Int Soc Neurochem; fel Am Acad Arts & Sci; Am Philos Soc. *Res:* Neurotransmitters; mechanism of action of psychotropic drugs. *Mailing Add:* 3801 Canterbury Rd Apt 1001 Baltimore MD 21218-2315. *Fax:* 410-955-3623; *E-Mail:* sol_snyder@qmail.bs.jhu.edu

SNYDER, STANLEY PAUL, VETERINARY PATHOLOGY, ONCOLOGY. *Current Pos:* DIR DIAG LAB & PROF, COL VET MED, ORE STATE UNIV. *Personal Data:* b Rifle, Colo, Sept 11, 42; m 66; c 2. *Educ:* Colo State Univ, DVM, 66, MS, 67; Univ Calif, Davis, PhD(comp path), 71. *Prof Exp:* Am Cancer Soc fel, Univ Calif, Davis, 71-72; asst prof vet med, Ore State Univ, 72-74; from asst prof to assoc prof path, Colo State Univ, 78- *Mem:* Am Vet Med Asn; Am Col Vet Path; Am Asn Cancer Res; Vet Cancer Soc. *Res:* Viral and comparative oncology; pathogenesis of viral diseases; leprology. *Mailing Add:* Diag Lab Ore State Univ PO Box 429 Corvallis OR 97339-0429

SNYDER, STEPHEN LAURIE, BIOLOGICAL CHEMISTRY. *Current Pos:* prof mgr biotechnol, 89-93, PROG MGR ENVIRON BIOCHEM, NAVAL RES LAB, 93- *Personal Data:* b Herkimer, NY, Oct 2, 42; m 66, Virginia Marie Holley; c Allison, Elizabeth & Sarah. *Educ:* Hobart Col, BS, 64; State Univ NY Binghamton, MA, 67; Univ Vt, PhD(chem), 70. *Prof Exp:* Res assoc biochem, Univ Colo, Boulder, 70-72; Nat Res Coun fel, Agr Res Serv, New Orleans, La, 72-75; biochemist, Armed Forces Radiobiol Res Inst, Bethesda, Md, 75-78; mem fac, Dept Chem, US Naval Acad, Annapolis, Md, 78-81; mem staff, Naval Med Res Inst, 81-83; chmn Radiation Biochem Dept, Armed Forces Radiobiol, Res Inst, 86-89. *Mem:* Am Chem Soc; Sigma Xi. *Res:* Reaction mechanisms; enzymology; charge-transfer complexes; radiation biology; pathophysiology of endotoxins; role of lysosomal hydrolases in inflammation; antifouling coatings. *Mailing Add:* PO Box 447 Clinton MD 20735

SNYDER, THOMA MEES, PHYSICS. *Current Pos:* res assoc, Res Lab, Gen Elec Co, 46-47, proj head preliminary pile assembly & mem intermediate breeder reactor staff, Knolls Atomic Power Lab, 47-49, asst mgr, physics sect, 49-52, mgr reactor sect, 52-54, mgr phys sect, 54-56, mgr res oper, 56-57, mgr phys sect, Vallecitos Atomic Lab, 57-64, consult, Res & Eng Prog, 64-69, CONSULT SCIENTIST, NUCLEAR ENERGY DIV, GEN ELEC CO, 70- *Personal Data:* b Baltimore, Md, May 21, 16; m 58; c 2. *Educ:* Johns Hopkins Univ, PhD(physics), 40. *Prof Exp:* Instr physics, Princeton Univ, 40-42; res assoc, Off Sci Res & Develop contract, 42-43; res assoc, Los Alamos Sci Lab, 43-45. *Concurrent Pos:* Mem cross sect adv group, US AEC, 48-56, secy, 48, mem adv comt reactor physics, 50-72, chmn, 54; tech adv, US AEC, Geneva Conf Peaceful Uses of Atomic Energy, 55 & 58; mem, Mission Atomic Energy, Eng & Belg, 56. *Mem:* Fel Am Nuclear Soc; fel Am Phys Soc. *Res:* Nuclear energy technology; processes and materials; nuclear and reactor physics; solid state and plasma physics; radiation effects. *Mailing Add:* 208 Kalkar Dr Santa Cruz CA 95060

SNYDER, VIRGIL W(ARD), STRUCTURAL DYNAMICS, FINITE ELEMENTS. *Current Pos:* prof, 65-, EMER PROF ENG MECH, MICH TECHNOL UNIV. *Personal Data:* b Midland, Mich, Mar 4, 34; m 58, 94, Margaret A Hope; c 2. *Educ:* Mich Technol Univ, BSCE, 56, MSCE, 62; Univ Ariz, PhD(aerospace eng), 68. *Prof Exp:* Stress engr, Northrup Aircraft, Inc, 56-58; struct engr, NAm Aviation, Inc, 58-60; instr eng mech, Mich Technol Univ, 60-62; consult, Kitt Peak Nat Observ, Univ Ariz, 63-65. *Concurrent Pos:* vis prof, Monash Univ, Australia, 83 & Curtin Univ, 93. *Mem:* Am Soc Eng Educ; Soc Exp Mech; Am Acad Mech. *Res:* Vibrations, dynamics, finite elements and rock mechanics; computer software developed for mechanics problems. *Mailing Add:* Dept Mech Eng Mich Technol Univ 1400 Townsend Dr Houghton MI 49931-1295

SNYDER, VIRGINIA, ELECTRON MICROSCOPY. *Current Pos:* ASSOC PROF BIOL, UNIV WIS-PLATTEVILLE, 88- *Personal Data:* b Coldwater, Ohio, July 30, 57. *Educ:* Defiance Col, BS, 79; Med Col Ohio, PhD, 88. *Prof Exp:* Res med technician, Med Col Ohio, 85-88. *Mem:* Human Anat & Physiol Soc; Sigma Xi; AAAS; Nat Asn Col & Teachers Agr; Am Asn Univ Women. *Res:* Physiology of animals; anatomy; effects of amiodarone on rat myocardium; instructional multimedia. *Mailing Add:* Dept Biol Univ Wis Rm 249 Gardner Platteville WI 53818-3099

SNYDER, WARREN EDWARD, MECHANICAL ENGINEERING. *Current Pos:* VPRES ENG, WAUKESHA ENG DIV, DRESSER INDUST, INC, 70- *Personal Data:* b Hutchinson, Kans, Feb 24, 22; m 43; c 3. *Educ:* Univ Kans, BS, 43; Univ Minn, MS, 48, PhD(mech eng), 50. *Prof Exp:* Mech engr, US Naval Res Lab, 43-46; instr mech eng & asst head, Univ Minn, 46-50; assoc prof & head, Univ Kans, 50-52; sr res engr, Res Labs, Gen Motors Corp, 52-57; dir eng div, Midwest Res Inst, 57-62; vpres eng, Cummins Eng Co, Ind, 62-66; vpres eng & res div, Am Bosch Arma Corp, Mass, 66-70. *Mem:* Am Soc Mech Engrs; Am Soc Eng Educ; Soc Automotive Engrs. *Res:* Design; analysis; mathematics; management. *Mailing Add:* 7032 W Hummingbird Ct Milwaukee WI 53223-2768

SNYDER, WESLEY EDWIN, ELECTRICAL ENGINEERING. *Current Pos:* asst prof, 76-81, ASSOC PROF ELEC ENG, NC STATE UNIV, 81- *Personal Data:* b Orlando, Fla, Nov 11, 46; m 68; c 3. *Educ:* NC State Univ, BS, 68; Univ Ill, Urbana-Champaign, MS, 70, PhD(elec eng), 75. *Prof Exp:* Vis asst prof elec eng, Univ Ill, Urbana-Champaign, 75. *Concurrent Pos:* Fel, Langley Res Ctr, NASA, 76; consult, UN, 75 & 77, IBM, Westinghouse, Gen Elec, & Res Triangle Inst; vis scientist, WGer Space Agency, 79. *Mem:* Sr mem Inst Elec & Electronics Engrs; Soc Mech Engrs; Asn Comput Mach; Robotics Inst Am. *Res:* Computer image analysis; machine vision; robotics. *Mailing Add:* 3603 Octavia St Raleigh NC 29606

SNYDER, WILBERT FRANK, PHYSICS, HISTORY OF SCIENCE. *Current Pos:* RETIRED. *Personal Data:* b Marion, Ohio, Apr 19, 04; m 33, 76, Dorothy J Norvell; c Elyse R & Tad W. *Educ:* NCent Col, BA, 26; Univ Ill, AM, 27. *Honors & Awards:* Bronze Medal for Superior Serv, Dept of Com, 68. *Prof Exp:* From jr physicist to physicist, Nat Bur Stand, 27-46, asst chief, Microwave Stand Sect, 46-54, asst to chief, Radio Stand Div, 54-56, asst chief, Electronic Calibration Ctr, 56-62, coordr calibration serv, Radio Stand Eng Div, 62-69, annuitant, Electromagnetics Div, 69-72, guest worker, 72-87. *Mem:* Fel Acoust Soc Am; Sigma Xi; sr mem Inst Elec & Electronics Engrs; sr mem Instrument Soc Am. *Res:* Acoustics of buildings and sound; standards and testing of hearing aids, audiometers and sixteen millimeter sound motion picture projectors; radar countermeasures; microwave standards; calibration of electronic standards; radio history. *Mailing Add:* 350 Ponca Pl Boulder CO 80303-3828

SNYDER, WILLARD MONROE, HYDROLOGY. *Current Pos:* RETIRED. *Personal Data:* b Lehighton, Pa, Sept 29, 18; m 48. *Educ:* Ursinus Col, BS, 40; Mass Inst Technol, MS, 48. *Prof Exp:* Engr hydrol, Fed-State Flood Forecasting Serv, Pa, 47-50; engr hydrol, Hydraul Data Br, Tenn Valley Authority, 50-55, head statist analytical unit, Hydrol Sect, 55-57, head hydrol sect, Hydraul Data Br, 57-60, staff res hydrologist, Off Tributary Area Develop, 60-62; prof hydrol, Ga Inst Technol, 63-69; res hydrol engr, Sci & Educ Admin-Agr Res, USDA, 69-75, res invest leader watershed eng, 70-73, res leader watershed hydrol, Southeast Watershed Res Ctr, Athens area, 74-80. *Concurrent Pos:* Consult, Oak Ridge Nat Lab, 67; consult hydrol, 80-. *Mem:* Am Soc Civil Eng; Am Geophys Union; Am Water Resources Asn; Sigma Xi. *Res:* Formulation and evaluation of hydrologic models based on statistical analysis and on explicit and implicit solution of watershed process equations. *Mailing Add:* 275 Gatewood Circle Athens GA 30607

SNYDER, WILLIAM JAMES, CHEMICAL ENGINEERING. *Current Pos:* from asst prof to assoc prof, 68-80, PROF CHEM ENG, BUCKNELL UNIV, 80- *Personal Data:* b Altoona, Pa, Nov 4, 41; m 64; c 1. *Educ:* Pa State Univ, BS, 63, MS, 65, PhD(chem eng), 67. *Prof Exp:* Fel, Lehigh Univ, 67-68. *Mem:* Am Inst Chem Engrs; Am Chem Soc; Am Soc Eng Educ. *Res:* Thermodynamic properties of solutions; heterogeneous catalysis; differential thermal analysis; polymers in solution; application of computers to chemical engineering plant design; mathematical modeling and simulation. *Mailing Add:* Rd No 1 Box 382 Lewisburg PA 17837-9553. *Fax:* 717-524-3760; *E-Mail:* bsnyder@Bucknell.edu

SNYDER, WILLIAM RICHARD, ORGANIC CHEMISTRY, POLYMER CHEMISTRY. *Current Pos:* Res specialist, 76-88, mgr, 3M Europe Healthcare, 88-93, TECH DIR, 3M CO, 93- *Personal Data:* b Brooklyn, NY, Jan 24, 47; m 69; c 3. *Educ:* Hamline Univ, BA, 69; Northwestern Univ, MS, 70, PhD(org chem), 74. *Concurrent Pos:* Res fel, Calif Inst Technol, 74-76. *Mem:* Am Chem Soc. *Res:* Organic synthesis of biologically active molecules. *Mailing Add:* 3M Center Bldg Bldg 230-3F-06 St Paul MN 55144

SNYDER, WILLIAM ROBERT, PHOSPHOLIPASE MECHANISMS, MEMBRANE ENZYMOLOGY. *Current Pos:* ASST PROF CHEM, NORTHERN ILL UNIV, 81- *Personal Data:* b Youngstown, Ohio, Mar 11, 46; m 77. *Educ:* Ohio State Univ, BS, 68; Univ Chicago, PhD(biochem), 72. *Prof Exp:* Res fel chem, Harvard Univ, 72-74; sr res scientist biochem, Armour Pharmaceut, 74-77; res fel neuropath, Ohio State Univ, 77-78; vis asst prof chem, Univ Ill, Chicago, 78-81. *Mem:* Am Chem Soc; AAAS; Sigma Xi. *Res:* Properties of enzymes involved in lipid metabolism; relationship of lipid hydrolysis to the structure and function of biological membranes; involvement of membrane alteration in biological processes. *Mailing Add:* 3N120 Springwood Lane Elburn IL 60134-3153

SNYDER, WILLIAM THOMAS, ENGINEERING MECHANICS. *Current Pos:* prof eng sci & mech & head dept, 70-83, DEAN ENG, UNIV TENN, KNOXVILLE, 83- *Personal Data:* b Knoxville, Tenn, Oct 18, 31; m 56; c 3. *Educ:* Univ Tenn, BS, 54; Northwestern Univ, MS, 56, PhD(mech eng), 58. *Prof Exp:* Asst prof mech eng, NC State Univ, 58-61; assoc prof thermal sci, State Univ NY, Stony Brook, 61-64; assoc prof aerospace eng, Space Inst, Univ Tenn, Tullahoma, 64-70. *Mem:* Am Soc Eng Educ; Am Soc Heating, Refrig & Air Conditioning Engrs; Am Acad Mech; Energy Conserv Soc; Asn Energy Engrs; Soc Eng Mgt. *Res:* Combustion; lubrication; magnetohydrodynamics; energy conservation. *Mailing Add:* Chancellor's Off Univ Tenn 527 Andy Holt Tower Knoxville TN 37996

SNYDERMAN, RALPH, IMMUNOLOGY & INFLAMMATION, RHEUMATOLOGY. *Current Pos:* from asst prof to prof med, Duke Univ Med Ctr, 72-77, from asst prof to prof immunol, 72-84, chief rheumatic & immunol dis, 75-84, FREDERIC M HANES PROF, DUKE UNIV, 84-, CHANCELLOR HEALTH AFFAIRS, DEAN, SCH MED, 89-, CHIEF EXEC OFFICER, DUKE UNIV MED CTR & HEALTH SYST, 89- *Personal Data:* b Brooklyn, NY, Mar 13, 40; m 67, Judith Ann Krebs; c Theodore Benjamin. *Educ:* Washington Col, BS, 61; State Univ NY, MD, 65; Am Bd Internal Med, dipl; Am Bd Allergy & Immunol, dipl. *Hon Degrees:* DSc, State Univ NY, Brooklyn, 96. *Honors & Awards:* Alexander von Humboldt Prize, 85; Givaudian lectr, Am Chemosensory Soc, 89; Ciba-Geigy Morris Ziff Award for Lifetime Achievements in Inflammation Res, 91; Bonzinga Award for Excellence in Leukocyte Biol Res, 93; Baruch Telchman Lectr, Sackler Med Sch, Tel Aviv, 95. *Prof Exp:* Intern med, Med Ctr, Duke Univ, 65-66, resident, 66-67; res assoc immunol, Lab Microbiol, Nat Inst Dent Res, 67-69, sr investr, 69-72. *Concurrent Pos:* Howard Hughes med investr; Alexander von Humboldt scientist award, Fed Repub Ger, 85; sr vpres, med res & develop, Genentech, Inc, 87-89; James B Duke prof med, 89. *Mem:* Inst Med-Nat Acad Sci; Am Soc Clin Invest; Am Asn Cancer Res; Soc Leukocyte Biol; Am Fedn Clin Res; Asn Am Physicians; Sigma Xi; Am Asn Pathologists; Am Soc Biochem & Molecular Biol; Am Col Rheumat; Soc Med Adminr. *Res:* Investigation of the biological effectors of inflammation; molecular and genetic techniques to define specific pathways for the regulation of inflammatory cells. *Mailing Add:* Duke Univ Med Ctr PO Box 3701 Durham NC 27710. *Fax:* 919-681-7020; *E-Mail:* snydeoo1@mc.duke.edu

SNYDERMAN, SELMA ELEANORE, INHERITED METABOLIC DISORDERS, PEDIATRIC NUTRITION. *Current Pos:* Fel pediat, 44-46, from instr to assoc prof, 46-67, PROF PEDIAT, SCH MED, NY UNIV, 67- *Personal Data:* b Philadelphia, Pa, July 22, 16; m 39, Joseph Schein; c Roland M & Oliver D. *Educ:* Univ Pa, AB, 37, MD, 40. *Honors & Awards:* Borden Award, Am Acad Pediat, 75. *Concurrent Pos:* Assoc attend physician, NY Univ Hosp, 52-60, attend pediatrician, 60-; attend physician, Wellowbrook State Univ, 57-70; attend physician, Bellevue Hosp, 58-; career scientist, Health Res Coun, City New York, 61-; mem nutrit study sect, NIH, 73-77; dir, Metab Dis Ctr, NY Univ, 68- *Mem:* Soc Pediat Res; Am Pediat Soc; fel Am Acad Pediat; Soc Inherited Metab Disorders (vpres & pres, 79). *Res:* Nutritional requirements of infants; investigation and treatment of inborn errors of metabolism, especially those of amino acid metabolism. *Mailing Add:* Dept Human Genetics Mt Sinai Med Ctr Fifth Ave & 100th St Box 1203 New York NY 10029. *Fax:* 212-263-8172

SNYGG, JOHN MORROW, APPLIED MATHEMATICS, CLIFFORD ALGEBRA. *Personal Data:* b Oswego, NY, Dec 2, 37; m 65; c 3. *Educ:* Harvard Univ, BA, 59; NY Univ, MA, 62, PhD(math), 67. *Honors & Awards:* Lindback Award, 77. *Prof Exp:* Lectr math, Hunter Col, 64-67; asst prof, Upsala Col, 67-76, assoc prof, 76-87, full prof math, 87-90. *Res:* Clifford algebra; quantum mechanics; population growth. *Mailing Add:* 433 Prospect St East Orange NJ 07017

SO, ANTERO GO, INTERNAL MEDICINE, HEMATOLOGY. *Current Pos:* asst prof, 68-73, assoc prof med, 68-74, ASSOC PROF BIOCHEM, UNIV MIAMI, 73-, PROF MED, 74- *Personal Data:* b Davao City, Philippines, Jan 3, 32; US citizen; m 65; c 2. *Educ:* Univ Santo Tomas, MD, 56; Univ Wash, PhD(biochem), 65. *Prof Exp:* USPHS fel, Western Reserve Univ, 60-62; USPHS trainee, Univ Wash, 62-65; Helen Hay Whitney Found res fel, Univ Geneva, 66-67; res instr biochem, Univ Wash, 67-68. *Concurrent Pos:* Estab investr, Am Heart Asn, 69, mem coun basic sci, 70; investr, Howard Hughes Med Inst, 74. *Mem:* Am Soc Clin Invest; Am Soc Biol Chemists. *Res:* Regulation of DNA and RNA synthesis in mammalian tissues. *Mailing Add:* Dept Med Univ Miami Sch Med PO Box 016960 Miami FL 33101-6960. *Fax:* 305-547-3549

SO, RONALD MING CHO, MECHANICAL ENGINEERING, AERONAUTICAL SCIENCES. *Current Pos:* CHAIR PROF & HEAD, HONG KONG POLYTECH UNIV, 96- *Personal Data:* b Hong Kong, Nov 26, 39; US citizen; m 68, Mabel Y Wu; c Winnie & Nelson. *Educ:* Univ Hong Kong, BSc, 62; McGill Univ, MEng, 66; Princeton Univ, MA, 68, PhD(mech sci), 71. *Hon Degrees:* DSc, Univ Hong Kong, 93. *Honors & Awards:* Dugald Clerk Prize, Inst Mech Eng, London; Lewis F Moody Award, Am Soc Mech Engrs. *Prof Exp:* Exec trainee, Shell Co, Hong Kong, 62-63; instr mech eng, Univ Hong Kong, 63-64; res scientist paper sci, Union Camp Corp, Res & Develop, 70-72; asst prof mech eng, Rutgers Univ, 72-76; mech engr res & develop, Gen Elec Corp, 76-81; assoc prof, Ariz State Univ, 81-83, prof mech & aero eng, 83-96. *Concurrent Pos:* Commonwealth scholar, 62-64; fluid physics consult, Res Cottrell Corp, 74-76; adj asst prof, Fairleigh Dickinson Univ, 74-76; adj assoc prof, Union Col, 77-78 & 79-81. *Mem:* Fel Am Soc Mech Engrs; assoc fel Am Inst Aeronaut & Astronaut; fel Inst Mech Engrs; fel Hong Kong Inst Engrs. *Res:* Fluid dynamics; energy and power generation research; wind power systems; combustion; nuclear reactors and gas turbines; flow induced vibrations; turbulent flows; heat transfer; atmospheric surface layers. *Mailing Add:* Mech Eng Dept Hong Kong Polytech Univ Hung Hom Howloon Hong Kong People's Republic of China. *Fax:* 852-2364-7183; *E-Mail:* mmmcso@polyu.edu.hk

SO, YING-HUNG, POLYMERS FOR ELECTRONIC APPLICATIONS, POLYMER DEGRADATION & STABILIZATION. *Current Pos:* Sr res chemist, Dow Chem Co, 81-84, proj leader, 85-89, res leader, 89-93, res assoc, 93-94, TECH LEADER, DOW CHEM CO, 95- *Personal Data:* b Hong Kong, Apr 8, 48; US citizen; m, Dora Dang; c Albert & Lisa. *Educ:* Chinese Univ, Hong Kong, BS, 71; Colo State Univ, PhD(org chem), 77. *Concurrent Pos:* Vis lectr indust org chem, Univ Hong Kong, 97- *Mem:* Am Chem Soc; Mat Res Soc; Microelectronics Soc. *Res:* Polymers for electronic applications; photosensitive polymers; polymer degradation and stabilization; high performance fibers; polymerization mechanism; photo chemistry; physical organic chemistry; organic synthesis. *Mailing Add:* Dow Chem Co 1712 Bldg Midland MI 48674. *Fax:* 517-636-6558; *E-Mail:* yinghso@dow.com, yinghso@concentric.net

SOARE, ROBERT I, MATHEMATICS. *Current Pos:* chmn, Dept Comput Sci, 83-87, PROF MATH, UNIV CHICAGO, 75- *Personal Data:* b Orange, NJ, Dec 22, 40; m 66; c 1. *Educ:* Princeton Univ, AB, 63; Cornell Univ, PhD(math), 67. *Prof Exp:* From asst prof to prof math, Univ Ill, Chicago Circle, 67-75. *Concurrent Pos:* NSF grant recursive anal, 68-70; prin investr, NSF grant recursive function theory, 70-; sr fel, Grad Col, Univ Ill, Chicago Circle, 71; assoc ed, Proc Am Math Soc, 71-74. *Mem:* Asn Comput Mach; Am Math Soc; Asn Symbolic Logic. *Res:* Mathematical logic, particularly recursive functions. *Mailing Add:* Dept Math Univ Chicago 5734 University Ave Chicago IL 60637-1514

SOARES, EUGENE ROBBINS, MAMMALIAN GENETICS. *Current Pos:* ASSOC, DOVER PEDIAT, 86- *Personal Data:* b New Bedford, Mass, Nov 22, 45; m 71. *Educ:* Univ RI, BS, 67, PhD(biol sci), 72. *Prof Exp:* NIH trainee, Jackson Lab, 72-73; staff fel, Nat Inst Environ Health Sci, 75-77; mammalian geneticist, Chem Indust Inst Toxicol, 76-86. *Mem:* AAAS; Environ Mutagen Soc; Genctics Soc Am; Am Genetic Asn; Sigma Xi. *Res:* Mammalian genetics; the genetic effects of chemical mutagens and electromagnetic radiation in mice; studies of chromosomal aberrations biochemical mutations, dominant and recessive lethal mutations and polygenic mutations in mice. *Mailing Add:* 9 Fairway Dr Dover NH 03820-5103

SOARES, JOSEPH HENRY, JR, NUTRITION, BIOCHEMISTRY. *Current Pos:* from asst prof to assoc prof, 72-79, chmn, Grad Prog Nutrit Sci, 84-89, PROF NUTRIT, UNIV MD, COLLEGE PARK, 79-, DIR GRAD PROG ANIMAL SCI, 96- *Personal Data:* b Fall River, Mass, July 30, 41; m, Janet M Kerr; c Deanna L & Keith M. *Educ:* Univ Md, BS, 64, MS, 66, PhD, 69. *Honors & Awards:* Res Award, Am Feed Mfrs Asn, 77. *Prof Exp:* Animal nutritionist, Bur Com Fisheries, US Dept Interior, 68-69; res nutritionist, Nat Marine Fisheries Serv, US Dept Com, 69-72. *Concurrent Pos:* Am Feed Mfrs res award, 77; vis prof, Human Nutrit Inst, USDA, 82; Dept Pediat Med, Univ SC, 89-90. *Mem:* World Aquacult Soc; Am Inst Nutrit; Nat Aquacult Soc; Am Soc Bone & Mineral Res; Striped Bass Growers Asn. *Res:* Micro nutrient nutrition; calcification and vitamin D hormones; nutrition of aquatic species; growth regulation in fin fish; N and P metabolism on striped bass. *Mailing Add:* Dept Animal Sci Univ Md College Park MD 20740. *Fax:* 301-314-9059; *E-Mail:* js89@umail.umd.edu

SOAVE, ROSEMARY, INFECTIOUS DISEASE, PARASITOLOGY-CRYPTOSPORIDIUM. *Current Pos:* med intern med, NY Hosp, Cornell Med Ctr, 76-77, med resident med, 77-79, fel infectious dis, 80-82, asst prof med, 82-89, asst prof pub health, 85-89, ASSOC PROF MED & PUB HEALTH, NY HOSP, CORNELL MED CTR, 89- *Personal Data:* b New York, NY, Jan 23, 49; m 91, Giacinto Grieco. *Educ:* Fordham Univ, BS, 70; Cornell Univ, MD, 76. *Honors & Awards:* Arthur Palmer Award, 76; Jean Roughgarden Frey Award, 76. *Prof Exp:* Chief resident med, Mem Hosp Sloan-Kettering Cancer Ctr, 79-80. *Concurrent Pos:* Lectr, Merck Sharp Dohme, 83-; prin investr, NIH res grant, 85-88; mem, NIH Study Sec, 93- *Mem:* Fel Am Col Physicians; Am Fedn Clin Res; NY Acad Sci; fel Infectious Dis Soc Am; Sigma Xi; AAAS. *Res:* Cryptosporidium; intestinal host defense mechanism against Cryptosporidium; treatment for cryptosporidiosis; infections in renal transplants; epidemiology of cryptosporidiosis and cyclosponiasis. *Mailing Add:* 525 E 68th St Box 125 New York NY 10021. *Fax:* 212-746-8978

SOBCZAK, THOMAS VICTOR, COMPETITIVE INTELLIGENCE, INFOWAR STRATEGIES. *Current Pos:* EXEC VPRES, APPLN CONFIGURED COMPUT, 87- *Personal Data:* b Brooklyn, NY, Aug 6, 37; m 60, Mary A Florio; c Thomas, Michael, Katherine, Elisabeth, Deanna & Jessica. *Educ:* St John's Univ, BA, 59; Hofstra Univ, MBA, 65; Sussex Col, Eng, PhD(mgt), 72. *Honors & Awards:* Eng Oscar, Inst Advan Eng, 85; Technol Award, USSBA, 86; Engr of the Year, Soc Mfg Engrs, 87. *Prof Exp:* Analyst, Sperry Gyroscope Co, 59-60; mgt specialist, Kollsman Instrument Co, 60-63; consult, Airborne Instrument Lab, 63-67; adminr, Citibank, 67-68; dept head, Computer Opers, Pic Design Corp, 68-70 & Waldes Kohinoor Inc, 70-79; vpres, Little Peoples Prod Ctr, 79-86. *Concurrent Pos:* Dir plans, Nat Defense Exec Reserve, Dept Com, 63-; adj prof, Hofstra Univ, 68-72 & NY Inst Technol, 73-76; aerospace appointee, Central Supply Agency, NATO, 87-95; chmn, Queensboro Correctional Facil adv bd, NY, 90- *Mem:* Fel Soc Mfg Engrs; fel Inst Advan Eng; fel Inst Prod Engrs; Data Processing Mgt Asn. *Res:* Manipulated equipment and software to create platform level security optimizing any operating system; software based radio frequency driven non-lethal weapons; create infowar methods; analyze intrusion psychology; disabling technologies. *Mailing Add:* PO Box 0433 Baldwin NY 11510-0433. *Fax:* 516-623-6295; *E-Mail:* tomsob@dorsai.org

SOBCZYNSKI, DOROTA, NEAR INFRARED SPECTROSCOPY, INSTRUMENTAL ANALYSIS IN CHEMISTRY. *Current Pos:* ASST PROF, INST BIOCYBERNETICS & BIOMED ENG, PAS, 96- *Personal Data:* b Warsaw, Poland, May 20, 56; m 80; c Sandra & Linda. *Educ:* Univ Warsaw, Poland, MS, 80; Polish Acad Sci, Warsaw, Poland, PhD(anal chem), 86. *Prof Exp:* Res asst, Polish Acad Sci, Warsaw, Poland, 80-86, adj res asst, 86-87; res assoc, Dept Food & Nutrit, Kans State Univ, 87-91; chem scientist, Dom Assocs Inc Int Hadamard Spectrometers, 92-96. *Res:* Non-invasive body fluid analytical techniques; interaction of carbohydrates in food development; chemically sensitive field effects transistors; chemometrics in chemical analysis (spectroscopy). *Mailing Add:* 574 Stone Hill Dr Orange KS 06477

SOBCZYNSKI, RADEK, HADAMARD SPECTROSCOPY, LASER SPECTROSCOPY. *Current Pos:* FT IR PRODUCT LINE MGR, ORIEL INSTRUMENTS, 96- *Personal Data:* b Warsaw, Poland, Nov 9, 56; m 80, Dorota Rosochacka; c Sandra & Linda. *Educ:* Univ Warsaw, Poland, MS, 80, PhD(phys chem), 86. *Prof Exp:* From jr to sr specialist, Plasma Diag Lab, Dept Chem, Univ Warsaw, 79-85, adj, 86-87; res assoc, Dept Chem Laser Lab, Kans State Univ, 87-90; optical design scientist, Dom Assocs Inc Int Hadamard Spectrometers, 90-92, res & develop mgr, 92-95. *Concurrent Pos:* Consult laser, Optimed, Poland, 82-86; res & develop mgr, Hadospectrum LTD Co, 96. *Mem:* Inst Elec & Electronics Engrs. *Res:* Fast chemical reactions in gas phase by laser spectroscopy; monitoring chemical agents with spectrometers; Hadamard and Fourier mathematics in optical instruments. *Mailing Add:* 574 Stone Hill Dr Orange CT 06477

SOBEL, ALAN, ELECTRONICS ENGINEERING, PHYSICS. *Current Pos:* CONSULT, 88- *Personal Data:* b New York, NY, Feb 23, 28; m 52, Marjorie Loebel; c Leslie & Edward. *Educ:* Columbia Univ, BS, 47, MS, 49; Polytech Inst Brooklyn, PhD(physics), 64. *Prof Exp:* Engr, Telectro Indust Corp, NY, 49-50; asst chief engr, Electronic Workshop, Inc, 50-51; electronic engr, Freed Radio Corp, 51-53; chief, Electronics Dept, Freed Electronics & Controls Corp, 53-55, head, Functional Eng Dept, Fairchild Controls Corp, 55-56; proj engr, Skiatron Electronics & TV Corp, 56-57; physicist, Zenith Radio Corp, 64-77; vpres, Lucitron Inc, 78-86, pres, 86-87. *Concurrent Pos:* NSF coop grad fel, 59-61; assoc ed, Inst Elec & Electronics Engrs Transactions Electron Devices, 70-77; contrib ed, Info Display, 90-; ed, J Soc Info Display, 91- *Mem:* Sr mem Inst Elec & Electronics Engrs; Am Phys Soc; fel Soc Info Display; Int Soc Optical Eng; Int Soc Optical Engrs. *Res:* Flat-panel displays; display systems and devices; gas discharges; electronic devices, circuits and systems. *Mailing Add:* 633 Michigan Ave Evanston IL 60202

SOBEL, EDNA H, PEDIATRICS, PEDIATRIC ENDOCRINOLOGY. *Current Pos:* from asst prof to prof, 56-68, EMER PROF PEDIAT, ALBERT EINSTEIN COL MED, 89- *Personal Data:* b New York, NY, Nov 2, 18. *Educ:* Univ Wis, BA, 39, MA, 40; Boston Univ, MD, 43; Am Bd Pediat, dipl, 54. *Prof Exp:* Intern, Montefiore Hosp, New York, 44; clin fel pediat, Harvard Med Sch & Mass Gen Hosp, 44-47, res fel, Harvard Med Sch, 47-49, res assoc, 55-56, clin & res fel, Mass Gen Hosp, 48-49; instr, Col Med, Univ Cincinnati, 50-53. *Concurrent Pos:* Commonwealth Fund fel advan med, Mass Gen Hosp, 49-50; Commonwealth Fund fel, 63-64; asst, Sch Pub Health, Harvard Univ, 44-46; vis physician, Children's Hosp, Cincinnati, Ohio, 50-53, asst physician, 55-56; res assoc, Children's Cancer Res Found, 53-56; asst vis pediatrician, Bronx Munic Hosp, Cent Res, 53-60, assoc vis pediatrician, 60-68, vis pediatrician, 68-; asst prof, Antioch Col & res assoc, Fels Res Inst, 51-53; consult, Misericordia Hosp, New York, 58-59; attend pediatrician, Lincoln Hosp, 59-70. *Mem:* AAAS; Am Pediat Soc; Endocrine Soc; Europ Soc Paediatric Endocrinol; Lawson Wilkins Pediat Endocrine Soc; Sigma Xi; fel Am Acad Pediat. *Res:* Endocrine function of normal and abnormal children; hormonal effects on growth and skeletal maturation of rats. *Mailing Add:* 1010 Waltham St D 233 Lexington MA 02173-8044

SOBEL, HENRY WAYNE, PARTICLE PHYSICS, COSMIC RAY PHYSICS. *Current Pos:* Asst res physicist, 69-74, Univ Calif, assoc res physicist, 74-80, res physicist, 80-86, PROF PHYSICS, UNIV CALIF, 86- *Personal Data:* b Philadelphia, Pa; m 65, Toni Choff; c Cindy & Mandy. *Educ:* Rensselaer Polytech Inst, BS, 62; Case Inst Technol, PhD(physics), 69. *Honors & Awards:* Bruno Rossi Prize, 89. *Mem:* Am Physics Soc; AAAS; am Soc Physics Teachers. *Res:* Neutrino physics; astrophysics; cosmic-ray physics; tests of conservation laws. *Mailing Add:* 3891 Cedron St Irvine CA 92606. *Fax:* 714-856-7478; *E-Mail:* hsobel@uci.edu

SOBEL, JAEL SABINA, CANCER RESEARCH, CELL MOTILITY. *Current Pos:* ASST PROF EMBRYOL & HISTOL, STATE UNIV NY BUFFALO, 79- *Personal Data:* b Israel, Nov 29, 35. *Educ:* Cornell Univ, BA, 57; Columbia Univ, MA, 62; Univ Wis-Madison, PhD(zool), 66. *Honors & Awards:* Rothschild Prize, Israel, 73. *Prof Exp:* Fel cancer res, Sloan-Kettering Inst, 68-70; lectr embryol, Med Sch, Tel-Aviv Univ, 72-76; res fel, Lab Radiobiol, Univ Calif, San Francisco, 77-79. *Concurrent Pos:* Consult, Lab Human Reproduction & Fetal Develop, Tel-Aviv Univ, 72-76. *Mem:* AAAS; Am Soc Cell Biol; Am Asn Anatomists. *Res:* Cell motility and characterization of cytoskeletal proteins during normal embryonic development and in developmental mutants; development of the trophoblast with emphasis on the regulation of invasive behavior. *Mailing Add:* Dept Anat Sci State Univ NY 17 Farber Hall Buffalo NY 14214

SOBEL, KENNETH MARK, MULTIVARIABLE CONTROL, ADAPTIVE CONTROL. *Current Pos:* assoc prof, 87-93, PROF, CITY COL NEW YORK, 93- *Personal Data:* b Brooklyn, NY, Oct 3, 54. *Educ:* City Col NY, BSEE, 76; Rensselaer Polytech Inst, MEng, 78, PhD(comput & syst eng), 80. *Prof Exp:* Res asst, Rensselaer Polytech Inst, 76-79, instr syst eng, 79-80; res scientist, Lockheed Calif Co, 80-87. *Concurrent Pos:* Adj res asst prof, Calif State Univ, Northridge, 81 & Univ Southern Calif, Los Angeles, 82-87; prin investr, USAF, 89 & 91. *Mem:* Sr mem Inst Elec & Electronics Engrs; Sigma Xi; assoc fel Am Inst Aeronaut & Astronaut. *Res:* Robust multivariable control; adaptive control; eigenstructure assignment; application of modern control theory to flight control design. *Mailing Add:* Elec Eng Dept City Col New York New York NY 10031

SOBEL, MARK E, MOLECULAR BIOLOGY. *Current Pos:* Sr investr path, 83-92, CHIEF, MOLECULAR PATH SECT, NAT CANCER INST, 92- *Personal Data:* b Brooklyn, NY, Apr 14, 49. *Educ:* Brandeis Univ, Mass, BA, 70; City Univ New York, PhD(biomed sci), 75; Mt Sinai Sch Med, MD, 75. *Honors & Awards:* Commendation Medal, USPHS, 89; Saul J Horowitz Jr Award, Mt Sinai Sch Med, 91. *Concurrent Pos:* Dir, Concepts Molecular Biol Course, Am Asn Pathologists, 87-96; counc, Am Soc Invest Path, 95- *Mem:* Am Soc Biochem & Molecular Biol; Am Soc Cell Biol; Asn Molecular Path (secy-tres, 95-97); AAAS; Am Asn Cancer Res; Am Soc Invest Path. *Res:* Tumor invasion and metastasis; connective tissue gene regulation; molecular diagnostics. *Mailing Add:* 9401 Bulls Run Pkwy Bethesda MD 20817-2405. *Fax:* 301-402-4094; *E-Mail:* molpath@helix.nih.gov

SOBEL, MICHAEL I, SCIENCE POLICY, SCIENCE EDUCATION. *Current Pos:* from asst prof to assoc prof, 64-72, PROF PHYSICS, BROOKLYN COL, 72- *Personal Data:* b Brooklyn, NY, Feb 5, 39; m 59; c Jonathan & Daniel. *Educ:* Swarthmore Col, BA, 59; Harvard Univ, MA, 61, PhD(physics), 64. *Prof Exp:* Res assoc physics, Northeastern Univ, 64. *Concurrent Pos:* NSF res grant, 65-72; res assoc, Harwell, Eng, 67-68; NATO fel, 73 & sr fel, 75; Woodrow Wilson Found fac develop award, 79; vis scientist, Princeton Univ, 88-89. *Mem:* AAAS; Am Phys Soc; Am Asn Physics Teachers; NY Acad Sci. *Res:* Nucleon-nucleon interactions; heavy ion reactions; author non-scientist publication; nuclear arms control. *Mailing Add:* Dept Physics Brooklyn Col Brooklyn NY 11210. *Fax:* 718-951-4407; *E-Mail:* msobel@brooklyn.cuny.edu

SOBELL, LINDA CARTER, TREATMENT RESEARCH, SUBSTANCE ABUSE PROBLEMS. *Current Pos:* PROF PSYCHOL FAMILY & COMMUNITY MED, BEHAVIOR SCI, UNIV TORONTO, 88-, CHIEF OF GUIDED SELF-CHANGE UNIT & ASST DIR RES & CLINICAL TRAINING, 91- *Personal Data:* b Reno, Nev, May 8, 48; m 69; c 2. *Educ:* Univ Calif, Riverside, BA, 70, Irvine, MA, 74, Riverside, PhD(psychol), 76. *Prof Exp:* Sr scientist, Addiction Res Found, 84-88. *Mem:* Asn Advan Behav Ther; Am Psychol Asn; Can Psychol Asn. *Res:* Published 70 articles in various journals and 4 books in the area of addictive behaviors research and treatment. *Mailing Add:* Addiction Res Found 33 Russell St Toronto ON M5S 2S1 Can

SOBELL, MARK BARRY, PSYCHOLOGY, ADDICTIONS. *Current Pos:* assoc prof, 80-87, PROF PSYCHOL FAMILY & COMMUNITY MED, BEHAV SCI, UNIV TORONTO, 87-, ASSOC DIR, TREATMENT RES & DEVELOP, INST ADDICTION RES FOUND. *Personal Data:* b Philadelphia, Pa, May 14, 44; US & Can citizen; m 69; c 2. *Educ:* Univ Calif, Los Angeles, AB, 66, Riverside, MA, 67, PhD(psychol), 70. *Prof Exp:* Res analyst II, Orange County Dept Mental Health, 72-74; assoc prof psychol, Vanderbilt Univ, 74-80. *Concurrent Pos:* Dir grad training on alcohol dependence, Dept Psychol, Vanderbilt Univ, 74-80, dir clin training, 79-80; sr scientist, Addiction Res Found, 80-; head, Sociobehav Res, Addiction Res Found, 88-90, chair, Treatment Res & Develop Dept, 90- *Mem:* Fel Am Psychol Asn; Asn Advan Behav Ther; Soc Psychologists in Addictive Behav. *Res:* Behavioral treatment of alcohol problems; conceptualizations of alcohol problems; models of addiction. *Mailing Add:* Addiction Res Found 33 Russell St Toronto ON M5S 2S1 Can

SOBER, DANIEL I(SAAC), EXPERIMENTAL NUCLEAR PHYSICS. *Current Pos:* from asst prof to assoc prof, 75-83, PROF PHYSICS, CATH UNIV AM, 83- *Personal Data:* b New York, NY, Sept 5, 42; m 73, Ingeborg Nachtigaeller; c Paul. *Educ:* Swarthmore Col, AB, 63; Cornell Univ, PhD(physics), 69. *Prof Exp:* Res asst physics, Princeton-Pa Accelerator, Princeton Univ, 68-70; adj asst prof, Univ Calif, Los Angeles, 70-75. *Concurrent Pos:* Vis prof, Polytech Inst Darmstadt, 81-82. *Mem:* Am Phys Soc. *Res:* Electromagnetic and weak interactions of elementary particles and nuclei; particle detectors; accelerators. *Mailing Add:* Dept Physics Cath Univ Am Washington DC 20064. *Fax:* 202-319-4448; *E-Mail:* sober@cua.edu

SOBERMAN, ROBERT K, ENVIRONMENTAL PHYSICS, ASTRONOMY. *Current Pos:* RETIRED. *Personal Data:* b NY, New York, Apr 8, 30; m 54, Diana H Gross; c Ellen S & June A. *Educ:* City Col New York, BS, 50; NY Univ, MS, 52, PhD(physics), 56; Temple Univ, MBA, 72. *Prof Exp:* Res physicist, Vallecitos Atomic Lab, Gen Elec Co, 55-57; sr scientist res & advan develop div, Avco Corp, 57-59; assoc prof elec eng, Northeastern Univ, 59-60; chief meteor physics br, Air Force Cambridge Res Labs, 60-66; mgr environ progs, Gen Elec Space Sci Lab, 66-76; vpres progs, Univ City Sci Ctr, 76-78; dir, Appl Sci Dept, Franklin Res Ctr, 78-88; lectr, Astron Dept, Univ Pa, 88-93. *Concurrent Pos:* Adj assoc prof, Northeastern Univ, 60-64; adj prof, Drexel Univ, 68-; mem, Post Apollo Sci Eval Comt, 65-; vchmn comn 22B, Int Astron Union; sect noctilucent cloud subcomn, Int Union Geod & Geophys & mem Cosmic Dust Panel, Comt Space Res, Int Coun Sci Unions. *Mem:* AAAS; Am Astron Soc; Int Astron Union; Am Geophys Union. *Res:* Micrometeoroid flux and composition; rocket sampling of noctilucent clouds and cosmic dust; artificial meteors; recoverable and nonrecoverable spacecraft studies of meteoroids; stellar evolution. *Mailing Add:* 2056 Appletree St Philadelphia PA 19103. *E-Mail:* rsoberma@mail.sas.upenn.edu

SOBEY, ARTHUR EDWARD, JR, PHYSICS, MATHEMATICS. *Current Pos:* INDEPENDENT AEROSPACE CONSULT, 91- *Personal Data:* b Shawnee, Kans, May 28, 24; m 48, Tommie N Holmberg; c Terry M, Karen A, Janet D & Mark E. *Educ:* Univ Tex, BS, 49, MA, 51, PhD(physics), 58. *Prof Exp:* Res scientist, Defense Res Lab, Univ Tex, 50-58; eng specialist, Chance Vought Aircraft Co, Tex, 58-59; mem tech staff, 59-66, mgr marine sci progs, 66-68, mgr signal processing progs, 69-71, mgr antisubmarine warfare surveillance progs, Tex Instruments Inc, 72-73; prog mgr, Electronic Sci, LTV Aerospace & Defense Co, 73-76, mgr electronics & optics res, 77-86, eng proj mgr, Vought Missiles & Advan Prog Div, 87-88, dep prog mgr, LTV Missiles & Electronics Group Missiles Div, & mgr, IR&D Planning, 88-91. *Res:* Underwater acoustics, including propagation and ambient noise; acoustic signal processing; space-time signal processing; infrared sensors and systems; electrooptic devices and subsystems; noise-cancelling microphones; atmospheric research; infrared scene simulation; mm-wave sensors. *Mailing Add:* 914 Northlake Dr Richardson TX 75080-4914

SOBIESKI, JAMES FULTON, PHOTORECEPTORS, TONERS. *Current Pos:* Sr res chemist, Microfilm Prod Lab, 68-85, PROCESS DEVELOP SPECIALIST, DOCUMENT SYSTS, 3M CO, ST PAUL, 85- *Personal Data:* b Berlin, Wis, Mar 18, 40; m 76; c 4. *Educ:* Univ Wis-Madison, BS, 61; Lawrence Univ, MS, 63, PhD(chem), 67. *Mem:* Soc Photog Sci & Eng. *Res:* Applications of photoconductors to imaging systems; imaging systems. *Mailing Add:* 225 Hickory St St Paul MN 55115

SOBIESZCZANSKI-SOBIESKI, JAROSLAW, APPLIED MECHANICS, OPTIMIZATION METHODS. *Current Pos:* Nat Acad Sci sr res fel, 70-71, aerospace engr, 71-73, sr res scientist, Struct Div, 73-80, br head multidisciplinary anal & optimization & struct dir, 80-84, dept head, Interdisciplinary Res Off, Struct Directorate, Langley Res Ctr, 84-93, CHIEF SCI, STRUCT DYNAMICS DIV, NASA, 93- *Personal Data:* b Wilno, Poland, Mar 11, 34; nat US; m 58; c 2. *Educ:* Warsaw Tech Univ, dipl aeronaut, 55, MS, 57, Dr Tech Sci(theory of thin shells), 64. *Honors & Awards:* Awards, Polish Soc Theoret & Appl Mech, 63-65; Medal for Except Eng Achievement, NASA, 88. *Prof Exp:* Asst aeronaut struct, Warsaw Tech Univ, 55-57, sr asst, 57 & 60-64, adj prof, 64-66; designer cranes & steel struct, Design Off Heavy Mach, Poland, 58-59; res fel, Inst Aeronaut, Norweg Inst Technol, 66; from asst prof to assoc prof aerospace eng, Parks Col Aeronaut Tech, St Louis, 66-71. *Concurrent Pos:* Cert expert stress & vibration, Polish Eng Asn, 62-64; Norweg Govt fel, Inst Aeronaut, Norweg Inst Technol, 64-65; NASA res grant nonlinear struct anal, 68-70; consult, Polish Aviation Indust, 61-64; assoc prof lectr, George Washinton Univ, 71-80, prof lectr, 80-87, res sci, Space Div, NASA. *Mem:* Assoc fel Am Inst Aeronaut & Astronaut; assoc fel Royal Aeronaut Soc. *Res:* Experimental and numerical stress analysis; development of finite element methods for analysis of nonlinear structures; development of automated methods for interdisciplinary systems analysis and design; optimization of structures. *Mailing Add:* 518 Elizabeth Lake Dr Hampton VA 23669

SOBIN, LESLIE HOWARD, PATHOLOGY. *Current Pos:* PROF PATH, UNIFORMED SERV UNIV HEALTH SCI, 84- *Personal Data:* b New York, NY, Feb 10, 34; m 62; c 1. *Educ:* Union Col, NY, BS, 55; State Univ NY, MD, 59; Am Bd Path, dipl anat path, 64. *Honors & Awards:* Pres Rank Award of Meritorious Exec, 91. *Prof Exp:* Res fel, Inst Cell Res, Karolinska Inst, Sweden, 58; asst path, Med Col, Cornell Univ, 60-62, from instr to asst prof, 62-66; prof, WHO, 65-68; assoc prof, Med Col, Cornell Univ, 68-70; pathologist, WHO, 70-81. *Concurrent Pos:* Vis prof, Fac Med, Kabul, Afghanistan, 65-68; mem, WHO Expert Adv Panel Cancer, 81-; head, WHO Ctr Int Histol Classification Tumors, 83-; co-ed, Atlas Tumor Path, Armed Forces Inst Path, 84-, dir, Sci Publ, 87-, chief gastrointestinal path, 91-; assoc ed, Cancer. *Mem:* Am Soc Invest Path; Int Acad Path; fel Royal Col Pathologists. *Res:* Histological classification of tumors; gastrointestinal pathology. *Mailing Add:* Div Gastrointestinal Path Armed Forces Inst Path Washington DC 20306-6000. *Fax:* 202-782-9020

SOBIN, SIDNEY S, PHYSIOLOGY, CARDIOVASCULAR. *Current Pos:* ADJ PROF PHYSIOL, UNIV CALIF, SAN DIEGO, 77- *Personal Data:* b Bayonne, NJ, Jan 1, 14; m 59; c 2. *Educ:* Univ Mich, BS, 35, MA, 36, PhD(physiol), 38, MD, 41; Am Bd Internal Med, cert, 51. *Honors & Awards:* Landis Award, Microcirculatory Soc, 80. *Prof Exp:* Asst physiol, Univ Mich, 34-38; resident med, Barnes Hosp, St Louis, Mo, 42-44; Nat Res Coun fel physiol, Harvard Med Sch, 44-46; assoc, Univ Southern Calif, 47-56, dir, Cardiovasc Lab, Childrens Hosp, 49-56; res prof med, Sch Med, Loma Linda Univ, 56-66; prof physiol, Sch Med, Univ Southern Calif, 66- *Concurrent Pos:* Res Career Awardee, NIH, 62-, mem, Cardiovasc A Study Sect, 66-70, exp cardiovasc sci, 82-86. *Mem:* Microcirculatory Soc; Soc Exp Biol & Med; Am Physiol Soc; fel Am Col Physicians. *Res:* Micro and peripheral circulation; pulmonary circulation and hypertension. *Mailing Add:* Dept Bio Eng Univ Calif San Diego 9800 Gilman Dr La Jolla CA 92093-0412. *Fax:* 619-481-7260

SOBKOWICZ, HANNA MARIA, NEUROLOGY. *Current Pos:* from asst prof to assoc prof, 66-79, PROF NEUROL, MED SCH, UNIV WIS-MADISON, 79- *Personal Data:* b Warsaw, Poland, Jan 1, 31; m 72. *Educ:* Med Acad, Warsaw, MD, 54, cert bd neurol, 59, PhD(med sci), 62. *Prof Exp:* From jr asst to sr asst neurol, Med Acad, Warsaw, 59-63; Nat Multiple Sclerosis Soc res fel tissue cult, Mt Sinai Hosp, 63-65; vis fel, Columbia Univ, 65-66. *Concurrent Pos:* Prin investr, NIH, 68- *Mem:* Soc Neurosci; Int Brain Res Orgn; Asn Res Otolaryngol; Int Soc Develop Neurosci; Electron Micros Soc Am. *Res:* Development and regeneration of nervous system in culture; organ of Corti; spinal cord; spinal ganglia; cerebellum. *Mailing Add:* Dept Neurol Univ Wis Med Sch 600 Highland Ave Madison WI 53792-0001

SOBOCZENSKI, EDWARD JOHN, INSECT TOXICOLOGY. *Current Pos:* RETIRED. *Personal Data:* b Exeter, NH, July 2, 29; m 53; c 2. *Educ:* Univ NH, BS, 52, MS, 54; Ohio State Univ, PhD(chem), 56. *Prof Exp:* Res chemist, Exp Sta, E I du Pont de Nemours & Co, Inc, 56-65, patent liaison chem & law, 65-70, res biologist, 70, res supvr insecticides, 70-81, supvr info resources, 81-90, personnel & admin, 90. *Concurrent Pos:* Consult, 90- *Mem:* Am Chem Soc. *Res:* Discovery and development of agricultural chemicals; inventor of Venzar R herbicide sold for control of weeds in sugarbeets in Europe and Demosan R soil fungicide. *Mailing Add:* 570 Pilottown Rd Lewes DE 19958

SOBOL, BRUCE J, MEDICINE, PHYSIOLOGY. *Current Pos:* RETIRED. *Personal Data:* b June 10, 23; US citizen; m 51; c Peter G & Scott D. *Educ:* Swarthmore Col, BS, 47; NY Univ, MD, 50; Am Bd Internal Med, dipl. *Prof Exp:* Intern med, Third Med Div, Bellevue Hosp, NY, 50-51, asst resident, 51-52; resident cardiol, Vet Admin Hosp, Boston, 52-53; dir, Cardiopulmonary Lab, Westchester Co Med Ctr, 59-78; res prof med, NY Med Col, 77-90, dir med res, 81-83. *Concurrent Pos:* Prof med, NY Med Col, 70-77; dir clin res, Boehringer Ingelheim Ltd, 78-83. *Mem:* Am Physiol Soc; fel Am Col Physicians; fel Am Col Chest Physicians; Am Heart Asn; fel NY Acad Sci. *Res:* Cardiac and pulmonary physiology. *Mailing Add:* 275 Ridgebury Rd Ridgefield CT 06877-1410

SOBOL, HAROLD, PHYSICAL ELECTRONICS, COMMUNICATIONS. *Current Pos:* dir prod develop, Collins Transmission Systs Div, 73-85, vpres eng & tech, 85-88, ASSOC DEAN ENG & PROF ELEC ENG, ROCKWELL INT, 88- *Personal Data:* b Brooklyn, NY, June 21, 30; m 57; c 4. *Educ:* City Col NY, BS, 52; Univ Mich, MSE, 55, PhD(elec eng), 60. *Prof Exp:* Res assoc radar, Willow Run Labs, Univ Mich, 52-55, res assoc phys electronics, Electron Physics Lab, 56-60; mem tech staff, Watson Res Ctr, Int Bus Mach Corp, 60-62; mem tech staff & group head, RCA Labs, 62-68, mgr microwave electronics, RCA Solid State Div, 68-70, mem, RCA Corp Res & Eng Staff, 70-72, group head, Commun Technol Res, 72-73. *Concurrent Pos:* Nat lectr, Inst Elec & Electronic Engrs, 70. *Mem:* Am Physics Soc; fel Inst Elec & Electronic Engrs, 70; Sigma Xi. *Res:* Radar propagation studies; electron devices; microwaves; superconductivity; plasmas; communications. *Mailing Add:* 7031 Hunters Ridge Dr Dallas TX 75248-5513

SOBOL, MARION GROSS, ECONOMICS OF COMPUTERIZATION. *Current Pos:* PROF & CHMN MGT INFO SYSTS, COX SCH BUS, SOUTHERN METHODIST UNIV, 74- *Personal Data:* b New York, NY, Dec 2, 30; m 57, Harold; c Diane, Neil, Jessica & Martin. *Educ:* Syracuse Univ, BA, 51; Univ Mich, MBA, 57, PhD(econ), 61. *Prof Exp:* Lectr econ, Univ Col, Rutgers, 64-71; assoc prof statist & dept chmn, Rider Col, 71-74. *Concurrent Pos:* Vpres & bd dirs, Decision Sci Inst, 87-89, treas, 94-96. *Mem:* Inst Mgt Sci; fel Decision Sci Inst; Int Reference Orgn Forensic Med & Scis. *Res:* Economics of computerization; economics of hospital computerization; management information systems in manufacturing; survey research. *Mailing Add:* Cox Sch Bus Southern Methodist Univ Dallas TX 75275. *Fax:* 214-768-4099; *E-Mail:* msobol@mail.cox.smu.edu

SOBOL, STANLEY PAUL, FORENSIC SCIENCE, RESEARCH ADMINISTRATION. *Current Pos:* LAB DIR CHEM, DRUG ENFORCEMENT ADMIN, SPEC TESTING & RES LAB, 73- *Personal Data:* b Boston, Mass, Oct 8, 37; m 63; c 2. *Educ:* Tufts Univ, BS, 59. *Honors & Awards:* Spec Achievement Award, Bur Narcotics & Dangerous Drugs, 73; Exceptional Serv Award, Drug Enforcement Admin, 75, Excellence of Performance Award, 77, Outstanding Performance Award, 87. *Prof Exp:* Biochemist, Pharmacol Dept, Arthur D Little Inc, 59-61; from chemist to res coordr, US Food & Drug Admin, Boston Dist, 61-69; forensic chemist, Bur Narcotics & Dangerous Drugs, Lab Div, 69-70, chief chemist, 70-73. *Concurrent Pos:* Consult, UN Div Narcotics, 73- & Pakistan Narcotic Control Bd, 81; mem forensic subcomt, Joint Comt Powder Diffraction Stand & Org Subcomt, 75-81; mem, Ed Bd, J Sci, 81-; fel, US Dept Com Sci & Technol Fel Prog, 83-84. *Mem:* Am Acad Forensic Sci; Int Asn Toxicologists; Am Mgt Asn; Asn Off Anal Chem; Am Soc Crime Lab Dirs. *Res:* Trace organic analysis; computer assisted correlations of drug exhibits and establishment of data base. *Mailing Add:* 7209 Sampal Pl Springfield VA 22153

SOBOLEV, IGOR, ORGANIC CHEMISTRY. *Current Pos:* SECT HEAD, CHEM, KAISER ALUMINUM & CHEM CORP, 70- *Personal Data:* b Zlin, Czech, July 31, 31; nat US; m 53; c 2. *Educ:* State Univ NY Col Forestry, Syracuse, BS, 54, MS, 55, PhD(org chem), 58. *Prof Exp:* Res chemist, Olympic Res Div, Rayonier, Inc, Wash, 58-61; chemist, Shell Develop Co, 61-64, sr technologist, Indust Chem Div, Shell Chem Co, NY, 64-66, chemist, 66-67, res supvr, Shell Develop Co, Calif, 67-70. *Mem:* Am Chem Soc; Tech Asn Pulp & Paper Indust. *Res:* Chemical process and product research and development involving raw materials and intermediates in aluminum production; reduction cell technology, organic polymers, fluorocarbons, atmospheric science, heterogeneous catalysis and flame retardants; fluorine chemistry. *Mailing Add:* C & P Technology Inc 5 Rita Way Orinda CA 94563-4131

SOBOLEV, NIKOLAI V, GEOPHYSICS. *Current Pos:* Dep dir, Siberian Br, Inst Geol & Geophys, 90, DIR, INST MINERAL & PETROG, RUSS ACAD SCI, 90- *Educ:* Lvov State Univ, 58. *Honors & Awards:* Alexander Humboldt Prize, 96. *Mem:* Nat Acad Sci; foreign assoc fel Nat Acad Sci; mem Nat Acad Europ; fel Russ Acad Sci. *Res:* Mineralogy, petrology and geochemistry of ultrahigh pressure rocks in the lithosphere; crystalline inclusions in diamonds; deep mantle xeniths in kimberlity; ultrahigh pressure metamorphic rocks; mineralogic approach of exploration for diamonds. *Mailing Add:* Inst Mineral & Petrog Novosjbirsk 630090 Russia. *Fax:* (3832) 35-26-92; *E-Mail:* sobolev@uiggm.nsc.ru

SOBOTA, ANTHONY E, BACTERIOLOGY. *Current Pos:* assoc prof, 68-77, PROF BIOL SCI, YOUNGSTOWN STATE UNIV, 77- *Personal Data:* b Bradenville, Pa, May 29, 38; m 62; c 1. *Educ:* Ind Univ Pa, BSEd, 60; Univ Pittsburgh, MS, 63, PhD(biol), 66. *Prof Exp:* NIH fel, Purdue Univ, 66-67; USDA grant, 67-68. *Mem:* Am Inst Biol Sci; Am Soc Microbiologists; Sigma Xi. *Res:* Importance of adherence in urinary tract infections. *Mailing Add:* Dept Biol Sci Youngstown State Univ 410 Wick Ave Youngstown OH 44555-0001

SOBOTA, WALTER LOUIS, NEUROPSYCHOLOGY, COGNITIVE ASSESSMENT. *Current Pos:* adj instr, 82-93, ADJ ASST PROF, WAYNE STATE UNIV MED SCH, 93-; PSYCHOLOGIST, SINAI HOSP, DETROIT, 73- *Personal Data:* b Detroit, Mich, Oct 30, 46; m 69, Dianne Brent; c Christopher & Jennifer. *Educ:* Univ Detroit, BA, 68, PhD (clin psychol), 73; Am Bd Prof Psychologists, dipl, 84; Am Bd Neuropsychol, dipl, 84. *Concurrent Pos:* Psychologist pvt pract, 77-; coun rep, Am Psychol Asn, 88-91. *Mem:* Am Psychol Asn; Int Neuropsychol Soc; AAAS; Nat Acad Neuropsychologists. *Res:* Neuropsychological sequelae of resuscitation from cardiac arrest; neuropsychological sequelae following anesthesia in the elderly; neuropsychological deficits associated with systemic lupus and chronic fatigue syndrome. *Mailing Add:* Dept Psychiat Sinai Hosp Detroit 14800 W McNichols Rd Suite 230 Detroit MI 48235. *Fax:* 313-493-7520

SOBOTKA, THOMAS JOSEPH, NEUROBEHAVIORAL TOXICOLOGY, BEHAVIORAL TERATOLOGY. *Current Pos:* Res pharmacologist, 69-78, actg chief, Whole Animal Toxicol Br, 81; SUPVRY PHARMACOLOGIST, LEADER NEUROBEHAV TOXICOL TEAM, 78- *Personal Data:* b Baltimore, Md, Aug 16, 42; m 64; c 2. *Educ:* Loyola Col, BS, 64; Loyola Stritch Sch Med, MS, 67, PhD(pharmacol), 69. *Honors & Awards:* Commemorative Medal, Polish Soc Internal Med, 76. *Concurrent Pos:* Mem organizing comt, Conf Nutrit & Behav, Franklin Res Found, 79-80; exec secy, Interagency Collab Group Hyperkinesis, Dept Health & Human Serv, 81-82; rep Interagency Comt Learning Disabilities, Food & Drug Admin, 86-87, Interagency Comt Neurotoxicol, 89, deleg, OECD ad hoc meeting Neurotoxicity test guidelines, 89-90; pres, Asn Gov & Toxicologists, 93- *Mem:* Am Soc Pharmacol & Exp Therapeut; Soc Neurosci; Behav Pharmacol Soc; Neurobehav Toxicol Soc; Asn Govt Toxicol; Neurobehav Teratology Soc; Int Brain Res Orgn; World Fedn Neurosci. *Res:* Neurotoxicity hazard of chemicals found in foods; effects of chemicals on the developing nervous system; development of testing guidelines for assessment of neurotoxicity; neurotoxicology; safety assessment. *Mailing Add:* Neurobehav Toxicol Team/HFS-507 Ctr for Food Safety & Appl Nutrit/ Food & Drug Admin 8301 Muir Kirk Rd Laurel MD 20708

SOBOTTKA, STANLEY EARL, PHYSICS. *Current Pos:* assoc prof, 64-71, PROF PHYSICS, UNIV VA, 71- *Personal Data:* b Plum City, Wis, Dec 20, 30. *Educ:* Univ Wis, BS, 55; Stanford Univ, MS, 57, PhD(physics), 60. *Prof Exp:* Mem tech staff, Sci Res Labs, Boeing Airplane Co, 59-60 & Watkins-Johnson Co, 60-63. *Mem:* Am Phys Soc. *Res:* High energy electron scattering; electron beam-plasma interactions; lasers; pion and muon interactions with nuclei; nuclear particle detectors; x-ray diffraction; x-ray detectors. *Mailing Add:* Dept Physics Univ Va Charlottesville VA 22903. *Fax:* 804-924-4576

SOBSEY, MARK DAVID, VIROLOGY, ENVIRONMENTAL MICROBIOLOGY. *Current Pos:* from asst prof to assoc prof, 74-84, dir environ health sci prog, 90-93, PROF ENVIRON MICROBIOL, SCH PUB HEALTH, UNIV NC, CHAPEL HILL, 84- *Personal Data:* b Lakewood, NJ, Sept 5, 43; m 65, 82, Edith M Alfano; c 2. *Educ:* Univ Pittsburgh, BS, 65, MS, 67; Univ Calif, Berkeley, PhD(environ health sci), 71. *Prof Exp:* Fel, Baylor Col Med, 71-72, from instr to asst prof, 72-74. *Concurrent Pos:* Res career develop award, Nat Inst Environ Health Sci, 77-82; vis scientist, Lab Infectious Dis, NIH, Bethesda, Md, 81, Nat Ctr Infectious Dis, Ctrs Dis Control & Prev, 96. *Mem:* Am Water Works Asn; Am Soc Microbiol; Water Pollution Control Fedn; Int Asn Water Qual. *Res:* Environmental microbiology; public health aspects of water and shellfish pollution; environmental virology; risk assessment of waterborne and foodborne infectious disease; molecular microbiology. *Mailing Add:* CB No 7400 Rosenau Hall Rm 106 Univ NC Sch Pub Health Chapel Hill NC 27599-7400. *Fax:* 919-966-4711; *E-Mail:* mark_sobsey@unc.edu

SOCHA, WLADYSLAW WOJCIECH, IMMUNOLOGY, PATHOLOGY. *Current Pos:* assoc dir, 77-80, DIR, PRIMATE BLOOD GROUP REF LAB & WHO COLLAB CTR HAEMATOL PRIMATE ANIMALS, 80-, RES PROF FORENSIC MED, LAB EXP MED & SURG PRIMATES, SCH MED, NY UNIV, 69- *Personal Data:* b Paris, France, July 3, 26; m 56, Adela-Katherine Zacharko. *Educ:* Jagiellonian Univ, MD, 52; Cracow Acad Med, Poland, DMedS(genetics), 59, habilitated Dozent (forensic med), 62. *Honors & Awards:* Polish Med Asn Award, 60; Polish Surg Asn Award, 60; Polish Acad Sci Award, 66. *Prof Exp:* Assoc path, Inst Oncol, Warsaw, Gliwice & Cracow, 52-61; asst prof forensic med, Cracow Acad Med, Poland, 55-64, dir inst pediat, 65-68. *Concurrent Pos:* Fr Asn Study Cancer fel, Regional Anticancer Ctr, Univ Montpellier, 59-60; US AID fel, 66; Fr Nat Inst Med Res fel, Ctr Hemotypology, Nat Ctr Sci Res, Toulouse, France, 71; mem comt human genetics, Polish Acad Sci, 65-68; vis scientist, Nat Inst Health & Med Res, Toulouse, France, 72; assoc ed, J Med Primatol, 73-77, ed, 77-; mem rev bd, J Human Evolution, 78-; vis scientist, Col France, Paris, 78, 84, 87; consult ed, Am Jour Primatol, 81- *Mem:* Am Soc Human Genetics; Am Soc Primatologists; Am Asn Lab Animal Sci; Int Primatol Soc; Int Soc Heart Transplant; NY Acad Sci. *Res:* Blood and serum groups; comparative serology; seroprimatology; population genetics; pathology of tumors; pathology of nonhuman primates; forensic pathology and serology. *Mailing Add:* Lab Exp Med & Surg Primates NY Univ Med Ctr New York NY 10016

SOCHER, SUSAN HELEN, CELL BIOLOGY. *Current Pos:* SR DIR INDUST & ACAD RELS, MERCK RES LABS, 83- *Personal Data:* b Chicago, Ill, June 19, 44. *Educ:* Mt Mary Col, BS, 66; Case Western Res Univ, PhD(cell biol), 70. *Prof Exp:* Univ res fel & NIH trainee, Sch Med, Vanderbilt Univ, 70-72, res assoc cell biol, 72; asst prof, Baylor Col Med, 72-83. *Mem:* AAAS; Am Soc Cell Biol; Develop Biol Soc. *Res:* Hormonal regulation of gene expression during mammary gland development and in mammary cancer; chromatin biochemistry. *Mailing Add:* Dept Indust & Academic Relations Merck Res Labs WP 42-217 West Point PA 19486. *Fax:* 215-652-3143

SOCIE, DARRELL FREDERICK, MECHANICAL BEHAVIOR OF MATERIALS. *Current Pos:* from asst prof to assoc prof, 77-85, PROF MECH ENG, UNIV ILL, 85- *Personal Data:* b Toledo, Ohio, Oct 29, 48; m 77; c 2. *Educ:* Univ Cincinnati, BS, 71, MS, 73; Univ Ill, PhD(mechs), 77. *Honors & Awards:* Ralph Teetor Award, Soc Automotive Engrs, 80. *Prof Exp:* Engr, Struct Dynamics, 71-74. *Concurrent Pos:* Pres, Somat Corp, 82; guest prof, Fed Tech Col, Zurich, 85. *Mem:* Soc Automotive Engrs; Am Soc Metals; Nat Soc Prof Engrs; Am Soc Testing & Mats. *Res:* Fatigue life prediction methods for structural design; cyclic deformation of cast materials; multiaxial fatigue and creep. *Mailing Add:* Dept Mech & Indust Eng Univ Ill 1206 W Green St Urbana IL 61801

SOCOLAR, SIDNEY JOSEPH, MEMBRANE PHYSIOLOGY, BIOPHYSICS. *Current Pos:* SR ASSOC, HEALTH ACTION RESOURCE CTR, NY, 86- *Personal Data:* b Baltimore, Md, Feb 10, 24; m 51; c 2. *Educ:* Johns Hopkins Univ, AB, 43, AM, 44, PhD(chem), 45. *Prof Exp:* Jr instr chem, Johns Hopkins Univ, 43-44, res chemist, 44-46; instr chem, Univ Ill, 47-48; from instr to asst prof phys sci, Univ Chicago, 50-57; math physicist, Heat & Mass Flow Analyzer Lab, Columbia Univ, 57-59, res assoc physiol, Col Physicians & Surgeons, 59-69, asst prof, 69-71; from asst prof to prof, 71-84, emer prof physiol & biophys, Sch Med, Univ Miami, 85- *Concurrent Pos:* Phillips fel, Pa State Col, 46-47. *Mem:* Soc Gen Physiologists; Biophys Soc; Am Pub Health Asn. *Res:* Cell-to-cell membrane channels: formation, permeability and permeability regulation; electrophysiology; membrane physiology. *Mailing Add:* 606 W 116th St Apt 122 New York NY 10027-7027

SOCOLOFSKY, MARION DAVID, MICROBIOLOGY. *Current Pos:* From asst prof to assoc prof microbiol, 61-68, chmn dept, 66-68 & 88-95, PROF MICROBIOL, LA STATE UNIV, BATON ROUGE, 68-, ALUMNI PROF, 91- *Personal Data:* b Marion, Kans, Sept 23, 31; m 53, Esther Green; c Kathleen & Mary S (Ingraham). *Educ:* Kans State Univ, BS, 53; Univ Tex, MA, 55, PhD(bact), 61. *Mem:* AAAS; Am Soc Microbiol; Electron Micros Soc Am; Brit Soc Gen Microbiol. *Res:* Electron microscopy; bacterial ultrastructure. *Mailing Add:* Dept Microbiol La State Univ Baton Rouge LA 70803. *Fax:* 504-388-2597; *E-Mail:* mbsoco@lsuvm.sncc.lsu.edu

SOCOLOW, ARTHUR A, ECONOMIC GEOLOGY, ENVIRONMENTAL GEOLOGY. *Current Pos:* CONSULT GEOLOGIST, 86- *Personal Data:* b New York, NY, Mar 23, 21; m 49, Edith Blumenthal; c Carl, Roy & Jeff. *Educ:* Rutgers Univ, BS, 42; Columbia Univ, MA, 47, PhD(econ geol), 55. *Honors & Awards:* Ralph Digman Award, Nat Asn Geol Teachers. *Prof Exp:* Asst field geologist, State Geol Surv, Va, 42; photogram engr, US Geol Surv, 42 & 46, geologist, 52 & Eagle Picher Mex, 47; asst econ geol, Columbia Univ, 47-48; instr geol & dir geol field camp, Colo, Southern Methodist Univ, 48-50; from instr to asst prof geol, Boston Univ, 50-55; from asst prof to prof geol, Univ Mass, 55-57; econ geologist, Pa Geol Surv, 57-61, state geologist & dir, 61-86; proj dir, Aggregate Resources New Eng Govs Conf, 90-95; prof environ geol, Salem State Col, 92-95. *Concurrent Pos:* Photogram, US Army Air Corps, 42-46; geologist, Defense Minerals Explor Authority, 52; geol adv, Boston Mus Sci, 55-57, lectr, 56; lectr, Pa State Univ, 59-73; mem, NSF Earth Sci Conf, 59; dir annual field conf Pa Geol, 61-86; ed, Pa Geol, 69-86; mem & past chmn, Am Comn Stratig Nomenclature; past chmn, Pa Water Resources Coord Comt; mem, Outer Continental Shelf Policy Comt, US Dept Interior; counr & fel, Geol Soc Am; gov rep & past chmn, Res Comt & Environ Protection Comt, Interstate Oil Compact Comn, 72-; Nat Acad Sci, Low Level Radioactive Waste Comt, 94-96. *Mem:* Fel AAAS; fel Mineral Soc Am; fel Am Geophys Union; Soc Econ Geologists; Nat Asn Geol Teachers; fel Geol Soc Am; Asn Am State Geologists (past pres); Sigma Xi. *Res:* Genesis and structural control of ore deposits; regional structure interpretation; alteration effects related to igneous rocks and ore deposits; geologic interpretation of aeromagnetic data; geologic impact on man's environment; geologic hazards; waste disposal siting; industrial minerals evaluation. *Mailing Add:* 26 Salt Island Rd Gloucester MA 01930-1945

SOCOLOW, ROBERT H(ARRY), ENERGY POLICY, ENVIRONMENTAL SCIENCES. *Current Pos:* assoc prof, 71-77, PROF ENVIRON SCI, PRINCETON UNIV, 77-, DIR, CTR ENERGY & ENVIRON STUDIES, 78- *Personal Data:* b New York, NY, Dec 27, 37; m 62, 86; c 2. *Educ:* Harvard Univ, BA, 59, MA, 61, PhD(physics), 64. *Prof Exp:* Asst prof physics, Yale Univ, 66-71, jr fac fel, 70-71. *Concurrent Pos:* NSF fel, 64-66; mem, Inst Advan Studies, 71; Guggenheim & Ger Marshall Fund fels, Energy Res Group, Cavendish Lab, Univ Cambridge, 77-78. *Mem:* Fel Am Phys Soc; Fedn Am Sci; fel AAAS. *Res:* Energy utilization; regional and global constraints on growth. *Mailing Add:* 34 Westcott Rd Princeton NJ 08540

SODAL, INGVAR E, CARDIOPULMONARY RESEARCH, PATIENT MONITORING IN ANESTHESIOLOGY & INTENSIVE CARE. *Current Pos:* PRES, MED PHYSICS, COLO, 91- *Personal Data:* b Norway, Feb 12, 34. *Educ:* Trondheim Tech Col, dipl elec eng, 59; Univ Colo, BS, 64. *Prof Exp:* Asst prof anesthesiol & head dept, Bioeng & Clin Res Div, Col Med, Ohio State Univ, 79-82; pres, Mastron Inc, 83-89; chief scientist, Paradym Sci & Technol, 89-90. *Mem:* Biomed Eng Soc; Asn Advan Med Instrumentation; Instrument Soc Am. *Mailing Add:* 1550 Moss Rock Pl Boulder CO 80304

SODANO, CHARLES STANLEY, NATURAL PRODUCTS CHEMISTRY. *Current Pos:* res chemist, Nabisco Brands Inc, 69-75, mgr anal systs res, 75-83, dir methods develop, 83-90, MGR, STRATEGIC SERV, NABISCO BRANDS INC, 90- *Personal Data:* b Newark, NJ, Nov 13, 39; c 5. *Educ:* Seton Hall Univ, BS, 61, MS, 63; Ariz State Univ, PhD(org chem), 67. *Prof Exp:* Res chemist cancer res, Pfizer Inc, 66-69. *Mem:* Am Chem Soc; Am Asn Cereal Chem; Am Soc Testing & Mat. *Res:* Structure elucidation of anti-tumor agents; fabricated foods development; catalytic hydrogenation; analytical methods for food analysis; process control; shelf life; lab robotics; technology assessment. *Mailing Add:* 15 Old Coach Rd Randolph NJ 07869

SODD, VINCENT J, NUCLEAR CHEMISTRY, NUCLEAR MEDICINE. *Current Pos:* RETIRED. *Personal Data:* b Toledo, Ohio, Nov 20, 34; m 56; c 4. *Educ:* Xavier Univ, Ohio, BS, 56, MS, 58; Univ Pittsburgh, PhD(nuclear chem), 64. *Prof Exp:* Asst instr chem, Xavier Univ, Ohio, 56-58; res chemist, Robert A Taft Sanit Eng Ctr, US Food & Drug Admin, 58-60, nuclear chemist, 64-66, dep chief nuclear med lab, 66-71, dir, Nuclear Med Lab, 71-84. *Concurrent Pos:* Asst clin prof, Col Med, Univ Cincinnati, 68-74, assoc prof, 74-77, prof, 77-86. *Mem:* Sigma Xi; Am Chem Soc; Soc Nuclear Med. *Res:* Nuclear medicine investigations involving clinic practice, radiation exposure reduction, dosimetry and instrumentation development; radiopharmaceutical production; cyclotron and linear accelerator research; activation analysis; semiconductor theory and use; development of analytical procedures for radionuclides regarded as being hazardous to our environment. *Mailing Add:* 5987 Turpin Hills Dr Cincinnati OH 45244

SODEMAN, WILLIAM A, GASTROENTEROLOGY. *Current Pos:* vchmn, Dept Med, 75-76, actg chmn, Dept Comprehensive Med, 76-77, med dir, Med Clins, 76-79, asst dir, Med Ctr, 80-84, dir, Pub Health Prog, 82-83, dep dean acad affairs, Col Med, 84-88, PROF, DEPT MED, COL MED, UNIV S FLA, TAMPA, 75-, PROF, DEPT COMPREHENSIVE MED, 76-, CHMN, 77-, ASSOC DEAN ACAD AFFAIRS, LSUMC-S COL MED, 88- *Personal Data:* b New Orleans, La, Mar 26, 36; c 2. *Educ:* Univ Mo, BA, 56; Univ Pa, MD, 60. *Prof Exp:* Assoc prof, dept internal med & chief, gastroenterol, Univ Ark, Little Rock, 70-73, assoc dir, Clin Res Ctr, 71-73; assoc prof, dept med & chief, div gastroenterol, Med Col Ohio, Toledo, 73-75. *Mem:* Sigma Xi; fel Am Col Physicians; Am Gastroenterol Asn; Am Soc Trop Med & Hyg; Am Soc Gastrointestinal Endoscopy. *Res:* Pathologic physiology; clinical parasitology; medical malacology; intermediate hosts in ecology. *Mailing Add:* Chief GI Sect Med Col Ohio PO Box 10008 Toledo OH 43699-0008

SODERBERG, LEE STEPHEN FREEMAN, HEMATOPOIESIS, DRUG ABUSE. *Current Pos:* from asst prof to assoc prof, 77-92, PROF IMMUNOL, COL MED, UNIV ARK MED SCI, 92-, DIR CELL & MOLECULAR IMMUNOL, IMMUNOPATH. *Personal Data:* b Chicago, Ill, Apr 17, 46; m 83, Georgiana McCormick; c Emily & Laura. *Educ:* Rutgers Univ, PhD(microbiol), 73. *Prof Exp:* Res fel immunol, Harvard Med Sch, 73-77. *Concurrent Pos:* Prin investr, NIH grant, 80-83, Alcohol, Drug Abuse & Mental Health Admin grant, 91-97; co-investr, NIH grants, 86-92. *Mem:* Am Asn Immunologists; Am Soc Microbiol; Sigma Xi; Soc Exp Biol Med; Soc Leukocyte Biol; AAAS. *Res:* Immunotoxicity of abused nitrite inhalants; immunotoxicology of commercial pesticides; immunity and vaccines to chlamydial genital infections; the role of bone marrow natural suppressor cells in immunodeficiencies. *Mailing Add:* Dept Microbiol & Immunol Univ Ark Col Med 4301 W Markham Slot 511 Little Rock AR 72205

SODERBERG, ROGER HAMILTON, ENVIRONMENTAL CHEMISTRY. *Current Pos:* From instr to assoc prof, 62-75, PROF CHEM, DARTMOUTH COL, 75- *Personal Data:* b Congress Park, Ill, June 19, 36; m 59, Mary Kincaid; c Daniel A & Timothy J. *Educ:* Grinnell Col, AB, 58; Mass Inst Technol, PhD(coord chem), 63. *Mem:* Am Chem Soc; AAAS. *Res:* Metal coordination chemistry. *Mailing Add:* Dept Chem Dartmouth Col 6128 Burke Lab Hanover NH 03755. *Fax:* 603-646-3946; *E-Mail:* soderberg@dartmouth.edu

SODERBLOM, LAURENCE ALBERT, PLANETARY GEOLOGY. *Current Pos:* Geophysicist, 70-78, SUPVR PHYS SCIENTIST, US GEOL SURV, 78- *Personal Data:* b Denver, Colo, July 17, 44; m 68; c 3. *Educ:* NMex Inst Mining & Technol, BS(geol) & BS(physics), 66; Calif Inst Technol, PhD(planetary sci & geophys), 70. *Concurrent Pos:* Assoc ed, J Geophys Res, 71-73; dep team leader, Voyager Imaging Sci Team, NASA, 72-, Comt Lunar & Planetary Explor, Space Sci Bd, 73-77, Viking Orbiter Imaging Team, 76-78, Galileo Near Infrared Mapping Spectrometer Team, 77- & Space Sci Adv Comt, 80- *Mem:* Am Geophys Union. *Res:* Global geologic histories of planets and satellites of the solar system employing earth-based and spacecraft remote-sensing data; established timescales for planetary evolution; computerized image processing. *Mailing Add:* 3940 N Paradise Rd Flagstaff AZ 86004

SODERLING, THOMAS RICHARD, PHYSIOLOGY, BIOCHEMISTRY. *Current Pos:* ASSOC DIR, VOLLUM INST & PROF BIOCHEM & MOLECULAR BIOL, ORE HEALTH SCI UNIV, 91- *Personal Data:* b Bonners Ferry, Idaho, May 25, 44; m 65; c 3. *Educ:* Univ Idaho, BS, 66; Univ Wash, PhD(biochem), 70. *Honors & Awards:* Andrew Mellon Found Scientist-Educr Award, 74. *Prof Exp:* NIH fel, Vanderbilt Univ, 71-72, Am Diabetes Asn fel, 72-73, from asst prof to prof physiol, Med Sch, 73-91. *Concurrent Pos:* Investr, Howard Hughes Med Inst, 76-89. *Mem:* Am Soc Biol Chemists; Soc Neurosci. *Res:* Regulation of protein phosphorylation in brain; mechanism of action of insulin; neuroscience. *Mailing Add:* Vollum Inst L-474 Ore Health Sci Univ 3181 Sam Jackson Park Rd Portland OR 97201-3098. *Fax:* 503-494-6934

SODERLUND, DAVID MATTHEW, ENTOMOLOGY, BIOCHEMICAL TOXICOLOGY. *Current Pos:* asst prof, 78-84, ASSOC PROF, DEPT ENTOMOL, NY STATE AGR EXP STA, CORNELL UNIV, 84- *Personal Data:* b Oakland, Calif, Oct 1, 50; m 72. *Educ:* Pac Lutheran Univ, BS, 71; Univ Calif, Berkeley, PhD(entomol), 76. *Prof Exp:* Vis res fel, insecticide biochem, Rothamsted Exp Sta, Harpenden, Eng, 76-77. *Concurrent Pos:* Rockefeller Found fel, 76-77; consult, Crop Chem Res & Develop, Mobil Chem Co, 78-81 & Agrochem Div, Rhone-Poulenc Inc, 82-85. *Mem:* Am Chem Soc; Entomol Soc Am; AAAS. *Res:* Biochemical and physiological interactions of insecticide chemicals and insect growth regulators in insects and mammals. *Mailing Add:* Dept of Entomol NY State Agr Exp Sta Geneva NY 14456

SODERMAN, J WILLIAM, GEOLOGY. *Current Pos:* RETIRED. *Personal Data:* b Helsinki, Finland, Oct 31, 35; US citizen; m 56; c 3. *Educ:* Columbia Univ, BA, 57; Univ Ill, MS, 60, PhD(geol), 62. *Prof Exp:* Geologist, Texaco Inc, 62-72, supvr geol res, 72-74, asst div geologist, 74-78; chief geologist, Monsanto Oil Co, BG Explor Am Inc, 78-79, dir domestic explor, 79-82, vpres, Explor, 82-88, vpres explor & prod, 88-93. *Mem:* Geol Soc Am; Am Asn Petrol Geol; Soc Econ Paleont & Mineral. *Res:* Geology of sedimentary rocks. *Mailing Add:* Drawer B Orchard TX 77464

SODERQUIST, DAVID RICHARD, PSYCHOACOUSTICS. *Current Pos:* asst prof, 68-72, assoc prof, 72-86, PROF PSYCHOL, UNIV NC, GREENSBORO, 86- *Personal Data:* b Idaho Falls, Idaho, June 26, 36; m 84. *Educ:* Utah State Univ, BS, 61, MS, 63; Vanderbilt Univ, PhD(psychol), 68. *Prof Exp:* Sr human factors specialist, Syst Develop Corp, 63-65. *Mem:* Acoust Soc Am; Sigma Xi. *Res:* Psychological acoustics; signal detection; pitch perception and temporal masking. *Mailing Add:* Dept Psychol Univ NC 296 Everhart Bldg Greensboro NC 27412

SODERSTROM, EDWIN LOREN, ENTOMOLOGY. *Current Pos:* RES ENTOMOLOGIST, AGR RES SERV, USDA, 62- *Personal Data:* b Riverside, Calif, Feb 8, 31; m 60; c 3. *Educ:* Calif State Polytech Col, BS, 57; Kans State Univ, MS, 59, PhD(entom), 62. *Prof Exp:* Res asst entom, Kans State Univ, 61-62. *Mem:* Entom Soc Am. *Res:* Entomological research on geographical populations of rice weevils; response of stored product insects to light; effects of pesticides on populations of dried fruit and tree nut insects; controlled atmosphere fumigation; insect attractants and repellents. *Mailing Add:* 7821 N Highland Ave Clovis CA 93611

SODERSTROM, KENNETH G(UNNAR), MECHANICAL ENGINEERING, SOLAR & WIND SYSTEMS ENERGY. *Current Pos:* PROF, SCH ENG, TURABO UNIV, PR, 91- *Personal Data:* b Red Bank, NJ, Apr 21, 36; m 62, Miriam Vega; c Karen & Kurt. *Educ:* Univ Fla, BME, 58, MSE, 59, PhD(mech eng), 72. *Prof Exp:* From asst prof to assoc prof mech eng, Univ PR, Mayaguez, 61-76, chmn dept, 63-68, prof mech eng, Dept Mech Eng, 76-91, sr scientist, Ctr Energy & Environ Res, 73-89, assoc dir, 79-82. *Concurrent Pos:* Res assoc, PR Nuclear Ctr, Univ PR, 62-68; consulting eng, energy syst, accident invest, 73-; vis prof, Mech Eng Dept, Univ Fla, Gainesville, 82-84. *Mem:* Am Soc Mech Engrs; Soc Automotive Engrs; Am Acad Forensic Sci. *Res:* Solar and energy, particularly experimental and analytical system studies; solar and wind data measurements and modeling of systems. *Mailing Add:* PO Box 5216 College Station Mayaguez PR 00681. *Fax:* 787-744-5476; *E-Mail:* ut_ksoderstr@feagm.feagm.clu.edu

SODETZ, JAMES M, PROTEIN BIOCHEMISTRY. *Current Pos:* ASSOC PROF BIOCHEM, UNIV SC, 83- *Personal Data:* b Chicago, Ill, Oct 9, 48. *Educ:* Univ Notre Dame, PhD(biochem), 75. *Mailing Add:* Dept Chem Univ SC Columbia SC 29208-0001. *Fax:* 803-777-9521

SODHI, NAVJOT SINGH, RAPTOR ECOLOGY, SONGBIRD ECOLOGY. *Current Pos:* RES ASSOC, UNIV ALTA, 92- *Personal Data:* b Nabha, India, Mar 18, 62; Can citizen; m 86, Charanjit Bhalla; c Ada & Darwin. *Educ:* Panjab Univ, India, BSc, 82, MSc, 83; Univ Sask, PhD(biol), 92. *Prof Exp:* Res fel, Panjab Univ, 84-86; teaching asst biol, Univ Sask, 88-92. *Concurrent Pos:* consult biologist, Terrestrial & Aquatic Environ Mgrs Ltd, 93; contract biologist, Can Wildlife Serv, 94. *Mem:* Am Ornithologists' Union; Cooper Ornith Soc; Can Soc Ornithologists. *Res:* Conservation of wild birds; effects of forest loss on birds. *Mailing Add:* Dept Zool Univ Alta Edmonton AB T6G 2E9 Can

SODICKSON, LESTER A, PHYSICS, ANALYTICAL INSTRUMENTS. *Current Pos:* PRES, CAMBRIDGE RES ASN, 85- *Personal Data:* b New York, NY, Oct 23, 37; m 63; c 3. *Educ:* Mass Inst Technol, BS, 58, PhD(physics), 63. *Prof Exp:* Sr scientist & dir new prod, Am Sci & Eng Inc, 63-70, pres, Biotech Diag, 70-71; prog mgr, Damon Corp, 71-72, vpres, Res & Eng Div, 72-74, res & develop, IEC Div, 75-81 & Inst Res, Damon Biotech, 81-83; dir appl res & sr res assoc, Corning Med, 84. *Mem:* AAAS; Am Phys Soc; Am Asn Clin Chem. *Res:* Electromagnetic sensing of molecular species for clinical chemistry; environmental pollution; infrared and optical physics; computer science; microencapsulation of living cells; cell culture; biotechnology. *Mailing Add:* 263 Waban Ave Waban MA 02168-1306

SODICOFF, MARVIN, ANATOMY, RADIATION BIOLOGY. *Current Pos:* PROF ANAT, MED SCH, TEMPLE UNIV, 66- *Personal Data:* b Brooklyn, NY, June 12, 37; m 60; c 3. *Educ:* Brooklyn Col, BS, 59; Univ Cincinnati, PhD(anat), 66. *Honors & Awards:* Lindback Award. *Mem:* Radiation Res Soc; Am Asn Anatomists. *Res:* Radiation biology. *Mailing Add:* Dept Anat & Cell Biol Temple Univ Med Sch 3420 N Broad St Philadelphia PA 19140

SOECHTING, JOHN F, BIOENGINEERING & BIOMEDICAL ENGINEERING. *Current Pos:* assoc, 72-74, lectr, 74-75, from asst prof to assoc prof, 75-85, PROF NEUROPHYSIOL, UNIV MINN, MINNEAPOLIS, 85- *Personal Data:* b Sept 27, 43; US citizen. *Educ:* Lehigh Univ, BS, 65; Cornell Univ, PhD(mech), 69. *Prof Exp:* Res assoc biomech, Brown Univ, 69-72. *Concurrent Pos:* NIH spec fel, 75-76. *Mem:* Soc Neurosci; Sigma Xi. *Res:* Motor control. *Mailing Add:* Dept Physiol 6-255 Millard Hall Univ Minn Med Sch 435 Delaware St SE Minneapolis MN 55455-0347

SOEDEL, WERNER, ENGINEERING MECHANICS, VIBRATIONS & ACOUSTICS. *Current Pos:* from asst prof to assoc prof, 67-75, PROF MECH ENG, PURDUE UNIV, 75- *Personal Data:* b Prague, Czech, Apr 24, 36; US citizen; m 61, Ann Greiber; c Sven M, Fritz P, Dirk T & Leni F. *Educ:* Frankfurt State Inst Eng, Ing Grad, 57; Purdue Univ, MSME, 65, PhD(mech eng), 67. *Honors & Awards:* Roe Award, Am Soc Eng Educ, 86. *Prof Exp:* Proj engr mech eng, Adam Opel AG, 57-63. *Concurrent Pos:* NAm ed J Sound & Vibration, 89- *Mem:* Am Acad Mech; Am Soc Mech Engrs; Am Acoustical Soc. *Res:* Vibrations of shell structures; dynamic interactions of solids and fluids; gas dynamics; acoustics; hydrodynamics. *Mailing Add:* 901 Allen St West Lafayette IN 47906

SOEDER, ROBERT W, ORGANIC CHEMISTRY. *Current Pos:* assoc prof, 67-72, PROF CHEM, APPALACHIAN STATE UNIV, 72- *Personal Data:* b Philadelphia, Pa, Oct 5, 35; m 59. *Educ:* Ursinus Col, BS, 57; Univ Del, MS, 59, PhD(org chem), 62. *Prof Exp:* Fel org chem, Univ Minn, 61-62; from asst prof to assoc prof, Wilkes Col, 62-67. *Mem:* Am Chem Soc. *Res:* Synthesis and reactions of heterocyclic compounds; reactions of B-diketones; chemical constituents of ferns. *Mailing Add:* Dept of Chem Appalachian State Univ Boone NC 28608-0001

SOEIRO, RUY, INFECTIOUS DISEASES, CELL BIOLOGY. *Current Pos:* From instr biochem to asst prof med, Albert Einstein Col Med, 67-73, assoc prof med & cell biol, 73-76, assoc prof immunol, 73-78, CO-DIR DIV INFECTIOUS DIS, ALBERT EINSTEIN COL MED, 73-, PROF MED & IMMUNOL, 78- *Personal Data:* b Boston, Mass, May 28, 32; m 66. *Educ:* Harvard Univ, AB, 54; Tufts Univ, MD, 58. *Concurrent Pos:* USPHS trainee bact, Harvard Med Sch, 62-65; USPHS spec fel biochem, Albert Einstein Col Med, 66-67; City New York career res scientist award, 68-73. *Mailing Add:* Dept Med Albert Einstein Col of Med Rm 418 Forchheimer Bldg Bronx NY 10461-1602. *Fax:* 718-597-5814

SOELDNER, JOHN STUART, DIABETES RESEARCH, GLUCOSE SENSOR. *Current Pos:* PROF MED, SCH MED, UNIV CALIF, DAVIS, 87- *Personal Data:* b Boston, Mass, Sept 22, 32; m 62, Elsie I Harnish; c Judith Marie (Gage), Elizabeth Marie (McCarthy) & Stephen J D (deceased). *Educ:* Tufts Univ, BSc, 54, Dalhousie Univ, MD, 59. *Hon Degrees:* LLD, Dalhousie Univ, Halifax, 96. *Honors & Awards:* Upjohn Award, Am Diabetic Asn, 86. *Prof Exp:* Assoc prof med, Harvard Med Sch, Boston; physician, Brigham & Womens Hosp, Boston; sr investr, Joslin Res Lab, Boston. *Concurrent Pos:* Active med staff, Davis Med Ctr, Univ Calif, Sacramento, 87. *Mem:* Am Physiol Soc; Am Diabetes Asn; Endocrine Soc; Am Soc Clin Invest. *Res:* Research pathogenesis of diabetes, type 1 and type 2; insulin secretions, genetics of type 1 and type 2 diabetes; study miniature implantable glucose sensor and implantable artificial beta cell for diabetes; study glycosylation proteins, particularly hemoglobin. *Mailing Add:* Univ Calif Davis Med Ctr 4301 "X" St-FOLB-2-C Sacramento CA 95817. *Fax:* 916-455-2772

SOERENS, DAVE ALLEN, PRESSURE-SENSITIVE ADHESIVES, NONWOVENS. *Current Pos:* SR RES CHEMIST, 3M CO, 78- *Personal Data:* b Sheboygan, Wis, Aug 26, 52; m 72; c 2. *Educ:* Calvin Col, BS, 74; Univ Wis-Milwaukee, PhD(chem), 78. *Mem:* Am Chem Soc; NAm Thermal Anal Soc. *Res:* Adhesives research and development; thermal analysis; nonwovens. *Mailing Add:* 736 Kensington Rd Neenah WI 54956-4908

SOERGEL, KONRAD H, INTERNAL MEDICINE, GASTROENTEROLOGY. *Current Pos:* from asst prof to assoc prof, 61-69, PROF MED, MED COL WIS, 69-, CHIEF DEPT GASTROENTEROL, 61- *Personal Data:* b Coburg, Ger, July 27, 29; US citizen; m 55; c 4. *Educ:* Univ Erlangen, MD, 54, DrMedSci, 57. *Prof Exp:* Res fel gastroenterol, Sch Med, Boston Univ, 58-60, instr med, 60-61. *Concurrent Pos:* Consult gastroenterologist, Wood Vet Admin Hosp, 67; consult, Vet Admin Res Serv Rev Bd, 69-71 & 72-74; mem gen med A study sect, NIH, 76-80. *Mem:* Am Fedn Clin Res; Am Gastroenterol Asn; Am Soc Clin Invest. *Res:* Absorption of water, electrolyte and sugar from the human small intestine. *Mailing Add:* Dept Med Gastroenterol Med Col Wis Frodtert Mem Lutheran Hosp 9200 W Wisconsin Ave Milwaukee WI 53226-3596. *Fax:* 414-259-1533

SOEST, JON FREDRICK, TECHNICAL MANAGEMENT, NUCLEAR MAGNETIC RESONANCE & MULTIVARIATE STATISTICS. *Current Pos:* DIR INDUST APPLNS, APPLIED RECOGNITION TECHNOLS INC, 94- *Personal Data:* b Santa Ana, Calif, Aug 3, 38; m 68, Sally Warren. *Educ:* Pomona Col, BA, 60; Univ Wash, MS, 62, PhD(physics), 67. *Prof Exp:* Assoc prof physics, Col William & Mary, 67-77; res scientist, Weyerhaeuser Co, 77-87; res eng, US Natural Resources, 87-95. *Concurrent Pos:* Affil assoc prof elec eng, Univ Wash, 84-96; consult, 94-97. *Res:* Developing a proprietary technology that combines magnetic resonance imaging or nuclear magnetic resonance with multivariate statistics, for medical and industrial applications. *Mailing Add:* 2055 43rd Ave E No 202 Seattle WA 98112. *Fax:* 206-860-3969

SOFER, SAMIR SALIM, CHEMICAL ENGINEERING, BIOENGINEERING. *Current Pos:* PROF & SPONSOR CHMN, DEPT BIOTECHNOL, NJ INST TECHNOL, 86- *Personal Data:* b Teheran, Iran, Oct 10, 45. *Educ:* Univ Utah, BS, 69; Tex A&M Univ, ME, 71; Univ Tex, PhD(chem eng), 74. *Honors & Awards:* First place, SCORE (Student Contest on Relevant Eng), 75. *Prof Exp:* Process design engr, Celanese Chem Co, 69-72; res assoc, Univ Tex, 73-74; from asst prof to assoc prof, Univ Okla, 74-80, dir, Sch Chem Eng & Mat Sci, 75-80, prof chem eng, 80-86. *Concurrent Pos:* Fel, Clayton Found Biochem Inst, 74-75. *Mem:* Am Inst Chem Engrs; AAAS; Am Soc Eng Educ. *Res:* Insolubilized enzyme technology and biochemical reactor design; reaction kinetics; process design. *Mailing Add:* NJ Inst Technol Chem Chem E Environ Sci 161 Warren St Newark NJ 07102-4370

SOFER, WILLIAM HOWARD, MOLECULAR GENETICS, GENETIC ALGORITHMS. *Current Pos:* dir, Grad Prog Microbiol & Molecular Genetics, 92-95, MEM FAC, WAKSMAN INST MICROBIOL, RUTGERS UNIV, 80- *Personal Data:* b Brooklyn, NY, Jan 14, 41; m 64; c Gregg & Douglas. *Educ:* Brooklyn Col, BS, 61; Univ Miami, PhD(cell physiol), 67. *Prof Exp:* NIH fel, John Hopkins Univ, 67-69, NSF fel, 69-71 from asst prof to assoc prof biol, 69-80. *Concurrent Pos:* NIH grant, 71-93; Dept Energy contract, 76-82; Nat Inst Environ Health Sci grant, 77-84; NSF grant, 93-; Howard Hughes Med Inst, 94- *Mem:* AAAS; Genetics Soc Am. *Res:* Genetic algorithms; protein structure determination; artificial intelligence. *Mailing Add:* Dept Molecular Biol & Biochem Rutgers Univ Piscataway NJ 08854-0759. *E-Mail:* sofer@mbcl.rutgers.edu

SOFFEN, GERALD A(LAN), BIOLOGY. *Current Pos:* proj scientist, Viking, Langley Res Ctr, 69-78, DIR LIFE SCI, HQ, NASA, 78- *Personal Data:* b Cleveland, Ohio, Feb 7, 26; m 79. *Educ:* Univ Calif, Los Angeles, BA, 49; Univ Southern Calif, MS, 56; Princeton Univ, PhD(biol), 60. *Prof Exp:* USPHS fel biol, Sch Med, NY Univ, 60-61; sr space scientist, Jet Propulsion Lab, Calif Inst Technol, 61-69. *Mem:* AAAS. *Res:* Physiology; biochemistry; growth, metabolism and physiology of the cell; effects of ultraviolet light; transport mechanisms; exobiology; muscle biochemistry; science administration. *Mailing Add:* 617 Fourth Pl SW Washington DC 20024

SOFFER, BERNARD HAROLD, PHYSICS. *Current Pos:* RETIRED. *Personal Data:* b Brooklyn, NY, Mar 2, 31; m 56, Reba Nusbaum; c Roger. *Educ:* Brooklyn Col, BS, 53; Mass Inst Technol, MS, 58. *Prof Exp:* Staff mem, Lab Insulation Res, Mass Inst Technol, 58-59; res physicist, Hughes Res Lab, Calif, 59-61 & Appl Physics Lab, Quanatron Inc, 61-62; sr scientist, Optical Physics Div, Korad Corp, Calif, 62-69; mem tech staff, Hughes Res Labs, 69-80, sr staff physicist, 80-87, sr scientist, 87-90, prin scientist, 90-96. *Concurrent Pos:* Consult. *Mem:* Am Phys Soc; Sigma Xi; sr mem Inst Elec & Electronics Eng; fel Optical Soc Am. *Res:* Optical, infrared and spin resonance spectroscopy of solids; laser physics and laser materials; optical physics; image and information processing; optical computing; neural networks; signal and data processing; foundations of physics. *Mailing Add:* 665 Bienveneda Ave Pacific Palisades CA 90272

SOFFER, RICHARD LUBER, BIOCHEMISTRY. *Current Pos:* prof, 76-94, EMER PROF MED & BIOCHEM, MED COL, CORNELL UNIV, 94- *Personal Data:* b Baltimore, Md, Oct 1, 32; m 68; c 2. *Educ:* Amherst Col, BA, 54; Harvard Univ, MD, 58. *Prof Exp:* Asst resident med, Sch Med, NY Univ, 61-62, resident, 64-65; fel biochem, Pasteur Inst, Paris, 62-64; asst mem enzymol, Inst Muscle Dis, New York, 65-67; from asst prof to assoc prof molecular biol, Albert Einstein Col Med, 72-76. *Concurrent Pos:* Career develop award, Nat Inst Arthritis & Metab Dis, 68; fac res award, Am Cancer Soc, 73. *Mem:* Am Soc Biol Chemists. *Res:* Post-translational protein modification catalyzed by aminoacyl-t RNA-protein transferases; angiotensin-converting enzyme and regulation of vasoactive peptides; enzymes involved in the metabolism of thyroid hormones by target cells; angiotensin receptors. *Mailing Add:* 12 Bonny Brook Trail Norwalk CT 06850

SOFIA, R DUANE, PHARMACOLOGY. *Current Pos:* sr res pharmacologist, 71-73, dir, Dept Pharmacol & Toxicol, 73-76, vpres biol res, 76-80, vpres res & develop, 80-82, VPRES PRE-CLIN RES, WALLACE LABS, CRANBURY, 82- *Personal Data:* b Ellwood City, Pa, Oct 8, 42; m 65; c 4. *Educ:* Geneva Col, BS, 64; Fairleigh-Dickinson Univ, MS, 69; Univ Pittsburgh, PhD(pharmacol), 71. *Prof Exp:* Res biologist, Lederle Labs, NY, 64-67; res assoc pharmacol, Union Carbide Corp, 67-69; sr pharmacologist, Pharmakon Labs, Pa, 69. *Concurrent Pos:* Consult, Pharmakon Labs, 69-71. *Mem:* Am Soc Pharmacol & Exp Therapeut; Soc Toxicol; Soc Neurosci; Int Soc Study Pain; Am Rheumatism Asn. *Res:* Pharmacology and toxicology of various constituents of marihuana; development of new drugs for cardiovascular, pulmonary and central nervous system diseases and pain relief. *Mailing Add:* Wallace Labs Half Acre Rd Cranbury NJ 08512-0181. *Fax:* 609-655-6779

SOFIA, SABATINO, ASTROPHYSICS. *Current Pos:* PROF ASTRON, YALE UNIV, 85-, DEPT CHMN, 93- *Personal Data:* b Episcopia, Italy, May 14, 39; m 63, Tara L Sibilia; c Tamara L (Cerilli) & Ulysses J. *Educ:* Yale Univ, BS, 63, MS, 65, PhD(astrophys), 67. *Prof Exp:* Nat Acad Sci-Nat Res Coun res assoc astrophys, Goddard Inst Space Studies, NASA, 66-67; from assoc prof to prof astron, Univ SFla, 67-73; vis fel, Joint Inst Lab Astrophysics, 73-74; sr res assoc, Univ Rochester, 74-75; staff scientist, Hq NASA, 75-77, sr res assoc solar phys, Nat Acad Sci-Nat Res Coun, 77-79, space scientist, Goddard Space Flight Ctr, 79-85. *Concurrent Pos:* Adj prof astron, Univ Fla, 75-79; mem, Space & Earth Sci Adv Comt, NASA, 85-88. *Mem:* Am Astron Soc; Int Astron Union; Am Geophys Union. *Res:* Solar physics, variability and evolution; stellar evolution; interstellar matter. *Mailing Add:* Dept Astron Yale Univ Observ PO Box 208101 New Haven CT 06520-8101. *Fax:* 203-432-5048; *E-Mail:* sofia@astro.yale.edu

SOFOS, JOHN N, FOODBORNE PATHOGENIC BACTERIA, MEAT SAFETY. *Current Pos:* from asst prof to assoc prof, 80-87, PROF FOOD MICROBIOL, COLO STATE UNIV, 87- *Personal Data:* b June 14, 48; m 78, Helen Stamatatos; c Marina & Elvera. *Educ:* Aristotelian Univ, Greece, 71; Univ Minn, MS, 75, PhD(food sci), 79. *Honors & Awards:* Distinguished Res Award, Am Meat Sci Asn, 94; Meats Res Award, Am Soc Animal Sci, 95. *Prof Exp:* Res assoc, Univ Minn, 78-80. *Concurrent Pos:* Sci adv microbiol, Food & Drug Admin, Denver, 89-; sci co-ed, J Food Protection, 95- *Mem:* Am Soc Microbiol; Am Soc Animal Sci; Am Meat Sci Asn; Int Asn Milk Food & Environ Sanitarians; AAAS; Inst Food Technologists; fel Am Acad Microbiol. *Res:* Behavior and control of spoilage of pathogenic microorganisms associated with food products; influence of food constituents and chemical agents on pathogenic bacteria; methodology for detection of pathogenic bacteria; influnce of environmental factors or foodborne pathogenic bacteria. *Mailing Add:* 1601 Sagewood Dr Ft Collins CO 80525. *E-Mail:* jsofos@ceres.agsci.colostate.edu

SOGAH, DOTSEVI YAO, HOST-GUEST CHEMISTRY, BIOMATERIALS. *Current Pos:* PROF CHEM, CORNELL UNIV, 91- *Personal Data:* b Ghana, West Africa, April, 19, 45; m 73; c 3. *Educ:* Univ Ghana, BSc, first class, 70, Hons, 71; Univ Calif, Los Angeles, MS, 74, PhD(chem), 75. *Honors & Awards:* Distinguished Bayer/Mobay Lectr, Cornell Univ; Waddell Prize, Univ Ghana, 74. *Prof Exp:* Fel chem, Univ Calif, Santa Barbara, 75-77; asst res chemist, Univ Calif, Los Angeles, 78-79, asst prof bio-org chem, 79-80; res chemist polymer chem, E I du Pont de Nemours & Co, Inc, 81-83, group leader, 83-84, res supv, 84-90, res mgr, 90-91. *Concurrent Pos:* Fel, African Am Inst, 71-75; mem, Bd Sci & Technol, Nat Res Coun, 88-89; mem, Nat Res Coun Briefing Panel Thin Films & Interfaces. *Mem:* Am Chem Soc; Sigma Xi; Int Soc African Scientists (pres, 87-88); NY Acad Sci; AAAS. *Res:* Synthesis and complexation of Macrocyclic Hosts; liquid-solid interface chemistry; asymmetric inductions and catalysis of Michael addition reactions; synthesis of optically active polymers; organosilicon chemistry; polymers for biomedical applications; drug delivery systems; group transfer polymerization; monolayers and surface interactions; fluoropolymers; living polymerizations. *Mailing Add:* Dept Chem Baker Lab Cornell Univ Ithaca NY 14853-1301

SOGANDARES-BERNAL, FRANKLIN, PARASITOLOGY. *Current Pos:* chmn dept, 74-77, prof, 74-96, EMER PROF BIOL, SOUTHERN METHODIST UNIV, 96-; PRES, CUSTOM ANTIBODIES, 96- *Personal Data:* b Panama, CZ, May 12, 31; div; c 3. *Educ:* Tulane Univ, BS, 54; Univ Nebr, MS, 55, PhD(zool), 58. *Honors & Awards:* Henry Baldwin Ward Medal, Am Soc Parasitol, 69. *Prof Exp:* Parasitologist, Marine Lab, State Bd Conserv, Fla, 58-59; from instr to prof zool, Tulane Univ, La, 59-71, mem grad fac, 61-71, exec officer biol, 62-65, univ coord sci planning, 65-67, dir, Lab Parasitol, 67-71; prof zool & chmn dept, Univ Mont, 71-72, prof microbiol, 72-74. *Concurrent Pos:* Guest investr, Lerner Marine Lab, Am Mus Natural Hist, 57 & 60; mem adv panel syst biol, Biomed Div, NSF, 63-66; mem bd sci adv, Saltwater Fish Div, Fla State Bd Conserv, 64-; consult path, Dept Path, Baylor Univ Med Ctr, 75-, med staff affil, 77-, dir, Ctr Infectious Dis Res, Baylor Res Fedn, 84-; asst to dean, Div Continuing Educ, Health Sci Ctr, Univ Tex, 77-80; consult engrs, SputterTex Corp. *Mem:* Am Asn Pathologists; Am Soc Zool; Am Soc Parasitol; Coun Biol Ed; Wildlife Dis Asn; Soc Social Biol. *Res:* Evolutionary biology of parasitism; immunopathology; photobiology. *Mailing Add:* Custom Antibodies Tex HC03 Box 70A Lampasas TX 76550

SOGN, JOHN ALLEN, IMMUNOLOGY, BIOCHEMISTRY. *Current Pos:* sr staff fel, NIH, 77-78, res chemist, Nat Inst Allergy & Infectious Dis, 78-87, prog dir, Cancer Immunol, Nat Cancer Inst, 87-90, CHIEF, CANCER IMMUNOL, NAT CANCER INST, NIH, 90- *Personal Data:* b Buffalo, NY, May 11, 46; m 69, Dorothy Deacon; c Amanda & Andrew. *Educ:* Brown Univ, AB, 68; Rockefeller Univ, PhD(biochem), 73. *Prof Exp:* Res assoc immunol & biochem, Rockefeller Univ, 73-76, asst prof, 76-77. *Mem:* Am Chem Soc; Harvey Soc; Am Asn Immunol; Sigma Xi; Am Asn Cancer Res. *Res:* Basic studies in molecular and cellular immunology relevant to the immune response to cancer. *Mailing Add:* 9208 Cedarcrest Dr Bethesda MD 20814

SOGNEFEST, PETER WILLIAM, GENERAL MANAGEMENT. *Current Pos:* PRES & CHIEF EXEC OFFICER, XYMOX TECHNOLOGIES, INC, 96- *Personal Data:* b Melrose Park, Ill, Feb 4, 41; m, Donna Stilwell; c Scott, Brian, Jennifer & Eric. *Educ:* Univ Ill, BSEE, 64, MS, 67. *Prof Exp:* Engr, Magnavox Co, 64-67; sr fel, Mellon Inst Sci, 67-71; gen mgr res & mfg, Essex Int Inc, 69-77; bus unit mgr, 77-80, vpres & gen mgr, Motorola, Inc, 80-84; chmn & chief exec officer, Digital Appliance Controls, Inc, 84-91; pres & chief exec officer, IRT Corp, 91-94; pres & chief exec officer, LH Res Inc, 94-96. *Concurrent Pos:* Vis fel, Mellon Inst Sci, 71-77; chancellor's assoc, Univ Calif, San Diego, 92- *Mem:* Inst Elec & Electronics Engrs. *Res:* Metal-Oxide-semiconductor integrated circuits as applied to automotive electrical systems; digital controls as applied to major appliances; microprocessor based instruments as applied to agriculture and construction equipment. *Mailing Add:* 9909 W Dean Rd Milwaukee WI 53224. *E-Mail:* kyym66a@prodigy.com

SOGO, POWER BUNMEI, PHYSICS. *Current Pos:* RETIRED. *Personal Data:* b San Diego, Calif, Feb 26, 25; m; c 3. *Educ:* San Diego State Col, AB, 50; Univ Calif, PhD(physics), 55. *Prof Exp:* Physicist, Radiation Lab, Univ Calif, 55-59; asst prof physics, San Diego State Col, 59-62; from asst prof to assoc prof physics, Pomona Col, 62-66; from assoc prof to prof, Calif State Col, San Bernardino, 66-71; prof physics, Univ Hawaii, Hilo, 71-86, chmn, Natural Sci Div, 78-80. *Res:* Electron paramagnetic resonance. *Mailing Add:* HC 3 Box 10008 Keaau HI 96749

SOH, CHAN, LIQUID CRYSTAL DISPLAYS, CLINICAL DIAGNOSTICS CHEMISTRY. *Current Pos:* sr chemist, Helipot Div, 75-82, MGR, DIAGNOSTICS SYSTS DIV, BECKMAN INSTRUMENTS, 82- *Personal Data:* b Kwangju, Korea, July 4, 38; m 68; c 2. *Educ:* Seoul Nat Univ, BS, 61; St John's Univ, MS, 67; PhD(org chem), 70. *Prof Exp:* Sr chemist, Columbia Pharmaceut Corp, 65-70; mem tech staff, David Sarnoff Res Ctr, 70-72; sr chemist, Helipot Div, Beckman Instruments, 72-74; mem tech staff, David Sarnoff Res Ctr, RCA Labs, 74. *Concurrent Pos:* Consult, Flat Panel Displays.

Mem: Am Chem Soc; Sigma Xi. *Res:* Organic synthesis; liquid crystal materials; liquid crystal display devices; immunochemistry; clinical chemistry. *Mailing Add:* Beckman Instruments Inc MS 553 200 S Kraemer Blvd Brea CA 92621-6209

SOH, SUNG KUK, POLYMER SCIENCE, POLYMER ENGINEERING. *Current Pos:* assoc prof chem eng, 86-, PROF CHEM ENG, UNIV DETROIT, MERCY. *Personal Data:* b Korea, Mar 5, 51; m 80, Kyung H Kim; c Jung Won & Jung In. *Educ:* Seoul Nat Univ, BS, 73, MS, 76; Univ NH, PhD(chem eng), 81. *Prof Exp:* Chem engr, Res & Develop, Yuyu Indust Co, 73-74; asst prof chem eng, Manhattan Col, 81-86. *Mem:* Soc Plastics Engrs. *Res:* Preform manufacturing process; plastics and SMC recycling. *Mailing Add:* Dept Chem Eng Univ Detroit Mercy 4001 W McNichols Rd Detroit MI 48219. *Fax:* 313-993-1409

SOHACKI, LEONARD PAUL, LIMNOLOGY, ZOOLOGY. *Current Pos:* Asst prof, 68-71, ASSOC PROF BIOL, STATE UNIV NY COL ONEONTA, 71- *Personal Data:* b Bay City, Mich, Aug 21, 33; m 60; c 5. *Educ:* Mich State Univ, BS, 61, MS, 65, PhD(limnol), 68. *Mem:* Am Soc Limnol & Oceanog; Sigma Xi; Water Pollution Control Fedn. *Res:* Eutrophication and productivity. *Mailing Add:* Dept of Biol State Univ NY Oneonta PO Box 4015 Oneonta NY 13820-4015

SOHAL, GURKIRPAL SINGH, NEUROEMBRYOLOGY. *Current Pos:* AT DEPT ANAT, MED COL GEORGIA. *Personal Data:* b Punjab, India, Oct 1, 48; m 75; c 1. *Educ:* Punjab Univ, BS, 69; La State Univ, PhD(anat), 73. *Prof Exp:* Asst prof anat, Fla Int Univ, 73-75; asst prof anat, Med Col Ga, 75-77, assoc prof, 77-80; mem fac, dept biol sci, Fla Int Univ, 80- *Concurrent Pos:* Res grant, Med Col Ga, 75; NIH res grant, 77- *Mem:* Am Asn Anatomists; AAAS; Soc Neurosci; Sigma Xi. *Res:* Factors responsible for cell death and cell differentiation in the developing brain. *Mailing Add:* Dept Cell Biol & Anat Med Col Ga Augusta GA 30912-2000

SOHAL, MANOHAR SINGH, THERMOFLUIDS, HEAT TRANSFER. *Current Pos:* PROJ MGR, IDAHO NAT ENG LAB, 80- *Personal Data:* b Ludhiana, India, June 1, 43; US citizen; m 75, Veena; c Vikaas & Ambika. *Educ:* Birla Inst Technol & Sci, India, BE, 65, ME, 67; Univ Houston, PhD(mech eng), 72. *Prof Exp:* Lectr mech eng & heat transfer thermodyn, Birla Inst Technol & Sci, India, 67-68; res fel, Eindhoven Univ Technol, Neth, 72-73; Univ Strathclyde, Scotland, 73-74; spec res asst, Univ Manchester Inst Sci & Technol, Eng; res assoc, Solar Energy Lab, Univ Houston, 75-76; develop engr, Res & Develop Lab, M W Kellogg, Houston, Tex, 76-80. *Concurrent Pos:* Lectr mech eng, Univ Houston, 76; proj mgr, Thermal Sci Prog. *Mem:* Am Soc Mech Engrs; Sigma Xi. *Res:* Analysis of transient thermohydraulic phenomena in nuclear reactors; heat transfer, fluid flow and two-phase flow problems; project management of advanced ceramic heat exchangers for high temperature applications; metal casting. *Mailing Add:* Idaho Nat Eng Lab PO Box 1625 Idaho Falls ID 83415-3875. *Fax:* 208-526-8883; *E-Mail:* sohalms@inel.gov

SOHAL, PARMJIT S, CARDIOVASCULAR DISEASE, DIABETES. *Current Pos:* FAC, INST HEALTH PROM RES, UNIV BC, 95-, RESIDENT FAMILY PRACT, 95- *Personal Data:* b Panjaur, India, Apr 6, 59; Can citizen; m 87, Neena; c Tanveer & Tanraj. *Educ:* Punjab Univ, BSc, 79; Punjab Agr Univ, MSc, 82; Univ Sask, PhD(biochem), 88; Univ Alta, MD, 95. *Honors & Awards:* Travel Award, Am Soc Biochem & Molecular Biol, 91. *Prof Exp:* Res fel biochem, Univ Delhi, India, 81-82; lab demonstr biochem, Univ Sask, 82-88; postdoctoral fel biochem, Simon Fraser Univ, Can, 88-90; postdoctoral fel biochem, Univ Alta, 90-91, res scientist nutrit biochem, 91-95. *Concurrent Pos:* Postdoctoral fel, Am Heart Asn, 89, Can Diabetes Asn, 91; travelling fel, NAm Soc Pacing & Electrophysiol, 93 & 95; res scientist, St George Hosp, London, UK, 93 & Hosp Jean Rostrand, Paris, 95. *Mem:* Can Biochem Soc; Can Soc Nutrit Sci; Can Med Asn; Col Family Physicians Can; fel Am Col Nutrit; fel Int Col Nutrit. *Res:* Nutrition and metabolic regulation; prevention and management of cardiovascular diseases and diabetes; disorders of lipid metabolism, particularly hypercholestolemia. *Mailing Add:* PO Box 3274 Vancouver BC V6B 3X9 Can

SOHAL, RAJINDAR SINGH, CELL BIOLOGY. *Current Pos:* from asst prof to assoc prof, 69-79, PROF BIOL, SOUTHERN METHODIST UNIV, 79- *Personal Data:* b Amritsar, India, July 1, 36; m 71, Barbara H Harris. *Educ:* Panjab Univ, BS, 60, MS, 61; Tulane Univ, PhD(biol), 65. *Hon Degrees:* Dr, Linkoping Univ, Sweden, 92. *Honors & Awards:* Life-Time Achievement Award Res, Am Aging Asn, 95; Irving Wright Award Am Fedn Aging Res, 97. *Prof Exp:* Asst prof biol, Xavier Univ, 65-66; from instr to asst prof, Dept Med, Sch Med, Tulane Univ, 66-69, Dept Med,. *Concurrent Pos:* Sr vis scholar, Zool Dept, Cambridge Univ, 75 & 79 & Univ Dusseldorf, Dept of Biochem, 84; vis prof, dept path, Linkoping Univ, Sweden, 87, 88, 90 & 94. *Mem:* Am Soc Cell Biol; fel Geront Soc Am; Oxygen Soc. *Res:* Differentiation and aging of cells; free radical biochemistry; relationship between life span and metabolic rate. *Mailing Add:* Dept Biol Sci Southern Methodist Univ Dallas TX 75275. *Fax:* 214-768-3955

SOHL, CARY HUGH, ACOUSTICS. *Current Pos:* PHYSICIST, E I DU PONT DE NEMOURS & CO, INC, 79- *Personal Data:* b Pittsfield, Mass. *Educ:* Renssalaer Polytech Inst, BS, 74; Northwestern Univ, MS, 76, PhD(physics), 79. *Res:* Plant process monitoring. *Mailing Add:* 32 Renee Lane Newark DE 19711

SOHL, NORMAN FREDERICK, paleontology; deceased, see previous edition for last biography

SOHLER, ARTHUR, BIOCHEMISTRY, MICROBIOLOGY. *Current Pos:* BIOCHEMIST, BRAIN BIOCENTER, 73- *Personal Data:* b New York, NY, Sept 23, 27; m 58; c 3. *Educ:* City Col New York, BS, 51; St John's Univ, NY, MS, 54; Rutgers Univ, PhD(microbiol chem), 57. *Prof Exp:* Asst, St John's Univ, NY, 53-54; res assoc, Inst Microbiol, Rutgers Univ, 57-58, asst res specialist biochem, 58-59; biochemist, Bur Res in Neurol & Psychiat, NJ Neuropsychiat Inst, 58-73. *Mem:* AAAS; Am Chem Soc; Am Soc Microbiol. *Res:* Biochemistry of mental illness; clinical and microbial biochemistry; chemistry of natural products. *Mailing Add:* 30 Hart Ave Hopewell NJ 08525-1425

SOHMER, BERNARD, GROUP THEORY. *Current Pos:* lectr, City Col NY, 53-57, from asst prof to assoc prof, 58-69, from assoc dean to dean students, 68-75, PROF MATH, CITY COL NY, 69- *Personal Data:* b New York, NY, July 16, 29; m 52, Margot Rosette; c Emily & Olivia. *Educ:* NY Univ, BA, 49, MS, 51, PhD(math), 58. *Prof Exp:* Mathematician, Army Signal Corps, 51-52; instr math, NY Univ, 52-53 & 57-58. *Concurrent Pos:* Chair, fac senate, City Col NY; chair, Prof Staff Cong; Ohmbudsman, gov, Math Asn Am; trustee, Univ Welfare Fund, vpres, Univ Fac Senate. *Mem:* AAAS; Am Math Soc; Math Asn Am. *Res:* Structure theory of groups; rings algebras. *Mailing Add:* Dept Math City Col NY 139th St & Convent Ave New York NY 10031. *E-Mail:* bescc@ccunyvm.cuny.edu

SOHMER, SEYMOUR H, SYSTEMATIC BOTANY. *Current Pos:* DIR, BOT RES INST TEX, 93- *Personal Data:* b Bronx, NY, Feb 27, 41; m 67, Sara Harrison; c Rebecca, Rose, Rachel & Adrienne. *Educ:* City Col New York, BS, 63; Univ Tenn, MS, 66; Univ Hawaii, PhD(bot), 71. *Honors & Awards:* Engler Silver Medal, 93. *Prof Exp:* Dir herbarium & assoc prof bot, Univ Wis-LaCrosse, 67-80; chmn, Dept Bot, Bernice P Bishop Mus, Honolulu, 80-91, asst dir, Res & Scholarly Studies, 85-91; sr biodiversity adv, Agency Int Develop, 91-93. *Concurrent Pos:* Res fel, Smithsonian Inst, 75-76 & partic Flora of Ceylon proj, 73-74; NSF assignment to assess status basic res trop biol, 77-78; forest botanist, Div Bot, Off Forests, Dept Primary Industs, Lae, Papua New Guinea, 79-; chmn, Standing Comt Bot, Pac Sci Asn, 83-95; adj prof pharmacol, Univ NTex Health Sci Ctr, Ft Worth, 93-; adj prof biol, Tex Christian Univ, 94- *Mem:* Am Inst Biological Scis; Asn Trop Biol; Int Asn Plant Taxon; Am Soc Plant Taxon; Soc Econ Bot. *Res:* Systematic revisionary work with selected angiosperms; ascertaining the identities and relationships among complex groups of flowering plants, particularly Psychotria (Rubiaceae). *Mailing Add:* Bot Res Inst Tex 509 Pecan St Ft Worth TX 76102-4060. *Fax:* 817-332-4112; *E-Mail:* ssohmer@brit.org

SOHN, CHANG WOOK, ENERGY STORAGE SYSTEMS, HEAT TRANSFER. *Current Pos:* MECH ENGR, US ARMY CONSTRUCT ENERGY RES LAB, 81-, PRIN INVESTR, 84- *Personal Data:* b Seoul, Korea, Jan 10, 47; US citizen; m 74, Han Chung-Hac; c Douglas & Sammy. *Educ:* Seoul Nat Univ, BS, 69; Tex Tech Univ, MS, 75; Univ Ill, Champaign, PhD(mech eng), 80. *Prof Exp:* Res assoc, Univ Ill, Urbana-Champaign, 80-81. *Concurrent Pos:* Adj assoc prof, Univ Ill, 92-; res fel, Korea Inst Energy Res, 95-96. *Mem:* Am Soc Mech Engrs; Am Soc Heating, Refrig & Air Conditioning Engrs; Asn Energy Engrs. *Res:* Building of energy systems, energy storage devices, advanced cooling systems, heat transfer and fluid mechanics in thermal systems and alternative energy sources. *Mailing Add:* 2910 Robeson Park Dr Champaign IL 61821. *E-Mail:* c_sohn@cecer.army.mil

SOHN, DAVID, PATHOLOGY, TOXICOLOGY. *Current Pos:* DIR LABS, GRACIE SQUARE HOSP, 65- *Personal Data:* b Far Rockaway, NY, Dec 5, 26; m 62, 85; c 6. *Educ:* Yeshiva Col, BA, 46; Columbia Univ, AM, 48; Polytech Inst Brooklyn, MA, 53; State Univ NY, Downstate Med Ctr, MD, 57. *Prof Exp:* Asst attend path, Montefiore Hosp & Med Ctr, NY, 62-63; asst pathologist, Maimonides Hosp & Med Ctr, NY, 63-65; attend path, Ctr Chronic Dis & assoc prof, NY Med Col, 65-88. *Concurrent Pos:* Mem, Comt Alcohol & Drug Abuse, Nat Safety Coun, 72-; mem, Toxicol Resource Comt, Col Am Pathologists, 73-81, chmn, 74-80, mem, Surv Comt, 74-81; assoc dean, NY Med Col, 73-88, asst clin prof dermat, 74-; consult, Toxicol Subcomt, Diag Devices Comt, US Food & Drug Admin, 75-, chmn, 80-81 & 85-86. *Mem:* Fel Col Am Pathologists; fel Am Soc Clin Pathologists; Am Asn Clin Chemists; fel Am Acad Forensic Sci; Am Chem Soc. *Res:* Methodology in the identification of drugs of abuse in biologic fluids, their quantitation and confirmed identification; quantitation of therapeutic drugs in body fluids. *Mailing Add:* Bendiner & Schlesinger 47 Third Ave New York NY 10003

SOHN, HONG YONG, PROCESS METALLURGY, REACTION ENGINEERING. *Current Pos:* from asst prof to assoc prof, 74-80, PROF METALL ENG, UNIV UTAH, 80- *Personal Data:* b Kaesung, Korea, Aug 21, 41; US citizen; m 71, Victoria Ngo; c Berkeley J & Edward J. *Educ:* Seoul Nat Univ, BS, 62; Univ NB, MSc, 66; Univ Calif, Berkeley, PhD(chem eng), 70. *Honors & Awards:* Fulbright Distinguished Lectr, 83; Extraction & Process Metall Lectr, Minerals, Metals & Mat Soc, Extraction & Process Metall Sci Award, 90 & 94, Champion H Mathewson Gold Metal Award, 93. *Prof Exp:* Res engr chem eng, Cheil Sugar Co, 61-64 & E I du Pont de Nemours & Co, 73-74. *Concurrent Pos:* Res assoc, State Univ NY, Buffalo, 71-73; consult, Lawrence Livermore Lab, 75-, Kennecott Co, Cabot Corp, 84-, Utah Power & Light Co, 87- & DuPont Co, 87-; Dreyfus Found teacher-scholar award, 77; adj assoc prof fuels eng, Univ Utah, 78-80, adj prof, 80- & adj prof chem eng, 87-; extractive metall lectr, Metall Soc, 90; hon vis prof, Kunming Inst Technol, Kunming, Yunnan, China. *Mem:* Am Inst Mining, Metall & Petrol Engrs (dir, 83-84); Am Inst Chem Engrs; Am Chem Soc; Sigma Xi; NAm Thermal Anal Soc. *Res:* Process metallurgy; self-propagating high temperature synthesis; oil shale conversion; gas-solid reactions; combustion of solids. *Mailing Add:* Dept Metall Eng Univ Utah Salt Lake City UT 84112-1183. *Fax:* 801-581-4937; *E-Mail:* hysohn@mines.utah.edu

SOHN, ISRAEL GREGORY, PALEONTOLOGY, MICROPALEONTOLOGY. *Current Pos:* Preparator, US Geol Surv, 41-42, geologist, 42-85, consult geologist, 85-91, EMER SCIENTIST, US GEOL SURV, 91- *Personal Data:* b Ukraine, Nov 12, 11; nat US; m 41, Bertha Schooler; c Vivian E & Daniel. *Educ:* City Col NY, BS, 35; Columbia Univ, AM, 38; Hebrew Univ, Israel, PhD, 66. *Concurrent Pos:* From assoc prof lectr to prof lectr, George Washington Univ, 58-68, adj prof, 69-; res assoc paleobiol, Smithsonian Inst, 60-; guest lectr, Hebrew Univ, Israel, 62-63 & Acad Sinica, Nanjing, Peoples Repub China, 79; res assoc, Smithsonian Inst, 68- *Mem:* Fel Geol Soc Am; Soc Econ Paleont & Mineral; Paleont Soc; Am Asn Petrol Geol. *Res:* Micropaleontology, especially post Devonian Ostracoda; video recording fossil and living ostracoda. *Mailing Add:* Nat Mus Natural Hist Rm E-308 MRC-13F Washington DC 20560. *Fax:* 202-343-8620

SOHN, KENNETH S (KYU SUK), ELECTRICAL ENGINEERING. *Current Pos:* asst prof, 66-69, ASSOC PROF ELEC ENG, NJ INST TECHNOL, 69- *Personal Data:* b Seoul, Korea, Aug 8, 33; m 62; c 2. *Educ:* Upsala Col, BS, 57; Stevens Inst Technol, MS, 59, ScD(elec eng), 67. *Prof Exp:* Instr elec eng, Stevens Inst Technol, 59-66. *Concurrent Pos:* Consult, NY Tel Co, 67-73. *Mem:* Inst Elec & Electronics Engrs; Sigma Xi. *Res:* Determination of the electrical conductivity of semi-conductors by optical method; non-magnetic-DC-DC converters; ultrasonic array scanner for non-invasively visualizing blood vessels; medical instrumentation; investigation of planar edge-contact Josephson Junction radiation detector and mixer. *Mailing Add:* Dept Elec Eng NJ Inst Technol 323 Martin L King Blvd Newark NJ 07102-1824

SOHN, YUNG JAI, CARDIOVASCULAR PHARMACOLOGY. *Current Pos:* CLIN PROF, UNIV CALIF, SAN FRANCISCO, 87- *Personal Data:* b Tokyo, Japan; US citizen; m 61, Vivian S Yim; c Andrew, Edward & Richard. *Educ:* Univ Rochester, BA, 58; State Univ NY, MD, 62. *Prof Exp:* From asst prof to assoc prof anesthesiol & pharmacol, Univ Miami, 70-75; assoc prof, Univ Calif, San Francisco, 75-87. *Concurrent Pos:* Sr scientist, Univ Groningen, Neth, 80-81; vis prof, Yonsei Univ, Korea, 85- *Mem:* NY Acad Sci; Sigma Xi; Am Surgical Asn; Am Soc Pharmacol & Exp Therapeut. *Res:* Neuromuscular pharmacology; autonomic neuropharmacology. *Mailing Add:* Dept Anesthesia Univ Calif Box 0648 San Francisco CA 94143-0648

SOHR, ROBERT TRUEMAN, CHEMICAL ENGINEERING, ENVIRONMENTAL HEALTH. *Current Pos:* TECH DIR & VPRES, ADA SYSTS, 88- *Personal Data:* b Green Bay, Wis, Apr 4, 37. *Educ:* Valparaiso Univ, BS, 60; Purdue Univ, BS, 61; Univ Chicago, MBA, 69. *Prof Exp:* Process engr, Natural Gas Pipeline Co Am, 60-67; cryogenic tech engr, Liquid Carbonic Div, Gen Dynamics, 67-69; regional mgr, US Stoneware Div, Norton, 69-72, Pollution Control Syst Div, Hormel, 72-75; exec vpres, Am Envirodyne Div, Pettibond, 75-78; US opers mgr, Tywood Industs, 78-79; tech dir, R T Sohr, PCHE, 79-88. *Concurrent Pos:* Nat speaker, Am Soc Heating, Refrig & Air Conditioning Engrs. *Mem:* Am Chem Soc; Am Inst Chemists; Am Inst Chem Engrs; Air Pollution Control Asn; Am Soc Heating, Refrig & Air Conditioning Engrs; Am Foundry Soc. *Res:* Development of a filtration system for solvent and heat recovery, and dust to allow recirculation; state of the art chemical absorbtion systems for foundry coreroom, corn wet milling and many other industrial applications; develop rubber deflashing with liquid N2 and blow molding with liquid CO2. *Mailing Add:* 4229 Grove Ave Gurnee IL 60031. *Fax:* 847-860-2934

SOICHER, HAIM, ELECTROMAGNETIC WAVE PROPAGATION, IONOSPHERIC PHYSICS. *Current Pos:* RES PHYS SCIENTIST, SPACE & TERRESTRIAL COMMUN DIRECTORATE, US ARMY COMMUN-ELECTRONIC COMMAND, 60- *Personal Data:* b Haifa, Israel, Dec 28, 36; US citizen; c Dean B, Neil E & Alan J. *Educ:* Brooklyn Col, BS, 59; NY Univ, MS, 61, PhD(physics), 72; Fairleigh Dickinson Univ, MBA, 79. *Concurrent Pos:* Prin, US Army Mem Study Group 3, Radio Commun Bur, Int Telecommun Union, 75-; mem & chmn, EM Wave Propagation Panel, NATO Adv Group Aerospace Res & Develop, 75-87, chmn, CECOM C3 Syst Directorate Res Coun, 85-95; US secy army fel, Technion-Israel Inst Technol, 80-81; assoc ed, Radio Sci, Am Geophys Union, 85-96; chmn, G/Int Union Radio Sci Comn, 90-93. *Mem:* Am Geophys Union; Int Union Radio Sci. *Res:* Conduct of both experimental and theoretical electromagnetics research with emphasis on electromagnetic wave propagation and ionospheric phenomena, modeling and predictions. *Mailing Add:* Attn AMSEL-RD-ST-WL-AA US Army CECOM Ft Monmouth NJ 07703-5203. *Fax:* 732-532-0456; *E-Mail:* soicher@doim6.monmouth.army.mil

SOIFER, ALEXANDER, COMBINATORIAL GEOMETRY, GIFTED EDUCATION. *Current Pos:* PROF MATH, ART HIST & FILM STUDIES, UNIV COLO, 79- *Personal Data:* b Moscow, Russia, Aug 14, 48; US citizen; m 90, Maya Kikoin; c Mark, Julia & Isabelle. *Educ:* Moscow State Pedagogical Univ, MS, 71, PhD(group theory), 73. *Prof Exp:* Assoc prof math, Karelsky Pedagogical Inst, 73-74; jr res staff, Inst Mach Theory, Moscow, 74-75; sr res staff, Inst Info, Moscow, 75-77; lectr, Univ Mass, 79. *Concurrent Pos:* Chair & founder, Colo Math Olympiad, 84-; secy, World Fedn Nat Math Competitions, 96-; mem, US Math Olympiad Subcomt, 96- *Mem:* World Fedn Nat Math Competitions; Math Asn Am. *Res:* Combinatorial geometry and Ramsey Theory and history of their emergence. *Mailing Add:* 885 Red Mesa Dr Colorado Springs CO 80906. *Fax:* 719-262-3140; *E-Mail:* asoifer@mail.uccs.edu

SOIFER, DAVID, CELLULAR & MOLECULAR NEUROBIOLOGY. *Current Pos:* PRIN, SOIFER ASSOCS, 95- *Personal Data:* b New York, NY, Sept 16, 37; m 60, Lea Yitshaki; c Hillel & Boaz. *Educ:* Swarthmore Col, Columbia Univ, BS, 61; Cornell Univ, PhD(anat), 69. *Prof Exp:* AMA fel regulatory biol, Inst Biomed Res, 68-70; sr res scientist, Inst Basic Res Develop Disabilities, 70-77, assoc res scientist, 77-86, dep dir, CSI/IBR Ctr Develop Neurosci & head, Lab Cell Biol, 87-95. *Concurrent Pos:* Vis asst prof anat, Col Med & vis asst prof cell biol, Grad Sch Med Sci, Cornell Univ, 70-77; assoc prof anat cell biol, State Univ NY Downstate Med Ctr, 77-86; prof biol, City Univ New York & Grad Ctr, 87-; writer & lectr. *Mem:* AAAS; Am Soc Cell Biol; Soc Neurosci; Am Soc Neurochem; Int Soc Neurochem. *Res:* Neurobiology; biology of microtubules; dynamics of the neuronal cytoskeleton; the molecular biology of neurofibrillary degeneration; function of cytoskeletal proteins in cells of the nervous system. *Mailing Add:* Soifer & Assocs 143 Nixon Ave Staten Island NY 10304. *Fax:* 718-727-1326; *E-Mail:* soifer@postbox.csi.cuny.edu

SOIFER, HERMAN, ENGINEERING. *Current Pos:* PARTNER, ALPERN & SOIFER CONSULT ENGRS, 71- *Personal Data:* US citizen. *Educ:* Cooper Union Sch Eng, BCE, 44. *Prof Exp:* From design engr to assoc, Consult Eng Firms, 46-71. *Concurrent Pos:* Adj instr, C W Post Sch Eng, 66-68. *Mem:* Am Soc Civil Engrs; Nat Soc Prof Engrs. *Res:* Sanitary and environmental engineering. *Mailing Add:* 1981 Carman Ct Merrick NY 11566

SOIKE, KENNETH FIEROE, VIROLOGY, CELL CULTURE. *Current Pos:* RETIRED. *Personal Data:* b Minneapolis, Minn, July 8, 27; m 78; c 3. *Educ:* Univ Minn, BA, 49; Ore State Univ, PhD(microbiol), 55. *Prof Exp:* Res assoc, Sterling Winthrop Res Inst, 55-61; assoc prof microbiol, Albany Med Col, 61-73; assoc dir res, Primate Res Inst, 73-75; sr res scientist, Delta Regional Primate Ctr, 75. *Concurrent Pos:* Adj prof, Primate Res Inst, NMex State Univ, 84-; consult. *Mem:* Am Soc Microbiol; Am Soc Virol; Int Soc Interferon Res; Int Soc Chemother; Int Soc Antiviral Res. *Res:* Evaluation of antiviral drugs and recombinant human interferons in the treatment of viral disease in nonhuman primates; pathogenesis of viral diseases in monkeys. *Mailing Add:* 17 Beth Dr Covington LA 70433

SOJKA, GARY ALLAN, MICROBIAL PHYSIOLOGY, GENETICS. *Current Pos:* prof biol, Bucknell Univ, 77, chmn, 78-84, dean arts & sci, 84-95, PRES, BUCKNELL UNIV, 95- *Personal Data:* b Cedar Rapids, Iowa, July 15, 40; m 62, Sandra K Smith; c 2. *Educ:* Coe Col, BA, 62; Purdue Univ, MS, 65, PhD(microbiol), 67. *Hon Degrees:* LLD, Lycomming Col, 96. *Prof Exp:* From res assoc to asst prof biol, Ind Univ, Bloomington, 67-72, assoc prof biol & assoc chmn dept, 72-78. *Concurrent Pos:* Comnr, Higher Educ Comt, Middle States Asn. *Mem:* AAAS; Am Soc Biochemists; Am Soc Microbiol. *Res:* Control of metabolism at a molecular level in photosynthetic bacteria. *Mailing Add:* Bucknell Univ Marts Hall Lewisburg PA 17837-2005. *Fax:* 717-524-3760

SOJKA, ROBERT E, SOIL & WATER CONSERVATION, CROP STRESS MANAGEMENT. *Current Pos:* soil scientist, USDA Agr Res Serv, SC, 78-86, SOIL SCIENTIST, USDA AGR RES SERV, ID, 86- *Personal Data:* b Chicago, Ill, Dec 28, 47. *Educ:* Univ Calif, Riverside, BA, 69, PhD(soil sci), 74. *Honors & Awards:* Technol Advan Award, Int Erosion Control Asn. *Prof Exp:* Lab asst, Soils Dept, Univ Riverside, 66-70, res asst, 70-74; res assoc, Agron Dept, Univ Ark, 74-76; asst prof soils, NDak State Univ, 76-78. *Concurrent Pos:* Adj assoc prof, Clemson Univ, 78-86; adj prof, Univ Idaho, 86-; tech ed, Soil Sci Soc Am J; assoc ed, Agron J, 85-89, Soil Sci Soc Am J, 86-91. *Mem:* Fel Am Soc Agron; fel Soil Sci Soc Am; Crop Sci Soc Am; Int Soc Soil Sci; Inst Soil & Tillage Res Orgn; Sigma Xi; Soil & Water Conserv Soc Am. *Res:* Physical edaphology, the study of the effects of soils physical properties on plant response, including the effects of soil compaction, aeration, temperature, flooding, and drought; conservation tillage; irrigation-induced erosion; surface water quality. *Mailing Add:* USDA-ARS 3793 N-3600 E Kimberly ID 83341. *E-Mail:* sojka@kimberly.ars.pn.usbr.gov

SOJKA, STANLEY ANTHONY, PHYSICAL ORGANIC CHEMISTRY. *Current Pos:* mgr environ technol, 80-85, DIR, NEW BUS DEVELOP, OCCIDENTAL CHEM CORP, 85- *Personal Data:* b Buffalo, NY, Nov 6, 46; m 70; c 2. *Educ:* Canisius Col, BS, 68; Ind Univ, Bloomington, PhD(org chem), 72. *Prof Exp:* Res assoc spectros, Nat Res Coun, 72-74; res chemist, Naval Res Lab, 74-76; sr res chemist, Hooker Chem & Plastics Corp, 76-80. *Mem:* Am Chem Soc; Com Develop Asn. *Res:* Using carbon-13 nuclear magnetic resonance spectroscopy to solve chemical problems; carbon-13 chemically induced dynamic nuclear polarization developed to gain knowledge about mechanism and kinetics of reactions. *Mailing Add:* Occidental Chem Corp PO Box 344 Niagara Falls NY 14302-0344

SOKAL, ROBERT REUVEN, POPULATION BIOLOGY, TAXONOMY. *Current Pos:* prof biol sci, State Univ NY, Stony Brook, 68-72, leading prof ecol & evolution, 71-91, chmn & dir grad studies, 80-83, actg vprovost res grad studies, 81-82, distinguished prof, 91-95, DISTINGUISHED EMER PROF ECOL & EVOLUTION, STATE UNIV NY, STONY BROOK, 95- *Personal Data:* b Vienna, Austria, Jan 13, 26; nat US; m 48; c 2. *Educ:* St John's Univ, China, BS, 47; Univ Chicago, PhD(zool), 52. *Hon Degrees:* DSc, Univ Crete, Iraklion, 90. *Prof Exp:* From instr to assoc prof entom, Univ Kans, 51-61, prof statist biol, 61-69. *Concurrent Pos:* Watkins scholar, Univ Ill, 56; NSF sr fel, Galton Lab, Univ Col, London, 59-60; Fulbright vis prof zool, Hebrew & Tel-Aviv Univs, Israel, 63-64; NIH career investr, 64-69; NATO sr fel, Cambridge Univ, 75; vis prof, Inst Advan Studies, Oeiras, Portugal, 71-80; vis distinguished scientist & Guggenheim Found fel, Univ Mich, 75-76; vis prof zool, Univ Vienna, 77 & 78, Fulbright vis prof human biol &

Guggenheim Found fel, 84; vis prof, Col France, Paris, 89; fel, Ctr Advan Study Behav Sci, Stanford, Calif, 92-93. *Mem:* Nat Acad Sci; hon fel Linnean Soc London; hon mem Soc Syst Zool; Am Soc Naturalists (ed, 69-74, pres, 84); Classification Soc (pres, 69-71); Soc Study Evolution (vpres, 67, pres, 77); fel AAAS; fel Am Acad Arts Sci; Int Fedn Classification Socs (vpres, 87, 90, pres, 88-89). *Res:* Geographic variation analysis; numerical taxonomy; theory of systematics; spatial models; human variation; European ethnohistory; human variation in relation to language and ethmohistory. *Mailing Add:* Dept Ecol & Evolution State Univ NY Stony Brook NY 11794-5245. *Fax:* 516-632-7626; *E-Mail:* sokal@life.bio.sunysb.edu

SOKATCH, JOHN ROBERT, BACTERIOLOGY. *Current Pos:* asst dean grad col, Univ Okla, 70, from asst prof to assoc prof, Sch Med, 58-67, assoc dean grad col, 71-77, assoc dir res admin, 73-77, prof microbiol, Sch Med, 67-84, PROF & CHMN, DEPT BIOCHEM & MOLECULAR BIOL, SCH MED, UNIV OKLA, 84- *Personal Data:* b Joliet, Ill, Dec 20, 28; m 57; c 3. *Educ:* Univ Mich, BS, 50; Univ Ill, MS, 52, PhD(bact), 56. *Prof Exp:* Res assoc chem, Wash State Univ, 56-58. *Concurrent Pos:* Fulbright sr res scholar, Sheffield, Eng, 63-64; USPHS res career develop award, 62-72; Fogarty sr int fel, Cambridge Univ, 79; vis prof, GBF, Graunschweig, Fed Rep Ger. *Mem:* Am Soc Microbiol; Am Soc Biol Chemists; Am Acad Microbiol; Sigma Xi. *Res:* Metabolism of branched chain amino acids by bacteria and regulation of catabolic pathways. *Mailing Add:* Dept Biochem BM 5B 953 Univ Okla Health Sci Ctr PO Box 26901 Oklahoma City OK 73190-0001. *Fax:* 405-271-3139

SOKOL, HILDA WEYL, NEUROENDOCRINOLOGY. *Current Pos:* res assoc, 61-63, from instr to prof, 63-95, EMER PROF PHYSIOL, DARTMOUTH MED SCH, 95- *Personal Data:* b St Louis, Mo, Dec 19, 28; m 51, Robert; c Kirstin, Niels & Heidi. *Educ:* Hunter Col, AB, 50; Harvard Univ, AM, 51, PhD, 57. *Prof Exp:* Instr sci, Boston Univ, 54-55; instr zool, Wellesley Col, 55-58; res assoc physiol, Harvard Med Sch, 60-61. *Concurrent Pos:* Adj prof biol & prof liberal studies, Dartmouth Col; sr int fel, NIH Fogarty Int Ctr, 75-76. *Mem:* Fel AAAS; Am Soc Zoologists; Endocrine Soc; Asn Women Sci. *Res:* Comparative endocrinology; cytology and physiology of the pituitary gland and hypothalamus; releasing factors, anterior and posterior pituitary hormones; diabetes insipidus; sexual dimorphism. *Mailing Add:* Dept Physiol Dartmouth Med Sch Hanover NH 03755-3836. *Fax:* 603-650-1130

SOKOL, ROBERT JAMES, OBSTETRICS & GYNECOLOGY, COMPUTER SCIENCE & MATERNAL-FETAL MEDICINE. *Current Pos:* dir, CS Mott Ctr Human Growth & Develop, Wayne State Univ, 83-89; chmn obstet & gynec, 83-89, interim dean, Sch Med, 88-89, PROF OBSTET & GYNEC, WAYNE STATE UNIV, 83-; DEAN, SCH MED, 89-, SR VPRES MED AFFAIRS, DETROIT MED CTR, 92- *Personal Data:* b Rochester, NY, Nov 18, 41; m 64, Roberta S Kahn; c Melissa A, Eric R & Andrew I. *Educ:* Univ Rochester, BA, 63, MD, 66; Am Bd Obstet & Gynec, dipl, 72, cert maternal-fetal med, 75. *Prof Exp:* Intern & resident obstet & gynec, Barnes Hosp, Wash Univ, 66-70; from obstetrician & gynecologist to chief obstetrician & gynecologist, USAF Hosp, Ellsworth AFB, 70-72; asst prof obstet & gynec, Sch Med & Dent, Univ Rochester, 72-73; from asst prof to prof obstet & gynec, Case Western Res Univ, 73-83; chief obstet & gynec, Hutzel Hosp, 83-89. *Concurrent Pos:* Buswell fel maternal-fetal med, Strong Mem Hosp, Sch Med & Dent, Univ Rochester, 72-73; asst prog dir, Perinatal Clin Res Ctr, Cleveland Metrop Gen Hosp, 73-78, co-prog dir, 73-81, prog dir, 81-83 & assoc dir, Dept Obstet & Gynec, 81-83; fel maternal-fetal med, Cleveland Metrop Gen Hosp & Case Western Res Univ, 74-75; consult, Nat Inst Child Health & Human Develop, 78-79 & 84-, Nat Inst Alcohol Abuse & alcoholism, 79-, Ctr Dis Control, 81, Nat Inst Health, 82-83, Health Resources & Serv Admin, 84; mem, Alcohol Psychosocial Res Rev Comt & Nat Inst Alcohol Abuse & Alcoholism, 82-; assoc examr, Am Bd Obstet & Gynec, 84-86; grad fac, Dept Physiol, Wayne State Univ, 84-, chmn med bd, Detroit Med Ctr, 84-, trustee, 90-; mem, Comt Study Fetal Alchol Syndrome, Inst Med-Nat Acad Sci, 94-96. *Mem:* Inst Med-Nat Acad Sci; Perinatal Res Soc; Res Soc Alcoholism; Soc Gynec Invest; Soc Perinatal Obstetricians; Am Col Obstet & Gynecologists; Behav Teratology Soc; Sigma Xi; Am Gynec & Obstet Soc; AMA. *Res:* Perinatal risk assessment; database management and statistical analysis; alcohol-related birth defects; low birth weight risks and outcomes; algorithmic diagnosis and management; medical informatics; fetal alcohol syndrome. *Mailing Add:* Deans Off Wayne State Univ Sch Med 540 E Canfield St Detroit MI 48201-1928. *Fax:* 313-577-8777; *E-Mail:* rsokol@moose.med.wayne.edu

SOKOL, RONALD JAY, PEDIATRIC GASTROENTEROLOGY & NUTRITION, PEDIATRIC LIVER DISEASE. *Current Pos:* asst prof, 83-88, assoc prof, 88-95, PROF PEDIAT, UNIV COLO SCH MED, 95- *Personal Data:* b Chicago, Ill, July 18, 50; m 89, Lori Lubman; c Skylar & Jared. *Educ:* Univ Ill, Urbana, BS, 72; Univ Chicago Pritzker Sch Med, MD, 76. *Honors & Awards:* First Award, NIH, 87; Mead Johnson Award, Am Inst Nutrit, 90. *Prof Exp:* Pediat resident, Univ Colo Health Sci Ctr, 76-79, chief resident, 79-80; fel pediat gastroenterol & nutrit, Childrens Hosp Res Found, Cincinnati, 80-83. *Concurrent Pos:* Grants Rev Comt, Am Liver Found, 85-88, mem, Children's Liver Coun, 96; chmn, Res Comt, NAm Soc Pediat Gastroenterol & Nutrit, 89-92; res grant, NIH, 93. *Mem:* Am Acad Pediat; Am Asn Study Liver Dis; Am Gastroenterol Asn; NAm Soc Pediat Gastroenterol & Nutrit (pres, 93-95); Am Inst Nutrit; Am Soc Clin Nutrit; Soc Pediat Res. *Res:* Causes, mechanisms and treatment of human vitamin E deficiency states; investigation of mechanisms of hepatocyte injury in cholestasis and copper overload states; mitochondrial function in liver injury; free radical injury in the liver. *Mailing Add:* Dept Pediat Div Pediat Gastroenterol & Nutrit Box B290 Children's Hosp 1056 E 19th Ave Denver CO 80218. *Fax:* 303-764-8025; *E-Mail:* sokol.ronald@tchden.org

SOKOLICH, WILLIAM GARY, SOUND & VIBRATION, MEASUREMENT & ANALYSIS. *Current Pos:* CONSULT SCIENTIST & ENGR, 85- *Personal Data:* b Mar 14, 46. *Educ:* Loyola Univ, BSEE, 69; Syracuse Univ, PhD(sensory sci), 77. *Prof Exp:* Elect serv technician, Goebel TV, 62-69; advan prog engr, Gen Elec Co, 69-70; postdoctoral fel, Johns Hopkins Univ, 76-77; grad res asst, Inst Sensory Res, 71-75; asst prof, Sch Med, Univ Calif, Los Angeles, 77-78, asst prof, 78-83; western regional appl engr, Bruel & Kjaer Instruments, 83-85. *Concurrent Pos:* NASA fel, 70; NIH fel, 77; Univ Calif, Los Angeles, Acad Grant, 79, Deafness Res Found Grant, 79-80, NIH Res Grant, 81-83. *Mem:* Inst Elec & Electronics Engrs; Acoust Soc Am; Audio Eng Soc; Soc Am Inventors. *Res:* Consulting scientist and engineer - sound and vibration measurements and analysis; two-channel FFT applications; transduced selection, design, evaluation. *Mailing Add:* 801 Kings Rd Newport Beach CA 92663. *E-Mail:* wgscse@earthlink.net

SOKOLOFF, ALEXANDER, ECOLOGICAL GENETICS. *Current Pos:* assoc prof, Natural Sci Div, 65-66, prof biol, 66-90, EMER PROF BIOL, CALIF STATE COL, SAN BERNARDINO, 90- *Personal Data:* b Tokyo, Japan, May 16, 20; nat US; m 56, Barbara B Bryant; c N Alexandra, Elaine A & Michael A. *Educ:* Univ Calif, Los Angeles, AB, 48; Univ Chicago, PhD(ecol), 54. *Prof Exp:* Res assoc cancer, Univ Chicago, 54, instr biol, 55; from instr to asst prof biol, Hofstra Col, 55-58; geneticist, William H Miner Agr Res Inst, NY, 58-60; assoc res botanist, Univ Calif, Los Angeles, 60-61, assoc res geneticist, Univ Calif, Berkeley, 61-66. *Concurrent Pos:* NSF res grant, Cold Spring Harbor Lab Quant Biol, 58-60; ed, Tribolium Info Bull, 60-; USPHS res grant, 61; res geneticist, Univ Calif, Berkeley, 66-68; NSF res grants, 67-75; assoc ed, Evolution, 72-74; chmn, Subcomt Insect Stocks, Comt for Maintenance of Genetic Stocks, Genetics Soc Am, 74-85; res grant, Army Res Off, 74-79; dir, Tribolium Stock Ctr, 61-; assoc ed, J Advan Zool, India, 80- *Mem:* Am Soc Zoologists; Am Soc Nat; Am Genetic Soc; Genetics Soc Am; Entom Soc Am; Soc Study Evolution; fel Royal Entom Soc London; Genetics Soc Can; Japanese Soc Pop Ecol; Sigma Xi. *Res:* Population ecological genetics of Tribolium; genetic control of flour beetles. *Mailing Add:* Dept Biol Calif State Univ San Bernardino CA 92407. *Fax:* 909-880-7005; *E-Mail:* asokolof@wiley.cscsb.edu

SOKOLOFF, JEFFREY BRUCE, SOLID STATE PHYSICS. *Current Pos:* PROF PHYSICS, NORTHEASTERN UNIV, 69- *Personal Data:* b New York, NY, Oct 7, 41; m 68; c 3. *Educ:* Queen's Col, NY, BS, 63; Mass Inst Technol, PhD(physics), 67. *Prof Exp:* Res assoc, Brookhaven Nat Lab, 67-69. *Concurrent Pos:* Vis mem staff, Weitzmann Inst, 79-80; vis prof, Ariz State Univ, 88. *Mem:* Am Phys Soc. *Res:* Magnetic and transport properties of metallic ferromagnets and ferrites; charge density wave conductivity in one-dimensional conductors; theory of ideal friction between sliding solid surfaces; excitations in crystals with two incommensurate periods; vibrations of DNA in solution. *Mailing Add:* Dept Physics Northeastern Univ Boston MA 02115

SOKOLOFF, LEON, PATHOLOGY. *Current Pos:* prof path, 73-89, EMER PROF PATH, STATE UNIV NY STONY BROOK, 89- *Personal Data:* b Brooklyn, NY, May 9, 19; m 71, Beverly Beinfeld; c Michael & Naomi. *Educ:* NY Univ, BA, 38, MD, 44. *Honors & Awards:* Philip Hench Award, 65; Van Breemen Award, Dutch Rheumatism Asn, 66. *Prof Exp:* Asst prof path, NY Univ, 50-52; chief sect rheumatic dis, Lab Exp Path, Nat Inst Arthritis, Metab & Digestive Dis, 53-73. *Concurrent Pos:* Mem, path study sect, NIH, 56-60, gen med A, 78-84; vis prof, Royal Soc Med, 85. *Mem:* AAAS; Harvey Soc; Am Soc Invest Path; master Am Col Rheumatism; hon mem Europ Soc Osteoarthrology; hon mem AmCol Vet Path. *Res:* Pathology of rheumatic diseases. *Mailing Add:* State Univ NY Stony Brook Health Sci Ctr Stony Brook NY 11794-8691. *Fax:* 516-444-3424; *E-Mail:* lsokolof@path.som.sunysb.edu

SOKOLOFF, LOUIS, PHYSIOLOGY, BIOCHEMISTRY. *Current Pos:* assoc chief sect cerebral metab, 53-56, chief, Lab Clin Sci, 56-68, CHIEF LAB CEREBRAL METAB, NIMH, 68- *Personal Data:* b Philadelphia, Pa, Oct 14, 21; m 47, Betty J Kaiser; c Kenneth L & Ann L. *Educ:* Univ Pa, BA, 43, MD, 46. *Hon Degrees:* MD, Univ Lund, 80, Univ Rome, 92; DSc, Albert Einstein Col Med, 82, Yeshiva Univ, 82, Univ Glasgow, 89, Georgetown Univ, 92, Mich State Univ, 93. *Honors & Awards:* F O Schmitt Award, 80; Albert Lasker Clin Med Res Award, 81; Karl Spencer Lashley Award, 87; Nat Acad Sci Award Neurosci, 88. *Prof Exp:* Intern, Philadelphia Gen Hosp, 46-47; res fel physiol, Grad Sch Med, Univ Pa, 49-51, instr physiol, 51-54, assoc, 54-56. *Concurrent Pos:* Vis prof, Col France, 68-69; clin prof, Georgetown Univ, 75- *Mem:* Nat Acad Sci; sr mem Inst Med-Nat Acad Sci; Am Soc Biol Chemists; Am Neurol Asn; Am Physiol Soc; Am Soc Neurochem; AAAS. *Res:* Cerebral circulation and metabolism; neurochemistry; biochemical basis of hormone actions; protein biosynthesis; thyroxine; functional brain imaging. *Mailing Add:* Lab Cerebral Metab NIMH Bldg 36 Rm 1A-05 Bethesda MD 20892

SOKOLOFF, VLADIMIR P, geochemistry; deceased, see previous edition for last biography

SOKOLOSKI, MARTIN MICHAEL, CONDENSED MATTER PHYSICS, MATHEMATICS. *Current Pos:* MGR ELECTRONICS, NASA, 79- *Personal Data:* b Freeland, Pa, Sept 7, 37; m 62; c 3. *Educ:* Bucknell Univ, BS, 59, MS, 60; Catholic Univ Am, PhD(physics), 69. *Prof Exp:* Mathematician, Dept Defense, Nat Security Agency, 60-61; aerospace technician, NASA Goddard Space Flight Ctr, 61-63, aerospace engr, 63-66; res assoc, Catholic Univ Am, 70-71; mem staff, Harry Diamond Labs, 71-79. *Mem:* Am Phys Soc; AAAS. *Res:* Determination of the nature of interface electronic states; theoretical studies of the static and dynamic properties of disordered systems; many body problems; basic research management. *Mailing Add:* 8515 Rhode Island Ave College Park MD 20740

SOKOLOSKI, THEODORE DANIEL, PHARMACY, PHYSICAL CHEMISTRY. *Current Pos:* from asst prof to assoc prof, 64-73, PROF PHARMACEUT & PHARMACEUT CHEM, OHIO STATE UNIV, 73- *Personal Data:* b Philadelphia, Pa, July 10, 33; m 61; c 3. *Educ:* Temple Univ, BS, 55; Univ Wis, Madison, MS, 59, PhD(pharm), 61. *Prof Exp:* Asst prof pharm, Wash State Univ, 61-64. *Mem:* Am Chem Soc; Am Pharmaceut Asn; Acad Pharmaceut Sci. *Res:* Application of physical chemistry to pharmaceutical systems. *Mailing Add:* R & D VW-2913 Smith Kline Beecham Pharmaceut 709 Swedeland Rd PO Box 1539 King of Prussia PA 19406-0939

SOKOLOVE, PHILLIP GARY, NEUROBIOLOGY, BIOPHYSICS. *Current Pos:* from asst prof to assoc prof, 72-83, PROF BIOL, UNIV MD, BALTIMORE COUNTY, 83-, ASSOC DEAN ARTS & SCI, 87- *Personal Data:* b Los Angeles, Calif, Aug 24, 42; div; c 1. *Educ:* Univ Calif, Berkeley, AB, 64; Harvard Univ, PhD(biophysics), 69. *Prof Exp:* Actg asst prof neurobiol, Stanford Univ, 71-72. *Concurrent Pos:* Res assoc, Stanford Univ, 72-74; consult, SRI Int, 72-79; Carnegie Sci fel, 82-83. *Mem:* Am Soc Zoologists; Soc Gen Physiologists; Soc Neurosci; Am Physiol Soc; AAAS; Sigma Xi. *Res:* Biological circadian rhythms; reproductive neuroendocrinology in molluscs; behavioral neurobiology. *Mailing Add:* Dept Biol Sci Univ Md Baltimore County 5401 Wilkens Ave Baltimore MD 21228-5329

SOKOLOW, MAURICE, MEDICINE. *Current Pos:* clin instr med, Univ Calif, San Francisco, 40-45, lectr, 45-46, from asst prof to prof, 46-78, chief, Electrocardiogram Dept, Univ Hosp, 46-78, chief, Cardiovasc Serv, Univ Hosp, 58-74, EMER PROF MED, SCH MED, UNIV CALIF, SAN FRANCISCO, 78- *Personal Data:* b New York, NY, May 19, 11; wid; c 2. *Educ:* Univ Calif, AB, 32, MD, 36; Am Bd Internal Med & Cardiovasc Dis, dipl. *Prof Exp:* Intern, San Francisco Hosp, Calif, 35-36; asst resident med, Univ Calif Hosp, 36-37; resident physician, New Eng Med Ctr, Boston, Mass, 37-38; researcher cardiovasc dis, Michael Reese Hosp, 38-39. *Concurrent Pos:* Res fel med, Sch Med, Univ Calif, San Francisco, 39-40, vis physician, 40-47; attend cardiologist, Langley Porter Clin, 46-; consult, Vet Admin Hosps, San Francisco & Oakland, Calif, 46-; researcher, Nat Heart Hosp, London, 53-54; mem, Coun Arteriosclerosis, Am Heart Asn. *Mem:* Fel Am Col Physicians; Am Soc Clin Invest; Asn Univ Cardiologists; hon fel Am Col Cardiol; Am Fedn Clin Res (vpres, 49). *Res:* Rheumatic fever; electrocardiography; hypertension; cardiac arrhythmias; cardiac failure. *Mailing Add:* M312 Box 0214 Univ Calif San Francisco CA 94143-0001

SOKOLOWSKI, DANNY HALE, SOLID STATE PHYSICS. *Current Pos:* GLOBAL PROJ MGR, WHIRLPOOL, 96- *Personal Data:* b Alton, Ill, June 1, 38; m 65; c 2. *Educ:* Southern Ill Univ, AB, 61; Univ Mo, Rolla, MS, 63; St Louis Univ, PhD(physics), 74. *Prof Exp:* Instr physics, Southern Ill Univ, 63-66, Marquette Univ, 69-71; assoc prof, Lewis & Clark Community Col, 71-81; corp mgr telecommun, Gen Dynamics Co, 83-89; mgr telecommun, Dow Corning Corp, 89-96. *Mem:* Am Phys Soc; Sigma Xi; Am Asn Physics Teachers. *Res:* Electrical and thermoelectrical properties of semiconductors. *Mailing Add:* 1905 Langley Ave St Joseph MI 49085-1738

SOKOLOWSKI, HENRY ALFRED, PHYSICS, MATHEMATICS. *Current Pos:* Physicist, 51-56, chief propellant physics, 56-61, chief Ballistics Lab, 61-71, chief Test Instrumentation Div, 71-74, chief Test & Eval Div, 74-76, DIR TECH SUPPORT DIRECTORATE, FRANKFORD ARSENAL, 77- *Personal Data:* b Hamtramck, Mich, Jan 21, 23; m 55; c 3. *Educ:* Univ Pa, AB, 57. *Mem:* Sigma Xi. *Res:* Ballistic, environmental materials test and evaluation utilizing the disciplines of physics, mathematics, metallurgy, chemistry, electrical engineering, mechanical engineering and associated specialized scientific fields. *Mailing Add:* 2731 Kirkbride St Philadelphia PA 19137

SOKOLSKI, WALTER THOMAS, MICROBIOLOGY. *Current Pos:* RETIRED. *Personal Data:* b Newark, NJ, Oct 29, 16; wid; c Thomas & Camille (Chartrand). *Educ:* Ind Univ, AB, 48; Purdue Univ, MS, 53, PhD(bact), 55. *Honors & Awards:* Award, Am Soc Microbiol, 52. *Prof Exp:* Serologist, Venereal Dis Res Lab, USPHS, 45-46; chemist, Parke, Davis & Co, 48-51; microbiologist, Upjohn Co, 54-59, head spec microbiol methods, Control Div, 59-67, head microbiol res, 67-70, mem staff infectious dis res, 70-78. *Concurrent Pos:* Consult antibiotic fermentation, Panlabs Taiwan Inc, Taiwan, 80-81; clin microbiol consult. *Mem:* Am Soc Microbiol; Am Soc Med Technol; Am Soc Clin Path; Soc Protozool; Soc Cryobiol. *Res:* Screening methods for new antibiotics; paper and column chromatography; microbiological assay for antibiotics; in vitro methodology in clinical research; environmental control. *Mailing Add:* 3304 Cranbrook Kalamazoo MI 49006-2020

SOLAND, RICHARD MARTIN, OPERATIONS RESEARCH. *Current Pos:* chair, Dept Opers Res, 89-92, assoc dean, Sch Eng, 92-95, PROF OPERS RES, GEORGE WASHINGTON UNIV, 78- *Personal Data:* b New York, NY, July 27, 40; m 79, My Linh Duong; c Caroline, Valerie, Francois, Peter & Myriam. *Educ:* Rensselaer Polytech Inst, BEE, 61; Mass Inst Technol, PhD(math), 64. *Prof Exp:* Mem tech staff, Advan Res Dept, Res Anal Corp, 64-71; assoc prof statist-opers res, Univ Tex, Austin, 71-76; assoc prof, Dept Indust Eng, Ecole Polytech, Univ Montreal, 76-78. *Concurrent Pos:* Asst prof lectr, Dept Bus Admin, George Washington Univ, 65-68, assoc prof lectr, Dept Eng Admin, 68-69; Fulbright lectr, Helsinki Sch Econ, Finland, 69-70; vis prof, Res Ctr, Inst d Admin des Enterprises, Univ Aix-Marseille, Aix-en-Provence, France, 73-74; vis prof, Carabobo Univ, Valencia, Venezuela, 75, Univ Copenhagen, Denmark, 82 & 88; conf chmn, Tenth Triennial Conf Oper Res, 84; consult, Inst Defense Anal, 83-85 & 90-95, Anal Serv Inc, 86-89, Logicon RDA, 90- *Mem:* Inst Opers Res & Mgt Sci; Inst Elec & Electronics Engrs; Math Programming Soc; Can Opers Res Soc; Inst Indust Engrs. *Res:* Multiple criteria decision making; branch-and-bound methods in mathematical programming; applications of mathematical programming; mathematical modeling; facility location; decision analysis; Bayesian statistics; missile defense models. *Mailing Add:* Dept Opers Res George Washington Univ Washington DC 20052. *Fax:* 202-994-0245; *E-Mail:* soland@seas.gwu.edu

SOLANKI, RAJ, FLAT-PANEL DISPLAYS, OPTICAL DEVICES. *Current Pos:* ASSOC PROF, ORE GRAD INST, 86- *Educ:* Dallas Univ, BS, 72; Univ Ill, MS, 75; Colo State Univ, PhD(physics), 82. *Prof Exp:* Fel, Johns Hopkins Univ, 82-83; asst prof, Colo State Univ, 83-86. *Res:* Optical properties of solid state devices; emissive flat-panel displays, electroluminescent displays. *Mailing Add:* PO Box 91000 Portland OR 97291-1000

SOLARI, MARIO JOSE ADOLFO, metallurgy, welding, for more information see previous edition

SOLARO, R JOHN, PROTEIN PHOSPHORYLATION & REGULATION. *Current Pos:* PROF PHYSIOL, SCH MED, UNIV CINCINNATI, 81- *Educ:* Univ Pittsburgh Sch Med, PhD(physiol), 71. *Res:* Calcium binding proteins. *Mailing Add:* Univ Ill-Chicago 835 S Wolcott Ave Rm E202 Chicago IL 60612-7342. *Fax:* 312-996-1414; *E-Mail:* Bitnet: u37241@uicvm

SOLBERG, JAMES J, INDUSTRIAL ENGINEERING, OPERATIONS RESEARCH. *Current Pos:* assoc prof, 72-81, PROF INDUST ENG, PURDUE UNIV, 81-, DIR, ENG RES CTR, 81- *Personal Data:* b Toledo, Ohio, May 27, 42; m 66. *Educ:* Harvard Col, BA, 64; Univ Mich, MA & MS, 67, PhD(indust eng), 69. *Prof Exp:* Asst prof indust eng, Univ Toledo, 68-72. *Mem:* Nat Acad Eng; Opers Res Soc Am; Inst Mgt Sci; Am Inst Indust Eng; Soc Mgf Eng; AAAS. *Res:* Graph theory; queueing theory; scheduling; probability; computer aided manufacturing. *Mailing Add:* Sch Indust Eng 114 Potter Purdue Univ West Lafayette IN 47907

SOLBERG, MYRON, FOOD SCIENCE, FOOD MICROBIOLOGY. *Current Pos:* from asst prof to assoc prof, 64-70, PROF FOOD SCI, RUTGERS UNIV, NEW BRUNSWICK, 70-, DIR, CTR ADVAN FOOD TECHNOL, 85-, ASOC DIR, NJ AGR EXPER STA, 91- *Personal Data:* b Boston, Mass, June 11, 31; m 56, Rona Bernstein; c Sara, Julie & Laurence. *Educ:* Univ Mass, BS, 52; Mass Inst Technol, PhD(food technol), 60. *Honors & Awards:* Distinguished Food Scientist, NY, Inst Food Technologists, 81, Nicholas Appert Medalist, Inst Food Technologists, 89. *Prof Exp:* Res asst food technol, Mass Inst Technol, 54-60; qual control mgr, Colonial Provision Co, 60-64. *Concurrent Pos:* Lectr, Meat Sci Inst, 65-72; vis prof food eng & biotechnol, Israel Inst Technol, 73-74; co-ed, J Food Safety, 77-87. *Mem:* Fel AAAS; fel Inst Food Technologists; Am Soc Qual Control; Am Soc Microbiol; Am Meat Sci Asn; fel Am Chem Soc. *Res:* Mode of action of microbial inhibition; assurance of microbiological safety in mass-feeding; regulation of toxinogenesis in clostridium perfringens; industry-university cooperative research systems development. *Mailing Add:* 415 Grant Ave Highland Park NJ 08904-2628. *Fax:* 732-932-8690

SOLBERG, RUELL FLOYD, JR, ELECTROMECHANICS, RESEARCH & DEVELOPMENT. *Current Pos:* res engr, 67-70, sr res engr, 70-87, PRIN ENGR, SIGNAL EXPLOITATION & GEOLOCATION DIV, SOUTHWEST RES INST, 87- *Personal Data:* b Norse, Tex, July 27, 39; m 59, Laquetta J Massey; c Chandra D (Hamilton) & Marla G (Dougherty). *Educ:* Univ Tex, Austin, BS, 62, MS, 67; Trinity Univ, MBA, 77. *Honors & Awards:* Centennial Medallion, Am Soc Mech Engrs, 80, Bd Gov Cert, 82, 83, 84, 85, 87, 89, 92, 95 & 96; Clifford H Shumaker Award, 90; Dedicated Serv Award, Am Soc Mech Engrs, 94. *Prof Exp:* Res engr & assoc II, Underwater Acoustics Div, Appl Res Labs, Univ Tex, 62-65, res engr, assoc III & asst supvr, Mech Eng Sect, 66-67. *Concurrent Pos:* Tech asst, Appl Mech Rev, 80-83. *Mem:* Sigma Xi; fel Am Soc Mech Engrs; Nat Soc Prof Engrs; Soc Allied Weight Engrs; Instrument Soc Am. *Res:* Structural optimization; mechanical design; response of structures to periodic and impulsive loading; behavioral science; flexible automation; material fatigue; environmental effects; zero-gravity in space flight; oceanography; management science; human factors; corrosion; mass measurement in microgravity. *Mailing Add:* 5906 Forest Cove San Antonio TX 78240-3429. *Fax:* 210-522-2709; *E-Mail:* rsolberg@swri.org

SOLBRIG, OTTO THOMAS, PLANT ECOLOGY. *Current Pos:* prof biol, Harvard Univ, 69-83, dir, Gray Herbarium & supvr, Bussey Inst, 78-83, Paul C Mangelsdorf prof natural sci, 83-87, BUSSEY PROF BIOL, HARVARD UNIV, 87- *Personal Data:* b Buenos Aires, Arg, Dec 21, 30; US citizen; m 56; c 2. *Educ:* Univ Calif, Berkeley, PhD(bot), 59. *Hon Degrees:* MA, Harvard Univ, 69. *Honors & Awards:* Cong Medal; Willdenow Medal, Berlin Bot Garden. *Prof Exp:* Botanist, Harvard Univ, 59-61, from asst cur to assoc cur, 61-66; from assoc prof to prof, Univ Mich, Ann Arbor & biosystematist, Bot Gardens, 66-69. *Concurrent Pos:* Hon travel fel, Univ Calif, Berkeley, 59-60; NSF & Am Acad Arts & Sci grants, 59-; lectr, Harvard Univ, 64-66; secy gen, Int Orgn Plant Biosysts, 64-69; mem, Int Orgn Biosysts & Orgn Trop Studies; dir, Struct Ecosystems Prog, US/IBP, 70-75; mem, IUBS Comt, Nat Acad Sci, 75-80; dir, Decade of the tropics prog. *Mem:* Int Union Biol Sci (pres, 85-88); Genetics Soc Am; Soc Study Evolution (secy, 73-78, pres, 81-82); Sigma Xi (secy-treas, 76-82); fel Am Acad Arts & Sci; fel AAAS; Latin Am Study Soc; Ecol Soc Am; Brit Ecol Asn. *Res:* Cytotaxonomical and cytogenetical studies of plant species; chemical and physiological studies of natural plant population; evolution of plants; plant population biology; resources and humans in Latin America; savana ecosystem. *Mailing Add:* Harvard Univ 26 Oxford St Cambridge MA 02138-2902

SOLC, KAREL, PHYSICAL CHEMISTRY. *Current Pos:* res scientist, 71-74, SR RES SCIENTIST, MICH MOLECULAR INST, 74-, PROF POLYMER CHEM, 84- *Personal Data:* b Nachod, Czech, July 25, 33; m 57, Jitka Hajna; c Charles & Paul. *Educ:* Inst Chem Technol, Prague, Czech, MSc, 56; Czech Acad Sci, PhD(macromolecular chem), 61. *Honors & Awards:* Josef Hlavka Mem Medal, Czechoslovak Acad Sci, 92. *Prof Exp:* From scientist to sr scientist, Inst Macromolecular Chem, Czech Acad Sci, 61-68; res instr chem, Dartmouth Col, 71. *Concurrent Pos:* NSF vis fel, Dartmouth Col, 68-70; Mich Found Advan Res vis fel, 70-71; fel, Japan Soc Promotion Sci Res, 85. *Mem:* AAAS; Am Chem Soc; Am Phys Soc; Sigma Xi. *Res:* Physical chemistry of polymers; statistical mechanics and thermodynamics; chain statistics; chemical kinetics; phase diagrams. *Mailing Add:* 4310 James Dr Midland MI 48642-3780. *Fax:* 517-832-5560

SOLDANO, BENNY A, PHYSICAL CHEMISTRY. *Current Pos:* prof chem, 71-77, PROF PHYSICS, FURMAN UNIV, 71- *Personal Data:* b Utica, NY, Nov 17, 21; m 46; c 2. *Educ:* Alfred Univ, BS, 43; Univ Wis, PhD(phys chem), 49. *Prof Exp:* From chemist to sr chemist, Oak Ridge Nat Lab, Tenn, 49-71. *Mem:* Am Chem Soc. *Res:* Ion exchange; thermodynamics; kinetics; solution chemistry. *Mailing Add:* 114 W Pasadana Lane Oakridge TN 37830-6301

SOLDAT, JOSEPH KENNETH, HEALTH PHYSICS, RADIOLOGICAL PHYSICS. *Current Pos:* RETIRED. *Personal Data:* b Chicago, Ill, May 4, 26; m 52, Mary Davis; c Kelvin L, Kathryn A & Dennis L. *Educ:* Univ Colo, BS, 48; Am Bd Health Physics, cert, 61. *Prof Exp:* Indust hyg engr, Med Ctr, Univ Colo, 48; from technician to sr engr, Gen Elec Co, Wash, 48-65; sr res scientist, Pac Northwest Labs, Battelle Mem Inst, 65-73, res assoc, 73-76, staff environ scientist, 77-96. *Concurrent Pos:* Bd dirs, Environ Radiation Sect, Health Physics Soc, 90-93. *Mem:* AAAS; Am Chem Soc; fel Health Physics Soc. *Res:* Human doses from environmental radiation sources; movement of radionuclides through the biosphere to man; radioactive waste management; surveillance of waste effluents and the environs for radioactive and nonradioactive materials. *Mailing Add:* Pac Northwest Labs 2408 Torbett St Battelle Mem Inst PO Box 999 Richland WA 99352

SOLDATI, GIANLUIGI, INORGANIC CHEMISTRY. *Current Pos:* sr synthetic chemist, Carter-Wallace, Inc, 70-75, sr res chemist, 75-78, group leader, 78-90, mgr, 90-93, DIR, CARTER PROD RES DIV, CARTER-WALLACE, INC, 93- *Personal Data:* b Bologna, Italy, Feb 17, 37; m 86, Doris Kowalski; c Lisa & Vanda. *Educ:* Univ Bologna, DSc(org chem), 61, Columbia Univ, Cosmetic Technol, dipl, 76-78. *Prof Exp:* Petrol Res Fund fel, Univ Mass, 62; lectr & res assoc org & anal chem, Univ Bologna, 63-64; phys & org chem, 64-65; sr res chemist, Agr Chem, Uniroyal, Inc, Conn, 65-70. *Mem:* Soc Cosmetic Chemists; Am Chem Soc. *Res:* Antihypertensive agents; inorganic antiperspirans; depilatory agents; polymers; synthesis of antiperspirant salts and complexes; synthesis and study of new anticalculus and anticaries materials; anticholinergics and antihypertensive agents; patent writing and liaison with Legal Department; surfactants; emulsion technology; product development cosmetics and toiletries; antiperspirant product development. *Mailing Add:* Carter Prod Res-POB 1001 Div Carter-Wallace Inc Cranbury NJ 08512. *Fax:* 609-655-6417

SOLDIN, STEVEN JOHN, CLINICAL CHEMISTRY, BIOCHEMISTRY. *Current Pos:* DIR CLIN CHEM, CHILDRENS NAT MED CTR & PROF PATH & PEDIAT, GEORGE WASHINGTON UNIV, 88- *Personal Data:* m 90, Offie Tsafriri; c Beverley, Elana, Belinda & Danielle. *Educ:* Univ Witwatersrand, BSc (Hons), 62, MSc, 65, PhD(biochem), 68; Univ Toronto, dipl clin chem, 76. *Honors & Awards:* Res Excellence Award, Can Soc Clin Chem, 93; Pippenger Award, Int Asn Therapeut Drug Monitoring & Clin Toxicol, 95; Alvin Dubin Award, Nat Acad Clin Biochem, 97. *Prof Exp:* Assoc biochemist & dir therapeut drug monitoring, Hosp Sick Children, Toronto, 75-87. *Concurrent Pos:* Co-ed chief, Therapeut Drug Monitoring, 90-; chmn, Capital Sect Am Asn Clin Chem, 95. *Mem:* Am Asn Clin Chem; Nat Acad Clin Biochem (pres, 88-90); Am Bd Clin Chem (pres, 90-91); Can Soc Clin Chem. *Res:* Pediatric clinical chemistry; immunosuppressive drug receptors and their application in the clinical laboratory. *Mailing Add:* 6308 Wolhonding Rd Bethesda MD 20816. *Fax:* 202-884-2007; *E-Mail:* ssoldin@cnmc.org

SOLDO, ANTHONY THOMAS, BIOCHEMISTRY, NUTRITION. *Current Pos:* RETIRED. *Personal Data:* b New York, NY, Sept 11, 27; m 51; c 3. *Educ:* Brooklyn Col, BS, 50, MA, 53; Ind Univ, PhD(biochem), 60. *Prof Exp:* Biochemist, Schering Corp, NJ, 59-62; res assoc, Inst Muscle Dis Inc, NY, 62-64; asst prof, Sch Med, Univ Miami, 65-72, assoc prof, 72-81, prof biochem, 81- *Concurrent Pos:* Res chemist, Vet Admin Hosp, 65- *Mem:* AAAS; Soc Protozool; NY Acad Sci; Am Inst Nutrit; Sigma Xi. *Res:* Nutrition and nucleic acid metabolism of Protozoa; biochemistry of endosymbiotes. *Mailing Add:* 11110 SW 125th Ave Miami FL 33186

SOLDO, BETH JEAN, DEMOGRAPHY, GERONTOLOGY. *Current Pos:* sr res scholar, 77-81, from asst prof to assoc prof, 81-85, PROF, 85-, CHAIR, DEPT DEMOG & DIR, CTR POP RES, GEORGETOWN UNIV, 86- *Personal Data:* b Binghamton, NY, Sept 30, 48; m 75, T Peter Bridge. *Educ:* Fordham Univ, BA, 70; Duke Univ, MA, 74, PhD(demog), 77. *Prof Exp:* Asst dir, Ctr Demog Studies, Duke Univ, 74-77. *Concurrent Pos:* Sr res scholar, Ctr Pop Res, Georgetown Univ, 77-, sr res fel, Kennedy Inst Ethics, 81-; consult, US Senate Comt Aging, Health Care & Financing Admin, Nat Inst Aging; mem, Comt Pop, Nat Acad Sci, 93- *Mem:* Geront Soc Am; Pop Asn Am; Am Pub Health Asn; Am Sociol Soc. *Res:* Implications of a changing age structure and disease profile for the organization, structure, and financing of health care facilities, particularly long-term care services. *Mailing Add:* Dept Demog 233 Poulton Hall Georgetown Univ 1437 37 St NW Washington DC 20007

SOLE, MICHAEL JOSEPH, NEUROCHEMISTRY, MOLECULAR BIOLOGY. *Current Pos:* DIR CARDIOL, TORONTO HOSP, 89- *Personal Data:* b Timmins, Ont, Mar 5, 40; m 64; c 2. *Educ:* Univ Toronto, BSc, 62, MD, 66; FRCP(C), 74. *Honors & Awards:* Res Award, Can Cardiovasc Soc, 75; William Goldie Prize, 80; Res Achievement Award, Can Cardiovasc Soc, 89. *Prof Exp:* Intern, Toronto Gen Hosp, 66-67, jr resident, 67-68, sr resident, 68-69, staff cardiologist, 74-89; cardiol fel, Cardiovasc Res Inst, 69-71 & Peter Bent Brigham Hosp, 71-74; res assoc nutrit, Mass Inst Technol, 73-74; from asst prof to assoc prof med, Univ Toronto, 74-83, prof med & physiol & dir cardiol res, 83-89, Heart & Stroke Found Ont distinguished res prof & dir, Ctr Cardiovasc Res, Univ Toronto, 89-95. *Concurrent Pos:* Fels, Ont Heart Found, 73-80, res assoc 80-; Med Review Comt, 78-; Sci Rev Comt, Can Heart Found, 76-; fels, Coun Clin Cardiol & Am Col Cardiol, 76-; Hon secy-treas, Banting Res Found, 78-81; staff, Inst Med Sci, Univ Toronto, 77-; vchmn, Can Heart Found, 80-; mem, Rev Comt, Gairdner Found, 80-; exec comt, Health Res Develop Coun, Ont, 84-86, exec, Basic Sci Coun Am Heart Asn, 87-, dir, Heart & Stroke Found Ont, 86- *Mem:* Am Heart Asn; Can Cardiovascular Soc; Am Fedn Clin Res; Int Soc Heart Res; Am Soc Clin Invest; Asn Am Physicians. *Res:* Central and peripheral neurotransmitter metabolism in cardiovascular disease; molecular biology of myocardial hypertrophy and failure. *Mailing Add:* Toronto Hosp EN 13-208 200 Elizabeth St Toronto ON M5G 2C4 Can

SOLECKI, ROMAN, SOLID MECHANICS. *Current Pos:* PROF MECH ENG, UNIV CONN, 68- *Personal Data:* b Lwow, Poland, Apr 6, 25; US citizen; m 48. *Educ:* Warsaw Polytech Inst, BS, 50, PhD(appl mech), 56; Inst Fund Technol Res, Warsaw, DSc, 60. *Prof Exp:* Asst prof civil eng, Warsaw Polytech Inst, 50-56, adj prof, 56-60; assoc prof continuum mech, Inst Fund Technol Res, Warsaw, 60-68. *Concurrent Pos:* Royal Norwegian Coun Sci Res fels, 62- & 64-; NSF sr foreign sci fel, Univ Conn, 68- *Mem:* Am Soc Mech Engrs; Sigma Xi; Am Acad Mech; Soc Eng Sci. *Res:* Wear; fracture mechanics; theory of elasticity. *Mailing Add:* Univ Conn U-37 Storrs CT 06268

SOLED, STUART, SOLID STATE CHEMISTRY. *Current Pos:* DIR MAT TECH, SUNSTONE INC, 87- *Personal Data:* b New York, NY, May 11, 48; m; c 1. *Educ:* City Col New York, BS, 69; Brown Univ, PhD(chem), 73. *Prof Exp:* Res assoc chem res, Brown Univ, 73-77; res chemist, Allied Chem Co, 77-80; Staff Exxon Res & Engr Co, 80-87. *Concurrent Pos:* Res assoc, Lab Inorg Chem, Univ Paris, 74-75. *Mem:* Am Chem Soc; Am Crystallog Asn. *Res:* Preparation, structure and properties of materials in solid state chemistry. *Mailing Add:* Cooks Cross Rd RD 1 Box 117 Pittstown NJ 08867-9407

SOLEM, JOHNDALE CHRISTIAN, EXPERIMENTAL & THEORETICAL PHYSICS. *Current Pos:* Group leader, Thermonuclear Weapons Physics Group, Los Alamos Nat Lab, 73-76, Neutron Physics Group, 77-79, High Power Density Group, 78, alt div leader, Physics Div, 78-80, assoc div leader, Theoret Div, 80-87, coordr, Advan concepts, 87-91, adv defense sci, 91-96, LAB FEL, LOS ALAMOS NAT LAB, 96- *Personal Data:* b Chicago, Ill, Nov 8, 41; m 65, Ann M Veirs. *Educ:* Yale Univ, BS, 63, MS, 65, PhD(physics), 68, MPhil, 67. *Concurrent Pos:* Mem, USAF Sci Adv Bd, 72-77 & Munitions & Armament Panel, 73-77. *Mem:* Am Phys Soc; AAAS. *Res:* Magnetism; transport theory; plasma physics; nuclear physics; nuclear explosive theory; equations of state; artificial intelligence and robotics; computational science; biomicroholography; antiproton science and technology; astrophysics; spacecraft propulsion; laser theory; author of more than 160 technical papers. *Mailing Add:* Los Alamos Nat Lab Theoret Div MS-B210 Box 1663 Los Alamos NM 87545

SOLEN, KENNETH A, CHEMICAL ENGINEERING, BIOMEDICAL ENGINEERING. *Current Pos:* from asst prof to assoc prof, 76-89, PROF CHEM ENG, BRIGHAM YOUNG UNIV, 89- *Personal Data:* b Calif, Feb 1, 47. *Educ:* Univ Calif, Berkeley, BS, 68; Univ Wis-Madison, MS, 72, PhD(chem eng), 74. *Prof Exp:* Res fel biomed eng, Univ Iowa Med Ctr, 74-76. *Concurrent Pos:* Res fel biomed eng, Univ Ore Health Sci Ctr, 75-76. *Mem:* Am Inst Chem Engrs; Asn Artificial Internal Organs; Biomed Eng Soc. *Mailing Add:* Chem Eng Dept 350 CB Brigham Young Univ Provo UT 84602

SOLENBERGER, JOHN CARL, INDUSTRIAL CHEMISTRY. *Personal Data:* b San Diego, Calif, Apr 2, 41; m 71. *Educ:* Univ NMex, BS, 63; Wash Univ, PhD(chem), 69. *Prof Exp:* Sr res chemist, Plastics Dept, E I du Pont de Nemours & Co, Inc, 69-80. *Mem:* Am Chem Soc; Sigma Xi. *Res:* Development of membranes for use as separators on chlor-alkali cells, polymeric coatings and binders, and general industrial process research. *Mailing Add:* 5 Wood Rd Wilmington DE 19806-2021

SOLEZ, KIM, PATHOLOGY, RENAL MEDICINE. *Current Pos:* asst prof, 77-83, ASSOC PROF PATH & MED, JOHNS HOPKINS UNIV, 83-; PATHOLOGIST, JOHNS HOPKINS HOSP, 77- *Personal Data:* b Washington, DC, June 20, 46; m 68; c 2. *Educ:* Oberlin Col, BA, 68; Univ Rochester, MD, 72. *Honors & Awards:* Res Career Develop Award, NIH. *Prof Exp:* Nat Kidney Found fel, 76-77. *Concurrent Pos:* NIH res career develop award. *Mem:* Am Soc Nephrology; Int Soc Nephrology. *Res:* Acute renal failure; renal circulation; renal transplantation; glomerul-onephritis; atherosclerosis. *Mailing Add:* Dept Path Univ Alberta W C Mackenzie HSC 5B402 Edmonton AB T6G 2R7 Can. *Fax:* 403-492-2253

SOLI, GIORGIO, MICROBIOLOGY. *Current Pos:* SCI CONSULT, 73- *Personal Data:* b Rome, Italy, Feb 3, 20; nat US; m 70, Karin Schneeweiss; c Giancarlo, Laura & Peter. *Educ:* Univ Rome, DSc(microbiol), 47. *Prof Exp:* Res asst microbiol, Med Sch, Univ Calif, Los Angeles, 49-50; res asst petrol explor & develop, Gen Petrol Corp, Calif, 51-53; microbiologist & consult, Soli Microbiol Labs, 53-59; microbiologist, US Naval Ord Test Sta, China Lake, 59-62, res microbiologist, Res Dept, 62-68; staff scientist, Naval Undersea Ctr, Hawaii, 68-70; res microbiologist, Michelson Labs, China Lake, 70-73. *Concurrent Pos:* Guest scientist, Oceanog Mus, Monaco, 66-67; resident scientist, Oceanic Inst, Hawaii, 68-70. *Mem:* AAAS; Am Soc Microbiol; Am Soc Limnol & Oceanog; Sigma Xi; NY Acad Sci. *Res:* Consulting in microbiology applied to diversified problems in marine pollution and petroleum technology. *Mailing Add:* PO Box 1679 Solvang CA 93464-1679

SOLIE, LELAND PETER, ACOUSTICS. *Current Pos:* SR MEM TECH STAFF, ELECTRONIC DECISION INC, 87- *Personal Data:* b Barron, Wis, July 19, 41; m 67; c 3. *Educ:* Stanford Univ, BS, 64, MS, 67, PhD(appl physics), 71. *Prof Exp:* Res asst microwave acoust, Hansen Lab, Stanford Univ, 65-70; vis prof & res assoc, Norwegian Tech Inst, 71-72; mem tech staff microwareacoust, Sperry Res Ctr, 73-87. *Mem:* Sigma Xi; Inst Elec & Electronics Engrs. *Res:* Signal processing with surface acoustic wave devices; particular emphasis on band pass filters, convolvers, surface wave amplifiers and wave propagation in layered media. *Mailing Add:* 2092 Cranberry Isles Way Apopka FL 32712

SOLIE, THOMAS NORMAN, PHYSICAL CHEMISTRY, BIOPHYSICS. *Current Pos:* asst prof, 67-74, ASSOC PROF BIOPHYS & CHEM, COLO STATE UNIV, 74- *Personal Data:* b Spring Grove, Minn, Sept 16, 31; m 59; c 2. *Educ:* Univ Minn, Minneapolis, BA, 59; Univ Ore, MA, 63, PhD(chem), 65. *Prof Exp:* Instr biophys, Med Ctr, Univ Colo, 65; USPHS fel, 65-66; res assoc molecular biol, Vanderbilt Univ, 66; asst prof chem, Luther Col, Iowa, 66-67. *Mem:* AAAS; Am Chem Soc; Biophys Soc; Sigma Xi; Inst Elec & Electronics Engrs. *Res:* Biophysical chemistry; instrumentation design; biological signal processing and spectral analysis. *Mailing Add:* Dept Chem Colo State Univ Ft Collins CO 80523-0001

SOLIMAN, AFIFI HASSAN, TRANSPORTATION, PHOTOGRAMMETRY. *Current Pos:* from asst prof to assoc prof, 69-75, exec secy, Ctr Transp Studies, 70-73, PROF CIVIL ENG & DIR CE COOP STUDIES PROG, UNIV MAN, 87- *Personal Data:* b Cairo, Egypt, Feb 2, 31; m 62; c 5. *Educ:* Ain-Shams Univ, Cairo, BSc, 58; Ohio State Univ, MSc, 62, PhD(geod sci), 68. *Prof Exp:* Design engr, Suez Canal Authority, Egypt, 58-60; res asst geod sci, Res Ctr Found, Ohio State Univ, 62-64; chief engr, Deleuw Cather & Brill Eng Co, Columbus, Ohio, 64-66; asst prof civil eng, McMaster Univ, 66-69. *Concurrent Pos:* Nat Res Coun Can & Can Transp Comn grants, Ctr Transp Studies, Univ Man; mem, Hwy Res Bd, Nat Acad Sci-Nat Res Coun; examr, Asn Man Land Surveyors, 73; assoc prof engrs, Prov of Man, 83-; vis prof civil eng, Univ Tex, 80-81; prof civil eng, Concordia Univ, Montreal, 83-85, adj prof, 85-87; consult, Can Aero Serv Ltd, Can Transp Comn & Transp Develop Ctr, Dept Transp, Air Serv Constr, Eng & Arch Br; chmn Tech Adv Comt, Energy Conserv, Man Dept Indust, 79-80; chmn Transp Div, Can Soc Civil Eng, 86-; coord & Tech chmn, annual CSCE Transp Prog, 87-, mem steering comt, N Am Conf on Microcomputers Transp, 87-, Can Conf Eng Educ, 87, chmn, Tech prog, 88. *Mem:* Am Soc Photogram; Eng Inst Can; Can Roads & Transp Asn; Am Cong Surv & Mapping; Inst Transp Engrs; Can Soc Civil Eng; Am Soc Eng Educ. *Res:* Transportation planning, especially public transportation in urban areas; transportation growth and demand; forecasting, methods and techniques for determining potential demand for highways; transportation energy conservation; systems approach to transportation problems; freight transport. *Mailing Add:* Dept Civil Eng Univ Man Winnipeg MB R3T 2N2 Can

SOLIMAN, KARAM FARAG ATTIA, NEUROENDOCRINOLOGY & ENDOCRINOLOGY, NEUROPHARMACOLOGY & NEUROTOXICOLOGY. *Current Pos:* PROF PHYSIOL & PHARMACOL, COL PHARM & PHARMACEUT SCIS, FLA A&M UNIV, 79-, CHMN DIV BASIC PHARMACEUT SCI, 81-, ASST DEAN, PHARM & PHARMACEUT SCIS, 93- *Personal Data:* b Cairo, Egypt, Oct 15, 44; US citizen; m 73, Samia Sidhom; c John, Gina, Mark & Mary. *Educ:* Cairo Univ, BS, 64; Univ Ga, MS, 71, PhD(endocrinol), 72. *Honors & Awards:* Lederl Res Achievement Award, 75. *Prof Exp:* Res asst physiol, Univ Ga, 68-72; asst prof, Sch Vet Med, Tuskegee Inst, 72-75, assoc prof, 75-79. *Concurrent Pos:* Prin investr grants, NASA, 76- & NIH, 76-81, 83-88; prog dir, Res Ctr Minority Inst, NIH, 94- *Mem:* Am Physiol Soc; Endocrine Soc; Neurosci Soc; Chronobiol Soc; Am Soc Pharmacol Exp Therap; Soc Exp Biol Med. *Res:* Investigate the role of peripheral nervous system in the regulation of the endocrine gland function; elucidate the physiology and the pharmacology of the role of the autonomic nervous system in the regulation of adrenal cortex function. *Mailing Add:* Div Basic Pharmaceut Sci Col Pharm Fla A&M Univ Tallahassee FL 32307. *Fax:* 850-599-3667

SOLIMAN, MAGDI R I, MOLECULAR PHARMACOLOGY, NEURO- & CHRONOPHARMACOLOGY. *Current Pos:* vis scientist, 80-82, from asst prof to assoc prof, 82-85, PROF PHARMACOL, COL PHARM, FLA A&M UNIV, 85-, DIR, CHRONOPHARMACOL RES LAB, 91- *Personal Data:* b Alexandria, Egypt, June 30, 42; m 67; c 2. *Educ:* Alexandria Univ, Egypt, BSc, 64, MS, 68; Univ Ga, PhD(pharmacol), 72. *Prof Exp:* Instr pharmacol, Fac Pharm, Alexandria Univ, Egypt, 64-69; teaching asst, Sch Pharm, Univ Ga, 69-72; res assoc biomed pharmacol, Penn State Col Med, 72-74; from asst prof to assoc prof, Fac Pharm, Alexandria Univ, 74-80. *Concurrent Pos:* Res grants, NIH & NASA. *Mem:* Sigma Xi; Egyptian Pharmaceut Soc; Egyptian Pharmacol Soc; Am Soc Pharmacol & Exp Therapeut. *Res:* Chronobiotic drugs to alleviate the deleterious symptomatology associated with internal rhythm desynchronization; elucidation of the neurochemical basis of motion and space sickness; toxicology. *Mailing Add:* Dept Pharmacol Fla A&M Univ Sch Pharm Tallahassee FL 32307. *Fax:* 850-599-3347

SOLIN, STUART ALLAN, SOLID STATE PHYSICS. *Current Pos:* MEM FAC, DEPT PHYSICS, MICH STATE UNIV, 80-, DIR, CTR FUNDAMENTAL MAT RES, 86- *Personal Data:* b Baltimore, Md, Sept 9, 42; m 64; c 3. *Educ:* Mass Inst Technol, BS, 63; Purdue Univ, MS, 66, PhD(physics), 69. *Prof Exp:* Asst physics, Purdue Univ, 64-69; from asst prof to assoc prof physics, Univ Chicago, 69-80. *Mem:* Am Phys Soc. *Res:* Solid state physics; laser Raman spectroscopy of solids; fundamental properties of lasers; superconductivity. *Mailing Add:* NEC Res Inst Inc Phys Sci Res Div 4 Independence Way Princeton NJ 08540. *Fax:* 609-951-2483

SOLINGER, ALAN M, IMMUNOLOGY, RHEUMATOLOGY. *Current Pos:* ASST DIR, ANTI-INFLAMMATORIES, DRUG DEVELOP DEPT, CIBA-GEIGY CORP, 91- *Personal Data:* b Nov 22, 48; m 83; c 2. *Educ:* Columbia Univ, BA, 70; Univ Cincinnati, MD, 74. *Prof Exp:* From asst prof to assoc prof med, Col Med, Univ Cincinnati, 81-91. *Mem:* AAAS; NY Acad Sci; Am Col Rheumatology; Am Col Physicians; Am Fedn Clin Res; Asn Clin Pathologists. *Res:* Clinical immunology; rheumatology; cellular immunology and its part in chronic synovitas. *Mailing Add:* Clin Therapy IDEC Pharm Corp 11011 Torreyana Rd San Diego CA 92121. *Fax:* 908-277-4795

SOLISH, GEORGE IRVING, OBSTETRICS & GYNECOLOGY, HUMAN GENETICS. *Current Pos:* From instr to asst prof, 57-68, assoc prof, 68-79, PROF OBSTET & GYNEC, STATE UNIV NY DOWNSTATE MED CTR, 79-; DIR MED GENETICS SERVS, MAIMONIDES MED CTR, 86- *Personal Data:* b Providence, RI, Jan 7, 20; m 46, Bernice Parvey; c Alfred M, Sharyn B (Seigel) & Samuel P. *Educ:* Providence Col, BS, 41; Tufts Univ, MD, 50; Univ Mich, MS, 61, PhD(human genetics), 68. *Concurrent Pos:* Consult, Margaret Sanger Res Bur, 64-79. *Mem:* Am Col Obstet & Gynec; Am Fertil Soc; Am Soc Human Genetics; Sigma Xi. *Res:* Population genetics; prezygotic selection and control of fertility; infertility; reproduction; prenatal genetic diagnosis. *Mailing Add:* 26 Barlow Dr N Brooklyn NY 11234-6720. *Fax:* 718-283-8351

SOLL, ANDREW H, CELL BIOLOGY, PHYSIOLOGY. *Current Pos:* PROF CLIN & PRECLIN MED, MED SCH, UNIV CALIF, LOS ANGELES, 75- *Personal Data:* b Mar 20, 45. *Educ:* Harvard Univ, MD, 70. *Res:* Cellular mechanisms underlying regulation of secretion and growth in gastric mucosa. *Mailing Add:* Dept GI Univ Calif Sch Med Vet Admin Med Ctr 115 Rm 15 11301 Wilshire Blvd Los Angeles CA 90073. *Fax:* 310-824-6752

SOLL, DAVID RICHARD, DEVELOPMENTAL BIOLOGY. *Current Pos:* asst prof, 72-77, ASSOC PROF ZOOL, UNIV IOWA, 77- *Personal Data:* b Philadelphia, Pa, Apr 29, 42; c 1. *Educ:* Univ Wis, BA, 64, MA, 68, PhD(zool), 70. *Prof Exp:* Fel develop biol, Univ Wis, 69-70, Brandeis Univ, 71-72. *Concurrent Pos:* Res grants, NSF, 74 & 76 & NIH, 78, 79 & 81; mem, Cell Biol Study Sect, NIH, 78-83. *Mem:* Soc Develop Biol; AAAS. *Res:* An analysis of the molecular mechanisms controlling cell differentiation and muticellular morphogenesis. *Mailing Add:* Dept Biol Univ Iowa Iowa City IA 52242-0001. *Fax:* 319-335-1069

SOLL, DIETER GERHARD, MOLECULAR BIOLOGY. *Current Pos:* from asst prof to assoc prof, 65-76, PROF MOLECULAR BIOPHYS, YALE UNIV, 76- *Personal Data:* b Stuttgart, Ger, Apr 19, 35; US citizen; m 64; c 3. *Educ:* Stuttgart Tech Univ, MSc, 60, PhD(chem), 62. *Honors & Awards:* Humboldt Prize, 88. *Prof Exp:* Fel, Inst Enzyme Res, Univ Wis-Madison, 62-65. *Concurrent Pos:* Guggenheim Found fel, 72 & 89. *Mem:* Nat Acad Sci; fel AAAS; Am Soc Biol Chem; Am Chem Soc; Am Soc Microbiol. *Res:* Regulation of gene expression; plant molecular biology. *Mailing Add:* Dept Biophys & Biochem Yale Univ Sch Med PO Box 208024 New Haven CT 06520-8024. *Fax:* 203-432-6202; *E-Mail:* soll@biomed.med.yale.edu

SOLLA, SARA A, STATISTICAL MECHANICS, COMPUTATIONAL NEUROSCIENCE. *Current Pos:* MEM TECH STAFF, AT&T BELL LABS, 86- *Personal Data:* b Buenos Aires, Arg, June 30, 50; m 74. *Educ:* Univ Buenos Aires, Arg, BS, 74; Univ Wash, PhD(physics), 82. *Prof Exp:* Lectr thermodyn, Nat Univ Technol, Buenos Aires, Arg, 74-76; teaching asst, Univ Wash, 76-77, res asst, 77-82; postdoctoral assoc, Lab Atomic & Solid State Physics, Cornell Univ, 82-84, lectr, 84; postdoctoral assoc, IBM Watson Res Ctr, 84-86. *Concurrent Pos:* Vis scientist, Boston Univ, 85; vis prof, ENS & ENSEA, Paris, France, 86, Ctr Telecommun Res, Columbia Univ, 87-88 & Nordic Inst theoret Atomic Physics, Copenhagen, 90. *Mem:* Am Phys Soc; Int Neural Network Soc; NY Acad Sci; AAAS. *Res:* Neural networks; statistical models to describe learning and adaptation in computational systems which are biologically inspired and try to mimic the parallel computation used by the brain for tasks such as associative memory and pattern recognition; author of various publications. *Mailing Add:* 175 W 12th St Apt 9B New York NY 10011

SOLLBERGER, ARNE RUDOLPH, BIOMETRY. *Current Pos:* prof, 72-88, VIS PROF PHYSIOL & INFO PROCESSING, MED SCH, SOUTHERN ILL UNIV, 88- *Personal Data:* b Dresden, Ger, Mar 17, 24; m 54; c 2. *Educ:* Caroline Inst, Stockholm, Sweden, MB, 49, MD, 57. *Honors & Awards:* Award, Biometeorol Res Found, 75. *Prof Exp:* From asst anat to assoc prof, Caroline Inst, Stockholm, Sweden, 48-62; prof pharmacol, Univ PR, 62-64; assoc med, Case Western Res Univ, 64-65; chief biomet, Eastern Res Supply

Ctr, Vet Admin Hosp, West Haven, Conn, 65-67; assoc prof psychiat, Med Sch, Yale Univ, 68-72. *Concurrent Pos:* Asst ward physician, Hosp Swed Diabetes Found, Stockholm, 54-62; lectr anat & physiol, two nursing schs & Sch Indust Art, Stockholm, 57-62; lectr biomet, Yale Univ, 66-72; chmn, Biol Rhythms StudyGroup, Int Soc Biometerol, 70-88; bd mem, Found Study Cycles, 75, pres, 76; ed-in-chief, J Interdisciplinary Cycle Res, 78-89. *Mem:* Hon mem Int Soc Chronobiol (secy, 55-67). *Res:* Cardiology and diabetes; biological rhythms, especially statistical problems; normal values in medicine; biomedical computer processing. *Mailing Add:* 1532 E Gary Dr Carbondale IL 62901

SOLLER, ROGER WILLIAM, PHARMACOLOGY, NEUROPHARMACOLOGY. *Current Pos:* sci assoc pharmacol, 79-81, VPRES DIR SCI AFFAIRS, GLENBROOK LABS, DIV STERLING DRUG INC, 81- *Personal Data:* b Bronxville, NY, Nov 18, 46. *Educ:* Colby Col, BA, 68; Cornell Univ, PhD(neurobiol), 73. *Prof Exp:* Fel pharmacol, Sch Med, Univ Pa, 73-75, instr & res assoc, 75-77, asst prof, 77-79. *Concurrent Pos:* Pharmaceut Mfrs Asn fel, 74-76; Pa plan scholar, Univ Pa, 76-79. *Mem:* Soc Neurosci; Sigma Xi. *Res:* Mechanisms of action of analgesics, hormones and neurotransmitter substances; clinical pharmacology. *Mailing Add:* NDMA 1150 Connecticut Ave NW Washington DC 20036-4104

SOLLEY, WAYNE B, HYDROLOGY. *Current Pos:* CHIEF, WATER USE INFO BR, US GEOL SURV, 84- *Personal Data:* b Baltimore, Md, July, 42. *Educ:* Univ Md, BS, 64. *Mem:* Am Water Res Asn; Am Inst Hydrol. *Mailing Add:* Water Resources Div US Geol Surv Nat Ctr MS 414 Reston VA 20192. *Fax:* 703-648-5722; *E-Mail:* wbsolley@usgs.gov

SOLLFREY, WILLIAM, PHYSICS. *Current Pos:* PHYS SCIENTIST, RAND CORP, 61- *Personal Data:* b New York, NY, Mar 8, 25; m 49. *Educ:* NY Univ, BA, 44, MS, 46, PhD(physics), 50. *Prof Exp:* Asst proj engr, Sperry Gyroscope Co, 44-47; res assoc, Math Res Group, NY Univ, 47-51; sr engr, W L Maxson Corp, 51-55; sr res engr, Chicago Midway Labs, 55-57; mgr syst anal, Mech Div, Gen Mills, Inc, 57-61. *Concurrent Pos:* Instr, Polytech Inst Brooklyn, 53-55. *Mem:* AAAS; Am Phys Soc. *Res:* Advanced analysis in military systems; mathematics; electrical engineering. *Mailing Add:* 633 Ocean Ave Apt 4 Santa Monica CA 90402

SOLLID, JON ERIK, APPLICATION OF LASERS TO MEDICINE, RESONATOR DESIGN. *Current Pos:* PRES & CHIEF EXEC OFFICER, SOLLID OPTICS, INC, 85- *Personal Data:* b Denver, Colo, Oct 1, 39; m 65, 80, 87 & 91, Dagne Helen Samuelson; c Sonje, Shije, Erika & Dahr. *Educ:* Univ Mich, Ann Arbor, BS, 61; NMex State Univ, MS, 65, PhD(physics), 67. *Prof Exp:* Physicist, White Sands Missile Range, 61-62; res assoc plasma physics, Los Alamos Sci Lab, 65-66; sr res scientist, Convair Aerospace Div, Gen Dynamics, 67-72 & Sci Res Lab, Ford Motor Co, 72-74; staff scientist, Los Alamos Nat Lab, 74-81, proj leader, 81-84; vpres & gen mgr, Los Alamos Div, Newport Corp, 84-86. *Concurrent Pos:* Adj prof, Tex Christian Univ, 68-72; instr, Northern NMex Community Col, 78-83; adj prof, Los Alamos Br, Univ NMex, 80- *Mem:* Am Phys Soc; Optical Soc Am; Soc Photo-Optical Instrumentation Engrs; fel Int Soc Optical Eng. *Res:* Development of optoelectronics technology for medical diagnostics and therapy, particularly the use of lasers and infrared spectroscopy; laser resonator design, optical beam transport and delivery systems; holography; process control; nondestructive testing. *Mailing Add:* 365 Valle Del Sol Rd Los Alamos NM 87544-3563. *Fax:* 505-672-1771; *E-Mail:* sollid@earthlink.net, jsollid@aol.com

SOLLITT, CHARLES KEVIN, PHYSICAL MODELING OF OCEAN WAVES, OCEAN & COASTAL STRUCTURES. *Current Pos:* asst prof, 72-78, ASSOC PROF, ORE STATE UNIV, 78-, DIR, OH HINSDALE WAVE RES LAB, 81- *Personal Data:* b Minneapolis, Minn, Aug 8, 43; m 67, Melissa A; c Katherine & Thomas. *Educ:* Univ Wash, BS, 66, MS, 68; Mass Inst Technol, PhD(civil eng), 72. *Prof Exp:* Res asst, Univ Wash, 66-68 & Mass Inst Technol, 68-72. *Mem:* Am Soc Civil Engr. *Res:* Analytical and experimental work in ocean wave-structure-foundation interaction; breakwater behavior; wave and current measurement systems analysis and interpretation; hydraulic modeling of ocean waves. *Mailing Add:* 113 NW 28th Corvallis OR 97330. *Fax:* 541-737-0485; *E-Mail:* sollittc@ccmail.orst.edu

SOLLMAN, PAUL BENJAMIN, ORGANIC CHEMISTRY. *Current Pos:* RETIRED. *Personal Data:* b Ft Branch, Ind, May 2, 20; m 41; c 4. *Educ:* Univ Ind, BS, 47; Univ Minn, PhD(org chem), 51. *Prof Exp:* res chemist, G D Searle Co, 51-80; res chemist, Regis Chem Co, 80-88. *Mem:* Am Chem Soc. *Res:* Organic synthesis; medicinal chemistry. *Mailing Add:* 549 Jupiter Dr Ft Myers FL 33908

SOLLNER-WEBB, BARBARA THEA, MOLECULAR BIOLOGY. *Current Pos:* FEL, DEPT EMBRYOL, CARNEGIE INST, WASHINGTON, 77- *Personal Data:* b Washington, DC, Dec 21, 48; m 73. *Educ:* Mass Inst Technol, BS, 70; Stanford Univ, PhD(biol), 76. *Prof Exp:* staff fel, Molecular Biol, Nat Inst Arthritis, Metab & Digestive Dis, NIH, 76-77. *Res:* Structure and function of chromatin; nuclease protease and polymerase action on nucleoprotein and nuclei; ribosomal RNA transcriptional control regions of xenopus laevis; DNA sequencing. *Mailing Add:* Dept Biol Chem Johns Hopkins Univ Sch Med 415 Hunterian Baltimore MD 21205-2105. *Fax:* 410-955-0192

SOLLOTT, GILBERT PAUL, ORGANIC CHEMISTRY. *Current Pos:* SR SCIENTIST, GEO CTR CORP, 87- *Personal Data:* b Philadelphia, Pa, July 12, 27; m 54; c 2. *Educ:* Univ Pa, BA, 49; Temple Univ, MA, 56, PhD(org chem), 62. *Honors & Awards:* Outstanding Achievement Award, US Dept Army, 64 & 82. *Prof Exp:* Chemist, R M Hollingshead Corp, 50-52 & Betz Labs, 52-53; org chemist, Pitman-Dunn Lab, Frankford Arsenal, 53-62, chief org chem group, 62-77; res chemist, US Army Armament Res & Develop Ctr, 77-87. *Mem:* AAAS; Am Chem Soc; Sigma Xi; NY Acad Sci; Royal Soc Chem. *Res:* Organic, organometallic and organometalloid chemistry including phosphorus, arsenic, boron, silicon and germanium; chemiluminescence research; new synthetic methods; mechanisms; ferrocene chemistry; polymers; nitrocompounds. *Mailing Add:* 618 Gawain Rd Plymouth Meeting PA 19462

SOLMAN, VICTOR EDWARD FRICK, ZOOLOGY, ECOLOGY. *Current Pos:* RETIRED. *Personal Data:* b Toronto, Ont, May 24, 16; m 54; c 2. *Educ:* Univ Toronto, BA, 38, MA, 39, PhD(biol), 42. *Honors & Awards:* Gold Medal, Prof Inst Pub Serv Can, 77; Kuhring Award, Bird Strike Comn, Europe, 86. *Prof Exp:* Asst zool, Univ Toronto, 36-42; limnologist, Nat Parks Bur, Dept Mines & Resources & Dom Wildlife Serv, 45-49, chief biologist, Dom Wildlife Serv, 49-50 & Can Wildlife Serv, 50-53, asst chief, 53-64, staff specialist, 64-81. *Mem:* Fel AAAS. *Res:* Cladocera of Costello Creek, Algonquin Park, Ontario; ecological relations of waterfowl, especially predatory fish; ecology; wildlife research and management; reduction of bird hazards to aircraft. *Mailing Add:* 614 Denbury Ave Ottawa ON K2A 2P1 Can

SOLMON, DONALD CLYDE, COMPUTED TOMOGRAPHY. *Current Pos:* asst prof, 77-81, ASSOC PROF MATH, ORE STATE UNIV, 81- *Personal Data:* b Fall River, Mass, Mar 28, 45; m 70; c 2. *Educ:* Southeastern Mass Tech Inst, BS, 67; Ore State Univ, MS, 73, PhD(math), 74. *Prof Exp:* Vis asst prof math, Univ Ore, 74-75; George William Hill res instr, State Univ NY at Buffalo, 75-77. *Concurrent Pos:* Vis lectr math, Univ des Saarlandes, 81. *Mem:* Am Math Soc; Math Asn Am. *Res:* Applications of analysis and functional analysis to obtain a deeper understanding of problems in medical radiology especially computed tomography. *Mailing Add:* Ore State Univ 368 Kidder Hall Corvallis OR 97331-4601

SOLN, JOSIP ZVONIMIR, THEORETICAL PHYSICS. *Current Pos:* PHYSICIST, NUCLEAR RADIATION EFFECTS LAB, HARRY DIAMOND LABS, 72- *Personal Data:* b Zagreb, Croatia, Mar 31, 34; m 66, Patricia M Stone; c Helen M. *Educ:* Univ Zagreb, BSc, 57, PhD(physics), 60. *Prof Exp:* Res assoc, Rudjer Boskovic Inst, Zagreb, 57-61, researcher particle physics & field theory, 62-64; fel high energy physics, European Ctr Nuclear Res, Geneva, Switz, 61-62; res assoc broken symmetries, Univ Calif, Los Angeles, 64-65, asst prof in residence, 65-66; asst prof particle physics, Univ Wis, Milwaukee, 66-70; vis asst prof, Univ Ill, Chicago Circle, 70-71; res assoc, Inst Theoret Sci, Univ Ore, 71-72. *Mem:* Sigma Xi; Am Phys Soc. *Res:* Nonconservation of parity in weak decays; quantum field theory; soluble models; particle production in pion-proton collision; high energy behavior of the scattering amplitude; broken symmetries; solid state devices; Cerenkov and stimulated radiations; free electron lasers; radiation propagation; unified gauge field theories; vacuum structure in Gauge Field Theories; supersymmetry; covariant perturbation theory; radiation shielding. *Mailing Add:* Army Res Lab Adelphi MD 20783. *Fax:* 703-281-5130; *E-Mail:* baton79@aol.com

SOLNIT, ALBERT J, PSYCHIATRY, PEDIATRICS. *Current Pos:* Sterling prof, 66-90, EMER STERLING PROF PEDIAT & PSYCHIAT & SR RES SCIENTIST, CHILD STUDY CTR, YALE UNIV, 90- *Personal Data:* b Los Angeles, Calif, Aug 26, 19. *Educ:* Univ Calif, BA, 40, MS, 42, MD, 43. *Hon Degrees:* MA, Yale Univ, 64. *Honors & Awards:* William C Menninger Award, Am Col Physicians, 79; Agnes Purcell McGavin Award, Am Psychiat Asn, 80; Andrew Rackow Mem Lectr, Abington Hosp Ment Health Ctr, 80; Lindemann Distinguished Lectr, NY Hosp, 83; Peter Blos Biennial Lectr, 83; C Anderson Aldrich Award, Am Acad Pediat, 89; Simon Wile Award, Am Acad Child & Adolescent Psychiat, 91. *Concurrent Pos:* Attend physician pediat & psychiat, Yale-New Haven Hosp, 52-; mem fac & supv analyst, Western New Eng Inst Psychoanal, 62 & NY Psychoanal Inst, 66-; fel, Branford Col, Yale Univ, 67-, chmn, Ctr Study Educ, Inst Social & Policy Studies, 71-73; managing ed, Psychoanal Study Child, 71-; vis prof psychiat & human develop, Ben-Gurion Univ Negev, 73-74; Sigmund Freud mem prof, Univ Col, London, 83-84; Sigmund Freud vis prof, Hebrew Univ, 85-87. *Mem:* Fel Inst Med-Nat Acad Sci; Inst Asn Child & Adolescent Psychiat (hon pres, 90-). *Res:* Child and adolescent psychiatry. *Mailing Add:* 107 Cottage St New Haven CT 06511-2465

SOLO, ALAN JERE, MEDICINAL CHEMISTRY, ORGANIC CHEMISTRY. *Current Pos:* from asst prof to assoc prof, 62-70, CHMN DEPT, STATE UNIV NY BUFFALO, 69-, PROF MED CHEM, 70- *Personal Data:* b Philadelphia, Pa, Nov 7, 33; m 63, Elma Mardirosian; c David M & Julia A. *Educ:* Mass Inst Technol, SB, 55; Columbia Univ, AM, 56, PhD(chem), 59. *Prof Exp:* Res assoc org chem, Rockefeller Inst, 58-62. *Concurrent Pos:* Consult, Westwood Pharmaceut Inc, 71-92. *Mem:* Am Chem Soc; NY Acad Sci. *Res:* Synthesis and structure-activity relationships of steroid hormones; investigations of mechanism of action of steroid hormones; synthesis of dihydropyridine-type calcium channel antagonists. *Mailing Add:* Dept Med Chem Sch Pharm State Univ NY Buffalo NY 14260-0001. *Fax:* 716-645-2393

SOLODAR, ARTHUR JOHN, ORGANIC CHEMISTRY, CATALYSIS. *Current Pos:* sr res chemist, 68-74, res specialist, 74-80, sr res specialist, 80-84, SR PROCESS CONSULT, MONSANTO CO, 84- *Personal Data:* b East Orange, NJ, Apr 18, 40; m 64; c 3. *Educ:* Swarthmore Col, BA, 62; Yale Univ, MS, 63, PhD(chem), 67. *Prof Exp:* Nat Cancer Inst fel, Mass Inst Technol, 67-68. *Mem:* Sigma Xi; Am Chem Soc. *Res:* Homogeneous catalysis; asymmetric synthesis; phase-transfer catalysis; exploratory process research. *Mailing Add:* 8135 Cornell Ct University City MO 63130-3639

SOLODAR, WARREN E, ORGANIC CHEMISTRY. *Current Pos:* INDEPENDENT CONSULT, 91- *Personal Data:* b New York, NY, Sept 29, 25; m 50, Betty Mogil; c Louise & Jessica. *Educ:* NY Univ, AB, 48; Stevens Inst Technol, MS, 53. *Prof Exp:* Assoc chemist, Hoffmann-La Roche, Inc, 48-54; chemist, Polaroid Corp, 54-64; scientist, Xerox Corp, 64-87; mem staff, DX Imaging, 87-91. *Concurrent Pos:* Res fel, Koor Chem Ltd, Beer Sheva, Israel, 74-75; vis prof, Hebrew Univ Jerusalem, 82. *Mem:* Am Chem Soc; Soc Imaging Sci & Technol; fel Am Inst Chemists; Asn Consult Chemists & Chem Engrs. *Res:* Pharmaceuticals; vitamins; hypertensive agents; analgesics; azo and anthraquinone dyes; photographic developers; organic photoconductors; pigments; photoelectrophoretic imaging materials; liquid xerographic inks; chemistry and applications of dyes, pigments, inks, imaging materials. *Mailing Add:* 480 Montgomery Ave Merion PA 19066-1213. *Fax:* 610-664-5321

SOLOFF, BERNARD LEROY, ANATOMY. *Current Pos:* RES PHYSIOLOGIST, LITTLE ROCK HOSP DIV, VET ADMIN, 65- *Personal Data:* b New York, NY, June 21, 31; m 61; c 2. *Educ:* Univ Cincinnati, BS, 53, MS, 56; Rice Univ, PhD(biol), 61. *Prof Exp:* Res asst trace metals, M D Anderson Hosp & Tumor Inst, 61; asst prof biol, Stephen F Austin State Col, 61-62; res assoc anat, Med Units, Univ Tenn, Memphis, 63-64. *Concurrent Pos:* Nat Heart Inst fel & training grant, Marine Lab, Inst Marine Sci, Univ Miami, 62-63; USPHS trainee, Med Units, Univ Tenn, Memphis, 64-65; instr, Med Ctr, Univ Ark, 65-70, asst prof, 70- *Mem:* NY Acad Sci; AAAS; Am Asn Anatomists; Tissue Cult Asn; Electron Micros Soc Am. *Res:* Ultrastructure of leukocytes; ultrastructure of hemoglobin interactions within erythrocytes; ultrastructure of lung; ultrastructure of bacteria and bacteriophage; ultrastructure of heart. *Mailing Add:* 8215 Reymere Dr Little Rock AR 72227

SOLOFF, LOUIS ALEXANDER, MEDICINE, CARDIOLOGY. *Current Pos:* From asst to assoc path & med, Temple Univ Hosp, 33-45, from asst prof to clin prof med, 45-54, prof clin med, 49-54, chief, Div Cardiol, Health Sci Ctr, 54-70, PROF MED, TEMPLE UNIV HOSP, 54-, BLANCHE P LEVY DISTINGUISHED SERV EMER PROF, 71- *Personal Data:* b Paris, France, Oct 2, 04; nat US; wid; c Joann (Green). *Educ:* Univ Pa, Ba, 26; Univ Chicago, MD, 30; Am Bd Internal Med, cert, 39. *Concurrent Pos:* Chief labs, St Joseph's & St Vincent's Hosps & Eagleville Sanatorium, 33-45; chief, Dept Cardiol, Episcopal Hosp, 49-56. *Mem:* Asn Univ Cardiol; Am Heart Asn; sr mem Am Fedn Clin Res; Am Col Cardiol; Sigma Xi. *Res:* Diseases of the heart; more than 400 scientific papers; contributor to numerous books in field. *Mailing Add:* Temple Univ Hosp Broad & Tioga Sts Philadelphia PA 19140. *Fax:* 215-707-2946

SOLOFF, MELVYN STANLEY, ENDOCRINOLOGY. *Current Pos:* asst prof biochem, 70-74, assoc prof, 74-79, PROF BIOCHEM, MED COL OHIO, 79- *Personal Data:* b Los Angeles, Calif, Oct 6, 38; m 68; c 2. *Educ:* Univ Calif, Los Angeles, AB, 62, MA, 64, PhD(zool), 68. *Prof Exp:* Res fel, Univ Calif, Los Angeles, 68-69; assoc res biologist, Sterling-Winthrop Res Inst, 69-70. *Mem:* Endocrine Soc; Am Soc Biol Chemists. *Res:* Hormone receptors; mechanisms of hormone action. *Mailing Add:* Dept Obstet-Gynec Univ Tex Med Br Med Res Bldg Galveston TX 77555-1062. *Fax:* 409-772-2261

SOLOMON, ALAN, HEMATOLOGY, ONCOLOGY. *Current Pos:* PROF MED, DEPT MED, UNIV TENN MED CTR, KNOXVILLE, 66-, HEAD, HUMAN IMMUNOL & CANCER PROG, 90-; CLIN RES PROF, CANCER SOC, 92- *Personal Data:* b New York, NY, May 16, 33; c David & Joseph. *Educ:* Bucknell Univ, BS, 53; Duke Univ, BSMed, 56, MD, 57; Am Bd Internal Med, dipl, 64. *Honors & Awards:* Laszlo Mem lectr, Montifiore Hosp, 84. *Prof Exp:* Intern, Mt Sinai Hosp, New York, 57-58, asst resident med, 59-60; asst resident, Montefiore Hosp, 58-59; clin assoc, Nat Cancer Inst, 60-62; chief resident, Mt Sinai Hosp, 62-63; asst attend physician, 65-66. *Concurrent Pos:* Res fel hemat, Mt Sinai Hosp, 63-65; Nat Inst Arthritis & Metab Dis spec fel, Rockefeller Inst, 63-65; USPHS res career develop award, 67-72; from asst physician to assoc physician, Rockefeller Inst, 63-66, guest investr, 63-66; prin investr, USPHS grant, 65-, mem rev comt, Nat Cancer Inst, Nat Cancer Prog Proj, 78-83; mem, Sci Counrs, Div Cancer Biol, Diag & Ctrs, Nat Cancer Inst, NIH, 93-95. *Mem:* Am Soc Clin Invest; fel Am Col Physicians; Am Soc Clin Oncol; Am Asn Cancer Educ; Am Soc Hemat. *Res:* Amyloidosis; human immunoglobulins; cancer; pathophysiology of the human light chain-associated renal and systemic diseases: myeloma (cast) nephropathy, light chain deposition disease and amyloidosis AL. *Mailing Add:* Univ Tenn Med Ctr 1924 Alcoa Hwy Knoxville TN 37920. *Fax:* 423-544-6865; *E-Mail:* asolomon@wizard.hosp.utk.edu

SOLOMON, ALVIN ARNOLD, MATERIALS SCIENCE, NUCLEAR MATERIALS. *Current Pos:* PROF NUCLEAR ENG, PURDUE UNIV, 74- *Personal Data:* b Chicago, Ill, Aug 17, 37; m 94, Jocelyne Quedru; c Danielle, Cathryne & Christopher. *Educ:* Univ Ill, BS, 59, MS, 61; Stanford Univ, PhD(mat sci), 68. *Honors & Awards:* Ceramographic Award, Am Ceramic Soc. *Prof Exp:* Develop engr, Advan Systs Develop Div, IBM Corp, 61-64; postdoctoral res, French Atomic Energy Comn, Saclay, 68-69; metallurgist, Argonne Nat Lab, 69-74. *Concurrent Pos:* Instr, San Jose State Col, 63-64; mem staff, Denver Res Inst, 66; Centre Nat de la Recherche Scientifique, 80-81. *Mem:* Fel Am Ceramic Soc; Am Nuclear Soc. *Res:* High temperature materials, nuclear and waste materials. *Mailing Add:* Purdue Univ Sch Nuclear Eng West Lafayette IN 47907-1290. *Fax:* 765-494-9570; *E-Mail:* solomon@ecn.purdue.edu

SOLOMON, ANNE G K, INTERNATIONAL SCIENCE. *Current Pos:* DEP ASST SECY STATE SCI, TECHNOL & HEALTH, BUR OCEANS & INT ENVIRON & SCI AFFAIRS, US COORDR, INT GLOBAL POSITIONING SYST POLICY. *Personal Data:* m, Richard H; c 3. *Educ:* Harvard Univ, MPA. *Prof Exp:* Dir, Comt Scholarly Commun Peoples Repub China, Nat Acad Sci, 71-77; sr policy anal int affairs, Off Sci & Technol Policy, 78-80; dir, US-Japan Technol & Trade Bilateral Discussion Group & Acad-Indust Prog, Nat Acad Sci, 83-88; dir govt & pub affairs, Carnegie Inst Wash, 88-92; consult, Rand Corp, 93. *Mem:* AAAS. *Mailing Add:* US Dept State Bur Oceans & Int Environ & Sci Affairs Washington DC 20520

SOLOMON, ARTHUR KASKEL, BIOPHYSICS. *Current Pos:* asst prof physiol chem, 46-56, from assoc to prof biophys prof, 57-83, EMER PROF BIOPHYS, HARVARD MED SCH, 83- *Personal Data:* b Pittsburgh, Pa, Nov 26, 12; m 72, Mariot Fraser; c Mark & Susanna. *Educ:* Princeton Univ, AB, 34; Harvard Univ, MA, 35, PhD(phys chem), 37; Cambridge Univ, PhD(physics), 47. *Hon Degrees:* ScD, Cambridge Univ, 64. *Honors & Awards:* Order Andres Bello, Govt of Venezuela, 74. *Prof Exp:* Res assoc physics & chem, Harvard Univ, 39-41, Exp Off, Brit Ministry Supply, 41-43 & Brit Admiralty, 43-45; mem staff, Radiation Lab, Mass Inst Technol, 45. *Concurrent Pos:* Assoc, Peter Bent Brigham Hosp, 50-72; chmn, Comt Higher Degrees Biophys, Harvard Univ, 59-80; mem, Radiation Study Sect, NIH, 60-63, Biophys Sci Training Comn, 63-68, chmn, 66-68; secy-gen, Int Union Pure & Appl Biophys, 61-72; mem bd, Int Orgn & Progs, Nat Res Coun, Nat Acad Sci, 67-80, chmn, 77-79; sci policy adv to Thai govt, UNESCO, 68-72, mem, US Nat Comt, 69-74. *Mem:* Fel AAAS; Am Chem Soc; Am Physiol Soc; Biophys Soc; fel Am Acad Arts & Sci; Soc Gen Physiol. *Res:* Permeability of cellular membranes and model systems. *Mailing Add:* Biophys Lab Harvard Med Sch 221 Longwood Ave Boston MA 02115

SOLOMON, DALE S, COMPUTER BASED MATHEMATICAL MODELS, FOREST MANAGEMENT & GROWTH. *Current Pos:* Res forester, 62-88, PROJ LEADER SUPVR, USDA FOREST SERV, 88- *Personal Data:* b Harmony, NJ, Apr 8, 39; m, Carol; c 3. *Educ:* Pa State Univ, BS, 61; Yale Sch Forestry, MF, 62; Univ Maine, PhD(forestry growth), 78. *Concurrent Pos:* Fac assoc, Univ Maine, 78, Syracuse Univ, 96- *Mem:* Soc Am Foresters; Sigma Xi; Int Union Forestry Res Orgns. *Res:* Development for forest growth models in Northeastern US; forest habitat types in New England; management, harvesting, regeneration, growth responses and species dynamics. *Mailing Add:* USDA Forest Serv NE-4104 PO Box 640 Durham NH 03824. *Fax:* 603-868-7604

SOLOMON, DAVID EUGENE, GENERAL MANAGEMENT, MATERIALS SCIENCE. *Current Pos:* PRES, SOLO HILL ENG, INC, 85- *Personal Data:* b Milton, Pa, June 22, 31; m 50; c 3. *Educ:* Susquehanna Univ, AB, 58; Bucknell Univ, MS, 60; Eastern Mich Univ, MBA, 75. *Prof Exp:* Sr engr, Electron Tube Lab, Westinghouse Elec Corp, Md, 59-65; sr res engr, Electron Physics Lab, Univ Mich, Ann Arbor, 65-67; chief engr, Electro Optics Div, Bendix Corp, Mich, 67-71, prog mgr Mars probe, Bendix Aerospace Systs Div, 71-72; dir laser fusion mat sci, KMS Fusion, Inc, 72-85, vpres opers, 80-85. *Mem:* Am Vacuum Soc; fel Inst Elec & Electronics Engrs. *Res:* Broad research in the material sciences aimed at laser thermonuclear fuel pellets, encompassing glass synthesis and fabrication, polymers, copolymers, cryogenics, thin film deposition biotechnology and others. *Mailing Add:* 3415 Woodlea Dr Ann Arbor MI 48103. *Fax:* 313-973-3029; *E-Mail:* solohill@ichet

SOLOMON, DAVID HARRIS, GERIATRICS, ENDOCRINOLOGY. *Current Pos:* from instr to prof, Sch Med, Univ Calif, Los Angeles, 52-93, chmn, Dept Med, 71-81, assoc dir, Multicampus Div Geriat Med, 82-90, dir, Ctr Aging, 91-96, EMER PROF MED/GERIAT, SCH MED, UNIV CALIF, LOS ANGELES, 93-, EMER DIR, CTR AGING, 96- *Personal Data:* b Mass, Mar 7, 23; m 46, Ronda Markson; c Patty (Sinaiko) & Nancy (Evans). *Educ:* Brown Univ, AB, 44; Harvard Med Sch, MD, 46. *Honors & Awards:* Distinguished Serv Award, Am Thyroid Asn, 86; Robert H Williams Distinguished Leadership Award, Endocrine Soc, 89; Wright Award of Distinction, Am Fedn Aging Res, 90; Milo Leavitt Award, Am Geriat Soc, 92, Distinguished Serv Award, 93. *Prof Exp:* House officer med, Peter Bent Brigham Hosp, 46-47, sr asst resident physician, 50-51; sr asst surgeon, NIH, 48-50; fel endocrinol, New Eng Ctr Hosp, 51-52. *Concurrent Pos:* Res fel, Peter Bent Brigham Hosp, 47-48; attend physician, Harbor Gen Hosp, Torrance, 52-66, chief, Dept Med, 66-71; attend physician, Vet Admin Ctr, 52-; mem, bd dirs, Am Geriat Soc & Am Fedn Aging Res; consult, Vet Admin Wadsworth Med Ctr, Los Angeles, 52-, Fresno Co Hosp, Fresno, 63-66, St Mary's Med Ctr, Long Beach, 68-71, Vet Admin Med Ctr, Sepulveda, Calif, 72-, Olive View Med Ctr, Van Nuys, 73-, Cedars-Sinai Med Ctr, 74 & Rand Corp, 88-94; ed-in-chief, J Am Geriat Soc, 88-93. *Mem:* Inst Med-Nat Acad Sci; Endocrine Soc; master Am Col Physicians; Am Thyroid Asn; Asn Am Physicians. *Res:* Thyroid hormone metabolism in animals and man; effect of illness and aging on thyroid hormone metabolism; appropriateness of surgical operations and other major procedures. *Mailing Add:* Ctr Aging Div Geriat Med Univ Calif 10945 Le Conte Ave Suite 3119 Los Angeles CA 90095-6980

SOLOMON, DONALD W, ANALYTICAL MATHEMATICS. *Current Pos:* from asst prof to assoc prof math, 66-74, assoc chmn dept, 75-78, PROF MATH, UNIV WIS-MILWAUKEE, 74-, CHMN, DIV NATURAL SCI, 76- *Personal Data:* b Detroit, Mich, Feb 6, 41; m 89; c 1. *Educ:* Wayne State Univ,

BS, 61, MA, 63, PhD(math), 66, MD, 68. *Prof Exp:* From teaching asst to instr math, Wayne State Univ, 63-66. *Concurrent Pos:* NSF res grants, 67-68 & 70-71; Univ Wis Grad Sch res grants, 69, 71-72 & 73-74. *Mem:* AAAS; Am Math Soc; Math Asn Am; Soc Indust & Appl Math; NY Acad Sci. *Res:* Measure, integration and differentiation. *Mailing Add:* Dept Math Univ Wis Milwaukee WI 53201-0413

SOLOMON, EDWARD I, PHYSICAL INORGANIC CHEMISTRY, BIOINORGANIC CHEMISTRY. *Current Pos:* prof, 82-92, MONROE E SPAGHT PROF CHEM, STANFORD UNIV, 92- *Personal Data:* b New York, NY, Oct 20, 46; m 84, Darlene Spira; c Mitchell & Paige E. *Educ:* Rensselaer Polytech Inst, BS, 68; Princeton Univ, MA, 70, PhD(chem), 72. *Honors & Awards:* O K Rice Lectr; Reilly Lectr; World Bank Lectr; First Glen Seaborg Lectr; Frontiers Chem Lectr; Taiwan Nat Sci Coun Lectr. *Prof Exp:* Danish Nat Sci Found fel chem, H C Orsted Inst, Univ Copenhagen, 73-74; NIH fel, Noyes Lab, Calif Inst Technol, 74-75; A P Sloan res fel, 76; from asst prof to prof, Mass Inst Technol, 75-81. *Concurrent Pos:* Sloan fel, 76-78; assoc ed, Inorg Chem; hon prof, Xiamen Univ, People's Repub China; invited prof, Univ Paris, Orasy, Univ LaPlata, Arg, Tokup Inst Technol. *Mem:* Am Chem Soc; Am Phys Soc; Sigma Xi; Am Asn Univ Profs; fel AAAS. *Res:* Inorganic spectroscopy and ligand field theory; spectral and magnetic studies on bioinorganic systems; interactions between metals in polynuclear complexes; spectroscopic studies of active sites in metalloprotein and heterogeneous catalysts; synchrotron spectroscopic studies of inorganic materials. *Mailing Add:* Dept Chem Stanford Univ Mudd Chem Bldg Stanford CA 94305. *Fax:* 650-725-0259; *E-Mail:* fb.eis@forsythe.binet

SOLOMON, FRANK I, ELECTROCHEMISTRY. *Current Pos:* PRES, ELECTROMEDIA, INC, 74- *Personal Data:* b Denver, Colo, Oct 7, 24; m 48; c 3. *Educ:* City Col New York, BChE, 47. *Prof Exp:* Asst vpres & tech dir, Yardney Elec Corp, 49-71; tech dir, Molecular Energy Corp, 71-74. *Mem:* Electrochem Soc. *Res:* Storage batteries, alkaline; gas diffusion electrodes. *Mailing Add:* 8 Hampton Ct Great Neck NY 11020

SOLOMON, GEORGE E, AERONAUTICAL & ASTRONAUTICAL ENGINEERING. *Current Pos:* RETIRED. *Personal Data:* b Seattle, Wash, July 14, 25. *Educ:* Univ Wash, BS, 49; Calif Inst Technol, MS, 50, PhD(aeronaut & physics), 53. *Prof Exp:* Res fel, Caltech, 53-54; tech consult re-entry body aerodyn, Ramo-Wooldridge Corp, 53-54, mem tech staff, Guided Missile Res Div, 54-58, dir, Syst Res & Anal Div, 58-62, vpres, Space Technol Labs, 62-65; vpres & dir, Syst Labs, TRW Syst Group, TRW Inc, 65-68, vpres & dir, mkt & requirements anal, 68-71, vpres & gen mgr, TRW Defense & Space Syst Group, 71-81, exec vpres & gen mgr, electronics & defense sector, 81-88. *Mem:* Nat Acad Eng; Sigma Xi; Aerospace Indust Asn. *Mailing Add:* 1903 Springbrook Lane Boise ID 83706

SOLOMON, GEORGE FREEMAN, PSYCHONEUROIMMUNOLOGY, FORENSIC PSYCHIATRY. *Current Pos:* Prof, 84-95, EMER PROF PSYCHIAT, UNIV CALIF, LOS ANGELES, 95- *Personal Data:* b Freeport, NY, Nov 25, 31; m 79, Susan Keran; c Joshua & Jared. *Educ:* Stanford Univ, AB, 52, MD, 55; FRCPsych, 89. *Prof Exp:* From asst to assoc prof psychiat, Stanford Univ, 62-73; chief psychiat, Valley Med Ctr Fresno, 74-83; prof, Univ Calif, San Francisco, 80-84. *Concurrent Pos:* Chief psychiat training & res, Palo Alto Vet Admin Hosp, 62-70; chief substance abuse treat unit, Sepulveda Vet Admin Med Ctr, 84-95. *Mem:* Fel Am Psychiat Asn; fel Acad Behav Med; fel Int Col Psychosomatic Med; Am Acad Psychiat & Law; fel Soc Behav Med; Am Psychosomatic Soc. *Res:* Psychoneuroimmunology, especially of AIDS and aging; criminal behavior, violence and aggression; post-traumatic stress syndrome in Vietnam veterans; normal behavior; psychosomatic medicine; immunity of schizophrenia. *Mailing Add:* 19054 Pac Coast Hwy Malibu CA 90265. *Fax:* 310-456-1854

SOLOMON, GORDON CHARLES, anatomy, pathology; deceased, see previous edition for last biography

SOLOMON, HARVEY DONALD, METALLURGY, MATERIALS SCIENCE. *Current Pos:* METALLURGIST & MAT SCIENTIST, RES & DEVELOP CTR, GEN ELEC CO, 68- *Personal Data:* b New York, NY, Dec 14, 41; m 66; c 2. *Educ:* NY Univ, BS, 63; Univ Pa, PhD(metall), 68. *Honors & Awards:* Joseph Vilella Award, Am Soc Testing & Mat, 79. *Concurrent Pos:* Adj assoc prof, Union Col, 89- *Mem:* Am Inst Mining, Metall & Petrol Engrs. *Res:* Physical and mechanical metallurgy; fatigue; fatigue crack propagation; creep-fatigue interactions; electrical interconnections; fatigue of solders; welding metallurgy; materials for advanced energy systems; superalloys; metallurgy of stainless steels; stress corrosion cracking. *Mailing Add:* Gen Elec Res & Develop Ctr PO Box 8 Schenectady NY 12301. *Fax:* 518-387-7495; *E-Mail:* solomon@crd.ge.com

SOLOMON, JACK, PHYSICAL CHEMISTRY. *Current Pos:* sr proj engr, Praxair Inc, 74-77, supvr, Gas Prod Develop Lab, 77-80, process mgr, Gas Prod Mkt Develop, 80-83, prod mgr, New Electronics Applns, 83-87, assoc dir develop, 87-90, mgr appln technol planning, 90-93, DIR TECHNOL PLANNING, PRAXAIR INC, 93- *Personal Data:* b Brooklyn, NY, July 26, 41; m 70, Janis Dollinger; c Sheri, Alyssa & Susan. *Educ:* Mass Inst Technol, BS, 63; Columbia Univ, PhD(phys chem), 67. *Prof Exp:* Res scientist, 67-72, proj scientist, Linde Res Lab, Union Carbide Co, 72-74. *Concurrent Pos:* Chmn tech sessions, Semicon West, 86; Reviewer Indust & Eng Chem Res; chmn, Tekcon, 88. *Mem:* Am Chem Soc; Sigma Xi; Semiconductor Equip & Mat Inst; Int Soc Hybrid Microelectronics. *Res:* Chemistry of oxygen in cryogenic, aqueous and other systems; atmospheres for carburizing; hardening and sintering; applications of oxygen in combustion; semiconductor fabrication technology; use of inert gas in polymer processing and other industrial processes; 4 US patents. *Mailing Add:* Praxair Inc 777 Old Saw Mill River Rd Tarrytown NY 10591. *Fax:* 914-345-6486

SOLOMON, JAMES DOYLE, FOREST ENTOMOLOGY. *Current Pos:* Res entomologist, Southern Forest Exp Sta, Asheville, NC, 60-61 & Stoneville, Miss, 61-75, prin res entomologist, 75-90, supvry res entomologist, 90-94, EMER SCIENTIST, SOUTHERN FOREST EXP STA, STONEVILLE, MISS, 94- *Personal Data:* b Bee Branch, Ark, May 18, 34; m 61; c 1. *Educ:* Univ Ark, BS, 56, MS, 60; Miss State Univ, PhD(entom), 71. *Honors & Awards:* US Dept Agr, Cert of Merit Award for Outstanding Res, 85. *Concurrent Pos:* Mem, Interagency Task Force, Cross-Fla Barge Canal Environ Impact Statement, 72-73; adj prof, Miss State Univ, 72-; mem, Task Force Long Range Forest Res Planning, Southern Region, USDA, 73-74, consult. *Mem:* Entom Soc Am; Sigma Xi; Poplar Coun US. *Res:* Hardwood insects with emphasis on the Cossid, Cerambycid and Sesiid Borers of living trees and shrubs; author of publication in field. *Mailing Add:* US Forest Serv PO Box 227 Stoneville MS 38776

SOLOMON, JAY MURRIE, COMPUTATION FLUID DYNAMICS, APPLIED MATHEMATICS. *Current Pos:* aerospace engr res viscous flows, 60-67, MATHEMATICIAN APPL MATH, WHITE OAK LAB, NAVAL SURFACE WEAPONS CTR, 67- *Personal Data:* b Washington, DC, June 6, 36; m 59; c 3. *Educ:* Univ Md, BS, 58, MS, 60, PhD(appl math), 68. *Prof Exp:* Res asst, Univ Md, 58-60. *Mem:* Soc Indust & Appl Math; Am Inst Aeronaut & Astronaut. *Res:* Development, analysis and application of finite difference methods to steady subsonic inviscid flows, incompressible Navier-Stokes equations and unsteady inviscid flows. *Mailing Add:* 2232 Hidden Valley Lane Silver Spring MD 20904-5240

SOLOMON, JEROME JAY, PHYSICAL CHEMISTRY, MASS SPECTROMETRY. *Current Pos:* assoc res scientist, NY Univ Med Ctr, 75-77, asst prof, Environ Med & Mass Spectrometry, Inst Environ Med, 77-83, res assoc prof, 83-90, PROF & DIR, LAB DNA CHEM & CARCINOGENESIS, INST ENVIRON MED, NY UNIV MED CTR, 90- *Personal Data:* b Brooklyn, NY, Apr 23, 45. *Educ:* Brooklyn Col, BS, 66; Cornell Univ, PhD(phys chem), 72. *Prof Exp:* Res assoc phys chem & ion-molecule reactions, Rockefeller Univ, 72-75. *Mem:* Am Soc Mass Spectrometry; Sigma Xi; Am Asn Cancer Res; AAAS. *Res:* Development of the analytical capability of mass spectrometry for use in biomedical research; emphasis on DNA chemistry. *Mailing Add:* Environ Med NY Univ Med Ctr Long Meadow Rd Tuxedo Park NY 10987

SOLOMON, JIMMY LLOYD, MATHEMATICS. *Current Pos:* assoc prof, 75-83, HEAD, DEPT MATH & STATIST, MISS STATE UNIV, 81-, PROF MATH, 83-, DEAN, COL ARTS & SCI, 91- *Personal Data:* b Milan, Tenn, Oct 3, 41; m 64; c Lloyd A & Marjorie D. *Educ:* Univ Miss, BS, 64; Miss State Univ, MS, 66; Tex A&M Univ, PhD(math), 72. *Prof Exp:* Asst mathematician, Dept Aerophys, Miss State Univ, 64-65, instr, 66-67; instr math, Tex A&M Univ, 71-72; asst prof, Tex A&I Univ, 72-75. *Concurrent Pos:* Consult. *Mem:* Am Math Soc; Math Assoc Am. *Res:* Fixed point theory, numerical analysis, and statistical pattern recognition. *Mailing Add:* Col Sci & Technol Ga Southern Univ Landrum Box 8044 Statesboro GA 30460-8044. *Fax:* 601-325-8740; *E-Mail:* jsolomon@math.msstate.edu

SOLOMON, JOEL MARTIN, IMMUNOGENETICS, IMMUNOHEMATOLOGY. *Current Pos:* RETIRED. *Personal Data:* b Malden, Mass, Dec 25, 32; m 84; c 3. *Educ:* Boston Col, BS, 53; Johns Hopkins Univ, ScM, 57; Univ Wis, PhD(med genetics), 63. *Prof Exp:* Immunohematologist, NIH, 57-60; sr res assoc, Am Nat Red Cross, 63-64; sr res assoc & training dir, 64-67; dir blood bank, Brooklyn-Cumberland Med Ctr, 67-70; blood prod dir, E R Squibb & Sons, Inc, 70-73; dep dir, Div Blood & Blood Prod, Bur Biologics, Food & Drug Admin, 74-77, dir, 78-81; policy coordr, Off Secy, Dept Health & Human Serv, 81-83; scientist adminr, Dept Transfusion Med, 83-85, spec asst to dir extramural affairs, 85-86, exec sec, HEM-2 study sect, NIH, 86-88; dir, Div Blood & Blood Prod, Ctr, Biologics, FDA, 88-91; exec dir, Am Asn Blood Banks, 91-94. *Concurrent Pos:* Clin instr pediat, Calif Col Med, 63-64; mem fac genetics & fac microbiol & immunol, Grad Sch, NIH, 64-67 & 74-; lectr, Sch Med, George Washington Univ, 66-67; clin assoc prof path, Sch Med, State Univ NY Downstate Med Ctr, 67-73. *Mem:* Int Soc Blood Transfusion; Am Asn Blood Banks. *Res:* Quantitative hemagglutination; genetics of human blood groups; immunochemistry of blood group antigens; parasite physiology. *Mailing Add:* 15714 Cherry Blossom Lane Gaithersburg MD 20878

SOLOMON, JOLANE BAUMGARTEN, PHYSIOLOGY, ENDOCRINOLOGY. *Current Pos:* vis lectr, 63-72, assoc prof, 74-80, PROF BIOL, BOSTON COL, 80- *Personal Data:* b New York, NY, Sept 23, 27; m 57; c 3. *Educ:* Hunter Col, BS, 52; Radcliffe Col, MS, 55, PhD(physiol), 58. *Prof Exp:* Teaching fel, biol, Harvard Univ, 53-55, sci news writer, 55-57; teaching fel, anat, Harvard Med Sch, 57-59; res assoc nutrit, Harvard Sch Pub Health, 60-63. *Concurrent Pos:* Dir, Off Resources, Boston Col, 70-72; Carnegie res fel, 72-74; grants, Nat Inst Drug Abuse, 75-76 & 76-78. *Mem:* AAAS; Am Diabetes Asn; Am Women Sci; Entomol Soc Am; Endocrine Soc. *Res:* Effect of THC on reproduction in male and female rats; effect of lighting regimens on growth of the American cockroach, P Americana; lipid metabolism in hyperglycemic ob/ob mice. *Mailing Add:* Dept Biol Boston Col 140 Commonwealth Ave Chestnut Hill MA 02167-3800

SOLOMON, JOSEPH ALVIN, PHYSICAL CHEMISTRY. *Current Pos:* RETIRED. *Personal Data:* b New Kensington, Pa, July 25, 25; m 53; c 1. *Educ:* Westminster Col, BS, 49; Carnegie-Mellon Univ, MS, 58, PhD, 59. *Prof Exp:* Analytical chemist, Us Steel Corp, NJ, 51-54; analyst, Gulf Res & Develop Co, 54-55; prof chem, St Joseph Col, Md, 58-61 & Marietta Col, 61-62; coal res engr, WVa Univ, 62-63; prof chem, St Joseph Col, Md, 63-65; from asst prof to prof chem, Philadelphia Col Pharm & Sci, 63-81. *Mem:* AAAS; Am Chem Soc. *Res:* Coal research, especially removal of sulfur both prior to and following combustion. *Mailing Add:* 44 S Lansdown Ave Lansdowne PA 19050

SOLOMON, JULIUS, HIGH ENERGY PHYSICS. *Current Pos:* from asst prof to assoc prof, 66-82, PROF PHYSICS, UNIV ILL, CHICAGO, 83- *Personal Data:* b Brooklyn, NY, Apr 14, 36; m 63; c 3. *Educ:* Columbia Univ, AB, 57; Univ Calif, Berkeley, PhD(physics), 63. *Prof Exp:* Res assoc, Lawrence Radiation Lab, Univ Calif, 63; instr, Princeton Univ, 63-66. *Mem:* Am Phys Soc. *Res:* Experimental high energy physics; k-zero meson decays; pion-proton scattering; k-zero regeneration; k-zero-k-zero bar mass differences; high transverse momentum scattering with Hadron beams; detection of I/4, B and chi decays. *Mailing Add:* Dept Physics MC 273 Univ Ill Chicago 845 W Taylor St Rm 2236 Chicago IL 60607-7059. *Fax:* 312-996-9016; *E-Mail:* solomon@ulcws.bitnet

SOLOMON, KENNETH, GERIATRICS, SEXUALITY. *Current Pos:* ASSOC PROF PSYCHIAT, ST LOUIS UNIV, 89-, ASSOC PROF MED, 93- *Personal Data:* b Brooklyn, NY, Oct 8, 47; c 2. *Educ:* NY Univ, BA, 67; State Univ NY, Buffalo, MD, 71. *Prof Exp:* Asst instr psychiat, Albany Med Col, 72-75, from instr to asst prof, 75-77; asst prof, Med Col Va, 77-79, asst dir residency training, 77-79; fac assoc geront, Va Ctr Aging, Va Commonwealth Univ, 78-79; asst prof psychiat, Univ Md, 79-81; assoc dir educ & planning, Levindale Hebrew Geriat Ctr & Hosp, 81-83; adj asst prof psychiat, Univ Md, 82-87, assoc mem grad fac, 80-89; chief geriatric psychiat, St Louis Dept Vet Affairs Med, 89-93. *Concurrent Pos:* Adj prof, Union Experimenting Cols & Univs, 81-90; assoc clin prof, geriat & psychiat, Univ Md, 87-90; chief, geriat & psychiat serv, Sheppard & Enoch Pratt Hosp, 83-89. *Mem:* Fel Am Psychiat Asn; fel Geront Soc Am; Am Pub Health Asn; fel Am Geriat Soc; AAAS; Am Asn Geriatric Psychiat. *Res:* Psychogeriatrics; depression; Alzheimer's disease; sterotyping the elderly; sexuality; men's issues; alcohol and drug abuse in elderly. *Mailing Add:* Howell & Haferkamp 7733 Forsyth Blvd St Louis MO 63105

SOLOMON, LAWRENCE MARVIN, DERMATOLOGY, PEDIATRIC DERMATOLOGY. *Current Pos:* from asst prof to prof, 66-76, actg dir, Univ Hosp, 69-70, PROF DERMAT & HEAD DEPT, UNIV ILL MED CTR, 74- *Personal Data:* b Montreal, Que, June 1, 31; div; c Marcus & Deborah. *Educ:* McGill Univ, BA, 53; Univ Geneva, MD, 59; FRCP(C), 64; Am Bd Dermat, dipl, 65. *Honors & Awards:* Gold Award, Am Acad Dermat & Am Acad Allergy, 64. *Prof Exp:* Intern, Jewish Gen Hosp, Montreal, 59-60; resident med, Queen Mary Vet Hosp, 60-61; resident dermat, Grad Hosp, Univ Pa, 61-64. *Concurrent Pos:* Res fel, Jewish Gen Hosp, Montreal, 64-66; consult, Vet Admin Hosp, Hines, Ill, 66-, 68- & West Side Vet Admin Hosp, 69-; chmn, comt dermat agents, Food & Drug Admin, 76-78; assoc chief ed, J Invest Dermat, 77-83; co-ed, J Pediat Dermat. *Mem:* Am Acad Dermat; Soc Invest Dermat; Int Soc Pediat Dermat (pres, 79-83); Am Soc Pediat Dermat; Am Dermat Asn. *Res:* Biochemical and pharmacological studies in atopic dermatitis; pharmacogenetic changes in hereditary skin diseases; catecholamines; congenital malformation of the skin. *Mailing Add:* 1775 Dempster Park Ridge IL 60068

SOLOMON, LOUIS, MATHEMATICS. *Current Pos:* PROF MATH, UNIV WIS-MADISON, 69- *Personal Data:* b New York, NY, June 20, 31; m 60; c 2. *Educ:* Harvard Univ, AB, 51, AM, 52, PhD(math), 58. *Prof Exp:* Asst prof math, Bryn Mawr Col, 58-59 & Haverford Col, 59-62, 63-64; vis mem, Inst Advan Study, 62-63; asst prof, Rockefeller Univ, 64-65; from assoc prof to prof, NMex State Univ, 65-69. *Concurrent Pos:* Vis prof, Univ London, 71-72. *Mem:* Am Math Soc; Math Asn Am. *Res:* Finite groups, especially groups generated by reflections and linear groups over finite fields; combinatorics. *Mailing Add:* Dept Math Univ Wis 480 Lincoln Dr Madison WI 53706-1313

SOLOMON, M MICHAEL, ORGANIC CHEMISTRY, POLYMER CHEMISTRY. *Current Pos:* RETIRED. *Personal Data:* b Philadelphia, Pa, Sept 20, 24; m 48, Selma Sion; c Mel & Jodee. *Educ:* Temple Univ, BA, 45, MA, 47; Purdue Univ, PhD, 51. *Prof Exp:* Asst, Temple Univ, 45-47 & Purdue Univ, 47-48; res assoc endocrine chem, Worcester Found Exp Biol, 51-52; sr develop chemist, Silicone Prod Dept, 52-60, mgr liaison & info, Space Sci Lab, Missile & Space Div, 60-66, mgr eng mat & tech lab, Lab Oper, Power Transmission Div, Pa, 66-71, mgr metall & fabrication lab oper, Power Delivery Group, Group Tech Resources Oper, Pittsfield, Mass, 71-75; mgr, Switchgear Resources Support Opers, Switchgear Distrib Transformer Div, Tech Resources Operators, Gen Elec Co, Philadelphia, 75-84. *Concurrent Pos:* Mgr environ technol, Power Delivery Div, King of Prussia, Pa, 79-84; consult mat & environ, Lawrence J Dove Assocs, Philadelphia, 85- *Mem:* Am Chem Soc; Inst Elec & Electronics Eng; Sigma Xi. *Res:* Management; metals; metal fabrication and equipment development; ceramics; electrochemistry for use in power delivery equipment; composite materials; dielectrics; silicone chemistry; biological metabolism of adrenocorticotrophic hormone and cortisone; organic chemistry; hazardous materials treatment and dispositions, fire and arson investigations. *Mailing Add:* 1871 Ambler Rd Abington PA 19001-2701

SOLOMON, MALCOLM DAVID, SOFTWARE SYSTEMS LAB MANAGEMENT & INSTRUMENTS. *Current Pos:* SOFTWARE ENG, HEWLETT-PACKARD, PALO ALTO, CA, 84- *Personal Data:* b Swansea, Wales, Oct 16, 42. *Educ:* Univ London, BSc, 64, PhD(org chem), 67; Univ Calif, Berkeley, AB, 83. *Prof Exp:* Res chemist, Med Ctr, Univ Calif, San Francisco, 67-69; fel genetics, Med Ctr, Stanford Univ, 70-71; res chemist, Ultrachem Corp, Walnut Creek, 71-73, tech dir, Sci Res Info Serv Inc, San Francisco, 73-74; toxiologist, Hine Inc, San Francisco, 74-79; software eng, Oxbridge, Mountain View, Ca, 83-84. *Mem:* Am Chem Soc; Royal Soc Chem; Asn Comput Mach. *Res:* Synthesis and chemistry of natural products; mass spectrometry; gas-liquid chromatography; narcotics and dangerous drugs; computer graphics; laboratory information management systems. *Mailing Add:* 535 Everett Ave Palo Alto CA 94301-1547

SOLOMON, MARVIN H, OPERATING SYSTEMS, PROGRAMMING LANGUAGES. *Current Pos:* instr, 76-77, asst prof, 77-82, ASSOC PROF COMPUT SCI, UNIV WIS-MADISON, 82- *Personal Data:* b Chicago, Ill, Mar 11, 49. *Educ:* Univ Chicago, BS, 70; Cornell Univ, MS, 74, PhD(comput sci), 77. *Prof Exp:* Vis instr comput sci, Aarhus Univ, 75-76. *Concurrent Pos:* Vis scientist, IBM Corp, 84-85. *Mem:* Asn Comput Mach; Inst Elec & Electronics Engrs. *Res:* Theory of programming languages; distributed operating systems; graph theory as applied to multiple-computer systems; computer networks; electronic mail. *Mailing Add:* Dept Comput Sci Univ Wis 1210 W Dayton St Madison WI 53706

SOLOMON, MORSE BARTT, MEAT SCIENCE & MUSCLE BIOLOGY, MUSCLE HISTOLOGY. *Current Pos:* Res scientist, 83-91, RES LEADER, MEAT SCI RES LAB, AGR RES SERV, USDA, 91- *Personal Data:* b Waterbury, Conn, Mar 9, 53; m 76, Betsy; c Neil & Andrea. *Educ:* Univ Conn, BS, 77; Univ Ky, MS, 79; Univ Fla, PhD(animal sci), 83. *Honors & Awards:* Northeast Young Scientist Award, Am Soc Animal Sci/Am Dairy Sci Asn, 91. *Concurrent Pos:* Chmn, Res Competition Comt, Am Meat Sci Asn, 86-87, Food/Meat Sci Sect, NE Am Soc Animal Sci/Am Dairy Sci Asn, 89. *Mem:* Am Soc Animal Sci (secy & treas, 92, vpres, 93, pres, 94); Am Meat Sci Asn; Inst Food Technologists; Am Inst Nutrit. *Res:* Regulation of growth and development of different biological slaughter animals for producing high lean/low fat meat; development of new technologies. *Mailing Add:* Meat Sci Res Lab USDA ARS Bldg 201 BARC-E 10300 Baltimore Ave Beltsville MD 20705-2350. *Fax:* 301-504-8438; *E-Mail:* msoloman@ggpl.arsusda.gov

SOLOMON, NEIL, PHYSIOLOGY, SCIENCE COMMUNICATIONS. *Current Pos:* CHMN, HEALTH, EDUC & SCI RES, 96- *Personal Data:* b Pittsburgh, Pa, Feb 27, 32; m 55; c 3. *Educ:* Western Res Univ, AB, 54, MD & MS, 61; Univ Md, PhD(physiol), 65. *Honors & Awards:* Schwentker Award, Johns Hopkins Hosp; Mental Health & Environ Health Hadassah Award, 73-; Act Award, 83. *Prof Exp:* Instr, Sch Med, Johns Hopkins Univ, 63-68, asst prof psychiat, 71-79; endocrinologist, Neil Solomon MD. *Concurrent Pos:* intern med, Johns Hopkins Hosp, 61-62, asst resident, 62-63, asst, 63-64, instr, 64-69; vis physician & asst chief med, Baltimore City Hosp, 63-68; consult, Vet Admin Hosp, Perry Pt, Md, 63-68; assoc prof physiol, Sch Med, Univ Md, Baltimore, 63-70; asst sr surgeon, Nat Inst Child Health & Human Develop, 64-65; vis physician, Univ Md Hosp, 65-68; Am Heart Asn res fel, 65-67; chmn, Comprehensive State Planning, MD, 68-69; secy, Md State Dept Health & ment Hyg, 69-79; clin prof pharmacol, Sch Med, Univ Miami, 79-81; chmn, Gov's Drug & Alcohol Abuse Comn, State Md, 91-93, Gov's Health Care Reform Comn, 92-93, Gov's AIDS Comn, 93; lectr med, Dept Med, Col Physicians & Surgeons, Columbia Univ, Presby Hosp, 93- *Mem:* Am Fedn Clin Res; Am Heart Asn; Am Physiol Soc; Fedn Am Socs Exp Biol; NY Acad Sci; hon mem Asn Ment Health Admin. *Res:* Aging and heart and endocrine function; social policy on health care reform, drug and alcohol abuse and acquired immune deficiency syndrome (AIDS); preventive medicine as a life enhancer. *Mailing Add:* 2209 Ken Oak Rd Baltimore MD 21209-4419. *Fax:* 410-664-6045; *E-Mail:* nsolomon@erols.com

SOLOMON, PAUL R, NEUROPSYCHOLOGY. *Current Pos:* From asst prof to assoc prof, 76-88, PROF PSYCHOL, WILLIAMS COL, 89-, CHAIR NEUROSCI, 91- *Personal Data:* b Brooklyn, NY, Aug 27, 48; m 70, Suellen Zablow; c Todd & Jessica. *Educ:* State Univ NY, BA, 70, MA, 72; Univ Mass, PhD(psychol), 75. *Concurrent Pos:* Adj asst prof, Dept Psychol, Univ Mass, Amherst, 76-78; fel, Univ Calif Irvine, 79-80; adj prof, Univ Vt Col Med, 86- *Mem:* Fel AAAS; fel Am Psychol Asn; fel Am Psychol Soc; Soc Neurosci; Int Brain Res Orgn. *Res:* Studies of the neurobiology of memory and memory disorders; development and testing of drugs to treat neurodegenerative disorders, especially Alzheimers disease; published over 100 articles. *Mailing Add:* Dept Psychol Williams Col Williamstown MA 01267. *Fax:* 413-597-4116; *E-Mail:* psolomon@williams.edu

SOLOMON, PETER R, SOLID STATE PHYSICS, COAL SCIENCE. *Current Pos:* PRES, ADVAN FUEL RES INC, 80- *Personal Data:* b New York, NY, Feb 19, 39; m 60, 75; c 3. *Educ:* City Col NY, BS, 60; Columbia Univ, MA, 63, PhD(physics), 65. *Honors & Awards:* Richard A Glean Award, Am Chem Soc. *Prof Exp:* Res asst physics, Watson Lab, IBM Corp, 63-65; exp physicist, United Technol Res Ctr, 65-68, prin scientist, 68-71, asst to dir res progs & technol, 71-73, prin physicist, 73-80. *Concurrent Pos:* Committeeman, Nat Acad Sci; chmn, Fuel Chem Div, Am Chem Soc, 84-85. *Mem:* Am Phys Soc; Sigma Xi; Am Chem Soc; Combustion Inst. *Res:* Low temperature physics; electrical instabilities in semiconductors; coal science; superconductivity; instabilities in solids. *Mailing Add:* Advan Fuel Res Inc PO Box 380379 East Hartford CT 06138-0379

SOLOMON, PHILIP M, ASTROPHYSICS, MOLECULAR PHYSICS. *Current Pos:* PROF ASTRON, STATE UNIV NY STONY BROOK, 74- *Personal Data:* b New York, NY, Mar 29, 39; m 58; c 1. *Educ:* Univ Wis, BS, 59, MS, 61, PhD(astron), 64. *Prof Exp:* Res assoc astrophys sci, Princeton Univ, 64-66, Univ Calif, San Diego, 70; lectr & sr res assoc astron, Columbia Univ, 66-70; from assoc prof to prof, Sch Physics & Astron, Univ Minn, Minneapolis, 71-73. *Concurrent Pos:* Vis scientist, Inst Theoret Astron, Univ Cambridge, 67-69 & 72; mem, Sch Natural Sci, Inst Advan Study, 73, 74 & 76, vis, 86; sr vis scientist, Inst Astron, Cambridge Univ, Eng, 81-82, overseas fel, Churchill Col, 81-82; Humboldt Sr Distinguished Scientist Award, Alexander von Humboldt Found, 88-89; invited prof, Ecole Normal Superieur, Paris, 89; vis astronr, Inst Astrophys, Paris, 93; sci team mem, Upper Atmospheric Prog & several review panels, NASA; mem, Astron & Astrophys Survey Comt, Adv panel on Infrared Astron, Nat Acad Sci, Comt Univ Radio Astron, NSF. *Mem:* Am Astron Soc; Int Astron Union. *Res:* Molecular opacities; interstellar matter; planetary atmospheres; interstellar chemistry; radioastronomy, masers; quasi-stellar objects. *Mailing Add:* Dept Earth Sci State Univ NY Stony Brook NY 11794-1400

SOLOMON, ROBERT DOUGLAS, PATHOLOGY. *Current Pos:* ADJ PROF BIOL, UNIV NC, WILMINGTON, 88- *Personal Data:* b Delavan, Wis, Aug 28, 17; m 43, Helen Fisher; c Susan, Wendy, James & William. *Educ:* Johns Hopkins Univ, MD, 42. *Prof Exp:* Pathologist, Kankakee State Hosp, 49-50; assoc dir, Terre Haute Med Lab, 50-54; assoc pathologist, Sinai Hosp, Baltimore, Md, 55-58; asst prof path, Univ Md, 58-60; assoc pathologist, City Hope Med Ctr, 60-63, dir path res, 63-67; dir labs, Doctors' Hosp San Leandro, Calif, 67-75; dir labs, Edgewater Hosp, Chicago, 75-76; assoc pathologist, Wilson Mem Hosp, Johnson City, 78-85; clin prof path, State Univ NY Upstate Med Ctr, 79-87. *Concurrent Pos:* Fel cancer res, Michael Reese Hosp, 47-49; trainee, Nat Cancer Inst, 58-60; consult, Regional Off US Vet Admin, Md, 58-60; assoc prof, Univ Southern Calif, 61-; fel coun arteriosclerosis, Am Heart Asn. *Mem:* Fel Royal Soc Med; Am Soc Clin Path; Am Chem Soc; Am Col Physicians; Col Am Path; Asn Clin Scientists; Sigma Xi. *Res:* Urinary pigments; nutritional influences on carcinogenesis; leukoplakia and vitamin A; experimental arteriosclerosis; vascular surgery; mechanisms of aging; reversal of atherosclerosis. *Mailing Add:* 113 S Belvedere Dr Hampstead NC 28443

SOLOMON, SAMUEL, BIOCHEMISTRY, ENDOCRINOLOGY. *Current Pos:* assoc prof, 60-67, PROF BIOCHEM OBSTETS & GYNECOL & EXP MED, MCGILL UNIV, 67-, DIR, MCGILL CTR, ENDOCRINE MECHANISMS, 87-; DIR, ENDOCRINE LAB, ROYAL VICTORIA HOSP, 65- *Personal Data:* b Brest Litovsk, Poland, Dec 5, 25; Can citizen; m 53, Augusta M Vineberg; c David, Peter & Jonathan. *Educ:* McGill Univ, BSc, 47, MSc, 51, PhD(biochem), 53. *Honors & Awards:* Price Orator; Am Soc Obstet & Gynecol; McLaughlin Gold Medal, Royal Soc Can. *Prof Exp:* Res asst, McGill Univ, 51-53; from res asst to res assoc, Columbia Univ, 53-57, assoc biochem, 58-59, asst prof, 59-60. *Concurrent Pos:* Chem Inst Can fel, 65; Can Soc Clin Invest Schering traveling fel, 65 & 69; consult, Ayerst Labs, 65-79 & Ortho Pharmaceut Co, 68-78; mem sen, McGill Univ, 69-71 & 74-77 & bd gov, 74-77; mem sci adv comt, Connaught Res Inst, 79-82; dir, Res Inst, Royal Victoria Hosp, 82-85; chmn steering comt, Int Study Group Steroid Hormones, Italy, 83-; mem var site vis teams, NSF, NIH & others; regional dir, Medicar Res Coun Can, 93-96; Daubin Comn, Drugs Athletics. *Mem:* AAAS; Soc Gynec Invest; fel Royal Soc Can; Perinatal Res Soc (pres, 75-76); Am Chem Soc; Sigma Xi; hon fel Am Gynec & Obstet Soc; fel Chem Inst Can; Endocrine Soc. *Res:* Hormones in pregnancy; endocrinology. *Mailing Add:* 239 Kensington Ave 804 Montreal PQ H3Z 2H1 Can

SOLOMON, SEAN CARL, GEOPHYSICS. *Current Pos:* DIR, DEPT TERRESTRIAL MAGNETISM, CARNEGIE INST WASHINGTON, 92- *Personal Data:* b Los Angeles, Calif, Oct 24, 45; m 93, Pamela Holter; c Maura & Erin. *Educ:* Calif Inst Technol, BS, 66; Mass Inst Technol, PhD(geophys), 71. *Prof Exp:* Fel, NSF, 71-72; from asst prof to prof geophys, 72-92. *Concurrent Pos:* Lunar Sample Analysis Planning Team, NASA, 74-76, mem, Venus Orbital Imaging Radar Sci Working Group, 77-78, mem, Lunar & Planetary Geosci Rev Panel, 80-88, chmn, 86-88, mem, Megellan Proj Sci Group, 81-94, chmn, Planetary Geol & Geophys Working Group, 84-86, mem, Space & Earth Sci Adv Comt, 84-87, mem, Solar Syst Explor Subcomt, 96-97; assoc ed, J Geophys Res, 76-78; Comt Planetary & Lunar Exploration, Nat Acad Sci-Nat Res Coun, 76-79, mem, Space Sci Bd, 78-82, chmn, Comt Earth Sci, 79-82, mem, Bd Earth Sci, 85-88; Alfred P Sloan res fel, 77-81; mem, Lunar & Planetary Sci Coun, Univ Space Res Asn, 78-80, 91-93; assoc ed, Eos Trans Am Geophys Union, 78-81; mem, Tech Rev Panel Nuclear Test Ban Treaty Verification, Defense Advan Projs Agency, 81-87; John Simon Guggenheim mem fel, 82-83; vis fac, Univ Calif, Los Angeles, 82-83; assoc, Space Sci Working Group, Am Univ, 84-91, chmn, 87-89; assoc ed, Geophys Res Lett, 86-88; Standing Comt, Global Seismic Network, Inc Res Insts Seismol, 87-90, chmn, 88-90; vis assoc, Calif Inst Technol, 90-91; mem, Vis Comt Nat Astron & Ionosphere Ctr, Cornell Univ, 95-98, pres-elect & pres, 94-98. *Mem:* Fel Am Geophys Union (pres-elect & pres, Planetology Sect, 84-88); Seismol Soc Am; AAAS; Geol Soc Am; Am Astron Soc; fel Am Acad Arts & Sci. *Res:* Earthquake seismology; marine geophysics; planetary geology and geophysics. *Mailing Add:* Dept Terrestial Magnetism Carnegie Inst Wash 5241 Broad Branch Rd NW Washington DC 20015. *Fax:* 202-364-8726; *E-Mail:* scs@dtm.ciw.edu

SOLOMON, SEYMOUR, HEADACHE. *Current Pos:* head EEG Dept, 55-71, ATTEND NEUROLOGIST, MONTEFIORE HOSP & MED CTR, 55-, DIR, HEADACHE UNIT, MED CTR, 80- *Personal Data:* b Milwaukee, Wis, May 27, 24; m 49, Ethel M Ross; c Robert & Debora. *Educ:* Marquette Univ, MD, 47. *Prof Exp:* Chief neurol, Philadelphia Gen Hosp, 52-53; attend neurologist, Bronx Munic City Hosp, 71-81. *Concurrent Pos:* Asst clin prof neurol, dept neurol, Col Physicians & Surgeons, Columbia Univ, 58-64; assoc prof neurol, 80-83, prof neurol, Albert Einstein Col Med, Yeshiva Univ, 83-; mem, Migraine Res Group, World Fedn Neurol, 85- *Mem:* Am Acad Neurol; Assoc Res Nervous & Mental Dis; Am Asn Study Headaches (treas & vpres, 88-92, pres, 92; Int Asn Study Pain; Am Pain Soc; Int Headache Soc; Am Neurol Asn. *Res:* Clinical research in the field of headache, particularly migraine, tension-type and cluster headache. *Mailing Add:* Montefiore Med Ctr 111 E 210th St Bronx NY 10467. *Fax:* 718-920-8341

SOLOMON, SOLOMON SIDNEY, MEDICINE, METABOLISM & ENDOCRINOLOGY. *Current Pos:* from asst prof to assoc prof, 69-77, PROF MED, UNIV TENN, MEMPHIS, 77-, ASSOC DEAN, RES COL MED, CTR HEALTH SCI, 83-, PROF PHARMACOL, 86-; CHIEF ENDOCRINOL & METAB, VET ADMIN HOSP, MEMPHIS, 71- *Personal Data:* b New York, NY, Dec 2, 36; m 62; c Joan G & Rebecca K. *Educ:* Harvard Univ, AB, 58; Univ Rochester, MD, 62. *Prof Exp:* Intern internal med, Med Ctr, Tufts Univ, 62-63, resident, Univ & Boston City Hosp, 63-65; fel, Endocrinol & Metab, Univ Wash Med Ctr, Seattle, 65-57; capt USAF MC, Chief of Med, Dyess AFB, Abilene, Tex, 67-69; res & educ assoc, Vet Admin Hosp, Memphis, 69-71. *Concurrent Pos:* Vet Admin Hosp career develop award, Univ Tenn, Memphis, 69-71; attend physician, City of Memphis Hosp, 71-; pres, Tenn Chap Am Diabetes Asn, 76; chair, Am Fedn Clin Res (South) & Southern Soc Clin Invest 77, 88, 90 & 92; chair, Am Diabetes Asn Metab, 83. *Mem:* Am Soc Clin Invest; Am Fedn Clin Res; Am Diabetes Asn; Endocrine Soc; Am Soc Pharmacol & Exp Therapeut; Cent Soc Clin Res. *Res:* Diabetes; intermediary metabolism; mechanism of action of insulin; role of second messenger's cyclic adenosine monophosphate in adipose tissue in normal and diabetic conditions; cyclic adenosine monophosphate phosphodiesterase, lipolysis; hormonal receptors diabetic animal models; molecular studies of 2nd messengers. *Mailing Add:* Vet Admin Hosp 1030 Jefferson Ave Memphis TN 38104. *Fax:* 901-577-7273

SOLOMON, SUSAN, PHOTOCHEMISTRY. *Current Pos:* RES CHEMIST, NAT OCEANIC & ATMOSPHERIC ADMIN, 81- *Personal Data:* b Chicago, Ill, Jan 19, 56; m 88. *Educ:* Ill Inst Technol, BS, 77; Univ Calif, Berkeley, MS, 79 & PhD(chem), 81. *Hon Degrees:* Dr, Tulane Univ, Williams Col, Univ Colo. *Honors & Awards:* J B MacElwane Award, Am Geophys Union, 85; Henry G Houghton Award, Am Meteorol Soc; Antarctic glacier named in honor, 94. *Concurrent Pos:* Assoc ed, J Atmospheric Sci, 83-86; mem, Comt Solar & Space Physics, NASA, 83-86, Space & Earth Sci Adv Comt, 85-88; adj prof, Univ Colo, Boulder, 85-; assoc ed, J Geophys Res, 85-; head proj scientist, Nat Ozone Exped, McMurdo Sta, Antarctica, 86-87. *Mem:* Nat Acad Sci; Royal Meteorol Soc; Am Geophys Union; foreign assoc Fr Acad Sci. *Res:* Photochemistry; transport processes in the earth's stratosphere and mesosphere; polar ozone; atmospheric chemistry; observations and interpretation of the chemistry of the Antarctic ozone hole. *Mailing Add:* ERL Aeron Lab Nat Oceanic & Atmospheric Admin 325 Broadway Boulder CO 80303. *Fax:* 303-497-5373

SOLOMON, SUSAN DIANE, SOCIAL PSYCHOLOGY. *Current Pos:* Res psychologist, Servs Res Br, Nat Inst Alcohol Abuse & Alcoholism, NIH, 80-83, chief, Disaster Res Prog, 83-90, chief, Violence & Traumatic Stress Res Br, NIMH, 90-95, SR ADV, OFF BEHAV & SOCIAL SCI RES, NIH, 95- *Personal Data:* b Minneapolis, Minn, May 2, 48. *Educ:* Univ Minn, BS, 71, MA, 75; Boston Univ, PhD(social psychol), 80. *Honors & Awards:* Pres Award, Int Soc Traumatic Stress Studies, 91. *Mem:* Int Soc Traumatic Stress Studies (secy & pres, 90-91); Am Psychol Asn. *Res:* Disaster; post-traumatic stress disorder; violence; behavioral science. *Mailing Add:* Off Dir NIH Fed Bldg Rm 8C16 7550 Wisconsin Ave Bethesda MD 20892. *Fax:* 301-480-8905; *E-Mail:* ssoloman@nih.gov

SOLOMON, THOMAS ALLAN, PHARMACOLOGY, CARDIOVASCULAR PHYSIOLOGY. *Current Pos:* assoc dir, Dept Clin Pharmacol, 87-90, ASSOC DIR, DEPT MED IMAGING, BERLEX LABS, 90- *Personal Data:* b New Kensington, Pa, Apr 3, 41; m 68. *Educ:* Westminster Col, Pa, BS, 64; WVa Univ, MA, 67; Univ Pittsburgh, PhD(pharmacol), 72. *Prof Exp:* From instr to asst prof psychiat & behav biol, Sch Med, 72-76, instr environ med, Sch Pub Health, 73-75, asst prof psychiat & behav biol, Sch Med, Johns Hopkins Univ, 74-76, instr environ med, Sch Pub Health, 73-75; head cardiovasc pharmacol, Pharmaceut Div, Sandoz, Inc, 74-80; assoc dir, Dept Clin Pharmacol, Revlon Health Care, 80-85, dir, 85-87. *Mem:* NY Acad Sci; Johns Hopkins Med Surg Soc; AAAS; Am Heart Asn; Sigma Xi. *Res:* Circulation; cardiovascular system and its regulation; control mechanisms involved in hypertension; cardiovascular pharmacology. *Mailing Add:* 265 Old Mill Rd Chester NJ 07930

SOLOMON, VASANTH BALAN, APPLIED STATISTICS. *Current Pos:* PROF STATIST, RADFORD UNIV, 88- *Personal Data:* b Nagercoil, Madras, India, Aug 8, 35; US citizen; m 60; c 2. *Educ:* Univ Madras, BSc, 58, MSc, 61; Iowa State Univ, PhD(statist), 70. *Prof Exp:* Statistician, Rubber Res Inst Ceylon, 62-64; biometrician, Dept Fisheries & Forestry, Govt of Can, 67-69; assoc prof statist, Drake Univ, 70-88. *Mem:* Am Statist Asn; Sigma Xi. *Res:* Statistical research in epidemiological problems. *Mailing Add:* 205 Wild Partridge Lane Radford VA 24141

SOLOMONOW, MOSHE, REHABILITATION ENGINEERING, NEUROSCIENCES. *Current Pos:* PROF & DIR BIOENG, LA STATE UNIV MED CTR, NEW ORLEANS, 83- *Personal Data:* b Tel-Aviv, Israel, Oct 24, 44; US & Israeli citizen; m 81, Susanne Nickerson; c Deborah & Esther. *Educ:* Calif State Univ, BS, 70, MS, 72; Univ Calif, Los Angeles, PhD(eng), 76. *Prof Exp:* Chief engr med eng, Calmag Electronics, 68-71, proj engr med eng, 72-73; res engr neuromuscular eng, Rancho Los Amigos Hosp, 71-72; clin intern prosthetics, Child Amputee Clin, Univ Calif, Los Angeles, 75, res engr, 73-80; assoc prof, Dept Biomed Eng, Tulane Univ, 80-83. *Concurrent Pos:* Consult, Olivetti Am Inc, 74-75 & Child Amputee Clin, Univ Calif, Los Angeles, 75-76; prin engr, Bennett Respiration Prod Inc, 77; consult, Lida Inc, 75-, Perceptronics Inc, 75-76, Vet Admin Hosp, Brentwood, 77-78, Vet Admin Hosp, Sepulveda, 78-80 & Dept Health, La, 81-85, NIH, 80-, NSF, 87-, Vet Admin, Washington, 87- *Mem:* Biomed Eng Soc; AAAS; Sigma Xi; Inst Elec & Electronics Engrs; Int Soc Biomechanics; Int Soc Electrophysiol Kinesiology; Orthop Res Soc. *Res:* Prosthetics, orthotics, biomechanics and electrophysiology of movement. *Mailing Add:* Dept Orthop La State Univ Med 433 Bolivar St New Orleans LA 70112. *Fax:* 504-599-1144

SOLOMONS, CLIVE (CHARLES), BIOCHEMISTRY, PEDIATRICS. *Current Pos:* assoc prof pediat, 63-75, PROF ORTHOP, DIR ORTHOP RES, ASSOC PROF ANAESTHESIOL, 75-, UNIV COLO MED CTR, DENVER, RES PROF, 85- *Personal Data:* b Johannesburg, SAfrica, June 6, 31; m 56; c 3. *Educ:* Univ Witwatersrand, BS, 52, PhD(biochem), 56. *Prof Exp:* Biochemist, SAfrican Inst Med Res, 52-55; biochemist, Dent Res Univ, Coun Sci & Indust Res & Univ Witwatersrand, 55-61; asst prof biochem,

McGill Univ, 61-63. *Concurrent Pos:* Fel radiation biol, Univ Rochester, 58-59; Can Med Res Coun grant, 61-63; NIH grant, 64-; NSF grant; Cystic Fibrosis Res Found grant. *Res:* Application of analytical biochemistry to clinical and basic science investigation, especially on the metabolism of connective tissue disorders; metals in the environment, cystic fibrosis and renal disease, and anaesthetic risk; Reyes syndrome; orthopedics anaesthesiology. *Mailing Add:* 164 S Fairfax Denver CO 80222-1141

SOLOMONS, GERALD, PEDIATRICS, CHILD GROWTH. *Current Pos:* RETIRED. *Personal Data:* b London, Eng, Feb 22, 21; US citizen; m 55; c 2. *Educ:* Royal Col Physicians & Surgeons, Edinburgh, LRCP, LRCS, 43; Royal Col Physicians & Surgeons Eng, dipl child health, 48; Am Bd Pediat, dipl, 52. *Prof Exp:* Asst supt, Charles V Chapin Hosp, Providence, RI, 52; pvt pract, 53-59; dep dir pediat, Inst Health Sci, Brown Univ, 59-62; asst mem, 60-62; from asst prof to prof pediat, Univ Iowa, 62-84, dir, Child Develop Clin, 63-84, actg head, Inst Child Behav & Develop, 75-84. *Concurrent Pos:* Consult, NIH, 59-; prog dir, Regional Ctr Child Abuse & Neglect, 75- *Mem:* Fel Am Acad Pediat; fel Am Acad Cerebral Palsy (pres, 77-78); Am Asn Ment Deficiency. *Res:* Child abuse; minimal brain damage, its diagnosis, drug therapy and effect on learning. *Mailing Add:* 319 Mullin Ave Iowa City IA 52246

SOLOMONS, NOEL WILLIS, CLINICAL NUTRITION, GASTROENTEROLOGY. *Current Pos:* SR SCIENTIST, CTR STUDIES SENSORY IMPAIRMENT, AGING & NUTRITION, GUATEMALA CITY, 85- *Personal Data:* b Boston, Mass, Dec 31, 44. *Educ:* Harvard Univ, AB, 66; Harvard Med Sch, MD, 70. *Prof Exp:* Instr med, Univ Chicago, 75-76, res assoc gastroenterol, 77-80; from asst to assoc prof clin nutrit, dept nutrit & food sci, Mass Inst Technol, 80-84. *Concurrent Pos:* Nutrit Found grant, 74-77; Josiah Macy Jr Found fac fel, 75-76; res assoc clin nutrit, Div Human Nutrit & Biol, Inst Nutrit Cent Am & Panama, 76-78, affil sci, 78-; mem, Comt Int Nutrit, Nat Acad Sci, 79-82. *Mem:* Am Gastroenterol Asn; Am Soc Clin Nutrit; Am Fedn Clin Res; Am Soc Nutrit; Latin Am Nutrit Soc. *Res:* Trace mineral nutrition; protein-energy malnutrition; trace mineral absorption, non-invasive and stable isotope technology in absorptive physiology. *Mailing Add:* CeSSIAM Hosp de Ojos y Oidos Dr Radolfo Robles V Diagonal 21 y 19 Calle, Zona 11 Guatemala City Guatemala. *Fax:* 502-2-5922-733906

SOLOMONS, THOMAS WILLIAM GRAHAM, ORGANIC CHEMISTRY. *Current Pos:* instr, 60-61, from asst prof to assoc prof, 61-73, PROF CHEM, UNIV S FLA, 73- *Personal Data:* b Charleston, SC, Aug 30, 34. *Educ:* The Citadel, BS, 55; Duke Univ, PhD(chem), 59. *Prof Exp:* Sloan Found fel, Univ Rochester, 59-60. *Mem:* Am Chem Soc. *Res:* Synthesis and reactions of heterocyclic aromatic compounds. *Mailing Add:* Hanging Birch House Hanging Birch Lane Horam Heathfield East Sussex TN21 0PA England

SOLOMONS, WILLIAM EBENEZER, MEDICINAL CHEMISTRY, ORGANIC CHEMISTRY. *Current Pos:* assoc prof, 76-83, PROF CHEM, UNIV TENN, MARTIN, 83- *Personal Data:* b Ridgeland, SC, Oct 2, 43; m 65; c 2. *Educ:* Berry Col, BA, 65; Univ Miss, PhD(pharmaceut chem), 70. *Prof Exp:* Res asst prof, Ctr Health Sci, Univ Tenn, Memphis, 70-73, res assoc prof med chem, 73-76. *Mem:* Am Chem Soc; Sigma Xi. *Res:* Synthetic organic chemistry; organic synthesis and structure determination; the relationships between molecular structure and biological activity; synthesis of novel analgesic and antipsychotic agents. *Mailing Add:* 107 Alberta Martin TN 38237-3501

SOLOMONSON, LARRY PAUL, BIOCHEMISTRY. *Current Pos:* asst prof, 76-79, assoc prof biochem, 80-86, prof & actg chmn, 86-88, CHMN, DEPT BIOCHEM & MOLECULAR BIOL, UNIV SOUTH FLA, 88- *Personal Data:* b Scarville, Iowa, June 26, 41; m 68; c 2. *Educ:* Luther Col, BA, 63; Univ Chicago, PhD(biochem), 69. *Prof Exp:* Res chemist res & develop, Borden Chem Co, 63-64; amanuensis, Physiol Inst, Univ Aarhus, Denmark, 69-70; scientist, Max Planck Inst, Berlin, Ger, 70-74; vis asst prof, Col Med, Univ Iowa, 74-76. *Mem:* AAAS; Am Chem Soc; Am Soc Biol Chemists; Am Soc Plant Physiologists; Sigma Xi. *Res:* Mechanism and regulation of nitrate assimilation; molecular properties and functions of the sodium pump. *Mailing Add:* Col Med Dept Biochem & Molecular Biol 12901 Bruce B Downs Blvd Tampa FL 33612-4799

SOLON, LEONARD RAYMOND, RADIOLOGICAL PHYSICS, RADIATION EPIDEMIOLOGY. *Current Pos:* HEALTH PHYSICS CONSULT & EDUCR, 91- *Personal Data:* b White Plains, NY, Sept 11, 25; m 46, Charlotte Rothman; c Miriam, Matthew & Emily. *Educ:* Hamilton Col, AB, 47; Rutgers Univ, MSc, 49; NY Univ, PhD(radiol health), 60. *Prof Exp:* Physicist, Nuclear Develop Assocs, 50-52; physicist, Radiation Br, Health & Safety Lab, US Atomic Energy Comn, 52-54, asst chief, 54-59, chief, 59-60; dir appl nuclear tech, Tech Res Group, Inc, NY, 60-64; mgr res & develop, Del Electronics Corp, mem vpres & tech dir, Hadron Inc, Westbury, 67-75; dir, Bur Radiation Control, Dept Health, NY, 75-91. *Concurrent Pos:* Lectr, Med Center, NY Univ, 56-60, from adj asst prof to adj assoc prof, 60-93; mem tech consults panel, Div Mil Appln, US Atomic Energy Comn, 57-60, consult, Health & Safety Lab, 62-65; prof health physics, US Merchant Marine Acad, 64. *Mem:* Am Phys Soc; Sigma Xi; Health Physics Soc; Am Nuclear Soc. *Res:* Radiation protection and health physics; environmental radiation measurements; laser physics and applications; biomedical instrumentation; radiation dosimetry; lead toxicity evaluation and abatement; application of lasers to thermonuclear fusion. *Mailing Add:* 1756 Lakefront Blvd Ft Pierce FL 34982

SOLORZANO, ROBERT FRANCIS, VIROLOGY, MEDICAL MICROBIOLOGY. *Current Pos:* RETIRED. *Personal Data:* b New York, NY, May 21, 29; div; c Jean L, Carolyn A & Robert S. *Educ:* Georgetown Univ, BS, 51; Pa State Univ, MS, 56, PhD(bact), 62. *Prof Exp:* Bacteriologist, Montefiore Hosp Chronic Dis, New York, 53-54; res asst virol, Children's Hosp, Philadelphia, Pa, 56-58; asst, Pa State Univ, 58-62; asst virologist, Coastal Plain Exp Sta, Univ Ga, 62-68; from assoc prof to prof vet microbiol, Col Vet Med, Univ Mo, Columbia, sr virologist, Vet Med Diag Lab, 68-95. *Concurrent Pos:* Mem, Am Asn & NCent Conf Vet Lab Diagnosticians; Fulbright res fel, Mex. *Mem:* AAAS; Am Soc Microbiol; Am Asn Vet Lab Diagnosticians; Am Leptosirosis Res Conf. *Res:* Japanese B encephalitis ecology; effect of sonic vibrations on Newcastle virus; entero-cytopathogenic human orphan virus serology; fluorescent antibody test for hog cholera; serology for leptospirosis; ecology of hog cholera virus; enteric virus diseases of swine; diagnostic virology, and serology; pseudorabies; turkey parvovirus. *Mailing Add:* Rte 6201 Molly Columbia MO 65203. *Fax:* 573-884-5050

SOLOTOROVSKY, MORRIS, bacteriology; deceased, see previous edition for last biography

SOLOVAY, ROBERT M, LOGIC, SET THEORY. *Current Pos:* Prof math, 86-96, EMER PROF MATH, UNIV CALIF, BERKELEY, 96- *Mem:* Nat Acad Sci. *Res:* Mathematics. *Mailing Add:* PO Box 5949 Eugene OR 97405

SOLOW, DANIEL, MATHEMATICAL PROGRAMMING. *Current Pos:* ASST PROF OPERS RES, CASE WESTERN RESERVE UNIV, 78- *Personal Data:* b Washington, DC, Nov 19, 49; m 80. *Educ:* Carnegie-Mellon Univ, BS, 70; Univ Calif, Berkeley, MS, 72; Stanford Univ, PhD(opers res), 78. *Mem:* Opers Res Soc; Math Prog Soc; Am Math Soc; Math Asn Am. *Res:* Development of computational algorithms for solving mathematical problems arising in combinatorial optimization, mathematical programming and operations research. *Mailing Add:* Dept Opers Res Case Western Res Univ 10900 Euclid Cleveland OH 44106-4901

SOLOW, MAX, PHYSICS, METALLURGY. *Current Pos:* RETIRED. *Personal Data:* b Philadelphia, Pa, Nov 20, 16; m 41; c 2. *Educ:* George Washington Univ, BEE, 43, MS, 50; Catholic Univ, PhD(physics), 57. *Prof Exp:* Radio engr, Nat Bur Stand, 46-49, electronic scientist, 49-53; physicist, US Naval Ord Lab, 53-60; sr scientist, Martin Co, 60-64; res coordr physics, US Navy Marine Eng Lab, 64-68 & Naval Ship Res & Develop Ctr, Annapolis, 68-71, sr res scientist/tech consult, 71-80; mem staff, Univ Md, College Park, Md, 81-85. *Mem:* Am Phys Soc; AAAS; Am Soc Metals; Inst Elec & Electronics Engrs; Am Inst Mining, Metall & Petrol Engrs; Sigma Xi. *Res:* Solid state physics; metals; electrochemistry; corrosion, materials; vacancy and dislocation technique and theory; random noise; explosion hydrodynamics; lasers; holography. *Mailing Add:* 725 Mt Wilson Lane Baltimore MD 21208

SOLOWAY, ALBERT HERMAN, MEDICINAL CHEMISTRY. *Current Pos:* prof med chem & dean, 77-88, PROF MED CHEM, COL PHARM, OHIO STATE UNIV, 88- *Personal Data:* b Worcester, Mass, May 29, 25; m 53, Barbara Berkowicz; c Madeleine (Carolan), Paul & Renee (Spiegler). *Educ:* Worcester Polytech Inst, BS, 48; Univ Rochester, PhD(org chem), 51. *Prof Exp:* USPHS fel, Sloan-Kettering Inst, 51-53; res chemist, Eastman Kodak Co, 53-56; res assoc surg, Harvard Med Sch, 56-63; from asst chemist to assoc chemist, Mass Gen Hosp, 56-73; assoc prof med chem, Northeastern Univ, 66-71, chmn dept med chem & pharmacol, Col Pharm & Allied Health Professions, 71-74, prof med chem & chem, 71-77, dir grad sch, Pharm & Allied Health Professions, 73-77, dean, Col Pharm & Allied Health Professions, 75-77. *Mem:* Fel AAAS; Am Chem Soc; Am Asn Cols Pharm; Am Asn Pharm Sci; Am Asn Cancer Res; Am Nuclear Soc. *Res:* Cancer therapy; development of drugs for chemoimmuno and chemoradiotherapy; use of Boron compounds in cancer. *Mailing Add:* Ohio State Univ Col Pharm 500 W 12th Ave Columbus OH 43210

SOLOWAY, HAROLD, organic chemistry, medicinal chemistry; deceased, see previous edition for last biography

SOLOWAY, S BARNEY, ORGANIC CHEMISTRY. *Current Pos:* RETIRED. *Personal Data:* b New York, NY, Jan 21, 15; m 38; c 2. *Educ:* City Col New York, BS, 36; Univ Colo, PhD(chem), 55. *Prof Exp:* Chemist, Div Insecticide Invests, USDA, 41-47; chemist & asst dir, Julius Hyman & Co, 47-52; supvr org res, Agr Res Div, Shell Develop Co, 52-64, head, Org Chem Div, Woodstock Agr Res Ctr, Shell Res Ltd, 64-67, head org chem, 67-80, asst to dir, Agr Res Div, Shell Develop Co, 80- 86. *Mem:* Am Chem Soc. *Res:* Synthesis; stereochemistry; agricultural chemicals. *Mailing Add:* 3401 Mansfield Lane Modesto CA 95350-1514

SOLOWAY, SAUL, ORGANIC CHEMISTRY. *Current Pos:* CONSULT CHEMIST, 73- *Personal Data:* b New York, NY, Apr 12, 16; m 44; c 3. *Educ:* City Col New York, BS, 36; Columbia Univ, AM, 38, PhD(chem), 42. *Prof Exp:* Hernschiem fel, Mt Sinai Hosp, New York, 40-41; mem staff, Nat Defense Res Comn, US Bur Mines, 41-43; Panel Chem Corp, 43-44 & Grosvenor Labs, 44-46; instr chem, City Col New York, 46-50, from asst prof to assoc prof, 50-73. *Concurrent Pos:* Consult, Faberge, Inc, 56-, dir res, 58-; consult, Revlon, 60-64. *Mem:* Am Chem Soc; NY Acad Sci. *Res:* Chelation; cosmetics; perfume; encapsulation of liquids; lipids; organic analysis; polymerization; thermochromism. *Mailing Add:* 180 Broadview Ave New Rochelle NY 10804. *Fax:* 914-636-6970

SOLOYANIS, SUSAN CONSTANCE, GLACIAL GEOLOGY, PETROLEUM GEOLOGY. *Current Pos:* HYDROGEOLOGIST, MITRE CORP, 89- *Personal Data:* b New York, NY, Jan 21, 52. *Educ:* Smith Col, AB, 72; Univ Mass, Amherst, MS, 75, PhD(geol), 78. *Prof Exp:* Geologist environ geol, Conn Valley Urban Area Proj, US Geol Surv, 71-75; teaching asst geol & geog, Univ Mass, Amherst, 74-78; geologist petrol geol, Amoco Prod Co, 78-89. *Concurrent Pos:* Teaching asst geol, Univ Ill, Urbana, 72-73. *Mem:* Geol Soc Am; Am Geophys Union; Sigma Xi; Soc Econ Paleontologists & Mineralogists. *Res:* Pleistocene paleomagnetic stratigraphy; magnetization of sediments; glacial sedimentation; petroleum exploration. *Mailing Add:* 4610 Fox Rd Cascade CO 80809

SOLSKY, JOSEPH FAY, ANALYTICAL CHEMISTRY. *Current Pos:* US ARMY CORPS ENGRS, 85- *Personal Data:* b Corning, NY, June 9, 49; m 70; c 2. *Educ:* State Univ NY, Buffalo, BA, 71, PhD(chem), 78. *Prof Exp:* Asst prof chem, Creighton Univ, 76-85. *Mem:* Am Chem Soc. *Res:* Investigations of stationary phases used in chromatographic systems including liquid crystal and permanently bound types. *Mailing Add:* US Army Corps Engrs 12565 W Center Rd Omaha NE 68144-3869

SOLT, DENNIS BYRON, ORAL PATHOLOGY. *Current Pos:* ASSOC PROF PATH, NORTHWESTERN UNIV MED & DENT SCHS, 82- *Educ:* Temple Univ, PhD(exp path), 78. *Mailing Add:* Dept Path 13280 WMB Northwestern Univ Med & Dent Schs 303 E Chicago Ave Chicago IL 60611-3072

SOLT, PAUL E, PNEUMATIC CONVEYING OF BULK MATERIALS. *Current Pos:* CONSULT, PNEUMATIC CONVEYING CONSULTS, 84- *Personal Data:* b Allentown, Pa, Feb 23, 29; m 50, Myrtle Schmoyer; c Timothy S & Patricia (Souders). *Educ:* Lehigh Univ, BS, 50. *Prof Exp:* Serv engr, Fuller Co, 50-52, res engr, 54-56; Lt, USAF, Korea, 52-54; proj engr, Mack Trucks, 56-62; res engr, Fuller Co, GATX, 62-68, mgr res, 68-84. *Concurrent Pos:* Course dir, Ctr Prof Advan, 72- & Am Inst Chem Engrs, 84-; consult, Teltech Resource Network, 87-; consult ed, Power & Bulk Eng, 89- *Mem:* Am Inst Chem Engrs. *Res:* Pneumatic conveying of bulk materials, including design, troubleshooting, engineering lectures and courses, expert witness and system modifications. *Mailing Add:* 529 S Berks St Allentown PA 18104-6647. *Fax:* 610-437-7935; *E-Mail:* pecsolt@itw.com

SOLTAN, HUBERT CONSTANTINE, MEDICAL GENETICS. *Current Pos:* RETIRED. *Personal Data:* b Wilno, Poland, Dec 16, 32; Can nat; m 62; c 3. *Educ:* Univ Toronto, BA, 55, PhD(human genetics), 59; Univ Western Ont, MD, 70. *Prof Exp:* Res fel genetics, Hosp Sick Children, Toronto, Ont, 55-58; asst prof biol, St Mary's Univ, NS, 58-61; from asst prof to assoc prof human genetics, Fac Med, Univ Western Ont, 61-77, clin assoc prof pediat, 71-77, prof human genetics, & clin prof pediat, 77-; med geneticist, Children's Hosp Western Ont, 77-97. *Mem:* Genetics Soc Can; Asn Genetic Counr Ont; Can Col Med Geneticists; Am Soc Human Genetics. *Mailing Add:* Children's Hosp Western Ont 800 Commissioners Rd E London ON N6C 2V5 Can

SOLTANI-GHASEMI, AZITA, BIOPHYSICS, MEDICAL PHYSICS. *Current Pos:* RES ASST, APPL PHYSICS LAB, UNIV WASH, 97- *Personal Data:* b Tehran, Iran, Apr 19, 63; Austrian citizen; m 95, Nader Noorfeshan. *Educ:* Tech Univ Vienna, MS, 93, PhD(med biophys), 96. *Prof Exp:* Res asst, Austrian Atomic Inst, 93-95. *Res:* Regulation effect of light on proliferation of human skin fibrosarcom and fibroblast cell cultures; x-ray fluorescence analysis of ancient ceramics; ultrasound increase the effect of thrombolysis. *Mailing Add:* 12032 53rd Ave SE Everett WA 98208. *Fax:* 425-316-7958; *E-Mail:* nader@halcyon.com

SOLTANPOUR, PARVIZ NEIL, SOIL FERTILITY, AGRONOMY. *Current Pos:* FROM ASST PROF TO PROF SOIL FERTILITY, COLO STATE UNIV, 66- *Personal Data:* b Tehran, Iran, Mar 21, 37; m 60; c 4. *Educ:* Am Univ Beirut, BS, 61, MS, 63; Univ Nebr, PhD(soil fertility), 66. *Concurrent Pos:* Consult, Egypt Water Mgt Proj, 78-83, Morocco Dryland Proj, 85-88, Asn Int Develop, Comn Int Develop & Colo State Univ; chmn, Coun on Soil Testing & Plant Anal, 83-84. *Mem:* Am Soc Agron; Soil Sci Soc Am; Int Soc Soil Sci; Sigma Xi. *Res:* Methods of soil testing for fertilizer recommendations; soil fertility and plant nutrition. *Mailing Add:* 3304 Shore Rd - Ft Collins CO 80524

SOLTER, DAVOR, DEVELOPMENTAL BIOLOGY. *Current Pos:* DIR, MAX PLANCK INST. *Personal Data:* b Zagreb, Yugoslavia, Mar 22, 41. *Educ:* Univ Zagreb, MD, 65, MSc, 68, PhD(biol), 71. *Prof Exp:* Instr anat, Med Sch, Univ Zagreb, 66-68, instr biol, 68-72, asst prof, 72-73. *Concurrent Pos:* Europ Molecular Biol Orgn scholar, 71; Damon Runyon Mem Cancer Fund fel, 73; assoc scientist, Wistar Inst, 73-75, assoc mem, 75-80, prof, 81-91, adj Wistar prof, 91-; assoc ed, Develop Biol, 80-87 & 92-95; mem, Study Sect Human Embryol & Develop, NIH, 81-85; Wistar prof biol, fac arts & sci, Univ Pa, 84-; scholar in residence, John E Fogarty Int Ctr, NIH, 94-98. *Mem:* Soc Develop Biol; foreign hon mem Am Acad Arts & Sci; Brit Soc Develop Biol; Ger Soc Develop Biol. *Res:* Development of early mouse embryo; role of membrane molecules in development of early mouse embryo; genetic control of development, nuclear transfer and transgenic animals; genomic imprinting. *Mailing Add:* Max Planck Inst Stubeweg 51 79108 Freiburg Germany. *Fax:* 43-761-5108-569; *E-Mail:* solter@immunbio.mpg.de

SOLTES, EDWARD JOHN, WOOD CHEMISTRY. *Current Pos:* assoc prof forest sci, Tex A&M Univ, 76-81, prof wood chem, 81-84, prof forest sci & plant physiol, Agr Exp Sta, 84-89, interim dept head, 89-90, assoc head acad affairs, 90-92, PROF FOREST SCI & PLANT PHYSIOL, TEX A&M UNIV, 92- *Personal Data:* b Montreal, Que, Mar 25, 41; m 87, Patty Patterson; c 4. *Educ:* McGill Univ, BSc, 61, PhD(carbohydrate chem), 65. *Honors & Awards:* Res Award, Tex Forestry Asn, 83. *Prof Exp:* Fel, Ohio State Univ, 65-66, lectr, 66; sr res chemist, Tech Ctr, St Regis Paper Co, 66-76, asst to dir res & develop, 70-71, responsibility Sylvachem Res & Develop, 73-75, responsibility wood chem, 75-76. *Concurrent Pos:* Chmn, Div Cellulose, Paper & Textile Chem, Am Chem Soc, 79, Tex A&M Sect, 86, 94 & Coun Comt Div Activ, 92-93; secy-gen, Macromolecular Secretariat, Am Chem Soc, 82, counr, 84-93. *Mem:* Am Chem Soc. *Res:* Wood chemistry, utilization of agricultural and forestry residues, pyrolysis, naval stores; physiology of tissue culture processes, molecular bases for host/pathogen interactions, photo bioreactor development and bioprocessing; resource sustainability. *Mailing Add:* 1884 Harris Dr College Station TX 77845. *Fax:* 409-845-6049

SOLTYSIK, EDWARD A, ATOMIC PHYSICS. *Current Pos:* assoc prof, 62-71, prof physics, 71-91, EMER PROF, UNIV MASS, AMHERST, 91- *Personal Data:* b Newark, NJ, Aug 23, 29; m 58; c 3. *Educ:* Lafayette Col, BS, 50; Ind Univ, MS, 52, PhD(nuclear physics), 56. *Prof Exp:* Lectr physics, Univ Nev, 55-56; physicist, Lawrence Radiation Lab, 56-62. *Concurrent Pos:* Consult, Lawrence Radiation Lab, 62-65 & Air Force Off Sci Res grants, 63- *Res:* Nuclear decay, shake off process and inner Bremsstrahlung; atomic physics, polarization of collisional radiation, especially radiation resulting from the collisions of electrons and protons on atoms. *Mailing Add:* La Clair Rd Churubusco NY 12923

SOLTZ, DAVID LEE, POPULATION ECOLOGY, ICHTHYOLOGY. *Current Pos:* from asst prof to assoc prof, 74-82, PROF BIOL, CALIF STATE UNIV, 82-, CHMN DEPT, 81- *Personal Data:* b La Cross, Wis, Nov 7, 46; m 78; c 2. *Educ:* Univ Calif, BA, 68, PhD(biol), 74. *Concurrent Pos:* NSF grant, 77-79; consult, Bur Land Mgr, US Fish & Wildlife Serv, Los Angeles County, Santa Barbara County, 78-; vis scientist, Univ Mich, 84. *Mem:* AAAS; Am Soc Ichthyologists & Herpetologists; Ecol Soc Am; Soc Study Evolution. *Res:* Population biology; evolutionary and reproductive ecology of fish populations; community ecology of isolated freshwater habitats. *Mailing Add:* Dept Biol Calif State Univ Long Beach 3702 Csulb Long Beach CA 90840-0004

SOLTZBERG, LEONARD JAY, PHYSICAL CHEMISTRY, CRYSTALLOGRAPHY. *Current Pos:* asst prof, 69-73, assoc prof, 73-79, PROF CHEM, SIMMONS COL, 79- *Personal Data:* b Wilmington, Del, July 10, 44. *Educ:* Univ Del, BS, 65; Brandeis Univ, MA, 67, PhD(phys chem), 69. *Prof Exp:* Nat Res Coun res assoc, Air Force Cambridge Res Lab, 69. *Mem:* Sigma Xi; Am Crystallog Asn; Am Chem Soc. *Res:* Chemical crystallography; optical and x-ray crystallography; phase transitions; microscopy; pedagogical computer application. *Mailing Add:* Dept of Chem Simmons Col 300 The Fenway Boston MA 02115

SOLURSH, MICHAEL, DEVELOPMENTAL BIOLOGY, CELL BIOLOGY. *Current Pos:* from asst prof to assoc prof, 69-79, PROF BIOL, UNIV IOWA, 79- *Personal Data:* b Los Angeles, Calif, Dec 22, 42; m 64, Victoria Raskin; c Elizabeth Libby. *Educ:* Univ Calif, Los Angeles, BA, 64; Univ Wash, PhD(zool), 69. *Prof Exp:* Teaching asst zool, Univ Wash, 64-66. *Mem:* Am Soc Cell Biol; Am Soc Zool; Soc Develop Biol; Tissue Culture Asn; Am Asn Anatomists. *Res:* Extracellular materials in morphogenesis and migration of primary mesenchyme cell in sea urchin embryos; cartilage cell differentiation and limb morphogenesis (heterotypic and homotypic cell interaction during chondrogenesis). *Mailing Add:* 819 N Linn St Iowa City IA 52245. *Fax:* 319-335-2077; *E-Mail:* michael_solursh@uiowa.edu

SOM, PRANTIKA, NUCLEAR MEDICINE, VETERINARY MEDICINE. *Current Pos:* from asst scientist to assoc scientist, 75-80, SCIENTIST, NUCLEAR MED, BROOKHAVEN NAT LAB, 80- *Personal Data:* b Silchar, Assam, India, Aug 31, 42; US citizen. *Educ:* Univ Calcutta, ISc, 60, DVM, 65; Johns Hopkins Univ, ScM, 69. *Honors & Awards:* Raymond Star Gold Medal. *Prof Exp:* Demonstr path, Bengal Vet Col, 65-66; investr, Marine Biol Lab, Wood's Hole, Mass, 67-68; asst pathobiol, Johns Hopkins Med Inst, 67-69, sr res fel, 73-74. *Concurrent Pos:* Reserve vet asst surgeon, Govt W Bengal, 65-66; jr res fel, Johns Hopkins Univ, 70-72, asst radiol, 73-74; mem vet serv comt, Brookhaven Nat Lab, 75-; mem educ comt, Soc Nuclear Med, 76-; res asst prof, State Univ NY, 79-86; consult, Vet Admin Hosp, Nathpat, 81-; res assoc prof, State Univ NY, 86- *Mem:* Soc Nuclear Med; Am Vet Med Asn; Radiol Soc NAm; Am Asn Lab Animal Sci. *Res:* Radiopharmaceutical development; evaluations and studies on their pharmacokinetics, metabolism and toxicology. *Mailing Add:* 2 Taylor Commons Yaphank NY 11980

SOMA, LAWRENCE R, ANESTHESIOLOGY. *Current Pos:* fel anesthesiol, Sch Med, 60-62, instr, Sch Vet Med, 62-64, from asst prof to assoc prof, 64-72, PROF ANESTHESIOL, SCH VET MED, UNIV PA, 72-, CHMN DEPT CLIN STUDIES, 75- *Personal Data:* b New York, NY, Feb 2, 33; m 55; c 3. *Educ:* Univ Pa, VMD, 57. *Prof Exp:* Intern vet med, Animal Med Ctr, NY, 57-58. *Concurrent Pos:* NIH career develop award, 67-72, staff mem, Dept Anesthesiol, Sch Med, 71-; spec fel, Heart Lung Inst, 74-75. *Mem:* Am Vet Med Asn; AAAS; Am Soc Vet Physiologists & Pharmacologists; Am Thoracic Soc; Am Soc Anesthesiol. *Res:* Veterinary anesthesiology; anesthesia and pharmacology; effects of respiratory stimulants in the dog; cardiovascular effects of local anesthetics; effects of anesthetics on the fetus, pathophysiology of shock lung; physiology of bronchial circulation. *Mailing Add:* Dept Clin Studies Univ Pa Sch Vet Med New Bolten Ctr Campus Kennett Square PA 19348. *E-Mail:* soma@corinbc.upenn.edu

SOMANI, ARUN KUMAR, PARALLEL COMPUTER SYSTEMS, FAULT-TOLERANT COMPUTING. *Current Pos:* from asst prof to assoc prof, 85-95, PROF ELEC ENG, UNIV WASH, SEATTLE, 95-, PROF, DEPT COMPUT SCI & ENG, 95- *Personal Data:* b Beawar, Raj, India, July 16, 51; m 76, 87, Manju Kankani; c Ashutosh, Paritosh & Anju. *Educ:* Birla Inst Technol & Sci, Pilani, India, BE Hons, 73; IIT, Delhi, ME, 79; McGill Univ, MSEE, 83, PhD(elec eng), 85. *Prof Exp:* Tech officer, Electronics Corps India, 73-74; sci officer, Dept Electronics, Syst Group, Govt India, 74-79, scientist D, 79-82. *Concurrent Pos:* Assoc prof, Dept Comput Sci & Eng, Univ Wash, 90-; consult, Boeing Com, 91-95, prof dept comput sci & eng, Univ Wash, 95- *Mem:* Sr mem Inst Elec & Electronics Engrs; Inst Elec & Electronics Engrs Comput Soc; Asn Comput Mach. *Res:* Design of fault tolerant parallel computer system; fault diagnosis algorithms; parallel computer algorithms; computer communication networks; modeling and analysis of computer systems. *Mailing Add:* 16609 126th Ave NE Woodinville WA 98072. *E-Mail:* somani@ee.washington.edu

SOMANI, PITAMBAR (PETER), CLINICAL PHARMACOLOGY, MEDICINE. *Current Pos:* asst dir health, 91-92, DIR HEALTH, STATE OF OHIO, 92- *Personal Data:* b Chirawah, India, Oct 31, 37; m 60, Kamlesh; c Anita, Alok & Jyoti. *Educ:* G R Med Col, Gwalior, India, MD, 60; Marquette Univ, PhD(pharmacol), 65. *Prof Exp:* Demonstr pharmacol, India Inst Med Sci, New Delhi, 60-62; from instr to asst prof, Sch Med, Marquette Univ, 65-69; assoc prof, Med Col Wis, 69-71, assoc clin prof, 71-74; prof pharmacol, Sch Med, Univ Miami, 74-80; dir clin pharmacol, Med Col Ohio, 80-90. *Concurrent Pos:* Wis Heart Asn res grants, 65-71; NIH res grants, 66-72 & 74-78; Fla Heart Asn grant, 75 & 78; consult, Selvi & Co, Italy, 65-66, Abbott Labs, 74-76, Riker Labs, 77 & Dupont Labs, 78; mgr gen pharmacol dept, Abbott Labs, 71-74, Pfizer Labs, 80-90, Merck, 81-90. *Mem:* AAAS; Am Soc Pharmacol & Exp Therapeut; Am Fedn Clin Res; fel Am Col Clin Pharmacol; Am Med Asn; Am Asn Physicians India. *Res:* Cardiovascular and autonomic pharmacology; drug-design; clinical pharmacology; public health; health care reform; granted 4 US patents. *Mailing Add:* Ohio Dept Health 246 N High St Columbus OH 43266-0588

SOMANI, SATU M, PHARMACOLOGY, BIOCHEMICAL PHARMACOLOGY. *Current Pos:* assoc prof, 74-82, PROF PHARMACOL & TOXICOL, SCH MED, SOUTHERN ILL UNIV, SPRINGFIELD, 82- *Personal Data:* b India, Mar 14, 37; m 66, Shipra Datta; c Indira & Sheila. *Educ:* Osmania Univ, BSc, 56; Univ Poona, MSc, 59; Duquesne Univ, MS, 64; Univ Liverpool, PhD(biochem pharmacol), 69. *Prof Exp:* Lectr chem, Vivek Vardhini Col, Osmania Univ, India, 59-61; scientist, Nuclear Sci & Eng Corp, Pa, 64-67; from instr to asst prof pharmacol, Univ Pittsburgh, 71-74. *Concurrent Pos:* Ellis T Davies fel, Liverpool Univ, Eng, 67-69; NIH fel, Univ Pittsburgh, 69-70; Health Res found grant, Univ Pittsburgh, 71; grant, Environ Protection Agency, 77-80, Am Heart Asn, 83-84 & 91-93, Dept Army, 84-91 & Deafness Res Found, 94- *Mem:* AAAS; Soc Toxicol; Am Soc Clin Pharmacol & Therapeut; Fedn Am Socs Exp Biol; NY Acad Sci; Am Col Sports Med. *Res:* Distribution, metabolism and excretion of anticholinesterases, caffeine, theophylline and pollutants in animals and man; competition of drugs for the plasma protein binding; biliary excretion of drugs; toxicology; analysis of water pollutants and mutagenicity; effects of exercise on pharmokinetics of drugs; mechanisms of activation of antioxidant enzymes; effect of age and exercise on expression of antioxidant enzymes; interaction of exercise, drugs and antioxidant system. *Mailing Add:* Southern Ill Univ Sch Med 801 N Rutledge Springfield IL 62702. *Fax:* 217-524-0145; *E-Mail:* ssomani@wpsmtp.siumed.edu

SOMASUNDARAN, P(ONISSERIL), SURFACE & COLLOID CHEMISTRY. *Current Pos:* from assoc prof to prof mineral eng, Henry Krumb Sch Mines, 70-83, LA VON DUDDLESON KRUMB PROF, SCH ENG & APPL SCI, COLUMBIA UNIV, 83-, CHMN, DEPT CHEM ENG & MAT SCI, HENRY KRUMB SCH MINES, 88- *Personal Data:* b Annallur, India, June 28, 39; m 66, Usha; c Tamara. *Educ:* Univ Kerala, BS, 58; Indian Inst Sci, Bangalore, BE, 61; Univ Calif, Berkeley, MS, 62, PhD(eng), 64. *Honors & Awards:* Antoine M Gaudin Award, Am Inst Mining Metall & Petrol Engrs, 82, Robert H Richards Award, 87, Arthur F Taggart Award, 87, Henry Krumb lectr, 88; Frank Aplan Award, Eng Found, 92. *Prof Exp:* Sr lab asst biochem, Nat Chem Lab, Poona, India, 58-59; res asst metall & mat sci, Univ Calif, Berkeley, 61-64; sr mineral res engr, Int Minerals & Chem Corp, 64-67; res chemist, Res Dept-Basic Sci, R J Reynolds Industs Inc, 67-70. *Concurrent Pos:* NSF grants; Am Iron & Steel Inst grants; consult, NIH, 73, Ill Inst Technol Res Inst, 74-77, Amoco Prod Co, 74-77, Int Paper Co, 75, NSF, 77, B F Goodrich Co, 77-81, Exxon Corp, 77-, Occidental Res, 77, Am Cyanamid, 78, Proctor & Gamble, 78-79, Union Carbide, 79, Colgate Palmolive, 79-, IBM, 84-85, UNESCO, 82 & DuPont, 88-; dir, Langmuir Ctr Colloid & Interfaces, 87-; hon prof, Cent S Univ Technol, China, 87-; Brahm Prakash chair, Indian Inst Sci, Bangalore, 90. *Mem:* Nat Acad Eng; Am Inst Mining, Metall & Petrol Engrs; Am Inst Chem Engrs; Int Asn Surface & Colloid Scientists; Am Chem Soc. *Res:* Surface and colloid chemistry; electrokinetics; flotation; flocculation; adsorption; mineral processing; enhanced oil recovery; superconductor processing; microbial surfaces; waste treatment; coal processing. *Mailing Add:* Sch Eng & Appl Sci Columbia Univ New York NY 10027. *Fax:* 212-854-3054; *E-Mail:* ps24@cunixf.cc.columbia.edu

SOMEKH, GEORGE S, CHEMICAL ENGINEERING. *Current Pos:* Proj engr, Plastics Div, 57-60, eng scientist, Chem Div, 60-77, RES ENGR, CHEM DIV, UNION CARBIDE CORP, 77- *Personal Data:* b Brussels, Belg, Apr 3, 35; US citizen; m 60; c 2. *Educ:* Mass Inst Technol, BS, 56, MS, 57. *Mem:* Am Inst Chem Engrs. *Res:* Separation and purification processes in petro-chemistry, petroleum refining and water pollution abatement; solvent extraction, azeotropic and extractive distillation; Rankine cycle fluids, lubricants and systems design. *Mailing Add:* 43 Winding Brook Rd New Rochelle NY 10804

SOMERO, GEORGE NICHOLLS, BIOCHEMISTRY, PHYSIOLOGY. *Current Pos:* DAVID & LUCILLE PACKARD PROF MARINE SCI, STANFORD UNIV, 95- *Personal Data:* b Duluth, Minn, July 30, 40; m 88, Amy Anderson. *Educ:* Carleton Col, BA, 62; Stanford Univ, PhD(biol), 67. *Prof Exp:* NSF fel, Univ BC, 67-69; I W Killam fel, 69-70; from asst prof to prof marine biol, Scripps Inst Oceanog, Univ Calif, San Diego, 80-91; prof zool, Ore State Univ, 91-95. *Concurrent Pos:* John Dove Isaacs prof natural philos, Univ Calif, San Diego, 84. *Mem:* Nat Acad Sci; AAAS; Am Soc Zool; Am Physiol Soc; Sigma Xi. *Res:* Comparative biochemistry of environmental adaptation. *Mailing Add:* Hopkins Marine Sta Stanford Univ Oceanview Blvd Pacific Grove CA 93950. *Fax:* 541-737-0501

SOMERS, ANNE R, ENVIRONMENTAL MEDICINE. *Current Pos:* RETIRED. *Personal Data:* b 1913. *Educ:* Vassar Col, BA, 35. *Hon Degrees:* DSc, Med Col Wis, 75. *Honors & Awards:* Charles H Mann MD Award, Nat Coun Aging, 96. *Prof Exp:* Adj prof, Dept Environ Community Med, Robert Wood Johnson Med Sch, 71-84. *Concurrent Pos:* Freelance writer & speaker, 54-; founder & co-dir, Geriat Prog in Geriat & Gerontol, 78-80. *Mem:* Sr mem Inst Med-Nat Acad Sci; fel Am Col Hosp Adminrs; hon mem Soc Teachers Family Med. *Res:* Geriatrics and long term care; health promotion and consumer health education; co-author of one book. *Mailing Add:* G205 Penswood Village Newtown PA 18940

SOMERS, GEORGE FREDRICK, JR, PLANT PHYSIOLOGY, PLANT BIOCHEMISTRY. *Current Pos:* assoc dir, Del Agr Exp Sta, 51-59, chmn dept agr biochem & food tech, 52-59, assoc dean, Sch Agr, 54-59, chmn dept biol, 59-71, H Fletcher Brown prof, 62-81, EMER PROF BIOL, UNIV DEL, 81- *Personal Data:* b Garland, Utah, July 9, 14; m 39, Beulah Morgan; c Ralph, Steven & Gary. *Educ:* Utah State Univ, BS, 35; Oxford Univ, BA, 38, BSc, 39; Cornell Univ, PhD(plant physiol), 42. *Prof Exp:* Instr biochem, Cornell Univ, 41-44, from asst prof to assoc prof, 44-51. *Concurrent Pos:* Plant physiologist, Plant, Soil & Nutrit Lab, USDA, 44-51, asst dir lab, 49-51; mem comt effects of atomic radiation on agr & food supplies, Nat Acad Sci-Nat Res Coun, 56-60; vis prof, Philippines, 58-59; ed, Gen Biochem Sect, Chem Abstr, 63-71; vis scientist, Brookhaven Nat Lab, 71; distinguished fac lectr, Univ Del, 80. *Mem:* Fel AAAS; Am Soc Plant Physiol; Bot Soc Am. *Res:* Enzymes; cell wall chemistry; physiological ecology; halophytes as potential food plants. *Mailing Add:* 22 Minquil Dr Newark DE 19713

SOMERS, KENNETH DONALD, MICROBIOLOGY. *Current Pos:* assoc prof, 74-78, PROF MICROBIOL, EASTERN VA MED SCH, 78- *Personal Data:* b Fremont, Mich, Mar 2, 38; m 61, Elizabeth A Ponstein; c Kara E, Lynn M & Christopher K. *Educ:* Univ Mich, BA, 60, MS, 62; Univ Chicago, PhD(microbiol), 69. *Prof Exp:* Res assoc virol, Ciba Pharmaceut Co, 63-65; res assoc biochem virol, Baylor Col Med, 69-70, asst prof, 70-74. *Mem:* AAAS; Am Soc Microbiol; Am Asn Cancer Res; Soc Exp Biol & Med. *Res:* Oncogenic RNA viruses; cancer biology. *Mailing Add:* Microbiol Dept Eastern Va Med Sch PO Box 1980 Norfolk VA 23501. *E-Mail:* somers@picard.evms.edu

SOMERS, MICHAEL EUGENE, NEUROBIOLOGY, HISTOLOGY. *Current Pos:* Instr, Univ Bridgeport, 55-59, from asst prof to assoc prof, 60-69, prof biol & chmn, 70-, EMER PROF BIOL, UNIV BRIDGEPORT. *Personal Data:* b Astoria, NY, Aug 11, 29; m 54; c 4. *Educ:* Univ Bridgeport, BA, 51; Clark Univ, MA, 55, PhD(animal morphol), 67. *Mem:* Am Soc Zool; Am Soc Ichthyol & Herpet; Am Micros Soc; Am Fisheries Soc. *Res:* Neuroanatomy of Crustacea; fine structure of invertebrate nervous systems; fish olfactory system. *Mailing Add:* 925 Longbrook Ave Stratford CT 06497

SOMERS, PERRIE DANIEL, BIOCHEMISTRY. *Current Pos:* Res chemist, 46-51, GROUP LEADER, LAB TECH CTR, INT MULTIFOODS CORP, 51- *Personal Data:* b Winona, Minn, Oct 18, 18; m 42; c 4. *Educ:* Wabash Col, AB, 41; Purdue Univ, MS, 43, PhD(biochem), 46. *Mem:* Am Chem Soc; Am Asn Cereal Chemists. *Res:* Enzymic reactions; biological food chemistry; new food product development; food process design; food product patents; new cereal products. *Mailing Add:* 13776 74th Pl N Osseo MN 55311-2762

SOMERSCALES, EUAN FRANCIS CUTHBERT, HEAT TRANSFER, FLUID MECHANICS. *Current Pos:* instr mech eng, 58-59, asst prof, 64-68, ASSOC PROF, RENSSELAER POLYTECH INST, 68- *Personal Data:* b London, Eng, Jan 23, 31; US citizen; m 64; c 2. *Educ:* Univ London, BSc, 53; Rensselaer Polytech Inst, MME, 61; Cornell Univ, PhD(heat transfer), 65. *Honors & Awards:* Bengough Medal & Prize, Inst Metals, 88. *Prof Exp:* Apprentice, NBrit Locomotive Co, 53-55. *Concurrent Pos:* Sr vis fel, Univ Manchester Inst Sci Technol, 75-76; sr vis scientist, Nat Phys Lab, London, 83. *Mem:* Am Soc Mech Eng; Nat Asn Corrosion Engrs; Sigma Xi. *Res:* Fluid mechanics and heat transfer with application to free convection and the fouling of heat transfer surfaces. *Mailing Add:* Mech Eng & Fluids Div Rensselaer Polytech Inst Troy NY 12180-3590

SOMERSET, JAMES H, MECHANICAL & AEROSPACE ENGINEERING. *Current Pos:* asst prof mech & aerospace eng, 65-69, assoc prof, 69-80, PROF MECH & AEROSPACE ENG, COL ENG, SYRACUSE UNIV, 80- *Personal Data:* b Philadelphia, Pa, Apr 19, 38; m 63; c 2. *Educ:* Drexel Inst Technol, BS, 61; Syracuse Univ, MS, 63, PhD(mech & aerospace eng), 65. *Prof Exp:* Engr, Scott Paper Co, 58-61. *Concurrent Pos:* NSF grant, 66-68; consult, Singer Publ Co, 66- *Mem:* Am Inst Aeronaut & Astronaut; Sigma Xi. *Res:* Stochastic response of structures; dynamic response of structures to periodic and impulse loads; dynamics; vibrations; stability of systems; plate and shell structures; biomechanics. *Mailing Add:* 307 Bradford Pkwy Syracuse NY 13224-1747

SOMERVILLE, CHRISTOPHER ROLAND, MOLECULAR GENETICS, LIPID BIOCHEMISTRY. *Current Pos:* DIR, CARNEGIE INST, 94-; PROF, STANFORD UNIV, 94- *Personal Data:* b Kingston, Ont, Can, Oct 11, 47; m 76. *Educ:* Univ Alta, BS, 74, MS, 76, PhD(genetics), 78. *Hon Degrees:* DSc, Queens Univ, 93. *Honors & Awards:* Young Presidential Investr Award, NSF, 84; Schull Award, Am Soc Plant Physiologists, 87; Gibbs Medal, Am Soc Plant Physiologist, 93. *Prof Exp:* Res assoc genetics, Univ Ill, 78-80; asst prof genetics, Univ Alta, 80-82; assoc prof molecular biol, Mich State Univ, 82-86, prof, 86-93. *Concurrent Pos:* Fel, Royal Soc London, 91, Royal Soc Can, 93; Humboldt sr res award, 92. *Mem:* Nat Acad Sci; Am Oil Chemists Soc; Int Soc Plant Molecular Biol; Am Soc Cell Biol; Am Soc Plant Physiologists. *Res:* Molecular genetics of Arabidopsis. *Mailing Add:* Carnegie Inst Washington 290 Panama St Stanford CA 94305. *Fax:* 650-325-6857; *E-Mail:* crs@andrew.stanford.edu

SOMERVILLE, GEORGE R, CHEMICAL ENGINEERING. *Current Pos:* RETIRED. *Personal Data:* US citizen; m 80, Clara Caldwell; c George, Donald & Charles. *Educ:* Tex A&M Univ, BS, 42; Trinity Univ, MBA, 79. *Prof Exp:* Plant engr, Chem Warfare Serv, US Army, 43-45; process engr, Neches Butane Prod Co, 46-53; assoc chem engr, Southwest Res Inst, 55-56, sr chem engr, 56-59, sr indust chemist, 59, asst mgr org & biol chem, 59-60, mgr encapsulation sect, 60-61, mgr spec projs, 61-64, actg dir, 64-65, asst dir, 65-74, dir, San Antonio Labs, Dept Chem & Chem Eng, 74-76, dir, Dept Appl Chem & Chem Eng, 76-81. *Mem:* Am Chem Soc; Sigma Xi. *Res:* Development of the process, materials and techniques for encapsulating various materials for commercial and military purposes. *Mailing Add:* 2519 Cedar Falls San Antonio TX 78232-4221

SOMERVILLE, MASON H, EDUCATIONAL ADMINISTRATION, MECHANICAL ENGINEERING. *Current Pos:* DEAN ENG & PROF MECH ENG, NORTHERN ARIZ UNIV, 94- *Personal Data:* m, Mary Huston; c 6. *Educ:* Worcester Polytech Inst, BS, 64; Northeastern Univ, MS, 66; Pa State Univ, PhD(mech eng, heat transfer & thermodyn), 72. *Honors & Awards:* Ralph R Teetor Award, 74. *Prof Exp:* Sr engr, Westinghouse Elec Co, 71-73; assoc prof mech eng, Univ NDak, 73-75, mgr, Eng Exp Sta, 75-77, dir, 77-80; prof & head, Dept Mech Eng & Eng Sci, Univ Ark, 80-84; dean eng & prof mech eng, Tex Tech Univ, 84-94. *Concurrent Pos:* Mem, Bd Eng Educ, Am Soc Mech Engrs, 90-94. *Mem:* Am Soc Mech Engrs; Am Soc Eng. *Res:* Coal gasification and its environmental impacts; alternate heat pump design and coupling of heat pumps to thermal sources; innovative wind turbine design. *Mailing Add:* PO Box 15600 Flagstaff AZ 86018-5600. *Fax:* 520-523-2300; *E-Mail:* mason.somerville@nau.edu

SOMERVILLE, PAUL NOBLE, STATISTICS. *Current Pos:* assoc prof, 72-79, PROF STATIST, UNIV CENT FLA, 79- *Personal Data:* b Vulcan, Alta, May 7, 25; nat US; m 54; c Deborah (Velez) & David Mackenzie. *Educ:* Univ Alta, BSc, 49; Univ NC, PhD(statist), 53. *Prof Exp:* Teacher, Lethbridge Sch Div, Can, 42-44; assoc prof statist, Va Polytech Inst & assoc statistician exten serv, Agr Exp Sta, 53-55; vis prof math, Am Univ, 55-57; asst proj dir, C-E-I-R, Inc, Ariz, 58-61, mgr, Utah Off, 61-62; mgr tech eval, RCA Corp, Patrick AFB, 62-72. *Concurrent Pos:* Guest scientist, Nat Bur Stand, 55-57; lectr, Univ Ariz, 58-61 & Brigham Young Univ, 62; chmn math dept, Fla Inst Technol, 63-72; adj prof, Univ Fla, Genesys, 68-72. *Mem:* Fel Am Statist Asn; Int Asn Statist Comput; Int Statist Inst. *Res:* Statistics; climatology; education; computer simulation; model building; multiple comparisons. *Mailing Add:* Dept Statist Univ Cent Fla Box 25000 Orlando FL 32816-0370

SOMERVILLE, RICHARD CHAPIN JAMES, METEOROLOGY, FLUID DYNAMICS. *Current Pos:* PROF METEOROL & HEAD, CLIMATE RES GROUP, SCRIPPS INST OCEANOG, UNIV CALIF, SAN DIEGO, 79- *Personal Data:* b Washington, DC, May 30, 41; m 65; c 2. *Educ:* Pa State Univ, BS, 61; NY Univ, PhD(meteorol), 66. *Prof Exp:* Res meteorologist, Geophys Fluid Dynamics Lab, Environ Sci Serv Admin, 67-69; res scientist, Courant Inst Math Sci, NY Univ, 69-72; meteorologist, Inst Space Studies, Goddard Space Flight Ctr, NASA, 71-74; scientist, Nat Ctr Atmospheric Res, 74-79. *Concurrent Pos:* Fel, Nat Ctr Atmospheric Res, 66-67; fel geophys fluid dynamics prog, Woods Hole Oceanog Inst, 67, staff mem, 70, 76; adj assoc prof, NY Univ, 71-73 & Columbia Univ, 71-74. *Mem:* Fel Am Meteorol Soc; Am Geophys Union. *Res:* Theoretical dynamic meteorology; numerical fluid dynamics; thermal convection; atmospheric general circulation; numerical weather prediction; parameterization of small-scale processes; climate modeling. *Mailing Add:* Scripps Inst Oceanog 9500 Gilman Dr 0224 La Jolla CA 92093-0224

SOMERVILLE, RONALD LAMONT, BIOCHEMISTRY, BIOTECHNOLOGY. *Current Pos:* assoc prof, 67-77, PROF BIOCHEM, PURDUE UNIV, WEST LAFAYETTE, 77- *Personal Data:* b Vancouver, BC, Feb 27, 35; nat US; m 55, Joyce E Crowe; c Gregory, Kenneth, Gordon, Victoria & Daniel. *Educ:* Univ BC, BA, 56, MSc, 57; Univ Mich, PhD, 61. *Honors & Awards:* C T Huang lectr, Univ Hong Kong, 83. *Prof Exp:* Res assoc biochem, Univ Mich, 60-61; asst prof, Univ Mich, Ann Arbor, 64-67. *Concurrent Pos:* Fel biol sci, Stanford Univ, 61-64. *Mem:* Am Soc Biochem & Molecular Biol; Genetics Soc Am; Am Soc Microbiol. *Res:* Transcriptional regulatory mechanisms; industrial production of proteins and small molecules by bacterial fermentation; genetic analysis; DNA-mediated redesign of proteins. *Mailing Add:* Dept of Biochem Purdue Univ West Lafayette IN 47907-1153. *Fax:* 765-494-7897; *E-Mail:* somerville@biochem.purdue.edu

SOMES, GRANT WILLIAM, STATISTICS AS APPLIED TO MEDICALLY RELATED DATA, CATEGORICAL & NONPARAMETRIC STATISTICS. *Current Pos:* assoc prof, 84-87, PROF STATIST, DEPT BIOSTATIST & EPIDEMIOL, UNIV TENN, MEMPHIS, 87-, CHMN DEPT, 84- *Personal Data:* b Bloomington, Ind, Jan 30, 47; m 67, Brenda S Weddle; c Anthony W, Joshua M & Meghan E. *Educ:* Ind Univ, AB, 68; Univ Ky, PhD(statist), 75. *Prof Exp:* Asst prof res design, Dept Commun Med, Univ Ky, 75-79, asst prof statist, Dept Statist, 76-79; postdoctoral epidemiol, Univ Minn, 76; assoc prof statist, Res Prog, E Carolina Univ, 79-84. *Concurrent Pos:* Statist consult, J Nuclear Med, 76-85; prin investr, Biomed Res Support grant, 76-79 & 81-84; co-prin investr, Nat Heart, Lung, Blood Inst & NIH, 85-; adj prof statist, Dept Math, Memphis State Univ, 88-, Dept Psychol, 90- *Mem:* Sigma Xi; Am Statist Asn; Biomet Soc; Am Soc Hypertension. *Res:* Cardiovascular risk factors, epilepsy, psychosocial factors and illness, smoking and behavior, blood pressure patterns; statistical theory, mainly in categorical data analysis and nonparametric statistics; author of numerous publications. *Mailing Add:* 340 Library Bldg Univ Tenn Health-Memphis Memphis TN 38163

SOMES, RALPH GILMORE, JR, AVIAN GENETICS, HUMAN NUTRITION. *Current Pos:* CONSULT, 91- *Personal Data:* b Melrose, Mass, Aug 15, 29; m 85; c 8. *Educ:* Univ Mass, BS, 60, PhD(poultry genetics), 63. *Prof Exp:* From asst prof to prof nutrit & genetics, Univ Conn, 63-91. *Mem:* Poultry Sci Asn; Am Genetic Asn; World Poultry Sci Asn. *Res:* Genetic investigations of feather pigment systems and new mutant traits in the domestic fowl; genetic-nutritional interaction. *Mailing Add:* 363 Fay Rd Pomfret Center CT 06259-1908

SOMJEN, GEORGE G, PHYSIOLOGY, PHARMACOLOGY. *Current Pos:* from asst prof to assoc prof, 63-71, PROF PHYSIOL & NEUROBIOL, DUKE UNIV, 71- *Personal Data:* b Budapest, Hungary, May 2, 29; m 76; c 4. *Educ:* Univ Amsterdam, MD, 56; Univ NZ, MD, 61. *Prof Exp:* Asst pharmacol, Univ Amsterdam, 53-56; lectr physiol, Univ Otago, NZ, 56-60, sr lectr, 61-62; res fel, Harvard Med Sch, 62-63. *Concurrent Pos:* Consult, Nat Inst Environ Health Sci, 71-75; invited speaker, XXVIIIth Int Cong Physiol, 81; vis prof, London, 75 & 85, Ibadan, Nigeria, 78. *Mem:* Am Asn Univ Professors; Am Soc Pharmacol Exp Therapeut; Soc Neurosci; Am Physiol Soc; hon mem Hungarian Physiol Soc; Sigma Xi. *Res:* Reflex function of spinal cord; mechanism of seizures; properties of neurons; effects of drugs and ions on central nervous system and on peripheral junctions; blood-brain barrier; hypoxia of central nervous system-stroke. *Mailing Add:* Dept Cell Biol Duke Univ Med Ctr Box 3709 Durham NC 27710-0001. *Fax:* 919-684-5481

SOMKAITE, ROZALIJA, PHARMACEUTICAL CHEMISTRY, ANALYTICAL CHEMISTRY. *Current Pos:* mgr anal res dept, 70-74, DIR ANAL SERV, REHEIS CHEM CO, 74- *Personal Data:* b Lithuania, Feb 10, 25; US citizen. *Educ:* St John's Univ, NY, BS, 54; Univ Wis, MS, 56; Rutgers Univ, PhD(pharmaceut sci), 62. *Prof Exp:* Assoc scientist, Warner-Chillcot Pharmaceut Co, 56-58; teaching asst, Rutgers Univ, 58-59, NIH res fel anal, 61-62; sr scientist, Ethicon, Inc, 62-70. *Mem:* Am Pharmaceut Asn; Am Chem Soc; Am Microchem Soc; Soc Appl Spectros. *Res:* Analytical research applying multiple technique systems. *Mailing Add:* 386 Hillside Pl South Orange NJ 07079-2903

SOMKUTI, GEORGE A, FERMENTATION BIOCHEMISTRY, APPLIED GENETICS. *Current Pos:* RES LEADER MICROBIOL & BIOCHEM, EASTERN REGIONAL RES CTR, USDA, 76- *Personal Data:* b Budapest, Hungary, Jan 6, 36; US citizen; m 59; c 2. *Educ:* Tufts Univ, BS, 59; Purdue Univ, MS, 63, PhD(microbiochem), 66. *Honors & Awards:* SIM Chas Porter Award, 88. *Prof Exp:* NIH fel, Purdue Univ, 66-68; asst prof microbiochem & immunol, Duquesne Univ, 68-69; res assoc cell biol, Purdue Univ, 69-73; sr res scientist, Res & Develop, Lederle Labs, Am Cyanamid Co, 73-76. *Concurrent Pos:* Mem, NSF Curric Develop Comt Univ Tex, San Antonio, 74-75 & NIH Spec Studies Sect, 76; ed, J Food Protection, 82-, J Indust Microbiol, 85-88, Appl Microbiol Biotechnol, 93-, J Daisy Sci, 93-, & Biotechnol Lett, 93-; NSF Spec Studies Sect, 83-90; mem, Bd Dirs, Soc Indust Microbiol, 84-87; Nat Acad Sci Spec Studies Sect, 92-93. *Mem:* Am Soc Microbiol; Soc Indust Microbiol (pres, 85-86); NY Acad Sci; Inst Food Technol; Am Dairy Sci Asn. *Res:* Microbial physiology and metabolism; plasmid function; applied enzymology. *Mailing Add:* 862 Gettysburg Dr Landsdale PA 19446. *Fax:* 215-233-6606

SOMLYO, ANDREW PAUL, PHYSIOLOGY, PATHOLOGY. *Current Pos:* from assoc prof to assoc prof, 64-71, PROF PATH, UNIV PA, 71-, PROF PHYSIOL, 73- *Personal Data:* b Budapest, Hungary, Feb 25, 30; US citizen; m 61; c 1. *Educ:* Univ Ill, Chicago, BS, 54, MS & Md, 56; Drexel Inst Technol, MS, 63. *Hon Degrees:* MA, Univ Pa, 81. *Prof Exp:* Intern, Philadelphia Gen Hosp, 56-57, resident, 57-58; asst resident med, Mt Sinai Hosp, New York, 58-59; sr asst resident, Bellevue Hosp, 59-60; asst physician, Columbia-Presby Med Ctr, 60-61; res assoc, Presby Hosp, 61-66. *Concurrent Pos:* Heart Asn Southeast Pa res fel, Philadelphia Gen Hosp, 57-58; NIH spec res fel, Presby Hosp, Philadelphia, 61-66; USPHS res career prog award, Presby-Univ Pa Med Ctr, 66-73; dir, Pa Muscle Inst; prof physiol & path, Univ of Pa Sch Med, 67-88; sr res pathologist, Presby-Univ Pa Med Ctr, 67-80; Charles Slaughter prof & chmn dept physiol & prof med cardiol, Univ Va, Sch Med, 88- *Mem:* Microbeam Anal Soc; AAAS; Soc Gen Physiol; Am Physiol Soc; Biophys Soc; Am Soc Cell Biol. *Res:* Development and application of quantitative electron optical techniques in biology including electron probe analysis and electron energy loss analysis; ultrastructure and cell physiology of vascular smooth muscle and skeletal muscle; pharmacology. *Mailing Add:* Dept Molecular & Biol Phys Univ Va Sch Med 1300 Jefferson Park Ave Jordan Hall Box 449 Charlottesville VA 22908-0001

SOMLYO, AVRIL VIRGINIA, CELL PHYSIOLOGY. *Current Pos:* Co prin investr, 68-79, from res assoc prof to res prof physiol, 82-89, PROF PHYSIOL, UNIV PA, 89- *Personal Data:* b Sask, Can, Apr 9, 39; m 61; c 1. *Educ:* Univ Sask, BA, 58, MSc, 61; Univ Pa, PhD, 76. *Concurrent Pos:* Mem, Biol Instrumentation Panel, NSF, 79-83; mem, Pharmacol Study Sect, NIH, 81-84, Physiol Study Sect, 90-93; mem, Nat Inst Heart, Lung & Blood Cardiol Adv Comt, 85-89; coun, Biophysics Soc, 84-87, exec coun, 85-87; coun, Cell & Gen Physiol Sect, Am Physiol Soc, 85-88, chmn, 87-88; mem, US Nat Comt, Int Union Physiol Soc, 88-91, Nat Acad Res Coun Deleg Gen Assembly, 89; mem, Sci Prog Comt, Int Physiol Cong, 88-93, Glasgow, 93; mem, Cell Transport & Metabolism Res Study Comt, Am Heart Asn, 89-92. *Mem:* Am Soc Pharmacol & Exp Therapeut; Biophys Soc; Sigma Xi; Soc Gen Physiologists; Am Physiol Soc. *Res:* Basic function and structure of striated and vascular smooth muscle, including excitation-contraction coupling, contractile proteins; the role of the in situ distribution of elements, especially calcium, within organelles, using high spatial resolution electron probe x-ray microanalysis and electron energy loss analysis. *Mailing Add:* Dept Physiol Univ Va Sch Med 1300 Jefferson Park Ave Box 449 Charlottesville VA 22908-0001. *Fax:* 804-982-1616

SOMMER, ALFRED, CHILD SURVIVAL, BLINDNESS PREVENTION. *Current Pos:* FROM ASST PROF TO PROF OPHTHAL, EPIDEMIOL & INT HEALTH, JOHNS HOPKINS UNIV, 80-, DEAN, SCH HYG & PUB HEALTH, 97- *Personal Data:* b New York, NY, Oct 2, 42; m 63; c 2. *Educ:* Union Col, BS, 63; Harvard Med Sch, MD, 67; Johns Hopkins Univ, MHS, 73. *Honors & Awards:* Helen Keller Blindness Prevention Award, Helen Keller Int, 80; Distinguished Serv Award for Contrib to Vision Care, Am Pub Health Asn, 88; Charles A Dana Award, Pioneering Achievements in Health, Charles A Dana Found, 88; E V McCollum Int Lectr Nutrit, Am Inst Nutrit, Fedn Am Soc Exp Biol, 88; Award for Distinguished Contrib World Ophthal, Int Fedn Ophthal Socs, 90; Gold Medal for Contrib to World Ophthal, Saudi Ophthal Soc, 91; Joseph E Smudel Award, Infectious Dis Soc Am, 92; Int Gold Medal Contrib to Ophthalmol, Singapore Nat Eye Ctr, 97. *Prof Exp:* Med epidemiologist, Ctrs Dis Control, 69-72; dir & prin investr clin epidemiol, Helen Keller Int Blindness Prev, 76-80; found dir, Int Ctr Epidemiol & Prev Ophthal, 80-90. *Concurrent Pos:* Med adv, Helen Keller Int, 73-; steering comt, Int Vitamin A Consultative Group, 75-; bd mem, Int Agency Prev Blindness, 78-; comt chmn, Nat Insts Health, 81-; bd dirs, Nat Soc Prev Blindness, 87-89; chmn, Prog Adv Group Blindness Prev, World Health Orgn, 88-90; comt mem, Nat Acad Sci, 89-96. *Mem:* Inst Med-Nat Acad Sci; Am Ophthal Soc; Soc Epidemiol Res; Asn Res in Vision & Ophthal; Am Pub Health Asn; Am Inst Nutrit; Am Acad Ophthal. *Res:* Epidemiologic assessment of blinding diseases; prevention of childhood mortality in developing countries and assessment of medical technology. *Mailing Add:* Sch Pub Hyg & Pub Health Johns Hopkins Univ 615 N Wolfe St Baltimore MD 21205-2179

SOMMER, ALFRED HERMANN, ELECTRON EMISSION. *Current Pos:* CONSULT, 78- *Personal Data:* b Frankfurt, Ger, Nov 19, 09; US citizen; m 38, Dorothy R Hulm; c Jane, Julia & Helen. *Educ:* Berlin Univ, Dr Phil(chem), 34. *Honors & Awards:* Gaede-Langmuir Award, Am Vacuum Soc, 82; Gold Medal, Int Soc Optical Eng, 93. *Prof Exp:* Res engr photo multipliers, Baird TV Co, London, 36-46; res engr TV camera tubes, EMI-Res Lab, Eng, 46-53; res engr electron emission, RCA-Res Labs, Princeton, NJ, 53-74; res engr, Thermo-Electron Co, Waltham, Mass, 74-78. *Mem:* Am Phys Soc; fel Inst Elec & Electronics Engrs. *Res:* New photoemissive materials; secondary emission; thermionic emission; photo multipliers; television camera tubes; image intensifier tubes; thermionic energy conversion. *Mailing Add:* Bayon Dr Apt 210 South Hadley MA 01075

SOMMER, CHARLES JOHN, STATISTICS, BIOMETRICS. *Current Pos:* ASST PROF, DEPT MATH & COMPUTER SCIENCE, STATE UNIV NY, BROCKPORT, 84- *Personal Data:* b New York, NY, Jan 12, 51. *Educ:* Manhattan Col, BS, 72; State Univ NY Buffalo, MA, 73, PhD(statist sci), 77. *Prof Exp:* Biostatistician, Sidney Farber Cancer Inst, 77-78; asst prof statist, Temple Univ, 78- *Mem:* Am Statist Asn. *Mailing Add:* 132 S Main St Brockport NY 14420

SOMMER, HARRY EDWARD, TREE BIOLOGY. *Current Pos:* ASSOC PROF TISSUE CULT, SCH FOREST RESOURCES, UNIV GA, 76- *Personal Data:* b Chatham, NY, July 25, 41; m 64; c 2. *Educ:* Univ Vt, BSAgr, 63; Univ Maine, MS, 66; Ohio State Univ, PhD(bot), 72. *Prof Exp:* Res assoc tissue cult, Sch Forest Resources, Univ Ga, 72-74; scientist, Weyerhaauser Forestry Res Ctr, 74-76. *Concurrent Pos:* Capt, US Army Chem Corps. *Mem:* Bot Soc Am; Sigma Xi; Scand Plant Physiol Soc; Tissue Cult Asn. *Res:* Tissue culture of trees. *Mailing Add:* Sch Forest Resources Univ Ga Athens GA 30602. *Fax:* 706-542-8356

SOMMER, HELMUT, ELECTRICAL ENGINEERING, ELECTRONICS. *Current Pos:* CONSULT, 80- *Personal Data:* b Ger, Aug 23, 22; nat US; m 46, Ethel K Benoist; c Richard J, Kathryn T, John R, Stephen A, Michel M & Michael T. *Educ:* Agr & Mech Col, Tex, BS, 44, MS, 47, PhD, 50. *Prof Exp:* Electronic scientist, Nat Bur Stand, 49-53 & Diamond Ord Fuze Labs, US Dept Army, 53-57; res prof electronics, Univ Fla, 57-58; chief, Microwave Br, Diamond Ord Fuze Labs, US Dept Army, 58-62, chief, Systs Res Lab, Harry Diamond Labs, 62-66, assoc tech dir, Harry Diamond Labs, 66-80. *Concurrent Pos:* Consult, Catholic Univ, 53-60. *Mem:* Inst Elec & Electronics Engrs. *Res:* Radar; microwaves; military electronics; proximity fuzes. *Mailing Add:* 9502 Hollins Ct Bethesda MD 20817

SOMMER, JOACHIM RAINER, PATHOLOGY. *Current Pos:* assoc, 58-59, from asst prof to assoc prof, 59-70, PROF PATH, MED CTR, DUKE UNIV, 70-, PROF PHYSIOL, 81- *Personal Data:* b Dresden, Ger, Apr 11, 24; nat US; m 51; c 2. *Educ:* Univ Munich, MD, 50; Am Bd Path, dipl, 58, cert anat & clin path, 69. *Prof Exp:* Asst, Path Inst, Munich, Ger, 51-52; asst, Med Clin Munich, 52-53; intern, Garfield Mem Hosp, Washington, DC, 53-54; resident path, Garfield Mem & De Paul Hosps, 54-58. *Mem:* Sigma Xi. *Res:* Histochemistry; cardiac ultrastructure and function; electron microscopy, cryotechniques. *Mailing Add:* Duke Univ Med Ctr PO Box 3548 Durham NC 27710. *Fax:* 919-286-6818

SOMMER, JOHN G, RUBBER & RUBBER PRODUCTS. *Current Pos:* PRES, ELASTECH, INC, 93- *Personal Data:* b Portsmouth, Ohio, Jan 28, 26; m 60, Nancy Lacher; c 4. *Educ:* Univ Dayton, BChE, 51; Univ Akron, MS, 65. *Honors & Awards:* Melvin Mooney Distinguished Technol Award, Rubber Div, Am Chem Soc, 88. *Prof Exp:* Lab mgr, Dayco Corp, 51-60; asst chief chemist, Precision Rubber Prod Corp, 60; sect head, Rubber Compounding & Processing, GenCorp Res, 60-88; lectr & consult, 88-93. *Concurrent Pos:* lectr, Univ Wis, Univ Akron & Indust Orgns. *Mem:* Am Chem Soc. *Res:* Molding of rubber; rubber part design; rubber use in aerospace applications; rubber dynamic properties; rubber materials science; physical testing and physical properties; rubber applications. *Mailing Add:* 5939 Bradford Way Hudson OH 44236-3905

SOMMER, LEO HARRY, ORGANIC CHEMISTRY. *Current Pos:* RETIRED. *Personal Data:* b New York, NY, Sept 21, 17; m 44; c 3. *Educ:* Pa State Univ, BS, MS, 42, PhD(org chem), 45. *Honors & Awards:* F S Kipping Award, Am Chem Soc, 63. *Prof Exp:* From instr to prof chem, Pa State Univ, 43-65; prof, Univ Calif, Davis, 65-86. *Concurrent Pos:* Consult, Dow Corning Corp, 47-; res fel, Harvard Univ, 50-51; Guggenheim fel, 60-61. *Mem:* Am Chem Soc; Royal Soc Chem. *Res:* Stereochemistry and reaction mechanisms of silicon centers in organosilicon compounds; chemistry of multiple-bonded unsaturated organosilicon compounds. *Mailing Add:* Dept Chem Univ Calif Davis CA 95616-5224

SOMMER, LEONARD SAMUEL, CARDIOLOGY. *Current Pos:* from asst prof to assoc prof, 56-74, PROF MED, SCH MED, UNIV MIAMI, 74- *Personal Data:* b Springfield, Mass, July 3, 24; m 63, Anita Friedman; c Babette & Anne. *Educ:* Yale Univ, BS, 44; Columbia Univ, MD, 47; Am Bd Internal Med, dipl, 57 & 77; Am Bd Cardiovasc Dis, dipl, 75. *Prof Exp:* Intern med, Peter Bent Brigham Hosp, 47-48; instr med, Med Sch, Georgetown Univ, 51-52; resident med, Peter Bent Brigham Hosp, 48-49 & 53-54; res fel, Harvard Med Sch, 54-55, asst, 55-56. *Concurrent Pos:* Teaching fel, Harvard Med Sch, 48-49; Am Heart Asn res fel cardiol, Columbia-Presby Med Ctr & NY Hosp, Cornell Univ, 49-50; Nat Heart Inst res fel cardiol, Hammersmith Hosp, London, Eng, 52-53; fel cardiol, Cardiovasc Lab, Children's Med Ctr, Boston, 54-56; consult cardiologist, Adolescent Unit, Children's Med Ctr, Boston, Mass, 54-56; asst physician, Peter Bent Brigham Hosp, 54-56; investr, Howard Hughes Med Inst, 56-59; mem coun clin cardiol, Am Heart Asn; dir, Cardiovasc Lab, Jackson Mem Hosp, 56-75 & dir, Exercise Labs, 78- *Mem:* Am Heart Asn; fel Am Col Cardiol; fel Am Col Physicians; Am Fedn Clin Res; Sigma Xi. *Res:* Cardiovascular physiology and diseases. *Mailing Add:* Univ Miami Sch Med Div Cardiol PO Box 016960 Miami FL 33101-6960. *Fax:* 305-585-7089

SOMMER, NOEL FREDERICK, PLANT PHYSIOLOGY, PATHOLOGY. *Current Pos:* asst pomologist, Univ Calif, Davis, 56-63, lectr & assoc pomologist, 63-67, lectr & pomologist, 67-75, chmn, Dept Pomol, 75-81, LECTR POMOL & POSTHARVEST PATHOLOGIST, UNIV CALIF, DAVIS, 81- *Personal Data:* b Scio, Ore, Jan 21, 20; m 46; c 1. *Educ:* Ore State Col, BS, 41; Univ Calif, MS, 52, PhD(plant path), 55. *Honors & Awards:* Bronze Medal, Agr Chamber, Vaucluse, France. *Prof Exp:* Co agr exten agent, Ore State Col, 46-51; res asst, Univ Calif, 52-55; plant pathologist, USDA, 55-56. *Mem:* Am Phytopath Soc; Am Soc Hort Sci; Am Soc Microbiol; Mycol Soc Am; NY Acad Sci; AAAS. *Res:* Physiology and pathology of fruits and vegetables after harvest; mycotoxins. *Mailing Add:* Dept of Pomology Univ of Calif Davis CA 95616

SOMMER, SHELDON E, GEOCHEMISTRY. *Current Pos:* SR RES ADV, MOBIL TECH CTR, DALLAS, 81- *Personal Data:* b New York, NY, Nov 3, 37; m 60. *Educ:* City Col New York, BS, 59; City Univ New York, MA, 61; Tex A&M, MS, 64; Pa State Univ, PhD(geochem), 69. *Prof Exp:* Sec sch teacher, Bd Ed, NY, 59-61; res asst geol, Kans Geol Surv, 61-62; oceanogr, Tex A&M, 62-63, res scientist, 63-64; asst geochem & mineral, Pa State Univ, 64-69; assoc prof geochem, Univ Md, College Park, 69-76, assoc prof geol, 76-81. *Mem:* Geochem Soc; Mineral Soc Am. *Res:* Geochemistry of marine sediments and sea water; low temperature mineral synthesis; study of geological materials by electron spectroscopy and electron microprobe spectroscopy; reservoir-fluid reaction chemical modeling. *Mailing Add:* 16806 Chepstow Ct Dallas TX 75248. *E-Mail:* sesommer@dal.mobil.com

SOMMERER, JOHN C, NOLINEAR DYNAMICS, STOCHASTIC PROCESSES. *Current Pos:* sr engr, Appl Physics Lab, Johns Hopkins Univ, 80-92, supvr, Oper & Tactics Sect, 85-89, prin staff physicist, 92-94, dep dir, Eisenhower Res Ctr, Appl Physics Lab, 94-96, DIR, EISENHOWER RES & TECHNOL DEVELOP CTR, APPL PHYSICS LAB, JOHNS HOPKINS UNIV, 96- *Personal Data:* b Milwaukee, Wis, Aug 5, 57; m 79, Suzette Jacques. *Educ:* Wash Univ, BS & MS, 79; Johns Hopkins Univ, MS, 89; Univ Md, PhD(physics), 91. *Prof Exp:* Res assoc, Dept Physiol & Biophys, Wash Univ, 79-80. *Concurrent Pos:* Mem, Nonacoust ASW Coord Comt, USN, 86-88; Nat Defense Sci & Eng fel, Air Force Off Sci Res, 89-91; adj prof physics, Whiting Sch Eng, Johns Hopkins Univ, 92-; tech consult, Nat Inst

Justice, 93- Mem: Soc Indust & Appl Math; Am Phys Soc. Res: Modeling of high-dimensional systems with nonlinear dynamics, as well as the effects of noise on nonlinear systems. Mailing Add: 1812 Tufa Terr Laurel MD 20904-5354. E-Mail: john.sommerer@jhuapl.edu

SOMMERFELD, JUDE T, CHEMICAL ENGINEERING. Current Pos: assoc prof, 70-75, assoc dir chem eng, 81-88, PROF CHEM ENG, GA INST TECHNOL, 75- Personal Data: b Elmwood Place, Ohio, Feb 4, 36; m 92, Elizabeth Ryder; c 4. Educ: Univ Detroit, BChE, 58; Univ Mich, MSE, 60, PhD(chem eng), 63. Prof Exp: Sr syst engr, Monsanto Co, 63-65, eng specialist, 65-66; sr syst engr, Wyandotte Chem Corp, 66-67, mgr syst eng, 67-68, dir process eng, 68-70. Mem: Am Chem Soc; Am Inst Chem Engrs; Nat Soc Prof Engrs. Res: Energy conservation; computer applications; applied mathematics; systems engineering; management science; thermodynamics; kinetics; catalysis. Mailing Add: Sch Chem Eng Ga Inst Technol Atlanta GA 30332. Fax: 404-894-2866

SOMMERFELD, MILTON R, PHYCOLOGY. Current Pos: from asst prof to assoc prof bot, 68-77, chair dept, 81-88, PROF BOT, ARIZ STATE UNIV, 78-, ASSOC DEAN, 89- Personal Data: b Thorndale, Tex, Nov 24, 40; m 63; c 2. Educ: Southwest Tex State Col, BS, 62; Wash Univ, PhD(bot), 68. Prof Exp: Teaching asst biol, Southwest Tex State Col, 61-62; teaching asst bot, Wash Univ, 64-65, instr, 65. Mem: AAAS; Bot Soc Am; Phycol Soc Am; Int Phycol Soc. Res: Morphogenesis and development of the algae; systematics; morphogenesis; life cycles; ecology of the algae; water quality; endolithic algae. Mailing Add: 49 W Secretariat Dr Tempe AZ 85284

SOMMERFELD, RICHARD ARTHUR, GEOCHEMISTRY, GEOLOGY. Current Pos: assoc geologist, 67-76, RES GEOLOGIST, ROCKY MOUNTAIN FOREST & RANGE EXP STA, US FOREST SERV, 77- Personal Data: b Chicago, Ill, July 4, 33. Educ: Univ Chicago, PhD(geophys), 65. Prof Exp: Micrometeorologist, Univ Wash, 61-64; fel geochem, Univ Calif, Los Angeles, 65-67, inst geophys fel, 66-67. Concurrent Pos: NSF fel, 65-66. Mem: Int Glaciol Soc; AAAS; Am Geophys Union. Res: Physical chemistry of mineral reactions, particularly the equilibria of quartz and water; metamorphism and solid mechanics of snow; ice crystallization from vapor; acoustic properties of snow; ice surface chemistry; snow chemistry. Mailing Add: 319 Pearl St Ft Collins CO 80521

SOMMERFELDT, THERON G, SOIL SCIENCE, PHYSICAL CHEMISTRY. Current Pos: RETIRED. Personal Data: b Cardston, Alta, Can, May 27, 23; m 48; c 5. Educ: Univ Alta, BSc, 50; Utah State Univ, MS, 52, PhD(soil chem), 61. Prof Exp: Asst agronomist, Can Sugar Factories, 51-53; asst soil scientist, NDak State Univ, 53-60; self employed, 60-61; asst soil scientist, Univ Idaho, 61-65; soil scientist, Can Dept Agr, 65-89. Mem: Am Soc Agron; Agr Inst Can; Can Soc Soil Sci; Prof Inst Pub Serv Can; Can Soc Agr Engrs. Res: Reclamation and drainage of saline and alkali soils; soil and water pollution from fertilizers and animal wastes; investigations, management and reclamation of dryland salinity; animal waste disposal and utilization. Mailing Add: 1705 20 St S Lethbridge AB T1K 2G1 Can

SOMMERFIELD, CHARLES MICHAEL, THEORETICAL PHYSICS, QUANTUM FIELD THEORY. Current Pos: from asst prof to assoc prof, 61-67, PROF PHYSICS, YALE UNIV, 67- Personal Data: b New York, NY, Oct 27, 33; m 69; c 2. Educ: Brooklyn Col, BS, 53; Harvard Univ, AM, 54, PhD(physics), 57. Hon Degrees: MA, Yale Univ, 67. Prof Exp: NSF fel physics, Univ Calif, 57-58, instr & jr res physicist, 58-59; res fel, Harvard Univ, 59-61, Corning lectr, 60-61. Concurrent Pos: Vis asst res mathematician, Univ Calif, 65; vis fel, Mass Inst Technol, 69-70; mem, Inst Advan Studies, 89. Mem: AAAS; Am Phys Soc. Res: Theories of quantized fields and elementary particle interactions. Mailing Add: Dept Physics Yale Univ 217 Prospect St Box 208120 New Haven CT 06511

SOMMERMAN, GEORGE M L, PHYSICS, DIELECTRICS. Current Pos: RETIRED. Personal Data: b Baltimore, Md, July 2, 09; m 34. Educ: Johns Hopkins Univ, BEE, 29, DEng, 33. Honors & Awards: Alfred Noble Prize, 38. Prof Exp: Fel engr, Westinghouse Elec, 54-74, consult, 74-82; consult, Oak Ridge Nat Lab, 74-82. Mem: Fel Inst Elec & Electronics Engrs. Res: Investigated stability properties of dielectric materials (resistance to oxidation and to electric discharges, including surface tracting) and correlated these with physical properties and chemical constitution. Mailing Add: 13801 York Rd Cockeysville MD 21030

SOMMERMAN, KATHRYN MARTHA, ENTOMOLOGY, PSOCOPTERA TAXONOMY-BIOLOGY. Current Pos: RETIRED. Personal Data: b New Haven, Conn, Jan 11, 15. Educ: Conn State Col, BS, 37; Univ Ill, MS, 41, PhD(entom), 45. Honors & Awards: Except Civilian Serv Award, Dept Army, 50; Sustained Super Performance Award, HEW, 60. Prof Exp: Artist entom, Univ Ill, 37-38, artist & asst entom, Ill Natural Hist Surv, 39-45; instr biol, Wells Col, 45; asst prof zool, Eastern Ill Col Educ, 46; entomologist, Army Med Dept Res & Grad Sch, Washington, DC, 46-51; entomologist, bur entom & plant quarantine, USDA, 51-53, collabr, Sect Insect Identification, Entom Res Br, Agr Res Serv, Md, 53-58; res entomologist, Arctic Health Res Ctr, 55-73, chief, Entom Unit, 60-73. Concurrent Pos: Entomologist, Alaskan Insect Proj, US Dept Army, 48; fel, Univ Ill, Urbana, 49; independent res & consult, 53-55; res consult, 73-77. Mem: Fel Entom Soc Am; Sigma Xi; Wilderness Soc. Res: Systematics and bionomics of Psocoptera; discovery that airborne pollen is the father of lichens and fungi. Mailing Add: MC 76 Box 384 Greenville ME 04441-9717

SOMMERS, ARMIGER HENRY, SCIENCE INFORMATION. Current Pos: RETIRED. Personal Data: b Clarksdale, Miss, June 15, 20; m 49, C Lenore Olson; c John, Richard, Robert, Mary & Elizabeth. Educ: Notre Dame Univ, BS, 42, MS, 43, PhD(org chem), 48. Prof Exp: Res chemist, Notre Dame Univ, 44-45 & Columbia Univ, 46; res chemist, Abbott Labs, 47-63, Licensing, 63-85. Mem: Am Chem Soc; Sigma Xi. Res: Organic synthesis of nitrogen compounds for medicinal use; new drug information and licensing. Mailing Add: 501 Oakwood 3A Lake Forest IL 60045

SOMMERS, ELLA BLANCHE, PHARMACY. Current Pos: From assoc prof to prof pharm, Univ Okla, 42-78, asst dean, 71-78, consult, Col Pharm & Off Develop, 78- Personal Data: b Lahoma, Okla, Mar 12, 08. Educ: Univ Okla, BS, 30, MS, 31; Ohio State Univ, PhD, 54. Mem: Am Chem Soc; Am Pharmaceut Asn; Sigma Xi. Res: Freeze drying. Mailing Add: 1805 S Virginia Norman OK 73071-4433

SOMMERS, HENRY STERN, JR, PHYSICS. Current Pos: RETIRED. Personal Data: b St Paul, Minn, Apr 21, 14; m 38; c 4. Educ: Univ Minn, AB, 36; Harvard Univ, PhD(physics), 41. Prof Exp: Instr, Harvard Univ, 41-42; mem staff, Mass Inst Technol, 42-45; asst prof physics, Rutgers Univ, 46-49; mem staff, Los Alamos Sci Lab, NMex, 49-54; fel, RCA Labs, RCA Corp, 54-84. Concurrent Pos: Fulbright lectr & Guggenheim fel, Hebrew Univ, Israel, 60-61. Mem: AAAS; fel Am Phys Soc; Fedn Am Sci. Res: Nuclear and semiconductor physics; instrumentation; cryogenics; photoconductivity; quantum electronics; experimental research on basic physics and control of power spectrum of injection lasers. Mailing Add: Pennswood Village No C201 Newtown PA 18940

SOMMERS, HERBERT M, PATHOLOGY. Current Pos: DIR CLIN MICROBIOL, NORTHWESTERN MEM HOSP, 72- Personal Data: b Colorado Springs, Colo, Sept 4, 25; m 55; c 4. Educ: Northwestern Univ, BS, 49, MD, 52. Prof Exp: Instr, 59-61, assoc, 61-62, from asst prof to assoc prof, 62-71, PROF PATH, MED SCH, NORTHWESTERN UNIV, CHICAGO, 71- Concurrent Pos: Res fel path, Med Sch, Northwestern Univ, Chicago, 54-58; attend pathologist, Chicago Wesley Mem Hosp, 58-68, Passavant Mem Hosp, 68-73 & Northwestern Mem Hosp, 73-; consult, Vet Admin Res Hosp; trustee, Am Bd Path, 82-88. Mem: Am Soc Clin Path; Am Asn Pathologists; Am Soc Microbiol; Am Thoracic Soc; Col Am Path; Sigma Xi. Res: Experimental pathology of ischemic myocardium and mechanisms of ventricular fibrillation; improvement of methods in clinical microbiology; laboratory methods for mycobacterial susceptiblity testing. Mailing Add: Dept Path Northwestern Univ Med Sch 303 E Chicago Ave Chicago IL 60611-3072

SOMMERS, JAY RICHARD, ORGANIC CHEMISTRY, TECHNICAL MANAGEMENT. Current Pos: dir feminine care res & develop, 83-87, dir res corp sci & technol, 87-90, MGR CLIN & SCI DOC, KIMBERLY-CLARK, 90- Personal Data: b Brooklyn, NY, May 19, 39; m 61, Eleanor Novak; c Craig, Eric & Marc. Educ: Brooklyn Col, BS, 61; Univ Pittsburgh, PhD(org chem), 65. Prof Exp: Res chemist, Org Chem Dept, E I du Pont de Nemours & Co, 65-69; sr res scientist & mgr, Surg Specialty Div, Johnson & Johnson Co, 69-74, mgr surg apparel & fabrics develop, Surgikos, 74-76, dir prod develop, Surgikos, 76-80, mgr fiber technol, Johnson & Johnson Prod, Inc, 80-81; dir prod develop, Int Playtex Inc, 81-83. Mem: Am Chem Soc; Asn Advan Med Instrumentation; Am Asn Textile Chem & Colorists; Sigma Xi; Asn Soc Testing & Mat; Nat Fire Protection Asn. Res: Textile chemicals; nonwoven fabrics and finishes; disposable apparel; fabric flammability; medical/surgical products; biomedical devices; internal and external sanitary protection; health and beauty aids; basic and long range research and development. Mailing Add: 1985 Willeo Creek Pt Marietta GA 30068. Fax: 770-587-8772; E-Mail: jsommers@kcc.com

SOMMERS, LAWRENCE M, DEVELOPMENT GEOGRAPHY, SCANDINAVIAN GEOGRAPHY. Current Pos: Instr, Mich State Univ, 49-51, from asst prof to prof, 51-89, head dept, 55-62, chmn, 62-79, asst provost acad serv, 87-89, EMER PROF GEOG, MICH STATE UNIV, 89- Personal Data: b Clinton, Wis; m 48, Marjorie S; c Laurie K. Educ: Univ Wis, BS, 41, PhM, 46; Northwestern Univ, PhD(geog), 50. Honors & Awards: res awards, Soc Sci Res Coun, Am Scand Found, Off Naval Res. Concurrent Pos: Mem, comt geog, adv geog br, off Naval Res-Nat Res Coun, 58-61; consult & examr, NCent Accrediting Asn, 63-79; vis scientist, NSF & Asn Am Geographers, 68-70; ed, Denoyer Geppert Co, 75-86; prof, Environ Qual Ctr, Mich State Univ, 79-81; US Deleg, study group, High Latitude Develop & Develop Issues Marginal Regions, Int Geog Union, 84-96, Dynamics of Marginal & Critical Regions, 96- Mem: AAAS; Asn Am Geographers; Am Geog Soc; Sigma Xi; Explorers Club. Res: Development issues in the state of Michigan, arid Southwest, and Scandanavian countries; Norwegian North Sea oil and gas developments; development problems and water quality in Norway; spatial analysis of Lake Michigan and the geography of Michigan; Marginal regions of Michigan and Norway. Mailing Add: Dept Geog Mich State Univ East Lansing MI 48824. Fax: 517-432-1671

SOMMERS, LEE EDWIN, SOIL MICROBIOLOGY, CHEMISTRY. Current Pos: PROF & DEPT HEAD, COLO STATE UNIV, 85- Personal Data: b Beloit, Wis, July 30, 44; m 66, 79; c 3. Educ: Wis State Univ, Platteville, BS, 66; Univ Wis-Madison, MS, 68, PhD(soil sci), 70. Honors & Awards: Environ Qual Res Award, Am Soc Agron. Prof Exp: Prof, Soil Microbiol, Purdue Univ, 70-85. Mem: Fel Am Soc Agron; fel Soil Sci Soc Am. Res: Effect of soil chemical and physical properties on microbial growth; microbial transformations of heavy metals; role of soils and sediments in eutrophication; plant nutrient and metal transformations in soils amended with industrial and municipal wastes. Mailing Add: 5101 Nelson Ct Ft Collins CO 80525. E-Mail: lsommers@ceres.agsci.colostate.edu

SOMMERS, RAYMOND A, ANALYTICAL CHEMISTRY. *Current Pos:* from asst prof to prof, 62-96, EMER PROF ANAL CHEM, UNIV WIS-STEVENS POINT, 96- *Personal Data:* b Marshfield, Wis, Nov 22, 31; m 54, Kathleen Hastings; c 14. *Educ:* Univ Wis-Stevens Point, BS, 53; Lawrence Univ, MS, 59, PhD(chem), 63. *Concurrent Pos:* NSF sci fac fel, Dept Chem, Mich State Univ, 68-69. *Mem:* Am Chem Soc. *Mailing Add:* Dept Chem Univ Wis Stevens Point WI 54481. *E-Mail:* rsommers@coredcs.com; rsommers@uwsp.edu

SOMMERS, SHELDON CHARLES, GASTROINTESTINAL PATHOLOGY, ENDOMETRIAL & ENDOCRINE PATHOLOGY. *Current Pos:* clin prof, 62-91, EMER PROF PATH, UNIV SOUTHERN CALIF, 92- *Personal Data:* b Indianapolis, Ind, July 7, 16; m 43, 90, Bernice Lang. *Educ:* Harvard Univ, BS, 37, MD, 41. *Prof Exp:* Assoc prof path, Sch Med, Boston Univ, 53-61; clin prof path, Univ Southern Calif, 62-88; from assoc prof to prof, Col Physicians & Surgeons, Columbia Univ, 63-68; clin prof, 68-90; lab dir, Lenox Hill Hosp, NY, 68-81, consult, 81-89. *Concurrent Pos:* Res assoc, Cancer Res Inst, New Eng Deaconess Hosp, 50-61; lectr, Harvard Med Sch, 53-61; pathologist, Mass Mem Hosps, 53-61; Scripps Hosp, 61-63 & Delafield Hosp, NY, 63-68; ed, Path Ann, 66-86 & Path Decenn, 66-75; sci dir, Coun Tobacco Res, 81-87, consult, 88; consult path, 81- *Mem:* Emer mem Am Soc Clin Pathologists; emer fel Am Asn Pathologists; emer fel Col Am Pathologists; emer mem US & Can Acad Path. *Res:* Investigations of pathogenesis and morphology of gastrointestinal diseases, particularly ulcerative colitis and Crohn's disease, hypertensive kidney disease, gynecologic pathology, particularly endometrial and ovarian cancers, endocrine pathology of hypothalamus, pituitary, thyroid, parathyroid, adrenal, gonadal and placental abnormalities. *Mailing Add:* Cambridge Way PO Box 1115 Alpine NJ 07620

SOMMERS, WILLIAM P(AUL), ENGINEERING, RESEARCH MANAGEMENT. *Current Pos:* RETIRED. *Personal Data:* b Detroit, Mich, July 22, 33; m 56, 78; c 5. *Educ:* Univ Mich, BSE, 55, MSE, 56, PhD(mech eng), 61. *Prof Exp:* Engr, Martin Co, 56-57, sr engr, 57-58; res assoc aeronaut eng, Inst Sci & Technol, Univ Mich, 59-61; chief chem propulsion, Martin Co, 61-63; proj scientist mech & aeronaut eng, Booz Allen & Hamilton, Inc, 63-65, res dir eng & sci mgt, 65-67, vpres & dir NASA progs, 67-71, pres & mem bd dirs, 71-73, pres, Technol Mgt Group, 73-79, sr exec vpres, 79-83. *Concurrent Pos:* Consult, Ethyl Corp, 60-61. *Mem:* Assoc fel Am Inst Aeronaut & Astronaut; sr mem Am Astron Soc; Sigma Xi. *Res:* Detonative combustion; fluid dynamics; heat transfer; propulsion and aerospace sciences. *Mailing Add:* 2181 Parkside Ave Hillsborough CA 94010-6452

SOMMERS SMITH, SALLY K, CELLULAR BIOLOGY. *Current Pos:* ASSOC PROF SCI, BOSTON UNIV, 84- *Personal Data:* b Menominee, Mich, Oct 2, 53; m 80, Dennis M Smith; c Matthew. *Educ:* Tufts Univ, PhD(cell biol & anat), 80. *Mem:* Am Soc Cell Biol; Am Thoracic Soc. *Res:* Cell-Cell interactions in pulmonary injury and repair; effect of beta-blockade on lung cell development. *Mailing Add:* Dept Sci Col Gen Studies Boston Univ Boston MA 02215

SOMMESE, ANDREW JOHN, COMPLEX ALGEBRAIC GEOMETRY. *Current Pos:* assoc prof, Univ Notre Dame, 79-83, co-dir, Ctr Appl Math, 87-92, chmn, Dept Math, 88-92, PROF MATH, UNIV NOTRE DAME, 83-, DUNCAN PROF MATH, 94- *Personal Data:* b New York, NY, May 3, 48; m 71, Rebecca DeBoer; c Rachel C & Ruth F. *Educ:* Fordham Univ, BA, 69; Princeton Univ, PhD(math), 73. *Honors & Awards:* Res Award for Sr US Scientist, Humboldt Found, 93. *Prof Exp:* Gibbs instr, Yale Univ, 73-75; asst prof, Cornell Univ, 75-79. *Concurrent Pos:* Sloan res fel, Alfred P Sloan Found, 73; mem, Inst Advan Study, NJ, 75-76; guest prof, Univ Gottingen, 77, Univ Bonn, 78-79 & Max Planck Inst Math, Bonn, wGer 84-85, 87 & 92-93; ed, Manuscripta Mathematica, 86-93; consult, Gen Motors Res Lab, 86- *Mem:* Am Math Soc; Soc Indust & Appl Math. *Res:* Numerical solution of polynomial systems arising in engineering; adjunction theory of projective varieties. *Mailing Add:* Dept Math Univ Notre Dame Notre Dame IN 46556. *E-Mail:* sommese.1@nd.edu

SOMOANO, ROBERT BONNER, SOLID STATE PHYSICS. *Current Pos:* MEM TECH STAFF, JET PROPULSION LABS, 69- *Personal Data:* b Houston, Tex, Sept 2, 40; m 62; c 3. *Educ:* Tex A&M, BS, 62, MS, 64; Univ Tex, PhD(physics), 69. *Mem:* Am Inst Physics; Am Phys Soc. *Res:* Liquid metals; polymer physics; superconductivity. *Mailing Add:* 835 Old Landmark Lane La Canada CA 91011-2526

SOMOGYI, LASZLO P, PLANT PHYSIOLOGY, HORTICULTURE. *Current Pos:* SR CONSULT, SRI INT, 89- *Personal Data:* b Budapest, Hungary, June 1, 31; US citizen; m 51, Marika Harmat; c Peter & George. *Educ:* Univ Agr Sci Hungary, BS, 56; Rutgers Univ, MS, 60, PhD(hort), 62. *Honors & Awards:* Outstanding Mem Award, Inst Food Technologist, Northern Calif, 84. *Prof Exp:* Jr res pomologist, Univ Calif, Davis, 62-64; proj leader, Hunt-Wesson Foods, Inc, 64-70; dir res & develop, Vacu-Dry Co, 70-74; tech dir, Biophys Res & Develop Corp, 74-76; sr food scientist, SRI Int, 76-79; vpres, Finn-Cal Prod, Inc, 79-81; pres, Etel, Inc, 81-89. *Mem:* Fel Inst Food Technologists; Am Asn Cereal Chem; Am Oil Chem Soc. *Res:* Food processing and product development; food dehydration; technoeconomic market studies of food ingredients and additives; environmental impact of food processing operations; harvesting and storage of fruits and vegetables. *Mailing Add:* 12 Highgate Ct Kensington CA 94707. *E-Mail:* laszlo_somogyi@qm.sri.com

SOMORJAI, GABOR ARPAD, PHYSICAL CHEMISTRY. *Current Pos:* from asst prof to assoc prof, 64-67, Miller prof, 77-78, DIR, SURFACE SCI & CATALYSIS PROG, LAWRENCE BERKELEY LAB, UNIV CALIF, BERKELEY, 64-, PROF CHEM, 72- *Personal Data:* b Budapest, Hungary, May 4, 35; m 57, Judith; c Nicole & John. *Educ:* Budapest Tech Univ, ChE, 56; Univ Calif, PhD(chem), 60. *Hon Degrees:* Dr, Univ Paris & Budapest Tech Univ, 89, Univ Pierre at Marie Curie, Paris, 90, Free Univ Brussels, Belg, 92. *Honors & Awards:* Emmett Award, Am Catalysis Soc, 77; Baker Lectr, Cornell Univ, 77; Colloid & Surface Chem Award, Am Chem Soc, 81, Peter Debye Award, 89, Ademson Award, 94; Pallodium Medal, 86; G N Lewis Lectr, Univ Calif, Berkeley, 87. *Prof Exp:* Mem res staff, Res Ctr, Int Bus Mach Corp, 60-64. *Concurrent Pos:* Guggenheim fel, 69-70; vis fel, Emmanuel Col, Cambridge, Eng, 69; Unilever vis prof, Bristol Univ, 71-72; chmn, Div Colloid & Surface Chem, Am Chem Soc, 75; Royal Soc lectr, 83. *Mem:* Nat Acad Sci; fel Am Phys Soc; Am Chem Soc; fel AAAS; Am Acad Arts & Sci. *Res:* Chemistry of surfaces and solids; catalysis; surface science of energy conversion; mechanism of catalysis of hydrocarbon reactions by metals and otides; structure of surfaces, tribology. *Mailing Add:* Dept Chem Univ Calif Berkeley CA 94720

SOMORJAI, RAJMUND LEWIS, THEORETICAL BIOLOGY, BIOPHYSICS. *Current Pos:* res officer, 65-91, HEAD, INFORMATICS GROUP, NAT RES COUN CAN, 91- *Personal Data:* b Budapest, Hungary, Jan 21, 37; Can citizen; m 70; c 2. *Educ:* McGill Univ, BSc, 60; Princeton Univ, PhD(physics, phys chem), 63. *Prof Exp:* NATO sci fel, Cambridge Univ, 63-65. *Concurrent Pos:* Adj prof, Dept Physiol & Biophys, Univ Ill Med Ctr, 75- *Mem:* Chem Inst Can; Am Phys Soc; Can Asn Physics. *Res:* Approximation methods; calculation of the dynamics of protein folding and enzyme action; structure-function relationships in biology; properties of complex, hierarchical systems; nonequilibrium phenomena; nonlinear problems. *Mailing Add:* Biodiagnostics Nat Res Coun Can 435 Ellice Ave Winnipeg MB R3B 1Y6 Can

SOMSEN, ROGER ALAN, pulp chemistry, for more information see previous edition

SON, CHUNG HYUN, FOOD PRODUCTS DEVELOPMENT. *Current Pos:* RETIRED. *Personal Data:* b Changyun, Korea, Mar 16, 17; US citizen; m 39, Insuk Kam; c Hoon, Myung He & Myung Sook. *Educ:* Rutgers State Univ NJ, BS, 56, MS, 57, PhD(food sci), 59. *Prof Exp:* Sr scientist, Del Monte Corp Res Ctr, 59-83, consult food processing, 84-89. *Mailing Add:* 782 Tiffany Pl Concord CA 94518

SONDAK, NORMAN EDWARD, COMPUTER SCIENCE, INFORMATION SYSTEMS. *Current Pos:* prof & chmn, 78-85, PROF, INFO & DECISION SYSTS, SAN DIEGO STATE UNIV, 85- *Personal Data:* b Cornwall, NY, Sept 1, 31; m 54; c 3. *Educ:* City Col NY, BE, 53; Northwestern Univ, MS, 54; Yale Univ, DEng(eng), 58. *Honors & Awards:* Kellog lectr, 79. *Prof Exp:* Sr technologist, Res Labs, Socony Mobil, 56-61; mgr data processing, Electronic Data Processing Div, RCA Corp, 61-63; vpres data processing, J Walter Thompson Co, NY, 63-68; prof comput sci & head dept, Worcester Polytech Inst, 68-78, dir comput ctr, 68-71. *Concurrent Pos:* Affil prof, Clark Univ, 69-78; mem coop staff, Worcester Found Exp Biol, 70-78; res prof, Med Sch, Univ Mass, 75-78. *Mem:* Data Processing Mgt Asn; Soc Indust & Appl Math; Asn Comput Mach; Inst Elec & Electronics Engrs; Am Soc Info Sci. *Res:* Programming languages; data base management systems; operating systems; social implications of computing; computer architecture; computer science education; computer networks; structured systems design; word processing; microcomputer systems; artificial intelligence; expert systems. *Mailing Add:* Info Systs Dept San Diego State Univ San Diego CA 92182-0001

SONDEL, PAUL MARK, TUMOR IMMUNOLOGY, IMMUNOGENETICS. *Current Pos:* asst prof pediat & human oncol, 80-84, asst prof med genetics, 81-84, assoc prof, 84-87, PROF, PEDIAT, HUMAN ONCOL & MED GENETICS, UNIV WIS-MADISON, 87- *Personal Data:* b Milwaukee, Wis, Aug 14, 50; m 73; c 2. *Educ:* Univ Wis-Madison, BS, 71, PhD(genetics), 75, Harvard Med Sch, MD, 77. *Prof Exp:* Res & teaching asst, Dept Genetics, Univ Wis-Madison, 71-72; res aide, Dept Immunol, Harvard Med Sch, 73-74; res assoc, Immunobiol Res Ctr, Univ Wis-Madison, 74-75; res fel tumor immunol, Sidney Farber Cancer Inst, 75-77; intern pediat, Univ Minn Hosp, 77-78; resident, Univ Wis Hosp, 78-80. *Concurrent Pos:* Scholar, Leukemia Soc Am, 81-86; fel, G A & J L Hartford Found, 81-84. *Mem:* Transplantation Soc; Am Asn Immunologists; Am Asn Clin Histocompatibility; Am Fedn Clin Res; Am Soc Clin Invest; Soc Pediat Res. *Res:* Tumor and transplantation immunogenetics: the in vitro responses of human lymphocytes to normal and abnormal cell populations to better define the role of human leucocyte antigen factors in immunoregulation. *Mailing Add:* Univ Wis Clin Sci Ctr 600 Highland Ave Rm K4-448 Madison WI 53792-0001. *Fax:* 608-263-8613; *E-Mail:* sundel%biostdecnet@ums.macc.wisc.edu

SONDER, EDWARD, PHYSICS, MATERIALS SCIENCE. *Current Pos:* RETIRED. *Personal Data:* b Ger, May 1, 28; nat US; m 53; c Karen A (Pawlo) & Leslie J. *Educ:* Queens Col, BS, 50; Univ Ill, MS, 51, PhD(physics), 55. *Prof Exp:* Res assoc solid state physics, Iowa State Col, 55-56; physicist, Oak Ridge Nat Lab, 56-95. *Concurrent Pos:* Vis prof physics, Okla State Univ, 74-75; adj prof, Vanderbilt Univ, 87-95. *Mem:* Am Phys Soc. *Res:* Imperfections in solids, radiation effects in insulators and semiconductors; color centers in alkali halides; electrical properties of insulators; varistors; high temperature superconductors. *Mailing Add:* Bldg 2652A MS 6290 Oak Ridge Nat Lab PO Box 2008 Oak Ridge TN 37831

SONDEREGGER, THEO BROWN, MEDICAL PSYCHOLOGY. *Current Pos:* from asst prof to prof psychol, 69-95, prof med psychol, 78-95, EMER PROF PSYCHOL, UNIV NEBR, LINCOLN, 95-, EMER PROF MED PSYCHOL, MED CTR, 95- *Personal Data:* b Brimingham, Ala, May 31, 25; m 47, Paul; c 3. *Educ:* Fla State Univ, BS, 46; Univ Nebr, Lincoln, MA, 48 & 60, PhD(clin psychol), 65. *Honors & Awards:* Outstanding Scientist Award, Sigma Xi, 91; Pound-Howard Award Career Achievement, 96. *Prof Exp:* Teaching asst psychol, Univ Nebr, Lincoln, 59-62, instr med psychol, Med Ctr, 65-69; asst prof psychol, Nebr Wesleyan Univ, 65-68. *Concurrent Pos:* Vis scholar, Dept Neurosci, Northwestern Univ, Evanston, 73-74; vis assoc res anatomist, Med Sch, Univ Calif, Los Angeles, 74, vis res psychol, Dept Psychiat, 79-80; vis res assoc biol, Calif Inst Technol, 79-80; vis prof, Brain Res Inst, Univ Calif, Los Angeles, 80-81. *Mem:* Fel Am Psychol Asn; Soc Neurosci; fel AAAS; Int Soc Develop Biol; Psychonomic Soc; fel Am Psychol Soc. *Res:* Neonatal narcotic addiction; fetal alcohol syndrome (animal model); intracranial self stimulation; catecholamines and the developing nervous system; psychology of women. *Mailing Add:* 1710 S 58th St Lincoln NE 68506. *Fax:* 402-488-2390; *E-Mail:* tbs@unlifo.unl.edu

SONDERGAARD, NEAL ALBERT, PHYSICAL CHEMISTRY, CHEMICAL PHYSICS. *Current Pos:* CHEMIST, NAVAL SHIP RES & DEVELOP CTR, ANNAPOLIS, 80- *Personal Data:* b Schenectady, NY, Mar 20, 49; m 77. *Educ:* Marist Col, BA, 70; Brown Univ, MSc, 73, PhD(chem), 77. *Prof Exp:* Fel, Wash Univ, 77; fel phys chem, Johns Hopkins Univ, 77-80. *Concurrent Pos:* Fel, Johns Hopkins Univ, 80- *Mem:* Sigma Xi. *Res:* Physical and chemical phenomena of high current density sliding electric contacts; techniques include molecular beams, ion cyclotron resonance and mass spectroscopy. *Mailing Add:* 423 Fernwood Dr Severna Park MD 21146-2817

SONDERGELD, CARL HENDERSON, GEOPHYSICS, ROCK MECHANICS. *Current Pos:* sr res scientist, 81-83, staff res scientist, 83-88, RES ASSOC, AMOCO PROD CO, 88- *Personal Data:* b Brooklyn, NY, Nov 4, 47; m 69; c 2. *Educ:* Queen's Col, NY, BA, 69, MA, 73; Cornell Univ, PhD(geophysics), 77. *Prof Exp:* Res assoc geothermal energy, Cornell Univ, 77; vis fel, Nat Oceanic & Atmospheric Admin, Univ Colo, 77-78, res assoc rock mech, Coop Inst Res Environ Sic, 78-81. *Concurrent Pos:* Adj prof, Univ Colo, 80-; vis scientist, Los Alamos Nat Lab. *Mem:* Am Geophys Union; Acoust Emission Soc; Sigma Xi. *Res:* Acoustic emissions in rock; elasticity of rocks and polycrystals; geothermal energy-two-phase convection in porous media; acoustic logging and shear wave anisotropy; acoustic magnetic and electrical properties of rock. *Mailing Add:* Amoco Prod Co PO Box 3385 Tulsa OK 74102

SONEA, SORIN I, BACTERIOLOGY. *Current Pos:* from asst prof to prof, 50-93, EMER PROF MICROBIOL, UNIV MONTREAL, 93- *Personal Data:* b Cluj, Romania, Mar 14, 20; Can citizen; m 46, Rodica Vlad; c Joana, Peter, Michael & Alexander. *Educ:* Univ Bucharest, MD, 44; Med Sch Paris Univ, dipl hyg, 49. *Hon Degrees:* Dr, Univ Que, 88. *Mem:* Fel Acad Sci, Royal Soc Can; fel Royal Col Physicians & Surgeons Can. *Res:* Nature of bacteria; shown the existence of solidarity among all bacteria based on an easy access at each other's genetic information; shown the presence of a general communication system among all bacteria at the global level supported when necessary by a bacterial biologic computer-like mechanism for solving problems. *Mailing Add:* 4282 Badgley Montreal PQ H4P 1N8 Can. *Fax:* 514-343-5701

SONENBERG, MARTIN, ENDOCRINOLOGY, BIOCHEMISTRY. *Current Pos:* from instr to assoc prof, 53-72, PROF MED, MED COL, CORNELL UNIV, 72-, PROF BIOCHEM, CORNELL GRAD SCH MED SCI, 66- *Personal Data:* b New York, NY, Dec 1, 20; m 56, Dellie Ellis; c Santha & Andrea. *Educ:* Univ Pa, BA, 41; NY Univ, MD, 44, PhD(biochem), 52. *Honors & Awards:* Van Meter Award, Am Thyroid Asn, 52; Sloan Award, 68. *Prof Exp:* Intern, Beth Israel Hosp, 44-45; asst resident med, Goldwater Hosp, 45-46. *Concurrent Pos:* Am Cancer Soc fel, Mem Ctr Cancer & Allied Dis, 52-57; Guggenheim fel, Carlsberg Lab, Copenhagen Univ, 57-58; clin asst, Mem Ctr Cancer & Allied Dis, 51-; assoc, Sloan-Kettering Inst Cancer Res, 52-60, assoc mem, 60-66, mem, 66-; assoc attend physician, Mem & James Ewing Hosps, 59-; attend physician, Mem Hosp, 69-; NIH endocrinol study sect, 83-87, chmn, 85-87. *Mem:* AAAS; Biophys Soc; Am Soc Biol Chem; Am Soc Clin Invest; Am Thyroid Asn; Endocrine Soc. *Res:* Chemistry and physiology of pituitary hormones; protein chemistry; mechanism of hormone action. *Mailing Add:* Mem Sloan-Kettering Cancer Ctr 1275 York Ave New York NY 10021. *Fax:* 212-639-5850; *E-Mail:* sonenbem@mskrc.org

SONENSHEIN, ABRAHAM LINCOLN, MICROBIOLOGY, MOLECULAR BIOLOGY. *Current Pos:* from asst prof to assoc prof, 72-82, PROF MOLECULAR BIOL & MICROBIOL, SCH MED, TUFTS UNIV, 82- *Personal Data:* b Paterson, NJ, Jan 13, 44; m 67, Gail Entner; c Dina & Adam. *Educ:* Princeton Univ, AB, 65; Mass Inst Technol, PhD(biol), 70. *Prof Exp:* Am Cancer Soc fel, Inst Microbiol, Univ Paris, 70-72. *Concurrent Pos:* Nat Inst Gen Med Sci res support grant, 72-; NSF res grant, 79-81. *Mem:* AAAS; Am Soc Microbiol; Fedn Am Sci; Am Soc Biochem & Molecular Biol. *Res:* Bacterial sporulation; control of transcription; RNA polymerase; genetics and physiology of Bacillus subtilis; phage infection of Bacillus subtilis. *Mailing Add:* Dept Molecular Biol Tufts Univ 136 Harrison Ave Boston MA 02111-1800

SONENSHINE, DANIEL E, ZOOLOGY. *Current Pos:* PROF MICROBIOL, EASTERN VA MED SCH, NORFOLK, 74- *Personal Data:* b New York, NY, May 11, 33; m 57. *Educ:* City Col NY, BA, 55; Univ MD, PhD(zool), 59. *Prof Exp:* Asst zool, Univ Md, 55-58, asst instr, 58-59; instr biol, Univ Akron, 59-61; mem staff, Old Dom Univ, 61-74. *Mem:* Am Soc Parasitol; Sigma Xi. *Res:* Acarology; parasitology; ecology and life history of ticks; physiology. *Mailing Add:* 1366 Little Neck Rd Virginia Beach VA 23452

SONETT, CHARLES PHILIP, PLANETARY & INTERPLANETARY PHYSICS. *Current Pos:* head, Dept Planetary Sci & dir, Lunar & Planetary Lab, 73-77, prof, 73-90, regents prof planetary sci, 90-93, EMER REGENTS PROF, LUNAR & PLANETARY LAB, UNIV ARIZ, 93- *Personal Data:* b Pittsburgh, Pa, Jan 15, 24; m 48; c Eric & Maria. *Educ:* Univ Calif, Berkely, BA, 49, Univ Calif, Los Angeles, MS, 52, PhD(physics), 54. *Honors & Awards:* Space Sci Award, Am Inst Aeronaut & Astronaut, 69; Except Sci Achievement Medal, NASA, 69 & 72. *Prof Exp:* From asst to assoc, physics, Univ Calif, 51-53; mem tech staff & head, Range Develop Group, Ramo Wooldridge Corp, 54-57; mem sr staff & head space physics, Space Technol Labs, Inc, 57-60; chief sci, Lunar & Planetary Prog, NASA, 60-62, chief, Space Sci Div, Ames Res Ctr, 62-70, dep dir astronaut, 71-73. *Concurrent Pos:* Lectr eng, Univ Calif, Los Angeles, 55-58; Guggenheim fel, Imp Col, Univ London, 68-69; ed, Cosmic Electrodynamics, 70-72; co-ed, Astrophys & Space Sci, 73-80; mem, Space Sci Steering Comt, NASA, chmn subcomts lunar sci & planetary & interplanetary sci, 60-62, mem subcomts planetology, 62-65 & particles & fields, 62-63, mem outer planets sci adv group, 71-72, mem, Outer Planets Sci Working Group, Post-Apollo Sci Planning Conf & ad hoc working group on planetary remote sensing, 72, mem NASA/Jet Propulsion Lab terrestrial bodies sci working group, 76, chmn NASA/Univs Space Res Asn, tethered satellite exp rev panel, 84, mem Mars Observer exp rev panel, 85; mem, Comn 17 & 49, Int Astron Union; consult, Jet Propulsion Lab & Rockwell Int; mem bd trustees, Univ Space Res Asn, 77-83; co-ed, Moon & Planets, 78-; mem Los Alamos br adv comn, Univ Calif Inst Geophys & Planetary Physics, 84-85; Carnegie fel, Univ Edinburgh, 85; fel, Inst Advan Studies, Univ Ind, 90. *Mem:* fel Am Geophys Union. *Res:* Planetary and interplanetary physics; physics of the moon; solar-terrestrial physics; solar wind; cosmogenic nuclides. *Mailing Add:* Dept Planetary Sci Univ Ariz Tucson AZ 85721

SONG, BYOUNG-JOON, PROTEIN BIOCHEMISTRY, MOLECULAR BIOLOGY. *Current Pos:* sr staff fel, 86-90, SECT CHIEF, LAB METAB & MOLECULAR BIOL, NAT INST ALCOHOL ABUSE & ALCOHOLISM, 90- *Personal Data:* b Mar 4, 50; US citizen; c 2. *Educ:* Seoul Nat Univ, BS, 72, MS, 76; Univ Minn, PhD(pharmacol, biochem), 83. *Prof Exp:* Res asst pharmacol, Univ Minn, 77-82; postdoctoral fel biochem, Lab Molecular Carcinogenesis, Nat Cancer Inst, NIH, 83-86. *Concurrent Pos:* Adj prof, Dept Pharmacol, Univ Md, 90- *Mem:* Am Soc Biochem & Molecular Biol; AAAS. *Res:* Molecular biology on ethanol inducible cytochrome P450; molecular biology on the pyruvate dehydrogenase multienzyme complex. *Mailing Add:* Molecular Biol Lab Neurogent NIAAA NIH 12501 Washington Ave Rockville MD 20852-1852. *Fax:* 301-443-5894

SONG, CHANG WON, RADIOBIOLOGY, IMMUNOLOGY. *Current Pos:* from asst prof to assoc prof, 70-78, PROF & DIR RADIATION BIOL, MED SCH, UNIV MINN, MINNEAPOLIS, 78- *Personal Data:* b Chun Chon City, Korea, Apr 10, 32. *Educ:* Seoul Nat Univ, BS, 57; Univ Korea, MS, 59; Univ Iowa, PhD(radiation biol), 64. *Prof Exp:* Res asst radiation biol, Univ Iowa, 60-64; asst mem, Res Labs, Albert Einstein Med Ctr, 64-69; asst prof, Med Col Va, 69-70. *Concurrent Pos:* Consult, Vet Admin & Nat Can Inst. *Mem:* Cell Kinetic Soc; AAAS; Radiation Res Soc; Am Asn Cancer Res; Europ Soc Hyperthermic Oncol; N Am Hyperthermia Group. *Res:* Relationship between vascular changes and curability of tumors by radiotherapy or hyperthermia; effect of radiation on immune system and feasibility of combination radio- and immuno-therapy for treatment of cancer; radiosensitization and radioprotection of tumors. *Mailing Add:* Dept Therapeut Rad Univ Minn Med Sch Box 494 MAYO 420 Delaware St SE Minneapolis MN 55455-0374

SONG, CHARLES CHIEH-SHYANG, CIVIL ENGINEERING, FLUID MECHANICS. *Current Pos:* From asst prof to assoc prof, 61-79, PROF CIVIL ENG, UNIV MINN, MINNEAPOLIS, 79- *Personal Data:* b Taiwan, China, Jan 12, 31; m 55; c 3. *Educ:* Nat Taiwan Univ, BS, 53; Univ Iowa, MS, 56; Univ Minn, Minneapolis, PhD(civil eng), 60. *Honors & Awards:* J C Stevens Award, 80. *Mem:* AAAS; Int Asn Hydraul Res; Soc Naval Archit & Marine Engrs; Am Soc Civil Engrs; Am Water Resources Asn. *Res:* Flows at large Reynolds numbers; computional hydrodymincs; turbulent flow modeling; drainage and water distribution system modeling; hydraulic transient; sediment transport; effect of ice on flooding. *Mailing Add:* 7042 Galpin Blvd Excelsior MN 55331

SONG, JIAKUN, COMPARATIVE NEUROANATOMY, ONTOGENY & PHYLOGENY OF VERTEBRATES. *Current Pos:* RES, DEPT ZOOL, UNIV MD, COLLEGE PARK. *Personal Data:* b Shanghai, China, Aug 27, 44. *Educ:* Shanghai Col Fisheries, BS, 67; Univ Mich, Ann Arbor, MS, 82, PhD(biol sci), 89. *Prof Exp:* Sci & technol dir aquaculture, Biol Stat Bur Fisheries, Ning-De Region Fujian Prov, China, 70-75; asst researcher ichthyol, Inst Zool, Academia Sinica, Beijing, 75-80; res assoc fish taxon, Mus Zool, Univ Mich, Ann Arbor, 81-83 & teaching asst & lab instr vertebrate biol, Dept Biol, 83-86; res assoc neurobiol, Neurobiol Unit, Scripps Inst Oceanog, Univ Calif San Diego, 87-89; postdoctoral res fel neurosci, Sch Life & Health Sci, Univ Del, 89- *Mem:* AAAS; Am Soc Ichthyologists & Herpetologists; Am Soc Zoologists; Chinese Soc Zoologists; Int Brain Res Orgn; Soc Neurosci. *Res:* Lateral line system of fishes; application of novel studies on organization of cranial nerves to questions of phylogenetic relationships of fishes. *Mailing Add:* 9117 St Andrews Pl College Park MD 20740

SONG, JOSEPH, PATHOLOGY. *Personal Data:* b Seoul, Korea, May 11, 27; nat US; m 58. *Educ:* Seoul Nat Univ, MD, 50; Univ Tenn, MS, 56; Univ Ark, MD, 65. *Honors & Awards:* Martin Luther King Med Achievement Award, 72; Statesman in Health Care Award, 87. *Prof Exp:* Instr path, Med Sch, Univ Tenn, 52-56; instr, Sch Med, Boston Univ, 56-61; assoc prof, Sch Med, Univ Ark, 61-65; dir dept path, Mercy Hosp, 65-92. *Concurrent Pos:* Assoc dir, RI State Cancer Cytol Proj, 56-59; sr instr, Med Sch, Tufts Univ, 59-61; assoc mem, Inst Health Sci, Brown Univ, 59-61; assoc pathologist, Providence Lying-In Hosp, 59-61; assoc med examr, State RI, 59-61; consult, St Joseph's Hosp, Providence, RI, 59-61 & Vet Admin Hosps, Little Rock & North Little Rock, Ark; clin prof, Sch Med, Creighton Univ. *Mem:* Fel Am Soc Clin Path; Am Asn Path & Bact; fel Am Col Path. *Res:* Hepatic pathology in sickle cell disease; exfoliative cytology in cancer of the cervix; splenic function and tumor growth, experimental cancer research. *Mailing Add:* 2345 Park Ave Des Moines IA 50321

SONG, JUNG HYUN, plastics processing technology, flame retardancy of polymers-plastics, for more information see previous edition

SONG, KONG-SOP AUGUSTIN, SOLID STATE PHYSICS. *Current Pos:* from asst prof to assoc prof, 69-80, PROF PHYSICS, UNIV OTTAWA, 80- *Personal Data:* b Korea, 1934. *Educ:* Chunpuk Nat Univ, Korea, 56, MS, 57; Univ Paris, Dr 3e Cycle, 64; Univ Strasbourg, Dr es Sci(physics), 67. *Prof Exp:* Jr researcher, Nat Ctr Sci Res, France, 63-69. *Concurrent Pos:* Instr, Univ Strasbourg, 65-69. *Mem:* Am Phys Soc. *Res:* Electronic and optical properties of semiconductors and insulators. *Mailing Add:* Dept Physics Univ Ottawa Ottawa ON K1N 6N5 Can

SONG, MOON K, formulate research proposal, for more information see previous edition

SONG, PILL-SOON, MOLECULAR BIOPHYSICS. *Current Pos:* PROF, DEPT CHEM, UNIV NEBR, LINCOLN, 87- *Personal Data:* b Osaka, Japan, Aug 5, 36; m 84; c 3. *Educ:* Univ Seoul, BS, 58, MS, 60; Univ Calif, PhD(biochem), 64. *Honors & Awards:* Outstanding Res Award, Am Soc Photobiol, 91. *Prof Exp:* Res assoc biochem & biophys, Iowa State Univ, 64-65; from asst prof to prof, Tex Tech Univ, 65-75, Paul W Horn prof, 75-87. *Concurrent Pos:* Grantee, NIH, 86-, Army Res Off, 91- *Mem:* Am Soc Biol Chemists; Am Soc Photobiol. *Res:* Photobiology of Phytochrome in plants and photosensory transduction in stentor; molecular spectroscopy and photochemistry of photoreceptor pigments, energy transduction, and quantum biology. *Mailing Add:* Dept Chem Univ Nebr Lincoln NE 68588-0304. *Fax:* 402-472-2094; *E-Mail:* pssong@unlinfo.unl.edu

SONG, SEH-HOON, BIOPHYSICS, CARDIOPULMONARY PHYSIOLOGY. *Current Pos:* lectr, 72-73, ASST PROF BIOPHYS, UNIV WESTERN ONT, 73- *Personal Data:* b Seoul, Korea, June 29, 36; Can citizen; m 62; c 4. *Educ:* Yonsei Univ, MD, 60; State Univ NY Buffalo, MA, 69; Univ Western Ont, PhD(biophys), 72. *Prof Exp:* Instr physiol, Sch Med, Yonsei Univ, 60-62 & 66-67; res assoc, State Univ NY Buffalo, 67-69. *Mem:* Biophys Soc; Am Physiol Soc; Can Physiol Soc. *Res:* Compartmentalization in the microcirculation of various organs, spleen, skeletal muscles and heart; transport of materials through the endothelial membranes. *Mailing Add:* Dept Med Biophysics Med Sci Bldg London ON N6A 5C1 Can

SONG, SUN KYU, NEUROPATHOLOGY. *Current Pos:* Asst prof, 65-71, ASSOC PROF NEUROPATH, MT SINAI SCH MED, 72- *Personal Data:* b Yonchon, Korea, May 15, 27; US citizen; m 56; c 3. *Educ:* Yonsei Univ, Korea, MD, 49. *Concurrent Pos:* USPHS spec fel, Mt Sinai Hosp, 59-63; asst attend neuropathologist, Mt Sinai Hosp, 63-; assoc attend physician, City Hosp Ctr, Elmhurst, NY, 64- *Mem:* Am Asn Neuropath; Histochem Soc; Am Asn Path & Bact; Am Soc Exp Path; Am Acad Neurol. *Res:* Histochemistry and electron microscopy of neuromuscular junction and pathology of neuromuscular diseases. *Mailing Add:* 1098 Anderson Ave Ft Lee NJ 07024-4249

SONG, WON-RYUL, POLYMER CHEMISTRY. *Current Pos:* SR STAFF CHEMIST, EXXON CHEM CO, 65- *Personal Data:* b Korea; US citizen; m 59; c 2. *Educ:* Yonsei Univ, Korea, BS, 52; McMaster Univ, MS, 58; Polytech Inst Brooklyn, PhD(polymer chem), 65. *Prof Exp:* Chemist, Am Cyanamide Co, 61-63. *Mem:* Am Chem Soc. *Res:* Fundamental studies on polymeric lube oil additives. *Mailing Add:* 1530 N Key Blvd Apt 608 Arlington VA 22209

SONG, YO TAIK, NUCLEAR ENGINEERING. *Current Pos:* PROG MGR NUCLEAR ENERGY, US DEPT ENERGY, GERMANTOWN, MD, 79- *Personal Data:* b Korea, Feb 23, 32; m 60; c 3. *Educ:* Yonsei Univ, Korea, BE, 54; Univ Ill, Urbana, MS, 62, PhD(nuclear eng), 68. *Prof Exp:* Nuclear engr, Korean Atomic Energy Res Inst, 59-60; nuclear physicist, US Naval Civil Eng Lab, 63-67; asst prof nuclear eng, Univ Tenn, Knoxville, 68-69; nuclear engr, Tenn Valley Authority, 69-70; assoc dir, Prof Adv Serv Ctr, Univ Colo, 70-72; res nuclear engr, US Naval Surface Weapons Ctr, White Oak Lab, 72-79. *Mem:* Am Nuclear Soc. *Res:* Radiation shielding; fast reactor physics; fuel management; nuclear weapons; radiation, neutral and charged; transport through various media; reactor and weapons safety. *Mailing Add:* 14209 Woodwell Terr Silver Spring MD 20906

SONGER, JOSEPH RICHARD, MICROBIOLOGY. *Current Pos:* CONSULT, BIOHAZARD CONTROL, 86- *Personal Data:* b South Charleston, WVa, Dec 20, 26; m 48; c 7. *Educ:* Eastern Nazarene Col, AB, 51; Iowa State Univ, MS, 65. *Prof Exp:* Bacteriologist, USDA, 51-60, vet microbiologist, Nat Animal Dis Ctr, Sci & Educ Admin, Agr Res Serv, 60-86. *Mem:* Am Soc Microbiol; Am Soc Safety Eng; Am Indust Hyg Asn; Sigma Xi; Am Biol Safety Asn (pres, 88-89). *Res:* Biological laboratory safety, disinfection, sterilization, air filtration and airborne infection; animal disease research, vesicular diseases; hog cholera; equine infectious anemia; biological hazard assessment; contamination control and euthanasia. *Mailing Add:* 419 Ninth St Ames IA 50010

SONGSTER, GERARD F(RANCIS), ELECTRICAL ENGINEERING. *Current Pos:* ELEC ENGR, GEN ELEC CO, TRANS DEVELOP ENG. *Personal Data:* b Darby, Pa, Aug 29, 27; m 53; c 2. *Educ:* Drexel Inst Technol, BSEE, 51; Univ Pa, MSEE, 65, PhD(elec eng), 62. *Prof Exp:* Res engr, Philco Corp, 51-52; instr digital comput, Moore Sch Elec Eng, Univ Pa, 52-56; asst prof elec eng, Drexel Inst Technol, 56-62, assoc prof & actg dir biomed eng prog, 63; sr scientist, Res Div, Melpar Inc, 63-64; elec engr, US Naval Res Lab, 64-65; NIH spec fel, Mass Inst Technol, 65-67; physiol studies, NASA Electronics Res Ctr, 67-70; prof elec eng & chmn dept, Old Dominion Univ, 70-75; elec engr, Naval Ship Eng Ctr, 75- *Mem:* AAAS; Am Soc Eng Educ; Sr mem, Inst Elec & Electronics Engrs; Sigma Xi. *Res:* Electrophysiology of nerve tissue; switching theory; computer simulation of living systems; underwater acoustics; automated measurement. *Mailing Add:* 190 Gardner Ave New London CT 06320

SONI, ATMARAM HARILAL, MECHANICAL ENGINEERING. *Current Pos:* res asst mech eng, 64-67, from asst prof to assoc prof, 67-77, PROF MECH ENG, OKLA STATE UNIV, 77- *Personal Data:* b Shihor, India, Oct 5, 35; m 64; c 3. *Educ:* Univ Bombay, BSc, 57; Univ Mich, BS, 59, MS, 61; Okla State Univ, PhD(mech eng), 67. *Prof Exp:* Res asst comput prog, Univ Mich, 61-64. *Concurrent Pos:* Prin investr, NSF grant, 68-69 & 70-72, dir appl mech conf, 69-71. *Mem:* Am Soc Mech Engrs; Am Soc Eng Educ. *Res:* Machine design; synthesis and analysis of mechanisms; fatigue; reliability. *Mailing Add:* 9934 Walnut Ridge Ct Cincinnati OH 45242

SONI, KUSUM, MATHEMATICAL ANALYSIS. *Current Pos:* from asst prof to assoc prof, 67-83, PROF MATH, UNIV TENN, KNOXVILLE, 83- *Personal Data:* b Hoshiarpur, India, Nov 14, 30; US citizen; m 58; c 2. *Educ:* Univ Panjab, India, BA, 49, MA, 51; Ore State Univ, PhD(math), 64. *Prof Exp:* Lectr math, Panjab Educ Serv, 52-59; asst prof, Ore State Univ, 66-67. *Concurrent Pos:* Vis mem, dept math sci, Univ Dundee, Scotland, 83; vis prof, Centre Math & Comput Sci, Amsterdam, 87, Indian Inst Sci Bangalore, 87- *Mem:* Math Asn Am. *Res:* Classical analysis, asymptotic expansions and approximation. *Mailing Add:* Dept Math Univ Tenn Knoxville TN 37916

SONI, MADHUSUDAN GHANSHYAM, BIOCHEMICAL TOXICOLOGY, HEPATOTOXICOLOGY. *Current Pos:* RES ASSOC, NORTHEAST LA UNIV, 96- *Personal Data:* b Feb 3, 55; m 84; Sandhya R Baheti; c Pooja & Sagar. *Educ:* Marathwada Univ, BSc, 77, MSc, 79, PhD(biochem), 84. *Prof Exp:* Res assoc, ICMR, Marathwada Univ, India, 84-85, CSIR, 85-86; res fel, Jichi Med Sch, Japan, 86-88; res assoc, Med Ctr, Univ Miss, 88-91; sci pool officer, Nat Inst Nutrit, India, 91-93, res officer, 93-95. *Concurrent Pos:* Lectr, LAISC, Nat Inst Nutrit, India, 93-95. *Mem:* Sigma Xi; Soc Biol Chemists India; Nutrit Soc India; Indian Asn Cancer Res; Int Soc Study Xenobiotics; Soc Toxicol. *Res:* Dose-response paradigm using injury and repair as two simultaneous but opposing responses in animals and its inclusion in predictive toxicology and risk assessment to increase the precision; establish sensitive molecular biomarkers which predispose smokers to the probable risk of cancer. *Mailing Add:* 2703 Sterlington Rd No 37 Monroe LA 71203. *Fax:* 318-342-1681; *E-Mail:* pyusoni@alpha.nlu.edu

SONI, PREM SARITA, OPTOMETRY. *Current Pos:* lectr optom, 76-78, asst prof optom, 78-92, PROF, IND UNIV, 92- *Personal Data:* b Kisumu, Kenya, Nov 17, 48; Brit citizen; m 74. *Educ:* Univ Manchester, BSc, 72; Ind Univ, OD, 75, MS 79. *Prof Exp:* Optometrist, Eng, 72-75. *Concurrent Pos:* Grant-in-aid, Ind Univ, 78-; Am Acad Optom grant, 78-; Wesley-Jassen, Inc grant, 78- *Mem:* Fel Brit Optical Asn; Am Acad Optom; Am Optom Asn; Contact Lens Educr Asn. *Res:* Corneal physiology and pathology with special reference to contact lens use. *Mailing Add:* 18 Churchill Ct Bloomington IN 47401

SONIN, AIN A(NTS), THERMO-FLUID SCIENCES. *Current Pos:* From asst prof to assoc prof, 65-74, PROF MECH ENG, MASS INST TECHNOL, 74- *Personal Data:* b Tallinn, Estonia, Dec 24, 37; US citizen; m 71; c 2. *Educ:* Univ Toronto, BASc, 60, MASc, 61, PhD(aerospace sci), 65. *Concurrent Pos:* Consult; sr scientist, Thermo Electron Corp, 81-82. *Mem:* AAAS; Am Phys Soc; Am Soc Mech Engrs; Am Nuclear Soc. *Res:* Fluid mechanics; thermodynamics; heat, mass and charge transport; electrochemistry. *Mailing Add:* Rm 3-256 Mass Inst Technol 77 Massachusetts Ave Cambridge MA 02139-4307

SONIS, MEYER, psychiatry, for more information see previous edition

SONIS, STEPHEN THOMAS, PERIODONTOLOGY, ORAL ONCOLOGY. *Current Pos:* CHIEF DENT SERV, BRIGHAM & WOMEN'S HOSP, BOSTON, 89-; PROF ORAL MED, HARVARD UNIV. *Personal Data:* b Oct 6, 45; c 2. *Educ:* Norwich, BS, 67; Tufts Univ, DMD, 72; Harvard Univ DMSc, 76. *Mem:* Am Asn Periodontology; Am Acad Oral Med; Am Acad Oral Path; Am Dental Asn. *Res:* Wound healing; stomatitis; oral medicine. *Mailing Add:* Dept Surg Brigham & Women's Hosp 75 Francis St Boston MA 02115

SONLEITNER, FRANK JOSEPH, POPULATION ECOLOGY. *Current Pos:* asst prof, 65-69, ASSOC PROF, DEPT ZOOL, UNIV OKLA, NORMAN, 69- *Personal Data:* b Chicago, Ill, Jan 23, 32; div; c Bonnie, Catherine & Carol. *Educ:* Univ Chicago, AB, 51, SB, 56, PhD(zool), 59. *Prof Exp:* Fel, Dept Zool, Univ Sydney, 59-61; lectr, Univ Calif, Berkeley, 61-62; asst prof entom, Univ Kans, Lawrence, 62-65. *Mem:* AAAS; Am Inst Biol Sci; Ecol Soc Am; Entom Soc Am; Sigma Xi. *Res:* Computer simulation models of population dynamics and ecogenetics (natural selection). *Mailing Add:* Dept Zool Univ Okla Norman OK 73019. *Fax:* 405-325-7560; *E-Mail:* zoology@aardvark.vcs.uoknor.edu

SONNEBORN, DAVID R, DEVELOPMENTAL BIOLOGY, MICROBIOLOGY. *Current Pos:* from asst prof to assoc prof, 64-72, PROF ZOOL, UNIV WIS-MADISON, 72- *Personal Data:* b Baltimore, Md, Oct 20, 36; m 62; c 2. *Educ:* Swarthmore Col, BA, 57; Brandeis Univ, PhD(biol), 62. *Prof Exp:* NIH fel virol, Univ Calif, Berkeley, 62-64. *Concurrent Pos:* Panel mem, Develop Biol Sect, NSF, 71-74. *Mem:* AAAS; Soc Develop Biol; Am Soc Microbiol; Am Soc Cell Biol. *Res:* Cell differentiation. *Mailing Add:* Zool Res Bldg Univ Wis 1117 W Johnson St Madison WI 53706

SONNEBORN, LEE MEYERS, MATHEMATICS. *Current Pos:* dir grad studies, 70-72, PROF MATH, MICH STATE UNIV, 67- *Personal Data:* b Baltimore, Md, Dec 27, 31; m 55, Vida Rodriguez; c Mary (Stiomgenst) & Tracey. *Educ:* Oberlin Col, BA, 51; Calif Inst Technol, PhD(math), 56. *Prof Exp:* Asst math, Calif Inst Technol, 53-56; fine instr, Princeton Univ, 56-58; from asst prof to assoc prof, Univ Kans, 58-67. *Concurrent Pos:* Math Asn Am vis lectr & NSF res grant, 65-67. *Mem:* Am Math Soc; Math Asn Am; Soc Indust & Appl; Sigma Xi. *Res:* Group theory; differential equation; topology. *Mailing Add:* 973 Rosewood East Lansing MI 48823. *E-Mail:* sonnebor@math.msu.edu

SONNEMANN, GEORGE, ENGINEERING MECHANICS, INFORMATION MANAGEMENT. *Current Pos:* PRES, SCONE ASSOC LTD, 95- *Personal Data:* b Munich, Germany, Feb 2, 26; nat US; m 54, Anneliese Jensen. *Educ:* NY Univ, BS, 47, MS, 49; Univ Mich, PhD(eng mech), 55. *Prof Exp:* Instr physics, Newark Col Eng, 47-48; instr eng mech, Univ Detroit, 48-49; asst prof aeronaut eng, Drexel Inst Tech, 49-52; res assoc, Univ Mich, 52-54; sr engr, Westinghouse Elec Corp, 54-55, Univ Pittsburgh-Westinghouse Elec Corp fel prog, 55-57; from assoc prof to prof mech eng, Univ Pittsburgh, 57-61, Westinghouse prof & dir grad studies mech eng, 57-61; dir staff eng & tech asst to gen mgr, Fecker Div, Am Optical Co, 61-63; chief adv design, United Aircraft Corp Systs Ctr, 63-66, mgr prod eng, 66-67, eng mgr, 67-69; mgr adv progs, Raytheon Co, Sudbury, 69-75; vpres-MIS, Com Union Assurance Co, 75-77; vpres, Conn Gen Life Ins Co, 77-78; vpres planning & mgt info, Nationwide Ins Co, 78-84; pres, Info, Finance & Technol Inc, 84-95. *Concurrent Pos:* Engr, Franklin Inst, 50; consult, Westinghouse Elec Corp, Am Optical Soc & Copes-Vulcan Div, Blaw-Knox Co, Warner Systs; adj prof, Ohio State Univ, 84-85; chief info officer, Robert Plan Co, 91-92. *Mem:* Am Soc Mech Engrs; Nat Asn Corp Dirs; Proj Mgt Inst. *Res:* Thermal stress analysis and fluid flow problems in reactor engineering; continuum mechanics; structural analysis; heat conduction; optical instrumentation; guidance systems; computer peripherals; manufacturing systems; management information systems; data processing; planning. *Mailing Add:* 543 Montgomery School Lane Wynnewood PA 19096

SONNENBERG, HARDY, EXPERIMENTAL PHYSICS, ENGINEERING PHYSICS. *Current Pos:* RETIRED. *Personal Data:* b Schoensee, Ger, Apr 12, 39; Can citizen; m 64; c 2. *Educ:* Univ Alta, BSc, 62; Stanford Univ, MS, 64, PhD(elec eng), 67. *Honors & Awards:* Charles G Ives Eng Award, Soc Photog Scientists & Engrs. *Prof Exp:* Eng specialist, GTE Sylvania, 66-73; mgr res & develop, Optical Diodes, Inc, 73-74; mem sci staff, Xerox Res Ctr Can, Ltd, 75-78, mgr physics & eng, 78-85, mgr res opers, 86-88, mgr technol & eng systs, 88-97. *Concurrent Pos:* Referee, Am Inst Physics, 70-; Arpa proposal consult, US Govt, 74-; grant appl consult, Can Govt; mem, Task Force Univ Indust, Can Mfrs Asn, 81 & Indust Adv Coun, McMaster Univ, 87-; adv comt, Ryerson Polytech Inst; pres, Sheridan Res Park Asn, 87-88. *Mem:* Sigma Xi; Inst Elec & Electronics Engrs; Am Phys Soc; Soc Photog Scientists & Engrs. *Res:* Investigations of the physics and systems aspects of photoactive-pigment-electrography and the coupling of such systems to high-speed channels; laser scanning in xerography; research management; management of technology. *Mailing Add:* 900 Hwy 97 Box 126 Freelton ON L0K 1K0 Can

SONNENBLICK, EDMUND H, CARDIOLOGY. *Current Pos:* OLFMAN PROF MED & DIR, CARDIOVASC CTR, ALBERT EINSTEIN COL MED, 84-, CHIEF, CARDIOL DIV, 75- *Personal Data:* b New Haven, Conn, Dec 7, 32. *Educ:* Harvard Univ, MD, 58. *Mailing Add:* Div Cardiol Albert Einstein Col Med 1300 Morris Park Ave Bronx NY 10461-1975

SONNENFELD, GERALD, INTERFERON, CYTOKINES. *Current Pos:* DIR RES IMMUNOL & SR SCIENTIST, CAROLINAS MED CTR, 94- *Personal Data:* b New York, NY, Oct 14, 49; div; c Jennifer. *Educ:* City Col New York, BS, 70; Univ Pittsburgh, PhD(microbiol & immunol), 75. *Prof Exp:* Fel infectious dis & immunol, Sch Med, Stanford Univ, 76-78; from asst prof to prof microbiol & immunol, Sch Med, Univ Louisville, 78-93, prof oral biol, Sch Dent, 84-93. *Concurrent Pos:* Assoc guest worker, NASA Ames Res Ctr, 76-78; sect ed immunol, J Interferon Res, 81-; dir, NASA space Biol Res Assoc Prog, 91-; adj prof, Univ NC, Chapel Hill, 94-; adj vis prof, Charlotte, 94-; adj prof, Clemson Univ, 95-, Univ Louisville, 95- *Mem:* Am Asn Immunologists; Am Soc Microbiol; Am Soc Gravitational Biol; Am Soc Virol; Int Soc Interferon Res. *Res:* Biological role of interferon; relationship of interferon to immune responses; resistance to infectious diseases and carcinogens. *Mailing Add:* Div Gen Surg Res Carolinas Med Ctr PO Box 32861 Charlotte NC 28232-2861

SONNENFELD, PETER, GEOLOGY. *Current Pos:* from assoc prof to prof geol, 66-89, head dept, 68-73, EMER PROF GEOL, UNIV WINDSOR, 89- *Personal Data:* b Berlin, Ger, Jan 20, 22; Can citizen; m 59, Jean E Brown; c Stephen & Margaret. *Educ:* Absoluturium, Univ Bratislava, 48; Dr rer nat(geol, geog), Charles Univ, Prague, 49. *Prof Exp:* Geologist, Falconbridge Nickel Mines, Nfld, 51-52; consult, Bennett & Burns, Sask, 52-53, Imp Oil Ltd, Alta, 53-58 & Shell Can Ltd, 58-63; asst prof geol & geog, Tex Col Arts & Indust, 63-66. *Res:* Sedimentology; genesis of sedimentary rocks; dolomitization; evaporite formation; petroleum geology. *Mailing Add:* 280 Simcoe St No 305 Toronto ON M5T 2Y5 Can. *Fax:* 416-598-4238

SONNENFELD, RICHARD JOHN, ORGANIC CHEMISTRY, SYNTHETIC INORGANIC CHEMISTRY. *Current Pos:* RETIRED. *Personal Data:* b Britton, Okla, Apr 29, 19; m 42, 75, Anita C Merrell; c Linda, Bruce, Carol & Barry. *Educ:* Univ Pittsburgh, BS, 41; Univ Okla, MS, 55, PhD(chem), 56. *Prof Exp:* Foreman, Weldon Spring Ord Works, 41-43; anal chemist, Phillips Petrol Co, 46-49, rubber chemist, 49-53, sr group leader, 56-63, sect mgr, 63-82. *Mem:* Am Chem Soc; AAAS. *Res:* Synthetic rubber by emulsion and stereospecific polymerization; chemicals from petroleum; free radicals; organo-metallic compounds. *Mailing Add:* 842 Concord Dr Bartlesville OK 74006

SONNENSCHEIN, CARLOS, CELLULAR BIOLOGY. *Current Pos:* PROF CELLULAR BIOL & CANCER, SCH MED, TUFTS UNIV, 80. *Educ:* Univ Buenos Aires, Arg, MD, 64. *Res:* Control of cellular proliferation; human breast tumors; diagnostic and therapeutic approaches. *Mailing Add:* Dept Anat Tufts Univ Sch Med 136 Harrison Ave Boston MA 02111-1800

SONNENSCHEIN, RALPH ROBERT, PHYSIOLOGY. *Current Pos:* from asst prof to prof, 51-88, EMER PROF PHYSIOL, UNIV CALIF, LOS ANGELES, 88- *Personal Data:* b Chicago, Ill, Aug 14, 23; m 52, Patricia Niddrie; c David, Lisa & Ann. *Educ:* Northwestern Univ, BS, 43, MS, 46, MD, 47; Univ Ill, PhD(physiol), 50. *Prof Exp:* Asst physiol, Northwestern Univ, 44-46; intern, Michael Reese Hosp, Chicago, Ill, 46-47; res asst psychiat, Univ Ill, 49-51, res assoc, 51. *Concurrent Pos:* USPHS res fel, 57-58; Swed Med Res Coun fel, 64-65; visiting scientist, Off Naval Res, London, 71-72. *Mem:* AAAS; Microcirc Soc; Am Physiol Soc; Soc Exp Biol & Med; Sigma Xi; hon mem Hungarian Physiol Soc. *Res:* Peripheral circulation. *Mailing Add:* Dept Physiol Univ Calif Sch Med Los Angeles CA 90095-1751. *Fax:* 310-206-5661

SONNER, JOHANN, MATHEMATICS. *Current Pos:* PROF MATH, UNIV NC, CHAPEL HILL, 67- *Personal Data:* b Munich, Ger, May 3, 24; nat US; m 57; c 2. *Educ:* Univ Munich, Dr rer nat, 54. *Prof Exp:* Asst prof, State Sch Eng, Ger, 56-57; tech consult, Wright Air Develop Ctr, Ohio, 57-58; prof math, Univ SC, 58-67. *Mem:* Am Math Soc; Math Asn Am; Ger Math Asn; Math Soc France. *Res:* Foundations of mathematics; general topology. *Mailing Add:* 3 Dogwood Acres Dr Chapel Hill NC 27516

SONNERUP, BENGT ULF OSTEN, SPACE PHYSICS, FLUID MECHANICS. *Current Pos:* assoc prof, 64-70, prof, 70-81, SYDNEY E JUNKINS PROF ENG SCI, DARTMOUTH COL, 81- *Personal Data:* b Malmo, Sweden, July 7, 31; m 55; c 3. *Educ:* Chalmers Inst Technol, Sweden, BME, 53; Cornell Univ, MAE, 60, PhD(fluid mech), 61. *Prof Exp:* Proj engr, Stal-Laval Steam Turbine Co, Sweden, 54-56; proj engr, Bofors Co, Sweden, 56-58; fel, Ctr Radiophys & Space Res, Cornell Univ, 61-62; fel, Inst Plasma Physics, Royal Inst Technol, Sweden, 62-64. *Concurrent Pos:* Lectr, Uppsala Univ, 63; Europ Space Res Orgn fel, Europ Space Res Inst, Italy, 70-71; vis scientist, Max Planck Inst Extraterrestrial Physics, Garching, Fed Repub Ger, 78-79, 86-87; ed, J Geophys Res, 82-85. *Mem:* AAAS; Am Geophys Union; Am Inst Aeronaut & Astronaut. *Res:* Plasma physics and magnetohydrodynamics applied to problems in space physics, particularly the structure of the magnetopause current layer and boundary layer; the magnetosphere and the nature of magnetic field merging. *Mailing Add:* Thayer Sch Eng Dartmouth Col Hanover NH 03755-2061

SONNET, PHILIP E, ORGANIC CHEMISTRY. *Current Pos:* res chemist, Agr Res Ctr, USDA, Beltsville, MD, 64-76, Laramie, WY, 76-78, Gainesville, Fla, 78-84, RES CHEMIST, AGR RES CTR, USDA, PHILADELPHIA, PA, 84- *Personal Data:* b New York, NY, Feb 6, 35; m 58; c 3. *Educ:* Columbia Univ, AB, 56; Rutgers Univ, PhD(org chem), 63. *Prof Exp:* NIH fel org chem, Mass Inst Technol, 63-64. *Concurrent Pos:* Instr, Univ Md, 72-76; adj, Temple Univ, 91- *Mem:* Am Chem Soc; Am Oil Chem Soc. *Res:* Lipids & Lipases; aliphatic synthesis. *Mailing Add:* 799 Spring Valley Rd Doylestown PA 18901. *Fax:* 215-233-6559; *E-Mail:* psonnet@errcars-gov

SONNICHSEN, GEORGE CARL, CHEMISTRY. *Current Pos:* res chemist, E I du Pont de Nemours & Co, 69-75, res supvr, 75-78, res assoc, 78-93, RES FEL, E I DU PONT DE NEMOURS & CO, 93- *Personal Data:* b Chicago, Ill, Nov 15, 41; m 70, Sally Burtun; c Laura & Andrew. *Educ:* DePauw Univ, BS, 63; Mich State Univ, PhD(chem), 67. *Prof Exp:* NSF fel chem, Univ Calif, Berkeley, 67-68, lectr, 68-69. *Mem:* Am Chem Soc. *Res:* Heterogeneous and homogeneous catalysis. *Mailing Add:* 614 Lindsay Rd Wilmington DE 19809-2231

SONNICHSEN, HAROLD MARVIN, ADHESIVES, ADHESIVE TAPE. *Current Pos:* PRES, H M SONNICHSEN & ASSOCS, 75- *Personal Data:* b Hancock, Minn, Apr 4, 12; m 39; c 2. *Educ:* Tex Col Mines, AB, 34; Harvard Univ, Phd(org chem), 39. *Prof Exp:* Res chemist, Electrochem Dept, E I du Pont de Nemours & Co, 39-40, supvr, Sales Res Sect, 40-43, plant supvr,

43-44; tech serv mgr, Permacel Tape Corp, 44-48, asst dir, 48-52, tech dir, 52-55, vpres, 55-60; dir fiber & saturant res, Dewey & Almy Chem Div, W R Grace & Co, 60-64, vpres, Precision Tech Prod, 65-75. *Concurrent Pos:* Consult, Adhesive Tape, 65- *Mem:* Am Chem Soc; fel Am Inst Chem; Am Soc Testing & Materials; Tech Asn Pulp & Paper Indust. *Res:* Properties and applications of synthetic high polymers; pressure sensitive adhesives; structural adhesives; latex; paper; artificial leather; paper and nonwoven disposable products. *Mailing Add:* 37 Robin Hood Rd Arlington MA 02174-1240

SONNINO, CARLO BENVENUTO, ELECTROCHEMISTRY, MATERIALS & MECHANICAL ENGINEERING. *Current Pos:* SR ENG SCIENTIST, SYSTS & ELECTRONICS INC, 82- *Personal Data:* b Torino, Italy, May 12, 04; US citizen; m 49, Matilde; c Patricia, Frederic & Bruno. *Educ:* Univ Milano, PhD(chem eng), 25. *Honors & Awards:* Klixon Award, Am Soc Heating, Refrigeration & Air Conditioning Engrs, 59; Knight Comdr, Italian Repub, 70. *Prof Exp:* Res mgr, Dept Flotation, Italian Aluminum Co, 28-33; mgr, Tonolli Co, 33-34; pres, Laesa-Milano, Italy, 34-43; dir res, Emballages Metalliques SA, Switz, 43-52; mgr & tech adv, Kreisler Co, 52-53; dir res, Anodal, Union City, 53-54; tech mgr, Alumacraft, St Louis, 53-56; dir res, Emerson Elec Co, St Louis, 56-82. *Concurrent Pos:* Consult, Monsanto, Wagner Elec, & Amax, 60-61; prof metall & mat sci, Washington Univ, 60-67; tech adv, Thompson Brand, Paris & Rouen, 70-75. *Mem:* Sigma Xi; Am Soc Testing Mat; fel Am Soc Metals; Soc Metal Engrs; AAAS. *Res:* Synthetic cryolite; anodizing of aluminum alloys. *Mailing Add:* 7206 Kingsbury Blvd St Louis MO 63130-4140

SONNTAG, BERNARD H, AGRICULTURAL ECONOMICS. *Current Pos:* economist, Econ Br, Agr Can, Sask, 62-68 & 79-80 & Lethbridge, 68-79, dir, Res Br, Brandon, 80-86 & Swift Current, 86-89, dir, Res Br, Agr Can, Lethbridge, 89-95, DIR GEN, PFRA, AGR CAN, REGINA, 96- *Personal Data:* b Goodsoil, Sask, June 27, 40; m 63, Mary Ortman; c Calvin, Galen & Courtney A. *Educ:* Univ Sask, BSA, 62, MSc, 65; Purdue Univ, PhD(agr econ), 71. *Honors & Awards:* Bell Can Leadership Award, 93. *Prof Exp:* Economist, O William Carr & Assoc, Ottawa, 66-68. *Concurrent Pos:* Dir, Can Agr Econ & Farm Mgt Soc, 83-85; pres, Man Inst Agrologists, 85. *Mem:* fel Agr Inst Can; Can Agr Econ & Farm Mgt Soc. *Res:* Production economics research in cereals, forages, special crops, beef, dairy, sheep, and soil and water resources. *Mailing Add:* 603-1800 Hamilton St Regina SK S4P 4L2 Can. *Fax:* 306-780-5018; *E-Mail:* pf10354@em.agr.ca

SONNTAG, NORMAN OSCAR VICTOR, ORGANIC CHEMISTRY, ANALYTICAL CHEMISTRY. *Current Pos:* CONSULT, 80- *Personal Data:* b Brooklyn, NY, Sept 10, 19; m 47; c 2. *Educ:* Polytech Inst Brooklyn, PhD(chem), 51. *Prof Exp:* Res chemist, Polytech Inst Brooklyn, 49-51 & Colgate Palmolive Co, 51-55; chief chemist, Chem Div, Celanese Corp Am, 55-56; res chemist, Emery Industs, Inc, 56-59; assoc mgr, Res & Develop Div, Nat Dairy Prod Corp, Ill, 59-66; mgr process res, Glyco Chem, Inc, 66-68; dir res, 68-77; tech dir chem div, Southland Corp, 78-80; asst prof, Bishop Col, Dallas, Tex, 81-84. *Mem:* Am Chem Soc; Am Oil Chem Soc (vpres, 78-79, pres, 79-80). *Res:* Reduction of highly arylated conjugated cyclic ketones; reactions of aliphatic acid chlorides; chemical utilization of fats; fatty chemicals; synthetic fatty acids; nitrogen derivatives; dibasic acids; hydantoin chemicals; agriculture and food chemistry. *Mailing Add:* 306 Shadowood Trail Red Oak TX 75154-1424

SONNTAG, RICHARD E, MECHANICAL ENGINEERING, THERMODYNAMICS. *Current Pos:* From asst prof to assoc prof, 60-67, PROF MECH ENG, UNIV MICH, ANN ARBOR, 67- *Personal Data:* b Chicago, Ill, Apr 17, 33; m 57; c 2. *Educ:* Univ Mich, BSE, 56, MSE, 57, PhD(mech eng), 61. *Mem:* Am Soc Mech Engrs; Am Soc Eng Educ; Sigma Xi. *Res:* Low temperature thermodynamics; phase equilibria; pressure-volume-temperature behavior. *Mailing Add:* 3925 Penberton Dr Ann Arbor MI 48105

SONNTAG, ROY WINDHAM, ORGANIC CHEMISTRY. *Current Pos:* from asst prof to assoc prof, 60-69, PROF CHEM, MCMURRY COL, 69- *Personal Data:* b Cleburne, Tex, Nov 17, 29; m 53; c 4. *Educ:* NTex State Col, BS, 53; Univ Tex, PhD(org chem), 59. *Prof Exp:* Res chemist, Monsanto Chem Co, 58 & Esso Res & Eng Co, 59-60. *Mem:* Am Chem Soc. *Res:* Molecular rearrangements of organic systems; conformational analysis. *Mailing Add:* Chem McMurray Univ 1400 Soyles Blvd Abilene TX 79697-0001

SONNTAG, WILLIAM EDMUND, AGING, ALCOHOLISM. *Current Pos:* Asst prof, 84-89, ASSOC PROF PHYSIOL, BOWMAN GRAY SCH MED, WAKE FOREST UNIV, 89-, ASSOC DIR BASIC SCI RES, J PAUL STICHT CTR AGING, 90- *Personal Data:* b Waterbury, Conn, Jan 1, 50; m 73; c 1. *Educ:* Tufts Univ, BS, 72; Univ Bridgeport, MS, 74; Tulane Univ, PhD(physiol psychol), 79. *Mem:* Endocrine Soc; Geront Soc; AAAS; Am Fedn Aging Res. *Res:* Molecular neuroendocrinology; effects of age and/or alcohol on the regulation of growth hormone and insulin-like growth factors. *Mailing Add:* Dept Physiol Bowman Gray Med Sch 300 S Hawthorne Winston-Salem NC 27157-0002

SONODA, RONALD MASAHIRO, PLANT PATHOLOGY. *Current Pos:* From asst prof to assoc prof, 69-81, PROF, INST FOOD & AGR SCI, INDIAN RIVER RES & EDUC CTR, UNIV FLA, 81- *Personal Data:* b Hilo, Hawaii, June 4, 39; m 66, Lorraine Itow; c G Koji & M Aiko. *Educ:* Sacramento State Col, AB, 63; Univ Calif, Davis, MS, 65, PhD(plant path), 69. *Concurrent Pos:* Fac develop grant, Univ Calif, Davis, 79-80; interim dir, Univ Fla Indian River Res & Educ Ctr, 94-95. *Mem:* Am Phytopath Soc. *Res:* Diseases of citrus; diseases of tropical forage legumes and grasses; diseases of tomatoes. *Mailing Add:* 1014 Caribbean Ave Ft Pierce FL 34982. *Fax:* 561-468-5668

SONS, LINDA RUTH, MATHEMATICS, COMPLEX ANALYSIS. *Current Pos:* From asst prof to assoc prof, 65-78, PROF MATH, NORTHERN ILL UNIV, 78-; PRESIDENTIAL TEACHING PROF, 94- *Personal Data:* b Chicago Heights, Ill, Oct 31, 39. *Educ:* Ind Univ, AB, 61; Cornell Univ, MS, 63, PhD(math), 66. *Concurrent Pos:* NSF grant, 70-72 & 74-75; mem bd gov, Math Asn Am, Comt Undergrad Prog, 89-92, chair, Subcomt Qual Literacy Requirements & Subcomt Assessment, 90-96. *Mem:* Math Asn Am; Am Math Soc; Asn Women Math; Nat Coun Teachers Math; Sigma Xi. *Res:* Mathematical analysis, especially complex function theory. *Mailing Add:* Dept Math Northern Ill Univ De Kalb IL 60115. *Fax:* 815-753-1112; *E-Mail:* sons@math.niu.edu

SONTAG, EDUARDO DANIEL, CONTROL THEORY, SYSTEMS THEORY. *Current Pos:* From asst prof to assoc prof, 77-87, PROF MATH, RUTGERS UNIV, NJ, 87-, MEM GRAD FAC COMPUT SCI, 85-, MEM GRAD FAC ELEC ENG, 88- *Personal Data:* b Buenos Aires, Arg, Apr 16, 51; US citizen; m 81, Frances David; c Laura & David. *Educ:* Univ Buenos Aires, Lic, 72; Univ Fla, PhD(math), 76. *Concurrent Pos:* Prin investr, Air Force Off Sci Res, 78-, NJ Dept Higher Educ, 85-86, NSF, 85-87 & 88-, Ctr Comput Aids Indust Prod, 86- *Mem:* Soc Indust & Appl Math; fel Inst Elec & Electronics Engrs. *Res:* Systems and control theory with applications to robotics and neural networks; related problems in mathematics, particularly in algebra; theory of computation. *Mailing Add:* Dept Math Rutgers Univ New Brunswick NJ 08903. *E-Mail:* sontag@math.rutgers.edu

SONTHEIMER, RICHARD DENNIS, DERMATOLOGY. *Current Pos:* PROF DERMAT & INTERNAL MED, HEALTH SCI CTR, UNIV TEX, 84- *Personal Data:* b Beaumont, Tex, Nov 3, 45. *Educ:* Univ Tex, MD, 72. *Mem:* Am Soc Clin Invest; Am Dermat Asn. *Mailing Add:* Dept Dermat Univ Tex Southwestern Med Ctr 5323 Harry Hines Blvd Dallas TX 75235-9069. *Fax:* 214-648-8275

SOO, SHAO-LEE, MECHANICAL ENGINEERING, MULTIPHASE FLUID DYNAMICS. *Current Pos:* PROF MECH ENG, UNIV ILL, URBANA, 59- *Personal Data:* b Peiping, China, Mar 1, 22; US citizen; m 52; c Shirley (Gorman), Lydia & David. *Educ:* Nat Chiaotung Univ, BS, 45; Ga Inst Technol, MS, 48; Harvard Univ, ScD, 51. *Honors & Awards:* Appl Mech Rev Award, Am Soc Mech Engrs, 72; Distinguished Lectr Award, Int Freight Pipeline Soc, 81; Alcoa Found Award, 85; Award for Creative Development, NASA, 92. *Prof Exp:* Teaching fel appl physics, Harvard Univ, 51; instr mech eng, Princeton Univ, 51-52, lectr, 52-54, from asst prof to assoc prof, 54-59. *Concurrent Pos:* Indust consult, 51-; mem consult team Skylab I, Univ Space Res Assoc, NASA, 71-72; Agard lectr, NATO, 73; distinguished lectr, Fulbright-Hays Prog, Buenos Aires, Arg, 74; mem sci adv bd, US Environ Protection Agency, 76-78; adv energy transp, World Bank, 79; dir, S L Soo Assocs Inc, Urbana, 80-; Int Powder Inst, 76-; UN Develop Prog, 85-92; hon prof, Academia Sinica, 88-; visit prof, Delft Univ Tuh, Netherlands, 92. *Mem:* Fel Am Soc Mech Engrs; Am Soc Eng Educ; Combustion Inst; Sigma Xi; Chinese Acad Sci; Int Freight Pipeline Soc. *Res:* Basic formulation of nonequilibrium fluid dynamics; experimental research in multi-phase flow; nonequilibrium ionized gases; gas-surface interaction; atmospheric transport of air pollutants and control by electrostatic precipitation; pneumatic conveying; laser, phase Doppler Anemometry. *Mailing Add:* 123 Mech Eng Bldg Univ Ill 1206 W Green St Urbana IL 61801. *E-Mail:* j.soo@uiuc.edu

SOOD, MANMOHAN K, PETROLOGY, GEOCHEMISTRY. *Current Pos:* from asst prof to assoc prof, Northeastern Ill Univ, 70-80, chmn dept, 74-82, dir, Univ Honors Prog, 85-91, PROF EARTH SCI, NORTHEASTERN ILL UNIV, 80-, DEAN, GRAD COL, 91-, DIR, INT PROF, 96- *Personal Data:* b Manpur Nagaria, India, Apr 17, 41; nat US; m 65; c 2. *Educ:* Panjab Univ, India, BSc, 60, MSc, 63; Univ Western Ont, MSc, 68, PhD(geol), 69. *Prof Exp:* Tech asst geol, Govt Punjab, 63-64; res assoc, Univ Western Ont, 69-70. *Concurrent Pos:* Geol consult, 79-; geochemist, Argonne Nat Lab, Ill, 82-83. *Mem:* Mineral Soc Am; Int Asn Advan Earth & Environ Sci(founding secy, 72-75). *Res:* Phase equilibrium related to alkaline igneous rocks; geochemistry and petrology of proterozoic granites, Wisconsin, USA; geological isolation of hazardous wastes; issues in science and math; education in schools and colleges. *Mailing Add:* 1807 Maine Dr Elk Grove Village IL 60007

SOOD, SATYA P, PHYSICAL CHEMISTRY, POLYMER CHEMISTRY. *Current Pos:* asst, Univ Hawaii, 57-62, res assoc physics, 62-63, from asst prof to assoc prof, 63-71, chmn, Div Sci, 71-80, PROF CHEM, UNIV HAWAII, HILO, 71- *Personal Data:* b Abohar, Punjab, India, Feb 4, 23; m 57, Hilegard L Koss; c Sneha L. *Educ:* Forman Christian Col, Punjab, BSc, 42; Acton Tech Col, London, API, 53; State Univ NY, MS, 56; Univ Hawaii, PhD(chem), 63. *Prof Exp:* Chemist various chem concerns, India, 42-49; tech asst, Indian High Comn, London, Eng, 50-53; teaching asst chem, State Univ NY, 53-55; res asst, Tex Tech Col, 55-57. *Concurrent Pos:* Lectr, Bahawal Col, Pakistan, 46-47; res fel, McMaster Univ, 68-69. *Res:* Chemical kinetics; synthetic organic chemistry; ultraviolet spectroscopy; dipole moments; radiation chemistry. *Mailing Add:* 969 Ainako Ave Hilo HI 96720-4091

SOODSMA, JAMES FRANKLIN, GAS CHROMATOGRAPHY-MASS SPECTROMETRY VOLATILE ORGANIC COMPOUND ANALYSIS. *Current Pos:* RES & DEVELOP CHEMIST, TRINITY ENVIRON TECHNOL, 90-, ANALYTICAL CHEMIST, 90- *Personal Data:* b Hull,

Iowa, Feb 3, 38; m 64, Mary Stevenson; c 2. *Educ:* Univ SDak, BA, 63; Univ NDak, MS, 65, PhD(biochem), 68; Univ Tulsa, MS, 81. *Prof Exp:* Chief scientist, William K Warren Med Res Ctr, Inc, 71-77; test engr, John Zink Co, 81-82. *Concurrent Pos:* AEC fel, Med Div, Oak Ridge Assoc Univs, 68-71. *Mem:* Am Chem Soc; Sigma Xi. *Res:* Studies on rat kidney glucose-6-phosphatase and associated phosphotransferase activities; rat liver enzyme system which cleaves glyceryl ethers; mammalian newborn phospholipid and carbohydrate metabolism; pollution control; polychlorinated biphenyl destruction in soil. *Mailing Add:* 20052 Harper Rd Mound Valley KS 67354-9608. *Fax:* 316-328-2033

SOOHOO, RONALD FRANKLIN, ELECTRICAL ENGINEERING, PHYSICS. *Current Pos:* chmn dept elec eng, 64-70, PROF ELEC ENG, UNIV CALIF, DAVIS, 64- *Personal Data:* b Kwangtung, China, Sept 1, 28; US citizen; m 57; c 2. *Educ:* Mass Inst Technol, SB, 48; Stanford Univ, MS, 52, PhD(elec eng, physics), 56. *Prof Exp:* Asst engr, Pac Gas & Elec Co, 48-51; dir res anal, Cascade Res Corp, 54-58; res physicist, Lincoln Lab, Mass Inst Technol, 58-61; assoc prof eng & appl sci, Calif Inst Technol, 61-64. *Concurrent Pos:* Consult, Space Technol Labs, 62-64, Ampex Corp, 62-64, Bunker-Ramo Corp, 62-64, E&M Labs, 67- & Lawrence Livermore Lab, 69-; NATO fel, Nat Ctr Sci Res, Bellevue, France, 70. *Mem:* Fel Inst Elec & Electronics Engrs; Am Inst Physics. *Res:* Magnetism and magnetic materials; solid state physics; microwave electronics; computer devices and systems; quantum electronics. *Mailing Add:* 568 Reed Dr Davis CA 95616

SOOKNE, ARNOLD MAURICE, TEXTILE CHEMISTRY, TEXTILE FLAMMABILITY. *Current Pos:* TEXTILE CONSULT, 83- *Personal Data:* b New York, NY, Oct 9, 15; m 39; c David & Judith. *Educ:* Brooklyn Col, BS, 35; George Washington Univ, MA, 42. *Honors & Awards:* Olney medal, Am Asn Textile Chem & Colorists, 60; Harold DeWitt Smith Award, Am Soc Test & Mat, 71; Inst Medal, Brit Textile Inst, 84. *Prof Exp:* Res assoc, Am Asn Textile Chemists & Colorists, Washington, DC, 36-37, Nat Res Coun, 37-38 & Textile Found, Nat Bur Stand, 38-44; assoc dir, Harris Res Labs Div, Gillette Res Inst, Inc, 44-65, vpres labs, 65-68, vpres, Inst, 68-69; dir chem develop, res ctr, Burlington Industs Inc, 69-77, asst dir corp res & develop, 78-83. *Concurrent Pos:* Vis prof, Univ NC, Greensboro, 79-89. *Mem:* Am Chem Soc; Am Asn Textile Chem & Colorists; Fiber Soc; Brit Textile Inst. *Res:* Physical chemistry of textiles; dyeing and finishing of textiles; flammability of textiles. *Mailing Add:* 3504 Flint St Greensboro NC 27405

SOOKY, ATTILA A(RPAD), FLUID MECHANICS. *Current Pos:* Asst prof, 64-71, ASSOC PROF POLLUTION CONTROL, UNIV PITTSBURGH, 71- *Personal Data:* b Rakoscsaba, Hungary, Aug 22, 32; US citizen; m 64; c 3. *Educ:* Budapest Tech Univ, BS, 55, MS, 56; Purdue Univ, PhD(fluid mech), 64. *Mem:* Am Soc Civil Engrs; Water Pollution Control Fedn; Sigma Xi. *Res:* Pollution control; fate of pollution in natural waters; health effects of pollutants. *Mailing Add:* Dept Civil & Environ Eng Grad Sch Pub Health Univ Pittsburgh Pittsburgh PA 15261

SOONG, TSU-TEH, CIVIL ENGINEERING, STRUCTURAL CONTROL & IDENTIFICATION. *Current Pos:* from asst prof to assoc prof eng sci, 63-68, chmn dept, 70-80, prof eng & civil eng, 68-89, SAMUEL P CAPEN PROF ENG, STATE UNIV NY, BUFFALO, 89- *Personal Data:* b Honan, China, Feb 10, 34; US citizen; m 59, Dorothy Tsai; c Karen, Stephen & Susan. *Educ:* Univ Dayton, BS, 55; Purdue Univ, MS, 58, PhD(eng sci), 62. *Honors & Awards:* Humboldt Found Sr US Scientist Award, 87. *Prof Exp:* Instr mech, Purdue Univ, 58-62; sr res engr, Jet Propulsion Lab, Calif Inst Technol, 62-63. *Concurrent Pos:* Lectr, Univ Calif, Los Angeles, 62-63; res mathematician, Cornell Aeronaut Lab, 64-; NSF res grants, 64-; sci faculty fel, Delft Technol Univ, 66-67. *Mem:* Nat Soc Prof Engrs; Am Soc Civil Engrs. *Res:* Stochastic processes with applications to analysis of engineering systems; identification and control of mechanical and structural systems. *Mailing Add:* Dept Civil Eng Ketter Hall State Univ NY Buffalo NY 14260

SOONG, YIN SHANG, PHYSICAL OCEANOGRAPHY. *Current Pos:* From asst prof to assoc prof, 77-89, PROF OCEANOG, MILLERSVILLE UNIV, 89- *Personal Data:* b Shanghai, Repub of China, July 14, 47; c 2. *Educ:* Nat Taiwan Univ, BS, 69; Fla State Univ, MS, 74, PhD(phys oceanog), 78. *Mem:* Am Meteorol Soc; Am Geophys Union. *Res:* Remote sensing; inertial currents; mesoscale oceanic phenomenon. *Mailing Add:* Dept Earth Sci Millersville Univ PO Box 1002 Millersville PA 17551-0302

SOONPAA, HENN H, SOLID STATE PHYSICS. *Current Pos:* assoc prof, 66-72, PROF PHYSICS, UNIV NDAK, 72- *Personal Data:* b Estonia, Mar 18, 30; nat US; m 59, Eunice M Refsell; c Nancy J & Mark H. *Educ:* Concordia Col, BA, 51; Univ Ore, MA, 53; Wayne State Univ, PhD(phys chem), 55. *Prof Exp:* Asst, Univ Ore, 51-52; res fel, Wayne State Univ, 52-54; res fel, Iowa State Univ, 56; sr scientist, Gen Mills, Inc, 57-58; assoc prof physics, Gustavus Adolphus Col, 58-59; sr & prin scientist, Gen Mills, Inc, 59-62 & Honeywell Corp Res Ctr, 62-66. *Mem:* Am Phys Soc; Am Asn Physics Teachers. *Res:* Solid state physics; transport phenomena; quantum size effects; two-dimensional systems. *Mailing Add:* Univ NDak Box 7129 Grand Forks ND 58202-7129. *Fax:* 701-777-3650; *E-Mail:* soonpaa@badlands.nodak.edu

SOORA, SIVA SHUNMUGAM, refractories-alumino silicate, fused, for more information see previous edition

SOOS, ZOLTAN GEZA, PHYSICAL CHEMISTRY. *Current Pos:* from asst to assoc prof, 66-74, PROF CHEM, PRINCETON UNIV, 74- *Personal Data:* b Budapest, Hungary, July 31, 41; US citizen; m 66. *Educ:* Harvard Col, AB, 62; Calif Inst Technol, PhD(chem, physics), 65. *Prof Exp:* NSF fel, Stanford Univ, 65-66. *Concurrent Pos:* Vis scientist, Sandia Corp, 71. *Mem:* Am Chem Soc. *Res:* Theory of molecular excitons; many-body methods in para magnetic crystals. *Mailing Add:* Dept of Chem Princeton Univ Princeton NJ 08544

SOOST, ROBERT KENNETH, GENETICS. *Current Pos:* From asst geneticist to assoc, 49-65, chmn, Dept Plant Sci, 69-75, geneticist, 65-86, EMER GENETICIST, UNIV CALIF, RIVERSIDE, 86- *Personal Data:* b Sacramento, Calif, Nov 13, 20; m 49; c 3. *Educ:* Univ Calif, PhD(genetics), 49. *Mem:* Fel Am Soc Hort Sci; Sigma Xi. *Res:* Citrus genetics and breeding. *Mailing Add:* PO Box 589 Inverness CA 94937-0589

SOOY, WALTER RICHARD, PHYSICS. *Current Pos:* SR STAFF SCIENTIST, LAWRENCE LIVERMORE NAT LAB, 81- *Personal Data:* b Boston, Mass, Dec 28, 32; m 82; c 2. *Educ:* Mass Inst Technol, BS, 56; Univ Southern Calif, MS, 58; Univ Calif, Los Angeles, PhD(physics), 63. *Prof Exp:* Mem tech staff, Hughes Aircraft Co, 56-62, staff physicist, 62-64, sr staff physicist, 64-66, sr scientist, 66-70, dept mgr, 68-70; supt optical sci div, Naval Res Lab, 70-75; vpres & chief scientist, Sci Applns Inc, 75-81. *Concurrent Pos:* Consult, Off Secy Defense & Naval Mat Command, 75- *Mem:* AAAS; Optical Soc Am; Am Phys Soc. *Res:* Superconductivity; microwave oscillators; nuclear physics; optics; lasers; systems. *Mailing Add:* Lawrence Livermore Nat Lab L-466 PO Box 808 Livermore CA 94551

SOPER, DAVISON EUGENE, THEORETICAL ELEMENTARY PARTICLE PHYSICS, QUANTUM CHROMODYNAMICS. *Current Pos:* from asst prof to assoc prof, 77-82, PROF PHYSICS, UNIV ORE, 82- *Personal Data:* b Milwaukee, Wis, Mar 21, 43; m 71; c 2. *Educ:* Amherst Col, AB, 65; Stanford Univ, PhD(physics), 71. *Prof Exp:* From instr to asst prof physics, Princeton Univ, 71-77. *Mem:* Am Phys Soc; fel AAAS. *Res:* Quantum field theory and particle physics; classical field theory; quantum chromodynamics. *Mailing Add:* Inst Theoret Sci Univ Ore Eugene OR 97403. *Fax:* 541-346-5217; *E-Mail:* soper@bovine.uoregon.edu

SOPER, GORDON KNOWLES, PLASMA PHYSICS. *Current Pos:* proj officer, HQ, 72-75, chief, Electronics Vulnerablity Div, 75-77, chief, Atmospheric Effects Div, 77-78, ASST TO DEP DIR SCI & TECHNOL EXP RES, DEFENSE NUCLEAR AGENCY, WASHINGTON, DC, 78- *Personal Data:* b Gunnison, Colo, July 25, 38; m 58; c 2. *Educ:* Univ Tenn, BS, 59, MS, 62, PhD(physics), 64. *Prof Exp:* From asst prof to assoc prof physics, US Air Force Inst Technol, 64-72. *Mem:* Am Phys Soc; Am Asn Physics Teachers. *Res:* Theoretical plasma physics, particularly stability theory. *Mailing Add:* 14824 N Ashdale Ave Woodbridge VA 22193

SOPER, JAMES HERBERT, BOTANY. *Current Pos:* chief botanist, 67-81, EMER CUR, BOT DIV, CAN MUS NATURE, 81- *Personal Data:* b Hamilton, Ont, Apr 9, 16; m 46; c 4. *Educ:* McMaster Univ, BA, 38, MA, 39; Harvard Univ, PhD(biol), 43. *Prof Exp:* Botanist, Can Dept Agr, 45-46; spec lectr bot, Univ Toronto, 46-47, from asst prof to prof bot, 47-67. *Concurrent Pos:* Curator, Herbarium Vascular Plants, Univ Toronto, 46-67. *Mem:* Royal Can Inst, (pres, 62-63); Can Bot Asn (pres, 82-83). *Res:* Flora of Ontario; distribution of vascular plants of North America; data-processing and automated cartography. *Mailing Add:* 621 Echo Dr Ottawa ON K1S 1P1 Can

SOPER, JON ALLEN, ELECTRICAL ENGINEERING. *Current Pos:* from asst prof to assoc prof, Mich Technol Univ, 68-79, asst dept head, 84-90, dept head, 91-97, PROF ELEC ENG, MICH TECHNOL UNIV, 79- *Personal Data:* b Wyandotte, Mich, Mar 7, 36; m 58; c 5. *Educ:* Mich Technol Univ, BS, 57, MS, 61; Univ Mich, Ann Arbor, PhD(elec eng), 69. *Prof Exp:* Instr elec eng, Mich Technol Univ, 57-60, asst prof, 60-63; design and develop engr, Raytheon Mfg Co, 63-64; asst prof elec eng, Mich Technol Univ, 64-65; asst res engr, Univ Mich, 67-68. *Concurrent Pos:* Actg assoc dean, Mich Tech Univ, 78-79, actg dept head, 90-91. *Mem:* Sr mem Inst Elec & Electronic Engrs; Am Soc Eng Educ. *Res:* Antenna theory and behavior; microwave networks; radar systems and navigation systems; electromagnetic interactions with snow; microwave coupling; electromagnetic compatibility and interference. *Mailing Add:* Dept Elec Eng Mich Technol Univ 1400 Townsend Dr Houghton MI 49931

SOPER, QUENTIN F(RANCIS), PHARMACEUTICAL CHEMISTRY, PESTICIDE CHEMISTRY. *Current Pos:* RETIRED. *Personal Data:* b Buhl, Minn, Dec 3, 19; m 46, Genevieve Lanrreth; c John, Julia, Dan & Jean. *Educ:* Univ Minn, BChem, 40; Univ Ill, PhD(org chem), 43. *Honors & Awards:* John Scott Award, Am Inst Chemists. *Prof Exp:* Asst chem, Univ Ill, 40-43, spec asst, Nat Defense Res Comt Contract, 43-44; sr org chem, Eli Lilly & Co, 44-65, head agr chem res, 65-72, agr sr assoc, 72-77, res adv, 77-84. *Mem:* Am Chem Soc; Weed Sci Soc Am. *Res:* Synthesis of new war gases; synthesis of new chemicals useful in the biosynthesis of new penicillins; quinoxaline formation and the ortho effect; hindrance at beta carbon atom; synthetic pharmaceuticals, herbicides and pesticides. *Mailing Add:* 2120 W 38th St Indianapolis IN 46208-3202

SOPER, RICHARD GRAVES, SURGICAL PATHOLOGY, CYTOPATHOLOGY. *Current Pos:* chair, Surg Dept, 92-93, PATHOLOGIST, MIDDLE TENN MED CTR, 90- *Personal Data:* b Trenton, Mich, Dec 10, 50; m 81, Deborah J Keselis; c Vanessa, Larissa, Cordell, Michael & Ashley. *Educ:* Univ Mich, BS, 70; Univ Tenn, MD, 77.

Honors & Awards: Physicians Recognition Award, AMA, 87, 90 & 93. *Prof Exp:* Instr path, Med Sch, Univ Tenn, 77-81; med dir, Roche Biomed Labs, Inc, 82-86 & CytoDiagnostics, 87-90; fel cytopath, Sch Med, Johns Hopkins Univ, 87. *Concurrent Pos:* Consult pathologist, CytoDiagnostics, Oklahoma City, Okla, 90-, Nat Ref Lab, Nashville, Tenn, 90- & Nat Health Labs, Birmingham, Ala, 90-; secy & treas, Stones River Med Acad, 92-93. *Mem:* Col Am Pathologists; Am Soc Clin Pathologists; Am Acad Path; Am Soc Cytol; Int Soc Anal Cytol; Fedn Am Soc Exp Biol. *Res:* Immunohistochemistry and static/flow cytometry of human neoplastic disease tissues. *Mailing Add:* Middle Tenn Med Ctr 400 N Highland Ave Murfreesboro TN 37130

SOPER, ROBERT JOSEPH, SOIL SCIENCE. *Current Pos:* From asst prof to assoc prof, 58-69, prof soils, Fac Agr, 69-92, EMER PROF, UNIV MAN, 92- *Personal Data:* b Weston, Ont, Aug 25, 27; m 57; c 2. *Educ:* Univ Sask, BA & BSA, 53, MSc, 55; McGill Univ, PhD(agr chem), 59. *Honors & Awards:* Queen's Jubilee Medal. *Concurrent Pos:* App sr officer P-5 head, Soils, Irrigation & Crop Prod Sect, Atomic Energy Food & Agr, Vienna, Austria. *Mem:* Fel Can Soc Soil Sci; fel Agr Inst Can; Int Soc Soil Sci; Am Soc Agron. *Res:* Soil fertility and chemistry. *Mailing Add:* 31 Fordham Bay Winnipeg MB R3T 3B8 Can

SOPER, ROBERT TUNNICLIFF, MEDICINE, PEDIATRIC SURGERY. *Current Pos:* resident, Univ Iowa Hosps, 54-57, instr, 57-58, assoc, 58-59, from asst prof to assoc prof, 59-67, PROF SURG, UNIV IOWA HOSPS, 67-, INTERIM HEAD DEPT SURG. *Personal Data:* b Iowa City, Iowa, Sept 16, 25; m 51, Helene Jolas; c John T, Robert M, Nathaniel J, Helen E, Timothy H & Margaret R. *Educ:* Cornell Col, BS, 49; Univ Iowa, MD, 52; Am Bd Surg, dipl, 59. *Prof Exp:* Intern med, Cleveland City Hosp, Ohio, 52-53. *Concurrent Pos:* Surg registr, Alder Hey Children's Hosp, Liverpool, Eng, 59-60. *Mem:* AMA; Am Col Surg; Brit Asn Pediat Surg; Am Pediat Surg Asn; Am Acad Pediat; Western Surg Asn. *Res:* Clinical pediatric surgery. *Mailing Add:* Dept Surg Univ Iowa Hosps Iowa City IA 52242

SOPHER, ROGER LOUIS, PATHOLOGY. *Current Pos:* PROF & CHMN DEPT PATH, UNIV NDAK, SCH MED, 88- *Personal Data:* b Long Beach, Calif, Oct 7, 36; m 72, Judith L Simon. *Educ:* St Mary's Col, BS, 58; Johns Hopkins Univ, MD, 62. *Prof Exp:* Intern path, Med Ctr, Univ Calif, Los Angeles, 62-63, resident, 63-64; resident, Sch Med, Univ NMex, 64-66, from asst prof to assoc prof path, 68-72, vchmn dept, 68-83; chief lab serv, Albuquerque Vet Admin Hosp, 69-83; prof path & dir clin labs, Hahnemann Univ, Philadelphia, Pa, 83-85; chmn path & lab med, Mercy Cath Med Ctr, Philadelphia, Pa, 85-88. *Mem:* AAAS; Col Am Path; Am Soc Clin Path; Am Asn Pathologists & Bacteriologists; AMA. *Res:* Pulmonary effects of altered atmospheres; computer applications to biomedicine. *Mailing Add:* Dept Pathol Box 9037 Univ NDak Sch Med Grand Forks ND 58202-9037. *Fax:* 701-777-3108; *E-Mail:* roger.sopher@medicine.und.nodak.edu

SOPHIANOPOULOS, ALKIS JOHN, BIOCHEMISTRY, BIOPHYSICS. *Current Pos:* ASSOC PROF BIOCHEM, EMORY UNIV, 68- *Personal Data:* b Athens, Greece, Aug 29, 25; US citizen; m 55; c 2. *Educ:* Drew Univ, AB, 53; Purdue Univ, MS, 57, PhD(chem), 60. *Honors & Awards:* Eli Lilly Med Fac Award, 65. *Prof Exp:* Trainee biophys, Dept Chem, Univ Ill, Urbana, 60-61; asst prof biochem, Univ Tenn Med Units, 61-68. *Mem:* Am Soc Biol Chemists; Biophys Soc; Am Chem Soc. *Res:* Physical chemistry of macromolecules; biophysical studies of relation of macromolecular structure to biological activity. *Mailing Add:* 2994 McCully Dr NE Atlanta GA 30345

SOPORI, MOHAN L, IMMUNOLOGY. *Current Pos:* ASST PROF MED MICROBIOL & IMMUNOL, MED CTR, UNIV KY, 80- *Personal Data:* b Kashmir, India, Dec 3, 42. *Educ:* All India Inst Med Sci, PhD(biochem), 70. *Mailing Add:* Dept Immunotoxicol Lovelace Inst 2425 Ridgecrest SE Albuquerque NM 87108. *Fax:* 505-262-7043

SOPPER, WILLIAM EDWARD, FORESTRY. *Current Pos:* Asst forestry, Pa State Univ, 54-55, instr, 55-60, from asst prof to assoc prof, 60-68, PROF FOREST HYDROL, FOREST RES LAB, PA STATE UNIV, 68-, HYDROLOGIST, INST RES LAND & WATER RESOURCES, 69- *Personal Data:* b Slatington, Pa, Aug 16, 28; m 51; c 3. *Educ:* Pa State Univ, BS, 54, MF, 55; Yale Univ, PhD(forest hydrol), 60. *Concurrent Pos:* Mem, Forest Influences & Watershed Mgt Sect, Int Union Forestry Res Orgns, 64-66. *Mem:* Soc Am Foresters; Water Pollution Contol Fedn. *Res:* Forest hydrology; watershed management; forest influences; land application of wastewater, strip mine reclamation with sludge. *Mailing Add:* 416 Outer Dr State College PA 16801

SORAUF, JAMES E, GEOLOGY. *Current Pos:* From asst prof to assoc prof, 62-75, chmn dept, 77-80, PROF GEOL, STATE UNIV NY, BINGHAMTON, 75-, CHMN DEPT, 86- *Personal Data:* b Milwaukee, Wis, May 19, 31; m 62; c 2. *Educ:* Univ Wis-Madison, BS, 54, MS, 55; Univ Kans, PhD(geol), 62. *Concurrent Pos:* Trustee, Paleont Res Inst, 83-, vpres, 86-88, pres, 88- *Mem:* Am Asn Petrol Geol; Geol Soc Am; Soc Econ Paleont & Mineral. *Res:* Permian stratigraphy; paleontology of Devonian corals. *Mailing Add:* Geol Sci State Univ NY PO Box 6000 Binghamton NY 13902-6000

SORBELLO, RICHARD SALVATORE, THEORETICAL SOLID STATE PHYSICS. *Current Pos:* from asst prof to assoc prof, 73-83, PROF PHYSICS, UNIV WIS-MILWAUKEE, 83- *Personal Data:* b New York, NY, Aug 10, 42. *Educ:* Mass Inst Technol, BS, MS, 65; Stanford Univ, PhD(appl physics), 70. *Prof Exp:* Res assoc low temperature physics, Swiss Fed Inst, Zurich, 71-73. *Concurrent Pos:* Vis prof, Vrije Univ, Amsterdam, 80. *Mem:* Am Phys Soc; AAAS. *Res:* Transport theory and atomic diffusion in solids; electromigration and thermomigration in metals; electronic structure of solids; dielectric response and transport properties of metallic microstructures. *Mailing Add:* Dept Physics Univ Wisc PO Box 413 Milwaukee WI 53201

SORBER, CHARLES ARTHUR, ENVIRONMENTAL ENGINEERING, CIVIL ENGINEERING. *Current Pos:* PRES, UNIV TEX-PERMIAN BASIN, 93- *Personal Data:* b Kingston, Pa, Sept 12, 39; m 62, Linda E (Babcock); c Kimberly & Kingsley. *Educ:* Pa State Univ, BS, 61, MS, 66; Univ Tex, Austin, PhD (environ eng), 71. *Honors & Awards:* Serv Award, Water Pollution Control Fedn, 85 & 89; Gordon Maskew Fair Award, Am Acad Environ Engrs, 93. *Prof Exp:* Proj engr, Harris, Henry & Potter, Inc, Pa, 65-66; chief, Gen Eng Br, USArmy Environ Hyg Agency, 66-69; comdr, US Army Med Environ Eng Res Univ, Md, 71-73; dir, Environ Qual Div, US Army Med Bioeng Res & Develop Lab, 73-75; asst dean, Col Sci & Math, Univ Tex, San Antonio, 76-77, assoc prof environ eng, Div Environ Studies, 75-80, acting dir, Div Earth & Phys Sci & dir, Ctr Appl Res & Technol, 76-80; prof civil eng & assoc dean, Col Eng, Univ Tex, Austin, 80-86, L B Meaders prof eng, 85-86; prof & dean, Sch Eng, Univ Pittsburgh, 86-93. *Concurrent Pos:* Prin investr, Fischer & Porter, Co, Pa, 76-78, Environmental Protection Agency grant, 76-86 & US Army & Mobility, Equip Res & Develop Command, 77-78; co-prin investr, Environmental Protection Agency grant, 77-79, NSF grant, 77-80 & Southwest Res Inst & Environmental Protection Agency grant, 78-83; grant, Environ Protection Agency, 84-86, 87-90 & 90-93; prin investr, MACME grant, 85-86, NSF grant, 89-91. *Mem:* Am Soc Eng Educ; Am Soc Civil Engrs; Am Water Works Asn; Nat Soc Prof Engrs; Water Environ Fedn (pres, 92-93); Am Acad Environ Engrs; Int Asn Water Qual. *Res:* Health effects associated with water and wastewater treatment processes including land application of wastewater and sludges; wastewater reuse including membrane processes and health effects; water-wastewater disinfection; kinetics and efficiency. *Mailing Add:* Univ Tex Permian Basin 4901 E University Blvd Odessa TX 79762. *Fax:* 915-552-2109; *E-Mail:* sorber_c@utpb.edu

SORBY, DONALD LLOYD, PHARMACY, PHARMACEUTICAL CHEMISTRY. *Current Pos:* RETIRED. *Personal Data:* b Fremont, Nebr, Aug 12, 33; m 59, Jacquelyn J; c 2. *Educ:* Univ Nebr, BS, 55; Univ Wash, Seattle, MS, 58, PhD(pharm), 60. *Prof Exp:* From asst prof to prof pharm & pharmaceut chem, Sch Pharm, Univ Calif, San Francisco, 60-72; prof pharm & chmn dept pharm pract, Col Pharm, Univ Wash, 72-74; dean, Sch Pharm, Univ Mo, Kansas City, 74-84; dean, Sch Pharm, Univ Pac, 84-93. *Concurrent Pos:* USPHS grant, 63-65. *Mem:* Am Pharmaceut Res & Sci; Acad Pharmaceut Sci; Am Acad Pharmaceut Scientists. *Res:* Interactions between drugs and adsorbent materials and how they affect action of various drug molecules; relationships between physical and chemical properties of drugs and their in vivo action. *Mailing Add:* 4362 Yacht Harbor Dr Stockton CA 95204. *Fax:* 209-946-2401

SORDAHL, LOUIS A, PHYSIOLOGY, BIOCHEMISTRY. *Current Pos:* assoc prof, 72-77, PROF BIOCHEM, UNIV TEX MED BR GALVESTON, 77- *Personal Data:* b Chicago, Ill, Aug 24, 36; m 62; c 2. *Educ:* Rutgers Univ, AB, 58, MS, 61, PhD(biochem), 64. *Honors & Awards:* Hektoen Gold Medal Award, AMA, 70. *Prof Exp:* Res asst biol, Rutgers Univ, 58-62, asst instr physiol, 63, instr, 63-64; from instr to asst prof pharmacol, Baylor Col Med, 66-72. *Concurrent Pos:* NIH staff fel geront, Baltimore City Hosps, Md, 64-66; vis prof cardiovasc med, Mayo Clin, 76-; co-adj prof exp med, Baylor Col Med, 78-; mem, Va Cardiovasc Merit Preview Panel, 87-91, chmn, 89-91, dir, Grad Prog Human Biol Chem & Genetics, 88-; mem, Vet Admin Career Develop Comt, 92-96. *Mem:* Int Soc Heart Res; fel Am Col Cardiol; Am Physiol Soc; Am Heart Asn; Biophys Soc; Am Soc Biochem & Molecular Biol. *Res:* Intermediary metabolism and metabolic diseases; cardiac bioenergetics; oxidative phosphorylation; enzymes and mechanisms of calcium transport in mitochondria; experimental surgery; coronary thrombosis. *Mailing Add:* Dept Human Biol Chem & Genetics Univ Tex Med Br Galveston TX 77555-0647. *Fax:* 409-747-0552; *E-Mail:* lsordahl@mspol.med.utmb.edu

SOREF, RICHARD ALLAN, ELECTROOPTICS. *Current Pos:* RES SCIENTIST, USAF ROME LAB, BEDFORD, 83- *Personal Data:* b Milwaukee, Wis, June 26, 36; m 69, Alice Rosen. *Educ:* Univ Wis, BS, 58, MS, 59; Stanford Univ, PhD(elec eng), 64. *Prof Exp:* Staff mem, Solid State Physics Div, Lincoln Lab, Mass Inst Technol, 64-65; res staff mem, Appl Physics Dept, Sperry Res Ctr, 65-83. *Mem:* Am Phys Soc; Optical Soc Am; sr mem Inst Elec & Electronics Engrs; Soc Photo-Optical Instrumentation Engrs; Mats Res Soc. *Res:* Electro-optical modulation in semiconductors; integrated optics; fiber optics; silicon optoelectronics; liquid crystal displays; infrared detectors; nonlinear optical effects in solids; optical communication; optical switching; sensors; quantum well and superlattice devices. *Mailing Add:* USAF Rome Lab (RL/ERO) Hanscom AFB MA 01731-5000. *Fax:* 781-377-4814; *E-Mail:* soref@maxwell.rl.plh.af.mil

SOREGAROLI, A(RTHUR) E(ARL), MINING, GEOLOGY. *Current Pos:* VPRES EXPLOR, WESTMIN RESOURCES LTD, VANCOUVER, 76- *Personal Data:* b Madrid, Iowa, Jan 4, 33; m 62, Rosalie A Lawrick; c Carla J & Brian A. *Educ:* Iowa State Univ, BSc, 59; Univ Idaho, MSc, 61; Univ Vancouver, PhD(geol), 68. *Honors & Awards:* Dist Proficiency Gold Medal, Can Inst Mining & Metall, 86, Julian Boldy Mem Award, 89; Duncan R Derry Gold Medal, Geol Asn Can, 87. *Prof Exp:* Geologist, Idaho Bur Mines & Geol, Moscow, 61-62; geologist, Noranda Explor Co Ltd, 63-68, chief geologist, Western Dist, 68-72; asst prof geol, Univ BC, Vancouver, 72-74; res scientist, Geol Surv Can, Ottawa, 74-76. *Concurrent Pos:* Chmn, Geol Div, Can Inst Mining & Metall, 78. *Mem:* Fel Geol Asn Can; Soc Econ Geologists; Asn Explor Geochemists (vpres, 87-88); Can Inst Mining & Metall; Geol Asn Can; Mineral Asn Can. *Res:* Geological exploration. *Mailing Add:* Westmin Resources Ltd Bentall Ctr PO Box 49066 Vancouver BC V7X 1C4 Can

SOREIDE, DAVID CHRISTIEN, ENGINEERING PHYSICS, AEROSPACE INSTRUMENTATION APPLICATIONS. *Current Pos:* Sr engr, Aerodyn Lab, Boeing Com Airplanes, 77-80, scientist, Laso Instrumentation Lab, 80-85, prin investr, 85-90, chief scientist, Lidar-air Data, High Technol Ctr, Boeing Defense & Space Group, 90-92, prin engr, Lidar Applns, Boeing Co, 92-95, NASA contractor, Lidar Applns, 95-96, PRIN ENGR, LIDAR APPLNS, BOEING DEFENSE & SPACE GROUP, 96- *Personal Data:* b Arlington, Va, July 20, 45; m 72, Nancy Niblett. *Educ:* Univ Colo, BS, 67; Univ Wash, MS, 68, PhD(physics), 78. *Mem:* Optical Soc Am; Int Soc Optical Eng; Am Inst Aeronaut & Astronaut. *Res:* Lidar systems to sense air velocities for airborne applications; including air data functions as well as gust alleviation, ride smoothing and turbulance deflection; granted 2 US patents. *Mailing Add:* 5113 48 NE Seattle WA 98105. *Fax:* 253-773-3698; *E-Mail:* david.soreide@pss.boeing.com

SORELL, HENRY P, ORGANIC CHEMISTRY. *Current Pos:* RETIRED. *Personal Data:* b Coeymans, NY, Nov 15, 23; m 70. *Educ:* Rensselaer Polytech Inst, BS, 48, MS, 50, PhD(chem), 54. *Prof Exp:* Teaching asst, Org Labs, Rensselaer Polytech Inst, 48-51; sr chemist coated abrasives, Behr-Manning Div, Norton Co, 51-55; fel dent mat res, Mellon Inst, 55-56, sr fel, 56-57; vpres dent res & mfg, Luxene, Inc, 57-58; sect leader adhesives develop, Hughson Chem Co, 58-61; group leader pressure sensitive tapes, Mystik Tape Div, Borden Chem Co, Ill, 63-65, sect leader, 65-70; tech dir, Pipeline Tapes, Plicoflex, Inc, 70-72; vpres res & develop, Anchor Continental, Inc, 70-85. *Concurrent Pos:* Admin fel dent plastics, Mellon Inst, 57-58. *Mem:* Am Chem Soc. *Res:* Organic adhesives; adhesion and effect of environmental factors on organic adhesives and on adhesion. *Mailing Add:* 125 Calhoun St Johnston SC 29832-1310

SOREM, MICHAEL SCOTT, LASER PHYSICS, PHOTOCHEMISTRY. *Current Pos:* STAFF PHYSICIST LASER RES, LOS ALAMOS SCI LAB, 74- *Personal Data:* b Berkeley, Calif, Apr 27, 45; div; c 2. *Educ:* Stanford Univ, BS, 67, MS, 68, PhD(physics), 72. *Prof Exp:* Physicist elastic-plastic flow codes, Lawrence Livermore Lab, 67; res asst high resolution spectros, Stanford Univ, 67-72; physicist, Nat Bur Standards, 72-74. *Concurrent Pos:* Nat Res Coun fel, Nat Bur Standards & Joint Inst Lab Astrophys, 72-74. *Res:* Tunable laser source development; sub-Doppler high resolution atomic and molecular spectroscopy; optically pumped ir lasers; excited-state spectroscopy; high average power solid state lasers. *Mailing Add:* Los Alamos Nat Lab MS E526 PO Box 1663 Los Alamos NM 87545

SOREM, RONALD KEITH, GEOLOGY, DEEP-SEA MINERAL RESOURCES. *Current Pos:* from asst prof to prof, Wash State Univ, 59-82, geol consult, 64-97, assoc dean sci, 80-81, dir, Marine Mineral Res Mus, 88-94, EMER PROF GEOL, WASH STATE UNIV, 83- *Personal Data:* b Northfield, Minn, June 18, 24; m 53, Judith LaFollete; c Kaia, Keith, Sam & Tom. *Educ:* Univ Minn, BA, 46, MS, 48; Univ Wis, PhD, 58. *Prof Exp:* Asst, State Geol Surv, Minn, 44-46; geol asst, Univ Minn, 47; field asst, US Geol Surv, Alaska, 47, geologist, 48-55; asst, Univ Wis, 56-57, fel econ geol, 58-59. *Concurrent Pos:* Strategic minerals adv, US For Opers Admin, 53-55; sr vis res fel, Univ Manchester, 70; co-investr, Int Decade Ocean Explor, Seabed Assessment Prog, NSF, 72-75; co-investr & co-chief scientist at sea, Deep Ocean Mining Environ Study Proj, Nat Oceanic & Atmospheric Admin, deep sea expeds, Pac Ocean, 75-79; grant, Nat Oceanic & Atmospheric Admin, US Geol Surv & US Bur Mines, 76-80; vpres, Comn Manganese, Int Asn Genesis Ore Deposits, 76-86, resource consult, 83-, pres, 86-90; consult Mineralogy Volcanic Ash Study Possible Health Hazards Eruption Mt St Helens Wash, Wash State Univ, 80-; vis res fel, Japan Soc Prom Sci, 81; field exam sulfide, tungsten & manganese deposits caucusus region, USSR, 82. *Mem:* Sigma Xi; sr fel Geol Soc Am; fel Mineral Soc Am; sr fel Soc Econ Geol; Int Asn Genesis Ore Deposits. *Res:* Mineralogy and origin of manganese deposits; application of micro x-ray analysis to ore and petrographic microscope studies; properties, texture and composition of ore minerals; exploration origin and evaluation of marine manganese nodule deposits; conservation of natural resources; manganese resources of Philippines; Ni-laterites of Cuba; promotion of international scientific cooperation by participation. *Mailing Add:* 925 SE Spring St Pullman WA 99163. *Fax:* 509-335-7237

SOREN, ARNOLD, ORTHOPEDIC SURGERY. *Current Pos:* asst prof, 63-67, assoc prof, 67-81, PROF ORTHOP SURG, SCH MED, NY UNIV, 81- *Personal Data:* b Vienna, Austria, Oct 30, 10; US citizen; m 61, Frieda Ernst. *Educ:* Univ Vienna, MD, 34, PhD(comp morphol), 51. *Honors & Awards:* City Vienna Prize, 52; Fed Pres Austria Prize, 55. *Prof Exp:* Resident orthop surg, Gen Hosp, Vienna, 34-47; asst, Univ Vienna, 47-51; asst, Univ Munich, 53-54. *Concurrent Pos:* Univ docent, Med Fac, Univ Vienna, 55-; USPHS grant, Sch Med, NY Univ, 62-; assoc attend physician, Univ Hosp, NY Univ, 62-; attend physician, Vet Admin Hosp, New York, 62-; asst admitting physician, Bellevue Hosp, New York, 64- *Res:* General orthopaedic surgery; rheumatic diseases and histopathology of arthritis; clinic, pathology, and treatment of arthritis. *Mailing Add:* Dept Orthop Surg NY Univ Sch Med 550 First Ave New York NY 10016

SOREN, DAVID, CLASSICAL ARCHAEOLOGY, CINEMA. *Current Pos:* dept head, 84-89, PROF ARCHAEOL, UNIV ARIZ, TUCSON, 82-; LECTR, AM MUS NATURAL HIST, NEW YORK, 83- *Personal Data:* b Philadelphia, Pa, Oct 7, 46; m 67, Noelle L Schattyn. *Educ:* Dartmouth Col, BA, 68; Harvard Univ, MA, 72, PhD, 73. *Prof Exp:* Cur coins, Foggs Art Mus, Cambridge Mass, 72; asst prof, Univ Mo, Columbia, 72-76, assoc prof & dept head, 76-81; creator dir, Am Excavations, Lugnano, Italy, 88-94; dir, Am Excavations, Chianciano, Italy, 95- *Concurrent Pos:* Pot consult & field dir, Tunisia Excavations, Chicago, Oriental Inst/Smithsonian Inst, 73-78; prin investr, Nat Endowment Humanities, 79 & 87, Fulbright, Lisbon, 83; dept rep, Am Sch Oriental Res, 81-85; creator dir, Kourion Excavations, Cyprus, 82-89, Port, 83-84; pres, Archaeol Inst Tucson, 83-86; proj dir, Nat Geog Soc, 83-84; guest cur, Am Mus Natural Hist, New York, 83-90; fel, Johns Hopkins Sch Int Affairs, 85; ed & founder, Roscius J, 93- *Mem:* Explorers Club; Archaeol Inst Am; Nat Geog Soc. *Res:* Archaeology; excavations; oriental research; discovered source/epicenter of the great Mediterranean earthquake of 365 AD; discovered oldest Celtic temple known at Mirobriga, Portugal; discovered the depressed pyramid vault, previously unknown type of ancient Roman vaulting; pioneered field of malaria studies through archaeology. *Mailing Add:* Univ Ariz Dept Classics 371 MLB Tucson AZ 85721. *Fax:* 520-621-3689; *E-Mail:* soren@u.arizona.edu

SORENSEN, ANDREW AARON, MEDICAL EDUCATION. *Current Pos:* prof & assoc dean, Sch Pub Health & exec dir, Acquired Immune Deficiency Syndrome Inst, 86-90, ADJ PROF, SCH PUB HEALTH, JOHNS HOPKINS UNIV, 90-; PROVOST & VPRES ACAD AFFAIRS, UNIV FLA, GAINESVILLE, 90- *Personal Data:* b Pittsburgh, Pa, July 20, 38; m 68; c 2. *Educ:* Univ Ill, BA, 59; Yale Univ, BD, 62, MPhil, 70, PhD(med sociol), 71; Univ Mich, MPub Health, 66. *Prof Exp:* Instr psychiat, Med Sch, Boston Univ, 70-71; asst prof community serv educ, Cornell Univ, 71-73; asst prof prev med, Univ Rochester, 73-76, assoc prof & assoc chmn prev med, Sch Med, 76-83; prof & dir, Sch Pub Health, Univ Mass, 83-86. *Concurrent Pos:* Vis assoc health serv res, Harvard Med Sch, 75-76; NSF fac sci fel, 75-76; vis fel, Univ Cambridge, 79-80; vis prof community med, Welsh Nat Sch Med, 81. *Mem:* Asn Teachers Prev Med; AAAS; Am Sociol Asn; Int Epidemiol Asn. *Res:* Health services; sociology of addictions. *Mailing Add:* Univ Fla 233 Tigert Hall Gainesville FL 32611-2073. *Fax:* 904-392-8735

SORENSEN, CHRISTOPHER MICHAEL, LIGHT SCATTERING. *Current Pos:* PROF PHYSICS, KANS STATE UNIV, 77-, ADJ PROF CHEM, 84- *Personal Data:* b Omaha, Nebr, Oct 1, 47; m 75, Georgia Gold; c Hali. *Educ:* Univ Nebr, BS, 69; Univ Colo, MS, 73, PhD(physics), 77. *Concurrent Pos:* Bd dirs, Am Asn Aerosol Res, 95- *Mem:* Am Phys Soc; Am Chem Soc; Am Asn Aerosol Res; German Soc Aerosol Res. *Res:* Optics and light scattering; combustion generated particulates; aerosol dynamics; phase transitions and critical phenomena. *Mailing Add:* Dept Physics Kans State Univ Manhattan KS 66506

SORENSEN, CRAIG MICHAEL, SUPPRESSOR T CELLS, IMMUNE RESPONSE GENES. *Current Pos:* SR RES SCIENTIST ONCOGENE SCI, MANHASSET, NY, 90- *Personal Data:* b May 29, 54. *Educ:* Washington Univ, St Louis, PhD(immunol), 80. *Prof Exp:* Asst prof immunol, Jewish Hosp Washington Univ Med Ctr, 81-90. *Mem:* Am Asn Immunologists; NY Acad Sci. *Res:* T cell regulation; oncogene expression; cell cycle regulation. *Mailing Add:* Prod Develop Cal Biochem 84 Rogers St Cambridge MA 02142

SORENSEN, DALE KENWOOD, VETERINARY SCIENCE. *Current Pos:* asst prof med, Univ Minn, 53-57, prof med, Col Vet Med, 58-94, head dept, 65-72, actg dean, 72-73, chmn, Dept Vet Clin Sci, 73-76, chmn, Dept Large Animal Clin Sci, 76-79, assoc dean, 80-87, EMER PROF, UNIV MINN, ST PAUL, 94- *Personal Data:* b Centuria, Wis, July 21, 24; m 48; c 3. *Educ:* Kans State Col, DVM, 46; Univ Wis, MS, 50, PhD(virol path), 53. *Prof Exp:* Consult vet, UNRRA, 46-47; instr vet sci & head, Sect Clin Med, Univ Wis, 47-53. *Concurrent Pos:* Med scientist, Brookhaven Nat Lab, 57-58; vet consult, AID, Dept of State, Philippine Island Mission, 66 & Indonesia, 74; prin vet, USDA-Coop State Res Serv, 85-86. *Mem:* Am Vet Med Asn. *Res:* Pneumonia of calves; radiation syndrome in dogs; diseases of swine and viral respiratory diseases of cattle; leukemia of cattle; animal pathology. *Mailing Add:* 460 Vet Hosp Bldg Univ Minn St Paul MN 55108

SORENSEN, DAVID PERRY, ORGANIC CHEMISTRY. *Current Pos:* RETIRED. *Personal Data:* b Spring City, Utah, Nov 1, 30; m 52, Mary L Pritchett; c Nadene & Bradley. *Educ:* Univ Utah, BS, 52, PhD, 55. *Honors & Awards:* 3M Carlton Soc, 88. *Prof Exp:* Res chemist, M W Kellogg Co, Pullman, Inc, 55-57; sr res chemist, 3M Co, 57-60, res supvr, 60-63, res specialist, 63-65, res mgr, 65-67, tech dir, Imaging Res Lab, 67-71, tech dir, Printing Prod Div, 71-81, dir, Corp Technol Assessment, 81-89, exec dir, Corp Tech Planning & Coord, 89-96. *Mem:* Am Chem Soc; Sigma Xi; Tech Asn Graphic Arts; Am Mgt Asn. *Res:* Imaging sciences; printing technology. *Mailing Add:* 4140 Lakewood Ave White Bear Lake MN 55110

SORENSEN, EDGAR LAVELL, PLANT BREEDING. *Current Pos:* prog specialist, Agr Conserv, Prod & Mkt Admin, 49-51, RES AGRONOMIST, AGR RES SERV, USDA, 55- *Personal Data:* b Mendon, Utah, Nov 26, 18; m 48; c 3. *Educ:* Utah State Univ, BS, 41, MS, 52; Univ Wis, PhD(agron), 55. *Prof Exp:* Soils technologist, Bur Reclamation, Utah, 46-47; state seed supvr, Utah State Dept Agr, 47-49. *Mem:* Am Soc Agron; Crop Sci Soc Am. *Res:* Breeding improved varieties of alfalfa; insect and disease resistance. *Mailing Add:* 1221 N Eighth St Manhattan KS 66502

SORENSEN, FREDERICK ALLEN, MATHEMATICAL STATISTICS. *Current Pos:* RETIRED. *Personal Data:* b Pittsburgh, Pa, July 18, 26. *Educ:* Carnegie Inst Technol, BS, 47, MS, 49, PhD(math), 59. *Prof Exp:* Instr, Carnegie-Mellon Univ, 51-54, 59-71. *Concurrent Pos:* Asst math, Carnegie Inst Technol, 47-51; statistician, Westinghouse Elec Corp, 51-54; statistician, Res Lab, US Steel Corp, 56-61, head, Oper Res Sect, 61-64, res mathematician, 64-77, assoc res consult, Math Div, 77-85; consult, 85-89. *Mem:* AAAS; Am Soc Qual Control; Am Statist Asn; Inst Math Statist. *Res:* Theory of control charts; design and analysis of industrial and engineering experiments. *Mailing Add:* 1074 Findley Dr Pittsburgh PA 15221

SORENSEN, HAROLD C(HARLES), STRUCTURAL ENGINEERING & DYNAMICS, ENGINEERING MECHANICS. *Current Pos:* asst prof civil eng, 66-75, ASSOC PROF CIVIL ENG, WASH STATE UNIV, 75- *Personal Data:* b Bancroft, Nebr, Dec 21, 34; m 60; c 2. *Educ:* Univ Nebr, BS, 57, MS, 62, PhD(eng mech), 66. *Prof Exp:* Jr engr, Dept Rds, State of Nebr, 57-59; instr eng mech, Univ Nebr, 59-65. *Concurrent Pos:* Consult, Palouse Prod, 77, Weyerhaeuser Corp, 78-80 & Wash Pub Power Supply Syst, 80. *Mem:* Am Soc Eng Educ; Am Concrete Inst; Earthquake Eng Res Inst. *Res:* Structural dynamics; earth sheltered homes; lateral buckling of parallel chord trusses; soil-structural interaction-AFWL. *Mailing Add:* 310 NW Brandon St Pullman WA 99163

SORENSEN, KELD, IMMUNOCHEMICAL REAGENTS, ASSAYS FOR BIOCHEMICALS. *Current Pos:* SR RES SCIENTIST, PIERCE CHEM CO, 91- *Personal Data:* b Copenhagen, Denmark, June 5, 53; m 76, Susan Hom; c Kasper. *Educ:* Univ Copenhagen, PhD(biochem), 80. *Prof Exp:* Researcher, Univ Bern, Switz, 80-87; dir biochem, NTD Labs, 87-90; lab dir, Equichem Res Inst, 90-91. *Concurrent Pos:* Asst prof biochem & immunol, Col Med, Univ Ill, 93- *Mem:* Am Asn Clin Chem. *Res:* Developed reagents and methods for immunochemical research and applications. *Mailing Add:* Pierce Chem Co Res & Develop PO Box 117 Rockford IL 61105. *Fax:* 815-968-7316; *E-Mail:* kelds@uic.edu

SORENSEN, KENNETH ALAN, ENTOMOLOGY. *Current Pos:* from exten asst prof to exten assoc prof, 70-84, EXTEN PROF ENTOM, NC STATE UNIV, 84- *Personal Data:* b Providence, RI, Aug 11, 44; m 69, Joyce Allegien; c Heather, Christina & Kylene. *Educ:* Univ RI, BS, 66; Kans State Univ, MS, 68, PhD(entom), 70. *Prof Exp:* Nat Defense Educ Act fel entom, Kans State Univ, 66-69, res asst, 69-70. *Mem:* Entom Soc Am. *Res:* Study of insect pest population dynamics and crop damage under grower conditions; evaluate new and review effectiveness of existing insecticides on vegetables and develop insect pest management programs for growers' use. *Mailing Add:* NC State Univ PO Box 7613 Raleigh NC 27695-0001. *Fax:* 919-515-7273; *E-Mail:* ksorense@ent.ncsu.edu

SORENSEN, LAZERN OTTO, MARINE PHYCOLOGY. *Current Pos:* assoc prof, Pan Am Univ, 56-63, dean sci & math, 68-75, head, Dept Biol, 65-68, PROF BIOL, PAN AM UNIV, 63-, DIR, MARINE LAB, 75- *Personal Data:* b Dannebrog, Nebr, Nov 1, 27; wid; c 1. *Educ:* Nebr State Univ, BS, 50; Univ Nebr, Lincoln, MS, 52, PhD(bot), 56. *Prof Exp:* Assoc prof, Nebr Wesleyan Univ, 53-56. *Mem:* Phycol Soc Am. *Res:* Physiology of macroscopic marine algae. *Mailing Add:* 112 Lakeshore Dr Brownsville TX 78521

SORENSEN, LEIF BOGE, MEDICINE, BIOCHEMISTRY. *Current Pos:* from instr to assoc prof, 58-70, PROF MED, UNIV CHICAGO, 70-, ASSOC CHMN, DEPT MED, 70- *Personal Data:* b Odense, Denmark, Mar 25, 28; US citizen; m 68; c 1. *Educ:* Copenhagen Univ, MD, 53, PhD(biochem), 60. *Prof Exp:* Instr anat, Copenhagen Univ, 50-51; resident, St Luke's Hosp, 54; intern, Copenhagen County Hosp, Hellerup, Denmark, 54-55; res asst geront, Med Sch, Wash Univ, 55-56; res asst med, Argonne Cancer Res Hosp, Univ Chicago, 56-57; resident, Copenhagen Munic Hosp, 57-58; resident, Copenhagen Univ Hosp, 58. *Concurrent Pos:* Fulbright scholar, Med Sch, Wash Univ, 55-56; lectr, Ill Acad Gen Pract, 62-63; fac mem, Am Col Physicians Postgrad Course, 62 & 69; sr fel, Fogarty Int Ctr, NIH, 80-81. *Mem:* AAAS; Am Rheumatism Asn; Am Soc Clin Invest; NY Acad Sci; Am Soc Geriat. *Res:* Gout; purine metabolism; aging of the immune system. *Mailing Add:* Dept Med Univ Chicago MC 6092 5841 Maryland Ave Chicago IL 60637-1463

SORENSEN, PAUL DAVIDSEN, BOTANY, TAXONOMY. *Current Pos:* from asst prof to assoc prof, 70-90, PROF PLANT TAXON, NORTHERN ILL UNIV, 90- *Personal Data:* b Seattle, Wash, Dec 4, 34; m 59, Marie L Eve; c Gerta, Everett & Eva. *Educ:* Univ Iowa, BA, 62, MS, 66, PhD(bot, plant taxon), 67. *Prof Exp:* Asst hort taxonomist, Arnold Arboretum, Harvard Univ, 67-68, asst cur, 68-70; vpres, Environ Consults & Planners, Encap Inc, 75-92. *Concurrent Pos:* Assoc prof bot, Univ Iowa, 78; vis scholar, Gray Herbarium, Harvard Univ, 86-87. *Mem:* Int Asn Plant Taxon; Am Soc Plant Taxon; Natural Areas Asn; Nature Conservancy. *Res:* Taxonomy of vascular plants; systematics and ecology of flowering plants; distributional relationships of plants and habitats of the Upper Midwest; taxonomic studies of Mexican and Central American floras; habitat restoration. *Mailing Add:* Dept Biol Sci Northern Ill Univ De Kalb IL 60115-2861. *Fax:* 815-753-0461

SORENSEN, PETER W, CHEMORECEPTION SCIENCE, CHEMICAL ECOLOGY. *Current Pos:* ASSOC PROF, UNIV MINN, 88- *Personal Data:* b Billings, Mont, Nov 27, 54. *Educ:* Bates Col, BA, 76; Univ RI, PhD(biol oceanog), 84. *Prof Exp:* Fel, Univ Alta, 84-88. *Mem:* Am Fisheries Soc; Asn Chemoreception Sci; AAAS. *Res:* Determining the identity and function of pheromones on the physiology and behavior of fishes; endocrinological basis of pheromone production; neural basis of olfactory and behavioral sensitivity to these compounds. *Mailing Add:* 200 Hodson Hall 1980 Folwell Ave St Paul MN 55108. *Fax:* 612-625-5299; *E-Mail:* pws@finsandfur.fw.umn.edu

SORENSEN, RALPH ALBRECHT, DEVELOPMENTAL BIOLOGY, IMMUNOLOGY. *Current Pos:* asst prof, 77-84, ASSOC PROF BIOL, GETTYSBURG COL, 84-, DEPT CHAIRPERSON, 90- *Personal Data:* b Lynwood, Calif, Apr 19, 45; m 84, Judith Haarsager; c Adam, Tracy & Peter. *Educ:* Univ Calif, Riverside, BA, 67; Yale Univ, PhD(biol), 72. *Prof Exp:* Res fel, Dept Physiol & Anat, Sch Med, Harvard Univ, 72-74; asst prof biol sci, DePaul Univ, 74-77. *Mem:* Soc Develop Biol; Soc Study Reproduction. *Res:* Early development of the sea urchin embryo; meiotic maturation and fertilization of the mammalian oocyte; preimplantation development of mammalian embryos. *Mailing Add:* Dept Biol Gettysburg Col 300 N Washinton St Gettysburg PA 17325-1400. *Fax:* 717-337-6157; *E-Mail:* rsorense@gettysburg.edu

SORENSEN, RAYMOND ANDREW, NUCLEAR PHYSICS. *Current Pos:* from asst prof to assoc prof, 61-68, chmn dept, 80-89, PROF PHYSICS, CARNEGIE-MELLON UNIV, 68- *Personal Data:* b Pittsburgh, Pa, Feb 27, 31; m 53; c 1. *Educ:* Carnegie Inst Technol, BS, 53, MS, 55, PhD(physics), 58. *Prof Exp:* NSF fel, Copenhagen Univ, 58-59; from instr physics to res assoc, Columbia Univ, 59-61. *Concurrent Pos:* NSF sr fel, Niels Bohr Inst, Copenhagen, Denmark, 65-66; Nordita prof, Res Inst Physics, Stockholm, 70-71 & 76-77; assoc ed, Nuclear Physics A, 72- *Mem:* Am Phys Soc; fel AAAS. *Res:* Theoretical nuclear structure physics. *Mailing Add:* Dept of Physics Carnegie-Mellon Univ Pittsburgh PA 15213. *E-Mail:* sorensen@cmu.edu

SORENSEN, RICARDO UWE, DEVELOPMENT OF CELLULAR & ANTIBODY MEDIATED IMMUNITY IN HUMANS, DIAGNOSIS & TREATMENT OF CLINICAL & ACQUIRED IMMUNODEFICIENCY DISEASES. *Current Pos:* PROF & HEAD, DIV ALLERGY, IMMUNOL & RHEUMATHOL, DEPT PEDIAT, LA STATE UNIV MED CTR, 89- *Personal Data:* b Valdivia, Chile, Mar 13, 39; m 70; c 3. *Educ:* Univ Chile, MD, 62. *Prof Exp:* Resident, Dept Pediat, Hosp Calvo MacKenna, Sch Med, Univ Chile, 64-65 & Univ Hosp, Bonn, Ger, 66-67; DAAD fel, Dept Pediat, Eppendorf Univ Hosps, Hamburg, Ger, 65-66; asst prof, Dept Pediat, Hosp Calvo MacKenna, Sch Med, Univ Chile, 71-74, assoc prof, Dept Pediat & Exp Med, 74-77; from asst prof to assoc prof, Div Immunol, Dept Pediat, Case Western Res Univ, 77-89, from asst prof to assoc prof, Dept Path, 79-89. *Concurrent Pos:* Staff pediatrician, Emergency Ward, Hosp Calvo MacKenna, Santiago, Chile, 67-71, clin consult immunol disorders, 68-74, developer & head, Div Clin Immunol, 74-76; developer & head, Div Immunopath, Inst Bacteriol Chile, 68-73, Dept Immunol, 73-76; actg head, Div Immunol, Dept Pediat, Case Western Res Univ, 77-89; dir, Clin Immunol Lab, Children's Hosp, New Orleans, La, 91- *Mem:* Am Asn Immunol; Am Col Allergy & Immunol; Clin Immunol Soc; Asn Med Lab Immunologists; Soc Pediat Res; Immunol Soc Chile. *Res:* Development of cellular and antibody mediated immunity in humans; diagnosis and treatment of congenital and acquired immunodeficiency diseases; cellular immunity in cystic fibrosis; biological pigments of P. aeruginosa phenazine pigments; BCG vaccination and immunity to tuberculosis in humans. *Mailing Add:* Dept Pediat La State Univ Med Ctr 1542 Tulane Ave New Orleans LA 70112-2865

SORENSEN, ROBERT CARL, SOIL CHEMISTRY. *Current Pos:* From asst prof to assoc prof, 64-75, PROF AGRON, UNIV NEBR, LINCOLN, 75- *Personal Data:* b Omaha, Nebr, July 24, 33; m 58; c 2. *Educ:* Univ Nebr, BS, 55, MS, 57; Iowa State Univ, PhD(soil chem), 64. *Mem:* Am Soc Agron; Soil Sci Soc Am; fel Nat Assoc Col Teachers Agr; Sigma Xi. *Res:* Reactions and movement of phosphorus in soils. *Mailing Add:* Dept Agron Univ Nebr Lincoln NE 68583

SORENSEN, THEODORE STRANG, PHYSICAL ORGANIC CHEMISTRY. *Current Pos:* from asst prof to assoc prof, 62-74, PROF CHEM, UNIV CALGARY, 74- *Personal Data:* b Dixonville, Alta, June 6, 34; m 66. *Educ:* Univ Alta, BSc, 56; Univ Wis, PhD(org chem), 60. *Prof Exp:* Imp Chem Industs fel, Univ Leicester, 60-62. *Mem:* AAAS; Am Chem Soc; Chem Inst Can. *Res:* Organic reaction mechanisms; stable aliphatic carbonium ions and their reactions; unusual organometallic compounds. *Mailing Add:* Dept of Chem Univ of Calgary Calgary AB T2N 1N4 Can

SORENSON, HAROLD WAYNE, CONTROL SYSTEMS ENGINEERING. *Current Pos:* VPRES BEDFORD GROUP & DIR AIR FORCE FED FUNDED RES & DEVELOP CTR, MITRE CORP, 90- *Personal Data:* b Omaha, Nebr, Aug 28, 36; m 58; c 3. *Educ:* Iowa State Univ, BS, 57; Univ Calif, Los Angeles, MS, 63, PhD(control systs eng), 66. *Prof Exp:* Sr res engr, Gen Dynamics/Astronaut, 57-62; head space systs group, AC Electronics Div, Gen Motors Corp, Calif, 63-66; guest scientist, Ger Exp Aerospace Facil, Inst Control Syst Technol, WGer, 66-67; asst prof systs dynamics & control, Univ Calif, San Diego, 68-71, from assoc prof to prof eng sci, 71-89; chief scientist, US Air Force, 85-88. *Concurrent Pos:* Consult, Adv Group Aerospace Develop, NATO, Paris, 66-67; Aerojet-Gen Corp, Azusa, Calif, 68-70 & Aerospace Corp, 71-75; pres, Orincon Corp, 74-81; mem, US Air Force Sci Adv Bd, 81-85. *Mem:* Fel Inst Elec & Electronics Engrs; Oper Res Soc Am; AAAS. *Res:* Control of stochastic and deterministic dynamical systems, including optimal deterministic control theory, numerical methods for optimal control, linear and nonlinear filtering for stochastic systems, optimal and suboptimal control of stochastic systems. *Mailing Add:* Mitre Corp Burlington Rd Bedford MA 01730

SORENSON, JAMES ALFRED, MEDICAL PHYSICS, MAGNETIC RESONANCE IMAGING. *Current Pos:* PROF MED PHYSICS, UNIV WIS, 89- *Personal Data:* b Madison, Wis, Aug 21, 38; m 61, Lucy Wagner; c James F, Julie, Kathleen & David. *Educ:* Univ Wis-Madison, BS, 63, MS, 64, PhD(radiol sci), 71. *Prof Exp:* Physicist, Sect Nuclear Med, Univ Wis-Madison, 66-71, asst prof med physics, Dept Radiol, 71-73; from assoc prof to prof radiol, Univ Utah, 80-87; dir res & develop, Lunar, Inc, Madison, Wis, 87-89. *Mem:* AAAS; Am Asn Physicists Med; Health Physics Soc; Soc Magnetic Resonance Med. *Res:* In vivo determination of body composition and elemental concentrations by radiation transmission measurements; magnetic resonance imaging. *Mailing Add:* Univ Wis 5117 Wiseman Ctr 1500 Highland Ave Madison WI 53705

SORENSON, JOHN R J, MEDICINAL CHEMISTRY, BIOCHEMISTRY & PHARMACOLOGY. *Current Pos:* assoc prof, 77-81, PROF MED CHEM, COL PHARM, UNIV ARK, LITTLE ROCK, 81- *Personal Data:* b Sturgeon Bay, Wis, June 13, 34; c Michael, Patrick, Paul, Anne, Joseph, Amy & Judith. *Educ:* Univ Wis, BS, 60; Univ Kans, PhD(med chem), 65. *Prof Exp:* Sr res chemist, G D Searle & Co, 65-70; asst prof environ health, Col Med, Univ Cincinnati, 70-76; adj asst prof med chem, Col Pharm, 76-77. *Concurrent Pos:* Corresp mem, UNESCO Int Ctr Trace Element Study, 84. *Mem:* Sigma Xi; Asn Bioinorg Sci; Am Chem Soc; Brit Pharmacol Soc. *Res:* Medicinal chemistry; pharmacology; syntheses and studies of the pharmacological and biochemical effects of essential metalloelement (copper, iron, manganese and zinc) complexes. *Mailing Add:* Univ Ark Med Sci 4301 W Markham St Little Rock AR 72205

SORENSON, JONATHAN PAUL, COMPUTER SCIENCES, MATHEMATICS. *Current Pos:* ASSOC PROF MATH & COMPUT SCI, BUTLER UNIV, 91- *Personal Data:* b Valparaiso, Ind, Feb 14, 64; m 86, Rachelle Leffert. *Educ:* Valparaiso Univ, BS, 86; Univ Wis, MS, 87, MA, 89, PhD(comput sci), 91. *Mem:* Asn Comput Mach; Am Math Soc; Math Asn Am. *Res:* Analysis and design of algorithms for solving problems from number theory; computing greatest common divisions, Jacobi symbols, lists of prime numbers and factoring large integers. *Mailing Add:* Dept Math & Comput Sci Butler Univ 4600 Sunset Ave Indianapolis IN 46208. *E-Mail:* sorenson@butler.edu

SORENSON, MARION W, ethology, zoology, for more information see previous edition

SORENSON, PAUL G, SOFTWARE SYSTEMS, ARTIFICIAL INTELLIGENCE. *Current Pos:* PROF & CHAIR, DEPT COMPUT SCI, UNIV ALTA, 89- *Personal Data:* b Stettler, Alta, Aug 30, 46. *Educ:* Univ Alta, BSc, 67, MSc, 69; Univ Toronto, PhD(comput sci), 74. *Prof Exp:* Vis scientist, IBM San Jose Res Lab, 79-80; prof & head, Dept Comput Sci, Univ Sask, 81-86. *Concurrent Pos:* Mem, Eng Res Coun, 81-83. *Mem:* Asn Comput Mach; Inst Elec & Electronics Engrs. *Res:* Software engineering environments, metasystems, computer-wired software design and requirements engineering. *Mailing Add:* Dept Comput Sci Univ Alta Edmonton AB T6G 2H1 Can. *Fax:* 403-492-1071; *E-Mail:* Sorenson@cs.valberta.ca

SORENSON, ROBERT LOWELL, ANATOMY, CELL BIOLOGY. *Current Pos:* From instr to assoc prof, 67-85, PROF CELL BIOL, UNIV MINN, MINNEAPOLIS, 85- *Personal Data:* b Albert Lea, Minn, Aug 3, 40. *Educ:* Univ Minn, BA, 62, PhD(anat), 67. *Concurrent Pos:* USPHS fel, Minn Med Res Found, 68-71, Univ Minn, 71-; res fel, Rigshospitalet, Copenhagen, Denmark, 68; investr, Minn Med Res Found, 67-70. *Mem:* AAAS; Am Anat Asn; Am Diabetes Asn. *Res:* Diabetes; islet cytology; protein synthesis and secretion; insulin secretion during pregnancy; Islet cell growth. *Mailing Add:* Dept Cell Biol & Neuroanat Univ Minn Sch Med 321 Church St SE Minneapolis MN 55455-0303. *Fax:* 612-624-8118; *E-Mail:* soren001@maroon.tc.umn.edu

SORENSON, WAYNE RICHARD, POLYMER CHEMISTRY, ORGANIC & INORGANIC CHEMISTRY. *Current Pos:* RETIRED. *Personal Data:* b St Paul, Minn, Dec 19, 26; m 54, Patricia Owen; c 3. *Educ:* Col St Thomas, BS, 49; Univ Md, PhD(org chem), 54. *Prof Exp:* Res chemist, E I du Pont de Nemours, 53-61; group leader Continental Oil Co, 61-64; sect leader, 64-67, mgr res & develop, 67-72, dir plastics res & develop, 72-77, coordr new ventures, 77-78; dir res & develop, Tenneco Chem, Inc, 78-79, vpres, 80-82; vpres res & develop, Church & Dwight Co Inc, 82-90. *Mem:* Am Chem Soc. *Res:* New polymer-forming reactions; properties of polymers; polymer applications; inorganic chemicals and detergents. *Mailing Add:* 29 Catskill Ct Belle Mead NJ 08502-4528

SORENSON, WILLIAM GEORGE, MYCOLOGY. *Current Pos:* ADJ PROF MICROBIOL & IMMUNOL, WVA UNIV, 77-; RES MYCOLOGIST, APPALACHIAN LAB OCCUP & SAFETY & HEALTH, 77- *Personal Data:* b Albert Lea, Minn, Oct 30, 35; m 57, Loretta Treptow; c Marshall B, Erich C, Matthew K & Kelly J. *Educ:* Univ Iowa, BA, 58, MS, 62; Univ Tex, PhD(bot), 64. *Prof Exp:* res microbiologist, Northern Utilization Res & Develop Div, USDA, 63-66; asst prof biol, Oklahoma City Univ, 66-68; NIH fel, Univ Okla, 68-70, asst prof bot & microbiol, 70-77. *Mem:* Mycol Soc Am; Am Soc Microbiol. *Res:* Physiology and taxonomy of fungi; mycotoxins; role of fungi in occupational lung disease. *Mailing Add:* NIOSH/DRDS 1095 Willowdale Rd Morgantown WV 26505

SORGER, GEORGE JOSEPH, BIOCHEMICAL GENETICS, MICROBIOLOGY. *Current Pos:* from asst prof to assoc prof, 66-78, PROF BIOL, MCMASTER UNIV, 78-, NAT RES COUN CAN FEL, 66- *Personal Data:* b Vienna, Austria, Sept 20, 37; Can citizen; m 61; c 2. *Educ:* McGill Univ, BS, 59; Yale Univ, PhD(microbiol), 64. *Prof Exp:* Res assoc bot, Ore State Univ, 64-66. *Concurrent Pos:* Exchange scientist, Chem Bact, Nat Ctr Sci Res, Marseille, 73-74; Cold Spring Harbor Lab, 81-82. *Mem:* Can Fedn Biol Soc; Can Soc Biochem; Can Soc Plant Molecular Biol. *Res:* Regulation and mechanism of action of nitrate reductase; nitrite reductase, studied using a molecular-genetical approach; isolation and study of genes concerned with nitrate assimilation and its regulation in neurospora; regulation of nitrate reductase in differnet organs of maize; developmental connections. *Mailing Add:* Dept Biol McMaster Univ 1280 Main St W Hamilton ON L8S 4K1 Can

SORIA, RODOLFO M(AXIMILIANO), TECHNICAL MANAGEMENT. *Current Pos:* RETIRED. *Personal Data:* b Berlin, Germany, May 16, 17; nat US; m 47, Faith McLeod; c Steven, Karen & David. *Educ:* Mass Inst Technol, SB, 39, SM, 40; Ill Inst Technol, PhD(elec eng), 47. *Prof Exp:* Instr electronics & microwave, US Army Sig Corps Training Prog, 42, lectr, 43, instr elec eng, 43-47, asst prof, 47; proj engr, Amphenol Corp, 46-49, dir res, 49-54, dir eng, 54-56, vpres res & eng, 56-68, dir corp res & eng, Bunker-Ramo Corp, 68, group vpres, Res & Eng, Amphenol Components Group, 69- 72; mgt consult, 72-85. *Concurrent Pos:* Pres, Nat Electronics Conf, 54; consult, Adv Group Electronic Parts, Off Dir Defense Res & Eng, 55-61; chmn, Electronic Components Conf, 57; mem comt, Radio Frequency Cables & Connectors & US deleg, Int Electrotech Comn; chmn eng panel, Microelectronics Subdiv, Electronic Indust Asn. *Mem:* Fel Inst Elec & Electronics Engrs; Sigma Xi. *Res:* Radio communications; wave propagation; microwaves; antennae; electronic components and systems. *Mailing Add:* RR1 PO Box 735 Kents Hill ME 04349-9502

SORIANO, DAVID S, HETEROCYCLIC SYNTHESIS & PHASE-TRANSFER CATALYSIS, CONFORMATIONAL ANALYSIS. *Current Pos:* ASSOC PROF CHEM, UNIV PITTSBURGH, BRADFORD, PA, 84- *Personal Data:* b Jersey City, NJ, June 3, 53; m 78; c 2. *Educ:* Fairleigh Dickinson Univ, Teaneck, NJ, BS, 75, MS, 77; Univ Nebr-Lincoln, PhD(chem), 80. *Prof Exp:* Res chemist, Buffalo Res Lab, Allied Corp, 80-82, sr res chemist, 82-84. *Concurrent Pos:* Asst ed, Internet J Sci Biol Chem. *Mem:* Sigma Xi; Am Chem Soc. *Res:* Immobilized enzymes as catalysts for organic synthesis; asymmetric organic synthesis; fermentation processes leading to chiral synthons for use in organic synthesis; computer aided molecular design. *Mailing Add:* Dept Chem Univ Pittsburgh Bradford PA 16701

SORKIN, BARBARA C, EPITHELIAL CELL INTERACTIONS, EPITHELIAL CELL FUNCTION. *Current Pos:* ASST MEM STAFF, RES INST FORSYTH DENT CTR, 93- *Personal Data:* b New York, NY, Sept 2, 56. *Educ:* Yale Univ, BS & MS, 78; Rockefeller Univ, PhD(develop & molecular biol), 85. *Prof Exp:* Fel, Rockefeller Univ, 85-88, asst prof, 88-92; asst mem, Scripps Res Inst, 92-93. *Concurrent Pos:* Lectr, Harvard Med Sch, 94- *Mem:* AAAS; Am Soc Cell Biol; Int Asn Dent Res; Sigma Xi. *Res:* Molecular basis of cell-cell interactions and the role of these interactions in biological processes including embryonic development, epithelial barrier function, tumor metastasis and bacterial infection. *Mailing Add:* Dept Cell Biol Forsyth Res Inst 140 Fenway Boston MA 02115-3799

SORKIN, HOWARD, ORGANIC CHEMISTRY, DISPLAY DEVICE CHEMISTRY. *Current Pos:* RETIRED. *Personal Data:* b New York, NY, Aug 29, 33; m 57, Marilyn Brode; c Linda & Rina. *Educ:* City Col New York, BS, 55; Cornell Univ, MS, 57, PhD(org chem), 59. *Prof Exp:* Sr res chemist, Cent Res Labs, Airco, 59-68; mem tech staff, Solid State Div, RCA Corp, Somerville, 68-76; sr chemist, Timex Components, Inc, Somerset, NJ, 76-80; prog mgr, Philips Labs, 80-96. *Concurrent Pos:* Adj prof, Rutgers Univ, 79-80. *Mem:* Am Chem Soc; Soc Info Display. *Res:* Synthesis and properties of liquid crystals and their application to electro-optic display devices; new polymers and polymerization processes; electrophoretic display devices; LCD device technology. *Mailing Add:* 241 Crescenzi Ct West Orange NJ 07052. *E-Mail:* hsorkin112@aol.com

SORKIN, MARSHALL, COSMETIC CHEMISTRY. *Current Pos:* dir toiletries res, 68-80, VPRES TOILETRIES DIV, CARTER PROD DIV, CARTER-WALLACE, INC, 80- *Personal Data:* b Chicago, Ill, July 12, 28; m 50; c 4. *Educ:* Roosevelt Univ, BS, 50; Northwestern Univ, MS, 59. *Prof Exp:* Chemist, Rock Island RR, 50-51; asst plant mgr, S Buchsbaum & Co, 51-52; res & develop group leader, Helene Curtis Ind Inc, 52-61, res dir, Toiletries Div, Alberto-Culver Co, 61-68. *Mem:* Am Chem Soc; Soc Cosmetic Chem. *Res:* Cosmetic and proprietary drug formulations; skin and hair physiology. *Mailing Add:* 48 Leeds Lane Jamesburg NJ 08831

SOROF, SAM, cellular biochemistry, cellular biology; deceased, see previous edition for last biography

SOROFF, HARRY S, SURGERY. *Current Pos:* CHMN DEPT SURG, MED SCH/HEALTH SCI CTR, STATE UNIV NY STONY BROOK, 74-, PROF SURG, 77- *Personal Data:* b Sydney, NS, Feb 2, 26. *Educ:* Temple Univ, MD, 48; Am Bd Surg, dipl, 60; Bd Thoracic Surg, dipl, 61. *Prof Exp:* Intern, Philadelphia Jewish Hosp, 48-49; asst resident surg, Montefiore Hosp, NY, 50-51; chief resident, Beth David Hosp, 51-52; chief, Metab Div, Surg Res Univ, Brooke Army Med Ctr, Ft Sam Houston, Tex, 53-56; resident surg, Lakeside Hosp, Cleveland, Ohio, 56-57; fel thoracic surg, Peter Bent Brigham Hosp, 57-61, chief thoracic lab, 60-61; from asst prof to prof surg, Sch Med, Tufts Univ, 68-74, dir Tufts Surg Serv, Boston City Hosp, 70-74. *Concurrent Pos:* Fel surg metab, Columbia-Presby Med Ctr, 52-53; res fel, Peter Bent Brigham Hosp, Boston, 57-60; fel thoracic surg, Mt Auburn & Malden Hosps, 57-60; asst surgeon, Boston City Hosp, 61-64; estab investr, Am Heart Asn, 61-66; assoc dir clin study unit, New Eng Ctr Hosp, Boston, 61-, asst surgeon, 61-64, surgeon, 64-; sr consult, Lemuel-Shattuck Hosp, Jamaica Plain, Mass, 67- *Mem:* Int Soc Burn Injuries; Am Soc Artificial Internal Organs; Int Cardiovasc Soc; Am Asn Thoracic Surg; Am Burn Asn. *Res:* Thoracic and cardiovascular surgery; surgical metabolism. *Mailing Add:* SUNY Stony Brook Health Sci Ctr Dept Surg T 19 Rm 028 Stony Brook NY 11790

SOROKIN, PETER, QUANTUM ELECTRONICS. *Current Pos:* Staff physicist, 57-68, IBM FEL, T J WATSON RES CTR, 68- *Personal Data:* b Boston, Mass, July 10, 31; m 77, Anita J Schell; c Elena & Paul. *Educ:* Harvard Univ, AB, 52, BS, 53, PhD(appl physics), 58. *Honors & Awards:* R W Wood Award, Optical Soc Am, 78; Comstock Award, Nat Acad Sci, 83; Schawlow Prize, Am Phys Soc, 91; Harvey Prize, Israel Inst Technol. *Mem:* Nat Acad Sci; NY Acad Sci; fel Am Optical Soc; fel Am Phys Soc Res Lasers; Am Acad Sci. *Res:* Development of ferntosecond ultra-violet and very ultra-violet laser sources. *Mailing Add:* T J Watson Res Ctr IBM Corp PO Box 218 Yorktown Heights NY 10598

SOROKIN, SERGEI PITIRIMOVITCH, HISTOLOGY, EMBRYOLOGY. *Current Pos:* asst prof, 70-77, ASSOC PROF CELL BIOL, SCH PUB HEALTH, HARVARD UNIV, 77- *Personal Data:* b Boston, Mass, Apr 13, 33. *Educ:* Harvard Univ, AB, 54, Harvard Med Sch, MD, 58. *Prof Exp:* Instr anat, Harvard Med Sch, 60-65, assoc & tutor, 65-69, asst prof, 69-70. *Concurrent Pos:* Res fel path, Harvard Med Sch, 58-59, fel anat, 59-60; vis asst prof, Cornell Univ, 62-63; mem pulmonary res eval comt, Vet Admin, 69-70; lung cancer adv group, Nat Cancer Inst, 71-74. *Mem:* Histochem Soc; Soc Cell Biol; Am Asn Anat. *Res:* Cell and biology; in vitro culturing techniques; cytological differentiation as studied with aid of electron microscopy, histochemistry and autoradiography; physiology; pulmonary morphology. *Mailing Add:* Dept Anat & Neurobiol Boston Univ Sch Med 80 E Concord St Boston MA 02118-2394

SOROOSHIAN, SOROOSH, HYDROLOGIC MODELLING, SURFACE HYDROLOGY. *Current Pos:* assoc prof, 83-87, PROF, DEPTS HYDROL & WATER RESOURCES & SYSTS & INDUST ENG, UNIV ARIZ, 87-, DEPT HEAD, HYDROL & WATER RESOURCES, 89- *Personal Data:* b Kerman, Iran, July 2, 48; US citizen; c 2. *Educ:* Calif State Polytech Univ, San Luis Obispo, BS, 71; Univ Calif Los Angeles, MS, 73, PhD(syst eng), 78. *Prof Exp:* Asst prof, Dept Systs Eng & Civil Eng, Case Western Reserve Univ, Cleveland, Ohio, 78-82. *Concurrent Pos:* Assoc ed, Water Resource Res, Am Geophys Union, 83-88, ed, 88-92; prog chmn, fall meetings, Hydrol Sect, Am Geophys Union, 84-87, mem, Hydrol Exec Comt, 84-; mem, Water Sci & Technol Bd, Comt Restoration Aquatic Ecosyts, Nat Res Coun, 90- *Mem:* Am Soc Civil Eng; Am Meteorol Soc; AAAS; Am Water Resources Asn. *Res:* Surface hydrology, including rainfall-runoff modeling, flood forecasting, application of remote sensing in hydrology of climate studies. *Mailing Add:* 6019 N Pinchot Rd Tucson AZ 85750

SORRELL, FURMAN Y(ATES), JR, FLUID DYNAMICS, HEAT TRANSFER. *Current Pos:* from asst prof to assoc prof eng mech, 68-75, dir grad prog, 70-74, PROF MECH & AEROSPACE ENG, NC STATE UNIV, 76-, HEAD MECH ENG, 96- *Personal Data:* b Wadesboro, NC, July 14, 38; m, Elizabeth Pearce; c Shannon C (Sorreto). *Educ:* NC State Univ, BS, 60; Calif Inst Technol, MS, 61, PhD(aeronaut), 66. *Prof Exp:* Res engr, Pratt & Whitney Aircraft, 61-62; res fel & asst prof aerospace eng sci, Joint Inst Lab Astrophys, 66-68. *Concurrent Pos:* Prof marine sci fac, NC State Univ, 72-, prof air conserv fac, 77-; assoc, Perry Assoc Consult Engrs, 74-75; co-chmn ocean panel, Comt Appln Rev High Resolution Passive Satellites, NASA, 76-78; Nat Oceanic & Atmospheric Admin grant, Nearshore Ocean Currents & Mixing, 76-81, chmn, Panel Marine Waste Disposal & mem, Steering Comt, Conf Marine Pollution, 79-80; grant Impact Off-Shore Pipelines, 80-82; mem, Prog Review Comt, Prog Phys & Chem Energy Storage, US Dept Energy, 81; tech dir, NC Alternative Energy Corp, 81-82; res contracts, IBM, 82-84, USAF, 85-88, Sematech, 88-, Semiconductor Res Corp, 88-, Army Res Off, 89- & Off Naval Res, 90-, NSF, 90- *Mem:* Am Phys Soc; Am Soc Mech Engrs. *Res:* Fluid dynamics; physics of fluids; heat transfer; laboratory and field measurements. *Mailing Add:* Dept Mech & Aerospace Eng NC State Univ Box 7910 Raleigh NC 27695-7910. *E-Mail:* fys@chaos.cc.ncsu.edu

SORRELL, GARY LEE, DECISION SUPPORT SYSTEMS, OPERATIONS RESEARCH. *Current Pos:* CHMN, CALIBRE SYST INC, 85- *Personal Data:* b Middletown, Ohio, Dec 7, 43; m 65; c 1. *Educ:* Park Col, BA, 65; Univ Okla, Norman, MA, 67. *Prof Exp:* Mathematician, Nat Security Agency, 67-73; opers dir, Teledyne Brown Eng, 73-74; sr opers analyst, US Postal Serv, 74-76; proj mgr, Genasys Corp, 76-77; sr assoc, J Watson Noah Assocs, 77-78; exec vpres, Mgt Consult & Res, Inc, 78-85. *Mem:* Opers Res Soc Am; Inst Cost Anal; Mil Opers Res Soc. *Res:* Computer systems design and development; decision support systems applications; resource management; cost analysis and estimation; economic analysis. *Mailing Add:* 5111 Leesburg Pike Suite 514 Falls Church VA 22041

SORRELL, MICHAEL FLOYD, GASTROENTEROLOGY. *Current Pos:* from asst prof to assoc prof, 71-76, PROF MED, UNIV NEBR MED CTR, OMAHA, 76-, CHMN DEPT INTERNAL MED, 81- *Personal Data:* b St Louis, Mo, July 4, 35; m 57; c 4. *Educ:* Univ Nebr, Omaha, BS, 57, MD, 59. *Prof Exp:* Intern med, Nebr Methodist Hosp, 59-60; pvt pract, 60-66; resident internal med, Col Med, Univ Nebr, Omaha, 66-68, fel gastroenterol, 68-69; NIH trainee liver dis & nutrit, Col Med & Dent, NJ, 69-71. *Concurrent Pos:* NIH acad career develop award, 71-76; dir, Liver Study Unit, 71- *Mem:* Am Fedn Clin Res; Am Gastroenterol Asn; Am Asn Study Liver Dis; Int Asn Study Liver Dis (secy-treas, 81-); fel Am Col Physicians; Asn Am Physicians. *Res:* Toxic effects of alcohol and its metabolites on protein fabrication and membrane repair; drug metabolism in liver disease. *Mailing Add:* Univ Nebr Med Ctr 600 S 42nd St Omaha NE 68198-3280

SORRELLS, FRANK DOUGLAS, DEVELOPMENT & DESIGN, STRESS ANALYSIS. *Current Pos:* CONSULT, DEVELOP & DESIGN, PVT PRACT, 76-; PRES, PEPE SOFTWARE, LLC, 96- *Personal Data:* b Toccoa, Ga, May 14, 31; m 54, Alma West; c Desiree G (Bright). *Educ:* Univ Tenn, BSME, 57, MS, 68. *Prof Exp:* Exec vpres res & develop, Charles A Lee Assocs, 67-76; Mgr technol transfer, Valmet Paper Mach, 88-93; mem, Design Team, Advan Toroidal Facil, Oak Ridge Nat Lab. *Mem:* Nat Soc Prof Engrs; Am Soc Mech Engrs. *Res:* Machinery and apparatus for various manufacturing industries; stress analysis; applied mathematics; computer codes; granted 22 patents. *Mailing Add:* 5516 Timbercrest Trail Knoxville TN 37909

SORRELLS, GORDON GUTHREY, SEISMOLOGY, GEOMECHANICS. *Current Pos:* RETIRED. *Personal Data:* b Dallas, Tex, Mar 5, 34. *Educ:* Southern Methodist Univ, BS, 55, MS, 61, PhD(geophysics), 71. *Prof Exp:* Res geophysicist seismol, Teledyne Geotech, 67-70; sr res assoc seismic measurement, Southern Methodist Univ, 70-71; prog mgr & prin investr geothermal, Teledyne Geotech, 71-74; dir, Senturion Sci, 74-75; consult hydraul fracturing, Teledyne Geotech, 75-76; tech dir geothermal & hydrocarbon, 76-81. *Concurrent Pos:* Consult, Dowell Div, Dow Chem Co, 75-76 & Dept of Energy, 78. *Mem:* Am Geophys Union; Seismol Soc Am. *Res:* Development of seismic techniques to assess and control environmental risk of induced seismicity associated with geothermal and hydrocarbon production. *Mailing Add:* 2714 Country Club Pkwy Garland TX 75043

SORRELLS, MARK EARL, PLANT BREEDING, GENETICS. *Current Pos:* ASST PROF PLANT BREEDING, CORNELL UNIV, 78- *Personal Data:* b Hillsboro, Ill, Mar 23, 50. *Educ:* Southern Ill Univ, BS, 73, MS, 75; Univ Wis, PhD (plant breeding), 77. *Prof Exp:* Fel, Dept Agron, Univ Wis, 77-78. *Mem:* Am Soc Agron; Crop Sci Soc Am; Genetic Soc Can; Am Genetic Asn; Sigma Xi. *Res:* Plant genetics; plant physiology. *Mailing Add:* Dept Plant Breeding & Biomet Cornell Univ 252 Emerson Hall Ithaca NY 14850

SORRELS, JOHN DAVID, PHYSICS, COMPUTER SCIENCE. *Current Pos:* GROUP DIR SPACECRAFT SYSTS ENG, AEROSPACE CORP, LOS ANGELES, 62- *Personal Data:* b Poteau, Okla, July 5, 27; m 51, Evelyn Young; c Sue (Steiminger) & Vanessa (Stothers). *Educ:* Mass Inst Technol, BS, 50; Rice Univ, MA, 51; Calif Inst Technol, PhD(physics), 56; Univ Juarez, MSc, 77. *Prof Exp:* Engr, Ramo-Wooldridge Corp, 55-62. *Mem:* AAAS; Am Phys Soc; Sigma Xi. *Res:* Cosmic rays; satellite orbit determination; control systems; data processing systems development; medical science. *Mailing Add:* 2738 Vista Mesa Dr Rancho Palos Verdes CA 90274-6324

SORRENTINO, SANDY, JR, NEUROENDOCRINOLOGY. *Current Pos:* Asst prof anat, 71-76, ASST CLIN PROF, SCH MED, UNIV ROCHESTER, 76- *Personal Data:* b Buffalo, NY, Dec 23, 43; m 65; c 3. *Educ:* Canisius Col, AB, 65; Univ Tenn, PhD(anat), 69; Univ Rochester, MD, 75. *Mem:* Am Asn Anat. *Mailing Add:* 1570 Long Pd Rd Rochester NY 14626-4117

SORROWS, HOWARD EARLE, physics; deceased, see previous edition for last biography

SORSCHER, ALAN J, MEDICINE. *Current Pos:* MED DIR, HOUSE STAFF & OCCUP HEALTH, HOLY CROSS HOSP, DETROIT, MICH, 86- *Personal Data:* b Flint, Mich, Sept 19, 34; m 57, 83; c David, Michael, Jonathan, Carly, Daniel & Natalie. *Educ:* Wayne State Univ, MD, 59; Am Bd Int Med, cert, 72. *Prof Exp:* Attend physician, Hurley Med Ctr, McLaren Hosp, 64-66 & 68-86; chief, Gastrointestinal Sect, USAF Hosp, Keesler AFB, Biloxi, 66-68. *Concurrent Pos:* Res asst, Univ Chicago, 60-61; clin instr, Univ Ill, 62-64; from clin asst prof to assoc prof, Col Human Med, Mich State Univ, 72-86; consult, Mich Atty Gen, 84 & Mich Dept Social Serv, 85-86. *Res:* Hormonal risk factors in breast carcinogenesis. *Mailing Add:* 351 Donegal Dr Rochester MI 48309

SORTER, PETER F, ORGANIC CHEMISTRY, INFORMATION SCIENCE. *Current Pos:* Info scientist, Hoffman-La Roche, 62-65, mgr, Sci Lit Dept, 66-79, dir, Res Serv, 80-84, dir, Info Ctr, 85-90, ASST VPRES, HOFFMAN-LA ROCHE, 91- *Personal Data:* b Vienna, Austria, Feb 8, 33; US citizen; m 65, Esther Cohen. *Educ:* Lafayette Col, BA, 54; DePauw Univ, MA, 56; Univ Iowa, PhD(chem), 62. *Concurrent Pos:* Mem bd dirs, Documentation Abstr, Inc, 70- *Mem:* Am Chem Soc; Chem Notation Asn (vpres, 72, pres, 73); Am Soc Info Sci; Drug Info Asn. *Res:* Storage retrieval of chemical and biological information, especially chemical structures. *Mailing Add:* 150 W End Ave New York NY 10023

SOSA, OMELIO, JR, ENTOMOLOGY, HOST PLANT RESISTANCE. *Current Pos:* RETIRED. *Personal Data:* b Camaguey, Cuba, Feb 2, 39; US citizen; m 61, Maria del C de Quesada; c 2. *Educ:* Okla State Univ, BS, 64; Purdue Univ, MS, 71, PhD(entom), 77. *Prof Exp:* Agr res tech emtom, Agr Res Serv, USDA, 65-73, entomologist, 73-76, res entomologist, 76-96. *Concurrent Pos:* Assoc ed, Fla Entomologist, 84-91; Hispanic employment prog mgr, USDA, ARS, South Atlantic Area (Va, NC & SC, Ga, Fla, PR, VI), 88-94; adj asst prof, Univ Fla; pres, Fla Div, Am Soc Sugar Cane Technol, 92; mem, Nat Plant Genetics Resources Bd, 91-92. *Mem:* Entom Soc Am; Am Soc Sugarcane Technol; Am Registry Prof Entom; Am Soc Agron. *Res:* Reduction of crop losses in sugarcane by controlling or suppressing insect population. *Mailing Add:* 2365 Palm Rd West Palm Beach FL 33406

SOSEBEE, RONALD EUGENE, PLANT PHYSIOLOGY, ECOLOGY. *Current Pos:* from asst prof to assoc prof, Tex Tech Univ, 69-79, assoc chmn, Dept Range, Wildlife & Fisheries Mgt, 80-90, chmn, 90-96, PROF DEPT RANGE, WILDLIFE & FISHERIES MGT, 96- *Personal Data:* b Abilene, Tex, July 2, 42; m 64; c 2. *Educ:* Abilene Christian Col, BS, 64; NMex State Univ, MS, 66; Utah State Univ, PhD(plant physiol), 70. *Prof Exp:* Instr range sci, Utah State Univ, 69. *Mem:* Am Soc Plant Physiol; Ecol Soc Am; fel Soc Range Mgt; Weed Sci Soc Am; Sigma Xi. *Res:* Photosynthesis of native plants; plant-soil water relationships; soil temperature and plant growth; carbohydrate relationships in plants; noxious plant control. *Mailing Add:* Dept Range & Wildlife Mgt Tex Tech Univ Lubbock TX 79409. *Fax:* 806-742-2280; *E-Mail:* c7res@tacs.ttu.edu

SOSKA, GEARY VICTOR, ROBOTICS. *Current Pos:* CONSULT ENG, GOODYEAR TIRE & RUBBER CO, 86- *Personal Data:* b Sewickley, Pa, June 30, 48; m 69, Carolyn Huppenthal; c Christopher & Aaron. *Educ:* Southwestern Univ, BS, 84; Univ Akron, BS, 90, MS, 93. *Honors & Awards:* Int Golden Robot Award, Int Fedn Robotics, 91. *Prof Exp:* Nuclear missile syst specialist, USAF, 68-72; field serv engr, Unimation Inc, 72-73; automation specialist robotics, Ford Motor Co, 73-79; mfg res & develop engr, John Deere, 79-81; dir mkt & sales, Cybotech Corp, 81-86. *Concurrent Pos:* Consult & prin appl robotics; lectr, Purdue Univ, 85-86; mem bd adv, Robotics Int, Soc Mfg Engrs, 89-90; instr robotics, Stark State Col Technol, 89-; indust curric adv, pub speaker, Univ Akron, 83-; bd dir, Robotic Indust Asn, 97- *Mem:* Soc Mfg Engrs; ROBOTIC INDUSTS ASN; Laser Inst Art; INST INDUST ENGRS. *Res:* Robotics and manufacturing engineering education; author of 22 publications; US patent for robot arm. *Mailing Add:* 7388 Ashburton Circle NW North Canton OH 44720

SOSLAU, GERALD, BIOCHEMISTRY, HEMATOLOGY. *Current Pos:* from asst prof to assoc prof, 75-89, PROF BIOCHEM & NEOPLASTIC DIS, MCP-HAHNEMANN MED COL, 89-, DIR, IMS, 96- *Personal Data:* b New York, NY, Jan 22, 44; m 66; c 4. *Educ:* Queens Col NY, BA, 65; Univ Rochester, PhD(biochem), 70. *Prof Exp:* Fel biochem, Med Sch, Univ Pa, 70-71, res assoc, 71-75. *Mem:* Sigma Xi; Am Soc Biol Chemists; Am Soc Cell Biol; Am Soc Hematol; Int Soc Thrombos Haemost. *Res:* Platelets and their receptors in hemostasis and vascular interactions; molecular biology of herpes simplex virus glycoproteins and their functional roles. *Mailing Add:* MCP-Hahnemann Med Sch Allegheny Univ MS344 Broad & Vine Philadelphia PA 19102-1192. *Fax:* 215-762-7434; *E-Mail:* soslaug@allegheny.edu

SOSNOVSKY, GEORGE, ORGANIC CHEMISTRY. *Current Pos:* lectr, 66-67, prof, 66-93, EMER PROF CHEM, UNIV WIS-MILWAUKEE, 93-, ADJ PROF, 93- *Personal Data:* b Petersburg, Russia, Dec 12, 20; US citizen; m 44. *Educ:* Univ Munich, dipl, 44; Univ Innsbruck, PhD(chem), 48. *Prof Exp:* Res assoc chem, Univ Innsbruck, 48-49; tech officer, Commonwealth Sci & Indust Res Orgn, Australia, 49-51; in-chg org process develop, Cent Res Lab, Imp Chem Industs, Ltd, 51-56; fel & res assoc, Univ Chicago, 56-59; sr scientist, Res Inst, Ill Inst Technol, 59-63, assoc prof chem, 63-66. *Concurrent Pos:* Res consult, Ill Inst Technol Res Inst, 63-66; USPHS spec sr res fel, Univ Col, London & Univ Tuebingen, 67-68; vis prof, Univ Tubingen, Ger, 67-68, Inst Toxicol & Chemother, Ger Cancer Ctr, Heidelberg, WGer, 85; ed, Synthesis, 69-85; regional dir, Nat Found Cancer Res, 80-85; James D & Dorothy Shaw grad sch discretionary fund awards, 83, 84, 85 & 86. *Mem:* Am Chem Soc. *Res:* Free radical chemistry; organometallic and organometalloid peroxides; metal ion-catalyzed and photochemical reactions of peroxides; phosphorus intermediates of biological interest; synthesis and biological applications of new phosphorus compounds containing a spin label; novel synthetic methods; medicinal chemistry; structure-activity relationship of anticancer drugs; syntheses and biological evaluation of new anticancer drugs; contrast enhancing agents for NMR-Imaging; NMR-Imaging for diagnostic assessment of tumors; radiation sensitizers; author/co-author of over 160 publications. *Mailing Add:* Dept Chem Univ Wis-Milwaukee PO Box 413 Milwaukee WI 53201-0413

SOSNOWSKI, THOMAS PATRICK, TELECOMMUNICATIONS. *Current Pos:* VPRES, DIR RES, FAX INT, 86- *Personal Data:* b Scranton, Pa, Aug 11, 36; m 64, Mary Staubach; c Thomas S, Jennifer J & Timothy P. *Educ:* Pa State Univ, BS, 62; Case Western Res Univ, MS, 65, PhD(eng), 67. *Prof Exp:* Mem tech staff, Bell Tel Labs, 68-80; tech mgr, GTE Labs, 80-84; dir eng, Eikonix, 84-86. *Concurrent Pos:* Ford Found fel, 62; consult, Sosnowski Assoc, 86- *Mem:* Sr mem Inst Elec & Electronics Engrs Eng Mgt Soc; Int Technol Inst. *Res:* Visual communication research; microprocessors; communication systems research; electronic imaging systems; lasers; electro-optics. *Mailing Add:* 58 Sears Rd Wayland MA 01778. *Fax:* 508-358-6687

SOSSONG, NORMAN D, ELEMENTARY PARTICLE PHYSICS, INTERNAL MEDICINE. *Current Pos:* PRIVATE PRAC INTERN MED, 79- *Personal Data:* b Wash, Mar 27, 39. *Educ:* Walla Walla Col, BS, 61; Univ Wash, MS, 66, PhD(physics), 69; Univ Chicago, MD, 75. *Prof Exp:* asst prof, Walla Walla Col, 69-72, assoc prof physics, Pacific Union Col, 79-83. *Mem:* Am Phys Soc; Am Med Asn. *Mailing Add:* PO Box 48297 Seattle WA 98148-0297

SOSULSKI, FRANK WALTER, GRAIN CHEMISTRY & PROCESSING TECHNOLOGY. *Current Pos:* Asst prof field husb, 58-66, assoc prof crop sci, 66-71, PROF CROP SCI, UNIV SASK, 71-, ASSOC MEM FOOD SCI, 90- *Personal Data:* b Weyburn, Sask, Dec 2, 29; m 81, Krystyna Elkowicz; c Tanya, Rena & David. *Educ:* Univ Sask, BSA, 54; Wash State Univ, MS, 56, PhD(agron), 59. *Honors & Awards:* Bronze Medal, Polish Acad Sci. *Concurrent Pos:* Vis prof, Food Sci, Univ Reading, UK, 78-79; vis scientist, Tex A&M Univ, 86-87. *Mem:* Am Asn Cereal Chemists; Agr Inst Can; Inst Food Technol; Am Oil Chemists Soc; Can Inst Food Sci & Technol; Can Seed Growers Asn. *Res:* Have 400 publications and conference presentations that encompass the chemistry, nutritive value, functional properties, processing and utilization of numerous cereal, oilseed and legume crops. *Mailing Add:* Dept Crop Sci Univ Saskatchewan Saskatoon SK S7N 5E5 Can. *Fax:* 306-966-5015

SOTERIADES, MICHAEL C(OSMAS), civil engineering, soil mechanics, for more information see previous edition

SOTHMANN, MARK STEVEN, EXERCISE PHYSIOLOGY, WORK PHYSIOLOGY. *Current Pos:* from asst prof to assoc prof appl physiol, Univ Wis-Milwaukee, 82-92, asst res prof, Milwaukee Clin Campus, 88-91, DIR, HUMAN PERFORMANCE RES LAB, UNIV WIS-MILWAUKEE, 85-, ASSOC PROF RES, MILWAUKEE CLIN CAMPUS, 91-, PROF APPL PHYSIOL, 92- *Personal Data:* b Davenport, Iowa, Nov 7, 49; m 79, Kathleen A Lally; c Stephen & Sarah. *Educ:* Univ Northern Iowa, BA, 71; Purdue Univ, PhD(appl physiol), 82. *Prof Exp:* Teacher hist, Danville Pub Schs, 71-76. *Concurrent Pos:* Consult, Wis Dept Transp, 85, City of Chicago, 85-, Lockheed Eng & Sci Co, 90; prin investr, Nat Inst Aging, 88-92; sci adv, NASA-Johnson Space Ctr, 89-, US Equal Employment Opportunity Comn, 90-91; assoc ed, Med & Sci in Sports & Exercise, 91- *Mem:* Fel Am Col Sports Med; Am Physiol Soc. *Res:* Physiological responses and adaptation to exercise; health and rehabilitation in medical settings; understanding human performance limitations in work settings. *Mailing Add:* Prof Ofc Res & Grad Studies Ind Univ Sch Allied Health Sci 1140 W Michigan St Coleman Hall 322 Indianapolis IN 46202-5119. *Fax:* 414-229-5100

SOTIRCHOS, STRATIS V, REACTION ENGINEERING, APPLIED NUMERICAL ANALYSIS. *Current Pos:* asst prof, 82-87, assoc prof, 87-92, PROF CHEM ENG, UNIV ROCHESTER, 92- *Personal Data:* b Mytilene, Greece, Feb 8, 56; m 83, Kalliopi; c Blaise & Elias. *Educ:* Nat Technol Univ Athens, dipl, 79; Univ Houston, PhD(chem eng), 82. *Mem:* Am Chem Soc; Am Inst Chem Engrs; Am Ceramic Soc; Mat Res Soc. *Res:* Applied mathematics and numerical analysis in chemical engineering; reaction engineering; combustion and gasification processes; transport and reaction in multiphase systems; ceramic material processing. *Mailing Add:* 11 Green Hill Lane Pittsford NY 14534. *Fax:* 716-442-6686; *E-Mail:* svs2@che.rochester.edu

SOTIRIOU-LEVENTIS, CHARIKLIA, BIORGANIC CHEMISTRY, PHYSICAL-ORGANIC CHEMISTRY. *Current Pos:* ASST PROF CHEM, UNIV MO, ROLLA, 94- *Personal Data:* b Nicosia, Cyprus, Jan 20, 60; m 88, Nicholas Leventis; c Theodora. *Educ:* Univ Athens, Greece, BS, 82; Mich State Univ, PhD(org chem), 87. *Honors & Awards:* Giessen Award, Barnett Inst Chem Anal & Mat Sci, 88. *Prof Exp:* Fel chem, Northeastern Univ, 87-89, Harvard Univ, 89-92; sr res scientist, Ciba Corning Diag Inc, 92-93. *Concurrent Pos:* Sohio fel, 87. *Mem:* Am Chem Soc; AAAS. *Res:* Design, synthesis and mechanistic studies of organic molecules with biological significance. *Mailing Add:* Dept Chem Univ Mo Rolla MO 65401. *Fax:* 573-341-6033; *E-Mail:* cslevent@umr.edu

SOTO, AIDA R, ORGANIC CHEMISTRY, BIOCHEMISTRY. *Current Pos:* MGR, BAXTER DIAGNOSTICS INC, 89- *Personal Data:* b Havana, Cuba, Dec 3, 31; US citizen. *Educ:* Univ Havana, BS, 53 & 55; Univ Miami, MS, 62, PhD(chem), 66. *Prof Exp:* Res chemist, Villanueva Univ, 55-58, asst prof, 58-61; fel, Dept Pharmacol, Univ Miami, 65-68, instr med, Sch Med, 68-69; supvr, Chem Res & Develop Dept, Baxter Int, 69-72, group leader, Biol Res & Develop Dept, 72-74, group leader immunochem res & develop, 74-84, sect head, Dade Div, 84-89. *Mem:* AAAS; Am Chem Soc; NY Acad Sci; Am Asn Clin Chemists. *Res:* Base promoted reactions of sulfonate esters in dipolar aprotic solvents; purification and characterization of proteolytic enzymes; clinical enzymology; radioimmunoassays; the use of immunologic techniques in clinical chemistry. *Mailing Add:* 14841 SW 159th St Miami FL 33187

SOTOMAYOR, RENE EDUARDO, genetics, mutagenesis, for more information see previous edition

SOTOS, JUAN FERNANDEZ, PEDIATRICS. *Current Pos:* from asst prof to assoc prof, 62-67, PROF PEDIAT, COL MED, OHIO STATE UNIV, 67-, DIR DIV ENDOCRINOL & METAB, DEPT PEDIAT, 63- *Personal Data:* b Tarazona, Spain, May 18, 27; US citizen; c 6. *Educ:* Univ Valencia, MD, 51. *Prof Exp:* Intern, Univ Valencia Hosp, 52-53; resident pediat path, St Christopher's Hosp, Philadelphia, Pa, 53-54; resident pediat, 54-55; resident pediat, Children's Hosp, Columbus, Ohio, 55-56, instr & chief resident, 56-57; instr, Mass Gen Hosp, 60-62. *Concurrent Pos:* Fel, Mass Gen Hosp, 57-60; dir, Clin Res Ctr, Children's Hosp, Columbus, 62-72. *Mem:* Endocrine Soc; Am Pediat Soc; Am Diabetes Asn; Soc Pediat Soc; Pediat Endocrine Soc. *Res:* Metabolic and endocrine disorders of children. *Mailing Add:* Children's Hosp 700 Childrens Dr Columbus OH 43205-2696

SOTTERY, THEODORE WALTER, GENERAL CHEMISTRY TEACHING. *Current Pos:* RETIRED. *Personal Data:* b Lebanon, Pa, Feb 8, 27; m 49; c 4. *Educ:* Dartmouth Col, BNS, 46; Clark Univ, cert chem, 49; Univ Maine, MS, 56, PhD(chem), 66. *Prof Exp:* Res vol endocrine res, Harvard Med Sch, 46-47; sci storekeeper, Mass-Ft Devens, 47; lab asst chem, Columbia Univ, 49-50; qual control group supvr pigments, E I du Pont de Nemours & Co, 50-51; instr sci, Finch Jr Col, 51-52; asst chem, Univ Maine,

Orono, 54-55, instr, 56-61; from asst prof to assoc prof, Univ S Maine, Portland, 61-73, prof chem, 73- *Concurrent Pos:* Consult, Howell Labs, Bridgton, Maine, Fairchild Camera & Instrument, South Portland, Maine, 66-; chem reviewer, several publ co; bk reviewer, J Chem Educ, 75- *Res:* Failure of the Darzans reaction to produce alpha-phenyl-substituted glycidic esters; reaction of sodium metal with dimethyl formamide. *Mailing Add:* 24 Chamberlain Ave Portland ME 04101

SOUBY, ARMAND MAX, HYDROGENATION & HYDROGENOLYSIS, CATALYTIC REACTIONS. *Current Pos:* CONSULT, 81- *Personal Data:* b Murfreesboro, Tenn, Jan 12, 17; m 47, Elizabeth Walters; c Susan, Anne, Margaret & Myra. *Educ:* Vanderbilt Univ, BS, 38. *Prof Exp:* res assoc, Exxon Res & Eng Co, 39-71; proj mgr, Univ NDak, 72-78, adj prof chem eng, 75-81, prin investr, 79-81. *Concurrent Pos:* Consult synthetic fuels, 82- *Mem:* Fel AAAS; fel Am Inst Chemists; Am Inst Chem Engrs; Am Chem Soc; Sigma Xi; Nat Soc Prof Engrs. *Res:* Conversion of coal to premium solid, liquid or gaseous fuels. *Mailing Add:* 103 Nichols San Marcos TX 78666. *E-Mail:* msouby@centuryinter.net

SOUCIE, WILLIAM GEORGE, FOOD CHEMISTRY, BIOTECHNOLOGY. *Current Pos:* ASSOC DIR, BIOTECHNOLOGY, KRAFT GEN FOODS, 88- *Personal Data:* b Missoula, Mont, Mar 20, 42; m 66; c 4. *Educ:* Carroll Col, BA, 64; Incarnate Word Col, MS, 68; NC State Univ, PhD(biochem), 73. *Prof Exp:* Res assoc, Chem Dept, Univ Colo, 73-76; res scientist, Protein Prods Lab, Kraft Res & Develop, 76-77, group leader, 77-83, group leader, Basic Food Sci Lab, 83-85, sr group leader, 85-87, mgr, biotechnol dept, 87-88. *Concurrent Pos:* Instr, chem dept, Col Lake County, 81-83. *Mem:* Am Chem Soc; Inst Food Technol; Am Oil Chemists Soc. *Res:* Investigations into the electrical, physical and chemical properties of proteins as a basis for the use of proteins in human foods; colloid chemistry of food constituents; emulsion science; biotechnology applications to fats & oils, cheese and crops. *Mailing Add:* 6135 Brookview Dr West Des Moines IL 50266

SOUDACK, AVRUM CHAIM, ELECTRICAL ENGINEERING. *Current Pos:* assoc prof, 66-71, PROF ELEC ENG, UNIV BC, 71- *Personal Data:* b July 5, 34; Can citizen; m 78; c 4. *Educ:* Univ Man, BScEE, 57; Stanford Univ, MS, 59, PhD(elec eng), 61. *Honors & Awards:* Marv Emerson Award, Soc Comput Simulation, 72. *Prof Exp:* Asst prof elec eng, Univ BC, 61-65; vis asst prof, Univ Calif, Berkeley, 65-66. *Concurrent Pos:* Vis assoc prof, Israel Inst Technol, 69-70; vis prof, Weizmann Inst Sci, Israel, 74-75. *Mem:* Simulation Coun; Inst Elec & Electronic Engrs. *Res:* Approximate solution of nonlinear differential equations; analog and hybrid simulation of nonlinear systems; stability of harvested predator-prey systems; analytical solutions of ecological models; choas in nonlinear dynamic systems. *Mailing Add:* Dept Elec Eng Univ BC Rm 434 2356 Main Mall Vancouver BC V6T 1W5 Can

SOUDEK, DUSHAN EDWARD, MEDICAL CYTOGENETICS. *Current Pos:* prof, 69-87, EMER PROF, DEPT PSYCHIAT & PEDIAT, QUEEN'S UNIV, 87- *Personal Data:* b Prague, Czech, May 4, 20; m 47, Vera Pistecka; c Stefan (deceased), Dushan Jr & Ivan. *Educ:* Univ Brno, Czech, MD, 49, CScbiol, 56. *Honors & Awards:* S Moravian Province Prize, 62; Mendel Medal, Mendel's Mus, Brno, 65. *Prof Exp:* Asst prof biol, Univ Brno, Czech, 53-62, privatdocent, 64, head dept genetics, 63-68; vis scientist dept anat, Univ Western Ont, 68-69. *Concurrent Pos:* Res assoc, Ont Ment Health Found, 69-85. *Mem:* Am Soc Human Genetics. *Res:* Human cytogenetics; mental defects, normal variants, chromosomal evolution; structure of chromosomes and cell nucleus. *Mailing Add:* 371 Elmwood St Kingston ON K7M 2Z2 Can

SOUDER, PAUL A, ELEMENTARY PARTICLE PHYSICS, NUCLEAR PHYSICS. *Current Pos:* PROF PHYSICS, SYRACUSE UNIV, 88- *Personal Data:* b New Jersey, May 26,44. *Educ:* Wheaton Col, BS, 66; Princeton Univ, PhD(physics), 71. *Prof Exp:* Res assoc physics, Princeton Univ, 71-72; res staff physicist, Yale Univ, 72-75, from instr to assoc prof physics, 75-82. *Concurrent Pos:* Vis assoc prof physics, Harvard Univ, 82-83. *Mem:* Am Phys Soc. *Mailing Add:* Dept Physics Syracuse Univ 201 Physics Bldg Rm 321 Syracuse NY 13244

SOUDER, WALLACE WILLIAM, NUCLEAR PHYSICS, GEOPHYSICS. *Current Pos:* SR RES PHYSICIST, RES CTR, PHILLIPS PETROL CO, 69- *Personal Data:* b Columbus, Kans, June 12, 37; m 65; c 3. *Educ:* Kans State Col, BS, 60; Iowa State Univ, PhD(physics), 69. *Mem:* Am Phys Soc; Soc Explor Geophys; Soc Prof Well Log Analysts. *Res:* New techniques for mineral exploration. *Mailing Add:* 601 Oakridge Dr Bartlesville OK 74006

SOUFER, ROBERT, NUCLEAR CARDIOLOGY, POSITRON EMISSION TOMOGRAPHY. *Current Pos:* res fel cardiol, 84-85, asst prof radiol & med, 85-86, ASSOC PROF DIAG RADIOL & MED, YALE UNIV SCH MED, 90-; DIR VET ADMIN PET CTR YALE UNIV, 85- *Personal Data:* b Bronx, NY, Aug 19, 53; c Edward W & Aaron R. *Educ:* NY Univ, BA, 74; NY Med Col, MD, 78; Am Bd Internal Med, dipl & dipl cardiovasc, Bd Nuclear Med, dipl. *Prof Exp:* Med resident, Kings Co Hosp, New York, 81, chief med resident, 82. *Concurrent Pos:* Attend radiol & med serv, Yale-New Haven Hosp, 85-; mem, Vet Admin Hosp Radioisotope Comt, 85-91, Sci Subcomt, 85-91 & Resource Mgt Comt, 88-89; med ground rounds, Yale Univ, 88-, Waterbury Hosp, 90-93, St Vincents Hosp, 93; chmn, Vet Admin Hosp Task Force Admis, 90-91; mem, Coun Cardiovasc Radiol, Am Heart Asn, 93- *Mem:* Assoc mem Am Col Physicians; Am Fedn Clin Res; Soc Nuclear Med; fel Am Col Cardiol; Am Soc Nuclear Cardiol. *Res:* Neuropsychology of mental stress induced ischemia. *Mailing Add:* 950 Campbell Ave No 115A New Haven CT 06516. *Fax:* 203-937-4509; *E-Mail:* rsoufer@lbm.com

SOUHRADA, FRANK, CHEMICAL ENGINEERING. *Current Pos:* PRES, PROCESS ENGINEERING INC, 86- *Personal Data:* b Sluknov, Czech, Sept 22, 37; m 62; c 2. *Educ:* Inst Chem Technol, Prague, Dipl Ing, 61; Czech Acad Sci, PhD(chem eng), 64. *Prof Exp:* Res scientist, Inst Chem Process Fundamentals, Czech Acad Sci, 64-68; Nat Res Coun Can fel dynamic simulation, Univ NB, Fredericton, 68-70; res assoc fluidization, McMaster Univ, 70-71; process engr, Int Nickel Co, 71-74; sr res engr process develop, Gulf Can Res & Develop, 74-86. *Mem:* Can Soc Chem Engrs; Chem Inst Can. *Res:* Mass transfer; liquid-liquid extraction; ion exchange; fluidization; dynamic simulation; optimization; alternate energy sources; heavy oil and tar sands; heat and mass transfer; optimization; feasibility studies; new technology; flare systems. *Mailing Add:* Seven Totteridge Rd Islington ON M9A 1Y9 Can

SOUKOULIS, COSTAS M, INTERNATIONAL PHYSICS. *Current Pos:* assoc physicist & asst prof, 84-86, phycisist & assoc prof, 86-90, SR PHYSICIST & PROF PHYSICS, AMES LAB & DEPT PHYSICS, IOWA STATE UNIV, 90- *Personal Data:* b Agios Ioannis Corinthias, Greece, Jan 15, 51. *Educ:* Univ Athens, BS, 74; Univ Chicago, MS, 75, PhD(physics), 78. *Prof Exp:* Res & teaching asst, Dept Physics & James Franck Inst, Univ Chicago, 74-78, res assoc, 78; vis asst prof, Dept Physics, Univ Va, 78-81; res physicist, Corp Res Sci Labs, Exxon Res & Eng Co, 81-84. *Concurrent Pos:* Vis prof physics, Res Ctr Crete & Dept Physics, Univ Crete, Greece, 86-87, 91, Univ Karlsruhe, Ger, 91; Alexander von Humboldt fel, 91. *Mem:* Fel Am Phys Soc; Greek Europ Phys Soc. *Res:* Development of theoretical understanding of the properties of disordered systems; electron and photon localization; photonic band gaps; spin glasses; random fields; superconductivity; effects of disorder on nonlinear systems. *Mailing Add:* Dept Physics Iowa State Univ Ames IA 50011

SOUKUP, RODNEY JOSEPH, SOLAR CELL & THIN FILMS. *Current Pos:* assoc prof, 76-80, PROF ELEC ENG, UNIV NEBR, 80-, CHMN DEPT, 78- *Personal Data:* b Faribault, Minn, Mar 9, 39; m 65, Theresa M Rockers; c Richard J, Michael H & Stephen R. *Educ:* Univ Minn, Minneapolis, BS, 61, MSEE, 64, PhD(elec eng), 69. *Prof Exp:* Prin develop engr, Univac, Sperry Rand Corp, 69-71; instr elec eng, Univ Minn, 72; asst prof elec eng, Univ Iowa, 72-76. *Concurrent Pos:* Rockwell Int; chmn, Nat Elec Eng Dept Heads Asn, 90-91, chmn cent states, 93-94. *Mem:* Am Vacuum Soc; fel Inst Elec & Electronics Engrs; Am Soc Eng Educ. *Res:* Solar cells and scanning electron microscopy; physical electronics; thin film devices with a study of materials used and methods of fabrication. *Mailing Add:* Dept Elec Eng 212 N WSEC Univ Nebr Lincoln NE 68588-0511. *Fax:* 402-472-4732; *E-Mail:* eerdrjs@engums.unl.edu

SOULE, DAVID ELLIOT, PHYSICS. *Current Pos:* PROF PHYSICS, WESTERN ILL UNIV, 71- *Personal Data:* b Norwalk, Conn, Feb 24, 25; m 49; c 3. *Educ:* DePauw Univ, AB, 49; Northwestern Univ, MS, 51, PhD(physics), 54. *Prof Exp:* Res physicist, Union Carbide Lab, 54-66 & Douglas Aircraft Advan Res Lab, Calif, 66-71. *Concurrent Pos:* NSF fel, Royal Soc Mond Lab, Univ Cambridge, 61-62; sr vis Dept Sci & Indust Res fel, Dept Physics, Univ Sussex, 65. *Mem:* Am Phys Soc. *Res:* Solid state physics; transport properties; photoconductivity; susceptibility; low-temperature electronic properties such as deHaas-vanAlphen effect. *Mailing Add:* Dept Physics Western Ill Univ 900 W Adams St Macomb IL 61455-1328

SOULE, DOROTHY (FISHER), MARINE BIOLOGY. *Current Pos:* res assoc marine biol, Univ Southern Calif, 67-71, marine biol & pollution, 71-76, sr res scientist, 76-86, dir, Harbors Res Lab, 76-84, sr res scientist, 76-86, RES PROF BIOL SCI, HANCOCK INST MARINE SCI, UNIV SOUTHERN CALIF, 86-, DIR, HARBORS ENVIRON PROJS, 71-, CUR BRYOZOA, 64- *Personal Data:* b Lakewood, Ohio, Oct 8, 23; m 43, John D; c 2. *Educ:* Miami Univ, BA, 45; Occidental Col, MA, 63; Claremont Grad Sch, PhD, 69. *Prof Exp:* Res assoc biochem, Allan Hancock Found, Univ Southern Calif, 45-47; cur & instr comp anat, biol & microbiol, Occidental Col, 61-63; asst prof embryol, invert biol & zool, Calif State Col, Los Angeles, 63-65. *Concurrent Pos:* Independent consult, 61-; coordr, Environ Qual Projs, Univ Southern Calif-Sea Grant, 72-78, assoc dir, 74-76; mem, Eng Panel, Nat Acad Sci, 73-75; adj prof environ eng, Univ Southern Calif, 74-; mem, marine fish adv comt, Dept Com, 76-79, sci adv bd, Environ Protection Agency, 78-81, consult, 81-; vpres, SOS Environ, Inc, 78-; res assoc, Los Angeles Co Mus Natural Hist, 85-, Santa Barbara Mus Natural Hist, 87-; lectr physiol, Calif Col Med, 65-66. *Mem:* AAAS; Int Bryozool Asn; Am Soc Zool; Western Soc Naturalists; Sigma Xi; Pac Sci Asn. *Res:* Ecology and pollution in urban harbors, beaches and estuaries; effluent and ocean dumping pollution; environmental impact assessment and coordination; coral reef ecology, systematics and ecology of tropical, temperate Bryozoa; bryozoan development. *Mailing Add:* Allan Hancock Found Univ Southern Calif Los Angeles CA 90089-0371. *Fax:* 213-740-8123

SOULE, JAMES, horticulture; deceased, see previous edition for last biography

SOULE, JOHN DUTCHER, ZOOLOGY. *Current Pos:* RETIRED. *Personal Data:* b Moline, Ill, Oct 11, 20; m 43; c 2. *Educ:* Miami Univ, AB, 42; Univ Southern Calif, MS, 48, PhD(zool), 52. *Prof Exp:* Asst zool, Univ Southern Calif, 47, from instr to prof histol & path, Sch Dent, 50-91, prof biol, 70-91. *Concurrent Pos:* Res assoc, Am Mus Natural Hist, 61-, Los Angeles Co Mus Natural Hist, 85-, Santa Barbara Mus Nat Hist, 87-; Hancock Found res scholar, Univ Southern Calif, 52-; asst dean, Sch Dent, 78. *Mem:* Fel AAAS; Am Micros Soc; Am Soc Zool; Am Inst Biol Sci; Sigma Xi. *Res:* Taxonomy, histogenesis, postlarval development, histology, anatomy, ecology and reef communities of Bryozoa; histology and histochemistry of tooth development in fish, amphibia and reptiles. *Mailing Add:* 5451 Godbey Dr La Canada Flintridge CA 91011

SOULE, OSCAR HOMMEL, ECOLOGY, BIOLOGY. *Current Pos:* Acad dean, 72-73, MEM FAC ECOL, EVERGREEN STATE COL, 71- *Personal Data:* b St Louis, Mo, Oct 6, 40; m 71; c 2. *Educ:* Colo Col, BA, 62; Univ Ariz, MS, 64, PhD(ecol), 69. *Concurrent Pos:* Ford Found fel, Mo Bot Garden, 70-71; sr ecologist, HDR Ecosci, 77-80; partner, Lidman & Soule, Consults, 78-; vis prof, Colo Col, 79. *Mem:* AAAS; Ecol Soc Am; Brit Ecol Soc; Sigma Xi. *Res:* Terrestrial aspects of applied environmental studies; special interests in desert biology, urban ecology and environmental education. *Mailing Add:* Environ Studies Div Evergreen State Col Olympia WA 98505-0001

SOULE, ROGER GILBERT, EXERCISE PHYSIOLOGY. *Current Pos:* PROF, BIOLA UNIV, LA MIRADA, 79- *Personal Data:* b Northport, NY, Feb 21, 35; m 59, Janet C Frew; c 3. *Educ:* State Univ NY Col, Cortland, BS, 57; Univ Ill, MS, 58; Wash State Univ, PhD(exercise physiol), 67. *Prof Exp:* Instr phys educ & health, Dutchess Community Col, 60-64; instr phys educ, Wash State Univ, 64-67; from asst prof to assoc prof exercise physiol, Sargent Col, Boston Univ, 71-76; prof, Liberty Baptist Col, Va, 76-79. *Concurrent Pos:* Res physiologist, Natick Labs, 68-74. *Mem:* AAAS; Am Physiol Soc; Am Col Sports Med. *Res:* Energy cost of exercise; physical fitness levels of various populations; metabolic substrate utilization during exercise; control of temperature under exercise and environmental stress; body composition studies of selected athletic populations. *Mailing Add:* Dept Phys Educ Biola Univ 13800 Biola Ave La Mirada CA 90639-0001. *Fax:* 562-903-4890

SOULEN, JOHN RICHARD, PHYSICAL CHEMISTRY. *Current Pos:* PRES, TECH & MGT SERV, INC, 83- *Personal Data:* b Milwaukee, Wis, June 19, 27; m 55; c 3. *Educ:* Carroll Col, Wis, BA, 50; Univ Wis, PhD(phys chem), 55. *Prof Exp:* Asst chem, Univ Calif, 50-52 & Univ Wis, 52-54; res chemist, Penwalt Chems Corp, 55-59, proj leader, inorg res dept, 59-63, group leader, contract res dept, 63-68, dir contract res, 68-73, assoc mgr res & develop, 73-82. *Concurrent Pos:* Lectr, Univ Pa, 60-61. *Mem:* AAAS; Am Chem Soc. *Res:* Inorganic, high temperature and ultrahigh pressure chemistry; thermodynamics; spectroscopy; kinetics. *Mailing Add:* 5333 Hickory Bend Bloomfield Hills MI 48304-3735

SOULEN, RENATE LEROI, MEDICINE, RADIOLOGY. *Current Pos:* PROF RADIOL, WAYNE STATE UNIV, 89- *Personal Data:* b Berlin, Ger, June 10, 33; US citizen; m 55; c 3. *Educ:* NY Univ, BA, 53; Med Col Pa, MD, 57; Am Bd Radiol, dipl, 63. *Prof Exp:* Intern, Albert Einstein Med Ctr, 57-58; from resident to instr, Hosp, Jefferson Med Col, 59-63; from instr to prof radiol, Health Sci Ctr, Med Sch, Temple Univ, 63-85; prof radiol, Johns Hopkins Univ, 85-88. *Concurrent Pos:* Nat Cancer Inst fel, Hosp, Jefferson Med Col, 61-62; mem coun cardiovasc radio, Am Heart Asn. *Mem:* Fel Am Heart Asn; fel Am Col Radiol; Asn Univ Radiol; Radiol Soc NAm; Am Inst Ultrasonics in Med; Soc Magnetic Resonance Med. *Res:* Cardiovascular system. *Mailing Add:* Harper Hosp 3990 John Rd Detroit MI 48201-2018

SOULEN, ROBERT J, JR, CRYOGENIC PHYSICS. *Current Pos:* HEAD SUPERCONDUCTING MAT SECT, NAVAL RES LABS, 86- *Personal Data:* b Phoenixville, Pa, July 16, 40; m 63; c 2. *Educ:* Rutgers Univ, BA, 62, PhD(physics), 66. *Prof Exp:* proj leader cryogenic physics, Nat Bur Standards, 67-86. *Mem:* Fel Am Phys Soc. *Res:* Very low temperature techniques, and low temperature thermometry; superconductivity. *Mailing Add:* Naval Res Lab Code 6344 4555 Overlook Ave SW Washington DC 20375. *Fax:* 202-767-1697

SOULEN, ROBERT LEWIS, ORGANOFLUORINE CHEMISTRY. *Current Pos:* RETIRED. *Personal Data:* b Chicago, Ill, Jan 19, 32; m 54, Lola Hendrickson; c Karin E, Stephen L & Julie K. *Educ:* Baker Univ, AB, 54; Kans State Univ, PhD(org chem), 60. *Prof Exp:* From res chemist to sr res chemist, Austin Res Labs, Jefferson Chem Co Inc, Tex, 60-64; Lillian Nelson Pratt prof chem & chmn dept, Southwestern Univ, Tex, 64-96. *Concurrent Pos:* NSF grant, 66-67; Robert A Welch grant, 66-88; consult, Tex Res Inst; chmn, Local Sect Activ Comt, Am Chem Soc, 85-87, chmn, Nominations & Elections Comt, 90-94, bd trustees, Mem Ins Prog, 90-; bd dir, Chem Heritage Found, 96- *Mem:* Sigma Xi; fel AAAS; Am Chem Soc. *Res:* Exploratory and applications research in rigid and flexible polyurethane foams; polyolefine polymerization; vinyl halogen displacement reactions; synthesis of organofluorine derivatives; fluoropolymers. *Mailing Add:* Dept Chem Southwestern Univ Georgetown TX 78626. *Fax:* 512-863-2326

SOULEN, THOMAS KAY, BIOCHEMISTRY. *Current Pos:* asst prof, Univ Minn, Minneapolis, 64-69, ASSOC PROF BOT, UNIV MINN, ST PAUL, 69- *Personal Data:* b Waukesha, Wis, Apr 7, 35; m 58; c 3. *Educ:* Univ Wis, BA, 57, MS, 61, PhD(biochem), 63. *Prof Exp:* Asst prof bot, Univ Wis, 63-64. *Mem:* AAAS; Am Chem Soc; Am Soc Plant Physiologists; Sigma Xi. *Res:* Nitrogen metabolism of higher plants, especially with reference to development; growth and flowering of Lemnaceae. *Mailing Add:* Plant Biol Dept Univ of Minn St Paul MN 55108

SOULES, JACK ARBUTHNOTT, PHYSICS. *Current Pos:* dean col arts & sci, 68-81, PROF PHYSICS, CLEVELAND STATE UNIV, 81- *Personal Data:* b Ashtabula, Ohio, Jan 26, 28; m 49, 70; c 3. *Educ:* Ohio State Univ, BS, 48, MSc, 50, PhD(physics), 54. *Prof Exp:* Res assoc & asst instr, Ohio State Univ, 54-55; from asst prof to prof physics, NMex State Univ, 55-68. *Concurrent Pos:* Am Coun Educ fel acad admin, 65-66. *Mem:* Am Phys Soc. *Res:* Solid state physics; x-rays; biophysics; laser physics. *Mailing Add:* 3009 Van Aken Blvd Cleveland OH 44120-2816

SOULSBY, MICHAEL EDWARD, MEDICAL PHYSIOLOGY, BIOPHYSICS. *Current Pos:* asst prof physiol & biophys, 77-83, ASSOC PROF PHYSIOL, BIOPHYS & TOXICOL, UNIV ARK MED SCI, 84- *Personal Data:* b Montgomery, WVa, Sept 4, 41; m 83, Ruth Steelman; c Michael Jr, Paul C, Sean P & Kevin T. *Educ:* WVa Univ, AB, 63, MS, 68, PhD(biophysics), 71. *Prof Exp:* USPHS fel, Appalachian Lab Occup Respiratory Dis, 71-72; from instr to asst prof physiol, Va Commonwealth Univ, 72-76. *Concurrent Pos:* Consult, Gen Med Corp, 76-; prin investr, Heart, Lung & Blood Inst, NIH, 76-78 & Ark Br, Am Heart Asn, 78- *Mem:* Am Heart Asn; Am Physiol Soc; Biophys Soc; Sigma Xi. *Res:* Myocardial and vascular smooth muscle physiological and biophysical properties during ischemia, cardiovascular shock and hypertension. *Mailing Add:* Dept Physiol & Biophys Univ Ark Med Sci 4301 W Markham St Little Rock AR 72205-7101

SOUNDARARAJAN, RENGARAJAN, COMPREHENSIVE REMEDIATION OF RADIOACTIVE WASTE FORMS, RESOURCE RECOVERY OF RADIOACTIVE & OTHER METALS. *Current Pos:* DIR RES & DEVELOP, RMC ENVIRON & ANALYTICAL LABS INC, 85- *Personal Data:* b Nagapattinam, Feb 18, 50; US citizen; m 83, Barrylyn S Cook; c Merrill K & Trevor S. *Educ:* Madras Univ, BSc, 70, MSc, 75; Indian Inst Sci, PhD, 79. *Prof Exp:* Asst prof chem, Madras Univ, 75-79; assoc prof, Southeast Mo State Univ, 82-83; consult, Agro K Corp, 83-85. *Concurrent Pos:* Lab dir, Greene Co Health Dept, 84-85; asst prof, Drury Col, 83-85; instr, Southwest Mo State Univ, 85-87; grantee, US Environ Protection Agency, 87- *Mem:* Am Chem Soc. *Res:* Stabilization/solidification, resource recovery, remediation of radioactive tank wastes. *Mailing Add:* 1905 Way Haven St West Plains MO 65775. *Fax:* 417-256-1103

SOUNG, WEN Y, SOLID-LIQUID SEPARATION, FLUIDIZATION. *Current Pos:* FEL ENG, WESTINGHOUSE ELEC CORP, 86- *Personal Data:* b Tainan, Taiwan, Feb 14, 45; m 75; c 3. *Educ:* Nat Cheng-Kung Univ Taiwan, BS, 67, MS, 69; WVa Univ, PhD(chem eng), 73. *Prof Exp:* Sr process engr, Catalytic Inc, Philadelphia, Pa, 73-75; chem engr, Hydrocarbon Res Inc, Lawrenceville, NJ, 75-79; sr staff engr, Exxon Res & Eng Co, Bayton, Tex, 79-86. *Mem:* Am Inst Chem Eng; Asn Am Chinese Prof. *Res:* Process development and improvement for catalytical coal gasification and liquefaction processes, involving catalyst recovery from spent char, solid-liquid separation, ash utilization and new catalyst development for coal liquefaction. *Mailing Add:* 426 Oak Lawn Dr Pittsburgh PA 15241

SOURES, JOHN MICHAEL, LASER-MATTER INTERACTION, ULTRA-HIGH-POWER LASER DEVELOPMENT. *Current Pos:* Res assoc, Univ Rochester, 70-72, group leader, Glass Laser Develop, 75-78, group leader, Laser Fusion Exp, 78-81, SR SCIENTIST, LAB LASER ENERGETICS, UNIV ROCHESTER, 72-, DIV DIR, EXP DIV, 79-, DEP DIR, 83- *Personal Data:* b Galati, Roumania, Jan 2, 43; US citizen; m 69, Dana Carrousos; c Mandy, Nicholas, Eleni, Alexander & Sophia. *Educ:* Univ Rochester, BS, 65, MS, 67, PhD(mech & aerospace sci), 70. *Honors & Awards:* Award for Excellence in Plasma Physics Res, Am Phys Soc, 93. *Concurrent Pos:* Consult, Oak Ridge Nat Lab, 70-71, Link Found, 83-84, Eastman Kodak, 84-85 & Lawrence Livermore Nat Lab, 88-90. *Mem:* Am Phys Soc; Optical Soc Am; AAAS; NY Acad Sci. *Res:* Laser-driven inertial fusion, including plasma physics of high-temperature, high-density fusion plasmas; development of plasma diagnostic techniques; high-power solid-state laser development; laser-beam smoothing systems; non-linear optics. *Mailing Add:* 146 E Brook Rd Pittsford NY 14534. *Fax:* 716-256-2586

SOURKES, THEODORE LIONEL, BIOCHEMISTRY. *Current Pos:* sr res biochemist, McGill Univ, 53-65, dir lab chem neurobiol, Allan Mem Inst Psychiat & prof psychiat, Fac Med, 65-91, prof biochem, 70-91 & prof pharmacol, 90-91, EMER PROF BIOCHEM & PHARMACOL, MCGILL UNIV, 91- *Personal Data:* b Montreal, Que, Feb 21, 19; m 43; c Barbara & Myra (Lewin). *Educ:* McGill Univ, BSc, 39, MSc, 46; Cornell Univ, PhD(biochem), 48. *Hon Degrees:* D U, Ottawa Univ, 90. *Honors & Awards:* Heinz-Lehmann Award, Can Col Neuropsychopharmacol, 82, Medal, 90; Jasper Pub Lecture, Can Assoc for Neurosci, 87, Order Andres Bello, Govt Venezuela, 87; Officer of the Order of Can, 93. *Prof Exp:* Chemist, Gen Eng Co, Ont, 42-44; biochemist, Frank W Horner, Ltd, Que, 44-45; asst biochem, Cornell Univ, 46-48; asst prof pharmacol, Med Sch, Georgetown Univ, 48-50; sr res assoc, Merck Inst Therapeut Res, NJ, 50-53. *Concurrent Pos:* From instr to assoc prof psychiat, Fac Med, McGill Univ, 54-65; assoc scientist, Royal Victoria Hosp, 70 & assoc dean med, 72-75; sr fel Award, Parkinson's Dis Found, NY, 63-66; Raven Press lectr, Int Soc Neurochem, Singapore & India, 86. *Mem:* Am Soc Neurochem; Am Soc Biol Chem; Am Soc Pharmacol & Exp Therapeut; Can Biochem Soc; Royal Soc Can; Int Soc Neurochem; Int Brain Res Orgn; Soc Neurosci; hon mem Can Physiol Soc. *Res:* Catecholamines and other biogenic amines; amino acid decarboxylases; amine oxidases; biochemistry of extrapyramidal syndromes; central pathways of response to stress; copper metabolism; biochemistry of mental diseases; history of biochemistry; imaging of brain serotonin. *Mailing Add:* Dept Psychiat McGill Univ 1033 Pine Ave W Montreal PQ H3A 1A1 Can. *Fax:* 514-398-4370

SOURS, RICHARD EUGENE, MATHEMATICAL ANALYSIS. *Current Pos:* Instr math, 65-68 & 71-77, ASSOC PROF MATH & COMPUT SCI, WILKES COL, 77- *Personal Data:* b Baltimore, Md, Sept 5, 41; m 64; c 1. *Educ:* Towson State Teachers Col, BS, 63; Mich State Univ, MS, 65; Univ Va, PhD(math), 71. *Mem:* Am Math Soc; Math Asn Am; Sigma Xi. *Res:* Some aspects of integral operators on hilbert spaces. *Mailing Add:* Dept Math Wilkes Univ Wilkes-Barre PA 18766

SOUSA, LYNN ROBERT, ORGANIC CHEMISTRY & PHOTOCHEMISTRY, CROWN ETHER CHEMISTRY. *Current Pos:* from asst prof to assoc prof, 78-85, PROF CHEM, BALL STATE UNIV, 85-, DEPT CHAIR, 92- *Personal Data:* b Oakland, Calif, Apr 14, 43; m 64; c 1. *Educ:* Univ Calif, Davis, BSc, 66; Univ Wis, PhD(org chem), 71. *Prof Exp:* Fel org chem, Univ Calif, Los Angeles, 71-73; asst prof, Mich State Univ, 73-78. *Concurrent Pos:* Bye fel, Robinson Col, Cambridge Univ, 91. *Mem:* Am Chem Soc. *Res:* Organic chemistry; synthesis and study of crown ether compounds applications of complexation by crown ethers in organic chemistry; especially those bearing chromophores that exhibit flurescence which is turned on or turned off by complexed actions. *Mailing Add:* Dept Chem Ball State Univ Muncie IN 47306

SOUTAS-LITTLE, ROBERT WILLIAM, BIODYNAMICS, TISSUE BIOMECHANICS. *Current Pos:* Assoc dir applied math, Mich State Univ, 65-67, chmn, dept mech eng, 72-77, chmn, dept biomech, 77-90, from asst prof to assoc prof, 65-70, prof, Dept Biomech, 70-93, DIR, PROF, DEPT MAT SCI & MECH, MICH STATE UNIV, 70-, BIOMECH EVAL LAB, 89- *Personal Data:* b Oklahoma City, Okla, Feb 25, 33; m 82, Patricia; c Deborah, Colleen, Karen, Catherine & Jennifer. *Educ:* Duke Univ, BS, 55; Univ Wis, MS, 59, PhD(mech), 62. *Concurrent Pos:* Consult, Lawrence Livermore Lab, Univ Calif, 77-78 & Biomech Interface, 84-; legal expert witness, 76- *Mem:* Sigma Xi; Am Soc Biomechanics; Soc Eng Sci; fel Am Soc Mech Eng; Am Col Sports Med. *Res:* Tissue mechanics; body dynamics; orthopedics; sports medicine and rehabilitation. *Mailing Add:* Dept Mat Sci & Mech Mich State Univ East Lansing MI 48824. Fax: 517-336-2767

SOUTH, FRANK E, PHYSIOLOGY. *Current Pos:* dir, 77-82, PROF, SCH LIFE & HEALTH SCI, UNIV DEL, 82- *Personal Data:* b Norfolk, Nebr, Sept 20, 24; m 46; c 2. *Educ:* Univ Calif, AB, 49, PhD(physiol), 52. *Prof Exp:* Jr res physiologist, Univ Calif, 52-53; asst prof physiol, Univ PR, 53-54, Col Med, Univ Ill, 54-61; from asst prof to prof, Colo State Univ, 61-65; prof physiol & investr, Dalton Res Ctr, Univ Mo-Columbia, 65-77. *Concurrent Pos:* NIH sr res fel, 61-65; co-dir, Hibernation Info Exchange, Off Naval Res; mem bd dirs, Int Hibernation Soc, 65- *Mem:* Fel AAAS; Am Physiol Soc; Am Soc Zool; Soc Cryobiol; Soc Gen Physiol; Int Hibernation Soc. *Res:* Environmental physiology; hibernation, hypothermia, acclimatization and adaptations to extreme environments; neurophysiology, thermoregulation and physiology of marine mammals; history of physiology and medicine. *Mailing Add:* 208 Sunset Rd Newark DE 19711-4525

SOUTH, GRAHAM ROBIN, PHYCOLOGY. *Current Pos:* DIR & PROF MARINE STUDIES, UNIV SPAC, 90-, DIR INT OCEAN INST OPER CTR, 93- *Personal Data:* b Thorpe, Eng, Oct 27, 40; m 66; c 2. *Educ:* Liverpool Univ, BS, 63, PhD(marine algal ecol), 66, DSc, 90. *Prof Exp:* NATO fel phycol, Univ BC, 66-67; from asst prof to assoc prof biol, Mem Univ Nfld, 67-76, assoc cur herbarium, 67-71, cur herbarium, 71-90, head, Dept Biol, 76-84, prof biol, 76-90. *Concurrent Pos:* Res fel, Edward Percival Marine Lab, Univ Canterbury, NZ, 73-74; ed, Phycologia, 77-82, assoc ed, 83-90; pres, Coun Can Univ Biol Chmn, 82-84; pres, Biol Coun Can, 82-84; assoc ed, Can J Bot, 83-89; dir, Huntsman Marine Sci Ctr, St Andrews, NB, Can, 85-90; chmn, Int Orgn Comt, Int Phycological Cong, 85-91; mem, Can Nat Comt, Int Union Biol Sci. *Mem:* Phycol Soc Am; Int Phycol Soc; Marine Biol Soc UK; Brit Phycol Soc; hon foreign mem, Societas pro Fauna et Flora Fennica. *Res:* Ecology, distribution, taxonomy biology and aquaculture of benthic marine algae; aquaculture. *Mailing Add:* Univ SPac Marine Studies Prog PO Box 1168 Suva Fiji. *Fax:* 679-301490; *E-Mail:* south_r@usp.ac.fj

SOUTH, HUGH MILES, DIGITAL SIGNAL PROCESSING, SONAR SYSTEMS ANALYSIS. *Current Pos:* Instr elec eng, Johns Hopkins Univ, 73-75, sr engr, Appl Physics Lab, 75-82, supvr, Span Lab, 79-85, PRIN ENGR, JOHNS HOPKINS UNIV, 82-, SUPVR, SIGNAL PROCESSING GROUP & LECTR ELEC ENG, 85-, MGR, AUTOMATED SURVEILLANCE PROJ, 90- *Personal Data:* b Houston, Tex, Nov 10, 47; m 76. *Educ:* Rice Univ, BA, 71; Johns Hopkins Univ, PhD(elec eng), 81. *Concurrent Pos:* Mem, Underwater Acoust Tech Comt, Inst Elec & Electronics Engrs Acoust, Speech & Signal Processing Soc. *Mem:* Inst Elec & Electronics Engrs; Acoust Soc Am; Sigma Xi. *Res:* Design of hardware and software systems for digital signal processing; beam forming; spectral estimation. *Mailing Add:* 11166 Woodelves Way Columbia MD 21044-1090. *E-Mail:* hugh.south@jhuapl.edu

SOUTH, MARY ANN, PEDIATRICS, IMMUNOLOGY & INFECTIOUS DISEASES. *Current Pos:* prof pediat, 86-89, DISTINGUISHED PROF PEDIAT, W K KELLOGG FOUND MEHARRY MED COL, 89- *Personal Data:* b Portales, NMex, May 23, 33; m 83; c 2. *Educ:* Eastern NMex Univ, BA, 55; Baylor Univ, MD, 59. *Prof Exp:* Intern, Presby-St Luke's Hosp, Chicago, 59-60; resident pediat, Baylor Univ, 60-62, fel, Infectious Dis, Col Med, 62-64; fel & instr immunol, Univ Minn, Minneapolis, 64-66; from asst prof to assoc prof, Col Med, Baylor Univ, 66-73; assoc prof pediat, Univ Pa, 73-77; chmn, dept pediat, Sch Med, Tex Tech Univ, 78-79, res prof pediat, 79-82; med officer, Neurol Inst, NIH, 82-85. *Concurrent Pos:* USPHS res career develop award, 68-73. *Mem:* Am Asn Immunol; Am Pediat Soc; Infectious Dis Soc Am; Am Med Women's Asn; Int Soc Exp Hemat; Soc Gnotobiol. *Res:* Pediatric immunology; immune deficiency diseases; congenital infections. *Mailing Add:* Dept Pediat Meharry Med Col 1005 D B Todd Blvd Nashville TN 37208

SOUTHAM, CHESTER MILTON, ONCOLOGY, GERIATRICS. *Current Pos:* head div med oncol, 71-79, PROF MED, JEFFERSON MED COL, 71- *Personal Data:* b Salem, Mass, Oct 4, 19; m 39; c 3. *Educ:* Univ Idaho, BS, 41, MS, 43; Columbia Univ, MD, 47. *Prof Exp:* Intern med, Presby Hosp, NY, 47-48; instr, Med Col, Cornell Univ, 51-52, from asst prof to assoc prof, Sloan-Kettering Div, 52-71. *Concurrent Pos:* Am Cancer Soc res fel, Mem Ctr Cancer & Allied Dis, 48-49; Damon Runyon Fund clin res fel, 49-51, sr res fel, 51-52; asst, Sloan-Kettering Inst, 49-52, assoc & head clin virol sect, 52-63, mem, 63-71; asst attend physician, Mem Hosp, New York City, 52-58, assoc attend physician, 59-71; asst vis physician, James Ewing Hosp, 52-59, assoc vis physician, 59-71; mem bd dirs, Am Asn Cancer Res, 66-70. *Mem:* Am Col Physicians; Am Asn Cancer Res (pres, 68-69); Am Fedn Clin Res; Am Asn Immunol; Am Soc Exp Path. *Res:* Clinical oncology; immunology; chemotherapy of cancer; oncolytic and oncogenic viruses; transplantation and tissue culture of human cancer; cancer immunology; carcinogenesis. *Mailing Add:* Jefferson Med Col 1025 Walnut St Philadelphia PA 19107-5001

SOUTHAM, DONALD LEE, MECHANICAL ENGINEERING. *Current Pos:* RETIRED. *Personal Data:* b Cleveland, Ohio, Aug 28, 29; m 52, Gloria Schadel; c Robert E & Linda (Merriam). *Educ:* Case Western Reserve Univ, BS, 51, MS, 54. *Prof Exp:* Designer eng, The Yoder Co, 51-53; chief engr, TRW, Inc, 53-66; vpres eng, Harris Corp, 66-74; vpres eng, Cast Equip Div, Combustion Eng, Inc, 74-82, pres, 82-91. *Res:* Research and development of aircraft fuel systems, space power systems, commercial printing presses and automated foundry equipment. *Mailing Add:* 10325 Whitewood Rd Cleveland OH 44141

SOUTHAM, FREDERICK WILLIAM, EXTRACTIVE METALLURGY OF ALUMINUM. *Current Pos:* RETIRED. *Personal Data:* b NS, July 2, 24; m 47, Merle E Shaver; c 3. *Educ:* Queen's Univ, Can, BSc, 46, MSc, 47; Mass Inst Technol, PhD(phys chem), 50. *Prof Exp:* Group leader, Electrometall Div, Aluminum Labs, Ltd, 50-71; sect head res lab, 71-72, Aluminum Co Can, sr tech consult, 72-85. *Concurrent Pos:* Mem, Grants Comt Chem & Metall Eng, Nat Res Coun Can, 70-73; consult, 85- *Mem:* Fel Chem Inst Can; Can Soc Chem Eng. *Res:* Processes associated with production of aluminum; heat and mass transfer; high temperature reaction kinetics; environmental control. *Mailing Add:* 36 Van Order Dr Kingston ON K7M 1B7 Can

SOUTHAM, JOHN RALPH, MARINE GEOLOGY. *Current Pos:* fel, 74, ASSOC PROF MARINE GEOL, ROSENSTIEL SCH MARINE & ATMOSPHERIC SCI, UNIV MIAMI, 75- *Personal Data:* b Youngstown, Ohio, Oct 30, 42. *Educ:* Purdue Univ, BSEE, 65, MSEE, 67; Univ Ill, MS, 69, PhD(physics), 74. *Prof Exp:* Aerospace scientist, Lewis Res Ctr, NASA, 67. *Mem:* AAAS; Am Geophys Union; Europ Geophys Soc; Int Asn Math Geol; Am Phys Soc. *Res:* Dynamic modelling of marine systems incorporating chemical, physical and biological processes; deep sea sedimentation and sedimentation processes in lakes and enclosed seas. *Mailing Add:* Univ Miami PO Box 248106 Miami FL 33124-8106

SOUTHARD, ALVIN REID, SOIL SCIENCE, GEOLOGY. *Current Pos:* from assoc prof to prof soil sci &biometeorol, 67-89, head dept, 83-89, EMER PROF, UTAH STATE UNIV, 89- *Personal Data:* b Centertown, Ky, June 30, 26; m 50; c 4. *Educ:* Utah State Univ, BS, 57, MS, 58; Cornell Univ, PhD(soil classification), 63. *Prof Exp:* From asst prof to assoc prof soils, Mont State Univ, 63-67. *Concurrent Pos:* Exp sta rep, Nat Coop Soil Surv, Mont, 63-67 & Utah, 67-; conservationist, US Agency Int Develop, Ecuador; Fulbright sr res scholar, Australia, 81; consult OICD, Peoples Repub China, 82. *Mem:* Am Soc Agron. *Res:* Soil genesis and classification in Utah, New York and Montana; soils of the alpine tundra in Alaska; soils of wet and dry tropics in Ecuador, Brazil, Mauritania, Hawaii & Australia. *Mailing Add:* 940 River Heights Blvd Logan UT 84321

SOUTHARD, JOHN BRELSFORD, GEOLOGY. *Current Pos:* from asst prof to assoc prof, 67-85, PROF GEOL, MASS INST TECHNOL, 85-; MAVICAR FAC FEL, 92- *Personal Data:* b Baltimore, Md, May 21, 38; m 60; c 2. *Educ:* Mass Inst Technol, SB, 60; Harvard Univ, MA, 63, PhD(geol), 66. *Prof Exp:* NSF fel, Calif Inst Technol, 66-67. *Mem:* AAAS; Geol Soc Am; Am Geophys Union; Int Asn Sedimentol; Soc Econ Paleontologists & Mineralogists. *Res:* Physical sedimentology; mechanics of sediment transport; marine geology; fluvial geomorphology. *Mailing Add:* Dept Earth Sci Mass Inst Technol 77 Massachusetts Ave Cambridge MA 02139-4307

SOUTHARD, WENDELL HOMER, BIOCHEMISTRY. *Current Pos:* from asst prof to prof, 67-89, EMER PROF PHARMACEUT CHEM, COL PHARM, DRAKE UNIV, 89- *Personal Data:* b Des Moines, Iowa, July 21, 27. *Educ:* Drake Univ, BS, 50; Univ Ill, MS, 53, PhD(biol chem), 60. *Prof Exp:* Asst pharm, Univ Ill, 50-51; instr mfg pharm, 51-55; pharm, 55-56. *Res:* Carbohydrate and microbial metabolism; manufacturing pharmacy. *Mailing Add:* 1542 Wilson Ave Des Moines IA 50316

SOUTHARDS, CARROLL J, NEMATOLOGY, PLANT PATHOLOGY. *Current Pos:* from asst prof to assoc prof plant path, 65-74, PROF AGR BIOL & HEAD DEPT, INST AGR, UNIV TENN, KNOXVILLE, 74- *Personal Data:* b Bryson City, NC, June 18, 32; m 56; c 3. *Educ:* NC State Univ, BS, 54, MS, 61, PhD(plant path), 65. *Prof Exp:* Asst county agr agent, NC Agr Exten Serv, 57-59; res asst hort, NC State Univ, 59-61, plant path, 61-65. *Mem:* Am Soc Phytopathologists; Soc Nematologists; Sigma Xi; Entom Soc Am. *Res:* Host-parasite relationships of tobacco, soybeans and vegetable crops and root-knot and cyst nematodes; host resistance; variability of root-knot nematodes. *Mailing Add:* Univ Tenn PO Box 1071 Knoxville TN 37901

SOUTHERLAND, WILLIAM M, SULFER METABOLISM. *Current Pos:* ASSOC PROF BIOCHEM, COL MED, HOWARD UNIV, 83- *Educ:* Duke Univ, PhD(biochem), 77. *Res:* Enzymology of sulfur metabolism; toxicity of sulfur oxides. *Mailing Add:* Dept Biochem Howard Univ Col Med 520 W St NW Washington DC 20059-0001. *Fax:* 302-806-5784

SOUTHERN, BYRON WAYNE, CONDENSED MATTER PHYSICS. *Current Pos:* PROF PHYSICS, UNIV MAN, 79- *Personal Data:* b Toronto, Ont, June 13, 46; m 71; c 3. *Educ:* York Univ, BSc, 69; McMaster Univ, MSc, 71, PhD(physics), 73. *Prof Exp:* Nat Res Coun Can fel physics, Imp Col Sci & Technol, London, Eng, 73-75; res physicist, Inst Laue Langevin, Grenoble, France, 75-79. *Mem:* Can Asn Physicists; Am Phys Soc. *Mailing Add:* Dept Physics Univ Man Winnipeg MB R3T 2N2 Can

SOUTHERN, L LEE, AMINO ACID & TRACE MINERAL NUTRITION OF PIGS & CHICKENS. *Current Pos:* from asst prof to assoc prof, 82-92, PROF ANIMAL SCI & NUTRIT, AGR CTR, LA STATE UNIV, 92- *Personal Data:* b Dobson, NC, Apr 11, 55; m 79, Denise Rossignol; c Michelle & Nicole. *Educ:* NC State Univ, BS, 77, MS, 79; Univ Ill, PhD(animal sci), 83. *Honors & Awards:* Award in Nonruminant Nutrit Res, Am Feed Indust Asn-Am Sci Animal Soc, 97. *Mem:* Am Soc Animal Sci; Poultry Sci Asn; Am Inst Nutrit. *Res:* Increasing the efficiency of lean meat production in nonruminant animals; evaluate the effect of chromium on glucose metabolism and to evaluate the use of amino acids in diets for nonruminants. *Mailing Add:* Dept Animal Sci La State Univ Baton Rouge LA 70803. *Fax:* 504-388-3279; *E-Mail:* lsouthern@agctr.lsu.edu

SOUTHERN, THOMAS MARTIN, TECHNICAL MANAGEMENT, QUALITY ASSURANCE STANDARDS. *Current Pos:* Chemist & qual control mgr, Tex Eastman Co, 69-80, mgr plastics prod develop & polyethylene qual mgr develop, 80-89, mgr polyethylene qual control & sr chemist analytical qual assurance, 89-91, prin chemist, Stand Lab, 91-93, PRIN CHEMIST QUAL ASSURANCES, PLASTICS DIV, TEX EASTMAN CO, 93- *Personal Data:* b Beaumont, Tex, June 19, 42; m 66, Barbara M Lewis; c Michellea & John W. *Educ:* Lamar Univ, BS, 64; Tex Tech Univ, MS, 66; Univ Houston, PhD(analytical chem), 69; Southern Methodist Univ, MBA, 77. *Concurrent Pos:* Pres & chmn, Cardinal Premium Finance, Longview, Tex. *Mem:* Am Soc Qual Control. *Res:* Liquid chromatography; thermoanalytical chemistry; application of computers dedicated to analytical instruments and data reduction; hot melt adhesives-formulation and application; computers; quality systems and standards. *Mailing Add:* Sr Chemist Qual Assurance PO Box 7444 Longview TX 75601. *E-Mail:* southern@eastman.com

SOUTHERN, WILLIAM EDWARD, ORNITHOLOGY, WETLAND SCIENCE. *Current Pos:* RETIRED. *Personal Data:* b Wayne Co, Mich, Dec 22, 33; m; c 3. *Educ:* Cent Mich Univ, BS, 55; Univ Mich, MA, 59; Cornell Univ, PhD(comp vert ethol, animal ecol, wildlife mgt), 67. *Honors & Awards:* Hann lectr, Biol Sta, Univ Mich, 73; Ernest P Edwards Prize, Wilson Ornith Soc, 75. *Prof Exp:* Pub sch teacher, Mich, 55-56 & 57-58; asst prof biol sci, Northern Ill Univ, 59-68,; assoc prof biol sci, Univ Mich Biol Sta, 68-72, prof ornith, 75-78; prof avian behav ecol, Northern Ill Univ, 72-90, dir coop educ prog, 84-90. *Concurrent Pos:* Grants, NSF, 59, 62 & 71-73, Frank M Chapman Mem Fund, 61-64 & 65, Sigma Xi, 61, 63-64 & 68-69, Northern Ill Univ, 62, 65, 67-68, 69, 72 & 76-77, Brown Fund, Cornell Univ, 63-64, sci fac fel, 63-64, desert biol fel, 65, Max McGraw Wildlife Found, 68-70, Off Naval Res, 71-72, Ill Dept Conserv, 73-74 & 81-85 & Nat Park Serv, 74-82; pres, Encap Inc, 74-94; mem, Ill Endangered Species Protection Bd, exec secy, 76-; USAF off sci res, 77-79; US Dept Educ, 84-90. *Mem:* Sigma Xi; Soc Wetland Scientists; Am Ornithologists Union; Nat Asn Environ Professionals; Wilson Ornith Soc; Cooper Ornithologists Soc. *Res:* Bird/ riveraft collision issues; avian behavior, ecology and population dynamics; environmental assessments; endangered species issues; wetland delineation; mitigation and management. *Mailing Add:* 400 E Hillcrest Dr De Kalb IL 60115

SOUTHGATE, PETER DAVID, PHYSICS. *Current Pos:* MEM TECH STAFF, DAVID SARNOFF RES CTR, 66- *Personal Data:* b Woking, Eng, July 20, 28; m 52; c 4. *Educ:* Univ London, BSc, 48, MSc, 52, PhD(physics), 59. *Prof Exp:* Res scientist, Mullard Res Labs, Eng, 48-58; res physicist, Res Inst, Ill Inst Technol, 59-65. *Mem:* Am Phys Soc. *Res:* Luminescence and recombination processes in semiconductors and organic materials; non-linear optical interactions in crystals; ferroelectric and pyroelectric phenomena and their application to radiation detection; acoustoelectric interactions in semiconductors; analysis of television tube and videodisc manufacturing processes. *Mailing Add:* David Sarnoff Res Ctr Princeton NJ 08543-5300

SOUTHIN, JOHN L, genetics, for more information see previous edition

SOUTHREN, A LOUIS, MOLECULAR BIOLOGY. *Current Pos:* From asst prof med & asst attend physician to assoc prof med & assoc attend physician, 61-69, PROF MED & ATTEND PHYSICIAN, NEW YORK MED COL, 69-, RES PROF OPHTHAL, 79-, CHIEF DIV ENDOCRINOL/ METABOLISM, 63-, PROF OBSTET & GYNEC (ENDOCRINOL). *Personal Data:* b New York, NY, Oct 12, 26; m 50; c 3. *Educ:* NY Univ, AB, 49; Chicago Med Sch, MD, 55. *Concurrent Pos:* Fel endocrinol, Mt Sinai Hosp, NY, 58-59; fel endocrine res, Jewish Hosp Brooklyn, 59-61; fel, training prog steroid biochem, Worcester Found Exp Biol, 61-62; USPHS res grants, 63-; career scientist, Health Res Coun of NY, 63-72 & 74-75; dir, USPHS Training Prog Endocrinol & Metab, 65-72; mem glaucoma panel, Nat Adv Eye Coun, 80-81; NY Med Col dean's distinguished res award, 93. *Mem:* AAAS; fel Am Col Physicians; Endocrine Soc; Soc Gynec Invest; Am Fertil Soc. *Res:* Glucocorticoid metabolism in glaucoma. *Mailing Add:* NY Med Col Valhalla NY 10595

SOUTHWARD, GLEN MORRIS, STATISTICS, SAMPLING. *Current Pos:* assoc prof, 75-80, PROF EXP STATIST, NMEX STATE UNIV, 80- *Personal Data:* b Boise, Idaho, Oct 8, 27; c 2. *Educ:* Univ Wash, BS, 49, MS, 56, PhD, 66. *Prof Exp:* Biologist, Int Pac Halibut Comn, 55-67; asst prof statist & asst statistician, Wash State Univ, 67-70 & Univ Wis, 70-71; biometrician, Int Pac Halibut Comn, 71-75. *Concurrent Pos:* Vis prof, Dept Statist, Univ Edinburgh, 81-82. *Mem:* Am Inst Fisheries Res Biologists; Am Statist Asn; Biomet Soc. *Res:* Biometry; experimental statistics, biomathematics, statistical consulting; sampling. *Mailing Add:* Dept Exp Statist NMex State Univ Dept 3130 Box 30003 Las Cruces NM 88003

SOUTHWARD, HAROLD DEAN, NUCLEAR PHYSICS, SOLID STATE PHYSICS. *Current Pos:* assoc prof, 63-69, dir, Bur Eng Res, 71-76, PROF ELEC ENG, UNIV NMEX, 69-, CHMN ELEC ENG & COMPUT SCI, 81- *Personal Data:* b Headrick, Okla, June 22, 30; m 54; c 4. *Educ:* WTex State Univ, BS, 51; Univ Tex, MA, 57, PhD(physics), 58. *Prof Exp:* Engr, Aircraft Armaments, Inc, 54-55; sr res technologist, Mobil Oil Corp, 58-63. *Mem:* Am Phys Soc; Inst Elec & Electronics Engrs. *Res:* Radiation effects of solid state electronics; radiation measurement; photovoltaic energy systems. *Mailing Add:* 1308 Evelyn Ct NE No NE Albuquerque NM 87112

SOUTHWELL, P(ETER) H(ENRY), MECHANICAL & AGRICULTURAL ENGINEERING. *Current Pos:* RETIRED. *Personal Data:* b Rochdale, Eng, Nov 29, 24; m 46; c 4. *Educ:* Royal Naval Eng Col, Eng, Engr, 45; Univ Sask, MSc, 60. *Honors & Awards:* Pilcher Mem Prize, Royal Aeronaut Soc, 52. *Prof Exp:* Eng officer, Nat Inst Agr Eng, Eng, 48-54; asst prof eng sci, Univ Guelph, 55-60, assoc prof, Sch Eng, 61-88. *Concurrent Pos:* Chmn, Assoc Comt Agr & Forestry Aviation, Nat Res Coun Can, 66-72; mem, Energy & Agr Policy Comt, Ont Govt, 80-81. *Mem:* Can Soc Agr Engrs; Am Soc Agr Engrs; assoc fel Royal Aeronaut Soc; Inst Mech Engrs. *Res:* Combustion engines and turbines; terrain-vehicle systems and terra-mechanics; agricultural aviation; pesticides application systems; energy analysis and energy ratios of food production; biomass fuels. *Mailing Add:* RR 1 Rockwood ON N0B 2K0 Can

SOUTHWICK, CHARLES HENRY, PRIMATE ECOLOGY. *Current Pos:* prof epo biol, 79-93, EMER PROF EPO BIOL, UNIV COLO, 93- *Personal Data:* b Wooster, Ohio, Aug 28, 28; m 52, Heather Milne Beck; c Steven & Karen. *Educ:* Col Wooster, BA, 49; Univ Wis, MS, 51, PhD(zool), 53. *Honors & Awards:* Distinguished Primatologist Award, Am Soc Primatol, 95. *Prof Exp:* Asst prof biol, Hamilton Col, 53-54; NSF fel, Bur Animal Pop, Oxford Univ, 54-55; from asst prof to assoc prof zool, Ohio Univ, 55-61; from assoc prof to prof pathobiol, Sch Hyg & Pub Health, Johns Hopkins Univ, 61-79. *Concurrent Pos:* Mem numerous primate expeds, Panama, India, Nepal, Indonesia, Malaysia, Burma, China, Kenya, 51-96; Fulbright fel, Aligarh Muslim Univ, India, 59-60; mem, Calif Primate Res Ctr, 74-76 & Gov Sci Adv Coun, Md, 75-77; mem, Primate Adv Cmt, Nat Acad Sci, Nat Res Coun & Adv Bd, Caribbean Primate Res Ctr, Cmt Res & Explor, Nat Geog Soc. *Mem:* Fel AAAS; Ecol Soc Am; Am Soc Mammal; Am Soc Zoologists; fel Animal Behav Soc (pres, 68); Am Soc Primate; Int Primate Soc; Sigma Xi; fel Acad Zool. *Res:* Vertebrate population dynamics; sociobiology and animal behavior, especially behavioral ecology; global ecology; primatology. *Mailing Add:* 6507 Baseline Rd Boulder CO 80303

SOUTHWICK, DAVID LEROY, PRECAMBRIAN GEOLOGY, TECTONICS. *Current Pos:* sr geologist, 77-89, ASST DIR & RES ASSOC, MINN GEOL SURV, 89- *Personal Data:* b Rochester, Minn, Aug 30, 36; m 59; c 3. *Educ:* Carleton Col, BA, 58; Johns Hopkins Univ, PhD(geol), 62. *Prof Exp:* Geologist, US Geol Surv, 62-68; from asst prof to prof geol, Macalester Col, 68-77. *Concurrent Pos:* Adj assoc prof, Univ Minn, 83- *Mem:* Am Geophys Union; fel Geol Soc Am; fel Geol Asn Can. *Res:* Petrology of metamorphic and igneous rocks; structural geology; stratigraphy and structural geology of the Precambrian rocks of Minnesota. *Mailing Add:* 764 Fairmount Ave St Paul MN 55105

SOUTHWICK, EDWARD E, GROUP INTELLIGENCE & ADAPTATION, SUPERORGANISMS. *Current Pos:* assoc prof, 77-85, PROF BIOL, STATE UNIV NY, BROCKPORT, 85- *Personal Data:* b Northampton, Mass. *Educ:* Univ Mich, BSME, 65, MS, 67; Wash State Univ, PhD(zool), 71. *Prof Exp:* Asst prof biol, Duquesne Univ, 71-73; lectr physiol ecol, Grad Sch, Georgetown Univ, 74-75; dir, Chippewa Nature Ctr, Inc, 75-77. *Concurrent Pos:* Prin investr, NSF res grant, 80; Mellon Found fel microclimate & pollination, 81-83; Alexander von Humboldt fel, 83, 84, 88; prin investr, NATO res, 88; fac exchange scholar, 90. *Mem:* Int Union Study Social Insects; Sigma Xi; Int Bee Res Asn; Entom Soc Am. *Res:* Melittology; nectar biology and nutrition; plant insect relationships; pollination ecology; microclimates; cold temperature physiology; animal energetics including energy balance; thermoregulation and metabolism, especially in social insects; superorganism attributes of social insects. *Mailing Add:* Dept Biol Sci State Univ NY Col Brockport 350 New Campus Dr Brockport NY 14420-2915. *Fax:* 716-395-2416; *E-Mail:* esouthwi@acspr1.acs.brockport.edu

SOUTHWICK, EVERETT WEST, ORGANIC CHEMISTRY. *Current Pos:* CHEMIST, PHILIP MORRIS USA, 80- *Personal Data:* b Providence, RI, Sept 19, 41; m 83; c 2. *Educ:* Univ RI, BA, 63; Univ NH, PhD(org chem), 73. *Prof Exp:* Fel org chem, State Univ NY, Buffalo, 72-74, Duke Univ, 73-74; sr chemist, Liggett & Myres Inc, 74-80. *Mem:* Am Chem Soc; Am Chem Soc. *Res:* Synthesis, isolation, purification and characterization of organic compounds of potential value as flavorants; structure-activity; relations in olfaction. *Mailing Add:* 1211 W 43rd St Richmond VA 23225

SOUTHWICK, FRANKLIN WALLBURG, POMOLOGY. *Current Pos:* RETIRED. *Personal Data:* b Boston, Mass, May 29, 17; m 40; c 4. *Educ:* Mass State Col, BS, 39; Ohio State Univ, MS, 40; Cornell Univ, PhD(pomol), 43. *Honors & Awards:* Gold Medal, Mass Soc Promoting Agr, 65. *Prof Exp:* Asst prof pomol, Univ Conn, 43-45 & Cornell Univ, 45-48; head, Dept Plant & Soil Sci, Univ Mass, Amherst, 64-77, dir grad prof, 73-80, prof pomol, 48-83. *Mem:* AAAS; fel Am Soc Hort Sci. *Res:* Fruit storage; respiration; growth regulating substances; nutrition. *Mailing Add:* 993 E Pleasant Amherst MA 01002

SOUTHWICK, HARRY W, surgery; deceased, see previous edition for last biography

SOUTHWICK, LAWRENCE, AGRONOMY, HORTICULTURE. *Current Pos:* RETIRED. *Personal Data:* b Worcester, Mass, Apr 6, 12; m 37; c 3. *Educ:* Univ Mass, BS, 33, MS, 38. *Prof Exp:* Instr, Univ Mass, 35-45; bioprod res & develop chemist & tech ed, Dow Chem Co, 45-80. *Mem:* Am Soc Agron; fel Weed Sci Soc Am; Am Soc Hort Sci; Sigma Xi. *Res:* Chemical weed control; plant nutrition; soils; dwarf fruit trees; growth substances; pest control; environmental science. *Mailing Add:* 4504 Bond Ct Midland MI 48640

SOUTHWICK, RICHARD ARTHUR, PLANT BREEDING, PLANT PROPAGATION. *Current Pos:* RETIRED. *Personal Data:* b White River Jct, Vt, Sept 16, 24; m 45, Mary E Rodriguez; c Richard A Jr & Evelyn H. *Educ:* Univ Vt, BS, 50, MS, 54. *Prof Exp:* Instr agron, Univ Mass, Amherst, 54-58, asst prof, 58-67; from assoc prof to prof plant sci, State Univ NY, Agr & Tech Col Cobleskill, 67-87. *Concurrent Pos:* Botanist, George Landis Arboretum, Esperance, 70-82, assoc dir, 82-84, trustee, 92-95, emer trustee, 95-; mem, Adv Comt Rare & Endangered Plants, State NY, 71-79; emer trustee, 95- *Mem:* Sigma Xi. *Res:* Plant propagation; improvement, evaluation, and collection of ornamental plant materials. *Mailing Add:* RR-1 2 Box 648 Cobleskill NY 12043

SOUTHWICK, RUSSELL DUTY, physics, for more information see previous edition

SOUTHWICK, WAYNE ORIN, ORTHOPEDIC SURGERY. *Current Pos:* assoc prof, 58-61, chief sect, 58-77, PROF ORTHOP SURG, SCH MED, YALE UNIV, 61-, CONSULT ORTHOP, UNIV HEALTH SERV, 69- *Personal Data:* b Lincoln, Nebr, Feb 6, 23; m 44; c 3. *Educ:* Univ Nebr, AB, 45, MD, 47; Am Bd Orthop Surg, dipl, 58. *Prof Exp:* Asst anat & histol, Col Med, Univ Nebr, 46-47; intern med, Boston City Hosp, 47-48, asst resident surg, Fifth Surg Div, 48-50; asst resident orthop surg, Hosp, Johns Hopkins Univ, 50-54, instr, Sch Med, Univ & chief resident, Hosp, 54-55, asst prof, Univ, 55-58. *Concurrent Pos:* Fel, Branford Col, Yale Univ, 70- *Mem:* Am Acad Orthop Surg; Am Orthop Asn; fel Am Col Surg; AMA; Orthop Res Soc. *Res:* Degenerative cervical disk disease; slipped epiphysis; experimental osteomyelitis; histology of cartilage. *Mailing Add:* PO Box 390 Old Lyme CT 06371-0390

SOUTHWORTH, RAYMOND W(ILLIAM), CHEMICAL ENGINEERING. *Current Pos:* dir, Comput Ctr, 66-81, prof math & comput sci, 66-85, EMER PROF MATH, COL WILLIAM & MARY, 85- *Personal Data:* b North Brookfield, Mass, Oct 23, 20. *Educ:* Worcester Polytech Inst, BS, 43; Yale Univ, MEng, 44, DEng, 48. *Prof Exp:* From asst instr to assoc prof chem eng, Yale Univ, 43-66. *Concurrent Pos:* Mem staff, Brookhaven Nat Lab, 48-49; mem, Inst Math Sci, NY Univ, 60-61; dir, Southeastern Va Regional Comput Ctr, 69-81. *Mem:* Am Chem Soc; Am Inst Chem Engrs; Asn Comput Mach; Am Math Soc; Soc Indust & Appl Math. *Res:* Digital computing; numerical methods. *Mailing Add:* 102 S Sulgrave Ct Williamsburg VA 23185

SOUTHWORTH, WARREN HILBOURNE, PUBLIC HEALTH, PREVENTIVE MEDICINE. *Current Pos:* assoc prof, 44-52, prof prev med, 77-81, prof curric & instr, 53-87, EMER PROF PREV MED, UNIV WIS-MADISON, 81- *Personal Data:* b Lynn, Mass, Feb 10, 12; m 37; c 2. *Educ:* Univ Mass, BS, 34; Boston Univ, MS, 35; Mass Inst Technol, DrPH, 44. *Honors & Awards:* William A Howe Award, 68. *Prof Exp:* Teacher biol, Whitman High Sch & Belmont High Sch, Mass, 36-39; res dir, Mass Dept Pub Health, 41-42; prof health sci, Panzer Col, 42-44; coordr sch health, Wis Dept Pub Instr, 44-48; coordr read team, Wis State Bd Health, 52-53. *Concurrent Pos:* Lectr pub health, NY Univ, 43-44; field rep, Fed Venereal Dis Prog, Am Social Hyg Asn, 44. *Mem:* AAAS; Am Pub Health Asn; Am Sch Health Asn (treas, 60-74); Soc Pub Health Educrs. *Res:* Community health education; school health education; occupational health education; patient health education; drug education; family life education. *Mailing Add:* 110 S Henry St Apt 615 Madison WI 53703-3160

SOUTO BACHILLER, FERNANDO ALBERTO, PHYSICAL ORGANIC CHEMISTRY, PHOTOCHEMISTRY. *Current Pos:* from asst prof to assoc prof chem, 79-88, DIR LAB, CRIL, UNIV PR, 84-, PROF CHEM, 88- *Personal Data:* b Andujar, Spain, Mar 27, 51; m 74; c 3. *Educ:* Univ Granada, Spain, Lic Sc, 74; Univ Alta, Can, PhD(chem), 78; Ministerio Educación, Madrid, Spain, 88. *Prof Exp:* Res assoc chem, Imp Col, London, 78-79. *Concurrent Pos:* Vis prof plant biol, Univ Granada, Spain, 87-88, vis prof chem, EPFL, Lausanne, Switz, 88-89 & Univ Malaga, Spain, 89-90. *Mem:* Sigma Xi; fel Royal Soc Chem; fel Am Inst Chemists; Electrochem Soc; Am Soc Pharmacog; Am Chem Soc. *Res:* Organic molecular photophysics; organic photochemistry; organic electrochemistry; tropical plant products, their isolation, characterization, photochemistry and in vitro biosynthesis; association of organic dyes in solution, equilibrium polymerization, absorption and emission of electronic excitation energy; excitation energy transfer; photochemistry of N-oxides. *Mailing Add:* Chem Dept Univ PR Mayaguez PR 00708. *E-Mail:* f__souto@rumac.upr.clu.edu

SOVEN, PAUL, PHYSICS. *Current Pos:* from asst prof to assoc prof, 67-76, PROF PHYSICS, UNIV PA, 77- *Personal Data:* b New York, NY, Sept 30, 39; m 61; c 3. *Educ:* City Col New York, BS, 60; Univ Chicago, MS, 61, PhD(physics), 65. *Prof Exp:* Mem staff, Bell Tel Labs, 65-67. *Mem:* Am Phys Soc. *Res:* Theory of metals. *Mailing Add:* Dept Physics Univ Pa Philadelphia PA 19174

SOVERS, OJARS JURIS, ASTROMETRY, SPACE GEODESY. *Current Pos:* AT JET PROPULSION LAB, CALIF INST TECHNOL, 76- *Personal Data:* b Riga, Latvia, July 11, 37; US citizen; m 59, Zinta A Aisters. *Educ:* Brooklyn Col, BS, 58; Princeton Univ, PhD(physics, phys chem), 62. *Prof Exp:* NSF fel chem, Oxford Univ, 61-62; fel, Columbia Univ, 62-63, res assoc, Watson Lab, 63-64; res engr, Gen Tel & Electronics Lab, Inc, 64-72, Sony Corp, 72-79. *Concurrent Pos:* Mem, Study Group Extragalactic Reference Frames, Int Astron Union. *Mem:* Am Phys Soc; AAAS; Am Geophys Union; Sigma Xi. *Res:* Applications of very long baseline radio interferometry to astrometric; geodetic measurements for spacecraft navigation. *Mailing Add:* 1367 La Solana Dr Altadena CA 91001-2624. *Fax:* 818-393-4965; *E-Mail:* ojs@logos.jpl.nasa.gov

SOVIE, MARGARET D, NURSING ADMINISTRATION, HOSPITAL ADMINISTRATION. *Current Pos:* assoc exec dir & chief nursing officer, Hosp Univ Pa, 88-94, assoc dep exec dir & chief nursing officer, 94-95, assoc hosp dir & chief nursing officer, 95-96, JANE DELANO PROF NURSING ADMIN & ASSOC DEAN NURSING PRACT, HOSP UNIV PA, 96- *Personal Data:* b July 7, 34; m 54, Alfred L; c Scot M. *Educ:* Syracuse Univ, BS, 64, MS, 68, PhD(educ), 72. *Hon Degrees:* DSc, State Univ NY, Syracuse, 89. *Prof Exp:* Supvr & instr nursing, Good Shepherd Hosp & State Univ Hosp, 63-66; assoc prof nursing, educ dir & coord nursing serv, Upstate Med Ctr Univ Hosp, State Univ NY, 66-71, assoc dean & dir continuing educ, 72-76; assoc dir, Strong Mem Hosp, 76-88; assoc dean nursing pract & prof nursing, Sch Nursing, Univ Rochester, 76-88. *Concurrent Pos:* Sr fel, Leonard Davis Inst Health Care Econs, Univ Pa. *Mem:* Inst Med-Nat Acad Sci; fel Am Acad Nursing. *Res:* Examining the relationship of mix of nursing staff, costs, and worked hours of nursing care to clinical outcomes of care; creating and testing nursing practice models that assure quality care at controlled costs; author of numerous publications. *Mailing Add:* Admin Sch Nursing Nursing Educ Bldg 420 Guardian Dr Philadelphia PA 19104-6096

SOVISH, RICHARD CHARLES, POLYMER CHEMISTRY, TECHNICAL MANAGEMENT. *Current Pos:* CONSULT, 91- *Personal Data:* b Cleveland, Ohio, July 22, 25; m 54, Amelia Martin; c Leslie, Linda & Eric. *Educ:* Ohio Univ, BS, 49; Case Western Res Univ, MS, 52,PhD(chem), 54. *Prof Exp:* Res chemist, Dow Chem Co, 54-62; res scientist, Lockheed Missile & Space Co, 62-63; staff mem, Raychem Corp, 63-67; res team leader, 67-70, mgr, Mfg Compounding Dept, 70-73, mgr eng, Thermofit Div, 73-75, tech mgr, Utilities Div, Raychem Belg, 75-78, int tech dir, Telecom Div, 78-80, tech dir Europe, 80-83, exec tech dir, Corp Res & Develop, 83-89, vpres, Corp Technol, 89-91. *Mem:* Am Chem Soc; Sigma Xi; Soc Plastics Engrs. *Res:* Irradiation effects on polymers; polymer cross-linking; graft copolymers; mechanical properties of polymers. *Mailing Add:* 1 Ashdown PL Half Moon Bay CA 94019. *Fax:* 650-726-0842

SOVOCOOL, G WAYNE, PHYSICAL-ORGANIC CHEMISTRY, ANALYTICAL CHEMISTRY. *Current Pos:* res chemist, 72-81, supvry phys scientist, 81-87, CHEM, US ENVIRON PROTECTION AGENCY, 87- *Personal Data:* b Cortland, NY, Oct 30, 42; m 71; c 2. *Educ:* Rochester Inst Technol, BS, 65; Cornell Univ, MS, 67, PhD(chem), 71. *Prof Exp:* Fel chem, Univ NC, Chapel Hill, 71-72. *Concurrent Pos:* Adj assoc prof, Biochem Lab, Bot Dept, Univ NC, Chapel Hill, 81-82. *Mem:* Am Chem Soc; Am Soc Mass Spectrometry. *Res:* Structure determination and quantitative measurement of organic chemical compounds occurring in complex mixtures, as human tissue and environmental samples, through the use of mass spectrometry; quality assurance of analytical data; predictive methods for chemical and physical properties of compounds. *Mailing Add:* 3155 Highview Dr Henderson NV 89014-2131

SOWA, JOHN ROBERT, ORGANIC CHEMISTRY. *Current Pos:* from asst prof to assoc prof, 67-90, PROF CHEM, UNION COL, NY, 77- *Personal Data:* b South Bend, Ind, Aug 21, 34; m 61; c 4. *Educ:* Univ Notre Dame, BS, 56; Univ Pa, PhD(org chem), 64. *Prof Exp:* Res asst chem, Sowa Chem Co, 58-59; res assoc, Univ Ariz, 64-66. *Concurrent Pos:* Henry Busche teaching fel, Univ Pa, 62; consult, Sowa Chem Co, 66-, decontamination res div, Edgewood Arsenal, 67 & Schenectady Chem Co, 68-; vis prof, Rensselaer Polytech Inst, 73-74 & Univ Albany, 81. *Mem:* Am Chem Soc; NY Acad Sci; Am Inst Chemists; Sigma Xi. *Res:* Nuclear magnetic resonance applied to mechanisms in organic chemistry; silicon-carbon d-pi/p-pi bonding; mustard reactions with purines; vinyl polymerizations; organophosphorous chemistry; acetylenes; liquid crystals; diazonium ions; undergraduate organic laboratory experiments. *Mailing Add:* Chem Dept Union Col 807 Union St Schenectady NY 12308-3103

SOWA, WALTER, organic chemistry, for more information see previous edition

SOWDER, LARRY K, MATHEMATICS EDUCATION. *Current Pos:* PROF, MATH SCI, SAN DIEGO STATE UNIV, 86- *Personal Data:* b Bedford, Ind, Mar 17, 38. *Educ:* Univ Wis, PhD(math), 69. *Mailing Add:* Math Sci Dept San Diego State Univ San Diego CA 92182-0001

SOWELL, JOHN BASIL, PLANT PHYSIOLOGICAL ECOLOGY. *Current Pos:* ASSOC PROF BOT, WESTERN STATE COL, 91- *Personal Data:* b Phoenix, Ariz, Oct 22, 58; m 83; c 3. *Educ:* Univ Calif, Davis, BS, 79; Univ Idaho, PhD(bot), 85. *Prof Exp:* Asst prof Biol, Southwest State Univ, Minn, 85-91. *Mem:* Am Soc Plant Physiologists; Ecol Soc Am. *Res:* Physiological ecology of alpine timberline trees; winter water relations; effects of low soil temperature on plant functioning; ecological modeling. *Mailing Add:* 5 Floresta St Gunnison CO 81230

SOWELL, JOHN GREGORY, PHARMACOLOGY, PHARMACY. *Current Pos:* assoc prof, 79-83, PROF, DEPT PHARMACEUT SCI, SAMFORD UNIV, 83- *Personal Data:* b Knoxville, Tenn, Jan 22, 41; m 67; c 1. *Educ:* Murray State Univ, BS, 63; Univ Tenn, MS, 67, PhD, 69; Samford Univ, BS, 89. *Prof Exp:* Instr pharmacol, Univ Tenn, 70-71; asst prof pharmacol & ophthal, Med Ctr, Univ Ala, Birmingham, 73-79. *Concurrent Pos:* Fel, Univ Southern Calif, 71-73. *Mem:* Am Soc Pharmacol & Exp Therapeut; Asn Am Col Pharm. *Res:* Mechanism of steroid action; pharmacy education. *Mailing Add:* Pharmaceut Sci Dept Samford Univ 800 Lakeshore Dr Birmingham AL 35229-0001. *Fax:* 205-870-2088

SOWELL, KATYE MARIE OLIVER, MATHEMATICS, HISTORY & PHILOSOPHY. *Current Pos:* from asst prof to assoc prof, 65-71, PROF MATH, ECAROLINA UNIV, 72- *Personal Data:* b Winston-Salem, NC, Apr 6, 34; wid; c David. *Educ:* Flora Macdonald Col, BA, 56; Univ SC, MS, 58; Fla State Univ, PhD(math educ), 65. *Honors & Awards:* W W Rankin Mem Award, 85. *Prof Exp:* Asst prof math, Elon Col, 58-60; instr, Univ Southern Miss, 60-63; instr & res assoc math educ, Fla State Univ, 65. *Concurrent Pos:* Dir, student teaching prog math & supvr student teachers, ECarolina Univ, 66-79 & math educ comput lab, 81-84; NSF grants, 68-74; consult, var bk pubis & city & co bds of educ, Eastern NC, 67-; consult, Ctr Individualized Instr Systs, Durham, NC, 71-73; mem, Adv Coun Math, NC State Dept Pub Instr, 70-72, Metric Educ, 74-76; pres, NC Coun Teachers Math, 75-77; vis scholar, Univ Mich, 80 & 81; co-ed, The Centroid, 83-85; dir, Eastern Carolina Educ Consults, 84- *Mem:* NY Acad Sci; Math Asn Am; Nat Coun Teachers Math; Asn Women Math; Sigma Xi. *Res:* Mathematics education; geometry; number theory; taxicab geometry. *Mailing Add:* 103 College Court Dr Greenville NC 27858-3926. *Fax:* 919-328-6414; *E-Mail:* masowell@ecuvm.cis.ecu.edu

SOWER, STACIA ANN, NEUROENDOCRINOLOGY, REPRODUCTION. *Current Pos:* asst prof zool, 83-87, assoc prof zool & biochem, 87-92, PROF BIOCHEM & MOLECULAR BIOL, UNIV NH, 92- *Personal Data:* b Ft Belvoir, Va, Nov 16, 50. *Educ:* Univ Utah, BA, 73; Ore State Univ, MS, 78, PhD(fisheries physiol), 81. *Honors & Awards:* Career Develop Award, NSF, 88, Fac Award, Women Scientists & Engrs, 91. *Prof Exp:* Fel endocrinol, Univ Wash, 80-83. *Concurrent Pos:* Consult, Sea Run, Inc, Maine, 85-; secy, Div Comp Endocrin, Am Soc Zoologists, 88-89; mem, Physiol Processes Panel, NSF, 88-92; prin investr, NSF grant, 89-94; mem, Tech Prog Comn for 2nd Int Fish Endocrinol Symp, France, 90-92; prog dir, Integrative Animal Biol Prog, NSF, 96-97. *Mem:* Am Soc Zoologists; Soc Neurosci; NY Acad Sci; AAAS; Am Soc Endocrinol. *Res:* Comparative reproductive physiology and endocrinology in fishes; structure and function of brain hormones, particularly lampreys. *Mailing Add:* Dept Biochem & Molecular Biol Univ NH Durham NH 03824. *Fax:* 603-862-4013; *E-Mail:* sasower@christa.unh.edu

SOWERS, ARTHUR EDWARD, MEMBRANE BIOLOGY. *Current Pos:* SCIENTIST II MEMBRANES, AM RED CROSS RES LAB, 82- *Personal Data:* b Chicago, Ill, Dec 20, 43; m 82. *Educ:* Univ Ill, Urbana, BS, 66; Tex A&M Univ, PhD(biol), 77. *Prof Exp:* Res fel membranes, Med Sch, Univ NC, 78-82. *Mem:* AAAS; Biophys Soc; Am Soc Cell Biol; Electron Micros Soc Am; Bioelectromagnetics Soc. *Res:* Electric field effects on membrane structure and function; electrofusion, electroporation and lateral diffusion of mobile membrane components; membrane structure-function relationships. *Mailing Add:* PO Box 489 Georgetown DE 19947-0489. *Fax:* 410-706-8341

SOWERS, EDWARD EUGENE, INDUSTRIAL ORGANIC CHEMISTRY. *Current Pos:* PATENT COUNR, 93- *Personal Data:* b Crawfordsville, Ind, Nov 26, 42; m 67, Margaret R Sayre; c William E & Jodi L. *Educ:* Wabash Col, AB, 64; Tufts Univ, PhD(org chem), 70; Ind Univ Law Sch, JD, 90. *Prof Exp:* Staff chemist res, Reilly Tar & Chem Corp, 69-75, mgr prod develop, 75-80, sr sect head, Reilly Industs Inc, 81-93. *Mem:* Am Chem Soc. *Res:* Synthesis and product development of nitrogen heterocycles; synthesis and characterization of linear and crosslinked polymers. *Mailing Add:* 3280 State Rd 39 Mooresville IN 46158

SOWERS, GEORGE F(REDERICK), civil & geological engineering; deceased, see previous edition for last biography

SOWINSKI, RAYMOND, BIOCHEMISTRY. *Current Pos:* RETIRED. *Personal Data:* b Hammond, Ind, Feb 8, 24; m 54. *Educ:* Ind Univ, BS, 49, PhD(biochem), 52. *Prof Exp:* Res asst phys chem, Yale Univ, 52-53; supvy biochemist, Mercy Hosp, Chicago, Ill, 53-55; res assoc biochem, Med Sch, Northwestern Univ, 55-58; res assoc biophys, Univ Pittsburgh, 58-60; sr res assoc hemat, Hektoen Inst Med Res, Cook Co Hosp, 60-63; asst prof microbiol, Albany Med Sch, 63-66; assoc prof biochem, Rochester Inst Technol, 66-87. *Mem:* AAAS; Am Chem Soc; NY Acad Sci. *Res:* Protein chemistry; physical biochemistry; neurochemistry. *Mailing Add:* 171 Brandywine Terr Rochester NY 14623-5251

SOWLS, LYLE KENNETH, WILDLIFE BIOLOGY. *Current Pos:* RETIRED. *Personal Data:* b Darlington, Wis, Feb 28, 16; m 74; c 6. *Educ:* Univ Wis, PhD(wildlife mgt), 51. *Honors & Awards:* Terrestial Publ Award, Wildlife Soc, 55 & 80; Thomas E McCullough Award, Ariz Wildlife Fedn, 82. *Prof Exp:* Biologist, Delta Waterfowl Res Sta, Wildlife Mgt Inst, Can, 46-50; leader coop Wildlife Res Unit, Univ Ariz, 50-86. *Concurrent Pos:* Fulbright vis lectr zool, Univ Col Rhodesia & Nyasaland, 62-63; wildlife consult, Food & Agr Orgn, Philippines, 67; mem, pigs & peccaries comt, Species Surv Comm, Int Union Conserv Nature. *Mem:* Wildlife Soc; Am Soc Mammal; Int Union Conserv Nature. *Res:* Game birds and mammals. *Mailing Add:* 3653 N Vine Ave Tucson AZ 85719

SOWMAN, HAROLD G, CERAMIC ENGINEERING. *Current Pos:* RETIRED. *Personal Data:* b Murphysboro, Ill, July 21, 23; m 45; c 2. *Educ:* Univ Ill, BS, 48, MS, 49, PhD(ceramic eng), 51. *Honors & Awards:* John Jeppson Medal & Award, Am Ceramic Soc, 85, Samuel Geijsbeek Award, 89. *Prof Exp:* Assoc ceramist, Titanion Alloy Div, Nat Lead Co, 51-52; res assoc, Knoll Atomic Lab, Gen Elec Co, 52-57; mgr & supvr nuclear mat res, 3M Co, 57-65, sr res specialist, 66-70, corp scientist, 70-87. *Mem:* Nat Acad Eng; fel Am Ceramic Soc; Nat Inst Ceramic Eng. *Res:* High temperature materials and ceramics; utilization of chemical ceramic on SOL-GEL technology for fibers, fabric, coatings and abrasive minerals. *Mailing Add:* 855 Towne Circle Stillwater MN 55082

SOX, HAROLD C, INTERNAL MEDICINE. *Current Pos:* instr, 70-73, JOSEPH HUBER PROF & CHMN, DEPT MED, DARTMOUTH MED SCH, 88- *Personal Data:* b Palo Alto, Calif, Aug, 18, 39; m 62, Carol H Hill; c Colin M & Lara K. *Educ:* Stanford Univ, BS, 61; Harvard Univ, MD, 66. *Hon Degrees:* MA, Dartmouth Col, 93. *Prof Exp:* Intern & resident, Mass Gen Hosp, Boston, 66-68; clin assoc, Nat Cancer Inst, Bethesda, 68-70; from asst prof to prof med, Stanford Univ Med Sch, 73-88; assoc chief staff ambulatory care, Vet Admin Med Ctr, Palo Alto, 76-88. *Concurrent Pos:* Chair, Comt Priority-Setting Health Tech, Assess Inst Med, 90-91, US Prev Serv Task Force, 90-95, Pre-test Writing Comt, Am Bd Internal Med, 92-94; chair, Inst Med Comt HIV & Blood Supply, 94-95. *Mem:* Fel Am Col Physicians (pres elect, 97-); Soc Gen Internal Med; Soc Med Decision Making (pres, 83-84); Am Fedn Clin Res; Asn Am Physicians; Asn Profs Med; Inst Med Nat Acad Sci. *Res:* Diagnostic tests and treatments, using techniques such as cost-effectiveness analysis and meta-analysis, and develop guidelines for their use in clinical medicine; author of 100 publications. *Mailing Add:* Dartmouth Hitchcock Med Ctr Lebanon NH 03756

SOYKA, LESTER F, CARDIOVASCULAR CLINICAL RESEARCH. *Current Pos:* CLIN DIR THERAPEUT AREA, BRISTOL-MYERS RESEARCH CENTER, 82- *Personal Data:* b Chicago, Ill, Mar 12, 31; div; c 4. *Educ:* Univ Ill, MD, 61. *Mem:* Soc Pediat Res; Endocrine Soc; Am Soc Clin Res; Am Soc Pharmacol & Exp Therapeut. *Mailing Add:* Bristol-Myers Squibb Ctr PO Box 4000 Princeton NJ 08543-4000. *Fax:* 203-284-6251

SOZEN, M(ETE) A(VNI), CIVIL ENGINEERING. *Current Pos:* PROF, SCH CIVIL ENG, PURDUE UNIV, 94- *Personal Data:* b Istanbul, Turkey, May 22, 30; m 56. *Educ:* Robert Col Istanbul, BS, 51; Univ Ill, MS, 52, PhD(civil eng), 57. *Hon Degrees:* Doctorate, Bogazici Univ, 89. *Honors & Awards:* Res Prize, Am Soc Civil Engrs, 63, R C Reese Prize, 70, Moisseiff Prize, 72, Howard Award, 87, Base Award, 88; J W Kelly Award, Am Concrete Inst, 74, Bloem Award, 85; Drucker Award, 86. *Prof Exp:* Engr, Kaiser Engrs, 52 & Hardesty & Hanover, 53; res assoc civil eng, Univ Ill, Urbana, 55-57, from asst prof to prof, 57-94. *Mem:* Nat Acad Eng; Am Soc Civil Engrs; Am Concrete Inst. *Res:* Reinforced and prestressed concrete structures; earthquake-resistant design. *Mailing Add:* Sch Civil Eng Purdue Univ 1284 Civil Eng Bldg West Lafayette IN 47907-1284

SPACH, MADISON STOCKTON, PEDIATRIC CARDIOLOGY. *Current Pos:* From instr to assoc prof, 57-68, PROF PEDIAT, SCH MED, DUKE UNIV, 68-, CHIEF PEDIAT CARDIOL, 60- *Personal Data:* b Winston Salem, NC, Nov 10, 26; c 4. *Educ:* Duke Univ, AB, 50, MD, 54. *Concurrent Pos:* Chmn, Nat Heart, Lung & Blood Inst Manpower Rev Comt, 82-85. *Mem:* Soc Pediat Res (pres, 74); Am Acad Pediat; fel Am Col Cardiol; Asn Europ Pediat Cardiol; NY Acad Sci; Int Soc Heart Res; Biomed Eng Soc. *Res:* Electrophysiology, determining the mechanisms by which antisotropic structural complexities of the cardiac muscle alters the kinetics of ionic channels during the propagation of action potentials. *Mailing Add:* Dept Pediat & Cell Biol Duke Univ Med Ctr Box 3475 Durham NC 27710

SPACIE, ANNE, AQUATIC TOXICOLOGY, POLLUTION BIOLOGY. *Current Pos:* from asst prof to assoc prof, 75-92, PROF FISHERIES, PURDUE UNIV, 92- *Personal Data:* b Boston, Mass, Aug 19, 45. *Educ:* Mt Holyoke Col, BA, 67; Univ Calif, San Diego, MS, 69; Purdue Univ, PhD(limnol), 75. *Prof Exp:* Researcher aquatic biol, Union Carbide Corp, 69-73. *Concurrent Pos:* Vis prof, Savannah River Ecol Lab, 79; consult, US Environ Protection Agency; Alexander von Humboldt fel, Ger, 84-85. *Mem:* Am Fisheries Soc; Am Soc Limnol & Oceanog; AAAS; Soc Environ Toxicol & Chem; Sigma Xi. *Res:* The accumulation and toxicity of synthetic organic compounds in fish and other aquatic organisms; effects of stream modifications on water quality and the distribution of fishes. *Mailing Add:* Forestry & Natural Resources Purdue Univ West Lafayette IN 47907-1159. *E-Mail:* aspacie@purdue.edu

SPACKMAN, DARREL H, BIOCHEMISTRY, CANCER. *Current Pos:* RETIRED. *Personal Data:* b Morgan, Utah, July 18, 24; m 47, Melva Hatch; c 5. *Educ:* Univ Utah, BA, 50, MA, 52, PhD, 54. *Prof Exp:* Res assoc, Rockefeller Inst, 54-59; sr biochemist, Spinco Div, Beckman Instruments, Inc, 59-62; res asst prof biochem, obstet & gynec, Univ Wash, 62-68; sr res biochemist, Pac Northwest Res Found, 68-82; chmn, Dept Microbiol, 82-85. *Concurrent Pos:* Res scientist, Fred Hutchinson Cancer Res Ctr, 75-85; asst prof, Rehab Med Dept, Univ Wash, 77-80. *Mem:* Am Asn Cancer Res; Am Soc Biol Chemists. *Res:* Amino acids, peptides and proteins of physiological fluids and tissues in hosts with malignancies; deprivation therapy in cancer research; methodology for automatic amino acid analysis. *Mailing Add:* 500 166th Ave NE Bellevue WA 98008-4049

SPACKMAN, WILLIAM, JR, PALEOBOTANY. *Current Pos:* from asst prof to assoc prof, Pa State Univ, 49-61, prof paleobot, 61-86, dir coal res sect, Earth & Mineral Sci Exp Sta, 86-87, EMER PROF PALEOBOT, PA STATE UNIV, 86- *Personal Data:* b Chicago, Ill, Sept 20, 19; m 42; c 3. *Educ:* Univ Ill, BS, 42; Harvard Univ, MA, 47, PhD(bot), 49. *Honors & Awards:* Joseph Becker Award, Am Inst Mining, Metall & Petrol Engrs; G H Cady Award, Geol Soc Am; Reinhardt Thiessen Medal, Int Comn Coal Petrol. *Prof Exp:* Assoc biologist, US Naval Shipyard, Pa, 44-45. *Concurrent Pos:* Mem, Int Comn Coal Petrol. *Mem:* Geol Soc Am. *Res:* Tertiary floras; fossil woods; plant phylogeny; coal petrology; modern phytogenic sediments; peat to coal transformation. *Mailing Add:* 120 Aaron Sq Aaronsburg PA 16820

SPADAFINO, LEONARD PETER, ORGANIC CHEMISTRY. *Current Pos:* ORG CHEMIST, TENN EASTMAN CO, 63- *Personal Data:* b Jersey City, NJ, Oct 25, 31; m 56; c 2. *Educ:* Univ Ga, BS, 58, PhD(chem), 63. *Mem:* Am Asn Textile Chemists & Colorists; Am Chem Soc. *Res:* Kinetics of the decomposition of peroxides in systems where stable free radicals function as scavengers of reactive radicals; anthraquinone and azo dyes for synthetic fibers and films. *Mailing Add:* 4413 Beechcliff Dr Kingsport TN 37664-9508

SPADONI, LEON R, OBSTETRICS & GYNECOLOGY, REPRODUCTIVE ENDOCRINOLOGY & INFERTILITY. *Current Pos:* resident obstet & gynec, Univ Integrated Hosp, 60-63, fel reprod endocrinol & infertil, 63-65, from instr to assoc prof, Sch Med, 63-74, PROF OBSTET & GYNEC, SCH MED, UNIV WASH, 74-, VCHMN, 77 - *Personal Data:* b Kent, Wash, Aug 11, 30; m 57, Yvonne Niemitz; c Mark, Janine & James. *Educ:* Univ Wash, BS, 53, MD, 57. *Prof Exp:* Intern med, Minn Gen Hosp, 57-58. *Concurrent Pos:* Attend physician, Univ & Harborview Med Ctr, 63-; consult, Univ Wash Hall Health Ctr, 63 -; consult, Madigan Gen Hosp, Tacoma, 69; pres, Pac Coast Fertil Soc, 83; examr, Am Bd Obstet & Gynec, 85; chief of staff, Univ Wash Med Ctr, 89-91. *Mem:* Am Fertil Soc; Am Col Obstet & Gynec; Soc Reproductive Surgeons; Am Bd Obstet & Gynec. *Res:* Infertility; gynecologic endocrinology. *Mailing Add:* Dept Obstet & Gynec RH-20 Univ Wash Med Ctr Seattle WA 98195. *Fax:* 206-543-3915

SPAEDER, CARL EDWARD, JR, METALLURGY. *Current Pos:* SR RES METALLURGIST, ARISTECH CHEM, 90- *Personal Data:* b Meadville, Pa, Mar 29, 35; m 62; c 3. *Educ:* Pa State Univ, University Park, BS, 57; Carnegie-Mellon Univ, MS, 63; Univ Pittsburgh, PhD(metall), 70. *Prof Exp:* Sr res metallurgist, US Steel Res Ctr, 57-90. *Mem:* Am Soc Metals; Am Soc Mech Engrs. *Res:* Elevated temperature; properties of metals; cryogenic properties; formability; material characteristics. *Mailing Add:* 3905 Princess Ct Murraysville PA 15668

SPAEPEN, FRANS, PHYSICAL METALLURGY, MATERIALS SCIENCE. *Current Pos:* Res fel, 75-77, from asst prof to assoc prof, 77-83, GORDON MCKAY PROF APPL PHYSICS, HARVARD UNIV, 83-, DIR MAT RES LAB, 90- *Personal Data:* b Mechelen, Belgium, Oct 29, 48; m 73; c 3. *Educ:* Univ Leuven, Belgium, ME, 71; Harvard Univ, PhD(appl physics), 75. *Concurrent Pos:* Vis prof, Univ Leuven, Belgium, 84-85; counr, Mat Res Soc, 86-89 & 90-93; chmn, Phys Metall Gordon Conf, 88. *Mem:* Am Soc Metals; fel Am Phys Soc; Mat Res Soc; Am Soc Mining & Metall Engrs; Bhmische Phys Soc; fel Metal Soc. *Res:* Atomic transport (viscosity, diffusivity, phase transformations) in amorphous materials: metals, semiconductors and oxides; thin films and multilayers: preparation, stability, mechanical properties; properties of interfaces: crystal/melt, amorphous/crystalline semiconductor, grain boundaries, grain growth, interface tension, interface stress; quasicrystals. *Mailing Add:* Div Eng & Appl Sci Harvard Univ Pierce Hall 29 Oxford St Cambridge MA 02138

SPAETH, GEORGE L, OPHTHALMOLOGY. *Current Pos:* ATTEND SURGEON OPHTHAL, CHESTNUT HILL HOSP, 75-; PROF OPHTHAL, THOMAS JEFFERSON UNIV, 74-, ATTEND SURGEON OPHTHAL, THOMAS JEFFERSON UNIV HOSP, 84- *Personal Data:* b Philadelphia, Pa, Mar 3, 32; m 58, Ann Ward; c Kristin (Crowley), George L & Eric E. *Educ:* Yale Univ, BA, 54; Harvard Med Sch, MD, 59; Am Bd Ophthal, dipl, 65. *Honors & Awards:* Award Merit, Am Acad Opthal & Otolaryngol, 73. *Prof Exp:* Intern, Univ Hosp, Ann Arbor, Mich, 60; resident ophthal, Wills Eye Hosp, 63; clin assoc, Nat Inst Neurol Dis & Blindness, 63-65; instr ophthal, Univ Pa, 65-68; clin instr ophthal, Temple Univ, 68, from assoc prof to prof, 68-74. *Concurrent Pos:* Asst ophthalmologist, Grad Hosp, Univ Pa, 65, assoc ophthalmologist, 66; clin asst, Wills Eye Hosp, 65, sr asst surgeon, 66, assoc surgeon, 68, dir glaucoma serv, 68, attend surgeon, 73, pres med staff, 84; grants, Nat Soc Prev Blindness, 67 & 68, Nat Coun Combat Blindness, 68, Nat Eye Inst, 72-75 & NIH, 88-94, 90- & 93-; consult ophthalmologist, Bryn Mawr Hosp, 93-; staff ophthalmologist, Miners Mem Hosp, Tamaqua, Pa, 93-; pres, Am Glaucoma Soc. *Mem:* Fel Am Ophthal Soc; fel Am Acad Ophthal; fel Danish Ophthal Soc; fel Royal Soc Med; fel Am Col Surgeons; fel Royal Soc Health; fel Royal Col Ophthalmologists; AMA; Asn Res Vision & Ophthal; AAAS; Pan-Am Ophthalmic Asn; Int Soc Pediat Ophthal. *Res:* Diagnosis, treatment and pathophysiology of glaucoma; metabolic diseases, their ocular aspects and treatment, especially homocystinuria; sociology of chronic disease; ocular surgery, especially of glaucoma; genetic aspects of glaucoma; effects of glaucoma on quality of life; development of nerve damage in glaucoma; change in optic nerve and visual field. *Mailing Add:* Wills Eye Hosp 900 Walnut St Philadelphia PA 19107-5598

SPAETH, RALPH, MEDICINE. *Current Pos:* From instr to prof, 36-72, EMER CLIN PROF, COL MED, UNIV ILL, CHICAGO, 72-; EMER CLIN PROF PEDIAT, RUSH MED COL, 72- *Personal Data:* b Cleveland, Ohio, Mar 21, 05; wid; c Virginia M & Howard W. *Educ:* Western Res Univ, AB, 27, MD, 31; Am Bd Pediat, dipl, 38. *Concurrent Pos:* Supvr physician, East Off, Chicago Div, State of Ill Children & Family Serv, 37-75; mem, Nat Comn Venereal Dis, 71-72; regional medical coordr, Proj Head Start to 78. *Mem:* Am Acad Pediat; AMA. *Res:* Immunology and clinical management of tetanus; immunology and immunization against mumps; prevention of rabies; therapy of poliomyelitis with convalescent serum; active immunization against measles. *Mailing Add:* 9030 S Bell Ave Chicago IL 60620-6118

SPAFFORD, EUGENE HOWARD, COMPUTER SECURITY, COMPUTER LAW & ETHICS. *Current Pos:* asst prof, 87-93, ASSOC PROF COMPUT SCI, PURDUE UNIV, 93-, DIR, COAST PROJ & LAB, 93- *Personal Data:* b Rochester, NY, Mar 26, 56. *Educ:* State Univ NY, Brockport, BA, 79; Ga Inst Technol, MS, 81, PhD(info & comput sci), 86. *Prof Exp:* Res scientist II, Software Eng Res Ctr, Ga Inst Technol, 86-87. *Concurrent Pos:* Bd dirs, Sun User Group, 96- *Mem:* Asn Comput Mach; Inst Elec & Electronics Engrs; Inst Elec & Electronics Engrs Comput Soc; Comput Security Inst; Sigma Xi; Usenix Asn. *Res:* Reliable computing and the consequences of computer failure and misuse; software validation, verification and debugging; computer and network security; reliable distributed computer systems; ethical and societal implications of computing; published several books and articles. *Mailing Add:* Dept Comput Sci Purdue Univ West Lafayette IN 47907-1398. *Fax:* 765-494-0739; *E-Mail:* spaf@cs.purdue.edu

SPAGNA, GEORGE FREDRIC, JR, RADIATION TRANSPORT IN INTERSTELLAR & CIRCUMSTELLAR CLOUDS. *Current Pos:* asst prof, 86-92, CHAIR, DEPT PHYSICS, RANDOLPH-MACON COL, 91-, ASSOC PROF PHYSICS & DIR KEEBLE OBSERV, 92- *Personal Data:* b Portland, Ore, Apr 8, 51; m 74, Sylvia M Beaudry; c Amy L & Kimberley A. *Educ:* Rensselaer Polytech Inst, BS, 73, MS, 82, PhD(physics), 86. *Prof Exp:* Lectr-demonstr, Dept Physics, Rensselaer Polytech Inst, 79-85, lectr astron, 85-86. *Mem:* Am Asn Physics Teachers; Sigma Xi; Am Astron Soc; Astron Soc Pac; AAAS; Am Asn Univ Profs; Am Physics Soc. *Res:* Numerical modelling of radiation transport in disk-shaped circumstellar and interstellar dust clouds; seeking observational signature of geometry as precursor to star formation. *Mailing Add:* Randolph-Macon Col Physics Dept PO Box 5005 Ashland VA 23005-5505. *Fax:* 804-752-4724; *E-Mail:* gspagna@rmc.edu

SPAHN, GERARD JOSEPH, MICROBIOLOGY. *Current Pos:* DIR SAFETY, SALK INST BIOL STUDIES, SAN DIEGO, 79- *Personal Data:* b Baltimore, Md, May 4, 38; m 61, Jane Skezilaj; c Sheila, Julie, David & Anne. *Educ:* Mt St Mary's Col, Md, BS, 60; St John's Univ, MS, 62; Univ Md, PhD(microbiol), 65. *Prof Exp:* Lab scientist rabies diag, Livestock Sanit Serv Lab, 65-66; virologist, Microbiol Assoc, Inc, Md, 66-72; sr scientist, Litton Bionetics, Inc, 72-76; virologist, Microbiol Assocs, Inc, 76-77; sr scientist, Environ Control, Inc, Rockville, Md, 77-79. *Mem:* Am Asn Lab Animal Sci; Am Biol Safety Asn; Sigma Xi. *Res:* Oncogenic virus expression in cell culture; tumorigenicity in vivo and transformation in vitro; studies on spontaneous neoplasms of rats and mice; environmental, occupational health, and safety program. *Mailing Add:* Salk Inst PO Box 85800 San Diego CA 92186. *Fax:* 619-824-1962; *E-Mail:* spahn@salk.edu

SPAHN, ROBERT JOSEPH, APPLIED MATHEMATICS. *Current Pos:* asst prof, 64-70, ASSOC PROF MATH, MICH TECHNOL UNIV, 70- *Personal Data:* b Chicago, Ill, July 2, 36; m 61; c 4. *Educ:* Mich Technol Univ, BS, 58; Mich State Univ, PhD(physics), 63. *Prof Exp:* Engr, NAm Aviation, Inc, Ohio, 63-64. *Mem:* Soc Indust & Appl Math. *Res:* Solutions of boundary value problems in partial differential equations. *Mailing Add:* RR 2 PO Box 5A Chassell MI 49916

SPAHR, SIDNEY LOUIS, AGRICULTURE, DAIRY SCIENCE. *Current Pos:* asst prof dairy husb, 64-70, from assoc prof to prof dairy sci, 72-85, PROF ANIMAL SCI, UNIV ILL, URBANA, 85- *Personal Data:* b Bristol, Va, Sept 5, 35; m 60, 75, Gladys Biggs; c Douglas E & Diane S (Krueger). *Educ:* Va Polytech Inst, BSc, 58; Pa State Univ, MSc, 60, PhD(dairy sci), 64. *Honors & Awards:* Am Dairy Sci Asn, 87. *Prof Exp:* Instr dairy sci, Pa State Univ, 62-64. *Concurrent Pos:* Staff officer, Nat Acad Sci, Washington, DC, 70-72. *Mem:* AAAS; Am Dairy Sci Asn; Am Soc Animal Sci; US Animal Health Asn. *Res:* Dairy cattle management and nutrition; dairy automation: electronic animal identification; automatic data acquisition; application of database management; expert systems and artificial intelligence techniques in dairy herd management. *Mailing Add:* 230 Animal Sci Lab Univ Ill 1207 W Gregory Dr Urbana IL 61801. *Fax:* 217-333-7088; *E-Mail:* spahr@uiuc.edu

SPAHT, CARLOS G, II, MATHEMATICS, OPERATIONS RESEARCH. *Current Pos:* from asst prof to assoc prof math, 72-85, prof math & comput sci, 81-85, chmn, Math & Comput Sci Dept, 85-88, PROF MATH & COMPUT SCI, LA STATE UNIV, SHREVEPORT, 88- *Personal Data:* b

New Orleans, La, June 22, 42; m 64; c 2. *Educ:* La State Univ, BS, 64, MS, 66, PhD(math), 70. *Prof Exp:* Asst math, La State Univ, Baton Rouge, 64-70, spec lectr, 70. *Concurrent Pos:* Instr & consult, Educ Ctr, Barksdale Air Force Base, 73-75. *Mem:* Am Math Asn; Am Math Soc; Nat Coun Teachers Math. *Res:* Abstract algebra; operation research field. *Mailing Add:* Dept Math La State Univ Shreveport LA 71115

SPAID, FRANK WILLIAM, FLUID DYNAMICS. *Current Pos:* chief scientist, McDonnell Douglas Res Labs, 72-92, prog dir, Exp Fluid Dynamics, McDonnell Douglas Res Labs, 92-93, GROUP MGR ENG, MCDONNELL DOUGLAS AEROSPACE, 93- *Personal Data:* b Pocatello, Idaho, Mar 7, 38; m 64, Maureen H Buck; c 2. *Educ:* Ore State Univ, BS, 59; Calif Inst Technol, MS, 61, PhD(mech eng), 64. *Prof Exp:* Assoc res engr, Jet Propulsion Lab, Pasadena, 59-60, res engr, 61; supvr, Douglas Aircraft Co, Inc, 64-67; asst prof aeronaut, Univ Calif, Los Angeles, 67-72. *Concurrent Pos:* Consult, McDonnell Douglas Corp, 67-72. *Mem:* Am Inst Aeronaut & Astronaut; Sigma Xi. *Res:* Interaction of a liquid or gaseous jet with a supersonic flow; boundary layer separation; hypersonic fluid dynamics; low-speed and transonic airfoil and wing flowfields. *Mailing Add:* 12963 Thornhill Dr St Louis MO 63131. *Fax:* 314-777-1328; *E-Mail:* spaid@mdcgwy.mdc.com

SPAIN, JAMES DORRIS, JR, BIOCHEMISTRY. *Current Pos:* PRES, ELECTRONIC HOMEWORK SYSTS, INC, 94- *Personal Data:* b Washington, DC, Feb 3, 29; m 52, Patricia Mann; c James, Caryn & Lisa. *Educ:* Mich Technol Univ, BS, 51; Med Col Va, MS, 53; Stanford Univ, PhD(chem), 56. *Honors & Awards:* Mich Tech Fac Res Award, 65. *Prof Exp:* Res fel biochem, Univ Tex, M D Anderson Hosp & Tumor Inst, 55-56; from asst prof to assoc prof chem, Mich Technol Univ, 56-62, head, Dept Biol Sci, 62-68, prof biochem, 62-84, dir, Instrnl Comput Ctr, Eastern Mich Univ, 84-85; vis prof chem, Clemson Univ, 85-94. *Concurrent Pos:* Emer prof, Mich Technol Univ. *Mem:* Am Chem Soc; Sigma Xi. *Res:* Computerized instruction design; computer modeling of biological systems; mixing of water masses in large lakes; simulation of biological and chemical systems; liver damage and azo dye carcinogenesis, histochemistry; precipitation chromatography; physical and chemical limnology; computer search and retrieval. *Mailing Add:* 129 Leslie Lane Boscobel Pendleton SC 29670. *Fax:* 864-646-9748; *E-Mail:* jspain@clemson.edu

SPALATIN, JOSIP, VIROLOGY. *Current Pos:* RES ASSOC VIROL, UNIV WIS-MADISON, 63- *Personal Data:* b Ston, Yugoslavia, Jan 29, 13; m 41; c 3. *Educ:* Univ Zagreb, BS, 38, DVM, 41; Univ Giessen, PhD(vet med), 44. *Prof Exp:* Teaching asst animal infectious dis, Univ Zagreb, 39-46; res assoc vaccine & sera prod, Vetserum Kalinovica, Yugoslavia, 46-53; from res assoc virol to assoc prof zoonoses, Sch Med, Univ Zagreb, 53-61; vis prof virol, Univ Sask, 61-63. *Concurrent Pos:* Yugoslav fel, Univ Wis-Madison, 56-59. *Mem:* Asn Yugoslav Microbiologists (treas, 40-45); Wildlife Dis Asn; Sigma Xi. *Res:* Epidemiology, diagnosis and immunology in groups of mixoviruses; arbor-viruses and psittacosis lymphogranuloma venereum agents. *Mailing Add:* 4505 Onaway Pass Madison WI 53711-2711

SPALL, HENRY ROGER, GEOPHYSICS. *Current Pos:* GEOPHYSICIST, US GEOL SURV, 73- *Personal Data:* b Newcastle upon Tyne, Eng, Oct 10, 38; US citizen; m 70, Juliet Ridley. *Educ:* Univ London, BSc, 62, PhD(geophys), 70; Southern Methodist Univ, MS, 68. *Prof Exp:* Res asst geophys, Cambridge Univ, 62-64 & Southwest Ctr Advan Studies, Univ Tex, Dallas, 64-67; lectr geol, Southern Methodist Univ, 67-68; geologist, Mobil Res Labs, 68-69; Coop Inst Res Environ Sci fel, Univ Colo, Boulder, 70-71; geophysicist, Environ Res Labs, Nat Oceanic & Atmospheric Admin, 71-73. *Concurrent Pos:* Mem working group 10, Comn Geodynamics, Int Union Geod & Geophys, 72-76; ed, Geol, 73-81 & Earthquakes & Volcanoes, 75-90; info handling panel, Ocean Drilling Prog, 88- *Mem:* Am Geophys Union; Seismol Soc Am; fel Geol Soc Am; fel Royal Astron Soc; Europ Asn Sci Ed; Geologists' Asn. *Res:* Paleomagnetism and plate tectonics. *Mailing Add:* 11319 French Horn Lane Reston VA 20191. *E-Mail:* hspall@usgs.gov

SPALL, WALTER DALE, ANALYTICAL CHEMISTRY. *Current Pos:* MEM STAFF, LOS ALAMOS SCI LAB, UNIV CALIF, NMEX, 75- *Personal Data:* b Greeley, Colo, Apr 23, 43; m 70. *Educ:* Colo Col, BA, 66; Univ NMex, PhD(analytical chem), 70. *Prof Exp:* Res chemist, Chem Div, Uniroyal, Inc, 70-75. *Concurrent Pos:* Part-time asst prof, Univ New Haven, 71-75. *Mem:* Am Chem Soc; Sigma Xi. *Res:* Chromatography; analytical instrumentation; computer automation of instrumentation; mass spectroscopy. *Mailing Add:* 365 Brighton Loop Los Alamos NM 87544

SPALLHOLZ, JULIAN ERNEST, BIOCHEMISTRY, NUTRITION. *Current Pos:* assoc prof, 78-84, PROF, DEPT FOOD & NUTRIT, TEX TECH UNIV, 84- *Personal Data:* b Boston, Mass, Oct 8, 43; m 64; c 2. *Educ:* Col State Univ, BS, 65, MS, 68; Univ Hawaii, PhD(biochem), 71. *Prof Exp:* Fel, Dept Biochem, Colo State Univ, 71-72, res assoc, 72-73, instr, 73-74; res chemist nutrit, Lab Exp Metab Dis, Vet Admin Hosp, 74-78; assoc res chemist, State Univ NY, Albany, 78. *Concurrent Pos:* Interim dir, Inst Nutrit Sci, 81-84, dir, 85-91; ed-in-chief, J Nutrit Immunol, 89- *Mem:* Sigma Xi; Am Inst Nutrit. *Res:* Nutritional importance of trace metals, especially selenium; immunology toxicology; free radical research; application of physical probes such as nitroxides, fluorescent molecules and radionuclide probes to biological, biochemical and immunological research. *Mailing Add:* Dept Food & Nutrit Tex Tech Univ Lubbock TX 79409. *Fax:* 806-742-3042

SPANDE, THOMAS FREDERICK, ORGANIC CHEMISTRY. *Current Pos:* Staff fel org chem, 64-66, RES CHEMIST, NIH, 66- *Personal Data:* b Madison, Wis, June 22, 37; m 68. *Educ:* St Olaf Col, BA, 59; Princeton Univ, PhD(org chem), 65. *Mem:* Am Chem Soc. *Res:* Steroid chemistry; amino acid and protein chemistry, particularly indole and tryptophan chemistry. *Mailing Add:* Lab 1A-18 Lab Bioorganic Chem Bldg Eight NIDDK Bethesda MD 20892

SPANDORFER, LESTER M, ELECTRICAL ENGINEERING, COMPUTER SCIENCE. *Current Pos:* PRES, DESIGN DATA, INT, 85- *Personal Data:* b Philadelphia, Pa, Oct 16, 25; m 56; c 2. *Educ:* Univ Mich, BSME, 47, MSEE, 48; Univ Pa, PhD(elec eng), 56. *Prof Exp:* Mem tech staff, Bell Tel Labs, 48-50; res asst dir comput ctr & proj mgr, Univ Pa, 50-57; sr engr, Sperry Univac Div, Sperry Rand Corp, 57-58, dept mgr, 58-60, staff consult, 60-65, dept mgr, 65-67, dir tech develop, 67-72, dir data entry, 72-77, off automation, 77-85. *Mem:* Fel Inst Elec & Electronics Engrs. *Res:* Computer design; application of semiconductor and magnetic devices. *Mailing Add:* 8012 Ellen Lane Cheltenham PA 19012

SPANEL, LESLIE EDWARD, SOLID STATE PHYSICS. *Current Pos:* asst prof, 68-74, ASSOC PROF PHYSICS, WESTERN WASH UNIV, 74- *Personal Data:* b St Louis, Mo, Mar 13, 37; m 61; c 2. *Educ:* Univ Mo-Rolla, BS, 59; Iowa State Univ, PhD(physics), 64. *Prof Exp:* Res asst physics, Ames Lab, AEC, Iowa State Univ, 60-64; res specialist, Microelectronics Orgn, Boeing Space Div, Boeing Co, 64-68. *Mem:* Am Phys Soc. *Res:* Fermi surface of magnetic and nonmagnetic metals; transport properties of semiconductors. *Mailing Add:* 901 Liberty St Bellingham WA 98225

SPANG, ARTHUR WILLIAM, MICROCHEMISTRY. *Current Pos:* OWNER, SPANG MICROANALYTICAL LAB, 54- *Personal Data:* b Detroit, Mich, Aug 16, 17; m 44, 67; c 5. *Educ:* Wayne State Univ, BS, 41. *Prof Exp:* Org microanalyst & head lab, Parke, Davis & Co, 41-48, med detailing, 48-49; mem analytical staff, Upjohn Co, 49-50; head microanalytical lab, Olin Mathieson Chem Corp, 50, supvr res analytical lab, 51-54. *Mem:* Am Chem Soc; Am Microchem Soc; Royal Soc Chem. *Res:* New methods for the microanalysis of new types of organic and organometallic compounds. *Mailing Add:* PO Box 2327 Red Lodge MI 59068

SPANG, H AUSTIN, III, CONTROL ENGINEERING. *Current Pos:* CONTROL ENGR, GEN ELEC RES & DEVELOP CTR, 60- *Personal Data:* b New Haven, Conn, July 16, 34; m 57; c 3. *Educ:* Yale Univ, BE, 56, MEng, 58, DEng (elec eng), 60. *Prof Exp:* Lab asst, Yale Univ, 56-58, res engr commun, 58-60. *Concurrent Pos:* Instr, New Haven Col, 58-60; lectr, Univ Calif, Los Angeles, 66-69; assoc ed, Automatica, Int Fedn Automatic Control, 67-80; assoc ed appln, Inst Elec & Electronics Engrs Trans Automatic Control, 77-79; ed, Automatica, Int Fedn Automatic Control, 80- *Mem:* Fel Inst Elec & Electronics Engrs; Soc Indust & Appl Math; Sigma Xi. *Res:* Applications of control and their digital implementation; multivariable control; real-time computer control; computer aided control system design. *Mailing Add:* 2525 Hilltop Rd Schenectady NY 12309-2406

SPANGENBERG, DOROTHY BRESLIN, ZOOLOGY, BIOCHEMISTRY. *Current Pos:* assoc prof, 77-80, RES PROF, EASTERN VA MED SCH, 80- *Personal Data:* b Galveston, Tex, Aug 31, 31; m 58; c 1. *Educ:* Univ Tex, BA, 56, MA, 58, PhD(zool), 60. *Prof Exp:* Dir, Spangenberg Labs, 60-62; res assoc, Med Ctr, Univ Ark, 62-65; assoc prof biol res, Univ Little Rock, 65-66; res scholar zool, Ind Univ, 66-69; res assoc, Water Resources Lab, Univ Louisville, 69-70; Dept Oral Biol, Sch Dent, 70-72; vis assoc prof molecular, cellular & develop biol, Univ Colo, Boulder, 72-77. *Concurrent Pos:* Grants, NSF, 64-66, Sigma Xi, 65-66, NIH, 66-, NIH & Nat Inst Dent Res, 78, NIH & Nat Inst Child Health & Human Develop & Dept Energy Contract, 77-82 & NASA, 84- *Mem:* Am Soc Zoologists; Am Soc Cell Biol; Sigma Xi; Electron Micros Soc Am; AAAS; Am Soc Gravity & Space Biol. *Res:* Development of coelenterate model systems for study of mechanisms of cellular and organismal development, especially metamorphosis, utilizing biochemical and cytological technics; effects of microgravity on development and behavior of jellyfish. *Mailing Add:* 6085 River Crescent Norfolk VA 23505-4706

SPANGLER, BRENDA DOLGIN, PROTEIN STRUCTURE-FUNCTION RELATIONSHIPS & BACTERIAL TOXINS, MACROMOLECULAR INTERACTION. *Current Pos:* instr, Dept Biol Sci, 65-69, ADJ ASST PROF BIOCHEM & MICROBIOL, DEPT CHEM & DEPT BIOL SCI, NORTHERN ILL UNIV, 91- *Personal Data:* b Philadelphia, Pa, Feb 14, 39; m 61, Charles W; c 2. *Educ:* Brandeis Univ, BS, 61; Ohio Wesleyan Univ, MS, 65; Northern Ill Univ, PhD(biochem), 84. *Prof Exp:* Res asst, NIH-Nat Cancer Inst, Lab Viral Oncol, 62-64; res assoc, Dept Chem, Univ Ill, Chicago, 84-86; appointee, Biol & Med Res Div, Argonne Nat Lab, 86-91. *Concurrent Pos:* Guest scientist, Biol Med Res Div, Argonne Nat Lab, 91- *Mem:* AAAS; Am Chem Soc; Am Crystallog Asn; Am Soc Microbiol. *Res:* Protein structure-function relationships; molecular recognition; bacterial protein toxins especially choleratoxin, pertussis toxin; protein crystallization; protein-ligand interaction. *Mailing Add:* 3425 Sourdough Rd Bozeman MT 59715. *Fax:* 815-753-4802; *E-Mail:* spangler@cz.chem.niu.edu

SPANGLER, CHARLES WILLIAM, PHYSICAL ORGANIC CHEMISTRY, POLYMER CHEMISTRY. *Current Pos:* from asst prof to assoc prof, 65-81, PROF ORG CHEM, NORTHERN ILL UNIV, 81- *Personal Data:* b Philadelphia, Pa, Feb 12, 38; m 61, Brenda Dolgin; c David R & Daniel L. *Educ:* Mass Inst Technol, BS, 59; Northeastern Univ, MS, 61; Univ Md, PhD(org chem), 64. *Prof Exp:* Great Lakes Cols Asn teacher intern org chem, Ohio Wesleyan Univ, 64-65. *Concurrent Pos:* Res Corp, NSF, Army Off Res, Air Force Off Sci Res, Eppley Found Petrol Res Fund, NATO Travel, res grants; presidential res prof, Northern Ill Univ, 91- *Mem:* Am Chem Soc; Royal Soc Chem; Mat Res Soc; Int Soc Optical Engr. *Res:* Chemistry of conjugated polyenes; electrophilic substitution; new organic materials for nonlinear optics; electrocyclic reactions; photochemistry of polyunsaturated systems; sigmatropic migrations; conjugated conducting polymers and monomers; superconducting polymers. *Mailing Add:* Chem Northern Ill Univ 1425 W Lincoln Hwy De Kalb IL 60115-2825. *Fax:* 815-753-4802; *E-Mail:* cws@marilyn.chem.nu.edu

SPANGLER, DANIEL PATRICK, GEOLOGY, HYDROLOGY & WATER RESOURCES. *Current Pos:* asst prof, 74-77, ASSOC PROF GEOL, UNIV FLA, 77- *Personal Data:* b Meadows of Dan, Va, Apr 22, 34; m 61; c 1. *Educ:* Berea Col, BA, 56; Univ Va, MS, 64; Univ Ariz, PhD(geol), 69. *Prof Exp:* Geologist, Va Hwy Dept, 57-59 & 61-63; asst, Univ Va, 63-65 & Univ Ariz, 65-67; geologist, Agr Res Serv, USDA, 67-69; asst prof geol, SFla Univ, 69-74. *Concurrent Pos:* Consult, hydrogeol, 69-; partic, NSF-Am Geol Inst Tenth Int Field Inst, Spain, 71; res award, Univ SFla & Penrose bequest res grant, Geol Soc Am, Tampa, Fla, 72; state & fed res grants, 74- *Mem:* Geol Soc Am; Am Water Resources Asn; Nat Asn Geol Teachers; Nat Water Well Asn; Am Inst Prof Geologists; Sigma Xi. *Res:* Hydrogeologic systems; wetlands and karst; engineering and economic geology. *Mailing Add:* Dept Geol Univ Fla 1212 Turlington Hall Gainesville FL 32611-2002. *Fax:* 352-392-9294; *E-Mail:* spang@nervm.nerdc.ufl.edu

SPANGLER, FRED WALTER, CHEMISTRY. *Current Pos:* RETIRED. *Personal Data:* b Park Ridge, Ill, Feb 27, 18; m 41, Margaret Thomas; c Janice & James. *Educ:* Carthage Col, AB, 40; Univ Ill, PhD(org chem), 44. *Prof Exp:* Res chemist, Eastman Kodak Co, 44-52, tech assoc, 52-59, asst supt, Film Emulsion Div, 59-81. *Mem:* Am Chem Soc; Soc Photog Sci & Eng. *Res:* Grignard reactions involving the naphthalene nucleus; organic chemicals used in photography; anthraquinone and related dyes; detergents and wetting agents; photographic emulsions. *Mailing Add:* 121 Nob Hill Rochester NY 14617

SPANGLER, GEORGE RUSSELL, AQUATIC ECOLOGY, POPULATION DYNAMICS. *Current Pos:* ASSOC PROF FISHERIES, UNIV MINN, 78- *Personal Data:* b Susanville, Calif, Oct 22, 42; m 62; c 4. *Educ:* Humboldt State Col, BS, 64; Univ Toronto, MS, 66, PhD(zool), 74. *Prof Exp:* Res scientist fisheries, Ont Dept Lands & Forests, 68-71; scientist-in-chg, Lake Huron Res Unit, Ont Ministry Natural Resources, 72-78. *Mem:* Am Fisheries Soc; Int Asn Great Lakes Res; Biomet Soc; Am Inst Fishery Res Biologists. *Res:* Population dynamics of fish stocks; predator-prey interactions; effects of exploitation on fish communities; efficiency and selectivity of fishing gear. *Mailing Add:* Dept Fisheries & Wildlife Univ Minn 200 Hodson Hall 1980 Folwell Ave St Paul MN 55108-1037

SPANGLER, GLENN EDWARD, forensic science, environmental detection technology, for more information see previous edition

SPANGLER, GRANT EDWARD, METALLURGICAL ENGINEERING, MATERIAL SCIENCES. *Current Pos:* res scientist, Reynolds Metals Co, 64-65, sect dir, 56-66, 65-66, dept dir, 66-78, GEN DIR METALL RES DIV, REYNOLDS METALS CO, 78- *Personal Data:* b Lebanon, Pa, Oct 17, 26; m 54; c 3. *Educ:* Lehigh Univ, BS, 50; Univ Pa, MS, 53. *Prof Exp:* Res scientist metall, Westinghouse Atomic Power Div, 50-52, Res Lab, Air Reduction Co, 53-56 & Franklin Inst Res Labs, 56-64. *Mem:* Fel Am Soc Metals; Am Inst Mining, Metall & Petrol Engrs. *Res:* Fuel element development; treatment of molten metals by powder injection; purification of reactive metals by floating zone refining; alloy development, physical metallurgy and process metallurgy of aluminum and aluminum alloys. *Mailing Add:* 307 Coal Port Rd Richmond VA 23229

SPANGLER, HAYWARD GOSSE, ENTOMOLOGY. *Current Pos:* RES ENTOMOLOGIST, CARL HAYDEN BEE RES CTR, AGR RES SERV, USDA, ARIZ, 67- *Personal Data:* b Redbank, NJ, July 6, 38; m 66; c 2. *Educ:* La Sierra Col, BS, 61; Univ Ariz, MS, 63; Kans State Univ, PhD(entom), 67. *Mem:* Entom Soc Am; Am Entom Soc; Int Union Study Social Insects. *Res:* Insect behavior; acoustical communication in bees, moths and beetles. *Mailing Add:* Carl Hayden Bee Res Ctr USDA-ARS 2000 E Allen Rd Tucson AZ 85719

SPANGLER, JOHN ALLEN, CHEMISTRY. *Current Pos:* assoc prof, 46-52, chmn dept, 55-58, PROF CHEM, SAN DIEGO STATE UNIV, 54- *Personal Data:* b Morgantown, WVa, Jan 1, 18; m 48; c 3. *Educ:* WVa Univ, AB, 39, PhD(chem), 42. *Prof Exp:* Res chemist, Am Viscose Corp, 42-44. *Mem:* Am Chem Soc. *Res:* Multiple-junction thermocouples for low freezing-point measurements; physical constants related to easier methods of analysis; ternary systems; physical methods of analysis; fiber chemistry. *Mailing Add:* 4959 Catactin Dr San Diego CA 92115-2608

SPANGLER, JOHN DAVID, PHYSICS. *Current Pos:* from asst prof to assoc prof, 65-80, PROF PHYSICS, KANS STATE UNIV, 80- *Personal Data:* b Lincoln, Nebr, Nov 18, 36; m 58; c 5. *Educ:* Kans State Univ, BS, 58; Duke Univ, PhD(physics), 61. *Prof Exp:* Res assoc physics, Duke Univ, 61-62; asst prof, DePauw Univ, 64-65. *Mem:* Am Phys Soc; Soc Indust & Appl Math; Am Asn Physics Teachers. *Res:* Theoretical applied physics. *Mailing Add:* 601 Brevoort Lane Green Bay WI 54301-2627

SPANGLER, LORA LEE, THERMAL ANALYSIS OF POLYMERS, POLYMER PHYSICS. *Current Pos:* SR RES ENGR, CHEM GROUP, MONSANTO CO, 92- *Personal Data:* b Lebanon, Pa, Oct 30, 64; m, J Scot Royal. *Educ:* Univ Del, BchE, 86; Northwestern Univ, PhD(chem eng), 92. *Prof Exp:* Engr, Mobil Oil Corp, 86-87. *Mem:* Am Chem Soc; Am Asn Univ Women; Nat Asn Female Execs. *Res:* Polymer diffusion; polymer crystallization; thermal analysis of polymer including degradation studies, structure-property relationships and rheology. *Mailing Add:* 39 Segur Lane Belchertown MA 01151. *E-Mail:* ilspan@wicken.monsanto.com

SPANGLER, MARTIN ORD LEE, ORGANIC CHEMISTRY, BIOCHEMISTRY. *Current Pos:* from assoc prof to prof, 66-93, chmn dept, 73-80, EMER PROF CHEM, ELIZABETHTOWN COL, 93- *Personal Data:* b Roanoke, Va, Sept 17, 28; m 56, Mary L Wampler; c Nancy, Julia, John & Susan. *Educ:* Bridgewater Col, BA, 50; Va Polytech Inst & State Univ, MS, 53, PhD(chem), 59. *Prof Exp:* Res assoc analyst biol fluids, Univ Mich Hosp, 53-55; instr chem, Va Polytech Inst & State Univ, 55-56; assoc prof, Waynesburg Col, 58-59 & King Col, 59-66. *Concurrent Pos:* Vis prof, Hershey Med Ctr, Pa State Univ, 72-73; lectr, Ohio State Univ, 80-81. *Mem:* AAAS; Am Chem Soc; Sigma Xi. *Res:* Organic synthesis and mechanisms of organic reactions; synthesis of antitumor agents and antibiotics from sugar derivatives. *Mailing Add:* Dept Chem 216 Musser Elizabethtown Col Elizabethtown PA 17022-2298

SPANGLER, PAUL JUNIOR, ENTOMOLOGY. *Current Pos:* CUR, DIV COLEOPTERA, NAT MUS NATURAL HIST, SMITHSONIAN INST, 62- *Personal Data:* b York, Pa, Nov 21, 24; m 50; c 1. *Educ:* Lebanon Valley Col, AB, 49; Ohio Univ, MS, 51; Univ Mo, PhD(entom), 60. *Prof Exp:* Mus asst entom, Univ Kans, 51-53; instr entom, Univ Mo, 53-57; fishery res biologist, US Fish & Wildlife Serv, 57-58; syst entomologist, Entom Res Div, Agr Res Serv, USDA, 58-62. *Concurrent Pos:* Lectr, Grad Fac, Univ Md. *Mem:* Entom Soc Am; Sigma Xi. *Res:* Systematics, biology and zoogeography of aquatic beetles. *Mailing Add:* Dept Entom MRC-169 Nat Mus Natural Hist Smithsonian Inst Washington DC 20560

SPANGLER, ROBERT ALAN, BIOPHYSICS. *Current Pos:* Res fel, 59-65, asst prof, 65-70, actg chmn dept, 70-77, ASSOC PROF BIOPHYS, SCH MED, STATE UNIV NY BUFFALO, 70- *Personal Data:* b Celina, Ohio, Apr 10, 33; m 59. *Educ:* Harvard Univ, AB, 55, MD, 59; State Univ NY Buffalo, PhD(biophys), 64. *Mem:* Biophys Soc; NY Acad Sci; AAAS. *Res:* Chemical kinetics in biological systems; non-equilibrium thermodynamics of biological systems; transport; models; medical diagnostic imaging. *Mailing Add:* Dept Biophys Sci State Univ NY at Buffalo 116 Cary Hall Buffalo NY 14214-3005. *Fax:* 716-329-2415; *E-Mail:* spangler@ubmed.buffalo.edu

SPANGLER, STEVEN RANDALL, RADIO ASTRONOMY, THEORETICAL ASTROPHYSICS. *Current Pos:* res assoc, 76-78, ASST SCIENTIST RADIO ASTRON, NAT RADIO ASTRON OBSERV, 78- *Personal Data:* b Stamford, Conn, Sept 25, 50; m 70; c 2. *Educ:* Univ Iowa, BA & MS, 72, PhD(physics), 75. *Prof Exp:* Res assoc space physics, Univ Iowa, 75-76. *Mem:* Am Astron Soc; Am Phys Soc. *Res:* Observations of extragalactic radio sources and their interpretation in terms of hydrodynamics, statistical physics and radiation theory. *Mailing Add:* 3217 Shamrock Dr Iowa City IA 52245-5131

SPANIER, ARTHUR M, PHYSIOLOGY, BIOCHEMISTRY. *Current Pos:* res physiologist, 85-86, LEAD SCIENTIST & RES PHYSIOLOGIST, USDA/ARG RES SERV SOUTHERN REGIONAL RES CTR, 86- *Personal Data:* b New York, NY, July 5, 48; m 72, Sharon Hoffman; c Adam J, Holly E, Rebecca L & David A. *Educ:* Herbert H Lehman Col City Univ New York, BA, 70, MA, 74; Rutgers State Univ NJ, PhD(physiol), 77. *Prof Exp:* MDAA postdoc fel, Dept Med, Univ Chicago, 77-79, NIH fel, 79-80,; res assoc & instr biophys, Med Col Va, 80-81; asst mem, Okla Med Res Found, 81-85. *Concurrent Pos:* Prin investr, Univ Chicago, 77-79 & Okla Res Found, NIH, 83-86; co-investr, 3 NIH grants to Okla Med Res Found, 81-85, Med Col Va, 80-81 & Univ Chicago, 79-80; adj asst prof physiol & biophys, Univ Okla Health Sci Ctr, 82-85; consult, George Washington Univ, 85-92; from adj asst prof to adj prof, Dept Food Sci, La State Univ, 86-; consult, 93- *Mem:* Am Physiol Soc; Am Chem Soc; Am Soc Cell Biol; Inst Food Technologists; Am Meat Sci Asn; Am Comt on Proteolysis. *Res:* Muscle & meat physiology; quality of fresh-cut fruit; food flavor chemistry and nutrition; protein, peptide and amino acid flavor; proteinase biochemistry; natural food product chemistry; lysosomes, lysosomal hydrolases of muscle and other tissue. *Mailing Add:* USDA/ARS-SRRC 1100 Robert E Lee Bldg New Orleans LA 70124. *Fax:* 504-286-4419; *E-Mail:* aspanier@nola.srrc.udsa.gov

SPANIER, EDWARD J, INORGANIC CHEMISTRY. *Current Pos:* RETIRED. *Personal Data:* b Philadelphia, Pa, May 13, 37; m 68, Helene M Moeltner; c Christopher E & David E. *Educ:* La Salle Univ, BA, 59; Univ Pa, PhD(inorg chem), 64. *Prof Exp:* Res chemist, E I du Pont de Nemours & Co, 64-65; assoc prof inorg chem, Seton Hall Univ, 65-72; asst dean sci & eng, Wright State Univ, 72-73, assoc dir planning health affairs, 73-74, asst dean admin, Sch Med, 74-75, assoc dean admin, Sch Med, 75-80, asst vpres health affairs, 80-81, asst vpres financial serv, 81-85, treas, 84-92, vpres bus & finance, 85-95. *Concurrent Pos:* Adj assoc prof chem, Wright State Univ, 72- *Mem:* AAAS; Am Chem Soc; Sigma Xi. *Res:* Chemistry of the hydrides of boron, silicon and germanium; nuclear magnetic resonance; reactions of metal carbides; chemistry of group V elements. *Mailing Add:* 1966 State Rd 65 Spring Valley OH 45370. *Fax:* 513-873-3711; *E-Mail:* espanier@desire.wright.edu

SPANIER, EDWIN HENRY, mathematics; deceased, see previous edition for last biography

SPANIER, GRAHAM BASIL, SOCIOLOGY, FAMILY RELATIONS. *Current Pos:* CHANCELLOR, UNIV NEBR, LINCOLN, 91- *Personal Data:* b Cape Town, SAfrica, July 18, 48; m 71, Sandra K Whipple; c Brian L & Hadley A. *Educ:* Iowa State Univ, BS, 69, MS, 71; Northwestern Univ, PhD, 73. *Honors & Awards:* Moran Award, Am Home Econ Asn, 87. *Prof Exp:* Assoc dean & prof in charge, Pa State Univ, University Park, 73-82; vprovost & prof, State Univ NY, Stony Brook, 82-86; vprovost & vpres acad affairs, Ore State Univ, 86-91. *Concurrent Pos:* Woodrow Wilson fel, 72-73; soc sci analyst, US Bur Census, 78; deleg, White House Conf Families, 80; chmn, Family Sect, Am Sociol Asn, 83-84; fel, Am Asn Marriage & Family Ther, 83-; chmn bd, Christian Childrens Fund, 92-94. *Mem:* Nat Coun Family Rels (pres, 87-88); Int Acad Sex Res; Pop Asn Am; Am Sociol Asn; Int Sociol Asn. *Res:* Quality and stability of marriage across the life course; family demography; measurement of marriage and family behavior. *Mailing Add:* Human Dev & Fam Univ Nebr E Campus PO Box 830809 Lincoln NE 68583-0809. *Fax:* 402-472-5110; *E-Mail:* gspanier@unl.edu

SPANIER, JEROME, NUMERICAL ANALYSIS, APPLIED PROBABILITY. *Current Pos:* dean, 82-88, vpres & dean, 86-88, PROF MATH, CLAREMONT GRAD SCH, 71- *Personal Data:* b St Paul, Minn, June 3, 30; m 52, Bernice Hoffman; c Stephen A, Adrienne E & Ruth A. *Educ:* Univ Minn, BA, 51; Univ Chicago, MS, 52, PhD(math), 55. *Prof Exp:* Asst, Univ Minn, 50-51; mathematician, Bettis Atomic Power Lab, Westinghouse Elec Corp, Pa, 55-67; mem tech staff, Math Group, NAm Rockwell Corp, Calif, 67-70, group leader math group, Sci Ctr, 70-71. *Concurrent Pos:* Fulbright sr scholar, Massey Univ, NZ, 90. *Mem:* Am Math Soc; Soc Indust & Appl Math; Math Asn Am; AAAS. *Res:* Monte Carlo methods; numerical analysis; random walk processes; transport theory; applications of numerical techniques to nuclear reactor design. *Mailing Add:* Prof Math Claremont Grad Sch Claremont CA 91711-3988

SPANIOL, CRAIG, ALTERNATIVE ENERGY SYSTEMS. *Current Pos:* assoc prof indust tech, 85-92, PROF, WVA STATE COL, 92- *Personal Data:* b Charleston, WVa, Feb 22, 44; m 63; c 3. *Educ:* WVa State Col, BS, 66; Ohio Univ, MS, 69; Rensselaer Polytech Inst, PhD(eng sci), 74. *Prof Exp:* Elec engr, E M Johnson Consult Eng, 62-66; elec engr, Chesapeake & Potomac Tel Co, 66-70; nuclear engr, Gen Elec Co, 70-73; prin engr nuclear eng, Babcock & Wilcox Co, 73-76; asst prof elec eng, WVa Inst Technol, 76-81; consult engr, Midwest Tech, Inc, 81- *Concurrent Pos:* Pvt legal consult, 76- *Mem:* Inst Elec & Electronics Engrs; Am Nuclear Soc. *Res:* High temperature furnace/autoclave development; high pressure gas encapulation; crystal technology; alternative energy systems. *Mailing Add:* Dept Indust Tech WVa State Col Institute WV 25112

SPANIS, CURT WILLIAM, NEUROPHYSIOLOGY, PSYCHOLOGY. *Current Pos:* RESEARCHER, DEPT PSYCHIAT, VET MEM HOSP, LA JOLLA, CALIF, 75- *Personal Data:* b Barrie, Ont, May 6, 32; US citizen; m 65. *Educ:* Queen's Univ, Ont, BA, 57; Univ Calif, Los Angeles, MA, 60, PhD(physiol), 62; Alvarez Soc Med, Mex, dipl, 75. *Prof Exp:* Asst prof biol, San Diego State Col, 62-63 & microbiol, Inst Marine Sci, Univ Miami, 64; fel biol clocks, Scripps Inst Oceanog, Univ Calif, San Diego, 64-65; from asst prof to assoc prof biol, 65-70, chmn dept, 66-72, prof biol, Univ San Diego, 72- *Concurrent Pos:* NIH grants, Univ Miami, 64, Scripps Inst Oceanog, Univ Calif, San Diego, 64-65, Univ San Diego, 69-72; NSF grants, 64 & 75; vis prof, Biol Inst, Helgoland, Germany, 64; mem NSF grants rev bd. *Mem:* Fel Am Inst Chem; hon mem Mex Soc Biol Psychiat; Soc Neurosci; Brit Brain Res Asn; Am Soc Microbiol; Int Brain Res Orgn-World Fedn Neuroscientists. *Res:* Sleep and the biochemistry of rapid eye movement sleep; memory; amnesia-electroshock; exercise physiology, sports medicine and nutrition. *Mailing Add:* Dept Biol Univ San Diego San Diego CA 92110-2429

SPANN, CHARLES HENRY, EXPERIMENTAL PATHOLOGY, HUMAN ANATOMY. *Current Pos:* ASSOC PROF BIOL & DIR HEALTH CAREERS, JACKSON STATE UNIV, 74- *Personal Data:* b Brandon, Miss, Sept 11, 39; m 63; c 3. *Educ:* Tougaloo Col BS, 62; Univ Miss Med Ctr, MS, 73, PhD(human anat & path), 74. *Prof Exp:* Instr biol & sci, Holtzclaw High Sch, 66-69 & Crystal Springs High Sch, Miss, 69-70. *Concurrent Pos:* Consult pre-nursing prog, Meridian Jr Col, Miss, 76-77; res trainer, Minority Biomed Res Support Prog, Jackson State Univ, 77-, dir, 81-, dir, Health Careers Training Prog. *Mem:* Am Soc Anatomists; AAAS. *Res:* Relationship and susceptibility to endotoxic shock, with emphasis on the histopathological effects of the general viscera and treatment modalities. *Mailing Add:* Dept Biol Jackson State Univ 1400 John R Lynch St Jackson MS 39217-0001

SPANN, JAMES FLETCHER, (JR), CARDIOLOGY. *Current Pos:* PROF MED, CHIEF CARDIOVASC SECT, HEALTH SCI CTR, TEMPLE UNIV, 70- *Personal Data:* b Dothan, Ala, Nov 21, 35; m 56; c 2. *Educ:* Emory Univ, MD, 61. *Prof Exp:* Intern med, Mass Gen Hosp, 61, asst resident, 62; sr investr, Cardiol Br, attend physician, Sr consult cardiologist & med coordr, Surg Br, Nat Heart Inst, 66-68; assoc prof med & physiol, chief cardiovasc diag & asst chief cardiovasc med, Sch Med, Univ Calif, Davis, 68-70. *Concurrent Pos:* Fel, Cardiol Br, Nat Heart Inst, 63-65, spec fel, 65-66. *Mem:* AAAS; Am Col Cardiol; Am Fedn Clin Res; NY Acad Sci; Am Soc Pharmacol & Exp Therapeut. *Res:* Clinical and investigative cardiology; cardiovascular physiology and pathophysiology; cardiac hypertrophy and congestive heart failure. *Mailing Add:* Cardiol Div Med Univ SCarolina 171 Ashley Ave Charleston SC 29401-5801

SPANNINGER, PHILIP ANDREW, ORGANIC CHEMISTRY. *Current Pos:* VPRES, INT, GENCORP, INC, 88- *Personal Data:* b Quakertown, Pa, May 31, 43; m 63; Detweiler; c 3. *Educ:* Philadelphia Col Textiles & Sci, BS, 65; Clemson Univ, MS, 67, PhD(org chem), 70. *Prof Exp:* NIH fel, Univ Tex, Austin, 70-71; sr res chemist, Polyester Res, Goodyear, 71-74, proj mgr, joint ventures & licensing technol, 74-77, mgr, Int Chem Div, 77-80, dir, technol & ventures mgt, 80-88. *Concurrent Pos:* Sch Indust Mgt, Carnegie-Mellon Univ. *Mem:* Am Chem Soc. *Res:* Organometallic chemistry; stereochemistry; reaction mechanisms; catalysis; boron-nitrogen heteroaromatic compounds; high temperature polymers; polyester chemistry. *Mailing Add:* 2555 Olentangy Dr Akron OH 44333

SPANO, FRANCIS A, ORGANIC CHEMISTRY, BIOCHEMISTRY. *Current Pos:* asst prof org chem, 66-72, PROF CHEM, MIDDLESEX COUNTY COL, 72-, DEAN DIV SCI, 73- *Personal Data:* b New York, NY, Jan 6, 31; m 59; c 3. *Educ:* City Col New York, BS, 53; Fordham Univ, PhD(org chem), 63. *Prof Exp:* Res chemist, Allied Chem Corp, 62-66; res specialist, Gen Aniline & Film Corp, 66. *Mem:* Am Chem Soc. *Res:* Illucidation of ozone oxidation of heterocyclic aeromatic compounds. *Mailing Add:* Dept Chem Middlesex County Col 155 Mill Rd PO Box 3050 Edison NJ 08818-3050

SPANOS, POL DIMITRIOS, MECHANICAL ENGINEERING. *Current Pos:* prof mech eng & civil eng, 84-88, L B RYON ENDOWED CHAIR ENG, RICE UNIV, HOUSTON, 88- *Personal Data:* b Messini, Peloponneuos, Greece, Feb 27, 50; c Demetri & Eudokia. *Educ:* Nat Tech Univ, Athens, dipl mech eng, 73; Calif Inst Technol, MS, 74, PhD(appl mech), 76. *Honors & Awards:* Pi Tau Sigma Gold Medal, Am Soc Mech Engrs, 82, G L Larson Mem Award, 91; W L Huber Civil Eng Res Prize, Am Soc Civil Engrs, 89, Alfred M Freudenthal Medal, 92. *Prof Exp:* Res fel, Calif Inst Technol, 76-77; from asst prof to assoc prof, Univ Tex, Austin, 81-84, P D Henderson assoc prof eng, 83-84. *Concurrent Pos:* Presidential young investr earthquake eng, NSF, 84-89; Humboldt res award sr sci, 95. *Mem:* Am Soc Mech Engrs; Am Soc Civil Engrs; Am Acad Mech; Earthquake Eng Res Inst, Int Asn Struct Safety & Reliability; Am Soc Eng Educ. *Res:* Analytical and numerical applications of theory of dynamics and vibrations. *Mailing Add:* Dept Mech Eng MS 321 Rice Univ 6100 Main St Houston TX 77005-1892. *Fax:* 713-285-5191; *E-Mail:* spanos@rice.edu

SPANSWICK, ROGER MORGAN, BIOPHYSICS, PLANT PHYSIOLOGY. *Current Pos:* asst prof, 67-73, assoc prof, 73-79, PROF PLANT PHYSIOL, CORNELL UNIV, 79- *Personal Data:* b Eng, June 24, 39; m 63; c 2. *Educ:* Univ Birmingham, BSc, 60; Univ Edinburgh, dipl biophys, 61, PhD(biophys), 64. *Prof Exp:* Asst lectr physics, Univ Edinburgh, 62-64; postdoctoral res fel plant biophys, Cambridge Univ, 64-67. *Concurrent Pos:* Sci Res Coun sr vis fel, Cambridge Univ, 73-74; John Simon Guggenheim Mem fel, Univ Calif, Davis, 81-82. *Mem:* Brit Soc Exp Biol; Biophys Soc; Am Soc Plant Physiologists; AAAS. *Res:* Transport of ions across plant cell membranes; intercellular and long distance transport of ions in plants; partitioning of photosynthetic assimilates in relation to seed development in crop plants. *Mailing Add:* Sect Plant Biol Cornell Univ 228 Plant Sci Bldg Ithaca NY 14853-5908. *Fax:* 607-255-5407; *E-Mail:* rms6@cornell.edu

SPAR, IRVING LEO, immunology; deceased, see previous edition for last biography

SPAR, JEROME, METEOROLOGY. *Current Pos:* RETIRED. *Personal Data:* b New York, NY, Oct 7, 18; wid; c Susan & Richard. *Educ:* City Col New York, BS, 40; NY Univ, MS, 43, PhD(meteorol), 50. *Prof Exp:* From instr to prof meteorol, NY Univ, 46-73; prof meteorol, City Col, City Univ New York, 73-84. *Concurrent Pos:* Dir meteorol res, US Weather Bur, 64-65. *Mem:* Fel Am Meteorol Soc. *Res:* Atmospheric radioactivity; numerical weather prediction; cyclogenesis; applied meteorology; climatic variations; synoptic and dynamic meteorology; general circulation and air-sea interactions. *Mailing Add:* 34 Chelsea Rd Essex Junction VT 05452-2615

SPARACINO, CHARLES MORGAN, ORGANIC CHEMISTRY. *Current Pos:* Nat Inst Gen Med Sci fel, 70-71, CHEMIST, RES TRIANGLE INST, RESEARCH TRIANGLE PARK, 71- *Personal Data:* b Charleston, WVa, Oct 18, 41; m 64; c 2. *Educ:* Emory Univ, BS, 65, PhD(org chem), 69. *Prof Exp:* NIH fel, Worcester Found Exp Biol, 69-70. *Mem:* Am Chem Soc. *Res:* Organic synthesis; natural product biosynthesis; drug metabolism. *Mailing Add:* 3209 Jennifer Dr Durham NC 27705-5223

SPARACINO, ROBERT R, ELECTRICAL ENGINEERING, INSTRUMENTATION. *Current Pos:* PRES, SPARACINO ASSOCS, INC, 81-, SPARACINO MGT CO, INC, 83- *Personal Data:* b New York, NY, Nov 6, 27; m 49; c 3. *Educ:* City Col New York, BEE, 50; Polytech Inst Brooklyn, MEE, 55; Mass Inst Technol, ScD, 61. *Prof Exp:* Proj engr, Atlantic Electronics Corp, 50-54; chief engr & asst secy to corp, Penn-East Eng Corp, 54-58; res asst instrumentation, Mass Inst Technol, 58-59 & 60-61; sect head res & develop systs eng, AC Electronics Div, Gen Motors Corp, Wakefield, Mass, 61-62, lab dir, 62-63, dir res & develop, Los Angeles, 63-64, dir res & develop, Milwaukee, 64-68, dir eng, 68-70; vpres & mgr qual assurance dept, Bus Prod Group, Xerox Corp, 70-71, vpres & mgr prod design & eng, 71-73, vpres technol & eng, 73, sr vpres, Copier Duplicator Develop Div, 73-74, pres, Info Technol Group, 75-78, pres, Reprographics Tech Group, 78-80, corp vpres, 74-80, sr vpres, Info Prod Group, 80-82. *Mem:* Inst Elec & Electronics Engrs; Sigma Xi. *Mailing Add:* 175 Blackberry Dr Stamford CT 06903-1207

SPARAPANY, JOHN JOSEPH, physical organic chemistry, for more information see previous edition

SPARBER, SHELDON B, NEUROPSYCHOPHARMACOLOGY, NEUROBEHAVIORAL TOXICOLOGY. *Current Pos:* PROF PHARMACOL & PSYCHIAT & ADJ PROF PSYCHOL, MED SCH, UNIV MINN, 78- *Personal Data:* b Brooklyn, NY, Sept 29, 38. *Educ:* Univ Minn, PhD(pharmacol), 67. *Mem:* Am Soc Pharmacol & Exp Therapeut; AAAS; Soc Neurosci; Soc Develop Psychobiol; Soc Behav Teratology; Sigma Xi. *Mailing Add:* Dept Pharmacol Univ Minn 3-249 Millard Hall 435 Delaware St SE Minneapolis MN 55455-0347. *Fax:* 612-625-8408; *E-Mail:* sparber@umnhsnve.bitnet

SPARBERG, ESTHER BRAUN, HISTORY OF SCIENCE, CHEMISTRY. *Current Pos:* spec instr chem, Hofstra Univ, 59-63, instr, 63-66, from asst prof to assoc prof, chem & hist sci, 66-77, prof hist sci, 77-80, prof, 77-92, EMER PROF, HOFSTRA UNIV, 92- *Personal Data:* b New York, NY, June 17, 22; m 44, Lester; c Andrew & Alice. *Educ:* Univ NC, BS, 43; Columbia Univ, MA, 45, EdD(sci educ), 58. *Prof Exp:* Technician, Rockefeller Inst, 43-44; teacher high sch, NY, 46-47. *Concurrent Pos:* Consult, NSF Coop Col Sch Sci Progs, dir prog, Hofstra-Uniondale Schs, 70-72, Hofstra-New Hyde Park-Herricks Schs, 72-74; dir, NSF proj, Hofstra-Farmingdale, Glen Cove, Wantagh, Queens, NY Schs, 75-76; dir, NSF, Pre-Col Teacher Develop in Sci Proj, Hofstra Univ, 77-79 & Honors Workshop for Teachers, 84-85. *Mem:* Am Chem Soc; Hist Sci Soc; Am Asn Physics Teachers; NY Acad Sci. *Res:* Plasma and serum studies with Tiselius electrophoresis equipment; history of science; physical sciences; chemistry. *Mailing Add:* 25 Emerson Dr Great Neck NY 11023

SPARGO, BENJAMIN H, PATHOLOGY, RENAL. *Current Pos:* From instr to assoc prof, 53-64, PROF PATH, SCH MED, UNIV CHICAGO, 64- *Personal Data:* b Six Mile Run, PA, Aug 18, 19; m 42, Barbara Scollard; c Janet & Patricia. *Educ:* Univ Chicago, BS, 48, MS & MD, 52. *Honors & Awards:* Distinguished Lifetime Achievement Award, Renal Path Soc, 96. *Concurrent Pos:* Res career award, Heart & Lung Inst, NIH, 64-; chmn, comt Diag Electron Micros, Vet Admin, 75- *Mem:* Am Soc Nephrology; Am Acad Path; Can Acad Path. *Res:* Pathology of renal diseases. *Mailing Add:* Dept Pathol BH P312 MC 30-30 Univ Chicago 5841 S Maryland Ave Chicago IL 60637-1463

SPARKES, ROBERT STANLEY, MEDICINE, HUMAN GENETICS. *Current Pos:* vchmn, Dept Med, 81-92, PROF MED & MED GENETICS, SCH MED, UNIV CALIF, LOS ANGELES, 64- *Personal Data:* b Niagara Falls, NY, June 20, 30; m 71; c 2. *Educ:* Antioch Col, BS, 52; Univ Rochester, MD, 56. *Prof Exp:* Assoc med, Sch Med, Univ Wash, 61-63; assoc physician, City of Hope Med Ctr, 63-64. *Mem:* AAAS; Am Soc Human Genetics; Am Fedn Clin Res; Asn Am Physicians. *Res:* Human-medical cytogenetics; human biochemical genetics; genetic linkage; tissue culture. *Mailing Add:* Univ Calif Med Ctr Los Angeles CA 90024

SPARKMAN, DENNIS RAYMOND, ALZHEIMERS DISEASE & DEMENTIA. *Current Pos:* Res assoc, Univ Tex Southwestern Med Ctr, 76-78, asst instr, 82-85, res instr neurol, Inst Path, 85-88, ASST PROF PATH, UNIV TEX SOUTHWESTERN MED CTR, DALLAS, 88- *Personal Data:* b Ennis, Tex, Jan 12, 54. *Educ:* Univ Tex, Arlington, BS, 76; Tex A&M Univ, PhD(cell & molecular biol), 82. *Mem:* AAAS; Am Soc Cell Biol; Sigma Xi; Soc Neurosci; Am Asn Neuropath. *Res:* Pathology of neurofibrillary degeneration and cytoskeletal alterations that occur in Alzheimer's disease, related dementias and Parkinson's disease through isolation of antibodies, cellular and ultrastructural studies and molecular cloning. *Mailing Add:* 161 Rugby Rd Apt D Newport News VA 23606. *Fax:* 214-688-2077

SPARKMAN, DONAL ROSS, MEDICINE. *Current Pos:* From clin asst prof to clin prof, 54-56, assoc prof med, 66-76, EMER ASSOC PROF, MED SCH, UNIV WASH, 76- *Personal Data:* b Seattle, Wash, June 7, 07; m 48; c 4. *Educ:* Univ Wash, BS, 30; Univ Pa, MD, 34; Am Bd Internal Med, dipl, 47. *Concurrent Pos:* Assoc dir, Cancer Control Prog, Fred Hutchinson Cancer Res Ctr, 76-79; at Am Cancer Soc, Seattle, 79-84. *Mem:* Am Heart Asn; Am Col Physicians. *Res:* Cardiac rehabilitation; relationship of stress to heart disease. *Mailing Add:* 6545 Park Point Way NE C-105 Seattle WA 98115-7800

SPARKMAN, MARJORIE FRANCES, PHYSIOLOGY. *Current Pos:* assoc prof, 72-77, PROF PHYSIOL & DIR CONTRACT GRANT ADMIN, COL NURSING, FLA STATE UNIV, 77- *Personal Data:* b McShan, Ala, Jan 25, 23. *Educ:* Fla State Col Women, BM, 45; Univ Ala, BS, 61; Ohio State Univ, MS, 62, PhD(physiol), 68. *Prof Exp:* Instr nursing, Southern Baptist Hosp, New Orleans, La, 51-56; head nurse, Nursing Serv, Wichita Falls Gen Hosp, Tex, 56-57; actg dir nursing, Southern Baptist Hosp Sch Nursing, New Orleans, 58-60; instr nursing, Col Med, Ohio State Univ, 62-64, asst prof physiol, 68-72. *Mem:* Sigma Xi. *Res:* Effects of 100 percent oxygen at atmospheric pressure in rats. *Mailing Add:* 306 Tallwood Dr Tallahassee FL 32312

SPARKMAN, ROBERT SATTERFIELD, surgery; deceased, see previous edition for last biography

SPARKS, ALTON NEAL, entomology, for more information see previous edition

SPARKS, ARTHUR GODWIN, MATHEMATICS, COMPUTER SCIENCES. *Current Pos:* instr math, Ga Southern Univ, 64-65, asst prof, 65-66 & 69-72, assoc prof math & comput sci, 72-80, prof math & comput sci, 80-88, PROF & HEAD, MATH & COMPUT SCI, GA SOUTHERN UNIV, 88- *Personal Data:* b Savannah, Ga, Feb 10, 38; m 58; c 3. *Educ:* Ga Southern Col, BS, 60; Univ Ga, MEd, 62; Univ Fla, MA, 64; Emory Univ, PhD(math), 69. *Prof Exp:* Instr math & physics, high sch, Ga, 60-61. *Mem:* Am Math Soc; Math Asn Am; Soc Indust Appl Math; Asn Comput Mach; Sigma Xi. *Res:* Analysis; convexity; computer science. *Mailing Add:* 125 Simmons Rd Statesboro GA 30458-5324

SPARKS, CECIL RAY, ACOUSTICS, FLUID DYNAMICS. *Current Pos:* asst dir, dept appl physics, 57-74, dir eng physics, 74-85, VPRES, SOUTHWEST RES INST, 85- *Personal Data:* b Lockwood, WVa, Nov 16, 30; m 56; c 3. *Educ:* Univ Tex, BS, 53; Univ Pittsburgh, MS, 56. *Prof Exp:* Develop engr, New Prod Dept, Westinghouse Elec Corp, 53-57. *Mem:* Acoust Soc Am. *Res:* Noise control; machinery and structure vibrations; fluid mechanics; instrumentation. *Mailing Add:* 10906 Janet Lee Dr San Antonio TX 78230

SPARKS, CHARLES EDWARD, LIPOPROTEIN METABOLISM & APOLIPOPROTEINS. *Current Pos:* assoc prof path, 82-87, PROF PATH & LAB MED, UNIV ROCHESTER, 88- *Personal Data:* b Peoria, Ill, July 29, 40; m 77; c 3. *Educ:* Mass Inst Technol, BS, 63; Jefferson Med Col, MD, 68; Am Bd Path, cert; Am Bd Clin Chem, cert. *Prof Exp:* Asst prof, Med Col Pa, 75-77, assoc prof biochem & physiol, 77-82. *Concurrent Pos:* Fel, Coun Arteriosclerosis, Am Heart Asn & Am Diabetes Asn, 89-; vis assoc prof biochem, Med Col Pa, 82- *Res:* Hormonal regulation of lipoprotein metabolism-relationships to diabetes and atherosclerosis. *Mailing Add:* 139 Tobey Rd Pittsford NY 14534

SPARKS, CULLIE J(AMES), JR, X-RAY DIFFRACTION. *Current Pos:* METALLURGIST & MAT SCIENTIST, OAK RIDGE NAT LAB, 58-, GROUP LEADER, 80- *Personal Data:* b Belpre, Ohio, May 8, 29; m 51, Janet Webb; c 5. *Educ:* Univ Ky, BS, 52, EngrD(metall), 57. *Prof Exp:* Res assoc metall, Univ Ky, 53-56. *Concurrent Pos:* Officer, USAF, Wright-Patterson AFB, Ohio-Mat Sci, 56-58. *Mem:* Fel Am Soc Metals; Sigma Xi; Am Crystallog Asn; fel Am Phys Soc. *Res:* Relationship between the geometrical structure of materials and their physical and chemical behavior; x-ray scattering measurements of the short-range order and atomic displacements; crystallographic distributions of lattice defects and relationship to solid solution strengthening; atomic structure of thin films, surfaces, interfaces, epitaxial mismatch, growth imperfections and reaction rate. *Mailing Add:* 804 W Outer Dr Oak Ridge TN 37830-8517

SPARKS, DARRELL, PLANT PHYSIOLOGY, HORTICULTURE. *Current Pos:* From asst prof to assoc prof, 65-76, PROF HORT RES, UNIV GA, 76- *Personal Data:* b Tipton Hill, NC, Apr 14, 38. *Educ:* NC State Col, BS, 61; Mich State Univ, MS, 62, PhD(hort), 65. *Mem:* AAAS; Am Soc Hort Sci; Am Soc Plant Physiol; Bot Soc Am. *Res:* Applied ecology; mineral nutrition and general physiology of tree fruit crops. *Mailing Add:* Dept Hort Univ Ga Athens GA 30602

SPARKS, DONALD, KINETICS OF SOIL CHEMICAL PROCESSES, SURFACE CHEMISTRY OF SOILS. *Current Pos:* From asst prof to assoc prof soil chem, 79-87, PROF ENVIRON SOIL CHEM, UNIV DEL, 87-, CHMN, DEPT PLANT & SOIL SCI, 89-, DISTINGUISHED PROF SOIL SCI, 94- *Personal Data:* b Paris, Ky, June 26, 53; m 84, Joy Gooden. *Educ:* Univ Ky, BS, 75, MS, 76; Va Polytech Inst & State Univ, PhD(soil phys chem), 79. *Honors & Awards:* Distinguished scientist Award, Sigma Xi, 83; Res Award, Am Soc Agron, 86; M L & CM Jackson Soil Sci Award, Soil Sci Soc Am, 91, Soil Sci Res Award, 94; F D Chesters Distinguished Res Award, Univ Del, 91; Francis Alison Award. *Concurrent Pos:* Consult, DuPont Co, 83- & Dept Energy, 87; assoc ed, Soil Sci Soc Am J, 83-86, tech ed, 86-93; vis prof, Univ Calif, Riverside, 86; ed, Soil Sci, 87- & Advances Agron, 90-; chmn soil chem, Soil Sci Soc Am, 89; co ed-in-chief, Geoderma, 94-; vchair, Comn II Soil Chem, Int Soc Soil Sci. *Mem:* Fel Soil Sci Soc Am; fel Am Soc Am; Clay Minerals Soc; Am Chem Soc; Geochem Soc. *Res:* Kinetics of soil chemical processes and surface chemistry of soils; authored or edited numerous publications including two textbooks. *Mailing Add:* Dept Plant & Soil Sci Univ Del Newark DE 19717-1303. *Fax:* 302-831-3651; *E-Mail:* esl09729@udelvm.udel.edu

SPARKS, HARVEY VISE, MEDICAL PHYSIOLOGY. *Current Pos:* chmn, Dept Physiol, 79-89, vprovost, Human Health Progs, 89-93, PROF PHYSIOL, MICH STATE UNIV, 79- *Personal Data:* b Flint, Mich, June 22, 38; m 69; c 4. *Educ:* Univ Mich, MD, 63. *Prof Exp:* USPHS fel physiol, Harvard Med Sch, 63-65 & Univ Goteborg, 65-66; from instr to prof, Univ Mich, 66-79. *Concurrent Pos:* Mem, Coun on Circulation, Am Heart Asn; mem, Nat Bd Med Examiners; Fulbright lectr, Univ Zimbabwe, 86-87; merit award, NIH, 88- *Mem:* Am Heart Asn; Microcirculatory Soc; Soc Exp Biol & Med; Am Physiol Soc (pres, 87-88). *Res:* Metabolic control of coronary and skeletal muscle blood flow using mathematical model simulations and experimental approaches. *Mailing Add:* Dept Physiol Mich State Univ 314 Giltner Hall East Lansing MI 48824-1101. *Fax:* 517-355-1525; *E-Mail:* sparks@pslvax.psl.msu.edu

SPARKS, MORGAN, CHEMISTRY. *Current Pos:* RETIRED. *Personal Data:* b Pagosa Springs, Colo, July 6, 16; m 49, Elizabeth MacEvoy; c Margaret Ellen (Potter), Patricia Rae (Fusting), Morgan MacEvoy & Gordon Kenneth. *Educ:* Rice Univ, BA, 38, MA, 40; Univ Ill, PhD(chem physics), 43. Hon

Degrees: DSc, Univ NMex, 80. *Honors & Awards:* Jack A Morton Award, Inst Elec & Electronics Engrs, 77. *Prof Exp:* Mem staff, Nat Defense Res Comt, Univ Ill, 41-43; res chemist, Bell Tel Labs, Inc, 43-48, mem semiconductor group, 48-53, dept head semiconductor device feasibility, 53-55, dir solid state electronics res, 55-58, dir, Transistor Dept, 58-59, exec dir, Components & Solid State Div, 59-68, exec dir, Semiconductor Components Div, 68-69, vpres tech info & personnel, 69-71, vpres electronics technol, 71-72; pres, Sandia Labs, 72-81; dean, R O Anderson Sch Mgt, Univ NMex, 81-84. *Concurrent Pos:* Vpres, Western Elec Co, Inc, 72-81. *Mem:* Nat Acad Eng; Am Chem Soc; fel Am Phys Soc; fel Inst Elec & Electronics Engrs; fel Am Inst Chemists. *Res:* Solid state physics and chemistry; electron device development; semiconductors; transistors; thin film devices; passive components; memory elements. *Mailing Add:* 904 Lamp Post Circle SE Albuquerque NM 87123

SPARKS, PETER ROBERT, WIND ENGINEERING, EARTHQUAKE ENGINEERING. *Current Pos:* assoc prof, 82-87, PROF CIVIL ENG & ENG MECH, CLEMSON UNIV, 87- *Personal Data:* b Bristol, Eng, July 29, 47; m 76; c 2. *Educ:* Univ Bristol, BSc, 68; Univ London, PhD(structural eng), 74. *Prof Exp:* Sci officer, Bldg Res Sta, Eng, 68-73, higher sci officer, 73-75, sr sci officer, 75-77; vis prof eng mech, Va Polytech Inst & State Univ, 77-79, assoc prof, 79-82. *Concurrent Pos:* Hurricane & Tornado damage surv, Nat Res Coun, 84-; Dir Wind Eng Res Coun, 88- *Mem:* Am Soc Civil Engrs; Am Soc Eng Educ; Sigma Xi. *Res:* The behavior of structures under wind and earthquake loading; full-scale and model investigations of structural performance and loading; architectural aerodynamics; mitigation of damage due to natural hazards. *Mailing Add:* 310 Upper Highland Dr Clemson SC 29631

SPARKS, RICHARD EDWARD, AQUATIC BIOLOGY, AQUATIC TOXICOLOGY. *Current Pos:* asst aquatic biologist, 72-77, assoc aquatic biologist, 77-80, AQUATIC BIOLOGIST, ILL NATURAL HIST SURV, 80- *Personal Data:* b Kingston, Pa, Apr 19, 42; m 66, Ruth Cole; c Amy M & Carolyn D. *Educ:* Amherst Col, BA, 64; Univ Kans, MS, 68; Va Polytech Inst & State Univ, PhD(biol), 71. *Prof Exp:* Teacher gen sci & biol, US Peace Corps, Univ Nigeria, Methodist Higher Elem Teacher Training Col, Nigeria, 64-66; res assoc, Ctr Environ Studies, Va Polytech Inst & State Univ, 71-72. *Concurrent Pos:* Consult, US Army Corps Engrs, 74-81, Ill Power Co, 75-78 & Upper Miss River Basin Comn, 79-80; lectr, Bradley Univ, 75-; adj prof, Western Ill Univ, 76- *Mem:* AAAS; Am Fisheries Soc; Ecol Soc Am; NAm Benthological Soc; Sigma Xi; Am Inst Biol Sci. *Res:* Biological monitoring for pollution control; restoration of degraded aquatic ecosystems; ecology of Illinois River and Mississippi River; effects of toxicants and contaminants on aquatic organisms; relationships between annual cycle of flood and low flow and populations and productivity. *Mailing Add:* Ctr Aquatic Ecol River Res Lab PO Box 599 Havana IL 62644

SPARKS, ROBERT EDWARD, CHEMICAL ENGINEERING. *Current Pos:* PROF CHEM ENG, WASH UNIV, 72- *Personal Data:* b Marshall, Mo, Sept 25, 30; m 55; c 3. *Educ:* Univ Mo, BS, 52; Johns Hopkins Univ, DEng, 60. *Prof Exp:* Res engr, Esso Res & Eng Co, 60-62, sr engr, 62-63; from asst prof to prof chem eng, Case Western Reserve Univ, 63-72. *Concurrent Pos:* Consult, Nat Inst Arthritis & Metab Dis, 65-74 & Goodyear Tire & Rubber Co, 66-74. *Mem:* AAAS; Am Inst Chem Engrs; Am Soc Artificial Internal Organs. *Res:* Medical engineering; design of the artificial kidney; membrane transport; emulsion breaking; velocity profile control; mass transfer and fluid mechanics in chemical reactors; microencapsulation; controlled drug release; inventive reasoning. *Mailing Add:* 1318 W Adams Ave Kirkwood MO 63122

SPARKS, STEVEN RICHARD, plant ecophysiology, global change, for more information see previous edition

SPARKS, WALTER CHAPPEL, HORTICULTURE. *Current Pos:* assoc horticulturist, 47-57, horticulturist, 57-68, res prof hort, 68-81, coordr potato progs, 76-81, co-dir, Postharvest Inst Perishables, 80-81, EMER PROF HORT, UNIV IDAHO, 81- *Personal Data:* b New Castle, Colo, Aug 22, 18; m 42; c 3. *Educ:* Colo State Univ, BS, 41, MS, 43. *Hon Degrees:* DSc, Univ Idaho, 84. *Honors & Awards:* Potato Hall of Fame-Brussels, Belgium, 77; Eldred L Jenne Res Fel Award, 57. *Prof Exp:* Instr agr, Pueblo Col, 41; asst hort, Colo State Univ, 41-43, from instr to assoc prof, 43-47. *Concurrent Pos:* Actg supt, Aberdeen Br Exp Sta, 52, 56 & 65; Jenne res fel, Univ Idaho & rep, Nat Inter-Regional Potato Introd & Preserv Proj, 57; consult, Corporacion De La Produccion Santiago, Chile, 66, Australian Govt & Commonwealth Sci & Indust Res Orgn, Venezuelan Corp of Agr Mkt, 75, Japan, 75, 76 & 77, Repub S Africa, 77; exchange res prof, Res Inst Com & Indust Plants, Kolding, Denmark, 72-73; guest lectr, ten Europ countries, 72-73, Greece, Israel, Australia & NZ, 73, Europ Asn Potato Res, Poland, 78 & Ger, 79; adv, Israeli Veg Bd, 80, PEI, Can, 80 & Philippines, 81; Int Potato Ctr, Lima Peru, 82, Moscow, Russia, 83, Jamaica, 88. *Mem:* AAAS; hon mem Am Potato Asn (pres, 64-65); Am Soc Hort Sci; Am Inst Biol Sci; Europ Asn Potato Res. *Res:* Mechanical injury and storage; cultural practices of potatoes. *Mailing Add:* 1100 Burnet Dr 513 D St Nampa ID 83651

SPARLIN, DON MERLE, SOLID STATE PHYSICS, SEMICONDUCTORS-INSULATORS. *Current Pos:* from asst prof to assoc prof, 68-90, PROF PHYSICS, UNIV MO-ROLLA, 90- *Personal Data:* b Joplin, Mo, Mar 29, 37; m 59; c 4. *Educ:* Univ Kans, BS, 59; Northwestern Univ, PhD(physics), 64. *Prof Exp:* Instr physics, Case Western Res Univ, 64-65, asst prof, 65. *Mem:* Am Asn Physics Teachers; Am Inst Physics; AAAS. *Res:* Electronic and magnetic properties of materials. *Mailing Add:* 702 Angus Valley Dr Rolla MO 65401

SPARLING, ARTHUR BAMBRIDGE, SANITARY ENGINEERING. *Current Pos:* ASSOC PROF CIVIL ENG, UNIV MAN, 71- *Personal Data:* b Rossburn, Man, Jan 3, 30; m 55; c 5. *Educ:* Univ Man, BSc, 53; Univ Toronto, MASc, 54; Wash Univ, DSc(environ & sanit eng), 68. *Prof Exp:* Pub health engr, Prov of Man, 54-67, chief engr, Clean Environ Comn, 67-71. *Mem:* Water Pollution Control Fedn; Am Water Works Asn. *Res:* Waste treatment; water pollution and treatment. *Mailing Add:* 709 South Dr Winnepeg MB R3T 0C2 Can

SPARLING, DALE R, GEOLOGY, DEVONIAN CONODONTS. *Current Pos:* from asst prof to prof, 68-95, chmn earth sci prog, 71-76, chmn, dept biol & earth/space sci, 87-89, EMER PROF GEOL, SOUTHWEST STATE UNIV, MINN, 95- *Personal Data:* b St Clair, Mich, Dec 19, 29; m 58, Jane Stoudt; c Linda, Patricia (Brandt) & Cynthia (Tobin). *Educ:* Univ Wyo, BS, 54; Wayne State Univ, MS, 56; Ohio State Univ, PhD(geol), 65. *Prof Exp:* Asst geol, Wayne State Univ, 54-56; petrol geologist, Creole Petrol Corp, 56-61; asst geol, Ohio State Univ, 62-65, instr, 65; lectr, West Wash State Col, 66; instr, Dayton Univ, 66-67; asst prof, Earlham Col, 67-68. *Mem:* Geol Soc Am; Pander Soc; Paleont Soc. *Res:* Stratigraphy; sedimentology; conodont taxonomy and biostratigraphy. *Mailing Add:* Earth Sci Prog Southwest State Univ Marshall MN 56258

SPARLING, DONALD WESLEY, JR, BIOMETRICS & BIOSTATISTICS, WILDLIFE TOXICOLOGY. *Current Pos:* statistician, Northern Prairie Wildlife Res Ctr, Jamestown, NDak, 82-86, RES BIOLOGIST, PATUXENT WILDLIFE RES CTR, NAT BIOL SURV, LAUREL, MD, 86- *Personal Data:* b Chicago, Ill, Sept 20, 49; m 71; c 2. *Educ:* Southern Ill Univ, Carbondale, BA, 71, MS, 74; Univ NDak, Grand Forks, PhD(biol), 79. *Prof Exp:* Instr natural resource, Univ Minn Tech Col, Crookston, 74-78; asst dir, Coop Wildlife Res Lab, Southern Ill Univ, 78-79; asst prof biol & ecol, Dept Biol, Ball State Univ, Muncie, Ind, 79-82. *Concurrent Pos:* Adj prof, Prince Georges Co Community Col, 90- *Mem:* Soc Environ Toxicol & Chem; Wilson Ornith Soc. *Res:* Population and ecological effects of contaminants on wildlife with emphasis on pesticides, acid precipitation; author of numerous technical publications. *Mailing Add:* 12706 Kincaid Ln Bowie MD 20715

SPARLING, MARY LEE, EMBRYOLOGY, MEMBRANES. *Current Pos:* lectr embryol, Calif State Univ, 66-68, from asst prof to assoc prof, 66-76, secy treas fac, 78-80, PROF BIOL, EMBRYOL & CELL PHYSIOL, CALIF STATE UNIV, NORTHRIDGE, 76- *Personal Data:* b Ft Wayne, Ind, May 20, 34; c Bonnie L Barber & Bradley P Barber. *Educ:* Univ Miami, BS, 55; Duke Univ, MA, 58; Univ Calif, Los Angeles, PhD(embryol, zool), 62. *Prof Exp:* Part-time lectr gen zool, Univ Calif, Los Angeles, 62-64. *Concurrent Pos:* Consult, Oak Ridge Nat Lab, 58-59; NSF grant, 71-73 & 81-83, NIH grant, 87-89; nat bd dir, Sigma Xi, 78-92; statewide acad sen, Calif State Univ, 96-99. *Mem:* Sigma Xi; Am Soc Cell Biol; Soc Develop Biol; Am Soc Zoologists. *Res:* Protein and lipid changes in cell membranes during early development in normal embryos and in those treated with agents producing abnormalities in development. *Mailing Add:* Dept Biol Calif State Univ Northridge CA 91330. *Fax:* 818-885-2034; *E-Mail:* vcbi000i@vax.csun.edu

SPARLING, PHILIP FREDERICK, MEDICINE, BACTERIOLOGY. *Current Pos:* from asst prof to assoc prof, 69-75, PROF MED & MICROBIOL, UNIV NC, CHAPEL HILL, 75-, CHMN, DEPT MICROBIOL IMMUNOL, 81- *Personal Data:* b Evanston, Ill, Sept 10, 36; m 63; c 4. *Educ:* Princeton Univ, AB, 58; Harvard Univ, MD, 62. *Prof Exp:* Resident physician, Mass Gen Hosp, 62-64; officer, Comn Corps Venereal Dis Res, Ctr Dis Control, 64-66; fel bacteriol, Harvard Med Sch, 66-68; fel infectious dis, Mass Gen Hosp, 68-69. *Concurrent Pos:* NIH res career develop award, 71-76; mem adv comt, Ctr Dis Control, 72-; reader bacteriol, Univ Bristol, 74-75; chief, Div Infectious Dis, Univ NC, 75-81; dir, NC Prog on Sexually Transmitted Dis, Sch Med, 78-; mem, microbiol comt, Nat Bd Med Examrs, 78-83, chmn, 81-83; mem, NIH Study Sect Bact, Mycol I, 80-84, chmn, 82-84. *Mem:* Am Soc Microbiol; Asn Am Phys; Am Clin Asn; Am Soc Clin Invest; Infectious Dis Am. *Res:* Infectious diseases; genetics and biochemistry of microbial antibiotic resistance; biochemical genetics of microbial pathogenicity; bacterial physiology; immunobiology of Neisseria gonorrhoeae. *Mailing Add:* 3033 Old Clin Bldg CB 7005 Univ NC Dept Med Mem Hosp Chapel Hill NC 27599-7005

SPARLING, REBECCA HALL, TROUBLE-SHOOTING PROBLEMS WITH MATERIALS, TECHNICAL WRITING & SPEAKING. *Current Pos:* RETIRED. *Personal Data:* b Memphis, Tenn, June 7, 10; m 35, 48; c 1. *Educ:* Vanderbilt Univ, BA, 30, MS, 31. *Honors & Awards:* Achievement Award, Soc Women Engrs; Outstanding Engr Award, Inst Advan Eng. *Prof Exp:* Metallurgist prod, Am Cast Iron Pipe Co, 31-32 & Lakeside Malleable Castings Co, 32-34; tech writer, William H Baldwin, NY, 34-35; consult, self-employed, 36-44; chief mat processing engr design, Turbodyne Corp, 44-51; design spec materials, prod mat, Gen Dynamics, Pomona, Calif, 51-68; consult mat energy, self-employed, Laguna Hills, Calif, 68- 84. *Concurrent Pos:* Metallurgist invest, Naval Gunn Factory, Wash, 42; prof engr, Calif, 50-; speaker, US Navy, USAF, Army Missile Command, 50-68, Univ Southern Calif, Los Angeles, Calif State Univ, TV, radio, etc, 65-85; mem tech comt, Aircraft Industs Asn, 51-60; mem var comts, Am Soc Metals, 52-68, Soc Women Engrs, 57-80 & Am Soc Nondestructive Testing, 54-87; expert witness, Environ Protection Agency, Calif Air Resources Bd, Pub Utilities Comm, etc, 69-84; co-chmn, San Bernardino County Sci Comt, 72; engr mem, San Bernardino County Air Pollution Bd, 73; intervenor, rep AAUW, AF, EI, Calif State Energy Comm, 75-85, Comt Power Plant Siting, 84. *Mem:* Fel Am Soc Metals; fel Soc Women Engrs; fel Inst Advan Eng; Am Soc Nondestructive Testing; Am Nuclear Soc. *Res:* Developed visible penetrant inspection for nondestructive examination of metal components and new techniques for short-time tests of structural elements at elevated temperatures. *Mailing Add:* 650 W Harrison Ave Claremont CA 91711

SPARLING, SHIRLEY, PHYCOLOGY. *Current Pos:* RETIRED. *Personal Data:* b Detroit, Mich, Oct 28, 29. *Educ:* Iowa State Univ, BS, 50, MS, 51; Univ Calif, PhD(bot), 56. *Prof Exp:* Instr bot, Cent Col, Iowa, 51-53, Univ BC, 56-59 & Univ Calif, Santa Barbara, 59-63; instr bot, Calif Polytech State Univ, San Luis Obispo, 63-80, prof biol sci, 80- *Mem:* Bot Soc Am. *Res:* Morphology, anatomy, reproduction and life cycles of marine algae, especially red algae. *Mailing Add:* 502 Stanford Dr San Luis Obispo CA 93405

SPARNINS, VELTA L, MEDICINE. *Current Pos:* Teaching asst, Univ Minn, 65-67, res specialist, 70-75, res fel, 75-77, res assoc, dept biochem, 77, scientist, 77-86, sr scientist, dept lab med & path, 86-89, lectr, 89-95, ADJ ASST PROF, UNIV MINN, 95- *Personal Data:* b Riga, Latvia, May 16, 28; m 49, Andrejs; c Rita V & Arnold J. *Educ:* Univ Minn, Minneapolis, BS, 65, MS, 68, PhD(biochem), 70. *Concurrent Pos:* J P Fridley scholar. *Mem:* Am Chem Soc. *Res:* Inhibition of chemical carcinogenesis by chemicals and components of food. *Mailing Add:* 3220 Rankin Rd NE Minneapolis MN 55418

SPARROW, D(AVID) A, NUCLEAR REACTIONS & SCATTERING, TECHNICAL RISKS IN SYSTEM DEVELOPMENT. *Current Pos:* RES STAFF MEM, INST DEFENSE ANALYSIS, 86- *Personal Data:* b Boston, Mass, June 30, 47. *Educ:* Princeton Univ, BA, 69; Mass Inst Technol, MS, 71, PhD(physics), 74. *Prof Exp:* Instr math, physics & chem, Univ Mass, 71-73; res assoc physics, Univ Colo, 74-77 & Univ Md, 77-78; asst prof physics, Univ Pa, 78-85. *Concurrent Pos:* Vis asst prof, Univ Md, 78; vis assoc prof, Temple Univ, 85-86. *Res:* Theoretical physics: nuclear reactions and scattering, analytic methods; data-to-data (purely empirical) relations; isospin violation; antinucleon interaction; algebraic and analytic techniques in nuclear and molecular scattering; ultra-short wavelength lasers; air vehicle detection and engagement; military application of modeling and simulation; impact of technol on military systems. *Mailing Add:* Inst Defense Analyses Sci & Tech Div 1801 N Beauregard St Alexandria VA 22311

SPARROW, E(PHRAIM) M(AURICE), MECHANICAL ENGINEERING, HEAT TRANSFER. *Current Pos:* chmn fluid mech prog, 68-80, PROF MECH ENG, UNIV MINN, MINNEAPOLIS, 59-, INST PROF, 94- *Personal Data:* b Hartford, Conn, May 27, 28; m 52, Ruthmay Saltman; c Rachel. *Educ:* Mass Inst Technol, BS, 48, MS, 49; Harvard Univ, MA, 50, PhD(mech eng), 56. *Hon Degrees:* Dr, Univ Brazil, 67. *Honors & Awards:* Heat Transfer Mem Award, Am Soc Mech Engrs, 62, Centennial Award, 80, Charles Russ Richards Mem Award, 85; Max Jakob Award for Eminence in Heat Transfer Res, Am Soc Mech Engrs/Am Inst Chem Engrs, 77; Ralph Coats Roe Award for Eminence in Eng Educ, Am Soc Eng Educ, 78, Sr Res Award, 89; Hawkins Mem lectr, Purdue Univ, 85; Worcester Reed Warner Medal, Am Soc Mech Engr, 86. *Prof Exp:* Res engr, Oak Ridge Nat Lab, 49; mech engr, Raytheon Mfg Co, 52-53; res scientist, Lewis Res Ctr, Nat Adv Comt Aeronaut, 53-59. *Concurrent Pos:* Lectr, Commonwealth Sci & Indust Res Orgn, Australia, 65; chief-of-party, US Agency Int Develop Prog Grad Educ in Brazil, 66-67; vis prof, Israel Inst Technol, 69; consult, Solar Energy Panel, US Off Sci & Technol, 72; ed, J Heat Transfer, 72-80, US Sci Comt, Fifth Int Heat Transfer Conf, 74, chmn, 78; mem adv panel, US Cong, Off of Technol Assessment, 75-77; vis prof, Xian Jiaotong Univ, 84; prog dir, 86, div dir, NSF, 86-88; distinguished lectr, Am Soc Mech Engrs, 86-91. *Mem:* Nat Acad Eng; fel Am Soc Mech Engrs; Sigma Xi. *Res:* Analytical and experimental research in heat transfer and fluid mechanics. *Mailing Add:* Dept Mech Eng Univ Minn Minneapolis MN 55455-0111. *Fax:* 612-624-1398; *E-Mail:* esparrow@maroon.tc.umn.edu

SPARROW, ELENA BAUTISTA, SOIL MICROBIOLOGY, ENVIRONMENTAL MICROBIOLOGY. *Current Pos:* SOIL SCIENTIST, AGR RES SERV, SUBARCTIC AGR UNIT, USDA, 88- *Personal Data:* b Col, Laguna, Philippines; m 72; c 2. *Educ:* Univ Philippines, BS, 62; Cornell Univ, MS, 66; Colo State Univ, PhD(agron, soil microbiol), 73. *Prof Exp:* Res asst soil chem & microbiol, Int Rice Res Inst, 62-64, asst soil microbiologist, 66-69; fel microbiol ecol, dept agron, Colo State Univ, 73; independent microbiologist, Arctic Environ Res Lab, 75-76; microbiologist, US Environ Protection Agency, Arctic Environ Res Sta, 76-77 & US Army Cold Regions Res & Eng Lab, Alaska Projs Off, 77-80; fel soil microbiol, Agr Forestry Exp Sta, Univ Alaska, 87. *Concurrent Pos:* Affil asst prof environ microbiol, Inst Water Resources, 75 & 81-83; adj researcher, soil sci sept, Univ Minn, 79; affil asst prof, Sch Agr & Land Resources Mgt, Univ Alaska, Fairbanks, 83-87, affil assoc prof soil microbiol, 85-, lectr, 86-; consult microbiologist, 81- *Mem:* Am Soc Microbiol; Int Soc Soil Sci; Soil Sci Soc Am; Sigma Xi; Asn Women Sci. *Res:* Ecology of microorganisms in terrestrial and freshwater environments; effects and degradation of organic pollutants; microbial transformations of minerals and nutrient cycling. *Mailing Add:* 1127 Park Dr Fairbanks AK 99709

SPARROWE, ROLLIN D, WILDLIFE BIOLOGY. *Current Pos:* Asst leader, Mo Coop Wildlife Res Unit, Wildlife Mgt Inst, 69-75, supvr, 76-79, chief, Div Coop Fish & Wildlife Res Units, 79-83, chief, Div Wildlife Res, 83-84, chief migratory bird mgt, 84-89, dep asst dir refuges & wildlife, 89-91, PRES, WILDLIFE MGT INST, WASHINGTON, 91- *Educ:* Humboldt State Col, BS, 64; SDak State Univ, MS, 66; Mich State Univ, PhD, 69. *Res:* Wildlife biology. *Mailing Add:* Wildlife Mgt Inst 1101 14th St NW Suite 801 Washington DC 20005

SPATOLA, ARNO F, BIO-ORGANIC CHEMISTRY, PEPTIDE CHEMISTRY. *Current Pos:* from asst prof to assoc prof, 73-83, PROF CHEM, UNIV LOUISVILLE, 83-, PROF BIOCHEM, 90- *Personal Data:* b Albany, NY, May 9, 44; m 82, Jacqulyn Browning; c Kimberly E. *Educ:* Cornell Univ, AB, 66; Univ Mich, MS, 69, PhD(chem), 71. *Honors & Awards:* Devoe-Raynolds Award, 90. *Prof Exp:* Lectr chem, Univ Mich, 70-71; assoc, Univ Ariz, 71-73. *Concurrent Pos:* Pres, Peptides Int, Inc, Louisville, Ky; vis prof, Univ Padova, 82; chmn, Gordon Conf on Peptides, 90; counr & chmn, Pub Comt, Am Peptide Soc. *Mem:* AAAS; Am Chem Soc; Sigma Xi; Am Peptide Soc. *Res:* Polypeptide synthesis, solution, solid phase methods and catalytic transfer hydrogenation; hormones and hormone analogues incorporating novel amino acids and amide bond replacements; LH-RH, opioid peptides; structure-function studies on peptide hormones; collagenase inhibitors; cholecystokinin analogs; enzyme mimetics; cyclic peptide libraries; pseudopeptide libraries; nuclear magnetic resonance; enzyme degradation studies. *Mailing Add:* Dept Chem Belknap Campus Univ Louisville Louisville KY 40292-0001. *Fax:* 502-852-8149; *E-Mail:* afspatol@ulkyvm.louisville.edu

SPATZ, DAVID MARK, ORGANIC CHEMISTRY, AGRICULTURAL CHEMISTRY. *Current Pos:* MANAGING DIR TECHNOL MKT, CHEVRON INT OIL, 92- *Personal Data:* b Pottstown, Pa, Oct 10, 46. *Educ:* Clarkson Col, BS, 68; Univ Mich, Ann Arbor, PhD(med chem), 72. *Prof Exp:* Fel nucleotide synthesis, Stanford Univ, 72-74; sr res chemist, Dow Chem Pharmaceut Res & Develop, 74-77; res chemist, Agr Res Div, Am Cyanamid Co, 77-80; staff mem, Chevron Chem Co, 80-92. *Mem:* Am Chem Soc; AAAS. *Res:* Synthetic organic chemistry; medicinal and pesticidal chemistry; drug design; heterocyclic and natural product synthesis including nucleotides and terpenes. *Mailing Add:* Chevron Intl Oil PO Box 7146 San Francisco CA 94120-7146

SPATZ, MARIA, NEUROCYTOBIOLOGY, TISSUE CULTURE. *Current Pos:* LAB CHIEF, NAT INST NEUROL & COMMUN DIS, NIH, 85- *Mailing Add:* Sec Neurocytobiol Lab Neuropath & Neuroanat Sci NINDS NIH Bldg 36 Rm 4D04 Bethesda MD 20892-0036

SPATZ, SIDNEY S, oral surgery; deceased, see previous edition for last biography

SPATZ, SYDNEY MARTIN, ORGANIC CHEMISTRY, ORGANIC SYNTHESES. *Current Pos:* RETIRED. *Personal Data:* b New York, NY, June 9, 12; m 36; c 1. *Educ:* Univ Iowa, BA, 35, MS, 37; Iowa State Col, PhD(org chem), 41. *Prof Exp:* Res assoc, Nat Defense Res Comt, Iowa State Col, 42-43; res chemist, Nat Aniline Div, Allied Chem & Dye Corp, 43-47; chief chemist, Polak's Frutal Works, Inc, 47-53; pres & mgr, Spatz Chem, Inc, 53-54; res supvr, Nat Aniline & Specialty Chem Div, Allied Chem Corp, 54-71; sr prod eng specialist, Mead Papers Div, Mead Corp, 72-74, res fel, Mead Cent Res Div, 74-77; consult, 77-84. *Mem:* Am Chem Soc; Sigma Xi. *Res:* Dicarboxylic anhydride chemistry; synthetic antimalarials; organometallics of lithium; ultraviolet absorbers; epoxy curing agents; polyester fire-retardant resins; cationic dyestuffs; color precursors for copy systems; carbonless copy; N-heterocyclic chemistry; infringement searches; perfume and flavorant syntheses. *Mailing Add:* 6698 Tenth Ave N Apt 321 Lake Worth FL 33467-1961

SPAULDING, HARRY SAMUEL, JR, ALLERGY, IMMUNOLOGY. *Current Pos:* ASST CLIN PROF PEDIAT, MED CTR, UNIV COLO, 75-, STAFF PEDIAT & ALLERGY, DENVER'S CHILDRENS HOSP, 93-, ALLERGIST, DEPT PEDIAT, FITZSIMONS ARMY MED CTR, 93- *Personal Data:* b Waterbury, Vt, Dec 12, 30; m 56; c 5. *Educ:* Albany Col Pharm, NY, BS, 53; Duquesne Univ, MS, 55; Univ Vt, Burlington, MD, 59. *Prof Exp:* Post surgeon, 24th Med Detachment, 61-63; resident pediat, Walter Reed Army Med Ctr, 63-65; chief pediat, US Army Hosp, Ft Carson, 66-68; pvt pract, Beverly Hosp, Mass, 68-71; chief, Dept Clin Admin, Reynolds Hosp, Ft Sill, 71-72; chief, Gen Pediat Serv, Fitzsimons Army Med Ctr, Denver, 74-77; asst chief, Allergy-Immunol Serv & Fitzsimons Army Med Ctr, Aurora, Colo, 77-80, dep comdr, dep med activ & med educ, 80-81, dep comdr clin serv & dir med educ, 86-88 & 88-89, staff pediat allergist, Dept Pediat, 86-93, comdr, 88, staff allergist, 89, chirf, allergy-immunol & consult to Surgeon Gen, 89-93. *Concurrent Pos:* Consult pediat, Colo State Hosp, Pueblo, 66-68; clin instr pediat, Med Ctr, Tufts Univ, 68-71; fel allergy-immunol, Fitzsimons Army Med Ctr & Nat Jewish Hosp, Denver, 72-74; staff affil, Nat Jewish Hosp & Res Ctr, 77- *Mem:* Am Acad Pediat; fel Am Acad Allergy; Asn Mil Allergists. *Res:* Association between gastroesophageal reflux and asthma; pharmacology of aminophylline with respect to coagulation problems and sensitivity through its ethylene, diamine fraction. *Mailing Add:* 2600 S Parker Rd Bldg 2 Suite 100 Aurora CO 80014

SPAULDING, LEN DAVIS, INORGANIC CHEMISTRY, ORGANOMETALLIC CHEMISTRY. *Current Pos:* AT PLATINA CATALYST LAB INC. *Personal Data:* b Spring Valley, Ill, Oct 31, 42. *Educ:* Antioch Col, BSc, 65; Univ Cincinnati, PhD(chem), 72. *Prof Exp:* Res assoc, Ga Inst Technol, 72-74; assoc scientist chem, Brookhaven Nat Lab, 74-80; with Exxon Chem Corp, 80-94. *Concurrent Pos:* Consult, Mad River Chem Co, 67-69; NIH fel, Ga Inst Technol, 73-74. *Mem:* Am Chem Soc; AAAS. *Res:* Catalysis; Fischer-Tropsch and related reaction; porphyrin chemistry; transition metal organometallic chemistry. *Mailing Add:* 5 Spring Water Way Newark DE 19711

SPAULDING, MALCOLM LINDHURST, OCEAN ENGINEERING. *Current Pos:* from asst prof to assoc prof, 73-83, PROF OCEAN ENG, UNIV RI, 83-, CHMN, 92- *Personal Data:* b Providence, RI, Feb 15, 47. *Educ:* Univ RI, BS, 69, PhD(mech eng), 72; Mass Inst Technol, MS, 70. *Prof Exp:* Asst prof eng mech, Old Dominion Univ, 72-73. *Concurrent Pos:* Consult var pvt industs, 75-; Royal Norweg Res Coun Fel, 82-83; Fulbright-Hayes fel,

Leningrad, USSR; panel mem, Nat Res Coun, 87-90 & 91-94. *Mem:* Am Soc Civil Engrs; Am Soc Mech Engrs; AAAS; Am Geophys Union; Marine Technol Soc. *Res:* Numerical modelling of coastal and shelf processes to include circulation, temperature, salinity and pollutant transport; computational fluid mechanics; oil spill fates and impact modeling. *Mailing Add:* Dept Ocean Eng Univ RI Narragansett RI 02882-1179. *Fax:* 401-792-6837; *E-Mail:* spaulding@mistral.oce.uri.edu

SPAULDING, STEPHEN WAASA, ENDOCRINOLOGY, MEDICAL RESEARCH. *Current Pos:* assoc prof, 76-81, PROF, STATE UNIV NY, BUFFALO, 81- *Personal Data:* b San Francisco, Calif, Aug 24, 40; m 69, Monica Buckley; c Kathleen & Deborah. *Educ:* Pomona Col, BA, 62; McGill Univ, MD & CM, 66. *Prof Exp:* Intern & asst res med, Osler Serv, Johns Hopkins Univ, 66-68; clin assoc endocrinol, NIH Geront Ctr, 68-70; from fel to asst prof endocrinol, Sch Med, Yale Univ, 70-76. *Concurrent Pos:* Attend physician, Yale New Haven Hosp & West Haven Vet Admin Hosp, 72-76; res scholar, Am Col Physicians, 72; NIH spec res fel, 73-74; clin investr, Vet Admin, 74; traveling scholar endocrinol, Am Col Physicians, 76; chief, Endocrine Unit, Buffalo Gen Hosp, 76-82; assoc chief staff res, Buffalo VA Med Ctr, 82-; sr Int Fogarty fel, 84-85. *Mem:* Am Thyroid Asn; Endocrine Soc; Am Fedn Clin Res; Am Col Physicians; Am Soc Clin Invest. *Res:* Actions of thyrotropin on chromatin structure and function; thyroid hormone metabolism; posttran scriptional regulation of gene expression by hormones. *Mailing Add:* 4280 Freeman Orchard Park NY 14215. *Fax:* 716-862-3419; *E-Mail:* medspaul@acsu.buffalo.edu

SPAULDING, THEODORE CHARLES, PHARMACY, PHARMACEUTICALS. *Current Pos:* DIR PHARM & PHARMACOL, HEALTH CARE GROUP, BRIT OXYGEN CO, DIV ANIQUEST, 85- *Educ:* Univ NC, PhD(pharmacol), 73- *Mailing Add:* Int OTC Antiviral Clin Develop Glaxo Wellcome Five Moore Dr Res Triangle Park NC 27709

SPAUSCHUS, HANS O, MATERIALS SCIENCE. *Current Pos:* DIR RES, GA INST TECHNOL, 80- *Personal Data:* b Liedemeiten, Ger, June, 15, 23; US citizen; m 59; c 2. *Educ:* Ill Col, AB, 46; Tulane Univ, MS, 48, PhD(phys chem), 50. *Honors & Awards:* Steinmetz Medal, Gen Elec Co, 73. *Prof Exp:* Chemist, Gen Elec Co, 50-53, mgr lab, 53-56, res assoc, 56-68, mgr lab, 68-80. *Concurrent Pos:* Consult indust, Spauschus Assocs, 80- *Mem:* AAAS; Inst Elec & Electronics Engrs; fel Am Soc Heating, Refrig & Air Conditioning Engrs. *Res:* Biomass conversion to fuels and chemicals; high temperature solar thermal systems; materials sciences; heat pumps; technology appraisal and transfer; vapor compression cooling science and technology. *Mailing Add:* Spaschus Assoc Inc 300 Corporate Ctr Ct Stockbridge GA 30281-6360

SPAYD, RICHARD W, ORGANIC CHEMISTRY. *Current Pos:* RETIRED. *Personal Data:* b Reading, Pa, Dec 10, 32; m 58, Mary A Ruoff; c Leigh A, Alicia & Tracy. *Educ:* Albright Col, BS, 58; Univ Del, MS, 60, PhD(org chem), 62. *Prof Exp:* From res chemist to sr res chemist, Eastman Kodak Co, 62-67, lab head, 67-89. *Mem:* Am Chem Soc; Am Asn Clin Chem. *Res:* Photographic systems; use of radioactive isotopes to study reaction mechanisms; dry multilayer films for clinical analysis. *Mailing Add:* 8395 Cypress Hollow Dr Sarasota FL 34238

SPAZIANI, EUGENE, NEUROENDOCRINOLOGY, REPRODUCTIVE PHYSIOLOGY. *Current Pos:* from instr to assoc prof, 59-68, chmn dept, 77-80, PROF ZOOL, UNIV IOWA, 68- *Personal Data:* b Detroit, Mich, July 22, 30; m 53; c 2. *Educ:* Univ Calif, Los Angeles, BA, 52, MA, 54, PhD(zool), 58. *Prof Exp:* Asst zool, Univ Calif, Los Angeles, 52-55; hon res asst physiol, Univ Col, London, 58-59. *Concurrent Pos:* Lalor Found fel, 60; grantee, USPHS, 60-74, Am Cancer Soc, 60, 64, 66 & 69, NSF, 74-77 & 85-; vis investr, Inst Biomed Res, AMA, 66-67; mem, Bd Examrs, Grad Record Exam, Advan Test Biol, Educ Testing Serv, Princeton, NJ, 66-70; mem, Panel Undergrad Sci Partic Prog, NSF & consult, Panel Preprof Training, Comn Undergrad Educ Biol Sci; vis prof physiol, Univ Calif, Sch Med, San Francisco, 81. *Mem:* fel AAAS; Am Soc Zoologists; Am Physiol Soc; Endocrine Soc; Soc Study Reproduction. *Res:* Mechanisms of steroid hormone action in vertebrate reproductive organs; hormonal control of cellular transport; pigmentation; invertebrate endocrinology; comparative endocrinology. *Mailing Add:* Dept Biol Sci Univ Iowa Iowa City IA 52242. *Fax:* 319-335-1069; *E-Mail:* eugene-spaziani@uiowa.edu

SPEAR, ANTHONY J, AEROSPACE ENGINEERING. *Current Pos:* PROJECT MGR MAGELLAN, NASA, PASADENA, CALIF. *Honors & Awards:* Laurels Award-Space/Missiles, Aviation Week & Space Technol, 91. *Mailing Add:* Jet Propulsion Labs NASA 4800 Oak Grove Dr Pasadena CA 91109-8001

SPEAR, BRIAN BLACKBURN, GENE STRUCTURE. *Current Pos:* AT DEPT BIOL SCI, NORTHWESTERN UNIV. *Personal Data:* b Los Angeles, Calif, July 1, 47; m 72; c 1. *Educ:* Amherst Col, AB, 69; Yale Univ, MPhil, 70, PhD(biol), 73. *Prof Exp:* Res assoc, Dept Molecular Cell & Develop Biol, Univ Colo, 73-75; asst prof biol sci, Northwestern Univ, 76-82; res scientist, dept molecular biol, Abbott Labs, 82- *Mem:* Sigma Xi; Am Soc Cell Biol; AAAS. *Res:* Gene and chromosome structure; polytene chromosome organization in Drosophila and protozoa; molecular biology of ciliated protozoa; structure and evolution of genes for ribosomal RNA and actin. *Mailing Add:* 699 Walden Rd Winnetka IL 60093

SPEAR, CARL D(AVID), METALLURGY. *Current Pos:* head, Dept Mech Eng, 66-77, PROF MECH ENG, UTAH STATE UNIV, 66- *Personal Data:* b Salt Lake City, Utah, Dec 6, 27; m 58; c 6. *Educ:* Univ Utah, BS, 55, PhD(metall), 60. *Prof Exp:* Res metallurgist, Corning Glass Works, 60-63; asst prof metall, Univ Idaho, 63-66. *Mem:* Soc Mfg Engrs; Am Soc Metals. *Res:* Behavior of materials in manufacturing processes; non-traditional processes. *Mailing Add:* 20 N 400 E Providence UT 84332

SPEAR, GERALD SANFORD, PATHOLOGY. *Current Pos:* PROF PATH & MEM MED STAFF, CALIF COL MED, UNIV CALIF, IRVINE, 77- *Personal Data:* b Providence, RI, Mar 3, 28; m 64; c 3. *Educ:* Harvard Univ, AB, 48; Johns Hopkins Univ, MD, 52; Am Bd Path, dipl, 59. *Prof Exp:* Asst med, Sch Med, Wash Univ, 52-53; asst, Johns Hopkins Univ, 53-54, instr, 54-56 & 58-59, from asst prof to assoc prof path, Sch Med, 64-77. *Concurrent Pos:* Intern, Barnes Hosp, St Louis, Mo, 52-53; from asst pathologist to asst resident, Johns Hopkins Hosp, 53-56, resident, 58-59, pathologist, 59-77; vis pathologist, Baltimore City Hosps, 59-60. *Mem:* Int Soc Nephrology; Am Asn Path; Am Soc Pediat Nephrology; Am Soc Nephrology; Int Acad Path; Soc Pediat Path. *Res:* renal and pediatric pathology. *Mailing Add:* Dept of Path Univ Calif 101 City Dr S Orange CA 92668-3298. *Fax:* 714-456-5873

SPEAR, IRWIN, PLANT PHYSIOLOGY, BIOLOGY. *Current Pos:* Asst prof bot & physiologist, Plant Res Inst, 53-59, assoc prof bot, 59-69, PROF BOT, UNIV TEX, AUSTIN, 69- *Personal Data:* b New York, NY, Jan 4, 24; m 49; c 5. *Educ:* Cornell Univ, BS, 47; Harvard Univ, AM, 49, PhD(biol), 53. *Concurrent Pos:* Mem biol advan placement comt, Col Entrance Exam Bd. *Mem:* AAAS; Am Soc Plant Physiol; Bot Soc Am; Soc Exp Biol & Med; Scand Soc Plant Physiol; Sigma Xi. *Res:* Physiology of growth and development, especially flowering; social consequences of biological discoveries. *Mailing Add:* Biol Labs Univ Tex 2615 Pecos Austin TX 78703-1633

SPEAR, JOSEPH FRANCIS, PHYSIOLOGY. *Current Pos:* Instr physiol, Sch Med, 70, Sch Vet Med, 70-72, from asst prof to assoc prof, 72-79, PROF PHYSIOL, SCH VET MED, UNIV PA, 79- *Personal Data:* b Baltimore, Md, May 3, 43; c 2. *Educ:* Loyola Col, Md, BS, 65; Univ Pa, PhD(physiol), 69. *Concurrent Pos:* Pa Heart Asn res fel, Univ Pa, 70-71 & res grant, 71-72, res fel physiol, Dept Med, Univ Pa Hosp, 71-72; mem, Coun Basic Sci, Am Heart Asn, 71, estab investr, 72. *Mem:* AAAS; fel Am Col Cardiol; Am Heart Asn; Soc Gen Physiologists; Cardiac Muscle Soc. *Res:* Cardiovascular physiology; cardiac electrophysiology. *Mailing Add:* Sch Vet Med Univ Pa 3800 Spruce St Philadelphia PA 19104. *Fax:* 215-898-1055

SPEAR, JO-WALTER, HYDROGEOLOGY, LANDFILL DESIGN. *Current Pos:* SR ENVIRON ENGR, CH2M HILL, 90- *Personal Data:* b Bridgeton, NJ, Nov 3, 42; m 66, Faith Ford; c Morger R & Jo-Walter Jr. *Educ:* Rutgers Univ, AB, 63; Univ Pa, MSc, 70. *Prof Exp:* Teacher chem, Vineland Sr High Sch, 69-72; proj mgr, Pandullo Quirk Assocs, 72-78; sanit engr, Del Basin Comn, 78-79; dir, Chem Process Div, John Sexton Contractors, 79-82, dir corp develop, 82-86; asst prof civil eng, Midwest Col Eng, 80-86; pres, Morgen Environmental, 86-87; sr civil eng, Rogers Golden & Halpern, 87-90. *Concurrent Pos:* Tech dir, Alternative Technol, 80-86. *Mem:* Nat Soc Prof Engrs; Am Inst Chem Engrs; Am Soc Civil Engrs; fel Am Inst Chemists; Am Pub Works Asn; Water Pollution Control Asn; Govt Refuse Control & Disposal Asn. *Res:* Numerical risk assessment of landfill liner design. *Mailing Add:* CHZM Hill 411 E Wisconsin Ave Ste 1600 Milwaukee WI 53202-4421. *Fax:* 215-563-3828

SPEAR, PATRICIA GAIL, VIROLOGY, CELL BIOLOGY. *Current Pos:* from asst prof to assoc prof, 73-82, PROF MOLECULAR GENETICS & CELL BIOL, UNIV CHICAGO, 82- *Personal Data:* b Chattanooga, Tenn, Dec 14, 42; m 83. *Educ:* Fla State Univ, BA, 64; Univ Chicago, PhD(virol), 69. *Prof Exp:* USPHS trainee & res assoc virol, Dept Microbiol, Univ Chicago, 69-71; Arthritis Found fel & res assoc biochem, Rockefeller Univ, 71-73. *Concurrent Pos:* USPHS res career develop award, 75; consult comt virol & cell biol, Am Cancer Soc, 75-78; consult human cell biol prog, NSF, 75-77; mem med adv bd, Leukemia Res Found, Inc, 80-84; consult, Microbiol & Infectious Dis Res Comn, Nat Inst Allergy & Infectious Dis, NIH, 83- *Mem:* AAAS; Am Soc Virol; Am Soc Microbiologists. *Res:* Virus-induced modifications of cell membranes. *Mailing Add:* Microbiol-Immunol MC W213 303 E Chicago Ave Chicago IL 60611

SPEAR, PAUL WILLIAM, MEDICINE. *Current Pos:* RETIRED. *Personal Data:* b Baltimore, Md, Nov 3, 08; m 44; c 3. *Educ:* Johns Hopkins Univ, BA, 30, MD, 34; Am Bd Internal Med, dipl, 41, recert, 74. *Prof Exp:* From asst to instr med, Johns Hopkins Univ, 37-41; chief med, Manhattan Beach Vet Admin Hosp, 47-50; from asst chief med to chief med, Brooklyn Vet Admin Hosp, 50-63; dir med, Montefiore-Morrisania Affil, 63-76; emer prof med, Albert Einstein Col Med, 76-; med dir, Queens County Div Island Peer Rev Orgn, 84-86. *Concurrent Pos:* Vis physician, Sinai Hosp, Baltimore, 37-41; clin assoc prof med, Col Med, State Univ NY Downstate Med Ctr, 51-63; attend physician, Kings County Hosp, 57-63, Maimonides Hosp, 58-63 & Montefiore Hosp, 63-; assoc prof med, Albert Einstein Col Med, 66-77. *Mem:* Am Soc Hemat; Int Soc Hemat; Am Fedn Clin Res; fel Am Col Physicians; fel NY Acad Med. *Res:* Hematology. *Mailing Add:* 55 Manhasset Woods Rd Manhasset NY 11030-2612

SPEAR, ROBERT CLINTON, ENVIRONMENTAL HEALTH. *Current Pos:* US Pub Health Serv fel, Univ Calif, Berkeley, 69-70, from asst prof to assoc prof, 70-80, dir, Northern Calif Occup Health Ctr, 79-89, assoc dean, 89-91, PROF ENVIRON HEALTH SCI, SCH PUB HEALTH, UNIV

CALIF, BERKELEY, 81-, DIR, CTR OCCUP ENVIRON HEALTH, 93- *Personal Data:* b Los Banos, Calif, June 26, 39; m 62, Patricia Warner; c Andrew & Jenna. *Educ:* Univ Calif, Berkeley, BS, 61, MS, 63; Cambridge Univ, PhD(eng), 68. *Prof Exp:* Mech engr, US Navy, Calif, 63-65, 68-69. *Concurrent Pos:* Sr int fel, Fogarty Int Ctr, NIH, 77-78. *Mem:* AAAS; Am Soc Mech Engrs; Am Indust Hyg Asn; Am Pub Health Asn. *Res:* Engineering aspects of occupational and environmental health. *Mailing Add:* Sch Pub Health Univ Calif Berkeley CA 94720. *E-Mail:* spear@uclink2.berkeley.com

SPEARE, EDWARD PHELPS, zoology, for more information see previous edition

SPEARING, ANN MARIE, PLANT BIOPHYSICS. *Current Pos:* CONSULT, 89- *Personal Data:* b Olean, NY, Jan 29, 47. *Educ:* State Univ NY Col Buffalo, BA, 69; State Univ NY Col Forestry, Syracuse Univ, MS, 71; Univ Md, PhD(plant biophys), 75. *Prof Exp:* Asst prof bot, Wheaton Col, 75-78; actg asst dir, Environ Prog, Univ Vt, 78-81, asst dean, 81-84, assoc dean, Grad Col, 84-89. *Concurrent Pos:* Assoc prof forestry, Univ Vt, 83-89. *Mem:* AAAS; Am Inst Biol Sci; Am Soc Plant Physiologists; Ecol Soc Am; Sigma Xi; Asn Women Sci. *Res:* All aspects of physiological ecology, particularly responses of plants to light; effects of physical aspects of environment such as temperature and light on physiology of plants. *Mailing Add:* 632 Covered Bridge Rd Stow VT 05672

SPEARING, CECILIA W, biochemistry, for more information see previous edition

SPEARS, ALEXANDER WHITE, III, ORGANIC CHEMISTRY, PHYSICAL CHEMISTRY. *Current Pos:* res assoc, Res Div, P Lorillard Co, 59-61, sr res chemist, 61-65, dir basic res, 65-68, dir res & develop, 68-71, vpres res & develop, 71-75, from sr vpres to exec vpres opers & res, 75-91, vchmn & chief opers officer, 91-95, CHMN & CHIEF EXEC OFFICER, LORILLARD TOBACCO CO, 95- *Personal Data:* b Grindstone, Pa, Sept 29, 32; m 51, 77, Shirley Pierce; c Craig. *Educ:* Allegheny Col, BS, 53; Univ Buffalo, PhD(chem), 60. *Honors & Awards:* Distinguished Achievement Award Tobacco Sci, Philip Morris, Inc, 70. *Prof Exp:* Res assoc chem, Univ Buffalo, 56-58; instr, Millard Fillmore Col, 58-59. *Concurrent Pos:* Asst prof, Guilford Col, 61-65; adv, Nat Cancer Inst, 68-79; mem, Sci Comn, 72-76, Coop Ctr Sci Res Tobacco, 72-, Coun Tobacco Res-Bd Dirs, 90-; mem, Tech Study Group, Cigarette Safety Act, 84 & 90, ISO Comt 126, 88, Ctr Indoor Air Res, 88-; Chmn bd dirs, Indoor Air Res, 91-95. *Mem:* AAAS; Am Chem Soc; Sigma Xi; NY Acad Sci. *Res:* Cancer chemotherapy; pyrolytic reactions and products; spectroscopy; chromatography; analytical methods: structure of natural products; tobacco; foods; author and patentee in field. *Mailing Add:* Lorillard Tobacco Co PO Box 21688 Greensboro NC 27420-1688. *Fax:* 910-373-6917

SPEARS, BRIAN MERLE, entomology, range science, for more information see previous edition

SPEARS, DAVID LEWIS, OPTOELECTRONICS, ELECTROOPTICS. *Current Pos:* Mem, res staff, 69-84, ASST HEAD, ELECTROOPTICAL DEVICES GROUP, LINCOLN LAB, MASS INST TECHNOL, 84- *Personal Data:* b Belvidere, Ill, July 22, 40; div; c 2. *Educ:* Monmouth Col, Ill, BA, 62; Dartmouth Col, MA, 64; Purdue Univ, PhD(physics), 69. *Mem:* Am Phys Soc; Inst Elec & Electronic Engrs. *Res:* Acoustoelectric effect in Gas; x-ray lithography; surface wave devices; integrated optics; optical waveguide modulators; heterodyne detection; infrared heterodyne radiometry; infrared detectors; diode lasers. *Mailing Add:* Lincoln Lab Mass Inst Technol 244 Wood St Lexington MA 02173-9108

SPEARS, JOSEPH FAULCONER, biology; deceased, see previous edition for last biography

SPEARS, KENNETH GEORGE, LASER PHOTOPHYSICS, MEDICAL IMAGING WITH LASERS. *Current Pos:* asst prof, Northwestern Univ, 72-78, assoc prof chem, 78-89, JOINT PROF BIOMED ENG, NORTHWESTERN UNIV, 87-, PROF CHEM, 89- *Personal Data:* b Erie, Pa, Oct 23, 43; m 66; c 1. *Educ:* Bowling Green State Univ, BS, 66; Univ Chicago, MS, 71, PhD(chem), 71. *Prof Exp:* Fel chem physics, Nat Res Coun, Nat Oceanic & Atmospheric Admin, Boulder, Colo, 70-72. *Concurrent Pos:* Alfred P Sloan Found fel, 74-76; mem adv bd, Midwest Bio-Laser Inst, 85-; consult, Laser Surg Syst, 81-84. *Res:* Molecular photophysics, electron and energy transfer in solution; picosecond and other laser techniques; medical imaging and corneal applications of lasers; photophysical probes of vesicles and peptides; picosecond infrared spectroscopy. *Mailing Add:* Dept Chem Northwestern Univ 2145 Sheridan Rd Evanston IL 60208-3113. *Fax:* 847-491-7713; *E-Mail:* spears@chem.nwu.edu

SPEARS, RICHARD KENT, ENGINEERING MATERIALS, ENGINEERING MECHANICS. *Current Pos:* PRES, LARGO SCI INC, FLA, 82- *Personal Data:* b Brush, Colo, Mar 28, 37; m 57; c 5. *Educ:* Colo Sch Mines, BS, 59; Univ Denver, MS, 64; Univ Fla, PhD(eng sci), 77. *Prof Exp:* Engr metall, Martin Co, Denver, 59-64; applns engr, Honeywell, Inc, Minneapolis, 64-66; design engr, Gen Elec Co, St Petersburg, Fla, 66-82. *Mem:* Am Soc Metals (treas, 77-78). *Res:* Ferroelectricity; glass ceramics; glass coated wire; polymer research; adhesive research; impact property of metals. *Mailing Add:* 3104 Roberta St Largo FL 33771

SPEARS, SHOLTO MARION, engineering; deceased, see previous edition for last biography

SPEAS, ROBERT DIXON, AERONAUTICAL ENGINEERING, AVIATION. *Current Pos:* PRES, PRC AVIATION, 84- *Personal Data:* b Davis County, NC, Apr 14, 16; m 44, Manette Lansing Hollingsworth; c Robert & Jay (Hollingsworth). *Educ:* Mass Inst Technol, BS, 40. *Hon Degrees:* DBA, Embry Riddle Aeronaut Univ, 95. *Honors & Awards:* Res Award, Am Transport Asn, 42; Int Award, William A Downes Airport Operators Coun, 92; William Littlewood Memorial Lect, Am Inst Aeronaut & Astronaut, 94. *Prof Exp:* Engr, Am Airlines, 40-44, asst to vpres, 44-46, dir maintenance & eng, Cargo Div, 46-47, spec asst to pres, 47-50; US rep, A V Roe Can Ltd, 50-51; pres & chmn bd, R Dixon Speas Assocs, Inc, 51-76; pres & chmn bd, Aviation Consult, Inc, 76-82, chmn bd, 82-84. *Concurrent Pos:* Bd gov, Am Soc Mech Engrs, 58-71 & 79-90, exec comt, Flight Safety Found, 79-90; coun, Inst Aeronaut Scis, 59-62, exec comt, 62; coun, Am Inst Aeronaut & Astronaut, 63-64, chmn ethics comt, 89-92; coun, Soc Automotive Engr, 64-66; trustee, Col Aeronaut, 67-; chmn & chief exec officer, Speas-Harris Airport Dev Inc, 74-76; mem, Aerospace & Space Engr Bd, Nat Res Coun, 80-84. *Mem:* Fel Am Inst Aeronaut & Astronaut (treas, 63-64); Royal Aeronaut Soc; Soc Automotive Engrs (vpres, 55); Am Soc Mech Engrs; Inst Aeronaut Sci; Soc Aircraft Investr (pres, 62). *Mailing Add:* 4771 E Country Villa Dr Tucson AZ 85718-2640

SPECHT, DONALD FRANCIS, NEURAL NETWORKS, ELECTRICAL ENGINEERING & MEDICAL ELECTRONICS. *Current Pos:* SR MEM, LOCKHEED PALO ALTO RES LAB, 88-, CONSULT SCIENTIST, 91- *Personal Data:* b Harvey, NDak, Oct 15, 33; m 60; c 2. *Educ:* Univ Santa Clara, BEE, 55; Carnegie-Mellon Univ, MS, 56; Stanford Univ, PhD(elec eng), 66. *Prof Exp:* Electronics engr, Radio Corp Am, NJ, 55-57; res engr, Lockheed Missiles & Space Co, 57-63, res specialist biomed data anal, 63-66, scientist, Lockheed Palo Alto Res Lab, 66-70; mgr prog develop, Gould, Inc, Palo Alto, 70-74; mgr res, Smithkline Instruments, 75-81; dir res, Ekoline Inc, 81-82; vpres, Xonics Imaging, 82-84; mgr, image processing, KLA Instruments, 84-88. *Concurrent Pos:* Assoc ed, Inst Elec & Electronics Engrs Trans on Neural Networks. *Mem:* Inst Elec & Electronics Engrs; Int Neural Networks Soc. *Res:* Neural networks, sonar, and ultrasonic imaging; medical instrumentation; adaptive pattern-recognition techniques; nonlinear regression techniques; nonparametric probability estimators; radar target discrimination; automatic analysis of electrocardiograms, mammograms; digital radiography. *Mailing Add:* 869 Terrace Dr Los Altos CA 94024

SPECHT, EDWARD JOHN, GEOMETRY. *Current Pos:* prof, 72-86, EMER PROF, MATH, IND UNIV, SOUTH BEND, 86- *Personal Data:* b Loveland, Colo, July 29, 15; m 38, Mary J Michel; c Lahna J & Frederick M. *Educ:* Walla Walla Col, BS, 39; Univ Colo, MS, 41; Univ Minn, PhD(math), 49. *Hon Degrees:* DSc, Andrews Univ, 84. *Prof Exp:* Prof math, Andrews Univ, 47-72. *Concurrent Pos:* Vis lectr math, Univ Minn, 57. *Mem:* Fel AAAS; Math Asn Am; Sigma Xi; Am Math Soc. *Res:* Axiomatic development of Euclidean geometry and its subgeometries, where the axioms used are selected from the incidence, parallel, betweenness, plane separation, reflection, and least upper bound axioms. *Mailing Add:* 1023 Oakland South Bend IN 46615

SPECHT, HAROLD BALFOUR, ENTOMOLOGY, ECOLOGY. *Current Pos:* RETIRED. *Personal Data:* b Schenectady, NY, May 13, 27; Can citizen; m 49; c 5. *Educ:* McGill Univ, BSc, 48; Univ Wis, MSc, 51; Rutgers Univ, PhD(entom), 59. *Prof Exp:* Res scientist & entomologist, Kentville Res Sta, Can Dept Agr, 48-91. *Mem:* Entom Soc Am; Entom Soc Can. *Res:* Fruit insect ecology; integrated control studies on insects affecting apples; factors affecting mite populations on apple trees; pea aphid ecology; apple aphid ecology; tobacco cutworm investigation. *Mailing Add:* 14 Lavinia St Kentville NS B4N 1V7 Can

SPECHT, HEINZ, PHYSIOLOGY. *Current Pos:* RETIRED. *Educ:* Johns Hopkins Univ, PhD(physiol), 33. *Prof Exp:* Administrator, NIH, 68-71. *Mailing Add:* Fairhaven C135 7200 Third Ave Sykesville MD 21784-5201

SPECHT, JAMES EUGENE, PLANT GENETICS, PLANT PHYSIOLOGY. *Current Pos:* From asst prof to assoc prof, 74-85, PROF AGRON, INST AGR & NATURAL RESOURCES, UNIV NEBR, 85- *Personal Data:* b Scottsbluff, Nebr, Sept 12, 45; m 69, Pamela S Hammers. *Educ:* Univ Nebr, BS, 67, PhD(genetics), 74; Univ Ill, MS, 71. *Mem:* Fel AAAS; fel Am Soc Agron; Sigma Xi; fel Crop Sci Soc Am. *Res:* Novel approaches to the genetic and physiological improvement of the soybean. *Mailing Add:* Univ Nebr 309 Keim Hall Lincoln NE 68503-0915

SPECHT, LAWRENCE W, GENETICS. *Current Pos:* PROF DAIRY SCI, PA STATE UNIV, 57- *Personal Data:* b Roscoe, NY, Aug 5, 28; m 51; c 6. *Educ:* Cornell Univ, BS, 51; Mich State Univ, MS, 55, PhD, 57. *Mem:* Am Dairy Sci Asn. *Res:* Dairy cattle genetics and breeding, especially progeny testing and sire selection in artificial insemination; electronic data processing of milk production records. *Mailing Add:* 1204 Kay St Boalsburg PA 16827

SPECHT, ROBERT DICKERSON, MATHEMATICS. *Current Pos:* RETIRED. *Personal Data:* b Seattle, Wash, May 11, 13; m 36; c 5. *Educ:* Univ Fla, AB, 36, MS, 38; Univ Wis, PhD(math), 42. *Prof Exp:* Instr math, Univ Fla, 36-38; asst, Univ Wis, 38-41; instr, Univ Fla, 41-42; asst, Brown Univ, 42; from asst physicist to assoc mathematician, David Taylor Model Basin, US Dept Navy, 42-45; asst prof math, Univ Wis, 45-49; mathematician, Rand Corp, Santa Monica, 49-79. *Concurrent Pos:* Consult, Rand Corp, 79- *Res:* Applied mathematics; mechanics. *Mailing Add:* 14930 McKendree Ave Pacific Palisades CA 90272

SPECIAN, ROBERT DAVID, CYTOLOGY, ANIMAL PHYSIOLOGY. *Current Pos:* from asst prof to assoc prof anat, 81-90, prof cellular biol & anat, 90-96, PROF MOLECULAR & CELLULAR PHYSIOL SCH MED, LA STATE UNIV, SHREVEPORT, 96- *Personal Data:* b Niagara Falls, NY, Apr 25, 50; m 94, Janis Gabriel; c Victoria & Robert Jr. *Educ:* Southern Methodist Univ, BS, 72, MS, 74; Tulane Univ, PhD(biol), 80. *Prof Exp:* Fel cell biol & anat, Med Sch, Harvard Univ, 78-81. *Concurrent Pos:* Adj prof, dept biochem & molecular biol, Sch Med, La State Univ, Shreveport, 85- *Mem:* AAAS; Am Asn Anatomists; Am Soc Cell Biol; Am Soc Parasitol; NY Acad Sci. *Res:* Regulation and mechanisms of mucin synthesis and secretion in the mammalian intestine; physiochemical behavior of high molecular weight glycoproteins and their interaction with the intestinal flora; ishemia/reperfusion and intestinal function. *Mailing Add:* Dept Molecular & Cellular Physiol La State Univ 1501 Kingshwy PO Box 33932 Shreveport LA 71130-3932. *Fax:* 318-674-5889; *E-Mail:* rspeci@lsumc.edu

SPECK, DAVID RALPH, LASER SCIENCE, INERTIAL CONFINEMENT FUSION. *Current Pos:* PHYSICIST, LAWRENCE LIVERMORE NAT LAB, UNIV CALIF, 56- *Personal Data:* b Lindsay, Calif, Oct 31, 27; m 52; c 1. *Educ:* Fresno State Col, BS, 51; Univ Calif, Berkeley, MA, 53, PhD(physics), 56. *Mem:* Am Phys Soc. *Res:* Development and use of high power glass laser systems for inertial confinement fusion research; plasma physics; interaction of high power optical radiation with materials including non-linear optics and optical damage to materials. *Mailing Add:* 12 Corwin Dr Alamo CA 94507

SPECK, JOHN CLARENCE, JR, BIOCHEMISTRY. *Current Pos:* res assoc, 45-46, from instr to prof, 46-87, EMER PROF BIOCHEM, MICH STATE UNIV, 87- *Personal Data:* b Indianapolis, Ind, Jan 6, 17; m 40, Mary Peyton Hover; c Mary Suzanne (Hudson), John Peyton, Samuel Hover, Linda Christine & James Stephen. *Educ:* Univ Ill, BS, 39; Univ NC, PhD(org chem), 43. *Prof Exp:* Asst chem, Univ NC, 39-40; chemist, US Naval Res Lab, 41-43; res assoc chem, Ind Univ, 43-45. *Concurrent Pos:* Adj prof biochem, Mich State Univ, 88- *Mem:* Am Chem Soc; Am Soc Biol Chemists. *Res:* Chemistry of enzymes and other natural products. *Mailing Add:* Mich State Univ 976 Lantern Hill Dr East Lansing MI 48823-5383. *Fax:* 517-332-1077

SPECK, MARVIN LUTHER, FOOD SCIENCE & TECHNOLOGY. *Current Pos:* from assoc prof to prof dairy bact, 47-57, William Neal Reynolds prof, 57-79, EMER PROF FOOD SCI & MICROBIOL, NC STATE UNIV, 79- *Personal Data:* b Middletown, Md, Oct 6, 13; m 40; c 3. *Educ:* Univ Md, BS, 35, MS, 37; Cornell Univ, PhD(bact), 40. *Honors & Awards:* Borden Award, Am Dairy Sci Asn, 59 & Pfizer Award, 67; Nordica Int Res Award, Am Cultured Dairy Prod Inst, 81; Nat Award for Agr Excellence in Sci, Nat Agr-Mkt Asn, 84. *Prof Exp:* Bacteriologist, Western Md Dairy, 35-36; instr bact, Univ Md, 40-41; asst chief bacteriologist, Nat Dairy Res Labs, 41-47. *Concurrent Pos:* Jr bacteriologist, USDA, 36; bacteriologist, Dairymen's League, 40; instr, Univ Md, 45; consult, USPHS, 50-51 & 53; WHO fel, Europe, 66; consult, 79- *Mem:* Am Soc Microbiol; fel Inst Food Technologists. *Res:* Nutrition and metabolism of lactic acid bacteria; injury and destruction of bacteria by physical and chemical agents; uses and functions of intestinal lactobacilli. *Mailing Add:* 3204 Churchill Rd Raleigh NC 27607

SPECK, RHOADS MCCLELLAN, ORGANIC CHEMISTRY. *Current Pos:* RETIRED. *Personal Data:* b Glenside, Pa, Apr 12, 20; m 46, Dorothy Clem; c Jonathan, Carolyn, Martha & Rosemary. *Educ:* Philadelphia Col Pharm, BSc, 42; Pa State Univ, MSc, 49, PhD(org chem), 52. *Prof Exp:* Asst chemist, Eastern Regional Res Ctr, Agr Res Serv, USDA, 42-44 & 46-47; asst analytical chem, Pa State Univ, 47-48; res chemist, Res Ctr, Hercules Inc, Wilmington, 52-75, sr res chemist, 75-81, res scientist, 81-83. *Concurrent Pos:* Consult, Hercules Inc, 86-87. *Mem:* Am Chem Soc; Sigma Xi. *Res:* Syntheses and physical properties of high molecular weight hydrocarbons; syntheses of agricultural chemicals; rosin and fatty acid chemistry; emulsion polymerization; free radical reactions. *Mailing Add:* 45 Westview Dr Berkeley Springs WV 25411

SPECKARD, DAVID CARL, ENZYMOLOGY, STRUCTURE & FUNCTION OF ENZYMES & ENZYME-SUBSTRATE COMPLEXES. *Current Pos:* PROF, LORAS COL, 81- *Personal Data:* b Valparasio, Ind, June 9, 48; m 71, Sharon Daugherty; c Douglas K Daugherty & Sara Daugherty. *Educ:* De Pauw Univ, BA, 70; Ohio State Univ, PhD(chem), 75. *Prof Exp:* Asst prof biochem, Clemson Univ, 76-81. *Concurrent Pos:* Vis prof biochem, Univ Wis, 85-; Fulbright prof, Max Planck Inst Exp Med, Goettingen, Ger, 88-89. *Mem:* Am Chem Soc; Sigma Xi. *Res:* Chemical mechanism of enzymes, focusing on dehydrogenases, polymerases and kinases; employ chemical probes to map active centers of kinases. *Mailing Add:* 1450 Alta Vista Blvd Dubuque IA 52004-0178. *E-Mail:* drdcs@lcac1.loras.edu

SPECKMANN, ELWOOD W, PHYSIOLOGY, NUTRITION. *Current Pos:* DIR RES PROG, SHRINERS HOSPS CHILDREN, 91- *Personal Data:* b Brooklyn, NY, Jan 10, 36; m 62, Lorelei E Jacobs; c Kim M, Lynne E, Mark T & Scott W. *Educ:* Rutgers Univ, BS, 57; Mich State Univ, MS, 59, PhD(nutrit physiol), 62. *Prof Exp:* Res asst nutrit physiol, Mich State Univ, 57-62; res scientist, Biospecialties Br, Physiol Div, Aerospace Med Res Labs, Wright-Patterson AFB, Ohio, 62-65; from asst dir to dir nutrit res, Nat Dairy Coun, 65-83, interim educ dir, 67-68, vpres, 83-85, pres, 85-89, vpres, Nutrit Res & Tech Serv, United Dairy Indus Assoc, 89-90. *Concurrent Pos:* Air Force liaison rep food & nutrit bd & working group nutrit & feeding probs, Man in Space Comt, Space Sci Bd, Nat Acad Sci-Nat Res Coun, 63-65; Salisbury res fel, 60-62. *Mem:* Am Burn Asn; Am Soc Nutrit Sci; Orthop Res Soc; Am Soc Bone & Mineral Res; Am Soc Clin Nutrit (treas, 82-86); Fedn Am Socs Exp Biol (treas, 86-88). *Res:* Physiology of circulation and heart; arteriosclerosis; physiology of burns; physiology of digestion and metabolism of foods; nutrient interactions; connective tissue biology. *Mailing Add:* Shriners Hosps for Children Hq 2900 Rocky Point Dr Tampa FL 33607-1435. *Fax:* 813-281-8113; *E-Mail:* ewspeck@aol.com

SPECKMANN, GUNTER WILHELM-OTTO, VETERINARY BACTERIOLOGY. *Current Pos:* RETIRED. *Personal Data:* b Ger, Oct 3, 34; Can citizen; m 62, Rosemarie Grundmann; c Susanne, Thomas & Barbara. *Educ:* Vet Col Hannover, Ger, DMV, 67; Univ Guelph, DVM, 68. *Prof Exp:* Vet poultry dis, Agr Can, 68-76, vet bact, Animal Path Div, 76-81; vet, Health & Welfare, Can, 81-94. *Concurrent Pos:* Drug evaluation; pvt pract, 94. *Res:* Epidemiological studies of Salmonella and Yersinia carriers in livestock. *Mailing Add:* 6435 Fallowfield Rd Stittsville ON K2S 1B8 Can

SPECTER, STEVEN CARL, VIROLOGY. *Current Pos:* asst prof, 79-84, ASSOC PROF MICROBIOL & IMMUNOL, COL MED, UNIV SFLA, 84- *Personal Data:* b Philadelphia, Pa, June 4, 47; m 69; c 2. *Educ:* Temple Univ, BA, 69, PhD(microbiol), 75. *Prof Exp:* Res fel microbiol, Albert Einstein Med Ctr, Philadelphia, 74-76, asst dir, 76-79. *Concurrent Pos:* Virol consult, Tampa Gen Hosp, 79. *Mem:* Am Soc Microbiol; AAAS; fel Am Acad Microbiol. *Res:* Immune suppression by viruses, tumors and drugs, most notably friend leukemia virus and marijuana; clinical virology studies on antivirals and herpesviruses. *Mailing Add:* 2008 Chickwood Ct Tampa FL 33618

SPECTOR, ABRAHAM, BIOCHEMISTRY. *Current Pos:* from asst prof to assoc prof of ophthal, 65-73, PROF OPHTHALMIC BIOCHEM, COL PHYSICIANS & SURGEONS, COLUMBIA UNIV, 73-, DIR, LAB BIOCHEM & MOLECULAR BIOL, 76- *Personal Data:* b Nyack, NY, Jan 14, 26; m 83; c 2. *Educ:* Bard Col, AB, 47; NY Univ, PhD(biochem), 57. *Hon Degrees:* MD, Univ Repub Uruguay, 81; DSc, Bard Col, 85. *Honors & Awards:* Int Award, Japanese Coop Cataract Res Group, 87; Bausch & Lomb Sci Medal, 44. *Prof Exp:* Res chemist, Lederle Labs, Am Cyanamid Corp, 48-52; from instr to assoc biochem, Howe Lab, Mass Eye & Ear Infirmary, Harvard Med Sch, 58-65; lectr biol chem, Northeastern Univ, 59-62. *Concurrent Pos:* Mem, Nat Eye Inst Vision Res, 70-71; mem, Nat Eye Inst Bd Sci Advisors, 74; mem, Nat Eye Inst, 76-80, chmn, 78-80; vis prof ophthal, Univ Puerto Rico, 82-; vis prof biochem, Med Univ Shangai, 86-; John Simon Guggenheim fel, 71-72, Fulbright, 81. *Mem:* Am Soc Biol Chem; Am Chem Soc; Asn Res Vision & Ophthal (pres, 76); AAAS; Harvey Soc. *Res:* Protein chemistry; ophthalmic biochemistry; enzymology; biosynthesis of proteins and nucleic acids; oxidative stress. *Mailing Add:* Dept Ophthal Columbia Univ Col Phys & Surg 630 W 168th St New York NY 10032. *Fax:* 212-305-6205

SPECTOR, ARTHUR ABRAHAM, BIOCHEMISTRY, INTERNAL MEDICINE. *Current Pos:* from asst prof to assoc prof, 68-75, PROF BIOCHEM & MED & DIR ARTERIOSCLEROSIS SCOR CTR, UNIV IOWA, 75- *Personal Data:* b Philadelphia, Pa, May 14, 36; m 60; c 3. *Educ:* Univ Pa, BA, 56, MD, 60. *Prof Exp:* Intern, Abington Mem Hosp, 60-61; res med officer, Nat Heart Inst, 63-68. *Concurrent Pos:* NIH res career develop award, 69-74; Nat Heart Inst fel biochem, 63-65; mem coun arteriosclerosis, Am Heart Asn; mem metab study sect, NIH, 73-77 & rev comt, Ischemic Heart Dis Ctr, 78-79; chmn res comt & mem bd dirs, Iowa Heart Asn, 75-77; chmn & mem, Great Plains Regional Res Comn, Am Heart Asn, 77-80; mem & chmn biomed adv comt, Oak Ridge Assoc Univ, 78-82. *Mem:* AAAS; Tissue Cult Asn; Am Asn Cancer Res; Am Soc Biol Chemists; Am Soc Clin Invest. *Res:* Lipid metabolism; membranes; fatty acids; prostaglandin. *Mailing Add:* Dept Pharmacol Univ Iowa Col Med 2-471 Bowen Sci Bldg Iowa City IA 52242-1109. *Fax:* 319-335-9570

SPECTOR, BERTRAM, ENVIRONMENTAL HEALTH, MEDICAL SYSTEMS. *Current Pos:* CONSULT MED ENGR, 87- *Personal Data:* b New York, NY, Nov 1, 21; m 45; c 2. *Educ:* City Col New York, BEE, 45; Hunter Col, MS, 57; Cornell Univ, PhD(med sci), 61. *Prof Exp:* Vpres, Seversky Electronatom, NY, 60-63; dean acad affairs, NY Inst Technol, 63-64, chmn life sci dept, 63-64 & 67-68, prof life sci, 63-87, vpres res, 66-87; vpres, Ctr Educ Technol, 85-87. *Concurrent Pos:* Prin investr grants, Off Educ, Dept Health, Educ & Welfare, Carnegie Corp, Ford Found Fund for Advan Educ & Proj ULTRA, 64-; prin co-investr, Dept Health, Educ & Welfare grant, 68-; adj prof, Shaw Univ, 68-70; consult, Pan Am Airlines, 68, Nova Univ Advan Technol & Hofstra Univ, 69 & Wash Univ, 69-; mem NSF panel, 69; mem bd trustees, Affiliated Cols & Univs, Inc; mem bd dirs, Afro-Am Coun Higher Educ; mem bd dirs & exec comt, Cancirco, Inc; chmn, Environ Control Comn, Town of Oyster Bay, 74- & Comt Energy & Natural Resources, 73-; vpres res, NY Chiropractic Col, Glen Head, 76-; pres, New Ctr Wholistic Health & Res, 81-; Sloan fel. *Mem:* Fel Am Inst Biol Sci. *Res:* Physics; educational technology; environmental sciences and technology; pattern electromyography; biofeedback; moire contourography; computer technology. *Mailing Add:* 303 Sea Oats Dr Apt A North Palm Beach FL 33408

SPECTOR, CLARENCE J(ACOB), ENGINEERING PHYSICS, MATERIALS SCIENCE. *Current Pos:* sr engr & mgr display components develop, 62-76, MGR THERMAL TECHNOL, IBM SYST PROD, IBM CORP, 76- *Personal Data:* b New York, NY, June 19, 27; m 50; c 3. *Educ:* Va Polytech Inst & State Univ, BS, 53; Stevens Inst Technol, MS, 57. *Prof Exp:* Mem tech staff, Bell Tel Labs, Inc, 53-62. *Mem:* AAAS; Inst Elec & Electronics Engrs. *Res:* Physics of dielectrics, magnetic and semiconductor materials; passive and magnetic thin film devices; metallurgy. *Mailing Add:* 6765 Lazy River Way 95120 CA 95193

SPECTOR, DAVID LAWRENCE, NUCLEAR STRUCTURE, RNA PROCESSING. *Current Pos:* sr staff investr, 85-92, SR STAFF SCIENTIST, COLD SPRING HARBOR LAB, 85- *Personal Data:* b New York, NY, Dec 6, 52; m 81, Mona Friedman. *Educ:* City Col New York, BS, 73; Rutgers Univ, PhD(cell biol), 80. *Prof Exp:* Asst prof, Baylor Col Med, 81-85. *Concurrent Pos:* Mem, Electron Micros Spec Study Sect, NIH, 88- *Mem:* Am Soc Cell Biol; Micros Soc Am; fel Royal Micros Soc. *Res:* Understanding the functional organization of the mammalian cell nucleus, particularly how the processes of transcription by RNA polymerase II and pre-mRNA splicing are coordinated. *Mailing Add:* Cold Spring Harbor Lab PO Box 100 1 Bungtown Rd Cold Spring Harbor NY 11724-2217

SPECTOR, HAROLD NORMAN, SOLID STATE PHYSICS, SEMICONDUCTOR PHYSICS. *Current Pos:* res physicist, IIT Res Inst, 63-66, assoc prof, 66-76, PROF, ILL INST TECHNOL, 76- *Personal Data:* b Chicago, Ill, Feb 26, 35; m 61, Sarah Daniel; c Benyaminia. *Educ:* Univ Chicago, SB, 57, SM, 58, PhD(physics), 61. *Prof Exp:* NSF fel physics, Hebrew Univ, Israel, 61-62; asst prof, Case Inst Technol, 62-63. *Concurrent Pos:* Vis prof, Hebrew Univ, Israel, 73-74; fel, GTE, 83 & consult, 83-86. *Mem:* Fel Am Phys Soc; Sigma Xi. *Res:* Solid state theory, optical and electronic properties of semiconducting quantum well systems phonon-electron interactions in solids, transport theory, effect of strong electric and magnetic fields on electronic processes in solids. *Mailing Add:* Dept Physics Ill Inst Technol Chicago IL 60616. *Fax:* 312-567-3396; *E-Mail:* inphysspector@minna.iit.edu

SPECTOR, JONATHAN M, COMPUTER SCIENCES. *Current Pos:* SR SCIENTIST, TECH TRAINING RES DIV, ARMSTRONG LAB, BROOKS AFB, 91- *Personal Data:* b Pensacola, Fla, July 28, 45. *Educ:* USAF Acad, BS, 67; Univ Tex, Austin, PhD, 78. *Prof Exp:* Sr analyst, Cuvic Corp, 81-83; sr programmer, Nat Solar Observ, 83-84; prof comput sci, Jacksonville Univ, 84-91. *Concurrent Pos:* Fulbright scholar, Univ Bergen, Norway, 95-96. *Mem:* Am Philos Asn; Asn Educ Commun Tech; Int Soc Performance. *Mailing Add:* Armstrong Lab 7909 Lindberg Dr Brooks AFB TX 78235. *Fax:* 210-536-2902; *E-Mail:* mike@ifi.uib.no

SPECTOR, LEO FRANCIS, PLANT ENGINEERING, MECHANICAL DESIGN ENGINEERING. *Current Pos:* CONSULT PLANT ENG, 90- *Personal Data:* b Kansas City, Mo, Nov 10, 23; m 68; c 5. *Educ:* Univ Kans, BSME, 49. *Honors & Awards:* Leo F Spector Award for Outstanding Contrib Field Plant Eng, 90. *Prof Exp:* Sr assoc ed mach design, Penton Publ Co, 51-62, regional ed, 67-70; ed assembly eng, Hitchcock Publ Co, 62-67; ed plant eng, Tech Publ Co, 70-86; vpres & ed dir plant eng, Cahners Publ Co, Div Reed Publ, USA, 86-90. *Concurrent Pos:* Secy, Comt Sintered Metal Brake Mat (Stand), Am Soc Testing & Mat, 56-66; mem, several Am Nat Stand Comts Fasteners, 64-70; chmn, Am Nat Stand Comt Interference Fits, 65-67 & Nat Ann Plant Eng Conf & Related Regional Confs, 75-89. *Mem:* Am Soc Mech Engrs. *Res:* Technical editor and writer, written on subjects relating to plant engineering, design engineering and technical article preparation. *Mailing Add:* 1800 Wakeman Ct Wheaton IL 60187

SPECTOR, NOVERA HERBERT, NEUROBIOLOGY, BIOPHYSICS & NEUROIMMUNOMODULATION. *Current Pos:* VPRES SCI RES, AM INST NEUROIMMUNOMODULATION RES, 95- *Personal Data:* b Cincinnati, Ohio, Aug 23, 19; m 41, 81; c Helene N, David A, Lisa B & Alida M (Gertz). *Educ:* City Col New York, BS, 41; Univ Pa, PhD(physiol), 67. *Honors & Awards:* Dir's Award, NIH, 88; Metalnikov Gold Medal, Italy, 90-; Physiol Soc Medal, Poland, 90. *Prof Exp:* Consult engr, 41-62; from res assoc to asst prof psychiat, Med Col Va, Va Commonwealth Univ, 66-68, asst prof physiol, 68-69; prof physiol, Fac Med, Univ Claude Bernard, France, 69-71; chief, Dept Neurophysiol & sr res physiologist, Walter Reed Inst Res, 71-76; dir, Neurobiol Prog, NSF, 76-77; health sci adminr, Fundamental Neurosci Prog, Nat Inst Neurol Dis & Stroke, NIH, 77-95. *Concurrent Pos:* Consult, NASA, 68-71; adj prof physiol & biophys & adj prof anat, Med Ctr, Georgetown Univ, Washington, DC, 78-; vis prof psychiat, Med Ctr, Univ Ala, Birmingham, 80-83, prof neurosci, Med Sch, 80-83, adj prof, microbiol & neurosic, 85-; vis prof neuroimmunol, Geront Res Ctr Italy, Ancona, 92- *Mem:* Sigma Xi; Soc Exp Biol & Med; Am Physiol Soc; Soc Neurosci; Tissue Cult Asn; Am Soc Microbiol; Int Soc Neuroimmunomodulation (pres, 87-90); Asn des Physiologists, Int Brain Res Orgn. *Res:* Physiology; neuroimmunomodulation; neural data processing; biophysics of neurons in vivo and in vitro; neural substrates of sensation and behavior; epistemology; central nervous system influences on host responses to antigens and diseases; neuropharmacology; alcoholism; psychophysics; hypothalamic control mechanisms; neuroanatomy; neuroimmunogenesis; neuroimmunomodulation; energy balance in mammals; central nervous system regulation of automatic functions; conditioned immune responses. *Mailing Add:* 4014-G Layang Circle Carlsbad CA 92008. *Fax:* 301-402-1501

SPECTOR, REYNOLD, PHARMACOLOGY, INTERNAL MEDICINE. *Current Pos:* EXEC DIR, VPRES, SR VPRES, MERCK RES LAB, RAHWAY, NJ, 87- *Personal Data:* b Boston, Mass, Nov 3, 40; m 73; c 2. *Educ:* Harvard Col, AB, 62; Yale Univ, MD, 66. *Honors & Awards:* Harry Gold Award, Am Soc Pharmacol & Exp Therapeut, 91. *Prof Exp:* Sr med adv, Army Med Corps, US Army, Repub Korea, 68-70; instr med, Sch Med, Harvard Univ & Peter Bent Brigham Hosp, 71-74, from asst prof to assoc prof, 74-78, chief, div clin pharmacol, 76-78; dir, div gen med, 80-85, prof internal med & pharmacol & dir, div clin pharmacol, Col Med, Univ Iowa, Iowa City, 78-87, dir, div gen med, 80-85; dir clin res ctr & med dir, Poison Control Ctr, Hosps & Clins, 85-87. *Concurrent Pos:* Vis prof biochem, Stanford Univ, 83-84. *Mem:* Asn Am Physicians; Am Soc Clin Invest; Am Soc Pharmacol & Exp Therapeut; fel Am Col Physicians. *Res:* Passage of drugs, vitamins and hormones in and out of brain; poison victim treatment; effect of diet on the pharmacokinetics of drugs; development of drugs for human use. *Mailing Add:* Merck Res Labs PO Box 2000 Rahway NJ 07065-0900

SPECTOR, RICHARD M, THEORETICAL PHYSICS. *Current Pos:* ASSOC, HONIGMAN, MILLER, SCHWARTZ & COHN, DETROIT, 81- *Personal Data:* b St Louis, Mo, Jan 13, 38; div; c 3. *Educ:* Harvard Univ, BA, 59; Oxford Univ, PhD(physics), 62; Wayne State Univ, JD, 76. *Prof Exp:* Vis scientist physics, Saclay Nuclear Res Ctr, France, 62; res assoc, Univ Rochester, 62-64; prof assoc, NSF, 64-65; from asst prof to assoc prof physics, Wayne State Univ, 65-78; assoc, Dykema, Gossett, Spencer, Goodwin & Trigg, Detroit, 78-81. *Mem:* Am Bar Asn; Am Phys Soc. *Res:* Singular potential theory; spectra of rapidly rotating stars; geophysical aspects of pleochroic halos; group theory of elementary particles. *Mailing Add:* 745 Coronado Ave Coral Gables FL 33143

SPECTOR, SAMUEL, PEDIATRICS. *Current Pos:* prof, 79-90, EMER PROF PEDIAT, UNIV CALIF, SAN DIEGO, 90- *Personal Data:* b Brooklyn, NY, Mar 11, 14; m 43, Lillian Hutchinson; c Judith, Susan & Michael. *Educ:* Columbia Univ, BS, 34; Long Island Col Med, MD, 37. *Prof Exp:* Intern, Beth El Hosp, 37-38; intern, Kingston Ave Hosp, 38; resident pediat, Willard Parker Hosp, 39-41; resident, Univ Hosp, Univ Mich, 41-42, instr, Med Sch, 42-43; from asst prof to prof, Sch Med, Case Western Res Univ, 46-70; prof pediat & chmn dept, Univ Chicago, 70-79,. *Concurrent Pos:* From assoc pediatrician to assoc dir pediat, Babies & Children's Hosp, 46-66; dir pediat, Children's Hosp of Akron, 67-70; dir pediat, Wyler Children's Hosp, Univ Chicago Hosps & Clins, 70-79 & LaRabida Children's Hosp & Res Ctr, 73-78; attending pediat, Univ Hosp, Med Ctr, Univ Calif, San Diego. *Mem:* Soc Pediat Res; Am Pediat Soc; Am Acad Pediat; Sigma Xi. *Res:* Metabolic and endocrine problems of childhood. *Mailing Add:* Med Ctr Univ Calif H814L 200 W Arbor San Diego CA 92103. *E-Mail:* sispector@ucsd.edu

SPECTOR, SHELDON LAURENCE, ALLERGY, IMMUNOLOGY. *Current Pos:* Fel allergy & clin immunol, 69-71, clin coordr, 71-72, HEAD SECT ALLERGY & CLIN IMMUNOL, NAT JEWISH HOSP & RES CTR, 72- *Personal Data:* b Detroit, Mich, Feb 13, 39; m 66; c 3. *Educ:* Wayne State Univ, MD, 64. *Honors & Awards:* Distinguished Serv Award, Am Acad Allergy, 94. *Concurrent Pos:* Asst med, Mt Sinai Hosp Sch Med, 65-66; asst prof, Med Sch, Univ Colo, 71-77, assoc prof, 77-; vis prof, Hebrew Univ, Jerusalem, 78; Lady Davis fel allergy, Hebrew Univ, William Beaumont Soc, 78. *Mem:* Am Thoracic Soc; Am Soc Internal Med; fel Am Acad Allergy; fel Am Col Physicians; fel Am Col Chest Physicians; distinguished fel Am Col Allergy. *Res:* Bronchial inhalation challenge techniques; new modalities of treatment of asthma and rhinitis including unmarketed preparation; how certain substances in the environment affect bronchial and/or nasal reactivity; how commonly used medications affect asthmatic patients. *Mailing Add:* Allergy Med Clin 11620 Wilshire Blvd Suite 200 Los Angeles CA 90025

SPECTOR, SYDNEY, PHARMACOLOGY. *Current Pos:* HEAD PHYSIOL CHEM & PHARMACOL, ROCHE INST MOLECULAR BIOL, 68- *Personal Data:* b New York, NY, Oct 28, 23; m 48; c 2. *Educ:* Univ Denver, BS, 48, MS, 50; Jefferson Med Col, PhD(pharmacol), 56. *Honors & Awards:* Amer Soc Exp Therapeut Award, 79; P K Smith Award, 87. *Prof Exp:* Asst physiol, Univ Denver, 47-50; asst pharmacol, Sch Med, Wash Univ, 50-52; res assoc, Wyeth Inst Med Res, Pa, 52-55; pharmacologist, Nat Heart Inst, Md, 56-68. *Concurrent Pos:* Instr, Hahnemann Med Col, 54; adj prof pharmacol, Howard Med Sch, 60- & New York Med Col, 68-; adj prof pharmacol & anesthesiol, Col Physicians & Surgeons, Columbia Univ, 70- *Mem:* AAAS; Am Soc Pharmacol & Exp Therapeut (pres, 79); Am Col Neuropsychopharmacol. *Res:* Biochemical pharmacoloy; correlation between pharmacological effects of drugs and chemical changes, particularly of the central nervous system; development of antibodies toward drugs. *Mailing Add:* Dept Pharmacol & Psych Vanderbilt Univ Med Ctr Rm AA2232 Nashville TN 37232. *Fax:* 615-343-7675

SPECTOR, THOMAS, BIOCHEMISTRY, CHEMOTHERAPY. *Current Pos:* RETIRED. *Personal Data:* b New Haven, Conn, July 20, 44; m 69, Jo-Anna Spiegel; c 1. *Educ:* Univ Vt, BA, 66; Yale Univ, PhD(pharmacol), 70. *Prof Exp:* Fel biochem, Univ Mich, 70-72; prin scientist & asst div dir, Wellcome Res Labs, 72-96. *Concurrent Pos:* Adj prof, Dept Pharmacol, Univ NC, 76- *Mem:* Am Soc Biochem & Molecular Biol; Am Soc Microbiol; Am Asn Cancer Res. *Res:* Enzymology, mechanisms of inhibition and substrate catalysis; inhibitor and substrate specificities; studies of the mechanisms of interactions of drugs and drug matabolites with chemotherapeutically important enzymes of the purine and pyrimidine metabolic pathways; studies of enzymes from human immunodefficiency and herpes viruses; cancer chemotherapy. *Mailing Add:* Glaxo-Wellcome Co N23209 5 Moore Dr Research Triangle Park NC 27709. *Fax:* 919-315-8597

SPEDDEN, H RUSH, MINING ENGINEERING. *Current Pos:* CONSULT MINERAL PROCESSING ENGR, 77- *Personal Data:* b Colville, Wash, May 31, 16; m 51; c 4. *Educ:* Univ Wash, BS, 39; Mont Sch Mines, MS, 40. *Hon Degrees:* MinDrE, 64. *Honors & Awards:* Robert H Richards Award, Am Inst Mining, Metall & Petrol Engrs, 71. *Prof Exp:* Asst, Mass Inst Technol, 40-41, instr mineral dressing, 41-42, asst prof, 46-52, res engr, 52-57; head, Minerals Res Dept, Metals Res Lab, Union Carbide Corp, 52-57, dir res, Union Carbide Ore Corp, 52-57, dir res, Union Carbide Ore Co, 57-64; res dir, Kennecott Copper Corp, Metal Mining Div, Res Ctr, 64-74, dir tech admin, 74-77. *Concurrent Pos:* Prod specialist, Foreign Econ Admin, 42-44; adj prof, Univ Utah. *Mem:* Am Inst Mining, Metall & Petrol Engrs; Soc Mining Engrs (pres, 70). *Res:* Minerals beneficiation; extractive metallurgy. *Mailing Add:* 4131 Cumorah Dr Salt Lake City UT 84124-4040

SPEDDING, ROBERT H, DENTISTRY. *Current Pos:* from instr to assoc prof, 63-72, PROF PEDIAT DENT, COL DENT, UNIV KY, 72- *Personal Data:* b Lockport, NY, Feb 8, 31; m 59; c 3. *Educ:* Ind Univ, AB, 53, DDS, 60, MSD, 63; Am Bd Pedodont, dipl, 67. *Prof Exp:* Teaching asst periodont, Sch Dent, Ind Univ, 62-63. *Mem:* Am Dent Asn; Am Acad Pediat Dent; Am Asn Dent Schs; Am Asn Univ Prof. *Res:* Effects of various materials on primary tooth pulps and periodontal tissues. *Mailing Add:* 246 Tahoma Rd Lexington KY 40503

SPEECE, HERBERT E, MATHEMATICS. *Current Pos:* Head, Dept Sci & Math Educ, 72-80, prof, 47-80, EMER PROF MATH, NC STATE UNIV, 80- *Personal Data:* b Meadowlands, Minn, Oct 29, 14; m 45; c 2. *Educ:* York Col, AB, 38; Tex Christian Univ, MA, 43; NC State Col, MS, 51; Univ NC, PhD(math), 56. *Concurrent Pos:* Dir, Nat Acad Sci-NSF Inserv Insts, NC, 59-, assoc dir, NSF Acad Year Inst, 65-67; dir, Eng Concepts Curric Proj Implementation Ctr Southeast, NSF, 71-72 & 72-73; chmn adv bd, NC Student Acad Sci; chmn selection comt, NC Jr Sci & Humanities Symp; dir, Comput Educ Ctr, Dept Math-Sci Educ, NC State Univ, 73-78. *Res:* Tensors and differential geometry. *Mailing Add:* 3408 Wade Ave Raleigh NC 27607

SPEECE, SUSAN PHILLIPS, ACQUIRED IMMUNE DEFICIENCY SYNDROME EDUCATION. *Current Pos:* DEAN, MATH SCI & ENG, FRESNO CITY COL, 95- *Personal Data:* b Chicago, Ill, Aug 13, 45; div; c 2. *Educ:* Purdue Univ, BS, 67, MS, 71; Ball State Univ, EdD, 78. *Honors & Awards:* Distinguished Serv Award, Hosier Asn Sci Teachers, 89. *Prof Exp:* Dept chair sci, Gosport Sch, 67-68, Wes Del High Sch, 71-76; instr biol, Purdue Univ, 68-70; from asst prof to prof biol, Anderson Univ, 77-95, chair, Anderson Univ, 84-95. *Concurrent Pos:* Adj fac biol, Ball State Univ, 80-84; dist dir, Nat Sci Teacher's Asn, 88-90; mem, Ind Pesticide Rev Bd, 88-, Col Comt, Nat Sci Teacher's Asn, 91-93; prin investr, Comn Higher Educ grant for Acquired Immune Deficiency Syndrome Educ, 89-90; mem, AID Syndrome Adv Bd, Ind Dept Educ, 90- *Mem:* Nat Asn Biol Teachers (pres, 89); Hoosier Asn Sci Teachers (pres, 86-89); AAAS; Int Soc Acquired Immune Deficiency Syndrome Educ; Indian Acad Sci; Nat Asn Res Sci Teaching; Asn Instrnl Adminr. *Res:* AIDS research and its interpretation for education; effective science teaching strategies; calcium transport protein biochemistry. *Mailing Add:* Dept Math Sci & Eng Fresno City Col 1101 E Univ Fresno CA 93741. *E-Mail:* speece__s@scccd.cc.ca.us

SPEED, EDWIN MAURICE, DENTISTRY, ANATOMY. *Current Pos:* RETIRED. *Personal Data:* b Enterprise, Miss, Aug 17, 18; m 42; c 2. *Educ:* Birmingham Southern Col, BA, 52; Univ Ala, DMD, 54, MS, 65. *Prof Exp:* Pvt pract, 54-61; resident periodont, Vet Admin Hosp, Birmingham, Ala, 63-65; mem, Fac Dent & asst to dean, Sch Dent, Univ Ala, Brimingham, 65-66, prof dent & asst dean, 66-79. *Concurrent Pos:* Consult, US Army, Ft Benning, Ga, 71-72; mem coun, Nat Bd Dent Examr, 75-77 & Dent Hyg Nat Bd, 75-76. *Mem:* Am Dent Asn; Am Acad Periodont; fel Am Col Dent; Am Asn Dent Schs (vpres, 74, pres, 75). *Res:* Wound healing. *Mailing Add:* 729 River Haven Circle Birmingham AL 35244

SPEED, RAYMOND A(NDREW), CHEMICAL ENGINEERING. *Current Pos:* RETIRED. *Personal Data:* b Muldoon, Tex, Sept 30, 22; m 53; c 2. *Educ:* Univ Tex, BSChE, 49. *Prof Exp:* From jr chemist to res specialist, Humble Oil & Refining Co, 49-63; res specialist, Esso Res & Eng Co, 63-71; sr staff engr, Enjay Chem Co, 71-78, eng assoc, Exxon Chem Co USA, 78-82. *Mem:* Am Chem Soc. *Res:* Polyolefin polymers; separations. *Mailing Add:* 16110 Peach Bough Lane Houston TX 77095-4061

SPEED, ROBERT CLARKE, GEOLOGY, GEOPHYSICS. *Current Pos:* from asst prof to assoc prof, 66-74, PROF GEOL, NORTHWESTERN UNIV, EVANSTON, 74- *Personal Data:* b Los Angeles, Calif, June 20, 33; m 54; c 2. *Educ:* Univ Colo, BS, 54; Stanford Univ, MS, 58, PhD(geol), 61. *Prof Exp:* Res supvr, Jet Propulsion Lab, Calif Inst Technol, 60-66. *Res:* Tectonics and structural geology; structure and evolution of accretionary prisms and forearcs; tectonics of southeastern Caribbean and US cardillera; fold and thrust belts; seismicity. *Mailing Add:* Geol 309 Lacy Hall Northwestern Univ Evanston IL 60208-0001

SPEED, STAN, CHEMISTRY. *Current Pos:* RES SCIENTIST, EXXON CHEM CO, HOUSTON. *Honors & Awards:* Coop Res in Polymer Sci & Eng Award, Am Chem Soc, 95. *Mailing Add:* Exxon Chem Corp 13501 Katy Freeway Houston TX 77079-1305

SPEEDIE, MARILYN KAY, BIOTECHNOLOGY, APPLIED MICROBIOLOGY. *Current Pos:* PROF & DEAN, COL PHARM, UNIV MINN, 96- *Personal Data:* b Salem, Ore, Nov 13, 47; m 68, Stuart M; c Andrea & Christopher. *Educ:* Purdue Univ, BS, 70, PhD(med chem & pharmacog), 73. *Honors & Awards:* Paul Dawson Biotechnol Award, Am Asn Cols Pharm, 94. *Prof Exp:* Asst prof, Sch Pharm, Ore State Univ, 73-75; from asst prof to assoc prof pharmacog, Univ Md, 75-88, chmn, Dept Biomed Chem, 88-93, prof, Dept Pharm Sci, Sch Pharm, 90-96, chmn, 93-96. *Concurrent Pos:* Vis assoc prof, Stanford Univ, 84-85; Found Microbiol lectr, Am Soc Microbiol, 83-84. *Mem:* Am Soc Pharmacog; Am Soc Microbiol; Soc Indust Microbiol; Am Chem Soc; Sigma Xi; AAAS. *Res:* Regulation and enzymology of secondary metabolism in streptomycetes; expression and secretion of proteins from heterologous genes cloned into streptomycetes; microbial degradation of pollutants. *Mailing Add:* Col Pharm Univ Minn 308 Harvard St SE Minneapolis MN 55455. *Fax:* 612-624-2974; *E-Mail:* mspeedie@mailbox.mail.umn.edu

SPEEN, GERALD BRUCE, HEAT TRANSFER, ENERGY CONSERVATION. *Current Pos:* PRES, G SPEEN & ASSOCS, CONSULTS IN ENERGY FIELD, 78- *Personal Data:* b Philadelphia, Pa, Oct 2, 30; m 54, Gloria Simon; c Mitchell, Cyndie & Jill. *Educ:* Univ Del, BS, 52; Univ Calif, Los Angeles, MS, 54. *Honors & Awards:* Inst Elec & Electronics Engrs Award, 63. *Prof Exp:* mem tech staff, Res & Develop Labs, Hughes Aircraft Co, 52-54; res physicist, Micronics Inc Div, Zenith Plastics Corp, 54-55; res engr, Summers Gyroscope Co, 55-56; exec engr, ITT Fed Labs, Int Tel & Tel Corp, 56-64; gen mgr, Western Develop Ctr, Conductron Corp, Subsid McDonnell-Douglas Corp, 64-68; pres, Data Instruments Co, 68-73, pres, Lanco-Supreme, Inc, Hyatt Corp, 73-75, pres, Supreme Aire & Elmet Corp, Santa Fe Springs, 73-77; group vpres, Elsters Inc, 77-78. *Concurrent Pos:* Mem tech coord comt gas lubrication, Off Naval Res, 58-66. *Mem:* Am Phys Soc; Am Inst Aeronaut & Astronaut; sr mem Inst Elec & Electronics Engrs. *Res:* Guidance and control systems; sensor design; gyroscopes; accelerometers; gas lubrication and bearing design; pneumatic systems; data acquisition; environmental control systems; energy conservation and recovery systems; heat and solar actuated systems; thermodynamics. *Mailing Add:* 17339 Halsted St Northridge CA 91325. *E-Mail:* gbs-gps@worldnet.att.net

SPEER, CLARENCE ARVON, COCCIDIOSIS, SARCOCYSTOSIS. *Current Pos:* assoc prof, 83-86, PROF & HEAD VET SCI, MONT STATE UNIV, 86- *Personal Data:* b Lamar, Colo, Feb 14, 45; m 77; c 2. *Educ:* Colo State Univ, BS, 67; Utah State Univ, MS, 70, PhD(zool), 72. *Prof Exp:* Asst prof histol, Univ Tex, Houston, 72-73; res assoc malaria res, Univ NMex, 73-75; from asst prof to assoc prof microbiol, Univ Mont, 75-83. *Concurrent Pos:* Consult, Nat Res Inst Amazon, Manaus, 77-83. *Mem:* Am Asn Immunologists; Am Soc Parasitologists; Can Soc Zoologists; Soc Protozoologists. *Res:* In vitro cultivation and biochemical, physiological and ultrastructural aspects of protozoan parasites that cause coccidiosis, malaria and Chagas' disease. *Mailing Add:* Dir Vet Molecular Biol Mont State Univ Bozeman MT 59717-0360. *Fax:* 406-994-4303

SPEER, FRIDTJOF ALFRED, SPACE PROPULSION, HIGH ENERGY ASTROPHYSICS. *Current Pos:* AEROSPACE CONSULT, 91- *Personal Data:* b Berlin, Ger, Aug 23, 23; US citizen; m 51, Margret Hillemann; c Sabine, Susanne & Beate. *Educ:* Tech Univ Berlin, Dipl Ing, 50, Dr Ing(physics), 53. *Honors & Awards:* Except Serv Medals, NASA, 69; Holger Toftoy Award, Am Inst Aeronaut & Astronaut, 79; Randolph Lovelace Award, Am Astronaut Soc, 79. *Prof Exp:* Asst prof physics, Tech Univ Berlin, 50-55; div chief missile develop, US Army, 55-60; div chief spacecraft develop, Marshall Space Flight Ctr, NASA, 60-65, mgr, mission opers, 65-71, mgr, sci projs, 71-83, assoc dir sci, 83-86; dir, Ctr Adv Space Propulsion, UTST, Tullahoma, Tenn, 87-91. *Concurrent Pos:* Ed, Sci Abstr Periodical, Berlin, 53-55. *Mem:* Assoc fel Am Inst Aeronaut & Astronaut; fel Am Astronaut Soc. *Res:* Science policy; high energy astronomy; space propulsion. *Mailing Add:* 4920 Canterwood Dr NW Gig Harbor WA 98332

SPEER, VAUGHN C, NUTRITION, BIOCHEMISTRY. *Current Pos:* assoc animal husb, Iowa State Univ, 53-57, from asst prof to assoc prof, 58-66, prof, 66-90, EMER PROF NUTRIT, IOWA STATE UNIV, 91- *Personal Data:* b Milford, Iowa, Apr 5, 24; m 47; c 4. *Educ:* Iowa State Univ, BS, 49, MS, 51, PhD, 57. *Prof Exp:* Asst nutrit, Iowa State Univ, 49-51; nutritionist, Ralston Purina Co, 51-53. *Mem:* Am Inst Nutrit; Am Soc Animal Sci. *Res:* Swine nutrition; nutritional effects on swine reproduction. *Mailing Add:* Dept Animal Sci Iowa State Univ 337 Kildee Hall Ames IA 50011-0001

SPEERS, GEORGE M, poultry nutrition, for more information see previous edition

SPEERS, MARJORIE A, PREVENTIVE MEDICINE. *Current Pos:* epidemiologist, Cancer Prev & Control Br, Ctr Dis Control & Prev, 88-89, chief, Aging & Statist Br, 89-91, dir, 91-96, COORDR, BEHAV & SOC SCI, CTR DIS CONTROL & PREV, 95- *Educ:* Dickinson Col, BA, 78; Yale Univ, MS, 80, MPhil, 81, PhD(psych/epidemiol), 84. *Honors & Awards:* Joseph Middleton & Helen Burns Norcross Prize. *Prof Exp:* Instr, Univ Conn, 81-83; asst prof, Dept Prev Med & Community Health, Univ Tex Med Br, 84-87. *Concurrent Pos:* Mem, Dept Prev Med & Community Health Safety Comt, 87, Dept Health & Human Serv Interagency Comt Res Aging, 89-91, Pub Health Serv Yr 2000, Health Objectives Workgroup, 91-96, Eval Taskforce, Coun Epidemiol & Prev, Am Heart Asn, 94; tech adv, Coord Comt Data Aging, Pub Health Serv, 89-91; consult ed, J Behav Med, 90- & Am J Pub Health, 94-; consult, Cardiovasc Dis Unit, WHO, 94-95; regional ed, Health Prom Int. *Mem:* Am Psychol Asn; Am Pub Health Asn; Soc Epidemiol Res. *Res:* Author of numerous published articles. *Mailing Add:* Off Dir Ctr Dis Control & Prev 1600 Clifton Rd NE MS-D50 Atlanta GA 30333

SPEERS, WENDELL CARL, SURGICAL PATHOLOGY, MEDICAL EDUCATION. *Current Pos:* ASSOC PROF PATH, UNIV COLO HEALTH & SCI CTR, 79- *Educ:* Johns Hopkins Univ, MD, 71. *Mailing Add:* 140 Kramerio St Denver CO 80220-5929

SPEERT, ARNOLD, PHYSICAL ORGANIC CHEMISTRY. *Current Pos:* From asst prof to assoc prof chem, William Paterson Col, 70-80, asst to vpres acad affairs, 71-78, assoc dean, 78-79, vpres, 79-85, PROF CHEM, WILLIAM PATERSON COL, NJ, 80-, PRES, 85- *Personal Data:* b Bronx, NY, June 19, 45; m 67, Myrna Goldstein; c Alan M & Debra B. *Educ:* City Col New York, BS, 66; Princeton Univ, PhD(chem), 71. *Mem:* AAAS; Am Chem Soc. *Res:* Aromaticity; nuclear magnetic resonance spectroscopy; stereochemistry; iron carbonyl complexes. *Mailing Add:* William Paterson Col Wayne NJ 07470

SPEES, STEVEN TREMBLE, JR, INORGANIC CHEMISTRY. *Current Pos:* assoc prof inorg chem, 67-77, PROF CHEM, LYMAN BRIGGS COL, MICH STATE UNIV, 77- *Personal Data:* b Earl Park, Ind, May 12, 33; m 53; c 3. *Educ:* Purdue Univ, BS, 56; Univ Southern Calif, PhD(phys chem), 61. *Prof Exp:* Instr chem, Ohio State Univ, 61-62; asst prof inorg chem, Univ Minn, Minneapolis, 62-67. *Mem:* AAAS; NY Acad Sci; Am Chem Soc; The Chem Soc; Sigma Xi. *Res:* Chemistry of coordination compounds; synthesis; molecular and electronic structures; kinetics; optical activity; stereochemistry; photochemistry; nuclear magnetic resonances. *Mailing Add:* Holmes Hall Mich State Univ East Lansing MI 48824

SPEHRLEY, CHARLES W, JR, ELECTROMECHANICAL SYSTEM DESIGN, MACHINE DESIGN. *Current Pos:* VPRES, SPECTRA INC, 86- *Personal Data:* b Pottsville, Pa, July 16, 44. *Educ:* Dartmouth Col, AB, 66, BEng, 67, ME, 70. *Prof Exp:* Proj engr, Rohm & Haas Co, 66-68; proj engr, Creare Inc, 68-72, dir, Mach Systs Eng Div, 72-76, vpres, Creare Innovations Inc, 76-86. *Mem:* Am Soc Mech Engrs. *Res:* Xerographic and ink-jet copiers and printers; precision dynamic drives and mechanisms; electromechanical and digital servo systems; paper handling, feeding and collation; optomechanical and raster imaging systems. *Mailing Add:* Spectra Inc PO Box 68C Hanover NH 03755

SPEICHER, BENJAMIN ROBERT, ZOOLOGY. *Current Pos:* from instr to prof, Univ Maine, 37-74, actg head dept, 42-45, head dept, 45-63, EMER PROF ZOOL, UNIV MAINE, ORONO, 74- *Personal Data:* b Swatow, China, Jan 23, 09; US citizen; m 32, Kathryn Gilmore. *Educ:* Denison Univ, AB, 29; Univ Pittsburgh, MS, 31, PhD(genetics), 33. *Hon Degrees:* ScD, Colby Col, 69. *Prof Exp:* Asst, Univ Pittsburgh, 29-33; visitor, Carnegie Inst Technol, 33-35; asst, Amherst Col, 35; Nat Res Coun fel, Columbia Univ, 35-36. *Concurrent Pos:* Consult, Oak Ridge Nat Lab, 55-65. *Mem:* AAAS; Genetics Soc Am; Am Soc Zool; Sigma Xi. *Res:* Genetics of Hymenoptera; cytology of parthenogenesis. *Mailing Add:* 2350 Redwood Rd No 324 Napa CA 94558

SPEICHER, CARL EUGENE, PATHOLOGY. *Current Pos:* PROF & DIR, CLIN LAB, OHIO STATE UNIV HOSP, 77-, VCHMN, DEPT PATHOL, 92- *Personal Data:* b Carbondale, Pa, Mar 21, 33; m 58; c 3. *Educ:* Kings Col, BS, 54; Univ Pa, MD, 58. *Prof Exp:* Rotating med internship, Hosp Univ Pa, 58-59, resident anat & clin path, 59-63; pathologist, US Air Force, 63-70; fel path, Upstate Med Ctr, State Univ NY, 70-71; pathologist, US Air Force, 71-77. *Concurrent Pos:* Clin assoc prof path, Univ Tex Health Sci Ctr, San Antonio, 71-77; chmn, Dept Path, Wilford Hall, Med Ctr, Lackland AFB, Tex, 75-77. *Mem:* Col Am Pathologists; Am Soc Clin Pathologists; Am Med Asn; Acad Clin Lab Physicians & Scientists. *Res:* Application of laboratory medicine to patient care, using problem solving approach and computer assistance; author. *Mailing Add:* Ohio State Univ Hosp Rm N-343 410 W Tenth Ave Columbus OH 43210-1236

SPEIDEL, DAVID H, GEOCHEMISTRY, APPLIED GEOLOGY. *Current Pos:* from asst prof to assoc prof geol, Queens Univ, NY, 66-70, from assoc dean to dean sci fac, 70-78, chmn dept geol, 80-88, PROF GEOL, QUEENS COL, NY, 70- *Personal Data:* b Pottsville, Pa, Aug 10, 38; m 62, Margaret Liebrecht. *Educ:* Franklin & Marshall Col, BS, 60; Pa State Univ, PhD(geochem), 64. *Prof Exp:* Res assoc geochem, Pa State Univ, 64-66. *Concurrent Pos:* Vis scholar, Cong Res Serv, 77-78; section head, Major Proj, Earth Sci Div, NSF, Washington, DC, 88-89. *Mem:* AAAS; Am Ceramic Soc; fel Geol Soc Am; Mineral Soc Am; Am Geophys Union; Soc Environ Geochem & Health; Natural Hazards Soc. *Res:* Environmental geochemistry; probability analysis of impact craters and near Earth asteroids; probability analysis of earthquake magnitude frequencies. *Mailing Add:* Dept Geol Queens Col Flushing NY 11367-0904. *E-Mail:* david_speidel@qc.edu

SPEIDEL, EDNA W, BIOCHEMISTRY. *Current Pos:* RETIRED. *Personal Data:* b Indianapolis, Ind, June 14, 08; wid; c T M, J J & A E (Ferren). *Educ:* Butler Univ, BS, 29; Univ Mich, MA, 30; Univ Iowa, PhD(biochem), 34. *Prof Exp:* Res fel biochem, Univ Tenn, 34-36; res assoc anat, Univ Minn, Minneapolis, 58-77. *Res:* Biochemistry of diabetes mellitus; microanalytical techniques; mineral metabolism; radioactive turnover. *Mailing Add:* 5443 41st Pl NW Washington DC 20015

SPEIDEL, JOHN JOSEPH, POPULATION BIOLOGY, PUBLIC HEALTH. *Current Pos:* VPRES, POP CRISIS COMT, 83- *Personal Data:* b Iowa City, Iowa, Sept 17, 37; m 67; c 1. *Educ:* Harvard Univ, AB, 59, MD, 63, MPH, 65. *Prof Exp:* Intern med, St Luke's Hosp, NY, 63-64; resident pub health, City of New York Dept Health, 65-67; dep dir maternal & infant care proj, 66-67; chief develop group, Off Surgeon Gen, US Army, 67-69; dep chief res div, Off Pop, AID, 69-70, chief res div, 77-78, assoc dir, 77-78, dep dir, 78-83. *Mem:* Am Pub Health Asn; Population Asn Am; Brit Soc Study Fertil. *Res:* Population research including demograph, social science, operational and contraceptive development. *Mailing Add:* William & Flora Hewlett Found 525 Middlefield Rd Suite 200 Menlo Park CA 94025-3495

SPEIDEL, T(HOMAS) MICHAEL, ORTHODONTICS. *Current Pos:* From instr to assoc prof, 66-77, PROF ORTHOD & DENT, SCH DENT, UNIV MINN, 77- *Personal Data:* b Memphis, Tenn, Apr 17, 36; div; c 2. *Educ:* State Univ Iowa, BA, 58; Loyola Univ, DDS, 63; Univ Minn, MSD, 67; Am Bd Orthod, dipl, 72. *Mem:* Am Asn Orthodontists; Am Dent Asn; Int Asn Dent Res. *Res:* Quantitation of occlusal function. *Mailing Add:* 7438 Park Ave Minneapolis MN 55423

SPEIER, JOHN LEO, JR, CHEMISTRY. *Current Pos:* RETIRED. *Personal Data:* b Chicago, Ill, Sept 29, 18; m 44; c 6. *Educ:* St Benedict's Col, BS, 41; Univ Fla, MS, 43; Univ Pittsburgh, PhD(chem), 47. *Honors & Awards:* Scientist of the Yr Award, Indust Res & Develop, 78; Frederick Stanley Kipping Award, Am Chem Soc, 90. *Prof Exp:* Asst, Univ Fla, 41-43; sr fel organo-silicon chem, Mellon Inst, 47-56; res supvr, Dow Corning Corp, 56-65, mgr org res, 65-69, scientist, 70-75, sr scientist, 75-93. *Mem:* Sigma Xi; AAAS; Am Chem Soc. *Res:* Resin acids in pine tree oleoresins; polymerization of silicones; organo-silicon compounds, especially synthesis, derivatives and properties; synthesis and applications of carbon functional silicones. *Mailing Add:* 525 N State St Alma MI 48801-1638

SPEIGHT, JAMES G, ORGANIC CHEMISTRY. *Current Pos:* CHIEF EXEC OFFICER, WESTERN RES INST, 84- *Personal Data:* b Durham, Eng, June 24, 40; m 63, Sheila Stout; c James. *Educ:* Univ Manchester, BSc, 61, PhD(chem), 65. *Prof Exp:* Imp chem indust res fel chem, Univ Manchester, 65-67; res officer, Res Coun Alta, 67-80; res assoc, Exxon Res & Eng Co, 80-84. *Concurrent Pos:* Adj prof, Chem & Chem Eng, Univ Wyo & Fuels Eng, Univ Utah; vis prof, Univ Akron. *Mem:* Fel Chem Inst Can; fel Royal Soc Chem; assoc Royal Inst Chem; Am Chem Soc; Sigma Xi; fel Am Inst Chemists. *Res:* Naturally occurring high molecular weight organic residues, especially coal, asphalt, and petroleum. *Mailing Add:* Western Res Inst 365 N Ninth St Laramie WY 82071-3380

SPEIL, SIDNEY, CERAMICS. *Current Pos:* RETIRED. *Personal Data:* b Revere, Mass, Feb 21, 17; m 40, 79; c 2. *Educ:* Mass Inst Technol, BS, 36, DSc(ceramics), 39. *Honors & Awards:* Electrochem Soc Award, 41. *Prof Exp:* Asst ceramics, Mass Inst Technol, 37-39; res engr, Ideal Tooth, Inc Mass, 39-40; engr nonmetals, US Bur Mines, Tenn, 40-46; sr res engr, Johns-Manville Corp, Denver, 46-52, chief aviation & spec thermal insulations res, 52-64, basic chem res, 64-66, dir corp res & develop, 67-76, dir appl technol & int div res, 76-80, sr scientist & vpres, 80-82. *Mem:* Am Ceramic Soc; Am Inst Aeronaut & Astronaut; Am Chem Soc. *Res:* Home, industrial and aerospace thermal insulations; cryogenic thermal insulation; fiberization of glass wool; high temperature ceramic compositions; fiber reinforcements and fiber reinforced composites; synthetic and natural silicates; asbestos. *Mailing Add:* 3425 S Race Englewood CO 80110

SPEISER, ROBERT DAVID, PURE MATHEMATICS. *Current Pos:* ASST PROF MATH, ILL STATE UNIV, 73- *Personal Data:* b New York, NY, Aug 28, 43; m 81, Page Peters; c 2. *Educ:* Columbia Col, AB, 65; Cornell Univ, PhD(math), 70. *Prof Exp:* Res assoc psychol, Ctr Res in Educ, Cornell Univ, 70-71; asst prof math, Univ Tex, Austin, 71-73. *Concurrent Pos:* Vis assoc prof math, Univ Minn, Minneapolis, 78-79. *Res:* Algebraic geometry; commutative algebra. *Mailing Add:* Brigham Young Univ TMCB 292 Provo UT 84602

SPEISER, THEODORE WESLEY, ASTROPHYSICS, GEOPHYSICS. *Current Pos:* from lectr to assoc prof astro-geophys, 67-85, PROF ASTROPHYS, PLANETARY & ATMOSPHERIC SCI, UNIV COLO, BOULDER, 85- *Personal Data:* b Del Norte, Colo, Nov 23, 34; m 56, Patricia McCrummen; c Tanya, Kelly & Tertia. *Educ:* Colo State Univ, BS, 56; Calif Inst Technol, MS, 59; Pa State Univ, PhD(physics), 64. *Prof Exp:* Res physicist, Nat Bur Stand, 59, 60-61; Nat Acad Sci res assoc earth-sun rels, Goddard Space Flight Ctr, NASA, Md, 64-66. *Concurrent Pos:* Fel, Imp Col, Univ London, 66-67; US sr scientist award, Alexander von Humboldt Found, Ger, 77-78. *Mem:* Am Geophys Union. *Res:* Theories of the aurora and magnetosphere configuration; particle motion and acceleration; magnetospheric and solar wind plasma dynamics. *Mailing Add:* 2335 Dartmouth Ave Boulder CO 80303. *E-Mail:* speiser@spot.colorado.edu

SPEISMAN, GERALD, THEORETICAL PHYSICS. *Current Pos:* RETIRED. *Personal Data:* b New York, NY, Feb 27, 30; m 57, Barbara Waddell; c Aaron J. *Educ:* City Col New York, BS, 51; Calif Inst Technol, PhD(physics), 55. *Prof Exp:* Mem sch math, Inst Adv Study, 55-56; instr asst prof to prof physics, Fla State Univ, 56-87. *Concurrent Pos:* Physicist, Avco-Everett Res Lab, Avco Corp, 56-57. *Mem:* Am Phys Soc. *Res:* Quantum field theory; many-body problem; statistical mechanics; mathematical physics. *Mailing Add:* 1805 Jean St Tallahassee FL 32308

SPEIZER, FRANK ERWIN, EPIDEMIOLOGY, ENVIRONMENTAL MEDICINE. *Current Pos:* assoc prof med, Sch Med, Harvard Univ, 70-76, chief, Div Clin Epidemiol, Channing Lab & assoc prof med, 76-85, assoc physician, Throndike Lab, 68-77, PROF MED & ENVIRON SCI, SCH MED, HARVARD UNIV, 87-, CO-DIR, CHANNING LAB, 89-, EDWARD H KASS, PROF MED, 93- *Personal Data:* b San Francisco, Calif, June 8, 35; m 57, Jeanne J; c 4. *Educ:* Stanford Univ, BA, 57, MD, 60. *Hon Degrees:* AM, Harvard Univ, 89. *Honors & Awards:* Alton Oschner Award, 89. *Prof Exp:* Actg instr med, Sch Med, Stanford Univ, 65-66; vis scientist epidemiol, Brit Med Res Coun, Statist Res Unit, 66-68. *Concurrent Pos:* Assoc vis physician, Boston City Hosp, 68-77 & Peter Brent Brigham Hosp, 77-; Edmund Livingston Traudeu fel, Am Thoracic Soc, 68-70; career develop award, Nat Inst Environ Health Sci, 70-76; mem prog comt, 2nd Task Force Res Plans Environ Res, NIH, mem, Task Force Epidemiol Lung Dis & consult, 79-81; chmn epidemiol sect, Workshops on Environmentally Related Non-Oncogenic Lund Dis, US Task Force on Environ Cancer & Heart & Lung Dis, 82-83; consult, Sci Adv Bd Long Range Planning, Environ Protection Agency, Washington, 84-; working group mem, clin appl, Nat Heart, Lung & Blood Inst, Washington, 84-86; mem, Policy Bd, Honolulu Heart Study, Nat Heart, Lung & Blood Inst, Washington, 85-; mem, Task Force on Asthma Morbidity and Mortality, Nat Heart, Lung & Blood Inst, Washington, 86-87; advisory Committee, Clean Air Scientific Adv Comt,

USEPA, 94; Assoc Ed, Environ Res; sr-physician, Dept Med, Brigham & Woman's Hosp, 92-, Beth Israel Hosp, 96-; physician, Dep Med, Brockton Vet Admin Hosp, 94- *Mem:* Am Epidemiol Soc; Am Soc Clin Invest; fel Am Col Epidemiol; fel Am Col Chest Physicians; Am Asn Physicians. *Res:* Epidemiological studies of chronic diseases associated with environmental exposure, particularly heart, lung and cancer. *Mailing Add:* Dept Med Harvard Med Sch 181 Longwood Ave Boston MA 02115-5804

SPEJEWSKI, EUGENE HENRY, NUCLEAR PHYSICS. *Current Pos:* VPRES & DIR, TRAINING & MGT SYSTS DIV, OAK RIDGE INST SCI & EDUC, 89- *Personal Data:* b East Chicago, Ind, Sept 15, 38; m 63, Norma B Seekins; c Maria S (LeTellier), Beverly A, Andrew J & Jeanette M (Phillips). *Educ:* Univ Notre Dame, BS, 60; Ind Univ, Bloomington, PhD(exp physics), 66. *Prof Exp:* Res assoc physics, Ind Univ, Bloomington, 65-67; res assoc, Princeton Univ, 67-69, instr, 69-71; asst prof, Oberlin Col, 71-72; dir univ isotope separator proj, Oak Ridge Nat Lab, Assoc Univs, 72-85, proj mgr, Navy SDS proj, 85-87, chmn spec proj div, 87-89. *Concurrent Pos:* Consult, Oak Ridge Nat Lab, 71-72; vis prof physics, Univ Tenn, 81-82. *Mem:* AAAS; Am Phys Soc; Sigma Xi; Am Mgt Asn; Am Soc Training Develop; Nat Soc Performance & Instr. *Res:* Nuclear physics. *Mailing Add:* Oak Ridge Assoc Univs PO Box 117 Oak Ridge TN 37831-0117. *Fax:* 423-576-9383; *E-Mail:* spejewski@orav.gov

SPELIOTIS, DENNIS ELIAS, SOLID STATE PHYSICS, MAGNETISM. *Current Pos:* PRES, DIGITAL MEASUREMENT SYSTS, 77- *Personal Data:* b Kalamata, Greece, Nov 27, 33; US citizen; m 58; c 3. *Educ:* Univ RI, BS, 55; Mass Inst Technol, MS, 57, EE, 58; Univ Minn, PhD(magnetism), 61. *Honors & Awards:* Fel, Inst Elec & Electronic Engrs. *Prof Exp:* Staff physicist, Int Bus Mach Develop Labs, 61-63, mgr recording physics, 63-66, adv physicist, 66-67; assoc prof elec eng, Univ Minn, Minneapolis, 67-69; dir eng, Micro-Bit Corp, 69-76. *Concurrent Pos:* Consult, Kodak, BASF, Hitachi, Gen Elec, Mitsubishi Kasei, Toda, Orient Chem, Nashua, Digital Equip, Seagate, NKK, TDK, 3M, Cabot, Vermont Res, Polaroid. *Mem:* Inst Elec & Electronics Engrs. *Res:* Hard magnetic materials and their applications to bulk magnetic storage devices; magnetic recording; electron beam addressable memories; digital computer memory architecture. *Mailing Add:* Digital Measurement Systs Burlington MA 01803

SPELKE, ELIZABETH SHILIN, COGNITIVE SCIENCE. *Current Pos:* PROF BRAIN & COGNITIVE SCI, MASS INST TECHNOL, 96- *Personal Data:* b New York, NY, May 28, 49; m 88; c 2. *Educ:* Harvard Univ, BA, 71; Cornell Univ, PhD(psychol), 78. *Honors & Awards:* Boyd McCendress Young Investr Award, Am Psychol Asn, 85. *Prof Exp:* From asst prof to assoc prof psychol, Univ Pa, 77-86. *Concurrent Pos:* Vis scientist, Ctr Cognitive Sci, Mass Inst Technol, 82-83 & Nat Ctr Sci Res, Paris, 84-85; Fulbright fel, 84; prof, Cornell Univ, 86-97; John Simon Guggenheim fel, 88; mem, Adv Panel Human Perception & Cognition, NSF, 90-92. *Mem:* AAAS; Soc Res Child Develop; Soc Philos & Psychol; Sigma Xi. *Res:* Perceptual development, cognitive development and conceptual change in human infants and children; physical phenomena. *Mailing Add:* Dept Brain & Cognitive Scis E10-246 Mass Inst Technol Cambridge MA 02139

SPELL, ALDENLEE, PHYSICAL CHEMISTRY. *Current Pos:* RETIRED. *Personal Data:* b Rayne, La, Feb 9, 20; m 52; c 2. *Educ:* Southwestern La Inst, BS, 41; Tulane Univ, MS, 43; Brown Univ, PhD(chem), 52. *Prof Exp:* Chemist, Shell Develop Co, 43-48; scientist, Signal Corps, US Dept Army, 51-52; res supvr, Rohm & Haas Co, 52-82. *Mem:* Am Chem Soc; Soc Appl Spectros. *Res:* Infrared absorption and reflection spectroscopy; fractionation and analysis of polymers; gas chromatography. *Mailing Add:* 180 Iron Hill Rd Doylestown PA 18901-2510

SPELLACY, WILLIAM NELSON, OBSTETRICS & GYNECOLOGY. *Current Pos:* PROF & HEAD, DEPT OBSTET & GYNEC, UNIV SFLA, 88- *Personal Data:* b St Paul, Minn, May 10, 34; m 81, Lynn Larsen; c Kimberly, William & Kathleen. *Educ:* Univ Minn, BA, 55, BS, 56, MD, 59; Am Bd Obstet & Gynec, dipl, 66, maternal & fetal med cert, 75. *Prof Exp:* Intern, Minneapolis Gen Hosp, Minn, 59-60; from instr to asst prof obstet & gynec, Univ Minn, 63-67; from assoc prof to prof, Med Sch, Univ Miami, 67-74; prof & chmn dept, Col Med, Univ Fla, 74-79; prof & head, Dept Obstet & Gynec, Col Med, Univ Ill, 79-88. *Concurrent Pos:* Fel obstet & gynec, Univ Minn, 60-63; NIH, Pop Coun & Food & Drug Admin grants, 64-69; Josiah Macy Jr Found fel, 66-69; examr, Am Bd Obstet & Gynec. *Mem:* Inst Med-Nat Acad Sci; Endocrine Soc; Am Fertil Soc; Asn Prof Gynec & Obstet; Am Fedn Clin Res. *Res:* Metabolism of pregnant woman and fetus; effects of ovarian steroids on carbohydrate and lipid metabolism; studies of placental function and fetal maturity; endocrinology of reproduction. *Mailing Add:* 845 Seddon Cove Way Tampa FL 33602-5704

SPELLENBERG, RICHARD (WILLIAM), PLANT TAXONOMY. *Current Pos:* From asst prof to assoc prof, 68-77, PROF BIOL, NMEX STATE UNIV, 77- *Personal Data:* b San Mateo, Calif, June 27, 40; m 64; c 2. *Educ:* Humboldt State Col, BA, 62; Univ Wash, PhD(bot), 68. *Concurrent Pos:* Consult, endangered & threatened plant species. *Mem:* Am Soc Plant Taxon; Int Asn Plant Taxon. *Res:* Systematics of Gramineae and Nyctaginaceae. *Mailing Add:* Dept Biol Box 3 AF NMex State Univ Las Cruces NM 88003

SPELLER, STANLEY WAYNE, WILDLIFE BIOLOGY. *Current Pos:* JACQUES WHITFORD ENVIRON, 93- *Personal Data:* b Victoria, BC, June 6, 42; m 67; c 1. *Educ:* Univ Victoria, BS, 65; Carleton Univ, MS, 68; Univ Sask, PhD(mammal), 72. *Prof Exp:* Biologist, Can Wildlife Serv, Environ Can, 72-75; biologist, Environ Assessment Sect, Dept Indian Affairs & Northern Develop, 75-77; chief, Wildlife Res & Interpretation, Can Wildlife Serv, Environ Can, 77-81; supvr, 81-89, mgr environ, safety & indust hyg, Explor Dept, Petrocanada, 89-93. *Mem:* Can Soc Environ Biol. *Res:* Management of research programs on effects of insecticides on wildlife; wildlife and limnology studies for parks Canada; wildlife research of rare and endangered species; wildlife interpretation programs in Atlantic region. *Mailing Add:* 308 Ranchridge Bay NW Calgary AB T3G 1V5 Can

SPELLICY, ROBERT L, INFRARED SPECTROSCOPY. *Current Pos:* SR PROG MGR, RADIAN CORP, 89- *Personal Data:* b Detroit, Mich, Sept 18, 44. *Educ:* Univ Windsor, BS, 66; Univ Mich, MS, 69, PhD(physics), 74. *Prof Exp:* Staff scientist, Optimetrics Co, 78-89. *Mem:* Am Phys Soc. *Mailing Add:* 10406 Lockerbie Dr Austin TX 78750

SPELLMAN, CRAIG WILLIAM, TUMOR BIOLOGY, CELLULAR IMMUNOLOGY. *Current Pos:* ASSOC PROF, DEPT INTERNAL MED & DEPT IMMUNOL, UNIV NTEX HEALTH SCI CTR, FT WORTH, 91- *Personal Data:* b Longview, Wash, Dec 15, 46; m 75; c 2. *Educ:* Univ Wash, BS, 69; Mont State Univ, Bozeman, MS, 76; Univ Utah, PhD(path), 78. *Honors & Awards:* Wilson S Stone Mem Award, Syst Cancer Ctr, M D Anderson Hosp, Univ Tex, Houston, 79. *Prof Exp:* NIH teaching fel, Univ NMex, 78-80, res asst prof path, 80-81, asst prof path & cell biol, Sch Med, 81-91. *Mem:* Am Asn Pathologists; AAAS. *Res:* T-cell immune circuits operative in anti-tumor immunity; UV-induced syngeneic skin tumors and UV-irradiated hosts exhibiting defined states of tumor susceptibility. *Mailing Add:* Dept Internal Med Tex Col Osteo Med 3500 Camp Bowie Blvd Ft Worth TX 76107-2644

SPELLMAN, JOHN W, MATHEMATICS. *Current Pos:* PROF MATH, SW TEX STATE UNIV, 80- *Personal Data:* b Ft Worth, Tex, Oct 3, 41; m 59; c 2. *Educ:* Tex Lutheran Col, BA, 63; Emory Univ, MA, 65, PhD(math), 68. *Prof Exp:* Fel math, Univ Fla, 68-69; asst prof, Tex A&M Univ, 69-71; assoc prof math, Pan Am Univ, 71-80, head dept, 75-80. *Mem:* Am Math Soc. *Res:* Functional analysis; semigroups of operators; real analysis. *Mailing Add:* Turkey Hollow San Marcos TX 78666

SPELLMAN, MITCHELL WRIGHT, SURGERY. *Current Pos:* prof surg & dean med serv, Med Sch & exec vpres, Med Ctr, 78-90, dir, Int Med Progs, 83-90, EMER PROF SURG, EMER DEAN MED SERV & EMER DEAN INT PROJS, MED SCH, HARVARD UNIV, 90- *Personal Data:* b Alexandria, La, Dec 1, 19; m 47; c 8. *Educ:* Dillard Univ, AB, 40; Howard Univ, MD, 44; Univ Minn, PhD(surg), 55; Am Bd Surg, dipl, 53. *Hon Degrees:* DSc, Georgetown Univ, 74; DSc, Univ Fla, 77; LLD, Dillard Univ, 83. *Honors & Awards:* William A Sinkler Award Surg, Nat Med Asn, 68; Warfield Award, Freedmen's Hosp, 69. *Prof Exp:* From intern to asst resident surg, Cleveland Metrop Gen Hosp, Ohio, 44-46; asst resident, Freedmen's Hosp, Howard Univ, 46-47; chief resident thoracic surg, 47-48 & surg, 49-50, asst physiol, Col Med, 48-49 & surg, 50-51; res asst, Exp Surg Lab, Univ Minn, 51-53, sr resident surg, Univ Hosp, Univ Minn, 53-54; from asst prof to prof, Col Med, Howard Univ, 54-68; prof & asst dean, Sch Med, Univ Calif, Los Angeles & dean, Charles R Drew Postgrad Med Sch, 69-78. *Concurrent Pos:* Dir, Exp Surg Lab, Col Med, Howard Univ, 54-61, res asst prof, Grad Fac Physiol, 55-69, chief med officer, Howard Univ Div, DC Gen Hosp, 61-68; Mem, DC Bd Exam Med & Osteop, 55-68; exec vpres & mem bd dirs, Nat Med Asn Found, 68-70; mem, Spec Adv Group, Vet Admin, 69-73, nat surg consult, Cent Off, 69-73; clin prof surg, Sch Med, Univ Southern Calif, 69-78; bd dirs, Sun Valley Forum Nat Health, 70; mem, Comn Study of Accreditation Selected Health Educ Progs, 70-72; mem bd visitors, Med Ctr, Duke Univ, 70-75; bd trustees, Occidental Col, 71-78, Kaiser Found Health Plan, Inc & Kaiser Found Hosps, 71- & Lloyds Bank Calif, 74-; mem, Vis Comt, Sch Med, Stanford Univ, 72-73 & Med Ctr, Univ Mass, 74-75; mem, Bd Overseer's Comt Visit Univ Health Serv, Harvard Col, 72-78; bd regents, Georgetown Univ, 72-78; fel, Ctr Advan Study Behav Sci, Stanford, 75-76; vis prof surg, Sch Med, Stanford Univ, 75-76; mem bd dirs, Monogram Indusrs, Inc, 81-83; mem, Epcot Life & Health Pavilion Adv Bd, 81-; bd dirs, Georgetown Univ, 86-; mem, Transitional Coun, United Arab Emirates Univ, Fac Med & Health Sci, 87-; hon sr surgeon, Beth Israel Hosp, 90- *Mem:* Inst Med-Nat Acad Sci; Am Asn Univ Professors; Soc Univ Surg; AMA; Am Surg Asn; Nat Med Asn; AAAS; Am Col Cardiol; Nat Acad Practice Med. *Res:* Radiation biology; cardiovascular physiology; evaluation of methods of closure of bronchial stump; blood volume. *Mailing Add:* Harvard Med Int Off Int Exchange Progs 138 Harvard St Brookline MA 02146-6418

SPELMAN, MICHAEL JOHN, METEOROLOGY, ATMOSPHERIC SCIENCE. *Current Pos:* RES METEOROLOGIST, GEOPHYS FLUID DYNAMICS LAB, NAT OCEANIC & ATMOSPHERIC ADMIN, 69- *Personal Data:* b Rochester, NY, Mar 28, 39; m 67; c 3. *Educ:* LeMoyne Col, BS, 62; Pa State Univ, MS, 69. *Mem:* Am Meteorol Soc. *Res:* Investigation of the structure and circulations of the atmosphere and oceans through numerical modeling on super computers. *Mailing Add:* 106 Mine Rd Pennington NJ 08534. *E-Mail:* ms@gfdl.gov

SPELSBERG, THOMAS COONAN, GENETICS, BIOCHEMISTRY. *Current Pos:* PROF BIOCHEM, MAYO MED SCH & MAYO GRAD SCH MED, 77- *Personal Data:* b Clarksburg, WVa, July 6, 40; m 67; c Sarah, Thomas & Nancy. *Educ:* WVa Univ, AB, 63, PhD(genetics, biochem), 67. *Prof Exp:* Fel biochem, Univ Tex M D Anderson Hosp & Tumor Inst, 67-68; res asst, 68-69; asst biochemist, Mayo Clin, 69-70; asst prof obstet, gynec & biochem, Sch Med, Vanderbilt Univ, 70-74; assoc prof biochem, Mayo Med Sch & Mayo Grad Sch Med, 74-77; prof & head biochem sect, 79-83, mem staff, dept cell biol, Mayo Clin, 74-, chmn dept biochem & molecular biol, 88- *Concurrent*

Pos: Nat Genetics Found fel; distinguished lectr, Univ Conn, Univ NJ Med Sch & Oral Roberts Med Sch; distinguished investr, Mayo Grad Sch Med. *Mem:* AAAS; Am Soc Biol Chemists; Am Soc Cell Biol; Endocrine Soc; Am Soc Reprod Biol; Am Soc Bone & Mineral Res. *Res:* Role of nuclear proteins and steroid hormones in regulation of gene activity; DNA-protein interactions; steroid receptor interaction with chromatin; steroid action in human bone cells. *Mailing Add:* Dept Biochem & Molecular Biol Mayo Clin Guggenheim 1601A Rochester MN 55905. *Fax:* 507-284-2053; *E-Mail:* spelsberg.thomas@mayo.edu

SPENADEL, LAWRENCE, PHYSICAL CHEMISTRY, POLYMER CHEMISTRY. *Current Pos:* Res chemist, Esso Res & Eng Co, 56-65, sr chemist, Enjay Polymer Labs, 66-70, RES ASSOC, EXXON CHEM CO, 70- *Personal Data:* b Brooklyn, NY, Apr 1, 32; m 55; c 2. *Educ:* Queens Col, NY, BS, 53; Univ Cincinnati, MS, 54, PhD(phys chem), 57. *Mem:* Inst Elec & Electronic Engrs; Am Chem Soc; Soc Plastics Eng. *Res:* Compounding of ethylene propylene terpolymer and polyethylenes for wire and cable applications; development of thermoelastic rubbers; combustion; formulation and testing of high energy solid propellants; dispersion measurements on platinum catalysts. *Mailing Add:* 2105 Winged Foot Dr League City TX 77573

SPENCE, ALEXANDER PERKINS, COMPARATIVE ANATOMY, EMBRYOLOGY. *Current Pos:* From asst prof to assoc prof, 61-78, PROF ANAT & EMBRYOL & CHMN DEPT, STATE UNIV NY, CORTLAND, 78- *Personal Data:* b St Louis, Mo, Apr 5, 29; m 55; c 3. *Educ:* Univ Mo, BS, 60, MS, 61; Cornell Univ, PhD(biol), 69. *Mem:* Sigma Xi; Am Soc Zoologists. *Res:* Ultrastructure of spermatogenesis in Rana pipiens; sperm-egg chemotaxis in amphibians. *Mailing Add:* 469 W State Rd Dryden NY 13053

SPENCE, DALE WILLIAM, EXERCISE PHYSIOLOGY. *Current Pos:* from instr to assoc prof, 63-74, PROF HUMAN PERFORMANCE & HEALTH SCI, RICE UNIV, 74- *Personal Data:* b Beaumont, Tex, Apr 8, 34; m 55; c 3. *Educ:* Rice Inst, BS, 56; NTex State Univ, MS, 59; La State Univ, EdD(phys educ), 66. *Prof Exp:* Instr phys educ, NTex State Univ, 58-59 & Hardin-Simmons Univ, 59-62; asst, La State Univ, 62-63. *Concurrent Pos:* Fel, Baylor Col Med, 68-69, vis assoc prof, 71-80, prof, 80-86; dir exercise rehab & res, St Joseph Hosp, 74-76; vis scientist, Manned Spacecraft Ctr, 69-70; mem staff, Houston Cardovasc Rehabilitation Ctr, 80-86; consult scientist, Sch Aerospace Med, 80-81; adj prof med, Baylor Col Med, 87- *Mem:* fel Am Col Sports Med; Aerospace Med Asn. *Res:* Cardiovascular physiology and cardiovascular rehabilitation. *Mailing Add:* Human Performance Rice Univ 6100 Main St Houston TX 77005-1892

SPENCE, DAVID, ATOMIC PHYSICS. *Current Pos:* asst physicist, 71-74, PHYSICIST, ARGONNE NAT LAB, 74- *Personal Data:* b Halifax, Eng, Sept 23, 41; m 62; c 4. *Educ:* Univ Durham, BSc, 63; Univ Newcastle-upon-Tyne, PhD(physics), 67. *Prof Exp:* Res staff appl scientist physics, Yale Univ, 67-71. *Res:* Atomic and molecular spectroscopy; physical and gaseous electronics. *Mailing Add:* Argonne Nat Lab 9700 S Cass Ave Argonne IL 60439

SPENCE, GAVIN GARY, ORGANIC CHEMISTRY. *Current Pos:* TECHNOL MGR, SOLUTION POLYMERS, CALLAWAY CHEM CO, 87- *Personal Data:* b St Paul, Minn, July 23, 42; m 65 Geraldine Riley; c Heather, G Gregory & Patrick. *Educ:* Williams Col, BA, 64; Princeton Univ, AM, 67, PhD(chem), 68. *Prof Exp:* Res chemist, Hercules Inc, 68-75, sr res chemist, 75-79, res scientist, 79-87. *Mem:* Am Chem Soc; Tech Asn Pulp & Paper Indust. *Res:* Synthetic organic chemistry, in particular synthesis and evaluations of organic polymers for use in paper, adhesives, textiles. *Mailing Add:* 7113 Stillwater Dr Columbus GA 31904-1958

SPENCE, HILDA ADELE, MICROBIOLOGY. *Current Pos:* instr med technol, 59-64, asst prof microbiol, 64-74, ASSOC PROF MICROBIOL, LA STATE UNIV MED CTR, 89-, ASST DEAN, SCH GRAD STUDIES, 93- *Personal Data:* b Chattanooga, Tenn, Oct 13, 29. *Educ:* Univ Tenn, Chattanooga, BS, 51; La State Univ, MS, 66, PhD(microbiol), 71. *Honors & Awards:* Am Soc Med Technol Res Award, 63. *Prof Exp:* Med technologist, Charity Hosp La, New Orleans, 51-59. *Concurrent Pos:* Mem rev bd, Nat Accrediting Agency Clin Lab Sci, 72-77. *Mem:* Am Soc Microbiol; Am Soc Med Technol (pres, 78-79); Am Soc Virol. *Res:* Neurotropic strains of influenza viruses; clinical microbiology; microcomputers in medical education and research. *Mailing Add:* Dept Microbiol Med Ctr La State Univ 1901 Perdido St New Orleans LA 70112-2865

SPENCE, JACK TAYLOR, ANALYTICAL CHEMISTRY, INORGANIC CHEMISTRY. *Current Pos:* RETIRED. *Personal Data:* b Salt Lake City, Utah, Nov 16, 29; m 51; c 3. *Educ:* Univ Utah, BS, 51, PhD(chem), 57. *Prof Exp:* Fel, Univ Ore, 57-58; from asst prof to prof chem, Utah State Univ, 58-89, dept head, 76-81. *Concurrent Pos:* USPHS res career develop award, Nat Inst Gen Med Sci, 68-73. *Mem:* AAAS; Am Chem Soc. *Res:* Organic chelating agents; coordination compounds; inorganic photochemistry; inorganic biochemistry; mechanisms of enzyme reactions. *Mailing Add:* PO Box 142 Teasdale VT 84773

SPENCE, JOHN CHARLES, SOLID STATE PHYSICS. *Current Pos:* PROF, DEPT PHYSICS, ARIZ STATE UNIV, 76- *Personal Data:* b Melbourne, Australia, 46. *Educ:* Melbourne Univ, Australia, BS, PhD(physics), 73. *Prof Exp:* Fel, Oxford Univ, UK, 73-76. *Mem:* Fel Am Phys Soc. *Res:* Solid state physics. *Mailing Add:* Dept Physics Ariz State Univ Tempe AZ 85287

SPENCE, JOHN EDWIN, ELECTRICAL ENGINEERING. *Current Pos:* assoc prof elec eng, 68-76, PROF ELEC ENG, UNIV RI, 76- *Personal Data:* b Fall River, Mass, Oct 26, 34; m 58; c 3. *Educ:* Bradford Durfee Col Technol, BS, 57; Univ Wis, MS, 60, PhD(elec eng), 62. *Prof Exp:* Mem staff, Digital & Analog Comput Labs, Allis-Chalmers Mfg Co, 57-59; asst, Univ Wis, 59-62; assoc prof elec eng, Univ RI, 62-67; tech dir antennas & propagation group, Electronics & Commun Div, Atlantic Res Corp, Va, 67-68. *Concurrent Pos:* Consult, Amecom Div, Litton Systs, Inc, Md, 65. *Mem:* Inst Elec & Electronics Engrs. *Res:* Electromagnetic theory; wave propagation. *Mailing Add:* 6 Springcove Rd Narragansett RI 02882

SPENCE, JOSEPH THOMAS, NUTRITION, BIOCHEMISTRY & MOLECULAR BIOLOGY. *Current Pos:* DIR, BELTSVILLE HUMAN NUTRIT RES CTR, 93- *Personal Data:* b Brooklyn, NY, May 7, 51; m 80, Marlene Kovacich; c Joseph A & Laura E. *Educ:* St Frances Col, NY, BS, 73; Cornell Univ, MNS, 75, PhD(nutrit), 77. *Prof Exp:* Postdoctoral fel, McArdle Lab Cancer Res, 77-80; asst prof biochem, State Univ NY, 80-85, assoc dean res & grad studies, 88-93, assoc prof, 92-93; health scientist adminr, Nat Heart Blood & Lung Inst, 85-88. *Mem:* Am Asn Cancer Res; Am Soc Nutrit Sci; AAAS; Soc Exp Biol & Med. *Res:* Regulation of synthesis of enzymes involved in metabolism of carbohydrates and lipids. *Mailing Add:* Bldg 308 Rm 223 Human Nutrit Res Ctr USDA Beltsville MD 20705. *E-Mail:* spence@bhnrc.arsusda.gov

SPENCE, KEMET DEAN, MICROBIOLOGY, BIOCHEMISTRY. *Current Pos:* from asst prof to assoc prof, 68-80, PROF MICROBIOL, WASH STATE UNIV, 81- *Personal Data:* b Portland, Ore, Jan 10, 37; m 58, V Mariel Elliott; c Rurik, Holt, Molly & Hayden. *Educ:* Ore State Univ, BS, 60, MS, 62, PhD(microbiol, biochem), 65. *Prof Exp:* Microbiologist, Ore Fish Comn, 62-64; res fel, Argonne Nat Lab, 65-68. *Mem:* Am Soc Microbiol; Soc Invert Path; Am Soc Zoologists. *Res:* Biochemical and applied studies of microbial pathogens and immunity of insects. *Mailing Add:* Dept Microbiol Wash State Univ Pullman WA 99164

SPENCE, LESLIE PERCIVAL, MICROBIOLOGY. *Current Pos:* RETIRED. *Personal Data:* b St Vincent, WI, Aug 16, 22; m 53; c 2. *Educ:* Bristol Univ, MB, ChB, 50; Univ London, dipl trop med & hyg, 51; FRCP, 72. *Prof Exp:* Med officer, Trinidad Govt Med Serv, 51-62; dir regional virus lab, Trinidad & prof virol, Univ West Indies, 62-68; prof microbiol, McGill Univ, 68-72; chmn dept, Univ Toronto, 72-88, prof microbiol, 72-90. *Concurrent Pos:* Rockefeller Found fel, Rockefeller Found Virus Labs, NY, 55-56; consult, Nat Inst Allergy & Infectious Dis, 69-73 & Pan-Am Health Orgn, 69-70. *Mem:* Am Soc Trop Med & Hyg; Can Soc Microbiol; Am Soc Microbiol. *Res:* Arboviruses; viral gastroenteritis. *Mailing Add:* 18 Inez Ct Willowdale ON M2M 1C2 Can

SPENCE, MARY ANNE, HUMAN GENETICS. *Current Pos:* From asst prof to assoc prof, 70-80, PROF PSYCHIAT & BIOMATH, SCH MED, UNIV CALIF, LOS ANGELES, 80- *Personal Data:* b Tulsa, Okla, Sept 8, 44; m 72. *Educ:* Grinnell Col, BA, 66; Univ Hawaii, PhD, 69. *Honors & Awards:* Woman of Sci Award, Univ Calif, 79. *Concurrent Pos:* NIH fel genetics curric, Univ NC, Chapel Hill, 69-70; mem, Ment Retardation Res Ctr, Neuropsychiat Inst, Univ Calif, Los Angeles, 74-, assoc dean, Grad Div, 88- *Mem:* Am Soc Human Genetics; Genetics Soc Am; Behav Genetics Asn. *Res:* Mathematical and computer models for family data analysis; applications for genetic counseling. *Mailing Add:* 10 Ashwood Apt 4 Irvine CA 92604

SPENCE, MATTHEW W, NEUROBIOCHEMISTRY, BIOCHEMICAL GENETICS. *Current Pos:* PRES, ALTA HERITAGE FOUND MED RES, 90- *Personal Data:* b Chatham, Ont, Nov 18, 34; m 61, Cynthia Wells; c David, Carolyn & Rachael. *Educ:* Univ Alta, MD, 59; McGill Univ, PhD(biochem), 66; Can Col Med Genetics, FCCMG, 83. *Prof Exp:* Asst prof exp med, McGill Univ, 66-70; from assoc prof to prof pediat & from asst prof to prof biochem, Dalhousie Univ, Halifax, 70-90; dir, Atlantic Res Ctr, Halifax, NS, 76-90. *Concurrent Pos:* Jr asst physician, Montreal Gen Hosp, 66-70; active med staff, Childrens Hosp, Halifax, 76-90, chief res, 86-90; vis prof, Dept Neurol, Johns Hopkins Univ, 78-79; mem, Med Res Coun Can, 79-85, vpres, 84-85; chmn, NS Newborn Screening Prog, 79-90; coun, Can Fedn Biol Socs, 86-89. *Mem:* Can Soc Clin Invest (pres, 88-89); Can Fedn Biol Socs; Am Soc Biochem & Molecular Biol; Am Soc Neurochem; Int Soc Neurochem; Can Med Asn. *Res:* Membrane metabolism with a particular interest in lipids and lipid metabolism; inherited metabolic diseases in children; research administration, planning for new research developments. *Mailing Add:* Alberta Heritage Found Med Res 3125 Manulife Pl Edmonton AB T5J 3S4 Can. *Fax:* 403-429-3509; *E-Mail:* ahfmt@dns.sns.ab.ca

SPENCE, ROBERT DEAN, ENGINEERING. *Current Pos:* from asst prof to prof physics & astron, Mich State Univ, 47-76, actg head Dept Physics, 56-57, prof physics, 76-86, EMER PROF PHYSICS, MICH STATE UNIV, 86- *Personal Data:* b Bergen, NY, Sept 12, 17; m 42; c 4. *Educ:* Cornell Univ, BS, 39; Mich State Col, MS, 42; Yale Univ, PhD(physics), 48. *Prof Exp:* Asst physics, Mich State Col, 41-42; instr elec commun, Mass Inst Technol, 42-45. *Concurrent Pos:* Vis prof & Guggenheim fel, Bristol Univ, 55-56; vis prof, Eindhoven Technol Univ, 64 & State Univ Leiden, 71. *Mem:* Nat Soc Prof Engrs; Am Soc Heating Refrig & Air Conditioning Engrs. *Res:* Mathematical and crystal physics; nuclear magnetic resonance. *Mailing Add:* 1849 Ann St East Lansing MI 48823

SPENCE, SYDNEY P(AYTON), CHEMICAL ENGINEERING. *Current Pos:* Jr tech rep, Union Carbide Corp, Halowax Prods Div, 43-44 & 46, mem tech staff, Bakelite Co Div, 46-51, chem engr, Res & Develop Dept, 51-56, proj engr, 56-57, group leader process res, Union Carbide Plastics Co Div, 57-67, process tech mgr phenolic & epoxy resins, Coatings Intermediates Div, 67-71, DEVELOP SCIENTIST, UNION CARBIDE CORP, BOUND BROOK, 71- *Personal Data:* b Yonkers, NY, Dec 30, 21; m 44; c 5. *Educ:* Univ Rochester, BS, 44. *Mem:* Am Inst Chem Engrs. *Res:* Development of commercial processes for epoxy resins, bisphenol A, phenolic resin, acrylonitrile-butadiene-styrene resins, di-paraxylylene, polyester resins, chlorinated hydrocarbons. *Mailing Add:* 2159 Bayberry Lane Westfield NJ 07090-4701

SPENCE, WILLARD LEWIS, BOTANY. *Current Pos:* from asst prof to assoc prof biol, 64-69, PROF BIOL, FRAMINGHAM STATE COL, 69- *Personal Data:* b Providence, RI, Mar 16, 35; m 58; c 3. *Educ:* Colby Col, BA, 57; Univ Iowa, MS, 59; Univ Calif, Berkeley, PhD(bot), 63. *Prof Exp:* Asst cur bot, NY Bot Gardens, 63-64. *Mem:* Am Soc Plant Taxon; Bot Soc Am; Sigma Xi. *Res:* Vascular plant taxonomy; local flora; economically valuable plants. *Mailing Add:* Dept Biol Framingham State Col Framingham MA 01701-2460

SPENCE, WILLIAM J, TECTONOPHYSICS, EARTHQUAKE PREDICTION. *Current Pos:* RES GEOPHYSICIST, US GEOL SURV, 73- *Personal Data:* b Peoria, Ill, July 11, 37; m 84, Susan Edelstein; c Andrew. *Educ:* State Univ NY, Albany, BS, 59, MS, 60; Pa State Univ, PhD(geophys), 73. *Prof Exp:* Instr phys chem, Spencer Cent High Sch, 61-62; res geophysicist, US Coast & Geol Surv, 62-70, Environ Res Lab, 71, Nat Oceanic & Atmospheric Admin, 72; adj prof, Colo Sch Mines, Golden, 85-87. *Concurrent Pos:* Prin investr, Seismicity & Tectonics Proj, 76-90, comp earthquake & tsunami hazard for zones, Circum-Pac Proj, 84-89 & deep hole desalinization of Dolores River, Colo Proj, 84-89; pres, Front Range Chap, Am Geophys Union, 89; investr earthquake prediction, Subduction Process, Western US Tectonics, 90- *Mem:* Seismol Soc Am; Am Geophys Union; AAAS; Geol Soc Am; Sigma Xi. *Res:* Causes and consequences of great earthquakes; plate tectonics; earthquakes induced by reservoirs or by fluid injection into substrata; aftershocks; seismic siting of critical facilities; tectonic development of western United States. *Mailing Add:* Box 25046 MS967 Denver CO 80225. *Fax:* 303-399-5178

SPENCER, ALBERT WILLIAM, ZOOLOGY. *Current Pos:* asst prof zool, 65-74, ASSOC PROF BIOL, FT LEWIS COL, 74- *Personal Data:* b Omaha, Nebr, Jan 1, 29; m 56; c 4. *Educ:* Colo State Univ, BS, 57, MS, 62, PhD(zool), 65. *Prof Exp:* Asst prof zool, Eastern NMex Univ, 64-65. *Mem:* Am Soc Mammal; Soc Study Evolution; Ecol Soc Am; Wildlife Soc; Genetics Soc Am. *Res:* Vertebrate population biology, particularly speciation. *Mailing Add:* 3077 E Fourth Ave Durango CO 81301

SPENCER, ALEXANDER BURKE, geology; deceased, see previous edition for last biography

SPENCER, ANDREW NIGEL, INVERTEBRATE NEUROBIOLOGY. *Current Pos:* PROF ZOOL & ASSOC CHMN DEPT, UNIV ALTA, 75-; DIR, BAMFIELD MARINE STA, BAMFIELD, BC, 93- *Personal Data:* b Fulmer, Eng, Feb 13, 45; c 4. *Educ:* Univ London, BSc, 67; Univ Victoria, PhD(zool), 71. *Honors & Awards:* McCalla Professorship. *Prof Exp:* Sci Res Coun fel zool, Univ Bristol, 71-72; vis asst prof, 72-73; lectr biol, Inst Biol, Univ Odense, 73-75. *Concurrent Pos:* Consult, New Can Encyclopedia; vis prof, Univ Pet M Curie, Villefranche, 74-75; Grant Selection Comt Animal Biol, Nat Sci & Eng Res Coun Can. *Mem:* Am Soc Zoologists; Can Soc Zoologists (pres, 95-96); Brit Soc Exp Biol; Soc Neurosci. *Res:* The behavioural neurophysiology of hydrozoans; central control of rhythmical behavior in invertebrates; function of neuropeptides; voltage-clamp analysis; evolution of channel proteins; molecular aspects of channel functional. *Mailing Add:* Dept Biol Sci Univ Alta Edmonton AB T6G 2M7 Can. *E-Mail:* aspencer@bms.bc.ca

SPENCER, ARMOND E, MATHEMATICS. *Current Pos:* assoc prof, 71-76, PROF MATH, STATE UNIV NY COL POTSDAM, 76- *Personal Data:* b Crandon, Wis, Oct 1, 33; m 58; c 4. *Educ:* Mich State Univ, BS, 58, MS, 61, PhD(math), 67. *Prof Exp:* High sch instr, Mich, 58-60; instr math, Lansing Community Col, 62-65; asst prof, Western Mich Univ, 66-67 & Univ Ky, 67-71. *Mem:* Am Math Soc; Math Asn Am. *Res:* Finite group theory. *Mailing Add:* Dept Mathematics State Univ NY Potsdam NY 13676

SPENCER, ARTHUR COE, II, APPLIED MATHEMATICS, ENGINEERING SCIENCE. *Current Pos:* RETIRED. *Personal Data:* b Pittsburgh, Pa, Dec 16, 39; m 60; c 2. *Educ:* Allegheny Col, BS, 61; Univ Pittsburgh, MS, 64. *Prof Exp:* Res mathematician, PPG Industs, Inc, 61-67; sr engr, Westinghouse Elec Corp, 67-73, fel engr, 73-76, mgr thermal hydraul methods, 76-94. *Mem:* Soc Indust & Appl Math. *Res:* Computational fluid dynamics; numerical methods for partial differential equations; two phase flow; heat transfer. *Mailing Add:* 2513 College Park Rd Allison Park PA 15101

SPENCER, ARTHUR MILTON, JR, FUEL ENGINEERING, SURFACE CHEMISTRY. *Current Pos:* RETIRED. *Personal Data:* b Salt Lake City, Utah, Jan 6, 20; m 48; c 7. *Educ:* Univ Utah, BS, 49, MS, 51, PhD(fuels eng), 62. *Prof Exp:* Tech asst, explosives res group, Univ Utah, 53-59; sr res chemist, Allegany Balistics Lab, Hercules Inc, Md, 62-63; sr res assoc oil well stimulation & cement, West Co, Tex, 64-71; chief chemist, Petrol Technol Corp, 71-78; sr res scientist, Rocket Res Co, 78-79; chief chemist, Petrol Technol Corp, 79-85. *Concurrent Pos:* Fel, Petrol Res Fund, 59-62; teacher, high sch math & sci, 89- *Mem:* Am Chem Soc; Soc Petrol Engrs. *Res:* Explosives for oil well stimulation; acid corrosion at high temperatures; fuel and water gels; high temperature retarders for oil well cementing; high temperature explosives for geothermal wells. *Mailing Add:* 13719 115th Ave NE Kirkland WA 98034-2165

SPENCER, BROCK, INORGANIC CHEMISTRY. *Current Pos:* From instr to assoc prof, 65-76, chmn dept, 80-93, PROF CHEM, BELOIT COL, 76- *Personal Data:* b Horton, Kans, Sept 25, 39; m 64, Barbara McBride; c 2. *Educ:* Carleton Col, BA, 61; Univ Calif, Berkeley, PhD(chem), 65. *Honors & Awards:* Catalyst Award, Chem Mfr Asn, 91. *Concurrent Pos:* Vis prof, Case Western Res Univ, 67-68, Uppsala Univ, 71-72, Univ Calif, Berkeley, 79, Univ Wis-Madison, 85, Cambridge Univ, 93 & Univ Lund, 93. *Mem:* Am Chem Soc; AAAS. *Res:* Molecular spectroscopy and x-ray diffraction determination of molecular structure and bonding; molecular orbital calculations. *Mailing Add:* Dept Chem Beloit Col Beloit WI 53511. *Fax:* 608-363-2718; *E-Mail:* spencer@beloit.edu

SPENCER, CHARLES WINTHROP, GEOLOGY. *Current Pos:* RETIRED. *Personal Data:* b Cambridge, Mass, Dec 25, 30; m 54; c 3. *Educ:* Colby Col, AB, 53; Univ Ill, MS, 55. *Honors & Awards:* A I Levorsen Award. *Prof Exp:* Res asst, Clay Mineral, State Geol Surv, Ill, 53-55; geologist, US Geol Surv, 55-59; geologist, Texaco, Inc, Mont, 59-66, from asst res dist geologist to dist geologist, 66-73, div lab mgr, Colo, 73-74; prog chief, US Geol Surv, 74-95. *Mem:* Am Asn Petrol Geologists; Soc Econ Paleontologists & Mineralogists; Soc Prof Well Log Analysts; Soc Petrol Engrs. *Res:* Geology of mineral deposits; petroleum exploration; stratigraphy of Paleozoic and Cretaceous; hydrodynamics; environmental interpretation of sandstones and carbonates; petrol geology of southern Brazil; geology of low permeability (tight) gas reservoirs; origins of overpressured and underpressured gas reservoirs. *Mailing Add:* 13528 W Alaska Dr Lakewood CO 80228. *Fax:* 303-236-8822

SPENCER, CHERRILL MELANIE, DESIGN MAGNETS FOR PARTICLE ACCELERATORS & MAGNETIC RESONANCE IMAGING, DESIGN PARTICLE DETECTORS FOR ELEMENTARY PARTICLE PHYSICS. *Current Pos:* PHYSICIST, STANFORD LINEAR ACCELERATOR CTR, 88- *Personal Data:* b Derbyshire, Eng, Feb 17, 48; m 89, Richard O Leder; c Sierra. *Educ:* Univ London, BSc 69, Univ Oxford, DPhil, 72. *Honors & Awards:* Spectrum Award, Inst Elec & Electronics Engrs, 93. *Prof Exp:* Royal Soc Europ fel elem particle physics, Italian Nat Lab, 72-74; res assoc elem particle physics, Univ Wis-Madison, 74-77; res assoc, Fla State Univ, 77-79; staff scientist, Sci Applns Inc, 79-84; physicist, Resonex Inc, 84-88. *Concurrent Pos:* Cont educ, Am Phys Soc, 93-95. *Mem:* Am Phys Soc; AAAS; Inst Physics UK; Asn Women Sci. *Res:* Design and build iron cored electromagnets for particle accelerators and magnetic resonance imaging; designed and built non-destructive coal analyzer using prompt neutron activation analysis; designed particle detectors for elementary particle physics. *Mailing Add:* Stanford Linear Accelerator Ctr PO Box 4349 MS 12 Stanford CA 94309

SPENCER, CHESTER W(ALLACE), METALLURGY. *Current Pos:* RETIRED. *Personal Data:* b Greeley, Kans, Nov 2, 24; m 48; c 4. *Educ:* Univ Kans, BS, 49, MS, 50; Univ Wis, PhD(metall), 52. *Prof Exp:* Sr engr atomic energy div, Sylvania Elec Prod, Inc, 52-54; res metallurgist, Carnegie Inst Technol, 54-56; asst prof metall eng, Cornell Univ, 56-58, assoc prof, 58-62; mgr mat res & develop, Res & Adv Develop Div, Avco Corp, Mass, 62-64; vpres, Chase Brass & Copper Co, 64-77; exec dir, Nat Mat Adv Bd, Nat Acad Sci, 77-84. *Concurrent Pos:* Consult, Res & Adv Develop Div, Avco Corp, 59- *Mem:* Am Soc Metals; Am Inst Mining, Metall & Petrol Engrs; Brit Inst Metals. *Res:* Eutectoid and peritectoid transformations in alloys; electrical and physical properties of semiconducting intermetallic compounds; reactions between liquids and solids. *Mailing Add:* 1472 Chrisman Mill Rd Christianburg VA 24073-5862

SPENCER, CLAUDE FRANKLIN, ORGANIC CHEMISTRY. *Current Pos:* RETIRED. *Personal Data:* b Athens, Pa, Feb 14, 19; m 44, Louise Wible; c Frederic, Karen & Richard. *Educ:* Univ Mich, BS, 42; Mass Inst Technol, PhD(chem), 50. *Prof Exp:* Res chemist, Merck & Co, Inc, 42-46 & 50-59; sr res chemist, Norwich Pharmacol Co, 59-65, group leader, 65-80, res assoc, Norwich-Eaton Pharmaceut, 80-83. *Mem:* Am Chem Soc; fel Am Inst Chemists; Sigma Xi; Int Soc Heterocyclic Chemists; AAAS. *Res:* Synthesis and structure determination of natural products; synthesis and transannular rearrangements in eight-membered ring compounds; synthesis of medicinal and veterinary products; design and synthesis of biologically active compounds. *Mailing Add:* Box 244 A Hall Quarry Mt Desert ME 04660-9802

SPENCER, DAVID R, COMPUTER PUBLISHING, COLOR PRINTING. *Current Pos:* PRES, SPENCER & ASSOCS PUBL LTD, 89- *Personal Data:* b New York, NY, Apr 24, 42; m 68, Pamela J; c 2. *Educ:* Mass Inst Technol, BSEE, 64, MSEE, 68. *Prof Exp:* Mgr, Graphics Eng, EG&G, Inc, 62-63; pres, Datalog Div, Litton Systs, Inc, 73-82; pres, Muirhead NAm, Inc, 82-83; chmn, Data Recording Systs, Inc, 83-89. *Concurrent Pos:* Dir, Long Island Forum Technol, 78-82; dir, Long Island Ventura Group, 88-93; dir, Pixel Craft Inc, 93- *Mem:* Inst Elec & Electronics Engrs. *Res:* Image processing, compression and hardcopy recording; high resolution xerography; color printing technology, including imaging engines and controller/rips. *Mailing Add:* 3 Giffard Way Melville NY 11747

SPENCER, DOMINA EBERLE (MRS PARRY MOON), MATHEMATICS, PHYSICS. *Current Pos:* assoc prof math, 50-60, PROF MATH, UNIV CONN, 60- *Personal Data:* b New Castle, Pa, Sept 26, 20; m 61; c 1. *Educ:* Mass Inst Technol, SB, 39, MS, 40, PhD(math), 42. *Honors & Awards:* Illum Eng Soc Gold Medal, 74. *Prof Exp:* Asst illum eng, Mass Inst Technol, 42; asst prof physics, Am Univ, 42-43; Tufts Col, 43-47 & Brown Univ, 47-50. *Mem:* Am Math Soc; fel Optical Soc Am; fel Illum Eng Soc; Math Asn Am. *Res:* Application of tensors to physics, field theory; nomenclature, color, calculation of illumination; design of lighting for vision; foundations of electrodynamics; mathematics of nutrition. *Mailing Add:* Dept Math Univ Conn Storrs CT 06269-0001

SPENCER, DONALD CLAYTON, MATHEMATICS. *Current Pos:* prof, 68-72, Henry Burchard Fine prof, 72-78, EMER HENRY BURCHARD FINE PROF MATH, PRINCETON UNIV, 78- *Personal Data:* b Boulder, Colo, Apr 25, 12; m 36, 51; c 3. *Educ:* Univ Colo, BA, 34; Mass Inst Technol, BSc, 36; Cambridge Univ, PhD(math), 39, ScD, 63. *Hon Degrees:* DSc, Purdue Univ, 71. *Honors & Awards:* Bocher Prize, Am Math Soc, 48; Nat Medal Sci, 89. *Prof Exp:* Instr math, Mass Inst Technol, 39-42; from assoc prof to prof, Stanford Univ, 42-50, prof, 63-68; from assoc prof to prof, Princeton Univ, 50-63. *Mem:* Nat Acad Sci; London Math Soc; Am Acad Arts & Sci. *Res:* Differential geometry; partial differential equations. *Mailing Add:* 943 County Rd 204 Durango CO 81301

SPENCER, DONALD JAY, laser physics, aerothermodynamics, for more information see previous edition

SPENCER, DWIGHT LOUIS, ANIMAL ECOLOGY. *Current Pos:* from lectr to prof, 72-86, assoc chmn dept, 74-86, EMER PROF BIOL, EMPORIA KANS STATE UNIV, 86- *Personal Data:* b Harveyville, Kans, June 24, 24; m 48; c 6. *Educ:* Kans State Teachers Col, BS, 52, MS, 55; Okla State Univ, PhD(zool), 67. *Prof Exp:* Instr high sch, Kans, 53-60. *Mem:* Am Soc Mammal. *Res:* Mammalian ecology and speciation; ecological speciation study of Neotoma floridana and Neotoma micropus in Kansas and Oklahoma. *Mailing Add:* 560 County Rd 220 Emporia KS 66801

SPENCER, E MARTIN, MEDICINE. *Current Pos:* DIR, LAB GROWTH & DEVELOP, CHILDREN'S HOSP, SAN FRANCISCO, 80- *Personal Data:* b Cleveland, Ohio, Dec 6, 29; c 3. *Educ:* Dartmouth Col, AB, 52; Harvard Univ, MD, 56; Rockefeller Univ, PhD(biochem), 69. *Prof Exp:* Res assoc, Beth Israel Hosp, Sch Med, Harvard Univ, 59-60; attend physician, Harlem Hosp, New York, 69-70; guest investr, Rockefeller Univ, 69-70; assoc clin prof med, Univ Calif, San Francisco, 70- *Concurrent Pos:* Rotating intern, San Francisco Gen Hosp, Univ Calif Serv, 56-57; sr resident med, Bellevue Hosp, Columbia Univ Serv, 60-61; chief resident med, Univ Calif Med Ctr, San Francisco, 62-63; vis asst, Cardiol Ctr, Cantonal Hosp & 1 Univ, Geneva, Switz, 61-62; policy bd mem, Sickle Cell Vaso-Occlusive Clin Trials, Nat Heart & Lung Inst, 72, mem, Ad Hoc Comt, Studies Sickle Cell Dis, 73-75; chmn, Workshop Extracorporeal Treatment Sickle Cell Dis, NIH, 74-75. *Mem:* Fel Am Col Physicians; Western Soc Clin Res; Am Soc Bone & Mineral Res. *Res:* Somatomedin, its role in the control of cellular proliferation and its physiologic role and regulation; hormonal regulation of vitamin D metabolism. *Mailing Add:* Lab Growth & Develop Davies Med Ctr Castro & Duboce Sts San Francisco CA 94118

SPENCER, EDGAR WINSTON, GEOLOGY. *Current Pos:* from asst prof to assoc prof, Washington & Lee Univ, 57-63, actg chmn dept, 57-59, chmn, 59-95, PROF GEOL, WASHINGTON & LEE UNIV, 63- *Personal Data:* b Monticello, Ark, May 27, 31; m 58, Elizabeth Humphris; c Elizabeth Shawn & Kristen Shannon. *Educ:* Washington & Lee Univ, BS, 53; Columbia Univ, PhD(geol), 57. *Prof Exp:* Lectr geol, Hunter Col, 54-56, instr, 57. *Concurrent Pos:* Prin investr, NSF grant, 59-62, sci fac fel tectonics in NZ & Australia, 65-66; res grant, Switz & Spain, 71-72; pres, Rockbridge Area Conserv Coun, 78 & 95-97; res grant, Am Chem Soc, 81-82, Greece, 82 & Western NAm, 90. *Mem:* Fel AAAS; fel Geol Soc Am; Am Asn Petrol Geologists; Nat Asn Geol Teachers; Am Inst Prof Geologists; Am Geophys Union. *Res:* Tectonics; regional structure; land use planning; author of 6 books. *Mailing Add:* Dept Geol Washington & Lee Univ Lexington VA 24450

SPENCER, EDSON WHITE, INFORMATION SCIENCE & SYSTEMS. *Current Pos:* mem staff, Honeywell Inc, Minneapolis, 54-58, far east regional mgr, Tokyo, 59-65, corp vpres internal opers, 65-69, exec vpres, 69-74, pres & chief exec officer, 74-78, chief exec officer, 78-87, CHMN BD, HONEYWELL INC, MINNEAPOLIS, 78- *Personal Data:* b Chicago, Ill, June 4, 26. *Educ:* Williams Col, BA, 48; Oxford Univ, MA, 50. *Prof Exp:* Staff, Sears Roebuck & Co, Chicago, 51-54. *Mailing Add:* Mayo Found Bd Trustees 200 First St SW Rochester MN 55905-0001

SPENCER, EDWARD G, MATERIALS SCIENCE ENGINEERING. *Current Pos:* RETIRED. *Personal Data:* b Lynchburg, Va, July 21, 20; m 46, Necia Jellison; c Edward G Jr & Thomas J. *Educ:* George Washington Univ, BSE, 45; Boston Univ, MA, 50. *Prof Exp:* Physicist, US Naval Res Lab, 43-46 & 49-53; physicist, Cambridge Air Force Res Lab, 46-49; physicist, Diamond Ordinance Fuze Lab & Dept Defense, 53-58 & AT&T Bell Labs, 58-87. *Concurrent Pos:* Co-ed, Conf Magnetism & Magnetic Mat, New York City, 64-68. *Mem:* Fel Am Phys Soc. *Res:* Microwave radar; upper atmospheric physics; semiconductor and ferrimagnetic materials for scanning phase array microwave radars; magnetic spin resonance; dielectric materials for electrooptic; elastooptic and microwave ultrasonic applications; superconducting metals and alloys. *Mailing Add:* 76 Roland Rd Murray Hill NJ 07974

SPENCER, ELAINE, BIOCHEMISTRY. *Current Pos:* instr, 56-59, from instr to asst prof chem, 59-74, ASSOC PROF CHEM, PORTLAND STATE UNIV, 74- *Personal Data:* b Portland, Ore, Aug 6, 19; m 42; c 5. *Educ:* Linfield Col, BA, 40; Mass Inst Technol, MS, 48; Univ Ore, PhD(biochem), 61. *Prof Exp:* Instr chem, Ore State Col, 46-47, instr math, 47. *Mem:* Sigma Xi; Am Chem Soc. *Res:* Oxidative enzymes; proteins; enzyme kinetics. *Mailing Add:* 4835 NE Broadway St Portland OR 97213-2153

SPENCER, ELVINS YUILL, ORGANIC CHEMISTRY, AGRICULTURAL CHEMISTRY. *Current Pos:* RETIRED. *Personal Data:* b Edmonton, Alta, Oct 2, 14; m 42, Hanna Fischl; c Erica & Martin. *Educ:* Univ Alta, BSc, 36, MSc, 38; Univ Toronto, PhD(chem), 41. *Prof Exp:* Chief chemist, Fine Chem Can, 41-42; res chemist, Gelatin Prod Corp, Ont & Mich, 42-43; res engr, Consol Mining & Smelting Co, BC, 43-46; res chemist, E B Eddy Paper Co, Que, 46; assoc prof chem, Univ Sask, 46-51; prin chemist, Res Inst, Can Dept Agr, Univ Western Ont, 51-60, dir, Res Inst, 60-78, sr scientist, Dept Agr, 78-79, chmn, Int Expert Comt Dioxins, Ont Ministry Environ, Can Dept Agr, 83-90. *Concurrent Pos:* Coordr res, Sask Res Coun, 49-51; hon lectr, Univ Western Ont, 51-61, hon prof, 61-91; consult, Dept Natural Resources, Sask on Potash & Sabbatical at Cambridge Univ, 56-57; mem expert comt pesticide residues, Food & Agr Orgn; vis scholar, Rockefeller Conf Ctr, Bellagio, Italy, 76; mem, Fed Pest Mgt Adv Bd, 85-89; fel, Agrochem Div, Am Chem Soc & Chem Inst Can. *Mem:* Am Chem Soc; Chem Inst Can. *Res:* Flotation agent; pharmaceuticals; cereal chemistry; synthetic polypeptides; oils and fats; organic chemistry and biochemistry of pesticides; pesticide biochemistry and physiology. *Mailing Add:* 7 Westview Dr London ON N6A 2Y2 Can

SPENCER, FRANK, PHYSICAL ANTHROPOLOGY, WITH A PARTICULAR INTEREST IN THE HISTORY OF THE DISCIPLINE. *Current Pos:* from asst prof to assoc prof, 79-86, chmn, 85-94, FULL PROF, DEPT ANTHROP, QUEENS COL, 86- *Personal Data:* b Rochester, Kent, Eng, 41. *Educ:* FIMLS, London, 65; Univ Windsor, BA, 73; Univ Mich, Ann Arbor, MA, 74, PhD(anthrop), 79. *Prof Exp:* Chief med tech path, St Bartholomew's Hosp, Kent, Eng, 65-69; tech dir, Hotel Dieu Hosp, Windsor, Ont, 69-73. *Concurrent Pos:* Adj prof, New Sch Social Res, New York, NY, 85-91. *Mem:* Am Asn Phys Anthropologists; Am Anthrop Asn; Am Soc Hist Med. *Res:* History of physical anthropology and medicine; paleoanthropology; Plio Pleistocene hominid evolution. *Mailing Add:* Dept Anthrop CUNY Queens Col 6530 Kissena Blvd Flushing NY 11367-1575

SPENCER, FRANK COLE, MEDICINE. *Current Pos:* PROF SURG & CHMN DEPT, SCH MED, NY UNIV, 65- *Personal Data:* b Haskell, Tex, Dec 21, 25; c 3. *Educ:* NTex State Col, BS, 44; Vanderbilt Univ, MD, 47; Am Bd Surg & Bd Thoracic Surg, dipl. *Prof Exp:* Intern surg, Johns Hopkins Hosp, 47-48; asst res surgeon, Univ Calif Med Ctr, Los Angeles, 49-50; from asst resident surg to surgeon, Johns Hopkins Hosp, 53-65, from instr to assoc prof surg, Sch Med, Johns Hopkins Univ, 54-61; prof, Sch Med, Univ Ky, 61-65. *Concurrent Pos:* Fel, Sch Med, Johns Hopkins Univ, 48-49; USPHS fel cardiovasc surg, Sch Med, Univ Calif, Los Angeles, 51; Markle scholar; consult, Walter Reed Army Hosp, 57. *Mem:* Soc Univ Surg; Soc Clin Surg; Am Asn Thoracic Surg; Am Surg Asn. *Res:* Cardiovascular and thoracic surgery. *Mailing Add:* NY Univ Med Ctr 550 First Ave New York NY 10016-6402

SPENCER, FREDERICK J, PREVENTIVE MEDICINE, PUBLIC HEALTH. *Current Pos:* assoc prof, Med Col Va, Va Commonwealth Univ, 62-63, prof prev med, 63-81, chmn dept, 62-81, asst dean student activ, Sch Med, 78-81, EMER PROF & ASSOC DEAN, MED COL VA, VA COMMONWEALTH UNIV, 81- *Personal Data:* b Newcastle-on-Tyne, Eng, June 30, 23; US citizen; m 54; c 2. *Educ:* Univ Durham, MB, BS, 45; Harvard Univ, MPH, 58. *Prof Exp:* Health dir, Va State Dept Health, 56-62, dir bur epidemiol, 62. *Concurrent Pos:* Walter Reed lectr, Richmond Acad Med, 66. *Mem:* Am Pub Health Asn. *Res:* Epidemiology and its application in administration of medical care; history of medicine. *Mailing Add:* 560 Lake Caroline Dr Ruther Glen VA 22546

SPENCER, GORDON REED, electrical engineering, for more information see previous edition

SPENCER, GREGORY FIELDER, MESOSCOPIC DEVICE PHYSICS, SUBMICRON & NANOFABRICATION TECHNIQUES. *Current Pos:* res scientist, Low Temperature Physics Lab, 88-90, RES SCIENTIST NANO FAB CTR, TEX A&M UNIV, 90- *Personal Data:* b Dade City, Fla, Sept 20, 53; m 86, Sheila Ann Fenelon; c Lucas & William. *Educ:* Univ SFla, BS, 75; Univ Ill, MS, 78; Univ Fla, PhD(physics), 86. *Prof Exp:* Res asst, Ultra-Low Temperature Physics Lab, Lancaster Univ, Eng, 86-88. *Mem:* Am Phys Soc; Mat Res Soc; Inst Elec & Electronics Engrs; Am Vacuum Soc. *Res:* Standard submicron fabrication methods to construct mesoscopic devices in semiconductors and other materials systems such as electron-beam lithography, plasma processing, epitary and new nanoscale fabrication methods. *Mailing Add:* Nano Fab Ctr Jonsson Sch Eng & Comput Sci PO Box 830688 M/S EC33 Univ Tex Dallas Richardson TX 75083-0688. *Fax:* 409-845-2590; *E-Mail:* spencer@ec.tamu.edu

SPENCER, GUILFORD LAWSON, II, MATHEMATICS. *Current Pos:* RETIRED. *Personal Data:* b Natick, Mass, Feb 21, 23; m 51; c 1. *Educ:* Williams Col, BA, 43; Mass Inst Technol, MS, 48; Univ Mich, PhD(math), 53. *Prof Exp:* Instr math, Univ Md, 51-53; from asst prof to prof, Williams Col, 53-70, Frederick Latimer Wells prof math, 70-89. *Res:* Topology and hyperbolic systems of partial differential equations. *Mailing Add:* 70 Hamel Ave Williamstown MA 01267-2910

SPENCER, HAROLD GARTH, PHYSICAL CHEMISTRY. *Current Pos:* From asst prof to assoc prof, Clemson Univ, 59-68, head, Dept Chem & Geol, 66-77, prof chem, 68-88, alumni prof, 88-93, DISTINGUISHED ALUMNI PROF, CLEMSON UNIV, 93- *Personal Data:* b Avon Park, Fla, May 19, 30; m 56, Mary D Wilkes; c Steve & Susan. *Educ:* Univ Fla, BS, 52, MS, 58, PhD(phys chem), 59. *Concurrent Pos:* Vis scientist, Imperial Col, 74; AID adv, Instituto Universitario da Beira Interior, Portugal, 82; consult, Vicellon Inc, 74-77, CARRE Inc, 77-88 & Du Pont, 89-; Fulbright res award, 95. *Mem:* Am Chem Soc; Sigma Xi; AAAS; NAm Membrane Soc. *Res:* Physical chemistry of polymers and polymer membranes, structure and properties; transport in polymers; inorganic thin film coatings. *Mailing Add:* Dept Chem Clemson Univ Clemson SC 29634-1905

SPENCER, HARRY EDWIN, PHYSICAL CHEMISTRY. *Current Pos:* VIS PROF & AFFIL SCHOLAR, OBERLIN COL, 85- *Personal Data:* b Friendship, NY, June 8, 27; m 53; c 4. *Educ:* Syracuse Univ, BA, 50; Univ Calif, PhD, 54. *Honors & Awards:* Hon mem, Soc Photographic Sci & Technol Japan. *Prof Exp:* Chemist, Navy Ord Div, 53-59, res assoc, Res Labs, 59-72, sr res assoc, Res Labs, Eastman Kodak Co, 72-85. *Concurrent Pos:* Adj fac chem, Rochester Inst Technol, 63-80; mem, NY State Rating Comt PhD Prog Chem, 73-74. *Mem:* Am Chem Soc; Am Phys Soc; Royal Photog Soc; fel Am Inst Chemists; fel Soc Photog Scientists. *Res:* Radiation chemistry; photoconductivity; infrared detectors; theory of photography; photochemistry. *Mailing Add:* Dept Chem Oberlin Col Oberlin OH 44074

SPENCER, HERBERT W, III, PHYSICS, AIR POLLUTION. *Current Pos:* EXEC VPRES, EC&C TECHNOL, 89-; PRES, HWS ENG & RES CO. *Personal Data:* b Louisville, Ky, June 12, 45; m 67, 84, Amy Robinson; c 2. *Educ:* Vanderbilt Univ, BA, 67; Auburn Univ, MS, 69, PhD(physics), 74. *Prof Exp:* Res physicist electrostatic precipitators, Southern Res Inst, 74-77; mem staff, Joy Mfg Co, 77-80, mgr, Adv Tech Dept, Western Precipitation Div, 80-88. *Mem:* Am Phys Soc; Sigma Xi; Air & Waste Mgt Asn; Am Inst Chem Engrs. *Res:* Expert cleaning industrial gases for particulates SO2, NOx using scrubber, electrostatic precipitators and fabric filters. *Mailing Add:* 23629 Mill Valley Valencia CA 91355-2638

SPENCER, HERTA, METABOLISM. *Current Pos:* Chief metab sect, Vet Admin Hosp, 61-; PROF INTERNAL MED, SCH MED, LOYOLA UNIV, 64- *Educ:* Case Western Reserve Univ, MD, 46. *Res:* Mineral and trace element metabolism. *Mailing Add:* Metab Res Vet Med Ctr Box 35 Hines IL 60141-0035. *Fax:* 708-216-2319

SPENCER, HUGH MILLER, physical chemistry, for more information see previous edition

SPENCER, JACK T, BOTANY, AGRONOMY. *Current Pos:* RETIRED. *Personal Data:* b Mantua, Ohio, Sept 23, 12; m 34; c 1. *Educ:* Kent State Univ, BS, 35; Univ Wis, MSc, 36; Ohio State Univ, PhD(bot, agron), 39. *Prof Exp:* Agt maize breeding, Bur Plant Indust, USDA, 36-40; res agronomist forage crops, Univ Ky, 40-42 & 46-49; consult foreign res, USDA, 49-61; prog dir, NSF, 61-68; exec dir, Orgn Trop Studies, 68-72; dir develop, Shippensburg Univ, 72-77; fed liaison consult, Cols & Univs, 78-91. *Mem:* AAAS; Am Inst Biol Sci; Bot Soc Am; Orgn Trop Studies. *Res:* Plant genetics; tropical science; science administration. *Mailing Add:* 1303 Azalea Lane De Kalb IL 60115-2329

SPENCER, JAMES ALPHUS, PLANT PATHOLOGY. *Current Pos:* RETIRED. *Personal Data:* b Clayton, Okla, Nov 5, 30; c 3. *Educ:* Univ Ark, BS, 53, MS, 62; NC State Univ, PhD(plant path), 66. *Prof Exp:* Res asst plant path, Univ Ark, 57-62; agr res technician, NC State Univ, USDA, 62-66; from asst prof to assoc prof plant path, Miss State Univ, 66-76, prof, 76. *Mem:* Am Phytopath Soc; Am Soc Hort Sci; Can Plant Path Soc; Am Rose Soc. *Res:* Host-parasite relationships; mycology; woody ornamental plants; diseases; rose disease. *Mailing Add:* 2700 Maple Dr Starkville MS 39759

SPENCER, JAMES BROOKES, HISTORY OF SCIENCE. *Current Pos:* asst prof, 63-70, ASSOC PROF HIST SCI, ORE STATE UNIV, 70- *Personal Data:* b Canton, China, July 16, 26; US citizen; m 48; c 4. *Educ:* Lawrence Col, BS, 48; Univ Wis, MS, 56, PhD(hist sci), 64. *Prof Exp:* Res physicist & proj leader, Bjorksten Res Labs, Wis, 54-57; asst prof physics, Augustana Col, Ill, 57-59. *Concurrent Pos:* Vis asst prof, Johns Hopkins Univ, 65-66; NSF res grant, 65-69; vis asst prof, Univ Wis, 69; amanuensis, Niels Bohr Inst, Copenhagen, Denmark, 70-71. *Mem:* Hist Sci Soc. *Res:* History of 19th and early 20th century physical science, particularly magnetooptics and the structure of matter spectroscopy. *Mailing Add:* 5745 NW Oak Creek Dr Corvallis OR 97330

SPENCER, JAMES EUGENE, NUCLEAR & ACCELERATOR PHYSICS, NEURAL NETWORKS & CONTROL THEORY. *Current Pos:* STAFF MEM, STANFORD LINEAR ACCELERATOR CTR, 78- *Personal Data:* b Kansas City, Mo, Jan 2, 38; m 64, Nancy Casella. *Educ:* Mass Inst Technol, BS, 64, PhD(physics), 69. *Honors & Awards:* Achievement Accelerator Physics & Technol, USPHS, 95. *Prof Exp:* Fel physics, Stanford Univ, 69-71; staff mem, Los Alamos Sci Lab, 71-78. *Concurrent Pos:* Consult, Lawrence Livermore Lab, 70-72; mem tech adv panel, Los Alamos Physics Facil, 73-75; reviewer, Phys Res & Phys Rev Letts, 74-; mem prog adv comt, Ind Cyclotron Lab, 76-78. *Mem:* Am Phys Soc; Sigma Xi. *Res:* Particle physics; magnetic optics; synchrotron radiation; quantum electronics; storage rings; adaptive control theory; brain/neural net computers complexity. *Mailing Add:* Stanford Linear Accelerator Ctr PO Box 4349 MS-26 Stanford CA 94309. *Fax:* 650-926-4999; *E-Mail:* jus@slacvm.stanford.edu

SPENCER, JAMES NELSON, PHYSICAL CHEMISTRY. *Current Pos:* MEM FAC, CHEM DEPT, FRANKLIN & MARSHALL COL, 80- *Personal Data:* b Rainelle, WVa, Nov 11, 41. *Educ:* Marshall Univ, BS, 63; Iowa State Univ, PhD(phys chem), 67. *Prof Exp:* Student chemist, Int Nickel Co, WVa, 61-63; assoc prof chem, Lebanon Valley Col, 67-80. *Mem:* Am Chem Soc. *Res:* Hydrogen bonding; thermodynamic properties of solutions. *Mailing Add:* Chem Dept Franklin & Marshall Col Lancaster PA 17604-3003

SPENCER, JAMES W(ENDELL), EDUCATIONAL ADMINISTRATION. *Current Pos:* Instr civil eng, Cornell Univ, 49-51, from asst prof to prof, 51-87, vdir coop exten, 70-73, assoc dean, NY State Col Agr & Life Sci, 73-78, spec asst to pres, 78-79, vprovost, 79-87, EMER PROF & VPROVOST, CORNELL UNIV, 87- *Personal Data:* b Ithaca, NY, Aug 3, 27; m 46, Dorothy Dye; c James W Jr, Karen (Smith) & Susan (Coin). *Educ:* Cornell Univ, BCE, 49, MCE, 51; Stanford Univ, PhD, 67. *Concurrent Pos:* Field engr, D J Belcher & Assocs, NY, 54; lectr & assoc res engr, Inst Transp & Traffic Eng, Calif, 57-58; consult, NY State Temp Comn Agr, 58 & Ford Found, Colombia, SAm, 63; NSF sci faculty fel, Stanford Univ, 64-65; admin bd, Cornell Lab Ornithol. *Res:* Highway engineering; engineering-economic planning. *Mailing Add:* 1071 Taughannock Blvd Ithaca NY 14850

SPENCER, JESSE G, PHYSICAL CHEMISTRY, INORGANIC CHEMISTRY. *Current Pos:* PROF CHEM & HEAD DEPT, VALDOSTA STATE UNIV, 84- *Personal Data:* b Farmville, NC, Apr 10, 35; m 73, Jeanne Thomas; c Jennifer, Jess & Frances. *Educ:* Univ NC, BS, 57; Univ Va, MS, 59, PhD(chem), 62. *Prof Exp:* Res assoc chem, Univ NC, 61-62; from asst prof to prof, Univ Charleston, 62-84, head dept, 65-76, prog dir, Med Lab Technol, 75-79, chmn, Div Health Serv, 76-79, dir comput serv & records, 81-84; dean arts & sci, 82-84. *Mem:* Am Chem Soc; Sigma Xi. *Res:* Solution thermochemistry and polarography of transition metals in aqueous and nonaqueous media; trace analysis. *Mailing Add:* Dept Chem Valdosta State Univ Valdosta GA 31698. *E-Mail:* jspencer@grits.valdosta.peachnet.edu

SPENCER, JOHN EDWARD, PHYSICAL CHEMISTRY. *Current Pos:* MEM TECH STAFF, TEX INSTRUMENTS INC, 80- *Personal Data:* b Panama, CZ, Mar 22, 49; US citizen; m 75; c 1. *Educ:* Millsaps Col, BS, 71; Rice Univ, PhD(chem), 75. *Prof Exp:* Res assoc chem, Univ Calif, Irvine, 75-77; res chemist, Lighting Bus Group, Gen Elec Co, 77-80. *Mem:* Am Chem Soc; AAAS; Electrochem Soc. *Res:* Plasma etching of semiconductor thin films; plasma spectroscopy; high temperature chemistry and combustion. *Mailing Add:* 1213 Balboa Circle Plano TX 75075

SPENCER, JOHN FRANCIS THEODORE, MICROBIOLOGY, MICROBIAL GENETICS OF YEASTS. *Current Pos:* RES ASSOC, DEPT BIOL, GOLDSMITH'S COL, UNIV LONDON & THAMES POLYTECH, LONDON, 74-; PRIN RES SCIENTIST, CONICET ARGENTINA, 88- *Personal Data:* b Magrath, Alta, Jan 18, 22; m 45, 73, 96, Alicia L Ragout; c Carla, Cathy, Margaret, John, Jane & Hugh. *Educ:* Univ Alta, BSc, 49, MSc, 51; Univ Sask, PhD(chem), 55. *Prof Exp:* Asst res officer, Prairie Regional Lab, Nat Res Coun Can, 51-59, assoc res officer, 59-63, sr res officer, Eng & Process Develop Sect, 63-74. *Concurrent Pos:* Mem, Int Yeast Coun, 69-, Argentina, 88; vis prof, Dept Microbiol & Biochem, Univ Nat de Tucuman. *Mem:* AAAS; Am Soc Microbiol; Sigma Xi. *Res:* Genetic improvement of industrial yeasts using protoplast fusion as a principal tool; intergenetic fusion of baking yeasts with osmotolerent species; role of mitochondria as well as nuclear genomes in yeast performance; yeast genetics and molecular biology; biochemical taxonomy of yeasts. *Mailing Add:* PRO1M1 Ave Belgrano Y Pasaje Caseros San Miguel De Tucuman 4000 Argentina. *Fax:* 54-81-30222; *E-Mail:* fspencer@pvoimi.edu.ar

SPENCER, JOHN HEDLEY, BIOCHEMISTRY. *Current Pos:* head dept, 78-90, PROF BIOCHEM, QUEEN'S UNIV, 78- *Personal Data:* b Stapleford, Eng, Apr 10, 33; Can citizen; m 58, Madeliene V Kulin; c Robin, David & Mark. *Educ:* St Andrews Univ, BSc, 55, Hons, 56; McGill Univ, PhD(biochem), 60. *Honors & Awards:* Ayerst Award, Can Biochem Soc, 72. *Prof Exp:* Res asst biochem, McGill Univ, 56-59, lectr & teaching fel, 61-63, from asst prof to prof biochem, 63-78; Damon Runyon Mem Fund Cancer Res vis fel, Columbia Univ, 59-61, res assoc, 61. *Concurrent Pos:* Sci Officer biochem comt, Med Res Coun Can, 73-79; mem grants panel, Nat Cancer Inst, 75-79; mem, adv panel Collab Res Grants Prog, NATO, 86-89; chmn, 88-89, mem, Comite Scientifique, Programme Des Actions Structurantes, FONDS, FCAR, 85-90; vis scientist, Nat Inst Child Health & Human Develop, NIH, 87-88; professeur invite, Univ Montreal, 92-93. *Mem:* Can Biochem Soc (treas, 66-69, vpres, 78-79, pres, 79-80); Am Soc Biochem & Molecular Biol; AAAS; Brit Biochem Soc; Can Fed Biol Soc (vpres, 80-81, pres, 81-82); Sigma Xi; fel Royal Soc Can. *Res:* Chemistry and primary structure of DNA; gene expression transcription and control; antibacterial peptides. *Mailing Add:* Dept Biochem Queen's Univ Kingston ON K7L 3N6 Can. *Fax:* 613-545-2497; *E-Mail:* spencerl@post.queensu.ca

SPENCER, JOHN LAWRENCE, TECHNICAL SERVICE, QUALITY CONTROL. *Current Pos:* prof chem, 88-90, JESSE BALL DUPONT PROF NAT SCI, FLA SOUTHERN COL, 90- *Personal Data:* b Sanford, Fla, Sept 10, 32; m 54, 79; c Deborah & Diane. *Educ:* DePauw Univ, AB, 54; Univ Mich, MS, 56, PhD(isoxazolines), 58. *Prof Exp:* Org chemist, Lederle Lab, Am Cyanamid Co, 58-60; sr org chemist, Eli Lilly & Co, 60-67, res scientist, 67-71, mgr antibiotic prod technol, 71-78, mgr sterile operations, 78-80, mgr tech serv & qual control, 78-85, res assoc, 85-86, sr res scientist, 86-88. *Mem:* Am Chem Soc; Parenteral Drug Asn. *Res:* Synthesis of heterocyclic systems, particularly isoxazolines, oxadiazoles, benzodiazepines and quinazolines; antibiotic modifications, particularly tetracyclines, penicillins and cephalosporins; antibiotic manufacturing including fermentation, purification, and bulk parenteral operations; analytical supervision and quality control supervisions; vancomycin process improvements production scale high pressure liquid chromatograph. *Mailing Add:* Dept Chem Fla Southern Col 111 Lake Hollingsworth Dr Lakeland FL 33801-5698

SPENCER, JOSEPH WALTER, GEOPHYSICS. *Current Pos:* RETIRED. *Personal Data:* b Salt Lake City, Utah, May 24, 21; m 48; c 5. *Educ:* Brigham Young Univ, BS, 47; Pa State Univ, PhD(physics), 52. *Prof Exp:* Asst math, Brigham Young Univ, 47-48; asst physics, Pa State Univ, 48-49; asst acoust, 49-50; res physicist, Calif Res Corp, Stand Oil Co Calif, 52-54, proj leader geophys, 54-56, group supvr, 56-60; sr geophysicist, Calif Oil Co, 60-65, staff geophysicist, Western Div, Chevron Oil Co, 65-69, chief geophysicist, 69-77, chief geophysicist, Cent Region, Chevron USA, 77-83. *Mem:* Soc Explor Geophysicists; Am Geophys Union. *Res:* Fluid dynamics; viscous behavior of high molecular weight hydrocarbons; wave propagation in earth materials; interpretation of geophysical data; electronic computer applications. *Mailing Add:* 6910 S Prince Way Littleton CO 80120-3510

SPENCER, LARRY T, AQUATIC ECOLOGY, INVERTEBRATE ZOOLOGY. *Current Pos:* from instr to assoc prof biol, 67-78, PROF BIOL, PLYMOUTH STATE COL, 78- *Personal Data:* b Palo Alto, Calif, Oct 15, 41; m 64; c Mark, Julie & Suzannne. *Educ:* Brigham Young Univ, BS, 63; Ore State Univ, MA, 65; Colo State Univ, PhD(zool), 68; Univ Calif, MLS, 75. *Prof Exp:* Teaching asst zool, Brigham Young Univ, 62-63, Ore State Univ, 65-67 & Colo State Univ, 65-67. *Concurrent Pos:* Vis prof, Univ Hawaii, 82. *Mem:* AAAS; Am Soc Limnol & Oceanog; Ecol Soc Am; Am Soc Zoologists; Hist Sci Soc. *Res:* Population biology of marine and fresh water invertebrates; biology of cephalopod molluscs; history of biology and American science; exploration and settlement of the trans-Mississippi west; evolution, its impact on biological and intellectual thought; data base management and information retrieval in the biological sciences. *Mailing Add:* Dept Natural Sci Boyd Hall Plymouth State Col Plymouth NH 03264

SPENCER, LORRAINE BARNEY, phycology; deceased, see previous edition for last biography

SPENCER, MARY EILEEN STAPLETON, PLANT BIOCHEMISTRY, ETHYLENE. *Current Pos:* from asst prof to assoc prof biochem, Univ Alta, 53-64, actg head, Dept Biochem, 60-61, prof plant sci, 64- 83, UNIV PROF, UNIV ALTA, 84- *Personal Data:* b Regina, Sask, Oct 4, 23; m 46, Henry; c Susan M (McLean). *Educ:* Univ Sask, BA, 45; Bryn Mawr Col, MA, 46; Univ Calif, PhD(agr chem), 51. *Honors & Awards:* Medal, Can Soc Plant Physiologists, 90. *Prof Exp:* Chemist, Ayerst, McKenna & Harrison, Ltd, 46-47; chemist, Nat Canners Asn, Calif, 48-49; asst food chem, Univ Calif, 50-51, instr, 51-53. *Concurrent Pos:* Mem, Nat Res Coun Can, 70-76; mem, Natural Sci & Eng Res Coun Can, 86-; mem bd gov, Univ Alta, 76-79; mem, Task Force on Post-Secondary Educ, Alberta Govt Comn on Educ Planning, 70-72; mem, Alta Premier's Coun Sci & Technol 90- *Mem:* Can Soc Plant Physiologists (pres, 71-72); Am Soc Plant Physiologists; Chem Inst Can; Plant Growth Regulator Soc Am; Royal Soc Can; Int Soc Plant Molecular Biol; Int Plant Growth Regulator Soc Am. *Res:* Biology of ethylene, its effects on plants, animals, microorganisms, its relationship to aging and to plant productivity, its biogenesis, cyanide-resistant respiration, post-harvest physiology of fruits and vegetables and plant respiration. *Mailing Add:* Dept Plant Sci Univ Alberta Edmonton AB T6G 2P5 Can. *Fax:* 403-492-4265; *E-Mail:* s.heathco@vm.vcs.ualberta.ca

SPENCER, MAX M(ARLIN), MECHANICAL ENGINEERING. *Current Pos:* RETIRED. *Personal Data:* b Rocky Ford, Colo, Jan 10, 35; m 55, Sherry Stoehr; c Paula, Jeff & Mike. *Educ:* Okla State Univ, BS, 56, MS, 57, PhD(eng), 60. *Prof Exp:* Res asst & lectr eng, Okla State Univ, 56-60; assoc engr, Boeing Co, Kans, 57, faculty assoc adv design group, 58, res specialist, 60; res specialist & stress consult, Ballistics Res Labs, Aberdeen Proving Ground, Md, 60-61; res specialist, Boeing Co, 61-62, stress res group chief, 62-63, res specialist & fatigue group head, 63-69, sr eng supvr, 69-78, struct technol mgr & stress unit chief, 78-80, struct technol chief, 80-87, tech chief, 87-88, chief engr struct, 88-93. *Concurrent Pos:* Guest lectr, Univ Wichita, 62; designated eng rep, Fed Aviation Admin, 74. *Mem:* Am Soc Mech Engrs. *Res:* Aircraft structural analysis; stress and fatigue. *Mailing Add:* PO Box 1757 Everett WA 98206

SPENCER, MERRILL PARKER, CARDIOVASCULAR PHYSIOLOGY. *Current Pos:* MED DIR, PAC VASCULAR INC, 87- *Personal Data:* b Pawnee, Okla, Feb 27, 22; m 44; c 4. *Educ:* Baylor Univ, MD, 45. *Prof Exp:* Intern, Herman Hosp, Tex, 45-46; med resident, Crile Vet Admin Hosp, 50-51; instr physiol & pharmacol, Bowman Gray Sch Med, 51-54, asst prof physiol, 54-59, assoc prof physiol & pharmacol, 59-63; dir, Va Mason Res Ctr, 63-71; pres & dir, Inst Appl Physiol & Med, 71-86. *Concurrent Pos:* USPHS fel, Western Reserve Univ, 48-50; mem coun circulation & coun basic sci, Am Heart Asn; pres, Oceanographic Inst Wash. *Mem:* Am Physiol Soc; Am Heart Asn. *Res:* Medical electronics; cardiopulmonary medicine. *Mailing Add:* Inst Appl Physiol & Med 701 16th Ave Seattle WA 98122-4525. *Fax:* 206-553-1717

SPENCER, PAUL ROGER, ELECTROPHOTOGRAPHY, COMPUTER PRINTING TECHNOLOGY. *Current Pos:* DEVELOP ENGR & MEM TECH STAFF, ELECTROPHOTOG, DISK DRIVE ENG, BOISE PRINTER DIV & DISK MECHANISM DIV, HEWLETT-PACKARD CORP, BOISE, IDAHO, 79- *Personal Data:* b Madison, Wis, Dec 24, 41; m 92, Susan Daniels; c Tim & Rebecca. *Educ:* Wash State Univ, BS, 63; Univ Ill, MS, 65, PhD(physics), 69. *Prof Exp:* Sci co-worker electron-nuclear double resonance, Second Phys Inst, Stuttgart, Ger, 69-70; mem res staff electrophotog, Xerographic Technol Lab & Cent Res Lab, Xerox Corp, Webster, NY, 70-79. *Mem:* Am Phys Soc. *Res:* Electrophotographic printing, ink jet printing, specialized sensor development print quality management; 5 professional articles and 8 patents in electrophotography and ink jet printing. *Mailing Add:* 6045 Becky Dr Meridian ID 83642-5333. *E-Mail:* pauls@hpbs2547.boi.hp.com

SPENCER, PETER SIMNER, NEUROBIOLOGY, NEUROTOXICOLOGY. *Current Pos:* fel path, 71-73, from asst prof to assoc prof, 73-83, ASSOC PROF PATH & DIR, INST NEUROTOXICOL, ALBERT EINSTEIN COL MED, 79-, PROF NEUROSCI, 83-; DIR, ORE HEALTH SCI UNIV. *Personal Data:* b London, Eng, Nov 30, 46; US citizen; m 69; c 2. *Educ:* Univ London, BSc, 68, PhD(path), 71. *Honors & Awards:* Weil Award, Am Asn Neuropathologists, 76. *Prof Exp:* Res asst, Nat Hosp Nervous Dis, Univ London, UK, 68-70, res fel, Royal Free Hosp Sch Med, 70-71. *Concurrent Pos:* Joseph P Kennedy Jr Found fel, 74-76; consult, Nat Inst Occup Safety & Health, 76-77 & Environ Protection Agency, 77-; assoc ed, J Neurocytol, 77-; chmn adv bd, J Neurotoxicol, 78-; mem adv bd, Rutgers Univ Toxicol Prog, 84, Howe & Assocs, 85 & Peripheral Nerve Repair & Regeneration, 85; mem, Bd Toxicol & Environ Health Hazards, Nat Acad Sci, 84, Safe Drinking Water Comt, 85; secy, Third World Med Res Found, 85- *Mem:* Am Asn Neuropathologists; Am Soc Cell Biol; AAAS; Anat Soc Gt Brit & Ireland; British Neuropath Soc; World Fedn Neurol; Royal Col Pathologists; hon mem Pan-Am Neuroepidemiology Found. *Res:* Cellular relationships in the nervous system and the effects of neurotoxic chemicals. *Mailing Add:* Croft L606 Oregon Health Sci Univ 3181 SW Sam Jackson Park Rd Portland OR 97201-3098

SPENCER, RALPH DONALD, ORGANIC CHEMISTRY. *Current Pos:* assoc prof, 67-85, SR FEL, MELLON INST, CARNEGIE-MELLON UNIV, 57-, EMER PROF CHEM, 85- *Personal Data:* b Kolambugan, Philippines, July 22, 20; US citizen; m 47; c 2. *Educ:* Col Wooster, BA, 41; Stanford Univ, MA, 42; Cornell Univ, PhD(org chem), 47. *Prof Exp:* Du Pont fel chem, Cornell Univ, 47-48; Goodrich Tire & Rubber Co Prog res assoc, 50-51; chemist, Pineapple Res Inst, Hawaii, 48-50; chemist, E I du Pont de Nemours & Co, 51-57. *Mem:* Am Chem Soc. *Res:* New approach to desalination of sea water; daylily research and hybridizing. *Mailing Add:* 1207 N Western Dr Monroeville PA 15146-4403

SPENCER, RANDALL SCOTT, PALEONTOLOGY, STRATIGRAPHY. *Current Pos:* From asst prof to assoc prof, Old Dominion Univ, 66-77, asst chmn dept, 74-76, assoc dean, 78-81, PROF GEOL SCI, OLD DOMINION UNIV, 78-, CHMN DEPT, 81- *Personal Data:* b Sept 29, 37; US citizen; m 66; c 2. *Educ:* Univ Wis-Madison, BS, 60; Univ Kans, MS, 62, PhD(geol), 68. *Concurrent Pos:* NSF grant, 70-; fel Cushman Found. *Mem:* Fel Geol Soc Am; Soc Econ Paleontologists & Mineralogists. *Res:* Upper Paleozoic brachiopods; Cenozoic foraminifera of Atlantic Coast; statistical studies in brachiopod evolution; marine Pleistocene stratigraphy and fauna of the mid-Atlantic seaboard. *Mailing Add:* Geol Sci Old Dominion Univ Norfolk VA 23529-1000

SPENCER, RICHARD L, BIOCHEMISTRY. *Current Pos:* RETIRED. *Personal Data:* b Dunlap, Iowa, Feb 11, 34; m 59; c 3. *Educ:* Fresno State Col, AB, 56; San Jose State Col, MS, 63; Univ Calif, Davis, PhD(biochem), 66. *Prof Exp:* Asst chemist, Calif Chem Co, 56-59; res assoc biochem, Univ Ill, Urbana, 65-66; NIH fel, Univ Minn, 66-68; from asst prof to assoc prof, SW State Univ, 68-74, prof chem, 74-96. *Mem:* Am Chem Soc. *Res:* Enzyme chemistry. *Mailing Add:* 415 S Fourth St Marshall MN 56258

SPENCER, RICHARD PAUL, NUCLEAR MEDICINE, BIOCHEMISTRY. *Current Pos:* PROF NUCLEAR MED & CHMN DEPT, SCH MED, UNIV CONN HEALTH CTR, FARMINGTON, 74 - *Personal Data:* b New York, NY, June 7, 29; m 56, Gwendolyn Williams; c 3. *Educ:* Dartmouth Col, AB, 51; Univ Southern Calif, MD, 54; Harvard Univ, MA, 58, PhD(biochem), 61. *Hon Degrees:* MA, Yale Univ, 68. *Prof Exp:* From asst prof to assoc prof biophys, Univ Buffalo, 61-63; from assoc prof to prof nuclear med, Sch Med, Yale Univ, 63-74. *Concurrent Pos:* NSF fel, Harvard Univ, 57-58, Helen Hay Whitney fel, 58-60. *Mem:* AAAS; Am Physiol Soc; Soc Nuclear Med; Biophys Soc. *Res:* Organ structure and function as studied by radiopharmaceuticals; models of biological growth and differentiation; intestinal metabolism and transport. *Mailing Add:* Dept Nuclear Med Univ Conn Health Ctr Farmington CT 06030. *Fax:* 860-679-2164; *E-Mail:* rspencer@adp.uchc.edu

SPENCER, SELDEN J, BIOLOGICAL SCIENCES. *Current Pos:* RETIRED. *Personal Data:* b Towanda, Pa, Apr 28, 23; m 51, Jean Mumford; c James & Paul. *Educ:* Mansfield State Col, BS, 48; Pa State Univ, MEd, 52, DEd(biol sci), 62. *Prof Exp:* High sch teacher, Pa, 48-49; chem technician, Sylvania Elec Prod, Inc, 50-52; admin asst, Educ Off, Pa State Col, 52-53; admin asst educ film res prog, 53-54; high sch teacher, Pa, 54-57; mem, Inst Sci Teachers, Pa, 57-58; prof biol, Goddard Col, 58-63; from asst prof to prof, State Univ NY Col New Paltz 63-88 chmn dept, 72-78. *Res:* Bird banding research; bank swallow nesting sites; Arctic wilderness exploration; west Indian cushion starfish. *Mailing Add:* 55 DuBois Rd New Paltz NY 12561

SPENCER, TERRY WARREN, GEOPHYSICS. *Current Pos:* chmn dept, 66-77, PROF GEOPHYS, TEX A&M UNIV, 66- *Personal Data:* b Los Angeles, Calif, Feb 10, 30; m 53; c 2. *Educ:* Univ Calif, Los Angeles, AB, 51; Calif Inst Technol, PhD(geophys), 56. *Prof Exp:* Sr res physicist, Chevron Res Co, Calif, 56-66. *Mem:* Soc Explor Geophys. *Res:* Elastic wave propagation theory; petroleum seismology. *Mailing Add:* Dept Geophys Tex A&M Univ College Station TX 77843-3114

SPENCER, THOMAS, MATHEMATICS. *Current Pos:* PROF, INST ADVAN STUDY, PRINCETON UNIV, 86- *Personal Data:* b Dec 24, 46. *Educ:* Univ Calif, Berkeley, BA, 68; NY Univ, PhD, 72. *Prof Exp:* Vis mem, Inst Advan Study, Princeton Univ, 72-74; fel, Harvard Univ, 74-75; assoc prof, Rockefeller Univ, 75-77; prof, Rutgers Univ, 78-80; prof, Courant Inst Math, NY Univ, 80-86. *Concurrent Pos:* Sloan fel. *Mailing Add:* Inst Advan Study Sch Math Princeton NJ 08540

SPENCER, THOMAS A, ORGANIC CHEMISTRY. *Current Pos:* from instr to prof & chmn dept, 60-72, NH PROF CHEM, DARTMOUTH COL, 72- *Personal Data:* b Orange, NJ, Mar 31, 34; m 56, Patricia A Judkins; c Karen, Robert, Jonathan & Melinda. *Educ:* Amherst Col, AB, 56; Univ Wis, PhD(chem), 60. *Prof Exp:* Res assoc chem, Univ Wis, 60. *Concurrent Pos:* Alfred P Sloan Found res fel, 65-68; mem Grants Prog Adv Comt, Res Corp, 72-78. *Mem:* AAAS; Am Chem Soc; Am Soc Biochem & Molecular Biol. *Res:* Organic chemical synthesis; steroid biosynthesis and regulation; biochemical reaction mechanisms. *Mailing Add:* Dept Chem Dartmouth Col Hanover NH 03755. *Fax:* 603-646-3946; *E-Mail:* Bitnet: taspen@dartmouth.edu

SPENCER, THOMAS H, metallurgy, heat treatments, for more information see previous edition

SPENCER, WALTER WILLIAM, CLINICAL CHEMISTRY. *Current Pos:* admin dir lab serv, 85-93, CLIN CHEMIST, ST ELIZABETH MED CTR, 61-, ADMIN DIR LAB SERV, 85- *Personal Data:* b Mansfield, Ohio, Nov 10, 33; m 64, Margaret; c Mary & Jim. *Educ:* Heidelberg Col, BS, 55; Purdue Univ, West Lafayette, MS, 58, PhD(biochem), 60. *Honors & Awards:* Katchman Award, Ohio Valley Sect, Am Asn Clin Chem, 78. *Prof Exp:* Purdue Res Found fel, Purdue Univ, West Lafayette, 60-61. *Concurrent Pos:* Clin asst prof, Univ Dayton, 70-74, clin assoc prof, 74-80; treas, Clin Chem Consult, Inc, 78; consult, Vet Admin Hosp, Dayton, 84- *Mem:* Fel AAAS; Am Asn Clin Chemists; Sigma Xi; Nat Registry Clin Chem. *Res:* Development of new procedures for use in the field of clinical chemistry. *Mailing Add:* 933 Ingersoll Dr Dayton OH 45429

SPENCER, WILLIAM ALBERT, REHABILITATION, PEDIATRICS. *Current Pos:* RETIRED. *Personal Data:* b Oklahoma City, Okla, Feb 16, 22; m 45; c 2. *Educ:* Georgetown Univ, BS, 42; Johns Hopkins Univ, MD, 46; Am Bd Pediat, dipl, 55. *Honors & Awards:* Gold Medal, Int Cong Phys Med, 72; Gold Key Award, Am Cong Rehab Med, 72, Coulter Award, 78. *Prof Exp:* Intern, Johns Hopkins Hosp, 46-47, resident, 47-48; from instr to asst prof pediat, Baylor Col Med, 50-57, asst prof physiol, 54-57, prof rehab & chmn dept, 57-89, emer prof, Dept Rehab, 89-96. *Concurrent Pos:* Med dir, Southwestern Poliomyelitis Respiratory Ctr, 50-59; pres, Inst Rehab & Res, Tex Med Ctr, 59-87; Horowitz vis prof, Inst Phys Med & Rehab, 64; asst attend physician, Ben Taub Gen Hosp; mem active staff, Tex Children's Hosp; mem consult staff, M D Anderson Hosp & Tumor Inst Houston; mem courtesy staff, St Luke's Hosp; chmn, Spec Med Adv Group, Vet Admin, 74-75; dep dir & actg dir, Nat Inst Handicapped Res, Washington, DC, 79-80, intermittent consult, 79-; mem, Panel Testing Handicapped, Nat Acad Sci, 80-81; mem, Comt Health Care Racial-Ethnic Minorities & Handicapped Persons, 80-81; mem, Sci Merit Rev Bd, Vet Admin Rehab, Res & Develop, 81. *Mem:* Inst Med-Nat Acad Sci; AMA; Am Acad Pediat; Am Physiol Soc; Am Cong Rehab Med (pres, 68-69); AAAS; Nat Rehab Asn; NY Acad Sci; Asn Comput Mach; Sigma Xi. *Res:* Development of principles of rehabilitation medicine; application of electronic technology to research in disabling chronic disease and injuries; planning health services for disabled at community and national level. *Mailing Add:* Tex Inst Res & Rehab 1333 Moursand Houston TX 77030

SPENCER, WILLIAM F, SOIL CHEMISTRY. *Current Pos:* ADJ PROF, UNIV CALIF, RIVERSIDE, 75- *Personal Data:* b Carlinville, Ill, Mar 4, 23; m 46, Marjorie Hall; c Barbara A, William F Jr & Gary A. *Educ:* Univ Ill, BS, 47, MS, 50, PhD(agron), 52. *Prof Exp:* Asst soil physics, Univ Ill, 48-49; asst chemist, Citrus Exp Sta, Univ Fla, 51-54; soil scientist, Agr Res Serv, USDA, Wyo, 54-55 & Calif, 55-57; assoc soil chemist, Citrus Exp Sta, Univ Fla, 57-62; supvry soil scientist, Agr Res Serv, USDA, 62-95. *Concurrent Pos:* Consult, Cent Univ Venezuela, 59. *Mem:* Fel AAAS; Am Chem Soc; fel Soil Sci Soc Am; fel Am Soc Agron; Soc Environ Toxicol Chem. *Res:* Soil chemistry of pesticides, nutrient enrichment, waste disposal on land as related to water quality and vapor behavior of pesticides and other toxic organic chemicals in the environment. *Mailing Add:* Agr Res Serv USDA Univ Calif 1278 Geol Bldg Riverside CA 92521. *Fax:* 909-342-4964

SPENCER, WILLIAM J, SOLID STATE PHYSICS. *Current Pos:* CHMN & CHIEF EXEC OFFICER, SEMATECH, 90- *Personal Data:* b Raytown, Mo, Sept 25, 30; m 53; c 2. *Educ:* William Jewell Col, AB, 52; Kans State Univ, MS, 56, PhD(physics), 59. *Hon Degrees:* DSc, William Jewel Col, 69 & 90. *Honors & Awards:* Electronic 100 Award, 72; CB Sawyer Award, Inst Elec & Electronics Engrs, 72. *Prof Exp:* Mem tech staff, Bell Tel Labs, Pa, 59-60, supvr, Piezoelec Devices Group, 60-68, head, Piezoelec Devices Dept, 68-72, dir univ rels & tech employ, 72-73; dir microelectronics, Sandia Labs, 73-78, systs develop, Livermore, 78-81; mgr, Integrated Circuit Lab, Xerox Corp, Palo Alto Res Ctr, 81-82, vpres, Sci Ctr, 82-86, mgr, 83-86, group vpres & sr tech officer, Corp Res Group, 86-90. *Concurrent Pos:* Pres, Solid State Circuits Coun, Inst Elec & Electronics Engrs, 78-79; res prof med, Sch Med, Univ NMex, 78-97; mem, Comput Sci & Technol Bd, 88-90 & Executone Bd Dirs meeting, 89- *Mem:* Nat Acad Eng; Am Phys Soc; fel Inst Elec & Electronics Engrs; AAAS; Sigma Xi. *Res:* Integrated circuits design and processing; biomedical applications. *Mailing Add:* Sematech 2706 Montopolis Dr Austin TX 78741

SPENDLOVE, JOHN CLIFTON, bacteriology, for more information see previous edition

SPENDLOVE, REX S, VIROLOGY, IMMUNOLOGY. *Current Pos:* RETIRED. *Personal Data:* b Hoytsville, Utah, Apr 29, 26; m 49; c 5. *Educ:* Brigham Young Univ, BS, 50, MS, 52; Ohio State Univ, PhD, 55; Am Bd Med Microbiol, dipl. *Hon Degrees:* Doctorate, Utah State Univ, 89. *Prof Exp:* Instr microbiol, Univ Conn, 55-58; res microbiologist, Viral & Rickettsial Dis Lab, Calif State Dept Pub Health, 58-66; head dept bact & pub health, Utah State Univ, 66-73, prof virol, 66-81. *Concurrent Pos:* Mem ed bd, Excerpta Medica; mem reovirus study group, Vert Virus Subcomt, Int Comn Nomenclature Viruses; pres, HyClone Labs, Inc, 75- *Mem:* AAAS; Am Soc Microbiol; NY Acad Sci; Soc Exp Biol & Med; Am Asn Immunol. *Res:* Reovirus replication and genetics; affinity of reovirus for host cell microtubules; enhancement of reovirus infectivity by capsid removal; effect of proteolytic enzymes on viral structure; viral pollution of water; Rotavirus Gastroenteritis. *Mailing Add:* Hyclone Labs 1725 S Hy Clone Rd Logan UT 84321-8209. *Fax:* 435-753-4589

SPENGER, ROBERT E, ORGANIC CHEMISTRY. *Current Pos:* from asst prof to prof, 64-88, EMER PROF CHEM, CALIF STATE UNIV, FULLERTON, 88- *Personal Data:* b Oakland, Calif, Sept 20, 24; m 59; c 1. *Educ:* Univ Calif, Berkeley, AB, 54; Univ Calif, Los Angeles, PhD(org chem), 62. *Prof Exp:* Chemist, Radiation Lab, Univ Calif, 54-57; asst, Univ Calif, Los Angeles, 57-62, asst res chemist, Univ Calif, Riverside, 62-64. *Mem:* Am Chem Soc. *Res:* Synthesis of isotopically-labelled compounds; synthesis of organo-arsenic compounds. *Mailing Add:* 1318 E Glenwood Ave Fullerton CA 92631-2845

SPENGLER, KENNETH C, METEOROLOGY. *Current Pos:* Exec dir, 46-88, EMER EXEC DIR, AM METEOROL SOC, 88- *Personal Data:* b Harrisburg, Pa. *Educ:* Dickinson Col, BA, 36; Mass Inst Technol, MS. *Hon Degrees:* DSc, Univ Nev, 66. *Mem:* AAAS; Coun Eng & Sci Soc; Am Inst Aeronaut & Astronaut; Am Geophys Union. *Mailing Add:* 189 Jason St Arlington MA 02174

SPENNER, FRANK J(OHN), ELECTRICAL ENGINEERING. *Current Pos:* from asst prof to assoc prof eng, 47-63, assoc prof elec eng, 63-71, EMER ASSOC PROF ENG DRAWING, UNIV WYO, 71- *Personal Data:* b Riverside, Iowa, July 4, 01; m 39; c 1. *Educ:* Univ Iowa, BS, 24, MS, 27. *Prof Exp:* Asst foreman, Potter Condenser Co, Ill, 27-28; asst engr, Western Elec Co, 28-32; survr, US Coast & Geod Surv, Iowa, 33-34 & Johnson Co, Iowa, 36-39; instr eng, drawing & math, Trinidad State Jr Col, 41-47. *Mem:* Inst Elec & Electronics Engrs. *Res:* Design, inspection and development on equipment for measuring electrical characteristics of cables, coils and condensers; basic circuits. *Mailing Add:* Dept Eng Drawing Wyo Univ Laramie WY 82071

SPENNY, DAVID LORIN, PHYSICS EDUCATION, UNDERGRADUATE RESEARCH. *Current Pos:* assoc prof, 80-89, PROF PHYSICS, UNIV SOUTHERN COLO, 89- *Personal Data:* b Covington, Ky, Nov 5, 43; m 82, Debrah J Veeder. *Educ:* Wittenberg Univ, BS, 65; Univ Colo, Boulder, PhD(physics), 70. *Prof Exp:* Lectr physics, Univ Colo, Denver, 70-71; asst prof phys sci, Univ Colo, Boulder, 71-74; asst prof, NMex Highlands Univ, 74-75; asst prof physics, Bemidji State Univ, 76-79. *Mem:* Am Asn Physics Teachers. *Res:* Supervise undergraduate student research in fields of physics, especially optics. *Mailing Add:* 1531 Lexington Rd Pueblo CO 81001-2034. *Fax:* 719-549-2732

SPENSER, IAN DANIEL, BIO-ORGANIC CHEMISTRY. *Current Pos:* from assoc prof to assoc prof biochem, 57-64, prof chem, 64-89, EMER PROF CHEM, MCMASTER UNIV, 89- *Personal Data:* b Vienna, Austria, June 17, 24; m 51, Anita Fuchs; c Helen R & Paul A. *Educ:* Univ Birmingham, BSc, 48; Univ London, PhD(biochem), 52, DSc, 69. *Honors & Awards:* Sr Scientist Award, NATO, 80; Can (Nat Sci & Eng Res Coun Can)-Japan (Japan Soc Prom Sci) Exchange Award, 82 & 83; John Labatt Ltd Award, Chem Inst Can, 82 & 83. *Prof Exp:* Demonstr biochem, Kings Col, Univ London, 48-52, asst lectr biochem & chem, Med Col, St Bartholomew's Hosp, 52-54, lectr, 54-57. *Concurrent Pos:* Fel, Nat Res Coun Can, 53-54; vis prof, Lab Org Chem, Eidgenoessische Tech Hochschule, Zurich, 71, 89; vis prof, Inst Org Chem, Techn. Univ Denmark, 77, Inst Org Chem Univ Karlsruhe, Fed Rep Ger, 81 & Inst Pharmaceut Biol Univ Bonn, Fed Rep Ger, 89. *Mem:* Am Soc Biol Chemists; fel Chem Inst Can; Royal Soc Chem; Brit Biochem Soc; fel Royal Soc Can; Phytochem Soc NAm; Am Soc Pharmacog. *Res:* Biosynthesis of alkaloids and of B vitamins; chemistry and metabolism of amino acids. *Mailing Add:* Dept Chem McMaster Univ Hamilton ON L8S 4M1 Can. *Fax:* 905-522-2509

SPERA, FRANK JOHN, MAGMA TRANSPORT, IRREVERSIBLE THERMODYNAMICS. *Current Pos:* Asst prof, 77-81, ASSOC PROF THERMODYNAMICS & PETROL, PRINCETON UNIV, 82- *Personal Data:* b Philadelphia, Pa, Dec 6, 50; m 77. *Educ:* Franklin & Marshall Col, BA, 72; Univ Calif, Berkeley, BA, 74, PhD(geol), 77. *Concurrent Pos:* Vis lectr, Univ Calif, Los Angeles, 81-82, vis res geophysicists, 81-82; prin investr, NSF, 79-82. *Mem:* Am Geophys Union; Geol Soc Am. *Res:* Application of thermodynamics and fluid dynamics to magnatic processes; eruption and ascent of magma; experimental rheology of magma; origin of compositional zonation in magma chambers. *Mailing Add:* 5309 Parejo Dr Santa Barbara CA 93111

SPERANDIO, GLEN JOSEPH, CLINICAL PHARMACY. *Current Pos:* from instr to assoc prof pharm, Purdue Univ, 46-60, head, Dept Clin Pharm, 71-78, assoc dean, 78-83, PROF PHARM, PURDUE UNIV, WEST LAFAYETTE, 60-; EXEC DIR, IND SOC HOSP PHARM, 83- *Personal*

Data: b Glen Carbon, Ill, May 8, 18; m 46, Dorys Bell; c James. *Educ:* St Louis Col Pharm, BS, 40; Purdue Univ, MS, 47, PhD(pharm), 50. *Honors & Awards:* Glen J Sperandio Award for Advan of Pharm, 84. *Prof Exp:* Anal chemist, Grove Labs, 40-42, chief control chemist, 44-46 & United Drug Co, 42-43; asst dept mgr, William R Warner, Inc, 43-44. *Concurrent Pos:* Consult, Vet Admin Hosps, 69-79, Surgeon Gen, US Army, 74-80. *Mem:* Am Soc Hosp Pharmacists; Am Pharmaceut Asn; Soc Cosmetic Chem; Am Asn Col Pharm; Sigma Xi; assoc AMA. *Res:* Product formulation; tablets; dermatological medication; cosmetics; pharmaceuticals; hospital pharmacy. *Mailing Add:* 1306 Northwestern Ave West Lafayette IN 47906

SPERANZA, GEORGE PHILLIP, ORGANIC CHEMISTRY, POLYMER CHEMISTRY. *Current Pos:* mgr, 68-82, res fel, 82-90, SR RES FEL, TEXACO CHEM CO, 90- *Personal Data:* b Johnston City, Ill, Aug 27, 24; m 44; c 4. *Educ:* Southern Methodist Univ, BS, 48; Univ Ill-Urbana, MS, 49, PhD(org chem), 51. *Prof Exp:* Res chemist, Jefferson Chem Co, 51-56, supvr, 56-68. *Mem:* Am Chem Soc. *Res:* Synthetic organic chemistry involving petroleum based chemicals; urethane chemistry; exploratory research and supervisory positions. *Mailing Add:* 2800 Silverleaf Circle Austin TX 78757-1605

SPERATI, CARLETON ANGELO, FLUOROPOLYMER SYSTEMS, POLYMER CHEMISTRY & SCIENCE OF TERMINOLOGY. *Current Pos:* CONSULT, 81- *Personal Data:* b Fergus Falls, Minn, Sept 1, 18; m 41, Eloise Morris; c C Robert, William E & Solveig (Kovte). *Educ:* Luther Col, AB, 38; Univ Ill, MA, 39, PhD(org chem), 41. *Honors & Awards:* Frank W Reinhart Award, Am Soc Testing & Mat, 91. *Prof Exp:* Res chemist, Plastics Dept, E I du Pont de Nemours & Co, 41-52, res supvr, Polychem Dept, 52-55, sr res supvr, 55-60, sr res chemist, 60-62, res assoc, 62-69, res fel, Plastics Prod & Resins Dept, 69-79; C Paul Stocker prof eng, Ohio Univ, 79-80. *Concurrent Pos:* C Paul Stocker adj prof chem eng, Ohio Univ; chmn subcomt terminology, Am Soc Testing & Mat, 84-92, chmn sect fluoropolymers, 86-96, mem comt terminology, 86-96; vis prof, interim prog, Luther Col, Decorah, Iowa, 88; mem, US tech adv group, tech comt plastics, Int Orgn Standardization, 86-, Standards for fluoropolymers, 88-, convenor, gen vocabulary, 89-94, chmn US tech adv group, terminology, 89-96. *Mem:* AAAS; Am Chem Soc; Soc Plastics Eng; Am Soc Testing & Mat; Sigma Xi. *Res:* Steric hindrance; stable vinyl alcohols; low reflection coatings; laminating resins; condensation polymers; photochromic systems; computers in polymer studies; synthesis conditions and molecular structure versus properties of fluorocarbon especially polytetrafluoroethylene and other polymers; thermal analysis of polymers; plastics terminology; principles of terminology. *Mailing Add:* 23 Mustang Acres Parkersburg WV 26101-8040. *Fax:* 304-485-2374; *E-Mail:* ptza00099@alpha.wvup.wvnet.edu

SPERBER, DANIEL, PHYSICS. *Current Pos:* assoc prof, 67-72, PROF PHYSICS, RENSSELAER POLYTECH INST, 72- *Personal Data:* b Vienna, Austria, May 8, 30; m 63, Ora; c Ron E. *Educ:* Hebrew Univ, Israel, MSc, 54; Princeton Univ, PhD(physics), 60. *Prof Exp:* Teaching asst physics, Hebrew Univ, Israel, 53-54 & Israel Inst Technol, 54-55; asst, Princeton Univ, 55-60; instr, Ill Inst Technol, 61-62, lectr, 62-64, assoc prof, 64-67. *Concurrent Pos:* From assoc physicist to sr physicist, IIT Res Inst, 60-66, sci adv, 66-67; Nordita prof, Niels Bohr Inst, Univ Copenhagen, 73-75; NATO res fel, Niels Bohr Inst, 76-80; vis prof, GSI Darmstadt, WGer, 83; Fulbright res scholar, Saha Inst Nuclear Physics, Calcutta, India, 87-88. *Mem:* Fel Am Phys Soc; Phys Soc Israel; NY Acad Sci. *Res:* Nuclear structure, reactions and decay modes; physics of fission and heavy ions, nuclear equation of state; atomic spectroscopy; application of group theory to quantum mechanics; heavy ion dynamics, properties of hot nuclear matter and hot nuclei. *Mailing Add:* Dept Physics Rensselaer Polytech Inst Troy NY 12180-3590. *Fax:* 518-276-6680; *E-Mail:* sperbd@rpi.edu

SPERBER, GEOFFREY HILLIARD, ANATOMY, DENTISTRY. *Current Pos:* from asst prof to assoc prof, anat & oral surg, 61-72, prof oral biol, Fac Dent, 72-96, EMER PROF ORAL BIOL, UNIV ALTA, 96- *Personal Data:* b Bloemfontein, SAfrica, Dec 26, 33; Can citizen; m 63, Robyn C Fox; c Heather L (Singer), Jacqueline G (Woolfson) & Steven M. *Educ:* Univ Witwatersrand, BSc, 54, Hons, 58, BDS, 56, PhD, 74; Univ Rochester, MSc, 62. *Hon Degrees:* For Assoc RSSAF, 88. *Prof Exp:* Jr lectr anat, Med Sch, Univ Witwatersrand, 57-58. *Concurrent Pos:* Nat Res Coun Can res grants, 64-66; Nat Res Coun Can sr res fel, Univ Witwatersrand, 69-70; ed, Asn Can Fac Dent Newslett, 72-85; pres, Midwest Sect, Can Asn Dent Res, 84-85; fel, Can Fund Dent Educ, 85; McCalla prof, Univ Alta, 90-91; secy-tres, Cranifacial Biol Group, Int Asn Dent Res, 90-97; sect ed, Cleft Palate-Craniofacial J, 90-; vis prof, Nat Univ Singapore, 97. *Mem:* Can Asn Anatomists; Can Asn Phys Anthrop; Can Dent Asn; Int Asn Dent Res; Int Dent Fedn; Am Asn Anatomists; AAAS; Craniofacial Genetics Soc; Am Cleft Palate Craniofacial Asn; fel Int Col Dentists. *Res:* Dental science; physical anthropology; embryology; skull growth; oral pathology and teratology; comparative odontology; craniofacial development and anomalies. *Mailing Add:* Fac Med & Oral Health Univ Alta Edmonton AB T6G 2N8 Can. *Fax:* 403-492-1624; *E-Mail:* gsperber@gpu.srv.ualberta.ca

SPERBER, STEVEN IRWIN, GEOMETRY. *Current Pos:* mem fac, 80-, PROF MATH, DEPT MATH, UNIV MINN. *Personal Data:* b Brooklyn, NY, May 25, 45; m 73. *Educ:* Brooklyn Col, BA, 66; Univ Pa, MA & PhD(math), 75. *Prof Exp:* Instr math, York Col, City Univ New York, 71-73, adj fac, Lehman Col, 74-75; lectr math, Univ Ill, Urbana, 75-77, asst prof, 77-80. *Mem:* Am Math Soc; Sigma Xi. *Res:* A study of the p-adic cohomology of the generalized hypergeometric functions and the associated Frobenius structure of the deformation equation. *Mailing Add:* Dept Math 127 Vincent Hall Univ Minn 206 Church St SE Minneapolis MN 55455-0488

SPERBER, WILLIAM H, MICROBIOLOGY, FOOD SAFETY. *Current Pos:* SR CORP MICROBIOLOGIST CORP FOOD SAFETY, CARGILL INC, 95- *Personal Data:* b Sturgeon Bay, Wis, Feb 15, 41; m 63; c 2. *Educ:* Univ Wis-Madison, BS, 64, MS, 67, PhD(bact), 69. *Prof Exp:* Chief microbiol sect, Best Foods Res Ctr Div, CPC Int, Inc, 69-72; scientist microbiol sect, Res & Develop Ctr, Pillsbury Co, 72-74, sr scientist, 74-77, res assoc, corp microbio, 77-85, dir, microbiol food safety, 85-95. *Mem:* Am Soc Microbiologists; Soc Appl Bacteriol; Inst Food Technol; Int Asn Milk, Food & Environ Sanitarians. *Res:* Food microbiology, lactics, osmophilics, food poisoning organisms, evolution, philosophy of science; food safety. *Mailing Add:* 5814 Oakview Circle Minnetonka MN 55345

SPERDUTO, ROBERT D, OPHTHALMOLOGY. *Current Pos:* CHIEF, EPIDEMIOL BR, NAT EYE INST, 86- *Personal Data:* b Bound Brook, NJ, Sept 16, 38. *Educ:* Univ Pa, MD, 64. *Prof Exp:* Pvt pract, 70-78. *Mem:* AMA; Am Acad Opthal. *Mailing Add:* Nat Eye Inst Bldg 31 Rm 6A52 31 Center Dr MSC 2510 Bethesda MD 20892. *Fax:* 301-496-2297; *E-Mail:* ros@b31.nei.nih.gov

SPERELAKIS, NICHOLAS, ELECTRO PHYSIOLOGY, MEMBRANE BIOPHYSICS. *Current Pos:* prof & dir, Dept Physiol, 83-93, Joseph Eichberg prof, 83-96, JOSEPH EICHBERG EMER PROF PHYSIOL & BIOPHYS, COL MED, UNIV CINCINNATI, 96- *Personal Data:* b Joliet, Ill, Mar 3, 30; m 60, Dolores Martinis; c Christine, Sophia, Anthony & Thomas. *Educ:* Univ Ill, BS, 54, MS, 55, PhD(physiol), 57. *Honors & Awards:* Res Excellence Award, Am Heart Asn, 95, Sam Kaplan Res Visionary Award, 96. *Prof Exp:* Asst physiol, Univ Ill, 54-57; from instr to assoc prof, Western Res Univ, 57-66; prof physiol, Sch Med, Univ Va, 66-83. *Concurrent Pos:* Estab investr, Am Heart Asn, 66; hon res assoc biophys, Univ Col, Univ London; vis prof, Ctr Advan Studies, Mex, 72 & Univ St Andrews, Scotland, 72-73; assoc ed, Circulation Res J, 70-75; chmn, Steering Comt Cell & Gen Physiol Sect, Am Physiol Soc, 81-82. *Mem:* Am Physiol Soc; Soc Gen Physiologists; Int Soc Heart Res; Cardiac Muscle Soc; Biophys Soc; Am Soc Pharmacol Exp Ther; Inst Elec & Electronics Engrs. *Res:* Electrophysiology of nerve muscle; transmission of excitation in cardiac and smooth muscles; excitation-contraction coupling; active ion transport; membrane properties; mechanism of action of calcium-antagonistic drugs; electrophysiology of cultured heart cells; developmental changes in electrical properties of the heart; electrical properties of myocardial slow channels; regulation of ion channels. *Mailing Add:* 12114 Paulmeadows Dr Cincinnati OH 45249-1330. *Fax:* 513-558-2668; *E-Mail:* sperelen@ucbeh.san.uc.edu

SPERGEL, DAVID NATHANIEL, ASTROPHSYICS, ELEMENTARY PARTICLE PHYSICS. *Current Pos:* ASST PROF ASTRON, PRINCETON UNIV, 87- *Personal Data:* b Rochester, NY, Mar 25, 61. *Educ:* Princeton Univ, AB, 82; Harvard Univ, MA, 84, PhD(astron), 85. *Prof Exp:* Res assoc astron, Harvard Univ, 86. *Concurrent Pos:* Mem staff, Inst Advan Study, 86-88; Sloan fel, Alfred P Sloan Found, 88. *Res:* Stellar dynamics; early universe; cosmic strings; dark matter detection. *Mailing Add:* Princeton Univ Peyton Hall Princeton NJ 08544. *Fax:* 609-258-1020

SPERGEL, MARTIN SAMUEL, ASTROPHYSICS, HIGH ENERGY PHYSICS. *Current Pos:* assoc prof, 67-80, PROF PHYSICS, YORK COL, GRAD SCH & UNIV CTR, CITY UNIV NEW YORK, 80-, CHMN DEPT, 85- *Personal Data:* b New York, NY, Sept 13, 37; m 59; c 3. *Educ:* Rensselaer Polytech Inst, BS, 59; Univ Rochester, MA, 61, PhD(physics), 64. *Prof Exp:* Physicist, Indust Nucleonics Corp, 56 & Xerox Corp, 60; recitation instr basic physics, Univ Rochester, 59-61, res asst elem particles, 61-63; res scientist, Grumman Aircraft Corp, 63-67. *Concurrent Pos:* Adj asst prof, C W Post Col, 65-; vis lectr astron, State Univ NY Stony Brook, 66-67; vis res scientist, Brookhaven Nat Labs, 75-; prin investr, NASA, 78-81. *Mem:* AAAS; Am Phys Soc; Am Geophys Union; Inst Elec & Electronics Eng. *Res:* Planetary physics; interactions of cosmic rays with interplanetary and interstellar matter; molecules in space; radiation environment of solar system; solid state. *Mailing Add:* 300 E 59th St Apt 2106 York Col New York NY 10022

SPERGEL, PHILIP, INSTRUMENTATION, ELECTRICAL ENGINEERING. *Current Pos:* RETIRED. *Personal Data:* b New York, NY, Mar 5, 26; m 48; c 2. *Educ:* City Col New York, BEE, 48; NY Univ, MEE, 51. *Prof Exp:* Proj engr, Sperry Gyroscope Co, 48-54; chief engr, Indust Nucleonics Corp, 54-57 & Epsco, Inc, 57-61; mem staff, Mitre Corp, 61-62; dir eng, Baird Atomic, Inc, 62-67; vpres res & develop, Instrumentation Lab Inc, 67-74, vpres corp qual assurance, 74-88. *Mem:* Am Soc Qual Control; Inst Elec & Electronics Engrs; Asn Advan Med Instrumentation. *Res:* Development of optical, electronic, nuclear, mechanical and chemical instruments to meet specific and general purpose applications. *Mailing Add:* Seven Wainwright Rd No 17 Ledges Winchester MA 01890

SPERLEY, RICHARD JON, ORGANIC CHEMISTRY. *Current Pos:* Res chemist, Res Ctr, Uniroyal Inc, NJ, 66-72, SR RES SCIENTIST, TIRE DIV, UNIROYAL INC, 72- *Personal Data:* b Staples, Minn, May 28, 39. *Educ:* Concordia Col, BA, 61; Univ Minn, Minneapolis, PhD(org chem), 66. *Mem:* Am Chem Soc; Sigma Xi. *Res:* Polymer and elastomer degradation. *Mailing Add:* 9166 NW 43 Ct Coral Springs FL 33065-1766

SPERLING, FREDERICK, TOXICOLOGY, TERATOLOGY. *Current Pos:* RETIRED. *Personal Data:* Jan 16, 13; wid; c Barry L. *Educ:* Univ Chicago, PhD(zool), 52. *Honors & Awards:* Educ Award, Soc Toxicol; Distinguished Scientist Award, Soc Exp Biol & Med. *Prof Exp:* Emer prof pharmacol & toxicol, Col Med, Howard Univ. *Concurrent Pos:* Vis prof pharmacol, Hedassah Med Sch; emer scientist, Soc Exp Biol Med, Wash, DC;

toxicologist, Sperling Lab, Dept Pharm, Howard Univ Col Med. *Mem:* Fel AAAS; Soc Toxicol; Soc Exp Biol Med; Am Soc Pharmacol & Exp Therapeut; Am Soc Zool; Am Chem Soc. *Res:* Toxicology; methodology; teratology. *Mailing Add:* 5902 Mt Eagle Dr No 407 Alexandria VA 22303-2516

SPERLING, GEORGE, VISION, HUMAN INFORMATION PROCESSING. *Current Pos:* DISTINGUISHED PROF COGNITIVE SCI, UNIV CALIF, IRVINE. *Personal Data:* US citizen. *Educ:* Univ Mich, BS(math & biophys), 55; Columbia Univ, MA, 56; Harvard Univ, PhD(psychol), 59. *Honors & Awards:* Distinguished Sci Contrib Award, Am Psychol Asn, 88. *Prof Exp:* Res asst psychol, Harvard Univ, 57-59; vis assoc prof, Dept Psychol, Washington Sq Col, NY Univ, 62-63; adj assoc prof, Dept Psychol, Columbia Univ, 64-65; actg assoc prof, Dept Psychol, Univ Calif, Los Angeles, 67-68; fel, John Simon Guggenheim Mem Found, 69-70; adj prof psychol, Grad Sch Arts & Sci, NY Univ, 70-80, prof, 80-92, dir, Human Info Processing Lab, 80-92. *Concurrent Pos:* Mem tech res staff, Acoust & Behav Res Ctr, AT&T Bell Labs, 59-70; hon res assoc, Dept Psychol, Univ Col, Univ London, 69-70; vis prof, Dept Psychol, Univ Col, Univ London, 69-70; founder & organizer, Ann Interdisciplinary Conf, 75-; mem, Exec Bd, Soc Math Psychol, 79-85, chmn, 83-84; mem, Bd Dirs Eastern Psychol Asn, 82-85; William James fel, Am Psychol Soc; vis scholar, Dept Psychol, Stanford Univ, 84, Res Unit Math Behav Sci, Univ Calif, Irvine, 91. *Mem:* Nat Acad Sci; fel AAAS; Asn Res Vision & Ophthal; fel Am Psychol Asn; Soc Comput in Psychol; fel Optical Soc Am; Am Psychol Soc; Psychonomic Soc; Soc Exp Psychologists; Soc Math Psychol; fel Am Acad Arts & Sci; Int Neural Network Sci. *Res:* Vision and visual perception; mathematical and theoretical psychology; computational vision and computer image processing; human information processing. *Mailing Add:* Dept Cognitive Sci Univ Calif 3151 Social Sce Plaza Irvine CA 92697-5100

SPERLING, HARRY GEORGE, VISION, PSYCHOPHYSICS. *Current Pos:* RETIRED. *Personal Data:* b New York, NY, Aug 26, 24; m 50, Susanna Ehrmann; c Linda & Diane S (Lauderdale). *Educ:* Univ Pa, AB, 44; New Sch Social Res, MSc, 46; Columbia Univ, PhD(psychol), 53. *Honors & Awards:* Merit Award Retina Res, Retina Res Found, 82. *Prof Exp:* Jr instr psychol, Johns Hopkins Univ, 47-48; res psychologist, US Naval Med Res Lab, 48-52, chief, Psychophys Res Sect, 52-58; chief, Colorimetry Sect, 58-59; from sr scientist to mgr manned systs sci, Systs & Res Div, Honeywell Inc, 59-67; prof neurosci & ophthal, Med Sch & dir, Sensory Sci Ctr, Univ Tex Health Sci Ctr, Houston, 67-96, prof neural sci, Grad Sch, 67-96. *Concurrent Pos:* Clin assoc prof, Univ Minn, 61-67; mem, Armed Forces-Nat Res Coun Comt Vision & chmn working group laser-eye effects, 66-70; adj prof, Baylor Col Med, 67- & Rice Univ, 72-; mem, Nat Adv Eye Coun, NIH, 75-79; dir, Prevent Blindness, Houston Chap, 90- *Mem:* Assoc Res Vision & Ophthal; fel Optical Soc Am; Psychonom Soc; Soc Neurosci; Int Res Group Color Vision Deficiencies. *Res:* Psychophysical, electrophysiological and anatomical studies of color and brightness vision; intense light effects on retina. *Mailing Add:* 6431 Fannin Houston TX 77030. *Fax:* 713-792-5413; *E-Mail:* hsperlin@gsbs.gs.uth.tmc.edu

SPERLING, JACOB L, PLASMA PHYSICS, MICROWAVE & RADIO FREQUENCY COMMUNICATIONS & RADAR. *Current Pos:* staff scientist, Jaycor, 78-80, sr scientist, 80-83, prin scientist energy, 83-88, DIV MGR SYSTS SURVIVABILITY GROUP, JAYCOR, 88- *Personal Data:* b Linz, Austria, Jan 3, 49; US citizen; m 78; c 2. *Educ:* Columbia Univ, BS, 71; Princeton Univ, MA, 73, PhD(plasma physics), 75. *Prof Exp:* Sr scientist plasma physics, Gen Atomic Co, 75-78. *Mem:* Am Phys Soc. *Res:* Theoretical and applied plasma physics; health physics aspects of radioactivity; coal physics; microwave and radio frequency communication; radar propagation; satellite operability; systems engineering. *Mailing Add:* 4933 Concannon Ct San Diego CA 92130-2723

SPERLING, LESLIE HOWARD, POLYMER SCIENCE & ENGINEERING. *Current Pos:* from asst prof to assoc prof, 67-77, PROF, DEPT CHEM ENG & MAT RES CTR, LEHIGH UNIV, 77-, PROF, MAT SCI ENG DEPT, 89- *Personal Data:* b Yonkers, NY, Feb 19, 32; m 57, Caroline Neill; c Reisa & Sheri. *Educ:* Univ Fla, BS, 54; Duke Univ, MA, 57, PhD, 58. *Prof Exp:* Res chemist, Buckeye Cellulose Corp, Procter & Gamble Co, 58-65; res assoc phys chem, Princeton Univ, 65-67. *Concurrent Pos:* Mem, Ctr Polymer Sci Eng, Lehigh Univ, Polymer Interfaces Ctr. *Mem:* Am Chem Soc; Am Inst Chem Engrs; Soc Plastics Eng. *Res:* Physical and mechanical properties of polymers; polymer blends, particularly interpenetrating polymer networks; triglyceride oil-based interpenetrating polymer networks; noise damping polymer systems; small-angle neutron scattering from polymer latexes; author; molecular basis of fracture in polymers. *Mailing Add:* Whitaker No 5 Lehigh Univ Bethlehem PA 18015. *Fax:* 610-758-4244; *E-Mail:* lhs0.lehigh.edu

SPERLING, MARK ALEXANDER, ENDOCRINOLOGY, DIABETES. *Current Pos:* PEDIAT-IN-CHIEF, CHILDREN'S HOSP PITTSBURGH, 89-; CHAIR, DEPT PEDIAT, SCH MED, UNIV PITTSBURGH, 89- *Personal Data:* b Lodz, Poland, Sept 6, 38; US citizen; m 66, Vera R Schreiber; c Lisa Nicole & Jonathan Michael. *Educ:* Univ Melbourne, MB & BS, 62; Am Bd Pediat, dipl, 70. *Prof Exp:* Prof pediat & dir, Div Endocrin & Diabetes, Col Med, Children's Hosp Med Ctr, 78-89; chmn, Dept Pediat, Sch Med, Univ Pittsburgh, 89- *Concurrent Pos:* Intern, resident & sr resident pediat, Royal Children's Hosp, Australia, 63-68; fel, Pediat Endocrin & Metabolism, Children's Hosp, Pittsburgh, 68-70; asst prof Pediat, Univ Calif Los Angeles, Harbor Gen Hosp Campus, 70-75, assoc prof pediat & chief, Div Pediat Endocrin, 75-78; res career develop award, NIH, 75-80; mem, Comt Sci Prog, Endocrine Soc, 84-87, Maternal & Child Health Res Comt, Nat Inst Child Health, 84-89; vchmn, Clin Res Children's Med Ctr, Cincinnati, 87-89. *Mem:* Am Soc Clin Invest; Endocrine Soc; Am Diabetes Asn; Soc Pediat Res; Am Pediat Soc; Am Fedn Clin Res. *Res:* Hormonal control of carbohydrate metabolism; perinatal glucose homeostasis; insulin and glucagon receptors; endocrinology of hypertension; endocrinology of growth and development; numerous publications including 120 original papers, approximately 40 book chapters, editor and co-editor 3 books and approximately 150 published abstracts. *Mailing Add:* Dept Pediat Children's Hosp Pittsburgh 3705 Fifth Ave at Desoto St Pittsburgh PA 15213-2583. *Fax:* 412-692-5946; *E-Mail:* wasp@med.pill.edu

SPERO, CAESAR A(NTHONY), JR, MECHANICAL & SYSTEMS ENGINEERING. *Current Pos:* RETIRED. *Personal Data:* b Newport, RI, Oct 3, 21. *Educ:* Mass Inst Technol, BS, 44; Univ Northern Colo, MS, 77. *Prof Exp:* Proj engr equip design, Owens-Corning Fiberglass Corp, 46-50, eng mgr, 50-52; staff sci asst, Naval Underwater Ord Sta, 52-55, head, Eng Dept, 55-60, head, Testing & Eval Dept, 60-61, head, Develop Dept, 61-64, head, Shipborne Equip Dept, 64-65, assoc dir, Systs Develop, 65-71, chief, Res & Develop, Newport Lab, 71, assoc dir, Weapons, 71-72, dir, Systs Develop, 72-76, assoc tech dir, Prod Lines, 76-78, dep tech dir, Naval Underwater Syts Ctr, 78-80; vpres, OSD Gould Inc, 80-86. *Concurrent Pos:* Consult. *Mem:* Math Asn Am. *Res:* Complex system development from conceptual stage through actual manufacture, installation and operational testing. *Mailing Add:* 325 Mail Coach Rd Portsmouth RI 02871

SPERO, LEONARD, BIOCHEMISTRY. *Current Pos:* CONSULT, 81- *Personal Data:* b New York, NY, May 30, 21; m 43, Charlotte Cohen; c Ellen, Deborah, Abby & Sally. *Educ:* City Col New York, BS, 41; Univ Wis, MS, 43, PhD(biochem), 48. *Prof Exp:* Asst, Univ Wis, 42-44 & 46-48; biochemist, US Army Med Res Inst Infectious Dis, 48-63, chief, Chem Br, 63-71, biochemist, Path Div, 71-75, asst chief, Path Div, 75-81. *Concurrent Pos:* Secy Army res & study fel, 60; lectr, Georgetown Univ, 65. *Mem:* Am Soc Biochem & Molecular Biol. *Res:* Protein chemistry; isolation and purification; reactive groups; immunochemistry; bacterial toxins. *Mailing Add:* 635 Schley Ave Frederick MD 21702-4157

SPERONELLO, BARRY KEVEN, HETEROGENEOUS CATALYSIS, MATERIALS SCIENCE. *Current Pos:* Res & proj leader, 76-81, RES GROUP LEADER, ENGELHARD CORP, 81- *Personal Data:* b Passaic, NJ, July, 29, 50; m 75. *Educ:* Rutgers Univ, BS, 72, MS, 75, PhD(ceramic eng), 76. *Mem:* Am Ceramic Soc; NAm Catalysis Soc. *Res:* Synthesis and properties of oxide materials; physical and catalytic properties of oxide catalysts. *Mailing Add:* 15 Carriage Trail Belle Mead NJ 08502

SPERRY, CLAUDE J, JR, ELECTRICAL ENGINEERING. *Current Pos:* From instr to assoc prof, 48-65, PROF ELEC ENG, TULANE UNIV, 65-, RES ASSOC PHYSIOL, 51- *Personal Data:* b Greenwood, SC, Aug 8, 25; m 48; c 1. *Educ:* Clemson Col, BEE, 48; Univ Ill, MS, 54. *Mem:* Inst Elec & Electronics Engrs; Sigma Xi. *Res:* Electricity in medical research, especially remote recording of subcortical potentials. *Mailing Add:* 33 Stilt St New Orleans LA 70124

SPERRY, THEODORE MELROSE, botany, ecology; deceased, see previous edition for last biography

SPERRY, WILLARD CHARLES, NUCLEAR STRUCTURE, GENERAL PHYSICS. *Current Pos:* from asst prof to assoc prof, 66-79, PROF PHYSICS, CENT WASH UNIV, 79-, CHAIR, DEPT PHYSICS, 93- *Personal Data:* b Dunsmuir, Calif, Nov 29, 31; m 66; c 2. *Educ:* Stanford Univ, BS, 54; Univ Calif, Davis, MA, 67, PhD(physics), 68. *Prof Exp:* Physicist, Aerojet-Gen Corp, 56-60. *Res:* Nuclear structure by means of mesic atoms; improvement of undergraduate physics laboratories. *Mailing Add:* 1006 N Water St Ellensburg WA 98926. *E-Mail:* sperryw@cwu.edu

SPESSARD, DWIGHT RINEHART, ORGANIC CHEMISTRY. *Current Pos:* from asst prof to assoc prof, 53-60, chmn dept, 58-61, PROF CHEM, DENISON UNIV, 60-, WICKENDEN CHAIR, 66- *Personal Data:* b Westerville, Ohio, July 6, 19; m 43; c 2. *Educ:* Otterbein Col, BS, 41; Western Reserve Univ, PhD(inorg & org chem), 44. *Prof Exp:* Group leader, Lubrication Sect, Chem Div, Naval Res Lab, 44-47; res assoc chem, Gen Elec Res Lab, 47-49; from asst prof to assoc prof, Muskingum Col, 49-53. *Mem:* Am Chem Soc. *Res:* Organophosphorus, organosilicon and organofluorine chemistry. *Mailing Add:* 228 Granview Rd Granville OH 43023-1248

SPESSARD, GARY OLIVER, SYNTHETIC ORGANIC CHEMISTRY. *Current Pos:* from asst prof to assoc prof, 73-86, PROF CHEM, ST OLAF COL, 86- *Personal Data:* b Orange, Calif, Sept 27, 44; m 68, Carol A Hagen; c Sarah. *Educ:* Harvey Mudd Col, BS, 66; Univ Wis-Madison, MS, 68; Wesleyan Univ, PhD(org chem), 71. *Prof Exp:* Fel org chem, Univ Alta, 70-72; vis res assoc, Ohio State Univ, 72-73. *Concurrent Pos:* vis asst prof chem, Univ Wis-Madison, 76, vis prof, 92; vis assoc prof chem, Univ Utah, 79-80; vis prof chem, Ore State Univ, 86-87. *Mem:* Am Chem Soc; Coun Undergrad Res. *Res:* Synthetic organic chemistry of small ring compounds; synthetic organic and natural products chemistry; chemistry of phytoalexins. *Mailing Add:* Dept Chem St Olaf Col 1520 St Olaf Ave Northfield MN 55057-1098. *Fax:* 507-646-3968; *E-Mail:* spessard@stolaf.edu

SPETNAGEL, THEODORE JOHN, ENVIRONMENTAL SCIENCES, COMPUTER SCIENCES. *Current Pos:* civil engr, Hq Ft McPherson, 78-79, Hq US Army Forces Command, 79-84, dep engr, Hq Second US Army, 84-91, chief, Environ Br, 91-96, CHIEF, INSTALLATION DIV, HQ US

ARMY RES COMMAND, 96- *Personal Data:* b Chillicothe, Ohio, May 26, 48; m 70; c 2. *Educ:* Clemson Univ, BS, 70; Ga Inst Technol, MS, 72. *Prof Exp:* Struct engr, Appalachian Consult Engrs, 67-70; res asst, Ga Inst Technol, 70-71; struct engr, Atlantic Bldg Systs, Inc, 71-78. *Mem:* Am Soc Civil Engrs; Nat Soc Prof Engrs; Soc Am Mil Engrs. *Res:* Structural engineering. *Mailing Add:* 2111 Jarrod Pl SE Smyrna GA 30080

SPEVACK, JEROME, CHEMICAL ENGINEERING. *Current Pos:* PRES, DEUTERIUM CORP, 60- *Personal Data:* b New York City, NY, Aug 21, 18. *Res:* Chemical engineering. *Mailing Add:* 160 W Pinebrook Dr New Rochelle NY 10804-4521

SPEYER, JASON L, GUIDANCE CONTROL AEROSPACE. *Current Pos:* PROF, SYST THEORY & GUID CONTROL AEROSPACE, UNIV TEX-AUSTIN, 76- *Personal Data:* b Boston, Mass, Apr 30, 38. *Educ:* Mass Inst Technol, BS, 60, MS, 65; Harvard Univ, PhD(appl math), 68. *Prof Exp:* Res engr, Child Stock Draper Lab, Cambridge, Mass, 70-76. *Mem:* Fel Am Inst Aeronaut & Astronaut; fel Inst Elec & Electronics Engrs. *Res:* Deterministic and stochastic optimum control theory. *Mailing Add:* 11358 Chalon Rd Los Angeles CA 90049-1721

SPHAR, RAYMOND LESLIE, RESEARCH ADMINISTRATION. *Current Pos:* dir, Med Res Serv, 91-92, DEP ASSOC CHIEF MED DIR RES & DEVELOP, DEPT VET AFFAIRS, 92- *Personal Data:* b Charleroi, Pa, July 27, 34; div; c Christina L. *Educ:* Westminister Col, Pa, BS, 56; Jefferson Med Col, MD, 61; Yale Univ, MPH, 72. *Prof Exp:* Commanding officer, Naval Submarine Med Res Lab, US Navy, 73-78, dir, Submarine & Radiation Med, 78-81, commanding officer, Navy Med Res & Develop Command, 81-83, commanding officer, Naval Med Res Inst, 83-86, mil asst life scis, Off Secy Defense, 86-89, dir res & develop, Bur Med Surg, 89-90. *Concurrent Pos:* US rep, NATO Panel VIII, 86-89; Dept Defense rep, NIH Res Resource Coun, 86-89; Dept Vet Affairs rep, NIH Nat Cancer Adv Bd, 91- *Mem:* Am Col Prev Med; Col Occup & Environ Med. *Res:* Epidemiological research on submarine crews; medical research administration. *Mailing Add:* 2475 Virginia Ave NW Washington DC 20037-2639. *Fax:* 202-535-7159

SPHON, JAMES AMBROSE, MASS SPECTROMETRY. *Current Pos:* Chemist, 65-67, res chemist, 67-75, SUPVY CHEMIST, MASS SPECTROMETRY LAB, FOOD & DRUG ADMIN, 75- *Personal Data:* b Luxor, Pa, Nov 4, 39; m 67; c 3. *Educ:* St Vincent Col, BS, 66; Wayne State Univ, PhD(org chem), 77. *Mem:* Am Chem Soc; Am Soc Mass Spectrometry. *Res:* Application of mass spectrometry to structure elucidation and method development for components of foods: pesticides, mycotoxins, direct & indirect food additives and veterinary drugs. *Mailing Add:* 9900 Worrell Ave Glenn Dale MD 20769-9260

SPIALTER, LEONARD, ORGANIC CHEMISTRY, COMPUTER SYSTEMS. *Current Pos:* DIR, INSTRUMENTORS I-V, 75- *Personal Data:* b Newark, NJ, Jan 18, 23; m 46; c 2. *Educ:* Rutgers Univ, BS, 44, PhD(chem), 49; Polytech Inst Brooklyn, MS, 48. *Prof Exp:* Res chemist, Montclair Res Corp, NJ, 44-47; instr org chem, Univ Col, Rutgers Univ, 48-49; fel free radicals, Harvard Univ, 49-51; from res chemist to sr scientist & head org sect, Chem Res Lab, Aerospace Res Labs, Wright-Patterson AFB, 51-75. *Mem:* AAAS; Am Chem Soc; Am Inst Chemists; The Chem Soc; Electrochem Soc; Sigma Xi. *Res:* Organosilanes; amines; molecular rearrangements; free radicals; laboratory automation; information storage-retrieval; computer-based nomenclature; liquid fuel/byproducts from agricultural residues; computer-based information systems; computer-aided manufacturing. *Mailing Add:* 2536 England Ave Dayton OH 45406-1324

SPICER, CLIFFORD W, METALLURGY. *Current Pos:* RETIRED. *Personal Data:* b LaGrange, Ohio, Mar 9, 19. *Educ:* Univ Cincinnati, BS, 42. *Prof Exp:* Metallurgist, Eastern Steel Div, US Steel Corp, 42-83. *Mem:* Fel Am Soc Metals Int; Am Inst Mining Metall & Petrol Engrs. *Mailing Add:* 99 Birdsong Way Hilton Head Island SC 29926

SPICER, DONALD Z, MATHEMATICS, COMPUTER SCIENCE. *Current Pos:* ASST PROVOST UNIV COMPUT & PROF MATH, UNIV NOTRE DAME, 88- *Personal Data:* b St Paul, Minn, Mar 15, 37; m 68, Sue Maggard; c Gwen, Amy & Greer. *Educ:* Univ Minn, BA, 59, PhD(math), 65; Columbia Univ, MA, 60; dipl, Cambridge Univ, 84. *Prof Exp:* From actg asst prof to asst prof math, Univ Calif, Los Angeles, 65-67; asst prof, Univ Ky, 67-70; from asst prof to assoc prof math, Vassar Col, 70-86, assoc dean col, 80-83; dir acad comput & adj prof, Dartmouth Col, 85-88. *Concurrent Pos:* Proj dir, Fund Improvement Postsecondary Educ, HEW; vis lectr, Univ Kent, Canterbury, Eng, 84-85. *Mem:* Am Math Soc; Math Asn Am; Asn Comput Mach. *Res:* Computer algebra. *Mailing Add:* 315 W North Shore Dr South Bend IN 46617. *E-Mail:* spicer.1@nd.edu

SPICER, LEONARD DALE, PHYSICAL BIOCHEMISTRY, BIOMACROMOLECULAR STRUCTURE. *Current Pos:* PROF BIOCHEM & RADIOL, DUKE UNIV, 83-, DIR DUKE NUCLEAR MAGNETIC RESONANCE CTR, 86-, DISTINGUISHED SERV PROF, 93- *Personal Data:* b Detroit, Mich, July 7, 42; m 68, Marianna Martin; c Sean & Brian. *Educ:* Univ Mich, BSCh, 64; Yale Univ, PhD(phys chem), 68. *Prof Exp:* Assoc chem kinetics, Univ Wash, 68-69; from asst prof to prof phys chem, Univ Utah, 69-83, assoc dean, Grad Sch, 80-83. *Concurrent Pos:* Dreyfus Found fel, 71-77; NIH Reviewers Res, 92-; NSF, Biol Scis IID Adv Panel. *Mem:* Fel AAAS; Am Chem Soc; Am Phys Soc; Fedn Am Socs Exp Biol; Soc Nuclear Med; Protein Soc; Soc Magnetic Resonance Med. *Res:* Biophysical nuclear magnetic resonance; protein structure and function; hot atom chemistry; high energy and thermal kinetics; photoassisted catalysis; intermolecular vibrational energy transfer; atmospheric chemistry; nuclear medicine with positron tomography. *Mailing Add:* Dept Biochem Duke Univ Med Ctr Box 3711 Durham NC 27710. *Fax:* 919-684-8885; *E-Mail:* spicer@frodo.biochem.duke.edu

SPICER, SAMUEL SHERMAN, JR, EXPERIMENTAL PATHOLOGY, HISTOCHEMISTRY & CELL BIOLOGY. *Current Pos:* PROF PATH, MED UNIV SC, 66- *Personal Data:* b Denver, Colo, Aug 12, 14; m 41, Gertrude E McRae; c Kenneth, Eleanor & Samuel Jr. *Educ:* Univ Colo, BS, 36, MD, 39. *Hon Degrees:* MD, Univ Linkoping, Sweden. *Honors & Awards:* Gomori Found Medal, Histochem Soc; Pioneer in Histochem Award, Eighth Int Congress Histochem & Cytochem; Glick Lectr, Ninth Int Cong Histochem & Cytochem, Maastricht. *Prof Exp:* Intern, Univ Hosp, Univ Wis, 39-40; from asst surgeon to med dir, Nutrit Lab, Lab Phys Biol & Lab Exp Path, NIH, 40-55, chief, Sect Biophys Histol, 61-66. *Mem:* Hon mem Histochem Soc; Am Soc Cell Biol; Am Soc Exp Path. *Res:* Nutrition; folic acid deficiency; malariology; industrial toxicology; biochemistry of erythrocytes; muscle protein chemistry; chemistry of glycoconjugates, basic proteins and enzymes; experimental pathology of genetic diseases (cystic fibrosis); cytology and cytochemistry of developing, adult and senescent inner ear; epithelial ion transport; histology and histochemistry of developing and adult lung. *Mailing Add:* Dept Path 171 Ashley Ave Charleston SC 29425-2645

SPICER, WILLIAM EDWARD, SOLID STATE PHYSICS. *Current Pos:* from assoc prof to prof elec eng, 62-78, dep dir, Stanford Synchrotron Radiation Proj, 73-75, PROF ELEC ENG & MAT SCI, STANFORD UNIV, 72-, CONSULT DIR, STANFORD SYNCHROTRON RADIATION LAB, 75-, STANFORD W ASCHERMAN PROF ENG, 78- *Personal Data:* b Baton Rouge, La, Sept 7, 29; m 51; c 3. *Educ:* Col William & Mary, BS, 49; Mass Inst Technol, SB, 51; Univ Mo, MS, 53, PhD(physics), 55. *Hon Degrees:* Dr Technol, Univ Linkoping, Sweden, 75. *Honors & Awards:* Oliver E Buckley Solid State Physics Prize, Am Phys Soc, 80; Medard W Welch Award, Am Vacuum Soc, 84. *Prof Exp:* Res physicist, RCA Labs, 55-62. *Concurrent Pos:* Consult, Varian Assocs; Japan Soc Prom Sci fel, 72; mem adv group electron devices, Dept Defense, 73; Guggenheim fel, 78-79; overseas fel, Churchill Col, Cambridge Univ, 79 & 84; vis prof, Fudan Univ, Shanghai, 83; ed, J Crystal Growth. *Mem:* AAAS; fel Am Phys Soc; fel Inst Elec & Electronics Engrs; Sigma Xi; fel Am Vacuum Soc. *Res:* Electronic structure and optical properties of solids and surfaces; photoelectric emission; semiconductors; alloys; amorphous solids; surface and interface states; surface science and catalysis. *Mailing Add:* Stanford Electronics Lab Stanford Univ McCullough Bldg Rm 228 Stanford CA 94305. *Fax:* 650-723-4659

SPICHER, JOHN L, MEDICAL TECHNOLOGY. *Current Pos:* SR ENGR HUMAN SCI, WESTINGHOUSE RES & DEVELOP, WESTINGHOUSE ELEC CORP, 68- *Personal Data:* b Belleville, Pa, Sept 12, 35; m 59; c 3. *Educ:* Eastern Mennonite Col, BS, 58; Geisinger Med Ctr, MT, 64. *Prof Exp:* Res asst endocrinol, Med Col Va, 60; res asst chromatog, Geisinger Med Ctr, 62-64, asst instr med technol, 64-66; res asst path, Sch Med, Univ Pittsburgh, 66-68. *Mem:* Am Asn Clin Chemists; Am Soc Clin Pathologists. *Res:* Development of planning methods for health care systems which relate to consumer need, demands and available resources. *Mailing Add:* RR 8 PO Box 208 A Irwin PA 15642

SPICHER, ROBERT G, SANITARY & ENVIRONMENTAL ENGINEERING. *Current Pos:* assoc dean grad studies, 79-80, PROF SANIT & CIVIL ENG, SAN JOSE STATE UNIV, 65- *Personal Data:* b Pittsburgh, Pa, Apr 24, 35; m 59, 81; c 2. *Educ:* Cornell Univ, BCE, 58; Univ Calif, Berkeley, MS, 59; Wash Univ, St Louis, ScD(environ & sanit eng), 63. *Honors & Awards:* Lincoln Arc Welding Struct Nat Grand Award, 58. *Prof Exp:* Prod engr, Shell Oil Co, Calif, 59-60; asst prof sanit & civil eng, Univ Miami, 63-65. *Mem:* Am Soc Civil Engrs; Am Water Works Asn; Water Pollution Control Fedn. *Res:* Environmental engineering; cannery waste treatment; sanitary engineering aspects of shelters; treatment of photographic wastes; sanitary landfill stabilization; radioactive contamination of water; fuel gas production from biomass. *Mailing Add:* 1524 Norman Ave San Jose CA 95125

SPICKERMAN, WILLIAM REED, APPLIED MATHEMATICS. *Current Pos:* assoc prof, 67-72, PROF MATH, EAST CAROLINA UNIV, 72- *Personal Data:* b Council Bluffs, Iowa, Dec 28, 25; m 57. *Educ:* Univ Omaha, BA, 49, MS, 53; Xavier Univ, MS, 58; Univ Ky, PhD(curriculum), 65. *Prof Exp:* Teacher high sch, Iowa, 49-50; engr aid, Omaha Dist, Mo River Div, Corps of Engr, 51-52; teacher high sch, Iowa, 52-56; tech engr, Jet Engine Dept, Gen Elec Co, Ohio, 56-57; teacher high sch, Ohio, 57-58; engr, Avco Corp, 58-61; specialist-engr, Goodyear Aircraft Corp, 61-62; sr scientist, Spindletop Res Inc, Ky, 65-67. *Mem:* Am Math Soc; Math Asn Am; Soc Indust & Appl Math; assoc Opers Res Soc Am; Sigma Xi; Nat Coun Teachers Math. *Res:* Mathematics education; recursive sequences. *Mailing Add:* Dept Math East Carolina Univ Greenville NC 27834

SPICZAK, GLENN MICHAEL, COSMIC RAYS, ASTROPARTICLE PHYSICS. *Current Pos:* POSTDOCTORAL FEL, BARTOL RES INST, 96- *Personal Data:* b Columbus, Ind, Apr 15, 64; m 96, Heather D Martin. *Educ:* Ind Univ, BS, 86, MA, 91, PhD(astrophys), 95. *Mem:* Am Astron Soc; Astron Soc Pac; Am Phys Soc. *Res:* Design, construction and analysis of high energy astro-particle physics experiments. *Mailing Add:* 936 Rue Madora Bear DE 19701. *Fax:* 302-831-1843; *E-Mail:* spiczak@bartol.udel.edu

SPIEGEL, ALLEN DAVID, PUBLIC HEALTH, COMMUNICATIONS. *Current Pos:* PROF PREV MED & COMMUNITY HEALTH, STATE UNIV NY HEALTH SCI CTR, COL MED, 69- *Personal Data:* b New York, NY, June 11, 27; m 55, Lila Rosenberg; c Merrill, Marc & Andrea. *Educ:* Brooklyn Col, AB, 47; Columbia Univ, MPH, 54; Brandeis Univ, PhD(social welfare), 69. *Prof Exp:* Health educr to chief, Radio & TV Unit, New York City Health Dept, 51-61; health educ assoc, Med Found, Inc, 61-66. *Concurrent Pos:* WHO fel, Israel Med Schs, 74; consult to comnr, Social & Rehab Serv, HEW, 70; commun consult, Health Info Syts, Inc, 70-71; curriculum consult, Grad Prog Health Care Admin, Baruch Col, 70-; health manpower consult, NJ Regional Med Prog, 72; adj prof, St Francis Col, 74-76; fac, Staff Col, NIMH, 79; consult, Cancer Proj, Urban Health Inst, 79 & Home Care Proj, Temple Univ, 81, Vet Admin Med Ctr, Booklyn Home Care, 83, Long Term Care Greater Dept Med Record Asn, 84, Clin Prev, Robert Wood Johnson Med Sch, Piscataway, NJ, 87, Home Health Care Tele Med, Inc, 88, High Tech Home Care, Case Western Res Med Sch, 88, Patient Educ, Hutchinson, Black, Mill & Cook, 90, Med Data Source, Inc, 91-92; Risk Mgt Epidemiol, Inst Med Law, Inc, 95-96 & Outsourcing, United Univ, Prof, 96-97. *Mem:* Am Pub Health Asn; Health Educ Media Asn; Am Social Asn; Am Teachers Prev Med; Soc Pub Health Educators. *Res:* Medical sociology; medical communications; public health education; patient education; curriculum development; mass media health program; health care administration. *Mailing Add:* Dept Prev Med & Community Health State Univ NY Health Sci Ctr Col Med 450 Clarkson Ave Box 43 Brooklyn NY 11203. *Fax:* 718-270-2533

SPIEGEL, ALLEN J, PHARMACY, PHARMACEUTICAL CHEMISTRY. *Current Pos:* Res assoc, Pharmaceut Res & Develop Dept, Chas Pfizer & Co, Inc, 57-66, mgr res coordr, New Prod Dept, Pfizer Int, 66-69, patent agt, Legal Div, 69-76, mgr foreign patents, 76-81, asst dir, 81-86, DIR FOREIGN PATENTS, PFIZER INC, 86- *Personal Data:* b New York, NY, Sept 17, 32. *Educ:* Columbia Univ, BS, 53, MS, 55; Univ Fla, PhD(pharm), 57. *Mem:* Am Pharmaceut Asn; Am Chem Soc; NY Acad Sci. *Res:* Pharmaceutical product development; research administration; patent law. *Mailing Add:* Legal Div Pfizer Inc 235 E 42nd St New York NY 10017

SPIEGEL, ALLEN M, PATHOPHYSIOLOGY. *Current Pos:* CHIEF, MOLECULAR PATHOPHYSIOL BR, NAT INST DIABETES DIGESTIVE & KIDNEY DIS, NIH, 86- *Mailing Add:* NIH Nat Inst Diabetes Digestive & Kidney Dis 7908 Radnor Rd Bethesda MD 20817-6286. *Fax:* 301-496-9943; *E-Mail:* Bitnet: aso@nihcu

SPIEGEL, EDWARD A, ASTROPHYSICS, APPLIED MATHS. *Current Pos:* prof astron, 69-80, RUTHERFORD PROF ASTRON, COLUMBIA UNIV, 80- *Personal Data:* b New York, NY, Mar 7, 31. *Educ:* Univ Calif, Los Angeles, BA, 52; Univ Mich, MS, 54, MA, 56, PhD(astron), 58. *Prof Exp:* From instr to asst prof astron, Univ Calif, 58-60; res scientist, Inst Math Sci, NY Univ, 60-65; from assoc prof to prof physics, 65-69. *Concurrent Pos:* Peyton advan fel, Princeton Univ, 59-60; assoc, Woods Hole Oceanog Inst, 59-; consult, Goddard Inst Space Studies, NASA, 60-69 & Int Coun Asn Sci Educ; NSF sr fel, 66-67. *Mem:* Int Astron Union; NY Acad Sci; Royal Astron Soc. *Res:* Astrophysical fluid dynamics; chaos. *Mailing Add:* Dept Astron Columbia Univ New York NY 10027

SPIEGEL, EUGENE, MATHEMATICS. *Current Pos:* from asst prof to assoc prof, 67-78, dept head, 81-84, PROF MATH, UNIV CONN, 78- *Personal Data:* b Brooklyn, NY, Sept 16, 41; m 68; c 3. *Educ:* Brooklyn Col, BS, 61; Mass Inst Technol, PhD(math), 65. *Prof Exp:* Instr math, Mass Inst Technol, 64-65; Bateman res fel, Calif Inst Technol, 65-66, instr, 66-67. *Concurrent Pos:* Vis prof, Ecole Polytechnique Federal, Lausanne, 73, Weizmann Inst, Rehovot, 81. *Mem:* Am Math Soc. *Res:* Algebra; combinatorics. *Mailing Add:* Dept Math Univ Conn Storrs CT 06269-0001

SPIEGEL, EVELYN SCLUFER, DEVELOPMENTAL BIOLOGY. *Current Pos:* res assoc prof, 62-78, res prof, 78-92, EMER RES PROF BIOL, DARTMOUTH COL, 92- *Personal Data:* b Philadelphia, Pa, Mar 20, 24; m 55, Melvin; c Judith E & Rebecca A. *Educ:* Temple Univ, BA, 47; Bryn Mawr Col, MA, 51; Univ Pa, PhD(zool), 54. *Prof Exp:* Asst prog dir regulatory biol, NSF, 54-55; instr, Colby Col, 55-59. *Concurrent Pos:* Lalor fel, Univ Pa, 52-53; Am Cancer Soc fel, 61-62; vis res assoc, Calif Inst Technol, 64-65; vis assoc res biologist, Univ Calif, San Diego, 70-71; vis res scientist, Nat Inst Med Res, Eng, 71; NIH guest investr, 75-76; mem, Corp Marine Biol Lab, 75-, bd trustees, 81-85, 88-92; vis prof, Bioctr, Univ Basel, 79-82, 85. *Mem:* Soc Develop Biol. *Res:* Ultrastructural and immunocytochemical studies of cell adhesion; extracellular matrix and microvilli. *Mailing Add:* Dept Biol Sci Dartmouth Col Hanover NH 03755

SPIEGEL, HERBERT ELI, BIOCHEMISTRY, CLINICAL CHEMISTRY. *Current Pos:* CHIEF CLIN CHEM, ST VINCENT'S HOSP & MED CTR, 89- *Personal Data:* b New York, NY, July 7, 33; m 58; c Girard, Michael, Lawrence, Richard, Paul & James. *Educ:* Brooklyn Col, BS, 56; George Wash Univ, MS, 61; Rutgers Univ, New Brunswick, PhD(biochem, physiol), 66, Fairleigh Dickinson Univ, MBA, 81. *Honors & Awards:* Am Asn Clin Chemists Awards, 72 & 77. *Prof Exp:* Sr asst health officer biochem pharmacol, NIH, 57-62; sr biochemist, Schering Corp, 62-64; clin chemist, Mountainside Hosp, 64-67; chief clin chemist, Hoffmann-La Roche Inc, 67-72, dir, Dept Clin Biochem, 72-80, dir, Dept Clin Lab Res, 80-85; chief sci off, Quadretek Assocs, 85-87; dir, BurChem, Hearst Corp, 87-89. *Concurrent Pos:* Mem comn toxicol, Int Union Pure & Appl Chem, 74-; spec adv majority state senate NJ, 83-, cong comt sci & technol, 87; chmn, NJ State Comn Cancer Res, 83-86, vchmn, 86-, mem comn sci & technol, 85-; mem panel kits & devices, Food & Drug Admin, 89-; assoc prof clin path, NY Med Col. *Mem:* Am Chem Soc; fel Am Asn Clin Chemists; fel Am Inst Chemists; fel Nat Acad Clin Biochemists (pres, 81-); Soc Toxicol. *Res:* Biochemical pharmacology, especially catecholamines; clinical chemistry methods, especially fluorimetry and radioactivity; drug effects on clinical chemistry. *Mailing Add:* 39 Greendale Rd Cedar Grove NJ 07009-1312. *Fax:* 973-857-0062

SPIEGEL, LEONARD EMILE, ECOLOGY. *Current Pos:* prof, 63-89, chmn dept, 74-81, EMER PROF BIOL, MONMOUTH COL, NJ, 89- *Personal Data:* b New York, NY, Sept 12, 24; m 50; c 5. *Educ:* Drew Univ, AB, 48; Northwestern Univ, MS, 50; Cornell Univ, PhD(wildlife mgt), 54. *Prof Exp:* Asst wildlife mgt, State Dept Conserv, NY & Cornell Univ, 51-53; game mgt supvr, Div Wildlife, Ohio Dept Natural Resources, 53-55; instr biol, Alpena Community Col, 55-57; from asst prof to assoc prof, Cent Mich Univ, 57-63; asst prof, Cornell Univ, 63. *Concurrent Pos:* Environ consult, 67-; mem, NJ State Mosquito Control Comn, 76-; admin asst, NJ Sea Grant, 83-, assoc dir, 88-89. *Mem:* Wildlife Soc; Am Inst Biol Sci; Sigma Xi; Am Mosquito Control Asn. *Res:* Ecology of game animals; plant ecology; plant soil wildlife interrelationships. *Mailing Add:* 56 Golf St West Long Branch NJ 07764

SPIEGEL, MELVIN, DEVELOPMENTAL BIOLOGY. *Current Pos:* from asst prof to assoc prof zool, Dartmouth Col, 59-66, chmn dept biol sci, 72-74, prof biol, 66-93, EMER PROF BIOL, DARTMOUTH COL, 93- *Personal Data:* b New York, NY, Dec 10, 25; m 55, Evelyn Sclufer; c Judith E & Rebecca A. *Educ:* Univ Ill, BS, 48; Univ Rochester, PhD(zool), 52. *Hon Degrees:* MA, Dartmouth Col, 66. *Prof Exp:* Res fel zool, Univ Rochester, 52-53; USPHS res fel biol, Calif Inst Technol, 53-55; asst prof, Colby Col, 55-59. *Concurrent Pos:* Mem, NIH Cell Biol Study Sect, 66-70; vis sr res biologist, Univ Calif, San Diego, 70-71; vis prof, Nat Inst Med Res, Eng, 71; corp mem & mem bd trustees, Marine Biol Lab, 75-79; prog dir develop biol, NSF, 75-76; mem exec comt, Bd Trustees, Marine Biol Lab, 78-79; vis prof, Bioctr, Univ Basel, 79-82, 85. *Mem:* Am Soc Cell Biologists; fel AAAS; Int Soc Develop Biologists (secy-treas, 77-81); Soc Develop Biol. *Res:* Developmental biology; protein synthesis; fertilization; cell reaggregation; specificity of cell adhesion. *Mailing Add:* Dept Biol Sci Dartmouth Col Hanover NH 03755

SPIEGEL, ROBERT, control systems, energy conservation systems, for more information see previous edition

SPIEGEL, STANLEY LAWRENCE, SPACECRAFT CHARGING. *Current Pos:* PROF MATH, UNIV LOWELL, 73- *Personal Data:* b New York, NY, Oct 27, 35; m 72; c 3. *Educ:* NY Univ, BS, 57; Harvard Univ, AM, 59, PhD(physics), 66. *Prof Exp:* Fel, meteorol dept, Mass Inst Technol, 66-68; res assoc, math dept, Northwestern Univ, 69-73. *Concurrent Pos:* Sr scientist, EG&G Environ Consult, 78-79, consult, 79-82; fac res fel, Air Force Off Sci Res, 81 & 82, prin investr, 82-83 & 85-88. *Mem:* Am Geophys Union; Am Meteorol Soc; AAAS; NY Acad Sci; Sigma Xi. *Res:* Derivation, analysis and testing of computer algorithms for the automatic real time determination of space vehicle potentials in various plasma environments, such as at geosynchronous and low earth orbits; numerical modeling of geophysical fluids; electrostatic analyzer measurements. *Mailing Add:* 39 Stetson St Brookline MA 02146-3406

SPIEGEL, ZANE, HYDROLOGY, GEOLOGY. *Current Pos:* CONSULT HYDROL, ZANE SPIEGEL INT, 71- *Personal Data:* b Middletown, NY, Nov 6, 26; div; c Austin & Evan. *Educ:* Univ Chicago, BS, 49, MS, 52; NMex Inst Mining & Technol, PhD(earth sci), 62. *Prof Exp:* Geologist hydrol, US Geol Surv, 49-53; water resources engr, NMex State Engr Off, 54-58; vis prof eng, Imp Col, Univ London, 63-64; proj mgr hydrol, UN Spec Fund, Arg, 64-66; water resources engr, NMex State Eng Off, 66-71. *Concurrent Pos:* Fulbright lectr grant, Univ de San Agustin, Arequipa, Peru, 58-59; NSF Coop fel, NMex Inst Mining & Technol, 60-61, vis assoc prof hydrol, 71; water resources res fel, Water Resources Dept, Harvard Univ, 62-63; vis lectr hydrol, Univ Minn, Minneapolis, 67-68; earth sci course coordr, Continuing Educ Dept, Col Santa Fe, 73-77, 85; US Environ Protection Agency Extramural Grant reviewer, 73-75; hydrologist, Ohio State Univ, 80-82; instr physics, Col Santa Fe, 88; adj prof earth sci, Westchester Community Col, 90-93; vol exec, Ukraine Int Exec Serv Corps, 94. *Mem:* Fel Geol Soc Am; fel Am Soc Civil Engrs; Nat Ground Water Asn; Am Geophys Union; Interdisciplinary Environ Asn. *Res:* Fundamental concepts of hydrology; impacts of wells on streamflow and estuary salinity; movement and removal of contaminants in fresh ground waters; Cenozoic geohydrology; environmental impact analysis; aquifer performance test analysis. *Mailing Add:* PO Box 1541 Santa Fe NM 87504-1541. *Fax:* 505-984-2530

SPIEGELBERG, HANS L, ALLERGY. *Current Pos:* PROF & HEAD DEPT PEDIAT, PEDIAT IMMUNOL & ALLERGY DIV, UNIV CALIF SAN DIEGO SCH MED, 90- *Personal Data:* b Basel, Switz, Jan 8, 33; c 3. *Educ:* Univ Basel, MD, 58. *Prof Exp:* Mem staff, Scripps Clin & Res Found, 63-90. *Mem:* Am Soc Clin Invest; Am Soc Exp Path; Am Asn Immunologists; Int Col Allergy; Am Acad Allergy; Swiss Soc Allergy & Immunol. *Res:* Immunology. *Mailing Add:* Dept Pediat Univ Calif San Diego Sch Med 0609D 9500 Gilman Dr La Jolla CA 92093-0609. *Fax:* 619-534-1087

SPIEGELBERG, HARRY LESTER, PAPER CHEMISTRY. *Current Pos:* RETIRED. *Personal Data:* b New London, Wis, Apr 24, 36; m 60, Bonnie; c Susan, Sharon, Stephen & Scott. *Educ:* Univ Wis, BSChE, 59; Inst Paper Chem, MS, 63, PhD(mech, physics), 66; Univ Chicago, MBA, 80. *Prof Exp:* Instr mech, Univ Wis, 57-59; design engr, Kimberly Clark Corp, 59-61, res chemist, 65-68, mgr corp res & eng, New Concepts Lab, 68-73, dir contract res, 72-73, dir res & develop, Feminine Care Prod, Consumer Bus Div, 73-96, vpres res, Consumer Tissue, 85-92, dir res & develop, Consumer & Serv Tissue Prod, 79-96, vpres tech transfer, 92-96. *Concurrent Pos:* Chmn, Gordon Res Conf Chem & Physics of Paper, 71 & Indust Liason Coun, Univ Wis, 87-93; mem vis comt, Dept Chem Eng, Univ Wis, 86-, chmn, 86-87. *Res:* Mechanical properties of pulp fibers; mathematical analysis of screening systems; innovative process; long range invention of new products; absorbent materials. *Mailing Add:* 3624 S Barker Lane Appleton WI 54915. *Fax:* 920-734-9085; *E-Mail:* bspiegel@athenet.net

SPIEGELHALTER, ROLAND ROBERT, ANALYTICAL CHEMISTRY. *Current Pos:* RETIRED. *Personal Data:* b Dubuque, Iowa, May 31, 23; m 46; c 2. *Educ:* Carroll Col, PhB, 48; Univ Kans, MA, 50. *Prof Exp:* Analytical chemist, Commercial Solvents Corp, 50-56; sr develop chemist, Chemstrand Corp, 56-64; asst plant chemist, Escambia Chem Corp, 64-69, chief chemist, Eschabia Plant, Air Prod & Chem, Inc, 69-84. *Mem:* Am Chem Soc. *Res:* Titrimetry in nonaqueous solvents. *Mailing Add:* 8411 Country Walk D Pensacola FL 32514-4632

SPIEGELMAN, BRUCE M, CELL DIFFERENTIATION, CELLULAR DEVELOPMENT. *Current Pos:* ASST PROF PHARMACOL, DANA FARBER CANCER INST, MED SCH, HARVARD UNIV, 82- *Personal Data:* b Bayshore, NY, Nov 14, 52. *Educ:* Princeton Univ, PhD(biochem), 78. *Prof Exp:* Fel biol, Mass Inst Technol, 78-82. *Mem:* Am Soc Cell Biol; AAAS. *Mailing Add:* Dept Cell & Molecular Biol Dana Farber Cancer Inst Harvard Univ Med Sch 44 Binney St Boston MA 02115-6084. *Fax:* 617-735-8971

SPIEGELMAN, GEORGE BOOLE, TRANSCRIPTION ENZYMOLOGY REGULATION, PROTEIN DNA INTERACTION. *Current Pos:* asst prof, 78-85, assoc prof, 85-93, PROF, UNIV BC, 93- *Personal Data:* b St Louis, Mo, Aug 18, 45; m 67, Helen Bandy; c Eli & Jonah. *Educ:* Univ Ill, BSc, 66; Univ Wis, PhD(molecular biol), 72. *Prof Exp:* Sr fel, Univ Wash, 72-74, res assoc, 74-77, res asst prof, 77-78. *Mem:* Am Soc Microbiol; AAAS. *Res:* Interactions of proteins and DNA which regulate gene expression; examine signal transduction pathways in both eucaryotes and procaryotes. *Mailing Add:* Dept Microbiol & Immunol Univ BC Vancouver BC V6T 1Z3 Can. *Fax:* 604-822-0041; *E-Mail:* spie@unixg.ubc.ca

SPIEGELMAN, GERALD HENRY, ORGANIC CHEMISTRY, INDUSTRIAL CHEMISTRY. *Current Pos:* SECT HEAD, FOSTER WHEELER DEVELOP CORP, 90- *Personal Data:* b New York, NY, Oct 22, 38; m 60, Jean Lucousky; c 3. *Educ:* City Col New York, BS, 59; Columbia Univ, MA, 60; Stevens Inst Technol, PhD(chem), 69. *Prof Exp:* Chemist, Ultra Div, Witco Chem Corp, 60-64, sr res chemist, 67-72, group leader, 72-76, mgr res & develop, 76-79, asst dir corp res & develop, 79-84. *Mem:* Am Chem Soc; Am Soc Testing & Mat. *Res:* Surfactants; detergents; organometallics; unit processes; process development; analytical chemistry; petroleum. *Mailing Add:* 211 Indian Rd Wayne NJ 07470-4915

SPIEGELMAN, MARTHA, EMBRYOLOGY, CYTOLOGY. *Current Pos:* LECTR, SMITH COL, 82- *Personal Data:* b New York, NY, May 22, 36; m 64. *Educ:* Albertus Magnus Col, BA, 58; Columbia Univ, PhD(biol), 71. *Prof Exp:* Res fel develop genetics, Dept Anat, Med Col, Cornell Univ, 70-71, instr micros anat, 72-74, asst prof anat, 74-76, assoc develop genetics, Mem Sloan-Kettering Cancer Ctr, 76-82. *Concurrent Pos:* Adj assoc prof anat, Med Col, Cornell Univ, 78-81; vis investr, Mem Sloan-Kettering Cancer Ctr, 82- *Mem:* Soc Develop Biol; Am Soc Zoologists; Sigma Xi. *Res:* Fine structural analysis of genetic abnormalities in mouse embryos, especially cellular motility and cell-cell interactions during development. *Mailing Add:* 185 Middle St Amherst MA 01002

SPIEGLER, KURT SAMUEL, DESALINATION TECHNOLOGY. *Current Pos:* EMER PROF MECH ENG, UNIV CALIF, BERKELEY, 78- *Personal Data:* b Vienna, Austria, May 31, 20; nat US; m 71, Annie E Lick; c 3. *Educ:* Hebrew Univ, Israel, MS & PhD(chem), 44. *Honors & Awards:* Sr Res Award, Japan Soc Prom Sci, 80; Achievement Award, Int Desalination Asn, 95. *Prof Exp:* Develop chemist, Anglo-Iranian Oil Co, 44-46; res physicist, Palestine Potash Co, 46-47; actg head water purification proj, Weizmann Inst Sci, 48-50; Weizmann Inst & AEC fel, Mass Inst Technol, 50-52; res chemist, Geol Div, Gulf Res & Develop Co, 53-55, sect head phys geochem, 55-59; prof chem, Israel Inst Technol, 59-62; sr scientist, Pratt & Whitney Aircraft Div, United Aircraft Corp, 62-64; prof mech eng in residence, Univ Calif, Berkeley, 64-78. *Concurrent Pos:* Consult, Bur Reclamation, 75-80; prof chem eng, Mich Technol Univ, 78-81; prof, Fromm Inst Lifelong Learning, Univ San Francisco, 89-92. *Mem:* Asn Energy Engrs; NAm Membrane Soc; Am Chem Soc. *Res:* Ion exchange; electrochemistry; thermodynamics; water purification; fuel cells; membrane physics; geochemistry. *Mailing Add:* Dept Mech Eng Univ Calif Berkeley CA 94720

SPIEKER, ANDREW MAUTE, HYDROLOGY. *Current Pos:* Geologist, US Geol Surv, Ohio, 57-65, hydrologist, Ill, 65-67, NY, 67-68, staff hydrologist, Water Resources Div, Washington, DC, 68-70, dep proj dir, San Francisco Bay Region Environ & Resources Planning Study, 70-75, western region rep, Lan Info & Anal Off, 76-79, asst dist chief, 79-81, STAFF HYDROLOGIST, WATER RESOURCES DIV, WESTERN REGION, US GEOL SURV, 81- *Personal Data:* b Columbus, Ohio, Aug 15, 32; m 61; c 2. *Educ:* Yale Univ, BS, 54; Stanford Univ, MS, 56, PhD(geol), 65. *Honors & Awards:* W R Boggess Award, Am Water Resources Asn, 74. *Mem:* AAAS; Geol Soc Am; Am Geophys Union. *Res:* Hydrology of the urban environment; environmental geology; geology and hydrology of ground water; application of earth sciences to urban and regional planning; stratigraphy. *Mailing Add:* 341 Linfield Dr Menlo Park CA 94025

SPIELBERG, NATHAN, X-RAYS, LIQUID CRYSTALS. *Current Pos:* PROF PHYSICS, KENT STATE UNIV, 69- *Personal Data:* b Philadelphia, Pa, Feb 2, 26; m 47, Alice Benator; c Sarina, Naomi & Johanan. *Educ:* Emory Univ, AB, 47; Ohio State Univ, MS, 48, PhD(physics), 52. *Prof Exp:* Asst physics, Ohio State Univ, 47-49, res assoc, 51-53, asst prof welding eng, 53-54; assoc physicist, Philips Labs, NAm Philips Co, Inc, 54-58, sr physicist, 58-60, staff physicist, 60-65, res physicist, 65-69. *Concurrent Pos:* Adj prof geosciences, Tex Tech Univ, 78; mem, Liquid Crystal Inst, Kent State Univ, 79-; vis prof, Weizmann Inst, 83-84. *Mem:* Am Phys Soc; Am Asn Physics Teachers; Am Crystallog Asn; Microprobe Anal Soc; Sigma Xi. *Res:* X-ray spectrochemical analysis; high resolution x-ray spectroscopy; x-ray physics; crystal perfection; x-ray interferometry; structure of liquid crystals. *Mailing Add:* 728 Ivan Dr Kent OH 44240. *Fax:* 330-672-2959; *E-Mail:* nspielbe@kentvm.kent.edu

SPIELBERG, STEPHEN E, MATHEMATICS. *Current Pos:* From asst prof to assoc prof, 63-93, EMER PROF MATH, UNIV TOLEDO, 93- *Personal Data:* b Philadelphia, Pa, June 7, 34. *Educ:* Univ Pa, BA, 56; Univ Minn, MA, 58, PhD(math), 63. *Mem:* Math Asn Am; Am Math Soc. *Res:* Probability; statistics; Wiener integrals. *Mailing Add:* Dept Math Univ Toledo 2801 W Bancroft St Toledo OH 43606. *E-Mail:* sspielbe@math.utoledo.edu

SPIELBERGER, CHARLES DONALD, CLINICAL & HEALTH PSYCHOLOGY, BEHAVIORAL MEDICINE. *Current Pos:* prof, 72-85, DISTINGUISHED UNIV RES PROF PSYCHOL, UNIV SFLA, 85- *Personal Data:* b Atlanta, Ga, Mar 28, 27; m 71, Carol Lee; c 3. *Educ:* Ga Inst Technol, BS, 49; Univ Iowa, BA, 51, MA, 53, PhD(psychol), 54. *Hon Degrees:* LHD, Pac Grad Sch Psychol, 90; Dr, Hungarian Univ Phys Educ, 91. *Honors & Awards:* Distinguished Contrib Community Psychol, Am Psychol Asn, 82, Distinguished Contrib Clin Psychol, 89, Distinguished Contrib to Knowledge in Appl Psychol, 93; Distinguished Contribution Personality Assessment, Soc Personality Assessments, 90. *Prof Exp:* Asst prof psychiat, Med Sch, Duke Univ, 55-58, from asst prof to assoc prof psychol, 55-63; prof psychol, Vanderbilt Univ, 63-67; training specialist, NIMH, 65-67; prof psychol, Flat State Univ, 67-72. *Concurrent Pos:* Dir, Ctr Res Behav Med & Health Psychol, Univ SFla, 77-; ed, Am J Community Psychol, 71-78. *Mem:* Fel Am Psychol Asn (treas, 87-90, pres, 91-92); Soc Personality Assessments (pres, 86-); Int Coun Psychologists (pres, 86-87); Int Soc Test Anxiety Res (pres, 82-84). *Res:* Nature and assessment of anxiety, anger, curiosity and job stress; anger expression and control; cross-cultural research on emotion; stress management, behavioral medicine and health psychology; mental health consultation; community psychology; personality and learning. *Mailing Add:* Dept Psychol Univ SFla Tampa FL 33620. *Fax:* 813-974-2340

SPIELER, HELMUTH, RADIATION DETECTORS FOR ELEMENTARY PARTICLE PHYSICS, PHYSICS OF SEMICONDUCTOR DEVICES. *Current Pos:* staff scientist, 82-87, SR STAFF SCIENTIST, LAWRENCE BERKELEY LAB, 87- *Personal Data:* b Irvington, NJ, Aug 25, 45; m 71; c 2. *Educ:* Tech Univ Munich, Ger, dipl physics, 71, Dr Rer Nat, 74. *Prof Exp:* Staff scientist, Tech Univ Munich, 73-75 & GSI Darmstadt, 75-82. *Mem:* Am Phys Soc; Inst Elec & Electronics Engrs. *Res:* Radiation detectors and electronics; semiconductor detector systems for high energy physics; physics of semiconductor devices; design and fabrication of integrated circuits. *Mailing Add:* Lawrence Berkeley Nat Lab 50B-6208 1 Cyclotron Rd Berkeley CA 94720. *Fax:* 510-486-5401; *E-Mail:* spieler@lbl.gov

SPIELER, RICHARD ARNO, GENETICS, ZOOLOGY. *Current Pos:* from asst prof to assoc prof, 68-77, PROF BIOL, CALIF STATE UNIV, FRESNO, 77- *Personal Data:* b Syracuse, NY, Apr 8, 32. *Educ:* Univ Chicago, BA, 52, PhD(zool), 62. *Prof Exp:* Asst prof zool, Ill Inst Technol, 62-68. *Mem:* AAAS. *Res:* Genetics of meiosis; parental care by reptiles and amphibians. *Mailing Add:* Dept Biol Calif State Univ 2555 E San Ramon Fresno CA 93740-0001

SPIELER, RICHARD EARL, CHRONOBIOLOGY, ICHTHYOLOGY. *Current Pos:* assoc prof, 92-, PROF OCEANOG, NOVA UNIV. *Personal Data:* b Washington, DC, Mar 11, 42; m 87; c 2. *Educ:* Univ Md, BA, 63; Ark State Univ, BS, 70, MS, 71; La State Univ, PhD(marine sci), 75. *Prof Exp:* Cur fishes, Milwaukee Pub Mus, 75-92. *Concurrent Pos:* Instr anat, fisheries biol & ichthyol, Ark State Univ, 70-71; adj prof, Univ Wis, Milwaukee, 75-; grants, numerous orgn, 76-; instr zool, Milwaukee Inst Art & Design, 85-87; actg head vertebrate zool, Milwaukee Pub Mus, 87-89. *Mem:* AAAS; Am Fisheries Soc; Am Soc Zoologists; Int Soc Chronobiol; World Aquacult Soc. *Res:* Temporal integration of fishes with emphasis on both basic and applied aspects; author of numerous publications. *Mailing Add:* Dept Oceanog Nova Univ 8000 N Ocean Dr Dania FL 33004

SPIELHOLTZ, GERALD I, ANALYTICAL CHEMISTRY. *Current Pos:* from asst prof to assoc prof, 68-75, PROF CHEM, LEHMAN COL, 75- *Personal Data:* b New York, NY, Mar 12, 37; m 78; c 1. *Educ:* City Col New York, BS, 58; Univ Mich, MS, 60; Iowa State Univ, PhD(analytical chem), 63. *Prof Exp:* From instr to asst prof chem, Hunter Col, 63-68. *Mem:* Am Chem Soc; Sigma Xi. *Res:* Atomic absorption spectroscopy; wet oxidation of materials prior to analysis; analytical chemistry applied to anthropology. *Mailing Add:* Dept of Chem Lehman Col Bronx NY 10468

SPIELMAN, ANDREW, PUBLIC HEALTH ENTOMOLOGY. *Current Pos:* from instr to assoc prof, 59-80, PROF TROP PUB HEALTH, SCH PUB HEALTH, HARVARD UNIV, 80- *Personal Data:* b New York, NY, Feb 24, 30; m 55; c David, Deborah, & Susan. *Educ:* Colo Col, BS, 52; Johns Hopkins

Univ, ScD(med entom), 56. *Hon Degrees:* MA, Harvard Univ, 91. *Honors & Awards:* Medal of Honor, Am Mosquito Control Asn, 88; Merit Award, Nat Inst Allergy & Infectious Dis, 89. *Prof Exp:* Biologist, Tenn Valley Authority, 53; dis vector control officer, US Navy, 56-59. *Mem:* Am Soc Trop Med & Hyg; Entom Soc Am; Am Mosquito Control Asn; AAAS. *Res:* Epidemiology of lyme disease, babesiosis and arthropod-borne diseases; physiology of salivation and reproduction in mosquitoes. *Mailing Add:* Dept Trop Pub Health 665 Huntington Ave Harvard Sch Pub Health Boston MA 02115. *Fax:* 617-738-4914; *E-Mail:* aspielma@hsph.harvard.edu

SPIELMAN, BARRY E, EDUCATIONAL & RESEARCH ADMINISTRATION, RESEARCH IN MICROWAVE ELECTROMAGNETICS. *Current Pos:* PROF ELEC ENG & CHMN, DEPT ELEC ENG, WASHINGTON UNIV, ST LOUIS, 87-, DIR, MICROELECTRONIC SYSTS RES LAB, 90- *Personal Data:* b Chicago, Ill, Oct 29, 42; m 66, Louise; c Michael & Liza. *Educ:* Ill Inst Technol, BS, 64; Pa State Univ, MS, 67; Syracuse Univ, PhD(elec eng), 71. *Honors & Awards:* N Walter Cox Award, 92. *Prof Exp:* Res electronics engr, Microwave Integrated Circuits, Naval Res Lab, 71-78, head, Solid State Circuits Sect, 78-84, head, Microwave Technol Br, 84-87. *Concurrent Pos:* Consult, McDonnell-Douglas Cent Res Lab, 88-89; rep, Nat comt Superconductivity, Inst Elec & Electronics Engrs, Microwave Theory & Tech Soc, 89-90, mem & chmn, Adcom Tech Comt, MTT-6; pace coordr, Inst Elec & Electronics Engrs-MTTS; adj prof, Univ Mo, St Louis. *Mem:* Sigma Xi; Inst Elec & Electronics Engrs Theory & Tech Soc (secy-treas 73, vpres 87, pres 88); fel Inst Elec & Electronics Engrs. *Res:* Microwave and millimeter-wave planar components including directional couplers, filters, phase shifters, modulators and switches; applied numerical solutions to electromagnetic problems pertinent to the packaging microwave components; experimental measurements verify computations. *Mailing Add:* Washington Univ One Brookings Dr Box 1127 St Louis MO 63130. *Fax:* 314-935-7500; *E-Mail:* bes@ee.wustl.edu

SPIELMAN, RICHARD SAUL, HUMAN GENETICS, QUANTITATIVE VARIATION. *Current Pos:* from asst prof to assoc prof, 74-89, PROF HUMAN GENETICS, MED SCH, UNIV PA, 89- *Personal Data:* b New York, NY, Feb 25, 46; div; c 1. *Educ:* Harvard Col, AB, 67; Univ Mich, Ann Arbor, PhD(human genetics), 71. *Prof Exp:* Res assoc human genetics, Med Sch, Univ Mich, Ann Arbor, 71-74. *Concurrent Pos:* Vis scholar, Imp Cancer Res Fund, London, 82-83. *Mem:* Sigma Xi; AAAS; Genetics Soc Am; Am Soc Human Genetics; Am Diabetes Asn. *Res:* Human variation; biometric genetics; genetics of disease susceptibility. *Mailing Add:* Dept Human Genetics Univ Pa Col Med Philadelphia PA 19104

SPIELMAN, WILLIAM SLOAN, CARDIOVASCULAR & RENAL PHYSIOLOGY, CELL & MOLECULAR BIOLOGY. *Current Pos:* from asst to assoc prof, 80-87, PROF PHYSIOL, MICH STATE UNIV, 87-, DIR GRAD STUDIES, 89- *Personal Data:* b Tulsa, Okla, Aug 7, 47; m 70; c 2. *Educ:* Westminster Col, BA, 69; Univ Mo, Columbia, PhD(physiol), 74. *Prof Exp:* Fel physiol, Univ NC, 75-77; fel & instr, Mayo Med Sch, 77-78, asst prof, 78-80. *Concurrent Pos:* NIH career develop award, 81. *Mem:* Am Physiol Soc; Sigma Xi; Am Fedn Clin Res; Am Soc Nephrology. *Res:* Normal and abnormal function of the kidney; receptors and signalling mechanisms. *Mailing Add:* Dept Physiol Giltner Hall Mich State Univ East Lansing MI 48824-1101

SPIELVOGEL, BERNARD FRANKLIN, INORGANIC CHEMISTRY. *Current Pos:* pres, 86-92, CHMN & FOUNDER, BORON BIOLOGICALS, INC, 92- *Personal Data:* b Ellwood City, Pa, Apr 23, 37; m 63, 81; c 3. *Educ:* Geneva Col, BS, 59; Univ Mich, PhD(chem), 63. *Honors & Awards:* NC Distinguished Chemist Award, Am Inst Chem, 84. *Prof Exp:* From instr to asst prof chem, Univ NC, 63-67; chief, Inorg Br, Chem Div, US Army Res Off, 67-88. *Concurrent Pos:* Vis sr res assoc, Duke Univ, 67-72; adj assoc prof chem, 72-81, adj prof chem, 81-; chmn, NC Sect, Am Chem Soc, 84. *Mem:* Am Chem Soc. *Res:* Boron hydride chemistry; synthesis of Boron analogs of amino acids; peptides, DNA and other biologically important molecules. *Mailing Add:* 620 Hutton St Suite 104 Raleigh NC 27606-1490

SPIELVOGEL, LAWRENCE GEORGE, FORENSIC ENGINEERING. *Current Pos:* PRES, LAWRENCE G SPIELVOGEL, INC, 70- *Personal Data:* b Newark, NJ, June 2, 38; m 91, Maralynne Flehner. *Educ:* Drexel Univ, BS, 62. *Honors & Awards:* Crosby Field Award, Am Soc Heating, Refrig & Air Conditioning Engrs, 81. *Prof Exp:* Assoc, Robert G Werden & Assoc, Inc, 59-70. *Concurrent Pos:* Asst post eng, Walter Reed Med Ctr, 63-65; eng, Utility Surv Corp, 65-66; adj instr, Evening Col, Drexel Univ, 68-84; instr, plumbing design course, Am Soc Sanit Engrs, 69-78; adj asst prof, Col Eng Technol, Temple Univ, 71-74; lectr, Grad Sch Fine Arts, Univ Pa, 71-78 & Sch Continuing Educ, NY Univ, 76-79; vis lectr, Grad Sch Archit, Yale Univ, 75-82. *Mem:* Am Soc Heating, Refrig & Air Conditioning Engrs; Illuminating Eng Soc; Am Consult Engrs Coun; Am Soc Mech Engrs; Chartered Inst Bldg Serv Eng. *Res:* Energy in buildings. *Mailing Add:* Lawrence G Spielvogel Inc 203 Hughes Rd King Of Prussia PA 19406-3785. *Fax:* 610-687-5370

SPIELVOGEL, LESTER Q, ABSTRACT WAVE THEORY, OCEANOGRAPHY. *Current Pos:* CHIEF SCIENTIST, SEACO, 81- *Personal Data:* b Brooklyn, NY, June 27, 37; m 69; c 2. *Educ:* Cooper Union, BME, 59; Columbia Univ, MS, 62; NY Univ, PhD(math), 69. *Prof Exp:* Mech engr, Sperry Rand Corp, 59-69; asst prof civil eng, Univ Hawaii, 69-70; asst physics, Nat Oceanic & Atmospheric Admin, US Dept Com, 70-71; physicist oceanog, 71-81. *Concurrent Pos:* Adj prof oceanog, Univ Hawaii, 74-83. *Mem:* Soc Indust Appl Math; AAAS. *Res:* Ocean waves and abstract wave theory; engineering analysis; engineering physics; mathematics. *Mailing Add:* 619 Kumukahi Pl Honolulu HI 96825-1116

SPIERS, DONALD ELLIS, TEMPERATURE REGULATION, ENVIRONMENTAL PHYSIOLOGY. *Current Pos:* ASST PROF EPIDEMIOL, YALE UNIV, 84- *Personal Data:* b Richmond, Va, 48; m 84; c 2. *Educ:* Va Polytech Inst & State Univ, BS, 70, MS, 72; Mich State Univ, PhD(physiol), 80. *Prof Exp:* Asst fel, John B Pierce Found, 82-90, assoc fel, 90- *Concurrent Pos:* Biologist, Peace Corps, 73-75. *Mem:* Am Physiol Soc; Am Soc Zool; Am Inst Biol Sci; Bioelectromagnetics Soc; Sigma Xi; NY Acad Sci. *Res:* Environmental physiology; development of temperature regulation in birds and mammals; neonatal responses to stress. *Mailing Add:* 114 ASRC Univ Mo Columbia MO 65211-0001

SPIERS, JAMES MONROE, PLANT PHYSIOLOGY, AGRONOMY. *Current Pos:* Res plant physiologist, 69-71, res plant physiologist-in-charge fruit & forage res, 71-73, RES HORTICULTURIST, LOCATION LEADER & RES LEADER, SMALL FRUIT RES STA, SCI & EDUC ADMIN-FED RES, USDA, 73- *Personal Data:* b Wiggins, Miss, July 31, 40; m 65; c 3. *Educ:* Miss State Univ, BS, 63, MS, 66; Tex A&M Univ, PhD(agron, crop physiol), 69. *Mem:* Am Soc Hort Sci; Am Soc Agron; Am Soc Hort Sci; Crop Sci Soc Am. *Res:* Nutrition and cultural requirements of blueberries, strawberries and blackberries; hormonal regulation of rooting, flowering and growth of blueberries. *Mailing Add:* 94 Spiers Rd Wiggins MS 39577

SPIES, HAROLD GLEN, NEUROENDOCRINOLOGY, REPRODUCTIVE BIOLOGY. *Current Pos:* RETIRED. *Personal Data:* b Mountain View, Okla, Mar 30, 34; wid; c Russell L & Terry W (deceased). *Educ:* Okla State Univ, BS, 56; Univ Wis, MS, 57, PhD(animal sci & genetics), 59. *Prof Exp:* From asst prof to assoc prof animal physiol, Kans State Univ, 59-66; res assoc anatomist, Univ Calif, Los Angeles, 67-68; res scientist, Delta Regional Primate Res Ctr, 68-72, chmn reproductive physiol, 72-83, assoc dir res, Ore Regional Primate Res Ctr, 83-95. *Concurrent Pos:* NIH spec fel neuroendocrinol res, Univ Calif, Los Angeles, 66-67; assoc prof, Tulane Univ, 68-72; prof, Med Sch, Univ Ore, 73-; interim dir, Ore Regional Primate Res Ctr, 80-81, 93-94. *Mem:* Endocrine Soc; Am Asn Anat; Soc Study Reproduction (vpres, 79-80, pres, 80-81); Am Physiol Soc; Am Soc Animal Sci; Neurosci Soc; Soc Study Exp Biol Med; Int Soc Neuroendocrinology. *Res:* Reproductive physiology and endocrinology of laboratory animals and primates; hypothalamo-hypophysial-gonadal interrelationships; neural regulation of endocrine changes in the menstrual cycle. *Mailing Add:* Ore Regional Primate Res Ctr 505 NW 185th Ave Beaverton OR 97006

SPIES, JOSEPH REUBEN, analytical chemistry, immunochemistry; deceased, see previous edition for last biography

SPIES, ROBERT BERNARD, MARINE BIOLOGY & ECOLOGY, ECOTOXICOLOGY. *Current Pos:* SR ENVIRON SCIENTIST, ENVIRON DIV, LAWRENCE LIVERMORE LAB, UNIV CALIF, 73- *Personal Data:* b Palo Alto, Calif, May 21, 43; m 63; c 3. *Educ:* St Mary's Col, BS, 65; Univ Pac, MS, 69; Univ Southern Calif, PhD(marine biol), 71. *Prof Exp:* Sr res officer marine ecol, Fisheries & Wildlife Dept, Victoria, Australia, 70-73. *Concurrent Pos:* Ed, Marine Environ Res, 87-; pres, Appl Marine Sci Inc, Livermore, Calif; chief scientist, Exxon Valdez Oil Spill Assessment, US Govt, Alaska. *Mem:* AAAS; Am Soc Limnol & Oceanog; Western Soc Naturalists; Am Chem Soc; Soc Environ Toxicol Chem. *Res:* Effects of xenobiotic compounds on reproduction in estuarine fish; effects of petroleum hydrocarbons in the marine benthos; dynamics of petroleum hydrocarbons, trace elements and radionuclides in benthic organisms; dynamic processes in marine benthos. *Mailing Add:* 2155 Las Positas Ct Suite S Livermore CA 94550. *Fax:* 510-373-7834; *E-Mail:* spies@amarine.com

SPIESS, ELIOT BRUCE, GENETICS. *Current Pos:* prof, 66-89, EMER PROF BIOL SCI, UNIV ILL, CHICAGO, 89- *Personal Data:* b Boston, Mass, Oct 13, 21; m 51, Luretta Davis; c Arthur & Bruce. *Educ:* Harvard Univ, AB, 43, AM, 47, PhD(genetics), 49. *Prof Exp:* Instr biol, Harvard Univ, 49-52; from asst prof to prof biol, Univ Pittsburgh, 52-66. *Concurrent Pos:* Am Acad Arts & Sci grant in aid, 53; AEC res grant, 55-72; dir NIH grad training grant genetics, Univ Pittsburgh, 63-66; NSF res grant, 72-83; ed, Evolution, Soc Study Evol J, 75-78; pres, Am Soc Naturalists, 81. *Mem:* Fel AAAS; Soc Study Evolution. *Res:* Genetics of adaptive mechanisms in populations of Drosophila; behavior genetics. *Mailing Add:* Dept Biol Sci 845 W Taylor St Univ Ill Chicago Chicago IL 60607-7060

SPIESS, FRED NOEL, OCEANOGRAPHY, MARINE GEOPHYSICS. *Current Pos:* res physicist, Marine Phys Lab, Scripps Inst Oceanog, Univ Calif, San Diego, 52-61, dir, 58-80, prof oceanog, 61-90, actg dir, 61-63, chmn dept oceanog, 63-64 & 76-77, dir, 64-65, assoc dir, 65-80, dir, Inst Marine Resources, Univ Calif, San Diego, 80-88, EMER PROF OCEANOG, MARINE PHYS LAB, SCRIPPS INST OCEANOG, UNIV CALIF, SAN DIEGO, 88- *Personal Data:* b Oakland, Calif, Dec 25, 19; m 42, Sarah Scott Whitton; c Katherine (Dallaire), Mary Elizabeth (DeJong), John Morgen, Helen (Shamble) & Peggy (DeLigio). *Educ:* Univ Calif, AB, 41, PhD(physics), 51; Harvard Univ, MS, 46. *Honors & Awards:* Ewing Medal, Am Geophys Union-US Navy, 83; Pioneers of Underwater Acoust Medal, Acoust Soc Am, 85; Marine Technol Soc-Lockheed Award, 85; Sigma Xi, 49; Franklin Inst, John Price Wetherill Medal, 65; AAAS Newcomb Cleveland Prize, 80; Conrad Medal, USN, 74. *Prof Exp:* Nuclear engr, Knolls Atomic Power Lab, Gen Elec Co, 51-52. *Mem:* Nat Acad Eng; fel Acoust Soc Am; fel Am Geophys Union; fel Marine Technol Soc. *Res:* Underwater acoustics; marine geophysics; ocean technology. *Mailing Add:* Scripps Inst Oceanog Univ Calif San Diego 9500 Gilman Dr La Jolla CA 92093-0205. *E-Mail:* fns@mpl.ucsd.edu

SPIESS, JOACHIM, PROTEIN CHEMISTRY, NEUROSCIENCES. *Current Pos:* PRES, SCI MEM & DIR, MAX PLANCK INST EXP MED, GOETTINGEN, 87- *Personal Data:* b Ludenscheid, Ger; m 67; c 3. *Educ:* Univ Munchen, MD, 73, PhD(chem) 76. *Prof Exp:* Wiss asst, Max Planck Inst Biochem, 73-76; fel, Salk Inst, 76-77, from res assoc to assoc res prof, 78-87. *Concurrent Pos:* Adj prof, Salk Inst, 90 & Dept Psychiat, Univ Calif, San Diego. *Mem:* Am Soc Cell Biol; Endocrine Soc; Am Chem Soc; Am Soc Biochem & Molecular Biol; Protein Soc. *Res:* Conducting biochemistry of hormonal peptides and neuro transmitter receptors. *Mailing Add:* Dept Molecular Neuroendocrinol Max Planck Inst Exp Med Hermann Rein Str 3 37075 Goettingen Germany

SPIETH, JOHN, MOLECULAR & DEVELOPMENTAL GENETICS, GENE EXPRESSION. *Current Pos:* RES ASSOC, DEPT BIOL, IND UNIV, 78- *Educ:* Univ Wash, PhD(zool), 78. *Mailing Add:* 1811 Hyde Park Circle Bloomington IN 47401

SPIETH, PHILIP THEODORE, POPULATION GENETICS, EVOLUTION. *Current Pos:* asst prof & asst geneticist, 71-76, ASSOC PROF & ASSOC RES GENETICIST, UNIV CALIF, BERKELEY, 76-, ASSOC DEAN, STUDENT AFFAIRS, COL NAT RES, 80- *Personal Data:* b New York, NY, June 10, 41; m 63; c 4. *Educ:* Univ Calif, Berkeley, AB, 62; Univ Ore, PhD(biol), 70. *Prof Exp:* Ford Found fel pop biol, Univ Chicago, 70-71. *Mem:* Genetics Soc Am; Soc Study Evolution; Mycol Soc Am. *Res:* Genetic variation of natural populations; empirical population genetics of fungi; microevolutionary processes of speciation. *Mailing Add:* ESPM-Div Forest Sci 145 Mulford Hall Univ Calif Berkeley CA 94720-3114

SPIGARELLI, STEVEN ALAN, FISH ECOLOGY, POLLUTION BIOLOGY. *Current Pos:* DIR CTR ENVIRON STUDIES, BEMIDJI STATE UNIV, 82- *Personal Data:* b Highland Park, Ill, Mar 26, 42. *Educ:* Northwestern Univ, BA, 64; Univ Ill, Urbana, MS, 66; Mich State Univ, PhD(aquatic ecol), 71. *Prof Exp:* Asst ecologist, Argonne Nat Lab, 71-74, ecologist aquatic ecol, 74-82. *Concurrent Pos:* Mem res comt, Int Atomic Energy Agency, 75-79; assoc ed, J Great Lakes Res, 77- *Mem:* Am Fisheries Soc; Fisheries Res Bd Can; Int Asn Great Lakes Res; Am Chem Soc. *Res:* Thermal ecology; radioecology; fish behavior; stress ecology. *Mailing Add:* Dept Environ Studies Bemidji State Unvi Bemidji MN 56601-2699

SPIKE, CLARK GHAEL, INORGANIC CHEMISTRY. *Current Pos:* assoc prof chem, Eastern Mich Univ, 58-61, head dept, 61-77, prof, 61-83, interim dean, Col Arts & Sci, 77-79, actg assoc vpres acad affairs, 79-80, EMER PROF CHEM, EASTERN MICH UNIV, 83- *Personal Data:* b Ypsilanti, Mich, Sept 15, 21; m 47, Avis R; c James & Susan. *Educ:* Mich State Norm Col, BS, 44; Univ Mich, PhD(chem), 52. *Prof Exp:* Instr chem, Mich State Norm Col, 46-48; res chemist, Ethyl Corp, 52-58. *Mem:* AAAS; Am Chem Soc; Sigma Xi. *Res:* Coordination complexes; metallo-organic compounds. *Mailing Add:* 18580 Grass Lake Rd Manchester MI 48158

SPIKER, STEVEN L, PLANT CHROMATIN STRUCTURE. *Current Pos:* assoc prof, 81-92, PROF MOLECULAR GENETICS, NC STATE UNIV, 92- *Personal Data:* b Omaha, Nebr, Nov 1, 41; m 71, Jennifer Swiatoviak; c Benjamin. *Educ:* Univ Iowa, BS, 64, MS, 67, PhD(plant physiol), 70. *Prof Exp:* Asst prof biol, Am Univ Beirut, 72-74; asst prof molecular biol, Dept Bot & Plant Path, Ore State Univ, 78-81. *Concurrent Pos:* Fulbright fel, Max Planck Inst, Zuchtungsforschung Kolu, Ger, 89-90. *Mem:* Am Soc Plant Physiologists; Int Soc Plant Molecular Biol; Am Soc Biochem & Molecular Biol. *Res:* Isolation, characterization and evolution of plant chromosomal proteins; physical and chemical studies of protein-protein interactions in the nucleosome; role of chromosomal proteins in forming transcribable or inert chromatin structure. *Mailing Add:* Genetics Dept NC State Univ Raleigh NC 27695-7614. *Fax:* 919-515-3355; *E-Mail:* steven_spiker@ncsu.edu

SPIKES, JOHN DANIEL, PHOTOBIOLOGY. *Current Pos:* From asst prof to assoc prof biol, Univ Utah, 48-55, head dept exp biol, 54-62, dean, Col Lett & Sci, 64-67, chmn dept biol, 74-85, prof biol, 55-88, EMER PROF BIOL, UNIV UTAH, 89- *Personal Data:* b Los Angeles, Calif, Dec 14, 18; m 42, Anne Dorland; c John, Daniel & Mary. *Educ:* Calif Inst Technol, BS, 41, MS, 46, PhD(chem, embryol), 48. *Honors & Awards:* distinguished Res Prof Award, Univ Utah, 72; Medal, Europe Soc Photobiol, 89; Lifetime Achievement Award, Am Soc Photobiol, 92. *Concurrent Pos:* Cell physiologist, US AEC, Washington, DC, 58-60, consult, 60-65; counr, Smithsonian Inst, 66-72; vis prof, Univ Padua, Italy. *Mem:* Am Chem Soc; Inter-Am Photochem Soc; Am Soc Photobiol (pres, 74-75); Europ Photochem Asn; Europ Soc Photobiol; fel Am Soc Advan Sci. *Res:* Photobiology; photosensitized reactions; mechanisms of the sensitized photooxidation of biomolecules; sensitized photo effects on cells; photosensitized reactions as a tool in biology and medicine. *Mailing Add:* Dept Biol Univ Utah Salt Lake City UT 84112

SPIKES, PAUL WENTON, MATHEMATICAL ANALYSIS. *Current Pos:* from asst prof to prof, 70-94, EMER PROF MATH, MISS STATE UNIV, 94- *Personal Data:* b Ft Worth, Tex, Mar 22, 31; m 53; c 2. *Educ:* Miss Southern Col, BS, 53, MA, 57; Auburn Univ, PhD(math), 70. *Prof Exp:* Instr math, Copiah-Lincoln Jr Col, 57-58; assoc prof, William Carey Col, 58-65; chmn, Div Sci & Math, Alexander City State Jr Col, 66-68, chmn, Eve Div, 69-70. *Mem:* Am Math Soc; Math Asn Am. *Res:* Qualitative theory of ordinary differential equations. *Mailing Add:* Dept Math Drawer MA Miss State Univ Mississippi State MS 39762

SPILBURG, CURTIS ALLEN, enzymology, lipids, for more information see previous edition

SPILHAUS, ATHELSTAN FREDERICK, METEOROLOGY, OCEANOGRAPHY. *Current Pos:* PRES, PAN/GEO, INC, 84- *Personal Data:* b Cape Town, SAfrica, Nov 25, 11; nat US; m 78, Kathleen FitzGerald; c A F Jr, Karl, Eleanor (Kluge), Mary Tilney & Margaret Morse. *Educ:* Univ Cape Town, BSc, 31, DSc, 48; Mass Inst Technol, SM, 33. *Hon Degrees:* DSc, Coe Col, 61, Univ RI, 68, Hahnemann Med Col, 68, Philadelphia Col Pharm & Sci, 68, Hamilton Col, 70, Southeastern Mass Univ, 70, Univ Durham, 70, Univ SC, 71, Southwestern at Memphis, 72; LLD, Nova Univ Advan Technol, 70, Univ Md, 79, Oklahoma City Univ, 91. *Honors & Awards:* Berzelius Medal, Sweden, 62; Proctor Prize, Sci Res Soc Am, 68; Compass Award, Marine Tech Soc, 81. *Prof Exp:* Vol engr, Junkers Airplane Works, Ger, 31-32; res engr, Sperry Gyroscope Co, NY, 33; asst meteorol, Mass Inst Technol, 34-35; asst dir tech serv, Dept Defense, Union SAfrica, 35-36; asst, Woods Hole Oceanog Inst, 36-37, phys oceanogr, 38-60; dean, Inst Tech, Univ Minn, Minneapolis, 49-66, prof geophys, 66-77; pres, Franklin Inst, Pa, 67-69 & Aqua Int, Inc, 69-71; fel, Woodrow Wilson Int Ctr Scholars, Smithsonian Inst, 71-74; spec asst to adminr, Nat Oceanic & Atmospheric Admin, US Dept Com, 74-80. *Concurrent Pos:* From asst prof to prof, NY Univ, 37-48, chmn, Dept Meteorol, 38-47, dir res eng & phys sci, 46-48; mem, Subcomt Meteorol, Nat Adv Comt, Aeronaut, 41-56; consult, Div Ten, Nat Defense Res Comt, 42-43, SAfrican Govt, 47, Brookhaven Nat Lab, 47-49, US Weather Bur, 47-56, Air Materiel Command & Sci Adv Bd, US Dept Air Force, 48-58, US Dept Defense & Res & Develop Adv Coun, Signal Corps, US Dept Army & Nat Oceanic & Atmospheric Admin, 80-; sci dir weapons effects, Atomic Tests, Nev, 51; cem, Baker Mission, Korea, 52; US rep exec bd, UNESCO, 54-58; comnr, US Sci Exhib, Seattle World's Fair, 61-63; mem, Comt Pollution, Nat Acad Sci; mem Nat Sci Bd, 66-; vis prof, Tex A&M Univ, 74-75; chmn, Sci Adv Comt, Am Newspaper Publ Asn; mem bd trustees, Aerospace Corp, El Segundo, Sci Serv, Inc, Int Oceanog Found, Pac Sci Ctr Found & Sea Educ Asn, 74-; lectr, Phi Beta Kappa, 76-77; distinguished vis prof, Univ Tex, 77-78; Annenberg scholar, Univ Southern Calif, 81, vis scholar, Inst Marine & Coastal Studies, 81-83. *Mem:* Fel AAAS (pres, 70); fel Am Geog Soc; Am Inst Aeronaut & Astronaut; fel Geog Soc; fel Royal Meteorol Soc; fel Am Geophys Union; Am Philos Soc. *Res:* Spilhaus space clock; bathythermograph; aircraft, meteorological and oceanographic instruments; physical oceanography; cartography (world maps). *Mailing Add:* PO Box 1063 Middleburg VA 22117. *Fax:* 540-687-5026

SPILHAUS, ATHELSTAN FREDERICK, JR, SCIENTIFIC SOCIETY, GEOPHYSICS. *Current Pos:* asst exec dir, 67-70, EXEC DIR, AM GEOPHYS UNION, WASHINGTON, DC, 70- *Personal Data:* b Boston, Mass, May 21, 38; m 60, Sharon Brown; c Athelson F III, Ruth E & Mary C. *Educ:* Mass Inst Technol, SB, 59, SM, 60, PhD(oceanog), 65. *Prof Exp:* Oceanogr, US Govt, 65-67. *Concurrent Pos:* Dir & vpres, Oceanic Educ Found, 70-74; treas, Renewable Natural Resources Found, 72-74, dir, 72-; secy, US Nat Comt, Union Geodesy & Geophys, 72-; chmn, Conv Liaison Coun, 81-82; dir, Asn Women Geoscientists Found, 84-88. *Mem:* Fel AAAS; hon fel Am Geophys Union; Am Soc Limnol & Oceanog; Coun Eng & Sci Soc Exec (pres, 80-81); Asn Earth Sci Ed (pres, 77); Soc Scholarly Publ (secy, 78-80). *Res:* Use of optical measurements in oceanography. *Mailing Add:* 10900 Picasso Lane Potomac MD 20854. *E-Mail:* fspilhaus@agu.org

SPILKER, BERT, DRUG DEVELOPMENT. *Current Pos:* CLIN PROF, DEPT MED, MED SCH, UNIV NC, 79- *Personal Data:* b Washington, DC, July 3, 41; m 67; c 2. *Educ:* Univ Pa, AB, 62; Downstate Med Ctr, State Univ NY, PhD(pharmacol), 67; Univ Miami, MD, 77. *Honors & Awards:* Spec Citation Orphan Med, Food & Drug Admin Commissioners, 93. *Prof Exp:* Asst pharmacol, Med Sch, Univ Calif, 67-68; sr pharmacologist, Pfizer Ltd, Kent, Eng, 68-70, Philips-Duphar, Weesp, Holland, 70-72 & Sterling-Winthrop Res Inst, 72-75; resident, Med Sch, Brown Univ, 77-78; sr med consult, JRB Assocs, Inc, McLean, Va, 78-79; sr clin scientist, 79-83, Burroughs Wellcome Co, head dept proj coord, 83-93. *Concurrent Pos:* Adj prof, Dept Pharmacol, Med Sch, Univ NC, 79-, clin prof, Sch Pharm; clin prof, Sch Pharm Univ Minn, 93-; exec dir, Orphan Med, Minnetonka, Minn; chmn, Soc Chronic Dis, Minnetonka, Minn. *Mem:* Am Soc Clin Pharmacol & Therapeut; Am Soc Pharmacol & Exp Therapeut; Am Epilepsy Soc; Licensing Exec Soc. *Res:* Drug development. *Mailing Add:* 2107 Windsong Circle Wayzata MN 55391. *Fax:* 612-541-4969

SPILKER, LINDA JOYCE, PLANETARY SCIENCE, PLANETARY RINGS. *Current Pos:* Voyager infrared eng rep, Voyager Proj, Jet Propulsion Lab, 79-90, photopolarimeter sci assoc, 84-90, infrared radiometer & spectrometer sci assoc, 88-90, CASSINI MISSION SCIENTIST, CASSINI PROJ, JET PROPULSION LAB, 88- *Personal Data:* b Minneapolis, Minn, Apr 26, 55; m 76, 97, Thomas R; c Jennifer & Jessica. *Educ:* Calif State Univ, Fullerton, BA, 77; Calif State Univ, Los Angeles, MS, 83; Univ Calif, Los Angeles, PhD(geophys & space physics), 92. *Honors & Awards:* Except Serv Medal, Voyager IRIS Neptune Encounter, NASA, 90. *Concurrent Pos:* Co-investr, Cassini Composite Infrared Spectrometer, Jet Propulsion Lab, 90-, prin investr, Hermes Proj, 93-; prin investr, Planetary Geol & Geophys Prog, NASA, 93- *Mem:* AAAS; Am Astron Soc; Div Planetary Sci. *Res:* Dynamics and structure of planetary ring systems; systematic study of wave-like structure in Saturn's rings; discovery of a possible satellite density wave in the Uranium delta ring; discovery of new satellite wakes in Saturn's A ring. *Mailing Add:* Jet Propulsion Lab 4800 Oak Grove Dr M/S 183-501 Pasadena CA 91109. *Fax:* 818-354-0966; *E-Mail:* linda.j.spilker@jpl.nasa.gov

SPILLENKOTHEN, MELISSA J, SCIENCE ADMINISTRATION. *Current Pos:* ASST SECY ADMIN, US DEPT TRANSP, 86- *Educ:* Goucher Col, BA; George Washington Univ, MS. *Prof Exp:* Mgt intern, Dept Navy, 68-75; staff, Dept Treasury, 75-79; mgt, Off Mgt & Budget, 79-86. *Mailing Add:* US Dept Transp 400 Seventh St SW Washington DC 20590

SPILLER, EBERHARD ADOLF, X-RAY OPTICS. *Current Pos:* staff mem, 68-93, EMER RES STAFF MEM, T J WATSON RES CTR, IBM CORP, 93- *Personal Data:* b Halbendorf, Ger, Apr 16, 33; m 64, Marga Dietz; c Michael & Bettina. *Educ:* Univ Frankfurt, MSc, 60, PhD(physics), 64. *Prof Exp:* Asst prof physics, Univ Frankfurt, 65-68. *Concurrent Pos:* Vis prof, Tech Univ Denmark, 94-95, Univ Cent Fla, 96 & Univ Md, 96-; vis scientist, Nat Inst Sci & Technol & Lawrence Livermore Nat Lab, 97- *Mem:* Fel Optical Soc Am; Ger Phys Soc; fel AAAS; Int Soc Optical Eng. *Res:* Solid state physics; coherence of light; lasers; holography; nonlinear optics; thin films; x-ray optics; x-ray astronomy; x-ray extra-ultraviolet. *Mailing Add:* 60 Lakeside Rd Mt Kisco NY 10549. *Fax:* 914-945-2141; *E-Mail:* spiller@waton.ibm.com

SPILLER, GENE ALAN, CHOLESTEROL & LIPIDS, DIETARY FIBER RESEARCH & WRITING. *Current Pos:* PRES, HEALTH RES & STUDIES CTR, LOS ALTOS, CALIF, 88-, SPHERA FOUND, LOS ALTOS, CALIF. *Personal Data:* b Milan, Italy, Feb 19, 27; US citizen; m 81, Monica Alton. *Educ:* Univ Milan, Dr(chem), 49; Univ Calif, Berkeley, MS, 68, PhD(nutrit), 72. *Prof Exp:* Res Chemist, Univ Calif, Berkeley, 66-67, assoc specialist physiol, 68-72; prin scientist, Syntex Res, Palo Alto, Calif, 73-80. *Concurrent Pos:* Lectr nutrit, Mills Col, Oakland, Calif, 71-81; consult, Clin Nutrit Res, 81-; lectr, Foothill Col, Los Altos, Calif, 74- *Mem:* Am Inst Nutrit; Am Soc Clin Nutrit; Am Asn Cereal Chemists; Am Diabetes Asn; Mediterranean Group; Am Col Nutrit. *Res:* Effects of dietary fiber on health and disease; effects of carbohydrates and fats in human physiology and health; effects of dietary patterns on diseases of aging; role of lesser known food components on human health; pharmacological effects of nutrients and methylxanthines; design and execution of clinical studies; author of medical and popular nutrition books. *Mailing Add:* Health Res & Studies Ctr PO Box 338 Los Altos CA 94023. *Fax:* 650-948-8540; *E-Mail:* hrscebter@aol.com

SPILLERS, WILLIAM R, CIVIL ENGINEERING, ENGINEERING MECHANICS. *Current Pos:* PROF & CHMN, DEPT CIVIL & ENVIRON ENG, NJ INST TECHNOL, 90-, DISTINGUISHED PROF, 96- *Personal Data:* b Fresno, Calif, Aug 4, 34; c 3. *Educ:* Univ Calif, Berkeley, BS, 55, MS, 56; Columbia Univ, PhD(continuum mech), 61. *Prof Exp:* Struct designer, John Blume Assoc, Calif, 56-57; from instr to assoc prof civil eng, Columbia Univ, 59-68, prof civil eng & eng mech, 68-76; prof civil eng, Rensselaer Polytech Inst, 76-90. *Concurrent Pos:* Guggenheim fel, NY Univ, 68-69; NSF fel, Univ Calif, Berkeley, 75-76. *Mem:* Am Soc Civil Engrs; Int Asn Bridge & Struct Engrs. *Res:* Problems of structural mechanics; optimization; fatigue of buried power transmission cables; environmental design of housing; design theory. *Mailing Add:* Dept Civil & Environ Eng NJ Inst Technol Newark NJ 17102

SPILLETT, JAMES JUAN, animal ecology, wildlife resources, for more information see previous edition

SPILLMAN, CHARLES KENNARD, AGRICULTURAL ENGINEERING. *Current Pos:* from asst prof to assoc prof, Kans State Univ, 69-79, prof struct & environ, 79-82, head dept agr eng, 82-87, PROF GRAIN PROCESSING, KANS STATE UNIV, 87- *Personal Data:* b Lawrence County, Ill, Feb 26, 34; m 59; c 1. *Educ:* Univ Ill, Urbana, BS, 60, MS, 63; Purdue Univ, PhD(agr eng), 69. *Honors & Awards:* Metal Bldgs Mfg Award, Am Soc Agr Engrs. *Prof Exp:* Asst waste mgt, Univ Ill, Urbana, 60-62; exten agr mgr, Mich State Univ, 62-66. *Mem:* Fel Am Soc Agr Engrs; Am Asn Cereal Chemists; Am Soc Eng Educ; Sigma Xi. *Res:* Physical properties of cereal grains. *Mailing Add:* Dept Biol & Agr Eng 147 Seaton Hall Kans State Univ Manhattan KS 66506-2906

SPILLMAN, GEORGE RAYMOND, PHYSICS. *Current Pos:* RETIRED. *Personal Data:* b Holdenville, Okla, Oct 21, 34; m 66; c 2. *Educ:* Univ Okla, BS, 56; Univ Calif, Berkeley, MA, 61, PhD(physics), 64. *Prof Exp:* Assoc engr, Gen Dynamics/Convair, 56; proj officer, Res Directorate, Spec Weapons Ctr, Kirtland AFB, USAF, 56-59, proj officer, Weapons Lab, 63-67; staff mem, Los Alamos Sci Lab, 67-71, group leader, 71-74, assoc div leader, 74-76, alt div leader, 76-79, asst div leader, 79-83, prog mgr, 83-87, staff mem, 87-93. *Concurrent Pos:* Consult, 81- *Res:* Nuclear explosion phenomenology; nuclear weapons effects; plasma physics; atomic processes in plasma; radiative transfer; spectral absorption coefficients; hydrodynamics. *Mailing Add:* Pajarito Village Espanola NM 87532

SPILLMAN, RICHARD JAY, FAULT TOLERANT COMPUTING. *Current Pos:* ASST PROF COMPUT SCI, PAC LUTHERN UNIV, 81- *Personal Data:* b Tacoma, Wash, Sept 13, 49. *Educ:* Western Wash Univ, BS, 71; Univ Utah, MA, 73; Utah State Univ, PhD(elec eng), 78. *Prof Exp:* Asst prof elec eng, Univ Calif, Davis, 78-80; specialist eng, Boeing Co, 80-81. *Mem:* Inst Elec & Electronics Engrs; Am Soc Comput Mach. *Res:* Development of highly fault tolerant computer systems; analysis of system testability. *Mailing Add:* Dept Comput Sci Pacific Luthern Univ 12180 Park Ave S Tacoma WA 98447-0001

SPILLMAN, ROBERT DANIEL, END-USER SYSTEMS, OFFICE AUTOMATED SYSTEMS. *Current Pos:* ASST PROF INFO SYSTS, RADFORD UNIV, 84- *Personal Data:* b Winston-Salem, NC, June 8, 52. *Educ:* Gardner-Webb Univ, BS, 74; Univ NC, Greensboro, MS, 78; Ohio State Univ, PhD(mkt & bus educ), 83. *Prof Exp:* Secondary mkt & distrib educ teacher coord, High Point City Schs, NC, 78-80; instr bus, High Point Univ, NC, 80; postdoctoral fel, Ohio State Univ, 83-84. *Mem:* Int Acad Info Mgt; Data Processing Mgt Asn. *Res:* Telecommuting; end-user interface development and design; information systems curriculum development; trends and issues in information systems. *Mailing Add:* Dept Acct Finance & Info Systs Radford Univ Radford VA 24142. *Fax:* 540-831-6626; *E-Mail:* rspillma@runet.edu

SPILLMAN, WILLIAM BERT, JR, FIBER OPTIC SENSORS, DEVICE MODELLING. *Current Pos:* mgr advan develop, 84-87, dir res, 87-90, CHIEF SCIENTIST, SIMMONDS PRECISION AIRCRAFT SYSTS, 91-; PRES, CATAMOUNT SCI, INC, 91- *Personal Data:* b Charleston, SC, Jan 21, 46; m 74; c 2. *Educ:* Brown Univ, AB, 68; Northeastern Univ, MS, 72, PhD(physics), 77. *Prof Exp:* Res asst, Northeastern Univ, 72-77; tech staff mem, Sperry Res Ctr, 77-83; sr scientist, Geo-Centers, Inc, 83-84. *Concurrent Pos:* Adj assoc prof elec eng, Univ Vt, 87-90; mem, Adv Bd, Smart Struct Inst, Univ Strathclyde, UK, 91-; adj prof physics, Univ Vt, 91- *Mem:* Optical Soc Am; Am Phys Soc; Inst Elec & Electronics Engrs; sr mem Instrument Soc Am; Int Soc Optical Eng. *Res:* Fiber optic sensing; fiber optic sensor multiplexing; ultrasonic sensing; magneto-optic materials; smart structures and skins for aerospace and civil applications; computer modelling of sensor and sensor systems. *Mailing Add:* Simmonds Precision Aircraft Systs Vergennes VT 05491

SPILMAN, CHARLES HADLEY, HIGH THROUGHPUT SCREENING. *Current Pos:* res scientist II, Upjohn Co, 72-76, sr res scientist III, 76-85, sr scientist IV, 85-92, sr scientist V, Upjohn Co, 92-94, DIR, DISCOVERY TECHNOLOGIES, PHARMACIA & UPJOHN INC, 94- *Personal Data:* b Westerly, RI, Mar 30, 42; m 62, 85, Susan B Choudoir; c Charles, Christina (deceased), Michelle, Jamie & John. *Educ:* Clark Univ, AB, 65; Univ Mass, Amherst, PhD(physiol), 69. *Prof Exp:* Res asst, Univ Mass, 65-69; res assoc, Cornell Univ, 69-71 & Worcester Found Exp Biol, 71-72. *Concurrent Pos:* Vis scientist, Univ Calif, San Francisco, 85-86. *Mem:* NY Acad Sci; Am Heart Asn, Arteriosclerosis Coun; AAAS; Soc Exp Biol Med; Am Soc Cell Biol. *Res:* Research management; high throughput screening; assay design and development; drug discovery; robotic screening systems; research compound collection management. *Mailing Add:* Discovery Technol Pharmacia & Upjohn Inc Upjohn Co Kalamazoo MI 49001. *Fax:* 616-833-2225; *E-Mail:* charles.h.spilman@am.pnu.com

SPINAR, LEO HAROLD, PHYSICAL CHEMISTRY. *Current Pos:* assoc prof, 66-69, PROF CHEM, SDAK STATE UNIV, 69- *Personal Data:* b Colome, SDak, Feb 20, 29; m 56; c 4. *Educ:* Univ SDak, BA, 51; Univ Wis, MS, 53, PhD(chem), 58. *Prof Exp:* From instr to asst prof chem, Colo State Univ, 57-62; assoc prof, Univ Mo, 62-66. *Concurrent Pos:* Dir planning, program & budget, SDak State Univ, 73-82, environ regulatory compliance officer, 91- *Mem:* Am Chem Soc. *Res:* Physical inorganic chemistry; high temperature properties of materials; thermodynamics; vapor pressure studies. *Mailing Add:* Chem Dept SDak State Univ Box 2202 Brookings SD 57007-2202. *Fax:* 605-688-6364

SPINDEL, WILLIAM, CHEMISTRY, SCIENCE POLICY. *Current Pos:* RETIRED. *Personal Data:* b New York, NY, Sept 9, 22; m 42, 67, Louise Hoodenpyl; c Robert A & Laurence M. *Educ:* Brooklyn Col, BA, 44; Columbia Univ, MA, 47, PhD(chem), 50. *Honors & Awards:* Prof Staff Award, Nat Res Coun, 85. *Prof Exp:* Jr scientist, Manhattan Proj, Los Alamos Sci Lab, Univ Calif, 44-45; instr, Polytech Inst Brooklyn, 49-50; asst prof, State Univ NY Teachers Col, Albany, 50-54; from assoc prof to prof, Rutgers Univ, 57-64; prof, Belfer Grad Sch Sci, Yeshiva Univ, 64-74; exec secy, Off Chem & Chem Technol, Nat Acad Sci-Nat Res Coun, 74-82, staff dir, Bd Chem Sci & Technol, 83-88, prin staff, Off Spec Proj, 88-90, sr consult, 90-96. *Concurrent Pos:* Res assoc, Columbia Univ, 54-56, vis assoc prof, 56-57, vis prof, 62-70, sr lectr, 70-74; Fulbright res scholar, 61; Guggenheim fel, 61-62; NSF vis scientist, Yugoslavia, 71-72. *Mem:* Fel AAAS; Am Chem Soc; Am Phys Soc. *Res:* Separation of stable isotopes; physical and chemical properties of isotopes; mass spectrometry. *Mailing Add:* 6503 Dearborn Dr Falls Church VA 22044. *Fax:* 703-750-9018

SPINDLER, MAX, CIVIL & AERONAUTICAL ENGINEERING. *Current Pos:* asst prof civil eng, 70-77, ASSOC PROF CIVIL ENG, UNIV TEX, ARLINGTON, 77- *Personal Data:* b Antwerp, Belg, Dec 19, 38; US citizen; m 67; c 1. *Educ:* Cooper Union, BCE, 61; Northwestern Univ, Ill, MS, 63, PhD(civil eng), 68. *Prof Exp:* Eng specialist, LTV Aerospace Corp, Tex, 67-70. *Mem:* Am Soc Civil Engrs; Am Inst Aeronaut & Astronaut; NY Acad Sci; Sigma Xi. *Res:* Noise spectra due to flow through stenosed heart valves; fluid mechanics; hydraulics; biomedical engineering. *Mailing Add:* 1708 Park Ridge Terr Arlington TX 76012-1933

SPINDT, CHARLES A (CAPP), VACUUM MICROELECTRONICS TECHNOLOGY, MICROFABRICATED FIELD-ELECTRON EMITTERS & FIELD IONIZERS. *Current Pos:* sr res engr, 70-87, PROG DIR, SRI INT, 87- *Personal Data:* b San Jose, Calif, July 20, 31; div; c Christopher, Susan D & Kimberly K. *Educ:* Calif State Univ, San Jose, BS, 61; Eurotech Res Univ, PhD(eng physics), 90. *Honors & Awards:* Jan Rajchman Prize, Soc Info Display, 96. *Prof Exp:* Fighter Pilot, USAF, 53-56; res engr, Stanford Res Inst, 61-70. *Concurrent Pos:* Vis lectr, Stanford Univ, Univ Calif, Univ Ill & Mich State, 85-, Univ Calif, Davis, 94; co-chmn, Inst Elect & Electronics Engrs Int Vacuum Microelectronics Conf, 88, gen chmn, 90; vis scientist & lectr, Academia Sinica Beijing China, 93; vchmn, Int Vacuum Microelectronics Conf, 93. *Mem:* Soc Info Display; Am Vacuum Soc; Sigma Xi; Inst Elec & Electronics Engrs; Electrochem Soc. *Res:* Invented and developed microfabricated field-emitter arrays that have become the enabling technology for the new field of vacuum microelectronics and the development of new devices such as field emission panel displays. *Mailing Add:* SRI Int 333 Ravenswood Ave Menlo Park CA 94025

SPINDT, RODERICK SIDNEY, ORGANIC CHEMISTRY. *Current Pos:* RETIRED. *Personal Data:* b Waupaca, Wis, Mar 5, 19; m 50; c 2. *Educ:* Ripon Col, BA, 41; Univ Wis, MS, 44; Univ Pittsburgh, PhD(chem), 49. *Prof Exp:* Jr chemist org synthesis, Gulf Res & Develop Co, 44-45; fel org anal,

Mellon Inst, 45-56; staff asst, Gulf Res & Develop Co, 56-58, sect head, 58-60, sr chemist, 60-65, from res assoc to sr res assoc, 65-80. *Concurrent Pos:* Lectr, Univ Pittsburgh, 52- *Mem:* Am Chem Soc; Soc Automotive Engrs; Air Pollution Control Asn. *Res:* Characterization of sulfur compounds; mechanism of engine deposit formation; mechanisms of combustion in engines; air pollution research; vehicle emissions; composition of gasoline. *Mailing Add:* 3957 Parkview Lane Allison Park PA 15101-3522

SPINELLI, JOHN, ANALYTICAL CHEMISTRY, FOOD CHEMISTRY. *Current Pos:* DIR, UTILIZATION RES DIV, NORTHWEST & ALASKA FISHERIES CTR, SEATTLE, 80- *Personal Data:* b Seattle, Wash, July 23, 25; m 49; c 1. *Educ:* Univ Wash, BS, 49. *Prof Exp:* Consult chemist, Food Chem & Res Labs, Wash, 49-62; res chemist, Technol Lab, Nat Marine Fisheries Serv, 62-80. *Mem:* NY Acad Sci; AAAS; Am Chem Soc; Inst Food Technol; Pac Fisheries Technologists. *Res:* Food process quality control, product analysis and development; biochemical changes in fish postmortem; protein isolates of marine origin; protein and nutritional requirements of salmonids; food uses for underutilized species; improvement of quality and safety of fishery products. *Mailing Add:* 10002 63rd Ave S Seattle WA 98178

SPINGOLA, FRANK, CHEMISTRY. *Current Pos:* Asst prof, 68-76, ASSOC PROF CHEM, DOWLING COL, 76- *Personal Data:* b Brooklyn, NY, Aug 3, 37; m 67. *Educ:* Adelphi Univ, AB, 59; Polytech Inst Brooklyn, MS, 63, PhD(chem), 68. *Res:* Physical chemistry of aqueous solutions. *Mailing Add:* 14 Haight St Deer Park NY 11729-3112

SPINK, CHARLES HARLAN, ANALYTICAL CHEMISTRY, PHYSICAL CHEMISTRY. *Current Pos:* from asst prof to assoc prof, 67-72, PROF ANALYTICAL CHEM, STATE UNIV NY COL, CORTLAND, 72- *Personal Data:* b Platteville, Wis, Apr 9, 36; wid; c 1. *Educ:* Univ Wis, BS, 58; Pa State Univ, PhD(phys chem), 62. *Prof Exp:* Fel, Univ Wash, 62-63; asst prof anal chem, Juniata Col, 63-67. *Concurrent Pos:* Am Chem Soc-Petrol Res Fund grant, 63-64; USPHS res grant, 65-68; NY State Res Found fel & grant-in-aid, 69-72; res assoc, Lund Univ, Sweden, 73-74, Yale Univ, 80-81; USPHS res grant, 77-79, 80-87; Nat Sci Found Res Award, Cornell Univ, 87-88. *Mem:* Biophys Soc; Am Chem Soc; Sigma Xi. *Res:* Thermochemical studies on solutes in bile salt solutions; thermochemical analysis of mixed organic-aqueous mixtures; heat capacities of model biochemical compounds; scanning calorimetry of micelles and lipid-detergent mixtures. *Mailing Add:* Dept Chem State Univ NY Cortland NY 13045. *Fax:* 607-753-5999; *E-Mail:* spink@snycorva

SPINK, D(ONALD) R(ICHARD), EXTRACTIVE METALLURGY & CHEMICAL ENGINEERING, AIR POLLUTION CONTROL. *Current Pos:* pres, 76-95, FOUNDER & CHMN BD, AIR POLLUTION CONTROL EXPERTS, TURBOTAK INC, 76- *Personal Data:* b Buffalo, NY, Mar 11, 23; m 46, Helen Forrestel; c Bob, Tom, Dave, Don Jr, Ed & Bill. *Educ:* Univ Mich, BS, 45; Univ Rochester, MS, 49; Iowa State Univ, PhD(chem eng), 52. *Prof Exp:* Chem engr, Gen Elec Co, 46-48; asst, Iowa State Univ, 49-52; res engr, E I du Pont de Nemours & Co, 52; sr res engr, Carborundum Metals Climax, Inc, NY, 52-59, asst to mgr, Tech Br & mgr, Res & Develop Dept, 59-61, mgr, Tech Br, 61-65, vpres technol, 65-68. *Concurrent Pos:* Prof chem eng, Univ Waterloo, 68-88, emer prof, 88- *Mem:* Am Inst Chem Engrs; Can Soc Chem Engrs; Am Inst Mining, Metall & Petrol Engrs; Can Inst Mining & Metall; fel Com Inst Chemists. *Res:* Extractive metallurgy of zirconium, hafnium and titanium; solvent extraction; extractive metallurgy; air pollution research; low energy scrubber development; coal treatment (sulfur removal); fly ash treatment (recovery of vanadium and nickel); zinc concentrate roasting without formation of ferrites; sulphur dioxide removal and regeneration process; nozzle design; granted 30 patents; VOC removal and regeneration process. *Mailing Add:* 323 Grant Crescent 550 Parkside Dr Suite A-14 Waterloo ON N2K 2A3 Can. *Fax:* 519-885-6992

SPINK, GORDON CLAYTON, MEDICAL EDUCATION, FAMILY MEDICINE. *Current Pos:* Instr, Mich State Univ, 63-66, asst prof, Biol Res Ctr, 66-68, dir, Electron Micros Lab, 67-72, asst prof entom, Univ, 68-71, prof staff scientist electron micros, Pesticide Res Ctr, 71-72, instr & dir, Electron Micros Lab, 72-75, clin asst prof, Col Osteopath Med, 75-76, asst prof, Dept Family Med, 76-78, unit III coordr, 77-79, co-dir, Preceptor Prog, Dept Family Med, 78-80, actg asst dean grad & continuing educ, 80, ASSOC PROF, DEPT FAMILY MED, MICH STATE UNIV, 78- *Personal Data:* b Lansing, Mich, Jan 6, 35; m 60; c 2. *Educ:* Mich State Univ, BS, 57, PhD(bot, cytol), 66, DO, 75. *Concurrent Pos:* Res collabr, Biol Dept, Brookhaven Nat Lab, 69; intern, Flint Osteopath Hosp, Mich, 75-76, dir med educ, 80-81; dir med educ, Lansing Gen Hosp, 82-84; dir med educ, Ingham Med Ctr, Lansing, Mich, 87-; med prac fel, Chicago Col Osteop Med, Chicago, Ill, 87-88. *Mem:* AAAS; Electron Micros Soc Am; Asn Hosp Med Educ; Asn Osteop Dirs Med Educ; Am Osteop Asn; Am Heart Asn; Am Med Soccer Asn. *Res:* Medical education. *Mailing Add:* 3910 Sandlewood Dr Okemos MI 48864

SPINK, WALTER JOHN, STRATIGRAPHY, STRUCTURAL GEOLOGY. *Current Pos:* GEOL CONSULT, 86- *Personal Data:* b Hackensack, NJ, May 4, 33; m 57; c 2. *Educ:* Lehigh Univ, BS, 57; Rutgers Univ, MS, 63, PhD(geol), 67. *Prof Exp:* Geologist, NJ Geol Surv, 60-66; from instr to asst prof, Rider Col, 66-69, chmn dept, 69-76, assoc prof geol, 69-80, chmn dept, 80-83. *Mem:* AAAS; Geol Soc Am; Asn Prof Geol Scientists. *Res:* Areal geologic mapping and gravity survey of northwestern New Jersey; structural geology; stratigraphy and sedimentation. *Mailing Add:* Passaconway Rd Conway NH 03818

SPINKA, HAROLD M, SPIN PHYSICS, NUCLEON-NUCLEON INTERACTIONS. *Current Pos:* Fel, 70-73, physicist, 76-87, SR PHYSICIST, ARGONNE NAT LAB, 87- *Personal Data:* b Chicago, Ill, Apr 2, 45; m 73; c 2. *Educ:* Northwestern Univ, BA, 66; Calif Inst Technol, PhD(physics), 70. *Concurrent Pos:* Adj asst prof physics, Univ Calif, Los Angeles, 73-76. *Mem:* Am Phys Soc; Sigma Xi. *Res:* Strong interactions using polarized beams and targets and nuclear beams and targets; nucleon-nucleon interactions. *Mailing Add:* 635 S Loomis St Naperville IL 60540-6611

SPINKS, DANIEL OWEN, SOIL CHEMISTRY. *Current Pos:* RETIRED. *Personal Data:* b Dallas, Ga, Sept 5, 18; m 40; c 3. *Educ:* Univ Ga, BS, 39, MSA, 47; NC State Col, PhD, 53. *Prof Exp:* Instr soils & physics, Abraham Baldwin Agr Col, 39-44; from instr to assoc prof, 47-61, prof soils & soil chemist, Agr Exp Sta, Univ Fla, 61-84, assoc dean resident instr, Inst Food & Agr Sci, 69-84. *Mem:* Nat Asn Cols & Teachers Agr; Soil Sci Soc Am. *Res:* Effect of organic matter on the availability of fixed soil phosphorus. *Mailing Add:* RR 1 Louisburg NC 27549

SPINKS, JOHN LEE, CONSULTING. *Current Pos:* PRES, ENVIRON EMISSIONS ENG CO, 83- *Personal Data:* b Central City, Ky, June 19, 24; m 51; c 2. *Educ:* Univ Ky, BSME, 51. *Hon Degrees:* PhD(eng), World Univ, 84. *Honors & Awards:* US Presidential Sports Award. *Prof Exp:* Dep dir, Eng Div & Lt Col, Space Div, USAF, 61-73; supv engr, SCoast Air Qual Mgr Dist, 56-83. *Concurrent Pos:* Hon mem, Nat Adv Bd, Am Biog Inst; instr rock & ice mountaineering; lectr, marathon running; consult, Govt Air Qual Agencies. *Mem:* Am Acad Environ Engrs; Inst Advan Eng; Am Soc Mech Engrs; Air Pollution Control Asn; Nat Soc Prof Engrs; Inst Environ Sci; Soc Environ Engrs; Am Soc Eng Educ; Soc Eng Sci; AAAS. *Res:* Pioneered development of engineering principles and technology for air pollution control techniques and adapted by other similar agencies throughout the world; developed air and water pollution control programs for US Air Force. *Mailing Add:* 26856 Eastvale Rd Palos Verdes Peninsula CA 90274

SPINKS, JOHN WILLIAM TRANTER, CHEMISTRY. *Current Pos:* Asst prof chem, Univ Sask, 30-39, prof phys chem, 39-74, head dept, 48-59, dean grad col, 49-59, pres, 59-74, EMER PROF PHYS CHEM & EMER PRES, UNIV SASK, 74- *Personal Data:* b Methwold, Eng, Jan 1, 08; m 39. *Educ:* Univ London, BSc, 28, PhD(photochem), 30. *Hon Degrees:* DSc, Univ London, 57; LLD, Carleton Univ, 58 & Assumption Col, 62. *Honors & Awards:* Order Brit Empire; Companion Can. *Mem:* Am Chem Soc; fel Royal Soc Can; fel Royal Inst Chem. *Res:* Photochemistry; molecular structure; radioactive tracers; radiation chemistry. *Mailing Add:* 932 University Dr No 10111 Saskatoon SK S7N 0K1 Can

SPINNER, IRVING HERBERT, chemical engineering, for more information see previous edition

SPINNLER, JOSEPH F, PHYSICAL CHEMISTRY. *Current Pos:* CONSULT, 96- *Personal Data:* b Greenwood, SC, July 8, 31; m 62; c 2. *Educ:* Lafayette Col, BS, 53; Yale Univ, MS, 58, PhD(chem), 60. *Prof Exp:* Scientist, Ballistics Sect, Rohm and Haas Co, 59-65, sr scientist, Chem Sect, 65-70; mem, Explor Develop Group, Micromedic Systs Inc, 70-71; sr scientist, Rohm & Haas Co, 71-96. *Mem:* Sigma Xi. *Res:* Development of hydrogen fluorine chemical laser; automation of spectrophotometric and electrophoretic clinical laboratory procedures; metabolite and residue analysis using liquid chromatography; gas chromatography/mass spectrometry; thin layer chromatography and electrophoresis. *Mailing Add:* 258 Lanford Circle Travelers Rest SC 29690

SPINOSA, CLAUDE, PALEONTOLOGY, GEOLOGY. *Current Pos:* assoc prof, 70-76, PROF GEOL, BOISE STATE UNIV, 76- *Personal Data:* b Italy, July 17, 37; US citizen; m 63; c 3. *Educ:* City Col, New York, BS, 61; Univ Iowa, MS, 65, PhD(geol), 68. *Prof Exp:* Asst prof geol, Ind Univ, Southeast, 68-70. *Mem:* Geol Soc Am; Paleont Soc. *Res:* Permian ammonoids; Permian stratigraphy; nautilus; biology. *Mailing Add:* Dept Geosci Boise State Univ Boise ID 83725. *Fax:* 208-385-4061; *E-Mail:* cspinosa@trex.idbsu.edu

SPINRAD, BERNARD ISRAEL, PHYSICS, NUCLEAR ENGINEERING. *Current Pos:* EMER PROF NUCLEAR ENG, ORE STATE UNIV, 83-; EMER PROF NUCLEAR ENG, IOWA STATE UNIV, 90- *Personal Data:* b New York, NY, Apr 16, 24; m 51, 83, Lois Ringstrom; c Alexandra A, Mark D, Jeremy P & Diana E. *Educ:* Yale Univ, BS, 42, MS, 44, PhD(phys chem), 45. *Prof Exp:* Sterling fel, Yale Univ, 45-46; physicist, Clinton Labs, Tenn, 46-49; from assoc physicist to sr physicist, Argonne Nat Lab, 49-72, dir, Reactor Eng Div, 57-63; dir, Div Nuclear Power & Reactors, Int Atomic Energy Agency, Vienna, 67-70; ad hoc prof, Univ Wis-Parkside, 71; Northwest energy prof, nuclear eng, Ore State Univ, 72-82; chmn dept nuclear eng, Iowa State Univ, 83-90. *Concurrent Pos:* Adv US deleg, Conf Peaceful Uses of Atomic Energy, Geneva, 55-58; consult, Int Atomic Energy Agency, 61, 63; mem, Europ-Am Reactor Physics Comt, 61-66, chmn, 61-62; vis prof, Univ Ill, 64; mem, Comt Nuclear & Alternative Energy Systs, Nat Acad Sci, 75-80; res scholar, Int Inst Appl Systs Anal, 78-79; mem comt Univ res reactors, Nat Res Coun, 86-88. *Mem:* AAAS; fel Am Phys Soc; fel Am Nuclear Soc; Sigma Xi; Am Chem Soc. *Res:* Physics of nuclear reactors; nuclear systems; energy systems and economics; nuclear reactor shutdown power; nuclear fuel cycle and nuclear safeguards. *Mailing Add:* 18803 37th Ave NE Seattle WA 98155. *E-Mail:* bspinrad@aol.com

SPINRAD, HYRON, ASTRONOMY. *Current Pos:* from asst prof to assoc prof, 64-68, PROF ASTRON, UNIV CALIF, BERKELEY, 68- *Personal Data:* b New York, NY, Feb 17, 34; m 58, Bette L Abrams; c 3. *Educ:* Univ Calif, Berkeley, PhD(astron), 61. *Honors & Awards:* Dannie Heineman Prize Astrophys. *Prof Exp:* Sr scientist, Jet Propulsion Lab, 61-64. *Mem:* Nat Acad Sci; Am Astron Soc. *Res:* Planetary atmospheres; spectroscopic investigations of old stars and nuclei of galaxies; astrophysics; spectroscopy of faint, distant radio and cluster galaxies; spectroscopic studies of comets. *Mailing Add:* Dept Astron Univ Calif Berkeley CA 94720. *E-Mail:* spinrad@bigz.berkeley.edu

SPINRAD, RICHARD WILLIAM, OPTICAL OCEANOGRAPHY, FLOW CYTOMETRY. *Current Pos:* from prog mgr ocean optics, 87-88, DIV DIR, OFF NAVAL RES, 88, RES SCIENTIST OCEANOG, BIGELOW LAB OCEAN SCI, 82- *Personal Data:* b New York, NY, Apr 6, 54; m 80, Alanna Thompson; c Gary B. *Educ:* Johns Hopkins Univ, BA, 75; Ore State Univ, MS, 78, PhD(geol oceanog), 82. *Prof Exp:* Pres mfg, Sea Tech, Inc, 84-86. *Concurrent Pos:* Consult, Calgary Dept Waterworks, 89- *Mem:* Am Geophys Union; Oceanog Soc; Am Soc Limnol & Oceanog; Optical Soc Am. *Res:* Optical properties of marine particles; light scattering characteristics of phytoplankton and bacteria. *Mailing Add:* 2407 N Illinois St Arlington VA 22205. *Fax:* 703-696-4884

SPINRAD, ROBERT J(OSEPH), COMPUTER SCIENCE. *Current Pos:* vpres, Sci Data Systs, Xerox Corp, 68-70, vpres, Xerox Data Systs, 70-71, dir info sci, 71-76, vpres, Systs Develop Div, 76-78, vpres res, Parc, 78-83, dir, Systs Technol, 83-86, dir, Corp Technol, 87-92, vpres technol anal & develop, 92-94, VPRES TECHNOL STRATEGY, XEROX CORP, 94- *Personal Data:* b New York, NY, Mar 20, 32; m 54, Verna Winderman; c Susan & Paul. *Educ:* Columbia Univ, BS, 53, MS, 54; Mass Inst Technol, PhD, 63. *Prof Exp:* Assoc engr, Bulova Res & Develop Lab, 54-55; from asst elec engr to assoc elec engr, Brookhaven Nat Lab, 55-63, elec engr, 63-66, head, Comput Systs Group, 65-68, sr elec engr, 66-67, sr scientist, 67-68. *Concurrent Pos:* Consult, Bell Tel Labs, 62-67, Rand Corp, 77-79 & Int Inst Appl Syst Anal, 78-80; educ comt, Comput Sci & Eng Bd, Nat Acad Sci, 68-70, mem, Software Intellectual Property Panel, 89; mem, Comput Elec Eng Comt, Nat Acad Eng, 69-72; mem, Math Dept Vis Comt, Mass Inst Technol, 70-74; gen chmn, 1972 Fall Joint Comput Conf, 71-72; mem, Comput Sci Adv Comt, Stanford Univ, chmn, 72 & 83; mem, Eng Adv Coun, Univ Calif, 77-85; Overseers Comt Info Technol, Harvard Univ, 79-85; Nat Res Coun panel, Nat Bur Stand, 80-83; bd trustees, Educom, 82-89; mem adv group, CSNET, 82-83; mem, Info Technol Workshop, NSF, 83; dir, Digital Pathways Inc, 83-86; AAAS panel, NSF Bilateral Progs, 84-85; consult ed-comput, McGraw-Hill Encycl Sci & Technol, 87-93; mem, Technol Assessment Adv Comt, Comn Preserv & Access, 89-; mem, Info Sci & Technol Study Group, Defense Advan Res Projs Agency, 90-96; coun foreign rels study group info technol, 95-; coun foreign rel study group info technol, 95-; Calif coun sci & technol, 96- *Mem:* Nat Acad Eng. *Res:* Electronics; computers; computer systems; science policy; technical management. *Mailing Add:* 461 Nevada Ave Palo Alto CA 94301-4122. *Fax:* 650-812-4274; *E-Mail:* rspinrad@parc.xerox.com

SPIRA, ARTHUR WILLIAM, DEVELOPMENTAL NEUROSCIENCE. *Current Pos:* from asst prof to assoc prof, 75-85, PROF ANAT, UNIV CALGARY, 85- *Personal Data:* b New Britain, Conn, Oct 18, 41; m 65; c 3. *Educ:* City Col New York, BS, 62; Univ Mich, MS, 64, USPHS fel & PhD(anat), 67. *Prof Exp:* USPHS fel anat, McGill Univ, 67-68; asst prof, Univ BC, 68-73. *Concurrent Pos:* Mem, Grants Review Comt, Med Res Coun Can, 78-81; actg dir, Lions Sight Ctr, 85-86. *Mem:* Soc Neurosci; Am Asn Anat; Can Asn Anat; Asn Res Vision Ophthal. *Res:* Structure and function of the retina; ocular development; retinal histogenesis; retinal neurotransmitters; cytochemistry; neurochemistry; transmission and scanning electron microscopy. *Mailing Add:* Dept Anat Univ Calgary 3330 Hospital Dr NW Calgary AB T2N 4N1 Can

SPIRA, JOEL SOLON, ENGINEERING PHYSICS. *Current Pos:* CHMN & DIR RES, LUTRON ELECTRONICS CO, INC, 61- *Personal Data:* b New York, NY, Mar 1, 27; m 54; c 3. *Educ:* Purdue Univ, BS, 48. *Prof Exp:* Jr engr, Glenn L Martin Co, 48-52; engr, Reeves Instrument Corp, 52-54, sr engr, 54-56, sr proj engr, 56-59; prin systs analyst, ITT Commun Systs Inc, 59-61. *Mem:* Nat Acad Eng; Am Phys Soc; sr mem Inst Elec & Electronics Engrs; fel AAAS. *Res:* Supersonic aerodynamics; microwaves; computers; electronic instruments; missile technology; weapons systems analysis; nuclear and military strategy; electronic and general technology; light dimming and electron power control; energy conservation. *Mailing Add:* 7200 Suter Rd Coopersburg PA 18036

SPIRA, MELVIN, MEDICINE, PLASTIC SURGERY. *Current Pos:* From instr to assoc prof, 61-70, PROF PLASTIC SURG, BAYLOR COL MED, 70-, HEAD, DIV PLASTIC SURG, 76- *Personal Data:* b Chicago, Ill, July 3, 25; m 52; c 3. *Educ:* Northwestern Univ, DDS, 47, MSD, 51; Med Col Ga, MD, 56. *Mem:* Am Soc Plastic & Reconstruct Surg; Am Soc Maxillofacial Surg (pres, 74-); fel Am Col Surg; Am Asn Plastic Surg; Plastic Surg Res Coun. *Res:* Maxillofacial and microvascular surgery. *Mailing Add:* Baylor Col Med One Baylor Plaza Houston TX 77030-3411

SPIRITO, CARL PETER, NEUROBIOLOGY, ETHOLOGY. *Current Pos:* chmn, 83-88, MEM FAC DEPT PHYSIOL, UNIV NEW ENG, 80- *Personal Data:* b Hartford, Conn, Apr 7, 41; m 64; c 3. *Educ:* Cent Conn State Col, BA, 65; Univ Conn, PhD(biol eng), 69. *Prof Exp:* Nat Inst Child Health & Human Develop trainee, Univ Miami, 69-70; asst prof biol, Univ Va, 70-77; assoc prof neurophysiol, Ohio Univ, 77-80. *Mem:* Soc Neurosci; Soc Exp Biol & Med. *Res:* Invertebrate neurobiology and behavior; neural control of locomotion. *Mailing Add:* Dept Physiol Univ New Eng Col Osteo Med 605 Pool Rd Biddeford ME 04005-9524

SPIRO, HERZL ROBERT, PSYCHIATRY, SOCIAL PSYCHOLOGY. *Current Pos:* PROF PSYCHIAT & CHMN DEPT, MED COL WIS, 76-; PROF PSYCHIAT, SINAI SAMARITAN MED CTR, 88- *Personal Data:* b Burlington, Vt, Apr 22, 35; m 55; c 3. *Educ:* Univ Vt, BA, 55, MD, 60. *Prof Exp:* Intern internal med, Cornell Univ, 60-61; resident psychiat, Johns Hopkins Univ, 61-64, from instr to assoc prof psychiat, 64-71; prof psychiat, Med Sch, prof social psychol, Grad Fac & dir ment health ctr, Rutgers Univ, 71-76. *Concurrent Pos:* Fel, Johns Hopkins Univ, 61-64; assoc physician-in-charge psychiat liaison serv, Johns Hopkins Hosp, 64-66, psychiatrist-in-charge Henry Phipps outpatient serv, 66-70, dir outpatient & community ment health progs & div group process, 69-71; consult, Bur Disability Ins, Social Security Admin, 64-69; consult, NIMH, 69-, mem ment health serv res rev comt, 71-, mem task force health maintenance orgn, 71-72; mem, Nat Task Force Psychiat Res, 72-73. *Mem:* AAAS; fel Asn Psychiat Asn; fel Am Col Psychiat; fel Am Pub Health Asn; Am Psychosom Soc. *Res:* Social psychiatry including epidemiology of and attitudes towards mental illness; small group theory and practice; health and mental health service delivery systems; psychosomatic medicine and liaison psychiatry. *Mailing Add:* Sinai Samaritan Med Ctr 2000 W Kilbourn Corp 4 Milwaukee WI 53233

SPIRO, HOWARD MARGET, GASTROENTEROLOGY. *Current Pos:* From asst prof to assoc prof, 56-67, PROF MED, SCH MED, YALE UNIV, 67- *Personal Data:* b Cambridge, Mass, Mar 23, 24; m 51; c 4. *Educ:* Harvard Univ, BA, 43, MD, 47. *Hon Degrees:* Yale Univ, MA, 67. *Mem:* Am Gastroenterol Asn; Am Soc Clin Invest. *Res:* Gastroenterology. *Mailing Add:* Yale Univ Sch Med 333 Cedar St Box 208019 New Haven CT 06520-8019. *E-Mail:* spirohm@umas.po3.mas.yale.edu

SPIRO, JULIUS, ELECTRONICS ENGINEERING. *Current Pos:* sr elec engr, Accelerator Dept, 54-86, CONSULT, BROOKHAVEN NAT LAB, 88- *Personal Data:* b New York, NY, Nov 20, 21; m 50; c 2. *Educ:* City Col New York, BS, 53. *Prof Exp:* Electronic engr, Nevis Cyclotron, Columbia Univ, 47-53, Hudson Labs, 53-54. *Mem:* Sr mem Inst Elec & Electronics Engrs. *Res:* Electronic engineering applied to high energy particle accelerator design; logic and control systems for particle accelerators. *Mailing Add:* Brookhaven Nat Lab Upton NY 11973

SPIRO, MARY JANE, BIOCHEMISTRY. *Current Pos:* from res assoc to prin assoc, 60-84, ASSOC PROF MED, HARVARD MED SCH, 84- *Personal Data:* b Syracuse, NY, Nov 15, 30; m 52, Robert G; c David J & Mark D. *Educ:* Syracuse Univ, AB, 52, PhD, 55. *Prof Exp:* Res assoc biochem, Col Med, State Univ NY Upstate Med Ctr, 55-56. *Concurrent Pos:* Res fel, Harvard Med Sch, 56-60; sr investr, Joslin Res Lab, 74- *Mem:* Am Soc Biol Chemists; Glycobiol Soc. *Res:* Glycoprotein biosynthesis, structure and change in disease states; extracellular matrix changes in diabetes. *Mailing Add:* Joslin Res Lab One Joslin Pl Boston MA 02215. *E-Mail:* mjspiro@joslab.harvard.edu

SPIRO, MELFORD ELLIOT, ANTHROPOLOGY. *Current Pos:* prof & chmn, 68-90, EMER PROF, DEPT ANTHROP, UNIV CALIF, SAN DIEGO, 90- *Personal Data:* b Cleveland, Apr 26, 20; m 50, Audrey Goldman; c Michael & Jonathan. *Educ:* Univ Minn, BA, 41; Northwestern Univ, PhD, 50. *Hon Degrees:* LHD, Univ Chicago, 90. *Prof Exp:* Mem fac, Univ Conn, 52-57, Univ Wash, 57-64; prof anthrop, Univ Chicago, 64-68. *Concurrent Pos:* Bd dirs, Soc Sci Res Coun, 60-62. *Mem:* Nat Acad Sci; fel Am Acad Arts & Sci; Am Anthrop Asn; Am Ethnol Soc (pres, 67-68); AAAS; Soc Psychol Anthrop (pres, 79-80). *Res:* Anthropology; social science; ethnology. *Mailing Add:* 2500 Torrey Pines Rd La Jolla CA 92037-3431

SPIRO, ROBERT CHRISTOPHER, BONE & CARTILAGE REGENERATION, PROTEOGLYCANS & EXTRACELLULAR MATRIX. *Current Pos:* DIR BONE & CARTILAGE RES, ORQUEST INC, 94- *Personal Data:* b Worcester, Mass, May 7, 55; m 94, Lisa Beth Dreisbach. *Educ:* McGill Univ, Montreal, BSc, 77; Univ Mass, Worcester, PhD(immunol), 84. *Prof Exp:* Postdoctoral fel, Scripps Res Inst, 84-87, sr res assoc, 87-89, asst mem, 89-91; prin scientist, Telios Pharmaceut Inc, 91-94. *Concurrent Pos:* Prin investr, Scripps Res Inst, 89-94, Orquest Inc, 96- *Mem:* Fel Am Soc Cell Biol; fel AAAS; fel Am Asn Immunologists; fel Connective Tissue Soc. *Res:* Role of extracellular matrix proteins, particularly the proteoglycan class of proteins in the development and regeneration of bone, cartilage and other soft skeletal tissues. *Mailing Add:* 365 Ravendale Dr Mountain View CA 94043

SPIRO, ROBERT GUNTER, BIOCHEMISTRY. *Current Pos:* res assoc med, 60-63, from assoc to assoc prof biol chem, 64-74, PROF BIOL CHEM, HARVARD MED SCH, 74- *Personal Data:* b Berlin, Germany, Jan 5, 29; nat US; m 52, Mary Jane Paisley; c David & Mark. *Educ:* Columbia Col, AB, 51; State Univ NY, MD, 55. *Hon Degrees:* AM, Harvard Univ, 75. *Honors & Awards:* Lilly Award, Am Diabetes Asn, 68; Claude Bernard Award, Europ Asn Study Diabetes, 75. *Prof Exp:* Intern, Syracuse Med Ctr, NY, 55-56. *Concurrent Pos:* Am Cancer Soc res fel biochem, Harvard Med Sch, 56-58 & res fel med, Mass Gen Hosp, 58-60; USPHS res fel, 58-59; Am Heart Asn advan res fel, 59-61; estab investr, Am Heart Asn, 61-66; sr investr & chief sect, Complex Carbohydrates & Biomembranes, Joslin Res Lab, 61- *Mem:* Am Diabetes Asn; Am Soc Biol Chem; Am Chem Soc; Soc Complex Carbohydrates (pres, 78). *Res:* Chemical structure and biosynthesis of glycoproteins; biochemistry and biology of cell surfaces and basement membranes; biochemistry of diabetes mellitus; regulatory action of insulin; chemistry of connective tissues and basement membranes. *Mailing Add:* Joslin Diabetes Ctr One Joslin Place Boston MA 02215-5397. *Fax:* 617-732-2569

SPIRO, THOMAS GEORGE, CHEMISTRY. *Current Pos:* from instr to assoc prof, 63-64, chmn dept, 79-88, PROF CHEM, PRINCETON UNIV, 74- *Personal Data:* b Aruba, Netherlands Antilles, Nov 7, 35; m 59; c 2. *Educ:* Univ Calif, Los Angeles, BS, 56; Mass Inst Technol, PhD(chem), 60. *Honors & Awards:* Bomem Michelson Award, 86; Merit Award, NIH, 89. *Prof Exp:* Fulbright student, Copenhagen, 60-61; res chemist, Calif Res Corp, 61-62; NIH fel, Royal Inst Technol Sweden, 62-63. *Concurrent Pos:* Guggenheim fel, 89. *Mem:* Fel AAAS; Am Chem Soc; Am Soc Biol Chemists; Biophys Soc. *Res:* Resonance Raman spectroscopy; applications to biological structure; role of metals in biology; bonding in inorganic molecules; environmental chemistry. *Mailing Add:* Dept Chem Princeton Univ Washington Rd Princeton NJ 08540

SPIROFF, BORIS E N, biology, embryology, for more information see previous edition

SPIRTAS, ROBERT, PUBLIC HEALTH. *Current Pos:* scientist, 88-92, CHIEF, CONTRACEPTIVE BR, NAT INST CHILD HEALTH & HUMAN DEVELOP, NIH, 92- *Personal Data:* b Bellville, Ill, Oct 5, 43. *Educ:* Univ Ill, BA, 65; Univ Iowa, MS, 67; Univ NC, Chapel Hill, PhD(pub health), 75. *Honors & Awards:* Statist Sect Award, Am Pub Health Asn, 92. *Prof Exp:* Math statistician, Nat Air Pollution, 67-69; br chief, Ctr Dis Control, 76-80; biostatician, Nat Cancer Inst, 80-88. *Mem:* Fel Am Col Epidemiol. *Mailing Add:* NIH-CHHD Rm 8B07 6100 Executive Blvd Bethesda MD 20892. *Fax:* 301-496-0962; *E-Mail:* robert_spirtas@nih.gov

SPITALNY, GEORGE LEONARD, IMMUNOBIOLOGY. *Current Pos:* VPRES RES & DEVELOP, TARGE TECH INC; PRES & CHIEF OPER OFFICER, SELECT THERAPEUT, 97- *Personal Data:* b Philadelphia, Pa, Mar 7, 47; c 3. *Educ:* Pa State Univ, BS, 69; NY Univ, PhD(immunol, parasitol), 73. *Prof Exp:* Asst res sci, Sch Med, NY Univ, 73, from instr to asst prof immunobiol, 73-75; res assoc, Trudeau Inst, 75-77, asst mem immunobiol staff, 77-82; dir immunol, Bristol-Myers Co, 83- *Concurrent Pos:* Nat Inst Allergy & Infectious Dis fel, Sch Med, NY Univ, 74-75; fel, Trudeau Inst, 75-76, fel, Cancer Res Inst, 77; prin investr, Trudeau Inst, Nat Cancer Inst grant, 78-81; prin investr, Grant Nat Inst Allergy & Infectious Dis, 81-84; coprin investr, Grant Nat Cancer Inst, 81-85; assoc mem, Trudeau Inst, 82-83; consult, Zoltic Ltd, 95-97. *Mem:* Am Assoc Immunol; AAAS; Am Assoc Cancer Res; Am Assoc Microbiol; Reticuloendothelial Soc. *Res:* Mechanisms of immunity to infectious and neoplastic diseases; tumor induced suppressor cells; regulation of immunity; delivery of cytotoxic drug via linkage to monoclonal antibodies. *Mailing Add:* 6 Brookfield Ct Cheshire CT 06410. *Fax:* 203-271-3245; *E-Mail:* glspitalny@aol.com

SPITLER, LYNN E, IMMUNOLOGY, INTERNAL MEDICINE. *Current Pos:* fel immunol, 67-69, instr, 69-71, ASST PROF MED, MED CTR, UNIV CALIF, SAN FRANCISCO, 71- *Personal Data:* b Grand Rapids, Mich, Sept 28, 38; m 67; c 2. *Educ:* Univ Mich, MD, 63. *Prof Exp:* Intern, Highland-Alameda County Hosp, 63-64; resident, Med Ctr, Univ Calif, San Francisco, 64-66; fel immunol, NY Univ, 66-67. *Concurrent Pos:* Res assoc, Cancer Res Inst, 73-; assoc ed, J Immunol, 74-78; dir res, Children's Hosp, San Francisco, 75-; mem allergy & immunol res comt, Nat Inst Allergy & Infectious Dis, NIH, 76-; mem immunol rev comt, Vet Admin, Washington, DC, 77- *Mem:* Am Asn Immunologists; AAAS; Am Fedn Clin Res. *Res:* Immunopotentiator therapy; transfer factor; levamisole; multiple sclerosis immunology; immunotherapy of malignant melanoma; monoclonal antibodies. *Mailing Add:* Northern California Melanoma Ctrs 1895 Mountain View Dr Tiburon CA 94920

SPITLER, MARK THOMAS, PHYSICAL CHEMISTRY. *Current Pos:* RES FEL, PHOTOM CTR, BOSTON UNIV, 96- *Personal Data:* b Rockford, Ill, Oct 19, 50. *Educ:* Stanford Univ, BS, 72; Univ Calif, Berkeley, PhD(phys chem), 77. *Prof Exp:* Guest scientist, Fritz Haber Inst, Max Planck Soc, 77-78; asst prof chem, Mount Holyoke Col, 79-84; staff mem, Polaroid Corp, 84-96. *Concurrent Pos:* Vis asst prof chem, Amherst Col, 78-79. *Mem:* Sigma Xi; Am Chem Soc; AAAS; Electrochem Soc. *Res:* Photoelectrochemistry; semiconductor electrochemistry; photochemical energy conversion photochemistry at electrified interfaces; amorphous semiconductors. *Mailing Add:* 110 Tarbell Spring Rd Concord MA 01742

SPITSBERGEN, JAMES CLIFFORD, THERMOSET POLYMER TECHNOLOGY, EPOXY RESIN TECHNOLOGY. *Current Pos:* POLYMER CONSULT, EPOXY CONSULT, INC, 85- *Personal Data:* b Washington, DC, Sept 1, 26; m 80; c 2. *Educ:* George Washington Univ, BS, 49; Univ Del, MS, 59, PhD(phys polymer chem), 62. *Prof Exp:* Chemist, Eng Res & Develop Labs, Army Eng Corp, 51; chemist, Elec Hose & Rubber Co, 51-57; sr chemist, 57-61; sr chemist, Elastomers Lab, E I du Pont de Nemours & Co, 62-68; proj leader, polymer res & develop, Corp Res & Develop Lab, Witco Chem Corp, 68-83; polymer consult, Unitrode Corp, 83-85. *Mem:* Am Chem Soc; Soc Plastics Eng; Int Electronics Packaging Soc; Soc Plastics Indust; Int Soc Hybrid Microelectronics; Soc Advan Mat & Process Eng. *Res:* Elastomer technology, particularly compositions for hose; molecular weight distribution-rheology relationships of elastomers, particularly neoprene; synthesis and characterization of thermosetting polymers, particularly epoxy resins; structure-property relationships of polymers; potting; transfer molding; powder coating; adhesion and laminating of electrical and electronic components. *Mailing Add:* 696 Knollwood Rd Franklin Lakes NJ 07417-1710

SPITTELL, JOHN A, JR, INTERNAL MEDICINE, CARDIOVASCULAR DISEASES. *Current Pos:* RETIRED. *Personal Data:* b Baltimore, Md, Apr 7, 25; m 49; c 5. *Educ:* Franklin & Marshall Col, BS, 44; Univ Md, MD, 49; Univ Minn, MS, 55. *Prof Exp:* From asst prof to prof, Mayo Med Sch, Univ Minn, 62-80, vchmn educ, Dept Med, Mayo Clin, 72-76, assoc dir continuing educ, Mayo Found, 78-84, Mary Lowell Leary prof med, 80-89. *Concurrent Pos:* NIH grant, 64-68; consult, Mayo Clin, 56-; mem spec ad hoc comt, Food & Drug Admin, 63; Nat Cardiovasc Conf Peripheral Vascular Dis, 64; bd regents, Am Col Physicians, 80-89. *Mem:* Fel Am Col Physicians; fel Am Col Cardiol. *Res:* Peripheral vascular disease; relationship of changes of blood coagulation and intravascular thrombosis; mechanism of action of Coumarin anticoagulants; aneurysmal disease; aortic dissection. *Mailing Add:* Mayo Clin Rochester MN 55901

SPITTLER, ERNEST GEORGE, CHEMISTRY. *Current Pos:* asst prof, 65-76, ASSOC PROF CHEM, JOHN CARROLL UNIV, 76- *Personal Data:* b Cleveland, Ohio, May 4, 28. *Educ:* Loyola Univ, Ill, AB, 51, PhL(philos), 53, ThL(theol), 63; Cath Univ Am, PhD(chem), 59. *Prof Exp:* Instr physics, Loyola Acad, Ill, 53-54. *Concurrent Pos:* Res assoc, Bushy Run Radiation Lab, Mellon Inst, 64-66; secy bd trustees, John Carroll Univ, 69-71, mem bd trustees, 80- *Mem:* Am Chem Soc; Hist Sci Soc. *Res:* Mercury-photosensitized reactions of hydrocarbon systems; use of carbon-14 tagged molecules as tracers in studying gas phase reactions; chemical effects of lasers and ultra-sound; photochemistry of inorganic complexes; history of periodic table; development of theories of chemistry. *Mailing Add:* Chem John Carroll Univ 20700 N Park Blvd Cleveland OH 44118-4520

SPITTLER, TERRY DALE, ORGANIC CHEMISTRY, PESTICIDE CHEMISTRY. *Current Pos:* LAB COORDR, PESTICIDE RESIDUES, NY STATE AGR EXP STA, CORNELL UNIV, 77- *Personal Data:* b Buffalo, NY, Apr 29, 43; m 74, Mary Stover; c Elizabeth J, Max F & Gretchen M. *Educ:* Bowling Green State Univ, BA, 65; State Univ NY, Buffalo, MS, 68; State Univ NY, Albany, PhD(org chem), 74. *Prof Exp:* Res assoc paper & pulp, State Univ NY Col Environ Sci & Forestry, 74-75; res assoc coal & asphalt, Mont State Univ, 75-77. *Mem:* Am Chem Soc. *Res:* Analytical organic methods development in pesticide residues; carbon and proton nuclear magnetic resonance; groundwater pollution and quality determination; pulp bleaching with alkaline hydrogen peroxide; pesticide worker exposure to second disposal. *Mailing Add:* Analytical Div NY State Agr Exp Sta Cornell Univ NY Geneva NY 14456. *Fax:* 315-787-2397; *E-Mail:* terry_spittler@cornell.edu

SPITZ, IRVING MANFRED, ENDOCRINOLOGY, METABOLISM. *Current Pos:* DIR CLIN RES, CTR BIOMED RES, POP COUN, NY, 82- *Personal Data:* b July 9, 39, Johannesburg, SAfrica; Israeli citizen; m 64; c 2. *Educ:* Witwatersrand Med Sch, Johannesburg, MB, BCh, 62, MD, 71; Royal Col Physicians, London, MRCP, 65. *Honors & Awards:* Albelheim Prize, 63. *Prof Exp:* Temp chief physician, dept chem endocrinol, Hadassah Univ Hosp, Jerusalem, 70-73, permanent chief physician, 73-74, actg chief dept, 75-76; assoc prof endocrinol, Hebrew Univ, 78-82. *Concurrent Pos:* Head dept endocrinol & metab, Shaare Zedek Med Ctr, Jerusalem, 77-82. *Mem:* Endocrine Soc; Am Soc Andrology; NY Acad Sci; AAAS; Am Soc Clin Invest. *Res:* Endocrine control of human reproduction, hormonal aspects of contraception; role of prolactin in reproduction; hormonal regulation of hypogonadal states; inappropriate TSH secretion. *Mailing Add:* 420 E 79th St New York NY 10021

SPITZ, TIBOR RICHARD, RESEARCH & DEVELOPMENT OF MAGNETIC RECORDING HEADS, RESEARCH & DEVELOPMENT OF GLASS TECHNOLOGY & SCIENCE. *Current Pos:* STAFF ENGR & SR DEVELOP ENGR, NAT MICRONETICS, 83- *Personal Data:* b Dolny Kubin, Slovakia, Aug 28, 29; US citizen; m 67, Noemi Eichler. *Educ:* Chem & Technol Univ, Prague, Czech Repub, MS, 53, PhD(ceramic eng), 58. *Prof Exp:* Res scientist, Inst Glass, 53-68; mgr, chief chemist & technologist, Domglas, Can, 69-78, glass technol, Nat Bottle Inc, 78-81, melting processes, Wheaton Glass Co, 81-83. *Concurrent Pos:* Lectr, Int Glass Cong, 65; instr post grad students, Inst Glass, 65-68. *Mem:* Can Ceramic Soc; Am Ceramic Soc. *Res:* Glass science and glass manufacturing technologies; magnet recording heads research and manufacturing; 21 published papers and 11 patents in seven countries. *Mailing Add:* 500 Washington Ave No 8G Kingston NY 12401. *E-Mail:* tibor@mhv.net

SPITZ, WERNER URI, PATHOLOGY, FORENSIC MEDICINE. *Current Pos:* PROF PATH, SCH MED, WAYNE STATE UNIV, 72- *Personal Data:* b Stargard, Ger, Aug 22, 26; US citizen; c 3. *Educ:* Hebrew Univ, Jerusalem, MD, 53; Am Bd Path, dipl & cert path anat, 61, cert forensic path, 65. *Prof Exp:* Resident path, Tel-Hashomer Govt Hosp, Israel, 53-56; resident forensic med, Hebrew Univ, Jerusalem, 56-59; asst forensic path, Free Univ Berlin, 61-63; assoc med examr, Md Med-Legal Found, 63-65; asst med examr, Off Chief Med Examr, Md, 65-69, dep chief med examr, 69-72; chief med examr, Wayne County, Mich, 72- *Concurrent Pos:* Consult path, Israel Ministry of Health, 57-59; Res fel forensic path, Univ Md, Baltimore City, 59-61; Nat Inst Gen Med Sci training & res grant forensic path, Md State Med Examr, 64-65, NIH grant, 64-66; lectr, Johns Hopkins Univ, 66, assoc prof, Sch Hyg & Pub Health, 67-72, consult, appl physics lab, 72-; asst prof, Sch Med, Univ Md, 66, clin assoc prof, 69-72, mem grad fac, Col Park, 70-; dir res & training, Md Med-Legal Found, 67-; mem ed bd, J Forensic Sci, J Legal Med, Excerpta Medica-Forensic Sci; adj prof chem, Univ Windsor, Ont, Can, 78- *Mem:* Fel Am Col Am Path; fel Am Soc Clin Path; AMA; Soc Exp Biol & Med; Nat Asn Med Examrs; hon mem Latin Am Asn Legal Med, 82- *Res:* Mechanism of death by drowning; pathology of vehicular trauma; wound patterns by firearms and other agents. *Mailing Add:* Dept Path 9374 Scott Hall Wayne State Univ Sch Med 540 E Canfield St Detroit MI 48201-1928

SPITZBART, ABRAHAM, MATHEMATICS. *Current Pos:* from instr to assoc prof, 45-61, PROF MATH, UNIV WIS-MILWAUKEE, 61- *Personal Data:* b New York, NY, Oct 13, 15. *Educ:* City Col New York, BS, 35; Harvard Univ, AM, 36, PhD(math), 40. *Prof Exp:* Instr math, Harvard Univ, 37-40, City Col New York, 40-41 & Univ Minn, 42; prof, Col of St Thomas, 42-43. *Mem:* Am Math Soc; Math Asn Am. *Res:* Approximation theory in complex variables; numerical analysis. *Mailing Add:* Dept Math Univ Wis Milwaukee WI 53201-0413

SPITZE, LEROY ALVIN, chemistry; deceased, see previous edition for last biography

SPITZE, ROBERT GEORGE FREDERICK, PUBLIC POLICY, INSTITUTIONAL ECONOMICS. *Current Pos:* PROF AGR ECON, UNIV ILL, URBANA, 60- *Personal Data:* b Berryville, Ark, Oct 12, 22. *Educ:* Univ Ark, BS, 47; Univ Wis, PhD(agr econ), 54. *Honors & Awards:* Distinguished Teaching Award, Am Agr Econ Asn, 72, Distinguished Policy Award, 81. *Prof Exp:* From asst prof to prof agr econ, Univ Tenn, 51-60. *Concurrent Pos:* Consult, Fed Intermediate Credit Bank, 56, Ill Gen Assembly Revenue, 63, Am Farm Bur Fedn, 71, Ill Govs Econ Coun, 74-76, Wharton Economet Forecasting, 77, Nat Rural Ctr, 79 & USDA, Res Rex Teams, 86, 87, 90 & 92; vis prof agr econ, Univ London, 67-69, USDA, 75-76. *Mem:* Am Agr Econ Asn; Am Econ Asn; Int Asn Agr Econ; AAAS; Sigma Xi; Coun Agr & Sci Technol. *Res:* Analysis of food and agricultural policies of United States and select trading countries; inquiry into the conceptual foundations of economic policy decision making and its determinants. *Mailing Add:* 1406 S Vine Urbana IL 61801

SPITZER, ADRIAN, NEPHROLOGY. *Current Pos:* PROF PEDIAT & DIR, DEPT NEPHROLOGY, ALBERT EINSTEIN COL MED, 73- *Personal Data:* b Dec 21, 27; m, Carole; c Vlad G. *Educ:* Med Sch Bucharest, Rumania, MD, 52. *Concurrent Pos:* Vis prof, Wilhelmena Children's Hosp, Ufrecht, Holland & Dept Biochem, Oxford, Eng; Christiansen vis fel, St Catherine Col, Oxford, Eng, 82; Prof C Donders rotating chair, Univ Utrecht, Holland, 90. *Mem:* Soc Pediat Res; Am Pediat Soc; Am Soc Nephrol; Am Soc Pediat Nephrol; Am Physiol Soc; Am Fedn Clin Res. *Res:* Developmental renal physiology; pediatric nephrology. *Mailing Add:* Dept Pediat Albert Einstein Col Med 1410 Pelham Pkwy S Bronx NY 10461. *Fax:* 718-824-2392; *E-Mail:* spitzer@aecom.yu.edu

SPITZER, CARY REDFORD, ELECTRONICS ENGINEERING, EARTH SCIENCES. *Current Pos:* Aerospace technologist, instrumentation, 62-69, exp mgr, planetary missions, 69-78, MGR PROG PLANS FLIGHT RES, NASA LANGLEY RES CTR, 78- *Personal Data:* b New Hope, Va, Jul 31, 37; m 60, Carrie L Logan; c Stiegel Logan. *Educ:* Va Polytechnic Inst & State Univ, BS, 59; George Washington Univ, MS, 70. *Honors & Awards:* Centennial Medal, Inst Elec & Electronics Engrs, 84. *Prof Exp:* USAF, 59-62. *Concurrent Pos:* Lectr, Univ Calif, Los Angeles, 89- *Mem:* AAAS; Am Inst Aeronaut & Astronaut; Inst Elec & Electronics Engrs. *Res:* Flight research and development and validation of advanced aircraft flight control laws; electronic displays; operating procedures. *Mailing Add:* 3409 Foxridge Rd Williamsburg VA 23188-2499

SPITZER, FRANK L, mathematics; deceased, see previous edition for last biography

SPITZER, IRWIN ASHER, SYSTEMS ENGINEERING, MECHANICAL ENGINEERING. *Current Pos:* RETIRED. *Personal Data:* b Los Angeles, Calif, July 4, 22; m 53, Lyllas Barnes; c David C & Andrew B. *Educ:* Univ Calif, BS, 44. *Prof Exp:* Sr engr, Kaiser Steel Corp, 47-56; prin engr, Grand Cent Rocket Co, 56-62; sr prog mgr, Lockheed Propulsion Co, 62-73; asst dir procurement, Amecom Div, Litton Indust, 73-75; sr staff engr, Ballistic Missile Div, TRW Systs, 75-88. *Mem:* Am Soc Qual Control; Am Inst Aeronaut & Astronaut; Air Force Asn. *Res:* Solid rocket propulsion systems; advanced inter-continental ballistic missile basing concepts. *Mailing Add:* 306 Marcia St Redlands CA 92373

SPITZER, JEFFREY CHANDLER, ORGANIC CHEMISTRY, SPECTROSCOPY. *Current Pos:* asst ed, 67-69, sr assoc indexer, 69-79, SR ED, CHEM ABSTRACTS SERV, 79- *Personal Data:* b Malden, Mass, Dec 1, 40; m 67; c 1. *Educ:* Mass Inst Technol, BS, 61; Univ Ariz, PhD(chem), 66. *Prof Exp:* Res assoc org chem, Univ Calif, 66-67. *Res:* Terpene and polyacetylene structure determination; synthesis of pyrrole derivatives. *Mailing Add:* 2279 Canterbury Rd Columbus OH 43221

SPITZER, JOHN J, PHYSIOLOGY. *Current Pos:* PROF PHYSIOL & HEAD DEPT, LA STATE UNIV MED CTR, NEW ORLEANS, 73- *Personal Data:* b Baja, Hungary, Mar 9, 27; m 51; c 2. *Educ:* Univ Munich, MD, 50. *Honors & Awards:* Christian R & Mary F Lindback Award, 61. *Prof Exp:* Demonstr physiol, Sch Med, Univ Budapest, 47-49; lectr, Sch Med, Dalhousie Univ, 51-52; asst prof, Fla State Univ, 52-54; res scientist, Div Labs & Res, NY State Dept Health, 54-57; from asst prof to prof physiol, Hahnemann Med Col, 57-73. *Concurrent Pos:* Vis scientist, Lab Physiol, Oxford Univ; Burroughs Wellcome Professorships, 83. *Mem:* AAAS; Am Physiol Soc; Soc Exp Biol & Med; Am Heart Asn; NY Acad Sci; Res Soc Alcoholism; Shock Soc. *Res:* Substrate metabolism in vivo; carbohydrate metabolism; hepatic non-parenchymal cells; shock and metabolism; sepsis-induced metabolic changes; oxygen free radical production; alcohol and host defense. *Mailing Add:* Dept Physiol La State Univ 1901 Perdido St New Orleans LA 70112

SPITZER, JUDY A, IMMUNOLOGY, BIOCHEMISTRY. *Current Pos:* assoc prof med & physiol, 73-79, PROF PHYSIOL MED, LA STATE UNIV MED CTR, NEW ORLEANS, 79- *Personal Data:* b Budapest, Hungary, Feb 25, 31; US citizen; m 51, John J; c Peter & Juliet. *Educ:* Fla State Univ, BA, 53; Albany Med Col, MS, 55; Hahnemann Med Col, PhD(microbiol, immunol), 63. *Prof Exp:* Res asst physiol, Fac Med, Dalhousie Univ, 51-52; asst biochem, Fla State Univ, 53-54; biochemist, Div Labs & Res, NY State Dept Health, 54-57; res assoc physiol, Hahnemann Med Col, 57-61 & 62-70, res asst prof physiol & biophys, 70-72, res assoc prof, 72-73. *Concurrent Pos:* Prin investr, Off Naval Res Contract, 73-82 & 89-93 & NIH grants, 82-; chmn, Am Physiol Soc Educ Comt, 82-87, Fedn Am Soc Exp Biol Educ Comt, 84-86; mem, Surg, Anesthesiol & Trauma Study Sect, NIH, 84-89, Metab Study Sect, 90. *Mem:* NY Acad Sci; Endotoxin Soc; Am Physiol Soc; Shock Soc (secy, 85-89); Soc Exp Biol Med; Am Soc Biochem & Molecular Biol. *Res:* Signal transduction mechanisms; metabolic and endocrine changes in shock; host defense mechanisms; intercellular communication in the liver. *Mailing Add:* Dept Physiol & Med La State Univ Med Ctr 1901 Perdido St New Orleans LA 70112-1328. *Fax:* 504-568-6158

SPITZER, LYMAN, JR, INTERSTELLAR MATTER, STELLAR DYNAMICS. *Current Pos:* SR RES ASTRONR, PRINCETON UNIV OBSERV. *Personal Data:* b Toledo, Ohio, June 26, 14; m 40, Doreen D Canaday; c Nicholas, Dionis (Griffin), Sarah & Lydia. *Educ:* Yale Univ, BA, 35; Princeton Univ, MA, 37, PhD(astrophys), 38. *Hon Degrees:* DSc, Yale Univ, 58, Case Inst Technol, 61 & Harvard Univ, 75; LLD, Univ Toledo, 63; DSc, Princeton Univ, 84. *Honors & Awards:* Rittenhouse Medal, Franklin Inst, 57; Bruce Gold Medal, Astron Soc Pac, 73; Henry Draper Medal, Nat Acad Sci, 74; James Clerk Maxwell Prize, Am Phys Soc, 75; Distinguished Pub Serv Medal, NASA, 76; Gold Medal, Royal Astron Soc, 78; Jules Janssen Medal, Soc Astron de France, 80; Franklin Medal, Franklin Inst, 80; Nat Medal of Sci, 80; Crafoord Prize, 85; James Madison Medal, Princeton Univ, 89; Franklin Medal, Am Philos Soc, 91. *Prof Exp:* Nat Res Coun fel, Harvard Univ, 38-39; instr physics, Yale Univ, 39-41, instr astron & physics, 41-42; scientist spec studies group, Div War Res, Columbia Univ, 42-44, dir sonar anal group, 44-46; assoc prof astrophys, Yale Univ, 46-47; prof, Princeton Univ, 47-52, Young prof astron, 52-82, chmn dept & dir observ, 47-79. *Concurrent Pos:* Dir, Proj Matterhorn, Princeton Univ, 53-61, chmn exec comt, Plasma Physics Lab, 61-66 & Univ Res Bd, 67-72, chmn, Asn Univ Res Astron Space Telescope Inst Coun, 81-90. *Mem:* Nat Acad Sci; Am Astron Soc (pres, 60-62); foreign corresp Royal Soc Sci, Liege; foreign mem Royal Soc London; foreign assoc Royal Astron Soc England; Am Acad Arts & Sci; Am Philos Soc. *Res:* Interstellar matter; dynamics of stellar systems; physics of fully ionized gases; controlled thermonuclear research; space astronomy. *Mailing Add:* Peyton Hall Princeton Univ Observ Princeton NJ 08544. *Fax:* 609-258-1020

SPITZER, NICHOLAS CANADAY, DEVELOPMENTAL NEUROBIOLOGY. *Current Pos:* From asst prof to prof biol, 73-82, chmn dept, 88-90, PROF BIOL, UNIV CALIF, SAN DIEGO, 82- *Personal Data:* b New York, NY, Nov 8, 42; m 67, Janet Lamborghini; c Julian & Hilary. *Educ:* Harvard Univ, BA, 64, PhD(neurobiol), 69. *Prof Exp:* NIH fel neurobiol, Harvard Univ, 69-70; NATO NSF fel biophysics, Univ Col London, 70-72. *Concurrent Pos:* Guggenheim fel, 90-91. *Mem:* Soc Neurosci; AAAS; Biophys Soc; Soc Develop Biol; Am Physiol Soc; Int Soc Develop Neurosci. *Res:* Mechanisms of neuronal differentiation; signal transduction; development of excitability. *Mailing Add:* 0357 Biol Dept Univ Calif San Diego 9500 Gilman Dr La Jolla CA 92093-0357. *Fax:* 619-534-7309; *E-Mail:* nspitzer@ucsd.edu

SPITZER, RALPH, CHEMISTRY, PATHOLOGY. *Current Pos:* clin instr, Univ BC, 58-65, assoc prof, 65-82, clin prof, 82-85, EMER CLIN PROF CHEM PATH, UNIV BC, 85- *Personal Data:* b New York, NY, Feb 9, 18; m 41, Therese Perles; c Eloise (Spitzer). *Educ:* Cornell Univ, AB, 38; Calif Inst Technol, PhD(chem), 41; Univ Man, MD, 57; FRCPath. *Prof Exp:* Assoc phys chemist, Nat Adv Comt Aeronaut, 42-43; res assoc, Woods Hole Oceanog Inst, 43-45; assoc prof chem, Ore State Col, 46-50 & Univ Kans City, 50-53; res assoc med, Univ Man, 53-54. *Concurrent Pos:* Dir, Biochem Labs, Royal Columbian Hosp, 58-81, chem pathologist, 81-88; vis sr lectr, Univ Otago, NZ, 62-63. *Mem:* Acad Lab Physicians & Scientists; Can Soc Clin Chem; sr mem Can Med Asn. *Res:* Chemical biology and pathology; endocrine effects of tumors; clinical enzymology; psychopharmacology. *Mailing Add:* 1911 Knox Rd Vancouver BC V6T 1S5 Can. *Fax:* 604-224-4950; *E-Mail:* ralphs@unixg.ubc.ca

SPITZER, ROBERT HARRY, BIOCHEMISTRY. *Current Pos:* from res assoc med to res assoc enzymol & exp hypersensitivity, 61-65, from asst prof enzymol & exp hypersensitivity to asst prof biochem, 65-70, assoc prof, 70-75, PROF BIOCHEM, CHICAGO MED SCH, 75- *Personal Data:* b Chicago, Ill, July 25, 29. *Educ:* Valparaiso Univ, BA, 51; Loyola Univ, Ill, MS, 53, PhD(biochem), 55. *Prof Exp:* Instr exp surg, Sch Med, Wash Univ, 55-56; res chemist, Gillette Co, 56-61. *Mem:* Am Asn Immunologists. *Res:* Cell biology; metabolism in lower vertebrates; immunobiology. *Mailing Add:* Dept Biol Chem & Struct Chicago Med Sch 3333 Green Bay Rd North Chicago IL 60064-3095. *Fax:* 847-578-3240

SPITZER, ROGER EARL, PEDIATRICS, IMMUNOLOGY & NEPHROLOGY. *Current Pos:* assoc prof, 73-77, PROF PEDIAT, UPSTATE MED CTR, STATE UNIV NY, 77- *Personal Data:* b Washington, DC, June 20, 35; m 62; c Scott, Neal & Amy. *Educ:* George Washington Univ, BS, 58; Howard Univ, MD, 62; Am Bd Pediat, dipl, 68, dipl pediat nephrology, 73. *Honors & Awards:* Jefferson Award, 94. *Prof Exp:* Intern, Gen Hosp, Cincinnati, 62-63; resident pediat, Children's Hosp, 63-65; NIH spec fel nephrol-immunol, Childrens Hosp Res Found, 67-69; asst prof pediat,

Col Med, Univ Cincinnati, 69-73. *Concurrent Pos:* Clinician pediat, Gen Hosp, 59-73; res assoc immunol, Children's Hosp Res Found & attend pediatrician, Children's Hosp Med Ctr, 69-73, attend nephrologist, 72-73; consult, pediatrician, Good Samaritan Hosp, 71-73. *Mem:* Fel Am Acad Pediat; Am Soc Pediat Nephrology; Am Soc Nephrology; Soc Pediat Res; Am Asn Immunol. *Res:* Biology of complement; pediatric renal disease; biology of antibody formation. *Mailing Add:* Dept Pediat State Univ NY Health Sci Ctr Syracuse NY 13210

SPITZER, WALTER O, EPIDEMIOLOGY. *Current Pos:* prof family med, McGill Univ, 75-83, chmn, Dept Epidemiol & Biostatist, 84-93, prof epidemiol & health, 75-95, prof med, 83-95, Strathcona prof prev med, 84-93, EMER PROF, MCGILL UNIV, 96-; SR EPIDEMIOLOGIST, GENENTECH INC, 96- *Personal Data:* b Asuncion, Paraguay, Feb 19, 37; Can citizen. *Educ:* Univ Toronto, MD, 62; Univ Mich, MHA, 66; Yale Univ, MHP, 70; FRCP(C). *Honors & Awards:* Nat Health Scientist of Can, 81. *Prof Exp:* Gen dir, Int Christian Med Soc, 66-69; assoc mem, Dept Family Med, McMaster Univ, 69-75, asst prof clin epidemiol & biostatist, 69-75. *Concurrent Pos:* Prin investr grants, Ont Min Health, 70-74, 71-72, Can Arthritis & Rheumat Soc, 72-74, Nat Cancer Inst Can, 72-74, 80-81 & 82, Health & Welfare Can, 76-78, Commonwealth of Australia, 79-80, Can Res Soc, 82, Toronto Dept Health, 83 & Govt Alta, 85-86; co-investr grants, Health & Welfare Can, 71-74, 72-74, NIH, 86-; attend physician, McMaster Univ Med Ctr, 71-75; mem, Task Force Demonstration Models, Comt Health Res, Ont Coun Health, 73-76; mem, Res Eval Panel Clin Res, Nat Cancer Inst Can, 74-78, Rev Panel Epidemiol Res, 80-81; vis prof epidemiol, Univ Buenos Aires, Arg, 75, Sydney Univ, Australia, 79-80, Newcastle Univ, Australia, 79-80; vis fac, Int Ctr Res Cancer, WHO, Lyons, France, 75; vis prof clin epidemiol, Nat Univ Chile, 75; sr physician, Dept Med, Montreal Gen Hosp, 75-, Royal Victoria Hosp, 85-; chmn, Task Force Eval of Periodic Health Exam, Health & Welfare Can, 76-85, mem, 85-, nat vis health scientist to Australia, 79-80; vis prof, Western Australia Inst Technol, 77, Univ Cologne, 87 & Shanghai Univ, Peoples Repub China, 87; dir, W K Kellogg Ctr Advan Studies in Primary Care, McGill Univ & Montreal Gen Hosp, 77-83, Div Clin Epidemiol, Dept Med, Montreal Gen Hosp, 79-86; John F McCleary vis prof, Univ BC, 78; prof, McGill Cancer Ctr, 78-, assoc dir, 79-; vis prof med & epidemiol, Royal North Shore Hosp, Sydney, Australia, 79-80; mem, Comt Study Pain, Disability & Chronic Illness Behav, Inst Med-Nat Acad Sci, 85-; ed, J Clin Epidemiol. *Mem:* Inst Med-Nat Acad Sci; fel Am Col Epidemiol; Can Oncol Soc (pres, 88-89); Soc Epidemiol Res; Int Epidemiol Asn; Col Family Physicians Can; Am Fedn Clin Res; Am Epidemiol Soc; fel Royal Col Physicians & Surgs Can. *Res:* Health manpower studies; causality in biomedical phenomena; epidemiology of clinical phenomena in primary care; clinical epidemiology of cancer; clinical epidemiology of rheumatic and arthritic complaints; randomized controlled trials; systematic error and bias in clinical and epidemiologic research; epidemiology of environmental health hazards; quality of life measurement and validation; pharmacoepidemiology; author or co-author of numerous publications. *Mailing Add:* Genentech Inc 460 Ft San Bruno Blvd South San Francisco CA 94080

SPITZER, WILLIAM CARL, ORGANIC POLYMER CHEMISTRY. *Current Pos:* RETIRED. *Personal Data:* b Chicago, Ill, Sept 15, 14; m 42; c 1. *Educ:* Univ Chicago, BS, 36, PhD(org chem), 40. *Prof Exp:* Org chemist, Sherwin-Williams Co, 40-47; org chemist, Paint Res Assoc Inc, 48-66, dir res, 66-75, dir res, PRA Labs, Inc, 75-81. *Concurrent Pos:* Instr, Ill Inst Technol, 50-51; lectr, DePaul Univ, 64; consult, 82-87. *Mem:* Am Chem Soc; Am Oil Chemists Soc; Am Soc Testing & Mat. *Res:* Organic coatings; synthetic resins; drying oils. *Mailing Add:* 221 White Fawn Trail Downers Grove IL 60516

SPITZER, WILLIAM GEORGE, PHYSICS. *Current Pos:* prof physics, elec eng & mat sci, Univ Southern Calif, 63-92, chmn, Dept Mat Sci, 67-69, chmn, Dept Physics, 69-72 & 78-81, dean natural sci, 72-73, vprovost res & dean grad studies, 83-85, dean lett, arts & sci, 85-89, ACTG PROVOST, UNIV SOUTHERN CALIF, 93- *Personal Data:* b Los Angeles, Calif, Apr 24, 27; m 49, Jenny Navsky; c 2. *Educ:* Univ Calif, Los Angeles, BA, 49; Univ Southern Calif, MS, 52; Purdue Univ, PhD(physics), 57. *Hon Degrees:* LHD, Hebrew-Union Col, 92. *Prof Exp:* Mem tech staff, Hughes Aircraft Co, 52-53, Bell Labs, Inc, 57-62 & Bell & Howell Res Ctr, 62-63. *Mem:* Fel Am Phys Soc; Inst Elec & Electronics Engrs; Sigma Xi. *Res:* Solid state and semiconductor physics; infrared properties of semiconductors and dielectrics. *Mailing Add:* Dept Mat & Sci Univ Southern Calif Vivian Hall Eng MC 4012 Los Angeles CA 90089-4012

SPITZIG, WILLIAM ANDREW, MECHANICAL METALLURGY, STRUCTURE-PROPERTY CORRELATIONS. *Current Pos:* PROG DIR, MECHS & MATS PROG, NSF, 93- *Personal Data:* b Cleveland, Ohio, Sept 12, 31; m 59, Marilyn Ferlin; c Andrew, Laura, William & Dawn. *Educ:* Cleveland State Univ, BS, 60; Case Western Res Univ, MS, 62, PhD(mat sci), 65. *Honors & Awards:* Energy Res Award, Dept Energy, 87. *Prof Exp:* Metallurgist, Thompson-Ramo-Wooldridge Inc, 60-62; mat engr, Lewis Res Ctr, NASA, 62-66; sr scientist, US Steel Res Labs, 66-84; sr metallurgist, Ames Lab, Iowa State Univ, 84-93. *Concurrent Pos:* Lectr, Univ Pittsburgh, 68-83; adj prof MS & E, Iowa State Univ, 84- *Mem:* Am Soc Metals; Am Inst Mining, Metall & Petrol Engrs; Mats Res Soc. *Res:* Structure-property relationships in body centered cubic single crystals, steels, titanium alloys, aluminum alloys, metal and ceramic composites and polymers; determination of quantitative correlations between the geometric properties of second phase populations and mechanical properties; computer controlled automatic image analysis techniques. *Mailing Add:* 4650 Washington Blvd Arlington VA 22201. *Fax:* 703-306-0291; *E-Mail:* wspitzig@nsf.gov

SPITZNAGEL, EDWARD LAWRENCE, JR, MATHEMATICAL STATISTICS, BIOMETRICS. *Current Pos:* assoc prof, 69-80, PROF MATH, WASH UNIV, 80- *Personal Data:* b Cincinnati, Ohio, Sept 4, 41; m 71, Alice McCaffrey; c Bridget, Edward, Michael, Sally & Casey. *Educ:* Xavier Univ, BS, 62; Univ Chicago, MS, 63, PhD(math), 65. *Prof Exp:* From instr to asst prof math, Northwestern Univ, Ill, 65-69. *Mem:* Sigma Xi; Math Asn Am. *Res:* Statistics; finite group theory. *Mailing Add:* Dept Math Wash Univ St Louis MO 63130. *E-Mail:* ed@math.wustl.edu

SPITZNAGEL, JOHN A, PULSE POWER ENGINEERING, DEFECTS IN CRYSTAL GROWTH. *Current Pos:* sr engr, Westinghouse Res & Develop Ctr, 70-74, fel engr, 74-80, adv engr, 80-91, CHIEF SCIENTIST, SYST PROCESSES & TECHNOL DIV, WESTINGHOUSE SCI & TECHNOL CTR, 91- *Personal Data:* b Pittsburgh, Pa, June 27, 41; m 72; c 4. *Educ:* Carnegie Inst Technol, BS, 63, MS, 64; Carnegie-Mellon Univ, PhD(metall & mat sci), 69. *Prof Exp:* Mem staff soil mech, US Army Waterways Exp Sta, 68-70; sr engr, 70-74, fel engr, 74-80, adv engr, Westinghouse Res & Develop Ctr, 80- *Concurrent Pos:* Prin investr ion beam effects in solids, NSF, 74-; prin investr irradiation response mat fusion, Dept Energy, 77-81; mem, Damage Analysis & Fundamental Studies Task Group, Dept Energy, 77-; ed, Advan Techniques Characterizing Microstruct, Am Inst Mining, Metall & Petrol Engrs, 80-82; adj prof, Dept Mat Sci & Eng, Univ Pittsburgh, 84-88. *Mem:* Am Inst Mining, Metall & Petrol Engrs; Am Soc Metals; Mats Res Soc. *Res:* Fundamental processes of ion beam, plasma and neutron interactions with solids; microstructural and microchemical effects of irradiation in metals and semiconductors; modification of surfaces by ion implantation; control of thermal stress induced defects during crystal growth. *Mailing Add:* Westinghouse Sci & Technol Ctr 1310 Beulah Rd Pittsburgh PA 15235

SPITZNAGEL, JOHN KEITH, MICROBIOLOGY, MEDICINE. *Current Pos:* chmn, Bact Mycol Study Sect, 77-79, CONSULT MEM, NIH, 85- *Personal Data:* b Peoria, Ill, Apr 11, 23; m 47; c 5. *Educ:* Columbia Univ, BA, 43, MD, 46; Am Bd Internal Med, dipl, 53. *Prof Exp:* Asst instr basic sci, US Army Med Sch, 47-49; asst med, Wash Univ, 49-52; vis investr, Rockefeller Inst, 52-53; from chief infectious dis serv to chief med serv, US Army Hosp, Ft Bragg, 53-57; from lectr to prof bact, immunol & med, Univ NC, Chapel Hill, 57-79; prof microbiol & immunol & chmn dept, Emory Univ, 79-93. *Concurrent Pos:* USPHS sr res fel, 58-68; vis investr, Nat Inst Med Res, Eng, 67-68; consult mem, Bact & Mycol Study Sect, USPHS-Dept Health, Educ & Welfare. *Mem:* Infectious Dis Soc; Am Soc Microbiol; Sigma Xi; fel Am Col Physicians; Am Asn Immunol. *Res:* Role of cationic proteins in oxygen-independent antimicrobial capacity of neutrophil granulocytic granules; mechanisms of resistance to cationic antimicrobial proteins in salmonella. *Mailing Add:* Dept Microbiol Emory Sch Med Rollins Res Ctr Atlanta GA 30322-3070

SPITZNAGLE, LARRY ALLEN, RADIOPHARMACEUTICAL CHEMISTRY, PHARMACEUTICAL DEVELOPMENT. *Current Pos:* assoc prof nuclear med, 81-86, assoc dir health physics, 86-91, SR PROJ MGR, SCH MED, UNIV CONN HEALTH CTR, 91- *Personal Data:* b Lafayette, Ind, Oct, 17, 43; m 61; c 2. *Educ:* Purdue Univ, BS, 65, MS, 66, PhD(bionucleonics), 69. *Prof Exp:* Asst prof bionucleonics, Sch Pharm, Univ Wash, 69-75; asst prof nuclear med, Sch Med, Univ Conn Health Ctr, 75-79; assoc prof med chem, Sch Pharm, Univ Md, Baltimore, 79-81. *Concurrent Pos:* NIH res grants, 71-74 & 75-85. *Mem:* AAAS; Am Chem Soc; Drug Info Asn. *Res:* Manage clinical development projects for phase 1-4 and Rx to OTC switch. *Mailing Add:* Merck Res Lab PO Box 4 BL1-2 Westpoint PA 19486. *E-Mail:* spitznag@merck.com

SPIVACK, HARVEY MARVIN, NAVAL SYSTEMS ANALYSIS, OCEAN ACOUSTICS. *Current Pos:* MEM PROF STAFF SYSTS ANALYSIS, CTR NAVAL ANALYSIS, 77- *Personal Data:* b Brooklyn, NY, Feb 3, 48; m 72; c 1. *Educ:* Brooklyn Col, BS, 68; Purdue Univ, MS, 70, PhD(physics), 76. *Prof Exp:* Res assoc physics, Purdue Univ, 76; asst physicist, Brookhaven Nat Lab, 77. *Mem:* Am Phys Soc. *Res:* Cost and effectiveness of military systems; neutrino physics; theory of weak interactions. *Mailing Add:* 3219 Parkwood Terr Falls Church VA 22042. *Fax:* 703-824-2955

SPIVAK, JERRY LEPOW, HEMATOLOGY. *Current Pos:* from asst prof to assoc prof med, 72-88, dir, Div Hemat, 80-92, PROF MED, SCH MED, JOHNS HOPKINS UNIV, 88-, PROF ONCOL, 90- *Personal Data:* b New York, NY, Jan 5, 38; m 67; c 2. *Educ:* Princeton Univ, AB, 60; Cornell Univ, MD, 64; Am Bd Int Med dipl, 71, cert hemat, 75. *Honors & Awards:* Borden Award; Res Career Develop Award, Merit Award, USPHS. *Prof Exp:* Intern, Johns Hopkins Hosp, 64-65, asst resident, 65-66, chief resident, 71-72; sr resident med, NY Hosp, 68-69. *Concurrent Pos:* Clin assoc, Nat Cancer Inst, 66-68; fel hemat, Johns Hopkins Hosp, 69-71; investr med, Howard Hughes Med Inst, 72-77. *Mem:* Am Fedn Clin Res; Am Soc Hemat; Soc Exp Biol & Med; fel Am Col Physicians; Int Soc Exp Hemat; Am Clin Climat Asn. *Res:* Erythropoietin and the regulation of erythropoiesis. *Mailing Add:* 4904 Roland Ave Baltimore MD 21210

SPIVAK, STEVEN MARK, TEXTILE ENGINEERING, FIRE & FLAMMABILITY. *Current Pos:* from asst prof to prof textiles & consumer econ, 70-92, PROF FIRE PROTECTION ENG, UNIV MD, 92- *Personal Data:* b New York, NY, Oct 11, 42; m 92, Loida Velilla. *Educ:* Philadelphia Col Textiles & Sci, BS, 63; Ga Inst Technol, MS, 65; Univ Manchester, PhD(polymer & fiber sci), 67. *Honors & Awards:* Geo S Wham Leadership Medal, Am Nat Stand Inst, 92; William J Slattery Award, Stand Eng Soc, 88. *Prof Exp:* Asst prof textiles & apparel res assoc, Philadelphia Col Textiles & Sci, 68-70. *Concurrent Pos:* Tech adv, ASCR Int, Annapolis Junction, Md, 75-; dir, Stantex Consults, Annapolis Junction, Md, 76- *Mem:* Am Asn

Textile Chemists & Colorists; fel Stand Engrs Soc; Soc Fire Protection Eng; fel Textile Inst; Fiber Soc; Am Soc Test Mat. *Res:* End-use performance aspects of textiles and related materials, including interior textiles (carpet, upholstery, draperies), flammability and fire resistance of textile materials; standards engineering and consumer product standards. *Mailing Add:* Dept Fire Protection Eng Univ Md College Park MD 20742-3031. *Fax:* 301-405-9383; *E-Mail:* ss60@umail.umd.edu

SPIVEY, BRUCE ELDON, OPHTHALMOLOGY, MEDICAL EDUCATION. *Current Pos:* dean, Sch Med, 71-76, PROF OPHTHAL & HEAD DEPT, PAC MED CTR, UNIV PAC, 71- *Personal Data:* b Cedar Rapids, Iowa, Aug 29, 34; m 56; c 2. *Educ:* Coe Col, BA, 55; Univ Iowa, MD, 59, MS, 64; Univ Ill, MEd, 69; Am Bd Ophthal, dipl, 65. *Prof Exp:* Intern, Highland-Alameda County Hosp, Oakland, Calif, 59-60; resident, Univ Hosps, Iowa City, 60-63; res assoc ophthal, Col Med, Univ Iowa, 63-64, from asst prof to assoc prof, 66-71. *Concurrent Pos:* Co-dir, NIH grants, 67 & 72. *Mem:* AMA; Am Col Surgeons; Am Acad Ophthal (vpres, 77-); Pan-Am Asn Ophthal; Asn Res Vision & Ophthal. *Res:* Strabismus; ophthalmologic genetics. *Mailing Add:* Northwestern Healthcare Net 980 N Michigan Ave No 1500 Chicago IL 60611

SPIVEY, GARY H, environmental epidemiology & occupational epidemiology, for more information see previous edition

SPIVEY, HOWARD OLIN, PHYSICAL BIOCHEMISTRY. *Current Pos:* from asst prof to assoc prof, 67-75, PROF BIOCHEM, OKLA STATE UNIV, 75- *Personal Data:* b Gainesville, Fla, Dec 10, 31; m 59, Dorothy E Luke; c Bruce A, Curt O & Diane E. *Educ:* Univ Ky, BS, 54; Harvard Univ, PhD(biochem), 63. *Prof Exp:* Res assoc phys chem, Rockefeller Univ, 62-64; NIH fel chem, Mass Inst Technol, 64-65; asst prof chem, Univ Md, College Park, 65-67. *Mem:* Am Chem Soc; Sigma Xi; Am Soc Biochem & Molecular Biol; AAAS. *Res:* Physical biochemistry; heterologous associations among the enzymes - studies of extents of formation, substrate channeling and other catalytic properties. *Mailing Add:* Dept Biochem & Molecular Biol 246NRC Okla State Univ Stillwater OK 74078-3035. *E-Mail:* biochos@okway.okstate.edu

SPIVEY, ROBERT CHARLES, geology, for more information see previous edition

SPIVEY, WALTER ALLEN, STATISTICS. *Current Pos:* From asst prof to assoc prof, 57-62, PROF STATIST, UNIV MICH, ANN ARBOR, 62- *Personal Data:* b Wilmington, NC, July 24, 26; m 52; c 2. *Educ:* Univ NC, AB, 50, MA, 52, PhD(statist), 56. *Concurrent Pos:* NSF fel, Stanford Univ, 57; vis assoc prof, Harvard Univ, 59-60; vis prof, London Sch Econ, 65-66, Doshisha Univ, 67; Claire E Aker distinguished prof bus admin. *Mem:* Fel Royal Statist Soc; fel Am Statist Asn; Soc Indust & Appl Math; Math Asn Am; Inst Mgt Sci. *Res:* Statistics and data analysis; optimization theory and applications; statistical forecasting. *Mailing Add:* Univ Mich Bus Sch 701 Tappan Rm 7214 Ann Arbor MI 48109-1234

SPIZIZEN, JOHN, MICROBIOLOGY, BIOCHEMISTRY. *Current Pos:* prof & head dept, 79-89, PROF EMER MICROBIOL & IMMUNOL, UNIV ARIZ, 89- *Personal Data:* b Winnipeg, Man, Feb 7, 17; US citizen; m 43, 68, Louise F Myers; c Gary S. *Educ:* Univ Toronto, BA, 39; Calif Inst Technol, PhD(bact), 42. *Prof Exp:* Asst biol, Univ Toronto, 38-39; Nat Res Coun fel med sci, Vanderbilt Univ, 42-43; instr bact, Med Sch, Loyola Univ, Ill, 43; assoc virus res, Sharp & Dohme, Inc, 46-54; from asst prof to assoc prof microbiol, Sch Med, Western Res Univ, 54-61; prof microbiol & head dept, Univ Minn, Minneapolis, 61-65; chmn dept microbiol, Scripps Clin & Res Found, 65-76, mem dept cellular biol, Res Inst Scripps Clin, 76-79. *Concurrent Pos:* Mem, Life Sci Comt, NASA; mem recombinant DNA adv comt, NIH; fel, Nat Res Coun, 42-43; res career develop award, NIH, 56-61; mem, Am Cancer Soc Coun, 74-, Nat Acad Sci & Res Coun, Am Cancer Soc, 74-; adj prof, Univ Calif, San Diego; consult, various co. *Mem:* Am Soc Microbiol; Am Soc Biol Chemists; AAAS. *Res:* Cloning of genes in bacillus species; identification and cloning of genes for insecticidal toxins. *Mailing Add:* Dept Microbiol & Immunol Univ Ariz Sch Med Tucson AZ 84724

SPJUT, HARLAN JACOBSON, PATHOLOGY. *Current Pos:* prof path, 62-83, actg chmn dept, 69-72 & 87-88, IRENE & CLARENCE PROF PATH, BAYLOR COL MED, 83- *Personal Data:* b Salt Lake City, Utah, May 3, 22; m; c 5. *Educ:* Univ Utah, BS, 43, MD, 46; Am Bd Path, dipl. *Prof Exp:* Intern, Jackson Mem Hosp, Miami, Fla, 46-47; asst resident path, Salt Lake Vet Hosp, Utah, 49-50; from asst resident to instr, Univ Utah, 50-53; from instr to assoc prof surg path & path, Sch Med, Wash Univ, 54-62. *Concurrent Pos:* Am Cancer Soc fel surg path, Sch Med, Wash Univ, 53-54; attend pathologist, St Louis Vet Hosp, 55-59; assoc pathologist, Barnes Hosp, 54-62; vis asst, Karolinska Hosp, Stockholm, Sweden, 59-60; attend pathologist, St Luke's Hosp, 71-80; consult, Houston Vet Admin Hosp; sr attend pathologist, Methodist Hosp, 80- *Mem:* Col Am Path; AMA; Int Acad Path; Int Skeletal Soc. *Res:* Carcinoma; bone and large bowel tumors; cytology in diagnosis of carcinoma of various sites. *Mailing Add:* Dept Path Baylor Col Med One Baylor Plaza Houston TX 77030-3611

SPLETTSTOESSER, JOHN FREDERICK, GEOMORPHOLOGY, ENVIRONMENTAL GEOLOGY. *Current Pos:* POLAR SCI CONSULT, 89- *Personal Data:* b Waconia, Minn, Oct 17, 33; c 2. *Educ:* Univ Minn, 62. *Honors & Awards:* Soviet Polar Medal, 74. *Prof Exp:* Ed, Am Geol Inst, 62-63; head, Sci & Tech Div, Libr Cong, 64-67; asst dir, Inst Polar Studies, Ohio State Univ, 67-69, assoc dir, 69-74; admin dir, Ross Ice Shelf Proj Mgt Off, Univ Nebr, 74-77; prog mgr, Minn Geol Surv, Univ Minn, St Paul, 77-89. *Concurrent Pos:* Sci coordr US remote field camps, Antarctica, 78-; staff lectr geol, tourist ships to Antarctica, 83-; spokesman, Int Asn Antarctica Tour Oper, 91-; vis fac, Col Atlantic Bar Harbor, Maine, 91-; mem deleg, Antarctic Treaty Consultative Meeting, US State Dept, 92. *Mem:* AAAS; Am Inst Mining, Metall & Petrol Eng; Soc Mining Eng; Arctic Inst NAm; Am Geophys Union; Geol Soc Am. *Res:* Geology of Antarctica; mining geology; scientific editing; mineral resource potential of Antarctica; tourism in polar regions. *Mailing Add:* 235 Camden St Suite 32 Rockland ME 04841

SPLIES, ROBERT GLENN, ORGANIC CHEMISTRY. *Current Pos:* RETIRED. *Personal Data:* b Bird Island, Minn, Oct 2, 25; m 52; c 1. *Educ:* Univ Wis, BS, 47, MS, 48, PhD, 51. *Prof Exp:* Instr, Wis State Col, Milwaukee, 51-52; chemist, Solvay Process Div, Allied Chem Corp, NY, 52-53; coordr, Bjorksten Res Lab, Wis, 53-55; chemist, Oscar Mayer & Co, 55-57; asst prof org chem, Univ NDak, 57-59; from asst prof to assoc prof, Univ Wis-Milwaukee, 59-67; from assoc prof to prof org chem, Univ Wis-Waukesha, 67-88. *Mem:* Am Chem Soc. *Res:* Nitro and amino derivatives of aromatic hydrocarbons; color reactions of alkaloids. *Mailing Add:* W 300N1102 McDowell Rd Waukesha WI 53188

SPLIETHOFF, WILLIAM LUDWIG, ORGANIC CHEMISTRY. *Current Pos:* MGT CONSULT, 86- *Personal Data:* b Matamoras, Pa, Apr 8, 26; m 49, 71, Marjorie A Johnson; c Christina (Hansen), Karen (Walker) & W Mark. *Educ:* Pa State Univ, BS, 46, MS, 48; Mich State Univ, PhD(org chem), 53. *Honors & Awards:* Com Develop Asn Honor Award, 82. *Prof Exp:* Asst fuel tech, Pa State Univ, 46-48; asst gen org & phys chem, Mich State Univ, 50-52; res chemist textile fibers dept, E I du Pont de Nemours & Co, 52-60; dir mkt res chem div, Gen Mills, Inc, Ill, 60-62, mgr com develop, 62-67; asst managing dir, Polymer Corp Ltd, Sydney, Australia, 67-69; dir opers indust chem, Chem Div, Gen Mills Chem, Inc, 69-70, vpres, 70-77; exec vpres & dir, Henkel Corp, 77-86; srvpres & dir, Henkel Am, 81-86. *Concurrent Pos:* Dir & officer subsid, Mex, Japan, Ireland, SAfrica, Venezuela, Italy & Pakistan, 70-86. *Mem:* Am Chem Soc; Com Develop Asn; Chem Mkt Res Asn. *Res:* Mechanism and kinetics of racemization of optically active halides by phenols; condensation polymers; new uses for synthetic fibers; market research and commercial development; general industrial chemical management. *Mailing Add:* 113 Sandy Hook Rd Chanhassen MN 55317

SPLINTER, WILLIAM ELDON, ENGINEERING. *Current Pos:* prof & head dept, Univ Nebr, 68-84, George Holmes distinguished prof & head, Dept Agr Eng, 84-88, assoc vchancellor for res, 88-90, interim vchancellor for res & dean grad studies, 90-91, vchancellor res, 91-93, George Holmes Distinguished Emer Prof, 93-94, Interim Dean, Col Eng Technol, 94, GEORGE HOLMES DISTINGUISHED EMER PROF, UNIV NEBR, 95- *Personal Data:* b North Platte, Nebr, Nov 24, 25; m 53, Eleanor L Peterson; c Kathryn L, William J, Karen A & Robert M. *Educ:* Univ Nebr, BSc, 50; Mich State Univ, MSc, 51, PhD(agr eng), 55. *Honors & Awards:* Massey Ferguson Medal, Am Soc Agr Engrs, 78; John Deere Gold Medal, Am Soc Agr Engrs, 95. *Prof Exp:* Instr agr eng, Mich State Univ, 53-54; res assoc prof, NC State Univ, 54-61, prof, 61-68. *Concurrent Pos:* Consult, Southern Rhodesia, Univ So Africa, 63, Ford Found, IIT Kharagpur, India, 66, Columbia, 68, Chile, 78, Peru, 78, Russia & Mexico, 80, China, 81 & 86, Ger, 83, Univ Melbourne, Australia, 85, Morocco, 86 & Ireland, 89; hon prof, Shenyang Agr Univ, 86,; mem, Nat Coun Res Adminrs, 88-93; consult on technol Park, Univ Nebr found; consult, Renewable Resources Res Inst. *Mem:* Nat Acad Eng; fel Am Soc Agr Engrs (vpres, 76-77, pres, 78-79); Soc Automotive Engrs; fel AAAS; Am Asn Eng Socs; Am Soc Agr Eng Found (pres, 87-89). *Res:* Bioengineering of plant systems; systems engineering of crop production; electrostatic application of agricultural pesticides; mathematical modeling of plants; machine design and development; human factors engineering. *Mailing Add:* 202 Biological Systems Eng Lab Univ of Nebr Lincoln NE 68583-0832. *Fax:* 402-472-8367; *E-Mail:* wsplinter@unl.edu

SPLITTER, EARL JOHN, VETERINARY PARASITOLOGY. *Current Pos:* RETIRED. *Personal Data:* b Lorraine, Kans, June 29, 20; m 43, Clara B Paris; c Gary A, Marianne & Elinor J. *Educ:* Kans State Col, DVM, 43, MS, 50. *Honors & Awards:* Res Award, Am Feed Indust Asn, 86. *Prof Exp:* Jr state vet, NC State Dept Agr, 43-46; from asst prof to assoc prof path, Kans State Col, 46-57; group leader & asst dep adminr, Coop State Res Serv, USDA, 77-81; priv vet, 57-86. *Mem:* Am Vet Med Asn; Nat Asn Fed Vets. *Res:* Blood parasitic diseases of domestic animals; research administration; veterinary pathology and medicine. *Mailing Add:* 7053 SE Bunker Hill Dr Hobe Sound FL 33455-7321

SPLITTER, GARY ALLEN, VETERINARY MEDICINE, IMMUNOPATHOLOGY. *Current Pos:* ASST PROF IMMUNOPATH, DEPT VET SCI, UNIV WIS-MADISON, 76- *Personal Data:* b Lumberton, NC, July 19, 45; m 67. *Educ:* Kans State Univ, BS, 67, DVM, 69, MS, 70; Wash State Univ, PhD(path), 76. *Prof Exp:* Instr path, Kans State Univ, 69-70; captain, Sch Aerospace Med, US Air Force, 70-72; NIH fel, Dept Vet Path, Wash State Univ, 72-76. *Concurrent Pos:* Ed reviewer, Am Vet Med Asn, 78- *Mem:* Am Vet Med Asn; Am Col Vet Toxicologists. *Res:* Pathology; immunology; mechanisms of host defense in chronic and viral diseases. *Mailing Add:* Dept Animal Health & Biomed Sci Univ Wis 1655 Linden Dr Madison WI 53706-1581. *Fax:* 608-262-7420; *E-Mail:* gas@zeusatlabs.wisc.edu

SPLITTGERBER, GEORGE H, INORGANIC CHEMISTRY. *Current Pos:* RETIRED. *Personal Data:* b Van Tassel, Wyo, Jan 25, 18; m 42; c 3. *Educ:* Univ Nebr, BSc, 39; Mich State Univ, MSc, 40; Kans State Univ, PhD(chem), 60. *Prof Exp:* Chemist, Victor Chem Works, 40-42 & Sinclair Res & Develop Co, 42-48; from instr to prof chem, Colo State Univ, 48-88. *Mem:* Am Chem Soc; AAAS; Sigma Xi. *Res:* Antioxidants and corrosion inhibitors; nonaqueous polarography. *Mailing Add:* 709 Birky Pl Ft Collins CO 80526-1907

SPLITTSTOESSER, CLARA QUINNELL, BACTERIOLOGY, INSECT PATHOLOGY. *Current Pos:* RETIRED. *Personal Data:* b Miles City, Mont, Jan 19, 29; m 59. *Educ:* Mont State Univ, BS, 50; Univ Wis, MS, 51, PhD(bact), 56. *Prof Exp:* Fel, Univ Wis, 56-57; assoc exp surg, Med Ctr, Univ Calif, 57-58; experimentalist, Cornell Univ, 59-62, res assoc insect path, NY Exp Sta, 62-77. *Mem:* Soc Invert Path. *Res:* Physiology of microorganisms; viral and bacterial pathogens of insects. *Mailing Add:* One Highland Ave Geneva NY 14456

SPLITTSTOESSER, DON FREDERICK, BACTERIOLOGY. *Current Pos:* RETIRED. *Personal Data:* b Norwalk, Wis, 27; m 59, Clara Quinnell. *Educ:* Univ Wis, BS, 52, MS, 53, PhD, 56. *Prof Exp:* Proj assoc bact, Univ Wis, 55-56; from asst prof to assoc prof bact, Cornell Univ, 58-69, prof microbiol, 69-95, chmn dept, 82-88. *Concurrent Pos:* Mem, Ad Hoc Subcomt Food Microbiol, Food Protection Comt, Nat Acad Sci-Nat Res Coun, 63 & Comt Microbiol Food, Adv, Bd Mil Personnel Supplies, Nat Res Coun, 72-75, chmn, Food Protection Comt, 82-86. *Mem:* Am Soc Microbiol; Inst Food Technol; Int Asn Milk, Food & Environ Sanitarians; Am Soc Enologists. *Res:* Sanitation in food processing; microbiology of frozen foods; physiology of spore germination; wine fermentation. *Mailing Add:* Dept Food Sci & Technol Cornell Univ Geneva NY 14456

SPLITTSTOESSER, WALTER E, PLANT PHYSIOLOGY, BIOCHEMISTRY. *Current Pos:* plant biochemist, Univ Ill, Urbana, 65-74, head, Div Veg Crops, 73-76, asst head, Dept Hort, 82-88, PROF VEG CROPS, UNIV ILL, URBANA, 75- *Personal Data:* b Claremont, Minn, Aug 27, 37; m 60, Shirley O'Connor; c Pamula, Sheryl & Riley. *Educ:* Univ Minn, BS, 58; SDak State Univ, MS, 60; Purdue Univ, PhD(plant biochem), 63. *Honors & Awards:* J H Gourley Award, Am Soc Hort Sci, 74; Outstanding Grad Educator, Am Soc Hort Sci, 90. *Prof Exp:* Plant physiologist, Shell Develop Co, 63-64; biochemist, Univ Calif, Davis, 64-65. *Concurrent Pos:* NIH fel, 64-65; prof bot & microbiol, Univ Col, London, 72-73; prof soil sci, Rothamsted Exp Sta, Harpenden, Eng, 80; distinguished vis prof, Nagoya Univ, Japan, 82; biotechnologist, Univ Col, Dublin, 87; prof agr, LaTrobe Univ, Australia, 95. *Mem:* Fel Am Soc Hort Sci; Japan Soc Plant Physiol; Plant Growth Reg Soc Am; Interam Soc Trop Hort. *Res:* Plant metabolism; biotechnology; tissue culture; plant regeneration and improvement. *Mailing Add:* 2006 Cureton Dr Urbana IL 61801-6226. *Fax:* 217-244-3219; *E-Mail:* splittst@uiuc.edu

SPOCK, ALEXANDER, PEDIATRICS, ALLERGY, PEDIATRIC PULMONOLOGY. *Current Pos:* from instr to assoc prof, 59-77, chief, Pediat Pulmonary Div, 75-92, PROF PEDIAT, MED CTR, DUKE UNIV, 77- *Personal Data:* b Shamokin, Pa, May 5, 29; m 70, Diana Stafford; c Christopher, Karen, Alexander & Diana. *Educ:* Loyola Col, Md, BS, 51; Univ Md, MD, 55. *Honors & Awards:* Davison Award, SEastern Allergy Asn 65 & 80; NC Thoracic Soc Award, 91. *Prof Exp:* From intern to resident pediat, Geisinger Mem Hosp, Danville, Pa, 55-58. *Concurrent Pos:* Fel pediat allergy, Med Ctr, Duke Univ, 60-62; vis res prof, Karolinska Inst, Stockholm, Sweden, 73-74. *Mem:* Am Acad Pediat; Am Acad Allergy; Am Col Allergists; Am Thoracic Soc; Soc Pediat Res. *Res:* Immunology; pulmonary physiology; lung disease and allergic problems in pediatric patients; cystic fibrosis. *Mailing Add:* Box 2994 Dept Pediat Duke Univ Med Ctr Durham NC 27710. *Fax:* 919-684-2292

SPOCK, BENJAMIN MCLANE, PEDIATRICS, PSYCHIATRY. *Current Pos:* RETIRED. *Personal Data:* b New Haven, Conn, May 2, 03; div; c Michael, John Cheney. *Educ:* Yale Univ, BA, 25; Columbia Univ, MD, 29. *Prof Exp:* Intern med, Presbyn Hosp, New York City, 29-31; intern pediat, NY Nursery & Childs Hosp, 31-32; intern psychiat, NY Hosp, 32-33; instr pediat, Cornell Med Col, 33-47; assoc prof psychiat, Mayo Found, Univ Minn, 47-51; prof child develop, Univ Pittsburgh, 51-55, Western Res Univ, 55-67. *Concurrent Pos:* Asst attend pediatrician, NY Hosp, 33-47; consult pediat psychiat, New York City, Health Dept, 42-47; consult psychiat, Mayo Clin & Rochester Child Health Proj, Rochester, Minn; USNR, 44-46; co-chmn, Nat Comt Sane Nuclear Policy, 62. *Res:* Pediatrics; psychiatry; child development. *Mailing Add:* PO Box 1268 Camden ME 04843

SPODICK, DAVID HOWARD, CARDIOLOGY. *Current Pos:* PROF MED, UNIV MASS, 76- *Personal Data:* b Hartford, Conn, Sept 9, 27; m 51, 69, Casrolyn Gosse; c Marjory, Nancy, Stephen & John. *Educ:* Bard Col, AB, 47; New York Med Col, MD, 50. *Prof Exp:* From instr to prof med, Tufts Univ, 57-76. *Concurrent Pos:* Nat Heart Inst spec fel, WRoxbury Vet Admin Hosp, NY, 56-57; Am Col Physicians Brower Traveling Scholar, 64; sr physician, Lemuel Shattuck Hosp, Boston, 57-76, chief cardiol div, 62-76; chief cardiac diag & res ctr, Boston Eve Clin, 60-; assoc med, Boston City Hosp, 65-, lectr, Sch Med, Boston Univ, 66- & Sch Med, Tufts Univ, 76-; attend cardiologist, Univ Mass Hosp, 76-; dir cardiol div, St Vincent Hosp, 76-84, dir clin cardiol, 85-; ed, Am J Noninvasive Cardiol, 85- *Mem:* Am Col Chest Physicians; Am Fedn Clin Res; Am Col Cardiol; Am Col Physicians; Am Heart Asn. *Res:* Noninvasive polycardiography; clinical pharmacology; exercise physiology; physical diagnosis; diseases of pericardium; electrocariography echo-doppler. *Mailing Add:* Cardiol Div St Vincent Hosp Worcester MA 01604. *Fax:* 508-798-1240

SPOEHR, ALBERT FREDERICK, CHEMISTRY. *Current Pos:* RETIRED. *Personal Data:* b Milwaukee, Wis, Feb 24, 18; m 47. *Educ:* Univ Wis, BS, 42. *Prof Exp:* Lab supvr, Hercules Powder Co, Del, 42-45; res chemist, Am Anode, Inc, 45-53; mgr tech servs, Latex Compounding Div, Polson Rubber Co, Garretsville, 53-70, tech dir, 70-79; prod mgr, Bearfoot Inc, Wadsworth, 79-82,. *Mem:* Am Chem Soc. *Res:* Rubber and latex compounding; explosives. *Mailing Add:* 1912 Phelps Ave Cuyahoga Falls OH 44223

SPOELHOF, CHARLES PETER, ENGINEERING PHYSICS, MATHEMATICS. *Current Pos:* RETIRED. *Personal Data:* b Hackensack, NJ, Aug 6, 30; m 53, Kay Maliepaard; c Beth, Philip, Gordon & Ronald. *Educ:* Univ Mich, BS(eng physics) & BS(eng math), 53, MS, 54. *Honors & Awards:* Apollo Achievement Award, NASA, 71. *Prof Exp:* Engr, EKCo, Camera Works, Navy Ord Div & Kodak Appartus Div, 54-62; tech asst to dir res & develop, Eastman Kodak Co, 62-64, proj mgr, 64-65, prog mgr, 66-68, asst to dir res & develop, 68-72, mgr govt prod, 72-73, dir res & eng, 73-75, mgr bus & prof prod, 75-82, vpres & asst gen mgr, 82-85, vpres & dir, tech assessment com & info systs, 85-86. *Concurrent Pos:* Mem sci adv comt, Defense Intel Agency; mem, Hubble Space Telescope Optical Systs Bd Invest, NASA; mem adv bd, NY Ctr Advan Optical Tech; mem tech adv bd, Microelectronics & Comp Tech Corp. *Mem:* Nat Acad Eng; Optical Soc Am; Soc Imaging Sci & Tech. *Res:* Optical and photographic systems; image evaluation; optical design; imaging sensors; optical measurements. *Mailing Add:* 5 Mullet Dr Pittsford NY 14534

SPOERLEIN, MARIE TERESA, PHARMACOLOGY, PHYSIOLOGY. *Current Pos:* prof, 68-87, EMER PROF PHARMACOL, COL PHARM, RUTGERS UNIV, NEW BRUNSWICK, 87- *Personal Data:* b Dormont, Pa, Nov 3, 25. *Educ:* Seton Hall Col, BA, 47; Rutgers Univ, MS, 54, PhD, 59. *Prof Exp:* Asst pharmacologist, Schering Corp, 47-54 & Maltbie Labs, Wallace & Tiernan, Inc, 54-56; asst physiol, Col Pharm, Rutgers Univ, Newark, 56-58, from asst prof to assoc prof pharmacol, 59-68. *Mem:* AAAS; Am Soc Pharmacol & Exp Therapeut; Am Pharmaceut Asn; NY Acad Sci; Sigma Xi. *Res:* Biochemical pharmacology, especially mechanism of drug action and nervous system pharmacology. *Mailing Add:* 252 Carol Jean Way Somerville NJ 08876-3350

SPOFFORD, JANICE BROGUE, GENETICS. *Current Pos:* assoc prof ecol & evolution, 70-96, EMER ASSOC PROF, UNIV CHICAGO, 96- *Personal Data:* b Chicago, Ill, Nov 14, 25; m 51, Richardson L; c John & George. *Educ:* Univ Chicago, PhB, 44, SB, 46, PhD(zool), 55. *Prof Exp:* Instr natural sci, Univ Col, 48-51, asst prof biol, 55-61, res assoc zool, 56-70, assoc prof biol, 61-96. *Mem:* AAAS; Genetics Soc Am; Soc Study Evolution; Am Soc Human Genetics; Am Soc Naturalists (secy, 71-74, pres, 79); Soc Molecular Biol & Evolution. *Res:* Population genetics; mechanism of position-effect variegation; multi-gene families in evolution. *Mailing Add:* Dept Ecol & Evol Univ Chicago Chicago IL 60637

SPOFFORD, SALLY HOYT, ORNITHOLOGY. *Current Pos:* RETIRED. *Personal Data:* b Williamsport, Pa, Apr 11, 14; m 42, 64, Walter R. *Educ:* Wilson Col, AB, 35; Univ Pa, MS, 36; Cornell Univ, PhD(ornith), 48. *Prof Exp:* Asst biol, Wilson Col, 37-39; med technician, Stark Gen Hosp, Charleston, SC, 42-44 & Kennedy Gen Hosp, Memphis, Tenn, 44-45; admin asst, Lab Ornith, Cornell Univ, 55-69, res collabr, 69-80. *Concurrent Pos:* Simon Henry Gage fel, Cornell Univ. *Mem:* Wilson Ornith Soc; Western Field Ornith; Am Geog Soc; Am Ornith Union; Raptor Res Found. *Res:* Life history and ecology of pileated woodpecker; population and distribution studies of Southeastern Arizona birds; public education in ornithology; conservation; food habits and behavior of roadrunners; feeding behavior of hummingbirds. *Mailing Add:* Rancho-Aguila PO Box J Portal AZ 85632

SPOFFORD, WALTER O, JR, ENVIRONMENTAL SCIENCES & ENGINEERING. *Current Pos:* res assoc, Resources for the Future, 68-74, dir Qual Environ Div, 74-80, dir hazardous waste mgt prog, 85-88, SR FEL, RESOURCES FOR THE FUTURE, 78-, DIR, ENVIRON & DEVELOP PROG, 89- *Personal Data:* b Swampscott, Mass, May 9, 36; m 61; c 3. *Educ:* Northeastern Univ, BS, 59; Harvard Univ, MS, 60, PhD(water resources eng), 65. *Prof Exp:* Res asst, Harvard Water Resources Group, Harvard Univ, 61-65, res fel water resources mgt, Sch Pub Health, 65-66. *Concurrent Pos:* Ford Found consult, Aswan Reg Develop Proj, Cairo, 65-66; WHO consult, Czech Res & Develop Ctr for Environ Pollution Control, 72-74 & Environmental Pollution Abatement Ctr, Poland, 76-78; mem panel on marine ecosyst anal, Nat Acad Sci-Nat Acad Eng, Sci & Eng Comt Adv to Nat Oceanic & Atmospheric Admin, 72-73; mem fac systs anal for environ pollution control, NATO Advan Study Inst, Baiersbronn, Ger, 72; consult, Los Alamos Sci Lab, 73-78, NSF, 73, World Bank, 74- 75, 79 & 89-, Ministry Conserv, Victoria, Australia, 74, Int Inst Appl Systs Anal, 78-79 & Asian Develop Bank, Manila, 80, 83, 86; res scholar water resources, Int Inst Appl Systs Anal, Austria, 74; mem subcomt on water resources adv comt, Int Inst Appl Systs Analysis, Nat Acad Sci, 74-76, mem & chmn, Liaison Subcomt on Resources & Environ, 78-82 & mem, Int Coop in Systs Analysis Res Exec Subcomt, 78-82; mem, Metro Study Task Force, Washington Ctr Metro Studies, Washington, DC, 77-78; mem bd dirs, Roy F Weston, Inc, Pa, 78-89; mem, US Nat Comt Scientific Hydrology, 78-; consult, Asian Develop Bank, Repub Korea 80, 83, Malaysia, 86, 87; consult, World Bank, Peoples Repub China, 89- *Mem:* Fel Am Inst Chemists; Am Soc Civil Engrs; Am Geophys Union; Pub Works Hist Soc; Sigma Xi; Asn Environ & Resource Economists. *Res:* Environmental economics and management; civil and sanitary engineering; water resources engineering and management; public health. *Mailing Add:* 3348 Beech Tree Lane Falls Church VA 22042

SPOFFORD, WALTER RICHARDSON, II, zoology, anatomy; deceased, see previous edition for last biography

SPOHN, HERBERT EMIL, EXPERIMENTAL PSYCHOPATHOLOGY. *Current Pos:* RETIRED. *Personal Data:* b Berlin, Ger, June 10, 23; US citizen; m 73; c Jessica & Madeleine. *Educ:* City Col New York, BSS, 49; Columbia Univ, PhD, 55; Am Bd Prof Psychologists, dipl clin psychol, 62. *Prof Exp:* Lectr, City Col New York, 49-52; res assoc, Sarah Lawrence Col, Bronxville, 50-54; res psychologist, Franklin D Roosevelt Vet Admin Hosp, Montrose, 55-61, chief, Res Sect, 61-64; sr res psychologist, Menninger Found, 65-80, dir, 81-93. *Concurrent Pos:* Prin investr & res scientist, USPHS res grants, 66-76. *Mem:* Sigma Xi; Am Psychol Asn; AAAS; Soc Res Psychopath; Am Psychopath Asn. *Res:* Experimental psychopathology; clinical and experimental psychopharmacology; schizophrenia; treatment evaluation research; mechanisms in schizophrenia. *Mailing Add:* 1906 SW Village Dr Topeka KS 66604-3714

SPOHN, RALPH JOSEPH, HOMOGENEOUS CATALYSIS, ORGANOMETALLIC CHEMISTRY. *Current Pos:* Chemist, Enjay Chem Lab, Exxon Chem Co, 70-72, res chemist, Corp Res Lab, 72-75, staff chemist & group leader, Chem Intermediate Technol Div, 75-79, sr staff chemist, 79-82, head synthesis gas process res, New Ventures Technol Div, 82-84, head, Chem Analysis Lab, 84-92, sect leader, Technol Support Serv, Paramins Technol Div, 92-95, OFFSITE PROCESSING MGR, PARAMINS, EXXON CHEM CO, 95- *Personal Data:* b New York, NY; m 89; c 2. *Educ:* Providence Col, BS, 65; Mass Inst Technol, PhD(inorg chem), 70; Rutgers Univ, MBA, 75. *Mem:* Am Chem Soc; NY Acad Sci. *Res:* Homogeneous and heterogeneous catalysis, especially that of the reactions of carbon monoxide and/or hydrogen with organic substrates and their industrial applications; analytical chemistry. *Mailing Add:* 10 Kings Ct Woodcliff Lake NJ 07675-8022. *Fax:* 732-434-7273

SPOHN, WILLIAM GIDEON, JR, MATHEMATICS. *Current Pos:* RETIRED. *Personal Data:* b Lancaster, Pa, Mar 8, 23; m 87, Claire Demant; c Susan, Peter, Kathleen & Mary. *Educ:* St John's Col, Md, BA, 47; Univ Calif, Berkeley, MA, 50; Univ Pa, PhD(math), 62. *Prof Exp:* Instr math, Temple Univ, 52-54, Univ Del, 54-56 & Bowling Green State Univ, 56-59; William S Parsons fel, Johns Hopkins Univ, 66-67, sr staff mathematician, Appl Physics Lab, 59-84. *Mem:* Math Asn Am. *Res:* Analytical mathematics; applied mathematics; mathematical analysis; number theory; numerical analysis; system analysis. *Mailing Add:* 5423 Storm Drift Columbia MD 21045

SPOHR, DANIEL ARTHUR, PHYSICS. *Current Pos:* RETIRED. *Personal Data:* b Meadville, Pa, Sept 13, 27; m 66; c 2. *Educ:* Allegheny Col, BS, 49; Oxford Univ, DPhil(physics), 58. *Prof Exp:* Res physicist, Cryogenics Br, US Naval Res Lab, 49-54 & 58-68, consult physicist, 68-89. *Mem:* AAAS; Am Phys Soc; Sigma Xi; Soc Photo-Optical Instrumentation Engrs. *Res:* Infrared, fiber optic and optical systems; data and signal processing; instrumentation systems analysis and development; computer application to structural, thermal and circuit analysis; applied superconductivity; low temperature physics; nuclear cooling and orientation; application of advanced materials. *Mailing Add:* 4477 Q St NW Washington DC 20007-2071

SPOKANE, ROBERT BRUCE, BIOSENSORS, ARTIFICIAL BLOOD. *Current Pos:* RES SCIENTIST, YELLOW SPRINGS INSTRUMENT CO, 90- *Personal Data:* b Cleveland, Ohio, Aug 5, 52; m 76, Linda C Wright; c Lea F, Hannah J & Tara M. *Educ:* Ohio Univ, BS, 75; Univ Colo, Boulder, MS, 78, PhD(biophys chem), 81. *Honors & Awards:* Merck Index Award. *Prof Exp:* Teaching asst chem, Univ Colo, Boulder, 75-77, res asst chem, 77-81; res asst chem, Procter & Gamble Co, 77-81, staff scientistt, 81-84; res scientist, Dept Neurophysiol, Childrens Hosp, 84-90. *Concurrent Pos:* Rescuer/treas, Boulder Emergency Squad, 80; consult, Synthetic Blood Int, 92- *Mem:* Am Chem Soc; Sigma Xi; Am Soc Internal Artificial Organs; Am Physiol Soc; Nat Speol Soc. *Res:* Industrial and implantable applications of biosensors, environmental monitoring in submerged aquifers, fluorocarbon based artificial blood, fluorocarbon based liquid breathing and hyperbaric medicine; submerged cave environmental monitoring. *Mailing Add:* 1715 Garry Dr Bellbrook OH 45305. *Fax:* 937-767-9353

SPOKAS, JOHN J, RADIATION PHYSICS, DOSIMETRY. *Current Pos:* assoc prof, 61-70, chmn dept, 67-72, prof physics & dir, Phys Sci Lab, 70-86, PROF PHYSICS, ILL BENEDICTINE COL, 86- *Personal Data:* b Lisle, Ill, Oct 15, 28; m 52, Elizabeth Beauvais; c John J, Joseph A, Anne E (Dawson), David M, Mary J, Janet M (Kappel) & Clare J. *Educ:* St Procopius Col, BS, 52; Univ Ill, MS, 54, PhD(physics), 58. *Prof Exp:* Mem tech staff, RCA Labs, 57-61. *Concurrent Pos:* Tech dir, Exradin, Inc, 87- *Mem:* Am Phys Soc; Am Asn Physics Teachers; Radiation Res Soc; Am Asn Physicists Med. *Res:* Radiation dosimetry; nuclear instrumentation; charge transport in insulators; conducting plastics; nuclear magnetic resonance relaxation. *Mailing Add:* Dept Physics Ill Benedictine Col Lisle IL 60532. *Fax:* 630-829-6551; *E-Mail:* jspokas@ben.edu

SPOKES, ERNEST M(ELVERN), mine safety, mining environment; deceased, see previous edition for last biography

SPOKES, G(ILBERT) NEIL, RESEARCH DIRECTION, ANALYTICAL CHEMISTRY. *Current Pos:* TECH DIR, CHEMETRICS INC, CALVERTON, VA, 88- *Personal Data:* b Isleworth, Eng, July 18, 35; m 69, Cynthia F White; c Jeffrey, Pauline, Judith & Peter. *Educ:* Univ London, BSc, 56, PhD(flame spectra), 59. *Prof Exp:* Res assoc chem, Univ Mich, 59-60 & Yale Univ, 60-61; chem physicist, Stanford Res Inst, 61-72; dir eng res & develop dept, Hycel Inc, 72; prin engr & dir res, Technicon Instruments Corp, 73-76; vpres, Chem Serv Div, US Testing Co, Inc, Hoboken, NJ, 76-81; group vpres, Chem Serv Group, 81-87. *Mem:* Am Soc Testing & Mat; Am Chem Soc; Am Soc Quality Control. *Res:* Emission and absorption spectra of flames and of negative ions; gaseous electronics; ion sampling; gas kinetics and thermochemistry; pyrolysis and oxidation of gases and solids using mass spectrometry; biomedical diagnostic instrumentation; Inorganic analytical instrumentation; environmental chemistry; water analysis. *Mailing Add:* 7267 Laurel Brook Lane Marshall VA 20115

SPOKOYNY, FELIX E, TURBULENT GAS-SOLIDS FLOWS, HEAT & MASS TRANSFER. *Current Pos:* SR RES SCIENTIST, WAHLCO ENVIRON SYSTS, INC, 89- *Personal Data:* b Odessa, Ukraine, June 20, 47; m 85, Eleonora S Desiatuik; c Ilanit & Jessica. *Educ:* Lomonosov's Inst Technol, MS, 69; Odessa Inst Techol, PhD(thermophys), 70. *Prof Exp:* Sr researcher, Dept Heat & Mass Transfer, Odessa Inst, 69-83, Dept Mineral Wool Technol, Thermoinsulation Inst, 83-89. *Concurrent Pos:* Lectr, Odessa Inst Technol, 76-83. *Mem:* Am Soc Mech Engrs; Fine Particle Soc. *Res:* Heat and mass transfer in turbulent flows with different sources of inhomogeneity; granted 32 US and Russian patents. *Mailing Add:* 1650 Samar Pl Costa Mesa CA 92626. *Fax:* 714-641-9014

SPOLJARIC, NENAD, SEDIMENTARY PETROLOGY, ENVIRONMENTAL GEOLOGY. *Current Pos:* SR SCIENTIST, DEL GEOL SURV, UNIV DEL, 65- *Personal Data:* b Zagreb, Croatia, July 3, 34; US citizen; m 64, Barbara Simunovic; c Raymond E. *Educ:* Univ Ljubljana, GE, 60; Harvard Univ, MA, 65; Bryn Mawr Col, PhD(sedimentary petrol), 70. *Honors & Awards:* Autometric Award, Am Soc Photogram, 76. *Prof Exp:* Explor geologist, Proizvodnja Nafte Co, Slovenia, 60-61; petrol geologist, Petrol Inst, Croatia, 62-63. *Concurrent Pos:* Mem Int Petrol Tech Deleg To People's Repub of China, 83 & Australia & Indonesia, 84. *Mem:* Am Asn Petrol Geologists. *Res:* Study of glauconitic sediments; geographic distribution, stratigraphy, correlation and origin of these sediments; study of clay-mineralogy of the Mid-Atlantic Coastal Plain, USA; study of New Zealand glauconitic sediments; geology of the mid-Atlantic coastal plain, USA. *Mailing Add:* Del Geol Surv Univ Del Newark DE 19716. *Fax:* 302-831-3579; *E-Mail:* iat-inc@juno.com

SPOLSKY, CHRISTINA MARIA, MITOCHONDRIAL DNA, EVOLUTION. *Current Pos:* RES SCIENTIST, ACAD NATURAL SCI, PHILADELPHIA, 78- *Personal Data:* b Reute, Austria, Mar 3, 45; Can citizen; m 75; c 2. *Educ:* Univ Toronto, BS, 67; Yale Univ, PhD(microbiol), 73. *Prof Exp:* Fel, Univ Pa, 73-75, Am Cancer Soc, 74; res assoc cell biol, Wistar Inst, 75-76; at dept ecol & evolution, Univ Ill. *Concurrent Pos:* Prin invstr, Whitehall Fedn grant, 81-84. *Mem:* Sigma Xi; Tissue Cult Asn; Am Soc Cell Biol; Am Soc Microbiol. *Res:* The relationship of chemical carcinogenesis to mutagenesis in cell cultures; the information content and biogenesis of mitochondrial DNA; use of mitochondrial DNA to determine toxonomic relationships of species; rate of evolution of mitochondrial DNA in vertebrates; origin of mitochondria as determined by rDNA sequences. *Mailing Add:* Acad Natural Sci 1900 Benjamin Franklin Pkwy Philadelphia PA 19103-1195

SPOLYAR, LOUIS WILLIAM, TOXICOLOGY. *Current Pos:* RETIRED. *Personal Data:* b Detroit, Mich, May 6, 08; m 35; c 3. *Educ:* DePauw Univ, AB, 31; Ind Univ, MD, 36; Am Bd Prev Med, dipl, 50. *Prof Exp:* Lectr indust med, Sch Med, Ind Univ, Indianapolis, 40-46, asst prof pub health, 46-78; asst health comnr, Ind State Bd Health, 69- *Concurrent Pos:* Dir div indust hyg, Ind State Bd Health, 37-56 & bur prev med, 56-68, asst comnr med opers, 68-69; dir prev med br, State Civil Defense, Ind, 50-, chmn opers br, Med Health Serv, 55; consult, Surgeon Gen, USPHS, 57. *Mem:* Am Med Asn; Indust Med Asn; Am Conf Govt Indust Hygienists (vpres, 48, pres 49). *Res:* Toxicology of cadmium and lead; toxicology and generation of arsine; industrial toxicology; chemotherapy of tuberculosis; laboratory determination of sickle cell anemia. *Mailing Add:* 9110 Mud Creek Rd Indianapolis IN 46256

SPOMER, GEORGE GUY, PLANT PHYSIOLOGY, ECOLOGY. *Current Pos:* ASSOC PROF BOT, UNIV IDAHO, 72- *Personal Data:* b Denver, Colo, Mar 2, 37; m 60; c 4. *Educ:* Colo State Univ, BS, 59, MS, 61, PhD(bot sci), 62. *Prof Exp:* From instr to asst prof bot, Univ Chicago, 62-68; from asst prof to assoc prof, Wash State Univ, 68-72. *Concurrent Pos:* NSF res grant, 65-67, 75-76 & 79-82; Nat Geog Soc res grant, 75. *Mem:* AAAS; Ecol Soc Am; Am Soc Plant Physiol. *Res:* Plant eco-physiology, environmental analysis, alpine plant ecology, water relations, tree physiology; sagebrush eco-physiology. *Mailing Add:* Dept Biol Univ Idaho 375 S Line St Moscow ID 83843-4140

SPOMER, LOUIS ARTHUR, PLANT PHYSIOLOGY, SOIL SCIENCE. *Current Pos:* asst prof plant physiol & hort, 72-75, assoc prof, 75-77, PROF PLANT PHYSIOL, UNIV ILL, URBANA, 77- *Personal Data:* b Apr 17, 40; US citizen; m 62. *Educ:* Colo State Univ, BS, 63; Cornell Univ, MS, 67, PhD(plant sci), 69. *Prof Exp:* Meteorologist, Deseret Test Ctr, US Army, 69-71, phys scientist, US Dept Defense, 71-72. *Mem:* Am Soc Plant Physiol; Am Soc Agron; Am Soc Hort Sci; Soil Sci Soc Am. *Res:* Soil-plant-water relationships; water stress and crop growth; plant and crop water requirement. *Mailing Add:* 704 E Burkwood Dr Urbana IL 61801

SPONGBERG, STEPHEN ALAN, SYSTEMATIC BOTANY. *Current Pos:* Asst cur bot, 70-76, CURATORIAL TAXONOMIST, ARNOLD ARBORETUM, HARVARD UNIV, 76- *Personal Data:* b Rockford, Ill, Oct 15, 42; m 72. *Educ:* Rockford Col, BA, 66; Univ NC, Chapel Hill, PhD(bot), 71. *Concurrent Pos:* Ed bd, J Arnold Arboretum, 71-, ed, 79- *Mem:* Bot Soc

Am; Am Soc Plant Taxonomists; Int Asn Plant Taxon; Linnean Soc London; Int Dendrol Soc. *Res:* Taxonomic revisions of woody angiosperm genera of eastern Asiatic-eastern North American distribution, particularly genera of ornamental importance; taxonomy; nomenclature of woody plants cultivated in the North Temperate Zone. *Mailing Add:* Harvard Univ-Herbaria 125 The Arborway Jamaica Plain MA 02130

SPONSEL, WILLIAM ERIC, GLAUCOMA, OCULAR CIRCULATION. *Current Pos:* CHIEF GLAUCOMA SERV & DIR CLIN RES LAB, DEPT OPHTHAL, UNIV TEX HEALTH SCI CTR, SAN ANTONIO. *Personal Data:* b Minneapolis, Minn, Jan 25, 55; m, Valerie M (Frydman); c Alistair W & Heather M. *Educ:* Bristol Univ, BSc, 79, MBChB, 83, Doct Med Sci(glaucoma), 86. *Prof Exp:* Anat instr, Univ Bristol, 84-85; res fel, Nat Eye Res Ctr, Eng, 85-86; hon fel, Univ Wis-Madison, 86-88; asst prof ophthal, Ind Univ, 91-, dir, Glaucoma Res & Diag Lab, 91- *Concurrent Pos:* Mem, Nat Glaucoma Adv Comt, Nat Soc Prev Blindness, 89-; mem sci adv comt, Glaucoma Found, 92- *Mem:* Asn Res Vision & Ophthal; Am Acad Ophthal; AMA; Am Col Eye Surgeons. *Res:* Etiology, diagnosis and management of glaucoma; retinal vascular physiology; diabetic retinopathy; human immunodeficiency virus. *Mailing Add:* 19733 La Sierra Blvd San Antonio TX 78256

SPONSELLER, D(AVID) L(ESTER), METALLURGICAL ENGINEERING. *Current Pos:* RES ENGR, ERIM TRANSP & ENERGY MAT CTR, 87- *Personal Data:* b Canton, Ohio, Oct 2, 31; m 55; c 7. *Educ:* Univ Notre Dame, BS, 53; Univ Mich, MSE, 58, PhD(metall eng), 62. *Prof Exp:* Instr marine eng, US Naval Acad, 55-57; res asst, Res Inst, Univ Mich, 57-60, instr metall eng, 60-62; asst prof, Univ Notre Dame, 62-65; staff metallurgist, Molybdenum Co, Mich, 65-87, res group leader, 67-70, res supvr, 70-79,. *Concurrent Pos:* Vis res metallurgist, Edgar C Bain Lab, US Steel Corp, 63. *Mem:* Am Soc Metals; Am Inst Mining, Metall & Petrol Engrs; Nat Asn Corrosion Engrs; Am Soc Mech Engrs; Soc Automotive Engrs. *Res:* Physical metallurgy and alloy development of steels and alloys for oil production and for elevated temperature service; corrosion in oil field environments; failure analysis of metals; differential thermal analysis; manufacturing metallurgy; mechanical testing; oxidation and sulfidation of metals; steel desulfurization; casting of metals; embrittlement of metals; issued five US patents. *Mailing Add:* 2648 Antietam Dr Ann Arbor MI 48105

SPONSLER, GEORGE C, MATHEMATICAL MODELS, SCIENCE & TECHNOLOGY POLICY. *Current Pos:* PRES, LAW, MATH & TECHNOL INC, 70-; LEGAL ATTY, 81- *Personal Data:* b Dec 2, 27; m 55, Bridget R Butcher; c Freda, Naomi & Curtis. *Educ:* Princeton Univ, BSE, 49, MA, 51, PhD, 52; George Washington Univ, JD, 81. *Prof Exp:* Chief scientist & dir, Tech Anal & Oper Res, Bur Ships US Navy, 60-63; dir, Ctr for Exp Studies, IBM/FSD, 63-68; exec secy, Nat Acad Sci, Div Eng, 68-70. *Concurrent Pos:* Congressional fel, 87-88. *Mem:* Fel Am Phys Soc; fel AAAS; Sigma Xi; sr mem Inst Elec & Electronics Engrs. *Res:* triggered-fusion theory; Subjective probability; science and technology policy. *Mailing Add:* 7804 Old Chester Rd Bethesda MD 20817-6280. Fax: 301-320-3431

SPOONER, BRIAN SANDFORD, DEVELOPMENTAL BIOLOGY, CELL & GRAVITATIONAL BIOLOGY. *Current Pos:* asst prof biol, Kans State Univ, 71-75, assoc dir res, Div Biol, 75-77, assoc prof, 75-79, PROF BIOL, KANS STATE UNIV, 79-; DIR, NASA SPECIALIZED CTR RES & TRAINING GRAVITATIONAL BIOL , 90- *Personal Data:* b St Louis, Mo, Dec 27, 37; m 63; c 4. *Educ:* Quincy Col, BS, 63; Temple Univ, PhD(biol), 69. *Prof Exp:* Teaching asst biol, Temple Univ, 63-65; USPHS trainee, Univ Wash, 69; NIH fel, Stanford Univ, 69-71. *Concurrent Pos:* Nat Inst Gen Med Sci grants, 72-75 & 75-80, Nat Heart, Lung & Blood Inst, 80-82 & 82-87, Am Heart Asn, 80-82 & 88-94, NASA, 91-; vis prof, MRC Lab Molecular Biol, Cambridge, Eng, 77-78. *Mem:* Soc Develop Biol; Am Soc Cell Biol; Am Soc Gravitation & Space Biol. *Res:* Control of differentiation during embryonic development; mechanism of cell movement; regulation of cytodifferentiation and morphogenesis; interactions in organogenesis; stability of the differentiated state. *Mailing Add:* Div Biol Kans State Univ 232 Ackert Hall Manhattan KS 66506-4901

SPOONER, CHARLES EDWARD, JR, NEUROPHARMACOLOGY, NEUROPHYSIOLOGY. *Current Pos:* RETIRED. *Personal Data:* b Boston, Mass, July 25, 32; m 62; c 2. *Educ:* Univ Calif, Los Angeles, BA, 56, MS, 61, PhD(neuropharmacol), 64. *Prof Exp:* Res pharmacologist, Riker Labs, Calif, 51-59; asst res pharmacologist, Med Sch, Univ Calif, Los Angeles, 65-68; from asst prof to assoc prof neurosci, Univ Calif, San Diego, 68-74, asst dean spec curricula, 69-71, asst dean admis & student affairs, 71-74, prof neurosci, Sch Med, assoc dean admis, 74- *Concurrent Pos:* NIMH fel, 63-65; consult, Psychobiol Labs, Sepulveda Vet Hosp, Calif & Neurochem Sect, Space Biol Labs, Univ Calif, Los Angeles, 68-80; vis prof, Harvard Med Sch, 76; vis prof, Oxford Univ Sch Med, 87; nat chair, group student affairs, Asn Am Med Col, 89-90. *Mem:* AAAS; Am Soc Pharmacol & Exp Therapeut; Asn Am Med Col; Soc Exp Biol & Med; Am Educ Res Asn. *Res:* medical education. *Mailing Add:* 3520 Wild River Dr Roseburg OH 97470

SPOONER, ED THORNTON CASSWELL, GEOLOGY. *Current Pos:* asst prof geol, 77-90, PROF GEOL, UNIV TORONTO, 90- *Personal Data:* b Blandford, Dorset, Eng, June 16, 50; m 72. *Educ:* Univ Cambridge, BA, 71, MA, 71; Oxford Univ, MA, 75; Univ Manchester, PhD(geol), 76. *Prof Exp:* Demonstr mineral, Oxford Univ, 73-77. *Concurrent Pos:* Lectr geol, Oriel & Pembroke Cols, Oxford Univ, 74-77; Can rep to Comn on Ore Forming Fluids in Inclusions, 78-; Natural Sci & Eng Res Coun Can grants, 78- *Mem:* Can Inst Mining & Metall; Brit Geol Asn. *Res:* Mineral deposits in geology, especially hydrothermal; geochemical methods of exploration for economic mineral deposits. *Mailing Add:* Dept Geol Univ Toronto Toronto ON M5S 3B1 Can

SPOONER, GEORGE HANSFORD, CLINICAL CHEMISTRY. *Current Pos:* CLIN CHEMIST, VET ADMIN HOSP, CHARLESTON, 73- *Personal Data:* b Henderson, NC, Feb 24, 27; m 53; c 3. *Educ:* Univ Miami, BS, 50; Univ NC, PhD(biochem), 58. *Prof Exp:* Res asst sanit eng, Sch Pub Health, Univ NC, 54-56, res asst, Sch Dent, 56-57, res assoc biochem, Sch Med, 57-58, instr, 58-61, USPHS trainee microbiol, 61-62, asst prof biochem, 62-65; asst prof path, Sch Med, Duke Univ, 65-73; assoc prof path, Med Univ SC, 73- *Concurrent Pos:* Res scientist, State Sanitorium Syst NC, 58-61; biochemist, Clin Res Unit, NC Mem Hosp, 62-65; clin chemist, Vet Admin Hosp, Durham, 65-73. *Res:* Serum enzyme levels in the diagnosis of disease; continuous flow kinetics. *Mailing Add:* 6914 Toogoodoo Rd Hollywood SC 29449

SPOONER, JOHN D, ZOOLOGY, ENTOMOLOGY. *Current Pos:* chmn div natural sci, 70-76, actg acad dean, 76, from asst prof to assoc prof, 70-78, PROF BIOL, UNIV SC, AIKEN, 78- *Personal Data:* b Hillsborough Co, Fla, Dec 18, 35; m 58; c 5. *Educ:* Ga State Univ, BS, 60; Univ Fla, MS, 62, PhD(entom), 64. *Prof Exp:* Asst prof biol, Ga Southern Col, 64-66 & Augusta Col, 66-70. *Concurrent Pos:* NSF grant, 66-68. *Mem:* Pan Am Acridiological Soc; Sigma Xi; Am Soc Zoologist; Entom Soc Am; Entom Soc Am. *Res:* Acoustical pair forming systems of Orthoptera, particularly phaneropterine katydids; geographic variation in orthopteran acoustical behavior; life history studies of phaneropterine katydids. *Mailing Add:* Dept Biol Univ SC Aiken 171 University Pkwy Aiken SC 29801-6309

SPOONER, M(ORTON) G(AILEND), ELECTRICAL ENGINEERING. *Current Pos:* RETIRED. *Personal Data:* b Eau Claire, Wis, Jan 16, 24; m 50; c 4. *Educ:* Univ Wis, BS, 48, MS, 54, PhD(elec eng), 56. *Prof Exp:* Elec engr, Standard Oil Co, Ind, 48-52; from instr to asst prof, Univ Wis, 52-56; res electronics engr, Cornell Aeronaut Lab Inc, 56-76, sr vpres tech opers, 56-76; dir strategic planning, Garland Div, E Systs, 76-91. *Mem:* Inst Elec & Electronic Engrs. *Res:* Technical management in high speed special purpose digital processing systems and large scale software systems; strategic planning. *Mailing Add:* 20534 Greentree Ct Estero FL 33928

SPOONER, PETER MICHAEL, ENDOCRINOLOGY, LIPID BIOCHEMISTRY. *Current Pos:* Sr staff fel lipid res, Nat Inst Arthritis, Metab & Digestive Dis, Nat Heart, Lung & Blood Inst, NIH, 74-79, physiologist & biochemist, 79-80, health sci adminr, 80-85, chief prog rev, 85-90, chief, Cardiac Functions Br, 90-95, DIR, RES GROUP, NAT HEART, LUNG & BLOOD INST, NIH, 95- *Personal Data:* b Newport, RI, Nov 11, 42; m 90. *Educ:* Bates Col, BS, 64; Univ Ill, Urbana-Champaign, MS, 66, PhD(physiol & biophys), 70. *Concurrent Pos:* Vis investr, Imp Cancer Res Found Labs, London, 72-74; physiologist & biochemist, Nat Inst Arthritis, Metab & Digestive Dis, NIH, 78-85; adj asst prof, Uniformed Serv, Univ Health Sci, 78-85 Dis, NIH, 77-79; lectr, Found Advan Educ Sci, 80-84; mem, Exec Comt, Basic Sci Coun, Am Heart Asn, 88- *Mem:* Am Soc Biol Chemists; Sigma Xi; Am Heart Asn. *Res:* Endocrine control of uptake, metabolism and deposition of lipids into cells in vivo and vitro using model cell culture systems, ion channels and transport systems. *Mailing Add:* 6701 Rockledge Dr Nat Heart Lung & Blood Inst NIH Bethesda MD 20892-7940

SPOONER, ROBERT BRUCE, CLINICAL ENGINEERING. *Current Pos:* RETIRED. *Personal Data:* b Cleveland, Ohio, Aug 7, 20; wid, Gloria M Hoffman; c Robert L, Holly R (Shafer), Wendy A (Stoner) & Laura C (Anderson). *Educ:* Hiram Col, BA, 41; Northwestern Univ, PhD(physics), 49. *Prof Exp:* Asst, Northwestern Univ, 46-48; head, Thermodyn Analysis Sect, Lewis Flight Propulsion Lab, Nat Adv Comt Aeronaut, 49-53; mgr, Adv Nuclear Design Dept, Martin Co, 53-55; mgr assoc res, Koppers Co, Inc, 55-62; coordr sci & res adv group, Regional Indust Develop Corp, 63-65; pres, Impac, 65-74; dir, Med Instrumentation Ctr, MPC Corp, 74-75; sr proj engr, Emergency Care Res Inst, 75-97. *Concurrent Pos:* Lectr, Case Western Res Univ, 50-52; chmn, Annual Res Conf Instrumentation Sci, 69-; vis lectr, Biomed Instrumentation, Bosphorus Univ, Istanbul, Turkey, 83; mem, Int Cert Exam Bd for clin eng and biomed technol; comt on stand for anesthesia and breathing equipment. *Mem:* Am Phys Soc; sr mem Instrument Soc Am; sr mem Inst Elec & Electronics Engrs; Asn Advan Med Instrumentation; Am Soc Testing & Mat. *Res:* Radioisotope and radiation applications; instrumentation and control; medical instrumentation; anesthesia and breathing systems; evaluations, investigations of accidents and incidents; study and correction of hazards, review and writing standards for equipment. *Mailing Add:* 534 Vista Rd Ambler PA 19002-2638

SPOONER, STEPHEN, MATERIALS SCIENCE, METALLURGY. *Current Pos:* RES SCIENTIST, OAK RIDGE NAT LAB, 82- *Personal Data:* b Worcester, Mass, Apr 2, 37; m 59; c 2. *Educ:* Mass Inst Technol, BS, 59, ScD(metall), 65. *Prof Exp:* Res asst, Mass Inst Technol, 59-65; from asst prof to assoc prof, 65-75, prof metall, 75-81, res scientist, eng exp sta, Ga Inst Technol, 65- *Concurrent Pos:* Consult, Oak Ridge Nat Lab, 73-77; res scientist, Ga Inst Technol, 82. *Mem:* Am Phys Soc; Am Inst Mining, Metall & Petrol Engrs; Am Crystallog Asn. *Res:* Materials science; phase transformations; magnetic materials. *Mailing Add:* 104 Hardwick Dr Oak Ridge TN 37830. Fax: 423-574-6268

SPOONHOWER, JOHN PHILIP, SPECTROSCOPY, SPECTROMETRY. *Current Pos:* RES ASSOC, EASTMAN KODAK, 79- *Educ:* Univ Notre Dame, BS, 72; Cornell Univ, MS, 75, PhD(appl physics), 77. *Prof Exp:* Res scientist, Sybron Corp, 77-79. *Res:* Luminescence spectroscopy of organic and inorganic materials. *Mailing Add:* Eastman Kodak Res Rochester NY 14650-2021

SPOOR, RYK PETER, BIOLOGY, PHARMACOLOGY. *Current Pos:* from asst prof to assoc prof pharmacol, Albany Med Col, 69-82, assoc prof, 82-90, PROF BIOL, ALBANY COL PHARM, 91- *Personal Data:* b Albany, NY, June 30, 35; m 57; c 2. *Educ:* State Univ NY Albany, BS, 57; Union Univ, NY, PhD(pharmacol), 62. *Prof Exp:* Instr physiol & pharmacol, Sch Med, Creighton Univ, 62-64; asst prof, Univ SDak, 64-67; fel pharmacol, Emory Univ, 67-69. *Mem:* AAAS; Sigma Xi. *Res:* Predation of korner blue butterfly eggs. *Mailing Add:* 1052 Brierwood Blvd Schenectady NY 12308

SPOOR, WILLIAM ARTHUR, ZOOLOGY, PHYSIOLOGY. *Current Pos:* RETIRED. *Personal Data:* b New York, NY, Dec 14, 08; m 34; c 2. *Educ:* Univ Wash, BS, 31; Univ Wis, PhD(zool), 36. *Prof Exp:* From instr to prof zool, Dept Biol Sci, Univ Cincinnati, 36-68, head dept biol sci, 58-64; res aquatic biologist, Environ Res Lab, 68-82. *Concurrent Pos:* Mem aquatic life adv comt, Ohio River Valley Water Sanit Comn, 52-68; consult physiol of aquatic animals, Nat Water Qual Lab, Dept Interior, Minn, 66-68; mem nat tech comt on water qual requirements for aquatic life, Fed Water Pollution Control Admin, 67-68; mem summer staff, F T Stone Lab, Ohio State Univ, 48-62. *Mem:* Sigma Xi. *Res:* Environmental requirements and oxygen requirements of fish; activity detectors for aquatic animals; physiology of aquatic animals. *Mailing Add:* 1053 Jackson Rd Covington KY 41011

SPOREA, TEOFIL, AUTOMATION ENGINEERING, SYSTEM ENGINEERING. *Current Pos:* SUPVR ENG SYSTS, FRIGIDAIRE CO, 89- *Personal Data:* b Resita, Romania, Apr 8, 55; US citizen; m 81, Ana Schintfte; c Teofil-Andrei. *Educ:* Electro-Mechanical, Romania, BA; Polytech Univ Brooklyn, MS; Kennedy Western Univ, PhD(comput sci). *Prof Exp:* Mfg engr, Leviton Co, 84-89. *Res:* Control and program electronic devices; combined analog and digital control circuitry. *Mailing Add:* 54 Gladiola Dr Howell NJ 07731. *Fax:* 908-287-2493

SPOREK, KAREL FRANTISEK, ANALYTICAL CHEMISTRY, ORGANIC CHEMISTRY. *Current Pos:* PRES, CONTRACT LABS ASSOC, INC, 82- *Personal Data:* b Bohumin, Czech, Oct 12, 19; US citizen; m 51, Jessie McCormick; c Caroline. *Educ:* St Andrews Univ, MA, 47. *Prof Exp:* Res chemist, Nobel Div, Imp Chem Indust Ltd, Scotland, 47-54, group leader anal res, Plant Protection Div, Eng, 54-57; res chemist, Eldorado Mining & Refining, Can, 57-58; head, Anal Dept, Bioferm Corp, Calif, 58-60; res chemist, Tech Ctr, Owens-Ill Inc, 60-61, chief org anal chem, 61-73, radiation officer, 73-82. *Mem:* Am Chem Soc; Am Nuclear Soc; Am Soc Testing & Mat; Sigma Xi; Am Soc Safety Engrs; Royal Soc Chem. *Res:* High explosives; detonators; fuses; cellulose derivatives; insecticides; fungicides; fertilizers; polymers; polyethylene; silicones; pharmaceuticals; vitamin B-12; uranium; radiation chemistry. *Mailing Add:* 7142 Erie St Sylvania OH 43560-1134

SPORER, ALFRED HERBERT, INK CHEMISTRY, PHOTO CHEMISTRY. *Current Pos:* staff chemist, IBM Corp, San Jose, 57-73, mgr appl sci, Res Div, 73-79, mem, Corp Tech Comt, 79-81, res staff mem, IBM Res, San Jose, 81-85, MGR, INK TECHNOL, IBM RES, IBM CORP, SAN JOSE, 85- *Personal Data:* b New York, NY, May 28, 29; m 55; c 2. *Educ:* City Col, BA, 51; Univ Calif, Los Angeles, MS, 53, PhD(phys org chem), 56. *Prof Exp:* Res chemist, Esso Res & Eng Corp, 56; fel photochem, Univ Southern Calif, 56-57. *Mem:* Am Chem Soc; Soc Imaging Sci & Technol; Sigma Xi; AAAS. *Res:* Electrophotography; organic photoconductors; physical organic chemistry; photochemistry of complex ions, chelates and organic compounds in condensed phases; mechanisms of organic reactions; chromatography; technical management of programs in electrophotography; photoconductors; non-impact printing; magnetic recording media; ink jet inks. *Mailing Add:* 1812 Kirkmont Dr San Jose CA 95124-1238

SPORN, MICHAEL BENJAMIN, CANCER, BIOCHEMISTRY. *Current Pos:* PROF PHARMACOL, DARTMOUTH MED SCH, 95- *Personal Data:* b New York, NY, Feb 15, 33; m 56, Catherine Daly; c 2. *Educ:* Univ Rochester, MD, 59. *Prof Exp:* Intern med, Sch Med, Univ Rochester, 59-60; staff mem, Lab Neurochem, Nat Inst Neurol Dis & Blindness, 60-64; staff mem, Nat Cancer Inst, 64-70, head, Lung Cancer Unit, 70-73, chief, Lung Cancer Br, 73-78, chief, Lab Chemoprev, 78-95. *Mem:* Am Asn Cancer Res; Am Soc Biol Chem. *Res:* Nucleic acids and cancer, vitamin A and related compounds; carcinogenesis studies; retinoids and cancer prevention; peptide growth factors, transforming growth factor-beta; cell biology. *Mailing Add:* Dept Pharmacol Dartmouth Med Sch Hanover NH 03755. *Fax:* 603-650-1129; *E-Mail:* michael.sporn@dartmouth.edu

SPORNICK, LYNNA, PHYSICS. *Current Pos:* RETIRED. *Personal Data:* b Oct 6, 47. *Educ:* Carnegie-Mellon Univ, BS, 69; Rutgers Univ, PhD(physics), 75; Johns Hopkins Univ, MS(comput sci), 81. *Prof Exp:* Fel, Dept Physics, Colo State Univ, 75-77; sr staff physicist, Appl Physics Lab, Johns Hopkins Univ, 77-92. *Concurrent Pos:* Lectr, Appl Physics Dept, Whiting Sch Eng, Johns Hopkins Univ, 85- *Mem:* Am Phys Soc; Am Asn Physics Teachers; Soc Comput Simulations. *Res:* Computer modeling of physical systems. *Mailing Add:* 9510 Dragonclaw Rd Columbia MD 21046

SPOSITO, GARRISON, GEOCHEMISTRY, SOIL CHEMISTRY. *Current Pos:* prof soil phys chem, 88-92, PROF ABOVE-SCALE, UNIV CALIF, BERKELEY, 92- *Personal Data:* b Los Angeles, Calif, July 29, 39; m 76, Mary E Campbell; c Douglas, Geraldine, Frank, Jennifer, Sara & Cristina. *Educ:* Univ Ariz, BS, 61, MS, 63; Univ Calif, PhD(soil sci), 65. *Honors & Awards:* Soil Sci Award, 82; Horton Award, 90. *Prof Exp:* From asst prof to prof physics, Sonoma State Univ, 65-74; from asst prof to assoc prof soil sci, Univ Calif, Riverside, 74-88, chmn, Div Environ Sci, 75-78. *Concurrent Pos:* Fulbright fel, 73; vis fel, Nat Inst Agron Res, France, 81 & St Cross Col, Oxford Univ, Eng, 84; Guggenheim fel, 84. *Mem:* Am Chem Soc; Am Geophys Union; fel Soil Sci Soc Am; Am Phys Soc; Geochem Soc; fel Am Soc Agron. *Res:* Environmental geochemistry, statistical mechanics, thermodynamics of soils and clays; surface chemistry of soils, transport in porous media. *Mailing Add:* Hilgard Hall No 3110 Univ Calif Berkeley CA 94720-3110. *E-Mail:* gsposito@nature.berkeley.edu

SPOSITO, VINCENT ANTHONY, operations research, statistics; deceased, see previous edition for last biography

SPOTNITZ, HENRY MICHAEL, MEDICAL SCIENCES, PHYSIOLOGY. *Current Pos:* ASSOC ATTEND SURGEON, PRESBY HOSP, NY, 80- *Personal Data:* b New York, NY, July 7, 40; m 77; c 2. *Educ:* Harvard Univ, BA, 62; Columbia Univ, MD, 66. *Prof Exp:* Intern surg, Bellevue Hosp, NY, 66-67; staff assoc cardiol, Nat Heart Inst, 67-69; resident surg, Presby Hosp, NY, 69-75; asst prof med sci, 75-80, asst attend surgeon, Presby Hosp, NY, 75-80, assoc prof surgery, Columbia Univ, 80-, lab dir cardiovasc surg, 76- *Concurrent Pos:* Estab investr, Am Heart Asn, 76-81; prin investr, Nat Heart Lung & Blood Inst, NIH res grant, 78-81; asst attend surgeon, Presby Hosp, NY, 75-80. *Mem:* AAAS; Am Heart Asn; fel Am Col Cardiol; fel Am Col Surgeons; Soc Univ Surgeons; Am Asn Thoracic Surg; Soc Thoracic Surg; Am Surg Asn. *Res:* Human left ventricular compliance and systolic mechanics; mechanical and pharmacologic circulatory support; open heart surgery; intraoperative echocardiography. *Mailing Add:* 161 Ft Washington Ave New York NY 10032-3713

SPOTTS, CHARLES RUSSELL, MICROBIOLOGY. *Current Pos:* from assoc prof to prof biol, 69-95, EMER PROF BIOL, CALIF STATE UNIV, NORTHRIDGE, 95- *Personal Data:* b Phoenix, Ariz, Oct 14, 33; m 54; c 4. *Educ:* Univ Calif, Berkeley, BA, 55, PhD(microbiol), 61. *Prof Exp:* NIH fel, 61-63; instr microbiol, Univ Wash, 63, asst prof, Sch Med, 63-69. *Mem:* Am Soc Microbiol. *Res:* Bacterial metabolism; physiology of bacterial sporulation. *Mailing Add:* Dept Biol Calif Sate Univ 18111 Nordhoff St Northridge CA 91330-0001

SPOTTS, JOHN HUGH, GEOLOGY. *Current Pos:* RETIRED. *Personal Data:* b Lauratown, Ark, Nov 2, 27; m 54; c 3. *Educ:* Univ Mo, BA, 50, MA, 51; Univ Western Australia, MSc, 56; Stanford Univ, PhD, 59. *Prof Exp:* Res geologist, Shell Develop Co, 52-53; geologist & geophysicist, Stand Oil Co, Calif, 53-56, gp geologist, 58-59, res geologist, La Habra Lab, Chevron Res Co, 59-68, mgr geol res, 68-70, div geologist, Stand Oil Co, Calif, 70-77, chief geologist, Chevron Resources Co, San Francisco, 77-81, vpres exploration res, Chevron Oil Field Res Co, La habra, Calif, 81-89. *Mem:* Mineral Soc Am; Am Asn Petrol Geologists; Soc Econ Paleontologists & Mineralogists; Int Asn Sedimentologists. *Res:* Mineralogy; sedimentary petrology; heavy minerals; geochemistry; carbonate petrography; petrofabrics. *Mailing Add:* 692 E 900 S Pleasant Grove UT 84062-3623

SPOTTS, M(ERHYLE) F(RANKLIN), MACHINE DESIGN. *Current Pos:* from asst prof to prof, 43-77, EMER PROF MECH ENG, TECHNOL INST, NORTHWESTERN UNIV, EVANSTON, 77- *Personal Data:* b Battle Creek, Iowa, Dec 5, 95; m 47; c 2. *Educ:* Ohio Northern Univ, BS, 23; Ohio State Univ, MA, 33; Univ Mich, PhD(appl mech), 38. *Hon Degrees:* DEng, Ohio Northern Univ, 80. *Honors & Awards:* Worcester Reed Warner Medal, Am Soc Mech Engrs, 68; Century II Medallion, Am Soc Mech Engrs, 81; Machine Design Award, Am Soc Mech Engrs, 81. *Prof Exp:* Engr, Brown Steel Co, Ohio, 27-32; designer, Jeffrey Mfg Co, 33-35; assoc mech eng, Johns Hopkins Univ, 38-41. *Mem:* Fel Am Soc Mech Engrs. *Res:* Applied mechanics; mechanical vibrations; stress analysis. *Mailing Add:* 2033 Sherman Ave No 305 Evanston IL 60201

SPOTTS, ROBERT ALLEN, PLANT PATHOLOGY. *Current Pos:* PROF PLANT PATH, ORE STATE UNIV, 78- *Personal Data:* b Philadelphia, Pa, June 10, 45; m 69; c 2. *Educ:* Colo State Univ, BS, 67, MS, 69; Pa State Univ, PhD(plant path), 74. *Prof Exp:* Chemist, Colo Dept Health, 69-71; asst prof plant path, Ohio Agr Res & Develop Ctr, 74-78. *Mem:* Am Phytopath Soc. *Res:* Epidemiology, physiology and control of diseases of fruit crops. *Mailing Add:* Dept Botany Ore State Univ 2082 Cordley Hall Corvallis OR 97331-2902

SPRADLEY, JOSEPH LEONARD, ENGINEERING PHYSICS, HISTORY OF SCIENCE. *Current Pos:* assoc prof, Wheaton Col, 59-72, chmn dept, 68-70, chmn sci div, 90-91 & 92-95, PROF PHYSICS, WHEATON COL, ILL, 72- *Personal Data:* b Baker, Ore, Oct 30, 32; m 55, Marilyn Carnett; c Joanna (Moffett), Daniel, Benjamin & Susanna (Smoak). *Educ:* Univ Calif, Los Angeles, BS, 54, MS, 55, PhD(eng physics), 58. *Prof Exp:* Mem tech staff, Hughes Aircraft Co, 54-58. *Concurrent Pos:* Consult, Sunbeam Corp, 60-61; prof, Haigazian Col, Lebanon, 65-68; US Agency Int Develop sci specialist, Ahmadu Bello Univ, Nigeria, 70-72; vis prof, Daystar Univ Col, Kenya, 88 & Am Univ, Cairo, Egypt, 91-92. *Mem:* Am Asn Physics Teachers; Am Sci Affil. *Res:* Microwave antenna arrays; laser communications; history of science; prewar Japanese particle physics; women in science. *Mailing Add:* Dept Physics Wheaton Col Wheaton IL 60187

SPRADLIN, JOSEPH E, BEHAVIOR ANALYSIS. *Current Pos:* res assoc, Bur Child Res, Univ Kans, 58-59, dir, Parsons Res Ctr, 59-69 & Kans Univ Affil Prog, 78-88, PROF HUMAN DEVELOP, UNIV KANS, 69-, DIR, PARSONS RES CTR, 87- *Personal Data:* b Bloom, Kans, July 12, 29; m 48; c 3. *Educ:* Univ Kans, BA, 51; Ft Hays State Col, MS, 54; George Peabody

Col, PhD(psychol), 59. *Prof Exp:* Teaching asst psychol, Ft Hays Col, 53-54; clin psychologist, Winfield State Sch, 54-56; res fel psychol, George Peabody Col, 56-58. *Concurrent Pos:* Consult ed, Am J Ment Retardation, 73-75 & J Speech & Hearing Dis, 75-78; mem, Ment Retardation Comt, Nat Inst Child Health & Human Develop, 74-78. *Mem:* Fel Am Psychol Asn; fel Am Psychol Soc. *Res:* Behavior analysis, with a special emphasis on stimulus control with persons with retardation. *Mailing Add:* Dept Family Life & Develop Univ Kans Lawrence KS 66045-0501

SPRADLIN, WILFORD W, PSYCHIATRY. *Current Pos:* PROF, PSYCHIAT & CHMN DEPT, MED CTR, UNIV VA, 78-; PROF, DEPT BEHAV MED & PSYCHIAT, MED CTR, WVA UNIV, 67- *Personal Data:* b Bedford Co, Va, Oct 4, 32; m 58; c 2. *Educ:* Univ Va, BA, 53, MD, 57. *Prof Exp:* Intern, Royal Victoria Hosp, McGill Univ, 58; resident psychiat, Eastern State Hosp, 58-59 & Med Ctr, Duke Univ, 60-62; staff psychiatrist, Vet Admin Hosp, Durham, 62; assoc psychiat, Med Ctr, Duke Univ, 62-63; asst chief, Vet Admin Hosp, Durham, 63-64; asst prof, Med Ctr, Duke Univ, 64-67, chief psychiat day unit, 65-67, asst head psychiat inpatient serv, 65-67; prof psychiat & chmn dept behav med & psychiat, Med Ctr, WVa Univ, 67-78. *Mem:* AAAS; fel Am Psychiat Asn; AMA; Sigma Xi. *Mailing Add:* Box 170 Ivy VA 22945-0170

SPRAFKA, ROBERT J, SYSTEMS INTEGRATION OF MAN-MACHINE SYSTEMS, COMPUTER ASSISTED MEASUREMENT. *Current Pos:* STAFF MEM, EAST OHIO GAS CO, 88- *Personal Data:* b Chicago, Ill, Nov 24, 38; m 90, Bonney George. *Educ:* Purdue Univ, BS, 59, PhD(physics), 65. *Prof Exp:* Res assoc high energy physics, Purdue Univ, 64-66; physicist, Lawrence Radiation Lab, Calif, 66-67; from asst prof to assoc prof physics, Mich State Univ, 67-74, assoc prof, & Off Health Serv Educ & Res, 74-76, assoc prof community health sci, 76-82; sr assoc, E F Technol Inc, 81-84; dir, Systs Design & Implementation, LAM Consult Inc, 84-88. *Mem:* Am Phys Soc; Sigma Xi; Am Soc Heating, Refrigerating & Airconditioning Engrs. *Res:* Use of microcomputers for process control and measurement in research and development environments; computer applications in music. *Mailing Add:* 5554 Ericson Lane Willoughby OH 44094-4123. Fax: 216-736-5355; E-Mail: rjsprafka@icgroup.net, rjsprafka@bigfoot.com

SPRAGG, JOCELYN, IMMUNOPHARMACOLOGY. *Current Pos:* ASSOC PROF MED & IMMUNOL, HARVARD MED SCH, 84-, FAC COORDR, PROGS MINORITY STUDENTS. *Personal Data:* b New York, NY, Sept 16, 40. *Educ:* Smith Col, AB, 62; Radcliffe Col, MA, 65; Harvard Univ, PhD(bact & immunol), 69. *Prof Exp:* Immunologist, Dept Rheumatology & Immunol, Brigham & Women's Hosp, 82- *Concurrent Pos:* Mem, Coun Kidney & Cardiovasc Dis & Coun Thrombosis, Am Heart Asn; course developer & prin lectr, Radcliffe Summer Prog Sci, Radcliffe Col, 89- *Mem:* Am Asn Immunol; NY Acad Sci; AAAS; Am Heart Asn. *Res:* Human kallikrein-kinin systems. *Mailing Add:* MEC 435 260 Longwood Ave Boston MA 02115

SPRAGGINS, ROBERT LEE, MASS SPECTROMETRY, ORGANIC CHEMISTRY. *Current Pos:* PRIN SCIENTIST, SCI CONSULTS COLO, DENVER, 91- *Personal Data:* b Sedalia, Mo, Feb 18, 39; m 63, 87, Gabriela A Solis; c Robin L, William R & Lesie B. *Educ:* La Tech Univ, BS, 63, MS, 66; Univ Okla, PhD(org chem), 70. *Honors & Awards:* Sigma Xi Res Award, 70. *Prof Exp:* Chemist, Cities Serv Oil Co, 63-64; res fel, Alza Corp, Calif, 70-71; sea grant, Stevens Inst Technol, 71-72, res scientist, 72-74; res scientist, Ctr Trace Characterization, Tex A&M Univ, 75-77; sr scientist, Radian Corp, 77-78, sr scientist & group leader mass spectros, , 79-81; sr scientist & mgr analytical chem, Sumx Corp, 81-82; prin chemist, Great Plains Gasification Assocs, 82-85; sr res chemist, Manville Tech Ctr, Denver, 85-91. *Mem:* Am Chem Soc; Sigma Xi; Am Soc Mass Spectrometry. *Res:* Mass spectroscopy; biomedical and natural products; analytical chemistry; environmental chemistry; organic chemistry. *Mailing Add:* 2612 W Berridge Lane C-124 Phoenix AZ 85017. Fax: 602-438-9709

SPRAGINS, MELCHIJAH, pediatrics, for more information see previous edition

SPRAGUE, ANN LOUISE, ATMOSPHERIC SCIENCE, PLANETARY SCIENCE. *Current Pos:* PLANETARY SCIENTIST, UNIV ARIZ, 92- *Personal Data:* b Bellfonte, PA, Feb 25, 46; c Barbara L. *Educ:* Syracuse Univ, BA, 69, Boston Univ, MA, 82; Univ Ariz, PhD(planetary sci), 90. *Honors & Awards:* Gerard Kuiper Mem Award, Univ Ariz. *Prof Exp:* Pub sch teacher, Selinsgrove Mid Sch, 74-80; Nat Res Coun fel, NASA Ames Res Ctr, 90-92. *Mem:* Int Astron Union; Am Astron Soc; Am Geophys Union. *Res:* Study the atmospheres of Mercury, the Moon, Mars and Jupiter; mid-infrared spectroscopy of the surfaces of the Moon, Mercury and asteroids to determine their composition. *Mailing Add:* 3445 W Foxes Den Dr Tucson AZ 85745. E-Mail: sprague@pirl.lpl.arizona.edu

SPRAGUE, BASIL SHELDON, MATERIALS SCIENCE, POLYMER PHYSICS. *Current Pos:* RETIRED. *Personal Data:* b Hartford, Conn, Aug 3, 20; m 44; c 2. *Educ:* Swarthmore Col, AB, 42; Polytech Inst Brooklyn, MChE, 44. *Hon Degrees:* ScD, Lowell Univ, 69. *Honors & Awards:* H DeWitt Smith Medal, 76. *Prof Exp:* Res engr plastics, Celanese Corp, 44-48, res engr textiles, 48-50, group leader textiles phys res, 50-52, head textile eval res, 52-56, head fiber physics & eval res, 56-64, mgr physics res dept, 64-65, mgr mat sci res dept, 65-68, dir mat sci res, 68-76, sr res fel, 76-82. *Mem:* AAAS; Am Chem Soc; Fiber Soc (vpres, 65, pres, 66). *Res:* Relationship of chemical constitution and morphology to physical properties of polymers and fibers; dyeing of synthetic fibers; materials research. *Mailing Add:* 356 Timber Dr Berkeley Heights NJ 07922-1764

SPRAGUE, CHARLES CAMERON, INTERNAL MEDICINE, HEMATOLOGY. *Current Pos:* pres, 86-88, chmn bd & pres, 88-95, EMER CHMN, SOUTHWESTERN MED FOUND, 95-; EMER PROF MED, HEALTH SCI CTR, UNIV TEX, 86- *Personal Data:* b Dallas, Tex, Nov 16, 16; m 41; c 1. *Educ:* Southern Methodist Univ, BBA & BS, 40; Univ Tex, MD, 43; Am Bd Internal Med, dipl. *Hon Degrees:* DSc, Southern Methodist Univ, 66, Univ Dallas, 83, Tulane Univ, 91, State Univ Ny, Syracuse, 92, Austin Col, 94, Baylor Col Dent, 94. *Prof Exp:* Intern, US Naval Hosp, Md, 43-44; from asst to prof med, Sch Med, Tulane Univ, 47-67, prof hemat, 54-63, dean div, 63-67; prof med & dean, Health Sci Ctr, Univ Tex, Dallas, 67-72, pres, 72-86. *Concurrent Pos:* Asst resident, Charity Hosp of La, 47-48, sr vis physician, 52-67; fel, Sch Med, Tulane Univ, 48-49; Commonwealth res fel hemat, Sch Med, Wash Univ, 50-52, Sch Med, Oxford Univ, 52; chmn, Gov Task Force Health Manpower, 81, Gov Med Educ Mgt Effectiveness Comt & Allied Health Educ Adv Comt, Coord Bd, Tex Col & Univ Syst; mem, coord bd, Tex Col & Univ, 88-, vchmn, 89- *Mem:* Inst Med-Nat Acad Sci; Am Soc Hemat (pres, 67); Am Fedn Clin Res; Int Soc Hemat; fel Am Col Physicians; AMA; Asn Am Med Col; Cent Soc Clin Res; Southern Soc Clin Res. *Res:* Hemoglobinopathies; leukemia; cancer chemotherapy. *Mailing Add:* PO Box 45708 Dallas TX 75245-0708

SPRAGUE, ESTEL DEAN, PHYSICAL CHEMISTRY. *Current Pos:* from asst prof to assoc prof, 74-93, ASST DEPT HEAD, UNIV CINCINNATI, 88-, PROF PHYS CHEM, 93- *Personal Data:* b Leavenworth, Kans, Oct 17, 44; m 67, Elsie Grantham; c Gail & Susan. *Educ:* Asbury Col, BA, 66; Univ Tenn, Knoxville, PhD(phys chem), 71. *Prof Exp:* Res kinetics & radiation chem, Max Planck Inst Coal Res, 71-73 & Dept Chem, Univ Wis-Madison, 73-74. *Mem:* Am Chem Soc. *Res:* Micelle chemistry; polymer models for micelles; computers in chemical education. *Mailing Add:* Dept Chem Univ Cincinnati Cincinnati OH 45221-0172. Fax: 513-556-9239; E-Mail: estel.sprague@uc.edu

SPRAGUE, G(EORGE) SIDNEY, POLYMER CHEMISTRY. *Current Pos:* sr chemist, 73-90, CONSULT, LOCTITE CORP, 91- *Personal Data:* b Lexington, Ky, Sept 9, 18; m 42, 74; c 3. *Educ:* Lehigh Univ, BS, 40; Univ Wis, MS, 43; NY Univ, PhD(chem), 50. *Prof Exp:* Res chemist, Sharples Chem Inc, 43-45 & Deering Milliken Res Trust, 47-49; from res chemist to sr res chemist, Am Cyanamid Co, 49-72. *Mem:* Am Chem Soc; Sigma Xi. *Res:* Adhesives and sealants; thermoplastics; solid rocket propellant and explosive binders; water soluble polymers; monomer synthesis. *Mailing Add:* 241 Avery Heights Hartford CT 06106-4200

SPRAGUE, GEORGE FREDERICK, AGRONOMY. *Current Pos:* prof, 73-87, EMER PROF AGR, UNIV ILL, URBANA, 87- *Personal Data:* b Crete, Nebr, Sept 3, 02; m; c 4. *Educ:* Univ Nebr, BSc, 24, MS, 26; Cornell Univ, PhD(genetics), 30. *Prof Exp:* Jr agronomist, Bur Plant Indust, USDA, Washington, DC, 24-28, from asst agronomist to agronomist, 28-42, from sr agronomist to prin agronomist, 42-58, head, Corn & Sorghum Sect, Crops Res Div, Agr Res Serv, 58-72. *Concurrent Pos:* Prof, Iowa State Univ, 48-58. *Mem:* Nat Acad Sci; fel Am Soc Agron (vpres, 59-60); Am Genetics Asn; Genetics Soc Am; Biomet Soc. *Res:* Corn breeding and genetics; statistics. *Mailing Add:* Washington Abbey 494 W 10th St Eugene OR 97401

SPRAGUE, ISABELLE BAIRD, ENTOMOLOGY, AQUATIC ECOLOGY. *Current Pos:* From instr to prof zool, Mt Holyoke Col, 45-64, chmn dept, 63-66, prof biol sci, 76-80, DAVID B TRUMAN PROF ZOOL & EMER PROF BIOL SCI, MT HOLYOKE COL, 80- *Personal Data:* b Manila, PI, May 30, 16; c James B. *Educ:* Mt Holyoke Col, AB, 37, MA, 39; Univ Kans, PhD(entom), 53. *Concurrent Pos:* NSF fac fel 58-59. *Mem:* Ecol Soc Am; Entom Soc Am. *Res:* Aquatic biology; endocrinology of insects; semi-aquatic hemiptera. *Mailing Add:* Dept Biol Sci Mt Holyoke Col South Hadley MA 01075

SPRAGUE, JAMES ALAN, SURFACE MODIFICATION, THIN FILMS. *Current Pos:* ADJ PROF, GEORGE WASHINGTON UNIV, 83- *Personal Data:* b Cleveland, Ohio, Aug 24, 43; m 68. *Educ:* Rice Univ, BA, 65, BS, 66, PhD(mat sci), 70. *Prof Exp:* res metallurgist, Naval Res Lab, 70- *Concurrent Pos:* NSF fel, Max Planck Inst Metall Res, 69-70. *Mem:* Am Inst Mining, Metall & Petrol Engrs; Am Ceramics Soc; Electron Micros Soc Am; Sigma Xi. *Res:* Electron microscopy of defects in solids; ion beam surface modification of materials; thin film processing, microstructure and properties. *Mailing Add:* Naval Res Lab Code 6671 Washington DC 20375

SPRAGUE, JAMES CLYDE, INDUSTRIAL ENGINEERING. *Current Pos:* from assoc prof to prof, 69-92, EMER PROF MECH ENG, UNIV ALTA, 92- *Personal Data:* b Gibbons, Alta, Aug 4, 28; m 52; c 1. *Educ:* Univ Okla, BSc, 60; Iowa State Univ, MSc, 67, PhD(indust eng), 69. *Prof Exp:* Chief economist, Hu Harries & Assocs, 60-61; chief engr, BJ Serv of Can, 61-65; dir eng eval, Gamma Eng, 65-66; asst prof indust eng, Iowa State Univ, 68-69. *Mem:* Am Soc Eng Educ; Am Inst Indust Engrs. *Res:* Engineering economy and capital budgeting, design of industrial systems; mass production of homes. *Mailing Add:* Dept Mech Eng 15944 Patricia Dr NW Edmonton AB T5R 5N4 Can

SPRAGUE, JAMES MATHER, NEUROANATOMY & NEUROSCIENCE, SENSORY PSYCHOPHYSICS. *Current Pos:* from asst prof to prof anat, Sch Med, Univ Pa, 50-73, mem, Inst Neurol Sci, 54-73, assoc dir, 57-60, chmn dept, 67-76, dir, 73-80, Joseph Leidy prof, 73-84, EMER CHAIR & EMER PROF ANAT, SCH MED, UNIV PA, 84- *Personal Data:* b Kansas City, Mo, Aug 31, 16; m 59, Dolores Eberhart; c James. *Educ:* Univ Kans, AB, 38, AM, 40; Harvard Univ, PhD(biol), 42. *Hon*

1158 / SPRAGUE

Degrees: MA, Univ Pa, 71. *Honors & Awards:* Lindbach Found Award, 66. *Prof Exp:* From asst mus mammals to asst instr zool, Univ Kans, 36-40; from asst to asst prof anat, Sch Med, Johns Hopkins Univ, 42-50. *Concurrent Pos:* John Simon Guggenheim fel, Cambridge Univ & Oxford Univ, 48-49; Josiah Macy found Scholar award, 74-75; vis investr, Med Sch, Northwestern Univ, 48, Rockefeller Inst, 55, Cambridge Univ, 56, Univ Pisa, Italy, 66, 68, 70 & 74, Univ Leuven, Belg, 83-93; consult, NIH, 57-58. *Mem:* Nat Acad Sci; Int Brain Res Orgn; Soc Neurosci; Am Asn Anat (vpres, 76-78). *Res:* neural mechanisms of vision and visual behavior; anatomy of visual cortex and subcortizal structures; psycho-physics of visual perception and discrimination. *Mailing Add:* Dept Cell & Develop Biol Sch Med Univ Pa Philadelphia PA 19104-6058. *Fax:* 215-898-9871

SPRAGUE, JOHN BOOTY, biology, for more information see previous edition

SPRAGUE, LUCIAN MATTHEW, FISHERIES POLICY STUDIES. *Current Pos:* ED, AQUATIC RESOURCES, 94- *Personal Data:* b Salt Lake City, Utah, Apr 14, 26. *Educ:* Univ Calif, AB, 50, PhD, 57. *Prof Exp:* Res asst, Univ Calif, 52-56; geneticist biol lab, Bur Commercial Fisheries, US Fish & Wildlife Serv, 56-60, chief subpop invest, 60-62, dep dir, Hawaii Area, 62-67; assoc dir med & natural sci, Rockefeller Found, 67-69; prof oceanog & dir, Int Ctr Marine Resource Develop, Univ RI, 69-72; sr fisheries specialist, Agr & Rural Develop Dept, Int Bank Reconstruction & Develop 72-88, Fisheries Consult, World Bank, 88-90; adj prof fisheries, Dept Fisheries & Aquacult, Sea Grant Col, Univ Fla, Gainesville, 90-94. *Concurrent Pos:* Res fel, Univ Uppsala, 66-67. *Mem:* AAAS; Genetic Soc Am; Sigma Xi. *Res:* Blood groups and genetics of natural populations of vertebrates, particularly teleosts; international fisheries resources and policy studies. *Mailing Add:* 4486 Occoquan View Ct Woodbridge VA 22192. *Fax:* 703-590-1699; *E-Mail:* lsprague@gte.net

SPRAGUE, NEWTON G, PHYSICS, ASTRONOMY. *Current Pos:* RETIRED. *Personal Data:* b Indianapolis, Ind, Feb 8, 14; m 37; c 2. *Educ:* Butler Univ, BS, 35; Ind Univ, MS, 51, EdD(educ psychol), 55. *Prof Exp:* Asst physics, Butler Univ, 47-48; phys chemist, Indust Oils Lab, 48-49; teacher pub sch, Ind, 49-51, asst visual prod, 51-56, consult, 56-60; from asst prof to prof physics & astron, Ball State Univ, 60-78, dir, Univ Observ & Planetarium, 65-78, emer prof physics & astron, 78- *Mem:* AAAS; emer mem Am Astron Soc. *Res:* Spectroscopic and photometric stellar measurements. *Mailing Add:* 1111 Whitlock Crossing Ct Charlotte NC 28273

SPRAGUE, RANDALL GEORGE, internal medicine, endocrinology; deceased, see previous edition for last biography

SPRAGUE, RICHARD HOWARD, MATHEMATICS. *Current Pos:* asst prof, 61-67, ASSOC PROF MATH, IOWA STATE UNIV, 67- *Personal Data:* b Cincinnati, Ohio, Nov 9, 24. *Educ:* Maryville Col, BS, 49; Univ KY, MA, 52, PhD(math), 61. *Prof Exp:* Asst math, Ohio State Univ, 49-50; asst, Univ Ky, 50-52, instr, 53-56; asst prof, NMex State Univ, 58-60. *Mem:* Am Math Soc. *Res:* Univalent functions; geometry; complex variables. *Mailing Add:* 2219 N Dakota Ave Ames IA 50014

SPRAGUE, ROBERT ARTHUR, OPTICS. *Current Pos:* mem res staff, 76-80, RES AREA MGR, PALO ALTO RES CTR, XEROX CORP, 80- *Personal Data:* US citizen. *Educ:* Univ Rochester, BS, 67, PhD(optics), 71. *Prof Exp:* Sr scientist, Itek Corp Cent Res Labs, 71-74, staff scientist, 74-76. *Concurrent Pos:* Comt mem, US Nat Comt, Int Comn Optics, 73-75. *Mem:* Optical Soc Am; Soc Photo-Optical Instr Engrs; Am Inst Physics. *Res:* Electro-optics, input/output systems, optical signal processing, coherent optical processing and acousto-optics. *Mailing Add:* Xerox Palo Alto Res Ctr 3333 Coyote Hill Rd Palo Alto CA 94304

SPRAGUE, ROBERT HICKS, organic chemistry, for more information see previous edition

SPRAGUE, ROBERT W, ENVIRONMENTAL SCIENCE. *Current Pos:* CONSULT, 88- *Personal Data:* b Omaha, Nebr, Aug 1, 23; m 78, Florence E Trippenseee; c Robert P & Marguerite A. *Educ:* Univ Calif, Los Angeles, BS, 44; Ohio State Univ, PhD(inorg chem), 57. *Prof Exp:* Sales engr, R E Cunningham & Son, 46-48; chemist, US Naval Ord Test Sta, Calif, 48-57; teaching asst & res fel chem, Ohio State Univ, 54-57; sr chemist, Min Mining & Mfg Co, 57-58; res specialist propulsion, Rocketdyne Div, NAm Aviation, Inc, 58-60; res scientist, Aeronutronic Div, Philco Corp, 60-65; sr res chemist, US Borax Res Corp, Anaheim, 65-83, sr scientist, 83-88. *Mem:* Fel AAAS; Am Chem Soc. *Res:* Inorganic chemistry of nonmetals; chemistry of boron oxides, sulfides, halides; chemistry of oxide systems; environmental chemistry; fire retardance. *Mailing Add:* 5753 Wildbriar Dr Rancho Palos Verdes CA 90275-1752

SPRAGUE, VANCE GLOVER, JR, PHYSICAL OCEANOGRAPHY. *Current Pos:* Oceanogr, Naval Oceanog Off, 65-72, sr scientist, 72-77, head, Analysis Sect, Phys Oceanog Br, 77-85, head, Phys Oceanog Br, 80-85, DIR, PHYS OCEANOG DIV, NAVAL OCEANOG OFF, 85- *Personal Data:* b Bellefonte, Pa, Oct 28, 41; m 89. *Educ:* Penn State Univ, BS, 63; Salve Regina Col, MS, 82; Naval War Col, MS, 83. *Mem:* Am Geophys Union. *Res:* Airborne and shipboard field programs; design and construction of oceanographic data bases and mathematical models; transition of numerical ocean models for operational use and implementation of satellite remote sensing techniques. *Mailing Add:* 114 Camelia Dr Pass Christian MS 39571

SPRAKER, HAROLD STEPHEN, MATHEMATICS. *Current Pos:* from asst prof to prof 60-92, chmn dept, 67-92, EMER PROF MATH, MID TENN STATE UNIV, 92- *Personal Data:* b Cedar Bluff, Va, May 13, 29; m 54, Betty Conley; c John S & Mark C. *Educ:* Roanoke Col, BS, 50; Univ Va, MEd, 55, DEd(math educ), 60. *Prof Exp:* Teacher high sch, Va, 53-55, asst prin, 55-57; res assoc, Univ Va, 56-60, instr math, 59-60. *Concurrent Pos:* Apprentice coordr, Va State Dept Labor, 53-57; dir, NSF In-Serv Inst & vis scientist lectr. *Mem:* Math Asn Am; Nat Coun Teachers Math. *Res:* Mathematical education; geometry; algebra; statistics. *Mailing Add:* 2148 Elam Rd Murfreesboro TN 37127

SPRANGLE, PHILLIP ALLEN, PHYSICS. *Current Pos:* scientist, Plasma Physics Div, 72-, CHIEF SCIENTIST, NAVAL RES LAB, 82- *Personal Data:* b Brooklyn, NY, Sept 27, 44. *Educ:* Polytech Inst Brooklyn, BEE, 67; Univ PR, MA, 69,; Cornell Univ, PhD(appl physics), 72. *Prof Exp:* Res asst, Cornell Univ, 69-72. *Mem:* Fel Am Phs Soc; Sigma Xi; sr mem Inst Elec & Electronics Engrs. *Res:* Linear and nonlinear collective wave-particle processes; collective particle acceleration mechanisms and radiation sources and processes based on relativistic electron beams; developing advanced concepts in accelerator physics and radiation source physics; free electron lasers; laser driven and plasma accelerators; electron cyclotron masers; advanced high current accelerators. *Mailing Add:* Plasma Physics Div Naval Res Lab 4555 Overlook Ave SW Washington DC 20375-5000

SPRATLEY, RICHARD DENIS, PHYSICAL CHEMISTRY. *Current Pos:* asst prof chem, 67-72, res adminr, 72-83, DIR RES SERVS, UNIV BC, 83- *Personal Data:* b Vancouver, BC, Apr 18, 38; m 64; c 3. *Educ:* Univ BC, BSc, 61; Univ Calif, Berkeley, PhD(chem), 65. *Prof Exp:* Res assoc chem, Brookhaven Nat Lab, 65-67. *Mem:* Can Asn Univ Res Adminr; Soc Univ Patent Adminr. *Res:* Infrared spectroscopy; x-ray and neutron diffraction; molecular structure and bonding. *Mailing Add:* Off Res Servs & Admin Univ BC IRC 323-2194 Health Sci Mall Vancouver BC V6T 1Z3 Can. *Fax:* 604-822-5093; *E-Mail:* rds@exchange.ubc.ca

SPRATT, BRIAN GEOFFREY, MICROBIOLOGY. *Current Pos:* lectr, 80-87, reader, 87-89, WELLCOME TRUST PRIN RES FEL, SUSSEX UNIV, BRIGHTON, ENG, 89-, PROF, 90- *Personal Data:* b Margate, Kent, Eng, Mar 21, 47; m, Jiaji Zhon; c Henry Jestyn. *Educ:* London Univ, BSc, 68, PhD, 72. *Honors & Awards:* Fleming Award, Soc Gen Microbiol, 82; Hoechst-Roussel Award, Am Soc Microbiol, 93. *Prof Exp:* Res assoc, Princeton Univ, NJ, 73-75; res fel, Leicester Univ, Eng, 75-80. *Mem:* Fel Royal Soc London. *Res:* Mechanisms of action and resistance to antibiotics. *Mailing Add:* Sussex Univ Sch Biol Brighton BN1 9QG England

SPRATT, JAMES LEO, PHARMACOLOGY. *Current Pos:* from asst prof to assoc prof, 61-71, PROF PHARMACOL, UNIV IOWA, 71- *Personal Data:* b Chicago, Ill, Jan 27, 32; c 2. *Educ:* Univ Chicago, AB, 53, PhD(pharmacol), 57, MD, 61. *Prof Exp:* Res assoc pharmacol, Argonne Cancer Res Hosp, Univ Chicago, 57-61. *Concurrent Pos:* USPHS res career develop award, 63-68; Markle scholar, 63-68. *Mem:* AAAS; Am Soc Pharmacol & Exp Therapeut. *Res:* Therapeutics; radioisotopic tracer methods in cardiac glycoside research; cardiac glycosides and neurotoxicity; biochemical neuropharmacology. *Mailing Add:* Dept Pharmacol Univ Iowa Iowa City IA 52240

SPRATT, JOHN STRICKLIN, SURGERY. *Current Pos:* PROF SURG ONCOL, UNIV LOUISVILLE, 76-; CLIN PROF SURG, UNIFORMED SERVS UNIV HEALTH SCI, 88- *Personal Data:* b San Angelo, Tex, Jan 3, 29; m 51; c 3. *Educ:* Univ Tex, Dallas, MD, 52; Univ Mo-Columbia, MSPH, 70; Southern Methodist Univ, BS, 76; Am Bd Surg, dipl, 60. *Prof Exp:* Asst physiol, Univ Tex Southwestern Med Sch Dallas, 52; intern surg, Barnes Hosp, 52-53, from asst resident to resident, 55-59; from instr to assoc prof, Sch Med, Washington Univ, 59-66; prof surg, Sch Med, Univ Mo-Columbia, 66-76, prof community health & med pract, 71-76. *Concurrent Pos:* USPHS cancer res fel radiother & surg, Mallinckrodt Inst Radiol, St Louis, 57-58; Am Cancer Soc fel, Barnes Hosp, 58-59; Am Cancer Soc advan clin fel, 60-63; from asst prof to assoc prof, Sch Med, Univ Mo, 61-66, dir clin res & mem sci adv comt, Cancer Res Ctr, 64, dir ctr, 65-76; med dir, Dept Surg, Ellis Fischel State Cancer Hosp, Columbia, 61-76; med adv bur hearings & appeals, Soc Security Admin, 64-; mem rev comt sr clin traineeships surg, Cancer Control Prog, USPHS, 64-68; coordr cancer control, State of Mo; mem study sect, Supportive Serv Rev, 75-77; prof clin oncol, Am Cancer Soc, 76- *Mem:* Am Surg Asn; Am Asn Cancer Res; Soc Head & Neck Surg; Soc Surg Oncol; Am Col Surgeons. *Res:* Surgical oncology; natural history of cancer; cancer growth rates. *Mailing Add:* Dept Surg & Cmty Health James Graham Brown Cancer Ctr 529 S Jackson St Louisville KY 40202-1621

SPRATTO, GEORGE R, PHARMACOLOGY. *Current Pos:* from asst prof to assoc prof pharmacol, 68-79, assoc head, Dept Pharmacol & Toxicol, 78-83, PROF PHARMACOL, PURDUE UNIV, 79-, ASSOC DEAN PROF PROGS, SCH PHARM, 84- *Personal Data:* b Waterbury, Conn, July 28, 40; m 68; c 2. *Educ:* Fordham Univ, BS, 61; Univ Minn, PhD(pharmacol), 66. *Honors & Awards:* Merck Sharp & Dohme Award Outstanding Achievement Prof Pharm, 89; Distinguished Serv Award, Am Sch Health Asn, 74. *Prof Exp:* Pharmacologist, Food & Drug Admin, 66-68. *Concurrent Pos:* mem, Instnl Rev Bd, Pharmadynamics, Inc, 79-87; adj prof, Sch Med, Ind Univ, 81-; secy, coun deans, Am Pharmaceut Asn, 87-90, coun faculties, 79-80. *Mem:* Am Soc Pharmacol & Exp Therapeut; Am Asn Col Pharm; Am Soc Hosp Pharmacists; Am Asn Pharmaceut Scientists; Am Pharmaceut Asn. *Res:* Assessment of the interation of acute or subchronic administration of acetylcholinesterase inhibitors and stress on endocrine parameters and glucose; interaction of central nervous system drugs in animals treated acutely or chronically with narcotics. *Mailing Add:* Dean WVa Univ Sch Pharm HSC 1136 HSN PO Box 9500 Morgantown WV 26506-9500. *Fax:* 765-494-7880

SPRAWLS, PERRY, JR, MEDICAL PHYSICS, BIOMEDICAL ENGINEERING. *Current Pos:* from instr to assoc prof,59-77, PROF RADIOL, EMORY UNIV, 77- *Personal Data:* b Williston, SC, Mar 2, 34; m 61; c 1. *Educ:* Clemson Univ, BS, 56, MS, 60, PhD, 68. *Prof Exp:* Engr, Bell Tel Labs, 56-58; physicist, Savannah River Labs, AEC, 59-60. *Mailing Add:* 2665 Laurel Ridge Dr Decatur GA 30033

SPRAY, CLIVE ROBERT, metabolic studies with radiolabeled substrates, for more information see previous edition

SPRAY, DAVID CONOVER, NEUROPHYSIOLOGY. *Current Pos:* Res fel, 73-77, ASST PROF NEUROSCI, ALBERT EINSTEIN COL OF MED, 77- *Personal Data:* b Pittsburgh, Pa, June 7, 46; div; c 1. *Educ:* Transylvania Col, BS, 68; Univ Fla, PhD(physiol), 73. *Concurrent Pos:* Trainee, Ctr Neurosci, 69-73; mem corp, Marine Biol Lab, Woods Hole, 74- *Mem:* Am Physiol Soc; Biophys Soc; Soc Neurosci; Soc Gen Physiologists; Sigma Xi. *Res:* General neurophysiology, especially the physiology of chemical and electrical synapses, electro- and cutaneous receptors, cellular excitability and intracellular communication and excitability during development. *Mailing Add:* Dept Neurosci Albert Einstein Col Med 1410 Pelham Parkway South Bronx NY 10461-1101. *Fax:* 718-825-3058; *E-Mail:* spray@aecomyu.edu

SPRECHER, DAVID A, MATHEMATICS. *Current Pos:* assoc prof, Univ Calif, 66-71, chmn, Dept Math, 72-75, actg dean, Col Lett & Sci, 78-79, dean, 79-80, provost & dean, Col Lett & Sci, 81-91, prof math, 71-91, EMER PROF, UNIV CALIF, SANTA BARBARA, 91- *Personal Data:* b Saarbrucken, Ger, Jan 12, 30; US citizen; m 79; c Lorraine C & Jeanne V. *Educ:* Univ Bridgeport, AB, 58; Univ Md, PhD(math), 63. *Prof Exp:* Instr math, Univ Md, 61-63; asst prof, Syracuse Univ, 63-66. *Concurrent Pos:* NSF grant, 65-67. *Mem:* Am Math Soc; Math Asn Am. *Res:* Structure of functions of several variables; superposition of functions and approximation theory. *Mailing Add:* Dept Math Univ Calif Santa Barbara CA 93106

SPRECHER, HOWARD W, BIOCHEMISTRY. *Current Pos:* from asst prof to assoc prof physiol chem, 64-72, PROF PHYSIOL CHEM, OHIO STATE UNIV, 72- *Personal Data:* b Sauk City, Wis, Oct 13, 36; m 64. *Educ:* NCent Col, BA, 58; Univ Wis, PhD(biochem), 64. *Prof Exp:* Fel biochem, Hormel Inst, Univ Minn, 63-64. *Mem:* AAAS; Am Chem Soc; Am Oil Chem Soc; Am Soc Biol Chemists. *Res:* Organic synthesis, metabolism and characterization of lipids. *Mailing Add:* Dept Med Biochem Ohio State Univ Sch Med 370 W 9th Ave Columbus OH 43210

SPREITER, JOHN R(OBERT), SPACE PLASMA PHYSICS, FLUID MECHANICS. *Current Pos:* lectr, 50-68, prof, 68-92, EMER PROF APPL MECH, MECH ENG & AERONAUT & ASTRONAUT, STANFORD UNIV, 92- *Personal Data:* b Oak Park, Minn, Oct 23, 21; m 53, Brenda; c Terry A, Janet L (Adler), Christine P & Hilary M. *Educ:* Univ Minn, BAeroE, 43; Stanford Univ, MS, 47, PhD(eng mech), 54. *Honors & Awards:* NASA Group Achievement Award, 83; Am Geophys Union Excellence in Reviewing, 88, 91. *Prof Exp:* Aeronaut engr, Flight Res Br, Ames Aeronaut Lab, Nat Adv Comt Aeronaut, 43-46, res scientist, Theoret Aerodyn Br, 47-58, res scientist, Theoret Br, Ames Res Ctr, NASA, 58-62, chief, Theoret Studies Br, Space Sci Div, 62-69. *Concurrent Pos:* Mem ionospheres & radio physics subcomt, Space Sci Steering Comt, NASA, 60-64; mem various comts, Int Asn Geomag & Aeronomy, 64-, Am Inst Aeronaut & Astronaut, 68-74; consult, Neilson Eng & Res, Inc, 68-85, Gen Motors, 75-76, RMA Aerospace, 85- *Mem:* Fel Am Geophys Union; Am Phys Soc; fel Am Inst Aeronaut & Astronaut; fel Royal Astron Soc; Sigma Xi; Planetary Soc. *Res:* Computer modeling of the interaction of the solar wind with the earth, other planets, the moon, and the interstellar medium; aerodynamics and fluid mechanics; magnetohydrodynamics. *Mailing Add:* 1250 Sandalwood Lane Los Altos CA 94024-6739

SPREITZER, ROBERT JOSEPH, CHLOROPLAST MOLECULAR GENETICS, PHOTOSYNTHESIS. *Current Pos:* from asst prof to assoc prof, 84-93, PROF BIOCHEM, UNIV NEBR, 93- *Personal Data:* b Cleveland, Ohio, Apr 12, 52; m 78, Nancy J Pitts. *Educ:* Cleveland State Univ, BS, 74; Case Western Res Univ, PhD(biol), 80. *Prof Exp:* Res assoc, Univ Ill, 79-80, vis scholar, 80-82; fel, Univ Geneva, Switz, 82-84. *Concurrent Pos:* Prin investr, US Dept Agr, 85-87, 89-92 & 94-97, NSF, 87-90 & 90-94; consult, US Dept Energy, 93, US Dept Agr, 95 & NSF, 96. *Mem:* Am Chem Soc; Am Soc Plant Physiol; Genetics Soc Am. *Res:* Genetically engineer the photo-synthetic rubisco enzyme as a means for increasing plant productivity; nuclear and chlorplast genes are changed by classical and molecular genetic methods to understand the structure-function relationships of enzyme catalysis. *Mailing Add:* Dept Biochem Univ Nebr Lincoln NE 68583-0718. *E-Mail:* rjs@unlinfo.unl.edu

SPREITZER, WILLIAM MATTHEW, AERONAUTICAL ENGINEERING, INTELLIGENT TRANSPORTATION SYSTEMS. *Current Pos:* from jr res engr to sr res engr, Eng Develop Dept, Gen Motors, 51-61, sr liaison engr, Exec Dept, 61-66, head transp res dept, 66-72 & 79-85, transp & urban anal dept, 72-78, operating systs res, 85-87, mgr planning, 87-89, mgr, Vehicle/Hwy Systs Coord, TECH DIR, INTELLIGENT TRANSP SYSTS PROG, GEN MOTORS RES & DEVELOP CTR, 91- *Personal Data:* b Highland Park, Mich, Aug 14, 29; m 52, Rose Marie Millek; c Barbara L (Berent) & Christopher J. *Educ:* Univ Detroit, BAeE, 51. *Hon Degrees:* AeE, Univ Detroit, 57. *Honors & Awards:* Roy W Crum Award, Transp Res Bd Nat Res Coun, 84; Delco Electronics ITS Award, Soc Automotive Engrs, 96. *Prof Exp:* Eng draftsman, Dept Aeronaut, State Mich, 49-51. *Concurrent Pos:* Mem, Comt on Transp, Nat Res Coun Assembly Eng, 70-81 & Bay Area Rapid Transit Impact Adv Comt, 72-79; mem, Transp Develop Adv Comt, Hwy Users Fedn Safety & Mobility, 70-72; deleg transp panel, White House Conf on Aging, 71; mem panel on urbanization, transp & commun, Nat Acad Sci-Nat Res Coun Study for 79 UN Conf on Sci & Technol for Develop, 77-78; chmn, div A group 5, Transp Res Bd, Nat Acad Sci, 86-93 & chair, Intelligent Vehicle Hwy Systs Soc Automotive Engrs, 85-; mem & chair, coord coun, Int Transp Hwy Soc Am, 91-; chair, US deleg, Tech Adv Group, Int Stand Orgn Tech Comt. *Mem:* Assoc fel Am Inst Aeronaut & Astronaut; fel Soc Automotive Engrs; Transp Res Forum. *Res:* Transportation and traffic science; automotive gas turbine engine research, development and applications; research administration. *Mailing Add:* Tech Dir Gen Motors ITS Prog MS 480 106 390 Warren MI 48090-9055

SPREMULLI, LINDA LUCY, CHEMISTRY. *Current Pos:* asst prof, 76-81, ASSOC PROF CHEM, UNIV NC, 81- *Personal Data:* b Corning, NY, Sept 6, 47. *Educ:* Univ Rochester, BA, 69; Mass Inst Technol, PhD(biochem), 73. *Prof Exp:* Assoc chem, Univ Tex, Austin, 73-74, fel, 74-76. *Concurrent Pos:* Mem, Biomed Sci Study Sect, NIH, 82-86, Biochem study sect, 87- *Mem:* Am Soc Biol Chemists; Am Chem Soc; AAAS; Asn Women Sci; Am Soc Microbiol; Int Soc Plant Molecular Biol. *Res:* Characterization of mammalian mitochondrial protein synthesis; characterization of the ribosomes and auxiliary factors required for chloroplast protein synthesis and induction of this system by light. *Mailing Add:* Dept Chem Univ NC CB 3290 Venable Chapel Hill NC 27599-3290. *Fax:* 919-962-2388; *E-Mail:* lls@oncuxi.bitnet

SPRENG, ALFRED CARL, STRATIGRAPHY. *Current Pos:* from asst prof to prof, 50-88, chmn, Dept Geol & Geophys, 71-75, EMER PROF GEOL, UNIV MO, ROLLA, 88- *Personal Data:* b Alliance, Ohio, Feb 2, 23; m 49, Wealthy Purrington; c Carl, Catherine & Lillian. *Educ:* Col Wooster, AB, 46; Univ Kans, AM, 48; Univ Wis, PhD(geol), 50. *Prof Exp:* Asst, Univ Wis, 48-50; asst prof, Tex Tech Inst, 50. *Concurrent Pos:* Consult limestone & shale raw mats, 55- *Mem:* Paleont Soc; Am Asn Petrol Geologists; Geol Soc Am; Soc Econ Paleontologists & Mineralogists; Am Inst Prof Geologists. *Res:* Stratigraphic paleontology; carbonate petrology; paleozoic stratigraphy. *Mailing Add:* Dept Geol & Geophys Univ Mo Rolla MO 65409-0410. *Fax:* 573-341-6935; *E-Mail:* aspreng@umr.edu

SPRENGNETHER, MICHELE M, CHEMICAL KINETICS. *Current Pos:* ASST PROF, WELLESLEY COL, 93- *Personal Data:* b Minneola, NY, Mar 28, 62; m 90, R G Gonzalez. *Educ:* Wellesley Col, BA, 84; Mass Inst Technol, PhD(phys chem), 92. *Mem:* Am Chem Soc; Am Geophys Union. *Res:* Chemical kinetics studies of reactions important in the troposphere. *Mailing Add:* 31 Chilton St No 2 Cambridge MA 02138-6801. *E-Mail:* msprengnethe@lucy.wellesley.edu

SPRENKEL, RICHARD KEISER, ENTOMOLOGY. *Current Pos:* asst prof, 79-84, ASSOC PROF ENTOM, UNIV FLA, 84- *Personal Data:* b York, Pa, July 10, 43; m 65. *Educ:* Pa State Univ, BS, 65, MS, 67; Univ Ill, PhD(entom), 73. *Prof Exp:* Res assoc entom, NC State Univ, 73-79. *Mem:* Entom Soc Am; Sigma Xi. *Res:* Development of integrated pest management programs on row crops in Florida. *Mailing Add:* Rte 3 PO Box 4370 Quincy FL 32351

SPRESSER, DIANE MAR, GRAPH THEORY & ALGORITHMS. *Current Pos:* From instr to assoc prof math, 67-80, actg head, Dept Math, 78-79, head dept, 79-94, assoc prof math & comput sci, 80-82, prof math & comput sci, 82-94, PROF MATH, JAMES MADISON UNIV, 94-; PROG DIR MATH TEACHER ENHANCEMENT, NSF, 94- *Personal Data:* b Welch, WVa, Dec 12, 43. *Educ:* Radford Col, BS, 65; Univ Tenn, Knoxville, MA, 67; Univ Va, PhD(math sci & educ), 77. *Concurrent Pos:* Lectr, Vis Scientists Prog, Va Acad Sci, 74-; mem, Nat Question Writing Comt, Math Counts Found, 93-96. *Mem:* Am Math Soc; Asn Comput Mach; Math Asn Am; Asn Women in Math; Nat Coun Teachers Math. *Res:* Properties of graphs and analysis of related computer algorithms; mathematical education at the collegiate level. *Mailing Add:* NSF 4201 Wilson Blvd Rm 885 Arlington VA 22230. *Fax:* 703-306-0412; *E-Mail:* dspresse@nsf.gov

SPRIGGS, ALFRED SAMUEL, ORGANIC CHEMISTRY. *Current Pos:* PROF CHEM & CHMN DEPT, CLARK COL, 55- *Personal Data:* b Houston, Tex, Aug 1, 22; m 49; c 4. *Educ:* Dillard Univ, AB, 42; Howard Univ, MS, 44; Washington Univ, PhD(chem), 54. *Prof Exp:* Asst prof chem, Tenn Agr & Indust State Col, 47-51; prof, Lincoln Univ, Pa, 54-55. *Mem:* Fel AAAS; Am Chem Soc; Sigma Xi. *Res:* Isotope tracers with carbon 14; carbohydrates; organic synthesis; radiochemistry; chromatography. *Mailing Add:* 4629 Boulder Park Dr SW Atlanta GA 30331-4511

SPRIGGS, RICHARD MOORE, MATERIALS RESEARCH, CERAMIC ENGINEERING. *Current Pos:* JOHN FRANCIS MCMAHON PROF CERAMIC ENG & DIR, NY STATE CTR ADV CERAMIC TECHNOL, NY STATE COL CERAMICS, ALFRED UNIV, 87-, DIR, OFF SPONSORED PROG, 88- *Personal Data:* b Washington, Pa, May 8, 31; m 53, Patricia Blaney; c Carolyn (Muchna), Richard Jr & Alan. *Educ:* Pa State Univ, BS, 52; Univ Ill, MS, 56, PhD(ceramic eng), 58. *Honors & Awards:* Ross Coffin Purdy Award, Am Ceramic Soc, 67; Hobart M Kramer Award, Am Ceramic Soc, 80; Orton Mem Lectr & McMahon Mem Lectr, Am Ceramic Soc, 88; Int Prize, Ceramic Soc Japan, 92; Mueller Mem Lect, Amalgamated Carriage & Wagon Soc, 96. *Prof Exp:* Asst ceramic eng, Univ Ill, 54-56; sr res engr ceramics, Ferro Corp, Ohio, 58-59; sr scientist, Res & Advan Develop Div, Avco Corp, Mass, 59-60, staff scientist, 60-62, sr staff scientist & ceramics res group leader, 62-64; assoc dir, Mat Res Ctr & dir, Phys Ceramics Lab, Lehigh Univ, 64-70, from assoc prof to prof metall & mat sci, 64-80, admin asst to pres, 70-71, asst vpres admin, 71-72, vpres admin,

72-78; vis sr staff assoc, 79-80, sr staff officer/staff scientist, Nat Mat Adv Bd, 80-87, staff dir bd assessment NBS Progs, 84-87. *Concurrent Pos:* Am Coun Educ fel, Lehigh Univ, 70-71; consult to var corps & govt labs; foreign mem, Serbian Acad Sci & Arts, 86-; consult prof, Univ Belgrade, Yugoslavia, 85- *Mem:* Fel Brit Inst Ceramics; fel Am Ceramic Soc (treas, 80-82, vpres, 82-83, pres-elect, 83-84, pres, 84-85); Nat Inst Ceramic Engrs; Brit Ceramic Soc; Int Inst Sci Sintering; Am Soc Eng Educ; Am Soc Testing & Mat; AAAS; NY Acad Sci; Int Acad Ceramics (secy, 93-96). *Res:* Physical ceramics; materials science; correlations among processing, internal structure and physical and mechanical properties of dense polycrystalline refractory ceramic oxide systems; author or coauthor of over 100 technical articles. *Mailing Add:* Alfred Univ NY State Ctr Adv Ceramic Technol Alfred NY 14802. *Fax:* 607-871-3469; *E-Mail:* spriggs@bigvax.alfred.edu

SPRINCE, HERBERT, biochemistry, pharmacology; deceased, see previous edition for last biography

SPRING, BONNIE JOAN, PSYCHIATRY, PHARMACOLOGY. *Current Pos:* PROF PSYCHOL, CHICAGO MED SCH, 88-; RES HEALTH SCIENTIST, HINES VET ADMIN MED CTR, 94- *Personal Data:* b Hackensack, NJ, Oct 9, 49; c Heidi K. *Educ:* Bucknell Univ, BA, 71; Harvard Univ, MA, 75, PhD(psychol), 77. *Prof Exp:* From asst prof to assoc prof psychol, Harvard Univ, 77-84; prof & dir psychol, Tex Tech Univ, Lubbock, 84-88; Health sci officer, Med Ctr, N Chicago Vet Admin, 88-94. *Concurrent Pos:* Vis lectr, Dept Nutrit & Food Sci, Mass Inst Technol, 79-84, lectr dept psychiat, Columbia Col, NY, 79-85; res assoc prof, Univ Md Sch Med, 84-89; comt mem, Nat Needs Biomed & Behav Res Personnel, Inst Med, Nat Acad Sci, 84-86, Nat Plan Res Schizophrenia Treat Panel, 87; field ed N & S Am, Psychopharmacol, Human Exp Studies, 87; mem, Behav Med Study Sect, NIH, 93- *Mem:* Fel Am Psychol Asn; Soc Biol Psychiat; Am Col Neuropharmacol; Am Psychopathol Asn; Soc Exp Psychopath; Soc Behav Med; AAAS; Sigma Xi. *Res:* State and trait aspects of brain-behavior relationships as manifested in the areas of psychopathology and health psychology; weight gain after smoking cessation; comorbidity among dysphoric mood, overeating and addictive disorders. *Mailing Add:* Dept Psychol Univ Health Sci Chicago Med Sch 3333 Green Bay Rd North Chicago IL 60064-3095. *Fax:* 847-578-3015; *E-Mail:* sprigb@mis.finchcms.edu

SPRING, JEFFREY H, INSECT ENDOCRINOLOGY, INSECT EXCRETORY PHYSIOLOGY. *Current Pos:* asst prof, 83-87, ASSOC PROF BIOL, UNIV SOUTHWESTERN LA, 87- *Personal Data:* b Galt, Ont, Mar 14, 50; m 91; c 1. *Educ:* Univ Waterloo, Can, BSc, 73, MSc, 76; Univ BC, Can, PhD(zool), 79. *Prof Exp:* NATO postdoctoral zool, Univ Cambridge, Eng, 79-81; univ res fel zool, La Trobe Univ, Melbourne, Australia, 82. *Mem:* AAAS; Am Soc Zoologists. *Res:* Salt and water balance in insects; structure of malpighian tubules and rectum; physiology of primary urine formation and reabsorptive processes; source, structure, release and function of neurohormones controlling diuresis; isolation and identification of neuropeptides. *Mailing Add:* Biol Univ Southwestern LA PO Box 42451 Lafayette LA 70504-9998

SPRING, RAY FREDERICK, MATHEMATICS. *Current Pos:* from asst prof to assoc prof, 55-66, PROF MATH, OHIO UNIV, 66- *Personal Data:* b Cincinnati, Ohio, Mar 28, 25; m 49; c 2. *Educ:* Univ Cincinnati, BS, 48; Univ Ill, MS, 52, PhD(math), 55. *Prof Exp:* Chem engr, US Playing Card Co, 48-50; asst math, Univ Ill, 52-54. *Mem:* Am Math Soc. *Res:* Modern abstract algebra; group and lattice theories; digital computer programming; characterization and classification of metabelian p-groups and other groups by means of their subgroup lattices. *Mailing Add:* 41 Carol Lane Athens OH 45701

SPRING, SUSAN B, VIROLOGY, IMMUNOCHEMISTRY. *Current Pos:* Exec secy, Microbiol & Infectious Dis Res Comt, Nat Inst Allergy & Infectious Dis, 81-84, prog dir DNA virus studies I, Biol Carcinogenesis Br, Div Cancer Etiology, 84-90, PROG OFFICER, PERSISTING VIRAL DIS, VIROL BR, DMID, NAT INST ALLERGY & INFECTIOUS DIS, NIH, 90- *Personal Data:* b New York, NY, May 1, 43. *Educ:* Univ Chicago, PhD(microbiol), 68. *Mem:* Am Soc Immunol; Am Soc Virol; Am Soc Microbiol; Sigma Xi; NY Acad Sci; Infectious Dis Soc Am. *Mailing Add:* Persisting Viral Dis VB DMID NI AID NIH Solar Bldg 3A-14 MSC 7630 Bethesda MD 20892-7630. *Fax:* 301-496-8030

SPRINGBORN, ROBERT CARL, POLYMER SCIENCE, BIORESEARCH. *Current Pos:* CHMN & CHIEF EXEC OFFICER, SPRINGBORN GROUP, INC, 85- *Personal Data:* b Geneva, Ill, Oct 19, 29; m 51; c 2. *Educ:* Univ Ill, BS, 51; Cornell Univ, PhD(org chem), 54. *Prof Exp:* Res chemist, Monsanto Chem Co, 54-58; tech dir, Marbon Chem Div, Borg-Warner Corp, 58-63; vpres & tech dir, Ohio Rubber Co, 63-65; gen mgr, Ionics, Inc, 65-67; vpres, W R Grace & Co, 67-69; chmn & pres, Gen Econ Corp, 69-71. *Concurrent Pos:* Mem, White House Conf Small Bus Com, 78- *Mem:* Am Chem Soc; AAAS; Soc Plastics Engrs; Plastics Inst Am; Nat Asn Life Sci Industs. *Res:* Polymer science including polymeric synthesis and processing; medical and health sciences, particularly related to bioresearch. *Mailing Add:* 4601 Gulfshore Blvd N No 7 Naples FL 34103

SPRINGER, ALAN DAVID, NEUROSCIENCE. *Current Pos:* assoc prof, 79-84, PROF ANAT, NY MED COL, 84- *Personal Data:* b Linz, Austria, Jan 6, 48; US citizen; m 69; c 2. *Educ:* Brooklyn Col, BS, 69; City Univ New York, PhD(psychol), 73. *Prof Exp:* Scholar neurosci, Univ Mich, 73-77; asst prof physiol, Univ Ill Med Ctr, 77-79. *Concurrent Pos:* Prin investr, Nat Inst Aging, NIH grant & NSF grant, 78-81 & Nat Eye Inst, NIH grant, 81-90. *Mem:* Soc Neurosci; Asn Res Vision & Ophthal; Am Asn Anatomists; NY Acad Sci; AAAS. *Res:* Vision and optic nerve regeneration in vertebrates, including conditions leading to abnormal and normal patterns of regeneration and the role of various brain structures in mediating vision; retinal development and retinal regeneration. *Mailing Add:* Dept Anat New York Med Col Valhalla NY 10595

SPRINGER, ALLAN MATTHEW, CHEMICAL ENGINEERING, PULP & PAPER TECHNOLOGY. *Current Pos:* from asst prof to assoc prof pulp & paper technol, 76-86, PROF PAPER SCI & ENG, MIAMI UNIV, 86- *Personal Data:* b Baraboo, Wis, Oct 2, 44; m 67. *Educ:* Univ Wis-Madison, BS, 66; Lawrence Univ, MS, 69, PhD(chem eng), 72. *Honors & Awards:* Environ Div Award, Tech Asn Pulp & Paper Indust, 89. *Prof Exp:* Process engr, Olin Mathieson Chem Corp, 67-68; res engr, Nat Coun Paper Indust Air & Stream Improvement, 72-76. *Concurrent Pos:* Sr Fulbright lectr, Univ Pertanian Malaysia, 79-80; sr Fulbright prof, Univ Sao Paulo, Brazil, 85. *Mem:* Tech Asn Pulp & Paper Indust; Am Inst Chem Engrs; Am Asn Environ Eng Prof; Sigma Xi; Int Asn Water Pollution Res & Control. *Res:* Water pollution abatement through process modification; wastewater treatment optimization; resource recovery and recycling in the pulp and paper industry. *Mailing Add:* 109 McKee Ave Oxford OH 45056

SPRINGER, BERNARD G, science policy, for more information see previous edition

SPRINGER, CHARLES EUGENE, MATHEMATICS. *Current Pos:* RETIRED. *Personal Data:* b Storm Lake, Iowa, Oct 25, 03; m 30; c 1. *Educ:* Univ Okla, AB, 25, AM, 26; Oxford Univ, BSc, 40; Univ Chicago, PhD(math), 38. *Prof Exp:* Instr math, Univ Okla, 26-27 & Iowa State Co, 30; from instr to prof, Univ Okla, 30-61, chmn, Dept Math, 46-55, form David Boyd prof to David Ross Boyd emer prof math, 61-77. *Concurrent Pos:* Chmn dept math, Oklahoma City Univ, 70-72. *Res:* Differential geometry; dual geodesics on a surface; metric geometry of surfaces by use of tensor analysis and in four-dimensional space; union curves and curvature. *Mailing Add:* 1617 Jenkins St Norman OK 73072

SPRINGER, CHARLES SINCLAIR, JR, BIOPHYSICAL CHEMISTRY. *Current Pos:* from asst prof to assoc prof, 68-85, PROF CHEM, STATE UNIV NY STONY BROOK, 85- *Personal Data:* b Houston, Tex, Nov 2, 40; m 63; c 2. *Educ:* St Louis Univ, BS, 62; Ohio State Univ, MSc, 64, PhD(chem), 67. *Honors & Awards:* US Air Force Res & Develop Award, 67. *Prof Exp:* Res chemist, Aerospace Res Labs, 65-68. *Concurrent Pos:* Vis assoc, Calif Inst Technol, 76-77; vis assoc prof, Med Sch, Harvard Univ, 83-84. *Mem:* AAAS; Am Chem Soc; NY Acad Sci; Biophys Soc; Int Soc Magnetic Resonance; Soc Magnetic Resonance in Med; Sigma Xi. *Res:* Nuclear magnetic resonance and electron paramagnetic resonance studies of living systems and biological membranes; physical properties, and ionophore- and protein- catalyzed metal ion membrane transport, metal ion binding to membrane surfaces, physical chemistry of micelle and inverse micelle solutions. *Mailing Add:* Dept Chem Brookhaven Natl Lab Bldg 555 Upton NY 11973-5000. *E-Mail:* cspringer@sbccmail

SPRINGER, DONALD LEE, SEISMOLOGY, PHYSICS. *Current Pos:* PHYSICIST SEISMOL, LAWRENCE LIVERMORE NAT LAB, 56- *Personal Data:* b Hampton, Iowa, Mar 15, 33; m 55, Georgia L Branscum; c D Scott, Victorine K & Brian W. *Educ:* Univ Calif, Santa Barbara, BA, 56. *Concurrent Pos:* Mem ground shock tech working group, Canal Studies, AEC, 66-70, mem ground shock subcomt, 69-70; mem seismic rev panel, US Air Force Tech Appl Ctr, 74-79 & Off Sci & Technol Policy, White House, 77-79; mem, US deleg, Ad Hoc Group Sci Experts Comt Disarmament, UN, 80-94. *Mem:* Seismol Soc Am. *Res:* Observational seismology; explosion seismology; geophysics; earth structure; earthquake prediction; seismic energy. *Mailing Add:* 27258 S Lillegard Ct Tracy CA 95376. *E-Mail:* springer@s31

SPRINGER, DWIGHT SYLVAN, CHEMICAL ENGINEERING, CHEMISTRY EDUCATION. *Current Pos:* exec officer, Dept Chem, 88-90, ASSOC PROF CHEM & CHEM ENG, US MIL ACAD, 81-, DEP HEAD, DEPT CHEM, 91- *Personal Data:* b Harrisburg, Pa, Oct 8, 43; m 64, Mary L George; c Kristin (Gustavsen), Kathryn & Mark P. *Educ:* Univ Del, BChE, 65; Univ Minn, PhD(chem eng), 71; Long Island Univ, MS, 90. *Honors & Awards:* Herbert W Alden Award, Am Defense Preparedness Asn, 75. *Prof Exp:* Chem engr power supplies, Harry Diamond Labs, US Army, Washington, DC, 72-74; instr, US Mil Acad, 74-77, asst prof chem, 77-79; chem officer, US Army, Berlin, 80-81. *Concurrent Pos:* Vis scholar chem, Stanford Univ, 90-91. *Mem:* Am Inst Chem Engrs; Am Chem Soc; Am Soc Eng Educ. *Res:* Chemical and conventional ammunition; chemical defense material; phosphorus and sulfur chemistry; lasers in chemical education. *Mailing Add:* Dept Chem US Mil Acad West Point NY 10996-1785

SPRINGER, EDWARD L(ESTER), PULP BLEACHING, WOOD DELIGNIFICATION-HYDROLYSIS-STORAGE. *Current Pos:* CHEM ENGR, FOREST PROD LAB, USDA, 58- *Personal Data:* b Baraboo, Wis, July 12, 31; m 61, Patricia Maher; c E Lucia & Catherine. *Educ:* Univ Wis, BS, 53, MS, 58, PhD(chem eng), 61. *Prof Exp:* Chem engr, Kimberly-Clark Corp, Wis, 55-56. *Concurrent Pos:* Fulbright fel, Finland, 61-62. *Mem:* Tech Asn Pulp & Paper Indust; Am Chem Soc. *Res:* Wood preservation; preservation of pulp chips; kinetics of wood hydrolysis and of the delignification of wood; nonconventional pulping and pulp bleaching using peroxymonosulfuric acid and peroxymonophosphoric acid. *Mailing Add:* Forest Prod Lab USDA Forest Serv 1 Gifford Pinchot Dr Madison WI 53705-2398. *Fax:* 608-231-9262

SPRINGER, GEORG F, CANCER INNUMOLOGY, BREAST CARCINOMA IMMUNOLOGY & IMMUNOCHEMISTRY. *Current Pos:* PROF MICROBIOL & IMMUNOL, MED SCH, NORTHWESTERN UNIV, EVANSTON, 63-, DIR IMMUNOCHEM RES, EVANSTON HOSP, 63- *Personal Data:* b Berlin, Ger, Feb 29, 24; nat US; m 51, Bligh; c Martin, Elizabeth & Julia. *Educ:* Univ Heidelberg, MA, 47; Univ Basel, MD, 51. *Hon Degrees:* DSc, FUHS, Chicago Med Sch, 94. *Honors & Awards:* Oehlecker Prize, Ger Soc Blood Transfusion, 66; John G Gibson II Lect, 66; Ernst Jung Prize Med, 77. *Prof Exp:* Res fel pediat, Sch Med, Univ Pa, 53, Woodward fel physiol chem, 52-53, asst instr path, Sch Med, 52-54, assoc clin path, 55-58, asst prof immunol, 56-61, assoc prof, 61-62, mem, Pepper Lab, 55-62. *Concurrent Pos:* Mem, Germ Free Res Unit, Walter Reed Army Med Ctr, 54-55; chief blood group, City Philadelphia, 57-63; ed var sci jour; Am Heart Asn estab investr, 58-63; mem, Evanston Hosp Res & Educ Comt & Protection Human Subjects Comt, Northwestern Univ Cancer Ctr; prof microbiol, immunol & surg, FUSH, Chicago Med Sch. *Mem:* AAAS; Am Soc Microbiol; Am Chem Soc; Am Heart Asn; NY Acad Sci; Am Soc Immunol. *Res:* cancer research and immunology; immunochemistry of blood-group active sustances; carbohydrate chemistry; virus action on blood groups; immunology of human breast cancer; infectious mononucleosis; shock; physical chemistry of antigen-antibody interactions; tumor virus receptors. *Mailing Add:* Sch Med Univ Health Sci Med 3333 Green Bay Rd North Chicago IL 60064-3037. *Fax:* 847-578-3432; *E-Mail:* springeg@mis.finchcms.edu

SPRINGER, GEORGE, MATHEMATICS. *Current Pos:* assoc dean res & develop, 73-80, actg dean res & grad develop, 80-82, PROF MATH, IND UNIV, BLOOMINGTON, 64-, PROF COMPUT SCI, 87- *Personal Data:* b Cleveland, Ohio, Sept 3, 24; m 50, Ann Marie Keiner; c Leonard, Claudia & Joel. *Educ:* Case Inst, BS, 45; Brown Univ, MS, 46; Harvard Univ, PhD(math), 49. *Prof Exp:* Moore instr math, Mass Inst Technol, 49-51; asst prof, Northwestern Univ, 51-54; vis prof & Fulbright lectr, Univ Münster, 54-55; from assoc prof to prof, Univ Kans, 55-64. *Concurrent Pos:* Vis prof, Univ Sao Paulo, 61; vis prof & Fulbright lectr, Univ Wurzburg, 61-62; ed, J Math & Mech, Ind Univ, 65-; consult, examr, N Cent Asn Cols & Univs, 68-; vis prof, Imp Col, Univ London, 71-72; consult ed, McGraw Hill Book Co, 71-; prog dir math sci sect, NSF, Washington, DC, 78-79. *Mem:* Am Math Soc; Math Asn Am; Asn Comput Mach. *Res:* Theory of functions of one and several complex variables; harmonic functions; conformal and quasiconformal mapping; programming languages. *Mailing Add:* 1026 S Mitchell St Bloomington IN 47401-5155. *Fax:* 812-855-4829; *E-Mail:* springer@cs.indiana.edu

SPRINGER, GEORGE HENRY, GEOLOGY. *Current Pos:* from instr to assoc prof, 46-56, DISTINGUISHED SERV PROF GEOL, UNIV DAYTON, 84- *Personal Data:* b Bristol, RI, Jan 16, 18; m 41; c 1. *Educ:* Brown Univ, AB, 38, ScM, 40. *Prof Exp:* Geologist, Tenn Valley Authority, 41. *Mem:* AAAS; Nat Asn Geol Teachers; Int Glaciol Soc; Sigma Xi. *Res:* Structural geology; petrography. *Mailing Add:* 2373 Shelterwood Dr Dayton OH 45409

SPRINGER, GEORGE S, AERONAUTICAL & ASTRONAUTICAL ENGINEERING. *Current Pos:* PAUL PIGOLT PROF, DEPT AERONAUT & ASTRONAUT, STANFORD UNIV, 83-, CHMN DEPT, 90- *Personal Data:* b Budapest, Hungary, Dec 12, 33; US citizen; m 63, Susan M Flary; c Elizabeth A (Greer) & Mary K (Zasio). *Educ:* Univ Sydney, BE, 59; Yale Univ, MEng, 60, MS, 61, PhD(mech eng), 62. *Honors & Awards:* Ralph E Teetor Award, Soc Automotive Engrs, 78; Pub Serv Achievement Award, NASA, 88; Delmonte Award, 91; Worcester Reed Warner Medal, 94; Engr Year Award, Am Inst Aeronaut & Astronaut, 95. *Prof Exp:* Ford Found fel & instr mech eng, Mass Inst Technol, 62-63, asst prof, 63-67; from assoc prof to prof mech eng, Univ Mich, Ann Arbor, 67-83. *Mem:* Nat Acad Eng; Am Phys Soc; fel Am Inst Aeronaut & Astronaut; Soc Automotive Engrs; fel Soc Adv Mech & Process Eng; fel Am Soc Mech Engrs; foreign mem Hungarian Acad Sci. *Res:* Composite materials. *Mailing Add:* Dept Aeronaut & Astronaut Stanford Univ Stanford CA 94305. *Fax:* 650-723-0062; *E-Mail:* springer@sierra.stanford.edu

SPRINGER, JOHN KENNETH, plant pathology, nematology; deceased, see previous edition for last biography

SPRINGER, JOHN MERVIN, CHEMICAL PHYSICS. *Current Pos:* Res assoc chem physics, 71-73, asst prof, 73-77, res assoc physics, 77-80, ASSOC PROF PHYSICS, FISK UNIV, 81- *Personal Data:* b Peoria, Ill, Apr 19, 41; m 66; c 3. *Educ:* Knox Col, BA; Vanderbilt Univ, MS, 65, PhD(physics), 72. *Mem:* Sigma Xi; Am Asn Physics Teachers. *Res:* Crystal structure determinations via infrared and Raman spectroscopy; optical analysis of crystal defects. *Mailing Add:* 1609 Ash Valley Dr Nashville TN 37215

SPRINGER, KARL JOSEPH, MECHANICAL ENGINEERING. *Current Pos:* sr engr, US Army Fuels & Lubricants Res Lab, 63-67, mgr, Emissions Res Lab, Dept Automotive Res, 67-72, asst dir automotive res, 72-74, DIR, DEPT EMISSIONS RES, ENGINES, EMISSIONS & VEHICLES RES DIV, SOUTHWEST RES INST, 74-, VPRES, AUTOMOTIVE PRODS & EMISSIONS RES DIV. *Personal Data:* b San Antonio, Tex, Apr 14, 35; m 57, Ann Andrews; c Karen, Erik & Kurt. *Educ:* Tex A&M Univ, BS, 57; Trinity Univ, MS, 66; Am Acad Engrs, dipl. *Honors & Awards:* S Honda Gold Medal, Am Soc Mech Eng, 91 & 96. *Prof Exp:* Res engr auto engines, Southwest Res Inst, 57-58; proj engr jet engines, Wright Air Develop Ctr, US Air Force, 58-60; field engr, E I du Pont de Nemours & Co, Inc, 60-62; proj engr, Automotive Res Assocs, 62-63. *Concurrent Pos:* Am Soc Mech Eng distinguished lectr, 91, 92-94. *Mem:* Nat Acad Eng; fel Soc Automotive Engrs; fel Am Soc Mech Engrs. *Res:* Emissions from diesel and gasoline vehicles; control of emissions from diesels and measurement of combustion odor. *Mailing Add:* 15614 Dove Meadow San Antonio TX 78248-1715

SPRINGER, MAXWELL ELSWORTH, SOIL MORPHOLOGY. *Current Pos:* CONSULT, 79- *Personal Data:* b Bourbon, Mo, Oct 21, 13; m 53, Jean Huston; c Steve, Kent & Scott. *Educ:* Univ Mo, BS, 35, AM, 46; Univ Calif, Berkeley, PhD(soils), 53. *Prof Exp:* Asst agr econ, Univ Mo, 36-37, asst soils, 37-40, instr, 40-42 & 46-49, asst prof, 53-57; assoc prof agron, Univ Tenn, Knoxville, 57-67, prof plant & soil sci, 67-79. *Concurrent Pos:* Soil surv specialist, Natural Resources Sect, Gen Hq, Supreme Comdr Allied Powers, Tokyo, 46-47; Fulbright Award, Univ Ghent, 66-67. *Mem:* Fel AAAS; Am Soc Agron. *Res:* Soil formation and classification; physical, chemical and mineralogical studies of soils. *Mailing Add:* 1600 Autry Way Knoxville TN 37909

SPRINGER, MELVIN DALE, MATHEMATICAL STATISTICS. *Current Pos:* prof, EMER PROF INDUST ENG, UNIV ARK, FAYETTEVILLE, 84- *Personal Data:* b Saybrook, Ill, Sept 12, 18; m 48; c 1. *Educ:* Univ Ill, BS, 40, MS, 41, PhD(math statist), 47. *Prof Exp:* Asst math, Univ Ill, 41-44 & 46-47, instr, 47-48; asst prof, Mich State Col, 48-50; math statistician, Res Dept, US Naval Ord Plant, Ind, 50-56; sr opers analyst, Tech Opers, Inc, Va, 56-59; sr res statistician, Defense Res Labs, Gen Motors Corp, 59-67, dir reliability res & educ, A C Electronics Div, 67-68. *Mem:* Am Statist Asn; Math Asn Am. *Res:* Reliability theory and analysis; Bayesian statistics; experimental design; sampling theory; integral transforms in stochastic models; algebra of random variables. *Mailing Add:* Dept Indust Eng Univ Ark Fayetteville AR 72701

SPRINGER, PAUL FREDERICK, WILDLIFE RESEARCH, ORNITHOLOGY. *Current Pos:* RETIRED. *Personal Data:* b Chicago, Ill, Apr 25, 22; m 49, Virginia Haggerty; c James, Thomas, William & Peter. *Educ:* Univ Ill, AB, 43; Univ Wis, MS, 48; Cornell Univ, PhD(wildlife conserv), 61. *Prof Exp:* Waterfowl res biologist, State Natural Hist Surv, Ill, 47-48; wildlife res biologist, US Fish & Wildlife Serv, 48-58, chief sect wetland ecol, Patuxent Wildlife Res Ctr, 58-63, leader, SDak Coop Wildlife Res Unit, 63-67, asst dir, Northern Prairie Wildlife Res Ctr, US Bur Sport Fisheries & Wildlife, 67-72, biologist-in-charge, Wildlife Res Field Sta, 73-84. *Concurrent Pos:* Mem comt agr pests, Agr Bd, Nat Res Coun, 56-58; secy, Nat Mosquito Control-Fish & Wildlife Mgt Coord Comt, 60-63, mem, 72-73; vpres, Raptor Res Found, 67-68; mem vector control comt, Water Resources Coun, 72-73; adj prof wildlife mgt, Humboldt State Univ, 73-; mem, Aleutian Can Goose Recovery Team, 75- *Mem:* Wildlife Soc; Am Ornithologists Union; Cooper Ornith Soc; Wilson Ornith Soc. *Res:* Wintering population; distribution and ecology of Aleutian Canada geese; Waterfowl and wetland ecology and management; effects of mosquito control and chemical pesticides on wildlife; wildlife-estuarine relationships. *Mailing Add:* 1610 Panorama Dr Arcata CA 95521. *Fax:* 707-826-5555; *E-Mail:* pfs7001@axe.humboldt.edu

SPRINGER, ROBERT HAROLD, GASEOUS ELECTRONICS. *Current Pos:* RES PHYSICIST, LIGHTING RES & TECH SERV OPER, GEN ELEC CO, 65- *Personal Data:* b Downsville, Wis, Nov 7, 32; m 54; c 7. *Educ:* Univ Minn, BS, 58, MS, 60, PhD(elec eng), 65. *Mem:* Am Phys Soc. *Res:* All aspects of electrical discharges in gases related to light production; specializing in electrodes. *Mailing Add:* 6524 Duneden Ave Cleveland OH 44139

SPRINGER, TIMOTHY ALAN, LEUKOCYTE ADHESION. *Current Pos:* from asst prof to assoc prof, 77-89, LATHAM FAMILY PROF PATH, HARVARD MED SCH, 89- *Personal Data:* b Ft Benning, Ga, Feb 23, 48. *Educ:* Univ Calif, Berkeley, BA, 71; Harvard Univ, PhD(biochem & molecular biol), 76. *Honors & Awards:* Harvey Lectr, 91; 14th Ann Jim McGinnis Mem Lectr, Duke Univ, 92; Medal, Royal Soc Med, 94; Second Ann Norman Heatley Lectr, Univ Oxford, 94; William B Coley Award, Cancer Res Inst, 95; Marie T Bonazinga Award, Soc Leukocyte Biol, 95. *Prof Exp:* NIH res fel, Univ Cambridge, Eng & Lab Molecular Biol, Med Res Coun, 76-77. *Concurrent Pos:* Vis prof, Univ Mich, 80; assoc ed, J Immunol, 81-85, Molecular Biol of Cell, 92-96; chief, Lab Membrane Biol, Dana Farber Cancer Inst, Boston, 81-88; mem, Allergy & Immunol Study Sect, NIH, 86-90; vpres, Ctr Blood Res, Boston, 88-92; Burroughs-Wellcome vis prof, Royal Soc Med, London, 94; immunol panel mem, Howard Hughes Med Inst, 96; Wellcome vis prof, Wayne State Univ, 97. *Mem:* Nat Acad Sci; Am Asn Immunologists; Am Soc Bio Chemists; An Asn Pathologists; Soc Leukocyte Biol. *Res:* Adhesion receptors of the immune system; differentiation and function of high endothelial venules. *Mailing Add:* Dept Pathol Harvard Med Sch Ctr Blood Res 200 Longwood Ave Boston MA 02115. *Fax:* 617-278-3232

SPRINGER, VICTOR GRUSCHKA, BIOLOGY, MARINE SCIENCES. *Current Pos:* res assoc, 61-62, assoc cur, 63-66, supvr, 70-71 & 84-86, CUR, DIV FISHES, NAT MUS NATURAL HIST, SMITHSONIAN INST, 67- *Personal Data:* b Jacksonville, Fla, June 2, 28; m 65, Shirley Silverman; c Jessica & Eden. *Educ:* Emory Univ, AB, 48; Univ Miami, MS, 54; Univ Tex, PhD(vert zool), 57. *Honors & Awards:* Stoye Award, 57; Robert H Gibbs Jr Mem Award, Am Soc Ichthyologists & Herpetologists, 93. *Prof Exp:* Ichthyologist, Marine Lab, State Bd Conserv, Fla, 57-61. *Concurrent Pos:* Ed, Proc Biol Soc Wash, 65-67; res assoc, Moore Lab, Occidental Col, 71-72 & Bishop Mus, 84-; Nat Geog Soc grant, 73-74; Max & Victoria Dreyfus Found Grant, 80, 82 & 86; bd dirs, Nat Aquarium Baltimore, 79-85. *Mem:* Fel AAAS; Am Soc Ichthyologists & Herpetologists (treas, 65-67); Soc Syst Zool (treas, 78-80); Sigma Xi; Biol Soc Wash (pres, 73). *Res:* Systematics; zoogeography; ecology; life histories of tropical marine fishes. *Mailing Add:* Div Fishes US Nat Mus Natural Hist MRC-159 Washington DC 20560. *Fax:* 202-357-2986; *E-Mail:* springer.v@nmnh.si.edu

SPRINGER, WAYNE RICHARD, ADHESION MECHANISMS. *Current Pos:* res biochemist, 79-92, RES SAFETY OFFICER, VET AFFAIRS MED CTR, SAN DIEGO, 88-, CHEM HYG OFFICER, 93- *Personal Data:* b Milwaukee, Wis, Nov 16, 46; m 72, Jane Bradley; c Matthew & Katherine. *Educ:* Northwestern Univ, BA, 68; Univ Calif, Berkeley, PhD(biochem), 77. *Prof Exp:* Fel, Univ Calif, San Diego, 77-79, res biochemist, 79-92. *Concurrent Pos:* assoc proj scientist, Univ Calif, San Diego, 92- *Mem:* Am Soc Biochem & Molecular Biol; Am Soc Cell Biol. *Res:* Mechanisms of cell to cell and cell to substrate adhesion; integrin function in prostate cancer growth and metastasis. *Mailing Add:* Vet Affairs Med Ctr 3350 La Jolla Village Dr San Diego CA 92161-0001. *Fax:* 619-552-7436

SPRINGETT, BRIAN E, PHYSICS, MATERIALS SCIENCE ENGINEERING. *Current Pos:* scientist, 74-77, TECH MGR, XEROX CORP, 77- *Personal Data:* b Chatham, Eng, Apr 24, 36; m 63; c 2. *Educ:* Cambridge Univ, BA, 60, MA, 64; Univ Chicago, MS, 63, PhD(physics), 66. *Prof Exp:* Res assoc physics, Univ Chicago, 66-67; asst prof, Univ Mich, Ann Arbor, 67-72; vis prof, Univ Que, 72-73 & Oakland Univ, 73-74. *Concurrent Pos:* Assoc ed, Info Display Ser. *Mem:* AAAS; Am Phys Soc; Soc Imaging Sci & Technol. *Res:* Low temperature physics, gas discharges, ion and electron transport in dielectric media, amorphous photoconductors; electrophotographic sciences,; imaging and printing technologies; research administration. *Mailing Add:* Xerox Corp Bldg 103 800 Phillips Rd Webster NY 14580. *Fax:* 716-422-9358; *E-Mail:* brian_springett@wb.xerox.com, besker@juno.com

SPRINGFIELD, J, CIVIL ENGINEERING. *Honors & Awards:* Can-Am Amity Award, Am Soc Civil Engrs, 90; A B Anderson Award for Struct Eng, Can Soc Civil Eng, 91. *Mailing Add:* 194 Bayview Heights Dr Toronto ON M4G 2Z2 Can

SPRING-MILLS, ELINOR JANE, BREAST & PROSTATE CANCER. *Current Pos:* PROF ANAT, CELL BIOL & UROL, STATE UNIV NY, SYRACUSE, 77- *Educ:* Vassar Col, AB, 60; Mt Holyoke Col, MA, 62; Harvard Univ, PhD(med sci), 68. *Prof Exp:* Asst chief, Cell Biol Sect, Vet Admin Hosp, San Francisco, 70-77; from asst prof to assoc prof anat, Med Sch, Univ Calif, San Francisco, 70-77. *Mailing Add:* Dept Anat Cell & Biol Health Sci Ctr State Univ NY Syracuse NY 13078

SPRINGSTEEN, KATHRYN ROSE MOONEY, EDUCATION. *Current Pos:* From asst prof to assoc prof, 77-78, PROF & CHAIR NAT SCI, COLBY-SAWYER COL, 78- *Personal Data:* b Logan WVa, July 6, 49; m 71, Arthur W; c Anne E. *Educ:* Marshall Univ, BS, 71; WVa Univ, PhD(inorg chem), 77. *Concurrent Pos:* Vis scholar, Sch Pub Health, Harvard Univ, 91. *Mem:* Am Chem Soc; Nat Sci Teacher's Asn. *Res:* Development of lab and new teaching techniques for general chemistry. *Mailing Add:* Colby-Sawyer Col 100 Main St PO Box 1076 New London NH 03257. *Fax:* 603-526-2135

SPRINKLE, JAMES (THOMAS), INVERTEBRATE PALEONTOLOGY, ECHINODERM EVOLUTION. *Current Pos:* from asst prof to prof, 71-86, YAGER PROF GEOL, UNIV TEX, AUSTIN, 86- *Personal Data:* b Arlington, Mass, Sept 2, 43; m 68, Gloria Klizicki; c David & Diana. *Educ:* Mass Inst Technol, SB, 65; Harvard Univ, MA, 66, PhD(geol), 71. *Honors & Awards:* Schuchert Award, Paleont Soc, 82. *Prof Exp:* Nat Res Coun-US Geol Surv assoc, Paleont & Stratig Br, US Geol Surv, Denver, 70-71. *Concurrent Pos:* Prin investr, NSF grant, 77-80, 89-91, 93-94. *Mem:* AAAS; Paleont Soc; Geol Soc Am; Palaeont Asn England; Soc Syst Biol; Soc Sedimentary Geol. *Res:* Primitive echinoderms; blastoids; Paleozoic stratigraphy and invertebrate paleontology; echinoderm biology and evolution. *Mailing Add:* Dept Geol Sci Univ Tex Austin TX 78712. *Fax:* 512-471-9245; *E-Mail:* echino@mail.utexas.edu

SPRINKLE, JAMES KENT, JR, APPLIED NUCLEAR PHYSICS. *Current Pos:* STAFF MEM, LOS ALAMOS NAT LAB, 78- *Personal Data:* b Cambridge, MA, Nov 1, 52; m 82; c 2. *Educ:* State Univ NY, BS, 74; Univ Rochester, 76, MS, 77. *Prof Exp:* Res assoc, Argonne Nat Lab, 77-78. *Mem:* Am Phys Soc. *Res:* Develop instrument based on nuclear radiation which determine the quantity (mass) of radioactive isotope in various containers and matrics; instrument uranium and plutonium. *Mailing Add:* N1 E540 Los Alamos Nat Lab PO Box 1663 Los Alamos NM 87545. *Fax:* 505-665-4433

SPRINKLE, PHILIP MARTIN, OTOLARYNGOLOGY. *Current Pos:* assoc prof, 65-68, PROF OTOLARYNGOL & CHMN DEPT, MED CTR, W VA UNIV, 68- *Personal Data:* b Greensboro, NC, Aug 5, 26; m 55; c 2. *Educ:* Univ Va, MD, 53. *Honors & Awards:* Prof Dr Ignacio Barroquer Mem Award. *Prof Exp:* Intern, Virginia Mason Hosp, Seattle, Wash, 53-54; pvt pract, Va, 54-60; resident gen surg, Watts Hosp, Durham, NC, 60-61; resident otolaryngol, Hosp, Univ Va, 61-64, asst prof, 64-65. *Concurrent Pos:* Physician consult, Vet Admin Hosp & WVa Rehabil Ctr, 69- *Mem:* AMA; Am Acad Gen Pract; Am Acad Ophthal & Otolaryngol; Am Col Surgeons; Royal Soc Med; Sigma Xi. *Mailing Add:* RR 6 Box 10 State Rd 220 Martinsville VA 24112-8806

SPRINKLE, ROBERT SHIELDS, III, ORGANOLEPTIC EVALUATION. *Current Pos:* Chemist, 57-63, mgr prod develop, 63-65, supvr new prod div, 65-68, coordr res & develop, 68-76, dep dir res & develop, 76-78, dir, 78-80, vpres res & develop, 80-86, SR VPRES, RES & DEVELOP, AM TOBACCO CO, 86- *Personal Data:* b Martinsville, Va, Apr, 8, 35; m 61; c 3. *Educ:* Emory and Henry Col, BS, 57. *Mem:* Am Chem Soc. *Res:* Chemistry and composition of tobacco and tobacco smoke; pyrolytic products of combustion; applications of radioactive assay techniques for identification of particulates and gas phase constituents of tobacco smoke; spectroscopy; gas and liquid phase chromatography. *Mailing Add:* 9217 Groomfield Rd Richmond VA 23236

SPRINSON, DAVID BENJAMIN, BIOCHEMISTRY. *Current Pos:* from res assoc to prof, 48-78, EMER PROF BIOCHEM & MOLECULAR BIOPHYS, COL PHYSICIANS & SURGEONS, COLUMBIA UNIV, 78- *Personal Data:* b Russia, Apr 5, 10; nat US; m 43, Helen Evans Yeargain; c Joan, Mary & John. *Educ:* City Col New York, BS, 31; NY Univ, MS, 36; Columbia Univ, PhD(biochem), 46. *Hon Degrees:* ScD, Columbia Univ, 91. *Prof Exp:* Asst thyroid biochem, Chem Lab, Montefiore Hosp, 31-42. *Concurrent Pos:* Fulbright fel, Univ Paris, 52; Guggenheim fels, Stanford Univ, 57 & Univ Oxford, 60-61; career investr, Am Heart Asn, 58-75; vis scientist, NIH, 65; Brown-Hazen lect, NY State Dept Health, Albany, 69. *Mem:* Nat Acad Sci; Am Soc Biochem & Molecular Biol; Brit Biochem Soc; Am Chem Soc. *Res:* Intermediary metabolism of amino acids; biosynthesis of methyl groups and purines, aromatic compounds and sterols; regulation of metabolic pathways; mechanism of enzymic reactions. *Mailing Add:* 111 Leonia Ave Leonia NJ 07605

SPRITZ, NORTON, BIOCHEMISTRY. *Current Pos:* PROF MED, NY UNIV, 69- *Personal Data:* b Baltimore, Md, June 19, 28; c 1. *Educ:* Johns Hopkins Univ, AB, 48; Univ Md, MD, 52. *Prof Exp:* Asst med, Med Col, Cornell Univ, 52-54, from instr to assoc prof, 56-66; assoc prof, Rockefeller Univ, 66-69. *Concurrent Pos:* Intern, 2nd Cornell Med Div, Bellevue Hosp, 52-53, asst res, 53-54, fel cardiol, 56-57, chief res, 57-58, asst vis physician, 58-63, attend cardiorenal lab, 58-60, dir lipid metab lab, 63-66, vis physician, 64-; estab investr, Health Res Coun New York, 59-; clin asst, Mem Hosp, 60-; asst vis physician, James Ewing Hosp, 60-; asst attend, NY Hosp, 60-65, assoc attend, 65-; guest investr & asst physician, Rockefeller Univ, 61-63, assoc physician, 66-; chief med, NY Vet Admin Hosp, 69-; chief med serv, Manhattan Vet Hosp, 69- *Mem:* Am Soc Clin Invest; Am Fedn Clin Res; Am Diabetes Asn. *Res:* Lipid metabolism as related to human disorders and particularly atherosclerosis. *Mailing Add:* Manhattan Vet Admin Hosp First Ave & 24th St New York NY 10010

SPRITZ, RICHARD ANDREW, MEDICAL GENETICS, PEDIATRICS. *Current Pos:* asst prof, 81-86, ASSOC PROF MED GENETICS & PEDIAT, SCH MED, UNIV WIS, 86- *Personal Data:* b Philadelphia, Pa, Dec 19, 50; div. *Educ:* Univ Wis, BS, 72; Pa State Univ, MD, 76. *Prof Exp:* Intern pediat, Children's Hosp Philadelphia, Univ Pa, 76-77; resident, 77-78; fel, Dept Human Genetics, Sch Med, Yale Univ, 78-80. *Mem:* Am Soc Human Genetics; AAAS. *Res:* Molecular aspects of the structure, organization and control of human genes; molecular mechanisms of RNA processing; the molecular basis of human genetic disorders. *Mailing Add:* Univ Wis Genetics Lab 317 445 Henry Mall Madison WI 53706-1501

SPRITZER, ALBERT A, MEDICINE. *Current Pos:* RETIRED. *Personal Data:* b Brooklyn, NY, Apr 2, 27; m 53; c 3. *Educ:* Col Wooster, BS, 48; Albany Med Col, MD, 52; Univ Pittsburgh, MPH, 56. *Prof Exp:* Asst prof occup health, Grad Sch Pub Health, Univ Pittsburgh, 57-89, prof radiation health, 73-89. *Concurrent Pos:* Dept Health, Educ & Welfare res grant, 65-; consult, Babcox & Wilcox, Duquesne Light; med dir, Nuclear Energy Systs, Westinghouse Elec Corp, 70- *Mem:* Am Indust Hyg Asn; Health Physics Soc; AMA; Am Occup Health Asn. *Res:* Radiation biology; industrial radiation health practice; occupational health and radiation health research in pulmonary clearance; physiology and radiation hazard evaluation. *Mailing Add:* 9 Churchill Rd Verona PA 15147

SPRITZER, MICHAEL STEPHEN, ANALYTICAL CHEMISTRY. *Current Pos:* asst prof, 66-77, PROF CHEM, VILLANOVA UNIV, 77- *Personal Data:* b New York, NY, July 15, 39; m 64; c 2. *Educ:* Polytech Inst Brooklyn, BS, 60; Univ Mich, MS, 62, PhD(chem), 65. *Prof Exp:* Instr, Univ Mich, 65-66. *Mem:* AAAS; Am Chem Soc; Sigma Xi. *Res:* Electrochemical analysis; electrochemistry in nonaqueous media; organic polarography and voltammetry; electrochemical and photoelectrochemical energy storage. *Mailing Add:* Dept Chem Villanova Univ Villanova PA 19085. *Fax:* 610-519-7167; *E-Mail:* mspritze@email.uill.edu

SPROKEL, GERARD J, PHYSICAL CHEMISTRY. *Current Pos:* adv chemist, IBM Corp, 58-65, adv solid state, 65-70, adv, Components Div, 70-74, MEM RES STAFF, RES DIV, IBM CORP, 74- *Personal Data:* b Valkenburg, Netherlands, Aug 14, 21; US citizen; m 49. *Educ:* State Univ Utrecht, PhD(phys chem), 52. *Prof Exp:* Res chemist, Am Viscose Corp, Pa, 54-58. *Mem:* AAAS; Am Chem Soc; Electrochem Soc; Inst Elec & Electronics Engrs. *Res:* Diffusion and surface properties in semiconductors; semiconducting and scintillation counters; injection lasers; liquid crystals; materials research. *Mailing Add:* 2831 Castle Dr San Jose CA 95125

SPROTT, DAVID ARTHUR, MATHEMATICAL STATISTICS. *Current Pos:* assoc prof, 58-70, chmn dept & dean fac, 67-72, prof math, 70-, DISTINGUISHED EMER PROF, UNIV WATERLOO. *Personal Data:* b Toronto, Ont, May 31, 30. *Educ:* Univ Toronto, BA, 52, MA, 53, PhD, 55. *Prof Exp:* Asst, Comput Ctr, Univ Toronto, 52-53, Defence Res Bd, 54 & Galton Lab, Eng, 55-56. *Mem:* Am Math Soc; Inst Math Statist; Math Asn Am. *Res:* Mathematical genetics; experimental design; statistical inference. *Mailing Add:* Dept Statist & Math Univ Waterloo Waterloo ON N2L 3G1 Can

SPROTT, GEORGE F, PHYSICS. *Current Pos:* COMPUT SOFTWARE PROGRAMMER, IRIS ASSOC, 93- *Personal Data:* b Berkeley, Calif, July 22, 40. *Educ:* Occidental Col, Los Angeles, BA, 61; Columbia Univ, PhD(physics), 68. *Prof Exp:* Staff scientist, GenRad 72-93. *Mem:* Am Phys Soc. *Mailing Add:* 43 White Ave Concord MA 01742

SPROTT, GORDON DENNIS, BIOCHEMISTRY, IMMUNOLOGY. *Current Pos:* Fel, 73-75, asst res officer, 75-81, SR RES OFFICER, NAT RES COUN CAN, 88- *Personal Data:* b Badjeros, Ont, Feb 27, 45; m 68; c 2. *Educ:* Univ Guelph, BS, 68, MS, 70; McGill Univ, PhD(microbiol), 73. *Honors & Awards:* Can Soc Microbiol Award, 89. *Concurrent Pos:* Sect ed, Can J Microbiol, 86-89; adj prof, Ottawa Univ, 85-90, Univ Guelph, 86-91; sect ed, Can J Microbiol, 86-90. *Mem:* Am Soc Microbiol; Can Soc Microbiol (vpres), 96-97, pres, 97-98). *Res:* structures and catabolism of ether lipids unique to Archaea including archaeal extremophiles, and their application in biotechnology; archaeal lipids to produce stable liposomes (archaeosomes) for drug and vaccine delivery. *Mailing Add:* Inst Biol Sci Nat Res Coun Rm 3017 100 Sussex Dr Ottawa ON K1A 0R6 Can. *Fax:* 613-592-9092; *E-Mail:* dennis.sprott@nrc.ca

SPROTT, JULIEN CLINTON, PLASMA PHYSICS, NONLINEAR DYNAMICS. *Current Pos:* from asst prof to assoc prof, 72-79, PROF PHYSICS, UNIV WIS-MADISON, 79- *Personal Data:* b Memphis, Tenn, Sept 16, 42; m 65. *Educ:* Mass Inst Technol, BS, 64; Univ Wis, MS, 66, PhD(physics), 69. *Prof Exp:* Lectr elec eng & proj assoc physics, Univ Wis-Madison, 69-70; physicist, Thermonuclear Div, Oak Ridge Nat Lab, 70-72. *Concurrent Pos:* Consult, Oak Ridge Nat Lab, 72, McDonnell Douglas Corp, 77-80, Elec Power Res Inst, 78, TRW, 78-79, Argonne Nat Lab, 79-80 & Honeywell, 81; prin investr, Plasma Physics Contract, Univ Wis, US Dept Energy, 80-86. *Mem:* Fel Am Phys Soc; Am Asn Physics Teachers; Sigma Xi. *Res:* Plasma confinement and heating in toroidal and magnetic mirror fields; toroidal multipoles; tokamaks; bumpy torii, reversed field pinches; computer simulation of plasmas; ionospheric and extra-terrestrial plasmas and cosmic rays; chaos; complex systems. *Mailing Add:* Dept Physics Univ Wis Madison WI 53706. *E-Mail:* sprott@juno.physics.wisc.edu

SPROTT, RICHARD LAWRENCE, AGING, BEHAVIOR GENETICS. *Current Pos:* health scientist admin & aging, 80-81, br chief aging, 81-84, ASSOC DIR AGING, NAT INST AGING, NIH, 84- *Personal Data:* b Tampa, Fla, Aug 9, 40; m 65, Margaret Weidel; c Lynn & Deborah. *Educ:* Univ NC, AB, 62, MA, 64, PhD(psychol), 65. *Prof Exp:* Fel behav genetics, Jackson Lab, 65-67, assoc staff scientist, 69-71, staff scientist, 71-80; asst prof psychol, Oakland Univ, 67-69. *Concurrent Pos:* Mem, Comt Animal Models for Aging, Nat Res Coun, 78-79; head, Off Res Resources, Nat Inst Aging, 81-85. *Mem:* Am Psychol Asn; Behav Genetics Asn; Geront Asn Am. *Res:* Study of genetic determinants of behavior from maturity to senescence; stimulation and development of biological research on aging and the development of animal models for such research. *Mailing Add:* 11514 Regency Dr Potomac MD 20854. *Fax:* 301-402-0010

SPROUL, GORDON DUANE, COORDINATION POLYMERS. *Current Pos:* from asst prof to assoc prof, 75-86, PROF CHEM, UNIV SC, BEAUFORT, 86- *Personal Data:* b Edgewood, Md, Mar 6, 44; m 75, Nancy E Klemann; c Elise C, Karen E & Lacy D. *Educ:* Harvey Mudd Col, BS, 66; Univ Ill, MS, 69, PhD(chem), 71. *Prof Exp:* Fel chem, Tulane Univ, 71-72 & Univ SC, 72-75. *Concurrent Pos:* Consult, 82-; pres, SC Acad Sci, 90-91. *Mem:* Am Chem Soc; Sigma Xi. *Res:* Design and synthesis of trans-coordinating bidentate tetradentate liqands for coordination polymer formation; studies of electronegativity relationships. *Mailing Add:* 980 Edith Lane Beaufort SC 29902. *Fax:* 803-521-4198

SPROUL, OTIS J, ENVIRONMENTAL ENGINEERING. *Current Pos:* DEAN, COL ENG & PHYS SCIS & PROF CIVIL ENG, UNIV NH, 82- *Personal Data:* b Dover Foxcroft, Maine, July 9, 30; m 52, Dorothy Estabrook; c Bryce J & Dana C (deceased). *Educ:* Univ Maine, BS, 52, MS, 57; Wash Univ, St Louis, ScD(sanit eng), 61. *Honors & Awards:* Rudolph Hering Award, Am Soc Civil Engrs, 71. *Prof Exp:* Instr civil eng, Univ Maine, 55-57, asst prof, 57-59; trainee sanit eng, Wash Univ, St Louis, 59-61; from assoc prof to prof civil eng, Univ Maine, 61-77; prof & chmn, Dept Civil Eng, Ohio State Univ, 77-82. *Concurrent Pos:* Consult engr, Environ Control Prob & Expert Witness. *Mem:* Am Water Works Asn; Int Ozone Assn; Water Environ Fed; Am Soc Eng Educ; Nat Soc Prof Engrs. *Res:* Virus, bacteria and cyst inactivation by water and wastewater treatment processes; industrial air and water pollution control. *Mailing Add:* Kingsbury Hall Col Eng/Phys Sci Univ NH Durham NH 03824. *Fax:* 603-862-2486

SPROUL, WILLIAM DALLAS, REACTIVE SPUTTERING, UNBALANCED MAGNETRON SPUTTERING. *Current Pos:* GROUP LEADER, BIRL, NORTHWESTERN UNIV, 87- *Personal Data:* b Fitchburg, Mass, Mar 14, 43; m 68; c 2. *Educ:* Brown Univ, ScB, 66, ScM, 68, PhD(mat eng), 75. *Prof Exp:* Scientist, Am Can Corp, 75-77; sr engr, Borg-Warner Corp, 77-87. *Concurrent Pos:* Co-ed, Physics & Chem Protective Coatings, 85; gen chmn, Int Conf Metall Coatings, 87-88 & 90; bd dir, Am Vacuum Soc, 90-91, chmn, Vacuum Metall Div, 91. *Mem:* Am Soc Metals Int. *Res:* Sputtering of hard, wear and corrosion resistant coatings; invented the high-rate reactive sputtering process. *Mailing Add:* 500 S Bristol Ct Palatine IL 60067

SPROULE, BRIAN J, MEDICINE, THORACIC DISEASES. *Current Pos:* from instr to prof, 59-91, head, Div Respiratory Dis, 70-91, EMER PROF MED, UNIV ALTA, 91- *Personal Data:* b Calgary, Alta, Oct 31, 25; m 55, Marnie MacKay; c Timothy, Shannon, John & Friol. *Educ:* Univ Alta, BSc, 49, MD, 51, MSc, 55; FRCPS(C). *Honors & Awards:* Achievement Award, Royal Col, 96. *Prof Exp:* Instr med, Southwestern Med Sch, Univ Tex, Dallas, 55-59. *Concurrent Pos:* Consult, Can Dept Vet Affairs, 60-; chmn, Dept Med, Am Col Chest Physicians, 75-76, gov, 76-78; gov, Am Col Physicians, 79-83. *Mem:* Fel Am Col Chest Physicians; fel Am Col Physicians; Am Fedn Clin Res; Can Soc Clin Invest; Royal Col Physicians & Surgeons Can (vpres). *Res:* Pulmonary mechanics; blood gas derangements in chronic lung disease. *Mailing Add:* Dept Med Sch Med Univ Alta 2E436 W C McKenzie Ctr Edmonton AB T6G 2B7 Can. *Fax:* 403-492-3606

SPROULL, ROBERT FLETCHER, COMPUTER SCIENCE. *Current Pos:* FEL, SUN MICROSYSTEMS, INC. *Personal Data:* b Ithaca, NY, June 6, 47; m 71, Lee Sonastine. *Educ:* Harvard Col, AB, 68; Stanford Univ, MS, 70, PhD(comput sci), 77. *Prof Exp:* Staff programmer artificial intel, Stanford Univ, 69-70; comput specialist, Div Comput Res & Technol, NIH, 70-72; mem res staff comput sci, Xerox Palo Alto Res Ctr, 73-77; from asst prof to assoc prof, Carnegie-Mellon Univ, 77-84; vpres, Sutherland, Sproull & Assoc, 79-90. *Concurrent Pos:* Mem tech adv coun, R R Donnelly & Sons, 81-89; adj prof comput sci, Carnegie-Mellon Univ, 84-92. *Mem:* Nat Acad Eng; Inst Elec & Electronic Engrs; Asn Comput Mach. *Res:* Computer graphics; large-scale integrated circuits. *Mailing Add:* Sun Microsysts Inc 2 Elizabeth Dr Chelmsford MA 01824. *E-Mail:* rsproull@east.sun.com

SPROULL, ROBERT LAMB, GENERAL PHYSICS. *Current Pos:* vpres & provost, Univ Rochester, 68-70, pres, 70-84, chief exec officer, 74-84, EMER PRES & PROF PHYSICS, UNIV ROCHESTER, 84- *Personal Data:* b Lacon, Ill, Aug 16, 18; m 42, Mary L Knickerbocker; c Robert F & Nancy M (Highbarger). *Educ:* Cornell Univ, BA, 40, PhD(exp physics), 43. *Hon Degrees:* LLD, Nazareth Col, 83. *Prof Exp:* Physicist, RCA Labs, NJ, 43-46; from asst prof to prof physics, Cornell Univ, 46-68, dir, Lab Atomic & Solid State Physics, 59-60, dir, Mat Sci Ctr, 60-63, vpres acad affairs, 65-68. *Concurrent Pos:* Part-time instr, Princeton Univ & Univ Pa, 43-45; pres, Telluride Asn, 45-47; mem, Solid State Sci Adv Panel, Off Naval Res & later Nat Acad Sci, 50-68; physicist, Oak Ridge Nat Lab, 52 & Europ Res Assocs, Belg, 58-59; ed, J Appl Physics, 54-57; trustee, Assoc Univs, Inc, 62-63; dir, Advan Res Projs Agency, Dept Defense, 63-65; mem, Bd Dirs, John Wiley Sons, Inc, NY, 65-89; mem, Lab Mgt Coun, Oak Ridge Nat Lab, 65-75, chmn coun, 71-73; mem, Defense Sci Bd, 66-70, chmn bd, 68-70; mem, Statutory Vis Comt, Nat Bur Stand, 66-71, chmn comt, 68-71; trustee, Deep Springs Col, 67-74 & 82-86; mem, Sci Adv Comt, Gen Motors Corp, 71-80, chmn, 73-80; mem, Bd Dirs, United Technol Corp, 72-89, Xerox Corp, 76-89, Sybron Corp, 72-85 & Bausch & Lomb Corp, 82-89; trustee, Cornell Univ, 72-77; mem, Bd Dir, Commonwealth Fund, 79-89 & Inst Defense anal, 85-91. *Mem:* Fel AAAS; Am Phys Soc; Am Acad Arts & Sci. *Res:* Thermionic electron emission; microwave radar; experimental solid state physics; imperfections in nonmetallic crystals, especially in barium oxide; low temperature physics; phonon scattering. *Mailing Add:* 16910 Bay St E402 Jupiter FL 33477

SPROUSE, GENE DENSON, ATOMIC & MOLECULAR PHYSICS. *Current Pos:* from asst prof to assoc prof, 73-77, PROF PHYSICS, STATE UNIV NY, STONY BROOK, 77- *Personal Data:* b Litchfield, Ill, May 7, 41; m 65; c 2. *Educ:* Mass Inst Technol, BS, 63; Stanford Univ, MS, 65, PhD(physics), 68. *Honors & Awards:* Humboldt Prize, Am Phys Soc. *Prof Exp:* Res assoc physics, Stanford Univ, 67-69, asst prof, 69-70. *Concurrent Pos:* Fel, Alfred P Sloan Found, 72-74; dir, Nuclear Struct Lab, 84-86, chmn, 90- *Mem:* Fel Am Phys Soc. *Res:* Hyperfine interactions; perturbed angular correlations; recoil implantation; laser spectroscopy. *Mailing Add:* Dept Physics State Univ NY Stony Brook NY 11794-3800. *Fax:* 516-632-8176; *E-Mail:* gsprouse@sunysb.edu

SPROW, FRANK BARKER, petroleum & synthetic fuels, for more information see previous edition

SPROWLES, JOLYON CHARLES, ELECTROPLATING, PHYSICAL INORGANIC CHEMISTRY. *Personal Data:* b Columbia, SC, July 6, 44; m 68; c 3. *Educ:* Princeton Univ, AB, 66; Cornell Univ, PhD(inorg chem), 73. *Prof Exp:* Asst prof chem, Williams Col, 70-72; res assoc, Purdue Univ, 72-74; vis asst prof, Univ Mo, Columbia, 74-75; asst prof, Bates Col, 75-82; process engr, Maine Electronics Inc, 82-89. *Mem:* Am Chem Soc. *Res:* Electroplating; uses of plasma in manufacturing; vibrational spectroscopic studies of equilibria and structure in solutions of organometallic cations and weak Lewis base anions. *Mailing Add:* 80 Boyer Rd Stafford Springs CT 06076-4108

SPROWLS, DONALD O(TTE), CHEMICAL ENGINEERING, METALLURGY. *Current Pos:* RETIRED. *Personal Data:* b Arnold, Pa, Sept 9, 19; m 44; c 4. *Educ:* Drexel Inst Technol, BS, 43. *Honors & Awards:* Sam Tour Award, Am Soc Testing & Mat. *Prof Exp:* Technician, Chem Metall Div, Alcoa Res Labs, Pittsburgh, 36-43, res engr, 43-64, head stress corrosion sect, 64-77, assoc engr, Alcoa Tech Ctr, 77-82. *Concurrent Pos:* Consult aluminum corrosion, 83- *Mem:* Am Soc Testing & Mat. *Res:* Corrosion and stress corrosion of aluminum alloys. *Mailing Add:* 4419 Seventh Street Rd New Kensington PA 15068

SPROWLS, RILEY CLAY, STATISTICS. *Current Pos:* from asst prof statist to prof bus statist, 51-71, PROF COMPUT & INFO SYSTS, UNIV CALIF, LOS ANGELES, 71- *Personal Data:* b Medina, NY, July 22, 21; m 50; c 2. *Educ:* Univ Chicago, PhD(statist), 51. *Prof Exp:* Instr statist, Univ Chicago, 49-51. *Mem:* Am Statist Asn. *Res:* Business statistics; electronic computers. *Mailing Add:* 12112 La Casa Lane Los Angeles CA 90049

SPRUCH, GRACE MARMOR, SCIENCE EDUCATION, SCIENCE WRITING. *Current Pos:* assoc prof physics, 69-75, PROF PHYSICS, RUTGERS UNIV, 75- *Personal Data:* b Brooklyn, NY, Nov 19, 26; m 50, Larry Spruch. *Educ:* Brooklyn Col, BA, 47; Univ Pa, MS, 49; NY Univ, PhD(physics), 55. *Prof Exp:* Res asst physics, Univ Pa, 47-48, asst instr, 48-49; res asst, NY Univ, 52-55, assoc res scientist, 55-56; instr physics, Cooper Union, 57-58; assoc res scientist, NY Univ, 58-63; Am Asn Univ Women fel, Oxford Univ, 63-64; vis assoc prof, Rutgers Univ, 64-65; assoc res scientist, NY Univ, 65-67, res scientist, 67-68. *Concurrent Pos:* Secy, Int Conf Luminescence, NY Univ, 61; writer, ed & translator; hon res assoc appl sci, Harvard Univ, 77-78; hon assoc, Neiman Found for Jour, 77-78; fel, Ctr Energy & Environ Studies, Princeton Univ, 81; mem, interview team for china, US Physics exam & appln prog, Peoples Repub China, 85-86; fel, Ctr Technol Studies, NJ Inst Technol, 86-87; NJ Humanities Grant, Dept Higher Educ, 90-91; partic, Andrew W Mellon Humanities Sem Vis Scholars, NY Univ, 90-91. *Mem:* Am Phys Soc. *Res:* Luminescence, photoconductivity and applications to biophysics; light scattering; science writing. *Mailing Add:* Dept Physics Rutgers Univ 101 Warren St Newark NJ 07102. *Fax:* 973-648-1434; *E-Mail:* spruch@andromeda.rutgers.edu

SPRUCH, LARRY, THEORETICAL PHYSICS. *Current Pos:* from asst prof to assoc prof, 50-61, PROF PHYSICS, FAC ARTS & SCI, NY UNIV, 61- *Personal Data:* b Brooklyn, NY, Jan 1, 23; m 50. *Educ:* Brooklyn Col, BA, 43; Univ Pa, PhD(physics), 48. *Honors & Awards:* von Humboldt Sr Award, 85 & 88. *Prof Exp:* From asst instr to instr physics, Univ Pa, 43-46, Tyndale fel, 46-48; Atomic Energy Comn fel, Mass Inst Technol, 48-50. *Concurrent Pos:* Consult, Lawrence Radiation Lab, 59-66; NSF sr fel, Univ London & Oxford Univ, 63-64; vis prof, Inst Theoret Phys, Univ Colo, 61 & 68; correspondent, Comments on Atomic & Molecular Physics, 72-; mem, Inst Advan Study, 81-82; deleg, China US Physics Exam & Appln, 85 & 86; mem adv bd, Inst Theoret Atomic & Molecular Physics, Harvard-Smithsonian Ctr Astrophys, 89-91. *Mem:* Fel Am Phys Soc. *Res:* Beta decay; nuclear moments; isomeric transitions; internal conversion; atomic and nuclear scattering; variational principles; astrophysics; charge transfer; Thomas-Fermi theory; radiative corrections; atoms in magnetic fields; Levinson's theorem; casimir interactions; semi-classical radiation theory. *Mailing Add:* Dept Physics Meyer Bldg NY Univ Four Washington Pl N New York NY 10003. *Fax:* 212-995-4016

SPRUGEL, DOUGLAS GEORGE, FOREST ECOLOGY, PHYSIOLOGICAL ECOLOGY. *Current Pos:* sr res assoc, 83-87, res assoc prof, 87-90, PROF, COL FOREST RES, UNIV WASH, 90- *Personal Data:* b Ames, Iowa, Feb 18, 48; m 84, Katherine S Hilliker; c Bennett G & Peter F. *Educ:* Duke Univ, BS, 69; Yale Univ, MPhil, 71, PhD(plant ecol), 74. *Honors & Awards:* Mercer Award, Ecol Soc Am, 77. *Prof Exp:* Lectr ecol, Univ Pa, 73-74; res assoc, Argonne Nat Lab, 74-76, asst ecologist, 76-79; asst prof, Dept Forestry, Mich State Univ, 79-82. *Mem:* Ecol Soc Am (vpres, 88, pres, 89); Am Inst Biol Sci; AAAS; Int Asn Veg Sci. *Res:* Effects of natural and human disturbance on natural ecosystems; tree ecophysiology; woody-tissue respiration; techniques for scaling physiological measurements up to stand level. *Mailing Add:* Col Forest Res AR-10 Univ Wash 3900 Seventh Ave NE Seattle WA 98195-0001. *E-Mail:* sprugel@u.washington.edu

SPRUGEL, GEORGE, JR, ZOOLOGY, ECOLOGY. *Current Pos:* chief, 66-80, EMER CHIEF, ILL NATURAL HIST SURV, 80- *Personal Data:* b Boston, Mass, Sept 26, 19; m 45, Catharine B Cornwell; c Douglas G. *Educ:* Iowa State Col, BS, 46, MS, 47, PhD(econ zool), 50. *Honors & Awards:* Distinguished Serv Citation, Ecol Soc Am, 76. *Prof Exp:* From instr to asst prof zool & entom, Iowa State Col, 46-54; spec asst to asst dir biol & med sci, NSF, 53-54, prog dir environ biol, 54-64; chief scientist, Nat Park Serv, 64-66. *Concurrent Pos:* Asst & actg head, Biol Br, Off Naval Res, 51-53; mem adv comt environ biol, NSF, 65 & Nat Res Coun, 68-71; prog dir conserv ecosyst, US Int Biol Prog, 69-72; mem life sci comt, NASA, 73-78. *Mem:* AAAS (vpres, biol sci, 71); Am Soc Zoologists (secy, 70-72); Ecol Soc Am (vpres, 68); Am Inst Biol Sci (vpres, 73, pres, 74). *Res:* Aquatic ecology; fish growth; animal population dynamics. *Mailing Add:* 2710 S First St Champaign IL 61820

SPRUIELL, JOSEPH E(ARL), MATERIALS SCIENCE, ENGINEERING. *Current Pos:* From asst prof to assoc prof metall eng, 63-71, PROF METALL ENG & POLYMER ENG, UNIV TENN, KNOXVILLE, 71-, HEAD DEPT MAT SCI & ENG, 85- *Personal Data:* b Knoxville, Tenn, Oct 13, 35; m 58, Rhonda P Ownby; c Teresa & Janet. *Educ:* Univ Tenn, BS, 58, MS, 60, PhD(metall eng), 63. *Concurrent Pos:* Consult, Metals & Ceramics Div, Oak Ridge Nat Lab, 60-77. *Mem:* Fel Am Soc Metals; Sigma Xi; fel Soc Plastics Engrs; Int Polymer Processing Soc; Fiber Soc. *Res:* X-ray diffraction; physical metallurgy; polymer science; polymer processing; structure/property/processing relationships. *Mailing Add:* Dept Mat Sci & Eng 434 Dougherty Eng Bldg Univ Tenn Knoxville TN 37996

SPRUILL, NANCY LYON, PLANNING, PROGRAMMING & BUDGETING. *Current Pos:* sr analyst planning, prog & budgeting, Manpower, Installations & Logistics, 83-85, assoc dir intergovernmental affairs, Force Mgt & Personnel, Off Asst Secy Defense, 85-94, OFF SECY DEFENSE ADI/AR, DEPT DIR ACQUISITION RESOURCE, 94- *Personal Data:* b Takoma Park, Md, Mar 24, 49; m 69. *Educ:* Univ Md, BS, 71; George Washington Univ, MA, 75, PhD(math statist), 80. *Honors & Awards:* Jerome Cornfield Award, 80. *Prof Exp:* Proj dir, Ctr Naval Anal, 71-83. *Concurrent Pos:* Assoc prof/lectr, Statist Dept, George Washington Univ, 78-79. *Mem:* Am Statist Asn. *Res:* Resource implications of changes in Department of Defense policies and procedures, including changes recommended by Congress and organizations outside of the Department; measures of defense capability; confidentiality of different kinds of data releases. *Mailing Add:* Rm 1E 474 3000 Defense Pentagon Washington DC 20301-3000

SPRULES, WILLIAM GARY, AQUATIC ECOLOGY. *Current Pos:* From asst prof to assoc prof, 70-84, vprin res & grad studies, 86-89, PROF ZOOL, ERINDALE COL, UNIV TORONTO, 84- *Personal Data:* b Hamilton, Ont, Nov 5, 44; m 67; c 3. *Educ:* Queen's Univ, Ont, BSc, 66; Princeton Univ, MA, 68, PhD(ecol), 70. *Concurrent Pos:* Operating grant, Nat Sci & Eng Res Coun Can, Donner Can Found, Wildlife Toxicol Fund. *Mem:* Ecol Soc Am; Am Soc Limnol & Oceanog; Int Asn Theoret & Appl Limnol; Freshwater Biol Asn, Eng; Can Soc Zoologists; Can Soc Limnologists. *Res:* Size structure of aquatic plankton communities; aquatic food webs; zooplankton behavior. *Mailing Add:* Erindale Col Univ Toronto 3359 Mississauga Rd Mississauga ON L5L 1C6 Can

SPRUNG, DONALD WHITFIELD LOYAL, NUCLEAR PHYSICS, NANOSCOPIC SYSTEMS. *Current Pos:* from asst prof to assoc prof physics, McMaster Univ, 62-71, dean fac sci, 75-84 & 89, chair, Dept Physics & Astron, 91-97, PROF PHYSICS, MCMASTER UNIV, 71- *Personal Data:* b Kitchener, Ont, June 6, 34; m 58, Hannah Sueko Nagai; c 2. *Educ:* Univ Toronto, BA, 57; Univ Birmingham, PhD(physics), 61, DSc, 77. *Honors & Awards:* Herzberg Medal, 72. *Prof Exp:* Instr physics, Cornell Univ, 61-62. *Concurrent Pos:* Mem res staff, Lab Nuclear Sci, Mass Inst Technol, 64-65; C D Howe fel, Orsay, France, 69-70; guest prof, Univ Tuebingen, Ger, 80-81; exchange prof, Univ Mainz, Ger, 90-91; vis prof, Univ Barcelona, Spain, 91 & 95; exchange prof, Sendai, Tokyo & Kyoto, 85, Melbourne, 86. *Mem:* Am Phys Soc; Can Asn Physicists; Brit Inst Physics; fel Royal Soc Can. *Res:* Nucleon-nucleon interaction; effective force in finite nuclei; nuclear structure and forces theory; theory of mesoscopic systems. *Mailing Add:* Dept Physics & Astron ABB-348 McMaster Univ 1280 Main St W Hamilton ON L8S 4M1 Can. *E-Mail:* dwsprung@mcmaster.ca

SPRUNG, JOSEPH ASHER, ORGANIC CHEMISTRY. *Current Pos:* RETIRED. *Personal Data:* b Wahpeton, NDak, Dec 25, 15; m 44, Helen Rochlin; c Laurel. *Educ:* Univ Minn, BChem, 38, MS, 39, PhD(org chem), 43. *Prof Exp:* Res chemist, Cent Res Lab, GAF Corp, Pa, 43-47, group leader photog sect, 47-51, sr res specialist, Photog Div, 51-61, mgr, Photog Emulsion Tech Dept, 61-62, assoc dir res & develop, 62-64, sr scientist, Photog Div, 64-80, tech consult photog sci & technol, 80. *Mem:* Fel AAAS; Am Chem Soc; Soc Imaging Sci & Technol. *Res:* Synthesis of vitamin E and vitamin A intermediates; color photography processes; photographic emulsions. *Mailing Add:* 16 Devon Blvd Binghamton NY 13903

SPRUNT, EVE SILVER, GEOPHYSICS, GEOLOGY. *Current Pos:* RES ASSOC, MOBIL RES & DEVELOP CORP, 78- *Personal Data:* b Brooklyn, NY, July 9, 51; m 73; c Alexander & Elsa. *Educ:* Mass Inst Technol, SB, 72, SM, 73; Stanford Univ, PhD(geophys), 77. *Prof Exp:* Res assoc, Stanford Univ, 76-78. *Concurrent Pos:* Chmn, API Subcomt Core Analysis, 89-; mem bd dirs, Soc Petrol Engrs, 91-94; sr tech ed, 93-96; columnist, 96-; Mass Inst Technol Vis Comt Sponsored Res; Color Sch Mines vis comt, Dept Petrol Engrs. *Mem:* Am Geophys Union; Geol Soc Am; Soc Explor Geophysicists; Soc Petrol Engrs; Soc Prof Well Log Analysts; Soc Core Analysts. *Res:* Rock physics, specifically solution transfer; quartz cathoduluminescence; porosity; permeability; velocity; scanning electron microscopy; hydraulic fracturing; core analysis; formation damage. *Mailing Add:* Mobil Oil Corp PO Box 650232 Dallas TX 75265-0232. *Fax:* 214-951-2104; *E-Mail:* essprunt@dal.mobil.com

SPRY, ROBERT JAMES, SOLID STATE PHYSICS, OPTICS. *Current Pos:* RES PHYSICIST, AIR FORCE MAT LAB, WRIGHT-PATTERSON AFB, 67-; ADJ PROF, WRIGHT STATE UNIV, 86- *Personal Data:* b Dayton, Ohio, Feb 12, 38; m 69; c 4. *Educ:* Univ Ill, Urbana, BS, 60, MS, 62, PhD(solid state physics), 67. *Prof Exp:* Res asst solid state physics, Univ Ill, Urbana, 62-67. *Mem:* Am Phys Soc; Sigma Xi. *Res:* Optical properties of semiconductors; radiation damage; infrared spectroscopy; optical sensors; laser technology; low temperature physics; electro-optics, patent law. *Mailing Add:* 5830 Worley Rd West Milton OH 45383

SPUDICH, JAMES ANTHONY, BIOCHEMISTRY. *Current Pos:* prof, Dept Cell Biol, Sch Med, Stanford Univ, 77-79, chmn & prof, 79-84, prof, 84-92, PROF, DEPT DEVELOP BIOL, SCH MED, STANFORD UNIV, 89-, PROF, DEPT BIOCHEM, 92-, CHMN & PROF, 94- *Personal Data:* b Collinsville, Ill, Jan 7, 42; m 64; c 2. *Educ:* Univ Ill, Urbana, BS, 63; Stanford Univ, PhD(biochem), 67. *Honors & Awards:* Basic Res Prize, Am Heart Asn, 91; Clayton S White Lectr, Okla Med Res Found, 91; First Ann Frank Pepe Lectr, Univ Pa, 93; Mayer Lectr, Mass Inst Technol, 95; John S Colter Lectr Biochem, 95; Lifetime Res Award Career Award, Biophys Soc, 95; Lewis S Rosenstiel Award, 96; Repligen Corp Award in Chem Biol Processes, Div Biol Chem, Am Chem Soc, 96. *Prof Exp:* USPHS trainee, Stanford Univ, 68; USAF Off Sci Res fel, Cambridge Univ, 69 & NSF fel, 70; from asst prof to prof, Dept Biochem & Biophys, Univ Calif, San Francisco, 71-77. *Concurrent Pos:* Am Cancer Soc res grant, Univ Calif, San Francisco, 70. *Mem:* Nat Acad Sci; AAAS; Am Soc Cell Biol (pres, 89); Am Soc Biol Chem & Molecular Biol;

Biophys Soc. *Res:* Molecular basis of mitosis, amoeboid movement and other forms of cell mobility; regulation of actin & myosin interaction & their assembly states; roles of actin and myosin in vivo; contraction of mammalian muscle. *Mailing Add:* Dept Biochem Beckman Ctr Rm 8400 Stanford Univ Sch Med Stanford CA 94305-5307

SPUDIS, PAUL D, PLANETARY SCIENCE, LUNAR GEOLOGY. *Current Pos:* STAFF SCIENTIST PLANETARY SCI, LUNAR & PLANETARY INST, 90- *Personal Data:* b Bowling Green, Ky, Aug 29, 52; m 82, Anne Seaborne; c Janelle & Diane. *Educ:* Ariz State Univ, BS, 76, PhD(geol), 82; Brown Univ, ScM, 77. *Prof Exp:* Res assoc, NASA-Ames Res Ctr, 77-78; geologist, US Geol Surv, 80-90. *Concurrent Pos:* Vis scientist, Univ Hawaii, 80, Univ Col, London, 80 & Nat Air & Space Mus, 91; explor sci planner, White House, 90-91; consult, Lawrence Livermore Nat Labs, 92-94; adj assoc prof geol, Rice Univ, 92- *Mem:* Am Geophys Union; Geol Soc Am; Sigma Xi. *Res:* Study of the geological history and evolution of the moon; geological processes of impact and volcanism on the terrestrial planets. *Mailing Add:* Lunar Planetary Inst 3600 Bay Area Blvd Houston TX 77058. *Fax:* 281-486-2162; *E-Mail:* spudis@lpi.jsc.nasa.gov

SPULLER, ROBERT L, PROTOZOOLOGY, PARASITOLOGY. *Current Pos:* asst prof, 68-70, assoc prof, 70-74, chmn div natural sci & math, 75-79, actg dean acad affairs, 77-78, PROF BIOL, LENOIR-RHYNE COL, 75-, CHMN DEPT, 68- *Personal Data:* b Shelbyville, Ind, Aug 21, 37; m 59; c 2. *Educ:* Purdue Univ, BS, 59, MS, 60; Univ Mich, MS, 63, PhD(zool), 68. *Prof Exp:* Teacher high sch, Ind, 60-62. *Mem:* AAAS; Soc Protozool; Sigma Xi; Am Soc Zool. *Res:* Electron microscopy of ciliated protozoa; ecological relationships in the protozoa. *Mailing Add:* Dean Acad Affairs Lenoir-Rhyne Col Hickory NC 28601-3976

SPURGEON, WILLIAM MARION, PHYSICAL CHEMISTRY. *Current Pos:* DIR MFG ENG PROG, UNIV MICH, DEARBORN, 85- *Personal Data:* b Quincy, Ill, Dec 5, 17; m 41, Richarda Neuberg; c William, Richard & Ben. *Educ:* Univ Ill, BS, 38; Univ Mich, MS, 39, PhD(phys chem), 41. *Honors & Awards:* Colwell Award, Soc Automotive Engrs, 67; Siegel Award, Soc Mfg Engrs, 81. *Prof Exp:* Res chemist, Tex Co, NY, 41-42 & 46; asst prof appl sci, Univ Cincinnati, 46-48; res dir & vpres, Am Fluresit Co, Ohio, 47-54; mgr phys chem unit, Flight Propulsion Lab Dept, Gen Elec Co, 54-59; mgr mat & processes dept, Res Labs, Bendix Corp, 59-73, dir mfg qual control, Home Systs Res, Res Labs, 73-78, sr res planner, 78-80; dir prod res prog, NSF, 80-85. *Concurrent Pos:* Mem, Nat Mat Adv Bd, 78-80. *Mem:* Am Chem Soc; Am Soc Metals; fel Soc Mfg Engrs; Sigma Xi; Soc Auto Engrs. *Res:* Catalysis; solubility; fluid flow; building materials; ophthalmology; corrosion; coatings; thermal properties; semiconductors; friction materials; composites; separation processes; manufacturing processes; unit operations of manufacturing. *Mailing Add:* 24799 Edgemont Rd Southfield MI 48034. *Fax:* 248-356-2609

SPURLOCK, CAROLA HENRICH, CHROMATOGRAPHY, SPECTROPHOTOMETRY. *Current Pos:* RETIRED. *Personal Data:* b Detroit, Mich, July 24, 26; m 54, Harry V; c Margaret A (Prince) & Charles F. *Educ:* Univ Detroit, BS, 48, MS, 50. *Prof Exp:* Asst chemist phys chem, Parke Davis & Co, 50-69, assoc chemist, 69-78; scientist anal serv, Warner-Lambert/Parke Davis, 78-86. *Mem:* Am Chem Soc. *Res:* Ultraviolet-visible spectrophotometry, chromatography, potentiometric titration and instrumental analytical methods. *Mailing Add:* PO Box 122 Hawks MI 49743

SPURLOCK, JACK MARION, CHEMICAL ENGINEERING, BIOMEDICAL ENGINEERING. *Current Pos:* EXEC VPRES, SPURLOCK INFO TECHNOL ASSOCS, 95- *Personal Data:* b Tampa, Fla, Aug 16, 30; m 52, 95, Diane Kluska; c 4. *Educ:* Univ Fla, BChE, 52; Ga Inst Technol, MSChE, 58, PhD(chem eng), 61. *Honors & Awards:* M A Ferst Res Award, 61. *Prof Exp:* Qual control engr, Auto-Lite Battery Co, Ga, 54-55; res engr, Eng Exp Sta, Ga Inst Technol, 55-58, asst prof chem eng, Sch Chem Eng, 58-62; mgr, Aerospace Sci Lab, Orlando Div, Martin Co, 62-64; chief, Eng Res Group, Atlantic Res Corp, 64-69; pres, Health & Safety Res Inst, 69-74; prin res engr, Eng Exp Sta & assoc dir, Appl Sci Lab, Ga Inst Technol, 74-79, dir, Off Interdisciplinary Prog, 79-83, assoc vpres res, 83-85; pres, Cetrest Corp, 85-88; pres, S&A Automated Systs, Inc, 90-95. *Concurrent Pos:* Biomed eng consult, T A Jones Assocs, 71-74. *Mem:* Am Inst Chem Eng; fel Royal Soc Health; Am Chem Soc; Aerospace Med Asn; fel Am Inst Chem. *Res:* Acoustical effects on transport phenomena; conduction and convection heat transfer; vacuum environmental effects on liquid propellants; biomedical transport phenomena and instrumentation; chemical process economics; energy conservation; research management; alcohol fuels technology; systems design and analysis; rehabilitation technology for the disabled; computer-based training; spacecraft life support systems. *Mailing Add:* PO Box 490143 Leesburg FL 34749-0143

SPURLOCK, LANGLEY AUGUSTINE, ORGANIC CHEMISTRY. *Current Pos:* dir biomed & environ, Spec Progs Div, 82-89, dir, 89-92, VPRES, CHEMSTAR DIV, CHEM MFRS ASN, 92- *Personal Data:* b Charleston, WVa, Nov 9, 39. *Educ:* WVa State Col, BS, 59; Wayne State Univ, PhD(org chem), 63. *Prof Exp:* Res chemist, Gen Chem Div, Allied Chem Corp, NJ, 63-65, sr res chemist, Nitrogen Div, 66; asst prof org chem, Temple Univ, 66-69; assoc prof org chem, Brown Univ, 69-76; fel, US Dept Health Educ & Welfare, 76-77; spec asst to dir, Off Audit & Oversight, NSF, 77-80, staff assoc spec proj, 80-81, sr staff assoc oper math & phys sci dir, 81-82. *Concurrent Pos:* Asst to pres, Am Coun Educ, 73-76. *Mem:* Am Chem Soc; AAAS; Am Soc Asn Execs. *Res:* Mechanistic organic chemistry, bridged polycyclic compounds, molecular rearrangements, free radical and ionic additions; synthetic organic chemistry, conformational analysis; organic ultrasonic chemistry, sonochemistry. *Mailing Add:* 2649 Woodley Rd NW Washington DC 20008-4105

SPURR, ARTHUR RICHARD, PLANT MORPHOLOGY & PLANT PHYSIOLOGY, PLANT ULTRASTRUCTURE & X-RAY MICROANALYSIS. *Current Pos:* instr truck crops, 48-53, from jr olericulturist to assoc olericulturist, 48-73, from asst prof to prof veg crops, 54-84, OLERICULTURIST, EXP STA, UNIV CALIF, DAVIS, 73-, EMER PROF VEG CROPS, 84- *Personal Data:* b Glendale, Calif, July 21, 15; m 42, Winifred M Blair; c Jeffrey B, John O, Douglas J & Pamela J. *Educ:* Univ Calif, Los Angeles, BS, 38, MA, 40; Harvard Univ, AM, 42, PhD(biol), 47. *Prof Exp:* Instr biol, Harvard Univ, 47-48. *Concurrent Pos:* NIH spec res fel, 60-61; NSF res grant, 71-72; French govt res grant, 77-78. *Mem:* AAAS; Electron Micros Soc Am; Microbeam Anal Soc; Am Inst Biol Scientists; Bot Soc Am. *Res:* Cytology and ultrastructure of vascular plants; electron microscopy and analytical techniques; pathology of physiological disorders; mineral nutrition; electron probe x-ray analysis; ion probe microanalysis; responses to salinity and boron toxicity; granted one US patent. *Mailing Add:* 617 Elmwood Dr Davis CA 95616-3514. *Fax:* 530-752-9659

SPURR, CHARLES LEWIS, medicine; deceased, see previous edition for last biography

SPURR, DAVID TUPPER, STATISTICS, BIOLOGY. *Current Pos:* res scientist statist, Statist Res Serv, 70-75, STATISTICIAN, RES STA, AGR CAN, 75- *Personal Data:* b Notikewin, Alta, May 21, 38; m 62; c 3. *Educ:* Univ Alta, BSc, 61, MSc, 65; Ore State Univ, PhD(genetics), 68. *Prof Exp:* Pub lands appraiser, Lands Br, Alta Dept Lands & Forests, 61-63; asst animal sci, Univ Alta, 63-65; asst genetics, Ore State Univ, 66-68; res assoc animal genetics, Comput Ctr, Univ Ga, Athens, 69-70. *Mem:* Am Statist Asn. *Res:* Biometrical genetics; experimental design theory; bioassay; sampling. *Mailing Add:* Agr & Agri-Food Can 107 Sci Pl Saskatoon SK S7N 0X2 Can

SPURR, GERALD BAXTER, PHYSIOLOGY, NUTRITION. *Current Pos:* PROF PHYSIOL, MED COL WIS, 68- *Personal Data:* b Cambridge, Mass, June 1, 28; m 52, Elizabeth Sullivan; c Michael, Karen, David & Ellen. *Educ:* Boston Col, BS, 50; Univ Iowa, PhD(physiol), 54. *Prof Exp:* From res asst to instr physiol, Univ Iowa, 51-54; from instr clin physiol to prof physiol & biophys, Col Med, Univ Tenn, Memphis, 56-68. *Concurrent Pos:* Am Heart Asn fel, Univ Iowa, 54-56; Markle scholar med sci, 58-63; vis prof, Univ Valle, Colombia, 61-62 & 79-; consult, Res Serv, Vet Admin Ctr, Wood, Wis, 68- *Mem:* Am Physiol Soc; fel Am Col Sports Med; Am Soc Nutrit Sci. *Res:* Environmental and cardiovascular physiology; cold heart; hypothermia; hyperthermia; electrolyte and fluid metabolism; peripheral circulation; respiration; exercise; nutrition; nutritional status; malnutrition. *Mailing Add:* Dept Physiol Med Col Wis Ctr 8701 Watertown Plank Rd Milwaukee WI 53226

SPURR, HARVEY WESLEY, JR, PLANT PATHOLOGY. *Current Pos:* assoc prof, 69-74, PROF PLANT PATH, NC STATE UNIV, 74-; RES PLANT PATHOLOGIST, OXFORD TOBACCO LAB, USDA, 69-, RES LEADER & LAB DIR, 88- *Personal Data:* b Oak Park, Ill, June 8, 34; m 56, Idamarie Thome; c 3. *Educ:* Mich State Univ, BS, 56, MS, 58; Univ Wis, PhD(plant path), 61. *Prof Exp:* NIH fel plant path, Univ Wis, 61-63; plant pathologist, Agr Res Sta, Union Carbide Corp, NC, 63-69. *Mem:* Am Phytopath Soc; Am Soc Microbiol. *Res:* Plant disease control research; biological and chemical control; biochemistry of plant disease. *Mailing Add:* 4185 Tommie Sneed Rd Oxford NC 27565

SPURR, ORSON KIRK, JR, PHYSICAL CHEMISTRY. *Current Pos:* CONSULT, 88- *Personal Data:* b Cambridge, NY, Sept 4, 30; m 53; c 2. *Educ:* Dartmouth Col, BA, 52; Cornell Univ, MS, 56, PhD(phys chem), 58. *Prof Exp:* Res polymer chemist, Chem & Plastics Div, Union Carbide Corp, 58-79, res polymer chemist, Specialty Chem & Plastic Div, 79-85; consult, Amoco Performance Prod Inc, 86-88. *Mem:* Am Chem Soc; Sigma Xi. *Res:* Epoxy resins. *Mailing Add:* 1270 Cornell Rd Bridgewater NJ 08807-2301

SPURRELL, FRANCIS ARTHUR, VETERINARY MEDICINE, RADIATION BIOLOGY. *Current Pos:* Instr vet anat, Univ Minn, 47-49, vet obstet, 49-55, assoc prof vet radiol, 55-62, dir summer inst radiation biol, 60-64, prof vet radiol, 62-68, prof theriogenol & genetics, 68-89 EMER PROF THERIOGENOL & GENETICS, UNIV MINN, ST PAUL, 89- *Personal Data:* b Independence, Iowa, Apr 13, 19; m 42; c 1. *Educ:* Univ Wis, BS, 41; Iowa State Col, DVM, 46; Univ Minn, PhD(vet med), 55; Am Bd Vet Radiol, dipl. *Concurrent Pos:* County livestock agt, 46-47. *Mem:* Am Soc Animal Sci; Am Vet Radiol Soc; Am Vet Med Asn; Educators Vet Radiol Sci; Sigma Xi. *Res:* Genetics; heritability of fertility in dairy cattle; gaiting inheritance in racing thoroughbreds, with applied computer data base management procudures; veterinary radiology; heredity and diseases of animals; theriogenology computer systems; "bleeders" in racing horses. *Mailing Add:* 1440 Midway Pkwy Apt 306 St Paul MN 55108-2449

SPURRIER, ELMER R, MICROBIOLOGY, PUBLIC HEALTH. *Current Pos:* RETIRED. *Personal Data:* b Ava, Mo, Aug 1, 20; m 41; c 3. *Educ:* Univ Mo, BS, 49; Univ Minn, MPH, 54; Univ NC, MSPH, 62, DrPH, 64. *Prof Exp:* Technologist, Landon-Meyer Labs, Ohio, 49-50; supvr serologist, Pub Health Lab, 50-53, supvr serol & virol, 54-60, asst lab dir, 64-66, dir labs, Mo Dept Health, 66-87. *Concurrent Pos:* Lectr microbiol, Sch Med, Univ Mo, 64- *Mem:* Am Soc Microbiol; Am Pub Health Asn; Conf Pub Health Lab Dirs; Asn State & Territorial Pub Health Lab Dirs. *Res:* Antigenic relationships among parainfluenza viruses. *Mailing Add:* Lookout Point Rte 3 Eldon MO 65026

SPURRIER, JOHN DAVID, SIMULTANEOUS INFERENCE, STATISTICS EDUCATION. *Current Pos:* From asst prof to assoc prof, 74-84, chmn, Dept Statist, 93-96, PROF STATIST, UNIV SC, 84- *Personal Data:* b Kansas City, Mo, Nov 16, 48; m 74, Pamela Greasor; c Katie & Ryan. *Educ:* Univ Mo, BA, 70, MA, 71, PhD(statist), 74. *Mem:* Fel Am Statist Asn; Inst Math Statist. *Res:* Statistical theory, including simultaneous inference and nonparametric statistics, applied statistical theory to environment research and made advances in statistical education; published 68 papers and 2 books. *Mailing Add:* Dept Statist Univ SC Columbia SC 29208. *E-Mail:* spurrier@stat.sc.edu

SPYHALSKI, EDWARD JAMES, ENTOMOLOGY. *Current Pos:* RETIRED. *Personal Data:* b Chase, Wis, Apr 13, 25; m 55; c 3. *Educ:* Univ Wis, BS, 50, MA, 51; NC State Col, PhD(entom), 59. *Prof Exp:* Res entomologist, Am Cyanamid Co, 51-55; mgr tech serv, Niagara Chem Div, FMC Corp, NY, 59-69; res biologist, Air Prod & Chem, Inc, 69-71; sr biochem field specialist, PPG Industs Inc, 71-88, Valent USA Corp, 89-90. *Mem:* Weed Sci Soc Am; Entom Soc Am; Soc Nematol. *Res:* Relationship of chemicals to pesticidal activity; pesticide formulation research; crop culture research; pest control procedures. *Mailing Add:* 348 Penn Ave Floyd VA 24091-2212

SQUATTRITO, PHILIP JOHN, X-RAY CRYSTALLOGRAPHY. *Current Pos:* asst prof, 89-94, ASSOC PROF CHEM, CENT MICH UNIV, 94- *Personal Data:* b Middletown, Conn, Dec 4, 60. *Educ:* Brown Univ, ScB, 82; Northwestern Univ, MS, 83, PhD(inorg chem), 87. *Prof Exp:* Assoc, Tex A&M Univ, 86-88, Robert A Welch fel, 88-89. *Concurrent Pos:* Vis assoc prof chem, Univ Tokyo, 96. *Mem:* Sigma Xi; Am Chem Soc; Am Crystallog Asn. *Res:* Synthesis and characterization of novel inorganic materials with low-dimensional or layered structures; determination of structure by x-ray methods; structural trends in inorganic compounds. *Mailing Add:* Dept Chem Cent Mich Univ Mt Pleasant MI 48859. *Fax:* 517-774-3883; *E-Mail:* 3clwp5s@cmuvm.csv.cmich.edu

SQUIBB, ROBERT E, TOXICOLOGY. *Current Pos:* SR PRIN SCIENTIST, SCHERING-PLOUGH CO, 82- *Personal Data:* b Sacramento, Calif, Sept 30, 42; m 71; c 2. *Educ:* Rutgers Univ, BA, 73, MS, 75, PhD(toxicol), 77. *Prof Exp:* Sr staff fel, Nat Inst Environ Health Sci, 77-81. *Mem:* Soc Toxicol; Am Soc Pharmacol & Exp Therapeut; Am Col Toxicol; NY Acad Sci. *Res:* Design, conduct and evaluate preclinical toxicity studies in support of drug discovery and development programs. *Mailing Add:* Dir Toxicol Hugh E Black & Assoc IPC 5126 Durham Rd E Columbia MD 21044. *Fax:* 703-759-6947

SQUIBB, SAMUEL DEXTER, ORGANIC CHEMISTRY. *Current Pos:* prof & dept chmn, 64-94, EMER PROF CHEM, UNIV NC, ASHEVILLE, 94- *Personal Data:* b Limestone, Tenn, June 20, 31; m 51, Jo Ann Kyker; c Sandra & Kevin. *Educ:* ETenn State Univ, BS, 52; Univ Fla, PhD(chem), 56. *Honors & Awards:* Charles H Stone Award for Chem Educ Achievements, Carolina-Piedmont Sect, Am Chem Soc, 79; Distinguished Chemist Award, Western Carolinas Sect, Am Chem Soc, 93. *Prof Exp:* Assoc prof chem, Western Carolinas Univ, 56-60; from asst prof to assoc prof chem, Eckerd Col, 60-64, dir chem prog, 60-64. *Concurrent Pos:* Vis prof chem, Univ NC, Chapel Hill, 76-95. *Mem:* Am Chem Soc; fel Am Inst Chem; Sigma Xi; Nat Col Sci, Teachers Asn. *Res:* Allyl-type optically active quaternary ammonium salts; aqueous solution chemistry. *Mailing Add:* 8 Honey Dr Asheville NC 28805-1217. *E-Mail:* sdsquibb@juno.com

SQUIER, DONALD PLATTE, MATHEMATICS. *Current Pos:* RETIRED. *Personal Data:* b Des Moines, Iowa, Aug 16, 29. *Educ:* Stanford Univ, BS, 51, PhD(math), 55. *Prof Exp:* Mathematician, Remington Rand Univac Div, Sperry Rand Corp, 55-57; asst prof math, San Diego State Col, 57-59; reservoir engr, Calif Res Corp, 59-64; assoc prof math, Colo State Univ, 64-69; prof math & statist, Univ West Fla, 69-83. *Res:* Elliptic partial differential equations; numerical analysis. *Mailing Add:* 136 Red Breast Lane Pensacola FL 32503

SQUIERS, EDWIN RICHARD, PLANT ECOLOGY, FIELD BOTANY. *Current Pos:* PROF BIOL & ENVIRON SCI, TAYLOR UNIV, 76-, DIR ENVIRON SCI PROG, 80- *Personal Data:* b Bath, NB, May 15, 48; US citizen. *Educ:* State Univ NY, Binghamton, BA, 70; Rutgers Univ, MS, 73; Ohio Univ, PhD(bot), 76. *Prof Exp:* Res assoc terrestrial veg, Jack McCormick & Assocs, Ecol Consults, 70-71, consult, 71-76. *Mem:* Ecol Soc Am; Am Inst Biol Sci; Sigma Xi; Bot Soc Am. *Res:* Organization and dynamics of secondary successsion succession systems; systems modeling; floristics; phenology of successional species; biogeography; wetlands survey and mapping. *Mailing Add:* Dept Biol Taylor Univ 500 W Reade Ave Upland IN 46989-1001

SQUILLACE, PAUL JEROME, OCCURENCE & TRANSPORT OF ORGANIC CHEMICALS IN GROUND WATER, GROUND WATER & SURFACE WATER INTERACTION. *Current Pos:* hydrologist, 84-94, RES HYDROLOGIST, US GEOL SURV, 94- *Personal Data:* m 79, Sandra Kessler; c Timothy, Anna, Joseph, Maria, Emily & Rosemary. *Educ:* Winona State Univ, BA, 77; Univ Minn, Duluth, MS, 80. *Prof Exp:* Cartogr, Aerospace Ctr, Defense Mapping Agency, 83-84. *Concurrent Pos:* Prin investr, Cedar River Proj Toxic Substances Hydrol Prog, US Geol Surv, 89-94, sr ground water mem, Nat Water Qual Assessment Prog, 94- *Mem:* Nat Ground Water Asn. *Res:* Sources, status and trends of organic contaminants in ground water and natural and anthropogenic factors that control the occurence of organic contaminants in ground water. *Mailing Add:* US Geol Sur 1608 Mt View Rd Rapid City SD 57702. *Fax:* 605-394-5373; *E-Mail:* pisquill@usgs.gov

SQUILLACOTE, MICHAEL EDWARD, PHOTOCHEMISTRY, NUCLEAR MAGNETIC RESONANCE. *Current Pos:* ASST PROF CHEM, BROWN UNIV, 80- *Personal Data:* b Washington, DC, Dec 27, 50. *Educ:* Univ Chicago, BS, 72; Univ Calif, Los Angeles, PhD(chem), 78. *Prof Exp:* Res fel chem, Calif Inst Technol, 78-80. *Mem:* Am Chem Soc; Sigma Xi. *Res:* Low temperature photochemical and nuclear magnetic resonance studies of reactive intermediates; potential surfaces of excited states; routes of intramolecular vibrational decay. *Mailing Add:* Dept Chem Auburn Univ Auburn AL 36849

SQUINTO, STEPHEN P, MOLECULAR BIOLOGY. *Current Pos:* SR DIR MOLECULAR SCI, ALEXION PHARMACEUT, 92- *Personal Data:* b Cook Co, Ill, Sept 19, 56; m 87, Adrienne Block; c 2. *Educ:* Loyola Univ BA, 78, PhD(biochem & biophys), 84. *Prof Exp:* Fel biochem, Loyola Univ, 78-84; fel Molecular biol, Northwestern Univ Med Sch, 84-86; asst prof biochem & molecular biol, La State Univ Med Ctr, 86-89; staff scientist cell & molecular biol, Regeneron Pharmaceut, 89-92. *Concurrent Pos:* Lectr natural sci, Loyola Univ, 84-86; ind nat res, NIH, 84-86; cancer res award, United Way & Cancer Asn, 87-89, Leukemia Soc, 88-89; consult, Nat Inst Drug Abuse, 89-90, NIH, 91-92. *Mem:* AAAS; Am Soc Microbiol; Am Soc Biochem & Molecular Biol; Am Soc Neurosci. *Res:* Discovery of novel neurotropic factor related to nerve growth factor; discovery that BNDF protects nerves from the neurotoxins that cause Parkinson's disease; engineering of porcine organs for transplantation into humans. *Mailing Add:* 11 Coachmans Lane Bethany CT 06524. *Fax:* 203-772-3655

SQUIRE, ALEXANDER, ENGINEERING ADMINISTRATION, NUCLEAR POWER. *Current Pos:* RETIRED. *Personal Data:* b Dumfrieshire, Scotland, 1917; m 45; c 9. *Educ:* Mass Inst Technol, SB, 39; Columbia Univ, PhD(exec mgt prog), 58. *Prof Exp:* Proj mgr, Bettis Automic Power Lab, 50-62; mgr, Plant Apparatus Div, Westinghouse Corp, 62-69, dir purchasing & traffic, Westinghouse Elec Corp, 69-71, pres, Westinghouse Hanford Co, 71-80; dep mgr dir, Wash Pub Power Supplies Syst, 80-85; consult, Nuclear Power & Contract Settlement, 85-92. *Concurrent Pos:* Dir, Tri City Nuclear Coun, Wash & Old Nat Bank, United Way; mem bd, Grad Ctr Richmond, Wash. *Mem:* Nat Acad Eng; Am Nuclear Soc; Am Soc Metals; Am Defense Preparedness Asn. *Res:* Development and construction of naval nuclear power plants; development and construction of breeder reactor facilities including fast flux test facility; construction of commercial nuclear power plants. *Mailing Add:* 2415 Winburn Ave Durham NC 27704

SQUIRE, CHARLES F, CHEMICAL PHYSICS. *Current Pos:* RETIRED. *Personal Data:* b Washington, DC, 1912. *Educ:* Johns Hopkins Univ, PhD(chem physics), 37. *Prof Exp:* Dean sci, Tex A&M Univ, 62-72; consult, 72-85. *Mem:* Fel Am Phys Soc. *Mailing Add:* 1014 River Bend Dr Houston TX 77063

SQUIRE, DAVID R, POLYMER CHEMISTRY, PHYSICAL CHEMISTRY. *Current Pos:* RETIRED. *Personal Data:* b Bartlesville, Okla, Mar 11, 35; m 56; c 4. *Educ:* Southern Methodist Univ, BS, 57; Rice Univ, PhD(theoret chem), 61. *Prof Exp:* Assoc chem, Duke Univ, 61-62; assoc prof chem & head dept, Nicholls State Col, 61-62; chief phys chem br, US Army Res Off, 62-77, assoc dir chem div, 77-88; mem staff, Defense Advan Res Proj Agency, 88-90; adj & dir res & develop, Loker Hydrocarbon Res Inst, Univ Southern Calif, Los Angeles, 90-92. *Concurrent Pos:* Vis asst prof, Duke Univ, 62-72; adj prof, NC State Univ, 70. *Mem:* Am Chem Soc; Am Phys Soc. *Res:* Theoretical chemistry; fundamental investigations in polymer chemistry; radiation chemistry of polymers; statistical mechanics of solids and liquids. *Mailing Add:* 1032 Diamond Crest Ct Santa Barbara CA 93110

SQUIRE, LARRY RYAN, NEUROSCIENCE, NEUROPSYCHOLOGY. *Current Pos:* From asst prof to assoc prof, 73-81, PROF PSYCHIAT, UNIV CALIF, SAN DIEGO, 81-; RES CAREER SCIENTIST, VET ADMIN MED CTR, 80- *Personal Data:* b Cherokee, Iowa, May 4, 41; c 1. *Educ:* Oberlin Col, BA, 63; Mass Inst Technol, PhD(psychol), 68. *Concurrent Pos:* NIMH interdisciplinary fel, Albert Einstein Col Med, 68-70; clin investr, Vet Admin Med Ctr, 73-76. *Mem:* Nat Acad Sci; Int Neuropsychol Soc; Soc Neurosci; Psychonomic Soc; fel AAAS; Int Brain Res Orgn; Fel Am Psychol Asn. *Res:* Organization and neurological foundations of memory in man and non-human primate; neural plasticity; memory disorders in man; electroconvulsive therapy and memory. *Mailing Add:* Dept Psychiat Med Sch Univ Calif San Diego 9500 Gilman Dr La Jolla CA 92093-0001

SQUIRE, RICHARD DOUGLAS, GENETICS, RADIATION BIOLOGY. *Current Pos:* from asst prof to assoc prof, 78-87, PROF BIOL, UNIV PR, MAYAGUEZ, 87- *Personal Data:* b New York, NY, Oct 9, 40; m 80, Marthe Auguste. *Educ:* Hofstra Univ, BA, 63, MA, 69; NC State Univ, PhD(genetics), 69. *Prof Exp:* Asst prof biol, Long Island Univ, Brooklyn Ctr, 69-73, adj assoc prof, 74-75, 76-78; res fel, Med Ctr, Cornell Univ, 75-76. *Concurrent Pos:* Consult, Lamont-Doherty Geol Observ, 73; adj assoc prof, Staten Island Community Col, 74-75, 77 & St John's Univ, 77. *Mem:* Genetics Soc Am; Soc Study Evolution; Am Genetic Asn. *Res:* Radiation genetics, ecological genetics, developmental genetics, cytogenetics and ecology of Artemia; chemically-induced polyploidy in animals; animal and human cytogenetics; genetics of color patterns in birds and fish. *Mailing Add:* Dept Biol Univ PR Mayaguez Campus Mayaguez PR 00681

SQUIRE, ROBERT ALFRED, COMPARATIVE PATHOLOGY. *Current Pos:* asst prof, 64-68, ASSOC PROF PATH, SCH MED, JOHNS HOPKINS UNIV, 68-, ASSOC PROF COMP MED, 77- *Personal Data:* b Dobbs Ferry, NY, July 1, 30; m 50; c 3. *Educ:* Univ Vt, BS, 52; Cornell Univ, DVM, 56,

PhD(vet path), 64; Am Col Vet Path, dipl. *Prof Exp:* Private practice, Vt, 56-60; asst path, Cornell Univ, 60-61, instr, 62-64. *Concurrent Pos:* Mem adv comt, Registry Comp Path, 68-; chmn comt lab animal dis, Nat Acad Sci-Nat Res Coun, 69-; mem adv coun, Morris Animal Found, 71-; chmn adv coun, NY State Vet Col, Cornell Univ, 71-; lectr, Armed Forces Inst Path; dir comp path, Johns Hopkins Univ, 66-76. *Mem:* Int Acad Path; Am Asn Cancer Res; Am Col Vet Path; Am Vet Med Asn. *Res:* Pathology of hematopoietic tissues; animal models of human disease, particularly lymphomas and immunologic diseases. *Mailing Add:* Dept Comp Med Johns Hokpins Univ Med Sch 720 Rutland Ave Baltimore MD 21205-2109

SQUIRE, WILLIAM, APPLIED MATHEMATICS, FLUID MECHANICS. *Current Pos:* prof, 61-86, EMER PROF, AEROSPACE ENG, WVA UNIV, 86- *Personal Data:* b New York, NY, Sept 22, 20; m 48; c 2. *Educ:* City Col New York, BS, 41; Univ Buffalo, MA, 59. *Prof Exp:* Inspector, Philadelphia Signal Corps Inspection Zone, US Dept Army, 42-43; jr physicist, Nat Bur Stand, 43-45; asst physicist, 45-48; assoc physicist, Cornell Aeronaut Lab, Inc, 48-57; aerodynamicist, Bell Aircraft Corp, 57-59; sr res engr, Southwest Res Inst, 59-61. *Concurrent Pos:* Vis lectr, UTA, 87-88. *Mem:* assoc fel Inst Aeronaut & Astronaut. *Res:* Turbulence; high temperature gas dynamics; boundary layer theory; numerical integration; computer algebra. *Mailing Add:* 449 Hillview Dr Morgantown WV 26505

SQUIRES, ARTHUR MORTON, CHEMICAL ENGINEERING. *Current Pos:* Frank C Vilbrandt prof, 76-82, distinguished prof, 78-86, EMER DISTINGUISHED PROF CHEM ENG, VA POLYTECH INST & STATE UNIV, 86- *Personal Data:* b Neodesha, Kans, Mar 21, 16. *Educ:* Univ Mo, AB, 38; Cornell Univ, PhD(phys chem), 47. *Honors & Awards:* Storch Award, Am Chem Soc, 73. *Prof Exp:* Asst chem, Univ Mo, 38 & Cornell Univ, 38-41; lab technician, E I Du Pont de Nemours & Co, NY, 41; phys chemist, M W Kellogg Co, 42-43 & Kellex Corp, 43-46; asst head, Process Develop Dept, Hydrocarbon Res, Inc, 46-51, head, 51-59; prof, City Col New York, 67-74, chmn dept, 71-74, distinguished prof chem eng, 74-76. *Concurrent Pos:* Process consult, 59-67; lectr, Am Inst Chem Eng, 77. *Mem:* Nat Acad Eng; Am Soc Mech Eng; Am Chem Soc; Am Inst Chem Eng; Am Acad Arts & Sci. *Res:* Physical chemistry of solutions; multistage fractionation; flow-properties of fluid-solids systems; hydrocarbon synthesis and cracking; iron ore reduction; coal and oil gasification; hydrogen production; power generation; dust collection; low-temperature processes; small-scale coal combustion; heat transfer in shallow vibrated and gas-fluidized beds of particles; government management of technological change; vibrated-bed microreactors. *Mailing Add:* Dept Chem Eng Va Polytech Inst & State Univ Blacksburg VA 24061

SQUIRES, CATHERINE L, MOLECULAR GENETICS, MICROBIOLOGY. *Current Pos:* from asst prof to assoc prof, 77-87, PROF, DEPT BIOL SCI, COLUMBIA UNIV, 87- *Personal Data:* b Sacramento, Calif, Apr 9, 41; m 66, Craig; c Sean & Ciaron. *Educ:* Univ Calif, Davis, BA, 63, MA, 67; Univ Calif, Santa Barbara, PhD(molecular biol & biochem), 72. *Prof Exp:* Fel, Stanford Univ, 72-74; asst prof, Dept Biol Sci, Dartmouth Col, 74-76, adj asst prof, Biochem Dept, 75-77, Gross Taylor/Cornelia Pierce Williams asst prof biol, Dept Biol Sci, 76-77. *Concurrent Pos:* Helen Hay Whitney Found fel; guest prof, Univ Inst Microbiol, Univ Copenhagen, 81, 84 & 90; mem, Microbial Physiol & Genetics Study Sect, NIH, 84-88; ed, Microbiol Rev, 92-; vis prof, Grad Sch, City Univ New York, 89, Div Oral Biol, Univ Calif, San Francisco, 63. *Mem:* Sigma Xi; AAAS; Am Soc Microbiol; Harvey Soc; Am Soc Biochem & Molecular Biol. *Res:* Expression of the transcription and translation machinery in prokaryotes. *Mailing Add:* Dept Molecular Biol & Microbiol Tufts Univ Sch Med 136 Harrison Ave Boston MA 02111-1800. *Fax:* 212-865-8246; *E-Mail:* cathy@cubmol.bio.columbia.edu

SQUIRES, DALE EDWARD, RESOURCE ECONOMICS, ECONOMICS OF REGULATION. *Current Pos:* INDUST ECONOMIST, NAT MARINE FISHERIES SERV, 82-; ASSOC ADJ PROF, ECON RESOURCES, DEPT ECON, UNIV CALIF, SAN DIEGO, 89- *Personal Data:* b San Diego, Calif, Aug 28, 50; m 86, Virginia Shirin Sharifzadeh; c Haleh & Phillip. *Educ:* Univ Calif, Berkeley, BSc, 73, MSc, 78; Cornell Univ, PhD(resource econ), 84. *Prof Exp:* Asst prof econ theory, Fac Econ & Mgt, Univ Agr Malaysia, 75-77; sr economist, Dept Fisheries, Sabah Malaysia, 77-78; intern, Agency Int Develop, 79. *Concurrent Pos:* Scholastic fel, Foreign Lang Area Studies, Indonesia, 78-79 & Sea Grant Scholar, 80-81; mem, Working Group Ltd Access Alternatives, Pac Fishery Mgt Coun, 84-86, Ltd Entry Tech Adv Group, 87-89, Ltd Entry Oversight Comt, 89-90 & Groundfish Mgt Team, 89-; vis prof, Dept Econ, Univ Queensland, Brisbane, Qld, Australia, 90; assoc adj prof, Pub Policy Anal, Grad Sch Int Rels & Pac Studies, Univ Calif, San Diego, 91- *Mem:* Am Econ Asn; Am Agr Econ Asn; Asian Fisheries Soc. *Res:* Analysis of markets for tradable quotas and property rights; productivity measurement; economics of quotas; measurement of capacity utilization. *Mailing Add:* Southwest Fisheries Sci Ctr PO Box 271 La Jolla CA 92038-0271. *Fax:* 619-546-7003; *E-Mail:* dsquires@its.ucsd.edu

SQUIRES, DONALD FLEMING, GENERAL MARINE & ENVIRONMENTAL SCIENCES. *Current Pos:* PROF MARINE SCI & DIR, MARINE SCI INST, UNIV CONN, 85- *Personal Data:* b Glen Cove, NY, Dec 19, 27; m 51; c 2. *Educ:* Cornell Univ, AB, 50, PhD, 55; Univ Kans, MA, 52. *Honors & Awards:* Secy's Gold Medal, Smithsonian Inst. *Prof Exp:* Asst cur paleont, Am Mus Natural Hist, 55-61, assoc cur, 61-62; assoc cur marine invert, Mus Natural Hist, Smithsonian Inst, 62-63, cur-in-chg, 63-64, chmn dept invert zool, 65, dep dir, 66-68; actg assoc provost grad studies & res, 72-73, prof biol sci, earth & space sci & dir, Marine Sci Res Ctr, State Univ NY Stony Brook, 68-85. *Concurrent Pos:* Fulbright res fel, NZ, 59; dir, NY Sea Grant Inst, 71-85. *Mem:* Fel AAAS; Sigma Xi; Marine Technol Soc. *Res:* Marine and coastal policy. *Mailing Add:* 19 Shady Lane Storrs CT 06268-1814

SQUIRES, LOMBARD, ENGINEERING. *Current Pos:* RETIRED. *Prof Exp:* Asst gen mgr, E I du Pont de Nemours & Co. *Mem:* Nat Acad Eng. *Mailing Add:* 100 Moorings Park Dr No F101 Naples FL 33940

SQUIRES, PAUL HERMAN, CHEMICAL ENGINEERING, POLYMER PROCESSING. *Current Pos:* RETIRED. *Personal Data:* b Sewickley, Pa, July 14, 31; m 53; c 6. *Educ:* Rensselaer Polytech Inst, BChE, 53, PhD(chem eng), 56; Univ Wis, MS, 54. *Honors & Awards:* Presidents' Cup, Soc Plastics Engrs, 89, Distinguished Serv Award, 89. *Prof Exp:* Engr, Plastics Dept, 56-59, supvr, 59-63, sr res engr, 63-67, res assoc, Eng Dept, 67-76, prin consult, Eng Dept, E I Du Pont De Nemours & Co, Inc, 76- *Mem:* Fel Soc Plastics Engrs; Am Inst Chem Engrs. *Res:* Energy and momentum transfer in viscous materials, especially translation of theory into design and development of plastics processing equipment; laminated safety glass interlayer; extrusion. *Mailing Add:* 1235 E Lake Shore Dr Landrum SC 29356

SQUIRES, RICHARD FELT, NEUROPHARMACOLOGY, NEUROCHEMISTRY. *Current Pos:* PRIN RES SCIENTIST, NATHAN KLINE INST PSYCHIAT RES, 79- *Personal Data:* b Sparta, Mich, Jan 15, 33; m 70, Else Saederup; c Iben. *Educ:* Mich State Univ, BS, 58. *Prof Exp:* Res biochemist, Pasadena Found Med Res, 61-62; head biochemist, Res Dept, Ferrosan A/S, Soeborg, Denmark, 63-78; group leader CNS biol, nerv res neurochem, Lederle Labs, Am Cyanamid, 78-79. *Mem:* Soc Neurosci; Europ Neurosci Asn; Am Soc Neurochem; Int Soc Neurochem; Am Soc Biol Chemists; Am Soc Pharmacol & Exp Therapeut. *Res:* Gamma aminobutyric acid; benzodiazepine; picrotoxin receptors in brain; biochemistry; characterization of receptors in central nervous system; development of novel psychotropic drugs; neurological and psychiatric disorders. *Mailing Add:* Nathan Kline Inst Orangeburg NY 10962. *Fax:* 914-365-6107; *E-Mail:* foldi@nki.rfmh.org

SQUIRES, ROBERT GEORGE, CHEMICAL ENGINEERING. *Current Pos:* From asst prof to assoc prof, 62-72, PROF CHEM ENG, PURDUE UNIV, WEST LAFAYETTE, 72- *Personal Data:* b Sewickley, Pa, Oct 1, 35; m 57; c 3. *Educ:* Rensselaer Polytech Inst, BChE, 57; Univ Mich, Ann Arbor, MSE, 58, MS, 60, PhD(chem eng), 63. *Mem:* Am Inst Chem Engrs; Am Chem Soc; Am Soc Eng Educ; Catalysis Soc. *Res:* Heterogeneous catalysis; adsorption; reaction kinetics. *Mailing Add:* 807 N Salisbury St West Lafayette IN 47906-2715

SQUIRES, ROBERT WRIGHT, FERMENTATION TECHNOLOGY. *Current Pos:* CONSULT, 90- *Personal Data:* b Barberton, Ohio, Aug 25, 21; m 48, Ruth Bixler; c David M & Kerry R. *Educ:* Kent State Univ, BS, 48; Purdue Univ, MS, 50, PhD(microbiol), 54. *Honors & Awards:* Charles Porter Award, Soc Indust Microbiologists, 66. *Prof Exp:* Instr gen bact, Purdue Univ, 49, instr food bact, 50-53; sr microbiologist, Eli Lilly & Co, 54-65, res scientist, 65-66, asst mgr pilot plant opers, 66-67, mgr antibiotic opers, 67-69, eng coordr antibiotic fermentations, 69-80; tech dir biomfg, Searle Chem, Inc, 81-83, dir biochem process technol, Nutrasweet Group, G D Searle, 84-89. *Mem:* Fel Soc Indust Microbiologists (treas, 61-66, pres, 68-69); Am Inst Biol Scientists; Sigma Xi; Am Soc Microbiol; Instrument Soc Am. *Res:* Antibiotic fermentation pilot plant operations; fermentation development and equipment design; continuous fermentation; process scaleup and fermentation process control dynamics; fermentor reactor design large airlift as well as agitated tanks. *Mailing Add:* 10105 Dorsey Hill Rd Louisville KY 40223

SQUYRES, STEVEN WELDON, PLANETARY GEOLOGY. *Current Pos:* NAT RES COUN ASSOC, AMES RES CTR, NASA, 81-; ASSOC PROF, DEPT ASTRON, CORNELL UNIV, 85- *Personal Data:* b Woodbury, NJ, Jan 9, 56. *Educ:* Cornell Univ, BA, 78, PhD(geol), 81. *Concurrent Pos:* Mem, Planetary Geol Working Group, NASA, 82- *Mem:* Am Geophys Union; AAAS. *Res:* Geomorphology and climatic evolution of Mars; formation, internal evolution, and surface geology of outer planet satellites; photometry of outer planet satellites. *Mailing Add:* 383 Hurd Rd Ithaca NY 14850

SRAMEK, RICHARD ANTHONY, RADIO ASTRONOMY. *Current Pos:* VLA SCIENTIST, NAT RADIO ASTRON OBSERV, 78- *Personal Data:* b Baltimore, Md, June 5, 43. *Educ:* Mass Inst Technol, BS, 65; Calif Inst Technol, PhD(astron), 70. *Prof Exp:* Res assoc, Nat Radio Astron Observ, 70-72, asst scientist, 72-74, assoc scientist, 74-75; res assoc, Arecibo Observ, 75-78. *Mem:* Am Astron Soc; Int Union Radio Sci. *Res:* Extra-galactic astronomy and experimental tests of general relativity. *Mailing Add:* 1005 Calle Del Sol Socorro NM 87801

SRB, ADRIAN MORRIS, GENETICS. *Current Pos:* from assoc prof to prof plant breeding, Cornell Univ, 48-65, prof, 65-76, Jacob Gould Schurman prof genetics, 76-84, JACOB GOULD SCHURMAN EMER PROF GENETICS, CORNELL UNIV, 84- *Personal Data:* b Howells, Nebr, Mar 4, 17; m 40; c 3. *Educ:* Univ Nebr, AB, 37, MS, 41; Stanford Univ, PhD(genetics), 46. *Hon Degrees:* DSc, Univ Nebr, 69. *Honors & Awards:* Darling Lectr, Allegheny Col, 64. *Prof Exp:* Asst prof biol, Stanford Univ, 46-47. *Concurrent Pos:* Nat Res Coun fel, Calif Inst Technol, 46-47; Guggenheim fel & Fulbright res fel, Univ Paris, 53-54; NSF sr res fel, 60-61; Univ Edinburgh, 67-68; dir, NIH & Pre-training Prog Genetics, Cornell Univ, 62-67; mem, Genetics Study Sect, NIH, 64-67 & Genetics Training Comt, 69-; vis scholar, Va Polytech Inst, 65; co-chmn, Prog Comt, XI Int Bot Cong; trustee, Cornell Univ, 75-80; mem, Educ Adv Bd, John Simon Guggenheim Mem Found, 76- *Mem:* Nat Acad Sci; fel AAAS; Genetics Soc Am; Am Soc Naturalists; fel Am Acad Arts & Sci. *Res:* Physiological genetics of fungi; mutagenesis; extranuclear heredity; developmental genetics. *Mailing Add:* 411 Cayuga Heights Rd Ithaca NY 14850

SREBNIK, HERBERT HARRY, GROSS & DEVELOPMENTAL ANATOMY, REPRODUCTIVE ENDOCRINOLOGY. *Current Pos:* from instr to prof anat, 57-89, chmn, Dept Biol, 87-89, EMER PROF ANAT, UNIV CALIF, BERKELEY, 90- *Personal Data:* b Berlin, Ger, Mar 25, 23; nat US; m 51; c 2. *Educ:* Univ Calif, BA, 50, MA, 55, PhD(anat), 57. *Prof Exp:* Asst anat, 53-57. *Mem:* AAAS; Soc Exp Biol & Med; Am Inst Nutrit; Am Asn Anat; Endocrine Soc. *Res:* Endocrine-nutrition interrelationships; physiology of reproduction; anterior pituitary function; investigations into hormonal and nutritional factors influencing the course and outcome of gestation in laboratory animals. *Mailing Add:* Dept Molecular & Cell Biol Univ Calif Berkeley 229 Stanley Hall Berkeley CA 94720

SREBRO, RICHARD, BIOENGINEERING. *Current Pos:* assoc prof ophthal & physiol, 77-87, PROF OPHTHAL, SOUTHWESTERN MED SCH, DALLAS, 87- *Personal Data:* b New York, NY, Jan 9, 36; m 67, Anne Murphy; c Nancy, Daniel & Julie. *Educ:* Wash Univ, MD, 59. *Honors & Awards:* Sr Sci Investn Award, Res to Prevent Blindness. *Prof Exp:* Intern, State Univ NY Upstate Med Ctr, 59-60; resident ophthal, Sch Med, Wash Univ, 60-62; sr asst surgeon, Lab Phys Biol, NIH, 62-64; res scientist biophys, Walter Reed Army Inst Res, 65-68; from res asst prof to assoc prof physiol, State Univ NY Buffalo, 68-77. *Concurrent Pos:* Nat Inst Neurol Dis & Blindness fel, 64-65. *Mem:* Am Asn Artificial Intel; Asn Res Vision & Ophthal; Soc Neurosci; Inst Elec & Electronics Engrs; Eng Med & Biol Soc. *Res:* Physiology of vision, functional brain imaging, evoked potentials, nonlinear analysis. *Mailing Add:* Dept Ophthal Southwestern Med Sch 5323 Harry Hines Blvd Dallas TX 75235

SREEBNY, LEO MORRIS, PATHOLOGY, BIOCHEMISTRY. *Current Pos:* dean, Sch Dent Med, 75-79, PROF ORAL BIOL, SCH DENT MED, STATE UNIV NY, STONY BROOK, 75- *Personal Data:* b New York, NY, Jan 8, 22; m 45; c 2. *Educ:* Univ Ill, AB, 42, DDS, 45, MS, 50, PhD(path), 54. *Honors & Awards:* Anat Sci Award, Int Asn Dent Res, 69; Silver Medal Dent Soc, Paris, France, 79; List of Honor, Fed Dent Int, 89. *Prof Exp:* Asst therapeut, Col Dent, Univ Ill, 49-50, instr, 51-53, from asst prof to assoc prof oral path, 53-57; from assoc prof to prof oral biol, Sch Dent, Univ Wash, 57-75, chmn dept, 57-75, prof path, Sch Med, 65-75. *Concurrent Pos:* Fulbright lectr & advan res award, Hebrew Univ Jerusalem, 63-64; dir, Ctr Res Oral Biol, Sch Med, Univ Wash, 68-75; chmn, Sci Prog, Int Dent Fed, 70-88; mem bd dirs, Am Asn Dent Res, 81. *Mem:* AAAS; Int Asn Dent Res; Am Dent Asn; Int Dent Fedn. *Res:* Secretory mechanism of salivary secretions; pathophysiology of diseases of the oral cavity; nutrition and oral diseases. *Mailing Add:* Family Med State Univ NY Health Sci Col Med 100 Nicholls Rd Stony Brook NY 11794-0001

SREE HARSHA, KARNAMADAKALA S, MATERIALS SCIENCE. *Current Pos:* asst prof mat sci, 66-77, chmn, Dept Mat Eng, 78-94, PROF MAT SCI, SAN JOSE STATE UNIV, 78-94. *Personal Data:* b India, May 25, 36; m 67; c 2. *Educ:* Univ Mysore, BSc, 55; Indian Inst Sci, Bangalore, dipl metall, 57; Univ Notre Dame, MS, 60; Pa State Univ, PhD(metall), 64. *Prof Exp:* Res fel, Iowa State Univ, 65-67. *Mem:* Am Soc Metals; Am Inst Mining, Metall & Petrol Engrs; Mat Res Soc. *Res:* Structure and transformations of solids; theory of dislocation; surfaces; thermodynamics; semiconductors. *Mailing Add:* Dept Mat Sci San Jose State Univ One Washington Sq San Jose CA 95192-0086

SREEKRISHNA, KOTI, KLUYVEROMYCES LACTIS GENE REGULATION, PICHIA PASTORIS GENE EXPRESSION. *Current Pos:* SCIENTIST, HOECHST MARION ROUSSEL INC, 93- *Personal Data:* b Bangalore, India, May 10, 53; m, Shailini Chitrapura; c Naetra & Nishant. *Educ:* Bangalore Univ, India, BSc, 71, MSc, 73; Indian Inst Sci, PhD(biochem), 78. *Prof Exp:* Res assoc, Biochem Dept, Baylor Col Med, 78-80, Univ Ky, 80-85; sr scientist, Phillips Petrol Co, 85-92. *Mem:* Am Soc Biochem & Molecular Biol. *Res:* Protein expression and secretion in pichia pastori; yeast to hybrid analysis of protein-protein interaction; fermentation optimization and scale up of recombinart protein production. *Mailing Add:* 5655 Bayberry Dr Cincinnati OH 45242-8015. *Fax:* 513-948-7345; *E-Mail:* tatacher@aol.com

SREENIVASAN, KATEPALLI RAJU, SCIENCE & SOCIETY, TEACHING OF SCIENCE & TECHNOLOGY. *Current Pos:* from asst prof to assoc prof, 82-85, PROF MECH ENG, YALE UNIV, 85-, CHMN DEPT, 87- & HAROLD W CHEEL PROF, 88- *Personal Data:* b Kolar, India, Sept 30, 47; m 80, Sudha; c Kartik & Aditya. *Educ:* Bangalore Univ, BE, 68; Indian Inst Sci, ME, 70, PhD(aeronaut eng), 75. *Hon Degrees:* MA, Yale Univ, 89. *Honors & Awards:* Narayan Gold Medal, Indian Inst Sci, 75; Oho Laport Award, Am Phys Soc, 95. *Prof Exp:* JRD Tata fel, Indian Inst Sci, 72-74, proj asst, 74-75; fel, Univ & Sydney, 75, Univ Newcastle, 76-77; res assoc, Johns Hopkins Univ, 77-79. *Concurrent Pos:* Vis scientist, Indian Inst Sci, 79, vis prof, 82; vis sci, DFVLR, Gottingen, WGer, 83; fel, Humboldt Found, 83; vis prof, Cal Inst Tech, Pasadena, 86; Guggeheim fel, 89; vis prof, Rockefeller Univ, 89- *Mem:* Fel Am Soc Mech Engrs; assoc fel Am Inst Astronaut & Aeronaut; fel Am Phys Soc; Am Math Soc; Sigma Xi; fel Am Soc Mech Engrs. *Res:* Origin and dynamics of turbulence; control of turbulent flows, especially drag reduction; chaotic dynamics; fractals. *Mailing Add:* Mech Eng M6 ML Yale Univ New Haven CT 06520-8286

SREENIVASAN, SREENIVASA RANGA, PHYSICS, ASTROPHYSICS. *Current Pos:* from asst prof to assoc prof, 67-75, PROF PHYSICS, UNIV CALGARY, 75- *Personal Data:* b Mysore, India, Oct 20, 33; m 63, Claire de Reineck; c Gopal, Govind, Gauri, Gayatri & Aravind. *Educ:* Univ Mysore, BS, 50, BS, 52; Gujarat Univ, India, PhD(physics), 58. *Prof Exp:* Res fel, Harvard Univ, 59-61; Nat Acad Sci res assoc, Goddard Inst Space Studies, New York, 61-64; vis scientist, Max Planck Inst Physics & Astrophys, 64-66. *Concurrent Pos:* Vis prof, Royal Inst Technol, Univ Stockholm & vis scientist, Swed Natural Sci Res Coun, 74-75. *Mem:* Am Astron Soc; Am Geophys Union; Am Phys Soc; fel Royal Astron Soc; Int Astron Union; Am Meteorol Soc; Astron Soc Japan. *Res:* Theoretical astrophysics; theoretical plasma physics; general relativity; nonlinear phenomena in physics. *Mailing Add:* 2110 30 Ave SW Calgary AB T2T 1R4 Can. *Fax:* 403-289-3331; *E-Mail:* srs@acs.ucalgary.ca

SREEVALSAN, THAZEPADATH, MICROBIOLOGY, VIROLOGY. *Current Pos:* asst prof, 69-73, assoc prof, 73-80, PROF MICROBIOL, MED & DENT SCH, GEORGETOWN UNIV, 80- *Personal Data:* b Kanjiramattom, India, Jan 25, 35. *Educ:* Univ Kerala, BSc, 53, MSc, 56; Univ Tex, PhD(microbiol), 64. *Prof Exp:* Teacher, St Ignatius High Sch, India, 53-54; res asst virol, Pasteur Inst, Coonoor, 56-61 & Univ Tex, 61-63, assoc res scientist, 64-66; res scientist virol, Cent Res Sta, E I du Pont de Nemours & Co, Inc, 66-69. *Mem:* AAAS; Am Soc Microbiol. *Res:* Viruses, replication of animal viruses, molecular biology of animal virus development, mode of RNA replication; interfrons their biological activity and mode of action in inhibiting cell growth and viral multiplication; control of proliferation in animal cells. *Mailing Add:* Dept Microbiol Georgetown Univ Sch Med 3900 Reservoir Rd NW Washington DC 20007-2187

SRERE, PAUL ARNOLD, ENZYMOLOGY, METABOLISM. *Current Pos:* PROF BIOCHEM, SOUTHWESTERN MED SCH, UNIV TEX HEALTH SCI CTR DALLAS, 66- *Personal Data:* b Davenport, Iowa, Sept 1, 25; m 53; c 4. *Educ:* Univ Calif, Los Angeles, BS, 47; Univ Calif, Berkley PhD(comp biochem), 51. *Hon Degrees:* Dr, Pecs Univ Hungary, 90. *Honors & Awards:* William S Middleton Award, 74. *Prof Exp:* Asst physiol, Univ Calif, 47-51; asst biochemist, Mass Gen Hosp, 51-53; from asst prof to assoc prof biochem, Univ Mich, 56-63; biochemist, Biomed Div, Lawrence Radiation Lab, Univ Calif, 63-66. *Concurrent Pos:* Childs Found Med Res fel, Yale Univ, 53-54; USPHS fels, Pub Health Res Inst, New York, 54-55 & Max Planck Inst Cell Biol, Ger, 55-56; chief basic biochem unit, Gen Med Res, Vet Admin Hosp, 69-72. *Mem:* Am Chem Soc; Fedn Am Soc Exp Biol. *Res:* Intermediary metabolism; enzymology; metabolic regulation. *Mailing Add:* Pre Clin Sci Vet Admin Med Ctr 4500 S Lancaster Rd Dallas TX 75216. *Fax:* 214-372-9534

SRETER, FRANK A, BIOCHEMISTRY. *Current Pos:* ASSOC, DEPT NEUROPATH, HARVARD MED SCH, 72-; SR RES SCIENTIST, DEPT MUSCLE RES, BOSTON BIOMED RES INST, 72- *Personal Data:* b Szanda, Hungary, Oct 2, 21; US citizen; m 44; c 2. *Educ:* Budapest Tech Univ, MS, 43, PhD(animal nutrit), 44; Vet Sch Budapest, DVM, 49; Med Univ Budapest, MD, 50. *Prof Exp:* From instr to assoc prof, Budapest Tech Univ, 44-51; assoc prof, E-tv-s Lorand Univ, Budapest, 51-56; from instr to asst prof, Univ BC, 57-63; res assoc, Dept Muscle Res, Retina Found, 63-72. *Concurrent Pos:* Can Muscular Dystrophy, Inc fel, 63-66; estab investr, Am Heart Asn, 66-71; assoc biochemist, Mass Gen Hosp. *Mem:* Am Physiol Soc; Biophys Soc. *Res:* Muscle physiology and biochemistry. *Mailing Add:* Dept Muscle Res Boston Biomed Res Inst 20 Staniford St Boston MA 02114-2500

SRIBNEY, MICHAEL, BIOCHEMISTRY. *Current Pos:* RETIRED. *Personal Data:* b Alta, Can, Feb 5, 27; m 54; c 2. *Educ:* Univ Alta, BSc, 52; McMaster Univ, MSc, 53; Univ Chicago, PhD, 57. *Prof Exp:* Fel, Enzyme Inst, Univ Wis, 58-60; asst prof biochem & psychiat, Yale Univ, 60-69; assoc prof biochem, Queen's Univ, 69-93. *Mem:* AAAS; Am Chem Soc. *Res:* Lipids. *Mailing Add:* 26 Edgehill St Kingston ON K7L 2T5 Can

SRIDARAN, RAJAGOPALA, REPRODUCTIVE ENDOCRINOLOGY. *Current Pos:* ADJ PROF BIOL, GA STATE UNIV, ATLANTA, 89- *Personal Data:* b Papireddipatti, India, Feb 22, 50; m 78; c 2. *Educ:* Univ Madras, India, BS, 70, MS, 72; Univ Health Sci, Chicago Med Sch, PhD(physiol), 77. *Prof Exp:* Instr zool, Madras Christian Col, 72-73; res assoc endocrinol, Univ Nebr Med Ctr, Omaha, 77-78, Univ Ill Med Ctr, 78-81; asst prof, 81-87, assoc prof physiol, Morehouse Sch Med, Atlanta, 87- *Mem:* Am Physiol Soc; Endocrin Soc; Soc Neurosci; Soc Study Reproduct; AAAS; Soc Exp Biol Med. *Res:* Corpus luteum function and maintenance of pregnancy; mechanism of antifertility action of gonadotropin-releasing hormone agonisk (GnRM-sq) during pregnancy in the rat; circadian rhythms in reproductive endocrinology. *Mailing Add:* Dept Physiol Morehouse Sch Med 720 Westview Dr SW Atlanta GA 30310-1495. *Fax:* 213-221-1235

SRIDHAR, CHAMPA GUHA, SOLID STATE PHYSICS. *Current Pos:* PVT CONSULT, 96- *Personal Data:* Indian citizen. *Educ:* Calcutta Univ, BSc, 63; Jadavpur Univ, Calcutta, MSc, 65; Northeastern Univ, MS, 68; Univ Conn, PhD(solid state physics), 73. *Prof Exp:* Teaching asst physics, Northeastern Univ, 66-68; asst, Univ Conn, 68-73; fel liquid crystal, 73; fel solid state physics, Stanford Univ, 74; Nat Res Coun fel theoret solid state physics, Ames Res Ctr, NASA, Moffett Field, 74-77; sr process engr, SX-70 film, Polaroid Corp, 77; develop engr precision frequency stand, Hewlett Packard Co, 78-83. *Mem:* Am Phys Soc; Sigma Xi. *Res:* Ban structure and optical properties calculation of solids; optical and electron spin resonance studies of radiation induced colour centers in solids; magnetic properties of liquid crystals. *Mailing Add:* 834 Hierra Ct Los Altos CA 94024

SRIDHAR, RAJAGOPALAN, BIOCHEMISTRY, CHEMISTRY. *Current Pos:* ASST MEM BIOMEMBRANE RES, OKLA MED RES FOUND, 78-; PROF, UNV SC. *Personal Data:* b Trichinopoly, Madras, India, July 29, 41; Can citizen. *Educ:* Univ Delhi, BSc, 61; Kurukshetra Univ, India, MSc, 63; Univ London, PhD(org chem), & DIC, 68. *Prof Exp:* Fel org chem, Res Inst for Med & Chem, Cambridge, 68-71; res assoc, Johns Hopkins Univ, 71-72;

assoc biochem, Univ Western Ont, 73-75; res fel radiobiol, Ont Cancer Treatment & Res Found, 75-78. *Concurrent Pos:* Consult biochem, Ont Cancer Treatment & Res Found, London Clin, Victoria Hosp, 78-; adj asst prof, Dept Radiol Sci, Okla Univ Health Sci Ctr, 81- *Mem:* Assoc mem Radiation Res Soc; Am Soc Photobiol; Biophys Soc; Am Asn Cancer Res; Sigma Xi. *Res:* Electron spin resonance studies in biological systems; DNA and membrane damage due to carcinogens and pharmaceuticals; radiosensitizers and other cytotoxic agents specific for hypoxic cells; multicell spheroids as a solid tumor model; nuclear magnetic resonance studies in biological systems. *Mailing Add:* Dept Radiation Therapy Howard Univ Hosp 2041 Georgia Ave NW Washington DC 20060. *Fax:* 213-221-1235

SRIDHARA, S, HORMONE ACTION, REGULATION TRANSCRIPTION. *Current Pos:* ASSOC PROF BIOCHEM, HEALTH & SCI CTR, TEX TECH UNIV, 82- *Educ:* Indian Inst Sci, Bangalora, India, PhD(biochem), 65. *Res:* Gene activity during insect metamorphosis. *Mailing Add:* Dept Biochem Tex Tech Univ Health Sci Ctr 3601 Fourth St Lubbock TX 79430-0001. *Fax:* 806-743-2990

SRIDHARAN, NATESA S, software process improvement, object technology, for more information see previous edition

SRIHARI, SARGUR N, ARTIFICIAL INTELLIGENCE, RECOGNITION. *Current Pos:* from asst prof to assoc prof, 78-87, PROF COMPUT SCI, STATE UNIV NY, BUFFALO, 87-, DIR, CTR DOCUMENT ANALYSIS & RECOGNITION, 91- *Personal Data:* b Bangalore, India, May 7, 50; m 77. *Educ:* Bangalore Univ, BSc, 68; Indian Inst Sci, BE, 70; Ohio State Univ, PhD(comput & info sci), 76. *Prof Exp:* Res asst, Ohio State Univ, 70-75; asst prof, Wayne State Univ, 76-78. *Concurrent Pos:* Assoc ed, Pattern Recognition J, 83-; prin investr, USPS Proj, 84-; consult, Xerox Corp, 85-; chmn, Cedartech, Inc, 96- *Mem:* Asn Comput Mach; fel Inst Elec & Electronics Engrs; Pattern Recognition Soc; Am Asn Artificial Intel; fel Int Asn Pattern Recognition. *Res:* Pattern recognition and artificial intelligence; document image analysis; handwriting recognition. *Mailing Add:* Cedar 520 Lee Entrance U B Commons Suite 202 Amherst NY 14228-2567. *E-Mail:* srihari@cedar.buffalo.edu

SRI-JAYANTHA, SRI MUTHUTHAMBY, MODELLING SIMULATION & IMPLEMENTATION OF SERVO SYSTEMS, MODELLING & SIMULATION OF ELECTRO-MECHANICAL SYSTEMS. *Current Pos:* RES STAFF MEM, TJ WATSON RES CTR, IBM, YORKTOWN HEIGHTS, 83- , MGR RES & DEVELOP, 89- *Personal Data:* b Eelam, Sri Lanka, Jan 24, 54; m, Avis Harrell; c Darren, Loren & Dylan. *Educ:* Univ Sri Lanka, BSc, 76; Pa State Univ, MS, 79; Princeton Univ, MA, 81 PhD(mech & aerospace eng), 83. *Prof Exp:* Res asst, Princeton Univ, 79-83. *Mem:* Inst Elec & Electronics Engrs. *Res:* Innovation of magnetic storage devices (hard disks) through modelling and simulation of precision mechanics and servo-system design; enhancing the ruggedness of these devices for mobile computer applications; granted 12 patents in field. *Mailing Add:* 32 Sherwood Ave Ossining NY 10562. *E-Mail:* msri@watson.ibm.com

SRIKANTH, SIVASANKARAN, ANTENNAS, MICROWAVES. *Current Pos:* ELECTRONICS ENGR, NAT RADIO ASTRON OBSERV, 84- *Personal Data:* b Thuckalay, Tamil Nadu India, Oct 3, 50; m 77, Viji Muthulakshmi; c Sushmita L & Shivshankar. *Educ:* Univ Madras, India, 85, 72, Indian Inst Technol, cert, 75, Ohio State Univ, MSEE, 84. *Prof Exp:* Aeronaut engr, Hindustar Aeronaut Ltd, Bangalore, India, 74-78; tech officer, State Bank India, 78-82. *Concurrent Pos:* mem, US Comn J, Int Union Radio Sci, 93. *Mem:* Inst Elec & Electronics Engrs. *Res:* Antennas and microwave passive components; Study of the effects of deformations in large reflector antennas using high frequency techniques and their compensation. *Mailing Add:* Nat Radio Astron Observ 2015 Ivy Rd Charlottesville VA 22903. *Fax:* 804-296-0324; *E-Mail:* ssrikant@nrao.edu

SRINATH, MANDYAM DHATI, ELECTRICAL ENGINEERING. *Current Pos:* assoc prof info & control sci, 67-76, PROF ELEC ENG, SOUTHERN METHODIST UNIV, 76- *Personal Data:* b Bangalore, India, Oct 12, 35; m 65; c 2. *Educ:* Univ Mysore, BSc, 54; Indian Inst Sci, DIISc, 57; Univ Ill, Urbana, MS, 59, PhD(elec eng), 62. *Prof Exp:* Asst prof elec eng, Univ Kans, 62-64; asst prof, Indian Inst Sci, 64-67. *Mem:* Inst Elec & Electronics Engrs; Soc Indust & Appl Math. *Res:* Control and estimation theory; digital signal processing; identification. *Mailing Add:* Dept Elec Eng Perkins Admin Bldg Southern Methodist Univ Dallas TX 75275

SRINIVASA, VENKATARAMANIAH, TECHNICAL MANAGEMENT, PLASTICS & PACKAGING ENGINEERING. *Current Pos:* sr packaging engr, Hosp Prods Div, 75-78, sr proj engr, Diag Div, 78-83, MGR, DIAG DIV, ABBOTT LABS, 83- *Personal Data:* b Mysore, India, Aug 30, 41; US citizen; m 72, Janakimala Muthiah; c Supreeth & Suman. *Educ:* Mysore Univ, BSc, 62, MSc, 64; Rutgers Univ, MS, 72, PhD(polymer sci & eng), 75. *Prof Exp:* Tech officer, Indian Inst Packaging, Bombay, 67. *Mem:* Am Chem Soc; Sigma Xi; Soc Plastics Engrs; Inst Packaging Profs. *Res:* Plastics and other packaging materials used in medical diagnostics products devices, kit designs, packaging, shipping and transportation. *Mailing Add:* 2729 Sallmon Ave Waukegan IL 60087-3514. *Fax:* 847-937-5810; *E-Mail:* vasa.srinivasa@add.ssw.abbott.com

SRINIVASAN, ASOKA, PHEROMONES. *Current Pos:* Asst prof biol, Tougaloo Col, 69-74, chmn, Biol Dept, 71-81, assoc prof, 74-80, chmn, nat sci div, 81-83, DIR BIOMED RES, TOUGALOO COL, 73- , PROF BIOL, 80- *Personal Data:* b Bangalore, India, May 13, 39, US citizen; m 67; c 2. *Educ:* Univ Mysore, India, BSc, 63; Univ Calif, Berkeley, PhD(entom), 70; MBA, Millsaps Col, 84. *Concurrent Pos:* Asst to pres, Miss Bio Asn, 87-, secy/treas, 88- *Mem:* Tissue Cult Asn; Entom Soc Am; Am Inst Biol Sci; AAAS; Sigma Xi. *Res:* Development and activity of the sex pheromone gland in Lepidoptera; tissue culture of sex pheromone gland of insects. *Mailing Add:* Dept Natural Sci Tougaloo Col Gen Delivery Tougaloo MS 39174-9999

SRINIVASAN, BHAMA, GROUP REPRESENTATIONS, ALGEBRA. *Current Pos:* PROF MATH, UNIV ILL, CHICAGO CIRCLE, 80- *Personal Data:* b Madras, India, Apr 22, 35; nat US. *Educ:* Univ Madras, BA, 54, MSc, 55; Univ Manchester, PhD(math), 59. *Prof Exp:* Lectr math, Univ Keele, 60-64; Nat Res Coun Can fel, Univ BC, 65-66; reader, Univ Madras, 67-70; assoc prof, Clark Univ, 70-80. *Mem:* Am Math Soc; London Math Soc; Indian Math Soc; Asn Women Math (pres, 81-83). *Res:* Representations of finite groups of lie type. *Mailing Add:* Dept Math M-C 249 Univ Ill Chicago IL 60607-7045. *Fax:* 312-996-1491; *E-Mail:* srinivas@uic.edu

SRINIVASAN, G(URUMAKONDA) R, THEORETICAL MODELING, RADIATION EFFECTS. *Current Pos:* adv engr, 74-82, sr eng mgr, Gen Technol Div, 82-96, RES SCIENTIST, ADVAN SEMICONDUCTOR TECHNOL LAB, IBM, 92- *Personal Data:* b Mysore, India; m 68, Alisan Snider; c Sandhya, Leela, Nina & Neil. *Educ:* Univ Mysore, BS, 54, Hons, 56; Indian Inst Sci, dipl metall, 58; Colo Sch Mines, MS, 61; Univ Ill, Urbana, PhD(metall), 66. *Prof Exp:* Res scholar metall, Indian Inst Sci, 58-59; res asst, Colo Sch Mines, 59-61, Univ Ill, Urbana, 61-66; res assoc mat sci, Cornell Univ, 66-68; from asst prof to assoc prof mat sci, Cath Univ Am, 68-74. *Concurrent Pos:* Europ affairs comt, Electrochem Soc, 84-92, tech exec comt, 82-, tech planning comt, 83; ed jour, Electronics Div, Electrochem Soc, 84-90. *Mem:* Metall Soc; Electrochem Soc. *Res:* Theoretical modeling; epitaxy; semiconductor devices; phase transformations, martensitic transformation in metals, spinodal decomposition in glasses; electron microscopy; x-ray diffraction and scattering; device physics; head of theoretical modeling group covering transistor processes and devices; cosmic ray and radiation effects; stress effects; ion implantation channeling theory and energy loss; epitaxy and diffusion; computer-aided device design; dislocation modeling; device physics; effects of cosmic rays on the soft error rate in integrated circuit chips. *Mailing Add:* 15 Mark Vincent Dr Poughkeepsie NY 12603. *Fax:* 914-892-3039; *E-Mail:* srinivas@Ffshvm1.vnet.ibm.com

SRINIVASAN, MAKUTESWARAN, MATERIALS SCIENCE, PHYSICAL METALLURGY & CERAMICS ENGINEERING. *Current Pos:* VPRES, MATS SOLUTIONS INT, INC, 90- *Personal Data:* b Tiruchirapalli, India, Jan 26, 45; m 71, Shantha; c Dipak M & Latha F. *Educ:* Univ Madras, India, BSc, 64; Indian Inst Sci, BE, 67; Univ Wash, MSinMetD, 69, PhD(metall), 72. *Prof Exp:* Res assoc mat sci, Univ Wash, 72-74; staff scientist graphite, Union Carbide Corp, 74-78; develop assoc silicon carbide, Carborundum Co, 78-79, sr res assoc struct ceramic, 79-83; mgr mat characterization & properties res, Sohio Engineered Mat Co, 84-88, res mgr, Struct & Refractory Prod, 88-89. *Mem:* Am Soc Metals; fel Am Ceramic Soc. *Res:* Mechanical properties of ceramics, mainly high temperature, high performance ceramics such as silicon carbide and silicon nitride; tribology; corrosion; advanced nondestructive evaluation; reliability and ceramic design; process yield improvement; materials selection. *Mailing Add:* 227 Deerwood Lane PO Box 663 Grand Island NY 14072. *Fax:* 716-839-1307

SRINIVASAN, P R, BIOCHEMISTRY. *Current Pos:* Fulbright-Smith Mundt fel Columbia Univ, 53-54, res fel, 53-57, res assoc , 57-58, from instr to assoc prof, 58-70, PROF BIOCHEM, COL PHYSICIANS & SURGEONS, COLUMBIA UNIV, 70- *Personal Data:* b Villupuram, India, Nov 24, 27. *Educ:* Univ Madras, BSc, 46, PhD(biochem), 53; Banaras Hindu Univ, MSc, 48. *Prof Exp:* Asst res officer biochem, Indian Coun Med Res, 52-53. *Concurrent Pos:* Fulbright Smith Mundt Scholar, 53-54; fel, John Simon Guggenheim Found, 67-68; Irma T Herschl Career Scientist Award, 73-77; sr int fel, Fogarty Int Ctr, 77-78; chmn, Conf Comt NY Acad Sci, 77 & 78. *Mem:* Am Chem Soc; Harvey Soc; Am Soc Microbiol; NY Acad Sci (pres, 80); Am Soc Biol Chemists; Sigma Xi. *Res:* Genetic analysis of nucleic acid biosynthesis in eucaryolic cells; drug induced gene amplification. *Mailing Add:* Dept Biochem & Molecular Biophys Columbia Univ Col P&S 630 W 168th St New York NY 10032-3702. *Fax:* 212-305-7932

SRINIVASAN, RAMACHANDRA SRINI, MATHEMATICAL MODELING & COMPUTER SIMULATION OF PHYSIOLOGICAL SYSTEMS, SPACEFLIGHT PHYSIOLOGY. *Current Pos:* SR RES SCIENTIST, KRUG LIFE SCI, INC, HOUSTON, 87- *Personal Data:* b Madurai, India, Mar 16, 39; US citizen; m 71, Prabha Venkataraman; c Karthik. *Educ:* Madras Univ, India, BE, 60; Indian Inst Sci, ME, 62; Purdue Univ, MSEE, 65; Calif Inst Technol, PhD(elec eng), 69. *Prof Exp:* Res assoc, Elec Eng Dept, Rice Univ, 70-72 & Baylor Col Med, Tex Med Ctr, 72-75; biomed engr, Abbott Labs, Chicago, 75-77; asst prof systs analysis, Dept Med & Biomet, Med Univ SC, 77-80; proj scientist & biomed engr, Gen Elec Govt Serv, 80-87. *Concurrent Pos:* Instr, Elec Eng Dept, Rice Univ, 74-75 & Univ Houston, 87-; prin investr, NASA, 87-, co-investr, 91-93. *Mem:* Sr mem Biomed Eng Soc; Inst Elec & Electronics Engrs; Sigma Xi. *Res:* Mathematical modeling and computer simulation of physiological systems and cardiovascular systems; spaceflight biomedical data. *Mailing Add:* Krug Life Sci Inc 1290 Hercules Dr Suite 120 Houston TX 77058-2769. *Fax:* 281-212-1316; *E-Mail:* srinivasan@plato.jsc.nasa.gov

SRINIVASAN, RANGASWAMY, OPTICS, CHEMICAL DYNAMICS. *Current Pos:* PRES, UV TECH, 90- *Personal Data:* b Madras, India, 1929; US citizen. *Educ:* Univ Madras, BSc Hons, 49, MSc, 51; Univ Southern Calif, PhD(phys chem), 56. *Prof Exp:* Mgr, T J Watson Res Ctr, IBM, 61-90. *Concurrent Pos:* Guggenheim fel, 65; vis prof, Ohio State Univ, 66-67, Columbia-Presby Med Ctr, 84-, Wellman Lab, Harvard Med Sch, 86-88. *Mem:* Fel AAAS; fel Am Phys Soc; fel Am Soc Laser Surg & Med; Am Chem Soc. *Res:* Photochemistry; laser interaction with matter; laser surger. *Mailing Add:* UVTECH Assoc 98 Cedar Lane Ossining NY 10562. *Fax:* 914-245-4763

SRINIVASAN, S, TELECOMMUNICATIONS, INFORMATION SYSTEMS MANAGEMENT. *Current Pos:* assoc prof, 87-96, PROF COMPUT INFO SYST, UNIV LOUISVILLE, 87- *Personal Data:* b Mayiladuturai, India, July 15, 48; US citizen; m 80, Lakshmi; c Sowmya & Harish. *Educ:* Annamalai Univ, India, MSc, 70; Univ Pittsburgh, MS, 75; Univ Akron, MS, 85; Univ Pittsburgh, PhD(math), 81. *Prof Exp:* Asst prof, Carlow Col, Pittsburgh, 81-82, Univ Akron, 82-84; assoc prof, Austin Peay State Univ, 84-87. *Mem:* Asn Comput Mach; sr mem Inst Elec & Electronics Engrs; sr mem Inst Elec & Electronics Engrs Commun Soc. *Res:* Electronic commerce and hospital information systems development. *Mailing Add:* Col Bus Univ Louisville Louisville KY 40292. *Fax:* 502-852-4875; *E-Mail:* srini@cbpa.louisville.edu

SRINIVASAN, SATHANUR RAMACHANDRAN, CHEMISTRY, BIOCHEMISTRY. *Current Pos:* PROF, DEPT APPL HEALTH & BIOCHEM, TULANE UNIV MED CTR, 93- *Personal Data:* b Madras, India, July 16, 38; m 67; c 1. *Educ:* Univ Madras, BSc, 58, BSc, 60, MSc, 62, PhD, 65. *Prof Exp:* Res assoc, Sch Med, La State Univ Med Ctr, New Orleans, 67-72, from asst prof to assoc prof, 72-81, prof, Dept Med & Biochem, 81-93. *Mem:* Am Heart Asn; Am Soc Biochem & Molecular Biol; Southern Soc Clin Invest. *Res:* Cardiovascular connective tissue and its relation to the pathogenesis of atherosclerosis; role of lipoproteins and lipoprotein-proteoglycans complexes in atherosclerosis; lipoprotein metabolism; lipoprotein epidemiology. *Mailing Add:* Ctr Cardiovasc Health SL 29 Tulane Univ Med Ctr New Orleans LA 70112-2699

SRINIVASAN, VADAKE RAM, BIOCHEMISTRY, MICROBIOLOGY. *Current Pos:* assoc prof, 65-70, PROF MICROBIOL, LA STATE UNIV, BATON ROUGE, 70- *Personal Data:* b Ponnani, India, Nov 18, 25; US citizen; m 57; c 2. *Educ:* Univ Madras, MA, 48, PhD(biol chem), 51; Univ Mainz, Dr rer Nat(org chem), 55. *Prof Exp:* Res assoc microbiol, Univ Ill, Urbana, 56-59; asst res prof biochem, Univ Pittsburgh, 59-60; res asst prof microbiol, Univ Ill, Urbana, 60-65. *Concurrent Pos:* Res grants, NIH, 66-, Am Cancer Soc, 66- & Am Sugarcane League, 68; partic, NSF Int Prog, 72; guest prof, Max Planck Inst Biochem, 72-73. *Mem:* Am Soc Microbiol; Am Chem Soc; Brit Biochem Soc; fel Am Inst Chem; NY Acad Sci. *Res:* Microbial biochemistry and molecular biology; intracellular differentiation in bacteria, control of macromolecular synthesis; single cell protein from cellulose wastes. *Mailing Add:* Dept Microbio La State Univ 602 Life Sci Bldg Baton Rouge LA 70803-0100

SRINIVASAN, VAKULA S, ELECTROCHEMISTRY, ANALYTICAL CHEMISTRY. *Current Pos:* assoc prof, 77-78, PROF CHEM, BOWLING GREEN STATE UNIV, 78- *Personal Data:* b Madras, India, Mar 25, 36; nat US; m 67, Malathi; c Sonja. *Educ:* Univ Madras, BSc, 56, MA, 58; La State Univ, Baton Rouge, PhD(chem), 65. *Prof Exp:* Archaeol chemist, Govt India, 57; scientist, Indian Atomic Energy Estab, 58-61; vis asst prof chem, La State Univ, Baton Rouge, 65; res fel, Case Inst Technol, 65-67; mem sci staff, TRW Systs, Calif, 67-71; res fel, Calif Inst Technol, 71. *Concurrent Pos:* Res fel, Purdue Univ, 73; consult, Gen Atomics Corp, 74, Energy Conversion Devices, Mich, Vulcan Mat, Ohio, Dinner Bell Inc, Henry Filters, Capitol Plastics, Ohio; vis prof, Tohoku Univ, Japan, 81; fac fel, NASA, 84-85, 85-86; res fel, Argonne Nat Lab, Ill, 84. *Mem:* Sigma Xi; Am Chem Soc; Royal Soc Chem. *Res:* Energy conversion; electrochemistry; space power systems; photopharmacology; enzyme electrodes. *Mailing Add:* Dept Chem Bowling Green State Univ Bowling Green OH 43403. *E-Mail:* vsriniv@bgnet.bgsu.edu

SRINIVASAN, VIJAY, COMPUTER AIDED DESIGN & MANUFACTURING, MODELING & SIMULATION. *Current Pos:* RES STAFF MEM, INT BUS MACH CORP RES DIV, T J WATSON RES CTR, 83-, MGR, 85- *Personal Data:* b Tamil Nadu, India, Oct 30, 54; m 84; c 1. *Educ:* Indian Inst Technol, BTech, 76, PhD(mech eng), 80. *Prof Exp:* Postdoctoral fel mech eng, Okla State Univ, 80-83. *Concurrent Pos:* Adj assoc prof, Dept Mech Eng, Columbia Univ, 86-90, adj prof, 91- *Mem:* Soc Indust & Appl Math. *Res:* Computer modeling and simulation of engineering systems in design and manufacturing; theories and algorithms in computer aided design and computer aided manufacturing. *Mailing Add:* Dept Mech Eng Columbia Univ 2960 New York NY 10027-6902

SRINIVASARAGHAVAN, RENGACHARI, environmental engineering, sanitary engineering, for more information see previous edition

SRIPADA, PAVANARAM KAMESWARA, SYNTHESIS OF MEMBRANE CONSTITUENTS. *Current Pos:* CONSULT, 89- *Personal Data:* b India, Jan 17, 33; US citizen; m 64; c 3. *Educ:* Anbhra Univ, BS,52, MSc,53,PhD(org chem), 58. *Hon Degrees:* Fel Royal Inst Chem, London, Eng, 69. *Prof Exp:* Lectr, Univ Toronto, 68-72; res assoc, Univ Rhode Island, 72-76 & Univ Conn Health Ctr, 76-81; res biochemist, Biophys Inst, Boston Univ, Med Sch, 81-89. *Concurrent Pos:* Vis scientist, Dept Org Chem, Nagarjuna Univ, India, 85-86. *Mem:* Am Chem Soc; NY Acad Sci; royal Inst Chem. *Res:* Synthesizing various labeled and unlabeled components of biomembranes to facilitate physical studies of their reconstituted molecular assemblies to probe into the mechanism of the progression of atherosclerosis. *Mailing Add:* 11421 Encore Dr Silver Spring MD 20901

SRIVASTAV, RAM PRASAD, APPLIED MATHEMATICS. *Current Pos:* assoc prof math, State Univ NY, Stony Brook, 67-73, actg chmn, 76-77, dir grad studies, 86-90, PROF APPL MATH, STATE UNIV NY, STONY BROOK, 73- *Personal Data:* b Khairabad, India, Oct 13, 34; m 59, Kusum Srivastava; c Raman, Divya & Mukta. *Educ:* Univ Lucknow, BSc, 53, MSc, 55, PhD(math), 58; Univ Glasgow, PhD(appl math), 63, DSc, 72. *Prof Exp:* Lectr math, Indian Inst Technol, Kanpur, 60-64; asst prof, 64-66; asst prof, Duke Univ, 66-67. *Concurrent Pos:* Assoc ed, J Appl Math, Soc Indust & Appl Math, 70-76; NSF grants, State Univ NY Stony Brook, 72, 74 & 89; vis mem, Math Res Ctr, Univ Wis-Madison, 73-74; US Army Res Off grant, 76-; vis fel, Princeton Univ, 81; IPA mathematician, US Army Res Off, 84-86; vis mem, Courant Inst Math Sci, NY Univ, 88; assoc ed, Comput & Math with Applications, 84-, Appl Numerical Math, 85- & Appl Math Lett, 87-; consult, UN Develop Prog, IIT, Madras, India, 89; US Army Res Off grant, 90-93. *Mem:* Am Math Soc; Soc Indust & Appl Math; fel Indian Nat Acad Sci; Math Asn Am; Am Acad Mech; Int Asn Math & Comput Simulation. *Res:* Integral equations; mixed boundary value problems in elasticity; numerical analysis and scientific computing; fracture mechanics. *Mailing Add:* Dept Appl Math & Statist State Univ NY Stony Brook NY 11794-3600. *E-Mail:* rsrivastav@ccmail.sunysb.edu, srivasta@ams.sunysb.edu

SRIVASTAVA, ARUN, PARVOVIRUSES & HUMAN DISEASE, PARVOVIRUS-BASED VECTORS FOR HUMAN GENE THERAPY. *Current Pos:* from asst prof to assoc prof, 85-94, PROF, IND UNIV SCH MED, 94- *Personal Data:* A Benjamin. *Educ:* Univ Allahabad, India, BS, 71, MS, 73; Indian Inst Sci, PhD(molecular biol), 79. *Honors & Awards:* Sreenivasaya Mem Medal, Univ Allahabad, India, 79. *Prof Exp:* Asst res, Mem Sloan Kettering Cancer Ctr, NY, 78-80; res assoc, Univ Fla, 80-82; asst prof, Univ Ark Med Sci, 82-85. *Concurrent Pos:* Consult, Baxter Healthcare Corp, 90-93. *Mem:* AAAS; Am Soc Microbiol (vpres, 90-91, pres, 91-92); Sigma Xi; Am Soc Hemat. *Res:* Parvoviruses and human disease; molecular biology of DNA replication; parvovirus-based vectors for human gene therapy-hemoglobinopathy, cancer and infectious diseases. *Mailing Add:* Ind Univ Sch Med Microbiol Dept MS-231 Indianapolis IN 46202-5120. *Fax:* 317-274-4090; *E-Mail:* arun_srivastava@hem_onc.iupui.edu

SRIVASTAVA, ASHOK KUMAR, GLYCOGEN METABOLISM-PROTEIN KINASES. *Current Pos:* ASST PROF, UNIV MONTREAL, 82- *Personal Data:* b Basti, India, July 5, 51; m 78; c 2. *Educ:* Lucknow Univ, India, BSc, 68, MSc, 70; Kanpur Univ, India, PhD(biochem), 74. *Prof Exp:* Fel, Univ Southern Calif, Los Angeles, 74-77; res assoc, Vanderbilt Univ, 77-80; sr investr, Clin Res Inst, Montreal, 81-93. *Mem:* Soc Exp Biol & Med; Can Biochem Soc; Am Soc Pharmacol & Exp Therapeut; Am Soc Biochem & Molecular Biol. *Res:* Regulation of cell function involving reversible protein phosphorylation dephosphorylation mechanisms; signal transduction in pathophysiological states. *Mailing Add:* Lab Dir Res Ctr Hotel Dieu Montreal Univ Montreal 3840 Rue St Urbain Jeanne Mance Pav Montreal PQ H2W 1T8 Can

SRIVASTAVA, BEJAI INDER SAHAI, BIOCHEMISTRY, MOLECULAR BIOLOGY. *Current Pos:* asst res prof biol, 66-74, ASST RES PROF BIOCHEM, STATE UNIV NY, BUFFALO, 75-; CANCER RES SCIENTIST V, ROSWELL PARK MEM INST, 77- *Personal Data:* b Shahjahanpur, India, June 1, 32; m 62; c 3. *Educ:* Agra Univ, BSc, 52; Univ Lucknow, MSc, 54; Univ Sask, PhD(plant physiol), 60. *Prof Exp:* Res asst plant physiol, Main Sugar Cane Res Sta, India, 54-55; lectr bot, Ramjas Col, Delhi, 55-57; res biochemist, Grain Res Lab, Winnepeg, Can, 61-63; assoc prof plant physiol, Carver Res Found, Tuskegee Inst, 63-65; sr cancer res scientist, Roswell Park Mem Inst, 65-68, assoc cancer res scientist, 68-77. *Concurrent Pos:* Res fel, Univ Sask, 60-61; NSF grants, 63-69 & 69-72; AEC grant, 66-69; NIH grant, 73-81. *Mem:* Am Soc Plant Physiol; Am Soc Biol Chemists; Am Asn Cancer Res; NY Acad Sci. *Res:* Biochemical markers for the differential diagnosis of leukemias; gene analysis for leukemia diagnosis; cytokines and cytokine receptors in human leukemias; human T-cell leukemia viruses. *Mailing Add:* Assoc Cancer Res Scientist Roswell Park Cancer Inst Buffalo NY 14263-0001

SRIVASTAVA, HARI MOHAN, MATHEMATICS, MATHEMATICAL PHYSICS. *Current Pos:* assoc prof, 69-74, PROF MATH, UNIV VICTORIA, BC, 74- *Personal Data:* b Ballia, India, July 5, 40; m 78, Panda; c Sapna & Gautam M. *Educ:* Univ Allahabad, BSc, 57, MSc, 59; Univ Jodhpur, PhD(math), 65. *Hon Degrees:* FNASc, India, 69; FRAS, London, UK, 68; FIMA UK, 75; C Math UK, 91; dipl, Univ Zulia, 91 & 96; FVPI, India, 93; FAAAS Washington, DC, 96. *Honors & Awards:* Hon Dip, La Universidad del Zulia, 92 & 96. *Prof Exp:* Lectr math, D M Govt Col, Gauhati Univ, India, 59-60 & Univ Roorkee, 60-63; lectr, Univ Jodhpur, 63-68, reader, 68-69; asst prof, WVa Univ, 67-69. *Concurrent Pos:* UGC grant, India, 65; vis prof numerous univs, sci acad & math insts around the world, 67-; grants, Natural Sci & Eng Res Coun Can, 69-; ed, Jnanabha, 72-; regional ed, Pure & Appl Math Sci, 76-; reviewer, Math Rev, Zentralblatt Fur Math & Appl Mech Rev; hon foreign mem, Royal Acad Sci, Lit & Fine Arts, Belg, 91-; hon prof, Inst Basic Res, Palm Harbor, Fla, 92-; hon adv prof, Fudan Univ, Shanghai, China, 93; assoc ed, J Math Anal & Applns, 93-; hon prof, Inst per la Ricerca di Base, Monteroduni, Molise, Italy, 95-, La Univ del Zulia, Marqcaibo, Venezuela, 96-; ed, PanAm J Kyungbook Math J, Soochow J Math. *Mem:* Am Math Soc; fel Inst Math & Appl; fel Royal Astron Soc London; fel Indian Nat Acad Sci; Can Math Soc; fel AAAS. *Res:* Special functions; operational calculus and related areas of differential and integral equations; Fourier analysis; combinatorial analysis; applied methematics; queuing theory; fractional calculus, complex analysis, mathematical physics and astrophysical applications; author, co-author or co-ed of 11 research monographs/books and over 400 journal articles. *Mailing Add:* Dept Math & Statist Univ Victoria Victoria BC V8W 3P4 Can. *Fax:* 250-721-8962; *E-Mail:* hmsri@uvvm.uvic.ca, harimsri@math.uvic.ca, harims@uvvm.uvic.ca

SRIVASTAVA, JAGDISH NARAIN, STATISTICS, MATHEMATICS. *Current Pos:* PROF STATIST & MATH, COLO STATE UNIV, 66- *Personal Data:* b Lucknow, India, June 20, 33; m 51; c 3. *Educ:* Univ Lucknow, BS, 51, MS, 54; Indian Statist Inst, Calcutta, dipl, 58; Univ NC, PhD(math statist), 61. *Honors & Awards:* Award, J Indian Soc Agr Statist, 61. *Prof Exp:* Statistician, Indian Inst Sugarcane Res, Lucknow, 55-57 & Indian Coun Agr Res, New Delhi, 58-59; res assoc, Univ NC, 61-63; assoc prof math, Univ Nebr, 63-66. *Concurrent Pos:* Consult, Lincoln State Hosp, Nebr, 63-64; res grants, Aerospace Res Labs, Air Force Base, Dayton, Ohio, 65-71, 74-, Nat Bur Standards, 69-72, 74-, Air Force Off Sci Res, 71- & NSF, 71-80; dir, Vis Lectr Prog Statist, US & Can, 73-75; founder & ed-in-chief, J Statist Planning & Inference, 75-84, chair gov bd, 84-; sessional pres, Indian Soc Agr Statist, 77. *Mem:* Fel Am Statist Asn; fel Inst Math Statist; Int Statist Inst; Indian Statist Inst; Forum Interdisciplinary Math (vpres, 75-77). *Res:* Multivariate analysis; combinatorial mathematics; weather modification statistics; foundations of statistics; sampling; design of experiments; co-authored one book, edited four books and published more than 100 papers. *Mailing Add:* 1318 Hillside Dr Denver CO 80524

SRIVASTAVA, KAILASH CHANDRA, MICROBIOLOGY. *Current Pos:* dir bioprocessing res, 92-94, vpres & dir bioprocessing res, 94-96, EXEC VPRES TECHNOL & COMMERCIALIZATION, ARCTECH INC, 96- *Personal Data:* b Varanasi, India, Sept 4, 47; m 77, Kumkum C Srivastava; c Mukta & Tarun K. *Educ:* Punjab Univ, BS, 68; Seton Hall Univ, MS, 71; Univ Col London, PhD, 75. *Honors & Awards:* Yusuf Ali Award, 72. *Prof Exp:* Dir, Lab Opers, Ivy Med Lab, NY, 75-78; assoc prof, Dept Food Sci & Technol, Londrina Brazil, 78-80; prof food microbiol & chmn dept, 80-84; researcher, Forest Prod Lab, Madison, Wis, 84-86; prof, Mich State Univ, East Lansing, 86-87; res scientist, Mich Biotech Inst, Lansing, 88-92. *Concurrent Pos:* Adj asst prof, Mich State Univ, 90- *Mem:* Am Soc Microbiol; NY Acad Sci; Soc Indust Microbiol. *Res:* Degradation of recalcitrant; xenobiotic compounds by microbes; several patents; bioconversion and upgrading of fossil fuels. *Mailing Add:* Arctech Inc 14100 Park Meadow Dr Suite 210 Chantilly VA 22021. *Fax:* 703-222-0299

SRIVASTAVA, KRISHAN, HIGH VOLTAGE ENGINEERING. *Current Pos:* PROF, DEPT ELEC ENG, UNIV WATERLOO, ONT, CAN, 66-, VPRES, STUDENT & ACAD SERVS, 83- *Personal Data:* b Kampur, India, July 9, 31; Can citizen; m; c 5. *Educ:* Agra Univ, India, BSc, 49; Roorkee Univ, India, BE, 52; Glasgow Univ, PhD(elec), 57. *Prof Exp:* Res assoc, Strathclyde Univ, Glasgow, 55-56; res engr, A Reyrolle & Co, 57-58; lectr, Univ Roorkee, India, 58-59; head, Elec Eng Dept, Eng Col, Univ Jodhpur, India, 59-60; sr res engr, Brush Elec Co, 61-62. *Concurrent Pos:* assoc chmn, 69-71, chmn, Dept Elec Eng, Univ Waterloo, 72-78. *Mem:* Fel Inst Elec & Electronics Engrs. *Res:* High Voltage Engineering; electrical insulation engineering; gaseous discharges. *Mailing Add:* Dept Elec Eng Univ BC Main Mall Mcleod Bldg Vancouver BC V6T 1Z1 Can

SRIVASTAVA, LALIT MOHAN, BIOLOGY. *Current Pos:* from asst prof to assoc prof, Simon Fraser Univ, 65-71, acad vpres, 69-70, chmn, 85-90, PROF BIOL SCI, SIMON FRASER UNIV, 71- *Personal Data:* b Gonda, India, Sept 7, 32; m 64. *Educ:* Univ Allahabad, BSc, 50, MSc, 52; Univ Calif, Davis, PhD(bot), 62. *Prof Exp:* Mercer res fel, Harvard Univ, 61-64, Maria Moors Cabot res fel, 64-65. *Concurrent Pos:* Mem, Mgt Adv Coun, Ministry Educ, BC, 78-81; pres, Enmar Res Corp, 81- *Mem:* Can Soc Plant Physiol; Can Fedn Biol Socs; Am Soc Plant Physiol; Plant Growth Regulator Soc Am. *Res:* Cambium, xylem and phloem; cell growth; gibberellins, receptors, mode of action; physiology of growth, nutritional requirements and chemical constituents of seaweeds. *Mailing Add:* Dept Biol Sci Simon Fraser Univ Burnaby BC V5A 1S6 Can

SRIVASTAVA, LAXMI SHANKER, ENDOCRINOLOGY. *Current Pos:* from asst prof to assoc prof, 69-78, PROF EXP MED, DEPT INTERNAL MED, MED CTR, UNIV CINCINNATI, 78-, DIR ENDOCRINOL & METAB LABS, 69- *Personal Data:* b Deoria, Uttar Pradesh, India, Mar 2, 38; m 60; c 3. *Educ:* Bihar Univ, BVSc & AH, 59; Univ Mo-Columbia, MS, 61, PhD(animal breeding), 64. *Prof Exp:* Vet surgeon, Bihar Govt, India, 59-60; instr endocrinol, Univ Mo-Columbia, 64-65, res assoc, Space Res Ctr, 67-68. *Concurrent Pos:* Univ Res Fund grant, St Louis Univ, 65-66; NIH grant, Wash Univ, 66-67. *Mem:* Endocrine Soc; Am Fedn Clin Res; Am Asn Clin Chemists. *Res:* Mammary cancer; neuroendocrine control of pituitary function; mammalian reproductive physiology. *Mailing Add:* 1868 Loisview Lane Cincinnati OH 45255

SRIVASTAVA, MUNI SHANKER, MATHEMATICAL STATISTICS. *Current Pos:* From asst prof to assoc prof math, 63-72, PROF MATH, UNIV TORONTO, 72- *Personal Data:* b Gonda, India, Jan 20, 36; m 64; c 4. *Educ:* Univ Lucknow, BSc, 56, MSc, 58; Stanford Univ, PhD(statist), 64. *Concurrent Pos:* Vis res staff, Princeton Univ, 65-66; assoc prof, Univ Conn, 70-71; vis prof, Univ Wis & Indian Statist Inst, 77-78. *Mem:* Fel Inst Math Statist; fel Am Statist Asn; fel Royal Statist Soc; fel Int Statist Inst. *Res:* Multivariate statistics; quality control; sequential analysis. *Mailing Add:* Dept Statist Univ Toronto Toronto ON M5S 1A7 Can

SRIVASTAVA, PRAKASH NARAIN, REPRODUCTIVE BIOCHEMISTRY. *Current Pos:* asst prof, 69-75, assoc prof, 75-81, PROF BIOCHEM, UNIV GA, 82- *Personal Data:* b Allahabad, India, Dec 7, 29; m 55, Krishna; c Sunita, Sujata, Shikha & Nalin. *Educ:* Lucknow Univ, India, BSc, 49, MSc, 51; Cambridge Univ, PhD(biochem), 65. *Prof Exp:* Asst res officer hormones, Indian Vet Res Inst, 58-68. *Mem:* Am Soc Biol Chemists; Am Physiol Soc; Soc Study Reproduction; Soc Study Fertil UK; Am Soc Cell Biol. *Res:* Sperm enzymes and their inhibitors in fertilization. *Mailing Add:* Dept Biochem Univ Ga Life Sci Bldg Athens GA 30602. *Fax:* 706-542-1738; *E-Mail:* srivas@bchiris.biochem.Uga.edu

SRIVASTAVA, PRAKASH NARAIN, insect physiology & biochemistry, aphid feeding & nutrition, for more information see previous edition

SRIVASTAVA, REKHA, APPLICABLE MATHEMATICS. *Current Pos:* res fel, Univ Victoria, 72-73, res assoc & vis scientist, 73-77, sessional lectr, 78-89, ADJ ASSOC PROF MATH, UNIV VICTORIA, 89-, ADJ PROF MATH, 97- *Personal Data:* b Chikati, Orissa, India, Feb 15, 45; m 78, Hari M; c Sapna & Gautam M. *Educ:* Utkal Univ, India, BSc, 62; Banaras Hindu Univ, MSc, 65, PhD(math), 67. *Prof Exp:* Lectr math, Khallikote Col, Berhampur Univ, 68-69, Rourkela Sci Col, 69-70, Women's Col, Berhampur Univ, 70-71 & Ravenshaw Col, Utkal Univ, India, 71-72. *Concurrent Pos:* Reviewer, Mathematical Reviews, Zentralblatt fur Mathematike; vis prof, McGill Univ, 90; vis prof & actg dir, Ctr Math Sci, Trivandrum, India, 92 & 94. *Mem:* Am Math Soc; Vijnana Parishad India; Asn Women Math; Indian Math Soc. *Res:* Special functions; operational calculus including integral transforms and related areas of integral equations; Fourier analysis; G H and the generalized Lauricella functions of several variables; fractional calculus; statistical applications; author or co-author of about 50 research papers in professional journals and conference proceedings, and cited in several books and monographs. *Mailing Add:* Dept Math & Statist Univ Victoria Victoria BC V8W 3P4 Can. *Fax:* 205-721-8962; *E-Mail:* rekhas@uvvm.uvic.ca

SRIVASTAVA, SANTOSH KUMAR, MASS SPECTROMETRY, CHEMICAL PHYSICS. *Current Pos:* RES SCIENTIST, JET PROPULSION LAB, 75- *Personal Data:* b Kanpur, India, Jan 10, 41; US citizen; div; c Shan, Shalini & Nisha. *Educ:* Univ Southern Calif, PhD(physics), 73. *Mem:* Fel Am Phys Soc. *Res:* Ion formation by electron impact; mass spectromeric studies related to atmospheric pollutant gases; development of instrumentation for planetary atmospheres; electron collision physics. *Mailing Add:* Jet Propulsion Lab 4800 Oak Grove Dr Pasadena CA 91109. *Fax:* 818-393-4605; *E-Mail:* santoshk.srivastava@scn1.jpl.nasa.gov

SRIVASTAVA, SATISH KUMAR, BIOCHEMISTRY, GENETICS. *Current Pos:* PROF HUMAN BIOL CHEM & GENETICS, UNIV TEX MED BR GALVESTON, 74- *Personal Data:* b Rae Bareli, India, July 21, 37; m 62; c 3. *Educ:* Univ Lucknow, India, BS, 56, MS, 58, PhD(biochem), 62. *Prof Exp:* Tutor biochem, Postgrad Med Sch, Chandigarh, India, 64-66; res scientist, City of Hope Nat Med Ctr, 66-74; asst prof pharmacol, Med Sch, Univ Southern Calif, 70-74. *Concurrent Pos:* Coun Sci & Indust Res India fel, Univ Lucknow, 62-64; NIH res grant, 71. *Mem:* Am Soc Hemat; Asn Res Vision & Ophthal. *Res:* Genetics of glycolipid storage diseases; glutathione metabolism in red cells and lens; enzyme kinetics and red cell metabolism; biochemical alterations in senile cataract formation. *Mailing Add:* Dept Human Biol Chem & Genetics Univ Tex Med Br Galveston TX 77555. *Fax:* 409-772-4001

SRIVASTAVA, SUDHIR, EARLY DETECTION DIAGNOSIS & SCREENING OF CANCER, PUBLIC HEALTH ISSUES COMPUTER APPLICATIONS FOR EARLY DETECTION & DIAGNOSIS OF CANCER. *Current Pos:* sr staff fel, Nat Heart Lung & Blood Inst, 87-88, cancer prev fel, Nat Cancer Int, 88-90, PROG DIR, NIH DEPT HEALTH & HUMAN SERV, US GOV, 90- *Personal Data:* m 83, Rashimi Gopal; c Aditi & Jigisha. *Educ:* Benaras Hindu Univ, PhD(biochem), 77; Va Commonwealth Univ, MS, 87. *Prof Exp:* Asst prof, Banaras Hindu Univ, India, 76-78; vis scientist, Univ Osaka, Japan, 78-79; NIH training fel, Univ Calif, San Francisco, 79-80; staff fel, Boston Biomed Res Inst, 80-81; res assoc, Univ Tucson, 81-83; instr, Med Col Va, 83-87. *Concurrent Pos:* Mombusho fel, Ministry Educ, Japan Gov, 77-78; sr investr, Am Heart Asn, 81; consult, Global Inst Nutrit Info, 94- *Mem:* Fedn Am Soc Exp Biol; Am Asn Cancer Res. *Res:* Development of molecular and genetic markers for early detection, risk assessment and diagnosis of cancer; investigating the factor(s) that predisposes individuals to cancer. *Mailing Add:* 8216 Brucar Ct Gaithersburg MD 20877

SRIVASTAVA, SURAT PRASAD, GEOPHYSICS. *Current Pos:* RES SCIENTIST, ATLANTIC GEOSCI CENTRE, BEDFORD INST OCEANOG, 65- *Personal Data:* b Allahabad, India, July 1, 37. *Educ:* Indian Inst Technol, Kharagpur, BSc, 58, MTech, 60; Univ BC, PhD(physics), 63. *Prof Exp:* Nat Res Coun Can res fel, Dom Observ, Can, 63-64; asst prof geophys, Univ Alta, 64-65. *Concurrent Pos:* Mem, Can Subcomt Geomagnetism, Assoc Comt Geod & Geophys, 66. *Mem:* Am Geophys Union. *Res:* Tectonic implications of the subsurface structures across the continental slope and margin obtained using gravity, magnetic and seismic measurements; application of magnetotelluric method on land and sea. *Mailing Add:* Bedford Inst Oceanog Regional Reconnaissance Div Atlantic Geosci Ctr PO Box 1006 Dartmouth NS B2Y 4A2 Can

SRIVASTAVA, SURESH CHANDRA, RADIOPHARMACEUTICAL SCIENCE, RADIO & NUCLEAR CHEMISTRY. *Current Pos:* assoc scientist, 75-78, scientist, 78-79, HEAD, RADIONUCLIDE & RADIOPHARMACEUT RES DIV, MED DEPT, BROOKHAVEN NAT LAB, 83-, SR SCIENTIST, 90-; RES PROF RADIOL, UNIV STONY BROOK, 93- *Personal Data:* b Aligarh, India, Jan 1, 39; US citizen; m 68, Maria; c Stephen & Neil. *Educ:* Agra Univ, BS, 55, MS, 57; Univ Allahabad, PhD(chem), 61. *Honors & Awards:* NATO Advan Study Inst Award, 85; Res & Develop 100 Award, 86; Spec Recognition Award, Chilean Soc Biol Nuclear Med, 89; Fed Lab Consortium Award, 88. *Prof Exp:* AEC fel, La State Univ, New Orleans, 62-65; res assoc, Brookhaven Nat Lab, 65-67; vis scientist, Sch Chem, Univ Paris, 67-69; res assoc, Ga Inst Technol, 69-71; chemist, Res Triangle Inst, NC, 71-74; clin asst prof radiol, Downstate Med Ctr, Brooklyn, NY, 74-75. *Concurrent Pos:* Consult, Northport Vet Admin Hosp, NY, 82-, Mem Sloan Kettering Cancer Res Ctr, NY, 83-86, Cremascoli Inc, Milan, 86-92, Mallinckrodt Med Inc, 90-94; int expert, Int Atomic Energy Agency, 83-, bd dir, Radiopharmaceut Sci Coun, 85-87; prin investr radionuclide & radiopharmaceut res prog, 83-; ed spec issue, Int J Nucl Med Biol, 86 & 91; ed bd, Int J Biol Markers, 86; subcomt nucl med, Dept Energy, Off Health Environ Res Adv Comt, 87-88; ed, NATO Advan Study Inst, Proc on Monoclonal Antibodies, 88. *Mem:* Am Chem Soc; Soc Nuclear Med; Radiopharmaceut Sci Coun (bd dirs, 85-87, pres, 93-94); AAAS; Indo-Am Soc Nuclear Med (vpres, 87-88, pres, 89-90); Int Asn Radiopharmacol; Int Isotope Soc; hon mem Asn Latin Am Soc Bio & Nuclear Med. *Res:* Radiopharmaceuticals; novel diagnostic reagents and therapeutic agents for in vitro and in vivo applications; radiolabeled monoclonal antibodies for imaging and therapy of cancer; chemistry and production of short-lived gamma and positron-emitting radionuclides and of beta emitters of interest to nuclear medicine; technetium chemistry and radiopharmaceuticals; blood cell labeling; radiopharmaceuticals for bone pain therapy; author of 160 articles, 170 abstracts, 20 book chapters and 1 book; granted 14 US and foreign patents on radiopharmaceuticals. *Mailing Add:* Dept Med Brookhaven Nat Lab PO Box 5000 Upton NY 11973-5000. *Fax:* 516-344-5962; *E-Mail:* srivast1@bnl.gov

SRIVASTAVA, TRILOKI N, PURE MATHEMATICS, MATHEMATICAL STATISTICS. *Current Pos:* ASSOC PROF MATH, CONCORDIA UNIV, 72- *Personal Data:* b Lucknow, India, June 1, 36; Can citizen; m 77, Zahida; c Yusuf & Alireza. *Educ:* Lucknow Univ, BS, 57, MS, 59; Gorakhpur Univ, PhD(math), 69; Sheffield Univ, PhD(statist). *Prof Exp:* Sr lectr math, Loyola Col Montreal, 63-64, from asst prof to assoc prof, 64-71; vis prof, Univ Isfahahan, Iran, 71-72. *Res:* Study of differential geometry of special Kawaguchi manifold, generalized statistical distributions and distributions of general functions of random variables; published 30 research articles in refereed journals; reviewer for mathematical reviews. *Mailing Add:* Dept Math Concordia Univ 1455 Demaisonneuve Blvd W Montreal PQ H3G 1M8 Can. *Fax:* 848-2831; *E-Mail:* sriv@vax2.concordia.ca

SRIVASTAVA, UMA SHANKER, MOLECULAR BIOLOGY, BIOCHEMISTRY. *Current Pos:* RETIRED. *Personal Data:* b Lucknow, Uttar Pradesh, India, Mar 13, 34; Can citizen; m 70; c Srivastava C. *Educ:* Lucknow Univ, India, BSc, 55, MSc, 57; Laval Univ, Can, DSc, 65. *Prof Exp:* From asst prof to assoc prof, Dept Nutrit, Univ Montreal, 68-79, prof nutrit & toxicol, 79-95, prof prog toxicol, 80-95. *Concurrent Pos:* Exchange fel, France & Can, 73; prof toxicol, Div Toxicol, Johns Hopkins Univ, 80; sr res scientist biochem & appl nutrit, Cent Food & Technol Res Inst, India, 80-81; prof pharmacol & physiol, San Luis, Patosi, Mexico, 89-90. *Mem:* NY Acad Sci; Am Inst Nutrit; fel Am Col Nutrit; Soc Environ Geochem & Health; Can Biochem Soc; Fr-Can Asn Advan Sci; Can Soc Nutrit. *Res:* Biochemical and molecular aspects of malnutrition in the development of the brain; modulation, translation and decoding of coding sequences in the messenger RNA of the brain of well fed and dietary restricted rats; toxic effects of heavy metals in the nutrition of animals and man; etiology of progressive muscular dystrophy; nutrients and minerals in North American diet; role of chemically defined diet on the growth of pea aphids. *Mailing Add:* 3920 Rue Beriot Brossard PQ J4Z 2W7 Can. *Fax:* 514-343-7395

SRIVASTAVA, VISHNU CHANDRA, APPLIED SUPERCONDUCTIVITY, CRYOGENICS. *Current Pos:* SR STAFF SCIENTIST, PICKER INT, 90- *Personal Data:* b Faizbad, India, Jan 21, 39; US citizen; m 63, Saroj; c Aseem, Nina, Ameet & Meena. *Educ:* Lucknow Univ, BSc, 59; McGill Univ, MSc, 65, PhD(solid state physics), 69. *Prof Exp:* Prof assoc, McGill Univ, Montreal, 70-73; prod mgr, Can Superconductor, 73-78; sr res engr, Magnetic Corp Am, 78-80; proj engr, Advan Energy Syst, Gen Elec, 80-84, sr engr, Med Systs, 85-90. *Mem:* Inst Elec & Electronics Engrs. *Res:* Magnetic resonance imaging systems utilizing superconducting magnets; interventional magnetic resonance imaging systems developed for diagnosis and therapy; open systems which cause no claustrophobic effects on patients. *Mailing Add:* Picker Int 595 Miner Rd Highland Heights OH 44143. *Fax:* 440-473-5728; *E-Mail:* vcs@mr.picker.com

SRIVATSAN, TIRUMALAI SRINIVAS, MATERIALS TESTING, SOLID & FRACTURE MECHANICS. *Current Pos:* asst prof, 87-92, assoc prof mat sci & mech, 92-, PROF MAT SCI & MECH UNIV AKRON, 97- *Personal Data:* b Madras, India, July 14, 57; US citizen; m 89. *Educ:* Univ Bangalore, BEng, 80; Ga Inst Technol, MS, 81, PhD(mech eng), 84. *Prof Exp:* Res fel, Ctr Computational Studies, 84-85; res fel & instr mat processing, Ga Tech Res Inst, 85-86; proj engr & mgr, Mat Modification Inc, 86-87. *Concurrent Pos:* Mem, Struct Mat Comt, Metals, Minerals & Mat Soc, 87-; distinguished lectr, Am Soc Mat Int, 88; ed-in-chief, Mat & Mfg Processes Int J, 89- *Mem:* Am Soc Mech Engrs; Am Soc Mat Int; Metals Minerals & Mat Soc. *Res:* Mechanical behavior of engineering materials; relationship between microstructure and mechanical properties; mechanical life-time failure prediction; thermal-mechanical fatigue; materials processing and characterization; electron microscopy; fracture mechanics; stress analysis; composite materials; author of over 150 technical publications. *Mailing Add:* Dept Mech Eng Univ Akron Akron OH 44325-3903

SRNKA, LEONARD JAMES, INVERSE THEORY, GEOPHYSICAL APPLICATIONS. *Current Pos:* mem staff, Long Range Res Div, Exxon Prod Res Co, 79-93, SUPVR, GRAVITY/MAGNETICS, EXXON EXPLOR CO, 93- *Personal Data:* b Cleveland, Ohio, Nov 17, 46; div; c 1. *Educ:* Purdue Univ, BS, 68; Univ Newcastle, UK, PhD(physics), 74. *Prof Exp:* Sci officer plasma physics, Culham Lab, UK Atomic Energy Authority, Eng, 70-73; fel, Lunar Sci Inst, Univ Space Res Asn, 74-75, staff scientist, Lunar & Planetary Inst, 75-79. *Concurrent Pos:* Vis scientist, Lunar & Planetary Inst, 79-; group leader, wave equation methods, Long Range Res Div, Exxon Prod Res Co, 84- *Mem:* Am Geophys Union; Am Phys Soc; Soc Explor Geophys. *Res:* Electromagnetic fields in planetary interiors; exploration geophysics, seismic and electromagnetic inversion; gravity and magnetic methods. *Mailing Add:* Exxon Explor Co 222 Benmar Rm 616 Houston TX 77060-2544. *E-Mail:* len.j.srnka@exxon.sprint.com

SROLOVITZ, DAVID JOSEPH, MICROSTRUCTURAL EVOLUTION, STRUCTURE OF DEFECTS. *Current Pos:* PROF MAT SCI & APPL PHYSICS, UNIV MICH, 87- *Personal Data:* b Milwaukee, Wis, Mar 13, 57; m 78, Carem Thomas; c Aron, Miriam & Noam. *Educ:* Rutgers Univ, BS, 78; Univ Pa, MSE, 80, PhD (mats sci & eng), 81. *Prof Exp:* Postdoctoral, Exxon Res & Eng Co, 82-84; staff mem, Los Alamos Nat Lab, 84-87. *Concurrent Pos:* Mem, Advan Res Projs Agency, Mat Res Coun, 86-88. *Mem:* Am Inst Mech Eng; Mat Res Soc; Am Phys Soc; Metall Soc. *Res:* Microstructural evolution; dislocation dynamics; structure and thermodynamics of interfaces; mechanics of defected materials; film growth; computer simulation. *Mailing Add:* Dept Mat Sci & Eng Univ Mich Dow Bldg Ann Arbor MI 48109-2136. *Fax:* 313-763-4788; *E-Mail:* srol@engin.umich.edu

SROOG, CYRUS EFREM, ORGANIC & POLYMER CHEMISTRY, THERMODYNAMICS & MATERIAL PROPERTIES. *Current Pos:* OWNER, POLYMER CONSULT, INC, 86- *Personal Data:* b New York, NY, Mar 25, 22; m 43, Irene Klein; c Katherine & Jeanne. *Educ:* Brooklyn Col, BA, 42; Univ Buffalo, PhD(chem), 50. *Prof Exp:* Instr chem, Univ Buffalo, 46-50; res chemist, E I du Pont de Nemours & Co, Inc, 50-54, res supvr, 54-61, develop mgr, 62-64, res mgr, 64-76, sr fel, 76-86. *Concurrent Pos:* Res fel, NY Acad Sci, 76-86; invited lectr, Germany, France, Eng, Japan & US; lectr, Oxford Univ, 89. *Mem:* Am Chem Soc; NY Acad Sci; The Chem Soc. *Res:* High temperature polymers; thermally stable polymers; heterocyclic, organic nitrogen, organic sulfur and metalloorganic compounds; aromatic polyimides; heterocyclic polymers. *Mailing Add:* 3227 Coachman Rd Surrey Park Wilmington DE 19803

SROUR, JOSEPH RALPH, solid state electronics, radiation effects, for more information see previous edition

SRYGLEY, FLETCHER DOUGLAS, MATERIALS SCIENCE ENGINEERING. *Current Pos:* assoc prof, 73-79, PROF PHYSICS, DAVID LIPSCOMB COL, 79- *Personal Data:* b Nashville, Tenn, Mar 27, 38; m 68, Gail L Gregory; c Perry A, Amy L & F Douglas. *Educ:* David Lipscomb Col, BA, 60; Duke Univ, PhD(physics), 66. *Prof Exp:* Asst prof physics, Stetson Univ, 66-73. *Mem:* Sigma Xi; Am Phys Soc; Am Asn Physics Teachers. *Res:* Electron spin resonance studies of radiation damage in single crystals; electron spin resonance and ultraviolet studies of color centers in magnesium oxide; fourier analysis of x-ray line shapes. *Mailing Add:* Dept Physics Box 4107 David Lipscomb Univ Nashville TN 37204-3951. *Fax:* 615-269-1830; *E-Mail:* srygleyfd@dlu.edu

SRYGLEY, ROBERT BAXTER, PHYSIOLOGICAL ECOLOGY, EVOLUTION. *Current Pos:* POSTDOCTORAL RES ASSOC, DEPT ZOOL, UNIV WASH. *Personal Data:* b Washington, DC, Nov 17, 59. *Educ:* Univ Wash, BA, 83; Univ Tex, PhD(zool), 91. *Honors & Awards:* Presidential Award, Am Naturalists Soc, 90. *Prof Exp:* Res assoc, Dept Ecol & Evolution, Univ Chicago, 91-93; NSF-NATO fel, Dept Zool, Univ Cambridge, 93- *Mem:* Asn Study Animal Behav. *Res:* Integrate the physiology of flight energetics with the evolutionary ecology of insects. *Mailing Add:* Dept Zool Univ Wash Box 351800 Seattle WA 98195

STAAL, GERARDUS BENARDUS, ENTOMOLOGY, BIOLOGY. *Current Pos:* dir biol res, 68-80, DIR INSECT RES, SANDOZ CROP PROTECTION RES DIV, 80- *Personal Data:* b Assen, Neth, Aug 19, 25; m 57; c 2. *Educ:* State Agr Univ, Wageningen, Ing, 57, PhD(insect physiol), 61. *Prof Exp:* Sr res officer, Neth Orgn Appl Sci Res, 61-68. *Concurrent Pos:* Neth Orgn Pure Res fel biol, Harvard Univ, 62-63. *Mem:* AAAS; Entom Soc Am; Am Chem Soc; Am Soc Zoologists; Am Orchid Soc. *Res:* Comparative insect endocrinology; insect bioassay of toxicants; juvenile hormone analogs; antagonists and other principles affecting growth and development of insects; neurohormones; neurotransmitters. *Mailing Add:* 635 Marion Ave Palo Alto CA 94301

STAAT, ROBERT HENRY, PATHOGENIC MECHANISMS, MICROBIAL ADHERENCE & INFECTION CONTROL. *Current Pos:* from asst to assoc prof, 76-83, PROF MICROBIOL, SCH DENT, UNIV LOUISVILLE, 83-, ASSOC PROF MICROBIOL, SCH MED, 76- *Personal Data:* b Denver, Colo, Apr 2, 42; m 79, Cynthia R Alfery; c Cynthia H, Barton C & Sarah C. *Educ:* Univ NMex, BS, 65, MS, 68; Univ Minn, PhD(microbiol), 75. *Prof Exp:* Res assoc, Univ NMex, 67-69; scientist, Sch Dent, Univ Minn, 71-73, res fel, 73-75; asst prof microbiol, Sch Dent, Med Univ SC, 75-76. *Concurrent Pos:* Prin investr, Sugar Asn grant, 79-82 & Nat Inst Dent Res, NIH, 76-83; dir, Sterilizer Monitoring Prog. *Mem:* AAAS; Am Soc Microbiol; Am Asn Dent Res; Sigma Xi; Am Asn Dent Sch. *Res:* Determination of the pathogenic mechanisms of oral Streptococci, specifically, definition of the adherence reaction of streptococcus mutans to the tooth surface and purification of the adherence factors for use in a dental caries vaccine; infection control principles as applied to dentistry. *Mailing Add:* Dept Biol Sci Sch Dent Univ Louisville Louisville KY 40292. *E-Mail:* rhstaa0l@ulkyum.louisville.edu

STAATS, GUSTAV W(ILLIAM), ELECTRICAL ENGINEERING. *Current Pos:* from asst prof to assoc prof, 65-77, PROF ELEC ENG, UNIV WIS-MILWAUKEE, 77- *Personal Data:* b Forest Park, Ill, Nov 30, 19; m 49, Evelyn Zars; c David & Mary. *Educ:* Ill Inst Technol, BS, 42, MS, 48, PhD(elec eng), 56. *Prof Exp:* Engr, Motor & Generator Dept, Allis-Chalmers Mfg Co, 42-56, staff engr, Thermal Power Dept, 56-63, res engr, Res Div, 63-65. *Mem:* Fel Inst Elec & Electronics Engrs. *Res:* Rotating electrical machinery; high strength magnetic fields; electric power systems. *Mailing Add:* 6124 N Lake Dr Whitefish Bay WI 53217

STAATS, PERCY ANDERSON, PHYSICAL CHEMISTRY, PHYSICS. *Current Pos:* RETIRED. *Personal Data:* b Belleville, WVa, Feb 20, 21; m 44, Julia Bourmorck; c Thomas, Ruth A, Nancy & Theresa. *Educ:* Marietta Col, AB, 43; Univ Minn, MS, 49. *Hon Degrees:* DS, Fisk Univ, 74. *Prof Exp:* Instr physics, Marietta Col, 43; tech supvr, Tenn Eastman Corp, 43-46; chemist, Rohm and Haas Co, Pa, 49-52; chemist, Oak Ridge Nat Lab, 52-85. *Concurrent Pos:* Guest lectr & lab dir, Infrared Spectros Inst, Fisk Univ, 57-75; traveling lectr, Oak Ridge Inst Nuclear Studies, 59-60, 62-63 & 65-66. *Mem:* Am Chem Soc. *Res:* Molecular structure by infrared spectroscopy; infrared spectra of gases as solids at low temperatures; inorganic ions in solid solution; isotopes, especially tritium; gas lasers; plasma diagnostics using far infrared submillimeter lasers. *Mailing Add:* 119 Manchester Rd Oak Ridge TN 37830

STAATS, WILLIAM R, CHEMICAL ENGINEERING. *Current Pos:* GEN MGR BASIC RES, GAS RES INST, 79- *Personal Data:* b Chicago, Ill, Sept 10, 35; m 80, Ann C Hulsey; c 2. *Educ:* Ill Inst Technol, BS, 57, MS, 60, PhD, 70. *Prof Exp:* Chem engr, Inst Gas Technol, 57-58; proj develop officer, Rome Air Develop Ctr, 59-62; chem engr, Inst Gas Technol, 62-69; vpres eng res, Polytech, Inc, 70-75; assoc dir, Inst Gas Technol, 75-79. *Mem:* AAAS; Am Inst Chem Engrs; Combustion Inst; Am Chem Soc. *Res:* Natural Gas technology. *Mailing Add:* 705 Timber Trail Dr Naperville IL 60565-2705. *Fax:* 773-399-8170

STAATZ, MORTIMER HAY, ECONOMIC GEOLOGY. *Current Pos:* RETIRED. *Personal Data:* b Kalispell, Mont, Oct 20, 18; m 52; c 3. *Educ:* Calif Inst Technol, BS, 40; Northwestern Univ, MS, 42; Columbia Univ, PhD(geol), 52. *Prof Exp:* Asst geol, Northwestern Univ, 41-42; geologist, US Geol Surv, 42-44 & 46-84. *Mem:* Geol Soc Am; Soc Econ Geologists; Mineral Soc Am. *Res:* Pegmatites of Colorado and South Dakota; geology of eastern Great Basin and Washington; beryllium, fluorspar and phosphate deposits; vein-type uranium and thorium deposits; thorium and rare earth resources in United States. *Mailing Add:* 13435 Braun Rd Golden CO 80401

STAATZ, WILLIAM D, INTEGRINS, CELL BIOLOGY & ADHESION. *Current Pos:* RES INSTR, SCH MED, WASH UNIV, 89- *Personal Data:* b Glendale, Calif; c 3. *Educ:* Univ Puget Sound, BS, 67; Wash State Univ, MS, 69; Univ Edinburgh, PhD(zool), 76. *Prof Exp:* Res asst, Max Planck Inst, 69-71; asst res scientist, City Hope Med Ctr, 76-78; res fel, Eye Inst, Med Col Wis, 78-80; res assoc develop biol, Univ Wis-Madison, 80-84; asst prof genetics & develop biol, State Univ NY, Fredonia, 84-89. *Concurrent Pos:* Fel, Robert E Cook Res Fund, 77; res fel, Wash Univ Sch Med, 87-89. *Mem:* Am Soc Cell Biol; Soc Develop Biol; AAAS. *Res:* Role of cell adhesion receptors and extracellular matrix molecules in normal and pathologic development and function of cells and tissues; protein chemistry. *Mailing Add:* Div Lab Med Wash Univ Sch Med 660 S Euclid Box 8118 St Louis MO 63110. *Fax:* 314-362-3016

STABA, EMIL JOHN, PHARMACOGNOSY. *Current Pos:* RETIRED. *Personal Data:* b New York, NY, May 16, 28; m 54; c 5. *Educ:* St John's Univ, NY, BS, 52; Duquesne Univ, MS, 54; Univ Conn, PhD(pharmacog), 57. *Honors & Awards:* Lunsford-Richardson Award, 58. *Prof Exp:* Prof pharmacog & chmn dept, Univ Nebr, Lincoln, 57-68; asst dean, Univ Minn, Minneapolis, 74-78, prof pharmacog & chmn dept, Col Pharm, 68-85. *Concurrent Pos:* Consult var indust & govt agencies; NSF sr foreign scientist, Poland, Hungary & Czech, 69; Fulbright-Hays res fel, Ger, 70; partic, US-Repub China Coop Sci Prog, Plant Cell & Tissue Culture, 74; mem, US Pharmacopeia Comt Rev-Natural Prod, 80- & Life Sci Adv Comt, NASA, 84-87. *Mem:* AAAS; Am Soc Pharmacog (pres, 71-72); Tissue Cult Asn; Am Pharmaceut Asn; Soc Econ Bot. *Res:* Cultivation, extraction and tissue culture of medicinal plants; herbal teas. *Mailing Add:* 2840 Stinson Blvd Minneapolis MN 55418

STABLEFORD, LOUIS TRANTER, biology, for more information see previous edition

STABLER, TIMOTHY ALLEN, DEVELOPMENTAL BIOLOGY, ENDOCRINOLOGY. *Current Pos:* asst prof biol & health professions, Ind Univ Northwest, 73-76, actg chmn biol, 81 & 87, chmn biol, 83-85, ASSOC PROF BIOL & HEALTH PROFESSIONS ADV, IND UNIV NORTHWEST, 76-, CHMN BIOL, 95- *Personal Data:* b Port Jervis, NY, Sept 27, 40; m, Kellee; c Ashlee. *Educ:* Drew Univ, BA, 62; DePauw Univ, MA, 64; Univ Vt, PhD(zool), 69. *Prof Exp:* Asst prof biol, Hope Col, 69-71. *Concurrent Pos:* NIH fel, Univ Minn, 68-69; mem, NSF workshop develop biol, Univ Calif, San Diego, 71; NIH trainee reproductive endocrinol, Sch Med, Boston Univ, 71-73; adj asst prof physiol, Northwest Ctr Med Educ, Ind Univ Sch Med, 74-76, adj assoc prof physiol, 76- *Mem:* AAAS; Am Soc Zool; Am Inst Biol Sci; NY Acad Sci; Tissue Cult Asn; Nat Asn Adv Health Prof; Cent Asn Adv Health Prof (treas, 80-); Int Electrophoresis Soc. *Res:* Steroid receptor biochemistry; tissue culture of steroid-producing tissues; two-dimensional electrophoresis of steroid tissues. *Mailing Add:* Dept Biol Ind Univ Northwest Gary IN 46408. *Fax:* 219-980-7125

STACEY, GARY, PLANT MOLECULAR BIOLOGY, PLANT-MICROBE INTERACTIONS. *Current Pos:* from asst prof to assoc prof, Dept Microbiol, 81-92, DIR, CTR LEGUME RES, UNIV TENN, 90-, PROF, DEPT MICORBIOL, 92- *Personal Data:* b Dayton, Ohio, Dec 28, 51. *Educ:* Bowling Green State Univ, Ohio, BS, 74; Univ Tex, Austin, PhD(micorbiol), 78. *Prof Exp:* Res assoc, Dept Bact, Univ Wis, 78-81. *Concurrent Pos:* Fel, NSF, 79; Alexander von Humboldt Fel, Max Planck Inst Plant Breeding, Koln, Ger, 88-89; Van der Klaauw vis chair plant molecular biol & vis prof, Leiden Univ, Holland, 90. *Mem:* AAAS; Am Soc Microbiol; Am Soc Plant Physiologists; Int Soc Plant Molecular Biol; Int Soc Molecular Plant-Microbe Interactions; Sigma Xi. *Res:* Molecular studies of the interaction of nitrogen fixing bacteria with leguminous plants resulting in a nitrogen fixing symbiosis. *Mailing Add:* Microbiol Dept M409 Walter Life Sci Bldg Univ Tenn Knoxville TN 37996. *Fax:* 615-374-4007; *E-Mail:* gstacey@utkvx.utk.edu

STACEY, JOHN SYDNEY, GEOPHYSICS. *Current Pos:* RETIRED. *Personal Data:* b June 15, 27; m 54; c 3. *Educ:* Univ Durham, BSc, 51; Univ BC, MASc, 58, PhD(physics), 62. *Prof Exp:* Engr, Marconi Wireless Tel Co, 51-55; lectr elec eng, Univ BC, 57-58; physicist, Isotope Geol Br, US Geol Surv, 62-88. *Mem:* Geol Soc Am; Am Soc Mass Spectrometry. *Res:* Mass spectrometry in geologic studies and related data processing techniques; lead isotope and U-Pb zitcon geochronology for ore genesis and crustal evolution. *Mailing Add:* 309 11th St Pacific Grove CA 93950-3520

STACEY, LARRY MILTON, PHYSICS. *Current Pos:* ASST PROF PHYSICS, ST LOUIS UNIV, 71- *Personal Data:* b Greensboro, NC, July 30, 40. *Educ:* Univ NC, Chapel Hill, BS, 62, PhD(physics), 68. *Prof Exp:* Fel physics, Rutgers Univ, New Brunswick, 67-70; chem engr, Calif Inst Technol, 70-71. *Mem:* Am Phys Soc; Am Asn Physics Teachers. *Res:* Applications of magnetic resonance to the study of solids and fluids; critical point phenomena. *Mailing Add:* 35 Willow Hill Rd St Louis MO 63124-2055. *Fax:* 314-658-2521

STACEY, WESTON MONROE, JR, REACTOR PHYSICS, FUSION PLASMA THEORY. *Current Pos:* CALLAWAY PROF NUCLEAR ENG, GA INST TECHNOL, 77- *Personal Data:* b US; div; c Helen, Bill & Lucia. *Educ:* Ga Inst Technol, BS, 59, MS, 63; Mass Inst Technol, PhD(nuclear eng), 66. *Honors & Awards:* Distinguished Assoc Award, Dept Energy, 90. *Prof Exp:* Nuclear engr, Knolls Atomic Power Lab, 62-64; mgr reactor kinetics, 66-69; sect head reactor theory, Argonne Nat Lab, 69-72, assoc dir, Appl Physics Div, 72-77, dir fusion prog, 73-77. *Mem:* Fel Am Nuclear Soc; fel Am Phys Soc; AAAS; Am Soc Eng Educ. *Res:* Nuclear reactor theory, fusion reactor technology, plasma physics; fusion reactor design. *Mailing Add:* Nuclear Eng Prog Ga Inst Technol Atlanta GA 30332. *E-Mail:* weston.stacey@me.gatech.edu

STACH, JOSEPH, SOLID STATE ELECTRONICS, ELECTRICAL ENGINEERING. *Current Pos:* PRES & CHIEF EXEC OFFICER, RF POWER PRODS, 91- *Personal Data:* b Wallington, NJ, Aug 21, 38; m 63, Kathleen J Kobscenski; c Kevin J & Marcy A. *Educ:* Newark Col Eng, BS, 60; Pa State Univ, MS, 62, PhD(elec eng), 66. *Prof Exp:* Instr elec eng, Pa State Univ, 62-65; mem tech staff, Bell Tel Labs, 66-67; from asst prof to prof elec eng, Pa State Univ, University Park, 67-91; exec dir, Mass Microelectronics Ctr, 84-87, Microelectronics Res Ctr, Univ SFla, 88-91; exec vpres, Plasma-Therm, 91. *Concurrent Pos:* Consult, Air Prod & Chem Carbrundum. *Mem:* Inst Elec & Electronics Engrs; Sigma Xi. *Res:* Investigation of avalanche breakdown in metal barrier diodes and surface properties of insulators on semiconductors; boron nitride processing, HCI oxidations and plasma etching. *Mailing Add:* RF Power Prods 1007 Laurel Oak Rd Voorhees NJ 08043

STACH, ROBERT WILLIAM, NEUROBIOCHEMISTRY, BIOCHEMISTRY. *Current Pos:* DIR RES & PROF CHEM, UNIV MICH, FLINT, 87- *Personal Data:* b Chicago, Ill, Feb 12, 45; m 66; c 1. *Educ:* Ill Wesleyan Univ, BA, 67; Univ Wis-Madison, PhD(org chem), 72. *Prof Exp:* Trainee neurobiochem, Depts Genetics & Biochem, Sch Med, Stanford Univ, 72-74; from asst prof to assoc prof biochem, molecular biol, anat & cell biol, State Univ NY Upstate Med Ctr, 74-87, assoc mem fac, Ctr Neurobehav Sci, 79-87. *Concurrent Pos:* Biomed res support grants, 74-75, 79, 81, 84-85 & 88-89; NIH res grants, 75-85 & 87-90. *Mem:* Am Soc Neurochem; AAAS; NY Acad Sci; Soc Neurosci; Am Soc Biochem & Molecular Biol; Int Soc Neurochem. *Res:* Factors involved in the growth, development and regeneration of the nervous system with special emphasis on the mechanism of the nerve growth. *Mailing Add:* Dept Chem Univ Mich Flint 556 Murchie Sci Bldg Flint MI 48502-2186. *Fax:* 313-766-6693; *E-Mail:* stachr@msbflint.umich.edu

STACHEL, JOHANNA, relativistic heavy ion physics, low & intermediate energy heavy ion physics, for more information see previous edition

STACHEL, JOHN JAY, RELATIVITY THEORY. *Current Pos:* from asst prof to prof, 64-96, EMER PROF PHYSICS & DIR CTR EINSTEIN STUDIES, BOSTON UNIV, 96- *Personal Data:* b New York, NY, Mar 29, 28; m 53, Evelyn Wassermann; c Robert, Laura & Deborah. *Educ:* City Univ NY, BS, 56; Stevens Inst Technol, MS, 59, PhD(physics), 62. *Prof Exp:* Instr physics, Lehigh Univ, 59-61; instr, Univ Pittsburgh, 61-62, res assoc, 62-64. *Concurrent Pos:* Vis res assoc, Inst Theoret Physics, Warsaw, 62; vis prof, King's Col, Univ London, 70-71; vis sr res fel, Dept Physics, Princeton Univ, 77-84; ed, Collection Papers Albert Einstein, Princeton Univ Press, 77-88; res assoc, Univ Calif, Berkeley, 94; vis prof, Max Planck Inst Hist Sci, Berlin, 94-95. *Res:* General relativity; foundations of quantum theory; history and philosophy of physics. *Mailing Add:* Ctr Einstein Studies Boston Univ 745 Commonwealth Ave Boston MA 02215

STACHOWIAK, MICHAL KACPER, GROWTH FACTORS, TRANSCRIPTIONAL REGULATION. *Current Pos:* STAFF SCIENTIST & LAB DIR, BARROW NEUROL INST, ARIZ, 89- *Personal Data:* b Suwalki, Poland, Jan 5, 50; US citizen; m 74, Ewa Lukaszkiewicz; c Rafal-M & Karina-O. *Educ:* Nicholaus Copernicus Univ, Poland, MSc, 73; Med Acad, Poland, PhD(neurochem), 80. *Prof Exp:* Adj prof physiol, Acad Med, Poland, 80-81; res assoc, Univ Pittsburgh, 81-86; sr staff fel, Nat Inst Environ Health Sci/NIH, NC, 86-89. *Concurrent Pos:* Adj prof biol psychol, Ariz State Univ, 85-; prin investr, NIH, NSF, Am Parkinson Dis Asn, Nat Parkinson's Found, Am Heart Asn, Ariz Dis Control Res Comn. *Mem:* Am Soc Neurosci; Am Soc Cell Biol; Polish Soc Neurosci. *Res:* Molecular mechanisms that control cell genesis, growth, differentiation and gene expression in the nervous system in relation to development, plasticity, regeneration, neurodegenerative disorders and brain cancer. *Mailing Add:* Barrow Neurol Inst 350 W Thomas Rd Phoenix AZ 85013. *Fax:* 602-406-4172; *E-Mail:* mstacho@mha.chw.edu

STACK (STACHIEWICZ), B(OGDAN) R(OMAN), ELECTRONICS ENGINEERING, SATELLITE COMMUNICATIONS. *Current Pos:* PRES, BRS ASSOCS, 86- *Personal Data:* b Lwow, Poland, Sept 16, 24; nat US; m 55, Mathilde M Norvell; c Thomas, Elisabeth,Joanna & Christina. *Educ:* Bristol Univ, BSEE, 47; McGill Univ, MEE, 53. *Prof Exp:* Engr, Radio Eng Prod, Ltd, Can, 47-52; proj engr, Lenkurt Elec Co, Calif, 52-55; asst sect head, Stromberg-Carlson Div, Gen Dynamics Corp, NY, 55-57; assoc lab dir, Int Tel & Tel Fed Labs, Calif, 57-62; dept mgr, Philco Corp, Ford Motor Co, 62-64; prog mgr, Stanford Res Inst, 64-68; mgr, Systs Design Dept, WDL Div, Ford Aerospace Corp, Palo Alto, 68-78; mgr, Aydin Satellite Commun, 77-80, vpres eng, 80-82, vpres & gen mgr, Aydin Systs Div, 82-86. *Concurrent Pos:* Expert witness, Dept Justice, ITT-ABC merger proc; vis lectr commun, Univ Alexandria, Egypt, lectr, Telecommun Cert Prog, San Francisco State Univ; consult various corps. *Mem:* Sr mem Inst Elec & Electronics Engrs. *Res:* Space and ground communications systems; signal analysis and detection; 6 US patents in the field of telecommunications. *Mailing Add:* 358 Toyon Ave Los Altos CA 94022

STACK, JOHN D, THEORETICAL PHYSICS. *Current Pos:* from asst prof to assoc prof, 66-81, PROF PHYSICS, UNIV ILL, URBANA, 82- *Personal Data:* b Los Angeles, Calif, July 24, 38; m 63; c 1. *Educ:* Calif Inst Technol, BSc, 59; Univ Calif, Berkeley, PhD(physics), 65. *Prof Exp:* Actg asst prof physics, Univ Calif, Berkeley, 65-66. *Concurrent Pos:* Vis assoc, Calif Inst Technol, 69-70, Standford Linear Accelerator Ctr, 73. *Mem:* Am Phys Soc. *Res:* Field theory; lattice gauge theory; Feynman path integrals. *Mailing Add:* 606 W Vermont Ave Urbana IL 61801-4825. *Fax:* 217-333-9819

STACK, STEPHEN M, CYTOLOGY. *Current Pos:* Asst prof, 69-74, ASSOC PROF BOT & PLANT PATH, COLO STATE UNIV, 74- *Personal Data:* b Monahans, Tex, Feb 12, 43; m 65; c 2. *Educ:* Univ Tex, Austin, BAS, 65, PhD(cytol, bot), 69. *Mem:* Am Soc Cell Biol; AAAS; Bot Soc Am. *Res:* Structure and function of chromosomes. *Mailing Add:* Dept Biol Colo State Univ Ft Collins CO 80523-0001. *Fax:* 970-491-0649

STACKELBERG, OLAF PATRICK, MATHEMATICS. *Current Pos:* PROF MATH & CHMN DEPT, KENT STATE UNIV, 76- *Personal Data:* b Munich, Ger, Aug 2, 32; US citizen; m 54; c 3. *Educ:* Mass Inst Technol, BS, 55; Univ Minn, MS, 60, PhD(math), 63. *Prof Exp:* Teaching asst math, Univ Minn, 58-63; from asst prof to assoc prof, Duke Univ, 63-76. *Concurrent Pos:* Alexander V Humboldt fel, Stuttgart Tech Univ, 65-66; vis assoc prof, Univ Ill, Urbana, 69-70 & Univ London, 74; ed, Duke Math J, 71-74. *Mem:* Am Math Soc; Math Asn Am; Inst Math Statist. *Res:* Probability; metric number theory. *Mailing Add:* Dept Math/Comput Sci Kent State Univ Kent OH 44242-0001

STACKMAN, ROBERT W, RESEARCH ADMINISTRATION, POLYMER CHEMISTRY. *Current Pos:* sr group leader, Adv Mat Corp Res & Develop, 84-89, sr sect mgr, Pioneering Polymer Res, 89-93, SR MGR, EXTERNAL TECHNOL, S C JOHNSON & SON INC, 93- *Personal Data:* b Dayton, Ohio, June 29, 35; m 62, Patricia Bugg; c Katherine J, Robet W Jr, & Michael C. *Educ:* Univ Dayton, BS, 57; Univ Fla, PhD(org chem), 61. *Prof Exp:* Res asst cyclopolymers of silanes, Univ Fla, 58-61; res chemist, Summit Labs, Celanese Corp, 61-65, sr res chemist, Celanese Res Co, 65-72, res assoc, 72-74, res supvr polymer flammability res, 74-76, res supvr polymer & specialty chem res, 76-80, res assoc, Celanese Res Co, 80-84. *Mem:* AAAS; Am Chem Soc; fel Am Inst Chem; NY Acad Sci. *Res:* Condensation polymerization; emulsion polymerization; high temperature polymers; cyclopolymerization; organic synthesis; organosilicon compounds; addition polymerization; polymer modification and stabilization; flammability of polymers; water soluble polymers; coatings and graphic arts polymers; liquid crystal polymers. *Mailing Add:* 100 Northwood Dr Racine WI 53402. *Fax:* 414-631-3954

STACKPOLE, JOHN DUKE, METEOROLOGY. *Current Pos:* Res meteorologist, 64-73, SUPVRY RES METEOROLOGIST, NAT WEATHER SERV, NAT OCEANIC & ATMOSPHERIC ADMIN, 73- *Personal Data:* b Boston, Mass, Dec 28, 35; m 60; c 3. *Educ:* Amherst Col, BA, 57; Mass Inst Technol, MS, 59, PhD(meteorol), 64. *Res:* Numerical weather prediction. *Mailing Add:* 11 Battersea Land Ft Washington MD 20744-7203

STACY, ANGELICA M, CHEMISTRY. *Current Pos:* PROF, DEPT CHEM, UNIV CALIF, BERKELEY. *Honors & Awards:* Francis P Garvan-John M Olin Medal, Am Chem Soc, 95. *Mailing Add:* Dept Chem Univ Calif 419 Latimer Hall Berkeley CA 94720-1401

STACY, CARL J, POLYMER SCIENCE. *Current Pos:* INDEPENDENT CONSULT POLYMERS, PLASTICS & RUBBER, 86- *Personal Data:* b Joplin, Mo, Jan 20, 29; m 51, Virginia Payne; c Carl C, John E & Nathan E. *Educ:* Pittsburg Kans State Univ, BA, 51; Purdue Univ, PhD(phys chem), 56. *Prof Exp:* Res fel starch, Purdue Univ, 55-56; res physicist, Phillips Petrol Co, 56-61, sr res chemist, 62-86. *Mem:* AAAS; Am Chem Soc; Sigma Xi. *Res:* Polymer molecular weight distribution and structure by light scattering, gel permeation chromatography, ultracentrifuge and other physical techniques. *Mailing Add:* 2929 Sheridan Rd Bartlesville OK 74006

STACY, DAVID LOWELL, ANGIOGENESIS, INFLAMMATION. *Current Pos:* CELL BIOL, TEX BIO-TECHNOL CORP. *Personal Data:* b Kansas City, Mo, Oct 7, 50. *Educ:* Oral Roberts Univ, BA, 78; Univ Nebr Med Ctr, PhD(physiol), 86. *Prof Exp:* Grad res assoc physiol, Univ Nebr Med Ctr, 80-85; postdoctoral fel physiol, Eastern Va Med Sch, 85-88, res asst prof, 88; sr scientist, Glaxo Inc, 88-89, res investr, 89- *Concurrent Pos:* Travel award, Japanese Soc Microcirculation, 87. *Mem:* Microcirculation Soc; Am Phys Soc; Am Diabetes Asn. *Res:* Physiology, pharmacology, and pathology of small blood vessels; therapeutics of hypertension, inflammation, diabetes and angiogenesis; compounds which inhibit tumor angiogenesis. *Mailing Add:* 5118 Blue Creek Dr Humble TX 77345

STACY, GARDNER W, organic chemistry, chemical education; deceased, see previous edition for last biography

STACY, T(HOMAS) D(ONNIE), PETROLEUM ENGINEERING. *Current Pos:* RETIRED. *Personal Data:* b Houston, Tex, Jan 13, 34; m 54; c 4. *Educ:* La Polytech Inst, BS, 57, MS, 62; Miss State Univ, PhD(eng), 66. *Prof Exp:* Petrol engr, Pan-Am Petrol Corp, 57-58 & 62-63; asst petrol eng, La Polytech Inst, 61-62; from instr to asst prof, Miss State Univ, 63-68; area engr, Pan Am Petrol Corp, 68-76; mgr res, Amoco Prod Co, 76-80, mgr prod, Amoco Int, 80-81, mgr prod serv, vpres prod, Amoco, pres & chmn, Amoco Can, 93, chmn & pres, Amoco Eurasia, 93-97. *Mem:* AAAS; Am Inst Mining, Metall & Petrol Engrs; Soc Petrol Engrs (treas, pres-elect, 81). *Res:* Petroleum engineering, surface chemistry and gas adsorption. *Mailing Add:* Amoco Eurasia PO Box 3092 Houston TX 77253

STADDON, JOHN ERIC RAYNER, PSYCHOLOGY, ZOOLOGY. *Current Pos:* from asst prof to prof, 67-83, J B DUKE PROF PSYCHOL, NEUROBIOL & ZOOL, DUKE UNIV, DURHAM, NC, 83- *Personal Data:* b Grayshott, Eng; m, Lucinda Paris. *Educ:* Univ Col London, BSc, 60; Harvard Univ, PhD, 64. *Honors & Awards:* Von Humboldt Prize, 85. *Prof Exp:* Asst prof psychol, Univ Toronto, Ont, Can, 64-67. *Concurrent Pos:* Assoc ed, J Exp Anal Behav, 79-82. *Mem:* Fel AAAS; NY Acad Scis; Soc Exp Psychol; Sigma Xi. *Res:* Psychology; zoology; neurobiology. *Mailing Add:* Duke Univ Dept Exp Psychol Durham NC 27706

STADELMAIER, H(ANS) H(EINRICH), PHYSICAL METALLURGY. *Current Pos:* from res assoc to res prof, 52-80, prof, 80-93, EMER PROF METALL, NC STATE UNIV, 93- *Personal Data:* b Stuttgart, Ger, Nov 14, 22; nat US; m 46, Gerda Schewe; c Christiane, Michael & Barbara. *Educ:* Univ Stuttgart, Dipl, 51, Dr rer nat, 56. *Prof Exp:* Interpreter, US Mil Govt, Ger, 45-47. *Concurrent Pos:* Vis scientist, Max Planck Inst Metall, Stuttgart, Ger, 85-96. *Mem:* Fel Am Soc Metals; Ger Mat Soc; Metall Soc; Am Inst Mining Engrs. *Res:* Alloy phases; x-ray crystallography; electronic materials; permanent magnet materials. *Mailing Add:* Mat Sci & Eng Dept NC State Univ Box 7907 Raleigh NC 27695-7907. *Fax:* 919-515-7724

STADELMAN, WILLIAM JACOB, FOOD SCIENCE, POULTRY PRODUCTS. *Current Pos:* from assoc prof to prof poultry sci, 55-62, prof, 62-83, EMER PROF FOOD SCI, PURDUE UNIV, WEST LAFAYETTE, 83-; CONSULT POULTRY INDUST, 83- *Personal Data:* b Vancouver, Wash, Aug 8, 17; m 42, Margaret; c Ralph & Paula. *Educ:* Wash State Univ, BS, 40; Pa State Univ, MS, 42, PhD(biochem), 48. *Honors & Awards:* Christie Award, Poultry & Egg Nat Bd, 55; Res Award, Am Egg Bd, 75; Sci Award, Inst Food Technol, 77; Poultry Hall of Fame, Am Poultry Hist Soc, 92. *Prof Exp:* Asst poultry husb, Pa State Univ, 40-42; from asst prof to assoc prof, Wash State Univ, 48-55. *Concurrent Pos:* Consult, Food & Poultry Int Indust; mem tech adv comt, Poultry & Egg Inst Am, 57-83, Nat Turkey Fedn, 71-83 & Am Egg Bd, 74-83; mem bd dirs, Res & Develop Assocs, Food & Container Inst, 66-69, 72-75; mem, Sci Adv Comt, Refrig Res Found, 67-; mem adv bd mil personnel supplies, Food Irradiation Comt, Nat Acad Sci, 67-69. *Mem:* Inst Food Technol; Poultry Sci Asn (pres, 77-78); Am Soc Heat, Refrig & Air-Conditioning Eng; World Poultry Sci Asn; Am Meat Sci Asn; Int Inst Refrig. *Res:* Effects of refrigeration and freezing on quality preservation of protein rich foods; poultry products quality evaluation and preservation; new product development. *Mailing Add:* Dept Food Sci Smith Hall Purdue Univ West Lafayette IN 47907-1160. *Fax:* 765-494-7953

STADELMANN, EDUARD JOSEPH, PLANT PHYSIOLOGY, CELL PHYSIOLOGY. *Current Pos:* from asst prof to prof, 64-90, EMER PROF PLANT PHYSIOL, UNIV MINN, ST PAUL, 91- *Personal Data:* b Graz, Austria, Sept 24, 20; m 95, Young A Lee. *Educ:* Innsbruck Univ, PhD(bot, philos), 53; Univ Freiburg, Venia Legendi, 57. *Hon Degrees:* Dr, Agr Univ Vienna, Austria, 89. *Honors & Awards:* Humboldt Award, Bonn, Ger, 73-75; Fulbright Award, 79 & 87. *Prof Exp:* Asst bot, Freiburg Univ, 54-61, privat docent, 57, sr asst, 62-64. *Concurrent Pos:* Muellhaupt scholar biol, Ohio State Univ, 58-59; res assoc, Univ Minn, 63-64; vis prof, Dept Bot, Seoul Nat Univ, Korea, 78-79, vis scientist, Shijiazhuang, Hebei, China, 85, 86, 87, 88-93 & 96; agr, Univ Vienna, Austria, 87. *Mem:* Ger Bot Soc; Swiss Bot Soc; Austrian Zool-Bot Soc; Am Inst Biol Sci; Sigma Xi; Am Soc Plant Physiologists. *Res:* Permeability; cytomorphology; salt resistance; protoplasmatology; radiation effects; desiccation resistance; drought resistance. *Mailing Add:* Dept Hort Sci 436 Univ Minn 1970 Folwell Ave St Paul MN 55108. *Fax:* 612-624-4341; *E-Mail:* estadelm@maroon.tc.umn.edu

STADLBAUER, JOHN MANNIX, EDUCATION, SOLUTION KINETICS. *Current Pos:* asst prof, 83-90, ASSOC PROF CHEM, HOOD COL, 90-, CHMN DEPT, 92- *Personal Data:* b Denver, Colo, May 21, 52. *Educ:* Univ Alaska, Fairbanks, BS, 74, MA, 75; NMex State Univ, MS, 79, PhD(phys chem), 81. *Prof Exp:* Chemist, Arctic Environ Res Sta, Environ Protection Agency, 74-76. *Concurrent Pos:* Vis scientist, Tri-Univ-Meson Facil, 84-; Wye fac fel, Wye Inst, 87. *Mem:* Am Chem Soc; fel Am Inst Chem; Nat Asn Advisors Health Professions; Am Asn Univ Profs; Sigma Xi. *Res:* Solution kinetics and spectroscopy of the atom-like particle muonium which behaves in a manner similar to a light isotope of hydrogen; addition reactions to vinyl monomers and aromatics, p 4 dependence, temperature dependence and free radical products. *Mailing Add:* Dept Chem Hood Col Frederick MD 21701-8575. *Fax:* 301-694-7653; *E-Mail:* stadlbauer@nimue.hood.edu

STADLER, DAVID ROSS, GENETICS. *Current Pos:* instr bot, Univ Wash, 56-57, from asst prof to prof, 57-95, EMER PROF GENETICS, UNIV WASH, 95- *Personal Data:* b Columbia, Mo, May 24, 25; m 52, Anne Morgan; c Michael, Susan, Aaron & Matthew. *Educ:* Univ Mo, AB, 48; Princeton Univ, MA, 50, PhD, 52. *Prof Exp:* Instr biol, Univ Rochester, 52; Gosney res fel genetics, Calif Inst Technol, 52-53, USPHS fel, 53-55. *Concurrent Pos:* Ed, Genetics, Genetics Soc Am, 73-76. *Mem:* Genetics Soc Am (treas, 69-71). *Res:* Genetics of microorganisms; mutation and recombination in Neurospora. *Mailing Add:* Dept Genetics Univ Wash Seattle WA 98195

STADLER, LOUIS BENJAMIN, PHARMACEUTICAL CHEMISTRY, ANALYTICAL CHEMISTRY. *Current Pos:* RETIRED. *Personal Data:* b Monroe, Mich, Feb 26, 26; m 51; c 3. *Educ:* Univ Mich, BS, 48, MS, 50, PhD(pharmaceut chem), 54. *Prof Exp:* Sr analytical chemist, Parke, Davis & Co, 53-63, mgr analytical stand, 63-64; asst head qual control, William S Merrell Co Div, Richardson-Merrell Inc, 64-65, head qual control, 66-71, Merrell Nat Labs, 71-73, Master Documents Admin, 73-75, mgr, Qual Opers Rec, systs & planning, Merrell-Nat Labs, 75-81, qual opers tech proj mgr, 81-83, qual assurance compliance coordr & qual opers compliance mgr, Merrell Dow Pharmaceut, 83-90. *Concurrent Pos:* Mem adv panel steroids, Nat Formulary, 60-65, comt specifications, 66-75, panel trypsin & chymotrypsin, 70-75; mem rev comt, US Pharmacopeia, 70-80, asst, 80-90. *Mem:* Am Pharmaceut Asn; Am Chem Soc; Am Soc Qual Control. *Res:* Analytical methodology for testing drug substances, pharmaceutical dosage forms and associated standards; improved control techniques for pharmaceuticals; technical management; regulatory compliance. *Mailing Add:* 508 Laramie Trail Cincinnati OH 45215-2504

STADNICKI, STANLEY WALTER, JR, RESEARCH ADMINISTRATION. *Current Pos:* ASST DIR TOXICOL, MED RES LABS, PFIZER, INC, 76- *Personal Data:* b Norwich, Conn, Sept 30, 43; m 65; c 4. *Educ:* Assumption Col, Mass, BA, 65; Clark Univ, Mass, MA, 70; Worcester Polytech Inst, PhD(biomed eng), 76. *Prof Exp:* Res scientist, E G & G Mason Res Inst, 67-76. *Mem:* Soc Toxicol; Am Soc Pharmacol & Exp Therapeut; Am Col Toxicol; Soc Toxicol Can; Inst Elec & Electronics Engrs. *Res:* Directing research for the purpose of testing the toxicological effects of new drug candidates; interpretation, analysis and documentation of research results. *Mailing Add:* Dept Drug Safety Eval Pfizer Cent Res Groton CT 06340-5196. *Fax:* 860-441-5499

STADNIK, ZBIGNIEW M, PHOTOEMISSION SPECTROSCOPY, MOSSBAUER SPECTROSCOPY. *Current Pos:* ASSOC PROF, DEPT PHYSICS, UNIV OTTAWA, 90- *Personal Data:* b Dobrodzien, Poland, May 1, 48; Can citizen. *Educ:* Univ Cracow, MSc, 71, PhD(solid state physics), 80; Dalhousie Univ, BEd, 90. *Prof Exp:* Fel, Univ Nijmegen, 80-82; res assoc, Univ Manitoba, 83-84, Dalhousie Univ, 86-89; asst prof, Univ Cracow, 85. *Concurrent Pos:* Vis prof, Univ Nijmegen, 83, 85 & 88, Univ Mainz, 86, Univ Bochum, 90, Tohoku Univ, 93 & Univ Neuchatel, 95. *Res:* Production of novel alloys (quasicrystals, amorphous) electronic structure and magnetism of novel alloys. *Mailing Add:* Dept Physics Univ Ottawa Ottawa ON K1N 6N5 Can. *Fax:* 613-562-5190; *E-Mail:* stadnik@joule.physics.uottawa.ca

STADTER, JAMES THOMAS, COMPUTER SIMULATION. *Current Pos:* Assoc engr, 60-65, sr engr, 65-81, PRIN PROF STAFF, APPL PHYSICS LAB, JOHNS HOPKINS UNIV, 81-, INSTR COMPUT SCI & APPLIED MATH, 80- *Personal Data:* b Baltimore, Md. *Educ:* Loyola Col, BS, 59; Univ Md, MA, 64; Am Univ, PhD(math), 75. *Res:* Aeroelasticity and structural analysis; applied mathematics; eigenvalue estimation procedure. *Mailing Add:* Appl Physics Lab Johns Hopkins Univ Johns Hopkins Rd Laurel MD 20723-6090

STADTHERR, LEON, bioinorganic chemistry, engineering, for more information see previous edition

STADTHERR, MARK ALLEN, CHEMICAL ENGINEERING. *Current Pos:* MEM STAFF, UNIV NOTRE DAME. *Personal Data:* b Austin, Minn, May 15, 50. *Educ:* Univ Minn, BChE, 72; Univ Wis-Madison, PhD(chem eng), 76. *Prof Exp:* From asst prof to assoc prof chem eng, Univ Ill, Urbana-Champaign, 76-94. *Mem:* Am Inst Chem Engrs; Am Chem Soc; Am Soc Eng Educ; Soc Indust & Appl Math. *Res:* Chemical process simulation, optimization and design; sparse matrix computations; resource management. *Mailing Add:* Dept Chem Eng Univ Notre Dame South Bend IN 46556. *E-Mail:* markst@uiuc.edu

STADTHERR, RICHARD JAMES, plant physiology, plant breeding; deceased, see previous edition for last biography

STADTMAN, EARL REECE, BIOCHEMISTRY. *Current Pos:* chemist, Lab Cellular Physiol & Metab, 50-58, chief, Enzyme Sect, 58-62, chief, Lab Biochem, 62-95, HEAD, ENZYME SECT, NAT HEART, LUNG & BLOOD INST, NIH, 58- *Personal Data:* b Carrizozo, NMex, Nov 15, 19; m 43, Thressa Campbell. *Educ:* Univ Calif, Berkeley, BS, 42, PhD(comp biochem), 49. *Hon Degrees:* DSc, Univ Mich, 87; PhD, Weizmann Inst Sci, 88. *Honors & Awards:* Lewis Award, Am Chem Soc, 53; Burroughs-Wellcome Lectr, Mass Gen Hosp, 68; Microbiol Award, Nat Acad Sci, 70; Distinguished Serv Award, HEW, 70; Plenary Lectr, Am Soc Biol Chemists, 76, Merck Award, 83; Nat Medal Sci, 79; Distinguished Camille & Henry Dreyfus Lectr, Northwestern Univ, 80; Presidential Rank Award, Sr Exec Serv, 81; Kamen Lectr, Univ Calif, 85; John Muntz Mem Lectr, Union Univ, 85; Seventh Robert E Olson Lectr, St Louis Univ, 90; Robert A Welch Award Chem, 91; Res Award, Am Aging Asn, 92; Glenn Found Award, 93. *Prof Exp:* Res asst, Dept Food Technol, Univ Calif, 43-46, Leopold Wrasse res assistantship, Div Plant Nutrit, 46-47, Leopold Wrasse grad res fel & sr lab technician, 47-78, res asst 48-49; AEC res fel, Mass Gen Hosp, 49-50. *Concurrent Pos:* Lectr, USDA Grad Sch, 54-, Georgetown Univ, 56-58 & Univ Md, 59-; lectr var socs & univs, 56-; vis scientist, Max Planck Inst, Ger, 59-60 & Pasteur Inst, France, 60; ed, J Biol Chem, 60-; exec ed, Archives Biochem, Biophys, 60-; chmn, Biochem Div, Found Advan Educ Sci, 64-; mem, Adv Comt, Oak Ridge Nat Lab, 63-66; chmn, Biochem Div, Found Advan Educ Sci, 64-; chmn, Comt Policy & Procedures, Am Soc Biol Chemists, 65-66, coun, 72-85; NIH lectr, 66; vis prof var univs, 67-; adv bd, Biochem, 69-76 & Trends Biochem Res, 76-79; Nat Acad Sci deleg, Int Union Biochem, 76; coun, Int Union Biochem, 76-82, chmn, Interest Group Comt, 79-84; coun mem, Oxygen Soc, 91-94. *Mem:* Nat Acad Sci; Am Chem Soc; Am Soc Biol Chemists (pres, 82-83); Am Soc Microbiol; Am Acad Arts & Sci; Int Union Biochem; Biophys Soc; Protein Soc; fel Oxygen Soc; Geront Soc. *Res:* Microbial and intermediary metabolism; enzyme chemistry; biochemical function of vitamin B12 and ferredoxin; metabolic regulation of biosynthetic pathways; membrane transport; oxygen radical mediated modification of enzymes; role of protein modification in aging; oxygen toxicity; author of various publications. *Mailing Add:* 16907 Redland Rd Rockville MD 20855-1954. *Fax:* 301-496-0599; *E-Mail:* earlstadman@nih.gov

STADTMAN, THRESSA CAMPBELL, BIOCHEMISTRY, MICROBIOLOGY. *Current Pos:* BIOCHEMIST, NAT HEART INST, 50- *Personal Data:* b Sterling, NY, Feb 12, 20; m 43. *Educ:* Cornell Univ, BS, 40, MS, 42; Univ Calif, PhD(microbiol), 49. *Honors & Awards:* Hillebrand Award, 79; Rose Award, 87; Klaus Schwary Award, 88. *Prof Exp:* Asst nutrit, Agr Exp Sta, Cornell Univ, 42-43; res assoc food microbiol, Univ Calif, 43-46; asst, Harvard Med Sch, 49-50. *Concurrent Pos:* Whitney fel, Oxford Univ, 54-55; Rockefeller grant, Inst Cell Chem, Univ Munich, 59-60; French govt fel, Inst Biol & Phys Chem, France, 60; ed-in-chief, Biofactors. *Mem:* Nat Acad Sci; Am Soc Biol Chemists (secy, 78-81); Brit Biochem Soc; Am Chem Soc; Am Soc Microbiol; Am Acad Microbiol; Int Soc Vitamins & Related Biofactors (pres-elect). *Res:* Amino acid intermediary metabolism; one-carbon metabolism; methane formation; microbial biochemistry; selenium biochemistry. *Mailing Add:* Nat Heart Lung & Blood Inst Bethesda MD 20892

STAEBLER, DAVID LLOYD, KINESCOPE DESIGN, PHOTOVOLTAIC CELLS. *Current Pos:* DIR, SARNOFF CORP, 95- *Personal Data:* b Ann Arbor, Mich, Apr 25, 40; m 61; c 2. *Educ:* Pa State Univ, BS, 62, MS, 63; Princeton Univ, MA, 67, PhD(elec eng), 70. *Prof Exp:* Mem tech staff, RCA Labs, 63-81, head, Kinescope Syst Group, 81-89; mgr, Mat Sci Br, Nat Renewable Lab, 92-95. *Concurrent Pos:* Vis prof, Inst Phys Chem Sao Carlos, Univ Sao Paulo, Brazil, 74-75; vis mem tech staff labs, RCA Ltd, Zurich, Switz, 79-80. *Mem:* Inst Elec & Electronics Eng; AAAS. *Res:* Electron gun and kinescope design; photovoltaic properties of amorphous silicon; hologram storage in electro-optic materials; photochromic and electrochromic phenomena; hologram storage in electro-optic materials; optical and electronic properties of amorphous silicon. *Mailing Add:* Sarnoff Corp CN-5300 Princeton NJ 08543-5300. *Fax:* 609-734-2886; *E-Mail:* dstaebler@sarnoff.com

STAEHELIN, LUCAS ANDREW, CELL BIOLOGY, CYTOKINESIS. *Current Pos:* asst prof, Univ Colo, 70-73, assoc chmn, Dept Molecular Cell & Develop Biol, 72-73, assoc prof, 73-78, PROF CELL BIOL, UNIV COLO, BOULDER, 79- *Personal Data:* b Sydney, Australia, Feb 10, 39; m 65, Margrit Weibel; c 3. *Educ:* Swiss Fed Inst Technol, DiplNatw, 63, PhD(biol), 66. *Honors & Awards:* Humboldt Award, 78. *Prof Exp:* Res scientist, Dept Sci & Indust Res, NZ, 66-69; res fel cell biol, Harvard Univ, 69-70. *Concurrent Pos:* Nat Inst Gen Med Sci grant, 71-; study sect cell biol, NIH, 80-84; vis prof, Inst Biol & Microbiol, Univ Freiburg, Ger, 78, cell biol, Swiss Fed Inst Technol, 84, 92; mem, Cell Biol Panel, NSF, 94-96; rev panel, Div Energy Biosci Prog, 88 & 92. *Mem:* AAAS; Am Soc Cell Biol; Am Soc Plant Physiol; Int Soc Plant Molecular Biol; Ger Acad Nat Scientists-Leopoldina. *Res:* Structure and function of biological membranes; freeze-etch electron microscopy; plant cytokinesis; plant cell walls; plant cell secretion. *Mailing Add:* Dept Molecular Cell Develop Biol Univ Colo Box 347 Boulder CO 80309. *Fax:* 303-492-7744

STAEHLE, ROGER WASHBURNE, METALLURGICAL ENGINEERING, CORROSION. *Current Pos:* dean, Inst Technol, 79-83, prof chem eng & mat sci, 83-84, ADJ PROF, UNIV MINN, 88- *Personal Data:* b Detroit, Mich, Feb 4, 34; div; c 4. *Educ:* Ohio State Univ, BMetE & MS, 57, PhD(metall eng), 65. *Honors & Awards:* Willis Rodney Whitney Award, Nat Asn Corrosion Engrs, 80. *Prof Exp:* Res asst corrosion, Ohio State Univ, 61-65, from asst prof to assoc prof metall eng, 65-70, prof, 70-79; pres & chmn, Automated Transp Systs, Inc, Minneapolis, 84-86. *Concurrent Pos:* Consult, 3M Co, Oak Ridge Nat Lab, Monsanto Co, Int Nickel Co, Inc, NUS Corp & Parameter Inc; mem adv panel, Mat Div, Nat Bur Stand; Int Nickel prof corrosion sci & eng, 71-76; ed, Corrosion J, 73-79; dir, Fontana Corrosion Ctr, 75-79; indust consult, North Oaks, Minn, 86- *Mem:* Nat Acad Eng; fel Am Soc Metals; Electrochem Soc; Sigma Xi; Am Concrete Inst; Am Soc Testing & Mat; Nat Asn Corrosion Eng. *Res:* Passivity of metals; stress corrosion cracking; process of fracture; fatigue; optical properties of surfaces; surface chemistry; author of various publications; granted one patent. *Mailing Add:* 22 Red Fox Rd North Oaks MN 55127

STAELIN, DAVID HUDSON, RADIO ASTRONOMY, METEOROLOGY. *Current Pos:* From instr to assoc prof, 65-76, PROF ELEC ENG, MASS INST TECHNOL, 76-, ASST DIR, LINCOLN LAB, 90- *Personal Data:* b Toledo, Ohio, May 25, 38; m 62, Ellen Mahoney; c Carl, Katharine & Paul. *Educ:* Mass Inst Technol, SB, 60, SM, 61, ScD(elec eng), 65. *Honors & Awards:* NASA Award, Voyager Sci Invest - Planetary Radio Astron, Uranus, 86, Neptune, 90; Alan Berman Res Publ Award, Naval Res Lab, 88; Sr Award, Inst Elec & Electronics Engrs Signal Processing Soc, 92. *Concurrent Pos:* Ford fel eng, 65-67; vis asst scientist, Nat Radio Astron Observ, 68-69; dir, Environ Res & Technol, Inc, 69-79; chmn, Nat Acad Sci Comn Radio Frequency Req Res, 83-86; mem, Space Appln Adv Comt, NASA, 83-86, prin invest spaceflight exp, Nimbus-E Microwave Spectrometer, 72, Scanning Microwave Spectrometer, 75, Tech Adv Comt, Comsat, 84-87; pres, Pictel Corp, 84, chmn 84-87. *Mem:* AAAS; Am Geophys Union; Inst Elec & Electronics Engrs; Am Meteorol Soc. *Res:* Space-based and ground-based meteorological observations using passive microwave techniques; design of experiments; microwave and optical instrumentation; atmospheric sensing; communications satellites; video image processing; planetary atmospheres; pulsars. *Mailing Add:* Dept Elec Eng & Comput Sci Mass Inst Technol Cambridge MA 02139

STAETZ, CHARLES ALAN, ECONOMIC ENTOMOLOGY. *Current Pos:* MEM STAFF, AGR CHEM GROUP, FMC CORP, 78- *Personal Data:* b North Platte, Nebr, July 12, 45; m 68; c 2. *Educ:* Chadron State Col, BS, 67; Univ Nebr, MS, 72, PhD(entom), 75. *Prof Exp:* Entomologist, Velsicol Chem Corp, 75-78. *Mem:* Entom Soc Am. *Res:* New insecticides; insecticide resistance-detection and countermeasures. *Mailing Add:* 85 Hickory Lane Newtown PA 18940

STAFFORD, BRUCE H(OLLEN), ELECTRICAL ENGINEERING, OPERATIONS RESEARCH. *Current Pos:* RETIRED. *Personal Data:* b North Platte, Nebr, Aug 25, 22; m 47; c 2. *Educ:* Univ Nebr, BSc, 43; Univ Md, MSc, 49. *Prof Exp:* Head dir systs sect, Oper Res Br, US Naval Res Lab, 43-54; opers analyst, Strategic Air Command, US Dept Air Force, 54-57, chief opers anal, 8th Air Force, 57-59, chief oper capability div, Opers Anal, 59-61, dep chief, Opers Anal, Strategic Air Command, 61-63, chief opers anal, HQ, 63-71, chief sci & res, 71-74. *Res:* Circuit analysis; servo-mechanisms; weapon control systems, including radar and computers; nuclear physics; electronic countermeasures; guided missiles; aircraft; operations research. *Mailing Add:* 3803 Chiswell Ct Greensboro NC 27410

STAFFORD, DARREL WAYNE, ZOOLOGY, MOLECULAR BIOLOGY. *Current Pos:* asst prof, 65-70, assoc prof, 70-77, PROF ZOOL, NUTRIT & BIOCHEM, UNIV NC, CHAPEL HILL, 78- *Personal Data:* b Parsons, Kans, Mar 11, 35; m, Sheve-Mei Wu; c 5. *Educ:* Southwest Mo State Col, BA, 59; Univ Miami, Fla, PhD(cellular physiol), 64. *Prof Exp:* NIH fel, Albert Einstein Col Med, 64-65. *Mem:* AAAS. *Res:* Molecular biology; coagulation; genes for related proteins. *Mailing Add:* Dept Biol Univ NC 442 Wilson Hall CB3280 Chapel Hill NC 27599-3280. *Fax:* 919-962-0597; *E-Mail:* stafford@uncvx1.oit.unc.edu

STAFFORD, FRED E, SCIENCE ADMINISTRATION & POLICY SOLID STATE CHEMISTRY. *Current Pos:* DIR SPEC PROJS, UNIV CHICAGO, 87- *Personal Data:* b New York, NY, Mar 30, 35; m 63, Barbara M Davis. *Educ:* Cornell Univ, AB, 56; Univ Calif, Berkeley, PhD(chem), 60. *Honors & Awards:* Palme Acad, FR Gov. *Prof Exp:* NSF fel, Free Univ Brussels, 59-61; from asst prof to assoc prof chem, Northwestern Univ, 61-74; prog officer sci develop progs, NSF, 74-75, prog dir solid state chem, 75-87. *Concurrent Pos:* Mem, Comt on High Temp Sci & Technol, Res Coun Can-Nat Acad Sci, 75-78; mem bd dirs, Chicago Unit Recording for the Blind. *Mem:* Am Chem Soc; Am Phys Soc; Asn Univ Technol Mgrs; Fed Exec Inst Alumni Asn; AAAS. *Res:* Solid state chemistry: administers research activities in a broad interdisciplinary area; oversees technology transfer. *Mailing Add:* Univ Chicago 970 E 58th St Chicago IL 60637-1475. *E-Mail:* f_stafford@uchicago.edu

STAFFORD, HELEN ADELE, PLANT PHYSIOLOGY. *Current Pos:* from asst prof to prof bot, 54-87, PROF BIOL, REED COL, 87- *Personal Data:* b Philadelphia, Pa, Oct 9, 22. *Educ:* Wellesley Col, BA, 44; Conn Col, MA, 48; Univ Pa, PhD, 51. *Honors & Awards:* C R Barnes Award, Am Soc Plant Physiologists. *Prof Exp:* Instr bot & res assoc biochem, Univ Chicago, 51-54. *Concurrent Pos:* Guggenheim fel, Harvard Univ, 58-59; NSF sr fel, Univ Calif, Los Angeles, 63-64. *Mem:* Bot Soc Am; Am Soc Plant Physiol; Am Soc Biol Chemists; Phytochem Soc NAm (pres, 77-78). *Res:* Plant biochemistry; metabolism of phenolic compounds; regulation of and metabolism of phenolic compounds in higher plants. *Mailing Add:* Dept Biol Reed Col 3203 SE Woodstock Blvd Portland OR 97202. *E-Mail:* helen.stafford@reed.edu

STAFFORD, JOHN WILLIAM, ELECTRONIC PHYSICAL DESIGN & SEMICONDUCTOR PACKAGING, ENGINEERING MECHANICS-STRESS & DYNAMIC ANALYSIS. *Current Pos:* lab head & sr mem tech staff, Schaumburg, Ill, 88-92, Tempe, Ariz, 92-96, SR MEM TECH STAFF & MGR, PROTOTYPE LAB, MOTOROLA INC, 97- *Personal Data:* b New York, NY, Mar 11, 32; m 58, Minerva L Genzinger; c Beth A & Brian J. *Educ:* Mass Inst Technol, BS, 54; Brooklyn Polytech Inst, MS, 59 & 70; Fairleigh Dickinson Univ, MBA, 79. *Prof Exp:* Struct engr, Grumman Aircraft, Bethpage, NY, 57-60 & Knolls Atomic Power Lab, Schenectady, 60-61; tech supvr & mem tech staff, Bell Tel Labs, Murray Hill, NJ, 61-82 & AT&T Info Systs, Holmdel, NJ, 82-84; tech dir & founder, Lytel Inc, Branchburg, NJ, 84-87. *Concurrent Pos:* Chmn, Prog Subcomt Packaging, Electronic Component & Technol Conf, 80-89; dir, Int Electronic Packaging Soc, 83-86; mem, Component Hybrids & Mfg Technol Admin Comn, Int Elec & Electronics Engrs, 86-89; prog chmn, 41st Electronic Component & Technol Conf, 90-91; gen chmn, 43rd Electronics Components & Technol Conf,92-93; vpres conf, Inst Elec & Electronics Engrs Components, Hybrids & Mfg Technol, 93- *Mem:* fel Inst Elec & Electronics Engrs; Int Elec Packaging Soc. *Res:* Electronics systems physical design and semiconductor packaging; development of precision equipment for electronic manufacturing; high volume low cost manufacturing technology; stress analysis; author/coauthor 39 scientific publications; granted 14 patents. *Mailing Add:* 15035 S 19th Way Phoenix AZ 85048. *Fax:* 602-897-5748

STAFFORD, MAGDALEN MARROW, gerontology, rehabilitation, for more information see previous edition

STAFFORD, ROBERT OPPEN, ENDOCRINOLOGY, NAUTICAL ARCHEOLOGY. *Current Pos:* RETIRED. *Personal Data:* b Milwaukee, Wis, Jan 28, 20; m 61, Dorothy Cooper; c 3. *Educ:* Univ Wis, BA, 41, MA, 48, PhD(zool), 49. *Prof Exp:* Res scientist, Upjohn Co, 49-60, asst dir biol res, 60-62, biochem res, 62-68, asst to exec vpres pharmaceut div, 68-71, chmn & chief exec officer, Upjohn Healthcare Serv, 76-82, vpres corp planning, Upjohn Co, 70-82. *Mem:* Soc Ocean Studies (vpres & treas). *Res:* Pharmacology, virology, pathology; metabolic diseases; management of research. *Mailing Add:* 353 Village Dr St Augustine Key Colony Beach FL 32095-9065

STAFFORD, THOMAS PATTEN, AERONAUTICS. *Current Pos:* RETIRED. *Personal Data:* b Weatherford, Okla, Sept 17, 30; m, Linda A Dishman; c Dionne & Karin. *Educ:* US Naval Acad, BS, 52. *Hon Degrees:* DSc, Oklahoma City Univ, 67; LLD, Western State Univ Col Law, 69, Univ Cordoba, Argentina; DrCommun, Emerson Col, 69; DrAero Eng, Embry-Riddle Aeronaut Inst, 70; LHD, Univ Okla, 94, MHL, Southwestern Univ, 94; HHD, Okla Christian Univ. *Honors & Awards:* Chanute Flight Award, Am Inst Aeronaut & Astronaut, 76; Nat Space Award, Vet Foreign Wars, 76. *Prof Exp:* Chief performance br, Aerospace Res Pilot Sch, Edwards AFB, Calif; staff mem, NASA, 62-75, chief astronaut off, 69-71, dep dir flight crew opers, Apollo-Soyuz Flight, 75; comdr, Air Force Flight Test Ctr, Edwards AFB, 75-79, lt gen & dep chief staff, Res, Develop & Acquisition, 79. *Mem:* Fel Am Astronaut Soc; Soc Exp Test Pilots; Am Inst Aeronaut & Astronaut. *Mailing Add:* 1006 Cameron St Alexandria VA 22314-2427

STAFSUDD, OSCAR M, JR, SOLID STATE SPECTROSCOPY. *Current Pos:* asst prof eng, 67-72, assoc prof eng, 74-80, assoc prof appl sci, 74-80, PROF ELEC ENG, UNIV CALIF, LOS ANGELES, 80- *Personal Data:* b Allison Park, Pa, Nov 10, 36; m 67; c 1. *Educ:* Univ Calif, Los Angeles, BA, 59, MS, 62, PhD(physics), 67. *Prof Exp:* Physicist, Atomics Int Div, NAm Aviation, Inc, 60-64 & Hughes Res Labs, 64-67. *Concurrent Pos:* Consult, Hughes Res Labs, 67- *Mem:* Am Phys Soc; Optical Soc Am; Am Soc Eng Educ. *Res:* Laser technology; crystal growth; solid state electronics. *Mailing Add:* Dept Elec Eng 58-113 Eng IV Bldg Univ Calif PO Box 9514-94 Los Angeles CA 90095-1594

STAGEMAN, PAUL JEROME, BIOCHEMISTRY. *Current Pos:* from asst prof to prof, 41-80, EMER PROF CHEM,UNIV NEBR, OMAHA, 80- *Personal Data:* b Persia, Iowa, June 21, 16; m 37, MaryJane Holmes; c paul J. *Educ:* Univ Omaha, AB, 39; Univ Iowa, MS, 50; Univ Nebr, PhD, 63. *Prof Exp:* Res chemist, Cudahy Packing Co, 39-41. *Mem:* AAAS; Am Chem Soc; Am Inst Chemists; Sigma Xi. *Res:* Ultracentrifugation; lipoproteins; atherosclerosis; plant pigments. *Mailing Add:* 308 W Oak St Council Bluffs IA 51503. *E-Mail:* stageman@cwis.unomaha.edu

STAGER, CARL VINTON, SOLID STATE PHYSICS. *Current Pos:* from asst prof to assoc prof, 63-72, PROF PHYSICS, MCMASTER UNIV, 72- *Personal Data:* b Kitchener, Ont, June 10, 35; m 62; c 4. *Educ:* McMaster Univ, BSc, 58; Mass Inst Technol, PhD(physics), 61. *Prof Exp:* Mem res staff, Francis Bitter Nat Magnet Lab, Mass Inst Technol, 60-63. *Mem:* Can Asn Physicists (treas, 64-68); Am Phys Soc. *Res:* Magnetism of insulating crystals; crystal fields spectra; electron paramagnetic resonance. *Mailing Add:* Dept Physics McMaster Univ 1280 Main St W Hamilton ON L8S 4M1 Can

STAGER, DONALD K, CIVIL ENGINEERING. *Current Pos:* CHMN, DILLINGHAM CONSTRUCT CORP. *Honors & Awards:* Roebling Award, Am Soc Civil Engrs, 95. *Mailing Add:* Dillingham Construct Corp 5960 Inglewood Dr Pleasanton CA 94588-8535

STAGER, HAROLD KEITH, GEOLOGY, MINING & EXPLORATION GEOLOGY. *Current Pos:* RETIRED. *Personal Data:* b Gardena, Calif, Dec 5, 21; m 49, 87, Kathryn Folliott; c Diana W, David M, Claire E & Karl E. *Educ:* Univ Calif, Los Angeles, BA, 48. *Prof Exp:* Geologist, Mineral Deposits Br, US Geol Surv, 48-63, Geol Br, 63-64, Base Metals Br, 64-65, field officer, Off Minerals Explor, 65-82. *Concurrent Pos:* Consult mining geologist, 82-. *Mem:* Fel Geol Soc Am. *Res:* Mining geology; mineral deposits; strategic and rare metals. *Mailing Add:* PO Box 1197 Bodega Bay CA 94923

STAGG, GLENN W, ELECTRIC POWER SYSTEMS. *Current Pos:* ENERGY SPECIALIST, INST INT EDUC. *Mem:* Nat Acad Eng. *Mailing Add:* Inst Int Educ 1400 K St NW Suite 650 Washington DC 20005

STAGG, RONALD M, PHYSIOLOGY, ENDOCRINOLOGY. *Current Pos:* assoc prof, 65-74, PROF BIOL, HARTWICK COL, 74- *Personal Data:* b Brooklyn, NY; m 52; c 5. *Educ:* Tusculum Col, BA, 50; Brooklyn Col, MA, 55; Rutgers Univ, PhD(endocrinol), 62. *Prof Exp:* Asst adminr, Willard F Greenwald, Med & Chem Consult, NY, 51-53; asst to med dir adminr, Warner-Chilcott Lab Div, Warner-Lambert Pharmaceut Co, NJ, 53-56; instr zool, Drew Univ, 59-60; instr physiol, Med Col Va, 60-65. *Concurrent Pos:* NIH grant, 63-65. *Mem:* Am Soc Zool. *Res:* Physiology, specifically mammalian; endocrinology, specifically the relationship between hormones and nutrition. *Mailing Add:* 51 Ford Ave Oneonta NY 13820

STAGG, WILLIAM RAY, PHYSICAL INORGANIC CHEMISTRY. *Current Pos:* SR RES CHEMIST, BABCOCK & WILCOX CO, 77- *Personal Data:* b Lexington, Ky, Sept 15, 37; m 62; c 2. *Educ:* Univ Ky, BS, 59; Iowa State Univ, PhD(chem), 63. *Prof Exp:* Res chemist, FMC Corp, NJ, 63-64; res assoc chem, Univ Ill, 66-67; asst prof, Colgate Univ, 67-72; assoc prof chem, Randolph-Macon Women's Col, 72-77. *Mem:* Am Nuclear Soc; Am Chem Soc. *Res:* Complex equilibria of lanthanide elements; heteroatom ring systems of sulfur, nitrogen and phosphorous; environmental chemistry; nuclear reactor coolant chemistry. *Mailing Add:* 3006 Sedgewick Dr Lynchburg VA 24503

STAGNO, SERGIO BRUNO, PEDIATRICS, INFECTIOUS DISEASES. *Current Pos:* res assoc pediat, Univ Ala, 72-73, asst prof, 73-77, asst prof microbiol, 75-81, assoc prof pediats, 77-80, assoc prof microbiol, 81-85, PROF PEDIAT, UNIV ALA, 80-, PROF MICROBIOL, 85- *Personal Data:* b Santiago, Chile, Oct 31, 41; m 68; c 1. *Educ:* Univ Chile, Bachelor, 60, MD, 67. *Prof Exp:* Instr pediat & parasitol, Sch Med, Univ Chile, 70-71. *Concurrent Pos:* Fel, Univ Ala, 71-72. *Mem:* Am Soc Microbiol; Soc Pediat Res; Chilean Pediat Soc; Chilean Parasitol Soc; Am Acad Pediats. *Mailing Add:* Childrens Hosp 1600 7th Ave S 600ACC Birmingham AL 35233

STAHEL, EDWARD P(AUL), CHEMICAL ENGINEERING. *Current Pos:* from asst prof to assoc prof, 62-74, prof & grad adminr, 66-72, PROF CHEM ENG, NC STATE UNIV, 74- *Personal Data:* b New York, NY, June 3, 34; m 57, 65; c 5. *Educ:* Princeton Univ, BSE, 55; Univ Notre Dame, MS, 57; Ohio State Univ, PhD(chem eng), 61. *Prof Exp:* Res engr, E I Du Pont de Nemours & Co, 61-62. *Mem:* AAAS; Am Chem Soc; Am Inst Chem Engrs; Am Soc Eng Educ. *Res:* Chemical engineering kinetics and reactor design; transport phenomena; polymer chemical engineering; biotechnological engineering. *Mailing Add:* 3900 Stratford Ct Raleigh NC 27609

STAHL, BARBARA JAFFE, COMPARATIVE ANATOMY, EVOLUTION. *Current Pos:* PROF BIOL, ST ANSELM COL, 54- *Personal Data:* b Brooklyn, NY, Apr 17, 30; m 51, David G; c 4. *Educ:* Wellesley Col, BA, 52; Radcliffe Col, AM, 53; Harvard Univ, PhD(biol), 65. *Hon Degrees:* DSc, St Anselm Col, 93. *Mem:* AAAS; Soc Vert Paleont; Sigma Xi. *Res:* Evolution of holocephali and early vertebrates. *Mailing Add:* Dept Biol St Anselm Col Manchester NH 03102-1310

STAHL, C(HARLES) D(REW), PETROLEUM ENGINEERING. *Current Pos:* Asst, 47-48, res assoc, 49-53, from asst prof to assoc prof, 53-61, PROF PETROL ENG, PA STATE UNIV, UNIVERSITY PARK, 61-, HEAD DEPT, 62- *Personal Data:* b Altoona, Pa, Aug 28, 23; m 48; c 1. *Educ:* Pa State Univ, BS, 47, MS, 50, PhD(petrol eng), 55. *Honors & Awards:* Am Asn Oilwell Drilling Contractors Award, 56. *Concurrent Pos:* Consult, Minerals Div, Pa State Dept Forests & Waters & Socony Mobil Oil Co, Venezuela, 58. *Mem:* Am Inst Mining, Metall & Petrol Engrs. *Res:* Displacement of immiscible fluids in porous media. *Mailing Add:* 209 Norle St State College PA 16801

STAHL, FRANK LUDWIG, CIVIL ENGINEERING. *Current Pos:* proj engr, Ammann & Whitney Consult Engrs, 55-67, assoc, 68-76, sr assoc, 77-81, CHIEF ENGR, TRANSP DIV, AMMANN & WHITNEY CONSULT ENGRS, NEW YORK, 82- *Personal Data:* b Fuerth Ger, 1920; nat US; m 47, Edith Cosmann; c David & Robert. *Educ:* Tech Inst Zurich, Switz, BSCE, 45. *Honors & Awards:* Thomas Fitch Rowland Prize, Am Soc Civil Engrs, 67, Roebling Award, 90; Gold Award, James F Lincoln Arc Welding Found, 86; John A Roebling Medal, Int Bridge Conf, 92. *Concurrent Pos:* Vchmn, Comt A-1 Steel, Stainless Steel & Related Alloys, Am Soc Testing & Mat, 78-83; mem, Res Coun Struct Connections, Eng Found. *Mem:* Am Inst Steel Construct; Int Asn Bridge & Struct Eng; Int Bridge Tunnel & Turnpike Asn; fel Am Soc Civil Engrs; fel Am Soc Testing & Mat. *Res:* Bridges. *Mailing Add:* Ammann & Whitney 96 Morton St New York NY 10014-3326

STAHL, FRANKLIN WILLIAM, GENETICS. *Current Pos:* res prof biol & res assoc, Inst Molecular Biol, 59-63, actg dir, 73-74, PROF BIOL & MEM, INST MOLECULAR BIOL, UNIV ORE, EUGENE, 63-; RES PROF MOLECULAR GENETICS, AM CANCER SOC, 85- *Personal Data:* b Boston, Mass, Oct 8, 29; m 55; c 2. *Educ:* Harvard Univ, AB, 51; Univ Rochester, PhD(biol), 56. *Hon Degrees:* DSc, Oakland Univ, 66 & Univ Rochester, 82. *Honors & Awards:* MacArthur Fel, John D & Catherine T MacArthur Found, 85- *Prof Exp:* Grad teaching asst & res asst, Univ Rochester, 51-54, NSF fel, 54-55; fel, NSF-Nat Res Coun, Div Med Sci, Calif Inst Technol, 55-57, res fel, 57-58; assoc prof zool, Univ Mo, 58-59. *Concurrent Pos:* Vol scientist, Div Molecular Genetics, Med Res Coun, Cambridge, Eng, 64-65; mem, Virol Study Sect, NIH, 68-71, spec fel, 69; vis scientist, Molecular Genetics Unit, Med Res Coun, Univ Edinburgh, Scotland & Int Lab Genetics & Biophys, Naples, 69-70; Guggenheim fel, 75 & 85; Lady Davis vis prof, Dept Genetics, Hebrew Univ, Jerusalem, 75-76. *Mem:* Nat Acad Sci; Am Acad Arts & Sci. *Res:* Genetics of bacteriophage. *Mailing Add:* Inst Molecular Biol Univ Ore Eugene OR 97403

STAHL, FRIEDA A, THERMAL PHYSICS. *Current Pos:* lectr physics, Calif State Univ, Los Angeles, 58-59, from asst prof to prof, 59-92, assoc dean acad planning, 70-75, EMER PROF PHYSICS, CALIF STATE UNIV, LOS ANGELES, 92- *Personal Data:* b Brooklyn, NY, May 27, 22; div; c Linda (Cofsky) & Richard. *Educ:* Hunter Col, BA, 42; Hofstra Col, MA, 57; Claremont Grad Sch, PhD(educ), 69. *Honors & Awards:* Coler-Maxwell Prize, Int Soc for the Arts, Sci & Technol, 87. *Prof Exp:* Jr physicist, US Army Signal Corps, NJ & Ala, 42-44 & Petty Labs, Petty Geophys Eng Co, Tex, 44-46; physicist, Hillyer Instrument Corp, NY, 46-48; sr physicist, Sylvania Res Labs, NY, 48-52; consult physicist, Gen Instrument Corp, NY, 56-57. *Concurrent Pos:* NSF sci fac fel, Harvey Mudd Col & Claremont Grad Sch, 66-68; res assoc chem, Harvey Mudd Col, 69-70, 75-76 & 90-91; consult ed, Col Teaching, 89- *Mem:* Am Phys Soc; Am Asn Physics Teachers; Sigma Xi; Asn Women Sci. *Res:* Electro-optical behavior in semiconductors; ultrasound propagation in solid methane and deuteromethane as a function of temperature, with particular interest in the lambda-type phase transitions of these substances; electro-optical phenomena in thin-film metal-insulator-metal structures. *Mailing Add:* Dept Physics & Astron Calif State Univ Los Angeles CA 90032. *Fax:* 213-343-2497; *E-Mail:* fstahl@calstatela.edu

STAHL, GLENN ALLAN, POLYMER CHEMISTRY. *Current Pos:* SR STAFF CHEMIST, EXXON CHEM CO, 87- *Personal Data:* b Snyder, Tex, Mar 14, 45; m 70; c 2. *Educ:* Univ Houston, PhD(polymer chem), 75. *Prof Exp:* Robert A Welch fel polymers, Univ Houston, 75-76; fel, Univ Ala, Tuscaloosa, 76-77; res chemist, Res & Develop Ctr, B F Goodrich Co, 77-80; sr chemist, Phillips Petrol Co, 80-87. *Concurrent Pos:* Grant adv, Paint Res Inst, 77-79. *Mem:* Am Chem Soc; Soc Plastic Engrs. *Res:* Water soluble polymers; polymers for oil recovery; science education through industry-academic cooperation; anchored organic reagents; application of polypropylene in textiles. *Mailing Add:* 8111 Hurst Forest Dr Humble TX 77346-1704

STAHL, JOEL S, PLASTICS IN BUILDING. *Current Pos:* PRES, STAHL INDUSTS, INC, 51-, CHIEF EXEC OFFICER, STAHL CO, 92- *Personal Data:* b Youngstown, Ohio, June 10, 18; wid. *Educ:* Ohio State Univ, BChE, 39. *Prof Exp:* Mgr spec prod, Ashland Oil, Inc, 39-50; pres, Cool Ray Co, 50-51. *Concurrent Pos:* Plastics-chem expert, US Trade Develop Mission, 63 & US Indust Develop Mission, 66. *Mem:* Soc Plastics Engrs; Soc Plastics Indust; Am Soc Testing & Mat; Asn Consult Chemists & Chem Engrs; NY Acad Sci. *Res:* Fire-resistant polymers; development of low-cost housing using plastic-foam cores and thin-skins sandwich construction; encasement of asbestos, lead paint and nuclear reactor site waste; plutonium and nuclear waste monitored retrievals storage. *Mailing Add:* 530 E Central 1504 Orlando FL 32801

STAHL, JOHN BENTON, LIMNOLOGY. *Current Pos:* asst prof, 66-72, ASSOC PROF BIOL, SOUTHERN ILL UNIV, 72- *Personal Data:* b Columbus, Ohio, Mar 28, 30; m 74, Lidia Claus; c Karl. *Educ:* Iowa State Univ, BS, 51; Ind Univ, AM, 53, PhD(zool), 58. *Prof Exp:* Sessional lectr biol, Queen's Univ, Ont, 58-59; asst prof, Thiel Col, 59-63; asst prof, Wash State Univ, 63-66. *Mem:* N Am Benthological Soc; Am Soc Limnol & Oceanog; Ecol Soc Am; Int Asn Theoret & Appl Limnol. *Res:* Chironomidae and Chaoborus; limnology of strip-mine lakes. *Mailing Add:* Dept Zool Southern Ill Univ Carbondale IL 62901-6501. *Fax:* 618-453-4110

STAHL, JOHN WENDELL, ANALYTICAL CHEMISTRY. *Current Pos:* ASSOC PROF CHEM, GENEVA COL, 85- *Personal Data:* b Wilkinsburg, Pa, Aug 24, 56; m 77; c 3. *Educ:* Geneva Col, BS, 79; Pa State Univ, PhD(chem), 83. *Prof Exp:* Asst prof chem, Bloomsburg Univ, Pa, 83-85. *Concurrent Pos:* Assoc mem, Comn VI, Int Union Pure & Appl Chem, 85-; vis prof, Univ Pittsburgh, 88. *Mem:* Am Chem Soc; Am Sci Affil. *Res:* Environmental analysis; inorganic sulfur chemistry; enthalpimetry; electrochemistry; computerization of instrumentation. *Mailing Add:* Dept Chem Geneva Col Beaver Falls PA 15010-3599

STAHL, LADDIE L, FLUID MECHANICS. *Current Pos:* RETIRED. *Personal Data:* b Terre Haute, Ind, Dec 23, 21; m 42, Beasley; c Stephanie, Laddie Jr & Craig. *Educ:* Purdue Univ, BS, 42; Johns Hopkins Univ, MS, 50. *Prof Exp:* Mgr prod planning & market res, Guided Missile Dept, Gen Elec Co, 54-55, Missile & Space Vehicle Dept, 55-59, mgr tech planning, 59-60, tech rels, 60-61, mgr spec prod, Gen Eng Lab, 61-62, adv technol appln, 62-64, mgr, Info Eng Lab, Adv Technol Labs, 64-65, res & develop appln, 65-70, adminr progs & systs, Res & Develop Ctr, 68-70, mgr res & develop appln, 70-74, planning & resources, electronics sci & eng, 74-76, Electronics Systs Progs Oper, electronics sci & eng, 76-84, mgr spec progs, proj develop oper res & develop appln oper, Corp Res & Develop, 84-90. *Concurrent Pos:* Alt mem, Gen Staff Comt Army Res Policy, 63; mem, Electronics Adv Group, US Army Electronics Command, 70-74, chmn, 71-74; mem Secy Labor Nat Adv Comt Jobs Ret, 71- & Nat Adv Coun Employer Support of Guard & Reserve, 72-; consult, US Army Aviation Systs Command sci adv group aviation systs, 73-75; mem, Army Reserve Forces Policy Comt, 73-76, chmn, Army Reserve Subcomt, 76; mem, US Army Sci Bd, 78-87; dir, Technol Transfer Prog, Data Storage Systs Ctr, Carnegie Mellon Univ, 90- *Mem:* Sr mem Inst Elec & Electronics Engrs; Am Inst Aeronaut & Astronaut; Am Defense Preparedness Asn. *Res:* Velocity fields induced by supersonic lifting surfaces; weapon system design and selection. *Mailing Add:* 29 Fairway Lane Rexford NY 12148

STAHL, NEIL, MATHEMATICAL ANALYSIS. *Current Pos:* PROF MATH, UNIV WIS CTR, FOX VALLEY CAMPUS, 76- *Personal Data:* b Sheridan, Ind, June 11, 42; m 67; c 1. *Educ:* Ind Univ, Bloomington, AB, 64; Brown Univ, PhD(appl math), 70. *Prof Exp:* Asst prof ecosysts anal, Univ Wis-Green Bay, Marinette Campus, 69-72, asst prof math, Univ Wis Ctr, Marinette Campus, 72-76. *Mem:* Math Asn Am. *Res:* Differential equations and their applications; educational software. *Mailing Add:* 921 Whittier Dr Appleton WI 54914. *E-Mail:* nstahl@worldnet.att.net

STAHL, PHILIP DAMIEN, PHYSIOLOGY, CELL BIOLOGY. *Current Pos:* From asst prof to assoc prof, 71-81, PROF PHYSIOL, MED SCH, WASH UNIV, 82-, HEAD, 84- *Personal Data:* b Wheeling, WVa, Oct 4, 41; m 68; c 3. *Educ:* WLiberty State Col, BS, 64; WVa Univ, PhD(pharmacol), 67. *Concurrent Pos:* Fel, Space Sci Res Ctr, Univ Mo, 67; Arthritis Found fel molecular biol, Vanderbilt Univ, 68-70. *Mem:* Brit Biochem Soc; Am Chem Soc; Am Physiol Soc; Am Soc Biol Chemists. *Res:* Lysosomes. *Mailing Add:* Dept Cell Biol & Physiol Wash Univ Med Sch 660 S Euclid Ave St Louis MO 63110-1093

STAHL, RALPH HENRY, EXPERIMENTAL PHYSICS. *Current Pos:* VPRES, JAYCOR, 77- *Personal Data:* b Berlin, Ger, Dec 29, 26; US citizen; m 55; c 3. *Educ:* Harvard Univ, AB, 49, MA, 50, PhD(nuclear physics), 54. *Prof Exp:* Mem tech staff, Radiation Lab, Univ Calif, 54-56; mem tech staff, Gen Atomic Div, Gen Dynamics Corp, 56-68; secy-treas, Systs, Sci & Software, 68-72; mem tech staff, IRT Corp, 72-77. *Concurrent Pos:* Vis prof, Univ Ill, Urbana, 61. *Mem:* Am Phys Soc; Am Nuclear Soc. *Res:* Nuclear weapons effects on military systems; electronics and electronics components; nuclear reactor physics. *Mailing Add:* 3060 Cranbrook Ct La Jolla CA 92037

STAHL, ROLAND EDGAR, ORGANIC CHEMISTRY. *Current Pos:* RETIRED. *Personal Data:* b Northumberland, Pa, Sept 2, 25; m 55; c 2. *Educ:* Bucknell Univ, BS, 50; Cornell Univ, PhD(chem), 54. *Prof Exp:* Asst org chem, Cornell Univ, 50-53; res chemist, Am Cyanamid Co, 54-56; res chemist, E I DuPont De Nemours & Co Inc, NY, 56-60, Tenn, 60-65, res chemist, 65-75, mkt res rep, 75-77, toxicol & regulatory affairs coordr, 77-78, sr regulatory affairs specialist, 73-83, regulatory affairs consult, Del, 83-90. *Mem:* Am Chem Soc. *Res:* Peroxide and radical chemistry; polymer applications; adhesives; textile finishing and applications. *Mailing Add:* 2619 Skylark Rd Wilmington DE 19808-1633

STAHL, SAUL, MATHEMATICS, COMBINATORICS. *Current Pos:* from asst prof to assoc prof, 77-86, PROF MATH, UNIV KANS, 86- *Personal Data:* b Antwerp, Belg, Jan 23, 42; US citizen; m 72, Susan Hogle; c Dan, Lynne & Amy. *Educ:* Brooklyn Col, BA, 63; Univ Calif, Berkeley, MA, 66; Western Mich Univ, PhD(math), 75. *Prof Exp:* Systs programmer, Int Bus Mach, 69-73; asst prof math, Wright State Univ, 75-77. *Mem:* Math Asn Am; Am Math Soc. *Res:* Graph theory; combinatorics. *Mailing Add:* Dept Math Univ Kans 603 Snow Lawrence KS 66045-0001

STAHL, WILLIAM J, BIOCHEMISTRY. *Current Pos:* asst prof, 65-74, ASSOC PROF BIOCHEM, JOHN JAY COL CRIMINAL JUSTICE, 74- *Personal Data:* b New York, NY, Jan 3, 39; m 64; c 3. *Educ:* Merrimack Col, AB, 60; Fordham Univ, MS, 61; St John's Univ, NY, PhD(biochem), 69. *Prof Exp:* Res asst biochem, Albert Einstein Med Ctr, 62-64; res chemist, Tenneco Chem Inc, 64-65. *Concurrent Pos:* Chief Coroner, Putnam County, NY, 79- *Mem:* AAAS; Am Soc Microbiol; Am Chem Soc. *Res:* Enzymes associated with invasive microbes and biochemical intermediates; development of vaccine for heroin and related alkaloids; ria-digoxin, amerod immunology. *Mailing Add:* PO Box 426 Brewster NY 10509-0426

STAHL, WILLIAM LOUIS, BIOCHEMISTRY, NEUROCHEMISTRY. *Current Pos:* res asst prof physiol & med, Univ Wash, 67-71, assoc prof, 71-77, PROF PHYSIOL & BIOPHYS & MED, SCH MED, UNIV WASH, 77-; CHIEF NEUROCHEM, VET AFFAIRS MED CTR, SEATTLE, 67- *Personal Data:* b Glen Dale, WVa, Aug 2, 36; m 59; c 2. *Educ:* Univ Notre Dame, BS, 58; Univ Pittsburgh, PhD(biochem), 63. *Prof Exp:* Res assoc biochem, NIH, 65-67. *Concurrent Pos:* United Cerebral Palsy Res & Educ Found fel, Biochem Dept, Inst Psychiat, Maudsley Hosp, Univ London, 63-65; exec dir, Histochem Soc, 97- *Mem:* Am Chem Soc; Am Soc Biochem & Molecular Biol; Am Soc Neurosci; Am Soc Neurochem; Int Soc Neurochem; Histochem Soc. *Res:* Transport homeostasis in the nervous system; intracellular signalling *Mailing Add:* Neurochem Lab 151 Vet Admin Med Ctr 1660 S Columbian Way Seattle WA 98108. *E-Mail:* wlstahl@u.washington.edu

STAHLMAN, MILDRED, PEDIATRICS, PHYSIOLOGY. *Current Pos:* From instr to asst prof pediat, Vanderbilt Univ, 51-59, from instr to asst prof physiol, 54-60, dir, Div Neonat, 61-89, assoc prof pediat, 64-70, PROF PEDIAT, SCH MED, VANDERBILT UNIV, 70-, PROF PATH, 82- *Personal Data:* b Nashville, Tenn, July 31, 22. *Educ:* Vanderbilt Univ, BA, 43, MD, 46; Am Bd Pediat, dipl, 54. *Hon Degrees:* MD, Univ Goteborg, Sweden, 73; Univ Nancy, France, 82. *Honors & Awards:* Apgar Award, 87; John Howland Award, 96. *Concurrent Pos:* Lederle med fac award, 61-62; dir, Div Neonatology, 61-89; USPHS career development award, 64-68; mem, Human Embryol & Develop Study Sect, USPHS, 64-68; perinatal biol, Infant Mortality Study Sect, 69-73; adv, Child Health & Human Develop Coun, 76-80. *Mem:* Inst Med-Nat Acad Sci; Am Pediat Soc; Am Physiol Soc; Am Fedn Clin Res; AAAS; Soc Pediat Res. *Res:* Newborn cardiorespiratory and fetal physiology; cardiology; rheumatic fever; lung development. *Mailing Add:* Dept Pediat Vanderbilt Univ Sch Med A-0109 Med Ctr N Nashville TN 37232-2370. *Fax:* 615-343-1763; *E-Mail:* mildredstahlman@mcmail.vanderbilt.edu

STAHLMAN, PHILLIP WAYNE, WEED SCIENCE, AGRONOMY. *Current Pos:* supt agron res, Harvey County Exp Field Agron, 75-76, RES WEED SCIENTIST, KANSAS STATE UNIV AGR RES CTR, HAYS, 76- *Personal Data:* b Shattuck, Okla, Jan 4, 48; m 69; c 2. *Educ:* Panhandle State Univ, BS, 70; NDak State Univ, MS, 73; Univ Wyo, PhD, 89. *Prof Exp:* Asst agronomist, NCent Br, NDak Agr Ecp Sta, 72-75. *Mem:* Weed Sci Soc Am; Am Soc Agron; Coun Agr Sci & Technol. *Res:* Weed control in dryland wheat and grain sorghum; chemical fallow and reduced tillage systems; control of field bindweed. *Mailing Add:* 506 W 31st St Hays KS 67601

STAHLY, DONALD PAUL, MICROBIOLOGY. *Current Pos:* from asst prof to assoc prof, 66-79, PROF MICROBIOL, UNIV IOWA, 79- *Personal Data:* b Columbus, Ohio, May 29, 37; m 59, Sally E Howard; c 2. *Educ:* Ohio State Univ, BS, 59, MS, 61; Univ Ill, PhD(microbiol), 65. *Prof Exp:* NIH fel, Univ Minn, 65-66. *Concurrent Pos:* Sabbatical, Scripp's Clin & Res Found, 77-78. *Mem:* AAAS; Am Soc Microbiol. *Res:* Bacterial sporulation; plasmids and bacteriophages in Bacillus species; Bacillus species pathogenic for insects; vitamin synthesis by bacillus subtiles. *Mailing Add:* Dept Microbiol Univ Iowa Iowa City IA 52242. *E-Mail:* donald-stahly@uiowa.edu

STAHLY, GLENN PATRICK, ORGANIC SYNTHESIS, CHIRAL MOLECULE PRODUCTION. *Current Pos:* SR RES & DEVELOP ADV, ALBEMARLE CORP, 94- *Personal Data:* b Washington, DC, Jan 24, 53; m 75, Barbara Clack; c Christopher P & Brian C. *Educ:* Univ Md, BS, 74, PhD(chem), 79. *Prof Exp:* Res chemist, Ethyl Corp, 80-83, sr res chemist, 83-88, sr res specialist, 88, new proj develop adv, 88-89, res & develop mgr, 89-91, res & develop adv, 91-92, sr res & develop adv, 92-94. *Mem:* AAAS; Am Chem Soc. *Res:* Organic synthesis and reaction mechanisms; organometallic synthesis; chiral molecule production (resolution and asymmetric synthesis); process development and scale-up; solid properties of organic crystals. *Mailing Add:* 3908 Sunnycroft Pl West Lafayette IN 47906. *Fax:* 504-587-5990; *E-Mail:* sn+stahly%g+pat%o+chemicals%albemarle@mcimail.com

STAHMANN, MARK ARNOLD, BIOCHEMISTRY, BOTANY-PHYTOPATHOLOGY. *Current Pos:* res assoc biochem, 46-47, from asst prof to prof, 47-82, EMER PROF BIOCHEM, UNIV WIS-MADISON, 82- *Personal Data:* b Spanish Fork, Utah, May 30, 14; m 41, Gertrude Harder; c 2. *Educ:* Brigham Young Univ, BA, 36; Univ Wis, PhD(biochem), 41. *Prof Exp:* Asst chem, Rockefeller Inst, 42-44; res assoc org chem, Mass Inst Technol, 44-45. *Concurrent Pos:* Guggenheim fel, Pasteur Inst, Paris, 55; Fulbright scholar, Nagoya, 67; FAO consult, Biol Inst, Sao Paulo, 74. *Mem:* AAAS; Am Chem Soc; Am Soc Biol Chemists; Soc Exp Biol & Med; Am Phytopath Soc. *Res:* Anticoagulant 4-hydroxycoumarins; warfarin; biochemistry of plant diseases; synthetic polypeptides; polypeptidyl proteins; virus diseases; plant proteins; molecular pathology of atherosclerosis. *Mailing Add:* 742 Hickman Dr Melbourne FL 32901-2729

STAHR, HENRY MICHAEL, VETERINARY TOXICOLOGY, MASS SPECTROSCOPY. *Current Pos:* PROF ANAL TOXICOL, IOWA STATE UNIV, 69- *Personal Data:* b White, SDak, Dec 10, 31; m 52; c Michael, John, Mary, Patrick & Matthew. *Educ:* SDak State Univ, Brookings, BS, 56; Union Col, Schnectady, NY, MS, 61; Iowa State Univ, Ames PhD(food chem), 76. *Prof Exp:* Anal develop chemist anal chem, Gen Elec Co, 56-65; sr scientist anal chem, Philip Morris Res, 65-69. *Mem:* Am Chem Soc; Soc Appl Spectros; Am Microchem Soc; Am Col Vet & Comp Toxicol; Am Asn Vet Lab Diagnostician; Asn Off Analytical Chemists; Sigma Xi; Soc Toxicol. *Res:* Analytical toxicology; develop techniques to analyze biological and environmental samples for toxic substances; natural intoxicants; man made chemicals; food contamination; safety considerations of contamination in foods; development of simple tests for field application and applying quantitative analytical procedures to provide quantitative data for toxicological assessments; veterinary medicine; mutagenic testing of substances-natural and synthetic. *Mailing Add:* Vet Diag Lab Vet Col Iowa State Univ Ames IA 50011-0061. *E-Mail:* hmstahr@jsu.edu

STAIB, JON ALBERT, COSMIC RAY PHYSICS, PHYSICS OF MUSIC. *Current Pos:* Asst prof, 69-70, ASSOC PROF PHYSICS, JAMES MADISON UNIV, VA, 70- *Personal Data:* b Toledo, Ohio, Mar 23, 40; m 67; c 2. *Educ:* Univ Toledo, BS, 63; Case Western Reserve Univ, MS, 67, PhD(physics), 69. *Concurrent Pos:* Consult, Case Western Reserve Univ, 69-73; lectr, Univ Ore, 81-82. *Mem:* Am Asn Physics Teachers; Int Planetarium Soc. *Res:* Gamma ray astronomy; atmospheric gamma radiation. *Mailing Add:* 114 Flint Ave Harrisonburg VA 22801

STAIFF, DONALD C, PHARMACEUTICAL CHEMISTRY, BIONUCLEONICS. *Current Pos:* CHIEF CHEMIST, WENATCHEE RES STA, ENVIRON PROTECTION AGENCY, 72- *Personal Data:* b Everett, Wash, Feb 26, 36; m 59; c 2. *Educ:* Univ Wash, BS, 59, PhD(pharmaceut chem), 63. *Prof Exp:* Asst prof pharmaceut chem, Ohio Northern Univ, 63-64; asst prof pharmaceut chem & bionucleonics, NDak State Univ, 64-67; anal res chemist, Western Pesticide Res Lab, Nat Commun Dis Ctr, USPHS, Wash, 67-72. *Concurrent Pos:* Mead-Johnson Labs grant, 64-65; NSF inst grant, 65-66; Soc Sigma Xi grant-in-aid res, 65-66; guest lectr, Training Prog, Perrine Primate Res Lab, Environ Protection Agency, Fla. *Mem:* Am Pharmaceut Asn; Am Chem Soc; Health Physics Soc. *Res:* Conformational and configurational studies of some substituted phenyl-cyclohexane compounds by modern instrumental methods; metabolism studies including use of radiotracer techniques; effect of pesticides on health and persistence in the environment. *Mailing Add:* 2017 N Western Ave Wenatchee WA 98801

STAIGER, ROGER POWELL, ORGANIC CHEMISTRY. *Current Pos:* RETIRED. *Personal Data:* b Trenton, NJ, Nov 23, 21; m 44; c 1. *Educ:* Ursinus Col, BS, 43; Univ Pa, MS, 48, PhD, 53. *Prof Exp:* From instr to assoc prof, Ursinus Col, 43-63, prof & chmn dept chem, 63-87. *Concurrent Pos:* Consult, Maumee Chem Co, 55-64; vis prof, Temple Univ, 63-82 & Alexandria Hosp, Nevis, 68-73. *Mem:* Am Chem Soc; Sigma Xi. *Res:* Synthesis of organic heterocyclic compounds. *Mailing Add:* 707 Chestnut St Collegeville PA 19426-2556

STAIKOS, DIMITRI NICKOLAS, ELECTROCHEMISTRY. *Current Pos:* RETIRED. *Personal Data:* b Piraeus, Greece, Dec 18, 19; m 47; c 2. *Educ:* Nat Univ Athens, dipl, 42; Western Reserve Univ, MS, 50, PhD(chem). 51. *Prof Exp:* Off Naval Res asst, Western Reserve Univ, 49-50; res chemist, Pa, 50-56, res engr, Eng Res Lab, 56-60, sr res phys chemist, 60-64, sr res phys chemist, Cent Res Dept, Exp Sta, E I Du Pont De Nemours & Co, Inc, 64-82. *Concurrent Pos:* Instr, St Joseph's Col, Pa, 54-55. *Mem:* Am Chem Soc; Electrochem Soc. *Res:* Fundamentals of electrochemical processes; corrosion; electronic instrumentation; ultrasonics; surface tension; fused salts; electrochemistry in nonaqueous solutions; electroless deposition; software systems programming. *Mailing Add:* 1306 Quincy Dr Green Acres Wilmington DE 19803-5146

STAINER, DENNIS WILLIAM, BIOCHEMISTRY, VACCINOLOGY, MICROBIOLOGY, BIOTECHNOLOGY. *Current Pos:* PRES, STAINER ASSOCS, 92- *Personal Data:* b Liverpool, Eng, Aug 25, 32; m 57, 84, Inge Winslow; c 3. *Educ:* Univ Liverpool, BSc, 54, Hons, 55, PhD(biochem), 58. *Prof Exp:* Asst dir, Connaught Labs Ltd, 60-83, dir, 83-88; vpres reg sci affairs, ConPharma Vaccines, 88-92. *Concurrent Pos:* Nat Res Coun Can fel biochem, Food & Drug Directorate, 57-59. *Mem:* Am Soc Microbiol; Int Asn Biol Standardization. *Res:* Production and control of diphtheria and tetanus toxoids and pertussis vaccine and studies on their immunogenicity; development of new bacteriological media and their application in bacterial fermentations; immunology; facility and equipment design. *Mailing Add:* 109 Regent St Richmond Hill ON L4C 9P3 Can. *Fax:* 905-884-8561; *E-Mail:* stainer@direct.com

STAINS, HOWARD JAMES, ZOOLOGY. *Current Pos:* RETIRED. *Personal Data:* b Frenchtown, NJ, Apr 16, 24; m 54; c 3. *Educ:* NC State Col, BS, 49, MS, 52; Univ Kans, PhD(zool), 55. *Prof Exp:* Lab instr econ zool, NC State Col, 48, res biologist, 49-51; res biologist, Univ Kans, 51-54, instr biol, 54-55; from asst prof to prof zool, Univ Southern Ill, 55-86. *Mem:* Wildlife Soc; Ecol Soc Am; Am Soc Mammal; Soc Study Evolution. *Res:* Furbearing mammals; osteology and ecology of mammals; wildlife techniques. *Mailing Add:* 1701 Pinedale Dr Raleigh NC 27603

STAINSBY, WENDELL NICHOLLS, PHYSIOLOGY OF RESPIRATION CIRCULATION & SKELETAL MUSCLE, MEMALIAN MUSCLE METABOLISM CIRCULATION & MECHANICS. *Current Pos:* from instr to prof, 57-97, EMER PROF PHYSIOL, COL MED, UNIV FLA, 97- *Personal Data:* b New York, NY, Nov 14, 28; m 52, Frances E Winterstreen; c Barbara E (Whitehill), Jane L (Ryals), Wendell L & Andrew W. *Educ:* Bucknell Univ, AB, 51; John Hopkins Univ, ScD, 55. *Honors & Awards:* Citation Award, Am Col Sports Med, 86. *Prof Exp:* Jr asst scientist, Cardiovasc Lab, Nat Heart Inst, NIH, Bethesda, Md, 55-56, asst scientist, 56-57. *Concurrent Pos:* NIH res grant, 58-93. *Mem:* Am Physiol Soc; Am Col Sports Med. *Res:* Circulatory and muscle physiology; muscle metabolism and circulation; tissue gas transport. *Mailing Add:* Dept Physiol Univ Fla Col Med Gainesville FL 32610. *Fax:* 352-846-0270

STAIR, PETER CURRAN, PHYSICAL CHEMISTRY, SURFACE SCIENCE. *Current Pos:* From asst prof to assoc prof, 77-87, PROF CHEM, NORTHWESTERN UNIV, 87- *Personal Data:* b Pasadena, Calif, Jan 25, 50; m 83, Thomson; c Jason & Neil. *Educ:* Stanford Univ, BS, 72; Univ Calif, Berkeley, PhD(chem), 77. *Mem:* Am Vacuum Soc; Am Phys Soc; Am Chem Soc; Catalysis Soc. *Res:* Structure and chemistry of metal and metal oxide surfaces, catalysis, and surface photochemistry. *Mailing Add:* Dept Chem Northwestern Univ Evanston IL 60208-3113. *Fax:* 847-491-7713; *E-Mail:* pstair@nwu.edu

STAIR, WILLIAM K(ENNETH), MECHANICAL ENGINEERING. *Current Pos:* from asst prof to assoc prof mech eng, Univ Tenn, Knoxville, 50-62, assoc dir eng exp sta, 70-76, asst dean res, 70-72, PROF MECH ENG, UNIV TENN, KNOXVILLE, 62-, ASSOC DEAN RES, COL ENG, 72- *Personal Data:* b Clinton, Tenn, Oct 1, 20; m 45; c 2. *Educ:* Univ Tenn, BS, 48, MS, 49. *Prof Exp:* Asst engr, Tenn Rwy Co, 39-41; eng aide, Tenn Valley Authority, 41-43; instr mech eng, Univ Tenn, 48-49; res participant nuclear eng, Oak Ridge Inst Nuclear Studies, 49-50. *Mem:* Fel Am Soc Lubrication Engrs; Am Soc Mech Engrs. *Res:* Lubrication and fluid dynamics; heat transfer; combustion phenomena. *Mailing Add:* 2317 Lakemoor Dr Knoxville TN 37920

STAIRS, GORDON R, INSECT PATHOLOGY. *Current Pos:* from asst prof to assoc prof, 65-73, PROF ENTOM, OHIO STATE UNIV, 73- *Personal Data:* b Millville, NB, May 18, 32; m 54; c 4. *Educ:* Univ NB, BSc, 54; McGill Univ, MSc, 58, PhD(entom), 63. *Prof Exp:* Res officer forest entom, Can Dept Agr, 54-58; res scientist, Insect Path Res Inst, 58-65. *Res:* Natural population biology and the effects of microorganisms on these populations; possible utilization of microorganisms in the control of pest populations; forest entomology and insect ecology. *Mailing Add:* 1070 Garden Rd Columbus OH 43224

STAIRS, ROBERT ARDAGH, SOLUTION PROPERTIES, ACID PRECIPITATION. *Current Pos:* actg chmn dept, Trent Univ, 66-67, from assoc prof to prof, 64-90, chmn dept, 86-89, EMER PROF CHEM, TRENT UNIV, 90- *Personal Data:* b Montreal, Que, June 10, 25; m 48, Sibyl Coulter; c Jennifer & Michael. *Educ:* McGill Univ, BSc, 48; Univ Western Ont, MSc, 51; Cornell Univ, PhD(inorg chem), 55. *Prof Exp:* Instr chem, Cornell Univ, 53-55; lectr, Queen's Univ, Ont, 55-58, asst prof, 58-64. *Concurrent Pos:* Pres, R & R Labs, Ltd, 85-86. *Mem:* Fel Chem Inst Can; AAAS; Am Chem Soc; Sigma Xi. *Res:* Physical properties of electrolyte solutions; viscosity of solutions; analysis acid precipitation; analytical methods. *Mailing Add:* Dept Chem Trent Univ Peterborough ON K9J 7B8 Can. *Fax:* 705-741-1625; *E-Mail:* rstairs@trentu.ca

STAKE, PAUL ERIK, ANIMAL NUTRITION. *Current Pos:* asst prof, 74-79, ASSOC PROF NUTRIT SCI, UNIV CONN, 79-, ACTG DEPT HEAD, 86 & 87- *Personal Data:* b Grandy, Minn, Jan 15, 44; m 66; c 3. *Educ:* Univ Minn, BS, 68; SDak State Univ, MS, 71; Univ Ga, PhD(nutrit biochem), 74. *Prof Exp:* Lab supvr dairy sci, SDak State Univ, 68-71; res asst animal nutrit, Univ Ga, 71-74. *Mem:* Am Dairy Sci Asn; Am Chem Soc; Am Soc Animal Sci; Nutrit Today Soc; Am Inst Nutrit. *Res:* Comparative metabolism of dietary essential and non-essential trace elements in animals and humans. *Mailing Add:* 166 Caroline Rd Bozrah CT 06334

STAKER, DONALD DAVID, ORGANIC CHEMISTRY, PHYSICAL ORGANIC CHEMISTRY. *Current Pos:* PVT CONSULT, 86- *Personal Data:* b Wheelersburg, Ohio, Jan 16, 26; m 47, Joan Lyon; c Diana, D Daniel, Deborah & Dorothy. *Educ:* Ohio Univ, BS, 47, MS, 48; Ohio State Univ, PhD(chem), 52. *Prof Exp:* Asst, Ohio Univ, 44-45 & 47-48; asst, Ohio State Univ, 48-49, res fel, 49-52; res chemist, Monsanto Chem Co, 52-56, res proj leader, 56-57, res group leader, 57-61; res sect leader, Nat Dist & Chem Corp, 61-67, res sect mgr, Fatty Acid Div, 67-78, Res Dept, Emery Chem Div, 78-86. *Mem:* Am Chem Soc. *Res:* Fatty acid chemistry, production processes, utilization; reaction mechanisms; rubber chemicals; polymer properties; lubricant additives; process development; metalworking lubricants; chemical business development and investment. *Mailing Add:* 591 Abilene Trail Cincinnati OH 45215-2554

STAKER, MICHAEL RAY, MATERIALS SCIENCE, METALLURGY. *Current Pos:* MAT RES ENGR, ARMY RES LAB, ABERDEN PROVING GROUND, MD, 94- *Personal Data:* b Dayton, Ohio, Nov 25, 47; m 76, Virginia Tien; c Nicholas T. *Educ:* Univ Dayton, BME, 70; Mass Inst Technol, MS, 71, PhD(metall), 75. *Prof Exp:* Mat engr, Gen Elec Aircraft Engine Group, 75-78; metallurgist, Army Mat Technol Lab, 78-93. *Concurrent Pos:* Lectr, Dept Mech Eng, Northeastern Univ, 80 & Dept Civil Eng, Tufts Univ, 84-86; lectr, Dept Civil Eng, Tufts Univ, 84-86. *Mem:* Am Soc Testing & Mat; Am Soc Metals Int. *Res:* Energy production by cold fusion, mechanism of nuclear reactions in metal lattices uranium metallurgy; high strain rate deformation and fracture; metal defects and structure by electron microscopy; structure and mechanical property relations in metals; fractography, fracture; dislocations; high temperature deformation of metals; super alloys; failure analysis. *Mailing Add:* 2817 Wesleyan Dr Churchville MD 21028

STAKER, ROBERT D, PHYCOLOGY, OPERATIONS RESEARCH. *Current Pos:* MGT ANALYST, WRIGHT-PATTERSON AFB, 81- *Personal Data:* b Newport, RI, July 3, 45; m 85, Carolyn R Kleinhenz; c Patrick J, Katrina L & Theresa R. *Educ:* Univ Dayton, BS, 67, MBA, 81, MA, 84; Univ Ariz, MS, 71, PhD(bot), 73. *Prof Exp:* Res asst phycol, Dept Biol, Univ PEI, 73-75; asst res scientist phytoplanktology, NY Ocean Sci Lab, 75-79; admin asst, Univ Dayton, 79-81. *Concurrent Pos:* Adj prof dept biol, Wright State Univ, 96-97. *Mem:* Am Soc Limnol & Oceanog; Phycol Soc Am; Int Soc Limnol; Sigma Xi; Nat Estimating Soc. *Res:* Marine and freshwater algal taxonomy and ecology; resource management; modeling using regression analysis and develop cost factors for planning and budget purposes; cost estimating for Air Force program office MIS modernization. *Mailing Add:* 3542 Woodgreen Dr Beavercreek OH 45434-5942. *Fax:* 937-257-0736; *E-Mail:* staker@wpdis01.wpafb.af.mil

STAKES, DEBRA SUE, marine geochemistry, geology, for more information see previous edition

STAKGOLD, IVAR, APPLIED MATHEMATICS. *Current Pos:* prof, 75-95, chmn, 75-91, EMER PROF, DEPT MATH SCI, UNIV DEL, 95- *Personal Data:* b Oslo, Norway, Dec 13, 25; nat US; m 64; c 1. *Educ:* Cornell Univ, BME, 45, MME, 46; Harvard Univ, MA, 48, PhD(appl math), 49. *Prof Exp:* From instr to asst prof appl math, Harvard Univ, 49-56; head math & logistics brs, US Off Naval Res, 56-59; assoc prof eng sci, Northwestern Univ, Evanston, 60-64, prof eng sci & math, 64-75, chmn dept eng sci, 69-75. *Concurrent Pos:* Vis asst prof, Stanford Univ, 53-54; liaison scientist, US Off Naval Res, London, 67-69; vis prof, Oxford Univ, 73-74, Univ Col, London, 78, Victoria Univ, Wellington, NZ, 81 & Polytech Inst, Lausanne, Switz, 81 & 84, Massey Univ, NZ, 87, Univ Bari, Italy, 87; consult, various indust & govt agencies; assoc ed, J Integral Equations, Int J Eng Sci, J Math Appl Analysis, 88-94, Siam Review, 88-95 chair ethics comn, Counc Sci Soc Pres, 90, Conf Bd Math Sci, 90-92; mem, Joint Policy Bd Math, 85-90; dir, Am Math Soc Wash Off, 94-95; dir, del Math Coalition, 96- *Mem:* Am Math Soc; Soc Indust & Appl Math (pres, 89-90); Math Asn Am; London Math Soc; Soc Natural Philos; Am Acad Mech. *Res:* Nonlinear boundary value problems. *Mailing Add:* Dept Math Sci Univ Del Newark DE 19716-2553. *Fax:* 302-831-4511; *E-Mail:* stakgold@math.udel.edu

STAKLIS, ANDRIS A, ORGANIC CHEMISTRY. *Current Pos:* mgr eng mat, Brake & Steering Div, 77-83, MGR FRICTION MAT DIV, BENDIX CORP, 84- *Personal Data:* b Valmiera, Latvia, Feb 4, 39; US citizen; m 61; c 1. *Educ:* Univ Nebr, BS, 61, PhD(org chem), 65. *Prof Exp:* Asst head met develop sect, Manned Spacecraft Ctr, NASA, 65-67; sr scientist, Bell Aerospace Co Div, Textron Inc, mgr mat develop, New Orleans Oper, 71-77. *Mem:* Am Chem Soc; Am Soc Test & Mat; Soc Automotive Engrs; Am Soc Metals; Sigma Xi. *Res:* Direct materials development for air cushion ships; development of flexible composites; corrosion protection of metallic materials; non-asbestos linings; brake lining development and processing; optimization. *Mailing Add:* Bendix Friction MTRLS Div 900 W Maple Troy MI 48084

STAKNIS, VICTOR RICHARD, MATHEMATICS. *Current Pos:* RETIRED. *Personal Data:* b Bridgewater, Mass, June 14, 20; m 42. *Educ:* Bridgewater Teachers Col, BS, 42; Mass Inst Technol, BS, 46; Boston Univ, MA, 50, PhD(math), 53. *Prof Exp:* Instr math, Ft Devens Br, Univ Mass, 46-49; lectr, Boston Univ, 51-52, instr, 52-53; from asst prof to assoc prof math, Northeastern Univ, 53-85. *Mem:* Am Math Soc. *Res:* Topology. *Mailing Add:* 90 Stoneleigh Rd Watertown MA 02172-1339

STAKUTIS, VINCENT JOHN, ATMOSPHERIC PHYSICS, OPTICS. *Current Pos:* RETIRED. *Personal Data:* b Boston, Mass, June 20, 20; m 47; c 4. *Educ:* Boston Col, BS, 43; Brown Univ, MS, 50, PhD(physics), 54. *Prof Exp:* Lab instr optics, Boston Col, 42-43; instr & asst to headmaster, Marianapolis Prep Sch, Conn, 46-48; asst optics, photog, atomic physics & acoust, Brown Univ, 48-53; res physicist, Geophys Res Dir, Air Force Cambridge Res Labs, 53-57, supvry physicist, 57-58, br chief atmospheric optics, 58-60; mem tech staff, 60-63, mem sr tech staff, Mitre Corp, Bedford, 63-87. *Concurrent Pos:* Private consult. *Mem:* AAAS; Sigma Xi; Am Geophys Union; Optical Soc Am; Acoust Soc Am. *Res:* Ultrasonic attenuation in aqueous suspensions; electromagnetic propagation; scattering processes in the atmosphere; high altitude sky luminance and albedo measurements; vision in the atmosphere; satellite reconnaissance systems; nuclear weapon environmental effects. *Mailing Add:* 160 Grant St Lexington MA 02173

STALCUP, MARVEL C, PHYSICAL OCEANOGRAPHY, GEOLOGY. *Current Pos:* RETIRED. *Personal Data:* b Mandan, NDak, Dec 30, 31; c 6. *Educ:* Univ Idaho, BS, 61. *Prof Exp:* Res specialist oceanog, Woods Hole Oceanog Inst, 61-92. *Concurrent Pos:* Consult oceanog, ECO-Zist, Teheran, Iran, 77-78. *Mem:* AAAS. *Res:* Identification and description of water masses and currents of the Atlantic and Indian Oceans and Caribbean Sea. *Mailing Add:* 25 Sierra Roja Circle Sedona AZ 86531

STALDER, KENNETH R, PHYSICS OF MATERIALS PROCESSING PLASMAS, PLASMA DIAGNOSTICS. *Current Pos:* RES PHYSICIST, MOLECULAR PHYSICS LAB, SRI INT, 86- *Personal Data:* b Palo Alto, Calif, Jan 9, 52; m 81, Patricia Nassos; c Katherine & Julia. *Educ:* Unif Calif, San Diego, AB, 74; Univ Calif, Berkeley, MA, 76, PhD(physics), 82. *Prof Exp:* Res asst, Physics Dept, Univ Calif, Berkeley-Lawrence Berkeley Lab, 76-82; res specialist, Physics Dept, Univ Calif, Irvine, 82-83; mem tech staff, Appl Mat Inc, 83-86. *Concurrent Pos:* Lectr physics, San Jose State Univ, 85; adj lectr physics, Santa Clara Univ, 86; distinguished vis scholar, Queen's Univ, Belfast, Northern Ireland, 92. *Mem:* Am Phys Soc. *Res:* Research in a wide variety of basic and applied physics research, but specialize in ionized gas phenomena and plasma physics; experimental diagnostic measurements of plasmas; applied diagnostic techniques to other problems such as found in acoustics or process industries. *Mailing Add:* SRI Int 333 Ravenswood Ave Menlo Park CA 94025. *Fax:* 650-859-6196; *E-Mail:* krs@mplvax.sri.com

STALEY, DAVID H, MATHEMATICS. *Current Pos:* from asst prof to assoc prof, 61-70, PROF MATH, OHIO WESLEYAN UNIV, 70- *Personal Data:* b Columbus, Ohio, Jan 30, 30; m 58; c 3. *Educ:* Oberlin Col, AB, 52; Ohio Univ, MS, 54; Ohio State Univ, PhD(math), 63. *Prof Exp:* Instr math, Henry Ford Community Col, 56-57 & Oberlin Col, 60-61. *Concurrent Pos:* Consult legal math questions, USDA; mem, N Cent Eval Team, USDA. *Mem:* Math Asn Am; Nat Coun Teachers Math. *Res:* Commutability of operators in a topological space; mathematical models of insect populations; mathematical models for temperature and heat accumulation. *Mailing Add:* Dept Math Sci Ohio Wesleyan Univ Delaware OH 43015

STALEY, DEAN ODEN, METEOROLOGY. *Current Pos:* RETIRED. *Personal Data:* b Kennewick, Wash, Oct 18, 26; m 63; c 5. *Educ:* Univ Wash, BS, 50, PhD(meteorol), 56; Univ Calif, Los Angeles, MA, 51. *Prof Exp:* From instr to asst prof, Univ Wis, 55-59; assoc prof & assoc meteorologist, Univ Ariz, 59-65, prof atmospheric sci & res prof, Inst Atmospheric Physics, 65-91. *Mem:* Am Meteorol Soc; Am Geophys Union. *Res:* Dynamic and synoptic meteorology. *Mailing Add:* 222 Sierra Vista Dr Tucson AZ 85719

STALEY, JAMES T, ALUMINUM ALLOYS. *Current Pos:* CHIEF SCIENTIST AEROSPACE & INDUST PROD GROUP & CORP CONSULT HIGH STRENGTH ALUM PROD, ALCOA LABS. *Personal Data:* b Pittsburgh, Pa, Oct 15, 34; m 57, Nora C Marion; c James Jr, Robert, Judith, Leila & Linda. *Educ:* Univ Pittsburgh, BS, 62, MS, 67; Drexel Univ, PhD(mat eng), 89. *Honors & Awards:* James Douglas Gold Medal, Am Inst Mining, Metall & Petrol Engrs, 92; Edgar C Bain Award, Am Soc Metals Int, 95. *Concurrent Pos:* Mem, Bergey's Manual Trust. *Mem:* Fel Am Soc Metals Int; Metall Soc Am Inst Mining Metall & Petrol Engrs; Sigma Xi. *Res:* Physical metallurgy; development of aluminum alloys and processes; applications of aluminum alloy mill products in the aerospace industry; over 40 publications; six patents. *Mailing Add:* Alcoa Tech Ctr Aluminum Co Am Alcoa Center PA 15069. *Fax:* 412-337-2166; *E-Mail:* james.staley@alcoa.com

STALEY, JAMES TROTTER, BACTERIAL TAXONOMY, MICROBIAL ECOLOGY. *Current Pos:* from asst prof to assoc prof, 71-82, PROF MICROBIOL, UNIV WASH, 82- *Personal Data:* b Brookings, SDak, Mar 14, 38; m 63, Erickson; c 2. *Educ:* Univ Minn, Minneapolis, BA, 60; Ohio State Univ, MS, 63; Univ Calif, Davis, PhD(bact), 67. *Honors & Awards:* Alexander von Humboldt Sr Scientist Award. *Prof Exp:* Instr microbiol, Mich State Univ, 67-69; asst prof environ sci & eng, Univ NC, Chapel Hill, 69-71. *Concurrent Pos:* Mem, Bergey's Manual Trust, 76-; ed, Bergey's Manual Syst Bacteriol, vol 3, 83-87; mem, Int Symp Environ Biochem, 85-; ed, Microbiol Rev, 90-; assoc ed, Intern J Syst Bacteriol, 91. *Mem:* Am Soc Microbiol; AAAS. *Res:* Biology of prosthecate, budding and gas vacuolate bacteria; aquatic bacteriology; fresh water microbiology; microbial ecology; microbiology of desert varnish formation; sea ice bacteriology; bacterial taxonomy. *Mailing Add:* Dept Microbiol Univ Wash Sch Med 3900 Seventh Ave NE Seattle WA 98195-0001. *Fax:* 206-543-8927

STALEY, JOHN M, PLANT PATHOLOGY, FORESTRY. *Current Pos:* AGR RES TECHNOLOGIST, DEPT PLANT PATH, WASH STATE UNIV, 83- *Personal Data:* b Three Rivers, Mich, Sept 12, 29; m 80; c 4. *Educ:* Univ Mont, BS, 51; WVa Univ, MS, 53; Cornell Univ, PhD(plant path), 62. *Prof Exp:* Asst forest path, WVa Univ, 51-53; plant pathologist, Pac Northwest Forest & Range Exp Sta, US Forest Serv, 53, Northeastern Forest Exp Sta, 56-62, res plant pathologist, Rocky Mountain Forest & Range Exp Sta, 62-82. *Concurrent Pos:* Res asst, Cornell Univ, 56-62; affil prof, Grad Fac, Colo State Univ, 67- *Mem:* Am Phytopath Soc; Mycol Soc Am. *Res:* Complex diseases of forest trees; vascular wilt diseases of forest trees; foliage diseases of coniferous trees; rust diseases of cereals. *Mailing Add:* Wash State Univ 7612 Pioneer Way E Puyallup WA 98371-4998

STALEY, L(EONARD) M(AURICE), agriculture, engineering; deceased, see previous edition for last biography

STALEY, RALPH HORTON, PHYSICAL CHEMISTRY. *Current Pos:* SR RES ASSOC, E I DU PONT DE NEMOURS & CO, INC, 81- *Personal Data:* b Boston, Mass, Mar 15, 45; m 83, Laura A Lewin; c Sasha, Hannah & Naomi. *Educ:* Dartmouth Col, AB, 67; Calif Inst Technol, PhD(chem), 76. *Prof Exp:* Res physicist, Feldman Res Labs, Picatinny Arsenal, 68-71; asst prof phys chem, Mass Inst Technol, 75-81. *Mem:* Am Chem Soc; AAAS. *Res:* Materials research. *Mailing Add:* Cent Res & Develop Dept E356 Dupont Co Wilmington DE 19880-0356

STALEY, ROBERT NEWTON, ORTHODONTICS, PHYSICAL ANTHROPOLOGY. *Current Pos:* from asst prof to assoc prof, 70-85, PROF ORTHOD, COL DENT, UNIV IOWA, 85- *Personal Data:* b Canova, SDak, Oct 15, 35; m 70, Kathleen Holmes; c 2. *Educ:* Univ Minn, Minneapolis, BS, 57, DDS, 59; Univ Chicago, MA, 67; State Univ NY, Buffalo, cert orthod, 69, MS, 70; Am Bd Orthod, dipl, 83. *Prof Exp:* Intern dent, Zoller Mem Dent Clin, Univ Chicago Hosp & Clins, 59-60, mem staff, 62-65. *Concurrent Pos:* Cap, Dent Corp, US Army, 60-62. *Mem:* Int Asn Dent Res; Am Dent Asn; Am Asn Orthodont; Am Cleft Palate Asn; Am Asn Phys Anthrop; fel Int Col Dentists. *Res:* Investigates the relations of craniofacial morphology to clinical orthodontics, growth and genetics; orthodontic biomechanics and materials testing. *Mailing Add:* Dept Orthod Univ Iowa Col Dsb S224 Iowa City IA 52242. *Fax:* 319-335-6847

STALEY, STUART WARNER, PHYSICAL & ORGANIC CHEMISTRY, STRUCTURE CHEMISTRY. *Current Pos:* PROF CHEM, CARNEGIE MELLON UNIV, 86- *Personal Data:* b Pittsburgh, Pa, July 11, 38; m 63, Mary Waugh; c Stuart W & Andrew W. *Educ:* Williams Col, BA, 59; Yale Univ, MS, 61, PhD (phys org chem), 64. *Prof Exp:* Res assoc phys org chem, Univ Wis, 63-64; from asst prof to prof chem, Univ Md, College Park, 64-78; prof chem, Univ Nebr, Lincoln, 78-85. *Concurrent Pos:* Vis prof, Swiss Fed Inst Technol, Zurich, 71-72, Univ Calif, Riverside, 84, Univ Umea, Sweden, 92 & Univ Marburg, Ger, 92. *Mem:* Am Chem Soc. *Res:* Photoelectron, electron transmission, and nuclear magnetic resonance spectroscopy of organic compounds; reaction mechanisms; carbanion chemistry; molecular orbital calculations; synthesis of theoretically interesting molecules; fullerenes; solid state organic chemistry. *Mailing Add:* Dept Chem Carnegie Mellon Univ 4400 Fifth Ave Pittsburgh PA 15213-2683. *E-Mail:* staley@cmchem.chem.cmu.edu

STALFORD, HAROLD LENN, APPLIED MATHEMATICS. *Current Pos:* PRES, PRACTICAL SCI, INC, 80- *Personal Data:* b Avery, Okla, July 22, 42; m 63; c 5. *Educ:* Okla State Univ, BS, 65; Univ Calif, Berkeley, MS, 66, PhD(appl mech), 70. *Prof Exp:* Asst res engr, Univ Calif, 70; opers res analyst, Radar Div, US Naval Res Lab, 70-71, math analyst, 71-76; sr analyst, Dynamics Res Corp, 76-80. *Concurrent Pos:* Sr analyst, Dynamics Res Corp, 76- *Mem:* Sigma Xi. *Res:* Estimation, control, system identification and differential games; design and evaluation of optimum survivability maneuvers for airborne applications; non-linear track filter sand predictors for shipboard applications; statistics; system identification and classification. *Mailing Add:* Ga Inst Tech Sch Aerospace Eng Atlanta GA 30332

STALHEIM, OLE H VIKING, VETERINARY HISTORY. *Current Pos:* assoc prof & collabr, Dept Hist, 85-93, ASSOC PROF & COLLABR, DEPT MICROBIOL, IMMUNOL & PREV MED, COL VET MED, IOWA STATE UNIV, AMES, 93- *Personal Data:* b Garretson, SDak, Sept 23, 17; m 42, Vivian Elverson; c 4. *Educ:* Tex A&M Univ, DVM, 41; Univ SDak, MA, 61; Univ Wis, PhD(bact), 63. *Honors & Awards:* E A Pope Award, 79; 12th Int Vet Congress Prize, Am Vet Med Asn, 84. *Prof Exp:* Vet practitioner, Vermillion, SDak, 41-58; NIH fel, Univ Wis, 60-63; res vet, Nat Animal Dis Ctr, Sci & Educ Admin-Agr Res, USDA, 63- *Concurrent Pos:* Fulbright-Hays award, 80-81 & 87-89. *Mem:* Am Vet Med Asn; Am Soc Microbiol; Conf Res Workers Animal Dis; US Animal Health Asn. *Res:* Microbial nutrition, metabolism and virulence; immunity to bacterial infection; veterinary history; chemotherapy. *Mailing Add:* 1918 George Allen Ave Ames IA 50010

STALICK, WAYNE MYRON, ORGANIC CHEMISTRY. *Current Pos:* from asst prof to assoc prof, 72-87, PROF ORG CHEM, GEORGE MASON UNIV, 87- *Personal Data:* b Oregon City, Ore, Aug 24, 42; c Jonathan. *Educ:* Univ Ore, BA, 64; Northwestern Univ, PhD(org chem), 69. *Prof Exp:* Asst prof org chem, Calif State Univ, San Jose, 69-70; fel, Ohio State Univ, 70-72, lectr, 72. *Concurrent Pos:* Sabbatical, Naval Res Lab, 85-86. *Mem:* Sigma Xi; Am Chem Soc. *Res:* Chemistry of petroleum products, in particular, catalytic reactions of hydrocarbons, pryrolosis of long chain alkylaromatic compounds; synthetic techniques in organic chemistry. *Mailing Add:* Dept Chem George Mason Univ Fairfax VA 22030. *Fax:* 703-993-1055; *E-Mail:* wstalick@gmu.edu

STALKER, ARCHIBALD MACSWEEN, GLACIAL GEOLOGY, PALEOENVIRONMENTS. *Current Pos:* RETIRED. *Personal Data:* b Montreal, Que, June 29, 24; m 51, Marion I Gilker; c David A, Jane M, Margaret I & Mary F. *Educ:* McGill Univ, BA, 45, MSc, 48, PhD(geol), 50. *Hon Degrees:* DSc, Univ Lethbridge, 84. *Prof Exp:* Geologist, Geol Surv Can, 50-87. *Concurrent Pos:* Adj prof, Univ Lethbridge, 87- *Mem:* Can Quaternary Asn; fel Geol Soc Am; Geol Asn Can; Am Quaternary Asn; Quaternary Res Asn (UK). *Res:* Glacial geology; geomorphology; relations of Cordilleran and Laurentide glaciations; preglacial drainage; early man in New World; climate, stratigraphy and mammals of Quaternary; Quaternary vertebrate paleontology. *Mailing Add:* 2126 Strathmore Blvd Ottawa ON K2A 1M7 Can

STALKER, HAROLD THOMAS, PLANT CYTOGENETICS, PEANUT BREEDING. *Current Pos:* Res assoc cytogenetics, NC State Univ, 77-79, asst prof crop sci, 79-83, assoc prof crop sci & biotechnol, 87-89, ASSOC PROF, NC STATE UNIV, 83-, PROF CROP SCI & BIOTECHNOL, 89- *Personal Data:* b Pittsburgh, Pa, Oct 27, 50; m 72, Helen Zaepful; c Michael T & Stephen E. *Educ:* Univ Ariz, BS, 72, MS, 73; Univ Ill, PhD(genetics), 77. *Mem:* Crop Sci Soc Am; Am Genetic Asn; fel Am Peanut Res & Educ Soc; Soc Econ Bot; Bot Soc Am. *Res:* Cytogenetics; genetics; speciation and biosystematics of wild and cultivated species of the genus Arachis; introgressing disease and insect resistances from arachis species to cultivated peanut; molecular markers. *Mailing Add:* 1206 Ivy Lane Cary NC 27511. *Fax:* 919-515-5657

STALKER, HARRISON DAILEY, genetics; deceased, see previous edition for last biography

STALKUP, FRED I(RVING), JR, CHEMICAL ENGINEERING. *Current Pos:* sr res adv, 83-97, DISTINGUISHED ADV, ARCO EXPLOR & PROD TECHNOL, 97- *Personal Data:* b Temple, Tex, Feb 3, 36; m 65; c 1. *Educ:* Rice Univ, BA, 57, PhD(chem eng), 62. *Honors & Awards:* Sigma Xi Res Award, 62; Lester C Uren Award, Soc Petrol Engrs, 85, Distinguished Lectr, 85, Anthony F Lucas Gold Medal, 95. *Prof Exp:* Sr res engr, Atlantic-Richfield Co, 61-65, prin res engr, 65-67, dir, Process Develop Res, 67-69, dir, Reservoir Eng Res, 69-71, dir, Reservoir Math Res, 71-77, dir recovery res, 77-79; consult, 79-83. *Mem:* Nat Acad Eng; Soc Petrol Engrs. *Res:* Hydrocarbon phase equilibria; miscible, immiscible and thermal methods of oil recovery; reservoir engineering; secondary and tertiary recovery; mathematical modeling; author, SPE monograph: Misable Displacement and 21 other publications; reservoir simulation. *Mailing Add:* Arco Explor & Prod Technol 2300 W Plano Pkwy Plano TX 75075

STALL, ROBERT EUGENE, PLANT PATHOLOGY. *Current Pos:* Res asst plant path, Ohio Agr Exp Sta, 57-63, assoc prof & assoc plant pathologist, 63-69, PROF PLANT PATH, UNIV FLA, 69- *Personal Data:* b Leipsic, Ohio, Dec 11, 31; m 52, Burkholder; c Ronald & David. *Educ:* Ohio State Univ, BSc, 53, MSc, 54, PhD(bot, plant path), 57. *Concurrent Pos:* Vis prof, Nat Inst Agr Technol, Bella Vista, Arg, 78-79. *Mem:* AAAS; fel Am Phytopath Soc; Am Soc Microbiol. *Res:* Bacterial phytopathology. *Mailing Add:* 2725 NW 62nd Terr Gainesville FL 32606

STALL, WILLIAM MARTIN, HORTICULTURE, WEED SCIENCE. *Current Pos:* PROF, EXTEN VEG SPECIALIST, HORT SCI DEPT, UNIV FLA, 80- *Personal Data:* b Bluffton, Ohio, Apr 14, 44; m 69, Donna Duncan. *Educ:* Ohio State Univ, BSA, 67; Univ Fla, MSA, 69, PhD(vegetable crops), 73. *Prof Exp:* Teacher biol, Southwestern City Sch, Grove City, Ohio, 69-71; exten agent veg, Fla Coop Exten Serv, 74-80. *Mem:* Am Soc Hort Sci; Weed Sci Soc Am; Nat Agr Plastics Asn; Coun Agr Sci & Technol. *Res:* Integrated pest management; herbicide efficacy and phytotoxicity; weed crop interference; herbicide and growth regulator residues for minor crop clearance. *Mailing Add:* 1010 SW 35th Pl Gainesville FL 32607. *Fax:* 352-392-5653; *E-Mail:* wms@gnv.ifas.ufl.edu

STALLARD, MICHAEL LEE, ORGANIC CHEMISTRY. *Current Pos:* PRES, AM WASTE MGT, INC, 93- *Educ:* Va Commonwealth Univ, BS, 76; Va Polytech Inst, MS, 86, PhD(civil eng), 90. *Prof Exp:* Dir environ eng, Envirotrol, Inc, 90-93. *Mem:* Nat Soc Prof Engrs; Am Soc Civil Engrs. *Res:* Polychlorinated biphenyl detoxification by photochemical techniques; synthesis of novel mineral processing surface active agents. *Mailing Add:* 824 Ohio River Blvd No 6 Sewickley PA 15143

STALLARD, RICHARD E, anatomy, periodontology, for more information see previous edition

STALLCUP, MICHAEL R, MOLECULAR BIOLOGY, GENETICS. *Current Pos:* assoc prof, Dept Path, 85-93, assoc prof, Dept Biochem, 85-93, PROF DEPT PATH & BIOCHEM, UNIV SOUTHERN CALIF, SCH MED, 93- *Personal Data:* b Dallas, Tex, Nov 6, 47; m 80, Terry Riemer. *Educ:* Yale Univ, BA, 69; Univ Calif, Berkeley, PhD(biochem), 74. *Prof Exp:* Fel biochem & biophysics, Univ Calif, San Francisco, 74-79; asst prof biol, Univ SC, 80-85. *Concurrent Pos:* NSF grad trainee award, 69-72; fel, Am Cancer Soc, 74-75, Nat Res Serv Award, NIH, 77-79; prin investr, NIH res grant, 80-, Am Cancer Soc res grant, 88-92 & 95-96; Res Career Develop Award, NIH, 83-88; mem Molecular Biol study sect, NIH, 84-88; mem, Tumor Biochem & Ednocrinol Study Sect, Am Cancer Soc, 94-98, chair, 97-98. *Mem:* Am Soc Cell Biol; Endocrine Soc; AAAS. *Res:* Biochemical and genetic studies on regulation of gene expression in mammalian cells by steroid hormones. *Mailing Add:* Dept Path HMR 301 Univ Southern Calif Sch Med 2011 Zonal Ave Los Angeles CA 90033-1034

STALLCUP, ODIE TALMADGE, NITROGEN METABOLISM, PHYSIOLOGY OF REPRODUCTION. *Current Pos:* from assoc prof to prof, 50-85, univ prof animal sci, 85-88, EMER UNIV PROF ANIMAL SCI, UNIV ARK, 89- *Personal Data:* b Paragould, Ark, Dec 2, 18; m 47; c 3. *Educ:* Univ Ark, BSA, 43; Univ Mo, AM, 47, PhD(nutrit/physiol), 50. *Prof Exp:* Instr dairy sci, Dept Dairy Husb, Univ Mo, 47-50. *Concurrent Pos:* Instr dairy sci, Dept Animal Indust, Univ Ark, 45-46. *Mem:* Am Soc Animal Sci; Am Dairy Sci Asn; Soc Study Reproduction; Histochem Soc; Am Inst Nutrit; fel AAAS; Int Fedn Soc Histochem & Cytochem. *Res:* Nutrition and physiology; nutritive value of forages for cattle; nitrogen in ruminants; histochemical studies on bovine embryo growth and reproduction in cattle. *Mailing Add:* Dept Animal Sci Univ Ark Fayetteville AR 72701. *Fax:* 501-575-7273

STALLCUP, WILLIAM BLACKBURN, JR, VERTEBRATE ZOOLOGY. *Current Pos:* RETIRED. *Personal Data:* b Dallas, Tex, Oct 18, 20; m 42, Marcile Patterson; c William B, Michael R, Jerre A, Cathy M & Lise G. *Educ:* Southern Methodist Univ, BA, 41; Univ Kans, PhD(zool), 54. *Prof Exp:* Instr biol, Southern Methodist Univ, 45-50; asst instr, Univ Kans, 50-53; from instr to assoc prof biol, Southern Methodist Univ, 53-62, prof, 62-89, chmn dept, 63-67, assoc dean, Sch Humanities & Sci, 71-74, assoc provost, 74-80 & 81-83, provost, ad interim, 80-81, actg provost, 86, pres ad interim, 86-87, dir, Smu-In-Taus Prog, 90-92, emer prof, 89-95. *Concurrent Pos:* Spec asst to pres, Southern Methodist Univ, 82-83. *Res:* Comparative myology and serology of birds; vertebrate natural history. *Mailing Add:* PO Box 1257 Ranchos De Taos NM 87557

STALLEY, ROBERT DELMER, NUMBER DENSITY, ADDITIVE MODULAR NUMBER THEORY. *Current Pos:* from asst prof to prof, 56-89, EMER PROF MATH, ORE STATE UNIV, 89- *Personal Data:* b Minneapolis, Minn, Oct 25, 24; m 50, Dorothy Ann Jeffery; c Mark Frederick, Jeffery Alan, John Michael & Lorena Ellen. *Educ:* Ore State Col, BS, 46, MA, 48; Univ Ore, PhD(math), 53. *Prof Exp:* Instr math, Univ Ariz, 49-51; instr, Iowa State Col, 53-54, asst prof, 54-55; instr, Fresno State Col, 55-56. *Concurrent Pos:* Prin investr, Nat Sci Found res contract, Addition Theorems Density Spaces, 67-71. *Mem:* Am Math Soc. *Res:* Has obtained extensions of the fundamental metric theorems of additive number theory, results for density spaces and results concerning the cardinality of zero sum subsets (submultisets) of certain sets (multisets) of residue classes. *Mailing Add:* 1405 NW Forest Dr Corvallis OR 97330-1705

STALLING, DAVID LAURENCE, MATERIAL SCIENCE-NEW ADSORBENTS, MULTIVARIATE ANALYSIS. *Current Pos:* VPRES RES & TECH SUPPORT, OI ANALYTICAL, 95- *Personal Data:* b Kansas City, Mo, Oct 24, 41; m 62, Dorothy Borgman; c Sheila, Mark & Michael. *Educ:* Mo Valley Col, BS, 62; Univ Mo, MS, 64, PhD(analytical biochem), 67. *Prof Exp:* Instr agr chem, Univ Mo, 62-66, NASA fel analytical chem, 67-68; chief chemist, Fish-Pesticide Res Lab, US Fish & Wildlife Serv, 68-86, sr res scientist, Columiba Nat Fisheries Res Ctr, 86-89; sr vpres res & develop, ABC Labs Inc, 89-93; vpres res & technol, Lab Automation Inc, 93-95. *Concurrent Pos:* Secy & mem bd dirs, ABC Labs Inc, 68-93, dir, 93-; partic, Exo-biol Consortium, NASA, 71-73. *Mem:* AAAS; Sigma Xi; Am Chem Soc; Am Asn Off Analytical Chemists. *Res:* Development of quantitative analytical methods for food and environmental pollutants, polychlorinated biphenyls, chlorinated dioxins and dibenzofurnas; study of chemical fate in aquatic ecosystems; developed and patented automated gelpermeation chromatography for containment enrichment; patented surface-linked fullerenes as a new chromatographic adsorbent and bis(trimethylsily) trifluoroacetamide novel silylating reagent; developed through technology transfer, a new liquid-liquid extractor using high voltage pulses. *Mailing Add:* OI Analytical Inc 555 Vandiver Dr Columbia MO 65202. *Fax:* 573-449-2988; *E-Mail:* dstall@oico.com

STALLINGS, CHARLES HENRY, PLASMA PHYSICS. *Current Pos:* Sr physicist, Physics Int Co, 70-77, dept mgr, 77-78, dir prog off, 79-81, dir prog develop, 81-82, vpres, 82-96, VPRES & GEN MGR, PRIMEX PHYSICS INT, 97- *Personal Data:* b Durham, NC, Dec 28, 41; m 65, Elizabeth Bright; c Deborah & Sharon. *Educ:* NC State Univ, BS, 63, MS, 64; Univ Wis-Madison, PhD(physics), 70. *Mem:* Am Phys Soc; Inst Elec & Electronics Eng. *Res:* Generation and propagation of intense relativistic electron beams and their interaction with background on target plasma; high density imploding plasmas and x-ray diagnostics. *Mailing Add:* PRIMEX Physics Int Co 2700 Merced St San Leandro CA 94577-0599

STALLINGS, JAMES CAMERON, ORGANIC CHEMISTRY. *Current Pos:* prof chem & dir dept, 59-78, dean, Col Sci, 78-81, EMER DEAN, SAM HOUSTON STATE UNIV, 81- *Personal Data:* b Denton, Tex, Jan 16, 19; m 49, Stelia Limmer; c Stephanie (Hoefar) & Deborah (Morgan). *Educ:* Univ Tex, PhD(org chem), 49. *Prof Exp:* Prof chem, Sam Houston State Col, 49-57; sr res chemist, Celanese Corp Am, 57-59. *Mem:* Am Chem Soc. *Res:* Steric hindrance; synthetic hypnotics; free radicals in solution; organic synthesis; chemical education. *Mailing Add:* 1912 18th St Huntsville TX 77340-4211

STALLINGS, JOHN ROBERT, JR, TOPOLOGY. *Current Pos:* PROF MATH, UNIV CALIF, BERKELEY, 67- *Personal Data:* b Morrilton, Ark, July 22, 35. *Educ:* Univ Ark, BS, 56; Princeton Univ, PhD(math), 59. *Honors & Awards:* Frank Nelson Cole Prize, Am Math Soc, 70. *Prof Exp:* NSF fel math, Oxford Univ, 59-60; from instr to assoc prof, Princeton Univ, 60-67. *Concurrent Pos:* Sloan Found fel, 62-65. *Mem:* Am Math Soc. *Res:* Three-manifolds; geometric topology; group theory from topological and homological viewpoints. *Mailing Add:* 1107 Keith Ave Berkeley CA 94708-1606

STALLKNECHT, GILBERT FRANKLIN, PLANT PHYSIOLOGY, PLANT BIOCHEMISTRY. *Current Pos:* SUPT, SOUTHERN AGR RES CTR, MONT STATE UNIV, RES SCIENTIST, CENT AGR RES CTR, 97- *Personal Data:* b Spooner, Minn, Sept 21, 35; m 58; c 4. *Educ:* Univ Minn, BS, 62, MS, 66, PhD(plant physiol), 68. *Prof Exp:* Agr res technician, USDA Sugar Beet Invests, Univ Minn, St Paul, 63-67; asst prof plant physiol, Univ Idaho, 68-72, assoc prof, 72-82. *Mem:* Am Soc Plant Physiol; Scand Soc Plant Physiol. *Res:* Fungus physiology; metabolic studies in host-parasite physiology; physiology of tuberization in potatoes; productivity and physiological age of potato tubers; physiology of seed crops. *Mailing Add:* RR 2 Box 2387A Lewiston MT 59457-9635

STALLMANN, FRIEDEMANN WILHELM, MATHEMATICS. *Current Pos:* assoc prof, 64-69, PROF MATH, UNIV TENN, KNOXVILLE, 69- *Personal Data:* b Koenigsberg, Germany, July 29, 21; m 53; c 2. *Educ:* Stuttgart Tech Univ, dipl math, 49; Univ Giessen, Dr rer nat, 53. *Prof Exp:* Asst math, Univ Giessen, 53-55, lectr, 55-59; asst, Brunswick Tech Univ, 59-60; chief math sect, Spec Res Unit Med Electronic Data Processing, Vet Admin, DC, 60-64. *Concurrent Pos:* Consult, Oak Ridge Nat Lab, 64- *Mem:* Am Math Soc. *Res:* Numerical analysis; conformal mapping and differential equations, lead field theory of electrocardiogram; computer analysis of electrocardiograms; complex variables. *Mailing Add:* 207-A Ayres Hall 140 Sunrise Dr Knoxville TN 37919-4122

STALLMEYER, J(AMES) E(DWARD), STRUCTURAL ENGINEERING. *Current Pos:* Res asst prof, 53-57, from assoc prof to prof, 57-91, EMER PROF CIVIL ENG, UNIV ILL, URBANA, 91- *Personal Data:* b Covington, Ky, Aug 11, 26; m 53, Mary K Davenport; c Cynthia M, James D, Michael J, Catherine A, John C & Gregory E. *Educ:* Univ Ill, BS, 47, MS, 49, PhD(civil eng), 53. *Honors & Awards:* Adams Mem Award, Am Welding Soc. *Mem:* Am Soc Civil Engrs; Am Soc Mech Engrs; Am Soc Testing & Mat; Soc Exp Stress Anal; Am Concrete Inst; Sigma Xi; Am Ry Eng Asn. *Res:* Fatigue of metals and structures; welded structures; brittle fracture; structural analysis, design and dynamics; research on fatigue strength of welded connections and plate girder bridges. *Mailing Add:* Dept Civil Eng Univ Ill 205 N Mathews St Urbana IL 61801. *Fax:* 217-333-9464

STALLONES, LORANN, AGRICULTURAL SAFETY & HEALTH, TEACHING. *Current Pos:* PROF EPIDEMIOL, COLO STATE UNIV, 86- *Personal Data:* b San Francisco, Calif, May 6, 52; m 85, John R Nuckols; c John B, Erin L & Jesse M. *Educ:* Univ Calif, Santa Barbara, BA, 74; Univ Tex, MPH, 75, PhD(epidemiol), 82. *Prof Exp:* Pub health analyst, Nat Heart Lung & Blood Inst, NIH, 77-78; res fel, Mary Imogene Bassett Hosp, 82-84; from asst prof to assoc prof epidemiol & prev med, Dept Environ Health & Prev Med, Univ Ky, 84-89. *Concurrent Pos:* Sect coun mem, Am Pub Health Asn, 88-93, Action Bd, 91-95, Joint Policy Comt, 94-; mem, Injury Res Grant Rev Comt, Ctrs Dis Control, 91-95; prin investr, Colo Farm Family Health & Hazard Surveillance. *Mem:* Soc Epidemiol Res (secy-treas, 91-93); Am Pub Health Asn; fel Am Col Epidemiol. *Res:* Injuries, mental health, environmental exposures to xenobiotics among agricultural population in rural areas; reproductive outcomes for surveillance in environmental health using geographic information systems; role of companion animals in human health. *Mailing Add:* Dept Environ Health Colo State Univ Ft Collins CO 80523-1676. *E-Mail:* lstallones@vines.colo.state.edu

STALLWOOD, ROBERT ANTONY, NUCLEAR PHYSICS. *Current Pos:* assoc prof physics, Thiel Col, 67-80. *Personal Data:* b Oxbow, Sask, June 15, 25. *Educ:* Univ Toronto, BASc, 49, MA, 50; Carnegie Inst Technol, PhD(physics), 56. *Prof Exp:* Physicist, Nuclear Sci Sect, Gulf Res & Develop Co, 56-64; physicist, Gen Elec Space Sci Ctr, 64-67. *Concurrent Pos:* Vis prof physics, Cleveland State Univ, 80-82 & Case Western Reserve Univ, 83- *Mem:* Am Phys Soc. *Res:* High energy nuclear physics; gamma ray and x-ray spectroscopy; neutron physics. *Mailing Add:* 12 Eagle St Greenville PA 16125

STALNAKER, CLAIR B, FISH BIOLOGY, GENETICS. *Current Pos:* LEADER, COOP INSTREAM FLOW SERV GROUP, US FISH & WILDLIFE SERV, FT COLLINS, 76- *Personal Data:* b Parkersburg, WVa, July 21, 38; m 63; c 2. *Educ:* WVa Univ, BSF, 60; NC State Univ, PhD(zool), 66. *Prof Exp:* Res asst fisheries biol, NC State Univ, 60-66; asst prof, Utah State Univ, 66-72, assoc prof fisheries biol, 72-76, asst unit leader, Utah Coop Fishery Unit, 66-75. *Mem:* AAAS; Am Fisheries Soc; Wildlife Soc; Am Soc Ichthyol & Herpet; Soc Am Nat; Sigma Xi. *Res:* Physiological-genetic studies of fishes; administration of multi-agency, interdisciplinary programs; physical aspects of stream ecology; aquatic environmental interactions. *Mailing Add:* 742 Cottonwood Dr Ft Collins CO 80524-1517

STALTER, RICHARD, BOTANY, PLANT ECOLOGY. *Current Pos:* from asst prof to assoc prof, 71-83, dir environ studies prog, 75-85, PROF BIOL, ST JOHN'S UNIV, NY, 83- *Personal Data:* b Jan 16, 42; US citizen; m 68. *Educ:* Rutgers Univ, BS, 63; Univ RI, MS, 66; Univ SC, PhD(biol), 68. *Prof Exp:* Asst prof biol, High Point Col, 68-69 & Pfeiffer Col, 69-70. *Mem:* Torrey Bot Club; Sigma Xi. *Res:* Barrier island ecology; flora of barrier islands; water relations of dune vegetation. *Mailing Add:* Dept of Biol St John's Univ Jamaica NY 11439-0001

STALVEY, JOHN ROBERT DIXON, REPRODUCTIVE ENDOCRINOLOGY, CELLULAR & MOLECULAR ENDOCRINOLOGY. *Current Pos:* asst prof, 87-92, ASSOC PROF, DEPT BIOL SCI, KENT STATE UNIV, 92- *Personal Data:* b Boston, Mass, Jan 9, 55; m 78, Marica Holmes; c Ross W & Connor W. *Educ:* Williams Col, BA, 77; Univ Southern Calif, MS, 78, PhD(physiol & biophys), 81. *Prof Exp:* Nat Res Serv Award Scholar, Univ Mich, 81-85, sr res fel, 85-87. *Concurrent Pos:* Asst dir molecular diag lab pediat, Univ Mich, 85-87; dir tissue & cell cult facil biol scis, Kent State Univ, 88-; prin investr, Nat Inst Diabetes & Digestive & Kidney Dis, 92-95; coordr grad studies, Biol Sci, 96- *Mem:* Endocrine Soc; Soc Study Reproduction; Sigma Xi; AAAS. *Res:* Tissue specific and hormonal regulation of the key steroidogenic enzymes, 3 beta-hydroxysteroid dehydrogenase-isomerase and P450 cholesterol side-chain-cleavage enzyme, expressed in all stereogenic tissue. *Mailing Add:* Dept Biol Sci Kent State Univ Kent OH 44242. *E-Mail:* jstalvey@ken.edu

STAM, JOS, ENVIRONMENTAL LAW, FOOD-CONTACT PLASTICS. *Current Pos:* INDEPENDENT CONSULT, ENVIRON AFFAIRS, 85- *Personal Data:* b Rotterdam, Neth, Apr 3, 24; m 59, Visser; c Simon, Pieternella, Jos & Margot. *Educ:* Tech Col, Dordrecht, BSc, 46; Delft Univ Technol, MS(chem eng), 52. *Prof Exp:* Chief engr, Unie Chem, Inc, 52-56; res engr, Carothers Res Lab & Textile Res Lab, E I Du Pont de Nemours & Co, 56-65; tech assoc, 65-70; staff engr, Neth, 70-72; prod environ mgr, 72-85. *Res:* Toxicology, ecology and health legislation of chemicals, in particular food-contact plastics. *Mailing Add:* 10 Chemin Sur Le Crets Troinex 1256 Switzerland. *Fax:* 41-22-784-2133

STAMATOYANNOPOULOS, GEORGE, MEDICAL GENETICS, HEMATOLOGY. *Current Pos:* res assoc med, 64-65, instr, 65-66, res asst prof, 65-69, assoc prof, 69-72, PROF MED, DIV MED GENETICS, UNIV WASH, 72- *Personal Data:* b Athens, Greece, Mar 11, 34; m 64; c 1. *Educ:* Nat Univ Athens, MD, 58, DSc, 60. *Prof Exp:* Asst med, Nat Univ Athens, 58-59, asst med & hemat, 61-64. *Concurrent Pos:* Royal Hellenic Res Found fel, 61-64. *Mem:* Am Soc Human Genetics; Am Soc Clin Invest; Europ Soc Human Genetics; Genetics Soc Am; Asn Am Physicians. *Res:* Developmental genetics-genetic hematology. *Mailing Add:* Dept Med Div Med Genetics Univ Wash 1959 NE Pacific Rm BB527A MS RG-25 Seattle WA 98195

STAMBAUGH, EDGEL PRYCE, hydrothermal hydrometallurgy technology, environmental management, for more information see previous edition

STAMBAUGH, JOHN EDGAR, JR, ONCOLOGY, CLINICAL PHARMACOLOGY. *Current Pos:* From instr to assoc prof, 68-82, PROF PHARMACOL, JEFFERSON MED COL, THOMAS JEFFERSON UNIV, 82- *Personal Data:* b Everrett, Pa, Apr 30, 40; m 61, Shirley Louise; c Lynn, Michele, Michael & Heather. *Educ:* Dickinson Col, BS, 62; Jefferson Med Col, MD, 66, Thomas Jefferson Univ, PhD(pharmacol), 68. *Honors & Awards:* Harry Gold Award, Am Soc Clin Pharmacol. *Concurrent Pos:* Resident and AMA spec scholar, Thomas Jefferson Univ Hosp, 68-70, fel oncol, 70-72; staff physician, Cooper Hosp, Camden, NJ, 72-, Underwood Hosp, Woodbury, 73-, W Jersey Hosp, 73- & JFK Health Syst, 78- *Mem:* Am Asn Cancer Res; Am Soc Clin Oncol; Am Soc Pharmacol & Exp Therapeut; Am Soc Clin Pharmacol; Am Pain Soc; Int Pain Soc. *Res:* Clinical drug metabolism and drug interactions; clinical oncology; cancer pain research-analgesic eval with pharmacokinetics. *Mailing Add:* 730 S Park Dr Collingswood NJ 08108-2236. *Fax:* 609-384-0275

STAMBAUGH, RICHARD L, BIOCHEMISTRY. *Current Pos:* ASSOC PROF, DIV REPRODUCTIVE BIOL, SCH MED, UNIV PA, 66- *Personal Data:* b Mechanicsburg, Pa, Aug 16, 36; m 56; c 2. *Educ:* Albright Col, BS, 53; Univ Pa, PhD(biochem), 59. *Prof Exp:* Res assoc biochem, Philadelphia Gen Hosp, 58-59; dir biochem, Elwyn Res & Eval Ctr; instr biochem in pediat, Univ Pa, 59-63; sr res investr, Fels Res Inst & instr biochem, Sch Med, Temple Univ, 63-66. *Concurrent Pos:* Consult, Penrose Res Lab, Zool Soc Philadelphia & Elwyn Res & Eval Ctr, 63-67. *Mem:* AAAS; Soc Study Reproduction; Fedn Am Socs Exp Biol. *Res:* Enzymology; biochemistry of reproduction. *Mailing Add:* 211 Redwood Rd King of Prussia PA 19406-1925

STAMBAUGH, RONALD D, PLASMA PHYSICS. *Current Pos:* RES SCIENTIST, GEN ATOMICS, 75- *Personal Data:* b May 24, 47. *Educ:* Univ Wis, BS 69; Yale Univ, MS, 72, PhD(physics), 75. *Mem:* Am Phys Soc. *Mailing Add:* MS 13/458 Gen Atomics PO Box 85608 San Diego CA 92186

STAMBAUGH, WILLIAM JAMES, FOREST PATHOLOGY. *Current Pos:* from asst prof to assoc prof, 61-72, PROF FOREST PATH, DUKE UNIV, 72-, ASSOC DEAN ACAD PROG, 84- *Personal Data:* b Allenwood, Pa, Dec 1, 27; m 52; c 3. *Educ:* Pa State Univ, BS, 51, MS, 52; Yale Univ, PhD(forest path), 57. *Honors & Awards:* Southern Forest Path Achievement Award, 82. *Prof Exp:* Instr bot, Pa State Univ, 53-57, asst prof forest path, 57-61. *Mem:* AAAS; Am Phytopath Soc; Sigma Xi; Am Inst Biol Sci. *Res:* Diseases of forest trees, with emphasis on forest pest management and biocontrol; microbiology of forest soils. *Mailing Add:* Sch Forestry Duke Univ Durham NC 27706-8001

STAMBROOK, PETER J, BIOLOGY. *Current Pos:* PROF ANAT & BIOCHEM, CELL & MOLECULAR BIOL, COL MED, UNIV CINCINNATI, 80-, PROF MOLECULAR GENETICS, BIOCHEM & MICROBIOL, 86- *Personal Data:* b London, Eng, July 24, 41; m 81; c 1. *Educ:* Rensselaer Polytech Inst, BSc, 63; Syracuse Univ, MSc, 65; State Univ NY Buffalo, PhD(biol), 69. *Prof Exp:* Fel cell biol, Med Ctr, Univ Ky, 69-71; investr cell, develop & molecular biol, Dept Embryol, Carnegie Inst Washington, 71-74; asst prof cell, develop & molecular biol, Case Western Reserve Univ, 74-80. *Concurrent Pos:* Assoc dir, Barrett Cancer Ctr; Sr Int Fogarty fel, 81-82. *Mem:* AAAS; Am Soc Cell Biol. *Res:* Regulation of cell cycle with particular focus on DNA replication; gene expression and mechanisms of mutation in eukaryotic cells and animals. *Mailing Add:* Dept Cell Biol, Neurobiol & Anat Univ Cincinnati Col Med 231 Bethesda Ave Cincinnati OH 45267-0521. Fax: 513-558-4454

STAMER, JOHN RICHARD, MICROBIOLOGY. *Current Pos:* from asst prof to assoc prof bact, 64-77, prof microbiol, 77-86, PROF MICROBIOL, NY STATE AGR EXP STA, CORNELL UNIV, 86- *Personal Data:* b Plankinton, SDak, May 19, 25; m 58; c 3. *Educ:* Dakota Wesleyan Univ, BA, 50; SDak State Col, MS, 53; Cornell Univ, PhD(bact), 62. *Prof Exp:* Res assoc bact, Univ Ill, 53-56; jr scientist, Smith Kline & French Labs, 56-58; asst bact, Cornell Univ, 58-62, NIH fel, 62-64. *Mem:* AAAS; Am Soc Microbiol. *Res:* Microbial physiology and nutrition. *Mailing Add:* 186 Nursery Ave Geneva NY 14456

STAMER, PETER ERIC, PHYSICS. *Current Pos:* from asst prof to assoc prof, 66-78, PROF PHYSICS, SETON HALL UNIV, 78- *Personal Data:* b New York, NY, June 4, 39; m 68. *Educ:* Stevens Inst Technol, BS, 61, MS, 63, PhD(physics), 66. *Prof Exp:* Instr physics, Upsala Col, 65-66. *Concurrent Pos:* Jr res assoc physics, Stevens Inst Technol, 66-68, res assoc, 68- *Mem:* AAAS; Am Asn Physics Teachers; Am Phys Soc. *Res:* Experimental elementary particle physics; pi-P, P-P, K-P interactions at 147 GeV/C and neutrino interactions at 2.0-5.0 GeV/C. *Mailing Add:* Box 347 Sparta NJ 07871-0347

STAMEY, THOMAS ALEXANDER, UROLOGY. *Current Pos:* assoc prof surg, 61-64, chmn, Dept Urol, 61-, PROF UROL, SCH MED, STANFORD UNIV, 64- *Personal Data:* b Rutherfordton, NC, Apr 26, 28; m 56; c 5. *Educ:* Vanderbilt Univ, AB, 48; Johns Hopkins Univ, MD, 52; Am Bd Urol, dipl, 61. *Honors & Awards:* Hugh Hampton Young Award, Am Urol Asn, 72; Sheen Award, Am Col Surgeons, 90; Kamon Gutera's Award, Am Urol Asn, 95. *Prof Exp:* Intern, Johns Hopkins Hosp, 52-53; mem, Brady Urol House Staff Residency Prog, Johns Hopkins Univ, 53-56; urol consult, US Armed Forces, UK, 56-58; from asst prof to assoc prof urol, Johns Hopkins Univ, 58-61. *Concurrent Pos:* Mem, Comt Renal Dis & Urol Training Grants, NIH, 67-72, chmn, 71-72; mem, Sci Adv Bd, Nat Kidney Found, Sci Adv Coun, Coop Study Pyelonephritis, USPHS; mem, Sci Adv Comt, Hosp Sick Children, Toronto, Can; mem, Study of Res in Nephrology & Urol, NIH; assoc ed, Campbell's Urol; Edmund L Keeney vis lectr, Scripps Clin & Res Found, 96. *Mem:* Inst Med-Nat Acad Sci; Am Urol Asn; Am Surg Asn; Soc Univ Urol; hon fel Royal Col Surgeons; Am Soc Nephrol; Clin Soc Genitaurinary Surgeons. *Res:* Renal physiology and disease and urinary tract infections; microbiology and hypertension; cancer of the prostate. *Mailing Add:* Dept Urol Stanford Univ Sch Med Stanford CA 94305

STAMEY, WILLIAM LEE, MATHEMATICS. *Current Pos:* from asst prof to assoc prof, Kans State Univ, 53-62, assoc dean, 63-69, dean, Col Arts & Sci, 69-87, PROF MATH, KANS STATE UNIV, 62- *Personal Data:* b Chicago, Ill, Oct 19, 22; m 45; c 3. *Educ:* Univ Northern Colo, AB, 47; Univ Mo, MA, 49, PhD(math), 52. *Prof Exp:* From asst instr to instr math, Univ Mo, 47-52; asst prof, Ga State Univ, 52-53. *Concurrent Pos:* Secy-treas, Coun Cols Arts & Sci, 78-87. *Mem:* Am Math Soc; AAAS; Math Asn Am. *Mailing Add:* 416 Edgerton Ave Manhattan KS 66502-3712

STAMFORD, BRYANT, EXCERCISE PHYSIOLOGY. *Current Pos:* DIR, EXERCISE PHYSIOL LAB, DIV ALLIED HEALTH, SCH MED, UNIV LOUISVILLE, 73-, PROF, 78-, ASST DEAN, GRAD SCH, 84-, DIR, HEALTH PROMOTION CTR. *Personal Data:* b Pittsburgh, Pa, Sept 10, 46. *Educ:* Univ Pittsburgh, PhD(excercise physiol & phys educ), 73. *Mem:* Am Physiol Soc; Sigma Xi; Am Col Sports Med; Am Alliance Health, Phys Educ & Recreation. *Mailing Add:* Health Promotion Ctr Crawford Gym, Rm 2 Univ Louisville Louisville KY 40292-0001

STAMLER, JEREMIAH, PREVENTIVE MEDICINE, PUBLIC HEALTH. *Current Pos:* from asst to assoc prof, 59-71, chmn Dept, Community Health & Prev Med, 72-86, Mem Hosp, 73-85, DINGMAN PROF CARDIOL, MED SCH, NORTHWESTERN UNIV, CHICAGO, 71-73, PROF MED 71- *Personal Data:* b New York, NY, Oct 27, 19; m 42; c 1. *Educ:* Columbia Univ, AB, 40; State Univ NY, MD, 43. *Honors & Awards:* Med J Award, Lasker Found, 65; Blakeslee Award, Am Heart Asn, 64; Donald Reid Medal, London Sch Hgy & Royal Col Physicians, London, England, 88. *Prof Exp:* Intern, Long Island Col Med Div, Kings County Hosp, 44; res assoc, Cardiovasc Dept, Med Res Inst, Michael Reese Hosp, Chicago, 49-55, asst dir dept, 55-58; dir heart dis control prog, Chicago Bd Health, 58-74, dir div adult health & aging, 63-74. *Concurrent Pos:* Fel path, Long Island Col Med, 47; res fel, Cardiovasc Dept, Med Res Inst, Michael Reese Hosp, Chicago, 48; Am Heart Asn estab investr, 52-58, fel coun arteriosclerosis, 63-64 & coun epidemiol, 64-66; dir chronic dis div, Chicago Bd Health, 61-63; chmn coun arteriosclerosis, Am Heart Asn, 63-64, mem exec comt, Coun Epidemiol, 64-66 & coun high blood pressure res; western hemisphere ed, Atherosclerosis, 63-75; exec dir, Chicago Health Res Found, 63-72; consult, St Joseph Hosp, 64-, Rush-Presby-St Luke's Hosp, 64- & Atherosclerosis Cardiol Drug Lipid Coop Study & Cardiovasc Res Prog Eval Comt, Vet Admin, 65; prof lectr med, Div Biol Sci, Pritzker Sch Med, Univ Chicago, 70-; vis prof, Dept Internal Med, Rush Presby-St Luke's Med Ctr, 72-; attend physician, Northwest Mem Hosp, 72-; sponsor, Nat Health Educ Comt; mem, Worcester Found Exp Biol; specialist clin nutrit, Am Bd Nutrit; chmn coun epidemiol & prev, Int Soc Cardiol, 74-78. *Mem:* Fel AAAS; fel Am Col Cardiol; Am Diabetes Asn; Am Fedn Clin Res; Asn Teachers Prev Med. *Res:* Cardiovascular physiology, medicine, epidemiology and preventive medicine, particularly atherosclerosis and hypertension; chronic disease, preventive medicine and public health. *Mailing Add:* 211 E Ohio St Apt 720 Chicago IL 60611-3222

STAMM, ROBERT FRANZ, SPECTROSCOPY, OPTICAL PHYSICS. *Current Pos:* CONSULT, CUBE-CORNER RETROREFLECTIVE SHEET HWY SIGNS, 87- *Personal Data:* b Mt Vernon, Ohio, Mar 28, 15; m 64. *Educ:* Kenyon Col, AB, 37; Iowa State Univ, PhD(phys chem), 42. *Prof Exp:* Res physicist, Am Cyanamid Co, 42-54, group leader, Basic Res Dept, 54-59 & Phys Res Dept, 59-61, res assoc, Chem Dept, 61-66, res fel, 66-72; sr res investr, Clairol, Inc, Div Bristol Myers Co, 73-82. *Mem:* Am Chem Soc; Am Phys Soc; Optical Soc Am; NY Acad Sci. *Res:* Raman spectroscopy; light scattering; fluorescence; radiation chemistry and sterilization; neutron activation analysis; spectroscopy of triplet molecules and excited transients; photochromism; flash photolysis; kinetic spectroscopy; retroreflectors; optical properties of human hair fibers; FTIR spectroscopy. *Mailing Add:* 158 Rufous Lane Sedona AZ 86336-7116

STAMM, STANLEY JEROME, MEDICINE. *Current Pos:* dir cardiac diag lab, 58-59, co-dir dept cardiol & attend, 59-63, co-dir cystic fibrosis clin, 63, dir cardiopulmonary res lab, 62-67, dir cardiol dept, 67-70, DIR CARDIOPULMONARY DEPT, CHILDREN'S ORTHOP HOSP, 70- *Personal Data:* b Seattle, Wash, July 14, 24; m; c 3. *Educ:* Seattle Univ, BS, 48; St Louis Univ, MD, 52; Am Bd Pediat, dipl, 58. *Prof Exp:* Intern, King County Hosp, Seattle, Wash, 52-53; resident pediat, Univ Wash, 53-55; instr, 57-58. *Concurrent Pos:* NIH cardiac trainee, Children's Orthop Hosp, 55-56, hosp cardiac fel, 56-57; clin assoc prof, Univ Wash, 66-69. *Mem:* Fel Am Acad Pediat; Am Heart Asn; fel Am Col Chest Physicians; fel Am Col Angiol. *Mailing Add:* Children's Orthop Hosp & Med Ctr 4800 Sand Point Way NE Seattle WA 98105-3916

STAMMER, CHARLES HUGH, ORGANIC CHEMISTRY, AMINO ACID CHEMISTRY. *Current Pos:* assoc prof, 62-80, PROF CHEM, UNIV GA, 80-, ASSOC DIR, SCH CHEM SCI, 85- *Personal Data:* b Indianapolis, Ind, Apr 1, 25; m 47; c 2. *Educ:* Univ Ind, BS, 48; Univ Wis, PhD(org chem), 52. *Prof Exp:* Res chemist, Merck & Co, Inc, NJ, 52-62. *Mem:* Am Chem Soc; AAAS. *Res:* Synthesis of cyclopropane amino acids and peptides. *Mailing Add:* 718 Riverhill Dr Athens GA 30606-4050

STAMMER, DETLEF BENIGNUS, SATELLITE ALTIMETRY, STATE ESTIMATION. *Current Pos:* res assoc, 93-95, res scientist, 95-97, PRIN RES SCIENTIST, MASS INST TECHNOL, 97- *Personal Data:* b Paderborn, Ger, July 25, 57; m 87, Barbel Hildebrand; c Peter J, Wolfgang T & Morite L. *Educ:* Kiel Univ, dipl, 87, PhD(phys oceanog), 92. *Prof Exp:* Res scientist, Inst Meereskunde, 92-93. *Res:* Climate-relevance of the low-frequency variability of the ocean, including its eddy component, from observation and numerical ocean circulation models, either separately or combined through state estimation procedures. *Mailing Add:* Mass Inst Technol MS 54-1518 Cambridge MA 02139. Fax: 617-253-4464; E-Mail: detlef@lagoon.mit.edu

STAMPER, EUGENE, MECHANICAL ENGINEERING, EDULATION ADMINISTRATION. *Current Pos:* CONSULT, 90- *Personal Data:* b New York, NY, Mar 24, 28; m 53, Sally Goldfeder; c Emily & Marcy. *Educ:* City Col New York, BME, 48; NY Univ, MME, 52. *Honors & Awards:* Distinguished Serv Award, Am Soc Heating, Refrig & Air- Conditioning Engrs. *Prof Exp:* Aeronaut res scientist, Nat Adv Comt Aeronaut, 48-49;

design engr, S Schweid & Co, 49-50, Karp Metal Prod Co, 50-51 & Seelye, Stevenson, Value & Knecht, 51-52; assoc prof mech eng, NJ Inst Technol, 52-69, prof, 69-88, asst dean acad affairs, 72-85; consult engr, J R Loring & Assoc, 88-90. *Concurrent Pos:* Consult, 56- *Mem:* Am Soc Mech Engrs; Am Soc Eng Educ; fel Am Soc Heating, Refrig & Air-Conditioning Engrs; NY Acad Sci; Sigma Xi; fel Am Soc Heating Refrigerating Air-Conditioning Engr. *Res:* Heat transfer; fluid mechanics; thermodynamics; refrigeration; air conditioning; building energy studies. *Mailing Add:* 73 Cranford Pl Teaneck NJ 07666. *Fax:* 201-833-1898; *E-Mail:* estam19460@aol.com

STAMPER, HUGH BLAIR, RESEARCH ADMINISTRATION, INFORMATION TECHNOLOGY. *Current Pos:* health scientist adminr, Div Lung Dis, Nat Heart, Lung & Blood Inst, NIH, 77-83, exec secy, Spec Rev Sect, Div Res Grants, 83-85, exec secy, Immunol Sci Study Sect, Div Res Grants, USPHS, 85-87, chief, Biol Sci Rev Sect & asst chief, Referrals & Rev Br, Div Res Grants, 87089, DIR, DIV EXTRAMURAL ACTIVITIES, NIMH, NIH, 89- *Personal Data:* b Warren, Ohio, Dec 13, 43; m 72, Gwen Demshok; c Lucy & Kevin. *Educ:* Ohio State Univ, BSc, 67, MSc, 68, PhD(microbiol), 72. *Prof Exp:* Bacteriologist, Clin Lab, Licking County Mem Hosp, Newark, Ohio, 68-69; asst prof microbiol & immunol, Biol Dept, Old Dominion Univ, Norfolk, Va, 72-75; asst instr & res assoc, Dept Microbiol & Immunol, Downstate Med Ctr, State Univ NY, Brooklyn, 75-77. *Mem:* AAAS; Am Asn Immunologists; Sigma Xi. *Res:* Research administration; lymphocyte biology. *Mailing Add:* Parklawn Bldg 5600 Fishers Lane Rm 17C20 Rockville MD 20857-0001. *Fax:* 301-443-6812; *E-Mail:* hstamper@nih.gov

STAMPER, JAMES HARRIS, MATHEMATICAL MODELING, HUMAN EXPOSURE TO PESTICIDES. *Current Pos:* RES ASSOC, UNIV FLA, 77- *Personal Data:* b Richmond, Ind, Sept 10, 38; div. *Educ:* Miami Univ, BA, 60; Yale Univ, MS, 62, PhD(physics), 65. *Prof Exp:* Asst prof physics, Elmira Col, 62-63, dir math & physics, 65-66; asst prof, Univ Fla, 67-70; prof & chmn, Dept Physics & Chem, Fla Southern Col, 70-79. *Concurrent Pos:* Consult, Battelle Mem Inst, 68-70; reader, advan placement exam physics, Educ Testing Serv, Princeton, NJ, 80-85; Consult, Tex Tech Univ Health Sci Ctr, San Benito, Tex, 84; Consult, Duphar BV, Crop Protection Div, Amsterdam, Holland, 86- *Mem:* Am Asn Physics Teachers. *Res:* Atomic and molecular physics; environmental sciences; theory of atomic collisions and quantum effects of interatomic exchange forces; mathematical modeling; environmental fate of pesticides; farm and greenhouse worker exposure to pesticides; pesticide drift. *Mailing Add:* 98 Imperial Southgate Lakeland FL 33803

STAMPER, JOHN ANDREW, PLASMA PHYSICS. *Current Pos:* RES PHYSICIST, NAVAL RES LAB, DC, 68- *Personal Data:* b Middletown, Ohio, Mar 28, 30; m 59, Patricia Cain; c Gregory, Lucia (deceased) & Julian. *Educ:* Ohio State Univ, BS, 53; Univ Ky, MS, 58; Univ Md, PhD(physics), 68. *Honors & Awards:* E O Hulburt Award, US Naval Res Lab, 74. *Prof Exp:* Mem tech staff semiconductor physics, Tex Instruments, Inc, 58-63. *Mem:* Fel Am Phys Soc. *Res:* Experimental plasma physics, including physics of laser-matter interactions; semiconductor physics, including thermal, thermoelectric and thermomagnetic effects; laser-produced plasmas; interaction of laser radiation with plasmas. *Mailing Add:* 5110 Mason Springs Rd Indian Head MD 20640. *Fax:* 202-767-0046; *E-Mail:* stamper@this.nrl.navy.mil

STAMPER, MARTHA C, ORGANIC CHEMISTRY. *Current Pos:* RETIRED. *Personal Data:* b Dawson Springs, Ky, May 7, 25. *Educ:* DePauw Univ, AB, 47; Univ Wis, PhD(org chem), 52. *Prof Exp:* Org chemist, Process Res Div, Eli Lilly & Co, 52-88. *Mem:* Am Chem Soc. *Res:* Antibiotics and pharmaceuticals. *Mailing Add:* 4833 Wilde Pointe Dr Sarasota FL 34233-3541

STAMPF, EDWARD JOHN, JR, INORGANIC CHEMISTRY. *Current Pos:* asst prof, Lander Col, 77-89, ASSOC PROF CHEM, LANDER UNIV, 89- *Personal Data:* b Evergreen Park, Ill, May 5, 49; m 72. *Educ:* Northern Ill Univ, BS, 72; Univ SC, PhD(chem), 76. *Prof Exp:* Fel, Univ SC, 76-77. *Mem:* Am Chem Soc; Sigma Xi. *Res:* Boron hydrides and organoboranes; compounds are synthesized using high vacuum technology and studied by nuclear magnetic resonance spectroscopy. *Mailing Add:* Rte 1 Box 470 Waterloo SC 29384

STAMPFER, JOSEPH FREDERICK, PERSONAL CHEMICAL PROTECTIVE EQUIPMENT. *Current Pos:* staff mem, 58-67 & 77-90, assoc staff mem, 91-94, GUEST SCIENTIST, LOS ALAMOS NAT LAB, 95- *Personal Data:* b Dubuque, Iowa, Mar 15, 30; m 53, Anne Hawkins; c 2. *Educ:* Dartmouth Col, AB, 52; Univ NMex, PhD(chem), 58. *Prof Exp:* Assoc prof chem, Univ Mo-Rolla, 67-77. *Mem:* AAAS; Am Chem Soc; Am Meteorol Soc; Am Indust Hyg Asn. *Res:* Personal protective clothing chemical permeation; respiratory protection; atmospheric chemistry; sorbent efficiency; self-contained breathing apparatus; generation, sampling and characterization of vapors and aerosols; surfactants; surface to atmosphere exchange; isotope separation; aircraft sampling. *Mailing Add:* Group ESH-5 MSK-553 Los Alamos Nat Lab Los Alamos NM 87545. *Fax:* 505-665-3689; *E-Mail:* stampfer@lanl.gov

STAMPFL, RUDOLF A, electrical engineering, electronic communications, for more information see previous edition

STAMPFLI, JOSEPH, SPECTRA SETS, HYPNONORMAL OPERATORS. *Current Pos:* assoc prof, 67-69, chmn dept, 80-83, PROF MATH, IND UNIV, 69- *Personal Data:* b Rochester, NY, Aug 9, 32; m 64; c 3. *Educ:* Univ Rochester, BA, 54; Univ Mich, MA, 55, PhD(math), 59. *Prof Exp:* Instr math, Yale Univ, 59-61; from asst prof to assoc prof, NY Univ, 61-67. *Concurrent Pos:* res fel, Off Naval Res, 64-65; prin investr, Nat Sci Found, 65-; Sherman Fairchild distinguished scholar, Calif Inst Technol, 74-75. *Mem:* Am Math Soc; AAAS; Am Asn Artificial Intelligence. *Res:* Operators on Hilbert Space; hyponormal operators, spectral sets, and local spectral theory. *Mailing Add:* Ind Univ Bloomington IN 47405-4301

STAMPS, JUDY ANN, ANIMAL BEHAVIOR, ECOLOGY. *Current Pos:* from actg asst prof to prof zool, 73-93, PROF EVOLUTION & ECOL, UNIV CALIF, DAVIS, 93- *Personal Data:* b San Francisco, Calif, Mar 13, 47. *Educ:* Univ Calif, Berkeley, BA, 69, MA, 71, PhD(zool), 74. *Honors & Awards:* Exemplar Award, Animal Behav Soc. *Mem:* Fel Animal Behav Soc; Am Soc Ichthyologists & Herpetologists; Ecol Soc Am; fel AAAS; Am Soc Naturalist. *Res:* Evolution of social systems, ecological determinates of variability of social behavior; lizard social behavior; territorial behavior; sexual size dimosphism. *Mailing Add:* Sect Evolution & Ecol Univ Calif Davis CA 95616

STANA, REGIS RICHARD, DATA ANALYSIS, STATISTICS. *Current Pos:* SR CONSULT ENG URANIUM RECOVERY PHOSPHATE FERTILIZERS, INT MINERALS & CHEM, 81- *Personal Data:* b Greensburg, Pa, Sept 7, 41; m 68, Angela Caironi; c Cynthia, Ronald, Rita & Diane. *Educ:* Univ Pittsburgh, BS, 63, MS, 65, PhD(chem eng), 67, PE, 88. *Prof Exp:* Fel engr water & waste treat, Westinghouse Res, 67-78; adv engr uranium recovery, Wyo Mineral Corp, 78-81. *Mem:* Am Inst Chem Engrs. *Res:* Reverse osmosis membranes; fabrication and utilization; process development for recovery of uranium from secondary sources, phosphate fertilizers process improvement; on-line expert systems; artificial intelligence. *Mailing Add:* 935 Heathercrest Lakeland FL 33813. *Fax:* 941-428-7312; *E-Mail:* rr_stana@imc-acrico.com

STANABACK, ROBERT JOHN, ORGANIC CHEMISTRY. *Current Pos:* SR CHEMIST, MAGRUDER COLOR CO, 85- *Personal Data:* b Weehawken, NJ, Dec 24, 30; m 57; c 1. *Educ:* Rutgers Univ, BA, 53; Seton Hall Univ, MS, 64, PhD(chem), 66. *Prof Exp:* Assoc scientist, Warner-Lambert Res Inst, 56-67; sr chemist, Tenneco Chem, Inc, Piscataway, 67-78; sr chemist org pigments res & develop, AM Cyanamid Co, 78-83; sr chem, Inmont Corp, 83-85. *Mem:* Am Chem Soc. *Res:* Synthetic organic medicinals; thyroxine analogs; central nervous depressants; biocides; plasticizers; synthetic polymers; vinyl chloride technology and additives. *Mailing Add:* 9 Union Grove Rd Gladstone NJ 07934-2040

STANACEV, NIKOLA ZIVA, BIOLOGICAL CHEMISTRY. *Current Pos:* RETIRED. *Personal Data:* b Milosevo, Yugoslavia, July 17, 28. *Educ:* Univ Zagreb, Chem E, 53, PhD(chem), 58. *Prof Exp:* Asst prof med, Univ Zagreb, 55-58; fel div biosci, Nat Res Coun Can, Ottawa, 58-59; res assoc chem & chem eng, Univ Ill, Urbana, 59-61; res assoc cell chem lab, Dept Biochem, Columbia Univ, 61-62; res assoc, Banting & Best Dept Med Res, Univ Toronto, 62-64, lectr, 64-65; res assoc biol chem, Harvard Med Sch, 65-67; from assoc prof to prof clin biochem, Univ Toronto, 67-94. *Res:* Organic biochemistry; chemistry and biochemistry of membrane lipids; isolation, determination of constitution and biosynthesis of complex lipids of membranes of animal and bacterial origin. *Mailing Add:* Dept Biochem Univ Toronto 1 Kings Col Circle Toronto ON M5S 1A5 Can

STANAT, DONALD FORD, COMPUTER SCIENCE. *Current Pos:* asst prof, 67-72, assoc prof, 72-82, PROF COMPUT SCI, UNIV NC, CHAPEL HILL, 82- *Personal Data:* b Jackson, Miss, Jan 10, 37; m 58, Sylvia Chi; c Gregory, Douglas & Melissa. *Educ:* Antioch Col, BS, 59; Univ Mich, Ann Arbor, MS, 62, PhD(commun sci), 66. *Prof Exp:* Assoc res mathematician, Univ Mich, 66-67. *Concurrent Pos:* Consult, IBM Corp, 67-71, Naval Res Lab, 81-84; vis scientist, IBM Corp, 79-80. *Mem:* AAAS; Asn Comput Mach; Sigma Xi. *Res:* Algorithm analysis; data structures and models of computation; parallel computation and cellular computers; research centers on the execution of functional language programs on highly parallel computers; algorithm design; programming language sematics; architecture of parallel computers. *Mailing Add:* 2516 Homestead Rd Chapel Hill NC 27516-9086. *Fax:* 919-962-1799; *E-Mail:* stanat@cs.unc.edu

STANBACK, MARK T, BEHAVIORAL ECOLOGY. *Current Pos:* ASST PROF, DEPT BIOL, DAVIDSON COL, 95- *Personal Data:* b Salsbury, NC, May 18, 62; m 90, Nancy Popkin; c Gray & Sylvie. *Educ:* Davidson Col, BS, 84; Univ Calif, Berkeley, PhD, 90. *Prof Exp:* Res assoc, Univ Wash, 91-94. *Concurrent Pos:* Participant, Orgn Trop Studies, Costa Rica, 88; grantee, Nat Geog Soc, 91, Am Philos Soc, 94 & Chicago Zool Soc, 94; Nat Res Serv award, NIH, 91-92; postdoctoral fel, Univ Wash, 92-94; Fulbright scholar, Namibia, Africa, 94-95; NSF int postdoctoral fel, Namibia, 95. *Mem:* Am Ornithologists Union; Am Soc Naturalists; Animal Behav Soc; Asn Field Ornithologists; Int Soc Behav Ecol. *Res:* Hatching asynchrony in acorn woodpeckers and hornbills; sperm storage in hornbills; endocrinology of cooperative breeding; reproductive strategies in bluebirds. *Mailing Add:* Biol Dept Davidson Col PO Box 1719 Davidson NC 28036. *E-Mail:* mastanback@davidson.edu

STANBERRY, LAWRENCE RAYMOND, VIROLOGY, PEDIATRIC INFECTIOUS DISEASES. *Current Pos:* asst prof, 82-87, ASSOC PROF PEDIAT, CHILDRENS HOSP RES FOUND, UNIV CINCINNATI COL MED, 87-, ALBERT B SABIN PROF PEDIAT. *Personal Data:* b Detroit,

Mich, Aug 27, 48; m 69, Elizabeth Thompson; c Lindsey E & David M. *Educ:* Southwestern Univ Georgetown, BS, 70; Univ Ill Med Ctr, Chicago, MD, 77, PhD (pharmacol), 79. *Prof Exp:* Intern pediat, Childrens Med Ctr, Dallas, 77-78; fel oncol & exp therapeut, Univ Ill Med Ctr, 78-79; resident pediat, Univ Utah Med Ctr, Salt Lake, 79-80, fel ped infections dis, 80-82. *Concurrent Pos:* Fel John Hartford Found, 84-87; chmn spec rev comt vitro antiviral screen, Nat Inst Allergy & Infectious Dis, 88-; mem Epidemiol & Dis Control #2 study sect, Nat Inst Health, 89-; prin investr, Nat Inst Allergy & Infectious Dis, 85-; Procter & Gamble Univ Explor grant, 85-88. *Mem:* Infectious Dis Soc Am; Soc Pediat Res; Int Soc Antiviral Res; Am Soc Virol; Pediat Infectious Dis Soc; Am Soc Microbiol. *Res:* Human herpes viruses, their vaccine development and anti-viral evaluation; analysis of latency and pathogenesis; vaginal microbicide development. *Mailing Add:* 3475 Whitfield Ave Cincinnati OH 45220-1556

STANBRIDGE, ERIC JOHN, CELL BIOLOGY, MICROBIOLOGY. *Current Pos:* from asst prof to assoc prof microbiol, 75-82, PROF MICROBIOL, COL MED, UNIV CALIF, IRVINE, 82- *Personal Data:* b London, Eng, May 28, 42; m 71; c 2. *Educ:* Brunel Univ, HNC, 62; Stanford Univ, PhD(med microbiol), 71. *Prof Exp:* Tech officer virol, Nat Inst Med Res, UK, 60-65; res asst cell biol, Wistar Inst Anat & Biol, 65-67; mem sci staff cell biol, Nat Inst Med Res, UK, 68-69; instr med microbiol, Sch Med, Stanford Univ, 73-75. *Concurrent Pos:* Spec fel, Leukemia Soc Am, 76-78; res career develop award, Nat Cancer Inst, 78-83; Eleanor Roosevelt Int Fel, 83,84. *Mem:* Am Soc Microbiol; Tissue Cult Asn; Int Orgn Mycoplasmologists; NY Acad Sci. *Res:* Cancer biology; somatic cell genetics; mycoplasmology. *Mailing Add:* Dept of Microbiol Univ of Calif - Irvine Irvine CA 92717-0001

STANBRO, WILLIAM DAVID, COMPUTATIONAL CHEMISTRY, SYSTEMS ANALYSIS. *Current Pos:* STAFF MEM, LOS ALAMOS NAT LAB, 89- *Personal Data:* b St Louis, Mo, Nov 29, 46; m 69, Helen F deChabert; c Jennifer M, Elizabeth M, Patrick W & William T. *Educ:* George Washington Univ, BS, 68, PhD(chem), 72; Johns Hopkins Univ, MS, 85. *Prof Exp:* Res asst, Geophys Lab, Carnegie Inst, Washington, 69-70; NSF presidential intern, 72-73, chemist & sr prof staff, Appl Physics Lab, Johns Hopkins Univ, 73-86; vpres res, Biotronic Systs Corp, 86-89. *Mem:* Am Chem Soc; Inst Nuclear Mat Mgt; fel Am Inst Chemists. *Res:* Chemical dynamics and photochemistry of oxidants in condensed media; development of chemical and biological sensors; development of arms control verification procedures. *Mailing Add:* Los Alamos Nat Lab MS E541 Los Alamos NM 87545. *E-Mail:* wds@lanl.gov

STANBROUGH, JESSE HEDRICK, JR, PHYSICS. *Current Pos:* exec secy, Undersea Warfare Res & Develop Planning Coun, Woods Hole Oceanog Inst, 60-61, tech asst to dir, 61-67, exec secy,Joint Oceanog Insts Deep Earth Sampling Prog, 66-67, exec asst, Ocean Eng Dept, 67-76, RES PHYSICIST, WOODS HOLE OCEANOG INST, 60- *Personal Data:* b Ruston, La, May 1, 18; c 1. *Educ:* Univ Tex, BS, 49, MA, 50. *Prof Exp:* Asst geophys, Univ Tex, 48-50, res physicist, Defense Res Lab, 50-60; tech staff asst, Naval Underwater Syst Ctr, Newport, RI, 79-88; corp dir, Benthos Corp, 68-88. *Concurrent Pos:* Co-founder, Tracor, Inc, 55-60; tech asst, Comt Undersea Warfare, Nat Acad Sci, 56; consult variable depth sonar, US Navy, 58-60, Washington Anal Servs Ctr Inc & EG&G Inc, 79-81. *Res:* Oceanography; underwater sound. *Mailing Add:* 36 Riddle Hill Rd Falmouth MA 02540

STANBURY, DAVID MCNEIL, INORGANIC CHEMISTRY. *Current Pos:* assoc prof, 87-94, PROF CHEM, AUBURN UNIV, 94- *Personal Data:* b Boston, Mass, May 9, 52; m 90, Lorraine Wolf. *Educ:* Duke Univ, BA, 74; Univ Southern Calif, PhD(chem), 78. *Prof Exp:* Fel, Stanford Univ, 78-80; asst prof chem, Rice Univ, 80-87. *Concurrent Pos:* Sloan Fel, 92-96. *Mem:* Am Chem Soc; Sigma Xi; AAAS. *Res:* Kinetics and mechanisms of inorganic redox reactions. *Mailing Add:* Dept Chem Auburn Univ 179 Chem Bldg Auburn AL 36849-5312

STANBURY, JOHN BRUTON, EXPERIMENTAL MEDICINE. *Current Pos:* RETIRED. *Personal Data:* b Clinton, NC, May 15, 15; m 45; c 5. *Educ:* Duke Univ, BA, 35; Harvard Med Sch, MD, 39; Am Bd Internal Med, dipl, 49. *Hon Degrees:* MD, Univ Leiden, 75. *Prof Exp:* House officer, Mass Gen Hosp, Boston, 40-41; asst in med, Harvard Med Sch, from asst to assoc clin prof, 56-66, lectr med, 66-; prof exp med, Mass Inst Technol, 66-81. *Concurrent Pos:* Res fel pharmacol, Harvard Med Sch, 47-48; chief med resident, Mass Gen Hosp, 48-49, asst in med, 49-50, chief thyroid clin & lab, 49-66, from asst physician to physician, 50-66, consult physician, 66-, sr physician, 81-86. *Mem:* Endocrine Soc; Am Soc Clin Invest; Asn Am Physicians; Am Thyroid Asn. *Res:* Endocrinology; metabolism; genetics; metabolic disease. *Mailing Add:* 43 Circuit Rd Chestnut Hill MA 02167-1802

STANCAMPIANO, CHARLES VINCENT, ELECTRICAL ENGINEERING, SUPERCONDUCTIVITY. *Current Pos:* Res assoc & asst prof, 75-76, ASST PROF ELEC ENG, UNIV ROCHESTER, 77-, SCIENTIST, LAB LASER ENERGETICS, 80- *Personal Data:* b Brooklyn, NY, Oct 27, 48; m 69; c 1. *Educ:* Rensselaer Polytech Inst, BS, 69; Univ Rochester, MS, 71, PhD(elec eng), 76. *Concurrent Pos:* Consult, Dept Radiation Biol & Biophys, Univ Rochester, 76-80; co-investr, Ctr Naval Anal grant, 78- *Mem:* Inst Elec & Electronics Engrs; Electron Devices Soc; Am Phys Soc. *Res:* Microwave applications of the Josephson effect; nonequilibrium superconductivity. *Mailing Add:* Eastman Kodak Co Kodak Res Lab Bldg 81 Device Dev Lab Rochester NY 14650

STANCEL, GEORGE MICHAEL, BIOCHEMISTRY, ENDOCRINOLOGY. *Current Pos:* ASSOC PROF PHARMACOL, UNIV TEX MED SCH HOUSTON, 72- *Personal Data:* b Chicago, Ill, Dec 29, 44; m 72. *Educ:* St Thomas Col, BS, 66; Mich State Univ, PhD(biochem), 70. *Concurrent Pos:* NIH fel endocrinol, Univ Ill, 71-72. *Mem:* Endocrine Soc; NY Acad Sci; Am Chem Soc; Tissue Cult Asn. *Res:* Biochemical endocrinology; steroid hormone action; hormone receptors; estrogen regulation of uterus and pituitary. *Mailing Add:* Dept Pharmacol Univ Tex Med Sch PO Box 20708 Houston TX 77225-0708. *Fax:* 713-792-5911; *E-Mail:* gstancel@farmr1.med.uth.tmc.edu

STANCELL, ARNOLD F, CHEMICAL ENGINEERING. *Current Pos:* PROF CHEM ENG, GA INST TECHNOL, 94- *Personal Data:* b New York, NY, Nov 16, 36. *Educ:* City Col NY, BS, 58; Mass Inst Technol, PhD & Sci(chem eng), 62. *Honors & Awards:* Marshall Lectr, Univ Wis, 90. *Prof Exp:* Vpres, Mobil Oil Corp, 62-93. *Concurrent Pos:* Vis prof, Mass Inst Technol, 70-71. *Mem:* Nat Acad Eng. *Mailing Add:* 15 Woodside Dr Greenwich CT 06830

STANCER, HARVEY C, PSYCHIATRY, NEUROCHEMISTRY. *Current Pos:* chief clin invest univ & head neurochem, Univ Toronto, 66-76, assoc prof, 69-72, prof psychiat, 72-91, prof psychiat res, 74-81, chief, Affective Disorders Unit, Clarke Inst Psychiat, 78-84, vchmn, Dept Psychiat, 80-85, EMER PROF PSYCHIAT, FAC MED, UNIV TORONTO, 91- *Personal Data:* b Toronto, Ont, Mar 6, 26; m 58, Magda Winter; c Claire & Karen. *Educ:* Univ Toronto, BA, 50, PhD(path chem), 53, MD, 55; Royal Col Physicians Can, cert psychiat, 62, fel, 72. *Honors & Awards:* Clarke Inst Prize, Univ Toronto, 70 & 74; McNeil Award, 72. *Prof Exp:* Head neurochem, Toronto Psychiat Hosp, 62-66. *Concurrent Pos:* McLean fel, Maudsley Inst, Univ London, 58-59; NY State Dept Hyg fel, Columbia Univ-Presby Med Ctr, 59-61; McLellan fel, Univ Toronto, 61-62; assoc, Med Res Coun Can, 62-64; vis prof, Univ Calif, Los Angeles, 83- *Mem:* Int Soc Neurochem; Neurochem Soc; Soc Biol Psychiat; Psychiat Res Soc; Can Endocrinol Soc & Metab. *Res:* Clinical psychiatric investigation and animal behavioral investigation of brain biogenic amines; genetics of affective disorders; psychopharmacology. *Mailing Add:* Clarke Inst of Psychiat Univ Toronto Toronto ON M5T 1R8 Can. *Fax:* 416-979-6902

STANCL, DONALD L, MATHEMATICS, OPERATIONS RESEARCH. *Current Pos:* PROF MATH, ST ANSELM COL, 85- *Personal Data:* b Oak Park, Ill, Feb 21, 40; m 66, Mildred Luzader. *Educ:* Knox Col, AB, 62; Univ Ill, PhD(math), 66; Nichols Col, MBA, 78. *Prof Exp:* Instr math, Princeton Univ, 67-69; asst prof, Univ Kans, 69-72; from assoc prof to prof math & statist, Nichols Col, 72-83; sr software engr, Sanders Assocs, 84-85. *Mem:* Math Asn Am; Sigma Xi. *Res:* Operations research and general applications of mathematics to problems of management. *Mailing Add:* 40 Briar Hill Rd New Boston NH 03070-4030

STANCL, MILDRED LUZADER, TOPOLOGY. *Current Pos:* assoc prof, 72-76, PROF MATH, NICHOLS COL, 76- *Personal Data:* b Parkersburg, WVa; m 66. *Educ:* Marietta Col, AB, 49; Univ Ill, AM, 62, PhD(math), 69. *Prof Exp:* Systs analyst, Sperry-Rand Corp, 54-57 & Radio Corp Am, 57-60; teaching asst math, Univ Ill, 61-66; asst prof, Trenton State Col, 68-69 & Kans Univ, 69-72. *Mem:* Am Math Soc; Math Asn Am; Sigma Xi. *Res:* Isomorphisms of smooth manifolds surrounding polyhedra. *Mailing Add:* 40 Briar Hill Rd New Boston NH 03070-4030

STANCYK, STEPHEN EDWARD, MARINE ECOLOGY, INVERTEBRATE ZOOLOGY. *Current Pos:* ASST PROF MARINE SCI & BIOL, UNIV SC, 75- *Personal Data:* b Denver, Colo, Apr 8, 46; m 78. *Educ:* Univ Colo, Boulder, BA, 68; Univ Fla, MS, 70, PhD(zool), 74. *Prof Exp:* Instr biol, Dept Zool, Univ Fla, 74-75. *Mem:* Am Soc Zoologists; AAAS; Ecol Soc Am; Southeastern Estuarine Res Soc; Sigma Xi. *Res:* Reproductive ecology of marine invertebrates; estuarine zooplankton dynamics; marine turtle conservation; systematics of Phoronids. *Mailing Add:* Dept Biol Sci Univ SC Columbia SC 29208

STANCZYK, FRANK ZYGMUNT, PERINATAL PHYSIOLOGY, STEROID BIOCHEMISTRY. *Current Pos:* ASSOC PROF, DEPT OBSTET & GYNEC, UNIV SOUTHERN CALIF, LOS ANGELES, 86- *Personal Data:* b Montreal, Que, July, 4, 36; m 70; c 1. *Educ:* Western Ill Univ, BS, 61; McGill Univ, MS, 67, PhD(exp med), 72. *Prof Exp:* Fel reproductive biol, Obstet & Gynec Dept, Univ Southern Calif, 72-74, from instr to asst prof, 74-76, asst prof, Obstet & Gynec Dept & Physiol Dept, 76-80; asst scientist perinatal physiol, Ore Regional Primate Res Ctr, 80-86; asst prof, Dept Obstet & Gynec, Ore Health Sci Univ, 80-86. *Mem:* Soc Gynec Invest; Endocrine Soc; Am Chem Soc; Can Biol Soc; Sigma Xi. *Res:* In vivo and in vitro studies of steroid hormone metabolism in pregnancy and endocrinopathies; pharmacokinetics and endocrine effects of contraceptive steroids; prediction and detection of ovulation; regulation of parturition and placental production of hormones. *Mailing Add:* 22258 James Alan Circle Chatsworth CA 91311

STANCZYK, MARTIN HENRY, EXTRACTIVE METALLURGY, RECYCLING TECHNOLOGY. *Current Pos:* SR VPRES OPERS & TECHNOL DEVELOP, SERI CORP, 90- *Personal Data:* b Jersey City, NJ, Jan 26, 30; m, Charlotte A Barger; c 7. *Educ:* Univ Ariz, BS, 57, MS, 58. *Honors & Awards:* Silver & Gold Medals from the Dept of the Interior for Meritorious & Distinguished Serv, 80, 87. *Prof Exp:* Bur Mines fel, US Bur Mines, Ariz, 57-58, extractive metallurgist, 57-60 & Ala, 60-61, res extractive metallurgist, 61-68, supvry metallurgist, College Park Metall Res Ctr, 68-72, res dir, Tuscaloosa Metall Res Ctr, 73-88. *Concurrent Pos:* Adj prof, Univ

Ala, 84-88; vpres, Tech Dev-wTe Corp, 88-90. *Mem:* Am Inst Mining, Metall & Petrol Engrs; Am Inst Mining Engrs; Sigma Xi; Soc Plastic Engrs. *Res:* Extractive metallurgy of nonmetallic minerals, including beneficiation studies, dewatering mineral wastes and developing new or improved ceramic and refractory materials; recycling plastics from municipal and curbside collection programs. *Mailing Add:* 4941 Red Oak Lane Tuscaloosa AL 35405. *Fax:* 205-554-0112

STANDAERT, FRANK GEORGE, pharmacology; deceased, see previous edition for last biography

STANDAERT, MARY L, PHOSPHOLIPIDS, INSULIN ACTION. *Current Pos:* RES BIOLOGIST, VET ADMIN HOSP, 75-; ASST PROF, UNIV SFLA, 93- *Personal Data:* b Seneca, SC, Oct 17, 47; m 69, Joseph; c Patricia E & Diane M. *Educ:* Winthrop Col, BA, 69; Yale Univ, MFS, 71; Univ SFla, PhD(biochem), 91. *Mem:* Am Diabetes Asn; Nat Endocrine Soc. *Res:* Investigation of the roles of phospholipids and protein kinase C as second messengers in the transduction of insulin action. *Mailing Add:* Vet Admin Hosp VAR151 13000 Bruce B Downs Blvd Tampa FL 33612. *Fax:* 813-972-7623

STANDEFER, JIMMY CLAYTON, biochemistry, clinical chemistry, for more information see previous edition

STANDER, JOSEPH W, ALGEBRA. *Current Pos:* from asst prof to assoc prof math, Univ Dayton, 60-74, dean, Grad Studies & Res, 67-74, vpres, Acad Affairs & Provost, 74-89, PROF MATH, UNIV DAYTON, 74- *Personal Data:* b Covington, Ky, Dec 2, 28. *Educ:* Univ Dayton, BS, 49; Cath Univ, MS, 57, PhD(math), 59. *Prof Exp:* Teacher, Hamilton Cath High Sch, 49-50 & Col Ponce, 50-55. *Mem:* Math Asn Am; Sigma Xi. *Res:* Matrix theory. *Mailing Add:* Univ Dayton Dayton OH 45469-0001

STANDIFER, LEONIDES CALMET, JR, PLANT PHYSIOLOGY. *Current Pos:* from asst prof to assoc prof, 61-74, prof bot, 74-77, PROF HORT, LA STATE UNIV, BATON ROUGE, 78- *Personal Data:* b Gulfport, Miss, Apr 24, 25; m 57; c 2. *Educ:* Miss State Univ, BS, 50, MS, 54; Univ Wis, PhD(bot), 59. *Prof Exp:* Plant physiologist, Firestone Plantations Co, 54-61. *Mem:* Bot Soc Am; Am Soc Plant Physiol; Weed Sci Soc Am. *Res:* Patterns of plant recovery from flame injury; histological responses of certain plants to herbicides, and physiology of herbicidal action. *Mailing Add:* 1244 Pasture View Dr Baton Rouge LA 70810

STANDIFER, LONNIE NATHANIEL, APICULTURE & POLLINATION, HONEY BEE NUTRITION. *Current Pos:* RETIRED. *Personal Data:* b Itasca, Tex, Oct 28, 26; div. *Educ:* Prairie View Agr & Mech Col, BS, 49; Kans State Col, MS, 51; Cornell Univ, PhD(med & vet entom & parasitol), 54. *Honors & Awards:* Award 120, Excellence Biol & Life Scis, Nat Consortium Black Prof Develop. *Prof Exp:* Instr biol sci & supvr campus pest control, Tuskegee Inst, 51-52; asst livestock insect control, Cornell Univ, 53-54; asst prof biol sci, Southern Univ, 54-56; res scientist & apiculturist, USDA, 56-70, dir, Bee Res Lab, 70-85, res leader, Honey Bee Pollination Lab, 72-85, tech adv apicult, Western Region, 73-85. *Mem:* AAAS; Entom Soc Am; Am Soc Parasitol; Am Beekeeping Fedn; Sigma Xi. *Res:* Medical and veterinary entomology and parasitology; control of insects of public health importance; insect physiology and nutrition; botany and plant pathology; honey bee physiology and nutrition, protein and lipids; pollen chemistry, fatty acids, sterols and hydrocarbons; honey bee pollination. *Mailing Add:* 1212 Galsgow Rd Ft Worth TX 76134-1626

STANDIL, SIDNEY, PHYSICS. *Current Pos:* From asst prof to assoc prof, 51-63, dean fac grad studies, 73-79, prof physics, 63-86, SR SCHOLAR, UNIV MAN, 86- *Personal Data:* b Winnipeg, Man, Oct 19, 26; m 50; c 4. *Educ:* Queen's Univ, Ont, BSc, 48, MSc, 49; Univ Man, PhD, 51. *Mem:* Am Phys Soc. *Res:* Cosmic ray and space physics. *Mailing Add:* Dept Physics Univ Man Winnipeg MB R3T 2N2 Can

STANDING, CHARLES NICHOLAS, chemical engineering, food science, for more information see previous edition

STANDING, KEITH M, VERTEBRATE ZOOLOGY. *Current Pos:* Assoc prof, 58-69, Chmn Dept, 69-72, PROF BIOL, CALIF STATE UNIV, FRESNO, 69-, CHMN DEPT, 82- *Personal Data:* b Ogden, Utah, Aug 2, 28; m 56; c 7. *Educ:* Brigham Young Univ, BS, 53, MS, 55; Wash State Univ, PhD(zool, bot), 60. *Concurrent Pos:* NSF res grants, 64-67; mem, NSF Conf Histochem-Its Appl in Res & Teaching, Vanderbilt Univ, 65; mem gov bd, Moss Landing Marine Labs; bd dirs, Ctr Urban & Regional Studies; vis scholar, Univ Calif, Berkeley & Univ Calif, Davis. *Mem:* AAAS; Am Soc Zool. *Res:* Histological analysis of reproductive organs of blue grouse; comparative histology of nephron units of kangaroo rats; isolation of nephron units of Dipodomys by various techniques; cytotaxonomy of Dipodomys; embryonic kidney development. *Mailing Add:* 1798 E Powers Ave Fresno CA 93720

STANDING, KENNETH GRAHAM, MASS SPECTROMETRY. *Current Pos:* from asst prof to prof, 53-95, EMER PROF PHYSICS, UNIV MAN, 95-- *Personal Data:* b Winnipeg, Man, Apr 3, 25; div; c 4. *Educ:* Univ Man, BSc, 48; Princeton Univ, AM, 50, PhD(physics), 55. *Concurrent Pos:* Nuffield Found Dom traveling fel, Wills Physics Lab, Bristol Univ, 58-59; dir, Cyclotron Lab, 59-67 & 68-74; Nat Res Coun Can sr res fel, Univ Grenoble, 67-68; vis prof, Inst Nuclear Physics, Orsay, 85-86. *Mem:* Am Phys Soc; Can Asn Physicists; Am Soc Mass Spectrometry; Chem Inst Can; Am Vacuum Soc. *Res:* Mass spectrometry of biomolecules and molecular clusters; nuclear physics and applications. *Mailing Add:* Dept Physics Univ Man Winnipeg MB R3T 2N2 Can. *Fax:* 204-269-8489; *E-Mail:* standin@cc.umanitoba.ca

STANDING, MARSHALL B, ENGINEERING. *Current Pos:* RETIRED. *Mem:* Nat Acad Eng. *Mailing Add:* 5434 Via Carrizo Laguna Hills CA 92653

STANDISH, CHARLES JUNIOR, MATHEMATICS. *Current Pos:* RETIRED. *Personal Data:* b Triangle, NY, Nov 10, 26. *Educ:* Hamilton Col, NY, BA, 49; Johns Hopkins Univ, MA, 51; Cornell Univ, PhD(math), 54. *Prof Exp:* Instr math, Hamilton Col, NY, 51-52; asst, Cornell Univ, 52-54; asst prof, Union Univ, NY, 54-57; mathematician, IBM Corp, 57-84. *Concurrent Pos:* Vis assoc prof, NC State Univ, 60-61; vis lectr, Sch Adv Technol, State Univ NY, Binghamton, 74-78, adj lectr, Dept Elec Eng, 84- *Mem:* Am Math Soc; Soc Indust & Appl Math. *Res:* Kalman filtering; control theory. *Mailing Add:* 397 Rathbun Hill Rd Greene NY 13778-2031

STANDISH, E MYLES, JR, ASTRONOMY. *Current Pos:* MEM TECH STAFF, JET PROPULSION LAB, 72- *Personal Data:* b Hartford, Conn, Mar 5, 39; m 68; c 3. *Educ:* Wesleyan Univ, BA, 60, MA, 62; Yale Univ, PhD(astron), 68. *Prof Exp:* Asst prof astron, Yale Univ, 68-72. *Mem:* Am Astron Soc-Div Dynamic Astron; Int Astron Union. *Res:* Celestial mechanics; numerical analysis; continuous improvement of the planetary, lunar and natural satellite ephemerides. *Mailing Add:* Jet Propulsion Lab 301-150 4800 Oakgrove Dr Pasadena CA 91109

STANDISH, NORMAN WESTON, TECHNICAL MANAGEMENT, ORGANIC CHEMISTRY. *Current Pos:* PRES, STANDISH HOUSE CONSULT, 95- *Personal Data:* b Marion, Iowa, Apr 4, 30; m 56; c Robin S (Hicks), Christopher B & Hilary A. *Educ:* Beloit Col, BS, 52; Purdue Univ, MS, 57, PhD(org chem), 59. *Prof Exp:* Chemist, Selectron Div, Pittsburgh Plate Glass Co, 52-53; res assoc biochem, Stand Oil Co, 60-65, tech dir plastics, Prophylactic Brush Div, 65-67, res supvr, Cleveland, 67-70, supvr develop, Tech Serv & Polymers, 70-75, mgr, Tech Serv, 75-80, lab dir, Explor Prod, 80-84, mgr, Strategic Planning, 84-87; mgr prog develop, Bp Am, Inc, Cleveland, 88-89, sr res assoc, 90-93; sr scientist, Epic Nat Polymer Lifecycle Ctr, 88-93, exec dir, 93-95. *Concurrent Pos:* Mem adv bd, Col Sci, Tex A&M Univ; nat coun, Cleveland Sect, Am Chem Soc, 95-; chair, Petrol Div Am Chem Soc, 97; chair, Employment Serv. *Mem:* Am Chem Soc; Soc Plastics Engrs; fel Am Inst Chemists; Soc Plastics Indust; Soc Petrol Engrs; Soc Mfg Engrs. *Res:* Computer modelling of fluid flow in reservoirs, enhanced oil recovery systems; polymer processing and fabrication plastic market development; technology strategic planning; technical program development and commercialization; director of state of Ohio funded program to recycle plastic waste; fuel technology and petroleum; environmental engineering; published a chapter on reinforced plastics. *Mailing Add:* 32250 Burlwood Dr Solon OH 44139. *Fax:* 440-248-7807; *E-Mail:* nstandish@aol.com

STANDISH, SAMUEL MILES, ORAL PATHOLOGY, FORENSIC ODONTOLOGY. *Current Pos:* Inst dent, Sch Dent, Ind Univ, Indianapolis, 52-57, from asst prof to assoc prof oral path, 57-67, asst dean grad & postgrad educ, 69-74, prof oral path, 67-88, assoc dean grad & postgrad educ, 74-88, EMER PROF, DENT DIAG SCI & ORAL PATH, SCH DENT, IND UNIV, INDIANAPOLIS, 88- *Personal Data:* b Campbellsburg, Ind, July 6, 23; m 49, Gertrude E Eberle; c Nancy (Bridgeforth) & Linda. *Educ:* Ind Univ, DDS, 45, MS, 56; Am Bd Oral Path, dipl, 59; Am Bd Forensic Odontol, dipl, 77. *Honors & Awards:* Odontol Award, Am Acad Forensic Sci. *Concurrent Pos:* Mem, Clin Cancer Educ Comt, Nat Cancer Inst, 69-79; consult, Coun Dent Educ, Am Dent Asn, 71-77; mem, Nat Bd Test Constructors Comt, Am Dent Asn, 66-75; pres, Am Bd Oral Path, 78-79 & Orgn Teachers Oral Diag, 87-88. *Mem:* Am Dent Asn; fel Am Acad Oral Path (pres, 72-73); Int Asn Dent Res; fel Am Acad Forensic Sci. *Res:* Salivary gland pathophysiology and experimental carcinogenesis; inflammatory mechanisms; striated muscle regeneration; muscle diseases; clinical oral pathology; forensic dentistry. *Mailing Add:* 4548 Manning Rd Indianapolis IN 46208

STANDISH, WILLIAM JOHN, ROLE OF HYDROGEN IN SUPERCONDUCTIVITY. *Current Pos:* asst prof, 83-95, CHAIR, DEPT PHYSICS & CHEM, SKIDMORE COL, 94-, ASSOC PROF PHYSICS, 95- *Personal Data:* b New York, NY, Oct 5, 45; m 77, Jacqueline Marie Cluff; c 7. *Educ:* Harpur Col, BA, 67; State Univ NY, Binghamton, MA, 76, PhD(physics), 78. *Prof Exp:* Asst prof physics, Hartwick Col, 78; res assoc, State Univ NY, Albany, 78-80, vis asst prof, 80-83, adj prof, 83-90. *Concurrent Pos:* Consult, Atomic Data & Nuclear Data Tables, 84- *Mem:* Am Phys Soc; Am Asn Physics Teachers; Coun undergrad res. *Res:* Study effects of composition and fabrication techniques on electronic properties of both low temperature and high temperature superconductors. *Mailing Add:* Dept Chem & Physics Skidmore Col Saratoga Springs NY 12866. *Fax:* 518-580-5139; *E-Mail:* wstandis@skidmore.edu

STANDLEE, WILLIAM JASPER, POULTRY NUTRITION. *Current Pos:* CONSULT POULTRY & ANIMAL NUTRIT, 79- *Personal Data:* b Zybach, Tex, May 2, 29; m 58; c 3. *Educ:* Tex Tech Univ, BS, 54, MS, 55; Tex A&M Univ, PhD(poultry sci), 63. *Prof Exp:* Animal nutritionist, Standard Milling Co, Tex, 55-57; salesman, Van Waters & Rogers, 57-58; res asst, Tex Agr Exp Sta, 58-63; dir nutrit & res, Darragh Co, Ark, 63-65; dir nutrit, Burrus Feed Mills, Tex, 65-68; dir nutrit & res, Food Div, Valmac Industs, Inc, Ark, 68-71; dir res & nutrit, B & D Mills, 71-79. *Res:* Nutrition and feeding management of turkey breeders; broiler chicken breeders, market turkeys and broilers and egg production chickens. *Mailing Add:* 815 N Lucas Dr Grapevine TX 76051-5063

STANDLEY, PAUL MELVIN, AUTOMOTIVE PRODUCTS. *Current Pos:* from res chemist to sr res chemist, Dayco Technol Ctr, Springfield, Mo, 74-81, mgr tech servs, 81-83, mgr advan tech group, 83-86, bus mgr auto accessories, Dayco Prods Plant, Springdale, Ariz, 86-89, VPRES RES & DEVELOP, DAYCO PRODS INC, DAYTON, OHIO, 89- *Personal Data:* b East Liverpool, Ohio, Nov 8, 43; m 69, 90, Monica L Sneller; c Celeste N, Matthew J & Zachary P. *Educ:* Kent State Univ, BS, 70. *Prof Exp:* Compounder, Gen Tire Develop, 70-74. *Concurrent Pos:* Mem, Rubber Div, Am Chem Soc. *Res:* Elastomer products; process equipment and product applications; pulleys; power transmission products; material compositions. *Mailing Add:* 8700 Centerridge Pt Dayton OH 45458-1004

STANDLEY, ROBERT DEAN, ELECTRICAL ENGINEERING. *Current Pos:* MEM TECH STAFF COHERENT OPTICS RES, BELL TEL LABS, INC, 66- *Personal Data:* b Findlay, Ill, Aug 25, 35; m 59; c 2. *Educ:* Univ Ill, BS, 57; Rutgers Univ, MS, 60; Ill Inst Technol, PhD(elec eng), 66. *Prof Exp:* Assoc engr, IIT Res Inst, 60-62, res engr, 62-64, asst mgr microwaves & antennas, 64-65, mgr electromagnetic compatibility, 65-66. *Mem:* Inst Elec & Electronics Engrs. *Res:* Microwave filters; antennas; electromagnetic compatibility; avalanche transit time diode oscillators; optical modulators; optical integrated circuits; fiber optics; satellite communications. *Mailing Add:* 4 Sunnybank Dr Shrewsbury NJ 07702

STANEK, ELDON KEITH, ELECTRICAL ENGINEERING. *Current Pos:* PROF & HEAD ELEC ENG, MICH TECH UNIV, 80- *Personal Data:* b Novinger, Mo, Dec 12, 41; m 69; c 2. *Educ:* Ill Inst Technol, BSEE, 64, MS, 65, PhD(elec eng), 69. *Prof Exp:* Asst prof elec eng, Ill Inst Technol, 68-70; from asst prof to assoc prof elec eng, 70-77, prof, 77-80. *Concurrent Pos:* NSF grant, WVa Univ, 71-73, Bur Mines grant, 72-79; consult, Dept Energy, 77- & Union Carbide Corp, 77- *Mem:* Inst Elec & Electronics Engrs; Am Soc Elec Engrs; Sigma Xi. *Res:* Electrical power systems; digital simulation and mathematical modeling; simulation of switching transients; inductive interference; induced voltage in cables. *Mailing Add:* Dept Elec Eng Univ Mo Rolla MO 65401-0249

STANEK, PETER, MATHEMATICS, SYSTEMS ANALYSIS. *Current Pos:* MEM STAFF, KETRON INC, 78- *Personal Data:* b Chicago, Ill, Dec 3, 37; m 60; c 2. *Educ:* Univ Chicago, MS, 58, PhD(math), 61. *Prof Exp:* Mem, Inst Defense Anal, 61-62; analyst, Opers Eval Group, 62-63; asst prof math, Univ Southern Calif, 63-65; sr scientist, Jet Propulsion Lab, 65-68 & Lear Siegler Inc, 68-72; mem staff, Systs Applns Inc, 72-78. *Mem:* Am Math Soc; Soc Indust & Appl Math; Human Factors Soc; Am Inst Aeronaut & Astronaut. *Res:* Algebra; operations research; communications engineering; human factors engineering; computer applications. *Mailing Add:* 1281 Idylberry Rd San Rafael CA 94903-1071

STANFIELD, JAMES ARMOND, ORGANIC CHEMISTRY. *Current Pos:* from asst prof to prof chem, 47-56-, asst dir sch chem, 65-85, res assoc, res inst, 51-85, EMER PROF, GA INST TECHNOL, 85- *Personal Data:* b Covington, Ky, Aug 28, 17; m 42, Marjorie Lively; c Elizabeth, Judith & Jane. *Educ:* Eastern Ky State Col, BS, 40; Univ Tenn, MS, 42, PhD(phys org chem), 47. *Prof Exp:* Instr chem, Univ Ky, 41-42; instr, Univ Tenn, 42-46. *Mem:* Am Chem Soc. *Res:* Organic synthesis; catalytic hydrogenation kinetics; spirobarbituric acids; chemistry of uramil. *Mailing Add:* 1065 Ferncliff Rd NE Atlanta GA 30324-2522

STANFIELD, KENNETH CHARLES, EXPERIMENTAL HIGH ENERGY PHYSICS. *Current Pos:* assoc head, Fermi Nat Accelerator Lab, 77-79, head, Proton Dept, 79-81, Exp Areas Dept, 82, Bus Sect, 84, HEAD, RES DIV, FERMI NAT ACCELERATOR LAB, 85- *Personal Data:* b Los Angeles, Calif, Sept 21, 42; c 1. *Educ:* Univ Tex, BS, 64; Harvard Univ, AM, 67, PhD(physics), 69. *Prof Exp:* Res assoc physics, Univ Mich, 69-71; asst prof physics, Purdue Univ, 71-77. *Concurrent Pos:* Mem prog adv comt, Zero Gradient Synchrotron, Argonne Nat Lab, 75- *Mem:* Sigma Xi. *Res:* Experimental research, using electronic techniques, into the nature of elementary particle properties. *Mailing Add:* MS 105 Fermilab PO Box 500 Batavia IL 60510

STANFIELD, MANIE K, BIOCHEMISTRY, NUTRITION. *Current Pos:* ASST PROF BIOCHEM, SCH MED, TULANE UNIV, 65- *Personal Data:* b St Petersburg, Fla, Feb 15, 31. *Educ:* Univ Chicago, BA, 54, MS, 57; Univ Calif, Los Angeles, PhD(org chem), 62. *Prof Exp:* Asst org chem, Mass Inst Technol, 62-63 & Rockefeller Univ, 63-65. *Mem:* AAAS; Am Chem Soc. *Res:* Nutrition in medicine; stability and polymerization of beta-lactam antibiotics. *Mailing Add:* 710 Park Blvd New Orleans LA 70114. *Fax:* 504-584-2739

STANFORD, AUGUSTUS LAMAR, JR, SOLID STATE PHYSICS. *Current Pos:* RETIRED. *Personal Data:* b Macon, Ga, Jan 20, 31; m 52; c 2. *Educ:* Ga Inst Technol, BS, 52, MS, 55, PhD(physics), 58. *Prof Exp:* Sr staff consult, Sperry Rand Corp, 58-64; from assoc prof to prof physics, Ga Inst Technol, 64-96. *Concurrent Pos:* NASA res grant, 64- *Mem:* Am Phys Soc. *Res:* Nuclear spectroscopy; ferroelectrics; pyroelectrics; phonon in solids. *Mailing Add:* 330 Eldon Dr Atlanta GA 30342

STANFORD, DENNIS JOE, ARCHAEOLOGY. *Current Pos:* Head, Div Archeol, Smithsonian Inst, Washington, 90-92, ARCHEOLOGIST & CUR, SMITHSONIAN INST, WASH, 72-, CHMN, DEPT ANTHROP, 92-; VPRES & DIR, TARAXACUM PRESS, 81- *Personal Data:* b Cherokee, Iowa, May 13, 43; m 88, Margaret Brierty; c Brandy L. *Educ:* Univ Wyo, BA, 65; Univ NMex, MA, 67, PhD, 72. *Concurrent Pos:* Res assoc, Denver Mus Natural Hist, 89-; mem, Anthrop Soc Wash. *Mem:* Soc Am Archeol; Am Quaternary Asn. *Res:* Archaeology; anthropology; research and publications on Paleo-Indian studies, North and South America, Northeast Asia (China and Siberia), especially Western United States. *Mailing Add:* Smithsonian Inst Washington DC 20560. *Fax:* 202-357-2208

STANFORD, GEOFFREY BRIAN, ENVIRONMENTAL MANAGEMENT. *Current Pos:* PRES, AGRO-CITY, INC, 74- *Personal Data:* b London, Eng, Mar 29, 16; m 59; c 3. *Educ:* Royal Col Physicians & Surgeons, MRCS & LRCP, 39; dip med radiol, 47. *Prof Exp:* Vis prof, Sch Archit & Environ Planning Calif State Polytech Col, San Luis Obispo. 70; adj prof, Environ Studies Ctr, Antioch Col, 71; vis prof & dir, Environics Ctr, St Edwards Univ, 71-72; biomed res scientist, Urban Health Module Sch Pub Health, Univ Tex, Houston, 72-74. *Concurrent Pos:* Adj prof, Sch Archit, Rice-Univ, 72-74; mem environ & eco-systs planning comt, Prep Planning Group, UN Environ Prog for 1976 Habitat Cont, 74; vis prof & resource recovery planning specialist, Inst Urban Studies, Univ Tex, Arlington, 74-; UN Environ Prog deleg, Sump on Develop Patterns of Humans Settlements in Developing Countries for Yr 2000, 75; proj dir res into effects of landmix, Environ Protection Agency; dir, Greenhills Environ Studies Ctr; trustee, Environic Found Int. *Mem:* Archit Asn Gt Brit; Am Soc Testing & Mat; fel Royal Photog Soc Gt Brit; Soil Asn; AAAS. *Res:* Use of municipal waste resources for restoring soil fertility and water characteristics; measurement of the effects of crop yield, water quality and climate application to regional environmental management. *Mailing Add:* 7171 Mountain Creek Pkwy Dallas TX 75249-1159

STANFORD, GEORGE STAILING, REACTOR PHYSICS. *Current Pos:* PHYSICIST, ARGONNE NAT LAB, 59- *Personal Data:* b Halifax, NS, July 23, 28; US citizen; m 56, Janet Clarke; c Susan, Rachel & Stephen. *Educ:* Acadia Univ, BSc, 49; Wesleyan Univ, MA, 51; Yale Univ, PhD(nuclear energy levels), 56. *Prof Exp:* Proj engr infrared instrumentation, Perkin-Elmer Corp, 55-59. *Mem:* AAAS; Fedn Am Scientists. *Res:* Experimental reactor physics; verification of arms-control treaties. *Mailing Add:* Argonne Nat Lab D208 9700 S Cass Ave Argonne IL 60439

STANFORD, JACK ARTHUR, LIMNOLOGY. *Current Pos:* DIR, FLATHEAD LAKE BIOL STA, 80-; BIERMAN PROF ECOL, UNIV MONT, 86- *Personal Data:* b Delta, Colo, Feb 18, 47; m, Bonnie Ellis; c Jake & Chriss. *Educ:* Colo State Univ, BS, 69, MS, 71; Univ Utah, PhD(limnol), 75. *Prof Exp:* Asst fish & wildlife, Colo State Univ, 65-69, asst zool, 69-72; res limnol, Univ Utah & Univ Mont, 72-74; from asst prof to assoc prof limnol & biol, NTex State Univ, 74-80. *Concurrent Pos:* Dir, Flathead Res Group, Biol Sta, Univ Mont, 77-; consult, Nature Conserv Nordic Coun Ecol; exec comt, NAm Bentho-logical Soc, 79, 87, 88; vis lectr, Norway, 80; fel, Nordic Coun Ecol, Oslo Univ, Bergen Univ & Tronheim Univ, Norway, 80; fel, Found Res Develop, Repub SAfrica, 89; vis lectr, SAfrica, 90. *Mem:* Sigma Xi; Int Soc Theoret & Appl Limnol; Am Soc Limnol & Oceanog; Ecol Soc Am; NAm Benthological Soc; AAAS; Am Inst Biol Sci. *Res:* All aspects of limnological study in lakes and streams with special interest in nutrient cycling by algae and heterotrophic bacteria; benthic ecology and life histories of the Plecoptera; hyporheic ecology. *Mailing Add:* Flathead Lake Biol Sta Univ Mont 311 Biol Sta Lane Polson MT 59860-9659. *E-Mail:* stanford@selway.umt.edu

STANFORD, JACK WAYNE, PLANT TAXONOMY. *Current Pos:* from asst prof to assoc prof, 66-74, PROF BIOL, HOWARD PAYNE UNIV, 74- *Personal Data:* b Eldorado, Tex, Dec 21, 35; m 58; c 2. *Educ:* Baylor Univ, BA, 58; Tex Tech Univ, MS, 66; Okla State Univ, PhD(bot), 71. *Prof Exp:* Teacher jr high sch, Tex, 60-62, high sch, 62-66. *Res:* Pollen morphology of the Mimosoideae; floristic studies of central Texas. *Mailing Add:* Dept Biol Howard Payne Univ 1000 Center Ave Brownwood TX 76801-2794

STANFORD, MARLENE A, FOOD CHEMISTRY, PHYSICAL CHEMISTRY. *Current Pos:* sr res scientist, Basic Res, Kraft Gen Foods, 86-87, Venture Prod, 87-89, Microwave Technol, 89-92, ASSOC TECHNOL PRINCIPAL, PHYS CHEM, KRAFT FOODS, 92- *Personal Data:* m 92, Robert J McGorrin. *Educ:* Ind Univ, BS, 74; Northwestern Univ, MS, 78, PhD(phys chem), 80. *Prof Exp:* Lab technician & res asst, Gibbs Labs, Wilmette, Ill, 75-76; res fel & teaching asst, dept chem, Northwestern Univ, Evanston, 76-80; mem staff, new prod develop, Pet Foods Res & Develop, Quaker Oats Co, Barrington, Ill, 80-82 & Cent Res & Develop, 82-84; scientist, Technol & New Bus Res & Develop, 84-86. *Concurrent Pos:* Mem, Prod Benchmarking Panel Participation, Kraft Gen Foods, 90-95, Sensory Spectrum Flav & Texture Profile Description Analysis Training, 90-95. *Mem:* Am Chem Soc; Inst Food Technologists; Int Microwave Power Inst; Soc Rheology. *Res:* Control of moisture migration through water activity and moisture barriers; thermal analysis, calorimetry, reaction kinetics, crystallization, flavor partitioning and volatile loss; microwave heating, dielectric relaxation, microwave oven dynamics, heat and mass transfer, water mobility and binding; extrusion, co-extrusion, precooked pasta, preacidified meat; thermal processing, aseptic processing and packaging, processed cheese technology; identification of new product opportunities; product concepts and innovative executions; rheology and texture of food systems; dairy protein functionality; food emulsions and suspensions. *Mailing Add:* Kraft Foods Inc 801 Waukegan Rd Glenview IL 60025-4391. *Fax:* 847-646-3864; *E-Mail:* mstanford@kraft.com

STANG, ELDEN JAMES, APPLIED PHYSIOLOGY, TEACHING. *Current Pos:* PROF POMOL, UNIV WIS-MADISON, 78- *Personal Data:* b Victoria, Kans, Jan 23, 40; m 63; c 3. *Educ:* Kans State Univ, BS, 67; Iowa State Univ, MS, 69, PhD(hort), 73. *Prof Exp:* Res asst hort, Iowa State Univ, 67-69, res assoc, 69-73, instr, 73; exten horticulturist pomol, Ohio State Univ, 73-78. *Concurrent Pos:* Peace Corps, Chile, 61-63; assoc ed, Am Soc Hort Sci, 80-84; Fulbright fel, Finland, 87. *Mem:* Am Soc Hort Sci; Int Soc Hort Sci. *Res:* Production of tree fruit and small fruit; weed control; plant nutrition; plant growth regulators. *Mailing Add:* 4293 Highway T Sun Prairie WI 53590. *E-Mail:* elderstary@aol.com

STANG, LOUIS GEORGE, REMOTELY OPERATED EQUIPMENT, COMPUTER SOFTWARE. *Current Pos:* PROPRIETOR, DORILOU ASSOC, 87-; COMPUT PROGRAMMER, SEVEN LOCKS SOFTWARE, 96- *Personal Data:* b Portland, Ore, Oct 25, 19; m 43, Dorian Heintz; c David, Steven & Mark. *Educ:* Reed Col, BA, 41. *Honors & Awards:* Distinguished Serv Award, Am Nuclear Soc, 69; Cert Appreciation, Am Nuclear Soc, 78. *Prof Exp:* Res chemist, Nat Defense Res Comt, Northwestern Univ, 42-43, Calif Inst Technol, 43, Clinton Labs, Tenn, 43-44, Metall Lab, Univ Chicago, 44-45, Monsanto Chem Co, Ohio, 45 & Universal Oil Prod Co, Ill, 45-47; div head, 47-80, chemist, Brookhaven Nat Lab, 47-82. *Concurrent Pos:* USAEC consult, Yugoslavia & Israel, 60 & rep, regional meetings utilization res reactors, Int Atomic Energy Agency, Manila, 63, Bombay, 64; Indian Atomic Energy Estab & Int Atomic Energy Agency lect prod radioisotopes, Bombay, 64; comput database ed, Norman Data Defense, 94-95. *Mem:* Emer mem Am Chem Soc; assoc mem Sigma Xi. *Res:* Production of radioisotopes; spallation reactions; radionuclide generators; design of radioactive laboratories and equipment; heuristic diagnosis of computer viruses; health effects of photovoltaic materials. *Mailing Add:* 13769 Exotica Lane Wellington FL 33414

STANG, PETER JOHN, ORGANIC CHEMISTRY. *Current Pos:* from asst prof to assoc prof, 69-79, chmn dept, 89-95, PROF CHEM, UNIV UTAH, 79-, DISTINGUISHED PROF CHEM, 92- *Personal Data:* b Nurnberg, Ger, Nov 17, 41; US citizen; m 69, Christine M E Schirmer; c Antonia & Alexandra. *Educ:* DePaul Univ, BS, 63; Univ Calif, Berkeley, PhD(chem), 66. *Hon Degrees:* Dr, Lomonosov Moscow State Univ, Russia, 92; DSc, Russ Acad Sci, Moscow, 92. *Honors & Awards:* Alexander von Humboldt US Sr Scientist Award, 77; Mendeleev Lectr, USSR, 89. *Prof Exp:* NIH fel chem, Princeton Univ, 66-68, instr, 68-69. *Concurrent Pos:* Assoc ed, J Am Chem Soc, 82; Lady Davis fel, Haifa, Israel; Fulbright sr scholar, Yugoslavia, 87-88. *Mem:* Am Chem Soc; Chem Soc; fel AAAS; fel Japan Soc Prom Sci. *Res:* Generation, nature and chemistry of unsaturated reactive intermediates (vinyl cations, carbenes, ylides and strained ring compounds); mechanism of metal mediated vinylic couplings, novel transition metal complexes; preparation and uses of alkynyl esters, and alkynyliodonium species, enzyme inhibition (new suicide substrates and their mode of action), novel antitumor agents; molecular architectual via coordination. *Mailing Add:* Dept Chem Univ Utah Salt Lake City UT 84112. *Fax:* 801-581-8433

STANG, ROBERT GEORGE, MATERIALS SCIENCE & ENGINEERING, MECHANICAL BEHAVIOR OF MATERIALS. *Current Pos:* asst prof, 73-79, ASSOC PROF, DEPT MAT SCI & ENG, UNIV WASH, 79- *Personal Data:* b Los Angeles, Calif, June 20, 38; m 64, Kathleen Desmond. *Educ:* Long Beach State Col, BS, 61; Univ Calif, Los Angeles, MS, 65; Stanford Univ, PhD(mat sci & eng), 72. *Prof Exp:* Instr mech eng, Long Beach State Col, 65-66; res asst mat sci, Dept Mat Sci & Eng, Stanford Univ, 66-71; asst prof, Inst Mil Engenharia, Rio de Janeiro, 71-72; res assoc, Dept Mat Sci & Eng, Stanford Univ, 72-73. *Concurrent Pos:* Inco fel, Dept Mat Sci & Eng, Stanford Univ, 66-68; consult, USCG, 78, Battelle Pac Northwest Labs, 78-83, Hewlett Packard, Boise Div, 79; sr Fulbright-Hayes researcher & lectr, Montanuniversitat, Austria, 80-81; assoc prog dir, Metall Prog, Div Mat Res, NSF, Washington, DC, 84-85, prog dir, 85-86. *Mem:* Am Soc Metals Int; Sigma Xi. *Res:* Structure-property relationships in materials; deformation at ambient and high temperatures in metals, alloys and ceramics; fatigue and fracture; effect of micro-structure on deformation and fracture. *Mailing Add:* Dept Mat Sci & Eng box 352120 Univ Wash Seattle WA 98195-2120. *E-Mail:* stang@u.washington.edu

STANGE, HUGO, ORGANIC CHEMISTRY, INORGANIC CHEMISTRY. *Current Pos:* RETIRED. *Personal Data:* b Elizabeth, NJ, June 24, 21; m 42, Margaret H Cox; c 5. *Educ:* Northwestern Univ, BS, 42, PhD(chem), 50. *Prof Exp:* Chemist, Pa Ord Works, US Rubber Co, 42; chemist res dept, Olin Mathieson Chem Corp, 50-52, sect leader, 52-55; mgr org res, FMC Corp, 55-60, mgr org & polymer res, 60-62, res mgr, 62-65, asst dir, Cent Res Dept, 65-72, dir, Princeton Ctr Tech Dept, 72-82. *Concurrent Pos:* Consult, 83-; pres, Princeton Chap Sigma Xi, 88-89. *Mem:* Asn Res Dirs (pres, 82-82); Am Chem Soc; Royal Soc Chem; Am Inst Chemists; Am Inst Chem Eng; Sigma Xi. *Res:* Thianaphthene and boron chemistry; industrial process and product development in organic and inorganic chemistry; agricultural pesticides; polymers; chemical research management; general technical management; government research contract management. *Mailing Add:* 19 Hamilton Ave Princeton NJ 08542

STANGE, LIONEL ALVIN, SYSTEMATIC ENTOMOLOGY. *Current Pos:* TAXON ENTOMOLOGIST, BUR ENTOM, DIV PLANT INDUST & CONSUMER SERV, DEPT AGR, FLA, 78- *Personal Data:* b Los Angeles, Calif, June 27, 35; m 67; c 2. *Educ:* Univ Calif, Berkeley, BS, 58; Univ Calif, Davis, MS, 60, PhD(entom), 65. *Honors & Awards:* Ellsworth Award, Am Mus Natural Hist, NY, 60; Nat Geog Soc Grant, 74-76. *Prof Exp:* Prof entom, Nat Univ Tucuman, Arg, 65-78. *Concurrent Pos:* Investr entom, Miguel Lillo Found, Tucuman, Arg, 65-78; grants, Sigma Xi, 68, Nat Coun Res Technol, Buenos Aires, 70-75 & Nat Geog Soc, 75-77; vis curator, Mus Comp Zool, Harvard Univ, 70; vis prof, North East Univ Corrientes, Arg, 74; Smithsonian fel, 89. *Mem:* Nat Geog Soc; Sigma Xi. *Res:* Biosystematics of the Neuroptera especially Myrmeleontidae (world) and of Hymenoptera (Eumenidae and Megachilidae) of the western hemisphere. *Mailing Add:* 610 NW 54th Terr Gainesville FL 32607

STANGEBY, PETER CHRISTIAN, FUSION ENERGY. *Current Pos:* PROF PLASMA PHYSICS & FUSION, INST AEROSPACE STUDIES, UNIV TORONTO, 72- *Personal Data:* b Can, Sept 6, 43; m 64; c 2. *Educ:* Univ Toronto, BSc, 66, MSc, 67; Oxford Univ, dipl sci, 68, DPhil(plasma physics), 71. *Concurrent Pos:* Sci consult, Princeton Plasma Physics Lab, 83-84 & 90-91, Joint Europ Torus Fusion Energy Proj Europ Community, 84- *Mem:* Can Asn Physicists; Am Phys Soc. *Res:* Fusion energy particularly edge studies of tokamaks; modeling impurity behavior. *Mailing Add:* Inst Aerospace Studies Univ Toronto 4925 Dufferin St Downsview ON M3H 5T6 Can

STANGEL, IVAN, ADHESION, INTERFACES. *Current Pos:* Lectr, Dept Oper Dent, McGill Univ, 77-78, asst prof, Dept Clin Dent, 78-80, asst prof, Sect Oper Dent, Div Prosthodontics, 80-82, ASSOC PROF, McGILL UNIV, 82-, DIR BIOMAT SCI, 95- *Personal Data:* b Kosice, Czech, Sept 8, 46; m 85, Cynthia S Palmer; c Jacob Louis. *Educ:* Univ Pa, DMD, 70. *Prof Exp:* Resident, Univ Col Hosp, Univ London, 70-71; clin staff, Lutheran Med Ctr/Sunset Park Family Health Ctr, 71-72, Polyclinique Dent, Univ Lousanne, 73; instr, Dept Oper Dent, Sch Dent Med, Tufts Univ, 74; pvt practice, Burlington, Vt, 74-77. *Concurrent Pos:* Asst dent surgeon, Montreal Gen Hosp, 78-; vis prof, Dept Biomat, Boston Univ, 83-84; guest researcher, Am Dent Asn Health Found, 92-95. *Mem:* Fel Acad Dent Mats; Adhesion Soc; Am Acad Oper Dent; Int Asn Dent Res; Int Col Dentists; Can Soc Biomats. *Res:* Contributed numerous articles to professional journals in the field of biomaterials science. *Mailing Add:* 5612 Glenwood Rd Bethesda MD 20817. *Fax:* 514-398-8242; *E-Mail:* stangel@medcor.mcgill.ca

STANGER, ANDREW L, COMPUTER SCIENCE, SOLAR PHYSICS. *Current Pos:* sci programmer solar physics, 75-85, ASSOC SCIENTIST SOLAR PHYSICS, HIGH ALTITUDE OBSERV, NAT CTR ATMOSPHERIC RES, 85- *Personal Data:* b Boulder, Colo, Apr 12, 48; m. *Educ:* Univ Colo, BA, 71. *Honors & Awards:* Res support Award, Solar Maximum Mission Satellite, Nat Ctr Atmospheric Res, 80. *Prof Exp:* Comput programmer signal processing, Naval Undersea Ctr, 71-72; res asst nuclear eng, Gen Atomic Co, 72-74; engr & scientist sci comput, TRW Systs Group, Inc, 74-75. *Res:* Image processing; scientific analysis of solar corona images; spacecraft control software. *Mailing Add:* 3685 Smuggler Pl Boulder CO 80303

STANGER, PHILIP CHARLES, ASTRONOMY. *Current Pos:* from instr to prof, 52-85, chmn dept, 59-85, EMER PROF ASTRON, OHIO WESLEYAN UNIV, 85- *Personal Data:* b Newark, NJ, Nov 11, 20; m 43; c 2. *Educ:* Montclair State Teachers Col, AB, 42; Okla Agr & Mech Col, MS, 49; Ohio State Univ, MA, 54. *Prof Exp:* Instr math, Okla Agr & Mech Col, 46-48; instr, Ohio Univ, 48-50. *Mem:* AAAS; Am Astron Soc. *Res:* Spectroscopic binaries; stellar atmospheres. *Mailing Add:* 22 Griswold St Delaware OH 43015

STANGHELLINI, MICHAEL EUGENE, PLANT PATHOLOGY. *Current Pos:* FAC MEM, UNIV CALIF, RIVERSIDE. *Personal Data:* b San Francisco, Calif, Mar 21, 40; m 66; c 2. *Educ:* Univ Calif, Davis, BA, 63; Univ Hawaii, MS, 65; Univ Calif, Berkeley, PhD(plant path), 69. *Prof Exp:* From asst prof to assoc prof, Univ Ariz, 69-81, res scientist plant path, Agr Exp Sta, 77-97, prof plant path, 81- *Mem:* Am Phytopath Soc; Sigma Xi. *Res:* Soil borne fungal pathogens. *Mailing Add:* Dept Plant Path Fawcett Lab Bldg Univ Calif Riverside CA 92507

STANGL, WALTER DAVID, HISTORY & PHILOSOPHY OF MATHEMATICS. *Current Pos:* ASSOC PROF MATH, BIOLA UNIV, 84-, DEAN SCI, 93- *Personal Data:* b Bethlehem, Pa, Apr 9, 49; m 72, Ann Middlebrook; c Deborah Ann & Rebecca Lynn. *Educ:* Lehigh Univ, BA, 70, MS, 72, PhD(math), 74; Denver Sem, MDiv, 84. *Prof Exp:* Lectr Math, Moravian Col, 74-75; assoc prof, Gordon Col, 75-80; asst prof, Rockmont Col, 80-84. *Mem:* Math Asn Am. *Res:* Elementary number theory; mathematics and mathematicians of the 17th and 18th centuries. *Mailing Add:* Dept Math & Comput Sci Biola Univ 13800 Biola Ave La Mirada CA 90639-0001. *E-Mail:* walt_stangl@peter.biola.edu

STANIFORTH, RICHARD JOHN, WEED SCIENCE & PLANT REPRODUCTION, ECOLOGY OF PIONEER PLANT SPECIES. *Current Pos:* from asst prof to assoc prof, 75-91, PROF, UNIV WINNIPEG, 91- *Personal Data:* b Sidmouth, Eng, Oct 2, 46; Brit & Can citizen; m 70, Diane S Parry; c Terry, Ian, Graham & Christopher. *Educ:* Univ Col NWales, BSc, 68; Univ Western Ont, PhD(plant sci), 75. *Prof Exp:* Lectr biol, Univ Western Ont, 73-75. *Concurrent Pos:* Sci dir, Field Sta, Churchill Northern Studies Ctr, Man, 80-81; adj prof, Dept Bot, Univ Man, 80-; vis prof, Nfld Forest Res Ctr, Environ Can, St Johns, 81-82. *Mem:* Ecol Soc Am; Can Bot Asn. *Res:* Seed ecology of Poygonum (smart weed) species; flouride air pollutants and seed production in boreal forest plants; reproduction and survival in Opuntia fragilis; ecology of subarctic estuaries; reproductive biology of white spruce at tree line; seed banks of arctic and subarctic plant communities. *Mailing Add:* Dept Biol Univ Winnipeg 515 Portage Ave Winnipeg MB R3B 2E9 Can. *Fax:* 204-786-1824; *E-Mail:* staniforth@uwpg02.uwinnipeg.ca

STANIFORTH, ROBERT ARTHUR, INORGANIC CHEMISTRY. *Current Pos:* RETIRED. *Personal Data:* b Cleveland, Ohio, Oct 5, 17; m 44; c 3. *Educ:* Case Western Reserve Univ, BA, 39; Ohio State Univ, MS, 42, PhD(inorg chem), 43. *Prof Exp:* Asst chem, Ohio State Univ, 39-43; res chemist, Monsanto Chem Co, Ohio, 44-46, group leader, 47, sect chief, AEC, Mound Lab, 48, res dir, 48-54, mgr chem develop, Inorg Chem Div, 54-59, asst dir develop, 59-62; mgr prod planning, Monsanto Indust Chem Co, 62-69, mgr commun & info, 69-75. *Concurrent Pos:* Res chemist, Gen Aniline & Film Corp, Pa, 43. *Mem:* Am Chem Soc; Electrochem Soc. *Res:* Ultramicrobalances; chelate compounds of the rare earth metals; radiochemistry; metals; semiconductors. *Mailing Add:* 1215 Walnut Hill Farm Dr Chesterfield MO 63005

STANIONIS, VICTOR ADAM, APPLIED MATHEMATICS, SCIENCE EDUCATION. *Current Pos:* Instr math & Physics, Iona Col, 61-66, from asst prof to assoc prof physics, 66-89, chmn dept, 75-82, DIR, SCI & TECHNOL LITERACY PROG & PROF PHYSICS, IONA COL, 90- *Personal Data:* b New York, NY, Dec 24, 38; m 60, Lydia Sobole; c Victor J & Christine A. *Educ:* Iona Col, BS, 60; NY Univ, MS, 64; Queen's Col, MA, 70; Columbia Univ, PhD(math), 75. *Mem:* Am Asn Physics Teachers; Math Asn Am; Nat Asn Sci Technol & Soc. *Res:* Computers in physics teaching; nature of problem solving in physics and mathematics; teaching science to liberal arts and business students using multimedia. *Mailing Add:* Dept Physics Iona Col 715 North Ave New Rochelle NY 10801. *Fax:* 914-633-2240; *E-Mail:* tahionis@cona.edu

STANISLAO, BETTIE CHLOE CARTER, NUTRITION, FOOD SERVICE SYSTEMS. *Personal Data:* b Alexandria, La, June 12, 34; m 60. *Educ:* Northwestern State Univ, La, BS, 56; Pa State Univ, MSc, 60; Case Western Reserve Univ, DPhil, 76. *Prof Exp:* Therapeut dietitian, Baptist Hosp, Alexandria, 56-57; asst hotel & inst admin, Pa State Univ, 57-59; dietetic intern, Barnes Hosp, St Louis, Mo, 59-60; chief therapeut dietitian, Pawtucket Mem Hosp, 61-63; therapeut dietitian, Good Samaritan Hosp, Phoenix, 63-64; nutrit asst, Coop Exten Serv, RI, 64-65; asst prof food & nutrit, Univ RI, 65-71; asst nutrit, Case Western Reserve Univ, 72-73; assoc prof food & nutrit & chairperson dept, NDak State Univ, 76-80, systs analyst & comput supvr, food servs, 84-93. *Concurrent Pos:* Nutrit adv, Child Develop Ctr, Univ RI, 65-71; support serv contract, Food & Nutrit Serv, Nutrit Educ & Training Prog, USDA, 78-80; dietition, Fargo Diabetes Educ Ctr, 80-84; instr, Col Eng & Mgt, NDak State Univ, 88-93. *Mem:* Am Dietetic Asn; Am Home Econ Asn; Soc Nutrit Educ; Am Asn Univ Women; Am Diabetes Asn; Am Asn Diabetes Educrs. *Res:* Food habits of college men; effectiveness of nutrition counseling in changing food habits of pedodontic patients; nutrition in preventive dentistry; nutrition in diabetic care; computer food service systems. *Mailing Add:* 8 Park Plaza Rd Bozeman MT 59715

STANISLAO, JOSEPH, INDUSTRIAL ENGINEERING. *Current Pos:* dean & prof, 75-94, EMER PROF ENG & MGT, COL ENG & ARCHIT, NDAK STATE UNIV, 94- *Personal Data:* b Manchester, Conn, Nov 21, 28; m 60. *Educ:* Tex Tech Col, BS, 57; Pa State Univ, MS, 59; Columbia Univ, DEngSc, 70. *Prof Exp:* Asst prof indust eng, NC State Col, 59-61; dir res & develop, Darlington Fabrics Corp, 61-62, actg plant mgr, 62; from asst prof to assoc prof indust eng, Univ RI, 63-71; prof & chmn dept, Cleveland State Univ, 71-75. *Concurrent Pos:* Res grants, Am Soc Mfg & Tool Eng, US Steel Co & Gen Elec Co, 65-66, Naval Air Syst Command, 68-71; lectr, Indust Eng Dept, Columbia Univ, 66-67; consult, Asian Productivity Orgn, 72. *Mem:* AAAS; sr mem Am Inst Indust Engrs; Am Soc Metals; Am Soc Mech Engrs; Am Soc Eng Educ; Sigma Xi. *Res:* Manufacturing engineering, technical aspects, economic considerations and organizational theory; machinability, instrumentation and nondestructive testing techniques. *Mailing Add:* 8 Park Pl Bozeman MT 59715

STANISZ, ANDRZEJ MACIEJ, NEUROIMMUNOLOGY, IMMUNOPHARMACOLOGY. *Current Pos:* asst prof med, 83-89, ASSOC PROF IMMUNOL & PATH, MCMASTER UNIV, 89- *Personal Data:* b Cracow, Poland, Nov 20, 51; Can citizen; m 78; c 2. *Educ:* Univ Cracow, MS, 74, PhD(immunol), 77; Med Acad Cracow, MD. *Prof Exp:* Asst prof cell biol, Univ Cracow, Poland, 77-79; res assoc immunol, Dept Micro & Immunol, Wash Univ, 79-83. *Mem:* Am Asn Immunologists; NY Acad Sci; Int Soc Immunopharmacol; Int Soc Neuroimmunomodulation (vpres); Soc Mucosal Immunol; Can Asn Gastroenterol. *Res:* Interactions between nervous and immune system in health and gastrointestinal and rheumatic diseases; mucosal immunity. *Mailing Add:* Health Sci Ctr 3N5C McMaster Univ 1200 Main St W Hamilton ON L8N 3Z5 Can. *Fax:* 505-522-3454; *E-Mail:* stanisz@fhs.mcmaster.ca

STANITSKI, CONRAD LEON, CHEMICAL EDUCATION. *Current Pos:* PROF & CHMN, CHEM DEPT, UNIV CENT ARK, 92- *Personal Data:* b Shamokin, Pa, May 3, 39; m 63, Barbara; c Susan B. *Educ:* Bloomsburg State Col, BSEd, 60; State Col Iowa, MA, 64; Univ Conn, PhD(inorg chem), 71. *Honors & Awards:* Gustav Ohauv Award, Creative Col Sci Teaching, 73. *Prof Exp:* Teacher high sch, Pa, 60-63 & Goshen Cent Sch, 64-65; instr chem, Edinboro State Col, 65-67; teaching fel, Univ Conn, 70-71; asst prof, Ga State Univ, 71-75; assoc prof chem, Kennesaw Jr Col, 75-76; from assoc prof to prof chem, Randolph-Macon Col, 76-85, chmn dept, 76-; exec asst, pres, Franklin & Marshall Col, 85-88; vpres acad affairs, Mt Union Col, 88-92. *Concurrent Pos:* W Nelson Gray Distinguished Prof, 83. *Mem:* Am Chem Soc; Sigma Xi; AAAS. *Res:* Solid state hydride synthesis and reaction studies; chemical education. *Mailing Add:* Chem Dept Univ Cent Ark Conway AR 72035

STANKIEWICZ, RAYMOND, INDUSTRIAL ENGINEERING DESIGN, DESIGN ENGINEERING FOR NEW PRODUCTS FOR INJECTION MOLDING. *Current Pos:* IN-HOUSE CONSULT ENGR, US AIR TOOL CO, INC, NY, 91-; CONSULT DESIGNER, NAT MOLDING CORP, 91- *Personal Data:* b Brooklyn, NY, Sept 3, 32; m 55, Ann F Carpenter; c Michael R, Raymond T & Stacy A. *Educ:* Allied Inst Technol, BS, 67; Am Western Univ, MS, 82. *Hon Degrees:* Dr Eng, World Univ, 91. *Honors & Awards:* Republican Presidential Legion of Merit, 86; Gen Elec Innovation Award, 87. *Prof Exp:* Founder, owner, engr & model & pattern maker, Am Eng Model Co, 59-84; prog mgr, tool design mgr & machine shop mgr, Russell Plastics Technol, 84-87; sr develop & tooling engr & qual control mgr, Symbol Technol Inc, 87-88; consult, design & manufacture new prods, Long Island, Manhattan, Conn & NJ, 88-91. *Mem:* Inst Indust Engrs; Soc Plastic Engrs; Soc Mech Engrs; Soc Am Mil Engrs; Soc Mfg Engrs. *Res:* Mold design for injection, compression, rotational, blow, bag, high-temp, etc; pattern making and model making; design of any new product. *Mailing Add:* Accurato Design & Model Co 866 Bohemia Pkwy Bohemia NY 11716. *Fax:* 516-589-5261

STANKO, JOSEPH ANTHONY, INORGANIC CHEMISTRY. *Current Pos:* ASSOC PROF CHEM, UNIV S FLA, TAMPA, 73- *Personal Data:* b Wilkes-Barre, Pa, July 2, 41; m 62; c 3. *Educ:* King's Col, BS, 62; Univ Ill, PhD(inorg chem), 66. *Prof Exp:* Asst prof chem, Pa State Univ, 66-73. *Mem:* Am Chem Soc; The Chem Soc; Am Crystallog Asn. *Res:* X-ray crystallography; chemistry of platinum anti-cancer drugs; synthesis of 1-dimensional conductors. *Mailing Add:* Dept Chem Sca 228 Univ SFla 4202 Fowler Ave Tampa FL 33620-9951

STANKOVIC, JOHN A, COMPUTER SCIENCE. *Current Pos:* B P AM PROF & CHMN, DEPT COMPUT SCI, UNIV VA, 97- *Personal Data:* b Brooklyn, NY, Sept 15, 48. *Educ:* Brown Univ, ScB, 70, ScM, 76, PhD(comput sci), 79. *Honors & Awards:* Meritorious Serv Award, Inst Elec & Electronics Engrs, 91. *Prof Exp:* Software engr, Western Elec Co, 70-74; from asst prof to assoc prof, Dept Elec & Comput Eng, Univ Mass, Amherst, 79-86, assoc prof, Dept Comput Sci, 86-90, prof, 90-96, dir, Ctr Autonomous Real-Time Systs, 91-96. *Concurrent Pos:* Invited speaker, Univ Distinguished Lectr Series, Univ Mich, Navat Postgrad Sch, Northeastern Tex A & M & Triangel CS Distinguished Lectr Series, Duke, NC & NC State; vis res scientist, Comput Scis Corp, 80, INRIA, France, 82; distinguished vis, Inst Elec & Electronics Engrs Comput Soc, 85-88; vis prof, Comput Sci Dept, Carnegie-Mellon Univ, 85-86, Scuola Super Studi Univ Santa Anna, Pica Italy, 92-93, Consiglio Nazionale delle Ricerche, Inst di Elaborazione dell'Info, Pisa, Italy, 92; ed, Inst Elec & Electronics Engrs Trans Comput, 86-90; co-ed-in-chief & co-founder, Int J Real Time Systs; dirs & exec comt, Appl Comput Inst Mass, 92-96; assoc ed, Inst Elec & Electronics Engrs Trans Parallel & Distrib Systs, 93-; bd dirs, Comput Res Asn, 96- *Mem:* Fel Asn Comput Mach; fel Inst Elec & Electronics Engrs; Sigma Xi. *Mailing Add:* PO Box 3 Ivy VA 22945

STANKOVICH, MARIAN THERESA, ELECTROCHEMISTRY, BIOCHEMISTRY. *Current Pos:* MEM FAC, CHEM DEPT, UNIV MINN, 80- *Personal Data:* b Houston, Tex, Nov 14, 47. *Educ:* Univ St Thomas, Tex, BA, 70; Univ Tex, Austin, PhD(analytical chem), 75. *Prof Exp:* Scholar biochem, Univ Mich, 75-77; asst prof analytical chem, Univ Mass, Amherst, 77-80. *Concurrent Pos:* Fac res grant, Univ Mass, 77-78; Cottrell Corp res grant, 78-79. *Mem:* Am Chem Soc; Electrochem Soc. *Res:* Spectral and electrochemical study of electron transfer in flavoproteins, riboflavin, and flavin analogs; parameters studied are redox potentials; number of electrons transferred in a reaction; kinetics of electron transfer. *Mailing Add:* 207 Pleasant St SE Chem Dept Univ Minn Minneapolis MN 55455-0431

STANLEY, DANIEL JEAN, GEO-ARCHAEOLOGY, ENVIRONMENTAL SCIENCE. *Current Pos:* assoc cur sedimentol, Smithsonian Inst, 66-68, supvr div, 68-71, cur sedimentol, 68-71, geol oceanogr, 71-79, SR SCIENTIST, SMITHSONIAN INST, 79- *Personal Data:* b Metz, France, Apr 14, 34; US citizen; m 60, Adrienne N; c Marc, Eric, Natalie, Brian & Susan. *Educ:* Cornell Univ, BSc, 56; Brown Univ, MSc, 58; Univ Grenoble, DSc, 61. *Honors & Awards:* Medaille, Alpes Maritimes, France, 76; Francis Shepard Medal Excellence Marine Geol, 90. *Prof Exp:* Res geologist, French Petrol Inst, 58-61; geologist, Pan-Am Petrol Corp, 61-62; asst to dir geol, US Army Engrs Waterways Exp Sta, 62-63; asst prof sedimentol, Univ Ottawa, 63-64; asst prof marine geol, Dalhousie Univ, 64-66; hon prof, EChina Univ, 95. *Concurrent Pos:* Postdoctoral fel, Woods Hole Oceanog Inst, 63; founder & ed, Maritime Sediments J, 64-66; Nat Res Coun Can travel award, USSR, 66; Nat Acad Sci exchange award, Poland, 67 & Romania, 76; adj prof, Univ Maine, Orono, 74-84, Nat Sch; Petrol, France, 78-84, Univ Quebec, 90; adv, Int Court Justice, Hague, 81; dir, Global Change prog. *Mem:* Fel AAAS; fel Geol Soc Am; Soc Econ Paleontologists & Mineralogists; Am Mineralogists; Am Asn Petrol Geologists; corresp mem Geol Soc Belg; Sigma Xi. *Res:* Sedimentology, marine geology and geo-archaeology, Mediteranean; directs multi-national studies of Nile delta of Egypt and other modern world deltas; author or co-editior of 8 books and over 250 articles in scientific journals. *Mailing Add:* Div Sedimentol E-206 NMNH Smithsonian Inst Washington DC 20560. *Fax:* 202-786-2832; *E-Mail:* stanley.daniel@nmnh.si.edu

STANLEY, DAVID WARWICK, FOOD SCIENCE. *Current Pos:* from asst prof to assoc prof, 70-79, PROF FOOD SCI, UNIV GUELPH, 79- *Personal Data:* b Muncie, Ind, Oct 12, 39. *Educ:* Univ Fla, BS, 62, MS, 63; Univ Mass, PhD(food sci), 67. *Honors & Awards:* Eva Award, Can Inst Food Sci & Technol, 92. *Prof Exp:* Res fel, Smith Col, 67-68; asst prof food sci, Univ Toronto, 68-70. *Concurrent Pos:* Ed, Can Inst Food Sci & Tech Jour, 76-82. *Mem:* Fel Inst Food Technol; fel Can Inst Food Sci & Technol. *Res:* Animal protein systems including meat texture and muscle protein biochemistry; cell membranes including structure and function; plant protein systems including food uses of plant proteins; food analysis; postharvest physiology of fruits and vegetables; food microstructure. *Mailing Add:* Dept Food Sci Univ Guelph Guelph ON N1G 2W1 Can

STANLEY, EDWARD ALEXANDER, forensic science, palynology, for more information see previous edition

STANLEY, EDWARD LIVINGSTON, CHEMISTRY. *Current Pos:* CONSULT, 76- *Personal Data:* b Orange, NJ, Sept 6, 19; m 43; c 2. *Educ:* Princeton Univ, AB, 40, MA, 43, PhD(chem), 47. *Prof Exp:* Asst, Princeton Univ, 40-41, res assoc analytical chem, Off Sci Res & Develop & Manhattan Dist Proj, 41-43; supvr, Analytical Lab, Rohm & Haas Co, 43-50, lab head, Res Div, 50-57, foreign area supvr, 57-76. *Mem:* AAAS; Am Chem Soc; Sigma Xi. *Res:* Analytical chemistry; facility is mass-burning, generating electricity. *Mailing Add:* 124 Plymouth Rd Gwynedd Valley PA 19437

STANLEY, EVAN RICHARD, CELL BIOLOGY, MEDICAL RESEARCH. *Current Pos:* from asst prof to prof, Depts Microbiol, Immunol & Cell Biol, 76-87, PROF & CHMN, DEPT DEVELOP & MOLECULAR BIOL, ALBERT EINSTEIN COL MED, 87- *Personal Data:* b Sydney, Australia, 1944; m 70, Pamela M Fetherstonhaugh; c Damian A & Robert F. *Educ:* Univ Western Australia, BSc, 67; Univ Melbourne, PhD(med biol), 70. *Honors & Awards:* Res Award, Soc Leukocyte Biol. *Prof Exp:* Fel med biol, Walter & Eliza Hall Inst Med Res, Melbourne, Australia, 70-72; lectr cell biol, Dept Med Biophys, Univ Toronto, 72-73; asst prof, 73-76. *Concurrent Pos:* Mem sr sci staff, Ont Cancer Inst, 72-76; mem, Study Sect Hemat, NIH. *Mem:* Am Soc Hemat; Soc Develop Biol; Harvey Soc; AAAS; Am Soc Microbiol. *Res:* Biochemical and genetic studies on growth factor biology and signal transduction id Drosophilia and mammals. *Mailing Add:* 380 Riverside Dr No 1H New York NY 10025. *E-Mail:* rstanley@aecom.yu.edu

STANLEY, GEORGE DABNEY, JR, INVERTEBRATE PALEONTOLOGY, TAXONOMY, PALEOECOLOGY OF MODERN & ANCIENT CORALS & REEF EVOLUTION. *Current Pos:* PROF PALEONT, DEPT GEOL, UNIV MONT, 82- *Educ:* Univ Tenn, BA, 70; Univ Kans, PhD(paleont), 77. *Honors & Awards:* Burlington Northern Achievement Award, 88. *Prof Exp:* Lectr geol, Univ Calif, Davis, 77-78; geologist & res assoc, Natural Hist Mus, Smithsonian Inst, 78-81; sr prof, Fulbright, Univ Erlangen, Ger, 81-82. *Concurrent Pos:* Fel, Orgn Trop Studies, 74; prin investr, NSF, 82-; hon res assoc, Smithsonian Inst, 86-; exchange fel, Univ Kumamoto, Japan, Univ Mont, 92-93; distinguished lectr, Paleont Soc, 93-94. *Mem:* Soc Sedimentary Geol; Paleont Soc; Int Soc Reef Studies; Geol Soc Am; Paleont Asn Gt Brit; Sigma Xi. *Res:* Study of living and fossil coral reefs and taxonomy of corals, especially of early Mesozoic age; evolution of corals and reef building fossils; paleobiogeographic distributions of fossil organisms, fossils and plate tectonic history. *Mailing Add:* Dept Geol Univ Mont Missoula MT 59812. *Fax:* 406-243-4028; *E-Mail:* fossil@selway.umt.edu

STANLEY, GEORGE GEOFFREY, HOMOGENEOUS CATALYSIS. *Current Pos:* from asst prof to assoc prof, 86-95, PROF, LA STATE UNIV, 95- *Personal Data:* b Palmerton, Pa, May 2, 53; m 85, Eileen Horn; c Edward & Eric. *Educ:* Univ Rochester, BS, 75; Tex A&M Univ, PhD(chem), 79. *Prof Exp:* Fel, Univ Louis Pasteur, France, 79-81; asst prof inorg, Washington Univ, St Louis, 81-86. *Concurrent Pos:* Fel, NATO, 79 & Nat Ctr Sci Res, France, 80. *Mem:* Am Chem Soc; AAAS; Sigma Xi. *Res:* Synthesis, structure and reactivity of bi-and poly-metallic transition metal compounds with particular emphasis on hydroformylation and carbonulation catalysis; organophospmine synthetic chemistry. *Mailing Add:* Dept Chem La State Univ Baton Rouge LA 70803-1804. *Fax:* 504-388-3458; *E-Mail:* george.stanley@chemgate.chem.lsu.edu

STANLEY, GEORGE M, HISTORY OF GREAT LAKES, DEATH VALLEY NAT PARK. *Current Pos:* RETIRED. *Personal Data:* b Detroit, Mich, Mar 15, 05. *Educ:* Univ Mich, BS, 28, MS, 32 & PhD(geol), 36. *Prof Exp:* Prof geol, Univ Mich, 32-48; prof geol, Univ Calif, Fresno, 48-67. *Mem:* Geol Soc Am; Sigma Xi. *Mailing Add:* 7321 Mesa Dr Aptos CA 95003-3311

STANLEY, GERALD R, POWER ELECTRONICS SIMULATION,TEF ANALYSIS. *Current Pos:* prin engr, 66-78, MGR RES & RESOURCES, CROWN INT INC, 78- *Personal Data:* b Niles, Mich, Nov 14, 43; m 66, Ellen G Cook; c Gerald R & Mark A. *Educ:* Mich State Univ, BS, 65; Univ Mich, MS, 66. *Mem:* Inst Elec & Electronics Engrs; Acoust Soc Am; Asn Comput Mach; Audio Eng Soc. *Res:* Developed and designed first commercially successful solid- state audio amplifier, the Crown DC300; and the first commercial TDS analyzer; designer of most commonly used gradient amplifiers for magnetic resonance imaging; granted 20 patents. *Mailing Add:* 59766 Beech Rd Osceola IN 46561. *Fax:* 219-294-8329; *E-Mail:* gstanley@crownintl.com

STANLEY, H(ARRY) EUGENE, STATISTICAL MECHANICS, BIOLOGICAL PHYSICS. *Current Pos:* PROF PHYSICS, BOSTON UNIV, 76-, PROF PHYSIOL, SCH MED & DIR, CTR POLYMER STUDIES, 78-, UNIV PROF, 79- *Personal Data:* b Norman, Okla, Mar 28, 41; m 67; c 3. *Educ:* Wesleyan Univ, BA, 62; Harvard Univ, PhD(physics), 67. *Hon Degrees:* PhD, Bar-Ilan Univ, Israel, 94. *Honors & Awards:* Joliot-Curie Medal, 79. *Prof Exp:* Staff mem solid state theory group, Lincoln Lab, Mass Inst Technol, 67-68; fel physics, Miller Inst Basic Res Sci, Univ Calif, Berkeley, 68-69; from asst prof physics to assoc prof, Mass Inst Technol, 71-76, Hermann von Helmholtz assoc prof health sci & technol, 73-76. *Concurrent Pos:* NSF fel theoret physics, 62-66; consult, Lincoln Lab, Mass Inst Technol, 69-71; vis prof physics, Osaka Univ, 75, Univ Toronto, 77, Sch Physics & Chem, 79 & Peking Normal Univ & Nanking Univ, 81; John Simon Guggenheim Mem fel, 79-81; consult, Sclumberge, 82-83 & Sandia Labs, 84-92. *Mem:* AAAS; fel Am Phys Soc. *Res:* Phase transitions and critical phenomena; biomedical physics; polymer physics; physics of random media; percolation; liquid state physics; cooperative functioning of polymers and other systems with no underlying lattice; fractals in biology and medicine. *Mailing Add:* Dept Physics Boston Univ 590 Commonwealth Ave Boston MA 02215. *Fax:* 617-353-3783; *E-Mail:* hes@bu.edu

STANLEY, HAROLD RUSSELL, ORAL PATHOLOGY. *Current Pos:* PROF PATH, UNIV FLA, 81-, CHMN DEPT ORAL MED, 70- *Personal Data:* b Salem, Mass, June 26, 23; m 46; c 3. *Educ:* Univ Md, DDS, 48; Am Univ, BS, 52; Georgetown Univ, MS, 53; Am Bd Oral Path, dipl, 57. *Honors & Awards:* Sci Award, Int Asn Dent Res, 78. *Prof Exp:* Intern, Marine Hosp, USPHS, Baltimore, Md, 48-49; resident oral path, Armed Forces Inst Path, 51-53; mem staff, Nat Inst Dent Res, 53-66, clin dir, 66-68. *Concurrent Pos:* Hon prof, San Carlos, Univ Guatemala, 60- *Mem:* Hon fel Am Asn Endodont; Int Asn Dent Res; Am Dent Asn; Am Acad Oral Path (pres, 67). *Res:* Diseases of the human dental pulp; periodontium; oral mucous membranes. *Mailing Add:* 2 Sea Oats Terr Ormond Beach FL 32176

STANLEY, HUGH P, ELECTRON MICROSCOPY, CELL BIOLOGY. *Current Pos:* from asst prof to assoc prof zool, 66-76, prof biol, 76-87, EMER PROF BIOL, UTAH STATE UNIV, 87- *Personal Data:* b Modesto, Calif, July 14, 26; m 59; c 2. *Educ:* Univ Calif, Berkeley, BA, 51; Ore State Univ, MA, 58, PhD(zool), 61. *Prof Exp:* NIH fel zool, Zool Sta, Naples, Italy, 61-63 & Cornell Univ, 63 & sr fel biol struct, Univ Wash, 63-65; asst prof anat, Univ Minn, 65-66. *Mem:* AAAS; Am Soc Zool. *Res:* Ultrastructure of developing cell systems, especially vertebrate spermatid differentiation. *Mailing Add:* 3310 D Bailer Hill Rd Friday Harbor WA 98250

STANLEY, JON G, AQUACULTURE. *Current Pos:* RETIRED. *Personal Data:* b Edinburg, Tex, Oct 28, 37; m 65, Carol L Heidebrecht; c 3. *Educ:* Univ Mo, AB, 60, BS, 63, PhD(zool), 66. *Prof Exp:* Asst prof biol, DePaul Univ, 66-69; from asst prof to assoc prof, Univ Wis-Milwaukee, 69-72; fisheries biologist & leader, Maine Coop Fishery Res Unit, Univ Maine, Orono, 72-83; supvr fisheries biologist, Coop Res Units, US Dept Interior Fish & Wildlife Servs, 83-85; ctr dir, US Fish & Wildlife Serv, Nat Fisheries Res Ctr, Great Lakes, 85-95. *Concurrent Pos:* Nat Acad Sci exchange scholar, Czech. *Mem:* Am Fisheries Soc. *Res:* Polyploidy and genetics in aquaculture; biology of Chinese fishes such as Grass Carp; gynogenesis and breeding of freshwater fish; environmental effects of pesticides on fishes. *Mailing Add:* 7500 W Mississippi Ave, Suite D-2 Denver CO 80226. *E-Mail:* stankyjon@aol.com

STANLEY, KENNETH EARL, BIOSTATISTICS. *Current Pos:* BIOSTATISTICIAN, SIDNEY FARBER CANCER CTR INST, 77-; ASST PROF BIOSTATIST, HARVARD UNIV, 77- *Personal Data:* b Auburn, NY, Nov 7, 47; m 71; c 2. *Educ:* Alfred Univ, BA, 69; Bucknell Univ, MA, 70; Univ Fla, PhD(statist), 74. *Prof Exp:* Res asst prof statist, State Univ Ny, Buffalo, 75-77. *Concurrent Pos:* Statistician, Ludwig Lung Cancer Study Group, 77-; coord statistician, Eastern Coop Oncol Group, 78-80; mem expert adv panel cancer, WHO, consult, 81-; co-dir, Collaborating Ctr Cancer Biostatistics Eval, Harvard Sch Pub Health, WHO. *Mem:* Am Statist Asn; Biomet Soc; Soc Clin Trials; Int Asn Study Lung Cancer. *Res:* Clinical trials in cancer. *Mailing Add:* 16 Sherwood Rd Nattock MA 01760

STANLEY, LUTICIOUS BRYAN, JR, TECHNICAL MANAGEMENT, REGIONAL PROJECT ADMINISTRATION. *Current Pos:* PRIN, L B S ENTERPRISES, 89- *Personal Data:* b Atlanta, Ga. *Educ:* Southern Tech Inst, BCET, 74, BMET, 82; Ga State Univ, MS, 86. *Prof Exp:* Field engr civil eng, Jordan Jones & Goulding, Inc, 74-79; proj engr, Mayes, Sudderth & Etheredge, Inc, 79-82; asst regional proj mgr, Westinghouse Elec Corp, 82-88. *Mem:* Am Soc Mech Engrs. *Res:* Improvement of the operation of turbines at nuclear power plants. *Mailing Add:* Pebble Brook Shores Rd Gainesville GA 30506

STANLEY, MALCOLM MCCLAIN, medicine, for more information see previous edition

STANLEY, MELISSA SUE MILLAM, MEDICAL TECHNOLOGY. *Current Pos:* from asst prof to assoc prof biol, 67-74, prog coordr, 68-69, PROF BIOL, GEORGE MASON UNIV, 74- *Personal Data:* b South Bend, Wash, June 23, 31; div. *Educ:* Univ Ore, BS, 53, MA, 59; Univ Utah, PhD(zool, entom), 65. *Prof Exp:* Med technologist, Hosps & Labs, 53-57; teaching asst biol, Univ Ore, 57-58; med technologist, Hosps & Labs, 58-59; instr, Westminster Col, Utah, 59-61, asst prof, 61-63, actg chmn dept 59-60, chmn dept, 60-63; res assoc, Pioneering Lab Insect Path, USDA, 65-67. *Mailing Add:* Dept Biol George Mason Univ Fairfax VA 22030. *Fax:* 703-993-1046; *E-Mail:* mstanle1@osf1.gmu.edu

STANLEY, NORMAN FRANCIS, CHEMISTRY. *Current Pos:* RETIRED. *Personal Data:* b Rockland, Maine, May 6, 16; m 63, Eleanor Payson; c Susan & Craig. *Prof Exp:* Res chemist, Algin Corp Am, 40-53, res dir, 53-59; asst tech dir, Marine Colloids, Inc, 59-64, res chemist, 64-75; sr scientist, Marine Colloids Div, FMC Corp, 74-85. *Mem:* AAAS; Am Chem Soc; Soc Rheol; Am Inst Aeronaut & Astronaut. *Res:* Polysaccharide chemistry; chemistry and technology of marine algae, algal products and watersoluble gums; design and analysis of experiments. *Mailing Add:* PO Box 723 Rockland ME 04841

STANLEY, PAMELA MARY, CARBOHYDRATE STRUCTURES, SOMATIC CELL GENETICS. *Current Pos:* from asst prof to assoc prof, 77-86, PROF CELL BIOLOGY, ALBERT EINSTEIN COL MED, NY, 86- *Personal Data:* b Melbourne, Australia, Mar 25, 47; m 70; c 2. *Educ:* Univ Melbourne, BSc Hons, 68, PhD(virol), 72. *Prof Exp:* Fel somatic cell, Univ Toronto, Int, 72-75, res assoc, 75-77. *Concurrent Pos:* Mem grant rev panel, Am Cancer Soc & Palhobiochem study sect, NIH. *Mem:* Am Soc Biol Chemists; Int Asn Women Biochemists. *Res:* Generation of animal cell mutants which express altered carbohydrates at the cell surface to isolate genes coding for glycosylation enzymes, to delineate glycosylation pathways and to study structure; function relationships of cell surface carbohydrates; glycosyltransferase genes; molecular genetics. *Mailing Add:* Dept Cell Biol Albert Einstein Col Med 1300 Morris Park Ave Bronx NY 10461-1975. Fax: 212-829-7619; *E-Mail:* stanley@aecom.yu.edu

STANLEY, PATRICIA MARY, MICROBIOLOGY, MICROBIAL ECOLOGY. *Current Pos:* prin microbiologist, 79-86, SCIENTIST, ECOLAB, INC, 86- *Personal Data:* b Oneonta, NY, Mar 28, 48; m 77. *Educ:* Cornell Univ, BS, 70; Univ Wash, MS, 72, PhD(microbiol), 75. *Prof Exp:* Res specialist, Dept Microbiol, Univ Minn, 76-79. *Mem:* Am Soc Microbiol; Soc Indust Microbiol; Am Soc Testing & Mat. *Res:* In situ metabolism of nitrifying and heterotrophic bacteria; biology of nitrifying bacteria; use of fluorescent antibody staining in microbial ecology; bacterial adhesion to surfaces; antimicrobial activity of biocides and disinfectants; industrial enzymology. *Mailing Add:* 4741 Hauge Circle St Paul MN 55122

STANLEY, RICHARD PETER, ALGEBRAIC COMBINATORICS, ENUMERATIVE COMBINATORICS. *Current Pos:* Moore instr, 70-71, from asst prof to assoc prof, 73-79, PROF APPL MATH, MASS INST TECHNOL, 79- *Personal Data:* b New York, NY, June 23, 44; m 71; c 2. *Educ:* Calif Inst Technol, BS, 66; Harvard Univ, PhD(math), 71. *Honors & Awards:* Polya Prize, Soc Indust & Appl Math, 75. *Prof Exp:* Miller fel math, Miller Inst Basic Res Sci, 71-73. *Concurrent Pos:* Res scientist & consult, Jet Propulsion Lab, 65-72; consult, Bell Tel Labs, 73-; Guggenheim, fel, 83-84. *Mem:* Nat Acad Sci; Math Asn Am; fel Am Acad Arts & Sci; Am Math Soc. *Res:* Development of a unified foundation to combinatorial theory; interactions between algebra and combinatorics. *Mailing Add:* Dept Math Mass Inst Technol Cambridge MA 02139-4307

STANLEY, RICHARD W, nutrition, biochemistry; deceased, see previous edition for last biography

STANLEY, ROBERT LAUREN, MATHEMATICS. *Current Pos:* assoc prof, 61-66, PROF MATH, PORTLAND STATE UNIV, 66- & HEAD DEPT MATH, 78- *Personal Data:* b Seattle, Wash, Dec 30, 21; m 47; c 2. *Educ:* Univ Wash, BS, 43, MA, 47; Harvard Univ, PhD, 51. *Prof Exp:* Guest lectr philos, Univ BC, 51-52, guest lectr math, 52-54; guest lectr, Univ SDak, 54-57; asst prof, Wash State Univ, 57-61. *Mem:* Am Math Soc; Asn Symbolic Logic; Math Asn Am. *Res:* Mathematical logic and foundations; logical analysis in philosophy of science. *Mailing Add:* Dept Math 3931 SW Idaho Terr Portland OR 97221-3355

STANLEY, ROBERT LEE, JR, AGRONOMY. *Current Pos:* Asst prof, 68-74, ASSOC PROF AGRON, UNIV FLA, 74- *Personal Data:* b Dodge Co, Ga, Mar 7, 40; m 68, Ruth Bowen; c Robert L III & Clayton G. *Educ:* Univ Ga, BSA, 63, PhD(agron), 69; Clemson Univ MSA, 64. *Mem:* Am Soc Agron; Crop Sci Soc Am; Soc Range Mgt. *Res:* Forage crops management and utilization. *Mailing Add:* North Fla Res Educ Ctr Rt 3 Box 4370 Quincy FL 32351-9529

STANLEY, ROLFE S, GEOLOGY. *Current Pos:* from asst prof to assoc prof, 64-72, instnl res grant, 64-66, chmn dept, 64-78, PROF GEOL, UNIV VT, 72- *Personal Data:* b Brooklyn, NY, Nov 4, 31; m 52; c 4. *Educ:* Williams Col, BA, 54; Yale Univ, MS, 55, PhD(geol), 62. *Prof Exp:* Geologist, Shell Oil Co, 57-59; NSF fel & lectr geol, Yale Univ, 62-64. *Concurrent Pos:* Res assoc, Ctr Technophysics, Tex A&M Univ, 71 & 72; prin investr, Northern Vt Serpentinite belt; res grant, Nat Res Coun, Repub China. *Mem:* Fel Geol Soc Am. *Res:* Structural geology; structural petrology; regional geology of western New England; compilation of the geological map of Massachusetts; metamorphic core of the central mountains of Taiwan. *Mailing Add:* Buck Hollow Rd Fairfax VT 05454

STANLEY, RONALD ALWIN, WETLANDS ECO-PHYSIOLOGY, ECOSYSTEM RESTORATION. *Current Pos:* BIOL FAC MEM, FROSTBURG STATE UNIV, 96- *Personal Data:* b Edinburg, Tex, June 18, 39; m 92, Mary Miller; c Ronald Jr, Cathy, David & Angela. *Educ:* Univ Ark, BS, 61, MS, 63; Duke Univ, PhD(plant physiol), 70; Univ Southern Calif, MPA, 81. *Prof Exp:* Botanist, Tenn Valley Authority, 64-75; asst prof biol, Univ SDak, Springfield, 75 & Univ Memphis, 75; plant physiologist, Environ Protection Agency, 76-94, policy analyst, 94-96. *Concurrent Pos:* Consult, WHO, 86-87; consult, AID, 89-91; prin/mgr, Blackberry Hills Farm, 92-; bd dir, Am Chestnut Found, 96- *Mem:* Ecol Soc of Am; Soc Wetland Scientists; Am Chestnut Found. *Res:* Synergistic interactions of chemical, physical and biological factors in the environment with aquatic macrophytes; adaptation to the aquatic environment; assessment of risk from toxic substances; wetlands restoration; restoration of trees to degraded habitat. *Mailing Add:* Rte 1 Box Clearville PA 15535

STANLEY, S J, CIVIL ENGINEERING. *Current Pos:* PROF CIVIL ENG, UNIV ALTA. *Honors & Awards:* T C Keefer Medal, Can Soc Civil Eng, 92. *Mailing Add:* Dept Civil Eng Univ Alta Edmonton AB T6G 2G7 Can

STANLEY, STEVEN MITCHELL, GEOBIOLOGY, MACROEVOLUTION. *Current Pos:* from asst prof to assoc prof, 69-74, PROF PALEOBIOL, JOHNS HOPKINS UNIV, 74- *Personal Data:* b Detroit, Mich, Nov 2, 41; m 69, Nell W Gilmore; c Svetlana. *Educ:* Princeton Univ, AB, 63; Yale Univ, PhD(geol), 68. *Honors & Awards:* Charles Schuchert Award, Paleont Soc, 77. *Prof Exp:* Asst prof paleont, Univ Rochester, 67-69. *Concurrent Pos:* Res assoc, Smithsonion Inst, 72-; Guggenheim fel, 80; bd earth sci, Nat Res Coun, 85-88, bd earth scis & resources, 88-90, comn geosci, environ & resources, 90-96. *Mem:* Nat Acad Sci; Geol Soc Am; Soc Study Evolution; Am Acad Arts & Sci; Paleont Res Assoc; Paleont Soc (pres 93-94). *Res:* Rates and patterns of evolution and extinction; geobiology and the history of ecosystems; functional morphology; paleoclimatology marine ecology and paleoecology; paleoceanography. *Mailing Add:* Dept Earth & Planetary Sci Johns Hopkins Univ 34th & Charles St Baltimore MD 21218. Fax: 410-516-7933; *E-Mail:* stanley@gibbs.eps.jhu.edu

STANLEY, THEODORE H, ANESTHESIOLOGY. *Current Pos:* PROF ANESTHESIOL, COL MED, UNIV UTAH, 79- *Personal Data:* b New York, NY, Feb 4, 40. *Educ:* Columbia Univ, MD, 65. *Mailing Add:* Dept Anesthesiol & Surg Univ Utah 50 N Medical Dr Salt Lake City UT 84132-1001

STANLEY, THOMAS P, ENGINEERING. *Current Pos:* chief scientist, 81-86, CHIEF ENGR OFF ENG & TECH, FED COMMUN COMN, WASHINGTON, 86- *Educ:* Johns Hopkins Univ, BSEE; Princeton Univ, MA & PhD. *Concurrent Pos:* Staff mem, Bell Tel Labs, US Army Singal Corps, Inst Defense Analysis. *Mailing Add:* FCC Sci & Tech 1919 M St NW Rm 7002 Washington DC 20554

STANLEY, WENDELL MEREDITH, JR, MOLECULAR BIOLOGY, BIOCHEMISTRY. *Current Pos:* asst prof, 67-70, ASSOC PROF BIOCHEM, UNIV CALIF, IRVINE-CALIF COL MED, 70- *Personal Data:* b New York, NY, Nov 9, 32; m 58; c 3. *Educ:* Univ Calif, Berkeley, AB, 57; Univ Wis-Madison, MS, 59, PhD(biochem), 63. *Prof Exp:* From instr to asst prof biochem, Sch Med, NY Univ, 65-67. *Concurrent Pos:* USPHS grant, Sch Med, NY Univ, 63-65; assoc dean, Undergrad Affairs, Sch Biol Sci, Univ Calif, Irvine, 80. *Mem:* AAAS; Am Soc Biol Chem. *Res:* Control of protein biosynthesis in eukaryotes. *Mailing Add:* Dept Molecular Biol & Biochem Univ Calif Irvine CA 92717-0001

STANLEY, WILLIAM DANIEL, ELECTRICAL ENGINEERING TECHNOLOGY. *Current Pos:* assoc prof, Old Dominion Univ, 66-72, chmn, Dept Eng Technol, 70-74, dir, Div Eng Technol, 74-76, grad prog dir, Dept Elec Eng, 76-79, chmn, Dept Elec Eng Technol, 79-90, PROF, OLD DOMINION UNIV, 72-, EMINENT PROF, 85-, CHMN, DEPT ENG TECHNOL, 91- *Personal Data:* b Bladenboro, NC, June 13, 37; m 62; c Karen. *Educ:* Univ SC, BS, 60; NC State Univ, MS, 62, PhD(elec eng), 63. *Prof Exp:* Develop engr, Electro-Mech Res, Inc, 63; asst prof elec eng, Clemson Univ, 64-66. *Concurrent Pos:* Consult, NASA, 67-69. *Mem:* Inst Elec & Electronics Engrs; Am Soc Elec Engrs. *Res:* Communications systems analysis and design; network synthesis; radiometer measurements. *Mailing Add:* Dept Eng Tech Old Dom Univ Col Eng & Tech Norfolk VA 23529

STANLEY, WILLIAM LYONS, ORGANIC CHEMISTRY. *Current Pos:* chief res chemist, Fruit & Veg Processing Lab, Western Regional Lab, 70-76, EMER CONSULT COLLABR, SCI & EDUC ADMIN-AGR RES, 76- *Personal Data:* b Teh Chou, China, May 30, 16; US citizen; m 41; c 3. *Educ:* Marietta Col, AB, 39; Univ Calif, PhD(chem), 48. *Prof Exp:* Chemist & asst group leader, Carbide & Carbon Chem Corp, WVa, 39-45; res chemist, Western Regional Res Lab, USDA, 48-51 & Res & Develop Ctr, Union Oil Co, 51-54; prin chemist, Fruit & Veg Chem Lab, USDA, 54-60, chief fruit lab, Western Utilization Res & Develop Div, Agr Res Serv, Calif, 60-68; UN develop prog citrus res technologist, Food Inst, Centre Indust Res, Haifa, Israel, 68-69. *Concurrent Pos:* Mem comt fruit & veg prod, Adv Bd Mil Personnel Supplies, Nat Res Coun-Nat Acad Sci; consult, Almond Bd Calif & Dried Fruit Asn, Calif. *Mem:* Fel Am Chem Soc; Phytochem Soc NAm. *Res:* Synthetic organic chemistry; petrochemicals; chemistry of natural products; flavor components of citrus fruits; immobilized enzymes in food processing. *Mailing Add:* 8545 Carmel Valley Rd Carmel CA 93923-9556

STANNARD, CARL R, JR, IN-SERVICE EDUCATION, WRITING MATERIALS AT VARIOUS LEVELS. *Current Pos:* Asst prof, 64-70, ASSOC PROF PHYSICS, STATE UNIV NY, BINGHAMTON, 70- *Personal Data:* b Syracuse, NY, July 24, 35; m 67, L Gay Hickox; c Kent G & Ross M. *Educ:* Syracuse Univ, BS, 56, PhD(physics), 64; Cornell Univ, MS, 60. *Concurrent Pos:* IBM prin investr, State Univ NY, Binghamton, 67-69, dir undergrad physics prog, 70-78, proj dir, Physics Technol Ctr, 71- 75, chair physics dept, 78-81; dir, Southern Tier Educators (K-12) Prog Understanding Physics (STEP UP), NY State Dept Educ, 88- *Mem:* Am Phys Soc; Sigma Xi; Am Asn Physics Teachers; Nat Sci Teachers Asn. *Res:* Pedagogy of physics: improvement of methods and structures to provide education physics to a broader population: at K-12 levels: increased awareness utility of principles of physics among teachers and students; encourage of interest in physics engineering technology among women, mi disabled, etc; at college level: courses in practical physics lit non-science students; inservice training for K-12 teachers to become more knowledgeable in science and help them make s exciting for their students, especially those underrepresent *Mailing Add:* Dept Physics State Univ NY PO Box 6016 F 13902-6016. Fax: 607-777-2546; *E-Mail:* stannard@bingb

STANNARD, J NEWELL, TOXICOLOGY, HF RADIOBIOLOGY. *Current Pos:* asst & instr physic Rochester, 35-39, asst dir educ, Atomic Er Radioactive Inhalation Sect, 52-59, assoc dir e studies, Med Sch, 59-75, EMER PROF RADIATIC

PHARMACOL & TOXICOL, SCH MED & DENT, UNIV ROCHESTER; ADJ PROF COMMUNITY MED & RADIOL, UNIV CALIF, SAN DIEGO, 78- *Personal Data:* b Owego, NY, Jan 2, 10; m, Helena Woodhouse; c Susan S (Frazier). *Educ:* Oberlin Col, BA, 31; Harvard Univ, MA, 34, PhD(gen physiol & biophys), 35. *Honors & Awards:* Distinguished Achievement Award, Health Physics Soc, 77; Parker Lectr, Battelle Pac Northwest Labs, 88; Taylor Lectr, Nat Coun Radiation Protection & Measurements, 90; Stannard Lect Ser, Health Physics Soc. *Prof Exp:* Asst prof pharmacol, Emory Univ Med Sch, 39-41; pharmacologist, USPHS, NIH, Bethesda, Md, 41-44, sr pharmacologist, 46-47; naval officer, Res Div, Bur Med & Surg, Navy Dept, Wash, DC, 44-46. *Concurrent Pos:* Consult, health physics, radiation protection, radiation biol & toxicol, several orgn; mem, Radiation Exposure Adv Comt, US Environ Protection Agency, Nat Res Coun Ocean Affairs Bd-Workshop Transuranics in Environ, Nat Acad Sci & Adv Comt Reactor Safeguards, US Nuclear Regulatory Comn, Wash, DC; chmn, Sci Comt-57, Nat Coun Radiation Protection & Measurements; lectr radiobiol, Traveling Lect Prog, Am Inst Biol Sci; hon mem, Nat Coun Radiation Protection. *Mem:* Am Physiol Soc; Soc Pharmacol & Exp Therapeut; Radiation Res Soc; fel AAAS; Soc Gen Physiologists; Am Indust Hyg Asn; fel Health Physics Soc (pres-elect, 68-69, pres, 69-70); Biophys Soc; Soc Toxicol; Sigma Xi. *Res:* Cellular radiobiology and metabolism and biological effects of radioisotopes in the body; setting of radiation protection standards for radioisotopes in workers, the general population, and the environment, particularly alpha emitters such as plutonium and uranium; history of radioactivity and health; author of over 150 publications. *Mailing Add:* Dept Community Med Univ Calif 17441 Plaza Dolores San Diego CA 92128-2243. *Fax:* 619-487-4670

STANNARD, WILLIAM A, mathematics, for more information see previous edition

STANNERS, CLIFFORD PAUL, MOLECULAR BIOLOGY, CELL BIOLOGY. *Current Pos:* PROF BIOCHEM, MCGIL UNIV 82-, DIR, CANCER CTR, 88- *Personal Data:* b Sutton Surrey, Eng, Oct 19, 37; Can citizen; m 59; c 3. *Educ:* McMaster Univ, BSc, 58; Univ Toronto, MSc, 60, PhD(med biophys), 63. *Prof Exp:* Fel molecular biol, Mass Inst Technol, 62-64; from asst prof to prof med biophys, Univ Toronto, 64-82; sr scientist biol res, Ont Cancer Inst, 64-82. *Concurrent Pos:* Grants, Med Res Coun & Nat Cancer Inst Can, 65-, US Nat Cancer Inst, 73-79 & Multiple Sclerosis Soc Can, 79-; assoc ed, J Cell Physiol, 73-, Cell, 75-84; mem grants panel, Nat Cancer inst Can, 76-81; sci adv, Amyotropic Lateral Sclerosis Soc Can, 77-79. *Mem:* Can Biochem Soc; Can Soc Cell Biol. *Res:* Growth control of animal cells; protein synthesis somatic cell genetics; molecular genetics; cell virus interactions; persistent infection with vesicular stomatitis virus; molecular genetics; human cancer; human carcinoembryonic antigen. *Mailing Add:* McGill Univ Cancer Ctr 3655 Drummond St Montreal PQ H3G 1Y6 Can

STANNETT, VIVIAN THOMAS, POLYMER CHEMISTRY. *Current Pos:* prof, 67-69, vprovost & dean grad sch, 75-82, CAMILLE DREYFUS PROF CHEM ENG, NC STATE UNIV, 69- *Personal Data:* b Langley, Eng, Sept 1, 17; nat US; m 46, Susanne Sulzbacher; c Rosemary. *Educ:* London Polytech Inst, BSc, 39; Polytech Inst Brooklyn, PhD(chem), 50. *Honors & Awards:* Borden Award & Payen Award, Am Chem Soc, 74; Int Award & Gold Medal, Soc Plastics Eng; Polymer Chem Award, Am Chem Soc, 87. *Prof Exp:* Plant chemist, Brit Celanese Co, 39-41; chief chemist, Utilex, Ltd, 44-47, dir, 50-51; asst group leader polymers, Koppers Co, 51-52; from asst prof to prof polymer chem, State Univ NY Col Forestry, Syracuse Univ, 52-61; assoc dir, Camille Dreyfus Lab, Res Triangle Inst, 61-67. *Concurrent Pos:* Res assoc, Mellon Inst, 51. *Mem:* Nat Acad Eng; Tech Asn Pulp & Paper Indust; fel NY Acad Sci; Am Chem Soc; fel Royal Soc Chem; Soc Chem Indust. *Res:* Physical chemistry and engineering properties of plastics; cellulosic plastics; plastics-paper combinations; radiation chemistry of polymers; membrane science. *Mailing Add:* Dept Chem Eng NC State Univ Box 7905 Raleigh NC 27695-7905

STANOJEVIC, CASLAV V, MATHEMATICS. *Current Pos:* PROF MATH, UNIV MO, ROLLA, 68- *Personal Data:* b Belgrade, Yugoslavia, June 23, 28; US citizen; m 70; c 1. *Educ:* Univ Belgrade, BS, 52, MS, 54, PhD(math), 55. *Prof Exp:* From asst prof to assoc prof math, Univ Belgrade, 58-61; from assoc prof to prof math, Univ Detroit, 62-68. *Concurrent Pos:* Vis prof, Ohio State Univ, 67-68 & La State Univ, New Orleans, 71-52. *Mem:* Am Math Soc; Math Asn Am; Inst Math Statist. *Res:* Fourier analysis; geometry of quantum states and normed linear spaces; applied probability; analysis; theory of probability. *Mailing Add:* Dept Math Univ Mo Rolla MO 65409-0020

STANONIS, DAVID J(OSEPH), BIOCHEMISTRY. *Current Pos:* VPRES, BENDAL, INC, METAIRIE, LA, 80- *Personal Data:* b Louisville, Ky, Mar 19, 26. *Educ:* Univ Ky, BS, 45; Northwestern Univ, PhD(chem), 50. *Prof Exp:* Instr chem, Northwestern Univ, 48-49; asst prof, Clark Univ, 49-50 & Loyola Univ, Ill, 50-54; res chemist, Southern Regional Res Lab, USDA, 56-79. *Mem:* Am Chem Soc; Sigma Xi; Am Inst Chem; Fiber Soc. *Res:* Stereochemistry; mechanisms of organic reactions; cellulose chemistry. *Mailing Add:* Bendal Inc 7809 Airline Hwy Suite 306-C Metairie LA 70003

STANONIS, FRANCIS LEO, MINERALOGY, PETROLOGY. *Current Pos:* assoc prof geol & geog, 69-74, chmn, Div Sci & Math, 73-79, PROF GEOL & GEOG, UNIV SOUTHERN IND, EVANSVILLE, 74-, DEAN SCH SCI & ENG TECHNOL, 88- *Personal Data:* b Louisville, Ky, July 9, 31; c 2. *Educ:* Univ Ky, BS, 51, MS, 56; Pa State Univ, PhD(mineral & petrol), 58. *Prof Exp:* Geologist, Carter Oil Co, 58-60 & George A Hoffman Co, 60-62; pres, Mitchell & Stanonis Inc, 62-67 & Int Pollution Control, Inc, 67-69. *Concurrent Pos:* Owner, Red Banks Oil & Gas Co, 60-69; pres, Enviro-Sci Corp, 70-76; mem environ comt, Interstate Oil Compact Comn, 76-; owner, Stanonis Mineral Explor Co, 69-; comnr environ protection, Commonwealth, Ky, 75-77; explor mgr, Wiseroil Co, Sisterville, WVa, 84-85. *Mem:* Geol Soc Am; Am Inst Prof Geol. *Res:* Archaeoastronomy. *Mailing Add:* 142 N Arlington Dr Henderson KY 42420

STANOVSKY, JOSEPH JERRY, ENGINEERING MECHANICS, CIVIL ENGINEERING. *Current Pos:* ASSOC PROF ENG MECH, UNIV TEX, ARLINGTON, 66- *Personal Data:* b Galveston, Tex, Mar 4, 28; wid; c 4. *Educ:* Southern Methodist Univ, BSCE, 48; Univ Tex, Austin, MSCE, 51; Pa State Univ, PhD(eng mech), 66. *Honors & Awards:* Ralph R Teetor Award, Soc Automotive Engrs, 74. *Prof Exp:* Steel detailer, Austin Bros Steel Co, Tex, 48-49; instr civil eng, Univ Tex, Austin, 50-51; sr struct test engr, Convair, Tex, 51-53; design supvr, Austin Co, Tex, 53-54; design engr supvr, Fluor Corp, Tex, 54-58; asst prof civil eng, Tex Technol Col, 58-59; design engr, Boeing Airplane Co, Wash, 59-60; instr eng mech, Pa State Univ, 61-66. *Concurrent Pos:* Vis assoc prof civil eng, Univ Petrol & Minerals, Dhahran, Saudi Arabia, 74-76. *Mem:* Soc Automotive Engrs; Soc Petrol Engrs; Am Inst Aeronaut & Astronaut; AAAS. *Res:* Shock response on nonlinear structures; structural dynamics; experimental mechanics; structures; plasticity. *Mailing Add:* 1816 Michael Ct Arlington TX 76010

STANSBERY, DAVID HONOR, ZOOLOGY, HYDROBIOLOGY. *Current Pos:* Fel, Stone Lab Hydrobiol, Ohio State Univ, 53-55, asst instr gen zool, 56-57, instr animal ecol, 58-60, from asst prof to assoc prof, 61-71, PROF ZOOL, OHIO STATE UNIV, 71- *Personal Data:* b Upper Sandusky, Ohio, May 5, 26; m 48; c 4. *Educ:* Ohio State Univ, BS, 50, MS, 53, PhD, 60. *Concurrent Pos:* Cur natural hist, Ohio State Mus, 61-72; dir mus zool, Ohio State Univ, 71-77. *Mem:* AAAS; Ecol Soc Am; Soc Syst Zool; Soc Study Evolution; Am Malacol Union (pres, 70-71); Sigma Xi. *Res:* Zoogeography, ecology, evolution and taxonomy of freshwater forms, especially bivalve molluscs and decapod crustaceans. *Mailing Add:* Mus Biol Diversity Ohio State Univ 1315 Kinnear Rd Columbus OH 43212-1192

STANSBREY, JOHN JOSEPH, PHYSICAL CHEMISTRY. *Current Pos:* CONSULT STATISTICIAN, RICERCA, INC, 88- *Personal Data:* b St Louis, Mo, Dec 30, 18; m 63; c 2. *Educ:* Washington Univ, AB, 41, MS, 43, PhD(chem), 47. *Prof Exp:* Asst chem, Washington Univ, 41-45, lectr, US Army Training Prog, 43-44; res chemist, Am Can Co, Ill, 45-47; res physicist, Anheuser-Busch, Inc, 47-53; mem tech staff, Bell Tel Labs, Inc, 53-56; mem group staff, Res Develop & Mfg Div, NCR Corp, 56-73; scientist, Glidden Coatings & Resins Div, D P Joyce Res Ctr, SCM Corp, 78-86. *Concurrent Pos:* Instr, Webster Col, 44-45, Cuyahoga Community Col W, 86, Ashland Col, 87 & Kent State Univ, 87-88; instr exten div, Univ Cincinnati, 56-57. *Mem:* Am Chem Soc; Am Statist Asn; Sigma Xi; Inst Mgt Sci. *Res:* Colloid chemistry; thixotropy; electrochemistry; conductance; electrophoresis; ultracentrifuge; light scattering and viscosity of protein solutions; emission and absorption spectra of biological materials; solid state physics and transistors; mathematical programming; statistical analysis and experimental design; computer automation of laboratory and production processes. *Mailing Add:* 137 Parmelee Dr Hudson OH 44236-3427

STANSBURY, E(LE) E(UGENE), PHYSICAL METALLURGY. *Current Pos:* from assoc prof to prof, 47-89, Alumni Distinguished Serv Prof, 76-89, EMER PROF METALL, UNIV TENN, KNOXVILLE, 89- *Personal Data:* b Indianapolis, Ind, Dec 14, 18; m; c 4. *Educ:* NC State Col, BChE, 40; Univ Cincinnati, MS, 42, PhD(metall), 46. *Prof Exp:* Asst, Univ Cincinnati, 40-42, from instr to asst prof metall, 42-47. *Concurrent Pos:* Consult, Oak Ridge Nat Lab, 47- *Mem:* Am Soc Metals; Metall Soc; Am Soc Eng Educ; Soc Hist Technol; Sigma Xi. *Res:* Thermodynamics of metal systems; kinetics of phase transformations; corrosion. *Mailing Add:* 5800 Woodburn Dr Knoxville TN 37919

STANSBURY, HARRY ADAMS, JR, CHEMISTRY. *Current Pos:* EXEC SECY, WVA ASN SCH ADMIN, 76- *Personal Data:* b Morgantown, WVa, Sept 14, 17; m 44; c 4. *Educ:* WVa Univ, AB, 40, MS, 41; Yale Univ, PhD(org chem), 44. *Prof Exp:* Group leader, Union Carbide Corp, WVa, 44-71; state dir comprehensive health planning, Gov Off, 71-76. *Mem:* Am Chem Soc. *Res:* Development of new pesticides; registration of pesticides; synthetic organic chemistry; residue analyses. *Mailing Add:* 220 Highland Ave South Charleston WV 25303-1910

STANSBY, MAURICE EARL, AGRICULTURAL & FOOD CHEMISTRY. *Current Pos:* Jr chemist, US Bur Commercial Fisheries, Mass, 31-35, Md, 35-37 & Wash, 38-40, technologist chg fishery prod lab, Alaska, 40-42, dir tech lab, 42-66, dir food sci, Pioneer Res Lab, Wash, 66-71, dir environ conserv div, 72-75, SCI CONSULT, NORTHWEST FISHERIES CTR, NAT MARINE FISHERIES SERV, 75- *Personal Data:* b Cedar Rapids, Iowa, Apr 25, 08; m 38, Belinda Lewis; c Lew(is). *Educ:* Univ Minn, BChem, 30, MSc, 33. *Concurrent Pos:* Lectr, Sch Fisheries, Univ Wash, 38-89. *Mem:* Am Chem Soc; Inst Food Technologists; Am Oil Chemists Soc. *Res:* Analysis, preservation and processing of fish; chemistry and nutritional properties of fish oils; effects of contaminants in the environment upon fish. *Mailing Add:* 5105 NE 75th St Seattle WA 98115-5209

STANSEL, JAMES WILBERT, PLANT BREEDING, PLANT GENETICS. *Current Pos:* Asst geneticist, Tex A&M Univ, 60-66, asst prof genetics, 66-70, asst prof agron, Agr Res & Exten Ctr Beaumont, 70-77, assoc prof agron, 78-82, RES DIR & PROF, TEX AGR EXP STA, TEX A&M UNIV, 82- *Personal Data:* b Angleton, Tex, Apr 8, 34; m 54; c 2. *Educ:* Tex A&M Univ, BS, 56, MS, 59; Purdue Univ, PhD(plant breeding & genetics), 65. *Concurrent*

Pos: Assoc prof genetics & environ & scientist in chg, Western Div, Tex A&M Univ, 72-77. *Mem:* Am Soc Agron; Soil Sci Soc Am; Am Asn Cereal Chemists; Am Genetics Asn. *Res:* Increasing rice yields by developing through genetic and cultural manipulation morphologically and physiologically superior rice plants which more effectively utilize available sunlight in intensified cultural practice systems. *Mailing Add:* 13595 Chimney Rock St Beaumont TX 77713. *Fax:* 409-752-5560

STANSEL, JOHN CHARLES, ENGINEERING, FUEL TECHNOLOGY. *Current Pos:* DIR PROG MGT, TRW VEHICLE SAFETY SYSTS INC, 89- *Personal Data:* b Spring Canyon, Utah, Nov 18, 35; m 60; c 7. *Educ:* Univ Utah, BS, 60; Calif Inst Technol, MS, 62. *Prof Exp:* Res engr rockets, Jet Propulsion Lab, 61; mem tech staff fluid flow, 62-66, sect head nuclear, 66-72, dept mgr lasers, 72-78, asst lab mgr lasers, 78-80, chief engr combustion & gasification, TRW Inc, 80-84; mgr, Eng & Res & Develop, CBU, 84-89. *Concurrent Pos:* Chmn nuclear space safety, Atomic Indust Forum, 67-70. *Res:* Application of physics and engineering principles to development of advanced chemical combustion and laser devices. *Mailing Add:* 6577 Hill Top Dr Troy MI 48098

STANSFIELD, BARRY LIONEL, plasma physics, for more information see previous edition

STANSFIELD, ROGER ELLIS, ORGANIC CHEMISTRY. *Current Pos:* RETIRED. *Personal Data:* b Sanford, Maine, July 16, 26; m 51, Audrey Hasselbacher; c Samuel & Harold. *Educ:* Northwestern Univ, BS, 50; Carnegie Inst Technol, PhD(chem), 55. *Prof Exp:* From asst prof to assoc prof chem, Baldwin-Wallace Col, 56-65, chmn dept, 71-74, prof, 65-91. *Concurrent Pos:* Fel, Duke Univ, 54-56; vis prof, Forman Christian Col, W Pakistan, 64-66. *Mem:* AAAS; Am Chem Soc; Am Asn Univ Prof. *Res:* Synthesis of peptides; alkaloids of nicotiana; esterification; chemistry of pyroles; computer interfacing. *Mailing Add:* 145 Beech St Berea OH 44017

STANSFIELD, WILLIAM D, GENETICS. *Current Pos:* instr, 63-92, EMER BIOL, CALIF POLYTECH STATE UNIV, SAN LUIS OBISPO, 92- *Personal Data:* b Los Angeles, Calif, Feb 7, 30; m 53; c 3. *Educ:* Calif State Polytech Col, BS, 52, MA, 58; Univ Calif, Davis, MS, 61, PhD(animal breeding), 63. *Mem:* Am Genetic Asn; Soc Study Evolution; Sigma Xi. *Res:* Writer. *Mailing Add:* Dept Biol Sci Calif Polytech State Univ San Luis Obispo CA 93407

STANSLOSKI, DONALD WAYNE, CLINICAL PHARMACY, MICROCOMPUTERS. *Current Pos:* CONSULT. *Personal Data:* b Big Rapids, Mich, June 22, 39; m 59; c 4. *Educ:* Ferris State Col, BS, 61; Univ Nebr-Lincoln, MS, 69, PhD(pharmaceut sci), 70. *Honors & Awards:* Merck Award. *Prof Exp:* Asst prof pharm, Col Pharm, Univ Nebr-Lincoln, 70-72; clin coordr, Raabe Col Pharm, Ohio Northern Univ, 72-95, dept chmn, 75-95. *Concurrent Pos:* Consult, Vet Admin Hosp, Lincoln, Nebr, 71, Ohio Dept Pub Welfare, 74-78 & var comput systs, 75- *Mem:* Am Pharmaceut Asn; Am Asn Cols Pharm. *Res:* Chemistry of mesoionic compounds and role of pharmacist in the provision of drug therapy; computer applications to health care; expanding the use of computers in the provision of health care. *Mailing Add:* 4775 W Cedar Lake Rd Greenbush MI 48738

STANSLY, PHILIP GERALD, ANTIBIOTIC RESEARCH, VIRAL ONCOLOGY. *Current Pos:* RETIRED. *Educ:* Univ Minn, PhD(biochem), 44, Univ Wis, PD,(enzyme chem), 54. *Prof Exp:* Prog dir biochem, Nat Cancer Inst, NIH, 68-80. *Mailing Add:* 3150 Fallen Oaks Ct 113 Rochester Hills MI 48309-2764

STANTON, BRUCE ALAN, RENAL PHYSIOLOGY, ION TRANSPORT. *Current Pos:* asst prof, 84-88, ASSOC PROF PHYSIOL, DARTMOUTH MED SCH, 88- *Personal Data:* b Providence, RI, Mar 31, 52. *Educ:* Univ Maine, BS, 74; Yale Univ, MS, 76, PhD(physiol), 80. *Prof Exp:* Teaching fel physiol, Sch Med, Yale Univ, 80-83, assoc res scientist, 83-84. *Concurrent Pos:* Prin investr, NIH grant, 85-88; mem, Kidney Coun, Am Heart Asn; established investr, Am Heart Asn; ed bd, Am J Physiol. *Mem:* Am Soc Nephrology; Int Soc Nephrology; Soc Gen Physiologists; Am Physiol Soc; Biophys Soc; Am Heart Asn. *Res:* Renal physiology; cellular mechanisms of ion transport studied by electrophysiological and ultrastructural techniques; regulation of sodium, potassium and hydrogen; ion transport by adrenal corticosteroids and acid-base disorders. *Mailing Add:* Dept Physiol Dartmouth Med Sch Hanover NH 03755-3830. *Fax:* 603-650-1130

STANTON, CHARLES MADISON, MATHEMATICS, COMPUTER SCIENCE. *Current Pos:* VIS ASSOC PROF COMPUT SCI, IND UNIV, SOUTH BEND, 85- *Personal Data:* b San Diego, Calif, July 2, 42; m 71. *Educ:* Wesleyan Univ, BS, 64; Stanford Univ, PhD(math), 69. *Prof Exp:* Lectr, Wesleyan Univ, 68-69, asst prof math, 69-76; asst prof math, Fordham Univ, 76-80; consult programmer, Comput Ctr, Univ Notre Dame, 84-85. *Concurrent Pos:* Vis assoc prof math, Wesleyan Univ, 80-81; adj assoc prof math, Univ Notre Dame, 81-82, IHES, 82 & Max Planck Inst Math, 83. *Mem:* Am Math Soc; Math Asn Am; Asn Comput Mach; Inst Elec & Electronics Engrs. *Res:* Complex analysis; algebras of analytic funtions; Riemann surfaces; symbolic manipulation. *Mailing Add:* Dept Math Sci Manchester Col North Manchester IN 46962

STANTON, GEORGE EDWIN, AQUATIC ECOLOGY, INVERTEBRATE ECOLOGY. *Current Pos:* from asst prof to assoc prof, 69-76, prof, 76-83, BIOL DEPT CHAIRPERSON, COLUMBUS COL, 82-, DISTINGUISHED PROF BIOL, 83- *Personal Data:* b Danville, Pa, Mar 28, 44; m 65, Susan Merritt; c Deborah & Kay. *Educ:* Bucknell Univ, BS, 66; Univ Maine, Orono, PhD(zool, entom), 69. *Prof Exp:* USDA res asst, Univ Maine, Orono, 66-69. *Concurrent Pos:* Adj assoc prof, Ga State Univ, 72-73; vis assoc prof biol, Mt Lake Biol Sta, 75; NSF sci fac fel, Auburn Univ, 75-78; Danforth fel, 79; mem, Muscogee County Bd Educ, 76-80, 82-87, first vpres, 85, pres, 86-87; dir, Oxbow Meadows Environ Learning Ctr, 95- *Mem:* Am Inst Biol Sci; Ecol Soc Am; Entom Soc Am; AAAS; Am Benthological Soc; Am Astacol Soc. *Res:* Distribution ecology of crayfish and other invertebretes. *Mailing Add:* Dept Biol Columbus State Univ Columbus GA 31907-5645. *Fax:* 706-569-3133; *E-Mail:* stanton__george@colstate.edu

STANTON, HUBERT COLEMAN, PHARMACOLOGY. *Current Pos:* CONSULT & MED WRITER, 87- *Personal Data:* b Orofino, Idaho, May 3, 30; m 50; c 2. *Educ:* Idaho State Col, BS, 51; Ore State Col, MS, 53; Univ Iowa, PhD(pharmacol), 58. *Prof Exp:* Asst pharmacol, Univ Iowa, 55-58; instr, Sch Med, Univ Colo, 58-60; sr pharmacologist & group leader, Mead Johnson & Co, 60-65; asst prof pharmacol, Col Med, Baylor Univ, 65-68; head, Dept Animal Physiol, Biol Res Ctr, Shell Develop Co, 68-79; dir biol res, Mead Johnson & Co, 79-82; dir cardiovascular preclin res, Pharmaceut Res & Develop, Bristol Myers Corp, 82-84. *Mem:* AAAS; fel Am Col Vet Pharmacologists; Soc Exp Biol & Med; Am Soc Pharmacol & Exp Therapeut; Am Asn Med Writers. *Res:* Autonomic pharmacology; neonatal physiology; cardiovascular pharmacology. *Mailing Add:* Vis Prof Univ Pac Sch Pharm 11028 Sycamore Ct Auburn CA 95603-8681

STANTON, K NEIL, ENGINEERING. *Current Pos:* pres & chief exec officer, 79-85, vpres, 85-90, CHMN BD, ESCA CORP, 90- *Educ:* Univ New South Wales, BE, 59, ME, 61, PhD(elec eng), 64. *Prof Exp:* Trainee engr, Australian Iron & Steel Co, 52-58; teaching asst, Univ New South Wales, Australia, 59-64; asst prof sch elec eng, Purdue Univ, 65-70; sr res eng, Syst Control, Inc, Palo Alto, Ca, 70-76; supvr, Consorcio Hidroservice-Sci, 76-78; pres, ENSYSCO, 76-78. *Mem:* Fel Inst Elec Electronics Engrs; Inst Elec & Electronics Engrs Power Eng Soc. *Res:* Author of several books and articles; developed medium term load forecasting programs for several electric utilities companies; developed the dynamic energy balance technique for simulation of long term power system dynamics. *Mailing Add:* ESCA Corp 11120 NE 33rd Pl Bellevue WA 98004

STANTON, MEARL FREDRICK, medicine; deceased, see previous edition for last biography

STANTON, NANCY KAHN, MATHEMATICS. *Current Pos:* assoc prof, 81-85, PROF MATH, UNIV NOTRE DAME, 85- *Personal Data:* b San Francisco, Calif, Mar 23, 48; m 71; c 2. *Educ:* Stanford Univ, BS, 69; Mass Inst Technol, PhD(math), 73. *Prof Exp:* Instr math, Mass Inst Technol, 73-74; lectr, Univ Calif, Berkeley, 74-76; Ritt asst prof math, Columbia Univ, 76-81. *Concurrent Pos:* Mem, Inst Advan Study, 79-80; Sloan res fel, 81-85; vis, Institut des Hautes 'Etudes Scientifiques, 82-83; Gast prof, Max Planck Inst, 83; vis prof, Univ Mich, 86-87. *Mem:* Am Math Soc; Math Asn Am; Asn Women Math. *Res:* Spectrum of the Laplacian on complex manifolds, geometry of complex manifolds with boundary; geometry of real hypersurfaces in complex space. *Mailing Add:* Dept Math Univ Notre Dame Notre Dame IN 46556

STANTON, NANCY LEA, COMMUNITY ECOLOGY, SOIL BIOLOGY. *Current Pos:* Asst prof, 72-80, actg dept head, 81-82, dept head, 82-85, ASSOC PROF ECOL, DEPT ZOOL, UNIV WYO, 81- *Personal Data:* b Casper, Wyo, Jan 13, 44; m 70; c 2. *Educ:* Creighton Univ, BS, 66; Univ Chicago, PhD(biol), 72. *Concurrent Pos:* Consult, Environ Protection Agency & NSF, 80-83; prog dir ecol, NSF. *Mem:* Ecol Soc Am; Sigma Xi; Soc Nematologists; AAAS; Am Inst Biol Sci; Am Soc Naturalists. *Res:* Community and evolutionary ecology including soil microarthropods and nematodes, plant and animal interactions, specifically on grasslands; pollination biology; parasite ecology. *Mailing Add:* Dept Zool & Physiol Box 3166 Univ Wyo Laramie WY 82071-3166

STANTON, NOEL RUSSELL, HIGH ENERGY PHYSICS. *Current Pos:* asst prof, 68-73, assoc prof, 73-77, PROF PHYSICS, OHIO STATE UNIV, 78- *Personal Data:* b Dover, NJ, Dec 29, 37; m 62; c 1. *Educ:* Rutgers Univ, BA, 60; Cornell Univ, PhD(exp physics), 65. *Prof Exp:* Res assoc exp high energy physics, Univ Mich, 65-68. *Mem:* Am Phys Soc. *Res:* Strong interactions of elementary particles at high energy. *Mailing Add:* Kans State Univ Cardwell Hall Manhattan KS 66506. *Fax:* 614-292-8261

STANTON, RICHARD EDMUND, THEORETICAL CHEMISTRY. *Current Pos:* ADJ PROF CHEM, STATE UNIV NY, BUFFALO, 96- *Personal Data:* b Brooklyn, NY, Aug 31, 31; m 57; c 5. *Educ:* Niagara Univ, BS, 52; Univ Notre Dame, PhD(phys chem), 57. *Prof Exp:* Fel, Cath Univ Am, 56-57; from asst prof to prof phys chem, Canisius Col, 57-96, chmn, Chem Dept, 81-96. *Concurrent Pos:* Consult, Union Carbide Res Inst, 61-63, Occidental Chem, 90-; Sloan fel, 69-71; vis prof, Univ Manchester, 70-71; vis scientist, Brookhaven Nat Lab, 85-86. *Mem:* Am Chem Soc; Am Phys Soc. *Res:* Quantum chemistry, especially self-consistent field convergence theory, methodology and electron correlation theory; group theory of transition states in chemical kinetics; relativistic techniques; carbon clusters. *Mailing Add:* State Univ NY Buffalo NY 14260-3000

STANTON, ROBERT E, RADIATION ONCOLOGY, MACHINE CALIBRATION & QUALITY ASSURANCE. *Current Pos:* SR CLIN PHYSICIST, COOPER HOSP/UNIV MED CTR, 75- *Personal Data:* b Philadelphia, Pa, Dec 5, 47; m 77. *Educ:* Univ Pa, BA, 69, MS, 69; Drexel Univ, PhD(biomed eng), 82. *Prof Exp:* Radiologist physicist, Univ Pa, 71-73; from jr physicist to sr physicist, Mem Sloan Kettering Hosp, 73-75. *Concurrent Pos:* Lectr, Gwynedd-Mercy Col Sch Radiation Tech, 78-85; partic consult, Am Col Radiol, 78-; mem ad hoc comt, Proposal Eval, Nat Cancer Inst, 83-85; adj assoc prof, Drexel Univ, 85-89; consult, Emer Care Res Inst, 85-; adj asst prof, Univ Med & Dent NJ-Robert Woods Johnson Med Sch, 85- *Mem:* Am Asn Physicists Med; Am Col Radiol; Health Physics Soc. *Res:* Clinical medical physics; radiation oncology; machine parameter measurement; quality assurance. *Mailing Add:* Cooper Hosp Univ Med Ctr Camden NJ 08103. *Fax:* 609-365-8504

STANTON, ROBERT JAMES, JR, GEOLOGY, PALEONTOLOGY. *Current Pos:* from assoc prof to prof, 67-85, head dept, 78-82, RAY C FISH PROF GEOL, TEX A&M UNIV, 85- *Personal Data:* b Los Angeles, Calif, June 17, 31; m 53, Patricia Burns; c John & Carol. *Educ:* Calif Inst Technol, BS, 53, PhD(geol), 60; Harvard Univ, MA, 56. *Prof Exp:* Res geologist, Shell Develop Co, 59-67. *Concurrent Pos:* Vis prof, Univ Erlangen-Nurnberg, Ger, 84. *Mem:* Fel Geol Soc Am; Soc Econ Paleontologists & Mineralogists; Paleont Soc; Paleont Res Inst. *Res:* Paleoecology-development of criteria and techniques for determining ancient environments from the fossil record; research focus on Cenozoic of California; modern of Texas Gulf coast; Triassic reefs of Austrian Alps, carboniferous of Southwest United States. *Mailing Add:* Dept Geol Tex A&M Univ College Station TX 77843

STANTON, ROBERT JOSEPH, MATHEMATICS. *Current Pos:* MEM FAC, DEPT MATH, OHIO STATE UNIV, 80- *Personal Data:* b Pottsville, Pa, Feb 5, 47; m 70; c 2. *Educ:* Drexel Inst Technol, BS, 69; Cornell Univ, MA, 71, PhD(math), 74. *Prof Exp:* Asst prof math, Rice Univ, 69-80. *Concurrent Pos:* NSF grant, 75-; mem, Sch Math, Inst Advan Study, 77-78. *Mem:* Am Math Soc. *Res:* Analysis on lie groups. *Mailing Add:* Dept Math Ohio State Univ 231 W 18th Ave Columbus OH 43210-1174

STANTON, THADDEUS BRIAN, ANAEROBIC BACTERIOLOGY, MICROECOLOGY. *Current Pos:* res microbiologist, 83-91, LEAD SCIENTIST SWINE DYSENTERY, PHYSIOPATH RES UNIT, NAT ANIMAL DIS CTR, AGR RES SERV, USDA, 91- *Personal Data:* b Cincinnati, Ohio, Nov 11, 51; m 72, Susan Pennington; c 2. *Educ:* Thomas More Col, BA, 71; Univ Mass, PhD(microbiol), 80. *Prof Exp:* NIH postdoctoral fel, Dept Microbiol, Univ Ill, 80-82; res microbiologist, Pfizer Cent Res, 82-83. *Concurrent Pos:* Consult, Pfizer Cent Res, Upjohn Co; assoc prof, collabr, Microbiol Dept, Iowa State Univ, 87- *Mem:* Am Soc Microbiol; Conf Res Workers Animal Dis; AAAS; Soc Microbiol Ecol & Dis; Sigma Xi. *Res:* Phylogenetic analysis of spirochetes based on 16S rRNA comparisons; DNA probes for swine pathogen Serpulina hyodysenteriae; identification of virulence-associated enzymes and proteins of S hyodysenteriae; one US patent. *Mailing Add:* Nat Animal Dis Ctr Agr Res Serv USDA PO Box 70 Ames IA 50010. *Fax:* 515-239-8458; *E-Mail:* tstanton@iastate.edu

STANTON, TONI LYNN, NEUROPEPTIDES, PINEAL MELATONIN. *Current Pos:* res asst, 78-81, ASST RES SCIENTIST, ALFRED I DU PONT INST, 81- *Personal Data:* b Johnstown, Pa, July 21, 44. *Educ:* Univ Md, BS, 68, MS, 71; Thomas Jefferson Univ, PhD(pharmacol), 81. *Prof Exp:* Res asst, Dept Physiol, Sch Med, Univ Pa, 72-78. *Concurrent Pos:* Lectr, Col Nursing, Univ Del; consult pychoneuroendocrinol, Michael R Babitts Fund, 81- *Mem:* Soc Neurosci; Int Hibernation Soc. *Res:* Behavioral and physiological aspects of neuropeptide action in the mammalian central nervous system; role of pineal melatonin in mechanisms that control the state of hibernation; control of central activity state. *Mailing Add:* Dept Biol Sci Calif State Univ Long Beach 1250 Bellflower Blvd Long Beach CA 90840-0001

STANTON, WILLIAM ALEXANDER, ORGANIC CHEMISTRY. *Current Pos:* RETIRED. *Personal Data:* b Washington, DC, Sept 9, 15; m 42, Mildred Hall; c 3. *Educ:* Univ Md, BS, 36, PhD(org chem), 41. *Honors & Awards:* J Award, Soc Motion Picture & TV Engrs, 70-80. *Prof Exp:* Res chemist, Tech Div, Photo Prod Dept, NJ, E I Du Pont de Nemours & Co, Inc, 41-45, group leader, 46-49, chief supvr, Plant Process Dept, Prod Div, 49-50, plant process supt, 50-52, prod supt, 53-56, asst plant mgr, NY, 57-58, dir, Parlin Res Lab, NJ, 58-63, mgr prod mkt, Del, 64-65, dir printing & indust sales, 66, dir int opers, 67-80. *Mem:* AAAS; Am Chem Soc; Sigma Xi. *Res:* Natural products; photographic emulsions and processing solutions; synthetic color-forming polymers for photographic emulsions. *Mailing Add:* 726 Loveville Rd No 28 Hockessin DE 19707-1521

STANWICK, GLENN, SOLID STATE PHYSICS, NUCLEAR PHYSICS. *Current Pos:* ENGR, ACCURATE AUTOMATIC INC, 53- *Personal Data:* b Milwaukee, Wis, Oct 17, 28. *Educ:* Northwestern Univ, BSc, 50, MSc, 51. *Prof Exp:* Res scientist, Johnsons Control, 51-53. *Mem:* Am Phys Soc; Soc Manufacturing Engrs. *Mailing Add:* 1325 Valley Ridge Rd Brookfield WI 53005

STANWICK, TAD, SYSTEMS ENGINEERING. *Current Pos:* RETIRED. *Personal Data:* b Severn, Md, May 4, 16; m 41, Wickliffe Shackleford; c Covington Philip, Wickliffe Mary & Wells Thomas. *Prof Exp:* from asst to pres & chmn bd, Am Mach & Foundry Co, 52-55, vpres, 55-57; vpres & dir, Cleveland Pneumatics Industs Inc, 57-62; pres, Pneumo Dynamics Corp, 59-62; pres & chmn bd, Stanwick Corp, 62-92. *Mem:* Philos Soc Am; Soc Naval Architects & Marine Engrs; Int Oceanog Found; Metaphys Soc Am; Inst Elec & Electronics Engrs. *Mailing Add:* 4715 Lipton St NW Washington DC 20016-2369

STAPELBROEK, MARYN G, INFRARED DETECTOR DEVELOPMENT, DETECTOR PHYSICS. *Current Pos:* mem tech staff, Res & Develop, 78-91, PRIN SCIENTIST, SILICON DEVICES FUNCTION, SCI CTR, ROCKWELL INT, 91- *Personal Data:* b Veghel, Neth, Aug 3, 47; US citizen; m 79, Marlys G Gengler; c Kelly A & Sara L. *Educ:* Univ Wis, Oshkosh, BS, 72; Univ Conn, MS 74, PhD (solid state physics), 76. *Prof Exp:* Resident res assoc, Naval Res Lab, Washington, DC, 76-78. *Mem:* Am Phys Soc; AAAS; Sigma Xi. *Res:* Invention and development of highly sensitive infrared detectors, based on impurity band conduction, specifically the blocked impurity band (BIB) detector, the solid state photomultiplier (SSPM) and visible light photon counter (VLPC). *Mailing Add:* 10611 Rockhurst Ave Santa Ana CA 92705-1413. *Fax:* 714-762-0844; *E-Mail:* mgstapel@science.remnet.ab.com

STAPH, HORACE E(UGENE), MECHANICAL ENGINEERING. *Current Pos:* RETIRED. *Personal Data:* b Petrolia, Tex, Jan 8, 21; m 50; c 3. *Educ:* Rice Univ, BSME, 43; Univ Tex, MSME, 51; Univ Minn, PhD(mech eng), 59. *Prof Exp:* Design engr hydraul, Douglas Aircraft Co, Inc, 43-44; asst prof mech eng, Univ Tex, 46-60; sr res engr, Southwest Res Inst, 60-85. *Mem:* Am Soc Mech Engrs; Am Soc Testing & Mats. *Res:* Lubrication; wear; friction phenomena, especially wet-brake studies. *Mailing Add:* 6526 Redbird Lane San Antonio TX 78240

STAPLE, PETER HUGH, HISTOCHEMISTRY. *Current Pos:* from assoc prof to prof, 63-87, EMER PROF ORAL BIOL, SCH DENT MED, STATE UNIV NY, BUFFALO, 87- *Personal Data:* b Tonbridge, Eng, Oct 15, 17; m 52, Joan Lorch; c Gregory & Alan. *Educ:* Univ London, BDS, 40, BSc, 49, PhD(sci, histochem), 52. *Prof Exp:* Mem sci staff, Med Res Coun, Eng, 51-57; lectr physiol, Univ Birmingham, 57; res assoc, Med Res Labs, Charing Cross Hosp, Univ London, 57-59; instr pharmacol, Univ Ala, 59-60, assoc prof, 60-63, assoc prof dent, Med Col & Sch Dent, 59-63. *Concurrent Pos:* Nuffield Found Dental Res Fel, 49-51; hon vis assoc prof, Univ BC, 71; vis prof, Univ Ill, 81-82. *Mem:* Histochem Soc; Int Asn Dent Res. *Res:* Detection of sulfated glycosaminoglycans in microsamples of biological fluids by cationic dyes used according to critical electrolyte concentration principles; phenytoin sodium and arthritis. *Mailing Add:* Dept Oral Biol State Univ NY Buffalo Sch Dent Med Buffalo NY 14214-3008. *Fax:* 716-829-3942

STAPLE, TOM WEINBERG, MEDICINE, RADIOLOGY. *Current Pos:* STAFF MEM, DEPT RADIOL, MEM HOSP, LONG BEACH, 75- *Personal Data:* b Hamburg, Ger, May 6, 31; US citizen; m 64; c 1. *Educ:* Univ Ill, Chicago, BS, 53, MD, 55. *Prof Exp:* From instr to prof radiol, Mallinckrodt Inst Radiol, Sch Med, Wash Univ, 73-75; adj prof radiol, Univ Calif, Irvine, 75. *Concurrent Pos:* Consult, VA Hosp, Long Beach, Calif. *Mem:* Fel Am Col Radiol; Asn Univ Radiol; assoc mem Am Acad Orthop Surg. *Res:* Bone growth and arthrography. *Mailing Add:* 2801 Atlantic Ave Box 1428 Long Beach CA 90806-1799

STAPLES, BASIL GEORGE, CORROSION TESTING, ELECTRICAL INSPECTION. *Current Pos:* RETIRED. *Personal Data:* b Eliot, Maine, Aug 13, 14; m 35, Jeannette Morgan; c John E & George D. *Educ:* Univ Maine, BS, 35, MS, 36. *Prof Exp:* Foreman, Gen Chem Co, 36-42; supt, US Rubber Co, 42-45; chemist, The Pfaudler Co, 45-64, engr, 64-79. *Mem:* Am Chem Soc; fel Am Ceramic Soc (vpres, 74-75); fel Am Soc Testing & Mat; Nat Asn Corrosion Engrs; Am Inst Chemists; Nat Inst Ceramic Engrs. *Res:* Glass coated vessels and other equipment, with special emphasis on practical design details, such as closures and gaskets. *Mailing Add:* 275 Colwick Rd Rochester NY 14624

STAPLES, JON T, ORGANIC CHEMISTRY, POLYMER CHEMISTRY. *Current Pos:* sr res chemist, 67-71, RES ASSOC, EASTMAN KODAK LABS, ROCHESTER, 71-, HEAD LAB, 75- *Personal Data:* b Waterville, Maine, Sept 14, 38; m 62; c 3. *Educ:* Bowdoin Col, AB, 61; Univ NC, Chapel Hill, PhD(org chem), 66. *Prof Exp:* Res assoc org chem, Mass Inst Technol, 66-67. *Mem:* Am Chem Soc. *Res:* Protecting group chemistry; peptide synthesis; monomer and polymer synthesis; photographic science. *Mailing Add:* 14 Ithaca Dr Pittsford NY 14534

STAPLES, LLOYD WILLIAM, MINING ENGINEERING. *Current Pos:* from instr to prof, 39-74, head dept, 58-68, EMER PROF GEOL, UNIV ORE, 74- *Personal Data:* b Jersey City, NJ, July 8, 08; m 41; c 3. *Educ:* Columbia Univ, AB, 29; Univ Mich, MS, 30; Stanford Univ, PhD(mineral), 35. *Honors & Awards:* Legion of Honor, Soc Mining Engr, 90. *Prof Exp:* Instr geol, Mich Col Mining & Technol, 31-33; res assoc mineral, Stanford Univ, 35-36; instr geol, Ore State Col, 36-37. *Concurrent Pos:* Chief geologist, Horse Heaven Mines, 37-41 & Cordero Mining Co, Nev, 41-45; Guggenheim fel, Mex, 60-61; consult, UNESCO, Paris, 68-71; mem, State Ore Bd Geologist Examrs, 77-80. *Mem:* Fel Geol Soc Am; fel Mineral Soc Am; distinguished mem Am Inst Mining, Metall & Petrol Engrs. *Res:* Mineralogy and crystallography; economic geology of quicksilver; microchemistry of minerals; mineral determination by microchemical methods; field and x-ray study of zeolites. *Mailing Add:* Dept Geol E 13th St Univ Ore Eugene OR 97403-1272

STAPLES, MARK, BIOCHEMISTRY, PROCESS DEVELOPMENT. *Current Pos:* GROUP LEADER, FORMULATION & ANALYTICAL, BIOGEN, 92- *Personal Data:* b Boston, Mass, July 19, 53. *Res:* Biochemistry; process development. *Mailing Add:* Biogen 14 Cambridge Ctr Cambridge MA 02142

STAPLES, RICHARD CROMWELL, phytopathology, for more information see previous edition

STAPLES, ROBERT, ENTOMOLOGY. *Current Pos:* assoc prof entom, 50-74, PROF ENTOM, UNIV NEBR, LINCOLN, 74-, ASSOC ENTOMOLOGIST, 50- *Personal Data:* b Philadelphia, Pa, Dec 9, 16; m 43; c 3. *Educ:* Univ Mass, BS, 40; Cornell Univ, PhD, 48. *Prof Exp:* Asst entomologist, Conn Agr Exp Sta, 49-50. *Mem:* Entom Soc Am. *Res:* Arthropod transmission of plant viruses; economic entomology. *Mailing Add:* 1040 N 65th St Lincoln NE 68505

STAPLETON, HARVEY JAMES, MAGNETIC RESONANCE. *Current Pos:* from asst prof to prof, Univ Ill, Urbana, 61-95, assoc dean, Grad Col, 80-95, assoc vchancellor res, 87-95, interim dean, Grad Col & interim vchancellor res, 92, EMER PROF PHYSICS, UNIV ILL, URBANA, 95- *Personal Data:* b Kalamazoo, Mich, Dec 22, 34; m 57, Joan Sylvander; c Patricia, Susan & Jeffrey. *Educ:* Univ Mich, BS, 57; Univ Calif, Berkeley, PhD(physics), 61. *Mem:* Sigma Xi; fel Am Phys Soc; Biophys Soc. *Res:* Paramagnetic resonance; electron spin-lattice relaxation; nuclear orientation; physics of solids, surfaces and biomolecules. *Mailing Add:* 3806 Gulf of Mexico Dr Apt 310 Longboat Key FL 34228. *E-Mail:* hstapleton@netsrq.com

STAPLETON, JAMES H, MATHEMATICAL STATISTICS. *Current Pos:* from asst prof to assoc prof, 58-73, chmn, dept statist & probability, 69-75, PROF STATIST, MICH STATE UNIV, 73- *Personal Data:* b Royal Oak, Mich, Feb 8, 31; m 63, Alicia Brown; c James B, Lara M & Sara L. *Educ:* Eastern Mich Univ, AB, 52; Purdue Univ, MS, 54, PhD(math statist), 57. *Prof Exp:* Statistician, Gen Elec Co, 57-58. *Concurrent Pos:* NSF fac sci fel, Univ Calif, Berkeley, 66-67; vis prof, Sch Econ, Univ Philippines, 78-79. *Mem:* Am Math Asn; Inst Math Statist; Am Statist Asn. *Res:* Linear models; log-linear models; simulation. *Mailing Add:* Dept Statist & Probability Mich State Univ East Lansing MI 48823. *Fax:* 517-336-1405; *E-Mail:* 20974jns@msu.edu

STAPLETON, JOHN F, MEDICINE. *Current Pos:* PROF MED & ASSOC DEAN, SCH MED, GEORGETOWN UNIV, 67-, MED DIR, UNIV HOSP, 67- *Personal Data:* b Brooklyn, NY, Jan 25, 21; m 50; c 5. *Educ:* Fordham Univ, AB, 42; Georgetown Univ, MD, 45; Am Bd Internal Med, dipl, 53; Am Bd Cardiovasc Dis, dipl, 57. *Hon Degrees:* DSc, Georgetown Univ, 83. *Prof Exp:* Intern, Providence Hosp, Washington, DC, 45-46; resident med, Georgetown Univ, 49-51, clin instr med, Hosp, 52-54, from instr to asst prof, 54-65; assoc prof med & chief cardiol, Woman's Med Col Pa, 65-67. *Concurrent Pos:* Nat Heart Inst res fel, Georgetown Univ, 51-52; dir med educ, St Vincent Hosp, Worcester, Mass, 54-65; attend physician, Philadelphia Vet Admin Hosp, 65-67; consult, Vet Admin Hosp, Wilmington, Del, 65-67. *Mem:* Am Heart Asn; Am Col Physicians; AMA. *Res:* Clinical cardiology; medical education; hospitals. *Mailing Add:* Dean Med NW 104 Med-Dent Georgetown Univ Hosp 3800 Reservoir Rd NW Washington DC 20007-2196

STAPLEY, EDWARD OLLEY, MICROBIOLOGY. *Current Pos:* RETIRED. *Personal Data:* b Brooklyn, NY, Sept 25, 27; m 49, Helen A; c Susan, Robin & Janice. *Educ:* Rutgers Univ, BS, 50, MS, 54, PhD(microbiol), 59. *Honors & Awards:* Waksman Award, 90. *Prof Exp:* From jr microbiologist to sr microbiologist, Merck Sharp & Dohme Res Labs, 50-66, res fel microbiol, 66-69; asst dir basic microbiol res, Merck Inst Therapeut Res, 69-74, dir microbial chemotherapeut, 74-76, dir, 76-78, sr dir basic microbiol, 78-83, exec dir, 84-93. *Mem:* AAAS; Am Acad Microbiol; Am Soc Microbiol; Soc Indust Microbiol (vpres, 74-75, pres, 76-77); NY Acad Sci; Infectious Dis Soc Am. *Res:* Isolation of microorganism; mutation; fermentation; ergosterol production by yeasts; microbial transformations of steroids; isolation and utility of antibiotic-resistant microorganisms; detection, characterization and evaluation of new antibiotics; microbial transformations of sulfur; detection and production of microbiol chemotherapeutics. *Mailing Add:* 110 Highland Ave Metuchen NJ 08840-1913

STAPP, HENRY P, PHYSICS. *Current Pos:* THEORET PHYSICIST, LAWRENCE BERKELEY LAB, UNIV CALIF, 59- *Personal Data:* b Cleveland, Ohio, Mar 23, 28. *Educ:* Univ Mich, BS, 50; Univ Calif, MA, 52, PhD, 55. *Prof Exp:* Theoret physicist, Lawrence Berkeley Lab, Univ Calif, 55-58 & Inst Theoret Physics, Swiss Fed Inst Technol, 58. *Res:* Elementary particle physics. *Mailing Add:* Univ Calif Lawrence Berkeley Lab 1 Cyclotron Blvd MS 50A-5101 Berkeley CA 94720

STAPP, JOHN PAUL, BIOPHYSICS. *Current Pos:* RETIRED. *Personal Data:* b Bahia, Brazil, July 11, 10; US citizen; m 57. *Educ:* Baylor Univ, BA, 31, MA, 32; Univ Tex, PhD(biophys), 40; Univ Minn, BM & MD, 44; Am Bd Prev Med, dipl, 56. *Hon Degrees:* DSc, Baylor Univ, 56, NMex State Univ, 79. *Honors & Awards:* Nat Medal of Technol, 91; Cheney Award Valor, 54; Gorgas Medal, Mil Surg Asn, 57; Cresson Medal, Franklin Inst, 73; Excalibur Award, Safety Adv Coun, US Dept Transp, 75; Honda Award Automotive Safety, Am Soc Mech Engrs, 85; FISITA Annual Medal, 90. *Prof Exp:* Instr zool, Decatur Col, 32-34; proj officer, Aero Med Lab, Wright Field, USAF, 46-53, chief, Aero Med Field Lab, Holloman AFB, 53-58, chief, Aero Med Lab, Wright AFB, 58-60, asst to comdr aerospace med, Aerospace Med Ctr, Brooks AFB, 60-65, resident biophys, Armed Forces Inst Path, 65-67; prin med scientist, Nat Hwy Safety Bur, 67-72; adj prof & consult, Safety & Systs Mgt Ctr, Univ Southern Calif, 72-76; chmn, Space Ctr Comn, Alamagordo, NMex. *Concurrent Pos:* Vpres, Int Astron Fedn, 60; consult, Nat Acad Sci, Nat Traffic Safety Agency, Gen Serv Admin & Nat Bur Stand; permanent chmn, Annual Stapp Car Crash Conf, Soc Automotive Engrs, 55- *Mem:* Fel Am Inst Aeronaut & Astronaut (pres, 59); fel Soc Automotive Engrs; Aerospace Med Asn (vpres, 57); AMA; Civil Aviation Med Asn (pres, 68); Sigma Xi. *Res:* Aerospace and industrial medicine; biodynamics of crashing and ditching; impact injury; medical biophysics. *Mailing Add:* PO Box 553 Alamogordo NM 88310-0553

STAPP, WILLIAM B, ENVIRONMENTAL SCIENCES. *Current Pos:* instr conserv, 59-61, lectr, 63-64, from asst prof to assoc prof, 64-72, PROF NATURAL RESOURCES & CHAIRPERSON BEHAV & ENVIRON PROG, SCH NAT RESOURCES, UNIV MICH, ANN ARBOR, 72- *Personal Data:* b Cleveland, Ohio, June 17, 29; m 55; c 3. *Educ:* Univ Mich, Ann Arbor, BA, 51, MA, 58, PhD(conserv), 63. *Honors & Awards:* Samuel Trask Dana Award Conserv, 62; Key Man Award, Conserv Educ Asn, 71; Lorado Taft Spec Recognition Award, 77; Walter Jeskie Award, 88. *Prof Exp:* Instr sci, Cranbrook Sch Boys, Mich, 51-52; instr biol, 54-58; conservationist, Aullwood Audubon Ctr, Ohio, 58-59. *Concurrent Pos:* Res assoc, Cranbrook Inst Sci, Mich, 55-57; consult conserv, Ann Arbor Pub Schs, 61-68, youth progs, Nat Audubon Soc, New York, 65-66; consult, Int Film Bur, Chicago, Kalamazoo Nature Ctr, Mich & Creative Visuals, Tex, 66-68; consult environ educ prog, University City Pub Schs, Mo, 66-67, DeKalb Pub Schs, Ill, 67-68, Grand Haven Pub Schs, Mich, 67-, Raleigh County Sch Syst, WVa, 68-69, Toledo Bd Educ, Ohio, 70- & State of Alaska, 72-; consult, Nat Youth Movement Natural Beauty & Conserv, Washington, DC, 67-69, NJ Environ Educ Prog, 67-69, High Rock Interpretive Ctr, NY, 68-70, Seven Ponds Nature Ctr, 69- & Tapes Unlimited, Div Educ Unlimited Corp, 72-; consult environ interpretive ctr, Dept of Interior, 67-69 & environ educ, Dept HEW, 68 & div col support, Off Educ, 70-; consult audio-cassette series ecol, Am Soc Ecol Educ, 72- & proj man & environ, Nat TV Learning Systs, Miami, Fla, 72-; mem conserv comt, Mich Dept Pub Instr, 65-68; mem bd dirs, Drayton Plains Interpretive Ctr, Pontiac, Mich, 67-; prog dir, Ford Found grant, 68-70; mem working comt, Ann Arbor Environ Interpretive Ctr, 69-; mem bd dirs, Mich Pesticide Coun, 69-71; mem comn educ, Int Union Conserv Nature & Natural Resources, 69-; mem bd adv, Gill Inst Environ Studies, NJ, 70-; mem, Ecol Ctr Commun Coun, Washington, DC, 71- & Educ Resources Info Ctr Sci, Math & Environ Educ, Columbus, Ohio, 71-; fac adv, Ecol Ctr Ann Arbor, 71-, vpres & mem bd dirs, 72-; mem, Pub Sanit Systs, Los Angeles, Calif, 72- & Mich Pop Coun, 72-; chmn Gov Task Force Develop State Environ Educ Plan, 72-; mem task force estab guidelines environ educ elem & sec schs, Mich Dept Educ, 72-; dir environ educ, UNESCO, Paris, France, 74-76; mem, US Deleg World Conf Environ Educ, Tbilisi, USSR, 77; consult, UN Environ Prog, Nairobi, Kenya, 77, Asian Conf Environ Educ, Sri Lanka, 78, Nat Leadership Conf Environ Educ, Washington, DC, 78, Nat Audubon Soc, 78, Consumer Dynamics, Inc 79, Int Union Conserv Nature & Natural Resources, Morges, Switz, 79-81, Unesco, 79-80, Morton Arboretum, 80, Environ Educ Plan Sri Lanka, Nat Park Ser, Int Br, 86-87, Annapurna Proj, King Mahendra Trust Nature Conserv, Katmandu, Nepal, 87, Mahaweli Environ Proj, Nat Park Serv, Colombo, Sri Lanka, 87, adv, govt Venezuela, Nat Environ Educ Plan, Caracas, 78; team dir, Nat Univ Benin, W Africa, 87; adv comt, Int Conf Environ Educ Teachers & Students, Hague, Neth, 87; proj dir, Kellogg Found Grant, 87-89, Ford Motor Co Grant, 87-89, Ohio Pub Interest Found Grant, 85-87. *Mem:* Am Nature Study Soc (vpres, 66-67, pres, 69-70); Conserv Educ Asn; Nat Audubon Soc; Asn Interpretive Naturalists (vpres, 69-71). *Res:* Environmental education and ecology; programs directed at helping man to develop a fuller understanding of environmental resource problems and his role in helping to resolve them. *Mailing Add:* 2050 Delaware Dr Ann Arbor MI 48103

STAPPER, CHARLES HENRI, ELECTRICAL ENGINEERING, SOLID STATE PHYSICS. *Current Pos:* INDEPENDENT INDUST CONSULT, 93- *Personal Data:* b Amsterdam, Neth, Mar 27, 34; US citizen; m 58, Ellen L Beck; c Solomon, Cossimo, Bentram, Winnie & Tiger. *Educ:* Mass Inst Technol, BS, 59, MS, 60; Univ Minn, Minneapolis, PhD(elec eng, physics), 67. *Honors & Awards:* P K McElroy Award. *Prof Exp:* Coop student elec eng, Gen Radio Co, 57-59; elec engr, IBM Corp, 60-65; teaching assoc elec eng, Univ Minn, Minneapolis, 66-67; eng mgr, IBM Corp, 67-69; adv scientist, 70-78, sr engr, 78-93. *Concurrent Pos:* Ed, J Electronic Testing, Theory & Applns. *Mem:* Fel Inst Elec & Electronics Engrs; Sigma Xi. *Res:* Application of mathematical theory to practical engineering and physics problems; statistical models for reliability, yields and manufacturing processes. *Mailing Add:* RR 2 Box 22 Jericho VT 05465

STAPRANS, ARMAND, ELECTRICAL ENGINEERING. *Current Pos:* engr, 57-59, sr eng mgr, Super Power Opers, 69-71, mgr eng, High Power Microwave Opers, 71-75, mgr, Coupled Cavity Traveling Wave Tube Opers, 75-78, CHIEF ENGR, PALO ALTO MICROWAVE TUBE DIV, VARIAN ASSOCS, 78- *Personal Data:* b Riga, Latvia, Feb 28, 31; nat US; m 55; c 3. *Educ:* Univ Calif, BS, 54, MS, 55, PhD(elec eng), 59. *Prof Exp:* Asst elec eng, Univ Calif, 54-55, res asst, Microwave Tube Lab, 55-58. *Mem:* Inst Elec & Electronics Engrs; Sigma Xi. *Res:* Microwave electronics; space-charge waves in periodic beams; electron optics; linear beam; super power tubes; coupled cavity traveling wave tubes; high power microwave windows; insulation of high voltages in vacuum; gyrotrons. *Mailing Add:* 445 Knoll Dr Los Altos CA 94024-4732

STAR, AURA E, BOTANY, NATURAL PRODUCTS CHEMISTRY. *Current Pos:* from asst prof to assoc prof, 67-75, PROF BIOL, TRENTON STATE COL, 75- *Personal Data:* b New York, NY, Mar 15, 30; m 50; c 2. *Educ:* Hunter Col, BA, 49; Mt Holyoke Col, MA, 51; Rutgers Univ, PhD(cytogenetics), 67. *Prof Exp:* Chemist, Baltimore Light & Power Co, Md, 51-52; instr biol, Morgan State Col, 52-53. *Concurrent Pos:* Sigma Xi res grant, 63. *Mem:* AAAS; Bot Soc Am; Am Inst Biol Sci; Phytochem Soc; Torrey Bot Club. *Res:* Biochemical systematics of ferns and grasses; flavonoid chemistry; chemical biogeography of Pityrogramma; physiology of flavonoids in ferns; carofenogenesis in algae. *Mailing Add:* 26 White Pine Lane Princeton NJ 08540

STAR, JEFFREY L, oceanography; deceased, see previous edition for last biography

STAR, JOSEPH, ELECTRONIC SYSTEMS ENGINEERING. *Current Pos:* INDEPENDENT CONSULT, 73- *Personal Data:* b Far Rockaway, NY, Sept 2, 16; m 46; c 2. *Educ:* Univ NC, BS, 37. *Prof Exp:* Engr, Radio Develop & Res Corp, 37-40; radio engr, Ft Monmouth Signal Lab, War Dept, 40-43; proj engr, Lab for Electronics, Inc, 46-48; staff engr, Hillyer Instrument Co, Inc, 48-51; chief electronics develop, Astrionics Div, Fairchild Engine & Aircraft Corp, 52-59; vpres eng, Instrument Systs Corp, 59-63; vpres & corp dir res & develop, Lundy Electronics & Systs, Inc, Glen Head, 63-73. *Mem:* Sr mem Inst Elec & Electronics Engrs; Water Pollution Control Fedn; Int Asn Pollution Control. *Res:* Complex electronics for military and commercial purposes; derivation and investigation of new electronic and electromechanical devices; pollution control devices and systems; environmental systems engineering. *Mailing Add:* 186 Parkway Dr Roslyn Heights NY 11577

STAR, MARTIN LEON, COMPUTER SCIENCE, APPLIED STATISTICS. *Current Pos:* ASSOC DIR MGT SERV, S D LEIDESDORF & CO, NEW YORK, 67- *Personal Data:* b Brooklyn, NY, May 3, 28; m 55; c 1. *Educ:* City Col New York, BBA, 48. *Prof Exp:* Qual control supvr, Sonotone Corp, 52-55; comput programmer, Remington Rand Univac, 55-56; systs analyst, Underwood Corp, 56-57; opers res analyst, Stevens Inst Technol, 57-59; asst programming mgr, Teleregister Corp, 59-61; programming supvr on-line systs, Nat Cash Register Co, 61-67. *Concurrent Pos:* Partner, Eisner & Lubin, 78- *Mem:* Data Processing Mgt Asn (treas, 70-). *Res:* Statistical techniques in auditing; on-line systems and programming techniques. *Mailing Add:* 25 Willow Lane Great Neck NY 11021. *Fax:* 516-487-3522

STARACE, ANTHONY FRANCIS, ATOMIC PHYSICS. *Current Pos:* from asst prof to assoc prof, 73-81, chmn, Dept Physics & Astron, 84-95, PROF PHYSICS, UNIV NEBR, LINCOLN, 81- *Personal Data:* b New York, NY, July 24, 45; m 68, Katherine A Fritz; c Alexander F & Anne K. *Educ:* Columbia Univ, AB, 66; Univ Chicago, MS, 67, PhD(physics), 71. *Prof Exp:* Res assoc physics, Imp Col, Univ London, 71-72. *Concurrent Pos:* Alfred P Sloan Found fel, 75-79; prin investr, Dept Energy res contract, 76-85, res grant, 85-; Alexander von Humboldt res fel, Freiburg Univ, Fed Repub Ger, 79-80; prin investr, NSF res grant, 81-; mem, Nat Res Coun Comt Atomic, Molecular & Optical Sci, 86-89, 90-91; chmn, Div Atomic Molecular & Optical Physics, Am Phys Soc, 90-91; vis prof, Univ Pierre Marie Curie, Paris, France, 92; vis fel, Joint Inst Lab Astrophys, Univ Colo, Boulder, 92; vis fel, Inst Theoret Atomic & Molecular Physics, Harvard-Smithsonian Ctr Astrophys, Cambridge, Mass, 95; assoc ed, Reviews Modern Physics, 96-99. *Mem:* Fel Am Phys Soc; Brit Inst Physics; fel AAAS. *Res:* Theory of single and multi-photon detachment and ionization processes; electron-atom and negative ion-atom collisions; atoms in high magnetic fields; coherent control of quantum processes with short-pulse lasers; harmonic generation processes. *Mailing Add:* Dept Physics & Astron Univ Nebr Lincoln NE 68588-0111. *Fax:* 402-472-2879; *E-Mail:* astarace@unl.info.unl.edu

STARBIRD, MICHAEL PETER, TOPOLOGY. *Current Pos:* From asst prof to assoc prof, 74-88, PROF MATH, UNIV TEX, AUSTIN, 88-, ASSOC DEAN, COL NATURAL SCI, 89- *Personal Data:* b Los Angeles, Calif, July 10, 48; m 78; c 2. *Educ:* Pomona Col, BA, 70; Univ Wis-Madison, MA, 73, PhD(math), 74. *Concurrent Pos:* Vis mem, Inst Advan Study, 78-79, Jet Propulsion Lab, 85-86. *Mem:* Am Math Asn; Math Asn Am. *Res:* Geometric topology. *Mailing Add:* Dept Math CNS/OFF Dean Univ Tex Austin TX 78712-1199

STARCHER, BARRY CHAPIN, NUTRITION, BIOCHEMISTRY. *Current Pos:* mem fac, Dept Home Econ, Austin, 80-84, PROF BIOCHEM, UNIV TEX HEALTH CTR, TYLER, 84- *Personal Data:* b Los Angeles, Calif, Dec 1, 38; m 60; c 3. *Educ:* Univ Calif, Davis, BS & MS, 62; NC State Univ, PhD(biochem), 65. *Prof Exp:* Asst mem biochem, Inst Biomed Res, 66-70; asst prof path, Univ Colo Med Ctr, 70-72; asst prof biochem, Med Ctr, Univ Ala, Birmingham, 72-74; res asst prof, Pulmonary Div, Sch Med, Washington Univ, 74-80. *Mem:* Am Nutrit Soc. *Res:* Studies on the biochemistry of copper and zinc metabolism; enzyme induction in relation to stress, and the chemistry of the crosslinking amino acids in elastin; connective tissue components of lung; the role of elastin in calcification and arteriosclerosis. *Mailing Add:* Dept Biochem 21 Texas Health Sci Ctr PO Box 2003 Tyler TX 77510-2003. *Fax:* 903-877-7558

STARCHMAN, DALE EDWARD, MEDICAL PHYSICS. *Current Pos:* PRES, MED PHYSICS SERV, INC, 71- *Personal Data:* b Wallace, Idaho, Apr 16, 41; m 69; c Ann, Cindy, Julie & Mark. *Educ:* Pittsburg State Univ, BS, 63; Univ Kans, MS, 65, PhD(radiation biophys), 68; Am Bd Radiol, cert; Am Bd Health Physics, cert; Am Bd Med Physics, cert. *Prof Exp:* Chief health physicist, Ill Inst Technol Res Inst & radiol physicist, Inst Radiation Therapy Mercy Hosp & Med Ctr, Chicago, 68-71. *Concurrent Pos:* Consult, Aultman Hosp & Timken Mercy Hosp, Canton, Ohio & Northeast Ohio Conjoint Radiation Oncol Ctr, 71-; mem bd, Mideast Region Radiol Physics Ctr Bd Adv & prof, Univ Akron, 73-; prof & chmn radiation biophys, Northeastern Ohio Univ Col Med, 74-; mem, Adv Staff, Akron Gen Med Ctr, 75-; bd dirs, Am Asn Physicists Med, 84-86. *Mem:* Am Asn Physicists Med; Soc Nuclear Med; Health Physics Soc; fel Am Col Radiol; Sigma Xi; Radiol Soc NAm. *Res:* Electron beam perturbation by cavities; radiation dosimetry; post irradiation atrophic changes of bone; information optimization with dose minimization in diagnostic radiology; radiation oncology treatment development. *Mailing Add:* 5942 Easy Pace Circle NW Canton OH 44718

STARE, FREDRICK J, NUTRITION. *Current Pos:* prof nutrit & chmn dept, 42-76, EMER PROF NUTRIT, SCH PUB HEALTH, HARVARD UNIV, 80- *Personal Data:* b Columbus, Wis, Apr 11, 10; m 84, Irene Mackey; c Fredrick A, David S & Mary S (Wilkinson). *Educ:* Univ Wis, SB, 28, SM, 30, PhD, 34; Univ Chicago, MD, 41. *Hon Degrees:* MA, Harvard Univ, 45; DSc, Suffolk Univ, 63, Univ Dublin, Ireland, 64, Muskingum Col, 77. *Honors & Awards:* Goldberger Award, AMA, 62; Henderson Award, Am Geriat Soc, 77; Medal Hon, Int Found Nutrit Res & Educ, 87; Award Excellence Med & Dent Nutrit Educ, Am Soc Clin Nutrit, 93. *Concurrent Pos:* Ed, Nutrit Rev, 42-68; co-founder & dir, Am Coun Sci & Health. *Mem:* Am Chem Soc; Am Soc Biol Chemists; fel Am Inst Nutrit; Biochem Soc; Am Soc Clin Invest; hon mem Am Dietetic Asn; Soc Nutrit Educ; fel Royal Irish Col Physicians. *Res:* Diet in relation to heart disease; exposing food faddism; heart disease and obesity. *Mailing Add:* PO Box 812085 Wellesley MA 02181-0013. *Fax:* 617-432-1833

STARFIELD, BARBARA HELEN, PEDIATRICS, MEDICAL SCIENCE. *Current Pos:* from instr to asst prof pediat, Sch Med, Johns Hopkins Univ, 63-73, instr pub health admin, Sch Hyg & Pub Health, 65-66, from asst prof to assoc prof med care & hosps, 66-75, PEDIAT, 73-, JOHNS HOPKINS UNIV, PROF & HEAD DIV HEALTH POLICY, SCH HYG & PUB HEALTH, 75-, PEDIAT, 73-, UNIV DISTINGUISHED SERV PROF, DEPT HEALTH POLICY & MGT, 94- *Personal Data:* b Brooklyn, NY, Dec 18, 32; m 55, Neil A Holtzman; c Robert, Jon, Steven & Deborah. *Educ:* Swarthmore Col, BA, 54; State Univ NY Downstate Med Ctr, MD, 59; Johns Hopkins Univ, MPH, 63. *Honors & Awards:* Award, Enuresis Found, 67; George Armstrong Award, Am Pediat Asn, 83; First Annual Res Award, Am Pediat Asn, 90; Distinguished Invest Award, Asn Health Serv Res, 95; Martha May Eliot Award, Am Pub Health Asn, 95. *Prof Exp:* Teaching asst anat, State Univ NY Downstate Med Ctr, 54-57; from intern to resident pediat, Harriet Lane Home, Johns Hopkins Hosp, 59-62. *Concurrent Pos:* Nat Ctr Health Serv Res & Develop res scientist develop award; med dir, Community Nursing Proj, Dept Pediat & dir, Pediat Med Care Clin, Johns Hopkins Hosp, 63-66, asst dir community health, Comprehensive Child Care Proj & mem, Comt Planning & Develop, 65-67, pediatrician, dir, Pediat Clin Scholars Prog, 71-76; mem spec rev comt, Exp Med Care Rev Orgns, Dept Health, Educ & Welfare, mem, Health Serv Res Study Sect, 74-78, Nat Ctr Health Serv Res & Develop, 82-85; mem, Nat Prof Standards Rev Coun, 80-81; chmn health serv develop grants study sect, 86-91; mem, Nat Adv Coun, Agency, Health Care Policy & Res, 90-; assoc ed, Ann Rev Pub Health, 96-, J Dev Behav Pediat, 94-, Health Serv Res, 96- *Mem:* Inst Med Nat Acad Sci; Am Pub Health Asn; Sigma Xi; Am Pediat Soc; Int Epidemiol Asn; Am Pediat Asn (pres, 80). *Res:* Cost effectiveness of health care; care of vulnerable population subgroups; epidemiology of child health and measurement of health status; primary care; health services research. *Mailing Add:* Sch Hyg & Pub Health Johns Hopkins Univ 624 N Broadway Baltimore MD 21205

STARICH, GALE HANSON, ENDOCRINOLOGY, BIOCHEMISTRY. *Current Pos:* ASST PROF ENDOCRINOL, ANDERSON MED SCH, UNIV NEV, 84- *Educ:* Univ Nev, PhD(biochem), 81. *Mailing Add:* Internal Med Anderson Bldg Rm 108 Nev Med Sch Reno NV 89557

STARK, ALLEN ROSS, PODIATRY. *Current Pos:* OWNER INSTR, SOUTHERN CALIF SCH PODIATRIC RADIOGRAPHY, 86- *Personal Data:* b Binghampton, NY, Mar 22, 37; m 61, Saundra Earkas; c Robert S & Janice L. *Educ:* Calif Col Podiatric Med, BS, 50, Dr Podiatric Med, 63. *Prof Exp:* Secy/treas, Orange Co Podiatric Med Asn, 68-70, pres, 70-72, treas, 84-89; clin prof, Calif Col Podiatric Med, 76-83. *Concurrent Pos:* Comnr, Bd Podiatric Med, 87-88; pres, Calif Podiatric Med Asn, 93-94. *Mem:* Am Podiatric Med Asn; Am Public Health Asn; Am Asn Hosp Podiatrists; Am Col Foot & Ankle Surgeons (secy/treas, 77-79, vpres, 79-81, pres, 81-83). *Mailing Add:* 555 N Tustin Orange CA 92867

STARK, ANTONY ALBERT, ATMOSPHERIC CHEMISTRY & PHYSICS. *Current Pos:* MEM TECH STAFF, AT&T BELL LABS, 79- *Personal Data:* b Seattle, Wash, Oct 29, 53; m 76. *Educ:* Calif Inst Technol, BS(physics) & BS(astron), 75; Princeton Univ, MA, 77, PhD(astrophys), 79. *Prof Exp:* Physicist, Lawrence Livermore Lab, 75-76. *Concurrent Pos:* Vis lectr, Princeton Univ, 80- *Mem:* Int Astron Union; Am Astron Soc. *Res:* Galactic dynamics; interstellar medium; sub-millimeter-wave observations; constructing a submillimeter telescope and remote observatory at the South Pole. *Mailing Add:* Smithsonian Astrophys Observ 60 Garden St MS 78 Cambridge MA 02138

STARK, BENJAMIN CHAPMAN, STRAIN IMPROVEMENT OF BACTERIA, RIBONUCLEASE P. *Current Pos:* from asst prof to assoc prof, 83-96, ASSOC CHAIR, DEPT BIOL, CHEM, PHYS SCIS, ILL INST TECH, 95-, PROF, 96- *Personal Data:* b Saginaw, Mich, Nov 22, 49; m 79, Carol A Hunt; c Rebecca & Sarah. *Educ:* Univ Mich, Ann Arbor, BS, 71; Yale Univ, MPh, 74, PhD(biol), 77. *Prof Exp:* Fel biochem, Dept Bot, Wash State Univ, 77-79; res assoc, Dept Biol, Ind Univ, 79-82, vis asst prof, 82-83. *Concurrent Pos:* NSF energy related fel, Wash State Univ, 77-78. *Mem:* AAAS; Sigma Xi. *Res:* Genetic engineering using the bacterial hemoglobin gene to produce bacteria that are superior in the production of valuable metabolites or as bioremediators; study of the structure and function of toxoplasma RNASI P. *Mailing Add:* Dept Biol, Chem & Phys Scis Ill Inst Tech ITT Ctr Chicago IL 60616. *Fax:* 312-567-3494; *E-Mail:* bstark@charlie.cns.iit.edu

STARK, DENNIS MICHAEL, LABORATORY ANIMAL SCIENCE, INVITRO TOXICOLOGY. *Current Pos:* EXEC DIR VET SCI, BRISTOL MYERS SQUIBB, 91- *Personal Data:* b Baltimore, Md, May 16, 42; m 88, Simone; c Nicolas & Madeline. *Educ:* Univ Ga, DVM, 66; Cornell Univ, PhD(immunol), 69. *Honors & Awards:* Griffin Award, Am Asn Lab Animal Sci. *Prof Exp:* Res asst immunol, Cornell Univ, 66-69; asst prof, C W Post Col, Long Island Univ, 69-73; assoc prof path & dir animal facil, Med Ctr, NY Univ, 73-76; assoc prof & dir, Lab Animal Res Ctr, Rockefeller Univ, 76-91. *Mem:* AAAS; Am Soc Microbiol; Am Asn Lab Animal Sci (pres, 87); Am Vet Med Asn; fel NY Acad Sci; Soc Toxicol. *Res:* Immunology of diseases of laboratory animals; in vitro measurement of cytotoxicity. *Mailing Add:* 72 Henry Ave Princeton NJ 08540. *Fax:* 609-252-6607

STARK, EGON, MICROBIOLOGY. *Current Pos:* prof biol, 66-87, EMER PROF BIOL, ROCHESTER INST TECHNOL, 87- *Personal Data:* b Vienna, Austria, Sept 28, 20; nat US; m 48; c 3. *Educ:* Univ Man, BS, 47, MS, 48; Purdue Univ, PhD(microbiol), 51. *Prof Exp:* Asst org chem, Univ Man, 44-47, asst microbiol, 45-48; asst bact, Purdue Univ, 48-51, Purdue Res Found Indust fel & res assoc microbiol, 51-53; consult microbiol, 53-54; sr res scientist, Joseph E Seagram & Sons, Ky, 54-66. *Mem:* AAAS; Am Soc Microbiol; Am Chem Soc. *Res:* Microbiology of bacteria, yeasts, fungi; taxonomy, physiology, enzymology, ecology, fermentations, water pollution, waste disposal; process of producing a heat-stable bacterial amylase. *Mailing Add:* 152 Wintergreen Way Rochester NY 14618

STARK, FORREST OTTO, ORGANOSILICON CHEMISTRY, SILICONE MATERIALS. *Current Pos:* Chemist, Anal Labs, 51-61, Phys Chem Labs, 61-71, mgr, Med Tech Serv & Develop, 71-76, Resins & Chem Res, 76-79 & Elastomers Res, 79-81, dir, Silicone Res, 81-86, DIR HEALTH & ENVIRON SCI, DOW CORNING CORP, 86- *Personal Data:* b Bay City, Mich, Mar 31, 30; m 58; c 6. *Educ:* Univ Pittsburgh, BS, 55; Pa State Univ, University Park, PhD(phys & organic chem), 61. *Concurrent Pos:* Mem, adv bd, Mich Molecular Inst, 84-85. *Mem:* Am Chem Soc; Soc Chem Indust. *Res:* Synthesis and characterization of silane, silicon and ceramic materials for a wide range of applications in high technology industries such as aerospace, automotive, construction, medical and electronics. *Mailing Add:* 1801 Sylvan Midland MI 48640-2535

STARK, FRANCIS C, JR, HORTICULTURE. *Current Pos:* From asst prof to prof veg crops, Univ Md, 45-64, prof hort & head dept, 64-74, chmn, Food Sci Fac, 66-73, provost, Div Agr & Life Sci, 74-80, actg vchancellor acad affairs, 81-82, EMER PROF HORT, UNIV MD, COLLEGE PARK, 80-, SPEC ASST TO VPRES ACAD AFFAIRS, 82- *Personal Data:* b Drumright, Okla, Mar 19, 19; m 41, Dorothy L Moore; c Carolyn (Reich) & Francis C III. *Educ:* Okla State Univ, BS, 40; Univ Md, MS, 41, PhD(hort), 48. *Concurrent Pos:* Chmn, Gov Comn Migratory Labor, Md, 63-77; trustee, Lynchburg Col, 70-79; dir, Coun Agr Sci & Technol, 76-79. *Mem:* Fel AAAS; fel Am Soc Hort Sci. *Res:* Nutrition, physiology, breeding and culture of vegetable crops. *Mailing Add:* 7318 Radcliffe Dr College Park MD 20740-3024

STARK, GEORGE ROBERT, BIOCHEMISTRY. *Current Pos:* CHMN, RES INST, CLEVELAND CLINIC FOUND, 92- *Personal Data:* b New York, NY, July 4, 33; m 56, Mary Beck; c Robert B & Janna E. *Educ:* Columbia Univ, AB, 55, MA, 56, PhD(chem), 59. *Honors & Awards:* Reilly lectr, Notre Dame Univ, 72; H A Sober Mem lectr, Am Soc Biol Chemists, 86. *Prof Exp:* Res assoc biochem, Rockefeller Inst, 59-61, asst prof, 61-63; from asst prof to prof, Sch Med, Stanford Univ, 63-83; sr scientist, Imp Cancer Res Fund, London, 83-85, asst dir res, 85-89, assoc dir res, 89-92. *Concurrent Pos:* Guggenheim fel, 70-71; invited lectr, Australian Biochem Soc, 81; rep, US Nat Comt Biochem, Am Soc Biochem & Molecular Biol, 95. *Mem:* Nat Acad Sci; Am Chem Soc; Am Soc Biochem & Molecular Biol; fel Royal Soc; Europ Molecular Biol Orgn. *Res:* Chemistry and reactions of proteins; control of mammalian gene expression. *Mailing Add:* Cleveland Clin Found 9500 Euclid Ave Cleveland OH 44195. *Fax:* 216-444-3279; *E-Mail:* starkg@cesmtp.ccf.org

STARK, HAROLD EMIL, ENTOMOLOGY. *Current Pos:* RETIRED. *Personal Data:* b San Diego, Calif, July 26, 20; m 44, 71; c 4. *Educ:* San Diego State Col, BA, 43; Univ Utah, MS, 48; Univ Calif, PhD, 65. *Prof Exp:* Asst, Univ Utah, 46-48; jr entomologist, USPHS, 48-49, med entomologist, 50-63, trainin officer health mobilization, 63-64, ecol & chief vert-vector unit, Commun Dis Ctr, Ga, 64-68, entomologist, Walter Reed Army Inst Res, US Army Med Component/SEATO, Bangkok, Thailand, 68-70, res entomologist, Ecol Invest, Ctr Dis Control, USPHS, 70-73; res zoologist, Environ & Ecol Br, Dugway Proving Ground, Utah, 73-79. *Mem:* Entom Soc Am. *Res:* Systematics of Siphonaptera; ecology of small wild rodents and fleas in relation to natural occurrence of plague and tularemia; preparation of training literature and audiovisuals for vector-borne diseases; preparation of environmental impact assessments and statements. *Mailing Add:* 1205N-400W Trenton UT 84338

STARK, HAROLD MEAD, NUMBER THEORY. *Current Pos:* assoc prof, 69-72, PROF MATH, MASS INST TECHNOL, 72- *Personal Data:* b Los Angeles, Calif, Aug 6, 39; m 64. *Educ:* Calif Inst Technol, BS, 61; Univ Calif, Berkeley, MA, 63, PhD(math), 64. *Prof Exp:* From instr to asst prof math, Univ Mich, Ann Arbor, 64-66; asst prof, Univ Mich, Dearborn Ctr, 66-67; from asst prof to assoc prof, Univ Mich, Ann Arbor, 67-68. *Concurrent Pos:* Off Naval Res fel, 67-68; Sloan fel, 68-70. *Mem:* Am Math Soc; Math Asn Am. *Res:* Analytic and elementary number theory with emphasis on zeta functions and applications to quadratic fields. *Mailing Add:* Univ Calif San Diego 9500 Gilman Dr La Jolla CA 92093-0112

STARK, HENRY, COHERENT OPTICS, PATTERN RECOGNITION. *Current Pos:* CHMN, ELEC ENG DEPT, ILL INST TECHNOL, 89- *Personal Data:* b Antwerp, Belg, May 25, 38; US citizen; m 60; c 2. *Educ:* City Col New York, BS, 61; Columbia Univ, MS, 64, DrEngSc(elec eng), 68. *Prof Exp:* Asst proj engr, Bendix Corp, 61-62; res engr, Columbia Univ, 62-69; sr lectr elec eng, Israel Inst Technol, 69-70; from assoc prof to prof, Yale Univ, 70-77; from assoc prof to prof, Rensselaer Polytech Inst, 78-89. *Concurrent Pos:* Lectr, City Col New York, 67 & 69; jr fel, Weizmann Inst Sci, 69; Frederick Gardner Cottrell grant, Res Corp, 71-72, NSF, 73- & Air Force Res & Develop Command, 78-; consult, Rome Air Develop Ctr & Gen Elec Corp Res, 78- *Mem:* Fel Optical Soc Am; Inst Elec & Electronics Engrs; NY Acad Sci; Sigma Xi. *Res:* Information science, coherent optics, image and data processing; systems; electrical communications; mathematical statistics. *Mailing Add:* Ill Inst Technol Elec Eng Dept Siegal Hall Chicago IL 60616

STARK, J(OHN) P(AUL), JR, PHYSICS, METALLURGY. *Current Pos:* From asst prof to assoc prof, 63-72, PROF MECH ENG, UNIV TEX, AUSTIN, 72- *Personal Data:* b Des Moines, Iowa, Nov 9, 38; m 59. *Educ:* Univ Okla, BS, 60, PhD(metall), 63. *Concurrent Pos:* Consult, Humble Oil & Refining Co, Tex, 63-67 & Tracor, Inc, 64-65; NSF res grant, 66-68 & 74-; Air Force Off Sci Res grant, 72-76. *Mem:* Am Inst Mining, Metall & Petrol Engrs; Am Soc Metals; Am Phys Soc. *Res:* Diffusion in solids; thermodynamics; phase transformations. *Mailing Add:* Dept Mech Eng Univ Tex Austin TX 78712

STARK, JAMES CORNELIUS, ORGANIC CHEMISTRY, BIOCHEMISTRY. *Current Pos:* ASSOC PROF CHEM, EASTERN NAZARENE COL, 68- *Personal Data:* b Port Jefferson, NY, Sept 1, 41; m 63; c 3. *Educ:* Eastern Nazarene Col, BS, 63; Purdue Univ, Lafayette, PhD(org chem), 69. *Mem:* Am Chem Soc. *Res:* Preparation and reactions of polyhalo-organic compounds. *Mailing Add:* Dept Chem Eastern Nazarene Col Quincy MA 02170-2999

STARK, JEREMIAH MILTON, MATHEMATICS. *Current Pos:* head dept, 56-77, PROF MATH, LAMAR UNIV, 56- *Personal Data:* b Norfolk, Va, Apr 1, 22; m 49, 62; c 3. *Educ:* US Coast Guard Acad, BS, 44; NTex State Col, BS, 46; Mass Inst Technol, SM, 49, PhD(math), 54. *Prof Exp:* Instr math, Mass Inst Technol, 49-52, mathematician instrumentation lab, 54-56. *Concurrent Pos:* NSF sci fac fel, Stanford Univ, 63-64. *Mem:* AAAS; Am Math Soc; Math Asn Am; Soc Indust & Appl Math. *Res:* Analysis; complex variables. *Mailing Add:* 304 W Dogwood St Woodville TX 75979

STARK, JOEL, SPEECH PATHOLOGY. *Current Pos:* assoc prof, 68-72, PROF COMMUN ARTS & SCI & DIR SPEECH & HEARING CTR, QUEENS COL, NY, 72- *Personal Data:* b New York, NY, Nov 18, 30; m 50; c 2. *Educ:* Long Island Univ, BA, 50; Columbia Univ, MA, 51; NY Univ, PhD(speech), 56. *Prof Exp:* Instr speech, Long Island Univ, 51-54; asst prof, City Col New York, 54-65; assoc prof speech path, Sch Med, Stanford Univ, 65-68. *Concurrent Pos:* Nat Inst Neurol Dis & Blindness fel, 62-64; mem coun except children. *Mem:* Am Speech & Hearing Asn; Am Asn Ment Deficiency. *Res:* Communications disorders; language development and disorders in children. *Mailing Add:* Dept Commun Arts & Sci City Univ NY Queens Col 6530 Kissena Blvd Flushing NY 11367-1575

STARK, JOHN, JR, CHEMICAL ENGINEERING. *Current Pos:* RETIRED. *Personal Data:* b Headland, Ala, Aug 26, 21; m 58; c 2. *Educ:* Univ Ala, BS, 48, MS, 61, PhD(chem eng), 64. *Prof Exp:* Chemist, Astilleros Dominicanos, 55-60; asst prof chem eng, Univ Ala, 64-65; assoc prof, Univ SAla, 65-77, prof chem eng & chmn dept, 77-86; mem fac, Univ Tex, Austin, 86- *Concurrent Pos:* Consult, NASA, Ala, 64-68. *Mem:* Am Chem Soc; Am Inst Chem Engrs. *Res:* Turbo grid-plate efficiencies; distribution of noncondensable gases in liquids; effect of surface waves on evaporation rates. *Mailing Add:* 5622 William & Mary St Mobile AL 36608

STARK, JOHN HOWARD, PAPERMAKING CHEMISTRY. *Personal Data:* b Port Jefferson, NY, Sept 1, 41; m 63, Patricia Reed; c Brenda, Douglas & Michelle. *Educ:* Eastern Nazarene Col, BS, 63; Purdue Univ, MS, 65, PhD(biochem), 69. *Honors & Awards:* Texaco Res Award, Am Chem Soc. *Prof Exp:* Sr res assoc mat res, Int Paper, 87-93. *Concurrent Pos:* Group mgr, fiber sci. *Mem:* Am Chem Soc; Sigma Xi; Tech Asn Pulp & Paper Indust. *Res:* Papermaking chemistry; application of new materials to improve product performance; chemistry and physics of pulp fibers. *Mailing Add:* Int Paper Long Meadow Rd Tuxedo Park NY 10987

STARK, LARRY GENE, PHARMACOLOGY. *Current Pos:* From asst prof to assoc prof, 69-82, asst dean curricular affairs, 80-83, PROF PHARMACOL, SCH MED, UNIV CALIF, DAVIS, 82-, CHMN DEPT, 83- *Personal Data:* b Abilene, Kans, Dec 31, 38; m 76; c 2. *Educ:* Univ Kans, BS, 61, MS, 63; Stanford Univ, PhD(pharmacol), 68. *Concurrent Pos:* NIH fel, Univ Chicago, 68-69; guest prof, Pharmacol Inst, Univ Bern, Switz, 83-84. *Mem:* Soc Neurosci; Am Soc Pharmacol & Exp Therapeut; Am Epilepsy Soc. *Res:* Anticonvulsant drugs and models of epilepsy. *Mailing Add:* Dept Pharmacol & Toxicol Univ Calif Davis Sch Med Davis CA 95616-5224. *Fax:* 530-752-7710; *E-Mail:* lostark@ucdavis.bitnet

STARK, LAWRENCE W, BIOENGINEERING. *Current Pos:* prof, 68-94, EMER PROF PHYSIOL OPTICS & ENG SCI, UNIV CALIF, BERKELEY, 94-, PROF, GRAD SCH, 94- *Personal Data:* b New York, NY, Feb 21, 26; m 49; c 3. *Educ:* Columbia Univ, AB, 45; Albany Med Col, MD, 48; Am Bd Psychiat & Neurol, dipl, 57. *Hon Degrees:* ScD(hon), SUNY, 88;

Dr, Tokushima Univ, Japan, 92. *Honors & Awards:* Morlock Award in Biomed Eng, 77; Franklin V Taylor Award, 89; Charles F Prentice Medal, Am Acad Optom, 95. *Prof Exp:* Intern, US Naval Hosp, St Albans, 48-49; res asst biochem, Oxford Univ & mem, Trinity Col, 49-50; res asst physiol, Univ Col, London, 50-51; asst prof physiol & pharmacol & res assoc neurophysiol & neuromuscular physiol, NY Med Col, 51; from instr to asst prof neurol & assoc physician, Yale Univ, 55-60; head neurol sect, Ctr Commun Sci, Res Lab Electronics & Electronic Systs Lab, Mass Inst Technol, 60-65; prof bioeng, neurol & physiol & chmn, Biomed Eng Dept, Univ Ill, Chicago Circle, 65-68. *Concurrent Pos:* Fel neurol & EEG, Neurol Inst, Columbia Univ & Presby Hosp, 51-52; fel neurol, Sch Med, Yale Univ, 54-55; fel, Mass Inst Technol, 60-65; fel neurol, Mass Gen Hosp, 60-65; Guggenheim fel, 68-70; vis app, Univ Col, London, 50-51, Nobel Inst Neurophysiol, Stockholm, 57, Harvard Univ, 63-65, Univ Calif, Los Angeles, 65 & Stanford Univ, 68 & 75; dir, Biosysts, Inc, Cambridge, 62-67 & Biocontacts, Inc, Berkeley, 69-73; chmn neurosci work session, Math Concepts of Cent Nerv Syst, 64, Gordon Conf Biomath, 65 & bioeng training comt, Nat Inst Gen Med Sci, 67-68; consult, NIH, NSF & var indust companies; assoc ed or ed bd mem, Math Biosci, Inst Elec & Electronics Eng-SMC, Brain Res, J Appl Physiol, J Neurosci & Comput in Biol & Med; emer prof neurol, Univ Calif, San Francisco, 74- *Mem:* Am Physiol Soc; Biophys Soc; Am Acad Neurol; fel Inst Elec & Electronic Engrs; Asn Comput Mach; fel Am Inst Med & Biol Eng, 92. *Res:* Application of communication and information theory to neurophysiology; normal and abnormal neurological control systems; cybernetics; pattern recognition and artificial intelligence; information flow in biological evolution and economic theory; neurological control theory, especially applied to ocular motor systems; robotic manipulation, locomotion and vision compared with biological mechanisms. *Mailing Add:* 485 Minor Hall Univ Calif Berkeley CA 94720-2020. *Fax:* 510-642-7196; *E-Mail:* stark@pupil.berkeley.edu

STARK, MARVIN MICHAEL, DENTISTRY. *Current Pos:* PROF OPER DENT & ORAL BIOL, SCH DENT, UNIV CALIF, SAN FRANCISCO, 53-; CHIEF DENT OFFICER, STATE CALIF DEPT HEALTH, 75- *Personal Data:* b Mich, Mar 14, 21; c 3. *Educ:* Univ Calif, Los Angeles, AB, 48, DDS, 52. *Concurrent Pos:* Res fel dent med, Sch Dent Med, Harvard Univ, 52-53. *Mem:* Am Asn Endodont; fel Int Col Dent; fel Am Col Dent; Am Dent Asn; Int Asn Dent Res. *Mailing Add:* Dept Dent Univ Calif Box 0758 San Francisco CA 94143

STARK, NATHAN JULIUS, HEALTH LAW. *Current Pos:* RETIRED. *Personal Data:* b Minneapolis, Minn, Nov 9, 20; m 43; c 4. *Educ:* US Merchant Marine Acad, BS, 43; Chicago Kent Col Law, JD, 48. *Hon Degrees:* LLD, Park Col, 69, Univ Mo; LHD, Hahnemann Univ. *Honors & Awards:* Trustee Award, Am Med Asn, 74. *Prof Exp:* Plant mgr, Englander Co, Inc, Chicago, 49-51; partner law firm, Downey, Abrams, Stark & Sullivan, Kansas City, 52-53; vpres, Rival Mfg Co, Kansas City, 54-59; sr vpres opers, Hallmark Cards, Inc, Kansas City, 59-74; vchancellor, Schs Health Professions & pres, Univ Health Ctr, Univ Pittsburgh, 74-79, prof health sci & sr vchancellor, Grad Sch Pub Health, 80-86; undersecy, US Dept Health & Human Serv, 79-80. *Concurrent Pos:* Secy, Eddie Jacobson Mem Found, 60-; pres & chmn, Kansas City Gen Hosp & Med Ctr, 62-74; vchmn, Health Ins Benefits Adv Comt, HEW, 65-70, secy, Task Force Medicaid, 69-70, chmn, Adv Comn Incentive Reimbursement Exp, 68-70, chmn, Capital Investment Conf, HEW-Health Resources Admin, 76; dir, Woolf Bros, Inc, ERC Corp & Nat Fidelity Ins Co Hallmark Continental Ltd, Ireland, 71-73; pres & chmn bd, Crown Ctr Redevelop Corp, Kansas City, 72-74; chmn community hosp-med staff group pract prog, Robert Wood Johnson Found, 74-79; mem, Med Malpract Adv Comt, Inst Med-Nat Acad Sci, 75-79; mem bd, Am Nurses Found, 75-79; mem tech bd, Milbank Mem Fund, 76-79; fel, Hastings Ctr, mem bd trustees, 81; mem exec bd, Nat Bd Med Examiners; consult & treas, Nat Acad Social Ins. *Mem:* Inst Med-Nat Acad Sci; hon mem Am Hosp Asn; hon mem Am Col Hosp Adminrs; AMA. *Mailing Add:* 4343 Westover Pl NW Washington DC 20016

STARK, NELLIE MAY, SOIL ECOLOGY, FORESTRY. *Current Pos:* COURTESY PROF, ORE STATE UNIV, 92- *Personal Data:* b Norwich, Conn, Nov 20, 33; m 62. *Educ:* Conn Col, BA, 56; Duke Univ, MA, 58, PhD(plant ecol, bot), 62. *Prof Exp:* Botanist, Pac Southwest Forest & Range Exp Sta, US Forest Serv, 58-64; res assoc, Lab Atmospheric Physics, Desert Res Inst, Univ Nev, Reno, 64-72; assoc prof, Univ Mont, 72-79, prof forestry, 79-92. *Concurrent Pos:* Mem, Alph Helix Res Exped for Desert Res Inst, Brazil & Peru, 67; Int Biol Prog grants & NSF grants, 72-73. *Mem:* Soc Am Foresters. *Res:* Nutrient cycling and soil ecology in tropical and temperate forests; fire and logging ecology; applied concept of the biological life of a soil to land use management; forest ecology; soil chemistry; xylem sap chemistry; chemical perturbation of forest ecosystems; aging in trees; survival ecology based on wild animal behavior. *Mailing Add:* 36053 Blakesley Creek Rd Philomath OR 97370

STARK, PAUL, PHARMACOLOGY, PHYSIOLOGY. *Current Pos:* PRES & CHIEF EXEC OFFICER, INT CLIN RES CORP, 84- *Personal Data:* b Philadelphia, Pa, Feb 1, 29; m 52; c 3. *Educ:* McGill Univ, BSc, 49; Univ Rochester, PhD(pharmacol), 63; Sch Law, Ind Univ, JD, 77. *Prof Exp:* Chief prod biochem, Gerber Prod Co, 52-55; res technician, Stromberg-Carlson Co, 55-57; res chemist, Allerton Chem, 57-60; sr pharmacologist, Eli Lilly & Co, 63-66, res scientist, 67-72, res assoc, 72-84. *Concurrent Pos:* Assoc prof, Sch Med, Ind Univ, Indianapolis. *Mem:* Int Col Neuropsychopharmacol; Am Soc Pharmacol & Exp Therapeut; Am Physiol Soc; Am Bar Asn; Soc Neurosci. *Res:* Neuropharmacological and psychopharmacological techniques in the study of neuro-transmitters within the central nervous system; clinical evaluation of psychotropic drugs. *Mailing Add:* 160 Olde Mill Circle S Dr Indianapolis IN 46260

STARK, PHILIP HERALD, PETROLEUM DATABASES. *Current Pos:* mgr geol applns, Petrol Info Corp, 69-74, dir tech applns, 74-77, vpres spec projs, 77-84, exec vpres int opers, 84-88, vpres tech mkt, 88-92, VPRES NEW VENTURES, PETROL INFO CORP, 93- *Personal Data:* b Iowa City, Iowa, Mar 2, 36; m 81, Christine K Baumgartner; c Johnathon P. *Educ:* Univ Okla, BS, 58; Univ Wis, MS, 61, PhD(geol), 63. *Prof Exp:* Explor geologist, Mobil Oil Corp, 63-65, sr explor geologist, 65-66, regional comput coordr, 66-69. *Concurrent Pos:* Lectr, Continuing Educ Prog, Am Asn Petrol Geologists. *Mem:* Soc Econ Paleontologists & Mineralogists; Am Asn Petrol Geologists. *Res:* Stratigraphy and micropaleontology of Paleozoic flysch facies; computer applications in geology for petroleum exploration; US natural gas productivity. *Mailing Add:* 2770 S Elmira St Denver CO 80231. *Fax:* 303-694-1754

STARK, RICHARD B, PLASTIC SURGERY. *Current Pos:* from instr to assoc prof, 55-73, PROF CLIN SURG, COL PHYSICIANS & SURGEONS, COLUMBIA UNIV, 73- *Personal Data:* b Conrad, Iowa, Mar 31, 15; m 67, Judy Thornton. *Educ:* Stanford Univ, AB, 36; Cornell Univ, MD, 41; Am Bd Plastic Surg, dipl, 52 & 78. *Honors & Awards:* Res Prize, Am Soc Plastic & Reconstruct Surg Found, 51; Medal of Honor, Vietnam, 67 & 69; Order of San Carlos, Colombia, 69; Dieffenbach Award, Ger, 92; Gold Medal, Nat Inst Social Scis, 92. *Prof Exp:* Intern, Peter Bent Brigham & Children's Hosps, Boston, Mass, 41-42; resident, Children's Hosp, 42; plastic surgeon, Northington Gen Hosp, Tuscaloosa, Ala, 45-46 & Percy Jones Gen Hosp, Battle Creek, Mich, 46; surgeon, Kingsbridge Vet Hosp & NY Hosp, 47-50; from inst to assoc prof clin surg, Cornell Med Col, 50-55. *Concurrent Pos:* Exchange scholar, Univ Heidelberg, Ger, 36-37; fel, Med Sch, Stanford Univ, 46-47; plastic surgeon, NY Hosp, 48-55; attend surgeon chg plastic surg, St Luke's Hosp, 58-77; vis prof, Univ Tex, 65, Univ Mich, 66, Walter Reed Med Ctr, 70, Univ Man, 71 & Univ Pa, 82, SAM, 73, France & Spain, 80; from vpres to pres, Am Bd Plastic Surg, 66-68; ed, Annals Plastic Surg, 77-82. *Mem:* AAAS; Soc Univ Surg; Am Soc Plastic & Reconstructive Surgeons; Am Asn Plastic Surg; Am Col Surgeons; Am Surg Asn. *Res:* Circulation in skin grafts; homologous transplants of skin; pathogenesis of harelip and cleft palate; aesthetic surgery; reconstruction of total face. *Mailing Add:* 35 E 75th St New York NY 10021

STARK, RICHARD HARLAN, COMPUTER SCIENCE. *Current Pos:* PROF COMPUT SCI, NMEX STATE UNIV, 69- *Personal Data:* b Ozawkie, Kans, Dec 5, 16; m 42; c 4. *Educ:* Univ Kans, AB, 38; Northwestern Univ, MS, 42, PhD(math), 46. *Prof Exp:* Jr physicist, US Naval Ord Lab, 42-43 & Los Alamos Sci Lab, 44-45; instr math, Northwestern Univ, 46-48; mathematician, Los Alamos Sci Lab, 48-51; mgr math analysis, Knolls Atomic Power Lab, Gen Elec Co, 52-56, mgr math & comput oper, Atomic Power Equip Dept, 56-61, consult analyst, Comput Dept, 62-64; from assoc prof to prof math & info sci, Wash State Univ, 64-69. *Mem:* Soc Indust & Appl Math; Asn Comput Mach. *Res:* Proofs of program validity. *Mailing Add:* 4119 Macaw Circle Las Cruces NM 88005

STARK, ROBERT M, OPERATIONS RESEARCH, CIVIL ENGINEERING. *Current Pos:* PROF CIVIL ENG & MATH SCI, UNIV DEL, 76- *Personal Data:* b New York, NY, Feb 6, 30; wid; c Bradley R, Timothy D, Steven M & Candice B (Combs). *Educ:* Johns Hopkins Univ, AB, 51; Univ Mich, MA, 52; Univ Del, PhD(appl sci), 65. *Prof Exp:* Instr physics, Rochester Inst Technol, 55-57; asst prof math & asst dean col eng, Cleveland State Univ, 57-62; from asst prof to assoc prof civil eng, statist & comput sci, Univ Del, 62-72; vis assoc prof civil eng, Mass Inst Technol, 72-73. *Concurrent Pos:* Res physicist, Bausch & Lomb Optical Co, 55-56; consult various industs & govt agencies. *Mem:* Fel AAAS; Opers Res Soc Am; Am Soc Civil Engrs; Am Soc Eng Educ; Nat Coun Teachers Math. *Res:* Civil engineering systems; applied probability; engineering management; applied mathematics. *Mailing Add:* Dept Math Sci Univ Del Newark DE 19716. *Fax:* 302-831-4456; *E-Mail:* start@math.udel.edu

STARK, RONALD WILLIAM, FOREST ENTOMOLOGY. *Current Pos:* RETIRED. *Personal Data:* b Can, Dec 4, 22; nat US; m 44; c 2. *Educ:* Univ Toronto, BScF, 48, MA, 51; Univ BC, PhD(forest entom), 58. *Honors & Awards:* Gold Medalist, Entom Soc Can. *Prof Exp:* Agr res officer, Div Forest Biol, Sci Serv, Can Dept Agr, 48-59; asst prof entom & asst entomologist, Agr Exp Sta, Univ Calif, Berkeley, 59-61, from assoc prof to prof, 61-70, entomologist, 61-70, vchmn, Dept Entom & Parasitol, 68-70; grad dean & coordr res, Univ Idaho, 70-77, prof forestry & entom, 78-, emer prof. *Concurrent Pos:* NSF sr fel, 67-68; collabr, Pac Southwest Forest & Range Exp Sta, US Forest Serv; Am rep & chmn working group forest entom, Int Union Forest Res Orgn; proj leader, Pest Mgt Prog Pine Back Beetle Ecosyst, Int Biol Prog; mem, USDA Comt Scientists, 76-78, dep prog mgr, USDA Expanded Douglas-fir Tussock Moth Prog, Portland, Ore, 77-78; prog mgr, Int Spruce Budworms Prog, Western Component, US Forest Serv. *Mem:* AAAS; Soc Am Foresters; fel Entom Soc Am; Ecol Soc Am; Entom Soc Can. *Res:* Population dynamics; integrated pest management; research management. *Mailing Add:* 520 S First Sandpoint ID 83864-1206

STARK, ROYAL WILLIAM, SOLID STATE PHYSICS, LOW TEMPERATURE PHYSICS. *Current Pos:* PROF PHYSICS, UNIV ARIZ, 72- *Personal Data:* b Wellington, Ohio, Apr 30, 37; m 62; c 2. *Educ:* Case Inst Technol, BS, 59, MS, 61, PhD(physics), 62. *Prof Exp:* Res assoc solid state physics, Case Inst Technol, 62; from instr to prof, Univ Chicago & Inst Study Metals, 63-72. *Concurrent Pos:* Alfred P Sloan res fel, 64-70. *Mem:* Am Phys Soc. *Res:* Electronic properties of metals; magnetic breakdown; Fermi surface and band structure; ferromagnetism; plasma effects. *Mailing Add:* 1285 N Speedway Pl Tucson AZ 85715

STARK, RUTH E, NUCLEAR MAGNETIC RESONANCE, MOLECULAR BIOPHYSICS. *Current Pos:* ASSOC PROF CHEM, COL STATEN ISLAND, CITY UNIV NY, 85- *Personal Data:* b Philadelphia, Sept 22, 50. *Educ:* Cornell Univ, AB, 72; Univ Calif, San Diego, PhD(phys chem), 77. *Prof Exp:* Res assoc fel, Nat Magnet Lab, Mass Inst Technol, 77-79; asst prof chem, Amherst Col, 79-85. *Mem:* Am Chem Soc; Sigma Xi; Am Women Sci; Biophys Soc. *Mailing Add:* Dept Chem 6S-220 Col Staten Island City Univ NY 2800 Victory Blvd Staten Island NY 10314. *Fax:* 718-816-9095; *E-Mail:* ressi@cunyvm.cuny.edu

STARK, WALTER A(LFRED), JR, PHYSICAL CHEMISTRY. *Current Pos:* STAFF MEM MATS SCI, LOS ALAMOS NAT LAB, 73- *Personal Data:* b San Antonio, Tex, Aug 30, 40; m 68, Charlotte Brown; c 1. *Educ:* Princeton Univ, AB, 62; Univ Calif, Berkeley, PhD(chem), 67; Univ NMex, MBA, 82. *Prof Exp:* Staff mem mat sci, Sandia Labs, 67-73. *Mem:* Am Phys Soc. *Res:* Transport properties of materials, especially diffusion and permeation; high temperature materials compatibility. *Mailing Add:* 275 Kimberly Los Alamos NM 87544. *Fax:* 505-665-1357

STARK, WILLIAM POLSON, AQUATIC ENTOMOLOGY, SYSTEMATICS. *Current Pos:* Asst prof, 76-80, assoc prof, 80-86, PROF BIOL, MISS COL, 86- *Personal Data:* b French Camp, Calif, Dec 30, 43; m 65; c 2. *Educ:* Southeastern Okla State Univ, BS, 65; NTex State Univ, MS, 72; Univ Utah, PhD(biol), 74. *Concurrent Pos:* Adj prof biol, NTex State Univ, 77-87; res assoc, Fla Collection Arthropods, 77-87. *Mem:* Entom Soc Am; NAm Benthological Soc; Soc Syst Zool. *Res:* Systematics and biology of Nearctic Plecoptera. *Mailing Add:* 1603 Laurelwood Dr Clinton MS 39056

STARK, WILLIAM RICHARD, DISTRIBUTED COMPUTATION & ALGEBRAIC ASPECTS OF COMPUTATION, BIOLOGICAL INFORMATION PROCESSING. *Current Pos:* assoc dir, Inst Construct Math, 87-91, CHMN, MATH DEPT, UNIV SFLA, 94-, PROF MATH, 95- *Personal Data:* b Lexington, Ky, Apr 28, 45; m 68, Judy Kay Ingrao; c Christopher Jon. *Educ:* Univ Ky, BS, 68; Univ Wis-Madison, PhD(math), 75. *Prof Exp:* Fel, Univ Wis-Madison, 69-74; instr math, Univ Tex, Austin, 74-78; asst prof, Calif State Univ, San Jose, 78-79; assoc prof math, Univ SFla, 78-85; sr scientist, AT&T Bell Labs, 85-88. *Mem:* Am Math Soc; Asn Symbolic Logic; Asn Comput Mach; Math Asn Am; Union Concerned Scientists. *Res:* Formal mathematical aspects of asynchronous distributed computation; biological information processing. *Mailing Add:* Math Dept Univ SFla Tampa FL 33620-5700. *Fax:* 813-974-2700; *E-Mail:* stark@math.usf.edu

STARKE, ALBERT CARL, JR, ORGANIC CHEMISTRY & BIOCHEMISTRY, INFORMATION SCIENCE. *Current Pos:* RETIRED. *Personal Data:* b Cleveland, Ohio, Jan 14, 16; m 41, Annette Jensen; c Robert C, Richard J & John M. *Educ:* Fla Southern Col, BS, 36; Northwestern Univ, PhD(chem), 40. *Prof Exp:* Lab instr, Dent Sch, Northwestern Univ, 37-40, Nat Defense Res Comt fel, 40-42; res chemist, GAF Corp, 42-46, patent searcher, 46-47, patent liaison, 48-50, patent agt, 50-55, supvr tech info serv, 55-66, mgr tech info, 66-72; res specialist, Univ Conn, 72-81; info mgr, New Eng Res Appln Ctr, 72-81. *Concurrent Pos:* Mem, Franklin Inst, Chem Abstr communicator, 66- *Mem:* Fel AAAS; Am Chem Soc; Am Soc Info Sci; fel Am Inst Chemists. *Res:* Physiological and synthetic organic chemistry; color photography; patent soliciting and prosecution; warfare agents; polymers; storage and retrieval of technical information; computer systems design; documentation; computer searching of major computerized scientific file. *Mailing Add:* 10 Carriage Cove Way Sanford FL 32773-6012

STARKE, EDGAR ARLIN, JR, PHYSICAL METALLURGY. *Current Pos:* dean, Sch Eng & Appl Sci, 84-94, EARNEST OGLESBY PROF MAT SCI, UNIV VA, 83- *Personal Data:* b Richmond, Va, May 10, 36; m 61, Donna Frazier; c John A & Karen (De Conti). *Educ:* Va Polytech Inst, BS, 60; Univ Ill, MS, 61; Univ Fla, PhD(metall), 64. *Prof Exp:* Res metallurgist, Savannah River Lab, E I du Pont de Nemours & Co, Inc, 61-62; from asst prof to prof metall, Ga Inst Technol, 64-82, dir, Fracture & Fatigue Res Lab, 78-82. *Concurrent Pos:* Consult, Lockheed Co, Northrop Corp, Reynolds Metals Co, Arco Metals Co, Kaiser Aluminum; vis scientist, Oak Ridge Nat Lab, 67 & Max Planck Inst Metall Res, 71; Sigma Xi res award, 70, Nonferrous Div Wire Asn, 72; mem res coun, Defense Advan Res Projs Agency, acad adv comt, Aluminum Asn, bd rev, Metall Trans Asn, adv bd, Nat Mat, panel, Agard, NATO, adv comt, Aeronaut, NASA. *Mem:* Fel Am Soc Metals Int; Am Inst Mining, Metall & Petrol Engrs. *Res:* Strengthening mechanisms; alloy theory; fracture and fatigue; aluminum alloys. *Mailing Add:* Sch Eng & Appl Sci Univ Va Charlottesville VA 22901. *E-Mail:* eas.1@virginia.edu

STARKEBAUM, WARREN L, BIOMEDICAL ENGINEERING. *Current Pos:* mgr, Heart Tissue Stimulation Prog, 83-85, prod develop mgr, 85-93, DIR TECH DEVELOP, NEUROL DIV, MEDTRONIC INC, 93- *Personal Data:* b Richland, Wash, Aug 29, 49. *Educ:* Univ Wash, BS, 71; Univ Pa, PhD(mat sci & biomed eng), 77. *Prof Exp:* Mat res lab mgr, Zimmer Corp, 77-81; tech dir, Kirschner Med, 81-83. *Mem:* Soc Biomat; Biomed Eng Soc; Asn Advan Med Instrumentation; Am Soc Testing & Mat. *Mailing Add:* 4230 Trentonlnn Minneapolis MN 55442

STARKEY, EUGENE EDWARD, DAIRY SCIENCE. *Current Pos:* RETIRED. *Personal Data:* b Yakima, Wash, July 14, 26; m 54; c 3. *Educ:* Calif State Polytech Col, BS, 52; Univ Wis, MS, 54, PhD(dairy husb, genetics), 58. *Prof Exp:* Res asst, Univ Wis, 52-55; dairy husbandman, Dairy Husb Res Br, Agr Res Serv, USDA, 55-57; asst prof dairy prod, Utah State Univ, 57-60; prof dairy prod, Univ Wis-Madison, 60-78; prof & head dept, Calif Polytech State Univ, 78-91, emer prof dairy sci, 91. *Mem:* Am Dairy Sci Asn. *Res:* Dairy cattle breeding sire selection and evaluation of environmental influences on production. *Mailing Add:* 1730 Portola San Luis Obispo CA 93405

STARKEY, FRANK DAVID, ORGANIC CHEMISTRY. *Current Pos:* HUMAN RES PROG MGR RES & DEVELOP, GE CORP, 80- *Personal Data:* b Indianapolis, Ind, Aug 6, 44; m 67; c 2. *Educ:* Wabash Col, AB, 66; Brown Univ, PhD(org chem), 73. *Prof Exp:* From asst prof to assoc prof chem, Wesleyan Univ, 71-80, head dept, 79-80. *Concurrent Pos:* Vis res assoc, Univ Minn, 77-78. *Mem:* Am Chem Soc; AAAS. *Res:* Carbonium ion chemistry; synthesis and reaction of various substrates that give carbonium ions. *Mailing Add:* 1274 Regent St Schenectady NY 12309-5351

STARKEY, JOHN, STRUCTURAL GEOLOGY, PETROFABRIC ANALYSIS. *Current Pos:* from asst prof to assoc prof, 65,79, PROF GEOL, UNIV WESTERN ONT, 79- *Personal Data:* b Manchester, Eng, Aug 11, 36; m 58; c 2. *Educ:* Univ Liverpool, BSc, 57, PhD(geol), 60. *Prof Exp:* NATO & Dept Sci & Indust Res Gt Brit res fels geol, Inst Crystallog & Petrol, Swiss Fed Inst Technol, 60-62; Miller res fel, Univ Calif, Berkeley, 62-65. *Concurrent Pos:* Leverhulme Europ fel, 60-61; Royal Soc bursary, Imp Col, Univ London, 71-72; vis prof geochem, Fed Univ Bahia, Salvador, Brazil, 75-77; vis prof geol, Monash Univ, Australia, 78; vis prof geol, Eidgenoessiche Technische Hochschule, Zurich, Switzerland, 78-79. *Mem:* Brit Mineral Soc; Am Mineral Soc; Mineral Soc Can; Geol Asn Can; Sigma Xi. *Res:* Petrofabric analysis of rocks, primarily by x-ray techniques image analysis, with particular reference to the microstructures of deformed rocks; crystallography of plagioclase feldspars and their twinning; crystal chemistry of rock forming minerals. *Mailing Add:* Dept Earth Sci Univ Western Ont London ON N6A 3B7 Can. *Fax:* 519-661-3198; *E-Mail:* jstarkey@julian.vwo.ca

STARKEY, PAUL EDWARD, pedodontics, dentistry, for more information see previous edition

STARKEY, WALTER L(EROY), MECHANICAL ENGINEERING. *Current Pos:* from instr to prof, 47-78, EMER PROF MECH ENG, OHIO STATE UNIV, 78- *Personal Data:* b Minneapolis, Minn, Oct 5, 20; m 49; c 2. *Educ:* Univ Louisville, BME, 43; Ohio State Univ, MSc, 47, PhD(mech eng), 50. *Honors & Awards:* Mach Design Award, Am Soc Mech Engrs, 71. *Prof Exp:* Instr mech eng, Univ Louisville, 43-46. *Concurrent Pos:* Consult, 50- *Mem:* Fel Am Soc Mech Engrs. *Res:* Fatigue of metals; mechanics of materials; machine dynamics; mechanical design of machinery. *Mailing Add:* 6503 Cook Rd Powell OH 43065-8969

STARKOVSKY, NICOLAS ALEXIS, ORGANIC CHEMISTRY. *Current Pos:* RETIRED. *Personal Data:* b Alexandria, Egypt, Jan 15, 22; US citizen; m 59, Lilia B. *Educ:* Univ Cairo, BS, 46, MS, 54, PhD(chem), 56. *Prof Exp:* Res chemist, Memphis Chem Co, Egypt, 51-60, Dow Chem Co, 61-64; fel, Columbia Univ, 60-61; dir res & develop, Collab Res, Inc, Mass, 64-70; dir proj develop, Ortho Res Found, NJ, 71-72; sr scientist, Wampole Div, Carter Wallace, Inc, Cranbury, 73-80; dir pro develop, Meloy Labs, Va, 80-82. *Concurrent Pos:* ESL teacher, Fairfax Co Pub Schs Adult Ed, 82- *Mem:* Am Chem Soc. *Res:* Immunology; clinical medicine. *Mailing Add:* 6352 Silas Burke Burke VA 22015-3447

STARKS, AUBRIE NEAL, JR, ANALYTICAL CHEMISTRY. *Current Pos:* MEM FAC, CHEM DEPT, NORTHEAST LOUISIANA UNIV, 80- *Personal Data:* b Dermott, Ark, Aug 20, 46. *Educ:* Southern Ill Univ, Carbondale, BA, 67; Univ Ark, Fayetteville, PhD(chem), 75. *Prof Exp:* Instr chem, Univ Ark, Fayetteville, 73-74; intern, Hendrix Col, 74-75; asst prof chem, Thiel Col, 75-80. *Mem:* Am Chem Soc. *Res:* Photovoltammetric investigation of transition metal complexes for photocurrents generated in optically-shielded electrode systems. *Mailing Add:* 2012 Elton Ft Worth TX 76117-6507

STARKS, FRED, DEVELOPMENT OF CANDIDATE DRUGS FOR CANCER & AIDS, RESEARCH ADMINISTRATION. *Current Pos:* CHMN & CHIEF EXEC OFFICER, STARKS ASSOCS, 57- *Personal Data:* b Milford, Ill, Aug 16, 21. *Res:* Development of candidate drugs for cancer and acquired immunodeficiency syndrome. *Mailing Add:* 742 Highland Ave Buffalo NY 14223-1645

STARKS, KENNETH JAMES, ENTOMOLOGY. *Current Pos:* RETIRED. *Personal Data:* b Ft Worth, Tex, July 27, 24; m 51; c 2. *Educ:* Univ Okla, BS, 50, MS, 51; Iowa State Univ, PhD(entom), 54. *Prof Exp:* Asst prof, Univ Ky, 53-61; mem staff, USDA, Uganda, 61-69; prof entom, Okla State Univ, 69; res & location leader, Agr Res Serv, USDA, 69-85. *Mem:* Entom Soc Am. *Res:* Grain insects investigations. *Mailing Add:* 724 W Ute Ave Stillwater OK 74075

STARKS, THOMAS HAROLD, ENVIRONMENTAL STATISTICS. *Current Pos:* RETIRED. *Personal Data:* b Owatonna, Minn, Aug 19, 30; m 59, Kathleen Boulden; c Clandia & Warren. *Educ:* Mankato State Col, BA, 52; Purdue Univ, MS, 54; Va Polytech Inst, PhD(statist), 59. *Honors & Awards:* Sci & Technol Achievement Award, 88 US Environ Protection Agency. *Prof Exp:* Spec serv engr, E I DuPont de Nemours & Co, 59-61; from assoc prof to prof math, Southern Ill Univ, Carbondale, 61-84; sr statistician, Environ Res Ctr, Univ Nev, Las Vegas, 84-89. *Mem:* Inst Math Statist. *Res:* Design of experiments; statistical inference; geostatistics. *Mailing Add:* 1954 Rockledge Dr Las Vegas NV 89119

STARKWEATHER, GARY KEITH, physical optics, electrooptics, for more information see previous edition

STARKWEATHER, HOWARD WARNER, JR, PHYSICAL CHEMISTRY. *Current Pos:* RETIRED. *Personal Data:* b Cambridge, Mass, July 20, 26; m 48, Elizabeth M; c Mary, John, & Catherine. *Educ:* Haverford Col, AB, 48; Harvard Univ, AM, 50; Polytech Inst Brooklyn, 50-52, PhD(chem), 53. *Honors & Awards:* Metler Award, NAm Thermal Anal Soc. *Prof Exp:* Chemist, Rayon Dept, E I du Pont de Nemours & Co, Inc, 47, res chemist, Ammonia Dept, 48-49 & Plastics Dept, 52-57, sr res chemist, 57-66, res assoc, Plastics Dept, 66-76, Cent Res & Develop Dept, 76-93. *Mem:* Am Chem Soc; fel NAm Thermal Analysis Soc. *Res:* Polymer chemistry; polymerization kinetics; polymer properties and molecular structure; polymer crystallography; dynamic mechanical and dielectric properties. *Mailing Add:* 3931 Heather Dr Wilmington DE 19807

STARKWEATHER, PETER LATHROP, AQUATIC ECOLOGY, INVERTEBRATE PHYSIOLOGY. *Current Pos:* from asst prof to assoc prof, 78-88, PROF AQUATIC ECOL, UNIV NEV, 88-, CHMN DEPT, 84- *Personal Data:* b Glen Ridge, NJ, Nov 7, 48; m 72; c 1. *Educ:* Union Col, NY, BS, 70; Dartmouth Col, PhD(biol sci), 76. *Prof Exp:* Teaching asst zool & ecol, State Univ NY Albany, 70-72; teaching fel biol sci, Dartmouth Col, 72-76, res assoc ecol, 76-78. *Concurrent Pos:* Co-prin investr biol sci, NSF grant, Dartmouth Col, 78-81, vis asst prof, 79 & 80; prin investr, NSF grant, Univ Nev, 81-84; Am Coun Educ fel, 87-88. *Mem:* Am Soc Limnol & Oceanog; Am Soc Zoologists; Ecol Soc Am; AAAS; Sigma Xi; Am Asn Higher Educ. *Res:* Feeding biology and behavior of microcrustacean zooplankton and rotifers; biological rhythms and invertebrate ecology; examination and analysis of feeding behavior and ecology of zooplankton, both freshwater and marine. *Mailing Add:* Univ Nev Las Vegas Dept Biol Sci 4505 S Maryland Pkwy Las Vegas NV 89154-9900

STARLING, ALBERT GREGORY, MATHEMATICS, COMPUTER SCIENCE. *Current Pos:* CHMN, COMP SCI DEPT, UNIV ARK, 88- *Personal Data:* b Joiner, Ark, Feb 24, 39. *Educ:* Univ Ark, BSEE, 61, MS, 64, PhD(math), 69. *Prof Exp:* Jr engr electronics, Int Bus Mach Corp, 61-62, assoc engr & mathematician appl math, 64-65; asst prof math, Univ Mass, Amherst, 69-71; ASSOC PROF MATH, WESTERN CAROLINA UNIV, 71- *Concurrent Pos:* Fel, Univ Mass, 69-71. *Mem:* Am Math Soc. *Res:* Directed graphs of finite groups. *Mailing Add:* Comp Sci Dept Sci Eng Bldg Univ Ark Rm 232 Fayetteville AR 72701-8331

STARLING, JAMES LYNE, PLANT BREEDING, STATISTICS. *Current Pos:* Asst forage crop breeding, 54-57, from instr to assoc prof agron, 57-69, prof agron & head dept, 69-85, assoc dean admin, 85-93, SR ASSOC DEAN, COL AGR SCI, PA STATE UNIV, 93- *Personal Data:* b Henry Co, Va, Aug 16, 30; m 68, Martha Lewis; c Elizabeth A. *Educ:* Va Polytech Inst, BS, 51; Pa State Univ, MS, 55, PhD(agron), 58. *Mem:* AAAS; Am Soc Agron; Sigma Xi. *Res:* Forage crop breeding; genetics and cytogenetics of forage crop species; experimental design. *Mailing Add:* 1736 Princeton Dr State College PA 16803

STARLING, JANE ANN, METABOLISM, PARASITE PHYSIOLOGY. *Current Pos:* asst prof, 76-83, ASSOC PROF BIOL, UNIV MO-ST LOUIS, 83- *Personal Data:* b Waco, Tex, Jan 4, 46. *Educ:* Rice Univ, BA, 67, PhD(physiol), 72. *Prof Exp:* Fel zool, Univ Mass, 72-75; vis asst prof biol, Univ Pittsburgh, 75-76. *Concurrent Pos:* NIH fel, 73-75. *Mem:* AAAS; Am Micros Soc; Am Soc Parasitol; Sigma Xi. *Res:* Trehalose metabolism; energy metabolism in intestinal helminths; host parasite integration; carbohydrate and amino acid transport in helminths; anaerobic energy metabolism. *Mailing Add:* Univ Mo Dept Biol 8001 Natural Bridge Rd St Louis MO 63121. *Fax:* 314-516-6233; *E-Mail:* sjastar@umslvmd.umsl.edu

STARLING, KENNETH EARL, CHEMICAL ENGINEERING. *Current Pos:* from asst prof to assoc prof, 62-77, PROF CHEM ENG, UNIV OKLA, 77- *Personal Data:* b Corpus Christi, Tex, Mar 9, 35; m 60; c 3. *Educ:* Tex A&I Univ, BS, 57 & 58; Ill Inst Technol, MS, 60, PhD(gas technol), 62. *Prof Exp:* Res engr, Inst Gas Technol, Ill Inst Technol, 62-63; Robert A Welch Found fel chem, Rice Univ, 63-64; sr res engr, Standard Oil Co, NJ, 64-66. *Concurrent Pos:* Consult, Standard Oil Co, NJ, 68-, Inst Gas Technol, Ill Inst Technol, 70- & J F Pritchard & Co, 71-; fel, Inst Low Temperature Physics, Cath Univ Louvain, 72-73. *Mem:* AAAS; Am Inst Chem Engrs; Am Chem Soc; Soc Petrol Engrs. *Res:* Energy conversion; fossil energy processes; thermodynamics; correlation of fluid properties. *Mailing Add:* 2611 Lynwood Circle Norman OK 73072

STARLING, THOMAS MADISON, PLANT BREEDING. *Current Pos:* From asst agronomist to assoc agronomist, Va Polytech Inst & State Univ, 44-60, prof agron, 60-70 & 71-85, assoc dean grad sch, 70-71, W G Wysor prof agr, 85-88, EMER PROF VA POLYTECH INST & STATE UNIV, 88- *Personal Data:* b Loneoak, Va, Aug 12, 23; m 61, Evelyn C Barker; c Sarah S (Moore) & Linda S (Lewis). *Educ:* Va Polytech Inst, BS, 44; Iowa State Univ, MS, 47, PhD, 65. *Mem:* Am Soc Agron; fel Crop Sci Soc Am. *Res:* Plant breeding and genetics of winter barley and wheat. *Mailing Add:* 618 Woodland Dr NW Blacksburg VA 24060

STARMER, C FRANK, PHARMACOLOGY, CARDIOLOGY. *Current Pos:* Res assoc med, Duke Univ, 63-65, assoc biomath, 66-68, asst prof, med & community health sci, 68-71, assoc prof comput sci, 71-77, assoc prof med, Med Ctr, 77-90, PROF COMPUT SCI, DUKE UNIV, 77-, PROF EXP MED, 90- *Personal Data:* b Greensboro, NC, Sept 4, 41; m 63; c 4. *Educ:* Duke Univ, BSEE, 63, MSEE, 65; Rice Univ, 65-66; Univ NC, PhD(biomath, bioeng), 68. *Concurrent Pos:* NIH career develop award, Duke Univ, 72-77; mem coun, Div Res Resources, NIH, 84-88; US-USSR exchange (sudden death), 87-90. *Mem:* AAAS; Asn Comput Mach; Am Heart Asn; Am Col Med Informatics. *Res:* Computer science; applied biostatistics; communication in cellular systems; pharmacology. *Mailing Add:* 1411 Gray Bluff Trail Chapel Hill NC 27710

STARNES, WILLIAM HERBERT, JR, POLYMER DEGRADATION, STABILIZATION. *Current Pos:* GOTTWALD PROF CHEM, COL WILLIAM & MARY, 89-, PROF APPL SCI, 90- *Personal Data:* b Knoxville, Tenn, Dec 2, 34; m 86, Maria S Molina. *Educ:* Va Polytech Inst, BS, 55; Ga Inst Technol, PhD(chem), 60. *Honors & Awards:* MA Ferst Award, Sigma Xi, 60; Honor Scroll Award, Am Inst Chemists, 89. *Prof Exp:* Res chemist, Humble Oil & Refining Co, Esso Res & Eng Co, 60-62, sr res chemist, 62-65, res specialist, 65-67, res assoc, 67-71; res assoc & instr, Dept Chem, Univ Tex, Austin, 71-73; mem tech staff, AT&T Bell Labs, 73-82; distinguished mem tech staff, Polytech Univ, Brooklyn, 82-85, prof chem, 85-89, head, Dept Chem & Life Sci, 85-88, assoc dir, Polymer Durability Ctr, 87-89. *Concurrent Pos:* Sect head, Humble Oil & Refining Co, Esso Res & Eng Co, 64; vis scientist, Tex Acad Sci, 64-67; consult, numerous indust co, 85-; adv bd & bd rev, J Vinyl Technol, 81-83; chmn, chem subpanel, AAAS proj 2061, 85-86; NSF grantee, 89-; distinguished vis prof, Beijing Inst Technol, 96. *Mem:* Fel AAAS; fel Am Inst Chemists; Am Chem Soc; NY Acad Sci; Soc Plastics Engrs. *Res:* Degradation, stabilization, microstructure, flammability and polymerization chemistry of synthetic polymers; physical organic studies of polymer reactions; free-radical chemistry; liquid-phase autoxidation; organic synthesis; applied carbon-13 nuclear magnetic resonance spectroscopy. *Mailing Add:* Col William & Mary Dept Chem PO Box 8795 Williamsburg VA 23187-8795. *Fax:* 757-221-2715; *E-Mail:* se@chem1.chem.wm.edu

STAROS, JAMES VAUGHAN, PROTEIN CHEMISTRY. *Current Pos:* from asst prof to prof biochem, 78-91, interim chmn, Dept Biochem, 88-91, PROF MOLECULAR BIOL & BIOCHEM & CHAIR, DEPT MOLECULAR BIOL, VANDERBILT UNIV, 91- *Personal Data:* b May 20, 47; US citizen; m 76, Alice C Harris; c Arwen, J Vaughan & Alice. *Educ:* Dartmouth Col, AB, 69; Yale Univ, PhD(molecular biophysics & biochem), 74. *Prof Exp:* Helen Hay Whitney fel, Dept Chem, Harvard Univ, 74-77. *Concurrent Pos:* Mem, Grad Fel Eval Panel in Biochem & Biophys, Nat Res Coun, 87, Cellular & Molecular Basis of Dis Rev Comn, NIH, 88-92, chair, 90-92; chair, Nat Inst Diabetes & Digestive & Kidney Dis Workshop on Membrane Protein Struct, 90; consult, CarboMed, Inc, 92-; chair, Nat Inst Gen Med Sci Spec Study Sect Training Progs Biol-Chem Interface, NIH, 93; magisterial lectr, Inter-Am Univ PR, 93. *Mem:* Am Chem Soc; Biophys Soc; Fedn Am Scientists; AAAS; Am Soc Biochem & Molecular Biol; Protein Soc. *Res:* Protein chemistry; structure and function of biomembrane proteins; design and synthesis of new chemical probes of biomembrane protein structure and function. *Mailing Add:* Dept Molecular Biol Vanderbilt Univ Box 1820 Sta B Nashville TN 37235-0001. *Fax:* 615-343-6707; *E-Mail:* starosjv@ctrvax.vanderbilt.edu

STARR, ALBERT, THORACIC SURGERY. *Current Pos:* from instr to assoc prof surg, 57-64, PROF CARDIOPULMONARY SURG, MED SCH, UNIV ORE, 64-, HEAD DIV, 63- *Personal Data:* b New York, NY, June 1, 26; m 55; c 2. *Educ:* Columbia Col, BA, 46; Columbia Univ, MD, 49. *Honors & Awards:* Award, Am Heart Asn, 63; Rene Le Riche Award Cardiovasc Surg, 65. *Prof Exp:* Asst surg, Columbia Univ, 56-57. *Mem:* Am Surg Asn; Am Asn Thoracic Surg; Am Col Cardiol; Int Cardiovasc Soc. *Res:* Prosthetic values for cardiac surgery. *Mailing Add:* 9155 SW Barnes Rd 240 Portland OR 97225-6629

STARR, ARNOLD, COGNITIVE DISORDERS. *Current Pos:* from assoc prof to prof med, Univ Calif, Irvine, 71-77, chief, Div Neurol, 73-77, founding chmn, Dept Neurol, 77-86, PROF NEUROL, PSYCHOBIOL & COGNITIVE SCI, UNIV CALIF, IRVINE, 77-, PROF PSYCHIAT, 83- *Personal Data:* b New York, NY, Aug 5, 32; c 3. *Educ:* Kenyon Col, Gambier, Ohio, AB, 53; NY Univ, MD, 57. *Prof Exp:* Asst prof med, Sch Med, Stanford Univ, 64-71. *Concurrent Pos:* Dir, Residency Prog, Univ Calif, Irvine, 73-90; vis prof, Dept Psychol, Univ London Nat Hosp, 85-86, 87 & 88, Dept Neurol, Univ Hanzhou, China, 86 & Dept Neurol, Vienna, Austria, 89; mem, Bd Sci Counr, NIH, 88-92, Comt Mapping & Evoked Potentials, Int Fed Soc EEG, 89 & Therapeut & Technol Assessment Subcomt, Am Acad Neurol, 90. *Mem:* Am EEG Soc; Am Neurol Asn; fel Am Acad Neurol; Soc Neurosci; fel Acoust Soc Am; Am Physiol Soc. *Res:* Auditory brainstem evoked potentials; magnetic stimulation; multiple sclerosis; memory and cognitive disorders; author of over 130 publications. *Mailing Add:* Dept Neurol Med Surg Rm 154 Univ Calif Irvine CA 92717-4290

STARR, C DEAN, METALLURGY. *Current Pos:* PRES, C DEAN STARR INC, 84- *Personal Data:* b Tulare, SDak, Apr 24, 21; m 46; c 4. *Educ:* SDak Sch Mines, BS, 43; Univ Utah, MS, 48, PhD(metall), 49. *Honors & Awards:* Sam Tour Award, Am Soc Testing & Mat, 66. *Prof Exp:* Jr metallurgist, AC Spark Plug Co Div, Gen Motors Corp, 43-44, spectrographer, 46-47; asst res prof metall, Univ Calif, Berkeley, 49-53; chief res metallurgist, Wilbur B Driver Co, Gen Tel & Electronics Corp, 54-60, tech dir eng, 60-66, vpres eng & tech dir eng, 66-71, vpres eng & res, 71-79, vpres eng & res, Amax Specialty Metals Corp, 79-84. *Concurrent Pos:* Vis sr lectr, Grad Sch Metall, Stevens Inst Technol, 61-84. *Mem:* Am Soc Metals; Am Inst Mining, Metall & Petrol Engrs; Electrochem Soc. *Res:* Alloy development for resistance, particularly heat resisting, thermocouple, corrosion and high strength alloys; thermodynamic and kinetic studies of simple and complex alloy systems. *Mailing Add:* 1621 Farr Rd Reading PA 19610

STARR, CHAUNCEY, ENGINEERING PHYSICS. *Current Pos:* pres, 72-78, vchmn, 78-87, EMER PRES, ELEC POWER RES INST, 87- *Personal Data:* b Newark, NJ, Apr 14, 12; m 38; c 2. *Educ:* Rensselaer Polytech Inst, EE, 32, PhD(physics), 35. *Hon Degrees:* DrEng, Rensselaer Polytech Inst, 64; DrEng, Swiss Inst Technol, Switz, 80; DSc, Tulane Univ, 86. *Honors & Awards:* Legion of Honor, French Govt, 78; Walter H Zinn Award, Am Nuclear Soc, 79; Rockwell Medal, 88; Pres Nat Med Tech, President US, 90. *Prof Exp:* Coffin fel & res fel physics, Harvard Univ, 35-37; res physicist, P R Mallory Co, Ind, 37-38; res assoc phys chem, Mass Inst Technol, 38-41; physicist, D W Taylor Model Basin, Bur Ships, US Dept Navy, 41-42, Radiation Lab, Univ Calif, 42-43 & Manhattan Dist, Oak Ridge, 43-46; dir atomic energy res dept, N Am Aviation, Inc, 46-55, vpres, 55-66, gen mgr, Atomics Int Div, 55-60, pres, 60-66; dean sch eng & appl sci, Univ Calif, Los Angeles, 67-72. *Concurrent Pos:* Consult, US Off Sci & Technol, NASA, AEC & USAF; dir, Atomic Indust Forum; mem, Rockefeller Univ Coun, Rockefeller Univ, NY. *Mem:* Nat Acad Eng (vpres); Am Inst Aeronaut & Astronaut; Sigma Xi; fel Am Phys Soc; Am Nuclear Soc (pres, 58-59); Royal Acad Eng Sci, Sweden. *Res:* Semiconductors; thermal conductivity of metals; high pressures; cryogenics; magnetic susceptibilities at low temperatures; gas discharge phenomena, solid state; Atomic energy and nuclear reactors; risk analysis. *Mailing Add:* Elec Power Res Inst 3412 Hillview Ave Palo Alto CA 94303. *Fax:* 650-855-2090; *E-Mail:* cstarr@epri.com

STARR, DAVID WRIGHT, MATHEMATICS. *Current Pos:* instr ground sch aviation, Southern Methodist Univ, 40-43, coordr war training serv, Civil Aeronaut Admin, 41-44, chmn dept, 63-77, EMER PROF MATH, SOUTHERN METHODIST UNIV, 78- *Personal Data:* b Anna, Tex, Dec 8, 12; wid; c David Jr & Sally. *Educ:* Southern Methodist Univ, AB, 33; Univ Ill, AM, 37, PhD(math), 41. *Prof Exp:* High sch instr, Tex, 33-37, prin, 34; asst math, Univ Ill, 38-40. *Mem:* Am Math Soc; Math Asn Am. *Res:* Analysis; Schrodinger wave equation from the point of view of singular integral equations. *Mailing Add:* 3503 Normandy Ave Apt 5 Dallas TX 75205-2290

STARR, DUANE FRANK, PHYSICAL CHEMISTRY. *Current Pos:* ENGR URANIUM ENRICHMENT, NUCLEAR DIV, OAK RIDGE GASEOUS DIFFUSION PLANT, UNION CARBIDE CORP, 77- *Personal Data:* b Pasadena, Calif, Oct 20, 42; m 65; c 2. *Educ:* Wesleyan Univ, BA, 64; Ore State Univ, PhD(phys chem), 73. *Prof Exp:* Resident res assoc lasers, Naval Res Lab, Nat Res Coun, 73-75; staff chemist propellant chem, Allegany Ballistics Lab, Hercules Inc, 75-77. *Mem:* Am Chem Soc; Am Phys Soc. *Res:* Economic assessment of advanced isotope separation methods. *Mailing Add:* 109 Woodridge Lane Oak Ridge TN 37830

STARR, JAMES LEROY, SOIL PHYSICS. *Current Pos:* RES SOIL SCIENTIST, USDA, 79- *Personal Data:* b Almont, Mich, Aug 14, 39; m 60; c 2. *Educ:* Mich State Univ, BS, 61, MS, 70; Eastern Baptist Theol Sem, MA, 66; Univ Calif, Davis, PhD(soil sci), 73. *Prof Exp:* Voc Agr teacher, Carson City Community Schs, Mich, 61-62 & Mayville Community Schs, 62-64; teaching asst, Mich State Univ, 67-68, instr soils & dir audiotutorial lab, 68-70; res asst, Univ Calif, 70-72, staff res assoc, 72-74; from asst res scientist to assoc scientist soil physics, Conn Agr Exp Sta, 74-78. *Mem:* Sigma Xi; Am Soc Agron; Soil Sci Soc Am; Int Soc Soil Sci; Am Geophys Union. *Res:* Soil water nitrogen relations; infiltration; movement of nutrients and agrochemicals to ground water. *Mailing Add:* USDA Agr Res Serv BARC-W B007 Rm 207 Beltsville MD 20705. *E-Mail:* jstarr@asrr.arsusda.gov

STARR, JASON LEONARD, oncology, biochemistry; deceased, see previous edition for last biography

STARR, JOHN EDWARD, PHOTOGRAPHY. *Current Pos:* RETIRED. *Personal Data:* b St Louis, Mo, July 12, 39; m 61; c 2. *Educ:* Colo Col, BA, 61; Stanford Univ, PhD(org chem), 65. *Prof Exp:* Sr chemist, Eastman Kodak Co, 65-69, lab head, Res Labs, 69-78, res assoc, 78-92. *Res:* Spectral sensitization of photographic emulsions by sensitizing dyes; color reproduction. *Mailing Add:* 582 Bending Bough Dr Webster NY 14580

STARR, MATTHEW C, CARDIOVASCULAR, MICROCIRCULATION. *Current Pos:* RETIRED. *Educ:* Univ Southern Calif, PhD(psychol), 74. *Prof Exp:* Health sci adminr, Nat Heart Lung & Blood Inst, NIH, 81-95. *Mailing Add:* 5607 Montgomery St Chevy Chase MD 20815-3401. *Fax:* 301-594-7407

STARR, NORMAN, MATHEMATICAL STATISTICS. *Current Pos:* RETIRED. *Personal Data:* b Scranton, Pa, Apr 14, 33; m 65. *Educ:* Univ Mich, BA, 55, MA, 60; Columbia Univ, PhD(math statist), 65. *Prof Exp:* Assoc math, Evans Res & Develop Corp, 61-65; asst prof statist, Univ Minn, 65-66; from asst prof to assoc prof, Carnegie-Mellon Univ, 66-68; assoc prof, Univ Mich, Ann Arbor, 68-73, prof math, Dept Statist, 68-86; heath prog consult, 86-95. *Concurrent Pos:* Contractor, 86-95. *Mem:* Inst Math Statist; Am Math Soc; Am Statist Asn. *Res:* Sequential analysis; optimal stopping; statistical allocation and theory; applied probability. *Mailing Add:* 4775 Waters Rd Ann Arbor MI 48103

STARR, NORTON, MATHEMATICS. *Current Pos:* asst prof, 66-71, assoc prof, 71-78, PROF MATH, AMHERST COL, 78- *Personal Data:* b Kansas City, Mo, June 18, 36; m 59; c 2. *Educ:* Harvard Col, AB, 58; Mass Inst Technol, PhD(math), 64. *Prof Exp:* Instr math, Mass Inst Technol, 64-66. *Concurrent Pos:* Vis asst prof, Univ Waterloo, 72-73. *Mem:* Am Math Soc; Math Asn Am. *Res:* Operator limit theory. *Mailing Add:* Dept Math Amherst Col PO Box 2239 Amherst MA 01002-5000

STARR, PATRICIA RAE, MICROBIOLOGY, HISTORY & PHILOSOPHY OF SCIENCE. *Current Pos:* chair, 80-83, instr, Sci Div, 77-93, EMER PROF, MT HOOD COMMUNITY COL, 93- *Personal Data:* b Hood River, Ore, Feb 28, 35. *Educ:* Ore State Univ, BS, 57, MS, 62; Univ Ore, Med Sch, PhD(microbiol), 68. *Prof Exp:* Instr microbiol, Dent Sch, Univ Ore, 68-69; assoc, Ore State Univ, 69-71; asst prof, Univ Ill, Urbana, 71-75; res assoc, Providence Hosp, 75-77. *Mem:* AAAS; Am Soc Microbiol; Hist Sci Soc. *Res:* Relationship of sterol synthesis to respiratory adaptation in yeast; amino acid uptake systems in yeast; white blood cell function. *Mailing Add:* Dept Sci Mt Hood Community Col 26000 SE Stark Gresham OR 97030-3300

STARR, PATRICK JOSEPH, MECHANICAL ENGINEERING, INTELLIGENT SYSTEMS. *Current Pos:* from asst prof to assoc prof, 71-94, PROF, INDUST ENG & OPERS RES DIV, DEPT MECH ENG, UNIV MINN, 94- *Personal Data:* b St Paul, Minn, Oct 24, 39. *Educ:* Univ Minn, Minneapolis, BME, 62, MSME, 66, PhD(mech eng), 70. *Prof Exp:* Develop eng, Honeywell Inc, 62-64, 68; teaching assoc, Univ Minn, Minneapolis, 64-70; control syst engr, Northern Ord Div, FMC Corp, 70-71. *Res:* Modeling of large scale socio-industrial systems; system dynamics; technology assessment; expert simulation; manufacturing system analysis. *Mailing Add:* 251 Bedford St SE Minneapolis MN 55413

STARR, PHILLIP HENRY, PSYCHIATRY. *Current Pos:* ASSOC PROF NEUROL & PSYCHIAT, SCH MED, UNIV NEBR, OMAHA, 57- *Personal Data:* b Poland, Nov 16, 20; nat US; div; c 3. *Educ:* Univ Toronto, MD, 44. *Prof Exp:* Asst prof neuropsychiat & pediat, Sch Med, Wash Univ, 52-55, dir community child guid clin, 52-56. *Concurrent Pos:* Chief psychiat consult, St Louis Children's Hosp, 51-56; chief children's outpatient serv, Nebr Psychiat Inst, 56-64, consult, 64-; consult, Offut Air Base Hosp & Immanuel Ment Health Ctr. *Mem:* Fel Am Psychiat Asn; fel AMA; Int Asn Child Psychiat; fel Am Acad Child Psychiat. *Res:* Child and adult psychiatry. *Mailing Add:* PO Box 5973 Scottsdale AZ 85261-5979

STARR, RICHARD CAWTHON, PHYCOLOGY. *Current Pos:* PROF BOT, UNIV TEX, AUSTIN, 76-, DIR CULT COLLECTION ALGAE, 76- *Personal Data:* b Greensboro, Ga, Aug 24, 24. *Educ:* Ga Southern Col, BS, 44; George Peabody Col, MA, 47; Vanderbilt Univ, PhD(biol), 52. *Honors & Awards:* US Sr Award, Alexander von Humboldt Found, 72; Gilbert Morgan Smith Medal, Nat Acad Sci, 85. *Prof Exp:* From instr to prof bot, Ind Univ, Bloomington, 52-76. *Concurrent Pos:* Guggenheim fel, 59. *Mem:* Nat Acad Sci; Bot Soc Am; AAAS; Phycol Soc Am. *Res:* Morphology and cultivation of green algae; genetics and development of Volvox. *Mailing Add:* Univ Tex Dept Botany Austin TX 78713. *Fax:* 512-471-3878

STARR, ROBERT I, CHEMISTRY, ENVIRONMENTAL SCIENCES. *Current Pos:* RETIRED. *Personal Data:* b Laramie, Wyo, Dec 11, 32; m 56; c 2. *Educ:* Univ Wyo, BS, 56, MS, 59, PhD(plant physiol), 72. *Prof Exp:* Res biochemist, US Fish & Wildlife Serv, Colo, 60-63; plant physiologist, Colo State Univ, 63-64; analytical chemist, US Food & Drug Admin, 64-65; chemist, Colo State Univ, 65-69; res chemist, Bur Sport Fisheries & Wildlife, US Dept Interior, 69-74; environ scientist, US Geol Surv, 74-77, chief, Environ-Tech Unit, 77-78; chief, Biol-Ecol Sci Br, US Dept Interior, 78-81; pvt consult environ chem, 81-84; consult environ chem, US Dept Interior, 84-89; sr res chemist, Pesticides, USDA, 89-93. *Concurrent Pos:* Res biochemist, Wildlife Res Ctr, US Fish & Wildlife Serv, Colo, 68-69; pvt consult environ chemist, 92- *Mem:* Am Chem Soc; fel Am Inst Chemists. *Res:* Pesticide chemistry as related to plant soil and water systems, including method development studies; plant, soil, and chemistry matters relating to mining operations; trace metals in soil and water systems. *Mailing Add:* 404 Tulane Dr Ft Collins CO 80521

STARR, THEODORE JACK, MICROBIOLOGY. *Current Pos:* RETIRED. *Personal Data:* b Plainfield, NJ, Aug 22, 24; m 54; c 3. *Educ:* City Col New York, BS, 49; Univ Mass, MS, 51; Univ Wash, PhD(microbiol), 53. *Prof Exp:* Res assoc microbiol, Haskins Labs, 48-49; instr biol, Univ Ga, 54-55; fishery res biologist, US Fish & Wildlife Serv, 55-57; McLaughlin fel virol, Med Br, Univ Tex, 57-60; assoc res scientist, Lab Comp Biol, Kaiser Found Res Inst, 60-62; assoc prof microbiol, Univ Notre Dame, 62-68; prof biol sci & assoc head dept, Col Arts & Sci, Univ Ill, Chicago Circle, 68-70; head dept, Col Brockport, State Univ NY, 70-80, prof biol sci, 70-97, asst vpres acad affairs, grad studies & res, 75-77. *Concurrent Pos:* Fac exchange scholar, State Univ NY, 75. *Mem:* Am Soc Microbiol; Soc Exp Biol & Med. *Res:* Cytochemistry; virology; marine and space biology; gnotobiology. *Mailing Add:* 4133 Oak Orchard Rd Albion NY 14411

STARR, THOMAS LOUIS, ANALYTICAL CHEMISTRY, PHYSICAL CHEMISTRY. *Current Pos:* sr res scientist, 80-87, PRIN RES SCIENTIST, GA INST TECHNOL, 87- *Personal Data:* b Cincinnati, Ohio, Mar 22, 49; m 70; c 3. *Educ:* Univ Detroit, BS, 70; Univ Louisville, PhD(phys chem), 76. *Honors & Awards:* J M Houchens Prize, Univ Louisville, 77. *Prof Exp:* Analytical chemist, Major Appliance Labs, Gen Elec Co, 77-80. *Concurrent Pos:* Pres scholar, Univ Detroit, 67-70; J B Speed fel, Univ Louisville, 76. *Mem:* Am Chem Soc; Am Ceramic Soc; Mat Res Soc. *Res:* Chemistry and physics of materials processing; ceramics and ceramic composites; high performance coatings; molecular and microstructure modeling. *Mailing Add:* Ga Tech Res Inst Ga Inst Technol Atlanta GA 30332. *Fax:* 404-894-5073; *E-Mail:* tom.starr@gtri.gatech.edu

STARR, WALTER L(EROY), PHYSICS. *Current Pos:* RETIRED. *Personal Data:* b Portland, Ore, Feb 9, 24; m 44; c 2. *Educ:* Univ Southern Calif, BS, 50; Calif Inst Technol, MS, 51. *Prof Exp:* Physicist, US Naval Missile Test Ctr, 50; res physicist, US Naval Civil Eng Lab, 51-55; res scientist, Phys Sci Lab, Lockheed Missiles & Space Co, 55-67; physicist, Ames Res Ctr, NASA, 67-88. *Mem:* AAAS; Am Phys Soc; Am Geophys Union. *Res:* Atomic and molecular physics; atmospheric processes; ionization and excitation; absorption cross sections. *Mailing Add:* 46747 Goodpasture Rd Vida OR 97488

STARRATT, ALVIN NEIL, NATURAL PRODUCTS CHEMISTRY. *Current Pos:* RES SCIENTIST, PEST MGT RES CTR, AGR & AGR-FOOD, CAN, 65- *Personal Data:* b Paradise, NS, Sept 18, 36; m 67, Sue Stewart; c John & Neil. *Educ:* Acadia Univ, BSc, 59; Univ Western Ont, PhD(org chem), 63. *Prof Exp:* Brit Petrol Co res fel, Imp Col, Univ London, 63-64; res fel, Res Inst Med & Chem, Mass, 64-65. *Mem:* Am Chem Soc; fel Chem Inst Can; Entom Soc Can. *Res:* Natural products influencing the behavior of insects and insect neuropeptides. *Mailing Add:* Res Ctr Agr Can 1391 Sandford St London ON N5V 4T3 Can. *Fax:* 519-457-3997; *E-Mail:* starratta@em.agr.ca

STARRETT, ANDREW, MAMMALOGY. *Current Pos:* assoc prof, 65-69, PROF BIOL, CALIF STATE UNIV, NORTHRIDGE, 69- *Personal Data:* b Greenwich, Conn, Mar 18, 30; m 51; c 3. *Educ:* Univ Conn, BS, 51; Univ Mich, MS, 55, PhD(zool), 58. *Prof Exp:* Instr zool, Univ Mich, 56-57; from instr to asst prof biol, Univ Southern Calif, 57-64; asst prof, Northeastern Univ, 64-65. *Concurrent Pos:* Res assoc, Los Angeles County Mus Natural Hist. *Mem:* AAAS; Soc Syst Zool; Soc Study Evolution; Am Soc Mammalogists. *Res:* Vertebrate and mammalian evolution and distribution; mammalian morphology and systematics, particularly Chiroptera. *Mailing Add:* 10601 Andora Ave Chatsworth CA 91311-2007

STARRETT, PRISCILLA HOLLY, HERPETOLOGY. *Current Pos:* RETIRED. *Personal Data:* b Hartford, Conn, Nov 1929; div; c David, Laurel & Bruce. *Educ:* Univ Conn, BA, 50, MS, 53; Univ Mich, PhD(herpet), 68. *Prof Exp:* Teaching asst, Univ Mich, 53-57; dir lab, Univ Southern Calif, 75-92. *Res:* Working on the life histories of tropical frogs. *Mailing Add:* 6517 Garth Ave Los Angeles CA 90056

STARRETT, RICHMOND MULLINS, BIOTECHNOLOGY, INDUSTRIAL MICROBIOLOGY. *Current Pos:* res chemist, 72-75, sr res chemist, 75-79, RES ASSOC, DEPT RES & DEVELOP, ETHYL CORP, 79- *Personal Data:* b Gardner, Mass, Oct 1, 43; m 66; c 3. *Educ:* Univ NC, BA, 66; Iowa State Univ, PhD(org chem), 70. *Prof Exp:* Res assoc, R A Welch Found, Tex Tech Univ, 71-72. *Mem:* Am Chem Soc; Org Reactions Catalysis Soc; Nat Asn Advan Sci; Soc Indust Microbiol. *Res:* Development of biological processes for industrial chemicals; investigation of fundamental microbiological methodology, including recombinant DNA techniques; study of novel synthetic and catalytic processes for chemical manufacture. *Mailing Add:* 939 Edmund Hawes Rd Baton Rouge LA 70810

STARRFIELD, SUMNER GROSBY, THEORETICAL & OBSERVATIONAL ASTROPHYSICS. *Current Pos:* from asst prof to assoc prof, 72-79, PROF ASTROPHYS, ARIZ STATE UNIV, 80- *Personal Data:* b Los Angeles, Calif, Dec 29, 40; m 66, Susan L Hutt; c Barry, Brian & Sara. *Educ:* Univ Calif, Berkeley, BA, 62; Univ Calif, Los Angeles, MA, 65, PhD(astron), 69. *Honors & Awards:* Philips lectr, Haverford Col, 78. *Prof Exp:* Lectr astron, Yale Univ, 67-69, asst prof, 69-71; scientist, Thomas J Watson Res Ctr, IBM Corp, 71-72. *Concurrent Pos:* Res grants, NSF, 74 & 75-89, NASA, 80-89; vis staff mem, Los Alamos Sci Lab, 74-; fels, Assoc Western Univ, 85 & Joint Inst Lab Astrophys, 86. *Mem:* Fel Royal Astron Soc; Int Astron Union; Am Astron Soc; Am Phys Soc. *Res:* Stellar structure and evolution; hydrodynamical studies of novae; stellar pulsation; ultraviolet studies of novae. *Mailing Add:* Ariz State Univ Dept Physics & Astron PO Box 871504 Tempe AZ 85287-1504. *Fax:* 602-965-7954; *E-Mail:* sumner. starrfield@asu.edu

STARUSZKIEWICZ, WALTER FRANK, JR, ANALYTICAL CHEMISTRY, FOOD CHEMISTRY. *Current Pos:* RES CHEMIST ANALYTICAL CHEM FOODS, US FOOD & DRUG ADMIN, 67- *Personal Data:* b Ellwood City, Pa, Jan 31, 39; m 63; c 3. *Educ:* Geneva Col, BS, 60; Univ Hawaii, MS, 65. *Prof Exp:* Res asst biochem, Pineapple Res Inst Hawaii, 64-66; chemist, Del Monte Corp, 66-67. *Mem:* Am Chem Soc; fel Asn Off Analytical Chemists. *Res:* Development of analytical methods for the detection of decomposition in foods; applications of gas and liquid chromatography for the determination of histamine, cadaverine and other biogenic amines in seafoods. *Mailing Add:* US Food & Drug Admin HFS-426 200 C St SW Washington DC 20204. *Fax:* 202-205-4881; *E-Mail:* wfs@fdacf. ssw.dhhs.gov

STARY, FRANK EDWARD, EPOXY POLYMER CHEMISTRY-CHEMILUMINESCENCE. *Current Pos:* from asst prof to assoc prof, 74-82, PROF CHEM, MARYVILLE UNIV, ST LOUIS, 82-, CHMN DEPT, 74- *Personal Data:* b St Paul, Minn, Jan 3, 41; m 64, Sonja G Dalsbo. *Educ:* Univ Minn, BChem, 63; Univ Cincinnati, PhD(inorg chem), 69. *Prof Exp:* Res asst nuclear magnetic resonance, Univ Cincinnati, 64-68 & Univ Calif, Irvine, 68-72; res assoc, Univ Mo, St Louis, 72-74. *Mem:* Am Chem Soc; Sigma Xi. *Res:* Mercaptan dissociation constants; organometallic electrochemistry; ozonation and singlet oxygen; pulsed nuclear magnetic resonance of solids to investigate molecular motions, mainly in plastic crystals; low field nuclear magnetic resonance; ternary phase diagrams; weak bases; cyclic voltammetry; chemical lasers; ozone and singlet oxygen; reverse burn char technology. *Mailing Add:* 13550 Conway Rd Creve Coeur MO 63141

STARZAK, MICHAEL EDWARD, BIOPHYSICAL CHEMISTRY. *Current Pos:* from asst prof to assoc prof, 70-88, PROF CHEM, STATE UNIV NY, BINGHAMTON, 88- *Personal Data:* b Woonsocket, RI, Apr 21, 42; m 67, Andrea L Zahorak; c Jocelyn, Alissa, Mark & Richard. *Educ:* Brown Univ, BS, 63; Northwestern Univ, PhD(chem), 68. *Prof Exp:* From actg instr to actg asst prof chem & grant, Univ Calif, Santa Cruz, 68-70. *Concurrent Pos:* Corp mem, Marine Biol Lab, 74-; Fulbright fel, Poland. *Mem:* Sigma Xi; Am Chem Soc; Am Phys Soc; Biophys Soc; NY Acad Sci. *Res:* Excitable membrane phenomena; photochemistry; stochastic processes; membrane channels. *Mailing Add:* Dept Chem State Univ NY Binghamton NY 13902-6000. *E-Mail:* starzak@bingvmb

STARZL, THOMAS E, TRANSPLANTATION, IMMUNOLOGY. *Current Pos:* PROF SURG, MED CTR, UNIV PITTSBURGH, 81-, DIR TRANSPLANTATION INST, 90- *Personal Data:* b Le Mars, Iowa, Mar 11, 26; m 81, Joy D Cooper; c Tom, Tim & Becky. *Educ:* Westminster Col, Mo, BA, 47; Northwestern Univ, MA, 50, PhD(anat) & MD, 52. *Hon Degrees:* DSc, Westminster Col, 68, NY Med Col, 70, Westmar Col, 74, Med Col Wis, 81, Northwestern Univ, 82, Bucknell Univ, 85, Muhlenberg Col, 85, Mt Sinai Sch Med, 88, Univ Pittsburg, 93; LLD, Univ Wyo, 71, Chatham Col, 93; DMed, Univ Louvain, Belg, 85, Univ Rennes, 88, Univ Bologna, 88, Univ Padua, 92; DHL, LaRoche Col, 88. *Honors & Awards:* WS Middleton Award, 68; Mod Med Distinguished Achievement Award, 69; Eppinger Prize, 70; Brookdale Award, 74; Robert L Stearns Award, 76; David M Hume Mem Award, 78; Medallion Sci Achievement, Am Surg Asn, 90; Distinguished Serv Award, Am Liver found, 91; William Beaumont Prize Gastroenterol, 91; Hugh R Butt Award, Am Gastroenterol Asn, 91; Distinguished Achievement Award, Am Asn Study Liver Dis, 91; Medawar Prize, Transplantation Soc, 92; William Ladd Medal, Acad Pediat, 93. *Prof Exp:* Intern surg, Johns Hopkins Hosp, 52-53, asst resident, 55-56; resident, Sch Med, Univ Miami, 56-58; resident & instr, Northwestern Univ, 58-59, assoc, 59-61, asst prof, 61; assoc prof surg, Sch Med, Univ Colo, Denver, 62-64, prof, 64-81, chmn dept, 72-81. *Mem:* Am Col Surg; fel Am Acad Arts & Sci; Soc Univ Surg; Am Surg Asn; Soc Vascular Surg; Fr Acad Med. *Res:* General and thoracic surgery; neurophysiology, cardiac physiology; transplantation of tissues and organs. *Mailing Add:* Univ Pittsburgh Sch Med Pittsburgh PA 15261-0001

STARZYK, MARVIN JOHN, MICROBIOLOGY. *Current Pos:* asst prof, 66-71, assoc prof, 71-85, chmn dept biol sci, 84, PROF MICROBIOL, NORTHERN ILL UNIV, 85- *Personal Data:* b Chicago, Ill, Feb 3, 35; m 58; c 4. *Educ:* Loyola Univ, Chicago, BS, 57; Univ Wis-Madison, PhD(microbiol), 62. *Honors & Awards:* Fulbright Sr Lectr, USSR, 83. *Prof Exp:* Asst prof natural sci, Northern Ill Univ, 61-64; group leader microbiol, Res Dept, Brown & Williamson Tobacco Corp Ky, 64-65, asst sect leader biol sci, 65-66. *Concurrent Pos:* Consult, Brown & Williamson Tobacco Corp, 66-67. *Mem:* Am Soc Microbiol; AAAS; Sigma Xi. *Res:* Aquatic Microbiology, the pathological ecology of microorganisms associated with contaminated waters. *Mailing Add:* Dept Biol Sci Northern Ill Univ 1425 W Lincoln Hwy De Kalb IL 60115-2825

STASHEFF, JAMES DILLON, MATHEMATICS, PHYSICAL MATHEMATICS. *Current Pos:* PROF MATH, UNIV NC, 76- *Personal Data:* b New York, NY, Jan 15, 36; m 59, Ann Pekarik; c Steven & Kim. *Educ:* Univ Mich, BA, 56; Princeton Univ, MA, 58, PhD(math), 61; Oxford Univ, DPhil(math), 61. *Prof Exp:* Moore instr math, Mass Inst Technol, 60-62; from asst prof to prof, Univ Notre Dame, 62-70; prof, Temple Univ, 70-78. *Concurrent Pos:* NSF grants, 64-; mem, Inst Advan Study, 64-65, 87, Sloan fel, 69-70; vis prof, Princeton Univ, 68-69, Univ Pa, 83 & 92, Rutgers Univ, 87, Lehigh Univ, 93. *Mem:* Am Math Soc; Math Asn Am. *Res:* Algebraic topology, especially higher homotopy theory; higher nomotopy algebra, chomological physics; homological algebra. *Mailing Add:* Math Dept Univ NC Chapel Hill NC 27599-3250. *Fax:* 919-962-2568; *E-Mail:* jds@math. umc.edu

STASIOR, WILLIAM F, ENGINEERING. *Current Pos:* staff mem, 67-90, PRES & CHIEF OPER OFFICER, BOOZ ALLEN & HAMILTON INC, 90-, CHIEF EXEC OFFICER & CHMN BD DIRS, 91- *Personal Data:* b 1941. *Educ:* Northwestern Univ, BSEE & MSEE. *Mailing Add:* Booz Allen & Hamilton Inc 8283 Greensboro Dr McLean VA 22102

STASIW, ROMAN OREST, CLINICAL CHEMISTRY, BIOCHEMISTRY. *Current Pos:* SCIENTIST, TECHNICON, 73- *Personal Data:* b Ukraine, May 3, 41; US citizen; m 68; c 1. *Educ:* Univ Rochester, BS, 63; State Univ NY Buffalo, PhD(inorg chem), 68. *Prof Exp:* Analyst, E I du Pont de Nemours & Co, summers 62 & 63; asst scientist, Cancer Res Ctr, Columbia, Mo, 68-73. *Mem:* Am Asn Clin Chem. *Res:* Inorganic and synthetic organic chemistry; enzymology; clinical automation. *Mailing Add:* 98 N Grant Ave Congers NY 10920

STASKAWICZ, BRIAN, PLANT BIOLOGY. *Current Pos:* PROF PLANT PATH, UNIV CALIF, BERKELEY. *Honors & Awards:* Ruth Allen Award, Am Phytopath Soc, 95. *Mailing Add:* Plant Biol Dept Univ Calif 111 Koshland Hall Berkeley CA 94720

STASKIEWICZ, BERNARD ALEXANDER, PHYSICAL CHEMISTRY. *Current Pos:* assoc prof, 58-62, PROF CHEM, WASHINGTON & JEFFERSON COL, 62-, CHMN DEPT, 67-, CHMN, DIV SCI & MATH, 88- *Personal Data:* b Monessen, Pa, Aug 20, 24; m 49; c 5. *Educ:* Washington & Jefferson Col, AB, 46; Carnegie Inst Technol, MS, 50, PhD(chem), 53. *Prof Exp:* Instr chem, Washington & Jefferson Col, 46-51; res chemist, Esso Res & Eng Co, Standard Oil Co, NJ, 53-56 & Rayonier, Inc, 56-58. *Mem:* Am Chem Soc. *Res:* Thermodynamics; cellulose chemistry; automotive lubricants. *Mailing Add:* Chem Washington Jefferson Col 60 S Lincoln St Washington PA 15301-4812

STASKO, AIVARS B, AQUATIC ECOLOGY & FISHERIES, RESEARCH MANAGEMENT. *Current Pos:* RETIRED. *Personal Data:* b Riga, Latvia, May 22, 37; Can citizen; m 63; c 3. *Educ:* Univ Toronto, BASc, 60, PhD(zool), 69. *Prof Exp:* Res assoc limnol, Univ Wis-Madison, 67-70; res scientist, St Andrews, Dept Fisheries & Oceans, Ottawa, Ont, 70-79, head, Crustaceans Sect, 77-79, assoc dir, fisheries res prog anal, 80- *Concurrent Pos:* Ed, Underwater Telemetry Newslett, 71-76. *Res:* Crab and lobster biology and fisheries; underwater biotelemetry; responses of fish to environmental factors. *Mailing Add:* 20 Corkstown Nepean ON K1A 0E6 Can

STASSIS, CONSTANTINE, NEUTRON SCATTERING. *Current Pos:* PROF, DEPT PHYSICS & AMES LAB, IOWA STATE UNIV, 71- *Personal Data:* b Athens, Greece. *Educ:* Univ Lausanne, Switz, BS, 60, MS, 61; Mass Inst Technol, PhD(physics), 70. *Mem:* Fel Am Phys Soc; Neutron scattering Soc Am. *Res:* Neutron Scattering. *Mailing Add:* Dept Physics & Astron Iowa State Univ Ames IA 50011

STASZAK, DAVID JOHN, ANIMAL PHYSIOLOGY, BIOCHEMISTRY. *Current Pos:* PROF BIOL & DEAN GRAD STUDIES, UNIV WIS, STEVENS POINT, 80- *Personal Data:* b Milwaukee, Wis, Mar 29, 44; m 65; c 2. *Educ:* Iowa State Univ, BS, 66, MS, 68, PhD(physiol), 71. *Prof Exp:* Res asst insect physiol, Iowa State Univ, 66-68, teaching asst human physiol, 68-69, res asst insect physiol, 69-71; asst prof physiol, Ill Col, 71-72; assoc prof physiol, Ga Col, 72-76, assoc prof biol & dir, Res Servs, 76-80. *Concurrent Pos:* USDA grant, Iowa State Univ, 66-71; asst prof, Dept Biol, MacMurray Col, 71-72; consult, Biochem Sect, Res Dept, Regional Ment Health Ctr, Cent State Hosp, 75-79. *Mem:* Am Inst Biol Sci; Sigma Xi; AAAS; Nat Coun Univ Res Adminrs. *Res:* Influence of low temperature on animals; chill-coma; thermal acclimation. *Mailing Add:* Rm 118 Main Bldg Univ Wis 2100 Main St Stevens Point WI 54481

STASZEKY, FRANCIS M, MECHANICAL ENGINEERING. *Current Pos:* CONSULT, 83- *Personal Data:* b Wilmington, Del, Apr 16, 18. *Educ:* Mass Inst Technol, BS & MS, 43. *Prof Exp:* Mech engr, Union Oil Co, Calif, 43-45, E I du Pont de Nemours, Wilmington, 46-48 & Boston Edison Co, 48-57; supt, eng & consult, 57-64; asst vpres, Boston Edison Co, 64-67, exec vpres, 67-69, dir, 68-83, pres & chief operating officer, 79-83,. *Mem:* Nat Acad Eng; Inst Elec & Electronics Engrs; Am Soc Mech Engrs. *Mailing Add:* 166 Bank St Harwich Port MA 02646-1321

STATE, DAVID, SURGERY. *Current Pos:* PROF SURG & VCHMN DEPT, UNIV CALIF, LOS ANGELES & CHMN, DEPT SURG, HARBOR GEN HOSP, 71- *Personal Data:* b London, Ont, Nov 13, 14; nat US; m 45; c 5. *Educ:* Univ Western Ont, BA, 36, MD, 39; Univ Minn, MS, 45, PhD(surg), 47; Am Bd Surg, dipl, 46; Bd Thoracic Surg, dipl, 52. *Prof Exp:* Intern, Victoria Hosp, Ont, 39-40; from intern to sr resident surg, Univ Minn Hosp, 41-45, res asst, Univ, 45-46, from instr to assoc prof, 46-52, dir cancer detection ctr, Univ Hosp, 48-52; clin assoc prof surg, Sch Med, Univ Southern Calif, 52-58; prof, Albert Einstein Col Med, 58-71, chmn dept, 59-71. *Concurrent Pos:* Fel path, St Luke's Hosp, Chicago, 40-41; dir surg, Cedars of Lebanon Hosp, Los Angeles, Calif, 53-58, Bronx Munic Hosp Ctr, New York, 59-71 & Hosp of Albert Einstein Col Med, 66-71. *Mem:* AAAS; Soc Exp Biol & Med; Am Thoracic Soc; Soc Univ Surg; AMA. *Res:* General, thoracic and open heart surgery; gastrointestinal physiology. *Mailing Add:* 1 Reata Lane Rolling Hills CA 90274

STATEN, RAYMOND DALE, agronomy, botany; deceased, see previous edition for last biography

STATES, JACK STERLING, MICROBIAL ECOLOGY, MYCOLOGY. *Current Pos:* from asst prof to assoc prof, 70-84, PROF BIOL, NORTHERN ARIZ UNIV, 84- *Personal Data:* b Laramie, Wyo, Nov 6, 41; m 65; c 2. *Educ:* Univ Wyo, BAEd, 64, MSc, 66; Univ Alta, PhD(bot), 69. *Prof Exp:* Res assoc bot, Univ Wyo, 69-70. *Concurrent Pos:* High sch instr, Wyo, 69-70; chmn comt teaching, Mycol Soc Am, 80-81; southwest regional dir, nat bd dirs, Sigma Xi, 86-88, mem nat comt membership, 86-88. *Mem:* Mycol Soc Am; Sigma Xi; Regist Forensics Experts. *Res:* Soil microfungi; ecological studies and effects of industrial pollutants; mycorrhizal fungi; mycophagy by mammals and insects. *Mailing Add:* Dept Biol Northern Ariz Univ PO Box 5640 Flagstaff AZ 86011

STATHOPOULOS, THEODORE, WIND ENGINEERING. *Current Pos:* res assoc, Concordia Univ, 79, from asst prof to assoc prof, 79-87, assoc dir, Ctr Bldg Studies, 83-95, PROF, CONCORDIA UNIV, 87-, ASSOC DEAN FAC ENG & COMPUT SCI, 93- *Personal Data:* b Athens, Greece, Sept 30, 47; Can citizen; m 79, Theodora Kourtelessi; c George & Helen. *Educ:* Nat Tech Univ, Athens, dipl, 70; Univ Western Ont, MS, 76, PhD(wind eng), 79. *Prof Exp:* Engr struct design, Stefanou & Assoc, Athens, 70-73. *Mem:* Tech Chamber Greece; fel Am Soc Civil Engrs; Can Soc Wind Eng; Wind Engr Res Coun. *Res:* Wind loads on buildings; wind tunnel testing techniques; economical measurements of area averaged wind loads on structures (pneumatic averaging technique); wind environmental problems; computational wind engineering. *Mailing Add:* Ctr Bldg Studies Concordia Univ 1455 De Maisonneuve Blvd W Montreal PQ H3G 1M8 Can. *Fax:* 514-848-7965; *E-Mail:* statho@cbs_engr.concordia.ca

STATLER, IRVING C(ARL), NEUROSCIENCES, BIOMATHEMATICS. *Current Pos:* CHIEF AEROSPACE, HUMAN FACTORS RES DIV, AMES RES CTR, NASA, 88- *Personal Data:* b Buffalo, NY, Nov 23, 23; m 53, Renee Roll; c William S & Thomas S. *Educ:* Univ Mich, BS(aeronaut eng) & BS(eng math), 45; Calif Inst Technol, PhD(aeronaut, math), 56. *Prof Exp:* Res engr, Cornell Aeronaut Lab, Inc, 46-53; sr res engr, Jet Propulsion Lab, Calif Inst Technol, 53-55; prin engr, Cornell Aeronaut Lab, Inc, 56-57, asst head, Appl Mech Dept, 57-63, head, 63-70; res scientist, US Army Mobility Res & Develop Lab, Ames Res Ctr, NASA, 70-72, dir, Dept Defense, Aeromech Lab, 72-85; dir, Adv Group Aerospace & Res Develop, NATO, 85-88. *Concurrent Pos:* Lectr, Univ Buffalo, 56-57; mem, Flight Mech Panel, Adv Group Aerospace Res & Develop, NATO. *Mem:* Fel AAAS; fel Am Inst Aeronaut & Astronaut; Am Helicopter Soc; fel Royal Aeronaut Soc; fel Ger Aerospace Soc. *Res:* Aerodynamics; dynamic stability and control; aeroelasticity; rotary wing aerodynamics; applied mathematics; human factors; aeronautical and astronautical engineering. *Mailing Add:* Ames Res Ctr NASA Mail Stop 262-1 Moffett Field CA 94035-1000. *Fax:* 650-969-0477; *E-Mail:* istatler@mail.arc.nasa.gov

STATON, ROCKER THEODORE, JR, MECHANICAL & INDUSTRIAL ENGINEERING. *Current Pos:* RETIRED. *Personal Data:* b McComb, Miss, Dec 6, 20; m 41; c 3. *Educ:* Miss State Col, BS, 41; Ga Inst Technol, MS, 49; Johns Hopkins Univ, PhD(indust eng), 55. *Prof Exp:* Instr mech eng, Miss State Col, 44-48 asst prof indust eng, Ga Inst Technol, 48-51 & Johns Hopkins Univ, 51-54; assoc prof, Ga Inst Technol, 54-58, asst dean col eng, 56-61, assoc dean, 61-66, dean undergrad div, 66-77, prof indust eng, 58-81, dir inst res, 77-81. *Mem:* Am Soc Mech Engrs; Am Soc Eng Educ. *Res:* Academic administration. *Mailing Add:* 106 B O'Parsons Rd Duluth GA 30136

STATT, TERRY G, REFRIGERATION & AIR CONDITIONING SYSTEMS, DEVELOPMENT & COMMERCIALIZATION OF NEW TECHNOLOGIES. *Current Pos:* PROG MGR, ELEC POWER RES INST, 92- *Personal Data:* b Rochester, NY, Apr 19, 53. *Educ:* Stevens Inst Technol, BE & ME, 75. *Honors & Awards:* Citation of Excellence, UN Envrion Prog, 89. *Prof Exp:* Assoc engr, Hittman Assocs, Inc, 75-77; sr engr, Automation Industs, Inc, 77-78; sr assoc, PRC Energy Anal Co, 78-80; mech engr, Energy Appl, Inc, 80-83; mech engr, US Dept Energy, 83-85; prog mgr refrig systs, 85-92. *Concurrent Pos:* Mem, Refrig Comt, Am Soc Heating, Refrig & Air Conditioning Engrs, 88-90, Task Group Halocarbon Emissions & Tech Comt Unitary Air Conditioners & Heat Pumps; mem bd dirs, US Nat Comt, Int Inst Refrig, 91- *Mem:* Am Soc Heating Refrig & Air Conditioning Engrs; Int Inst Refrig. *Res:* Directing research activities among industry, government and utilities to foster the development of highly efficient refrigeration and air conditioning systems. *Mailing Add:* 5139 Capitola Way Union City CA 94587-5156

STATTON, GARY LEWIS, POLYMER CHEMISTRY, SURFACTANT CHEMISTRY. *Current Pos:* CONSULT, MACH I INC, 92- *Personal Data:* b New Brighton, Pa, Nov 4, 37; m 79, Kathleen R Sammartino; c Cathleen A, Robert M, Debbie M, Debra L, Denise & Darelene. *Educ:* Geneva Col, BS, 59; Univ Fla, PhD(org chem), 64. *Prof Exp:* Res chemist, Atlantic Richfield Co, 64-66, sr res chemist, 66-91. *Mem:* Am Chem Soc; Royal Soc Chem. *Res:* Organometallics; polymers; polyurethanes. *Mailing Add:* 1392 Bittersweet Lane West Chester PA 19380-1314

STATZ, HERMANN, PHYSICS, SOLID STATE PHYSICS. *Current Pos:* group leader, Raytheon Co, 53-58, asst gen mgr, 58-69, div gen mgr, Res Div, 88-92, ASST GEN MGR & TECH DIR, RAYTHEON CO, 69-; EXEC DIR, SCI & TECHNOL, XMX CORP, 93- *Personal Data:* b Herrenberg, Ger, Jan 9, 28; nat US; m 53, Ilse Dobler; c Eva & Ingrid. *Educ:* Stuttgart Tech Univ, MS, 49, Dr rer nat(physics), 51. *Prof Exp:* Res assoc, Max Planck Inst Metal Res, Ger, 49-50; Ger Res Asn fel physics, Stuttgart Tech Univ, 51-52; mem solid state & molecular theory group, Mass Inst Technol, 52-53. *Mem:* Nat Acad Eng; fel Inst Elec & Electronics Engrs; fel Am Phys Soc. *Res:* Semiconductor physics, surfaces and devices; noise in electronic devices, device modeling ferromagnetism; paramagnetic resonance; exchange interactions in solids; masers and lasers; new electronic printing concepts. *Mailing Add:* 10 Barney Hill Rd Wayland MA 01778-3602

STAUB, FRED W, HEAT TRANSFER, FLUID DYNAMICS. *Current Pos:* Heat transfer engr, Gen Eng Lab, 53-61, proj engr, Res & Develop Ctr, 61-67, mgr two phase processes, Gen Eng Lab, 67-68, mgr heat transfer unit, 68-82, CONSULT ENGR, CORP RES DEVELOP CTR, GEN ELEC CO, 82- *Personal Data:* b Apr 5, 28; US citizen; m 65; c 3. *Educ:* Rensselaer Polytech Inst, BME, 52, MME, 53. *Honors & Awards:* Melville Medal, Am Soc Mech Engrs, 80. *Concurrent Pos:* US Atomic Energy Comn-Europ Atomic Energy Comn personnel exchange rep, France, 66; vis fel, Cambridge Univ, 79; Coolidge Fel, Gen Elec Co, 76. *Mem:* Fel Am Soc Mech Engrs; Am Inst Chem Engrs. *Res:* Applied research and development in convective heat transfer and fluid flow radiation exchange processes; adiabatic and diabatic two phase flow processes. *Mailing Add:* 1186 Godfrey Lane Schenectady NY 12309

STAUB, HERBERT WARREN, NUTRITIONAL BIOCHEMISTRY. *Current Pos:* CONSULT, 90- *Personal Data:* b Brooklyn, NY, Aug 31, 27; m 55; c 1. *Educ:* Syracuse Univ, AB, 49; Rutgers Univ, MS, 54, PhD(biochem, physiol), 60. *Prof Exp:* Asst, Rutgers Univ, 57-60; sr res specialist, Gen Foods Corp, 60-80, prin scientist, Nutrit Tech Ctr, 80-90. *Concurrent Pos:* Mem coun arteriosclerosis, Am Heart Asn; adj prof nutrit, Pace Univ Westchester, 75-81. *Mem:* Am Inst Nutrit; fel Am Col Nutrit; Am Chem Soc; Soc Nutrit Educ; Inst Food Technologists; fel Am Inst Chemists. *Res:* Nutritional biochemistry; atherosclerosis; proteins; carbohydrates; relationship of dietary carbohydrates to metabolic activity; protein quality evaluation and protein nutrition; dietary fiber. *Mailing Add:* 41 Clover Lane Hightstown NJ 08520-3401. *Fax:* 609-443-1737

STAUB, NORMAN CROFT, PHYSIOLOGY. *Current Pos:* vis asst prof, 58-59, asst res physiologist, 59-60, from asst prof to assoc prof physiol, 60-70, PROF PHYSIOL, CARDIOVASC RES INST, MED CTR, UNIV CALIF, SAN FRANCISCO, 70-, MEM SR STAFF, 58- *Personal Data:* b Syracuse, NY, June 21, 29; m 53; c 5. *Educ:* Syracuse Univ, AB, 50; State Univ NY, MD, 53. *Prof Exp:* Intern, Walter Reed Army Med Ctr, Washington, DC, 54; instr physiol, Grad Sch Med, Univ Pa, 57-58. *Concurrent Pos:* Res fel physiol, Grad Sch Med, Univ Pa, 56-58. *Mem:* AAAS; Am Physiol Soc; Microcirc Soc (pres, 78-79); Int Soc Lymphology; Am Thoracic Soc. *Res:* Pulmonary physiology; pulmonary structure-function relations; kinetics of reaction of oxygen and hemoglobin; diffusion of oxygen and carbon monoxide; pulmonary capillary bed; pulmonary edema and blood flow; pulmonary lymph and lymphatics. *Mailing Add:* Dept Physiol CVRI Box 0130 Univ Calif San Francisco CA 94143-0130. *Fax:* 415-476-2283

STAUB, ROBERT J, ecology, botany, for more information see previous edition

STAUBER, WILLIAM TALIAFERRO, PHYSIOLOGY. *Current Pos:* asst prof, 79-81, assoc prof, 79-85, PROF, WVA UNIV, 85- *Personal Data:* b East Orange, NJ, June 15, 43; m 70; c 1. *Educ:* Ithaca Col, BS, 67; Rutgers Univ, MS, 69, PhD(physiol), 72. *Prof Exp:* NSF fel, Univ Iowa, 72-73, Muscular Dystrophy Asn fel physiol, 74-75, assoc physiol, 76-79; NSF fel 72-73, muscular dystrophy asn fel physiol, 74-75, assoc physiol, Univ Iowa, 76-79. *Mem:* Sigma Xi; Am Physiol Soc. *Res:* Physiology-pathology of skeletal muscle protein breakdown; muscle injury and repair; cumulative trauma disorders; eccentric muscle action. *Mailing Add:* Dept Physiol WVa Univ PO Box 9229 Morgantown WV 26506-9229. *Fax:* 304-293-3850

STAUBITZ, WILLIAM JOSEPH, MEDICINE, UROLOGY. *Current Pos:* RETIRED. *Personal Data:* b Buffalo, NY, Mar 19, 15; m 44; c 4. *Educ:* Gettysburg Col, AB, 38; Univ Buffalo, MD, 42. *Prof Exp:* Chmn urol, Roswell Park Mem Inst, 49-60; prof urol & chmn dept, Sch Med, State Univ NY Buffalo, 60-89. *Concurrent Pos:* Chmn dept urol, Buffalo Gen Hosp, Buffalo Children's Hosp & Edward J Meyer Mem Hosp, 60-; consult, Roswell Park Mem Inst, 60-; consult & mem dean's comt, Vet Admin Hosp, 65-; mem, Residency Rev Comt Urol, 68- *Mem:* Can Urol Asn; Am Urol Asn; Am Col Surg; Am Acad Pediat; Am Asn Genito-Urinary Surg. *Res:* Carcinoma of the prostate; carcinoma of the testes; urinary tract infections. *Mailing Add:* 13 Stonecraft Lane Buffalo NY 14226-4129

STAUBUS, ALFRED ELSWORTH, PHARMACOKINETICS, FORENSIC TOXICOLOGY. *Current Pos:* ASSOC PROF PHARMACEUT & PHARMACEUT CHEM, COL PHARM, OHIO STATE UNIV, 74- *Personal Data:* b San Jose, Calif, Nov 20, 47; m 72; c 1. *Educ:* Univ Calif, San Francisco, PharmD, 71, PhD(pharmaceut chem), 74. *Concurrent Pos:* Co-dir clin pharmacokinetic lab, Interdisciplinary Oncol Unit, Ohio State Univ Comprehensive Cancer Ctr, 77-; vis prof, Abbott Labs, North Chicago, 76. *Mem:* Am Pharmaceut Asn; Acad Pharmaceut Sci; Am Soc Hosp Pharmacists; Am Asn Cancer Res; Am Asn Pharmaceut Scientists; Am Acad Forensic Sci. *Res:* Forensic pharmacokinetics and toxicology; clinical pharmacology of phase I-II. *Mailing Add:* Col Pharm Ohio State Univ 500 W 12th Ave Columbus OH 43210-1214. *Fax:* 614-451-0174

STAUBUS, JOHN REGINALD, DAIRY SCIENCE. *Current Pos:* RETIRED. *Personal Data:* b Cissna Park, Ill, Mar 21, 26; m 51, Lorene Lawrence; c Anna Marie (Jones). *Educ:* Univ Ill, BS, 50, MS, 56, PhD(dairy sci), 59. *Prof Exp:* Asst dairy sci, Univ Ill, 54-59, res assoc, 59-60; from asst prof to assoc prof dairy sci, Ohio State Univ, 60-69, prof dairy sci, 69-87, exten specialist, 60-87, emer prof dairy sci, 87. *Mem:* Am Dairy Sci Asn; Sigma Xi; Am Soc Animal Sci. *Res:* Nutrition in dairy science; ruminant nutrition and physiology; bacteriology of silage; forage plant physiology and composition. *Mailing Add:* 915 Brentford Dr Columbus OH 43220

STAUDENMAYER, RALPH, CEMENTED CARBIDES. *Current Pos:* DIR ENG, HUGHES TOOL CO, 80- *Personal Data:* b July 28, 42; US citizen. *Educ:* Univ Calif, Los Angeles, BS, 66; Univ Ariz, MS, 68; Univ Ark, PhD(chem), 73. *Prof Exp:* Chief chemist metall, TRW Inc, Wendt Sonis, 73-80. *Concurrent Pos:* Cert Calif Jr Col Instr. *Mem:* Am Powder Metall Inst; Am Soc Testing & Mat. *Res:* Powder metallurgy and gas deposition on cemented carbides; fracture mechanics of oil and gas drilling. *Mailing Add:* Hughes Tool Div 4435 W 12th St Houston TX 77055. *Fax:* 713-957-7114

STAUDENMAYER, WILLIAM J(OSEPH), CHEMICAL ENGINEERING. *Current Pos:* Develop engr, Mfg Exp Div, 57-59, res engr, Res Labs, 62-69, res assoc, 69-86, SR RES ASSOC, EASTMAN KODAK, 86-, LAB HEAD, IMAGE FIXING, 89- *Personal Data:* b Rochester, NY, Jan 4, 36; m 63; c 2. *Educ:* Clarkson Col Technol, BS, 57; Cornell Univ, PhD(chem eng), 63. *Mem:* Soc Photog Sci & Eng. *Res:* Electrophotography; photo receptors; high temperature elastomers. *Mailing Add:* 47 Greylock Ridge Pittsford NY 14534

STAUDER, WILLIAM, GEOPHYSICS, SEISMOLOGY. *Current Pos:* from instr to assoc prof geophys, St Louis Univ, 60-66, chmn dept earth & atmospheric sci, 72-75, dean Grad Sch/Univ Res Adminr, 75-88, prof, 66-92, ASSOC ACAD VPRES, ST LOUIS UNIV, 89-, EMER PROF GEOPHYS, 92- *Personal Data:* b New Rochelle, NY, Apr 23, 22. *Educ:* St Louis Univ, AB, 43, MS, 48; Univ Calif, PhD(geophys), 59. *Prof Exp:* Instr, Marquette Univ High Sch, 48-49; res asst geophys, Univ Calif, 57-59. *Concurrent Pos:* Mem geophys adv panel, Air Force Off Sci Res, 61-71; mem panel seismol, Comt Alaska Earthquake, Nat Acad Sci-Nat Res Coun, 64-72; mem adv panel, Nat Ctr Earthquake Res, 66-76; mem ad hoc comt triggering of earthquakes, AEC, 69-72. *Mem:* Fel Am Geophys Union; Seismol Soc Am (vpres, 64, pres, 65). *Res:* Focal mechanism of earthquakes; crustal structure in central United States; seismicity of southeastern Missouri. *Mailing Add:* 3601 Lindell Blvd St Louis MO 63108

STAUDHAMMER, JOHN, ELECTRICAL ENGINEERING, COMPUTER GRAPHICS. *Current Pos:* PROF ELEC ENG, UNIV FLA, 80- *Personal Data:* b Budapest, Hungary, Mar 15, 32; US citizen; m 60; c 2. *Educ:* Univ Calif, Los Angeles, BS, 54, MS, 56, PhD(eng), 63. *Prof Exp:* From asst to assoc eng, Univ Calif, Los Angeles, 54-59; sr syst engr, Syst Develop Corp, 59-64; prof eng, Ariz State Univ, 64-67; prof elec eng, NC State Univ, 67-80. *Concurrent Pos:* Consult var industs, 57-; designer, Douglas Aircraft Co, 59; tech adv, US Army Comput Systs Command, 76-77; nat lectr, Asn Comput Mach, 76-79; comput engr, US Army Res Off, 78-79; adv prof, Zhejiang Univ, Hangzhou, PRC, 85-; expert witness comput graphics & systs, 87- *Mem:* Nat Acad Eng; sr mem Inst Elec & Electronics Engrs; Asn Comput Mach; Am Soc Eng Educ. *Res:* Use of computers in circuit design; design and analysis of computer systems; system engineering of graphics displays. *Mailing Add:* Dept Elec & Comput Eng Univ Fla 216 Larson Hall PO Box 116200 Gainesville FL 32611-6200

STAUDHAMMER, KARL P, MATERIALS SCIENCE. *Current Pos:* staff sci, Los Alamos Nat Lab, 78-83, sect leader phys metall, 83-84, sect leader characterization sect, 84-87, spec proj, MST Div Off, 87-88, staff sci mat technol, 89-90, mat res & processing sci, 90-92, DEP GROUP LEADER MAT RES & PROCESSING, LOS ALAMOS NAT LAB, 92- *Personal Data:* b Budapest, Hungary, Mar 1, 42. *Educ:* Calif State Univ, Los Angeles, BS, 66; Univ Southern Calif, MS, 70 & 73; NMex Inst Mining & Tech, PhD(metall), 75. *Prof Exp:* Electron microscopist, Rockwell Atomics Int, Canoga Park, Calif, 72-73; asst prof mat sci & eng, Wash State Univ, Pullman, 75-78. *Concurrent Pos:* Secy, Am Soc Metals & Mat, Los Alamos Chap, 82, treas, 83, vchmn, 84, chmn, 85; adj prof, Univ NMex, 84-88; Alexander von Humboldt sr scientist. *Mem:* Am Inst Mining & Metall Eng; Am Soc Metal & Mat; Electron Micros Soc Am; fel Am Soc Metals. *Res:* Shock and high strain rate effects on materials including powder compaction and martensitic transformation in steels; materials characterization, alloy development, materials compatibility and metal matrix composites. *Mailing Add:* 534 Ridgecrest Los Alamos NM 87544

STAUDHAMMER, PETER, ENGINEERING, TECHNICAL MANAGEMENT. *Current Pos:* head, Chem Sect, TRW, Inc, 59-60, mgr, Propulsion Res Dept, 60-63, chief engr, Apollo Lunar Descent Engine, 63-74, mgr, Res Lab, 75-81, mgr energy systs opers, 81-87, vpres, Defense Proj Div, 87-90, vpres, Ctr Automotive Technol, 90-93, VPRES, SCI & TECHNOL, TRW INC, 93- *Personal Data:* b Budapest, Hungary, Mar 4, 34; US citizen; m 58, June A Fochler; c 3. *Educ:* Univ Calif, Los Angeles, BS, 55, MS, 56, PhD(eng, phys chem), 57. *Honors & Awards:* Engr Achievement Award for Viking Biol Inst, Inst Advan Eng, 76; Group Achievement Award for Pioneer Venus Sci Team, NASA, 80, Award for Voyager Jupiter-Saturn Ultra-violet Spectrometer, 81; NASA Group Achievement Award for Pioneer Venus Sci Team, 80. *Prof Exp:* Res engr, Univ Calif, Los Angeles, 55-57; sr res engr, Jet Propulsion Lab, Calif Inst Technol, 57-59. *Concurrent Pos:* Magnetic Fusion Adv Comt, 86-; mem, Navy Studies Bd, 89. *Mem:* Nat Acad Eng; Combustion Inst; Soc Automotive Engrs; assoc fel Am Inst Aeronaut & Astronaut. *Res:* After burning of automobile exhaust; regenerable fuel cells; combustion and chemical kinetics of rocket propellants; developer of Apollo lunar module descent engine; space science instruments; fusion research; spacecraft and ground systems engineering; automotive technology; technology management. *Mailing Add:* 2201 Landerhaven MayField Heights OH 44124. *E-Mail:* pete.staudhammer@trw.com

STAUFFER, ALLAN DANIEL, ATOMIC PHYSICS. *Current Pos:* fel, York Univ, 66-67, asst prof, 67-71, assoc prof, 71-80, PROF PHYSICS, YORK UNIV, 81- *Personal Data:* b Kitchener, Ont, Mar 11, 39; m 62; c 2. *Educ:* Univ Toronto, BSc, 62; Univ London, PhD(appl math), 66. *Prof Exp:* Asst lectr math, Royal Holloway Col, 64-66. *Concurrent Pos:* Vis prof, Royal Holloway Col, London, 74-75; vis fel, Joint Inst Lab Astrophys, Boulder, Co, 89-90. *Mem:* Fel Am Phys Soc; Can Oper Res Soc; Opers Res Soc Am; Brit Inst Physics; Can Asn Physicists. *Res:* Theoretical atomic collisions; atomic structure problems. *Mailing Add:* Dept Physics & Astron York Univ 4700 Keele St Downsview ON M3J 1P3 Can. *Fax:* 416-736-5516; *E-Mail:* stauffer@yorku.ca

STAUFFER, CHARLES HENRY, PHYSICAL CHEMISTRY. *Current Pos:* prof & chmn Div Natural Sci, 65-77, EMER PROF, BATES COL, 77- *Personal Data:* b Harrisburg, Pa, Apr 17, 13; m 39; c Charles R, Anne E & John E. *Educ:* Swarthmore Col, AB, 34; Harvard Univ, AM, 36, PhD(chem), 37. *Prof Exp:* Lab asst org chem, Harvard Univ, 34-36, from instr to assoc prof chem, Worcester Polytech Inst, 37-58; prof & head dept, St Lawrence Univ, 58-65. *Concurrent Pos:* Dir chem kinetics data proj, Nat Acad Scis, 54-64. *Mem:* Am Chem Soc; fel AAAS; Sigma Xi. *Res:* Enolization of unsymmetrical ketones; gaseous formation and decomposition of tertiary alkyl halides; reaction kinetics; experimental and theoretical calculations of rates of reaction in gas and liquid phases. *Mailing Add:* 10 Champlain Ave Lewiston ME 04240-5217

STAUFFER, CLYDE E, BAKING. *Current Pos:* OWNER, TECH FOOD CONSULTS, 82- *Personal Data:* b Duluth, Minn, Nov 8, 35; m 58; c Grant & Katherine. *Educ:* NDak State Univ, BS, 56, MS, 58; Univ Minn, PhD(biochem), 63. *Prof Exp:* Res chemist, Procter & Gamble Co, 63-76; dir,

Kroger Baked Foods Res & Develop, 76-81; dir res & develop, Colso Prods Inc, 81-82. *Mem:* AAAS; Am Asn Cereal Chemists; Am Soc Biol Chemists; Sigma Xi; Inst Food Technologists. *Res:* Protein biophysical chemistry; enzymology; surface and interfacial adsorption from solution; edible fats and oils. *Mailing Add:* 631 Christopal Dr Cincinnati OH 45231. *Fax:* 513-522-9641; *E-Mail:* cestafr@eos.net

STAUFFER, EDWARD KEITH, MEDICAL PHYSIOLOGY. *Current Pos:* ASSOC PROF PHYSIOL, SCH MED, UNIV MINN, DULUTH, 75- *Personal Data:* b Logan, Utah, July 6, 41; m 65, 79, Regis Fichtner; c Stacy, Brenda, Jessica (Hurst) & William (Hurst). *Educ:* Utah State Univ, BS, 64, MS, 69; Univ Ariz, PhD(physiol), 74. *Prof Exp:* Assoc, Col Med, Univ Ariz, 74-75. *Mem:* Am Physiol Soc; Soc Neurosci; Sigma Xi; AAAS. *Res:* Neurophysiological studies of motor control with emphasis on afferent, central and efferent mechanisms found in the spinal cord; electrophysiology of neurons in tissue culture. *Mailing Add:* Sch Med Univ Minn 10 Univ Dr Duluth MN 55812-2487. *E-Mail:* estauffe@d.umn.edu

STAUFFER, GARY DEAN, FISHERIES. *Current Pos:* FISHERY BIOLOGIST NAT MARINE FISHERY SERV, 73- *Personal Data:* b Wenatchee, Wash, Feb 26, 44; m 68; c 2. *Educ:* Univ Wash, BS, 66, MS, 69, PhD(fisheries & statist), 73. *Prof Exp:* Fishery biologist salmon res, Quinault Resource Develop Proj, Quinault Tribal Coun, 71-72. *Res:* Stock assessment and fishery evaluation of pacific coast fisheries for developing management information including groundfish species of Alaska and small pelagic species off the coast of California. *Mailing Add:* 7600 Sand Point Way NE BIN C15700 Seattle WA 98115

STAUFFER, GEORGE FRANKLIN, ASTRONOMY. *Current Pos:* RETIRED. *Personal Data:* b Hanover, Pa, Oct 23, 07; m 31. *Educ:* Millersville State Col, BS, 32; Univ Pa, MS, 38, EducD, 63. *Prof Exp:* Teacher pub sch, Pa, 26-27 & high schs, 29-57; prof astron, Millersville State Col, 57-80. *Mem:* AAAS; Am Astron Soc; Nat Sci Teachers Asn. *Mailing Add:* Willow Valley Manor Lancaster PA 17602

STAUFFER, HOWARD BOYER, APPLIED STATISTICS APPLICATIONS TO FORESTRY & WILDLIFE MANAGEMENT. *Current Pos:* PROF MATH, HUMBOLDT STATE UNIV, 83- *Personal Data:* b Philadelphia, Pa, Aug 10, 41; m 84, Rebecca Chwelos; c Sarah & Noah. *Educ:* Williams Col, BA, 64; Univ Calif, Berkeley, PhD(math), 69. *Prof Exp:* Fel, Univ Chicago, 68-69; fel, Univ BC, 69-70; asst prof math, Calif State Univ, Hayward, 70-80; biometrician, BC Ministry Forests, 80-83. *Concurrent Pos:* Fulbright prof, Nat Univ Malaysia, 74-75; res fel, Pac Forest Res Ctr, Victoria, BC, 75-76; vis instr, Univ BC, 78-80; mgr, image processing, NASA-Ames Res Ctr; statist consult, US Forest Serv, B C Ministry Forests, Nature Conservancy. *Res:* Applied statistics; forestry and wildlife management applications. *Mailing Add:* Math Dept Humboldt State Univ Arcata CA 95521. *Fax:* 707-826-3140; *E-Mail:* hbs2@axe.humboldt.edu

STAUFFER, JACK B, TRANSPORTATION SYSTEM DEVELOPMENT. *Current Pos:* PRES, ENG CONSULT GROUP, 91- *Personal Data:* b Newton, Iowa, May 19, 28; m 53, Marion Montgomery; c James, Julie & Nancy. *Educ:* Univ Ill, BSME, 54. *Prof Exp:* Design engr, ACF Industs, Inc, 55-59, proj engr, 59-69; proj mgr, US AEC, 62-69 & Westinghouse Elec Corp, 69-72; dir, Transp Test Ctr, US Dept Transp, 72-76; asst dir indust eng, Consol Rail Corp, 77-79, dir, Technol Serv Lab, 79-82 & appl res, 82-87; dir test eng, Transp Test Ctr, Asn Am Railroads, 87-91. *Concurrent Pos:* Pvt consult, 76-77. *Mem:* Nat Soc Prof Engrs. *Res:* Development of nuclear, space, underwater and transportation projects. *Mailing Add:* ESP Assocs 821 Cottonwood Dr Evergreen CO 80439. *Fax:* 719-545-4435

STAUFFER, JAY RICHARD, JR, AQUATIC ECOLOGY, ICHTHYOLOGY. *Current Pos:* assoc prof, 84-88, PROF FISHERY SCI, PENN STATE UNIV, 88- *Personal Data:* b Lancaster, Pa, Apr 8, 51. *Educ:* Cornell Univ, BS, 72; Va Polytech Inst & State Univ, PhD, 75. *Prof Exp:* Asst prof, 75-80, assoc prof aquatic ecol, Appalachian Environ Lab, Univ Md, 80-84. *Concurrent Pos:* Mem, Pa Rare & Endangered Fishes Coun, 77- *Mem:* Am Inst Fishery Res Biologists; Am Fisheries Soc; Am Soc Ichthyologists & Herpetologists. *Res:* Zoogeography of freshwater fishes; status of rare and endangered fishes; temperature behavior of fishes; assessment of environmental stresses; systematics of African cichlids. *Mailing Add:* Sch Forest Resources Penn State Univ 101 Ferguson Bldg University Park PA 16802

STAUFFER, JOHN RICHARD, STELLAR EVOLUTION, SPECTROSCOPY. *Current Pos:* AT DOMINION ASTROPHYS OBSERV. *Personal Data:* b Findlay, Ohio, Oct 27, 52; m 80. *Educ:* Case Western Reserve Univ, BS, 74; Univ Calif, Berkeley, MS, 77, PhD(astron), 82. *Prof Exp:* Fel, Harvard-Smithsonian Ctr Astrophys, 81- *Mem:* Am Astron Soc. *Res:* Emperical pre-main sequence evolutionary tracks for low mass stars; observational constraints on the physical process at work in active galaxy nuclei. *Mailing Add:* 11332 Rocoso Rd Lakeside CA 92040

STAUFFER, MEL R, STRUCTURAL GEOLOGY. *Current Pos:* From asst prof to assoc prof, 65-75, PROF STRUCT GEOL, UNIV SASK, 75- *Personal Data:* b Edmonton, Alta, July 16, 37; m 58, 72, Sharlene Savage; c 6. *Educ:* Univ Alta, BSc, 60, MSc, 61; Australian Nat Univ, PhD(geol), 64. *Concurrent Pos:* Vis lectr, Univ Alta, 64-65; Nat Res Coun fel, Univ BC, 65-66. *Mem:* Geol Asn Can. *Res:* Structures in rocks, both primary and secondary; shear zones, geotectonics, Canadian shield. *Mailing Add:* Dept Geol Sci Univ Sask Saskatoon SK S7N 0W0 Can. *Fax:* 306-966-8593; *E-Mail:* mel.stauffer@sask.usask.ca

STAUFFER, ROBERT ELIOT, physical chemistry; deceased, see previous edition for last biography

STAUFFER, THOMAS MIEL, FISH BIOLOGY. *Current Pos:* BIOLOGIST IN CHARGE FISH RES, MARQUETTE FISHERIES RES STA, 64- *Personal Data:* b Edmore, Mich, June 24, 26; m 54; c 2. *Educ:* Mich State Univ, Lansing, BS, 49, MS, 66. *Prof Exp:* From fisheries technol fish res to supvr sea lamprey res, Mich Dept Conserv, 50-64. *Concurrent Pos:* Head, Great Lakes Res, Mich Dept Natural Resources, 64-72, anadromous fisheries res, 72-; assoc ed, Transactions of Am Fisheries Soc, 77-; mem bd tech experts, Great Lakes Fishery Comn, 80-81. *Mem:* Am Fisheries Soc; Am Inst Fisheries Res Biologists. *Res:* Determination of the cause of reproductive failure of planted lake trout and assessment of reproduction by coho and chinook salmon in the Great Lakes. *Mailing Add:* 193 Lakewood Lane Marquette MI 49855

STAUFFER, TRUMAN PARKER, SR, PHYSICAL GEOGRAPHY. *Current Pos:* from asst prof to assoc prof, 75-77, PROF GEOSCI, PROF GEOG, UNIV MO, KANSAS CITY, 77- *Personal Data:* b Illmo, Mo, May 29, 19; m 45; c 1. *Educ:* Univ Kansas City, BA, 61; Univ Mo, Kansas City, MA, 64; Univ Nebr, PhD(geog), 72. *Prof Exp:* From teacher geog to admin supt aide, Ft Osage Sch Dist, 61-68. *Concurrent Pos:* Coun mem, Underground Construct Res Coun, Am Soc Civil Engrs, 74-; consult, Union Carbide of AEC, 75. *Mem:* Asn Am Geogr; fel Geog Soc Am; Sigma Xi; Nat Coun Geog Educ; Int Conf Bldg Off. *Res:* Utilization and economic development of underground space for the conservation of space and energy by planned excavation and conversion of mined areas preserving the qualities of the surface. *Mailing Add:* Geosci Univ Mo 5100 Rockhill Rd Volker MO 64110-2446

STAUM, MUNI M, RADIOCHEMISTRY, PHARMACEUTICAL CHEMISTRY. *Current Pos:* RETIRED. *Personal Data:* b New York, NY, Oct 30, 21; m 46; c 2. *Educ:* City Col New York, BS, 42; Columbia Univ, BS, 51; Univ Fla, PhD(pharmaceut chem), 61. *Prof Exp:* Develop chemist, Am Cyanamid Co, 53-57; sr res scientist, Olin Mathieson Chem Corp, 61-67; asst prof radiol, Sch Med, Univ Pa, 67-87. *Concurrent Pos:* Am Found Pharmaceut Educ fel. *Mem:* Am Chem Soc; Am Pharmaceut Asn; Soc Nuclear Med. *Res:* Organic reaction mechanisms; pharmaceutical drug development; development of radioactive pharmaceuticals for diagnostic nuclear medicine. *Mailing Add:* 822 Kings Croft Rd Cherry Hill NJ 08034

STAUNTON, JOHN JOSEPH JAMESON, INSTRUMENTATION, PATENTS. *Current Pos:* TECH CONSULT 78- *Personal Data:* b Binghamton, NY, July 4, 11; m 39; c 6. *Educ:* Univ Notre Dame, BSEE, 32, MS, 34, MSEE, 41. *Hon Degrees:* DEng, Midwest Col Eng, 69. *Prof Exp:* Jr engr mfg, Bantam Ball Bearings Co, Ind, 35-36; head, physics dept, DePaul Univ, 36-38; engr instruments, Coleman Elec Co, Maywood, Ill, 38-44, dir res, Coleman Instruments, Inc, 44-56, sr staff scientist, 56-64; sr staff scientist instruments, Perkin-Elmer Corp, Ill, 64-78. *Mem:* Fel Inst Elec & Electronic Engrs; Optical Soc Am; Sigma Xi. *Res:* Optical, electronic, thermal control and electrochemical instrumentation for clinical and chemical analysis. *Mailing Add:* 310 Wesley Ave Oak Park IL 60302

STAUSS, GEORGE HENRY, PHYSICS. *Current Pos:* PHYSICIST, US NAVAL RES LAB, 61- *Personal Data:* b East Orange, NJ, Mar 25, 32; m 59; c 2. *Educ:* Princeton Univ, AB, 53; Stanford Univ, MS, 58, PhD(physics), 61. *Mem:* Am Phys Soc. *Res:* Nuclear magnetic resonance and electron paramagnetic resonance, principally in magnetically ordered compounds and semiconductors. *Mailing Add:* 7701 Tauxemont Rd Alexandria VA 22308-1056

STAUT, RONALD, CERAMICS, PHYSICAL CHEMISTRY. *Current Pos:* VPRES SALES & MKT, APC INT LTD, 96- *Personal Data:* b New York, NY, Mar 30, 41; m 73, Rebecca; c Scott, Tara, Doug & Kenny. *Educ:* Rutgers Univ, BS, 63, MS, 66, PhD(ceramics), 67. *Prof Exp:* Res assoc inorg chem & ceramics, Mat Res Group, Gen Refractories Co, 67-73, mgr, 73-81, dir corp res & develop, 81-82, vpres res & develop, US Refractories Div, 82-83; pres, Becron Inc, 84-95. *Concurrent Pos:* Consult, 83- *Mem:* Am Ceramic Soc; Can Ceramic Soc. *Res:* Inorganic chemistry; glass-ceramics; refractories; glass; technical and electronic ceramics; piezoeurtric ceramics. *Mailing Add:* 1249 Haymaker Rd State College PA 16801. *Fax:* 717-726-6961; *E-Mail:* ronstaut@esrlink.com

STAVCHANSKY, SALOMON AYZENMAN, PHARMACY, PHARMACEUTICS. *Current Pos:* asst prof, 74-80, ASSOC PROF PHARM, UNIV TEX, AUSTIN, 80-, BIOPHARMACEUT COORDR, DRUG DYNAMICS INST, 75- *Personal Data:* b Mexico City, Mex, May 7, 47; m 70; c 2. *Educ:* Nat Univ Mex, BS, 69; Univ Ky, PhD(pharmaceut sci), 74. *Prof Exp:* Anal chemist, Nat Med Ctr, Mex, 68-69; develop pharmacist, Syntex Labs, Mex, 69-70; vis scientist, Sloan Kettering Inst Cancer Res, 74. *Concurrent Pos:* Consult, Alcon Labs, 75- & Dept Health, Educ & Welfare, 76- *Mem:* Am Pharmaceut Asn; Am Chem Soc; Mex Pharmaceut Asn. *Res:* Analytical chemistry of pharmaceutical systems; protein binding; application of short lived isotopes for the identification of neoplastic tumors. *Mailing Add:* Col Pharm Univ Tex Austin TX 78712

STAVELY, JOSEPH RENNIE, PLANT PATHOLOGY. *Current Pos:* res plant pathologist, Tobacco Lab, Plant Genetics & Germplasm Inst, 66-80, RES PLANT PATHOLOGIST, MICROBIOL & PLANT PATH LAB, PLANT SCI INST, AGR RES SERV, USDA, 80- *Personal Data:* b

Wilmington, Del, May 28, 39; m 65; c 1. *Educ:* Univ Del, BS, 61; Univ Wis-Madison, MS, 63, PhD(plant path, bot), 65. *Prof Exp:* Fel plant path, Univ Wis-Madison, 65-66. *Concurrent Pos:* Pres, Potomac Div Am Phytopath Soc, 79-80; assoc ed, Phytopathology, 87-90. *Mem:* Am Genetic Asn; Crop Sci Soc Am; Am Phytopath Soc; Am Soc Hort Sci. *Res:* Disease resistance in Phaseolus beans; bean diseases, especially rust, pathogenic specialization, genetics of resistance, development of comprehensive and stable resistance for United States green, wax and dry Phaseolus beans. *Mailing Add:* 2206 Apple Tree Lane Silver Spring MD 20905

STAVER, ALLEN ERNEST, SYNOPTIC METEOROLOGY. *Current Pos:* asst prof, 69-72, ASSOC PROF METEOROL, NORTHERN ILL UNIV, 72- *Personal Data:* b Scribner, Nebr, Dec 5, 23; m 65; c 4. *Educ:* Univ Nebr, Omaha, BGen Ed, 56; NY Univ, MS, 59; Univ Wis-Madison, PhD(meteorol), 69. *Prof Exp:* Weather officer, Air Weather Serv, US Air Force, 43-67. *Mem:* Am Meteorol Soc; Nat Weather Asn; Sigma Xi. *Res:* Dynamic and synoptic meteorology utilizing satellite data; computerized meteorological models. *Mailing Add:* 1626 Huntington Rd De Kalb IL 60115. *E-Mail:* astaver@geog.niu.edu

STAVINOHA, WILLIAM BERNARD, PHARMACOLOGY, TOXICOLOGY. *Current Pos:* assoc prof pharmacol, 68-72, PROF PHARMACOL, UNIV TEX MED SCH SAN ANTONIO, 72- *Personal Data:* b Temple, Tex, June 11, 28; m 56, 67; c 4. *Educ:* Univ Tex, BS, 51, MS, 54, PhD(pharmacol), 59. *Honors & Awards:* Sigma Xi res award, Univ Tex Med Br, Galveston. *Prof Exp:* From instr to asst prof pharmacol & toxicol, Med Br, Univ Tex, 58-60; chief toxicol res, Civil Aeromed Inst, Fed Aviation Agency, Okla, 60-68. *Concurrent Pos:* Asst res prof, Med Ctr, Univ Okla, 60, adj prof, 62. *Mem:* Soc Neurochem; Am Soc Pharmacol & Exp Therapeut; Int Soc Neurochem. *Res:* Neurochemistry; insecticides; adaptive mechanisms; study of rapidly metabolized compounds in the CNS; anti-inflammatory drug development. *Mailing Add:* Dept Pharmacol Univ Tex Med Sch San Antonio 7703 Floyd Curl Dr San Antonio TX 78284-6200. *Fax:* 210-567-4303

STAVIS, GUS, ELECTRICAL ENGINEERING. *Current Pos:* RETIRED. *Personal Data:* b New York, NY, June 5, 21; m 44; c 3. *Educ:* City Col New York, BEE, 41; Fairleigh Dickinson Univ, MBA, 79. *Honors & Awards:* Thurlow Award, Inst Navig, 87. *Prof Exp:* Mem staff, Fed Telecommun Labs, Int Tel & Tel Corp, 41-44, assoc head, Air Navig Dept, 46-52; res assoc, Radio Res Lab, Harvard Univ, 45-46; mgr radar advan develop, Kearfott Div, Singer Co, 69-85. *Mem:* Fel Inst Elec & Electronics Engrs; Inst Navig. *Res:* Navigation and radar electronics techniques and systems, including microwave, sonar and optical radiation devices, propagation, transmitters, receivers and signal processing. *Mailing Add:* 2021 SW 17th Ave Boynton Beach FL 33426

STAVITSKY, ABRAM BENJAMIN, IMMUNOLOGY. *Current Pos:* asst prof immunol, Sch Med, Case Western Reserv Univ, 47-49, from asst prof to prof microbiol, 49-83, prof molecular biol & microbiol, 83-89, EMER PROF, SCH MED, CASE WESTERN RESERV UNIV, 89- *Personal Data:* b Newark, NJ, May 14, 19; m 42; c 2. *Educ:* Univ Mich, AB, 39, MS, 40; Univ Minn, PhD(bact-immunol), 43; Univ Pa , VMD, 46. *Prof Exp:* Asst bact, Med Sch, Univ Minn, 42; bacteriologist, Dept Pediat, Univ Pa, 44-46. *Concurrent Pos:* Res fel immunochem, Calif Inst Technol, 46-47; NSF fel, Nat Inst Med Res, Eng, 58-59; bacteriologist, State Dept Health, Minn, 42 & Children's Hosp, Philadelphia, Pa, 44-46; estab investr, Am Heart Asn, 54-59; mem microbiol fel panel, USPHS, 60-63; expert comts immunochem & teaching immunol, WHO, 63-; ed, J Cellular Physiol, Wistar Inst, 66-74 & J Immunol Methods, Immunopharmacology; mem microbiol test comt, Nat Bd Med Examr, 70-74. *Mem:* Fel AAAS; Am Soc Microbiol; Am Asn Immunol. *Res:* Induction and regulation of cellular and humoral immunity in schistosomiasis japonica. *Mailing Add:* Dept Molecular Biol & Microbiol Case Western Res Univ Cleveland OH 44106. *Fax:* 216-368-3055

STAVN, ROBERT HANS, OCEANOGRAPHY, GEOPHYSICS. *Current Pos:* asst prof, 71-77, ASSOC PROF BIOL, UNIV NC, GREENSBORO, 77- *Personal Data:* b Palo Alto, Calif, July 30, 40. *Educ:* San Jose State Col, BA, 63; Yale Univ, MS, 65, PhD(ecol), 69. *Prof Exp:* Lectr biol, City Univ New York, 67-70, instr, 70-71. *Concurrent Pos:* Grant-in-aid, Univ NC, Greensboro, Res Coun, 71-85, univ res assignment leave, 79; res grant, NC Bd Sci & Technol, 74-75; consult hydrospheric optics, Water Qual & Watershed Res Lab, USDA, Durant, Okla, 83; vis prof, Univ Southern Calif, 86, Naval Ocean Res & Develop Activ, 87-89, Naval Oceanic & Atmospheric Res Lab, 90-91 & Naval Res Lab, 92-94; researcher, Univ NC, Greensboro & Off Naval Res, 86-87; Off Naval Res grants, 88-94. *Mem:* Am Soc Limnol & Oceanog; Am Geophys Union; Ecol Soc Am; Biomet Soc; Optical Soc Am; Oceanog Soc. *Res:* Aquatic ecology; physiological ecology; oceanographic optics; theory of the ecological niche; transmission and absorption of light by the ocean; energy-balance of air water interface. *Mailing Add:* Dept Biol Univ NC Greensboro NC 27412-0001. *Fax:* 910-334-5839; *E-Mail:* stavnrh@iris.uncg.edu

STAVRIC, BOZIDAR, FOOD TOXICOLOGY, NATURAL PRODUCTS. *Current Pos:* res scientist biochem, Health Protection Br, 65-72, res scientist toxicol, 72-80, RES SCI FOOD RES, FOOD DIRECTORATE, HEALTH PROTECTION BR, HEALTH & WELFARE CAN, 80- *Personal Data:* b Skopje, Macedonia, Oct 31, 26; Can citizen; m 58, Stanislava Vicic; c Branka & Verna. *Educ:* Univ Zagreb, BSc, 50, PhD(org chem), 58. *Prof Exp:* Lectr org chem, Univ Zagreb, 50-63, asst prof, 63. *Concurrent Pos:* Nat Res Coun Can fel biosci, 63-65; vis prof, Univ Ottawa, 86-92. *Mem:* AAAS; Am Chem Soc; Soc Exp Biol & Med; Soc Toxicol; Am Col Toxicol; NY Acad Sci. *Res:* Isolation and identification of mutagens and other naturally occuring toxic components in foods; experimentally induced hyperuricemia in animals for studies in the fields of hyperuricemia and hyperuricosuria; isolation of biologically active impurities in food additives; caffeine metabolism in monkey; human exposure to polyaromatic hydrocarbons; bioavailability of benzopyrene from foods; toxicity of methylxanthines (caffeine, theoffiline) to humans; health significance from naturally occurring antimutagens/anticarcinogens in foods; carcinogenic heterocyclic aromatic amines in human diet. *Mailing Add:* 37 Charkay St Nepean ON K2E 5N5 Can. *Fax:* 613-941-4775

STAVRIC, STANISLAVA, BIOCHEMISTRY, MICROBIOLOGY. *Current Pos:* RETIRED. *Personal Data:* b Celje, Yugoslavia, Nov 13, 33; Can citizen; m 58; c 2. *Educ:* Univ Zagreb, BSci, 59, PhD(biochem), 62. *Prof Exp:* Technician org synthesis, Fac Biochem & Pharm, Univ Zagreb, 56-57, technician radiobiol, Inst Rudjer Boskovic, 57-59, res assoc, 59-63; fel org synthesis, Dept Chem, Univ Ottawa, 64-65; res scientist, Bur Microbiol Hazards, Health Protection Br, Health & Welfare Can, 65-, head, Ecol Sect, 89-96. *Mem:* Can Soc Microbiol; Soc Appl Microbiol UK; Inst Food Techologists; Int Soc Toxinology. *Res:* Effects of irradiation on the metabolism of nucleic acids in bacteria; detection methods for bacterial enterotoxins; isolation and characterization of bacterial enterotoxins; pathogenicity of campylobacter species; competitive exclusion of salmonella from young chicks; isolation and characterization of chickens gut flora; development of defined mixture of bacterial isolates for protection of poultry against salmonella; pathogenicity of vibrio species. *Mailing Add:* 37 Charkay St Nepean ON K2E 5N5 Can. *Fax:* 613-941-0280

STAVROUDIS, ORESTES NICHOLAS, MATHEMATICS, OPTICS. *Current Pos:* INVESTR, CENTRO INVEST OPTICA, 92- *Personal Data:* b New York, NY, Feb 22, 23; m 49, Dorothea; c Christopher & Gregory. *Educ:* Columbia Univ, AB, 48, MA, 49; Imp Col, dipl & Univ London, PhD, 59. *Prof Exp:* Asst math, Rutgers Univ, 50-51; mathematician, US Dept Navy, 51; mathematician, Nat Bur Stand, 51-54, in chg lens anal & design, 57-67; prof, Optical Sci Ctr, Univ Ariz, 67-88; sr staff scientist, Fairchild Space Co, 88-90; sr staff engr, Lockheed Missile & Space Co, 90-91. *Concurrent Pos:* Fac fel, Stanford Univ, 76; vis prof, Nat Chiao Tung Univ, Hsinchu, Taiwan, 82-83; Sistema nat investr, 93-96 & 97. *Mem:* Fel AAAS; Soc Hist Technol; Am Math Soc; Soc Indust & Appl Math; Math Asn Am; Hist Sci Soc; fel Optical Soc Am. *Res:* Geometric and physical optics; differential equations; differential geometry; diffraction; micro computers; geometrical and physical optics; optical design; applied mathematics. *Mailing Add:* Circunvavacion OTE 504-16 Jardines del Moral Leon GTO 37160 Mexico. *Fax:* 52-47-17-50-00; *E-Mail:* ostavro@foton.cio.mx

STAY, BARBARA, INSECT MORPHOLOGY, PHYSIOLOGY. *Current Pos:* assoc prof, 67-77, PROF BIOL, UNIV IOWA, 77- *Personal Data:* b Cleveland, Ohio, Aug 31, 26. *Educ:* Vassar Col, AB, 47; Radcliffe Col, MA, 49, PhD(biol), 53. *Prof Exp:* Asst biol, Harvard Univ, 52; Fulbright Scholar, Commonwealth Sci & Indust Res Orgn, Australia, 53-54; entomologist, Qm Res & Eng Ctr, US Dept Army, 54-59; Lalor fel, Harvard Univ, 59; vis asst prof zool, Pomona Col, 60; asst prof biol, Univ Pa, 61-67. *Mem:* Entom Soc Am; Am Soc Zoologists; Am Soc Cell Biol; fel AAAS; Sigma Xi; Am Inst Biol Sci. *Res:* Histochemistry of blowfly during metamorphosis and larval blowfly midgut; histology of scent glands, physiology and fine structure of accessory reproductive glands in cockroaches; control of reproduction in cockroaches; regulation of corpora allata; neuropeptides (allatostatins). *Mailing Add:* Dept Biol Sci Univ Iowa Iowa City IA 52242

STEAD, EUGENE ANSON, JR, MEDICINE. *Current Pos:* Florence McAlister prof, 47-78, EMER PROF MED, SCH MED, DUKE UNIV, 78- *Personal Data:* b Atlanta, Ga, Oct 6, 08; m 40; c 3. *Educ:* Emory Univ, BS, 28, MD, 32. *Honors & Awards:* Abraham Flexmer Award, Am Med Cols, 70; Gold Heart Award, Am Heart Asn, 76; Kaber Medal, Asn Am Physicians, 80. *Prof Exp:* Intern med, Peter Bent Brigham Hosp, Boston, 32-33, intern surg, 34-35; instr, Univ Cincinnati, 35-37; asst, Harvard Med Sch, 37-39, instr, 39-41, assoc, 41-42; prof, Sch Med, Emory Univ, 42-46, dean, 45-46. *Concurrent Pos:* Fel, Harvard Univ, 33-34; from asst resident to resident, Cincinnati Gen Hosp, 35-37; resident physician, Thorndike Mem Lab & asst, Boston City Hosp, 37-39; assoc med, Peter Bent Brigham Hosp, 39-42, actg physician-in-chief, 42; physician-in-chief, Univ Div, Grady Hosp, 42-46 & Duke Hosp, 47-67; distinguished physician, Vet Admin, 78-85; ed, NC Med J, 82. *Mem:* Inst Med-Nat Acad Sci; Am Soc Clin Invest (secy, 46-48); Asn Am Physicians (secy, 62-67, pres, 71-72); Am Fedn Clin Res. *Res:* Cardiovascular studies. *Mailing Add:* 5113 Townsville Rd Bullock NC 27507

STEAD, FREDERICK L, NATURAL GAS EXPLORATION & DEVELOPMENT, DISPOSAL OF HAZARDOUS WASTE. *Current Pos:* PRES, F L STEAD & ASSOC, INC, 79- *Personal Data:* b Toledo, Ohio, Dec 20, 23; m 47, Betty Leonard; c Michele, Patricia, Ashley & Lee. *Educ:* Col Wooster, BA, 47; Univ Tex-Austin, MA, 50. *Prof Exp:* Instr geol, Univ Tex, 48-50; staff geologist, Continental Oil Co, Midland, Tex, 50-53, dist geologist, 53-54; div mgr, Ada Oil Co, Midland, Tex, 54-56; chief geologist, McAlester Fuel Co, Magnolia, Ark, 56-60; pres, Great Lakes Gas Corp, Dallas & Houston, Tex, 63-67; pres, Coastline Petrol Corp, Los Angeles, 70-72, Malibu Mining Corp, Los Angeles, 72-74 & Helmet Petrol Corp, Denver, Colo, 75-76; consult, 76-79. *Concurrent Pos:* Pres, Tri-Coast Petrol Corp, Los Angeles, 70-72 & Discovery Develop Corp, Los Angeles, 70-72; pres, Malibu Mining Co, 72-74; pres, Calif Sect, Am Inst Prof Geologists, 75; presidents coun, Am Inst Mgr, 77- *Mem:* Am Asn Petrol Geologists; Am Inst Prof Geologists (vpres, 76-77); fel Geol Soc Am. *Res:* Exploration in frontier areas, preferably basin margins, looking for major deposits of natural gas for clients. *Mailing Add:* 14803 Le Grande Dr Dallas TX 75244

STEAD, WILLIAM WALLACE, MEDICAL INFORMATICS, HOSPITAL INFORMATION SYSTEMS. *Current Pos:* Intern med, Duke Univ Med Ctr, 73-74, asst resident, 74-75, fel nephrology, 75-77, assoc med & nephrology, 77-80, asst prof, 80-83, ASSOC PROF MED & NEPHROLOGY, DUKE UNIV MED CTR, 84-, ASSOC PROF COMMUNITY & FAMILY MED, 85- *Personal Data:* b Durham, NC, Aug 23, 48; m 77; c 1. *Educ:* Duke Univ, BA, 70, MD, 73; Am Bd Internal Med, dipl, 77 & 80. *Concurrent Pos:* Dir med ctr info systs, Duke Univ Med Ctr, 85-; dir ctr dialysis, Durham Vet Admin Med Ctr, 77-83, chief nephrology, 83-85; mem biomed libr rev comt, NIH, 87-; prin investr, Nat Libr Med Grant, 87- *Mem:* Am Col Med Informatics; Am Soc Nephrology; Int Soc Nephrology; Am Fedn Clin Res. *Res:* Medical informatics database design, computer-based medical records, practice and hospital information systems and consultation systems; co-developer of the TMR medical information system; testing a model of an integrated academic information management system based upon integration of distributed resources. *Mailing Add:* Vanderbilt Univ 2209 Garland Ave Nashville TN 37232-8340

STEAD, WILLIAM WHITE, INTERNAL MEDICINE, PULMONARY DISEASES. *Current Pos:* PROF PULMONARY DIS, UNIV ARK, LITTLE ROCK, 72-; DIR TUBERC PROG, ARK DEPT HEALTH, 73- *Personal Data:* b Decatur, Ga, Jan 4, 19; m 75, M Joan Jordan; c Richard B. *Educ:* Emory Univ, AB, 40, MD, 43. *Honors & Awards:* James D Bruce Award, Am Col Physicians, 88; Edward Livingston Trudeau Medal, Am Thoracic Soc, 88; Robert T Howell Award, Southern Health Asn, 93. *Prof Exp:* Resident med, Emory Univ, 44-45, Univ Cincinnati, 46-47 & Univ Minn, 48-49; chief serv pulmonary dis, Vet Admin Hosp, Minneapolis, Minn, 54-57; assoc prof, Col Med, Univ Fla, 57-60; prof, Med Col Wis, 60-72; chief pulmonary dis, Vet Admin Hosp, Little Rock, Ark, 72-73. *Concurrent Pos:* Fel cardiol, Univ Cincinnati, 47-48; med dir, Muirdale Sanatorium, Milwaukee, 60-72; consult, Dept Med, Vet Admin Hosp, Little Rock, 73- & Arthur D Little Co, Mass, 74. *Mem:* AAAS; Am Soc Clin Invest; Am Fedn Clin Res (secy, 55-58, vpres, 58-59, pres, 59-60); Am Thoracic Soc; Am Col Chest Physicians; Am Col Physicians. *Res:* Pulmonary physiology, development of spirometers; clinical and public health aspects of tuberculosis; history of tuberculosis as a global epidemic. *Mailing Add:* Ark Dept Health 4815 W Markham St Little Rock AR 72205-3867

STEADMAN, JAMES ROBERT, PLANT PATHOLOGY. *Current Pos:* From asst prof to assoc prof, 69-75, FULL PROF PLANT PATH, UNIV NEBR, LINCOLN, 75- *Personal Data:* b Cleveland, Ohio, Feb 7, 42; m 64, 89, Terri Spoutz; c Cyndy, Leslye, Jai & Tracey. *Educ:* Hiram col, BA, 64; Univ Wis-Madison, MS, 68, PhD(plant path), 70. *Prof Exp:* NIH WARF fel, Univ Wis-Madison, 64-69. *Concurrent Pos:* Bean Indust, USDA & Chem Co grants, 80-; consult, Latin Am, Africa & Australia, 80-91; US AID title XII grants-bean improv, Dominican Repub, 81-, Honduras, 87-, & Jamaica, 89- *Mem:* Am Phytopath Soc; Sigma Xi; Int Soc Plant Path. *Res:* Epidemiology; vegetable diseases; white mold disease; bean rust; plant disease and microclimate interaction; disease resistance; disease management. *Mailing Add:* Dept Plant Path Univ Nebr 406 Plant Sci Lincoln NE 68583-0722. *Fax:* 402-472-2853

STEADMAN, JOHN WILLIAM, ELECTRICAL ENGINEERING, BIOENGINEERING. *Current Pos:* from asst to assoc prof, 71-81, PROF BIOENG & ELEC ENG, UNIV WYO, 81-, ASSOC DEAN ENGR, 83- *Personal Data:* b Cody, Wyo, Oct 13, 43; m 83; c 2. *Educ:* Univ Wyo, BS, 64, MS, 66; Colo State Univ, PhD(elec eng), 71. *Prof Exp:* Res engr life sci res, Convair Div, Gen Dynamics Corp, Calif, 66-68. *Mem:* Inst Elec & Electronics Engrs; Am Soc Eng Educ. *Res:* Machine analysis of electroencephalograms; information processing in the nervous system; digital system design; microprocessor and microcomputer systems; electrical safety; microprocessor design. *Mailing Add:* Elec Eng Dept Wyo Univ Univ Sta Box 3295 Laramie WY 82071

STEADMAN, THOMAS REE, ORGANIC CHEMISTRY, HIGH PERFORMANCE FIBERS. *Current Pos:* RETIRED. *Personal Data:* b Erie, Pa, Mar 15, 17; m 41; c 2. *Educ:* Rensselaer Polytech Inst, BS, 37; Harvard Univ, AM, 38, PhD(org chem), 41. *Prof Exp:* Sr chemist org chem, B F Goodrich Co, 41-51; res assoc process res, Nat Res Corp, 51-57; mgr org chem res admin, W R Grace & Co, 57-68 & Allied Chem Corp, 68-72; sr chem economist consult, Battelle Mem Inst, 72-73. *Concurrent Pos:* Hormel Found fel, Univ Minn, 40-41; dir org chem res, Signal Oil & Gas Co, 68; adj prof chem eng, Ohio State Univ, 74. *Mem:* Am Chem Soc; Sigma Xi. *Res:* Beta-propiolactone; chemistry of formaldehyde; synthesis of amino acids; methionine and tryptophane; polyvinyl chloride additives; process chemistry; catalysts; water and air pollution; chemical economics; composite materials; high performance fibers; plastic composites. *Mailing Add:* 12401 N 22nd St Apt H304 Tampa FL 33612-4630

STEAR, EDWIN BYRON, SYSTEMS SCIENCE, BIOMEDICAL ENGINEERING. *Current Pos:* EXEC DIR, WASH TECHNOL CTR, UNIV WASH. *Personal Data:* b Peoria, Ill, Dec 8, 32; div; c 2. *Educ:* Bradley Univ, BSME, 54; Univ Southern Calif, MS, 56; Univ Calif, Los Angeles, PhD(control & info systs), 61. *Prof Exp:* Mem tech staff missile syst design, Hughes Aircraft Co, 54-59; assoc res engr, Univ Calif, Los Angeles, 59-61; mgr, Control & Commun Lab, Lear Siegler, Inc, 63-64; assoc prof info systs, Univ Calif, Los Angeles, 64-69; prof elec eng, Univ Calif, Santa Barbara, 69-, chmn dept elec eng & comput sci, 75- *Concurrent Pos:* Mem, Am Automatic Control Coun, 63-; consult, several indust orgn, 64-; sr consult, US Air Force Space & Missile Test Ctr, 69-; mem, Sci Adv Bd, 71- *Mem:* Am Inst Aeronaut & Astronaut; fel Inst Elec & Electronics Engrs; NY Acad Sci. *Res:* Control systems theory; optimum filtering and data processing; biological control systems; computer analysis of electroencephalogram signals; technology for continuing education. *Mailing Add:* Boeing Co PO Box 3707 MS 13-43 Seattle WA 98124

STEARMAN, ROEBERT L(YLE), systems analysis; deceased, see previous edition for last biography

STEARMAN, RONALD ORAN, AEROSPACE ENGINEERING. *Current Pos:* assoc prof aerospace eng, 66-77, PROF AEROSPACE ENG & ENG MECH, UNIV TEX, AUSTIN, 77- *Personal Data:* b Wichita, Kans, June 8, 32; m 57; c 2. *Educ:* Okla State Univ, BS, 55; Calif Inst Technol, MS, 56, PhD(aeronaut), 61. *Prof Exp:* Res fel aeronaut, Calif Inst Technol, 61-62; sr analyst math & physics, Midwest Res Inst, 62-66; assoc prof mech & aerospace eng, Univ Kans, 64-66. *Concurrent Pos:* Air Force Off Sci Res res grant, 66- *Mem:* Am Inst Aeronaut & Astronaut; Soc Exp Stress Analysis; Am Helicopter Soc; Am Soc Engr Educ. *Res:* Aeroelastic and structural dynamics; reliability engineering. *Mailing Add:* Aerospace Eng Dept Univ Tex Austin TX 78712

STEARN, COLIN WILLIAM, PALEONTOLOGY, STRATIGRAPHY. *Current Pos:* From asst prof to prof geol, McGill Univ, 52-68, asst dean fac grad studies & res, 60-63, chmn, Dept Geol Sci, 69-74 & 80-84, Logan Prof Geol, 68-93, EMER PROF GEOL, MCGILL UNIV, 93- *Personal Data:* b Bishops Stortford, Eng, July 16, 28; Can citizen; m 53, M J Mackenzie; c Patricia, Virginia & Andrew. *Educ:* McMaster Univ, BSc, 49; Yale Univ, PhD(geol), 52. *Honors & Awards:* Billings Medal, Geol Asn Can. *Mem:* Geol Soc Am; Paleont Soc; Geol Asn Can; Royal Soc Can; Can Soc Petrol Geologists; Soc Sedimentary Geol. *Res:* Lower Paleozoic stratigraphy and paleontology of Canada; historical geology of North America; fossil stromatoporoids; organisms of Caribbean and Paleozoic reefs. *Mailing Add:* Dept Earth & Planetary Sci McGill Univ 3450 University St Montreal PQ H3A 2A7 Can

STEARNER, SIGRID PHYLLIS, CARDIOVASCULAR PHYSIOLOGY, RADIOBIOLOGY. *Current Pos:* RETIRED. *Personal Data:* b Chicago, Ill, Jan 10, 19. *Educ:* Univ Chicago, BS, 41, MS, 42, PhD(zool), 46. *Prof Exp:* Biologist, Div Biol & Med Res, Argonne Nat Lab, 46-82. *Mem:* AAAS; Sigma Xi. *Res:* Late effects of ionizing radiations on the heart and vascular system, physiological and ultrastructural studies; other physiological effects of radiations on biological systems; pigmentation changes. *Mailing Add:* 1141 Iroquois Ave Naperville IL 60563

STEARNS, BRENTON FISK, ENERGY CONVERSION. *Current Pos:* RETIRED. *Personal Data:* b Chicago, Ill, July 28, 28; m 57, 74, 78; c 2. *Educ:* Pomona Col, BA, 49; Washington Univ, PhD(physics), 56. *Prof Exp:* Asst prof physics, Univ Ark, 54-57; from asst prof to assoc prof, Tufts Univ, 57-68; chmn, Dept Physics, Hobart & William Smith Cols, 68-74, assoc provost, 74-75, prof physics, 68-93. *Mem:* AAAS; Am Phys Soc; Am Asn Physics Teachers. *Res:* Applications of energy storage and efficient use. *Mailing Add:* 478 Washington St Geneva NY 14456

STEARNS, CHARLES EDWARD, GEOLOGY. *Current Pos:* from assoc prof to prof, Tufts Univ, 54-87, dean, Col Lib Arts, 54-69, actg provost, 66-67, EMER PROF GEOL, TUFTS UNIV, 87- *Personal Data:* b Billerica, Mass, Jan 20, 20; wid, Helen Louise Hurley; c Jonathan, Martha, Rebecca, Carola, Jeremie & Kate. *Educ:* Tufts Univ, AB, 39; Harvard Univ, MA, 42, PhD(geol), 50. *Hon Degrees:* LLD, Southeastern Mass Technol Inst, 62. *Prof Exp:* Asst geol, Tufts Univ, 41, instr, 41-42, 45, 46-48, asst prof, 48-51; asst prof, Harvard Univ, 51-54. *Mem:* AAAS; Geol Soc Am; Sigma Xi. *Res:* Pleistocene stratigraphy; shoreline geomorphology; tertiary stratigraphy. *Mailing Add:* 6444 Tahawash Cochiti Lake NM 87083-6042

STEARNS, CHARLES R, METEOROLOGY. *Current Pos:* asst meteror, Univ Wis, 55-56, res assoc meteorol, 57-65, asst prof, 65-69, chmn, Inst Environ Studies, 72-74, PROF METEOROL, UNIV WIS-MADISON, 69- *Personal Data:* b McKeesport, Pa, May 21, 25. *Educ:* Univ Wis, BS, 50, MS, 52, PhD(meteorol), 67. *Prof Exp:* Chief physicist, Winzen Res, Inc, 56-57. *Concurrent Pos:* Consult, Aberdeen Proving Ground, Md, 69-; consult, Red Stone Arsenal, Ala; consult, Argonne Nat Lab, Ill. *Mem:* Am Meteorol Soc; Am Geophys Union; AAAS. *Res:* Micrometeorology, particularly boundary layer problems; evaporation from lakes; diffusion from power plants; antarctic meteorology; automatic weather stations. *Mailing Add:* Meteorol Univ Wis 1225 W Dayton St Madison WI 53706-1695. *E-Mail:* chucks@ssec.wisc.edu

STEARNS, DONALD EDISON, ZOOPLANKTON BEHAVIORAL ECOLOGY, ESTUARINE ECOLOGY. *Current Pos:* ASST PROF BIOL, DEPT BIOL, RUTGERS UNIV, 89- *Personal Data:* b Columbus, Ohio, Nov 1, 48; div; c 1. *Educ:* Dartmouth Col, AB, 70; Univ NH, MS, 74; Duke Univ, PhD(zool), 83. *Prof Exp:* Catedratico biol, Escuela Super Cieucias Marinas, Univ Autonoma Baja Calif, 74-76; postdoctoral res assoc, Skidaway Inst Oceanog, 84-86; res assoc, Dauphin Island Sea Lab, 86-88; res scientist assoc, Marine Sci Inst, Univ Tex, 88-89. *Concurrent Pos:* Adj res assoc & adj asst prof, Dept Biol, Univ Ala, Birmingham, 86-88; adj asst prof, Dept Zool & Wildlife Sci, Auburn Univ, 86-88; grad fac assoc, Univ SAla, 86-88; prin investr, Nat Oceanic & Atmospheric Admin, 88-89. *Mem:* Am Soc Limnol & Oceanog; Nat Marine Educators Asn; Estuarine Res Fedn. *Res:* Marine and estuarine plankton ecology; zooplankton and ichthyoplankton behaviors, photobehavior, feeding, migration, egg production, endogenous rhythms; predator-prey interactions and sublethal pollution detection. *Mailing Add:* Dept Biol Sci Wagner Col Biol Dept 631 Howard Ave Staten Island NY 10301-4428

STEARNS, EDWIN IRA, physical chemistry; deceased, see previous edition for last biography

STEARNS, EUGENE MARION, JR, BIOCHEMISTRY, MANAGEMENT. *Current Pos:* RETIRED. *Personal Data:* b Evanston, Ill, May 3, 32; wid; c 3. *Educ:* Denison Univ, BA, 54; Purdue Univ, West Lafayette, MS, 61, PhD(biochem), 65. *Prof Exp:* Res fel, Hormel Inst, Univ Minn, 65-67, res assoc lipid biochem, 67-70, asst prof, 70-76; sect leader, Conklin Co Inc, 76-81, group mgr biochem 81-83, prod develop mgr life sci, 83-93. *Mem:* AAAS; Am Chem Soc; Plant Growth Regulator Soc Am; Am Inst Biol Sci. *Res:* Animal health and nutrition; microbial- or enzyme-containing materials for home, agricultural and industrial uses; plant tissue culture; microbial biochemistry; plant growth regulators; plant protection. *Mailing Add:* 5383 Flagstaff Circle SE Prior Lake MN 55372-2011

STEARNS, FOREST, ECOLOGY, BOTANY. *Current Pos:* prof, 68-87, EMER PROF BOT, UNIV WIS, MILWAUKEE, 87- *Personal Data:* b Milwaukee, Wis, Sept 10, 18; m 43, 56; c 4. *Educ:* Harvard Univ, AB, 39; Univ Wis, PhM, 40, PhD(bot), 47. *Prof Exp:* Asst bot, Univ Wis, 40-42 & 46-47; instr bot exp sta, Purdue Univ, 47-49, asst prof, 49-57; botanist, Vicksburg Res Ctr, US Forest Serv, 57-60, proj leader forest wildlife habitat res, NCent Forest Exp Sta, 61-68. *Mem:* AAAS; Ecol Soc Am (pres, 75-76); Bot Soc Am; Wildlife Soc; Am Inst Biol Sci (pres, 81-82). *Res:* Autecology of trees and shrubs; seed germination; early succession and productivity; wetland, urban and landscape ecology and phenology. *Mailing Add:* PO Box 1516 Rhinelander WI 54501-1516

STEARNS, H(ORACE) MYRL, ENGINEERING. *Current Pos:* exec vpres & gen mgr, Varian Assocs, 48-57, dir & consult to bd dirs, 48-89, pres, 57-64, EMER DIR, VARIAN ASSOCS, 89- *Personal Data:* b Kiesling, Wash, Apr 24, 16; m 39; c 4. *Educ:* Univ Idaho, BS, 37; Stanford Univ, MSEE, 39. *Hon Degrees:* DSc, Univ Idaho, 60. *Honors & Awards:* Fel AAAS. *Prof Exp:* Asst to chief engr, Gilfillan Bros, 39-41; mem eng staff, Sperry Gyroscope Co, 41-43, head, Doppler Radar Develop Prog, 43-45; res engr in charge klystron res & develop mfg, 45-48. *Concurrent Pos:* Dir, Idaho Res Found, Univ Idaho, 90- *Mem:* Am Mgt Asn; fel Inst Elec & Electronics Engrs. *Res:* Automatic frequency control and ranging; radar; microwave tubes; engineering management. *Mailing Add:* PO Box 947 Bolinas CA 94924-0947

STEARNS, MARTIN, physics, for more information see previous edition

STEARNS, MARY BETH GORMAN, magnetism, multilayer films, for more information see previous edition

STEARNS, RICHARD EDWIN, COMPUTATIONAL COMPLEXICITY, ALGORITHRIS. *Current Pos:* PROF COMPUT SCI, STATE UNIV NY, ALBANY, 78- *Personal Data:* b Caldwell, NJ, July 5, 36; m 63; c 2. *Educ:* Carleton Col, BA, 58; Princeton Univ, PhD(math), 61. *Prof Exp:* Mathematician, Res Lab, Gen Elec Corp, 61-65, Res & Develop Ctr, 65-71, Corp Res & Develop, 71-78. *Concurrent Pos:* Vis prof, Hebrew Univ, 75, Math Sci Res Inst, 85; ed, Siam J Comput, 72- *Mem:* Math Asn Am; Asn Comput Mach. *Res:* Computational complexity; algorithms; game theory. *Mailing Add:* Dept Comput Sci State Univ NY 1400 Washington Ave Albany NY 12222-0001

STEARNS, RICHARD GORDON, GEOLOGY, GEOPHYSICS. *Current Pos:* from asst prof to assoc prof, 61-68, chmn dept, 67-76, PROF GEOL, VANDERBILT UNIV, 68- *Personal Data:* b Buffalo, NY, Apr 28, 27; m 50; c 2. *Educ:* Vanderbilt Univ, AB, 48, MS, 49; Northwestern Univ, PhD(geol), 53. *Prof Exp:* Asst state geologist, State Div Geol, Tenn, 53-61. *Mem:* AAAS; Geol Soc Am; Am Asn Petrol Geol; Am Geophys Union. *Res:* Stratigraphy; structure; geophysics; hydrogeology. *Mailing Add:* 304 Binkley Dr Nashville TN 37211

STEARNS, ROBERT INMAN, INORGANIC CHEMISTRY. *Current Pos:* from asst prof to assoc prof, 66-78, PROF CHEM, EVE DIV, UNIV MO-ST LOUIS, 78- *Personal Data:* b Atlanta, Ga, Feb 26, 32; m 66; c 2. *Educ:* Loyola Univ, La, BS, 53; Tulane Univ, MS, 55, PhD(inorg chem), 58. *Prof Exp:* Res specialist, Cent Res Dept, Monsanto Co, Mo, 59-68; from asst prof to assoc prof chem, Eve Div, Univ Mo-St Louis, 66-78; DIR RES, LORVIC CORP, 68- *Res:* Physical chemistry of fluorides in preventive dentistry; dental materials, cements and polymers; semiconductor materials research, particularly vapor phase depositon of single crystal thin films. *Mailing Add:* 2396 Wesglen Est Dr Maryland Heights MO 63043

STEARNS, ROBERT L, PHYSICS. *Current Pos:* RETIRED. *Personal Data:* b New Haven, Conn, July 28, 26; m 58; c 2. *Educ:* Wesleyan Univ, BA, 50; Case Inst Technol, MS, 52, PhD(physics), 55. *Prof Exp:* Instr physics, Case Inst Technol, 52-55 & Queens Col, 55-58; dean freshman, Vassar Col, 74-77, from asst prof to prof physics, 58-93, chmn dept, 62-64, 66-69, 78-81 & 85-93. *Concurrent Pos:* Res collabr, Brookhaven Nat Lab, 57-, vis assoc physicist, 64-65; vis scientist, Europ Orgn Nuclear Res, Geneva, 70-71; vis staff mem, Los Alamos Nat Lab, 72-80. *Mem:* Am Phys Soc; Am Asn Physics Teachers. *Res:* Neutron physics; scattering of cold neutrons from crystals and liquids; nuclear structure physics using high energy proton scattering; nuclear structure-mesic atoms and hypernuclear physics. *Mailing Add:* 11 Carriage Hill Lane Poughkeepsie NY 12603

STEARNS, RONALD C, PHYSICS. *Current Pos:* STAFF SCIENTIST, NEWPORT CORP, 74- *Educ:* Univ Pac, BS, 70; Univ Calif, Los Angeles, MS, 72, PhD(physics), 82. *Mem:* Am Phys Soc. *Mailing Add:* Newport Klinger Corp PO Box 19607 Fountain Valley CA 92713

STEARNS, S(TEPHEN) RUSSELL, GEOTECHNICAL TRANSPORTATION. *Current Pos:* instr, Thayer Sch Eng, Dartmouth Col, 43-45, asst prof civil eng, 45-53, assoc dean, 73-75 & 80-82, PROF, 53-80, EMER PROF CIVIL ENG, THAYER SCH ENG, DARTMOUTH COL, 80- *Personal Data:* b Manchester, NH, Feb 28, 15; m 39, Eulalie Holmes; c Marjorie E, Stephen J & Jonathan D. *Educ:* Dartmouth Col, AB, 37, CE, 38; Purdue Univ, MS, 49. *Hon Degrees:* AM, Dartmouth Col, 70. *Prof Exp:* Jr engr, Gannett, Eastman & Fleming, Pa, 38-40; jr prof engr, Navy Yard, Philadelphia, 40-41, eng, Dry Docks Assoc, 41-43; consult engr, US Army CEngrs, 54-60. *Concurrent Pos:* Field engr, Boston Univ, Alaska, 53; chief, Appl Res Br, Snow, Ice, Permafrost Res Estab, US Dept Army, 54-55, consult, 55-60; sr res engr, Oper Res Inc, 62-64; mem, NH Transp Comn, 66, 68; chmn Lebanon, NH Airport Authority, 66-69; mem, NH Tomorrow Exec Comn, 70-72; mem hwy res bd, Nat Acad Sci; dir, NH Bd Regist Prof Engrs, 73-82 & Am Soc Civil Engrs, 78-81; consult engr, UN Develop Prog, Poland, 74, 78, 80- & TAMS, 74-82; forensic engr, 80- *Mem:* Nat Soc Prof Engrs; Am Soc Eng Educ; fel Am Soc Civil Engrs (pres, 83-84). *Res:* Transportation engineering, environmental planning and design; soil mechanics and foundations; permafrost engineering; forensic engineering. *Mailing Add:* Thayer Sch Eng Dartmouth Col Hanover NH 03755

STEARNS, THOMAS W, BIOCHEMISTRY. *Current Pos:* asst prof chem, Univ Fla, 46-49, assoc prof agr chem, 49-55, prof chem & asst chmn dept, 55-74, EMER PROF CHEM & ASST CHMN DEPT, UNIV FLA, 74- *Personal Data:* b New York, NY, June 17, 09; wid; c 2. *Educ:* Univ Fla, BS, 34, MS, 37; Univ Minn, PhD(biochem), 40. *Prof Exp:* Asst, Univ Minn, 38-40; asst prof vet res, Iowa State Col, 40-46. *Mem:* Am Chem Soc. *Res:* Physical chemistry bacteria; biochemistry foods; biosynthesis riboflavin. *Mailing Add:* 171 E Burgess Rd Pensacola FL 32503

STEBBINGS, JAMES HENRY, ENVIRONMENTAL EPIDEMIOLOGY, OCCUPATIONAL EPIDEMIOLOGY. *Current Pos:* CHIEF SCIENTIST, MIDWEST EPIDEMIOL ASSOCS, 91- *Personal Data:* b Grand Rapids, Mich, 1937; m 89; c 1. *Educ:* St Louis Univ, BS, 60; Johns Hopkins Univ, ScD(epidemiol), 69. *Prof Exp:* Asst prof epidemiol, Univ Minn, 70-73; staff scientist, US Environ Protection Agency, Res Triangle Park, NC, 74-77; group leader, Los Alamos Nat Lab, 77-79; assoc prof, Univ Minn, 80-81; group leader, Argonne Nat Lab, 81-90. *Concurrent Pos:* Asst epidemiol, Sch Pub Health & Admin Med, Columbia Univ, 68-69, instr, 69-70; adj asst prof environ med, NY Univ, 68-70; adj assoc prof, Dept Epidemiol, Sch Pub Health, Univ NC, 75-77; clin assoc, Dept Family, Community & Emergency Med, Sch Med, Univ NMex, 77-78; mem, Inhalation Toxicol Comt, Nat Ctr Toxicol Res, Jefferson, Ark, 77-78, Sci Adv Group, Power Plant Siting Dept, Environ Qual Bd, St Paul, Minn, Sci Adv Panel, Overhead Power Lines Proj, Dept Health, Albany, NY, 81-86 & Adv Bd Great Lakes Ctr Occup Safety & Health, Col Med, Univ Ill, Chicago, 86-90; consult, Dept Health & Environ Sci, Helena, Mont, 79-80, Comt Fed Res on Biol & Health Effects of Ionizing Radiation, Nat Res Coun, NIH, 80 & Nat Comn Air Qual, Washington, DC, 81; pract supvr, Occup Med Residency Prof, Great Lakes Ctr Occup Safety & Health, Col Med, Univ Ill, Chicago, 82-90, adj assoc prof, Epidemiol & Biomet Prog, Sch Pub Health, 82-97, adj full mem, Grad Col, 82-, adj prof, Epidemiol & Biomet Prog, Sch Pub Health, 91- *Mem:* Soc Epidemiol Res; Int Epidemiol Asn; Soc Environ Geochem & Health; Health Physics Soc. *Res:* Environmental and occupational epidemiology; health effects of radium, plutonium, and other radionuclides. *Mailing Add:* Midwest Epidemiol Assocs 24W571 Mallard Ct Naperville IL 60540-3737. *E-Mail:* 75022.3263@compuserve.com

STEBBINGS, RONALD FREDERICK, PHYSICS. *Current Pos:* vpres student affairs, 83-92, PROF PHYSICS & ASTRON, RICE UNIV, 68- *Personal Data:* b London, Eng, Mar 20, 29; m 52; c 2. *Educ:* Univ Col, Univ London, BSc, 52, PhD(atomic physics), 56. *Prof Exp:* Scientist, Atomic Physics Lab, San Diego, Calif, 58-65; reader physics, Univ Col, Univ London, 65-68. *Concurrent Pos:* Chmn, Dept Space Sci, 69-74. *Mem:* Fel Am Phys Soc; Am Geophys Union. *Res:* Experimental atomic physics, particularly as it relates to problems of astrophysical or aeronomic interest. *Mailing Add:* Dept Space Physics & Astron Rice Univ MS 108 Houston TX 77005-1892

STEBBINGS, WILLIAM LEE, ANALYTICAL CHEMISTRY. *Current Pos:* Sr chemist, 3M Co, 72-77, res specialist, 77-82, analytical mgr, 82-90, SR RES SPECIALIST, 3M CO, 90- *Personal Data:* b Santa Ana, Calif, Mar 1, 45; m 68, Deanna Harlow; c Kenneth. *Educ:* Iowa State Univ, BS, 66; Univ Wis, PhD(org chem), 72. *Mem:* Am Chem Soc; Am Soc Mass Spectrometry; NAm Thermal Anal Soc; Soc Appl Spectros. *Res:* Applications of mass spectrometry chromatography, raman, infrared and thermal analysis in analytical chemistry. *Mailing Add:* 3M Co PO Box 33221 St Paul MN 55133-3221. *E-Mail:* wlstebbings@mmm.com

STEBBINS, DEAN WALDO, PHYSICS, ACADEMIC ADMINISTRATION. *Current Pos:* RETIRED. *Personal Data:* b Billings, Mont, Jan 14, 13; m 37; c 1. *Educ:* Mont State Col, BS, 35; Iowa State Univ, PhD(appl physics), 38. *Prof Exp:* Instr physics, State Col Wash, 38-39 & Agr & Mech Col Tex, 39-41; asst prof, Lehigh Univ, 46-47; from assoc prof to prof, Iowa State Univ, 47-60; physicist, Rand Corp, Calif, 60-63; prof physics & head dept, Mich Technol Univ, 63-65, dean fac, 65-66, vpres acad affairs, 66-76. *Concurrent Pos:* Consult, Opers Anal Off, Hq, US Dept Air Force, 50-60, Radiation Lab, Univ Calif, 56-58, Westinghouse Elec Corp, Pa, 57 & Ramo-Wooldridge Corp, 59. *Mem:* AAAS; Am Phys Soc; Am Asn Physics Teachers. *Res:* Classical physics; geophysics; presence and distribution of matter; interplanetary and interstellar space. *Mailing Add:* RR 4 Box 169 Ames IA 50014-9804

STEBBINS, GEORGE LEDYARD, BOTANY. *Current Pos:* jr geneticist, 35-39, from asst prof to prof, 39-73, EMER PROF GENETICS, UNIV CALIF, DAVIS, 73- *Personal Data:* b Lawrence, NY, Jan 6, 06; m 31, 58; c 3. *Educ:* Harvard Univ, AB & AM, 28, PhD(biol), 31. *Hon Degrees:* Dr, Univ Paris, 62, Ohio State Univ, 82 & Carleton Col, 83. *Honors & Awards:* Jesup Lectr, Columbia Univ, 46; Lewis Prize, Am Philos Soc, 60; Nat Medal Sci, 80. *Prof Exp:* Asst bot, Harvard Univ, 29-31; instr biol, Colgate Univ, 31-35. *Concurrent Pos:* Guggenheim fels, 54 & 60; secy gen, Int Union Biol Sci, 59-64; fac res lectr, Univ Calif, Davis, 62; hon fel, Smithsonian Inst, 82. *Mem:* Nat Acad Sci; Am Soc Naturalists (pres, 69); Bot Soc Am (pres, 62); Soc Study Evolution (vpres, 47, pres, 48); Am Philos Soc. *Res:* Cytogenetics of parthenogenesis in the higher plants; production of hybrid and polyploid types of forage grasses; natural selection, developmental genetics and morphogenesis of higher plants; mechanisms of evolution. *Mailing Add:* Molecular & Cellular Biol Sect 149 Briggs Hall Univ Calif Davis CA 95616

STEBBINS, JONATHAN F, NUCLEAR MAGNETIC RESONANCE SPECTROSCOPY, HIGH TEMPERATURE MATERIALS CHEMISTRY. *Current Pos:* asst prof, 85-90, ASSOC PROF, STANFORD UNIV, 90- *Educ:* Harvard Univ, AB, 77; Univ Calif, Berkeley, MS, 80, PhD(geol sci), 83. *Honors & Awards:* Presidential Young Investr, NSF, 87; Mineral Soc Am Award, 92. *Res:* High temperature materials chemistry. *Mailing Add:* Dept Geol & Environ Sci Bldg 320 Rm 118 Stanford CA 94305-2115

STEBBINS, RICHARD GILBERT, PHYSICAL CHEMISTRY. *Current Pos:* Asst prof, 70-76, ASSOC PROF CHEM, BETHANY COL W VA, 76- *Personal Data:* b Providence, RI, May 20, 43; m 77; c 3. *Educ:* Wesleyan Univ, BS, 65; Tex A&M Univ, PhD(phys chem), 70. *Concurrent Pos:* Vis prof, Mont State Univ, 75-76. *Res:* Analysis of trace organics by API mass spectrometry and the electron capture detector. *Mailing Add:* Dean Arts & Sci Univ Southern Maine 96 Falmouth St Portland ME 04103-4864

STEBBINS, ROBERT CYRIL, ZOOLOGY. *Current Pos:* From instr to prof zool, 58-78, cur herpet, Mus Vet Zool, 48-78, EMER PROF ZOOL, UNIV CALIF, BERKELEY, 78- *Personal Data:* b Chico, Calif, Mar 31, 15; m 41, Anna-rose Cooper; c 3. *Educ:* Univ Calif, MA, 41, PhD(zool), 43. *Concurrent Pos:* Guggenheim fel, 49; ed, Am Soc Ichthyol & Herpet J, 55; NSF sr fel, 58-59. *Mem:* Soc Syst Zool; Am Soc Ichthyol & Herpet; fel Am Acad Zool. *Res:* Natural history and factors in the evolution of amphibians and reptiles; population studies of amphibians and reptiles; function of pineal apparatus; research development of biological science topics for schools; scientific illustrations. *Mailing Add:* Mus Vert Zool Univ Calif Berkeley Berkeley CA 94720-3160

STEBBINS, ROBERT H, GENERAL EARTH SCIENCES. *Current Pos:* CONSULT & ADJ INSTR, J S ARGENT REYNOLDS COMMUNITY COL, 92- *Personal Data:* b Boston, Mass, Nov 14, 24; m 50; c 3. *Educ:* Mass Inst Technol, BS, 50; Columbia Univ, MA, 57. *Prof Exp:* Explor geologist, US Steel, 54-59; gen mgr, Hunting Geophys Surv Inc, 59-63; pres, Stebbins Mineral Surv Inc, 63-66; vpres, Gulf Resources & Chem Corp, 67-72; mgr, Minerals Div, Exxon Corp, 73-76; consult, Robert H Stebbin, 76-80; sr vpres, Int Energy Corp, 80-84; vpres, O'Connor Res Inc, 84-86; pres, Sci Bank Inc, 86-90. *Concurrent Pos:* Founder, Fourm Resources, 79. *Mem:* AAAS; Am Asn Petrol Geologists; Geol Soc Am; Soc Econ Geologists. *Res:* Development and application of models ore deposit formation to exploration programs world wide; application of rubber sheet algorithms to transference of data from one map or engineering drawing to another. *Mailing Add:* 9207 Venetian Way Richmond VA 23229

STEBBINS, ROBIN TUCKER, SOLAR PHYSICS, PHYSICS. *Current Pos:* SR RES ASSOC, JOINT INST LAB ASTROPHYS, UNIV COLO, 86- *Personal Data:* b Philadelphia, Pa, July 9, 48; m 85; c 1. *Educ:* Wesleyan Univ, BA, 70; Univ Colo, Boulder, MS, 73, PhD(physics), 75. *Prof Exp:* Fel, Advan Study Prog, Nat Ctr Atmospheric Res, 75-76; res assoc, Sacramento Peak Nat Observ, 76-77, asst astronr, 77-82, assoc astronr solar physics, 82-86. *Mem:* Am Phys Soc; Optical Soc Am; Am Astron Soc; AAAS; Int Astron Union. *Res:* Global properties of the sun; relativity; fundamental tests. *Mailing Add:* 2530 Kohler Dr Boulder CO 80303. *Fax:* 303-492-5235

STEBBINS, WILLIAM COOPER, BIOACOUSTICS, COMPARATIVE PERCEPTION. *Current Pos:* from asst prof to assoc prof, 63-70, PROF PSYCHOL & OTORHINOLARYNGOL, LITERARY COL & MED SCH, UNIV MICH, ANN ARBOR, 70- *Personal Data:* b Watertown, NY, June 6, 29; m 53; c 3. *Educ:* Yale Univ, BA, 51; Columbia Univ, MA, 54, PhD(psychol), 57. *Prof Exp:* Res assoc otol, NY Univ Med Ctr, 57; asst prof psychol, Hamilton Col, 57-61; fel neurophsyiol, Med Sch, Univ Wash, 61-63. *Concurrent Pos:* Prin investr, Sigma Xi res grants, 60-61; prin investr, NIH res grants, 60-61 & 64-; fel, Univ Wash, 61-63; prin investr, NSF res grants, 74-; mem, Commun Dis Rev Comt, Nat Inst Neurol & Commun Dis & Stroke, 76-80; mem, Comt Hearing, Bioacoust & Biomech, Nat Res Coun, 80- *Mem:* Fel AAAS; fel Acoust Soc Am; Int Primatol Soc; Asn Res Otolaryngol (pres elect, pres, past pres, 83-86); fel Am Psychol Soc. *Res:* Comparative bioacoustics and the evolution of hearing, animal psychophysics, hearing and auditory perception in nonhuman primates. *Mailing Add:* 340 Orchard Hills Dr Ann Arbor MI 48104

STEBELSKY, IHOR, ENVIRONMENTAL SCIENCES, AGRICULTURAL GEOGRAPHY OF THE SOVIET UNION. *Current Pos:* from asst prof to assoc prof, 68-82, chmn, 82-89, PROF, DEPT GEOG, UNIV WINDSOR, 82- *Personal Data:* b Krakow, Poland, Sept 6, 39; Can citizen; m 63, Anne Kuzemka; c Stephan, Andrew & Lesia. *Educ:* Univ Toronto, BA, 62, MA, 64; Univ Wash, PhD(geog), 67. *Prof Exp:* Res asst geog, Univ Wash, 65-67, res assoc, 68. *Concurrent Pos:* Russian & Far Eastern Inst res assoc, Univ Wash, Moscow & Leningrad, USSR, 68; Ont Dept Univ Affairs grant, Univ Windsor, 70-71; Can Coun res grant, 74; Can Coun-Acad Sci USSR travel grant, 76; External Affairs travel grant, UK, 77; Woodrow Wilson Int Ctr for Scholars fel, 83; Geog ed, Encycl Ukraine, 88-93; Acad Sci USSR travel grant, Asn Univ & Cols Can, 90, Russ Acad Sci travel grant, 92; consult, Univ Kiev-Mohyla Acad, Ukraine, 96. *Mem:* Asn Am Geog; Can Asn Geog; Can Asn Slavists; Int Ukrainian Econ Asn; Shevchenko Sci Soc; Int Agribus Mgt Asn. *Res:* Geography of agricultural resources, food production and consumption in the Soviet Union; historical geography of the Soviet Union, with emphasis on population migration to Siberia; land use and occupance in Ukraine; environmental impact in Ukraine; Ukrainian post World War II refugees and their immigration to Canada. *Mailing Add:* Dept Geog Univ Windsor Windsor ON N9B 3P4 Can. *Fax:* 519-973-7050

STEBEN, JOHN D, COMPUTER SCIENCE, ENGINEERING PHYSICS. *Current Pos:* SR PHYSICIST, VITRO CORP, 93- *Personal Data:* b Hinsdale, Ill, Feb 27, 36; m 59, 92, Lynn A Weer; c Amy, Sarah & Jessica. *Educ:* Univ Ill, BS, 58, MS, 59, PhD(physics), 65. *Prof Exp:* Physicist, Midwest Univs Res Asn, 65-67; physicist, Phys Sci Lab, Univ Wis-Madison, 67-74, lectr nuclear eng, 70-74; asst prof radiation ther, Thomas Jefferson Univ, 74-77, lectr radiation technol, 78, sr systs analyst mgr serv, 76-84; sr mem eng staff, RCA-ESD Systs Eng, Moorestown, NJ, 84-91; sr systs engr, GSI, Cherry Hill, NJ, 92. *Concurrent Pos:* Adj asst prof, Dept Neurol, Thomas Jefferson Univ, 79- *Mem:* Sr mem Inst Elec & Electronics Engrs; Sigma Xi; Am Phys Soc. *Res:* Nuclear physics, particle accelerator physics; plasma and medical physics, neurologic studies; radar studies; computer methods in these areas. *Mailing Add:* Vitro Corp 4002 Lincoln Dr W Marlton NJ 08053. *Fax:* 609-988-6086; *E-Mail:* jsteben@ccgate.motown.lmco.com

STEBER, GEORGE RUDOLPH, ELECTRICAL ENGINEERING. *Current Pos:* From instr to asst prof, 63-71, ASSOC PROF ELEC ENG, UNIV WIS-MILWAUKEE, 71-, ASST DEAN SCH ENG & APPL SCI, 77- *Personal Data:* b West Milwaukee, Wis, Sept 25, 38; m 64; c 2. *Educ:* Univ Wis-Milwaukee, BS, 63, MS, 66; Marquette Univ, PhD(elec eng), 69. *Concurrent Pos:* Grants, NSF & Wis Dept Natural Resources. *Mem:* Inst Elec & Electronics Engrs; Simulation Coun; Am Soc Eng Educ. *Res:* Control theory; hybrid computers and systems; electronic circuits; minicomputer interfacing; air pollution control. *Mailing Add:* Dept Elec Eng Univ Wis Milwaukee WI 53201

STECHER, EMMA DIETZ, organic chemistry, for more information see previous edition

STECHER, MICHAEL, MATHEMATICS. *Current Pos:* ASST PROF MATH, TEX A&M UNIV, 73- *Personal Data:* b Milwaukee, Wis, Feb 8, 42; m 64; c 3. *Educ:* Univ Wis-Milwaukee, BS, 64, MS, 65; Ind Univ, PhD(math), 73. *Mem:* Am Math Soc; Soc Indust & Appl Math. *Res:* Partial differential equations; integral equations. *Mailing Add:* Dept Math Tex A&M Univ College Station TX 77843-1246

STECHER, THEODORE P, ASTRONOMY, ASTROPHYSICS. *Current Pos:* Head, Observ Astron Br, NASA Goddard Space Flight Ctr, 72-77, astronomer, 59-76, discipline scientist for astron, Space Shuttle Spacelab Proj, 76-82, SR SCIENTIST, NASA GODDARD SPACE FLIGHT CTR, 77- *Personal Data:* b Kansas City, Mo, Dec 15, 30; m 56, Elizabeth Olmey; c Alan, Martin, Sarah & Byron. *Educ:* Univ Iowa, BA, 53, MS, 56. *Honors & Awards:* John C Lindsay Mem Award, NASA, 66, Except Sci Achievement Medal, 85, 93. *Concurrent Pos:* Mem space sci sub-comt astron, NASA, 68-70; independent res fel, Goddard Space Flight Ctr, 71-72; vis fel, Joint Inst Lab Astrophys, Univ Colo/Nat Bur Stand, 71-72; US proj scientist, Astron Neth Satellite; prin investr, Ultraviolet Imaging Telescope for Astro Missions, Spacelab, 79-82 & mission scientist, OSS-3 payload & flight, 81-82. *Mem:* Am Astron Soc; Int Astron Union; fel Royal Astron Soc. *Res:* Ultraviolet stellar spectrophotometry from rockets; stellar physics; interstellar grains and molecules; space instrumentation; gum nebula; gaseous nebulae; galaxies; globular clusters. *Mailing Add:* Goddard Space Flight Ctr Code 680 Greenbelt MD 20771. *E-Mail:* stecher@uit.gsfc.nasa.gov

STECHSCHULTE, AGNES LOUISE, BIOLOGY, MICROBIOLOGY. *Current Pos:* Chmn dept, 61-72, FROM INSTR TO PROF BIOL, BARRY COL, 60- *Personal Data:* b Owosso, Mich, Jan 9, 24. *Educ:* Siena Heights Col, BS, 47; Detroit Univ, MS, 53; Cath Univ, PhD(biol), 61. *Concurrent Pos:* NIH res grant, 62-65. *Mem:* AAAS; Am Soc Microbiol; Nat Asn Biol Teachers; NY Acad Sci. *Res:* Lysozyme resistant mutants. *Mailing Add:* 11300 NE Second Ave Barry Univ Miami FL 33161-6695

STECK, DANIEL JOHN, RADON & NATURAL RADIOACTIVITY. *Current Pos:* asst prof, 77-83, assoc prof physics, 83-90, PROF PHYSICS, ST JOHNS UNIV, 90- *Personal Data:* b Calumet, Mich, Mar 2, 46; m 70, Joan Orr. *Educ:* Univ Mich, BS, 68; Univ Wis-Madison, MS, 70, PhD(physics), 76. *Prof Exp:* Staff physics, Los Alamos Sci Lab, 68; asst, Univ Wis-Madison, 68-69, res asst nuclear physics, 69-76. *Mem:* Am Phys Soc; Health Physics Soc; Am Asn Physics Teachers. *Res:* Environmental radioactivity; radon; historical radiation dose reconstruction; radioactive contamination. *Mailing Add:* 31148 County Rd 50 Avon MN 56310. *Fax:* 320-363-3202; *E-Mail:* dsteck@csbsju.edu

STECK, EDGAR ALFRED, ORGANIC CHEMISTRY, PARASITOLOGY. *Current Pos:* RETIRED. *Personal Data:* b Philadelphia, Pa, Dec 24, 18; m 50, Mildred Anselment; c Marlene D & Alfred E. *Educ:* Temple Univ, AB, 39; Univ Pa, MS, 41, PhD(org chem), 42. *Prof Exp:* Asst bact, Temple Univ, 36-39; sr res org chemist, Winthrop Chem Co, 42-46; assoc mem, Sterling-Winthrop Res Inst, 46-56, mem, 56-58; med res group leader, Res Ctr, Johnson & Johnson, 58-60; dir res, Wilson Labs, 60-61; sr scientist, Nalco Chem Co, 61-65; dir res, McKesson Labs, 65-67; proj dir parasitic dis, Walter Reed Army Inst Res, 67-81. *Concurrent Pos:* Consult chemother parasitic dis, WHO, 77-93. *Mem:* Am Soc Trop Med & Hyg; Am Chem Soc; Royal Soc Chem; Royal Soc Trop Med & Hyg; Swiss Chem Soc. *Res:* Chemotherapy of parasitic diseases; liposomes; nitrogen heterocyclic compounds. *Mailing Add:* 1913 Edgewater Pkwy Silver Spring MD 20903-1207

STECK, THEODORE LYLE, BIOCHEMISTRY. *Current Pos:* asst prof med, Univ Chicago, 70-73, asst prof biochem, 73-74, from assoc prof to prof biochem & med, 74-84, chmn biochem, 79-84, PROF BIOCHEM & MOLECULAR BIOL, UNIV CHICAGO, 84-, CHMN, ENVIRON STUDIES PROG, 93- *Personal Data:* b Chicago, Ill, May 3, 39; m 61, 82, Yvonne Lange; c David B & Oliver M. *Educ:* Lawrence Col, BS, 60; Harvard Univ, MD, 64. *Honors & Awards:* Robert A Welch Found lectr, 89. *Prof Exp:* Intern med, Beth Israel Hosp, Boston, 64-65; res fel, Sch Med, Harvard Univ, 65-66, 68-70 & Mass Gen Hosp, 68-70; res assoc, Nat Cancer Inst, 66-68. *Concurrent Pos:* Schweppe Found fel, 71-74; fac res award, Am Cancer Soc, 75-80, mem adv comt biochem & chem carcinogenesis, 75-78; publ comt, Am Soc Biochem & Molecular Biol, 83-86; bd sci counr, Nat Heart, Lung & Blood Inst, NIH, 84-88; res council, NY Heart Asn, 84-86; coun invest awards, Am Cancer Soc, 86-89; mem adv comt, Can Inst Advan Res, 96- *Mem:* AAAS; Am Soc Biol Chemists. *Res:* Membrane biochemistry; cell biology of the erythrocyte and of dictyostelium; cholesterol cell biology. *Mailing Add:* 920 E 58th St Chicago IL 60637. *Fax:* 773-702-0439

STECK, WARREN FRANKLIN, ORGANIC CHEMISTRY, ENTOMOLOGY. *Current Pos:* asst res officer, Nat Res Coun Can, 64-70, assoc res officer, 70-76, sr res officer, 76-80, asst dir, 80-81, assoc dir, 82-83, dir plant biotech inst, 83-90, DIR GEN PLANT BIOTECH INST, NAT RES COUN CAN, 91- *Personal Data:* b Regina, Sask, May 10, 39; m 63; c 2. *Educ:* McGill Univ, BEng, 60; Univ Sask, PhD(org chem), 64. *Prof Exp:* Res assoc, Okla Univ Res Inst, 63-64. *Mem:* Phytochem Soc NAm; Can Asn Conifer Biotech; Int Asn Plant Tissue Cult; Int Soc Chem Ecol; Can Res Mgt Asn. *Res:* Insect sex attractants and pheromones; chemical ecology. *Mailing Add:* 1326 Conn Saskatoon SK S7H 3L1 Can

STECKEL, RICHARD J, MEDICAL & HEALTH SCIENCES. *Current Pos:* PROF RADIOL SCI, UNIV CALIF, LOS ANGELES, 67- *Personal Data:* b Scranton, Pa, Apr 17, 36; m 61; c 2. *Educ:* Harvard Univ, BA, 57, MD, 61. *Prof Exp:* Clin res assoc, Nat Cancer Inst, 65-67. *Concurrent Pos:* Pres & chmn bd, Asn Am Cancer Insts. *Mem:* Fel Am Col Radiol; Radiol Soc NAm; Am Roentgen Ray Soc; Asn Univ Radiologists; Asn Am Cancer Insts; Soc Cancer Imaging. *Res:* Diagnostic imaging in cancer management. *Mailing Add:* Radiol Sci UCLA Sch Med 10833 Le Conte Ave Los Angeles CA 90024-1300. *Fax:* 310-794-6613

STECKER, FLOYD WILLIAM, PHYSICS, ASTRONOMY. *Current Pos:* astrophysicist, Lab Theoret Studies, 68-71, & Lab Space Physics, 71-77, SR ASTROPHYSICIST, LAB HIGH ENERGY ASTROPHYS, GODDARD SPACE FLIGHT CTR, NASA, 77- *Personal Data:* b New York, NY, Aug 12, 42; m 65; c 2. *Educ:* Mass Inst Technol, SB, 63; Harvard Univ, AM, 65, PhD(astrophys), 68. *Prof Exp:* Res assoc astrophys, NASA-Nat Res Coun, 67-68. *Concurrent Pos:* Lectr, Univ Md, 85-; mem, Comt Cosmology & Galactic Struct, Int Astron Union; adj prof, Univ Utah, 93- *Mem:* Am Astron Soc; fel Am Phys Soc; Int Astron Union. *Res:* High-energy astrophysics; cosmic-ray physics; gamma-ray astronomy and cosmology; infrared astrophysics; neutrino astrophysics; galaxy structure. *Mailing Add:* High Energy Astrophys Lab Code 660 Goddard Space Flight Ctr NASA Greenbelt MD 20771

STECKL, ANDREW JULES, SEMICONDUCTOR DEVICES, INTEGRATED CIRCUITS. *Current Pos:* ASSOC PROF INFRARED DETECTORS & SOLID STATE DEVICES, RENSSELAER POLYTECH INST, 76- *Personal Data:* US citizen. *Educ:* Princeton Univ, BSE, 68; Univ Rochester, MS, 70, PhD(eng), 73. *Prof Exp:* Sr res engr, Honeywell Radiation Ctr, 72-73; mem tech staff, Rockwell Electronics Res Ctr, 73-76. *Concurrent Pos:* Fac fel, T J Watson Res Ctr, IBM, 77. *Mem:* Am Phys Soc; Inst Elec & Electronics Engrs; Electron Devices Soc. *Res:* Semiconductors and solid state devices; integrated circuits and infrared detectors. *Mailing Add:* ML 30 Univ Cinncinnati 899 Rhodes Hall MI Cincinnati OH 45221

STECKLER, BERNARD MICHAEL, organic chemistry, educational administration, for more information see previous edition

STEDINGER, JERY RUSSELL, WATER RESOURCES PLANNING. *Current Pos:* PROF ENVIRON ENG, CORNELL UNIV, 77- *Personal Data:* b Oakland, Calif, June 22, 51; m 73; c 2. *Educ:* Univ Calif, Berkeley, AB, 72; Harvard Univ, AM, 74, PhD(eng), 77. *Honors & Awards:* Huber Res Prize, Am Soc Civil Engrs, 89. *Mem:* Am Geophys Union; Am Soc Civil Engrs; Inst Mgt Sci; Sigma Xi; Soc Risk Anal. *Res:* Application of statistics and scientific management techniques to problems in environmental engineering and water resources planning; reservoir operation and management; risk management. *Mailing Add:* Hollister Hall Cornell Univ Ithaca NY 14853-3501

STEDMAN, DONALD HUGH, ATMOSPHERIC CHEMISTRY. *Current Pos:* PROF CHEM, UNIV DENVER, 83- *Personal Data:* b Dundee, Scotland, Feb 8, 43; m 64, Hazel M Cooke; c Kenneth M, Roy W & Ian D. *Educ:* Cambridge Univ, BA, 64; Univ EAnglia, MSc, 65, PhD(chem), 67. *Honors & Awards:* Am Chem Soc Award, 96; Frank A Chambers Award, Air & Waste Mgt Asn, 96. *Prof Exp:* US Dept Health Educ & Welfare grant, Kans State Univ, 67-69; sr res scientist air pollution chem, Sci Res Labs, Ford Motor Co, 69-72; vis lectr atmospheric chem, Inst Environ Qual, Univ Mich, Ann Arbor, 72-73, asst prof, 73-80, assoc prof chem & atmospheric & oceanic sci, 80-83. *Mem:* AAAS; Chem Soc; Am Chem Soc; Am Phys Soc. *Res:* Gas phase chemical kinetics and spectroscopy of small molecules, particularly as related to aeronomy, atmospheric chemistry and air pollution; trace analysis of atmospheric pollutants, remote sensing of emissions, particularly automobile exhaust. *Mailing Add:* 2620 S Fillmore St Denver CO 80210-6213

STEDMAN, JAMES MURPHEY, CLINICAL PSYCHOLOGY. *Current Pos:* From asst prof psych to assoc prof psychol, 69-85, PROF & COORD, PSYCHOL TRAINING PROG, HEALTH SCI CTR, SAN ANTONIO, 85- *Personal Data:* b Lockhart, Tex, July 6, 38; m 61, Susan Bradley; c James, Mary, Matthew & Anne. *Educ:* Rockhurst Col, BA, 61; St Louis Univ, MA, 62, PhD (psych), 66; Am Bd Prof Psychol, dipl. *Concurrent Pos:* Secy & treas, Asn Psychol Internship Ctrs, 87-88; regional chair, Am Asn Psychiat Invest Children, 77-79. *Mem:* Fel Am Psychol Assoc; Behavior Therapy & Res Soc. *Res:* Children and family clinical issues; psychology internship issues. *Mailing Add:* Dept Psychiat Univ Tex Health Sci Ctr 7703 Floyd Curl Dr San Antonio TX 78284-7792

STEDMAN, ROBERT JOHN, ORGANIC CHEMISTRY. *Current Pos:* assoc prof phys org chem, 69-76, PROF MED CHEM, SCH PHARM, TEMPLE UNIV, 76- *Personal Data:* b Marlow, Eng, Jan 28, 29; wid; c 2. *Educ:* Cambridge Univ, BA, 49, MA & PhD(chem), 52. *Prof Exp:* Fel chem, Nat Res Coun Can, 52-54; res assoc, Med Col, Cornell Univ, 54-56; res assoc, Banting Inst, Univ Toronto, 57-58; res chemist, Chas Pfizer & Co, Conn, 58-60 & Smith Kline & French Labs, Pa, 60-69. *Concurrent Pos:* Consult, Smith Kline & French Labs, Pa, 79- *Mem:* AAAS; Am Chem Soc; The Chem Soc. *Res:* Natural products and medicinals; nuclear magnetic resonance spectroscopy. *Mailing Add:* 90 Birch Lane Paoli PA 19301

STEEGE, DEBORAH ANDERSON, BIOCHEMISTRY, MOLECULAR BIOLOGY. *Current Pos:* from asst prof to assoc prof, 77-93, PROF BIOCHEM, DUKE UNIV, 93- *Personal Data:* b Boston, Mass, Oct 2, 46; m 82, Robert L. *Educ:* Stanford Univ, BA, 68; Yale Univ, PhD(molecular biophys, biochem), 74. *Prof Exp:* Fel molecular biophys & biochem, Yale Univ, 74-76, fel biol, 76-77. *Concurrent Pos:* Am Cancer Soc fel, 74-76. *Mem:* Sigma Xi; Am Soc Microbiol; AAAS; Am Soc Biochem & Molecular Biol. *Res:* Post-transcriptional controls of gene expression; ribonucleic acid, messenger processing/stability; translational coupling; control strategies. *Mailing Add:* Dept Biochem Duke Univ Med Ctr Durham NC 27710-0001. *Fax:* 919-684-8885

STEEGMANN, ALBERT THEODORE, JR, BIOLOGICAL ANTHROPOLOGY, PHYSICAL ANTHROPOLOGY. *Current Pos:* CONSULT, 86- *Personal Data:* b Cleveland, Ohio, Aug 15, 36; m 63; c 2. *Educ:* Univ Kans, BA, 58; Univ Mich, MA, 61, PhD(anthrop), 65. *Prof Exp:* From instr to asst prof anthrop, Univ Mo, Columbia, 64-66; from asst prof to assoc prof, State Univ NY, Buffalo, 66-74, chmn, Anthrop Dept, 79-86, prof anthrop, 74-86. *Concurrent Pos:* Vis colleague, Univ Hawaii, 67-68; NSF res grants, 67-70, 73-75, 78-80, 91-92 & 95; State Univ NY Buffalo fac res grants, 69-72; res assoc, Royal Ont Museum, 70-; vis prof, Inst Occup Med, Beijing, 89. *Mem:* AAAS; Am Anthrop Asn; Am Asn Phys Anthrop (secy & treas, 85-89); Soc Study Human Biol; Human Biol Asn (secy & treas, 74-77). *Res:* Human cold response, physiological and behavioral; cranio-facial evolution; American sub-arctic; nutritional anthropology; behavior, biology, health and work capacity. *Mailing Add:* Dept Anthrop 380 MFAC Buffalo NY 14261

STEEL, COLIN, PHYSICAL CHEMISTRY. *Current Pos:* from asst prof to assoc prof, 63-77, PROF CHEM, BRANDEIS UNIV, 77- *Personal Data:* b Aberdeen, Scotland, Feb 7, 33; m 58; c 3. *Educ:* Univ Edinburgh, BSc, 55, PhD(chem), 58. *Prof Exp:* Res assoc chem, State Univ NY Col Forestry, Syracuse Univ, 58-59; res assoc, Brandeis Univ, 59-60; asst prof, Univ Toronto, 60-61; res scientist, Itek Corp, 61-63. *Mem:* Am Chem Soc; Royal Soc Chem. *Res:* Reaction kinetics and photochemistry. *Mailing Add:* Chem Brandeis 415 Univ South St Waltham MA 02154-2700

STEEL, COLIN GEOFFREY HENDRY, INVERTEBRATE PHYSIOLOGY, COMPARATIVE ENDOCRINOLOGY. *Current Pos:* res assoc, 75-78, from asst prof to assoc prof, 78-91, PROF, DEPT BIOL, YORK UNIV, 92- *Personal Data:* b London, Eng, June 15, 46; m 70. *Educ:* Univ Cambridge, BA, 67, MA, 71; Queen's Univ, PhD(zool), 71; Univ London, FRESL, 71, DIC, 75. *Prof Exp:* Fel insect physiol, Imp Col, Univ London, 71-72, res fel, 72-75. *Concurrent Pos:* Sci consult, Ont Educ Commun Authority. *Mem:* Fel Royal Entom Soc London; Soc Exp Biol; Europ Soc Comp Endocrinol; Am Soc Zoologists; Can Soc Zool. *Res:* Neurosecretion in insects and crustacea; nervous and hormonal mechanisms controlling development; circadian rhythms, photoperiodism and endocrine aspects; circadian regulation of the endocrine system. *Mailing Add:* Dept Biol York Univ 4700 Kele St North York ON M3J 1P3 Can

STEEL, HOWARD HALDEMAN, ORTHOPEDIC SURGERY. *Current Pos:* chief staff, 65-86, EMER CHIEF, SHRINERS HOSP CHILDREN, 86-; PROF ORTHOP SURG, MED CTR, TEMPLE UNIV, 65- *Personal Data:* b Philadelphia, Pa, Apr 17, 21; m 64, Betty J Clack; c Michael, Patrick, Kathy, Turner, Townsend, Celia, Josh & Anna. *Educ:* Colgate Univ, BA, 42; Temple Univ, MD, 45, MS, 51; Am Bd Orthop Surg, dipl, 52; Univ Wash, PhD(anat), 65. *Prof Exp:* Resident, Temple Univ Hosp & Shriners Hosp Children, 48-52. *Concurrent Pos:* Staff surgeon, Med Ctr, Temple Univ, 51-; assoc prof, Div Grad Med, Univ Pa, 55-; clin prof, Med Sch, Univ Wash, 64-65; consult, Vet Admin Hosp, Philadelphia, 67- & Walson Army Hosp, Ft Dix, NJ, 67-; attend surgeon, St Christopher's Hosp Children; clin prof ortho surg, Med Col Pa, 85- *Mem:* Orthop Res Soc; AMA; Am Acad Orthop Surg; Am Orthop Asn; Am Fedn Clin Res; Eastern Orthop Asn; Scoliosis Res Soc. *Res:* Clinical investigation of hip problems in the child; clinical and bacteriological investigations of nosocomial infections; studies of the C1-C2 articulations in humans; studies on Protrusio acetabuli in the child with closure of the triraplate epiphysis; effect of gluteus medius and minimus advancement in cerebral palsied patient; rib resection in scoliosis; correlation of appearance of the face with skeletal diseases; studies on etiology of palsy in lower extremity after proximal tibial osteotomy. *Mailing Add:* Shriners Hosp Children 8400 Roosevelt Blvd Philadelphia PA 19152

STEEL, R KNIGHT, INTERNAL MEDICINE. *Current Pos:* ASSOC PROF MED, BOSTON UNIV, 77-, CHIEF GERIAT & DIR GERONT CTR, 77- *Personal Data:* b New York, NY, Dec 1, 39; m 65; c 1. *Educ:* Yale Univ, BA, 61; Columbia Univ, MD, 65. *Prof Exp:* From intern to chief resident med, Univ NC, Chapel Hill, 65-71; asst prof, 71-72; asst prof med, Univ Rochester, 72-77; assoc dir, Monroe Community Hosp, 72-77. *Mem:* Sigma Xi. *Res:* Medical education; geriatrics; health care delivery. *Mailing Add:* World Orgn Care Home Hospice 519 C St NE Washington DC 20002

STEEL, ROBERT, MICROBIOLOGY. *Current Pos:* res assoc, 58-71, HEAD MICROBIOL & CHEM SERV, UPJOHN CO, 71-, PROD MGR FERMENTATION OPERS, 76-, ASSOC DIR BIOCHEM ENG, 83- *Personal Data:* b Winnipeg, Man, Mar 17, 23; m 52; c 2. *Educ:* Univ Man, BS, 49, MS, 51; Univ Manchester, PhD(microbiol, biochem), 56. *Prof Exp:* Jr res officer, Div Appl Biol, Nat Res Coun Can, 51-54; Imp Chem Industs res fel, Univ Manchester, 55-58. *Mem:* Am Soc Microbiol; Can Soc Microbiol; Am Chem Soc. *Res:* Steroid bioconversions; utilization of agricultural wastes by fermentation; production of 2, 3-butanediol, citric acid; biochemical engineering; agitation aeration studies in fermentation; mixing and scale-up of antibiotic fermentations. *Mailing Add:* 3505 Pinegrove Lane Kalamazoo MI 49008-2027

STEEL, ROBERT GEORGE DOUGLAS, STATISTICAL ANALYSIS. *Current Pos:* prof statist & grad adminr, 60-82, EMER PROF STATIST, NC STATE UNIV, 83- *Personal Data:* b St John, NB, Sept 2, 17; m 41, Jennie Cole; c Jonathan C (deceased) & Marcia R. *Educ:* Mt Allison Univ, BA, 39, BSc, 40; Acadia Univ, MA, 41; Iowa State Univ, PhD(statist), 49. *Prof Exp:* Asst prof math, Univ Wis & statistician, Agr Exp Sta, 49-52; assoc prof biol statist, Cornell Univ, 52-60. *Concurrent Pos:* Mem math res ctr, US Dept Army, Univ Wis, 58-59. *Mem:* Fel Am Statist Asn. *Res:* Nonparametric statistics; experimental design; data analysis. *Mailing Add:* 2106 Coley Forest Pl Raleigh NC 27607

STEELE, ARNOLD EDWARD, ZOOLOGY, NEMATOLOGY. *Current Pos:* RETIRED. *Personal Data:* b Estherville, Iowa, June 21, 25; m 54; c 3. *Educ:* Iowa State Univ, BA, 53, MS, 57. *Prof Exp:* Parasitologist, Animal Parasite & Dis Div, USDA, 55-56, zoologist plant nematol, Tifton, Ga, 55-59, zoologist plant nematol, Sci & Educ Admin-Fed Res, Calif, 59-86. *Concurrent Pos:* Assoc ed, Soc Nematologists, 75-77. *Mem:* Soc Nematologists; Am Phytopath Soc; Sigma Xi. *Res:* Biology; host-parasite relationships and control of nematodes affecting production of sugarbeet and vegetable crops. *Mailing Add:* 1118 Briarwood Pl Salinas CA 93901. *Fax:* 408-422-5764

STEELE, CHARLES RICHARD, APPLIED MECHANICS, BIO-MEDICAL ENGINEERING. *Current Pos:* assoc prof, 66-71, PROF APPL MECH, STANFORD UNIV, 71- *Personal Data:* b Royal, Iowa, Aug 15, 33; m 69; c 4. *Educ:* Tex A&M Univ, BS, 56; Stanford Univ, PhD(appl mech), 60. *Prof Exp:* Eng specialist aircraft struct, Chance-Vought Aircraft, Dallas, 59-60; res scientist shell theory, Lockheed Res Lab, Palo Alto, 60-66. *Concurrent Pos:* Lectr, Univ Calif, Berkeley, 64-65; vis prof, Swiss Fed Inst Technol, Zurich, 71-72; Univ Lule, Sweden, 82 & Chung Kung Univ, Taiwan, 85; tech dir, Shelltech Assoc; chmn, Exec Comt, Appl Mech Div, Am Soc Mech Engrs, 83-84; ed-in-chief, Int J Solids Struct, 85- *Mem:* Nat Acad Eng; fel Am Soc Mech Engrs; Acoust Soc Am; fel Am Acad Mech (pres, 89-90); Am Inst Aeronaut & Astronaut. *Res:* Asymptotic analysis in mechanics; thin shell theory; mechanics of the inner ear; noninvasive determination of bone stiffness. *Mailing Add:* Stanford Univ Durand Blvd Rm 3558 Bldg 500 Stanford CA 94305-4040

STEELE, CRAIG WILLIAM, ICHTHYOLOGY, AQUATIC BEHAVIORAL TOXICOLOGY. *Current Pos:* asst prof biol, 90-94, ASSOC PROF BIOL, DEPT BIOL & HEALTH SERV, EDINBORO UNIV, 94-, HEAD, GRAD PROG, 94-, ASST DEPT CHMN, 96- *Personal Data:* b Port Arthur, Tex, Mar 22, 54; m 96, Kitty Mathewson. *Educ:* Pa State Univ, BS, 76; Tex A&M Univ, MS, 78, PhD(zool), 86. *Prof Exp:* Fel aquatic toxicol, Dept Zool, Miami Univ, Ohio, 86-89. *Concurrent Pos:* Adj asst prof, Greenwich Univ, Hawaii, 85-; vis scientist, Santa Fe Inst, 89. *Mem:* Am Soc Testing & Mat; Nat Marine Educ Asn; Soc Environ Toxicol & Chem. *Res:* Ethology and behavioral ecology of aquatic animals, primarily fishes; chemoreception; hierarchical organization of food search and feeding behavior; behavioral toxicology; development of methodologies for the quantitative study of behavior; mathematical modelling of behavioral processes. *Mailing Add:* Dept Biol & Health Serv Edinboro Univ Edinboro PA 16444. *Fax:* 814-732-2422; *E-Mail:* csteele@edinboro.edu

STEELE, DAVID GENTRY, ZOOARCHAEOLOGY, PHYSICAL ANTHROPOLOGY. *Current Pos:* ASSOC PROF ANTHROP, TEX A&M UNIV, 79- *Personal Data:* b Beeville, Tex, Feb 8, 41; m 80; c 1. *Educ:* Univ Tex, Austin, BA, 67; Univ Kans, PhD(anthrop), 70. *Prof Exp:* Fel anthrop, Smithsonian Inst, 70-71; from asst prof to assoc prof, Univ Alta, Edmonton, 71-79. *Mem:* Am Soc Phys Anthrop; Soc Am Archaeologists. *Res:* Predator/prey relationships of man; human adaptations to the Texas coast; animal remains from a Roman farm site in southern Italy; human osteology; mammalian paleontology of the Texas Quaternary. *Mailing Add:* Dept Anthropol Tex A&M Univ College Station TX 77843-4352

STEELE, DONALD HAROLD, ZOOLOGY. *Current Pos:* from asst prof to assoc prof, 62-75, PROF BIOL, MEM UNIV NFLD, 75- *Personal Data:* b London, Ont, Nov 5, 32; m 59; c 1. *Educ:* Univ Western Ont, BSc, 54; McGill Univ, MSc, 56, PhD(zool), 61. *Prof Exp:* Technician, Biol Sta, St Andrews, NB, 55-56; lectr biol, Sir George Williams Univ, 60-62, asst prof, 62. *Mem:* AAAS; Ecol Soc Am; Brit Ecol Soc; Int Asn Ecol; Can Soc Zool. *Res:* Marine ecology; zoogeography; systematics of marine amphipoda. *Mailing Add:* Dept Biol Mem Univ Nfld St John's NF A1B 3X9 Can

STEELE, EARL L(ARSEN), SOLID STATE PHYSICS, ELECTRICAL ENGINEERING. *Current Pos:* chmn dept, 71-80, PROF ELEC ENG, COL ENG, UNIV KY, 69- *Personal Data:* b Denver, Colo, Sept 24, 23; m 53; c 6. *Educ:* Univ Utah, BS, 45; Cornell Univ, PhD(physics), 52. *Prof Exp:* Lab asst physics, Univ Utah, 44-45; asst, Cornell Univ, 45-51; res physicist, Gen Elec Co, 51-56; chief res dept, Semiconductor Div, Motorola, Inc, Ariz, 56-58; asst lab mgr, Semiconductor Div, Hughes Aircraft Co, 58-59, lab mgr, 59-63; staff scientist, Res & Eng Div, Autonetics Div, N Am Aviation, Inc, Calif, 63-69. *Concurrent Pos:* Ed, Trans Electron Devices, Inst Elec & Electronics Engrs, 54-61; assoc prof, Ariz State Univ, 57-58; lectr, Univ Calif, Los Angeles, 59; phys sci coordr, Southern Calif Col, 62-63; affil prof & lectr, Univ Calif, Irvine, 67-69; officer, Southeastern Ctr Elec Eng Educ, 74- *Mem:* Am Phys Soc; Am Soc Eng Educ; Sigma Xi; Am Asn Physics Teachers; fel Inst Elec & Electronics Engrs; Int Soc Hybrid Microelectronics. *Res:* Semiconductor p-n junction theory and device design; solid state theoretical studies of band structure of barium oxide; transistors and parametric devices; microelectronics; lasers and electrooptics; computer aided electronic circuit design; quantum electronics. *Mailing Add:* Dept Elec Eng Univ Ky 567 Anderson Hall Lexington KY 40506

STEELE, GLENN DANIEL, JR, SURGICAL ONCOLOGY. *Current Pos:* from instr to assoc prof surg, 76-84, WILLIAM V MCDERMOTT PROF SURG, MED SCH, HARVARD UNIV, 85-; DEAN, MED DEPT UNIV, CHICAGO. *Personal Data:* b Baltimore, Md, June 23, 44; m, Lisa; c Joshua, Kirsten & Lara. *Educ:* Harvard Univ, AB, 66; NY Univ, MD, 70; Lund Univ, Sweden, PhD, 75. *Prof Exp:* From intern to resident, Med Ctr, Univ Colo, Denver, 70-76. *Concurrent Pos:* NIH fel immunol, Univ Lund, Sweden, 73-75; asst surgeon, Sidney Farber Cancer Inst, Boston, 76-78, clin assoc surg oncol, 78-79, asst physician surg oncol, 79-82; jr assoc surg, Peter Bent Brigham Hosp, 76-82; Am Cancer Soc fel, 76-79; consult surgeon, Boston Hosp Women, 77-80; surgeon, Brigham & Womens Hosp, 82-84; assoc physician surg oncol, Dana-Farber Cancer Inst, 82-84, physician, 84-; chmn, Dept Surg, Deaconess Harvard Surg Serv, New Eng Deaconess Hosp, Boston, 85-95; assoc ed, J Clin Oncol, 86-, J Hepatobiliary-Pancreatic Surg, 93-; mem, Patient Care & Res Comt Cancer, Am Col Surgeons, 89-91, chmn, Comt Cancer, 91-93. *Mem:* Fel Am Col Surgeons; Am Asn Immunologists; Am Bd Surg; Am Bd Med Specialties; Am Soc Clin Oncol; Am Surg Asn; Int Surg Cols; Int Surg Group. *Res:* Cancer; oncology. *Mailing Add:* 5841 Maryland Ave MC 1000 Chicago IL 60037-1470

STEELE, IAN MCKAY, LEAD CHEMICALS, COMPUTER CONTROL OF INSTRUMENTS. *Current Pos:* RES ASSOC GEOPHYSICS, UNIV CHICAGO, 71- *Personal Data:* b Syracuse, NY, June 19, 44; div; c Brian, Andrew, Catherine & Brenda. *Educ:* Rensselaer Poly Inst, BS, 66; Univ Ill, PhD(geol), 71. *Concurrent Pos:* Consult, Hammond Lead Corp, 86- *Mem:* fel Mineral Soc Am; Geochem Soc; fel Meteoritical Soc; Am Geophys Union; Mineral Soc Gt Brit; Microbeam Anal Soc. *Res:* Crystallograph, mineralogy and chemical processes of phases in lead acid batteries; analytical techniques of chemical and structural analysis; computer application to analysis techniques. *Mailing Add:* Univ Chicago 5734 S Ellis Ave Chicago IL 60637. *Fax:* 773-702-9505; *E-Mail:* steele@geol.uchicago.edu

STEELE, JACK, INORGANIC CHEMISTRY, PHYSICAL CHEMISTRY. *Current Pos:* from asst prof to assoc prof, 70-80, chmn, dept chem & physics, 81-85, PROF CHEM, ALBANY STATE COL, 80- *Personal Data:* b Indianapolis, Ind, Jan 22, 42; m 68; c 3. *Educ:* DePauw Univ, BA, 64; Univ Ky, PhD(inorg chem), 68. *Prof Exp:* Am Chem Soc Petrol Res Fund grant & teaching intern, Wash State Univ, 68-70. *Concurrent Pos:* NSF col sci improv prog mem, Albany State Col, 72-73, minority sch biomed support prog mem, 72-76; Minority Access to Res Career, 88- *Mem:* Am Chem Soc. *Res:* Stereochemistry of metal chelates of biologically important compounds; science education; analysis of environmental samples. *Mailing Add:* Dept Natural Sci Albany State Col 504 College Dr Albany GA 31705-2717

STEELE, JACK ELLWOOD, BIONICS, INTELLIGENT SYSTEMS. *Current Pos:* PRES, GEN BIONICS CORP, 79- *Personal Data:* b Lacon, Ill, Jan 27, 24; m 55, Ruth E Kelley; c Jill (Mayer) & Suzy. *Educ:* Northwestern Univ, BM, 49, MD, 50; Wright State Univ, MS, 77. *Prof Exp:* Intern, Cincinnati Gen Hosp, 49-50; fel neuroanat, Med Sch, Northwestern Univ, 50-51; ward officer, USAF, 2750 US Air Force Hosp, Wright-Patterson AFB, 51-53, proj officer, Aerospace Med Lab, 53-71; pvt pract, 71-73; physician, Dayton Mental Health Ctr, 73-75, med dir, Drug Treatment Unit, 75-78. *Concurrent Pos:* Physician, Buda Narcotics Clinic, 78-81; med dir, Nova House, 81-90. *Mem:* Inst Elec & Electronics Engrs; AMA; Asn Comput Mach; Am Soc Clin Hypnosis. *Res:* Analysis and design of systems with lifelike behavior, intelligence in particular; logic of human mind; protologic; psychotherapy; motion sickness. *Mailing Add:* 2313 Bonnieview Ave Dayton OH 45431-1987

STEELE, JAMES HARLAN, VETERINARY MEDICINE & PUBLIC HEALTH, ZOONOSES & FOOD IRRADIATION. *Current Pos:* prof, 71-83, EMER PROF ENVIRON SCI, SCH PUB HEALTH, UNIV TEX, HOUSTON, 83- *Personal Data:* b Chicago, Ill, Apr 3, 13; m 41, 69, Maria-Brigitte Meyer; c James, David & Michael. *Educ:* Mich State Univ, DVM, 41; Harvard Univ, MPH, 42; Am Bd Vet Pub Health, dipl, Am Col Vet Med, dipl. *Honors & Awards:* Janes H Steele Vet Pub Health Award, World Vet Epidemiol Soc, 75 & 93; Int Vet Award, Am Vet Med Asn, 84, Pub Serv Award, 93; Int Award for Contrib to World Health, Ger Health Serv, 88, Medal of Merit, 93; Distinguished Serv Award, Am Vet Hist Soc, 95. *Prof Exp:* State Health Dept, Ohio, 42-43; vet, USPHS, 43-45, chief vet pub health, Nat Commun Dis Ctr, 45-68, asst surgeon gen vet affairs, 68-71. *Concurrent Pos:* Consult, Pan-Am Sanit Bur, 44, WHO, 50-, Food & Agr, 60-, & White House Comt Consumer Protection; founder, Am Bd Vet Pub Health, 50-52; chmn, WHO-Food & Agr Orgn & Expert Comt Zoonoses, 3rd Report, 67; hon dipl, Tenth World Vet Cong, 75; ed-in-chief, CRC Handbk Zoonoses, 78-94; Conf Emer Mem, Pub Health Asn; vis prof, Tex A&M Univ, 76-, all univ prof, 81-82; consult, Ger Health Serv, 86-93; trustee, Nat Found Infectious Dis; professorship, UISPH, 96. *Mem:* Emer mem Am Soc Trop Med & Hyg; Asn Mil Surg US; Am Vet Med Asn; emer mem Am Vet Epidemiol Soc (pres, 88-90); hon mem World Vet Cong; hon mem World Vet Asn; emer mem Am Pub Health Asn; Nat Acad Health Practrs; hon mem World Vet Asn; hon mem Philippines Vet Med Asn; hon mem Peru Vet Med Asn; emer mem Infectious Dis Soc Am; emer mem Inst Epidemiol Soc; Am Col Epidemiol; Am Col Vet Prev Med; World Vet Epidemiol Soc (pres, 71); hon mem Mil Surgeons Asn. *Res:* Veterinary public health; epidemiology of zoonoses and chronic diseases common to animals and man; cost benefits of international veterinary public health programs; tuberculosis in animals; food irradiation and hygiene; contributed articles to professional journals. *Mailing Add:* Sch Pub Health Univ Tex Houston TX 77225

STEELE, JAMES PATRICK, radiology, for more information see previous edition

STEELE, JOHN EARLE, ENDOCRINOLOGY, CELL BIOLOGY. *Current Pos:* from asst prof to assoc prof, 64-75, PROF ZOOL, UNIV WESTERN ONT, 75- *Personal Data:* b St John's, Nfld, Jan 29, 32; m 57; c 3. *Educ:* Dalhousie Univ, BSc, 54; Univ Western Ont, MSc, 56; Univ Sask, PhD(biol), 59. *Prof Exp:* Res officer, Can Dept Agr, 59-64. *Mem:* Can Soc Zool; Entom Soc Ont. *Res:* Hormonal control of metabolism, water transport and growth and development in insects; effect of stress in insects. *Mailing Add:* Dept Zool Univ Western Ont London ON N6A 5B7 Can

STEELE, JOHN H, OCEANOGRAPHY. *Current Pos:* dir, 77-89, pres, 83-91, EMER PRES, WOODS HOLE OCEANOG INST, 91- *Personal Data:* b Edinburgh, UK, Nov 15, 26; m 56; c 1. *Educ:* Univ Col, London, BSc, 46, DSc, 64. *Honors & Awards:* Alexander Agassiz Medal, Nat Acad Sci, 73. *Prof Exp:* Scientist, Marine Lab, Scotland, 51-77, dep dir, 73-77; dir, Exxon Corp, 89-97. *Concurrent Pos:* Trustee, Bermuda Biol Sta Res Inc, 77-95, Univ Corp Atmospheric Res, 85-89, & Rob Wood Johnson Found, 90-; mem, bd govs, Joint Oceanog Inst Inc, 77-89; mem, Nat Res Coun, Nat Acad Sci, 78-88, chmn ocean sci bd, 81-82; mem comt res explor, Nat Geog Soc, 87- *Mem:* Fel Royal Soc; fel Royal Soc Edinburgh; Am Acad Arts & Sci; fel AAAS. *Res:* Dynamics of marine ecosystems. *Mailing Add:* Woods Hole Oceanog Inst Woods Hole MA 02543. *E-Mail:* jsteele@whoi.edu

STEELE, JOHN WISEMAN, PHARMACEUTICAL CHEMISTRY. *Current Pos:* Lectr, Univ Man, 58-59, from asst prof to assoc prof, 59-81, dean fac pharm, 81-92, PROF, UNIV MAN, 81- *Personal Data:* b Motherwell, Scotland, May 27, 34; m 58; c 4. *Educ:* Glasgow Univ, BSc, 55, PhD(pharmaceut chem), 59. *Concurrent Pos:* Fel, Chelsea Col Sci & Technol, 65-66; mem, Med Res Coun Can, 70-72; vis scientist, Med-Chem Inst, Univ Bern, 72-73; mem, Man Drug Stand & Therapeut Comt, 78-86. *Mem:* Can Pharmaceut Asn; Asn Faculties Pharm Can (pres, 75-76); Royal Soc Chem. *Res:* Drug metabolism, especially of anabolic steroids and other drugs likely to be abused by athletes; methods of drug analysis, including gas-liquid chromatography. *Mailing Add:* Fac Pharm Univ Man 50 Fifton Rd Winnipeg MB R3T 2N2 Can. *Fax:* 204-275-7509

STEELE, KENNETH F, WATER QUALITY, WATER CHEMISTRY. *Current Pos:* From instr to assoc prof, 70-83, PROF GEOL, UNIV ARK, FAYETTEVILLE, 83-, DIR ARK WATER RESOURCES RES CTR, 88- *Personal Data:* b Statesville, NC, Jan 16, 44; m 66, Sheila Stumpf; c Krista & Celisa. *Educ:* Univ NC, Chapel Hill, BS, 62, PhD(geol), 71. *Honors & Awards:* Oak Ridge Assoc Univs fel. *Concurrent Pos:* Mem, S Cent Mgt Bd, Geol Soc Am, 80-82, 84-86, prog chmn, 85; bd dirs, Ark Ground Water Asn, 88-90 & 93-, vpres, 91, pres, 92; reg dir, Nat Insts Water Resources, 90-93; bd dirs, Am Water Resources Asn, 91-94. *Mem:* Int Asn Hydrogeologists; Int Asn Geochem & Cosmochem; Soc Environ Geochem & Health; Am Water Resources Asn; Asn Explor Geochemists; Asn Groundwater Sci & Engrs; Am Inst Hydrol. *Res:* Major and trace element geochemical investigations applied to environmental geochemistry, especially water. *Mailing Add:* 1115 Valley View Dr Fayetteville AR 72701. *Fax:* 501-575-3846

STEELE, LAWRENCE RUSSELL, CHEMICAL ENGINEERING. *Current Pos:* SR RES ENGR, E R SQUIBB & SONS, INC, 66-, SECT HEAD, 75-, ASST DEPT HEAD, 81-, DIR, 83- *Personal Data:* b Manhattan, Kans, Nov 7, 35; m 59; c 3. *Educ:* Ohio State Univ, BChE & MSc, 58, PhD(chem eng), 62; Fairleigh-Dickinson Univ, MBA, 83. *Prof Exp:* Sr res engr, NAm Aviation, Inc, 62-63; res scientist, Columbia Univ, 63-66. *Mem:* Am Inst Chem Engrs; Am Chem Soc. *Res:* Chemical process development of pharmaceuticals. *Mailing Add:* 55 Cherry Brook Dr Princeton NJ 08540-7710

STEELE, LENDELL EUGENE, NUCLEAR ENGINEERING, MATERIALS SCIENCE. *Current Pos:* chemist, Naval Res Lab, 50-51, anal chemist, 53-57, sect head & br head, 57-66, br head & assoc supt mat sci & technol, 67-80, BR HEAD, RES MGR, NAVAL RES LAB, 80- *Personal Data:* b Kannapolis, NC, May 5, 28; m 49; c 4. *Educ:* George Washington Univ, BS, 50; Am Univ, MA, 59. *Honors & Awards:* Wash Acad Sci Eng Award, 62; Appl Sci Award, Naval Res Labs-Sigma Xi, 66; Spec Annual Prize Award, Am Nuclear Soc, 72; Dudley Medal, Am Soc Testing & Mat, 73, Award of Merit, 78. *Prof Exp:* Chemist phys sci, Res Mgt, Agr Res Ctr, 49-50; res & develop officer radiol safety, US Air Force, 51-53; metall eng, US Atomic Energy Comn, 66-67. *Concurrent Pos:* Consult, Metal Properties Coun, 67-; US deleg, Int Atomic Energy Agency, Vienna, 67-; task group leader, Metals Properties Coun, ed, 67-; consult nuclear engr, 86- *Mem:* Fel Am Soc Metals; Am Nuclear Soc; fel Am Soc Testing & Mat; Res Soc Am; Fed Mat Soc (vpres, 83 pres, 84). *Res:* Fundamental and applied research on materials for advanced energy conversion systems, especially gas turbine materials but including response of nuclear structural material to nuclear effects for light water, breeder and fusion reactors as well. *Mailing Add:* 7624 Highland St Springfield VA 22150

STEELE, LEON, plant breeding; deceased, see previous edition for last biography

STEELE, MARTIN CARL, SOLID STATE ELECTRONICS. *Current Pos:* DIR, INST AMORPHOUS STUDIES, 85- *Personal Data:* b New York, NY, Dec 25, 19; m 41; c 4. *Educ:* Cooper Union, BChE, 40; Univ Md, MS, 49, PhD, 52. *Prof Exp:* Physicist & chief cryomagnetics sect, US Naval Res Lab, 47-55; res physicist, Res Lab, Radio Corp Am, 55-58, head semiconductor res group, 58-60, dir res labs, Japan, 60-63, head solid state electron physics group, 63-72; head semiconductor mat & device res, 72-81, staff res scientist, Electronics Dept, Res Labs, Gen Motors Corp, 81-85. *Concurrent Pos:* Vis lectr, Princeton Univ, 65-66; adj prof elec eng, Wayne State Univ, 76-85. *Mem:* Fel Am Phys Soc; Electrochem Soc; fel Inst Elec & Electronics Engrs. *Res:* Solid state physics; superconductivity; galvanomagnetic effects in metals and semiconductors; high electric field effects in semiconductors; solid state plasma effects; microwave devices; infrared detection; integrated circuits; MOS devices; semiconductor surfaces. *Mailing Add:* 1098 Welsh Rd Huntington Valley PA 19006

STEELE, RICHARD, CHEMISTRY, POLYMER CHEMISTRY. *Current Pos:* CONSULT, 82- *Personal Data:* b Charlotte, NC, Sept 6, 21; m 49, Virginia Miller; c Caroline & Ann. *Educ:* Univ NC, SB, 42; Princeton Univ, MA, 48, PhD(chem), 49. *Honors & Awards:* Olney Medal, Am Asn Textile Chemists & Colorists, 64; Harold DeWitt Smith Award, Am Soc Testing & Mat, 78. *Prof Exp:* Res chemist, Rohm and Haas Co, 42-46; res chemist & head phys org chem sect, Textile Res Inst, 50-53; lab head, Rohm and Haas Co, 53-65; dir appln & prod develop, Celanese Int Co, NY, 65-66, vpres & tech dir, 66-71; sr vpres technol & admin, Celanese Fibers Mkt Co, 71- 73 & Celanese Fibers Co, 73-76, sr vpres mfg & technol, Celanese Fibers Int Co, 76-79, exec vpres, 80 -82. *Mem:* AAAS; Am Chem Soc; Am Asn Textile Chemists & Colorists; Brit Textile Inst; Fiber Soc; Sigma Xi. *Res:* Structure of natural and synthetic fibers; chemistry of textile wet-finishing processes; cellulose chemistry; research administration and management. *Mailing Add:* Strafford Rd Tunbridge VT 05077

STEELE, RICHARD HAROLD, BIOCHEMISTRY. *Current Pos:* PROF BIOCHEM, TULANE UNIV, 57- *Personal Data:* b Buffalo, NY, Aug 1, 19; m 52; c 3. *Educ:* Univ Ala, BS, 48; Tulane Univ, PhD(biochem), 53. *Prof Exp:* Vis investr, Inst Muscle Res, Marine Biol Lab, 54-57. *Concurrent Pos:* Lederle Med Fac Award, 57-60; NIH sr res fels, 60 & 65. *Mem:* Am Chem Soc; Am Soc Biol Chemists. *Res:* Energy generation and transfer; spectroscopy; chemiluminescence and bioluminescence; copper metabolism; alcholism. *Mailing Add:* 3905 Cleveland Pl Metairie LA 70003-1436

STEELE, ROBERT, PREVENTIVE MEDICINE, EPIDEMIOLOGY. *Current Pos:* assoc prof prev med, Fac Med & dir res, 64-68, prof community health & epidemiol & head dept, 68-94, EMER PROF COMMUNITY HEALTH & EPIDEMIOL, QUEENS UNIV, ONT, 94- *Personal Data:* b Scotland, Jan 16, 29; m 55; c 2. *Educ:* Univ Edinburgh, DPH, 56; Univ Sask, MD, 60; FRCP(C); FFCM; FRCP(ED). *Prof Exp:* Asst prof prev med, Col Med, Univ Sask, 58-62; med officer, Scottish Health Dept, 62-64; assoc prof prev med, Fac Med & dir res, Queen's Univ, Ont, 64-68, prof community health & epidemiol & head dept, 68-94. *Concurrent Pos:* Consult, Kingston Gen Hosp, Ont. *Mem:* Asn Teachers Prev Med; fel Int Epidemiol Asn; fel Am Pub Health Asn; Royal Med Soc; Can Asn Teachers Social & Prev Med. *Res:* Cancer; medical care; community health, AIDS, international health. *Mailing Add:* 231 Alwington Pl Kingston ON K7L 4P9 Can

STEELE, ROBERT DARRYL, INTERMEDIARY METABOLISM, PROTEIN METABOLISM. *Current Pos:* DEAN, COL AGR SCI, PA STATE UNIV. *Personal Data:* b New Eagle, Pa, Dec 5, 46; m 79. *Educ:* Univ Ariz, BS, 70, MS, 73; Univ Wis-Madison, PhD(nutrit & biochem), 78. *Honors & Awards:* Bio-Serve Award, Am Inst Nutrit. *Prof Exp:* Prof, Dept Nutrit Sci, Univ Wis. *Mem:* Am Inst Nutrit; Am Physiol Soc; Sigma Xi. *Res:* Investigating the central role of the liver in amino acid and protein metabolism in mammals; blood-brain barrier transport; folic acid metabolism. *Mailing Add:* Dean Col Agr Sci Pa State Univ University Park PA 16802. *Fax:* 608-262-5860

STEELE, ROBERT WILBUR, FOREST MANAGEMENT. *Current Pos:* CONSULT, FORESTRY ASSOC INT INC, 81- *Personal Data:* b Denver, Colo, Aug 13, 20; m 42, 61; c 6. *Educ:* Colo State Univ, BSF, 42; Univ Mich, MSF, 49; Colo State Univ, PhD(forest fire sci), 75. *Prof Exp:* Forest guard, US Forest Serv, Ore, 42-43, forester, Pac Northwestern Exp Sta, 46-55; forest mgr, SDS Lumber Co, 55-56; asst prof forestry, Univ Mont, 56-67, assoc prof, 67-70, prof, 70-81. *Mem:* Soc Am Foresters; Am Meteorol Soc. *Res:* Forest fire control; development of techniques and machinery for fire detection and control; use and effects of prescribed fire in the forest; forest fire science; land surveying; sagebrush burning. *Mailing Add:* 1165 Hamilton Heights Corvallis MT 59828

STEELE, RONALD EDWARD, PHYSIOLOGY, ENDOCRINOLOGY. *Current Pos:* sr scientist endocrinol, Ciba-Geigy Corp, 74-86, admin mgr, 86-89, dir arthroscoloris, 89-93, DISTINGUISHED RES FEL, CIBA-GEIGY CORP, 93- *Personal Data:* b Pittsburgh, Pa, May 19, 43; m 69, Sara Huff. *Educ:* Pa State Univ, BS, 65; Univ Ky, PhD(physiol), 70. *Prof Exp:* Fel physiol, Worcester Found Exp Biol, 69-72; asst prof pediat endocrinol, Johns Hopkins Hosp, 72-74. *Concurrent Pos:* CIBA fel, Basle, Switz, 94. *Mem:* Endocrine Soc; Am Soc Andrology; Am Heart Asn; AAAS. *Res:* Male and female reproductive endocrinology and corticosteroid physiology; lipid metabolism; granted 5 US patents. *Mailing Add:* Pharmaceut Div Ciba-Geigy Corp 556 Morris Ave Summit NJ 07901. *Fax:* 908-277-5949; *E-Mail:* ronald.steele@ussu.mns.ciba.com

STEELE, SIDNEY RUSSELL, CHEMISTRY. *Current Pos:* RETIRED. *Personal Data:* b Toledo, Ohio, June 30, 17; m 44; c 2. *Educ:* Univ Toledo, BS, 39; Ohio State Univ, PhD(chem), 43. *Prof Exp:* Res chemist, Girdler Corp, Ky, 43-47; from assoc prof to prof chem, Eastern Ill Univ, 47-84, head dept, 67-77 & 78-79. *Mem:* Am Chem Soc. *Res:* Polarography; abnormal diffusion currents; water gas-shift catalysis; methanation of carbon monoxide. *Mailing Add:* 6 Woodfield Lane Charleston IL 61920-3839

STEELE, TIMOTHY DOAK, HYDROLOGY, RESOURCE MANAGEMENT. *Current Pos:* DIR HYDORL, HSI GEOTRANS, GOLDEN, COLO, 96- *Personal Data:* b Muncie, Ind, Apr 12, 41; m 92, Inge la Cour; c Tolan D & Karina K. *Educ:* Wabash Col, AB, 63; Stanford Univ, MS, 65, PhD(hydrol), 68; USDA Grad Sch, advan cert acct, 73. *Prof Exp:* Res hydrologist, Water Resources Div, Menlo Park, US Geol Surv, Colo, 66-68, res hydrologist, Systs Lab Group, Washington, DC, 68-72, hydrologist, Qual Water Br, 72-74, proj chief & hydrologist, Yampa River Basin Assessment Study, 75-80; sr proj hydrologist & chief, Water Qual Group, Woodward-Clyde Consult, Denver, 80-83; water resources mgr, In-Situ Inc, Denver, 83-89; mgr, Water Res/Phys-Sci Dept, Advan Sci Inc, Lakewood, 89-94; prin water resources/Denver off mgr, Balloffet & Assoc, 94-96; pres, TDS Consult Inc, 96. *Concurrent Pos:* Water qual specialist, US AID, Pakistan, 72; Alex von Humboldt res fel, Univ Bayreuth, WGer, 79; affiliated fac mem & guest lectr, Colo State Univ, Ft Collins, 79-; Fulbright study grant; Woodrow Wilson fel; mem Colo Ground Water Asn. *Mem:* Am Geophys Union; Int Asn Hydrol Sci; Int Water Res Asn; Am Chem Soc; Am Inst Hydrol. *Res:* Design of hydrologic data-collection networks; statistical analysis of data; hydrologic simulation and modeling; water resources planning and systems analysis; hydrogeochemistry; water quality; assessments of environmental impacts of energy-resource development; regional water-resources assessments; ground water contamination and resource conservation and recovery act regulations. *Mailing Add:* 1274 Country Rd 65 No 217 Evergreen CO 80439-9603. *Fax:* 303-279-7988; *E-Mail:* tdscons@aol.com

STEELE, VERNON EUGENE, CANCER PREVENTION. *Current Pos:* PROG DIR, DIV CANCER PREV & CONTROL, NAT CANCER INST, NIH, 89- *Personal Data:* b Blairsville, Pa, July 23, 46; m 68, MaryAnn Buchanon; c Michael & Carrie. *Educ:* Bucknell Univ, BS, 68; Univ Rochester, MS, 74, PhD(radiation biol), 75; Johns Hopkins Univ, MPH, 96. *Prof Exp:* Investr carcinogenesis, Biol Div, Oak Ridge Nat Lab, 75-77; mem staff, Nat Inst Environ Health Sci, NIH, 77-82. *Concurrent Pos:* Res supvr, Northrop Serv, Inc, 82- *Mem:* Soc In Vitro Biol; Sigma Xi; Am Asn Cancer Res. *Res:* Preclinical development of cancer chemopreventive agents; mechanisms of cancer prevention; computer assisted image analysis. *Mailing Add:* 3017 Vandever St Brookville MD 20833. *Fax:* 301-402-0553

STEELE, VLADISLAVA JULIE, INVERTEBRATE PHYSIOLOGY, HISTOLOGY. *Current Pos:* vis lectr, Mem Univ Nfld, 62-63, lectr histol & embryol, 63-65, from asst prof to assoc prof, 65-91, dept head biol, 80-82, PROF HISTOL DEVELOP BIOL CELL BIOL, MEM UNIV NFLD, 91- *Personal Data:* b Prague, Czech, July 8, 34; m 59, Donald; c Sean. *Educ:* McGill Univ, BSc, 57, MSc, 59, PhD(zool), 65. *Prof Exp:* Lectr histol, McGill Univ, 60-61. *Mem:* Am Inst Biol Sci; Can Soc Zool; Crustacean Soc Can; Soc Cell Biologists; Am Soc Zool. *Res:* Photoperiod, neurosecretion and steroid production in marine amphipods; influence of environmental factors on the reproduction of boreo-arctic intertidal amphipods; sensory receptors crustaceans. *Mailing Add:* Dept Biol Mem Univ Nfld St John's NF A1B 3X9 Can. *Fax:* 709-737-3018

STEELE, WARREN CAVANAUGH, PHYSICAL CHEMISTRY. *Current Pos:* lab dir, 85-87, SR CONSULT, CLAYTON ENVIRON CONSULTS, INC, 87- *Personal Data:* b Pocatello, Idaho, Oct 25, 29; m 55. *Educ:* Ore State Col, BA, 51, PhD(phys chem), 56. *Prof Exp:* Res chemist, Dow Chem Co, 56-58; res assoc chem, Tufts Univ, 58-60 & 62-64; res fel, Harvard Univ, 60-62; sr staff scientist, Space Systs Div, Avco Corp, Wilmington, 64-75; prin scientist, Energy Resources Co Inc, Cambridge, 75-78; proj leader, Foremost Res Ctr, Foremost-McKesson, Inc, Dublin, 78-86. *Mem:* AAAS; Am Chem Soc. *Res:* Mass spectrometry; gas-surface reaction kinetics; high temperature thermochemistry; environmental chemistry. *Mailing Add:* 1854 San Ramon Ave Berkeley CA 94707

STEELE, WILLIAM A, PHYSICAL CHEMISTRY. *Current Pos:* Fel, Cryogenic Lab, 54-55, from asst prof to assoc prof, 55-66, PROF PHYS CHEM, PA STATE UNIV, UNIVERSITY PARK, 66- *Personal Data:* b St Louis, Mo, June 4, 30; m 55; c 2. *Educ:* Wesleyan Univ, BA, 51; Univ Wash, PhD(phys chem), 54. *Concurrent Pos:* NSF fel, 57-58, sr fel, 63-64; mem comt colloid & surface chem, Nat Acad Sci-Nat Res Coun, 66-72; mem adv comt, Chem Div, NSF, 72-76; Unilever vis prof, Univ Bristol, 77; Guggenheim fel, 77; Fulbright fel, Univ Vienna, 79; assoc ed, J Phys Chem, 80- *Mem:* Am Chem Soc; Am Phys Soc. *Res:* Thermodynamics and statistical mechanics of liquids and physical adsorption of gases on solids. *Mailing Add:* Dept Chem Pa State Univ 152 Davey Lab University Park PA 16802. *Fax:* 814-865-3314

STEELE, WILLIAM F, mathematics; deceased, see previous edition for last biography

STEELE, WILLIAM JOHN, biochemical pharmacology, for more information see previous edition

STEELE, WILLIAM KENNETH, GEOLOGY, GEOPHYSICS. *Current Pos:* From asst prof to assoc prof, 70-82, PROF GEOL, EASTERN WASH UNIV, 82- *Personal Data:* b Ft Wayne, Ind, Nov 2, 42; m 85, Carol I Lewis; c Steven W. *Educ:* Case Western Res Univ, BS, 65, PhD(geol), 70. *Mem:* Am Geophys Union; Sigma Xi. *Res:* General geophysics, especially gravity and magnetic modeling, paleomagnetism. *Mailing Add:* Dept Geol Eastern Wash Univ Cheney WA 99004. *Fax:* 509-359-4386

STEELINK, CORNELIUS, ORGANIC CHEMISTRY. *Current Pos:* from asst prof to assoc prof chem, 57-70, PROF CHEM, UNIV ARIZ, 70- *Personal Data:* b Los Angeles, Calif, Oct 1, 22; m 49; c 2. *Educ:* Calif Inst Technol, BS, 44; Univ Southern Calif, MS, 50; Univ Calif, Los Angeles, PhD(chem), 56. *Prof Exp:* Lectr chem, Univ Southern Calif, 49-50 & Orange Coast Col, 50-53; asst, Univ Calif, Los Angeles, 53-56; res fel, Univ Liverpool, 56-57. *Mem:* Am Chem Soc. *Res:* Structure of lignin; electron spin resonance studies on naturally-occurring compounds; isolation and structural elucidation of plant terpenoids; structures and reactions of aquatic humic acids. *Mailing Add:* Dept Chem Univ Ariz Tucson AZ 85721-0002

STEELMAN, CARROL DAYTON, VETERINARY ENTOMOLOGY. *Current Pos:* From asst prof to assoc prof, 65-73, PROF MED & VET ENTOM, LA STATE UNIV, BATON ROUGE, 73-, PROF ENTOM, 79- *Personal Data:* b Vernon, Tex, Dec 9, 38; m 79, Pamela Murtough; c Buell, Mary, Travis, Tyler & Todd. *Educ:* Okla State Univ, BS, 61, MS, 63, PhD(entom), 65. *Concurrent Pos:* Asst dir, La Agr Exp Sta, 79-83; assoc dir, Ark Agr Exp Sta, 83-87; prof, Dept Entom, Univ Ark, 87- *Mem:* Entom Soc Am; Am Mosquito Control Asn; Sigma Xi. *Res:* External parasites of domestic animals and poultry; disease-vector-host biological, ecological and control relationships; effects of insect parasites on animal hosts and resistance of animals to arthropod ectoparasites. *Mailing Add:* Dept Entom 321 Agr Bldg Univ Ark Fayetteville AR 72701-1202. *Fax:* 501-575-2452; *E-Mail:* dsteelm@uafsysb.uark.edu

STEELMAN, SANFORD LEWIS, CLINICAL PHARMACOLOGY. *Current Pos:* RETIRED. *Personal Data:* b Hickory, NC, Oct 11, 22; m 45; c 2. *Educ:* Lenoir-Rhyne Col, BS, 43; Univ NC, PhD(biol chem), 49. *Prof Exp:* Biochemist, Armour & Co Labs, 49-50, head endocrinol sect, 51-53, head dept biochem res, 53-56; assoc prof biochem, Baylor Col Med, 56-58; dir endocrinol, Merck Inst Therapeut Res, 68-70, sr clin assoc, Merck Sharp & Dohme Res Labs, Rahway, 70-76, dir clin pharmacol, 76-78, sr investr, 78-86. *Concurrent Pos:* Assoc prof, Postgrad Sch Med, Univ Tex, 56-58. *Mem:* AAAS; Am Chem Soc; Soc Exp Biol & Med; Endocrine Soc; Am Soc Exp Therapeut. *Res:* Isolation and biological and physicochemical properties of protein and peptide hormones; physiology, pharmacology and bioassay of steroidal hormones; analgesics; hypothalamic hormones; clinical pharmacology. *Mailing Add:* PO Box 5358 Hickory NC 28603-5358

STEEN, EDWIN BENZEL, parasitology; deceased, see previous edition for last biography

STEEN, JAMES SOUTHWORTH, BIOLOGY, IMMUNOLOGY. *Current Pos:* From asst prof to assoc prof, 68-77, PROF BIOL, DELTA STATE COL, 77- *Personal Data:* b Vicksburg, Miss, Oct 26, 40; m 60; c 2. *Educ:* Delta State Col, BS, 62; Univ Miss, MS, 64, PhD(biol), 68. *Mem:* Am Soc Microbiol. *Res:* Carbohydrate metabolism in bacteria; tissue transplantation and immunosuppression as related to the enhancement phenomenon in inbred strains of mice. *Mailing Add:* 208 N Leflore Ave Cleveland MS 38732

STEEN, LYNN ARTHUR, SCIENCE WRITING, MATHEMATICS EDUCATION. *Current Pos:* From asst prof to assoc prof, 65-75, PROF MATH, ST OLAF COL, 75- *Personal Data:* b Chicago, Ill, Jan 1, 41; m 63, Mary Frost; c Margaret & Catherine. *Educ:* Luther Col, BA, 61; Mass Inst Technol, PhD(math), 65. *Hon Degrees:* DSc, Luther Col, 86, Wittenberg Univ, 91, Concordia Co, Minn, 96. *Honors & Awards:* Lester R Ford Award, Math Asn Am, 73 & 75; Bd Dirs Spec Award, Sigma Xi, 89; Distinguished Serv Award, Math Asn Am, 92. *Concurrent Pos:* Assoc ed, Am Math Monthly, 70-92; NSF sci faculty fel, Mittag-Leffler Inst, Sweden, 71-72; ed, Math Mag, 76-80; mem bd gov, Math Asn Am, 76-92; contrib ed, Sci News, 77-82; proj dir, NSF comput grants, 78-83; assoc dir acad comput, St Olaf Col, 82-84; mem, Math Sci Educ Bd, Nat Res Coun, 85-91; chmn, Conf Bd Math Sci, 88-90, Coun Sci Soc Pres, 89; chmn, Conf Bd Math Sci, 88-90, Coun Sci Soc Pres, 89; exec dir, Math Sci Educr Bd, 92-94. *Mem:* Am Math Soc; Math Asn Am (vpres, 80-81, pres, 85-86); AAAS; Nat Coun Teachers Math. *Res:* Analysis; mathematical logic; general topology; mathematics education. *Mailing Add:* Dept Math St Olaf Col Northfield MN 55057. *Fax:* 507-646-3968; *E-Mail:* steen@stolaf.edu

STEEN, PAUL H, STABILITY OF FLUID FLOWS & HYDRODYNAMIC SYSTEMS, INTERFACIAL & NONLINEAR DYNAMICS. *Current Pos:* From asst prof to assoc prof, 82-94, PROF, CORNELL UNIV, 94- *Personal Data:* b Meadville, Pa, June 22, 52; m 89, Kyra Stephanoff; c Julia Anastasia & Frances Alexandra. *Educ:* Brown Univ, ScB, 75, AB, 75; Johns Hopkins Univ, PhD(fluid dynamics), 81. *Concurrent Pos:* Consult, law firms, 81-84, Alcoa Corp, 86-90 & 96-; res fel, Alexander Von Humboldt, 90 & 96. *Mem:* Fel Am Phys Soc; Am Inst Chem Engrs; Soc Indust & Appl Math. *Res:* Dynamics and instability of fluid flows in the presence of heat transfer and/or fluid interface; spin-casting of molten metals; break-up/stabilization of fluid columns, bridges and jets; spatio-temporal complexity in flows driven by natural convection. *Mailing Add:* 8 Fox Hollow Rd Ithaca NY 14850

STEEN, R GRANT, PHYSIOLOGICAL MECHANISMS OF CANCER RESISTANCE TO THERAPY. *Current Pos:* KARNOFSKY FEL DIAG IMAGING, ST JUDES CHILDRENS HOSP, 93- *Personal Data:* b Montreal, Que, Sept 14, 54; m 82, Wil O'Loughlin; c Alena & Mariel. *Educ:* McGill Univ, BSc, 77; Univ Southern Calif, MS, 81; Univ Calif, Los Angeles, PhD(biol), 85. *Prof Exp:* Fel radiol, Johns Hopkins Med Sch, 86-88, fel environ health, 87-88; asst prof radiol, Univ Wash, 88-92, adj asst prof bioeng, 91-93. *Concurrent Pos:* Adj asst prof radiol & bioeng, Univ Tenn, 95- *Mem:* AAAS; Am Asn Cancer Res; Soc Magnetic Resonance Med. *Res:* Characterization of physiological mechanisms of tumor resistance to therapy, using quantitative magnetic resonance imaging of edema to measure tumor blood perfusion and to predict tumor drug delivery; use of quantitative magnetic resonance imaging to characterize physiology of the human brain in healthy and in various disease states, including cancer, sickle cell disease and hypoxia. *Mailing Add:* Dept Diag Imaging St Jude Children's Hosp 332 N Lauderdale Memphis TN 38101-0318. *Fax:* 901-527-0054

STEEN, ROBERT FREDERICK, electrical engineering, computer science, for more information see previous edition

STEEN, STEPHEN N, ANESTHESIOLOGY. *Current Pos:* dir training & res, Harbor Gen Hosp, 71-75, PROF ANESTHESIOL & DIR RES, SCH MED, UNIV CALIF, LOS ANGELES, 71- *Personal Data:* b London, Eng, Sept 6, 23; US citizen; wid. *Educ:* Mass Inst Technol, SB, 43; Univ Geneva, ScD(med biochem), 51, MD, 52; Am Bd Anesthesiol, dipl, 60. *Prof Exp:* Intern Abbot Hosp, Minneapolis, Minn, 53-54; res anesthetist, Columbia-Presby Ctr, 54-56; instr, Albert Einstein Med Sch, 56-60; from asst prof to assoc prof, State Univ NY Downstate Med Ctr, 61-69; physician-in-chief anesthesia res, Cath Med Ctr Brooklyn & Queens, Inc, NY, 69-71. *Concurrent Pos:* Actg dir, Delafield Hosp, NY, 56, attend anesthesiologist, 56-61; instr, Bronx Munic Hosp Ctr, 56-60 & Columbia Univ, 57-61; physician, Beth Israel Hosp, 57-61; attend anesthesiologist, Cent Islip State Hosp & St Francis Hosp, 58-, Misericordia Hosp, 58-62, Vet Admin 62- & St Barnabas Hosp, Bronx, NY, 56-61, dir anesthesiol, 60-61; vis attend anesthesiologist, Brooklyn Vet Admin Hosp, 61-66; from assoc vis anesthesiologist to vis anesthesiologist, Kings County Hosp Ctr, 61-; attend anesthesiologist, Harbor Gen Hosp & Torrance Mem Hosp, Univ Calif, Los Angeles; dir, Pulmonary Function Labs, Meditrina Med Ctr, 79-; physicians specialist anesthesia, Los Angeles City Col-Univ Southern Calif, 81- *Mem:* Fel Am Col Anesthesiol; sr mem Am Chem Soc; AMA; Am Soc Anesthesiol. *Res:* Anesthesiology. *Mailing Add:* 1900 Ocean Blvd 1802 Long Beach CA 90802. *Fax:* 562-435-7545

STEENBERGEN, JAMES FRANKLIN, MICROBIOLOGY. *Current Pos:* asst prof, 70-75, assoc prof, 75-79, PROF MICROBIOL, SAN DIEGO STATE UNIV, 80- *Personal Data:* b Glasgow, Ky, May 11, 39; m 82. *Educ:* Western Ky State Col, BS, 62; Ind Univ, MA, 65, PhD(microbiol), 68. *Prof Exp:* Res assoc marine microbiol, Ore State Univ, 68-69, vis asst prof microbiol, 69-70. *Mem:* Am Soc Microbiol; World Mariculture Soc. *Res:* Microbial ecology and physiology; diseases of crustaceans and fish; invertebrate immunology. *Mailing Add:* 235 S Lucas Rd Lucas KY 42156

STEENBURG, RICHARD WESLEY, SURGERY. *Current Pos:* RETIRED. *Personal Data:* b Aurora, Nebr, Feb 3, 25; m 50; c 2. *Educ:* Harvard Univ, MD, 48; Am Bd Surg, dipl. *Prof Exp:* Assoc prof surg, Johns Hopkins Univ, 65-69; prof surg, Col Med, Univ Nebr, Omaha, 69. *Concurrent Pos:* Surgeon in chief, Baltimore City Hosps, 67-69. *Mem:* Soc Univ Surg. *Res:* General surgery; surgical endocrinology; vascular disease; renal physiology. *Mailing Add:* 2824 SE Dune Dr 2102 Stuart FL 34996-1926

STEEN-MCINTYRE, VIRGINIA CAROL, TEPHROCHRONOLOGY. *Current Pos:* CONSULT TEPHROCHRONOLOGIST, 77- *Personal Data:* b Chicago, Ill, Dec 3, 36; m 67, David H. *Educ:* Augustana Col, Ill, 59; Wash State Univ, MS, 65; Univ Idaho, PhD(geol), 77. *Prof Exp:* Asst geologist, George H Otto, Consult Geologist, Chicago, 59-61; jr geologist, Lab Anthrop, Wash State Univ, 64-66; phys sci technician, US Geol Surv, Denver, 70-75; res affil dept anthrop, Colo State Univ, 77-83. *Concurrent Pos:* Corresp mem, Int Asn Quaternary Res Comn Tephrochronology, 73-77; tephrochronologist, Valsequillo Early Man Proj, Mex, 66- & El Salvador Protoclassic Proj, 75-; guest lectr, NATO Advanced Studies Inst, Iceland, 80. *Mem:* Sigma Xi; Am Asn Quaternary Res. *Res:* Volcanic ash chronology; archaeological site stratigraphy; petrography of friable Pleistocene deposits; tephra hydration dating; weathering of volcanic ejecta; human origins; christian metaphysics, occult. *Mailing Add:* Box 1167 Idaho Springs CO 80452

STEENSEN, DONALD H J, FOREST ECONOMICS. *Current Pos:* asst prof, 65-73, ASSOC PROF FOREST ECON & MENSURATION, SCH FOREST RESOURCES, NC STATE UNIV, 73- *Personal Data:* b Clinton, Iowa, Apr 26, 29; m 54. *Educ:* Iowa State Univ, BS, 58; Duke Univ, MF, 60, PhD(forest econ), 65. *Prof Exp:* Asst prof forest econ & sampling, Auburn Univ, 60-65. *Mem:* Soc Am Foresters; Sigma Xi. *Res:* Forest mensuration. *Mailing Add:* 912 Merwin Rd Raleigh NC 27606

STEENSON, BERNARD O(WEN), ELECTRICAL ENGINEERING. *Current Pos:* RETIRED. *Personal Data:* b Crosby, NDak, Aug 2, 22; m 51; c 3. *Educ:* Ill Inst Technol, BS, 44; Calif Inst Technol, MS, 48, PhD(elec eng), 51. *Prof Exp:* Lab technician, Calif Inst Technol, 50-51; res physicist, Hughes Aircraft Co, 51-58, sr staff engr, 58-62, sr scientist, Space Systs Div, 62-71, Space & Commun Group, 71-88, chief scientist, 88-89. *Res:* Radar systems and communication satellites design and analysis. *Mailing Add:* 2878 W 230th St Torrance CA 90505

STEEPLES, DONALD WALLACE, ENVIRONMENTAL GEOPHYSICS, SEISMOLOGY. *Current Pos:* MCGEE DISTINGUISHED PROF GEOPHYS, UNIV KANS, 93- *Personal Data:* b Hays, Kans, May 15, 45; m 67, Tammy Gaynier; c Flint & Brad. *Educ:* Kans State Univ, BS, 69, MS, 70; Stanford Univ, MS, 74, PhD(geophys), 75. *Prof Exp:* Geophysicist seismol, US Geol Surv, 72-75; res assoc geophys, State Geol Surv, Kans, 75-92, dep dir, 87-91. *Concurrent Pos:* Chmn, Geophys Prog, Univ Kans; pres, Great Plains Geophys, Kans; ed, Geophys, J Soc of Explor Geophysicists, 89-91; pres, Near-Geophys Sect, Soc Explor Geophysicists, 93-94; mem, Geotech Bd, Nat Acad Sci, Nat Res Coun. *Mem:* Am Geophys Union; Soc Explor Geophysicists; Seismol Soc Am; AAAS; Am Asn Petrol Geologists. *Res:* Crust and upper mantle structure of central North America; use of seismic methods for shallow exploration; environmental geophysics; engineering geophysics; ground water geophysics; midcontinent earthquake seismology. *Mailing Add:* 2913 Westdale Rd Lawrence KS 66049

STEER, MARTIN WILLIAM, TIP GROWTH, SECRETION-ENDOCYTOSIS. *Current Pos:* PROF & DEPT HEAD BOT, UNIV COL DUBLIN, 84- *Personal Data:* b Chelmsford, Essex, UK, Aug 19, 42; m 84, Jill; c 3. *Educ:* Univ Bristol, UK, BSc Hons, 63, DSc(plant cell biol), 86; Queen's Univ Belfast, UK, PhD(cell biol), 66. *Prof Exp:* Res assoc bot, Univ Wis-Madison, 66-68; res asst bot, Queen's Univ Belfast, 63-66, lectr, 68-79, reader, 79-84. *Concurrent Pos:* Mem, Finance Comt & Cell Biol Comt, Soc Exp Biol, 77-80; consult, Gallagher's Tobacco Co, Belfast, 80-84; assoc ed, J Exp Bot, 83-89; dir, Electron Micros Lab, Univ Col Dublin, 86-90. *Mem:* Fel Royal Micros Soc; Am Soc Cell Biol; Soc Exp Biol; Royal Irish Acad. *Res:* Structure and function of plant cells, using mainly light and electron microscope techniques to record effects of physiological and biochemical perturbations; quantitative and stereological image analysis; secretory and endocytotic mechanisms and pollen tube tip growth. *Mailing Add:* Dept Bot Univ Col Dublin Belfield Dublin 4 Ireland. *Fax:* 353-1-7061153

STEER, MAX DAVID, SPEECH & HEARING SCIENCES. *Current Pos:* from instr to prof speech sci, 35-70, dir, Speech & Hearing Clin, 46-70, head dept 63-70, Hanley distinguished prof, 70-77, DISTINGUISHED PROF EMER AUDIOL & SPEECH SCI, PURDUE UNIV, WEST LAFAYETTE, 77- *Personal Data:* b New York, NY, June 14, 10; m 42. *Educ:* Long Island Univ, 32, LLD, 57; Univ Iowa, MA, 33, PhD(psychol), 38. *Prof Exp:* Asst speech path, Univ Iowa, 33-35. *Concurrent Pos:* Consult, State of Ind Hearing Comn, 66-, US Off Educ, NIH, NSF & Ind State Training Sch Ment Retarded; consult, Neurol & Sensory Dis Control Prof, USPHS, Pan-Am Health Orgn, 72-, Latin Am Fedn Logopedics, Phoniatrics, Audiol, 72- & Univ Bogota, 74; mem nat res adv comt, Bur Educ Handicapped, US Off Educ, 72-; consult & vis lectr, Nat Rehab Inst, Panama, 74. *Mem:* AAAS; Acoust Soc Am; Am Psychol Asn; fel Am Speech & Hearing Asn (vpres, 49, pres, 51); Int Asn Logopedics & Phoniatrics (vpres, 63-65, 71-77 & 80-83); Sigma Xi. *Res:* Speech disorders and acoustics; audiology; clinical psychology; neurology; physiology and psychology of communication. *Mailing Add:* 342 Westview West Lafayette IN 47906

STEER, MICHAEL BERNARD, MICROWAVE ENGINEERING, ANALOG COMPUTER AIDED DESIGN. *Current Pos:* ASSOC PROF ELEC ENG, NC STATE UNIV, 83- *Personal Data:* b Brisbane, Australia, Apr 26, 55; m 80, Mary C Kelly; c 2. *Educ:* Univ Queensland, BE, 78, PhD(elec eng), 83. *Concurrent Pos:* NSF presidential young investr award, 87. *Mem:* Sr mem Inst Elec & Electronics Engrs. *Res:* Simulation, measurement and computer aided design of nonlinear microwave circuits, high speed multi-chip modules, parameter extraction, and millimeter-wave quasi-optical techniques; author of more than 90 publications. *Mailing Add:* Elec & Comput Eng Dept NC State Univ Box 7911 Raleigh NC 27695. *E-Mail:* mbs@ncsu.edu

STEER, RONALD PAUL, LASER CHEMISTRY, PHOTOCHEMISTRY. *Current Pos:* from asst prof to prof, 69-93, THORVALDSON, PROF CHEM, UNIV SASK, 93- *Personal Data:* b Regina, Sask, Mar 7, 43; m 64, Sheilagh L Cameron; c David A & Jennifer A. *Educ:* Univ Sask, BA, 64, PhD(chem), 68. *Hon Degrees:* DSc, Univ Sask, 95. *Prof Exp:* USPHS fel, Univ Calif, Riverside, 68-69. *Concurrent Pos:* Vis fel, Univ Southampton, 75-76; vis scientist, Nat Res Coun Can, 84-85 & 91-92; mem, Natural Sci & Eng Res Coun Can, 90-96; NAm ed, Sect A, J Photochem & Photobiol, 90- *Mem:* Fel Chem Inst Can; Inter-Am Photochem Soc. *Res:* Laser chemistry, photochemistry, photophysics and spectroscopy of small molecules; fluorescence probe techniques in biological systems; chemistry and spectroscopy of van der Waals clusters; picosecond and femtosecond spectroscopy. *Mailing Add:* Dept Chem Univ Sask 110 Science Pl Saskatoon SK S7N 5C9 Can. *Fax:* 306-966-4730; *E-Mail:* steer@.usask.ca

STEERS, EDWARD, JR, biological chemistry, for more information see previous edition

STEEVES, HARRISON ROSS, III, HISTOCHEMISTRY, TAXONOMY. *Current Pos:* asst prof histol & histochem, 66-68, ASSOC PROF ZOOL, VA POLYTECH INST & STATE UNIV, 68- *Personal Data:* b Birmingham, Ala, July 2, 37; m 57; c 4. *Educ:* Univ of the South, BS, 58; Univ Va, MS, 60, PhD(biol), 62. *Honors & Awards:* Andrew Fleming Award Biol Res, 61. *Prof Exp:* Instr zool, Univ Va, 62; fel histol, Med Ctr, Univ Ala, 62-65, instr, 65-66. *Mem:* AAAS. *Res:* Invertebrate histochemistry; taxonomy, ecology and physiology of cave crustaceans and histochemistry of digestion in these forms. *Mailing Add:* Dept Biol Va Polytech Inst & State Univ PO Box 0406 Blacksburg VA 24063-0001

STEEVES, JOHN DOUGLAS, NEUROBIOLOGY, DEVELOPMENTAL BIOLOGY & SPINAL CORD REPAIR. *Current Pos:* asst prof, 79-85, assoc prof neurobiol, Dept Zool, 85-92, assoc prof, Grad Prog Neurosci, 85-92, PROF, UNIV BC, 92-, DIR, CORD, 95-, ASSOC DEAN EXTERNAL AFFAIRS & FAC SCI, 96- *Personal Data:* b Calgary, Alta, Mar 25, 52; m, Lucia Fuentes; c Kristy, Lorena & Alexander. *Educ:* Univ Man, BSc, 73, PhD(physiol), 79. *Prof Exp:* Fel neurophysiol, Dept Physiol, Univ Alta, 78-79. *Concurrent Pos:* Consult, Can Broadcasting Corp, 81-83; vis prof, Jinan Univ, Guagzhou (Canton), People's Repub China, 85; assoc mem, Dept Anat, Univ BC, 87-, Dept Surg, 95- *Mem:* Soc Neurosci; Can Asn Neurosci; Brain Res Orgn; Int Soc Develop Neurosci. *Res:* Central nervous system mechanisms in vertebrates, specifically birds and mammals; pertaining to promoting repair of neurotrauma injuries such as spinal cord injury. *Mailing Add:* CORD C/O Depts Zool, Anat & Surg Univ BC 6270 University Blvd Vancouver BC V6T 1Z4 Can. *Fax:* 604-822-2924; *E-Mail:* steeves@bcu.ubc.ca

STEEVES, RICHARD ALLISON, ONCOLOGY, VIROLOGY. *Current Pos:* from asst prof to assoc prof, 80-93, PROF HUMAN ONCOL, UNIV WIS-MADISON, 93- *Personal Data:* b Fredericksburg, Va, Feb 2, 38; m 65; c 3. *Educ:* Univ Western Ont, MD, 61; Univ Toronto, PhD(med biophys), 66. *Prof Exp:* From sr cancer res scientist to assoc cancer res scientist, Roswell Park Mem Inst, 67-72; assoc prof develop biol & cancer, 72-77, vis assoc prof genetics, Albert Einstein Col Med, 77-80. *Concurrent Pos:* Nat Cancer Inst Can fel, Dept Biol, McMaster Univ, 66-67; resident therapeut radiol, Albert Einstein Col Med, 77-80. *Mem:* Am Asn Cancer Res; Radiol Soc NAm; Am Endocurietheray Soc; Am Soc Therapeut Radiol. *Res:* Interaction of radiation and hyperthermin in cancer therapy; genetic control of target cells for murine leukemia viruses. *Mailing Add:* 600 Highland Ave Madison WI 53792

STEEVES, TAYLOR ARMSTRONG, BOTANY. *Current Pos:* from assoc prof to prof, Univ Sask, 59-85, head dept, 76-81, Rawson prof biol, 85-94, EMER PROF, UNIV SASK, 94- *Personal Data:* b Quincy, Mass, Nov 29, 26; m 56, Margaret Wolfe; c Elizabeth, Timothy & Thomas. *Educ:* Univ Mass, BS, 47; Harvard Univ, AM, 49, PhD(biol), 51. *Hon Degrees:* DCnL, Emmanuel Col, Sask; DSc, Univ Sask, 92. *Honors & Awards:* Lawson Medal, Can Bot Asn, 78; Mary E Elliott Award, 90. *Prof Exp:* Jr fel, Soc Fels, Harvard Univ, 51-54, asst prof bot, Biol Labs, 54-59. *Concurrent Pos:* Ed, Bot Gazette, 69-75, Can J Bot, 79-88. *Mem:* Bot Soc Am; fel Royal Soc Can; Can Bot Asn (pres, 72-73); Am Fern Soc. *Res:* Morphogenesis of vascular plants; plant tissue culture and growth hormones; plant architecture. *Mailing Add:* Dept Biol Univ Sask Saskatoon SK S7N 0W0 Can

STEFAN, HEINZ G, HYDROMECHANICS, WATER RESOURCES ENGINEERING. *Current Pos:* from asst prof to assoc prof, 67-77, PROF CIVIL ENG, UNIV MINN, MINNEAPOLIS, 77- *Personal Data:* b Landskron, CSR, June 12, 36; m 62; c 3. *Educ:* Munich Tech Univ, Dipl Ing, 59; Univ Toulouse, Ing Hydraulicien, 60, DrIng(hydromech), 63. *Prof Exp:* Res fel hydraul, Univ Minn, 63-64; chief engr, Inst Water Resources & Hydraul Eng, Tech Univ, Berlin, 65-67. *Concurrent Pos:* Consult, Power Co; UN expert, India, 81, 92 & Brazil, 90; lectr, foreign countries; assoc dir, St Anthony Falls Hydrol Lab, 74- *Mem:* Am Soc Civil Engrs; Am Geophys Union; Int Asn Hydrol Res; Am Water Resources Asn; Int Water Resources Asn; Int Asn Limnol. *Res:* River and lake hydromechanics; thermal pollution; aquatic systems; water resources; hydraulic structures. *Mailing Add:* Dept Civil Eng Univ Minn 122 Eng Bldg 500 Hillsberry Dr SE Minneapolis MN 55455. *Fax:* 612-627-4609

STEFANAKOS, ELIAS KYRIAKOS, ENGINEERING SCIENCE, SOLAR ENERGY. *Current Pos:* assoc prof, 77-80, PROF ELEC ENG, NC A&T STATE UNIV, 80- *Personal Data:* b Athens, Greece, Sept 30, 40; m 68; c 1. *Educ:* Wash State Univ, BS, 64, MS, 65, PhD(eng sci), 69. *Prof Exp:* Res asst elec eng, Wash State Univ, 66-68; from asst prof to assoc prof elec eng, Univ Idaho, 68-77. *Concurrent Pos:* Fel, 71-72, int travel grant, NSF, 78; vis prof, Greek Atomic Energy Comn, 75. *Mem:* AAAS; Inst Elec & Electronics Engrs; Am Soc Eng Educ; Int Solar Energy Soc. *Res:* Semiconductor materials and devices; photovoltaics; solar energy utilization. *Mailing Add:* 5110 E Longboat Blvd Tampa FL 33615

STEFANCSIK, ERNEST ANTON, ORGANIC CHEMISTRY. *Current Pos:* RETIRED. *Personal Data:* b Brooklyn, NY, Sept 10, 23. *Educ:* St John's Univ, NY, BS, 43; NY Univ, MS, 47, PhD(chem), 53. *Prof Exp:* Chemist, Am Cyanamid Co, 43-46; teaching fel, NY Univ, 47-49, asst, 50-52; from res chemist to res assoc, Pigments Dept, E I du Pont de Nemours & Co, Inc, Newark, 52-82. *Mem:* AAAS; Am Chem Soc; Sigma Xi. *Res:* Physics and chemistry of organic pigments. *Mailing Add:* 162 Voorhees Corner Rd Flemington NJ 08822

STEFANESCU, DORU MICHAEL, METAL CASTING, SOLIDIFICATION OF ALLOYS. *Current Pos:* assoc prof metall, 80-84, PROF METALL, UNIV ALA, 84-, UNIV RES PROF, 88- *Personal Data:* b Sibiu, Romania, Nov 15, 42; m 71; c 2. *Educ:* Polytech Inst Bucharest, BEng, 65, DEng, 73. *Prof Exp:* Jr researcher metal casting, Technol Inst Hot Processes, Bucharest, 68-70, sr res, 70-72, group head, 72-80; vis prof, Univ Wis-Madison, 80. *Concurrent Pos:* Prof, Polytech Inst Bucharest, 73-80. *Mem:* Metall Soc; Am Soc Metals; Am Foundrymens Soc. *Res:* Solidification processing; physical chemistry of surface and interface reactions; metal matrix composites, superconductivity; numerical modeling of solidification; thermal analysis of alloys; cast metals technology. *Mailing Add:* PO Box 870202 Tuscaloosa AL 35487-0202

STEFANI, ANDREW PETER, ORGANIC CHEMISTRY, PHYSICAL CHEMISTRY. *Current Pos:* from asst prof to assoc prof, 63-68, PROF CHEM, UNIV MISS, 68-, CHMN DEPT, 77- *Personal Data:* b Cyprus, July 10, 26; US citizen; m 55; c 1. *Educ:* Mich State Univ, BA, 56; Univ Colo, PhD(chem), 60. *Prof Exp:* Res assoc chem, State Univ NY Col Forestry, Syracuse Univ, 60-62; asst prof, Purdue Univ, 62-63. *Concurrent Pos:* Res grants, Res Corp, 64, Petrol Res Fund & NSF, 64-68. *Mem:* AAAS; Am Chem Soc. *Res:* Chemical kinetics; free radical reactivity; solvent effects in chemical reactions; high pressure chemistry. *Mailing Add:* Box 174 University MS 38677-0174

STEFANI, STEFANO, radiotherapy, radiobiology, for more information see previous edition

STEFANOU, HARRY, POLYMER PHYSICS. *Current Pos:* mgr mat res, 85-86, MGR POLYMER APPLN, ARCO CHEM, 86- *Personal Data:* b New York, NY, June 16, 47; m 69; c 1. *Educ:* City Col New York, BS, 69; City Univ New York, PhD(phys chem), 73. *Prof Exp:* Res assoc polymer physics, Princeton Univ, 72-73; sr res chemist, Pennwalt Corp, 73-79, res scientist, 79-82, proj leader, 82, tech mgr, 82-85. *Mem:* AAAS; Am Chem Soc; Am Phys Soc; Sigma Xi. *Res:* The areas of polymer crystallization kinetics; polymer viscoelasticity and solution thermodynamics; piezo- and pyro-electric polymers. *Mailing Add:* 201 Country Gate Rd Wayne PA 19087-5321

STEFANSKI, RAYMOND JOSEPH, PHYSICS. *Current Pos:* STAFF PHYSICIST, SUPERCONDUCTING SUPERCOLLIDER LAB, 90- *Personal Data:* b Buffalo, NY, July 22, 41; m 69; c 1. *Educ:* State Univ NY Buffalo, BA, 63; Yale Univ, PhD(physics), 69. *Prof Exp:* Res assoc physics, Yale Univ, 68-69; physicist, Fermi Nat Accelerator Lab, 69-90. *Mem:* Am Phys Soc; Opers Res Soc Am; Europ Phys Soc. *Res:* High energy physics and cosmic rays; neutrino interactions. *Mailing Add:* MS 200 Fermilab PO Box 500 Batavia IL 60510. *Fax:* 630-840-2939

STEFANSSON, BALDUR ROSMUND, PLANT BREEDING. *Current Pos:* Res assoc, 52-66, from assoc prof to prof, 66-91, EMER PROF PLANT SCI, UNIV MAN, 91- *Personal Data:* b Vestfold, Man; m, Sigridar Jonina Margaret Westdal; c Paul, Bjorguin & Helga. *Educ:* Univ Man, BSA, 50, MS, 52, PhD(plant sci), 66. *Honors & Awards:* Queen's Jubilee Medal, 77; Grindley Medal, Agr Inst Can, 78; Officer Order Can, 85; McAnsh Award, 89. *Mem:* Fel Agr Inst Can; hon mem Can Seed Growers Asn. *Res:* Plant breeding and related research with oilseed crops, formerly soybeans, currently rapeseed; compositional changes in rapeseed, including low erucic acid, low glucosinolate and low fibre content, induced by breeding. *Mailing Add:* 923 Crescent Dr Winnipeg MB R3T 1X6 Can

STEFFAN, WALLACE ALLAN, entomology, for more information see previous edition

STEFFEK, ANTHONY J, dentistry, pharmacology, for more information see previous edition

STEFFEN, DANIEL G, SCIENCE COMMUNICATION & POLICY. *Current Pos:* MGR SCI REL, KRAFT GEN FOODS, 90- *Personal Data:* b St Louis, Mo, Feb 9, 48; m 74, Kathleen Peterson; c Maegan, Danika, Mollie & Daniel. *Educ:* Univ Notre Dame, BS, 70; Univ Mo, PhD(physiol), 74. *Prof Exp:* Fel swine lipid metab, Shell Develop Co, 74-76; res scientist nutrit, Gen Foods Corp, 76-90. *Mem:* Inst Food Technologists; Am Inst Nutrit; Sigma Xi. *Res:* Age and diet effects on physiological systems; application of technical strategies to development of regulatory policies. *Mailing Add:* Mar Sci Rels Tech Ctr Kraft Foods 250 North St White Plains NY 10625-0001. *Fax:* 914-335-6239

STEFFEN, JUERG, LASERS, LASER-MATERIALS PROCESSING. *Current Pos:* MANAGING DIR LASERS & APPLN, OERLIKON PRECISION LASER SA, GLAND, SWITZ, 89- *Personal Data:* b Zurich, Switz, Dec 11, 42; m 70, Anne-Marie Schwab; c Daniel, Gabriela, Reto & Marc. *Educ:* Swiss Fed Inst Technol, Zurich, dipl, 66; Univ Berne, Switz, PhD(physics), 70. *Prof Exp:* Group leader lasers, Inst Appl Physics, Univ Berne, 70-72; head laser appln, Res Inst, Pierres Holding SA, 72-74; res & develop mgr, Lasag AG, Thun, 74-81; group leader lasers & appln, Asulab SA, Neuchatel, 81-89. *Concurrent Pos:* Vis prof, Inst Appl Physics, Univ Darmstadt, 78-84, Physics Dept, Univ Kaiserslautern, 81-82. *Mem:* Swiss Phys Soc; Europ Phys Soc; fel Optical Soc Am; Int Soc Optical Eng. *Res:* Development of industrial Nd-YAG- and CO2- lasers; development of applications procedures of lasers in materials processing and optical metrology; author of 70 technical and review papers. *Mailing Add:* Le Bon Pirouz Vich CH-1267 Switzerland. *Fax:* 22-364-39-54

STEFFEN, ROLF MARCEL, NUCLEAR PHYSICS. *Current Pos:* From asst prof to prof, 49-82, EMER PROF PHYSICS, PURDUE UNIV, WEST LAFAYETTE, 82- *Personal Data:* b Basel, Switz, June 17, 22; m 49; c 2. *Educ:* Cantonal Col, Zurich, BS, 41; Swiss Fed Inst Technol, PhD, 48. *Concurrent Pos:* Vis staff mem, Los Alamos Sci Lab, 64-; Sigma Xi Res Award, 64. *Mem:* Fel Am Phys Soc; Swiss Phys Soc. *Res:* Nuclear spectroscopy; angular correlations of nuclear radiation; influence of extranuclear fields on angular correlation; beta decay; nuclear structures studies by muonic x-rays; muonic atoms; hyperfine fields; heavy ion nuclear reactions. *Mailing Add:* PO Box 220 Tesuque NM 87574

STEFFENS, DAVID LEE, DNA SEQUENCING. *Current Pos:* RES SCIENTIST MOLECULAR BIOL, LI-COR, INC, 90- *Personal Data:* b Miami, Okla, Mar 28, 57. *Educ:* Okla State Univ, BS, 79, PhD(biochem), 84. *Prof Exp:* Chemist, Sigma Chem Co, 84-87; res assoc, Wash Univ, Sch Med, 87-90. *Mem:* Am Soc Biochem & Molecular Biol; AAAS. *Res:* Development of new DNA sequencing methodology; molecular biology of plant viruses and intracellular signal transduction. *Mailing Add:* R&D Li-Cor Inc PO Box 4000 Lincoln NE 68504-5000. *Fax:* 402-467-0819

STEFFENS, GEORGE LOUIS, PLANT PHYSIOLOGY, PLANT GROWTH REGULATION. *Current Pos:* RETIRED. *Personal Data:* b Bryantown, Md, June 13, 30; m 59, Jean M Gemmill; c Christopher L, Lisa M. *Educ:* Univ Md, BS, 51, MS, 53, PhD(agron), 56. *Honors & Awards:* Philip Morris Award, 72; Cert Merit, USDA, 82, Achievement Award, 84, Career Achievement Award, 92; Silver Medal, Japanese Soc Chem Regulation Plants, 87. *Prof Exp:* Biochemist, US Army, Army Chem Ctr, Md, 56-58; aqron biochemist, Gen Cigar Co, Inc, Lancaster, Pa, 58-61; plant psychologist, Coastal Plain Exp Sta, USDA, Ga, 61-63, plant physiologist, 63-74, lab chief, 74-82, plant physiologist, Fruit Lab, Plant Sci Inst, Beltsville Agr Res Ctr, Agr Res Serv, 82-92. *Concurrent Pos:* Vis prof, Agron Dept, Cornell Univ, 81-82; chmn, Plant Growth Reg Soc Am, 86-87; emer collabr, Agr Res Ctr, Agr Res Serv, USDA, 93- *Mem:* Fel AAAS; Am Soc Plant Physiologists; Am Chem Soc; Scand Soc Plant Physiologists; Plant Growth Regulator Soc Am; Am Soc Hort Sci. *Res:* Natural and synthetic plant growth regulating chemicals, their development and physiological effects, especially tree crops (apple). *Mailing Add:* 101 W Marengo St St Michaels MD 21663. *Fax:* 301-504-5062

STEFFENSEN, DALE MARRIOTT, GENETICS. *Current Pos:* prof genetics & develop, PROF AGRON, UNIV ILL, URBANA, 84-, PROF CELL BIOL, 87- *Personal Data:* b Salt Lake City, Utah, Apr 17, 22; m 50, 70; c 3. *Educ:* Univ Calif, Los Angeles, AB, 48; Univ Calif, Berkeley, PhD(genetics), 52. *Prof Exp:* Asst res geneticist, Univ Calif, 52; from assoc geneticist to geneticist, Brookhaven Nat Lab, 52-61. *Concurrent Pos:* USPHS spec fel, Naples, Italy, 67-68. *Mem:* Genetics Soc Am; Am Soc Cell Biol; Soc Develop Biol. *Res:* Nuclear structure, developmental genetics and cell biology; biochemistry of nuclear structures; gene mapping on chromosomes by RNA-DNA hybridization; molecular development of maize. *Mailing Add:* 2102 S Race St Urbana IL 61801

STEFFEY, EUGENE P, ANESTHESIOLOGY. *Current Pos:* Chmn, Dept Surg, 80-93, VET ANESTHESIOL ASST TO PROF, SCH VET MED, UNIV CALIF, DAVIS, 74- *Personal Data:* b Reading, Pa, Oct 27, 42; c Michele A, Bret E, Michael R & Brian T. *Educ:* Univ Pa, VMD, 67; Univ Calif, Davis, PhD(comp path), 73. *Concurrent Pos:* Intern, Univ Calif, Davis, 68; pvt pract, Reading, Pa, 69. *Mem:* Am Physiol Soc; Am Soc Pharmacol & Exp Therapeut; Int Anesthesia Res Soc; Am Soc Anesthesiol; Am Vet Med Asn; Am Col Vet Anesthesiol. *Res:* Comparative anesthesiology; pharmacology of inhalation anesthetics and opioids; comparative cardiopulmonary pathophysiology. *Mailing Add:* Dept Surg & Radiol Univ Calif Davis Sch Vet Med Davis CA 95616-5224. *Fax:* 530-752-6042; *E-Mail:* epsteffey@ucdavis.ucdavis.edu

STEFFEY, ORAN DEAN, INDUSTRIAL HYGIENE, HEALTH PHYSICS. *Current Pos:* RETIRED. *Personal Data:* b Billings, Okla, May 19, 21; m 43; c 2. *Educ:* Phillips Univ, AB, 48; Okla State Univ, MS, 50, PhD(bot), 53. *Prof Exp:* Asst zool, Phillips Univ, 42, asst bot & zool, 47-48; res assoc, Res Found, 50-53, from instr to asst prof bot & plant path, 53-56; radiol health physics officer, Radiation Lab, Continental Oil Co, 56-72, indust hygienist, med dept, Conoco Inc, 72-85. *Concurrent Pos:* Mem, Okla State Radiation Adv Comt, 72-85. *Res:* Variations of the fruits of Quercus Macrocarpa; development of an autoradiographic technique for use in botanical investigations; cyto-morphogenetic studies in sorghum. *Mailing Add:* 2001 Wildwood Ave Ponca City OK 74604

STEFFGEN, FREDERICK WILLIAMS, FUEL SCIENCE, SURFACE CHEMISTRY. *Current Pos:* RETIRED. *Personal Data:* b San Diego, Calif, Nov 21, 26; m 49, 86, Mary Schneiders; c Frederick K & Kristin E. *Educ:* Stanford Univ, BS, 47; Northwestern Univ, Evanston, MS, 49; Univ Del, PhD(org chem), 53. *Prof Exp:* Res chemist, Cutter Labs, Calif, 49-50; res chemist, Esso Res & Eng Co, Stand Oil Co (NJ), La, 52-56; sr res chemist, Union Oil Res, Union Oil Co Calif, 56-60; res assoc, Richfield Res Ctr, Atlantic Richfield Co, 60-69; mgr process develop, Antox, Inc, WVa, 70-71; supvry res chemist, Pittsburgh Energy Res Ctr, US Bur Mines, 71-75, res supvr chem, Pittsburgh Energy Res Ctr, US Energy Res & Develop Admin, 75-77 & US Dept Energy, 77-79, dir, advan res contracts proj, mgt div, Pittsburgh Energy Tech Ctr, Dept Energy, 79-89. *Mem:* Am Chem Soc; Am Inst Chem Engr; Catalysis Soc. *Res:* Heterogeneous catalysis, processes and catalyst preparation; conversions to produce low sulfur, clean fuels from coal, petroleum and organic wastes; support of grants and contracts in advanced coal research. *Mailing Add:* 2363 Caminito Eximio San Diego CA 92107-1524

STEFFY, JOHN RICHARD, ARCHAEOLOGY, ANTHROPOLOGY. *Current Pos:* from lectr to prof, 76-91, EMER PROF ANTHROP, TEX A&M UNIV, 91- *Personal Data:* b Lancaster, Pa, May 1, 24; m 51, Esther L Koch; c David A & Loren C. *Prof Exp:* Partner, M G Steffy & Sons, Denver, Pa, 50-72. *Concurrent Pos:* Lectr, Ship Construct; secy, Denver Bor Auth, Pa, 62-72; ship reconstructor, Kyrenia Ship Proj, Cyprus, 72-73 & Inst Nautical Archaeol, College Station, Tex, 73-; MacArthur Found fel, 85. *Mem:* Archaeol Inst Am; Soc Nautical Res; NAm Soc Oceanic Hist. *Res:* Archaeology; anthropology. *Mailing Add:* 1307 Sussex Dr College Station TX 77845

STEG, L(EO), ENGINEERING MECHANICS, PHYSICS. *Current Pos:* PRES, STEG, RAY & ASSOC, 82- *Personal Data:* b Vienna, Austria, Mar 30, 22; nat US; m 47, Ray; c Paula, Leslie & Audrey. *Educ:* City Col New York, BS, 47; Univ Mo, MS, 48; Cornell Univ, PhD(mech, math, physics), 51. *Prof Exp:* Chief engr, Fed Design Co, 46-47; instr mech eng, Univ Mo, 47-48; from instr to asst prof mech & mat, Cornell Univ, 48-55; syst engr, Missile & Space Div, Gen Elec Co, 55-56, mgr, GE Space Sci Lab, 56-80; sr vpres, Res Inst Div, Univ City Sci Ctr, 81-82; sci & pub policy fel, Brooking Inst, Washington, DC, 83-84. *Concurrent Pos:* Consult, Fed Design Co, 48-53, Lincoln Lab, Mass Inst Technol, 52-55, Ramo-Wooldridge Corp, 54-55 & US Dept Defense, 67-71; res engr, Boeing Airplane Co, 54; ed-in-chief, Am Inst Aeronaut & Astronaut J, 62-67; adj prof, Drexel Univ, 70-; mem, Bd Managers, Franklin Inst, 72-82; chmn, Comt Space Res Working Group-Mat Sci Space, 75-80; chmn, Gordon Conf Fundamentals of Cybernetics, 84; chmn, Gordon Conf Gravitational Effects Mat Separation & Living Systs, 85; lectr, United States Info Agency, 83-84. *Mem:* Fel AAAS; fel Am Inst Aeronaut & Astronaut; Sigma Xi. *Res:* Nonlinear mechanics; stability in dynamical systems; applied mechanics; space and reentry technology and applications; research administration; science policy; defense conversion. *Mailing Add:* 1616 Hepburn Dr Villanova PA 19085. *Fax:* 215-525-5838; *E-Mail:* clearn@aol.com

STEGELMANN, ERICH J, ELECTROOPTICS. *Current Pos:* RETIRED. *Personal Data:* b Lutjenburg, Ger, Mar 28, 14; m 51; c 3. *Educ:* Tech Univ, Berlin, Dipl Ing, 38, Dr Ing, 39. *Prof Exp:* Develop engr, Rheinmetall-Borsig, Ger, 44-45; scientist, Tech Off USSR, Berlin, 46-48; sr res engr, Can Aviation Electronics, Montreal, 52-54; design & res specialist, Lockheed Calif Corp, 54-60, sr res scientist, 60-63, mem tech staff, Northrop Space Lab, 63-64; sr tech specialist, Space Div, NAm Aviation, Inc, Calif, 64-68, mem tech staff, Autonetics Div, NAm Rockwell Corp, 68-70; mem tech staff, Electro-Optical Labs, Hughes Aircraft Co, Culver City, 72-80. *Mem:* Optical Soc Am. *Res:* Space physics; propagation of light in atmosphere. *Mailing Add:* 18559 Chatsworth St Northridge CA 91326-3141

STEGEMAN, GEORGE I, NONLINEAR OPTICS. *Current Pos:* PROF PHYSICS, UNIV CENT FLA, 90- *Personal Data:* b Edinburgh, Scotland, Aug 4, 42; Can citizen; m 67; c 3. *Educ:* Univ Toronto, BSc, 65, MSc, 66, PhD(physics), 69. *Honors & Awards:* Hertzberg Medal, Can Asn Physicists, 80. *Prof Exp:* Prof physics, Univ Toronto, 69-80; prof optics, Univ Ariz, 80-90. *Concurrent Pos:* Vis prof, Univ Calif, Irvine, 79-80 & Stanford Univ, 80. *Mem:* Fel Optical Soc Am; Can Asn Physicists; Inst Elec & Electronics Engrs; Am Phys Soc. *Res:* Propagation charecteristics of various waves guided by surfaces or films, their nonlinear interactions with matter and one another and their potential applications. *Mailing Add:* Univ Cent Fla Creol 400 Central Florida Blvd PO Box 162700 Orlando FL 32816-2700

STEGEN, GILBERT ROLLAND, FLUID MECHANICS. *Current Pos:* mgr, 76-80, ASST VPRES, SCI APPLNS INC, 80- *Personal Data:* b Long Beach, Calif, Aug 19, 39; m 66. *Educ:* Mass Inst Technol, BS, 61; Stanford Univ, MS, 62, PhD(aeronaut, astronaut), 67. *Prof Exp:* Develop engr, United Tech Ctr, United Aircraft Corp, 62-63; vis sr res fel, Col Aeronaut Eng, 67; asst res engr, Univ Calif, San Diego, 67-69; asst prof civil eng, Colo State Univ, 69-70; asst prof geol & geophys sci, Princeton Univ, 70-74; div mgr & sr res scientist, Flow Res Co, 74-76. *Mem:* Am Meteorol Soc; Sigma Xi; Am Phys Soc; Am Geophys Union. *Res:* Experimental fluid mechanics; experimental studies in atmospheric and oceanic turbulence. *Mailing Add:* Sci Applns Inc Corp 18706 N Creek Pkwy Suite 100 Bothell WA 98011

STEGENGA, DAVID ALLAN, HARDY SPACE THEORY, COMPLEX ANALYSIS. *Current Pos:* from asst prof to assoc prof, 80-88, PROF MATH, UNIV HAWAII, 88- *Personal Data:* b Chicago, Ill, Aug 20, 46; m 71, Bridgit Folstad. *Educ:* Purdue Univ, BS, 68; Univ Wis, MA, 71, PhD(math), 73. *Prof Exp:* Teaching asst math, Univ Wis, 68-73; mem, Inst Advan Study,

Princeton, 73; asst prof, Ind Univ, 73-80. *Concurrent Pos:* Prin investr, NSF, 75-86 & Alfred P Sloan Found, 87-88; vis prof, Univ NC, 87 & Univ Tenn, 88; vis researcher, Bar Ilan Univ, Israel, 91 & 94, Inst Study, Catalan, Spain, 94. *Mem:* Am Math Soc; Math Asn Am. *Res:* Duality theory of Hardy spaces and related spaces of analytic functions in complex analysis. *Mailing Add:* Dept Math Univ Hawaii Honolulu HI 96822. *Fax:* 808-956-4680; *E-Mail:* steganga@math.hawaii.edu

STEGER, RICHARD WARREN, NEUROENDOCRINOLOGY, NEUROCHEMISTRY. *Current Pos:* assoc prof physiol, 85-90, PROF PHYSIOL, MED SCH, SOUTHERN ILL UNIV, 90- *Personal Data:* b Richmond, Calif, Aug 4, 48; m 79; c 3. *Educ:* Univ Wyo, BA, 70, PhD(physiol), 74. *Prof Exp:* Asst obstet & gynec, Wayne State Univ, 74-77; asst physiol, Mich State Univ, 77-79; asst prof gynec, Health Sci Ctr, Univ Tex, 80-85. *Mem:* Endocrine Soc; Soc Study Reproduction; Am Physiol Soc; Sigma Xi; Int Soc Neuroendocrinology; Soc Neuroscience. *Res:* Transduction of environmental signals into hormonal signals; age related changes in neuroendocrine function; prolactin & gonadotropin regulation; diabetes and neuroendocrine function. *Mailing Add:* Dept Physiol Southern Ill Univ Me Sch PO Box 19230 Springfield IL 62794-9230

STEGINK, LEWIS D, BIOLOGICAL CHEMISTRY. *Current Pos:* Fel biochem, 63-65, asst prof pediat, 65-71, from asst prof to assoc prof biochem, 68-76, PROF PEDIAT & BIOCHEM, UNIV IOWA, 76- *Personal Data:* b Holland, Mich, Feb 8, 37; m 62, Carol Kallio; c David W & Daniel E. *Educ:* Hope Col, BA, 58; Univ Mich, MS & PhD(biol chem), 63. *Honors & Awards:* Mead Johnson Award, Am Inst Nutrit, 76. *Mem:* Soc Pediat Res; Am Chem Soc; Am Inst Nutrit; Am Soc Biochem & Molecular Biol; Am Pediat Soc; Sigma Xi. *Res:* Biochemistry of normal and abnormal growth and development; amino acids; parental nutrition; acetylated proteins; nutritional toxicology. *Mailing Add:* Dept Pediat & Biochem Univ Iowa S-385 Hosp Sch Iowa City IA 52242-1011

STEHBENS, WILLIAM ELLIS, PATHOLOGY, VASCULAR PATHOLOGY. *Current Pos:* prof, 74-92, EMER PROF PATH, WELLINGTON SCH MED, UNIV OTAGO, NZ, 92- *Personal Data:* b Australia, Aug 6, 26; m 61, Jean S Raeside; c Gilbert, Rachel, Bronwyn, Philippa & Rohan. *Educ:* Univ Sydney, MB & BS, 50, MD, 62; Oxford Univ, DPhil(path), 60; FRCP(A), 62; FRCPath, 61. *Honors & Awards:* R T Hall Res Prize, Cardiac Soc Australia & NZ, 65. *Prof Exp:* From lectr to sr lectr path, Univ Sydney, 53-62; from assoc prof to prof, Wash Univ, 66-68; prof, Albany Med Col, 68-74. *Concurrent Pos:* Teaching fel path, Univ Sydney, 52; Nuffield Dom travelling fel, Univ Oxford, 58; sr res fel, Australian Nat Univ, 62-66, sr fel, 66; pathologist-in-chief & dir, Dept Path & lab med, Jewish Hosp St Louis, 66-68; dir, Electron Micros Unit, Vet Admin Hosp, Albany, 68-74; dir, Malaghan Inst Med Res, 74-93; Alexander Von Humboldt Res Prize, 93- *Mem:* Royal Col Pathologists UK; Royal Col Pathologists Australasia; Int Col Angiol; Am Asn Cardiovascr Pathologists. *Res:* Relationship of intimal thickening, thrombosis and hemodynamics to the pathogenesis of atherosclerosis and cerebral aneurysms; epidemiology of coronary heart disease. *Mailing Add:* Dept Path Wellington Sch Med PO Box 7343 Wellington South New Zealand. *Fax:* 64-4-389-5725

STEHLE, PHILIP MCLELLAN, QUANTUM ELECTRONICS. *Current Pos:* asst prof, Univ Pittsburgh, 47, dept chmn, 70-75 & 82-85, prof, 53-89, EMER PROF PHYSICS, UNIV PITTSBURGH, 89- *Personal Data:* b Philadelphia, Pa, Mar 3, 19; m 42; c 3. *Educ:* Univ Mich, AB, 40, AM, 41; Princeton Univ, PhD(physics), 44. *Prof Exp:* Asst, Univ Mich, 40-41; instr physics, Princeton Univ, 41-44; instr, Harvard Univ, 46-47. *Concurrent Pos:* Fulbright prof, Univ Innsbruck, 59-60, 65 & 85; vis prof, Univ Munich, 69. *Mem:* Am Phys Soc. *Res:* Quantum theory; quantum optics. *Mailing Add:* 714 Delafield Rd Pittsburgh PA 15215

STEHLI, FRANCIS GREENOUGH, GEOLOGY. *Current Pos:* RETIRED. *Personal Data:* b Montclair, NJ, Oct 16, 24; m 48; c 4. *Educ:* St Lawrence Univ, BS, 49, MS, 50; Columbia Univ, PhD(geol), 53. *Prof Exp:* Asst prof invert paleont, Calif Inst Technol, 53-56; res engr, Pan Am Petrol Corp, 57, tech group supvr, 58-60; prof geol, Case Western Reserve Univ, 60-74, chmn dept, 61-73, Samuel St John prof earth sci, 74-80, actg dean sci, 75- 76, actg dean sci & eng, 76-77, dean sci & eng, 77-79; pres, Dicar Corp of Case Western Reserve, 78-80; dean grad studies & res, Univ Fla, 80-82; dean, Col Geosci, 82-86, dir, Weather Ctr, Univ Okla, 84-86; chmn, Sci Adv Comt, DOSECC Inc, Gainesville, Fla, 86-88. *Concurrent Pos:* Mem, NSF Earth Sci Adv Panel, 67-69, chmn, 69; chmn comt ocean drilling, Nat Res Coun, 81-82, chmn coun on Continental Sci Drilling, 83-86; pres, Appl Systs Inst, Norman Okla, 83-86; mem, Energy Res Adv Bd, Dept Energy, 84- *Mem:* Paleont Soc (pres, 77-80); fel Geol Soc Am; Geochem Soc; fel AAAS; Am Soc Eng Educ. *Res:* Paleozoic brachiopods; Mesozoic stratigraphy of Gulf Coast and western Mexico; paleoecology; carbonate rock formation and diagenesis; continental drift, polar wandering and paleoclimatology. *Mailing Add:* 11240 Stratford Ridge Dr Chardon OH 44024-8652

STEHLIN, JOHN SEBASTIAN, JR, ONCOLOGY. *Current Pos:* CLIN ASSOC PROF SURG, BAYLOR COL MED, 67-; SCI DIR, STEHLIN FOUND CANCER RES, 69- *Personal Data:* b Brownsville, Tenn, June 16, 23; div; c Mary C. *Educ:* Med Col Wis, MD, 47; Am Bd Surg, dipl. *Prof Exp:* Intern, Milwaukee Hosp, 47-48; resident surg, 49-52; resident path, Baptist Hosp, Milwaukee, 48-49; fel surg, Lahey Clin, Boston, 52-53 & 56; sr fel surg, M D Anderson Hosp & Tumor Inst, Univ Tex 55-56, from asst prof to assoc prof, Postgrad Sch, 57-63, assoc prof, Grad Sch, Biomed Sci, 63-67. *Concurrent Pos:* Mem surg staff, M D Anderson Hosp & Tumor Inst, Univ Tex, 57-67 & asst surgeon, 57-60, assoc surgeon, 61-67; hon prof, Fac Med, Univ Repub Uruguay, 65; mem surg staff, St Joseph Hosp, Houston, 67- *Mem:* Fel Am Col Surgeons; Am Asn Cancer Res; AAAS; AMA; hon mem Cancer Asn Arg; hon mem Cancer Soc Chile; Soc Surg Oncol; Pan Am Med Asn; Royal Soc Med; NY Acad Sci; hon mem Soc Dermat Uruguay; hon mem Surg Soc Chile. *Res:* Cancer. *Mailing Add:* Stehlin Found Cancer 1315 Calhoun St Suite 1800 Houston TX 77002

STEHLING, FERDINAND CHRISTIAN, POLYMER PHYSICS, PHYSICAL CHEMISTRY. *Current Pos:* Res assoc, 58-80, SR RES ASSOC POLYMERS, EXXON CHEM CO, 80- *Personal Data:* b Fredericksburg, Tex, Feb 18, 30; c 4. *Educ:* St Mary's Univ, Md, BS & BA, 50; Univ Tex, MA, 57, PhD(phys chem), 58. *Honors & Awards:* Prof Progress Award, Soc Prof Engrs & Chemists, 73. *Mem:* Am Chem Soc; Sigma Xi. *Res:* Polymer morphology and properties; mass spectroscopy. *Mailing Add:* 4123 Bee Creek Rd Spicewood TX 78669

STEHLY, DAVID NORVIN, INORGANIC CHEMISTRY. *Current Pos:* From instr to assoc prof, 60-75, PROF CHEM, MUHLENBERG COL, 75- *Personal Data:* b Bethlehem, Pa, Oct 3, 33; m 61; c 2. *Educ:* Moravian Col, BS, 59; Lehigh Univ, MS, 62, PhD(inorg chem), 67. *Mem:* Am Chem Soc. *Res:* Metal chelates of substitued amides; trace metal ions in surface waters. *Mailing Add:* 1254 Lehigh St Allentown PA 18103-3861

STEHNEY, ANDREW FRANK, RADIOCHEMISTRY, RADIOBIOLOGY. *Current Pos:* assoc chemist, Argonne Nat Lab, 50-71, sr chemist, 71-85, assoc div dir, 76-84, SCIENTIST, ARGONNE NAT LAB, 85- *Personal Data:* b Chicago, Ill, May 4, 20; m 43; c 3. *Educ:* Univ Chicago, BS, 42, PhD(chem), 50. *Prof Exp:* Instr chem, Univ Chicago, 49-50. *Concurrent Pos:* Lectr, Univ Chicago, 56-61; vis scientist, Europ Orgn Nuclear Res, 61-63; mem subcomt radiochem, Nat Res Coun, 69-77; mem, Safe Drinking Water Comt, Nat Acad Sci, 76; mem subcomt, radiation adv comt, Environ Protection Agency, 86-90. *Mem:* Fel AAAS. *Res:* Toxicity of radium and other internal emitters; applications of radiochemistry to environmental studies; nuclear reactions. *Mailing Add:* 1132 Curtiss St Downers Grove IL 60515. *E-Mail:* avasteh@aol.com

STEHNEY, ANN KATHRYN, CRYPTOLOGY. *Current Pos:* RES STAFF MEM, CTR COMMUN RES, INST DEFENSE ANALYSIS, 83- *Personal Data:* b Oak Ridge, Tenn, June 30, 46; c 2. *Educ:* Bryn Mawr Col, AB, 67; State Univ NY, Stony Brook, MA, 69, PhD(math), 71. *Prof Exp:* From asst prof to prof math, Wellesley Col, 71-85, chmn dept, 77-78 & 80-81. *Concurrent Pos:* Vis scholar, Enrico Fermi Inst, Univ Chicago, 74-75; vis assoc prof, State Univ NY, Stony Brook, 81-82. *Mem:* Am Math Soc; Math Asn Am; Soc Indust & Appl Math. *Res:* Cryptology, analysis and statistical studies in communication. *Mailing Add:* 385 Walnut Lane Princeton NJ 08540-3466

STEHOUWER, DAVID MARK, ORGANIC CHEMISTRY. *Current Pos:* tech adv fuels & lubricants, 81-85, MGR FUELS, LUBRICANTS & ORG MAT, CUMMINS ENGINE CO, 85- *Personal Data:* b Grand Rapids, Mich, July 14, 43; m 68; c 3. *Educ:* Hope Col, BA, 65; Univ Mich, Ann Arbor, MS, 67, PhD(org chem), 70. *Prof Exp:* Sr chemist res labs, Texaco Inc, 70-76; sr res scientist, Gen Motors Res Labs, 76-81. *Mem:* Am Soc Testing & Mat; Soc Automotive Engrs; Am Chem Soc. *Res:* Lubricant additive chemistry; mechanisms of lubricant performance; corrosion mechanisms; engine oil wear protection; engine oil consumption; oil conservation and recycling. *Mailing Add:* Fleetguard Inc Box 3005 MC 41502 Columbus IN 47202-3005

STEHR, FREDERICK WILLIAM, SYSTEMATICS, BIOCONTROL. *Current Pos:* from asst prof to assoc prof, 65-76, PROF ENTOM, MICH STATE UNIV, 76-, ASST CHMN DEPT, 79-, CUR, CTR ARTHROPOD DIVERSITY STUDY. *Personal Data:* b Athens, Ohio, Dec 23, 32; m 59; c 2. *Educ:* Univ Ohio, BS, 54; Univ Minn, MS, 58, PhD(entom), 64. *Honors & Awards:* Karl Jordan Medal, Lepidop Soc, 74; Thomas Say Award, Entom Soc Am. *Prof Exp:* Res fel entom, Univ Minn, 62-65. *Mem:* Entom Soc Am; Soc Syst Zool; Lepidop Soc; Entom Soc Can; Soc Conserv Biol; Willi Hennig Soc. *Res:* Systematics of Lepidoptera and immature insects; biological control; ecology. *Mailing Add:* Dept Entom Mich State Univ East Lansing MI 48824

STEHSEL, MELVIN LOUIS, ORGANIC CHEMISTRY, PLANT PHYSIOLOGY. *Current Pos:* assoc prof biol, 65-72, PROF BIOL, PASADENA CITY COL, 72- *Personal Data:* b Long Beach, Calif, Oct 3, 24; m 57; c 2. *Educ:* Univ Calif, Berkeley, BS, 45, MS, 47, PhD(plant physiol), 50. *Prof Exp:* Off Naval Res fel biochem genetics, 50-51; French Govt fel, 51; res chemist, Socony Mobil Oil Co, 51-56; chief phys lab, Aerojet-Gen Corp, 56-65. *Mem:* AAAS; Bot Soc Am; Am Chem Soc. *Res:* High temperature mechanical properties of graphite for nuclear rockets; action of natural and synthetic plant growth hormones; stimulation and cause of cell differentiation in plant tissue culture; plant biochemistry. *Mailing Add:* 1049 Rancho Rd Arcadia CA 91006-2225

STEICHEN, RICHARD JOHN, environmental engineering, computer applications, for more information see previous edition

STEIDEL, ROBERT F(RANCIS), JR, MECHANICAL ENGINEERING. *Current Pos:* assoc, Univ Calif, Berkeley, 54-55, from asst prof to prof, 55-91, chmn, Div Mech Design, 61-64, chmn dept, 69-74, EMER PROF MECH ENG, UNIV CALIF, BERKELEY, 91- *Personal Data:* b Goshen, NY, July

6, 26; m 46; c 4. *Educ:* Columbia Univ, BS, 48, MS, 49; Univ Calif, DEng, 55. *Honors & Awards:* Chester F Carlson Award, 74. *Prof Exp:* From instr to asst prof mech eng, Ore State Col, 49-54; eng adv, John Wiley & Sons, 73-87. *Concurrent Pos:* Consult, Bonneville Power Admin, 50-53, Missile & Space Div, Lockheed Aircraft Corp, 59-63, Jet Propulsion Lab, Calif, 61-68 & Sandia Corp, 67; consult, Lawrence Radiation Lab, Univ Calif, 55-88, proj engr, 58-60; fac athletic rep, Univ Calif, 72-90, assoc dean eng, 81-86. *Mem:* Am Soc Mech Engrs; Am Soc Eng Educ; Inst Mech Engrs. *Res:* Engineering mechanics; mechanical vibration, systems analysis and design. *Mailing Add:* 1877 San Pedro Ave Berkeley CA 94707-1934

STEIDTMANN, JAMES R, GEOLOGY. *Current Pos:* PROF GEOL & GEOPHYS, UNIV WYO, 68- *Personal Data:* b Toledo, Ohio, Oct 14, 38. *Educ:* Bowling Green State Univ, BS, 60; Dartmouth Univ, MA, 62; Mich State Univ, PhD(geol), 68. *Honors & Awards:* A I Leaderson Mem Award, Am Asn Petrol Geologists. *Mem:* Soc Econ Paleontologists & Mineralogists; Geol Soc Am; Int Asn Sedimentologist. *Mailing Add:* 6597 Picot Peak Rd Laramie WY 82070

STEIER, WILLIAM H(ENRY), ELECTRICAL ENGINEERING, OPTICS. *Current Pos:* assoc prof, 68-76, co-chmn dept, 70-84, PROF ELEC ENG, UNIV SOUTHERN CALIF, 76- *Personal Data:* b Kendallville, Ind, May 25, 33; m 55; c 4. *Educ:* Evansville Col, BS, 55; Univ Ill, MS, 57, PhD(elec eng), 60. *Prof Exp:* Asst elec eng, Univ Ill, Urbana, 55-60, asst prof, 60-62; mem tech staff, Bell Tel Labs, NJ, 62-68. *Concurrent Pos:* Consult, Space Technol Labs, 61-62 & Northrop Corp Labs, 68- *Mem:* Fel Inst Elec & Electronics Engrs; AAAS. *Res:* Propagation of electromagnetic energy; millimeterwave detectors and transmission lines; optical transmission systems, modulators and components; lasers; optical signal processing; polymer electro-optic materials and devices. *Mailing Add:* Univ Southern Calif SSC 502 Mail Code 0483 Los Angeles CA 90089

STEIGBIGEL, ROY THEODORE, INFECTIOUS DISEASES. *Current Pos:* PROF, STATE UNIV NY, STONY BROOK, 83-; DIR, COMPREHENSIVE AIDS CTR, 85- *Personal Data:* b Brooklyn, NY, Nov 23, 41; m 67, 85, Sidonie A Morrison; c Keith D, Glenn N & Andrew M. *Educ:* Carleton Col, BA, 62; Univ Rochester, MD, 66; Am Bd Internal Med, dipl. *Honors & Awards:* Howard M Temin Award. *Prof Exp:* Resident, Univ Rochester, 66-68, from assoc prof to prof, 73-83; resident, Stanford Univ, 70-71, fel, 71-73, grantee, 85-; mem, Adv Bd Infectious Dis, US Pharmacopea, 80- *Mem:* Fel Am Col Physicians; fel Infectious Dis Soc Am; Am Soc Microbiol. *Res:* Infectious disease; host defense mechanisms; immunopathogenesis of HIV, therapy of HIV. *Mailing Add:* Sch Med HSC-T-15-080 State Univ NY Stony Brook NY 11794-8153. *Fax:* 516-444-7518; *E-Mail:* rsteigb@epo.com.sunysb.edu

STEIGELMANN, WILLIAM HENRY, engineering, for more information see previous edition

STEIGER, FRED HAROLD, APPLIED CHEMISTRY, ABSORBENT STRUCTURES. *Current Pos:* CONSULT, 88- *Personal Data:* b Cleveland, Ohio, May 11, 29; m 52, 91, Estelle Dubin; c Eden L (Fisher) & Susan L (Baron). *Educ:* Univ Pa, BA, 51; Temple Univ, MA, 56. *Prof Exp:* Res chemist, Rohm & Haas Co, Pa, 51-60; group leader sanit protection, Johnson & Johnson, 60-62, sr res chemist, 62-68, sr res assoc, 68-74, sr res assoc, 74-76, prod develop mgr, Personal Prod Co Div, 76-85, technol assessment mgr, 85-88. *Concurrent Pos:* Abstractor, Chem Abstr, 53-68, ed, Textile Sect, 68-85; vpres prof affairs, NJ Inst Chemists, 75-77. *Mem:* Am Chem Soc; Am Asn Textile Chem & Colorists; fel Am Inst Chem; Fiber Soc. *Res:* Textile chemistry; fibers and polymers; sanitary protection; absorption of liquids; cosmetics and toiletries; household products; technology assessment; competitor assessment. *Mailing Add:* 10 Tompkins Rd East Brunswick NJ 08816-1709

STEIGER, ROGER ARTHUR, HIGH TEMPERATURE CHEMISTRY. *Current Pos:* sr res chemist indust chem div, 67-79, sr res assoc, 79-81, SR RES ASSOC, PPG INDUSTS INC, 81- *Personal Data:* b Potosi, Wis, Dec 29, 39; m 67; c 3. *Educ:* Wis State Univ-Platteville, BS, 61; Univ Iowa, PhD(phys chem), 67. *Mem:* AAAS; Am Chem Soc; Am Ceramic Soc. *Res:* Thermodynamics of refractory compounds; plasma chemical reactions; powder metallurgy of fine-grained cemented carbides; preparation, fabrication and properties of sinterable submicron ceramic powders. *Mailing Add:* 105 Heritage Circle Greensburg PA 15601-9172

STEIGER, WALTER RICHARD, PHYSICS. *Current Pos:* from asst prof to assoc prof, 53-65, PROF PHYSICS, UNIV HAWAII, 65-, CHMN DEPT PHYSICS & ASTRON, 72- *Personal Data:* b Colo, Sept 4, 23; m 46; c 2. *Educ:* Mass Inst Technol, BS, 48; Univ Hawaii, MS, 50; Univ Cincinnati, PhD(physics), 53. *Prof Exp:* Asst physics, Univ Hawaii, 48-50; instr, Univ Cincinnati, 51-52. *Concurrent Pos:* Vis researcher high altitude observ, Univ Colo, 59-60; Fulbright res scholar, Tokyo Astron Observ, 66-67. *Mem:* AAAS; Am Phys Soc; Am Asn Physics Teachers. *Res:* Upper atmosphere physics, ionosphere; airglow. *Mailing Add:* 30 Kiele Pl Hilo HI 96720-1732

STEIGER, WILLIAM LEE, LINEAR OPTIMIZATION. *Current Pos:* assoc prof, 74-84, PROF COMPUT SCI, RUTGERS UNIV, 84- *Personal Data:* b New York, NY, Nov 17, 39; m 71; c 2. *Educ:* Mass Inst Technol, SB, 61, SM, 63; Australian Nat Univ, PhD(statist), 69. *Concurrent Pos:* Assoc prof, Princeton Univ, 79-81, vis prof, 83-84; res fel, Australian Nat Univ, 79-81. *Mem:* Am Math Soc; Inst Math Statist; Australian Math Soc. *Res:* Computer sciences, theory; statistical computing; linear optimization. *Mailing Add:* Dept Comp Sci Rutgers Univ Hill Ctr Res Campus Piscataway NJ 08855

STEIGLITZ, KENNETH, COMPUTER SCIENCE, ELECTRICAL ENGINEERING. *Current Pos:* From asst prof to prof elec eng, 63-73, PROF COMPUT SCI, PRINCETON UNIV, 73- *Personal Data:* b Weehawken, NJ, Jan 30, 39; m 65; c 1. *Educ:* NY Univ, BEE, 59, MEE, 60, EngScD(elec eng), 63. *Honors & Awards:* Tech Achievement Award, Inst Elec & Electronics Engrs, 81, Centennial Medal, 84; Soc Award, Acoust, Speech & Signal Processing Soc, 86. *Concurrent Pos:* Assoc ed, J Asn Comput Mach, 78-81 & Networks, 80- *Mem:* Fel Inst Elec & Electronics Engrs; Asn Comput Mach. *Res:* Algorithms; digital signal processing. *Mailing Add:* Dept Comput Sci Princeton Univ Princeton NJ 08544

STEIGMAN, GARY, ASTROPHYSICS, COSMOLOGY. *Current Pos:* PROF PHYSICS & ASTRON, OHIO STATE UNIV, 86- *Personal Data:* b New York, NY, Feb 23, 41; div. *Educ:* City Col New York, BS, 61; NY Univ, MS, 63, PhD(physics), 68. *Honors & Awards:* Alexander Von Humboldt Award, 86; Gravity Res Found Prize, 80. *Prof Exp:* Instr physics, New York Univ, 67-68; vis fel, Inst Theoret Astron, Cambridge, Eng, 68-70; res fel, Calif Inst Technol, 70-72; asst prof astron, Yale Univ, 72-78; assoc prof, Univ Del, 78-80, prof, Bartol Res Found, 80-86. *Concurrent Pos:* Vis scientist, Nat Radio Astron Observ, 75; vis scholar, Stanford Univ, 79; vis scientist, Inst Theoret Physics, Santa Barbara, 81; George Ellery Hale Distinguished Vis Prof, Enrico Fermi Inst, Univ Chicago, 83; vis theorist, Fermi Nat Accelerator Lab, 84, 85. *Mem:* Am Astron Soc; Int Astron Union; fel Am Phys Soc. *Res:* Cosmology: primarily the early evolution of the universe; connections between elementary particle physics, cosmology, and astrophysics; big bang nucleosynthesis; astrophysical constraints on the properties of elementary particle candidates for the dark matter in the universe. *Mailing Add:* Dept Physics Ohio State Univ 174 W 18th Ave Columbus OH 43210

STEIGMANN, FREDERICK, MEDICINE. *Current Pos:* RETIRED. *Personal Data:* b Austria, Apr 25, 05; nat US; m 37; c 3. *Educ:* Univ Ill, BS, 28, MD, 30, MS, 38. *Prof Exp:* Asst, Col Med, Univ Ill, 33-34, from instr to assoc prof, 34-72, clin prof med, 72. *Concurrent Pos:* Pvt pract, 33-; dir depts therapeut & gastroenterol & attend physician, Cook County Hosp, 40- *Mem:* Fel Soc Exp Biol & Med; fel Am Soc Pharmacol & Exp Therapeut; fel Am Fedn Clin Res; fel Am Col Physicians; Am Gastroenterol Asn; Sigma Xi. *Res:* Gastroenterology; liver; vitamin A; protein metabolism. *Mailing Add:* 1205 W Kirby Ave Champaign IL 61821-5102

STEILA, DONALD, climatology, meteorology & pedogenesis; deceased, see previous edition for last biography

STEIMAN, HENRY ROBERT, DENTISTRY, PHYSIOLOGY. *Current Pos:* Asst prof, 69-73, chmn dept physiol, 70-77, dir div biol sci, 73-77, ASSOC PROF PHYSIOL, DENT SCH, UNIV DETROIT, 73-, CHMN DEPT ENDODONTICS, 80- *Personal Data:* b Winnipeg, Man, Aug 2, 38; m 73; c 2. *Educ:* NDak State Univ, BS, 64; Wayne State Univ, MS, 67, PhD(physiol), 69; Univ Detroit, DDS, 73; Indiana Univ, MSD, 79. *Concurrent Pos:* Mich Asn Regional Med Progs grant, Dent Sch, Univ Detroit, 74-76; consult, Hypertension Coordinating & Planning Comt, Southeastern Mich, 74-77; consult, Detroit Receiving Hosp, 80-, Vet Admin Hosp, Allen Park, 81- *Mem:* Am Dent Asn; Am Asn Endodontics. *Mailing Add:* 255 Hillcrest Ave Grosse Pointe MI 48236

STEIMLE, TIMOTHY C, ATOMIC PHYSICS, MOLECULAR PHYSICS. *Current Pos:* ASST PROF CHEM, ARIZ STATE UNIV, 85- *Personal Data:* b Benton Harbor, Mich, May 6, 51; m 74. *Educ:* Mich State Univ, BS, 73; Univ Calif, Santa Barbara, PhD(chem), 78. *Prof Exp:* Fel, Rice Univ, 78-80; fel, Univ Southampton, Eng, 80-81; res asst, Univ Ore, 81-85. *Mem:* Am Phys Soc. *Res:* High resolution spectroscopy of gas phase free radials and ionic species. *Mailing Add:* Dept Chem Ariz State Univ Tempe AZ 85287-0001

STEIN, ABRAHAM MORTON, BIOCHEMISTRY. *Current Pos:* chmn dept, 71-74, PROF BIOL SCI, FLA INT UNIV, 71- *Personal Data:* b Chicago, Ill, Aug 9, 23; m 43; c 1. *Educ:* Univ Calif, Los Angeles, AB, 49, MA, 51; Univ Southern Calif, PhD(biochem), 57. *Prof Exp:* NIH res fel biochem, Brandeis Univ, 57-59; res assoc, Univ Pa, 59-65, sr res investr, 65-67; assoc prof col med, Univ Fla, 67-71. *Concurrent Pos:* Adj prof col med, Univ Miami, 71- *Mem:* AAAS; Am Soc Biol Chem; Am Chem Soc; NY Acad Sci. *Res:* Chemical carcinogenesis; monoclonal antibodies to DHA adducts. *Mailing Add:* Div Med Genet D-870 Univ Miami Sch Med 1601 NW 12th Ave Miami FL 33136-1005

STEIN, ALAN H, ANALYTIC NUMBER THEORY, MICROCOMPUTERS. *Current Pos:* From instr to asst prof, 72-80, ASSOC PROF MATH, UNIV CONN, 80- *Personal Data:* b New York, NY, Apr 2, 47; m 69; c 1. *Educ:* Queen's Col, BA, 68; NY Univ, MS, 70, PhD(math), 73. *Mem:* Am Math Soc; Math Asn Am. *Res:* Analytic number theory; additive number theory; binary numbers. *Mailing Add:* Dept Math Univ Conn 32 Hillside Ave Waterbury CT 06710-2288. *E-Mail:* stein@mathinconn.edu

STEIN, ALLAN RUDOLPH, PHYSICAL ORGANIC CHEMISTRY. *Current Pos:* from asst prof to assoc prof chem, 65-75, PROF CHEM, MEM UNIV, NFLD, 75- *Personal Data:* b Edmonton, Alta, Nov 14, 38. *Educ:* Univ Alta, BSc, 60; Univ Ill, Urbana, PhD(org chem), 64. *Prof Exp:* Asst org chem, Univ Ill, Urbana, 60-61; res scientist, Domtar Cent Res Labs, Senneville, Que, 64-65. *Concurrent Pos:* Nat Res Coun Can res grants, 65-69, 75-78 & 78-81; vis prof, King's Col, Univ London, Univ Umea, Sweden, 72-73; Univ Alta, 86, U Western Ont, 93-94; res grant, Swed Res Coun, 73; hon prof chem, Univ

Auckland, NZ, 80-81; scientist, Atomic Energy Can, 81. *Mem:* Am Chem Soc; Brit Chem Soc; Chem Inst Can. *Res:* Organic reaction mechanism studies, especially reactions of ambident ions, the isonitriles and of phenol alkylation; ion-pair mechanism of nucleophilic displacement; set process; deuterium kinetic isotope effects. *Mailing Add:* Dept Chem Mem Univ St John's NF A1B 3X7 Can. *Fax:* 709-737-3702; *E-Mail:* arstein@morgan.ucs.mun.ca

STEIN, ARTHUR, mathematical statistics; deceased, see previous edition for last biography

STEIN, ARTHUR A, MEDICINE, PATHOLOGY. *Current Pos:* instr path & bact, Albany Med Col, 49-52, from asst prof to assoc prof path, 52-59, dir res inst exp path & toxicol, 65-69, PROF PATH, ALBANY MED COL, 59- *Personal Data:* b Toronto, Ont, Mar 12, 22; nat US; m 48; c 3. *Educ:* Univ Toronto, MD, 45; Am Bd Path, dipl, 52. *Prof Exp:* Intern, Victoria Hosp, London, Ont, 45-46; asst resident med, Jewish Hosp, St Louis, Mo, 47; asst resident path, City Hosp, 47-48; resident, Sch Trop Med, Univ PR, 48-49. *Concurrent Pos:* Surg pathologist, Albany Hosp, 55-; sci adv, Ky Tobacco & Health Bd, Commonwealth of Ky, 71-; dir Micros Biol Res, Inc, 67- *Mem:* Am Soc Clin Path; AMA; Col Am Path; Am Acad Clin Toxicol; Soc Toxicol. *Res:* Toxicology. *Mailing Add:* 38 Colonial Ave Albany NY 12203-2012

STEIN, BARRY EDWARD, NEUROPHYSIOLOGY, DEVELOPMENTAL PHYSIOLOGY. *Current Pos:* asst prof, 75-76, assoc prof, 76-82, PROF PHYSIOL, MED COL VA, VA COMMONWEALTH UNIV, 82- *Personal Data:* b New York, NY, Dec 3, 44; m 68. *Educ:* Queens Col, BA, 66, MA, 69; City Univ New York, PhD(neuropsychol), 70. *Prof Exp:* Fel neurophysiol & neuroanat, Univ Calif, Los Angeles, 70-72, asst res anatomist, 72-75. *Mem:* Sigma Xi; Int Brain Res Orgn; AAAS; Am Psychol Asn; Soc Neurosci; Am Physiol Soc. *Res:* Multisensory integration; the ontogenesis of sensory systems; neurophysiological, neuroanatomical and behavioral changes during early life. *Mailing Add:* Neurobiol & Anat Bowman Gray Sch Med Wake Forest Univ Med Ctr Blvd Winston-Salem NC 27157-1010. *E-Mail:* Bitnet: bstein@vcuvax

STEIN, BARRY FRED, SOLID STATE PHYSICS. *Current Pos:* dir, device res, Univ City Sci Ctr, 83, spec asst to pres, 84, dir res & develop, 84, vpres, res & develop, 88-89, sr vpres, Res & Develop, 89-92, SR VPRES & CHIEF OPERATING OFFICER, BEN FRANKLIN TECHNOL CTR, UNIV CITY SCI CTR, 92- *Personal Data:* b Philadelphia, Pa, Nov 2, 37; m 62; c 3. *Educ:* Univ Pa, BA, 59, MS, 61, PhD(physics), 65. *Prof Exp:* Staff physicist, Univac Div, Sperry Rand Corp, 65-79, mgr, magnetic device res, Sperry Univac Div, 79-82. *Concurrent Pos:* Adj prof, Grad Exten, Pa State Univ, 65-76. *Mem:* Am Phys Soc; Inst Elec & Electronics Engrs. *Res:* Electrical properties of gallium arsenide; chemical vapor deposition and magnetic and optical properties of gadolinium iron garnet; liquid phase epitaxial growth of garnets; magnetic bubble device fabrication; high resolution x-ray lithography; Josephson junction devices. *Mailing Add:* Ben Franklin Technol Ctr Univ City Sci Ctr 3624 Market St Philadelphia PA 19104

STEIN, BENNETT M, NEUROSURGERY. *Current Pos:* PROF, CHEM DEPT NEUROSURG, COLUMBIA PRESBYTERIAN MED CTR, COL PHYSICIANS & SURGEONS, COLUMBIA UNIV, 80- *Personal Data:* b New York, NY, Feb 2, 31; m 55, 87; c 3. *Educ:* Dartmouth Col, BA, 52; McGill Univ, MD, 55; Am Bd Neurol Surg, cert, 66. *Prof Exp:* Intern, US Naval Hosp, St Albans, NY, 58-59; surg resident, Columbia Presby Hosp, New York, 59-60, from asst resident to chief resident neurosurg, 60-64; asst prof, Neurol Inst, Columbia Univ, 68-71; prof neurosurg & chmn dept, New Eng Med Ctr, Tufts Univ, 71-80. *Concurrent Pos:* Fulbright scholar neurol, Nat Inst, Queens Sq, London, Eng, 58-59; NIH spec fel neuroanat, Columbia Univ, 64-66; consult, US Naval Hosp, Chelsea, Lemuel Shattuck Hosp, Boston & Vet Admin Hosp, Boston, 71- *Mem:* Fel Am Col Surg; Am Asn Anat; Soc Neurol Surg; Cong Neurol Surg; Am Acad Neurol Surg; Sigma Xi. *Res:* Cerebrovascular reactions, specifically cerebrovasospasm in response to subarachnoid hemorrhage; neuroanatomical problems. *Mailing Add:* Neurol Inst 710 W 168th St New York NY 10032

STEIN, BLAND ALLEN, AEROSPACE ENVIRONMENTAL EFFECTS ON MATERIALS, AEROSPACE MATERIALS & STRUCTURES. *Current Pos:* PROG MGR, AS&M, INC, 93- *Personal Data:* b New York, NY, Feb 27, 34; m 56, Shirley Nestler; c David M, Lynne M (Benzion) & Ellen P. *Educ:* City Col New York, BME, 56; Va Polytech Inst & State Univ, MMetE, 64. *Prof Exp:* Mat res engr, Langley Res Ctr, NASA, 56-68, head, Metals Sect, 68-74, asst head, Mat Res Br, 74-81, head, Advan Mat Br, 81-82, head, Polymeric Mat Br, 82-84, head, Appl Mat Br, 84-85, asst chief, Mat Div, 85-92, chmn, LDEF Spec Inv Group/Mat, 89-92. *Concurrent Pos:* Failure anal consult var govt agencies, 63-; educ pub mgt fel, Univ Va, 77-78; asst prof & lectr, George Washington Univ, 77-; adj prof, Christopher Newport Col, 80- *Mem:* Am Soc Testing & Mat; Soc Advan Mat & Process Eng; Am Inst Aeronaut & Astronaut. *Res:* Materials for space vehicle applications (directed LDEF materials analyses); materials for subsonic, supersonic and hypersonic aircraft; environmental effects of aerospace environments on materials, structures and systems; adhesives, coatings, thermal protection system materials research and development; structural material research and development. *Mailing Add:* 732 Jouett Dr Newport News VA 23602-1914

STEIN, CAROL B, ZOOLOGY, FRESHWATER MALACOLOGY. *Personal Data:* b Columbus, Ohio, Jan 1, 37. *Educ:* Lake Erie Col, AB, 58; Ohio State Univ, MSc, 63, PhD(zool), 73. *Prof Exp:* Asst, Dept Bot, Ohio State Univ, 60, asst, Dept Zool & Entom, 60-61; mus technician natural hist, Ohio Hist Soc, Ohio State Mus, 64-66; teaching assoc, Biol Core Prog, Ohio State Univ, 68-69; mus technician natural hist, Ohio Hist Soc, Ohio State Mus, 69-70; asst curator, Ohio State Univ, 70-72, curator Mus Zool, 72-90. *Mem:* Am Malacological Union; Am Inst Biol Sci; Sigma Xi; Nature Conservancy. *Res:* Systematics, zoogeography, and life history of the freshwater mollusks, especially the endangered species of eastern North America. *Mailing Add:* 13633 Fancher Rd Johnstown OH 43031-9325

STEIN, CHARLES M, MATHEMATICS. *Current Pos:* EMER PROF STATIST, STANFORD UNIV. *Mem:* Nat Acad Sci. *Mailing Add:* 821 Santa Fe Stanford CA 94305

STEIN, CHARLES W C, ORGANIC CHEMISTRY. *Current Pos:* RETIRED. *Personal Data:* b Philadelphia, Pa, Apr 28, 14; m 38, Elizabeth Eisenhardt. *Educ:* Univ Pa, BS, 36, MS, 39, PhD(org chem), 42. *Prof Exp:* Asst instr chem, Lehigh Univ, 37; asst instr, Drexel Inst, 37-42; res chemist, Gen Aniline & Film Corp, 42-46; process develop chemist, Calco Div, Am Cyanamid Co, 46-51; tech assoc, GAF Corp, 51-79. *Mem:* AAAS; emer mem Am Chem Soc. *Res:* Dyestuff chemistry; pigments; organic synthesis; plastics. *Mailing Add:* 910 Summit Ave Westfield NJ 07090

STEIN, DALE FRANKLIN, METALLURGY, SURFACE CHEMISTRY. *Current Pos:* prof metall eng & dept head, Mich Technol Univ, 71-77, vpres acad affairs, 77-79, pres, 79-91, EMER PRES, MICH TECHNOL UNIV, HOUGHTON, 91- *Personal Data:* b Kingston, Minn, Dec 24, 35; m 58; c Derek & Pamela. *Educ:* Univ Minn, BS, 58; Rensselaer Polytech Inst, PhD(metall), 63. *Hon Degrees:* DSc, Cent Mich Univ. *Honors & Awards:* Hardy Gold Medal, Am Inst Mining, Metall & Petrol Engrs, 65; Giesler Award, Am Soc Metals, 67. *Prof Exp:* Asst plant metallurgist, Metall Inc, 57-58; prog metallurgist, Gen Elec Co, 58-59, metallurgist, Res & Develop Ctr, 59-67; assoc prof, Sch Mineral & Metall Eng, Univ Minn, Minneapolis, 67-70, assoc prof mech eng, chem eng & mat sci, 70-71. *Concurrent Pos:* Consult, Dept Energy; bd mem, Ctr Nuclear Waste Regulatory Anal, 92-; chmn, Nat Acad Eng, Nat Res Ctr, Comt Decontamination & Decommissioning of Uranium Enrichment Facil, 93- *Mem:* Nat Acad Eng; fel Am Inst Mining, Metall & Petrol Engrs (pres elect, 79); Am Soc Metals; Sigma Xi; fel Metall Soc; fel AAAS. *Res:* Application of Auger spectroscopy to metallurgical problems, including brittle fracture, corrosion and structure stability, cleavage fracture, dislocation dynamics and high purity metals; author of over 60 publications; materials and the environment; nuclear waste. *Mailing Add:* 6387 E Placita Divina Tucson AL 85715

STEIN, DANIEL L, STATISTICAL MECHANICS OF DISORDERED SYSTEMS, BIOPHYSICS OF PROTEINS. *Current Pos:* assoc prof, 87-93, PROF PHYSICS, UNIV ARIZ, 93-, HEAD, DEPT PHYSICS, 95- *Personal Data:* b New York, NY, Aug 19, 53; m 86, Bernadette Klimashousky; c 2. *Educ:* Brown Univ, ScB, 75; Princeton Univ, MS, 77, PhD(physics), 79. *Prof Exp:* Instr, Princeton Univ, 80, asst prof physics, 80-87. *Concurrent Pos:* Consult, Xerox Palo Alto Res Labs, 80 & AT&T Bell Labs 84-86; fel, Alfred P Sloan Found, 85; mem, Space Launch Strategy Task Force & Defense Sci Bd, Aspen Ctr Physics, 88-89, secy, 89-90, trustee, 92-94, asst treas, 95-97, treas, 97-; external fac, Sante Fe Inst, 89-, sci bd mem, 91- *Mem:* Am Phys Soc; Ny Acad Sci; AAAS. *Res:* Statistical mechanics and dynamics of spin glasses, glasses, and related disordered systems; large fluctuations and escape problem in irreversible systems; dynamics of fully folded, globular proteins. *Mailing Add:* Dept Physics Univ Ariz Tucson AZ 85721. *Fax:* 520-621-4721; *E-Mail:* dls@physics.arizona.edu

STEIN, DARYL LEE, ORGANIC CHEMISTRY. *Current Pos:* TECH MGR NEW PROD, DOVER CHEM, 96- *Personal Data:* b Canton, Ohio, Aug 27, 49; m 71. *Educ:* Bowling Green State Univ, BS, 71, MS, 73; Mich State Univ, PhD(chem), 78. *Prof Exp:* Res scientist, Continental Oil Co, 77-80; res scientist, Lucidol Div, Pennwalt Corp, 80-89; sr res chemist, Akzo Chem, 89-91; res specialist, Quantum Chem, 91-93. *Mem:* Am Chem Soc. *Res:* Catalysts for polymers; additives for polymers. *Mailing Add:* 6125 Sandy Ridge Circle NW North Canton OH 44720-6689

STEIN, DAVID MORRIS, OPERATIONS RESEARCH, COMPUTER SCIENCE. *Current Pos:* Res scientist comput sci, 77-81, MEM TECH PLANNING STAFF, IBM CORP, 81-, DIR INVEST RES. *Personal Data:* b Johannesburg, SAfrica; m 75. *Educ:* Univ Witwatersrand, BSc, 72, MSc, 74; Harvard Univ, PhD(eng), 77. *Res:* Application of mathematical techniques to industrial problems; optimization, decision and control methods applied to transportation problems; performance and storage organizations for future computer systems. *Mailing Add:* 5 Sipperleys Hill Rd Westport CT 06880

STEIN, DIANA B, BOTANY, MOLECULAR EVOLUTION. *Current Pos:* from asst prof to assoc prof, 80-91, PROF BIOL SCI, MOUNT HOLYOKE COL, S HADLEY, MASS, 91-, CHAIR, 97- *Personal Data:* b New York, NY, July 5, 37; m 58, Otto L Stein; c Deborah Lee, Judith Ann, Suzanne Beth & Jonathan Henri Richard. *Educ:* Barnard Col, AB, 58; Univ Mont, MA, 61; Univ Mass, Amherst, PhD(molecular biol), 76. *Prof Exp:* Instr bot, Univ Mass, 64-69, instr plant physiol, 78, res assoc molecular biol, 76-79. *Concurrent Pos:* Mem, DNA Study Comn Amherst, 77-78, Biohazards Comn, Amherst Col, 78- & Amherst Bd Health, 84-93. *Mem:* Bot Soc Am; Am Soc Plant Physiol; Sigma Xi; AAAS; Soc Plant Molecular Biol; Soc Develop Biol. *Res:* DNA sequence comparisons; DNA protein interactions; molecular evolution of pterophyta (ferns). *Mailing Add:* Dept Biol Sci Mt Holyoke Col South Hadley MA 01075. *E-Mail:* dstein@mhc.mtholyoke.edu

STEIN, DONALD GERALD, PSYCHOPHYSIOLOGY, BIOPSYCHOLOGY. *Current Pos:* asst prof psychol & co-dir animal lab, 66-69, assoc prof psychol, 69-73, PROF PSYCHOL, CLARK UNIV, 73-, DIR, BRAIN RES FACIL, 73-; DEAN GRAD SCH & ASSOC PROVOST RES, RUTGERS UNIV, NEWARK, 88- *Personal Data:* b New York, NY, Jan 27, 39; m 60, Darel Hammer; c 2. *Educ:* Mich State Univ, BA, 60, MS, 62; Univ Ore, PhD(psychol), 65. *Prof Exp:* NIMH res fel, Mass Inst Technol, 65-66; prof neurol, Univ Mass Med Ctr, Worcester, 78-87. *Concurrent Pos:* USPHS res contract, 67; NSF res contract, 67-71; USPHS biomed sci grant, 69-, Fulbright awards, 71-75; NIMH res career develop award, 72-78; prof, Univ Nice, France, 77; vis scientist, Nat Inst Health & Med Res, Lyon, 75-76, Paris, 79; France Nat Inst Aging res contract, 76-79; vis scientist, Nat Asn Health & Med Res, Paris, 78, Univ L Pasteur, Strasbourg, France, 81-; Congressional fel sci & eng, AAAS, 80-81. *Mem:* Sigma Xi; Soc Neurosci; Psychonomic Soc; Europ Brain & Behav Soc; Int Soc Neuropsychol; fel AAAS. *Res:* Recovery from brain damage; aging and brain function; nerve growth factor and behavior; neuroplasticity. *Mailing Add:* Rutgers Univ Newark Campus 175 University Ave Newark NJ 07102-1814

STEIN, ELIAS M, MATHEMATICS. *Current Pos:* chmn dept, 68-71, PROF MATH, PRINCETON UNIV, 63- *Personal Data:* b Antwerp, Belg, Jan 13, 31; nat US; m 59; c 2. *Educ:* Univ Chicago, AB, 51, MS, 53, PhD, 55. *Prof Exp:* Instr, Mass Inst Technol, 56-58; mem fac, Univ Chicago, 58-62, assoc prof math, 61-62; mem, Inst Advan Study, 62-63. *Concurrent Pos:* Sloan Found res fel, 61-63; NSF sr fel, 62-63 & 71-72; sr vis fel, Sci Res Coun, Gt Brit, 68. *Mem:* Nat Acad Sci; Am Math Soc. *Res:* Topics in harmonic analysis related to the Littlewood-Paley theory; singular integrals and differentiality properties of functions. *Mailing Add:* Dept Math Princeton Univ Princeton NJ 08544

STEIN, FRANK S, PHYSICS. *Current Pos:* CONSULT, 87- *Personal Data:* b Lancaster, Pa, Jan 11, 21; m 47, Eleanor Bankoff; c Robert B, Joan (Jenkins) & William M. *Educ:* Franklin & Marshall Col, BS, 42; Columbia Univ, MA, 47; Univ Buffalo, PhD(physics), 51. *Honors & Awards:* Award of Excellence, Electronic Indust Asn, 85. *Prof Exp:* Res physicist, Manhattan Proj, Columbia Univ, 44-46; instr physics, Univ Buffalo, 48-51; res physicist res labs, Westinghouse Elec Corp, 51-55, mgr semiconductor dept electronic tube div, 55, mgr power devices develop sect semiconductor dept, 55-60; mgr eng semiconductor div, Gen Instrument Corp, NJ, 60-61, dir res appl res lab, 61-63; sr scientist semiconductor dept, Delco Radio Div, 63-66, chief engr solid state prod, Div, 66-75, chief engr advan eng, 75-83, mgr res & devel, Delco Electronics Div, Gen Motors Corp, 83-86. *Concurrent Pos:* Chmn joint electron device eng coun, Solid State Prod Eng Coun, 69-70 & 73-75; mem, Nat Acad Sci/Nat Acad Eng/Nat Res Coun Eval Panel Electronic Technol Div, Nat Bur Standards, 75-79. *Mem:* Inst Elec & Electronics Eng. *Res:* Mass spectrometry; properties of semiconductors and semiconductor devices; solid state electronics; microelectronics. *Mailing Add:* 3204 Tallyho Dr Kokomo IN 46902. *Fax:* 765-453-4792; *E-Mail:* fsstein@aol.com

STEIN, FRED P(AUL), THERMODYNAMIC PROPERTIES. *Current Pos:* from asst prof to assoc prof, 63-71, assoc chmn, 83-89, PROF CHEM ENG, LEHIGH UNIV, 71-, ASSOC CHMN, 91- *Personal Data:* b Dallastown, Pa, Nov 22, 34; m 56, Monica Bieri; c 3. *Educ:* Lehigh Univ, BS, 56; Univ Mich, MSE, 57, PhD(chem eng), 61. *Prof Exp:* Sr chem engr, Air Prod & Chem Inc, 60-61. *Concurrent Pos:* Consult, Picatinny Arsenal, 63-65; Gardner Cryogenics, 65-69, Hershey Foods Corp, 71-72 & Air Prod & Chem, 76-89; vis prof, Monash Univ, Melbourne, Australia, 73, Univ Queensland, Brisbane, 74 & Univ Canterbury, Christchurch, NZ, 89-90. *Mem:* Am Inst Chem Engrs; Am Chem Soc. *Res:* Phase equilibria at cryogenic temperatures, at supercritical conditions, and at high temperatures; thermodynamic properties of mixtures; air preheaters in power plants; equations of state for electrolyte mixtures. *Mailing Add:* Dept Chem Eng Lehigh Univ 111 Research Dr Bethlehem PA 18015-4791

STEIN, FREDERICK MAX, MATHEMATICS. *Current Pos:* assoc prof, 55-63, PROF MATH, COLO STATE UNIV, 63- *Personal Data:* b Wyaconda, Mo, Feb 17, 19; m 43; c 2. *Educ:* Iowa Wesleyan Col, AB, 40; Univ Iowa, MS, 47, PhD(math), 55. *Prof Exp:* Instr high schs, Iowa, 40-43; instr math, Univ Iowa, 43-44 & 53-54, asst, 46-47; assoc prof, Iowa Wesleyan Univ, 47-53. *Mem:* Am Math Soc; Math Asn Am. *Res:* Approximation; orthogonal functions; differential and integro-differential equations; Sturm-Liouville Systs. *Mailing Add:* 1212 W Olive St Ft Collins CO 80521-2450

STEIN, GARY S, GENE EXPRESSION. *Current Pos:* PROF & CHMN, DEPT CELL BIOL, UNIV MASS MED CTR, 87-; DEP DIR, UNIV MASS COMPREHENSIVE CANCER CTR. *Personal Data:* b Brooklyn, NY, July 30, 43; m 74. *Educ:* Hofstra Univ, BA, 65, MA, 66; Univ Vt, PhD(cell biol), 69. *Honors & Awards:* Elizabeth Uruston Lanier-Kappa Delta Award, Am Acad Orthop Surgeons & Orthop Res Soc, 93. *Prof Exp:* Res assoc biochem, Temple Univ, 71-72; prof biochem & molecular biol, 78-87, from asst prof to assoc prof biochem, Sch Med, Univ Fla, 72-78, assoc chmn dept, 81-87. *Concurrent Pos:* NIH fel, Sch Med, Temple Univ, 69-71; Damon Runyon Mem Fund cancer res grant, Sch Med, Univ Fla, 71-73; Am Cancer Soc, NSF & NIH grants, 74- *Mem:* AAAS; Am Soc Biol Chemists; Am Asn Cancer Res; Am Soc Cell Biol; Orthop Res Soc; Am Soc Bone & Mineral Res. *Res:* Molecular, biochemical, and cellular approaches to control of cell proliferation and differentiation in normal and tumor cells. *Mailing Add:* Dept Cell Biol Univ Mass Med Ctr 55 Lake Ave N Worcester MA 01655

STEIN, GEORGE NATHAN, RADIOLOGY. *Current Pos:* resident radiol, Grad Hosp, 47-49, assoc radiologist, 49-51, from instr to assoc prof, Div Grad Med, 51-61, assoc dir dept, Ctr, 67-71, dir dept radiol, Presby-Univ Pa Med Ctr, 71-84, prof, 61-88, EMER PROF RADIOL, SCH MED, UNIV OF PA, 88- *Personal Data:* b Philadelphia, Pa, Aug 11, 17; m 48; c 3. *Educ:* Univ Pa, BA, 38; Jefferson Med Col, MD, 42; Am Bd Radiol, dipl, 49. *Prof Exp:* Intern, Jewish Hosp, Philadelphia, 43. *Concurrent Pos:* Hon prof, Pontif Univ Javeriana, Colombia, 60. *Mem:* Radiol Soc NAm; Am Roentgen Ray Soc; fel Am Col Radiol. *Res:* Gastrointestinal radiology. *Mailing Add:* Dept Radiol Presby-Univ Pa Med Ctr 51 N 39th St Philadelphia PA 19104-2640

STEIN, GRETCHEN HERPEL, CELL BIOLOGY. *Current Pos:* res assoc cell biol & molecular biol, 74-81, ASSOC PROF, ATTEND RANK, DEPT MOLECULAR, CELLULAR & DEVELOP BIOL, UNIV COLO, 82- *Personal Data:* b Asbury Park, NJ, Mar 27, 45; m 66; c 1. *Educ:* Brown Univ, AB, 65; Stanford Univ, PhD(molecular biol), 71. *Prof Exp:* NIH fel cell biol, Sch Med, Stanford Univ, 71-73, res fel cell biol & molecular biol, 73-74. *Concurrent Pos:* Vis scientist, Cancer Biol Prog, Frederick Cancer Res Ctr, 80-81; consult health scientist adminr & mem, aging planning panel, Nat Inst Aging, 81, mem aging rev comt, 81-83, cell adv comt, 82- *Mem:* Am Soc Cell Biol; Tissue Cult Asn; Int Cell Cycle Soc. *Res:* Control of cellular proliferation in normal and neoplastic human cells; mechanism for cessation of proliferation in senescent cells. *Mailing Add:* Dept Biol Box 347 Univ Colo Boulder Boulder CO 80309-0347. *Fax:* 303-492-7744; *E-Mail:* stein@boulder.colorado.edu

STEIN, HARVEY PHILIP, ORGANIC CHEMISTRY, PUBLIC HEALTH. *Current Pos:* sr scientist, 75-83, SCIENTIST DIR, USPHS, 83- *Personal Data:* b Brooklyn, NY, May 4, 40; m 65; c 3. *Educ:* Queens Col, NY, BS, 61; Mass Inst Technol, PhD(org chem), 67. *Prof Exp:* Chemist, Stamford Res Labs, Am Cyanamid Co, summer 61; asst, Mass Inst Technol, 61-65; instr chem, Pa State Univ, 65-67, asst prof, 67-68; asst prof, Trenton State Col, 68-71; prof, Western Col, 71-75. *Res:* Reaction mechanisms; use of isotopes; biomedical effects of ethanol; public health; identification of previously unrecognized occupational hazards. *Mailing Add:* 11705 Silent Valley Lane Gaithersburg MD 20878-2433

STEIN, HERMAN H, BIOCHEMISTRY, PHARMACOLOGY. *Current Pos:* assoc fel, 72-76, RES FEL, PHARMACEUT PROD DIV, ABBOTT LABS, 76- *Personal Data:* b Chicago, Ill, May 27, 30; m 51; c 2. *Educ:* Univ Ill, BS, 51; Univ Minn, MS, 53; Northwestern Univ, PhD(chem), 56. *Prof Exp:* Lab asst, Northwestern Univ, 53-54; res chemist, Toni Co Div, Gillette Co, 56-61; sr res chemist, Abbott Labs, 61-66, group leader, 66, sect head, 67-72. *Mem:* Am Chem Soc; Am Soc Pharmacol & Exp Therapeut. *Res:* Enzymology; automated metabolic and enzymic analyses; antianginal agents; cyclic adenosine monophosphate metabolism; pharmacology of nucleosides; beta-adrenergic blocking agents; lipid metabolism; inhibitors of renin. *Mailing Add:* 240 Hastings Ave Highland Park IL 60035-5141

STEIN, HOLLY JAYNE, RHENIUM-OSMIUM ISOTOPE GEOCHEMISTRY, ISOTOPIC STUDIES OF ORE DEPOSITS. *Current Pos:* GEOLOGIST, US GEOL SURV, 82- *Personal Data:* b Memphis, Tenn, Oct 4, 54. *Educ:* Western Ill Univ, BS, 76; Univ NC, Chapel Hill, MS, 78, PhD(geol-geochem), 85. *Prof Exp:* Geologist, Climax Molybdenum Co, 78-80. *Concurrent Pos:* Adj fac, Univ Vt, 90-; assoc ed, Econ Geol, 91-95; Gilbert fel, US Geol Surv, 92-93; affil fac, Col State Univ, 95- *Mem:* Fel Soc Econ Geologists; Geol Soc Am; Geochem Soc & Meteoritical Soc; Sigma Xi; Am Geophys Union; Soc Geol Appl Mineral Deposits. *Res:* Application of rhenium-osmium isotopes to dating ore deposits; timing and duration of mineralizing events. *Mailing Add:* US Geol Surv 910 National Ctr Reston VA 20192. *Fax:* 703-648-6683; *E-Mail:* hstein@vsgs.gov

STEIN, HOWARD JAY, RESEARCH & DEVELOPMENT, CELL PHYSIOLOGY. *Current Pos:* assoc prof, 65-71, chmn dept, 66-68 & 71-75, PROF BIOL, GRAND VALLEY STATE COL, 71-, DIR RES & DEVELOP, 79 - *Personal Data:* b Baltimore, Md, May 28, 33; m 57; c 5. *Educ:* Temple Univ, BA, 54; Univ Mich, MA, 58, PhD(bot). 61. *Prof Exp:* From asst prof to assoc prof biol, Kans State Col, Pittsburg, 60-65. *Concurrent Pos:* NSF grant, 62-64; staff biologist, Off Biol Educ, Am Inst Biol Sci, 69-71, vis biologist, 71-72, curric consult bur, 71-74; NSF Grants, 68-70, 68-69, 79-80, 80-81; EESA Title II Grants, 86, 87, 88. *Mem:* AAAS; Nat Sci Teachers Asn; Sigma Xi; Nat Asn Biol Teachers; Fedn Am Scientists. *Res:* Amino acid metabolism in plant roots; metabolism in plant mitochondria; development of geoglossum. *Mailing Add:* Biol Grand Valley State Univ 1 Campus Dr Allendale MI 49401

STEIN, IRVING F, JR, SURGERY. *Current Pos:* Asst prof, 54-93, EMER PROF SURG, MED SCH, NORTHWESTERN UNIV, 93- *Personal Data:* b Chicago, Ill, July 6, 18; m 50; c 2. *Educ:* Dartmouth Col, AB, 39; Northwestern Univ, MS, 41, MD, 43, PhD, 51; Am Bd Surg, dipl, 50. *Concurrent Pos:* Attend surgeon, Cook County Hosp; chief surg, Highland Park Hosp. *Mem:* AAAS; fel AMA; fel Am Col Surg; Am Fedn Clin Res. *Res:* Gastrointestinal and surgical research; author of 50 papers. *Mailing Add:* Finch Univ Chicago Med Sch 3333 Green Bay Rd North Chicago IL 60064-3037

STEIN, IVIE, JR, MATHEMATICS. *Current Pos:* Asst prof, 71-75, ASSOC PROF MATH, UNIV TOLEDO, 75- *Personal Data:* b Orange, Calif, Dec 31, 40; m 79, Barbara E Schrader. *Educ:* Long Beach State Univ, BS, 62, MA, 63; Univ Calif, Los Angeles, CPhil, 70, PhD(math), 71. *Concurrent Pos:* Pac Missle Ctr, 66, 67, 68 & 74; Argonne Nat Lab, 72. *Mem:* Am Math Soc; Soc

Appl & Indust Math; Sigma Xi. *Res:* Calculus of variations; optimal control theory; numerical analysis; differential equations; optimization. *Mailing Add:* Dept Math Univ Toledo Toledo OH 43606-3390. *E-Mail:* istein@uoft02.utoledo.edu

STEIN, JACK J(OSEPH), ELECTRICAL ENGINEERING. *Current Pos:* ASSOC PROF ELEC ENG, GT VALLEY GRAD CTR, PA STATE UNIV, 67- *Personal Data:* b New York, NY, Feb 14, 38; m 59, Paula Korn; c 3. *Educ:* City Col New York, BEE, 59; Columbia Univ, MSEE, 60; NY Univ, DrEngSci, 65. *Prof Exp:* Res staff mem, IBM Res Div, Int Bus Mach Corp, 60-62; lectr, City Col New York, 62-63; instr, NY Univ, 63-65; systs engr, IBM Data Processing Div, Int Bus Mach Corp, 65-66; engr, Hughes Aircraft Co, 66-67. *Concurrent Pos:* Consult, Gen Elec, 68-69, Burroughs, 73-74. *Mem:* Inst Elec & Electronics Engrs. *Res:* Network theory; digital computers; solid state devices; biomedical simulation. *Mailing Add:* Pa State Great Valley 30 E Swedesford Rd Malvern PA 19355. *Fax:* 610-889-1334

STEIN, JAMES D, JR, MATHEMATICS. *Current Pos:* assoc prof, 74-79, PROF MATH, CALIF STATE UNIV, LONG BEACH, 90- *Personal Data:* b New York, NY, Aug 29, 41. *Educ:* Yale Univ, BA, 62; Univ Calif, Berkeley, MA & PhD(math), 67. *Prof Exp:* Asst prof math, Univ Calif, Los Angeles, 67-74, NSF grant, 70-74. *Mem:* Am Math Soc. *Res:* Banach algebras; continuity and boundedness problems in Banach spaces; measure theory; fixed points. *Mailing Add:* 13930 NW Passage Apt 210 Marina Del Rey CA 90291

STEIN, JANET LEE SWINEHART, GENE EXPRESSION, TRANSCRIPTION. *Current Pos:* PROF CELL BIOL, UNIV MASS MED CTR, 87- *Personal Data:* b Danville, Pa, Apr 3, 46; m 74, Gary S. *Educ:* Elizabethtown Col, BS, 68; Princeton Univ, MA, 71, PhD(chem), 75. *Prof Exp:* Res assoc biochem, 74-76, from asst prof to prof immunol & med microbiol, Univ Fla, 76-87. *Concurrent Pos:* Res grants, NSF, 75-90, Am Cancer Soc, 77-78, March of Dimes, 78- & NIH, 88-; mem, Physiol Chem Sect, NIH, 86-90, chair, 88-90; ed, Critical Rev Eukaryotic Gene Expression, 90- *Mem:* Am Soc Cell Biol; Am Chem Soc; AAAS; Am Soc Biochem Molecular Biol. *Res:* Regulation of gene expression, especially at the transcriptional level, in eukaryotic cells; structure and regulation of human histone genes; cell cycle and cell growth regulation. *Mailing Add:* Dept Cell Biol Univ Mass Med Ctr 55 Lake Ave N Worcester MA 01655-0106. *Fax:* 508-856-6800; *E-Mail:* jlstein@umassmed.ummed.edu

STEIN, JERRY MICHAEL, CONTACT LENSES, CARDIOVASCULAR PHYSIOLOGY. *Current Pos:* sr clin res assoc, 81-85, asst dir clin sci, 86-94, ASSOC DIR CLIN VISION CARE, ALCON LABS, FT WORTH, TEX, 94- *Personal Data:* b Brooklyn, NY, Jan 9, 52; m 74. *Educ:* Brooklyn Col, BA, 73; Syracuse Univ, MS & PhD(psychol), 77. *Prof Exp:* Res assoc physiol & biophys, Reg Primate Res Ctr, Univ Wash, 78-79; res assoc, Cardiovasc Ctr & Dept Psychol, Univ Iowa, Iowa City, 79-81. *Concurrent Pos:* Teaching asst, Syracuse Univ, 77; lectr psychol, Univ Wash, 78-, fel, Regional Primate Res Ctr, 78-79. *Mem:* Soc Neurosci; Assocs Clin Pharmacol. *Res:* Clinical testing of medical devices and ethical drugs; central nervous system control of cardiovascular physiology and renal functions. *Mailing Add:* Alcon Labs Mail Code R6-35 6201 S Freeway Ft Worth TX 76134-2099

STEIN, JOHN MICHAEL, SURGERY. *Current Pos:* DIR, BURN & TRAUMA CTR ARIZ, 89- *Personal Data:* b Vienna, Austria, May 29, 35; US citizen; m 69; c 4. *Educ:* Harvard Univ, AB, 57, MD, 61; Am Bd Surg, dipl, 68. *Prof Exp:* Assoc surg, New York Hosp-Cornell Med Ctr, 62-63; asst instr, Albert Einstein Col Med, 66-67; chief, Burn Study Br, US Army Inst Surg Res, Tex, 67-69; assoc prof surg & burns, Albert Einstein Col Med, 69-79; dir, Burn Unit, Aricopa Co Hosp, 79-89. *Concurrent Pos:* NIH fel surg, Albert Einstein Col Med, 64-65; pres med bd, Bronx Munic Hosp Ctr, 74-76; co-chmn burn comt & mem bd dirs Regional Emergency Med Servs, Coun of New York, 77- *Mem:* Am Burn Asn; NY Surg Soc; fel Am Col Surg; Am Trauma Soc; Asn Acad Surg. *Res:* Surgical training and research, expecially metabolic care of surgical and burned patients. *Mailing Add:* 3501 N Scottsdale Rd Ste 348 Scottsdale AZ 85251-5627

STEIN, KATHRYN E, IMMUNOCHEMISTRY, BIOCHEMISTRY. *Current Pos:* RES CHEMIST, OFF BIOL RES REV, US FOOD & DRUG ADMIN, 80- *Educ:* Albert Einstein Col Med, PhD(microbiol & immunol), 76. *Mailing Add:* Div Monoclonal Antibodies FDA CBER 8800 Rockville Pike Bethesda MD 20892-0029. *Fax:* 301-402-5943; *E-Mail:* stein@aicber.fda.gov

STEIN, LARRY, NEUROSCIENCE, BEHAVIOR. *Current Pos:* PROF & CHMN, DEPT PHARMACOL, COL MED, UNIV CALIF, IRVINE, 79- *Personal Data:* b New York, NY, Nov 10, 31; m 60, Marsha Kessler; c Richard & Charles. *Educ:* NY Univ, BA, 52; Univ Iowa, MA, 53, PhD, 55. *Honors & Awards:* Bennett Award, Soc Biol Psychiat, 61. *Prof Exp:* Res psychologist, Walter Reed Army Inst Res, 55-57 & Vet Admin Res Labs Neuropsychiat, 57-59; sr res scientist, Wyeth Labs, 59-64, mgr, Dept Psychopharmacol, 64-79. *Concurrent Pos:* Res assoc, Bryn Mawr Col, 61-72, adj prof, 72-; adj prof med sch, Univ Pa. *Mem:* Am Psychol Asn; Am Physiol Soc; Am Soc Pharmacol & Exp Therapeut; Soc Neurosci; Am col Neuropsychopharmacol. *Res:* Cellular mechanisms of reward and punishment, psychopharmacology, biological basis of schizophrenia and depression. *Mailing Add:* Dept Pharm Col Med MSII 360 Univ Calif Irvine CA 92717-0001. *Fax:* 714-824-4855; *E-Mail:* lstein@uci.edu

STEIN, LAWRENCE, INORGANIC CHEMISTRY, FLUORINE CHEMISTRY. *Current Pos:* RETIRED. *Personal Data:* b Hampton, Va, July 21, 22; m 52, Shirley Nerman; c Rachel & Susan. *Educ:* George Washington Univ, BS, 48; Univ Wis, PhD(chem), 52. *Prof Exp:* Anal chemist, Nat Bur Stands, 48; asst, Univ Wis, 50-51; chemist, Argonne Nat Lab, 51-88. *Concurrent Pos:* Adv panelist comt biol effects atmospheric pollutants, Nat Res Coun, 71-72; consult, Nat Inst Occup Saftey & Health, 73; consult, Gould, Inc, 83, Chicago Sanit Dist, 92, Air Liquide, 93. *Mem:* Fel AAAS; Am Chem Soc. *Res:* Fluorine chemistry; interhalogen compounds; chemistry of noble gases, particularly radon; environmental radiation; biologic effects of atmospheric pollutants; infrared spectroscopy; chemistry of actinide elements; laser raman spectroscopy. *Mailing Add:* 1223 Gilbert Ave Downers Grove IL 60515-4516

STEIN, LYNN ANDREA, ARTIFICIAL INTELLIGENCE. *Current Pos:* ASSOC PROF, DEPT ELEC ENG & COMPUT SCI, MASS INST TECHNOL. *Educ:* Harvard & Radcliffe Cols, AB, 86; Brown Univ, ScM, 87, PhD(comput sci), 90. *Honors & Awards:* Fac For Future Award, Gen Elect Found, 92; Young Investr Award, Nat Sci Found, 93. *Concurrent Pos:* From assoc chair to chair, Symposium Comt, Am Asn Artificial Intel, 91-96. *Mem:* Am Asn Artificial Intel. *Res:* Cognitive robotics; commonsense reasoning; software agents; human-computer interaction and collaboration; object-oriented programming. *Mailing Add:* Artificial Intel Lab Mass Inst Technol 545 Technology Sq No 811 Cambridge MA 02139. *Fax:* 617-253-5060; *E-Mail:* las@ai.mit.edu

STEIN, MARJORIE LEITER, PROBLEM SOLVING, NETWORK ANALYSIS. *Current Pos:* sr math statistician, US Postal Serv, 75-76, sr opers res analyst, 76-77, mgt analyst/prog mgr, 77-79, prin economist, 79-86, prog dir, Opers Res, 86-92, customer serv analyst, 92-96, STRATEGIC PLANNING SPECIALIST, US POSTAL SERV, 96- *Personal Data:* b New York, NY. *Educ:* Barnard Col, AB, 68; Princeton Univ, MA, 71, PhD(math), 72. *Prof Exp:* Res assoc, Math Res Ctr, Univ Wis, Madison, 72-73; lectr computer sci, Univ Wis, 73; res assoc, Nat Bur Standards, 73-75. *Concurrent Pos:* Vis lectr, Math Asn Am, 75-78; docent, Nat Mus Natural Hist, Smithsonian Inst, 76-96; gov-at-large, Math Asn Am, 77-80 & 88-91; mem coun, Asn Women Math, 78-91. *Mem:* Math Asn Am; Asn Women Math; Nat Geog Soc. *Res:* Combinatorial theory; networks; linear programming; applications to economics; managed development of decision support systems for postal management; long-term strategic planning. *Mailing Add:* US Postal Serv 475 L'Enfant Plaza West W Washington DC 20260-1520. *Fax:* 202-268-6269; *E-Mail:* mstein3@email.usps.gov

STEIN, MARVIN, PSYCHIATRY. *Current Pos:* Klingenstein Prof, 87-95, KLINGENSTEIN EMER PROF, MT SINAI SCH MED, 95- *Personal Data:* b St Louis, Mo, Dec 8, 23; m 50, Ann Hackman; c Leslie, David & Lisa. *Educ:* Washington Univ, BS & MD, 49. *Prof Exp:* Intern, St Louis City Hosp, 49-50; asst resident psychiat, Sch Med, Washington Univ, 50-51; asst instr, Sch Med, Univ Pa, 53-54, res assoc, 54-56, from asst prof to assoc prof, 56-63; prof, Med Col, Cornell Univ, 63-66; prof & chmn dept, Downstate Med Ctr, State Univ NY, 66-71; prof psychiat & chmn dept, Mt Sinai Sch Med, psychiatrist-in-chief, 71-87. *Concurrent Pos:* USPHS fel clin sch, Sch Med, Univ Pittsburgh, 51-53; fel psychiat, Sch Med, Univ Pa, 53-54; ment health career investr, NIMH, 56-61, mem, Ment Health Fels Rev Panel, 61-64, Ment Health Res Career Award Comt, 63-65, chmn, 65-67; mem, Behav Med Study Sect, 81-83 & Geriat Rev Comt, 86-88, NIH; chmn, Spec Rev Comt, Ment Health Aspects of Acquired Immune Deficiency Syndrome, 87-88, & chmn, Ment Health Acquired Immune Deficiency Syndrome Res Rev Comt, NIMH, 88-90; mem, NY Acad Med Acad Behav Med Res. *Mem:* Am Psychiat Asn (chmn res coun, 81-84); Asn Res Nerv & Ment Dis; Soc Biol Psychiat. *Res:* Brain and behavior; immunity; investigation of interaction of brain, endocrine and immune systems with an emphasis on the hypothalamic-pituitary-adrenal axis. *Mailing Add:* 5700 Arlington Ave 11J Riverdale NY 10471. *E-Mail:* ms7@doc.mssm.edu

STEIN, MARVIN L, MATHEMATICS, COMPUTER SCIENCE. *Current Pos:* from asst prof to prof math, Univ Minn, Minneapolis, 55-70, dir, Univ Comput Ctr, 58-70, actg head, Comput Info & Control Sci Dept, 70-71, dir grad studies, 87-90, PROF COMPUT SCI, UNIV MINN, MINNEAPOLIS, 70- *Personal Data:* b Cleveland, Ohio, July 15, 24; m 44; c 3. *Educ:* Univ Calif, Los Angeles, BA, 47, MA, 49, PhD, 51. *Prof Exp:* Asst math, Univ Calif, Los Angeles, 47-48, mathematician inst numerical anal, 48-52; sr res engr, Consol-Vultee Corp, 52-55. *Concurrent Pos:* Lectr, Univ Calif, Los Angeles, 54-55; Guggenheim fel, 63-64; vis prof, Tel Aviv Univ & Hebrew Univ, Jerusalem, 71-72. *Mem:* Am Math Soc; Soc Indust & Appl Math; Asn Comput Mach. *Res:* Numerical analysis; applications of super computers; parallel computer systems. *Mailing Add:* 8803 W 102nd Pl Apt D Overland Park KS 66212

STEIN, MICHAEL ROGER, ALGEBRAIC K-THEORY. *Current Pos:* Asst prof math, 70-74, assoc prof, 74-80, PROF MATH, NORTHWESTERN UNIV, EVANSTON, 80- *Personal Data:* b Milwaukee, Wis, Mar 21, 43; m 67; c 2. *Educ:* Harvard Univ, BA, 64; Columbia Univ, PhD(math), 70. *Concurrent Pos:* Fel, Hebrew Univ, Jerusalem, 72-73; Sci Res Coun sr vis fel, King's Col, Univ London, 77-78; vis scientist, Weizmann Inst Sci, 78; vis scholar, Univ Chicago, 84. *Mem:* Am Math Soc. *Res:* Algebraic K-theory; algebra. *Mailing Add:* Northwestern Univ 2033 Sheridan Rd Evanston IL 60208-2730

STEIN, MYRON, PHYSIOLOGY, MEDICINE. *Current Pos:* DIR PULMONARY DIV, BROTMAN MEM HOSP, 73- *Personal Data:* b East Boston, Mass, May 27, 25; m 53; c 4. *Educ:* Dartmouth Col, BA, 48; Tufts Univ, MD, 52. *Prof Exp:* Instr med, Harvard Med Sch, 57-64, assoc, 64-65; from assoc prof to prof med sci, Brown Univ, 69-73; prof med, Univ Calif, Los Angeles, 73- *Concurrent Pos:* Consult, Mass Rehab Comt, 60-65, Vet Admin Hosps, West Roxbury, 63- & Davis Park, RI, 65- *Mem:* Am Fedn Clin Res; Am Physiol Soc. *Res:* Pulmonary physiologic effects of pulmonary embolism; relationship of acid-base states and thyroid hormone transport; physiologic studies in clinical lung diseases. *Mailing Add:* 1156 San Ysidro Beverly Hills CA 90210

STEIN, OTTO LUDWIG, PLANT MORPHOGENESIS. *Current Pos:* head dept, 70-74, from assoc prof to prof, 64-90, EMER PROF BOT, UNIV MASS, AMHERST, 90- *Personal Data:* b Augsburg, Ger, Jan 14, 25; nat US; m 58, Diana Borut; c Deborah L, Suzanne B, Judith A & Jonathan H. *Educ:* Univ Minn, BS, 49, MS, 52, PhD(bot), 54. *Prof Exp:* Asst bot, Univ Minn, 48-53; instr, Univ Mo, 55; USPHS res fel, Brookhaven Nat Lab, 55-58; from asst prof to assoc prof bot, Mont State Univ, 58-64. *Concurrent Pos:* Res collab, Brookhaven Nat Lab, 58-70; vis asst prof, Univ Calif, 61-62; sr NATO res fel, Imp Col, Univ London, 71-72; dir, Univ Mass-Univ Freiburg, WGer, Exchange Prog, 79. *Mem:* Bot Soc Am; Soc Study Develop Biol; Soc Exp Biol & Med; Linnaean Soc, London. *Res:* Genetics; cytology; developmental anatomy of apical meristems and their derivatives. *Mailing Add:* Morrill Sci Ctr Amherst MA 01003

STEIN, PAUL DAVID, CARDIOLOGY, BIOENGINEERING. *Current Pos:* DIR CARDIOVASC RES, HENRY FORD HOSP, DETROIT, 76- *Personal Data:* b Cincinnati, Ohio, Apr 13, 34; m, Janet Tucker; c 3. *Educ:* Univ Cincinnati, BS, 55, MD, 59. *Prof Exp:* Fel cardiol, Col Med, Univ Cincinnati, 62-63 & Mt Sinai Hosp, New York, 63-64; res fel med, Peter Bent Brigham Hosp, Harvard Med Sch, Boston, 64-66; asst dir, catheterization lab, Baylor Univ Med Ctr, Dallas, 66-67; asst prof med, Creighton Univ, Omaha, 67-69; assoc prof, Col Med, Univ Okla, 69-73, res prof, 73-76. *Concurrent Pos:* Adj prof physics, Oakland Univ, Rochester, Mich, 85- *Mem:* Fel Am Col Cardiol; fel Am Col Chest Physicians (pres, 93); Am Heart Asn; Am Physiol Soc; Laennec Soc (pres); Cent Soc Clin Res; fel Am Col Physicians; fel Am Soc Mech Engrs; Int Acad Chest Physicians & Surgeons (pres, 93). *Res:* Cardiovascular research and bioengineering; left ventricular function; mechanisms of heart sounds; disturbances of fluid flow; bioprosthetic valves; pulmonary embolism. *Mailing Add:* Cardiac Wellness Ctr 6525 Second Ave Detroit MI 48202-3006. *Fax:* 313-972-1921

STEIN, PAUL JOHN, BIOCHEMISTRY, CHEMICAL EDUCATION. *Current Pos:* ASSOC PROF CHEM, COL ST SCHOLASTICA, 78- *Personal Data:* b Pittsburgh, Pa, Sept 28, 50; m 74, Molly Keating; c David, Mary & Peter. *Educ:* Bethany Col, WVa, BS, 72; Duke Univ, PhD(bioinorg chem), 76. *Prof Exp:* Res biochem, Inst Cancer Res, Fox Chase Cancer Inst, Philadelphia, 76-77. *Mem:* Am Chem Soc. *Res:* Fluorescence and nuclear magnetic resonance studies of enzymes; structure-function relationships of lectins. *Mailing Add:* Col St Scholastica 1200 Kenwood Ave Duluth MN 55811-4101. *E-Mail:* pstein@cssi.css.edu

STEIN, PAUL S G, NEUROBIOLOGY, MOTOR CONTROL. *Current Pos:* from asst prof to assoc prof, 71-86, PROF BIOL, WASHINGTON UNIV, 86- *Personal Data:* b New York, NY, Apr 3, 43. *Educ:* Harvard Univ, BA, 64; Univ Calif, Berkeley, MA, 65; Stanford Univ, PhD(neurosci), 70. *Prof Exp:* Fel neurosci, Univ Calif, San Diego, 69-71. *Mem:* Soc Neurosci; Int Soc Neuroethology. *Res:* Spinal cord control of limb movement; scratch reflex in turtles; neuronal pattern generation. *Mailing Add:* Dept Biol Washington Univ St Louis MO 63130-4899. *Fax:* 314-935-4432; *E-Mail:* stein@biodec.wustl.edu

STEIN, PHILIP, PHYSIOLOGY. *Current Pos:* ASSOC PROF BIOL, STATE UNIV NY COL, NEW PALTZ, 68- *Personal Data:* b New York, NY, Apr 28, 32. *Educ:* Brooklyn Col, BA, 53; George Washington Univ, MS, 54; Columbia Univ, MA, 59; Univ Geneva, PhD(biochem), 61. *Prof Exp:* Instr chem, Brooklyn Col, 60-62; instr, New York Community Col, 62-64; asst prof biol, Fairleigh Dickinson Univ, 64-68. *Concurrent Pos:* USPHS grant, 62-64; NSF grant, 64-; consult biochemist, Nat Sugar Industs; consult, Sugar Refinery, Pepsi Cola, 72- *Mem:* Fel Am Inst Chem; Am Chem Soc; Am Soc Biol Chemists. *Res:* Chemical composition of the thyrotropic hormone secreted by the anterior pituitary gland; role of hypothalamus in regulation of thyroid function. *Mailing Add:* Dept Biol State Univ NY Col New Paltz NY 12561. *Fax:* 914-257-3791; *E-Mail:* steind@matrix.newplatz.edu

STEIN, REINHARDT P, ORGANIC CHEMISTRY. *Current Pos:* res chemist, Wyeth Labs, Inc, 64-87, RES SCIENTIST, WYETH AYERST RES INC, 87- *Personal Data:* b New York, NY, Dec 19, 35; m 62; c 2. *Educ:* Rensselaer Polytech Inst, BS, 58; Ohio State Univ, PhD(org chem), 63. *Prof Exp:* Res chemist, Dow Chem Co, 63-64. *Mem:* Am Chem Soc; Sigma Xi; Molecular Graphics Soc. *Res:* Total synthesis of natural products; new totally synthetic steroids; structural elucidation of natural products; synthesis of new drugs; design of new drugs; computer graphics of drugs; molecular modeling of drugs; computer systems management; computational chemistry. *Mailing Add:* Wyeth-Ayerst Res Inc CN 8000 Princeton NJ 08543-8000

STEIN, RICHARD ADOLPH, ELECTRICAL ENGINEERING. *Current Pos:* assoc prof, 68-74, assoc dean, Fac Eng, 75-79, PROF ELEC ENG, UNIV CALGARY, 74- *Personal Data:* b Edmonton, Alta, May 17, 37. *Educ:* Univ Alta, BS, 58; Univ Ill, Urbana, MS, 61; Univ BC, PhD(elec eng), 68. *Prof Exp:* Asst prof elec eng, Univ Alta, 61-65. *Mem:* Inst Elec & Electronics Engrs; Am Soc Eng Educ. *Res:* Electrical circuit theory; electrical filter design; digital image processing. *Mailing Add:* Dept Elec Eng Univ Calgary 2500 Univ Dr NW Calgary AB T2N 1N4 Can

STEIN, RICHARD BALLIN, extractive metallurgy of light refractory metals, engineering design & construction of oil refineries & petrochemical plants, for more information see previous edition

STEIN, RICHARD BERNARD, NEUROPHYSIOLOGY, BIOPHYSICS. *Current Pos:* assoc prof physiol, 68-72, PROF PHYSIOL, UNIV ALTA, 72- *Personal Data:* b New Rochelle, NY, June 14, 40; m 62; c 2. *Educ:* Mass Inst Technol, BS, 62; Oxford Univ, MA & DPhil(physiol), 66. *Hon Degrees:* DSc, Univ Waterloo. *Prof Exp:* Res fel med res, Exeter Col, Oxford Univ, 65-68. *Concurrent Pos:* USPHS fel, 66-68. *Mem:* Brit Physiol Soc; Can Physiol Soc; Neurosci Soc. *Res:* Motor control; information processing by nerve cells; sensory feedback; neural models. *Mailing Add:* Dept Physiol Univ Alberta Fac Med Edmonton AB T6G 2R7 Can

STEIN, RICHARD JAMES, POLYMER CHEMISTRY. *Current Pos:* RETIRED. *Personal Data:* b Palmerton, Pa, Aug 10, 30; m 53. *Educ:* Pa State Univ, BS, 58; Univ Akron, MS, 60, PhD(polymer chem), 67. *Prof Exp:* Res chemist, Goodyear Tire & Rubber Co, 60-63, sr res chemist, 66-71; polymer specialist, Insulating Mat Dept, Gen Elec Co, 71-85, staff chemist, 85-88; staff chemist, Insulating Mat Inc, 88-89, chief chemist, 89-96. *Mem:* Am Chem Soc; AAAS. *Res:* Polymer synthesis and properties. *Mailing Add:* 239 Pinewood Dr Schenectady NY 12303

STEIN, RICHARD JAY, GLOW-DISCHARGE PROCESSES, EQUIPMENT DESIGN. *Current Pos:* OWNER, R J STEIN ASSOCS, 86- *Personal Data:* b New York, NY, Jan 22, 46. *Educ:* Mass Inst Technol, SB, 67; Polytech Inst Brooklyn, MS, 70, PhD(physics), 72. *Prof Exp:* Res Scientist, Nat Bur Stand, 72-76; sr staff, Tex Instruments Res, 76-80 & GTE Labs, 80-81; mgr res & develop, Balzers Inc, 82-83; sr scientist, Perkin-Elmer Corp, 84-86. *Res:* Microelectronic and coating equipment and process. *Mailing Add:* PO Box 252 West Redding CT 06896

STEIN, RICHARD LOUIS, DRUG DESIGN USING COMPUTER MODELING. *Current Pos:* From asst prof to assoc prof, Germanna Community Col, 70-75, prog head, Sci Dept, 70-84, actg div chmn technol, 79-80, PROF CHEM, GERMANNA COMMUNITY COL, 75- *Personal Data:* b Washington, DC, July 7, 44; m 68, Jane T Taylor. *Educ:* George Washington Univ, BS, 66; Med Col Va, PhD(med chem), 70. *Concurrent Pos:* Vis Scientist, Va Acad Sci, 80-; grants, Inst Instrnl Excellence, 85. *Mem:* Fel Am Inst Chemists; Am Chem Soc; AAAS; Sigma Xi. *Res:* Molecular design and synthesis of new pharmacological agents using computer assisted molecular modeling and structure activity relationships. *Mailing Add:* Germanna Community Col 15015 Gen Longstreet Ave Culpeper VA 22701. *E-Mail:* gesteid@gc.cc.va.us

STEIN, RICHARD STEPHEN, POLYMER CHEMISTRY. *Current Pos:* from asst prof to prof, Univ Mass, Amherst, 50-61, commonwealth prof, 61-80, Goessman prof chem & dir, Polymer Res Inst, 80-91, EMER GOESSMAN PROF CHEM, UNIV MASS, AMHERST, 91- *Personal Data:* b Far Rockaway, NY, Aug 21, 25; m 51, Judith Belise; c Linda, Anne, Carol & Lisa. *Educ:* Polytech Inst Brooklyn, BS, 45; Princeton Univ, MA, 48, PhD(phys chem), 49. *Hon Degrees:* DSc, Univ Ulm & Univ Mass. *Honors & Awards:* Int Award, Soc Plastics Eng, 69; Borden Award, Am Chem Soc, 72, Award in Polymer Chem, 83; Bingham Medal, Soc Rheol, 72; High Polymer Physics Award, Am Phys Soc, 76. *Prof Exp:* Asst, Polytech Inst Brooklyn, 45; asst, Princeton Univ, 49-50. *Concurrent Pos:* Fulbright vis prof, Kyoto Univ, 68; Ecole Super physics & chem, Paris, 86 & Univ Ulm, 88; vis prof, Syracuse Univ, 88, Lavol Univ, 52. *Mem:* Nat Acad Sci; Nat Acad Eng; Soc Rheol; Soc Polymer Sci Jap; Am Chem Soc; AAAS; Mat Res Soc; Am Phys Soc; Am Acad Arts & Sci. *Res:* Molecular structure; light scattering; mechanical and optical properties of high polymers. *Mailing Add:* Conte Polymer Ctr Univ Mass Amherst MA 01003. *Fax:* 413-545-0082; *E-Mail:* stein@ecs.umass.edu

STEIN, ROBERT ALFRED, WEAPON SYSTEM ANALYSIS, ENGINEERING MECHANICS. *Current Pos:* Prin physicist, Dept Physics & Metall, Columbus Labs, Battelle Mem Inst, 55-60, sr physicist, 60-63, prog mgr, 63-66, assoc div chief, 66-70, asst sect mgr, 72-73, sect mgr, Defense Anal, 73-76, div chief, 70-76, assoc dir, Advan Syst Lab, 76-86, PROG MGR, ADV TECHNOL OFF, BATTELLE MEM INST, 86- *Personal Data:* b Chicago, Ill, Feb 20, 33; m 56; c 2. *Educ:* Univ Ill, BS, 55; Ohio State Univ, MS, 58, PhD, 67. *Concurrent Pos:* Guest ed, J Defense Res, 77. *Mem:* AAAS; Am Defense Preparedness Asn. *Res:* Hypervelocity impact phenomena and development of hypervelocity accelerators; weapon systems analysis; non-nuclear kill mechanisms; naval ordnance systems; army combat vehicle systems; terminal ballistics. *Mailing Add:* 11521 Danville Dr Rockville MD 20852

STEIN, ROBERT FOSTER, ASTROPHYSICAL FLUID DYNAMICS. *Current Pos:* assoc prof astrophys, 76-81, PROF ASTROPHYS, MICH STATE UNIV, 81- *Personal Data:* b New York, NY, Mar 4, 35; m 58, Laura Cooper; c Karen & Tamara. *Educ:* Univ Chicago, BS, 57; Columbia Univ, PhD(physics), 66. *Prof Exp:* Res fel, Carnegie Inst Wash Mt Wilson & Palomar Observs, 66-67; res fel, Harvard Observ, 67-69; asst prof astrophys, Brandeis Univ, 69-76. *Concurrent Pos:* Consult, Smithsonian Astrophys

Observ, 69-78; vis fel joint inst lab astrophys, Nat Bur Stand & Univ Colo, 73-74; vis scientist, Observatoire de Nice, 81, Univ St Andrews, 84, Nordita, 86; consult, Jet Propulsion Lab, 83-85. *Mem:* Am Astron Soc; Int Astron Union; Norwegian Acad Sci & Letters. *Res:* Astrophysical fluid dynamics; solar chromosphere and corona; radiative hydrodynamics; convection; computational magneto-hydrodynamics. *Mailing Add:* Dept Physics & Astron Mich State Univ East Lansing MI 48824. *E-Mail:* stein@msu.edu

STEIN, ROBERT G, LOGISTICS MANAGEMENT, SYSTEMS MANAGEMENT. *Current Pos:* DEAN, ARTS, MGT & LOGISTICS, COLO TECH, 89- *Personal Data:* b Bedford, Ohio, Nov 5, 34; m 59, Arlene Patterson; c Robert G, Robyn & Gifford. *Educ:* Ohio State Univ, BS, 56; Univ Detroit, MBA, 66; Univ Utah, PhD (educ admin), 75; Weber State Univ, BS, 78. *Honors & Awards:* Eccles Medal, Soc Logistics Engrs, 86. *Prof Exp:* Logistics engr, USAF, 57-70; prof logistics, Weber State Univ, 70-84; sr logistics engr, Res Anal Corp, 85-87; prof logistics & dir, Nat Univ, 87-88; Brig Gen, USAFR, 87-92. *Concurrent Pos:* Dist dir, Soc Logistics Engrs, 79-85; vpres, Decision Visability Assocs, 80-85; vis prof logistics, Hughes Aircraft Corp, 85. *Mem:* Fel Soc Logistics Engrs; Logistics Educ Found (vpres, 84-86); Am Prod & Inventory Control Soc; Nat Defense Transp Asn; Armed Forces Communs & Electronics Asn. *Res:* Futuristic logistics; nontraditional adult general education; total quality management and university education. *Mailing Add:* 5965 Wilson Rd Colorado Springs CO 80919. *Fax:* 719-598-3740; *E-Mail:* astein1752@aol.com

STEIN, ROY ALLEN, ZOOLOGY, AQUATIC ECOLOGY. *Current Pos:* ASST PROF ZOOL, OHIO STATE UNIV, 76- *Personal Data:* b Warren, Ohio, Aug 28, 47; m 73. *Educ:* Univ Mich, BS, 69; Ore State Univ, MS, 71; Univ Wis, PhD(zool), 75. *Prof Exp:* Partic scientist fisheries, Smithsonian Inst, 72; res assoc zool, Univ Wis, 76. *Mem:* Am Fisheries Soc; Am Inst Biol Sci; AAAS; Ecol Soc Am; Sigma Xi. *Res:* Behavioral ecology with a major emphasis on intra- and inter-specific interactions among aquatic organisms, specifically fish; examining how two important processes (predation and competition) structure fresh water communities. *Mailing Add:* Ohio State Univ 1314 Kinnear Rd Columbus OH 43212

STEIN, RUTH E K, MEDICINE. *Current Pos:* From instr to assoc prof, 70-83, PROF, DEPT PEDIAT, ALBERT EINSTEIN COL MED, 83-, VCHMN, 92- *Personal Data:* b New York, NY, Nov 2, 41; m 63, H David; c Lynn, Sharon & Deborah. *Educ:* Columbia Univ, New York, BA, 62; Albert Einstein Col, New York, MD, 66. *Honors & Awards:* Schick Medalist, Dept Pediat, 90, Ambulatory Pediat Asn Res Award, 95. *Concurrent Pos:* Jacob I Berman & Dora B Friedman fel pediat, Albert Einstein Col Med, 76, 77-83, dir, Pediat Ambulatory Care Treatment Study, 77-83, Prev Intervention Res Ctr Child Health, 83-93; vis scholar Robert Woods Johns Clin Scholars Prog, Sch Med, Yale Univ, New Haven, Conn, 86-87, vis prof pub health, Dept Epidemiol & Pub Health, 86-87; mem, Pediat Emer Serv Comt, Inst Med, 91-92; dir radiat, Jacolni Med Ctr, 92- *Mem:* Ambulatory Pediat Asn (pres, 87-88); Am Acad Pediat; Am Pub Health Asn; Am Pediat Soc; Soc Pediat Res; Soc Behav Pediat. *Res:* Medical and health sciences; child health especially psychological and social consequences of chronic conditions and measurement of child health status. *Mailing Add:* Albert Einstein Col Med 1300 Morris Park Ave Bronx NY 10461-1924. *Fax:* 718-918-5007; *E-Mail:* rstein@aecom.yu.edu

STEIN, SAMUEL H, PHOTOGRAPHIC SCIENCE & PHYSICAL ORGANIC CHEMISTRY, GRAPHIC ARTS. *Current Pos:* TECH DIR, THERIMAGE DIV, AVERY DENNISON, 89- *Personal Data:* b New York, NY, Jan 6, 37; m 57; c 3. *Educ:* City Col New York, BS, 57; Boston Univ, PhD(org chem), 67. *Prof Exp:* Res chemist, Nat Cash Register Co, Ohio, 57-59; res chemist, Itek Corp, summer 60, sr res chemist & proj leader org chem, Lexington Res Labs, 65-68, mgr paper develop group, Lexington Develop Labs, 68-69, mgr sci staff negative lithographic plate group, 69-71, mgr positive lithographic plate group, 71-72, mgr lithographic systs res dept, Lithographic Technol Lab, 72-74; mgr emulsion res, Chemco PhotoProd, 74-79, mem staff, New Prod Comt & Strategic Planning Comt, 79-84, dir emultion res & develop, 80-84; consult, Sesame Assocs, 84-87; tech dir, Citiplate, Inc, 87-89. *Concurrent Pos:* Consult, Sesame Assocs. *Mem:* AAAS; Am Chem Soc; Soc Photog Sci & Eng; Sigma Xi; Am Soc Qual Control. *Res:* Photochemistry, including unconventional photographic process and silver halide photo processes; silver halide emulsions for positive and negative systems; photoconductors, photopolymers and heterogeneous catalysis; graphic arts. *Mailing Add:* Nine Mathieu Dr Westborough MA 01581-3560

STEIN, SAMUEL RICHARD, PHYSICS. *Current Pos:* Physicist time & frequency, 74-80, CHIEF PROG OFF, NAT BUR STANDARDS, 80- *Personal Data:* b New York, NY, Jan 7, 46; m 66. *Educ:* Brown Univ, ScB & ScM, 66; Stanford Univ, PhD(physics), 74. *Concurrent Pos:* Nat Res Coun fel, Nat Bur Standards, 74-76. *Mem:* Am Phys Soc. *Res:* Frequency standards; frequency metrology; superconductivity; lasers; quartz crystal oscillators. *Mailing Add:* 1180 Poplar Ave Boulder CO 80304

STEIN, SETH AVRAM, SEISMOLOGY, PLATE TECTONICS. *Current Pos:* from asst prof to assoc prof, 79-87, chmn, 89-92, PROF GEOL SCI, NORTHWESTERN UNIV, 87- *Personal Data:* b Middletown, Conn, July 12, 53; m 82, Carol A Geller; c David & Rachel. *Educ:* Mass Inst Technol, SB, 75; Calif Inst Technol, MS, 77, PhD(geophys), 78. *Honors & Awards:* UNESCO lectr, Int Inst Seismol, Japan, 85; J B Macelwayne Medal, Am Geophys Union, 89. *Prof Exp:* Res affil geophys, Stanford Univ, 78-79. *Concurrent Pos:* Assoc ed, J Geophys Res, 86, Geophys Res Lett, 86, ed, 86-89; vis sr scientist, Goddard Space Flight Ctr, NASA, 93-94. *Mem:* Fel Am Geophys Union; Seismol Soc Am; fel Royal Astron Soc. *Res:* Investigation of plate tectonic processes using seismology; space based geodesy; marine geophysics; thermal/mechanical modeling of the lithosphere. *Mailing Add:* Dept Geol Sci Northwestern Univ 309 Locy Hall Evanston IL 60201-5096. *Fax:* 847-491-8060; *E-Mail:* seth@earth.nwu.edu

STEIN, SEYMOUR NORMAN, PHYSIOLOGY. *Current Pos:* PROF PHYSIOL, SAN JOSE STATE UNIV, 77- *Personal Data:* b Chicago, Ill, Nov 23, 13; m 36; c 1. *Educ:* Univ Ill, BS, 41, MD, 43. *Honors & Awards:* Aerospace Contribution to Soc Medal, Am Inst Aeronaut & Astronaut, 80. *Prof Exp:* From res asst to res assoc neurophysiol, Univ Ill, 46-49, asst prof & res physiologist, 49-51; head neurophysiol br & submarine & diving med br, Naval Med Res Inst, 52-60, head physiol div, 53-57; dep bio-sci officer, Pac Missile Range, US Dept Navy, 61-63; chief life sci officer, NASA-Ames Res Ctr, 64-65, chief med officer, 66-71, guest scientist, 71- *Concurrent Pos:* Consult, Surgeon Gen, US Dept Army, 47-, NIMH, 53-; mem panel underwater swimmers, Nat Res Coun, 54-55; ed, J Biol Photog Asn, 56; pres, The Perham Found, 74-82, bd dirs, 75- *Mem:* Fel AAAS; Am Physiol Soc; Soc Exp Biol & Med; Biol Photog Asn; assoc fel Am Inst Aeronaut & Astronaut; Sigma Xi. *Res:* Basic and clinical studies on convulsions; effects of acute and chronic exposure to hypernormal amounts of carbon dioxide and oxygen; space medicine; bioinstrumentation. *Mailing Add:* 13080 Lorene Ct Mountain View CA 94040

STEIN, SHERMAN KOPALD, MATHEMATICS. *Current Pos:* RETIRED. *Personal Data:* b Minneapolis, Minn, Aug 11, 26; m 50, Hannah Dunitz; c Joshua, Rebecca & Suzanna. *Educ:* Calif Inst Technol, BSc, 46; Columbia Univ, MA, 47, PhD(math), 52. *Hon Degrees:* DH, Marietta Col, 75. *Honors & Awards:* L R Ford Award, Math Asn Am, 75. *Prof Exp:* Prof math, Univ Calif, Davis, 53-93. *Mem:* Am Math Soc; Math Asn Am. *Res:* Algebraic applications to geometry. *Mailing Add:* Dept Math Univ Calif Davis CA 95616. *E-Mail:* stein@math.ucdavis.edu

STEIN, STEPHEN ELLERY, PHYSICAL CHEMISTRY, CHEMICAL KINETICS. *Current Pos:* RES CHEMIST, NAT BUR STANDARDS, 82-, ACTG CHIEF, CHEM KINETICS DIV. *Personal Data:* b New York, NY, Dec 13, 48; m 74. *Educ:* Univ Rochester, BS, 69; Univ Wash, PhD(phys chem), 74. *Prof Exp:* Res assoc, SRI Int, 74-75; phys chemist, 75-76; asst prof, Dept Chem, WVa Univ, 76-81, assoc prof, 81-82. *Mem:* NAm Photochem Soc; Am Chem Soc. *Res:* Thermochemistry and kinetics of elementary chemical reactions; rate and thermochemical estimation methods; unimolecular reactions; high temperature free radical reactions; gas-surface reactions; liquid-phase pyrolysis; analysis of complex reacting systems; coal conversion chemistry; combustion; ignition processes. *Mailing Add:* A111/221 Nat Inst Stand & Technol Gaithersburg MD 20899

STEIN, T PETER, BIOCHEMISTRY. *Current Pos:* PROF SURG & NUTRIT, SCH MED, UNIV MED & DENT OF NJ, 86- *Personal Data:* b London, Eng, Apr 27, 41; m 67. *Educ:* Univ London, BSc, 62; MSc, 63; Cornell Univ, PhD(chem), 67. *Prof Exp:* Asst chem, Cornell Univ, 63-67; instr res surg & biochem, Sch Med, Univ Pa, 69-72, assoc prof surg, 72-86. *Concurrent Pos:* NIH fel biochem, Univ Calif, Los Angeles, 67-69; adj prof surg, Univ Pa; adj prof nutrit, Rutgers Univ. *Mem:* AAAS; Am Chem Soc; Royal Soc Chem; Am Inst Nutrit; Am Soc Clin Nutrit; Am Physiol Soc; Am Col Nutrit; Am Soc Parenteral & Enteral Nutrit. *Res:* Protein metabolism during spacelift; lipid metabolism, clinical nutrition, nutritional assessment; nitrogen-15 metabolism and rates of protein synthesis in man; lung biochemistry. *Mailing Add:* UMDNJ Sch Osteo Med 106 Sci Ctr 2 Med Ctr Dr Stratford NJ 08084

STEIN, TALBERT SHELDON, POSITRON-ATOM SCATTERING EXPERIMENTS. *Current Pos:* from asst prof to assoc prof, 70-82, PROF PHYSICS, WAYNE STATE UNIV, 82- *Personal Data:* b Detroit, Mich, Jan 6, 41; m 63; c 2. *Educ:* Wayne State Univ, BS, 62; Brandeis Univ, MA, 64, PhD(physics), 68. *Prof Exp:* Res assoc physics, Univ Wash, 67-70. *Concurrent Pos:* Alfred P Sloan res fel, 76-80. *Mem:* Fel Am Phys Soc; Am Asn Physics Teachers. *Res:* Experimental atomic physics including low energy positron-atom interactions; precision measurement of the g factor of the free electron; studies of effects of electric fields on neutral atoms. *Mailing Add:* 26707 Humber Huntington Woods MI 48070. *Fax:* 313-577-3932; *E-Mail:* stein@hal.physics.wayne.edu

STEIN, THEODORE ANTHONY, PHOSPHOLIPIDS, CELL SIGNAL TRANSMISSION. *Current Pos:* DIR RES, LI VASCULAR CTR, 94- *Personal Data:* b St Louis, Mo, Aug 30, 38; m, Virginia Loos. *Educ:* St Louis Univ, BS, 60; Southern Ill Univ-Carbondale, MS, 70; City Univ NY, PhD(biochem), 88. *Prof Exp:* From res asst to res instr biochem, Sch Med, Wash Univ, 72-75; res supvr biochem, Long Island Jewish Med Ctr, 75-77, res coordr, biochem/physiol, 77-88, res scientist, biochem/physiol & surg, 88-94. *Concurrent Pos:* Res asst prof, State Univ NY, Stony Brook, 78-89; asst prof, Albert Einstein Col Med, 89-94. *Mem:* Sigma Xi; Am Pub Health Asn; Am Asn Clin Chem; Am Gastroenterol Asn; Am Fedn Clin Res; AAAS. *Res:* Role of prostaglandins and leukotrienes in inflammatory bowel disease, gastric ulcer and motility; regulation of liver regeneration after partial hepatic resection; changes in pancreatic physiology associated with pharmacological agents; development of chromatographic methodologies to measure chemotherapeutic agents in tissue and tumor factors affecting graft failure after vascular bypass procedures; reduction of stroke rate. *Mailing Add:* LI Vascular Ctr 1050 Northerd Blvd Roslyn NY 11576

STEIN, WAYNE ALFRED, ASTROPHYSICS. *Current Pos:* FAC, UNIV CALIF, 94- *Personal Data:* b Minneapolis, Minn, Dec 6, 37. *Educ:* Univ Minn, BPhys, 59, PhD(physics), 64. *Prof Exp:* Res assoc astrophys, Princeton Univ, 64-66; asst res physicist, Univ Calif, San Diego, 66-69, asst prof to prof; from asst prof to assoc prof astrophys, Univ Minn, 69-74, prof physics, 74-94. *Concurrent Pos:* Alfred P Sloan Found fel, Univ Minn, Minneapolis & Univ Calif, San Diego, 69- *Mem:* Am Astron Soc; Am Phys Soc. *Res:* Infrared astronomy; active galaxies. *Mailing Add:* Univ Calif CASS-0111 La Hoya CA 92093

STEIN, WILLIAM EARL, ELECTRON PHYSICS, NUCLEAR PHYSICS. *Current Pos:* PHYSICIST, KIRK MAYER, 82- *Personal Data:* b Rochester, NY, May 30, 24; m 47; c 4. *Educ:* Univ Va, BEE, 46; Stanford Univ, MS, 50; Univ NMex, PhD(physics), 62. *Prof Exp:* Physicist, Los Alamos Sci Lab, 49-82. *Mem:* Am Phys Soc. *Res:* Electron-photon interactions and production of nearly monochromatic soft x-rays by the inverse Compton effect. *Mailing Add:* 124 Monte Rey Dr N Los Alamos NM 87544

STEIN, WILLIAM EDWARD, OPERATIONS RESEARCH. *Current Pos:* ASSOC PROF BUS, TEX A&M UNIV, 82- *Personal Data:* b Cleveland, Ohio, June 18, 46. *Educ:* Case Western Res Univ, BS, 68; Purdue Univ, MS, 70; Univ NC, PhD(opers res), 75. *Prof Exp:* Asst prof math, Univ Ill, Chicago, 74-77; assoc prof math, Tex Christion Univ, 77-82. *Mem:* Opers Res Soc; Inst Mgt Sci; Asn Comput Mach. *Res:* Applied probability; fuzzy sets; stochastic dominance. *Mailing Add:* Dept Bus Analysis Tex A&M Univ 322 Wehner College Station TX 77843-4217

STEIN, WILLIAM IVO, REFORESTATION, FOREST ECOLOGY. *Current Pos:* Forester timber mgt res, Pac Northwest Res Sta, US Forest Serv, 48-52, asst res forester, 52-63, prin plant ecologist, 63-80, res forester, 80-90, VOL, PAC NORTHWEST RES STA, US FOREST SERV, 90- *Personal Data:* b Wurzburg, Ger, July 22, 22; nat US; m 48, Dorothy E Palmblad; c Clifford, Kathleen, Roderick, Bradford, Benjamin, Lawrence, Margaret, Randolph, Nicholas, Clarence, Patricia & Charlene. *Educ:* Pac Col, BS, 43; Ore State Univ, BF, 48; Yale Univ, MF, 52, PhD(forest ecol), 63. *Concurrent Pos:* Mem, Western Forest Tree Seed Coun, Western Forestry & Conserv Asn, 53-90, Exec Comt, 68-78, secy, 68-71, chmn, Western Reforestation Comt, 72-75; Mem, Nat Tree Seed Comt, Soc Am Foresters, 67-71, Comt Nursery Stock Measurement Procedures, 67-68. *Mem:* Fel Soc Am Foresters; Nature Conservancy; Am Forestry Asn; Sigma Xi. *Res:* Study of ecology and physiology of Pacific Northwest species for the purpose of improving reforestation practices; reforestation research. *Mailing Add:* Forestry Sci Lab USDA Forest Serv 3200 SW Jefferson Way Corvallis OR 97331

STEINBACH, LEONARD, ORGANIC CHEMISTRY. *Current Pos:* Group leader org res, 56-62, prod mgr, 63-64, dir res & develop, 65, dir corp develop, 66-67, gen mgr, 67-69, vpres, 69-74, VPRES CORP DIR PURCHASING, INT FLAVORS & FRAGRANCES, INC, HAZLET, 74- *Personal Data:* b New York, NY, Feb 26, 27; m 51; c 3. *Educ:* City Col New York, BS, 47; Polytech Inst Brooklyn, MS, 54. *Concurrent Pos:* Mem chm fac, Monmouth Col, 56-61. *Mem:* AAAS; Am Chem Soc; NY Acad Sci. *Res:* Organic synthesis and development in aromatic chemicals, perfumes and flavor materials. *Mailing Add:* 10 Ramsgate Rd Cranford NJ 07016

STEINBECK, KLAUS, FORESTRY, SILVICULTURE. *Current Pos:* asst prof, 69-72, assoc prof, 72-81, PROF FOREST RESOURCES, UNIV GA, 81- *Personal Data:* b Munich, Ger, Dec 11, 37; US citizen; m 60; c 4. *Educ:* Univ Ga, BSF, 61, MS, 63; Mich State Univ, PhD(forestry), 65. *Prof Exp:* Res plant physiologist, US Forest Serv, 65-68. *Mem:* Soc Am Foresters. *Res:* Biomass production of short-rotation forests. *Mailing Add:* Sch Forest Resources Univ Ga 1180 E Broad St Athens GA 30602-3040

STEINBERG, ALFRED DAVID, IMMUNOLOGY, RHEUMATOLOGY. *Current Pos:* MED DIR, US PUB HEALTH SERV, 78- *Personal Data:* b New York, NY, Nov 4, 40; m; c 4. *Educ:* Princeton Univ, AB, 62; Harvard Univ, MD, 66. *Honors & Awards:* Philip Hench Award, 74; Hollister-Stiers lectr, Wash State Univ, 85; Nelson lectr, Univ Calif, 87. *Prof Exp:* Intern & resident internal med, Bronx Munic Hosp Ctr, 66-68; clin assoc, 68-70, NIH, sr staff fel, 70-71, sr investr, 71-81, chief, Cellular Immunol Sect, Nat Inst Arthritis, Diabetes & Digestive & Kidney Dis, 81-86, Chief, Immunol Sect, Arthritis & Rheumatism Br, Nat Inst Arthritis, Metab & Digestive Dis, NIH, 86- *Concurrent Pos:* Clin Res Comt, NIH, 71-72, Peer Rev Comt, 72-74; USA-USSR Coop in Rheumatol & Immunol, 74-87; Lupus Study Group, Arthritis Found, 82-89, pres, 86-87; vis prof, Yale Univ, 81, Univ Calif, 82, 84 & 88, Univ Vienna, Austria, 83. *Mem:* NY Acad Sci; Am Fedn Clin Res; Am Rheumatism Asn; Am Asn Immunologists; Am Soc Exp Path; Am Soc Clin Invest; fel Am Col Physicians; Soc Exp Biol & Med; Transplantation Soc. *Res:* Autoimmunity; immune regulation. *Mailing Add:* 8814 Bells Mill Rd Potomac MD 20854. *Fax:* 703-883-1951

STEINBERG, ARTHUR GERALD, MEDICAL GENETICS, HUMAN GENETICS. *Current Pos:* prof biol, Case Western Reserve Univ, 56-72, from asst prof to assoc prof, Dept Prev Med, 56-70, prof human genetics, Dept Reproductive Biol, 70-75, Francis Hobart Herrick prof biol, 72-82, prof human genetics, Dept Med, 75-82, FRANCIS HOBART HERRICK EMER PROF BIOL, 82- *Personal Data:* b Port Chester, NY, Feb 27, 12; m 39; c 2. *Educ:* City Col New York, BSc, 33; Columbia Univ, MA, 34, PhD(zool), 41. *Prof Exp:* Lectr genetics, McGill Univ, 40-44; mem opers res group, Off Sci Res & Develop, US Dept Navy, 44-46; assoc prof genetics, Antioch Col & chmn dept genetics, Fels Res Inst, 46-48; consult div biomet & med statist, Mayo Clinic, 48-52; geneticist, Children's Cancer Res Found & res assoc, Children's Hosp, Boston, Mass, 52-56. *Concurrent Pos:* Mem permanent comt int human genetics cong, NIH, 66-71; chmn med adv bd, Nat Genetics Found, 68-81; consult ed, Transfusion; adj staff mem, Cleveland Clin, 83-; consult, WHO. *Mem:* Fel AAAS; Am Soc Human Genetics (pres, 64); Genetics Soc Am; Am Asn Immunol; hon mem Japanese Soc Human Genetics. *Res:* Immunogenetics; study of genetic control of human immunoglobulins; population genetics; genetics of diabetes. *Mailing Add:* 20300 N Park Blvd No 4B Shaker Heights OH 44118

STEINBERG, BERNARD ALBERT, MICROBIOLOGY, VIROLOGY. *Current Pos:* RETIRED. *Personal Data:* b New York, NY, Oct 2, 24; m 46; c 3. *Educ:* NY Univ, AB, 47; Univ Ill, MS, 48, PhD(bact), 50. *Prof Exp:* Head sect bact & mycol, Squibb Inst Med Res, NJ, 50-56; head virus & cancer res, Wm S Merrell Co, 56-63; group leader, Chemother Sect, Sterling-Winthrop Res Inst, 63-87. *Mem:* AAAS; Am Soc Microbiol; Sigma Xi. *Res:* Antiviral chemotherapy; upper respiratory viruses; veterinary viruses; virus vaccines and immunology of viruses; viral etiology of cancer. *Mailing Add:* 10 Dykeman Rd Delmar NY 12054

STEINBERG, BERNARD D, ELECTRICAL ENGINEERING, ULTRAHIGH RESOLUTION IN MICROWAVE IMAGING & DIAGNOSTIC ULTRASOUND IMAGING. *Current Pos:* PROF ELEC ENG & DIR, VALLEY FORGE RES CTR, UNIV PA. *Personal Data:* b New York, NY, Oct 19, 24; m 49, Jacqueline Zeinbarg; c 4. *Educ:* Mass Inst Technol, BE, MS; Univ Pa, PhD(elec eng). *Prof Exp:* Co-found & vpres res & eng, Gen Atonics Corp; co-found & emer chmn bd, Interspec, Inc, Philadelphia, Pa, 78-89. *Concurrent Pos:* Distinguished lectr, Antennas & Propagation Soc, Inst Elec & Electronics Engrs; vis prof, Tel Aviv Univ, Stanford Univ & Univ Paris. *Mem:* Fel Inst Elec & Electronics Engrs; Sigma Xi; AAAS; Int Union Radio Sci. *Res:* High resolution microwave imaging based upon self calibration of huge distorted antenna arrays; high resolution medical ultrasound imaging in inhomogeneous and refractive media; the arrays may be real, synthetic or combinations of both; author of 2 publications. *Mailing Add:* Moore Sch Elec Eng Univ Pa Philadelphia PA 19104

STEINBERG, BERNHARD, pathology; deceased, see previous edition for last biography

STEINBERG, BETTIE MURRAY, CELL-VIRUS INTERACTIONS. *Current Pos:* res scientist, 80-83, head sect otolaryngol res, 83-92, CHIEF, DIV OTOLARYNGOL MED, LONG ISLAND JEWISH MED CTR, 92- *Personal Data:* b Price, Utah, June 13, 37; m 60, Walter Steinberg; c 3. *Educ:* Univ Calif, Riverside, BA, 59; Adelphi Univ, MS, 67; State Univ NY Stony Brook, PhD(microbiol), 76. *Prof Exp:* Fel, Dept Microbiol, State Univ NY Stony Brook, 76-78; res assoc, Dept Biol Sci, Columbia Univ, 78-80. *Concurrent Pos:* Lectr, Dept Biol Sci, Columbia Univ, 79-80; adj asst prof, Dept Surg, State Univ NY Stony Brook, 80-90, adj assoc prof microbiol, oral biol & path, 90-; assoc prof otolaryngol, Albert Einstein Col Med, 90- *Mem:* Am Soc Microbiol; AAAS; NY Acad Sci; Am Acad Otolaryngol-Head & Neck Surg; Asn Res Otolaryngol. *Res:* Interaction between human papillomavirus type 11 (HPV 11) and laryngeal epithelial cells; major focus is on cellular and viral regulation of viral expression, using cells cultured in vitro and various cloned viral DNA mutants. *Mailing Add:* 270-05 76th Ave Dept Otolaryngol Long Island Jewish Med Ctr New Hyde Park NY 11040. *Fax:* 718-342-2320

STEINBERG, DANIEL, BIOCHEMISTRY. *Current Pos:* PROF MED, HEAD & DIR, SPECIALIZED CTR RES ARTERIOSCLEROSIS, SCH MED, UNIV CALIF, SAN DIEGO, 68- *Personal Data:* b Windsor, Ont, July 21, 22; US citizen; m 91, Mary Stratthaus; c Jonathan H, Anne B & David E. *Educ:* Wayne State Univ, BS, 42, MD, 44; Harvard Univ, PhD(biochem), 51. *Hon Degrees:* MD, Univ Gothenburg, 92. *Honors & Awards:* Mayo Soley Award, 84; Distinguished Achievement Award, Am Heart Asn, 88; Bristol-Myers Squibb Award Outstanding Cardiovascular Res, 95; Conner Lectr, Am Heart Asn, 95. *Prof Exp:* Intern internal med, Boston City Hosp, 44-45; resident, Detroit Receiving Hosp, 45-46; instr physiol, Med Sch, Boston Univ, 47-48; res scientist, Sect Cellular Physiol, Nat Heart Inst, 51-54, from actg chief to chief sect metab, 54-68. *Concurrent Pos:* Vis scientist, Carlsberg Labs, Copenhagen, 52-53; pres, Found Advan Educ in Sci, 59; ed-in-chief, J Lipid Res, 61-64; chmn coun arteriosclerosis, Am Heart Asn, 68-69. *Mem:* Nat Acad Sci; Inst Med-Nat Acad Sci; Am Soc Biol Chem; Am Chem Soc; Am Oil Chem Soc; Soc Exp Biol & Med; AAAS. *Res:* Mechanisms of hormone action; biochemistry of lipid and lipoprotein metabolism and its relation to atherosclerosis. *Mailing Add:* Div Endocrinol & Metab Dept Med 0682 Univ Calif Sch Med La Jolla CA 92093-0682. *Fax:* 619-534-2005; *E-Mail:* dsteinberg@ucsd.edu

STEINBERG, DANIEL J, thermodynamics, hydrodynamics, for more information see previous edition

STEINBERG, DAVID H, ORGANIC CHEMISTRY. *Current Pos:* res chemist Res Div, Geigy Chem Corp, 59-72, res assoc, 72-83, SR STAFF SCIENTIST ADDITIVES RES, CIBA-GEIGY CHEM CORP, 80-, RES MGR, 83- *Personal Data:* b Bronx, NY, Nov 24, 29; m 52; c 4. *Educ:* Yeshiva Univ, BA, 51; NY Univ, MS, 56, PhD(org chem), 60. *Prof Exp:* Res asst biochem, Montefiore Hosp, NY, 52-53; res assoc org chem res div, NY Univ, 53-59. *Mem:* Am Chem Soc; Royal Soc Chem. *Res:* Organic chemistry encompassing synthesis, reaction mechanism, stereochemistry and structure-activity relationships. *Mailing Add:* 2216 Wilson Ave Bronx NY 10469-5811

STEINBERG, DAVID ISRAEL, OPERATIONS RESEARCH, APPLIED MATHEMATICS. *Current Pos:* assoc prof, 72-78, dir assessment, 90-91, PROF MATH, SOUTHERN ILL UNIV, EDWARDSVILLE, 78-, ASSOC DEAN, SCH ARTS & SCI, 91- *Personal Data:* b St Louis, Mo, July 18, 42; m 65, Dale Katy; c Marc & Reuven. *Educ:* Washington Univ, BS, 64, MS, 66, DSc, 68. *Prof Exp:* Asst prof appl math, Washington Univ, 67-72. *Concurrent Pos:* Affil assoc prof, Washington Univ, 74-77, vis assoc prof comput sci, 77-78, affil prof, 78-81. *Mem:* Opers Res Soc Am; Am Asn Univ Professors; Inst Mgt Sci; Nat Coun Teachers Math. *Res:* Mathematical programming; numerical linear algebra. *Mailing Add:* Col Arts & Sci Southern Ill Univ PO Box 1608 Edwardsville IL 62026-1608

STEINBERG, ELIOT, ORGANIC CHEMISTRY, RESEARCH ADMINISTRATION. *Current Pos:* RETIRED. *Personal Data:* b New York, NY, June 5, 23; m 47; c 3. *Educ:* Polytech Inst Brooklyn, BS, 43, MS, 47. *Prof Exp:* Res chemist, Johnson & Johnson, NJ, 43-44; res chemist, Chilcott Labs Div, Maltine Co, 47-52; res adminr, Warner-Chilcott Labs, 52-58, dir res admin, 58-77, dir admin opers, Warner-Lambert Co, 77-81; mgr mem serv, Indust Res Inst, 81-88; consult, Rutgers Univ, 88-91. *Mem:* AAAS; Am Chem Soc; Am Soc Asn Execs; Coun Eng & Sci Soc Execs. *Res:* Information retrieval. *Mailing Add:* 20 Sherwood Dr Morristown NJ 07960-6366

STEINBERG, GEORGE MILTON, PHARMACOLOGY. *Current Pos:* RETIRED. *Educ:* Purdue Univ, PhD(org chem), 45. *Prof Exp:* Head, Pharmacol Prog, NIH, 80-85. *Mailing Add:* 1730 Sunrise Dr Potomac MD 20854-2670

STEINBERG, GUNTHER, SURFACE CHEMISTRY, PHYSICAL CHEMISTRY. *Current Pos:* mgr, media res & mgr advan develop, 72-76, PRES & DIR, STEINBERG ASSOCS, 77- *Personal Data:* b Cologne, Ger, Apr 14, 24; nat US; m 49; c 2. *Educ:* Univ Calif, Los Angeles, BS, 48, MS, 50, PhD(physiol chem), 56. *Prof Exp:* Res assoc, Scripps Metab Clin, Calif, 50; biochemist atomic energy proj, Univ Calif, Los Angeles, 50-56; res chemist, Martinez Res Lab, Shell Oil Co, 56-61, res chemist, Shell Develop Co, 61-64; res chemist, Stanford Res Inst, 64-67; sr staff chemist, Memorex Corp, 67-77. *Mem:* Am Chem Soc; Int Asn Colloid & Interface Scientists; NAm Thermal Analysis Soc. *Res:* Surface and physical chemistry of polymer composites; physical and chemical measurements; magnetic media processing and surface calorimetry development; electrical contact phenomena; heterogeneous catalysis; radiotracer applications. *Mailing Add:* 95 Lerida Ct Menlo Park CA 94025-3446

STEINBERG, HERBERT AARON, MATHEMATICS. *Current Pos:* RETIRED. *Personal Data:* b Bronx, NY, Sept 19, 29; m 55, Bernice Schneck; c Terry & David. *Educ:* Cornell Univ, BA, 50; Yale Univ, MA, 51, PhD(math), 55. *Prof Exp:* Aerodynamicist, Repub Aviation Corp, 55-56; digital systs engr, Sperry Gyroscope Co, 56; sr mathematician, TRG Div, Control Data Corp, 56-68; dir sci serv, Math Applns Group, Inc, 68-76, res & develop dir, 76-85; dir res & develop, Interactive Solid Design, Cadam, 85-92. *Concurrent Pos:* Adj prof math, Polytech Inst, NY, 81-82. *Mem:* Soc Indust & Appl Math; Inst Elec & Electronics Engrs; Math Asn Am; Am Math Soc; Sigma Xi. *Res:* Systems engineering; signal processing; Monte Carlo methods; computer simulation; radiation transport; random noise; stochastic processes; numerical analysis, computer generated imagery; computer aided design. *Mailing Add:* 25 N Lake Rd Armonk NY 10504

STEINBERG, HOWARD, ORGANIC CHEMISTRY. *Current Pos:* res chemist, Pac Coast Borax Co, 54, mgr org res, US Borax Res Corp, 55-58, asst dir chem res, 58, from assoc dir to dir, 59-63, vpres, 63-69, PRES, US BORAX RES CORP, 69-, VPRES US BORAX & CHEM CORP, 69-, MEM BD DIRS, 73- *Personal Data:* b Chicago, Ill, Aug 23, 26; m 46; c 3. *Educ:* Univ Ill, BS, 48; Univ Calif, Los Angeles, PhD(chem), 51. *Prof Exp:* AEC fel, Mass Inst Technol, 51-52; res chemist, Aerojet-Gen Corp, 52; res assoc org synthesis, Univ Calif, Los Angeles, 52-53; collabr natural prod, USDA, 53-54. *Mem:* Am Chem Soc. *Res:* Boron and synthetic organic chemistry; reaction mechanisms; kinetics. *Mailing Add:* 17 Dorchester Green Laguna Nigel CA 92677-9377

STEINBERG, JOSEPH, MATHEMATICAL STATISTICS, PROBABILITY SAMPLING. *Current Pos:* STATIST CONSULT, 94- *Personal Data:* b New York, NY, Mar 22, 20; m 49, Ruth Cohen; c Steven L & Seth M. *Educ:* City Col NY, BS, 39. *Honors & Awards:* Distinguished Serv Award, US Dept Health Educ & Welfare, 68. *Prof Exp:* Statistician pop div, US Bur Census, 40-42; math statistician, Social Security Bd, 42-44; statistician statist res div, US Bur Census, 44-45, chief statist; chief math statistician, Social Security Admin, 63-72; dir off surv methods res & asst comnr surv design, Bur Labor Statist, 72-75; pres, Surv Design, Inc, 75-94 methods br pop & housing div, 45-59, chief statist methods off, 59-60, chief statist methods div, 60-63. *Concurrent Pos:* Lectr, USDA Grad Sch, 42-74; consult, Orgn Am States, Chile, 65 & 67; vis prof surv res ctr, Inst Social Res, Univ Mich, 68, 69, 70 & 72; mem assembly behav & soc sci, Nat Acad Sci-Nat Res Coun, 72-77, mem comt Fed Agency Eval Res, 71-75, mem comt energy consumption measurement, 75-77; mem comt eval res, Social Sci Res Coun, 77-79; assoc ed, Am Statistician, 77-84. *Mem:* Hon fel AAAS; hon fel Am Statist Assn. *Res:* Sample survey design and statistical analysis; evaluation of non-sampling errors; response variance and bias; data linkage; computer analysis; quality control; operations research; cost functions and optimization. *Mailing Add:* 1011 Roswell Dr Silver Spring MD 20901-2131

STEINBERG, KAREN K, MOLECULAR BIOLOGY. *Current Pos:* CHIEF, MOLECULAR BIOL BR, NAT CTR ENVIRON HEALTH, CTR DIS CONTROL, 91- *Personal Data:* b Atlanta, Ga, June 17, 44. *Educ:* Ga Col, BS, 66; Ga State Univ, MS, 76; Emory Univ, PhD(exp path), 80. *Honors & Awards:* Special Recognition Award, USPHS, 92, Award for Breast Cancer Work, 96. *Mailing Add:* Nat Ctr Environ Health CDC 4770 Buferd Hwy MS F24 Atlanta GA 30341. *Fax:* 770-488-4005; *E-Mail:* kks1@cehehl1.em.cdc.gov

STEINBERG, M(ORRIS) A(LBERT), METALLURGY. *Current Pos:* RETIRED. *Personal Data:* b Hartford, Conn, Sept 24, 20; m 51; c 3. *Educ:* Mass Inst Technol, BS, 42, MS, 46, DSc(metall), 48. *Prof Exp:* Instr metall, Mass Inst Technol, 45-48; head, Metall Dept, Horizons, Inc, 48-58; with Micrometric Instrument Co, 49-51; chief metallurgist, Horizons Titanium Corp, 51-55; secy & dir, Diwolfram Corp, 51-58; consult scientist, Lockheed Missiles & Space Co, 58-59, mgr mat, propulsion & ord res, Lockheed Aircraft Corp, Burbank, 59-62, lab dir, Mat Sci Lab, 62-64; mgr mat sci lab, Res & Develop Div, 64-65, dep chief scientist, 65-72, dir technol applns, 72-83, vpres sci, 83-86. *Concurrent Pos:* S K Wellman fel, Mass Inst Technol, 47-48; mem adv comt, US Israeli Bi-Nat Res Found, 75-; mem, Nat Mat Adv Bd, Nat Res Ctr, Nat Acad Sci, 75-; adj prof mat sci dept, Sch Eng, Univ Calif Los Angeles, 77-; pres, PVD Corp; mem bd dirs, HCC Industs, Encino, Calif, 80-87, Cadam Inc, Dialog Info Serv, Inc & Dataplan, 80-85; mem, Aeronaut Space Eng Bd, 83-86; chmn, Panel Continuing Educ & Utilization Engr NRC, Nat Acad Eng, 83-84; Air Force Studies Bd NRC Comt Nat Shape Technol, 84-85 & Aeronaut Space & Eng Bd Comt NASA/Univ Retionships Aero/ Space, 84-; mem, Nat Acad Eng Ad Hoc Comt Evaluate Prog NSF's Directorate Eng; mem, Aeronaut & Space Eng Bd Comt, Nat Res Coun, Nat Acad Eng, 87 & Air Force Specification Bulletin Comt, 87-89. *Mem:* Nat Acad Eng; fel Am Soc Metall; fel Am Inst Chem; fel Am Inst Astronaut & Aeronaut; fel Inst Advan Eng; fel AAAS; Sigma Xi. *Res:* Missile and spacecraft materials; extractive metallurgy of reactive metals; powder metallurgy; high strength steels. *Mailing Add:* 348 Homewood Rd Los Angeles CA 90049

STEINBERG, MALCOLM SAUL, DEVELOPMENTAL BIOLOGY, CELL BIOLOGY. *Current Pos:* prof, 66-75, HENRY FAIRFIELD OSBORN PROF BIOL, PRINCETON UNIV, 75- *Personal Data:* b New Brunswick, NJ, June 1, 30; m 83; c 4. *Educ:* Amherst Col, BA, 52; Univ Minn, MA, 54, PhD(zool), 56. *Prof Exp:* Instr zool, Univ Minn, 55; fel embryol, Carnegie Inst, Washington, 56-58; from asst prof to assoc prof biol, Johns Hopkins Univ, 58-66. *Concurrent Pos:* Instr-in-charge embryol course, Woods Hole Marine Biol Lab, 67-72, trustee, 69-77; chmn, Div Develop Cell Biol, Am Soc Zool, 83-84; chmn, Gordon Res Conf Cell Contact & Adhesion, 85; mem bd biol, Nat Res Coun, Nat Acad Sci, 86-92. *Mem:* Fel AAAS; Am Soc Cell Biol; Am Soc Zool; Soc Develop Biol (secy, 70-73); Int Soc Develop Biol; Int Soc Differentiation. *Res:* Mechanisms of animal morphogenesis; identification and analysis of cell adhesion systems; role of cell adhesion in malignant invasion. *Mailing Add:* Dept Molecular Biol Princeton Univ Princeton NJ 08544-1014. *Fax:* 609-258-5323

STEINBERG, MARCIA IRENE, ION TRANSPORT, ENZYMOLOGY. *Current Pos:* PROG DIR, MOLECULAR BIOCHEM PROG, NSF, 90- *Personal Data:* b Brooklyn, NY, Mar 7, 44; c Eric F. *Educ:* Brooklyn Col, BS, 64, MA, 66; Univ Mich, PhD(biochem), 73. *Prof Exp:* From asst prof to assoc prof pharmacol, Health Sci Ctr, State Univ NY, Syracuse, 85-90. *Mem:* Am Soc Biochem & Molecular Biol; Asn Women in Sci; AAAS. *Res:* Mechanism of action of ion transport ATPases. *Mailing Add:* NSF Rm 655 4201 Wilson Blvd Arlington VA 22230. *E-Mail:* msteinbe@nsf.gov

STEINBERG, MARSHALL, PHARMACOLOGY, TOXICOLOGY. *Current Pos:* vpres & dir sci oper, 78-83, VPRES & SCI DIR, HAZLETON LABS CORP, 83- *Personal Data:* b Pittsburgh, Pa, Sept 18, 32; m 62; c 3. *Educ:* Georgetown Univ, BS, 54; Univ Pittsburgh, MS, 56; Univ Tex Med Br Galveston, PhD(pharmacol, toxicol), 66; Nat Registry Clin Chem, cert, 70; dipl, Acad Toxicol Sci, 81. *Prof Exp:* Asst dir, Trop Testing, Univ Pittsburgh, 55-56; chief clin path lab, 97th Gen Hosp, Med Serv Corps, US Army, Frankfurt, Ger, 56-60, chief, Biochem & Toxicol Div, 4th Army Med Lab, San Antonio, Tex, 61-63, chief toxicol div, Environ Hyg Agency, 66-71, dir, Lab Serv, US Army Environ Hyg Agency, 72-75; consult to US Army surg gen, Lab Sci, 75-76; vpres & dir, Bioassay Prog, Tracor Jitco, 77-78. *Concurrent Pos:* Liaison mem, Armed Forces Pest Control Bd, 67-75; mem, Pesticide Monitoring Panel, Fed Working Group Pesticide Mgt, Coun Environ Quality, 71-72 & safety panel, 72-; adj prof, Am Univ, 81; mem, Prof Accreditation Bd, Acad Toxicol Sci, 82-85; secy, Toxicol Lab Accreditation Bd, 84-85; pres, Nat Capital Area Chap, Soc Toxicol, 84-85. *Mem:* Soc Toxicol, (secy, 83-85); Am Soc Pharmacol & Exp Therapeut; Am Conf Govt Indust Hygienists; Am Col Toxicol (pres elect, 84-85); Am Indust Hyg Asn. *Res:* Applied research in industrial and environmental toxicology, insect repellants, pesticides and fire extinguishants, particularly in regard to hazards owing to skin penetration or irritation as well as toxic effects due to inhalation. *Mailing Add:* Hercules Inc One Hercules Plaza Wilmington DE 19894-0001. *Fax:* 302-594-5400

STEINBERG, MARTIN, PHYSICAL CHEMISTRY. *Current Pos:* RETIRED. *Personal Data:* b Chicago, Ill, Apr 18, 20; m 42; c 3. *Educ:* Univ Ill, BS, 41; Univ Chicago, PhD(chem), 49. *Prof Exp:* Res chemist, Continental Carbon Co, 41-45; res assoc rest nuclear studies, Univ Chicago, 49-51; res chemist, Gen Elec Co, 51-56; sr scientist, Armour Res Found, 56-61; head chem physics, Delco Electronics Div, Gen Motors Corp, 61-74; res chemist, Quantum Inst, Univ Calif, Santa Barbara, 74-90. *Mem:* AAAS; Am Chem Soc; Am Phys Soc; Combustion Inst. *Res:* Carbon black formation and properties; electrochemistry in fused salts; stable isotope geochemistry; reentry physics; high temperature kinetics; air pollution; chemical lasers; gaseous radiation and spectroscopy; flame chemistry. *Mailing Add:* 345 N Ontare Rd Santa Barbara CA 93105-2536

STEINBERG, MARTIN H, MOLECULAR BIOLOGY, GENETICS & HEMATOLOGY. *Current Pos:* from asst prof to assoc prof, 74-77, PROF MED, MED SCH, UNIV MISS, 77- *Personal Data:* b New York, NY, July 2, 36; m 73, Susan McDaniel; c Elizabeth A. *Educ:* Cornell Univ, AB, 58; Tufts Univ, MD, 62. *Prof Exp:* Med intern, Cornell Med Serv, 62-63; med resident, New Eng Med Ctr, 66-68, fel hemat, 68-70. *Concurrent Pos:* Mem, Res Rev Comt, Am Heart Asn, 81-84; prin investr, NIH, Vet Admin, 73-; assoc chief staff res, Jackson Vet Admin Med Ctr, 73-; asst dean, Sch Med, Univ Miss, 73-; vis prof med, Tufts Univ, 87. *Mem:* Am Fedn Clin Res; Am Soc Clin Invest; Am Soc Hemat; Asn Am Physicians; fel AAAS. *Res:* Intrinsic factors which may determine the clinical course of sickle cell anemia; interactions of structural variants of hemogoblin with the thalassemia syndromes; fetal hemoglobin synthesis. *Mailing Add:* Vet Admin Med Ctr 151 Jackson MS 39216. *Fax:* 601-364-1390; *E-Mail:* mhs@fiona.umsmed.edu

STEINBERG, MARVIN PHILLIP, agricultural & food chemistry; deceased, see previous edition for last biography

STEINBERG, MELVIN SANFORD, THEORETICAL PHYSICS. *Current Pos:* assoc prof, 62-86, PROF PHYSICS, SMITH COL, 86- *Personal Data:* b Canton, Ohio, Mar 28, 28; m 54; c 2. *Educ:* Univ NC, BS, 49, MS, 51; Yale Univ, PhD(physics), 55. *Prof Exp:* Asst physics, Yale Univ, 54-55; asst prof, Stevens Inst Technol, 55-59; assoc prof, Univ Mass, 59-62. *Concurrent Pos:* Res assoc, Woods Hole Oceanog Inst, 56-58 & 62; res assoc, Air Force Cambridge Res Lab, 60-61; NSF sci fac fel, 66-67. *Mem:* Am Phys Soc; Sigma Xi; Am Asn Phys Teachers. *Res:* Theory of solids; acoustics; electrodynamics; physics education; student's problems of comprehension in electricity and mechanics; new apparatus and instructional strategies; comparison of student's and historical learning. *Mailing Add:* Dept Physics Smith Col Northampton MA 01063

STEINBERG, MEYER, CHEMICAL ENGINEERING & CHEMISTRY, ENERGY. *Current Pos:* CHEM ENGR & HEAD, PROCESS SCI DIV, DEPT ENERGY & ENVIRON, BROOKHAVEN NAT LAB, 57- *Personal Data:* b Philadelphia, Pa, July 10, 24; m 50; c 2. *Educ:* Cooper Union, BChE, 44; Polytech Inst Brooklyn, MChE, 49. *Prof Exp:* Jr chem engr, Manhattan Dist, Kellex Corp, 44-46; asst chem engr process develop, Deutsch & Loonam, NY, 47-50; assoc chem engr, Guggenheim Bros, Mineola, NY, 50-57. *Mem:* Fel Am Inst Chem Engrs; Am Chem Soc; Sigma Xi; AAAS; fel Am Nuclear Soc. *Res:* New processes for energy conversion, nuclear, fossil, geothermal and solar; development of materials for conservation and energy storage; process research and development in energy conversion. *Mailing Add:* 15 Alder Field Lane Melville NY 11747

STEINBERG, MITCHELL I, PHARMACOLOGY. *Current Pos:* sr pharmacologist, Eli Lilly Res Labs, 72-77, res scientist, 77-80, res assoc, 80-89, RES ADV, ELI LILLY RES LABS, 90- *Personal Data:* b Philadelphia, Pa, Jan 22, 44; m 66; c 3. *Educ:* Philadelphia Col Pharm & Sci, BSc, 66; Univ Mich, PhD(pharmacol), 70. *Prof Exp:* Res fel, Univ Conn Health Ctr, 70-71, instr pharmacol, 71-72. *Mem:* AAAS; Am Soc Pharmacol & Exp Therapeut; NY Acad Sci. *Res:* Interactions of pharmacological agents with excitable membranes of mammalian cardiac & neuronal tissues; antiarrhythmic drug research; cardiac electrophysiology. *Mailing Add:* Eli Lilly & Co Lilly Res Labs Lilly Corp Ctr MC 304 Indianapolis IN 46285-0001. *Fax:* 317-277-0892

STEINBERG, RICHARD, ELECTRICAL ENGINEERING. *Current Pos:* staff engr, 72-80, SR STAFF ENGR, LOCKHEED MISSILES & SPACE CO, SUNNYVALE, 80- *Personal Data:* b Brooklyn, NY, Feb 22, 30; m 53; c 3. *Educ:* City Col New York, BEE, 52; Univ Pa, MSEE, 58. *Prof Exp:* Jr engr, Govt & Indust Div, Philco Corp, 52-54; engr, Decker Corp, 54-56; sr engr, Electronics Div, Parsons Corp, 56-59; mem tech staff, Hughes Aircraft Co, 59-61; asst sect head elec eng, TRW Systs Group, Calif, 61-71; dept staff engr, Western Develop Labs Div, Philco-Ford Corp, 71. *Concurrent Pos:* Instr, Univ Calif, Los Angeles, 61-64 & Calif State Col, Los Angeles, 61-68. *Res:* Scattering from random surfaces; acoustical and electromagnetic waves; nonlinear differential equations. *Mailing Add:* 2714 Preston Dr Mountain View CA 94040

STEINBERG, ROBERT, MATHEMATICS. *Current Pos:* from instr to prof, 48-92, EMER PROF MATH, UNIV CALIF, LOS ANGELES, 92- *Personal Data:* b Stykon, Rumania, May 25, 22; m 52. *Educ:* Univ Toronto, PhD(math), 48. *Prof Exp:* Lectr math, Univ Toronto, 47-48. *Mem:* Nat Acad Sci; Am Math Soc; Math Asn Am. *Res:* Group representations; algebraic groups. *Mailing Add:* Dept Math Univ Calif 6364 Math Sci Bldg Los Angeles CA 90024

STEINBERG, RONALD T, CHEMICAL ENGINEERING. *Current Pos:* RETIRED. *Personal Data:* b New York, NY, Apr 18, 29; m 50; c 3. *Educ:* Polytech Inst Brooklyn, BChE, 49; Clarkson Col Technol, MChE, 51. *Prof Exp:* Process engr, Schwarz Labs, Inc, 51-52; plant engr, 52-61; plant engr, Alcolac Inc, 61-66, mgr process research, 66-84. *Concurrent Pos:* Environ consult. *Mem:* Am Chem Soc. *Res:* Process development; specialty surfactants and monomers; ethoxylations, sulfations, and esterifications; diffusional operations and solids handling. *Mailing Add:* 2107 Cedar Circle Dr Catonsville MD 21228-3748

STEINBERG, ROY HERBERT, NEUROPHYSIOLOGY. *Current Pos:* asst res physiologist, 69-72, assoc prof physiol, 72-77, PROF PHYSIOL & OPHTHAL, SCH MED, UNIV CALIF, SAN FRANCISCO, 78- *Personal Data:* b New York, NY, Dec 9, 35; m 59; c 1. *Educ:* Univ Mich, BA, 56, MA, 57; NY Med Col, MD, 61; McGill Univ, PhD(neurophysiol), 65. *Prof Exp:* Intern med, Mass Mem Hosp, 61-62; USPHS fel, NIMH, 62-65; head Neurophysiol Br, Neurol Sci Div, Naval Aerospace Med Inst, Fla, 68-69. *Concurrent Pos:* USPHS career develop award, 71-; William C Bryant, Bernard C Spiegel & Harpuder awards, NY Med Col. *Mem:* Soc Neurosci; Asn Res Vision & Ophthal; Am Phys Soc. *Res:* Physiology of the nervous system; vision, especially physiology and anatomy of the retina. *Mailing Add:* Dept Physiol Univ Calif S-762 San Francisco CA 94143-0730. *Fax:* 415-476-6289

STEINBERG, SETH MICHAEL, CLINICAL TRIALS, DATA ANALYSIS. *Current Pos:* actg head, 86-90, HEAD, BIOSTATIST & DATA MGT SECT, DIV CLIN SCI, NAT CANCER INST, 90- *Personal Data:* b Washington, DC, June 5, 58; m 89; c 2. *Educ:* Johns Hopkins Univ, BA, 79; Univ NC, Chapel Hill, MS, 81, PhD(biostatist), 83. *Prof Exp:* Statistician, EMMES Corp, 83-86. *Mem:* Am Statist Asn; Biometric Soc. *Res:* Design, monitoring, and evaluation of clinical trials for treatment of cancer and AIDS; identification of prognostic factors for patients treated on studies; development and use of methods for evaluation of data from clinical trials. *Mailing Add:* 12002 Pineapple Grove Dr North Potomac MD 20878

STEINBERG, STANLY, APPLIED MATHEMATICS. *Current Pos:* ASSOC PROF MATH, UNIV NMEX, 74- *Personal Data:* b Traverse City, Mich, Mar 10, 40; m 60. *Educ:* Mich State Univ, BS, 62; Stanford Univ, PhD(math), 68. *Prof Exp:* Asst prof math, Purdue Univ, Lafayette, 67-74. *Res:* Partial differential equations. *Mailing Add:* Dept Math Univ NMex Albuquerque NM 87131

STEINBERG, STUART ALVIN, MATHEMATICS. *Current Pos:* from asst prof to assoc prof, 71-80, PROF MATH, UNIV TOLEDO, 80- *Personal Data:* b Chicago, Ill, Feb 3, 41; m 66; c 3. *Educ:* Univ Ill, Urbana, BS, 63, PhD(math), 70; Univ Chicago, MS, 65. *Prof Exp:* Asst prof math, Univ Mo, St Louis, 70-71. *Mem:* Am Math Soc. *Res:* Algebra, especially ring theory and ordered algebraic structures. *Mailing Add:* Dept Math Univ Toledo 2801 W Bancroft Toledo OH 43606-3390

STEINBERGER, ANNA, CELL BIOLOGY, IMMUNOLOGY. *Current Pos:* prof reproductive biol, 71-94, EMER PROF, DEPT OBSTET, GYNEC & REPRODUCTION SCI, MED SCH, UNIV TEX, HOUSTON, 94-, ASST DEAN FAC AFFAIRS, 95- *Personal Data:* b Radom, Poland, Jan 1, 28; US citizen; m 50, Emil Steinberger; c Pauline & Meffe. *Educ:* State Univ Iowa, MS, 52; Wayne State Univ, PhD(microbiol), 61. *Honors & Awards:* Distinguished Andrologist Award, Am Soc Andrology, 93. *Prof Exp:* Bacteriologist, State Univ Iowa, 53-55; res virologist, Parke, Davis & Co, Mich, 55-56 & 58-59; asst mem, Albert Einstein Med Ctr, 61-71. *Concurrent Pos:* USPHS res grant, Albert Einstein Med Ctr, 61-71. *Mem:* Endocrine Soc; Soc Study Reproduction; Tissue Cult Asn; hon mem Polish Andrology Soc; Am Soc Andrology (vpres, 84-85, pres, 85-86). *Res:* Endocrine and paracrine regulation of spermatogenesis in male mammalian gonads; hormonal control of spermatogenesis; secretion of gonadotropins; cell interactions in the testis; tissue culture. *Mailing Add:* Univ Tex Med Sch PO Box 20708 Houston TX 77225-0708. *Fax:* 713-500-0614; *E-Mail:* steinbez@dean.med.uth.tme.edu

STEINBERGER, JACK, PHYSICS. *Current Pos:* physicist, Europ Ctr Nuclear Res, 68-86, PROF, SCHOLA NORMALE SUP, PISA, ITALY, 86- *Personal Data:* b Bad Kissingen, Ger, May 25, 21; nat US; m 61, Cynthia E Alff; c 2. *Educ:* Univ Chicago, BS, 42, PhD, 48. *Hon Degrees:* Dr, Ill Inst Technol, 89, Univ Glasgow, 90, Dortmund Univ, 90, Columbia Univ, 90, Univ Autonoma Barcelona, 92. *Honors & Awards:* Nobel Prize in Physics, 88; Nat Medal of Sci, 88; Mateuzzi Medal, Ital Phys Soc, 89. *Prof Exp:* Mem, Inst Advan Study, Princeton, 48-49; res asst, Univ Calif, Berkeley, 49-50; Higgins prof physics, Columbia Univ, 50-71. *Concurrent Pos:* Mem, Inst Advan Study, Princeton, 59-60; hon prof, Univ Heidelberg. *Mem:* Nat Acad Sci; Am Acad Arts & Sci; Heidelberg Acad Sci. *Res:* Mesons, spin, parity and other properties of pions; particle, spins, other properties of strange particles; two neutrinos; CP violating properties of kaons; interactions of neutrinos at high energies; quark structure of nucleons. *Mailing Add:* Europ Ctr Nuclear Res (CERN) Geneva CH 1211 Switzerland. *Fax:* 41-22-783-0672; *E-Mail:* steinberger@vxcern.decknet.cern.ch

STEINBRECHER, LESTER, INORGANIC CHEMISTRY. *Current Pos:* res chemist, 58-70, dir res, 70-88, SR TECHNOL CONSULT, HENKEL CORP-P & A, 88- *Personal Data:* b Philadelphia, Pa, Sept 17, 27; m 51, Michaelis; c Linda, Theodore & Beth. *Educ:* Temple Univ, BA, 50; Drexel Inst, MS, 57, Univ Pa, PhD, 68. *Prof Exp:* Chemist, Socony Mobil Oil Corp, 52-58. *Mem:* Nat Asn Corrosion Eng; Am Soc Electroplaters; Am Chem Soc. *Res:* Solid state reactions; inorganic metallic coatings; analytical chemistry; coatings for metals; twenty-one US patents. *Mailing Add:* Henkel Corp P & A Ambler PA 19002

STEINBRENNER, ARTHUR H, MATHEMATICS EDUCATION. *Current Pos:* from instr to prof math & edu, 53-83, EMER PROF MATH, UNIV ARIZ, 84- *Personal Data:* b New York, NY, July 23, 17; div; c 2. *Educ:* Columbia Univ, AB, 40, AM, 41, PhD, 55. *Prof Exp:* Instr math & physics, Graham-Eckes Sch, Fla, 41-46; asst math, Teachers Col, Columbia Univ, 46-48; asst prof, US Naval Acad, 48-53. *Concurrent Pos:* Coordr, Sch Math Study Group, 58-61, Ariz Ctr Minn Math & Sci Teaching Proj, 63-65; Fulbright lectr, Australia, 63. *Mem:* Math Asn Am; Sch Sci & Math Asn; Nat Coun Teachers Mathematics. *Res:* Mathematics curricula experiments; math learning by the blind. *Mailing Add:* 2254 E Mitchell St Tucson AZ 85719

STEINBRENNER, EUGENE CLARENCE, FORESTRY, SOILS. *Current Pos:* RETIRED. *Personal Data:* b St Paul, Minn, Sept 3, 21; m 44; c 4. *Educ:* Univ Minn, BS, 49; Univ Wis, MS, 51; Univ Wash, Seattle, PhD(forest soils), 54. *Prof Exp:* Asst, Univ Wis, 49-51; asst, State Conserv Dept, Wis, 49-50; forest soils specialist, Forestry Res Ctr, Weyerhaeuser Co, 52-81. *Concurrent Pos:* Weyerhaeuser fel, 51-52, affil prof forest soils, Univ Wash, 74- Bullard fel, Harvard Univ, 68. *Mem:* Fel Soil Sci Soc Am; Soc Am Foresters; fel Am Sci Affil. *Res:* Soil classification and mapping; nutrition; productivity; soil management for site protection, rehabilitation and improvement; nursery soils. *Mailing Add:* 1205 Marion St Centralia WA 98531

STEINBRUEGGE, KENNETH BRIAN, ADVANCED SENSORS & SMART SENSORS. *Current Pos:* Assoc engr laser applications res & develop, Res & Develop Ctr, Westinghouse Elec Corp, 63-65, scientist laser mat & systs, 65-69, sr scientist laser-optical res & develop, 69-85, fel scientist optical-anal instrumentation, 85-86, mgr sensor appl, optical-nuclear sensors, 82-86, mgr fiber optics, Mach Technol Div, 86-89, SR ADV ENGR HEALTH PHYSICS INSTRUMENTATION & MACH CONTROL SENSORS, MECH TECHNOL DIV, WESTINGHOUSE ELEC CORP, 89- *Personal Data:* b St Louis, Mo, Dec 9, 39; m 66, Eileen Kelly; c Terri, Craig & Steven. *Educ:* Univ Mo, Rolla, BS, 62, MS, 63. *Honors & Awards:* IR-100 Award, 68. *Concurrent Pos:* Technol advocate, Westinghouse Elec Corp, 81-87. *Mem:* Health Physics Soc; Am Soc Testing & Mat; Inst Elec & Electronics Engrs. *Res:* Development of advanced microprocessor based continuous air monitors for radiological monitoring; research and development on networking radiological instrumentation, analysis of radiological data for improved sensitivity and trending; use of nuclear techniques for sensing and analysis, such as detection of plastic explosives; optical analytical instrumentation; fiber optic sensors and communications; granted 12 US patents. *Mailing Add:* 3496 Ivy Lane Murrysville PA 15668

STEINBRUGGE, KARL V, ENGINEERING SEISMOLOGY. *Current Pos:* prof, 50-78, EMER PROF STRUCT DESIGN, UNIV CALIF, BERKELEY, 78-, CONSULT ENGR, 80- *Personal Data:* b Tucson, Ariz, Feb 8, 19; m 42; c 2. *Educ:* Ore State Univ, BS, 41. *Honors & Awards:* Alfred E Alquist Medal, 87. *Prof Exp:* Struct designer, Austin Co, 42-47; sr struct engr, Calif Div Archit, 48-50. *Concurrent Pos:* Chief engr, Earthquake Dept, Pac Fire Rating Bur, 50-71, mgr, Earthquake Dept, Insurance Serv Off, 71-80; vpres, Earthquake Eng Res Inst, 62, pres, 68-70; mem US comt, Int Asn Earthquake Eng, 69, US chmn, 66-73; chmn task force earthquake hazard reduction, Off Sci & Technol, Washington, DC, 70; chmn adv group, Calif Legis Joint Comt Seismic Safety, 70-73; chmn eng criteria rev bd, San Francisco Conserv & Develop Comn, 71-72; chmn earthquake hazard reduction, Exec Off Pres, 77-78; chmn, Calif Seismic Safety Comn, 74-77, mem, 77-80; invited keynote speaker, foreign international conferences, Turkey, 68, 73, Peru, 73, NZ, 75, 89, Malaysia, 83; chmn, US Working Group Earthquake Related Casualties, 89-90 & Working Group on Risk, Int Asn Seismol & Physics Earth's Interium, 88- *Mem:* Seismol Soc Am (vpres, 66-67, pres, 67-68); hon mem Earthquake Eng Res Inst (pres, 67-68). *Res:* Earthquake engineering; author or co-authored 98 published scientific papers on earthquake engineering and earthquake damage. *Mailing Add:* 6851 Cutting Blvd El Cerrito CA 94530

STEINDLER, MARTIN JOSEPH, NUCLEAR FUEL CYCLE, RESEARCH ADMINISTRATION. *Current Pos:* assoc chemist, Argonne Nat Lab, 53-74, assoc dir, Chem Eng Div, 77-84, dir, Chem Tech Div, 84-92, SR CHEMIST, ARGONNE NAT LAB, 74-, SR TECH ADV, 93- *Personal Data:* b Vienna, Austria, Jan 3, 28; nat US; m 52; c 2. *Educ:* Univ Chicago, PhB, 47, BS, 48, MS, 49, PhD(chem), 52. *Honors & Awards:* Robert E Wilson Award, Am Inst Chem Eng, 90. *Prof Exp:* Res asst, USN Inorg Proj, Univ Chicago, 48-52, consult, 53. *Concurrent Pos:* Consult, Adv Comt Reactor Safeguards, 67-87, Lawrence Livermore Lab, 78-90, Oak Ridge Gas Diffusion Plant, 80-88; mem, Atomic Safety & Licensing Bd Panel, 72-90; mem, Adv Comt Reactor Safeguards, Nuclear Regulatory Comn, 87-88, Adv Comt Nuclear Waste, 88-96. *Mem:* Am Nuclear Soc; Am Chem Soc; Sigma Xi; AAAS; Am Inst Chem Eng. *Res:* Nuclear fuel cycle; radiological safety; nuclear waste disposal; fluorine chemistry of the actinide elements and fission product elements; reactor fuel reprocessing; non-aqueous inorganic chemistry. *Mailing Add:* Argonne Nat Lab Bldg 205 9700 S Cass Ave Argonne IL 60439-4837

STEINECK, PAUL LEWIS, MICROPALEONTOLOGY, BIOLOGICAL SYSTEMATICS. *Current Pos:* From asst prof to assoc prof, 71-87, PROF NATURAL SCI, STATE UNIV NY COL, PURCHASE, 87- *Personal Data:* b Yonkers, NY, Jan 20, 42; m 88. *Educ:* NY Univ, BA, 63, MS, 66; La State Univ, PhD(geol), 73. *Concurrent Pos:* chmn, Div Nat Sci, Suny, Purchase, 81-85. *Mem:* Geol Soc Am; Paleont Soc; Soc Econ Paleontologists & Mineralogists; Int Paleont Union; Micropaleont Soc. *Res:* Deep sea ostracoda from the Pacific and Caribbean and Southern ocean; emphasis on taxonomy and pale oceanography and evolution; deep sea ostracoda from eutrophic habitat islands (taxonomy, origin and ecology); ostracoda of tidal wetlands in the Hudson River. *Mailing Add:* State Univ NY Col Purchase 735 Anderson Hill Rd State Univ NY Purchase NY 10577-1445

STEINER, ANNE KERCHEVAL, MATHEMATICS. *Current Pos:* from asst prof to assoc prof, 68-72, PROF MATH, IOWA STATE UNIV, 72- *Personal Data:* b Warrensburg, Mo, Aug 5, 36. *Educ:* Univ Mo, AB, 58, MA, 63; Univ NMex, PhD(math), 65. *Prof Exp:* Eng asst, Am Tel & Tel Corp, 58-59; asst prof math, Tex Tech Col, 65-66; asst prof, Univ NMex, 66-68. *Concurrent Pos:* Vis assoc prof, Univ Alta, 70-71; chair, Math Dept, Iowa State Univ, 82-86. *Mem:* Am Math Soc; Math Asn Am; Sigma Xi. *Res:* Point set topology. *Mailing Add:* Dept Math Iowa State Univ Ames IA 50011

STEINER, BRUCE, OPTICS. *Current Pos:* SCIENTIST, NAT INST STAND & TECHNOL, 61- *Personal Data:* b Oberlin, Ohio, May 14, 31; m 60, Ruth Piette; c Jonathan & Miriam. *Educ:* Oberlin Col, AB, 53; Princeton Univ, PhD, 57. *Prof Exp:* Res assoc physics, Univ Chicago, 58-61. *Mem:* AAAS; Am Phys Soc; Inst Elec & Electronic Engrs; Optical Soc Am. *Res:* Structure of materials, optical properties of materials; breakdown of molecules under impact; electron detachment phenomena in ions and molecules; optical radiation measurement. *Mailing Add:* Bldg Mat Rm A256 Nat Inst Stand & Technol Gaithersburg MD 20899. *Fax:* 301-990-8729

STEINER, DONALD FREDERICK, BIOCHEMISTRY, ENDOCRINOLOGY. *Current Pos:* from asst prof to prof biochem, Univ Chicago, Ill, 60-70, A N Pritzker prof biochem & med, 70-74, actg chmn, Dept Biochem, 72-73, chmn, 73-79, dir, Diabetes-Endocrinol Ctr, 74-78, assoc dir, Diabetes & Res Training Ctr, 77-81, A N PRITZKER DISTINGUISHED SERV PROF BIOCHEM & MOLECULAR BIOL & MED, UNIV CHICAGO, 84-, SR INVESTR, HOWARD HUGHES MED INST, 85- *Personal Data:* b Lima, Ohio, July 15, 30. *Educ:* Univ Cincinnati, BS, 52; Univ Chicago, MS & MD, 56. *Hon Degrees:* DSc, Royal Univ Umea, Sweden, 73 & Univ Ill Chicago, 84; MD, Rhenische-Westfalische Tech Sch, Aachen, Ger, 92; DrMedSci, Univ Uppsala, Sweden, 93. *Honors & Awards:* Bordon Award, Asn Am Med Cols, 56 & 80; Lilly Award, Am Diabetes Asn, 69, Banting Medal, 76; Ernst Oppenheimer Award, Endocrine Soc, 70, Fred C Koch Award, 90; Hans Christian Hagedorn Medal, Steensen Mem Hosp, Copenhagen, 70; Gairdner Award, Gairdner Found, Can, 71; Diaz-Cristobal Award, Span Soc Study Diabetes, 73; Elliott P Joslin Medal, New Eng Diabetes Asn, 76; Boris Pregal Award, NY Acad Sci, 76; Passano Found Award, 79; E F F Copp Mem lectr, La Jolla, Calif, 71; Mellon lectr, Pittsburgh, Pa, 79; Pachkis lectr, Philadelphia Endocrinol Soc, 79; Banting Mem lectr, Brit Diabetic Soc, 81; David Rumbough Award, Juv Diabetes Found, 82; Rolf Luft Award & lectr, Stockholm, Sweden, 84; Wolf Found Prize Med, 85; Ray A & Robert Kroc lectr, Dept Med Cell Biol, Univ Uppsala, Sweden, 93. *Prof Exp:* Intern, King Co Hosp, Seattle, Wash, 56-57; asst med, Univ Wash, 57-60, med resident, 59-60. *Concurrent Pos:* Res fel med, Univ Wash, 57-59; res career develop award, USPHS, 62-72; mem, Metab Study Sect, USPHS, 65-70; coun, Am Soc Biochem & Molecular Biol, 86-91; consult, Eli Lilly & Co, Indianapolis, Ind, 87-, Biohybrid Technol, 89- & Khepri Corp, San Francisco, 93-; mem bd coun, Nat Inst Diabetes & Digestive & Kidney Dis, 90- *Mem:* Nat Acad Sci; AAAS; Am Soc Biol Chemists; Biochem Soc; Am Diabetes Asn; Am Acad Arts & Sci; Sigma Xi; Int Diabetes Fedn; Endocrine Soc; Protein Soc. *Res:* Discovery, isolation, structural analysis and biosynthesis of proinsulin; mechanism of conversion of proinsulin to insulin; insulin binding to tissues and mechanism of action; evolutionary development of insulin and related hormones; study of normal and mutant insulin and insulin receptor genes; author of various publications. *Mailing Add:* Dept Biochem & Howard Hughes Med Inst Univ Chicago 5841 S Maryland Ave Chicago IL 60637. *Fax:* 773-702-0271

STEINER, ERICH E, GENETICS. *Current Pos:* From instr to assoc prof, 58-61, Univ Mich, chmn dept. 68-71 & 79-81, dir, Matthaei Bot Gardens, 71-77, 89-91. PROF BOT, UNIV MICH, ANN ARBOR, 61- *Personal Data:* b Thun, Switz, Apr 9, 19; nat US; m 44, Dorothy White; c Kurt E, Karl R & Kim E. *Educ:* Univ Mich, BS, 40; Ind Univ, PhD(bot), 50. *Concurrent Pos:* NSF sr fel, 60-61. *Mem:* Bot Soc Am; Genetics Soc Am; Soc Study Evolution; Am Soc Naturalists; Soc Econ Bot. *Res:* Genetics and evolutionary biology of Oenothera; genetics of incompatibility; ecological genetics. *Mailing Add:* Dept Biol Univ Mich Ann Arbor MI 48109. *Fax:* 313-747-0884

STEINER, EUGENE FRANCIS, MATHEMATICS. *Current Pos:* RETIRED. *Personal Data:* b St Louis, Mo, July 15, 34; m 63; c 1. *Educ:* Univ Mo, BS, 56, MA, 60, PhD(math), 63. *Prof Exp:* Asst prof physics, Southwestern La Inst, 56-57; eng physicist, McDonnell Aircraft Corp, 58-59; asst prof math, Univ NMex, 63-65; assoc prof, Tex Tech Col, 65-66; assoc prof, Univ NMex, 66-68; from assoc prof to prof math, Iowa State Univ, 68-93. *Concurrent Pos:* Vis prof, Univ Alta, 70-71. *Mem:* Am Math Soc; Math Asn Am. *Res:* General topology. *Mailing Add:* PO Box 575 Bisbee AZ 85603

STEINER, GEORGE, ENDOCRINOLOGY & METABOLISM. *Current Pos:* dir, Lipid Res Clin, Toronto Gen Hosp, 66-80, dir, Diabetes Clin, 66-83, dir, Div Endocrinol & Metab, 80-91, DIR, DIABETES ATHEROSCLEROSIS INTERVENTION STUDY, TORONTO GEN HOSP, 91- *Personal Data:* b Czech, Mar 11, 36; Can citizen; m 66; c 2. *Educ:* Univ BC, BA, 56, MD, 60; FRCP(C), 65. *Honors & Awards:* MDS Award, Can Soc Clin Chem; Pfizer lectureship, Clin Res Inst, Montreal. *Prof Exp:* Resident med, Royal Victoria Hosp, McGill Univ, 60-62; fel, Harvard Med Sch, Peter Bent Brigham Hosp & Joslin Clin Res Lab, 62-64; resident med & endocrinol, Royal Victoria Hosp, McGill Univ, 64-66; from lectr to assoc prof med & physiol, Univ Toronto, 66-80. *Concurrent Pos:* Med Res Coun Can scholar, 67-72. *Mem:* Am Diabetes Asn; Am Fedn Clin Res; Am Physiol Soc; Endocrine Soc; Can Soc Clin Invest; Am Heart Asn. *Res:* Interaction of carbohydrate and lipid metabolism; hyperlipemia and atherosclerosis; diabetes and atherosclerosis. *Mailing Add:* Dept Med & Physiol Toronto Gen Hosp Rm NUW9-112 200 Elizabeth St Toronto ON M5G 2C4 Can. *Fax:* 416-340-3473

STEINER, GEORGE, THEORY OF SCHEDULING, ALGORITHMIC ORDER THEORY. *Current Pos:* from asst prof to assoc prof, 81-92, chair, Mgt Sci & Info Systs Area, 89-93, PROF, PROD & MGT SCI, MCMASTER UNIV, 92- *Personal Data:* b Budapest, Hungary, Sept 11, 47; Can citizen; m 74, Judit Csizmazia; c Adam & David. *Educ:* Eotvos Univ, Budapest, Hungary, MSc, 71; Univ Waterloo, Can, PhD(math), 82. *Prof Exp:* Systs analyst, Infelor Syst Eng Inst, Hungary, 71-73, Steel Co Can, 74-80. *Concurrent Pos:* Vis prof, Univ Bonn, Ger, 87; vis res dir, Univ Montpellier

II, France, 93. *Mem:* Fel Inst Combinatorics & Applns; Soc Indust & Appl Math; Inst Mgt Sci & Opers Res; Math Prog Soc; Can Oper Res Soc. *Res:* Scheduling; combinatorial optimization; algorithmic order theory; operations research; author of various publications; graph theory. *Mailing Add:* Fac Bus McMaster Univ Hamilton ON L8S 4M4 Can. *Fax:* 905-521-8995; *E-Mail:* steiner@mcmaster.ca

STEINER, GILBERT, MATHEMATICS, ALGEBRA. *Current Pos:* from asst prof to assoc prof, 68-79, PROF MATH, FAIRLEIGH DICKINSON UNIV, TEANECK CAMPUS, 79- *Personal Data:* b Moscow, USSR, Jan 19, 37; US citizen; m 71; c 2. *Educ:* Univ Mich, BS, 58, MS, 59; Univ Calif, Berkeley, PhD(math), 62. *Prof Exp:* Instr math, Reed Col, 62-64; asst prof, Dalhousie Univ, 64-68. *Mem:* Am Math Soc; Math Asn Am. *Res:* Functional analysis. *Mailing Add:* Dept Math Fairleigh Dickinson Univ Teaneck NJ 07666-1914

STEINER, HENRY M, ENGINEERING ECONOMICS, HIGHWAY ECONOMICS. *Current Pos:* PROF ENG ECON, GEORGE WASHINGTON UNIV, 76- *Personal Data:* b San Francisco, Calif, Aug 20, 23; m, Altagracia Landeros; c Richard, Maria C, Jessie A & Henry A. *Educ:* Stanford Univ, BA, 44, MS, 50, PhD(civil eng), 65. *Prof Exp:* Engr, War Dept, Korea, 46-47, Utah Construct Co, 50-51 & Aramco, Saudi Arabia, 53-55; asst prof sci, Univ Americas, 59-63; prof econ, Escuela Administracion Graduados, 65-67; assoc prof mgt, Univ Tex, Austin, 68-76. *Concurrent Pos:* Vis prof, Stanford Univ, 67-68 & Univ Calif, Berkeley, 87; consult, World Bank, Ecuador, Panama & Mex, 69, 77, 91, 93 & 94, Army CEngr, 88-89 & many pvt co. *Mem:* Am Soc Civil Engrs; Transp Res Forum. *Res:* Engineering economics; surface transportation, particularly roads. *Mailing Add:* 5315 Wehawken Rd Bethesda MD 20816. *Fax:* 202-994-4606

STEINER, HERBERT M, PARTICLE PHYSICS. *Current Pos:* Lectr, 57-60, from asst prof to assoc prof, 61-67, PROF PHYSICS, UNIV CALIF, BERKELEY, 67-, PHYSICIST, LAWRENCE BERKELEY LABS, 53- *Personal Data:* b Goppingen, Ger, Dec 8, 27; nat US. *Educ:* Univ Calif, Berkeley, BS, 51, PhD(physics), 56. *Concurrent Pos:* Guggenheim fel, 60-61; vis scientist, Europ Ctr Nuclear Res, 60-61, 64 & 68-69; Alexander von Humboldt sr scientist, 76-77; guest scientist, Max Planck Inst Physics & Astrophysics, Munich, 76-78; vis prof, Japan Soc Promotion Sci, 78. *Mem:* Am Phys Soc. *Res:* High energy physics; elementary particle interactions. *Mailing Add:* Lawrence Berkeley Nat Lab 1 Cyclotron Rd MS 50-208 Berkeley CA 94720. *Fax:* 510-643-8497

STEINER, JAMES W(ESLEY), ELECTRICAL ENGINEERING. *Current Pos:* dept mgr systs design, Western Develop Labs Div, Philco-Ford Corp, 68-69, mgr systs design, 69-70, mgr systs eng activ, 70-78, mgr, equip prog activ, 78-80, MGR, SYSTS INTEGRATION ACTIV, ESD DIV, FORD AEROSPACE & COMMUN CORP, 80- *Personal Data:* b Lexington, Ky, Oct 3, 26; m 51; c 3. *Educ:* Univ Ky, BSEE, 48; Purdue Univ, MSEE, 50; Columbia Univ, EE, 60; NY Univ, MBA, 68. *Prof Exp:* Asst proj engr flight simulators, Curtiss-Wright Corp, 50-52; sr engr Lacrosse Missile, Fed Labs Div, Int Tel & Tel Corp, 52-55, develop engr, 55-56, proj engr, 56-58, sr proj engr Dew Line, 58-60, exec engr courier satellite, 60-66, proj mgr commun, Telemetry & Command Subsyst Develop, Intelsat III Commun Satellite, 66-68. *Mem:* Sr mem Inst Elec & Electronics Engrs. *Res:* Range measurement by continuous wave phase shift measurements; digital command for satellite communications; telemetry and master timing systems; satellite ground support systems; telemetry, tracking and commanding; digital communications. *Mailing Add:* 14195 Wild Plum Lane Los Altos Hills CA 94022

STEINER, JEAN LOUISE, agroclimatology, for more information see previous edition

STEINER, JOHN EDWARD, AERONAUTICAL ENGINEERING MANAGEMENT. *Current Pos:* RETIRED. *Personal Data:* b Seattle, Wash, Nov 7, 17; m 42; c 3. *Educ:* Univ Wash, BS, 40; Mass Inst Technol, MS, 41. *Hon Degrees:* Summa Laude Dignatus, Univ Wash, 78. *Honors & Awards:* Elmer A Sperry Award, 80; Thulin Medal, Sweden; Sir C Kingsford Smith Award, Australia; Wright Brothers Mem Lectr, 82. *Prof Exp:* Aerodynamist com & mil airplane, Boeing Airplane Co, 41-44, chief aerodynamist, 44-48, sr group engr, 48-55, proj engr, 55-58, prog mgr 727 prog, 58-60, chief proj engr, 60-65, chief engr all com opers, 65-66, vpres eng & prod develop, 66-68, vpres mkt, Boeing Com Airplane Co, 68-70, vpres & div gen mgr, 70-73, vpres all opers, 73-74, vpres prog develop, 74-76, vpres, corp prod develop, 76-83; chmn, Aeronaut Policy Rev Comt, Exec Off President of US, 83-89. *Concurrent Pos:* Trustee & mem exec comt, Pac Sci Ctr, 75- *Mem:* Nat Acad Eng; fel Am Inst Aeronaut & Astronaut; fel Royal Aeronaut Soc. *Res:* High technology research involving aerodynamic efficiency of swept wings and total commercial and military configurations; structural efficiency and durability; propulsion integration; computer aided productivity improvement research in engineering and manufacturing. *Mailing Add:* 3425 Evergreen Pt Rd Medina WA 98039

STEINER, JOHN F, ELECTROCHEMISTRY. *Current Pos:* RETIRED. *Personal Data:* b Milwaukee, Wis, July 21, 08; m 49. *Educ:* Univ Wis, BS, 29, MS, 32, PhD(chem), 33. *Prof Exp:* Instr chem, Univ Wis, 29-33, Alumni Asn fel, 33-34; develop chemist, Milwaukee Gas Specialty Co, 35-36; res chemist, Globe-Union, Inc, Wis, 36-37 & Miner Labs, Ill, 38-53; head food lab, Guardite Corp, 53-56; dir, Chem Res Labs, 56-85. *Concurrent Pos:* Dir develop, Sound Recording Serv, 47-; mem staff, Univ Ill & Wilson Col, 59-; consult, Ill Dept Revenue, 64- & US Dept Internal Revenue, 65- *Mem:* AAAS; Am Chem Soc; Electrochem Soc. *Res:* Limnology; ceramics; dentifrices; cereals; food technology; sound recording; information storage-retrieval. *Mailing Add:* 2748 S Superior Milwaukee WI 53207-2328

STEINER, JOSEPH PERRY, NEUROBIOLOGY OF NEURODEGENERATIVE DISEASES. *Current Pos:* SR SCIENTIST, GUILFORD PHARMACEUT INC, 94- *Personal Data:* b Allentown, Pa, Sept 15, 61; m 83, Alice M Domitrovits; c Hayley J. *Educ:* Lehigh Univ, BS, 83, MS, 84; Johns Hopkins Univ, PhD(cell biol), 89. *Prof Exp:* Postdoctoral fel, Duke Univ Med Ctr, 89-90, Sch Med, Johns Hopkins Univ, 90-94. *Concurrent Pos:* Vis scientist, Sch Med, Johns Hopkins Univ, 94- *Mem:* Soc Neurosci; AAAS; NY Acad Sci. *Res:* Evaluating novel small molecule neurotrophic factors (neuroimmunophilia ligands) for the treatment of neurodegenerative diseases of the peripheral nervous system. *Mailing Add:* Guilford Pharmaceut Inc 6611 Tributary St Baltimore MD 21124. *Fax:* 410-631-6804; *E-Mail:* steiner_j@guilfordpharm.com

STEINER, KIM CARLYLE, FOREST GENETICS. *Current Pos:* PROF FOREST GENETICS, PA STATE UNIV, 87- *Personal Data:* b Alton, Ill, Nov 21, 48; m 70; c 3. *Educ:* Colo State Univ, BS, 70; Mich State Univ, MS, 71, PhD(forest genetics), 75. *Mem:* Sigma Xi; Soc Am Foresters. *Res:* Genetics and ecology of forest trees; genetic adaptation of trees to environmental stresses; taxonomy, distribution and geographic variation of forest trees. *Mailing Add:* Dept Forestry Pa State Univ 313 Forest Resources University Park PA 16802-1009

STEINER, KURT EDRIC, DIABETES, ATHEROSCLEROSIS. *Current Pos:* res scientist metabolic dis, Wyeth Labs, 84-88, sect head, Wyeth-Ayerst Res, 88, assoc dir, 88-91, DIR CARDIOVASC & METAB DIS, WYETH-AYERST RES, 91- *Personal Data:* b Roanoke, Va, July 24, 46; m 80; c 3. *Educ:* Col Wooster, BA, 68; Univ Calif, Davis, PhD(biochem), 76. *Prof Exp:* From instr to asst prof physiol, Vanderbilt Med Sch, 81-84. *Mem:* Am Diabetes Asn; Am Heart Asn. *Res:* Hormonal regulation of metabolism; mechanisms of insulin resistance in diabetes mellitus and the discovery of novel pharmacological interventions. *Mailing Add:* 15 Woodlane Rd Trenton NJ 08648

STEINER, LISA AMELIA, IMMUNOLOGY. *Current Pos:* From asst prof to assoc prof, 57-80, PROF BIOL, MASS INST TECHNOL, 80- *Personal Data:* b Vienna, Austria, May 12, 33; US citizen. *Educ:* Swarthmore Col, BA, 54; Radcliffe Col, MA, 56; Yale Univ, MD, 59. *Concurrent Pos:* Helen Hay Whitney res fel microbiol med sch, Wash Univ, St Louis, 62-65; Am Heart Asn res fel immunol, Wright-Fleming Inst, London, 65-67; mem allergy & immunol study sect, NIH, 74-78; mem bd overseers, Rosenstiel Basic Med Sci Res Ctr, 76-80, chmn, 80-; mem personnel comt, Am Cancer Soc, 79-84; mem bd sci counsrs, Nat Cancer Inst, 80-83; bd trustees, Helen Hay Whitney Found, 84-; mem-at-large, Biol Sci Comt, AAAS, 85-87. *Mem:* Am Asn Immunol; Am Soc Biol Chem; fel AAAS. *Res:* Structure and function of immunoglobulins; phylogeny and ontogeny of immune response; protein chemistry. *Mailing Add:* Dept Biol Mass Inst Technol 77 Massachusetts Ave Cambridge MA 02139. *Fax:* 617-253-8699; *E-Mail:* lsteiner@mit.edu

STEINER, MANFRED, PLATELETS, BIOCHEMISTRY. *Current Pos:* PROF HEMAT, BROWN UNIV, 68-, DIR, DIV HEMAT & ONCOL, BROWN UNIV MEM HOSP, 82- *Educ:* Univ Vienna, Austria, MD, 55; Mass Inst Technol, PhD(biochem), 67. *Concurrent Pos:* Vis scientist, Roche Fund. *Mem:* Am Physiol Soc; Am Soc Biochem & Molecular Biol; Am Asn Path; Am Soc Hemat. *Mailing Add:* Dept Med Hematol & Oncol E Carolina Univ Sch Med Bio op 3E-127 Greenville NC 27858-4354. *Fax:* 401-722-0198

STEINER, MARION ROTHBERG, BIOCHEMISTRY, ONCOLOGY. *Current Pos:* asst prof exp path, 78-83, ASSOC PROF MICRO IMMUNOL, UNIV KY, 83- *Personal Data:* b New York, NY, May 23, 41; m 63; c 2. *Educ:* Smith Col, BA, 62; Univ Ky, PhD(biochem), 68. *Prof Exp:* Instr biochem, Univ Ky, 68-70; fel, Baylor Col Med, 71-73, asst prof virol, 73-78. *Mem:* Am Chem Soc; Am Soc Microbiologists; Am Asn Cancer Res. *Res:* Examination of the structure and function of the surface membrane of oncogenic cells, utilizing mouse mammary carcinomas and dysplasias as a model system. *Mailing Add:* Dept Microbiol Univ Ky Med Schh 800 Rose St Lexington KY 40536-0001

STEINER, MORRIS, pediatrics; deceased, see previous edition for last biography

STEINER, PINCKNEY ALSTON, III, SOLID STATE PHYSICS, MAGNETIC RESONANCE. *Current Pos:* asst prof, 66-77, ASSOC PROF PHYSICS, CLEMSON UNIV, 77-, ASSOC DEPT HEAD. *Personal Data:* b Athens, Ga, Apr 5, 38; m 60, Billie Peebles; c Pinckney A & Susan (Stoddard). *Educ:* Univ Ga, BS, 59; Duke Univ, PhD(physics), 65. *Prof Exp:* Res fel chem physics, H C Orsted Inst, Copenhagen Univ, 64-66. *Mem:* Am Phys Soc; Sigma Xi; Am Asn Physics Teachers. *Res:* Electron paramagnetic resonance applied to various problems in solid state physics and in biophysics. *Mailing Add:* Dept Physics & Astron Clemson Univ 302A Kinard Lab Clemson SC 29634

STEINER, RAY PHILLIP, NUMBER THEORY. *Current Pos:* Asst prof, 68-72, assoc prof, 72-78, PROF MATH, BOWLING GREEN STATE UNIV, 78- *Personal Data:* b Bronx, NY, Apr 28, 41; m 72, Carol M Cooper. *Educ:* Univ Ariz, BSEE, 63, MS, 65; Ariz State Univ, PhD(math), 68. *Mem:* Fibonacci Asn; Am Math Soc; Math Asn Am; Nat Coun Teachers Math. *Res:* Finding the units and class numbers of algebraic number fields by linear programming techniques, Diophantine equations and Fibonacci numbers; Diophantine approximation; Catalan's problem. *Mailing Add:* Dept Math Bowling Green State Univ Bowling Green OH 43403-0001. *Fax:* 419-372-6092; *E-Mail:* steiner@math.ugsu.edu

STEINER, ROBERT ALAN, NEUROENDOCRINOLOGY, REPRODUCTIVE PHYSIOLOGY. *Current Pos:* Sr fel endocrinol, Univ Wash, 75-77, asst prof physiol, 77-80, assoc prof, 80-85, PROF OBSTET & GYNEC, PHYSIOL & BIOPHYS, UNIV WASH, 85- *Personal Data:* b Chicago, Ill, Mar 9, 47. *Educ:* Univ Pac, BA, 69; Univ Ore, PhD(physiol), 75. *Concurrent Pos:* Res affil, Regional Primate Res Ctr, Univ Wash, 77-, Diabetes Res Ctr, 78- *Mem:* Am Physiol Soc; Soc Study Reproduction; Am Soc Zoologists; Am Endocrine Soc; Intl Neuroendocrine Soc; Soc Neurosci. *Res:* Control of neuropeptide gene expression; neuroendocrine control of the onset of puberty and growth. *Mailing Add:* Dept OB/GYN Physiol & Biophys RH 20 Univ Wash Sch Med Box 357290 Seattle WA 98195-7290

STEINER, ROBERT FRANK, PHYSICAL BIOCHEMISTRY. *Current Pos:* chmn dept, 74-82, prof, 70-95, EMER PROF CHEM, UNIV MD, BALTIMORE COUNTY, 95- *Personal Data:* b Manila, Philippines, Sept 29, 26; US citizen; m 56, Ethel Fisher; c Victoria & Laura. *Educ:* Princeton Univ, AB, 47; Harvard Univ, PhD(phys chem), 50. *Prof Exp:* Fel, US Naval Med Res Inst, 50-51, phys chemist, 51-70. *Concurrent Pos:* Jewett fel, 50-51; lectr, Georgetown Univ, 57-58 & Howard Univ, 58-59 & 60-61; mem, US Civil Serv Bd Exam, 58-; mem, Molecular Biol Panel, NSF, 67-70; ed, Res Commun Chem Path & Pharmacol, 70- & Biophys Chem, 73-95; mem, biophys & biophys chem study sect, NIH, 76-80; fel, Japanese Soc Prom Sci, 91. *Mem:* Am Chem Soc; Biophys Soc; Am Soc Biol Chem; NY Acad Sci. *Res:* Light scattering; fluorescence; protein interactions; nucleic acids; synthetic polynucleotides; statistical thermodynamics. *Mailing Add:* 2609 Turf Valley Rd Ellicott City MD 21043-2021. *Fax:* 410-455-2608

STEINER, RUSSELL IRWIN, INDUSTRIAL ORGANIC CHEMISTRY. *Current Pos:* RETIRED. *Personal Data:* b Lebanon, Pa, July 21, 27; m 56, Rosemary; c Robert, Jane, James & Peter. *Educ:* Lebanon Valley Col, BS, 49; Univ Conn, MS, 52, PhD(chem), 55. *Prof Exp:* Res chemist, Nat Aniline Div, Allied Chem Corp, 55-63, group leader, 63-65, res supvr, Indust Chem Div, 65-67; res assoc, Crompton & Knowles, 67-74, group leader disperse dyes, 74-80, dir process develop, 80-86, res & develop, 86-89, vpres res & develop, Dyes & Chem Div, 89-92. *Mem:* Am Chem Soc; Am Asn Textile Chem & Colorists; Sigma Xi. *Res:* Textile dyes; food colors. *Mailing Add:* 3905 Kline Ave Reading PA 19606-2804

STEINER, SHELDON, BIOCHEMISTRY. *Current Pos:* assoc prof biol sci, 78-83, PROF BIOL SCI, UNIV KY, LEXINGTON, 83- *Personal Data:* b Bronx, NY, Apr 23, 40; m 63; c 2. *Educ:* Drew Univ, BA, 61; Univ Ky, MS, 64, PhD(microbiol), 67. *Prof Exp:* Instr, Baylor Col Med, 71-73, from asst prof to assoc prof virol, 73-78. *Concurrent Pos:* NIH grant, Univ Ky, 69-71; NIH spec fel, Baylor Col Med, 72-75; fac res award, Am Cancer Soc, 75-80. *Mem:* AAAS; Am Soc Biol Chemists; Am Soc Microbiol; Am Soc Cell Biol; Soc Complex Carbohydrates. *Res:* Structure and function of procaryotic and eucaryotic membranes; biochemical characterization of membranes of malignant cells; role of eicosanoids in myoblast differentiation. *Mailing Add:* Dept Biol Sci Univ Ky Lexington KY 40506-0001. *Fax:* 606-257-1717; *E-Mail:* biui66@ukcc

STEINER, WERNER DOUGLAS, ORGANIC CHEMISTRY. *Current Pos:* RETIRED. *Personal Data:* b Milwaukee, Wis, Oct 8, 32; m 61; c 3. *Educ:* Univ Karlsruhe, BA, 56, MA, 58; Univ Pa, PhD(org chem), 64. *Prof Exp:* Res & develop chemist, Org Chem Dept, Jackson Lab, E I DuPont de Nemours & Co, Deepwater, NJ, 63-65, process develop chemist, 67-68 & dyes & intermediates, 68-75, sr chemist, 62-80. *Mem:* AAAS; Am Chem Soc. *Res:* Research and development of dyes for natural and man-made fibers; research and development of fluorine compounds for use as aerosol propellants, hydraulic fluids, instrument fluids, convective coolants and working fluids; process development of dyes and fluorine compounds; dye process development, manufacture, intermediates. *Mailing Add:* 1135 Mainsail Dr Tarpon Springs FL 34689

STEINERT, LEON ALBERT, QUANTUM PHYSICAL SYSTEMS, ELECTROMAGNETIC RADIATION. *Current Pos:* RES DIR, PHYS SYNERGETICS INST, 81- *Personal Data:* b Shattuck, Okla, May 2, 30; m 88, Emanuela Montauti. *Educ:* La Sierra Col, BA, 52; Univ Colo, MS, 56, PhD(physics), 62. *Prof Exp:* Physicist, Nat Bur Standards, 53-65; theoret physicist, Lawrence Radiation Lab, 66-67; sr scientist, McDonnell Douglas Corp, 67-70; sr res engr-scientist, Lockheed Corp, 72-79; res engr, Systs Control, Inc, 79; consult, IRT Corp & Miss State Univ, 80-81. *Concurrent Pos:* Lectr, Loma Linda Univ, 68. *Mem:* Am Phys Soc; Am Math Soc; Soc Indust & Appl Math. *Res:* Theoretical physics of quantum physical systems; applications of quantum statistical condensed-matter physics theory in microelectronics; electromagnetic fields scattering theory. *Mailing Add:* PO Box 8634 Riverside CA 92515-8634

STEINERT, PETER MALCOLM, EPIDERMIS, KERATIN. *Current Pos:* SR INVESTR, NAT CANCER INST, 73- *Educ:* Univ Adelaide, Australia, PhD(biochem), 72. *Mem:* Am Soc Cell Biol; Am Soc Biochem & Molecular Biol; Soc Invest Dermat. *Res:* Studies the structure, function and expression of keratin intermediate filaments of the epidemus and their associated proteins, including filagrin and the cornified cell envelop. *Mailing Add:* Br Lab Skin Biol NIAMS NIH 6425 Bethesda MD 20892-0001. *Fax:* 301-402-2886; *E-Mail:* pemast@helix.nih.gov

STEINETZ, BERNARD GEORGE, JR, ENDOCRINOLOGY, REPRODUCTIVE PHYSIOLOGY. *Current Pos:* assoc prof, 84-90, PROF FORENSIC MED, LAB EXP MED & SURG PRIMATES, MED CTR, NY UNIV, TUXEDO, 90- *Personal Data:* b Germantown, Pa, May 30, 27; m 49, Jane Nash; c Scott & Ann. *Educ:* Princeton Univ, AB, 49; Rutgers Univ, PhD(zool), 54. *Prof Exp:* Asst org res chemist, Irving Varnish & Insulator Co, 47; asst, Rutgers Univ, 52-54; sr scientist physiol res, Warner-Lambert Res Inst, 54-62, sr res assoc, 62-67; head reproductive physiol & fel, Ciba Res, Ciba Pharmaceut Co, NJ, 67-71, mgr endocrinol & metab, Pharmaceut Div, Ciba-Geigy Corp, Ardsley, NY 71-84. *Concurrent Pos:* Res assoc prof, NY Univ Sch Med, 74- *Mem:* Endocrine Soc; Am Physiol Soc; Orthop Res Soc; fel NY Acad Sci; Soc Exp Biol & Med; Soc Study Reproduction. *Res:* Reproductive physiology; hormone metabolism; hormones and connective tissue; hormones and aging; hormone interactions; role of mediators in osteoarthritis; hip dysplasia; milk-borne hormones. *Mailing Add:* 336 Longbow Dr Franklin Lakes NJ 07417. *Fax:* 914-351-5258

STEINFELD, JEFFREY IRWIN, PHYSICAL CHEMISTRY. *Current Pos:* from asst prof to assoc prof, 66-79, PROF CHEM, MASS INST TECHNOL, 80- *Personal Data:* b Brooklyn, NY, July 2, 40. *Educ:* Mass Inst Technol, BS, 62; Harvard Univ, PhD(chem), 65. *Prof Exp:* NSF fel, 65-66. *Concurrent Pos:* Alfred P Sloan res fel, 69-71; John Simon Guggenheim fel, Univ Calif, Berkeley & Kammerlingh-Onnes Lab, Leiden, 72-73; consult, Aerospace Corp, 74-80, Los Alamos Nat Lab, 75-85 & KOR, Inc, 80-85; mem, Sci Adv Bd, Laser Technics, Inc, 82-; vis prof, Joint Inst Lab Astrophys, 83 & 86; prof invite, Univerite de Bourgogne, Dijon, France, 91. *Mem:* AAAS; fel Am Phys Soc; Fedn Am Sci; Sigma Xi; Union Concerned Scientists. *Res:* Molecular spectroscopy; energy transfer in molecular collisions; applications of lasers to chemical kinetics, atmospheric and environmental chemistry. *Mailing Add:* Dept Chem Rm 2-221 Mass Inst Technol Cambridge MA 02139. *E-Mail:* jisteinf@athena.mit.edu

STEINFELD, JESSE LEONARD, CANCER, MEDICINE. *Current Pos:* RETIRED. *Personal Data:* b West Aliquippa, Pa, Jan 6, 27; m 53, Gen M Stokas; c Mary Beth, Jody K & Susan F. *Educ:* Univ Pittsburgh, BS, 45; Western Res Univ, MD, 49; Am Bd Internal Med, dipl, 58. *Hon Degrees:* LLD, Gannon Col, 72. *Prof Exp:* Instr med, Univ Calif, 52-54 & George Washington Univ, 54-58; asst dir, Blood Hosp, City of Hope, Duarte, Calif, 58-59; from asst prof to prof med, Sch Med, Univ Southern Calif, 59-68, cancer coordr, 66-68; dep dir, Nat Cancer Inst, 68-69; dep asst secy health & sci affairs, HEW, 69-72; surgeon gen, USPHS, 69-73; prof med & dir, Dept Oncol, Mayo Clin & Mayo Med Sch, Rochester, Minn, 73-74; prof med, Univ Calif, Irvine, 74-76; chief med serv, Long Beach Vet Admin Hosp, 74-76; prof med & dean, Sch Med, Med Col Va, 76-83; pres, Med Col Ga, 83-87. *Concurrent Pos:* AEC fel med, Univ Calif, 52-53; clin investr, Nat Cancer Inst, 54-58, mem, Krebiozen Rev Comt, 63- & Clin Studies Panel, 64-66, consult, 66-, mem chemother adv comt, 67 & cancer spec prog adv comt, 67; consult, Vet Admin Hosp, Long Beach, Calif, 59-, City of Hope Med Ctr, 60- & Kern County Gen Hosp, Bakersfield, 64-; mem, Calif State Cancer Adv Coun, 61-68. *Mem:* Soc Nuclear Med; Am Asn Cancer Res; AMA; fel Am Col Physicians; Am Fedn Clin Res. *Res:* Cancer chemotherapy; hematology; health administration. *Mailing Add:* 18676 Avenida Cordillera San Diego CA 92128. *Fax:* 619-485-0468; *E-Mail:* jlsondsd@pachell.net

STEINFELD, LEONARD, MEDICINE. *Current Pos:* assoc prof, 66-69, PROF PEDIAT, MT SINAI SCH MED, 69- *Personal Data:* b New York, NY, Nov 16, 25; m 65; c 4. *Educ:* Hofstra Col, BA, 49; State Univ NY Downstate Med Ctr, MD, 53. *Prof Exp:* Intern, Los Angeles County Gen Hosp, 53-54; resident pediat, Mt Sinai Hosp, NY, NY, 54-56, instr pediat, Col Physicians & Surgeons, Columbia Univ, 58-68. *Concurrent Pos:* NIH fel pediat cardiol, Mt Sinai Hosp, NY, 56-57, NY Heart Asn fel, 57-58; from asst attend pediatrician to assoc attend pediatrician, Mt Sinai Hosp, 59-69, attend pediatrician, 69-; consult, USPHS Hosp, Staten Island, 60- & Perth Amboy Gen Hosp, NY, 70- *Mem:* Am Acad Pediat; Am Col Cardiol; Am Heart Asn; NY Acad Sci. *Res:* Heart disease in infants and children. *Mailing Add:* Dept Pediat Mt Sinai Hosp 5th Ave & 100th St New York NY 10029

STEINFINK, HUGO, MATERIALS SCIENCE & ENGINEERING. *Current Pos:* assoc prof, 60-63, PROF CHEM ENG, UNIV TEX, AUSTIN, 63-, T BROCKETT HUDSON PROF ENG, 81- *Personal Data:* b Vienna, Austria, May 22, 24; nat US; m 48; c 2. *Educ:* City Col New York, BS, 47; Columbia Univ, MA, 48; Polytech Inst Brooklyn, PhD(chem), 54. *Prof Exp:* Res chemist, Shell Develop Co, 48-51 & 54-60. *Mem:* Am Chem Soc; Mineral Soc Am; Am Crystallog Asn; Am Inst Chem Engrs; Mat Res Soc. *Res:* Crystal structures of silicate minerals and silicate-organic complexes; crystal chemistry and physical properties of semiconductor and superconductor materials; materials science research. *Mailing Add:* Mat Sci & Eng Prog Univ Tex Ete 9104 Austin TX 78712. *Fax:* 512-471-7060; *E-Mail:* hugo@utxvm.cc.utexas.edu

STEINGISER, SAMUEL, CHEMISTRY. *Current Pos:* COMPUTER CONSULT, 85- *Personal Data:* b Springfield, Mass, June 6, 18; m 46; c 3. *Educ:* City Col New York, BS, 38; Polytech Inst Brooklyn, MS, 41; Univ Conn, PhD, 49. *Prof Exp:* Chemist, Rockefeller Inst, 41-42; asst atom bomb proj S A M Labs, Columbia Univ, 42-43; asst, Carbide & Carbon Chems Corp, NY, 44-46; res assoc, Metall Lab, Univ Chicago, 43-44; group leader phys chem, Publicker Industs, Pa, 46; res assoc, US Off Naval Res, Conn, 46-50; group leader & res scientist, Cent Res Dept, Monsanto Chem Co, 50-54; group leader, Mobay Chem Co, 54-59, asst res dir, 59-65; scientist, Monsanto Res Corp, Ohio, 66-70, sci fel, Lopac Proj, Monsanto Co, Bloomfield, Conn, 70-77, res mgr & sr fel, 77-83. *Concurrent Pos:* Mem mat adv bd, Nat Res Coun, 61-63; mem, Int Standardization Orgn; ed, J Cellular Plastics, J Elastomer & Plastics. *Mem:* Fel AAAS; Am Chem Soc; Soc Plastics Indust; Am Soc Test & Mat; Soc Rheol. *Res:* Mass spectroscopy; corrosion; electrolysis; nuclear chemistry; high-vacuum phenomena; magneto-optics; magnetic susceptibility; high polymer physics; mechanical properties; foams and elastomers; advanced composites; instrumentation design; plastics processing and development; computer technology. *Mailing Add:* Five Fox Chase Rd Bloomfield CT 06002-2107

STEINGLASS, PETER JOSEPH, ALCOHOLISM, CHRONIC ILLNESS. *Current Pos:* DIR, ACKERMAN INST FAMILY THER, 90-; CLIN PROF PSYCHIAT, CORNELL UNIV MED COL, 93- *Personal Data:* b New York, NY, Mar 1, 39; m 62, Abbe Stahl; c Matthew A & Joanna E. *Educ:* Union Col, AB, 60; Harvard Univ, MD, 65; Am Bd Psychiat & Neurol, dipl. *Prof Exp:* Head clin res prog, Nat Inst Alcohol Abuse & Alcoholism, 71-74; asst prof psychiat, George Washington Univ, 74-77, assoc prof, 77-81, prof psychiat & behav sci, 81-90. *Concurrent Pos:* Vis prof psychiat, Hebrew Univ, Jerusalem, 81-82. *Mem:* Fel Am Psychiat Asn; fel Am Asn Marriage & Family Ther; fel Asn Clin Psychosocial Res; Am Family Ther Acad (vpres, 89-91); fel Am Orthopsychiat Asn; Am Psychosom Soc; AAAS. *Res:* Family therapy; psychiatry. *Mailing Add:* Ackerman Inst Family Ther 149 E 78th St New York NY 10021-0405. *Fax:* 212-744-0206

STEINGOLD, HAROLD, ENGINEERING. *Current Pos:* RETIRED. *Personal Data:* b Providence, RI, May 7, 29; m 57; c 3. *Educ:* Brown Univ, AB, 49; Univ Calif, Los Angeles, MS, 60, PhD(eng), 64. *Prof Exp:* Engr, Hughes Aircraft, 59-63, Rand Corp, Calif, 63-70, Visualtek, 70-72; eng specialist, Actron Corp, 72-77; eng survr, Hughes Helicopters, 77-82, sr scientist, Hughes Aircraft, 82-89. *Concurrent Pos:* Lectr, exten, Univ Calif, Santa Barbara, 64-, Los Angeles, 65 & San Fernando Valley State Col, 70- *Mem:* Sr mem Inst Elec & Electronics Engrs; Am Inst Mining Engrs. *Res:* Applications of computer technology and coherent electromagnetic sources to communications imaging and data processing; infrared and microwave imaging systems; protheses for the physically handicapped. *Mailing Add:* 407 16th St Santa Monica CA 90402

STEINHAGEN, WILLIAM HERRICK, INHALATION TOXICOLOGY TECHNOLOGY. *Current Pos:* TECH SALES MGR, ALL TECH ASSOC, INC, 89- *Personal Data:* b Dayton, Ohio, May 25, 48; m 68, Cheryl Strader; c Lorre & Bryan. *Educ:* NC State Univ, Raleigh, BS, 83. *Prof Exp:* Inhalation tech, Wright-Patterson AFB, 68-74; inhalation toxicologist, Becton-Dickinson Res Ctr, 74-78; sr res asst inhalation toxicol, Chem Indust Inst Toxicol, 78-79, res assoc, 79-81, sr res assoc, 81-84, assoc scientist inhalation toxicol, 84-89. *Concurrent Pos:* Consult, Northrop Serv, Inc, 85. *Mem:* Soc Toxicol; Wildlife Soc; Waterfowl USA, Inc. *Res:* Inhalation technology associated with the generation and analysis of gas, vapor, liquid aerosol and particulate test atmospheres for inhalation toxicology studies; author or co-author of over 40 articles and abstracts in the field of inhalation toxicology. *Mailing Add:* 412 Oak Ridge Rd Cary NC 27511. *Fax:* 919-469-5334

STEINHARDT, CHARLES KENDALL, ORGANIC CHEMISTRY, MATHEMATICAL STATISTICS. *Current Pos:* SR CHEMIST, MOBAY CHEM CORP, 77- *Personal Data:* b Milwaukee, Wis, Mar 1, 35; m 70; c 2. *Educ:* Univ Wis, BS, 57; Univ Ill, PhD(org chem), 63. *Prof Exp:* Instr chem, Univ Wash, Seattle, 63-65; chemist, Lubrizol Corp, Ohio, 65-71 & Napko Corp, Tex, 73-77. *Mem:* Am Chem Soc; Am Soc Qual Control. *Mailing Add:* 5206 Valerie Bellaire TX 77401-4827

STEINHARDT, EMIL J, MECHANICAL ENGINEERING. *Current Pos:* asst prof, 65-69, assoc prof, 69-81, PROF MECH ENG, WVA UNIV, 81- *Personal Data:* b Pittsburgh, Pa, Aug 19, 37; m 60. *Educ:* Univ Pittsburgh, BS, 59, MS, 61, PhD(mech eng), 65. *Prof Exp:* Instr mech eng, Univ Pittsburgh, 63-65. *Mem:* Am Soc Eng Educ; Am Soc Mech Engrs; Am Inst Aeronaut & Astronaut. *Res:* Satellite systems design; engineering systems design; rural systems and housing systems design. *Mailing Add:* 672 Westview Dr Morgantown WV 26505

STEINHARDT, GARY CARL, SOIL SCIENCE, AGRONOMY. *Current Pos:* asst, 71-74, from instr to assoc prof, 74-91, PROF AGRON, PURDUE UNIV, 91- *Personal Data:* b Lansing, Mich, Sept 13, 44; m 73, Thinh T Nguyen; c Angela A & Sarah J. *Educ:* Mich State Univ, BS, 66, MS, 68; Purdue Univ, PhD(agron), 76. *Prof Exp:* Asst soil sci, Mich State Univ, 66-68. *Mem:* Am Soc Agron; fel Soil & Water Conserv Soc; Coun Agr Sci & Technol. *Res:* Effects of soil management and tillage practices on the physical properties of soil; agricultural aspects of land use planning. *Mailing Add:* Dept Agron Purdue Univ 1150 Lilly Hall West Lafayette IN 47907-1150. *Fax:* 765-496-2926; *E-Mail:* gsteinhardt@dept.agry.purdue.edu

STEINHARDT, PAUL JOSEPH, INFLATIONARY UNIVERSE, QUASICRYSTALS. *Current Pos:* from asst prof to prof, 81-89, MARY AMANDA WOOD PROF PHYSICS, UNIV PA, 89- *Personal Data:* b Washington, DC, Dec 25, 52; m 79, Nancy R Shatzman; c Charles, Joseph & William. *Educ:* Caltech Univ, BS, 74; Harvard Univ, MA, 75, PhD(physics), 78. *Honors & Awards:* Second Award, Gravitational Res Found, 90, First Award, 93; Loeb lectr, Harvard Univ, 91; Welsh lectr, Univ Toronto, 96; Cita lectr, Can Inst Theoret Astrophys, 96. *Prof Exp:* Jr fel Harvard Univ, 78-81. *Concurrent Pos:* Consult, IBM Res, Yorktown Heights, NY, 78-91, Mass Inst Technol Res Estab Corp, 87-91; Sloan fel, 82-86; Monell fel, Inst Adv Study, 89-90, Dyson fel, 95; lectr, Phi Beta Kappa, 89-90; Guggenhein fel, 94-95. *Mem:* Fel Am Phys Soc; Sigma Xi; Am Astron Soc; Mat Res Soc. *Res:* Particle cosmology, especially phase transitions in the early universe; quasicrystals (theory of physical properties); amorphous solids and glasses; cosmic microwave background; granted 3 patents. *Mailing Add:* Dept Physics Univ Pa Philadelphia PA 19104. *Fax:* 215-898-2010; *E-Mail:* steinh@steinhardt.hep.upenn.edu

STEINHARDT, RICHARD ANTONY, CELL BIOLOGY. *Current Pos:* from asst prof to assoc prof, 67-78, PROF ZOOL, UNIV CALIF, BERKELEY, 79-, PROF MOLECULAR & CELL BIOL, 89- *Personal Data:* b Washington, DC, Sept 23, 39; m 77; c 2. *Educ:* Columbia Univ, AB, 61, PhD(biol sci), 66. *Honors & Awards:* Miller Res Prof, Univ Calif, Berkeley, 79. *Prof Exp:* NSF fel, Agr Res Coun Inst Animal Physiol, Babraham & Plymouth Marine Sta, Eng, 66-67. *Concurrent Pos:* Overseas fel, Churchill Col, Cambridge, Eng, 81. *Mem:* Fel AAAS; Soc Develop Biol; Am Soc Cell Biol. *Res:* Cell biology related to intracellular signals; developmental biology; ion transport; membrane permeability. *Mailing Add:* Dept Molecular & Cell Biol 391 LSA Univ Calif Berkeley CA 94720-3200. *Fax:* 510-643-6791; *E-Mail:* rick_steinhardt@maillink.berkeley.edu

STEINHART, CAROL ELDER, AGRICULTURAL & ENVIRONMENTAL SCIENCE, FOOD SAFETY. *Current Pos:* specialist, Biodata Sect, Dept Human Oncol, 77-80, proj assoc, Water Resources Ctr, 80-81, researcher, Food Res Inst, 91-96, ASST ED, JOUR CHEM EDUC, DEPT CHEM, UNIV WIS, 96- *Personal Data:* b Cleveland, Ohio, Mar 27, 35; div; c Gail S, Martha R & Geoffrey B. *Educ:* Albion Col, AB, 56; Univ Wis, PhD(bot), 60. *Prof Exp:* Biologist, Lab Gen & Comp Biochem, NIMH, 61-66; sci analyst div res grants, NIH, Md, 66-68; biologist, 68-70. *Concurrent Pos:* Freelance sci writer & ed, 70-83; res analyst, Wis Dept Agr, Trade & Consumer Protection, 81-83; tech writer & ed, Middleton Mem Vet Hosp, 83-90. *Res:* Growth, differentiation and nutrition of plant tissue cultures; hormonal control of enzyme synthesis in plants; ecology and environmental problems; environmental indices; soil erosion control; medical science; nutrition, food safety, diet and health; foodborne illness. *Mailing Add:* 104 Lathrop St Madison WI 53705. *Fax:* 608-262-7145; *E-Mail:* cstein@chem.wisc.edu

STEINHART, WILLIAM LEE, VIROLOGY. *Current Pos:* from asst prof to assoc prof, 75-91, PROF GENETICS, BOWDOIN COL, 91- *Personal Data:* b Philadelphia, Pa, May 31, 42; m 67, Sydnae Rouse; c Siri M. *Educ:* Univ Pa, AB, 64; Johns Hopkins Univ, PhD(biochem), 68. *Prof Exp:* Res assoc, Dept Biol Chem, Col Med, Pa State Univ, 71-75. *Concurrent Pos:* Mem bd dirs, Found Blood Res, 80-82; grant reviewer, Am Heart Asn, 83-85; mem med adv comt, Bd Pesticides Control, State of Maine, 85- *Mem:* AAAS; Am Soc Plant Physiologists; Am Soc Microbiol; Int Soc Plant Molecular Biol. *Res:* molecular genetics of virus replication; molecular biology of plant development. *Mailing Add:* Dept Biol Bowdoin Col Brunswick ME 04011. *Fax:* 207-725-3405

STEINHAUER, ALLEN LAURENCE, ENTOMOLOGY, ECOLOGY. *Current Pos:* from asst prof to assoc prof entom, Univ Md, 58-66, assoc prof, 69-71, prof, 71-93, chmn dept, 75-93, EMER PROF ENTOM, UNIV MED, COLLEGE PARK, 93- *Personal Data:* b Winnipeg, Man, Oct 17, 31; US citizen; m 58; c 2. *Educ:* Univ Man, BSA, 53; Ore State Univ, MS, 55, PhD(entom), 58. *Prof Exp:* Assoc prof, Ohio State Univ, 66-69. *Concurrent Pos:* Entom specialist, Ohio State Univ-US Agency Int Develop, Brazil, 66-69; ed, Environ Entom, 71-75. *Mem:* AAAS; Entom Soc Am; Int Orgn Biol Control; Brazilian Entom Soc. *Res:* Applied ecology; forage crop insects; biological control; pest management; insect behavior; graduate training. *Mailing Add:* Dept Entom Univ Md 4112 Plant Sci Bldg c/o Shirley Donkis College Park MD 20742-0001

STEINHAUER, PAUL DAVID, CHILD PSYCHIATRY. *Current Pos:* dir training child psychiat, 64-89, PROF PSYCHIAT, UNIV TORONTO, HOSP SICK CHILDREN, 65-, STAFF PSYCHIATRIST, 65- *Personal Data:* b Toronto, Ont, Nov 29, 33; m 56; c 4. *Educ:* Univ Toronto, MD, 57; FRCP(C), 62. *Honors & Awards:* Weiler Award. *Concurrent Pos:* Psychiat consult, Halton Co Children's Aid Soc, 63-75, Toronto Cath Children's Aid Soc, 64 & Children's Aid Soc Metrop Toronto, 65-; chmn, Sparrow Lake Alliance; chair, Voices for Children; mem, Ont Med Asn. *Mem:* Can Psychiat Asn; Can Acad Child Psychiat (pres, 81-82). *Res:* Development of process model of family functioning and the family assessment measure based on that model; relative effectiveness of two models of foster care on protecting children's adjustment and development and foster parent satisfaction; development of an instrument for assessing/predicting parenting capacity. *Mailing Add:* Dept Psychiat Hosp Sick Children 555 University Ave Toronto ON M5G 1X8 Can

STEINHAUS, DAVID WALTER, ATOMIC PHYSICS, SPECTROCHEMISTRY. *Current Pos:* RETIRED. *Personal Data:* b Neillsville, Wis, July 29, 19; m 49, Jean C Carryer; c Eric D, Bruce M, Kurt A & Karl E. *Educ:* Lake Forest Col, AB, 41; Johns Hopkins Univ, PhD(physics), 52. *Prof Exp:* Physicist, Cent Sci Co, 41-45, Cenco Indust fel, 41-42; res asst inst coop res, Johns Hopkins Univ, 46-52; mem staff & physicist, Los Alamos Nat Lab, 52-73, sect leader, 69-79; assoc prof physics, Memphis State Univ, 83-84; adj assoc prof physics & astron, Univ MNex, 84-93. *Concurrent Pos:* Mem comt line spectra of the elements, Nat Acad Sci-Nat Res Coun, 66-70; consult, Los Alamos Nat Lab, 79-83; distinguished US prof physics, Southwestern Memphis Col (now Rhodes Col), 79-83. *Mem:* AAAS; Optical Soc Am; Am Asn Physics Teachers; Soc Appl Spectros. *Res:* Instrument development; visible and ultraviolet spectroscopy; time resolution of spectra from spark discharges; high resolution spectroscopy; optical spectra of the heavy elements; spectrochemical analysis. *Mailing Add:* 2925 Candelita Ct NE Albuquerque NM 87112-2108

STEINHAUS, JOHN EDWARD, ANESTHESIOLOGY. *Current Pos:* assoc prof, 58-59, prof & chmn dept, 59-85, EMER PROF ANESTHESIOL, SCH MED, EMORY UNIV, 87- *Personal Data:* b Omaha, Nebr, Feb 23, 17; m 43, Jean; c 5. *Educ:* Univ Nebr, BA, 40, MA, 41; Univ Wis, MD, 45,

PhD(pharmacol), 50; Am Bd Anesthesiol, dipl, 59. *Honors & Awards:* Distinguished Serv Award, Am Soc Anesthesiol, 82. *Prof Exp:* Asst prof pharmacol, Marquette Univ, 50-51; assoc prof, Univ Wis, 51-54, asst prof anesthesiol, 54-58. *Mem:* Am Soc Anesthesiol (pres, 70); Asn Univ Anesthetists (pres, 71); Am Soc Pharmacol & Exp Therapeut; AMA. *Res:* Drug reactions and intoxications; antiarrhythmic agents; cough mechanism and suppression; depression of respiratory reflexes. *Mailing Add:* 836 Castle Falls Dr NE Atlanta GA 30329

STEINHAUS, RALPH K, ANALYTICAL CHEMISTRY. *Current Pos:* from asst prof to assoc prof, 68-82, PROF CHEM, WESTERN MICH UNIV, 82- *Personal Data:* b Sheboygan, Wis, June 21, 39; m 65, Nancy Hoover; c Kirk & Karen. *Educ:* Wheaton Col, BS, 61; Purdue Univ, PhD(anal chem), 66. *Prof Exp:* Asst prof chem, Wis State Univ-Oshkosh, 65-68. *Concurrent Pos:* Res assoc, Ohio State Univ, 75-76. *Mem:* Am Chem Soc; Sigma Xi. *Res:* Kinetics and mechanisms of transition metal chelates; factors affecting stability of metal chelates. *Mailing Add:* Dept Chem Western Mich Univ Kalamazoo MI 49008

STEINITZ, MICHAEL OTTO, SOLID STATE PHYSICS, MATERIALS SCIENCE. *Current Pos:* from asst prof to assoc prof, 73-83, PROF PHYSICS, ST FRANCIS XAVIER UNIV, 83- *Personal Data:* b New York, NY, June 12, 44; m 65, Heidi Maenz; c Daniel & Susanna. *Educ:* Cornell Univ, BE, 65; Northwestern Univ, Evanston, PhD(mat sci), 70. *Prof Exp:* Coop student comput logic, Philco Corp, 62-63, coop student radio propagation, 63; Nat Res Coun Can fel, Dept Physics, Univ Toronto, 70-72, proj scientist solid state physics, Dept Metall, 72-73. *Concurrent Pos:* Instr, Scarborough Col, 70-72; Lady Davis prof physics, Isreal Inst Technol, 77-78 & 80-81. *Mem:* Am Phys Soc; Can Asn Physicists (vpres, 97-98). *Res:* Magnetic properties of metals; thermal expansion; magnetostriction; neutron diffraction; ultrasonic attenuation; phase transitions; chromium; charge and spin density waves; layered structures; rare-earth metals; incommen surate structures. *Mailing Add:* Dept Physics St Francis Xavier Univ PO Box 5000 Antigonish NS B2G 2W5 Can. *Fax:* 902-867-2414; *E-Mail:* msteinit@juliet.stfx.ca

STEINITZ-KANNAN, MIRIAM R, PALEOLIMNOLOGY, DIATOM TAXONOMY. *Current Pos:* from asst prof to prof, 80-93, REGENTS PROF BIOL, ECOL, MICROBIOL, MICROBIOL ECOL, LIMNOL & TROPICAL ECOL, NORTHERN KY UNIV, 93- *Personal Data:* b Quito, Ecuador, Nov 17, 51; US citizen; m, Ramamurthi; c Geetha. *Educ:* Rider Univ, BA, 73; Ohio State Univ, Columbus, MSc, 77, PhD(zool), 79. *Prof Exp:* Lectr biol, Clermont Col, Univ Cincinnati, 79-80. *Mem:* Am Quaternary Asn; Int Soc Dietom Res; Sigma Xi; AAAS; Int Limnol Soc. *Res:* Reconstructing climatic histories using fossil diatoms from lake cores; reconstruction of El Nino events in the past 6000 years from cores in Galapagos Islands and mainland Equador. *Mailing Add:* Dept Biol Sci Northern Ky Univ Highland Heights KY 41099-0400. *Fax:* 606-572-5639; *E-Mail:* kannan@nku.edu

STEINKE, FREDERICH H, POULTRY NUTRITION. *Current Pos:* RETIRED. *Personal Data:* b Wilmington, Del, Nov 26, 35; m 60; c 2. *Educ:* Univ Del, BS, 57, MS, 59; Univ Wis, PhD(biochem), 62. *Prof Exp:* Asst mgr poultry nutrit, Ralston-Purina Co, 62-63, mgr turkey res, 63-72, mgr nutrit res, Cent Res Lab, 72-91. *Mem:* Poultry Sci Asn; Am Inst Nutrit; Inst Food Technol. *Res:* Poultry nutrition including broilers, laying hens and turkeys; nutrition evaluation; human nutrition. *Mailing Add:* 9713 Fall Ridge Trail St Louis MO 63127. *Fax:* 314-982-3960

STEINKER, DON COOPER, PALEOBIOLOGY. *Current Pos:* from asst prof to assoc prof, 67-78, PROF GEOL, BOWING GREEN STATE UNIV, 78- *Personal Data:* b Seymour, Ind, Oct 6, 36; m 70, Paula Dziak. *Educ:* Ind Univ, BS, 59; Univ Kans, MS, 61; Univ Calif, Berkeley, PhD(paleont), 69. *Prof Exp:* Res paleontologist, Univ Calif, Berkeley, 62-63, teaching asst paleont, 62-65, instr, 66-67; asst prof geol, San Jose State Col, 65-66; lectr, Univ Calif, Davis, 66. *Concurrent Pos:* Managing ed, J Paleont, 88-94; nat ed, Compass, 90- *Mem:* Paleont Soc; Nat Asn Geol Teachers; Sigma Xi. *Res:* Foraminiferal biology and ecology; paleobiology. *Mailing Add:* Dept Geol Bowling Green State Univ Bowling Green OH 43403. *Fax:* 419-372-7205

STEINKRAUS, DONALD CURTISS, MYCOLOGY, INSECT PATHOLOGY. *Current Pos:* ASST PROF MORPHOL & BIOCONTROL, DEPT ENTOM, UNIV ARK, FAYETTEVILLE, 89- *Personal Data:* b Ames, Iowa, Sept 25, 50; m 87; c 2. *Educ:* Cornell Univ, BA, 75, PhD(entom), 87; Univ Conn, MS, 79. *Prof Exp:* Res assoc, Dept Entom, Cornell Univ, 87-89. *Mem:* Entom Soc Am; Sigma Xi. *Res:* Insect pathogenic microorganisms, particularly entomopathogenic fungi; biological control of filth flies and litter beetles on poultry and dairy farms and of lepidopterous pests of cotton, soybean and grain sorghum. *Mailing Add:* Entomol 321 Agr Bldg Univ Ariz Fayetteville AR 72701-1202

STEINKRAUS, KEITH HARTLEY, MICROBIOLOGY, BIOCHEMISTRY. *Current Pos:* from asst prof to prof bact, 51-88, EMER PROF MICROBIOL, NY STATE COL AGR, CORNELL UNIV, 88- *Personal Data:* b Bertha, Minn, Mar 15, 18; m 41, Maxine Grace Curtiss; c Bonnie, Nancy, Donald, Anna & Karen. *Educ:* Univ Minn, BA, 39; Iowa State Col, PhD(bact), 51. *Honors & Awards:* Int Award, Inst Food Technologists, 85; Fel, Inst Food Technologists, 87. *Prof Exp:* Chemist, Am Crystal Sugar Co, Minn, 39; microbiologist, Jos Seagram & Sons, Inc, 42; instr electronics, US Army Air Force Tech Training Sch, SDak, 42-43; res microbiologist, Gen Mills, Inc, Minn, 43-47 & Pillsbury Mills, Inc, 51. *Concurrent Pos:* Food & agr specialist, US Nutrit Surv, Ecuador & Vietnam, 59, Burma, 61 & 64, Malaya, Thailand & Korea, 64; spec consult interdept comt nutrit for nat defense, NIH, 59-60, spec consult off int res, 67-68; vis prof microbiol col agr, Univ Philippines, 67-69 & Polytech South Bank, London, 72-73; vis prof, UNESCO-Int Cell Res Orgn-UN Environ Prog Training Course Appl Microbiol, Inst Technol, Bandung, Indonesia, 74 & Inst Microbiol, Univ Gottingen, Germany, 80; int organizer Symp Indigenous Fermented Foods, Bangkok, 77; vis prof UNESCO/ICRO Training Course Appl Microbiol, Kasetsart Univ, Bangkok, 76; res scientist, Nestle Prod Tech Assistance Co, Ltd, La-Tour-de-Peilz, Switzerland, 79-80; consult, UN Ind Develop Orgn, 83-84; mem panel microbiol, UN Environ Prog-UNESCO-Int Cell Res Orgn, 84-; team dir, Ind Study Mission Japan, Tech Transfer Inst, 85; vis res scientist, Eastreco, Nestle, Singapore, 86-87, consult, Nestec-Westreco (Nestle), New Milford, Conn, 88-93. *Mem:* Fel AAAS; fel Am Acad Microbiol; Am Soc Microbiol; Inst Food Technol; Sigma Xi. *Res:* Biochemical, microbial and nutritional changes in fermented protein-rich foods; biological and chemical transformations by yeasts, molds and bacteria; biological control of insects with parasitic spore-forming bacteria; extraction of plant proteins; protein hydrolysis; nutrition. *Mailing Add:* Cornell Univ 15 Cornell St Ithaca NY 14850

STEINLAGE, RALPH CLETUS, MATHEMATICS, FUZZY SETS & SYSTEMS. *Current Pos:* From asst prof to assoc prof, 66-79, PROF MATH, UNIV DAYTON, 79- *Personal Data:* b St Henry, Ohio, July 2, 40; m 62, Mary Rammel; c Cynthia, Victoria & Laara. *Educ:* Univ Dayton, BS, 62; Ohio State Univ, MS, 63, PhD(math), 66. *Concurrent Pos:* Woodrow Wilson Fac Develop grant, 82, fel, Ohio State Univ, 62-63. *Mem:* Math Asn Am; Am Math Soc; NAm Fuzzy Info Processing Soc; Int Fuzzy Systs Asn. *Res:* Measure theory and topology; Haar measure on locally compact Hausdorff spaces; function spaces; conditions related to equicontinuity; non-standard analysis; fuzzy topological spaces; experiential training in mathematics programs; applications of fuzzy sets; author of various books. *Mailing Add:* Dept Math Univ Dayton Dayton OH 45469-2316. *Fax:* 937-229-4000; *E-Mail:* steinlag@dayton.bitnet

STEINLE, EDMUND CHARLES, JR, ORGANIC CHEMISTRY. *Current Pos:* CHEMIST, PLASTICS & CHEM RES & DEVELOP LAB, UNION CARBIDE CORP, 55- *Personal Data:* b Scranton, Pa, Feb 7, 24; m 47; c 3. *Educ:* DePauw Univ, AB, 47; Univ Iowa, MS, 49, PhD(org chem), 52. *Prof Exp:* Chemist, Ethyl Corp Res Lab, 52-55. *Mem:* AAAS; Am Chem Soc; Am Oil Chemists Soc; fel Royal Soc Chem; Sigma Xi. *Res:* Fatty alchohols; biodegradable surfactants; surfactant intermediates. *Mailing Add:* 1220 Ridge Dr South Charleston WV 25309-2418

STEINMAN, ALAN DAVID, ALGAL-HERBIVORE INTERACTIONS, NUTRIENT CYCLING IN STREAM ECOSYSTEMS. *Current Pos:* SUPV PROF SCIENTIST, SFLA WATER MGT DIST, 93- *Personal Data:* b New York, NY, May 20, 57; c Seth. *Educ:* Univ Vt, BS, 80; Univ RI, MS, 83; Ore State Univ, PhD(bot), 87. *Prof Exp:* Fel, Ore State Univ, 87; res assoc, Oak Ridge Nat Lab, 87-92; sr scientist, Sci Applns Int Corp, 92-93. *Concurrent Pos:* Adj fac stream ecol, Univ Tenn, 91-92; assoc ed, J NAm Benthological Soc, 92-; adj fac biol, San Diego State Univ, 93; invited scientist, Univ Minn, Duluth, 93. *Mem:* Am Soc Limnol & Oceanog; Ecol Soc Am; Phycol Soc Am; AAAS; NAm Benthological Soc; Nature Conservancy. *Res:* Nutrient cycling in aquatic ecosystems, the evolution of ecosystem integrity on river restoration, diagnosis of periphyton assembloges in aquatic ecosystems and assessment of trophic status in phosphorus-impacted lakes. *Mailing Add:* Dept Res SFla Water Mgt Dist PO Box 24680 West Palm Beach FL 33416-4680. *E-Mail:* al.steinman@sfwmd.gov

STEINMAN, CHARLES ROBERT, RHEUMATOLOGY, BIOCHEMISTRY. *Current Pos:* dir div rheumatol & prof, Dept Med, Downstate Med Sch, 83-90, RES ASSOC PROF MED, STATE UNIV NY, STONEY BROOK, 90- *Personal Data:* b New York, NY, Aug 3, 38. *Educ:* Princeton Univ, AB, 59; Columbia Univ, MD, 63. *Prof Exp:* From intern to resident med, Presby Hosp, Columbia Univ, 63-65 & 68-69; assoc biochem, Nat Inst Arthritis, Metab & Digestive Dis, NIH, 65-67; fel rheumatology, Presby Hosp, Columbia Univ, 67-68 & 69-70; vis fel rheumatology, The London Hosp, 70; asst prof med, Mt Sinai Sch Med, 70-77, assoc prof, 77-82. *Concurrent Pos:* Asst attend physician, Mt Sinai Hosp, 70-77, assoc attend physician, 77-82; asst attend physician, Beth Israel Hosp, 71; consult rheumatol, Bronx Vet Admin Hosp, 77-83; dir rhem, 83-88, Kings County Hosp, attend physician, 83-90; attend physician, State Univ NY, Stony Brook, NY State Hosp, Northports Vet Admin Hosp, 90- *Mem:* Harvey Soc; Am Fed Clin Res; AAAS; Am col Reum; Am Asn Immunol; NY Acad Scis. *Res:* Study of rheumatoid arthritis; systemic lupus erythematosus and related disorders to determine their pathogenesis by biochemical, immunological and microbiological approaches. *Mailing Add:* Dept Rheumatol SUNY Stony Brook Health Sci Ctr T16-040 Stony Brook NY 11794-8161

STEINMAN, HARRY GORDON, ORGANIC CHEMISTRY. *Current Pos:* From biochemist to head sect biochem, Lab Clin Invest, Nat Inst Allergy & Infectious Dis, 38-66, chief viral reagents, Nat Cancer Inst, 66-69, Off Res Safety, 69-77, CONSULT, NAT CANCER INST, 77- *Personal Data:* b Trenton, NJ, Jan 5, 13; m 36; c 1. *Educ:* Mass Inst Technol, BS, 33; Rutgers Univ, MS, 36; Columbia Univ, PhD(chem), 42. *Mem:* Am Chem Soc; Soc Exp Biol & Med; Am Soc Biol Chem; Am Soc Microbiol; Tissue Cult Asn. *Res:* Cell-mediated immunity; chemotherapy of infectious diseases; penicillins and penicillinases; drug-protein interactions; viral oncology. *Mailing Add:* 1040 Deer Ridge Dr Apt 413 Baltimore MD 21210

STEINMAN, HOWARD MARK, OXYGEN TOXICITY, PROTEIN STRUCTURE. *Current Pos:* asst prof, 76-81, ASSOC PROF BIOCHEM, ALBERT EINSTEIN COL MED, 81- *Personal Data:* b Detroit, Mich, Feb 18, 44; m 81; c 2. *Educ:* Amherst Col, BA, 65; Yale Univ, PhD(molecular biophys), 70. *Prof Exp:* Assoc biochem, Duke Univ, 72-75, asst med res prof, 75-76. *Concurrent Pos:* Fel, Dept Biochem, Duke Univ, 70-72. *Mem:* Sigma Xi; Am Soc Biochem & Molecular Biol. *Res:* Biochemical mechanisms of oxygen toxicity; structure, function and relationships among enzymes. *Mailing Add:* Dept Biochem Albert Einstein Col Med 1300 Morris Park Ave Bronx NY 10461-1975. Fax: 718-892-0703

STEINMAN, IRVIN DAVID, MICROBIOLOGY. *Current Pos:* mem staff, Fed Trade Comn, 69-74, actg asst dir, Div Sci Opinion, 74-76, spec asst sci affairs, 76-80, sci adv & res analyst, Bur Consumer Protection, 81-87, NW BR COORDR, INTERSTATE COMN POTOMAC RIVER BASIN, FED TRADE COMN, 88- *Personal Data:* b New York, NY, Nov 7, 24; m 54; c 2. *Educ:* Brooklyn Col, AB, 48; Univ Chicago, MS, 49; Rutgers Univ, PhD(microbiol), 58. *Prof Exp:* Instr microbiol, Col Dent, NY Univ, 51-54; asst instr biol, Rutgers Univ, 54-58; mem fac, Monmouth Jr Col, NJ, 58-59; dir biol serv, US Testing Co, 59-61; dir prof serv, White Labs, 61-67; head med commun, Bristol Labs Int Corp, 67-68; clin res assoc, Ciba Pharm Co, 68-69. *Concurrent Pos:* Pvt consult fed regulatory matters relating to sci. *Mem:* AAAS; Am Soc Microbiol; Am Med Asn; Asn Mil Surg US; fel Am Acad Microbiol. *Res:* Microbial genetics; metabolism; pigmentation and production of antibiotics; scientific evaluation of false and misleading advertising claims; health sciences administration. *Mailing Add:* 14601 Notley Rd Silver Spring MD 20905

STEINMAN, MARTIN, MEDICINAL CHEMISTRY, ORGANIC CHEMISTRY. *Current Pos:* From chemist to sr chemist, Schering Corp, 65-70, prin scientist, 70-73, sect leader, 73-76, mgr, 76-79, assoc dir, 79-89, DIR, SCHERING-PLOUGH RES, SCHERING CORP, 89- *Personal Data:* b Passaic, NJ, Feb 16, 37; m 61; c 2. *Educ:* Rutgers Univ, BS, 58, MS, 62; Univ Kans, PhD(med chem), 65. *Concurrent Pos:* Vis assoc prof pharmaceut chem, Rutgers Univ. *Mem:* Am Chem Soc; NY Acad Sci; fel Am Inst Chemists; Sigma Xi. *Res:* Stereochemistry; new heterocyclic ring systems; synthesis of potentially useful medicinal agents; chemical and antibiotic process research; structure-activity relationships. *Mailing Add:* Schering Corp 1011 Morris Ave Union NJ 07083

STEINMAN, ROBERT, INORGANIC CHEMISTRY, ORGANIC CHEMISTRY. *Current Pos:* VPRES RES & DEVELOP, WHITTAKER CORP, 67- *Personal Data:* b New York, NY, Mar 30, 18; m 39; c 4. *Educ:* Carnegie Inst Technol, BS, 39; Univ Ill, MS, 40, PhD(chem), 42. *Prof Exp:* Res chemist, Owens-Corning Corp, 42-47; dir res, Waterway Projs, 47-48; pres, Garan Chem Corp, Calif, 48-67. *Mem:* AAAS; Am Chem Soc; Soc Plastics Eng; Soc Plastics Indust. *Res:* Phosphorus nitrogen chemistry; surface chemistry of glass; reinforced plastics. *Mailing Add:* 4122 Pindar Way Oceanside CA 92056-7403

STEINMEIER, ROBERT C, HEMEPROTEINS, KINETICS. *Current Pos:* asst prof, 78-83, ASSOC PROF CHEM, UNIV ARK, 83- *Personal Data:* b Glendale, Calif, Apr 16, 43; m 68, 87; c 2. *Educ:* Univ Nebr, Lincoln, BS, 65, PhD(biochem), 75. *Prof Exp:* Immunochemist, Hyland Div, Travenol Labs, 67-69; res assoc bioenergetics, State Univ NY Buffalo, 74-76, Nat Cancer Inst fel, 75-76; *Mem:* Am Chem Soc. *Res:* Structure-function studies on hemeproteins and enzymes by various chemical and kinetic methods. *Mailing Add:* Dept Chem Univ Ark 2801 S University Ave Little Rock AR 72204

STEINMETZ, CHARLES HENRY, OCCUPATIONAL HEALTH. *Current Pos:* RETIRED. *Personal Data:* b Logansport, Ind, Oct 5, 29; m 71, 88; c 4. *Educ:* Ind Univ, AB, 50, PhD(comp physiol), 53, MBA, 92; Univ Cincinnati, MD, 60; Johns Hopkins Univ, MPH, 72; Am Bd Prev Med, cert gen prev med, 73. *Prof Exp:* Asst physiol, Ind Univ, 49-50, anat, 50-51 & zool, 51-53; asst chief space biol, Aero Med Field Lab, Holloman AFB, NMex, 53-56; epidemiologist, Off of Dir, Robert A Taft Sanit Eng Ctr, USPHS, Ohio, 58-60; intern, Staten Island Marine Hosp, NY, 60-61; asst gen mgr, Life Sci Opers, NAm Aviation, Inc, 62-68; dir, Systemed Corp, Md, 68-72; vpres, Nat Health Serv, 72-74; clin instr pub health, Med Col, Cornell Univ, 75-79; med dir, Marathon Oil Co, 79-87 & Indiana Bell Tell Col, 87-92; consult, Methodist Occup Health Ctrs, 92-96. *Concurrent Pos:* Chmn, Occup Med Sect Methodist Hosp, 88-89. *Mem:* Fel Aerospace Med Asn; fel Am Acad Occup Med; fel Am Occup Med Asn; fel Am Col Prev Med. *Res:* General preventive medicine; occupational health; systems analysis. *Mailing Add:* 5959 Cape Cod Ct Indianapolis IN 46250-1845

STEINMETZ, MICHAEL ANTHONY, NEUROPHYSIOLOGY, CEREBRAL CORTEX. *Current Pos:* Res fel physiol, Johns Hopkins Univ, 82-83, res fel neurosci, 83-85, asst prof, 85-89, ASSOC PROF, DEPT NEUROSCI, SCH MED, JOHNS HOPKINS UNIV, 89- *Personal Data:* b Ft Belvoir, Va, Nov 9, 51; m 73. *Educ:* Univ Mich, BS, 73; Mich State Univ, MS, 74, PhD(physiol), 82. *Mem:* AAAS; Am Physiol Soc; Soc Neurosci. *Res:* Neurophysiology of the cerebral cortex in primate behavior. *Mailing Add:* Dept Neurosci Sch Med Johns Hopkins Univ 338 Krieger Hall 3400 N Charles St Baltimore MD 21218. Fax: 410-955-8883; *E-Mail:* steinmetz@hubard.bitnet

STEINMETZ, PHILIP R, KIDNEY PHYSIOLOGY, EPITHELIAL TRANSPORT. *Current Pos:* PROF MED, UNIV CONN, 81- *Personal Data:* b De Bilt, Neth, 27; m, Micheline Osmont; c Jan P & Mark C. *Educ:* Univ Leiden, Neth, MD, 54, PhD, 75. *Honors & Awards:* Homer Smith Award, Renal Physiol, 85. *Concurrent Pos:* Fac, Harvard Med Sch, 65-73; prof med, Univ Iowa, 73-81; fac scholar, Josiah Macy Jr Found. *Mem:* Am Soc Clin Invest; Am Soc Nephrology; Am Physiol Soc; Soc Gen Physiol; Asn Am Physicians. *Res:* Cellular mechanisms of urinary acidification. *Mailing Add:* Dept Med Univ Conn Farmington CT 06030

STEINMETZ, WALTER EDMUND, ORGANIC CHEMISTRY. *Current Pos:* RETIRED. *Personal Data:* b Washington, DC, Jan 12, 21; m 47; c 2. *Educ:* St Ambrose Col, BS, 43; Univ Iowa, MS, 47, PhD(org chem), 49. *Prof Exp:* Res chemist, Nalco Chem Co, 48-49, group leader org chem, 49-53, dir, 53-57, sr tech adv, 57-60; sect leader, El Paso Natural Gas Prod Co, 60-65; sect leader, Pennzoil Co, 65-69, mgr chem res div, 69-75, sr tech adv, 75-83. *Mem:* Am Chem Soc. *Res:* Herbicides; oil treatment chemicals; petrochemicals. *Mailing Add:* 2070 Holly Oak Dr Shreveport LA 71118

STEINMETZ, WAYNE EDWARD, PHYSICAL CHEMISTRY, MOLECULAR SPECTROSCOPY & MODELING. *Current Pos:* from asst prof to prof, 73-92, CARNEGIE PROF CHEM, POMONA COL, 92- *Personal Data:* b Huron, Ohio, Feb 16, 45. *Educ:* Oberlin Col, AB, 67; Harvard Univ, AM, 68, PhD(chem), 73. *Prof Exp:* Instr phys sci, St Peter's Boys' High Sch, 69-70; lab instr, Oberlin Col, 70-71. *Concurrent Pos:* Guest prof, Eidgenossische Tech Hochschule, Zurich, 79-80 & 87-88; consult, Abbott Labs, Abbott Park, Ill, 93-94. *Mem:* Am Chem Soc; AAAS; Sigma Xi. *Res:* Molecular structure and spectroscopy; application of molecular moding and nuclear magnetic resonance spectroscopy to conformational analysis; nuclear magnetic resonance spectroscopy of peptides and antibiotics; three dimensional quantitative structure-activity relationship. *Mailing Add:* Seaver Chem Lab Pomona Col Claremont CA 91711-6338. Fax: 909-624-5509; *E-Mail:* wsteinmetz@pomona.edu

STEINMETZ, WILLIAM JOHN, APPLIED MATHEMATICS. *Current Pos:* from asst prof to assoc prof, 70-81, PROF MATH, ADELPHI UNIV, 81- *Personal Data:* b Wheeling WVa, Nov 14, 39; m 71. *Educ:* St Louis Univ, BS, 60; Ga Inst Technol, MS, 62; Rensselaer Polytech Inst, PhD(math), 70. *Prof Exp:* Res scientist aeronaut eng, NASA Ames Res Ctr, 61-66. *Mem:* Soc Indust & Appl Math; Sigma Xi. *Res:* Applied mathematics, in particular singular perturbations of ordinary and partial differential equations; stochastic differential equations. *Mailing Add:* 14 Elfmere Ave Oakdale NY 11769

STEINRAUF, LARRY KING, BIOCHEMISTRY, PHYSICAL CHEMISTRY. *Current Pos:* assoc prof biochem, 64-68, PROF BIOCHEM & BIOPHYS, SCH MED, IND UNIV, INDIANAPOLIS, 68- *Personal Data:* b St Louis, Mo, June 8, 31; m 68; c 1. *Educ:* Univ Mo, BS & MA, 54; Univ Wash, PhD(biochem), 57. *Prof Exp:* Asst prof phys chem, Univ Ill, Urbana, 59-64. *Concurrent Pos:* Res fel chem, Calif Inst Technol, 57-58; USPHS fel crystallog, Cavendish Lab, Cambridge, 58-59. *Mem:* Am Crystallog Asn. *Res:* Relation of molecular structure to biological activity. *Mailing Add:* Dept Biochem Ind Univ Sch Med 1120 South Dr Indianapolis IN 46202-5135

STEINSCHNEIDER, ALFRED, PEDIATRICS. *Current Pos:* PRES, AM SUDDEN INFANT DEATH SYNDROME, ATLANTA, GA, PORTLAND, ORE. *Personal Data:* b Brooklyn, NY, June 11, 29; m 50, Rosalind Glassman; c Mitchell & Janice. *Educ:* NY Univ, BA, 50; Univ Mo, MA, 52; Cornell Univ, PhD(psychol), 55; State Univ NY, MD, 61. *Prof Exp:* Asst psychol, Univ Mo, 50-52; asst, Cornell Univ, 52-54; engr, Advan Electronics Ctr, Gen Elec Co, NY, 54-57; res assoc, State Univ NY Upstate Med Ctr, 58-64, from asst prof to assoc prof pediat, 64-77; prof pediat & dir, Sudden Infant Death Syndrome Inst, Sch Med, Univ Md, 77-83. *Mem:* Am Psychosom Soc; Soc Res Child Develop; Soc Psychophysiol Res; Am Acad Pediat. *Res:* Sudden infant death syndrome; child development; psychophysiology. *Mailing Add:* Am Sudden Infant Death Syndrome Inst 6065 Roswell Rd Atlanta GA 30328

STEIN-TAYLOR, JANET RUTH, botany, horticulture, for more information see previous edition

STEINWACHS, DONALD MICHAEL, PUBLIC HEALTH ADMINISTRATION. *Current Pos:* Res mgr, Health Serv Res & Develop Ctr, Johns Hopkins Univ, 72-79, asst prof, Dept Health Serv, 73-79, asst dir, 79-81, dept dir, 81-82, assoc prof, Dept Health Serv Admin, 79-85, DIR, HEALTH SERV RES & DEVELOP CTR, SCH PUB HEALTH, JOHNS HOPKINS UNIV, 82-, PROF, DEPT HEALTH POLICY & MGT, 86-, CHAIR, 94- *Personal Data:* b Boise, Idaho, Sept 9, 46; m 72. *Educ:* Univ Ariz, BS, 68, MS, 70; Johns Hopkins Univ, PhD(opers res), 73. *Honors & Awards:* Ment Health Sect Award, Am Pub Health Asn, 94; Eli Lilly Lectr, 96. *Concurrent Pos:* Dir, Ctr Res Servs Severe Mental Illness, Johns Hopkins Univ & Univ Md, 87-; mem, Comt Res Personnel Needs Biomed & Behav Sci, Inst Med-Nat Acad Sci, 93- *Mem:* Inst Med-Nat Acad Sci; Opers Res Soc Am; Inst Mgt Sci; Am Pub Health Asn; fel Asn Health Serv Res (treas, 85-87, pres, 88-89); AAAS; Found Health Serv Res (treas, 85-87, secty, 87-88, pres, 89-90); Int Soc Technol Assessment Health Care. *Res:* Primary medical care; effects of availability, access, continuity, organization and financing on cost and quality; information systems; impact of hospital cost containment strategies; models for health resource allocation; health manpower planning and evaluation; author of numerous articles. *Mailing Add:* Johns Hopkins Univ Sch Hygiene & Pub Health Dept Health Policy & Mgt 624 N Broadway Rm 482 Baltimore MD 21205-1996

STEITZ, JOAN ARGETSINGER, BIOCHEMISTRY, MOLECULAR BIOLOGY. *Current Pos:* From asst prof to assoc prof, 70-78, PROF MOLECULAR BIOPHYS & BIOCHEM, YALE UNIV, 78-, INVESTR, HOWARD HUGHES MED INST, 86-, HENRY FORD II PROF MOLECULAR BIOPHYS & BIOCHEM, 92- *Personal Data:* b Minneapolis, Minn, Jan 26, 41; m 66, Thomas A; c 1. *Educ:* Antioch Col, BS, 63; Harvard Univ, MA, 67, PhD(biochem, molecular biol), 68. *Hon Degrees:* DSc, Lawrence Univ, 81, Sch Med, Univ Rochester, 84, Mt Sinai Sch Med, 89, Bates Col, 90, Trinity Col, 92, Harvard Univ, 92. *Honors & Awards:* Passano Award, 75; Eli Lilly Award, 76; US Steel Award, 82; Lee Halley Sr Award, Arthritis Res, 84; Nat Medal of Sci, 86; Radcliffe Grad Soc Medal, 87; Dickson Prize for Sci, 88; Warren Triennial Prize, 89; Christopher Columbus Discovery Award, 92; Eleventh Ann Keith Porter lectr, 92; Weizmann Women & Sci Award, Am Comt for Weizmann Inst, 94. *Concurrent Pos:* NSF fel, Med Res Coun Lab Molecular Biol, Cambridge, Eng, 68-69, Jane Coffin Childs Fund med res fel, 69-70; assoc mem, Europ Molecular Biol Orgn, 87; dir, Jane Coffin Child Mem Fund Med Res, 91-; trustees, Cold Spring Harbor Lab, 92- *Mem:* Nat Acad Sci; Am Soc Biol Chemists; fel AAAS; Am Philos Soc; Am Acad Arts & Sci. *Res:* Control of transcription and translation; RNA and DNA sequence analysis; structure and function of small ribonucleoproteins from eukaryotes; RNA processing. *Mailing Add:* Dept Molecular Biophys & Biochem Yale Univ Howard Hughes Med Inst 295 Congress Ave New Haven CT 06536. *Fax:* 203-624-8213

STEITZ, THOMAS ARTHUR, MOLECULAR BIOLOGY. *Current Pos:* from asst prof to assoc prof, 70-79, actg dir, Div Biol Sci, 81, PROF MOLECULAR BIOPHYS & BIOCHEM, YALE UNIV, 79-, EUGENE HIGGINS PROF, 94-; INVESTR, HOWARD HUGHES MED INST, 86- *Personal Data:* b Milwaukee, Wis, Aug 23, 40; m 66, Joan Argetsinger; c 1. *Educ:* Lawrence Univ, BA, 62; Harvard Univ, PhD(molecular biol & biochem), 66. *Hon Degrees:* DSc, Lawrence Univ, 81. *Honors & Awards:* Pfizer Award, Am Chem Soc, 80. *Prof Exp:* NIH grant, Harvard Univ, 66-67; Jane Coffin Childs Mem Fund med res fel, Med Res Coun, Lab Molecular Biol, Cambridge Univ, 67-70. *Concurrent Pos:* Macy fel, Max Planck Inst Biophys Chem, Goettingen, Ger & Med Res Coun, Lab Molecular Biol, Cambridge, Eng, 76-77; actg dir, Div Biol Sci, Yale Univ, 81; Fairchild scholar, Calif Inst Technol, 84-85. *Mem:* Nat Acad Sci; Am Soc Biol Chem; Biophys Soc Am; Am Crystallog Asn; Protein Soc; Am Acad Arts & Sci; RNA Soc. *Res:* Protein and nucleic acid x-ray crystallography; structural basis of enzyme mechanisms; protein-nucleic acid interaction. *Mailing Add:* Yale Univ Dept Molecular Biophys & Biochem 226 Whitney Ave PO Box 208114 New Haven CT 06520-8114

STEJSKAL, EDWARD OTTO, PHYSICAL CHEMISTRY, NUCLEAR MAGNETIC RESONANCE. *Current Pos:* PROF CHEM, NC STATE UNIV, 86- *Personal Data:* b Chicago, Ill, Jan 19, 32; m 57, Anita Lasher. *Educ:* Univ Ill, BS, 53, PhD(chem), 57. *Prof Exp:* Asst phys chem, Univ Ill, 53-56; NSF fel, Harvard Univ, 57-58; Wis Alumni Res Found fel, Univ Wis, 58-59, from instr to asst prof phys chem, 58-64; res specialist, Monsanto Co, 64-67, sr res specialist, 67-80, fel, 80-86. *Mem:* Am Phys Soc; Am Chem Soc. *Res:* Molecular structure; spectroscopy; nuclear magnetic resonance; molecular motion in solids, liquids and gases; nuclear spin relaxation and diffusion phenomena; high-resolution nuclear magnetic resonance in solids; fluid rheology; lubrication. *Mailing Add:* NC State Univ Box 8204 Raleigh NC 27695-8204. *Fax:* 919-515-5079; *E-Mail:* edward_stejskal@ncsu.edu

STEJSKAL, RUDOLF, PATHOLOGY. *Current Pos:* ASSOC DIR PATH, BIO-RES LABS, CAN, 83- *Personal Data:* b Budejovice, Czech, Apr 16, 31; m 68; c 2. *Educ:* Charles Univ, Czech, DDS, 56; Univ Chicago, MS, 69; Chicago Med Sch-Univ Health Sci, PhD(path), 72. *Prof Exp:* Trainee path, Univ Chicago, 67-69; res assoc exp path, Mt Sinai Hosp Med Ctr, Chicago, 70-72; res assoc & asst prof path, Univ Chicago, 72-73; sr res investr, Searle Res & Develop, 73-75, sr res scientist, Searle Labs, 75-78, dir path, France, 78-83. *Concurrent Pos:* Clin assoc path, Chicago Med Sch, 70-72. *Mem:* Europ Soc Toxicol; Soc Toxicol Pathologists; Int Acad Path; Am Asn Path. *Res:* Fate of blood group substances in human cancer; drug-induced carcinogenesis; toxicologic pathology. *Mailing Add:* Dept Pathol Bio Res Labs Ltd 87 Senneville Rd Senneville PQ H9X 3R3 Can. *Fax:* 514-457-3883

STEKEL, FRANK D, SCIENCE EDUCATION, PHYSICS. *Current Pos:* From instr to assoc prof, 65-77, PROF PHYSICS, UNIV WIS-WHITEWATER, 77- *Personal Data:* b Hillsboro, Wis, Aug 26, 41; m 67, Shirley L Dow; c Sharon & Sandra. *Educ:* Univ Wis-La Crosse, BS, 63, Univ Wis-Madison, MS, 65; Ind Univ, Bloomington, EdD(sci educ), 70. *Mem:* fel AAAS; Am Asn Physics Teachers; Nat Asn Res Sci Teaching; Nat Sci Teachers Asn; Sch Sci & Math Asn. *Res:* Development, implementation and evaluation of physical science instruction at all levels, from the elementary school up to the college and university level; archaeostronomy and effigy mounds. *Mailing Add:* N 997 Cold Spring Rd Ft Atkinson WI 53538. *E-Mail:* stekelf.uwwvax.uww.edu

STEKIEL, WILLIAM JOHN, BIOPHYSICS. *Current Pos:* USPHS fel & instr physiol, 57-60, asst prof biophys, 60-66, assoc prof, 66-77, PROF PHYSIOL, MED COL WIS, 77- *Personal Data:* b Milwaukee, Wis, Jan 1, 28; m 55; c 2. *Educ:* Marquette Univ, BS, 51; Johns Hopkins Univ, PhD(biophys), 57. *Honors & Awards:* Goldblatt Award, Am Heart Asn. *Concurrent Pos:* Res exchange prof, Med Univ, Budapest, 63; fel, coun circulation, Am Heart Asn, coun high blood pressure, Cardiovasc Sect, APS. *Mem:* Biophys Soc; Am Physiol Soc; Microcirc Soc. *Res:* Electrophysiology; circulatory physiology; hypertension. *Mailing Add:* Dept Physiol Med Col Wis 8701 Watertown Plank Rd Milwaukee WI 53226-4801. *Fax:* 414-257-8215; *E-Mail:* wstekiel@post.its.mcw.edu

STEKLY, Z J JOHN, MECHANICAL ENGINEERING. *Current Pos:* VPRES ADVAN PROGS, INTERMAGNETICS GEN CORP, 87- *Personal Data:* b Czech, Oct 11, 33; US citizen. *Educ:* Mass Inst Technol, BA, MA(mech eng) & MA(elec eng), 55, ScD, 59. *Prof Exp:* Chmn bd & tech dir, Magnetic Corp Am, 69-86. *Concurrent Pos:* Mem, Comt Magnetic Fusion, Nat Res Coun, 81-82, Comt Elec Energy Systs, 84-86, Comt Crit Mat, US Army, 84-86, Comt Space Based Power, 87-90; mem peer rev comt & mem comt, Nat Acad Eng, 82-84. *Mem:* Nat Acad Eng; Inst Elec & Electronics Engrs; Sigma Xi; Am Phys Soc; Soc Magnetic Resonance Med. *Mailing Add:* c/o Field Effects Intermagnetics Gen Corp 300 Vesper Executive Park Tyngsboro MA 01879

STEKOLL, MICHAEL STEVEN, BIOCHEMISTRY. *Current Pos:* Res fel marine pollution, 76-78, from asst prof to assoc prof, 78-91, PROF CHEM & BIOCHEM, UNIV ALASKA, SE & FAIRBANKS, 91- *Personal Data:* b Tulsa, Okla, May 7, 47; m 76, Deborah Hansen; c Justin, Skye, Spencer & Kokii. *Educ:* Stanford Univ, BS, 71; Univ Calif, Los Angeles, PhD(biochem), 76. *Concurrent Pos:* Asst, Univ Calif, Los Angeles, 72-76, res trainee, 72-76; res biochemist, Nat Marine Fisheries Serv, 79; assoc res biologist, Univ Calif, Santa Barbara, 86-87. *Mem:* AAAS; Phycol Soc Am. *Res:* Purification and properties of phytoalexin elicitors; effects of marine pollution on intertidal and subtidal biota, mariculture; algal physiology & ecology; salmon biochemistry and physiology. *Mailing Add:* Juneau Ctr Fisheries & Ocean Sci 11120 Glacier Hwy Juneau AK 99801. *E-Mail:* jfmss@acad1.alaska.edu

STELCK, CHARLES RICHARD, CRETACEOUS, MICROPALEONTOLOGY. *Current Pos:* lectr, 48-53, from assoc prof to prof, 54-82, EMER PROF, UNIV ALTA, 82- *Personal Data:* b Edmonton, Alta, May 20, 17; m 45; c 4. *Educ:* Univ Alta, BSc, 37, MSc, 41; Stanford Univ, PhD(geol), 50. *Honors & Awards:* Logan Medal, Geol Asn Can, 81. *Prof Exp:* Lab asst, Univ Alta, 37-41; well site geologist, BC Dept Mines, 40-42; field geologist, Canol Proj, 42-44 & Imp Oil Co, 44-48. *Mem:* Geol Soc Am; Paleont Soc; fel Royal Soc Can; Geol Asn Can. *Res:* Stratigraphic paleontology of western Canada. *Mailing Add:* Geol Dept Univ Alta Edmonton AB T6G 2E3 Can

STELL, GEORGE ROGER, STATISTICAL MECHANICS. *Current Pos:* from assoc prof to prof mech, State Univ NY, Stony Brook, 68-77, prof mech eng, 77-85, prof chem, 79-85, LEADING PROF CHEM & MECH ENG, STATE UNIV NY, STONY BROOK, 85- *Personal Data:* b Glen Cove, NY, Jan 2, 33; m 52, Ann Thurlow; c Susan. *Educ:* Antioch Col, BS, 55; NY Univ, PhD(math), 61. *Honors & Awards:* Creativity Exten Award, NSF, 87; Joel Henry Hildebrand Award Theoret Exp Chem Liquids, Am Chem Soc, 96. *Prof Exp:* Instr physics, Univ Ill, Chicago, 55-56; assoc res scientist, Inst Math Sci, NY Univ, 61-64, Belfer Grad Sch Sci, Yeshiva Univ, 64-65; from asst prof physics to assoc prof physics, Polytech Inst Brooklyn, 65-68. *Concurrent Pos:* Consult, Lawrence Radiation Lab, Univ Calif, 63-66; vis prof, Lab Theoret & High Energy Physics, Nat Ctr Sci Res, France, 67-68; prin investr, NSF grants, 70-, Guggenheim Fel, 84-85; prin investr, Dept Energy contract, 79-87, Dept Energy grant, 87- *Mem:* Am Math Soc; fel Am Phys Soc; Royal Norweg Soc Sci & Lett. *Res:* Statistical mechanics; especially molecular theory of fluids and lattice systems; mathematics associated with statistical mechanics, especially graph theory; generating functionals and non-linear integral equations; theory of critical phenomena and thermodynamics; dielectric, structural and transport properties of fluids; percolation and composite-media theory. *Mailing Add:* 9 Bobs Lane Setauket NY 11733. *Fax:* 516-632-7960

STELL, WILLIAM KENYON, RETINAL NEUROBIOLOGY, MYOPIA. *Current Pos:* chmn, 80-85, PROF ANAT & DIR, LION'S SIGHT CTR, UNIV CALGARY, 80-; PROF SURG & OPHTHAL, 93- *Personal Data:* b Syracuse, NY, Apr 21, 39; m 74, 96, Kathie L MacDonald; c Jennifer S & Sarah R. *Educ:* Swarthmore Col, BA, 61; Univ Chicago, PhD(anat), 66, MD, 67. *Prof Exp:* Staff assoc, Lab Neurophysiol, Nat Inst Neurol Dis & Stroke, 67-68, staff assoc neurocytol, Lab Neuropath & Neuroanat Sci, 68-69 & Lab of the Dir, 69, sr staff fel, Off Dir Intramural Res, 69-71 & Lab Neurophysiol, Sect Cell Biol, 71-72; assoc prof ophthal, Jules Stein Eye Inst, Univ Calif, Los Angeles, 72-76, prof, 76-80, assoc dir, 78-80. *Concurrent Pos:* Mem bd dirs, RP Res Found Fighting Blindness. *Mem:* Asn Res Vision & Ophthal; Soc Neurosci. *Res:* Neurocytology, ultrastructure and functional interconnections in vertebrate retina; neuropeptide chemistry and function; developmental neurobiology; experimental myopia; visual control of ocular growth. *Mailing Add:* Dept Anat Univ Calgary 3330 Hosp Dr NW Calgary AB T2N 4N1 Can. *Fax:* 403-283-2700; *E-Mail:* wstell@acs.ucalgary.ca

STELLA, PAUL M, MATERIALS SCIENCE ENGINEERING, MECHANICAL ENGINEERING. *Current Pos:* TECH GROUP LEADER, JET PROPULSION LAB, CALIF INST TECHNOL, 78- *Personal Data:* b Hartford, Conn, Dec 13, 44; m 79; c 1. *Educ:* Princeton Univ, BA, 66; Calif State Univ-Northridge, MS, 71. *Prof Exp:* Sr engr, Spectrolab, Inc, Hughes Aircraft Co, 67-78. *Concurrent Pos:* Aerospace Power Comt, Am Inst Aeronaut & Astronaut, 84-87. *Mem:* Inst Elec & Electronics Engrs; Am Inst Aeronaut & Astronaut. *Res:* Design and development of advanced photovoltaic solar array systems for space applications; development of appropriate photovoltaic cell technology to satisfy requirements for operation near sun and far sun. *Mailing Add:* Jet Propulsion Lab Calif Inst Technol MS303-308 4800 Oak Grove Dr Pasadena CA 91109

STELLA, VALENTINO JOHN, PHARMACY. *Current Pos:* from asst prof to assoc prof, 73-81, PROF PHARMACEUT CHEM, SCH PHARM, UNIV KANS, 81-, DIR, CTR DRUG DELIVERY RES, 89-, UNIV DISTINGUISHED PROF, 90- *Personal Data:* b Melbourne, Australia, Oct 27, 46; m 69, Mary E Roeder; c Catherine M, Anne E & Elise V. *Educ:* Victorian Col Pharm, Melbourne, BPharm, 67; Univ Kans, PhD(anal pharmaceut chem, pharmaceut), 71. *Honors & Awards:* Lederle Labs Award 72 & 75; Dolph Simons Award, 90. *Prof Exp:* Pharmacist, Bendigo Base Hosp, Australia, 67-68; asst prof pharm, Univ Ill, Med Ctr, 71-73. *Concurrent Pos:* Consult, Oreao Lab, 88-, Allergan, 89- & Cydex, 93-; victorian intersearch prof, Victorian Col Pharm, Melbourne, Australia, 80- *Mem:* Am Chem Soc; Am Asn Col Pharm; Victorian Pharmaceut Soc; fel Acad Pharmaceut Sci; fel AAAS; fel AM Asn Pharmaceut Scientists; Controlled Release Soc. *Res:* Physical pharmacy; pro-drugs and drug latentiation; drug stability; ionization kinetics; biopharmaceutics and pharmacokinetics; preformulation of anticancer drugs; development of novel cyclodextrins; lymphatic transport of drugs. *Mailing Add:* Dept Pharmaceut Chem Univ Kans Lawrence KS 66045-1500. *Fax:* 785-864-5389; *E-Mail:* stella@kuhub.cc.ukans.edu

STELLER, KENNETH EUGENE, ORGANIC CHEMISTRY. *Current Pos:* Res chemist, 67-74, SR RES CHEMIST, HERCULES INC, 74- *Personal Data:* b Lancaster, Pa, Mar 14, 41; m 64; c 2. *Educ:* Franklin & Marshall Col, BS, 63; Northwestern Univ, PhD(org chem), 67. *Mem:* Am Chem Soc. *Res:* Polyether polymerization; elastomers; polymer modification; thermoplastic elastomers; peroxide research and development. *Mailing Add:* 13 Lamatan Rd Newark DE 19711-2315

STELLINGWERF, ROBERT FRANCIS, STELLAR STRUCTURE & STABILITY. *Current Pos:* res scientist, 80-84, DIV LEADER, MISSION RES CORP, 84- *Personal Data:* b Hawthorne, NJ, Apr 22, 47. *Educ:* Rice Univ, BA, 69; Univ Colo, MS, 71, PhD(astrophys), 74. *Prof Exp:* Res assoc, Columbia Univ, 74-77; asst prof astron, Rutgers Univ, 77-80. *Concurrent Pos:* Vis staff mem, Los Alamos Sci Lab, 76-; prin investr, NSF, 78- *Mem:* Am Astron Soc. *Res:* Stellar structure and stability; pulsation theory; astrophysical gas flow. *Mailing Add:* 2229 Loma Linda Dr Los Alamos NM 87544. *Fax:* 505-665-3389

STELLNER, KEVIN, PHYSICAL CHEMISTRY, TECHNICAL SALES. *Current Pos:* RESEARCHER CHEM & SALES, GIST-BROCADES, 89- *Personal Data:* b Washington, DC, 1959. *Educ:* Univ Okla, BS, 81, PhD(chem eng), 87. *Prof Exp:* Scientist res & develop, Lever Brothers, 87. *Mem:* Am Chem Soc; Am Inst Chem Engrs. *Mailing Add:* 2046 Lawton Bluff Rd Charlotte NC 28226-2941

STELLWAGEN, EARLE C, BIOCHEMISTRY. *Current Pos:* from asst prof to assoc prof, 64-72, PROF BIOCHEM, UNIV IOWA, 72- *Personal Data:* b Joliet, Ill, June 14, 33; m 58, Nancy; c Anne, John & David. *Educ:* Elmhurst Col, BS, 55; Northwestern Univ, MS, 58; Univ Calif, Berkeley, PhD(biochem), 63. *Prof Exp:* NIH res fel biochem, Univ Vienna, 63-64. *Concurrent Pos:* NIH career develop award, 67-72; mem, Biophysics & Biophysical Study Sect B, NIH, 70-, chmn, 72-; vis scientist, Bell Labs, 71-72. *Mem:* Am Soc Biol Chem; Biophys Soc. *Res:* Relationship of structure of proteins to their biological function. *Mailing Add:* Dept Biochem 4-612BSB Univ Iowa Iowa City IA 52242-0001. *Fax:* 319-335-9570; *E-Mail:* cmdste@vaxa.weeg.uiowa.edu

STELLWAGEN, ROBERT HARWOOD, BIOCHEMISTRY. *Current Pos:* from asst prof to assoc prof, 70-80, interim chmn, 80-86, PROF BIOCHEM, SCH MED, UNIV SOUTHERN CALIF, 80- *Personal Data:* b Joliet, Ill, Jan 6, 41; m 63, Joanne Kovacs; c Robert H Jr & Alisa A (Kirksey). *Educ:* Harvard Univ, AB, 63; Univ Calif, Berkeley, PhD(biochem), 68. *Prof Exp:* Res biochemist, Univ Calif, Berkeley, 68; staff fel molecular biol, Nat Inst Arthritis & Metab Dis, 68-69. *Concurrent Pos:* USPHS fel biochem, Univ Calif, San Francisco, 69-70; vis scientist, Nat Ins Med Res, London, 79. *Mem:* AAAS; Am Soc Biochem & Molecular Biol. *Res:* Biochemical control mechanisms in animal cells; enzyme induction by hormones; control of protein degradation. *Mailing Add:* 2011 Zonal Ave Univ S Calif Sch Med Los Angeles CA 90033-4526

STELLY, MATTHIAS, SOIL FERTILITY. *Current Pos:* RETIRED. *Personal Data:* b Arnaudville, La, Aug 7, 16; m 40, Thelma L Thoreson; c Mary L, Julie M, David M & Carol A. *Educ:* Univ Southwestern La, BS, 37; La State Univ, MS, 39; Iowa State Univ, PhD(soil fertil), 42. *Prof Exp:* Asst agronomist, Exp Sta, La State Univ, 42-43; from assoc prof to prof soils, Univ Ga, 46-57; prof in chg soil testing serv, La State Univ, 57-59, prof soil chem, 59-61; exec secy & treas, ASA Publs, Am Soc Agron, 61-70, exec vpres & ed-in-chief, 70-82. *Concurrent Pos:* Soil specialist, USDA, EAfrica, 52-53; Am secy, Comn Soil Fertil & Plant Nutrit, 7th Cong, Int Soc Soil Sci, 58-60; prog dir transl & printing, Soviet Soil Sci; ed, Agron J, 61-82; dir Am Soc Agron vis scientist prog, 63-72 & Agron Sci Found, 67-82; consult, Int Inst Tropical Agr, Nigeria, 84-85; Tropical Agr Res Fund, 85. *Mem:* Fel AAAS; fel Am Soc Agron; Crop Sci Soc Am; Soil Sci Soc Am; Int Soc Soil Sci. *Res:* Soil chemistry; identification of inorganic soil phosphorus compounds; radioactive materials as plant stimulants; crop rotation; radioactive phosphorus; fertilizer requirements and chemical composition of Bermuda grasses; methodology of soil testing; chemical and mineralogical investigations of Louisiana soils. *Mailing Add:* 2113 Chamberlain Ave Madison WI 53705

STELOS, PETER, IMMUNOLOGY, IMMUNOCHEMISTRY. *Current Pos:* CONSULT, 88- *Personal Data:* b Lowell, Mass, May 17, 23. *Educ:* Berea Col, AB, 48; Univ Chicago, PhD(microbiol), 56. *Prof Exp:* Res assoc microbiol, Univ Chicago, 56-57; cancer res scientist, Roswell Park Mem Inst, 59-60, from sr cancer res to assoc cancer res scientist, 60-65; assoc prof microbiol, Hahnemann Med Col, 65-73; assoc surg & immunol, Peter Bent Brigham Hosp & Harvard Med Sch, 73-79, assoc med & biochem, Harvard Med Sch, 80-88. *Concurrent Pos:* Fel chem, Yale Univ, 57-59. *Mem:* AAAS; Am Asn Immunol; Am Chem Soc; Sigma Xi. *Res:* Separation and properties of immunoglobulins and urinary proteins. *Mailing Add:* 83 Garden St West Roxbury MA 02132-4929

STELSON, ARTHUR WESLEY, AEROSOL THERMODYNAMICS & CHEMISTRY, URBAN AIR POLLUTION. *Current Pos:* environ engr, 95-96, SR ENVIRON ENGR, GA DEPT NAT RESOURCES, 96- *Personal Data:* b Pittsburgh, Pa, May 12, 55. *Educ:* Ga Inst Technol, BS, 75, MS, 76,; Calif Inst Technol, PhD(chem eng), 82. *Prof Exp:* Proj engr, Exxon Res & Eng Co, 81-84; sr res scientist, Atlanta Univ Ctr, Inc, 85-90; assoc prof chem, Clark Atlanta Univ, 90-91; sr res scientist, Ga Inst Technol, 91-95. *Concurrent Pos:* Adj prof chem, Clark Atlanta Univ, 85-90. *Mem:* Fel Am Inst Chemists; Am Inst Chem Engrs; Am Chem Soc; Nat Soc Prof Engrs; Air & Waste Mgt Asn; Am Acad Environ Engrs. *Res:* Application of thermodynamics, chemical engineering, mathematics and kinetics to urban air quality problems. *Mailing Add:* 1101 Stoney Creek Lane Austell GA 30001. *Fax:* 404-363-7100; *E-Mail:* 201-3233@mcimail.com

STELSON, T(HOMAS) E(UGENE), civil engineering, for more information see previous edition

STELTENKAMP, ROBERT JOHN, ORGANIC CHEMISTRY. *Current Pos:* RETIRED. *Personal Data:* b Dayton, Ky, Sept 13, 36; m 57; c 2. *Educ:* Xavier Univ, Ohio, BS, 58; Purdue Univ, PhD(org chem), 62. *Prof Exp:* Sr res chemist perfumery res, Colgate Palmolive Co, NJ, 62-67, sec head var res & develop sections, 67-80, res assoc res & develop, 80-84, sr assoc, 84-87, assoc res fel, 87-96. *Mem:* Am Chem Soc; Sigma Xi; NY Acad Sci. *Res:* Identification of the composition of essential oils; structural identification of natural components and the toxicology of fragrance raw materials; organic synthesis. *Mailing Add:* 92 Emerson Rd Somerset NJ 08873

STELTS, MARION LEE, NUCLEAR PHYSICS. *Current Pos:* PHYSICIST, LOS ALAMOS NAT LAB, 80- *Personal Data:* b Oregon City, Ore, Mar 28, 40; m 61; c 2. *Educ:* Univ Ore, BA, 61; Univ Calif, Davis, MS, 70, PhD(appl sci), 75. *Prof Exp:* Physicist, Lawrence Livermore Lab, 61-75; physicist nuclear physics, Brookhaven Nat Lab, 75-80. *Mem:* Am Phys Soc. *Mailing Add:* 3660 Ridgeway Dr Los Alamos NM 87544. *Fax:* 505-667-1507

STEMBRIDGE, VERNIE A(LBERT), PATHOLOGY. *Current Pos:* assoc prof, Univ Tex Southwestern Med Ctr, Dallas, 59-61, chmn dept, 66-88, actg dean, 88-91, PROF PATH, UNIV TEX SOUTHWESTERN MED CTR, DALLAS, 61- *Personal Data:* b El Paso, Tex, June 7, 24; m 44; c 3. *Educ:* Tex Col Mines, BA, 43; Univ Tex, MD, 48; Am Bd Path, cert anat & clin path, 53. *Honors & Awards:* Ward Burdick Outstanding Award, Am Soc Am Path, 81. *Prof Exp:* Intern, Marine Hosp, Norfolk, Va, 48-49; resident path, Med Br, Univ Tex, 49-52, assoc clin labs & from asst prof to assoc prof, 52-56; chief, Aviation Path Sect, Armed Forces Inst Path, 56-59. *Concurrent Pos:* Consult, Vet Admin Hosp, Dallas, 59-, Civil Air Surgeon, Fed Aviation Agency, DC, 59-70 & Surgeon Gen, US Air Force, 62-70; trustee, Am Bd Path, 69-80, secy 77-79, pres, 80; mem sci adv bd, Armed Forces Inst Path, DC, 71-75, chmn, 74-75, Residency Rev Comt Path, 72-78, chmn, 74-75, 77-78; pres, Dallas County Med Soc, 85; secy, Am Registry Path, 86, pres, 89-90. *Mem:* AMA; Am Asn Path; Col Am Path; Am Soc Clin Path (pres, 77-78); Int Acad Path; Asn Clin Lab Physicians & Scientists; Am Registry Path. *Res:* Neoplasms, environment and immunopathology. *Mailing Add:* Dept Path Univ Tex Southwestern Med Ctr 5323 Harry Hines Blvd Dallas TX 75235-9072

STEMKE, GERALD W, MICROBIOLOGY. *Current Pos:* PROF MICROBIOL, UNIV ALTA, 70- *Personal Data:* b Watseka, Ill, Oct 7, 35; m; c 2. *Educ:* Ill State Univ, BS, 57; Univ Ill, PhD(chem), 63. *Prof Exp:* Teaching asst, Univ Ill, 59-60; trainee microbiol, NY Univ Med Ctr, 60-62, res assoc, 62-63; NIH fel, Pasteur Inst, Paris, 63-64; asst prof biol, Univ Pittsburgh, 65-66, asst prof microbiol & molecular biol, 66-67, assoc prof biophys & microbiol, 67-70. *Concurrent Pos:* Nat Res Coun Can res grant, 70-74; Nat Sci Eng, Res Coun Can res grant. *Mem:* AAAS; Int Org Mycoplasmol; Am Soc Microbiol; Can Soc Immunol. *Res:* Mycoplasma; ureaplasma surface antigens; pylogeny; I6S-RNA. *Mailing Add:* Dept Biol Sci Univ Alta Edmonton AB T6G 2E2 Can. *E-Mail:* gw.stemke@ualberta.ca

STEMLER, ALAN JAMES, PLANT PHYSIOLOGY. *Current Pos:* PROF, SECT PLANT BIOL, UNIV CALIF, DAVIS, 78- *Personal Data:* b Chicago, Ill, July 29, 43; m 85, Elisabeth Creach; c 2. *Educ:* Mich State Univ, BS, 65; Univ Ill, Urbana, PhD(plant physiol), 74. *Prof Exp:* Instr plant physiol, Univ Ill, Urbana, 74-75; fel, Dept Plant Biol, Carnegie Inst Wash, 75-78. *Mem:* Am Soc Photobiol; Am Soc Plant Physiologists. *Res:* Photochemical events of photosynthesis. *Mailing Add:* Sect Plant Biol Univ Calif Davis CA 95616. *Fax:* 530-752-5410; *E-Mail:* ajstemler@ucdavis.edu

STEMMER, EDWARD ALAN, THORACIC SURGERY. *Current Pos:* asst prof in residence, 66-70, assoc prof, 70-76, PROF SURG, UNIV CALIF, IRVINE, 76-; CHIEF SURG SERV, LONG BEACH VET ADMIN HOSP, 65- *Personal Data:* b Cincinnati, Ohio, Jan 20, 30; m 54, Lois Moss; c Susan, Paul, Linda, Nancy & Carol. *Educ:* Univ Chicago, BA, 49, MD, 53; Am Bd Surg, dipl, 62; Am Bd Thoracic Surg, dipl. *Prof Exp:* Intern med, Univ Chicago Clins, 53-54, res asst surg, Sch Med, 54-55, from asst resident to sr resident, 54-60, instr, 59-60; chief resident, Stanford Univ, 60-61, clin teaching asst, 61; chief resident, Palo Alto Vet Admin Hosp, 61-62, asst chief surg serv, 62-64; asst prof surg, Univ Utah, 64-65. *Concurrent Pos:* Responsible investr, Vet Admin Hosp, 62-; attend surgeon, Salt Lake County Hosp, Utah, 64-65; prin investr, NIH, 64-70. *Mem:* Fel Am Col Surg; Am Asn Thoracic Surg; Soc Thoracic Surg; Am Surg Asn; Soc Vascular Surg. *Res:* Vascular surgery; metabolism of plasma proteins; myocardial function; control of regional blood flow. *Mailing Add:* Long Beach Vet Admin Hosp 5901 E Seventh St Long Beach CA 90822-5201. *Fax:* 562-494-5666

STEMMLER, EDWARD J, MEDICINE. *Current Pos:* RETIRED. *Personal Data:* b Philadelphia, Pa, Feb 15, 29; m 58; c 5. *Educ:* La Salle Col, BA, 50; Univ Pa Sch Med, MD, 60; Am Bd Intern cert, 67; subspecialty Bd Pulmonary Dis, cert, 72. *Hon Degrees:* DSc, Ursinus Col, 77, La Salle Univ, 83, Philadelphia Col Pharm & Sci, 89; LHD, Rush Univ, 86. *Honors & Awards:* Frederick A Packard Award, 60; Albert Einstein Med Ctr Staff Award, 60; Roche Award, 60; Laureate Award, Am Col Physicians; Roland Holroyd Lectr, La Salle Univ, 80; Aaron Brown Lect, Univ Pittsburgh Sch Med, 83; Gus Carroll Mem Lectr, Asn Am Med Cols, 88; Kiskadden Lectr, Am Asn Plastic Surgeons, 91. *Prof Exp:* Exec vpres, Asn Am Med Cols, 90-94; intern, Univ Pa, 60-61, med resident, 61-63, fel cardiol, Hosp Pa, 63-64, instr med, 64-66, assoc, 66-67, assoc physiol, Grad Div Med, 67-72, assoc prof, 70-74, prof, 74-81, Robert G Dunlop prof, 80-; sr adv to pres, Asn Am Med Cols, 94- *Concurrent Pos:* Chief med resident, Hosp Univ Pa, 66-67, chief med, Vet Admin, 67-73, assoc dean, Univ Hosp, 73, actg dean, Sch Med, 74-75, dean, 75-86, exec vpres & dean, Med Ctr, 86-88, exec vpres, 88-89, emer dean, Sch Med, 89-; mem, Lower Merion Township Bd, Sch Dir, 73-74; dean comt, Philadelphia Vet Admin Hosp, 74-; mem, Gov Comt Health Educ, 74-77; comt dean, Pa Sch Med, 75, chmn; chmn, Invest Comt, 75-81; mem, Educ Policy Comt, Nat Fund Med Educ, 75-78; dir, Rorer Group Inc, 78-; mem, Sci Affairs Comt, 78; mem, Select Comt Med Prospective Prog, 78-80; mem, Task Force Support Med Educ, 77-81, chmn, 79-81; mem coun deans admin bd, 80, chmn, 82-84; chmn, Mgt Educ Prog, 83-85, Comt Practice Plan, 85-86; lectr, higher educ & health, Western Higher Educrs, 84; vchmn, Nat Bd Med Examr, 87-; invitational lectr, Asn Med Dean Europe, 86, Japan Med Educ Found, Japan, 87; AMA, 87, Am Med Asn & Annenberg Ctr Health Sci, 88. *Mem:* Inst Med-Nat Acad Sci; Am Col Physicians (treas, 75-81); Am Fed Clin Res; Am Heart Asn; AMA; Am Thoracic Soc; Asn Am Med Col; Am Clin & Climat Asn; fel AAAS. *Res:* Author of numerous scientific publications. *Mailing Add:* Rural Rte 1 Box 363 Roseland VA 22967

STEMNISKI, JOHN ROMAN, ORGANIC CHEMISTRY. *Current Pos:* RETIRED. *Personal Data:* b Nanticoke, Pa, Apr 29, 33; m 59; c 3. *Educ:* Fordham Univ, BS, 55; Carnegie Inst Technol, MS, 59, PhD(org chem), 60. *Honors & Awards:* STRATOSPHERIC OZONE PROTECTION AWARD, ENVIRON PROTECTION AGENCY. *Prof Exp:* Res chemist, Monsanto Res Corp, 59-65; staff chemist, Mass Inst Technol, 65-69, prin chemist polymer prod, 69-73, chief mat & process control lab, 73-84, sr technologist, C S Draper Lab, 84-94. *Concurrent Pos:* Mem, United Nation Environ Protection Solvents Comt. *Mem:* Am Chem Soc; Royal Soc Chem; Am Soc Testing and Mat; Sigma Xi. *Res:* Synthesis of medicinal compounds; synthesis of oil additives; lubricant systems; oxidation mechanism; high density fluids; gel permeation chromatography; fluorine containing fluids, materials science studies; fiber optics instrumentation; chloro fluoro carbon alternatives; strat ozone protection. *Mailing Add:* C S Draper Lab-MS 25 555 Technology Sq Cambridge MA 02139-3539

STEMPAK, JEROME G, ANATOMY. *Current Pos:* Instr, 63-66, asst prof, 66-77, ASSOC PROF ANAT, STATE UNIV NY DOWNSTATE MED CTR, 77- *Personal Data:* b Chicago, Ill, Dec 24, 31; m 61; c 2. *Educ:* Roosevelt Univ, BS, 58; Univ Ill, MS, 60, PhD(teratology), 62. *Concurrent Pos:* USPHS fel, 62-63. *Mem:* Am Asn Anat; Am Soc Cell Biol. *Res:* Electron microscopy of differentiating cells and tissues; electron microscopic investigations on generation of cell organelles. *Mailing Add:* Dept Anat & Cell Biol SUNY Health Sci Col Med 450 Clarkson Ave Brooklyn NY 11203-2012

STEMPEL, ARTHUR, CHEMISTRY. *Current Pos:* CONSULT, SCR ASSOC, 85- *Personal Data:* b Brooklyn, NY, June 8, 17; m 50; c 2. *Educ:* City Col New York, BS, 37; Columbia Univ, MA, 39. PhD(chem), 42. *Prof Exp:* Asst, Col Physicians & Surgeons, Columbia Univ, 38-39, org chem, Col Pharm, 40-41, res assoc, Chem Labs, 42-43; tutor & fel chem, Queens Col, 41-42; sr chemist, Hoffman-LaRoche, Inc, 43-68, from res group chief to sr res group chief, chem res dept, 69-85. *Mem:* Am Chem Soc. *Res:* Isolation of natural products of animal and plant origin; antibiotics; organic synthesis of pharmaceuticals; investigations on loco weeds; synthesis of benzodiazepines; cholinesterase inhibitors; anticurare compounds. *Mailing Add:* 1341 River Rd Teaneck NJ 07666

STEMPEL, EDWARD, PHARMACY. *Current Pos:* RETIRED. *Personal Data:* b Brooklyn, NY, Mar 7, 26; m 59; c 1. *Educ:* Brooklyn Col Pharm, BS, 49; Columbia Univ, MS, 52, MA, 55, EdD, 56. *Prof Exp:* From instr to prof pharm, Arnold & Marie Schwartz Col Pharm & Health Sci, 49-92, chmn dept, 64-79, assoc dean, 79-83. *Mem:* Am Pharmaceut Asn; Am Asn Col Pharm. *Res:* Dispensing pharmacy; long-acting dosage forms. *Mailing Add:* 1817 E 29th St Brooklyn NY 11229

STEMPEL, ROBERT C, AUTOMOTIVE PRODUCTION ADMINISTRATION. *Current Pos:* RETIRED. *Personal Data:* b 1933. *Prof Exp:* Var positions, Gen Motors Corp, 58-90, chmn & chief exec officer, 90-93. *Mem:* Nat Acad Eng. *Mailing Add:* Gen Motors Corp 14-132 Gen Motors Bldg 3044 W Grand Blvd Detroit MI 48202

STEMPEN, HENRY, MICROBIOLOGY. *Current Pos:* asst prof biol, 62-63, ASSOC PROF MICROBIOL, RUTGERS UNIV, CAMDEN, 63- *Personal Data:* b Phila, Pa, May 10, 24; m 54; c 4. *Educ:* Phila Col Pharm, BS, 45; Univ Pa, PhD(microbiol), 51. *Prof Exp:* Res asst cytol, Lankenau Hosp Res Inst, Phila, Pa, 45-46; from instr to asst prof, bact, Jefferson Med Col, 50-57, assoc prof microbiol, 57-62. *Concurrent Pos:* NIH grants, 59-60 & 64-66. *Mem:* AAAS; Am Soc Microbiol; Mycol Soc Am. *Res:* Bacterial cytology and genetics; morphogenesis of myxomycetes. *Mailing Add:* 2364 Geneva Rd Glenside PA 19038-4216

STEMPIEN, MARTIN F, JR, BIOCHEMISTRY. *Current Pos:* Res assoc & sr investr bio-org chem, 60-66, ASST TO DIR & BIO-ORG CHEMIST, OSBORN LABS, MARINE SCI, NY AQUARIUM, NY ZOOL SOC, 66- *Personal Data:* b New Britain, Conn, Sept 2, 30. *Educ:* Yale Univ, BS, 52, MS, 53, PhD(org chem), 57; Cambridge Univ, PhD(org chem), 60. *Concurrent Pos:* Consult, Off Naval Res, 68; fel, NY Zool Soc, 68- *Mem:* AAAS; Am Chem Soc; NY Acad Sci; Am Soc Zool; The Chem Soc; Sigma Xi. *Res:* Physiologically active materials from extracts of marine invertebrates, particularly Porifera and Echinodermata; bio-chemical taxonomy of Phylum Porifera. *Mailing Add:* 343 Eighth Ave Apt 13G New York NY 10001

STEMPLE, JOEL G, MATHEMATICS. *Current Pos:* Asst prof, 66-70, ASSOC PROF MATH, QUEENS COL, NY, 70- *Personal Data:* b Brooklyn, NY, Feb 3, 42; m 68. *Educ:* Brooklyn Col, BS, 62; Yale Univ, MA, 64, PhD, 66. *Res:* Theory of graphs. *Mailing Add:* 46 Old Brook Rd Dix Hills NY 11746

STEMSHORN, BARRY WILLIAM, INFECTIOUS DISEASES, SCIENCE ADMINISTRATION. *Current Pos:* dir, Animal Path Lab, Saskatoon, 81-83, dir, Animal Dis Res Inst, 83-92, DIR ANIMAL HEALTH, NEPEAN, AGR CAN, 92- *Personal Data:* b Montreal, Que, Dec 15, 47; m 80. *Educ:* McGill Univ, BSc, 69; Univ Montreal, DMV, 74; Univ Guelph, PhD(microbiol & immunol), 79. *Prof Exp:* Staff scientist, Animal Dis Res Inst, Ont, 75-81. *Concurrent Pos:* Assoc grad fac mem, Dr Vet Sci prog, Dept Vet Microbiol & Immunol, Univ Guelph, 81-; mem, Brucellosis Sci Adv Comt, US Animal Health Asn & Subcomt on Taxon the Genus Brucella; consult, UN Univ; coordr, Caribbean Animal & Plant Health Prog, Inter-Am Inst Coop Agr, Trinidad & Tobago, 88-90. *Mem:* Am Vet Med Asn; Can Vet Med Asn; US Animal Health Asn; Am Asn Vet Lab Diagnosticians. *Res:* Management of diagnostic service and research programs related to livestock diseases; microbiological and serological methods for diagnosis of brucellosis and other bacterial diseases. *Mailing Add:* 2748 Howe Nepean ON K2B 6W9 Can. *Fax:* 613-993-4336

STENBACK, WAYNE ALBERT, MICROBIOLOGY, ELECTRON MICROSCOPY. *Current Pos:* electron microscopist, Tex Children's Hosp, 75- AT DEPT PATH, BAYLOR COL MED,. *Personal Data:* b Brush, Colo, June 12, 29; m 54; c 1. *Educ:* Univ Colo, BS, 55; Univ Denver, MS, 57; Univ Mo, PhD(microbiol), 62. *Prof Exp:* Instr exp biol, 62-66, asst prof exp biol, Dept Surg, Baylor Col Med, 66-75. *Concurrent Pos:* Mem, Int Asn Comp Res on Leukemia & Related Dis. *Mem:* AAAS; Am Soc Microbiol; Am Asn Cancer Res; Electron Micros Soc Am. *Res:* Density gradient studies of Newcastle disease virus; control of endemic microorganisms in mouse colonies; electron microscopy, biological and biophysical studies of viruses associated with neoplasms. *Mailing Add:* 5518 Lymbar Dr Houston TX 77096

STENBAEK-NIELSEN, HANS C, AURORAL PHYSICS. *Current Pos:* PROF GEOPHYS, UNIV ALASKA, 67- *Personal Data:* b Slagelse, Denmark. *Educ:* Tech Univ Denmark, MSc, 65. *Mem:* Am Geophys Union. *Res:* Space and auroral physics; optical observations of auroras and upper atmosphere chemical releases. *Mailing Add:* Geophys Inst Univ Alaska Fairbanks AK 99775-7320

STENBERG, CHARLES GUSTAVE, PHYSICS, COMPUTER SCIENCE. *Current Pos:* PHYSICIST REACTOR PHYSICS, ARGONNE NAT LAB, 69- *Personal Data:* b Chicago, Ill, Apr 11, 35; m 66. *Educ:* Univ Ill, Urbana, BS, 59, MS, 60, PhD(physics), 68. *Mem:* Am Nuclear Soc; Sigma Xi. *Res:* Method and code development of models and computer codes for reactor physics calculations. *Mailing Add:* Reactor Physics-Nat Lab 9700 S Cass Ave Argonne IL 60439-4803

STENBERG, PAULA E, HEMATOLOGY. *Current Pos:* FEL PATH, ORE HEALTH SCI UNIV SCH MED, 89- *Personal Data:* b Montreal, Que, Can, June 25, 53. *Educ:* Univ Calif, San Francisco, PhD(path), 89. *Prof Exp:* Fel path, Vet Admin Med Ctr, 84-89. *Mem:* Am Soc Women Sci; Am Soc Cell Biol. *Mailing Add:* Ore Health Sci Univ Sch Med 3181 SW Sam Jackson Park Rd L-113 Portland OR 97201-3098

STENBERG, VIRGIL IRVIN, ORGANIC CHEMISTRY. *Current Pos:* From asst prof to assoc prof, 60-67, PROF CHEM, UNIV NDAK, 67- *Personal Data:* b Grygla, Minn, May 18, 35; m 56; c 4. *Educ:* Concordia Col, Moorhead, Minn, BA, 56; Iowa State Univ, PhD(org chem), 60. *Honors &*

Awards: Sigma Xi Res Award, 74; Chester Fritz Prof Award, 77. *Concurrent Pos:* Res grants, Res Corp, 60-62; Petrol Res Fund, 61-63, NIH, 61-64, 68-71 & 74-76, career develop award, 70-75; NSF res grant, 66-68; vis prof, Imp Col, Univ London, 71-72; Energy Res Develop Admin contract, 75-78 & Dept Energy contract, 78-87. *Mem:* Am Chem Soc; Sigma Xi. *Res:* Natural products; medicinal chemistry of inflammation. *Mailing Add:* 1866 W 15th Lane Apache Junction AZ 85220

STENCEL, ROBERT EDWARD, ASTRONOMY, SPECTROSCOPY. *Current Pos:* WOMBLE PROF ASTROPHYS, UNIV DENVER, 92- *Personal Data:* b Wausau, Wis, Apr 16, 50; m 77, Susan Conat; c 1. *Educ:* Univ Wis-Madison, BS, 72; Univ Mich, Ann Arbor, MS, 74, PhD(astron), 77. *Prof Exp:* Res asst solar physics, Sacramento Peak Observ, 75; res assoc astron, NASA Johnson Space Ctr, 77-78; res assoc astron, Nat Acad Sci & NASA, Goddard Space Flight Ctr, 78-80; res assoc astron, Joint Inst Lab, Astrophys, Univ Colo, 80-82; staff scientist, NASA Hq, 82-85; exec dir, Ctr Astrophys Space Astron, Univ Colo, Boulder, 85-92. *Concurrent Pos:* Res assoc, Nat Res Coun/Nat Acad Sci, 77-; mem adv coun, Archeoastron Ctr, Univ Md, 78-82; NSF & NASA grants; vis prof, Dept Physics, Univ Mich-Ann Arbor, 92-93. *Mem:* Am Phys Soc; Am Astron Soc; Int Astron Union; Int Dark-Sky Asn. *Res:* High resolution spectroscopy of the outer atmospheres of low temperature supergiant stars; radiative transfer studies; infrared astronomy. *Mailing Add:* Univ Denver 2112 E Wesly Ave Denver CO 80208. *E-Mail:* rstencel@diana.cair.du.edu

STENCHEVER, MORTON ALBERT, HEALTH CARE OF OLDER WOMEN, UROGYNECOLOGY & REPARATIVE PELVIC SURGERY. *Current Pos:* prof & chmn, Dept Obstet & Gynec, 77-96, EMER PROF, DEPT OBSTET & GYNEC, UNIV WASH, 96- *Personal Data:* b Paterson, NJ, Jan 25, 31; m 55, Diane; c Michael, Marc & Douglas. *Educ:* NY Univ, AB, 51; Univ Buffalo, MD, 56; Am Bd Obstet & Gynec, cert 65 & 85. *Honors & Awards:* Wyeth Distinguished Serv Award, Asn Prof Gynec & Obstet. *Prof Exp:* Intern med, Mt Sinai Hosp, NY, 56-57; resident, Columbia-Presby Med Ctr, 57-60; from instr to assoc prof obstet & gynec, Case Western Res Univ, 64-70, dir, Tissue Cult Lab, 64-70, assoc, Dept Med Educ, 68-70; prof obstet & gynec & chmn dept, Univ Utah, 70-77. *Concurrent Pos:* NIH res training fel genetics, 62-64; Oglebey res fel, Case Western Res Univ, 64; chief obstet & gynec serv, Malmstrom AFB Hosp, Mont; pres, Asn Prof Gynec & Obstet, 83-84, Seattle Gynec Soc, 83-84; dir, vpres & treas, Am Bd Obstet & Gynec, 88, chmn, 96; mem, Residency Rev Comt Obstet & Gynec, 93- *Mem:* AAAS; AMA; fel Am Col Obstet & Gynec; fel Am Soc Obstet & Gynec; Soc Cryobiol; Asn Prof Gynec & Obstet. *Res:* Male infertility; human reproduction; health care for older women. *Mailing Add:* Dept Obstet & Gynec Univ Wash Seattle WA 98195. *Fax:* 206-543-3915

STENDELL, REY CARL, POLLUTION BIOLOGY. *Current Pos:* asst dir, Northern Prairie Wildlife Res Ctr, 79-81, dir, 81-89, DIR, NAT ECOL RES CTR, NAT BIOL SURV, 89- *Personal Data:* b San Francisco, Calif, Aug 12, 41; m 66, Marlynn Smith; c Brett & Nicole. *Educ:* Univ Calif, Santa Barbara, BA, 63, MA, 67; Univ Calif, Berkeley, PhD(zool), 72. *Prof Exp:* Res biologist, US Fish & Wildlife Serv, 72-73, res coordr, Patuxent Wildlife Res Ctr, 73-77, prog coordr pollution biol, Washington, DC, 77-79. *Mem:* Am Ornithologists Union; Cooper Ornithol Soc. *Res:* Evaluation of the effects of environmental pollutants on wildlife, particularly birds. *Mailing Add:* 2819 Zendt Dr Ft Collins CO 80526. *Fax:* 970-226-9230

STENESH, JOCHANAN, MOLECULAR BIOLOGY, MICROBIOLOGY. *Current Pos:* RETIRED. *Personal Data:* b Magdeburg, Ger, Dec 19, 27; US citizen; m 57; c 2. *Educ:* Univ Ore, BS, 53; Univ Calif, Berkeley, PhD(biochem), 58. *Prof Exp:* Res assoc biochem, Weizmann Inst, 58-60 & Purdue Univ, 60-63; from asst prof to assoc prof, Western Mich Univ, 63-71, prof chem, 71-90. *Concurrent Pos:* Res grants, Nat Inst Allergy & Infectious Dis, 64-70, Am Cancer Soc, 65-67. *Mem:* AAAS; Am Chem Soc; Am Soc Biochem & Molecular Biol; Am Soc Microbiol. *Res:* Physical biochemistry; enzymology; protein synthesis; DNA replication and transcription. *Mailing Add:* Dept Chem Western Mich Univ Kalamazoo MI 49008-3804

STENGEL, ROBERT FRANK, AEROSPACE ENGINEERING, MECHANICAL ENGINEERING. *Current Pos:* assoc prof, 77-82, PROF MECH & AEROSPACE ENG, PRINCETON UNIV, ASSOC DEAN ENG, 94-, DIR, TOPICAL PROG ROBOTICS & INTEL SYSTS. *Personal Data:* b Orange, NJ, Sept 1, 38; m 61; c Brooke & Christopher. *Educ:* Mass Inst Technol, BS, 60; Princeton Univ, MSE, 65, MA, 66, PhD(aerospace & mech sci), 68. *Prof Exp:* Aerospace technologist rockets, NASA, 60-63; mem tech staff & group leader guid & control, Draper Lab, Mass Inst Technol, 68-73; mem tech staff & sect leader, Anal Sci Corp, 73-77. *Concurrent Pos:* Mem, Aerospace Guid & Control Systs Comt, Soc Automotive Engrs; assoc ed-at-large, Transactions on Automatic Control, Inst Elec & Electronics Engrs, 91-; NAm ed, Cambridge Univ Press Aerospace Ser. *Mem:* Fel Am Inst Aeronaut & Astronaut; fel Inst Elec & Electronics Engrs. *Res:* Atmospheric flight mechanics; optimal control and estimation; nonlinear dynamical systems; human factors; artificial intelligence. *Mailing Add:* D-202 Eng Quadrangle Princeton Univ Princeton NJ 08544. *Fax:* 609-258-6109; *E-Mail:* stengel@pucc.princeton.edu

STENGER, FRANK, APPLIED MATHEMATICS. *Current Pos:* from assoc prof to prof math, 69-89, PROF COMPUT SCI, UNIV UTAH, 89- *Personal Data:* b Veszprem, Hungary, July 6, 38; m 61; c 2. *Educ:* Univ Alta, BSc, 61, MSc, 63, PhD(math), 65. *Prof Exp:* Guest worker, Nat Bur Stand, Washington, DC, 63-64; asst prof comp sci, Univ Alta, 65-66; asst prof math, Univ Mich, 66-69. *Concurrent Pos:* NSF grant, Univ Utah, 70-71 & 76-78; vis math res ctr, Univ Montreal, 71-72; US Army res grant, Univ Utah, 74-76 & 77-80; distinguished vis prof, Univ Tsukuba, 87. *Mem:* Am Math Soc; Can Math Cong; Soc Indust & Appl Math; Asn Comput Mach. *Res:* Quadrature; numerical solution of differential and integral equations; asymptotic approximation of functions and integrals; asymptotic solution of differential equations; numerical solution of inverse probles in ultrasonic tomography and in geophysics; sine numerical methods, parallel computation. *Mailing Add:* 680 Terrace Hills Dr Salt Lake City UT 84103

STENGER, RICHARD J, PATHOLOGY, ELECTRON MICROSCOPY. *Current Pos:* DIR PATH & LABS, BETH ISRAEL MED CTR, 72-, PROF PATH, MT SINAI SCH MED, 72- *Personal Data:* b Cincinnati, Ohio, Dec 13, 27; m 51; c 2. *Educ:* Col of the Holy Cross, AB, 49; Univ Cincinnati, MD, 53. *Prof Exp:* Intern, Cincinnati Gen Hosp, 53-54; resident path, Mass Gen Hosp, 54-55, 57-58, fel 58-59, asst, 59-60; asst prof, Col Med, Univ Cincinnati, 60-64; from asst prof to assoc prof path, Case Western Reserve Univ, 64-68; prof, New York Med Col, 68-72. *Concurrent Pos:* Chief, Lab Serv, W Point Army Hosp, 55-57; Nat Inst Arthritis & Metab Dis res grant & Nat Inst Gen Med Sci career develop award, 64-68; instr, Harvard Med Sch, 59-60; attend pathologist, Cincinnati Gen Hosp, 60-64; assoc pathologist, Cleveland Metrop Gen Hosp, 64-68; attend pathologist, Flower & Fifth Ave Hosps, NY & vis pathologist, Metrop Hosp Ctr, NY, 68-72. *Mem:* AAAS; Am Asn Path; Am Asn Study Liver Dis. Int Acad Path; Sigma Xi. *Res:* Light and electron microscopic studies of the liver, especially with regards to toxic effects. *Mailing Add:* Path & Labs Dept Nassau County Med Ctr 2201 Hempstead Tpke East Meadow NY 11554-5400. *Fax:* 516-542-5792

STENGER, VERNON ARTHUR, INORGANIC CHEMISTRY, GEOCHEMISTRY. *Current Pos:* anal res chemist, 35-53, dir spec serv lab, 53-61, anal scientist, 61-73, CONSULT, DOW CHEM CO, 73- *Personal Data:* b Minneapolis, Minn, June 11, 08; m 96, Eleanor Miller; c Robert, Emilie (York), Alan, Gordon & David. *Educ:* Univ Denver, BS, 29, MS, 30; Univ Minn, PhD(anal chem), 33. *Hon Degrees:* DSc, Univ Denver, 71. *Honors & Awards:* Anachem Award, 70; Midland Sect Award, Am Chem Soc, 79. *Prof Exp:* Asst, Eastman Kodak Co, 29-30; anal chemist, Univ Minn, 33-35. *Mem:* Am Chem Soc; Sigma Xi; Geochem Soc; NY Acad Sci; fel Am Inst Chem. *Res:* Purity of reagents; technology of bromine and its compounds; instrumentation for water analysis; methods for environmental analysis. *Mailing Add:* 1108 E Park Dr Midland MI 48640-4249

STENGER, VICTOR JOHN, PHYSICS, PARTICLE ASTROPHYSICS. *Current Pos:* assoc prof, 63-74, PROF PHYSICS & ASTRON, UNIV HAWAII, 74- *Personal Data:* b Bayonne, NJ, Jan 29, 35; m 62, Phyllis M Black; c Noelle & Victor A. *Educ:* Newark Col Eng, BS, 56; Univ Calif, Los Angeles, MS, 58, PhD(physics), 63. *Prof Exp:* Mem tech staff, Hughes Aircraft Co, 56-59; asst physics, Univ Calif, Los Angeles, 59-63. *Concurrent Pos:* Vis prof, Univ Heidelberg, 69, Oxford Univ, 78 & Nat Inst Nuclear Physics, Frascuti, Italy, 87. *Res:* Elementary physics; particle astrophysics. *Mailing Add:* 508 Pepeekeo Pl Honolulu HI 96825. *Fax:* 808-956-2930; *E-Mail:* vjs@uhhepg.phys.hawaii.edu

STENGER, WILLIAM, MATHEMATICS. *Current Pos:* asst prof, 69-72, PROF MATH, AMBASSADOR UNIV, 72- *Personal Data:* b Bayonne, NJ, Jan 25, 42; wid; c Laura (Plummer) & Serena (Seifried). *Educ:* Stevens Inst Technol, BS, 63; Univ Md, PhD(math), 67. *Prof Exp:* Asst comput, Davidson Lab, Stevens Inst Technol, 62-63; res asst, Univ Md, 66-67; asst prof math, Am Univ, 67-68 & Georgetown Univ, 68-69. *Concurrent Pos:* Res grantee, Air Force Off Sci Res, 67-68 & NSF, 68-69. *Mem:* Math Asn Am; Am Math Soc; Soc Indust Appl Math. *Res:* Variational theory of eigenvalues and related inequalities. *Mailing Add:* Dept Math Ambassador Univ Big Sandy TX 75755. *Fax:* 903-636-2083; *E-Mail:* william_stenger@ambassador.edu

STENGER, WILLIAM J(AMES), SR, occupational health, environmental affairs, for more information see previous edition

STENGLE, WILLIAM BERNARD, WOOD CHEMISTRY. *Current Pos:* RETIRED. *Personal Data:* b Lancaster, Pa, Feb 21, 23; m 48; c 3. *Educ:* Franklin & Marshall Col, BS, 43; State Univ NY, Syracuse, MS, 49. *Prof Exp:* Chemist, Animal Trap Co Am, 47; asst, Col Forestry, State Univ NY, Syracuse, 49; res chemist, Crossett Co, Ark, 49-58, asst tech serv dir, Paper Mill Div, 58-62; tech dir, Tenn River Pulp & Paper Co, Counce, 62-82. *Concurrent Pos:* Officer, USMCR, 43-82; mem, Tenn Air Pollution Control Bd, 76-80. *Mem:* Am Chem Soc; Tech Asn Pulp & Paper Indust; Air Pollution Control Asn. *Res:* Hydroxy acids; alkaline pulping; bleaching; paper manufacture; tall oil; corrugated paperboard; water and air pollution abatement. *Mailing Add:* 116 College Ave Lancaster PA 17603-3316

STENKAMP, RONALD EUGENE, BIOINORGANIC CHEMISTRY, PROTEIN CRYSTALLOGRAPHY. *Current Pos:* res assoc crystallog, 78-81, ASSOC PROF, DEPT BIOL STRUCT, UNIV WASH, 81- *Personal Data:* b Bend, Ore, May 14, 48; m 70. *Educ:* Univ Ore, BA, 70; Univ Wash, MSc, 71, PhD(chem), 75. *Prof Exp:* Fel crystallog, Dept Molecular Biophys & Biochem, Yale Univ, 75-76; Am Cancer Soc fel, Dept Molecular Biophys & Biochem, Yale Univ & Dept Biol Struct, Univ Wash, 77. *Mem:* Am Crystallog Asn; Am Chem Soc; AAAS. *Res:* Crystallographic studies of molecules of biological interest, including metallo proteins, cellular recognition proteins, enzymes and nucleic acids. *Mailing Add:* Dept Biol Struct Univ Wash SM-20 Seattle WA 98195-7428

STENKEN, JULIE ANN, BIOANALYTICAL CHEMISTRY. *Current Pos:* ASST PROF CHEM, RENSSELAER POLYTECH INST, 96- *Personal Data:* b Cincinnati, Ohio, Jan 15, 67. *Educ:* Univ Akron, BS, 90; Univ Kans, PHD(bioanal chem), 95. *Prof Exp:* Res assoc, Dept Pharmacol, Med Ctr, Univ Kans, 95-96. *Mem:* Am Chem Soc; Sigma Xi; AAAS; NAm Membrane Soc; Oxygen Soc. *Res:* Development of microdialysis technology to study in vivo metabolism; development of bioanalytical methods for determining pharmaceutical and biotechnology products. *Mailing Add:* Dept Chem Rensselaer Polytech Inst 110 Eighth St Troy NY 12180-3590. *Fax:* 578-276-4887; *E-Mail:* stenkj@rpi.edu

STENN, KURT S, BIOLOGY OF SKIN. *Current Pos:* PROF DERMAT & PATH, YALE UNIV, 71- *Personal Data:* b Chicago, Ill, Apr 6, 40; m 64; c 2. *Educ:* Univ Chicago, BS, 61; Univ Rochester, NY, MD, 65. *Hon Degrees:* MS, Yale Univ, 83. *Mem:* Am Acad Dermat; Soc Invest Res Med; Am Soc Cell Biol; Am Soc Dermat Path; Sigma Xi; AAAS. *Res:* Epithelial mesenchymal interactions and the control of hair growth. *Mailing Add:* Skin Biol Res Ctr Johnson & Johnson 199 Grandview Rd Skillman NJ 08558-9418. *Fax:* 908-874-1254

STENSAAS, LARRY J, NEUROANATOMY, PLANT PHYSIOLOGY. *Current Pos:* from asst prof to assoc prof, 68-80, PROF PHYSIOL, UNIV UTAH, 80- *Personal Data:* b Nov 13, 32; US citizen; m 62; c 1. *Educ:* Univ Calif, Berkeley, BA, 55, MA, 57; Univ Calif, Los Angeles, PhD(neuroanat), 65. *Prof Exp:* Stratigrapher, Richmond of Columbia, 57-58; head, Paleont Sect, Cuba Calif Oil Co, 58-59; micropaleontologist, Standard of Calif, 59-60. *Concurrent Pos:* Cerebral Palsy Educ & Res Found fel, 65-67; NIH fel, 67-68; distinguished scientist, Armed Forces Inst Path, 84-85. *Mem:* AAAS; Am Asn Anat; Soc Neurosci. *Res:* Light and electron microscopy of normal and regenerating central nervous tissue; fertilization of plant communities by municipal wastes and rock phosphate solubilized by thermophyllic microorganisms. *Mailing Add:* Dept Physiol Univ Utah Sch Med 410 Chipeta Way Salt Lake City UT 84108

STENSAAS, SUZANNE SPERLING, NEUROANATOMY. *Current Pos:* Instr, 71-75, ASST PROF ANAT, COL MED, UNIV UTAH, 75- *Personal Data:* b Oakland, Calif, Mar 15, 39; m 62; c 1. *Educ:* Pomona Col, BA, 59; Univ Calif, Los Angeles, MA, 62; Univ Utah, PhD(anat), 75. *Mem:* Soc Neurosci; AAAS. *Res:* Biological compatability of materials with the brain; development of neuroprostheses; effects of electrical stimulation on the brain; problems of development and regeneration of the central nervous system. *Mailing Add:* 2460 Lynwood Dr Salt Lake City UT 84109

STENSETH, RAYMOND EUGENE, ORGANIC CHEMISTRY, PHARMACY. *Current Pos:* RETIRED. *Personal Data:* b Ludlow, SDak, Aug 5, 31; m 65; c 1. *Educ:* Univ Mich, BS, 53, MS, 57, PhD(pharmaceut chem), 61. *Prof Exp:* Sr res chemist, Monsanto Co, 60-68, res specialist, 68-85. *Mem:* Am Chem Soc; Sigma Xi. *Res:* Organic syntheses; nitrogen heterocycles; organophosphorus chemistry; food chemicals; pharmaceuticals; bacteriostats; fungistats; chemical processes. *Mailing Add:* 805 Westwood Dr St Louis MO 63105

STENSON, WILLIAM F, GASTROENTEROLOGY. *Current Pos:* From asst prof to assoc prof, 79-91, PROF MED, SCH MED, WASH UNIV, 91- *Personal Data:* b Rome, NY, Dec 2, 45; m 68, Janet Breaugh; c Catherine, Karen & Thomas. *Educ:* Providence Col, BS, 67; Washington Univ, MD, 71. *Mem:* Am Asn Immunologists; Am Soc Clin Invest; Am Gastroenterol Asn. *Res:* Intestinal inflammation; immunology and physiology. *Mailing Add:* Dept Gastroenterol Sch Med Washington Univ Sch Med 660 S Euclid Ave Box 8124 St Louis MO 63110. *Fax:* 314-362-8959

STENSRUD, HOWARD LEWIS, GEOLOGY, GEOCHEMISTRY. *Current Pos:* asst prof, 70-77, PROF GEOL, CALIF STATE UNIV, CHICO, 77- *Personal Data:* b Minneapolis, Minn, Nov 16, 36; div, Eileen Hopkins; c Richard & Paul. *Educ:* Univ Minn, Minneapolis, BA, 58; Univ Wyo, MA, 63; Univ Wash, PhD(geol), 70. *Prof Exp:* Explor geologist, Humble Oil & Ref Co, 60; asst prof geol, Univ Minn, Morris, 61-66. *Mem:* Geol Soc Am; Soc Mining Engrs; Nat Assoc Geol Teachers; Soc Explor Geologists. *Res:* Metamorphic petrology and Precambrian geology; economic geology. *Mailing Add:* Geosci Calif State Univ 101 Orange St Chico CA 95929-0001

STENSTROM, MICHAEL KNUDSON, ENVIRONMENTAL ENGINEERING. *Current Pos:* from asst prof to assoc prof, 77-84, PROF ENVIRON ENG, UNIV CALIF, LOS ANGELES, 84-, DEPT CHAIR, 91- *Personal Data:* b Anderson, SC, Nov 28, 48. *Educ:* Clemson Univ, SC, BS, 71, MS, 72, PhD(environ systs eng), 76. *Honors & Awards:* Best Dissertation Prize, Asn Environ Eng Prof, 75, 76; Huber Res Prize, Am Soc Civil Engrs, 89; Harrison Prescott Eddy Medal, Water Environment Fedn, 92. *Prof Exp:* Instr environ eng, Clemson Univ, 75; res engr, Amoco Oil Co, Stand Oil, Ind, 75-77. *Concurrent Pos:* Consult, Amoco Oil Co, 77-79, Exxon Res & Develop, 80, Sohio, 82-84, Chevron, 84-, City of Los Angeles, 87- *Mem:* Am Soc Civil Engrs; Water Environ Fedn; Asn Environ Eng Prof; Int Asn Water Quality; Am Chem Soc. *Res:* Wastewater and water treatment processes, including real time control of the activated sludge process, oxygen transfer, anaerobic treatment systems, hazardous waste control; urban runoff control; stormwater quality. *Mailing Add:* 4173 Eng I Univ Calif-Los Angeles Los Angeles CA 90095-1593. *Fax:* 310-206-5476; *E-Mail:* stenstro@seas.ucla.edu

STENSTROM, RICHARD CHARLES, GEOLOGY. *Current Pos:* from instr to assoc prof, 65-77, PROF GEOL, BELOIT COL, 77-, CHMN, 87- *Personal Data:* b Elkhorn, Wis, June 19, 36; m 60; c 1. *Educ:* Beloit Col, BS, 58; Univ Chicago, MS, 62, PhD(geophys sci), 64. *Prof Exp:* Am Chem Soc res fel geophys sci, Univ Chicago, 64-65. *Concurrent Pos:* Coun-at-large, Nat Asn Geol Teachers, 85-87. *Mem:* Nat Asn Geol Teachers; fel Geol Soc Am; Geochem Soc; Am Geophys Union. *Res:* Diffusion rates through sediments; hydrologic effects of urbanization; environmental geology; basin behavior and water quality; effects of urbanization versus agricultural use; sediment load, surface and subsurface character, general water quality; chemical analysis of geochemical systems, using field, AA, and EDS-SEM techniques. *Mailing Add:* Geol Beloit Col 700 College St Beloit WI 53511-5595

STENT, GUNTHER SIEGMUND, MOLECULAR BIOLOGY, NEUROBIOLOGY. *Current Pos:* asst res biochemist & lectr bact, Univ Calif, Berkeley, 52-56, assoc prof bact, 56-59, prof molecular biol, 59-94, prof arts & sci 67-68, chmn molecular biol & dir, Virus Lab, 80-86, chmn molecular & cell biol, 87-92, EMER PROF, UNIV CALIF, BERKELEY, 94- *Personal Data:* b Berlin, Ger, Mar 28, 24; nat US; wid; c Stefan L. *Educ:* Univ Ill, BS, 45, PhD(phys chem), 48. *Hon Degrees:* DSc, York Univ, Toronto, 84. *Honors & Awards:* Runnstrom Medal, 86; Urania Medal, 90. *Prof Exp:* Asst chem, Univ Ill, 44-48; Merck fel, Calif Inst Technol, Nat Res Coun, 48-50, Am Cancer Soc fel, Univ Copenhagen, 50-51, Pasteur Inst, Paris, 51-52. *Concurrent Pos:* Doc analyst, Field Intel Agency Tech, 46-47; mem, Genetics Study Sect, NIH, 59-64; sr fel, NSF, Univ Kyoto & Cambridge, 60-61; mem, Genetic Biol Panel, NSF, 65-69; external mem, Max Planck Inst Molecular Genetics, 66-; Guggenheim fel, Med Sch, Harvard Univ, 69-70; hon prof, Fac Sci, Univ Chile, 80; mem, Adv Bd, Basel Inst Immunol, 80-85; fel, Inst Advan Study, Berlin, 85-90; Inst Advan Study fel, 85-; chmn, Neurobiol Sect, Nat Acad Sci, 86-89; Fogarty scholar residence, NIH, Bethesda, 90-91. *Mem:* Nat Acad Sci; Soc Neurosci; Am Acad Arts & Sci; Am Philos Soc; fel AAAS; Europ Acad Sci & Arts. *Res:* Nervous control of behavior; developmental biology; philosophy of science; author of various publications. *Mailing Add:* Dept Molecular & Cell Biol Univ Calif Berkeley CA 94720. *Fax:* 510-643-6791; *E-Mail:* stent@uclink4.berkeley.edu

STENUF, THEODORE JOSEPH, chemical engineering; deceased, see previous edition for last biography

STENZEL, KURT HODGSON, NEPHROLOGY, MEDICINE. *Current Pos:* res fel, Cornell Univ Med Col, 63-64, from instr to assoc prof, 64-75, chief, Div Nephrology, 75-91, PROF MED, SURG & BIOCHEM, CORNELL UNIV MED COL, 75-; MED DIR, ROGOSIN INST, 83- *Personal Data:* b Stamford, Conn, Nov 3, 32; m 57; c 3. *Educ:* NY Univ, BA, 54; Cornell Univ, MD, 58. *Honors & Awards:* Hoening Award Excellence Renal Med, Nat Kidney Found. *Prof Exp:* Intern med, Second Cornell Med Div, Bellevue Hosp, NY, 58-59, asst resident, 59-60, cardio-renal resident, 62-63. *Concurrent Pos:* NY Heart Asn res fel, 63-66 & investr, 66-70; attend physician, NY Hosp, 75- *Mem:* Am Soc Biol Chemists; fel Am Col Physicians; Am Fedn Clin Res; Am Soc Artificial Internal Organs; Am Soc Nephrology; Am Asn Immunol & Transplantation Soc. *Res:* Dialysis; biomaterials; transplantation immunology; lymphocyte activation; renal cancer. *Mailing Add:* Rogosin Inst 505 E 70th St New York NY 10021

STENZEL, REINER LUDWIG, LABORATORY PLASMAS, PLASMA DIAGNOSTICS. *Current Pos:* assoc prof, 77-81, PROF PHYSICS, UNIV CALIF, LOS ANGELES, 81- *Personal Data:* b Breslau, Germany, Feb 18, 40; m 67; c 3. *Educ:* Calif Inst Technol, MS, 66, PhD(elec eng), 70. *Prof Exp:* Res fel plasma physics, Calif Inst Technol, 69-70; adj asst prof, Univ Calif, Los Angeles, 70-73; mem physics staff, TRW Systs, Calif, 72-77. *Concurrent Pos:* Vis prof, Univ Tokyo, 80 & Univ Paris-Sud, 95. *Mem:* Am Geophys Union; fel Am Phys Soc. *Res:* Experimental plasma physics on basic properties of plasmas such as waves, instabilities, beam-plasma interactions, double layers and magnetic reconnection; electron magnet hydrodynamics development of new laboratory plasma devices and diagnostic techniques; electron magnetohydrodynamics. *Mailing Add:* Dept Physics & Astron Univ Calif 405 Hilgard Ave Los Angeles CA 90095-1547. *Fax:* 310-825-4057; *E-Mail:* stenzel@physics.ucla.edu

STENZEL, WOLFRAM G, PHYSICS. *Current Pos:* prin engr physics, Ford Instrument Co Div, 55-69, SR ENGR, SYSTS MGT DIV, SPERRY RAND CORP, 69- *Personal Data:* b Berlin, Ger, May 24, 19; nat US; m 43; c 1. *Educ:* City Col New York, BS, 39, MS, 41. *Prof Exp:* Asst biochem, Warner Inst Therapeut Res, 42; res scientist phys chem, Nuodex Prod Co, Inc, 46-48; instr physics & math, Bloomfield Col, 48-51; physicist, B G Corp, 51-55. *Concurrent Pos:* Lectr, Adelphi Col, 57-60. *Mem:* Am Phys Soc. *Res:* Nuclear reactors and effects; mathematical physics; thermionics; traffic control; rocket trajectories. *Mailing Add:* 7721 250th St Jamaica NY 11426

STEPAN, ALFRED HENRY, ORGANIC CHEMISTRY. *Current Pos:* RETIRED. *Personal Data:* b St Paul, Minn, Jan 2, 20; m 44, Jane Thomsen; c Carol, Jean, Connie, Alyssa & Pala. *Educ:* Col St Thomas, BS, 42; Univ Nebr, MS, 45, PhD(org chem), 51. *Prof Exp:* Chemist, Tenn Eastman Corp, 44-46; sr chemist, Continental Oil Co, 48-56; sr res chemist, Minn Mining & Mfg Co, 56-60, supvr, 60-63, mgr, 63-81, chem specialist, 81-82. *Mem:* Am Chem Soc. *Res:* Carbonless papers; dielectric paper; imaging systems involving dry silver. *Mailing Add:* 1952 Oak Knoll Dr White Bear Lake MN 55110

STEPANISHEN, PETER RICHARD, ACOUSTICS. *Current Pos:* from asst prof to assoc prof, 74-82, PROF OCEAN ENG, UNIV RI, 83- *Personal Data:* b Boston, Mass, Jan 20, 42; m 70, Lee; c Kent & Mark. *Educ:* Mich State Univ, BS, 63; Univ Conn, MS, 66; Pa State Univ, PhD(eng acoust), 69. *Honors & Awards:* A B Wood Medal & Prize, Inst Acoust Eng, 77. *Prof Exp:* Sonar systs engr, Elec Boat Div, Gen Dynamics Corp, 63-66, sr systs engr, 66-70, res specialist acoust, 70-74. *Concurrent Pos:* Acoust consult, Naval Underwater Systs Ctr, 75- & Raytheon Co, 76-; res grant prin investr, NIH, 76-82, Off Naval Res, 83-92; vis prof, Cambridge Univ, 82, Stanford Univ, 89 & Univ S Hampton, 96. *Mem:* Fel Acoust Soc Am; Sigma Xi; Inst Elec & Electronics Engrs. *Res:* Underwater acoustics; mechanical vibrations and wave phenomena; ultrasonics; system theory and signal analysis; structural acoustics; noise and vibration control; sonar systems. *Mailing Add:* Dept Ocean Eng Univ RI Kingston RI 02881. *Fax:* 401-792-6837; *E-Mail:* stepanishen@mistral.oce.uri.edu

STEPENUCK, STEPHEN JOSEPH, JR, ENVIRONMENTAL CHEMISTRY. *Current Pos:* from asst prof to assoc prof, 70-79, PROF CHEM, KEENE STATE COL, 79- *Personal Data:* b Salem, Mass, Oct 12, 37; m 68, Therese Lamontagne; c Kathleen, Kristine & Scott. *Educ:* Merrimack Col, BS, 59; Col of the Holy Cross, MS, 61; Univ NH, PhD(phys chem), 71. *Prof Exp:* Instr chem, Merrimack Col, 61-65; teaching fel, Univ NH, 66-68, instr, 69-70. *Concurrent Pos:* Consult, indust, environ chem & chem safety. *Mem:* Am Chem Soc; Sigma Xi; AAAS. *Res:* Radiation chemistry; environmental analyses; occupational health. *Mailing Add:* Dept Chem Keene State Col 229 Main St Keene NH 03435-2001. *Fax:* 603-358-2897; *E-Mail:* sstepenu@keene.edu

STEPHAN, DAVID GEORGE, ENVIRONMENTAL & CHEMICAL ENGINEERING, POLLUTION PREVENTION. *Current Pos:* dir res prog mgt, Environ Protection Agency, 71-75, dir, Indust Environ Res Lab, 75-84, dir, Hazardous Waste Eng Res Lab, 84-85, SR ENG ADV, HAZARDOUS WASTE ENG RES LAB, ENVIRON PROTECTION AGENCY, 86- *Personal Data:* b Columbus, Ohio, Feb 8, 30; m 51, Dorothy V Spetnagel; c Douglas K, Donn P & Dean D. *Educ:* Ohio State Univ, BChE & MSc, 52, PhD(chem eng), 55. *Honors & Awards:* Ann Environ Div Award, Am Inst Chem Engrs, 83. *Prof Exp:* Res assoc heat transfer, Battelle Mem Inst, 52-55; technologist, Nat Lead Co Ohio, 55; chief air pollution control equip res, USPHS, 55-60, chief extramural res unit, Adv Waste Treatment Res Prog, 60-64, dep chief prog, 64-65, dep chief basic & appl sci br, 65-66; dir div res, Fed Water Pollution Control Admin, 66-68, asst comnr res & develop, Fed Water Qual Admin, 68-70. *Concurrent Pos:* Mem water reuse comt, Water Pollution Control Fedn, 64-71; mem water panel & spec consult comt pollution, Nat Acad Sci, 65; mem comt water resources res, Off Sci & Technol, 68-71; mem bd dirs, Marine Tech Soc, 70-73, Environ Div, Am Inst Chem Engrs, 83-85; mem policy bd, Nat Ctr Toxicol Res, 72-74; mem gov bd, Int Asn Water Pollution Res, 74-84; vchmn, USA Nat Comt, Int Asn Water Pollution Res, 74-80; adj prof chem eng, Univ Cincinnati, 76-89. *Mem:* Fel Am Inst Chem Engrs; Am Acad Environ Engrs. *Res:* Heat transfer from vibrating plates; fabric air filtration; air pollution control equipment; advanced waste treatment; waste water renovation and reuse; water pollution control; pollution prevention progress measurement. *Mailing Add:* 6435 Stirrup Rd Cincinnati OH 45244. *Fax:* 513-569-7680

STEPHANAKIS, STAVROS JOHN, PHYSICS, ELECTRICAL ENGINEERING. *Current Pos:* Electronics engr, 68-72, RES PHYSICIST, US NAVAL RES LAB, 72- *Personal Data:* b Salonica, Greece, Apr 15, 40; US citizen; m 66; c 2. *Educ:* NC State Univ, BS, 63, MEE, 65, PhD(elec eng), 69. *Mem:* Am Phys Soc; Inst Elec & Electronics Engrs; Sigma Xi. *Res:* Study of hot, dense plasma discharges, x-ray and neutron emissions from such discharges; diagnostics. *Mailing Add:* Naval Res Lab Code 6773 Washington DC 20375-0001

STEPHANEDES, YORGOS JORDAN, MODELING SIMULATION & CONTROL DESIGN OF TRAFFIC & INCIDENT MANAGEMENT SYSTEMS. *Current Pos:* from asst prof to assoc prof, 84-89, dir grad studies, 91-95, PROF CIVIL ENG, UNIV MINN, 89- *Personal Data:* b Athens, Greece, Sept 15, 51. *Educ:* Dartmouth Col, BA, 73, PhD(eng sci), 80; Carnegie-Mellon Univ, MS, 75. *Honors & Awards:* D Grant Mickle Award, Nat Res Coun, 93. *Prof Exp:* Res asst, Carnegie-Mellon Univ, 73-74; res & teaching assoc stat eng sci, Dartmouth Col, 75-78. *Concurrent Pos:* Res assoc, Oak Ridge Nat Labs, 75; mem, Transp Res Bd, Nat Acad Sci, 76-; prin investr, Univ Minn, 78-; consult, Hennepin Co, 80, Metrop Transp Comn, 84- & Wilbur Smith Assoc, 87; dir res & develop, United Eng, 82-86; referee sci manuscripts, NSF, 84- & Am Soc Civil Engrs, 84-; chmn, Comt Adv Technol Appln in Urban Transp, Am Soc Civil Engrs, 90-94. *Mem:* Inst Elec & Electronics Engrs; Am Soc Civil Engrs; Inst Transp Engrs; Fr Asn Cybernet, Econ & Technol. *Res:* Modeling, simulation, estimation and optimal control design in traffic engineering systems; integrated freeway ramp metering; adaptive control of urban traffic networks; automatic incident detection and management; advanced traveler information systems; traffic sensors and wide-area detection; accident analysis. *Mailing Add:* Dept Civil Eng 122 Civil Eng Bldg Univ Minn 500 Pillsbury Dr SE Minneapolis MN 55455

STEPHANOPOULOS, GREGORY, CHEMICAL ENGINEERING. *Current Pos:* assoc prof, 83-85, PROF CHEM ENG, MASS INST TECHNOL, 85- *Personal Data:* b Kalamata, Greece, Mar 10, 50; m, Miretta; c Nicholas-Odysseas, Alexander & Rona-Elisa. *Educ:* Nat Tech Univ, Greece, BS, 73; Univ Fla, MS, 75; Univ Minn, PhD, 78. *Prof Exp:* Asst prof chem eng, Calif Inst Technol, 78-83. *Concurrent Pos:* Camille & Henry Drefus teaching scholar, 82; prog coordr, Am Inst Chem Engrs, 83; grantee, NSF, 80-, pres young investr, 84. *Mem:* Am Inst Chem Engrs; Am Chem Soc; Soc Indust Microbiol; fel Int Asn Med & Biol Environ; Am Microchem Soc. *Res:* Kinetics and thermodynamics of biological systems. *Mailing Add:* Dept Chem 56-469C Mass Inst Technol 77 Massachusetts Ave Cambridge MA 02139-4307

STEPHANS, RICHARD A, SYSTEM SAFETY ENGINEERING ANALYSIS, QUALITY ASSURANCE ENGINEERING. *Current Pos:* PRIN CONSULT, ERC ENVIRON & ENERGY SERV CO, 91- *Personal Data:* b Newark, NJ, May 29, 35; m 60; c 3. *Educ:* Purdue Univ, BS, 57; NMex State Univ, MS, 62. *Prof Exp:* Mgr safety & qual assurance eng, BDM Int, 81-91. *Concurrent Pos:* Pvt consult, United Space Boosters, Inc, 81; mem, Risk Anal Task Force, Am Soc Mech Engrs, 87- *Mem:* Syst Safety Soc; Am Soc Qual Control; Am Soc Mech Engrs. *Res:* Safety analysis and assessments of chemical and nuclear facilities; hazards analysis of engineering development programs; quality audit of organizations; planning for systems engineering projects; technical proposal preparation; environmental assessments. *Mailing Add:* 13724 Pruitt NE Albuquerque NM 87112

STEPHANY, EDWARD O, MATHEMATICS, STATISTICS. *Current Pos:* RETIRED. *Personal Data:* b Rochester, NY, July 6, 16; m 41, Arline A Eckert; c Ann M (Mahon). *Educ:* Univ Rochester, AB, 37, AM, 38; Syracuse Univ, PhD(statist), 56. *Prof Exp:* Chmn, Dept Math, State Univ NY Col, Brockport, 47-77, prof math, 77-80. *Mem:* Nat Coun Teachers Math. *Res:* Technique for comparing factors obtained through factor analysis; mathematics education. *Mailing Add:* 229 West Brockport NY 14420

STEPHAS, PAUL, PHYSICS. *Current Pos:* PROF PHYSICS, EASTERN ORE STATE COL, 69- *Personal Data:* b New York, NY, Aug 31, 29; m 59; c 1. *Educ:* Univ Wash, Seattle, BS, 56; Rensselaer Polytech Inst, MS, 59; Univ Ore, PhD(physics), 66. *Prof Exp:* Asst res lab, Gen Elec Co, 56-58; metallurgist & ceramist, Vallecitos Atomic Lab, 58-62; asst prof physics, Univ BC, 66-69. *Mem:* Am Phys Soc; Am Asn Physics Teachers; AAAS; Sigma Xi. *Res:* Atomic effects associated with beta decay; low energy nuclear physics; special relativistic mechanics. *Mailing Add:* 15550 NW Willis Rd McMinnville OR 97128

STEPHEN, CHARLES RONALD, ANESTHESIOLOGY. *Current Pos:* RETIRED. *Personal Data:* b Montreal, Que, Mar 16, 16; nat US; m 41; c 3. *Educ:* McGill Univ, BSc, 38, MD & CM, 40. *Prof Exp:* Chief, Dept Anesthesia, Montreal Neurol Inst, 46-47; asst prof anesthesia, McGill Univ, 48-50; prof, Sch Med & chief div, Univ Hosp, Duke Univ, 50-66; prof, Univ Tex Southwest Med Sch Dallas, 66-71; head, Dept Anesthesia, Barnes Hosp, St Louis, 71-80; chief anesthesiology, St Luke's Hosp, St Louis, 80-85. *Concurrent Pos:* Chief, Dept Anesthesia, Childrens Mem Hosp, Montreal, 47-50; ed, Surv Anesthesiol, 56-; anesthesiologist, Parkland Mem Hosp, Dallas, 66-71; chief anesthesia, Children's Med Ctr, Dallas, 66-71; fel fac anesthetists, Royal Col Surgeons, 64. *Mem:* Am Soc Anesthesiol; Acad Anesthesiol; Inst Anesthesia Res Soc. *Res:* Pharmacology and physiology of clinical anesthesiology. *Mailing Add:* 15801 Harris Ridge Ct Chesterfield MO 63017-8725

STEPHEN, FREDERICK MALCOLM, JR, FOREST ENTOMOLOGY, INSECT ECOLOGY. *Current Pos:* from asst prof to prof, 74-92, UNIV PROF ENTOM, UNIV ARK, 92- *Personal Data:* b Oakland, Calif, May 11, 43; m 84, Judy Rogers; c Dan, Alison & Mac. *Educ:* San Jose State Univ, BA, 67; Univ Calif, Berkeley, PhD(entom), 74. *Honors & Awards:* A D Hopkins Outstanding Contrib to Southern Forest Entomol, 90; John W White Outstanding Res Award, 90; Burlington Northern Outstanding Fac-Sch Res Award, 90. *Prof Exp:* Res asst, Univ Calif, Berkeley, 67-74. *Concurrent Pos:* Vis scientist, Oxford Univ, 87. *Mem:* Entom Soc Am; Int Union Forestry Res Orgn. *Res:* Forest insect ecology and population dynamics of southern pine beetle and its natural enemy complex; biological control. *Mailing Add:* Dept Entom A-320 Univ Ark Fayetteville AR 72701. *Fax:* 501-575-2452; *E-Mail:* fstephen@comp.uark.edu

STEPHEN, KEITH H, INORGANIC CHEMISTRY. *Current Pos:* SR RES CHEMIST, EASTMAN KODAK CO, 64- *Personal Data:* b Ft Wayne, Ind, Jan 3, 34; m 59; c 2. *Educ:* Wabash Col, BA, 59; Northwestern Univ, PhD(inorg chem), 65. *Mem:* Am Chem Soc; Soc Photog Scientists & Engrs. *Res:* Coordination compounds; electron transfer reactions; photographic chemistry. *Mailing Add:* 186 Heritage Circle Rochester NY 14615-1110

STEPHEN, MICHAEL JOHN, PHYSICS. *Current Pos:* PROF PHYSICS, RUTGERS UNIV, 68- *Personal Data:* b Johannesburg, SAfrica, Apr 7, 33; m 66. *Educ:* Univ Witwatersrand, BS, 52, MS, 54; Oxford Univ, PhD(phys chem), 56. *Prof Exp:* Ramsey fel, 56-58; res assoc chem, Columbia Univ, 58-60; Imp Chem Industs res fel math, Oxford Univ, 60-62; from asst prof to assoc prof, Yale Univ, 62-68. *Concurrent Pos:* Consult, Bell Tel Labs, 64-66; vis prof, Mass Inst Technol, 67-68. *Mem:* Am Phys Soc. *Res:* Low temperature, solid state and molecular physics. *Mailing Add:* Dept Physics Rutgers State Univ New Brunswick NJ 08903

STEPHEN, RALPH A, SEISMOLOGY. *Current Pos:* Asst scientist, 78-82, assoc scientist, 82-90, SR SCIENTIST GEOPHYS, WOODS HOLE OCEANOG INST, 90- *Personal Data:* b Toronto, Ont, Feb, 18, 51; m 74; c 2. *Educ:* Univ Toronto, BASc, 74; Univ Cambridge, PhD(geophys), 78. *Mem:* Royal Astron Soc; Am Geophys Union; Soc Explor Geophysicists; Seismol Soc Am; Acoust Soc Am. *Res:* Borehole seismic experiments in oceanic crust; seismic structure of oceanic crust and synthetic seismogram development. *Mailing Add:* PO Box 567 West Falmouth MA 02574

STEPHEN, WILLIAM PROCURONOFF, ENTOMOLOGY. *Current Pos:* from asst prof & asst entomologist to assoc prof & assoc entomologist, 53-63, PROF ENTOM, ORE STATE UNIV, 63- *Personal Data:* b St Boniface, Man, June 6, 27; nat US; m 52; c 4. *Educ:* Univ Man, BSA, 48; Univ Kans,

PhD, 52. *Prof Exp:* From asst entomologist to assoc entomologist, Sci Serv, Can Dept Agr, 48-53. *Concurrent Pos:* Consult, Orgn Am States, Chile, 70-71 & Food & Agr Orgn, UN, Arg, 72-75; mem, Bee Res Inst. *Mem:* AAAS; Entom Soc Am; Animal Behav Soc; Soc Study Evolution; Soc Syst Zool; Sigma Xi. *Res:* Insect behavior; systematic zoology; development physiology; population genetics; pollination. *Mailing Add:* Dept Entom Ore State Univ Corvallis OR 97331. *Fax:* 541-737-3643

STEPHENS, ARTHUR BROOKE, NUMERICAL ANALYSIS. *Current Pos:* ASSOC PROF COMPUT SCI & ELEC ENG, UNIV MD, BALTIMORE CO, 83-, ASSOC DEAN, COL ENG, 97- *Personal Data:* b Dinuba, Calif, July 6, 42; m 68. *Educ:* Univ Colo, BA, 64; Univ Md, PhD(math), 69. *Prof Exp:* Asst prof math, Univ Hawaii, 69-71; asst prof, St Mary's Col, 73-77, assoc prof math, 77-78; mathematician, Naval Surface Weapons Ctr, 78-83. *Mem:* Am Math Soc; Math Asn Am. *Res:* Optimization problems in functional analysis; estimates for complex eigenvalues of positive matrices. *Mailing Add:* Dept Comput Sci & Elec Eng Univ Md Baltimore Co 1000 Hilltop Circle Baltimore MD 21250

STEPHENS, CHARLES ARTHUR LLOYD, JR, INTERNAL MEDICINE. *Current Pos:* DIR RES, SOUTHWESTERN CLIN & RES INST, INC, UNIV ARIZ, 46-, PRES, 71-, ASSOC PROF INTERNAL MED, COL MED, 70-, ADJ PROF MICROBIOL, 80- *Personal Data:* b Brooklyn, NY, Apr 4, 17; m 39, 64; c 2. *Educ:* Cornell Univ, AB, 38, MD, 42; Am Bd Internal Med, dipl, 52. *Concurrent Pos:* Sr consult, Tucson Med Ctr, St Joseph's & Palo Verde Hosps, Ariz; pvt pract; chmn med adv comt, Southern Chap, Am Red Cross; mem bd dirs & pres, Southwest Chap, Arthritis Found; adj prof microbiol, Univ Ariz, 76- *Mem:* AMA; fel Am Col Physicians; Am Rheumatism Asn; NY Acad Sci; Am Heart Asn; Sigma Xi. *Res:* Tissue culture research in rheumatic diseases. *Mailing Add:* 5265 E Knight Dr Tucson AZ 85712-2147

STEPHENS, CHRISTINE TAYLOR, plant pathology, for more information see previous edition

STEPHENS, CLARENCE FRANCIS, MATHEMATICS. *Current Pos:* prof & chmn dept, 69-87, EMER PROF MATH, STATE UNIV NY COL POTSDAM, 87- *Personal Data:* b Gaffney, SC, July 24, 17; m 42, Harriette J Briscoe; c Harriette J & Clarence F Jr. *Educ:* J C Smith Univ, BS, 38; Univ Mich, MS, 39, PhD(math), 43. *Hon Degrees:* DSc, J C Smith Univ, 54; LHD, Chicago State Univ, 90. *Prof Exp:* Instr math, Prairie View Col, 40-42, prof, 46-47; prof & head dept, Morgan State Col, 47-62; prof, State Univ NY Col Geneseo, 62-69. *Concurrent Pos:* Ford fel & mem, Inst Advan Study, 53-54. *Mem:* Assoc mem Am Math Soc; assoc mem Math Asn Am; Sigma Xi. *Res:* Non-linear difference equations analytic in a parameter. *Mailing Add:* 7244 Rte 255 Rural Delivery 2 Conesus NY 14435-9536

STEPHENS, DALE NELSON, ORGANIC CHEMISTRY. *Current Pos:* asst prof, 68-71, assoc prof, 71-77, PROF CHEM, BETHEL COL, MINN, 77- *Personal Data:* b Los Angeles, Calif, Dec 20, 41; m 64; c 2. *Educ:* Westmont Col, BA, 63; Univ Ariz, PhD(org chem), 67. *Prof Exp:* Res chemist, Corn Prod Co, 67-68. *Mem:* AAAS; Am Chem Soc. *Res:* Urethanes; epoxies; natural product synthesis; x-ray crystallography; organic synthesis. *Mailing Add:* Dept Chem Bethel Col 3900 Bethel Dr St Paul MN 55112-6999

STEPHENS, DOUGLAS ROBERT, CHEMICAL ENGINEERING, MATERIALS SCIENCE. *Current Pos:* PROJ LEADER, LAWRENCE LIVERMORE LAB, 61- *Personal Data:* b Portland, Ore, May 10, 35; m 61, Mary L Herweg; c Kathryn & Heidi. *Educ:* Univ Wash, BS, 57; Univ Ill, MS, 59, PhD(chem eng), 61. *Honors & Awards:* Spec Award Excellence Technol Transfer, Fed Lab Consortium, 86. *Concurrent Pos:* Consult & lectr, short course organizer. *Mem:* Fel Am Inst Chem Engrs; Am Chem Soc. *Res:* Experimental high pressure equation of state and phase transformation measurements; electrical properties of solids at high pressures; in-situ chemical processing; systems studies of nuclear weapon safety and counter proliferation. *Mailing Add:* Lawrence Livermore Lab PO Box 808 L-182 Livermore CA 94550. *E-Mail:* stephens2@llnl.gov

STEPHENS, FRANK SAMUEL, NUCLEAR CHEMISTRY. *Current Pos:* Res chemist, 55-57, SR SCIENTIST, LAWRENCE RADIATION LAB, UNIV CALIF, BERKELEY, 57- *Personal Data:* b Ind, June 30, 31; m 59. *Educ:* Oberlin Col, AB, 52; Univ Calif, PhD(chem), 55. *Concurrent Pos:* Ford Found grant, Inst Theoret Physics, Copenhagen, Denmark, 59-60; guest prof, Physics Sect, Univ Munich, 70-71. *Mem:* Am Phys Soc. *Res:* Coulomb excitation; nuclear structure; heavy ion physics. *Mailing Add:* Lawrence Berkeley Nat Lab Univ Calif Bldg 88 Berkeley CA 94720

STEPHENS, GEORGE ROBERT, FOREST ECOLOGY, FOREST-INSECT RELATIONS. *Current Pos:* Asst forester, Conn Agr Exp Sta, 61-65, assoc forester, 65-75, forester, 75-79, CHIEF FORESTER, CONN AGR EXP STA, 80- *Personal Data:* b Springfield, Mass, Nov, 10, 29; m 51; c 7. *Educ:* Univ Mass, BS, 52; Yale Sch Forestry, Yale Univ, MF, 58, PhD(forestry), 61. *Concurrent Pos:* Secy, Conn Tree Protection Exam Bd, 61-78, mem, 79- *Mem:* Soc Am Foresters. *Res:* Natural succession in forest; effects of insects on tree mortality; forest management; fiber flax production. *Mailing Add:* 182 Rimmon Rd New Haven CT 06473

STEPHENS, GREGORY A, CARDIOVASCULAR PHYSIOLOGY, RENAL PHYSIOLOGY. *Current Pos:* asst prof, 78-84, prog dir physiol & anat, 88-90, ASSOC PROF PHYSIOL, SCH LIFE & HEALTH SCI, UNIV DEL, 84-, ASSOC DIR, 90- *Personal Data:* b Salina, Kans, Dec 20, 47. *Educ:* Univ Kans, BA, 69, PhD(physiol & cell biol), 76. *Prof Exp:* Res fel, Dept Physiol, Sch Med, Univ Mo, 75-78. *Concurrent Pos:* NIH grant. *Mem:* Am Physiol Soc; Am Soc Zoologists; Am Heart Asn. *Res:* Control and functions of the renin angiotensin system in nonmammalian vertebrates. *Mailing Add:* Biol Dept Univ Del Newark DE 19716-2590. *Fax:* 302-831-2281; *E-Mail:* gregory.stephens@mvs.udel.edu

STEPHENS, GROVER CLEVELAND, ZOOLOGY. *Current Pos:* prof organismic biol, 64-69, chmn Dept Organismic Biol, 64-69, PROF DEVELOP & CELL BIOL, UNIV CALIF, IRVINE, 69- *Personal Data:* b Oak Park, Ill, Jan 12, 25; m 49; c 3. *Educ:* Northwestern Univ, BS, 48, MA, 49, PHD(biol), 52. *Prof Exp:* Asst philos, Northwestern Univ, 48-49, asst zool, 49-51; instr biol, Brooklyn Col, 52-53; asst zool, Univ Minn, Minneapolis, 53-55, from asst prof to prof, 55-64. *Concurrent Pos:* Mem corp, Marine Biol Lab, Woods Hole, 53-, instr, 53-60, in-charge invert zool, 58-60; NSF sr fel, 59-60; NATO sr fel, 74. *Mem:* AAAS; Am Physiol Soc; Mar Biol Asn, UK; Am Soc Zool; Am Soc Limnol & Oceanog. *Res:* Invertebrate physiology; biological rhythms; feeding mechanisms in invertebrates; algal physiology; amino acid transport. *Mailing Add:* Dept Ecol & Evolution Biol Univ Calif Irvine CA 92697. *Fax:* 714-725-2181

STEPHENS, HAROLD W, MATHEMATICS. *Current Pos:* from assoc prof to prof, 60-89, EMER PROF MATH, UNIV MEMPHIS, 89- *Personal Data:* b Trenton, NJ, Mar 16, 19; m 46, Rosemary Carswell; c Diane. *Educ:* Trenton State Col, BS, 41; Columbia Univ, MA, 44, EdD, 64. *Prof Exp:* Head dept math, Farragut Naval Acad, 44-46; instr, Univ Fla, 46-48, Univ Md, 48-49 & McCoy Col, Johns Hopkins Univ, 49-50; asst prof, Ball State Univ, 52-55 & Univ Tenn, 55-60. *Concurrent Pos:* Lectr, NSF insts & workshops, Univ Tenn, Memphis State, Murray State Univ, Univ Amc, Austin Peay State Univ & Southwestern at Memphis, 57- *Mem:* Math Asn Am; Am Math Soc. *Res:* Mathematics courses for teacher training; algebra. *Mailing Add:* 64 N Yates Rd Memphis TN 38120

STEPHENS, HOWARD L, POLYMER CHEMISTRY. *Current Pos:* Res chemist, Rubber Res Labs, Univ Akron, 49-52, Inst Rubber Chem, 53-56 & Inst Rubber Res, 56-57, admin asst, 57-65, from instr to assoc prof chem, 57-73, mgr appl res, Inst Polymer Sci, 66-81, PROF CHEM & POLYMER SCI, 73-, HEAD DEPT POLYMER SCI, 78-, EMER PROF, UNIV AKRON. *Personal Data:* b Akron, Ohio, Oct 9, 19; m 45; c 1. *Educ:* Univ Akron, BS, 49, MS, 50, PhD(polymer chem), 60. *Mem:* Am Chem Soc. *Res:* Polymer oxidation; preparation and structure of graft polymers; emulsion polymerization; vulcanization. *Mailing Add:* Dept Polymer Sci Univ Akron Akron OH 44325-3909

STEPHENS, JACK E(DWARD), HIGHWAY ENGINEERING, CONSTRUCTION MATERIALS. *Current Pos:* from asst prof to prof civil eng, 50-88, head dept, 65-72, EMER PROF CIVIL ENG, UNIV CONN, 89-, DIR, CONN ADVAN PAVEMENT LAB, 95- *Personal Data:* b Eaton, Ohio, Aug 17, 23; m 48, Virginia M Ives; c Jay E, Jerry E, Jill L & Jana L. *Educ:* Univ Conn, BS, 47; Purdue Univ, MS, 55, PhD(civil eng), 59. *Honors & Awards:* H Jackson Tibbet Award, Am Soc Civil Engrs, 72, Benjamin Wright Award, 89; George Westinghouse Award, Am Soc Eng Educ, 74. *Prof Exp:* Jr engr, State Hwy Dept, Conn, 48-50. *Concurrent Pos:* Owner, Jack E Stephens Soil Lab, 58-; dir, Joint Hwy Res Adv Coun, Univ Conn, 61-, NETTCP, 94-; consult, state Hwy Dept, Conn, 64-66, Conn Resource Recovery Agency, 92- & Vt Agency Trasp, 93-94; mem comts, Transp Res Bd, Nat Acad Sci-Nat Res Coun; mem, Mat Sci Inst, Univ Conn, 68-; vpres, Elasphalt, 83- *Mem:* Am Soc Civil Engrs; Am Rd Builders Asn (pres, 77); Asn Asphalt Paving Technologists; Sigma Xi; Am Soc Prof Engrs. *Res:* Highway pavement; bituminous and portland cement concrete mixes; aging of biuminous mixes; use of wastes in construction; implimentation and application of SHRP to bituminous concrete. *Mailing Add:* 270 S Eagleville Rd Storrs CT 06268-2010. *Fax:* 860-486-2399

STEPHENS, JAMES BRISCOE, ATMOSPHERIC PHYSICS, SPACE PHYSICS. *Current Pos:* Scientist remote sensing, 66-69, scientist statist physics, 70-72, TASK TEAM LEADER TERRESTRIAL DIFFUSION, MARSHALL SPACE FLIGHT CTR, NASA, 73- *Personal Data:* b San Francisco, Calif, Mar 5, 36; m 67; c 2. *Educ:* Univ Okla, BS, 64, MS, 66, PhD(eng physics), 71. *Concurrent Pos:* Mem, Atmos Effects Panel, NASA Hq, 74- *Mem:* Am Phys Soc; Sigma Xi. *Res:* The environmental effects from aerospace effluents. *Mailing Add:* 6800 Jones Valley Dr SE Huntsville AL 35802-1920

STEPHENS, JAMES FRED, POULTRY SCIENCE, MICROBIOLOGY. *Current Pos:* RETIRED. *Personal Data:* b Lexington, Tenn, Sept 29, 32; m 72; c 3. *Educ:* Univ Tenn, BS, 54, MS, 59, PhD(bact), 64. *Prof Exp:* Asst poultry, Univ Tenn, 56-62; from asst prof to assoc prof poultry sci, Clemson Univ, 62-68; assoc prof, Ohio State Univ, 68-74, prof, 74-95. *Mem:* Poultry Sci Asn; Am Soc Microbiol; World Poultry Sci Asn. *Res:* Poultry disease; nutrition relationships; pathogenecity of Salmonellae; drug resistance in enteric bacteria. *Mailing Add:* 1063 Havendale Dr Columbus OH 43220

STEPHENS, JAMES REGIS, ORGANIC CHEMISTRY, POLYMER CHEMISTRY. *Current Pos:* RETIRED. *Personal Data:* b Pittsburgh, Pa, Mar 16, 25; m 55, Beatrice Johnson; c James, Andrew, Paul & Rhea. *Educ:* St Vincent Col, BS, 47; Univ Pittsburgh, MS, 49; Northwestern Univ,

PhD(chem), 53. *Honors & Awards:* Glycerine Award, Glycerine Producer's Asn, 54; Outstanding Achievement Award, Soc Plastics Engrs, 87. *Prof Exp:* Res chemist, Sinclair Ref Co, 50 & Am Cyanamid Co, 53-57; sr res scientist, Amoco Chem Corp, 57-67, group leader res dept, 67-70, sect leader res & develop, 70-80, sr res assoc, 80-87. *Mem:* Am Chem Soc; Soc Plastics Engrs. *Res:* Organic nitrogen compounds; stereochemistry of dioxanes; alkyd resins; heterocyclic and aromatic polymers for high temperature service; magnet wire enamels; polyoxadazoles. *Mailing Add:* 7-S-361 Arbor Dr Naperville IL 60540

STEPHENS, JEFFREY ALAN, molecular photoionization processes, for more information see previous edition

STEPHENS, JESSE JERALD, PHYSICAL METEOROLOGY. *Current Pos:* RETIRED. *Personal Data:* b Oklahoma City, Okla, June 3, 33; m 55; c 3. *Educ:* Univ Tex, BS, 58, MA, 61; Tex A&M Univ, Nat Defense Educ Act fel & PhD(meteorol), 66. *Prof Exp:* Meteorologist, US Weather Bur, 57-59; lectr meteorol, Univ Tex, 59-61, from instr to asst prof, 64-66; assoc prof, Univ Okla, 66-67; from assoc prof to prof meteorol, Fla State Univ, 67-94, chmn dept, 75-77 & 81-85, dir, Univ Comput Ctr, 83, assoc dir, Supercomput Comput Res Inst, 85. *Mem:* Fel Am Meteorol Soc. *Res:* Scattering processes in the atmosphere; geophysical data processing. *Mailing Add:* 6125 Borderline Dr Tallahassee FL 32312

STEPHENS, JOHN C(ARNES), AGRICULTURE ENGINEERING, GEOLOGY. *Current Pos:* RETIRED. *Personal Data:* b Attalla, Ala, Sept 22, 10; m 36, Ophelia Welker; c John O, Mary Louise & Margret Editha. *Educ:* Univ Ala, BS, 31, Stanford Univ, 32. *Honors & Awards:* John Deere Gold Medal Award, Am Soc Agr Eng. *Prof Exp:* Agr engr, soil conserv serv, USDA, Ala, 33-39, asst proj engr, Everglades Proj, 39-46; chief water control engr, Dade County, 46-49; supvr, Everglades Proj, Soil & Water Conserv Res Div, 49-61, leader regional invests, watershed eng, S Br, Ga, 61-65, dir, SE Watershed Res Ctr, Ga, 65-69, chief, NW Br, Soil & Water Conserv-Agr Res Serv, USDA, Boise, ID, 69-72, area dir, Lower Miss Valley Area, Stoneville, Miss, 72-76. *Concurrent Pos:* Consult geohydrologist, US AID, Asia, Nat Res Coun, Washington, DC, pvt eng firms, Miami, FL, 76-88; collabr, Sci & Educ Admin, Agr Res Serv, USDA, 76- *Mem:* Am Soc Agr Eng; Am Geophys Union; Am Soc Civil Eng. *Res:* Peat and muck investigations; drainage; irrigation; weed control; hydrology of agricultural watersheds. *Mailing Add:* 4550 Middleton Park Circle W Jacksonville FL 32224

STEPHENS, JOHN STEWART, JR, MARINE BIOLOGY, FISH BIOLOGY. *Current Pos:* from instr to prof biol, 59-74, JAMES IRVINE PROF ENVIRON BIOL, OCCIDENTAL COL, 74- *Personal Data:* b Los Angeles, Calif, May 12, 32; m 53; c 1. *Educ:* Stanford Univ, BS, 54; Univ Calif, Los Angeles, MA, 57, PhD, 60. *Prof Exp:* Asst zool, Univ Calif, Los Angeles, 54-58, assoc biol, Santa Barbara, 58-69. *Concurrent Pos:* Dir, Vantuna Oceanog Prog, Occidental Col, 69- *Mem:* Am Soc Ichthyologists & Herpetologists; Soc Syst Zool; Am Fisheries Soc; Am Inst Fishery Res Biologists; Sigma Xi. *Res:* Systematics and distribution of blenniod fishes; especially Chaenopsidae; osteology of tropical blennies; ecology of nearctic fishes of California, including effects of pollution and habitat destruction. *Mailing Add:* Dept Environ Biol Occidental Col 1600 Campus Rd Los Angeles CA 90041-3384

STEPHENS, LAWRENCE JAMES, ORGANIC CHEMISTRY, SCIENCE EDUCATION. *Current Pos:* dean students, Elmira Col, 81-82, dir acad advising, 88-93, chair, Div Math & Natural Sci, 77-86, 90-94, PROF CHEM, ELMIRA COL, 73- *Personal Data:* b Chicago, Ill, Aug 11, 40; m 64, Theresa Duster; c 3. *Educ:* Loyola Univ Chicago, BS, 63; Univ Nebr, Lincoln, PhD(org chem), 69. *Prof Exp:* Res assoc, Stanford Univ, 68-69; asst prof chem, Findlay Col, 69-73. *Concurrent Pos:* Res chemist, Corp Res & Develop Ctr, Gen Elec Co, Schnectady, NY, 84 & 85; Nat Asn Adv Health Professions. *Mem:* Am Chem Soc; Nat Sci Teachers Asn; Am Asn Univ Prof. *Res:* Curriculum development in the natural sciences; soil chemistry. *Mailing Add:* Dept Chem Elmira Col One Park Pl Elmira NY 14901. *Fax:* 607-735-1701; *E-Mail:* larryst@servtech.com

STEPHENS, LEE BISHOP, JR, EMBRYOLOGY. *Current Pos:* from asst prof to assoc prof, 62-70, PROF BIOL, CALIF STATE UNIV, LONG BEACH, 70-; EMER PROF BIOL, SCH NATURAL SCI, 83- *Personal Data:* b Atlanta, Ga, Oct 22, 25; m 58; c 3. *Educ:* Morehouse Col, BS, 47; Atlanta Univ, MS, 50; Univ Iowa, PhD, 57. *Prof Exp:* Instr biol, Dillard Univ, 50-53; instr, NC Col Durham, 53-54; assoc prof, Southern Univ, 57-62. *Concurrent Pos:* Assoc dean, Sch Natural Scis, 75-83. *Mem:* Am Soc Zool; Am Micros Soc; Sigma Xi. *Res:* Neuroembryology; regeneration; endocrinology and development of the nervous system. *Mailing Add:* 505 E Collamer Dr Carson CA 90746

STEPHENS, MARVIN WAYNE, environmental chemistry, for more information see previous edition

STEPHENS, MICHAEL A, MATHEMATICAL STATISTICS, APPLIED STATISTICS. *Current Pos:* PROF MATH & STATIST, SIMON FRASER UNIV, 76- *Personal Data:* b Bristol, Eng, Apr 26, 27; m 62; c 1. *Educ:* Bristol Univ, BSc, 48; Harvard Univ, AM, 49; Univ Toronto, PhD(math), 62. *Honors & Awards:* Gold Medal, Statist Soc Can, 89. *Prof Exp:* Instr math, Tufts Col, 49-50; lectr, Woolwich Polytech, Eng, 52-53 & Battersea Col Technol, 53-56; instr, Case Western Res Univ, 56-59; lectr, Univ Toronto, 59-62, asst prof, 62-63; from asst prof to prof, McGill Univ, 63-70; prof, Univ Nottingham & Univ Grenoble, 70-72; prof, McMaster Univ, 72-76. *Concurrent Pos:* Consult, Can Packers Ltd, 62-63 & various Montreal Drs, 63-67; fel UK Sci Res Coun, 80-81; mem adv comt, Statist Can, 86- *Mem:* Fel Am Statist Asn; Statist Soc Can (pres, 83); Int Statist Inst; fel Inst Math Statist; Royal Statist Soc. *Res:* Mathematical statistics, distributions on a circle or a hyper-sphere; analysis of continuous proportions; goodness of fit statistics, robustness, density approximations. *Mailing Add:* Dept Math & Statist Simon Fraser Univ Burnaby BC V5A 1S6 Can

STEPHENS, N(OLAN) THOMAS, ENVIRONMENTAL SCIENCES, GENERAL. *Current Pos:* AT DEPT CHEM & ENVIRON ENG, FLA INST TECHNOL. *Personal Data:* b Mountainair, NMex, Oct 20, 32; m 53; c 3. *Educ:* Univ NMex, BS, 55; NMex State Univ, BS, 61; Univ Fla, MSE, 67, PhD(environ eng), 69. *Prof Exp:* Res engr, Rocketdyne Div, NAm Rockwell Inc, 61-64; mgr saline water conversion opers, Struthers Sci & Int Corp, 64-66; sr environ engr, Southern Res Inst, 69-70; prof civil eng & air pollution specialist, Va Polytech Inst & State Univ, 70- *Mem:* Air Pollution Control Asn. *Res:* Fundamental and applied research on causes, effects, and control of air and water pollutants; research and development on processes for saline water conversion. *Mailing Add:* Sch Aeronaut Fla Inst Technol 150 University Blvd Melbourne FL 32901-6988

STEPHENS, NEWMAN LLOYD, PHYSIOLOGY, BIOSTATISTICS & BIOCHEMISTRY. *Current Pos:* from asst prof to assoc prof, 67-73, PROF PHYSIOL, FAC MED, UNIV MAN, 73- *Personal Data:* b Kanth, India, Feb 28, 26; Can citizen; m 67, Maria Carla Concone; c Alexander M & Daniel L. *Educ:* Univ Lucknow, India, MB & BS, 50, DM, 53; FRCP, London, 84. *Prof Exp:* Resident med officer, King George's Med Col, Univ Lucknow, 50-53; head, Sect Med, Clara Swain Hosp, Bareilly, India, 55-58; med registr, Univ Col Hosp, London, Eng, 59-61. *Concurrent Pos:* Res fel cardiol, Res & Educ Hosp, Univ Ill, 62-64; res fel physiol, Sch Hyg, Johns Hopkins Univ, 64-65; res fel med, Winnipeg Gen Hosp, Man, 65-66; Can Heart Found scholar & Med Res Coun Can grant, Fac Med, Univ Man, 67-; mem, Soc Scholars, Johns Hopkins Univ, 84. *Mem:* Fel Royal Soc Med; Am Physiol Soc; Biophys Soc; Can Physiol Soc; Can Soc Clin Invest; Am Thor Soc. *Res:* Smooth muscle, biophysics, biochemistry and ultrastructure of normal muscle, effects of acidosis and hypoxia on these parameters; airway smooth muscle in asthma. *Mailing Add:* Dept Physiol Fac Med 425 Basic Med Sci Bldg Univ Man 730 William Ave Winnipeg MB R3E 3J7 Can. *Fax:* 204-783-2788; *E-Mail:* stephens@bldghsc.lan1.umanitoba.ca

STEPHENS, NOEL, JR, ANIMAL SCIENCE, ANIMAL NUTRITION. *Current Pos:* From instr to assoc prof, 56-69, PROF ANIMAL SCI, BEREA COL, 69- *Personal Data:* b Richmond, Ky, Dec 27, 28; m 58; c 4. *Educ:* Univ Ky, BS, 55, MS, 56, PhD(animal sci), 64. *Mem:* Am Soc Animal Sci. *Res:* Amino acids and trace mineral research in swine nutrition. *Mailing Add:* Dept Agr Berea Col 101 Chestnut St Berea KY 40404-0001

STEPHENS, OLIN JAMES, II, MARINE ENGINEERING. *Current Pos:* RETIRED. *Personal Data:* b New York, NY, Apr 13, 08; m 30, Florence Reynolds; c Olin J III & Samuel R. *Hon Degrees:* MS, Stevens Inst Tech; MA, Brown Univ; D laurea ad honorem, Univ Archit, Venice, Italy. *Honors & Awards:* David Taylor Medal, Soc Naval Archit & Marine Engrs, 59; Beppe Circle Award, Int Yacht Racing Union, 92; Gibbs Bros Medal, Nat Acad Sci, 93. *Prof Exp:* Draftsman, Henry J Gielow, New York, 27-28 & P L Rhodes, 28; chief designer, Sparkman & Stephens, Inc, 29-78. *Concurrent Pos:* Fac mem, Royal Designers for Ind, London. *Mem:* Nat Acad Eng; Am Boat & Yacht Coun (pres, 59-60); NAm Yacht Racing Union; Fel Soc Naval Archit & Marine Engrs. *Mailing Add:* 80 Lyme Rd Apt 160 Hanover NY 03755. *Fax:* 603-643-3457

STEPHENS, PETER WESLEY, SOLID STATE PHYSICS. *Current Pos:* asst prof, 80-86, assoc prof, 86-92, PROF PHYSICS, STATE UNIV NY, STONY BROOK, 92- *Personal Data:* b Evanston, Ill, Jan 30, 51; m 78; c 2. *Educ:* Univ Calif, Berkeley, BA, 73; Mass Inst Technol, PhD(physics), 78. *Prof Exp:* Asst, Mass Inst Technol, 78-80. *Concurrent Pos:* Assoc prof physics, Tohoku Univ, Japan, 88-89. *Res:* Use of x-ray and neutron scattering to study unusual states of condensed matter; phase transitions; surface structure; fullerenes; synchrotron radiation; powder diffraction. *Mailing Add:* Dept Physics State Univ NY Stony Brook NY 11794. *E-Mail:* pstephens@sunysb.edu

STEPHENS, PHILIP J, SPECTROSCOPY, TRANSITION-METAL CHEMISTRY. *Current Pos:* from asst prof to assoc prof, 67-76, PROF CHEM, UNIV SOUTHERN CALIF, 76- *Personal Data:* b West Bromwich, Eng, Oct 9, 40; m 62; c 1. *Educ:* Oxford Univ, BA, 62, DPhil(chem), 64. *Prof Exp:* Res fel chem, Univ Copenhagen, 64-65; res fel, Univ Chicago, 65-67. *Concurrent Pos:* Sci Res Coun fel, 64-66; Alfred P Sloan res fel, 68-70; John Simon Guggenheim Fel, 84-85. *Mem:* Am Chem Soc; Royal Soc Chem; Am Phys Soc. *Res:* Magneto-optical and spectroscopic properties of matter. *Mailing Add:* Dept Chem Univ Southern Calif Los Angeles CA 90089

STEPHENS, RALPH IVAN, MECHANICS. *Current Pos:* from asst prof to assoc prof, 65-72, PROF MECH ENG, UNIV IOWA, 72- *Personal Data:* b Chicago, Ill, June 3, 34; m 58; c 3. *Educ:* Univ Ill, BS, 57, MS, 60; Univ Wis, PhD(eng mech), 65. *Prof Exp:* Asst gen eng, Univ Ill, 57-59, instr theoret & appl mech, 59-60; instr eng mech, Univ Wis, 60-65. *Concurrent Pos:* Indust consult, prod viability, 76- *Mem:* Am Soc Testing & Mat; Soc Automotive Engrs. *Res:* Fracture mechanics; fatigue of engineering materials; mechanical behavior; mechanics of solids; failure analysis; products liability. *Mailing Add:* Mech Eng Dept Univ Iowa Iowa City IA 52242. *Fax:* 319-335-5669; *E-Mail:* stephens@icaen.uiowa.edu

STEPHENS, RAYMOND EDWARD, CELL BIOLOGY, PROTEIN CHEMISTRY. *Current Pos:* PROF PHYSIOL, SCH MED, BOSTON UNIV, 93- *Personal Data:* b Pittsburgh, Pa, Mar 5, 40. *Educ:* Geneva Col, BS, 62; Univ Pittsburgh, MS, 63; Dartmouth Med Sch, PhD(molecular biol), 65. *Prof Exp:* Fel, Univ Hawaii, 66; NIH fel, Harvard Univ, 66-67; from asst prof to assoc prof biol, Brandeis Univ, 67-77; investr, Marine Biol Lab, 70-93. *Concurrent Pos:* Mem, Cell Biol Study Sect, NIH, 71-75 & 83-87; vis prof biol, Univ Pa, 77; adj prof physiol, Sch Med, Boston Univ, 78-93. *Mem:* AAAS; Am Chem Soc; NY Acad Sci; Soc Gen Physiol; Am Soc Cell Biol; Biophys Soc. *Res:* Protein subunit association; bio-chemistry of cell division and cell movement; microtubules; comparative physiology of motile systems; ionic control of ciliary movement. *Mailing Add:* Boston Univ Sch Med 80 E Concord St Boston MA 02118-2394. *E-Mail:* rstephen@bu.edu

STEPHENS, RAYMOND WEATHERS, JR, PETROLEUM GEOLOGY. *Current Pos:* from asst prof to assoc prof, 72-90, EMER PROF EARTH SCI, UNIV NEW ORLEANS, 90-; CONSULT. *Personal Data:* b Marietta, Ga, Apr 20, 28; m 51; c 2. *Educ:* Univ Ga, BS, 51; La State Univ, MS, 56, PhD(geol), 60. *Prof Exp:* Geologist, Shell Oil Co, 59-66; dist geologist, Pubco Petrol Co, 66-72. *Mem:* Am Asn Petrol Geologists. *Res:* Stratigraphic and paleontologic geology. *Mailing Add:* 4920 James Dr Metairie LA 70003

STEPHENS, ROBERT ERIC, NEUROANATOMY, SPORTS MEDICINE. *Current Pos:* from asst prof to assoc prof, 81-92, DIR SPORTS MED, UNIV HEALTH SCIS, 85-, PROF & CHAIR ANAT, 92- *Personal Data:* b Kansas City, Kans, July 15, 52; m 92, Christine L Kingman; c Ryan & Trent. *Educ:* Washburn Univ, BS, 74; Kans Univ Med Ctr, PhD(anat), 80. *Prof Exp:* Instr, Kans Univ Med Ctr, 80-81. *Concurrent Pos:* Nat fac mem, US Sports Acad, 89-; bd dirs, Int Asn Dance Med & Sci, 92- *Mem:* Am Asn Clin Anatomists; Am Col Sports Med; Sigma Xi; Int Asn Dance Med & Sci (vpres, 93-). *Res:* Sports medicine, dance medicine and science, and fitness with a primary emphasis upon etiology of injuries, epidemiology and optimal human performance; clinical neurosciences. *Mailing Add:* Univ Health Scis 2105 Independence Blvd Kansas City MO 64124. *Fax:* 816-283-2303

STEPHENS, ROBERT JAMES, CELL BIOLOGY, BIOCHEMISTRY. *Current Pos:* DIR CELL BIOL, SRI INT, 66- *Personal Data:* b June 6, 31; m, Lola M Mathews; c Robert L, Susan L & James W. *Educ:* Pepperdine Col, BA, 54; Cornell Univ, MSc, 59; Univ Southern Calif, PhD(cell biol), 65. *Prof Exp:* Postdoctoral fel, Yale Univ, 65-66. *Concurrent Pos:* Lect, Yale Univ, Univ Southern Calif. *Mem:* Int Soc Eye Res; Soc Free Radical Res; Electron Micros Soc Am; Am Soc Cell Biol; Asn Res Vision & Ophthal; Am Soc Anat. *Res:* Ultrastructural and cytochemical description of the placenta and fetal membranes in the bat; injury and repair mechanisms in the lung resulting from oxidant gas exposure; mechanisms of retinal degeneration. *Mailing Add:* 343 Lexington Dr SRI Int 333 Ravenswood Ave Menlo Park CA 94025

STEPHENS, ROBERT LAWRENCE, biochemistry, microbiology, for more information see previous edition

STEPHENS, STANLEY LAVERNE, MATHEMATICS. *Current Pos:* asst prof, 71-80, ASSOC PROF MATH, ANDERSON COL, 80- *Personal Data:* b Niagara Falls, NY, Apr 23, 43; m 64; c 1. *Educ:* Anderson Univ, BA, 65; Lehigh Univ, MS, 67, PhD(math), 72. *Prof Exp:* Instr, Moravian Col, 68-71. *Mem:* Am Math Soc. *Res:* Prime power groups, particularly the autormorphism group of p-groups. *Mailing Add:* Dept Math Anderson Univ Anderson IN 46012-3462

STEPHENS, TIMOTHY LEE, NUCLEAR WEAPONS EFFECTS, RESEARCH MANAGEMENT. *Current Pos:* VPRES, VISIDYNE INC, 91- *Personal Data:* b Bellingham, Wash, June 27, 44; m 84, Ruth Ann Muirhead; c David. *Educ:* Calif Inst Technol, BS, 66; Harvard Univ, AM, 67, PhD(physics), 71. *Prof Exp:* Res fel physics, Smithsonian Astrophys Observ, 69-70; physicist, Gen Elec Co-Tempo, 70-81; prog mgr, Kaman Sci Corp, 81-83; vpres & dir res, Phys Res Inc, 83-91. *Res:* Optical emission processes of atoms and molecules; synthetic virtual reality environments for simulation and training; chemical and hydrodynamic properties of the atmosphere; environmental effects of nuclear weapons. *Mailing Add:* Visidyne Inc 3322 S Memorial Pkwy Ste 223 Huntsville AL 35801. *Fax:* 205-880-3284; *E-Mail:* stephens@visidyne.com

STEPHENS, TRENT DEE, DEVELOPMENTAL BIOLOGY, MORPHOGENESIS. *Current Pos:* asst prof, 81-86, assoc prof, 86-91, PROF ANAL & EMBRYOL, IDAHO STATE UNIV, 91- *Personal Data:* b Wendell, Idaho, Aug 14, 48; m 71, Kathleen Brown; c Summer, Rhett, Brittani, Derek & Blake. *Educ:* Brigham Young Univ, BS, 73, MS, 74; Univ Pa, PhD(anat), 77. *Prof Exp:* Sr fel, Univ Wash, 77-79, res assoc pediat & anat, 79-81. *Concurrent Pos:* Adj asst prof, Creighton Univ, 82-91, adj prof, 91- *Mem:* Teratology Soc; Am Asn Anatomists; Sigma Xi; AAAS; Soc Develop Biol. *Res:* Developmental biology; limb field induction; size and location of the limb field as related to overall body plan; characteristics of limbness; comparative and evolutionary morphogenesis; limb defects. *Mailing Add:* Dept Biol Sci Idaho State Univ Pocatello ID 83209. *Fax:* 208-236-4570; *E-Mail:* steptren@isu.edu

STEPHENS, VERONICA G, NURSING. *Current Pos:* CHIEF NURSE, FED BUR PRISONS, 96- *Educ:* Med Col Ga, BSN, 74. *Prof Exp:* Dir nurses & adminr, Cent Ga, Home Health Serv, Macon, 74-75; dir nursing serv, Riverside Clin Hosp, Macon, 75-76; dir, Student Health Serv, Austin Peay State Univ, Tenn, 76-77; nurse practr, US Army, Ft Stewart, Ga, Darnell Army Regional Hosp, 77-80, Health Resources & Serv Admin, Hawkins Co Primary Care Bd, Tenn, 80-84; Nursing Home Care Unit, Vet Admin Med Ctr, Washington, DC, 85-86; USN, Quontico Marine Base, 86-91; adminr, Attentive Care Home Health Serv, Rogersville, Tenn, 84-85; clin nurse specialist & nurse practr, Health Resources & Serv Admin, Div Fed Occup & Beneficiary Health Serv, Health Serv Support Br, Detail Dept Com, Norfold, Va, 91-92; sr clin nurse specialist & nurse practr, Int Health Soc & Santa Fe Serv Unit, Field Health Serv, NMex, 92-94; prog mgt officer & recruiter, Health Resources & Serv Admin, Dept Justice, Bur Opers & Prog, Washington, DC, 94-96. *Mem:* Asn Military Surgeons US; Uniformed Nurse Practr Asn. *Mailing Add:* Fed Bur Prisons 320 First St NW Rm 1000 Washington DC 20534. *Fax:* 908-771-8736

STEPHENS, WILLIAM D, ORGANIC CHEMISTRY. *Current Pos:* DIR ROCKET PROPULSION, US ARMY MISSILE COMMAND, 83- *Personal Data:* b Paris, Tenn, Nov 17, 32; div; c 3. *Educ:* Western Ky State Col, BS, 54; Vanderbilt Univ, PhD(chem), 60. *Prof Exp:* Group leader high energy oxidizers, Thiokol Chem Corp, 59-61, sect chief org chem, 61-63; group leader basic mat, Goodyear Tire & Rubber Co, 63-66; prin chemist, Thiokol Chem Corp, 66-78; chief chemist, Atlantic Res Corp, 78-83. *Concurrent Pos:* Adj assoc prof, Univ Ala, Huntsville, 70-78. *Mem:* Am Chem Soc. *Res:* Solid propellant research; explosives, burning-rate catalysts; organometallic, organic nitrogen, sulfur and cyclic compounds; polymer chemistry; adhesives; bonding agents; urethane catalysts; antioxidants. *Mailing Add:* PO Box 12652 Huntsville AL 35815-2652

STEPHENS, WILLIAM LEONARD, microbiology, for more information see previous edition

STEPHENS, WILLIAM POWELL, NEW SYNTHETIC METHODS. *Current Pos:* Chmn, dept nat sci, 81-83, asst prof, 79-87, dean sci & technol, 83-87, ASSOC PROF CHEM, INTERAM UNIV, PR, 87- *Personal Data:* b Rio de Janeiro, Brazil, Feb 18, 48; US citizen; m 76. *Educ:* Nasson Col, BS; Univ Vt, PhD(chem), 79. *Mem:* Am Chem Soc. *Res:* New synthetic methods; novel closure to the oxazoline ring system, the possibility of chiral induction upon closure and the subsequent reactions of these compounds. *Mailing Add:* Dept Chem Inter Am Univ Box 5100 San German PR 00683

STEPHENS-NEWSHAM, LLOYD G, BIOPHYSICS. *Current Pos:* from assoc prof to prof physiol, 66-74, prof, 74-86, EMER PROF PHARMACY & PHARMACEUT SCI, FAC PHARM, UNIV ALTA, 86- *Personal Data:* b Saskatoon, Sask, Apr 30, 21; m 50, Lois Rae Brown; c Joan & Helen. *Educ:* Univ Sask, BA, 43; McGill Univ, PhD(nuclear physics), 48. *Prof Exp:* Asst prof physics, Dalhousie Univ, 48-51; from asst prof to assoc prof, Fac Med, McGill Univ, 52-66. *Concurrent Pos:* Consult, Victoria Gen Hosp, 48-51; radiation physicist, Royal Victoria Hosp, Montreal, 52-66. *Mem:* Can Physiol Soc; Can Asn Physicists; Biophys Soc; Sigma Xi; fel Can Col Physicists Med. *Res:* Effects of ionizing radiation; neutron activation analysis. *Mailing Add:* 1791 Brymea Lane Victoria BC V8N 6B7 Can

STEPHENSON, ALFRED BENJAMIN, POULTRY HUSBANDRY. *Current Pos:* from assoc prof to prof poultry breeding, 53-82, EMER PROF, UNIV MO-COLUMBIA, 82- *Personal Data:* b Unity, Va, May 24, 12; m 41, Mary Olney; c Gary W, Blair O & Laura A. *Educ:* Va Polytech Inst, BS, 33; Rutgers Univ, MS, 34; Iowa State Col, PhD, 49. *Prof Exp:* Asst poultry breeding, Iowa State Col, 46-49; from asst prof to assoc prof, Utah State Agr Col, 49-53. *Mem:* Poultry Sci Asn. *Res:* Quantitative inheritance in poultry breeding. *Mailing Add:* 21 Bingham Rd Columbia MO 65203

STEPHENSON, ANDREW GEORGE, PLANT REPRODUCTIVE ECOLOGY. *Current Pos:* From asst prof to assoc prof, 78-86, PROF BIOL, PA STATE UNIV, 86- *Personal Data:* b Marion, Ohio, Dec 4, 50; m 77, Susan Tyzenhouse; c Lydia & Gabriel. *Educ:* Miami Univ, BA, 73; Univ Mich, MS, 75, PhD(bot), 78. *Concurrent Pos:* Vis researcher, Found Agr Plant Breeding, Wageningen, Neth; vis fel, MagDalen Col, Univ Oxford, 94-95; chair, Plant Pop Bil Sect, Ecol Soc Am, 96-97. *Mem:* Soc Study Evolution; Ecol Soc Am; Am Soc Naturalists; Bot Soc Am; Am Soc Plant Physiologists; AAAS. *Res:* Microgametophyte competition; ecology and evolution of plant reproduction; plant-animal coevolution in pollination, herbivory and dispersal. *Mailing Add:* 208 Mueller Lab Pa State Univ University Park PA 16802. *Fax:* 814-865-9131; *E-Mail:* as4@psu.edu

STEPHENSON, CHARLES BRUCE, ASTRONOMY. *Current Pos:* RETIRED. *Personal Data:* b Little Rock, Ark, Feb 9, 29; m 52, Elizabeth Griffith. *Educ:* Univ Chicago, BS, 49, MS, 51; Univ Calif, PhD(astron), 58. *Prof Exp:* Asst astron, Dearborn Observ, Northwestern Univ, 51-53 & Univ Calif, 56-57; from instr to prof astron, Case Western Res Univ, 58-88, Worcester R & Cornelia B Warner prof astron, 88-94. *Mem:* AAAS; Am Astron Soc; Int Astron Union. *Res:* Stellar spectra; galactic structure; positional astronomy. *Mailing Add:* 14205 Washington Blvd University Heights OH 44118

STEPHENSON, CHARLES V, SOLID STATE PHYSICS. *Current Pos:* chmn dept, 67-74, PROF ELEC ENG, VANDERBILT UNIV, 62- *Personal Data:* b Centerville, Tenn, Oct 1, 24; m 48; c 3. *Educ:* Vanderbilt Univ, BA, 48, MA, 49, PhD(physics), 52. *Prof Exp:* Res physicist, Sandia Corp, 52-56; asst prof physics, Ala Polytech Inst, 56-58; head physics sect, Southern Res Inst, 58-62. *Concurrent Pos:* Consult, Sandia Corp, 56-58. *Mem:* AAAS; fel Am Phys Soc; Acoust Soc Am; Am Asn Physics Teachers; sr mem Inst Elec & Electronics Eng. *Res:* Molecular spectroscopy; solid state physics. *Mailing Add:* 871 Rodney Dr Nashville TN 37205

STEPHENSON, DANNY LON, ORGANIC CHEMISTRY, SPECTROSCOPY. *Current Pos:* ADMINR, BEREAN BAPTIST SCH, 80- *Personal Data:* b Ft Worth, Tex, Nov 7, 37; m 63; c 1. *Educ:* Tex Christian Univ, BA, 59, MA, 60; Rice Univ, PhD(org chem), 64. *Prof Exp:* Res chemist, Phillips Petrol Co, 64-65; prof chem, Howard Payne Univ, 65-80, head dept & chmn, Div Sci & Math, 74-80. *Mem:* Am Chem Soc. *Res:* Mechanistic study of various condensation reactions with zinc chloride as the catalyst; natural products. *Mailing Add:* 16218 Autumn Wind Dr Houston TX 77090-4701

STEPHENSON, DAVID ALLEN, MOLECULAR PHYSICS. *Current Pos:* MEM TECH STAFF, SANDIA NAT LABS, 78- *Personal Data:* b Denver, Colo, Nov 23, 42; m 63; c 2. *Educ:* NMex State Univ, BS, 64; Univ Mich, Ann Arbor, MS, 65, PhD(physics), 68. *Prof Exp:* Nat Res Coun-Environ Sci Serv Admin res fel, Environ Sci Serv Admin Res Labs, Colo, 68-70; assoc sr res physicist, Gen Motors Res Labs, 70-78. *Mem:* Optical Soc Am. *Res:* Raman spectroscopy of gases; gas phase reactions. *Mailing Add:* 967 Lynn St Livermore CA 94550

STEPHENSON, DAVID TOWN, ELECTRICAL ENGINEERING. *Current Pos:* asst prof, 66-70, ASSOC PROF ELEC ENG, IOWA STATE UNIV, 70- *Personal Data:* b Colfax, Wash, Jan 28, 37; m 57; c 3. *Educ:* Wash State Univ, BS, 58; Univ Ill, MS, 62, PhD(elec eng), 65. *Prof Exp:* Asst elec eng, Univ Ill, 60-65, res assoc, 65-66. *Mem:* Inst Elec & Electronics Engrs; Am Soc Eng Educ. *Res:* Antennas; application to radio astronomy, spacecraft, and communications systems; microwave measurements; teaching in field theory and measurements. *Mailing Add:* 322 Hickory Dr Ames IA 50010-3431

STEPHENSON, EDWARD JAMES, MEDIUM ENERGY REACTIONS, POLARIZATION. *Current Pos:* from asst prof to assoc prof, 79-85, PROF, CYCLOTRON FAC, IND UNIT, 85- *Personal Data:* b Birmingham, Ala, Aug 13, 47; m 71, Linda Mangum; c Alan. *Educ:* Rice Univ, BA, 69; Univ Wis-Madison, MS, 71, PhD(physics), 75. *Prof Exp:* Fel nuclear physics, Lawrence Berkeley Lab, 75-78; fel nuclear physics, Argonne Nat Lab, Ill, 78-79. *Mem:* Am Phys Soc; AAAS. *Res:* Polarization; accelerator mass spectrometry; medium energy nuclear physics. *Mailing Add:* Ind Univ Cyclotron IUCS Fac 2401 Milo B Sampson Lane Bloomington IN 47408. *Fax:* 812-855-6645; *E-Mail:* stephenson@iucf.indiana.edu

STEPHENSON, EDWARD LUTHER, ANIMAL NUTRITION. *Current Pos:* RETIRED. *Personal Data:* b Calhoun, Tenn, May 5, 23; m 47; c 2. *Educ:* Univ Tenn, BS, 46, MS, 47; State Col Wash, PhD(poultry nutrit), 52. *Prof Exp:* From asst prof to prof animal nutrit, Col Agr, Univ Ark, Fayetteville, 49-64, head dept, 64-87. *Mem:* Am Soc Animal Sci; Soc Exp Biol & Med; fel Poultry Sci Asn; Am Inst Nutrit. *Res:* Poultry nutrition. *Mailing Add:* 1923 E Joyce Apt 107 Fayetteville AR 72703

STEPHENSON, EDWARD T, PHYSICAL METALLURGY. *Current Pos:* CONSULT, 92- *Personal Data:* b Atlantic City, NJ, Nov 7, 29; m 53, Irma P Geiger; c 4. *Educ:* Lehigh Univ, BS, 51, PhD(metall), 65; Mass Inst Technol, MS, 56. *Honors & Awards:* Grossman Award, Am Soc Metals, 64, Stoughton Award, 88. *Prof Exp:* From res engr to sr res engr, Bethlehem Steel Corp, 56-80, sr scientist, 80-88, res fel, Homer Res Labs, 88-92. *Concurrent Pos:* Fac, Metals Eng Inst, Am Soc Metals, 87-94. *Mem:* Fel Am Soc Metals; Am Inst Mining, Metall & Petrol Engrs; Sigma Xi. *Res:* Relation of strength and toughness to composition, processing and microstructure; electron microstructure, electrical resistivity, mechanical and magnetic properties, and internal friction of steel. *Mailing Add:* 1852 Levering Pl Bethlehem PA 18017. *E-Mail:* ed__stephenson@compuserve.com

STEPHENSON, EDWIN CLARK, DEVELOPMENTAL BIOLOGY. *Current Pos:* asst prof, 91-93, ASSOC PROF BIOL SCI, UNIV ALA, 93- *Personal Data:* b Charlotte, NC, May 28, 53; m 81, Karen M Tenbarge; c 2. *Educ:* Univ NC, BS, 75; Yale Univ, MPhil, 78, PhD(biol), 81. *Prof Exp:* NIH fel, Yale Univ, 76-81, Ind Univ, 81-83; asst prof biol, Univ Rochester, 84-91. *Mem:* Soc Develop Biol; Genetics Soc Am; AAAS. *Res:* Early embryonic development, especially egg structure and organization and embryonic determination; genetic, molecular and cytoskeletal mechanisms of RNA localization in Drosophila oocytes; evolution of developmental mechanisms. *Mailing Add:* Dept Biol Sci Univ Ala Tuscaloosa AL 35487. *Fax:* 205-348-1786; *E-Mail:* estephen@biology.as.ua.edu

STEPHENSON, ELIZABETH WEISS, MUSCLE, CALCIUM REGULATION. *Current Pos:* ASSOC PROF PHYSIOL, UNIV MED & DENT, NJ MED SCH, 81- *Personal Data:* b Newark, NJ, Apr 1, 27; m 46; c 3. *Educ:* Univ Chicago, BS, 47; George Washington Univ, PhD(physiol), 64. *Prof Exp:* Res asst, Ill Neuropsychiat Inst, 47-49; from instr to assoc prof physiol, Sch Med, George Washington Univ, 64-71; sr staff fel, Lab Phys Biol, Nat Inst Arthritis, Metab & Digestive Dis, 71-77, res biologist, 77-81. *Concurrent Pos:* Mem coun & exec bd, Biophys Soc, 83- *Mem:* AAAS; Am Physiol Soc; Biophys Soc (treas, 79-92); Soc Gen Physiol. *Res:* Ion transport across cellular and intracellular membranes; excitation-contraction coupling in skeletal muscle. *Mailing Add:* Dept Physiol Univ Med & Dent NJ Med Sch 185 S Orange Ave Newark NJ 07103. *Fax:* 973-504-7950

STEPHENSON, FRANCIS CREIGHTON, PHYSICS. *Current Pos:* from asst prof to assoc prof, 65-93, chmn, Physics Dept, 89-93, EMER ASSOC PROF PHYSICS, CLEVELAND STATE UNIV, 93- *Personal Data:* b Brantford, Ont, Mar 24, 24; m 48, Shirley L Wilkes; c Wendy, Paul, Grant & Sara. *Educ:* Univ Toronto, BASc, 49, MA, 51, PhD(physics), 54. *Prof Exp:* Res physicist, Lamp Develop Dept, Gen Elec Co, 53-65. *Mem:* Am Asn Physics Teachers. *Res:* Molecular spectroscopy; incandescent radiation; vibration; gas discharge. *Mailing Add:* Dept Physics Cleveland State Univ Euclid Ave E 24 St Cleveland OH 44115

STEPHENSON, FREDERICK WILLIAM, ELECTRONICS ENGINEERING. *Current Pos:* assoc prof, 78-83, assoc dean, res grad studies, 86-90, PROF ELEC ENG, VA POLYTECH INST & STATE UNIV, 83-, DEPT HEAD, 90- *Personal Data:* b Tynemouth, Eng, Sept 25, 39; m 68, Sarah Smith; c Sara K. *Educ:* Kings Col, Univ Durham, BSc, 61; Univ Newcastle Upon Tyne, PhD(elec eng), 65. *Prof Exp:* Tech mgr, Microelectronics Div, Electrosil Ltd, 65-67; sr res assoc, Univ Newcastle Upon Tyne, 67-68; lectr, Univ Hull, UK, 68-75, sr lectr, 75-78. *Concurrent Pos:* R T French vis prof, Univ Rochester, 76-77; consult, Frequency Devices Inc, Haverhill, Mass, 79-; vis prof, Univ Cape Town, summer, 82 & 84. *Mem:* Fel Inst Elec & Electronics Engrs; fel Inst Elec Engrs. *Res:* Synthesis and sensitivity evaluation of active resistance capacitance and switched-capacitor filters; applications of hybrid microelectronics. *Mailing Add:* Bradley Dept Elec Eng Va Polytech Insts State Univ Blacksburg VA 24061. *Fax:* 540-231-3362; *E-Mail:* mfregy@vfvmii.bitnet

STEPHENSON, GERARD J, JR, THEORETICAL NUCLEAR PHYSICS, THEORETICAL PARTICLE PHYSICS. *Current Pos:* ADJ PROF PHYSICS, UNIV NMEX, 78- *Personal Data:* b Yonkers, NY, Mar 4, 37; m 60, Barbera Wertz; c Thomas. *Educ:* Mass Inst Technol, BS, 59, PhD(physics), 64. *Prof Exp:* Res fel physics, Calif Inst Technol, 64-66; from asst prof to assoc prof physics, Univ Md, College Park, 69-74; staff mem, Los Alamos Sci Lab, 74-93, group leader, 78-82 & 84-85, dep div leader, 85-93. *Concurrent Pos:* Guggenheim mem fel, Los Alamos Sci Lab, 72-73. *Mem:* Am Phys Soc. *Res:* Neutrino physics, theoretical studies of nuclear structure and of low and intermediate energy nuclear reactions, quark models applied to low energy nuclear physics. *Mailing Add:* Dept Physics & Astron Univ NMex Albuquerque NM 87131. *Fax:* 505-277-1520; *E-Mail:* gjs@hepv1.unm.edu

STEPHENSON, HAROLD PATTY, MOLECULAR SPECTROSCOPY. *Current Pos:* from assoc prof to prof, 60-90, head dept, 60-83, EMER PROF PHYSICS, PFEIFFER COL, 90- *Personal Data:* b Angier, NC, Dec 22, 25; m 56, Sarah Kincaid; c Ellen (Frazer) & Mark. *Educ:* Duke Univ, BSME, 47, MA, 49, PhD(physics), 52. *Prof Exp:* Instr physics, Duke Univ, 48-49 & 51-52; asst, Appl Physics Lab, Johns Hopkins Univ, 51; assoc prof physics, Ill Wesleyan Univ, 52-53, prof & chmn dept, 53-57; assoc prof mech eng, Duke Univ, 57-60. *Concurrent Pos:* Vis instr physics, Univ NC, Charlotte, 83 & Livingstone Col, 83-84. *Mem:* Am Asn Physics Teachers. *Res:* Near ultraviolet absorption spectra of poly-atomic molecules. *Mailing Add:* 1325 Mawbridge Rd Central SC 29630

STEPHENSON, HUGH EDWARD, JR, THORACIC SURGERY, CARDIOVASCULAR SURGERY. *Current Pos:* from asst prof to assoc prof, Sch Med, Univ Mo, Columbia, 53-55, chmn dept, 56-60, interim dean, 87-88, PROF SURG, SCH MED, UNIV MO, COLUMBIA, 56-, CHIEF, GEN SURG DIV, 76-, CHIEF OF STAFF, UNIV HOSP & CLIN, 82- *Personal Data:* b Columbia, Mo, June 1, 22; m 64, Sarah N Dickinson; c Hugh E III & Ann (Dunlop). *Educ:* Univ Mo, AB & BS, 43; Washington Univ, MD, 45; Am Bd Surg, dipl, 53; Bd Thoracic Surg, dipl, 63. *Prof Exp:* Instr surg, Sch Med, NY Univ, 51-53. *Concurrent Pos:* Chair-elect coun med educ, AMA, liason comt med educ; mem, Southern Med Asn. *Mem:* Soc Vascular Surg; AMA; Am Asn Surg Trauma; Am Col Surg; Am Col Chest Physicians. *Res:* Cardiovascular research; oncology-melonoma; cardiac arrest resuscitation; over 130 publications. *Mailing Add:* 204H Health Sci Ctr Univ Mo Sch Med Columbia MO 65201. *Fax:* 573-884-4808

STEPHENSON, J(OHN) GREGG, ELECTRONICS ENGINEERING. *Current Pos:* RETIRED. *Personal Data:* b Kansas City, Mo, Sept 21, 17; m 48; c 2. *Educ:* Yale Univ, BE, 39; Stanford Univ, Engr, 41. *Prof Exp:* Asst engr, Ohio Brass Co, 41-42; res assoc, Radio Res Lab, Harvard Univ, 42-45; engr, Airborne Instruments Lab, 45-55, sect head appl electronics, 55-57, sect head, Appl Res Div, 57-58, dep dir, Proj Star, 58-61, tech asst to dir, Res & Eng Div, 61-63, prog dir, 63-68, dep dir, Reconnaissance & Surveillance Div, Cutler-Hammer, Inc, 68-69, dir, Tech Support, AIL Div, Eaton Corp, 70-81. *Mem:* Sr mem Inst Elec & Electronic Engrs; Am Inst Aeronaut & Astronaut; Sigma Xi. *Res:* Ultrahigh frequency and microwave receiving and transmitting equipment; space technology; ionospheric propagation; systems management. *Mailing Add:* 80 Lyme Rd Hanover NH 03755

STEPHENSON, JOHN, THEORETICAL PHYSICS. *Current Pos:* res assoc physics, Univ Alta, 68-70, vis asst prof, 70-71, from asst prof to assoc prof, 71-81, PROF PHYSICS, UNIV ALTA, 81- *Personal Data:* b Chichester, Eng, 1939; m 65; c 3. *Educ:* Univ London, BSc, 61, PhD(theoret physics), 64, DSc, 90. *Prof Exp:* Lectr math, Univ Adelaide, 65-68. *Mem:* Can Asn Physicists; Am Phys Soc. *Res:* Statistical mechanics and critical phenomena in fluids and magnetic systems; non-linear dynamics, including the Mandelbrot Set. *Mailing Add:* Dept Physics Univ Alta Edmonton AB T6G 2J1 Can

STEPHENSON, JOHN CARTER, PHYSICAL CHEMISTRY. *Current Pos:* SCIENTIST, NAT BUR STANDARDS, 71- *Personal Data:* US citizen. *Educ:* Mass Inst Technol, BS, 66; Univ Calif, PhD(phys chem), 71. *Prof Exp:* Scientist, Avco Everett Res Lab, 70-71. *Mem:* Am Chem Soc; InterAm Photochem Soc. *Res:* Lasers; chemical kinetics; spectroscopy; energy transfer; air and water pollution. *Mailing Add:* Molecular Physics Div NIST Gaithersburg MD 20899

STEPHENSON, JOHN LESLIE, BIOMATHEMATICS. *Current Pos:* PROF BIOMATH PHYSIOL, CORNELL UNIV MED COL, 84- *Personal Data:* b Farmington, Maine, Dec 4, 21; m 46; c 3. *Educ:* Harvard Univ, BS, 43; Univ Ill, MD, 49. *Prof Exp:* Asst theoret physics, Metall Lab, Univ Chicago, 43-45; physicist, US Naval Ord Lab, 45; intern, Staten Island Marine Hosp, NY, 49-50; from res assoc to asst prof, Univ Chicago, 52-54; scientist, Nat Heart & Lung Inst, 54-73, 73-83, chief, Sect Theoret Biophys. *Concurrent Pos:* USPHS fel anat, Univ Chicago, 50-52; vis prof, Inst Fluid Dynamics & Appl Math, Univ Md, College Park, 73-74. *Mem:* Am Phys Soc; Am Physiol Soc; Int Soc Nephrology; Soc Math Biol (pres, 83-85); Biophys Soc; Am Soc Nephrology; Soc Gen Physiologists. *Res:* Mathematical theory of transport in biological systems; theory of renal function. *Mailing Add:* Dept Physiol & Biophysics Carnell Univ Med Col D-503 1300 York Ave New York NY 10021-4896. *Fax:* 212-746-8690; *E-Mail:* john@pipmed.cornell.edu

STEPHENSON, KENNETH EDWARD, accelerator physics, nuclear detector technology, for more information see previous edition

STEPHENSON, LANI SUE, NUTRITION, PARASITOLOGY. *Current Pos:* from res asst to res assoc, Cornell Univ, 73-80, vis prof, 80-83, asst prof, 83-88, ASSOC PROF INT NUTRIT, DIV NUTRIT SCI, CORNELL UNIV, 88- *Personal Data:* b Honolulu, Hawaii, July 31, 48; m 74. *Educ:* Cornell Univ, BS, 71, MNS, 73, PhD(gen nutrit), 78. *Honors & Awards:* Student Res Award, Am Inst Nutrit, 78. *Prof Exp:* Exten aide, Dept Human Nutrit Food, Col Human Ecol, Cornell Univ, 71. *Concurrent Pos:* Co-investr, World Bank, Brit Overseas Develop Ministry & Cornell Health & Nutrit Proj, Kenya, 78-81; prin investr, Clark Found Urinary Schistosomiasis Growth & Anemia Proj, Kenya, 81-83, 84- *Mem:* Am Pub Health Asn; Am Soc Parasitologists; Am Dietetic Asn; Am Inst Nutrit; Am Soc Trop Med Hyg; Soc Int Nutrit Res. *Res:* Maternal and child health; protein-calorie malnutrition in young children; relationships between intestinal parasites, schistosomiasis and nutritional status; dietary methodologies; international nutrition problems; nutritional anemias. *Mailing Add:* Savage Hall Cornell Univ Ithaca NY 14853-0001. *Fax:* 607-255-7906

STEPHENSON, LEE PALMER, GEOPHYSICS. *Current Pos:* RETIRED. *Personal Data:* b Fresno, Calif, Oct 21, 23; m 48; c 3. *Educ:* Fresno State Col, AB, 47; Univ Ill, MS, 49, PhD(physics), 53. *Prof Exp:* Asst physics, Univ Ill, 47-53; res physicist, Calif Res Corp, Stand Oil Co, Calif, 53-57, group supvr, 57-59, res assoc geophys, 59-63, sr res assoc, Chevron Oil Field Res Co, 63-86. *Mem:* AAAS; Am Phys Soc; Sigma Xi. *Res:* Exploration seismology; seismic signal detection, data processing and interpretation; physical properties of earth materials; compaction and cementation of clastic sediments; optics; astronomy; astronomical instrumentation. *Mailing Add:* 1248 N Stanford Ave Fullerton CA 92631

STEPHENSON, LOU ANN, TEMPERATURE REGULATION, BIOLOGICAL TIMEKEEPING. *Current Pos:* RES PHYSIOLOGIST, US ARMY RES INST ENVIRON MED, 83- *Personal Data:* b Logansport, Ind, Apr 7, 54. *Educ:* Ind Univ, PhD(human performance), 81. *Mem:* Am Physiol Soc; AAAS. *Mailing Add:* US Army Res Inst Environ Med Kansas St Natick MA 01760-5007

STEPHENSON, MARY LOUISE, MOLECULAR BIOLOGY. *Current Pos:* RETIRED. *Personal Data:* b Brookline, Mass, Feb 23, 21. *Educ:* Conn Col, AB, 43; Radcliffe Col, PhD(biochem), 56. *Prof Exp:* Res fel, Mass Gen Hosp, Harvard Med Sch, 56-59, asst biochemist, 59-66, assoc biol chem, 66- 74, assoc biochemist, 74-92, Prin res assoc, 69-83. *Mem:* Am Soc Biochem & Molecular Biol; Am Asn Cancer Res; Am Soc Cell Biol; Am Soc Bone & Mineral Res. *Res:* Biosynthesis of proteins and nucleic acids. *Mailing Add:* 308 Ocean Ave Marblehead MA 01945-3706

STEPHENSON, NORMAN ROBERT, biochemistry, science administration; deceased, see previous edition for last biography

STEPHENSON, PAUL BERNARD, PHYSICS. *Current Pos:* from asst prof to assoc prof, 66-75, PROF PHYSICS, LA TECH UNIV, 75- *Personal Data:* b Jena, La, Dec 16, 37; m 59; c 3. *Educ:* La Polytech Inst, BS, 60, MS, 61; Duke Univ, PhD(physics), 66. *Prof Exp:* Engr, Tex Instruments Inc, 61-62; res asst physics, Duke Univ, 62-66. *Mem:* Am Asn Physics Teachers; Am Phys Soc. *Res:* Solid state physics, particularly luminescence of organic crystals. *Mailing Add:* Dept Physics La Tech Univ Ruston LA 71272-0001

STEPHENSON, RICHARD ALLEN, COASTAL GEOMORPHOLOGY, ENVIRONMENTAL PLANNING. *Current Pos:* asst prof phys geog, ECarolina Univ, 62-67, assoc prof phys geog, 71-74, dir, Inst Coastal & Marine Resources, 74-77, prof, Dept Geog & planning, 77-94, PROF, DEPT PLANNING, ECAROLINA UNIV, 94- *Personal Data:* b Cleveland, Ohio, June 8, 31; m 52; c 3. *Educ:* Kent State Univ, BA, 59; Univ Tenn, MS, 61; Univ Iowa, PhD(geog, geol), 67. *Prof Exp:* asst prof phys geog & earth sci, Univ Ga, 67-71. *Mem:* Asn Am Geog; Geol Soc Am; Sigma Xi. *Res:* Geomorphology; water resources; environmental resources; environmental planning. *Mailing Add:* Dept Planning E Carolina Univ 139 Rawl Annex Greenville NC 27858-4353. *Fax:* 973-328-1269; *E-Mail:* gestephe@ecuum.cis.ecu.edu

STEPHENSON, ROBERT BAIRD, NUCLEAR ENGINEERING. *Current Pos:* pres & chief exec officer, Bellevue, 91-92, PRES, CHIEF EXEC OFFICER & BD DIR, SIEMENS POWER CORP, MILWAUKEE, 92- *Personal Data:* b Washington, Jan 20, 43; m 67, Sheryl Ann Fish; c Brie Danielle & Eric Baird. *Educ:* Purdue Univ, BS, 65; Univ Mich, MS, 70, MBA, 72. *Prof Exp:* Engr, Jersey Nuclear Co, Inc, 72-74; engr mgr, Exxon Nuclear Co, Inc, Wash, 74-80, managing dir, Exxon Nuclear GmBH, Germany, 80-83, mkt & sales staff, Exxon Nuclear Co Inc, Wash, 83-85, vpres admin, 86, vpres com div, 87; pres, chief exec officer & chmn, Epid Inc, 85-86; pres & chief exec officer, Advanced Nuclear Fuels Corp, 88-91. *Mem:* Am Nuclear Soc. *Mailing Add:* 10503 N Woodcrest Dr Mequon WI 53092

STEPHENSON, ROBERT BRUCE, HUMAN PHYSIOLOGY, CARDIOVASCULAR PHYSIOLOGY. *Current Pos:* ASST PROF PHYSIOL, MICH STATE UNIV, 79- *Personal Data:* b Colfax, Wash, Feb 15, 46; m 68; c 3. *Educ:* Wash State Univ, BS, 68; Univ Wash, PhD(physiol & biophysics), 76. *Prof Exp:* Assoc res engr, Boeing Co, 68-70; fel, Univ Wash, 70-76 & Mayo Clin & Found, 77-79. *Res:* Cardiovascular physiology; neural control of the circulation, particularly reflex regulation of blood pressure in normotension and hypertension. *Mailing Add:* Dept Physiol Mich State Univ Giltner Hall East Lansing MI 48824-0001

STEPHENSON, ROBERT CHARLES, geology; deceased, see previous edition for last biography

STEPHENSON, ROBERT E(LDON), ELECTRICAL ENGINEERING, GENERAL COMPUTER SCIENCES. *Current Pos:* RETIRED. *Personal Data:* b Nephi, Utah, Aug 7, 19; m 42, Frances Call; c Jill, Robert A, Jane & Ned E. *Educ:* Univ Utah, BS, 41; Calif Inst Technol, MS, 46; Purdue Univ, PhD(elec eng), 52. *Prof Exp:* From instr to prof elec eng & comput sci, Univ Utah, 46-71, assoc dean, Col Eng, 71-89. *Concurrent Pos:* Instr, Purdue Univ, 50-52; engr, Hughes Aircraft Co, 55, Sperry Utah Eng Labs, 59; consult, Sandia Corp, 59-64, Utah Power & Light, 81- *Mem:* Inst Elec & Electronics Engrs; Sigma Xi. *Res:* Computers; data systems; computer simulation; electric power. *Mailing Add:* 4144 S 660 E Salt Lake City UT 84107

STEPHENSON, ROBERT L, RAW MATERIALS BENEFICATION, COKE MANUFACTURE. *Current Pos:* RETIRED. *Personal Data:* b Pittsburgh, Pa, Feb 11, 13; m 38; c 3. *Educ:* Princeton Univ, AB, 35. *Honors & Awards:* T L Joseph Award, Iron & Steel Soc, Am Inst Mining, Metall & Petrol Engrs, 79. *Prof Exp:* Observer, Duquesne Works, US Steel Corp, 33-37, metallurgist, 37-40, lab foreman, 40-45, chief metallurist, 45-51; from res engr to chief res engr, US Steel Res Lab, 51-78; consult, 78-86. *Concurrent Pos:* Distinguished mem, Iron & Steel Soc, Am Inst Mining, Metall & Petrol Engrs, 83. *Mem:* Fel Am Soc Metals; Am Inst Mining Metall & Petrol Engrs; Am Iron & Steel Inst; Am Iron & Steel Engrs; mem Am Inst Mech Engrs. *Res:* Developed slide rule for accurately predicting the hardenability of steel from its chemical composition; developed methods for injecting hydrocarbon fuels through blast furnace tuyeres to decrease coke consumption and increase hot-metal production rate; determined methods for eliminating the harmful effects of alkalies on blast furnace performance. *Mailing Add:* 1309 Shady Ave Pittsburgh PA 15217-1339

STEPHENSON, ROBERT MOFFATT, JR, MATHEMATICS. *Current Pos:* assoc prof, 73-78, chmn dept, 76-79, PROF MATH, UNIV SC, 78-, CHMN DEPT, 94- *Personal Data:* b Atlanta, Ga, Dec 25, 40; m 65; c 2. *Educ:* Vanderbilt Univ, BA, 62; Tulane Univ, MS, 65, PhD(math), 67. *Prof Exp:* Asst prof math, Univ NC, Chapel Hill, 67-73. *Mem:* Am Math Soc. *Res:* General topology. *Mailing Add:* Dept Math Univ SC Columbia SC 29208-0001

STEPHENSON, ROBERT STORER, NEUROPHYSIOLOGY, VISION RESEARCH. *Current Pos:* ASSOC PROF, DEPT BIOL SCI, WAYNE STATE UNIV, 81- *Personal Data:* b Corpus Christi, Tex, Apr 30, 43; m 69; c 2. *Educ:* Princeton Univ, AB, 65; Mass Inst Technol, SM, 67, PhD(neurophysiol), 73. *Prof Exp:* Lectr physiol, Fac Sci, Rabat, Morocco, 73-76; res assoc physiol, Dept Biol Sci, Purdue Univ, 76- *Concurrent Pos:* Fel, Purdue Univ, 76. *Mem:* AAAS; Sigma Xi; Biophys Soc; Asn Res Vision Ophthalmol. *Res:* Invertebrate photoreceptors and phototransduction; nerve regeneration; morphogenesis. *Mailing Add:* Dept Biol Sci Wayne State Univ 210 Science Hall Detroit MI 48202-3940. *Fax:* 313-577-6891

STEPHENSON, SAMUEL EDWARD, JR, MEDICINE, ORGANIC CHEMISTRY. *Current Pos:* PROF SURG, UNIV FLA, 67- *Personal Data:* b Bristol, Tenn, May 16, 26; m 50, 70, Janet Spotts; c Sam E III, William Douglas, Dorothea Louise (Rogers) & Judith Maria (Anderson). *Educ:* Univ SC, BS, 46; Vanderbilt Univ, MD, 50; Am Bd Surg & Bd Thoracic Surg, dipl, 57. *Prof Exp:* Asst surg, Sch Med, Vanderbilt Univ, 53-55; from instr to asst prof, 55-61, assoc prof, Sch Med & assoc dir, Clin Res Ctr, 61-67, dir, S R Light Lab Surg Res, 59-62; chmn dept surg, Univ Hosp Jacksonville, 67-78; chief gen surg, Baptist Med Ctr, 79-86. *Concurrent Pos:* Consult, Regional Respiratory & Rehab Ctr, 58 & Thayer Vet Admin Hosp, 59. *Mem:* Am Surg Asn; Southern Surg Asn; Am Asn Thoracic Surg; fel Am Col Surgeons; Soc Univ Surgeons. *Res:* Medical electronics, especially physiological control of respiration and cardiac rate; experimental atherogenesis; malignant disease; cardiovascular surgery and neoplasms. *Mailing Add:* 1501 San Marco Blvd Jacksonville FL 33207

STEPHENSON, STANLEY E(LBERT), ELECTRICAL & NUCLEAR ENGINEERING. *Current Pos:* RETIRED. *Personal Data:* b Ogden, Utah, Mar 12, 26; m 49; c 6. *Educ:* Univ Colo, BS, 48; Tex A&M Univ, MS, 61, PhD(elec eng), 64. *Prof Exp:* Engr, Lago Oil & Transport, 48-52; sr engr, Stand Oil Co, Ohio, 52-54; engr, Am Petrofina, 54-59; asst supvr, Nuclear Sci Ctr, Tex A&M Univ, 59-61, asst res engr, Activation Anal Lab, 61-62; from assoc prof to prof elec eng, Univ Ark, Fayetteville, 64-90. *Mem:* Am Soc Eng Educ; Inst Elec & Electronics Engrs. *Res:* Digital control systems; optimal control systems. *Mailing Add:* 1726 Carolyn Dr Fayetteville AR 72701

STEPHENSON, STEPHEN NEIL, BOTANY, ECOLOGY. *Current Pos:* asst prof, 65-72, ASSOC PROF BOT, MICH STATE UNIV, 72- *Personal Data:* b Hayden Lake, Idaho, Feb 3, 33; m 53; c 4. *Educ:* Idaho State Univ, BS, 55; Rutgers Univ, MS, 63, PhD(bot), 65. *Prof Exp:* Park ranger, Nat Park Serv, 57-61; instr bot, Douglass Col, Rutgers Univ, 62-63. *Concurrent Pos:* Mem eastern deciduous forest biome coord comt, Int Biol Prog, 68- *Mem:* AAAS; Am Soc Mammal; Ecol Soc Am; Am Inst Biol Sci. *Res:* Community structure and organization; biosystematics of Gramineae; biogeography of North America, especially arid and semiarid regions. *Mailing Add:* Dept Bot Mich State Univ 166 Plant Biol East Lansing MI 48824-1312

STEPHENSON, STEVEN LEE, MYCOLOGY, FOREST ECOLOGY. *Current Pos:* PROF BOT, FAIRMONT STATE COL, 76- *Personal Data:* b Washington, DC, Mar 28, 43; m 72; c 1. *Educ:* Lynchburg Col, BS, 68; Va Polytech Inst & State Univ, MS, 70, PhD(bot), 77. *Prof Exp:* Sec teacher biol, Bedford County Pub Schs, 70-74. *Concurrent Pos:* Adj prof, WVa Univ, 82-85; res fel, Univ Va, 82; Fulbright scholar, Himachal Pradesh Univ, India, 87; vis prof, Univ Alaska, 89. *Mem:* Mycol Soc Am; Brit Mycol Soc; Torrey Bot Club; NAm Mycol Asn. *Res:* Distribution and ecology of Myxomycetes in temperate forest ecosystems; upland forests of the mid-Appalachian region of eastern North America. *Mailing Add:* Fairmont State Col 1201 Locust Ave Fairmont WV 26554-2451

STEPHENSON, THOMAS E(DGAR), ADSORPTION. *Current Pos:* CONSULT, 97- *Personal Data:* b Dahlgren, Ill, Oct 19, 22; m 46, Helen Mizzoni; c Thomas P, Joan P, Timothy J & Michael D. *Educ:* Southern Ill Univ, BS, 45; Univ Tenn, MS, 50. *Prof Exp:* Physicist, Manhattan Dist, Atomic Energy Comn, 46-47, Oak Ridge Nat Lab, 47-54; nuclear engr, Convair Div, Gen Dynamics Corp, 54-55; design engr, Nuclear Div, Martin Co, 55-56; physicist, Sci Res Staff, Repub Aviation Corp, 56-65, Brookhaven Nat Lab, 65-70, S M Stoller Corp, 70-73; nuclear applications engr, Va Elec & Power Co, 73-76; sr nuclear engr, Burns & Roe, Inc, 76-80; sr engr, Stone & Webster, 80-89; consult, physics & eng, 89-90; proj engr, Brookhaven Nat Lab, 90-97. *Concurrent Pos:* Adj assoc prof, Long Island Univ, 68-70. *Mem:* Am Phys Soc; Am Nuclear Soc. *Res:* Neutron and reactor physics; radiation effects and shielding; power reactor safety analysis and environmental effects; neutron cross section measurement and evaluation; nuclear fuel evaluation; nuclear licensing; neutron and nuclear polarization; low temperature physics; nuclear polarization. *Mailing Add:* 16 Briarfield Lane Huntington NY 11743. Fax: 516-427-8095

STEPHENSON, WILLIAM KAY, PHYSIOLOGY. *Current Pos:* RETIRED. *Personal Data:* b Chicago, Ill, Apr 6, 27; m 51; c 3. *Educ:* Knox Col, AB, 50; Univ Minn, PhD, 55. *Prof Exp:* Phys chemist, Nat Bur Stand, 49-50; asst zool, Univ Minn, 50-53, instr, 54; from asst prof to prof biol, Earlham Col, 54-94, chmn dept, 64-77. *Mem:* AAAS; Am Soc Zool; Am Soc Cell Biol. *Res:* Ion distribution; active transport; bioelectric phenomena; cnidarian behavior. *Mailing Add:* Dept Biol Earlham Col Richmond IN 47374

STEPIEN, CAROL ANN, FISHERIES POPULATION GENETICS, MOLECULAR SYSTEMATICS OF FISHES. *Current Pos:* MAYER ASST PROF BIOL, CASE WESTERN RES UNIV, 92- *Personal Data:* b Cleveland, Ohio, Apr 21, 58; m 95, James Callahan; c Andrew N & Anna B. *Educ:* Bowling Green Univ, BS, 79; Univ Southern Calif, MS, 80, PhD(biol), 85. *Prof Exp:* Lectr marine biol, Univ San Diego, 84-86; NSF researcher, 86-88; Sloan fel molecular evolution, 88-90; Nat Res Coun res assoc, 90-92. *Concurrent Pos:* Nat Geog Soc researcher, SAm, 87; adj researcher, Scripps Inst Oceanog, 94- *Mem:* Am Fisheries Soc; Soc Syst Biologists; Am Soc Ichthyologists & Herpetologists; Ecol Soc Am; Soc Study Evolution; Soc Molecular Biol & Evolution; AAAS; Int Asn Great Lakes Res. *Res:* Population genetics of freshwater and marine fishes based on DNA sequencing; population genetics of the zebra mussel; molecular systematics of fishes. *Mailing Add:* Dept Biol Case Western Res Univ Cleveland OH 44106-7080. Fax: 216-368-4672; E-Mail: cas20@pop.cwrj.edu

STEPKA, WILLIAM, PLANT PHYSIOLOGY, PLANT BIOCHEMISTRY. *Current Pos:* plant physiologist in chg, Radiol Nutriculture Lab, Med Col Va, Va Commonwealth Univ, 55-68, prof, 68-82, EMER PROF PHARMACOG, HEALTH SCI DIV, VA COMMONWEALTH UNIV, 82- *Personal Data:* b Veseli, Minn, Apr 13, 17; m 48; c 1. *Educ:* Univ Rochester, AB, 46; Univ Calif, PhD, 51. *Prof Exp:* Asst, Univ Rochester, 46-47 & Univ Calif, 48-49; res assoc bot, Univ Pa, 51-54, asst prof, 54-55. *Concurrent Pos:* Plant physiologist & biochemist, Am Tobacco Co, 55-68. *Mem:* Am Soc Plant Physiol; Am Soc Pharmacognosy; Am Asn Cols Pharm. *Res:* Discovery and isolation of cardioactive, hypotensive and contraceptive compounds from natural sources. *Mailing Add:* 715 Glendale Dr Richmond VA 23229

STEPLEMAN, ROBERT SAUL, MATHEMATICS. *Current Pos:* group head sci comput, Exxon Res & Eng Co, 80-85, group head comput & info support, 85-86, sect head res comput, 86-90, res & tech comput adv, 90-91, comput planner, 91-95, SECT HEAD NETWORK COMPUT, EXXON RES & ENG, 95- *Personal Data:* b New York, NY, Nov 2, 42; m 67, Barbara Weinberg; c 2. *Educ:* State Univ NY, Stony Brook, BS, 64; Univ Md, College Park, PhD(math), 69. *Prof Exp:* Res assoc numerical anal, Inst Fluid Dynamics & Appl Math, Univ Md, College Park, 69; asst prof appl math & comput sci, Sch Eng & Appl Sci, Univ Va, 69-73; mem tech staff, David Sarnoff Res Ctr, RCA, 73-80. *Concurrent Pos:* Adj assoc prof comput sci, Rutgers Univ, 78-81; ed, Appl Numerical Math, 84-91. *Mem:* Math Asn Am; Asn Comput Mach; Soc Indust & Appl Math. *Res:* Numerical analysis; convergence of numerical methods; solution of elliptic partial differential equations; solution of singular Fredholm integral equations of the first kind; stopping criteria for numerical processes. *Mailing Add:* Exxon Res Eng PO Box 180 Florham Park NJ 07932-0101. Fax: 973-765-2530; E-Mail: robert.s.stepleman@ere.exxon.sprint.com

STEPLEWSKI, ZENON, cell biology, immunotherapy, for more information see previous edition

STEPONKUS, PETER LEO, CRYOBIOLOGY, PLANT PHYSIOLOGY. *Current Pos:* asst prof, 68-72, Cornell Univ, assoc prof hort, 72-77, assoc prof crop physiol, 77-79, prof, 79-87, LIBERTY HYDDE BAILEY PROF CROP PHYSIOL, CORNELL UNIV, 87- *Personal Data:* b Chicago, Ill, Sept 18, 41; c Peter C, Dana S, Karen M & Kristen E. *Educ:* Colo State Univ, BSc, 63; Univ Ariz, MSc, 64; Purdue Univ, PhD(plant physiol), 66. *Honors & Awards:* Kenneth Post Award, Am Soc Hort Sci, 71, 73. *Prof Exp:* Asst prof hort & asst horticulturist, Univ Ariz, 66-68. *Mem:* AAAS; Am Soc Plant Physiol; Soc Cryobiol. *Res:* Stress physiology; biochemical mechanisms of cold acclimation; freezing injury; cryopresentation of plant germplasm; cryopreservation of Drosophila embryos. *Mailing Add:* 611 Bradfield Hall-SCAS Cornell Univ Ithaca NY 14853. Fax: 607-255-2644; E-Mail: pls4@cornell.edu

STEPTO, ROBERT CHARLES, OBSTETRICS & GYNECOLOGY, PATHOLOGY. *Current Pos:* prof, 79-90, EMER PROF OBSTET & GYNEC, UNIV CHICAGO, 90- *Personal Data:* b Chicago, Ill, Oct 6, 20; m 42; c 2. *Educ:* Northwestern Univ, BS, 41; Howard Univ, MD, 44; Univ Chicago, PhD(path), 48. *Prof Exp:* Asst, Col Med, Univ Chicago, 41; clin instr obstet & gynec, Stritch Sch Med, Loyola Univ Chicago, 50-60; from clin asst prof to clin assoc prof, Univ Ill, 60-70; chmn dept, Chicago Med Sch, 70-74, prof obstet & gynec, 70-75; prof obstet & gynec, Rush Med Col, 75-79; vpres, Chicago Bd Health, 64-88, pres, 88-90. *Concurrent Pos:* USPHS fel, Inst Res, Michael Reese Hosp, 48-50; chmn, Dept Obstet & Gynec, Provident Hosp, 53-63 & Mt Sinai Hosp & Med Ctr, 70-; dir obstet & gynec, Cook County Hosp, 72-75; mem, Food & Drug Adv Comt Obstet & Gynec, 72-76; mem maternall & preschool nutrit comt, Nat Acad Sci, 75; mem, Family Planning Coord Coun, 76. *Mem:* Fel AMA; Am Col Obstet & Gynec; Am Col Surg; hon fel Int Col Surg; Am Fertil Soc. *Res:* Endocrine pathology; oncology; sex hormones influence on tissue synthesis; laser surgery; gynecological/urology. *Mailing Add:* 5201 S Cornell Ave Chicago IL 60615

STERANKA, LARRY RICHARD, NEUROPHARMACOLOGY, AMPHETAMINES. *Current Pos:* DIR, TECHNOL TRANSFER, VANDERBILT UNIV. *Educ:* Vanderbilt Univ, PhD(pharmacol), 76. *Prof Exp:* Sect head, CNS Pharmaceut Inc, Baltimore, 84- *Res:* Opiates. *Mailing Add:* 5311 Williamsburg Rd Brentwood TN 37027. Fax: 410-633-4366

STERBENZ, FRANCIS JOSEPH, BIOCHEMICAL PHARMACOLOGY. *Current Pos:* asst dept head, Bristol-Myers Co, 65-70, dept head biochem, 70-75, sr res investr clin res, 75-85, SR RES INVESTR MED SERV, RES & DEVELOP LAB, BRISTOL-MYERS PROD, HILLSIDE, 85- *Personal Data:* b Queens, NY, May 11, 24; m 56; c 3. *Educ:* St John's Univ, NY, BS, 50, MS, 52; NY Univ, PhD, 57. *Prof Exp:* Asst bacteriologist, New York City Dept Hosps, 51-52; res assoc protozool, St John's Univ, NY, 52-56; instr physiol, NJ Col Med & Dent, 56-58, instr microbiol, 58-59; sr res microbiologist, Squibb Inst Med Res, 59-65. *Mem:* AAAS; Soc Protozool; NY Acad Sci; Am Soc Microbiol; Sigma Xi. *Res:* Bio-availability and biochemistry of analgesic, sedative and related drugs; immunochemistry; mechanisms involved in microbial pathogenicity; chemotherapy; nutritional physiology of microorganisms. *Mailing Add:* 60 Drake Rd Somerset NJ 08873

STERE, ATHLEEN JACOBS, HISTOCHEMISTRY. *Current Pos:* from res asst to asst prof, 63-77, ASSOC PROF BIOL, PA STATE UNIV, UNIVERSITY PARK, 77- *Personal Data:* b Boston, Mass, Feb 1, 21; m 43, Hassell L; c David W Bishop II, Deborah Bishop (Crist) & Robert H. *Educ:* Bryn Mawr Col, AB, 41; Radcliffe Col, MA, 42; Pa State Univ, University Park, PhD(biol), 71. *Honors & Awards:* Christian R & Mary F Lindback Found Award, 80. *Prof Exp:* Res asst immunol, Sch Med, Boston Univ, 44-46; res asst microbiol, Res Div, Albert Einstein Med Ctr, Philadelphia, 59-63. *Mem:* AAAS; Sigma Xi. *Res:* Histochemistry; effect of oxygen deprivation on cellular metabolism in cardiac muscle. *Mailing Add:* Dept Biol Pa State Univ Altoona PA 16601-3760

STERGIS, CHRISTOS GEORGE, PHYSICS. *Current Pos:* physicist, 51-58, chief Space Physics Lab, 59-63, chief aeronomy div, 63-83, SR SCIENTIST, AIR FORCE GEOPHYS LAB, 83- *Personal Data:* b Greece, Dec 19; US citizen; m 48, Grace; c Robin & Heidi. *Educ:* Temple Univ, AB, 42, AM, 43; Mass Inst Technol, PhD(physics), 48. *Prof Exp:* Physicist, Radiation Lab, Mass Inst Technol, 44-45, res asst physics, 45-48; asst prof, Temple Univ, 48-51. *Concurrent Pos:* Hon res asst, Univ Col, Univ London, 64-65; mem, comt high altitude rocket & balloon res, Nat Acad Sci, 63-66, comt Int Quiet Sun Yr, 63-67, comt solar-terrestrial res, 71-78, Aeronomy Panel, Interdept

Comt Atmospheric Sci, 71-77. *Mem:* Am Phys Soc; Am Geophys Union; Sigma Xi. *Res:* Structure of the earth's upper atmosphere by means of rockets and satellites; scattering of solar radiations by the atoms and molecules of the upper atmosphere; solar and atmospheric ultraviolet radiations. *Mailing Add:* 32 Salt Pond Rd Falmouth MA 02540

STERIADE, MIRCEA, NEUROPHYSIOLOGY. *Current Pos:* assoc prof, 68-69, PROF PHYSIOL, FAC MED, UNIV LAVAL, 69- *Personal Data:* b Bucharest, Romania, Aug 20, 24; c 2. *Educ:* Col Culture, Bucharest, BA, 44; Fac Med, Bucharest, MD, 52; Inst Neurol, Acad Sci, Bucharest, DSc(neurophysiol), 55. *Honors & Awards:* Claude Bernard Medal, Univ Paris, 65; Distinguished Scientist Award, Sleep Res Soc, 89. *Prof Exp:* Sr scientist, Inst Neurol, Acad Sci, Bucharest, 55-62, head lab, 62-68. *Mem:* AAAS; Int Brain Res Orgn; Can Physiol Soc; Fr Neurol Soc; Fr Asn Physiol; Soc Neurosci; fel Royal Soc Can. *Res:* Neuronal circuitry of thalamic nuclei and cortical areas; responsiveness of thalamic and cortical relay cells; thalamic and cortical inhibitory mechanisms during sleep and waking; ascending reticular systems; neuronal organization and properties related to shifts in vigilance states; cellular bases of thalamic and cortical oscillations. *Mailing Add:* Dept Physiol Univ Laval Fac Med Quebec PQ G1K 7P4 Can. *Fax:* 418-656-7898; *E-Mail:* mircea.steriade@phs.ulaval.ca

STERLING, ARTHUR MACLEAN, COMBUSTION. *Current Pos:* assoc prof chem eng, La State Univ, 75-80, actg chmn, 87-88, assoc dean, Col Eng, 89-95, PROF DEPT CHEM ENG, LA STATE UNIV, 80-, CHMN, DEPT CHEM ENG, 95- *Personal Data:* b Ronan, Mont, June 21, 38; m 61; c Patrick, Michelle, Kari & Jay. *Educ:* Gonzaga Univ, Spokane, Wash, BS, 61; Univ Wash, Seattle, PhD(chem eng), 69. *Prof Exp:* NIH spec fel, Univ Wash Sch Med, 69-72; wetenschappelijk medewerker, Acad Hosp Leiden, Neth, 72-75. *Concurrent Pos:* Assoc res engr, Boing Co, 66; instr, Dept Urol, Univ Wash Sch Med, 69-71, res assoc, Dept Chem Eng, 71-72; head, Urodynamic Lab, Acad Hosp Leiden, Neth, 73-75. *Mem:* Am Inst Chem Engrs; Combustion Inst. *Res:* Combustion phenomena, especially multi-phase processes; hazardous waste incineration; fluid mechanics and heat transfer; biomechanics; computational fluid mechanics. *Mailing Add:* 110 Chem Eng Bldg La State Univ Baton Rouge LA 70803. *Fax:* 504-388-1476; *E-Mail:* egster@lsuvm.sncc.lsu.edu

STERLING, CLARENCE, botany; deceased, see previous edition for last biography

STERLING, LEON SAMUEL, LOGIC PROGRAMMING, EXPERT SYSTEMS. *Current Pos:* asst prof, 85-89, ASSOC PROF COMPUT SCI, DEPT COMPUT ENG & SCI, CASE WESTERN RES UNIV, 89- *Personal Data:* b Melbourne, Australia, May 17, 55; m 82; c 2. *Educ:* Univ Melbourne, BSc, 76; Australian Nat Univ, PhD(math), 81. *Prof Exp:* Res fel, Dept Artificial Intel, Univ Edinburgh, UK, 80-83; Don Biegun postdoctoral fel, Dept Appl Math & Computer Sci, Weizmann Inst Sci, Israel, 83-85. *Concurrent Pos:* Vis lectr, Computer Sci, Univ Melbourne, 87; dir, Ctr Automation & Intel Systs Res, 89-91. *Mem:* Am Asn Artificial Intel; Asn Comput Mach; Inst Elec & Electronics Engrs; Asn Automated Reasoning. *Res:* Development of a methodology for prolog programming; build expert system tools and expert system applications; explore alternative foundations for artificial intelligence. *Mailing Add:* Dept Comput Eng & Sci Case Western Res Univ Cleveland OH 44106

STERLING, NICHOLAS J, MATHEMATICS. *Current Pos:* Asst prof, 66-70, ASSOC PROF MATH, STATE UNIV NY, BINGHAMTON, 70- *Personal Data:* b Cooperstown, NY, Nov 7, 34; m 62; c 2. *Educ:* Williams Col, BA, 56; Syracuse Univ, MS, 61, PhD(math), 66. *Mem:* Am Math Soc; Sigma Xi. *Res:* Non-associative ring theory. *Mailing Add:* Dept Math State Univ NY Binghamton NY 13901

STERLING, PETER, NEUROANATOMY, NEUROPHYSIOLOGY. *Current Pos:* From asst prof to assoc prof, 69-80, PROF NEUROANAT, SCH MED, UNIV PA, 80- *Personal Data:* b New York, NY, June 28, 40; m 61; c 2. *Educ:* Western Res Univ, PhD(biol), 66. *Honors & Awards:* C Judson Herrick Award, Am Asn Anat, 71. *Concurrent Pos:* NSF fel, Med Sch, Harvard Univ, 66-68; NIH fel, 68-69; NSF grant, Sch Med, Univ Pa, 69-71; NIH grant, 71- *Mem:* Am Asn Anat; Soc Neurosci. *Res:* Relation between form of nerve cells and their physiological functioning, particularly in the visuo-motor system. *Mailing Add:* Dept Neurosci Univ Pa Sch Med Philadelphia PA 19104-6058

STERLING, RAYMOND LESLIE, UNDERGROUND CONSTRUCTION & TUNNELING, ROCK MECHANICS & BUILDING SCIENCE. *Current Pos:* from asst prof to assoc prof civil eng, 77-83, DIR, UNDERGROUND SPACE CTR, UNIV MINN, 77-, SHIMIZU PROF CIVIL ENG, 88- *Personal Data:* b London, Eng, Apr 19, 49; m 70, 83, Janet; c Paul, Juliet, Erika & Zoey. *Educ:* Univ Sheffield, BEng, 70; Univ Minn, Minneapolis, MS, 75, PhD(civil eng), 77. *Honors & Awards:* Appl Rock Mechs Award, US Nat Comm Rock Mech, Nat Res Coun, 93. *Prof Exp:* Construct engr, Egil Wefald & Assoc, Minneapolis, 70-71; Husband & Co, Eng, 71-73 & Setter, Leach & Lindstrom, Inc, Minneapolis, 76-77. *Concurrent Pos:* Prin investr res proj, Univ Minn, 77-; consult archit & eng firms, 77-; lectr, 77-; vchmn, US Nat Comt on Tunneling Technol, chmn, 92-94. *Mem:* Am Soc Civil Eng; Inst Struct Engrs; Nat Soc Prof Engrs; Am Underground Space Asn; Inst Civil Engrs; US Nat Comt on Tunneling Technol. *Res:* Underground construction and underground space use; tunneling; rock mechanics; earth-sheltered building design. *Mailing Add:* PO Box 10348 TTC Ruston LA 71272. *E-Mail:* sterling@maroon.tc.umn.edu

STERLING, REX ELLIOTT, BIOCHEMISTRY. *Current Pos:* RETIRED. *Personal Data:* b Eldorado, Kans, Sept 5, 24; m 48; c 2. *Educ:* Cent Mo State Col, BS, 48; Univ Ark, MS, 49; Univ Colo, PhD(biochem), 53. *Prof Exp:* Clin biochemist, Los Angeles County Gen Hosp, 53-71; from instr to assoc prof, biochem, Univ southern Calif, 53-88; head clin biochemist, Los Angeles County Gen Hosp, 71-88. *Mem:* Am Asn Clin Chem. *Res:* Diabetes and carbohydrate in cataract formation; carbohydrate metabolism and adrenal cortical function; prophyrins and porphyria; clinical biochemical methodology and automation. *Mailing Add:* 454 S Woodward Blvd Pasadena CA 91107

STERLING, THEODOR DAVID, COMPUTER SCIENCE, BIOMETRY. *Current Pos:* prof comput sci & fac interdisciplinary studies, 72-81, UNIV RES PROF, SIMON FRASER UNIV, 81- *Personal Data:* b Vienna, Austria, July 3, 23; nat US & Can; m 48; c 2. *Educ:* Univ Chicago, AB, 49, MA, 53; Tulane Univ, PhD, 55. *Prof Exp:* Instr math, Univ Ala, 54-55, asst prof statist, 55-57; asst prof statist, Mich State Univ, 57-58; asst prof prev med, Col Med, Univ Cincinnati, 58-66, assoc prof biostatist, 61-63, prof & dir med comput ctr, 63-66; prof comput sci, Wash Univ, 66-72. *Concurrent Pos:* Consult, NSF, 67, Environ Protection Agency, 71 & Fed Trade Comn, 72; vis prof statist, Princeton Univ, 78. *Mem:* Am Comput Mach; fel AAAS; fel Am Statist Asn; fel Am Col Epidemiol; Comput Sci Asn Can (pres, 75-80). *Res:* Humanizing effects of automation; errors and foibles in investigations, especially medical; artificial intelligence. *Mailing Add:* Sch Comput Sci Simon Fraser Univ Burnaby BC V5A 1S6 Can

STERLING, WARREN MARTIN, OPTICS, COMPUTER SCIENCES. *Current Pos:* DIR ENG, TERADATA CORP, 82 - *Personal Data:* b Chicago, Ill, Jan 4, 47; m 77; c 1. *Educ:* Univ Ill, BS, 68; Carnegie-Mellon Univ, MS, 70, PhD(elec eng), 74. *Prof Exp:* Engr numerical control, Westinghouse Elec Corp, 68-74; engr elec eng, Xerox Corp, El Segundo, Calif, 74-82. *Concurrent Pos:* Res instr elec eng, Carnegie-Mellon Univ, 72; instr eng, Univ Calif, Los Angeles, 77-82. *Mem:* Inst Elec & Electronics Engrs. *Res:* Design of high performance multi-microprocessor systems for very large relational databases; automated inspection and manufacturing; digital image processing; optical computing. *Mailing Add:* Att/Teradata Corp 100 N Sepulveda Blvd Rm 15-110 El Segundo CA 90245

STERLING, WINFIELD LINCOLN, ENTOMOLOGY. *Current Pos:* RETIRED. *Personal Data:* b Edinburg, Tex, Sept 18, 36; m 61; c 3. *Educ:* Pan Am Col, BA, 62; Tex A&M Univ, MS, 66, PhD(entom), 69. *Prof Exp:* Res assoc entom, Tex A&M Univ, 64-66, asst prof, 69-74, assoc prof, 74-81, prof, 81- *Concurrent Pos:* AID consult, Univ Calif, Berkeley, 74-75; postdoctoral fel, Univ Queensland, 75-76. *Mem:* Entom Soc Am; Entom Soc Can; Am Inst Biol Sci; Sigma Xi. *Res:* Insect ecology, pest management and population dynamics. *Mailing Add:* Dept Entom Tex A&M Univ College Station TX 77843-2475

STERMAN, MELVIN DAVID, COLLOID CHEMISTRY, POLYMER CHEMISTRY. *Personal Data:* b Brooklyn, NY, Sept 19, 30; m 56; c 4. *Educ:* City Col New York, BS, 51; Purdue Univ, PhD(phys chem), 55. *Prof Exp:* Teaching asst, Iowa State Univ, 51-52; from res chemist to sr res chemist, Eastman Kodak Co, 55-62, res assoc, Res Labs, 63-78, res assoc, Mfg Technol Div, 79-93. *Mem:* Am Chem Soc. *Res:* Characterization of polymers by physical chemical techniques; electrical properties of polymers; chemistry of cross-linking of polymers; properties of cross-linked polymer works; polymer adsorption on surfaces; preparation and stability of lyophobic colloids in non-aqueous solvents; electrophoretic mobility of colloidal particles. *Mailing Add:* 51 Braeloch Crossing Penfield NY 14526

STERMAN, SAMUEL, PHYSICAL CHEMISTRY. *Current Pos:* RETIRED. *Personal Data:* b Buffalo, NY, June 6, 18; m 53; c 4. *Educ:* Univ Buffalo, BS, 39. *Honors & Awards:* Award, Soc Plastics Indust, 61. *Prof Exp:* Develop chemist, Nat Carbon Co Div, Union Carbide Corp, 40-45, res chemist, Linde Co Div, 45-50, supvr spec prod develop, Silicone Div, 50-66, asst dir res & develop, Chem & Plastics, 66-73, assoc dir res & develop, Union Carbide Tech Ctr, 73-88. *Mem:* Am Chem Soc; Soc Plastics Indust; AAAS. *Res:* Textile chemicals; protective coatings; water repellants; surface active agents; composites; interface bonding; organofunctional silanes; urethane foam; high temperature polymers; surface chemistry; elastomers; patent management. *Mailing Add:* 56 Commodore Rd Chappaqua NY 10514-2628

STERMER, RAYMOND A, AGRICULTURAL ENGINEERING, OBJECTIVE QUALITY MEASUREMENT USING UNIQUE INSTRUMENTATION. *Current Pos:* Conserv aid, Soil Conserv Serv, USDA, 43-47, agr engr, 50-55, res engr, Agr Mkt Serv, 55-63 & Agr Res Serv, 63-65, invests leader qual eval, Mkt Qual Res Div, 65-73, res agr engr, Grain Qual & Instrumentation Res Group, 73-76, res agr engr, 76-89, RES AGR ENGR, TEX AGR EXP STA, TEX A&M UNIV, USDA, 89- *Personal Data:* b Barclay, Tex, July 22, 24; m 48; Gladys Hoelscher; c Linda G & Nancy L. *Educ:* Tex A&M Univ, BS, 50, MS, 58, PhD, 71. *Concurrent Pos:* Consult agr eng. *Mem:* Am Soc Agr Engrs; Sigma Xi. *Res:* Instruments or techniques for rapid, objective measurement of quality of agricultural products; biomedical radio telemetry for monitoring physiological parameters in cattle; control of bacteria in meats; measurement and control of contaminants in soil and water using gamma irradiation; image analysis and environmental control; experiments in radiation systems. *Mailing Add:* Tex Agr Exp Sta Agr Eng Bldg College Station TX 77843-2117. *E-Mail:* ras0447@acs.tamu.edu

STERMER, ROBERT L, JR, ELECTRONICS ENGINEERING. *Current Pos:* PHYSICIST, ELECTRONICS MAT, LANGLEY RES CTR, NASA, 60- *Personal Data:* b Wilmington, Del, Jan 27, 35; m 57; c 4. *Educ:* Univ Va, BEE, 60, MEE, 65; Duke Univ, PhD(elec eng), 71. *Concurrent Pos:* Lectr, George Washington Univ, 73- *Mem:* Inst Elec & Electronics Engrs; Am Phys Soc; Sigma Xi. *Res:* Development of electronic device technology for spacecraft; early work in hybrid circuits using film technology and semiconductor devices; development of spacecraft memory systems using bubble technology. *Mailing Add:* Three Drammen Ct Williamsburg VA 23188

STERMITZ, FRANK R, ORGANIC CHEMISTRY. *Current Pos:* assoc prof, 67-69, CENTENNIAL PROF CHEM, COLO STATE UNIV, 69- *Personal Data:* b Thermopolis, Wyo, Dec 3, 28; m 54; c 5. *Educ:* Univ Notre Dame, BS, 50; Univ Colo, MS, 51, PhD(chem), 58. *Prof Exp:* Res chemist, Merck & Co, Inc, NJ, 51-53 & Lawrence Radiation Lab, Univ Calif, Berkeley, 58-61; from asst prof to assoc prof chem, Utah State Univ, 61-67. *Concurrent Pos:* USPHS res career develop award, 63-67; vpres, Elars Biores Labs, 74-76; Fulbright sr fel, Argentina, 73; Fogarty sr fel, Peru, 82. *Mem:* Am Chem Soc; Am Soc Pharmacog; Phytochem Soc NAm; Int Soc Chem Ecol; AAAS. *Res:* Alkaloid and other natural product isolation, structure proof and biosynthesis; medicinal chemistry; ecology; chemotaxonomy. *Mailing Add:* Dept Chem Colo State Univ Ft Collins CO 80523-1872. *Fax:* 970-491-5610; *E-Mail:* frslab@tamar.colostate.edu

STERN, ALBERT VICTOR, ASTRONOMY, SYSTEMS ENGINEERING. *Current Pos:* RETIRED. *Personal Data:* b New York, NY, Apr 26, 23; div; c 2. *Educ:* Univ Calif, Berkeley, AB, 47, PhD(astron), 50. *Prof Exp:* Sect head digital subsysts, Hughes Aircraft Co, Fullerton, 54-57, sr scientist, 57-59, lab mgr adv systs, 59-66, asst div mgr, 66-69, chief scientist, Syst Div, 69-73, prog mgr, Missile Systs Group, Canoga Park, 73-76, prog mgr, Radar Systs Group, Culver City, 76-79. *Res:* Celestial mechanics; weapons systems analysis; systems engineering. *Mailing Add:* 279 Ravenna Dr Long Beach CA 90803

STERN, ARTHUR IRVING, PLANT PHYSIOLOGY, PHOTOBIOLOGY. *Current Pos:* from asst prof to assoc prof, 65-88, PROF BIOL, UNIV MASS, AMHERST, 89- *Personal Data:* b New York, NY, Dec 8, 30; m 62; c 3. *Educ:* City Col New York, BS, 53; Brandeis Univ, PhD(biol), 62. *Prof Exp:* NIH fel develop biol, Brandeis Univ, 62-63; Kettering fel photosynthesis, Weizmann Inst, 63-64, USPHS fel, 64-65. *Concurrent Pos:* Secy-treas, NE sect, Am Soc Plant Physiol, 78-91. *Mem:* Sigma Xi; Am Soc Plant Physiol; Am Soc Photobiol. *Res:* Chloroplast structure and function; chloroplast development; photophosphorylation; proton excretion in plant protoplasts and intact cells; plasma membrane redox. *Mailing Add:* 119 Huntington Rd Hadley MA 01035-9610. *Fax:* 413-545-3243; *E-Mail:* astern@bio.umass.edu

STERN, ARTHUR PAUL, ELECTRONICS ENGINEERING. *Current Pos:* PRES, EASTERN BEVERLY HILLS CORP, 91- *Personal Data:* b Budapest, Hungary, July 20, 25; nat US; m 52, Edith M Samuel; c Daniel, Claude & Jacqueline. *Educ:* Univ Lausanne, BS, 46; Swiss Fed Inst Technol, dipl, 48; Syracuse Univ, MEE, 56. *Honors & Awards:* Centennial Medal, Inst Elect & Electronics Engrs, 84. *Prof Exp:* Res engr, Jaeger, Inc, Switz, 48-50; instr, Swiss Fed Inst Technol, 50-51; res engr electronics lab, Gen Elec Co, 51-52, proj leader semiconductor appins, 52-54, mgr adv circuits, 54-57, mgr electronic devices & applications lab, 57-61; dir eng, Electronics Div, Martin Marietta Corp, Md, 61-64; dir opers, Defense Systs Div, Bunker-Ramo Corp, 64-66; vpres & gen mgr, Magnavox Res Labs, Magnavox Advan Prod & Systs Co, 66-70, vpres & gen mgr, Advan Prod Div, 70-79, pres, 80-90, vchmn, Magnavox Electronic Systs Co, 87-90. *Concurrent Pos:* Non-res staff mem, Mass Inst Technol, 56-59; mem, Int Solid State Circuits Conf, 54-68, chmn, 59-60; chmn, numerous prof comts. *Mem:* Fel Inst Elec & Electronics Engrs (secy, 72, treas, 73, vpres 74, pres, 75); Sigma Xi; fel AAAS. *Res:* Applications of modern solid state physics; design, application and electronic circuit behavior of solid state electronic components; solid state circuit engineering; synthesis of electronic systems - defense, navigation; author of 20 publications and granted 12 patents. *Mailing Add:* 606 N Oakhurst Dr Beverly Hills CA 90210-3531. *Fax:* 310-278-3251

STERN, DANIEL HENRY, LIMNOLOGY, ECOLOGY. *Current Pos:* from asst prof to assoc prof, 69-75, chmn dept, 86-92, PROF BIOL & NURSING, UNIV MO, KANSAS CITY, 75- *Personal Data:* b Richmond, Va, June 18, 34; m 63, 83, Ann Binswanger; c Jeffrey, Brian, John & Alexander. *Educ:* Univ Richmond, BS, 55, MS, 59; Univ Ill, PhD(zool), 64. *Prof Exp:* Asst prof biol, Tenn Technol Univ, 64-66 & La State Univ, New Orleans, 66-69. *Mem:* Ecol Soc Am; Am Soc Limnol & Oceanog; Phycol Soc Am; Micros Soc Am; NAm Benthological Soc. *Res:* Ecology of aquatic organisms; invertebrate ecology; applied ecology and environmental impacts; asbestos analysis. *Mailing Add:* Sch Biol Sci Univ Mo Kansas City MO 64110-2499. *Fax:* 816-235-5158

STERN, DAVID P, SPACE PHYSICS. *Current Pos:* Nat Acad Sci-Nat Res Coun resident res assoc, 61-63, PHYSICIST, GODDARD SPACE FLIGHT CTR, NASA, 63- *Personal Data:* b Decin, Czech, Dec 17, 31; US citizen; m 61, Audrey Jackson; c Ilana, Oren & Allon. *Educ:* Hebrew Univ, Israel, MSc, 55; Israel Inst Technol, DSc(physics), 59. *Prof Exp:* Res assoc physics, Univ Md, 59-61. *Concurrent Pos:* Chmn, AGU Comt, Hist Geophysics, 82-88. *Mem:* Am Phys Soc; Am Geophys Union. *Res:* Geomagnetic field, its structure, configuration and dynamics; geomagnetic plasmas and particle motion; theory of magnetospheric electric fields; field-aligned currents and associated processes. *Mailing Add:* Code 695 Goddard Space Flight Ctr NASA Greenbelt MD 20771. *Fax:* 301-286-1683

STERN, EDWARD ABRAHAM, CONDENSED MATTER SCIENCE. *Current Pos:* PROF PHYSICS, UNIV WASH, 66- *Personal Data:* b Detroit, Mich, Sept 19, 30; m 55, Sylvia R Sidell; c Hilary, Shari & Miri. *Educ:* Calif Inst Technol, BS, 51, PhD(physics), 55. *Honors & Awards:* Warren Diffraction Physics Award, Am Crystal Asn, 79. *Prof Exp:* Res fel solid state physics, Calif Inst Technol, 55-57; from asst prof to prof, Univ Md, 57-66. *Concurrent Pos:* Guggenheim fel, 63-64; NSF sr res fel, 70-71; Fulbright fel, 86-87. *Mem:* Fel Am Phys Soc; fel AAAS. *Res:* Electronic structure of metals and alloys; collective effects; structural phase transition; atomic structure of amorphous and biological matter; ferromagnetism. *Mailing Add:* Dept Physics Box 351560 Univ Wash Seattle WA 98195. *Fax:* 206-685-0635; *E-Mail:* stern@dirac.phys.washington.edu

STERN, ELIZABETH KAY, general academic pediatrics, for more information see previous edition

STERN, ERIC WOLFGANG, CHEMISTRY. *Current Pos:* CONSULT, 96- *Personal Data:* b Vienna, Austria, Nov 4, 30; nat US; m 60; c 1. *Educ:* Syracuse Univ, BS, 51; Northwestern Univ, PhD(chem), 54. *Prof Exp:* Res chemist, Texaco, Inc, 54-57; res chemist, M W Kellogg Co Div, Pullman, Inc, NJ, 58-63, res assoc, 63-70; sect head res & develop, Englehard Corp, 70-87, sr res assoc, 87-96. *Concurrent Pos:* Co-adj prof, Rutgers Univ, 65-74; res assoc, Seton Hall Univ, 96- *Mem:* AAAS; Am Chem Soc; NAm Catalysis Soc; NY Acad Sci; Royal Chem Soc; Sigma Xi. *Res:* Heterogeneous and homogeneous catalysis; coordination chemistry; reaction mechanisms; molecular structure; catalyst characterization; medical application of precious metals; organometallics. *Mailing Add:* 234 Oak Tree Rd Mountainside NJ 07092

STERN, ERNEST, SOLID STATE PHYSICS, ACOUSTICS. *Current Pos:* staff mem, 64-68, group leader acoustics, 68-82, ASSOC HEAD, SOLID STATE DIV, LINCOLN LAB, MASS INST TECHNOL, 82- *Personal Data:* b Wetter, Ger, June 5, 28; US citizen; m 53; c 4. *Educ:* Columbia Univ, BS, 53. *Honors & Awards:* Fel, Inst Elec & Electronics Engrs. *Prof Exp:* Sr engr, Sperry Gyroscope Co, 55-57; mem staff, Electronics Lab, Gen Elec Co, 58-62, vpres, Microwave Chem Lab, 62-64. *Concurrent Pos:* Consult, US Dept Defense. *Mem:* Sigma Xi; Am Phys Soc. *Res:* Gyromagnetic phenomena; microwave frequencies; nonlinear magnetic phenomena; surface acoustics and acousto-electric phenomena; components and devices; x-ray lithography; superconducting devices; electronic engineering. *Mailing Add:* 31 Oxbow Rd Concord MA 01742

STERN, FRANK, LOW-DIMENSIONAL ELECTRON SYSTEMS. *Current Pos:* Zurich Res Lab, T J Watson Res Ctr, 65-66, mgr semiconductor electronic properties, 73-81, mgr device theory & modeling, 85- 90, res staff mem, IBM Res Div, 62-93, EMER RES STAFF MEM, T J WATSON RES CTR, 93- *Personal Data:* b Koblenz, Ger, Sept 15, 28; nat US; m 55, Shayne Nemerson; c David & Linda. *Educ:* Union Col, NY, BS, 49; Princeton Univ, PhD(physics), 55. *Honors & Awards:* John Price Wetherill Medal, Franklin Inst, 81; Jack A Morton Award, Inst Elec & Electronics Engrs, 88; Res Award for Sr US Scientists, Alexander von Humboldt, Found, 93. *Prof Exp:* Physicist, US Naval Ord Lab, Md, 53-62. *Concurrent Pos:* Lectr, Univ Md, 55-58, part-time prof, 59-62; chmn, Organizing Comt, Electron Properties Two-Dimensional Systs Int Conf, New London, NH, 81; vis scientist, Cavendish Lab, Cambridge, 71 & 95, Max Planck Inst Fur Festkorperforschung, 80, 88 & 93-96; mem at large, Exec Comt, Am Phys Soc Div Condensed Matter Physics, 87-90; Walter Schottlay Inst, Tech Univ Munich, 95 & 96. *Mem:* Fel Am Phys Soc; Sigma Xi. *Res:* Cohesive energy of iron; semiconductors; injection lasers; optical properties of solids; quantum effects and transport in low dimensional electron systems. *Mailing Add:* IBM Res Div T J Watson Res Ctr Yorktown Heights NY 10598-0218. *Fax:* 914-945-2141

STERN, HERBERT, CELL BIOLOGY. *Current Pos:* chmn dept, 67-76, EMER PROF BIOL, UNIV CALIF, SAN DIEGO, 65- *Personal Data:* b Can, Dec 22, 18; m 53; c 3. *Educ:* McGill Univ, BSc, 40, MSc, 42, PhD, 45. *Hon Degrees:* DSc, McGill Univ. *Prof Exp:* Royal Soc Can fel, Univ Calif, 46-48; lectr cell physiol, Med Sch, Univ Witwatersrand, 48-49; assoc, Rockefeller Inst Med Res, 49-55; head biochem cytol, Plant Res Inst, Can Dept Agr, 55-60; prof bot, Univ Ill, Urbana, 60-65. *Concurrent Pos:* Mem, Develop Biol Panel, NSF; mem, Cell Biol Panel, NIH; mem, Spec Subcomt Cellular & Subcellular Struct & Function, Nat Acad Sci. *Mem:* Am Soc Plant Physiol; Soc Develop Biol (pres, 64-65); Am Soc Cell Biol; fel Am Soc Biol Chem; Genetics Soc Am; Sigma Xi. *Res:* Cell biology and biochemistry. *Mailing Add:* Dept Biol B-022 Box 109 Univ Calif San Diego La Jolla CA 92093-0322. *Fax:* 619-534-0053

STERN, IRVING B, DENTISTRY, CELL BIOLOGY. *Current Pos:* RETIRED. *Personal Data:* b New York, NY, Sept 12, 20; m, Charlotte Sapsowitz; c Andrea (White) & Wendy (Russell). *Educ:* City Col New York, BS, 41; NY Univ, DDS, 46; Columbia Univ, cert, 56. *Prof Exp:* Lectr periodont, Sch Dent, Univ Wash, 59-60, from asst prof to prof, 60-75; prof periodont & chmn dept, Sch Dent Med, Tufts Univ, 75-77. *Concurrent Pos:* Spec res fel anat, Sch Med, Univ Wash, 61-62; USPHS grant. *Mem:* AAAS; Am Dent Asn; Am Acad Periodont; Am Soc Cell Biol; Int Asn Dent Res. *Res:* Ultrastructure and biology of oral epithelium and epithelial derivatives; ultrastructure of dento-gingival junction and cementum; keratinization. *Mailing Add:* 247 84th Ave NE Medina WA 98039

STERN, JACK TUTEUR, JR, BIOMECHANICS, HUMAN EVOLUTION. *Current Pos:* assoc prof, 74-81, PROF ANAT, STATE UNIV NY STONY BROOK, 81-, CHAIR, 90- *Personal Data:* b Chicago, Ill, Jan 18, 42; m 67; c 2. *Educ:* Univ Chicago, PhD(anat), 69. *Prof Exp:* Instr anat, Univ Chicago, 69-70, asst prof, 70-74. *Concurrent Pos:* Assoc ed, Anat Rec, 72-80, Am J Phys Anthrop, 81-87; USPHS res career develop award, 73. *Mem:* Am Asn Phys Anthrop; Am Asn Anat; AAAS; Sigma Xi. *Res:* Functional anatomy of primates; evolution of erect posture; biomechanics and evolution of muscles. *Mailing Add:* Dept Anat Sci Health Sci Ctr Univ NY Stony Brook NY 11794-8081. *Fax:* 516-444-3947; *E-Mail:* jstern@epo.som.sunysb.edu

STERN, JOHN HANUS, PHYSICAL CHEMISTRY. *Current Pos:* From asst prof to assoc prof, 58-67, PROF CHEM, CALIF STATE UNIV, LONG BEACH, 67- *Personal Data:* b Brno, Czech, May 21, 28; nat US; m 49. *Educ:* Univ Calif, BS, 53; Univ Wash, MS, 54, PhD(chem), 58. *Concurrent Pos:* Am Chem Soc-Petrol Res Found int fac fel, Univ Florence, 64-65; vis prof, Hebrew Univ, Jerusalem, 71-72, Univ London, 79-80. *Mem:* Am Chem Soc. *Res:* Thermodynamics of electrolytes and non-electrolytes in aqueous solutions. *Mailing Add:* 7151 Carlton Ave Westminster CA 92683

STERN, JOSEPH AARON, food science & technology, for more information see previous edition

STERN, JUDITH S, NUTRITION. *Current Pos:* from asst prof to assoc prof, 75-82, DIR, FOOD INTAKE LAB, UNIV CALIF, DAVIS, 80-, PROF NUTRIT, 82-, PROF, DIV CLIN NUTRIT & METAB, DEPT INT MED, 86- *Personal Data:* b Brooklyn, NY, Apr 25, 43; m 64, Richard C; c Daniel. *Educ:* Cornell Univ, BS, 64; Harvard Univ, MS, 66, ScD, 70. *Honors & Awards:* H Brooks James Mem Lectr, NC State Univ, 84; Lydia Roberts Mem Lectr, Univ Chicago, 92; Egyptian Med Syndicate Medal, 95. *Prof Exp:* From res assoc to asst prof, Rockefeller Univ, 69-74. *Concurrent Pos:* Mem, Nutrit Comt, Med Ctr, Sch Med, Univ Calif, Davis, 79-84 & co-dir, Core Lab, Clin Nutrit Res Unit, 85-, Human Nutrit Bd Sci Counr, NIH, 88 & Obesity Task Force, Nat Inst Diabetes & Digestive & Kidney Dis, 95-; mem, Nutrit Labeling Comt, Inst Med-Nat Acad Sci, 89-90, chair, Comt Develop Criteria Eval Outcomes Approaches Prev & Treat Obesity, 93-94. *Mem:* Inst Med-Nat Acad Sci; Am Inst Nutrit; Am Dietetic Asn; AAAS; Sigma Xi; Am Physiol Soc; Am Soc Clin Nutrit (vpres, 95-96, pres, 96-97); NAm Asn Study Obesity (secy, 84-88, vpres, 90-91, pres elect, 91-92, pres, 92-93); Inst Food Technologists; Int Asn Study Obesity (treas, 93-); Am Diabetes Asn; Geront Soc Am; NY Acad Sci; Sigma Xi; Soc Ingestive Behav. *Res:* Studies of some critical factors involved in the development of obesity which include adipose cellularity, food intake, diet composition, exercise, hyperinsulinemia and tissue resistance in muscle and adipose. *Mailing Add:* Dept Nutrit Univ Calif Rm 3150 B Meyer Hall Davis CA 95616

STERN, KINGSLEY ROWLAND, TAXONOMIC BOTANY. *Current Pos:* from asst prof to assoc prof, 59-68, PROF BOT, CALIF STATE UNIV, CHICO, 68- *Personal Data:* b Port Elizabeth, SAfrica, Oct 30, 27; nat US; m 56; c 2. *Educ:* Wheaton Col, Ill, BS, 49; Univ Mich, MA, 50; Univ Minn, PhD(bot), 59. *Prof Exp:* Asst, Univ Mich, 49-51 & Univ Ill, 54-55; asst, Univ Minn, 55-56 & 57-58, instr bot, 58-59; instr biol, Hamline Univ, 57-58. *Concurrent Pos:* NSF res grants, 59, 60 & 63-71; consult, Bot Field Surveys; vis prof, Univ Hawaii, 87. *Mem:* Am Soc Plant Taxon; Bot Soc Am. *Res:* Taxonomy of vascular plants, especially pollen grains, anatomy, cytology and morphogenesis. *Mailing Add:* One Spinnaker Way Chico CA 95926

STERN, KURT, PATHOLOGY, CANCER. *Current Pos:* prof & pathologist, Res & Educ Hosp, 60-70, EMER PROF PATH, UNIV ILL COL MED, 70-; RES PROF, LAUTENBERG CTR IMMUNOL, HEBREW UNIV-HADASSAH MED SCH, JERUSALEM, 81- *Personal Data:* b Vienna, Austria, Apr 3, 09; nat US; wid; c Elsa L, Josey J & David M. *Educ:* Univ Vienna, MD, 33. *Honors & Awards:* John Elliott Mem Award, Am Asn Blood Banks, 72. *Prof Exp:* Instr biochem, Inst Med Chem, Univ Vienna, 30-33, res assoc, 33-38; jr physician, State Inst Study & Treatment Malignant Dis, Buffalo, 43-45; asst pathologist, Mt Sinai Hosp, 45-48, from asst to assoc dir, Mt Sinai Med Res Found, 48-60, dir, Blood Ctr, 50-60. *Concurrent Pos:* Res fel, NY Cancer Hosp & Div Cancer, Bellevue Hosp, 39-40; from assoc to assoc prof, Chicago Med Sch, 49-60; sci ed, Bull Am Asn Blood Banks, 60; prof life sci, Bar-Ilan Univ, Israel, 69-80. *Mem:* Fel Am Soc Clin Path; Soc Exp Biol & Med; Am Soc Exp Path; Am Asn Immunol; Am Asn Cancer Res. *Res:* Experimental cancer research; immunology; experimental pathology; blood groups and immunohematology; physiopathology of reticulo-endothelial system. *Mailing Add:* Lautenberg Ctr Immunol Hebrew Univ Hadassah Med Sch POB 12272 Jerusalem 91120 Israel. *E-Mail:* kstern@md2.huji.oc.il

STERN, KURT HEINZ, PHYSICAL INORGANIC CHEMISTRY, HIGH TEMPERATURE ELECTROCHEMISTRY. *Current Pos:* RETIRED. *Personal Data:* b Vienna, Austria, Dec 26, 26; nat US; m 60, Faith Bueltmann; c Karen R & Alan J. *Educ:* Drew Univ, AB, 48; Univ Mich, MS, 50; Clark Univ, PhD(chem), 53. *Honors & Awards:* Turner Prize, Electrochem Soc, 51, Blum Award, 71. *Prof Exp:* Asst, Univ Mich, 50; instr chem, Clark Univ, 50-52; from instr to assoc prof, Univ Ark, 52-60; res chemist, Electrochem Sect, Nat Bur Stand, 60-68; res chemist, Inorg & Electrochem Br, 74-90, consult, 90-92. *Concurrent Pos:* Res assoc, Nat Acad Sci-Nat Res Coun, 59-60; mem fac, Grad Sch, NIH, 63-88. *Mem:* Am Chem Soc; Electrochem Soc; Royal Soc Chem; fel AAAS. *Res:* High temperature electrochemistry; molten salts; vaporization and thermal decomposition of inorganic salts; refactory coating. *Mailing Add:* Surface Chem Br Naval Res Lab Washington DC 20375-5000

STERN, LEO, PERINATAL BIOLOGY, CLINICAL PHARMACOLOGY. *Current Pos:* PROF PEDIAT & CHMN DEPT, BROWN UNIV, 73- *Personal Data:* b Montreal, Que, Jan 20, 31; m 55; c 4. *Educ:* McGill Univ, BSc, 51; Univ Man, MD, 56; FRCPS(C), 64; Brown Univ, MA, 74. *Hon Degrees:* Dr, Univ Nancy, 77. *Honors & Awards:* Queen Elizabeth II Res Scientist Award, 66. *Prof Exp:* Demonstr, McGill Univ, 62-66, lectr, 66-67, from asst prof to assoc prof pediat, 67-73. *Concurrent Pos:* Mead Johnson res fel, Karolinska Inst, Sweden, 58-59; Nat Res Coun Can med res fel, 59-60; Queen Elizabeth II scientist for res in dis of children, McGill Univ, 66-72; mem, Comn Study Perinatal Mortality, Prov of Que, 67-73; dir, Dept Newborn Med, Montreal Childrens Hosp, 69-73; pediatrician-in-chief, RI Hosp, 73- *Mem:* Perinatal Res Soc; Soc Pediat Res; Am Pediat Soc; Am Soc Clin Nutrit; Am Soc Clin Pharmacol & Therapeut. *Res:* Development pharmacology; perinatal biology, adaptation to extrauterine life, thermoregulation and bilirubin metabolism in the new born, respiratory adaptation in the normal and abnormal newborn infant. *Mailing Add:* RI Hosp 202 President Ave Providence RI 02906

STERN, MARSHALL DANA, RUMEN MICROBIOLOGY, PROTEIN NUTRITION. *Current Pos:* ASSOC PROF RUMINANT NUTRIT, UNIV MINN, ST PAUL, 81- *Personal Data:* b New York, NY, Mar 18, 49; m 74; c 1. *Educ:* State Univ NY, Farmingdale, AAS, 70; Cornell Univ, BS, 72; Univ RI, MS, 75; Univ Maine, PhD(animal nutrit), 77. *Prof Exp:* Res assoc fel, Univ Wis-Madison, 77-81. *Concurrent Pos:* Ed, J Animal Sci, 82-84. *Mem:* Am Soc Animal Sci; Am Dairy Sci Asn; Nutrit Soc. *Res:* Protein (amino acid) requirements and nitrogen utilization in high producing dairy cows; metabolism of nutrients in gastro intestinal tract of ruminants; factors affecting fermentation and microbiol populations in the rumen. *Mailing Add:* Dept Animal Sci 122 Peters Hall Univ Minn St Paul 1404 Gortner Ave St Paul MN 55108-6160

STERN, MARTIN, ORAL SURGERY. *Current Pos:* INSTR, NAVAL HOSP, SAN DIEGO, 94- *Personal Data:* b New York, NY, Jan 9, 33; m 69; c 1. *Educ:* Harvard Univ, DMD, 56; Am Bd Oral Surg, dipl, 63. *Prof Exp:* Attend surgeon in chg oral surg, Long Island Jewish Med Ctr/Queens Hosp Ctr Affiliation, 67-94, assoc dir dent, 72-94; prof oral surg, Sch Dent Med, State Univ NY Stony Brook, 71-94. *Concurrent Pos:* Asst clin prof, Sch Dent, Columbia Univ, 68-70. *Mem:* Am Dent Asn; Am Soc Oral Surg. *Mailing Add:* 4129 Pindar Way Oceanside CA 92056

STERN, MARVIN, PSYCHIATRY. *Current Pos:* from fel to prof psychiat, Univ Hosp, 40-79, Menas S Gregory prof psychiat, 79-86, exec chmn dept, 76-86, attend psychiatrist, 52-95, prof, 86-95, EMER PROF, UNIV HOSP, 95- *Personal Data:* b New York, NY, Jan 6, 16; m 42, Libby Rifkin; c Carol S, Robert M & Theodore A. *Educ:* City Col NY, BS, 35; NY Univ, MD, 39. *Concurrent Pos:* Consult, US Vet Admin Regional Off, Brooklyn, 51-66, Manhattan Vet Admin Hosp, 66-, & Brookdale Hosp, Brooklyn, 76-94, emer consult, 94-; assoc vis neuropsychiatrist, Bellevue Hosp, 52-62, vis neuropsychiatrist, 62- *Mem:* Psychosom Soc; Am Psychopath Asn; Am Psychiat Asn. *Res:* Psychosomatic medicine; altered brain function in organic disease. *Mailing Add:* 300 E 33rd St New York NY 10016

STERN, MELVIN ERNEST, HYDRODYNAMICS. *Current Pos:* PROF OCEANOG, GRAD SCH, UNIV RI, 64- *Personal Data:* b New York, NY, Jan 22, 29; m 56; c 2. *Educ:* Cooper Union, BEE, 50; Ill Inst Technol, MS, 51; Mass Inst Technol, PhD(meteorol), 56. *Prof Exp:* From res assoc meteorol to physicist, Woods Hole Oceanog Inst, 51-64. *Concurrent Pos:* Guggenheim fel, 70-71. *Mem:* Fel Am Acad Arts & Sci, 75. *Res:* Oceanic circulation and turbulence; non-linear stability theory. *Mailing Add:* Dept Oceanog Fla State Univ Tallahassee FL 32306

STERN, MICHELE SUCHARD, LIMNOLOGY, AQUATIC ECOLOGY. *Current Pos:* ENVIRON SCIENTIST, BLACK & VEATCH, 92- *Personal Data:* b Chicago, Ill, Mar 17, 43; div; c Alexander. *Educ:* Univ Ill, Urbana, BS, 64; Tenn Technol Univ, MS, 66; Tulane Univ, PhD(biol), 69. *Prof Exp:* Asst prof biol, Univ Mo, Kansas City, 69-82, assoc prof, 85-92. *Concurrent Pos:* Capt & nuclear med sci officer, US Army, Ft Sam, Houston, Tex, 82-85. *Mem:* AAAS; Am Chem Soc; Ecol Soc Am; Am Soc Limnol & Oceanog; Soc Environ Toxicol & Chem; NAm Benthological Soc. *Res:* Environmental impact assessments and NEPA documentation; performance of ecological risk assessments and toxicity testing of various types of effluents and sediments; water pollution; aquatic toxicology; ecology; environmental science. *Mailing Add:* Black & Veatch 11401 Lamar Overland Park MO 66211

STERN, MIKLOS, FIBER-OPTIC COMMUNICATIONS, DIGITAL DATA COMMUNICATION. *Current Pos:* Mem tech staff, Bell Tel Labs, 82-84, mem tech staff, 84-91, SR SCIENTIST, SYMBOL TECHNOL, BELL COMMUN RES, 91- *Personal Data:* b Budapest, Hungary, May 31, 57; US citizen. *Educ:* Polytech Inst NY, BS, 81; Columbia Univ, MS, 82, PhD(elec eng), 90. *Concurrent Pos:* Consult, Start Up Co Radio Commun. *Mem:* Inst Elec & Electronics Engrs. *Res:* High-speed digital fiber-optic communication systems; gigabit computer system based on Sonet/ATM protocols; optoelectronics; radio communications. *Mailing Add:* Symbol Tech Inc 116 Wilbur Pl Bohemia NY 11716. *Fax:* 516-244-4618

STERN, MILTON, CHEMICAL ENGINEERING, PHYSICAL METALLURGY. *Current Pos:* DIR MERGERS & ACQUISITIONS, STERN & ASSOC, 84- *Personal Data:* b Boston, Mass, Apr 20, 27; m 49; c 3. *Educ:* Northeastern Univ, BS, 49; Mass Inst Technol, MS, 50, PhD(phys metall, corrosion), 52. *Honors & Awards:* Willis R Whitney Award, 63. *Prof*

Exp: Res scientist, Metals Div, Union Carbide Corp, NY, 54-60, mgr res, Linde Div, Ind, 60-65, mgr mat res, NY, 65-67, mgr corp res 67, dir technol, Mat Systs Div, 67-68, vpres, Electronics Div, 68-69, exec vpres, Mining & Metals Div, 69-73; vpres, Kennecott Corp, 73-76, sr vpres, 76-78, exec vpres, 78-82; vchmn, Stauffer Chem Co, 83-86. *Mem:* Nat Asn Corrosion Eng; Electrochem Soc; Am Inst Mining, Metall & Petrol Eng. *Res:* Electrochemistry; corrosion; kinetics; plasma technology; crystal growth; welding. *Mailing Add:* 24 Cayman Pl Palm Beach Gardens FL 33418-8047

STERN, MORRIS, COMPUTATIONAL MECHANICS, SOLID MECHANICS. *Current Pos:* assoc prof, 66-80, PROF ENG MECH, UNIV TEX, AUSTIN, 80- *Personal Data:* b St Louis, Mo, Nov 26, 30; m 52; c 2. *Educ:* Wash Univ, BS, 52; Univ Ill, MS, 57, PhD(eng mech), 62. *Prof Exp:* Teaching & res assoc theoret appl mech, Univ Ill, 56, asst prof, 62-66. *Concurrent Pos:* Vis asst prof, Univ Colo, 65-66. *Mem:* Am Soc Eng Sci; Am Acad Mech. *Res:* Solid mechanics; continuum mechanics; computational fracture mechanics; boundary element methods. *Mailing Add:* 6820 Cypress Point N No 22 Austin TX 78746

STERN, PAULA HELENE, PHARMACOLOGY. *Current Pos:* from asst prof to assoc prof, 66-77, PROF PHARMACOL, MED SCH, NORTHWESTERN UNIV, 77- *Personal Data:* b New Brunswick, NJ, Jan 20, 38; m 59. *Educ:* Univ Rochester, BA, 59; Univ Cincinnati, MS, 61; Univ Mich, PhD(pharmacol), 63. *Prof Exp:* Instr pharmacol, Univ Mich, 65-66. *Concurrent Pos:* Fel pharmacol, Rochester Univ, 63-64 & Marine Biol Lab, Woods Hole, Mass, 64; res career develop award, NIH; consult, Food & Drug Admin; Am Inst Biol Sci/NASA mem, Gen Med B Study Sect, NIH. *Mem:* Am Soc Pharmacol & Exp Therapeut; Endocrine Soc; Asn Women Sci; Am Soc Bone & Mineral Res; Soc Exp Biol & Med. *Res:* Calcium metabolism; mechanisms of action of drugs and hormones on bone. *Mailing Add:* Dept Pharmacol Northwestern Univ Med Sch 303 E Chicago Ave Chicago IL 60611-3072. *Fax:* 312-503-5349

STERN, RAUL A(RISTIDE), PLASMA PHYSICS, GAS DYNAMICS. *Current Pos:* prof astrophys sci & phys, 78-96, PROF PHYSICS, UNIV COLO, BOULDER, 96- *Personal Data:* b Bucharest, Romania, Dec 26, 28; US citizen; m 53; c 2. *Educ:* Univ Wis, BS, 52, MS, 53; Univ Calif, Berkeley, PhD(aeronaut sci), 59. *Prof Exp:* Res assoc, Univ Calif, Berkeley, 59-60; mem tech staff, Bell Labs, 60-81. *Concurrent Pos:* Vis prof, New York Univ, 69-70, Univ Calif, Los Angeles, 77-78, Ctr Res Plasma Physics, Fed Polytech Sch, Lausanne, Switz, 82-83, Univ Calif, Irvine, 85 & Univ Provence, Marseille, France, 94; vis res physicist, Univ Calif, Irvine, 75-, Ctr Res Plasma Physics, 83-, Ecole Polytechnique, Palaiseau, France, 86-; assoc ed, Physics of Fluids, 84-87; Sherman Fairchild Found distinguished scholar, Calif Inst Technol, 86. *Mem:* Fel Am Phys Soc. *Res:* Plasma waves, instabilities, transport, turbulence; shock and detonation waves; gas discharge physics; microwave and laser interactions with plasmas; diagnostics; nonlinear plasma properties; negative ion plasmas; laser fluorescence techniques. *Mailing Add:* Dept Physics Univ Colo Boulder CO 80309

STERN, RICHARD, ACOUSTICS. *Current Pos:* assoc dir res, 84-94, ASSOC DIR OCEAN & ATMOSPHERIC SCI, APPL RES LAB, PA STATE UNIV, 94- *Personal Data:* b Paterson, NJ, Nov 27, 29; m 58, 80; c William D, Alan W & Evan G. *Educ:* Univ Calif, Los Angeles, BA, 52, MS, 56, PhD(physics), 64. *Prof Exp:* Asst res physicist, Univ Calif, Los Angeles, 64-65, from asst prof to assoc prof eng, 66-76, prof, 76-84, asst dean undergrad studies, 75-84. *Concurrent Pos:* Exchange fel, Imp Col, Univ London, 64-65. *Mem:* Fel Acoust Soc Am. *Res:* Experimentation in physical, engineering and medical acoustics. *Mailing Add:* 1150 Linden Hall Rd Boalsburg PA 16827

STERN, RICHARD CECIL, CHEMICAL PHYSICS, ISOTOPE SEPARATION. *Current Pos:* CHEMIST, LAWRENCE LIVERMORE LAB, UNIV CALIF, 74- *Personal Data:* b New York, NY, Jan 4, 42; m 64; c 1. *Educ:* Cornell Univ, AB, 63; Harvard Univ, AM, 65, PhD(chem), 68. *Prof Exp:* From asst prof to assoc prof chem, Columbia Univ, 68-74. *Mem:* Am Chem Soc; Am Phys Soc. *Res:* Laser isotope separation; photochemical kinetics; scattering and chemical reactions of low energy electrons; molecular beam and time-of-flight technology. *Mailing Add:* Lawrence Livermore Lab L468 PO Box 808 Livermore CA 94550-0808

STERN, RICHARD MARTIN, JR, AUDITORY PERCEPTION, AUTOMATIC SPEECH RECOGNITION. *Current Pos:* asst prof elec & biomed eng, 77-82, ASSOC PROF ELEC & COMPUT ENG, CARNEGIE MELLON UNIV, 82- *Personal Data:* b New York, NY, July 5, 48; m 88, Lauren D Lazar; c Sarah. *Educ:* Mass Inst Technol, SB, 70, PhD(elec eng), 77; Univ Calif, Berkeley, MS, 72. *Concurrent Pos:* Vis prof speech & commun sci, Nippon Telegraph & Telephone, Tokyo; secy, ARPA Spoken Lang Coord Comt, gen chmn, Speech & Natural Lang Workshop, 90, Technol Workshop, 94. *Mem:* Acoust Soc Am; Inst Elec & Electronics Engrs; Audio Eng Soc. *Res:* Auditory perception of binaural and monaural sounds; robust automatic speech recognition. *Mailing Add:* Dept Elec & Comput Eng Carnegie-Mellon Univ 5000 Forbes Ave Pittsburgh PA 15213-3890. *Fax:* 412-268-3890; *E-Mail:* rms@cs.cmu.edu

STERN, ROBERT, PATHOLOGY, BIOCHEMISTRY. *Current Pos:* ASSOC PROF, DEPT PATH, UNIV CALIF, SAN FRANCISCO, 77- *Personal Data:* b Bad Kreuznach, Ger, Feb 11, 36; US citizen; m 63; c 3. *Educ:* Harvard Univ, BA, 57; Univ Wash, MD, 62. *Prof Exp:* USPHS officer, Nat Inst Dent Res, 63-65; sr scientist, Nat Inst Dent Res, 67-77; resident anat path, Nat Cancer Inst, 74-76. *Concurrent Pos:* Nat Cancer Inst spec fel, Weizmann Inst Sci, 65-67. *Mem:* AAAS; Am Soc Biol Chem; Am Soc Microbiol. *Res:* Transcriptional, translational controls in animal cells; translation of collagen messenger RNA; anatomic pathology; pathologic fibrosis. *Mailing Add:* Dept Path Univ Calif San Francisco Med Sch 513 Parnassus San Francisco CA 94122-2722. *Fax:* 415-476-9672

STERN, ROBERT LOUIS, ORGANIC CHEMISTRY. *Current Pos:* ASSOC PROF CHEM, OAKLAND UNIV, 68-, CO-CHMN DEPT, 74- *Personal Data:* b Newark, NJ, Apr 10, 35; m 58; c 3. *Educ:* Oberlin Col, AB, 57; Johns Hopkins Univ, MA, 59, PhD(org chem), 64. *Prof Exp:* Asst prof chem, Northeastern Univ, 62-65, assoc prof, 65-68. *Mem:* AAAS; Am Chem Soc; Sigma Xi. *Res:* Organoanalytical chemistry; organic reaction mechanisms; biosynthesis; separation mechanisms of structurally related organic molecules; organic photochemistry. *Mailing Add:* Dept Chem Oakland Univ Rochester MI 48309

STERN, ROBERT MORRIS, GASTROINTESTINAL PSYCHOPHYSIOLOGY. *Current Pos:* from asst prof to prof, 65-78, head dept, 78-87, DISTINGUISHED PROF PSYCHOL, PA STATE UNIV, 92- *Personal Data:* b New York, NY, June 18, 37; m 60, Wilma Olch; c Jessica Leigh & Alison Rachel. *Educ:* Franklin & Marshall Col, AB, 58; Tufts Univ, MS, 60; Ind Univ, PhD, 63. *Honors & Awards:* Nat Media Award, Am Psychol Found, 78. *Prof Exp:* Res assoc, Dept Psychol, Ind Univ, 63-65. *Mem:* Am Psychol Soc; Aerospace Med Asn; Soc Psychophysiol Res; Am Gastroenterol Asn; Int EGG Soc. *Res:* Contributed articles to professional journals. *Mailing Add:* 512 Moore Building Pa State Univ University Park PA 16802

STERN, RONALD JOHN, TOPOLOGY. *Current Pos:* PROF MATH, UNIV CALIF, IRVINE, 89- *Personal Data:* b Chicago, Ill, Jan 20, 47; m 85; c 2. *Educ:* Knox Col, BA, 68; Univ Calif, Los Angeles, MA, 70, PhD(math), 73. *Prof Exp:* Mem, Inst Advan Study, 73-74; instr math, Univ Utah, 74-76, asst prof, 76; mem, Inst High Sci Studies, 77-78; from assoc prof to prof math, Univ Utah, 79-89. *Concurrent Pos:* Assoc prof math, Univ Hawaii, 79. *Mem:* Am Math Soc; Math Asn Am; AAAS. *Res:* Geometrical topology emphasizing the structure of topological manifolds especially of low dimension. *Mailing Add:* Dept Math Univ Calif Irvine CA 92697-3875

STERN, SAMUEL T, mathematics; deceased, see previous edition for last biography

STERN, SILVIU ALEXANDER, CHEMICAL ENGINEERING, PHYSICAL CHEMISTRY. *Current Pos:* RETIRED. *Personal Data:* b Bucharest, Romania, June 18, 21; US citizen; m 73, Renee E; c 2. *Educ:* Israel Inst Technol, BS, 45; Ohio State Univ, MS, 48, PhD(phys chem), 52. *Honors & Awards:* Inst Award Exxcellence Indust Gases Technol, Am Inst Chem Engrs, 93. *Prof Exp:* Res assoc chem eng, Ohio State Univ, 52-55; res engr, Linde Div, Union Carbide Corp, NY, 55-58, group leader, 58-61, res supvr, 61-67; prof chem eng, Syracuse Univ, 67-90, Donald Gage Stevens distinguished prof membrane sci & eng, 90-92, Donald Gage Stevens distinguished res prof, 92-93. *Concurrent Pos:* Mem, US Nat Comt, Int Inst Refrig, 62-69, Subcomt Gas Permeability, Am Soc Testing & Mat, 65-71, Comt Cryogenics, Am Inst Chem Engrs, 68-75 & Comt Vacuum Technol, Am Vacuum Soc, 69-77; Acad vis, Chem Dept, Imp Col Sci & Technol, London, 75; adj prof chem, Col Environ Sci & Forestry, 79-94, assoc mem, Inst Polymer Res, Col Environ Sci & Forestry, 79-94; bd dirs, NAm Membrane Soc, 85-89; co-chmn, Sci & Orgn Comt, 85-87, Int Cong Membranes & Membrane Processes, Orgn Comt, 89-90; assoc dir, Res Ctr Membrane Eng & Sci, Syracuse Univ, 87-; sci adv, Fourth & Fifth Int Conf, Pervaporation Processes Chem Indust, 88-89 & 90-91; consult numerous corps. *Mem:* Am Chem Soc; fel Am Inst Chem Engrs; AAAS; Sigma Xi; Am Asn Univ Prof; Int Union Pure & Appl Chem; NAm Membrane Soc. *Res:* Transport phenomena in polymers; separation processes, particularly membrane separation processes; surface phenomena; biomedical engineering. *Mailing Add:* c/o Sarenski 472 S Salina St No 620 Syracuse NY 13202-2401

STERN, THEODORE, NUCLEAR ENGINEERING. *Current Pos:* CONSULT, 92- *Personal Data:* b Frankfurt am Main, Ger, Aug 27, 29; nat US; m 51; c 2. *Educ:* Pratt Inst, BME, 51; NY Univ, MS, 56. *Prof Exp:* Engr, Foster Wheeler Corp, NY, 52-55, proj mgr, 55-56, head, Res Reactor Sect, 56-58; asst to tech dir, Atomic Power Dept, Westinghouse Elec Corp, 58, mgr adv develop, 58-59, mgr plant develop, 59-62, mgr, Projs Dept, 62-66, gen mgr, Pressurized Water Reactor Plant Div, 66-71, vpres & gen mgr, Nuclear Fuel Div, 71-72 & Water Reactor Div, 72-74, exec vpres, 74-90, sr exec vpres, 90-92. *Mem:* Nat Acad Eng; Am Soc Mech Engrs; Am Nuclear Soc. *Res:* Application of nuclear energy to commercial generation of electric power. *Mailing Add:* 2210 One Pittsburgh Plate Glass Pl Pittsburgh PA 15222. *Fax:* 412-434-1981

STERN, THOMAS WHITAL, GEOCHRONOLOGY. *Current Pos:* RETIRED. *Personal Data:* b Chicago, Ill, Dec 12, 22; m 55, Lyn Crost; c Julia (Kennedy). *Educ:* Univ Chicago, SB, 47; Univ Tex, MA, 48. *Prof Exp:* Geologist, US Geol Surv, 48-68, 71-88, chief, Isotope Geol Br, 68-71. *Concurrent Pos:* Docent, Nat Air & Space Mus, Smithsonian Inst. *Mem:* AAAS; Geol Soc Am; Mineral Soc Am; Am Geophys Union. *Res:* Geochemistry; mineralogy; lead-uranium age determinations; isotope geology; autoradiography. *Mailing Add:* 2400 Foxhall Rd NW Washington DC 20007-1148

STERN, VERNON MARK, ENTOMOLOGY. *Current Pos:* asst entomologist, Univ Calif, Riverside, 56-62, assoc prof, 62-68, prof entom, 68-93, assoc res entomologist, Lab Nuclear Med & Radiation Biol, Los Angeles, 66-93, EMER PROF, UNIV CALIF, 93- *Personal Data:* b Sykeston, NDak, Mar 28, 23; m 47; c 2. *Educ:* Univ Calif, Berkeley, BS, 49, PhD, 52. *Prof Exp:* Res asst entom, Univ Calif, Berkeley, 49-52; entomologist, Producers Cotton Oil Co, Ariz, 52-56. *Concurrent Pos:* Collabr, USDA, 53-56; vpres, Ariz State Bd Pest Control, 53-56; coordr, Producers Agr Found, 54-56; NSF res grants, 61-69; Cotton Producers Inst res grant, 63-69; consult, US AEC, 65-66 & UN Food & Agr Orgn, 66-; Cotton Inst res grant, 69-; USDA res grant, 71-; int biol prog, NSF res grant, 72- *Mem:* Entom Soc Am; Ecol Soc Am; Sigma Xi. *Res:* Insect ecology; integrated control of arthropod pests; environmental radiation; radioecology; arthropods; population dynamics; insect migration and biology of insects. *Mailing Add:* 2808 Pinkerton Pl Riverside CA 92506

STERN, W EUGENE, SURGERY. *Current Pos:* Instr neurol surg, Univ Calif, 51-52, chief neurosurg div, 52-84, from asst prof to prof, 52-87, chmn dept surg, 81-87, EMER PROF SURG, SCH MED, UNIV CALIF, LOS ANGELES, 87- *Personal Data:* b Portland, Ore, Jan 1, 20; m 46; c 4. *Educ:* Univ Calif, AB, 41, MD, 43. *Concurrent Pos:* Consult, Los Angeles Vet Admin Hosp, 52-; vchmn, Am Bd Neurol Surgeons. *Mem:* AMA; Am Surg Asn; Am Asn Neurol Surg (pres, 78); Soc Neurol Surg (past pres, 76); Am Col Surgeons (secy). *Res:* Cerebral swelling; intracranial circulatory dynamics and intracranial mass dynamics. *Mailing Add:* 435 Georgina Ave Santa Monica CA 90402-1909

STERN, WARREN C, neuropharmacology, drug development, for more information see previous edition

STERN, WILLIAM, BIOCHEMISTRY. *Current Pos:* CONSULT, 86- *Personal Data:* b Berlin, Germany, Jan 27, 46; m 74; c 1. *Educ:* NY Univ, BA, 67; Univ Mich, MS, 69, PhD(biochem), 72. *Prof Exp:* Asst, Pub Health Res Inst, 72-76, assoc, 76-83; scientist, Warner-Lambert, 83-84; sr scientist, 84-85; sr scientist, Organon Teknika, 85-86. *Mem:* Am Acad Sci; Am Chem Soc. *Res:* Purify Endoproteases and develop inhibitors of them. *Mailing Add:* 113 Surrey Lane Tenafly NJ 07670-2515

STERN, WILLIAM LOUIS, PLANT ANATOMY. *Current Pos:* chmn dept, 79-85, PROF DEPT BOT, UNIV FLA, GAINESVILLE, 79- *Personal Data:* b Paterson, NJ, Sept 10, 26; m 49, Floraet Tanis; c Paul E & Susan M (Fennell). *Educ:* Rutgers Univ, BS, 50; Univ Ill, MS, 51, PhD(bot), 54. *Honors & Awards:* Merit Award, Bot Soc Am, 87. *Prof Exp:* From instr to asst prof wood anat, Sch Forestry, Yale Univ, 53-60; cur, Samuel James Record Mem Collection, 53-60; cur, Div Plant Anat, Smithsonian Inst, 60-64, chmn, Dept Bot, 64-67; prof bot, Univ Md, College Park, 67-79, cur herbarium, 73-76. *Concurrent Pos:* Ed, Trop Woods, 53-60, Plant Sci Bull, 61-64 & Biotropica, 68-73; expert, UN Food & Agr Orgn, Philippines, 63-64; mem sci adv comt, Nat Trop Bot Garden, 69-80 & H P du Pont Winterthur Mus, 73-86; ed, Memoirs, Torrey Bot Club, 72-75; mem comt, Visit Arnold Arboretum, Harvard Univ, 72, vchmn comt, 73; prog dir syst biol, NSF, 78-79; mem bd trustees, Kampong Fund, 85-95; bd dir, Am Inst Biol Sci, 88; res assoc, Kampong, 96-; assoc ed, Phytomorphol, 96- *Mem:* Bot Soc Am (pres, 85, 86); Am Soc Plant Taxon (pres, 81); Am Inst Biol Sci; fel Linnean Soc; Soc Econ Bot (treas, 88-91). *Res:* Plant anatomy and its relationship to systematic botany; plant morphology and phylogeny; orchid and wood anatomy and systematics tropical dendrology; natural history of tropical plants; history of botany and horticulture. *Mailing Add:* Dept Bot Univ Fla Gainesville FL 32611-8526. *Fax:* 352-392-3993

STERNBACH, DANIEL DAVID, ORGANIC CHEMISTRY. *Current Pos:* PRIN RES INVESTR, GLAXO INC, 88- *Personal Data:* b Montclair, NJ, May 28, 49; m 78; c 3. *Educ:* Univ Rochester, BS, 71; Brandeis Univ, PhD(org chem), 76. *Prof Exp:* Swiss Nat Sci Found res asst, Swiss Fed Inst Technol, 76-77; res fel, Harvard Univ, 77-79; asst prof, Duke Univ, 79-86; SR SCIENTIST, GLAXO INC, 86-; ADJ PROF, UNIV NC, CHAPEL HILL, 88- *Mem:* Am Chem Soc. *Res:* Synthesis of interesting and biologically significant organic compounds and investigation of new synthetic methods. *Mailing Add:* Glaxo Inc 5 Moore Dr Research Triangle Park NC 27701-4613

STERNBACH, LEO HYNRYK, ORGANIC CHEMISTRY. *Current Pos:* RETIRED. *Personal Data:* b Abbazia, Austria, May 7, 08; m 41, Herta M Kreuzer; c Michael K & Daniel D. *Educ:* Jagiellonian Univ, MA, 29, PhD(org chem), 31. *Hon Degrees:* Dr Tech Sci, Tech Univ, Austria, 71; DSc, Centenary Col, NJ, 84; PhD, Johann Wolfgang Goethe Univ, Ger, 86. *Honors & Awards:* Seventh Award Med Chem, Div Med Chem, Am Chem Soc, 78, Cecil Brown, lectr, 79; Chem Pioneer Award, Am Inst Chemists, 79; Charles W Hartman Mem lectr, Univ Miss, 84; Carl Mannich Medal, Ger, Pharmaceut Soc, 84; Hoffmann-LaRoche lectr & Leo H Sternbach lectr, Yale Univ, 89. *Prof Exp:* Res asst, Jagiellonian Univ, 31-37; res fel, Swiss Fed Inst Tech, Zurich, Switz, 37-40; res chemist, Hoffmann-La Roche, Besol Switz, 40-41, group chief, sr group chief & sect chief, 41-66, dir med chem, 66-73. *Concurrent Pos:* Consult, 73- *Mem:* Am Chem Soc. *Res:* Study of 1,4-beuzodiazepines; synthesis of libriam and valium, they are psychoterapeutic agents; author and co-author over 120 publications; 5 monographs; granted 230 US patents. *Mailing Add:* 10 Woodmont Rd Upper Montclair NJ 07043-2536

STERNBERG, HILGARD O'REILLY, ALLUVIAL GEOMORPHOLOGY, ENVIRONMENTAL IMPACT OF ECONOMIC DEVELOPMENT IN THE TROPICS. *Current Pos:* prof, 64-88, EMER PROF GEOG, UNIV CALIF, BERKELEY, 88- *Personal Data:* b Rio de Janeiro, Brazil, July 5, 17; m 42, Carolina D Lobo; c Hilgard O Jr, Maria I (Mangiola), Ricardo D, Leonel D, Cristina S (Rauch). *Educ:* Univ Brazil, Rio de Janeiro, BA, 40, Licenciado, 41, Dr, 58; La State Univ, PhD(geog), 56. *Hon Degrees:* Dr, Univ Toulouse, France, 64. *Honors & Awards:* Nat Order Merit, Fed Repub Brazil, 56, Order Rio Branco, 67. *Prof Exp:* Teaching asst geog, Col Pedro II, Rio de Janeiro, 38-42; asst prof, Univ Brazil, 42-44, prof, 44-64; prof, Inst Rio Branco, 47-56. *Concurrent Pos:* Prof, Cath Univ, Rio de Janeiro, 41-44; consult, Nat Geog Coun, Brazil, 50-66; dir, Ctr Geog Studies Brazil, 51-64; mem, UNESCO Adv Comt Arid Zones Res, 55-56; vis prof, Univ Heidelberg, 61; Columbia Univ, 63-64, Univ Peking, 84; consult, Max-Planck Soc, 75-78; mem, Comt Res Priorities Trop Biol, Nat Res Coun, Nat Acad Sci, 78-80. *Mem:* Brazilian Acad Sci; Royal Geog Soc; Geog Soc Finland; Int Geog Union (vpres, 52-60); Leopoldina German Acad Natural Researchers; Soc Earth Sci Berlin; Serbian Soc Geog; fel AAAS. *Res:* Melding physico-biotic, cultural and historical geography; interface of human communities and their environments, and dysfunctions that occur on that interface, particularly as a consequence of development policies in the Neotropics, Brazil and Amazonia; climatic change and variability in Amazonia. *Mailing Add:* Dept Geog Univ Calif 501 McCone Hall Berkeley CA 94720. *Fax:* 510-524-8542; *E-Mail:* hilgards@violet.berkeley.edu

STERNBERG, JOSEPH, FLUID MECHANICS, AERODYNAMICS. *Current Pos:* DEPT PHYSICS, NAVAL POSTGRAD SCH. *Personal Data:* b Brooklyn, NY, Nov 24, 21; m 46; c 4. *Educ:* Calif Inst Technol, BS, 42, MS, 43; Johns Hopkins Univ, PhD(aeronaut), 55. *Honors & Awards:* Arthur S Flemming Award, 59. *Prof Exp:* Res supvr supersonic flow, Calif Inst Technol, 43-46; aerodynamicist, US Army Ballistic Res Labs, 46-49, chief, Supersonic Wind Tunnels Br, 50-58 & Exterior Ballistics Lab, 58-62; consult aerodyn, Baltimore Div, Martin Marietta Corp, 62-63; mgr res & develop, 63-65, asst dir eng, 65-66, dir adv syst, Aerospace Hq, 66-70; sci adv to supreme allied comdr Europe, Supreme Hq Allied Powers Europe, 71-76; dir, Aerospace Group, Martin Marietta Corp, 76- *Concurrent Pos:* Mem, Subcomt Fluid Mech, Nat Adv Comt Aeronaut, 50-58; mem, Res Adv Comt Fluid Mech, NASA, 58-62; mem, Res Adv Subcomt Fluid Mech, 67-69; mem consult panel, Chief Naval Opers, Opers Eval Group, 60-62; mem, fluid dynamics panel, Adv Group Aeronaut Res & Develop, NATO, 60-64; mem ground warfare panel, President's Sci Adv Comt, 69-70; mem, Army Sci Adv Panel, 70. *Mem:* Assoc fel Am Inst Aeronaut & Astronaut; Am Phys Soc. *Res:* Boundary layer phenomena; shock wave reflections and structure; turbulent shear flows; missile and reentry systems. *Mailing Add:* Dept Physics Naval Postgrad Sch Monterey CA 93943

STERNBERG, MOSHE, BIOCHEMISTRY, PLASMA PRODUCTS. *Current Pos:* SR VPRES RES & DEVELOP, MILES INC BIOTECHNOL, 86- *Personal Data:* b Marculesti, Rumania, Sept 3, 29; m 55; c 2. *Educ:* Parhon Univ, Bucharest, Rumania, MS 52, PhD(org chem), 61. *Prof Exp:* Lab chief, Chem Pharmaceut Res Inst, Bucharest, Rumania, 55-57; res fel, Israel Inst Technol, 61-62; dir protein & carbohydrate res, Miles Labs, Inc, 62-80; vpres res & develop, Cutter Labs Inc, 80-86. *Mem:* Am Chem Soc; AAAS; Am Soc Microbiol. *Res:* Separation of industrial enzymes; proteins separation and characterization; human plasma proteins; biotechnology. *Mailing Add:* 12101 Tartan Way Oakland CA 94619

STERNBERG, PAUL WARREN, C ELEGANS MOLECULAR GENETICS, NEMATODE CELL LINEAGE. *Current Pos:* from asst prof to assoc prof, 87-96, PROF BIOL, CALIF INST TECHNOL, 96- *Personal Data:* b Queens, NY, June 14, 56; 91, Jane Elizabeth Mendel; c Clara. *Educ:* Hampshire Col, BS, 78; Mass Inst Technol, PhD(biol), 84. *Prof Exp:* Postdoctoral fel, Univ Calif, 84-87. *Concurrent Pos:* Fel, Jane Coffin Childs Found Med Res, 84-87; pres young investr, NSF, 88-93; asst investr, Howard Hughes Med Ctr, 89-92, assoc investr, 92-97, investr, 97-; adj asst prof, Univ S Calif, Sch Med, 89; Eppley vis prof oncol, Univ Nebr Med Sch, 95. *Mem:* Fel AAAS; Am Soc Cell Biol; Genetics Soc Am; Soc Develop Biol; Soc Nematologists. *Res:* Molecular genetics of nemotode developments, behavior and evolution; use of C elegans to study proto-oncogenes and candidate tumor suppressors; roles of intercellular signaling in developmental pattern formation. *Mailing Add:* Caltech 156-29 1200 E California Blvd Pasadena CA 91125. *Fax:* 626-568-8012; *E-Mail:* pws@cco.caltech.edu

STERNBERG, RICHARD WALTER, GEOLOGICAL OCEANOGRAPHY, MARINE SEDIMENTATION. *Current Pos:* asst prof, 68-73, assoc prof, 73-75, actg chmn dept, 78-79, PROF OCEANOG, UNIV WASH, 75- *Personal Data:* b Mt Pleasant, Iowa, Nov 21, 34; m 57; c 3. *Educ:* Univ Calif, Los Angeles, BA, 58; Univ Wash, MSc, 61, PhD(oceanog), 65. *Prof Exp:* Assoc oceanog, Univ Wash, 63-65, res asst prof, 65-66; fel, Geomorphol Lab, Uppsala Univ, 66; res geophysicist, Univ Calif, San Diego, 67-68. *Concurrent Pos:* Adj assoc prof environ studies, Univ Wash, 73-90. *Mem:* Am Geophys Union. *Res:* Geological oceanography, especially processes of sediment transport and boundary-layer flow near the seafloor. *Mailing Add:* Sch Oceanog WB10 Univ Wash 3900 Seventh Ave NE Seattle WA 98195-0001

STERNBERG, ROBERT JEFFREY, THINKING STYLES, CREATIVITY. *Current Pos:* From asst prof to prof, 75-86, IBM PROF PSYCHOL & EDUC, YALE UNIV, 86- *Personal Data:* b Newark, NJ, Dec 8, 49; m 91, Alejandra Campos; c Seth & Sara. *Educ:* Yale Univ, BA, 72; Stanford Univ, PhD(psychol), 75. *Hon Degrees:* Dir, Complutense Univ, Madrid, Spain, 94. *Honors & Awards:* Early Career Award, Am Psychol Asn, 81, McCandless Award, 82; Cattell Award, Soc Multivariate Exp Psychol, 82; Distinguished

Scholar Award, Nat Asn Gifted Children, 85; Res Rev Award, Am Educ Res Asn, 86, Sylvia Scribner Award, 96; Int Award, Asn Port Psychologists, 91. *Concurrent Pos:* Prin investr, Contracts Naval Res, 77-82 & 85-88, Off Naval Res & Army Res Inst, 82-85, Army Res Inst, 85-98, Spencer Found, 82-84, 88-91, McDonnell Found, 87-90 & Dept Educ, Off Educ Res & Improv, 90-; sr fac fel, Yale Univ, 82-83, Guggenheim fel, 85-86; consult, Air Force Off Sci Res, 86-88, Psychol Corp, 86-89, Harcourt Brace Jovanovich, 89- & Nat Comn Coop Educ, 90-; ed, Psychol Bull, 91 & 96, Contemp Psychol, 98- *Mem:* fel Am Psychol Asn; fel AAAS; Psychonomic Soc; Soc Multivariate Exp Psychol; Soc Res Child Develop; fel Am Psychol Soc; fel Am Acad Arts & Sci. *Res:* Triarchic theory of human intelligence; theory of mental self-government (styles of thinking); investment theory of creativity; componential theories of reasoning; triangular theory of love; intelligence. *Mailing Add:* Dept Psychol PO Box 208205 New Haven CT 06520-8205. *Fax:* 203-432-8317; *E-Mail:* sterobj@yalevm.cis.yale.edu

STERNBERG, SHMUEL MOOKIE, MEMBRANE TECHNOLOGY, BIOSEPARATION & PURIFICATION. *Current Pos:* TECH DIR APPL SCI, BAXTER HEALTHCARE CORP, 90- *Personal Data:* b Haifa, Israel, Dec 6, 38; US citizen. *Educ:* Ga Tech, BCHE, 62; Carnegie Mellon Univ, MSc, 64; Case Western Res Univ, PhD(polymer sci & eng), 67. *Prof Exp:* Sr res scientist, Amicon Corp, 67-69; mgr mat develop, Koch Membranes, Abcor, 69-76; res mgr, Millipore Corp, 76-81; dir res, Chomerics, Inc, 81-83; vpres res & develop, Memtek Corp, 83-90. *Res:* Membrane development including microfiltration, ultrafiltration, reverse osmosis, affinity and specialty; membranes and devices in bioseparation in biotechnology, medical devices and diagnostics. *Mailing Add:* Baxter Healthcare Corp 4240 Yorkshire Lane Baxter Technol Park Northbrook IL 60062-2923

STERNBERG, STEPHEN STANLEY, PATHOLOGY, ONCOLOGY. *Current Pos:* ATTEND PATH, MEM HOSP, 49-; PROF PATH, MED COL, CORNELL UNIV, 79- *Personal Data:* b New York, NY, July 30, 20; m 58, Norma Wollner; c Alessandra & Susan. *Educ:* Colby Col, BA, 41; NY Univ, MD, 44. *Prof Exp:* Resident path, Sch Med, Tulane Univ, 47-49; *Concurrent Pos:* Mem, Sloan-Kettering Inst, 49-; mem, Sci Adv Comt, Sch Med, Stanford Univ, 78-81; consult pathologist, Food & Drug Admin, 71-73 & NSF, Div Problem-Focused Res, 75-79; ed-in-chief, Am J Surg Path, 76-; ed, Human Path, 77-81; pres med bd, Mem Hosp, NY, 78-81, pres gen staff, 81-83; sci adv panel, Environ Protection Agency, 82-84; bd dir, Am Coun Sci & Health, 83-85; chmn bd dir, Am Coun Sci, 85-89; mem, NY Sci Policy Asn, 86-; mem of bd sci adv world health orgn collaborating ctr for the prev of colorectal cancer, 88- *Mem:* Am Asn Cancer Res; Int Acad Path; Soc Toxicol; NY Acad Med. *Res:* Carcinogenesis; surgical pathology; toxicology of cancer chemotherapeutic agents. *Mailing Add:* Mem Sloan-Kettering Cancer Ctr 1275 York Ave New York NY 10021. *Fax:* 212-794-6233

STERNBERG, VITA SHLOMO, MATHEMATICS. *Current Pos:* asst prof, 59-63, chmn dept, 75-78, PROF MATH, HARVARD UNIV, 63-, GEORGE PUTNAM PROF PURE & APPL MATH, 81- *Personal Data:* b New York, NY, Jan 20, 36; m; c 5. *Educ:* Johns Hopkins Univ, BA, 53, MA, 55, PhD, 56. *Hon Degrees:* Dr, Univ Mannheim, WGer, 90. *Prof Exp:* Vis fel, Inst Math Sci, NY Univ, 56-57; instr, Univ Chicago, 57-59. *Concurrent Pos:* Fel, Mortimer & Raymond Sackler Inst Advan Studies, Tel Aviv Univ, 80- *Mem:* Nat Acad Sci; Am Acad Arts & Sci. *Res:* Author of numerous technical publications. *Mailing Add:* Dept Math Harvard Univ Cambridge MA 02138

STERNBERG, YARON MOSHE, GROUND WATER HYDROLOGY. *Current Pos:* assoc prof, 70-74, PROF CIVIL ENG, UNIV MD, COLLEGE PARK, 74- *Personal Data:* b Tel Aviv, Israel, May 26, 36; m 61; c 2. *Educ:* Univ Ill, BS, 61; Univ Calif, MS, 63, PhD(eng), 65. *Prof Exp:* From asst prof to assoc prof geol, Ind Univ, Bloomington, 65-70. *Mem:* Am Soc Civil Engrs; Am Geophys Soc; Am Inst Mining, Metall & Petrol Engrs. *Mailing Add:* 11905 Viewcrest Terr Silver Spring MD 20902

STERNBERGER, LUDWIG AMADEUS, MEDICINE. *Current Pos:* PROF NEUROL, PATH & ANAT, UNIV MD SCH MED, 86- *Personal Data:* b Munich, Ger, May 26, 21; nat US; m 62. *Educ:* Am Univ, Beirut, MD, 45. *Honors & Awards:* Paul A Siple Award, 72; Laureate of Alexander Von Humboldt Prize, 81. *Prof Exp:* Sr med bacteriologist, Div Labs & Res, State Dept Health, NY, 50-52, sr med biochemist, 52-53; asst prof med, Med Sch & assoc dir, Allergy Res Lab, Northwestern Univ, 53-55; chief, Path Br, US Army Chem Res & Develop Labs, 55-67, chief, Basic Sci Dept, Med Res Labs, Army Chem Ctr, 67-77; asst prof microbiol, Sch Med, Johns Hopkins Univ, 66-77; prof brain res, Sch Med & Dent, Univ Rochester, 78-86. *Concurrent Pos:* Fel exp path, Mem Cancer Ctr, New York, 48-50; assoc surg res, Sinai Hosp Baltimore, 66-; consult, Univ Iowa; neurosci investr award, 84. *Mem:* Soc Exp Biol & Med; Am Asn Immunologists; Am Acad Allergy; Histochem Soc; Am Soc Neurochem; Am Soc Neuropathologists. *Res:* Immunocytochemistry; neuroscience. *Mailing Add:* Hopkins Bayview Res Campus 5210 Eastern Ave Baltimore MD 21224. *Fax:* 410-550-2643

STERNBURG, JAMES GORDON, ENTOMOLOGY. *Current Pos:* Res assoc entom, 52-54, from asst prof to prof, 54-88, EMER PROF ENTOM, UNIV ILL, URBANA, 88- *Personal Data:* b Chicago, Ill, Feb 22, 19; wid, Eileen Mayer; c Virginia, Thomas & Janet. *Educ:* Univ Ill, AB, 49, MS, 50, PhD(entom), 52. *Concurrent Pos:* Affil mem, Biodiversity Ctr, Ill Nat Hist Surv, Urbana, ILL. *Mem:* Entom Soc Am; Lepidop Soc. *Res:* Insect physiology and toxicology of insecticides; enzymatic detoxication of dichloro-diphenyl-trichloro-ethane by resistance house flies; effects of insecticides on neuroactivity in insects; behavior of nearctic and neotropical Lepidoptera; mimicry by insects; biology of saturniid moths; spawning behavior of Phoxinus sp (Cyprinidae) and other fishes. *Mailing Add:* Dept Entom-320 Morrill Hall Univ Ill 505 S Goodwin Ave MC118 Urbana IL 61801

STERNER, CARL D, INORGANIC CHEMISTRY, PHYSICAL CHEMISTRY. *Current Pos:* Chair chem dept, 80-86, PROF CHEM, UNIV NEBR, 87- *Personal Data:* b Wellman, Iowa, Oct 15, 35; m 61; c 3. *Educ:* Kearney State Col, BS, 60; Univ Tex, Austin, MA, 67; Univ Nebr, Lincoln, PhD(chem), 73. *Concurrent Pos:* NSF fel, 71-72. *Mem:* Am Chem Soc. *Res:* Inorganic syntheses; solid state chemistry; electron spectroscopy chemical applications; materials science; GC/MS. *Mailing Add:* Dept Chem Kearney State Col Kearney NE 68849-0001

STERNER, JAMES HERVI, medicine; deceased, see previous edition for last biography

STERNER, ROBERT WARNER, LIMNOLOGY, PHYCOLOGY. *Current Pos:* ASST PROF BIOL, UNIV TEX, ARLINGTON, 88- *Personal Data:* b Elmhurst, Ill, Jan 15, 58; m 83; c 1. *Educ:* Univ Ill, Urbana, BS, 80, Univ Minn, PhD(ecology), 86. *Prof Exp:* Fel, Nat Sci Found, 80, Max Planck Inst, WGer, 87, Nat Sci Found/NATO, 88. *Mem:* Am Soc Limnol & Oceanog; Ecol Soc Am. *Res:* Ecological and physiological aspects of zooplankton/phytoplankton dynamics, combining herbivory and resource competition into one conceptual framework. *Mailing Add:* Univ Minn Dept Ecol 100 Ecol Bldg 1987 Upper Buford Circle St Paul MN 55108

STERNFELD, LEON, MEDICAL ADMINISTRATION, RESEARCH ADMINISTRATION. *Current Pos:* RETIRED. *Personal Data:* b Brooklyn, NY, June 15, 13; m 34, Ruth Schwartz; c Kay & Barbara. *Educ:* Univ Chicago, SB, 32, MD, 36, PhD(biochem), 37; Columbia Univ, MPH, 43. *Prof Exp:* Intern pediat, Johns Hopkins Univ, 38-39 & Sydenham Hosp, 39-40; asst res, Jewish Hosp, Brooklyn, 40-41; epidemiologist-in-training, State Dept Health, NY, 41-42, jr epidemiologist, 42, asst dist state health officer, 43-44, dir med rehab, 44-50, dist health officer, 50-51; asst dir, Tuberc Div, State Dept Pub Health, Mass, 51-52; assoc dir, Field Training Unit, Harvard Univ, 52-53, lectr, Sch Pub Health, 53-57, from asst clin prof to assoc clin prof maternal & child health, 58-70, vis lectr maternal & child health, 70-74; med dir, United Cerebral Palsy Asns, Inc, 71-93. *Concurrent Pos:* Chief Pub Health Admin, Korean Civil Asst Command, 53-55; chief prev med, Ft Devons, US Army, 55; City health comnr, Cambridge, Mass, 55-61; lectr, Simmons Col, 56-69; assoc physician, Children's Med Ctr, Boston, 57-69; dep health comnr, Mass Dept Pub Health, 61-69. *Mem:* Am Pub Health Asn; Am Asn Ment Deficiency; Am Acad Cerebral Palsy & Develop Med. *Res:* Chemical properties of essential bacterial growth factor; essential fructosuria; pathophysiology; medical and public health aspects of cerebral palsy and mental retardation; public health methodology and community health; bacterial breakdown of sugars; pathophysiology of fructosuria; epidemiology of cerebral palsy. *Mailing Add:* 1385 York Ave New York NY 10021

STERNFELD, MARVIN, ORGANIC CHEMISTRY. *Current Pos:* PRES, RES ORGANICS INC, 66- *Personal Data:* b Cleveland, Ohio, Feb 24, 27; m 50; c 3. *Educ:* Western Reserve Univ, BS, 49, MS, 51, PhD(chem), 53. *Prof Exp:* Pres, Cleveland Chem Labs, 53-66. *Concurrent Pos:* Head, Chem Dept, Ohio Col Podiat Med, 53-69. *Mem:* Am Chem Soc; Sigma Xi. *Res:* Synthesis of biochemicals, including biological buffers, fluorescent labels, brain research biochemicals, enzyme substrates and test reagents; amino acid derivatives, peptides, special biological dyes. *Mailing Add:* 4353 E 49th St Cleveland OH 44125-1003

STERNGLANZ, ROLF, MOLECULAR BIOLOGY, BIOCHEMISTRY. *Current Pos:* asst prof, 69-76, ASSOC PROF BIOCHEM, STATE UNIV NY STONY BROOK, 76- *Personal Data:* b Sewell, Chile, May 18, 39; US citizen; m 64. *Educ:* Oberlin Col, AB, 60; Harvard Univ, PhD(phys chem), 67. *Prof Exp:* NIH res fel biochem, Sch Med, Stanford Univ, 66-68. *Concurrent Pos:* Am Cancer Soc res grants, State Univ NY Stony Brook, 69- *Mem:* AAAS. *Res:* Mechanism of DNA replication; physical chemistry of DNA. *Mailing Add:* Dept Biochem & Cell Biol State Univ NY Stony Brook NY 11794-5215. *Fax:* 516-632-8575

STERNGLASS, ERNEST JOACHIM, PHYSICS. *Current Pos:* prof radiation physics, Univ Pittsburgh, 67-80, EMER PROF RADIOLOGICAL PHYSICS, 80- *Personal Data:* b Berlin, Ger, Sept 24, 23; nat US; m 57; c 2. *Educ:* Cornell Univ, BEE, 44, MS, 51, PhD(eng physics), 53. *Prof Exp:* Asst physics, Cornell Univ, 44, res assoc, 51-52; physicist, US Naval Ord Lab, 46-52; res physicist, Res Labs, Westinghouse Elec Co, Pa, 52-60, adv physicist, 60-67. *Concurrent Pos:* Assoc, George Washington Univ, 46-47; Westinghouse Res Lab fel, Inst Henri Poincare, Paris, 57-58; vis prof, Inst Theoret Physics, Stanford Univ, 66-67. *Mem:* AAAS; fel Am Phys Soc; Am Astron Soc; Fedn Am Sci; Am Asn Physicists in Med. *Res:* Secondary electron emission; physics of electron tubes; electron and elementary particle physics; electronic imaging devices for astronomy and medicine; radiation physics; biological effects of radiation. *Mailing Add:* 4601 Fifth Ave Apt 824 Pittsburgh PA 15253. *Fax:* 212-362-1334

STERNHEIM, MORTON MAYNARD, PHYSICS, SCIENCE EDUCATION. *Current Pos:* from asst prof to assoc prof, 65-71, PROF PHYSICS, UNIV MASS, 71-; DIR, INTERNET SERV, 93-; DIR, SCI TECHNOL ENG & MATH EDUC INST, 95- *Personal Data:* b Scranton, Pa, July 19, 33; m 55, Helen F Rothenberg; c 3. *Educ:* City Col, NY, BS, 54; NY Univ, MS, 56; Columbia Univ, PhD(physics), 61. *Prof Exp:* Fel physics, Brookhaven Nat Lab, 61-63; res assoc lectr, Yale Univ, 63-65. *Concurrent Pos:* Prin investr, NSF res grant, 65; consult, Las Alamos Nat Lab, 67-; visitor, Brookhaven Nat Lab, 66 & 68. *Mem:* Am Phys Soc; Am Asn Physics Teachers. *Res:* Theoretical nuclear physics; pion scattering and production;

exotic atoms; incoherent processes involving nucleons and mesons at intermediate energies; nucleon-nucleon interactions; skyrmion models. *Mailing Add:* Nuclear Physics LGRT Univ Mass Amherst MA 01003. *Fax:* 413-545-4884

STERNHEIMER, RUDOLPH MAX, ATOMIC PHYSICS, NUMBER THEORY. *Current Pos:* from assoc physicist to sr physicist, 52-92, GUEST SR PHSYCIST, BROOKHAVEN NAT LAB, 92- *Personal Data:* b Saarbruecken, Ger, Apr 26, 26; nat US; m 52; c Elizabeth A Pieczur. *Educ:* Univ Chicago, BS, 43, MS, 46, PhD, 49. *Prof Exp:* Jr scientist, Div War Res, Metall Lab, Columbia Univ, 45-46; instr physics, Univ Chicago, 46-48; asst & instr, Yale Univ, 48-49; mem staff, Los Alamos Sci Lab, 49-51. *Mem:* Fel Am Phys Soc; Math Asn Am; Fibonacci Asn. *Res:* Atomic and nuclear physics; theory of solids; theory of nuclear quadrupole coupling; theory of ionization loss and Cerenkov radiation; focusing magnets; polarization of nucleons; theory of meson production; electronic polarizabilities of ions; k-ordering of atomic and ionic energy levels; problems in number theory. *Mailing Add:* 240 E 76th St Apt 10M New York NY 10021

STERNICK, EDWARD SELBY, MEDICAL PHYSICS. *Current Pos:* assoc clin prof therapeut radiol, 78-87, CLIN PROF RADIATION ONCOL & DIR MED PHYSICS DIV, TUFTS-NEW ENGLAND MED CTR, 87- *Personal Data:* b Cambridge, Mass, Feb 10, 39; m 60; c 3. *Educ:* Tufts Univ, BS, 60; Boston Univ, MA, 63; Univ Calif, Los Angeles, PhD(med physics), 68; Northeastern Univ, MBA, 85. *Prof Exp:* Res scientist biophys, Nat Aeronaut & Space Admin, 63-64; instr radiol, Dartmouth-Hitchcock Med Ctr, 68-72, asst prof clin med, 72-78. *Concurrent Pos:* Prof, NH Voc Tech Inst, 72-78; adj asst prof bioeng, Thayer Sch Eng, Dartmouth Univ, 73-78; consult, Vet Admin Hosp, 74- *Mem:* Fel Am Asn Physicists in Med; Soc Nuclear Med; Sigma Xi; Health Physics Soc; fel Am Col Med Physics; fel Am Col Radiol. *Res:* Application of computer technology to radiation medicine. *Mailing Add:* 19 Cross St Charleston MA 02129-2504

STERNLICHT, B(ENO), ENERGY, PROPULSION. *Current Pos:* PRES, AMEAST TRADING CORP, 76-; PRES, BENJOSH MGT CORP, 80- *Personal Data:* b Poland, Mar 12, 28; nat US; m 55, 75; c 3. *Educ:* Union Col, BSEE, 49; Columbia Univ, PhD(appl mech), 54. *Hon Degrees:* DSc, Union Col, 70. *Honors & Awards:* Mach Design Award, Am Soc Mech Engrs, 66. *Prof Exp:* Engr, Gen Elec Co, 47-50; off mgr, Ameast Distribr Corp, 50-51; develop engr, Gen Elec Co, 51-53; res engr, AEC, 53-54; eng specialist, Gen Eng Lab, Gen Elec Co, 54-58, consult engr hydrodyn, 58-61; tech dir & chmn bd, Mech Technol Inc, 61-85. *Concurrent Pos:* Lectr, Union Col, 56-57 & Mass Inst Technol, 57 & 59; mem mat panel, Nat Acad Sci; founder sci based indust, Mamash, Israel; pres & chmn bd, Vols in Tech Assistance, 66-72; chmn, Comt Power & Propulsion, NASA; adv to energy, Pres Carter & Pres Reagan; bd mem, Vol in Tech Assistance; mem, Energy Policy Task Force, 81. *Mem:* Nat Acad Eng; Am Soc Lubrication Engrs; Inst Elec & Electronics Engrs; Am Inst Aeronaut & Astronaut; Am Soc Mech Engrs. *Res:* Turbomachinery; energy conversion; conservation diagnostic systems; automotive propulsion; separation systems; energy conversion, propulsion, separation and enrichment systems. *Mailing Add:* 123 Partridge Run Schenectady NY 12309. *Fax:* 718-378-4669; *E-Mail:* fkbjm@aol.com

STERNLICHT, HIMAN, PHYSICAL CHEMISTRY. *Current Pos:* ASSOC PROF PHARMACOL, CASE WESTERN RESERVE UNIV, 76- *Personal Data:* b New York, NY, May 31, 36; m 58; c 3. *Educ:* Columbia Univ, BA, 57, BS, 58; Calif Inst Technol, PhD(chem), 63. *Prof Exp:* Mem tech staff, Bell Tel Labs, NJ, 63-65; asst prof chem, Univ Calif, Berkeley, 65-70; mem tech staff, Bell Labs, Inc, 70-76. *Concurrent Pos:* NIH res grant, 66-69. *Mem:* Am Phys Soc; Am Chem Soc. *Res:* Magnetic resonance studies, including small and macromolecular systems. *Mailing Add:* Dept Pharmacol Case Western Res Univ Sch Med Rd W348 Cleveland OH 44106-4965. *Fax:* 216-368-3395

STERNLIEB, IRMIN, ELECTRON MICROSCOPY, HEPATOLOGY. *Current Pos:* asst instr, Albert Einstein Col Med, 56-57, instr & assoc, 57-61, from asst prof to assoc prof, 61-72, prof, 72-93, EMER PROF MED, ALBERT EINSTEIN COL MED, 93-; SR RES ASSOC, ST LUKE'S-ROOSEVELT HOSP. *Personal Data:* b Czernowitz, Rumania, Jan 11, 23; US citizen; m 53, Anne Lloyd. *Educ:* Univ Geneva, MSc, 49, MD, 52. *Honors & Awards:* Andrew Sass-Kortsak Award, Can Asn Study Liver, 90. *Prof Exp:* Intern, Morrisania City Hosp, Bronx, NY, 52-53; resident internal med, Bronx Munic Hosp Ctr, New York, 55-57. *Concurrent Pos:* Fel internal med & gastroenterol, Mt Sinai Hosp, New York, 53; USPHS fel, 58-60 & spec fel, Lab Atomic Synthesis & Proton Optics, Ivry, France, 64-65. *Mem:* Am Soc Clin Invest; Int Asn Study Liver; Am Gastroenterol Asn; Am Asn Study Liver Dis; Am Soc Cell Biol. *Res:* Clinical, genetic, biochemical, diagnostic and morphologic aspects of human, rodent and canine inherited copper toxicosis; electron microscopy of human liver. *Mailing Add:* Nat Ctr Study Wilson's Dis 432 W 58th St Suite 614 New York NY 10019. *Fax:* 212-523-8708

STERNLING, CHARLES V, ENGINEERING RESEARCH. *Current Pos:* RETIRED. *Personal Data:* b Pocatello, Idaho, Nov 15, 24. *Prof Exp:* Sr res assoc, Shell Develop Co, 49-89. *Mem:* Nat Acad Eng; Am Inst Chem Engrs; Am Chem Soc. *Mailing Add:* 1400 Stony Lane North Kingstown RI 02852. *E-Mail:* abcsternling@juno.com

STERNSTEIN, MARTIN, MATHEMATICS. *Current Pos:* From asst prof to assoc prof, 70-82, chmn dept, 72-76, 81-83, PROF MATH, ITHACA COL, 82- *Personal Data:* b Chicago, Ill, Apr 25, 45; m 80, Faith Mayu; c Jonathan & Jeremy. *Educ:* Univ Chicago, BS, 66; Cornell Univ, PhD(math), 71. *Concurrent Pos:* Vis lectr, Col VI, 78-79; Fulbright prof, Univ Liberia, 79-80, 83-84. *Res:* Algebraic topology. *Mailing Add:* Dept Math Ithaca Col Ithaca NY 14850

STERNSTEIN, SANFORD SAMUEL, POLYMER PHYSICS & ENGINEERING, COMPOSITES. *Current Pos:* From asst prof to prof polymers, 61-73, WILLIAM WEIGHTMAN WALKER PROF POLYMER ENG, RENSSELAER POLYTECH INST, 73-, DIR, CTR COMPOSITE MAT & STRUCT. *Personal Data:* b New York, NY, June 19, 36; m 58, Gail Golden; c Deborah & Alan. *Educ:* Rensselaer Polytech Inst, PhD(chem eng), 61. *Concurrent Pos:* Pioneering res grants, NSF & Inst Paper Chem, 63-65; Nat Inst Dent Res grant, 65-70; NSF res grants, 73-78, NASA grants, 77-85 & Advan Res Proj Agency grants, 87-; GE/Ford/Nat Inst Stand & Technol grant, 92-; pres, Dynastatics Instruments Corp. *Mem:* Am Inst Chem Eng; Soc Rheol; fel Am Phys Soc; Am Chem Soc. *Res:* Rheology; fracture; dynamic mechanical properties of polymers; polymer-solvent interactions and crazing; polymer network mechanics and rubber elasticity; composites. *Mailing Add:* Ctr Composite Mat & Struct Rensselaer Polytech Inst Troy NY 12180. *Fax:* 518-276-8784

STERRETT, ANDREW, MATHEMATICS. *Current Pos:* from asst prof to assoc prof, 53-65, chmn dept math, 60-63 & 65-68, dir comt undergrad prog in math, 70-72, dean col, 73-78, PROF MATH, DENISON UNIV, 65- *Personal Data:* b Pittsburgh, Pa, Apr 3, 24; m 48; c 2. *Educ:* Carnegie Inst Technol, BS, 48; Univ Pittsburgh, MS, 50, PhD(math), 56. *Prof Exp:* Lectr math, Univ Pittsburgh, 48-50; instr, Ohio Univ, 50-53. *Concurrent Pos:* NSF fac fel statist, Stanford Univ, 59-60; vis scholar statist, Univ Calif, Berkeley, 66-67 & Univ NC, 78-79; dir comt on undergrad prog in math, Math Asn Am, 70-72. *Mem:* Am Math Soc; Math Asn Am; Am Statist Asn; Sigma Xi; Nat Coun Teachers Math. *Mailing Add:* 222 N Granger St Granville OH 43023. *Fax:* 423-587-6417

STERRETT, FRANCES SUSAN, environmental sciences; deceased, see previous edition for last biography

STERRETT, JOHN PAUL, PLANT PHYSIOLOGY. *Current Pos:* CONSULT PLANT PHYSIOLOGIST, 90- *Personal Data:* b Springfield, Ohio, Dec 14, 24; m 49; c 2. *Educ:* Univ WVa, BS, 50; Va Polytech Inst, MS, 61, PhD(plant physiol), 66. *Honors & Awards:* Elaneo Pioneer Award, 89. *Prof Exp:* Co forester, WVa Conserv Comn, 50-53; forester, Bartlett Tree Expert Co, 53-59; res asst plant physiol, Va Polytech Inst, 59-61, asst prof, 61-69; plant physiologist, Veg Control Div, Ft Detrick, US Army, 69-74; plant physiologist, Sci Res Lab, Agr Res Serv, USDA, 74-86, plant physiologist, Foreign Dis-Weed Res Lab, 86-90. *Mem:* Plant Growth Regulators Soc Am. *Res:* Plant growth regulators for the control of weeds; determine physiological responses of woody plants to growth inhibitors. *Mailing Add:* 11935 Beaver Dam Rd Union Bridge MD 21791

STERRETT, KAY FIFE, GEOPHYSICS, SIGNAL PROCESSING. *Current Pos:* STAFF SPECIALIST, ENVIRON QUAL, OFF DIR DEFENSE RES & ENG, 92- *Personal Data:* b McKeesport, Pa, May 20, 31; m 60; c Margaret Baker; c David K, Emily K & Rebecca A. *Educ:* Univ Pittsburgh, BS, 53, PhD(phys chem), 57; Dartmouth Col, MS(eng sci), 85. *Prof Exp:* Asst, Univ Pittsburgh, 53-57; phys chemist, Nat Bur Stand, 57-61; mem res staff, Northrop Space Labs, 62-64, head, Space Physics & Chem Lab, 64-66; head, Phys Chem Lab, Northrop Space Labs, 66-67; chief, Res Div, US Army Cold Regions Res & Eng Lab, 67-89, tech staff, Hq Dept Army, 89-92. *Concurrent Pos:* Neth Govt fel, Kamerlingh Onnes Lab, Univ Leiden, 57-58; mem exten teaching staff, Univ Calif, Los Angeles, 65-66; mem Army res coun, Dept Army, 67-68; spec asst to cmndg gen, US Army Elec Res & Develop Command, 77; chief, Eng Div, US Army Cold Regions Res & Eng Lab, 84, tech dir, 84. *Mem:* Fel AAAS; Am Chem Soc; Am Phys Soc; Royal Soc Chem; Sigma Xi; Inst Elec & Electronics Engrs. *Res:* Technical management; digital signal processing; environmental quality research and development; low temperature physics. *Mailing Add:* 18004 Lickey Mill Rd Purcellville VA 20132

STERZER, FRED, ELECTRONICS ENGINEERING. *Current Pos:* PRES, MMTC, INC, 88- *Personal Data:* b Vienna, Austria, Nov 18, 29; nat US; m 64. *Educ:* City Col New York, BS, 51; NY Univ, MS, 52, PhD(physics), 55. *Prof Exp:* mem staff, RCA Corp, 54-87, dir, Microwave Technol Ctr, RCA Labs, 72-87; dir, med syst, David Sorwoff Res Ctr, 87-88. *Mem:* Nat Acad Eng; fel Inst Elec & Electronics Engrs; Am Phys Soc. *Res:* Microwave spectroscopy, tubes and solid state devices; medical devices. *Mailing Add:* MMTC Inc 12 Roszel Rd Suite A-203 Princeton NJ 08540. *Fax:* 609-520-9859

STETKA, DANIEL GEORGE, CYTOGENETICS. *Current Pos:* DIR & VPRES, DIAGENETICS OF FREDERICKSBURG, 94- *Personal Data:* b Baltimore, Md, Jan 8, 45; m 67, Mary L Johnson; c Breton S. *Educ:* Cornell Univ, BS, 66, MS, 67; Univ Mass, PhD(cell biol), 75. *Prof Exp:* Res biologist, Allied Corp, 79-84; dir cytogenetics, Children's Hosp, Buffalo, 84-91; asst prof pediat, State Univ NY, Buffalo, 84-91; dir, Amniocentesis Lab, Genetics & IVF Inst, 91-94. *Mem:* Am Soc Human Genetics. *Res:* Mechanisms and consequences of meiotic and mitotic non-disjunction in humans; applications of flourescence in situ hybridization in clinical cytogenetics. *Mailing Add:* 5619 Sirius Ct Atlantic Beach FL 32233. *Fax:* 703-876-3850

STETLER, DAVID ALBERT, PLANT CYTOLOGY. *Current Pos:* asst prof, 73-77, ASSOC PROF BOT, VA POLYTECH INST & STATE UNIV, 77-, ASSOC DEAN, 93- *Personal Data:* b Pasadena, Calif, June 17, 35; m 65, Paula Finch; c Tom & Dan (deceased). *Educ:* Univ Southern Calif, BSc, 59; Univ Calif, Berkeley, PhD(bot), 67. *Prof Exp:* Asst prof bot, Univ Minn, 67-69; asst prof biol, Dartmouth Col, 69-73. *Res:* Organelle development in plant cells; ultrastructure of plant tissues; ultrastructure of stressed animal tissues in the environment. *Mailing Add:* Off Dean Col Arts & Sci Va Polytech Inst & State Univ PO Box 0406 Blacksburg VA 24063-0405. *Fax:* 540-231-3380

STETLER, DEAN ALLEN, MOLECULAR BIOLOGY. *Current Pos:* asst prof biochem & molecular biol, 85-89, ASSOC PROF BIOCHEM, UNIV KANS, 89-, CHMN, GENETICS PROG, 86- *Personal Data:* b Beloit, Kans, Nov 25, 54; m 72; c 3. *Educ:* Univ Kans, BA, 76, PhD(microbiol), 80. *Prof Exp:* Res assoc molecular pharmacol, Pa State Col Med, 80-82, asst prof, 82-85. *Concurrent Pos:* Consult, Immunodiagnostics & Molecular Genetics. *Res:* Control of gene transcription; role of poly(A) polymerase in ultimate gene expression; role of protein phosphorylation in formation of autoimmunogenic nuclear proteins in rheumatic disease. *Mailing Add:* Dept Biochem Univ Kans 3043 Haworth Hall Lawrence KS 66045-2106. *Fax:* 785-864-5321

STETLER-STEVENSON, WILLIAM GEORGE, EXTRACELLULAR MATRIX, CELL INVASION. *Current Pos:* MED OFFICER, LAB PATH, NAT CANCER INST, 91-, CHIEF, EXTRACELLULAR MATRIX PATH SECT, 93- *Personal Data:* b Trenton, NJ, Nov 27, 53; m 75, Maryalice; c Margaret. *Educ:* Northwestern Univ, PhD(biochem), 83, MD, 84. *Honors & Awards:* Warner Lambert/Parke Davis Award, Am Soc Investigative Path, 96. *Mem:* Am Soc Investigative Path; Am Soc Biochem & Molecular Biol; US & Can Acad Path; Metastatis Res Soc (pres, 96-). *Res:* Invasion and remodelling of the extracellular matrix. *Mailing Add:* Bldg 10 Rm ZA33MSC1500 10 Center Dr Bethesda MD 20892-1500

STETSON, ALVIN RAE, HIGH-TEMPERATURE COATINGS. *Current Pos:* RETIRED. *Personal Data:* b San Diego, Calif, July 23, 26; m 47; c 2. *Educ:* San Diego State Col, AB, 48. *Prof Exp:* Anal chemist, Solar Turbine Inc, Caterpillar Tractor Co, 48-50, phys chemist, 50-53, from staff engr to sr res staff engr, 53-66, chief process res, 66-72, chief mat engr, 72-80, chief mat technol, 80-85, consult high temperature, 85-90. *Mem:* Am Chem Soc; Nat Asn Corrosion Eng; Am Soc Metals. *Res:* Fused salt plating; high temperature metallic and ceramic protective coatings; reaction of materials at high temperatures; reentry and gas turbine environment simulation; braze joining of dissimilar metals; plasma arc testing and spraying; abrasive and abradable turbine tip seals; materials research supervision; thirteen US patents in the proctive field. *Mailing Add:* 4834 Lucille Dr San Diego CA 92115

STETSON, HAROLD W(ILBUR), CERAMICS, INORGANIC CHEMISTRY. *Current Pos:* PRES, CERAMIC SCI ASSOC, 86- *Personal Data:* b Bristol, Pa, July 2, 26; m 52, Grace Leister; c Edith, Robert & Harold. *Educ:* Pa State Univ, BS, 50, MS 52, PhD(ceramics), 56. *Honors & Awards:* S J Geijsbeek Award, Am Ceramic Soc, 88, Founders Award, 90. *Prof Exp:* Sr engr, Corning Glass Works, 56-59 & Radio Corp Am, 59-62; sr engr, Western Elec Co, Princeton, 62-66, res leader ceramics, 66-69; dir res, Ceramic Metal Systs, Inc, 69-70; sr engr, Eastern Res Labs, TRW, 70-86. *Concurrent Pos:* Vis assoc prof ceramic eng, Rutgers Univ, 71-72; trustee, Am Ceramic Soc, 92- *Mem:* Fel Am Ceramic Soc; Nat Inst Ceramic Engrs (pres, 88-90); fel Am Inst Chemists; Int Soc Hybrid Microelectronics. *Res:* Ceramic materials for electronic uses; sintering theory of oxides; application of modern ceramic technology to archeological problems. *Mailing Add:* 222 N Chancellor St Newtown PA 18940

STETSON, KARL ANDREW, HOLOGRAM INTERFEROMETRY, VIBRATION THEORY. *Current Pos:* HEAD, KARL STETSON ASSOC, COVENTRY, CONN, 94- *Personal Data:* b Gardener, Mass, Oct 16, 37; m 59. *Educ:* Lowell Technol Inst, BSEE, 59; Univ Mich, MSE, 60; Royal Inst Technol, Stockholm, Sweden, PhD(phys optics), 69. *Honors & Awards:* Hefenji Award, Soc Exp Mech, 79, B J Lazan Award, 83. *Prof Exp:* Elec engr, Bell Aerosysts, 61-62; res scientist, Inst Sci & Technol, Univ Mich, 62-65; engr, GCA, 66-67; prin res fel, Nat Phys Lab, UK, 69-71; res scientist, Ford Motor Co Res Labs, 71-73; sr scientist, United Technol Res Ctr, 73-94. *Concurrent Pos:* Privat docent, Royal Inst Technol, 69-; adj prof, Worcester Polytech Inst, 80- *Mem:* Optical Soc Am; Soc Exp Mech. *Res:* Coherent optical metrology with emphasis on holography and laser methods. *Mailing Add:* 2060 South St Coventry CT 06238. *Fax:* 203-742-8414

STETSON, KENNETH F(RANCIS), AERODYNAMICS, AEROPHYSICS. *Current Pos:* RETIRED. *Personal Data:* b Winthrop, Maine, May 2, 24; m 48; c 2. *Educ:* Univ Maine, BS, 49; USAF Inst Technol, BS, 52; Ohio State Univ, MS, 56. *Prof Exp:* Proj engr, Aircraft Lab, Wright-Patterson AFB, Ohio, 50-51, aeronaut engr, Aeronaut Res Labs, 52-56; sr staff scientist, Everett Res Lab, Avco Corp, Mass, 56-61, sr proj engr, Res & Develop Div, 61-66, sr staff scientist, Space Systs Div, 66-68; Ohio State Univ Res Found vis res assoc, Wright-Patterson AFB, 68-69, aerospace engr, Aerospace Res Labs, 69-75, aerospace engr, Flight Dynamics Lab, 75-90. *Mem:* Assoc fel Am Inst Aeronaut & Astronaut. *Res:* Hypersonic, aerodynamic and aerophysics research. *Mailing Add:* 7104 Hartcrest Lane Dayton OH 45459

STETSON, LAVERNE ELLIS, ELECTRICAL WIRING & SAFETY FOR RURAL APPLICATIONS, ENERGY & ELECTRICAL DEMANDS OF RURAL INDUSTRIES. *Current Pos:* AGR ENGR, AGR RES SERV, USDA, 62- *Personal Data:* b Crawford, Nebr, Aug 26, 33; m 56, Shirley R Wasserburger; c Patricia, Erwin, Ronald & Helen. *Educ:* Univ Nebr, BS, 62, MS, 68. *Honors & Awards:* George W Kable Award, Am Soc Agr Engrs, 87, Packer Eng Safety Award, 90. *Concurrent Pos:* Mem, Panels 13 & 19, Nat Fire Protect Asn, 91- *Mem:* Fel Am Soc Agr Engrs; fel Inst Elec & Electronics Engrs; Irrig Asn; Int Asn Elec Inspectors; Nat Fire Protection Asn; Int Asn Elect Inspection. *Res:* Radio frequency electric fields for improving seed germination and controlling stored grain insects; safety, electrical requirements and load management of irrigation and farmstead equipment. *Mailing Add:* 252 Chase Hall Univ Nebr Lincoln NE 68583-0934. *Fax:* 402-472-6338; *E-Mail:* lstetson@unlinfo.unl.edu

STETSON, MILTON H, REPRODUCTIVE ENDOCRINOLOGY, BIOLOGICAL RHYTHMS. *Current Pos:* from asst prof to assoc prof biol & health sci, 73-80, prof life & health sci & assoc dir, Grad Progs & Res, 81-86, DIR, SCH LIFE & HEALTH SCI, UNIV DEL, 87- *Personal Data:* b Springfield, Mass, Nov 25, 43; m 66; c 2. *Educ:* Cent Conn State Col, BA, 65; Univ Wash, MS, 68, PhD(zool), 70. *Prof Exp:* NIH fel, 66-70; res fel reproduction, Univ Tex, Austin, 71-73. *Mem:* Am Physiol Soc; Am Soc Zool; fel AAAS; Soc Study Reproduction; Am Asn Univ Profs; Endocrine Soc; Soc Res Biol Rhythms. *Res:* Role of the circadian system in the timing of reproductive events; neural and neuroendocrine generation of female reproductive cyclicity; comparative endocrinology of the thyroid gland; ontogeny of puberty; pineal physiology. *Mailing Add:* Dept Biol Sch Life-Health Sci Univ Del 117 Wolf Hall Newark DE 19716. *Fax:* 302-831-2281

STETSON, PETER BRAILEY, PHOTOMETRY ASTRONOMY, STAR CLUSTERS STELLAR POPULATIONS. *Current Pos:* res assoc, 83-84, SR RES OFFICER, DOMINION ASTROPHYS OBSERV-HERZBERG INST ASTROPHYS-NAT RES COUN, 84-, HEAD COMPUT, 96- *Personal Data:* b Middleboro, Mass, Aug 30, 52; m 79, Frances Bogucki; c Whitney, Brailey, Garrett & Leete. *Educ:* Wesleyan Univ, BA & MA, 74; Yale, MSc, 75, PhD(astron), 79. *Honors & Awards:* Petrie Prize, Can Astron Soc, 91; Gold Medal, Sci Coun BC, 94. *Prof Exp:* Fel astron, Yale Univ, 79-80; Carnegie fel, Carnegie Inst Wash, 80-83; adj prof physics & astron, Univ Victoria, 88- *Mem:* Int Astron Union; Am Astron Soc; Can Astron Soc; Sigma Xi; Astron Soc USSR. *Res:* Measurement of stellar brightnesses, colors, and velocities through space - determine distance, ages, and motions of both star clusters and individual stars; provide direct information on age of galaxy, manner formed and how it continues to evolve; development of related computer software. *Mailing Add:* Dominion Astrophys Observ 5071 W Saanich Rd Victoria BC V8X 4M6 Can. *E-Mail:* peter.stetson@hia.nrc.ca

STETSON, ROBERT F, METALLURGICAL ENGINEERING. *Current Pos:* RETIRED. *Personal Data:* b New York, NY, Oct 20, 28. *Prof Exp:* Tech specialist, Gen Atomics, 58-90. *Mem:* Fel Am Soc Metals Int. *Res:* Design and construction of specialty testing equipment for materials; awarded one patent in plasma orifice nossel. *Mailing Add:* 6754 El Banquero Pl San Diego CA 92119

STETSON, ROBERT FRANKLIN, BIOMATHEMATICS, PLASMA PHYSICS. *Current Pos:* assoc prof, Fla Atlantic Univ, 64-69, dir fac scholars prog, 71-84, dir degree prog, 71-84, PROF PHYSICS, FLA ATLANTIC UNIV, 69- *Personal Data:* b Lewiston, Maine, Apr 17, 32; m 67, Dorothy McBride. *Educ:* Bates Col, BS, 54; Wesleyan Univ, MA, 56; Univ Va, PhD(physics), 59. *Prof Exp:* Asst physics, Wesleyan Univ, 54-56; instr, Univ Va, 56-58; asst prof, Univ Fla, 59-64. *Concurrent Pos:* Proj scientist, Air Force Off Sci Res, 62-64; consult, Col Entrance Exam Bd; dir, South Regional Ctr for Excellence, 86-; chmn physics, Fla Atlantic Univ, 91-94. *Mem:* Am Phys Soc; Am Asn Physics Teachers; fel AAAS. *Res:* Angular correlation of gamma rays; neutron scattering; non-traditional higher education; computer simulation of plasma and thermodynamic problems; computer simulation in biomathematics. *Mailing Add:* Dept Physics Fla Atlantic Univ Boca Raton FL 33431

STETTENHEIM, PETER, ORNITHOLOGY. *Current Pos:* COORD ED, RECENT ORNITH LIT, 96- *Personal Data:* b New York, NY, Dec 27, 28; m 65, Sandy Byers; c Wendy S (Jones) & Joel. *Educ:* Haverford Col, BS, 50; Univ Mich, MA, 51, PhD(zool), 59. *Honors & Awards:* Co-recipient, Tom Newman Mem Int Award, Brit Poultry Breeders & Hatcheries Asn, 73. *Prof Exp:* Res zoologist, USDA, Avian Anat Proj, 58-69; book rev ed, Wilson Bull, 70-74; ed, Condor, 74-85, ed, Biographies of North Am Birds, 85-95. *Concurrent Pos:* Mem, Int Comt Avian Anat Nomenclature; secy, bd dirs, Montshire Mus Sci; bd dirs, Soc Protection NH Forests. *Mem:* Wilson Ornith Soc; hon mem Cooper Ornith Soc; fel Am Ornith Union. *Res:* Growth, structure and functions of feathers; supervise production of a quarterly classified list of abstracts of worldwide ornithological literature. *Mailing Add:* HC 64, Box 255 Lebanon NH 03766-7607. *E-Mail:* peter.stettenheim@valley.net

STETTER, JOSEPH ROBERT, PHYSICAL CHEMISTRY, ELECTROCHEMISTRY. *Current Pos:* ADJ PROF, ILL INST TECHNOL, CHICAGO, 85-; INDEPENDENT INDUST CONSULT, 97- *Personal Data:* b Buffalo, NY, Dec 15, 46; m 72, M Francine Wroblewski; c Thomas, Edward & Suzanne. *Educ:* State Univ NY Buffalo, BA, 69, PhD(phys chem), 75. *Honors & Awards:* IR-100 Awards for Instrument Develop, 77, 84 & 94; New Tech Award, NASA, 79, 93; Tech Transfer Award, Fed Lab Consortium, 87. *Prof Exp:* Res asst, Linde Div, Union Carbide Corp, 66-68, chemist, 69; sr res chemist, Becton Dickinson & Co, 74-77, dir chem res, 77-80; scientist & sect head & group leader, Argonne Nat Lab, 80-85; pres, Transducer Res, Inc, Naperville, Ill, 83-97. *Concurrent Pos:* Trustee, Lakeland Cent Sch Dist, 77-80; mem gov bd, Fedn Anal Chem & Spectros Soc, 80-; comt mem, Nat Acad Sci, 87-91; secy/treas, Sensor Div, Electrochem Soc, 96- *Mem:* Am Chem Soc; AAAS; Int Soc Exposure Anal; Instrument Soc Am; Sigma Xi; Electrochem Soc; Am Conf Govt Indust Hygienists; Air & Waste Mgt Asn; Planetary Soc. *Res:* Chemical sensors, physical adsorption, chemisorption, heterogeneous catalytic systems, surface chemistry, environmental chemistry, electrochemistry, analytical chemistry and instrumentation. *Mailing Add:* 1228 Olympus Dr Naperville IL 60540. *E-Mail:* jrstetter@aol.com

STETTLER, JOHN DIETRICH, LASER PHYSICS, PROPAGATION. *Current Pos:* RETIRED. *Personal Data:* b Cleveland, Ohio, Mar 15, 34; m 57; c 5. *Educ:* Univ Notre Dame, BS, 56; Mass Inst Technol, PhD(physics), 62. *Prof Exp:* Res asst physics, Mass Inst Technol, 57-60; asst prof, Univ Mo-Rolla, 60-64; res physicist, US Army Missile Command, 64-76, mgr laser signature measurements, 76-79, chief, Optics Group, 79-80; sr scientist, Appl Res Inc, 81-82. *Concurrent Pos:* Adj prof physics, Univ Ala, Huntsville, 70-. *Mem:* AAAS; Am Phys Soc; Am Asn Physics Teachers. *Res:* Eximer lasers and Raman shifting; propagation of submillimeter to visible radiation through a turbulent atmosphere; application of lasers to ballistic missile defense; particle beam optics. *Mailing Add:* 175 Stoneway Madison AL 35758

STETTLER, REINHARD FRIEDERICH, FOREST GENETICS. *Current Pos:* from asst prof to assoc prof, 63-74, PROF FOREST GENETICS, UNIV WASH, 74- *Personal Data:* b Steckborn, Switz, Dec 27, 29; m 55; c 1. *Educ:* Swiss Fed Inst Technol, dipl, 55; Univ Calif, Berkeley, PhD(genetics), 63. *Prof Exp:* Res officer silvicult, Res Div, BC Forest Serv, Can, 56-58; res assoc forest mgt, Fed Inst Forest Res, Switz, 58-59. *Concurrent Pos:* Alexander von Humboldt fel, Inst Forest Genetics, Schmalenbeck, Ger, 69-70; vis scholar, Abegg Found, Berne, 76; guest lectr, Dept Bot, Univ Nijmegen, Neth, 77. *Mem:* AAAS; Sigma Xi. *Res:* Genetic control of morphogenesis in higher plants; reproductive biology of forest trees; genetic and physiological studies in short-rotation culture for fiber and energy; induction of haploid parthenogenesis. *Mailing Add:* Col Forestry Resources Univ Wash Seattle WA 98105

STETTNER, ROGER, PLASMA, PHYSICS. *Current Pos:* OWNER, ADVAN SCI CONCEPTS INC, 87- *Personal Data:* b New York, NY, July 29, 40. *Educ:* City Col New York, BS, 62; Columbia Univ, MS, 64; Univ Chicago, PhD(physics), 71. *Prof Exp:* Res scientist, Mission Res Corp, 74-87. *Mem:* Am Phys Soc. *Mailing Add:* 2441 Foothill Lane Santa Barbara CA 93105

STEUCEK, GUY LINSLEY, PLANT PHYSIOLOGY. *Current Pos:* from asst prof to assoc prof, 69-77, PROF BIOL, MILLERSVILLE UNIV, 77- *Personal Data:* b New Haven, Conn, Jan 22, 42; c 2. *Educ:* Univ Conn, BS, 63, PhD(plant physiol), 68; Yale Univ, MF, 65. *Prof Exp:* Nat Res Coun Can fel, Forest Prod Lab, BC, 64-65; vis scholar, Univ BC, 68-69. *Mem:* AAAS; Am Soc Plant Physiol; Scan Soc Plant Physiol; Ecol Soc Am; Am Inst Biol Sci. *Res:* Influence of mechanical stress on plant growth and development; phloem transport and mineral nutrition. *Mailing Add:* Dept Biol Millersville Univ Millersville PA 17551

STEUDEL, HAROLD JUDE, TOTAL QUALITY MANAGEMENT, COMPUTER SIMULATION. *Current Pos:* assoc prof indust eng, 82-85, assoc dir, Univ Indust Res, 82-91, PROF INDUST ENG, UNIV WIS-MADISON, 85- *Personal Data:* b Milwaukee, Wis, Jan 3, 45. *Educ:* Univ Wis-Madison, BS, 68, PhD(mech eng), 74, Milwaukee, MS, 71. *Prof Exp:* From asst prof to assoc prof mgt, Marquette Univ, 74-82. *Concurrent Pos:* Pres, H J Steudel & Assoc Inc, 74-; mem, Col-Indust Coun for Mat Handling Educ, 80-84. *Mem:* Sr mem Inst Elec & Electronics Engrs; sr mem Soc Mfg Engrs; Am Soc Qual Control. *Res:* Computer simulation and statistical modeling for the design and analysis of computer integrated manufacturing systems; design and evaluation of cellular manufacturing layout configurations for just-in-time operations; job sequencing and control strategies for flexible machining workcells. *Mailing Add:* 1309 Farwell Dr Madison WI 53704

STEUER, MALCOLM F, ATOMIC & MOLECULAR PHYSICS, NUCLEAR PHYSICS. *Current Pos:* asst prof, 58-63, assoc prof, 63-77, PROF PHYSICS, UNIV GA, 77- *Personal Data:* b Marion, SC, Dec 16, 28; m 58; c 3. *Educ:* US Merchant Marine Acad, BS, 50; Clemson Col, MS, 54; Univ Va, PhD(physics), 57. *Prof Exp:* Res fel, Univ Va, 57-58. *Concurrent Pos:* NSF sci fac fel, Univ Wis, 64-65; sci fac fel, Argonne Nat Lab, 80-81. *Mem:* Am Phys Soc. *Res:* Interactions of MeV projectiles with matter; interactions of neutrons with nuclei. *Mailing Add:* Dept Physics Univ Ga Athens GA 30602

STEUNENBERG, ROBERT KEPPEL, INORGANIC CHEMISTRY. *Current Pos:* RETIRED. *Personal Data:* b Caldwell, Idaho, Sept 18, 24; m 47, Jean Smylie. *Educ:* Col Idaho, BA, 47; Univ Wash, PhD(chem), 51. *Hon Degrees:* DSc, Col Idaho, 87. *Prof Exp:* Mem staff, Argonne Nat Lab, 51-67, sr chemist, 67-86. *Mem:* Am Chem Soc; Sigma Xi; Am Nuclear Soc; Electrochem Soc. *Res:* Fluorocarbons; interhalogen compounds; pyrometallurgical methods for processing nuclear reactor fuels; nuclear technology; high-temperature batteries; energy conversion; molten salt chemistry. *Mailing Add:* 60 Golden Larch Dr Naperville IL 60540-7407

STEVEN, ALASDAIR C, ELECTRON MICROSCOPY, IMAGE PROCESSING & STRUCTURAL BIOLOGY. *Current Pos:* vis scientist, 78-85, sect chief, 85-90, LAB CHIEF, NIH, 90- *Personal Data:* b Alyth, Scotland, June 27, 47; US citizen; m 71, Ray E; c Mairi C & Andrew. *Educ:* Edinburgh Univ, Scotland, MA, 69, Cambridge Univ, PhD(theoret physics), 73; Basel Univ, Switz, SKMB, 75. *Prof Exp:* Res asst, Basel Univ, 73-78. *Mem:* Electron Micros Soc Am; Biophys Soc; Am Soc Microbiol. *Res:* Structural basis of molecular biology; high resolution electron microscopy; computer image analysis and model building; assembly properties of proteins, nucleoproteins, viruses, crystals and polymers; virus structure; macromolecular assembly. *Mailing Add:* Bldg 6 Rm B2-34, MSC 2717 NIH Bethesda MD 20892. *Fax:* 301-480-7629; *E-Mail:* alasdair.steven@.nih.gov

STEVENS, ALAN DOUGLAS, OCCUPATIONAL HEALTH, VETERINARY MEDICINE. *Current Pos:* RETIRED. *Personal Data:* b Nashua, NH, Aug 17, 26; m 49; c 5. *Educ:* Cornell Univ, DVM, 47. *Prof Exp:* Pvt pract, Ga, 47-50; prog officer res grants, Div Environ Eng & Food Protection, USPHS, 63-66, chief res grants, 66-67, chief res & training grants rev, Nat Ctr Urban & Indust Health, 67-68, environ control admin, 68-69, chief res grants, Bur Safety & Occup Health, Environ Control Admin, 69-70, asst dir to dir extramural progs, 70-75, dir training & man power develop, Nat Inst Occup Safety & Health, Ctr Dis Control, Dept Health, Educ & Welfare, 75-86. *Mem:* AAAS; Am Inst Chemists; Am Conf Govt Indust Hygienists. *Res:* Food chemistry and microbiology; irradiation of foods; virology; laboratory animal medicine; research administration; information retrieval. *Mailing Add:* 100 Silver Ave Ft Mitchell KY 41017

STEVENS, ANN REBECCA, BIOCHEMISTRY, CELL BIOLOGY. *Current Pos:* PROF BIOCHEM & ASSOC VPRES RES, EMORY UNIV, 85- *Personal Data:* b Huntington, WVa, July 22, 39; m 65, 77; c 2. *Educ:* Univ Ala, Tuscaloosa, BS, 61; Univ Colo, Denver, PhD(biochem), 66. *Prof Exp:* Res assoc cell biol, Inst Cellular, Molecular & Develop Biol, Univ Colo, Boulder, 66-68; res investr & dir electron micros labs, Vet Admin Hosp, 68-81; from asst prof to assoc prof, Univ Fla, 68-82, from asst dean to assoc dean, res div, sponsored res, 81-85, prof biochem, 82-85. *Concurrent Pos:* Nat Inst Allergy & Infectious Dis res grants, 70-76; Fulbright awardee, Pasteur Inst, Lille, France; assoc vpres acad affairs & dir sponsored progs, Emory Univ, 85- *Mem:* AAAS; Am Soc Cell Biol; Soc Exp Biol & Med; NY Acad Sci; Am Soc Biol Chemists; Nat Soc Res Admin (secy-treas, 83-84); Soc Res Admin. *Res:* Aspects of nucleic acid metabolism during growth and differentiation in pathogenic and nonpathogenic strains of Acanthamoeba and Naegleria; biochemical mechanism of the pathogenicity of free-living amoebae. *Mailing Add:* Sponsored Progs Emory Univ 1784 N Decatur Rd Suite 510 Atlanta GA 30322

STEVENS, AUDREY L, BIOCHEMISTRY, MICROBIOLOGY. *Current Pos:* MEM RES STAFF, BIOL DIV, OAK RIDGE NAT LAB, 66- *Personal Data:* b Leigh, Nebr, July 21, 32; m 64; c 2. *Educ:* Iowa State Univ, BS, 53; Western Reserve Univ, PhD(biochem), 58. *Prof Exp:* NSF fel, 58-60; instr pharmacol, Sch Med, Univ St Louis, 60-62; asst prof, 62-63; from asst prof to assoc prof biochem, Sch Med, Univ Md, Balitmore City, 63-66. *Concurrent Pos:* NSF res grants, 60-66. *Mem:* Am Soc Biol Chem. *Res:* Nuclear acid biosynthesis. *Mailing Add:* Biol Div Oak Ridge Nat Lab 4-12 Plant Bldg 9211 Rm 2025 Oak Ridge TN 37831-8080. *Fax:* 423-574-1274

STEVENS, BRIAN, PHOTOCHEMISTRY. *Current Pos:* prof chem, 67-89, GRAD RES PROF, UNIV SFLA, 89- *Personal Data:* b South Elmsall, Eng, July 22, 24; m 53; c 2. *Educ:* Oxford Univ, BA & MA, 50, DPhil(phys chem), 53. *Hon Degrees:* DSc, Oxford Univ, 77. *Prof Exp:* Fel, Nat Res Coun Can, 53-55; res asst chem, Princeton Univ, 55-56, res assoc, 56-57; res assoc tech off chem eng, Esso Res & Eng Co, NJ, 57-58; lectr chem, Univ Sheffield, 58-65, reader photochem, 65-67. *Concurrent Pos:* Askounes-Ashford distinguished scholar, 86. *Mem:* Am Chem Soc; Am Soc Photobiol. *Res:* Molecular luminescence and electronic energy transfer in complex molecules; photosensitized peroxidation of unsaturated molecules and reduction of dyes; solute re-encounter effects; electron donor acceptor orbital correlations. *Mailing Add:* Dept Chem Univ South Fla Tampa FL 33620

STEVENS, BRUCE RUSSELL, MEMBRANE TRANSPORT, GASTROINTESTINAL ABSORPTION & BRAIN BIOCHEMISTRY. *Current Pos:* asst prof physiol, Dept Physiol, 84-89, assoc prof physiol & surg, 89-96, PROF PHYSIOL, COL MED, UNIV FLA, 96- *Personal Data:* b Ogden, Utah, Apr 1, 52; m 75. *Educ:* Valparaiso Univ, BS, 74; Ill State Univ, MS, 77, PhD(physiol), 80. *Prof Exp:* Res asst, Ill State Univ, 75-80, instr, 78; fel, Med Sch, Univ Calif, Los Angeles, 80-83, res physiologist, 83-84. *Concurrent Pos:* Vis scientist, Pavlov Inst Physiol, Leningrad; mem, Ad Hoc Rev Comt, NSF grant rev; grant reviewer, Am Heart Asn. *Mem:* Am Physiol Soc. *Res:* Biomembrane transport mechanisms for amino acids and sugars; enzymatic hydrolysis of peptides and carbohydrates. *Mailing Add:* Dept Physiol Univ Fla Col Med Box 100274 Gainesville FL 32610. *Fax:* 352-846-0270; *E-Mail:* stevens@phys.med.ufl.edu

STEVENS, CALVIN H, PALEOECOLOGY, STRATIGRAPHY. *Current Pos:* from asst prof to assoc prof, 66-72, PROF GEOL, SAN JOSE STATE UNIV, 72- *Personal Data:* b Sheridan, Wyo, Apr 3, 34; m 61, Frances; c Clark & Sarah. *Educ:* Univ Colo, AB, 56, MA, 58; Univ Southern Calif, PhD(geol), 63. *Prof Exp:* Geologist, Res Lab, Humble Oil Co, 58-60; asst prof geol, San Jose State Col, 63-65 & Univ Colo, 65-66. *Mem:* Am Asn Petrol Geologists; fel Geol Soc Am; Soc Econ Paleont & Mineral; Paleont Soc. *Res:* Late Paleozoic paleoecology and paleontology; Great Basin geology and stratigraphy; permian corals and fusulinids. *Mailing Add:* 1263 Clark Way San Jose CA 95125. *Fax:* 408-924-5053; *E-Mail:* stevens@sjsuvm1.sjsu.edu

STEVENS, CALVIN LEE, CHEMISTRY. *Current Pos:* from asst prof to assoc prof, 48-54, PROF ORG CHEM, WAYNE STATE UNIV, 54- *Personal Data:* b Edwardsville, Ill, Nov 3, 23; m 47; c 1. *Educ:* Univ Ill, BS, 44; Univ Wis, PhD(org chem), 47. *Hon Degrees:* Dr, Univ Nancy, France, 82. *Prof Exp:* Asst org chem, Univ Wis, 44-47; Du Pont fel, Mass Inst Technol, 47-48. *Concurrent Pos:* Guggenheim fel, Univ Paris, 55-56; sci liaison officer, Off Naval Res, London, 59-60; Fulbright fels, Sorbonne, 64-65, Univ Paris, 71-72. *Mem:* Am Chem Soc; The Chem Soc; Swiss Chem Soc; Chem Soc France. *Res:* Organic chemistry; epoxyethers and nitrogen analogs of ketenes; natural products; amino-sugars; amino-ketone rearrangements. *Mailing Add:* 200 Riverfront Park Apt 23K Detroit MI 48226-4525

STEVENS, CHARLES DAVID, BIOCHEMISTRY. *Current Pos:* from assoc prof to prof, 65-80, EMER PROF BIOMET, EMORY UNIV, 80- *Personal Data:* b Pittsburgh, Pa, Feb 1, 12; m 37, 79, Virginia A Larkin; c David, Sally, Susan, Robert, James & Constance. *Educ:* Univ Cincinnati, AB, 33, MSc, 34, PhD(biochem), 37. *Prof Exp:* Res assoc biochem, Cardiac Lab, Sch Med, Univ Cincinnati, 38-42 & Lab Aviation Med, 42-45; biochemist, Dow Chem Co, 45-46; res assoc biochem, Gastric Lab, Univ Cincinnati, 46-50, asst prof, Dept Prev Med & Indust Health, 50-65. *Concurrent Pos:* Fel, Med Col Va, 61-62. *Mem:* Fel AAAS; Soc Exp Biol & Med; Am Asn Cancer Res. *Res:* Selective localization of chemicals in acidic cancer tissue; respiration; biomathematics; synthesis and metabolism of organolead compounds. *Mailing Add:* 1519 Thornhill Ct Dunwoody GA 30338-4226

STEVENS, CHARLES EDWARD, VETERINARY PHYSIOLOGY, COMPARATIVE PHYSIOLOGY OF DIGESTIVE SYSTEM. *Current Pos:* assoc dean res & grad studies, 80-92, PROF PHYSIOL, COL VET MED, NC STATE UNIV, 92- *Personal Data:* b Minneapolis, Minn, June 5, 27; m, Barbara Cox; c Leslee, Judith, Laura & David. *Educ:* Univ Minn, BS, 51, DVM & MS, 55, PhD(vet physiol & pharmacol), 58. *Hon Degrees:* Hon Prof, San Marcos Univ, Peru, 72. *Prof Exp:* Instr vet anat, Univ Minn, 51-52, asst vet physiol, 52-55, res assoc, 58-60; vet physiologist, Agr Res Serv, USDA, 60-61; assoc prof vet physiol, NY State Vet Col, Cornell Univ, 61-66, prof, 66-79, chmn, Dept Physiol, Biochem & Pharmacol, 73-79. *Concurrent Pos:* NIH spec res fel, 62-63, dir training prog comp gastroenterol, 71-76; field rep grad physiol, Cornell Univ, 68-70; mem, Gen Med Study Sect, NIH, 69-73; Fulbright lectr, 72; mem, Nat Agr Res Coun, 90-92. *Mem:* Am Soc Vet Physiol & Pharmacol (pres, 67-68); Am Physiol Soc; Am Vet Med Asn; Conf Res Workers Animal Dis; Comp Gastroenterol Soc; Am Gastroenterol Asn. *Res:* Comparative physiology of the vertebrate digestive system; mechanisms of secretion, absorption and digesta transit. *Mailing Add:* Col Vet Med NC State Univ Raleigh NC 27650

STEVENS, CHARLES F, NEUROBIOLOGY. *Current Pos:* INVESTR, HOWARD HUGHES MED INST, 90-; PROF, SALK INST, 90- *Personal Data:* b Chicago, Ill, Sept 1, 34; m 56; c 3. *Educ:* Harvard Univ, BA, 56; Yale Univ, MD, 60; Rockefeller Univ, PhD, 64. *Honors & Awards:* Spencer Award, 79. *Prof Exp:* From asst prof to prof physiol & biophys, Sch Med, Univ Wash, 63-75; prof physiol, Sch Med, Yale Univ, 75-83, prof & chmn molecular neurobiol, 83-90. *Mem:* Nat Acad Sci; Soc Neurosci; Am Acad Arts & Sci. *Res:* Synaptic transmission; properties of excitable membranes. *Mailing Add:* Salk Inst Molecular Neurobiol 10010 N Torrey Pines Rd La Jolla CA 92037

STEVENS, CHARLES LE ROY, BIOPHYSICAL CHEMISTRY. *Current Pos:* RETIRED. *Personal Data:* b Chicago, Ill, Aug 8, 31; c 4. *Educ:* Valparaiso Univ, BA, 53; Univ Pittsburgh, MS, 60, PhD(biophys), 62. *Prof Exp:* Physicist, US Army Biol Labs, 55-56; NIH res fel, 62-64; from asst prof to assoc prof biophys, Univ Pittsburgh, 67-95. *Concurrent Pos:* NATO sr fel, Univ Uppsala, 69. *Mem:* AAAS; NY Acad Sci; Biophys Soc. *Res:* Physical chemistry of proteins and nucleic acids; the role of water in the structure of biological macromolecules; self-association of proteins; cell motility. *Mailing Add:* 851 N Meadow Cross Ave Pittsburgh PA 15216

STEVENS, CLARK, MICROBIOLOGY, CELL PHYSIOLOGY. *Current Pos:* prof & head Dept Biol, 66-88, PRO EMER, ABILENE CHRISTIAN COL, 88- *Personal Data:* b Richland, Tex, Mar 24, 21; m 44; c 2. *Educ:* Harding Col, BS, 49; Univ Ark, MA, 51; Vanderbilt Univ, PhD(biol), 56. *Prof Exp:* Instr sci, Beebe Jr Col, 47-49; asst prof biol, Harding Col, 50-52, prof, 55-66; instr, Vanderbilt Univ, 54-55. *Concurrent Pos:* NIH res fel, 62-63. *Res:* Bacterial physiology and biochemistry; animal virology; microbiology of water. *Mailing Add:* 902 Scott Pl Abilene TX 79601

STEVENS, DALE JOHN, PHYSICAL GEOGRAPHY. *Current Pos:* assoc prof, 66-80, PROF GEOG, BRIGHAM YOUNG UNIV, 80-, DEPT CHAIR, 89- *Personal Data:* b Ogden, Utah, June 27, 36; m 62, Mary Lasson; c Clarke, Alan, Jill, SueAnn, Kaylene, Cherie. *Educ:* Brigham Young Univ, BA, 61; Ind Univ, MA, 63; Univ Calif, Los Angeles, PhD(geog), 69. *Prof Exp:* Instr geog, Univ Wyo, 63-64. *Concurrent Pos:* Univ develop grant, Brigham Young Univ, 71-72, 84 & Austria, 77, 85 & 91; dir, Natural Arch & Bridge Soc. *Mem:* Asn Am Geog; Natural Arch & Bridge Soc. *Res:* Morphometric analysis of land forms, natural arches and bridges; climatology; Utah geography. *Mailing Add:* Geog Brigham Young Univ 690 SWKT Provo UT 84602-1130. *Fax:* 801-378-5978; *E-Mail:* stevensd@fhs.byu.edu

STEVENS, DAVID KING, WASTEWATER TREATMENT, CONTAMINANT TRANSPORT MODELING. *Current Pos:* ASSOC PROF ENVIRON ENG, UTAH STATE UNIV, 86- *Personal Data:* m 85, Margaret M Cashell; c Michael & Abby. *Educ:* Tufts Univ, BSCE, 76; Univ Wis, PhD(environ eng), 83. *Prof Exp:* Irrig engr, US Peace Corps, Malaysia, 76-78. *Concurrent Pos:* Adj prof biol & irrig engr, Utah State Univ, 93. *Mem:* Sigma Xi; Am Soc Civil Engrs; Water Environ Fedn; Am Water Works Asn. *Res:* Chemical, physical and biological treatment of water and wastewater; mathematical modeling of treatment processes and natural environmental systems. *Mailing Add:* 1525 E 1220 N Logan UT 84341. *E-Mail:* stevens@quito.cee.usu.edu

STEVENS, DAVID ROBERT, TECHNICAL MANAGEMENT, IMMUNOLOGY. *Current Pos:* CONSULT, 89- *Personal Data:* b Logan, Utah, Apr 4, 49; m 81; c 3. *Educ:* Wash State Univ, BS, 72, DVM, 74; Univ Calif, Davis, PhD(comput path), 77; Am Col Vet Pathologists, dipl, 79. *Prof Exp:* Prin scientist immunol, Advan Genetics Res Inst, Agrion Corp, 82-85, dir res & develop, 85-86, vpres res & develop, Diamond Sci Co, Agrion Corp, 86-87; at Hills Pets Prod, 88-89. *Concurrent Pos:* Mem, Nat Agr Res & Exten Users Adv Bd, 85-87; Nebr Res & Develop Authority, 86- *Mem:* AAAS; Am Vet Med Asn; Am Asn Vet Lab Diagnosticians. *Res:* Industrial research and development management; animal and human health products. *Mailing Add:* David Brown 40 New Hampshire St Lawrence KS 66044

STEVENS, DEAN FINLEY, ZOOLOGY, CELL BIOLOGY. *Current Pos:* RETIRED. *Personal Data:* b Derby, Conn, Oct 19, 23; m 51; c 3. *Educ:* Boston Univ, AB, 49, AM, 50; Clark Univ, PhD(cell biol), 64. *Prof Exp:* Res asst biol, Boston Univ, 50-51; teaching master, Mt Hermon Sch Boys, 51-54; staff scientist, Worcester Found Exp Biol, 54-67; assoc prof zool, Univ Vt, 67-88. *Concurrent Pos:* Fels, USPHS, Am Cancer Soc & NIH; Ortho Res Found spec grant. *Mem:* Am Soc Cell Biol; Am Asn Cancer Res. *Res:* Vascular physiology; cancer; mechanisms of cell division. *Mailing Add:* PO Box 686 Colchester VT 05446

STEVENS, DONALD KEITH, SOLID STATE PHYSICS. *Current Pos:* RETIRED. *Personal Data:* b Troy, NY, July 30, 22; m 45, 65, 74; c 2. *Educ:* Union Col, BS, 43; Univ NC, PhD(chem), 53. *Prof Exp:* Physicist, US Naval Res Lab, 43-49; consult radiation effects in solids, Oak Ridge Nat Lab, 49-51, physicist, 53-57; chief, Metall & Mat Br, Div Res, USAEC, 57-60, asst dir, Res Metall & Mat Progs, 60-74, asst dir res mat sci, ERDA-Dept Energy, 74-81; dep assoc dir, Off Energy Res, Dept Energy, 81-85, assoc dir basic energy sci, 85-91. *Concurrent Pos:* Mem mat adv bd, Nat Acad Sci-Nat Res Coun, 59-62. *Mem:* Fel, AAAS; Sci Res Soc Am; Am Phys Soc. *Res:* Radiation effects in solids. *Mailing Add:* 9709 W Bexhill Dr Kensington MD 20895-3508

STEVENS, DONALD MEADE, NUCLEAR PHYSICS, COMPUTER SCIENCE. *Current Pos:* sr res engr nuclear physics, Lynchburg Res Ctr, 74-79, group supvr, Diag evelop Group, 80-81, group supvr data processing & diagnostics, 81-85, mgr, Nondestructive Methods & Diagnostics Sect, 85-94; CONSULT ENGR, LYNCHBURG RES CTR, BABCOCK & WILCOX CO, 94- *Personal Data:* b Lynchburg, Va, May 9, 47; m 70, Mary A Henry. *Educ:* Va Polytech Inst & State Univ, BS, 69, MS, 70, PhD(physics), 74. *Prof Exp:* Res asst physics, Va Polytech Inst, 70-74. *Concurrent Pos:* Guest res asst, Brookhaven Nat Lab, 70-73; guest scientist, Fermi Nat Accelerator Lab, 73-74. *Mem:* Am Phys Soc; Am Soc Mech Engrs; Am Soc Nondestructive Testing; Am Soc Testing & Mat. *Res:* Applications in monitoring power plants and designing computer systems; data processing and diagnostic systems; nondestructive methods and diagnostics; acoustics. *Mailing Add:* Lynchburg Res Ctr PO Box 11165 Lynchburg VA 24506-1165. *Fax:* 804-522-6196

STEVENS, ERNEST DONALD, PHYSIOLOGY, ZOOLOGY. *Current Pos:* PROF ZOOL, UNIV GUELPH, 88- *Personal Data:* b Calgary, Alta, July 5, 41; m 64, Elinor Hagborg; c Ken & Wendy. *Educ:* Victoria Univ, BSc, 63; Univ BC, MSc, 65, PhD(zool), 68. *Prof Exp:* Assoc prof zool, Univ Hawaii, 68-75. *Concurrent Pos:* Vis prof, St Andrews, 75, Tohoku, Japan, 82, Tex A&M, 89 & Univ Mich, 96. *Mem:* Can Soc Zool; Soc Exp Biol. *Res:* Physiology, primarily of fish; mechanisms of respiration, especially as affected by muscular exercise; comparative physiology of muscle contraction. *Mailing Add:* Dept Zool Univ Guelph Guelph ON N1G 2W1 Can. *Fax:* 519-767-1656; *E-Mail:* dstevens@uoguelph.ca

STEVENS, FRED JAY, MACROMOLECULAR INTERACTIONS, COMPUTER MODELING. *Current Pos:* fel, Argonne Nat Lab, 77-81, asst scientist, 81, asst biophysicist, 84, BIOPHYSICIST, ARGONNE NAT LAB, 87- *Personal Data:* b St Paul, Minn, June 10, 49. *Educ:* Hamline Univ, BA, 71; Northwestern Univ, MS, 74, PhD(biophys), 76. *Prof Exp:* Res assoc, Mich State Univ, 76-77; res biochemist, Abbott Labs, 81-83. *Mem:* AAAS; Biophys Soc; Protein Soc. *Res:* Interactions of proteins, antibody-antigen, amyloid formation; computer simulation. *Mailing Add:* Ctr Mech Biol & Biotechnol A-141 BIM 202 Argonne Nat Lab Argonne IL 60439

STEVENS, FRITS CHRISTIAAN, BIOCHEMISTRY, PROTEIN CHEMISTRY. *Current Pos:* from asst prof to assoc prof, 67-78 assoc dean, 84-87, PROF BIOCHEM, UNIV MAN, 78-, DEPT HEAD, 87- *Personal Data:* b Ghent, Belg, Sept 18, 38; m 65; c 2. *Educ:* Univ Ghent, Lic chem, 59; Univ Calif, Davis, PhD(biochem), 63. *Prof Exp:* Asst biochem, Pharmaceut Inst, Univ Ghent, 59-60 & Univ Calif, Davis, 60-63; sr researcher, Univ Brussels, 63-64; fel, Univ Calif, Los Angeles, 65-67. *Concurrent Pos:* Exec dir, Manitoba Health Res Coun, 82- *Mem:* Can Biochem Soc; Am Soc Biochem & Molecular Biol. *Res:* Structure-function relationships in proteins. *Mailing Add:* Dept Biochem Univ Man Fac Med 770 Bannatyne Ave Winnipeg MB R3E 0W3 Can. *Fax:* 204-783-0864; *E-Mail:* stevens@bldghsc.lanl.umanitoba.ca

STEVENS, GLADSTONE TAYLOR, JR, ECONOMIC ANALYSIS, QUALITY CONTROL. *Current Pos:* PROF & CHMN DEPT INDUST ENG, UNIV TEX, ARLINGTON, 75- *Personal Data:* b Brockton, Mass, Dec 16, 30; wid; c Robert & Bartlett. *Educ:* Univ Okla, BS, 56; Case Inst Technol, MS, 62, PhD(indust eng & mgt), 66. *Honors & Awards:* Eugene L Grant Award, Am Soc Eng Educ, 74; Wellington Award, Inst Indust Eng, 92. *Prof Exp:* Proj engr, E I du Pont de Nemours & Co, 56-59; res engr, Thompson-Ramo-Wooldridge Co, 60-62; asst prof mech eng, Lamar State Col, 62-64; from asst prof to assoc prof indust eng & mgt, Okla State Univ, 66-75. *Concurrent Pos:* NASA res grant, 67-68; consult, Pub Serv Co of Okla, 73-75 & Standard Mfg Co of Dallas, 76- *Mem:* Am Inst Indust Engrs. *Res:* Allocation of capital funds; probabilistic models; in-plant service courses in areas of production control, operations research and quality control. *Mailing Add:* Dept Indust Eng Univ Tex Box 19017 Arlington TX 76019. *Fax:* 817-272-3406; *E-Mail:* stevens@imse.uta.edu

STEVENS, HAROLD, NEUROLOGY. *Current Pos:* PROF NEUROL, SCH MED, GEORGE WASHINGTON UNIV, 54- *Personal Data:* b Salem, NJ, Oct 18, 11; m 38; c 2. *Educ:* Pa State Univ, BS, 33; Univ Pa, AM, 34, PhD, 37, MD, 41. *Concurrent Pos:* Consult pediat neurol, DC Health Dept, 46-; sr attend neurologist, Children's Hosp, 51-; consult, Vet Hosp, 54- & Walter Reed Hosp & NIH, 57-; nat consult to Surg Gen, US Air Force; consult, FDA; distinguished prof neurol, Uniformed Serv Univ Health Sci. *Mem:* Am Asn Neurol Surg; Am Neurol Asn; Am Electroencephalog Soc; fel Am Col Physicians; fel Am Acad Neurol. *Res:* Clinical and pediatric neurology. *Mailing Add:* 4835 Del Ray Ave Bethesda MD 20814-3013

STEVENS, HENRY CONRAD, ORGANIC CHEMISTRY. *Current Pos:* ADJ PROF, UNIV AKRON, 86- *Personal Data:* b Vienna, Austria, Apr 17, 18; nat US; m 41, Joan Gordon; c Kathleen & James. *Educ:* Columbia Univ, BS, 41; Western Res Univ, MS, 49, PhD(chem), 51. *Prof Exp:* Res chemist, H Kohnstamm & Co, 41-42; res supvr, Chem Div, Pittsburg Plate Glass Co, 42-72, sr res supvr, 72-77, mgr, Univ & Govt Res Develop, 77-84, sr res assoc, PPG Indust, Inc, Barberton, 84-86. *Mem:* Am Chem Soc. *Res:* Chemistry of phosgene derivatives; free radical polymerization; polycarbonate resins; cycloadditions; tropolone syntheses; peroxides; epoxides; phase transfer catalysis; technology transfer; academic-industrial interface. *Mailing Add:* 1990 Brookshire Rd Akron OH 44313-5350

STEVENS, HERBERT H(OWE), JR, META-PHYSICS & COSMOLOGY. *Current Pos:* CONSULT RES & DEVELOP, 80- *Personal Data:* b Gardiner, Maine, May 12, 13; m 46, Elaine Goldberg; c Jane, India & Charlotte. *Educ:* Ga Inst Technol, BSME, 36; New Sch Social Res, MALS, 69; Southeastern Mass Univ, MS, 86; Univ Mass Dartmouth, MA, 93. *Prof Exp:* Engr & dir res aircraft seats, W McArthur Corp, 39-41; consult res & develop engr, 41-47; chief engr rolling steel doors, W Balfour Co, 47-53; supv engr elec shaver res, Schick, Inc, 53-55; chief engr paint sprayer develop, Champion Implement Co, 55-56; consult, 56-58; sr statist engr, M & C Nuclear, Inc, Div Tex Instruments, Inc, 58-65; consult engr, Walter Balfour & Co, Long Island City, 65-80. *Concurrent Pos:* Res Engr, 81- *Mem:* Am Soc Mech Engrs; AAAS; Philos Sci Asn; Inst Relig Age Sci. *Res:* Air-supported roofs; cooperative housing; philosophy; finitism; restoring minds and creative process to quantum physics; theoretical physics; professional writing; hypersphere accretion cosmology in place of Big Bang; healing 350 year split between humanities and science. *Mailing Add:* 218 Hix Bridge Road Westport MA 02790

STEVENS, HOWARD ODELL, (JR), PHYSICS, ELECTRICAL ENGINEERING. *Current Pos:* Physicist sensors & systs, 62-65, sr proj engr magnetic countermeasures, 65-69, sr proj engr superconducting mach, 69-79, head, Elec Propulsion & Mach Syst Br, 79-84, HEAD, ELEC SYSTS DIV, DAVID W TAYLOR NAVAL SHIP RES & DEVELOP CTR, 84- *Personal Data:* b Canonsburg, Pa, May 29, 40; m 62; c 2. *Educ:* Carnegie Inst Technol, BS, 62; Univ Md, MS, 67. *Honors & Awards:* Solberg Award, Am Soc Naval Engrs, 84. *Mem:* Am Soc Naval Engrs. *Res:* Superconducting and advanced electrical machinery; high current switchgear; advanced current collection systems; superconducting magnets and cryogenic systems; electrical power and distribution systems. *Mailing Add:* 228 Wiltshire Lane Severna Park MD 21146-4039

STEVENS, J(AMES) I(RWIN), CHEMICAL ENGINEERING. *Current Pos:* PVT CONSULT, 87- *Personal Data:* b Valley Station, Ky, July 15, 20; m 47; c 4. *Educ:* Univ Louisville, BChE, 42, MChE, 43. *Prof Exp:* Instr, Univ Louisville, 43-44, res assoc, Inst Indust Res, 45-46; instr, Univ Del, 46-48; asst prof chem eng, Vanderbilt Univ, 48-52; engr, Phillips Petrol Co, Okla, 52-56, group leader, Idaho, 56-59, sect head, 59-62; chem engr Infilco/Fuller, 62-66, tech dir, 66-67; staff engr, 67, sr engr, 67-76, mgt staff assoc, 77-80, mgt staff, Arthur D Little, Inc, 80-87. *Mem:* Am Chem Soc; fel Am Inst Chem Engrs; Air & Waste Mgt Asn; Water Pollution Control Fedn. *Res:* Technical and social aspects of environmental management. *Mailing Add:* 9 Glen Terrace Bedford MA 01730-2047

STEVENS, JACK GERALD, ANIMAL VIROLOGY, EXPERIMENTAL PATHOLOGY. *Current Pos:* from asst prof to assoc prof med microbiol & immunol, 63-73, prof microbiol, immunol & neurol, 73-80, PROF MICROBIOL, IMMUNOL, NEUROBIOL & NEUROL, SCH MED, COL LETTERS & SCI, UNIV CALIF, LOS ANGELES, 80-, CHMN, DEPT MICROBIOL & IMMUNOL, 81- CO CHIEF DIV INFECTIOUS DIS DEPT MED, 92- *Personal Data:* b Port Angeles, Wash, Nov 3, 33; m 84; c 2. *Educ:* Wash State Univ, DVM, 57; Colo State Univ, MS, 59; Univ Wash, PhD(virol), 62. *Prof Exp:* Asst prof microbiol, Wash State Univ, 62-63. *Concurrent Pos:* Mem, Infectious Dis Merit Rev Bd, Vet Admin Med Res Serv, 76-79; mem, Virol Study Sect, Div Res Grants, NIH, 78-82; mem, Fel Review Bd, Nat Multiple Sclerosis Soc, 81-86; mem nat bd, Med Exam, Microbiol & Immunol, 85-89. *Mem:* AAAS; Am Soc Microbiol; Am Asn Immunologists; Am Soc Exp Pathologists; Am Soc Virol. *Res:* Viral pathogenesis, particularly latent infections; diseases of the nervous system; viral vectors. *Mailing Add:* Dept Neurol Univ Calif Sch Med 108336 Le Conte Ave Los Angeles CA 90024-1602

STEVENS, JAMES EVERELL, plasma processing of materials, radio frequency heating of plasmas, for more information see previous edition

STEVENS, JAMES LEVON, ALUMINUM FOIL TECHNOLOGY, PASSIVE COMPONENTS. *Current Pos:* sr physicist, 89-92, MGR PROD DEVELOP, PHILIPS COMPONENTS, 92- *Personal Data:* b Startex, SC, Dec 17, 47; m 76, Bonnie Ellisor. *Educ:* Wofford Col, BS, 70; Univ SC, PhD(physics), 75, MBA, 92. *Prof Exp:* Res assoc physics, Case Western Res Univ, 76-77; asst prof physics, NGa Col, 77-78; develop physicist, Mepco-Electra Inc, 78-85, sr physicist, Mepco-Centralab Inc, 85-89. *Mem:* Am Phys Soc; Electrochem Soc; Sigma Xi; fel NSF. *Res:* Materials and processes for aluminum electrolytic capacitors; the technologies of etching, anodizing, fabrication and theoretical modeling; product development from materials and process perspective; including analysis, benchmarking and modeling; holder of 3 US patents. *Mailing Add:* 2820 Kennerly Rd Irmo SC 29063. *Fax:* 803-772-2445

STEVENS, JAMES T, INHALATION TOXICOLOGY, BIOCHEMICAL PHARMACOLOGY. *Current Pos:* DIR TOXICOL, CIBA GEIGY CORP, 89- *Personal Data:* b Wellsboro, Pa, June 23, 46; m; c 3. *Educ:* WVa Univ, PhD(pharmacol), 72. *Mem:* Soc Toxicol; Am Soc Pharmacol & Exp Therapeut. *Res:* General toxicology; risk assessment and biokinetics; 40 publications. *Mailing Add:* Ciba-Geigy Corp R 1058-4-660 Basel CH 4002 Switzerland. *Fax:* 919-632-2192

STEVENS, JANICE R, NEUROLOGY, PSYCHIATRY. *Current Pos:* resident, Univ Ore, 54-55, from instr to assoc prof, 55-71, assoc prof psychiat, 74-77, PROF NEUROL, MED SCH, UNIV ORE, PORTLAND, 71-, PROF PSYCHIAT, 77- *Personal Data:* b Portland, Ore; m 46; c 2. *Educ:* Reed Col, BA, 44; Boston Univ, MD, 49. *Prof Exp:* Intern med, Mass Mem Hosp, 49-50; resident neurol, Boston City Hosp, 50-51; researcher neurol & assoc physician, Sch Med, Yale Univ, 51-54. *Concurrent Pos:* Vis prof psychiat, Harvard Med Sch & Mass Gen Hosp, 71-73; NIMH guest worker, St Elizabeth's Hosp, Washington, DC, 75-76, mem staff, 80- *Mem:* AAAS; Am Acad Neurol; Am Electroencephalog Soc (pres, 73-74); Soc Neurosci; Am Epilepsy Soc; Am Pub Health Asn; Soc Biol Psychiat; Am Orthopsychiat Asn. *Res:* Neurology and electroencephalography of behavior; epilepsy; schizophrenia. *Mailing Add:* Dept Neurol & Psychol Ore Health Sci Univ 3181 SW Sam Jackson Park Rd Portland OR 97201

STEVENS, JOHN A(LEXANDER), CIVIL ENGINEERING. *Current Pos:* RETIRED. *Personal Data:* b Baltimore, Md, Mar 25, 21; m 53; c 3. *Educ:* Princeton Univ, BS, 43; Univ Miami, BSCE, 50; Putney Grad Sch Teacher Ed, MA, 51; Pa State Univ, MSCE, 52. *Prof Exp:* Proj engr, Am Dist Tel Co, NY, 46-49; from asst prof to assoc prof civil eng, Univ Miami, 52-, dir, Soils Eng Lab, 56- *Mem:* Am Soc Civil Engrs; Am Photogram; Am Forestry Asn. *Res:* Soils engineering; engineering geology; foundation engineering structure and properties of Florida marls and lime muds; air photo interpretation. *Mailing Add:* 9430 SW 93rd Ave Miami FL 33176-2924

STEVENS, JOHN BAGSHAW, VETERINARY MICROBIOLOGY. *Current Pos:* res scientist swine dis, 74-83, head microbiol serv, Health Animals Directorate, Animal Path Div, 83-92, ASSOC DIR, ANIMAL DIS RES INST, AGR CAN, 92- *Personal Data:* b Toronto, Ont, June 26, 41; m 72; c 3. *Educ:* Univ Toronto, BSc, 64; Univ Guelph, DVM, 69, MSc, 71; Iowa State Univ, PhD(vet microbiol), 75. *Prof Exp:* Res asst vet bacteriol, Dept Vet Microbiol & Immunol, Univ Guelph, 69; res assoc vet microbiol, Vet Med Res Inst, Iowa State Univ, 71-74. *Mailing Add:* Animal Dis Res Inst 3851 Fallowfield Rd Nepean ON K2H 8P9 Can

STEVENS, JOHN G, APPLIED MATHEMATICS, COMPUTER SCIENCE. *Current Pos:* From asst prof to assoc prof, 69-80, PROF MATH, MONTCLAIR STATE UNIV, 80- *Personal Data:* b Kansas City, Mo, Aug 7, 43; m 66, Mary L Beilstein; c Sarah & Rachel. *Educ:* Ind Univ, BS, 65; NY Univ, PhD(math), 72. *Concurrent Pos:* Consult, Exxon Res & Eng Co, 75-, Energia Inc, 83-; co-prin investr, Hazardous Substance Mgt Res Ctr, Newark, NJ, 92- *Mem:* Am Math Soc; Soc Indust & Appl Math; Soc Comput Simulation. *Res:* Mathematical modeling of physical systems, especially catalytic and photochemically enhanced combustion; pollution control technologies; patentee in field. *Mailing Add:* Dept Math & Comput Sci Montclair State Univ Valley Rd Upper Montclair NJ 07043. *Fax:* 973-655-7686; *E-Mail:* stevensj@alpha.montclair.edu

STEVENS, JOHN GEHRET, PHYSICAL CHEMISTRY, INFORMATION SCIENCE. *Current Pos:* From asst prof to assoc prof, 63-79, PROF CHEM, UNIV NC, ASHEVILLE, 79- *Personal Data:* b Mount Holly, NJ, Dec 16, 41; m 63, Virginia Entwistlg; c Sybil M, Robert J & John G. *Educ:* NC State Univ, BS, 64, PhD(chem), 69. *Concurrent Pos:* Dir, Mossbauer Effect Data Ctr, 69-; mem ad hoc comt Mossbauer spectros data & conv, Nat Acad Sci, 70-73; ed Mossbauer Effect Data Index, Univ NC & Nat Bur Standards, 70-78; res assoc, Max Planck Inst Solid State Physics, 73; res prof, Inst Molecular Spectroscopy, Univ Nijmegen, Neth, 76-77, 78, 79, 80 & 81; co-ed, Mossbauer Effect Reference & Data J, 78-; recipient over 50 grants, NSF, Nat Standard Ref Data Syst, NATO Off Sci Res, Am Chem Soc, Res Corp; dir undergrad res prog, 84-91; Nat Exec Officon, Coun Undergrad Res, 91- *Mem:* AAAS; Am Chem Soc; Am Phys Soc; Sigma Xi; Fedn Am Scientists. *Res:* Mossbauer spectroscopy; antimony chemistry; information sciences; evaluation of data. *Mailing Add:* Dept Chem Univ NC Asheville NC 28804. *Fax:* 704-251-6002; *E-Mail:* stevens@unca.edu

STEVENS, JOHN JOSEPH, CANCER. *Current Pos:* RES ADMINR, DEPT RES, AM CANCER SOC. *Personal Data:* b London, Eng, July 16, 41. *Educ:* Univ Buenos Aires, MD, 64. *Prof Exp:* Res physician, Inst Biol & Exp Med, Buenos Aires, 64-67, Nat Acad Med, Arg, 65-67; res fel, Res Inst, Hosp Joint Dis, New York, 67-70, res assoc, 70- *Concurrent Pos:* Instr, Dept Biochem, Mt Sinai Sch Med, City Univ New York, 70-73, res asst prof, 73-; spec fel, Leukemia Soc Am, 74-76, scholarship, 76-81. *Mem:* Endocrine Soc; Am Asn Cancer Res. *Res:* Mechanism of steroid hormone action; studies on glucocorticoid-induced lymphocytolysis of malignant lymphocytes; chemotherapy of cancer. *Mailing Add:* Am Cancer Soc Inc 1599 Clifton Rd NE Altanta GA 30327-3633. *Fax:* 404-321-4669

STEVENS, JOSEPH ALFRED, MEDICAL MYCOLOGY, MEDICAL MICROBIOLOGY. *Current Pos:* RETIRED. *Personal Data:* b Cleveland, Ohio, Jan 3, 27. *Educ:* Univ Dayton, BS, 49; Mich State Univ, MS, 53, PhD(microbiol), 57. *Prof Exp:* Res instr & fel, Mich State Univ, 57-59, res assoc, 59-61; from instr to prof microbiol, Chicago Col Osteop Med, 61-87, actg chmn dept, 70-74. *Concurrent Pos:* Consult microbiol & pub health, Nat Bd Exam, Osteop Physicians & Surgeons Inc, 79-86. *Mem:* Am Soc Microbiol; Mycol Soc Am; NY Acad Sci; Int Soc Human & Animal Mycol; Am Asn Univ Professors; Sigma Xi. *Res:* Fungal serology; immune responses to major fungal pathogens; development of fungal antigens and antisera; fungal diagnostic-serologic tests. *Mailing Add:* 7447 S South Shore Dr, Apt 33G Chicago IL 60649-3862

STEVENS, JOSEPH CHARLES, PSYCHOPHYSICS, SENSORY PSYCHOLOGY. *Current Pos:* res assoc & lectr, 66-77, SR RES SCIENTIST & LECTR PSYCHOL, YALE UNIV, 77- *Personal Data:* b Grand Rapids, Mich, Feb 28, 29. *Educ:* Calvin Col, AB, 51; Mich State Univ, MA, 53; Harvard Univ, PhD(psychol), 57. *Prof Exp:* From instr to asst prof psychol, Harvard Univ, 57-66. *Concurrent Pos:* Fel, John B Pierce Found, 66- *Mem:* Soc Neurosci; Acoust Soc Am; Optical Soc Am; fel AAAS; fel NY Acad Sci. *Res:* Psychophysics of sensory and perceptual processes, especially somatosensory and chemical sensory modalities. *Mailing Add:* John B Pierce Found Lab 290 Congress Ave New Haven CT 06519

STEVENS, KARL KENT, ENGINEERING MECHANICS, VIBRATIONS STRUCTURAL DYNAMICS. *Current Pos:* prof ocean eng, 78-83, chmn dept, 81-83 & 91-93, PROF MECH ENG, FLA ATLANTIC UNIV, 83-, ASSOC DEAN ENG, 93- *Personal Data:* b Topeka, Kans, Jan 24, 39; m 60; c 3. *Educ:* Kans State Univ, BS, 61; Univ Ill, MS, 63, PhD(theoret & appl mech), 65. *Prof Exp:* Staff mem, Sandia Corp, NMex, 61-62; from asst prof to prof eng mech, Ohio State Univ, 65-78. *Concurrent Pos:* Vis scientist, US Army Ballistic Res Labs, 72-73. *Mem:* Am Soc Mech Engrs; An Soc Eng Educ; Soc Exp Mechs. *Res:* Modal analysis, vibrations, finite element methods, and viscoelasticity. *Mailing Add:* Col Engrs Fla Atlantic Univ Boca Raton FL 33431. *Fax:* 561-367-2659; *E-Mail:* stevens@acc.fau.edu

STEVENS, KENNETH N(OBLE), ACOUSTICS, ELECTRICAL ENGINEERING. *Current Pos:* asst elec eng, Mass Inst Technol, 48-51, instr, 51-52, mem res staff commun acoust, 52-54, from asst prof to assoc prof, 54-63, PROF ELEC ENG, MASS INST TECHNOL, 63-, CLARENCE JOSEPH LEBEL PROF, 76- *Personal Data:* b Can, Mar 23, 24; m 94, Sharon Manuel; c Rebecca, Andrea, Michael & John. *Educ:* Univ Toronto, BASc, 45, MASc, 48; Mass Inst Technol, ScD(elec eng), 52. *Honors & Awards:* Silver Medal, Acoust Soc Am; Quintana Award, Voice Found; Gold Medal, Acoust Soc Am Medal of European Speech Communication Asn; Medal Europ Speech Commun Asn. *Prof Exp:* Instr appl physics, Univ Toronto, 46-48. *Concurrent Pos:* Consult & engr, Bolt Beranek & Newman, 52-88; Guggenheim fel, 62-63; NIH spec fel & vis prof, Univ Col, Univ London, 69-70; mem, Nat Adv Coun Neurol & Commun Dis & Stroke, NIH, 81-85; consult, Sensimetrics Inc, 87- *Mem:* Nat Acad Eng; Acoust Soc Am (pres, 76-77); Inst Elec & Electronics Engrs; Am Acad Arts & Sci. *Res:* Speech communication; psycho-acoustics; acoustics. *Mailing Add:* Dept Elec Eng Mass Inst Technol Cambridge MA 02139

STEVENS, LEROY CARLTON, JR, DEVELOPMENTAL BIOLOGY. *Current Pos:* res fel, 52-55, res assoc, 55-57, staff scientist, 57-67, SR STAFF SCIENTIST, JACKSON LAB, 67- *Personal Data:* b Kenmore, NY, June 5, 20; m 42; c 3. *Educ:* Cornell Univ, BS, 42; Univ Rochester, PhD, 52. *Prof Exp:* Asst, Univ Rochester, 48-52, instr, Univ Sch, 51-52. *Concurrent Pos:* Guggenheim fel, Exp Embryol Lab, Col of France, 61-62. *Res:* Experimental embryology; cancer; mammalian embryology and teratocarcinogenesis. *Mailing Add:* Pretty Marsh Rd Mt Desert ME 04660

STEVENS, LEWIS AXTELL, BIOPHYSICS, CHAOS ATTRACTOR-NONLINEAR DYNAMICS. *Current Pos:* CONSULT PHYSICIST, 70- *Personal Data:* b Butte, Mont, Nov 17, 13; m 35; c 3. *Educ:* San Jose State Col, AB, 50. *Prof Exp:* Meteorol aid, Sci Serv Div, US Weather Bur, 51-52; physicist, Aviation Ord Dept, US Naval Ord Test Sta, 52-56, electronic scientist, 56-57, electronic scientist, Fuze Eval Div, Test Dept, 57-60; gen engr & head, Measurements Br, Propulsion Develop Dept, 60-61, gen proj engr, 62, res physicist, Explosives & Pyro-Tech Div, 62-70. *Concurrent Pos:* Mem fuze field tests subcomt, Joint Army-Navy-Air Force, 61-64. *Mem:* AAAS; Am Phys Soc; Am Inst Aeronaut & Astronaut. *Res:* Development of new medical tools and techniques; nuclear physics; meteorological aspects of health physics; technology of high speed aerial tow targets; technology of soft lunar landings; effects of microwave radiation on enzyme systems in living organisms; in vivo pathology of varying magnetic fields; investigate possible combination of chaos attractor with transcuteneous electrical nerve stimulation to remedy cardiac arrhythmias non-invasively. *Mailing Add:* LASTEV Lab 5037 Kenneth Ave Carmichael CA 95608

STEVENS, LLOYD WEAKLEY, SURGERY. *Current Pos:* Assoc surg, Grad Sch Med, 46-49, assoc prof, Sch Med, 53-60, prof, 60-79, EMER PROF CLIN SURG, SCH MED, UNIV PA, 79- *Personal Data:* b Philadelphia, Pa, Jan 14, 14; m 71, Eleanor Van Dyke; c Mary-Ellen, Carol A (Hovey) & Susan (Plaza). *Educ:* Univ Pa, AB, 33, MD, 37; Am Bd Surg, dipl, 44. *Honors & Awards:* Roth Award Gastroenterol, 74; Citation Dominican Repub, Gastroenterol Soc, 74. *Concurrent Pos:* Assoc prof, Women's Med Col Pa, 46-49; dir surg, Presby-Univ Pa Med Ctr & assoc surgeon, Univ Hosp; chief surg, Philadelphia Gen Hosp. *Mem:* Am Col Surgeons; Soc Surg Alimentary Tract. *Res:* Acute cholecystitis; peptic ulcer; ulcerative colitis. *Mailing Add:* The Hermitage 1204 Round Hill Rd Bryn Mawr PA 19010

STEVENS, MALCOLM PETER, ORGANIC POLYMER CHEMISTRY. *Current Pos:* assoc prof, 71-78, chmn dept, 78-81, PROF CHEM, UNIV HARTFORD, 78- *Personal Data:* b Birmingham, Eng, Apr 3, 34; US citizen; m 60, Marcia Reed; c Jeffrey & Philip. *Educ:* San Jose State Col, BS, 57; Cornell Univ, PhD(org chem), 61. *Prof Exp:* Res chemist, Chevron Res Co, Stand Oil Co Calif, 61-64; asst prof chem, Robert Col, Istanbul, 64-67; asst prof, Univ Hartford, 67-68; from asst prof to assoc prof, Am Univ Beirut, 68-71. *Concurrent Pos:* Vis prof, Univ Sussex, Eng, 77, Colo State Univ, 85. *Mem:* Sigma Xi; Am Chem Soc. *Res:* Photopolymerization; thermal polymerization; polymer modification; synthesis of novel polymer systems, historical writing. *Mailing Add:* Dept Chem Univ Hartford West Hartford CT 06117-0395. *Fax:* 860-768-5244; *E-Mail:* stevens@uhavax.hartford.edu

STEVENS, MARION BENNION, CLINICAL NUTRITION & FOOD SCIENCE. *Current Pos:* INSTR HEALTH OCCUPATIONS, EL PASO COMMUNITY COL, 82- *Educ:* Univ Wis, PhD(food sci), 56. *Mailing Add:* 2320 Gene Littler Dr El Paso TX 79936

STEVENS, MICHAEL FRED, INDUSTRIAL CHEMISTRY, TOXICOLOGY. *Current Pos:* From res assoc to sr res assoc, Appleton Papers Inc, 70-74, staff res assoc, 74-86, proj mgr prod develop, 86-89, PROD SAFETY SPECIALIST, APPLETON PAPERS INC, 89- *Personal Data:* b Urbana, Ill, May 17, 41; m 65; c 2. *Educ:* Eastern Ill Univ, BS, 64; Univ Ill, Urbana, MS, 66; Univ Nebr, Lincoln, PhD(org chem), 70. *Mem:* Am Chem Soc; TAPPI. *Res:* Corporate liaison with government relative to toxic substances in control act matters; management of corporate toxicity testing programs; corporate consultant on chemical health and safety matters; air sampling work in plant mills for contaminants; advisor in product safety issues. *Mailing Add:* 314 E Glendale Ave Appleton WI 54911-2907

STEVENS, PETER FRANCIS, SYSTEMATIC BOTANY. *Current Pos:* asst cur Arnold Arboretum, 73-80, assoc cur, 80-83, from asst prof to assoc prof, 77-83, PROF BIOL & CUR ARNOLD ARBORETUM & GRAY HERBARIUM, HARVARD UNIV, 83- *Personal Data:* b Teignmouth, Eng, Nov 13, 44. *Educ:* Oxford Univ, BA, 66, MA, 72; Univ Edinburgh, PhD(bot), 70. *Prof Exp:* Forest botanist, Dept Forestry, Lae, Papua, New Guinea, 70-73. *Mem:* Fel Linnean Soc London; Soc Study Evolution; Bot Soc Am; Int Asn Plant Taxonomists. *Res:* Morphology; systematics and evolution of Indo-Malesian plants and the Ericaceae and Clusiaceae of the world; biogeography; tropical ecology; theory and history of systematics. *Mailing Add:* Dept Org/Edolut Biol Harvard Univ 26 Oxford St Cambridge MA 02138-2902

STEVENS, RICHARD EDWARD, microscopy, for more information see previous edition

STEVENS, RICHARD F, power engineering design; deceased, see previous edition for last biography

STEVENS, RICHARD JOSEPH, NEUROSCIENCES. *Current Pos:* asst prof, 70-75, ASSOC PROF HUMAN ADAPTABILITY, COL HUMAN BIOL, UNIV WIS-GREEN BAY, 75- *Personal Data:* b Rochester, NY, Oct 31, 41; m 65; c 3. *Educ:* Univ Rochester, BS, 63; Univ Ill, Urbana, MS, 65, PhD(biophysics), 69. *Prof Exp:* Aerospace technologist, NASA-Lewis Res Ctr, 63; res asst, Dept Physics, Univ Ill, 64-65, teaching asst human & cellular physiol, 66-67; res fel neuroanat, Dept Anat, Brain Res Inst, Univ Calif, Los Angeles, 69-70. *Concurrent Pos:* Consult, Med Col Wis Pain Clin & Green Bay Childbirth Educ Asn, 75-; Presidents teaching improvement grant, Univ Wis, 72. *Mem:* AAAS; Sigma Xi. *Res:* Neurophysiology of vision, neuro-behavioral aspects of environmental contaminants; neuro-behavioral aspects of pain perception; innovative teaching of biology. *Mailing Add:* Dept Biol Sci Univ Wis Green Bay, 2420 Nicolet Dr Green Bay WI 54311-7003

STEVENS, RICHARD S, marine geology, physical oceanography; deceased, see previous edition for last biography

STEVENS, RICHARD STONINGTON, DISTRIBUTED PROCESSING, DATA FLOW. *Current Pos:* mathematician, 80-83, COMPUT SCIENTIST, NAVAL RES LAB, 83- *Personal Data:* b Boston, Mass, Jan 14, 40; m 68, Kathleen Russell; c Neal R & Hilary J. *Educ:* Univ Colo, BA, 61, MA, 63; Colo State Univ, PhD(math), 72. *Prof Exp:* Asst prof math, Univ Mich, Flint, 72-76; mem tech staff, Anser Serv Inc, 77-80. *Concurrent Pos:* Vis scholar, Univ Calif, Berkeley, 96- *Mem:* Math Asn Am; Sigma Xi. *Res:* Standardize the processing graph method, a data-flow based architecture independent computer language; to develop a toolset for efficient production of compliers of processing graph method for distributed computer systems. *Mailing Add:* 8611 Ordinary Way Annandale VA 22003-4431. *E-Mail:* stevens@ait.nrl.navy.mil

STEVENS, ROGER TEMPLETON, ELECTRICAL ENGINEERING, SYSTEMS ENGINEERING. *Current Pos:* RETIRED. *Personal Data:* b Syracuse, NY, Jan 11, 27; m 48, 79; c 2. *Educ:* Union Col, BA, 49; Boston Univ, MA, 59; Blackstone Sch Law, LLB, 56; Va Polytech Inst & State Univ, MEng, 76; Calif Western Univ, PhD(elec eng), 78. *Prof Exp:* Tech writer, Raytheon Mfg Co, 50-51; engr, Lab Electronics Inc, 51-55; sr engr electronic design, Spencer Kennedy Labs, 55-56, AVCO Mfg Co, 56-57 & Electronics Systs Inc, 57-60; sect supvr, Sanders Assoc Inc, 60-65; group leader systs engr, Mitre Corp, 65-67, 70-74; leading scientist systs engr, Dikewood Indust Inc, 67-70, 74-81; eng specialist II, EG & G, Inc, 81-83; mem tech staff, Mitre

Corp, 83-94. *Mem:* Soc Old Crows; Asn Comput Mach. *Res:* Operational test and evaluation; computer design and software development; display design; radar system design; auth of numerous books. *Mailing Add:* 17 SE Castle Rock Rd Rio Rancho NM 87124

STEVENS, RONALD HENRY, CELLULAR IMMUNOLOGY, HUMAN IMMUNOBIOLOGY. *Current Pos:* ASSOC PROF MICROBIOL & IMMUNOL, UNIV CALIF, LOS ANGELES, 74- *Personal Data:* b Philadelphia, Pa, Dec 3, 46. *Educ:* Ohio Wesleyan Univ, BA, 68; Harvard Univ, PhD(microbiol), 71. *Prof Exp:* Fel immunol, Nat Inst Med Res, London, 71-74. *Mem:* Am Asn Immunologists; Am Fedn Clin Res; AAAS; NY Acad Sci. *Res:* Cellular and molecular interactions responsible for the successful initiation, maintenance, and termination of normal and abnormal humoral immune responses in humans. *Mailing Add:* Dept Microbiol & Immunol 43-319 CHS Univ Calif 405 Hilgard Los Angeles CA 90024-7009

STEVENS, ROSEMARY ANNE, HISTORY OF MEDICINE, PUBLIC HEALTH. *Current Pos:* prof hist & sociol sci, Univ Pa, 79-89, chmn dept, 80-83, chmn, Dept Hist & Social Sci, 86-93, UPS Found prof social sci, 90-93, SR FEL, LEONARD DAVIS INST HEALTH ECON, UNIV PA, 80-, DEAN, 93- *Personal Data:* b Bourne, Eng, Mar 18, 35; US citizen; m, Jack Barchas; c 2. *Educ:* Oxford Univ, BA, 57, MA, 61; Univ Manchester, dipl social admin, 59; Yale Univ, MPH, 63, PhD(epidemiol), 68. *Hon Degrees:* LHD, Hahnemann Univ, 88; Dr, Med Col Pa, 95, Rutgers Univ, 92; DSc, NE Ohio Univ, 95. *Honors & Awards:* Fulton Lectr, Yale Univ, 87; Arthur Viseltear Award, Am Pub Health Asn, 90; Welch Medal, Am Asn Hist Med, 90. *Prof Exp:* Res asst pub health, Sch Med, Yale Univ, 62-65, res assoc, 66-68, from asst prof to prof, 68-76; prof health systs mgt, Sch Pub Health & Trop Med, Tulane Univ, 76-79. *Concurrent Pos:* Hon res officer, London Sch Econ & Polit Sci, 62-63, vis lectr, 63-64 & 73-74; lectr, Sch Pub Health, Johns Hopkins Univ, 67-68; guest scholar, Brookings Inst, 67-68; consult, Bur Budget, Off Pres, 69, Ctr Res & Develop, AMA, 72, WHO, 74 & Brit Nat Health Serv, 81; mem, Comt Design Health Care Delivery Systs, Am Sociol Asn, 73, Subcomt Health, Comt Ways & Means, Adv Panel Nat Health Ins, US House Rep, 75, Comt Vital & Health Statist, 78-80 & US Nat Comt Int Union Hist & Philos Sci, Nat Acad Sci, 81-87; Rockefeller humanities fel, 82-83; Guggenheim fel, 84-85; Bellagio Study & Conf Ctr scholar, 84; Frohlich prof, Royal Soc Med, London, 86. *Mem:* Inst Med-Nat Acad Sci; fel Am Pub Health Asn; Am Sociol Asn; AMA; Sigma Xi; fel Am Acad Arts & Sci; Am Hist Asn. *Res:* History of medicine; comparative studies in health care policy; history of hospitals; medical education and manpower policies. *Mailing Add:* Dept Hist & Sociol Sci 3440 Market St Suite 500 Philadelphia PA 19104

STEVENS, ROY HARRIS, ORAL MICROBIOLOGY, DENTAL PULP BIOLOGY. *Current Pos:* PROF & CHMN, DEPT ENDONTOLOGY, SCH DENT, TEMPLE UNIV, 93- *Personal Data:* b New York, NY, Jan 8, 48; div; c Alexander M & Jocelyn N. *Educ:* Adelphi Univ, BA, 69; Rutgers Univ, MS, 72; Columbia Univ, DDS, 76. *Honors & Awards:* Waerhaug Prize. *Prof Exp:* Fel, Univ Pa, 77-79, from res assoc to res asst prof, Dept Microbiol, Sch Dent Med, 80-89; assoc prof, Sch Dent & Oral Surg, Columbia Univ, 89-93. *Concurrent Pos:* Co-prin investr, Nat Inst Dent Res Grants, 79-; ed consult, J Infectious Dis, 85, Oral Microbiol & Immunol, Endodontics & Dent Traumatology; vis teacher, Albert Einstein Med Ctr, 87-89. *Mem:* Am Soc Microbiol; Int Asn Dent Res; Sigma Xi. *Res:* Oral microbiology; epidemiology, taxonomy, virulence and ecological interactions of oral bacteria; viruses of oral bacteria. *Mailing Add:* 2083 Harts Lane Conshohocken PA 19428. *Fax:* 215-707-2802; *E-Mail:* rstevens@hal.dental.temple.edu

STEVENS, ROY WHITE, MEDICAL MICROBIOLOGY, LABORATORY METHODS. *Current Pos:* CONSULT, BIOMED RESOURCE GROUP, 91- *Personal Data:* b Troy, NY, Sept 4, 34; m 56, Shirley Brehm; c Scott & Mark. *Educ:* State Univ NY Albany, BS, 56, MS, 58; Albany Med Col, PhD(microbiol), 65; Am Bd Med Microbiol, dipl, 71. *Prof Exp:* Bacteriologist, NY State Dept Health, 58-61, sr bacteriologist, 62-65, assoc bacteriologist, 65-67, sr assoc prin res scientist immunol, 67-73, prin res scientist immunol, 73-79, dir labs diag immunol, 79-89, dir labs retrovirol/immunol, 89-91. *Concurrent Pos:* Adj assoc prof, Dept Microbiol & Immunol, Albany Med Col, NY, 82-91; ed, Diag Devices Manual & Directory; assoc prof, Biomed Sci Div, Sch Public Health, State Univ NY, Albany, 89- *Mem:* AAAS; Am Soc Microbiol; fel Am Acad Microbiol; Asn Med Lab Immunologists (pres, 89). *Res:* Diagnostic immunology, serology; medical microbiology; immunodiagnosis of infectious diseases; development of diagnostic devices. *Mailing Add:* 507 Acre Dr Schenectady NY 12303. *Fax:* 518-356-8160

STEVENS, STANLEY EDWARD, JR, GENETICS, ENZYMOLOGY OF NITROGEN ASSIMILATION & BIOTECHNOLOGY. *Current Pos:* chair, Dept Biol, 96, PROF & W HARRY FEINSTONE CHAIR EXCELLENCE MOLECULAR BIOL, UNIV MEMPHIS, 88-, CHAIR, DEPT MICROBIOL & MOLECULAR CELL SCI, 96-, DIR, FEINSTONE INST MOLECULAR BIOL, 96- *Personal Data:* b Ringgold, Tex, June 25, 44; m 69, Catherine L Reifel; c Kathleen M, Heather L & Nathan E. *Educ:* Univ Tex, Austin, BA, 66, MA, 68, PhD(bot), 71. *Prof Exp:* Teaching asst microbiol, Univ Tex, Austin, 67-68, res asst, 68, environ health trainee, 69-70, NIH fel protein chem, 71-73 & photosynthesis, 74-75; from asst prof to prof microbiol & molecular biol, Pa State Univ, 75-88, dir, Coop Prog Recombinant DNA Technol, 82-86, assoc dir, Biotechnol Inst, 84-87, dir, Coop Prog Biotechnol & chmn, Marine Sci Prog, 86-88. *Concurrent Pos:* Vis scientist, Los Alamos Sci Lab, 75-76; consult, US Environ Protection Agency, 79, Gulf & Western Corp, 80-83, Stand Oil Co & Coulter Immunol, 84-86, Aluminum Co Am, 86 & Celgene Corp, 87; mem, NSF Grad Fel Panel & Competitive Res Grants Off Biol Nit-Fix Panel, USDA, 83-85, Dept Energy Res Instr Panel, 85, NIH Acad Res Enhancement Panel, 86, NIH Biomed Res Shared Instr Panel, 90 & NIH Microbiol Physiol & Genetics Study Sect, 91 & 94; prog mgr, Competitive Res Grants Off Biol Nit-Fix, USDA, 87. *Mem:* Fel Am Acad Microbiol; AAAS; Am Soc Biochem & Molecular Biol; Am Soc Microbiol; Am Soc Plant Physiologists; Phycol Soc Am; Sigma Xi. *Res:* Molecular biology of nitrogen assimilation and of the light harvesting antenna in cyanobacteria; fouling of marine structures by algae; biotechnology of cyanobacteria and algae; biological desulfurization of coal. *Mailing Add:* Dept Microbiol & Molecular Cell Sci Univ Memphis 509 Life Sci Bldg Memphis TN 38152. *Fax:* 901-678-4457; *E-Mail:* estevens@adminl.memphis.edu

STEVENS, SUE CASSELL, BIOCHEMISTRY. *Current Pos:* RETIRED. *Personal Data:* b Roanoke, Va. *Educ:* Goucher Col, BA, 30; Columbia Univ, MA, 31, PhD(chem), 40. *Prof Exp:* Res biochemist, NY Skin & Cancer Hosp, NY, 32-35; biochemist, Fifth Ave Hosp, 35; res chemist, Col Physicians & Surgeons, Columbia Univ, 35-39, NY Orthop Hosp, 40-41 & Calif Milk Prod Co, 41-43; res dairy chemist, Golden State Co, Ltd, 43-46 & Swift & Co, 46-47; dir res & qual control, Steven Candy Kitchens, 47-48; assoc prof chem & biol, MacMurray Col, 48-49; chief biochemist, US Vet Admin Ctr, Dayton, Ohio, 49-52, res biochemist, 52-56, suprv res lab Hosp, Lincoln, Nebr, 56-65; dir, Div Endocrine Chem, Jewish Hosp St Louis, 65-79. *Concurrent Pos:* Asst prof path, Sch Med, Wash Univ, 67-79. *Mem:* Fel AAAS; Am Inst Chem; Am Soc Qual Control; NY Acad Sci; Am Chem Soc; Sigma Xi. *Res:* Clinical chemistry methods; electrolytes in biological fluids; steroids; hormones; automation. *Mailing Add:* PO Box 30206 Lincoln NE 68503-0206

STEVENS, THOMAS MCCONNELL, VIROLOGY, ENTOMOLOGY. *Current Pos:* RETIRED. *Personal Data:* b Plainfield, NJ, May 25, 27; m 54; c 4. *Educ:* Haverford Col, BA, 50; Rutgers Univ, MS, 55, PhD(entom), 57. *Prof Exp:* Fel microbiol, St Louis Univ, 57-58, from instr to asst prof, Sch Med, 58-63; asst prof, Med Sch, Rutgers Univ, NB, 63-66; assoc prof exp med & from assoc dir to dir teaching labs, Rutgers Med Sch, Col Med & Dent, NJ, 66-72, asst dean, 68-86, prof microbiol, 72-86. *Mem:* Am Soc Microbiol. *Res:* Physical and chemical nature of the togaviruses using dengue virus as a model. *Mailing Add:* Rte 2 Box 95 Heathsville VA 22473

STEVENS, TODD OWEN, ANAEROBIC MICROBIOLOGY OF SOILS & SEDIMENT-BIOREMEDIATION, BIOGEOCHEMISTRY & ECOLOGY OF THE TERRESTRIAL SUBSURFACE. *Current Pos:* RES SCIENTIST, PAC NW LAB, 91- *Personal Data:* b The Dalles, Ore, Jan 27, 62. *Educ:* Ore State Univ, BS, 84; Mich State Univ, MS, 87; Univ Idaho, PhD(bact), 89. *Prof Exp:* Scientist, NW Col & Univ Asn Sci, Wash State Univ, 89-91. *Mem:* Am Soc Microbiol; Soil Sci Soc Am; AAAS. *Res:* Physiological ecology of microbial ecosystems, primarily anaerobic sediments; periodically investigate bioremediation potential in these systems and the fate of anthropogenic chemicals. *Mailing Add:* Pac NW Nat Lab MS P7-54 P O Box 999 Richland WA 99352. *E-Mail:* to_stevens@pnl.gov

STEVENS, TRAVIS EDWARD, ORGANIC CHEMISTRY. *Current Pos:* sr res chemist, 55-75, RES SECT MGR, ROHM & HAAS CO, 75- *Personal Data:* b Leigh, Nebr, Dec 22, 27; m 61; c 4. *Educ:* Wayne State Col, AB, 51; Iowa State Col, PhD(chem), 55. *Prof Exp:* Asst, Iowa State Col, 51-53. *Concurrent Pos:* Vis prof, Ind Univ, 65. *Mem:* Am Chem Soc. *Res:* Synthesis and properties of high-energy compounds; molecular rearrangements; polymer synthesis; paper chemicals; coatings and textile chemistry. *Mailing Add:* 724 Buckley Rd Ambler PA 19002-2504

STEVENS, VERNON LEWIS, BIOCHEMISTRY, ANALYTICAL CHEMISTRY. *Current Pos:* RETIRED. *Personal Data:* b Tacoma, Wash, Oct 10, 30; m 54; c 4. *Educ:* Cent Wash State Col, BS, 57; Ore State Univ, MS, 60. *Prof Exp:* Res asst & biochemist, William S Merrell Co Div, Richardson-Merrell, Inc, 59-67; head anal chem, Enzomedic Lab, Inc, Wash, 67-69; chemist, Puget Sound Plant, Texaco Inc, 69-94, sr proj chemist, 94. *Res:* Development of analytical procedures for gas-liquid and thin layer chromatography, autoanalyzer, radioisotopes and spectronic equipment; lipid synthesis in animals; nucleotides; clinical, environmental and petroleum chemistry. *Mailing Add:* 844 Sneeoosh Rd La Conner WA 98257

STEVENS, VINCENT LEROY, BIOCHEMISTRY. *Current Pos:* asst prof chem & biochem, 59-62, assoc prof chem, 62-67, PROF CHEM, EASTERN WASH STATE COL, 67-, CHMN DEPT, 70-, DEAN, DIV HEALTH SCI, 74- *Personal Data:* b Boston, Mass, July 14, 30; m 58. *Educ:* Univ Calif, Berkeley, AB, 53, PhD(biochem), 57. *Prof Exp:* Jr res biochemist, Med Ctr, Univ Calif, San Francisco, 57-59. *Concurrent Pos:* Consult, Deaconess Hosp, Spokane, 62- *Mem:* Am Chem Soc. *Res:* Organic and physical chemistry of nucleic acids and their derivatives. *Mailing Add:* 3124 S Lamonte St Spokane WA 99203

STEVENS, VIOLETE L, paint & coatings, photochemistry, for more information see previous edition

STEVENS, WALTER, ANATOMY, RADIOBIOLOGY. *Current Pos:* From instr to prof anat, 62-97, head, Chem Group, Radiobiol Lab, 70-82, ASSOC DEAN RES, UNIV UTAH, 81-, INTERIM DEAN, 88- *Personal Data:* b Salt Lake City, Utah, Dec 6, 33; div; c 4. *Educ:* Univ Utah, BS, 56, PhD(anat, radiobiol), 62. *Concurrent Pos:* Dir, Nat Inst Gen Med Sci Training Grant, 74-77; vis prof, Stanford Univ, 77. *Mem:* Endocrine Soc; Am Asn Anatomists; Soc Neurosci; Am Physiol Soc; Radiation Res Soc. *Res:* Mechanism of action of glucocorticoids in lymphoid tissues, central nervous system and lung;

interaction of transuranic elements with biological systems; effect of radioactive fallout in humans; relationship to thyroid disease and leukemia. *Mailing Add:* Deans Office Sch Med Univ Utah 50 N Med Dr Salt Lake City UT 84132. *Fax:* 801-581-3300; *E-Mail:* stevens@dean.smedutah.edu

STEVENS, WALTER JOSEPH, THEORETICAL & PHYSICAL CHEMISTRY, CHEMICAL PHYSICS. *Current Pos:* CHIEF BIOTECHNOL DIV, NAT INST STAND & TECHNOL, 95-, PHYSICIST, PHYS & CHEM PROPERTIES DIV, 97- *Personal Data:* b Atlantic City, NJ, Apr 29, 44; m 66, Linda A Mescanti; c 2. *Educ:* Drexel Univ, BS, 67; Ind Univ, Bloomington, PhD(chem physics), 71. *Honors & Awards:* Silver Medal, Dept Com, 84, Gold Medal, 90. *Prof Exp:* NSF fel, Argonne Nat Lab, 71-72, lab fel, 72-73; physicist, Lawrence Livermore Lab, 73-75; mem staff, Time & Frequency Div, Nat Bur Stand, 75-77, mem staff, Molecular Spectros Div, 77-78; assoc dir, Ctr Adv Res Biotechnol, 88-91, actg dir, 92, res scientist, 93-95. *Concurrent Pos:* Adj prof, Univ Md Biotechnol Inst, 90- *Mem:* Am Chem Soc; Am Phys Soc; AAAS; Sigma Xi. *Res:* Quantum chemistry; ab initio calculation of molecular wavefunctions and properties; chemical reactions, condensed phase chemistry; biophysics. *Mailing Add:* Phys & Chem Properties Div Nat Inst Stand & Technol Gaithersburg MD 20899

STEVENS, WARREN DOUGLAS, BOTANY. *Current Pos:* B A KRUKOFF CUR CENT AM BOT, MO BOT GARDEN, 77-, DIR RES. *Personal Data:* b Long Beach, Calif, Sept 15, 44; m 63; c 1. *Educ:* Humboldt State Col, AB, 68; Mich State Univ, MS, 71, PhD(bot), 76. *Prof Exp:* Asst bot & plant path, Mich State Univ, 71-74; consult, Cyrus William Rice Div, NUS Corp, 75-77; res assoc bot & plant path, Mich State Univ, 76-78. *Concurrent Pos:* Collabr, Smithsonian Hassan Flora Proj, 69; consult, Ingham Co Circuit Court, 75-77. *Mem:* Am Soc Plant Taxonomists; Asn Trop Biol; Bot Soc Am; Int Asn Plant Taxon; Sigma Xi. *Res:* Flora of Nicaragua; systematics of Asclepiadaceae. *Mailing Add:* Mo Bot Garden PO Box 299 St Louis MO 63166

STEVENS, WILLIAM D, ENGINEERING. *Current Pos:* vpres equip dir, Foster Wheeler Corp, 62-73, sr vpres, 72-74, exec vpres, 74-78, chmn bd, 78-81, dir, 74-86, emer dir, 86-90, CONSULT, FOSTER WHEELER CORP, 88- *Personal Data:* b Bayonne, NJ, Aug 4, 18. *Educ:* Rensselaer Polytech Inst, BS, 40. *Hon Degrees:* DSc, NJ Inst Technol, 86. *Prof Exp:* Eng & mgt positions, Babcock & Wilcox Co, 40-62. *Mem:* Nat Acad Eng; Am Soc Macro Eng; fel Am Soc Mech Engrs. *Mailing Add:* 4 Stony Brook Dr North Caldwell NJ 07006

STEVENS, WILLIAM F(OSTER), CHEMICAL ENGINEERING. *Current Pos:* from res assoc to assoc prof, Northwestern Univ, Evanston, 51-64, assoc dean, Grad Sch, 65-72 & 86-88, chmn dept, 76-79, prof, 64-88, EMER PROF CHEM ENG, NORTHWESTERN UNIV, EVANSTON, 88- *Personal Data:* b Detroit, Mich, Oct 7, 22; m 62, Lillian Janda; c Francine (Derby), Susan (Pierce), Alan, Martha (Freeman) & Karin (Friese). *Educ:* Northwestern Univ, BS, 44; Univ Wis, MS, 47, PhD(chem eng), 49. *Prof Exp:* Chem engr, Res Ctr, B F Goodrich Co, 49-51. *Concurrent Pos:* Consult, Vern E Alden Co, Ill, 52-59, Pure Oil Co, 58-63, Argonne Nat Lab, 59-61, Chicago Bridge & Iron Co, 64-70, TecSearch, Inc, 65-71 & Chicago Mortgage Co, 91-93. *Mem:* Am Soc Eng Educ; Am Chem Soc; Am Inst Chem Engrs. *Res:* Applied mathematics and computers; process control and dynamics; process optimization. *Mailing Add:* Dept Chem Eng Northwestern Univ Evanston IL 60201. *Fax:* 847-724-2127; *E-Mail:* w-stevens@nwu.edu

STEVENS, WILLIAM GEORGE, ELECTROCHEMISTRY, ANALYTICAL CHEMISTRY. *Current Pos:* SR RES ENGR, SOLAR GROUP, INT HARVESTER, 76-, CHIEF CHEMIST, 78- *Personal Data:* b Champaign, Ill, Sept 20, 38; m 61; c 3. *Educ:* Mass Inst Technol, BS, 61; Univ Wis-Madison, PhD(chem), 66, PE(corrosion), 78. *Prof Exp:* Sr chemist, Corning Glass Works, 66-69; res specialist nonaqueous batteries, Res & Develop Div, Whittaker Corp, 69-72, res specialist anal chem, 72-76. *Concurrent Pos:* QA mgr, S-Cubed, 81; consult, 88- *Mem:* Am Chem Soc; Electrochem Soc; Inst Elec & Electronics Engrs. *Res:* Polymer characterization and physical properties of materials; hot corrosion, QA (EPA protocols). *Mailing Add:* PO Box 2157 Julian CA 92036-2157

STEVENS, WILLIAM Y(EATON), COMPUTER SYSTEM DESIGN. *Current Pos:* RETIRED. *Personal Data:* b South Portland, Maine, Nov 5, 31; m 66, Gwendolyn L Hamilton; c Emily & Guy. *Educ:* Bates Col, BS, 53; Cornell Univ, MS, 55, PhD(eng physics), 58. *Prof Exp:* Physicist, Gen Elec Co, 53; asst elec eng, Cornell Univ, 54-58; assoc engr, Int Bus Mach Corp, 58-60, staff systs planner, 60-63, adv engr, 63-69, sr engr, 69-93. *Mem:* AAAS; Asn Comput Mach; Inst Elec & Electronics Engrs. *Res:* System design of digital computing and data processing systems; data communications, system reliability and maintainability. *Mailing Add:* 5 Channingville Rd Wappingers Falls NY 12590

STEVENSON, BRUCE R, EPITHELIAL CELL BIOLOGY. *Current Pos:* ASSOC BIOL, YALE UNIV, 83- *Personal Data:* b Buffalo, NY, Sept 28, 52. *Educ:* Harvard Univ, PhD(med sci), 83. *Mem:* Am Soc Cell Biol. *Res:* Biochemical characterization of tight junction. *Mailing Add:* Dept Anat & Cell Biol Univ Alta Edmonton AB T6G 2H7 Can. *Fax:* 403-492-0450; *E-Mail:* earnuserbrus@valtamts.ca

STEVENSON, DAVID AUSTIN, materials science; deceased, see previous edition for last biography

STEVENSON, DAVID JOHN, PLANETARY PHYSICS. *Current Pos:* from assoc prof to prof, 80-95, chmn, Div Geol & Planetary Sci, 89-94, GEORGE VAN OSDOL PROF PLANETARY SCI, CALIF INST TECHNOL, 95- *Personal Data:* b Wellington, New Zealand, Sept 2, 48. *Educ:* Victoria Univ, BSc, 71, MS, 72; Cornell Univ, PhD(physics), 76. *Honors & Awards:* Fullbright Scholar, 71-76; Urey Prize, 84. *Prof Exp:* Res fel, Earth Sci, Australian Nat Univ, 76-78; asst prof, Univ Calif, 78-80. *Mem:* Fel Am Geophys Union; fel Royal Soc London. *Res:* Origin, evolution and structure of planets, including Earth. *Mailing Add:* Caltech 170-25 Pasadena CA 91125. *Fax:* 626-585-1917; *E-Mail:* djs@gps.caltech.edu

STEVENSON, DAVID MICHAEL, electrical engineering, physics; deceased, see previous edition for last biography

STEVENSON, DAVID P(AUL), chemistry, for more information see previous edition

STEVENSON, DAVID STUART, SOIL PHYSICS. *Current Pos:* RETIRED. *Personal Data:* b Virden, Man, Jan 23, 24; m 46, Doreen M Evans; c David P & Kathryn C. *Educ:* Univ BC, BSA, 51; Ore State Univ, MSc, 56, PhD(soils), 63. *Prof Exp:* Res officer, Dom Exp Farm, Can Dept Agr, Sask, 56-57, Agr Res Sta, Alta, 62-66, res scientist, 66-78, sect head, Soil Sci & Agr Eng, Summerland Res Sta, 78-89. *Concurrent Pos:* Assoc ed, Can Jour Soil Sc, 79-84; mem Can Expert Comt on Soil & Water, 81-87. *Mem:* Sigma Xi; Can Soc Soil Sci. *Res:* Irrigation; soil-water-plant growth relationship. *Mailing Add:* 48-3333 S Main St Penticton BC V2A 8J8 Can

STEVENSON, DENNIS A, HEALTH PHYSICS, ENVIRONMENTAL MONITORING. *Current Pos:* process physicist, Du Pont, Savannah River Plant, 83, area supvr, 83-84, tech supvr, 84-86, chief supvr, 86-88, mgr environ monitoring, 88-89, mgr, Health Protection Opers, Westinghouse Savannah River Co, 89-90, mgr, Health Protection Dept, 90-93, sr adv scientist solid waste & environ restoration, 93-94, MGR, TRANSITION, DECONTAMINATION & DECOMMISSIONING DEPT, WESTINGHOUSE SAVANNAH RIVER CO, 94- *Personal Data:* b Mt Holly, NJ, Jan 25, 44; m 66, Sandra L Davis; c Nancy A (Youmans), Donna G (Lann) & Joseph A. *Educ:* Gettysburg Col, BA, 66; Univ Del, MS, 68, PhD(physics), 72; Am Bd Health Physics, cert, 80. *Prof Exp:* Teaching res asst physics, Univ Del, 66-72; res assoc biophys, Univ Pittsburgh, 72-73; asst prof physics, Northeast La Univ, 73-77; asst health physics officer, Walter Reed Army Med Ctr, 77-80, health physics officer, 80-81; health physics officer/radiation protection officer, Dwight D Eisenhower Army Med Ctr, 81-83. *Concurrent Pos:* Mem health physics, ANSI Stand Comt Mult Dosimetry. *Mem:* Health Physics Soc; Am Acad Health Physics; Sigma Xi; Sci Res Soc NAm. *Res:* Physical studies of biologically important macromolecules, protein-nucleic acid interactions, virology, effects of various ionizing radiations on macromolecules and living systems; applied health physics; radiation accident emergency preparedness; environmental monitoring; decontamination and decommissioning. *Mailing Add:* 11628 Bermuda Dr Knoxville TN 37922

STEVENSON, DON R, FLAME RETARDANTS. *Current Pos:* TECH DIR DEVELOP, DOVER CHEM, 79- *Personal Data:* b Syracuse, NY, Dec 19, 44; m 66; c 3. *Educ:* Syracuse Univ, BA, 66; Univ Ariz, PhD(organic polymers), 71. *Prof Exp:* fel, Univ mass, 71-72; researcher plastics, Glidden, 72-76; tech dir, Union Camp, 76-79. *Mem:* Am Chem Soc. *Res:* Polymers and industrial polymer applications for reverse osmosis membranes, low profile plastics and coatings and flame retardant additives. *Mailing Add:* ICC Indust Inc Dover Chem Corp W 15th St PO Box 40 Dover OH 44622-9712

STEVENSON, DONALD THOMAS, SOLID STATE PHYSICS. *Current Pos:* Asst physics, Mass Inst Technol, 49-50, res assoc, 50-51, mem staff, Lincoln Lab, 51-53, asst group leader solid state physics, 53-57, group leader, 57-61, asst dir, 60-88, VIS SCIENTIST, FRANCIS BITTER MAGNET LAB, MASS INST TECHNOL, 88- *Personal Data:* b Washington, DC, Sept 8, 23; m 46, Marjory Mordoff; c Richard, Mary & Katherine. *Educ:* Cornell Univ, AB, 44; Mass Inst Technol, PhD(physics), 50. *Mem:* AAAS; Am Phys Soc. *Res:* Semiconductors; high magnetic fields. *Mailing Add:* Francis Bitter Magnet Lab Mass Inst Technol Rm NW14-3214 Cambridge MA 02139. *E-Mail:* dtsteven@mit.edu

STEVENSON, ELMER CLARK, HORTICULTURE. *Current Pos:* prof, assoc dean agr & dir resident instruct, 67-80, EMER PROF HORT, EMER ASSOC DEAN & EMER DIR RESIDENT INSTR AGR, ORE STATE UNIV, 80- *Personal Data:* b Pine City, Wash, Aug 20, 15; m 39; c 6. *Educ:* Univ Md, BS, 37; Univ Wis, PhD(agron, plant path), 42. *Prof Exp:* Asst plant path, Univ Wis, 38-42; from asst plant pathologist to assoc plant pathologist, Drug Plant Invests, US Dept Agr, 42-48; from assoc prof to prof hort, Purdue Univ, 48-67, head dept, 58-67. *Concurrent Pos:* Consult, US Dept Agr & Univ Ky, 58, US Agency Int Develop, Brazil, 62 & US Dept Agr & Miss State Univ, 64. *Mem:* Fel Am Soc Hort Sci. *Res:* Corn diseases and breeding; diseases of medicinal and special crops; mint breeding and production; vegetable breeding and genetics. *Mailing Add:* 8240 NW Chaparral Dr Corvallis OR 97330

STEVENSON, ENOLA L, PLANT PHYSIOLOGY. *Personal Data:* b Feb 20, 39; US citizen. *Educ:* Southern Univ, BS, 60; Univ NH, MS, 62, PhD(plant physiol), 68. *Prof Exp:* Res asst plant physiol, Univ NH, 60-62 & 67-68; instr bot, Southern Univ, 62-64; asst prof biol, Atlanta Univ, 68-72, assoc prof, 72-81; Southern Univ, Baton Rouge, La, 82-83. *Res:* Effects of light quality and intensity on plant growth and metabolism. *Mailing Add:* 188 W Flanacher Rd Zachary LA 70791

STEVENSON, F DEE, CHEMICAL ENGINEERING. *Current Pos:* RETIRED. *Personal Data:* b Ogden, Utah, June 7, 33; m 51; c 5. *Educ:* Univ Utah, BS, 55; Ore State Univ, PhD, 62. *Prof Exp:* Asst eng, Calif Res Corp, Stand Oil Co Calif, 55-57; from asst prof to prof chem eng, Iowa State Univ, 62-74; prof term with Chem Off, Div Phys Res, AEC, 72-74; prog mgr, Mat Sci & Molecular Sci Off, Div Basic Energy Sci, ERDA, 74-77; br chief, Chem Sci Div, Off Energy Res, Dept Energy, 77-94. *Mem:* Am Chem Soc; Am Inst Chem Engrs. *Res:* Kinetics of reactions; statistical application to data analysis and sequential experimental design; anhydrous separation and purification metals; thermodynamics of solutions, including liquid metals; high temperature and vacuum processing. *Mailing Add:* 3367 E Bernada Dr Salt Lake City UT 84124

STEVENSON, FORREST FREDERICK, PLANT MORPHOLOGY. *Current Pos:* from asst prof to prof biol, Ball State Univ, 55-82. *Personal Data:* b Kismet, Kans, Nov 12, 16; m 47; c 1. *Educ:* Cent Mo State Col, BS, 46; Univ Mo, MA, 48; Univ Mich, PhD(bot), 56. *Prof Exp:* Instr biol, Univ Kans City, 48-50 & McCook Jr Col, 50-51. *Mem:* Bot Soc Am; Am Bryol & Lichenological Soc. *Res:* Experimental plant morphology. *Mailing Add:* 1806 N Forest Ave Muncie IN 47304

STEVENSON, FRANK JAY, SOILS. *Current Pos:* From asst prof to assoc prof, 53-62, PROF SOIL CHEM, UNIV ILL, 62- *Personal Data:* b Logan, Utah, Aug 2, 22; m 56, Leda Jensen; c Mark (deceased), Diana & Frank E. *Educ:* Brigham Young Univ, BS, 49; Ohio State Univ, PhD(agron), 52. *Honors & Awards:* Agron Res Award, Am Soc Agron, 80; Soil Sci Res Award, Soil Sci Soc Am, 83, Bouyoucos Soil Sci Distinguished Career Award, 91, Distinguished Serv Award, 92, Wolf Prize in Agr, 95. *Mem:* Soil Sci Soc Am; Am Soc Agron; Int Soil Sci Soc; Humic Substances Soc. *Res:* Biochemical properties of soils; chemistry of soil organic matter. *Mailing Add:* Dept, Natural Resources & Environ Sci Univ Ill Urbana IL 61801

STEVENSON, FRANK ROBERT, SOLID STATE PHYSICS, ACOUSTICS. *Current Pos:* ENVIRON CONSULT, 87- *Personal Data:* b Brooklyn, NY, Aug 29, 31; m 56, Joyce Rieger; c 6. *Educ:* Polytech Inst Brooklyn, BS, 53, MS, 59. *Prof Exp:* Physicist, Sperry Gyroscope Co, NY, 53-56 & Curtis Wright Corp, Pa, 56-58; res assoc, RIAS Div, Martin Co, Md, 58-63; physicist, Lewis Res Ctr, NASA, Ohio, 63-71; environ scientist, Ford Motor Co, 71-87. *Concurrent Pos:* Lectr, Goucher Col, 61-62 & John Carroll Univ, 64-65. *Mem:* Am Phys Soc; Inst Noise Control Engrs. *Res:* Radiation damage; microwave electronics; low temperature physics; accelerators; air pollution; industrial noise control; energy conservation; water pollution management. *Mailing Add:* 18807 Ironwood Ave Cleveland OH 44110

STEVENSON, G W, PEDIATRIC ANESTHESIA. *Current Pos:* Assoc, 81-86, ASST PROF CLIN ANESTHESIA, NORTHWESTERN UNIV MED SCH, 86- *Personal Data:* b LaPorte, Ind, Sept 7, 51. *Educ:* DePauw Univ, BA, 73; Ind Univ, Indianapolis, MD, 77; Am Bd Med Examr, dipl, 78; Am Bd Anesthesiol, dipl, 81. *Concurrent Pos:* Fel pediatric anesthesia, Children's Mem Hosp Chicago, 80-81 & Philadelphia, 81; provisional attend staff anesthesiologist, Children's Mem Hosp, Chicago, 81-82, Med co-dir, Outpatient Surg, 83-, dir anesthesia res, 87-, mem, Disaster Planning Comt, 85, Code Comt, 85 & Operating Room Mgt Comt, 86-; mem, Resident Eval Comt, Northwestern Univ Med Sch, 85-89; fel Am Acad Pediat, 89. *Mem:* Int Anesthesia Res Soc; Am Soc Anesthesiologists; Soc Ambulatory Anesthesia; Soc Pediat Anesthesia; Soc Leukocyte Biol; Am Fedn Clin Res; Am Asn Immunologists. *Res:* Effects of anesthetic agents on immunologic function; co-author of numerous publications. *Mailing Add:* Dept Anesthesia Children's Mem Hosp 2300 Children's Plaza Box 19 Chicago IL 60614-3394

STEVENSON, GEORGE FRANKLIN, pathology; deceased, see previous edition for last biography

STEVENSON, HARLAN QUINN, CYTOGENETICS, RADIOBIOLOGY. *Current Pos:* from asst prof to assoc prof, 64-72, chmn dept, 75-84, PROF BIOL, SOUTHERN CONN STATE UNIV, 72- *Personal Data:* b Waynesboro, Pa, Apr 1, 27; m 60; c 2. *Educ:* Pa State Univ, BS, 50; Univ Fla, PhD(radiation bio), 63. *Prof Exp:* Asst bot, Pa State Univ, 50-51 & Cornell Univ, 51-56; res assoc biol, Brookhaven Nat Lab, 56-60; asst prof, Univ Fla, 63-64. *Mem:* AAAS; Soc Study Evolution; Am Inst Biol Sci; Am Soc Human Genetics; Genetics Soc Am; NY Acad Sci. *Res:* Chemical and radiation induced chromosomal aberrations; genetic and radiation effects in plant tumors; evolutionary and practical significance of multiple allopolyploidy; genetic counseling; bioethics. *Mailing Add:* 71 Doolittle Dr Bethany CT 06524

STEVENSON, HAROLD WILLIAM, PSYCHOLOGY. *Current Pos:* PROF PSYCHOL & FEL, CTR HUMAN GROWTH & DEVELOP, UNIV MICH, ANN ARBOR, 71- *Personal Data:* b Dines, Wyo, Nov 19, 24; m 50, Nancy Guy; c Peggy, Janet, Andrew & Patricia. *Educ:* Univ Colo, BA, 47; Stanford Univ, MA, 48, PhD, 51. *Hon Degrees:* ScD, Univ Minn, 96. *Honors & Awards:* Stanley Hall Award, Am Psychol Asn, 88, William James Award, 96, Bronfenbrenner Award, 97; Distinguished Res Award, Soc Res Child Develop, 93. *Prof Exp:* Asst prof psychol, Pomona Col, 50-53; from asst prof to assoc prof, Univ Tex, Austin, 53-59; prof child develop & psychol & dir, Inst Child Develop, Univ Minn, Minneapolis, 59-71. *Concurrent Pos:* Mem, Training Comt, Nat Inst Child Health & Human Develop, 64-67; fel, Ctr Advan Studies Behav Sci, 67-68, 82-83 & 89-90; mem deleg early childhood, Peoples Repub China, 73; mem, Personality & Cognition Study Sect, NIMH, 75-79; dir, Prog Child Develop & Social Policy, Univ Mich, 78-93; adj prof, Tohoku Fukushi Col, Japan, 89-, Peking Univ, 90-; Cattell fel award, Am Psychol Soc, 94. *Mem:* Fel Am Acad Arts & Sci; fel Nat Acad Educ; Am Psychol Asn; Soc Res Child Develop (pres, 69-71); Int Soc Study Behav Develop (pres, 87-91); Sigma Xi. *Res:* Child health and development. *Mailing Add:* 1030 Spruce Dr Ann Arbor MI 48104-2847. *Fax:* 313-936-9288

STEVENSON, HENRY C, CANCER IMMUNOLOGY. *Current Pos:* SR INVESTR, FCRF, NAT CANCER INST, 80- *Personal Data:* b Long Island, NY, Sept 18, 48. *Educ:* Stanford Univ, MD, 75. *Mem:* Am Col Physicians; Am Col Allergists; Soc Biol Ther; Am Fedn Clin Res. *Mailing Add:* 11223 Valley View Ave Kensington MD 20895-1929

STEVENSON, IAN, MEDICINE, PSYCHIATRY. *Current Pos:* prof & chmn dept neurol & psychiat, 57-67, CARLSON PROF PSYCHIAT, SCH MED, UNIV VA, 67- *Personal Data:* b Montreal, Que, Oct 31, 18; nat US; m 47. *Educ:* McGill Univ, BSc, 40, MD, CM, 43. *Prof Exp:* Intern & asst resident med, Royal Victoria Hosp, Montreal, 44-45; from intern to resident, St Joseph's Hosp, Phoenix, Ariz, 45-46; fel internal med, Ochsner Med Found, New Orleans, La, 46-47; Commonwealth fel med, Med Col, Cornell Univ, 47-49; asst prof med & psychiat, Sch Med, La State Univ, 49-52, assoc prof psychiat, 52-57. *Concurrent Pos:* Consult, New Orleans Parish Sch Bd, 49-52, State Dept Pub Welfare, 50-52 & Southeast La State Hosp, Mandeville, 52-57; vis physician, Charity Hosp, New Orleans, 52-57; hon mem staff, DePaul Hosp, 52-57; psychiatrist-in-chief, Univ Va Hosp, 57-67. *Mem:* AAAS; Am Psychosom Soc; Am Soc Psychical Res; Am Psychiat Asn; AMA; Soc Sci Explor. *Res:* Experimental psychoses; psychotherapy; paranormal phenomena. *Mailing Add:* Dept Psychiat Univ Va Health Sci Ctr Box 152 Charlottesville VA 22908-0001

STEVENSON, J(OSEPH) ROSS, EFFECTS OF STRESS ON ENDOCRINE & IMMUNE SYSTEMS. *Current Pos:* from instr to assoc prof, 60-71, assoc dean grad col, 73-74, PROF BIOL SCI, KENT STATE UNIV, 71- *Personal Data:* b Canton, China, Sept 4, 31; US citizen; m 54, Nancy Hanson; c Peter, Philip & Jay. *Educ:* Oberlin Col, BA, 53; Northwestern Univ, MS, 55, PhD, 60. *Prof Exp:* Asst zool & chem, Oberlin Col, 52-53; asst biol, Northwestern Univ, 53-55; instr, Chatham Col, 56-59; res assoc zool, Univ Wash, 59-60. *Concurrent Pos:* Jacques Loeb assoc, Rockefeller Univ, 63-64. *Mem:* AAAS; Sigma Xi; Am Soc Cell Biol; Am Asn Immunologists; Psychoneuroimmunol Res Soc Int Soc; Psychoneuroendocrinol. *Res:* Effects of stress and hormones on the immune system; lymphocyte functions. *Mailing Add:* Dept Biol Sci Kent State Univ Kent OH 44242. *E-Mail:* jstevens@kent.edu

STEVENSON, JAMES FRANCIS, POLYMER PROCESSING. *Current Pos:* res scientist, 77-79, group leader, 79-81, sect head, 81-86, MGR GENCORP, INC, 86- *Personal Data:* b Greenville, Pa, July 15, 43; m 71, Stetanie Handelman; c Daniel & Jason. *Educ:* Rensselaer Polytech Inst, BChE, 65; Univ Wis, Madison, MS, 67, PhD(chem eng), 70. *Prof Exp:* NIH fel, Columbia Univ, 70-71; from asst prof to assoc prof chem eng, Cornell Univ, 71-77. *Mem:* Am Inst Chem Engrs; Am Chem Soc; Soc Plastics Engrs; Polymer Processing Soc (treas, 85-88). *Res:* Innovation, optimization, and control of processes for thermoplastic and thermoset composite materials; processes include extrusion, coating, injection, transfer and compression molding; invention of net shape processes for efficient manufacturing; polymer rheology. *Mailing Add:* 24 Wood Rd Morristown NJ 07960. *Fax:* 330-794-6375

STEVENSON, JAMES RUFUS, SURFACE PHYSICS. *Current Pos:* asst prof, Ga Inst Technol, 55-62, actg dir, 68-69, assoc prof physics, 62-68, dir, Sch Physics, 69-78, actg vpres acad affairs, 79-81, exec asst pres, 81-88, EMER PROF PHYSICS & EMER EXEC ASST PRES, GA INST TECHNOL, 88- *Personal Data:* b Trenton, NJ, May 19, 25; m 55, Adelyn Stegall; c Alicia L (Steele), Maryhelen (Waugh) & Jana L (Waln). *Educ:* Mass Inst Technol, SB, 50; Univ Mo, PhD(physics), 58. *Prof Exp:* Res partic, Oak Ridge Nat Lab, 55. *Concurrent Pos:* Physicist, US Naval Res Lab, DC, 58, consult, 60-67; Fulbright-Hays vis prof, Univ Sci & Technol, Ghana, 65-66; NATO sr fel, Desy Hamburg, WGer, 72; mem comt applns physics, Am Phys Soc, 75-78; pres, Ionic Atlanta Inc, 88-91. *Mem:* Am Phys Soc; Am Asn Physics Teachers; Optical Soc Am; Am Soc Eng Educ; Sigma Xi. *Res:* Synchrotron radiation, Auger spectroscopy and optical surface studies of metals, metal oxides, and semiconductors with applications to corrosion and optical properties; science administration. *Mailing Add:* Sch Physics Ga Inst of Technol Atlanta GA 30332. *Fax:* 404-853-9958

STEVENSON, JEAN MOORHEAD, surgery; deceased, see previous edition for last biography

STEVENSON, JEFFREY SMITH, REPRODUCTIVE PHYSIOLOGY, REPRODUCTIVE ENDOCRINOLOGY. *Current Pos:* from asst prof to assoc prof, 80-91, PROF ANIMAL SCI, KANSAS STATE UNIV, 91- *Personal Data:* b Salt Lake City, Utah, June 15, 51; m 74, Barta Morrill. *Educ:* Utah State Univ Logan, BS, 75; Mich State Univ, Lansing, MS, 77; NC State Univ, Raleigh, PhD(animal physiol), 80. *Honors & Awards:* Young Scientist Award, Am Dairy Sci Asn, 90. *Prof Exp:* Grad res asst dairy sci, Mich State Univ, 75-77, animal sci, NC State Univ, 77-80. *Concurrent Pos:* Prin investr, Kans Agr Exp Sta, 80-; contrib columnist, Hoard's Dairyman, 92-; adj res prof, Utah State Univ, 96-98. *Mem:* Am Soc Animal Sci; Am Dairy Sci Asn; Soc Study Reproduction; Sigma Xi. *Res:* Physiologic and endocrinological factors associated with postpartum fertility of cattle including suckling-induced anestrus, estrous behavior, estrous detection, function of corpus luteum and other hormonal treatments that may improve conception rates. *Mailing Add:* Dept Animal Sci Kans State Univ Manhattan KS 66506-0201. *Fax:* 785-532-7059; *E-Mail:* jstevens@oz.oznet.ksu.edu

STEVENSON, JOANNE SABOL, ADULT HEALTH CARE, GERONTOLOGY & GERIATRICS. *Current Pos:* instr, Ohio State Univ, 64-67, from asst prof to prof, 70-95, dir, Ctr Nursing Res, 72-84, chairperson, Dept Life Span, 84-85, EMER PROF, OHIO STATE UNIV, 95- *Personal Data:* b Steubenville, Ohio, June 8, 39; m 66, Robert J; c James J & Michael J. *Educ:* Ohio State Univ, BS, 63, MS, 64, PhD, 70. *Prof Exp:* Nurse practitioner, Canton & Columbus, Ohio. *Concurrent Pos:* Prin investr, NIH, 66-68 & 80-84, Ohio State Univ Res Contingency Fund, 71-75 & 76-78, Ohio Dept Health, 74-75, Biomed Res develop grant, 79-82, Women's Health Res Prog, 80-84, Univ Small Grants Prog & Col Nursing Dir Support Funds, 86-87, Am Assoc Retired Persons Andrus Found, 94-96, Nat Inst Alcoholism & Alcohol Abuse, 94-98; res assoc, NIH, 72-75 & Nat Cancer Inst, 74-78; prog dir, Res Develop Prog, Div Nursing, 72-75, NIH, 72-77 & 79-82, Dept Health & Human Servs, 75-77 & 80-84, Health Res & Serv Admin, 91-95; co-dir, Health Clin Older Adults, 77-93; fac fel, Nat Inst Alcoholism & Alcohol Abuse, 90-95; Fulbright sr scholar, Univ Fed Santa Catarina, Brazil, 95-96. *Mem:* Am Nurses Asn; AAAS; fel Am Acad Nurses; Am Asn Univ Profs. *Res:* Health promotion and optimal functioning in middle age and older adulthood focused on women; exercise, strength training; contributed articles to professional journals. *Mailing Add:* Dept Adult Health & Illness Ohio State Univ 1585 Neil Ave Columbus OH 43210-1289

STEVENSON, JOHN CRABTREE, MATHEMATICS. *Current Pos:* From instr to assoc prof, 68-74, chmn dept, 72-78, PROF MATH, C W POST COL, LONG ISLAND UNIV, 74- *Personal Data:* b Everett, Wash, Feb 24, 37; m 60; c 3. *Educ:* NY Univ, BA, 63, MS, 63; Adelphi Univ, PhD(math), 70. *Concurrent Pos:* C W Post Col grant, dept physics, Imp Col, Univ London, 70-71. *Mem:* AAAS; Math Asn Am; Am Math Soc; Soc Indust & Appl Math. *Res:* Numerical solution of hyperbolic partial differential equations; plasma physics in the solar atmosphere and magnetosphere; multiple pool analysis of metabolic pathways. *Mailing Add:* 266 Southdown Rd Huntington Rd Huntington NY 11743-1706

STEVENSON, JOHN DAVID, HEAVY-ION REACTION MECHANISMS, EXOTIC NUCLEI. *Current Pos:* STAFF SCIENTIST, SCI APPLNS INT CORP, 90- *Personal Data:* b St Louis, Mo, Aug 12, 50; m 88. *Educ:* Univ Ill, Urbana, BS, 72; Univ Calif, Berkeley, PhD(physics) 77. *Prof Exp:* Asst prof physics, Physics & Astron Dept & Nat Superconducting Cyclotron Lab, Mich State Univ, 84-91. *Mem:* Am Phys Soc. *Res:* Heavy ion reaction mechanisms at intermediate energies; study of the properties of nuclei far from stability. *Mailing Add:* Sci Applns Int Corp 2950 Patrick Henry Dr Santa Clara CA 95054

STEVENSON, JOHN RAY, IMMUNOLOGY, MEDICAL MICROBIOLOGY. *Current Pos:* vis asst prof, 80-83, asst prof, 83-87, ASSOC PROF MICROBIOL, MIAMI UNIV, OHIO, 87- *Personal Data:* b Ordway, Colo, May 10, 43; m 80, P Helen Stevko. *Educ:* Kans State Teachers Col, BA, 65, MS, 67; Case Western Res Univ, PhD(microbiol), 72. *Prof Exp:* Fel, Johns Hopkins Univ, 72-74; asst prof biol & med, Biol Dept, Univ Mo, Kansas City, 74-80. *Concurrent Pos:* Univ Sanitarian, Miami Univ, 80-83. *Mem:* AAAS; Am Soc Microbiol; Sigma Xi; Am Asn Immunologists. *Res:* Mechanisms of immunodeficiency induced by protein and/or zinc malnutrition; immune system development; cytokines in immune responses; cell-mediated immunity and host-parasite relationships; heparin activity. *Mailing Add:* Dept Microbiol Miami Univ Oxford OH 45056. *Fax:* 513-529-2431; *E-Mail:* stevenjr@muohio.edu

STEVENSON, KENNETH EUGENE, food microbiology, for more information see previous edition

STEVENSON, KENNETH JAMES, PROTEIN CHEMISTRY. *Current Pos:* from asst prof to assoc prof, 69-82, PROF BIOCHEM, UNIV CALGARY, 82- *Personal Data:* b Calgary, Alta, Apr 16, 41; m 64; c 2. *Educ:* Univ Alta, BSc, 62, PhD(biochem), 66. *Prof Exp:* Med Res Coun fel, Lab Molecular Biol, Cambridge Univ, 66-67; Killam fel, Univ BC, 67-69. *Mem:* Can Biochem Soc; Brit Biochem Soc; Am Soc Biol Chemists; Sigma Xi; Protein Soc; NY Acad Sci. *Res:* Structure and function of dithiol reductases from Protozoa and archaebacteria; trivalent arsenicals. *Mailing Add:* Dept Biol Sci Univ Calgary 2500 University Ave Calgary AB T2N 1N4 Can. *Fax:* 403-289-9311; *E-Mail:* Bitnet: stevenson@ucdasumi__12092

STEVENSON, KENNETH LEE, PHOTOCHEMISTRY. *Current Pos:* from asst prof to assoc prof chem, 68-78, actg dean, Sch Sci & Humanities, 86-87, PROF CHEM, PURDUE UNIV, FT WAYNE, 78-, CHMN CHEM DEPT, 79-86 & 87- *Personal Data:* b Ft Wayne, Ind, Aug 1, 39; m 59, 92, Carmen Kmety; c Melinda & Jill. *Educ:* Purdue Univ, BS, 61, MS, 65; Univ Mich, PhD(phys chem), 68. *Honors & Awards:* Chemist of the Year, Am Chem Soc, 79, 93. *Prof Exp:* Teacher high schs, Ind & Mich, 61-65. *Concurrent Pos:* Fel, Chem Dept, NMex State Univ, 75-76; sabbatical vis, Solar Energy Res Inst, Colo, 80. *Mem:* Sigma Xi; Am Chem Soc; Inter-Am Photochem Soc. *Res:* Photochemistry and spectra of coordination compounds; kinetics and thermodynamics of ligand exchange reactions; induction of optical activity using light; photochemical conversion of solar energy; laser flash photolysis. *Mailing Add:* Dept Chem Ind Univ-Purdue Univ Ft Wayne IN 46805-1499. *Fax:* 219-481-6880; *E-Mail:* stevenso@cvax.pifw.indiana.edu

STEVENSON, L HAROLD, MICROBIOLOGY. *Current Pos:* Asst prof, 67-71, ASSOC PROF BIOL, UNIV SC, 71, ASSOC PROF MARINE SCI & MICROBIOL, 73-; AT DEPT BIOL & ENVIRON SCI, MCNEESE STATE UNIV. *Personal Data:* b Bogalusa, La, Mar 18, 40; m 61; c 1. *Educ:* Southeastern La Col, BS, 62; La State Univ, MS, 64, PhD(microbiol), 67. *Mem:* AAAS; Am Soc Microbiol. *Res:* Bacterial ecology; distribution, activity and taxonomy of estuarine bacteria; marsh ecology. *Mailing Add:* Dept Biol & Environ Sci McNeese State Univ PO Box 92000 Lake Charles LA 70609-2000

STEVENSON, LOUISE (STEVENS), MINERALOGY. *Current Pos:* mus assoc geol, 51-57, cur, 57-80, HON CUR GEOL, REDPATH MUS, McGILL UNIV, 80- *Personal Data:* b Seattle, Wash, July 28, 12; Can citizen; wid; c John S & Robert F. *Educ:* Univ Wash, BS, 32; Radcliffe Col, AM, 33; Harvard Univ, AM33. *Prof Exp:* Res asst climat, US Weather Bur, Seattle, 34; lectr geol & geog, Victoria Col, BC, 48-49. *Concurrent Pos:* Convener sect 17, Int Geol Cong, 70-72; mem bd dirs, Redpath Mus, 92- *Mem:* Fel Geol Asn Can; Mineral Soc Am; Mineral Asn Can; Sigma Xi (hon secy, 73-84). *Res:* Petrogenesis of rare minerals; mineralogy applied to medicine and dentistry; petrology of siliceous lavas; geological education through university museums; origin of the Sudbury, Ontario orebody; history of Canadian geology. *Mailing Add:* Redpath Mus McGill Univ 859 Sherbroket W Montreal PQ H3A 2K6 Can. *Fax:* 514-398-3185

STEVENSON, MARY M, GENETIC CONTROL OF HOST RESISTANCE. *Current Pos:* asst prof, 82-88, ASSOC PROF, DEPT MED, MCGILL UNIV, 88-, ASSOC MEM, DEPT PHYSIOL, 84- *Personal Data:* b Philadelphia, Pa, Sept 10, 51; m 90. *Educ:* Hood Col, BA, 73; Cath Univ, MS, 77, PhD(microbiol), 79. *Prof Exp:* Res asst, Nat Cancer Inst, NIH, 74-79; res fel, Montreal Gen Hosp Res Inst, 79-81, res assoc, 81-82. *Concurrent Pos:* Scholar, Med Res Coun, Can, 82-87. *Mem:* Sigma Xi; Reticuloendothelial Soc; Am Soc Microbiol; Am Asn Immunologists; Am Asn Trop Med & Hyg. *Res:* Role of cell-mediated immunity and cytokines and mediators produced by T cells and macrophages in host resistance to pathogenic microorganisms in the spleen, lung and gut. *Mailing Add:* Montreal Gen Hosp Res Inst 1650 Cedar Ave Montreal PQ H3G 1A4 Can

STEVENSON, MERLON LYNN, PARTICLE PHYSICS. *Current Pos:* From asst to lectr, 48-58, from asst prof to prof, 58-91, FAC SR SCIENTIST, LAWRENCE BERKELEY LAB, UNIV CALIF, 51-, EMER PROF, 91- *Personal Data:* b Salt Lake City, Utah, Oct 31, 23; m 48, Lois Griffin; c Leslie A, Scott, Jeffery, Conrad & Cybele M. *Educ:* Univ Calif, AB, 48, PhD(physics), 53. *Concurrent Pos:* NSF sr fel & vis prof physics, Inst High Energy Physics, Univ Heidelberg, 66-67. *Mem:* Am Phys Soc; AAAS; NY Acad Sci. *Res:* Neutrino physics and new particle search; electron-positron physics; High energy neutrino astrophysics. *Mailing Add:* Lawrence Berkeley Lab Univ Calif Rm 5239 Bldg 50B Berkeley CA 94720

STEVENSON, MICHAEL GAIL, NUCLEAR ENGINEERING. *Current Pos:* RETIRED. *Personal Data:* b Little Rock, Ark, Jan 10, 43; m 64. *Educ:* Univ Tex, Austin, BEngSc, 64, PhD(nuclear eng), 68. *Prof Exp:* Reactor safety analysis, Babcock & Wilcox Co, 68-71; mem staff & sect mgr, Argonne Nat Lab, 71-74; mem staff & group leader fast reactor safety, Los Alamos Nat Lab, 74-76, asst energy div leader, 76-79, assoc leader reactor safety, 79-81, dep energy div leader, 81-83, energy div leader, 83-86, dep assoc dir, energy & technol, 87-93. *Mem:* Am Nuclear Soc. *Res:* Development of computational methods for analysis of reactor accidents; design and analysis of experiments related to reactor safety analysis; research program planning and management. *Mailing Add:* One Mariposa Ct White Rock NM 87544

STEVENSON, NANCY ROBERTA, PHYSIOLOGY, NUTRITION. *Current Pos:* Nat Inst Arthritis, Metab & Digestive Dis fel, Univ Med & Dent NJ, RW Johnson Med Sch, 69-71, instr physiol, 71-72, asst prof, 72-78, ASSOC PROF PHYSIOL, UNIV MED & DENT NJ, RW JOHNSON MED SCH, 78- *Personal Data:* b Vinton, Iowa, Feb 14, 38; m 73, John Lenard; c Steven, Karen, Keith & Eric. *Educ:* Univ Northern Iowa, BS, 60; Rutgers Univ, MS, 63, PhD(nutrit), 69. *Honors & Awards:* Simon Kamorov Award. *Mem:* AAAS; Am Gastroenterol Asn; Am Dietetic Asn; Am Physiol Soc; Int Soc Chronobiol; Am Diabetes Asn. *Res:* Gastrointestinal digestion and absorption, intestinal blood flow; circadian rhythms. *Mailing Add:* Dept Physiol & Biophysics Univ Med & Dent NJ RW Johnson Med Sch Piscataway NJ 08854. *Fax:* 732-235-5038; *E-Mail:* stevenso@umdnj.edu

STEVENSON, PAUL MICHAEL, RENORMALIZATION, NONPERTURBATIVE QUANTUM FIELD THEORY. *Current Pos:* from asst prof to assoc prof, 84-93, PROF PHYSICS, PHYSICS DEPT, RICE UNIV, 93- *Personal Data:* b Denham, Eng, Oct 10, 54. *Educ:* Cambridge Univ, BA, 76; Imp Col, London, DIC, 79; London Univ, PhD(theoret physics), 79. *Prof Exp:* Res assoc, Dept Physics, Univ Wis-Madison, 79-81 & 83-84; Europ Orgn Nuclear Res fel, 81-83. *Res:* Theoretical elementary particle physics; optimization of perturbative quantum; chromodynamics calculations using renormalization-group invariance; nonperturbative quantum field theory; Gaussian effective potential; triviality and the Higgs mechanism. *Mailing Add:* Bonner Lab MS 315 Rice Univ 6100 Main St Houston TX 77005-1892

STEVENSON, RICHARD MARSHALL, ELECTROPLATING, ORGANIC CHEMISTRY. *Current Pos:* RES DIR, DETROIT PLASTIC MOLDING CO, 78- *Personal Data:* b Detroit, Mich, July 2, 23; m 43, Marion I Byrne; c Michael R & Mark A. *Educ:* Detroit Inst Technol, BS, 48. *Prof Exp:* Mfg chemist, Parke Davis & Co, 48-52; anal chemist, Difco Labs, 52-53, Cadillac Motor Car Div, Gen Motors Corp, 53-58; sr org res chemist, div oxy metal indusrs, Udylike Corp, 58-75, McGean Chem Co, 75-77. *Concurrent Pos:* Pres, Richard M Stevenson & Co Consult Chemists, 77- *Mem:* Fel Am Inst Chemists; Am Chem Soc; Am Electroplaters Finishers Soc. *Res:* Electroplating plastics; electroless copper and nickel processes; electroplating acid cooper, nickel and zinc. *Mailing Add:* 2179 Allard Ave Grosse Point MI 48236-1911

STEVENSON, ROBERT EDWIN, MICROBIOLOGY, SCIENCE ADMINISTRATION. *Current Pos:* DIR, AM TYPE CULT COLLECTION, 80- *Personal Data:* b Columbus, Ohio, Dec 2, 26. *Educ:* Ohio State Univ, BSc, 47, MSc, 50, PhD(bact), 54; Am Bd Microbiol, dipl. *Honors & Awards:* IR 100 Award, 70. *Prof Exp:* Res assoc, USPHS, 52-54, virologist, 54-58; head tissue cult div, Tissue Bank Dept, US Naval Med Sch, 58-60; head, Cell Cult & Tissue Mat Sect, Virol Res Resources Br, Nat Cancer Inst, 60-62, actg chief, 62-63, chief, 63-66, chief, Viral Carcinogenesis Br, 66-67; mgr biol sci, Develop Dept, Union Carbide Res Inst, NY, 67-71; vpres, Litton Bionetics & gen mgr, Nat Cancer Inst-Frederick Cancer Res Ctr, 72-80. *Concurrent Pos:* Mem, Nat Inst Allergy & Infectious Dis, bd virus reference reagent, 63-65; cell cult comt, Int Asn Microbiol Soc, 63-67; comt transplantation, Nat Acad Sci-Nat Res Coun, 66-70; chmn cell cult comt, Am Type Cult Collection, 71-75, mem bd trustees, 72-; founding mem Am Asn Tissue Banks, chmn Cell & Tumor Coun, 77-81; fel Hastings Inst; vpres, World Fedn Cult Collections, 81-; chmn, Biotechnol Tech Adv Comt, US Dept Comm, 87- *Mem:* AAAS; Am Soc Microbiol; Soc Cryobiol; Tissue Cult Asn; Am Asn Tissue Banks; Fed Culture Collections (pres, 88-90); Tissue Culture Asn (pres, 88-90). *Res:* Viral oncology; biomedical instrumentation; biological standardization. *Mailing Add:* 1200 La Ranbla Santa Fe NM 87501-5970. *Fax:* 505-986-8175

STEVENSON, ROBERT EVANS, OCEANOGRAPHY. *Current Pos:* RETIRED. *Personal Data:* b Des Moines, Iowa, May 5, 16; m 48; c 2. *Educ:* Univ Hawaii, BS, 39; State Col Wash, MS, 42; Lehigh Univ, PhD(geol), 50. *Prof Exp:* Asst, Univ Hawaii, 39; lab asst, State Col Wash, 39-42; geologist, Wash State Div Geol, 42-44; field geologist, Venezuelan Atlantic Ref Co, 44-46; instr geol, Lehigh Univ, 46-50; geologist, State Geol Surv, SDak, 50-51; from asst prof to prof geol, Univ SDak, 51-71, chmn dept geol, 57-67, prof earth sci, 71-80, cur geol, Mus, 73-80. *Concurrent Pos:* Geologist, NY State Sci Serv, 47-48. *Mem:* AAAS; fel Geol Soc Am; Am Asn Petrol Geol; Paleont Soc. *Res:* Stratigraphy, sedimentation and paleontology of South Dakota; paleoecology. *Mailing Add:* 1225 Valley View Dr Vermillion SD 57069

STEVENSON, ROBERT EVERETT, OCEANOGRAPHY. *Current Pos:* EXEC SECY, VEGA SOC, 96-; TRUSTEE & CHIEF FINANCIAL OFFICER, INT FOUND APPL RES NAT SCI, 96- *Personal Data:* b Fullerton, Calif, Jan 15, 21; m 48, Jeani Wetzel; c Michael & Robert. *Educ:* Univ Calif, AB, 46, AM, 48; Univ Southern Calif, PhD(marine geol), 54. *Honors & Awards:* Golden EGS Badge, 95. *Prof Exp:* Instr geol, Compton Col, 47-49; lectr, Univ Southern Calif, 49-51; dir inshore res oceanog, Hancock Found, 53-59, 60-61; res scientist, Off Naval Res, London, 59; dir, Marine Lab, Tex A&M Univ, 61-63; assoc prof meteorol & geol, Fla State Univ, 63-65; res oceanogr & asst dir, Biol Lab, US Bur Commercial Fisheries, 65-70; sci liason officer, Off Naval Res, Scripps Inst Oceanog, 70-85, dep dir space oceanog & fleet liaison, 85-88, consult oceanog, 88-96. *Concurrent Pos:* Distinguished lectr, Am Asn Petrol Geologists, 69-72. *Mem:* Fel Geol Soc Am; Am Geophys Union. *Res:* Space oceanography; surface layer oceanography as related to meteorology and climatology. *Mailing Add:* PO Box 689 Del Mar CA 92014-0689. *Fax:* 619-481-6938

STEVENSON, ROBERT JAN, PHYCOLOGY, STREAM BIOLOGY. *Current Pos:* from asst prof to assoc prof, 81-93, PROF BIOL, UNIV LOUISVILLE, 93- *Personal Data:* b Cleveland, Ohio, Jan 3, 52; m 74. *Educ:* Bowling Green State Univ, BS, 74, MS, 76; Univ Mich, PhD(natural resources), 81. *Prof Exp:* Scientist, Nalco Environ Sci, 76-77; res asst, Great Lakes Res Div, Univ Mich, 77-81. *Concurrent Pos:* Dir, Water Resources Lab, Univ Louisville & chair, Ctr Environ Sci. *Mem:* Phycol Soc Am; Ecol Soc Am; NAm Benthological Soc; Am Soc Limnol & Oceanog; Am Inst Biol Sci. *Res:* Algae systematics and ecology; benthic diatom systematics; utilization of algae for environmental monitoring; studies of benthic algal ecology. *Mailing Add:* Dept Biol Univ Louisville Louisville KY 40292-0001

STEVENSON, ROBERT LOUIS, MATHEMATICS, COMPUTER SCIENCE. *Current Pos:* RETIRED. *Personal Data:* b Princeton, NJ, Jan 15, 32; m 57; c 3. *Educ:* Hobart Col, BS, 54; Rutgers Univ, MEd, 60; NY Univ, PhD(math educ). *Prof Exp:* Teacher pub sch, NJ, 56-66; assoc prof, William Paterson Col, 66-80, prof math, 80-95. *Res:* Number theory and coding theory. *Mailing Add:* Dept Math William Patterson Col 300 Pompton Rd Wayne NJ 07470-2103

STEVENSON, ROBERT LOVELL, ANALYTICAL CHEMISTRY. *Current Pos:* V PRES RES, ALTEX SCIENTIFIC, 77- *Personal Data:* b Long Beach, Calif. *Educ:* Reed Col, BA, 63; Univ Ariz, PhD(chem), 66. *Prof Exp:* Sr chemist, Shell Develop Co, 66-69; sr chemist, Varian Aerograph, 69-75, mgr liquid chromatography-res & develop, Varian Assocs, 75-77. *Mem:* Am Chem Soc. *Res:* Managing a research and development group developing high speed liquid chromatographs and accessories. *Mailing Add:* 3338 Carlyle Lab 201 Lafayette CA 94549-5202

STEVENSON, ROBERT THOMAS, biology; deceased, see previous edition for last biography

STEVENSON, ROBERT WILLIAM, ORGANIC CHEMISTRY. *Current Pos:* RETIRED. *Personal Data:* b Philadelphia, Pa, Oct 22, 30; m 55, Marian Irvine; c Marian E, Robert W Jr & Eric R. *Educ:* Univ Pa, BS, 54; Ga Inst Technol, PhD(org chem), 58. *Prof Exp:* Res chemist, Celanese Corp Am, 58-61; sr res chemist, Mobil Chem Co, 62-69; chmn, Dept Phys Sci, Cheyney Univ, 74-75 & 85-88, asst chmn, Dept Sci & Allied Health, 88-89, prof sci, 69-93. *Concurrent Pos:* Sabbatical, Fats & Proteins Res Found, 76-77. *Mem:* Am Chem Soc; Sigma Xi. *Res:* Synthesis of linear polyamides and polyesters, polyacetals and polyolefins; modification of fats. *Mailing Add:* 316 W Virginia Ave West Chester PA 19380-2220

STEVENSON, ROBIN, AERONAUTICAL ENGINEERING, SPACE SYSTEMS INTEGRATION. *Current Pos:* CONSULT, 87- *Personal Data:* b Concepcion, Chile, Mar 4, 23; US citizen; m 48; c 1. *Educ:* Mass Inst Technol, BS, 47, MS, 48. *Prof Exp:* Proj officer, Air Force Air Mat Command, 48-52, chief engr, B-36 Prog Off, Wright-Patterson AFB, 52-53, chief, Prod Div, Air Force Plant Rep Off, Gen Dynamics/Convair, Tex, 53-55, chief ground systs, Atlas Prog Off, Western Develop Div, Air Force, 55-59; vpres eng, Nat Aeronaut & Space Eng Inc, 59-61; asst div mgr, Missile & Space Systs Eng Div, Ling-Temco-Vought, Inc, 61-62, mem tech staff, Space Tech Labs Div, Thompson-Ramo-Wooldridge, Inc, 62-63; assoc dir standard launch vehicles, Aerospace Corp, 63-72, dir-systs eng, 72-87. *Mem:* AAAS; Am Inst Aeronaut & Astronaut. *Res:* Systems engineering and operations research studies in support of classified military missile systems and space vehicle development. *Mailing Add:* 5003 Kingspine Rd Rolling Hills Estates CA 90274

STEVENSON, ROBIN, METALLURGY. *Current Pos:* Staff res engr, Gen Motors Res Labs, 73-83, supvr, Sheet Forming GP, 83-85, prog mgr, Gen Motors Advan Eng Staff, 85-88, SR STAFF RES ENG, GEN MOTORS RES LABS, 88- *Personal Data:* b Falkirk, Scotland, Dec 25, 46; m 75. *Educ:* Glasgow Univ, Scotland, BSc, 67; Mass Inst Technol, PhD(metall), 72. *Concurrent Pos:* Adj fac, Lawrence Technol Univ & Wayne State Univ. *Mem:* Am Soc Metals; Am Soc Mech Engrs; Minerals, Metals & Mat Soc. *Res:* Physics and mechanics of machining processes; sheet metal deformation and manufacturing; deformation mechanisms in solids. *Mailing Add:* Mfg & Design Systs Dept GM Res & Develop Ctr Warren MI 48090-9055. *Fax:* 810-986-9356

STEVENSON, THOMAS DICKSON, MEDICINE. *Current Pos:* assoc prof, 61-71, PROF PATH, COL MED, OHIO STATE UNIV, 71- *Personal Data:* b Columbus, Ohio, Sept 23, 24; m 52; c 3. *Educ:* Ohio State Univ, BA, 45, MD, 48; Am Bd Internal Med, dipl, 56; Am Bd Path, dipl, 64. *Prof Exp:* Intern med, Johns Hopkins Hosp, 48-49; asst resident, Univ Minn Hosps, 50-51; from asst resident to resident, Ohio State Univ Hosps, 51-53; investr clin gen med & exp therapeut, Nat Heart Inst, 53-55; asst prof med & assoc dir div hemat, Sch Med, Univ Louisville, 55-61. *Mem:* Am Fedn Clin Res; Am Soc Clin Path; Am Soc Cytol. *Res:* Biochemical aspects of erythropoiesis; vitamin B-12 metabolism. *Mailing Add:* 2061 N Old State Rd Delaware OH 43015-9450

STEVENSON, WALTER ROE, PLANT PATHOLOGY. *Current Pos:* assoc prof, 79-84, VAUGHAN-BASCOM PROF PLANT PATH, UNIV WIS-MADISON, 84- *Personal Data:* b Cortland, NY, Sept 16, 46; m 69, Judy Phelps; c 2. *Educ:* Cornell Univ, BS, 68; Univ Wis-Madison, PhD(plant path), 72. *Honors & Awards:* Exten Award, Am Phytopath Soc, 89. *Prof Exp:* Res asst plant path, Univ Wis, 68-72; asst prof, Purdue Univ, 72-77, assoc prof, 77-79. *Concurrent Pos:* Ind liaison rep, Interregional Proj No 4, 74-79; mem assessment team, Pentachloronitrobenzene, Nat Agr Pesticide Impact Assessment Prog, 77-80; mem, Tech-Adv Comt, North Cent Comput Inst, 82-86; mem, ECOP-IPM Task Force, 84-87, Ecop-Database Task Force, 87-88. *Mem:* Fel Am Phytopath Soc; Potato Soc Am. *Res:* Diseases of vegetable crops, including potato and mint crops; development of disease resistant cultivars; chemical control; epidemiology. *Mailing Add:* Dept Plant Path Univ Wis Madison WI 53706. *E-Mail:* wrs@plantpath.wisc.edu

STEVENSON, WARREN H, APPLIED OPTICS. *Current Pos:* from asst prof to assoc prof, 65-74, PROF APPL OPTICS, SCH MECH ENG, PURDUE UNIV, LAFAYETTE, 74-, ASST DEAN ENG, 93- *Personal Data:* b Rock Island, Ill, Nov 18, 38; m 59, Judith Ann Fleener; c Kathleen, Kevin & Kent. *Educ:* Purdue Univ, BSME, 60, MSME, 63, PhD(mech eng), 65. *Honors & Awards:* US Sr Scientist Award, Alexander von Humboldt Found WGer, 73. *Prof Exp:* Engr, Martin Co, Colo, 60-61. *Concurrent Pos:* Guest prof, Univ Karlsruhe, Ger, 73-74; vis prof, Ariz State Univ, 87, Ibaraki Univ, Hitachi Japan 93. *Mem:* Am Soc Mech Engrs; Am Soc Eng Educ; Optical Soc Am; fel Laser Inst Am (pres-elec, 88, pres, 89). *Res:* Application of advanced optical measurement techniques such as laser velocimetry and holography in the fields of fluid mechanics, heat transfer, combustion and automated manufacturing. *Mailing Add:* Sch Mech Eng Purdue Univ Lafayette IN 47907

STEVENSON, WILLIAM CAMPBELL, BIOCHEMISTRY. *Current Pos:* RETIRED. *Personal Data:* b Brooklyn, NY, Jan 22, 31; m 55; c 3. *Educ:* St John's Col, BS, 52. *Prof Exp:* Chemist, Quaker Maid Co, 54-57 & Nat Biscuit Co, 57-58; chemist, Mead Johnson Co, 58-67, sr scientist, 67-87. *Res:* Drug metabolism, isolation and identification of metabolites; assay of drugs in tissue. *Mailing Add:* 3520 Laurel Lane Evansville IN 47720

STEVER, H GUYFORD, AERONAUTICAL ENGINEERING. *Current Pos:* TRUSTEE & SCI CONSULT, 77- *Personal Data:* b Corning, NY, Oct 24, 16; m 46; c 4. *Educ:* Colgate Univ, AB, 38, ScD, 58; Calif Inst Technol, PhD, 41. *Hon Degrees:* Numerous from US univs, 58-81. *Honors & Awards:* Nat Medal of Sci, 91; Vannevar Bush Award, Nat Sci Bd, 97. *Prof Exp:* Mem staff, Radiation Lab, Mass Inst Technol, 41-42, from asst prof to prof aero eng, 46-65; pres, Carnegie Mellon Univ, 65-72; dir, NSF, 72-76; sci adv to Pres US, 73-77; dir, White House Off Sci & Technol Policy, 76-77. *Concurrent Pos:* Assoc dean eng, Mass Inst Technol, 56-59, head naval archit & marine eng, Dept Mech Eng, 61-65; chmn, Nat Acad Eng, 84-; chmn, Policy Div, Nat Res Coun, 95- *Mem:* Nat Acad Eng; Nat Acad Sci; AAAS; Am Phys Soc; Am Acad Arts & Sci. *Mailing Add:* 588 Russell Ave Gaithersburg MD 20877. *Fax:* 301-216-5345

STEVERMER, EMMETT J, ANIMAL SCIENCE, BIOCHEMISTRY. *Current Pos:* From asst prof to assoc prof, 62-74, PROF ANIMAL SCI, IOWA STATE UNIV, 74- *Personal Data:* b Wells, Minn, Aug 13, 32; m 70; c 3. *Educ:* Univ Wis, BS, 58, MS, 60, PhD(animal sci, biochem), 62. *Honors & Awards:* Extension Award, Am Soc Animal Sci. *Mem:* Am Soc Animal Sci. *Res:* Swine nutrition and reproductive physiology. *Mailing Add:* 2607 Tyler Ave Ames IA 50010

STEVINSON, HARRY THOMPSON, ELECTRICAL ENGINEERING. *Current Pos:* RETIRED. *Personal Data:* b Passburg, Alta, Mar 5, 15; m 44; c 3. *Educ:* Univ Alta, BSc, 44. *Honors & Awards:* Can Aeronaut & Space Inst Baldwin Award, 56, McCurdy Award, 66. *Prof Exp:* Officer, Signal Div, Can Navy, 44-45; res officer flight, Nat Res Coun Can, 45-79. *Mem:* Can Aeronaut & Space Inst. *Res:* Communications; flight instrumentation; specialized aerial delivery problems; aircraft crash recovery systems. *Mailing Add:* 3558 Revelstoke Dr Ottawa ON K1V 7C1 Can

STEWARD, JOHN P, MEDICAL MICROBIOLOGY, IMMUNOLOGY. *Current Pos:* Nat Inst Allergy & Infectious Dis fel med microbiol, Sch Med, Stanford Univ, 58-60, from instr basic med sci to asst prof exp med, 60-70, actg dir, Fleischmann Labs Med Sci, 70-74, assoc dean, Sch Med, 71-90, EMER PROF MICROBIOL & IMMUNOL, SCH MED, STANFORD UNIV, 90- *Personal Data:* b Huntington Park, Calif, Oct 9, 27. *Educ:* Stanford Univ, AB, 48, MD, 55. *Concurrent Pos:* Lectr, Sch Pub Health, Univ Calif, Berkeley, 63. *Mem:* Am Asn Immunologists; Am Soc Microbiol. *Res:* Host-parasite relationship between enterobacteriaceae and experimental animals. *Mailing Add:* 2070 Webster St Palo Alto CA 94301

STEWARD, KERRY KALEN, weed science, for more information see previous edition

STEWARD, OMAR WADDINGTON, ORGANOMETALLIC CHEMISTRY, INORGANIC CHEMISTRY. *Current Pos:* from asst prof to assoc prof, 64-72, PROF INORG CHEM, DUQUESNE UNIV, 72- *Personal Data:* b Woodbury, NJ, May 28, 32; m 58; c 3. *Educ:* Univ Del, BS, 53; Pa State Univ, PhD(chem), 57. *Prof Exp:* Proj leader fluorine & organosilicon chem, Dow Corning Corp, 57-62; NSF fel, Univ Leicester, 62-63; instr inorg chem, Univ Ill, 63; asst prof, Southern Ill Univ, 63-64. *Mem:* Am Chem Soc; Sigma Xi. *Res:* Structure, bonding and reaction mechanisms of group 14 organometallic compounds; bonding and reaction mechanisms of coordination compounds. *Mailing Add:* Dept of Chem Duquesne Univ Pittsburgh PA 15282

STEWARD, ROBERT F, MATHEMATICS. *Current Pos:* prof, 63-86, chmn dept, 67-73, EMER PROF MATH, RI COL, 86- *Personal Data:* b Springboro, Pa, June 2, 23; m 46; c 2. *Educ:* Wheaton Col, Ill, BS, 47; Rutgers Univ, MS, 49; Auburn Univ, PhD(math), 61. *Prof Exp:* Instr math, Va Mil Inst, 49-53; asst prof, Drexel Inst Technol, 53-57; instr, Auburn Univ, 57-58 & 59-60; assoc prof, Western Carolina Col, 60-61, prof & chmn dept, 61-63. *Mem:* Math Asn Am. *Res:* Numerical analysis. *Mailing Add:* 1003 Inverness Rd Southern Pines NC 28387

STEWARD, W(ILLIS) G(ENE), MECHANICAL ENGINEERING, SOLAR ENGINEERING. *Current Pos:* FLUID, THERM CO. *Personal Data:* b Hastings, Nebr, June 11, 30; m 58, Marcia Fenske; c Daniel E, David A, Darlene M & Deborah J (Valerio). *Educ:* Univ Colo, BS, 52, MS, 58; Colo State Univ, PhD, 69. *Prof Exp:* Engr, Gas Turbine Div, Gen Elec Co, 52-54; engr, Nat Bur Stand, 58-85. *Concurrent Pos:* Consult energy cryog, fluid mechanics, heat transfer. *Mem:* Sigma Xi; Am Soc Mech Engrs. *Res:* Thermodynamics; heat transfer; fluid mechanics; cryogenics; solar energy; gas turbine. *Mailing Add:* Sugarloaf Rd 169 S Peak Lane Boulder CO 80302. *E-Mail:* 72622.1607@compuserve.com

STEWART, ALBERT CLIFTON, RADIATION CHEMISTRY. *Current Pos:* dir univ rels, Western Conn Univ, 82-84, assoc dean & assoc prof, 84-87, actg dean, 87-89 & 91-92, ASSOC PROF MKT, AN CELL SCH BUS, WESTERN CONN UNIV, 89- *Personal Data:* b Detroit, Mich, Nov 25, 19; m 49. *Educ:* Univ Chicago, SB, 42, SM, 48; St Louis Univ, PhD(chem), 51. *Prof Exp:* Chemist, Sherwin-Williams Paint Co, Ill, 43-44; asst inorg chem, Univ Chicago, 47-49; instr & res assoc, St Louis Univ, 49-51; sr chemist, Oak Ridge Nat Lab, 51-56; group leader, Res Lab, Nat Carbon Co Div, Union Carbide Corp, 56-59, asst dir res, Consumer Prod Div, 60-63, asst develop dir, 63-65, planning mgr new mkt develop, 65-66, mkt develop mgr, Chem & Plastics Develop Div, 66-69, mkt mgr rubber chem, Mkt Area, 69-71, mkt mgr chem coatings solvents, 71-73, int bus mgr, Chem & Plastics Div, 73-77, dir sales, Chem & Plastics Div, 77-79, nat sales mgr, Solvents & Intermediates Div, 79-82, corp dir univ rels, 82-84. *Concurrent Pos:* Prof, Knoxville Col, 53-56; lectr, John Carroll Univ, 56-63; consult, Pub Affairs Div, Ford Found, 63; adminstr officer, NASA, 63 & Agency Int Develop, 64-69; treas, NY State Dormitory Authority, 71-76; consult, Union Carbide Corp, 84-; vpres, Found Social Justice S Africa, 86-93. *Mem:* AAAS; Am Chem Soc; Am Nuclear Soc. *Res:* Physical inorganic and radiation chemistry; research, development and general administration; marketing management; sales management; professor marketing; boron hydride synthesis; radiation investigations involving chemical results of absorption of gamma rays and alpha particles in matter. *Mailing Add:* 28 Hearthstone Dr Brookfield CT 06804-3006

STEWART, ALEC THOMPSON, SOLID STATE PHYSICS. *Current Pos:* head dept, 68-74, PROF PHYSICS, QUEEN'S UNIV, ONT, 68- *Personal Data:* b Can, June 18, 25; m 63, Alta Kennedy; c A James, Hugh & Duncan. *Educ:* Dalhousie Univ, BSc, 46, MSc, 49; Cambridge Univ, PhD(physics), 52. *Hon Degrees:* LLD, Dalhousie, 86. *Honors & Awards:* Can Asn Phys Medal, 92; Can 125 Medal, 92. *Prof Exp:* From asst res officer to assoc res officer, Atomic Engr Can Ltd, 52-57; assoc prof physics, Dalhousie Univ, 57-60; from assoc prof to prof, Univ NC, Chapel Hill, 60-68. *Concurrent Pos:* J S Guggenheim fel & Kenan travelling prof, 65-66; consult, res granting agencies, US & Can; NATO fel, 82-83; vis prof, many univs in Can, Eng, Ger, Switz, Japan & Hong Kong. *Mem:* Fel Am Phys Soc; Can Asn Physicists (pres, 72-73); fel Royal Soc Can (pres, 84-87). *Res:* Motion of electrons, positrons, positronium in crystals and liquids; two books and 100 publications in professional journals; general subjects reactor safety, possible hazard of power frequency electric and magnetic fields; emergency measures for populations near nuclear reactor accidents. *Mailing Add:* Dept Physics Queen's Univ Kingston ON K7L 3N6 Can. *Fax:* 613-545-6463

STEWART, ARTHUR VAN, DENTISTRY. *Current Pos:* asst dean acad affairs & dir grad affairs, 75-88, spec asst to Univ Provost, 84-89, PROF DEPT GROWTH & SPEC CARE DENT, SCH DENT, UNIV LOUISVILLE, 88-, DIR GERONT STUDIES, 88- *Personal Data:* b Buffalo, NY, July 25, 38; m 65; c 3. *Educ:* Univ Pittsburgh, BS, 60, MEd, 64, DMD, 68, PhD(educ admin), 73. *Prof Exp:* USPHS postdoctoral fel, Sch Dent, Univ Pittsburgh, 68-70; chair Dept Community Dent & Dir Learning Res, Continuing Educ & Auxiliary training, Fairleigh Dickinson Univ, 70-75, asst dean for students, 71-74, exec asst dean, 74-75, dir, Dent Sch Accredited Self Study, 75-77. *Concurrent Pos:* Consult, Headstart Prog, 70-75, Lutheran Nursing Home, 70-75, Ringwood Dent Prog, 72-75, Patterson Child Dent Care Prog, 73-75, Am Dent Asn Comn Dent Accreditation, 90-; mem task force Curric, Am Asn Dent Sch, 90-, task force Outcomes Assess, 88-90; dir Univ Accreditation, 84-87; chair Spec Int Group Geriatrics, Am Asn Dent Sch, 89-90, Univ Senate Exec Comt, 89-92; dir, Quest Excellence Dent Educ Proj, Am Asn Dent Sch, 88-; chmn, Educ Prog LIFESPAN Forum, 92-94. *Mem:* NY Acad Sci; Am Dent Asn; Am Asn Dent Schs; Am Soc Geriat Dent; Geront Soc Am; Sigma Xi; fel Am Col Dent; Am Pub Health Asn; Int Am Asn Dent Res. *Res:* Outcomes assessment/quality assurance; geriatric dentistry; health manpower; dental care in long term care facilities; geriatrics/gerontology; professional education outcomes measures; elderly and child abuse; homeless care programs; interdisciplinary health care services. *Mailing Add:* Pediat & Geront Dent Dept Univ Louisville Sch Dent 501 S Preston St Louisville KY 40292

STEWART, BARBARA YOST, BIOLOGY. *Current Pos:* From lectr to assoc prof, 75-96, ASSOC CHMN DEPT, SWARTHMORE COL, 85-, EMER PROF BIOL, 96- *Personal Data:* b Johnstown, Pa, Oct 12, 32; m 54, 91, Robert S Chase; c Russell R & Douglas W. *Educ:* Swarthmore Col, BA, 54; Bryn Mawr Col, MA, 72, PhD(biochem), 75. *Honors & Awards:* Course Develop Award, Sloan Found, 88; Res Collab Award, Pew Found, 89. *Concurrent Pos:* Evaluator, Biol Dept, Ursinus Col, 85 & 90 & Biol Dept, Juniata Col, 91; vis prof, Lafayette Col, 88 & 89; NSF reviewer, 90. *Mem:* Sigma Xi; Nat Sci Teachers Asn. *Res:* Effect of temperature on fatty acids; isozymes of lactate dehydrogenase in fish; investigative laboratories; writing in the sciences. *Mailing Add:* 10 Pilot Pl Winter Haven FL 33881. *E-Mail:* bstewar2@cc.swarthmore.edu

STEWART, BOBBY ALTON, WATER MANAGEMENT, SOIL CONSERVATION. *Current Pos:* DIR, DRYLAND AGR INST & DISTINGUISHED PROF SOIL SCI, WTEX A&M UNIV, CANYON, 93- *Personal Data:* b Erick, Okla, Sept 26, 32; m 56; c 3. *Educ:* Okla State Univ, BS, 53, MS, 57; Colo State Univ, PhD(soil sci), 61. *Honors & Awards:* Superior Serv Award, US Dept Agr, 86; Hugh Hammond Bennett Award, Soil & Water Conserv Soc, 94. *Prof Exp:* Soil scientist, Agr Exp Sta, USDA, Stillwater, Okla, 53-57, soil scientist, Agr Res Serv, Fort Collins, Colo, 57-68, dir & soil scientist, Agr Res Serv, Conserv & Prod Res Lab, Bushland, Tex, 68-93. *Concurrent Pos:* Instr, Colo State Univ, 62 & Tex A&M Univ, 72; ed, Advan in Soil Sci, 84- *Mem:* Fel Soil Conserv Soc Am; fel Am Soc Agron; fel Soil Sci Soc Am (pres, 81); Int Soil Sci Soc; Coun Agr Sci & Technol. *Res:* Conservation and production problems associated with agriculture in the Southern Great Plains of the United States; water-use efficiency; control of soil erosion. *Mailing Add:* Dryland Agr Inst WTex A&M Univ WTAMU Box 278 Canyon TX 79016

STEWART, BONNIE MADISON, mathematics; deceased, see previous edition for last biography

STEWART, BRENT SCOTT, DEMOGRAPHY & FORAGING ECOLOGY OF MARINE MAMMALS & SEABIRDS. *Current Pos:* SR STAFF SCIENTIST, HUBBS SEA WORLD RES INST, 77- *Personal Data:* b Fairbanks, Alaska, Nov 19, 54; m 89. *Educ:* Univ Calif, Los Angeles, BA, 77, PhD(biol), 89; San Diego State Univ, MS, 81. *Concurrent Pos:* Soc Expeds, 82-86; res assoc, Univ San Diego, 88-; adj fac mem, San Diego State Univ, 89- *Mem:* Fel Explorers Club; Ecol Soc Am; AAAS; Am Soc Zoologists; Am Soc Mammalogists; Soc Marine Mammal. *Res:* Population biology and ecology of marine mammals and seabirds; migrations, foraging ecology, demography, diving behavior and physiology of marine mammals and seabirds. *Mailing Add:* Hubbs Seaworld Res Inst 2595 Ingraham St San Diego CA 92109

STEWART, BURCH BYRON, CHEMICAL ANALYSIS & PHYSICAL TESTING OF MATERIALS. *Current Pos:* TECH DIR, APPL CONSUMER SERV, 86- *Personal Data:* b Chattanooga, Tenn, May 7, 29; m 67, Shirley Hamm; c Steven, Neal & Daryl. *Educ:* Univ Tenn, Knoxville, BS, 55, MS, 57, PhD(phys chem), 59. *Prof Exp:* Teaching asst, Univ Tenn, 55-57; res fel, Atomic Energy Comn, 57-59; sr engr, Western Elec, NJ, 59-60; res chemist, Allied Chem, 60-67; asst dir, Ciba-Geigy Corp, 67-72; dir chem, Appl Res Labs, 72-86. *Concurrent Pos:* Pres, Friends of Physics, 91-93, pres-elect, 93-94. *Mem:* Am Chem Soc; Sigma Xi; Asn Official Analytical Chemists. *Res:* Determination of properties of various new products, creation of new products, and testing performance; spectroscopy projects involving infrared radiation, nuclear magnetic resonance, mass spectrometry and energy dispersive spectroscopy. *Mailing Add:* 1394 NW 192nd Lane Pembroke Pines FL 33029-4521

STEWART, CAMERON LEIGH, DIOPHANTINE APPROXIMATION, ANALYTIC NUMBER THEORY. *Current Pos:* from asst prof to assoc prof, 78-86, PROF MATH, UNIV WATERLOO, 86- *Personal Data:* m 80, Ellen Papachristoforou; c Elisa M & Andrew R. *Educ:* Univ BC, BSc, 71; McGill Univ, MSc, 72; Univ Cambridge, PhD(math), 76. *Honors & Awards:* Jeffery Mem Lectr, Acadia Univ, 90. *Prof Exp:* Res assoc, Mathematisch Centrum, 76-77, Inst Advan Sci Studies, 77-78. *Concurrent Pos:* Vis prof, Univ Strasbourg, 81, Univ Leiden, 84, Univ Ulm, 84, IHES & Math Inst, Hunganan Acad Sci, 85, Univ Colo, 92, MSRI, 93; res fel, Killam Found, 90. *Mem:* Can Math Soc; Am Math Soc. *Res:* Number theory; diophantine equations and diophantine approximation. *Mailing Add:* Dept Pure Math Univ Waterloo Waterloo ON N2L 3G1 Can. *Fax:* 519-725-0160; *E-Mail:* cstewart@wat.semv1.uwaterloo.ca

STEWART, CARLETON C, IMMUNOLOGY, BIOPHYSICS. *Current Pos:* DIR FLOW CYTOMETRY, ROSWELL PARK CANCER INST, 88- *Personal Data:* b Schenectady, NY, July 13, 40; m 63, Sigrid; c Gregory & Cynthia. *Educ:* Hartwick Col, BA, 62; Univ Rochester, MA, 64, PhD(radiation), 67. *Prof Exp:* Atomic Energy Proj res asst & instr radiation physics, Univ Rochester, 62-67; instr immunol, Univ Pa, 67-69; sr scientist, Smith Kline & French Labs, 69-70; asst, Sch Med, Wash Univ, 70-78, assoc prof cancer biol in radiol, 78-81; group leader, Exp Path, Los Alamos Nat Labs, 81-88. *Concurrent Pos:* USPHS fel & grant, 67-69; Am Cancer Soc grant, 68-69; Cancer Ctr grant, Nat Cancer Inst, 70-78; NIH grants, 78-; ed-in-chief, J Leukocyte Biol, 80- *Mem:* AAAS; Soc Analytical; Am Asn Exp Pathologists; NY Acad Sci; Soc Leukocyte Biol; Sigma Xi. *Res:* Cellular immunology; tumor immunology; flow cytometry; application of multiparameter flow cytometry in studies dealing with the cellular and molecular biology of hemopoiesis. *Mailing Add:* Dept Flow Cytometry Roswell Park Cancer Inst Elm & Carlton St Buffalo NY 14263-0001. *Fax:* 716-845-8806; *E-Mail:* stewart@sc3101.med.buffalo.edu

STEWART, CECIL R, PLANT PHYSIOLOGY. *Current Pos:* asst prof, 68-71, assoc prof, 71-76, prof bot, 76-95, EMER PROF BOT, IOWA STATE UNIV, 96- *Personal Data:* b Monmouth, Ill, Mar 11, 37; m 58, Phyllis Murphy; c Christine & Shari. *Educ:* Univ Ill, BS, 58; Cornell Univ, MS, 63, PhD(plant physiol), 67. *Prof Exp:* NIH fel plant physiol, Purdue Univ, 66-68. *Res:* Plant metabolism; metabolic and molecular responses of plants to environmental conditions. *Mailing Add:* 3439 G W Carver Ave Ames IA 50010. *E-Mail:* csterwart@iastate.edu

STEWART, CHARLES JACK, BIOCHEMISTRY. *Current Pos:* from instr to assoc prof, San Diego State Univ, 55-65, prof chem, 65-92, chmn, Chem Dept, 67-70, actg chmn, 80-81, chmn, Chem Dept, 86-89, chair-fac senate, 90-91, EMER PROF, SAN DIEGO STATE UNIV, 92- *Personal Data:* b Rawlins, Wyo, June 17, 29; m 71, Nancy M Carmichael; c 3. *Educ:* San Diego State Col, BA, 50; Ore State Univ, MS, 52, PhD(biochem), 55. *Prof Exp:* Fulbright grant biochem, Inst Org Chem, Univ Frankfurt, 54-55. *Concurrent Pos:* NIH res grant, 62-; spec rch, 63-64; guest prof chem, Max Planck Inst Med Res, Heidelberg, Ger, 75-76, res fel, 79-80. *Mem:* AAAS; Am Soc Biol Chemists; Am Chem Soc. *Res:* Mechanism of enzymes and antimetabolites; synthesis and enzymatic properties of coenzyme A analogs. *Mailing Add:* Dept Chem San Diego State Univ San Diego CA 92182-0328. *Fax:* 619-594-4634; *E-Mail:* cstewart@sciences.sdsu.edu

STEWART, CHARLES NEWBY, CHEMICAL SENSES, PSYCHOPHARMACOLOGY. *Current Pos:* assoc prof, 65-72, PROF PSYCHOL, FRANKLIN & MARSHALL COL, 72-, CHARLES A DANA CHAIR PSYCHOL, 89- *Personal Data:* b New Westminster, BC, Can, May 16, 31; m 55, Ruth Nyhaug; c 5. *Educ:* Seattle Pac Univ, BA, 53; Univ Ore, MS, 56, PhD(psychol), 63. *Prof Exp:* Res psychologist, Dept Pub Health, Prov Sask, 52-62. *Concurrent Pos:* Affiliated scientist, Monell Chem Senses Ctr, 81-; assoc dean, Franklin & Marshall Col, 90-92. *Mem:* Sigma Xi; Psychonomics Soc; Asn Chemoreception Sci; AAAS; Soc Study Ingestive Behav; Am Inst Nutrit; Soc Neurosci. *Res:* Chemical senses; influence of molecular structure on taste perception; influence of nutritional state upon salt appetite; hormonal factors in sensory processes. *Mailing Add:* Dept Psychol Franklin & Marshall Col Lancaster PA 17604-3003. *Fax:* 717-291-4387; *E-Mail:* c__stewart@acad.fandm.edu

STEWART, CHARLES RANOUS, MICROBIAL GENETICS, BACTERIOPHAGE MOLECULAR BIOLOGY. *Current Pos:* from asst prof to prof biol, 69-89, PROF BIOCHEM & CELL BIOL, RICE UNIV, 89- *Personal Data:* b La Crosse, Wis, Aug 6, 40; m 88, Elizabeth A Lufburrow. *Educ:* Univ Wis, BS, 62; Stanford Univ, PhD(genetics), 67. *Prof Exp:* Am Cancer Soc fel biochem, Albert Einstein Col Med, 67-69. *Mem:* AAAS; Am Soc Micriobiol. *Res:* Genetics and biochemistry of Bacillus subtilis and its virulent bacteriophages. *Mailing Add:* Dept Biochem & Cell Biol Rice Univ Houston TX 77251. *Fax:* 713-285-5154; *E-Mail:* crs@biocl.rice.edu

STEWART, CHARLES WINFIELD, SR, THEORETICAL CHEMISTRY. *Current Pos:* Res chemist, Elastomer Chem Dept, 66-80, RES ASSOC POLYMER PROD DEPT, E I DU PONT DE NEMOURS & CO, INC, WILMINGTON, 80- *Personal Data:* b Wilmington, Del, Jan 27, 40; m 62; c 3. *Educ:* Univ Del, BS, 62, PhD(chem), 66. *Res:* Polymer physics. *Mailing Add:* Four Jobs Lane Newark DE 19711

STEWART, DANIEL ROBERT, GLASS TECHNOLOGY, CERAMICS. *Current Pos:* RETIRED. *Personal Data:* b New Kensington, Pa, July 25, 38; m 60; c 2. *Educ:* Pa State Univ, BS, 60, MS, 62, PhD(ceramic technol), 64. *Prof Exp:* Sr scientist glass res, Owens-Ill, Inc, 64-67; sect chief glass sci, 67-70, dir glass & ceramics res, 70-72, dir, Corp Res Labs, 72-73, vpres corp staff & dir glass & ceramic technol, 73-83; pres, Dura Temp Corp, 83-94. *Mem:* Fel Am Ceramic Soc; Sigma Xi; Brit Soc Glass Technol. *Res:* Glass and ceramic materials and processing; research and development. *Mailing Add:* 2718 River Rd Maumee OH 43537

STEWART, DAVID BENJAMIN, GEOLOGY, MINERALOGY. *Current Pos:* Geologist, US Geol Surv, 51-81, chief, Br Exp Geochem & Mineral, 76-80, prog coordr radioactive waste mgt, 78-80, sr policy analyst high level radioactive waste, State Planning Coun Radioactive Waste Mgt, 80-81, res geologist, 81-90, sr res geologist, 90-95, Pecora fel, 95-97, EMER, US GEOL SURV, 97- *Personal Data:* b Springfield, Vt, July 18, 28; m 52, 80, Odette Brilmont James; c Douglas N, Diane A & Jeffrey B. *Educ:* Harvard Univ, AB, 51; AM, 52, PhD(petrol), 56. *Concurrent Pos:* Guest prof, Univ Toronto, 68 & Swiss Fed Inst Technol, 71; mem, Lunar Sample Rev Bd, 70-72; prin investr, lunar feldspar Apollo 11-15, 69-72, lunar metamorphism, 73-76. *Mem:* Fel Geol Soc Am; fel Mineral Soc Am (pres, 88); Am Geophys Union. *Res:* Crustal structure of Maine by reflection seismology and three-dimensional digitized geoscience information systems; radioactive waste management; metamorphic recrystallization of lunar and terrestrial minerals; geochemistry of Maine coastal volcanic belt; crystal chemistry and phase relations of feldspar, silica and rock-forming silicates. *Mailing Add:* Nat Ctr 926A US Geol Surv Reston VA 20192. *Fax:* 703-648-6953; *E-Mail:* dbstewart@usgs.gov

STEWART, DAVID PERRY, geomorphology, for more information see previous edition

STEWART, DONALD BORDEN, ENVIRONMENTAL MANAGEMENT. *Current Pos:* RETIRED. *Personal Data:* b Sask, Can, Mar 15, 17; nat US; m 52; c 2. *Educ:* Univ Wash, BS, 39. *Prof Exp:* Chemist, B F Goodrich Co, 39-41, mgr, Gen Chem Lab, 41-42, oper mgr, Res Div, 42-48, opers mgr, Res Ctr, 48-56; bus mgr, Cent Labs, Gen Foods Corp, 56-57, dir admin serv, Res Ctr, 57-61; vpres, Sterling Forest Corp, 61-66; admin officer, Palisades Interstate Park Comn, 66-67, supt, 67-74, asst gen mgr, 74-78, dep gen mgr, 78-90. *Mem:* AAAS; Am Chem Soc; fel Am Inst Chem. *Res:* Analytical methods; industrial safety and hygiene. *Mailing Add:* 3522 Fishtrap Loop NE Olympia WA 98506-4605

STEWART, DONALD CHARLES, radiochemistry; deceased, see previous edition for last biography

STEWART, DONALD GEORGE, MATHEMATICS. *Current Pos:* asst prof, 64-72, ASSOC PROF MATH, ARIZ STATE UNIV, 72- *Personal Data:* b Pocatello, Idaho, Jan 9, 33. *Educ:* Univ Utah, BA, 59, MS, 61; Univ Tenn, PhD, 63. *Prof Exp:* Asst prof math, Univ Tenn, 63-64. *Mem:* Am Math Soc. *Res:* Point-set topology. *Mailing Add:* Dept Math Ariz State Univ Tempe AZ 85287-1804

STEWART, DOROTHY ANNE, METEOROLOGY, PHYSICS. *Current Pos:* res physicist atmospheric physics, 66-89, METEOROLOGIST, MISSILE COMMAND, 89- *Personal Data:* b Beech Grove, Ind, June 2, 37. *Educ:* Univ Tampa, BS, 58; Fla State Univ, MS, 61, PhD(meteorol), 66. *Prof Exp:* Teacher sci, Suwannee High Sch, 58-59; asst meteorol, Fla State Univ, 59-66. *Mem:* Am Meteorol Soc; Am Geophys Union; AAAS; Sigma Xi. *Res:* Evaluate atmospheric conditions which affect storage and performance of military equipment. *Mailing Add:* PO Box 12067 Huntsville AL 35815-2067

STEWART, DORIS MAE, zoology, physiology, for more information see previous edition

STEWART, EDWARD WILLIAM, METALLURGICAL ENGINEERING, CHEMISTRY. *Current Pos:* RETIRED. *Personal Data:* b Cardiff, Mo, Sept 17, 31; m 54; c 3. *Educ:* Wash Col, BS, 52; Lehigh Univ, MS, 54. *Prof Exp:* Tech supvr silicon, E I DuPont de Nemours & Co, Inc, 58-62, tech supt, 62-65, prof mgr titanium dioxide, 65-68, dist sales mgr, 68-73, lab dir chem, 73-83, bus mgr, 83-85. *Mem:* Sigma Xi. *Res:* Titanium dioxide and color pigment product development. *Mailing Add:* 229 Plymouth Rd Wilmington DE 19803

STEWART, ELWIN LYNN, MYCOLOGY, PLANT PATHOLOGY. *Current Pos:* PROF, DEPT PLANT PATH, PA STATE UNIV, 93- *Personal Data:* b Ellensburg, Wash, July 22, 40; c 1. *Educ:* Eastern Wash State Col, BA, 69; Ore State Univ, PhD(mycol), 74. *Prof Exp:* Fel mycol, Dept Bot & Plant Path, Ore State Univ, 74-75; from asst prof to prof mycol, Dept Plant Path, Univ Minn, 75-93, mycologists, 75-93. *Mem:* Mycol Soc Am; Am Phytopath Soc. *Res:* Fungal systematics; selection and utilization of mycorrhizal fungi in harsh site revegetation. *Mailing Add:* Dept Plant Path Pa State Univ 212 Buckout Lab University Park PA 16802-4506

STEWART, FRANK EDWIN, PHYSICS, CHEMISTRY. *Current Pos:* RETIRED. *Personal Data:* b Dallas, Tex, July 9, 41; m 72. *Educ:* Univ Tex, Arlington, BS, 61; Tex A&M Univ, MS, 64, PhD(physics), 66. *Prof Exp:* Instr physics, Tex A&M Univ, 64-66; Nat Acad Sci resident res assoc chem physics, Jet Propulsion Lab, Univ Calif, 66-67; asst prof physics, Northeast La Univ, 67-71; prof math, physics & astron & dir planetarium, Cooke Co Jr Col, 71-77; dir data processing, Cooke Co Col Comput Ctr, 77-96. *Concurrent Pos:* Nat Defense Title IV fel, Tex A&M, 61-66, R A Welch Found postdoctoral fel, Chem Dept, 66. *Mem:* Am Asn Physics Teachers; Am Phys Soc; Sigma Xi; Soc Physics Students. *Res:* Electron paramagnetic resonance; charge-transfer complexes. *Mailing Add:* 11 Quail Run Gainesville TX 76240

STEWART, FRANK MOORE, BIOMATHEMATICS. *Current Pos:* From instr to prof, 47-87, EMER PROF MATH, BROWN UNIV, 87- *Personal Data:* b Beirut, Lebanon, Dec 27, 17; US citizen; m 46; c 1. *Educ:* Princeton Univ, AB, 39; Harvard Univ, MA, 41, PhD(math), 47. *Mem:* AAAS. *Res:* Mathematical models in biology; population genetics. *Mailing Add:* Dept of Math Box 1917 Brown Univ Providence RI 02912

STEWART, GARY FRANKLIN, GEOLOGY. *Current Pos:* asst prof, 71-73, ASSOC PROF GEOL, OKLA STATE UNIV, 73- *Personal Data:* b Okmulgee, Okla, Apr 3, 35; m 56; c 3. *Educ:* Okla State Univ, BS, 57; Univ Okla, MS, 63; Univ Kans, PhD(geol), 73. *Prof Exp:* Geologist, Humble Oil & Refining Co, 58-60; geologist, Kans State Geol Surv, Univ Kans, 62-71. *Concurrent Pos:* Consult, Oak Ridge Nat Lab, 70-72. *Mem:* Am Asn Petrol Geologists; Sigma Xi. *Res:* Geomorphology; stratigraphy; geologic mapping for environmental purposes; depositional environments of sedimentary rocks. *Mailing Add:* 1102 N Payne St Stillwater OK 74075

STEWART, GEORGE HUDSON, PHYSICAL CHEMISTRY. *Current Pos:* chmn dept, 70-76, PROF CHEM, TEX WOMAN'S UNIV, 70- *Personal Data:* b Brooklyn, NY, May 13, 25; m 58; c 5. *Educ:* Univ Calif, Berkeley, BS, 49; Univ Utah, PhD(phys chem), 58. *Prof Exp:* Res asst chem, Univ Utah, 58-59; from instr to asst prof chem, Gonzaga Univ, 59-64, assoc prof chem & chmn dept chem & chem eng, 64-70, dean grad sch, 67-70. *Mem:* AAAS; Sigma Xi; Am Chem Soc. *Res:* Physical chemistry of chromatography; dynamics of gas-liquid interface; flow in porous media. *Mailing Add:* 2003 W Oak St Denton TX 76201-3720

STEWART, GEORGE LOUIS, PARASITOLOGY. *Current Pos:* ASST PROF PARASITOL, UNIV TEX, ARLINGTON, 77- *Personal Data:* b Washington, DC, Oct 30, 44; m 69. *Educ:* Tulane Univ, BS, 69; Rice Univ, PhD(parasitol), 73. *Prof Exp:* Fel parasitol, Rice Univ, 73-74, res assoc, 74, lectr, 75-77. *Concurrent Pos:* Consult, Phillips-Roxane, Inc, 73-78; Bellaire Blvd Animal Clin, 73-78 & Fielder Animal Clin, 77-; res grant, Phillips-Roxane, Inc, 73-78; fac res grant, Univ Tex, Arlington, 77-; NIH res grant, 79-82. *Mem:* Am Soc Parasitologists; Am Heartworm Soc. *Res:* Pathophysiology; host-parasite interactions; veterinary parasitology. *Mailing Add:* Dept Biol Univ Tex Arlington Box 19498 Arlington TX 76019-0001

STEWART, GERALD WALTER, PHYSICAL CHEMISTRY. *Current Pos:* PRES & CHIEF EXEC OFFICER, INDUST TECHNOL INC, 92- *Personal Data:* b Hamilton, Ohio, Oct 8, 44; m 82; c 2. *Educ:* Wilmington Col, Ohio, BS, 65; SDak Sch Mines & Technol, Rapid City, MS, 67; Univ Idaho, Moscow, PhD(phys chem), 71. *Prof Exp:* Res assoc, Washington Univ, St Louis, 71-73, Mass Inst Technol, 73-74; asst prof chem, WVa Univ, 74-77; chief, Supporting Res, US Dept Energy, 77-79; dir, Ctr Chem & Environ Physics, Aerodyne Res, Inc, 79-84, pres, Aerodyne Prod Corp, 84-92. *Concurrent Pos:* Adj assoc prof chem, WVa Univ, 77-81, Boston Col, 82-; mem, res comt corrosion & deposits, Am Soc Mech Engrs, 84- *Mem:* Am Chem Soc; Sigma Xi; Combustion Inst. *Res:* Theoretical and experimental investigations on the chemistry of coal combustion; evaluation and measurement of kinetic and thermodynamic parameters controlling pollutant formation; chemiluminescence studies of reactions involving inorganic hydrides with strong oxidizing agents; ion-molecule reactions by ion cyclotron resonance spectroscopy. *Mailing Add:* Indust Technol Inc One Trefoil Dr Trumbull CT 06611

STEWART, GLENN ALEXANDER, SOLID STATE PHYSICS, SURFACE PHSYICS. *Current Pos:* asst prof physics, 72-76, ASSOC PROF PHYSICS & DIR HONORS PROG, 76- *Personal Data:* b Ellensburg, Wash, Jan 14, 41; m 62; c 2. *Educ:* Amherst Col, BA, 62; Univ Wash, MSE, 65, PhD(physics), 69. *Prof Exp:* Fel physics, Univ Wash, 69-70; res fel physics, Calif Inst Technol, 70-72. *Mem:* Am Phys Soc. *Res:* Phase transitions in surface films, particularly in physically absorbed noble gas monolayers. *Mailing Add:* 1521 Williamsburg Pl Pittsburgh PA 15235

STEWART, GLENN RAYMOND, VERTEBRATE ZOOLOGY, NATURAL HISTORY. *Current Pos:* From asst prof to assoc prof, 63-73, PROF ZOOL, CALIF STATE POLYTECH UNIV, 73- *Personal Data:* b Riverside, Calif, Feb 7, 36; div; c Clifford & Michael. *Educ:* Calif State Polytech Col, BS, 58; Ore State Univ, MA, 60, PhD(zool), 64. *Honors & Awards:* Ralph W Ames Res Award, 85. *Mem:* Herpetologists's League; Am Soc Ichthyol & Herpet; Am Soc Mammal; Am Inst Biol Sci; Soc Study Amphibians & Reptiles. *Res:* Ecology, taxonomy and behavior of reptiles, amphibians and mammals; status of endangered and rare species. *Mailing Add:* Dept Biol Sci Calif State Polytech Univ Pomona CA 91768

STEWART, GORDON ARNOLD, dairy science, for more information see previous edition

STEWART, GORDON ERVIN, MICROWAVE PHYSICS, PLASMA PHYSICS. *Current Pos:* mem tech staff, Plasma Res Lab, 62-70, SECT HEAD, AEROSPACE CORP, 70- *Personal Data:* b San Bernardino, Calif, June 25, 34; m 59; c 3. *Educ:* Univ Calif, Los Angeles, BS, 55, MS, 57; Univ Southern Calif, PhD(elec eng), 63. *Prof Exp:* Mem tech staff, Hughes Aircraft Co, 55-62. *Concurrent Pos:* Asst prof, Univ Southern Calif, 62-66; mem comn 6, Int Union Radio Sci. *Mem:* Inst Elec & Electronic Engrs; Am Phys Soc. *Res:* Radar scattering; antenna theory; wave propagation in plasmas; acoustic holography. *Mailing Add:* Aerospace Corp PO Box 92957 Los Angeles CA 90009-2957

STEWART, GREGORY RANDALL, HEAVY FERMION SYSTEMS. *Current Pos:* PROF, PHYSICS, UNIV FLA, 85- *Personal Data:* b Glendale, Calif, Apr 27, 49; m; c 2. *Educ:* Calif Inst Tech, BS, 71; Stanford, MS, 73, PhD, 75. *Prof Exp:* Res asst, Univ Konstanz, WGer, 76-77; staff mem, Los Alamos Nat Lab, 77-85. *Concurrent Pos:* Vis prof, Inst fur Tech Physik, Kernforschungszentrum Karlsruhe, 83, 85, Tech Hochschule, Darmstadt/Transuranium Inst, Karlsruhe, WGer, 87; consult, Westinghouse, Res & Develop, 78, 80, MIT, 84, 85, Los Alamos Nat Lab, 85- *Mem:* Am Phys Soc. *Res:* Superconductivity; heavy fermions; specific heat; actinides. *Mailing Add:* Dept Physics Williamson Hall Univ Fla Gainesville FL 32611. *Fax:* 904-392-0524

STEWART, GWENDOLYN JANE, CELL ADHESION. *Current Pos:* PROF, TEMPLE UNIV MED SCH, 71- *Personal Data:* Nov 12, 26; m 48; c 4. *Educ:* WVa Univ Med Sch, PhD(microbiol & biochem), 62. *Mailing Add:* Thrombosis Res Ctr Temple Univ Med Sch Rm 413 Old Med Sch Bldg 3401 N Broad St Philadelphia PA 19140

STEWART, H(OMER) J(OSEPH), AERONAUTICAL ENGINEERING. *Current Pos:* Asst, Calif Inst Technol, 36-38, instr meteorol, 38-40, from instr to asst prof aeronaut & meteorol, 40-46, chief Res Anal Sect, Jet Propulsion Lab, 44-56, assoc prof aeronaut, 46-49, chief, Liquid Propulsion Systs Div, Jet Propulsion Lab, 56-58, spec asst to dir lab, 60-62, mgr Advan Studies Off, 62-68, prof aeronaut, 49-80, advan tech studies adv, Jet Propulsion Lab, 68-76, EMER PROF AERONAUT, CALIF INST TECHNOL, 80- *Personal Data:* b Elba, Mich, Aug 15, 15; m 40, Frieda Klassen; c Robert, Katherine & Barbara. *Educ:* Univ Minn, BAeroE, 36; Calif Inst Technol, PhD(aeronaut), 40. *Honors & Awards:* I B Laskowitz Award, NY Acad Sci, 85. *Concurrent Pos:* Mem tech eval group, Guided Missiles Comt, Res & Develop Bd, 48-52; mem, Sci Adv Bd, USAF, 49-55, 58-64; mem adv group artificial cloud nucleation, US Dept Defense, 51-55, chmn adv group on spec capabilities, 55-58; consult, Aerojet-Gen Corp, 51-58, 60-70, 75-84, Preparedness Invest Subcomt, US Senate, 57-58 & Rand Corp, 60-68; mem sci adv comt, Ballistics Res Lab, 58-77; dir, Off Prog Planning & Eval, NASA, 58-60; mem bd dirs, Meteorol Res Inc, 62-66 & Sargent Industs, Inc, 66-79. *Mem:* Am Meteorol Soc; fel Am Inst Aeronaut & Astronaut; Int Astronaut Fedn. *Res:* Dynamic meteorology; theoretical aerodynamics; fluid and supersonic flows; guided missiles; space and planetary exploration systems. *Mailing Add:* Dept Aeronaut Eng Calif Inst Technol Pasadena CA 91125

STEWART, HAROLD BROWN, BIOCHEMISTRY. *Current Pos:* From assoc prof to prof, 55-86, chmn dept, 65-72, dean fac grad studies, 72-86, EMER PROF BIOCHEM, UNIV WESTERN ONT, 86- *Personal Data:* b Chatham, Ont, Can, Mar 9, 21; m 50, Blake; c Ann. *Educ:* Univ Toronto, MD, 44, PhD, 50; Cambridge Univ, PhD, 55. *Concurrent Pos:* Med Res Coun vis scientist, Cambridge Univ, 71-72. *Mem:* Am Soc Biol Chem; Can Physiol Soc; Can Biochem Soc; Brit Biochem Soc. *Res:* Intermediary metabolism in animals and microorganisms. *Mailing Add:* 118 Base Line Rd E London ON N6C 2N8 Can

STEWART, HAROLD L, EXPERIMENTAL CARCINOGENICS. *Current Pos:* CLIN PROF PATH, GEORGETOWN UNIV, 65-; ORGANIZER REGISTRY EXP CANCERS, NIH, 70-, EMER SCIENTIST, 76- *Personal Data:* b Houtzdale, Penn, Aug 6, 99; wid, Cecelia E Finn; c Robert & Janet. *Educ:* Jefferson Med Col, MD, 26, DSc, 64; Univ Perugia, MD, 65; Univ Turku, Finland, MD, 70; Am Bd Path, dipl; Pan Am Med Asn, dipl. *Honors & Awards:* Ward Burdick Award, Am Soc Clin Pathologists, 57; Distinguished Serv Award, Dept Health, Educ & Welfare, 66; Lucy Wortham James Award, James Ewing Soc, 67; F K Mostofi Award, Int Acad Path, 76; Gold-headed Cane Award, Am Asn Pathologists, 78; Fund for Exp Path & lectureship named in Honor, Uniformed Serv Univ Health Sci, Bethesda, Md, 86. *Prof Exp:* Intern, Fitzsimons Gen Hosp, Denver, 26-27, med staff, 27-29; asst pathologist, Philadelphia Gen Hosp, 29-37; from instr to asst prof path, Jefferson Med Col, 30-37, res fel, 29-30; pathologist, Off Cancer Invest, Harvard Univ & USPHS, 37-39; chief, Lab Path, Nat Cancer Inst, USPHS, 39-67; chief, Dept Path & Anat, Clin Ctr, NIH, 54-69. *Concurrent Pos:* Mem, Subcomt Oncol, Nat Res Coun, 47-65, Comt Cancer Diag & Ther, 51-57, Comt Path, 58-66, Comt Animal Models & Genetic Stocks, 72-75; consult, Armed Forces Inst Path, 50-, Food & Drug Admin, 69-71, Nat Cancer Inst, 70-76; chmn, US Nat Comt, Int Union Against Cancer, 53-59, US Comt, Int Coun Soc Path, 57-62; mem study group, WHO, 57-81, prin investr, Head Collaborating Ctr Res Tumors Lab Animals, 76-; mem, Comt Advan World-Wide Fight Against Cancer, Am Cancer Soc, 63-76; chmn, Comt Histol Classification Lab Animal Tumors, 75-79, Subcomt Classification Rat Liver Tumors, 76-79. *Mem:* Am Soc Clin Pathologists; Am Asn Cancer Res (pres, 58-59); Am Soc Exp Path (hon pres, 55); Am Asn Pathologists (pres, 50-51); Col Am Pathologists; Int Acad Path (pres, 53-55); Int Union Against Cancer (vpres, 62); Int Coun Socs Path (pres, 62); Int Soc Geog Path. *Mailing Add:* 119 S Adams St Rockville MD 20850-2315

STEWART, HARRIS BATES, JR, OCEANOGRAPHY. *Current Pos:* RETIRED. *Personal Data:* b Auburn, NY, Sept 19, 22; m 88, Louise Conant; c Dorothy & Harry. *Educ:* Princeton Univ, AB, 48; Univ Calif, MS, 52, PhD(oceanog), 56. *Prof Exp:* Hydrographer, US Naval Hydrographic Off, 48-50; instr, Hotchkiss Sch, Conn, 50-51; res asst oceanog, Scripps Inst Oceanog, Univ Calif, 51-56; chief oceanogr, US Coast & Geod Surv, 57-65; dir, Inst Oceanog, Environ Sci Serv Admin, 65-70, dir, Atlantic Oceanog & Meteorol Labs, Nat Oceanic & Atmospheric Admin, 70-78; dir, Ctr Marine Studies, Old Dominion Univ, 80-85. *Concurrent Pos:* chmn, Ocean Surv Panel, Interagency Comt Oceanog, 62-66 & Int Progs Panel, 65-67; US nat coordr, Coop Invest of Caribbean & Adjacent Regions, 68-75; chmn adv coun, Dept Geol & Geophys Sci, Princeton Univ, 73-76; pres, Dade Marine Inst, 77-78; vchmn, Intergovt Oceanog Comn, Regional Asn for Caribbean, 78-82, US nat assoc, 76- *Mem:* Fel AAAS; fel Geol Soc Am; Am Geophys Union; fel Marine Technol Soc (vpres, 74-76); fel Int Oceanog Found (vpres, 82-86). *Res:* Coastal lagoons; marine geology; physical oceanography. *Mailing Add:* 720 Shadow Lake Lane Naples FL 34108. *Fax:* 305-443-6971

STEWART, HERBERT, SCIENCE EDUCATION, PLANT PHYSIOLOGY. *Current Pos:* PROF SCI EDUC, FLA ATLANTIC UNIV, 67- *Personal Data:* b Stanton, Ky, July 18, 28; m 53; c 3. *Educ:* Univ Conn, BA, 54, MS, 56; Columbia Univ, EdD, 58. *Prof Exp:* Teacher pub sch, Ky, 51-53; instr bot, Univ Conn, 54-56; instr biol, Teachers Col, Columbia Univ, 57-58; prof sci educ & biol, Md State Teachers Col, Towson, 58-59; asst prof biol, Sch Com, NY Univ, 59-60; asst prof sci educ, Rutgers Univ, 60-61; assoc prof, Univ SFla, 61-67. *Concurrent Pos:* Sci Manpower fel, Columbia Univ, 59-60; dir, NSF In-Serv Inst, 66-67; biol consult, Inst Univ Kerala, Trivandrum, S India, 66. *Mem:* Fel AAAS; Asn Comput Math & Sci Teaching; Asn Educ Teachers Sci; Asn Comput Math & Sci Teaching; Nat Asn Biol Teachers. *Res:* Synthesis and function of polymeric plant growth regulators. *Mailing Add:* Dept Biol Sci Fla Atlantic Univ 777 Glades Rd Boca Raton FL 33431-0991

STEWART, IVAN, PLANT CHEMISTRY. *Current Pos:* RETIRED. *Personal Data:* b Stanton, Ky, July 24, 22; m 47; c 3. *Educ:* Univ Ky, BS, 48, MS, 49; Rutgers Univ, PhD(soils), 51. *Prof Exp:* From asst biochemist to biochemist, Citrus Exp Sta, Univ Fla, 51-89. *Res:* Mineral nutrition of plants. *Mailing Add:* 1851 Peninsular Dr Haines City FL 33844

STEWART, J DANIEL, AIR FORCE DEVELOPMENT & TESTING. *Current Pos:* div chief, Air Force Armament Div, Eglin AFB, 81-83, dir, Drone Control Prog Off, 83-85, joint dir, US/Allied Munitions Prog Off, 85-86, tech dir res develop & acquisitions, Air Force Armament Div, 86-88, asst to comdr, 88-90, tech dir, Air Force Develop & Test Ctr, 90-93, EXEC DIR, AIR FORCE DEVELOP & TEST CTR, EGLIN AFB, 93- *Personal Data:* b Savannah, Ga, June 20, 41; m, Rebecca M Smith; c Daniel & Laura. *Educ:* Ga Inst Technol, BS, 63, MS, 65, PhD(aero eng), 67; Stanford Univ, MS, 79. *Honors & Awards:* Presidential Meritorious Rank Award, Pres US, 93; Lewis B Bereton Award, Air Force Asn, 94. *Prof Exp:* Mem tech staff, Appl Mech Div, Aerospace Corp, 67-74; br chief, Tech Div, Air Force Rocket Propulsion Lab, Edwards AFB, 74-78, asst to res & develop mgr, 79-81. *Concurrent Pos:* mem policy coun, Scientist & Eng Career Prog, Randolph AFB, 94-, chmn, Career Develop Panel, 94-96; mem, Eng Adv Bd, Univ Fla, 88- *Mem:* Am Defense Preparedness Asn. *Mailing Add:* AFDTC CD 101 W D Ave Suite 123 Eglin AFB FL 32542-5490

STEWART, J(AMES) R(USH), JR, CHEMICAL ENGINEERING. *Current Pos:* RETIRED. *Personal Data:* b Orange, Tex, Dec 28, 26; m 51, Elaine M Johnson; c Carol J, Linda K, James R III & Patricia A. *Educ:* La Polytech Inst, BS, 50; Ill Inst Technol, MGT, 52. *Prof Exp:* Engr, Pennzoil Co, 52-56, sect supvr chem eng, Res Dept, 56-60, admin asst res, 60-68, sr res assoc, 68-84, mgr process res and safety & environ officer, 84-90. *Concurrent Pos:* Instr, Centenary Col, 57-62; vpres sci & res, Houston Audubon Soc, 92- *Mem:* Am Chem Soc; Am Inst Chem Engrs; Am Ornith Union; Cooper Ornith Soc. *Res:* Hydrocarbon and chemical processing; gas engineering; petrochemicals; fuel cells; solar energy; fertilizers; lube oil refining. *Mailing Add:* 519 Pine Edge Dr The Woodlands TX 77380-2056

STEWART, J W, PSYCHOPHARMALOCOGY. *Current Pos:* RES PSYCHIATRIST, NY STATE PSYCHIATRIC INST, 78-, ASSOC PROF, COLUMBIA UNIV, 88- *Personal Data:* b Neosho, Missouri, Jan 18, 46; m 73; c 2. *Educ:* Swarthmore Col, BA, 67; Yale Univ, MD, 71. *Prof Exp:* Staff psychiatrist, Brookdale Hosp, 76-78; asst prof, Columbia Univ Col Physicians, 80-88. *Mem:* Am Psychiat Asn. *Res:* Nosology, biology and psychopharmacology of affective disorders. *Mailing Add:* 127 Berkeley Pl Brooklyn NY 11217-3603

STEWART, JACK LAUREN, DENTISTRY. *Current Pos:* RETIRED. *Personal Data:* b Covington, Okla, Apr 3, 24; m 48, Mary Frances Pulley; c Jay L, Jill L, David M & James W. *Educ:* Univ Kansas City, DDS, 52. *Prof Exp:* Pvt pract, 52-62; from asst prof to prof dent, Univ Mo-Kans City, 63-70, coordr res, 67-70, asst dean, 70-82, assoc dean, Sch Dent, 82-89. *Concurrent Pos:* Investr, US Army res contract, 63-67, co-responsible investr, 67-70; consult, Leavenworth Vet Admin Ctr, 64- & Kansas City Vet Admin Hosp, 67-; abstractor, Oral Res Abstr, Am Dent Asn; chmn sect comput appln, Am Asn Dent Schs, 68-69, from vchmn to chmn sect learning resources, 69-72. *Mem:* Am Asn Dent Schs; Am Dent Asn; Int Asn Dent Res. *Res:* Research administration; maxillofacial injuries; oral lesions. *Mailing Add:* 9724 Russell Overland Park KS 66212

STEWART, JAKE W, HIGH ENERGY PHYSICS. *Current Pos:* DIR, S & T ASSESSMENT, OFF NAVAL RES, 95- *Personal Data:* b Sherman, Tex, Oct 1, 39; m 65, Carolyn Pope; c Amy & Jeffrey. *Educ:* Ga Tech, BS, 62; Naval Postgrad Sch, PhD(high energy phsycis), 70. *Prof Exp:* Sr staff mem, Nat Security Coun, White House, 78-80; chief, Naval Opers Exec Panel, US Dept Navy, 80-84; asst undersecy defense res & eng, Off Secy Defense, Dept Defense, 84-87; prin, Logos Mythos, 87-92; exec dir & secy energy, US Dept Energy, 92-95. *Mem:* AAAS; Am Inst Aeronaut & Astronaut. *Res:* Government support. *Mailing Add:* 800 N Quincy St Arlington VA 22217

STEWART, JAMES A, ELECTRONICS ENGINEERING. *Current Pos:* PRIN ENGR, GTE LENKURT, INC. *Personal Data:* b Burnaby, BC, May 30, 20; m 50; c 2. *Educ:* Univ BC, BASc, 50; Stanford Univ, MSc, 59. *Prof Exp:* Prod engr, Lenkurt Elec Co Can, 51-54; sr electronics engr, Avro Aircraft, Ltd, 54-55; engr, Westinghouse Elec Corp, 55-56; res engr, Lenkurt Elec Co, Inc, 56-60; mem tech staff, West Coast Lab, Gen Tel & Electronics Labs, 60-63; sr staff engr, GTE Lenkurt Inc, 64-80; mem staff, Data Terminals Div, Hewlett-Packard, 80- *Mem:* Sr mem Inst Elec & Electronics Engrs. *Res:* Electronic circuitry; communication system design. *Mailing Add:* 839 Chesterton Ave Redwood City CA 94061

STEWART, JAMES ALLEN, PHYSICAL CHEMISTRY, CHEMICAL KINETICS & THERMODYNAMICS. *Current Pos:* RETIRED. *Personal Data:* b Pembroke, Ont, Can, Jan 7, 27; m 81, Ruth Deavitt; c Andrew, Catherine & Shelagh. *Educ:* Queen's Univ, Ont, BA, 51, MA, 53; Univ Ottawa, PhD(phys chem), 59. *Prof Exp:* Analytical res chemist, Dept Nat Health & Welfare, Can, 54-59; from asst prof to prof phys chem, Univ NDak, 59-87, emer prof chem, 87- *Mem:* Am Chem Soc; Sigma Xi. *Res:* Chemical kinetics of hydrolytic enzyme systems, ester hydrolyses and excited alkali metal reactions; solvent isotope effects on reaction rates. *Mailing Add:* 596 Elizabeth St Pembroke ON K8A 1X2 Can

STEWART, JAMES ANTHONY, BIOCHEMISTRY. *Current Pos:* from asst prof to assoc prof, Univ NH, 68-78, prof & chmn dept, 78-85, coord, 85-86, int vpres res, 90-91, ASSOC DEAN, RES COL LIFE SCI & AGR, UNIV NH, 86- *Personal Data:* b Manchester, NH, Aug 2, 38; m 63; c 3. *Educ:* St Anselm Col, BA, 63; Univ Conn, PhD(biochem), 67. *Prof Exp:* Investr, Biol Div, Oak Ridge Nat Lab, 67-68. *Concurrent Pos:* Vis prof, Univ Tex Med Br, Galveston, 81-82; assoc dir, NH Agr Exp Sta, 86-; coordr Biol Sci prog, 85. *Mem:* AAAS; Soc Develop Biol; Am Inst Biol Sci; Am Biochem & Molecular Biol. *Res:* Regulation of protein and nucleic acid synthesis during development and differentiation of the mouse central nervous system. *Mailing Add:* Taylor Hall Univ NH Durham NH 03824. *Fax:* 603-862-1585; *E-Mail:* j_stewart@unhh.unh.edu

STEWART, JAMES DREWRY, MATHEMATICAL ANALYSIS. *Current Pos:* asst prof, 69-74, ASSOC PROF MATH, MCMASTER UNIV, 74- *Personal Data:* b Toronto, Ont, Mar 29, 41. *Educ:* Univ Toronto, BSc, 63, PhD(math), 67; Stanford Univ, MS, 64. *Prof Exp:* Nat Res Coun Can fel, Univ London, 67-69. *Mem:* Am Math Soc; Math Asn Am; Can Math Soc. *Res:* Abstract harmonic analysis, functional analysis, history of mathematics. *Mailing Add:* Dept Math McMaster Univ Hamilton ON L8S 4L8 Can

STEWART, JAMES EDWARD, BACTERIAL PHYSIOLOGY, MICROBIOLOGY. *Current Pos:* Scientist, Fisheries Res Bd Can, Maritimes Region, Dept Fisheries & Oceans, 58-74, Res & Develop Directorate, 74-76 & Resource Br, 76-80, dir, Fisheries Res Br, 80-87 & Biol Sci Br, 87-88, RES SCIENTIST, BIOL SCI BR, SCOTIA-FUNDY REGION, DEPT FISHERIES & OCEANS, NS, 88- *Personal Data:* b Anyox, BC, Aug 3, 28; m 67; c 1. *Educ:* Univ BC, BSA, 52, MSA, 54; Univ Iowa, PhD, 58. *Mem:* Soc Invert Path; Sigma Xi; Can Soc Microbiol. *Res:* Microbial oxidation of hydrocarbons; enzymes; bacterial metabolism; defense mechanisms and diseases of marine animals; research management, microbial ecology and marine biotoxins. *Mailing Add:* Bedford Inst Oceanog Habitat Ecol Div-Biol Sci Br Scotia-Fundy Region PO Box 1006 Dartmouth NS B2Y 4A2 Can

STEWART, JAMES JOSEPH PATRICK, DEVELOPMENT OF MOPAC. *Current Pos:* CONSULT, STEWART COMPUTATIONAL CHEM, 91- *Personal Data:* b Glasgow, Scotland, July 26, 46; US citizen; m 84, Anna Carlson. *Educ:* Univ Strathclyde, Glasgow, Scotland, BSc, 69, PhD(chem), 72. *Hon Degrees:* DSc, Univ Strathclyde, Glasgow, Scotland, 95. *Prof Exp:* Asst prof, Glasgow Univ, Scotland, 72-75; assoc prof, Univ Strathclyde, Scotland, 75-85; res chemist, USAF, 87-91. *Concurrent Pos:* Res fel, Univ Tex Austin, 80-84; assoc, Nat Res Coun, 84-87. *Mem:* Am Chem Soc. *Res:* Semiempirical quartum chemistry software for predicting chemical properties. *Mailing Add:* 15210 Paddington Circle Colorado Springs CO 80921. *Fax:* 719-488-9758; *E-Mail:* jstewart@fai.com

STEWART, JAMES MCDONALD, PLANT PHYSIOLOGY, GERMPLASM DEVELOPMENT. *Current Pos:* PROF & ALTHEIMER CHAIR COTTON RES & DEVELOP, DEPT AGRON, UNIV ARK, 86- *Personal Data:* b Taft, Tenn, Sept 22, 41; m 86, Sherry Cunningham; c Heather, Jason, Loni, Calon & Gabrion. *Educ:* Okla State Univ, BS, 63, PhD(plant physiol), 68. *Prof Exp:* Plant physiologist, Agr Res Serv, USDA, 68-85. *Concurrent Pos:* Co-ed, Cotton Physiol, Cotton Found, Memphis, Tenn, 86; mem, Cotton Crop Germplasm Comt, USDA, 91-; consult, Agracetus Inc, 89-96. *Mem:* Crop Sci Soc Am; Agron Soc Am. *Res:* Basic and applied research on cotton concerning the effects of environment and heritable traits thereon; evaluation and enhancement of exotic germplasm; development of host plant resistance through biotechnology. *Mailing Add:* Dept Agron Univ Ark Fayetteville AR 72701. *Fax:* 501-575-7465; *E-Mail:* jstewart@comp.uark.edu

STEWART, JAMES MONROE, SPEECH PERCEPTION, STATISTICS. *Current Pos:* ASSOC PROF SPEECH, TENN TECH UNIV, 85- *Personal Data:* b Chicago, Ill, Feb 26, 46; m 69; c 2. *Educ:* Howard Univ, BA, 70, MA, 71; Ohio Univ, PhD(hearing & speech sci), 76. *Prof Exp:* Instr speech, Howard Univ, 70-71; teaching & res asst speech sci, Ohio Univ, 71-74; res assoc speech sci, Univ Tex Health Sci Ctr, Houston, 75-76; mem staff speech path & audiol, Tenn State Univ, 76-79, asst prof hearing & speech sci, 79-83. *Concurrent Pos:* Teacher eng & math, Washington DC Pub Sch, 70-73; teacher, Nashville Pub Sch, 84-85. *Mem:* Int Soc Phonetic Sci; Am Asn Phonetic Sci; Phonetic Soc Japan; Acoust Soc Am; Inst Acoust. *Res:* Psychological reality of speech perception; saliency of perceptual judgments; prevalence of communicative disorders. *Mailing Add:* Dept Eng Tenn Tech Univ PO Box 5204 Cookeville TN 38505

STEWART, JAMES R, INDUSTRIAL ENGINEERING. *Current Pos:* ASSOC PROF, NORTHERN ILL UNIV, 89- *Personal Data:* b Oct 19, 39; m 62, Barbra Ann Szabunia. *Educ:* NJ Inst Technol, BSME, 62; Univ Mo, MPA, 73; Okla State Univ, MSIE, 81; Tex A&M Univ, PhD, 90. *Prof Exp:* Engr consult, Gen Instruments, Selangor, 81; mgr indust eng, Centralab, Juarez, 82-84, Productos Magneticos, Zenith, 85-87. *Concurrent Pos:* Co-prin investr, Chicagoland Construct Safety Coun, 92; prin investr, McGraw Qual Acad, 94; Fulbright scholars prog, 95. *Mem:* Sr mem Inst Indust Engrs; sr mem Am Soc Qual Control; Soc Work Sci. *Res:* Study of the organization of work. *Mailing Add:* Dept Technol Col Eng Technol Northern Ill Univ 110 Still Hall DeKalb IL 60115-2854. *Fax:* 815-753-3702; *E-Mail:* stewart@ceet.niv.edu

STEWART, JAMES RAY, CELL BIOLOGY, MICROBIOLOGY. *Current Pos:* from asst prof to assoc prof, 74-86, PROF BIOL & CHEM, UNIV TEX, TYLER, 86- *Personal Data:* b Beeville, Tex, Aug 5, 37; m 68, Jeanette Kershaw; c Kelly D & Gregory A. *Educ:* NTex State Univ, BS, 59; Univ Ala, Tuscaloosa, MS, 65; Univ Tex, Austin, PhD(biol sci), 70. *Prof Exp:* NIH fel, Dept Biochem, Univ Tex Health Sci Ctr, San Antonio, 70-74. *Mem:* Am Soc Microbiol; Phycol Soc Am. *Res:* Bacterial and algae physiology; bacterial anatomy and taxonomy; bioremediation and biotransformation of petroleum. *Mailing Add:* Dept Biol Univ Tex Tyler 3900 University Blvd Tyler TX 75799. *Fax:* 903-566-7189; *E-Mail:* jstewart@mail.uttyl.edu

STEWART, JAMES T, PHARMACEUTICAL CHEMISTRY. *Current Pos:* From asst prof to assoc prof, 67-78, PROF & HEAD MED CHEM, UNIV GA, 78- *Personal Data:* b Birmingham, Ala, Dec 1, 38; m 63, Ella; c Elisa, Cathryn & Sharyn. *Educ:* Auburn Univ, BS, 60, MS, 63; Univ Mich, PhD(pharmaceut chem), 67. *Honors & Awards:* Justin L Powers Res Achievement Award, Pharmaceut Analysis, 93; Res Achievement Award in Analytical & Pharmaceut Qual, Am Asn Pharmaceut Scientists, 91. *Concurrent Pos:* Mead-Johnson res grant, 67-68; NIH biomed sci grant, 68-69; Food & Drug Admin contracts, 77-80 & 81-84; grants, Knoll Pharmaceut, 78 & 79, Boots Pharmaceut, 80 & Hoffman-La Roche, Inc, 81; mem, US Pharmacopeial Rev Comt, 80-85, 85-90 & 90-; res grants, Glaxo Inc, 86, 90-96, Upjohn, 86 & Burroughs Wellcome, 87, Microbiological Assocs, 93, Pharmacia, 95-96. *Mem:* Am Chem Soc; Am Pharmaceut Asn; Acad Pharmaceut Sci; Am Asn Pharmaceut Scientists; Sigma Xi. *Res:* Fluorometric analysis of pharmaceuticals; liquid chromatography; supercritical fluid extraction/chromatography. *Mailing Add:* 380 Woodhaven Pkwy Athens GA 30606-1958. *Fax:* 706-542-5358; *E-Mail:* jstewart@rx.uga.edu

STEWART, JANE, PSYCHOLOGY. *Current Pos:* prof & chmn, SGW Univ, 69-75, dir, Ctr Studies Behav Neurobiol, 90-97, PROF PSYCHOL, CONCORDIA UNIV, MONTREAL, 90-97. *Personal Data:* b Ottawa, Ont, Apr 19, 34; wid. *Educ:* Queens Univ, Ont, BA, 56; Univ London, PhD, 59. *Hon Degrees:* DSc, Queens Univ, 92. *Prof Exp:* Sr res biologist, Ayerst Labs, Montreal, 59-63; instr psychol, Sir George, 62-63; assoc prof, Williams Univ, Montreal, 63-69. *Mem:* Fel AAAS; fel Am Psychol Asn; fel Can Psychol Asn; Soc Neurosci; NY Acad Sci; Sigma Xi. *Res:* Behavioral neurobiology. *Mailing Add:* Concordia Univ 1455 de Maisonneuve Blvd W Montreal PQ H3G 1M8 Can

STEWART, JEFFREY GRANT, INTEGRATED PEST MANAGEMENT, BIOLOGICAL CONTROL OF INSECT & WEED PESTS. *Current Pos:* scientist-in-training, 83-87, RES SCIENTIST ENTOM, AGR CAN, RES STA, 87- *Personal Data:* b Ottawa, Ont, Apr 23, 55; m 77, Ann McKee; c Sara, Katie, Michael, & Jamie. *Educ:* Univ Ottawa, BSc, 78, MSc, 81; Univ Guelph, PhD(entom), 87. *Honors & Awards:* President's Prize, Entom Soc Ont, 86. *Prof Exp:* Pesticide eval biologist, Environ Can, Environ Protection Serv, 81-83. *Concurrent Pos:* Prof Agrologist, PEI Inst Agrologists, 87-93; adj prof biol, Univ PEI, 90-; adj prof entom, Univ Guelph, 91-; adj prof biol, Univ NB, 92- *Mem:* Entom Soc Can; Acadian Entom Soc (pres, 91-93). *Res:* Study of the impact of pest damage on yield (action thresholds); sampling methodology; management of insect pests with alternatives to synthetic insecticides in potatoes and cole crops. *Mailing Add:* Agr Can Res Ctr PO Box 1210 Charlottetown PE C1A 7M8 Can. *Fax:* 902-566-6821; *E-Mail:* stewartj@em.agr.ca

STEWART, JENNIFER KEYS, NEUROSCIENCE, MOLECULAR BIOLOGY. *Current Pos:* asst prof, 81-85, ASSOC PROF BIOL, VA COMMONWEALTH UNIV, 85- *Personal Data:* b Rome, Ga, May 15, 47; m 91, John S Ellett III. *Educ:* Emory Univ, BS, 68, MS, 69, PhD(physiol), 75. *Prof Exp:* Instr biol, Mercer Univ, 69-71; res fel endocrinol, Harborview Med Ctr, 75-78; res assoc, Univ Wash & Howard Hughes Med Inst, 79-80, res asst prof, 80-81. *Mem:* Am Physiol Soc; Am Endocrine Soc; AAAS; Asn Women Sci; Am Diabetes Asn. *Res:* Modulation of brain neurotransmitters and neuropeptides. *Mailing Add:* Dept Biol Va Commonwealth Univ Richmond VA 23284-2012

STEWART, JOAN GODSIL, MARINE BOTANY. *Current Pos:* RETIRED. *Educ:* Pomona Col, BA, 53; Calif State Univ, San Diego, MA, 67; Univ Calif, Irvine, PhD(biol), 73. *Prof Exp:* Instr marine bot, Calif State Univ, San Diego, 67-68; res fel marine algae, Scripps Inst Oceanog, Univ Calif, 73- 75; scientist intertidal ecol, Lockheed Marine Biol Lab, 76; consult algal develop, 77-78; assoc res marine biologist, marine algae, Scripps Inst Oceanog, Univ Calif, 78-92. *Mem:* Int Phycol Soc; Phycol Soc Am. *Res:* Developmental morphology and nearshore ecology of Rhodophyta. *Mailing Add:* 4996 Mt Alamagosa Dr San Diego CA 92111

STEWART, JOHN, ELECTRICAL ENGINEERING. *Current Pos:* PRES, QUAL QUAN, INC. *Personal Data:* b Redding, Calif, Dec 10, 29; m 56; c 4. *Educ:* Univ Calif, BSEE, 52. *Prof Exp:* Proj engr, Univac Div, Sperry-Rand Corp, Minn, 54-56, sr engr, 56-60; sr scientist, Systs Res Labs, Inc, 60-61, chief engr, 61-68, vpres res & develop, 68-72, group vpres, 72- *Mem:* Inst Elec & Electronics Engrs. *Res:* Digital computers and data processing systems. *Mailing Add:* 73 College St Cedarville OH 45314

STEWART, JOHN ALLAN, SOIL SCIENCE. *Current Pos:* AGRON CONSULT, 87- *Personal Data:* b Saskatoon, Sask, Feb 18, 24; m 48; c 5. *Educ:* Univ BC, BSA, 50, MSA, 53; Univ Wis, PhD, 64. *Prof Exp:* Lectr soils, Univ BC, 50-51 & 52-54; plant physiologist, Can Dept Agr, 54-65; agronomist, Can Int Minerals & Chem Corp, 65-67, res agronomist, Ill, 67-68, mgr fertilizers & cropping systs res, Res & Develop Div, 68-70, mgr agr res, 70-72, dir res & develop, 72-78, dir agron serv, 79-87. *Concurrent Pos:* Mem, Coun Agr Sci & Technol. *Mem:* Fel Am Soc Agron; Can Soc Soil Sci; Agr Inst Can; AAAS; fel Soil Sci Soc Am. *Res:* Mineral nutrition of agricultural crops; environmental aspects of agricultural technology; industrial minerals applications. *Mailing Add:* 15158 W Redwood Libertyville IL 60048

STEWART, JOHN HARRIS, GEOLOGY. *Current Pos:* GEOLOGIST, US GEOL SURV, 51- *Personal Data:* b Berkeley, Calif, Aug 7, 28; m 62; c 2. *Educ:* Univ NMex, BS, 50; Stanford Univ, PhD, 61. *Mem:* Geol Soc Am. *Res:* Stratigraphy; sedimentology; regional stratigraphy of Triassic rocks in Utah, Colorado, Nevada, Arizona and New Mexico and of late Precambrian and Cambrian in Nevada and California; regional and local mapping in Nevada; compilation of geologic map of Nevada. *Mailing Add:* 345 Middlefield Rd MS 901 Menlo Park CA 94025

STEWART, JOHN JOSEPH, PHARMACOLOGY. *Current Pos:* assoc prof, 77-86, PROF PHARMACOL, MED CTR, LA STATE UNIV, 86- *Personal Data:* b Paterson, NJ, July 27, 46. *Educ:* Duquesne Univ, BS, 69; Univ Wis-Madison, MS, 72, PhD(pharm), 75. *Prof Exp:* USPHS fel physiol, Med Sch, Univ Tex, Houston, 75-77. *Concurrent Pos:* Nat Inst Gen Med Sci grant, Med Sch, La State Univ, Shreveport, 78-81. *Mem:* Sigma Xi; Am Soc Pharmacol & Exp Therapeut; Soc Neurosci. *Res:* Central nervous system control of gastrointestinal function. *Mailing Add:* LSU Med Ctr PO Box 33932 Shreveport LA 71130-3932. *Fax:* 318-674-7857; *E-Mail:* jstewa@nomuslsumcedu

STEWART, JOHN L(AWRENCE), ELECTRICAL ENGINEERING. *Current Pos:* PRES, SET, INC, 89- *Personal Data:* b Pasadena, Calif, Apr 19, 25; m 51; c 2. *Educ:* Stanford Univ, BS, 48, MS, 49, PhD(elec eng), 52. *Prof Exp:* Res engr, Jet Propulsion Lab, Calif Inst Techol, 49-51; res assoc, Stanford Univ, 52-53; asst prof elec eng, Univ Mich, 53-56; assoc prof, Calif Inst Technol, 56-57 & Univ Southern Calif, 57-60; prof, Univ Ariz, 60-62; pres, Santa Rita Technol Inc, Calif, 62-71; pres, Av-Alarm Corp, 71-89; pres, Couox, Inc, 82-89. *Concurrent Pos:* Vert pest control res, 65-68. *Mem:* AAAS; sr mem Inst Elec & Electronics Engrs; Acoust Soc Am. *Res:* Electronic network simulations of animal sensory systems; bionics; speech and hearing; speech processing and recognition; acoustic control and cuing; artificial intelligence; signal analysis. *Mailing Add:* SET Inc 3205 SE Spyglass Dr Vancouver WA 98683

STEWART, JOHN MATHEWS, ORGANIC CHEMISTRY. *Current Pos:* RETIRED. *Personal Data:* b Vermillion, SDak, Apr 5, 20; m 43; c 1. *Educ:* Univ Mont, BA, 41; Univ Ill, PhD(org chem), 44. *Prof Exp:* Res chemist, War Prod Bd, Univ Ill, 43-45 & Calif Res Corp, 45-46; from asst prof to prof chem, Univ Mont, 46-77, chmn dept, 59-67, dean grad sch, 68-77, actg acad vpres, 75-77. *Concurrent Pos:* Asst acad vpres, Univ Mont, 78- *Mem:* Am Chem Soc; Sigma Xi. *Res:* Reactions of olefin sulfides; additions to unsaturated nitriles; participation of cyclopropane rings in conjugation, ring-opening reactions of cyclopropanes; use of diazomethane in synthesis of heterocyclic compounds. *Mailing Add:* 111 Crestline Missoula MT 59803

STEWART, JOHN MORROW, PEPTIDE CHEMISTRY & BIOLOGY, ENDOCRINOLOGY. *Current Pos:* PROF BIOCHEM, MED SCH, UNIV COLO, DENVER, 68- *Personal Data:* b Guilford Co, NC, Oct 31, 24; wid; c Ellen, Susan & David. *Educ:* Davidson Col, BS, 48; Univ Ill, MS, 50, PhD(org chem), 52. *Honors & Awards:* Gold Medal, Frey-Werle Found, Ger, 91. *Prof Exp:* Instr chem, Davidson Col, 48-49; asst, Rockefeller Univ, 52-57, from asst prof to assoc prof biochem, 57-68. *Mem:* Am Chem Soc; Am Soc Pharmacol & Exp Therapeut; NY Acad Sci; Am Soc Biochem & Molecular Biol; Endocrine Soc; Soc Neuroscience. *Res:* Chemistry and pharmacology of peptide hormones, methods of peptide synthesis, antimetabolites and amino acids; synthetic organic chemistry. *Mailing Add:* Dept Biochem Univ Colo Med Sch Denver CO 80262. *Fax:* 303-315-8215; *E-Mail:* john.stewart@uchsc.edu

STEWART, JOHN WESTCOTT, PHYSICS. *Current Pos:* Res fel, Univ Va, 54-56, asst prof, 56-60, assoc prof, 60-74, asst dean col, 70-91, EMER PROF PHYSICS, UNIV VA, 94- *Personal Data:* b New York, NY, Nov 15, 26; m 54; c 1. *Educ:* Princeton Univ, AB, 49; Harvard Univ, MA, 50, PhD(physics), 54. *Mem:* Fel Am Phys Soc; Am Asn Physics Teachers. *Res:* Properties of matter under combined field of high pressure and low temperature; meteorology. *Mailing Add:* 2205 Dominion Dr Charlottesville VA 22901

STEWART, JOHN WOODS, NUCLEAR ENGINEERING. *Current Pos:* Nuclear engr, E I Du Pont de Nemours & Co, Inc, 68-71, res supvr, 71-75, res mgr, 75-80, dept supt, 78-81, gen supt employee rels, Savannah River Plant, 81-82, sect dir, 83, tech mgr, Petrochem Dept, Atomic Energy Div, 84-87, design mgr, Eng Dept, 87-88, mgr, advan technol, Imaging Systs Dept, 88-90, CONSULT MGR, DUPONT ENG, E I DUPONT DE NEMOURS & CO, INC, 90- *Personal Data:* b Henderson, Tenn, Apr 5, 42; m 65; c John III & Jennifer. *Educ:* Univ Tenn, BS, 65, MS, 67, PhD(nuclear eng), 69. *Concurrent Pos:* Res assoc nuclear eng, Mass Inst Technol, 74-75. *Mem:* Am Nuclear Soc. *Res:* Nuclear reactor physics and engineering; equipment development; computer applications. *Mailing Add:* Dupont PO Box 80840 MS BEC 16/2004 Wilmington DE 19880-0840

STEWART, JOHN WRAY BLACK, SOIL SCIENCE, CHEMISTRY & ENVIRONMENTAL SCIENCES. *Current Pos:* fel, Univ Sask, 64-65, from asst prof to assoc prof, 65-76, prof, 76-81, dir, Sask Inst Pedol & head, Dept Soil Sci, 81-89, DEAN, COL AGR, UNIV SASK, 89- *Personal Data:* b Coleraine, NIreland, Jan 16, 36; Can citizen; m 65; Ann Poole; c Matthew & Hannah. *Educ:* Queen's Univ, Belfast, BSc, 58, BAgr, 59, PhD(soil sci), 63, DSc, 88. *Prof Exp:* From sci officer to sr sci officer soil sci, Chem Res Div, Ministry Agr, NIreland, 59-64. *Concurrent Pos:* Tech expert, Int Atomic Energy Agency, Vienna, 71-72; tech expert, UN Brazil Proj, 74-75; proj coordr, Can Int Develop Agency, Brazil, 76-; secy-gen, Scope/ICSU, 84-91, pres, 92-; fel, Berlin Inst Advan Studies, 89. *Mem:* Agr Inst Can; Brit Soc Soil Sci; Int Soil Sci Soc; fel Am Soc Agron; fel Can Soc Soil Sci; fel Soil Sci Soc Am. *Res:* Soil chemistry and fertility; cycling of macro and micro nutrients and heavy metals in the soil plant system. *Mailing Add:* Col Agr Univ Sask 51 Campus Dr Saskatoon SK S7N 5A8 Can. *Fax:* 306-966-8894; *E-Mail:* tiistewartj@sask.usask.ca

STEWART, JOSEPH LETIE, ANTHROPOLOGY. *Current Pos:* CONSULT, DEPT ELEC & COMPUT ENG, UNIV NMEX, 93- *Personal Data:* b Salida, Colo, Aug 2, 27; m 50, Valdee Balling; c Valley, Kathryn & Patricia. *Educ:* Univ Denver, BA, 49, MA, 50; Univ Iowa, PhD(speech path, audiol, anthrop), 59. *Prof Exp:* Res assoc speech path, Univ Iowa, 58-59; asst prof audiol & dir, Hearing Ctr, Univ Denver, 59-65; consult audiol & speech path, Neurol & Sensory Dis Control Prog, Nat Ctr Chronic Dis Control, USPHS, 65-70, chief, Sensory Disabilities Prog, Indian Health Serv, 70-93. *Concurrent Pos:* Hon res fel, Inst Speech Path & Exp Phonetics, Belgrade, Yugoslavia, 91. *Mem:* Fel Am Acad Audiol. *Res:* Application of acoustic phonetics and selective amplification to digital signal processing in hearing aid design. *Mailing Add:* Dept Elec & Comput Eng Univ NMex Albuquerque NM 87131. *Fax:* 505-277-1439

STEWART, KENNETH WILSON, ENTOMOLOGY, AQUATIC ECOLOGY. *Current Pos:* from instr to prof biol, Univ NTex, 61-79, prof & chmn biol sci, 79-83, chmn, Div Environ Sci, 88-90, FAC RES GRANTS, UNIV NTEX, 63-, REGENT'S PROF, 94- *Personal Data:* b Walters, Okla, Mar 5, 35; m 56; c 4. *Educ:* Okla State Univ, BS, 58, MS, 59, PhD(entom, zool), 63. *Honors & Awards:* Benthic Sci Excellence Award, NAm Benthological Soc, 97. *Prof Exp:* Entomologist, Rocky Mt Forest & Range Exp Sta, US Forest Serv, 58-59; head, dept biol, Coffeyville Col, 60-61. *Concurrent Pos:* NIH Res grant, 66-88; consult investr, US Corps Engrs; vis prof, Univ Okla, 66, 91 & 93; NSF res grants, 77-; fac affil, Univ Montana, 81, 85, 87 & 89 & Univ Denver, 84. *Mem:* Entom Soc Am; Am Entom Soc; NAm Benthological Soc (pres, 78-79). *Res:* Stream benthos community structure and dynamics; North American Plecoptera nymphs; passive dispersal of Algae and Protozoa by aquatic insects; food habits and life histories of aquatic insects and spiders; drumming behavior of Plecoptera. *Mailing Add:* Dept Biol Sci Univ NTex Box 5218 Denton TX 76203-0218

STEWART, KENT KALLAM, ANALYTICAL CHEMISTRY, BIOCHEMISTRY. *Current Pos:* head, Food Sci Dept, 82-85, PROF, DEPT BIOCHEM, VA POLYTECH INST, 85- *Personal Data:* b Omaha, Nebr, Sept 5, 34; m 56, Margaret Reiber; c 4. *Educ:* Univ Calif, Berkeley, AB, 56; Fla State Univ, PhD(chem), 65. *Prof Exp:* USPHS guest investr biochem, Rockefeller Univ, 65-67, res assoc, 67-68, asst prof, 68-69; res chemist, Nutrient Compos Lab, Nutrit Inst, Agr Res Serv, USDA, 70-75, lab chief, 75-82. *Concurrent Pos:* Ed, J Food Compos & Analysis, 87- *Mem:* Fel AAAS; Am Chem Soc; fel Inst Food Technologists; Asn Off Analytical Chemists. *Res:* Automated analyses, especially flow injection analyses; nutrient composition of foods; food and diet assay. *Mailing Add:* 3900 Glengarry Dr Austin TX 78731. *Fax:* 512-458-1078; *E-Mail:* kkstewart@mail.utexas.edu

STEWART, KENTON M, LIMNOLOGY, AQUATIC ECOLOGY. *Current Pos:* from asst prof to assoc prof biol, 66-92, dir Environ & Org Div Biol, 78-80, PROF BIOL, STATE UNIV NY, BUFFALO, 92- *Personal Data:* b Withee, Wis, Aug 28, 31; m 54; c 3. *Educ:* Wis State Univ, Stevens Point, BS, 55; Univ Wis-Madison, MS, 59, PhD(zool), 65. *Honors & Awards:* Chandler Meisner Award, Inst Asn Great Lakes Res, 89. *Prof Exp:* Asst limnol, ecol & invert zool, Univ Wis-Madison, 58-61, asst limnol, 61-65, fel, 65-66. *Concurrent Pos:* Vis, Max Planck Inst Limnol, Ger, 72-73, Cold Regions Res Environ Lab, NH, 80-81, Great Lakes Environ Lab, Mich, 87, 94-95; Coop Inst Res Environ Sci Fel, Univ Colo, 80; assoc ed, Int Rev Hydrobiol. *Mem:* Am Soc Limnol & Oceanog; Ecol Soc Am; Int Asn Theoret & Appl Limnol; Int Asn Gt Lakes Res; Am Geophys Res. *Res:* Physical limnology and eutrophication; comparative limnology of Finger Lakes of New York; climate change. *Mailing Add:* Dept Biol Sci State Univ NY Buffalo NY 14260. *Fax:* 716-645-2935

STEWART, LAWRENCE COLM, DATA COMPRESSION, SIGNAL PROCESSING. *Current Pos:* res staff mem, Digital Equip Systs Res Ctr, 84-89, RES STAFF MEM, DIGITAL EQUIP CAMBRIDGE RES LAB, 89- *Personal Data:* b Mineola, NY, July 12, 55; m 91, Catherine A Briasco. *Educ:* Mass Inst Technol, SB, 76; Stanford Univ, MS, 77, PhD(elec eng), 81. *Prof Exp:* Res staff mem, Xerox Palo Alto Res Ctr, 77-84. *Concurrent Pos:* Vis lectr, Stanford Univ, 82; vis scientist, Mass Inst Technol, 89- *Mem:* Inst Elec & Electronics Engrs; Asn Comput Mach. *Res:* Multiprocessor computer systems; voice input and voice output systems for computers and multimedia. *Mailing Add:* Open Market Inc 245 First St Cambridge MA 02142. *Fax:* 617-621-6650; *E-Mail:* stewart@crl.dec.com

STEWART, LELAND TAYLOR, STATISTICS, ARTIFICIAL INTELLIGENCE. *Current Pos:* MATHEMATICIAN, LOCKHEED MARTIN ADVAN TECHNOL CTR, 65- *Personal Data:* b San Francisco, Calif, Nov 24, 28; m 56; c 2. *Educ:* Stanford Univ, BS, 51, MS, 57, PhD(statist), 65. *Prof Exp:* Res engr, Autonetics Div, NAm Aviation, Inc, 51-56 & Electronic Defense Labs, Sylvania Elec Prod, Inc, 58-61; statistician, C-E-I-R Inc, 61-65. *Res:* Bayesian statistics and decision theory. *Mailing Add:* 152 Ferne Ct Palo Alto CA 94306

STEWART, MARGARET MCBRIDE, VERTEBRATE ECOLOGY, HERPETOLOGY. *Current Pos:* from asst prof to prof vert biol, 56-77, DISTINGUISHED TEACHING PROF, STATE UNIV NY ALBANY, 77- *Personal Data:* b Greensboro, NC, Feb 6, 27; m 69, George E Martin. *Educ:* Univ NC, AB, 48, MA, 51; Cornell Univ, PhD(vert zool), 56. *Hon Degrees:* DSc, Univ PR, Mayaguez, 96. *Prof Exp:* Lab instr anat & physiol, Woman's Col, Univ NC, 50-51; instr biol, Catawba Col, 51-53; asst bot & taxon, Cornell Univ, 53-56. *Concurrent Pos:* Res Found grant-in-aid, 58-61, 65-71, 73-74 & 84-85; grants, Am Philos Soc, 75 & 81 & NSF, 78-80; fac partic, Oak Ridge Assoc Univrs, 83-91; ed gen herpet, Am Soc Ichthyol & Herpet, 83-85; dir, Prog Biodiversity, Conserv & Policy, State Univ NY, Albany, 95- *Mem:* Ecol Soc Am; Asn Trop Biol; Am Soc Ichthyol & Herpet (pres, 96); Soc Study Amphibians & Reptiles (pres, 79); fel Herpetologists' League; Soc Study Evolution. *Res:* Competition in tropical and temperate frogs; pattern polymorphism; population dynamics of Adirondack frogs; ecology and behavior of Eleutherodactylus, Puerto Rico and Jamaica; population ecology and behavior of frogs; Eleutherodactylus in Puerto Rico, ranid frogs in upstate New York; fire ecology in the Albany Pine Bush, an endangered community. *Mailing Add:* Dept Biol Sci State Univ NY Albany NY 12222. *Fax:* 518-442-4767; *E-Mail:* mstewart@csc.albany.edu

STEWART, MARK ARMSTRONG, BIOCHEMISTRY, PSYCHIATRY. *Current Pos:* RETIRED. *Personal Data:* b Yeovil, Eng, July 23, 29; US citizen; m 55; c 3. *Educ:* Cambridge Univ, BA, 52; Univ London, LRCP & MRCS, 56. *Prof Exp:* Asst psychiat, Sch Med, Washington Univ, 57-61, instr, 61-63, asst prof psychiat & pediat, 63-67, from assoc prof to prof psychiat, 67-72, assoc prof pediat, 68-72; Ida P Haller prof child psychiat, Col Med, Univ Iowa, 72-90. *Concurrent Pos:* NIMH res career develop award, 61-71; dir psychiat, St Louis Children's Hosp. *Mem:* Int Soc Res Aggression; Am Soc Biol Chem; fel Am Acad Child Psychiat; fel Am Psychiat Asn; Soc Res Child Develop. *Res:* Genetic influences on children's aggressive and antisocial behavior. *Mailing Add:* 2012 Kestrel Ridge SW Oxford IA 52322

STEWART, MARK THURSTON, HYDROGEOLOGY, APPLIED GEOPHYSICS. *Current Pos:* PROF GEOL, UNIV SFLA, TAMPA, 76-, CHAIR GEOL DEPT, 89- *Personal Data:* b Montclair, NJ, Apr 27, 48. *Educ:* Cornell Univ, AB, 70; Univ Wis-Madison, MS(geol) & MS(water resources mgt), 74, PhD(geol), 76. *Mem:* Asn Ground Water Scientists & Engrs; Soc Exploration Geophys; Geol Soc Am; Environ & Eng Geophys Soc. *Res:* Applications of geophysical techniques to ground water resource investigations; interactions of hydrologic and geologic systems; karst hydrogeology; numerical modeling. *Mailing Add:* Dept Geol SCA 203 Univ SFla 4202 Fowler Ave Tampa FL 33620-9951. *Fax:* 813-974-2654

STEWART, MARY E, SKIN LIPIDS. *Current Pos:* asst res scientist, 78-81, ASSOC RES SCIENTIST, DEPT DERMAT, UNIV IOWA COL MED, 81- *Personal Data:* b Wilmington, Del, Oct 24, 39. *Educ:* Univ Del, BS, 61; Purdue Univ, MS, 64, PhD(biochem), 68. *Prof Exp:* Post doctorate trainee, Boston Biomed Res Found, 67-69; fel biochem, Boston Univ Sch Med, 69-71, res assoc, dept dermat, 71-78. *Mem:* Soc Invest Dermat; AAAS. *Res:* Epidermal and sebaceous lipds of human skin. *Mailing Add:* 270 ML Univ Iowa City IA 52242. *Fax:* 319-335-9559

STEWART, MELBOURNE GEORGE, PHYSICS. *Current Pos:* chmn dept, 63-73, assoc provost, 73-86, PROF PHYSICS, WAYNE STATE UNIV, 63- *Personal Data:* b Detroit, Mich, Sept 30, 27; m 54, Charlotte Ford; c Jill K, John H & Kevin G. *Educ:* Univ Mich, AB, 49, MS, 50, PhD(physics), 55. *Prof Exp:* Res assoc, Iowa State Univ, 55-56, from asst prof to assoc prof physics, 56-63. *Concurrent Pos:* Res fel, Dept Physics & Astron, Univ Col London, UK, 86-87 & 93. *Mem:* Am Phys Soc. *Res:* Solid state positron physics. *Mailing Add:* Dept Physics Wayne State Univ Detroit MI 48202. *Fax:* 313-577-3932

STEWART, PAUL ALVA, ecology, ornithology; deceased, see previous edition for last biography

STEWART, PHILIP S, CHEMICAL ENGINEERING. *Current Pos:* ASST PROF CHEM ENG, CTR BIOFILM ENG, MONT STATE UNIV, 91- *Educ:* Stanford Univ, PhD(chem eng), 88. *Honors & Awards:* Early Career Award, NSF, 96. *Prof Exp:* Res & develop engr, Lonza AG, Switz, 82-83; NATO postdoctoral fel, Inst Jacques Monod, France, 88-89; sr chem engr, Bechtel Environ, Calif, 90-91. *Res:* Biofilm control with antimicrobial agents; chemical and biological waste treatment technologies. *Mailing Add:* Ctr Biofilm Eng 366 EPS Bldg Mont State Univ PO Box 173980 Bozeman MT 59717-3980

STEWART, REGINALD BRUCE, ANALYTICAL CHEMISTRY. *Current Pos:* ANALYTICAL CHEM CONSULT, 85- *Personal Data:* b Moose Jaw, Sask, May 30, 28; m 50; c 1. *Educ:* Univ Man, BSc, 50. *Prof Exp:* Res chemist, Hudson Bay Mining & Smelting Co, 50-55; asst chief chemist, Noranda Mines Ltd, 55-62; res off analytical chem, Atomic Energy Can, 62-69, head analytical sci br, 69-85. *Concurrent Pos:* Analytical chem consult, 85-, lab mgt consult, World Bank, Peoples Repub China, 87. *Mem:* Fel Chem Inst Can. *Res:* Analytical sciences, particularly nuclear power research and development and environmental monitoring. *Mailing Add:* One McWilliams Pl Pinawa MB R0E 1L0 Can

STEWART, RICHARD BYRON, MECHANICAL ENGINEERING. *Current Pos:* chmn dept, 69-74, prof, 69-87, EMER PROF MECH ENG, UNIV IDAHO, 87- *Personal Data:* b Waterloo, Iowa, Aug 22, 24; m 44, Carol Entz; c Richard & Betty. *Educ:* Univ Iowa, BSME, 46, MS, 48, PhD(mech eng), 66; Univ Colo, ME, 59. *Prof Exp:* Instr mech eng, Univ Iowa, 46-48; from asst prof to assoc prof, Univ Colo, 48-60; supvry mech engr, Cryogenics Div, Nat Bur Stand, 60-66; prof mech eng, Worcester Polytech Inst, 66-69. *Concurrent Pos:* Fulbright lectr, Col Eng, Univ Baghdad, 56-57. *Mem:* Am Soc Heat, Refrig & Air-Conditioning Engrs. *Res:* Thermodynamic properties and processes; cryogenics; thermodynamic properties of cryogenic fluids. *Mailing Add:* 1415 Chinook St Moscow ID 83843

STEWART, RICHARD DONALD, INTERNAL MEDICINE, MEDICAL TOXICOLOGY. *Current Pos:* RETIRED. *Personal Data:* b Lakeland, Fla, Dec 26, 26; m 52, Mary Leeuw; c Richard S, Gregory D & Mary E. *Educ:* Univ Mich, AB, 51, MD, 55, MPH, 62; Am Bd Internal Med, dipl, 74; Am Bd Med Toxicol, dipl, 76; Univ Wis, Mailwaukee, MA, 79, PhD, 97. *Honors & Awards:* Weisfeldt Mem Award, 75; Dialysis Pioneering Award, Nat Kidney Found, 82. *Prof Exp:* Staff physician, Med Dept, Dow Chem Co, 56-59, dir, Med Res Sect, Biochem Res Lab, 62-66; resident internal med, Med Ctr, Univ Mich, 59-62; asst prof internal med & assoc prof prev med & toxicol, Sch Med, Med Col Wis, 66-69, chmn, Dept Environ Med, 66-78, prof environ med in internal med & toxicol & environ med, 69-78; corp med dir, S C Johnson & Son, 78-90. *Concurrent Pos:* Corp med adv, S C Johnson & Son, 71-78; clin prof pharmacol & toxicol, Med Col Wis, 78-; adj prof, Univ Wis Parkside, 78-; vis prof, Med Sch, Univ Hawaii, 80-; sect ed, Clin Med; dir med toxicol fel, Dept Environ Med, Med Col Wis, 89-91, med dir, Poison Ctr, 89-93. *Mem:* Fel Am Col Physicians; Am Soc Artificial Internal Organs; Soc Toxicol; fel Am Acad Clin Toxicol; fel Am Occup Med Asn; fel Acad Toxicol Sci. *Res:* Human toxicology; development of the hollow fiber artificial kidney; air pollution epidemiological studies; experimental human exposures to artificial environments; tropical diseases; author of 125 scientific publications; author of medical biographies. *Mailing Add:* 5337 Windpoint Rd Racine WI 53402-2322

STEWART, RICHARD JOHN, GEOLOGY. *Current Pos:* Asst prof, 69-77, ASSOC PROF GEOL, UNIV WASH, 77- *Personal Data:* b Duluth, Minn, May 30, 42; m 67. *Educ:* Univ Minn, BA, 65; Stanford Univ, PhD(geol), 70. *Concurrent Pos:* Geologist, Olympia Mts, US Geol Surv, 70; sedimentologist deep sea drilling proj, NSF, 71, res grant, Univ Wash, 72-73. *Mem:* Mineral Soc Am; Geol Soc Am; Am Asn Petrol Geologists; Soc Econ Paleontologists & Mineralogists; Am Geophys Union; Sigma Xi. *Res:* Sedimentary petrology; structural geology; geological and tectonic history of the northeast Pacific Ocean and its continental margin. *Mailing Add:* Dept Geol Sci AJ20 Univ Wash 3900 Seventh Ave NE Seattle WA 98195-0001

STEWART, RICHARD WILLIAM, SYSTEM SURVIVABILITY. *Current Pos:* RETIRED. *Personal Data:* b Ames, Iowa, Oct, 22, 46; m 71; c 2. *Educ:* Mich State Univ, BS, 70; Iowa State Univ, MS, 73, PhD(elec eng), 77. *Prof Exp:* Staff engr, Johns Hopkins Appl Physics Lab, 77-79; group leader, IRT Corp, 79-89; div vpres, SQ Corp, 89-90, vpres & group mgr, Div Maxwell Labs, 90-91. *Mem:* Inst Elec & Electronics Engrs; Soc Photo-Optical Instrumentation Engrs. *Res:* Evaluation and enhancement of the survivability of military and civil systems operating in hostile environments; electromagnetic coupling, nonlinear propagation and stochastic estimation. *Mailing Add:* Maxwell Labs S-Cubed Div 3020 Callan Rd San Diego CA 92121

STEWART, RICHARD WILLIS, ATMOSPHERIC PHYSICS. *Current Pos:* Res assoc atmospheric physics, 67-69, staff scientist, Goddard Inst Space Studies, 69-78, RES SCIENTIST, NASA GODDARD SPACE FLIGHT CTR, 78- *Personal Data:* b Atlanta, Ga, Dec 27, 36; m 64; c 2. *Educ:* Univ Fla, BS, 60; Columbia Univ, MA, 63, PhD(physics), 67. *Concurrent Pos:* Asst prof, Rutgers Univ, 68 & City Col New York, 69- *Mem:* Am Meteorol Soc; Am Geophys Union; AAAS. *Res:* Atmospheric chemistry. *Mailing Add:* 5359 Red Lake Columbia MD 21045-2433

STEWART, ROBERT ARCHIE, II, PLANT ECOLOGY. *Current Pos:* from asst prof to assoc prof, 70-80, PROF BIOL, DELTA STATE UNIV, 80- *Personal Data:* b Houston, Miss, Jan 23, 42; m 74; c 2. *Educ:* Miss State Univ, BS, 65, MS, 67; Ariz State Univ, PhD(bot), 71. *Prof Exp:* Partic, NSF advan seminar trop bot, Univ Miami, 68. *Mem:* Am Inst Biol Sci. *Res:* Plant ecology; flora of Mississippi. *Mailing Add:* Dept Biol Sci Delta State Univ Cleveland MS 38733

STEWART, ROBERT BLAYLOCK, plant pathology, for more information see previous edition

STEWART, ROBERT BRUCE, ANIMAL VIROLOGY. *Current Pos:* from assoc prof to prof bact, 63-93, EMER PROF MICROBIOL IMMUNOL, QUEEN'S UNIV, ONT, 93- *Personal Data:* b Toronto, Ont, May 2, 26; m 45; c 2. *Educ:* Mt Allison Univ, BSc, 49; Queen's Univ, Ont, MA, 51, PhD(bact), 55. *Prof Exp:* Res officer, Defence Res Bd, Can, 51-55; from instr to asst prof bact, Sch Med & Dent, Univ Rochester, 55-63. *Concurrent Pos:* Head dept, Queen's Univ, Ont, 71-86. *Mem:* Am Soc Microbiol; Can Soc Microbiol; Can Soc Microbiologists (pres, 85-86). *Res:* Virology; regulation of virus growth; infectious disease. *Mailing Add:* Dept Microbiol & Immunol Queen's Univ Kingston ON K7L 3N6 Can

STEWART, ROBERT CLARENCE, MATHEMATICS. *Current Pos:* from instr to prof, 50-76, CHARLES A DANA PROF MATH, TRINITY COL, CONN, 76- *Personal Data:* b Sharon, Pa, Sept 23, 21; m 59. *Educ:* Washington & Jefferson Col, BA, 42, MA, 44; Yale Univ, MA, 48. *Prof Exp:* Instr math, Washington & Jefferson Col, 42-44, 45-46; asst, Yale Univ, 46-50. *Mem:* Am Math Soc; Math Asn Am. *Res:* Modern algebra; matrix theory; differential equations. *Mailing Add:* Dept Math Trinity Col Hartford CT 06106-3186

STEWART, ROBERT DANIEL, PHYSICAL CHEMISTRY, METALLURGICAL CHEMISTRY. *Current Pos:* RETIRED. *Personal Data:* b Salt Lake City, Utah, June 15, 23; m 47; c 4. *Educ:* Univ Utah, BS, 50; Univ Wash, PhD(phys chem), 54. *Prof Exp:* Sr res chemist, Am Potash & Chem Corp, 54-56, group leader, 56-58, sect head, 58-68; group leader, Garrett Res & Develop Co, 68-75; group leader, Occidental Res Corp, 75-82; supvr, Cyprus Indust Minerals, 83-88. *Mem:* Am Chem Soc; Electrochem Soc; Am Inst Mining, Metall & Petrol Engrs. *Res:* Gas phase kinetics; thermodynamics; inorganic polymers; extractive hydrometallurgy; minerals beneficiation. *Mailing Add:* 17052 El Cajon Ave Yorba Linda CA 92886

STEWART, ROBERT EARL, FLUID MECHANICS, MICROMETEOROLOGY. *Current Pos:* ASSOC PROF MECH & ENVIRON ENG, UNIV LOUISVILLE, 70- *Personal Data:* b Campbellton, NB, Feb 17, 35; m 60; c 2. *Educ:* NS Tech Col, BEng, 57; Univ BC, MEng, 63; Univ Waterloo, PhD(mech), 66. *Prof Exp:* Design engr, BC Hydro, 57-58, res engr, 58-61; demonstr mech eng, Univ BC, 61-63; res asst, Univ Waterloo, 63-66; asst prof environ eng, Univ Fla, 66-70. *Mem:* Am Meteorol Soc; Can Meteorol Soc; fel Royal Meteorol Soc. *Res:* Diffusion of gases and particulates released into the atmosphere. *Mailing Add:* Dept Mech Eng Univ Louisville 200 Sackett Hall Louisville KY 40292

STEWART, ROBERT F, PHYSICAL CHEMISTRY. *Current Pos:* fel, 64-69, ASSOC PROF CHEM, CARNEGIE-MELLON UNIV, 69- *Personal Data:* b Seattle, Wash, Dec 31, 36; m 59; c 2. *Educ:* Carleton Col, AB, 58; Calif Inst Technol, PhD(chem), 63. *Prof Exp:* NIH fel, Univ Wash, 62-64. *Concurrent Pos:* Alfred P Sloan fel, 70-72. *Res:* Ultraviolet absorption of single crystals; valence structure from x-ray scattering; x-ray diffraction. *Mailing Add:* Dept Chem Carnegie-Mellon Univ Warner Hall 5000 Forbes Ave Pittsburgh PA 15213-3890

STEWART, ROBERT FRANCIS, NUCLEAR CHEMISTRY, FUEL TECHNOLOGY. *Current Pos:* head radioisotope lab, 63-69, RES CHEMIST, US BUR MINES, 54- *Personal Data:* b Birmingham, Ala, Oct 31, 26; m 58; c 4. *Educ:* Univ Ala, BS, 49, MS, 50. *Prof Exp:* Jr chemist, Nat Southern Prod Corp, 50-52; res supvr, Morgantown Energy Res Ctr, 69-82. *Concurrent Pos:* Pres, Five Four Three Co. *Mem:* Am Chem Soc; Am Soc Testing & Mat; Instrument Soc Am. *Res:* Nuclear methods of continuous analysis of bulk materials for process control based on neutron interactions in matter. *Mailing Add:* Rte 8 Box 228E Morgantown WV 26505-9024

STEWART, ROBERT HENRY, PHYSICAL OCEANOGRAPHY, SPACE SCIENCE. *Current Pos:* PROF, TEX A&M UNIV, 89- *Personal Data:* b York, Pa, Dec 26, 41; m 86, Tracy Bertolucci; c Alethea, Farrar (Clee) & Margaret. *Educ:* Univ Tex, Arlington, BS, 63; Univ Calif, San Diego, PhD(oceanog), 69. *Honors & Awards:* Pub Serv Medal, NASA, 94. *Prof Exp:* Asst res oceanogr, Scripps Inst Oceanog, 69-77, assoc res oceanogr & assoc adj prof, 77-83, res oceanogr & adj prof, 83-89; sr res scientist, Jet Propulsion Lab, Calif Inst Technol, 83-89. *Concurrent Pos:* Consult, NASA, 75-77; Topex proj scientist, 79-88; mem, Comt Earth Sci, Nat Acad Sci, Nat Res Coun, 87-89; res scientist, Jet Propulsion Lab, Calif Inst Technol, 79-83. *Mem:* Am Geophys Union; Int Union Radio Sci. *Res:* Satellite oceanography; currents; ocean waves; radio scatter from the sea; numerous publications in general field of satellite oceanography plus experience in designing the Topex/Poseidon satellite mission. *Mailing Add:* Dept Oceanog Tex A&M Univ College Station TX 77843-3146. *Fax:* 409-847-8879; *E-Mail:* rstewart@ocean.tamu.edu

STEWART, ROBERT MURRAY, JR, COMPUTER SCIENCE. *Current Pos:* Instr elec eng, Iowa State Univ, 46-48, res assoc physics, 48-54, from asst prof to assoc prof, 54-58, engr in charge, Cyclone Comput Lab, 56-67, assoc prof elec eng, 58-60, chmn, Dept Comput Sci, 69-83, prof physics & elec eng, 60-88, assoc dir, Comput Ctr, 63-88, prof comput sci, 69-88, EMER PROF PHYSICS, ELEC ENG & COMPUT SCI, IOWA STATE UNIV, 88- *Personal Data:* b Washington, DC, May 6, 24; m 45; c 2. *Educ:* Iowa State Col, BS, 45, PhD(physics), 54. *Concurrent Pos:* Sr physicist, Ames Lab, AEC; mem bd ed consults, Electronic Assocs, Inc; consult, Midwest Res Inst; mem educ comt, Am Fedn Info Processing Socs, 68-; mem, Comput Sci Bd, 72-; vchmn, Comput Sci Conf Bd, 75-76, chmn, 76-77. *Mem:* Am Phys Soc; Asn Comput Mach; Inst Elec & Electronics Eng; AAAS. *Res:* Design of logical control systems and digital computer systems; pattern recognition and adaptive logic. *Mailing Add:* 2233 Hamilton Dr Ames IA 50014-8210

STEWART, ROBERT WILLIAM, PHYSICS. *Current Pos:* from assoc prof to prof, 55-70, hon prof physics, 70-94, ADJ PROF EARTH & OCEAN SCI, UNIV BC, 94- *Personal Data:* b Smoky Lake, Alta, Aug 21, 23; div; c 3. *Educ:* Queen's Univ, Ont, BSc, 45, MSc, 47; Cambridge Univ, PhD(physics), 52. *Hon Degrees:* DSc, McGill Univ, 72. *Honors & Awards:* Patterson Medal, Can Meteorol & Oceanog Soc, 73; Sverdrup Gold Medal, Am Meteorol Soc, 76. *Prof Exp:* Lectr physics, Queen's Univ, Ont, 46; defence sci serv officer, Pac Naval Lab Can, 50-55; dir-gen, Pac Region, Ocean & Aquatic Sci, Can Dept Fisheries & Oceans, 70-79. *Concurrent Pos:* Vis prof, Dalhousie Univ, 60-61 & Harvard Univ, 64; distinguished vis prof, Pa State Univ, 64; Commonwealth vis prof, Cambridge Univ, 67-68; chmn, Joint Organizing Comt, Global Atmospheric Res Prog, 72-78; mem, Comt Climatic Changes & Ocean, 78-, chmn, 83-87; dep min, BC Ministry Univ, Sci & Comm, 79-84; pres, Alta Res Coun, 84-87; interim dir, Ctr Earth & Ocean Physics, Univ Victoria, BC, 87- *Mem:* Fel Royal Soc Can; fel Royal Soc; Can Asn Physicists; Can Meteorol Soc; Int Asn Phys Sci Ocean (pres, 77). *Res:* Turbulence; physical oceanography; air-sea interaction. *Mailing Add:* 4249 Thornhill Crescent Victoria BC V8N 3G6 Can. *Fax:* 250-721-7715, 477-3725

STEWART, ROBERTA A, SYNTHETIC ORGANIC & NATURAL PRODUCTS CHEMISTRY. *Current Pos:* RETIRED. *Personal Data:* b Rochester, NH, Aug 24, 23. *Educ:* Univ NH, BS, 44; Smith Col, MA, 46, PhD, 49. *Prof Exp:* Res assoc chem, Smith Col, 48-49; instr, Wellesley Col, 49-53; from asst prof to prof, Hollins Col, 53-93, chmn, Dept Chem, 63-66 & 69-73, chmn, Div Natural Sci & Math, 67-73 & 85-88, asst to pres, 69-75, dean col, 75-83, assoc dean student acad affairs, 90-92. *Concurrent Pos:* NSF fel, Radcliffe Col, 60-61; Am Coun on Educ fel acad admin, Univ Del, 66-67. *Mem:* Sigma Xi; Am Chem Soc. *Res:* Synthetic experiments in direction of morphine; some reactions of beta tetralone; derivatives of cyclohexanone. *Mailing Add:* 2 Harding St Rochester NH 03867-3721

STEWART, ROBIN KENNY, ANIMAL ECOLOGY. *Current Pos:* from asst prof to assoc prof, 66-77, coordr biol sci div, 72-75, PROF ENTOM & ZOOL, MACDONALD COL, MCGILL UNIV, 77-, CHMN DEPT ENTOM, 75- *Personal Data:* b Ayr, Scotland, May 22, 37; m 64; c 3. *Educ:* Glasgow Univ, BS, 61, PhD(entom), 66. *Prof Exp:* Asst lectr agr zool, Glasgow Univ, 63-64. *Concurrent Pos:* Consult, Can Pac Investment, 74-75 & UN Develop Proj, 75- *Mem:* Can Entom Soc; British Ecol Soc. *Res:* Agricultural zoology; ecology; entomology; integrated control. *Mailing Add:* National Resources MacDonald Stewart Bldg Rm M52-083 MacDonald Col 21111 Lakeshore Rd Ste Anne de Bellevue PQ H9X 3V9 Can

STEWART, ROSS, PHYSICAL ORGANIC CHEMISTRY. *Current Pos:* RETIRED. *Personal Data:* b Vancouver, BC, Mar 16, 24; m 46; c 2. *Educ:* Univ BC, BA, 46, MA, 48; Univ Wash, PhD, 54. *Prof Exp:* Lectr chem, Univ BC, 47-49; lectr, Can Serv Col, Royal Roads, 49-51, from asst prof to assoc prof, 51-55; from asst prof to prof, Univ BC, 55-94. *Mem:* Fel Royal Soc Can; fel Chem Inst Can. *Res:* Organic oxidation mechanisms; protonation of weak organic bases; general acid catalysis; ionization of weak acids in strongly basic solution. *Mailing Add:* Dept Chem Univ BC 2075 Westbrook Pl Vancouver BC V6T 1W5 Can

STEWART, RUTH CAROL, MATHEMATICS. *Current Pos:* PROF MATH, MONTCLAIR STATE UNIV, 64- *Personal Data:* b Englewood, NJ, Dec 18, 28. *Educ:* Rutgers Univ, AB, 50, MA, 63, EdD(math educ), 69. *Prof Exp:* Dir music, High Sch, NJ, 50-53; instr, Wiesbaden Am High Sch, Ger, 54-57; chmn dept math, Frankfurt Am High Sch, Ger, 58-62 & 63-64. *Mem:* Math Asn Am. *Res:* Mathematics in areas of algebra and analysis; mathematics education in areas of curriculum and instruction. *Mailing Add:* Dept Math Montclair State Univ Upper Montclair NJ 07043

STEWART, SCOTT DAVID, INTEGRATED PEST MANAGEMENT, BEHAVIORAL ECOLOGY. *Current Pos:* ASST ENTOM SPECIALIST, MISS STATE UNIV, 95- *Personal Data:* b Norfolk, Nebr, Apr 1, 62; m 84, Marilyn G Moore; c Jake. *Educ:* Univ Northern Iowa, BA, 84; Tex A&M Univ, MS, 87; Auburn Univ, PhD(entom), 93. *Prof Exp:* Fel, Auburn Univ, 93-95. *Mem:* Entom Soc Am; Am Peanut Res & Educ Soc; Sigma Xi. *Res:* Behavioral ecology of insects and how it pertains to management of crop pests; developing pest management strategies based on population ecology of pests and natural enemies. *Mailing Add:* Miss State Univ Cent Miss Res & Ext Ctr 1320 Seven Springs Rd Raymond MS 39154. *Fax:* 334-844-5005

STEWART, SHELTON E, BOTANY, ZOOLOGY. *Current Pos:* PROF BIOL, LANDER COL, 66- *Personal Data:* b Sanford, NC, Oct 1, 34; m 65; c 1. *Educ:* ECarolina Col, BS, 56; Univ NC, MA, 59; Univ Ga, PhD(bot), 66. *Prof Exp:* Teacher, Pine Forest High Sch, 56-57; prof sci, Ferrum Jr Col, 59; prof biol, Lander Col, 59-63; instr bot, Univ Ga, 64-65. *Mem:* AAAS. *Res:* Plant taxonomy; plant biosystematics. *Mailing Add:* 125 W Laurel Ave Greenwood SC 29649

STEWART, T BONNER, VETERINARY PARASITOLOGY. *Current Pos:* PROF PARASITOL, SCH VET MED, LA STATE UNIV, 79- *Personal Data:* b Sao Paulo, Brazil, Nov 24, 24; US citizen; m 56; c 4. *Educ:* Univ Md, BS, 49; Auburn Univ, MS, 53; Univ Ill, Urbana, PhD(vet med sci), 63. *Prof Exp:* Parasitologist, USDA, Ala, 50-53 & Ga Coastal Plain Exp Sta, 53-60; fel, Univ Ill, Urbana, 60-62; res parasitologist, Animal Parasite Res Lab, Ga Coastal Plain Exp Sta, USDA, 63-64, supvry zoologist, 64-79. *Concurrent Pos:* Vis prof, Rural Fed Univ, Rio de Janeiro, 86, Fed Univ, Rio Grande du Sol, Brazil, 86. *Mem:* AAAS; World Asn Advan Vet Parasitol; Am Soc Parasitol; Soc Protozool; Wildlife Dis Asn. *Res:* Life history of Cooperia punctata; gastrointestinal parasites of cattle; eradication of the kidneyworm of swine; beetles as intermediate hosts of nematodes; strongyloides ransomi of swine; ecology of swine parasites; perinatal infection of host by nematode parasites; anthelmintics for swine; host nutrition and parasite interaction. *Mailing Add:* Dept Microbiol & Parasitol Sch Vet Med La State Univ Baton Rouge LA 70803

STEWART, TERRY SANFORD, ANIMAL BREEDING, SYSTEMS ANALYSIS. *Current Pos:* PROF ANIMAL SCI, PURDUE UNIV, 77- *Personal Data:* b West Palm Beach, Fla, Feb 28, 51; m 74; c 3. *Educ:* Univ Fla, BSA, 72, MSA, 74; Tex A&M Univ, PhD(animal genetics), 77. *Prof Exp:* Grad asst animal genetics, dept animal sci, Univ Fla, 73-74; res asst, Animal Sci Dept, Tex A&M Univ, 74-77. *Mem:* Am Soc Animal Sci; Am Genetics Asn; Biomet Soc; Am Regist Cert Animal Scientists. *Res:* Animal systems analysis; animal genetics; biometrics; species, beef cattle and swine. *Mailing Add:* Dept Animal Sci Purdue Univ West Lafayette IN 47907-1968

STEWART, THOMAS, ORGANIC CHEMISTRY. *Current Pos:* SR SCIENTIST ORG SYNTHESIS, RES DIV, ROHM & HAAS CO, 68- *Personal Data:* b Leith, Scotland, Nov 25, 40. *Educ:* Heriot-Watt Univ, BS, 63; Glasgow Univ, PhD(org chem), 66. *Prof Exp:* Fel org synthesis, Calif Inst Technol, 66-67 & Glasgow Univ, 67-68. *Concurrent Pos:* Res sect mgr, Polymer Technol Res. *Mem:* Am Chem Soc. *Res:* Synthesis of acrylic monomers and polymerization inhibition. *Mailing Add:* 4984 Gayman Rd Doylestown PA 18901

STEWART, THOMAS HENRY MCKENZIE, INTERNAL MEDICINE, IMMUNOLOGY. *Current Pos:* lectr, Univ Ottawa, 64-66, asst prof, 66-72, assoc prof, 72-77, PROF MED, UNIV OTTAWA, 77- *Personal Data:* b Hertfordshire, Eng, Aug 17, 30; Can citizen; m 60; c 4. *Educ:* Univ Edinburgh, MB, ChB, 55; FRCP(C), 62. *Prof Exp:* House officer surg, All Saints Hosp, Chatham, Eng, 55-56; house officer med, Eastern Gen Hosp, Edinburgh, Scotland, 56 & Westminster Hosp, London, Ont, 58-60; resident, Ottawa Gen Hosp, 61-62; lectr nuclear med, Univ Mich, Ann Arbor, 63-64. *Concurrent Pos:* Teaching fel, Path Inst, McGill Univ, 60-61; res fel hemat, Univ Ottawa, 62-63. *Mem:* Can Soc Immunol; Can Soc Clin Invest; Soc Nuclear Med; Am Asn Cancer Res. *Res:* Immunology of cancer; host-tumor relationships; immunochemotherapy of human cancer; immunology of inflammatory bowel disease. *Mailing Add:* 1 Mt Pleasant Ave Ottawa ON K1S 0L6 Can

STEWART, W(ARREN) E(ARL), TRANSPORT PHENOMENA, NUMERICAL METHODS. *Current Pos:* from asst prof to assoc prof, 56-61, chmn dept, 73-78, PROF CHEM ENG, UNIV WIS-MADISON, 61- *Personal Data:* b Whitewater, Wis, July 3, 24; m 47, Jean Potter; c Marilyn, David, Douglas, Carol, Margaret & Mary J. *Educ:* Univ Wis, BS, 45, MS, 47; Mass Inst Technol, ScD(chem eng), 51. *Honors & Awards:* Alpha Chi Sigma Res Award, Am Inst Chem Engrs, 81, Comput Chem Eng Award, 85; Chem Eng Div Lectr Award, Am Soc Eng Educ, 83; E V Murphree Award in Indust & Eng Chem, Am Chem Soc, 89. *Prof Exp:* Instr chem eng, Mass Inst Technol, 48; proj chem engr, Sinclair Res Labs, Inc, 50-56. *Concurrent Pos:* Consult & vis prof, Univ Nac de La Plata, 62; mem, Math Res Ctr, Univ Wis, 78-86; McFarland-Bascom Prof, 83- *Mem:* Nat Acad Eng; fel Am Inst Chem Engrs; Sigma Xi; Am Soc Eng Educ; Am Chem Soc. *Res:* Transport phenomena; chemical reactor modelling; multicomponent mass transfer; modelling of distillation systems; weighted residual methods; parameter estimation; boundary layer theory; pulmonary perfusion/ventilation distribution estimation; fusion reactor engineering; ventilation and energy transport in animal fur; heat and mass transfer. *Mailing Add:* 2004 Eng Hall 1415 Eng Dr Univ Wis Madison WI 53706. *Fax:* 608-262-5434

STEWART, WILLIAM ANDREW, NEUROSURGERY. *Current Pos:* ASST PROF, DEPT NEUROSURG, HEALTH SCI CTR, STATE UNIV NY, SYRACUSE, 67- *Personal Data:* b Liberty Center, Ohio, Apr 6, 33; m 60; c 6. *Educ:* Miami Univ, AB, 54; Ohio State Univ, MD, 58. *Prof Exp:* Chief neurosurg, USS Repose AH 16, 66-67; reader neurosurg, Fac Health Sci, Univ Ife, Nigeria, 74-75. *Concurrent Pos:* Clin assoc prof, Dept Neurosurg, Health Sci Ctr, State Univ NY, Syracuse; chmn bd prof med conduct, NY Dept Health. *Mem:* Cong Neurol Surgeons; fel Am Col Surgeons; Am Asn Neurol Surgeons. *Res:* Trigeminal nerve; head injury. *Mailing Add:* 725 Irving Ave Syracuse NY 13210-1603

STEWART, WILLIAM C, MEDICAL & SURGICAL TREATMENT OF GLAUCOMA, GLAUCOMA RESEARCH. *Current Pos:* ASSOC PROF OPHTHAL, MED UNIV SC, 87- *Personal Data:* b New Orleans, La, June 14, 55; m 81, Jeanette Adams. *Educ:* Southern Methodist Univ, BA, 77; Southwestern Med Sch, MD, 81. *Mem:* Fel Am Acad Ophthal; Am Glaucoma Soc; Asn Res Vision & Ophthal; Prevent Blindness Am. *Res:* Clinical and basic science investigations of the results of glaucoma surgery (both conventional and laser surgery); Studies of visual function, mechanisms of chronic open-angle and low-tension glaucoma and glaucoma drug study trials (management and development). *Mailing Add:* Med Univ SC Storm Eye Inst 171 Ashley Ave Charleston SC 29425-2236. *Fax:* 803-792-4854

STEWART, WILLIAM HENRY, APPLIED STATISTICS. *Personal Data:* b Okalahoma City, Okla, Feb 9, 49; m 72; c 3. *Educ:* Univ Okla, BA, 71, MA, 74; Ore State Univ, PhD(statist), 79. *Prof Exp:* Asst prof statist, Okla State Univ, 78-84. *Mem:* Am Statist Asn; Biomet Soc. *Res:* Development of statistical methods for survival experiments with grouped data; general methods for categorical data with ordered classifications. *Mailing Add:* 4104 NW 75th St Kansas City MO 64151

STEWART, WILLIAM HOGUE, JR, PHYSICS. *Current Pos:* Res physicist, Milliken Res Corp, 66-71, sr res physicist, 71-74, res assoc, 74-79, SR SCIENTIST, MILLIKEN RES CORP, 79- *Personal Data:* b Mullins, SC, Dec 25, 36; m 59, Anne E Rogers; c Joyce E (Tambe), William H III & LeRoy M. *Educ:* The Citadel, BSEE, 59; Univ Cincinnati, MS, 61; Clemson Univ, PhD(physics), 64. *Prof Exp:* Physicist, Lewis Res Ctr NASA, 64-66. *Mem:* Electromagnetics Soc. *Res:* Fiber physics; static electricity and ion physics; paramagnetic resonance spectroscopy; solid state diffusion; x-ray diffraction and spectroscopy; nonlinear servomechanisms; digitally controlled machine design; Millitron ink jet printers. *Mailing Add:* PO Box 1927 Spartanburg SC 29304-1927. *Fax:* 864-573-2417

STEWART, WILLIAM HUFFMAN, MEDICINE. *Current Pos:* chancellor, 69-74, prof pediat & head dept, 73-77, HEAD DEPT PREV MED & PUB HEALTH, MED CTR, LA STATE UNIV, NEW ORLEANS, 77- *Personal Data:* b Minneapolis, Minn, May 19, 21; m 46; c 2. *Educ:* Univ Minn, 39-41; La State Univ, MD, 45; Am Bd Pediat, dipl, 52. *Hon Degrees:* Numerous from US univs & insts, 66-69. *Prof Exp:* Resident pediatrician, Charity Hosp, New Orleans, 48-50; pvt pract, 50-51; epidemiologist, Commun Dis Ctr, USPHS, 51-53, actg chief heart dis control prog, 54-55, chief, 55-56, asst dir, Nat Heart Inst, 56-57, asst to surgeon gen, 57-58, chief div pub health methods, Off Surgeon Gen, 57-61 & div community health serv, 61-63, asst to spec asst to secy health & med affairs, 63-65, dir, Nat Heart Inst, 65, surgeon gen, 65-69. *Concurrent Pos:* Mem tech adv bd, Milbank Fund & adv med bd, Leonard Wood Mem; secy, Dept of Health & Human Resources, State of La, 74-77. *Mem:* AAAS; Am Pub Health Asn; Am Acad Pediat; Am Col Prev Med; Asn Teachers Prev Med. *Res:* Epidemiology; medical administration. *Mailing Add:* 219 W Gatehouse Dr Apt B Metairie LA 70001-2030

STIBBS, GERALD DENIKE, dentistry; deceased, see previous edition for last biography

STIBITZ, GEORGE ROBERT, medical research; deceased, see previous edition for last biography

STICH, HANS F, cell biology, genetics; deceased, see previous edition for last biography

STICHA, ERNEST AUGUST, METALLURGICAL ENGINEERING. *Current Pos:* RETIRED. *Personal Data:* b Baltimore, Md, Mar 27, 11; m 39, Helen Koberna; c Philip E & Paul J. *Educ:* Ill Inst Technol, BS, 33; Univ Mich, MSE, 36. *Prof Exp:* Supv engr, Crane Co, 36-59; chief metallurgist, Edward Valves, Inc Div, Rockwell Mfg Co, 59-65; sr res engr, Amoco Corp, 65-76. *Concurrent Pos:* Consult, 76- *Mem:* Am Soc Testing & Mat; Am Soc Metals; Sigma Xi. *Res:* Creep of metals; metallurgy of high temperature materials. *Mailing Add:* 715 N Kensington Ave LaGrange Park IL 60526

STICHT, FRANK DAVIS, PHARMACOLOGY. *Current Pos:* From instr to prof, 61-84, EMER PROF PHARMACOL, UNIV TENN, MEMPHIS, 84- *Personal Data:* b Plattsburg, Miss, June 14, 19; m 41; c 2. *Educ:* Univ Miss, BS Pharm, 48; Baylor Univ, DDS, 56; Univ Tenn, Memphis, MS, 65. *Mem:* Am Soc Pharmacol & Exp Therapeut. *Res:* Autonomic and cardiovascular pharmacology; influence of drugs on the blood pressure within the tooth pulp; relationship of prostaglandins to periodontal disease; actions of calcium antagonists on veins. *Mailing Add:* 1795 Juniper Valley Dr Apt 3 Cordova TN 38018-5022

STICKEL, DELFORD LEFEW, SURGERY. *Current Pos:* Asst surg, 57-59, from instr to assoc prof, 59-72, PROF SURG, MED CTR, DUKE UNIV, 72-, ASSOC DIR HOSP, 72- *Personal Data:* b Falling Waters, WVa, Dec 12, 27; m 52; c 1. *Educ:* Duke Univ, AB, 49, MD, 53; Am Bd Surg, dipl, 63; Bd Thoracic Surg, dipl, 63. *Concurrent Pos:* Markle scholar & NIH career develop award, 62; attend physician, Durham Vet Admin Hosp, 65-66, chief surg serv, 66-68, chief staff, 70-72; consult, Watts Hosp, Durham, 66-70 & NC Eye & Human Tissue Bank, 69. *Mem:* AMA; Soc Univ Surgeons; Am Col Surgeons; Southern Surg Asn; Transplantation Soc; Am Soc Transplant Surg. *Res:* Clinical renal transplantation. *Mailing Add:* Dept Surg Duke Hosp Box 3917 Durham NC 27710

STICKELS, CHARLES A, METALLURGICAL ENGINEERING. *Current Pos:* CONSULT, ENVIRON RES INST MICH, 91- *Personal Data:* b Detroit, Mich, Apr 6, 33; m 57, Patricia J Forbes; c Charles F. *Educ:* Univ Mich, BS, 56, MS, 60, MA, 62, PhD(metall eng), 63. *Prof Exp:* Mem staff, Ford Motor Co, 63-85, prin res engr, 85-91. *Mem:* Fel Am Soc Metals Int; Am Inst Mining Metall & Petrol Engrs; Sigma Xi; Soc Automotive Engrs. *Res:* Metals processing including heat treatment. *Mailing Add:* 4620 Cottonwood Dr Ann Arbor MI 48108

STICKER, ROBERT EARL, ORGANIC CHEMISTRY. *Current Pos:* res chemist, 65-76, SR RES CHEMIST, NIAGARA CHEM DIV, FMC CORP, 76- *Personal Data:* b New York, NY, Mar 4, 30; m 57; c 3. *Educ:* Cornell Univ, AB, 53; Columbia Univ, AM, 57; Univ Kans, PhD(pinane chem), 65. *Prof Exp:* Res chemist, Eastman Kodak Co, 57-60. *Mem:* Am Chem Soc; Int Soc Heterocyclic Chem. *Res:* Terpenes; heterocycles; surfactants; herbicides; plant regulators; fungicides. *Mailing Add:* 514 Edgewood Pl Ithaca NY 14850-4426

STICKLAND, DAVID PETER, ELEMENTARY PARTICLE PHYSICS. *Current Pos:* Res asst, 80-81, instr, 81-82, ASST PROF PHYSICS, PRINCETON UNIV, 82-; RES, GENEVA, SWITZ. *Personal Data:* b Norwich, Eng, Aug 22, 54; m 79; c 1. *Educ:* Univ Bradford, BTech, 77; Univ Bristol, PhD(physics), 81. *Mem:* Am Phys Soc. *Mailing Add:* Dept Physics Princeton Univ PO Box 708 Princeton NJ 08544

STICKLE, GENE P, PROCESS ENGINEERING, PROJECT ENGINEERING. *Current Pos:* RETIRED. *Personal Data:* b New Castle, Pa, Apr 11, 29; m 54, Cecil Pressnell; c William & Douglas. *Educ:* Univ Tenn, BS, 53, MS, 54. *Prof Exp:* Res engr, Squibb Inst Med Res, Olin Mathieson Chem Corp, 54-61, sect head, Fermentation Mfg Dept, 61-62, sect head microbiol develop pilot plant, Squibb Inst Med Res, E R Squibb & Sons, Inc, 62-66, sect head chem develop pilot plant, 67-69, asst dept dir chem develop, 69-74, antibiotics mfg develop mgr, 74-77, dir antibiotics process eng, 77-81, tech eng dir, 81-90. *Concurrent Pos:* Lectr, Ctr Prof Advan, 81-85. *Mem:* Am Chem Soc; Am Inst Chem Eng; Sigma Xi. *Res:* Fermentation technology, scaleup, process design and development; plant start-up and manufacture of antibiotics, steroids, vitamins and enzymes; technical liaison; organic synthetics manufacture; pharmaceutical process engineering. *Mailing Add:* 754 Shade Pressnell Rd Tazewell TX 37879

STICKLER, DAVID BRUCE, COMBUSTION, FLUID MECHANICS. *Current Pos:* res scientist, 73-78, chmn aerophys, 78-82, CHIEF SCIENTIST, ENERGY TECHNOL, 82-, DIR, INNOVATIVE RES, AVCO RES LAB, INC, 87- *Personal Data:* b Taunton, Mass, Nov 17, 41; m 64; c 3. *Educ:* Mass Inst Technol, SB & SM, 64, PhD(hybrid combustion), 68. *Prof Exp:* Asst prof aeronaut & astronaut, Mass Inst Technol, 68-73. *Concurrent Pos:* Consult lasers & energy, 68-73. *Mem:* Combustion Inst; assoc fel Am Inst Aeronaut & Astronaut. *Res:* Heterogeneous combustion; turbulent combustion and flow; coal combustion and gasification; hybrid combustion; slag flow in power systems; polymer pyrolysis; pollution control; glass manufacture; metal refining. *Mailing Add:* 15 Indian Hill Carlisle MA 01741

STICKLER, DAVID COLLIER, ACOUSTICS, APPLIED MATHEMATICS. *Current Pos:* sr res scientist, 77-80, RES PROF, NY UNIV, 80- *Personal Data:* b Piqua, Ohio, Apr 12, 33; c 4. *Educ:* Ohio State Univ, BSc, 56, MSc, 59, PhD(elec eng), 64. *Prof Exp:* Res assoc elec eng, Ohio State Univ, 55-65; mem tech staff, Bell Tel Labs, Inc, 65-72; sr engr, Systs Control, Inc, 72-73; sr res assoc, Pa State Univ, 73-77. *Res:* Electromagnetic theory; heat transfer; thermoelastic effects mechanics. *Mailing Add:* Math Dept NJ Inst Technol 323 Martin Luther King Blvd Newark NJ 07102-1824

STICKLER, FRED CHARLES, AGRONOMY, CROP ECOLOGY. *Current Pos:* res agronomist, Deere & Co, 64-71, prod planner, 71-73, mgr agr equip planning, 73-76, dir, Tech Ctr, 76-80, DIR, PROD & MKT PLANNING, DEERE & CO, 80- *Personal Data:* b Villisca, Iowa, Dec 11, 31; m 55; c 3. *Educ:* Iowa State Univ, BS, 53, PhD, 58; Kans State Univ, MS, 55. *Prof Exp:* From asst prof to assoc prof agron, Kans State Univ, 58-64. *Mem:* Sigma Xi. *Res:* Ecological aspects of crop production and management; crop management for improved mechanization. *Mailing Add:* 7108 36th Ave B Ct Moline IL 61265-8045

STICKLER, GUNNAR B, PEDIATRICS, PEDIATRIC NEPHROLOGY. *Current Pos:* RETIRED. *Personal Data:* b Peterskirchen, Ger, June 13, 25; US citizen; m 56, Duci M Kronenbitter; c Katarina (Lovaas) & George D. *Educ:* Univ Munich, MD, 49; Univ Minn, PhD(pediat), 58; Am Bd Pediat, cert, 57, cert pediat & nephrol, 74. *Honors & Awards:* Founders Awawrd, Midwest Soc Ped Res, 96. *Prof Exp:* Resident clin path, Krankenhaus III Orden, Munich, 50; resident path, Univ Munich, 50-51; intern, Mountainside Hosp, Montclair, 51-52; resident fel pediat, Mayo Found Grad Sch, 53-56; chief pediat, US Army Hosp, Munich, 56; sr res scientist, Roswell Park Mem, Buffalo, 56-57; instr pediat, Univ Buffalo, 57; asst to staff, Mayo Found Grad Sch, Mayo Clin, 57-58, from instr to prof pediat, 58-73, sect head pediat, 69-74, prof pediat & chmn dept, 74-80, consult pediat, Mayo Clin, 58-89. *Mem:* Am Acad Pediat; Am Soc Pediat. *Res:* Hypophosphatemic and various other forms of rickets; nephrotic syndrome; immunology of renal disease; growth failure in various disease processes; treatment of acute otitis media; hereditary bone diseases; urinary tract infection; natural history studies in chronic diseases; inflammatory bowel disease; study of anxieties in parents and children; surveys of parents concerns and children's concerns; hereditary progressive axthrophtalmopathy. *Mailing Add:* Emer Off Mayo Clinic Rochester MN 55902. *Fax:* 507-284-5036

STICKLER, WILLIAM CARL, ORGANIC CHEMISTRY. *Current Pos:* from asst prof to assoc prof chem, Univ Denver, 47-63, prof, 63-83, actg chmn dept, 71-72 & 83-84, mem teaching fac, 83-86, EMER PROF CHEM, UNIV DENVER, 83- *Personal Data:* b Stuttgart, Ger, Jan 25, 18; nat US; m 42, 58, 68, Margarete Schmidt; c 4. *Educ:* Columbia Univ, AB, 41, AM, 44, PhD(chem), 47. *Prof Exp:* Asst chem, Columbia Univ, 41-44, 46-47. *Concurrent Pos:* Instr, Sarah Lawrence Col, 43-44 & Hofstra Col, 46-47; vis prof & lectr, Univ Munich & Munich Tech Univ, 56-58; NSF fac fel, 57-58;

vis prof, Univ Hamburg, 71 & 80; adj fac, Front Range Community Col, Westminster, Colo, 88- *Mem:* Am Chem Soc; Royal Soc Chem; Soc Ger Chem; Sigma Xi. *Res:* Organic nitrogen chemistry; stereochemistry; reaction mechanisms; natural products and physiologically important compounds; sterane synthesis. *Mailing Add:* Dept Chem Univ Denver Denver CO 80208-2436. Fax: 303-871-2254

STICKLEY, C(ARLISLE) MARTIN, ELECTRO-OPTICS, MATERIALS. *Current Pos:* PROF ELEC & COMPUT ENG, UNIV CENT FLA, 90- *Personal Data:* b Washington, DC, Oct 30, 33; m 58; c 3. *Educ:* Univ Cincinnati, BSEE, 57; Mass Inst Technol, MSEE, 58; Northeastern Univ, PhD, 64. *Prof Exp:* Mem, Transistor Circuits Br, Commun Sci Lab, Air Force Cambridge Res Lab, Laurence G Hanscom Field, Mass, 58-62 & Laser Physics Br, 62-65, chief, Laser Physics Br, Optical Physics Lab, 65-71; dir, Mat Sci Off, Defense Advan Res Proj Agency, Dept Defense, 71-76; dir inertial confinement fusion, US Dept Energy, 76-79; vpres & gen mgr advan technol, BDM Corp, 79-90. *Concurrent Pos:* Assoc mem, Spec Group Optical Lasers, comt laser coord, Dept Defense, 64-71; vis prof, Univ Rio Grande do Sul, Brazil, 66; prog chmn, Third Classified Conf Laser Tech, 67; co-chmn, Conf Laser Eng & Appln, 71; chmn, Inst Elec & Electronics Engrs, OSA Conf Inertial Fusion, 78; subcomt prog chmn, Optical Mats at CLEO, 89. *Mem:* Fel Inst Elec & Electronics Engrs; Sigma Xi; Soc Photo-Optical Instrumentation Engrs. *Res:* Optical fibers, sources and couplers; inertial confinement fusion; electro optical and semiconductor materials; laser devices; optical processing; communications technol; optical fiber sensors; advanced nuclear reactors. *Mailing Add:* 181 Stovin Ave Winter Park FL 32789

STICKNEY, ALAN CRAIG, USE OF CALCULATORS & COMPUTERS IN TEACHING OF MATHEMATICS. *Current Pos:* from asst prof to assoc prof math, 79-91, chmn, Dept Math & Comput Sci, 82-88, PROF MATH, WITTENBERG UNIV, 91- *Personal Data:* b Columbus, Ohio, Apr 28, 47; m 70, Ellen Rector; c Carolyn & Laura. *Educ:* Mich State Univ, BS, 69; Univ Mich, MS, 70, PhD(math), 75. *Prof Exp:* Instr math, Mich State Univ, 75-77; hons lectr math, Univ Del, 77-79. *Concurrent Pos:* Prin investr, NSF ILI grant, Math Dept, Wittenberg Univ, 90-91. *Mem:* Am Math Soc; Math Asn Am; Sigma Xi. *Res:* Use of graphing calculators and computers in the teaching of mathematics; undergraduate mathematics and computer science education; mathematics placement. *Mailing Add:* Dept Math & Comput Sci Wittenberg Univ Springfield OH 45501-0720. E-Mail: acs@wittenberg.edu

STICKNEY, ALDEN PARKHURST, MARINE ECOLOGY. *Current Pos:* RETIRED. *Personal Data:* b Providence, RI, Sept 7, 22; m 51; c 2. *Educ:* Univ RI, BSc, 48; Harvard Univ, MA, 51. *Prof Exp:* Fishery aide, US Fish & Wildlife Serv, 51-53; res asst, Stirling Sch Med, Yale Univ, 53-54; chief, Atlantic Salmon Invest, US Fish & Wildlife Serv, 54-60, fishery res biologist, Fishery Biol Lab, Bur Com Fisheries, Maine, 60-72 & Biol Lab, Nat Marine Fisheries Serv, 72-73; marine resources scientist, Maine Dept Marine Resources, 74-82. *Mem:* Ecol Soc Am; Am Fisheries Soc. *Res:* Estuarine ecology; shellfish biology; physiology of larval shellfish; behavior and ecology of sea herring and pandalid shrimp. *Mailing Add:* Cameron Point Rd West Southport ME 04576

STICKNEY, JANICE LEE, PHARMACOLOGY, CARDIOVASCULAR PHYSIOLOGY. *Current Pos:* DIR REGULATORY AFFAIRS, STERITECH, INC, CONCORD, CALIF, 92- *Personal Data:* b Tallahassee, Fla, July 21, 41. *Educ:* Oberlin Col, AB, 62; Univ Mich, PhD(pharmacol), 67. *Prof Exp:* Acad Senate grants, Univ Calif, San Francisco, 68 & 69; from instr to asst prof pharmacol, Sch Med, 69-72; from asst prof to prof, Mich State Univ, 72-81; sr scientist, GD Searle & Co, 81-83, dir, Cardiovas Prod, Off Sci Affairs, 87-92. *Concurrent Pos:* Training fel, 67-68; Bay Area Heart Asn grant, Univ Calif, San Francisco, 69-70; Nat Heart & Lung Inst, Nat Inst Drug Abuse & Mich Heart Asn grants, consult, Food & Drug Admin, 71-75 & 76-80 & Nat Inst Drug Admin, 87; mem, Special Study Sect, NIH, 78-79, Nat Adv Environ Health Sci Coun, 79-82; panelist, NSF, 76 & 81; pharmacol rev comt, Nat Inst Gen Med Sci, 84-87. *Mem:* AAAS; Pharmacol Soc Can; NY Acad Sci; Am Soc Pharmacol & Exp Therapeut. *Res:* Cardiovascular pharmacology, especially role of the sympathetic nervous system in the cardiac arrhythmias produced by large doses of digitalis, with emphasis on the mechanisms by which cardiac glycosides produce sympathetic effects; general cardiovascular effects of opiate agonists; antiarrhythmic drugs; calcium channel blocking agents; cardiac toxicology; cardiotorics. *Mailing Add:* JLS Assoc 6114 La Salle Ave Suite 263 Oakland CA 94611

STICKNEY, PALMER BLAINE, POLYMER CHEMISTRY. *Current Pos:* RETIRED. *Personal Data:* b Columbus, Ohio, Nov 1, 15; m 37; c 4. *Educ:* Ohio State Univ, AB, 38, PhD(phys chem), 49. *Prof Exp:* Res engr, Battelle Mem Inst, 40-42, 46, 49-52, asst chief, Rubber & Plastics Div, 52-60, chief polymer res, 60-68, tech adv, 68-73; prof, Wilberforce Univ, 73-81. *Mem:* Am Chem Soc; Am Asn Univ Profs. *Res:* Polymerization and processing of polymers. *Mailing Add:* 2870 Halstead Rd Columbus OH 43221

STICKSEL, PHILIP RICE, METEOROLOGY. *Current Pos:* RETIRED. *Personal Data:* b Cincinnati, Ohio, Feb 15, 30; m 53, Ann Huffman; c Rosalyn (Ries) & Kirsti (Contreras). *Educ:* Univ Cincinnati, BS, 52; Fla State Univ, MS, 59, PhD(meteorol), 66. *Prof Exp:* Jr develop engr, Goodyear Aircraft Corp, 53-54; res assoc meteorol, Fla State Univ, 64-65; res meteorologist, Environ Sci Serv Admin, 65-69 & Nat Air Pollution Control Admin, 67-69; sr meteorologist to prin res scientist, Battelle Mem Inst, 69-96. *Concurrent Pos:* Consult, Battelle Memorial Inst, 96- *Mem:* Am Meteorol Soc; Sigma Xi. *Res:* Air pollution meteorology and education; upper atmosphere ozone; air quality management; ozone transport; visible emissions; science education. *Mailing Add:* 1636 Park Trail Westerville OH 43081

STIDD, BENTON MAURICE, PALEOBOTANY, HORTICULTURE. *Current Pos:* chmn, 80-89, PROF BIOL SCI, WESTERN ILL UNIV, 70- *Personal Data:* b Bloomington, Ind, June 30, 36; m 58; c Beth, Laura, Kelly, Faye & Reva. *Educ:* Purdue Univ, BS, 58; Emporia State Univ, MS, 63; Univ Ill, PhD(bot), 68. *Prof Exp:* Teacher, Wheatland High Sch, 58-62; partic, NSF Acad Year Inst & Res Participation Prog Teachers, Emporia State Univ, 62-63; teacher, NKnox High Sch, 63-64; asst prof anat, morphol & paleobot, Univ Minn, Minneapolis, 68-70. *Concurrent Pos:* Univ Minnesota Grad Sch res grant, 68-69; Sigma Xi res grants-in-aid, 69-70; res coun grant, Western Ill Univ, 71-72, 80-81 & 85-86; NSF res grant, 74 & 76, NSF res grant, Res Undergrad Inst, 86; Nat Endowment Humanities, 82; US Dept Educ, 87. *Mem:* Nat Ctr Sci Educ; Paleontogical Soc; Bot Soc Am; Int Orgn Paleobot; Int Soc Hist, Philos & Social Studies of Biol; Soc Syst Biol. *Res:* Paleozoic paleobotany, especially Carboniferous coal ball plants. *Mailing Add:* Dept Biol Sci Western Ill Univ Macomb IL 61455

STIDD, CHARLES KETCHUM, METEOROLOGY. *Current Pos:* CONSULT, 79- *Personal Data:* b Independence, Ore, Aug 12, 18; m 42, Barbara Jean Mills; c John M & Charles W. *Educ:* Ore State Univ, BS, 41. *Prof Exp:* Res forecaster, US Weather Bur, 47-55; self employed, 55-62; res assoc meteorol & hydrol, Univ Nev, Reno, 62-71; specialist meteorol, Scripps Inst Oceanog, Univ Calif, San Diego, 71-79. *Mem:* Am Geophys Union; Sigma Xi. *Res:* Rainfall and climatic probabilities; general circulation of the atmosphere; moisture, energy and momentum balances; long-range forecasting; el nino. *Mailing Add:* 4005 Carmel View Rd No 61 San Diego CA 92130. E-Mail: stidd@juno.com

STIDHAM, HOWARD DONATHAN, PHYSICAL CHEMISTRY. *Current Pos:* from asst prof to assoc prof, 56-90, PROF CHEM, UNIV MASS, 90- *Personal Data:* b Memphis, Tenn, Sept 14, 25; div. *Educ:* Trinity Col, BS, 50; Mass Inst Technol, PhD, 55. *Prof Exp:* Spectroscopist, Dewey & Almy Chem Co, 55-56. *Mem:* AAAS; Optical Soc Am; Am Phys Soc; Am Chem Soc. *Res:* Molecular spectroscopy; statistical mechanics. *Mailing Add:* Chem Dept Lederle GRC Tower Univ Mass Box 34510 Amherst MA 01003-4510

STIDHAM, SHALER, JR, QUEUEING THEORY, DYNAMIC PROGRAMMING. *Current Pos:* chair, Dept Opers Res, 90-95, PROF OPERS RES, UNIV NC, 86- *Personal Data:* b Washington, DC, Dec 4, 41; m 68, Carolyn Noble; c Christiane W, Dana C & Ann-Elise S. *Educ:* Harvard Col, BA, 63; Case Inst Technol, MS, 64; Stanford Univ, PhD(opers res), 68. *Honors & Awards:* Young Scientist Res Award, Sigma Xi, 78. *Prof Exp:* Asst prof opers res & environ eng, Cornell Univ, 68-75; assoc prof, NC State Univ, 75-79; prof indust eng & opers res, 79-86. *Concurrent Pos:* Consult, Stanford Res Inst, Calif, 68-70; vis prof, Aarhus Univ, 71-72 & Tech Univ Denmark, 77; prin investr, NSF, 73-75, 79-82 & 88-91, NATO, 77 & US Army Res Off, 82-85; vis scholar, Stanford Univ, 75, 79; assoc ed, Operations Res, 76-85, area ed, 85-90, Mgt Sci, 75-81 & Queueing Systems Theory & Applications, 85-; consult, Bell Tel Lab, NJ, 81; vis res fel, Statist Lab, Univ Cambridge, 82-83; overseas fel, Churchill Col, Cambridge; prof invite, INRIA, Sophia-Antipolis, France, 91-92. *Mem:* Inst Oper Res Mgt Sci; Sigma Xi. *Res:* Queueing theory; optimal design and control of queueing systems; applications in manufacturing; transportation and public service systems; computer and communication systems. *Mailing Add:* Opers Res CB 3180 Smith Bldg Chapel Hill NC 27599. E-Mail: sandy_stidham@unc.edu

STIDWORTHY, GEORGE H, BIOCHEMISTRY. *Current Pos:* RETIRED. *Personal Data:* b Viborg, SDak, May 28, 24; m 48, Eloise Burchfield; c Kathryn, Kristin, Sharon & Robin. *Educ:* Univ SDak, BA, 49, MA, 51; Univ Okla, PhD(biochem), 61. *Prof Exp:* Res asst biochem, Okla Med Res Found, 51-53; asst chief, Gen Med Res Lab, Vet Admin Hosp, Oklahoma City, 53-57, chief biochemist, 57-59; chief biochemist, Cancer Res Lab, Vet Admin Hosp, Martinsburg, WVa, 59-64; supvr, Med Res Lab, Vet Admin Hosp, 64-72, chief, Gen Med Res Lab, 72-; asst prof biochem, Sch Med, Boston Univ, 64-84. *Concurrent Pos:* Nat Cancer Inst grant, Vet Admin Hosp, Martinsburg, WVa, 61-65. *Mem:* AAAS; Geront Soc; Tissue Cult Asn; Am Aging Asn. *Res:* Aging effects upon connective tissues; chemistry and biology of the intracellular matrix; in vitro aging of cells in culture; environmental effects in cell metabolism. *Mailing Add:* 48 S Sea Pines Dr Hilton Head Island SC 29928

STIEBER, MICHAEL THOMAS, systematic botany, agrostology, for more information see previous edition

STIEF, LOUIS J, PHOTOCHEMISTRY, ASTROCHEMISTRY. *Current Pos:* sr res fel, Nat Acad Sci-Nat Res Coun, 68-69, aerospace technol chemist, 69-74, head, Space Chem Sect, 74-76, head, Astrochem Br, 76-90, SR SCIENTIST, GODDARD SPACE FLIGHT CTR, NASA, 90- *Personal Data:* b Pottsville, Pa, July 26, 33; div; c Andrew & Lorraine. *Educ:* La Salle Col, BA, 55; Cath Univ, PhD(chem), 60. *Prof Exp:* Asst chem, Cath Univ, 55-59; Nat Acad Sci-Nat Res Coun res fel, Nat Bur Stand, 60-61; NATO fel, Univ Sheffield, 61-62; Dept Sci & Indust Res fel, 62-63; sr chemist, Res Div, Melpar, Inc, 63-65, sr scientist, 65-68. *Concurrent Pos:* Adj prof, Dept Chem, Cath Univ Am, DC, 75-; Res fel, Queen Mary Col, London Univ, 81-82. *Mem:* Am Chem Soc; Royal Soc Chem; Sigma Xi; Am Geophys Union; Am Astron Soc (Div Planetary Sci). *Res:* Vacuum-ultraviolet photochemistry; flash photolysis; interstellar molecules; upper atmosphere studies; planetary atmospheres; chemical kinetics; mass spectrometry of free radicals. *Mailing Add:* Code 690 NASA/Goddard Space Flight Ctr Greenbelt MD 20771

STIEFEL, EDWARD, TRANSITION METAL COORDINATION CHEMISTRY. *Current Pos:* group head, Sect Molecular & Biol Chem, 82-89, SCI AREA LEADER INORG & BIOL CHEM, EXXON RES & ENG CO, 89- *Personal Data:* b Brooklyn, NY, Jan 3, 42; m 65, Jeannette Musco; c Karen. *Educ:* NY Univ, BA, 63; Columbia Univ, MS, 64, PhD(chem), 67. *Prof Exp:* Sr investr, C F Kettering Res Lab, 74-80. *Concurrent Pos:* Vis prof, Princeton Univ, 83, Columbia Univ, 86. *Mem:* Am Chem Soc; Am Soc Biol Chemists; AAAS; NY Acad Sci. *Res:* Metalloenzymes; transition metal sulfide centers; biological nitrogen fixation; internal redox reactions, catalysis, lubrication. *Mailing Add:* Exxon Res & Eng Co Rte 22E Clinton Township Annandale NJ 08801. *Fax:* 908-730-3279; *E-Mail:* eistief@erenj.com

STIEFEL, ROBERT CARL, WASTEWATER MANAGEMENT. *Current Pos:* assoc prof, 71-73, prof & dir, Water Res Ctr, 73-95, EMER PROF CIVIL ENG, OHIO STATE UNIV, 95- *Personal Data:* b Camden, NJ, Feb 12, 34; m 57; c 3. *Educ:* Drexel Univ, BSCE, 57; State Univ Iowa, MS, 59; Rensselear Polytech Inst, PhD(environ eng), 68. *Prof Exp:* From asst prof to assoc prof civil eng, Drexel Inst Technol, 59-66; assoc prof, Northeastern Univ, 66-71. *Concurrent Pos:* Process engr, Roy F Weston & Assoc, 60-66; consult, Domey & Stiefel, 67-71; consult, 71-; chmn, Nat Asn Water Inst Dirs, 81-83. *Mem:* Nat Asn Water Inst Dirs. *Res:* Treatment of industrial wastewaters, water supplies and municipal waste waters. *Mailing Add:* 1491 London Dr Columbus OH 43221

STIEGLER, JAMES O, HIGH TEMPERATURE MATERIALS. *Current Pos:* Res asst, Solid State Div, Oak Ridge Nat Lab, 56-61, res staff mem, Metals & Ceramics Div, 61-63, group leader electron micros, 63-73, group leader radiation effects & microstruct analysis, 73-78, mgr, Mat Sci Sect, 78-81, mgr, Processing Sci & Technol Sect, 81-83, dir, Metals & Ceramics Div, 84-92, ASSOC DIR, OAK RIDGE NAT LAB, 92- *Personal Data:* b Valparaiso, Ind, July 25, 34; m 66, Patricia Burd; c Erik & Karl. *Educ:* Purdue Univ, BS, 56; Univ Tenn, PhD(metall eng), 71. *Honors & Awards:* William Sparagen Award, Am Welding Soc, 75; McKay-Helm Award, Am Welding Soc, 79. *Mem:* Fel Am Soc Metals; Am Ceramic Soc; Am Welding Soc; Am Soc Mech Engrs. *Res:* Design and production of metallic and ceramic materials for high temperature applications through control of processing variables. *Mailing Add:* Oak Ridge Nat Lab PO Box 2008 Oak Ridge TN 37831-6248. *E-Mail:* soj@ornl.gov

STIEGLER, T(HEODORE) DONALD, PROCESS ENGINEERING, MECHANICAL ENGINEERING. *Current Pos:* RETIRED. *Personal Data:* b Baltimore, Md, May 28, 34; m 57, Beth Sutton; c Linda & Sally. *Educ:* Duke Univ, BSME, 56. *Prof Exp:* Engr, E I du Pont de Nemours & Co, 58-63, res engr, 63-65, tech supvr, 65-66, res engr, Spruance Film Tech Lab, 66-73, sr engr, Imaging Systs Dept, 73-92, tech assoc, Films SBU, 92-96. *Res:* Mechanical development associated with the chemical industry; design and development of high speed web handling machinery and equipment for the coating of plastic films; process development associated with the manufacture of packaging films; process safety; process hazard evaluation. *Mailing Add:* 8700 Brown Summit Rd Richmond VA 23235. *E-Mail:* tdstiegler@aol.com

STIEGLITZ, RONALD DENNIS, ENVIRONMENTAL SCIENCE, EDUCATIONAL ADMINISTRATION. *Current Pos:* from asst prof to assoc prof, 76-89, PROF ENVIRON SCI & ASSOC DEAN GRAD STUDIES & RES, UNIV WIS-GREEN BAY, 89- *Personal Data:* b Milwaukee, Wis, Aug 25, 41; m 65, Beverly A Krowas; c Gina, Amy, Tari & Ryan. *Educ:* Univ Wis-Milwaukee, BS, 63; Univ Ill, Urbana, MS, 67, PhD(geol), 70. *Prof Exp:* Teaching asst geol, Univ Wis-Milwaukee, 63-64 & Univ Ill, 64-69; lectr, Univ Wis-Milwaukee, 71-72; geologist, Ohio State Geol Surv, 72-74, head, Regional Geol Sect, Ohio State Geol, 74-76. *Concurrent Pos:* Consult, 81- *Mem:* Asn Ground Water Scientists & Engrs; Soc Econ Paleont & Mineral; Sigma Xi. *Res:* Paleozoic stratigraphy; waste disposal and ground water pollution in Karst areas; quaternary geology. *Mailing Add:* Natural & Appl Scis Univ Wis ES-317 Green Bay WI 54311-7001. *Fax:* 920-465-2718; *E-Mail:* stieglir@uweb.edu

STIEHL, R(OY) THOMAS, JR, ORGANIC CHEMISTRY, SPANDEX CHEMISTRY. *Current Pos:* RETIRED. *Personal Data:* b Hay Springs, Nebr, Jan 27, 28; m 54, June Wade; c Thomas, Patricia & Richard. *Educ:* Univ Nebr, BS, 50, MS, 51; Univ Ill, PhD(org chem), 53. *Prof Exp:* Asst, Univ Nebr, 49-51 & Off Rubber Reserv, Univ Ill, 51-53; res chemist, E I du Pont de Nemours & Co, Inc, 53-68, sr res chemist, 68-85. *Res:* Spandex chemistry; butadiene copolymerization; vinyl monomer synthesis; organophosphorous compounds; textile compounds; textile chemistry; fiber additive chemistry. *Mailing Add:* 400 Ridge Circle Waynesboro VA 22980-5430

STIEHL, RICHARD BORG, BIOLOGY. *Current Pos:* ASST PROF BIOL, SOUTHEAST MO STATE UNIV, 84- *Personal Data:* b Chicago, Ill, Jan 10, 42; m 67; c 1. *Educ:* Southern Ore State Col, BS, 69, MS, 70; Portland State Univ, PhD(environ sci & biol), 78. *Prof Exp:* Instr biol, Mt Hood Community Col, 72-73; lectr, Lewis & Clark Col, 74-75; lectr biol, Univ Wis, Green Bay, 77-80, asst prof biol, 80- *Concurrent Pos:* Researcher, US Fish & Wildlife Serv, 75-77; fel, Lilly Endowment, Inc, 78-79. *Mem:* Am Inst Biol Sci; Am Soc Mammalogists; Am Ornithologists Union. *Res:* Wildlife ecology; corvid biology; predator-prey interactions. *Mailing Add:* 2323 Sublette Ave St Louis MO 63110

STIEHLER, ROBERT D(ANIEL), THERMODYNAMICS & MATERIAL PROPERTIES. *Current Pos:* chemist, Nat Bur Stand, 46-47, chief, Testing & Specif Sect, 47-64, Ploymer Eval Sect, 64-74, reemployed annuitant, 74-81, GUEST WORKER, NAT INST STAND & TECHNOL, 81- *Personal Data:* b Springfield, NY, July 16, 10; m 49, Grace L Vanorder; c Margaret S (Bacon) & John R. *Educ:* Johns Hopkins Univ, PhD(chem), 33. *Honors & Awards:* Silver Medal, US Dept Com, 63; Merit Award, Am Soc Test Mat, 68. *Prof Exp:* Nat Res Coun fel, Calif Inst Technol, 33-34; res fel & asst opthal, Johns Hopkins Med Sch, 34-38; sr scientist, B F Goodrich Co, 39-42; chemist, US Army Quarter master Corps, 42-43; tech asst, Reconstruction Finance Corp, 43-46. *Concurrent Pos:* Consult. *Mem:* Fel AAAS; emer mem Am Chem Soc; emer mem Am Soc Mech Engrs; emer mem Am Soc Qual Control; hon mem Am Soc Test & Mat; emer mem Am Soc Eng Educ. *Res:* Thermal properties of purines; formation of intraocear fluids; rubber vulcanization, rubber test methods; polymer evaluation; US metric study; standards for consumer products. *Mailing Add:* 3234 Quesada St NW Washington DC 20015-1663

STIEHM, E RICHARD, PEDIATRICS, ALLERGY IMMUNOLOGY. *Current Pos:* assoc prof, 69-72, PROF PEDIAT, SCH MED, UNIV CALIF, LOS ANGELES, 72- *Personal Data:* b Milwaukee, Wis, Jan 22, 33; m 58; c 3. *Educ:* Univ Wis-Madison, BS, 54, MD, 57. *Honors & Awards:* Ross Res Award Pediat Res, 71; E Mead Johnson Award Pediat Res, 74. *Prof Exp:* USPHS fels, physiol chem, Univ Wis, 58-59 & pediat immunol, Univ Calif, San Francisco, 63-65; from asst prof to assoc prof pediat, Med Sch, Univ Wis, 65-69. *Concurrent Pos:* Markle scholar acad med, 67. *Mem:* Am Acad Pediat; Am Soc Clin Invest; Soc Pediat Res; Am Asn Immunologists; Am Pediat Soc; Am Acad Allergy & Immunol. *Res:* Pediatric immunology, immunodeficiency disease; newborn defense mechanisms; human gamma globulin; immunology of malnutrition; clinical immunology; pediatric AIDS. *Mailing Add:* Dept Pediat Univ Calif Los Angeles Med Ctr 10833 LeConte Ave Rm 22-387 MDCC Los Angeles CA 90095-1752

STIEL, EDSEL FORD, MATHEMATICS. *Current Pos:* from asst prof to assoc prof, 62-72, chmn dept, 62-74, PROF MATH, CALIF STATE UNIV, FULLERTON, 72- *Personal Data:* b Los Angeles, Calif, Dec 19, 33. *Educ:* Univ Calif, Los Angeles, AB, 55, MA, 59, PhD(math), 63. *Prof Exp:* Math analyst, Douglas Aircraft Co, Calif, 55-56, comput analyst, 57-59; sr math analyst, Lockheed Missiles & Space Co, 60. *Mem:* Am Math Soc; Math Asn Am. *Res:* Isometric immersions of Riemannian manifolds; differential geometry. *Mailing Add:* Dept Math Calif State Univ 800 N State Col Blvd Fullerton CA 92631-3547

STIEL, LEONARD IRWIN, APPLIED PHYSICAL CHEMISTRY, THERMODYNAMICS. *Current Pos:* ASSOC PROF CHEM ENG, POLYTECH INST NY, 80- *Personal Data:* b Paterson, NJ, Sept 17, 37; m 75, Lily Yuan; c 2. *Educ:* Mass Inst Technol, SB, 59; Northwest Univ, MS, 60, PhD(chem eng), 63. *Prof Exp:* From asst prof to assoc prof chem eng, Syracuse Univ, 62-69; assoc prof, Univ Mo, Columbia, 69-72; res chem engr, Spec Chem Div, Allied Chem Corp, 72-79; sr process engr, APV Co, Inc, 79-80. *Concurrent Pos:* Vis scholar, Northwestern Univ, 62 & Oak Ridge Nat Lab, 84. *Mem:* Am Inst Chem Eng; Am Chem Soc. *Res:* Energy conversion; properties of fluids; equations of state. *Mailing Add:* Dept Chem Eng 6 Metrotech Ctr Brooklyn NY 11201-2907. *Fax:* 716-260-3776; *E-Mail:* lstiel@photon.poly.edu

STIELER, CAROL MAE, GENETICS, IMMUNOBIOLOGY. *Current Pos:* BREEDER, FARIS FARMS, 80- *Personal Data:* b Albert Lea, Minn, June 18, 46; m 73; c 2. *Educ:* Iowa State Univ, BS, 68, MS, 70, PhD(immunobiol), 78. *Prof Exp:* Res dir, Hy-Vigor Seeds Inc, 78-80. *Mem:* Am Genetic Asn; AAAS. *Res:* Genetics of laboratory mice, horses and humans; immunology, typing, inheritance and structure of dog and human red cell antigens; antibody formation; lectins; soybean variety development. *Mailing Add:* RR1 Rembrandt IA 50576

STIEMER, SIEGFRIED F, CIVIL ENGINEERING. *Honors & Awards:* LePrix E Whitman Wright Award, Can Soc Civil Eng, 91. *Mailing Add:* 5731 137A St Surrey BC V3W 5E7 Can

STIEN, HOWARD M, ZOOLOGY, PHYSIOLOGY. *Current Pos:* assoc prof, 65-72, PROF BIOL, WHITWORTH COL, WASH, 72-, CHMN DEPT, 65- *Personal Data:* b Montevideo, Minn, Apr 11, 26; m 47; c 2. *Educ:* Northwestern Col, Minn, BA, 56; Macalester Col, MA, 58; Univ Wyo, PhD(physiol), 63. *Prof Exp:* Instr biol, Pepperdine Col, 58-60; asst prof zool, Univ Wyo, 61-64; assoc prof biol, Northwestern Col, Minn, 64-65. *Mem:* AAAS; Sigma Xi. *Res:* Immunogenetics, especially the ontogeny of molecular individuality. *Mailing Add:* Dept Biol Whitworth Col Spokane WA 99251-3902

STIENING, RAE FRANK, HIGH ENERGY PHYSICS. *Current Pos:* physicist, Stanford Linear Accelerator Ctr, 78-83, dep dir, SLC Proj, 83-88, head, Accelerator Dept, 88-89, HEAD, INTERACTION REGIONS MACH GROUP, SSC LAB, 89- *Personal Data:* b Pittsburgh, Pa, May 26, 37; m 69, Nancy Foss; c John M. *Educ:* Mass Inst Technol, SB, 58, PhD(physics), 62. *Prof Exp:* Physicist, Lawrence Berkeley Lab, Univ Calif, 63-71; physicist, Fermi Nat Accelerator Lab, 71-78. *Res:* Weak interactions; fast stellar oscillations; far infrared astronomy; particle accelerators. *Mailing Add:* 2750 Falcon Way Midlothian TX 76065. *E-Mail:* stiening@sscux1.ssc.gov

STIENSTRA, WARD CURTIS, PLANT PATHOLOGY. *Current Pos:* From asst prof to assoc prof, 70-80, PROF PLANT PATH, UNIV MINN, ST PAUL, 80- *Personal Data:* b Holland, Mich, June 19, 41; m 63; c 2. *Educ:* Calvin Col, ABGen, 63; Mich State Univ, MS, 66, PhD(plant path), 70. *Mem:* Am Phytopath Soc; Am Inst Biol Sci. *Res:* Diseases of turf corn, soybeans and alfalfa; soil borne diseases. *Mailing Add:* Plant Path 495 Borlaugh Hall Univ Minn St Paul 1991 Upper Buford Circle St Paul MN 55108-6024

STIER, ELIZABETH FLEMING, biochemistry; deceased, see previous edition for last biography

STIER, HOWARD LIVINGSTON, HORTICULTURE, PLANT PHYSIOLOGY. *Current Pos:* RETIRED. *Personal Data:* b Delmar, Del, Nov 28, 10; c 5. *Educ:* Univ Md, BS, 32, MS, 37, PhD(plant physiol), 39. *Prof Exp:* Agent potato breeding, USDA, 33-35; res asst hort, Univ Md, 35-39, instr & asst prof, 39-41, exten prof mkt & head dept, 46-51; dir div statist & mkt res, Nat Food Processors Asn, 51-61; dir qual control, United Fruit Co, 61-71, dir develop & prod supporting serv, United Brands Co, 72-73, vpres qual control, 73-74, vpres res develop & qual control, 74-77, corp vpres, 78-79; consult, 79-81. *Concurrent Pos:* Prof lectr, George Washington Univ, 57-61; chmn, adv comt, Bur Census, 57-67; mem res adv comt, USDA, 62-64; mem adv comt, Dept Defense, 63; mem task group statist qual control of foods, Nat Acad Sci, 64. *Mem:* Fel AAAS; fel Am Soc Qual Control (vpres, 66-68, 73-74, pres, 74-75); Am Statist Asn; Am Soc Hort Sci; Inst Food Tech. *Res:* Plant breeding; factors affecting quality and growth and development of horticultural crops, food processing, statistical control of quality. *Mailing Add:* Carolina Meadows Villa 230 Whippoorwill Lane Chapel Hill NC 27514

STIER, PAUL MAX, physics, for more information see previous edition

STIERMAN, DONALD JOHN, SEISMOLOGY, ENVIRONMENTAL SCIENCES. *Current Pos:* asst prof, 84-87, ASSOC PROF GEOL, UNIV TOLEDO, 87- *Personal Data:* b Dubuque, Iowa, Oct 27, 47; m 70; c 4. *Educ:* State Univ NY Col Brockport, BS, 69; Stanford Univ, MS, 74, PhD(geophys), 77. *Prof Exp:* Physics instr, Teacher Training Col, Tegucigalpa, Honduras, 69-72; geophysicist, US Geol Surv, 74-75; res asst, Stanford Univ, 75-77; asst prof, Univ Calif, Riverside, 77-84. *Concurrent Pos:* Consult, Environ & Eng Geophys. *Mem:* Am Geophys Union; Seismol Soc Am; Geol Soc Am; Soc Explor Geophysicists. *Res:* Physical properties of the shallow crust; microearthquake studies; induced seismicity; crustal velocity structure; geophysical characterization of existing and proposed waste disposal sites; fracture hydrology; earthquake prediction. *Mailing Add:* 2226 Meadow Wood Dr Toledo OH 43606

STIFEL, FRED B, DIETARY REGULATION OF METABOLIC ENZYMES. *Current Pos:* ASSOC PASTOR, FAITH PRESBY CHURCH, 80- *Personal Data:* b St Louis, Mo, Jan 30, 40. *Educ:* Iowa State Univ, PhD(biochem & nutrit), 67. *Prof Exp:* Res biochemist, Dept Med, Letterman Army Res Inst, San Francisco, 74-76. *Mem:* Am Inst Nutrit; Am Asn Clin Nutrit. *Mailing Add:* Faith Presby Church 3492 S Blackhawk Way Aurora CO 80014-3909

STIFEL, PETER BEEKMAN, PALEONTOLOGY, STRATIGRAPHY & SEDIMENTATION. *Current Pos:* ASSOC PROF GEOL, UNIV MD, COLLEGE PARK, 66- *Personal Data:* b Wheeling, WVa, Feb 9, 36; c 2. *Educ:* Cornell Univ, BA, 58; Univ Utah, PhD(geol), 64. *Prof Exp:* Res asst, Univ Utah, 60-63. *Mem:* Soc Econ Paleont & Mineral; Paleontol Soc. *Res:* Paleontology, stratigraphy and sedimentation. *Mailing Add:* 9636 Old Spring Rd Kensington MD 20895

STIFF, ROBERT H, DENTISTRY. *Current Pos:* RETIRED. *Personal Data:* b Pittsburgh, Pa, Apr 23, 23; m 45; c 3. *Educ:* Univ Pittsburgh, BS, 43, DDS, 45, MEd, 53. *Prof Exp:* Instr oper dent, Sch Dent, Univ Pittsburgh, 45-58, asst prof oral med, 56-57, assoc prof oral genetic path & microbiol, 58-59, from assoc prof to prof oral med, 60-85, asst dean, 79-81, assoc dean, 81-84, chmn dept, 65-85, dir, outpatient serv, Hosp, 78-85. *Concurrent Pos:* Consult, USPHS, 62-66 & Dent Div, Pa Dept Health, 64-66. *Mem:* Am Acad Oral Path; fel Am Col Dent. *Res:* Task analysis of dental practice; dental education; dental treatment for the handicapped; attitudes of dental students towards treatment of chronically ill and aged; caries inhibiting effectiveness of a stannous fluoride-insoluble sodium metaphosphate dentifrice in children. *Mailing Add:* 4601 Doverdell Dr Pittsburgh PA 15236

STIFFEY, ARTHUR V, ENVIRONMENTAL SCIENCE, MICROBIOLOGY. *Current Pos:* VPRES, LUMITOX GULF LC, 93- *Personal Data:* b Burgettstown, Pa, Apr 16, 18; m 41, Helen Jancsik; c 6. *Educ:* Univ Pittsburgh, BS, 40; Lehigh Univ, MS, 47; Fordham Univ, PhD(biol), 81. *Prof Exp:* Chemist analytical chem, US Steel Co, 47-48; res assoc microbiol, Am Cyanamid Co, 48-74; asst prof microbiol, Ladycliff Col, 74-81, chmn, Dept Biol, 77-78, chmn, Dept Natural Sci, 79-81. *Concurrent Pos:* Sr scientist oceanog, US/USSR Bering Sea Exped, 77; proj dir instrnl sci equip prog, NSF grant, 77-78; staff scientist, Naval Ocean Res & Develop Activ, US Navy. *Mem:* AAAS; Sigma Xi; Phycol Soc; Am Inst Biol Sci. *Res:* Microbiological assays; metal determinations; uptake of metals by algae; chemical oceanography; antibiotics; bioluminescence; oceanography; bioluminescence assays; granted several patents. *Mailing Add:* 811 Freedom Lane Slidell LA 70458. *Fax:* 504-643-5588; *E-Mail:* jani@communique.net

STIFFLER, DANIEL F, INTEGRATIVE BIOLOGY, COMPARATIVE PHYSIOLOGY. *Current Pos:* from asst prof to assoc prof, Calif State Polytech Univ, 75-83, assoc dean sci, 83-85, PROF PHYSIOL & ZOOL, CALIF STATE POLYTECH UNIV, POMONA, 83- *Personal Data:* b Los Angeles, Calif, Nov 27, 42; m 67, Gail Clark; c 3. *Educ:* Univ Calif, Santa Barbara, BA, 68; Ore State Univ, MS, 70, PhD(physiol), 72. *Prof Exp:* NIH-USPHS trainee physiol, Health Sci Ctr, Univ Ore, 72-74; lectr animal physiol, Univ Calif, Davis, 74-75. *Mem:* AAAS; Am Physiol Soc; Soc Integrative & Comp Biol; Sigma Xi; Can Soc Zoologists. *Res:* Comparative physiology of systems involved in the evolution of terrestriality; changes necessitated in body fluid balance and its endocrine controls. *Mailing Add:* Dept Biol Sci Calif State Polytech Univ Pomona CA 91768

STIFFLER, JACK JUSTIN, HARDWARE SYSTEMS, ELECTRONICS ENGINEERING. *Current Pos:* EXEC VPRES, SEQUOIA SYSTS INC, 81- *Personal Data:* b Mitchellville, Iowa, May 22, 34; m 55, 89; c 1. *Educ:* Harvard Univ, BA, 56; Calif Inst Technol, MS, 57, PhD(elec eng), 62. *Prof Exp:* Mem tech staff, Jet Propulsion Lab, 59-67; consult scientist, Raytheon Co, 67-81. *Concurrent Pos:* Vis prof, Calif Inst Technol, Univ Calif, Los Angeles, Univ Southern Calif & Northeastern Univ; consult, var corps; ed, Trans Commun, 68-72, Trans Computers, 84-88. *Mem:* Fel Inst Elec & Electronics Engrs; Sigma Xi. *Res:* Defining computer architectures for high-performance on-line transaction processing and investigating fault-tolerance techniques for electronic circuitry. *Mailing Add:* Sequoia Systs Inc 400 Nickerson Rd Marlborough MA 01752

STIGLER, STEPHEN MACK, STATISTICS. *Current Pos:* PROF STATIST, UNIV CHICAGO, 79-, ERNEST DEWITT BURTON DISTINGUISHED SERV PROF, 92- *Personal Data:* b Minneapolis, Minn, Aug 10, 41; m 64, Virginia Lee; c Andrew, Geoffrey, Margaret & Elizabeth. *Educ:* Carleton Col, BA, 63; Univ Calif, Berkeley, PhD(statist), 67. *Prof Exp:* From asst prof to prof statist, Univ Wis-Madison, 67-79. *Concurrent Pos:* Ed, J Am Statist Asn, 79-82; mem bd trustee, Ctr Advan Study in Behav Sci, 86- *Mem:* Fel AAAS; fel Am Statist Asn; fel Inst Math Statist (pres, 93-94); Hist Sci Soc; fel Am Acad Arts & Sci. *Res:* Order statistics; experimental design; history of statistics; author one book and over 90 professional articles. *Mailing Add:* Dept Statist Univ Chicago 5734 University Ave Chicago IL 60637. *Fax:* 773-702-9810; *E-Mail:* stigler@galton.uchicago.edu

STIGLITZ, IRVIN G, ELECTRONICS ENGINEERING, ENGINEERING. *Current Pos:* res teaching asst statist commun theory, 58-63, asst prof elec eng, 63-64, staff mem, 64-71, GROUP LEADER, LINCOLN LAB, MASS INST TECHNOL, 71- *Personal Data:* b Cambridge, Mass, July 31, 36; m 60; c 2. *Educ:* Mass Inst Technol, SB & SM, 60, PhD(commun sci), 63. *Prof Exp:* Electronic engr, US Naval Ord Lab, 55-58; electronic eng, Gen Atronics Co, 60-61. *Concurrent Pos:* Consult, Guillemin Res Lab, 61, Joseph Kaye & Co, 63; Melpar Inc, 62 & Nat Acad Sci-Nat Res Coun, 70; Ford fel, 63-64. *Mem:* Inst Elec & Electronics Engrs. *Res:* Guidance and control technology; tactical systems technology; air traffic control; communications systems design; information theory; system design and analysis; adaptive array processing; interference suppression; surveillance. *Mailing Add:* Lincoln Lab Mass Inst Technol 244 Wood St PO Box 73 Boston MA 02173

STILES, A(LVIN) B(ARBER), CATALYST DEVELOPMENT, PROCESS DEVELOPMENT. *Current Pos:* RETIRED. *Personal Data:* b Springfield, Ohio, July 16, 09; m 34, Julia K Orr; c 3. *Educ:* Ohio State Univ, BChE, 31, MS, 33. *Prof Exp:* Indust engr, E I du Pont de Nemours & Co, Inc, NY, 31-32, res assoc, WVa, 33-58, sr res assoc, 58-65, res fel, Del, 65-74; assoc dir, Ctr Catalytic Sci & Technol, Dept Chem Eng, Univ Del, Newark, 74-86, res prof appl catalyst, 74-86. *Concurrent Pos:* Res fel, E I du Pont de Nemours, 34-74. *Mem:* Am Chem Soc; fel Am Inst Chemists; Am Inst Chem Engrs; AAAS; NY Acad Sci. *Res:* Industrial catalysis; synthesis of organic chemicals plastics, alcohols, intermediate and synthesis gas; author of 2 books, many articles and chapters; granted 65 US patents. *Mailing Add:* 1301 Grayson Rd Wilmington DE 19803

STILES, CHARLES DEAN, CANCER, ONCOGENES. *Current Pos:* PROF MICORBIOL & MOLECULAR GENETICS, SCH MED, HARVARD UNIV, 76- *Personal Data:* b Nov 18, 46; m; c 2. *Educ:* Harvard Univ, MA; Univ Tenn, PhD(biochem), 73. *Mem:* Am Asn Cancer Res. *Res:* Regulation of cell growth and development by polypeptide growth factors. *Mailing Add:* Dana-Farber Cancer Inst Harvard Med Sch 44 Binney St Boston MA 02115-6084. *Fax:* 617-735-0582

STILES, DAVID A, ANALYTICAL CHEMISTRY OF NON METALS, ENVIRONMENTAL CHEMISTRY. *Current Pos:* from asst prof to assoc prof, 66-77, head dept, 81-88, PROF CHEM, ACADIA UNIV, 77-, ACTG DIR, RES & GRAD STUDIES, 94- *Personal Data:* b Harrow, Eng, Apr 28, 38; m 66, Victoria J Walker; c John D, Mark E & Susan P. *Educ:* Univ Birmingham, BSc, 60, PhD(electron spin resonance spectros), 63. *Prof Exp:* Asst prof chem, Univ Calgary, 63-64; univ fel, Univ Alta, 64-66. *Mem:* Fel Chem Inst Can; Royal Soc Chem London; Can Soc Chem. *Res:* Agricultural pollution; fate of pesticides in sandy soils; applications of molecular emission cavity analysis to analysis of non-metals. *Mailing Add:* Dept Chem Acadia Univ Wolfville NS B0P 1X0 Can. *Fax:* 902-585-1114

STILES, GARY L, RECEPTOR MECHANISMS. *Current Pos:* From asst prof to assoc prof, 83-89, PROF MED, DUKE UNIV, 90-, PROF PHARMACOL, 90-, CHIEF, DIV CARDIOL, VCHAIR, DEPT MED, 95- *Personal Data:* b New York, NY, May 22, 49; m 71, Jane Black; c Heather & Wendy. *Educ:* St Lawrence Univ, BS, 71; Vanderbilt Univ, MD, 75. *Honors & Awards:* Louis N Katz Prize Basic Sci, 83; Young Investr Award, Southern Soc, Am Fedn Clin Res, 89; Established Investr Award, Am Heart Asn. *Concurrent Pos:* young investr award, Am Col Cardiol, 83; Mem, Basic Sci Coun, Am Heart Asn, 86-; Circulation Coun, 87-; mem, Pharmacol Study Sect, NIH, 87-90. *Mem:* Am Soc Clin Invest; Am Soc Biol Chemists; Am Heart Asn; Am Fedn Clin Res; Am Asn Physicians. *Res:* The mechanisms of transmembrane signalling with particular interest in adenosine receptor systems; structure function relationships at the biochemical and molecular biological levels. *Mailing Add:* Dept Med Div Cardiovasc Duke Univ Med Ctr Box 3444 Durham NC 27710

STILES, JOHN CALLENDER, applied physics, for more information see previous edition

STILES, LYNN F, JR, ENERGY CONSERVATION, UTILITY CONSERVATION ASSESSMENT. *Current Pos:* PROF PHYSICS, RICHARD STOCKTON COL NJ, 73- *Personal Data:* b Brooklyn, NY, July 4, 42; m 67, Sandra Larson; c Eric & Jon. *Educ:* State Univ NY, Stony Brook, BS, 64; Cornell Univ, MS, 67, PhD(physics), 70. *Prof Exp:* Instr physics, Hobart & William Smith Cols, 66-68; res physicist optics, E I du Pont de Nemours & Co, Inc, 69-73. *Concurrent Pos:* Vis lectr, Swarthmore Col, 72-; dir tech assessment, Atlantic County, 74-76; pres, Solar Alternatives, Inc, 78-81; consult energy systs design, 79-; pres, New Bus Incubator, 89-90. *Mem:* Am Asn Physics Teachers; Am Soc Heating Refrig & Air Conditioning Engrs. *Res:* Energy conservation in buildings - air filtration and envelope loss mechanisms; energy system designs and utility conservation program assessment; interferometric holography; geothermal heat pump systems. *Mailing Add:* 104 Arlington Ave Linwood NJ 08221. *Fax:* 609-748-5515; *E-Mail:* lynn@odin.stockton.edu

STILES, MARK DAVID, ELECTRONIC STRUCTURES OF INTERFACES, ULTRATHIN MAGNETIC FILMS. *Current Pos:* PHYSICIST, NAT INST STAND & TECHNOL, 88- *Personal Data:* b Philadelphia, Pa, Jan 7, 59; m 87, Barbara Weis; c Daniel & Christina. *Educ:* Yale Univ, BS & MS, 81; Cornell Univ, MS, 84, PhD(physics), 86. *Prof Exp:* Mem tech staff, A&T Bell Labs, 86-88. *Mem:* Am Phys Soc. *Mailing Add:* Metrol B206 Nat Inst Stand & Technol Gaithersburg MD 20899

STILES, MICHAEL EDGECOMBE, FOOD MICROBIOLOGY, MICROBIOLOGY. *Current Pos:* assoc prof food microbiol, 69-77, PROF FOOD MICROBIOL, UNIV ALTA, 77- *Personal Data:* b Brit, Dec 28, 34; Can citizen; m 59; c 5. *Educ:* Univ Natal, BScAgr, 56, MScAgr, 59; Univ Ill, PhD(food microbiol), 63. *Prof Exp:* Dairy researcher, S African Dept Agr, 57-59; from lectr to sr lectr dairy sci, Univ Natal, 59-69. *Concurrent Pos:* Killam fel, Univ Alta, 68-69; adj prof, Dept Microbiol, Univ Alta, 74- *Mem:* Can Inst Food Sci & Technol; Inst Food Technologists; Int Asn Sanitarians; Am Soc Microbiol. *Res:* Food microbiology for quality control and safety especially meats; consumer acceptance and awareness of foods and food safety. *Mailing Add:* Agr Food & Nutrit Sci 4-10 Agr Forestry Ctr Univ Alberta Edmonton AB T6G 2P5 Can

STILES, PHILIP GLENN, FOOD TECHNOLOGY, POULTRY SCIENCE. *Current Pos:* PROF POULTRY SCI & FOOD TECHNOL, ARIZ STATE UNIV, 69-, CHMN DEPT AGR INDUST, 78- *Personal Data:* b Terre Haute, Ind, Nov 24, 31; m 56; c 1. *Educ:* Univ Ark, BS, 53; Univ Ky, MS, 56; Mich State Univ, PhD(food tech), 58. *Prof Exp:* Assoc prof food tech, Univ Conn, 59-69. *Concurrent Pos:* Fel, Univ Calif, Davis, 66-67; consult, Nixon Baldwin Div, Tenneco Co, 67-, AID projs in Iran, Malaysia & Philippines, 73-75 & Saudia Arabia Agr Bank, 80-85. *Mem:* Inst Food Technol; Soc Int Develop. *Res:* Food technology as applied to poultry products and food packaging; food processing in developing nations. *Mailing Add:* Dept Agr Ariz State Univ Tempe AZ 85287-0002

STILES, PHILLIP JOHN, SOLID STATE PHYSICS. *Current Pos:* PROVOST & VCHANCELLOR, NC STATE UNIV, 93-, PROF PHYSICS, 93- *Personal Data:* b Manchester, Conn, Oct 31, 34; m 56, Elise Reichert; c Lauren P (Thissell), Lissa P, Mark D, Robert B, Cory T (MacLean) & Pat A. *Educ:* Trinity Col, Conn, BS, 56; Univ Pa, PhD(physics), 61. *Honors & Awards:* John Price Wetheral Medal, Franklin Inst, 81; Oliver E Buckley Prize, Am Phys Soc, 88. *Prof Exp:* Fel & res assoc physics, Univ Pa, 61-62; NSF fel, Cambridge Univ, 62-63; mem res staff, Thomas J Watson Res Ctr, Int Bus Mach Corp, NY, 63-70; prof physics, Brown Univ, 70-93, chair dept, 74-80, dean, Grad Sch & dean res, 86-93. *Concurrent Pos:* Humboldt Sr US Scientist award, 76; vis scientist, Tech Univ Munich, 76-77; vis sr fel, Univ Cambridge, 83-84. *Mem:* Fel Am Phys Soc. *Res:* Experimental investigation of the electronic properties of semiconductors and metals to determine what physics dominates behaviors; electronic properties of metals, semiconductors and lower dimensional systems. *Mailing Add:* PO Box 7101 Raleigh NC 27659-7101

STILES, ROBERT NEAL, PHYSIOLOGY. *Current Pos:* asst prof physiol & biophys, 68-75, ASSOC PROF PHYSIOL & BIOPHYS, UNIV TENN CTR HEALTH SCI, MEMPHIS, 75- *Personal Data:* b Mar 15, 33; m 59; c 3. *Educ:* Univ Mo, BS, 59, MA, 63; Northwestern Univ, PhD, 66. *Prof Exp:* Asst prof zool & physiol, Butler Univ, 66-68. *Concurrent Pos:* USPHS grant, Univ Tenn Ctr Health Sci, Memphis, 69- *Mem:* AAAS; Sigma Xi; Am Physiol Soc; Soc Neurosci. *Res:* Human limb tremor; muscle mechanics; motor control system. *Mailing Add:* Univ Tenn Memphis Col Med 894 Union Ave Memphis TN 38163-0001

STILES, SHEILA SUZANNE (JEWELL), CYTOGENETICS, ECOLOGY. *Current Pos:* fishery biologist, 71-84, RES GENETICIST FISHERIES & MARINE BIOL, US DEPT COM, NAT OCEANIC & ATMOSPHERIC ADMIN, NAT MARINE FISHERIES SERV, 85- *Personal Data:* b Memphis, Tenn, Sept 28, 42; wid. *Educ:* Xavier Univ, BS, 64; Univ Conn, MS, 73; Univ Mass, PhD(fish genetics), 94. *Prof Exp:* Biologist, US Dept Interior, US Fish & Wildlife Serv, 67-70. *Concurrent Pos:* Mem, NE Fish Ctr Res Coun, NE Fisheries Sci Ctr, 86-87, spec asst ctr dir, 87; co-prin investr, Environ Protection Agency grant, 87-88; vis scientist fish genetics, Jackson State Univ, 94 & 95. *Mem:* Genetics Soc Am; Genetics Soc Can; Am Fisheries Soc; Sigma Xi; Int Coun Explor Sea; Nat Tech Asn. *Res:* Planning, directing and conducting research on genetics and breeding (as well as population genetics, cytogenetics and chromosome engineering) of commercial shellfish. *Mailing Add:* 90 Lakeview Terr New Haven CT 06515

STILES, WARREN CRYDER, ORCHARD NUTRITION, ORCHARD MANAGEMENTS. *Current Pos:* assoc prof, 80-84, PROF POMOL, CORNELL UNIV, 84- *Personal Data:* b Dias Creek, NJ, June 16, 33; wid; c Matthew, Elizabeth, Kathleen & Steven. *Educ:* Rutgers Univ, BS, 54, MS, 55; Pa State Univ, PhD(hort), 58. *Prof Exp:* Asst prof pomol, Rutgers Univ, 58-63; from assoc prof to prof, Univ Maine, 63-80, exten fruit specialist, 63-80, supt, Highmoor Farm, 66-80. *Mem:* Am Soc Hort Sci. *Res:* Nutrition; soil management; weed control; physiology of fruit. *Mailing Add:* 120 Plant Sci Bldg Cornell Univ Ithaca NY 14853. *Fax:* 607-255-0599

STILES, WILBUR J, MATHEMATICS. *Current Pos:* ASSOC PROF MATH, FLA STATE UNIV, 65- *Personal Data:* b Suffern, NY, Jan 12, 32; m 56; c 2. *Educ:* Lehigh Univ, BS, 54; Ga Inst Technol, BS, 60, MS, 62, PhD(math), 65. *Mem:* Am Math Soc; Math Asn Am. *Res:* Functional analysis, geometry of Banach spaces. *Mailing Add:* 3106 W Lakeshore Dr Tallahassee FL 32312

STILL, CHARLES NEAL, NEUROLOGY. *Current Pos:* prof, 78-81, clin prof, 81-88, PROF NEUROPSYCHIAT & BEHAV SCI, SCH MED, UNIV SC, 89-; SR STAFF NEUROLOGIST, WJB DOWN VET ADMIN MED CTR, COLUMBIA, SC, 92- *Personal Data:* b Richmond, Va, Apr 15, 29; m 58, Dorothy Varn; c Charles, Carl & Sara. *Educ:* Clemson Univ, BS, 49; Purdue Univ, MS, 51; Med Col SC, MD, 59. *Prof Exp:* Instr chem, Clemson Univ, 51-52 & US Mil Acad, 53-55; intern, Univ Chicago Clins, 59-60; resident neurol, Baltimore City Hosps & Johns Hopkins Hosp, 60-63; chief, Neurol Serv, William S Hall Psychiat Inst, 65-81. *Concurrent Pos:* Fel neurol med, Sch Med, Johns Hopkins Univ, 60-63; Nat Inst Neurol Dis & Blindness spec res fel neuropath, Res Lab, McLean Hosp & Harvard Med Sch, 63-65; fel neurol, Seizure Unit, Children's Hosp Med Ctr, Boston, 66; assoc clin prof neurol, Med Univ SC, 73-91; chmn, Grants Rev Bd, SC Dept Ment Health, 73-78; mem, Huntington's Chorea Res Group, World Fedn Neurol; dir, C M Tucker Jr Human Resources Ctr, 81-88; dep comnr, Long Term Care Div, SC Dept Mental Health, 81-86; assoc dir gen psychiat & neurol, William S Hall Psychiat Inst, 89-92. *Mem:* Fel Am Acad Neurol; fel Am Geriat Soc; fel Am Inst Chemists; fel Geront Soc Am; AMA; Am Chem Soc. *Res:* Clinical neurology with special interest in the dementias. *Mailing Add:* 2 Culpepper Circle Columbia SC 29209-2234

STILL, EDWIN TANNER, RADIOBIOLOGY, ENVIRONMENTAL PROTECTION. *Current Pos:* sr phys scientist, 82-83, vpres Environ Affairs Dept, 83-84, VPRES & DIR, ENVIRON HEALTH & MGT DIV, KERR-MCGEE CORP, 84- *Personal Data:* b Monroe, Ga, Nov 2, 35; m 59; c 2. *Educ:* Univ Rochester, MS, 64; Univ Ga, DVM, 59. *Prof Exp:* Res scientist, Sch Aerospace Med, USAF, Brooks AFB, Tex, 64-67 & Naval Radiol Defense Lab, Calif, 67-69; res contracts adminr, Div Biol & Med, US AEC, 69-75; chmn, Radiation Biol Dept, Armed Forces Radiobiol Res Inst, 75-79; biomed adv, Defense Nuclear Agency, 79-81. *Mem:* Sigma Xi. *Res:* Low-level radiation effects; beneficial applications of radiation. *Mailing Add:* 2104 Thrush Circle Edmond OK 73074

STILL, EUGENE UPDIKE, physiology; deceased, see previous edition for last biography

STILL, GERALD G, BIOCHEMISTRY, ORGANIC CHEMISTRY. *Current Pos:* PRES, RES TECHNOL ASSESSMENT, AGR FUTURES, 94- *Personal Data:* b Seattle, Wash, Aug 13, 33; m 54; c 3. *Educ:* Wash State Univ, BS, 59; Ore State Univ, MS, 63, PhD(biochem), 65. *Prof Exp:* Res biochemist, Radiation & Metab Res Lab, Agr Res Serv, USDA, 65-77, staff scientist, Nat Prog Staff, 77-80, chief scientist, Sci & Educ Admin-Agr Res, 80-82, dir crop productivity, USDA-ARS, 83-84, dir, Plant-Gene Expression Ctr, USDA/ Univ Calif Berkeley, 84-94. *Concurrent Pos:* Mem, Sr Exec Serv, USDA, 84- *Mem:* Am Soc Plant Physiol; Am Chem Soc. *Res:* Metabolism of pesticides; isolation and characterization of pesticide metabolites; photosynthesis; biological nitrogen fixation; plant cell culture; field crop bioregulation. *Mailing Add:* 2832 Frayne Lane Concord CA 94518

STILL, IAN WILLIAM JAMES, SYNTHETIC METHODS, ORGANOSULFUR CHEMISTRY. *Current Pos:* from asst prof to assoc prof, 65-82, PROF CHEM, UNIV TORONTO, 82-, ASST CHAIR, 92-94 & 96- *Personal Data:* b Rutherglen, Scotland, July 5, 37; UK & Can citizen; m 64, Jillian Witt; c Ian & Alastair. *Educ:* Glasgow Univ, BSc, 58, PhD(chem), 62, DSc, 92. *Prof Exp:* Res assoc, Univ Toronto, 62-63; sci officer, Allen & Hanburys Ltd, Eng, 63-64; from asst lectr to lectr chem, Huddersfield Col Tech Eng, 64-65. *Concurrent Pos:* Dir, Can Soc Chem, 85-87. *Mem:* Am Chem Soc; fel Chem Inst Can; assoc mem Royal Soc Chem; Can Soc Chem. *Res:* Synthetic organic chemistry; new synthetic methods; organic sulfur chemistry; synthesis of naturally occurring antibiotics and antivirals; eudistomins and eudistomidins; varacin and lissoclinotoxin A and related polysulfides. *Mailing Add:* Univ Toronto 3359 Mississauga Rd Mississauga ON L5L 1C6 Can. *Fax:* 902-828-5425; *E-Mail:* istill@credit.erin.utoronto.ca

STILL, W CLARK, JR, SYNTHETIC ORGANIC CHEMISTRY. *Current Pos:* fel synthetic org chem, Columbia Univ, 73-75, asst prof, 77-80, assoc prof, 80-81, PROF, COLUMBIA UNIV, 81- *Personal Data:* b Augusta, Ga, Aug 31, 46; m 93, Carol. *Educ:* Emory Univ, BS, 69, PhD(org chem), 72. *Honors & Awards:* Alan T Waterman Award, NSF, 81; Buchman Award, Calif Inst Technol, 82; Stieglitz Award, 84; Cope Scholar Award, Am Chem Soc, 87; Japan Soc Promotion Sci Fel, 87; Comput Chem Award, Am Chem Soc, 93. *Prof Exp:* IBM fel theoret org chem, Princeton Univ, 72-73; asst prof org chem, Vanderbilt Univ, 75-77. *Concurrent Pos:* Alfred P Sloan Fel, 78-80; John Simon Guggenheim Fel, 81-82; Ruth & Arthur Sloan vis prof, Harvard,

82; Alexander Todd vis prof, Cambridge, 86; Rolf Sammet vis prof, Frankfurt, 92. *Mem:* Am Chem Soc; fel Am Acad Arts & Sci; fel Japan Soc Prom Sci. *Res:* Organic synthesis; new synthetic methods; computational chemistry; molecular recognition; combinatorial chemistry. *Mailing Add:* Dept Chem Columbia Univ Broadway & W 116th St New York NY 10027-2399. Fax: 212-854-5429

STILL, WILLIAM JAMES SANGSTER, PATHOLOGY. *Current Pos:* assoc prof, 65-70, PROF PATH, MED COL VA, 70- *Personal Data:* b Aberdeen, Scotland, Sept 16, 23; m 51; c 2. *Educ:* Univ Aberdeen, MB, ChB, 51, MD, 60. *Prof Exp:* Lectr path, Univ London, 57-60; asst prof, Sch Med, Washington Univ, 60-62; sr lectr, Univ London, 62-65. *Concurrent Pos:* Fel coun arteriosclerosis, Am Heart Asn, 65. *Mem:* Col Am Path; Path Soc Gt Brit & Ireland. *Res:* Cardiovascular disease, particularly arterial disease. *Mailing Add:* 5875 Bremo Rd Suite 201 Richmond VA 23226

STILLE, JOHN KENNETH, organometallic chemistry, polymer chemistry; deceased, see previous edition for last biography

STILLE, JOHN ROBERT, PEPTIDE MIMETICS, ZIEGLER-NATTA CATALYSIS. *Current Pos:* HEAD CHEM PROCESS, RES & DEVELOP, LILLY RES LAB, LILLY CORP CTR, ELI LILLY & CO, 94- *Personal Data:* b Iowa City, Iowa, Feb 22, 59; m, Aleta A Mungal; c Nicole & Joelle. *Educ:* Univ Colo, Boulder, BA(chem), & BA(molecular, cellular & develop biol), 81; Calif Inst Technol, PhD(chem), 86. *Prof Exp:* Res asst, Calif Inst Technol, 81-86; NIH fel, Columbia Univ, 86-87; asst prof org & organometall, Mich State Univ, 87-94. *Concurrent Pos:* Counr, Am Chem Soc, 88-92. *Mem:* Am Chem Soc; Sigma Xi. *Res:* Development of synthetic organic methodology for use in the construction of alkaloid natural products and biologically active peptide mimetics; mechanistic investigation and catalyst design in Ziegler-Natta polymerization systems. *Mailing Add:* Lilly Res Lab Eli Lilly & Co Lilly Corp Ctr Indianapolis IN 41285. Fax: 517-355-9715

STILLER, CALVIN R, IMMUNOLOGY, MEDICINE. *Current Pos:* DIR IMMUNOL, ROBARTS RES INST, LONDON, ONT, 84- *Personal Data:* b Naicam, Sask, Can, Feb 12, 41; m 62, 88; c 6. *Educ:* Univ Sask, MD, 65; FRCP(C), 70. *Prof Exp:* Med Res Coun fel biochem, Univ Western Ont, London, 67-69, from asst prof to assoc prof med, 72-82; chief nephrol, 73-84, DIR TRANSPLANT LAB, UNIV HOSP, LONDON, 73-, CHIEF TRANSPLANTATION, 84-; PROF MED, UNIV WESTERN ONT, 82- *Concurrent Pos:* Res assoc transplantation, Transplant Unit, Med Res Coun, Edmonton, 71-72; chmn, Ctr Transplant Studies, London, Ont, 81-; co-chmn, Ministers Task Force Organ Donation, Govt of Ontario, 83-85; chmn, Can-Europ Diabetes Study Group, 84-; mem, Task Force Indust-Acad Res Inst, Govt of Can, 85-; vis prof, over 50 univs; consult, NIH, Ways & Means Comt, Med Res Coun, Govt of Can & pharmaceut indust. *Mem:* Can Soc Nephrol (secy-treas & pres, 76-82); Transplantation Soc; Transplant Int Can; Can Soc Immunol; Med Res Coun Can. *Res:* Immune response in transplantation and autoimmune diesase; immunogenetic and molecular biologic aspects of diabetes and its possible prevention. *Mailing Add:* 14142 Medway Rd RR1 Arva ON N0M 1C0 Can

STILLER, DAVID, MEDICAL & VETERINARY ENTOMOLOGY. *Current Pos:* RES ENTOMOLOGIST VET ENTOM, AGR RES SERV, UNIV IDAHO, USDA, 75- *Personal Data:* b Seattle, Wash, Sept 9, 31; m 62; c 2. *Educ:* Whittier Col, BA, 53, MSc, 57; Univ Calif, Berkeley, PhD(parasitol), 73. *Prof Exp:* Staff res assoc med entom, George Williams Hooper Found, Univ Calif, San Francisco, 62-73, res parasitologist & res assoc med entom & acarol, Dept Int Health, 73-75. *Concurrent Pos:* Actg head, Int Ctr Med Res, Div Acarol, Inst Med Res, Kuala Lumpur, Malaysia, 73-75; consult scientist, Spec Foreign Currency Prog, Pub Law 480; vet entom coordr, Nat Emergency Prog Vet Serv, USDA, 78-; adj prof, Dept Vet Med, Univ Idaho & Dept Vet Micro-Path, Washington State Univ, 81- *Mem:* Entom Soc Am; Am Soc Trop Med & Hyg; AAAS; Wildlife Dis Asn; Sigma Xi. *Res:* Acarology; vector-pathogen relationships; arthropod-borne diseases; acarine biology and parasitism; tick-borne hemoparasitic diseases of livestock; epizootiology of these diseases. *Mailing Add:* Agr Res Serv Univ Idaho USDA Holm Res Ctr W Sixth St Extn Moscow ID 83843

STILLER, MARY LOUISE, PLANT PHYSIOLOGY, BIOCHEMISTRY. *Current Pos:* asst prof, 62-66, assoc prof, 66-96, EMER PROF BIOL SCI, PURDUE UNIV, LAFAYETTE, 96- *Personal Data:* b Salem, Ohio, Nov 29, 31. *Educ:* Purdue Univ, BS, 54, MS, 56, PhD(plant physiol), 59. *Prof Exp:* NSF fel biochem, Univ Chicago, 58-60, USPHS trainee, 60-61; fel, Univ Pa, 61-62. *Concurrent Pos:* NIH career develop award, 65- *Mem:* AAAS; Am Soc Plant Physiol. *Res:* Biochemistry of photosynthesis, photoreduction and respiration. *Mailing Add:* Dept of Biol Sci Purdue Univ West Lafayette IN 47907

STILLER, PETER FREDERICK, ALGEBRAIC GEOMETRY. *Current Pos:* asst prof math, Tex A&M Univ, 77-79, asst prof, 80, from asst prof to assoc prof math, 82-86, PROF MATH, TEX A&M UNIV, 87-, PROF COMPUT SCI, 94-, ASST DIR, INST SCI COMPUT, 95- *Personal Data:* b Green Bay, Wis. *Educ:* Mass Inst Technol, SB(econ) & SB(math), 73; Princeton Univ, MA, 74, PhD(math), 77. *Prof Exp:* Asst prof math, Tex A&M Univ, 77-79; NATO fel, Inst des Hautes Etudes Scientifiques, 79-80; asst prof, Tex A&M Univ, 80; res prof math, Sci Res Inst, Berkeley, Calif, 86-87; mem, Sch Math, Inst Advan Study, 87-90. *Concurrent Pos:* NATO fel, Inst des Hautes Etudes Sci, 79-80; res fel math, Univ Bonn, WGer, 81; NSF US France exchange grant, Inst Higher Sci Studies, 82-83; assoc prof math, La State Univ, 86- *Mem:* Am Math Soc; Math Res Fance; Math Assoc Am. *Res:* Families of algebraic varieties, algebraic cycles and Dirichlet series; applications of algebraic geometry to robotics and image processing. *Mailing Add:* Tex A&M Univ College Station TX 77843-3368. Fax: 409-845-6028

STILLER, RICHARD L, biochemistry; deceased, see previous edition for last biography

STILLINGER, FRANK HENRY, LIQUID STATE THEORY, PHASE TRANSITION THEORY. *Current Pos:* MEM TECH STAFF, BELL LABS, INC, 59- *Personal Data:* b Boston, Mass, Aug 15, 34; m 56; c 2. *Educ:* Univ Rochester, BS, 55; Yale Univ, PhD(chem), 58. *Honors & Awards:* Elliott Cresson Medal, Franklin Inst, 78; Hildebrand Award, Am Chem Soc, 86; Langmuir Prize, Am Phys Soc, 89; Trumbull lectr, Yale Univ, 84; Peter J Debye Award, Am Chem Soc, 92; Pitzer Lectr, Univ Calif, Berkeley, 96. *Prof Exp:* Fel chem, Yale Univ, 58-59. *Concurrent Pos:* Lectr, Welsh Found, 74; mem evaluation panel, Heat Div, Nat Bur Stand, 75-78; mem policy comt, Chem Div, NSF, 80-83 & Off Adv Sci Comput, 84-88; vis fac mem, Princeton Univ, 96- *Mem:* Nat Acad Sci; Am Phys Soc; AAAS. *Res:* Molecular theory of water and its solutions; theory of phase transitions; quantum chemistry. *Mailing Add:* Bell Labs 600 Mountain Ave Murray Hill NJ 07974

STILLINGS, BRUCE ROBERT, NUTRITION. *Current Pos:* VPRES SCI AFFAIRS, AM COCOA RES INST, 93- *Personal Data:* b Portland, Maine, May 18, 37; m 59; c 4. *Educ:* Univ Maine, BS, 58; Pa State Univ, MS, 60, PhD(animal nutrit), 63. *Prof Exp:* NIH fel, Cornell Univ, 63-66; supvry res chemist, food res prog leader & dep lab dir, US Nat Marine Fisheries Serv, 66-74; nutrit coordr, dir food safety, dir res activities, dir res & vpres res & develop, Nabisco Brands Inc, 74-89; vpres res & develop, Durkee-French Foods, 89-92; dep asst secy sci & educ, USDA, 92-93. *Mem:* Am Asn Cereal Chemists; AAAS; Am Inst Nutrit; Inst Food Technologists. *Res:* Nutritional studies on metabolism and utilization of minerals and amino acids; nutritive value of food-proteins and protein concentrates; factors affecting protein quality of foods. *Mailing Add:* AM Cocoa Res Inst 7900 West PK Dr Suite A320 McLean VA 22102. Fax: 703-790-5752

STILLIONS, MERLE C, LABORATORY ANIMAL SCIENCE, NUTRITION. *Current Pos:* RES DIR, AGWAY INC, 72- *Personal Data:* b Bedford, Ind, Feb 15, 29; m 53; c 5. *Educ:* Purdue Univ, BS, 57, MS, 58; Rutgers Univ, PhD(nutrit), 62. *Prof Exp:* Instr nutrit, Rutgers Univ, 58-62, chmn, Dairy Dept, Chico State Univ, 62-63; dir nutrit, Morris Res Lab, 63-72. *Concurrent Pos:* Mem, Equine Comt, Nat Res Coun, 69-73. *Mem:* Am Soc Animal Sci; Am Asn Lab Animal Soc. *Res:* Laboratory animal and fish nutrition and feed control programs. *Mailing Add:* 1342 Agard Rd Trumansburg NY 14886

STILLMAN, BRUCE WILLIAM, DNA REPLICATION, CELL CYCLE RESEARCH. *Current Pos:* Fel, 79-80, staff investr, 81-82, sr staff investr, 83-85, sr scientist, 85-90, asst dir, 90-93, DIR, COLD SPRING HARBOR CANCER CTR, 92- & COLD SPRING HARBOR LAB, 94- *Personal Data:* b Melbourne, Australia, Oct 16, 53; m, Grace Begley; c Keith & Jessica. *Educ:* Univ Sydney, BSC Hons I, 75; Australian Nat Univ, PhD(microbiol), 79. *Honors & Awards:* Niewland Lectr, Univ Notre Dame, 93. *Concurrent Pos:* Fel, Damon-Runyon Walter Winchell Cancer Fund, 79; scholar, Rita Allen Found, 82; adj prof microbiol, State Univ Ny, Stony Brook, 82-, adj prof biochem & cell biol, 88-; mem & chmn, Exp Virol Study Sect, NIH, 86-88; lectr, Harvey Soc, 93. *Mem:* Am Soc Virol; Am Soc Microbiol; Am Soc Biochem & Molecular Biol; fel Royal Soc (London). *Res:* Study of the mechanism of DNA replication in eukaryotic cells and the process of inheritance of chromatin during cell proliferation. *Mailing Add:* PO Box 100 Cold Spring Harbor Lab 1 Bungtown Rd Cold Spring Harbor NY 11724-1100

STILLMAN, GREGORY EUGENE, COMPOUND SEMICONDUCTOR MICROELECTRONICS. *Current Pos:* dir, Compound Semiconductor Microelectronics Lab, 84-87, assoc dir, Coordr Sci Technol, 85-86, PROF, DEPT ELEC ENG, UNIV ILL, 75- *Personal Data:* b Scotia, Nebr, Feb 15, 36; m 56; c 3. *Educ:* Univ Nebr, Lincoln, BS, 58; Univ Ill, Urbana, MS, 65, PhD(elec eng), 67. *Honors & Awards:* Jack Morton Award, Inst Elec & Electronics Engrs, 90; Heinrich Welker Medal, 90. *Prof Exp:* Res staff assoc solid state physics, Lincoln Lab, Mass Inst Technol, 67-75. *Concurrent Pos:* Vis scientist, Lab Elettronica dello Stato Solido, 72. *Mem:* Nat Acad Eng; fel Inst Elec & Electronics Engrs; Electron Devices Soc (pres, 84-86); Am Phys Soc. *Res:* Semiconductor physics; transport properties, photoconductivity; spectroscopy; luminescence. *Mailing Add:* 151 Microelectronics Lab Univ Ill 208 N Wright St Urbana IL 61801. Fax: 217-244-6375; E-Mail: gstill@ux1.cso.uiuc.edu

STILLMAN, JOHN EDGAR, QUALITY ASSURANCE, ENVIRONMENTAL CHEMISTRY. *Current Pos:* indust hygienist, Biomed Sci Div, Exxon Corp, 79-80, actg head, 80-81, sect head, Indust Hyg Lab, 81-91, SECT HEAD QUAL ASSURANCE, EXXON BIOMED SCIENCE DIV, EXXON CORP, 91- *Personal Data:* b Syracuse, NY, May 21, 45. *Educ:* State Univ NY Col Forestry at Syracuse Univ, BS, 67; Univ NC Sch Pub Health, MSPH, 69; NC State Univ, MAgri, 72; Am Bd Indust Hyg, cert, 80. *Prof Exp:* Analytic chem supvr, Div Health Serv, Occup Health Lab Unit, NC Dept Human Resources, 72-79. *Concurrent Pos:* Consult analytical chem, var pvt industs, 74-79; comt mem, Lab Accreditation, Am Indust Hyg Asn, 85-87; mem, Analytic Chem Comt, 87-92; mem, Asbestos Analysts Registry, 88-92, chair, 91. *Mem:* Am Indust Hyg Asn; Am Conf Govt Indust Hygienists; Am Acad Indust Hyg; Soc Qual Assurance; Am Soc Qual Assurance. *Res:* Occupational, industrial and environmental pollutants; quality assurance, for petrochemical analytical laboratory, laboratory administration, management and oversight; gas chromatography; microscopy; method evaluation and development; field hazards surveys; asbestos; kinetics of cholinesterase, anaerobic sludge digestion; industrial hygiene. *Mailing Add:* 2 Three Acre Lane Bunker Hill Rd Princeton NJ 08540. Fax: 732-873-6009

STILLMAN, MARTIN JOHN, BIOINORGANIC CHEMISTRY, SPECTROSCOPY. *Current Pos:* from asst prof to assoc prof, 75-86, PROF CHEM, UNIV WESTERN ONT, 86- *Personal Data:* b London, Eng, June 4, 47; Can citizen. *Educ:* Univ EAnglia, BSc, 69, MSc, 70, PhD(chem), 73. *Prof Exp:* Fel chem, Univ Alta, 73-75. *Mem:* Chem Soc; Can Inst Chem; Am Chem Soc. *Res:* Spectroscopic studies of metallothionein; computer assisted analytical chemistry; expert systems in analytical chemistry, electrochemistry and photochemistry of inorganic and biological systems; magnetic circular dichroism of heme proteins, porphyrins, phthalocyanines; binding of cadmium, copper and mercury in biological systems. *Mailing Add:* Dept Chem Univ Western Ont London ON N6A 5B7 Can. *Fax:* 519-661-3022; *E-Mail:* stillman@uwo.ca

STILLMAN, RICHARD ERNEST, mathematics, chemical engineering, for more information see previous edition

STILLMAN, RONA BARBARA, ANALYSIS OF MAJOR INFORMATION SYSTEMS, COMMUNICATIONS & NETWORKING OF SYSTEMS. *Current Pos:* CHIEF SCIENTIST, US GEN ACCT OFF, 84- *Personal Data:* b New York, NY, Apr 16, 44; m 65, Neil J. *Educ:* City Univ New York, BA, 64; Yeshiva Univ, MA, 67; Syracuse Univ, PhD(comput sci), 72. *Prof Exp:* Proj mgr, Nat Bur Stand, 72-75; asst to chief scientist for comput, Defense Commun Agency, 77-81; assoc dir technol, USAF, 81-84. *Mem:* Asn Comput Mach; Inst Elec & Electronics Engrs. *Res:* Technical content of testimonies; evaluating major federal information and communications systems and recommending improvements. *Mailing Add:* US Gen Acct Off 441 G St NW AIMD Washington DC 20548

STILLWAY, LEWIS WILLIAM, BIOCHEMISTRY. *Current Pos:* assoc chem, 69-71, from asst prof to assoc prof biochem, 71-83, PROF BIOCHEM, MED UNIV, SC, 83- *Personal Data:* b Casper, Wyo, Feb 27, 39; m 59; c 2. *Educ:* Col Idaho, BS, 62; Univ Idaho, MS, 65, PhD(biochem), 68. *Prof Exp:* Fel, Inst Marine Sci, Univ Miami, 68-69. *Concurrent Pos:* Ed, Med Biochem Question Bank, 78-; vis prof, Col Charleston Gov Sch, 88- *Mem:* Am Soc Biochem & Molecular Biol. *Res:* Science educational methods; lipid chemistry and metabolism. *Mailing Add:* Dept Biochem Med Univ SC 171 Ashley Ave Charleston SC 29425-0002. *Fax:* 803-792-4322

STILLWELL, EDGAR FELDMAN, PHYSIOLOGY. *Current Pos:* ASSOC PROF BIOL, OLD DOM UNIV, 68- *Personal Data:* b Staten Island, NY, Nov 2, 29. *Educ:* Wagner Mem Lutheran Col, BS, 51; Duke Univ, MA, 53, PhD(zool), 57. *Prof Exp:* Asst zool, Duke Univ, 52-56, res assoc, 56-57; asst prof biol, Longwood Col, 57-60 & Univ SC, 60-61; assoc prof zool, E Carolina Univ, 61-68. *Concurrent Pos:* NASA-Am Soc Eng Educ fac res fel, Langley Res Ctr, 69-70; NASA res grant, 71-72. *Mem:* AAAS; Am Soc Cell Biol. *Res:* Mitogenetic control mechanisms in central nervous system neurons in tissue culture. *Mailing Add:* 413 Warner Circle Norfolk VA 23509

STILLWELL, EPHRAIM POSEY, JR, SOLID STATE PHYSICS. *Current Pos:* RETIRED. *Personal Data:* b Sylva, NC, Aug 29, 34; m 60; c 2. *Educ:* Wake Forest Col, BS, 56; Univ Va, MS, 58, PhD(physics), 60. *Prof Exp:* From asst prof to prof physics, Clemson Univ, 60-90, head dept, 71-74. *Concurrent Pos:* US Air Force Off Sci Res grant, 63-69. *Mem:* Am Asn Physics Teachers; Am Phys Soc; AAAS. *Res:* Magnetoresistance in metals; superconductivity. *Mailing Add:* Gates Community Six Mile SC 29682

STILLWELL, GEORGE KEITH, PHYSICAL MEDICINE. *Current Pos:* RETIRED. *Personal Data:* b Moose Jaw, Sask, July 11, 18; m 43; c 2. *Educ:* Univ Sask, BA, 39; Queen's Univ, Ont, MD, CM, 42; Univ Minn, PhD(phys med & rehab), 54; Am Bd Phys Med & Rehab, dipl, 52. *Prof Exp:* Instr, Mayo Med Sch, 50-54, from asst prof to prof, Mayo Grad Sch Med, 55-73, chmn dept, 73-81, emer prof phys med rehab, 83- *Concurrent Pos:* Consult, Mayo Clin, 54-83. *Mem:* Cong Rehab Med; Am Acad Phys Med & Rehab. *Res:* Rehabilitation; physiologic effects of therapeutic procedures; edema of peripheral origin. *Mailing Add:* Emer Staff Mayo Clin 200 1st St SW Rochester MN 55905-0001

STILLWELL, HAROLD DANIEL, PHYSICAL GEOGRAPHY, BIOGEOGRAPHY. *Current Pos:* PROF GEOG, APPALACHIAN STATE UNIV, 71- *Personal Data:* b Staten Island, NY, Mar 21, 31; m 64; c 2. *Educ:* Duke Univ, BS, 52, MF, 54; Mich State Univ, PhD, 61. *Prof Exp:* Forestry aid, US Forest Serv, NC, 52; asst, Ore Forest Res Ctr, 54-57; asst geog, Mich State Univ, 57-59; asst prof, Eastern Mich Univ, 60-61 & Univ Tex, 61-62; assoc prof, ECarolina Univ, 62-71. *Mem:* Asn Am Geographers; Sigma Xi; Int Geog Union. *Res:* Natural hazards of mountain areas, particularly avalanche prediction; mountain geo-ecology with analysis of tree line location; remote sensing. *Mailing Add:* 123 Hawthorne Lane Boone NC 28607

STILLWELL, RICHARD NEWHALL, ORGANIC CHEMISTRY, COMPUTER SCIENCE. *Current Pos:* CONSULT, 84- *Personal Data:* b Princeton, NJ, Nov 22, 35. *Educ:* Princeton Univ, BA, 57; Harvard Univ, MA, 59, PhD(chem), 64. *Prof Exp:* From instr to prof chem, Baylor Col Med, 63-84. *Mem:* Am Chem Soc; Am Soc Mass Spectrometry; Asn Comput Mach. *Res:* Chemistry of natural products; chemical modelling; analytical systems. *Mailing Add:* 10 Daniels Dr Bedford MA 01730-1202

STILLWELL, WILLIAM HARRY, BIOCHEMISTRY, BIOPHYSICS. *Current Pos:* asst prof, 78-81, assoc prof, 82-92, PROF BIOL, IND UNIV-PURDUE UNIV, INDIANAPOLIS, 93- *Personal Data:* b Albany, NY, Mar 30, 46; m 78, Penelope Jordon; c 2. *Educ:* State Univ NY, Albany, BS, 67; Pa State Univ, MS, 73, PhD(biochem), 74. *Prof Exp:* Res asst prof origin life, Inst Molecular & Cellular Evolution, 74-75; res assoc membrane biophys, Mich State Univ, 76-78. *Mem:* AAAS; NY Acad Sci; Biophys Soc; Am Soc Plant Physiol. *Res:* Membrane biochemistry and biophysics; artificial membrane systems; action of plant hormones on membranes; origin of life; action of retinoids on membranes; affects N-3 fatty acids on membranes. *Mailing Add:* SL 2380A Dept Biol Ind Univ Purdue Indianapolis IN 46202-5132

STILWELL, BRIAN DAVID, POLYMER FOAMING. *Current Pos:* process engr extrusion, 81-87, res & develop process develop engr, 87-95, RES & DEVELOP PROD DEVELOP ENGR, OWENS-ILL, 96- *Personal Data:* b Monticello, Ind, Aug 21, 56; m 77, Benedetta French; c Tanya & Benjamin. *Educ:* Eastern Ky Univ, BS, 79. *Prof Exp:* Chem instr, Wayne Co Bd Educ, 79-81; prod engr extrusion, Mabex Universal, 95-96. *Concurrent Pos:* Int tech consult polymer foam extrusion, Owens-Ill, 87- *Mem:* Soc Plastic Engrs; sr mem Soc Mfg Engrs. *Res:* Development of new polymer process and products; carbon dioxide gas injection and extrusion; polymer blending for low yield material. *Mailing Add:* 1400 Cecil Lane Bardstown KY 40004. *Fax:* 502-348-7675; *E-Mail:* brians@bardstown.com

STILWELL, DONALD LONSON, ANATOMY. *Current Pos:* from instr to asst prof, 49-59, asst dean, 64-65, ASSOC PROF ANAT, SCH MED, STANFORD UNIV, 60- *Personal Data:* b Detroit, Mich, Dec 29, 18. *Educ:* Wayne State Univ, AB, 41, MD, 44. *Prof Exp:* Intern, Harper Hosp, Detroit, 44-45, resident surg, 45-56. *Concurrent Pos:* Fel anat, Wayne State Univ, 58-59. *Mem:* AAAS; Am Asn Anat. *Res:* Anatomy; experimental pathology; vascularization of vertebral column; innervation of hand, foot, joints, spine and eye; blood supply of brain. *Mailing Add:* 2244 Santa Ana Palo Alto CA 94303-3137

STILWELL, KENNETH JAMES, MATHEMATICS. *Current Pos:* from assoc prof to prof, 66-93, EMER PROF MATH, NE MO STATE UNIV, 93- *Personal Data:* b Poughkeepsie, NY, Apr 4, 34; m 56; c 3. *Educ:* Bob Jones Univ, BS, 56; Ariz State Univ, MA, 59; Univ Ariz, MS, 64; Hunter Col, MA, 65; Univ Northern Colo, EdD(math educ), 71. *Prof Exp:* Instr high schs, Ariz, 57-64; asst prof math, King's Col, NY, 65-66. *Concurrent Pos:* Comput specialist Carrolltom Sch, 84-85. *Mem:* Math Asn Am; Nat Coun Teachers Math; Sch Sci & Mat Asn. *Res:* Mathematics education; effect of video-tape and critique on attitude of pre-service mathematics teachers. *Mailing Add:* Truman State Univ Kirksville MO 63501

STIMMEL, GLEN LEWIS, CLINICAL PHARMACY, PSYCHOPHARMACOLOGY. *Current Pos:* asst prof clin pharm, Sch Pharm, 74-78, assoc prof, 79-84, PROF CLIN PHARM & PSYCHIAT, SCHS PHARM & MED, UNIV SOUTHERN CALIF, 84- *Personal Data:* b Lynwood, Calif, Mar 18, 49; m 89, Susan Wogoman; c Andrea & Nathan. *Educ:* Univ Calif, San Francisco, DPhar(pharm), 72. *Honors & Awards:* Clin Pract Award, Am Col Clin Pharm, 91. *Prof Exp:* Clin pharmacist psychopharm, Dept Health, San Francisco, 73-74. *Concurrent Pos:* Chmn, Pharm Sect, Am Pharmaceut Asn, 76-78; consult, Div Ment Health Servs, NIMH, Md, 80-85, Health Care Finance Admin, Health & Human Servs, DC, 85-90; panel mem, defined diets & childhood hyperactiv, NIH, 82; bd mem, Pharm Coun Mental Health, 91- *Mem:* Fel Am Col Clin Pharm (pres, 83-84); Am Soc Hosp Pharmacists; Am Pharmaceut Asn; Am Asn Col Pharm. *Res:* Clinical pharmacology; psychopharmacy education; health manpower utilization, expanded clinical poles for pharmacists; prescriptive authority for pharmacists. *Mailing Add:* 362 Tamarac Dr Pasadena CA 91105

STIMMELL, K G, engineering, for more information see previous edition

STIMSON, MIRIAM MICHAEL, ORGANIC CHEMISTRY. *Current Pos:* dir, Grad Studies Off, 78-91, EMER PROF, SIENA HEIGHTS COL, 91- *Personal Data:* b Chicago, Ill, Dec 24, 13. *Educ:* Siena Heights Col, BS, 36; Inst Divi Thomae, MS, 39, PhD(chem), 48. *Honors & Awards:* Charles Williams Award, 42. *Prof Exp:* Head res lab, Siena Heights Col, 36-68, instr chem, 39-46, asst prof, 46-50, prof natural sci & head div, 50-69; chmn dept, Keuka Col, 69-74, prof chem, 69-78. *Concurrent Pos:* Exec Comt, bd dirs Mich Consortium Substance Abuse Educ, 83-88, pres, 87-88; mem, SCent Mich Substance Abuse Comn, 91-93. *Mem:* Am Chem Soc; Nat Asn Women Deans & Counselors; Am Asn Coun & Develop. *Res:* Infrared and ultraviolet absorption in the solid state by potassium bromide disks; effect of irradiation on pyrimidines in the solid state. *Mailing Add:* Grad Studies Off Siena Heights Col Adrian MI 49221. *Fax:* 517-265-3380

STINAFF, RUSSELL DALTON, ELECTRICAL ENGINEERING, CYBERNETICS. *Current Pos:* CONSULT, 94- *Personal Data:* b Akron, Ohio, Mar 17, 40; m 68; c 1. *Educ:* Univ Akron, BSEE, 62; Purdue Univ, Lafayette, MSEE, 63; Univ Ill, Urbana, PhD(elec eng), 69. *Prof Exp:* Electronic engr, Nat Security Agency, 64-65; asst prof elec eng, Clemson Univ, 69-76; mem staff, Honeywell, Inc, 80-94. *Concurrent Pos:* US Off Sci Res grant, 71-73. *Mem:* AAAS; Simulation Coun; Am Soc Eng Educ; Inst Elec & Electronics Engrs; Asn Comput Mach. *Res:* Artificial intelligence; application of computers to education; simulation of large systems. *Mailing Add:* 615 W Braeside Dr Arlington Heights IL 60004

STINCHCOMB, THOMAS GLENN, RADIATION PHYSICS, MEDICAL PHYSICS. *Current Pos:* chmn dept, De Paul Univ, 68-76, head, Nat Sci & Math Div, 84-87, prof, 68-71, EMER PROF PHYSICS, DE PAUL UNIV, 71- *Personal Data:* b Tiffin, Ohio, Sept 12, 22; m 45, Maxine Orr Kohler; c James A, William T, David G & Dan T. *Educ:* Heidelberg Col, BS, 44; Univ Chicago, MS, 48, PhD(physics), 51. *Prof Exp:* From instr to asst prof physics, State Col Wash, 51-54; from assoc prof to prof & head dept, Heidelberg Col, 54-61; res physicist, Nuclear & Radiation Physics Sect, IIT Res Inst, 61-65, sr physicist & group leader, 65-68. *Concurrent Pos:* Actg mgr, Nuclear & Radiation Physics Sect, IIT Res Inst, 66-67; vis res assoc, Radiol Dept, Univ Chicago, 76-; mem, Task Group 18, Fast Neutron Beam Dosimetry, Am Asn Physicists Med, 79-85, Comt Continuing Educ, 82-85, vpres & prog chmn, Midwest Sect, 87-89, pres, 90-92. *Mem:* Sigma Xi; Am Asn Physics Teachers; Am Nuclear Soc; Fed Am Scientists; Am Asn Physicist Med; Am Inst Physics. *Res:* Medical applications of nuclear radiation physics, mainly the application of microdosimetric methods to assess the effects of neutron and alpha particle irradiations. *Mailing Add:* Dept Physics De Paul Univ Lincoln Park Campus Chicago IL 60614-3504. *Fax:* 773-325-7334; *E-Mail:* tstinchc@wppost.depaul.edu

STINCHCOMB, WAYNE WEBSTER, composite materials, mechanics; deceased, see previous edition for last biography

STINCHFIELD, CARLETON PAUL, adhesives & resin bonding, hazardous materials handling; deceased, see previous edition for last biography

STINE, GERALD JAMES, HUMAN GENETICS, MICROBIAL GENETICS. *Current Pos:* PROF GENETICS & MICROBIOL, UNIV NFLA, 72- *Personal Data:* b Johnstown, Pa, May 29, 35; m 62, Delores Calcagri; c 2. *Educ:* Southern Conn State Col, BS, 61; Dartmouth Col, MA, 63; Univ Del, PhD(biol-genetics), 66. *Prof Exp:* Geneticist, Oak Ridge Nat Lab, 66-68; asst prof microbiol genetics, Univ Tenn, Knoxville, 68-72. *Concurrent Pos:* Union Carbide fel, 66-68; consult, Oak Ridge Nat Lab, 68-; dir cytogenetics, Regional Genetic Ctr, Jacksonville, Fla, 82-85. *Mem:* Genetics Soc Am; Sigma Xi; Am Soc Human Genetics; assoc Inst Soc Ethics & Life Sci; Asn Cytogenetic Technologists; Nat Soc Genetic Counr. *Res:* Association of human blood groups and behavior. *Mailing Add:* Dept Natural Sci Univ N Fla 4567 St Johns Bluff S Jacksonville FL 32224-2646

STINE, PHILIP ANDREW, METALLURGICAL ENGINEERING, SHEET METAL FORMING. *Current Pos:* metall engr, Appl Res & Design Ctr, Gen Elec Co, 71-75, sr res metallurgist, 82-84, prog mgr, 84-85, mgr, Metall Lab, 84-85, mgr, Metall & Ceramics Lab, 85-89, staff metall, Appl Res & Design Ctr, 89-91, SR METALLURGIST, APPLIANCE TECHNOL, GEN ELEC CO, 91- *Personal Data:* b Detroit, Mich, Aug 12, 44; m 67, Carol Lynn Summers; c Laurie A & Philip A II. *Educ:* Wayne State Univ, BSME, 67; Purdue Univ, MS, 68, PhD(metall eng), 72. *Prof Exp:* Advan res projs agency res asst, Purdue Univ, Lafayette, 68-71. *Concurrent Pos:* Lectr sheet metal forming technol, Am Soc Metals, 80-89; hon fac mem, Acad Metal & Mat. *Mem:* Am Inst Metall Engrs; Am Soc Metals; Am Deep Drawing Res Group (treas, 76-78, secy, 78-80, pres, 80-82). *Res:* Formability research including methods and techniques that allow forming difficulty determination for given die, steel and lubricant conditions, allowing definition of optimum forming conditions; implemented computer analysis that predicts forming fractures at concept phase of new sheet metal designs. *Mailing Add:* 3326 Webb Rd Simpsonville KY 40067

STINE, WILLIAM H, JR, CHEMICAL ENGINEERING, TEXTILE ENGINEERING. *Current Pos:* engr, Carother Res Lab, E I du Pont de Nemours & Co, Inc, 55-58, res engr, 58-62, sr res engr, Textile Res Lab, 62-65, res supvr, 65-81, res assoc indust prod res, Textile Fibers Dept, 81-83. *Personal Data:* b Cincinnati, Ohio, Mar 23, 26; m 48; c 3. *Educ:* Univ Cincinnati, ChemE, 50. *Prof Exp:* Res technician, Chem Res Lab, Nat Cash Register Co, Ohio, 49; engr, Res & Develop Lab, Champion Paper & Fibre Co, 50-55. *Res:* Fiber technology; physical, physico-chemical, chemical and statistical relationships between fibers and end uses; polyamides and melt spinning processes. *Mailing Add:* Coffee Run Hockessin DE 19707

STINE, WILLIAM R, ORGANIC CHEMISTRY, BIOCHEMISTRY. *Current Pos:* From asst prof to assoc prof, 65-78, PROF CHEM, WILKES COL, 78- *Personal Data:* b Schenectady, NY, Dec 14, 38; c 1. *Educ:* Union Col, BS, 60; Syracuse Univ, PhD(chem), 66. *Mem:* Am Chem Soc; AAAS; Am Asn Univ Prof. *Res:* Structure of pentavalent phosphorus compounds; reactions of tertiary phosphines with positive halogen compounds; natural product synthesis. *Mailing Add:* Dept Chem Wilkes Col Wilkes-Barre PA 18766-0002

STINGELIN, RONALD WERNER, COAL & MINING GEOLOGY, REMOTE SENSING. *Current Pos:* GEOTECH CONSULT & REGIST PROF GEOLOGIST, 84- *Personal Data:* b New York, NY, May 29, 35; m 73, Janet L Hummel; c Jennifer L & Ronald D. *Educ:* City Col New York, BS, 57; Lehigh Univ, MS, 59; Pa State Univ, PhD(geol), 65. *Prof Exp:* Res geologist, HRB Singer Inc, 65-67, sr res geologist, 67 -68, mgr, Environ Sci Br, 68-72, prin geologist, Energy & Natural Resource Systs Dept, 72-80; vpres tech serv, Resource Technol Corp, 80-84. *Concurrent Pos:* NSF-Am Soc Photogram vis scientist, 68-71. *Mem:* Fel Geol Soc Am; Am Inst Prof Geologists. *Res:* Application of remote sensing to environmental problems; energy, resources and technology assessment studies with emphasis on fossil fuels; subsidence, seam interaction and prediction of roof hazards in coal mining; Appalachian coal geology, abandoned mined land problems, and mineral resource evaluation; Pennsylvania anthracite resources; mineral resource estimation and site investigations. *Mailing Add:* 120 Ronan Dr State College PA 16801-7809. *Fax:* 814-237-1769; *E-Mail:* rws@resourcetec.com

STINGER, HENRY J(OSEPH), ENGINEERING PHYSICS. *Current Pos:* RETIRED. *Personal Data:* b Minneapolis, Minn, Nov 22, 20; m 51; c 3. *Educ:* Univ Minn, BEE, 42; Mass Inst Technol, cert, 43. *Prof Exp:* Electronic engr, Control Corp, 46-47; supvr res lab, Gen Mills, Inc, 47-51; chief reactors br, Savannah River Oper Off, US Atomic Energy Comn, 51-52; res supvr, E I Du Pont De Nemours & Co, Inc, 53-62, res assoc, 62-85. *Concurrent Pos:* Pvt consult, 85-. *Mem:* Inst Elec & Electronics Engrs. *Res:* Tribiology; electronic properties of materials; electronic devices; electromagnetic shielding & materials; instrumentation & controls. *Mailing Add:* 119 Devonwood Lane Devon PA 19333

STINGL, GEORG, IMMUNODERMATOLOGY, DERMATOLOGIC MICROBIOLOGY. *Current Pos:* staff, 81-92, PROF DERMAT & HEAD, DIV IMMUNOL, ALLERGY & INFECTIOUS DIS, DEPT DERMAT UNIV VIENNA MED SCH, 92- *Personal Data:* b Vienna, Austria, Oct 28, 48; m 80, Laura A. *Educ:* Univ Vienna, MD, 73; Am Acad Dermat, dipl, 82. *Honors & Awards:* Montagna Award, Soc Investigative Dermat, 86; Karl Landsteiner Award, Austrian Soc Immunol, 88, Clemens von Pirquet Award, 92. *Prof Exp:* Res, Dept Dermat I, Univ Vienna, 73-76; fel dermat, Nat Cancer Inst, 77-78; staff, Dept Dermat, Univ Innsbruck, 78-81. *Concurrent Pos:* Vis scientist, Nat Inst Allergy & Infectious Dis, Lab Immunol, NIH, 85-86. *Mem:* Soc Investigative Dermat; Am Asn Immunologists; Am Fedn Clin Res; Ger Dermat Soc; Am Dermat Asn; Am Acad Derm. *Res:* Immunology of the epidermis; langerhans cells; skin T-cells; acquired immunodeficiency syndrome; Kaposi's sarcoma; tumor vaccines; skin allergy. *Mailing Add:* Univ Vienna Med Sch Dept Dermat Waehringer Guertel 18-20/7J Vienna A-1090 Austria. *Fax:* 43-1-4031900

STINGL, HANS ALFRED, INDUSTRIAL ORGANIC CHEMISTRY. *Current Pos:* res & develop chemist, 58-75, DEVELOP ASSOC, CIBA-GEIGY CORP-TOMS RIVER PLANT, 75- *Personal Data:* b Eger, Czech, Oct 13, 27; US citizen; m 54; c 2. *Educ:* Univ Erlangen, dipl, 54, PhD(org chem), 56. *Prof Exp:* Res assoc org chem, Univ Ill, Urbana, 56-58. *Mem:* Fel Am Inst Chem; Am Chem Soc; NY Acad Sci. *Res:* Organic dyestuffs and intermediates. *Mailing Add:* 852 Ocean View Dr Toms River NJ 08753-2797

STINI, WILLIAM ARTHUR, HUMAN BIOLOGY, PHYSICAL ANTHROPOLOGY. *Current Pos:* PROF ANTHROP, UNIV ARIZ, 76-, PROF FAMILY & COMMUNITY MED, 79- *Personal Data:* b Oshkosh, Wis, Oct 9, 30; m 50, Mary R Kalous; c 3. *Educ:* Univ Wis, BBA, 60, MS, 67, PhD(human biol), 69. *Prof Exp:* From asst prof to assoc prof anthrop, Cornell Univ, 68-73; assoc prof, Univ Kans, 73-76. *Concurrent Pos:* Mem rev panel, Anthrop Prog, NSF, 76-78; field ed, Phys Anthrop, Am Anthropologist, 79-82; mem, Gov Adv Coun on Aging, 80-83, Ariz Cancer Ctr, 94-; ed-in-chief, Am J Phys Anthrop, 83-; fel, Linacre Col & Univ of Oxford, 85; pres, Am Asn Phys Anthropologists, 89-91; vis fel, Univ London, 91; chair, Anthrop, Social & Ling Rev Panel; NSF grad fel prog, 93-94. *Mem:* Fel AAAS; Am Asn Phys Anthrop; fel NY Acad Sci; Am Anthrop Asn; Am Inst Nutrit; Sigma Xi. *Res:* Effects of stress on human development including growth and maturation as measured by gross morphological and serological parameters; evaluation of stress as evolutionary force; nutrition and aging; alterations in bone mineral metabolism associated with aging. *Mailing Add:* Dept Anthrop Univ Ariz Tucson AZ 85721-0001. *Fax:* 520-621-2088; *E-Mail:* stini@ccit.arizona.edu

STINNER, RONALD EDWIN, POPULATION ECOLOGY. *Current Pos:* res assoc, NC State Univ, 70-73, from asst prof to assoc prof, 73-83, dir, Biomath Grad Prog, 88-91, PROF ENTOM & BIOMATH, NC STATE UNIV, 83-; DIR, CTR INTEGRATED PEST MGT, NSF, 93- *Personal Data:* b New York, NY, July 27, 43; m 84, Karen Asbury; c Michelle & Chad. *Educ:* NC State Univ, BS, 65; Univ Calif, Berkeley, PhD(entom), 70. *Prof Exp:* Res assoc entom, Tex A&M Univ, 70. *Concurrent Pos:* Ed, Environ Entom, 87-97. *Mem:* Entom Soc Am; Entom Soc Can; Int Orgn Biol Control. *Res:* Modeling of population dynamics of agricultural pest insects and pathogens; internet dissemination of pest management information. *Mailing Add:* NSF Ctr IPM Suite 1100 Partners I / N Campus Dr Raleigh NC 27606. *Fax:* 919-515-2824; *E-Mail:* ron_stinner@ncsu.edu

STINNETT, HENRY ORR, CARDIOPULMONARY PHYSIOLOGY, BIOMATHEMATICS. *Current Pos:* asst prof, 76-81, ASSOC PROF PHYSIOL, SCH MED, UNIV NDAK, 81- *Personal Data:* b San Francisco, Calif. *Educ:* Calif State Univ, Sacramento, AB, 63; Univ Calif, Davis, 69, MS, 69, PhD(physiol), 74. *Prof Exp:* Lab technician III res, Dept Avian Sci, Univ Calif, Davis, 64-69, res physiologist, 76-80. *Concurrent Pos:* Fel pharmacol, Health Sci Ctr, Univ Tex, 74-75, asst lectr, 75-76; Am Heart Asn grant, Univ Tex Health Sci Ctr, 75-76 & Sch Med, Univ NDak, 77-83. *Mem:* Sigma Xi; Am Physiol Soc; Nat Asn Underwater Instr; Soc Exp Biol Med. *Res:* Cardiovascular, pulmonary physiology; modulatory interactions of the cardiopulmonary mechanoreceptors on the systemic cardiovascular baroreflexes during lung inflation; models, mathematical of carotid sinus wall strain and Sororeceptor transduction of wall strain to fiber activity. *Mailing Add:* Dept Acad Affairs Sch Med Univ NDak Grand Forks ND 58202-9037

STINO, FARID KAMAL RAMZI, BIOMETRICS, BIOSTATISTICS. *Current Pos:* PROF BIOSTATIST, FLA A&M UNIV, 88- *Personal Data:* m 68, Zandra Hargrove; c Ramzi, Farida, Karim & Magdi. *Educ:* Cairo Univ, Egypt, BSc, 64; Univ Ga, MSc, 68, PhD(pop genetics), 71. *Prof Exp:* Postdoctoral fel, Univ Ga, 71-72; asst prof pap genetics, Cairo Univ, Egypt, 72-77, assoc prof, 77-82, prof, 82-88. *Concurrent Pos:* Consult, Stino Agriconsults, 77-88. *Mem:* Fel Am Statist Asn; fel Biomet Soc; fel Am Soc Animal Sci; fel AAAS; fel Poultry Sci Asn; fel Sigma Xi. *Res:* Pharmacogenetic lines of mice that are sensitive and resistant to pentobarbital. *Mailing Add:* 6579 Montrose Trail Tallahassee FL 32308-1607. *Fax:* 850-894-3366; *E-Mail:* fstino@famu.edu

STINSKI, MARK FRANCIS, MICROBIOLOGY, BIOCHEMISTRY. *Current Pos:* asst prof, 73-78, ASSOC PROF VIROL, DEPT MICROBIOL, UNIV IOWA, 78- *Personal Data:* b Appleton, Wis, Jan 6, 41; m 68; c 2. *Educ:* Mich State Univ, BS, 64, MS, 66, PhD(microbiol & biochem), 69. *Prof Exp:* Instr microbiol, Dept Biol Sci, Western Mich Univ, 67; res virologist, US Army Med Sci Lab, Ft Detrick, 69-71; NIH fel virol, Dept Microbiol, Univ Pa, 71-73. *Concurrent Pos:* Am Cancer Soc grant, Dept Microbiol, Univ Iowa, 74-77; grant reviewer, Nat Found, 77-79, NSF, 78, 79 & 81, NIH, 78 & 80; NIH grant, 79-84, NIH res career develop award, 80-85. *Mem:* Am Soc Microbiol; Sigma Xi; AAAS; Soc Exp Biol & Med. *Res:* Transcription of the human cytomegalovirus genome; cytomegalovirus genome regulation; herpes virus cellular transformation and replication. *Mailing Add:* Dept of Microbiol Univ Iowa Col Med 3403 Bowen Sci Iowa City IA 52242-1109

STINSON, AL WORTH, ANIMAL BEHAVIOR. *Current Pos:* asst prof, 64-68, assoc prof, 68-73, PROF VET ANAT, MICH STATE UNIV, 73- *Personal Data:* b Monroe, NC, Aug 5, 26; m 60; c 4. *Educ:* NC State Col, BS, 49; Univ Ga, DVM, 56; Univ Minn, MS, 60. *Prof Exp:* Instr vet anat, Univ Minn, 56-60; asst prof vet anat, Cornell Univ, 60-64. *Mem:* Am Asn Vet Anatomists; Am Asn Anatomists. *Res:* Histology of domestic animals. *Mailing Add:* 1915 Epley Rd Williamston MI 48895

STINSON, DONALD CLINE, ELECTRICAL ENGINEERING. *Current Pos:* MEM TECH STAFF, HUGHES AIRCRAFT CO, 69- *Personal Data:* b Malta, Idaho, Dec 7, 25; m 54; c 5. *Educ:* Iowa State Col, BS, 47; Calif Inst Technol, MS, 49; Univ Calif, EE, 53, PhD, 56. *Prof Exp:* Test engr, Gen Elec Co, NY, 47-48; asst elec eng, Univ Calif, 50-52, asst, Electronic Res Lab, 53-56; sr scientist, Missile Systs Div, Lockheed Aircraft Corp, 56-57, group leader microwaves, 57-58, res scientist, 58; prof elec eng, Univ Ariz, 58-68 & Univ Tex, Arlington, 68-69. *Concurrent Pos:* Consult, McGraw-Hill Bk Co, 59- & Tex Instruments Inc, 68- *Mem:* Inst Elec & Electronics Engrs. *Res:* Electromagnetic theory; microwave engineering and networks; evaluation of intrinsic properties of and frequency multiplying in microwave ferrites; parametric amplifiers; damping mechanism of ferrimagnetic resonance in ferrites. *Mailing Add:* Lockheed Aircraft Service Co PO Box 33 1-304 15 Ontario CA 91762

STINSON, DONALD LEO, PETROLEUM ENGINEERING, CHEMICAL ENGINEERING. *Current Pos:* CONSULT, 86- *Personal Data:* b Hominy, Okla, Oct 8, 30; m 51; c 6. *Educ:* Univ Okla, BS, 50; Univ Mich, MS, 51, PhD(chem eng), 57. *Prof Exp:* Res engr, Phillips Petrol Co, 53-58; proj engr, Gulf Res & Develop Co, 58-60; prof petrol eng & head dept, Univ Wyo, 60-72, head dept mineral eng, 72-79, prof petrol eng, 79-81; vpres eng, Arnjac Corp, 81-86. *Concurrent Pos:* Consult, 62-, Petrol Res Ctr, US Bur Mines, 63- & Cooper Estate, 64- *Mem:* Am Chem Soc; Am Inst Chem Engrs; Am Inst Mining, Metall & Petrol Engrs; Nat Soc Prof Engrs; Soc Petrol Eng Eval. *Res:* Thermodynamics; waste disposal; water treatment; power recovery. *Mailing Add:* 1074 Alta Vista Dr Laramie WY 82070-5004

STINSON, DOUGLAS G, OPTICAL DATA STORAGE, MAGNETO-OPTICS. *Current Pos:* Sr res scientist, Res Lab, Diversified Technol Group, 81-90, MGR, ERASABLE OPTICAL MEDIA DEVELOP, MASS MEMORY DIV, EASTMAN KODAK CO, 90- *Personal Data:* b Manchester, NH, Nov 14, 53. *Educ:* New Col, Sarasota, FL, BA, 75; Univ Ill MS, 76, PhD(physics), 81. *Mem:* Am Phys Soc; Inst Elec & Electronics Engrs. *Res:* Materials, processes and systems for erasable optical data storage. *Mailing Add:* 26 Little Spring Run Fairport NY 14450-3204

STINSON, EDGAR ERWIN, ORGANIC CHEMISTRY, BIOCHEMISTRY. *Current Pos:* RES CHEMIST, AGR & FOOD CHEM, USDA, 57- *Personal Data:* b Auburn, Ind, May 14, 27; m 74; c 4. *Educ:* Purdue Univ, BS, 48; Iowa State Univ, MS, 51, PhD(biochem), 53. *Prof Exp:* Asst prof org chem, Villanova Univ, 53-56; asst prof, Mass Col Pharm, 56-57. *Mem:* Am Chem Soc; Inst Food Technologists. *Res:* Mycotoxins; mold metabolism. *Mailing Add:* 7810 Lafayette Ave Melrose Park Philadelphia PA 19126-1406

STINSON, GLEN MONETTE, EXPERIMENTAL NUCLEAR PHYSICS. *Current Pos:* Fel physics, Univ Alta, 66-68, res assoc, Tri/Univ Meson Facility, 68-69, asst res physicist, 69-71, asst prof, 71-76, ASSOC PROF PHYSICS, TRI-UNIV MESON FACILITY, UNIV ALTA, 76-, SR SCIENTIST. *Personal Data:* b Sarnia, Ont, Dec 27, 39; m 62; c 3. *Educ:* Univ Toronto, BASc, 61; Univ Waterloo, MSc, 62; McMaster Univ, PhD(nuclear physics), 66. *Concurrent Pos:* Lectr, Univ Alta, 66-68. *Mem:* Am Phys Soc; Can Asn Physicists. *Res:* Proton induced reactions; design and use of high precision magnetic spectrometers; design of charged particle beam transport systems. *Mailing Add:* Dept Physics Univ Alta Edmonton AB T6G 2J1 Can

STINSON, HARRY THEODORE, JR, GENETICS. *Current Pos:* chmn dept bot, 64-65, chmn sect genetics, develop & physiol, 65-77, PROF GENETICS, CORNELL UNIV, 62-, ASSOC DIR DIV BIOL SCI, 77-, DIR UNDERGRAD STUDIES, 80- *Personal Data:* b Newport News, Va, Oct 26, 26; m 49; c 3. *Educ:* Col William & Mary, BS, 47; Ind Univ, PhD(cytogenetics), 51. *Prof Exp:* Asst prof biol, Col William & Mary, 51-52; res asst genetics, Conn Agr Exp Sta, 52-53, res assoc, 53-60, chief geneticist, 60-62. *Mem:* AAAS; Soc Study Evolution; Bot Soc Am; Genetics Soc Am; Am Soc Nat (treas, 63-66); Sigma Xi. *Res:* Cytology. *Mailing Add:* 118 Stimson Hall Cornell Univ Ithaca NY 14853-7101

STINSON, MARY KRYSTYNA, CHEMICAL ENGINEERING, WATER RESOURCES SCIENCE. *Current Pos:* PHYS SCIENTIST, US ENVIRON PROTECTION AGENCY, 74- *Personal Data:* b Bydgoszcz, Poland; US citizen; m 65; c 2. *Educ:* Silesia Tech Univ, Poland, MS, 59; Univ Mich, Ann Arbor, MS, 69. *Honors & Awards:* Gold Medal award, Am Electroplaters Soc, 77; Bronze Medal Awards, Environ Protection Agency, 79 & 82. *Prof Exp:* Chem engr coal chem, Cent Mining Inst, Poland, 58-65; analytical chemist, Owens-Ill Tech Ctr, 66-67; res chemist, Univ Mich, Ann Arbor, 67-68. *Mem:* Am Chem Soc. *Res:* Development of new technologies for treatment of emissions generated by metal finishing, inorganic chemicals and asbestos industries; evaluation of innovative technologies for cleanup of superfund sites. *Mailing Add:* 37 Beacon Hill Dr Metuchen NJ 08840-1603

STINSON, MICHAEL ROY, ATMOSPHERIC SOUND PROPAGATION, PHYSICAL ACOUSTICS. *Current Pos:* from asst res officer to assoc res officer, 79-92, SR RES OFFICER, NAT RES COUN CAN, 93- *Personal Data:* b Vancouver, BC, Aug 9, 49; m 74, Susan E Thompson; c Kevin M, Cheryl A, Valerie G & Christopher E. *Educ:* Simon Fraser Univ, BSc, 71, MSc, 73; Queens Univ, PhD(physics), 79. *Concurrent Pos:* Vis assoc res scientist, Dept Otolaryngol, Columbia Univ, NY, 86- *Mem:* Fel Acoust Soc Am; Can Acoust Asn; Inst Noise Control Eng. *Res:* Study of the propagation of sound through a real turbulent atmosphere and the implications for long-range acoustical sensing; sound propagation in porous materials, modelling of acoustical transducers and microphone arrays and modelling of the acoustical properties of the human ear canal and middle ear. *Mailing Add:* Bldg M36 Inst Microstruct Sci Nat Res Coun Ottawa ON K1A 0R6 Can. *Fax:* 613-952-1362

STINSON, PERRI JUNE, operations research, statistics, for more information see previous edition

STINSON, RICHARD FLOYD, FLORICULTURE, SCIENCE EDUCATION. *Current Pos:* from assoc prof to prof, 67-89, EMER PROF AGR, EDUC & HORT, PA STATE UNIV, UNIV PARK, 90- *Personal Data:* b Cleveland, Ohio, Feb 4, 21; m 54, Lois Decker; c 5. *Educ:* Ohio State Univ, BS, 43, MS, 47, PhD, 52. *Honors & Awards:* Outstanding Serv Award, Am Asn Teachers Educ Agr. *Prof Exp:* Instr floricult, State Univ NY Sch Agr Alfred, 47-48; asst prof, Univ Conn, 48-55; from asst prof to assoc prof hort, Mich State Univ, 55-67. *Mem:* Am Soc Hort Sci; Nat Asn Col Teachers Agr; Sigma Xi; Am Asn Agr Educ. *Res:* Horticultural and natural resources instruction material in agricultural education. *Mailing Add:* 1041 Greenfield Circle State College PA 16801

STINSON, ROBERT ANTHONY, CLINICAL BIOCHEMISTRY. *Current Pos:* from asst prof to assoc prof, 71-81, PROF PATH, UNIV ALTA, 81-, DIR, MED LAB SCI, 88- *Personal Data:* b Hamilton, Ont, Sept 30, 41; m 91; c Sarah Mae & Caroline Sue. *Educ:* Univ Toronto, BScA, 64; Univ Alta, PhD(plant biochem), 68. *Prof Exp:* Med Res Coun Can fel molecular enzym, Bristol Univ, 68-71. *Concurrent Pos:* Sci & res assoc med staff, Univ Alta Hosp, 73-; hon vis sr lectr biochem med, Univ Dundee, 77-78. *Mem:* Can Soc Clin Chemists; Can Biochem Soc. *Res:* Studies of human alkaline phosphatase; to establish through hydrolytic, phosphotransferase, protein phosphatase, membrane attachment mechanism and clinical association studies, to establish a biochemical role for the enzyme. *Mailing Add:* B 117 Sci Clin Sci Bldg Univ Alta Edmonton AB T6G 2G3 Can. *Fax:* 403-492-7794; *E-Mail:* rstinson@gpu.srv.ualberta.ca

STINSON, ROBERT HENRY, BIOPHYSICS, PHYSICS. *Current Pos:* RETIRED. *Personal Data:* b Toronto, Ont, Sept 17, 31; m 54; c 3. *Educ:* Univ Toronto, BSA, 53, MSA, 57; Univ Western Ont, PhD(biophys), 60. *Prof Exp:* Mem faculty physics dept, Ont Agr Col, 53-63; prof physics, State Univ NY Col Potsdam, 63-67; assoc prof physics, Univ Guelph, 67-88. *Mem:* Biophys Soc. *Res:* Structural changes in plant membranes due to environmental stress and protection against such damage. *Mailing Add:* Dept Physics Univ Guelph Guelph ON N1G 2W1 Can

STINSON, WILLIAM SICKMAN, JR, NEW PRODUCT DEVELOPMENT, PRODUCT IMPROVEMENT. *Current Pos:* SR DIR PROD DEVELOP, HERSHEY FOODS INC, 87- *Personal Data:* b Massillon, Ohio, May 23, 39; m 63, Ruby Roush; c William III, Christine & Mary. *Educ:* Ohio State Univ, BSc, 61, MSc, 64, PhD(food technol), 66; Xavier Univ, MBA, 76. *Prof Exp:* Group leader new prods, Gen Foods, 66-70; vpres res & develop, Frank Foods, 70-77; dir new prods, Campbell Soup Co, 77-83; vpres res & develop, Celestial Seasoning, 83-87. *Mem:* Inst Food Technol; Am Asn Candy Technologists. *Res:* Total breadth of confectionary products; aseptic products. *Mailing Add:* 2021 Crown Ct Lakeland FL 33813

STIPANOVIC, BOZIDAR J, CHEMISTRY. *Current Pos:* TECH DIR, HBS ENTERPRISES, INC, 87- *Personal Data:* b Zagreb, Yugoslavia, Jan 9, 33; m 59; c 1. *Educ:* Univ Belgrade, BS, 60, PhD(org chem), 65. *Prof Exp:* Teaching asst org chem, Univ Belgrade, 61-65; fel, Ipatieff High Pressure & Catalytic Lab, Northwestern Univ, 66-69; vis assoc prof org chem, Cent Univ Venezuela, 69-70; dir res & develop, Coral Chem Co, Waukegan, 70-76; tech dir, Res & Tech Serv, Santek Chem, 76-87. *Mem:* Am Chem Soc; Sigma Xi. *Res:* Organic catalytic reactions; surfactants; polymers; base catalyzed alkylations; conversion and chemical coatings on metals; corrosion inhibitors; paper making chemicals. *Mailing Add:* 608 Longwood E Lake Forest IL 60045-4016

STIPANOVIC, ROBERT DOUGLAS, NATURAL PRODUCT CHEMISTRY. *Current Pos:* res chemist, 71-87, RES LEADER, USDA, 87- *Personal Data:* b Houston, Tex, Oct 28, 39; m 76; c 6. *Educ:* Loyola Univ, La, BS, 61; Rice Univ, PhD(chem), 66. *Prof Exp:* Res assoc chem, Stanford Univ, 66-67; asst prof, Tex A&M Univ, 67-71. *Mem:* Am Chem Soc; Phytochem Soc NAm; Royal Soc Chem. *Res:* Natural product synthesis' biosynthesis and structure determination; mass spectroscopy structure determination and reaction mechanisms; nuclear magnetic resonance studies. *Mailing Add:* 1103 Esther Blvd Bryan TX 77802-1924. *Fax:* 409-260-9232

STIPANOWICH, JOSEPH JEAN, MATHEMATICS. *Current Pos:* RETIRED. *Personal Data:* b Canton, Ill, Apr 14, 21; m 47, Mary L Forsythe; c Thomas J & James W. *Educ:* Western Ill Univ, BS, 46; Univ Ill, MS, 47; Northwestern Univ, EdD(math), 56. *Prof Exp:* Prof math, Western Ill Univ, 47-85, head dept, 58-68. *Concurrent Pos:* Mem bd, Nat Coun Teachers Math, 70-71, chmn, Ext Affairs Comt, 71-72 & Financial Policies comt, 75; pres, Elem Math Sect & mem bd, Cent Asn Sci & Math Teachers; pres, Ill Coun Teachers Math. *Mem:* Nat Coun Teachers Math; Math Asn Am; Cent Asn Sci & Math Teachers. *Res:* History of mathematics; mathematics education. *Mailing Add:* 613 Memorial Dr Macomb IL 61455-3034

STIREWALT, HARVEY LEE, AQUATIC BIOLOGY, ICHTHYOLOGY. *Current Pos:* instr biol, 59-60, chmn, Biol Dept, 59-65, asst prof, 60-73, ASSOC PROF BIOL, AUGUSTA COL, 73- *Personal Data:* b Douglas, Ga, Jan 9, 32; m 46; c 3. *Educ:* Univ Miss, BA, 53, MS, 58; Univ Tenn, PhD(zool), 72. *Prof Exp:* Teacher biol, Acad Richmond County, 57-58, teacher physics, 58-59. *Concurrent Pos:* Grad teaching asst zool, Univ Tenn, 68-70; consult, Ga Dept Natural Resources, 71-; res supvr, Augusta Col Found Fac Res Fund, 74-75 & 77-78. *Mem:* Am Fisheries Soc. *Res:* Taxonomy, especially fishes and immature insects; pollution of aquatic systems, especially organic, inert suspended particles such as dam construction and dredging and thermal loading. *Mailing Add:* 4070 Danielle Dr Augusta GA 30907

STIRLING, ANDREW JOHN, NUCLEAR PHYSICS, INSTRUMENTATION. *Current Pos:* prof electronics, Accelerator Bus Unit, 71-77, head, Instrument Develop Br, 77-80, dir, Electronics, Instrumentation & Control Div, Atomic Energy Can Ltd, 81-85, GEN MGR, ACCELERATOR BUS UNIT, 85- *Personal Data:* b Adelaide, S Australia, Dec 23, 44; Can citizen; m 67; c 1. *Educ:* Univ Adelaide, BSc(sci), 65, BSc(physics), 66; Flinders Univ, S Australia, PhD(physics), 70. *Honors & Awards:* Outstanding Achievement Award, Can Nuclear Soc, 92. *Prof Exp:* Fel physics, Nat Res Coun Can, 69-71. *Mem:* Can Nuclear Soc. *Res:* Nuclear power instrumentation; nuclear safeguards; environmental instrumentation; linear accelerators. *Mailing Add:* AECL Accelerators 10 Hearst Way Kanata ON K2L 2P4 Can. *Fax:* 613-599-7909

STIRLING, CHARLES E, PHYSIOLOGY, BIOPHYSICS. *Current Pos:* asst prof, 68-74, ASSOC PROF PHYSIOL, UNIV WASH, 74- *Personal Data:* b Havelock, NC, Nov 30, 33; m 62; c 3. *Educ:* George Washington Univ, BA, 61; State Univ NY, PhD(physiol), 67. *Prof Exp:* Instr physiol, State Univ NY Upstate Med 66-67. *Mem:* Am Physiol Soc; ARVO; Biophys Soc; Am Soc Cell Biol. *Res:* Active transport. *Mailing Add:* Dept Physiol & Biophys Univ Wash Sch Med 3900 Seventh Ave NE Seattle WA 98195-0001

STIRLING, IAN G, ZOOLOGY, WILDLIFE MANAGEMENT. *Current Pos:* RES SCIENTIST POLAR BEARS & SEALS, CAN WILDLIFE SERV, 70- *Personal Data:* b Nkana, Zambia, Sept 26, 41; Can citizen. *Educ:* Univ BC, BSc, 63, MSc, 65; Univ Canterbury, PhD(zool), 68. *Prof Exp:* Lectr zool, Univ Canterbury, 68-69; res assoc seals, Univ Adelaide, 69-70. *Concurrent Pos:* Chmn, Fed-Prov Tech Comt Polar Bear Res Can, 71-; mem, Polar Bear Specialists Group, Int Union Conserv Nature & Natural Resources, 74- & Polar Res Bel, 83-; adj prof, Univ Atla, 79. *Mem:* Can Soc Zoologists; Can Soc Environ Biologists; Am Soc Mammalogists; Marine Mammal Soc. *Res:* Ecology, behavior, evolution and management of marine mammals in polar marine ecosystems. *Mailing Add:* 7811 144ST Edmonton AB T5R 0R1 Can

STIRN, RICHARD J, ENERGY CONVERSION, ELECTRON DEVICES. *Current Pos:* RETIRED. *Personal Data:* b Milwaukee, Wis, Dec 5, 33; m 67; c 3. *Educ:* Univ Wis, BS, 61; Purdue Univ, MS, 63, PhD(physics), 66. *Prof Exp:* Mem tech staff, Jet Propulsion Lab, Calif Inst Technol, 66-93. *Concurrent Pos:* Ed, Appl Physics Commun. *Mem:* Am Phys Soc; sr mem Inst Elec & Electronics Engrs; Am Vacuum Soc. *Res:* Solid oxide fuel cells for energy conversion; chemical vapor deposition of III-V and II-VI semiconductors; conducting high temperature ceramic fabrication; sputtering of ceramic materials. *Mailing Add:* 10941 E Minnesota Ave Sun Lakes AZ 85248-7960

STITCH, MALCOLM LANE, lasers, laser isotope separation; deceased, see previous edition for last biography

STITELER, WILLIAM MERLE, III, STATISTICS, FORESTRY. *Current Pos:* STATISTICIAN, SYRACUSE RES CORP, 88- *Personal Data:* b Kane, Pa, July 30, 42; m 64; c 1. *Educ:* Pa State Univ, BS, 64, MS, 66, PhD(statist), 70. *Prof Exp:* Asst prof statist, Pa State Univ, University Park, 70-73; from assoc prof to prof, State Univ NY Col Forestry, 73-88. *Concurrent Pos:* Consult comput models. *Mem:* Inst Math Statist; Am Statist Asn; Int Asn Ecol; Biomet Soc; Sigma Xi. *Res:* Spatial patterns in ecological populations; modeling and simulation of biological populations; computer models for response to toxic substances. *Mailing Add:* Stevens Rd Tully NY 13159

STITES, JOSEPH GANT, JR, INORGANIC CHEMISTRY, ORGANIC CHEMISTRY. *Current Pos:* RETIRED. *Personal Data:* b Hopkinsville, Ky, Mar 29, 21; m 43; c 4. *Educ:* Univ Ky, BS, 43; Mich State Univ, PhD(inorg chem), 49. *Prof Exp:* Dir new process technol, Monsanto Co, 49-73; dir process technol, Res Cottrell, Inc, 73-75; dir res & develop, Air Correction Div, UOP Inc, 75-82. *Mem:* Am Chem Soc; Environ Indust Coun; Air Pollution Control Asn. *Res:* Environmental control-gaseous and particulate collection systems, heavy chemicals, phosphates, nitrogen chemicals, explosives, rare-earths and separation techniques. *Mailing Add:* 203 Barley Mill Rd Old Hickory TN 37138

STITH, BRADLEY JAMES, DEVELOPMENTAL BIOLOGY. *Current Pos:* Res assoc, Univ Colo Health Sci Ctr, 82-87, ASST PROF, UNIV COLO, DENVER, 87- *Personal Data:* b Columbus, Ohio, Nov 14, 52. *Educ:* Wash State Univ, PhD(zoophysiol), 82. *Mem:* Am Soc Develop Biol; Am Soc Cell Biol; Int Soc Develop Biologists. *Res:* PI turnover in cell division. *Mailing Add:* Univ Colo Denver Biol Dept Campus PO Box 173364 Denver CO 80217-3364. *Fax:* 303-556-4352; *E-Mail:* Bitnet: %bstith@cudnur

STITH, JAMES HERMAN, PHYSICS, PHYSICS EDUCATION. *Current Pos:* PROF PHYSICS, OHIO STATE UNIV, 93- *Personal Data:* b Brunswick Co, Va, July 17, 41; m 65, Alberta Hill; c Adrienne, Andrea & Alyssa. *Educ:* Va State Univ, BS, 63, MS, 64; Pa State Univ, DEd(physics), 72. *Hon Degrees:* LHD, Va State Univ, 92. *Honors & Awards:* Archie L Lacey Mem Award, NY Acad Sci. *Prof Exp:* Asst instr physics, Va State Univ, 64-65; assoc engr, RCA, 67-69; from asst prof to prof physics, US Mil Acad, 72-93. *Concurrent Pos:* Instr, Far East Div, Univ Md, 65-66; vis assoc prof, USAF Acad, 76-77; proposal reviewer, Dept Educ, Minority Insts Sci Improv Prog, 81; prin investr, Mat Technol Lab, 85-87; chmn, Minorities in Physics Educ Comt, Am Asn Physics Teachers, 86-88; vis scientist, Lawrence Livermore Nat Lab, 86-87; chmn, Comt Sci for Pub, Am Asn Physics Teachers, 89-90; int adv bd, Second Inter-Am Conf on Physics Educ, 90-91. *Mem:* Am Asn Physics Teachers (vpres, 90, pres elect, 91, pres, 92); fel Am Phys Soc; fel Nat Soc Black Physicists; AAAS; Coun Sci Soc Pres (treas, 94). *Res:* Improvement of the writing of examinations and the understanding of how students assimilate the concepts of physics; inquiry based teaching and its implications for student understanding. *Mailing Add:* Ohio State Univ Dept Physics 174 W 18th Ave Columbus OH 43210-1106. *E-Mail:* stith@mps.ohio-state.edu

STITH, JEFFREY LEN, ATMOSPHERIC SCIENCES, CLOUD PHYSICS. *Current Pos:* res assoc, 80-84, assoc prof, 84-92, CHAIR ATMOSPHERIC SCI DEPT, UNIV NDAK, 90-, PROF, 92- *Personal Data:* b Seattle, Wash, July 15, 50; m 79. *Educ:* Western Wash State Col, BA, 71; Rensselaer Polytech Inst, MS, 74; Univ Wash, PhD(atmospheric sci), 78. *Prof Exp:* Res scientist, Meteorol Res Inc, 78-80. *Concurrent Pos:* Mem, Comt Cloud Physics, Am Meterol Soc. *Mem:* Am Meteorol Soc; Am Geophys Union. *Res:* Aerosol and cloud physics research. *Mailing Add:* Atmospheric Sci Box 8216 Univ Sta Univ NDak Grand Forks ND 58202-8216

STITH, LEE S, PLANT BREEDING, AGRONOMY. *Current Pos:* RETIRED. *Personal Data:* b Tulia, Tex, Aug 30, 18; m 47, Bettye J Stevens; c Peggy L. *Educ:* NMex State Univ, BS, 40; Univ Tenn, MS, 42; Iowa State Univ, PhD(crop breeding), 55. *Prof Exp:* Asst co supvr, Farm Security Admin, DeBaca Co, NMex, 40-41; res asst agr econ, Univ Tenn, 41-42; agronomist, El Paso Valley Substa 17, Tex A&M Univ, 46-47, cotton breeder, 47-55; plant breeder & prof plant breeding, Univ Ariz, 55-83, dir, Hybrid Cotton Res Proj, 72-83, dir res instr, Plant Sci Dept, 76-83; consult, Agrigenetics Res Corp, 83-86; pvt consult, 86-88. *Concurrent Pos:* Consult & plant breeder, B&M Cotton Co, San Simon, Ariz, 88- *Mem:* Am Soc Agron; Crop Sci Soc; Am Genetics Asn; Sigma Xi. *Res:* Crop breeding; plant pathology and physiology; statistics; cotton and grain sorghum; cytoplasmic male sterility to produce hybrid cotton; revolutionary concept in cotton breeding. *Mailing Add:* 4311 E Seventh St Tucson AZ 85711-2909

STITH, REX DAVID, ENDOCRINOLOGY. *Current Pos:* asst prof, 72-75, ASSOC PROF PHYSIOL, HEALTH SCI CTR, UNIV OKLA, 75- *Personal Data:* b Hominy, Okla, Dec 11, 42; m 64; c 2. *Educ:* Okla State Univ, BS, 64, MS, 66; Purdue Univ, PhD(physiol), 71. *Prof Exp:* Instr biol, Southeast Mo State Col, 66-68; vet physiol, Purdue Univ, 68-71; res assoc pharmacol, Univ Mo-Columbia, 71-72. *Concurrent Pos:* Vis assoc prof, Dept Physiol, Univ Calif, San Francisco, 79; Guest lectr, Univ St Georges Sch Med, Grenada, West Indies. *Mem:* AAAS; Sigma Xi; Soc Exp Biol & Med; Am Physiol Soc; Endocrine Soc. *Res:* Mechanisms of action of glucocorticoids; interactions of steroids in target cells; effects of glucocorticoids on intracellular functions; mechanisms of action of steroid hormones on target tissues, especially brain tissues and biochemical interactions of steroids in these tissues. *Mailing Add:* Dept Phys Univ Okla Col Med PO Box 26901 Oklahoma City OK 73126-0901

STITH, WILLIAM JOSEPH, BIOCHEMISTRY. *Current Pos:* STAFF MEM, CORNING CLIN LAB, 91- *Personal Data:* b Oklahoma City, Okla, Feb 7, 42; m 66; c 3. *Educ:* Phillips Univ, BA, 64; Univ Okla, PhD(biochem), 72; Tex Wesleyan Sch Law, JD, 94. *Prof Exp:* Chief microbiol, US Naval Hosp, Philadelphia, 66-67, chief blood bank & serol, 67-68; asst officer in-chg, Armed Serv Whole Blood Processing Lab, McGuire AFB, NJ, 68-69; fel human biol chem & genetics, Univ Tex Med Br, Galveston, 72-73; scientist prod explor, Fenwal Div, Baxter Labs, Inc, 73-77; vpres affairs, Med Eng Corp, 77-81; mgr, Bioeng Dept, Lord Corp, Erie, Pa, 81-86; staff mem, Tex Black Inst, 86-91. *Mem:* Asn Advan Med Instrumentation; Am Soc Qual Control; Am Chem Soc; Sigma Xi. *Res:* Quality control; product reliability; regulatory affairs; product development, and clinical studies. *Mailing Add:* 2809 Boone Court Plano TX 75023

STITT, JAMES HARRY, GEOLOGY, PALEONTOLOGY. *Current Pos:* From asst prof to assoc prof, Univ Mo, Columbia, 68-77, dir grad studies, 70-77, chmn dept, 77-80, PROF GEOL, UNIV MO, COLUMBIA, 77-, DIR GRAD STUDIES, 82- *Personal Data:* b Sellersville, Pa, Dec 13, 39; m 64, Betty MaGee; c Tanya & Merrilee. *Educ:* Rice Univ, BA, 61; Univ Tex, Austin, MA, 64, PhD(geol), 68. *Mem:* Paleont Soc; Geol Soc Am. *Res:* Late Cambrian and early Ordovician trilobites; invertebrate paleontology and biostratigraphy; paleoecology. *Mailing Add:* Dept Geol Sci Univ Mo Columbia MO 65211. *E-Mail:* geoscjs@showme.missouri.edu

STITT, JOHN THOMAS, PHYSIOLOGY, NEUROPHYSIOLOGY. *Current Pos:* Can Med Res Coun fel, Med Sch, 69-72, asst fel, 69-73, asst prof environ physiol, 72-76, ASSOC FEL PHYSIOL, JOHN B PIERCE FOUND LAB, YALE UNIV, 73-, ASSOC PROF EPIDEMIOL & PHYSIOL, MED SCH, 76- *Personal Data:* b Belfast, Northern Ireland, Nov 7, 42; m 66; c 2. *Educ:* Queens Univ Belfast, BSc, 65; Queens Univ, Ont, MSc, 67, PhD(physiol), 69. *Mem:* Am Physiol Soc; Can Physiol Soc; Soc Neurosci. *Res:* Physiology of thermoregulation in mammals; role of the hypothalamus in the homeostasis of body temperature; neurophysiological mechanisms of fever. *Mailing Add:* Epidemiol-Physiol John B Pierce Found Lab Yale Univ 290 Congress Ave New Haven CT 06519-1403

STITZEL, ROBERT ELI, PHARMACOLOGY. *Current Pos:* from asst prof to assoc prof, WVa Univ, 67-73, dir grad studies, Dept Pharmacol, 73-76, asst chmn dept, 76-79, PROF PHARMACOL, WVA UNIV, 73-, ASSOC CHMN DEPT, 79-, INTERIM DIR, UNIV GRAD STUDIES, 92- *Personal Data:* b New York, NY, Feb 22, 37; m 61, Judith Gold; c David. *Educ:* Columbia Univ, BS, 59, MS, 61; Univ Minn, PhD(pharmacol), 64. *Prof Exp:* Res asst pharmacol, Univ Minn, 61-64; asst prof, WVa Univ, 65-66; Swed Med Res Coun fel, 66-67. *Concurrent Pos:* USPHS fel, 64-65; USPHS res career develop award, 70-75; vis prof, Univ Adelaide, Australia, 73 & Univ Innsbruck, Austria, 77; Danforth Found assoc, 75-; hon res fel anat & embryol, Univ Col London, 77; Fogarty Sr Int fel, NIH, 77; actg chmn dept pharmacol, WVa Univ, 78-87; chmn, Neurol Sci Study Sect, NIH, 83-85; vis res scholar, Commonwealth Sci & Indust Res Orgn, Adelaide, Australia, 87; ed-in-chief, Pharmacol Rev, 89- *Mem:* AAAS; Am Soc Pharmacol & Exp Therapeut; Int Soc Biochem Pharmacol; Am Soc Neurochem. *Res:* Physiological and pharmacological factors affecting catecholamine release; hypertension. *Mailing Add:* Dept Pharmacol & Toxicol WVa Univ Health Sci Ctr Morgantown WV 26506. *Fax:* 304-293-6854; *E-Mail:* rstitzel@mail.hsc.wvu.edu

STITZINGER, ERNEST LESTER, ALGEBRA, GEOMETRY. *Current Pos:* From asst prof to assoc prof, 69-78, PROF MATH, NC STATE UNIV, 78- *Personal Data:* b Chester, Pa, May 9, 40; m 67; c 3. *Educ:* Temple Univ, BA, 63, MA, 65; Univ Pittsburgh, PhD(math), 69. *Mem:* Am Math Soc; Math Asn Am. *Res:* Lie algebras, other non-associative algebras and group theory. *Mailing Add:* Dept Math Box 8205 NC State Univ Raleigh NC 27607-8205

STIVALA, SALVATORE SILVIO, PHYSICAL CHEMISTRY. *Current Pos:* from asst prof to assoc prof phys & polymer chem, 59-64, instr chem eng, 52-57, PROF PHYS & POLYMER CHEM, STEVENS INST TECHNOL, 64-, RENE WASSERMAR PROF CHEM & CHEM ENG, 79- *Personal Data:* b New York, NY, June 23, 23; m 50; c 2. *Educ:* Columbia Univ, AB, 48; Stevens Inst Technol, MSChE, 52, MS, 58; Univ Pa, PhD(chem), 60. *Hon Degrees:* MEng, Stevens Inst Technol, 64. *Honors & Awards:* Ottens Res Award, 68; Med Soc Sendai (Japan) Award, 69; Honor Scroll, Am Inst Chemists, 77. *Prof Exp:* Res engr, US Testing Co, 49-50; mat engr, Picatinny Arsenal, 50-51, 54-57; NSF sci fac fel, Univ Pa, 57-59. *Concurrent Pos:* Consult, 52-57, 59-, indust, 60-; vis scientist, Inst Phys Chem, Graz Univ, 66 & dept ultra-struct biochem, Cornell Med Col, 69. *Mem:* Am Chem Soc; Sigma Xi; Am Soc Testing & Mat; Soc Plastics Eng. *Res:* Physical chemistry of high polymers; solution properties; kinetics of polymer degradation; physico-chemical aspects of biopolymers. *Mailing Add:* Chem Eng Stevens Inst Technol 1 Castle Point Terr Hoboken NJ 07030-5906

STIVEN, ALAN ERNEST, ECOLOGY, POPULATION BIOLOGY. *Current Pos:* From asst prof to assoc prof zool, Univ NC, Chapel Hill, 62-71, chmn dept, 67-72, chmn ecol curric, 71-86, assoc chmn, Biol Dept, 92-97, PROF BIOL, UNIV NC, CHAPEL HILL, 71- *Personal Data:* b St Stephen, NB, Nov 12, 35; m 72, Julia A Heeb; c Terry, Kim, Alan, Lauri, Mike & Jeff. *Educ:* Univ NB, BSc, 57; Univ BC, MA, 59; Cornell Univ, PhD(ecol), 62. *Concurrent Pos:* NSF res grants, 63-95; USPHS ecol training grant, 66-69; ed, Ecol Monogr, 67-73, Ecol, 72-73; res fel, Univ BC, 70; panel mem, Nat Acad Sci Environ Educ, Phillipines, 73-74; res grant, Sea Grant, Nat Oceanog & Atmos Asn, 74-76; US Forest Serv grant, 82-85; study comt, Ecol Soc Am, 82-; chmn biol panel, Nat Sci Found/Nat Res Coun, fel prog, 85-89; vchmn, Div Natural Sci, Univ NC, 87-90; chmn bd dirs, Highlands Biol Sta, 87-; panel mem, Postdoctoral Res Assoc Prog, Nat Res Coun, 90-94; NC Wildlife Resource Comm Grants, 90-95; fel, Environ Protection Agency, 95- *Mem:* Ecol Soc Am; Am Soc Naturalists; Soc Study Evolution. *Res:* population biology; ecological genetics of mollusk populations; experimental analysis of salt marsh benthic community structure; stream and salt marsh population and community ecology. *Mailing Add:* Dept Biol CB#3280 Coker Hall Univ NC Chapel Hill NC 27599-3280. *Fax:* 919-962-1625; *E-Mail:* alan_stiven@unc.edu

STIVENDER, DONALD LEWIS, DYNAMIC CONTROL, INTERNAL COMBUSTION ENGINES. *Current Pos:* PRIN, STIVENDER ENG ASSOC, 80- *Personal Data:* b Chicago, Ill, May 8, 32; m 56, Margaret Lourim; c Anne, Robert & Carole. *Educ:* US Coast Guard Acad, BS, 54; Univ Mich, MS, 59. *Honors & Awards:* Arch T Colwell Awards, Soc Automotive Engrs, 68, 69 & 79. *Prof Exp:* Mem staff res & develop, Res Labs, Gen Motors Corps, 59-92, sr res engr, 68-92. *Concurrent Pos:* Consult, pub domain disciplines; consult, Nat Acad Sci, 78- & mem, Naval Studies Bd, 90-93. *Mem:* Fel Soc Automotive Engrs; Am Soc Mech Engrs; Combustion Inst; Sigma Xi; Asn Advan Invention & Innovation. *Res:* Gas turbine, diesel spark ignition and alternative engine combustion, emission, construction and control aspects; internal combustion engines; engine and vehicle dynamometer control and transient optimization. *Mailing Add:* Stivender Eng Assoc 1730 Hamilton Dr Bloomfield Hills MI 48302-0221. *Fax:* 248-334-7622; *E-Mail:* stive@pepmline.com

STIVER, JAMES FREDERICK, MEDICINAL CHEMISTRY, BIONUCLEONICS. *Current Pos:* adminr environ regulatory affairs, 81-88, patent liaison scientist, 88-92, SR PATENT LIAISON SCIENTIST, UPJOHN CO, 92-94. *Personal Data:* b Elkhart, Ind, Jan 27, 43; m 65, Joan Trudle; c Gregory, Richard, Kristin & Elizabeth. *Educ:* Purdue Univ, BS, 66, MS, 68, PhD(med chem, bionucleonics), 70. *Prof Exp:* From asst prof to assoc prof pharmaceut chem & bionucleonics, Col Pharm, NDak State Univ, 69-76, radiol safety officer, 70-76; radiol safety officer, KMS Fusion, Inc, 76-80. *Concurrent Pos:* Pharmacist, Meder, Inc. *Mem:* AAAS; Am Chem Soc; Am Pharmaceut Asn; Health Physics Soc; Am Biol Safety Asn; Sigma Xi. *Res:* Radioisotope labeling synthesis of organic compounds and drugs; radioisotope tracer techniques and tracer methodology development; metabolism of drug and toxic chemicals; radioactive nuclide levels in the environment; applied health physics and patent information research. *Mailing Add:* 505 Skyview Dr Middlebury IN 46540-9427

STIVERS, RUSSELL KENNEDY, SOIL FERTILITY, CROP CULTURAL PRACTICES. *Current Pos:* RETIRED. *Personal Data:* b Marshall Co, Ill, May 9, 17; m 47, Martha J Craig; c Barbara J (Traub), Nancy L (Arllen) & Mary J. *Educ:* Univ Ill, BS, 39; Purdue Univ, MS, 48, PhD, 50. *Prof Exp:* Assoc agronomist, Va Polytech Inst, 50-55; assoc prof agron, Purdue Univ, Lafayette, 55-82, emer prof, 82-87. *Concurrent Pos:* Teacher voc agr & biol, Normantown High Sch, Normantown, Gilmer Co, WVa, 39-41, Field Crop Sci, Philippine Inst, Manila, Philippine Island, 45; 4-H leader vol, Normontown High Sch, WVa. *Mem:* Am Soc Agron; Soil Sci Soc Am. *Res:* Soils and soil science; soil and plant nutrition field plot and crop sampling studies; small grain (wheat, oat and barley) varieties and fertilization were conducted for State of Indiana research bulletins and field days. *Mailing Add:* 451 Littleton West Lafayette IN 47906

STIX, THOMAS HOWARD, PLASMA PHYSICS. *Current Pos:* RETIRED. *Personal Data:* b St Louis, Mo, July 12, 24; m 50, Hazel Sherwin; c Susan (Fisher) & Michael Sherwin. *Educ:* Calif Inst Technol, BS, 48; Princeton Univ, PhD(physics), 53. *Honors & Awards:* James Clerk Maxwell Prize, Am Phys Soc, 80. *Prof Exp:* Res asst, Princeton Univ, 53-54, res assoc, 54-56, assoc head, Exp Div, 56-61, co-head, Exp Div, 61-78, prof astrophys sci, 62-96, assoc dir acad affairs, Plasma Physics Lab, 78-93, assoc chmn, Dept Astrophys Sci, 81-91. *Concurrent Pos:* NSF sr fel, 60-61; chmn, Div Plasma Physics, Am Phys Soc, 62-63; Comm Int Freedom Scientists, 85; mem adv comt, thermonuclear div, Oak Ridge Nat Lab, 66-68; John Simon Guggenheim Mem Found fel, 69-70; assoc ed, Phys Rev Letters, 74-77. *Mem:* Fel Am Phys Soc. *Res:* Controlled fusion; waves and instabilities; plasma heating and confinement. *Mailing Add:* 231 Brookstone Dr Princeton NJ 08540. *Fax:* 609-243-2299

ST-JEAN, GUY, power electrical circuit design, diagnostic power circuit breakers, for more information see previous edition

STJERNHOLM, RUNE LEONARD, BIOCHEMISTRY. *Current Pos:* PROF BIOCHEM & CHMN DEPT, MED SCH, TULANE UNIV, 71- *Personal Data:* b Stockholm, Sweden, Apr 25, 24; nat US; m 53; c 2. *Educ:* Stockholm Tech Inst, BS, 44; Western Reserve Univ, PhD(biochem), 58. *Prof Exp:* From asst prof to prof biochem, Case Western Reserve Univ, 58-71. *Mem:* Am Chem Soc; Am Soc Microbiol; Am Soc Biol Chemists; Swed Chem Soc. *Res:* Chemotherapeutics; carbohydrate metabolism in leukocytes. *Mailing Add:* Dept Biochem Tulane Univ Med Sch 1430 Tulane Ave New Orleans LA 70112

ST-MAURICE, JEAN-PIERRE, IONOSPHERIC PHYSICS. *Current Pos:* assoc prof physics, 87-90, PROF PHYSICS, UNIV WESTERN ONT, 90- *Personal Data:* b Valleyfield, Que, Mar 25, 49; m 72; c 4. *Educ:* Col Valleyfield, Que, BA, 68; Univ Montreal, BSc, 71; Yale Univ, PhD(geophys), 75. *Prof Exp:* Res asst geophys, Dept Geol & Geophys, Yale Univ, 71-74; scholar ionospheric physics, atmospheric & oceanic sci, Univ Mich, Ann Arbor, 74-76; from res asst prof to res prof physics, Utah State Univ, 77-87. *Concurrent Pos:* Vis scientist, Max Planck Inst fur Aeromie, WGer, 82 & ISAS, Tokyo, Japan, 87; SERC vis fel, Eng, 89; vis scientist, Nat Ctr Sci & Res, France, 92. *Mem:* Am Geophys Union; Can Asn Physics. *Res:* Theory and measurement of non-equilibrium ion velocity distributions in the ionosphere; transport properties of the ionosphere; neutral winds near auroral regions; anomalous ionospheric heating; ionospheric irregularities and waves; ionospheric electrodynamics; radar measurements in the ionosphere. *Mailing Add:* Dept Physics Univ Western Ont London ON N6A 3K7 Can. *Fax:* 519-661-2033; *E-Mail:* stmaurice@canlon.physics.uwo.ca

STOB, MARTIN, ANIMAL SCIENCE. *Current Pos:* Asst, Purdue Univ, 49-53, asst prof animal husb, 53-58, assoc prof, 58-63, prof, 63-92, EMER PROF ANIMAL SCI, PURDUE UNIV, WEST LAFAYETTE, 92- *Personal Data:* b Chicago, Ill, Feb 20, 26. *Educ:* Purdue Univ, PhD(physiol), 53. *Mem:* AAAS; Am Soc Animal Sci; Endocrine Soc; Soc Study Fertil; Soc Study

Reproduction. *Res:* Hormonal regulation of growth; occurrence of compounds with estrogenic activity in plant material; microbiological synthesis and metabolism of estrogens; reproductive physiology. *Mailing Add:* Dept Animal Sci Purdue Univ West Lafayette IN 47907-1151

STOB, MICHAEL JAY, RECURSION THEORY. *Current Pos:* asst prof, 81-83, assoc prof, 83-87, PROF MATH, CALVIN COL, 87- *Personal Data:* b Chicago, Ill, Aug 2, 52; m 74; c 1. *Educ:* Calvin Col, BS, 74; Univ Chicago, SM, 75, PhD(math), 79. *Prof Exp:* C L E Moore instr math, Mass Inst Technol, 79-81. *Concurrent Pos:* Prin investr, NSF grant; vis assoc prof math, Univ Wis, 83-84. *Mem:* Am Math Soc; Asn Symbolic Logic; Math Asn Am. *Res:* Mathematical logic especially recursion theory; recursively enumerable sets and degrees. *Mailing Add:* Calvin Col Grand Rapids MI 49546

STOBAUGH, ROBERT EARL, INFORMATION SCIENCE. *Current Pos:* from asst ed to sr assoc ed, Chem Abstr, 54-61, from asst dept head to dept head, 61-65, tech adv, Registry Div, 65-67, mgr res, 67-92, DIR RES, CHEM ABSTR, 92-, CONSULT, 93- *Personal Data:* b Humboldt, Tenn, June 24, 27; m 56. *Educ:* Southwestern at Memphis, BS, 47; Univ Tenn, MS, 49, PhD(chem), 52. *Prof Exp:* Res assoc, Ohio State Univ, 52-54. *Mem:* Am Soc Info Sci; Am Chem Soc. *Res:* Steroids; chemical literature; chemical information storage and retrieval; chemical structural data; chemical information science. *Mailing Add:* 4006 Kioka Ave Columbus OH 43220-4578

STOBBE, ELMER HENRY, AGRONOMY, WEED SCIENCE. *Current Pos:* VPRES, INTEGRATED CROP MGMT SERV INC, 85- *Personal Data:* b Matsqui, BC, Jan 26, 36; m 62; c 2. *Educ:* Univ BC, BSA, 61, MSA, 65; Ore State Univ, PhD(crop sci), 69. *Prof Exp:* From asst prof to assoc prof weed sci, Univ Man, 68-78, prof agron, 78-95. *Concurrent Pos:* Agron res, Weed Sci, NJORO, Kenya, 82-84; vis lectr, Huaghong Agr Univ, Waham, China, 91; vis scientist, INIA, Colonia, Uruguay, 92-93. *Mem:* Weed Sci Soc Am; Agr Inst Can; Am Soc Agron; Sigma Xi. *Res:* Weed control under reduced tillage systems; agronomy, especially integrated cereal management, use of plant growth regulators in cereals, winter wheat production, zero tillage research and effect of cultivation on crop yield; seed production and seed quality. *Mailing Add:* 2267 Taylor Way Abbotsford BC V2S 4T2 Can. *Fax:* 604-853-5704; *E-Mail:* stobbe@icms-inc.com

STOBER, HENRY CARL, ANALYTICAL CHEMISTRY, PHARMACEUTICAL CHEMISTRY. *Current Pos:* sr scientist, 71-74, SR STAFF SCIENTIST, CIBA-GEIGY CORP, SUFFERN, NY, 74-, SR RES FEL, 83- *Personal Data:* b Brooklyn, NY, June 20, 35; m 61; c 2. *Educ:* City Col New York, BS, 58; Seton Hall Univ, MS, 69, PhD(chem), 71. *Prof Exp:* Res asst biol chem, Letterman Army Hosp, US Army, 58-60; chemist, Ciba Pharmaceut Corp, 60-66, supvr anal chem, 66-70; teaching asst chem, Seton Hall Univ, 70-71. *Mem:* Am Chem Soc. *Res:* Analysis and solid state characterization of pharmaceuticals and related chemicals. *Mailing Add:* 124 Madison Ave Madison NJ 07940-1450

STOBER, QUENTIN JEROME, ECOTOXICOLOGY, FISHERIES MANAGEMENT. *Current Pos:* US ENVIRON PROTECTION AGENCY, REGION IV FISHERIES EXPERT, ECOL SUPPORT BR ENVIRON SERVS DIV, ATHENS, GA, 86- *Personal Data:* b Billings, Mont, Mar 25, 38; m 65; c 2. *Educ:* Mont State Univ, BS, 60, MS, 62, PhD(zool), 68. *Honors & Awards:* W F Thompson Award, Am Inst Fisheries Res Biol, 71; Bronze Medal, US Environ Protection Agency, 89. *Prof Exp:* Aquatic biologist, Southeast Water Lab, Div Water Supply & Pollution Control, USPHS, Ga, 62-65; res asst prof estuarine ecol, Fisheries Res Inst, 69-72, res assoc prof estuarine, stream ecol & marine toxicol, 72-77, res prof & prog mgr marine baseline studies, stream, reservoir ecol & marine toxicol, Univ Wash, 77-86. *Concurrent Pos:* Admin judge, Atomic Safety & Licensing Bd Panel, US Nuclear Regulatory Comn, 74-86; environ consult, 68-86; Joint Sci Comt, Wash Water Res Ctr, 75-86. *Mem:* AAAS; Am Fisheries Soc; Am Soc Limnol & Oceanog; Am Inst Fisheries Res Biol; Sigma Xi. *Res:* Fisheries problems related to hydro and thermal nuclear energy production; estuarine ecology of effects of municipal and industrial wastes; fish toxicology and behavior; stream ecology, instream flow needs and reservoir ecology; bioaccumulation of chemical contaminants in fish and risk assessment. *Mailing Add:* 1841 Daniels Bridge Rd Athens GA 30606-6204

STOBO, JOHN DAVID, IMMUNOLOGY. *Current Pos:* dir & physician-in-chief, 85-94, PROF MED, JOHNS HOPKINS UNIV, 85-, VDEAN CLIN SCI & ASST VPRES MED, JOHNS HOPKINS SCH MED, 94-, VPRES, JOHNS HOPKINS HEALTH SYST, 94-, CHMN & CHIEF EXEC OFFICER. *Personal Data:* b Somerville, Mass, Sept 1, 41; m 64; c 3. *Educ:* Dartmouth Col, AB, 63; State Univ NY, Buffalo, MD, 68. *Prof Exp:* Res assoc immunol, NIH, 70-72; chief resident med, Johns Hopkins Hosp, 72-73; asst prof immunol, Mayo Med Sch & Found, 73-76; assoc prof med & head, Sect Rheumatology/Clin Immunol, Moffitt Hosp, Univ Calif, San Francisco, 76-85. *Concurrent Pos:* Sr investr, Am Arthritis Asn, 73; rep, Nat Heart Asn, 75-77; chmn, Johns Hopkins HealthCare. *Mem:* Inst Med-Nat Acad Sci; Am Arthritis Asn; Am Asn Immunologists; Am Col Physicians. *Res:* Cellular immunology; forces involved in the regulation of cell mediated and humoral immune responses. *Mailing Add:* 601 N Caroline St Suite 2080 Baltimore MD 21287

STOBO, WAYNE THOMAS, FISHERIES BIOLOGY, SEAL BIOLOGY. *Current Pos:* Biologist fisheries, Dept Environ, Fed Govt, Can, 72-73; res scientist, 73-76, sect head pop dynamics, 76-77, pop dynamics & biostatist, 77-78, coordr, Marine Fish Div, 79-83, RES SCIENTIST, DEPT FISHERIES & OCEANS, FED GOVT CAN, 84- *Personal Data:* b Sudbury, Ont, June 16, 44; Can citizen. *Educ:* Laurentian Univ, BSc, 65; Univ Ottawa, MSc, 71; Dalhousie Univ, PhD(ecol), 73. *Concurrent Pos:* Chmn, Pelagic Subcomt, Can Atlantic Fisheries Sci Adv Comt, 79-81. *Mem:* Soc Marine Mammal. *Res:* Optimizing the biological productivity of commercially exploited finfish stocks; populations dynamics and migration of finfish and marine mammals. *Mailing Add:* Marine Fish Div Bedford Inst Oceanog PO Box 1006 Dartmouth NS B2Y 4A2 Can

STOCK, CARL WILLIAM, STROMATOPOROID SYSTEMATICS & TAXONOMY, STROMATOPOROID PALEOBIOGEOGRAPHY. *Current Pos:* From instr to assoc prof, 76-90, PROF GEOL, UNIV ALA, 90- *Personal Data:* b Oceanside, NY, May 5, 45; m 93, Judith A Mesnick. *Educ:* Hartwick Col, BA, 67; State Univ NY, Binghamton, MA, 74; Univ NC, Chapel Hill, PhD(geol), 77. *Concurrent Pos:* Prin investr, NSF, 84-87, Nat Acad Sci, 94; tech ed, J Paleont, 92-93. *Mem:* Paleontological Soc; Soc Sedimentary Geol; Geol Soc Am; Paleont Asn; Paleont Res Inst; Int Paleont Asn. *Res:* Paleontology of the stromatoporoid, including taxonomy, paleoecology and paleobiogeography, especially for the Silurian and Devonian periods. *Mailing Add:* Dept Geol Univ Ala Tuscaloosa AL 35487-0338. *E-Mail:* cstock@ua1vm.ua.edu

STOCK, CHARLES CHESTER, CHEMOTHERAPY. *Current Pos:* EMER PROF BIOCHEM, SLOAN-KETTERING DIV, MED COL, CORNELL UNIV, 76- *Personal Data:* b Terre Haute, Ind, May 19, 10; wid. *Educ:* Rose-Hulman Inst Technol, BS, 32; Johns Hopkins Univ, PhD(physiol chem), 37; NY Univ, MS, 41. *Hon Degrees:* ScD, Rose-Hulman Inst, 54. *Honors & Awards:* Alfred P Sloan Award, 65; C Chester Stock Award Cancer Res, 80. *Prof Exp:* Instr bact, Col Med, NY Univ, 37-41; vol worker, Rockefeller Hosp Med Res, 41-42; tech aide, Comt Treatment Gas Casualties, Div Med Sci, Nat Res Coun, 42-45, exec secy, Insect Control Comt, 45-46, chmn chem coding panel chem-biol, Coord Ctr, 46-52; assoc, Sloan-Kettering Inst Cancer Res, 46-50, chief, Div Exp Chemother, 47-72, mem, 50-80, assoc dir inst, 57-60, dir, 59-80, sci dir, 60-61, vpres, 61-72, vpres inst affairs, Cancer Ctr, 74-80, vpres & assoc dir admin & acad affairs, 76-80, emer mem & dir, Walker Lab, Rye Sloan-Kettering Inst Cancer Res, 80- *Concurrent Pos:* Prof biochem, Sloan-Kettering Div, Med Col, Cornell Univ, 51-75; mem comt tumor nomenclature & statist, Int Cancer Res Comn, 52-54; chmn screening panel, Cancer Chemother Nat Serv Ctr, NIH, 55-58 & drug eval panel, 58-; mem sci adv bd, Roswell Park Mem Inst, 57-66; mem chemother rev bd, Nat Adv Cancer Coun, 58-59; mem US nat comt, Int Union Against Cancer, 67-80, chmn, 75-80; mem bd dirs, Am Cancer Soc, 72-, hon mem, 85- *Mem:* Emer mem Am Chem Soc; emer mem Am Soc Biol Chemists; Soc Exp Biol & Med; Am Asn Cancer Res; hon mem Japanese Cancer Asn; hon fel Hungarian Cancer Soc; Europ Inst Ecol & Cancer (hon pres, 77-); foreign corresp mem, Cancer Soc Italy. *Res:* Enzymes; hypertension; experimental chemotherapy of cancer. *Mailing Add:* 27900 Fairmount Blvd Pepper Pike OH 44124-4616

STOCK, DAVID ALLEN, MICROBIOLOGY, GENETICS. *Current Pos:* from asst prof to assoc prof, 70-90, PROF BIOL, STETSON UNIV, 90- *Personal Data:* b Elyria, Ohio, Feb 8, 41; m 64; c 2. *Educ:* Mich State Univ, BS, 63; NC State Univ, MS, 66, PhD(genetics), 68. *Prof Exp:* Instr microbiol, Sch Med, Univ Miss, 67-68; USDA fel, Baylor Col Med, 68-69, NIH fel, 69-70. *Concurrent Pos:* Instr, Life Long Learning Prog, Daytona Beach Community Col; consult, Environ Mgt Div, Volusia Co Govt. *Mem:* Am Soc Microbiol; Am Soc Photobiol. *Res:* Physiology and pathogenesis of Candida albicans; radiobiology of foodstuffs; breeding behavior of limpkins; repair of radiation damage by plants. *Mailing Add:* Dept Biol Stetson Univ De Land FL 32720. *Fax:* 904-822-8170; *E-Mail:* dstock@tophat.stetson.edu

STOCK, DAVID EARL, FLUID MECHANICS, MULTIPHASE FLOW. *Current Pos:* from asst prof to assoc prof, 72-83, PROF MECH ENG, WASH STATE UNIV, 83- *Personal Data:* b Baltimore, Md, Feb 2, 39; m 62, Mary Roland Wilford; c Joseph & Katerine. *Educ:* Pa State Univ, BS, 61; Univ Conn, MS, 65; Ore State Univ, PhD(mech eng), 72. *Prof Exp:* Test engr, Pratt & Whitney Aircraft, 61-65; Peace Corps volunteer, Ghana, WAfrica, 66-68; teaching asst, Ore State Univ, 68-72. *Concurrent Pos:* Vis fel, Cornell Univ, 81-82, Univ Canterbury, NZ; Freeman scholar, Am Soc Mech Engrs, 94. *Mem:* Fel Am Soc Mech Engrs; Am Phys Soc. *Res:* Experimental fluid mechanics which includes the use of laser Dopper and thermal anemometry applied to gas particle flow; computation and measurement of flow and dispersion about buildings and hills. *Mailing Add:* Sch Mech & Mats Eng Wash State Univ Pullman WA 99164-2920. *Fax:* 509-335-4662; *E-Mail:* stock@mme.wsu.edu

STOCK, JOHN THOMAS, HISTORY OF CHEMISTRY. *Current Pos:* from assoc prof to prof, 56-79, EMER PROF CHEM, UNIV CONN, 79- *Personal Data:* b Margate, Eng, Jan 26, 11; nat US; m 45, Eileen L Terry; c Mavis L (McKeown). *Educ:* Univ London, BSc, 39 & 41, MSc, 45, PhD(chem), 49, DSc, 65. *Honors & Awards:* Dexter Award, Hist Chem, 92. *Prof Exp:* Sci off chem, Ministry Supply, Gt Brit, 40-44; actg chief chemist, Fuller's Ltd, 44-46; lectr chem, Norwood Tech Col, 46-51, head dept, 51-56. *Concurrent Pos:* Consult, 50-; London Co Coun Blair fel, Univ Minn, 53-54. *Mem:* Fel Am Chem Soc; fel Royal Soc Chem; Soc Chem Indust; Royal Inst Gt Brit; Sci Instrument Soc. *Res:* Design of automated and general scientific apparatus; history of scientific instruments. *Mailing Add:* Dept Chem Univ Conn Storrs CT 06269-4060

STOCK, LEON M, ORGANIC CHEMISTRY. *Current Pos:* dir, Chem Div, 88-96, RES ASSOC, ARGONNE NAT LAB, 96-; EMER PROF CHEM UNIV CHICAGO, 96- *Personal Data:* b Detroit, Mich, Oct 15, 30; m 61, Mary K Elmblod; c Katherine L (Bensching) & Ann V. *Educ:* Univ Mich, BS,

52; Purdue Univ, PhD, 59. *Honors & Awards:* Storch Award, Am Chem Soc, 87. *Prof Exp:* from instr to prof chem, Univ Chicago, 58-96. *Concurrent Pos:* Consult, Phillips Petrol Co, 64-95, Fujor Daniel Hanford, Co, 95-, Paci NW Nat Lab, 96- *Mem:* Am Chem Soc; Royal Soc Chem; Europ Org Geochemists. *Res:* Electrophilic aromatic substitution reactions; influences of structure and solvents on reactivity; models for evaluation of inductive influences of substituents; electron paramagnetic resonance spectra of organic radicals; the structure of coal; the chemistry of coal, its structure, liquefaction, gasification and pyrolysis reactions; hanford waste chemistry. *Mailing Add:* Chem Div Argonne Nat Lab 9700 S Cass Ave CHM/200 Argonne IL 60439. *Fax:* 503-977-2437; *E-Mail:* lstock6022@aol.com

STOCK, MOLLY WILFORD, ENTOMOLOGY, POPULATION GENETICS. *Current Pos:* asst prof entom, 76-78, from asst prof to assoc prof, 80-84, PROF FOREST RESOURCES & COMPUTER SCI, UNIV IDAHO, 84- *Personal Data:* b Glen Ridge, NJ, Aug 17, 42; m 62; c 2. *Educ:* Univ Conn, BA, 64, MS, 65; Ore State Univ, PhD(entom), 72. *Prof Exp:* Res asst entom, Ore State Univ, 68-69; res assoc insect biochem, Wash State Univ, 72-73, res collabr entom, 73-75; proj leader, 75-77. *Mem:* Entom Soc Am; Soc Am Foresters; Am Asn Artificial Intel. *Res:* Biosystematics; population dynamics of forest insects; expert systems for natural resource management. *Mailing Add:* Dept Forest Resources Univ Idaho Moscow ID 83844-1133

STOCKBAUER, ROGER LEWIS, SURFACE SCIENCE. *Current Pos:* PROF PHYSICS, LA STATE UNIV, 89- *Personal Data:* b Victoria, Tex, Feb 3, 44; m 72; c 3. *Educ:* Rice Univ, BA, 66; Univ Chicago, MS, 68, PhD(physics), 73. *Honors & Awards:* Silver Medal, US Dept Com, 83. *Prof Exp:* From res asst to res assoc physics, Univ Chicago, 66-73; res physicist, Nat Bur Stand, 73-89. *Concurrent Pos:* Teaching asst physics, Univ Chicago, 69-70; Nat Res Coun-Nat Acad Sci res assoc, Nat Bur Stand, 73-75. *Mem:* Fel Am Phys Soc; Sigma Xi; Am Vacuum Soc; Mat Res Soc; AAAS; Am Asn Univ Prof. *Res:* Geometric and electronic properties of materials especially thin film metal overlayer systems of interest in catalysis and magnetic systems; techniques include synchrotron based angle resolved photoemission and scanning tunneling microscopy. *Mailing Add:* Dept Physics La State Univ Baton Rouge LA 70803-4001. *Fax:* 504-388-5855; *E-Mail:* stockbau@rouge.phys.lsu.edu

STOCKBRIDGE, ROBERT R, ANIMAL HUSBANDRY, POULTRY HUSBANDRY. *Current Pos:* RETIRED. *Personal Data:* b Worcester, Mass, Aug 21, 10; m 37; c 1. *Educ:* Univ Mass, BVA, 34; Hofstra Col, MS, 46. *Prof Exp:* From instr to assoc prof, State Univ NY Agr & Tech Col Farmingdale, 38-60, prof poultry sci & chmn, Agr Dept, 60-80. *Mem:* Poultry Sci Asn; World Poultry Sci Asn. *Mailing Add:* Five Stephen Dr Farmingdale NY 11735

STOCKBURGER, GEORGE JOSEPH, INDUSTRIAL ORGANIC CHEMISTRY. *Current Pos:* RETIRED. *Personal Data:* b Philadelphia, Pa, May 23, 27; m 61, Barbara Trotz; c George Jr & Edward. *Educ:* St Joseph's Col, Pa, BS, 50; Univ Pa, MS, 52, PhD, 55. *Prof Exp:* Sr res chemist, Anal & Phys Chem Sect, ICI Americas Inc, 55-79, supvr gen anal, 79-86. *Concurrent Pos:* Consult, Moretech Consult Indust Chemists. *Mem:* Am Chem Soc. *Res:* Reaction kinetics and mechanism; catalysis. *Mailing Add:* 2211 Pennington Dr Brandywood Wilmington DE 19810

STOCKDALE, FRANK EDWARD, DEVELOPMENTAL BIOLOGY, ONCOLOGY. *Current Pos:* sr resident, Univ Hosp, Stanford Univ, 66-67, from instr to asst prof med, 68-74, asst prof biol, 70-74, assoc prof, 74-81, Josephine Knotts Knowles prof human biol, 90-96, PROF MED & BIOL SCI, SCH MED, STANFORD UNIV, 81-, LYLE D'AMBROGIO PROF MED, 96- *Personal Data:* b Long Beach, Calif, Mar 15, 36; c 3. *Educ:* Yale Univ, AB, 58; Univ Pa, MD & PhD(develop biol), 63. *Prof Exp:* Intern internal med, Univ Hosps, Western Reserve Univ, 63-64; staff assoc, Nat Inst Arthritis & Metab Dis, 64-66. *Mem:* Am Soc Clin Invest; AAAS; Soc Develop Biol; Am Soc Clin Oncol; Am Soc Cell Biol; Asn Am Physicians. *Res:* Cellular and molecular mechanisms for control of cell differentiation and growth during embryogenesis; medical oncology; breast cancer. *Mailing Add:* Dept Med Rm M211 Stanford Univ Sch Med Stanford CA 94305-5306

STOCKDALE, HAROLD JAMES, ECONOMIC ENTOMOLOGY. *Current Pos:* RETIRED. *Personal Data:* b Aplington, Iowa, Dec 3, 31; m 51; c 2. *Educ:* Iowa State Univ, BS, 58, MS, 79, PhD(entom), 64. *Prof Exp:* Exten entomologist & prof entom, Iowa State Univ, 61-82, chmn dept, 82-92. *Mem:* Entom Soc Am. *Res:* Field crop insect management; household and structural insect control. *Mailing Add:* 2721 Cleveland Ames IA 50010

STOCKDALE, JOHN ALEXANDER DOUGLAS, PHYSICS. *Current Pos:* DEVELOP STAFF, MARTIN MARIETTA, 93- *Personal Data:* b Ipswich, Australia, Mar 15, 36; m 57; c 3. *Educ:* Univ Sydney, BSc, 57, MSc, 60; PhD(physics), Univ Tenn, 69. *Prof Exp:* Res scientist, Australian AEC, 58-66; physicist, Health & Safety Res Div, Oak Ridge Nat Lab, 66-88; cofounder & pres, Com Stock, Inc, 79-90; physicist, Lawrence Livermore Nat Lab, 88-93. *Concurrent Pos:* John Simon Guggenheim fel, 70; vis prof, NY Univ, 75-76, Univ Crete, 85, 87. *Mem:* Am Phys Soc. *Res:* Atomic and molecular physics; laser physics. *Mailing Add:* 12309 North Fox Den Dr Knoxville TN 37922

STOCKDALE, WILLIAM K, civil engineering, structural dynamics, for more information see previous edition

STOCKELL-HARTREE, ANNE, BIOCHEMISTRY. *Current Pos:* RETIRED. *Personal Data:* b Nashville, Tenn, Jan 11, 26; m 59; c David & William. *Educ:* Vanderbilt Univ, BA, 46, MS, 49; Univ Utah, PhD(biochem), 56. *Hon Degrees:* MA, Cambridge Univ, 62. *Honors & Awards:* Silver Plate, Soc Endocrinol Eng, 90. *Prof Exp:* Asst biochem, Vanderbilt Univ, 46-51; fel USPHS Johnson Res Found, Univ Pa, 56-58; mem, Med Res Coun Unit Molecular Biol, Cavendish Lab, Cambridge Univ, 58-59, fel, Jane Coffin Childs Fund, 59-60, res worker, Dept Biochem, 60-80; res worker, Inst Animal Physiol, Agr Res Coun, Cambridge, Eng, 80-90. *Concurrent Pos:* Res fel, Girton Col, 62-65; fel, Lucy Cavendish Col, 69-; external mem sci staff, Med Res Coun, 70-90. *Mem:* Brit Biochem Soc; sr mem Brit Soc Endocrinol; Am Soc Biol Chemists; Endocrine Soc. *Res:* Amino acid analysis; enzyme kinetics; protein structure and function; pituitary protein hormones. *Mailing Add:* 4487 Post Pl Nashville TN 37205-1607

STOCKER, DONALD V(ERNON), ELECTRICAL ENGINEERING. *Current Pos:* RETIRED. *Personal Data:* b Detroit, Mich, Jan 5, 27; m 50; c 2. *Educ:* Wayne State Univ, BSEE, 49; Univ Mich, MSE, 50. *Prof Exp:* Jr engr, Magnetron Develop Lab, Raytheon Mfg Co, Mass, 50-51; from instr to asst prof, Wayne State Univ, 51-69, appln engr, Appl Sci & Technol Ctr, 64-68, assoc prof elec engr, 60-75, mgr admin serv, Col Eng, 69-75, assoc prof eng technol, 75-88, dir, Div Eng Technol, 81-87. *Concurrent Pos:* Consult, Detroit Edison Co, 76-80. *Mem:* Inst Elec & Electronics Engrs; Am Soc Eng Educ; Sigma Xi. *Res:* Load management. *Mailing Add:* 7772 Wexford Dr Onsted MI 49265-9594

STOCKER, FRED BUTLER, ORGANIC CHEMISTRY. *Current Pos:* Assoc prof, 58-69, chmn dept chem, 70-80, PROF CHEM, MACALESTER COL, 69- *Personal Data:* b Kenyon, Minn, Jan 31, 31; m 53; c 2. *Educ:* Hamline Univ, BS, 53; Univ Minn, MS, 55; Univ Colo, PhD(org chem), 58. *Concurrent Pos:* Consult, 59- *Mem:* Am Chem Soc. *Res:* Imidazole derivatives. *Mailing Add:* Dept Chem Macalester Col St Paul MN 55105-1899

STOCKER, JACK H(UBERT), ORGANIC CHEMISTRY, GENERAL CHEMISTY. *Current Pos:* from assoc prof to prof, 58-91, admin asst to dean, Col Sci, 65-67, EMER PROF CHEM, UNIV NEW ORLEANS, 91- *Personal Data:* b Detroit, Mich, May 3, 24; wid; c Daniel & David. *Educ:* Olivet Col, BS, 44; Ind Univ, MA, 47; Tulane Univ, PhD(org chem), 55. *Prof Exp:* Control chemist, R P Scherer Corp, Mich, 48-50, Atlas Pharmaceut Co, 50; Fulbright traveling fel, Heidelburg Univ, 55-56; assoc prof chem, Univ Southern Miss, 56-58. *Concurrent Pos:* Res partic, Oak Ridge Inst Nuclear Studies, 59; consult, Food & Drug Admin, 71-82; res assoc, Gulf South Res Inst; vis prof chem, Univ Lund, Sweden, 74-75; mem, Comt Meetings & Exposition, Am Chem Soc, 72-74, 76-81, chmn, 80-81, Sci Comn, 80-81, Coun Policy Comt, 82-87 & 95-, chmn, Div Hist Chem, 89-91, Comt Nomenclature, 76-; assoc mem, comt organic nomenclature, Int Union Pure Applied Chem, 91. *Mem:* Am Chem Soc; Sigma Xi. *Res:* Acetals and ketals; organometallics; stereoselective reactions; organic photochemistry and electrochemistry. *Mailing Add:* Dept of Chem Univ New Orleans Lakefront New Orleans LA 70148. *Fax:* 504-280-6860

STOCKERT, ELISABETH, IMMUNOGENETICS. *Current Pos:* Res assoc cancer, 73-76, ASSOC MEM, SLOAN-KETTERING CANCER CTR, 76-, LUDWIG INST, 90- *Personal Data:* b Vienna, Austria, Sept 29, 30. *Educ:* Univ Vienna, BS, 59; Univ Paris, Dr(immunol), 74. *Res:* Experimental tumor immunobiology, serology and genetics; cell surface antigens of normal and malignant cells. *Mailing Add:* 435 E 77th St New York NY 10021

STOCKHAM, THOMAS GREENWAY, JR, COMPUTER SCIENCE. *Current Pos:* assoc prof comput sci, 68-70, PROF COMPUT SCI, UNIV UTAH, 70-, PROF ELEC ENG, 76- *Personal Data:* b Passaic, NJ, Dec 22, 33; m 63; c 4. *Educ:* Mass Inst Technol, SB, 55, SM, 56, ScD(elec eng), 59. *Honors & Awards:* Audio & Electroacoust Sr Award, Inst Elec & Electronics Engrs, 68. *Prof Exp:* Teaching asst elec eng, Mass Inst Technol, 55-57, from instr to asst prof, 57-66, staff mem comput res, Lincoln Lab, 66-68. *Concurrent Pos:* Vis asst prof, Univ NMex, 62; consult, Data Div, Comput Group, Lincoln Lab, Mass Inst Technol, 64-66. *Mem:* Inst Elec & Electronics Engrs; Asn Comput Mach. *Res:* Digital signal processing of images and sound by non-linear methods; electrical communications; electrical circuit and systems theory; computer graphics; sensory information processing. *Mailing Add:* Dept Elect Eng Univ Utah 3280 Meb Salt Lake City UT 84112

STOCKHAMMER, KARL ADOLF, ZOOLOGY, ENTOMOLOGY. *Current Pos:* from asst prof to assoc prof, 59-92, EMER PROF CELL BIOL & PHYSIOL, UNIV KANS, 92- *Personal Data:* b Ried, Austria, July 19, 26; m 56; c 3. *Educ:* Graz Univ, PhD(zool), 51. *Prof Exp:* Res assoc zool, Univ Munich, 51-58; instr, Univ Gottingen, 58-59. *Mem:* Entom Soc Am. *Res:* Detection of e-vector of polarized light in insects; behavioral and physiological aspects of nesting in native bees. *Mailing Add:* 2434 Princeton Blvd Lawrence KS 66049

STOCKING, CLIFFORD RALPH, PLANT PHYSIOLOGY. *Current Pos:* assoc, Exp Sta, Univ Calif, Davis, 45-46, asst prof bot, Univ & asst botanist, Exp Sta, 46-52, assoc prof & assoc botanist, 52-58, actg chmn, Dept Bot, 66-67, chmn dept, 68-74, prof & botanist, Exp Sta, 58-81, EMER PROF, UNIV CALIF, DAVIS, 81- *Personal Data:* b Riverside, Calif, June 22, 13; wid; c Kathleen (Cropper) & Margery (Stocking). *Educ:* Univ Calif, BS, 37, MS, 39, PhD(plant physiol), 42. *Prof Exp:* Asst plant physiol, Univ Calif, 38-39, assoc bot, 39-42; food chemist, Puccinelli Packing Co, 42-45. *Concurrent Pos:* Merck sr fel biochem, Univ Wis, 55-56; NSF fel, Imp Col, Univ London, 63-64, vis fel, King's Col, 70-71. *Mem:* Fel AAAS; Am Soc Plant Physiol. *Res:* Biochemistry of chloroplasts; plant water relations; intracellular distribution of enzymes and phosynthetic products. *Mailing Add:* Plant Biol LSA Bldg Univ Calif-Davis Davis CA 95616

STOCKING, GORDON GARY, VETERINARY MEDICINE. *Current Pos:* RETIRED. *Personal Data:* b Axin, Mich, Jan 12, 24; m 47; c 2. *Educ:* Mich State Univ, DVM, 46. *Prof Exp:* Res vet, Upjohn Farms, 46-49, from asst vet to assoc vet, Upjohn Co, 49-57, dir, Vet Div, 57-64, asst dir, Agr Div, 65-69, prod mgr, 69-73, sr staff, Vet Agr Div, 73-90. *Concurrent Pos:* Ranch mgr & vet, Kellogg Ranch, Calif State Polytech Col, 51-52. *Mem:* Am Vet Med Asn; Indust Vet Asn; US Animal Health Asn; Am Asn Lab Animal Sci; Am Asn Equine Practr. *Res:* Equine reproduction and disease; bovine respiratory disease. *Mailing Add:* 3107 Audubon Dr Kalamazoo MI 49008

STOCKLAND, ALAN EUGENE, MICROBIOLOGY. *Current Pos:* PROF MICROBIOL, WEBER STATE COL, 70- *Personal Data:* b Huron, SDak, July 18, 38; m 68; c 2. *Educ:* Univ Nebr, BS & BA, 61; Mich State Univ, MS, 67, PhD(microbiol), 70. *Prof Exp:* Teacher secondary Sch, Malaysia, 62-64. *Mem:* AAAS; Am Soc Microbiol; Sigma Xi. *Res:* Microbiological control of insect pests; effect of trauma on the immune system. *Mailing Add:* Dept Microbiol Weber State Col Ogden UT 84403

STOCKLAND, WAYNE LUVERN, NUTRITION. *Current Pos:* res nutritionist & statist mgr, 70-76, dir, Animal Nutrit Res, 76-87, DIR, TECH OPERS INTERNATIONAL MULTIFOODS CORP, 87- *Personal Data:* b Lake Lillian, Minn, May 4, 42; m 71; c 3. *Educ:* Univ Minn, BS, 64, PhD(nutrit), 69. *Prof Exp:* Res asst nutrit, Univ Minn, 69, res fel, 69-70. *Mem:* Am Soc Animal Sci; Am Dairy Sci Asn; Poultry Sci Asn; Am Inst Nutrit; NY Acad Sci; Asn Off Analysis Chemists. *Res:* Swine, poultry and ruminant nutrition and management, especially the protein and amino acid requirements and the effect of energy level, temperature and other nutrients on these requirements. *Mailing Add:* Dir Tech Balchem Corp PO Box 175 Slate Hill NY 10973

STOCKLI, MARTIN P, ELECTRON BEAM ION SOURCES, ION-ATOM COLLISIONS. *Current Pos:* res assoc, Physics Lab, Kans State Univ, 81-83, staff physicist, 84-86, assoc scientist, 86-89, asst res prof, 89-95, ASSOC RES PROF, J R MCDONALD LAB, KANS STATE UNIV, 95- *Personal Data:* b Solothurn, Switz, June, 30, 49; m 83. *Educ:* Swiss Fed Inst Technol, Master, 74, PhD(physics), 78. *Honors & Awards:* First Prize, Schlatter-Pfaeler Found, Solothurn, 67. *Prof Exp:* Res asst, Physics Lab, Swiss Fed Inst Technol, 74-79, res assoc, 79-80; res assoc, Physics Lab, Western Mich Univ, 80-81. *Concurrent Pos:* Consult, Smithsonian Inst Astrophys Observ, 83, Inst Nuclear Physics, Univ Frankfurt, 84, 87. *Mem:* Am Phys Soc; Am Vacuum Soc. *Res:* Accelerator based atomic physics; ionisation and x-ray emmision in slow heavy ion collisions; electron beam ion sources. *Mailing Add:* Physics Dept Kans State Univ Cardwell Hall Manhattan KS 66506-2604. *Fax:* 785-532-6806

STOCKMAN, CHARLES H(ENRY), MANUFACTURING PROCESSES FOR RUBBER PRODUCTS, AEROSPACE TECHNOLOGIES. *Current Pos:* CONSULT, C H STOCKMAN ASSOCS, 82- *Personal Data:* b Oak Park, Ill, Sept 5, 22; m 48, 81; c Alan C, Judith L (Dininny) & David E. *Educ:* Purdue Univ, BS, 47, PhD(chem eng), 50. *Prof Exp:* Res engr, Res Ctr, B F Goodrich Co, 50-52, sr res engr, 52-56, sect leader, 56-58, mgr res opers, 58-61, tech dir, Aerospace & Defense Prod Div, 62-68, dir develop & new prod, 68-70; vpres & gen mgr, Goodrich High Voltage Astronaut, subsid B F Goodrich & High Voltage Eng Corp, 60-62; vpres, E A Butler Assocs, Inc, 70-76; dir res, develop & qual control, Rubber Group, H K Porter Co, 76-82. *Concurrent Pos:* Spec sci employee, Argonne Nat Lab, 53-54, consult, 54-56; lectr nuclear chem, Case Western Res Univ, 55-56; prin investr, Food & Drug Admin Hemodialysis Proj, Ohio Dept Health, 84-86. *Mem:* Am Chem Soc. *Res:* Chemical process thermodynamics; nuclear fuel processing; zone melting; solid propellant an ion rocket motors; antisubmarine warfare; marine fouling prevention; mosquito and schistosomiasis control; rubber hose manufacturing processes; rubber extrusion; hemodialysis. *Mailing Add:* 342 Glen Meadow Ct Dublin OH 43017

STOCKMAN, GEORGE C, COMPUTER SCIENCE. *Current Pos:* AT DEPT COMPUT SCI, MICH STATE UNIV. *Personal Data:* b Brooklyn, NY, Dec 16, 43; m 69; c 2. *Educ:* E Stroudsburg State Col, BS, 66; Harvard Univ, MAT, 67; Pa State Univ, MS, 71; Univ Md, PhD(comput sci), 77. *Prof Exp:* Instr math, Va Union Univ, 68-70; res asst comput sci, Univ Md, 73-75; res scientist comput sci, LNK Corp, 75-; assoc prof comput sci, American Univ, 79- *Concurrent Pos:* Vis lectr, Univ Md, 77-79. *Mem:* Asn Comput Mach; sr mem Inst Elec & Electronics Engrs. *Res:* Artificial intelligence; image processing; pattern recognition. *Mailing Add:* Dept Comput Sci Mich State Univ East Lansing MI 48824

STOCKMAN, HARRY E, electronics engineering, physics; deceased, see previous edition for last biography

STOCKMAN, HERVEY S, JR, ASTROPHYSICS, OPTICAL ASTRONOMY. *Current Pos:* DEPT DIR, SPACE TELESCOPE SCI INST, 88- *Personal Data:* b New York, NY, Mar 2, 46. *Educ:* Columbia Univ, MS, 70, PhD(physics), 73. *Prof Exp:* Proj officer, USAF, 73-75; res assoc, Univ Ariz, 75-79; asst astronomer, Starard Observ, 79-83, chief res support, 79-83. *Mem:* AAAS; Am Astron Soc; Am Phys Soc. *Res:* Astrophysical properties of binary systems; magnetic white dwarfs and active galactic nuclei. *Mailing Add:* Space Telescope Sci Inst 3700 San Martin Dr Baltimore MD 21218. *Fax:* 410-338-2519

STOCKTON / 1283

STOCKMAYER, WALTER H(UGO), POLYMER CHEMISTRY. *Current Pos:* chmn dept, 63-67 & 73-76, prof, 61-79, EMER PROF CHEM, DARTMOUTH COL, 79- *Personal Data:* b Rutherford, NJ, Apr 7, 14; m 38, Sylvia Bergen; c Ralph & Hugh. *Educ:* Mass Inst Technol, SB, 35, PhD(chem), 40; Oxford Univ, BSc, 37. *Hon Degrees:* Dr, Univ Louis Pasteur, 72; LHD, Dartmouth Col, 83; DSc, Univ Mass, Amherst, 96. *Honors & Awards:* Award, Mfg Chem Asn, 60; Polymer Chem Award, Am Chem Soc, 66, Peter Debye Award Phys Chem, 74, High Polymer Physics Prize, 75; Nat Medal Sci, 87; Richards Medal, Northeast Sect, Am Chem Soc, 88; Polymer Chem Div Award, 88; Int Award, Soc Plastics Engrs, 91; Procter Prize, 93. *Prof Exp:* Instr chem, Mass Inst Technol, 39-41 & Columbia Univ, 41-43; asst prof, Mass Inst Technol, 43-46, from assoc prof to prof phys chem, 46-61. *Concurrent Pos:* Consult, E I du Pont de Nemours & Co, Inc, 45-; Guggenheim fel, 54-55; trustee, Gordon Res Conf, 63-66; assoc ed, Macromolecules, 68-73 & 76-95; hon fel, Jesus Col, Oxford, 76; Humboldt fel, 78-79. *Mem:* Nat Acad Sci; Am Chem Soc; fel Am Phys Soc; fel Am Acad Arts & Sci. *Res:* High polymers; applied statistical mechanics; dynamics and statistical mechanics of macromolecules. *Mailing Add:* Dept Chem Dartmouth Col Hanover NH 03755. *Fax:* 603-646-3946; *E-Mail:* walter. stockmayer@dartmouth.edu

STOCKMEYER, LARRY JOSEPH, COMPUTATIONAL COMPLEXITY, DISTRIBUTED COMPUTING. *Current Pos:* Mem res staff, Thomas J Watson Res Ctr, 74-83, MEM RES STAFF, ALMADEN RES CTR, IBM CORP, 83- *Personal Data:* b Evansville, Ind, Nov 13, 48. *Educ:* Mass Inst Technol, SB & SM, 72, PhD(comput sci), 74. *Mem:* Asn Comput Mach; Sigma Xi. *Res:* Computational complexity; analysis of algorithms; distributed computing. *Mailing Add:* 5221 Adalina Ct San Jose CA 95124. *Fax:* 408-927-2100; *E-Mail:* stock@almaden.ibm.com

STOCKMEYER, PAUL KELLY, MATHEMATICS. *Current Pos:* Asst prof math, 71-77, assoc prof comput sci, 77-88, PROF COMPUT SCI, COL WILLIAM & MARY, 88- *Personal Data:* b Detroit, Mich, May 1, 43; m 66, Bonita L Karels; c Elizabeth (Cohen) & Andrea (Lofgren). *Educ:* Earlham Col, AB, 65; Univ Mich, Ann Arbor, MA, 66, PhD(math), 71. *Mem:* Math Asn Am; Am Math Soc; Asn Comput Mach; Fibonacci Asn. *Res:* Combinatorial analysis; graph theory; analysis of algorithms; recreational mathematics. *Mailing Add:* Dept Comput Sci Col William & Mary Williamsburg VA 23185. *Fax:* 757-221-1717; *E-Mail:* stockmeyer@cs.wm.edu

STOCKNER, JOHN G, LIMNOLOGY, ECOLOGY. *Current Pos:* limnologist, Freshwater Inst, Fisheries Res Bd Can, 68-71 & Pac Environ Inst, 71-81, ASSOC DIR FISHERIES RES, PAC REGION, CAN FISHERIES & OCEANS. *Personal Data:* b Kewanee, Ill, Sept 17, 40; m 62; c 2. *Educ:* Augustana Col, Ill, 62; Univ Wash, PhD(zool), 67. *Prof Exp:* Fel phytoplankton ecol, Windermere Lab, Freshwater Biol Asn, Eng, 67-68. *Mem:* Am Soc Limnol & Oceanog; Int Asn Theoret & Appl Limnol. *Res:* Phytoplankton ecology and paleolimnology; marine plankton ecology and benthic algal and phytoplankton production. *Mailing Add:* 2614 Mathers Ave West Vancouver BC V7V 2J4 Can

STOCKS, DOUGLAS ROSCOE, JR, MATHEMATICS. *Current Pos:* ADJ PROF MATH, UNIV ALA, BIRMINGHAM, 69- *Personal Data:* b Dallas, Tex, Sept 4, 32; m 51; c 4. *Educ:* Univ Tex, BA, 58, MA, 60, PhD(math), 64. *Prof Exp:* Spec instr math, Univ Tex, 60-64; from asst prof to assoc prof, Univ Tex, Arlington, 64-69. *Concurrent Pos:* Mathematician, US Navy Electronics Lab, 63; Tex Col & Univ Syst res grant, 66-67; vis prof, Auburn Univ, 78-79 & Univ Reading, Eng, 85-86. *Mem:* Am Math Soc; Math Asn Am. *Res:* Lattice paths and graph theory; foundations of mathematics; geometry; topology; point set theory. *Mailing Add:* Univ Ala Birmingham AL 35294-2060. *Fax:* 205-934-9025; *E-Mail:* stocks@math.uab.edu, D.R. Stocks@reading.ac.uk

STOCKS, GEORGE MALCOLM, SOLID STATE PHYSICS. *Current Pos:* RES STAFF MEM THEORET SOLID STATE PHYSICS, OAK RIDGE NAT LAB, 76- *Personal Data:* b Thurnscoe, Eng, June 5, 43; m 67; c 2. *Educ:* Univ Bradford, Eng, BTech, 66; Univ Sheffield, Eng, PhD(theoret physics), 69. *Prof Exp:* Res staff mem theoret solid state physics, Oak Ridge Nat Lab, 69-72; res assoc physics, Univ Bristol, Eng, 72-76. *Mem:* Am Phys Soc; Inst Physics, UK. *Res:* Theory of electronic states in ordered and disordered metals and alloys; bank theory; disordered systems theory; phase stability; transport; excitation processes in solids; photo electron spectroscopies; soft x-ray spectroscopy. *Mailing Add:* 171 Whippoorwill Dr Oak Ridge TN 37830. *Fax:* 423-574-7467

STOCKTON, BLAINE, AGRICULTURE. *Current Pos:* ASST ADMIN, ELEC PROG, USDA, 94- *Personal Data:* b Mar 7, 45. *Educ:* Pa State Univ, BS; George Washington Univ, MS. *Mailing Add:* USDA 14th Independence Ave SW Rm 40375 Washington DC 20250

STOCKTON, DORIS S, MATHEMATICS. *Current Pos:* asst prof, 58-73, ASSOC PROF MATH, UNIV MASS, AMHERST, 73- *Personal Data:* b New Brunswick, NJ, Feb 9, 24; m 48; c 2. *Educ:* Rutgers Univ, BSc, 45; Brown Univ, MSc, 47, PhD(math), 58. *Prof Exp:* Instr, Brown Univ, 52-54. *Mem:* Am Math Soc; Math Asn Am. *Res:* Functional analysis. *Mailing Add:* RFD 2 19 N Washington St Belchertown MA 01007-9803

STOCKTON, JAMES EVAN, ELECTRICAL ENGINEERING. *Current Pos:* Res engr, 60-64, supvr, Submarine Sonar Sect, 64-69, dep div head, Electroacoust Div, 69-70, HEAD ENG SERV DIV, APPL RES LABS, UNIV TEX, 70- *Personal Data:* b Goliad, Tex, Feb 28, 31; m 51; c 2. *Educ:* Univ Tex, Austin, BS, 60. *Mem:* Inst Elec & Electronics Engrs; Am Inst Physics; Acoust Soc Am. *Res:* Underwater acoustics; instrumentation for underwater acoustics; sonar systems. *Mailing Add:* 1508 Weyford Dr Austin TX 78757

STOCKTON, JOHN RICHARD, RESEARCH MANAGEMENT. *Current Pos:* PRES, MGT CATALYSTS, 74- *Personal Data:* b Jarrell, Tex, Feb 19, 17; m 38, 53, Norma Boyd; c James, Douglas, Alexandra, Joyce, J Richard & Robert D. *Educ:* Univ Tex, BSc, 38, MA, 41, PhD(microbiol), 51. *Prof Exp:* Pharmacist, Baylor Hosp, 38-39; tutor pharm, Univ Tex, 39-41, asst prof, 41-46; dir res, Hyland Labs, 46-50; tech asst to dir biol prod, Merck Sharp & Dohme, 50-54; mgr res & qual control, Pillsbury Co, 54-62, dir res & develop, 62-66, dir sci activities, 66-68; mgr res & develop Corn Prod Food Technol Inst, 68-70, assoc dir res & qual control, Best Foods, CPC Int, Inc, 70-73; vpres res & develop, Nutri Co, 73-74. *Mem:* AAAS; Inst Food Technol; Am Chem Soc; Am Soc Microbiol; NY Acad Sci. *Res:* Antimicrobial agents; structure-activity relationships; biological products; food science; product development; nutrition; research management. *Mailing Add:* Mgt Catalysts PO Box 70 Ship Bottom NJ 08008-0227. *Fax:* 609-597-2860

STOCKWELL, CHARLES WARREN, NEUROSCIENCES. *Current Pos:* PRES, STOCKWELL & ASSOC, 96- *Personal Data:* b Port Angeles, Wash, Dec 31, 40; m 66; c 2. *Educ:* Western Wash State Col, BA, 64; Univ Ill, MA, 66, PhD(psychol), 68. *Prof Exp:* Res psychologist, Naval Aerospace Med Ctr, 69-71; from asst prof to prof otolaryngol, Ohio State Univ, 72-84; prof otolaryngol, Wayne State Univ, 84-86, dir, Vestibular Lab, Providence Hosp, 86-96. *Res:* Vestibular function and testing. *Mailing Add:* 853 Rivard Blvd Grosse Pointe MI 48230

STOCKWELL, NORMAN D, PHYSICS OF BEAMS. *Current Pos:* SR PROJ ENGR, TRW, 82- *Personal Data:* b Detroit, Mich, Apr 6, 41; m, Helen Shepard. *Educ:* Tulane Univ, BS, 62; Rice Univ, MA, 65, PhD(physics), 67. *Mem:* Am Phys Soc; Sigma Xi. *Mailing Add:* 1816 Armour Lane Redondo Beach CA 90278

STOCUM, DAVID LEON, regeneration, tissue restoration, for more information see previous edition

STODDARD, JAMES H, MATHEMATICS. *Current Pos:* RETIRED. *Personal Data:* b Saginaw, Mich, June 17, 30; m 57, Nancy L Garland; c Kimberly J (Howard) & Robert J. *Educ:* Univ Mich, BS, 52, PhD(math), 61. *Prof Exp:* Instr math, Univ Mich, 60-61; asst prof, Oakland Univ, 61-62, Syracuse Univ, 62-66, Univ of the South, 66-67; assoc prof, Kenyon Col, 67-70; prof, Upsala Col, 70-72; prof math, Montclair State Col, 72-97. *Mem:* Am Math Soc; Math Asn Am. *Res:* Computer software; application to management sciences. *Mailing Add:* 204 Woodlawn Way North Chatham MA 02650

STODDARD, LELAND DOUGLAS, PATHOLOGY. *Current Pos:* chmn dept, 54-73, PROF PATH, EUGENE TALMADGE MEM HOSP, MED COL GA, 54- *Personal Data:* b Hillsboro, Ill, Mar 15, 19; m 46. *Educ:* DePauw Univ, AB, 40; Johns Hopkins Univ, MD, 43. *Prof Exp:* Asst & asst resident path, 47-48, instr & resident, 49-50, assoc, Sch Med Duke Univ, 50-51; from asst prof to assoc prof, Med Sch, Univ Kans, 51-54. *Concurrent Pos:* Chief staff, Eugene Talmadge Mem Hosp, 64-65; chief res path, Atomic Bomb Casualty Comn Japan, 61-62; vis prof, Med Sch, Osaka Univ, 66; mem path training comt, Vet Admin, 69-72; mem, Intersoc Path Coun, Int Coun Socs Path, US Nat Comt & Sci Adv Bd of Consult, Armed Forces Inst Path, 70-75. *Mem:* Am Asn Cancer Res; Asn Hist Med; Am Asn Pathologists; Int Acad Path (vpres, 74-78, treas, 78-); Int Acad Path (secy-treas, 70-79, pres, 81-82). *Res:* Cervical carcinoma; gynecological and reproductive endocrine pathology; knowledge theory in pathology and medicine. *Mailing Add:* Dept Path Med Col Ga 1120 15th St Augusta GA 30912-0001

STODDARD, STEPHEN D(AVIDSON), CERAMIC ENGINEERING, MATERIALS SCIENCE. *Current Pos:* RETIRED. *Personal Data:* b Everett, Wash, Feb 8, 25; wid; c Stephanie K & Dorcas (Avery). *Educ:* Univ Ill, BS, 50. *Honors & Awards:* PACE Award, Am Ceramic Soc, 64, Greaves-Walker Award, 84. *Prof Exp:* From asst ceramic engr to asst prod supvr, Coors Porcelain Co, Colo, 50-52; ceramics sect leader, Los Alamos Sci Lab, Univ Calif, 52-74, ceramics-powder metall sect leader, 74-80, consult, vpres & secy, Mat Technol Assocs, 77-80, pres & treas, 80-96. *Concurrent Pos:* Consult, 56-; consult ed, Ceramic Age, 58-60; mem, Mat Adv Bd, Dept Defense, Nat Acad Sci, 62-63; consult, Mat Technol Assocs, 77-80, pres & treas, 80- *Mem:* AAAS; fel Am Inst Chem; Nat Inst Ceramic Engrs; fel Am Ceramic Soc (vpres, 71-72, treas, 72-74, pres, 76-77); Sigma Xi; Am Soc Metals. *Res:* Fabrication techniques for refractory oxides, rare earth oxides, refractory metals, metal-oxide mixtures, ceramic-metal seals and electronic ceramics and their application in energy and nuclear weapon, power and propulsion studies. *Mailing Add:* 4557 Trinity Dr Los Alamos NM 87544

STOEBE, THOMAS GAINES, MATERIALS SCIENCE, ELECTRONIC MATERIALS. *Current Pos:* from asst prof to assoc prof, 66-75, assoc dean, Col Eng, 82-87, chmn, Dept Mat Sci & Eng, 87-96, PROF, UNIV WASH, 75-, PROF, MAT SCI & ENG, 96- *Personal Data:* b Upland, Calif, Apr 26, 39; m 82, Janet Dumm; c Brian, Paul & Diane. *Educ:* Stanford Univ, BS, 61, MS, 63, PhD(mat sci), 65. *Honors & Awards:* Western Elec Award, Am Soc Eng Educ, 77. *Prof Exp:* Vis lectr metall & res assoc, Imp Col, London, 65-66. *Concurrent Pos:* Vis prof, Atomic Energy Inst, Sao Paulo, Brazil, 72-73. *Mem:* Am Soc Eng Educ; Am Ceramic Soc; Am Phys Soc; Metall Soc; Am Soc Metals Int. *Res:* Influence of lattice imperfections on physical properties of solids; electronic and optical properties in semiconductors and insulators. *Mailing Add:* 9309 Vineyard Crest Bellevue WA 98004

STOECKENIUS, WALTHER, CYTOLOGY. *Current Pos:* prof, 67-92, EMER PROF CELL BIOL, SCH MED, UNIV CALIF, SAN FRANCISCO, 92- *Personal Data:* b Giessen, Ger, July 3, 21; m 52; c 3. *Educ:* Univ Hamburg, MD, 50. *Prof Exp:* Intern, Pharmacol Inst, Univ Hamburg, 51, intern internal med, 51 & obstet & gynec, 52, researcher virol, Inst Trop Med, 52-54, res asst path, 54-58, pvt docent, 58; guest investr, Rockefeller Inst, 59, from asst prof to assoc prof cytol, 59-67. *Concurrent Pos:* Biophys, Max Planck Inst, Ger, 93- *Mem:* Nat Acad Sci; AAAS; Am Soc Biol Chem; Am Soc Cell Biol; Biophys Soc; Harvey Soc. *Res:* Fine structure of cells at the molecular level; energy transducing membranes; photobiology; halobacteria. *Mailing Add:* 24 Southridge E Tiburon CA 94920

STOECKER, DIANE KASTELOWITZ, MARINE PROTISTS, MICROZOOPLANKTON PHYSIOLOGY & ECOLOGY. *Current Pos:* ASSOC PROF, HORN POINT ENVIRON LAB, UNIV MD, 91- *Educ:* Univ NH, BS, 69; Univ Hawaii, MS, 70; State Univ NY, Stony Brook, PhD(ecol & evol), 79. *Honors & Awards:* Hutner Award, Soc Protozoologists, 91. *Prof Exp:* Scholar, Woods Hole Oceanog Inst, 79-80, asst scientist, 80-84, assoc scientist, 84-91. *Concurrent Pos:* Fel, Japanese Soc Prom Sci, 91. *Mem:* AAAS; Am Soc Limnol & Oceanog; Soc Protozoologist; Sigma Xi. *Res:* Ecology and physiology of marine protists, including their role in food web dynamics and nutrient cycling; mixotrophy among the plankton; planktonic ciliates in marine food webs. *Mailing Add:* PO Box 775 Univ Md Syst Cambridge MD 21613. *Fax:* 410-476-5490; *E-Mail:* Stoecker@hpel.umd.edu

STOECKLE, JOHN DUANE, MEDICINE. *Current Pos:* CHIEF MED CLIN, MASS GEN HOSP, 54-, PHYSICIAN, 69- *Personal Data:* b Highland Park, Mich, Aug 17, 22; m 47; c 4. *Educ:* Antioch Col, BS, 48; Harvard Med Sch, MD, 48; Am Bd Internal Med, dipl, 58. *Honors & Awards:* Glazer Award, Soc Gen Internal Med, 89. *Prof Exp:* Intern med, Mass Gen Hosp, Boston, 48-49, asst resident, 49-50, resident, 51-52; panel dir med aspects of atomic energy, Comt Med Sci, Res & Develop Bd, Dept Defense, 52-54; from instr to assoc prof, 54-82, PROF MED, HARVARD MED SCH, 82- *Concurrent Pos:* mem comt on coal miner's safety & health, Dept Health, Educ & Welfare, 71-73; book rev ed, Soc Sci & Med, 72-89. *Mem:* Fel Am Pub Health Asn; assoc mem Am Sociol Asn; fel Am Anthrop Asn; fel Am Psychosom Soc; Soc Appl Anthrop; fel Am Col Physicians. *Res:* Medical care administration and health and illness behavior; longitudinal study of occupational lung diseases. *Mailing Add:* Mass Gen Hosp Fruit St Boston MA 02114

STOECKLER, JOHANNA D, CELLULAR SIGNAL TRANSDUCTION, NUCLEOSIDE TRANSPORT & METABOLISM. *Current Pos:* From instr to asst prof, 77-85, ASSOC PROF BIOCHEM PHARMACOL, BROWN UNIV, 85- *Educ:* Rutgers Univ, BA, 63, PhD(biochem), 73. *Mem:* Am Soc Biochem & Molecular Biol; Am Asn Cancer Res; AAAS; Am Asn Women Cancer Res. *Res:* Preclinical pharmacology involving transport and metabolism of purines; enzymology; signal transduction in cultured cell systems via adenylate cyclase and phospholipase C. *Mailing Add:* 62 Perryville Rd PO Box 747 Rehoboth MA 02769-0747. *Fax:* 401-863-1595

STOECKLEY, THOMAS ROBERT, ASTRONOMY. *Current Pos:* SR STAFF SCIENTIST, CONOCO INCORP, 83- *Personal Data:* b Ft Wayne, Ind, Dec 6, 42; m 73, Kathleen V; c Andrew J & Heidi N. *Educ:* Mich State Univ, BS, 64; Cambridge Univ, PhD(astron), 67. *Prof Exp:* From asst prof to assoc prof astron, Mich State Univ, 67-83. *Mem:* Soc Explor Geophysicists. *Res:* Seismic data processing. *Mailing Add:* 2303 Skylark St Ponca City OK 74604-2828

STOECKLY, ROBERT E, ATMOSPHERIC PHYSICS. *Current Pos:* Physicist, 83-85, RES SCIENTIST, KAMAN SCI CORP, 92- *Personal Data:* b Schenectady, NY, June 9, 38; m 69; c 2. *Educ:* Princeton Univ, PhD(astrophys sci), 64. *Prof Exp:* Res fel astron, Mt Wilson & Palomar Observs, 64-65; asst prof physics & astron, Rensselaer Polytech Inst, 65-72; physicist, Mission Res Corp, 72-83; res scientist, Phy Res Inc, 85-90. *Mem:* Asn Comput Mach. *Res:* Fluid dynamics; plasma physics; atmospheric physics. *Mailing Add:* 3229 Calle Cedro Santa Barbara CA 93105-2730. *Fax:* 805-963-8420

STOEHR, ROBERT ALLEN, METALLURGICAL ENGINEERING. *Current Pos:* asst prof, 68-74, ASSOC PROF METALL & MAT ENG, UNIV PITTSBURGH, 74- *Personal Data:* b Pittsburgh, Pa, July 10, 30. *Educ:* Hiram Col, BA, 52; Carnegie Inst Technol, MS, 65; Carnegie-Mellon Univ, PhD(metall & mat sci), 69. *Prof Exp:* Metall engr, Reactive Metals, Inc, Ohio, 54-60; res engr, Alcoa Res Labs, Aluminum Co Am, Pa, 60-67. *Mem:* Metall Soc; Am Inst Mining, Metall & Petrol Engrs; Am Soc Metals; Electrochem Soc. *Res:* Process and chemical metallurgy; casting and solidification; high temperature electrochemistry and corrosion; computer simulation of metallurgical processes. *Mailing Add:* Dept Mat Sci & Eng 848 Benedum Hall Univ Pittsburgh 4200 Fifth Ave Pittsburgh PA 15261

STOENNER, HERBERT GEORGE, BACTERIOLOGY, VIROLOGY. *Current Pos:* RETIRED. *Personal Data:* b Levasy, Mo, June 17, 19; m 46; c 4. *Educ:* Iowa State Col, DVM, 43. *Honors & Awards:* K F Meyer Gold Headed Cane Award, 74. *Prof Exp:* Asst scientist, Commun Dis Ctr, USPHS, Ga, 47-50, sr asst vet, 50-52, vet, 52-56, sr vet, 56-61, asst dir lab, 62-64, dir, Rocky Mountain Lab, Nat Inst Allergy & Infectious Dis, 64-82, vet officer dir, 61-82. *Concurrent Pos:* Fac affil, Univ Mont. *Mem:* Am Vet Med Asn; Am Pub Health Asn; US Animal Health Asn; Conf Res Workers Animal Dis. *Res:* Zoonoses; leptospirosis; rickettsioses; brucellosis; psittacosis. *Mailing Add:* 1102 S Second St Hamilton MT 59840

STOERMER, EUGENE F, PHYCOLOGY, LIMNOLOGY. *Current Pos:* assoc res algologist, Univ Mich, 66-71, lectr, Biol Sta, 69-77, assoc prof, 77-84, RES ALGOLONIST, GREAT LAKES RES DIV, UNIV MICH, ANN ARBOR, 71-, RES SCIENTIST, HERBARIUM, 73-, PROF, SCH NAT RES, 85- *Personal Data:* b Webb, Iowa, Mar 7, 34; m 60, Barbara Ryder; c Eric F & Karla J. *Educ:* Iowa State Univ, BS, 58, PhD(bot), 63. *Honors & Awards:* Darbaker Prize, Phycol Soc Am, 93. *Prof Exp:* NIH fel phycol, Iowa State Univ, 63-65. *Concurrent Pos:* McHenry fel, Acad Natural Sci, Philadelphia, Pa, 59; vis prof bot, Mich State Univ, 67-68; adj prof biol, City Univ New York, 74 & Bowling Green State Univ, 77-80; mem grad fac, Univ Maine, Orono, 81-; res fel, Acad Natural Sci Philadelphia; NFR res fel, Univ Lund, Sweden, 83; vis scholar, Ministry Educ, People's Repub China, 85; mem, Col Environ Sci & Forestry, Syracuse, 90. *Mem:* AAAS; Am Soc Limnol & Oceanog; Int Phycol Soc; Phycol Soc Am (pres, 88); Am Quaternary Asn; Sigma Xi. *Res:* Taxonomy and ecology of Bacillariophyta and Laurentian Great Lakes algal flora; paleoecology and algal evolution. *Mailing Add:* 4392 Dexter Rd Ann Arbor MI 48109-2099. *E-Mail:* Stoermer@umich.edu

STOESZ, JAMES DARREL, BIOPHYSICAL CHEMISTRY, BIOCHEMISTRY. *Current Pos:* sr chemist biosci, Cent Res Labs, 78-82, supvr, Biotechnol Lab, Life Sci Sect Lab, 82-85, mgr, Asepsis & Infection Control Lab, Med-Surg Div, 85-88, MGR, BIOTECHNOL LAB, LIFE SCI SECTOR LAB, 3M CO, 88- *Personal Data:* b Mountain Lake, Minn, July 3, 50; m 71; c 3. *Educ:* Bethel Col, BA, 72; Univ Minn, Minneapolis, PhD(biophys chem), 77. *Prof Exp:* Res fel biochem, Brandeis Univ, 76-78. *Mem:* Am Chem Soc. *Res:* Protein and polypeptide structure and function; enzyme mechanisms; nuclear magnetic resonance; lipid bilayer membranes; liposomes; immunodiagnostics; chemiluminescence. *Mailing Add:* 3M Co Bldg 260-6B-16 St Paul MN 55144

STOETZEL, MANYA BROOKE, ENTOMOLOGY. *Current Pos:* presidential intern, 73-74, res entomologist, Syst Entom Lab, Agr Res Serv, 74-94, RES LEADER, USDA, 94- *Personal Data:* b Houston, Tex, Apr 11, 40; c 2. *Educ:* Univ Md, College Park, BS, 66, MS, 70, PhD(entom), 72. *Prof Exp:* Entomologist, First US Army Med Lab, Ft Meade, Md, 66-68. *Concurrent Pos:* Ed, Entom Soc Wash, 77-79, pres, 83; gov bd, Enton Soc Am, 92-94; mem, Entom Soc Wash, SW Entom Soc, Fla Entom Soc, Ga Entom Soc. *Mem:* Entom Soc Am; Am Asn Zool. *Res:* Morphology and taxonomy of aphids, phylloxerans, adelgids and armored scale insects. *Mailing Add:* Syst Entom Lab USDA Bldg 046 Beltsville MD 20705

STOEVER, EDWARD CARL, JR, SCIENCE EDUCATION, GENERAL EARTH SCIENCES. *Current Pos:* RETIRED. *Personal Data:* b Milwaukee, Wis, Mar 13, 26; m 54, Norma E Johnson; c Gregory E & Catherine A (Bohrer). *Educ:* Purdue Univ, BS, 48; Univ Mich, MS, 50, PhD(geol), 59. *Prof Exp:* Res geologist, Int Minerals & Chem Corp, 52-54; from asst prof to assoc prof geol, Sch Geol & Geophys, Univ Okla, 56-69, assoc dir undergrad studies, Univ Okla, 70-72, prof geol & geophys, 69-78; prof geol & chmn dept earth sci, Southeast Mo State, 78-85, dir, Ctr Sci & Math Educ, 83-86; exec dir, Mo Alliance Sci, 87-92. *Concurrent Pos:* Fel, NSF, 55-56 & 57-58, dir, Okla Geol Camp, 64-69; dir inst earth sci, NSF, 65-69 & 70-72; assoc dir, Earth Sci Curriculum Proj, 69; assoc prog dir teacher educ sect, NSF, 69-70; sr staff consult, Earth Sci Teacher Prep Proj, 70-72; dir, Okla Earth Sci Educ Proj, 72-74; dir, Nat Asn Geol Teachers Crustal Evolution Educ Proj, NSF, 76-80; co dir, K6 Sci & Math Improv Proj, Southeast Mo, 85-91. *Mem:* Nat Asn Geol Teachers (vpres, 74-75, pres, 75-76); fel AAAS; fel Geol Soc Am; Nat Sci Teachers Asn; Am Asn Supvry & Current Develop. *Res:* Statewide elementary, secondary and college educational improvement in science, mathematics and technology through education; business-government partnerships. *Mailing Add:* 84 Edgewater Rhinelander WI 54501

STOEWSAND, GILBERT SAARI, FOOD TOXICOLOGY. *Current Pos:* from asst prof to assoc prof, 67-79, PROF TOXICOL, EXP STA, NY STATE COL AGR & LIFE SCI, CORNELL UNIV, 79- *Personal Data:* b Chicago, Ill, Oct 20, 32; m 57, Ellen Barby; c 2. *Educ:* Univ Calif, Davis, BS, 54, MS, 58; Cornell Univ, PhD, 64. *Prof Exp:* Res assoc poultry sci, Cornell Univ, 58-61; res nutritionist, US Army Natick Lab, Mass, 63-66; res assoc, Inst Exp Path & Toxicol, Albany Med Col, 66-67. *Concurrent Pos:* WHO fel, 72; consult, Toxicol Info Prog, Nat Libr Med, 77-85; vis scholar, Indonesia, 88 & 92. *Mem:* Am Soc Enology & Viticult; Inst Food Technol; Am Inst Nutrit; Soc Toxicol; Soc Exp Biol & Med. *Res:* Cancer and food; food additives; natural food toxicants and toxicant inhibitors. *Mailing Add:* Dept Food Sci & Technol NY State Agr Exp Sta Cornell Univ Geneva NY 14456. *Fax:* 315-757-2397

STOFFA, PAUL L, MARINE GEOPHYSICS, SIGNAL PROCESSING. *Current Pos:* AT INST FOR GEOPHYSICS, UNIV TEX, AUSTIN; CONSULT, GULF SCI TECHNOL, 81- *Personal Data:* b Palmerton, Pa, July 9, 48; m 68; c 2. *Educ:* Rensselaer Polytech Inst, BS, 70; Columbia Univ, PhD(geophys), 74. *Prof Exp:* Res assoc marine geophys, Lamont-Doherty Geol Observ, 74-81. *Concurrent Pos:* Adj asst prof, Columbia Univ, 78- *Mem:* Am Geophys Union; Soc Explor Geophys; Inst Elec & Electronics Engrs; Sigma Xi. *Res:* Marine seismology; wave propagation; numerical analysis. *Mailing Add:* Geol Sci Univ Tex Austin TX 78712-1026

STOFFELLA, PETER JOSEPH, VEGETABLE CROPS, ROOT SYSTEM FUNCTIONS. *Current Pos:* asst prof, 80-85, assoc prof, 85-90, PROF, UNIV FLA, 90- *Personal Data:* b Montreal, Que, Nov 21, 54; US citizen; m 87, Celina Zemora; c Sylvia & Anthony. *Educ:* Delaware Valley Col, BS, 76; Kansas State Univ, MS, 77, Cornell Univ, PhD(vegetable crops), 80. *Prof Exp:* Teaching asst, Kans State Univ, 77. *Concurrent Pos:* Vis prof, Univ Pisa, 87. *Mem:* Am Soc Horticult Sci; Am Soc Agron; Crop Sci Soc Am; Sigma Xi. *Res:* Cultural and management practices of commercial vegetable crops; development and functions of plant root systems. *Mailing Add:* Univ Fla Agricult Res & Educ Ctr PO Box 248 Ft Pierce FL 34954. *Fax:* 561-468-5668

STOFFER, JAMES OSBER, ORGANIC CHEMISTRY, POLYMER CHEMISTRY. *Current Pos:* from asst pro to assoc prof, 63-82, PROF CHEM, UNIV MO-ROLLA, 82-, SR INVESTR, MAT RES CTR, 85- *Personal Data:* b Homeworth, Ohio, Oct 16, 35; m 57; c 2. *Educ:* Mt Union Col, BS, 57; Purdue Univ, PhD(org chem), 61. *Prof Exp:* Res asst, Purdue Univ, 57-59; res assoc, Cornell Univ, 61-63. *Mem:* Am Chem Soc. *Res:* Beta deuterium isotope effects; trace organic analysis; small ring compounds; polymer synthesis and characterization. *Mailing Add:* 16 Laird Rolla MO 65401-3735

STOFFER, RICHARD LAWRENCE, AQUATIC ECOLOGY, SYSTEMATICS OF DIPTERA FAMILY CHIRONOMIDAE. *Current Pos:* from asst prof to assoc prof, 80-87, PROF BIOL, ASHLAND UNIV, 87- *Personal Data:* b Cleveland, Ohio, Dec 13, 48; m 71; c 2. *Educ:* Ashland Univ, BS, 70; Ohio State Univ, MS, 75, PhD(zool), 78. *Prof Exp:* Instr sci, Urbana Univ, 78-80. *Mem:* Am Inst Biol Sci; Am Soc Zoologists; Entom Soc Am. *Res:* Ecology of aquatic environments with a specific interest in the systematics (behavior, ecology, and taxonomy) of the Diptera family Chironomidae. *Mailing Add:* Dept Biol & Toxicol Ashland Univ 401 College Ave Ashland OH 44805-3702

STOFFER, ROBERT LLEWELLYN, INDUSTRIAL HYGIENE, ANALYTICAL CHEMISTRY. *Current Pos:* RETIRED. *Personal Data:* b North Georgetown, Ohio, Sept 16, 27; m 51, Joanne Selby; c Lisa, Eric & Wayne. *Educ:* Ashland Col, AB, 50; Ohio State Univ, PhD(analytical chem), 54. *Prof Exp:* Analytical chemist, Amoco Corp, 54-56, from asst proj chemist to sr proj chemist, 56-72, indust hyg chemist, Environ Affairs & Safety Dept, 72-92. *Mem:* Am Indust Hyg Asn; Am Chem Soc; Am Acad Indust Hygiene. *Res:* Development of new analytical methods in the industrial hygiene field. *Mailing Add:* 1237 Barbara Ct Naperville IL 60540-7801

STOFFOLANO, JOHN GEORGE, JR, ENTOMOLOGY, NEUROBIOLOGY. *Current Pos:* From asst prof to assoc prof, 69-80, PROF ENTOM, UNIV MASS, AMHERST, 80- *Personal Data:* b Gloversville, NY, Dec 31, 39; m 65; c 2. *Educ:* State Univ NY Col Oneonta, BS, 62; Cornell Univ, MS, 67; Univ Conn, PhD(entom), 70. *Concurrent Pos:* NSF fel neurobiol, Princeton Univ, 70-71; NIH fel, Univ Mass, Amherst, 72-75. *Mem:* AAAS; Entom Soc Am; Am Inst Biol Sci; Soc Nematol. *Res:* Integrative studies on the ecology, neurobiology and physiology of diapausing, nondiapausing and aging flies of the genus Musca and Phormia. *Mailing Add:* Montague Rd Entomol Univ Mass Amherst Fernald Hall Amherst MA 01003-0002

STOHLER, RUDOLF, ZOOLOGY. *Current Pos:* RETIRED. *Personal Data:* b Basel, Switz, Dec 5, 01; nat US; m 29; c 5. *Educ:* Univ Basel, MA & PhD(zool), 28. *Prof Exp:* Inst Student Exchange fel, Univ Calif, Berkeley, 28-30, res assoc zool, 32-34, instr, 34-35, res assoc, 35-41, instr zool & biol, Exten, 35-69, prin lab tech, 41-69, assoc res zoologist, 55-66, res zoologist, 66-69, emer res zoologist, 69- *Mem:* Swiss Soc Natural Sci; hon mem Swiss Zool; Sigma Xi. *Res:* Cytology of toads; sex reversal in fish; genetics of human twinning; Gastropoda of California coast; laboratory techniques. *Mailing Add:* 1584 Milvia St Berkeley CA 94709

STOHLMAN, STEPHEN ARNOLD, MICROBIOLOGY, VIROLOGY. *Current Pos:* ASST PROF NEUROL & MICROBIOL, UNIV SOUTHERN CALIF, 75- *Personal Data:* b Long Beach, Calif, Oct 4, 46. *Educ:* Calif State Univ, BS, 70, MS, 72; Univ Md, PhD(microbiol), 75. *Concurrent Pos:* Co-investr, NIH grant, 77-81; prin investr, Nat Multiple Sclerosis Soc grant, 79-81. *Mem:* Am Soc Microbiol; Tissue Cult Asn; Soc Gen Microbiol. *Res:* Neurovirology; molecular biology; immunology. *Mailing Add:* Dept Neurol & Microbiol Univ Southern Calif 2025 Zonal 142 McKibben Hall Los Angeles CA 90033. *Fax:* 213-225-2369

STOHR, JOACHIM, STRUCTURE OF SURFACES, THIN FILM MAGNETISM. *Current Pos:* res staff mem surface sci, IBM Res Div, Almaden Res Ctr, 85-89, mgr condensed matter sci, 89-91, mgr magnetic mat & phenomena, 91-94, MGR, SYNCHROTRON RADIATION STUDIES, IBM RES DIV, ALMADEN RES CTR, 94- *Personal Data:* b Meinerzhagen, WGer, Sept 28, 47; m 97, Linda Buckman; c Megan. *Educ:* Rheinische Friedrich Wilhelms Univ Bonn, Vordiplom, 69; Wash State Univ, MSc, 71; Tech Univ Munchen, Dr rer nat, 74. *Prof Exp:* Scientist solid state physics, Lawrence Berkeley Lab, 76-77; sr res assoc surface sci, Stanford Synchrotron Radiation Lab, 77-81; sr staff physicist surface sci, Exxon Res & Eng Co, 81-85. *Concurrent Pos:* Mem, Steering Comt, Advan Photon Source, 84-89,

Int Organizing Comt, Int Conf X-Ray Absorption Fine Struct, 86-, Dept Energy Synchrotron Radiation Facil Rev Comt, 87-88, Tenure Proposal Rev Comt, Nat Synchrotron Light Source, 89; consult prof elec eng, Stanford Univ, 89-, Synchotron Radiation Lab, 93-; adj prof physics, Uppsala Univ, Sweden, 94- Mem: Fel Am Phys Soc; Am Vacuum Soc. Res: Development of new synchrotron radiation based surface x-ray absorption techniques and their use for the determination of the geometric arrangement of atoms and molecules on surfaces and of the magnetic properties of surfaces and interfaces and thin films. Mailing Add: IBM Res Div Almaden Res Ctr 650 Harry Rd K11/802 San Jose CA 95120-6099. Fax: 408-927-3311; E-Mail: stohr@almaden.ibm.com

STOHRER, GERHARD, ORGANIC CHEMISTRY, BIOCHEMISTRY. Current Pos: Assoc biochem, 66-80, ASST PROF, BIOCHEM UNIT, KETTERING LAB, SLOAN-KETTERING INST CANCER RES, 80- Personal Data: b Heidelberg, Ger, May 28, 39. Educ: Univ Heidelberg, dipl chem, 62, PhD(chem), 65. Mem: Am Chem Soc; Ger Chem Soc. Res: Molecular biology of oncogenesis. Mailing Add: 20 Stafford Pl Larchmont NY 10538-2722

STOHS, SIDNEY J, MOLECULAR MECHANISMS & TOXICITY OF ENVIRONMENTAL CONTAMINANTS, FREE RADICALS & REACTIVE OXYGEN SPECIES. Current Pos: asst dean, 89-91, DEAN & PROF, CREIGHTON UNIV, 89- Personal Data: b Ludell, Kans, May 24, 39; m 60, Susan Stehl; c Sarah & Tim. Educ: Univ Nebr, Lincoln, BS, 62, MS, 64; Univ Wis-Madison, PhD(biochem), 67. Prof Exp: From asst prof to assoc prof, Univ Nebr, 67-74, prof, Med Ctr, 74-89, asst dean, 85-87. Concurrent Pos: Mem, Comt Struct & Process, Am Asn Cols Pharm, 95-; consult, US Asst Secy Health, 96. Mem: Sigma Xi; Soc Toxicol; Am Pharmaceut Asn; Am Asn Cols Pharm. Res: Cascade of molecular events associated with the toxicities of environmental contaminants including polyhalogenated cyclic hydrocarbons, heavy metal ions and tobacco smoke. Mailing Add: Creighton Univ 2500 California Plaza Omaha NE 68178

STOIBER, RICHARD EDWIN, VOLCANOLOGY, ECONOMIC GEOLOGY. Current Pos: RETIRED. Personal Data: b Cleveland, Ohio, Jan 28, 11; m 41; c 2. Educ: Dartmouth Col, AB, 32; Mass Inst Technol, PhD(econ geol), 37. Prof Exp: Instr geol, Dartmouth Col, 35-36 & 37-50, from asst prof to prof, 40-71, Frederick Hall prof, 71-89. Concurrent Pos: Mem, Nfld Geol Surv Pvt Mining Indust & US Geol Surv; govt-sponsored volcanic res, Worldwide, espec Cent Am; consult, UN; pvt consult. Mem: Mineral Soc Am; Soc Econ Geol; Geol Soc Am; Am Inst Mining, Metall & Petrol Eng. Res: Volcanoes; ore deposits; optical crystallography. Mailing Add: McKenna Rd Norwich VT 05055. Fax: 603-646-3922

STOIBER, SUSANNE A, HEALTH POLICY. Current Pos: dep asst secy health/planning & eval, health/dis prev & health prom, DEP ASST SECY, PLANNING & EVAL PROG SYSTS, DEPT HEALTH & HUMAN SERV. Prof Exp: Dir, Div Social & Econ Studies, Nat Res Coun, Nat Acad Sci, 90-94; hosp adminr, Warren Grant Magnuson Clin Res Ctr, NIH. Res: Health policy and management; workforce policies. Mailing Add: Off Asst Secy Planning & Eval 200 Independance Ave SW Room 447-D Washington DC 20201

STOICHEFF, BORIS PETER, LASERS, ATOMIC & MOLECULAR SPECTROSCOPY & STRUCTURE. Current Pos: prof physics, Univ Toronto, 64-77, chmn, eng sci, 72-77, univ prof, 77-90, dir, Ont Laser & Lightwave Res Ctr, 88-91, EMER UNIV PROF PHYSICS, UNIV TORONTO, 90- Personal Data: b Bitol, Macedonia, Yugoslavia, June 1, 24; nat Can; m 54, Lillian J Ambridge; c Richard P. Educ: Univ Toronto, BASc, 47, MA, 48, PhD(physics), 50. Hon Degrees: DSc, Univ Skopje, 81, York Univ, 82, Univ Windsor, 89, Univ Toronto, 94. Honors & Awards: Gold Medal, Can Asn Physicists, 74; William F Meggers Award, Optical Soc Am, 81; Officer of the Order of Can, 82, Frederic Ives Medal, 83; H L Welsh lectr, Univ Toronto, 84; Elizabeth Laird lectr, Univ Western Ont, 85; UK-Can Rutherford lectr, 89; Henry Marshall Tory Medal, Royal Soc Can, 89. Prof Exp: McKee-Gilchrist fel, Univ Toronto, 50-51; fel, Nat Res Coun Can, 52-53, res officer, Div Pure Physics, 53-64. Concurrent Pos: Vis scientist, Mass Inst Technol, 63-64; I W Killam mem scholar, 77-79; mem, Coun Nat Res, Coun Can, 77-83, Coun Assoc Prof Engr Ont, 86-91, Res Coun Can Inst Advan Res, 89-; vis scientist, Stanford Univ, 87; sr fel, Massey Col, 79-; Geoffrey Frew fel, Australian Acad Sci, 80; res fel, Japan Soc Prom Sci, 86; vpres, Int Union Pure & Appl Physics, 94-96; Mem: Fel Am Phys Soc; hon fel Indian Acad Sci; fel Royal Soc London; fel Royal Soc Can; fel Optical Soc Am (pres-elect, 75, pres, 76); Can Asn Physicists (pres, 83); hon fel Macedonian Acad Sci & Arts; hon foreign fel Am Acad Arts & Sci. Res: Molecular spectroscopy and structure; Rayleigh, Brillouin and Raman scattering; lasers and their applications in spectroscopy; stimulated scattering processes and two photon absorption; elastic constants of rare gas single crystals; vacuum ultraviolet laser spectroscopy, nonlinear optics. Mailing Add: Dept Physics Univ Toronto Toronto ON M5S 1A7 Can. Fax: 416-971-2068

STOJILKOVIC, STANKO S, NEUROENDOCRINOLOGY, CELLULAR & MOLECULAR SIGNALING. Current Pos: Guest researcher, 85-88, vis scientist, 88-93, INVESTR, NAT INST CHILD HEALTH & HUMAN DEVELOP, NIH, 93- Personal Data: b Karavukovo, Vojvodina, Yugoslavia, Aug 25, 50; m 78, Marina Francelj; c Kosta. Educ: Univ Novy Sad, BA, 74, PhD(endocrinol), 82; Univ Belgrade, MSci, 78. Concurrent Pos: Vis prof, Univ Belgrade, 90- Mem: Endocrine Soc; Am Soc Biochem & Molecular Biol. Res: Calcium signaling; inositol phosphate-diacylglycerol signaling; calcium-protein kinase C interactions; plasma-membrane signaling; primary and sustained gene responses; exocytosis in endocrine and neuronal cells. Mailing Add: Endocrinol & Reprod Res Br NICHD NIH Bldg 49 Rm 6A-36 Bethesda MD 20892-4510. Fax: 301-480-8010; E-Mail: stankos@helix.nih.gov

STOKELY, ERNEST MITCHELL, BIOMEDICAL ENGINEERING. Current Pos: asst prof, 73-80, ASSOC PROF RADIOL, UNIV TEX HEALTH SCI CTR, DALLAS, 80- Personal Data: b Greenwood, Miss, Mar 26, 37; m 64; c 2. Educ: Miss State Univ, BSEE, 59; Southern Methodist Univ, MSEE & EE, 68, EE, 71, PhD(biomed eng), 73. Prof Exp: Sr elec engr, Tex Instruments, Inc, 59-69. Concurrent Pos: Adj prof, Southern Methodist Univ, 73- & Univ Tex, Arlington, 73- Mem: Inst Elec & Electronic Engrs; Nat Asn Biomed Engrs. Res: Medical image and signal processing; biological system modeling. Mailing Add: Dept Biomed Eng Univ Ala Birmingham AL 35294

STOKER, HOWARD STEPHEN, INORGANIC CHEMISTRY. Current Pos: Assoc prof, 68-77, PROF INORG CHEM, WEBER STATE UNIV, 77- Personal Data: b Salt Lake City, Utah, Apr 16, 39; m 64, Sharon R Stevenson; c 7. Educ: Univ Utah, BA, 63; Univ Wis-Madison, PhD(chem), 68. Mem: Am Chem Soc. Res: Writer of 17 textbooks on general chemistry, liberal arts chemistry, organic chemistry, and biochemistry. Mailing Add: Dept Chem Weber State Univ Ogden UT 84408

STOKER, WARREN C, ELECTRICAL ENGINEERING. Current Pos: From instr to prof elec eng, Rensselaer Polytechnic Inst, Conn, 34-96, vpres, 61-74, trustee, 61-96, pres, 74-76, EMER PRES, RENSSELAER POLYTECHNIC INST CONN, 76- Personal Data: b Union Springs, NY, Jan 30, 12; m 34; c 3. Educ: Rensselaer Polytech Inst, EE, 33, MEE, 34, PhD(physics). Concurrent Pos: Chief engr, Radio Sta WHAZ, 44-51; head, Comput Lab, Hartford Grad Ctr, Rensselaer Polytechnic Inst Conn, 51-55, dir, 55-57, dean, 57-70; mem, Res Sci Adv Comt, United Aircraft Corp. Mem: AAAS; fel Inst Elec & Electronics Engrs; Am Soc Eng Educ; Newcomen Soc NAm. Res: Electronic instrumentation; electromagnetic shielding and noise measurements; leakage and radiation; servomechanisms; analog computing; automatic control systems. Mailing Add: 188-C Main St Manchester CT 06040

STOKES, ARNOLD PAUL, PURE MATHEMATICS. Current Pos: chmn dept, 67-70, PROF MATH, GEORGETOWN UNIV, 65- Personal Data: b Bismarck, NDak, Jan 24, 32; m 57, Gaye Wims; c Michael, Jonathan, Thomas, Katherine, Christopher & Peter. Educ: Univ Notre Dame, BS, 55, PhD(math), 59. Prof Exp: Staff mathematician, Res Inst Adv Study, 58-60; NSF fel math, Johns Hopkins Univ, 60-61; from asst prof to assoc prof, Catholic Univ, 61-65. Concurrent Pos: Sr res assoc, Nat Res Coun-Nat Acad Sci, Goddard Space Flight Ctr, NASA, 74-75; consult ocean acoustics, SAI, McLean, Va, 80- Res: Scattering from random surfaces; acoustical and electromagnetic waves; nonlinear differential equations. Mailing Add: Dept Math Georgetown Univ 37th & O Sts NW Washington DC 20057-0002

STOKES, BARRY OWEN, BIOLOGICAL STAINING, FUEL ALCOHOL PRODUCTION FROM CELLULOSE. Current Pos: SR SCIENTIST, WESCOR INC, LOGAN, UTAH, 86- Personal Data: b San Francisco, Calif, Jan 10, 45; div; c Diedre A, Darren S, Holly L, David L & Bradley G. Educ: Utah State Univ, Logan, BA, 69; Univ Calif, Los Angeles, PhD(biochem), 74. Prof Exp: Sr scientist, Jet Propulsion Lab, Pasadena, Calif, 74-82; vpres res & develop, Biomass Int Inc, Ogden, Utah, 82-86. Concurrent Pos: Consult, Biomass Int Inc, Ogden, Utah, 88- Res: Applied microbiology with emphasis on energy production through fermentation; biotechnology; developing instrumentation and reagents for medical invitro diagnostics. Mailing Add: 459 S Main Logan UT 84321

STOKES, BRADFORD TAYLOR, NEUROPHYSIOLOGY, DEVELOPMENTAL NEUROBIOLOGY. Current Pos: asst prof, 73-77, ASSOC PROF PHYSIOL, OHIO STATE UNIV, 78- Personal Data: b Beverly, Mass, Jan 22, 44; m 67; c 2. Educ: Univ Mass, BA, 66; Univ Rochester, PhD(physiol), 73. Prof Exp: Res assoc physiol, Univ Rochester, 69-73. Concurrent Pos: Proj investr, Muscular Dystrophy Asn, 75-, NIH, 78-83 & NSF, 79-81. Mem: AAAS; Am Physiol Soc; Int Soc Oxygen Transp Tissue; Neurosci Soc. Res: Developmental neurophysiology; the development of motor systems; bioelectrical activity in normal and abnormal spinal cords; the effects of acute changes in blood gases on fetal neurogenesis. Mailing Add: Dept Physiol Oh State Univ Col Med 370 W Ninth Ave Columbus OH 43210-1238. Fax: 614-292-4888; E-Mail: ts6055@ohstu.marcc.ohiostate.edu

STOKES, CHARLES ANDERSON, FUELS & PETROCHEMICALS VENTURE CONSULTANTS, AIR POLLUTION CONTROL & ABATEMENT. Current Pos: PRES, CHARLES H STOKES, SCD INC, 69- Personal Data: b Mohawk, Fla, Oct 28, 15; m 39, Constance Currier; c Harry C, Jeffrey A & Christopher A. Educ: Univ Fla, BS, 38, ChE, 51; Mass Inst Technol, ScD, 51. Prof Exp: Instr & assoc prof chem eng, Mass Inst Technol, 40-45; consult, War Prod Bd, 44-45; dir res & develop, Cabot Corp, 45-55; vpres & tech dir, Tex Butodiene & Chem Corp, 55-59; vpres technol & planning, Columbia Div, Cities Serv Co, 60-69. Concurrent Pos: Vpres & dir, Petrocarb, 45-55; mem bd dirs, Columbian Carbon Co, Petrol Chem, Inc & Columbian Carbon Int, 60-69; adj prof chem eng, Univ Pittsburgh, 80-81. Mem: Am Chem Soc; fel Am Inst Chem Engrs; Nat Soc Prof Engrs; Am Solar Energy Soc. Res: Air conditioning by solar energy; recovery of volatile organics; zero residue municipal solid waste processing. Mailing Add: 2355 Kingfish Rd Naples FL 34102-1539. Fax: 941-775-3438

STOKES, CHARLES SOMMERS, PHYSICAL CHEMISTRY. *Current Pos:* mgr, Elvenson Test Facil, Franklin Res Ctr, 80-84, head spec proj, 84-87, head Appl Sci Dept, 87-89, DIR, FRANKLIN RES CTR, 90- *Personal Data:* b Philadelphia, Pa, Apr 24, 29; m 54; c 2. *Educ:* Ursinus Col, BS, 51; Temple Univ, MA, 53. *Prof Exp:* Res chemist, Germantown Labs, Inc, 53-56, res assoc, 56-61, mgr test site, 61-72, vpres, 72-80. *Mem:* Am Chem Soc; Am Inst Aeronaut & Astronaut; Am Inst Chem; Combustion Inst; Sigma Xi. *Res:* Fluorine chemistry; propellants; high temperatures; energy research; plasma jet chemistry. *Mailing Add:* 127 Madison Rd Willow Grove PA 19090-2699

STOKES, DAVID KERSHAW, JR, FAMILY MEDICINE. *Current Pos:* MED DIR, CAMPHAVEN NURSING HOME, INMAN, SC, 65- *Personal Data:* b Camden, SC, Feb 3, 27; m 50; c 3. *Educ:* Clemson Univ, BS, 48; Univ Ga, MS, 52; Tex A&M Univ, PhD, 56; Med Univ SC, MD, 57. *Prof Exp:* Assoc prof, 72-80, clin assoc & prof family pract, Med Univ SC, 72- *Concurrent Pos:* Mem, bd dir, Am Geriat Soc, 85- *Mem:* AMA; Am Heart Asn; Am Acad Family Physicians; Am Rheumatism Asn; Am Med Dir Asn; Am Geriat Soc. *Res:* Geriatric medicine. *Mailing Add:* 34 Chestnut Ridge Dr Spartanburg SC 29303-9799

STOKES, DONALD EUGENE, nematology, for more information see previous edition

STOKES, GERALD MADISON, ENERGY USE IN BUILDINGS. *Current Pos:* Fel astron, Battelle Mem Inst, 76-78, res scientist, 78-80, sr res scientist space sci, 80-83, sect mgr, 83-85, prof mgr, End Use Load & Conserv Assessment Prog, Pac Northwest Labs, 85-86, dept mgr computational sci, 86-88, cent mgr appl physics, 88-90, DIR, GLOBAL STUDIES PROG & ASSOC LAB DIR, BATTELLE MEM INST, 89- *Personal Data:* b Burlington, Vt, Aug 16, 47; m 71; c 2. *Educ:* Univ Calif, Santa Cruz, BA, 69; Univ Chicago, MS, 71, PhD(astron), 77. *Concurrent Pos:* Tech dir, Atmospheric Radiol Measurement Prog, Dept Energy, 90- *Mem:* Am Astron Soc; AAAS; Am Geophys Union. *Res:* Formation and destruction of interstellar grains; polarimetry of x-ray binaries; abundances of atmospheric trace gases; electrical end use in buildings. *Mailing Add:* Pac NW Nat Lab PO Box 999 MS K9-95 Richland WA 99352

STOKES, GERALD V, MICROBIOLOGY. *Current Pos:* asst prof, 78-80, ASSOC PROF, DEPT MICROBIOL & IMMUNOL, SCH MED & HEALTH SCI, GEORGE WASH UNIV, 80- *Personal Data:* b Chicago, Ill, Mar 25, 43; c 2. *Educ:* Southern Ill Univ, BA, 67; Univ Chicago, PhD(microbiol), 73. *Prof Exp:* Fel & res assoc, dept molecular, cellular & develop biol, Univ Colo, Boulder, 73-76; asst prof, dept microbiol, Meharry Med Col, 76-78. *Concurrent Pos:* Fel, Am Can Soc, 74-76 & NIH, 76; res grants, NIH, 77-78 & NSF, 77-81. *Mem:* Am Soc Microbiol; Electron Micros Soc Am; Sigma Xi. *Res:* Developmental processes and molecular biology of the chlamydial organisms and fine structure electron microscopy; attachment receptors and virulence factors of Chlamydia psittaci and C trachomatis. *Mailing Add:* Microbiol George Washington Univ Med Sch 2300 First NW Washington DC 20037-2337

STOKES, GORDON ELLIS, COMPUTER SCIENCE, PHYSICS. *Current Pos:* asst dean phys & eng sci, 69-70, asst dir comput sci, 70-73, FAC COMPUT SCI, BRIGHAM YOUNG UNIV, 73-, ASSOC CHAIRPERSON, COMPUT SCI DEPT, 93- *Personal Data:* b Ogden, Utah, Feb 11, 33; m 55; c 9. *Educ:* Brigham Young Univ, BS, 61, EdD, 81; Univ Idaho, MS, 69. *Prof Exp:* Physicist, Phillips Petrol Corp, 61-66; sr res physicist, Idaho Nuclear Corp, 66-69. *Concurrent Pos:* Consult, State Ark, 75-81, Weidner Commun Corp, 77-, Geneal Dept, Latter-Day Saint Church, 77-81, Winnebago Indust, 78-82, Eyring Res Inst, 78-86 & Boeing Corp, 88- *Mem:* Asn Comput Mach; Inst Elec & Electronics Engrs. *Res:* Distributed data base systems; small computer applications; computer management; computer systems in business, government and industry. *Mailing Add:* Dept Comput Sci Brigham Young Univ 3368 TMCB Provo UT 84602. *Fax:* 801-378-7775

STOKES, HAROLD T, NUCLEAR MAGNETIC RESONANCE, PHASE TRANSITIONS. *Current Pos:* asst prof, 81-85, ASSOC PROF PHYSICS, BRIGHAM YOUNG UNIV, 85- *Personal Data:* b Long Beach, Calif, Jan 27, 47; m 74; c 4. *Educ:* Brigham Young Univ, BS, 71; Univ Utah, PhD(physics), 77. *Prof Exp:* Instr physics, Univ Utah, 77-78; res assoc, Univ Ill, 78-81. *Mem:* Am Phys Soc; Am Asn Physics Teachers. *Res:* Molecular and atomic motions in solids; platinum catalysts; phase transitions in solids. *Mailing Add:* Dept Physics & Astron Brigham Young Univ 296 ESC Provo UT 84602-1022. *Fax:* 801-378-2265

STOKES, JACOB LEO, microbiology; deceased, see previous edition for last biography

STOKES, JIMMY CLEVELAND, science education, for more information see previous edition

STOKES, JOSEPH FRANKLIN, MATHEMATICS. *Current Pos:* assoc prof, 62-80, PROF MATH, WESTERN KY UNIV, 80- *Personal Data:* b Havana, Ark, Feb 27, 34; m 59, Maxine Dean; c John & Janice. *Educ:* Univ Ark, Fayetteville, BS, 56, MA, 57; George Peabody Col, PhD(math), 72. *Prof Exp:* Instr math, Kans State Univ, 58-61; instr, Auburn Univ, 61-62. *Concurrent Pos:* Res partic, Oak Ridge Assoc Univ, 67. *Mem:* Math Asn Am; Sch Sci & Math Asn; Nat Coun Teachers Math. *Res:* Author of several books and journals in calculus, linear algebra statistics. *Mailing Add:* Dept Math Western Ky Univ Bowling Green KY 42101. *Fax:* 502-745-6471

STOKES, PAMELA MARY, TOXICOLOGY. *Current Pos:* PROF, BIOL DEPT, TRENT UNIV. *Personal Data:* b Hertford, UK, June 24, 35; m 58; c 2. *Educ:* Univ Bristol, BSc, 56, PhD(bot), 59. *Prof Exp:* Fel mycol, Imperial Col, London, 59-60; lectr bot, Sir John Cass Col, London, 60-63; res assoc plant pathol, Univ Ill, 64-65; instr biol, Univ Toronto, 69-70, assoc prof, 73-82, prof bot, 82-, dir, Inst Environ Studies, 84- *Mem:* Can Bot Asn; Am Phycol Soc; Am Mycol Soc; Am Soc Limnol & Oceanog; Am Soc Geochem & Health. *Res:* The response of aquatic organisms to high concentrations of metals and low pH; community response in the field; adaptations of algae which confer tolerance to metals; biological monitoring, metal cycling in aquatic systems. *Mailing Add:* Trent Univ PO Box 4800 Peterborough ON K9J 7B8 Can

STOKES, PETER E, ENDOCRINOLOGY, BIOLOGICAL PSYCHIATRY. *Current Pos:* instr med in endocrinol, 57-59, asst prof med in psychiat, 59-63, ASSOC PROF PSYCHIAT & MED, MED COL, CORNELL UNIV, 69-, PROF PSYCHIAT, 82- & PROF MED, 87- *Personal Data:* b Haddonfield, NJ, Aug 27, 26; m 56; c 3. *Educ:* Trinity Col, BS, 48; Cornell Univ, MD, 52; Am Bd Internal Med, dipl, 57; Am Bd Psychiat & Neurol, dipl, 71; Am Bd Radiol, dipl & cert nuclear med, 72. *Prof Exp:* Intern med, NY Hosp, 52-53, asst resident, 53-54, asst resident med & endocrinol, 54-55; trainee fel endocrinol, NIH, 55-57, clin trainee psychiat, 67-70. *Concurrent Pos:* Physician, Outpatient Clin, NY Hosp, 55-56, from asst attend to assoc attend physician, 61-86, attend physician, 87-; dir clin res labs, Payne Whitney Psychiat Clin, NY Hosp-Cornell Med Ctr, 57-, dir, Psychobiol Lab & Study Unit, 67, assoc attend psychiatrist, 69-82, attend psychiatrist, 82-; assoc vis physician, Cornell Div, Bellevue Hosp, 62-70; pvt pract consult, 59- *Mem:* Endocrine Soc; Am Soc Nuclear Med; fel Am Psychiat Asn; fel Am Col Neuropsychopharmacol; fel Am Col Physicians. *Res:* Neuroendocrine function in emotional disorders; hypothalamic pituitary adrenocortical function control systems in animals; effects of alcohol on neuroendocrine function; clinical endocrine problems including growth and thyroid; adrenal and ovarian function; clinical studies of affective disorders; lithium metabolism and physiological effects of lithium isotopes on manic behavior, renal, thyroid and cognitive function. *Mailing Add:* Dept Med/Psychiat Cornell Univ Med Col 1300 York Ave New York NY 10021

STOKES, RICHARD HIVLING, EXPERIMENTAL PHYSICS, ACCELERATOR PHYSICS. *Current Pos:* RETIRED. *Personal Data:* b Troy, Ohio, Apr 30, 21; m 56, Evelyn Hight; c Grant H & Laura (Burns). *Educ:* Case Univ, BS, 42; Iowa State Univ, PhD(physics), 51. *Prof Exp:* Staff mem, Underwater Sound Ref Lab, Nat Defense Res Comt, 42-44; res assoc, Inst Atomic Res, Iowa State Col, 46-51; group leader, Los Alamos Sci Lab, 67-77 & 81-84, staff mem, 51-67 & 84-88. *Concurrent Pos:* US deleg, Conf Peaceful Uses Atomic Energy, Geneva, 58; lectr, Univ Minn, 60-61. *Mem:* Fel Am Phys Soc; Sigma Xi. *Res:* Nuclear physics; accelerator research; fission; spectroscopy of light nuclei; nuclear detectors; heavy ion accelerators; heavy ion reactions. *Mailing Add:* 2450 Club Rd Los Alamos NM 87544

STOKES, ROBERT ALLAN, astrophysics, for more information see previous edition

STOKES, ROBERT MITCHELL, COMPARATIVE PHYSIOLOGY. *Current Pos:* From asst prof to assoc prof, 63-77, PROF BIOL SCI, KENT STATE UNIV, 77- *Personal Data:* b Vandalia, Ill, May 21, 36; m 59; c 3. *Educ:* Mich State Univ, BS, 58, MS, 59, PhD(physiol), 63. *Concurrent Pos:* Consult, Great Lakes Basin Comn Water Qual Task Force, 68-70. *Mem:* Am Soc Zool. *Res:* Biochemical and biophysical aspects of membrane transport phenomena in fish, especially glucose transport by intestine; fish physiology, metabolism and toxicology. *Mailing Add:* 1074 Elno Ave Kent OH 44240-3360

STOKES, RUSSELL AUBREY, MATHEMATICS. *Current Pos:* From asst prof to assoc prof, 56-66, PROF MATH, UNIV MISS, 66- *Personal Data:* b Preston, Miss, May 1, 22; m 59. *Educ:* Miss State Univ, BS, 48; Univ Miss, MA, 51; Univ Tex, PhD(math), 63. *Mem:* Am Math Soc; Math Asn Am. *Res:* Measure and integration. *Mailing Add:* 207 Colonial Rd Oxford MS 38655-2634

STOKES, WILLIAM GLENN, MATHEMATICS. *Current Pos:* head dept math, 55-57, PROF MATH & COMPUT SCI & CHMN DEPT, AUSTIN PEAY STATE UNIV, 74- *Personal Data:* b Corsicana, Tex, Dec 26, 21; c 2. *Educ:* Sam Houston State Col, BS, 46, MA, 47; Peabody Col, PhD(math), 57. *Prof Exp:* Head dept math, Navarro Jr Col, 47-53; instr appl math, Vanderbilt Univ, 54-55; assoc prof, Northwestern State Col, 57-59 & East Tex State Univ, 59-60. *Mem:* Math Asn Am; Am Math Soc. *Mailing Add:* 10800 Culberson Dr Austin TX 78748-1843

STOKES, WILLIAM LEE, stratigraphy, popularizing earth science; deceased, see previous edition for last biography

STOKES, WILLIAM MOORE, ORGANIC CHEMISTRY. *Current Pos:* RETIRED. *Personal Data:* b Cleveland, Ohio, Sept 18, 21. *Educ:* Franklin & Marshall Col, BS, 44; Yale Univ, PhD(chem), 52. *Hon Degrees:* MA, Providence Col, 61. *Prof Exp:* Chemist, Hamilton Watch Co, 44-46; lab asst, Yale Univ, 46-48, 49-51; from asst prof to assoc prof med res, Providence Col, 51-59, prof chem & dir med res lab, 59-65. *Mem:* Fel AAAS; Am Chem Soc; Am Oil Chem Soc; NY Acad Sci. *Res:* Neurochemistry; isolation of natural products; steroid metabolism; correlation of optical activity with molecular structure. *Mailing Add:* 16 Quoquonset Lane Little Compton RI 02837

STOKEY, W(ILLIAM) F(ARMER), MECHANICAL ENGINEERING. *Current Pos:* Asst prof, 49-55, ASSOC PROF MECH ENG, CARNEGIE-MELLON UNIV, 55- *Personal Data:* b Cincinnati, Ohio, Apr 19, 17; m 46; c 3. *Educ:* Ga Inst Technol, BS, 38; Mass Inst Technol, MS, 47, ScD(mech eng), 49. *Mem:* Am Soc Mech Engrs; Soc Exp Stress Anal; Sigma Xi. *Res:* Stress analysis; dynamic shock; vibrations. *Mailing Add:* 136 Columbia Dr Pittsburgh PA 15236-4429

STOKINGER, HERBERT ELLSWORTH, TOXICOLOGY. *Current Pos:* RETIRED. *Personal Data:* b Boston, Mass, June 19, 09. *Educ:* Harvard Univ, AB, 30; Columbia Univ, PhD(biochem), 37. *Honors & Awards:* Donald E Cummings Mem Award, Am Indust Hygiene Asn, 69; S C Weisfeld Mem Lect Award, 75; HE Stokinger Lectr, Am Conf Govt Ind Hygienists, 79; Inhalation Toxicol Award, Soc Toxicol, 83. *Prof Exp:* Instr chem, City Col New York, 32-39; res assoc bact, Sch Med & Dent, Univ Rochester, 39-43, chief indust hyg sect, AEC, 43-51, from asst prof to assoc prof pharm & toxicol, 45-51; chief toxicologist, Nat Inst Occup Safety & Health, USPHS, 51-77. *Concurrent Pos:* Res assoc, Col Physicians & Surgeons, Columbia Univ, 37-39; res assoc, Atomic Bomb Test, Bikini, 46; mem subcomt toxicol, Nat Res Coun, 46, chmn comt, 70-73; chmm subcomt toxicol, USPHS Drinking Water Stas, 58-70; chmn threshold limits comt, Am Conf Govt Indust Hygienists, 62-77. *Mem:* AAAS; Am Indust Hyg Asn; Am Asn Immunol; fel Soc Toxicol, 83. *Res:* Pharmacology and toxicology of atomic energy materials; bacteriological chemistry of gonococcus; toxins; chemotherapy of sulfonamides and arsenicals; prophylaxis of industrial poisons; industrial, water and air pollution toxicology. *Mailing Add:* Nine Twin Hills Ridge Dr Cincinnati OH 45228

STOKOE, KENNETH H, II, GEOTECHNICAL ENGINEERING. *Current Pos:* from asst prof to prof, 73-85, BRUNSWICK-ABERNATHY REGENTS PROF SOIL DYNAMICS & GEOTECH ENG, UNIV TEX, AUSTIN, 85- *Educ:* Univ Mich, BS, 66, MS, 67, PhD, 72. *Honors & Awards:* Distinguished Achievement Award, Grad Stud Civil Eng, 71; Aervin Sewell Perry Stud Appreciation Award, 77; Eng Found Award, 77; Outstanding Serv Award, Am Soc Civil-Engrs, 79, 86, Walter L Huber Civil Eng Res Prize, 83. *Prof Exp:* Instr, Univ Mich, 71; asst prof, Univ Mass, 72-73. *Concurrent Pos:* Appt vis prof, Univ Naples, 87; mem, Nat Geotech Bd, Nat Res Coun, 88-92; dir, Environ & Eng Geophys Soc, 92- *Mem:* Nat Acad Eng; Am Soc Civil Engrs; Int Soc Soil Mech & Found Engrs; Seismol Soc Am; Soc Explor Geophysicists; Am Soc Testing & Mats; Am Soc Nondestructive Testing; Environ & Eng Geophys Soc; Asn Drilled Shaft Contractors; Sigma Xi. *Res:* Situ seismic measurements; laboratory measurements of dynamic material properties; dynamic soil-structure interaction; published over 75 articles. *Mailing Add:* Dept Civil Eng Univ Tex Austin TX 78712

STOKOWSKI, STANLEY E, SOLID STATE PHYSICS, OPTICS. *Current Pos:* SR RES SCIENTIST, LAWRENCE LIVERMORE LAB, 77- *Personal Data:* b Lewiston, Maine, Dec 28, 41. *Educ:* Mass Inst Technol, SB, 63; Stanford Univ, PhD(physics), 68. *Prof Exp:* Physicist, Nat Bur Stand, 68-70; mem tech staff, Bell Tel Labs, NJ, 70-72; prin investr, Res Inst Advan Studies Div, Martin Marietta Corp, 72-77. *Mem:* Am Phys Soc; Am Optical Soc. *Res:* Crystal field theory; phase transitions; ferroelectricity; color centers; optical properties of crystals; laser glass; infrared detectors. *Mailing Add:* 755 Contada Circle Danville CA 94526. *Fax:* 650-968-9482

STOKSTAD, EVAN LUDVIG ROBERT, biochemistry; deceased, see previous edition for last biography

STOKSTAD, ROBERT G, NUCLEAR PHYSICS. *Current Pos:* SR SCIENTIST, PHYSICS, NUCLEAR SCI DIV, LAWRENCE BERKELEY LAB, 80- *Personal Data:* b Berkeley, Calif, June, 28, 40. *Educ:* Yale Univ, BS, 62; Calif Inst Technol, PhD(physics), 67. *Honors & Awards:* Alexander von Humboldt Award, 88-89. *Prof Exp:* Asst prof, physics, Yale Univ, 70-74; staff physicist, Oak Ridge Nat Lab, 74-80. *Concurrent Pos:* Chmn, Div Nuclear Physics, Am Physics Soc, 86-87. *Mem:* Fel Am Phys Soc. *Res:* Study of nuclear structure and heavy iron nuclear reaction mechanisms; experimental studies of nuclear structure. *Mailing Add:* Inst NUCL Part Astr Lawrence Berkeley Lab MS 50-208 Univ Calif Berkeley CA 94720. *Fax:* 510-486-7983

STOLARIK, EUGENE, AERODYNAMICS. *Current Pos:* ASSOC PROF AERONAUT ENG, UNIV MINN, MINNEAPOLIS, 47- *Personal Data:* b Zilina, Czech, Mar 27, 19; nat US; m 44; c 2. *Educ:* Prague Tech Univ, dipl, 39; Carleton Col, BA, 40; Univ Minn, MA, 42, MS, 44. *Honors & Awards:* Cert Appreciation, Off Sci Res & Develop, 45. *Prof Exp:* Asst physics, Univ Minn, 41-42, instr aerodyn & aircraft, 42-44; chief proj engr, Lawrance Aeronaut Corp, NJ, 44-45; chief engr, Off Res & Inventions Lab, US Dept Navy, 45-47. *Concurrent Pos:* US deleg, 2nd Int Cong Aeronaut Sci, Zurich; civilian with Nat Defense Res Comt & War Prod Bd, 45; consult, Boeing Co, Wash, 52-60, 62 & 68, Northrop Corp, Calif, 58, 64 & 66, Univac Div, Sperry Rand Corp, 64-66 & Honeywell Corp, 68-69; sr staff engr, Aeronca Mfg Corp, 60; eng staff specialist, Astronaut Div, Gen Dynamics Corp, Calif, 61 & 65; sr staff engr, Lockheed Missiles & Space Co, Calif, 63; dir res & develop, Control Technol Corp, 71; res analyzer, Am Inst Res. *Mem:* Assoc fel Am Inst Aeronaut & Astronaut; Am Helicopter Soc; Am Soc Eng Educ; Royal Aeronaut Soc. *Res:* Mechanics of flight; pneumatics; control and guidance of aerospace vehicles; convective heat transfer; interference effects; reentry of aerospace vehicles; engineering education. *Mailing Add:* 5529 Wooddale Ave Minneapolis MN 55424

STOLARSKY, KENNETH B, MATHEMATICS. *Current Pos:* asst prof, 69-73, ASSOC PROF MATH, UNIV ILL, URBANA, 73- *Personal Data:* b Chicago, Ill, May 9, 42; m 69. *Educ:* Calif Inst Technol, BS, 63; Univ Wis-Madison, MS, 65, PhD(math), 68. *Prof Exp:* Fel math, Inst Advan Study, 68-69. *Mem:* Am Math Soc; Math Asn Am; Sigma Xi. *Res:* Number theory; combinatorics; geometric inequalities. *Mailing Add:* Dept Math Univ Ill Urbana IL 61801

STOLBACH, LEO LUCIEN, ONCOLOGY, INTERNAL MEDICINE. *Current Pos:* ONCOLOGIST, NEW ENG DEACONESS HOSP BOSTON, 86-, MEM STAFF BEHAV MED, 86-; DIR, DIV HEMAT & ONCOL, ST VINCENT HOSP, WORCESTER, MASS, 91- *Personal Data:* b Geneva, Switz, Feb 25, 33; US citizen; m 61, Jeanne Garelick; c Deborah & Bradley. *Educ:* Harvard Univ, BA, 54; Univ Rochester, MD, 58; Am Bd Internal Med, cert, 67. *Prof Exp:* Chief med oncol, Ottawa Clin, Ont Cancer Found & Ottawa Civic Hosp, 81-84; oncologist, Boston Univ Med Ctr & Boston Vet Admin Med Ctr, 84-85. *Concurrent Pos:* From instr to assoc prof, Sch Med, Tufts Univ, 64-91; from assoc prof med, Sch Med, Univ Ottawa, 81-84; clin prof, Boston Univ Sch Med, 84-; lectr, Harvard Univ Med Sch, 85-; prof, Sch Med, Univ Mass, Worcester, Mass, 92-; chief, Pondville Hosp, Walpole, Mass. *Mem:* Am Asn Cancer Res; Am Soc Clin Oncol; fel Am Col Physicians; fel Royal Col Physicians & Surgeons Can; Int Soc Study Lung Cancer; Soc Behav Med; Int Soc Psychooncol. *Res:* Clinical chemotherapy; tumor immunology; tumor markers; behavioral medicine. *Mailing Add:* 38 Morseland Ave Newton Center MA 02159. *Fax:* 508-798-6190

STOLBERG, HAROLD JOSEF, MATHEMATICS. *Current Pos:* prog mgr, 80-86, sr prog mgr for western Europe & Latin Am, 86-91 PROG COORD FOR THE AMERICAS, NSF, 91- *Personal Data:* b San Juan, PR, Aug 4, 40; m 71; c 2. *Educ:* Univ PR, Rio Piedras, BS, 62; Cornell Univ, PhD(math), 69. *Prof Exp:* Asst prof math, Ithaca Col, 67-68; fel, Carnegie-Mellon Univ, 68-69, asst prof, 69-71; assoc prof math & chmn dept, Univ PR, Rio Piedras, 71-80. *Concurrent Pos:* Adj prof, George Washington Univ, 94-96. *Mem:* Am Math Soc; Math Asn Am; AAAS. *Res:* Commutative algebra; algebraic geometry; mathematics education. *Mailing Add:* 5052 N 36th St Arlington VA 22207-2947

STOLBERG, MARVIN ARNOLD, ORGANIC CHEMISTRY. *Current Pos:* RETIRED. *Personal Data:* b New York, NY, Oct 29, 25; m 49; c 2. *Educ:* Columbia Univ, BS, 50; Univ Del, MS, 54, PhD(chem), 56. *Prof Exp:* Org chemist, Chemother Br, US Army Chem Ctr, Md, 50-53, asst br chief, 54-56; head, Chem Dept, Tracerlab, Inc, Mass, 56-60; tech dir-vpres, New England Nuclear Corp, 60-72, pres & chief exec officer, 72-85. *Concurrent Pos:* Vpres, E I Dupont de Nemours, 83-85. *Mem:* Am Chem Soc; Soc Nuclear Med. *Res:* Organic and inorganic synthesis with radioactive isotopes; radioactive pharmaceuticals and assay of labeled compounds; tracer techniques for solving problems concerning food and drug acceptability criteria; product evaluation; organic reaction mechanisms. *Mailing Add:* 11253 Boca Woods Lane Boca Raton FL 33428-1840

STOLC, VIKTOR, ENDOCRINOLOGY, HEMATOLOGY. *Current Pos:* RETIRED. *Personal Data:* b Bratislava, Slov, Oct 5, 32; m 73; c 2. *Educ:* Univ Comenius Bratislava, RNDr, 56; Slovak Acad Sci, Slov, CSc(biochem), 63. *Prof Exp:* Biochemist, Endocrine Sta, Inst Health, Czech, 56-57; independent scientist, Inst Endocrinol, Slovak Acad Sci, 57-68; res assoc, Univ Pittsburgh, 65-66 & 68-70, from asst res prof to assoc res prof path, Sch Med, 70-95. *Mem:* AAAS; Endocrine Soc; Am Soc Biol Chemists; NY Acad Sci; Reticuloendothelial Soc. *Res:* Gene rearrangement in leukemia; endocrine factors in normal and leukemic leukocytes. *Mailing Add:* Dept Path 5940 CHP Main Tower Univ Pittsburgh Pittsburgh PA 15261-0001

STOLDT, STEPHEN HOWARD, ORGANIC CHEMISTRY, FUELS UTILIZATION. *Current Pos:* RES SUPVR, FUEL PROD, LUBRIZOL CORP, 84- *Personal Data:* b New York, NY, Dec 17, 38; m 65; c 2. *Educ:* Queens Col, NY, BS, 60; City Col New York, MA, 62, PhD(org chem), 68. *Prof Exp:* Res assoc org chem, Univ Wis, 67-68; res chemist fuels & lubricants, Shell Oil Co, 68-73; supvr chem res coal utilization, Apollo Chem Corp, 73-83; lab mgr, SCA Chem Serv, 83-84. *Mem:* Nat Asn Corrosion Engrs; Am Chem Soc; Soc Automotive Engrs. *Res:* Combustion; power generation; fuels; lubricants; coal utilization. *Mailing Add:* 7390 Southmeadow Dr Concord Township OH 44077

STOLEN, JOANNE SIU, IMMUNOLOGY. *Current Pos:* OWNER, SOS PUBL, 88-; ASST PROF, RUTGERS UNIV, 96- *Personal Data:* b Chicago, Ill, June 22, 43; m 72; c 1. *Educ:* Univ Mich, BS, 65; Seton Hall Univ, MS, 68; Rutgers Univ, PhD(biochem), 72. *Prof Exp:* Res intern immunol, Inst Microbiol, Rutgers Univ, 69-72; fel, Dept Serol & Bact, Univ Helsinki; res immunol, Sandy Hook Lab & Univ Helsinki, 74-85. *Concurrent Pos:* Adj prof, Drew Univ, 82- *Mem:* Sigma Xi; AAAS; Am Fisheries Soc; Am Soc Zoologists; NY Acad Sci. *Res:* Cellular immunology; thymus derived and bone marrow derived cell function in the mouse and presently in lower animals such as the fish; immunoregulation and the effect of stress on the immune system of fish; immunology of marine fishes; publisher and editor of scientific manuals and books. *Mailing Add:* 43 Normandie Ave Fair Haven NJ 07704-3303

STOLEN, ROGERS HALL, SOLID STATE PHYSICS. *Current Pos:* MEM TECH STAFF SOLID STATE OPTICS, BELL LABS, 66- *Personal Data:* b Madison, Wis, Sept 18, 37. *Educ:* St Olaf Col, BA, 59; Univ Calif, Berkeley, PhD(physics), 65. *Prof Exp:* Fel, Univ Toronto, 64-66. *Mem:* Am Phys Soc; Optic Soc Am. *Res:* Nonlinear properties of optical fibers; polarization preserving optical fibers; light scattering in glass. *Mailing Add:* AT&T Bell Labs Rm 4D-335 101 Crawfords Corner Rd Holmdel NJ 07733. *Fax:* 732-949-6010

STOLER, PAUL, NUCLEAR & PARTICLE PHYSICS, ELECTROMAGNETIC. *Current Pos:* PROF PHYSICS, RENSSELAER POLYTECH INST, 66- *Personal Data:* b Brooklyn, NY, June 8, 38; m 66, Janet Cohen; c Lisa & David. *Educ:* Brooklyn Col, BS, 60; Rutgers Univ, MS, 62, PhD(physics), 66. *Concurrent Pos:* Vis scientist, Cen-Saclay, France, 74-75, 92; CEBAF, 96. *Mem:* Fel Am Phys Soc. *Res:* Nuclear and particle physics using electromagnetic probes; structure of nucleons and nucleon resonances; properties of few-body systems. *Mailing Add:* Dept Physics Rensselaer Polytech Inst Troy NY 12181

STOLFI, ROBERT LOUIS, TUMMOR IMMUNOLOGY, TUMOR THERAPY. *Current Pos:* dir transplantation immunol, 69-78, ASST DIR CANCER RES, DEPT SURG, CATH MED CTR BROOKLYN & QUEENS INC, 78- *Personal Data:* b Brooklyn, NY, Sept 16, 38; m 68. *Educ:* Brooklyn Col, BS, 60; Univ Miami, PhD(microbiol), 67. *Prof Exp:* Bact technician, Jewish Hosp Brooklyn, 60-61; asst bacteriologist, Bellevue Hosp, 61-62; res assoc immunochem, Howard Hughes Med Inst, 63-67; from instr to asst prof microbiol, Sch Med, Univ Miami, 67-71. *Concurrent Pos:* Res assoc immunochem, Variety Children's Res Found, Fla, 67-71; res assoc, Cancer Inst, Univ Columbia, 80- *Mem:* AAAS; Am Asn Immunologists; Am Soc Microbiol; Am Cancer Soc; Sigma Xi; Soc Anal Cytol. *Res:* Therapeutic methods for the alteration of immunological reactivity in the tumor-bearing host, or in the recipient of a histoincompatible normal tissue transplant; analysis of the interactions among drugs; tumor and host immune systems during cancer chemotherapy. *Mailing Add:* 9 Union Ave Harrison NY 10528-2110

STOLFO, SALVATORE JOSEPH, COMPUTER SCIENCE, INTELLIGENT SYSTEMS. *Current Pos:* asst prof, 79-84, ASSOC PROF COMPUT SCI, COLUMBIA UNIV, 84- *Personal Data:* b Brooklyn, NY, Feb 21, 54; m 79; c 3. *Educ:* Brooklyn Col, BS, 74; NY Univ, MS, 76, PhD(comput sci), 79. *Prof Exp:* Lectr comput sci, Brooklyn Col, 74-78. *Concurrent Pos:* Consult, AT&T Bell Labs, 80-85, lectr, 85; prin investr, Defense Advan Res Projs Agency, 81-86, Off Navel Res, 82-84 & NY State Sci & Technol Found, 84-97; chief sci adv, Fifth Generation Comput Corp, 85-; consult, Citicopr Technol Off, 88097. *Mem:* Sr mem Inst Elec & Electronics Engrs; Sigma Xi; NY Acad Sci; Am Asn Artificial Intel; Asn Comput Mach. *Res:* Principal architect of an advanced parallel computer called DADO to accelerate artificial intelligence programs and speech recognition tasks; knowledge-based expert systems applied to conventional data base and management information systems; JAVA agents for distributed data mining. *Mailing Add:* Dept Comput Sci Columbia Univ 450 Comput Sci Bldg New York NY 10027. *Fax:* 212-666-0140; *E-Mail:* sal@cs.columbia.edu

STOLINE, MICHAEL ROSS, STATISTICAL ANALYSIS. *Current Pos:* Assoc prof, 67-77, PROF MATH, WESTERN MICH UNIV & STATIST, 77- *Personal Data:* b Jefferson, Iowa, Sept 17, 40; m 60; c 4. *Educ:* Univ Iowa, BA, 62, MA, 64, PhD(statist), 67. *Mem:* Am Statist Asn; Inst Math Statist. *Res:* Problems in the analysis of variance and regression; intervention time series; multiple comparisons. *Mailing Add:* Dept Math Western Mich Univ 1201 Oliver St Kalamazoo MI 49008-3804

STOLK, JON MARTIN, PSYCHIATRY, PHARMACOLOGY. *Current Pos:* PROF PSYCHIAT, SCH MED, UNIV MD, 78- *Personal Data:* b Englewood, NJ, Oct 15, 42; m 73. *Educ:* Middlebury Col, AB, 64; Dartmouth Col, PhD(pharmacol), 69; Stanford Univ, MD, 72. *Prof Exp:* Fel psychiat, Sch Med, Stanford Univ, 69-71; asst prof pharmacol, Dartmouth Med Col, 72-73; asst prof psychiat, 74-76, assoc prof, 76-78. *Mem:* Am Soc Pharmacol & Exp Therapeut; Int Soc Psychoneuroendocrinol; Am Col Neuropsychopharmacology. *Res:* Biogenic amines and behavior; psychopharmacology; neurochemistry and genetics. *Mailing Add:* 3620 Sweeten Creek Dr Chapel Hill NC 27514

STOLL, MANFRED, MATHEMATICAL ANALYSIS. *Current Pos:* From asst prof to assoc prof, 71-84, PROF MATH, UNIV SC, 85- *Personal Data:* b Calw, Ger, Aug 24, 44; US citizen; m 66, 90; c 3. *Educ:* State Univ NY Albany, BS, 67; Pa State Univ, MA, 69, PhD(math), 71. *Mem:* Am Math Soc. *Res:* Harmonic, holomorphic and plurisubharmonic function theory on bounded symmetric domains and generalized half planes; spaces and algebras of holomorphic functions of one and several complex variables. *Mailing Add:* Dept Math Univ SC Columbia SC 29208-0001. *E-Mail:* stoll@math.sc.edu

STOLL, PAUL JAMES, ELECTRICAL ENGINEERING, BIOENGINEERING. *Current Pos:* MEM STAFF, AEROSPACE CORP, 80- *Personal Data:* b Grass Valley, Calif, June 23, 33; m 59; c 1. *Educ:* Wesleyan Univ, BA, 55; Mass Inst Technol, SB, 57, SM, 58; Univ Wash, PhD(elec eng), 68. *Prof Exp:* Teaching asst, Mass Inst Technol, 57-58; res engr guid systs, Autonetics Div, NAm Rockwell Corp, 58-61, consult, 61-62; NIH fel, Sch Med, Univ Wash, 68-69; asst prof elec eng, Univ Calif, Davis, 69-80, lectr, 76-80. *Mem:* AAAS; Inst Elec & Electronics Engrs; Biomed Eng Soc. *Res:* Control system engineering; regulation of breathing in man and domestic fowl; physiological control system analysis and modeling. *Mailing Add:* 2559 Leafwood Dr Camarillo CA 93010-2220

STOLL, ROBERT D, SOIL MECHANICS. *Current Pos:* From instr to assoc prof, 56-71, PROF CIVIL ENG, COLUMBIA UNIV, 71- *Personal Data:* b Lincoln, Ill, Aug 12, 31; c 3. *Educ:* Univ Ill, BSCE, 53; Columbia Univ, MSCE, 56, EngScD(civil eng, eng mech), 62. *Concurrent Pos:* Chmn comt mech earth masses & layered systs, Hwy Res Bd, Nat Acad Sci-Nat Res Coun, 67-; vis sr res assoc, Lamont-Doherty Geol Observ, 69- *Mem:* Am Soc Civil Engrs. *Res:* Static and dynamic response of granular soils; wave propagation in granular media and ocean sediments; general constitutive relationships for granular media. *Mailing Add:* Civil Eng Columbia Univ 2960 Broadway New York NY 10027-6902

STOLL, SARAH LOUISE, SOLID STATE MATERIALS. *Current Pos:* ASST PROF CHEM, OBERLIN COL, 96- *Educ:* Smith Col, BA, 88; Univ Calif, Berkeley, PhD(inorg chem), 93. *Honors & Awards:* Award, Am Chem Soc, 88. *Prof Exp:* Postdoctoral fel, Harvard Univ, 94-95, Rice Univ, 95-96. *Mem:* AAAS; Am Chem Soc; Sigma Xi. *Res:* Synthesis of new magnetic materials. *Mailing Add:* Dept Chem Oberlin Col 130 W Loramist Oberlin OH 44074. *E-Mail:* fstoll@oberlin.edu

STOLL, WILHELM, MATHEMATICS. *Current Pos:* prof, Univ Notre Dame, 60-88, head, Dept Math, 66-68, Vincent F Duncan & Anna Marie Micus Duncan prof, 88-94, EMER PROF MATH, UNIV NOTRE DAME, 94- *Personal Data:* b Freiburg, Ger, Dec 22, 23; m 55, Marilyn Kremser; c Bob, Dieter, Elisabeth & Rebecca. *Educ:* Univ Tubingen, Dr rer nat, 53, Dr habil, 54. *Prof Exp:* Asst math, Univ Tubingen, 53-59, docent, 54-60, appl prof, 60. *Concurrent Pos:* Vis lectr, Univ Pa, 54-55; mem, Inst Adv Study, 57-59; vis prof, Stanford Univ, 68-69, Tulane Univ, 73, Kyoto Univ, 83, Univ Sci & Technol, Hefei, China, 86. *Mem:* Am Math Soc; Math Asn Am; Ger Math Asn; AAAS. *Res:* Complex analysis; value distribution in several variables, modifications meromorphic maps; families of divisors; continuation of analytic sets and maps; algebraic dependence of meromorphic functions; parabolic spaces. *Mailing Add:* 54763 Merrifield Dr Mishawaka IN 46545-1519

STOLL, WILLIAM FRANCIS, FOOD SCIENCE. *Current Pos:* DISTRIB MGR, AGR UTILIZATION RES INST, 88- *Personal Data:* b Lamoni, Iowa, July 21, 32; m 56; c 2. *Educ:* Iowa State Univ, BS, 55, MS, 57; Univ Minn, St Paul, PhD(dairy sci), 66. *Prof Exp:* Asst prof dairy sci, SDak State Univ, 57-67; sr food scientist, Prod Develop Dept, Green Giant Co, 67-79; sr scientist, frozen foods res & develop, Pillsbury Co, 79-82; assoc prof, Univ Minn, Waseca, 82-88. *Mem:* Inst Food Technologists; Am Dairy Sci Asn. *Res:* Use of physical, chemical, microbiological principles for design and fabrication of new food products. *Mailing Add:* Agr Utilization Res Inst St Paul MN 55105

STOLL, WILLIAM RUSSELL, PHARMACOLOGY, CHEMISTRY. *Current Pos:* From instr to assoc prof, 56-70, RES ASSOC PHARMACOL, ALBANY MED COL, 64- *Personal Data:* b Los Angeles, Calif, July 8, 31; m 55; c 2. *Educ:* Union Univ, NY, BS, 52; Univ Rochester, PhD(pharmacol), 56. *Res:* Chemical nature of sodium and carbonate in bone mineral; autonomic pharmacology; nature of 2-halo-2-phenethylamines; applications of nucleonics in biological research. *Mailing Add:* 478 Friars Gate Clifton Park NY 12065

STOLLAR, BERNARD DAVID, IMMUNOLOGY, BIOCHEMISTRY. *Current Pos:* asst prof pharmacol, 64-67, from asst prof to assoc prof, 67-74, PROF BIOCHEM, HEALTH SCI, TUFTS UNIV, 74-, CHMN, DEPT, TUFTS UNIV, 86- *Personal Data:* b Saskatoon, Sask, Aug 11, 36; m 56, Carol Singer; c Lawrence, Michael & Suzanne. *Educ:* Univ Sask, BA, 58, MD, 59. *Prof Exp:* Res fel biochem, Brandeis Univ, 60-62; dep chief, Biol Sci Div, Air Force Off Sci Res, 62-64. *Concurrent Pos:* NSF grant, 64-86, NIH grants, 77-; consult, Biol Sci Div, Air Force Off Sci Res, 66-69; sr fel, Weizmann Inst Sci, 71-72; vis prof, Univ Tromso, Norway, 81; consult, Cetus Corp, 82-85, Seragen, Inc, 83-88, Gene-Trak Systs, 86-89, Alkermes, Inc, 89-; Dozor vis prof, Ben-Gurion Univ Sch Med, Beersheba, Israel, 86; alumni lectr, Univ Sask, 89; mem, NIH Allergy Immunol & Transplantation Res Comt, 90-94. *Mem:* AAAS; Am Asn Immunologists; Am Soc Biochem & Molecular Biol; Am Col Rheumatology; Clin Immunol Soc; NY Acad Sci. *Res:* Immunochemistry of nucleic acids and nucleoprotein, especially in relation to auto-immune disease; use of antibodies to study structure of nucleic acids; molecular genetics of anti-nucleic acid antibodies. *Mailing Add:* Dept Biochem Tufts Univ Health Sci Campus 136 Harrison Ave Boston MA 02111. *Fax:* 617-636-6409; *E-Mail:* dstollar@opal.tufts.edu

STOLLAR, VICTOR, MICROBIOLOGY, VIROLOGY. *Current Pos:* from asst prof to assoc prof, Rutgers Med Sch, 65-75, PROF MICROBIOL, ROBERT WOOD JOHNSON MED SCH, UNIV MED & DENT, NJ, 75- *Personal Data:* b Saskatoon, Sask, Dec 6, 33; div; c Lisa, Miriam & Anna. *Educ:* Queen's Univ, Ont, MDCM, 56. *Prof Exp:* Fel, Brandeis Univ, 58-62; fel, Weizmann Inst Sci, 62-65. *Concurrent Pos:* Assoc ed, Virology, 76-; mem, Virol Study Sect, NIH, 80-83. *Mem:* AAAS; Am Soc Microbiol; Am Asn Immunologists; Am Soc Virol. *Res:* Replication of arthropod-borne viruses in vertebrate and in insect cells; genetics and biochemistry of cultured mosquito cells. *Mailing Add:* Dept Molecular Genetics & Microbiol Robert Wood Johnson Med Sch Univ Med & Dent NJ Piscataway NJ 08854. *Fax:* 732-235-5223; *E-Mail:* stollar@umdnj.edu

STOLLBERG, ROBERT, SCIENCE EDUCATION. *Current Pos:* RETIRED. *Personal Data:* b Toledo, Ohio, May 27, 15; m 43; c 4. *Educ:* Univ Toledo, BS, 35, BEd, 36; Columbia Univ, MA, 40, EdD(sci ed, electronics), 47. *Prof Exp:* Instr, Rossford High Sch, Ohio, 36-39; asst prof physics, Wabash Col, 46-47; ed, Purdue Univ, 47-49; assoc prof physics, San Francisco State Univ, 49-54, chmn, Dept Interdisciplinary Phys Sci, 67-69, assoc dean & actg dean, Sch Natural Sci, 69 & 71-75, prof physics, 54-83. *Concurrent Pos:* Mem, Harvard Univ Conf Prob Sci Ed, 53; chmn, Nat Conf Prob High Sch Sci, 59; mem, President's Comt Develop Scientists & Engrs; sci adv, Columbia Univ team, India, 65-66; Columbia Univ-USAID contract lectr, Inst Educ, Makerere Univ, Uganda, 69-71; vis prof, Columbia Univ. *Mem:* Fel AAAS; Am Asn Physics Teachers; Nat Sci Teachers Asn (pres, 55-56); Am Inst Physics. *Mailing Add:* 3028 Oak Knoll Dr Redwood City CA 94062

STOLLER, EDWARD W, PLANT PHYSIOLOGY, WEED SCIENCE. *Current Pos:* PLANT PHYSIOLOGIST, NORTH CENT REGION, AGR RES, USDA, 65- *Personal Data:* b McCook, Nebr, Jan 9, 37; m 60; c 2. *Educ:* Univ Nebr, BS, 58; Purdue Univ, MS, 62; NC State Univ, PhD(soil fertil), 66. *Mem:* Am Soc Plant Physiol; Am Soc Agron; Weed Sci Soc Am. *Res:* Weed physiology and control. *Mailing Add:* RR 3 No 33 Monticello IL 61856

STOLLERMAN, GENE HOWARD, MEDICINE, INFECTIOUS DISEASE. *Current Pos:* prof, 81-96, distinguished physician, Vet Admin, 86-92, EMER PROF, SCH MED, BOSTON UNIV, 97- *Personal Data:* b New York, NY, Dec 6, 20; m 45, Corynne Miller; c Lee (Meyburg), Anne (Dizio) & John E. *Educ:* Dartmouth Col, AB, 41; Columbia Univ, MD, 44; Am Bd Internal Med, dipl, 52. *Honors & Awards:* Bruce Mem Award, Am Col Physicians; Bicentennial Award Med, Columbia; Tewliss Award, Am Geriat Soc. *Prof Exp:* From intern to chief med resident, Mt Sinai Hosp, NY, 44-49; res fel microbiol, Col Med, NY Univ, 49-50, instr med, 51-55; instr, Col Med, Downstate Med Ctr, State Univ NY, 50-51; from asst prof to prof, Med Sch, Northwestern Univ, 55-64; prof med & chmn dept, Col Med, Univ Tenn, Memphis, 65-81. *Concurrent Pos:* Med dir, Irvington Hosp, NY, 51-55; prin investr, Sackett Found Res Rheumatic Fever & Allied Dis, 55-64; mem training grants comt, Nat Inst Arthritis & Metab Dis, US Pub Health Serv, 60-64, mem res career prog, 67-70, chmn, Rev Panel Bact Vaccines & Toxoids, Bur Biologics, Food & Drug Admin, 73-78; physician-in-chief, City Memphis Hosps, 65-81; consult, Memphis Vet Admin Hosp, 65-81; ed-in-chief, J Am Geriat Soc, 85-; mem, Expert Comt Cardiovasc Dis, WHO, 66-81; mem, Am Bd Internal Med, 67-73, chmn, Written Exam Comt, 69-73 & Exec Comt, 71-73; ed, Advan Internal Med, 68-; pres, Cent Soc Clin Res, 74-75; co-chmn, Educ Work Group Nat Comn Arthritis, 75-76; chmn, Panel Prod & Supply Work Group, HEW & Goodman prof, Univ Tenn, 77; co-ed, Hosp Pract, 77-; consult, Methodist Hosp, Memphis, St Joseph Hosp & LeBonheur Children's Hosp; mem, Adv Comt, Nat Inst Allergy & Infectious Dis, NIH, 79-83 & Nat Adv Comt Vaccines, Nat Immunization Prog, 88. *Mem:* Asn Profs Med (pres, 75-76); Asn Am Physicians; fel Am Col Physicians (vpres, 82-83); Am Soc Clin Invest; Am Asn Immunologists; Infectious Dis Soc Am; Cent Soc Clin Res. *Res:* Infectious and rheumatic diseases; biology of streptococcus; etiology of rheumatic fever; geriatrics health services outcomes research. *Mailing Add:* Dept Med Boston Univ 10 Willow Spg Lane Apt No 21 Hanover NH 03755. *Fax:* 603-643-3326

STOLLERY, ROBERT, ENGINEERING. *Current Pos:* chmn bd, 79-93, CHMN, PCL CONSTRUCT HOLDINGS, 93- *Personal Data:* b Edmonton, Alta, May 1, 24; m 47, Shirley Jean Hopper; c Carol, Janet & Douglas. *Educ:* Univ Alta, BSc, 49. *Hon Degrees:* LLD, Univ Alta, 85, Concordia Univ & Montreal, 86. *Honors & Awards:* Frank Spragins Mem Award, Asn Prof Engrs, 81; Julian C Smith Medal, Eng Inst Can, 90. *Prof Exp:* Field engr, Poole Construct Ltd, 49-54, proj mgr, 54-64, vpres, 64-69, pres, 69-81. *Mem:* Fel Can Acad Eng; Asn Prof Engrs; Eng Inst Can. *Mailing Add:* 99 Westbrook Dr Edmonton AB T6J 2C8 Can

STOLLEY, PAUL DAVID, PUBLIC HEALTH, EPIDEMIOLOGY. *Current Pos:* PROF & CHMN PREV MED, SCH MED, UNIV MD, 91- *Personal Data:* b Pawling, NY, June 17, 37; m 59, Jo Ann Goldenberg; c Jonathan, Dorie & Anna. *Educ:* Lafayette Col, AB, 57; Med Col, Cornell Univ, MD, 62. *Hon Degrees:* MA, Univ Pa, 76. *Honors & Awards:* Johns Hopkins Soc Scholars. *Prof Exp:* From asst prof to assoc prof epidemiol, Sch Pub Health, Johns Hopkins Univ, 68-79; prof med, Sch Med, Univ Pa, 76-85, Herbert C Rorer prof med sci, 85-91. *Mem:* Inst Med-Nat Acad Sci; Soc Epidemiol Res (pres, 82-83); Int Epidemiol Asn (treas, 81-84); Am Col Epidemiol (pres, 89-90). *Res:* Epidemiology of cancer; adverse drug reactions; prevention of heart disease; epidemiology of uterine diseases. *Mailing Add:* Sch Med Univ Md 655 W Redwood St Baltimore MD 21201. *E-Mail:* pstolley@umabnet.ab.edu

STOLOFF, IRWIN LESTER, MEDICINE. *Current Pos:* fel med, 57-58, from instr to asst prof, 59-69, ASSOC PROF MED & PREV MED, JEFFERSON MED COL, 69 - *Personal Data:* b Philadelphia, Pa, May 9, 27; m 52; c 3. *Educ:* Jefferson Med Col, MD, 51; Am Bd Internal Med, dipl, 58. *Prof Exp:* From intern to resident med, Jefferson Med Col Hosp, 51-53; resident, Baltimore City Hosps, Md, 53-54 & Mt Sinai Hosp, New York, 56-57. *Mem:* Fel Am Col Physicians; fel Am Col Chest Physicians. *Res:* Immunology; autoimmune diseases; cancer immunology; epidemiology of chronic lung disease. *Mailing Add:* New Jefferson Hosp Bldg Rm 4001 111 S 11th St Philadelphia PA 19107-5084

STOLOFF, LEONARD, BIOCHEMISTRY, AGRICULTURE & FOOD CHEMISTRY. *Current Pos:* RETIRED. *Personal Data:* b Boston, Mass, Mar 24, 15; m 40. *Educ:* Mass Inst Technol, BS, 36. *Honors & Awards:* Wiley Award, Asn Off Analytical Chemists, 81. *Prof Exp:* Chemist, Granada Wines, Inc, 36-37; self employed, 38-41; chemist, US Dept Navy, 41; chemist, Consumer's Union, 42; res chemist, Agar Substitute Prog, US Fish & Wildlife Serv, 42-44; res chemist, Krim-Ko Corp, 44-51; res dir, Seaplant Chem Corp, 51-59; asst tech dir, Marine Colloids, Inc, 59-63; chief, Mycotoxins & Enzymes Sect, Div Food Chem, Bur Foods, Food & Drug Admin, 63-71, natural toxicants specialist, 71-82. *Concurrent Pos:* Asn off analytical chemists, Gen Referee Mycotoxins, 66-82; ed, Newsletter Div Agr Food Chem, Am Chem Soc, 65-82. *Mem:* Am Chem Soc; Inst Food Technol; Asn Off Analytical Chemists. *Res:* Chemistry, toxicology and occurrence of natural poisons in foods. *Mailing Add:* 815 NW 21st Way Delray Beach FL 33445-2625

STOLOFF, NORMAN STANLEY, METALLURGY. *Current Pos:* from asst prof to assoc prof, 65-70, PROF ENG, RENSSELAER POLYTECH INST, 70- *Personal Data:* b Brooklyn, NY, Oct 16, 34; m 71; c Michael, Linda, David & Stephen. *Educ:* NY Univ, BMetE, 55; Columbia Univ, MS, 56, PhD(metall), 61. *Prof Exp:* Jr engr metall, Pratt & Whitney Aircraft Div, United Aircraft Corp, 56-58; staff scientist, Ford Motor Co, 61-65. *Concurrent Pos:* Fulbright sr res fel, Univ Birmingham, 67-68; vis prof, Eurat Joint Res Ctr, Ispra, Italy, 76-77, Technion, Israel Inst Technol, 80, Swiss Fed Inst, Lausanne, 81; vis scientist, Atomic Energy Res Estab, Harwell, 85 & Pac Northwest Nat Lab, Richland, Wash, 95 & 96. *Mem:* Am Inst Mining, Metall & Petrol Engrs; Mat Res Soc; Am Soc Metals Int. *Res:* Physical metallurgy; relationship between microstructure and plastic deformation of metals; environmental effects; strength and fracture of intermetallic compounds; powder processing of composites; fatigue of high temperature alloys. *Mailing Add:* Dept Mat Eng Rensselaer Polytech Inst Troy NY 12180-3590. *Fax:* 518-276-8554; *E-Mail:* stolon@rpi.edu

STOLOV, HAROLD L, PHYSICS, METEOROLOGY. *Current Pos:* from asst prof to assoc prof, 59-70, PROF PHYSICS, CITY COL NEW YORK, 70- *Personal Data:* b New York, NY, May 27, 21; m 81. *Educ:* City Col New York, BS, 42; Mass Inst Technol, MS, 47; NY Univ, PhD(physics, meteorol), 53. *Prof Exp:* Asst radio & electronics, Signal Corps, US Dept Army, 42; instr physics, City Col New York, 47-50; lectr, Hunter Col, 50-51; res assoc, NY Univ, 50-53; instr, Douglass Col, Rutgers Univ, 51-53, asst prof, 53-59. *Concurrent Pos:* Consult, Martin Co, 56-59; consult, Res & Adv Develop Div, Avco Corp, 60-61; Nat Acad Sci-Nat Res Coun sr res associateship, Inst Space Studies, New York, 65-67. *Mem:* Nat Sci Teachers Asn; Am Meteorol Soc; Am Asn Physics Teachers; Am Geophys Union. *Res:* Physics of the upper atmosphere; tidal oscillations; physics education; magnetosphere; solar-terrestrial physics. *Mailing Add:* 2575 Palisade Ave Apt 146 New York NY 10463

STOLOW, NATHAN, CHEMISTRY. *Current Pos:* CONSERV CONSULT, 79- *Personal Data:* b Montreal, Que, May 4, 28; m 50; c 2. *Educ:* McGill Univ, BSc, 49; Univ Toronto, MA, 52; Univ London, PhD(conserv), 56. *Honors & Awards:* Can Medal, Govt Can, 67. *Prof Exp:* Res chemist, Nat Res Coun Can, 49-50; vis lectr chem & physics, Sir John Cass Col, Univ London, 52-55, res assoc conserv, Courtauld Inst Art, 55-56; dir conserv, Nat Gallery Can, 56-72; dir, Can Conserv Inst, 72-75; spec adv conserv, Nat Mus Can, 76-79. *Concurrent Pos:* Carnegie travel grant, Nat Gallery Can, 56-57; rapporteur, Comt Conserv, Int Coun Mus, 64-, chmn Can nat comt, 70-; mem coun, Int Inst Conserv Hist & Artistic Works, 72- *Mem:* Fel Chem Inst Can; fel Can Mus Asn. *Res:* Museum conservation; problems of deterioration in works of art related to conservation; solution of museological problems by chemical and physical approaches; interaction of art history and scientific research; exhibition conservation research. *Mailing Add:* 100 Lexington Dr Williamsburg VA 23188

STOLOW, ROBERT DAVID, ORGANIC CHEMISTRY. *Current Pos:* From instr to assoc prof org chem, 58-76, PROF CHEM, TUFTS UNIV, 76- *Personal Data:* b Boston, Mass, Mar 9, 32; m 53; c 3. *Educ:* Mass Inst Technol, SB, 53; Univ Ill, PhD(chem), 56. *Concurrent Pos:* Fel, Calif Inst Technol, 67-68; vis res fel, Harvard, 76. *Mem:* Am Chem Soc. *Res:* Physical organic chemistry; stereochemistry; conformational analysis; nuclear magnetic resonance spectroscopy; computational chemistry. *Mailing Add:* Dept Chem Tufts Univ Medford MA 02155. *E-Mail:* rstolow@pearl.tufts.edu

STOLPER, EDWARD MANIN, EXPERIMENTAL PETROLOGY. *Current Pos:* From asst prof to prof geol, 79-90, WILLIAM E LEONHARD PROF GEOL, CALIF INST TECHNOL, 90-, CHMN, DIV GEOL & PLANETARY SCI, 94- *Personal Data:* b Boston, Mass, Dec 16, 52; m 73; c 2. *Educ:* Harvard Col, AB, 74; Univ Edinburgh, MPhil, 76; Harvard Univ, PhD(geol sci), 79. *Honors & Awards:* Nininger Meteorite Award, 76-77; Newcomb Cleveland Prize, AAAS, 84; F W Clarke Medal, Geochem Soc, 85; J B Macelwane Award, Am Geophys Union, 86; Arthur Holmes Medal, Europ Union Geosci, 97. *Concurrent Pos:* Marshall scholar, 74-76; mem, Basaltic Volcanism Study Proj, 77-80; assoc ed, J Geophys Res, 83-86; mem, Planetary Geosci, Strategy Comt, NASA, 86-88, Earth Sci Rev Panel, NSF, 90-93; Bateman vis scholar, Yale Univ, 88; Miller vis res prof, Univ Calif, Berkely, 90; ed, Chem Geol, 95- *Mem:* Nat Acad Sci; fel Am Geophys Union; fel Meteoritical Soc; fel Mineral Soc Am; fel AAAS; fel Am Acad Arts & Sci; Geol Soc Am; Sigma Xi; fel Geochem Soc; fel Europ Asn Geochem. *Mailing Add:* Div Geol Planet Sci 170-25 Calif Inst Technol Pasadena CA 91125. *E-Mail:* ems@expet.gps.caltech.edu

STOLTE, CHARLES, ELECTRICAL ENGINEERING, SOLID STATE PHYSICS. *Current Pos:* mem tech staff, 66-76, lab proj mgr, Solid State Lab, 76-84, RES & DEVELOP SECT MGR, MICROWAVE TECHNOL DIV, HEWLETT-PACKARD LAB, 84- *Personal Data:* b Blue Earth, Minn, Apr 20, 33; m 54; c 4. *Educ:* Univ Minn, BS, 55, MS, 58, PhD(elec eng), 66. *Prof Exp:* Res asst diffusion study, Univ Minn, 55-58. *Mem:* Inst Elec & Electronic Engrs. *Res:* Oxide coated cathode, schottky barriers, III-V materials and devices including ion implantation, LEP's, solid state lasers and microwave devices and GaAs integrated circuit technology; materials science engineering. *Mailing Add:* Microwave Technol Div Hewlett-Packard Co 1412 Fountaingrove Rd Santa Rosa CA 95403

STOLTENBERG, CARL H, FOREST ECONOMICS. *Current Pos:* RETIRED. *Personal Data:* b Monterey, Calif, May 17, 24; m 49; c 5. *Educ:* Univ Calif, BS, 48, MF, 49; Univ Minn, PhD(agr econ), 52. *Prof Exp:* Instr forestry, Univ Minn, 49-51; asst prof forest econ, Duke Univ, 51-56; head resource econ res, Northwest Forest Exp Sta, US Forest Serv, Pa, 56-58, chief, Div Forest Econ Res, 58-60; prof forestry & head dept, Iowa State Univ, 60-67; prof forestry, dean, Col Forestry & dir, Forest Res Lab, Ore State Univ, 67-90, emer prof & dean, 90-94. *Concurrent Pos:* Mem forestry res comn, Nat Acad Sci, 63-65; mem, Nat Adv Bd Coop Forestry Res, 62-66 & 86-, Ore Bd Forestry, 67-87, chmn, 74-84; mem Secy Agr State & Pvt Forestry Adv Comn, 70-74; chmn, Ore & Calif adv bd, Bur Land Mgt, 72-76. *Mem:* Fel Soc Am Foresters; Am Econ Asn; Forest Prod Res Soc; Sigma Xi; AAAS. *Res:* Economic analysis of forest management alternatives; forest policy; resource allocation in forestry; natural resource policy. *Mailing Add:* 14720 N Summerstar Blvd Tucson AZ 85737

STOLTZ, LEONARD PAUL, HORTICULTURE. *Current Pos:* from asst prof to assoc prof, 65-90, EMER PROF HORT, UNIV KY, 91- *Personal Data:* b Kankakee, Ill, Dec 5, 27; div; c 5. *Educ:* Agr & Mech Col, Tex, BS, 55; Ohio State Univ, MS, 56; Purdue Univ, PhD(hort), 65. *Honors & Awards:* Kenneth Post Award, Cornell Univ, 67; L M Ware Award, Am Soc Hort Sci, Southern Region, 68, 72. *Prof Exp:* Res assoc floricult, Rutgers Univ, 57-60; asst prof hort, Univ RI, 60-62. *Concurrent Pos:* USDA res grant, 66-70; ed, Eastern Region, Int Plant Propagators Soc, 68-78; lectr, Indonesia, 88; lectr & consult, Ecuador, 90. *Mem:* Fel Int Plant Propagators Soc (vpres, 82-83, pres, 83-84). *Res:* Plant propagation; Ginseng culture; tissue and embryo culture. *Mailing Add:* 3281 Squire Oak Dr Lexington KY 40515

STOLTZ, ROBERT LEWIS, ENTOMOLOGY. *Current Pos:* EXTEN SPECIALIST ENTOM, COOP EXTEN SERV, UNIV IDAHO, 75- *Personal Data:* b Bakersfield, Calif, May 15, 45. *Educ:* Univ Calif, Davis, BS, 67; Univ Calif, Riverside, PhD(entom), 73. *Prof Exp:* Fel entom, Univ Calif, Riverside, 73-74 & Univ Mo-Columbia, 74-75. *Mem:* Entom Soc Am; Sigma Xi. *Res:* Insect control, particularly in potatoes, sugar beets, beans, peas, and alfalfa hay; black fly control; livestock insects. *Mailing Add:* 339 Heyburn Ave W Twin Falls ID 83301. *Fax:* 208-736-0843; *E-Mail:* bstoltz@uidaho.edu

STOLTZFUS, NEAL W, ALGEBRAIC TOPOLOGY, KNOT THEORY. *Current Pos:* From asst prof to assoc prof, 73-84, PROF MATH, LA STATE UNIV, 84- *Personal Data:* b Lancaster, Pa, Aug 29, 46. *Educ:* Princeton Univ, PhD(math), 73. *Concurrent Pos:* Col dir, comp serv, La State Univ, 85-88. *Mailing Add:* Math Dept La State Univ Baton Rouge LA 70803-4918

STOLTZFUS, WILLIAM BRYAN, entomology; deceased, see previous edition for last biography

STOLWIJK, JAN ADRIANUS JOZEF, BIOPHYSICS. *Current Pos:* chmn, Dept Epidemiol & Pub Health, 82-89, PROF EPIDEMIOL, SCH MED, YALE UNIV, 75- *Personal Data:* b Amsterdam, Netherlands, Sept 29, 27; nat US; m 92, Deborah Rose; c Sarah Leia. *Educ:* State Agr Univ, Wageningen, MS, 51, PhD, 55. *Prof Exp:* Cabot res fel biol, Harvard Univ, 55-57; from assoc fel to fel biol, John B Pierce Found, 57-74, assoc dir, 74-88. *Concurrent Pos:* Mem, Comt Indoor Pollutants, Nat Res Ctr/Nat Acad Sci, 80-81; dir grad studies, Dept Epidemiol & Public Health, Yale Univ, 79-82 & 90-; vchmn comt, indoor air qual & total human exposure, Sci Adv Bd, Environ Protection Agency, 88-93. *Mem:* Aerospace Med Asn; Int Soc Biometeorol; Am Physiol Soc; Am Pub Health Asn; Biophys Soc; Health Physics Soc; Soc Occup Environ Health. *Res:* Body temperature regulation; regulatory systems in physiology; indoor air quality; radiant heat exchange with environment; environmental health; occupational health; risk assessment; construction and application of mathematical models for study of complex physiological systems; environmental physiology; environmental epidemiology. *Mailing Add:* Dept Epidemiol & Pub Health 60 College St PO Box 3333 New Haven CT 06510. *Fax:* 203-785-6103

STOLZ, WALTER S, DIABETES RESEARCH. *Current Pos:* educ prog dir, Arthritis Musculoskeletal & Skin Prog, Nat Inst Arthritis Diabetes Digestive & Kidney Dis, 77-78, NIH, prog dir, Manpower Develop & Res Resources, 78-80, prog dir, Metab Dis & Res Resource, 80-83, actg dep dir, Div Diabetes, Endocrinol & Metab Dis, 81-83, dir, Div Extramural Activ, 83-86, DIR DIV EXTRAMURAL ACTIVITIES, NAT INST DIABETES DIGESTIVE & KIDNEY DIS, NIH, 86- *Personal Data:* b Milwaukee, Wis, Dec 12, 38. *Educ:* Univ Wis-Madison, BS, 60, MS, 62, PhD(mass commun), 64. *Prof Exp:* Tech writer, Int Bus Mach Data Systs Div, 60-61CF; res asst, Mass Commun Res Ctr, Univ Wis-Madison, 61-64; NSF postdoctoral fel, Ctr Cognitive Studies, Harvard Univ, 64-65; asst prof psychol, Univ Tex, Austin, 65-71; from asst prof to assoc prof psychol, Earlham Col, Richmond, Ind & chmn dept, 71-75; sr res assoc & proj dir, Ctr Appl Ling, Arlington, Va, 75-76; grants assoc, Div Res Grants, 76-77. *Mem:* Am Psychol Asn. *Res:* Psychology; arthritis; metabolic diseases. *Mailing Add:* 14504 Falling Leaf Dr Gaithersburg MD 20878

STOLZBERG, RICHARD JAY, ANALYTICAL CHEMISTRY. *Current Pos:* ASST PROF, DEPT CHEM, UNIV ALASKA, FAIRBANKS, 78- *Personal Data:* b Winthrop, Mass, Feb 5, 48. *Educ:* Tufts Univ, BS, 69; Mass Inst Technol, PhD(analytical chem), 73. *Prof Exp:* Res assoc & prin investr, Harold Edgerton Res Lab, New Eng Aquarium, 73-77. *Mem:* Am Chem Soc; Sigma Xi; AAAS; Chemomets Soc. *Res:* Characterization of trace metal-organic interactions in natural waters; effect of metal speciation on bioavailability; chemometrics; chromatography; electrochemistry; spectroscopy. *Mailing Add:* Dept of Chem Univ of Alaska Fairbanks AK 99775

STOLZENBACH, KEITH DENSMORE, CIVIL & HYDRAULIC ENGINEERING. *Current Pos:* asst prof, 74-76, ASSOC PROF CIVIL ENG, MASS INST TECHNOL, 76- *Personal Data:* b Washington, DC, Aug 23, 44. *Educ:* Mass Inst Technol, SB, 66, SM, 68, PhD(civil eng), 71. *Prof Exp:* Asst prof civil eng, Mass Inst Technol, 70-71; res engr, Eng Lab, Tenn Valley Authority, 71-74. *Mem:* Am Soc Civil Engrs; Am Geophys Union; Int Asn Hydraul Res. *Res:* Hydraulic modeling techniques; environmental heat transfer; pollutant dispersal in natural waters; field survey techniques. *Mailing Add:* Dept Civil/Environ Eng Univ Calif Los Angeles CA 90095-1593

STOLZENBERG, GARY ERIC, PESTICIDE CHEMISTRY, FORMULATION AGENTS. *Current Pos:* RES CHEMIST, METAB & RADIATION RES LAB, USDA, 68- *Personal Data:* b Southampton, NY, Dec 1, 39; m 69. *Educ:* Rensselaer Polytech Inst, BS, 62; Kans State Univ, PhD(biochem), 68. *Prof Exp:* Asst biochem, Kans State Univ, 62-68. *Mem:* Am Chem Soc. *Res:* Xenobiotics metabolism in plants; behavior and fate of formulation agents; surfactant analysis. *Mailing Add:* Chem Dept Box 5516 NDak State Univ Fargo ND 58105-5516

STOLZENBERG, SIDNEY JOSEPH, REPRODUCTIVE PHYSIOLOGY, TOXICOLOGY. *Current Pos:* PHYSIOLOGIST, BUR DRUGS, CTR DRUGS & BIOLOGICS, FOOD & DRUG ADMIN, ROCKVILLE, MD, 80- *Personal Data:* b New York, NY, Nov 30, 27; m 58, Leah Schneider; c Rachael & Ethan. *Educ:* NY Univ, BA, 50; Univ Mo, MS, 54; Cornell Univ, PhD(reproductive physiol), 66. *Prof Exp:* Biochemist, Lederle Labs Div, Am Cyanamid Co, 54-59, Agr Div, 59-63; endocrinologist, SRI Int, 66-72, endocrinologist, Life Sci Div, 72-78; toxicologist, Dept Pharmacol, Sch Med, Univ Calif, San Francisco, 78-80. *Mem:* Teratology Soc; Am Physiol Soc; Soc Toxicol. *Res:* Reproductive physiology and toxicology; review animal research data for new drug applications with Food and Drug Administration. *Mailing Add:* Div Cardio Renal Drug Prod FDA HFD-110 5600 Fisher's Lane Rockville MD 20857-0001. *Fax:* 301-594-5494

STOLZY, LEWIS HAL, SOIL PHYSICS. *Current Pos:* asst irrig engr, 54-61, assoc soil physicist, 61-66, assoc prof, 66-78, PROF SOIL PHYSICS, UNIV CALIF, RIVERSIDE, 78- *Personal Data:* b Mich, Dec 11, 20; m 47; c 3. *Educ:* Mich State Col, BS, 48, MS, 50, PhD, 54. *Prof Exp:* Actg proj supvr, Soil Conserv Serv, USDA, 50-52; asst, Mich State Univ, 52-54. *Concurrent Pos:* Fulbright sr res scholar, Univ Adelaide, 64-65; prof, Nat Univ Agr, Chapingo, Mex, AID & Africa; agronomic res award, Int Soc Soil Sci. *Mem:* Fel Soil Sci Soc Am; Int Soc Soil Sci; Int Cong Plant Path; Am Phytopath Soc; fel Am Soc Agron. *Res:* Soil moisture and aeration. *Mailing Add:* 5510 Fargo Rd Riverside CA 92506

STOMBAUGH, TOM ATKINS, BIOLOGY. *Current Pos:* RETIRED. *Personal Data:* b Vancouver, Wash, Aug 22, 21; m 44; c 4. *Educ:* Ill State Norm Univ, BEd, 41; Univ Ill, MS, 46; Ind Univ, PhD, 53. *Prof Exp:* Asst prof zool, Eastern Ill State Col, 48-50; prof biol, Southwest Mo State Univ, 53-77, prof sci, 77-84. *Mem:* Am Soc Mammal. *Res:* Taxonomy of the voles of sub-genus Pedomys; mammalian taxonomy and ecology. *Mailing Add:* 801 S Kickapoo Springfield MO 65804

STOMBLER, MILTON PHILIP, EXPERIMENTAL SOLID STATE PHYSICS. *Current Pos:* dir technol transfer & spons activ, 83-87, DIR PROG DEVELOP, GA INST TECHNOL, 87- *Personal Data:* b New York, NY, Dec 19, 39; m 67; c 3. *Educ:* Univ Md, College Park, BS, 62; Univ SC, MS, 66, PhD(physics), 69. *Prof Exp:* Asst engr, Aerospace Div, Westinghouse Elec Corp, 64-65; fel, Univ Del, 69-71; asst prof physics, State Univ NY Col Potsdam, 71-73, dir spon prog, 73-77; assoc dean res, Polytech Inst & State Univ, 77-83. *Mem:* Sigma Xi; AAAS. *Res:* Electron paramagnetic resonance. *Mailing Add:* CEISMC Ga Inst Technol Atlanta GA 30332-0282

STOMS, DAVID MICHAEL, GEOGRAPHIC INFORMATION SYSTEMS, CONSERVATION PLANNING. *Current Pos:* ASST RESEARCHER, INST COMPUTATIONAL EARTH SYST SCI, UNIV CALIF, SANTA BARBARA, 92- *Personal Data:* b Cincinnati, Ohio, Dec 25, 48; m 87, Enid F Pritikin; c Joshua Pritikin & Noah Pritikin. *Educ:* Rice Univ, BA, 70; Univ Calif, Santa Barbara, MA, 86, PhD(geog), 91. *Prof Exp:* Asst planner, US Forest Serv, Lake Tahoe Basin, 75-84. *Mem:* Am Soc Photogram & Remote Sensing; Ecol Soc Am; Soc Conserv Biol; Natural Areas Asn. *Res:* Application of geographic information systems to assessment of the conservation status of biodiversity; sensitivity analysis of the effects of map scale and accuracy; validation of mapped biogeographic data. *Mailing Add:* Dept Geog Univ Calif Santa Barbara CA 93106-4060. *E-Mail:* stoms@geog.ucsb.edu

STONE, A DOUGLAS, TRANSPORT THEORY, MESOSCOPIC PHYSICS. *Current Pos:* PROF APPL PHYSICS & PHYSICS, YALE UNIV, 86- *Educ:* Harvard Univ, BA, 76; Balliol Col, Oxford, MA, 78; Mass Inst Technol, PhD(theoret solid state physics), 83. *Honors & Awards:* MacMillian Award, Univ Ill, 87; Presidential Young Investr Award, NSF, 87. *Mem:* Fel Am Phys Soc. *Res:* Theory of conducting properties of microstructures; mesoscopic phenomena; quantum chaos. *Mailing Add:* Appl Physics Yale Univ PO Box 208284 New Haven CT 06520-8284

STONE, ALBERT MORDECAI, PLASMA PHYSICS, MICROWAVE PHYSICS. *Current Pos:* tech asst to dir appl physics lab, 49-72, head tech info div, 62-80, dir advan res projs, Appl Physics Lab, 72-81, SR FEL, JOHNS HOPKINS UNIV, 81- *Personal Data:* b Boston, Mass, Dec 24, 13; m 41, 68; c 3. *Educ:* Harvard Univ, AB, 34; Mass Inst Technol, PhD(physics), 38. *Prof*

Exp: Res assoc, Mass Inst Technol, 38-39, staff mem, Radiation Lab, 42-46; instr, Middlesex Col 36-38; physicist, US Naval Torpedo Sta, 40-41; from asst prof to assoc prof physics, Mont State Col, 41-46; sci liaison officer, US Embassy, London, Eng, 46-48; assoc mem comt electronics & comt basic phys sci, Res & Develop Bd, US Dept Defense, 48-49. *Concurrent Pos:* mem, Fed Emergency Mgt Agency Adv Bd; fel mem, Hudson Inst; dir, energy fund, Gen Instrument Corp. *Mem:* Fel AAAS; fel Am Phys Soc; sr mem Cosmos Club. *Res:* Electronics; gaseous discharges; radar signal thresholds; guided missiles; countermeasures; controlled thermonuclear plasmas; geothermal energy; nuclear effects. *Mailing Add:* 4932 Sentinal Dr No 403 Bethesda MD 20816

STONE, ALEXANDER GLATTSTEIN, MATHEMATICS. *Current Pos:* RETIRED. *Personal Data:* b Hungary, Jan 30, 16; nat US; m 58, Susan Tarjan; c Peter & Victor. *Educ:* Univ Debrecen, Hungary, Dr Laws, 40; George Washington Univ, MS, 61. *Prof Exp:* Mathematician, Repub Aviation Corp, 55-56; mathematician appl physics lab, Johns Hopkins Univ, 56-69, supvr programmers digital comput, 66-69, lectr, univ, 59-60, instr, eve col, 66-67; mem tech staff, Jet Propulsion Lab, Calif Inst Technol, 69-91. *Mem:* Math Asn Am; Asn Comput Mach. *Res:* Programming for automatic digital computers; Boolean algebra. *Mailing Add:* 3554 Alginet Dr Encino CA 91436-4126

STONE, ALEXANDER PAUL, MATHEMATICS. *Current Pos:* assoc prof, 70-75, PROF MATH, UNIV NMEX, 76-, CHMN, DEPT MATH, 91- *Personal Data:* b West New York, NJ, June 28, 28; m 60, Mary Ann Majeski; c Christopher B. *Educ:* Columbia Univ, BS, 52; Newark Col Eng, MS, 56; Univ Ill, Urbana, PhD(math), 65. *Prof Exp:* Engr, Western Elec Co, 52-56; instr elec eng, Manhattan Col, 56-58; asst prof physics, Dickinson Col, 58-60; asst prof math, Univ Ill, Chicago Circle, 65-69, assoc prof, 69-70. *Mem:* Am Math Soc; Math Asn Am; Int Union Radio Sci. *Res:* Differential geometry; applied mathematics; electromagnetic theory. *Mailing Add:* Dept Math & Statist Univ NMex Albuquerque NM 87131. *Fax:* 505-277-5505; *E-Mail:* astone@math.unm.edu

STONE, ARTHUR HAROLD, PURE MATHEMATICS. *Current Pos:* prof, 61-87, EMER PROF MATH, UNIV ROCHESTER, 87-; ADJ PROF, NORTHEASTERN UNIV, 88- *Personal Data:* b London, Eng, Sept 30, 16; m 42, Dorothy Maharam; c David A & Ellen R. *Educ:* Cambridge Univ, BA, 38; Princeton Univ, PhD(math), 41. *Prof Exp:* Mem, Inst Advan Study, 41-42; instr math, Purdue Univ, 42-44; math physicist, Geophys Lab, Carnegie Inst, 44-46; fel, Trinity Col, Cambridge Univ, 46-47; lectr math, 47-56, sr lectr, Univ Manchester, 56-61. *Mem:* Am Math Soc; Math Asn Am; Sigma Xi. *Res:* Point-set topology; aerodynamics; graph theory; general topology; descriptive set theory. *Mailing Add:* Dept Math Northeastern Univ Boston MA 02115

STONE, BENJAMIN P, PLANT PHYSIOLOGY. *Current Pos:* assoc prof biol, 69-72, PROF BIOL, AUSTIN PEAY STATE UNIV, 72-, CHMN DEPT, 77-, DIR, CTR EXCELLENCE FIELD BIOL, 86- *Personal Data:* b Dover, Tenn, Aug 28, 35; m 56; c 1. *Educ:* Austin Peay State Univ, BS, 59; Univ Tenn, Knoxville, MS, 61, PhD(bot), 68. *Prof Exp:* Asst prof biol, Austin Peay State Univ, 61-65; res partic radiation biol, Cornell Univ, 65-66; asst prof plant physiol, Purdue Univ, West Lafayette, 69. *Concurrent Pos:* Fel hort, Purdue Univ, West Lafayette, 69. *Mem:* Am Soc Plant Physiol; Am Inst Biol Sci; Sigma Xi. *Res:* Nucleic acid; protein synthesis. *Mailing Add:* Dept Biol Austin Peay State Univ 601 College St Clarksville TN 37044-0001

STONE, BOBBIE DEAN, SOLID STATE CHEMISTRY, INORGANIC CHEMISTRY. *Personal Data:* b Paulton, Ill, June 11, 27; m 50, June Morgan; c Mark E & Pamela (Goldkamp). *Educ:* Univ Southern Ill, BS, 49; Northwestern Univ, PhD(chem), 52. *Prof Exp:* Res chemist, Mound Lab, Monsanto Electronic Mats Co, 52-53, Cent Res Dept & Res & Eng Div, 53-62 & Inorg Chem Div, 62-65, res group leader, Semiconductor Mat Dept, 65-69, silicon res mgr, 69-72, sr res specialist, Electronics Prod Div, 72-74, fel, 74-88. *Mem:* Am Chem Soc. *Res:* Semiconductor grade silicon; neutron transmutation doping; III-V compounds; polycrystalline silicon processes. *Mailing Add:* 415 Monticello Dr Ballwin MO 63011-2531

STONE, CHARLES DEAN, FOOD SCIENCE, BIOCHEMISTRY. *Current Pos:* RETIRED. *Personal Data:* b Athens, Ga, Sept 6, 26; m 50; c 1. *Educ:* Univ Ga, BS, 49, PhD(food sci), 64; Fla State Univ, MS, 59. *Prof Exp:* Partner, Stone's Ideal Bakery, 50-53; instr baking sci & mgt food serv bakery, Fla State Univ, 53-59, asst prof baking sci & mgt, 59-61; sect mgr food res, Quaker Oats Co, 64-69, mgr cereal res, 69-72, mgr cereals, mixes & corn goods res, 72-74; sr prod res scientist, Res & Develop, Mars Inc, 74-77 & 80-92, sr res scientist, Sci Affairs, 77-80. *Mem:* Am Asn Cereal Chemists; Am Soc Bakery Eng; Inst Food Technologists; Soc Nutrit Educ. *Res:* Cereal and confectionery; flavor, nutrition, rheology, structural, crystallization, stability, cariogenicity, new products; fermentation; ion-protein interactions as affected by fermentation; scientific affairs; venture technology. *Mailing Add:* 5 Hickory Trail Sparta NJ 07871

STONE, CHARLES JOEL, MATHEMATICS, STATISTICS. *Current Pos:* from asst prof to assoc prof, Univ Calif, Berkeley, 64-69, prof, 69-81, prof biomath, Los Angeles, 75-81, PROF STATIST, UNIV CALIF, BERKELEY, 81- *Personal Data:* b Los Angeles, Calif, July 13, 36; m 66; c 2. *Educ:* Calif Inst Technol, BS, 58; Stanford Univ, PhD(math statist), 61. *Honors & Awards:* Invited Wald Lectr, Inst Math Statist, 94. *Prof Exp:* Instr math, Princeton Univ, 61-62; asst prof, Cornell Univ, 62-64. *Concurrent Pos:* NSF grant, Univ Calif, Los Angeles, 64-; consult, Rand Corp, 66-67, Planning Res Corp, 66-68, Gen Elec Tech Mil Planning Oper, 68-70, Fed Aviation Admin, 70-74, Consol Analysis Ctr Inc, 71-74, Urban Inst, 75-76 & Technol Serv Corp, 77-80; Guggenheim fel, 80-81. *Mem:* Nat Acad Sci; Am Math Soc; Am Statist Asn; fel Inst Math Statist. *Res:* Probability and statistics, including random walks, birth and death, diffusion and infinitely divisible processes; potential theory; renewal theory; infinite particle systems; nonparametric estimation, classification and regression. *Mailing Add:* Dept Statist Univ Calif Berkeley CA 94720

STONE, CHARLES PORTER, WILDLIFE RESEARCH, WILDLIFE ECOLOGY. *Current Pos:* RES SCIENTIST, NAT PARK SERV, 80- *Personal Data:* b Owatonna, Minn, Sept 16, 37; m 85; c 4. *Educ:* Univ Minn, BA, 60; Colo State Univ, MS, 63; Ohio State Univ, PhD(zool), 73. *Prof Exp:* Res biologist, Patuxent Wildlife Res Ctr, 63-66; asst leader, Ohio Coop Wildlife Res Unit, 66-70; lectr, Ohio State Univ, 70; res biologist, Denver Wildlife Res Ctr, US Fish & Wildlife Serv, 71-73, asst dir, 73-75, supvry wildlife biologist, 73-80, chief wildlife ecol pub lands, 75-80. *Concurrent Pos:* Instr wildlife biol, Ohio State Univ, 66-70; mem adj fac, Colo State Univ, 73- *Mem:* AAAS; Wildlife Soc; Am Soc Mammalogists. *Res:* Effects of energy development, forest and range management practices, and other land disturbances upon wildlife abundance, distribution and behavior; ecology of animal damage to crops. *Mailing Add:* Hawaiian Volcanoes Nat Park PO Box 44 Hawaii National Park HI 96718

STONE, CHARLES RICHARD, AERODYNAMICS. *Current Pos:* res engr, Honeywell Inc, 55-58, proj engr, 58-61, res supvr automatic control, 61-64, STAFF ENGR, HONEYWELL INC, 65- *Personal Data:* b Portland, Ore, Sept 8, 21; m 47; c 3. *Educ:* Univ Minn, BSAero, 51; Univ Wash, MSAero, 58. *Prof Exp:* Aerodynamicist, Boeing Airplane Co, 51-55. *Mem:* Am Inst Aeronaut & Astronaut. *Res:* Automatic, optimal and adaptive control; aerodynamics of vertical takeoff airplanes; dynamics and control of flexible vehicles. *Mailing Add:* 4955 Sorell Ave Minneapolis MN 55422

STONE, CLEMENT A, PHARMACOLOGY. *Current Pos:* RETIRED. *Personal Data:* b Hastings, Nebr, May 23, 23; m 52; c 3. *Educ:* Univ Nebr, BSc, 46; Univ Ill, MS, 48; Boston Univ, PhD(physiol), 52. *Prof Exp:* From instr to asst prof physiol, Sch Med, Boston Univ, 51-54; res assoc, Res Div, Sharp & Dohme, Inc, 54-57, dir pharmacodynamics, Merck Inst Therapeut Res, 56-57, from assoc dir to dir, 58-66, exec dir, 66-71, vpres, 71-78, sr vpres, Merck Sharp & Dohme Res Labs, 78-88. *Concurrent Pos:* Lectr, St Andrews, 53. *Mem:* AAAS; Am Soc Pharmacol & Exp Therapeut; Am Chem Soc; Soc Exp Biol & Med; NY Acad Sci. *Res:* Pharmacology of adrenergic, ganglionic blocking drugs, antihypertensive agents and antiglaucoma agents. *Mailing Add:* 8 Farrier Lane Blue Bell PA 19422

STONE, CONNIE J, TOXICOLOGY. *Current Pos:* MGR, LIFE SCI, COCA-COLA, 85- *Personal Data:* b Michigan City, Ind, Oct 30, 43. *Educ:* Ind Univ, BA, 68, MS, 70, PhD(toxicol), 76; Am Bd Toxicol, dipl, 81; NC Cent Univ, JD, 85; NC Bar, 85; DC Bar, 87. *Prof Exp:* Mgr, Dept Toxicol, Becton Dickinson Res Ctr, 76-79; assoc dir, Life Sci Div, Clement Assoc, Inc, 79-81; mgr, Life Sci, Lorillard Res Ctr, 81-85. *Mem:* Am Col Toxicol; NY Acad Sci; Sigma Xi; Am Bar Asn. *Res:* Inhalation toxicology: chronic inhalation studies involving exposure of rodents to aluminum chlorhydrate, asbestos, fibrous glass, ozone, sulfuric acid, or vinyl chloride; general toxicology. *Mailing Add:* Coca-Cola Co PO Drawer 1734 Atlanta GA 30301

STONE, DANIEL BOXALL, INTERNAL MEDICINE, ENDOCRINOLOGY. *Current Pos:* RETIRED. *Personal Data:* b Gravesend, Eng, May 15, 25; US citizen; m 49; c Rodney E & Matthew R. *Educ:* Univ London, BS & MD, 48, dipl psychiat, 50. *Prof Exp:* Intern & resident internal med, Univ London, 48-56; from asst prof to prof, Col Med, Univ Iowa, 59-71, exec assoc dean, 67-71; Milard prof med, Univ Nebr, 71-73, clin prof, 75-89. *Concurrent Pos:* Fel internal med, Univ London, 48-56; fel internal med & endocrinol, Col Med, Univ Iowa, 57-59; Markle scholar acad med, 60-; consult, Vet Admin Hosp, Iowa City, 63-71 & Coun Drugs, AMA, 66-73. *Mem:* Fel Am Col Physicians; Am Diabetes Asn; Am Heart Asn; Endocrine Soc; Royal Soc Med. *Res:* Influence of diet on serum lipids; geographic pathology of diabetes; metabolism of adipose tissue; influence of hypoglycemic drugs on lipolysis in adipose tissue. *Mailing Add:* 26354 Valley View Ave Carmel CA 93923-9102

STONE, DANIEL JOSEPH, MEDICINE. *Current Pos:* fel internal med, NY Med Col, 46-47, prof med, 75-93, dir, Pulmonary Sect, 75-93, EMER PROF, NY MED COL, 93- *Personal Data:* b Passaic, NY, Dec 19, 18; m 50; c 3. *Educ:* Johns Hopkins Univ, BA, 39; George Washington Univ, MD, 43; Am Bd Internal Med, dipl, 51. *Prof Exp:* asst chief, Pulmonary Dis Serv, Bronx Vet Admin Hosp, 49-54, assoc, Cardiopulmonary Lab, 50-54, chief, Pulmonary Dis Serv & dir, Respiration Lab, 54- *Concurrent Pos:* Adv ed res, Handbk Biol Sci, Nat Acad Sci, 59; assoc prof, Mt Sinai Sch Med, 68; dir, Univ Sleep Breathing Dis Ctr, NY Med Col, 87-; chmn, Inhalation Ther Comt, Bronx Vet Admin Hosp, 60- *Mem:* Am Physiol Soc; fel Am Col Physicians; fel AMA; Am Fedn Clin Res; fel Am Thoracic Soc. *Res:* Pulmonary diseases; lung mechanics and the mechanisms of pulmonary failure. *Mailing Add:* 673A Heritage Hill Somers NY 10589

STONE, DAVID B, GEOPHYSICS. *Current Pos:* assoc prof, 66-77, head, Geol/Geophys Prog, 77-80, EMER PROF GEOPHYS, UNIV ALASKA, 77- *Personal Data:* b Guernsey, UK, Sept 14, 33; m 60; c 3. *Educ:* Univ Keele, BA, 56; Univ Newcastle, PhD(geophys), 63. *Prof Exp:* Sr demonstrator geophys, Univ Newcastle, 63-66. *Concurrent Pos:* Asst dir, Geophys Inst, Univ Alaska, 84-87. *Mem:* Fel Royal Astron Soc; Am Geophys Union; fel Geol Soc Am. *Res:* Geomagnetism; paleomagnetism; geotectonics. *Mailing Add:* Geophys Inst Univ Alaska Fairbanks AK 99775-7320. *E-Mail:* dstone@dino.alaska.edu

STONE, DAVID ROSS, ALGEBRA. *Current Pos:* PROF MATH, GA SOUTHERN COL, 68- *Personal Data:* b Little Rock, Ark, Aug 30, 42; m 65; c 3. *Educ:* Ga Inst Technol, BS, 64; Univ SC, PhD(math), 68. *Mem:* Am Math Soc; Math Asn Am; Asn Comput Mach. *Res:* Rings and modules; torsion theory; problem solving. *Mailing Add:* LB 8093 Ga Southern Univ Statesboro GA 30460-8093

STONE, DEBORAH BENNETT, PHYSICAL BIOCHEMISTRY, CONTRACTILITY. *Current Pos:* USPHS trainee phys biochem, Cardiovasc Res Inst, 66-68, lectr physiol, 68-77, asst res biochemist, 68-76, assoc res biochemist, 76-91, SPECIALIST, CARDIOVASC RES INST, UNIV CALIF, SAN FRANCISCO, 91- *Personal Data:* b Portchester, NY, Oct 26, 38; div; c James M & Jonathan B. *Educ:* Smith Col, BA, 60; Yale Univ, PhD(pharmacol), 65. *Prof Exp:* Res assoc pharmacol, Sch Med, Stanford Univ, 64-66. *Concurrent Pos:* USPHS res career develop award, 68-73. *Mem:* Biophys Soc. *Res:* Serotonin metabolism in the developing rat brain; regulation of phosphofructokinase activity; molecular mechanisms in muscle contraction; production of deuterated contractile proteins for neutron scattering experiments. *Mailing Add:* Cardiovasc Res Inst Box 0130 Univ Calif San Francisco CA 94143-0130. *E-Mail:* stone@musl.ucsf.edu

STONE, DONALD EUGENE, BOTANY, GENETICS. *Current Pos:* from asst prof to assoc prof, 63-70, PROF BOT, DUKE UNIV, 70- *Personal Data:* b Eureka, Calif, Dec 10, 30; m 52, Beverly Larson; c Jerry, Janne & Diane. *Educ:* Univ Calif, AB, 52, PhD(bot), 57. *Honors & Awards:* Distinguished Serv Sci, Am Inst Biol Sci, 88. *Prof Exp:* Asst cytol, biosyst & gen bot, Univ Calif, 54-57; from instr to asst prof bot, Tulane Univ, 57-63. *Concurrent Pos:* Assoc prog dir syst biol, NSF, 68-69; exec dir, Orgn Trop Studies, Inc, 76-96. *Mem:* Bot Soc Am; Soc Study Evolution; Am Soc Naturalists; Am Soc Plant Taxonomists (secy, 73-75); Orgn Trop Studies; Sigma Xi; fel AAAS; hon fel Asn Trop Biol. *Res:* Biosystematics of temperate and tropical plants. *Mailing Add:* Duke Univ Dept Bot Box 90338 Durham NC 27708. *Fax:* 919-660-7293; *E-Mail:* dstone@acpub.duke.edu

STONE, DOROTHY MAHARAM, MEASURE THEORY. *Current Pos:* prof, 61-87, EMER PROF MATH, UNIV ROCHESTER, 87-; ADJ PROF, NORTHEASTERN UNIV, 88- *Personal Data:* b Parkersburg, W Va, July 1, 17; m 42, Arthur H; c David A & Ellen R. *Educ:* Carnegie Inst Technol, BSc, 37; Bryn Mawr Col, PhD(math), 40. *Prof Exp:* Asst lectr math, Univ Manchester, 52-61. *Concurrent Pos:* NSF fel math, 65-66. *Mem:* Am Math Soc; Math Asn Am. *Res:* Measure theory; ergodic theory; probability; linear operators. *Mailing Add:* Dept Math Northeastern Univ Boston MA 02115

STONE, DOUGLAS ROY, OPTICAL MICROLITHOGRAPHY. *Current Pos:* mem tech staff, AT & T Bell Labs, 80-89, distinguished mem tech staff, 89-92, supvr, 92-96 DISTINGUISHED MEM TECH STAFF, LUCENT TECHNOL, 96- *Personal Data:* b Minneapolis, Minn, Nov 10, 48; m 72, 85, Joan R Gugliuzza; c Ryan & Kathryn (Marriner). *Educ:* Univ Minn, BChE, 70; Univ Wis, MS, 72, PhD(chem eng), 75. *Prof Exp:* Res engr med equip, Air Prod & Chem, Inc, 75-77, res engr chem eng, 77-80. *Concurrent Pos:* NIH grant, Dept Bioeng, Univ Pa, 77-81. *Mem:* Soc Photo Optical & Instrumentation Engrs. *Res:* Microlithographic process development for future integrated circuit manufacture; characterization and optimization of optical step-and-repeat lithography. *Mailing Add:* 1663 Westview Dr Coopersburg PA 18036. *E-Mail:* dougstone@lucent.com

STONE, EARL LEWIS, JR, FOREST SOILS, ATOLL SOILS. *Current Pos:* from asst prof to assoc prof forest soils, 48-62, Charles Lathrop Pack prof, 62-79, EMER PROF FOREST SOILS, CORNELL UNIV, 79- *Personal Data:* b Phoenix, NY, July 12, 15; m 41; c 3. *Educ:* State Univ NY, BS, 38; Univ Wis, MS, 40; Cornell Univ, PhD(soils), 48. *Hon Degrees:* DSc, State Univ NY, 90. *Honors & Awards:* Barrington Moore Award, Soc Am Foresters, 73. *Prof Exp:* Field asst & jr forester, Southern Forest Exp Sta, US Forest Serv, 40-41. *Concurrent Pos:* Collabr & consult, Southern Forest Exp Sta, US Forest Serv, 47-48 & 52; soil scientist, Pac Sci Bd, Nat Acad Sci, Marshall Islands, 50; Am-Swiss Found fel, 54-55; vis prof, Philippines, 58-60; Fulbright res fel, Forest Res Inst, NZ, 62; ed, Forest Sci, Soc Am Foresters, 65-71; Bullard fel, Harvard Univ, 69-70; consult, Biotrop, Indonesia, 70; mem Adv Panel Ecol, NSF, 70-; mem adv comn, Ecol Sci Div, Oak Ridge Nat Lab, 71-; mem, forest studies team, Nat Res Coun, 73-74, Comt Evaluate Int Biol Prog, 74-75 & comt scientist, Nat Forest Mgt Act, 77-; vis prof, Dept Soil Sci & Forestry, Univ Fla, Gainesville, 79-82, adj prof, 82-; mem, Bikini Atoll Rehab Comn, 83-89. *Mem:* Fel AAAS; fel Soc Am Foresters; fel Soil Sci Soc Am; Ecol Soc Am; fel Am Soc Agron. *Res:* Forest nutrition; ecology; Pacific tropics; atoll soils. *Mailing Add:* 1726 NW Tenth Terr Gainesville FL 32609. *Fax:* 352-392-3902

STONE, EDWARD, ORGANIC CHEMISTRY, POLYMER CHEMISTRY. *Current Pos:* tech mgr new prod res & develop, 65-80, dir polymer res & chem analysis, 80-85, DIR CHEM RES, BASF INMONT, 85- *Personal Data:* b Fall River, Mass, Dec 7, 32; m 56; c 4. *Educ:* Southeastern Mass Univ, BS, 55; Univ Md, PhD(org chem), 62. *Prof Exp:* Teaching asst, Univ Md, 55-57; chemist, Metals & Controls Corp, 56; analytical res chemist, Nat Inst Drycleaning, 57-61, consult, 61; sr res chemist, Tex-US Chem Co, NJ, 61-65. *Mem:* Am Chem Soc; Sci Res Soc Am; Fedn Soc Coatings Technol. *Res:* Radiation curing of inks and coatings; polymer research and development; block and graft copolymers; polyurethanes, polyesters, polyolefins, acrylics; structure-property correlations; organic synthesis; instrumental analysis. *Mailing Add:* 4 Inwood Rd Morris Plains NJ 07950-2193

STONE, EDWARD CARROLL, JR, PHYSICS. *Current Pos:* Res fel, Calif Inst Technol, 64-67, sr res fel, 67, from asst prof to assoc prof, 67-76, vpres, Astro Facil, 88-90, chmn, Div Physics, Math & Astron, 88-90, VPRES & DAVID MORRISROE PROF PHYSICS, CALIF INST TECHNOL, 76-, DIR, JET PROPULSION LAB, 91- *Personal Data:* b Knoxville, Iowa, Jan 23, 36; m 62, Alice Wickliffe; c Susan & Janet. *Educ:* Univ Chicago, SM, 59, PhD(physics), 64. *Hon Degrees:* DSc, Wash Univ, St Louis, Univ Chicago & Harvard Univ, 92. *Honors & Awards:* Am Educ Award, Am Asn Sch Adminr, 81; Dryden Lectr, Am Inst Aeronaut & Astronaut, 83, Space Sci Award, 84; Sci Award, Nat Space Club; Leroy Randle Grumman Medal, 92; Golden Plate Award, Am Acad Achievement, 92; Magellanic Award, Am Philos Soc, 92; Cospar Award, 92; Von Kamman Wings Award, 96; Asteroid named in honor, Int Astron Union, 96; Am Astronaut Soc Space Flight Award, 97. *Concurrent Pos:* Mem, Particles & Fields Adv Comt, NASA, 69-71, consult, 71-, proj scientist, NASA Voyager Mission, 72-, mem high energy astrophys mgt operating working group, 76-, mem, Comt Space Astron & Astrophys, Space Sci Bd, 79-82; Alfred P Sloan res fel, Calif Inst Technol, 71-73; mem, Jet Propulsion Lab Adv Coun, 80-82; mem, NASA Cosmic Ray Prog Working Group, 80-82, Outer Planets Working Group, Solar Syst Explor Comt, 81-82 & 83, Space Sci Bd, 82-85, Univ Rel Study Group, 83, Steering Group, Space Sci Bd Study Maj Directions Space Sci 1995-2015, 84-85, Adv Comt, NASA/JPL, Vis Sr Scientist Prog, 86-; bd dir, Calif Asn Res Astron, 85-, vchmn, 87-88 & 92-94, chmn, 88-91 & 94-; mem, Comn Phys Sci, Math & Resources, Nat Res Coun, 86-89, Comt Space Policy, 88-; dir, WM Keck Found, 93- *Mem:* Nat Acad Sci; AAAS; fel Am Phys Soc; fel Am Astron Soc; Int Astron Union; fel Am Geophys Union; Int Acad Astronaut; fel Am Inst Aeronaut & Astronaut; Astron Soc Pac. *Res:* Solar and galactic cosmic rays; planetary magnetospheres; interplanetary medium; solar system exploration; satellite and balloon instrumentation. *Mailing Add:* Jet Propulsion Lab M/S 180-904 4800 Oak Grove Dr Pasadena CA 91109. *E-Mail:* edward.c.stone@jpl.nasa.gov

STONE, EDWARD CURRY, plant physiology, for more information see previous edition

STONE, ERIKA MARES, MATHEMATICS. *Current Pos:* programmer, comput ctr, Duke Univ, 77-81, PROGRAMMER, CAROLINA POP CTR, UNIV NC, CHAPEL HILL, 81- *Personal Data:* b Prague, Czech, Jan 26, 38; US citizen; c 1. *Educ:* Pa State Univ, BA, 60, MA, 62, PhD(math), 64. *Prof Exp:* Instr math, Swarthmore Col, 64-65; sr res mathematician, HRB-Singer, Inc, Pa, 65-68, lectr, Dept Comput Sci, Pa State Univ, 68; vis asst prof, Dept Math & Comput Sci, Univ SC, 73-75. *Mem:* Am Math Soc. *Res:* Structure theory of semiperfect rings and the generalization of theory for modules. *Mailing Add:* 2106 Strebor Rd Durham NC 27705

STONE, GORDON EMORY, CELL BIOLOGY. *Current Pos:* PROF BIOL SCI & CHMN DEPT, UNIV DENVER, 72- *Personal Data:* b Sioux City, Iowa, July 12, 33; m 55; c 2. *Educ:* Univ Iowa, BA, 56, MSc, 58, PhD(zool), 61. *Prof Exp:* Res fel, NIH, 61-63 & AEC, 63-64; from asst prof to assoc prof anat, Sch Med, Univ Colo, 64-72. *Concurrent Pos:* NIH career develop award, 65-70. *Mem:* AAAS; Am Soc Cell Biol; Soc Protozool; Am Soc Zool; Sigma Xi. *Res:* Cytochemical studies on cell growth and division, especially the sequential macromolecular events during the interdivision interval leading to division with emphasis on microtubule protein synthesis. *Mailing Add:* Dept Biol Sci Univ Denver 2101 E Wesley Ave Denver CO 80210-5210

STONE, H NATHAN, CHEMICAL ENGINEERING. *Personal Data:* b Claremont, NH, May 8, 20; m 42; c 2. *Educ:* Univ NH, BS, 43; Univ Ill, MS, 47, PhD(chem eng), 50. *Prof Exp:* Group leader org res, Norton Co, 50-52; asst dir res, Bay State Abrasive Prod Co, 52-58, dir res & develop, 58-64, vpres & dir res & eng, Bay State Abrasives, Div Dresser Indust, Inc, 64-86. *Mem:* AAAS; Am Chem Soc; Am Ceramic Soc; Nat Soc Prof Engrs; Am Inst Chem Engrs. *Res:* Reaction kinetics in fluidized beds; solid state physics, especially the creation of new surfaces during abrasive machining; resins and polymers applicable to abrasive bonding. *Mailing Add:* 38 Sun Valley Dr Worcester MA 01609

STONE, HAROLD S, computer architecture, for more information see previous edition

STONE, HARRIS B(OBBY), electronics engineering; deceased, see previous edition for last biography

STONE, HENRY E, ENGINEERING. *Current Pos:* CONSULT, 87- *Personal Data:* b Munich, Ger, Feb 10, 22; US citizen; m 48, Joan; c David, Linda, Howard & Peter. *Educ:* Union Col, BS, 55; Univ Buffalo, BS, 55. *Prof Exp:* Mgr, Atomic Power Lab, Schenectady, NY, 50-68; gen mgr, Knoll Atomic Power Lab, 68-74; mgr, Strategic Planning Oper, Gen Elec Co, San Jose, 74-75, gen mgr, Boiling Water Syst Div, 75-77, mgr, 77-84, vpres, Nuclear Energy Bus Opers, 78-87, chief eng officer, 84-87. *Mem:* Nat Acad Eng; Am Nuclear Soc; fel Am Soc Mech Engrs. *Mailing Add:* 6805 Castle Rock Dr San Jose CA 95120

STONE, HENRY OTTO, JR, VIROLOGY, GENETIC ENGINEERING. *Current Pos:* ASSOC PROF MICROBIOL & IMMUNOL, SCH MED, E CAROLINA UNIV, 82- *Personal Data:* b Spartanburg, SC, Apr 10, 36; m 60; c 1. *Educ:* Wofford Col, BS, 59; Duke Univ, PhD(zool), 64. *Prof Exp:* Am Cancer Soc fel biochem, Duke Univ, 64-66; res chemist, E I du Pont de Nemours & Co, Inc, Del, 66-70; NIH spec res fel animal virol, St Jude Children's Res Hosp, 70-72; from asst prof to assoc prof microbiol, Univ Kans,

72-82. *Concurrent Pos:* Am Cancer Soc scholar, Duke Univ, 80-81. *Mem:* Am Soc Microbiol; Am Soc Biol Chemists; Soc Gen Microbiol; Am Soc Virol. *Res:* Paramyxoviruses; viral RNA synthesis; genome transcription; viral proteins; cloning sequence and expression of viral genes; complementary DNA copies of newcastle disease, virus genes were cloned into bacterial plasmids; DNA copies sequenced and inserted into procaryotio and eucargotic expression vectors. *Mailing Add:* Dept Microbiol & Immunol Sch Med E Carolina Univ Brody Bldg Greenville NC 27858-4354. *Fax:* 919-816-3104

STONE, HERBERT, NUTRITION. *Current Pos:* PRES, TRAGON CORP, 74- *Personal Data:* b Washington, DC, Sept 14, 34; m 64; c 2. *Educ:* Univ Mass, BSc, 55, MSc, 58; Univ Calif, Davis, PhD(nutrit), 62. *Prof Exp:* Specialist, Exp Sta, Univ Calif, Davis; food scientist, Stanford Res Inst, 62-64, dir dept food & plant sci, 67-74. *Concurrent Pos:* Pres, Sensory Eval Div, Inst Food Technol, 77-78, exec comt, 84-; assoc ed, J Food Sci, 77-80. *Mem:* AAAS; Sigma Xi; Am Soc Enol; fel Inst Food Technologists; Am Soc Testing & Mat. *Res:* Management consultant in product development, food, beverage, cosmetic products and product acceptance measurement; taste and odor research. *Mailing Add:* Tragon Corp 365 Convention Way Redwood City CA 94063-1402. *Fax:* 650-365-3737; *E-Mail:* tragonc@aol.com

STONE, HERBERT L(OSSON), CHEMICAL ENGINEERING. *Current Pos:* PRES, STONE ENG, 89- *Personal Data:* b Eddy, Tex, Nov 6, 28; m 47, 80, Beverly Evans; c 2. *Educ:* Rice Inst, BS, 50; Mass Inst Technol, ScD(chem eng), 53. *Prof Exp:* Asst process engr, Vulcan Copper & Supply Co, 53; res adv, Exxon Prod Res Co, 53-88. *Mem:* Am Inst Chem Engrs; Am Inst Mining, Metall & Petrol Engrs; Sigma Xi. *Res:* Numerical analysis; petroleum resevoir engineering; enhance petroleum recovery. *Mailing Add:* Box 22781 Houston TX 77227. *Fax:* 713-965-9544; *E-Mail:* stonehl@hal-pc.org

STONE, HERMAN, ORGANIC CHEMISTRY. *Current Pos:* dir foam develop, 74-95, TECH CONSULT ENVIRON & LEGAL, GEN FOAM CORP, 96- *Personal Data:* b Munich, Ger, Nov 3, 24; nat US; m 49; c 6. *Educ:* Bethany Col, WVa, BSc, 44; Ohio State Univ, PhD(chem), 50. *Prof Exp:* Analytical chemist, Nat Aniline Div, Allied Chem Corp, 44-45, analytical res chemist, 51-53, res chemist, 53-61, group leader appln res chem, 61-63, mgr chem res, Indust Chem Div, 63-68, dir res, Specialty Chem Div, 68-69, res assoc, Corp Chem Res Lab, 69-72; dir chem res, Malden Mills Inc, 72-74. *Concurrent Pos:* Consult, environ regulatory flammability & patents. *Mem:* AAAS; Am Chem Soc; Sigma Xi; Am Inst Chem. *Res:* Analytical and exploratory research on polymer intermediates; flammability of plastics; urethane polymer technology. *Mailing Add:* Gen Foam Corp Valmont Indust Park 1330 Roberts Ave Hazleton PA 18201

STONE, HOWARD ANDERSON, GENETICS, VIROLOGY. *Current Pos:* AT OMEGA CHICKS. *Personal Data:* b Claremont, NH, Nov 21, 40; m 62; c 3. *Educ:* Univ NH, BS, 62, MS, 65; Mich State Univ, PhD(poultry), 72. *Prof Exp:* Asst poultry extension, Univ NH, 62-65; res geneticist, agr res serv, USDA, 65- *Mem:* Poultry Sci Asn. *Res:* Investigations of the genetic control of Marek's disease and lymphoid leukosis in chickens; maintenance and development of highly inbred lines of chickens. *Mailing Add:* 1827 Lyndhurst Haslett MI 48840

STONE, IRVING CHARLES, JR, FORENSIC SCIENCE. *Current Pos:* criminalist, 72-74, CHIEF PHYS EVIDENCE SECT, INST FORENSIC SCI, 74- *Personal Data:* b Chicago, Ill, Dec 18, 30; m 55; c 3. *Educ:* Iowa State Univ, BS, 52; George Washington Univ, MS, 61, PhD(geochem), 67. *Honors & Awards:* Paul L Kirk Award, Outstanding Criminalist, Am Acad Forensic Sci, 90; Vision Award, Int Asn Forensic Nurses, 96. *Prof Exp:* Spec agt-microscopist, Fed Bur Invest, 55-61; res chemist, Res Div, W R Grace & Co, 61-63, proj leader, 63-64, res supvr, 64-68; vpres, Geochem Surv, Tex, 68-72. *Concurrent Pos:* Lectr police sci, Montgomery Jr Col, 67-70; instr forensic sci, Univ Tex Health Sci Ctr Dallas, 72-77, asst prof path, 77-85, dir grad prog forensic sci, Grad Sch Biomed Sci, 77-, assoc prof clin path, 85-; adj prof law, Baylor Univ Sch Law. *Mem:* Am Soc Firearms & Toolmark Examrs; fel Am Acad Forensic Sci; Int Asn Bloodstain Pattern Analysts. *Res:* Analytical chemistry, especially x-ray diffraction, spectrometry, light microscopy; applied research in forensic sciences, specifically glass, firearm residues, instrumental analytical applications, crime scene reconstruction. *Mailing Add:* Inst Forensic Sci Box 35728 Dallas TX 75235-0728

STONE, J(ACK) L(EE), ELECTRICAL ENGINEERING. *Current Pos:* sr scientist, Solar Energy Res Inst, 78-79, chief, Advan Silicon Br, 79-81, dep div dir, Solar Elec Conversion Res Div, 81-86, DIV DIR SOLAR ELEC RES DIV, SOLAR ENERGY RES INST, 86- *Personal Data:* b Taylor, Tex, July 12, 41; m 65; c 3. *Educ:* Univ Tex, BSEE, 63, MSEE, 64, PhD(elec eng), 68. *Prof Exp:* Res asst appl superconductivity, Univ Tex, 62-65, res asst elec eng, 65-66, teaching assoc, 66-67, asst prof, 67-68; res engr, Mesa Instruments Inc, 68-69; from asst prof to assoc prof elec eng, Tex A&M Univ, 69-77. *Concurrent Pos:* Co-prin investr, NASA res grant, 68-69; prin investr, Army Res Off-Durham res grant, 70-72; vis prof, Inst Nac Astrofisica, Optica, Electronics, 75-76. *Mem:* Inst Elec & Electronics Engrs; Am Inst Physics; Electrochem Soc. *Res:* Applied superconductivity; optical properties of semiconductors at low temperatures; high Q resonant circuit techniques; amorphous semiconductors; ion implantation; integrated circuit device processing; photovoltaic devices. *Mailing Add:* Nat Renewable Energy Lab 1617 Cole Blvd Bldg 16-3 Photovoltaics Div Golden CO 80401

STONE, JAY D, ENTOMOLOGY. *Current Pos:* from asst prof to assoc prof entom, 76-87, PEST MGT SERV, TEX A&M UNIV, 87- *Personal Data:* b Littlefield, Tex, Oct 14, 44; m 65; c 2. *Educ:* West Tex State Univ, BS, 68; Iowa State Univ, MS, 70, PhD(entom), 73. *Prof Exp:* Res assoc entom, Iowa State Univ, 72-73; asst prof, Kans State Univ, 73-76. *Mem:* Sigma Xi; Entom Soc Am. *Res:* Biology and control of urban insect pests of far west Texas. *Mailing Add:* 6613 Quincy Ave Lubbock TX 79424

STONE, JOE THOMAS, PHYSICAL ORGANIC CHEMISTRY, PHOTOGRAPHIC CHEMISTRY. *Current Pos:* sr res chemist, 68-92, SR PROCESS ENGR, EASTMAN KODAK CO, 92- *Personal Data:* b Miami, Okla, June 25, 41; m 63; c 2. *Educ:* Harvey Mudd Col, BS, 63; Univ Wash, PhD(org chem), 67. *Prof Exp:* NIH res fel, Univ Wash, 67-68. *Concurrent Pos:* Mem, Webster Conserv Bd. *Mem:* NY Acad Sci; Royal Soc Chem; Am Chem Soc. *Res:* Organic reaction mechanisms; application of physical-organic techniques to biological processes, enzyme kinetics and mechanism; homogeneous and heterogeneous catalysis and reaction kinetics; photographic science - film structure, process chemistry, development mechanisms. *Mailing Add:* 595 Drumm Rd Webster NY 14580-1512

STONE, JOHN AUSTIN, NUCLEAR WASTE MANAGEMENT, SCIENCE ENGINEERING EDUCATION. *Current Pos:* RETIRED. *Personal Data:* b Paintsville, Ky, Nov 30, 35; m 68, Helen Reynolds; c Philip, Tracye & Suzanne. *Educ:* Univ Louisville, BS, 55; Univ Calif, Berkeley, PhD(nuclear chem), 63. *Prof Exp:* Chemist, Savannah River Lab, E I Du Pont de Nemours & Co, Inc, 63-68, staff chemist, 68-74, res staff chemist, 74-81, res assoc, 81-89, mgr, Univ Relations, 89-90; mgr educ progs, Savannah River Technol Ctr, Westinghouse Savannah River Co, 90-92. *Concurrent Pos:* Traveling lect, 64-74; consult, Int Atomic Energy Agency, Vienna, 65 & 86; Assoc ed, Mat Lett, 83-89. *Mem:* Am Phys Soc; Am Chem Soc; Mat Res Soc; Am Soc Eng Educ. *Res:* Radioactive waste management; nuclear fuel cycle; solid state and chemical properties of the actinides; Mossbauer spectroscopy. *Mailing Add:* 2221 Morningside Dr Augusta GA 30904-3441

STONE, JOHN BRUCE, ANIMAL SCIENCE. *Current Pos:* RETIRED. *Personal Data:* b Forfar, Ont, Can, Sept 23, 30; m 54; c 4. *Educ:* Ont Agr Col, BSA, 53, MSA, 54; Cornell Univ, PhD, 59. *Prof Exp:* Asst prof animal husb, Ont Agr Col, 54-62; asst prof animal sci, Cornell Univ, 62-66; prof, Univ Guelph, 66-95, assoc dean, Col Agr, 83-95. *Mem:* Am Dairy Sci Asn; Agr Inst Can; Am Soc Animal Sci; Sigma Xi. *Res:* Dairy cattle nutrition; forages for dairy cattle rations; calf-raising programs; systems analyses for dairy production. *Mailing Add:* 11 Mayfield Ave Guelph ON N1G 2L9 Can

STONE, JOHN ELMER, GEOLOGY. *Current Pos:* RETIRED. *Personal Data:* b Montgomery, Ala, Aug 12, 31; m 59; c 2. *Educ:* Ohio Wesleyan Univ, BA, 53; Univ Ill, MS, 58, PhD(geol), 60. *Prof Exp:* Asst prof geol, Univ Tex, 60-62; geologist, Minn Geol Surv, 62-67; prof geol, Okla State Univ, 67-89, head dept, 67-77. *Concurrent Pos:* Res grants, Univ Tex Excellence Found, 61 & grad sch, Univ Minn, 62, 67; NSF summer grants, 68-72, sci equip grant, 69; Okla State Univ Res Found res grant, 70. *Mem:* AAAS; fel Geol Soc Am; Nat Asn Geol Teachers; Am Quaternary Asn; Soc Econ Paleont & Mineral. *Res:* Glacial and engineering geology. *Mailing Add:* 1024 W Eskridge Ave Stillwater OK 74075

STONE, JOHN FLOYD, SOIL PHYSICS. *Current Pos:* from asst prof to prof, 57-94, EMER PROF AGRON, OKLA STATE UNIV, 94- *Personal Data:* b York, Nebr, Oct 13, 28; m 53; c 4. *Educ:* Univ Nebr, BSc, 52; Iowa State Univ, MS, 55, PhD, 57. *Prof Exp:* Res assoc, Dept Agron & Inst Atomic Res, Iowa State Univ, 56-57. *Concurrent Pos:* Assoc ed, Soil Sci Soc Am, 68-75; vis scientist lectr, Am Geophys Union, 72; mem, Agr Adv Panel, US Dept Defense, 77-78, Comt Irrigation Water, Am Soc Civil Engrs, 85-88, Comt Water Resources, Soil Sci Soc Am & Comt Unsaturated Zone, 64-73, Am Geophys Union, 78-88; assoc ed, Am Soc Agron, 82-85; chmn, Comt Unsaturated Zone, Am Geophys Union, 86-88. *Mem:* Am Soc Agron; Soil Sci Soc Am; Am Geophys Union; Int Soc Soil Sci; Sigma Xi; Am Soc Civil Engrs. *Res:* Water conservation, evapotranspiration; water flow in plants; electronic instrumentation. *Mailing Add:* 1114 Frances Stillwater OK 74075

STONE, JOHN GROVER, II, GEOLOGY. *Current Pos:* RETIRED. *Personal Data:* b Pueblo, Colo, Aug 6, 33; m 64; c 5. *Educ:* Yale Univ, BS, 55; Stanford Univ, PhD(geol), 58. *Prof Exp:* Staff geologist, Hanna Mining Co, M A Hanna Co, 58-69, asst chief geologist, 69-77, proj mgr, 77-79, mgr, Pilot Knob Mine & Pellet Plant, 80-81, chief geologist, 86. *Mem:* Geol Soc Am; Soc Econ Geologists. *Res:* Genesis of ore deposits; ore reserve estimation. *Mailing Add:* 300 Mottsville Gardnerville NV 89410

STONE, JOHN PATRICK, ENDOCRINOLOGY, RADIOBIOLOGY. *Current Pos:* STAFF PHARMACIST, LYNCHBURG GEN HOSP, 86- *Personal Data:* b Algood, Tenn, Sept 5, 39; m 64; c 3. *Educ:* Wayne State Univ, BS, 61, PhD(biol), 72; Purdue Univ, Lafayette, MS, 64. *Prof Exp:* Teaching asst bionucleonics, Purdue Univ, Lafayette, 62-64; teaching asst endocrinol & radiobiol, Wayne State Univ, 65-68; fel radiobiol, Div Biol & Med Res, Argonne Nat Lab, 72-74; asst scientist, Brookhaven Nat Lab, 74-75, assoc scientist, 76-79, scientist, 79-86. *Concurrent Pos:* Assoc clin prof, State Univ NY, Stony Brook, 78; consult, Inner Radiation Belt Res Consults, 82- *Mem:* Endocrine Soc; Int Pigment Cell Soc; Radiation Res Soc; Am Soc Zoologists; Sigma Xi; Am Asn Career Res. *Res:* Hormonal control of radiation and chemically induced mammary tumorigenesis; effects of chronic gamma irradiation upon endocrine and hematopoietic systems; pigment cell biochemistry and physiology; pathophysiology of peptide toxins, retinoid inhibition of mammary carcinogenesis. *Mailing Add:* 3400 Ivy Link Pl Lynchburg VA 24503

STONE, JOSEPH, biochemistry, pharmacology; deceased, see previous edition for last biography

STONE, JULIAN, PHYSICS. *Current Pos:* mem tech staff, 69-83, DISTINGUISHED MEM TECH STAFF, BELL LABS, 83- *Personal Data:* b New York, NY, Apr 12, 29; m 51; c 3. *Educ:* City Col New York, BS, 50; NY Univ, MS, 51, PhD(physics), 58. *Honors & Awards:* David Richardson Award, Optical Soc Am. *Prof Exp:* Electronic scientist, Naval Mat Lab, 52; tutor physics, City Col New York, 52-53; res scientist, Hudson Lab, Columbia Univ, 53-69, assoc dir physics, 66-69. *Concurrent Pos:* Tutor physics, City Col New York, 56-57; assoc ed, Optics Lett, Optical Soc Am. *Mem:* Fel Optical Soc Am. *Res:* Lasers; spectroscopy; underwater sound propagation. *Mailing Add:* Bell Labs Rm L121 Box 400 Holmdel NJ 07733

STONE, KATHLEEN SEXTON, RESEARCH ADMINISTRATION. *Current Pos:* asst prof, 79-84, dir res, Ctr Nursing Res, 85-88, ASSOC PROF NURSING, GRAD EDUC, DEPT LIFE SPAN PROCESS, OHIO STATE UNIV COL NURSING, 84- *Personal Data:* b Lakewood, Ohio, March 29, 47; m 76; c 2. *Educ:* Ohio State Univ Sch Nursing, Columbus, BS, 72; Ohio State Univ Grad Sch, Columbus, PhD(physiol), 77. *Honors & Awards:* Res Award, Am Asn Critical Care Nurses, Nat Teaching Inst, 86. *Prof Exp:* Asst prof, grad & undergrad educ, Univ Cincinnati, 77-78. *Concurrent Pos:* Prin investr, endotracheal suctioning in acutely ill adults, Nat Ctr Nursing Res, 87-95 & Div Nursing, PHS, 84-87; group chair, Conf Res Priorities Nursing, Nat Ctr Nursing Res, 88; mem, Consensus Conf, Am Lung Assoc, 88; chair, Nat Study Group Endotracheal Suctioning, Am Asn Critical Care Nurses, 84-; lectr, Am Asn Critical Care Nurses Nat Teaching Inst, 88. *Mem:* Am Thoracic Soc; Am Lung Asn; Am Asn Critical Care Nurses; Sigma Xi. *Res:* Investigating the effects of lung hyperinflation and hyperoxygenation during endotracheal suctioning testing open vs closed techniques on mean arterial pressure, heart rate, cardiac output, pulmonary arterial pressure and airway pressure in critically ill adults. *Mailing Add:* 1227 Drumbarton Ct West Worthington Station OH 43235-5121

STONE, LAWRENCE DAVID, MATHEMATICS, OPERATIONS RESEARCH. *Current Pos:* SR VPRES, METRON, 86-, CHIEF OPERATING OFFICER, 95- *Personal Data:* b St Louis, Mo, Sept 2, 42; m 67, Harriet Williams; c Julia & David. *Educ:* Antioch Col, BS, 64; Purdue Univ, West Lafayette, MS, 66, PhD(math), 67. *Honors & Awards:* Lancaster Prize, Opers Res Soc, 75. *Prof Exp:* From assoc to sr assoc, Daniel H Wagner Assocs, 67-74, vpres, 74-81, br mgr, 81-86. *Concurrent Pos:* Off Naval Res grant, 69-76; assoc ed, Operations Res, 81- *Mem:* Am Math Soc; Inst Opers Res & Mgt Sci; Oper Res Soc. *Res:* Theory of search for stationary and moving targets; constrained extremal problems; threshold crossing problems for markov and semi-markov processes; optimal stochastic control of semi-markov processes; non-linear filtering; non-linear filtering and data fusion. *Mailing Add:* Metron 11911 Freedom Dr Suite 800 Reston VA 20190-5602. *Fax:* 703-787-3518; *E-Mail:* stone@metsci.com

STONE, LOYD RAYMOND, soil physics, soil & water management, for more information see previous edition

STONE, M(ORRIS) D, engineering; deceased, see previous edition for last biography

STONE, MARGARET HODGMAN, plant taxonomy; deceased, see previous edition for last biography

STONE, MARTHA BARNES, FOOD SCIENCE. *Current Pos:* PROF, DEPT FOOD SCI & HUMAN NUTRIT, COLO STATE UNIV, 89- *Personal Data:* b Paris, Tenn, Nov 20, 52; m 73; c 2. *Educ:* Univ Tenn, Martin, BS, 74; Univ Tenn, Knoxville, MS, 75, PhD(food sci), 77. *Prof Exp:* Res asst foods & nutrit, Univ Tenn, 74-77; from asst prof to assoc prof foods & nutrit, Kans State Univ, 78-89. *Concurrent Pos:* NSF grant, 78; mem regional commun, Inst Food Technologists, 81-, nat chmn, 85-; sci adv, Am Coun Sci & Health. *Mem:* Inst Food Technologists (secy, 76-77); Sigma Xi; Am Dietetics Asn; Am Assoc Cereal Chemists. *Res:* Formulated foods; quality evaluation of fruits and vegetables; food preservation soybean. *Mailing Add:* Dept Food Sci & Human Nutrit Colo State Univ Ft Collins CO 80523-0001

STONE, MARTIN JOSEPH, PROTEIN NUCLEAR MAGNETIC RESONANCE SPECTROSCOPY. *Current Pos:* ASST PROF CHEM, IND UNIV, 95- *Personal Data:* b Auckland, NZ, Aug 4, 65. *Educ:* Univ Auckland, NZ, BSc, 85, MSc, 87; Univ Cambridge, Eng, PhD(chem), 90. *Prof Exp:* Res assoc, Scripps Res Inst, 91-94, sr res assoc, 94-95. *Concurrent Pos:* Postdoctoral fel, Am Heart Asn, 93-95. *Res:* Protein nuclear magnetic resonance spectroscopy; structure-function relationships of the pro-inflammatory chemotactic cytokines (chemokines); relationship of active site dynamics and enzyme activity; influence of structural features on protein flexibility. *Mailing Add:* Chem Dept Ind Univ Bloomington IN 47405. *E-Mail:* mastone@indiana.edu

STONE, MARTIN L, OBSTETRICS & GYNECOLOGY. *Current Pos:* RETIRED. *Personal Data:* b New York, NY, June 11, 20; m 43; c 1. *Educ:* Columbia Univ, BS, 41; NY Med Col, MD, 44, MMSc, 49; Am Bd Obstet & Gynec, dipl, 52. *Prof Exp:* Prof obstet & gynec & chmn dept, NY Med Col, 56-78; prof obstet & gynec & chmn dept, Sch Med, State Univ NY, Stony Brook, 78-88. *Concurrent Pos:* Attend, Flower & Fifth Ave Hosps, Metrop & Bird S Coler Hosps, 56-; consult, Southampton Hosp, 60-, Deepdale Gen Hosp, 66- & Long Island Jewish-Hillside Med Ctr, 78. *Mem:* Fel Am Gynec Soc; fel Am Pub Health Asn; fel Am Asn Obstetricians & Gynecologists; assoc fel Royal Soc Med; fel Am Col Obstetricians & Gynecologists (secy, 71-78, pres-elect, 78 pres, 79). *Mailing Add:* Isle Water Mill NY 11976

STONE, MARVIN J, ONCOLOGY & HEMATOLOGY, IMMUNOLOGY. *Current Pos:* CHIEF ONCOL, DIR IMMUNOL & DIR CHARLES A SAMMONS CANCER CTR, BAYLOR UNIV MED CTR, 76- *Personal Data:* b Columbus, Ohio, Aug 3, 37; m 58, Jill Feinstein; c Nancy & Rob. *Educ:* Univ Chicago, MS, 62, MD, 63; Am Bd Internal Med, dipl, 70, cert hemat, 72, cert med oncol, 73. *Prof Exp:* Intern & asst resident, Ward Mem Serv, Barnes Hosp, St Louis, 63-65; clin assoc, Arthritis & Rheumatism Br, Nat Inst Arthritis & Metab Dis, NIH, 65-68; resident med, Parkland Mem Hosp, Dallas, 68-69; fel hematol-oncol, Univ Tex Southwestern Med Sch, 69-70, from instr to asst prof internal med, 70-73, assoc prof, 74-76. *Concurrent Pos:* Estab investr, Am Heart Asn, 70-75; mem fac & steering comt, Immunol Grad Prog, Grad Sch Biomed Sci, Univ Tex Health Sci Ctr Dallas, 75-76, adj mem, 76-; clin prof internal med, Univ Tex Southwestern Med Sch, 76-; co-dir div hemat-oncol, Baylor Univ Med Ctr, 76-, outstanding fac mem, 77-78 & 86-87; adj prof biol, Southern Methodist Univ, 77- *Mem:* Am Asn Cancer Res; Am Soc Hemat; Am Soc Clin Oncol; Am Asn Immunologists; fel Am Col Physicians; fel Int Soc Hemat; Sigma Xi. *Res:* Plasma cell dyscrasias and monoclonal immunoglobulins. *Mailing Add:* Baylor Univ Med Ctr Charles A Sammons Cancer Ctr 3500 Gaston Ave Dallas TX 75246-2088. *Fax:* 214-820-2780

STONE, MAX WENDELL, COMPUTER SCIENCES. *Current Pos:* RETIRED. *Personal Data:* b Petersburg, Tenn, Mar 6, 29; m 50, Muriel Franklin. *Educ:* Union Univ, Tenn, BS, 49; Peabody Col, MA, 50. *Prof Exp:* High sch teacher, Ark, 50-51; scientist & supvr comput & data reduction, Rohm & Haas Co, Redstone Res Labs, 53-64; mgr corp data processing, Sci Systs, Inc, 64-73; sr prog mgr, Unisys Corp, 73-94. *Concurrent Pos:* Teacher eve div, Univ Ala, Huntsville, 54-65; founder & dir, Fiscal Systs Inc, 83- *Res:* Digital computer applications to problems in engineering, science and business, including management information systems, accounting functions, inventory control and data reduction; solid rocket propellant grain design; operation of large computers; management of computer center operations; management of systems software; project management. *Mailing Add:* 1431 Chandler Rd SE Huntsville AL 35801-1407

STONE, MICHAEL GATES, MATHEMATICS. *Current Pos:* From asst prof to assoc prof math, 69-81, PROF MATH & STATIST, UNIV CALGARY, 81- *Personal Data:* b Midland, Tex, Oct 9, 38; div; c 1. *Educ:* Wesleyan Univ, BA, 60; La State Univ, Baton Rouge, MS, 62; Univ Colo, Boulder, PhD(math), 69. *Mem:* Am Math Soc; Math Asn Am; Sigma Xi. *Res:* Universal algebra; lattice theory. *Mailing Add:* Dept Math Statist Univ Calgary Calgary AB T2N 1N4 Can

STONE, ORVILLE L, ELECTRICAL ENGINEERING. *Current Pos:* CONSULT, 86- *Personal Data:* b New Albany, Ind, June 4, 21; m 45, Ida Whittinghill; c Christopher, Laura & Nancy. *Educ:* Rose-Hulman Inst Technol, BS, 48; Mass Inst Technol, SM, 50. *Prof Exp:* Asst, Mass Inst Technol, 48-50; mem staff, Los Alamos Sci Lab, Univ Calif, 50-53; assoc res staff mem, Raytheon Mfg Co, 53-57; proj engr, Schlumberger Well Serv, 57-86. *Concurrent Pos:* Lectr, Univ Houston, 65-68. *Mem:* Inst Elec & Electronics Engrs; AAAS. *Res:* Instrumentation for nuclear research; radiation detection; semiconductor devices; instrumentation for well logging. *Mailing Add:* 5119 Glenmeadow Houston TX 77096

STONE, PETER H, CARDIOLOGY, CORONARY ARTERY DISEASE. *Current Pos:* assoc dir med, Samuel A Levine Cardiac Unit, 81-93, DIR CLIN TRIALS, CARDIOVASC DIV, BRIGAM & WOMEN'S HOSP, 90-, CO-DIR, SAMUEL A LEVINE CARDIAC UNIT, 93-; ASSOC PROF MED, HARVARD MED SCH, 93- *Personal Data:* b New York, NY, Mar 31, 48; m 83, Lisa Vosburgh; c Emily, Michael & Benjamin. *Educ:* Princeton Univ, BA, 70; Cornell Univ Med Col, MD, 74. *Prof Exp:* From instr to asst prof, Harvard Med Sch, 79-91. *Mem:* Fel Am Heart Asn; fel Am Col Cardiol; Coun Clin Cardiol; Am Fedn Clin Res. *Res:* Stable and unstable coronary artery disease. *Mailing Add:* Dept Med Div Cardiovasc Brigham & Womens Hosp Sch Med 75 Francis St Boston MA 02115

STONE, PETER HUNTER, ATMOSPHERIC DYNAMICS, CLIMATE MODELING. *Current Pos:* head, Dept Meteorol, 81-83, dir, Ctr Meteorol & Phys Oceanog, 83-89, PROF METEOROL, MASS INST TECHNOL, 74- *Personal Data:* b Brooklyn, NY, May 10, 37; m 87, Paola Malanotte-Rizzoli. *Educ:* Harvard Univ, BA, 59, PhD(appl math), 64. *Prof Exp:* Lectr meteorol, Harvard Univ, 64-66, from asst prof to assoc prof, 66-72; staff scientist, NASA, 72-74. *Concurrent Pos:* Ed, Dynamics Atmospheres & Oceans, Elsevier, 88-, J Climate, Am Meterol Soc, 90-92. *Mem:* Fel Am Meteorol Soc; Am Geophys Union. *Res:* Dynamics of planetary atmospheres; climate modeling. *Mailing Add:* Dept Earth Atmospheric & Planetary Sci Rm 54-1718 Mass Inst Technol Cambridge MA 02139. *Fax:* 617-253-6208

STONE, PHILIP M, ATOMIC SCATTERING CALCULATERS, SCIENTIFIC COMPUTING. *Current Pos:* br chief, 78-87, exec asst to dir energy res, 87-88, DIR OFF PLANNING & ANALYSIS, US DEPT ENERGY, 87- *Personal Data:* b Wilkinsburg, Pa, Nov 23, 33; m 55, 80, Annie Lee; c 3. *Educ:* Univ Mich, BSE, 55, MSE, 56, PhD(nuclear eng), 62. *Prof Exp:* Staff mem, Los Alamos Sci Lab, 56-63, mem advan study prog, 59-60, grad thesis prog, 60-62; staff mem, Sperry Rand Res Ctr, 63-68, head radiation sci dept, 67-68; assoc prof, Div Interdisciplinary Studies, State Univ NY Buffalo, 68-69; liaison scientist, Sperry Rand Res Ctr, 69-71, mgr systs studies dept, 71-75; physicist, Energy Res & Develop Admin, 75-77. *Concurrent Pos:* Fel, Univ Col, Univ London, 65-66; vis scientist, Univ Pittsburgh, 67-68; vis scientist, Ctr d'Etudes Nucleaires de Saclay, 74. *Mem:* AAAS; Am Phys Soc; Sigma Xi; NY Acad Sci; Inst Elec & Electronic Engrs. *Res:* Theoretical atomic and plasma physics; electron-atom scattering, photoabsorption, recombination, line shapes and intensities, nonequilibrium populations, microwave radiation from plasmas; signal processing and system analysis; atomic radiation from plasmas; nuclear reactor design; fusion reactor design. *Mailing Add:* 7507 Whittier Blvd Bethesda MD 20817. *E-Mail:* pstone@erds.com

STONE, RICHARD SPILLANE, PHYSICS. *Current Pos:* PRES, FIRST LEXINGTON GROUP, INC, 86- *Personal Data:* b Huntington, NY, Sept 14, 25; m 48; c 3. *Educ:* Rensselaer Polytech Inst, BS, 49, MS, 50, PhD(physics), 52. *Prof Exp:* Asst physics, Rensselaer Polytech Inst, 49-52; res assoc nuclear physics instrumentation, Knolls Atomic Power Lab, Gen Elec Co, 52-57; physicist in chg, TRIGA Proj & sect mgr, HTGR Proj, Gen Atomic Div, Gen Dynamics Corp, 57-63; vpres eng & sales, Tech Measurement Corp, 63-64; head, Physics Sect, Arthur D Little, Inc, 64-86. *Mem:* Am Phys Soc; Am Nuclear Soc. *Res:* Underwater acoustics; computer applications; system analysis instrumentation design and development; reactor physics; design, construction and operation of experimental reactors; critical assemblies and in-pile experiments; nuclear power plant analysis and test. *Mailing Add:* 60 Baskin Rd Lexington MA 02173-6929

STONE, ROBERT EDWARD, JR, SPEECH & HEARING SCIENCES, SPEECH PATHOLOGY. *Current Pos:* assoc prof otolaryngol, Sch Med, 87-97, DIR, VANDERBILT VOICE CTR, VANDERBILT UNIV, 92- *Personal Data:* b Spokane, Wash, Feb 20, 37; m 62; c 3. *Educ:* Whitworth Col, BS, 60; Univ Ore, MEd, 64; Univ Mich, PhD(speech path & speech sci), 71. *Prof Exp:* Instr speech, Ore State Syst Higher Educ, 64-66; speech pathologist & res asst otorhinolaryngol, Univ Mich, Ann Arbor, 70-71; from asst prof to assoc prof otolaryngol, Sch Med, Ind Univ, 78-92. *Mem:* Fel Am Speech & Hearing Asn; assoc Acoust Soc Am. *Res:* Laryngeal physiology and effects of aberrant production of voice; indices of hypernasality. *Mailing Add:* Vanderbilt Voice Ctr Village Vanderbilt 1500 21st Ave S Suite 2700 Nashville TN 37212

STONE, ROBERT K(EMPER), mechanical engineering, for more information see previous edition

STONE, ROBERT LOUIS, microbiology, for more information see previous edition

STONE, ROBERT P(ORTER), electrical engineering; deceased, see previous edition for last biography

STONE, ROBERT SIDNEY, SYSTEMS ANALYSIS, NUCLEAR ENGINEERING. *Current Pos:* RETIRED. *Personal Data:* b Fond du Lac, Wis, Feb 16, 23; m 48, Barbara Furstenberg; c Robin & Thomas. *Educ:* Calif Inst Technol, BS, 48. *Prof Exp:* Jr elec engr, Oak Ridge Nat Lab, 48-50, develop engr, 50-54, physicist, 54-64, group leader dynamic analysis, 64-88; consult, Pai Corp, 88-95. *Mem:* Am Nuclear Soc. *Res:* Reactor design reviews; computer analysis of systems interactions; technical management; control studies of energy systems; reactor dynamics as related to safety and control. *Mailing Add:* 118 Canterbury Rd Oak Ridge TN 37830-7737

STONE, SAM, III, PHYSICS. *Current Pos:* student physicist, 62-69, PHYSICIST, THEORET PHYSICS DIV, LAWRENCE LIVERMORE NAT LAB, 69- *Personal Data:* b Louisville, Ky, Feb 11, 35. *Educ:* Univ Richmond, BS, 56; Univ Calif, Los Angeles, MS, 59; Univ Calif, Berkeley, PhD, 69. *Prof Exp:* Engr, Storage Tube Div, Hughes Aircraft Co, 56-58; physicist, Comput Div, US Naval Weapons Lab, 59-60; teaching asst, Dept Physics, Univ Calif, Berkeley, 61. *Mem:* Am Phys Soc. *Mailing Add:* Lawrence Livermore Nat Lab L-298 PO Box 808 Livermore CA 94550

STONE, SANFORD HERBERT, IMMUNOLOGY. *Current Pos:* RETIRED. *Personal Data:* b New York, NY, Sept 9, 21; m 53, Audrey Larack; c Andrew L, Leland S & Roger M. *Educ:* City Col NY, BS, 47; Univ Paris, DSc, 51. *Prof Exp:* NIH res fel, Sch Med, Johns Hopkins Univ, 51-52; res asst immunol, NY Med Col, 53; asst, Appl Immunol Div, Pub Health Res Inst, NY, 54-57; head sect natural & acquired resistance, Lab Immunol, Nat Inst Allergy & Infectious Dis, 57-62, head, Sect Allergy & Hypersensitivity, 63-69, head, Immunol Sect, Lab Microbiol, 70-74, OSD, 74-79, head, Exp Autoimmunity Sect, Lab Microbiol Immunity, 79-88, Immunol Allergy & Immunol Dis Prog, 88-89, Div Microbiol Infectious Dis, 89-90, Off of Dir, Div Intramural Res, 90-94. *Concurrent Pos:* Prof lectr, Howard Univ, 61-75. *Mem:* AAAS; Am Asn Immunologists; Reticuloendothelial Soc. *Res:* Tissue antigens and antibodies; mechanism of hypersensitivity; autoimmunity; transplantation immunity. *Mailing Add:* 1801 Long Corner Rd Mt Airy MD 21771. *E-Mail:* sstone@nih.gov

STONE, SHELDON LESLIE, HIGH ENERGY PHYSICS. *Current Pos:* PROF, SYRACUSE UNIV, 91- *Personal Data:* b Brooklyn, NY, Feb 14, 46; m 71; c 3. *Educ:* Brooklyn Col, BS, 67; Univ Rochester, PhD(physics), 72. *Prof Exp:* Res assoc, dept physics, Vanderbilt Univ, 72-73, asst prof, 73-79; sr res assoc, Lab Nuclear Studies, Cornell Univ, 79-91. *Concurrent Pos:* Vis fel, Lab Nuclear Studies, Cornell Univ, 77-79, adj prof, 88-91. *Mem:* Am Phys Soc; Sigma Xi. *Res:* Elementary particle interactions. *Mailing Add:* Physics Dept Syracuse Univ Syracuse NY 13244. *Fax:* 315-443-9103

STONE, SIDNEY NORMAN, OPTICAL PHYSICS, ASTROPHYSICS. *Current Pos:* RETIRED. *Personal Data:* b Rochester, NY, May 11, 22; m 51, Marcia McClain; c Susan (Mather) & Wendy (Shray). *Educ:* Univ Calif, BA, 51, MA, 52, PhD(astron), 57. *Prof Exp:* Physicist, Ballistic Res Lab, Aberdeen Proving Ground, Md, 44-49; asst astron, Univ Calif, 53-54, Lick Observ fel, 54-56; staff mem, Los Alamos Nat Lab, 57-84, consult, 84-90. *Concurrent Pos:* Teaching asst astron, Univ Calif, Berkeley, 51-53; consult, Los Alamos Tech Assocs, 84-86. *Mem:* Am Astron Soc; Astron Soc Pac; Sigma Xi. *Res:* Spectroscopy; optical instrumentation; spectroscopic binary stars; physics of the upper atmosphere; photographic sensitometry; high speed photography; radiation dosimetry. *Mailing Add:* 9112 Haines Ave NE Albuquerque NM 87112-3924

STONE, STANLEY S, BIOCHEMISTRY, IMMUNOCHEMISTRY. *Current Pos:* biochemist, Plum Island Animal Dis Lab, 57-62 & 64-66, EAfrican Vet Res Lab, 62-64, EAfrican Vet Res Orgn, 66-70 & Plum Island Animal Dis Lab, 70-71, head biochem biophys, Nat Animal Dis Ctr, 72-78, DIR, FAR EASTERN REGIONAL RES OFF, USDA, INDIA, 78- *Personal Data:* b Old Forge, Pa, Apr 4, 21; m 50; c 4. *Educ:* Loyola Col, Md, BS, 50; Georgetown Univ, MS, 53, PhD(biochem), 57. *Prof Exp:* Biochemist, USDA, 49-52; biochemist, NIH, 52-57. *Concurrent Pos:* Proj mgr, Vet Res Inst, Foreign Agr Orgn, Pakistan, 81, India. *Mem:* Am Chem Soc; Am Soc Microbiol. *Res:* Isolation and characterization of immunoglobulins from farm domestic animals, particularly immunoglobulins of the exocrine secretions; reactions of immunoglobulins with viral antigens; nutrition; biochemistry of nutrition. *Mailing Add:* 1702 Mexico Ave Tarpon Springs FL 24689-2226

STONE, WILLIAM C, mathematics; deceased, see previous edition for last biography

STONE, WILLIAM ELLIS, physiology; deceased, see previous edition for last biography

STONE, WILLIAM HAROLD, IMMUNOGENETICS & IMMUNOREPRODUCTION, MOLECULAR GENETICS. *Current Pos:* COWLES DISTINGUISHED PROF BIOL & GENETICS, TRINITY UNIV, SAN ANTONIO, 82- *Personal Data:* b Boston, Mass, Dec 15, 24; m 71, Carmen Maqueda; c Susan (Van Sidden), Debra (Nusshaum) & Alexander. *Educ:* Brown Univ, AB, 48; Univ Maine, MS, 49; Univ Wis-Madison, PhD(genetics & biochem), 53. *Hon Degrees:* ScD, Univ Cordoba, Spain, 84. *Honors & Awards:* I I Ivanov Medal, Ministry Agr, USSR, 74. *Prof Exp:* Res asst genetics, Univ Wis-Madison, 48-50, instr, 50-53, from asst prof to prof, 54-83; vis researcher immunochem, Columbia Univ, 53-54; NIH fel, Calif Inst Technol, 60-61. *Concurrent Pos:* Vis prof, Univ Barcelona, Spain, 70-71, Univ Zaragoza, 73; staff scientist, Wis Regional Primate Res Ctr, 78-83, Southwest Found Biomed Res, 83-; adj prof, Univ Tex Health Sci Ctr, San Antonio, 84-; mem, Study Sects, NIH & Pub Affairs Comt, Fed Am Socs Exp Biol. *Mem:* Genetics Soc Am; Am Genetics Asn; Soc Am Immunologists; Int Soc Animal Blood Group Res (pres, 65-68); Am Soc Primatologists; Int Primatological Soc; Transplant Soc; Am Aging Asn. *Res:* Immunogenetic research on nonhuman primates and marsupials; immunoreproduction and genetic polymorphism using molecular genetic techniques. *Mailing Add:* Dept Biol Trinity Univ 715 Stadium Dr San Antonio TX 78212-7200. *E-Mail:* wstone@vml.tucc.trinity.edu

STONE, WILLIAM JACK HANSON, plant pathology, weed science, for more information see previous edition

STONE, WILLIAM JOHN, NEPHROLOGY. *Current Pos:* PROF MED, VANDERBILT UNIV, 80- *Educ:* Johns Hopkins Univ, MD, 62. *Prof Exp:* CHIEF NEPHROL, DEPT MED, VET ADMIN MED CTR, 72- *Mailing Add:* Dept Med Vet Admin Med Ctr 1310 24th Ave S Nashville TN 37212-2637. *Fax:* 615-327-5357

STONE, WILLIAM LAWRENCE, LIPID METABOLISM. *Current Pos:* ASSOC PROF PEDIAT, E TENN STATE UNIV, JOHNSON CITY, 89-, DIR, PEDIAT RES, 89-, ADJ ASSOC PROF BIOCHEM, 90-, ADJ ASSOC PROF PHYSIOL, 91- *Personal Data:* b New York, NY, Oct 26, 44; m 68, Virginia C Richardson; c Isaac W & Nora M. *Educ:* State Univ NY, Stony Brook, BS, 55, PhD(biol), 73; Marshall Univ, WVa, MS, 68. *Prof Exp:* Phys chemist thermodyn, Dow Chem Co, Mich, 65; teacher chem, Marshall Univ Lab Sch, WVa, 58; grad asst biol, State Univ NY, Stony Brook, 68-72, grad res fel protein chem, 73; res assoc biochem, Med Sch, Duke Univ, NC, 73-75; asst res chemist nutrit, Univ Calif, Santa Cruz, 75-78; asst prof biomed sci, Meharry Med Col, Nashville, 78-89, from asst prof to assoc prof pediat & dir, Pediat Res, 84-89. *Concurrent Pos:* Am Heart Asn investr, Meharry Med Col, Nashville, 80-, prin investr, NIH grant, 80-; Nat Asn Sickle Cell Dis, Inc grant, 85; fel, USAF Summer Fac Res Prog, 84 & 85; NIH res career develop award, 86-91. *Mem:* Biophys Soc; AAAS; Am Inst Nutrit; NY Acad Sci; Soc Exp Biol; Sigma Xi. *Res:* Oxidative metabolism and its pathophysiological consequences in animals, humans and in in-vitro tissue cultures; lipid peroxidation and antioxidant nutrients on cardiovascular disease, particularly atherosclerosis; hyperbaric oxygen therapy and toxicity; enzymatic detoxification mechanisms. *Mailing Add:* Dept Pediatrics ETenn Univ James H Quillen Col Med Johnson City TN 37614-0578. *Fax:* 423-929-6158

STONE, WILLIAM ROSS, APPLIED PHYSICS, TELECOMMUNICATIONS & COMPUTER SCIENCE. *Current Pos:* PROF, STONEWARE LTD, 76- *Personal Data:* b San Diego, Calif, Aug 26, 47; m 70; c 1. *Educ:* Univ Calif, San Diego, BA, 67, MS, 73, PhD(appl physics

& info sci), 78. *Prof Exp:* Sr physicist electromagnetic field interaction, Gulf Gen Atomic Co, 69-72; sr engr computerized mgt info syst, 72-73; sr scientist ionospheric physics, Optical Propagation & Inverse Scattering Theory, Megatek Corp, 73-80; prin physicist & leader, Comput Ctr & Inverse Scattering Groups, Optical Propagation, Electromagnetic & Ionospheric Physics, Automated Inspection Appln, IRT Corp, 80-87; chief scientist, McDonnell Douglas Technologies, 89-90 & Expersoft Corp, 90-91. *Concurrent Pos:* Mem, Comn B, US Nat Comt, Int Union Radio Sci, 76, Comn G, 78, Comn F, 85, Comn A, 87; ed-in-chief, Inst Elec & Electronics Engrs Antennas & Propagation Mag, 84- *Mem:* Optical Soc Am; fel Inst Elec & Electronics Engrs; Asn Comput Mach; Soc Explor Geophysicists; Acoust Soc Am; Soc Indust & Appl Math. *Res:* Electromagnetic wave and optical propagation in the atmosphere, ionosphere and inhomogeneous and scattering media; electromagnetic theory and inverse scattering; geophysical remote probing; nuclear electromagnetic pulse generation and interaction; interactive computer systems for computation, display, management, and control. *Mailing Add:* Stoneware Ltd 1446 Vista Claridad La Jolla CA 92037

STONEBRAKER, MICHAEL R, DATA BASE MANAGEMENT SYSTEMS, OPERATING & EXPERT SYSTEMS. *Current Pos:* From asst prof to assoc prof, 71-81, PROF ELEC ENG & COMPUT SCI, UNIV CALIF, BERKELEY, 81- *Educ:* Princeton Univ, BS, 65; Univ Mich, MS, 66, PhD, 71. *Concurrent Pos:* Vis engr, Nat Bur-Stand, 72; vis prof, Pontifico Cath Univ, Brazil, 76, Univ Calif, Santa Cruz, 77-78 & Univ Grenoble, France, 84-85; United Nations Develop Prog lectr, Rangoon, Burma, 77, Bombay, India, 84; founder, consult & bd dir, Relational Technol Inc, 80-, vpres eng, 84; chmn, Asn Comput Mach Spec Interest Group Mgt of Data, 80-83. *Mem:* Nat Acad Eng. *Res:* Data base management systems; support for visualization environments and next generation distributed data base management systems. *Mailing Add:* Elec Eng & Comput Sci Dept Univ Calif Berkeley CA 94704

STONEBRAKER, PETER MICHAEL, LUBRICANT FORMULATION TECHNOLOGY, TOXICOLOGY LUBRICANTS. *Current Pos:* Res chemist, Chevron Res Co, Chevron Corp, 73-76, prod develop specialist oronite additives, Chevron Chem Co, 76-78, supvr, Engine Lubrication Div, 78-80, sr prod specialist, 80-82, area rep Latin Am, 82-84, supvr strategic analysis, 84-87, supvr prod servs, 87-91, PROD COMPLIANCE COORDR, CHEVRON CHEM CO, 91- *Personal Data:* b Glendale, Calif, Apr 18, 45; m 86, Jacqueline Bridges; c Emily, Tracy & Peter II. *Educ:* Whitworth Col, Spokane, Wash, BS, 67; Univ Wash, PhD(org chem), 73. *Concurrent Pos:* Ford Found fel, 65-67. *Mem:* Soc Automotive Engrs; Am Chem Soc; Soc Tribology & Lubrication Engrs; Soc Environ Chem & Toxicol. *Res:* Synthesis lubricating oil additives; additive formulation of crankcase engine oils; analysis of used oils; toxicology of lubricants and additives; global chemical registration; preparatuin of material safety data sheets. *Mailing Add:* Chevron Chem Co 100 Chevron Way Richmond CA 94802. *Fax:* 510-242-1054; *E-Mail:* pems@chevron.com

STONEBURNER, DANIEL LEE, MARINE SCIENCE, ZOOLOGY. *Current Pos:* SR RES ECOLOGIST, NAT PARK SERV, COLO STATE UNIV, 81- *Personal Data:* b Zanesville, Ohio, July 4, 45; m 71; c 2. *Educ:* Ind State Univ, BS, 67; Iowa State Univ, PhD(plant ecol), 70. *Prof Exp:* Regional ecologist, Nat Park Serv, Southeast Region, 74-78; res ecologist, Nat Park Serv, Univ Ga, 78-81. *Concurrent Pos:* Invited consult, Nat Marine Fisheries Sea Turtle Recovery Team 79- *Mem:* Ecol Soc Am; Am Soc Limnol & Oceanog; Am Soc Ichthyologists & Herpetologists; Int Asn Crenobiologists. *Res:* Development and application of biotelemetry equipment and techniques for marine freshwater and terrestrial organisms; heavy metal analyses of marine, terrestrial and freshwater organism tissues; freshwater and marine ecology; animal behavior and ecosystems modeling. *Mailing Add:* 185 Longview Dr Athens GA 30605

STONECYPHER, ROY W, FORESTRY, GENETICS. *Current Pos:* quant geneticist, Forestry Res Ctr, Weyerhauser Co, 72-80. *Personal Data:* b Atlanta, Ga, Mar 20, 33; m 54; c 3. *Educ:* NC State Univ, BS, 59, PhD(forestry), 66. *Prof Exp:* Proj leader, Int Paper Co, 63-67, res forester, 67-70; assoc prof forest genetics, Okla State Univ, 70-72. *Concurrent Pos:* Adj asst prof, NC State Univ, 67-70, adj prof, 76-; affil assoc prof, Univ Wash, 73-80, affil prof, 80- *Mem:* Soc Am Foresters; Sigma Xi. *Res:* Quantitative genetics work in pine populations; applied forest tree breeding; statistical analyses of forestry related research using electronic computers. *Mailing Add:* 116 NE Hillside Dr Chehalis WA 98532

STONECYPHER, THOMAS E(DWARD), CHEMICAL ENGINEERING. *Current Pos:* DIR ENG, ENG LABS, ROHM & HAAS CO, 76- *Personal Data:* b Savannah, Ga, June 20, 34; m 56; c 3. *Educ:* Ga Inst Technol, BS, 55, PhD(chem eng), 61. *Prof Exp:* Res asst, Eng Exp Sta, Ga Inst Technol, 55-58; engr, Redstone Res Labs, Rohm & Haas Co, 58-61, head appl thermodyn, 61-66, head eng serv, 66-69; prod mgr, Micromedic Systs, Inc, 70-76. *Res:* Medical instrumentation; engineering design; management. *Mailing Add:* 821 Tanna Hill Dr SE Huntsville AL 35802

STONEHAM, RICHARD GEORGE, mathematics, for more information see previous edition

STONEHILL, ELLIOTT H, MICROBIAL GENETICS, CELL BIOLOGY. *Current Pos:* geneticist & planning adminstr, 75-81, ASST DIR, NAT CANCER INST, NIH, 81- *Personal Data:* b Brooklyn, NY, Sept 22, 28; m 51; c 2. *Educ:* Col City New York, BS, 50; Brooklyn Col, MA, 56; Cornell Univ, PhD(microbiol), 65. *Prof Exp:* Res fel genetics, Gustave-Roussy Inst, France, 65-66; teaching fel microbiol genetics, Univ Sussex, Eng, 66-67; res assoc cell biol, Sloan-Kettering Inst, NY, 67-75; asst prof microbiol, Grad Sch Med Col, Cornell Univ, 68-75. *Mem:* Am Soc Microbiol; Am Soc Cell Biol; NY Acad Sci; AAAS; Am Soc Preventive Oncol; Am Asn Cancer Res. *Res:* Cellular genetic expression and the anachronistic appearance of fetal specific proteins in cancer cells of adults. *Mailing Add:* 2900 Connecticut Ave NW Washington DC 20008. *Fax:* 301-402-1508

STONEHILL, ROBERT BERRELL, INTERNAL MEDICINE, PULMONARY DISEASES. *Current Pos:* PROF MED, SCH MED, IND UNIV, INDIANAPOLIS, 67- *Personal Data:* b Philadelphia, Pa, Feb 14, 21; m 78; c 3. *Educ:* Temple Univ, BA, 42, MD, 45; Am Bd Internal Med, dipl, 56, re-cert, 74 & 80, cert pulmonary dis, 65; Am Bd Prev Med, dipl, 57. *Prof Exp:* Chief pulmonary physiol lab, Samson AFB Hosp, NY, 55-56, chief pulmonary dis serv, Wilford Hall, US Air Force Hosp, Lackland AFB, Tex, 56-61, chmn dept med, 61-67. *Concurrent Pos:* Rep to Surgeon Gen, Combined Vet Admin Armed Forces Comt Pulmonary Physiol, 56-57; rep to Surg Gen & mem exec comt, Vet Admin Armed Forces Coccidioidomycosis Coop Study Group, 58-65; gov, Am Col Chest Physicians, 62-67. *Mem:* Fel Am Col Physicians; fel Am Col Chest Physicians; fel Royal Soc Med; fel Am Col Prev Med. *Res:* Aerospace medicine; pulmonary diseases. *Mailing Add:* Ind Univ Sch Med 1100 W Michigan St Indianapolis IN 46223-0601

STONEHOCKER, GARTH HILL, SOLAR WIND, IONOSPHERE. *Current Pos:* SCIENTIST & CONSULT, UPPER ATMOSPHERIC TELECOMMUN, LIAHONA GEOCOM, 86- *Personal Data:* b Rigby, Idaho, Mar 19, 25; m 50, Jeannette Ridgway; c Anne (Pierce), Barbara (Shelton), Mark & Edward. *Educ:* Ore State Univ, BS, 53. *Honors & Awards:* Super Performance Award, Nat Oceanic & Atmospheric Admin, 63, 68 & 78; Antarctic Serv Medal, Nat Acad Sci, 66; Presidential Citation, Atomic Energy Comn, 66. *Prof Exp:* Physicist nuclear, Argonne Nat Lab, 51-55, nuclear instrument, Martin Co, 55-56, upper atmosphere, Nat Bur Stand, 56-60; elec engr, Nat Bur Stand, Inst Telecom Sci, 60-80, Army Foreign Sci & Tech Ctr, 80-87. *Concurrent Pos:* Consult, Ctr Atmospheric & Space Sci, Utah State Univ, 87- *Mem:* Am Geophys Union. *Res:* The ionospheres structure and its variation are studied and measured with the goal of benefiting radio propagation of telecommunication systems by analyzing and forecasting reliable operation for voice and data service; magnetosphere; telecommunication systems; high frequency radio propagation; expert computer system development. *Mailing Add:* PO Box 608 Hyde Park UT 84318

STONEHOUSE, HAROLD BERTRAM, geochemistry, for more information see previous edition

STONEKING, JERRY EDWARD, ENGINEERING MECHANICS, COMPUTATIONAL MECHANICS. *Current Pos:* from assoc prof to prof eng sci & mech, Univ Tenn, 75-84, head, 84-91, interim dean eng, 92-93, DEAN ENG, UNIV TENN, 93- *Personal Data:* b Cincinnati, Ohio, July 12, 42; m 67, Kaye Parnell; c Jennifer & Jeff. *Educ:* Ga Inst Technol, BS, 65; Univ Ill, Urbana, MS, 66, PhD(mechanics), 69. *Prof Exp:* Asst prof gen eng, Univ Ill, 69-70; asst prof civil eng, Clarkson Col Technol, 70-74. *Mem:* Am Soc Civil Engrs; Am Soc Mech Engrs; Sigma Xi; Soc Eng Sci; Nat Soc Prof Engrs; Am Soc Eng Educ. *Res:* Computational solid mechanics with emphasis on the analysis of ultra high precision machined structures; ultra-high-precision machining technology. *Mailing Add:* 720 Scenic Dr Knoxville TN 37919. *Fax:* 423-974-2669; *E-Mail:* stonekin@utkvx.utk.edu

STONEMAN, DAVID MCNEEL, MATHEMATICAL STATISTICS. *Current Pos:* from asst prof to prof math, 66-90, chair, Math Dept, 86-90, ASSOC DEAN, COL LETTERS & SCI, UNIV WIS, WHITEWATER, 90- *Personal Data:* b Madison, Wis, Oct 11, 39; m 64; c 2. *Educ:* Univ Wis, BS, 61, MS, 63, PhD(statist), 66. *Prof Exp:* Math statistician, Forest Prod Lab, Forest Serv, USDA, 64-66. *Mem:* Am Statist Asn. *Res:* Experimental design. *Mailing Add:* Univ Wis Whitewater 800 W Main Whitewater WI 53190

STONEMAN, WILLIAM, III, PLASTIC SURGERY. *Current Pos:* from assoc dean to dean, 73-94, prof surg & community med, 84-94 EMER DEAN, ST LOUIS UNIV SCH MED, 94-, EMER PROF SURGERY & COMMUNITY MED, 94- *Personal Data:* b Kansas City, Mo, Sept 8, 27; m 51, Bette Jo Wilson; c William Laurence, Sidney Camdon, Cecily Anne, Elizabeth Wilson & John Spalding. *Educ:* St Louis Univ, BS, 48, MD, 52. *Prof Exp:* Dir, Bi-State Reg Med Prog, 69-74. *Concurrent Pos:* Assoc vpres, St Louis Univ Med Ctr, 83-94; chmn, Midwest/Great Plains Sect Coun Deans, Asn Am Med Cols, 86-94; mem, sect Med Sch Gov Coun, AMA, 86-94, chmn, 88, Sect Med Sch Task Force Sect Planning, 87-88. *Mem:* Am Col Surgeons; Am Soc Plastic & Reconstructive Surgeons; AMA. *Res:* Plastic and reconstructive surgery; health care delivery issues. *Mailing Add:* St Louis Univ Sch Med 1402 S Grand Blvd St Louis MO 63104-1004. *Fax:* 314-367-3370; *E-Mail:* stoneman@slovca.slu.edu

STONER, ADAIR, ENTOMOLOGY. *Current Pos:* RETIRED. *Personal Data:* b Oklahoma City, Okla, Oct 15, 28; m 53; c 2. *Educ:* Okla State Univ, BS, 56, MS, 60. *Prof Exp:* Entomologist, Pest Control Div, USDA, 58-60, entomologist, Western Cotton Insect Invests, Cotton Insect Br, Entom Res Div, 60-67, res entomologist, 67-72, res entomologist, Western Cotton Res Lab, 72-75, res entomologist, Honey Bee Pesticides/Dis Res, Sci & Educ Admin-Agr Res Serv, 75-85. *Mem:* Entom Soc Am. *Res:* Effects of pesticides on honey bees. *Mailing Add:* 702 S 24th St Laramie WY 82070-4919

STONER, ALLAN K, HORTICULTURE. *Current Pos:* Horticulturist, Crops Res Div, Plant Indust Sta, USDA Agr Res Ctr, 65-71, Veg Lab, Agr Res Ctr, 71-88, chmn, Plant Genetics & Germplasm Inst, 81-88, RES LEADER, NAT GERMPLASM RESOURCES LAB, USDA AGR RES CTR, 88- *Personal Data:* b Muncie, Ind, July 6, 39; m 62; c 2. *Educ:* Purdue Univ, West Lafayette, BS, 61, MS, 63; Univ Ill, PhD(hort), 65. *Mem:* Fel Am Soc Hort Sci. *Res:* Vegetable breeding and production; breeding of tomatoes; plant germplasm collection and maintenance. *Mailing Add:* Nat Germplasm Resources Lab USDA Agr Res Ctr-W Beltsville MD 20705-2350

STONER, ALLAN WILBUR, PHYSICAL CHEMISTRY. *Current Pos:* SR VPRES, POWER TRANSMISSION DIV, GATES CORP. *Personal Data:* b Tipton, Ind, Sept 15, 31; m 58; c 3. *Educ:* Ind Univ, BS, 53; Univ Calif, PhD(chem), 56. *Prof Exp:* Res scientist, Res Ctr, Uniroyal, Inc, 56-58, res scientist, Indust Reactor Labs, 58-60, fiber develop mgr, Fiber & Textile Div, 60-66, plant mgr, NC, 66-69, mgr res & develop, Plastic Prod, Ind, 69-71, dir res & develop, Plastic & Indust Prod Div, Oxford Mgt & Res Ctr, 71-73, dir mkt, Indust Prod Div, Oxford Mgt & Res Ctr, 73- *Mem:* Am Chem Soc. *Res:* Nuclear physics and spectroscopy; radiochemistry; application of tracers; radiation and polymer chemistry; physical properties of fibers and elastomeric materials. *Mailing Add:* Gates Corp PO Box 5887 Denver CO 80209-5887

STONER, CLINTON DALE, BIOCHEMISTRY. *Current Pos:* asst prof, 65-69, ASSOC PROF BIOCHEM RES, DEPT SURG, OHIO STATE UNIV, 69- *Personal Data:* b Mellette, SDak, Feb 8, 33; m 65, Elaine Blatt; c Robert & Michael. *Educ:* SDak State Univ, BS, 57, MS, 60; Univ Ill, PhD(agron), 65. *Prof Exp:* Trainee biochem res, Inst Enzyme Res, Univ Wis, 64-65. *Mem:* Am Soc Biochem & Molecular Biol; Biochem Soc; AAAS; Am Phys Soc. *Res:* Structure and function of mitochondria; steady-state kinetics of multienzyme reactions; relationships between kinetics and thermodynamics in multienzyme reactions; nature of free energy and entropy. *Mailing Add:* Ohio State Univ 400 W 12th Ave Columbus OH 43210-1218

STONER, ELAINE CAROL BLATT, PHYSICAL CHEMISTRY. *Current Pos:* asst ed electrochem & anal chem elec phenomena, 65-68, from assoc ed to sr ed elec phenomena, 68-85, SR ED PATENT SERV PHYS CHEM, CHEM ABSTR SERV, AM CHEM SOC, 85- *Personal Data:* b New York, NY, Dec 31, 39; m 65, Clinton D; c Robert & Michael. *Educ:* Brooklyn Col, BS, 61; Univ Calif, Berkeley, PhD(chem), 65. *Prof Exp:* NIH fel, Univ Wis, 64-65. *Mem:* Am Chem Soc; Sigma Xi. *Res:* Nuclear magnetic resonance of exchange rates of ligands in coordination complexes. *Mailing Add:* Chem Abstr Serv Dept 57 Columbus OH 43210

STONER, GARY DAVID, CHEMICAL CARCINOGENESIS, CHEMOPREVENTION. *Current Pos:* dir, Basic Sci Prog, Comprehensive Cancer Ctr, 93, PROF & CHAIR, DIV ENVIRON HEALTH SCI, SCH PUB HEALTH, OHIO STATE UNIV, 92- *Personal Data:* b Bozeman, Mont, Oct 25, 42; m 69, Natalie Moser; c Jason & Sean. *Educ:* Mont State Univ, BS, 64; Univ Mich, MS, 68, PhD(microbiol), 70. *Honors & Awards:* Young Investr Award, NIH, Merit Award; Simson Award. *Prof Exp:* Asst res scientist, Univ Calif, San Diego, 70-72, assoc res scientist, 72-75; cancer expert, Nat Cancer Inst, 76-79; assoc prof path, Med Col Ohio, 79-84, prof, 84-92, asst dean spec prog, 87-92. *Concurrent Pos:* Consult, Nat Heart Lung & Blood Inst, 74-79, Environ Protection Agency, 81-, Food & Drug Admin, 90-, Chinese Acad Med Sci, 92-; lectr, W Alton Jones Cell Sci Ctr, 78-; mem, Am Cancer Soc Study Sect, Ohio, 82-91, NIH Study Sect, 88-92, 95-; prin investr grants, Nat Cancer Inst, Environ Protection Agency & US Army Res & Develop Command. *Mem:* Am Asn Cancer Res; Am Tissue Cult Asn; Am Asn Pathologists; Am Soc Cell Biol; AAAS; Europ Asn Cancer Res; Soc Toxicol. *Res:* Carcinogenesis studies in human and animal model respiratory and esophageal tissues; molecular events in tumor development; chemoprevention of lung and esophageal cancer. *Mailing Add:* Div Environ Health Sci Sch Pub Health Ohio State Univ 1148 CHRI 300 W Tenth Ave Columbus OH 43210. *Fax:* 614-293-3333; *E-Mail:* stoner.21@osu.edu

STONER, GEORGE GREEN, modern metric system; deceased, see previous edition for last biography

STONER, GLENN EARL, ELECTROCHEMISTRY. *Current Pos:* res assoc prof mat sci, ASSOC PROF, UNIV VA, 77- *Personal Data:* b Springfield, Mo, Oct 26, 40; m 62; c 3. *Educ:* Univ Mo-Rolla, BS, 62, MS, 63; Univ Pa, PhD(chem), 68. *Honors & Awards:* Cert Recognition, NASA, 75. *Prof Exp:* Sr scientist mat sci, Sch Eng, Univ Va, 68-71; vis assoc prof chem, Univ Mo-Rolla, 71; lectr chem eng, Univ Va, 71-72; sr scientist mat sci, 72-73; vis assoc prof electrochem, Fac Sci, Univ Rouen, France, 73-74. *Concurrent Pos:* Consult, Owens-Ill, Inc, 75- *Mem:* Electrochem Soc. *Res:* Applied research in bioelectrochemistry and biomaterials research; interaction with industry towards development of innovative concepts. *Mailing Add:* Mat Sci Thornton Hall Univ Va Charlottesville VA 22903

STONER, GRAHAM ALEXANDER, ANALYTICAL CHEMISTRY, AGRICULTURAL CHEMISTRY. *Current Pos:* PRES, AGTROL CHEM PROD, 85- *Personal Data:* b Saginaw, Mich, June 13, 29; m 55; c 4. *Educ:* Univ Mich, BS, 51, MS, 52; Tulane Univ La, PhD(chem), 56. *Prof Exp:* Chemist, Dow Chem Co, 55-58, proj leader, 58-60; chemist, Ethyl Corp, 60-62; mgr analytical chem, Bioferm Div, Int Minerals & Chem Corp, Calif, 62-64, assoc dir analytic labs, Chem Div, 64-67; dir analytical & tech serv, IMC Growth Sci Ctr, Ill, 67-69; plant mgr, Infotronics Corp, Tex, 69-70; dir res & develop spec prod div, Kennecott Copper Corp, 70-74; vpres technol, 74-75, vpres, 75-79, sr vpres mkt & develop, Kocide Chem Corp, 79-85. *Concurrent Pos:* Guest scientist, Brookhaven Nat Lab, 56-57. *Mem:* AAAS; Am Chem Soc; Sigma Xi; NY Acad Sci. *Res:* Pesticide research, testing, registration, formulation; governmental regulations; analytical-physical chemistry; enzymatic methods of analysis; automated analysis; radiochemistry. *Mailing Add:* 6606 Redding Rd Houston TX 77036

STONER, JOHN CLARK, veterinary medicine, for more information see previous edition

STONER, JOHN OLIVER, JR, ATOMIC SPECTROSCOPY. *Current Pos:* from asst prof to assoc prof, 67-76, PROF PHYSICS, UNIV ARIZ, 76- *Personal Data:* b Milton, Mass, Oct 4, 36; m 60; c 4. *Educ:* Pa State Univ, BS, 58; Princeton Univ, MA, 59, PhD(physics), 64. *Prof Exp:* Res assoc physics, Univ Wis, 63-66, asst prof, 66-67. *Mem:* Am Phys Soc; Int Soc Optical Eng; Soc Vacuum Coaters; Mat Res Asn. *Res:* Properties of, and techniques for, producing ultra-thin metal and carbon foils. *Mailing Add:* Ariz Carbon Foil Co Inc 2239 E Kleindale Rd Tucson AZ 85719

STONER, LARRY CLINTON, RENAL PHYSIOLOGY. *Current Pos:* PROF RENAL PHYSIOL, STATE UNIV NY HEALTH SCI CTR, 88- *Personal Data:* b Mt Union, Pa, May 17, 43; m 66, Louise Wian; c Michael & Christopher. *Educ:* Juniata Col, BS, 65; Syracuse Univ, PhD(zool), 70. *Prof Exp:* Fel renal physiol, Nat Heart & Lung Inst, 70-72, staff fel, 72-75. *Concurrent Pos:* Fel, USPHS, 70-72; investr, Am Heart Asn grant, 75-; prin investr, Nat Inst Arthritis, Metab & Digestive Dis, grant, 77- *Mem:* Am Physiol Soc; Am Soc Nephrology. *Res:* Mechanisms of ion transport. *Mailing Add:* Dept Physiol State Univ NY Health Sci Ctr 766 Irving Ave Syracuse NY 13210. *Fax:* 315-464-7712

STONER, MARSHALL ROBERT, ORGANIC CHEMISTRY. *Current Pos:* From asst prof to assoc prof, 64-81, PROF CHEM, UNIV SDAK, 81- *Personal Data:* b Kenesaw, Nebr, Sept 24, 38. *Educ:* Hastings Col, BA, 60; Iowa State Univ, PhD(chem), 64. *Concurrent Pos:* Adj vis prof, Univ Kans, 82-83. *Mem:* AAAS; Am Chem Soc; Royal Soc Chem; Sigma Xi. *Res:* Synthesis and rearrangements of bicyclic compounds; photochemical reactions of alcohols with unsaturated acids; photochemistry of benzyl phosphates. *Mailing Add:* Dept Chem Univ SDak Vermillion SD 57069. *E-Mail:* rstoner@sundance.usd.edu

STONER, MARTIN FRANKLIN, PLANT PATHOLOGY, MYCOLOGY. *Current Pos:* From asst prof to assoc prof, 67-75, PROF BOT, CALIF STATE POLYTECH UNIV, POMONA, 75- *Personal Data:* b Pasadena, Calif, Jan 19, 42; m 63. *Educ:* Calif State Polytech Col, BS, 63; Wash State Univ, PhD(plant path), 67. *Concurrent Pos:* vis prof, researcher & exten path, Univ Hawaii, 80-81. *Mem:* AAAS; Am Phytopath Soc; Bot Soc Am; Mycol Soc Am. *Res:* Agroecosystems; soil-borne fungi; microbial ecology; general plant pathology and mycology; diseases of nursery crops; mycology of sewage sludge; biotechnology. *Mailing Add:* Dept Biol Sci Calif State Polytech Univ 3801 W Temple Ave Pomona CA 91768

STONER, RICHARD DEAN, IMMUNOLOGY. *Current Pos:* Jr scientist, 50-52, assoc med bacteriologist, 52-54, from asst scientist to scientist, 52-62, SR SCIENTIST, MED DEPT, BROOKHAVEN NAT LAB, 62- *Personal Data:* b Newhall, Iowa, Mar 29, 19; m 45; c 2. *Educ:* Univ Iowa, BA, 40, PhD(zool), 50. *Concurrent Pos:* Consult, Off Surgeon Gen & Dep Dir Comn on Radiation & Infection, Armed Forces Epidemiol Bd, 63- *Mem:* Am Inst Biol Sci; Am Soc Microbiol; Radiation Res Soc; Am Soc Parasitol; Am Soc Exp Pathologists. *Res:* Radiation effect upon immune mechanisms; antibody formation; cellular defense mechanism; anaphylaxis; immunity to parasitic infections. *Mailing Add:* Med Dept Brookhaven Nat Lab Upton NY 11973-9999

STONER, RONALD EDWARD, THEORY ACTIVE GALAXIES. *Current Pos:* From asst prof to assoc prof, 66-74, chmn dept, 76-80, PROF PHYSICS, BOWLING GREEN STATE UNIV, 74- *Personal Data:* b Indianapolis, Ind, Nov 25, 37; m 60, Jeanne Smith; c Gwynne S (Rife) & Holly S (Bielawa). *Educ:* Wabash Col, BA, 59; Purdue Univ, MS, 61, PhD(physics), 66. *Honors & Awards:* Fulbright lectr, Sri Lanka, 80-81. *Concurrent Pos:* NASA Grant. *Mem:* Am Astron Soc; Am Phys Soc; Sigma Xi; Am Asn Univ Professors; AAAS. *Res:* Astrophysics; computational physics; theoretical physics. *Mailing Add:* Dept Physics & Astron Bowling Green State Univ Bowling Green OH 43403. *Fax:* 419-372-9938

STONER, WILLIAM WEBER, OPTICAL PHYSICS, REMOTE SENSING. *Current Pos:* mem staff analog & digital signal processing, 77-87, SR SCIENTIST, SCI APPLNS INT CORP, 87- *Personal Data:* b Columbus, Ohio, June 4, 44; m 78, Joan L Sauter; c Pamela K & Julia C. *Educ:* Union Col, NY, BS, 66; Princeton Univ, PhD(physics), 75. *Prof Exp:* Scientist radiol, Machlett Labs, Raytheon, Inc Stamford, Conn, 73-75, scientist nuclear med, Raytheon Res Div, 75-76. *Mem:* Optical Soc Am; Int Soc Optical Eng; AAAS. *Res:* Remote sensing in visible and infrared spectral bands; imaging spectrometry; optical system design. *Mailing Add:* Sci Applns Int Corp 20 Burlington Mall Rd Suite 130 Burlington MA 01803-4126. *E-Mail:* wotoner@bos.saic.com

STONES, ROBERT C, ENVIRONMENTAL PHYSIOLOGY. *Current Pos:* From asst prof to assoc prof, 64-70, head, Dept Biol Sci, 70-81, PROF PHYSIOL, MICH TECHNOL UNIV, 70-, VOC REHAB COUNR, 87- *Personal Data:* b Portland, Ore, May 19, 37; m 57; c 8. *Educ:* Brigham Young Univ, BS, 59, MS, 60; Purdue Univ, West Lafayette, PhD(environ physiol),

64. *Concurrent Pos:* Mem, Hibernation Info Exchange, 64-; NSF res grants, 67-71. *Mem:* Am Asn Higher Educ; Nat Asn Biol Teachers; Am Forestry Asn; Am Soc Mammal; Australian Soc Mammal. *Res:* Thermal regulation of hibernating species of bats; comparative and animal physiology; comparative anatomy. *Mailing Add:* 6396 SW McVey Ave Redmond OR 97756

STONEY, SAMUEL DAVID, JR, NEUROSCIENCE. *Current Pos:* NIH res grant, 70, asst prof, 70-74, ASSOC PROF PHYSIOL, MED COL GA, 74- *Personal Data:* b Charleston, SC, Dec 20, 39; m 59; c 2. *Educ:* Univ SC, BS, 62; Tulane Univ, PhD(physiol), 66. *Prof Exp:* From instr to asst prof physiol, New York Med Col, 66-70. *Mem:* Am Physiol Soc. *Res:* Electrophysiological studies of the organization of motor sensory cortex and pyramidal motor systems. *Mailing Add:* Dept Physiol Med Col Ga Sch Med 1120 15th St Augusta GA 30901-3181

STONG, DAVID BRUCE, DRUG METABOLISM, PHARMACO & TOXICO KINETICS. *Current Pos:* ASSOC DIR, DRUG SAFETY & DISPOSITION, CEPHALON INC, 91- *Personal Data:* b Lafayette, Ind, May 24, 52; m 74, Saundra L Dunlavey; c Hillary L & Ryan D. *Educ:* Purdue Univ, Lafayette, BS, 74; Univ Cincinnati, PhD(toxicol), 84. *Prof Exp:* Techserv chemist, Eli Lilly & Co, 74-79; sr scientist drug metab, Pennwalt Pharmaceut, 84-86; sr biochemist, Eastman Kodak-Eastman Pharmaceut, 86-88; prin res scientist, Sterling Drug, 88-91. *Res:* Mechanistic aspects of toxicology, especially as related to in vivo blood or tissue concentrations and the relationship of toxicity or to the metabolism and biochemistry of the toxicant. *Mailing Add:* RD 7 Reid Rd PO Box 193B Coatesville PA 19320

ST-ONGE, DENIS ALDERIC, GEOMORPHOLOGY. *Current Pos:* dir, Terrain Sci, 87-91, RES SCIENTIST, GEOL SURV CAN, 84-, SR SCIENTIST, POLAR CONTINENTAL SHELF PROJ, 91- *Personal Data:* b Ste-Agathe, Man, May 11, 29; m 55, Jeanne M Behaegel; c Marc Robert & Nicole J M. *Educ:* St-Boniface Col, Man, BA, 51; Cath Univ, Louvain, LicSc, 57, DocSc(geog), 62. *Hon Degrees:* DSc, Univ Man, 90. *Honors & Awards:* Recipient Medal, Queen Elizabeth II, 79; Medal A Cailleux, 91; Medal Can 125, 92; Medal Royal Scottish Geog Soc, 94. *Prof Exp:* Teacher elem sch, Sask, 51-52; teacher high sch, Ethiopia, 53-55; teacher, Col Jean de Brebeuf, Montreal, 57-58; geographer, Geog Br, Dept Mines & Technol Surv, 58-65; res scientist, Geol Surv Can, 65-68; prof geomorphol, Univ Ottawa, 68-70, 73-77 & 80-84, vdean, Grad Sch, 77-80; res scientist, Geol Surv Can, 70-73. *Concurrent Pos:* Nat Res Coun Can-NATO fel, 61-62; prof, Dept Geog, Univ Ottawa, 70-74. *Mem:* Fel Geol Asn Can; Can Asn Geog; Int Geog Union; Royal Can Geog Soc (pres, 92-); Artic Inst N Am. *Res:* Quaternary geology; geology and planning; geomorphology. *Mailing Add:* Polar Continental Shelf Proj 615 Booth St Ottawa ON K1A 0E9 Can. *Fax:* 613-947-1611; *E-Mail:* dst-orge@gse.nrean.gc.ca

STONIER, TOM TED, EVOLUTION OF SOCIETY, COMPUTER APPLICATIONS. *Current Pos:* CHMN, VALIANT TECHNOL, 88- *Personal Data:* b Hamburg, Ger, Apr 29, 27; nat US; m 72; c 5. *Educ:* Drew Univ, AB, 50; Yale Univ, MS, 51, PhD, 55. *Prof Exp:* Asst, Yale Univ, 51-52; jr res assoc biol, Brookhaven Nat Lab, 52-54; vis investr, Rockefeller Inst, 54-57, res assoc, 57-62; assoc prof biol, Manhattan Col, 62-71; prof biol & dir peace studies prog, 71-75; prof & chmn sci & soc, Univ Bradford, 75-90, pres, Appl Systs Knowledge, 82-85. *Concurrent Pos:* USPHS fel, 54-56; Damon Runyon Mem fel, 56-57; consult, Living Sci Labs, 61-62, Hudson Inst, 65-69, MacMillan Co, 68, Environ Defense Fund, 68-70 & Drew Univ, 69-71; instr, New Sch Social Res, 68-70 & State Univ NY Col Purchase, 72; vis prof, Bradford Univ, 90- *Mem:* AAAS; Am Soc Plant Physiol; Fedn Am Sci (secy, 66-67); NY Acad Sci; fel Royal Soc Arts; Sigma Xi; Soc Develop Biol. *Res:* Impact of science and technology on society; use of computers in education; information theory; technological forecasting; cell physiology of plant growth, cancer and aging; information theory. *Mailing Add:* 5 The Ave South Egremont MA 01258

STOOKEY, GEORGE K, DENTISTRY. *Current Pos:* Dir lab res, 63-64, asst dir, Prev Dent Res Inst, 69-72, exec secy, Oral Health Res Inst, 72-74, from asst prof to assoc prof, 64-78, assoc dir, Oral Health Res Inst, 74-81, PROF PREV DENT, SCH DENT, IND UNIV-PURDUE UNIV, INDIANAPOLIS, 64-, DIR, ORAL HEALTH RES INST, 81-, ASSOC DEAN RES, 87- *Personal Data:* b Waterloo, Ind, Nov 6, 35; m 55; c Lynda M (Howard), Lisa A (Hoover), Laura J (Bone) & Kenneth R. *Educ:* Ind Univ, AB, 57, MS, 62, PhD, 71. *Honors & Awards:* Eldon B Cox Mem Award, Am Asn Lab Animal Sci, 91. *Mem:* Am Asn Lab Animal Sci; Int Asn Dent Res; Am Dent Asn; Europ Orgn Caries Res; Fed Dent Int. *Res:* Metabolism of fluoride and other trace elements in experimental animals and humans; various types of dental caries preventive measures, including fluorides and various aspects of nutrition. *Mailing Add:* Ind Univ Sch Dent Oral Health Res Inst 415 Lansing St Indianapolis IN 46202-2876. *Fax:* 317-274-5425; *E-Mail:* gstookey@iusd.iupui.edu

STOOKEY, STANLEY DONALD, PHYSICAL CHEMISTRY, GLASS-CERAMICS. *Current Pos:* RETIRED. *Personal Data:* b Hay Spring, Nebr, May 23, 15; wid; c Robert, Margaret & Donald. *Educ:* Coe Col, AB, 36; Lafayette Col, MS, 37; Mass Inst Technol, PhD(phys chem), 40. *Hon Degrees:* DSc, Coe Col, SC Alfred Univ. *Honors & Awards:* Nat Medal of Technol, 76. *Prof Exp:* Res chemist, Corning Inc, Glass Works, 40-58, mgr fundamental chem res, 58-62, dir fundamental chem res, 60-79. *Mem:* Nat Acad Eng; Am Ceramic Soc; Am Chem Soc. *Res:* Glass composition; photosensitive, photochromic and opal glasses; glass ceramics; 64 patents, numerous publication and awards. *Mailing Add:* 714 Helmsman Lane Edgewater FL 32132

STOOLMAN, LEO, aerospace engineering, for more information see previous edition

STOOLMILLER, ALLEN CHARLES, BIOCHEMISTRY, RESEARCH ADMINISTRATION. *Current Pos:* health scientist adminr, Div Res Grants, 79-89, HEALTH SCIENTIST ADMINR, SCI REV PROG, NAT INST ALLERGY & INFECTIOUS DIS, NIH, 90- *Personal Data:* b Battle Creek, Mich, Nov 3, 40; m 92, Marilyn A Ward; c Scott A & Amy L (Lott). *Educ:* Western Res Univ, AB, 61; Univ Mich, MA, 64, PhD(biochem), 66. *Prof Exp:* Fel, Chicago & Ill Heart Asns, 66-68; instr pediat, Univ Chicago, 68-69, asst prof pediat & res assoc biochem, Dept Pediat & La Rabida Inst, 69-76; assoc biochemist, Eunice Kennedy Shriver Ctr Ment Retardation, 76-79. *Mem:* Am Soc Biochem & Molecular Biol; AAAS; Am Soc Neurochem; Sigma Xi; Nat Coun Univ Res Adminr. *Res:* Supervise review of research grant applications and contract proposals for research programs and special developmental programs supported by the National Institute of Allergy and Infectious Diseases. *Mailing Add:* Nat Inst Allergy & Infectious Dis NIH Solar Bldg Rm 4C-05 Bethesda MD 20892. *Fax:* 301-402-2638; *E-Mail:* as30q@nih.gov

STOOPS, CHARLES E(MMET), JR, NUCLEAR ENGINEERING. *Current Pos:* from assoc prof to prof, 67-85, actg chmn & chmn dept, 67-72, EMER PROF CHEM ENG, UNIV TOLEDO, 85- *Personal Data:* b Grove City, Pa, Dec 17, 14; m 43; c 3. *Educ:* Ohio State Univ, BChE, 37; Purdue Univ, PhD(chem eng), 42. *Prof Exp:* Plant & develop engr, Oldbury Electrochem Co, NY, 41-42; asst prof chem eng, Lehigh Univ, 42-44; process engr, Publicker Alcohol Co, Pa, 44; sr chem engr, Phillips Petrol Co, Okla, 44-47; prof chem eng & head dept, Clemson Col, 47-48; sr chem engr, Phillips Petrol Co, 48-52, proj engr, 52-54, chief chem eng develop, Atomic Energy Div, Idaho Falls, 54-55, mgr radiation chem sect, 55-67. *Mem:* AAAS; Am Chem Soc; Am Inst Chem Engrs; Nat Soc Prof Engrs; Am Soc Eng Educ. *Res:* Mixing; aromatic alkylation; nitrogen compounds; catalysis; nuclear engineering; photochemistry; radiation chemistry. *Mailing Add:* 371 Beryl Ave Mansfield OH 44907

STOOPS, JAMES KING, BIOCHEMISTRY. *Current Pos:* ASSOC PROF, UNIV TEX HEALTH SCI CTR, HOUSTON, 90- *Personal Data:* b Charleston, WVa, Sept 15, 37; m 62, Pamela A Moore; c Mary & Timothy. *Educ:* Duke Univ, BS, 60; Northwestern Univ, Evanston, PhD(chem), 66. *Prof Exp:* Sr demonstr biochem, Univ Queensland, 66-67, Australian Res Comt grants fel biochem, 67-70; NIMH fel, Duke Univ, 70-71; from asst prof to assoc prof, Baylor Col Med, 71-90. *Concurrent Pos:* Adj assoc prof, Baylor Col Med, 90- *Mem:* Am Chem Soc; Am Soc Biol Chemists; AAAS; NY Acad Sci. *Res:* Enzymology and protein chemistry; electron microscopy of macromolecules. *Mailing Add:* Dept Path Univ Tex Health Sci Ctr Houston TX 77030. *Fax:* 713-794-4149; *E-Mail:* stoops@casper.med.uth.tmc.edu

STOOPS, R(OBERT) F(RANKLIN), CERAMIC ENGINEERING, MATERIALS SCIENCE. *Current Pos:* RETIRED. *Personal Data:* b Winona, WVa, June 16, 21; m 44, Martha S Sprouse; c Carol (LaFone) & Robert F Jr. *Educ:* NC State Col, BSc, 49; Ohio State Univ, MSc, 50, PhD(ceramic eng), 51. *Prof Exp:* Res engr, Harbison-Walker Refractories Co, 51-52; res engr, Metall Prod Dept, Gen Elec Co, 52-57, sr res engr, 58; res prof ceramic eng, NC State Univ, 58-81, dir, Eng Res Servs Div, 67-81, prof & assoc head, Dept Mat Eng, 81-85. *Mem:* fel Am Ceramic Soc; Inst Ceramic Engrs. *Res:* Refractory oxides and carbides and combinations of these with metals; self-glazing ceramic-metal systems; effect of structure on properties of materials; nuclear fuel materials; ceramic forming processes. *Mailing Add:* 200 W Cornwall Rd Cottage No 123 Cary NC 27511-3802

STOPFORD, WOODHALL, INTERNAL MEDICINE, CLINICAL TOXICOLOGY. *Current Pos:* CLIN ASST PROF, DUKE MED CTR, 73- *Personal Data:* b Jersey City, NJ, Feb 25, 43; m 66. *Educ:* Dartmouth Col, BA, 65; Dartmouth Med Sch, BMS, 67; Harvard Univ, MD, 69; Univ NC, MSPH, 80. *Concurrent Pos:* Mem, Am Conf Govt Indust Hyg. *Mem:* Fel Am Col Occup Med; Am Indust Hyg Asn; AMA. *Res:* Clinical toxicologic studies of heavy metal and chlorinated hydrocarbon exposures; art hazards; airway reactivity after irritant gas exposures. *Mailing Add:* Duke Med Ctr PO Box 3834 Durham NC 27710-0001. *Fax:* 919-286-5647; *E-Mail:* stopf001@mc.duke.edu

STOPHER, PETER ROBERT, CIVIL AND TRANSPORTATION. *Current Pos:* dir, La Transp Res Ctr, 90-93, PROF CIVIL & ENVIRON ENG, LA STATE UNIV, 90-; FOUNDING PARTNER & CHIEF FINANCIAL OFFICER, PLANTRANS, 94- *Personal Data:* b Crowborough, Eng, Aug 8, 43; m 90, Cathy Jones; c Helen M (Metcalf) & Claire. *Educ:* Univ London, BSc, 64, PhD(traffic studies), 67. *Honors & Awards:* Fred Burgraaf Award, Hwy Res Bd, Nat Acad Sci-Nat Res Coun, 70; Jules Dupuit Prize, World Conf Transp Res, 92. *Prof Exp:* Res officer hwy & transp, Greater London Coun, 67-68; asst prof transp planning, Northwestern Univ, 68-70 & McMaster Univ, 70-71; assoc prof, Dept Environ Eng, Cornell Univ, 71-73; assoc prof civil eng, Northwestern Univ, 73-77, prof, 77-80; vpres, Schimpler-Corradino Assoc, 80-87; dir transp planning & econ studies, Eval & Training Inst, 87-90; prin, Appl Mgt & Planning Group, 89-90. *Concurrent Pos:* Consult various industs, 69-; Nat Res Coun Can & Dept Univ Affairs Ont grants, McMaster Univ, 70-71; chmn comt on traveler behav & values, Hwy Res Bd, Nat Acad Sci-Nat Res Coun, 71-77, consult, Planning Res Corp & Int Bank Reconstruct & Develop, 72-80, mem Transp Res Forum; consult, US Environ Protection Agency, 74; dir res, Transp Ctr, Northwestern Univ, 75-77; transp adv, Nat Inst Transp & Rd Res, SAfrica, 77-78; US area ed, Transp Rev, 79-84 & 91- *Mem:* Am Soc Civil Engrs; Inst Transp Engrs; Transp Res Forum; Am Statist Asn; Transp Res Bd. *Res:* Transportation planning techniques; mathematical modeling of travel demand; applied statistics; survey techniques; impact of transportation facilities on communities and the environment. *Mailing Add:* Dept Civil & Environ Eng L A State Univ Baton Rouge LA 70803-6405. *Fax:* 504-388-8652; *E-Mail:* tpstop@unix1.sncc.lsu.edu, ptrans__stop@msn.com

STOPKIE, ROGER JOHN, MICROBIOLOGY, BIOCHEMISTRY. *Current Pos:* DIR, DRUG DEVELOP, ZENECA PHARMACEUT GROUP, 86- *Personal Data:* b Perth Amboy, NJ, July 17, 39; m 62, Joelle; c Marc V. *Educ:* St Lawrence Univ, BS, 61; St Louis Univ, PhD(microbial physiol), 68. *Prof Exp:* Res asst biochem & microbiol, Merck & Co, 62-64; res biochemist, ICI US Inc, 69-75, sr res & info scientist, 75-76, pharmaceut develop coordr, 76-79, drug develop mgr, Stuart pharmaceut, ICI Americas Inc, 79-86. *Mem:* AAAS; Am Soc Microbiologists; Am Chem Soc; Sigma Xi; Drug Info Asn; Proj Mgt Inst; NY Acad Sci. *Res:* Biology of mycoplasma; information systems; enzyme regulation; pharmaceutical project management and administration; drug development. *Mailing Add:* Zeneca Pharmaceut Group 1800 Concord Pike Wilmington DE 19897. Fax: 302-886-2462

STOPPANI, ANDRES OSCAR MANUEL, ENZYMOLOGY, CELL BIOENERGETICS. *Current Pos:* PRIN CAREER INVESTR, SUPER CLASS, NAT RES COUN, ARG, 60-, DIR, BIOENERGETICS RES CTR, 80-; EMER PROF BIOCHEM, SCH MED, UNIV BUENOS AIRES, ARG, 81- *Personal Data:* b Buenos Aires, Rep Arg, Aug 19, 15; m 67, Antonia Delius. *Educ:* Univ Buenos Aires, MD, 41, PhD(chem), 45; Univ Cambridge, PhD(biochem), 53. *Honors & Awards:* Weissman Prize, Nat Res Coun, Arg, 62, Campomar Prize, 70; Bunge-Born Prize, Bunge-Born Found, Arg, 80; J J Kyle Prize, Arg Chem Soc, Arg, 87; B A Houssay Inter Am Sci Prize, Am States Orgn, 89; Nat Sci Prize, Arg, 93. *Prof Exp:* Prof biochem, Univ La Plata, Arg, 48-49; prof biochem, Sch Med, Univ Buenos Aires, Arg, 49-81, dir, Dept Physiol Sci, 70-80. *Concurrent Pos:* Vis profr, Inst Ciencias, Paraguay, Multinat Prog Biochem, Org Am States, 72; dir, Energy-Transducing Membranes Course, ICRO-UNESCO, 75, Bioenergetics Res Ctr, Nat Res Coun, Arg, 81-; mem, Chemother Chagas Dis Comt, TDR, WHO, 79-82, adv res coun, Pan Am Health Orgn, 80-83; exec secy, Nat Prog Endemic Dis, Secy State Sci & Technol, Arg, 83-88; pres, Nat Acad Med, Buenos Aires; past-pres, Nat Acad Exact, Physical & Nature Sci, 90-92. *Mem:* Fel AAAS; Am Chem Soc; Arg Asn Advan Sci (pres, 60-62); Arg Soc Protozoologists (pres, 80-81); Arg Soc Biol (pres, 70-76 & 80-84); Soc Exp Biol & Med; Am Soc Biol Chemists; NY Acad Sci; Int Physicians Prev Nuclear War; Int Cell Res Orgn; Am Soc Biochem & Molecular Biol; Am Soc Cell Biol; Am Soc Microbiol; Oxygen Soc. *Res:* Enzymology of Trypanosoma cruzi (the agent of American trypanosomiasis) and related organisms, in connection with the effect of oxy-radicals as a basis for the development of new trypanocidal agents; enzymology and transport phenomena in the yeast Saccharomyces and on the effect of steroid hormones on mitochondrial bioenergetics; author of over 300 research papers and several books. *Mailing Add:* Viamonte 2295 Buenos Aires 1056 Argentina

STORAASLI, JOHN PHILLIP, medicine; deceased, see previous edition for last biography

STORB, URSULA, IMMUNOBIOLOGY, MOLECULAR BIOLOGY. *Current Pos:* PROF, DEPT MOLECULAR GENETIC & CELL BIOL, UNIV CHICAGO, 86- *Personal Data:* b Stuttgart, Ger. *Educ:* Univ Tubingen, MD, 60. *Honors & Awards:* Quantrell Award, 91. *Prof Exp:* Assoc, Northwestern Univ, 51-55, from asst prof to prof urol, 56-86; from asst prof to prof microbiol, Univ Wash, 72-86, head, Div Immunol, 80-86. *Concurrent Pos:* NIH res grants, 72-; Prof, Comts Immunol, Develop Biol, Undergrad Col & Genetics, Univ Chicago. *Mem:* Am Asn Immunol; Am Soc Cell Biol; Asn Women in Sci; fel Am Acad Arts & Sci. *Res:* Organization of immunoglobulin genes; control of antibody gene expression; control and role of DNA methylation; mechanism of somatic hypermutation of immunoglobulin genes. *Mailing Add:* Dept Molecular Genetic & Cell Biol Univ Chicago 920 E 58th St Chicago IL 60637. Fax: 773-702-3172; E-Mail: stor@midway.uchicago.edu

STORCH, RICHARD HARRY, ENTOMOLOGY. *Current Pos:* Temp asst prof, USDA, 65-66, from asst prof to assoc prof, 66-80, PROF ENTOM, UNIV MAINE, ORONO, 80- *Personal Data:* b Evanston, Ill, Mar 16, 37; m 63; c Carl & Anita. *Educ:* Carleton Col, BA, 59; Univ Ill, MS, 61, PhD(entom), 66. *Mem:* Entom Soc Am; Entom Soc Can; Sigma Xi; Acadian Entom Soc. *Res:* Embryonic and postembryonic development of cervicothoracic structure and musculature; behavior and ecology of Coccinellidae; pests of potatoes. *Mailing Add:* Dept Entom Deering Hall Univ Maine Orono ME 04469. Fax: 207-581-2969

STORELLA, ROBERT J, JR, NEUROMUSCULAR PHYSIOLOGY & PHARMACOLOGY. *Current Pos:* res instr anesthesiol, 86-89, SR INSTR ANESTHESIOL & PHYSIOL/BIOPHYSIOL, HAHNEMANN UNIV, PHILADELPHIA, PA, 89- *Personal Data:* b Brighton, Mass, Sept 26, 56; m 83; c 2. *Educ:* Wesleyan Univ, BA, 78; Cornell Univ, PhD(pharmacol), 84. *Prof Exp:* Fel pharmacol, Med Sch, Univ Nev, 84-86. *Mem:* AAAS; Am Soc Pharmacol & Exper Therapeut; NY Acad Sci; Sigma Xi; Soc Neurosci; Am Soc Anesthesiologists. *Mailing Add:* Dept Anesthesiol Allegheny Univ Health Sci Broad & Vine Philadelphia PA 19102-1192

STORER, JAMES E(DWARD), COMPUTER DESIGN, APPLIED PHYSICS. *Current Pos:* CHIEF SCIENTIST COMPUT DESIGN, CSP, INC, 77- *Personal Data:* b Buffalo, NY, Oct 26, 27; m 49; c 3. *Educ:* Cornell Univ, AB, 47; Harvard Univ, AM, 48, PhD(appl physics), 51. *Prof Exp:* Fel, Electronics Res Lab, Harvard Univ, 51-52, lectr appl physics, 52-53, asst prof, 53-57; sr eng specialist, Appl Res Lab, Sylvania Elec Prod, Inc, Gen Tel & Electronics Corp, Mass, 57-60, sr scientist, 60-70, dir, 61-69; pres, Symbionics Consults, Inc, 70-76. *Concurrent Pos:* Guggenheim fel, 56; mem naval warfare panel, President's Sci Adv Comt. *Mem:* Am Asn Physics Teachers; fel Inst Elec & Electronics Engrs. *Res:* Electromagnetic theory; antennas and scattering; random processes; passive network synthesis. *Mailing Add:* CSP Inc 40 Linnell Circle Billerica MA 01821

STORER, JOHN B, RADIOBIOLOGY. *Current Pos:* RETIRED. *Personal Data:* b Rockland, Maine, Oct 16, 23; m 45; c 4. *Educ:* Univ Chicago, MD, 47. *Honors & Awards:* E O Lawrence Award, 68. *Prof Exp:* Intern, Mary Imogene Bassett Hosp, Cooperstown, NY, 47-48; USPHS res fel path, Univ Chicago, 48-49, res assoc, Toxicity Lab, 49-50; staff mem, Biomed Res Group, Los Alamos Sci Lab, 50-58; staff scientist, Jackson Mem Lab, 58-67; dep dir div biol & med, AEC, Md, 67-69; sci dir path & immunol, Oak Ridge Nat Lab, 69-75, dir, Biol Div, 75-80, sr scientist, 80-86. *Concurrent Pos:* Alt leader, Biomed Res Group & Leader Radiobiol Sect, Los Alamos Sci Lab, 52-58; mem subcomt relative biol effectiveness, Nat Coun Radiation Protection, 57-62; consult, Argonne Nat Lab, 59-67; mem, Radiation Study Section, NIH, 62-66 & 71-75, chmn, 72-75; mem adv comt, Atomic Bomb Casualty Comn, 69-74; mem subcomt radiobiol, Nat Coun Radiation Protection & Measurements, 69-, mem bd dirs, 75-80, mem sci comt, Biol Aspects of Basic Radiation Criteria, 72-80, Basic Radiation Criteria, 75-85 & Apportionment of Radiation Exposure, 78-86; mem adv comt biol & med to AEC Sci Secy, 69-73; mem sci adv bd, Nat Ctr Toxicol Res, 72-75; mem adv comt, Radiation Effects Res Found, Nat Acad Sci, 75-80, mem sci coun, 77-80; mem, UN Sci Comt Effects Atomic Radiation, 78-80. *Mem:* Radiation Res Soc; Am Soc Exp Path; Am Asn Cancer Res; Geront Soc; Soc Exp Biol & Med. *Res:* Late effects of ionizing radiation; aging. *Mailing Add:* 592 Eagle Point Rd Rockwood TN 37854

STORER, ROBERT WINTHROP, ZOOLOGY, BIOLOGY OF GREBES. *Current Pos:* RETIRED. *Personal Data:* b Pittsburgh, Pa, Sept 20, 14; wid; c Robert H & David W. *Educ:* Princeton Univ, AB, 36; Univ Calif, MA, 42, PhD(zool), 49. *Prof Exp:* Tech asst, Mus Vert Zool, Univ Calif, 41-42, mus technician, 48-49, assoc, Div Entom & Parasitol, Exp Sta, 45, asst zool, Univ, 46-48; from instr to prof zool, Univ Mich, Ann Arbor, 49-85, asst cur birds, Mus Zool, 49-56, cur, 56-85, actg dir, 79-82. *Concurrent Pos:* Ed, The Auk, Am Ornith Union, 53-57, ed, Ornith Monogr, 63-70; mem comt, Int Ornith Cong, 58-82; mem, Comt Classification & Nomenclature NAm Birds, Am Ornith Union, 63- *Mem:* Wilson Ornith Soc; hon mem Cooper Ornith Soc (vpres, 70); fel Am Ornith Union (pres, 70-72); Brit Ornith Union. *Res:* Avian morphology; systematics of Birds; distribution; paleontology; avian behavior. *Mailing Add:* 2020 Penncraft Ct Ann Arbor MI 48103

STORER, THOMAS, mathematics, for more information see previous edition

STOREY, ARTHUR THOMAS, ORTHODONTICS, PHYSIOLOGY. *Current Pos:* PROF & CHAIR, DEPT ORTHOD, SCH DENT, UNIV TEX HEALTH SCI CTR, SAN ANTONIO, 86- *Personal Data:* b Sarnia, Ont, July 8, 29; m 64; c 3. *Educ:* Univ Toronto, DDS, 53; Univ Mich, MS, 60, PhD(physiol), 64. *Prof Exp:* From instr to asst prof orthod, Sch Dent & Physiol & Sch Med, Univ Mich, 62-66; assoc prof, Fac Dent & asst prof physiol, Fac Med, Univ Toronto, 66-70, prof dent, fac dent & assoc prof physiol, 70-77; prof & head, Dept Prev Dent, Fac Dent, Univ Man, 77-86. *Concurrent Pos:* Ed, J Craniomandibular Disorders Facial Oral Pain, 87-; mem oral biol med, No 1 Study Sect, NIH, 88. *Mem:* Am Asn Orthod; Int Asn Dent Res; Soc Neurosci; Am Dent Asn; Am Acad Craniomandibular Disorders. *Res:* Oral, pharyngeal and laryngeal receptors and reflexes; temporomandibular disorders; forms of adaptation to malocclusion. *Mailing Add:* 66 Blyth Hill Rd Toronto ON M4N 3L8 Can

STOREY, BAYARD THAYER, CELL PHYSIOLOGY, PHYSICAL BIOCHEMISTRY. *Current Pos:* Nat Inst Gen Med Sci spec fel, Johnson Res Found, Univ Pa, 65-67, asst prof phys biochem, 67-73, assoc prof obstet & gynec, physiol & phys biochem, 73-84, prof reproductive biol & physiol in obsted & gynec, 84-96, EMER PROF, REPRODUCTIVE BIOL & PHYSIOL, UNIV PA, 96- *Personal Data:* b Boston, Mass, July 13, 32; m 58, Frances M Elliot; c Gwendolen M, Bayard T Jr, John M & Frances R. *Educ:* Harvard Univ, AB, 52, PhD(phys org chem), 58; Mass Inst Technol, MS, 55. *Prof Exp:* Res chemist, Ion Exchange Lab, Rohm and Haas Co, 58-60, head ion exchange synthesis lab, 60-65. *Concurrent Pos:* Mem, REB Study Sect, Div Res Grants, NIH, 86-90 & 90-94. *Mem:* Am Physiol Soc; Soc Study Reproduction; Am Soc Cell Biol; Am Soc Biochem & Molecular Biol; Am Soc Andrology; Biophys Soc. *Res:* Fertilization mechanisms in mammals; lipid peroxidation; mitochondrial ion movements; reproductive biology. *Mailing Add:* Dept Obstet & Gynec John Morgan Bldg 339 Univ Pa Philadelphia PA 19104-6080. Fax: 215-349-5118

STOREY, GARY GARFIELD, AGRICULTURAL STUDIES. *Current Pos:* asst prof, 70-72, PROF AGR ECON, UNIV SASK, SASKATOON, 77-, ASST DEAN AGR, 92- *Personal Data:* b Davidson, Sask, Mar 9, 39; m 65, Joelle Herbert; c Kristin J & Lauren C. *Educ:* Univ Sask, BSA, 63, MSc, 66; Univ Wis, MA, 68, PhD, 70. *Prof Exp:* Res economist, Govt Sask, 64-66. *Concurrent Pos:* Mem, Nat Coun, Agr Inst Can, 80-82; fel, Agr Inst Can, 91. *Mem:* Can Agr Econ & Farm Mgt Soc (pres, 77-78); Agr Inst Can; Asn Fac Agr Can (pres, 86-87). *Res:* Political economy of agricultural trade and policy. *Mailing Add:* Dept Agr Econ Univ Sask Saskatoon SK S7N 0W0 Can

STOREY, JAMES BENTON, POMOLOGY, PLANT PHYSIOLOGY. *Current Pos:* from asst prof to assoc prof, 57-74, PROF HORT, TEX A&M UNIV, 74- *Personal Data:* b Avery, Tex, Oct 25, 28; m 48, Marie Cox Storey; c Mark A & Lisa A. *Educ:* Tex A&M Univ, BS, 49, MS, 53; Univ Calif, Los Angeles, PhD(bot sci), 57. *Honors & Awards:* J H Henry Award, Federated Pecan Growers Asn US, 79. *Prof Exp:* Asst agr agt, Tex Agr Exten Serv, 49-52, asst hort, 52-53; asst plant physiol, Univ Calif, Los Angeles, 53-57. *Concurrent Pos:* Exec dir, Tex Pecan Producer's Bd; chair, USDA-ARS Pecan Genetics Prog, 95-96, Nat Pecan Breeding adv comt, 96-; vpres, Tex Pecan Growers Asn, 96-98. *Mem:* Fel Am Soc Hort Sci (pres-elect, 92-93, pres, 93-94); Int Soc Hort Sci; Am Pomol Soc; Sigma Xi. *Res:* Control of vegetative and fruiting responses in pecans; nutrition, salinity and post-harvest studies in pecans; coordinator pecan research program in Texas; vivipariry problem resulting in loss of nuts in Winter Garden area of Texas; author of numerous publications. *Mailing Add:* Hort Sci Dept Tex A&M Univ College Station TX 77843-2133. *Fax:* 409-845-0627; *E-Mail:* jbstorey@tamu.edu

STOREY, KENNETH BRUCE, COMPARATIVE BIOCHEMISTRY, ENZYMOLOGY. *Current Pos:* assoc prof, 79-85, PROF BIOCHEM, DEPTS BIOL & CHEM, INST BIOCHEM, CARLETON UNIV, 85- *Personal Data:* b Taber, Alta, Oct 23, 49; m 75, Janet Collicutt; c Jennifer & Kate. *Educ:* Univ Calgary, BSc, 71; Univ BC, PhD(zool), 74. *Honors & Awards:* Steacie Award, Nat Soc Eng Res Coun, 83; Ayerst Award, Can Biochem Soc, 89. *Prof Exp:* Asst prof physiol, Dept Zool, Duke Univ, 74-79. *Concurrent Pos:* Fel, Dept Biochem, Sheffield Univ, 76-77; EWR Steacie Mem fel, 84-86; Killam sr res fel, Nat Soc Eng Res Coun, 93-95. *Mem:* Am Soc Biol Chemists; Can Biochem Soc; Soc Cryobiol; AAAS; Can Soc Zool; fel Royal Soc Can. *Res:* Molecular adaptations of animals to environment, including adaptations of intermediary metabolism for living without oxygen and survival of freezing. *Mailing Add:* Dept Biol Carleton Univ Ottawa ON K1S 5B6 Can. *Fax:* 613-520-4389; *E-Mail:* kbstorey@ccs.carleton.ca

STOREY, RICHARD DRAKE, PLANT METABOLISM, NITROGEN FIXATION. *Current Pos:* HORT BUS CONSULT, 79- *Personal Data:* b Roswell, NMex, Dec 2, 44; m 71; c 2. *Educ:* Univ NMex, BS, 68; Univ Okla, MNS, 73, PhD(bot), 77. *Prof Exp:* Teacher biol, Manzano High Sch, Albuquerque, 68-73; res assoc plant physiol, Univ Okla, 73-77; vis scientist biochem, C F Kettering Res Lab, 77-78. *Concurrent Pos:* prin investr, grants in plant physiol, 80-85; dir, Inst Human Nutrit, Colo Col, 80-86. *Mem:* Am Soc Plant Physiologists; AAAS; Am Soc Agronomists; Nat Asn Biol Teachers; Am Asn Univ Prof. *Res:* Control of plant metabolism, particularly protein turnover and proteolysis as it influences growth and development, senescence and nitrogen fixation; physiology of potential crop plants. *Mailing Add:* Biol Dept Colo Col 14 E Cache La Poudre Colorado Springs CO 80903-3294

STOREY, THEODORE GEORGE, forestry; deceased, see previous edition for last biography

STORFER, STANLEY J, ORGANIC CHEMISTRY. *Current Pos:* chemist, Esso Res & Eng Co, 60-63, from sr chemist to sr res chemist, 63-73, RES ASSOC, EXXON CHEM-TECHNOL DEPT, 73- *Personal Data:* b Brooklyn, NY, July 31, 30; m 56; c 2. *Educ:* Polytech Inst Brooklyn, BS, 54, PhD(org chem), 60. *Prof Exp:* Jr chemist, Am Cyanamid Co, 54-56. *Mem:* Am Chem Soc. *Res:* Rheology of water-soluble polymer solutions; new product applications; statistical design of experiments; solvents technical service and market development. *Mailing Add:* 24 Ten Eyck Pl Edison NJ 08820-3223

STORHOFF, BRUCE NORMAN, INORGANIC CHEMISTRY. *Current Pos:* From asst prof to assoc prof, 68-79, admin asst head dept, 77-79, PROF CHEM, BALL STATE UNIV, 79-, HEAD DEPT, 79- *Personal Data:* b Lanesboro, Minn, Jan 2, 42. *Educ:* Luther Col, Iowa, BA, 64; Univ Iowa, PhD, 69. *Concurrent Pos:* Fel, Ind Univ, 69-70. *Mem:* Am Chem Soc. *Res:* Organic derivatives of transition metals; chemistry of carboranes. *Mailing Add:* Dept Chem Ball State Univ Muncie IN 47306-1099

STORK, DONALD HARVEY, HIGH ENERGY PHYSICS. *Current Pos:* from asst prof to assoc prof, 56-64, prof, 64-, EMER PROF PHYSICS, UNIV CALIF, LOS ANGELES. *Personal Data:* b Minn, Mar 22, 26; m 48; c 6. *Educ:* Carleton Col, BA, 49; Univ Calif, PhD(physics), 53. *Prof Exp:* Asst physics, Univ Calif, 48-51, asst, Lawrence Radiation Lab, 51-53, res assoc, 53-56. *Concurrent Pos:* Fel, Guggenheim Found, 65-66; guest scientist, Univ Oxford, Eng, 68 & Univ Res Asn, 85-86. *Mem:* Fel Am Phys Soc; AAAS; Am Asn Univ Profs. *Res:* Pions; K mesons; hyperons and antiprotons; production; beams; interactions; decay; high-energy electron-positron collisions; quark-antiquark and two-photon interactions; high-energy proton-proton collider design. *Mailing Add:* 21421 Encina Rd Topanga CA 90290

STORK, GILBERT (JOSSE), SYNTHETIC ORGANIC CHEMISTRY. *Current Pos:* from assoc prof to prof, Columbia Univ, 53-67, chmn dept, 73-76, Eugene Higgins prof, 67-93, EMER EUGENE HIGGINS PROF CHEM, COLUMBIA UNIV, 93- *Personal Data:* b Brussels, Belg, Dec 31, 21; nat US; wid; c Diana, Linda, Janet & Philip. *Educ:* Univ Fla, BS, 42; Univ Wis, PhD(chem), 45. *Hon Degrees:* DSc, Lawrence Col, 61, Univ Pierre et Marie Curie, Paris, 79, Univ Rochester, 82, Emory Univ, 88, Columbia Univ, 93. *Honors & Awards:* Pure Chem Award, Am Chem Soc, 57, Baekeland Medal, 61, Creative Work Synthetic Org Chem Award, 67, Nichols Medal, 80, Arthur C Cope Award, 80, Edgar Fahs Smith Award, 82, Willard Gibbs Medal, 82, Remsen Award, 86; Harrison Howe Award, 62; Franklin Mem Award, 66; Synthetic Org Chem Mfg Asn Gold Medal, 71; Roussel Steroid Prize, 78; Nat Acad Sci Chem Award, 82; Nat Medal Sci, 83; Pauling Award, 83; Tetrahedron Prize, Synthetic Chem, 85; Roger Adams Award, 91; George Kenner Award, 92; Robert Robinson Award, 92; Robert Welch Award, 92; Allan R Day Award, 94. *Prof Exp:* Sr res chemist, Lakeside Labs, Inc, 45-46; instr chem, Harvard Univ, 46-48, asst prof, 48-53. *Concurrent Pos:* Consult, NSF, 58-61, US Army Res Off, 66-69, NIH, 67-71, Sloane Found, 74-77, Syntex Corp & IFF Corp; var lectureships & professorships, US & abroad, 58-; Guggenheim fel, 59; mem comt org chem & comt postdoctoral fels, Nat Res Coun, 59-62; mem adv bd, Petrol Res Fund, 63-66. *Mem:* Nat Acad Sci; Am Acad Arts & Sci; Am Chem Soc; Swiss Chem Soc; hon fel Royal Soc Chem; hon mem Pharm Soc Japan; Am Philos Soc. *Res:* Total synthesis of complex structures; design of new synthetic reactions. *Mailing Add:* 459 Next Day Hill Dr Englewood NJ 07631-1921. *Fax:* 212-932-1289; *E-Mail:* gjs8@columbia.edu

STORM, CARLYLE BELL, CHEMISTRY. *Current Pos:* DIR, GORDON RES CONF, 93- *Personal Data:* b Baltimore, Md, Mar 2, 35; m 57, Lee Anzaldi; c Carol, Michael & Christy. *Educ:* Johns Hopkins Univ, BA, 61, MA, 63, PhD(chem), 65. *Prof Exp:* NIH res fel chem, Stanford Univ, 65-66; staff fel biochem, NIMH, 66-68; from asst prof to prof chem, Howard Univ, 68-86; chief scientist, Explosive Technol & Appl, Los Alamos Nat Lab, 85-93. *Concurrent Pos:* NIH res career develop award, 73-78; sr visitor, Inorg Chem Lab, Oxford Univ, 74-75; vis staff mem, Stable Isotope Res Resource, Los Alamos Nat Lab, NMex, 81-82; sr Fulbright Hays fel, Univ Trondheim, Norway, 77. *Mem:* Am Chem Soc; Royal Soc Chem; AAAS. *Res:* Nuclear magnetic resonance spectroscopy; research administration; energetic materials. *Mailing Add:* PO Box 984 Univ RI West Kingston RI 02892. *E-Mail:* cbstorm@grcmail.grc.wri.edu

STORM, DANIEL RALPH, BIOCHEMISTRY. *Current Pos:* ASSOC PROF PHARMACOL, UNIV WASH, 78- *Personal Data:* b Hawarden, Iowa, June 21, 44; m 66; c 3. *Educ:* Univ Wash, BS, 66, MS, 67; Univ Calif, Berkeley, PhD(biochem), 71. *Prof Exp:* Res asst biochem, Univ Calif, Berkeley, 67-71, NIH res fel, Harvard Univ, 71-72, NSF fel, 72-73; asst prof, Univ Ill, Urbana, 73-78. *Concurrent Pos:* Indust consult, Pharmaco Inc, 75- *Mem:* Am Chem Soc; Am Soc Biol Chemists; Am Soc Microbiol. *Res:* Structure and function of biological membranes; mechanism of enzymatic catalysis; membrane active antibiotics and molecular pharmacology at the membrane level. *Mailing Add:* Dept Pharmacol SJ-30 Univ Wash Seattle WA 98195-0001

STORM, EDWARD FRANCIS, computer science, mathematics, for more information see previous edition

STORM, LEO EUGENE, COMPUTER SCIENCE, STATISTICS, MINI COMPUTERS. *Current Pos:* RETIRED. *Personal Data:* b Valeda, Kans, Aug 29, 28. *Educ:* Okla Agr & Mech Col, BA, 53. *Prof Exp:* Seismic engr, Seismic Eng Co, 53-54; meteorologist, US Weather Bur, 54-55; mathematician, Northwestern Univ, 55; qual control engr, Metro Bottle Glass Co, 55-56; jr engr, US Testing Co, 56; assoc staff mem, Gen Precision Lab, Inc, 56-57; sr statistician, Nuclear Fuel Oper, Olin Mathieson Chem Corp, 57-61; statist qual control supvr, United Nuclear Corp, 61-62; opers analyst, United Aircraft Corp Systs Ctr, 62-67; sr sci programmer, NY Med Col, 67-70; syst analyst, Texaco Inc, 70-71; programmer analyst, Data Develop, Inc, 71-73; sr syst analyst, Nabisco Brands, Inc, 73-89. *Res:* Digital computer programming for management systems; statistical sample surveys; programming analysis for statistical accounting and biomedical applications; mini-computer systems for process control; material handling and management applications. *Mailing Add:* 1325 Viewtop Dr Clearwater FL 34624

STORM, ROBERT MACLEOD, ZOOLOGY. *Current Pos:* RETIRED. *Personal Data:* b Calgary, Alta, July 9, 18; US citizen; m 43, 59; c 6. *Educ:* Northern Ill State Teachers Col, BE, 39; Ore State Col, MS, 41, PhD(zool), 48. *Prof Exp:* From instr to prof zool, Ore State Univ, 48-84. *Mem:* Assoc Am Soc Ichthyologists & Herpetologists. *Res:* Natural history of cold-blooded land vertebrates. *Mailing Add:* 1623 SW Brooklane Dr Corvallis OR 97333

STORMER, HORST LUDWIG, SOLID STATE PHYSICS. *Current Pos:* consult, 77-78, mem tech staff physics, 78-83, DEPT HEAD, BELL LABS, AT&T, 83- *Personal Data:* b Frankfurt-Main, Ger, Apr 6, 49. *Educ:* Univ Frankfurt, BS, 70, dipl physics, 74; Univ Stuttgart, Ger, PhD(physics), 77. *Honors & Awards:* Oliver E Buckley Prize; Otto Klung Prize. *Prof Exp:* Mem tech staff physics, High Magnetic Field Lab, Max Planck Inst Solid State Res, 77. *Mem:* Am Phys Soc. *Mailing Add:* 11 Knob Hill Dr Summit NJ 07901. *Fax:* 908-582-3260

STORMER, JOHN CHARLES, JR, IGNEOUS PETROLOGY, GEOCHEMISTRY. *Current Pos:* CARY CRONEIS PROF GEOL, RICE UNIV, 83-, CHAIR GEOL, 88- *Personal Data:* b Englewood, NJ, Oct 28, 41; m 63; c 2. *Educ:* Dartmouth Col, BA, 63; Univ Calif, Berkeley, PhD(geol), 71. *Prof Exp:* Asst geologist, Climax Molybdenum Co, Colo, 67; from asst prof to assoc prof geol, Univ Ga, 71-83. *Concurrent Pos:* Vis prof, Inst Geosci, Univ Sao Paulo, 73; IPA, US Geol Surv, Reston, 82-83. *Mem:* Fel Mineral Soc Am; Geochem Soc; Am Geophys Union; Brazilian Geol Soc; Microbeam Analytical Soc. *Res:* Mineralogy and geochemistry of igneous rocks as applied to petrology; thermochemical data and methods of investigating the origin of igneous rocks, and applications to various rock suites and petrographic provinces. *Mailing Add:* Dept Geol & Geophys Rice Univ 6100 Main St Houston TX 77005-1892

STORMONT, CLYDE J, GENETICS, IMMUNOLOGY. *Current Pos:* asst prof, 50-54, assoc prof vet med & assoc seriologist, Exp Sta, 54-59, prof, 59-82, EMER PROF IMMUNOGENETICS & CHMN DEPT, UNIV CALIF, DAVIS, 82- *Personal Data:* b Viola, Wis, June 25, 16; m 40; c 5. *Educ:* Univ Wis, BA, 38, PhD(genetics), 47. *Prof Exp:* Instr genetics, Univ Wis, 46-47, lectr, 47, asst prof, 48-53. *Concurrent Pos:* E B Scripps fel, San Diego Zool Soc, 56-57 & 66-67; chmn & dir lab serv, Stormont Labs, Inc, Woodland, Calif. *Mem:* Genetics Soc Am; Am Soc Human Genetics; Soc Exp Biol & Med; hon mem Int Soc Animal Genetics; Am Soc Nat; hon mem Nat Buffalo Asn. *Res:* Blood groups; animal blood groups and biochemical polymorphisms; genetic markers in animal blood. *Mailing Add:* Stormont Labs Inc 1237 E Beamer St Suite D Woodland CA 95776-6000

STORMS, LOWELL H, NEUROPSYCHOLOGY. *Current Pos:* RETIRED. *Personal Data:* b Schenectady, NY, Feb 14, 28; m 55, 93, Joan McEcoy; c Christopher, Karen & Bruce. *Educ:* Univ Minn, BA, 50, MS, 51, PhD(clin psychol), 56. *Prof Exp:* Psychologist, Hastings State Hosp, Minn, 54-56; Fulbright grant, Inst Psychiat, Univ London, 56-57; from instr to prof psychiat, Neuropsychiat Inst, Univ Calif, Los Angeles, 57-71; prof psychiat, Sch Med, Univ Calif, San Diego, 71-96, clin psychologist, Vet Admin Med Ctr, 75-96. *Concurrent Pos:* Instr prof, Sch Med, Univ Calif, Los Angeles, 57-71; consult, Vet Admin, 64-71 & Encounters Unlimited, 68-71; Fulbright scholar. *Mem:* AAAS; Am Psychol Asn; Sigma Xi; Western Psychol Asn. *Res:* Behavior of schizophrenics; behavior therapy; clinical psychology. *Mailing Add:* PO Box 952 Rancho Santa Fe CA 92067. *E-Mail:* lstorms@ucsd.edu

STORMSHAK, FREDRICK, REPRODUCTIVE ENDOCRINOLOGY. *Current Pos:* from asst prof to assoc prof physiol, Ore State Univ, 68-79, actg head, Dept Animal Sci, 74 & 94-95, PROF PHYSIOL, ORE STATE UNIV, 79-, AFFIL PROF BIOCHEM BIOPHYS, 85- *Personal Data:* b Enumclaw, Wash, July 4, 36; m 63, Alice M Burk; c Elizabeth & Laurie. *Educ:* Wash State Univ, BSc, 59, MSc, 60; Univ Wis, PhD(endocrinol), 65. *Honors & Awards:* Ferguson Distinguished Prof of Agr Sci, 89; Animal Physiol & Endocrinol Award, Am Soc Animal Sci, 93; Earl Price Excellence in Res Award, Ore State Univ, 93. *Prof Exp:* Res physiologist, USDA, 65-68. *Concurrent Pos:* Postdoctoral trainee endocrinol, Univ Wis, 74-75; sect ed, J Animal Sci, 75-77, ed-in-chief, 82-85; actg assoc dir, Ore Agr Exp Sta, 85; NIH Study Sect Reprod Biol, 82-86; USDA grant rev panel, 88-90; bd dirs, Soc Study Reproduction, 92-95. *Mem:* Fel Am Soc Animal Sci; Soc Study Fertility; Endocrine Soc; Soc Study Reproduction (pres-elect, 96-97, pres, 97-98). *Res:* Quantitative measurement of steroid hormones of ovarian origin; factors affecting the regression and maintenance of the corpus luteum; pituitary, ovarian and uterine interrelationships in reproduction; hormone action. *Mailing Add:* Dept Animal Sci Ore State Univ Corvallis OR 97331-6702. *Fax:* 541-737-4174; *E-Mail:* stormshf@ccmail.orst.edu

STORRIE, BRIAN, BIOCHEMISTRY, CELL BIOLOGY. *Current Pos:* from asst prof to assoc prof, 76-86, PROF BIOCHEM, VA POLYTECH INST & STATE UNIV, 86- *Personal Data:* b East Cleveland, Ohio, Mar 9, 46; m 71, Muriel Lederman; c 2. *Educ:* Cornell Univ, BS, 68; Calif Inst Technol, PhD(biochem), 73. *Prof Exp:* NSF fel, Calif Inst Technol, 68-72; NIH fel, Univ Colo Med Ctr, 72, Am Cancer Soc fel, 73-74; res assoc, Mem Sloan-Kettering Cancer Ctr, 74-75; asst res biologist, Univ Calif, Berkeley, 75-76. *Concurrent Pos:* Prin investr, NSF grants, 78-85, 91- & NIH grants, 80-83 & 84-91; co-instr, Marine Biol Lab, 80; mem, cell biol panel, NSF, 82; consult, Gilford Systs, Ciba Corning, 82 & Collins & Assocs, 84-86; vis scientist, Europ Molecular Biol Lab, 88 & 91-92; fel, Fogarty Int Ctr, NIH, 91-92. *Mem:* Am Soc Cell Biol; Sigma Xi. *Res:* Intraorganelle protein exchange in animal cells; mechanisms for selective targeting of membrane vesicles arising from endocytosis; mechanisms of protein segregation during membrane trafficking; assembly of lysosomes. *Mailing Add:* Dept Biochem & Anaerobic Microbiol Va Polytech Inst & State Univ Blacksburg VA 24061-0308. *Fax:* 540-231-7070

STORROW, HUGH ALAN, PSYCHIATRY. *Current Pos:* PROF PSYCHIAT, COL MED, UNIV KY, 66 - *Personal Data:* b Long Beach, Calif, Jan 13, 26; m 53; c 3. *Educ:* Univ Southern Calif, AB, 46, MD, 50; Am Bd Psychiat & Neurol, dipl, 55. *Prof Exp:* Intern, USPHS Hosp, Baltimore, 49-50; resident, Sheppard & Enoch Pratt Hosp, Towson, Md, 50-51; staff psychiatrist, US Penitentiary Hosp, Leavenworth, Kans, 51-52; resident, USPHS Hosp, Lexington, Ky, 52-53; staff psychiatrist, 53-54; resident, Brentwood Vet Admin Hosp, Los Angeles, 54-55; instr psychiat, Sch Med, Yale Univ, 55-56; asst prof, Sch Med, Univ Calif, Los Angeles, 56-60, attend psychiatrist, Med Ctr, 57-60; assoc prof, Col Med, Univ Ky, 60-65; prof psychiat, Univ Minn, 65-66. *Concurrent Pos:* Attend psychiatrist, Brentwood Vet Admin Hosp, Calif, 57-60; consult, United Cerebral Palsy Asn, Los Angeles Co, Calif, 57-60; USPHS & Vet Admin Hosps, Ky, 60 - *Mem:* Am Psychiat Asn; AMA; Asn Am Med Cols. *Res:* Behavior modification; teaching methods for psychiatry. *Mailing Add:* Dept Psychiat Univ Ky Sch Med Lexington KY 40536

STORRS, CHARLES LYSANDER, NUCLEAR ENGINEERING, TECHNICAL MANAGEMENT. *Current Pos:* RETIRED. *Personal Data:* b Shaowu, Fukien, China, Oct 25, 25; US citizen; m 57; c 3. *Educ:* Mass Inst Technol, BS, 49, PhD, 52. *Prof Exp:* Mem staff, Aircraft Nuclear Propulsion Dept, Gen Elec Co, 52-56, supvr initial engine test opers, 56-59, supvr flight engine test opers, 59-61, mgr reactor test opers, Nuclear Propulsion Dept, 61, SL-1 Proj, Nuclear Mat & Propulsion Opers, 61-62 & 710 Proj, 62-65; dir heavy water organic cooled reactor, Atomics Int-Combustion Eng Joint Venture, Calif, 65-67; asst dir advan reactor eng, Combustion Eng, Inc, 67-69, dir advan reactor develop, 69-71, dir projs, 71-73, dir prod eng & develop, 73-75, dir fast breeder reactor develop, 75-80, dir advanced develop, Nuclear Power Systs, 80-86. *Mem:* AAAS; Am Nuclear Soc; Am Phys Soc. *Res:* Engineering, design and development of technology leading to the application of nuclear energy to power generation and desalination; reactor test operations; management of technical enterprises. *Mailing Add:* 76 Adams Rd Bloomfield CT 06002

STORRS, ELEANOR EMERETT, LEPROSY, ARMADILLO RESEARCH. *Current Pos:* RETIRED. *Personal Data:* b Cheshire, Conn, May 3, 26; m 63; c 2. *Educ:* Univ Conn, BS, 48; NY Univ, MS, 58; Univ Tex, PhD(biochem), 67. *Honors & Awards:* Charles A Griffin Award, Am Asn Lab Animal Sci, 75; Spec Recognition, Gerald B Lambert Awards, 75. *Prof Exp:* Asst, Boyce Thompson Inst Plant Res, 48-59, asst biochemist, 59-62; res scientist, Clayton Found Biochem Inst, Univ Tex, 62-65; res chemist, Pesticides Res Lab, USPHS, Fla, 65-67; res chemist, Gulf S Res Inst, 67-71, dir, Dept Comp Bioichem, 71-77c; dir, Div Comp Mammal & Biochem, Med Res Inst, Fla Inst Technol, 77-85, dir, Div Comp Mammol & Dept Biol Sci, 86-94. *Mem:* Fel AAAS; Am Soc Mammal; Am Asn Lab Animal Sci; Sigma Xi; Int Leprosy Asn; fel NY Acad Sci. *Res:* Armadillo in biomedical research; leprosy; biochemical individuality; analytical methods for biochemical, environmental and residue analyses; drug metabolism; mode of fungicidal, insecticidal action; armadillo reproduction. *Mailing Add:* 72 Riverview Terr Indialantic FL 32903

STORRY, JUNIS O(LIVER), ELECTRICAL POWER ENGINEERING. *Current Pos:* from instr to assoc prof, SDak State Univ, 46-64, actg dean, 71-72, prof elec eng, 64-85, dean eng, 72-82, EMER PROF ELEC ENG & EMER DEAN, SDAK STATE UNIV, 85- *Personal Data:* b Astoria, SDak, Mar 16, 20; m 50, Laurel Davis; c Cheryl (Greenhagen) & David. *Educ:* SDak State Col, BS, 42, MS, 49; Iowa State Univ, PhD, 67. *Prof Exp:* Mem student prog, Westinghouse Elec Corp, Pa, 42; elec engr, Bur Ships, Navy Dept, Washington, DC, 42-46; design engr, Reliance Elec & Eng Co, Ohio, 46. *Mem:* Inst Elec & Electronics Engrs; Am Soc Eng Educ; Nat Soc Prof Engrs. *Res:* Digital analysis of power systems using hybrid parameters. *Mailing Add:* 3132 Sunnyview Dr Brookings SD 57006-4281

STORTI, ROBERT V, MOLECULAR BIOLOGY, BIOCHEMISTRY. *Current Pos:* ASST PROF BIOCHEM, MED CTR, UNIV ILL, 78- *Personal Data:* b Providence, RI, May 14, 44. *Educ:* RI Col, BA, 68; Ind Univ, MA, 70, PhD(biol), 74. *Prof Exp:* Fel biol, Mass Inst Technol, 74-78. *Concurrent Pos:* NIH fel, 74-76; Muscular Dystrophy Soc fel, 77-78; Biomed Found Res fel, 78. *Mem:* Am Soc Cell Biol; AAAS; Soc Develop Biol. *Res:* Molecular biology of gene expression during eukaryotic cell growth and differentiation; transcriptional and translation control of protein synthesis. *Mailing Add:* Dept Biochem Univ Ill Col Med 1819 W Polk St Chicago IL 60612. *Fax:* 312-413-0364

STORTS, RALPH WOODROW, VETERINARY PATHOLOGY. *Current Pos:* from asst prof to assoc prof, 66-73, PROF VET PATH, TEX A&M UNIV, 73- *Personal Data:* b Zanesville, Ohio, Feb 5, 33; m 60; c 3. *Educ:* Ohio State Univ, DVM, 57, PhD(vet path), 66; Purdue Univ, West Lafayette, MSc, 62. *Prof Exp:* Instr vet microbiol, Purdue Univ, West Lafayette, 57-60; instr vet path, Ohio State Univ, 61-66. *Mem:* Am Vet Med Asn; Am Col Vet Path; Int Acad Path; Conf Res Workers Animal Dis. *Res:* Veterinary neuropathology including electron microscopy and cytology of normal and infected tissue cultures of nervous tissue. *Mailing Add:* 1006 Village Dr College Station TX 77840

STORTZ, CLARENCE B, MATHEMATICS. *Current Pos:* assoc prof, 68-72, head dept, 72-76, PROF MATH, NORTHERN MICH UNIV, 72- *Personal Data:* b Marlette, Mich, July 23, 33; m 56; c 5. *Educ:* Wayne State Univ, BS, 55; Univ Miami, MS, 58; Univ Mich, Ann Arbor, DEd(math), 68. *Prof Exp:* Asst prof math, Northern Mich Univ, 63-66 & Cent Mich Univ, 66-68. *Res:* General topology; history of mathematics. *Mailing Add:* Dept Math Northern Mich Univ Marquette MI 49855-5301

STORVICK, CLARA A, NUTRITION. *Current Pos:* from assoc prof to prof, Ore State Univ, 45-72, head home econ res, 55-72, dir, Nutrit Res Inst, 65-72, EMER PROF NUTRIT, ORE STATE UNIV, 72- *Personal Data:* b Emmons, Minn, Oct 31, 06. *Educ:* St Olaf Col, AB, 29; Iowa State Univ, MS, 33; Cornell Univ, PhD(nutrit, biochem), 41. *Honors & Awards:* Borden Award, Am Home Econ Asn, 52. *Prof Exp:* Instr chem, Augustana Acad, 30-32; asst, Iowa State Univ, 32-34; nutritionist, Fed Emergency Relief Admin, Minn, 34-36; asst prof nutrit, Okla State Univ, 36-38; asst, Cornell Univ, 38-41; asst prof nutrit, Univ Wash, 41-45. *Concurrent Pos:* Sigma Xi Lectr, Ore State Univ, 53; sabbatical leaves, Chem Dept, Columbia Univ & Inst Cytophysiol, Denmark, 52, Lab Nutrit & Endocrinol, NIH, 59 & Div Clin Oncol, Med Sch, Univ Wis, 66. *Mem:* Am Home Econ Asn; Am Dietetic Asn; fel Am Pub Health Asn; fel Am Inst Nutrit; fel AAAS; Am Chem Soc. *Res:* Calcium, phosphorus, nitrogen, ascorbic acid, thiamine and riboflavin metabolism; nutrition and dental caries; vitamin B-6. *Mailing Add:* 124 NW 29th St Corvallis OR 97330-5343

STORVICK, DAVID A, MATHEMATICS. *Current Pos:* from asst prof to assoc prof, 57-66, PROF MATH, UNIV MINN, MINNEAPOLIS, 66-, ASSOC HEAD, SCH MATH, 64- *Personal Data:* b Ames, Iowa, Oct 24, 29; m 52; c 3. *Educ:* Luther Col, Iowa, AB, 51; Univ Mich, MA, 52, PhD(math), 56. *Prof Exp:* From instr to asst prof math, Iowa State Univ, 55-57. *Concurrent Pos:* Res assoc, US Army Math Res Ctr, Wis, 62-63. *Mem:* Am Math Soc; Math Asn Am. *Res:* Complex function theory. *Mailing Add:* Univ Minn Minneapolis MN 55455-0100

STORVICK, TRUMAN S(OPHUS), CHEMICAL ENGINEERING, MOLECULAR PHYSICS. *Current Pos:* from asst prof to prof, 59-72, Robert Lee Tatum prof, 72-75, Black & Veatch prof, 75-82, EMER PROF ENG, UNIV MO, COLUMBIA, 96- *Personal Data:* b Albert Lea, Minn, Apr 14, 28; m 52, Arlyn Abrahamson; c Ruth (Hornig), Jan, Kris (Burg) & David O. *Educ:* Iowa State Univ, BS, 52; Purdue Univ, PhD(chem eng), 59. *Prof Exp:* Res engr, Res Dept, Westvaco Chloro-Alkali Div, FMC Corp, 52-55; instr chem eng, Purdue Univ, 58-59. *Concurrent Pos:* NSF fac fel, 65-66; fel, Royal Norweg Coun Sci & Indust Res, 72-73. *Mem:* AAAS; Am Chem Soc; Am Inst Chem Engrs; Am Phys Soc; Electrochem Soc. *Res:* Measurement and prediction of thermodynamic and transport properties of fluids; chemistry and electrochemistry of heavy metal chlorides in molten salt and liquid metals. *Mailing Add:* 2210 Ridgefield Rd Columbia MO 65203

STORWICK, ROBERT MARTIN, ELECTRICAL ENGINEERING, APPLIED MATHEMATICS. *Current Pos:* PATENT ATTY, SEED & BERRY, 79- *Personal Data:* b Seattle, Wash, Oct 14, 42; m 67; c 2. *Educ:* Calif Inst Technol, BS, 64; Univ Southern Calif, MSEE, 65, PhD(elec eng), 69; Detroit Col Law, JD, 82. *Prof Exp:* Mem tech staff, Radar & Data Processing Dept, Gen Res Corp, Calif, 69-70; staff res engr, Electronics Dept, Gen Motors Res Labs, 70-79. *Mem:* AAAS; sr mem Inst Elec & Electronics Engrs. *Res:* Signal processing; short-range and long-range radar systems; radar cross-section studies and analyses; statistical pattern recognition; information, coding and communication theory; networks and combinatorial systems; graph theory. *Mailing Add:* PO Box 386 Mercer Island WA 98040

STORY, ANNE WINTHROP, ENGINEERING PSYCHOLOGY. *Current Pos:* CONSULT, 78- *Personal Data:* b Haverhill, Mass. *Educ:* Smith Col, AB, 34; Univ Calif, Berkeley, PhD(exp psychol), 57. *Prof Exp:* Assoc engr, Turbine Div, Gen Elec Co, 42-44; instr, Stoneleigh Jr Col, 45-46, Greenbrier Col, 46-47 & Pa State Univ, 47-50; res assoc animal behav, Jackson Mem Lab, 50-51; res analyst flight safety, Norton AFB, 51-52; teaching asst statist & psychol, Univ Calif, Berkeley, 52-57; res psychologist flight safety & space psychol, Hanscom AFB, 58-66 & NASA, 66-70; eng psychologist man-machine syst, US Dept Transp, 70-78. *Concurrent Pos:* Assoc prof, Dept Psychol, Univ Mass, 72-76. *Mem:* AAAS; Sigma Xi; Am Psychol Asn; Am Psychol Soc. *Res:* Aviation collision pilot-warning; vehicle driver safety devices; visual perception; attention; man-machine systems. *Mailing Add:* 29 Newbury Neck Rd Newbury MA 01951

STORY, HAROLD S, SOLID STATE PHYSICS, NUCLEAR MAGNETIC RESONANCE. *Current Pos:* from assoc prof to prof physics, 59-80, physics dept chmn, 81-82, PROF ASTRON & SPACE SCI, STATE UNIV NY ALBANY, 80- *Personal Data:* b Catskill, NY, Oct 5, 27; m 51; c 2. *Educ:* NY State Col Teachers, BA, 49, MA, 50; Univ Maine, Orono, MS, 52; Case Inst Technol, PhD(physics), 57. *Prof Exp:* Mem tech staff, Bell Tel Labs, NJ, 56-59. *Mem:* Am Phys Soc; Sigma Xi; Am Asn Physics Teachers. *Res:* Structure, defects and conduction processes in superionic conductors, utilizing nuclear magnetic resonance. *Mailing Add:* Dept Physics State Univ NY 1400 Wash Ave Albany NY 12222-0001

STORY, JIM LEWIS, NEUROSURGERY. *Current Pos:* PROF NEUROSURG, UNIV TEX HEALTH SCI CTR SAN ANTONIO, 67-, PROF ANAT, 77- *Personal Data:* b Alice, Tex, July 30, 31; m 58; c 4. *Educ:* Tex Christian Univ, BS, 52; Vanderbilt Univ, MD, 55. *Prof Exp:* From instr to asst prof neurosurg, Med Sch, Univ Minn, 61-67. *Concurrent Pos:* Univ fels neurol surg, Univ Minn, 56-59 & 60-61; USPHS fels anat, Univ Calif, Los Angeles, 59-60 & Univ Minn, 60-62. *Mem:* Am Asn Neurol Surgeons; Soc Neurol Surgeons; Am Col Surgeons; Neurosurg Soc Am; Am Acad Neurol Surgeons. *Res:* Intracranial pressure monitoring; etiology of brain tumors. *Mailing Add:* Univ Tex Med Sch San Antonio 7703 Floyd Curl Dr San Antonio TX 78284-6200

STORY, JON ALAN, BIOCHEMISTRY, NUTRITION. *Current Pos:* assoc prof foods & nutrit, 77-80, assoc dean consumer & family sci, 88-95, PROF NUTRIT PHYSIOL, PURDUE UNIV, WEST LAFAYETTE, 80- *Personal Data:* b Odebolt, Iowa, Apr 7, 46; m 69, Margaret Gossard; c Emilie, Julia & William. *Educ:* Iowa State Univ, BS, 68, MS, 70, PhD(zool), 72. *Prof Exp:* Instr zool, Iowa State Univ, 71-72; trainee lipid metab, Wistar Inst Anat & Biol, 72-74, asst prof lipid metab, 74-77. *Mem:* Am Inst Nutrit; Nutrit Soc; Sigma Xi; Soc Exp Biol & Med. *Res:* Investigation into the effects of several dietary components on cholesterol and bile acid metabolism as involved in development of experimental atherosclerosis. *Mailing Add:* Dept Foods & Nutrit Purdue Univ 1264 Stone Hall West Lafayette IN 47907-1264. *E-Mail:* story@cfs.purdue.edu

STORY, TROY L, JR, CHEMICAL PHYSICS. *Current Pos:* from asst prof to assoc prof, 71-83, PROF & CHAIR DEPT CHEM, MOREHOUSE COL, 83- *Personal Data:* b Montgomery, Ala, Nov 11, 40. *Educ:* Morehouse Col, BS, 62; Univ Calif, Berkeley, PhD(chem), 68. *Prof Exp:* Mem staff & fel chem, Univ Calif, Berkeley, 69-70; fel physics, Chalmers Univ Technol, Sweden, 70-71. *Mem:* Am Chem Soc; Am Phys Soc; Math Asn Am. *Res:* Experimental determination of dipole moments using molecular beam resonance and deflection techniques; theoretical quantum mechanical model for the analysis of rotational distributions for reactive scattering experiments; topological analysis of composite particles; thermodynamics on 1-forms; characteristic differential equation for electromagnetic and Yang-Mills gauge. *Mailing Add:* Dept Chem Morehouse Col 830 Westview Dr Atlanta GA 30314-3799

STORZ, JOHANNES, VIROLOGY, MICROBIOLOGY. *Current Pos:* PROF & DEPT HEAD, DEPT VET MICROBIOL & PARASITOL, LA STATE UNIV, 82- *Personal Data:* b Hardt/Schramberg, Ger, Apr 29, 31; US citizen; m 59, Hannelore Roeber; c Gisela T, J Peter K & Heidi E. *Educ:* Vet Col, Hannover, dipl, 57; Univ Munich, Dr Med Vet, 58; Univ Calif, Davis, PhD(comp path), 61; Am Col Vet Microbiol, dipl, 69. *Hon Degrees:* Dr, Univ Zurich, Switz. *Prof Exp:* Res assoc, Fed Res Inst Viral Dis Animals, Tubingen, Ger, 57-58; lectr vet microbiol, Univ Calif, Davis, 58-61; from asst prof to assoc prof vet virol, Utah State Univ, 61-65; from assoc prof to prof vet virol, Colo State Univ, 65-82. *Concurrent Pos:* USPHS res grant, Utah State Univ, 62-65; res grants, USPHS, Colo State Univ, 66-72, 72-77 & 79-82, WHO, 72-77 & USDA, 80-85, 86-92 & 93-98; vis scientist, Univ Giessen, 71-72 & 78-79; consult, WHO, Geneva, 71 & Munich, 76, 86-92 & 93-98; Alexander Humboldt award, Ger, 78. *Mem:* AAAS; Am Soc Microbiol; Am Vet Med Asn; Conf Res Workers Animal Dis; World Asn Buiatrics; Am Soc Virol. *Res:* Chlamydiology; pathogenic mechanisms in intrauterine viral and chlamydial infections; chlamydial polyarthritis; intestinal corona and parvoviral infections; cell biology of chlamydial infections. *Mailing Add:* Dept Vet Microbiol & Parasitol Sch Vet Med La State Univ Baton Rouge LA 70803. *Fax:* 504-346-5715; *E-Mail:* storz@vt8200.vetmed.lsu.edu

STOSICK, ARTHUR JAMES, CHEMISTRY. *Current Pos:* CONSULT, 80- *Personal Data:* b Milwaukee, Wis, Dec 1, 14; m 37; c 3. *Educ:* Univ Wis, BS, 36; Calif Inst Technol, PhD(struct chem), 39. *Prof Exp:* Fel, Calif Inst Technol, 39-40, instr gen chem, 40-41, Nat Defense Res Comt res assoc, 41-43, res chemist, Jet Propulsion Lab, 44-46, chief, Rockets & Mat Div, 50-56; res chemist, Aerojet Eng Corp, 43-44; assoc prof phys chem, Iowa State Col, 46-47; prof, Univ Southern Calif, 47-50; asst dir, Union Carbide Res Inst, 56-59; asst vpres, Gen Atomic Div, Gen Dynamics Corp, 59-60; sr scientist, Aerojet-Gen Corp, 60-71; asst sr vpres, United Technol Corp, 72-80. *Concurrent Pos:* Mem, rocket eng subcomt, Nat Adv Comt Aeronaut, 52-56; staff scientist, Adv Res Proj Agency, Off Secy Defense, 58-59. *Mem:* Am Chem Soc; Am Phys Soc; Am Crystallog Asn. *Res:* Molecular structures by diffraction; physical chemistry as related to molecular structures; propellants; high temperature chemistry; metallurgy. *Mailing Add:* 1153 Lime Dr Sunnyvale CA 94087-2021

STOSKOPF, MICHAEL KERRY, AQUATIC MEDICINE, AQUATIC TOXICOLOGY. *Current Pos:* asst prof, 79-86, ASSOC PROF COMP MED, SCH MED, JOHNS HOPKINS UNIV, 86-; CHIEF MED, NAT AQUARIUM, BALTIMORE, 81-; COL VET MED, NC STATE UNIV, 94- *Personal Data:* b Garden City, Kans, March 21, 50; m 81. *Educ:* Colo State Univ, BS, 73, DVM, 75; Am Col Zool Med, dipl; Johns Hopkins Univ, PhD, 86. *Prof Exp:* Staff vet comp med, Overton Park Zoo & Aquarium, 75-77. *Concurrent Pos:* Consult, Nat Inst Exp Progs, Antivenom Inst, Columbia, 79; staff vet, Baltimore Zool Soc, 77-81; adj prof path, Sch Med, Univ Md, 81-; chmn exam comt, Am Col Zoo Med, 86-88. *Mem:* Int Asn Aquatic Animal Med (pres, 88); Am Asn Zoo Veterinarians; Am Col Zoo Med; Wildlife Dis Asn; Am Vet Med Asn. *Res:* Investigation of new animal models for human disease with particular interest in the effects of environmental factors on the physiology and biochemistry of living organisms. *Mailing Add:* NC State Univ 4700 Hillsborough St Raleigh NC 27606

STOSKOPF, N C, CROP BREEDING & CROP PRODUCTION. *Current Pos:* asst prof crop sci, Ont Agr Col, 62-66, assoc prof, 66-69, PROF CROP SCI, UNIV GUELPH, 69-, DIR, DIPL PROG AGR, 74- *Personal Data:* b Mitchell, Ont, June 11, 34; m 60; c 2. *Educ:* Univ Toronto, BSA, 57, MSA, 58; McGill Univ, PhD(agron), 62. *Honors & Awards:* Friendship Award, China, 95. *Prof Exp:* Lectr agron, Ont Agr Col, 58-59; instr & exten specialist, Kemptville Agr Sch, 59-60. *Mem:* Agr Inst Can. *Res:* Winter wheat breeding given a physiological basis with yield as main objective; plants selected for upright leaves to achieve a high optimum leaf area, a high net assimilation rate and a long period of grain filling; cereal physiology. *Mailing Add:* Dept Crop Sci Univ Guelph Guelph ON N1G 2W1 Can

STOSSEL, THOMAS PETER, HEMATOLOGY, CELL BIOLOGY. *Current Pos:* PROF MED, HARVARD MED SCH, 82-; CHIEF, DIV EXP MED, BRIGHAM & WOMEN'S HOSP, 91- *Personal Data:* b Chicago, Ill, Sept 10, 41; m 65; c 2. *Educ:* Princeton Univ, AB, 63; Harvard Med Sch, MD, 67. *Hon Degrees:* MD, Univ Linkoping, Sweden. *Honors & Awards:* Damashek Prize, Am Soc Hemat, 83, Thomas Prize, 93. *Prof Exp:* House staff med, Mass Gen Hosp, 67-69; staff assoc, NIH, 67-71; from fel to sr assoc, Med Ctr, Children's Hosp, Boston, 71-76; chief hematol & oncol unit, Mass Gen Hosp, 76-91. *Concurrent Pos:* Fel, Harvard Med Sch, 71-78; ed, J Clin Invest, 82-87; scientific bd, Biogen Corp, 87-; clin res prof, Am Cancer Soc, 87- *Mem:* Nat Acad Sci; Am Soc Clin Investigation (pres, 87); Am Soc Hematol (pres, 97); Am Soc Cell Biol; Asn Am Physicians; fel Am Acad Arts & Sci; Am Fedn Clin Res. *Res:* Molecular basis of cell movements; education in clinical hematology; sociology of biomedical research. *Mailing Add:* Hematol & Oncol Dept Med Brigham/Womens' Hosp Francis St Boston MA 02115

STOTHERS, JOHN BAILIE, ORGANIC CHEMISTRY. *Current Pos:* lectr chem, Univ Western Ont, 59-61, from asst prof to prof, 61-96, chmn, 76-86, EMER PROF CHEM, UNIV WESTERN ONT, 96- *Personal Data:* b London, Ont, Apr 16, 31; m 53, Catherine; c Marta & Margot. *Educ:* Univ Western Ont, BSc, 53, MSc, 54; McMaster Univ, PhD(org chem), 57. *Honors & Awards:* Merck, Sharp & Dohme Lect Award, 71. *Prof Exp:* Res chemist, Res Dept, Imp Oil, Ltd, 57-59. *Mem:* Royal Soc Can; fel Chem Inst Can. *Res:* Nuclear magnetic resonance spectroscopy; applications of deuterium and carbon-13 nuclear magnetic resonance to organic structural, stereochemical and mechanistic problems and biosynthesis; deuterium exchange processes and molecular rearrangements. *Mailing Add:* 45 Mayfair Dr London ON N6A 2M7 Can

STOTLER, RAYMOND EUGENE, BOTANY. *Current Pos:* asst prof, 69-74, ASSOC PROF BOT, SOUTHERN ILL UNIV, 74- *Personal Data:* b Peoria, Ill, Mar 30, 40; m 69. *Educ:* Western Ill Univ, BS, 62; Southern Ill Univ, MA, 64; Univ Cincinnati, PhD(bot), 68. *Honors & Awards:* Dimond Award, NSF & Bot Soc Am, 75. *Prof Exp:* Fel bot, Univ Wis-Milwaukee, 68-69. *Mem:* Am Bryol & Lichenological Soc; Am Fern Soc; Am Soc Plant Taxon; Int Soc Plant Taxon; Int Asn Bryologists. *Res:* Nomenclature and biosystematics of hepatics, hornworts, and mosses. *Mailing Add:* Dept Plant Biol Southern Ill Univ Carbondale IL 62901-6509

STOTLER, RAYMOND T, GEOLOGY. *Current Pos:* CONSULT PETROL GEOLOGIST, 39- *Personal Data:* b Cincinnati, Ohio, June 1, 16. *Educ:* Princeton Univ, BS, 39. *Mem:* Am Asn Prof Geologists; fel Geol Soc Am. *Mailing Add:* 3238 Citation Dr Dallas TX 75229

STOTSKY, BERNARD A, PSYCHOLOGY, PSYCHIATRY. *Current Pos:* DIR, SCRANTON COUN SERV, 96- *Personal Data:* b New York, NY, Apr 8, 26; m 52; c 5. *Educ:* City Col New York, BS, 48; Univ Mich, MA, 49, PhD(psychol), 51; Western Res Univ, MD, 62. *Prof Exp:* Staff psychologist, Ment Hyg Clin, Vet Admin, Detroit, 51-53; instr & assoc, Boston Univ, 54-56, asst prof psychol, 56-57; asst prof, Duke Univ, 57-58; staff psychologist, Vet Admin Hosp, Brockton, Mass, 58-61; intern, George Washington Univ Hosp, 62-63; fel psychiat & resident psychiat, Mass Ment Health Ctr, 63-65 & Boston State Hosp, 65-66; from lectr to prof psychol, Boston State Col, 64-82, head dept, 72-73; chief psychiat, Northeastern Univ, 78-89; prof psychol, Univ Mass, Boston, 82-90. *Concurrent Pos:* Chief coun psychologist, Vet Admin Hosp, Brockton, Mass, 53-56, consult, 56-57 & 70- & chief psychologist, Durham, NC, 57-58; consult, Brockton Family Serv, 54, Hayden Goodwill Inn, 54-57, Mass Dept Pub Health, 67 & Boston State Hosp, 63-65, 68-75; prin investr, psychiat consult & lectr, Northeastern Univ, 64-88; assoc psychiat, Tufts Univ, 66-67, from asst prof to assoc prof, 67-88, lectr, Clark Univ, 69-70 & Mt Sinai Sch Med, 69-72; consult, Food & Drug Admin, 72-75 & Nat Inst Child Health & Human Develop, 73-77; prof psychiat & behav sci, Univ Wash, 73-77; dir, Outpatient Psychiat Clin, St Elizabeth's Hosp Boston, 73, assoc dir psychiat educ, 74-81, dir psychiat educ, 81-84; consult, Campus Sch, Boston Col, 74-84; adj prof psychol, Univ Mass, 92-94, Salem State Col, 92-96. *Mem:* Fel Am Psychol Asn; Am Psychiat Asn; Am Psycolog Soc. *Res:* Psychopharmacology; diagnosis and treatment of mental disease; personality and organic factors in rehabilitation of chronically ill patients; geriatrics. *Mailing Add:* Forum Towers 220 Linden St Ste 605 Scranton PA 18503

STOTT, BRIAN, COMPUTER CONTROL METHODS. *Current Pos:* PRES, POWER COMPUT APPLN CORP, MESA, ARIZ, 84- *Personal Data:* b Manchester, Eng, Aug 5, 41. *Educ:* Univ Manchester, BSc, 62, MSc, 63, PhD(elec eng), 71. *Prof Exp:* Lectr elec power eng, Univ Manchester Sci & Technol, 68-74; assoc prof, Univ Waterloo, Ont, Can, 74-76; consult, Brazilian Inst Elec Power Res, 76-83; prof, Ariz State Univ, Tempe, 83-84. *Mem:* Fel Inst Elec & Electronics Engrs. *Mailing Add:* 1921 S Alma School Rd Suite 207 Mesa AZ 85210

STOTT, DONALD FRANKLIN, GEOLOGY. *Current Pos:* RETIRED. *Personal Data:* b Reston, Man, Apr 30, 28; m 60; c 3. *Educ:* Univ Man, BSc, 53, MSc, 54; Princeton Univ, AM, 56, PhD, 58. *Honors & Awards:* Miller Medal, Royal Soc Can, 83. *Prof Exp:* geologist, Geol Surv Can, 57-72, head, Regional Geol Subdiv, 72-73, dir, 73-80; res scientist, inst Sedimentary & Petrol Geol, 73-89. *Mem:* Fel Geol Soc Am; Can Soc Petrol Geologists; Geol Asn Can. *Res:* Physical stratigraphy and sedimentation, particularly of Cretaceous system of Rocky Mountain foothills, Canada. *Mailing Add:* 8929 Forest Park Dr Sidney BC V8L 5A7 Can

STOTT, KENHELM WELBURN, JR, mammalogy, ornithology; deceased, see previous edition for last biography

STOTT, PAUL EDWIN, ANTIOXIDANTS-INHIBITORS, CHEMICAL BLOWING AGENTS. *Current Pos:* SCI REP TO FORMER SOVIET UNION, 91- *Personal Data:* b Springfield, Mass, Jan 18, 48; m 70; c 3. *Educ:* Brigham Young Univ, BS, 71, PhD(chem), 79, Univ Mass, MS, 72. *Prof Exp:* Gen mgr, res chem, Parish Chem Co, 74-79; res chem, Uniroyal Inc, 79-80, sr group leader, 80-82; tech dir, Lubritex Inc, 72-84; dir res, Texmark Resins, 82-85; sect mgr, Chem Div, Uniroyal Chem Co Inc, 85-86, res mgr, 86-91. *Mem:* Sigma Xi; Com Develop Asn. *Res:* Heterocyclic chemistry; development of antioxidants, inhibitors & stabilizers for petroleum, plastics & monomers. *Mailing Add:* 48 Coniston Ave Waterbury CT 06708

STOTTLEMYRE, JAMES ARTHUR, GEOPHYSICS, RESERVOIR ENGINEERING. *Current Pos:* MGR, EARTH SCI SECT, BATTELLE PAC NORTHWEST LABS, 76- *Personal Data:* b Juneau, Alaska, Jan 4, 48; m 70; c 2. *Educ:* Univ Wash, BS, 71, MS, 74, PhD, 80. *Prof Exp:* Resource engr energy resources, Wash Water Power Co, 74-76. *Mem:* Soc Explor Geophys; Soc Petrol Engrs; Am Geophys Union. *Res:* Underground fluid and heat storage, disposal of hazardous waste; geohydrochemical modeling; waste management. *Mailing Add:* 2205 Carriage Ave Richland WA 99352

STOTTS, JANE, IMMUNOLOGY, MICROBIOLOGY. *Current Pos:* RETIRED. *Personal Data:* b Dallas, Tex, Sept 15, 39. *Educ:* Univ Tex, Austin, BA, 61; Baylor Univ, MS, 64. *Prof Exp:* Res mgr microbiol & immunol, Proctor & Gamble Co, 64- *Res:* Allergic contact dermatitis, predictive testing and identification of allergens; primary irritant dermatitis; microflora of skin; hospital infection control. *Mailing Add:* 9 Falling Brook Cincinnati OH 45241

STOTZ, ROBERT WILLIAM, RESEARCH ADMINISTRATION. *Current Pos:* MGR, VALIDATION, JACOBS ENG GROUP, 91- *Personal Data:* b Monroe, Mich, July 18, 42; m 71, Sandra L Johnston; c Jason. *Educ:* Univ Toledo, BS, 64, MS, 66; Univ Fla, PhD(inorg chem), 70. *Prof Exp:* Res assoc, Mich State Univ, 70-71; instr chem, Eastern Mich Univ, 72-72; asst prof, Mercer Univ, 72-73; asst prof, Tri-State Col, 73-74; srpvr inorg anal res, Inst Gas Technol, 74-76; mgr anal chem, 76-79; mgr, validation, Upjohn Co, 79-90. *Mem:* Am Chem Soc; Parenteral Drug Asn. *Res:* Development and modification of various instrumental methods for determination of pharmaceutical constituents. *Mailing Add:* Jacobs Eng Group Sabine & Essex Ave Narberth PA 19072. *Fax:* 513-595-7860

STOTZKY, GUENTHER, MICROBIAL ECOLOGY. *Current Pos:* assoc prof biol, NY Univ, 68-70, adj assoc prof, 67-68, chmn dept, 70-77, PROF BIOL, NY UNIV, 70- *Personal Data:* b Leipzig, Ger, May 24, 31; nat US; m 58, Kayla Baker; c Jay, Martha & Deborah. *Educ:* Calif Polytech State Univ, BS, 52; Ohio State Univ, MS, 54, PhD(agron & microbiol), 56. *Honors & Awards:* Selman A Waksman Hon Lect Award, Theobald Smith Soc, 89; Fisher Sci Co Award for Appl Environ Microbiol, Am Soc Microbiol, 90. *Prof Exp:* Res asst soil biochem & microbiol, Ohio State Univ, 53-56; res assoc bot & plant nutrit, Univ Mich, 56-58; head soil microbiol, Cent Res Labs, United Fruit Co, 58-63; microbiologist & chmn, Kitchawan Res Lab, Brooklyn Bot Garden, 63-68. *Concurrent Pos:* Spec scientist, Argonne Nat Lab, 55; mem, Am Inst Biol Sci-NASA Regional Coun, 65-68; regional ed, Soil Biol & Biochem, 69-; assoc ed, Appl Environ Microbiol, 71-77 & Can J Microbiol, 71-75; mem ad hoc comt rev biomed & ecol effects of extremely low frequency radiation, Bur Med & Surg, Dept Navy, 72-75; vis prof, Inst Advan Studies, Polytech Inst, Mex, 73; Cath Univ, Santiago, Chile, 81, & Moscow State Univ, 90; mem, Comn Human Res, Nat Res Coun, 75-77; mem, Environ Biol Rev Panel, US Environ Protection Agency, 80-; mem, Controlled Ecol Life Support Systs Prof Rev Panel, NASA, Am Inst Biol Sci, 80-87; res assoc, Nat Ctr Sci Res, Poitiers Univ, France, 82; guest lectr, Australian Soc Microbiol Found, 84; distinguished vis scientist, US Environ Protection Agency, 86-89; ser ed, Marcel Dekker Inc, 86-92. *Mem:* Fel AAAS; Soc Environ Geochem & Health; Am Soc Microbiol; Can Soc Microbiol; Int Soil Sci Soc; fel Am Acad Microbiol; fel Soil Sci Soc Am; fel Am Soc Agron; Bot Soc Am; Am Inst Biol Sci. *Res:* Microbial ecology; surface interactions; soil, water and air pollution; environmental microbiology, virology and immunology; ecotoxicology; fate gene transfer and effects of genetically engineered microbes in natural habitats; clinical microbiology. *Mailing Add:* Dept Biol NY Univ Wash Sq New York NY 10003

STOUDT, EMILY LAWS, GEOLOGY. *Current Pos:* MGR GEOLOGIC RES, TEXACO HOUSTON RES CTR, 84- *Personal Data:* b Columbus, Ohio, Apr 5, 43; m 67, 77; c 2. *Educ:* Ohio State Univ, BA, 66, PhD(geol), 75; La State Univ, MS, 68. *Prof Exp:* Geologist, Spec Proj Br, US Geol Surv, 68-70; geologist, Explor & Prod Res Lab, Getty Oil Co, 75-81, geologic supvr, Getty Res Ctr, 81- *Mem:* Geol Soc Am; Am Asn Petrol Geologists; Soc Econ Paleontologists & Mineralogists. *Res:* Carbonate petrology; regional geology of the mid-continent Silurian, western United States Permian, Gulf Coast Jurassic-Cretaceous systems, Guatemalan Jurassic-Cretaceous. *Mailing Add:* 11710 Primwood Dr Houston TX 77070

STOUDT, HOWARD WEBSTER, HUMAN FACTORS, ERGONOMICS. *Current Pos:* prof & chmn dept community med, Col Osteop Med, 73-77, prof, 78-88, EMER PROF COMMUNITY HEALTH SCI, MICH STATE UNIV, 88-; CONSULT, 88- *Personal Data:* b Pittsburgh, Pa, May 13, 25; m 53; c Katherine (Robson) & Roberta (Lackie). *Educ:* Harvard Univ, AB, 49, SM, 62; Univ Pa, AM, 53, PhD(anthrop), 59. *Prof Exp:* Res asst, Sch Pub Health, Harvard Univ, 52-55; res & educ specialist, Air Univ, 55-57; res assoc phys anthrop, Sch Pub Health, Harvard Univ, 57-66, asst prof, 66-73. *Concurrent Pos:* Consult, Nat Health Exam Surv, USPHS Ctr Dis Control, Soc Automotive Engrs, Vet Admin, NASA US Army, US Air Force, Nat Res Coun, Nat Acad Sci. *Mem:* Am Asn Phys Anthrop; Human Factors Soc; AAAS; Human Biol Asn; Ergonomics Soc; Am Col Epidemiol. *Res:* Physical anthropology; anthropometry and biomechanics, epidemiology of accidents; application of human biological data to the design of equipment and workspaces with special reference to safety and health. *Mailing Add:* 4 Schooner Ridge Rd Bath ME 04530

STOUDT, THOMAS HENRY, MICROBIOLOGY. *Current Pos:* PRES, STOUDT ASSOCS, 84- *Personal Data:* b Temple, Pa, Apr 6, 22; m 43; c 3. *Educ:* Albright Col, BS, 43; Rutgers Univ, MS, 44; Purdue Univ, West Lafayette, PhD(org chem), 49. *Prof Exp:* Asst chem, Rutgers Univ, 43-44 & Purdue Univ, West Lafayette, 46-47; sr microbiologist, 49-58, Merck & Co, Inc, from sect head to sr sect head, 58-69, dir appl microbiol, 69-75, sr dir appl microbiol & nat prod isolation, 75-77, exec dir, 77-84. *Concurrent Pos:* Mem adv bd, Health & Environ, Union County, NJ. *Mem:* Am Chem Soc; AAAS; Am Soc Microbiologists; NY Acad Sci. *Res:* Microbial transformations; microbial biosyntheses; antibiotics; microbial physiology and genetics, rumen microbiology; oral microbiology; microbial enzymology; vaccines and immunology; scale-up of industrial fermentation processes. *Mailing Add:* 857 Village Green Westfield NJ 07090-3515

STOUFER, ROBERT CARL, INORGANIC CHEMISTRY. *Current Pos:* ASSOC PROF INORG CHEM, UNIV FLA, 58- *Personal Data:* b Ashland, Ohio, Nov 3, 30; m 54, Virginia Knight; c Michael & William. *Educ:* Otterbein Col, BA & BS, 52; Ohio State Univ, PhD, 59. *Mem:* Am Chem Soc; Sigma Xi. *Res:* Synthesis of inorganic complexes and their characterization, particularly of spectroscopic and magnetic properties; investigations of Jahn-Teller prone systems. *Mailing Add:* Dept Chem Univ Fla Gainesville FL 32611

STOUFFER, DONALD CARL, ENGINEERING MECHANICS. *Current Pos:* from asst prof to assoc prof eng sci, 69-77, fac fel, 71, PROF ENG SCI, UNIV CINCINNATI, 77- *Personal Data:* b Philadelphia, Pa, May 15, 38; m 62; c 2. *Educ:* Drexel Univ, BSME, 61, MSME, 65; Univ Mich, Ann Arbor, PhD(eng mech), 68. *Prof Exp:* Engr, Philco-Ford Corp, 61-63 & Westinghouse Elec Corp, 63-65; instr mech, Univ Mich, Ann Arbor, 66-68, lectr, 68-69. *Concurrent Pos:* US-Australian Coop Sci fel, Univ Melbourne, 76; vis scientist, Wright-Patterson AFB, Ohio, 75-; res grants, NSF & Air Force Wright Aeronaut Lab, NASA Lewis Res Ctr, GE Aircraft Engrs. *Mem:* Soc Rheol; Soc Nat Philos; Am Soc Mech Engrs; Am Acad Mech. *Res:* Theoretical and applied mechanics; rheology; constitutive equations; life prediction. *Mailing Add:* 6982 Driftwood Cincinnati OH 45241-1039

STOUFFER, JAMES L, AUDIOLOGY, PSYCHOACOUSTICS. *Current Pos:* asst prof audiol, Univ Western Ont, 69-70, dir, Commun Dis & Chief Speech & Hearing Serv, Univ Western Ont & Univ Hosp, London, Ont, 72-81, ASSOC PROF, SCH COMMUN SCI & DIS, UNIV WESTERN ONT, 82- *Personal Data:* b Harrisburg, Pa, Sept 25, 35; m 68. *Educ:* State Univ NY Col Buffalo, BSc, 64; Pa State Univ, MSc, 66, PhD(audiol, statist), 69. *Prof Exp:* Clin audiologist, Pa State Univ, 64-69. *Concurrent Pos:* NIH fel psychoacoust, Commun Sci Lab, Univ Fla, 69-70; consult, Oxford County Ment Health Centre, 70-; ed asst, Ont Speech & Hearing Asn, 71- *Mem:* Am Speech & Hearing Asn; Acoust Soc Am. *Res:* Tinnitus measurement and handicap; central auditory processing disorders. *Mailing Add:* Sch Commun Sci & Dis Univ Western Ont London ON N6G 1H1 Can

STOUFFER, JAMES RAY, ANIMAL SCIENCE. *Current Pos:* asst prof animal husb, 56-62, assoc prof animal sci, 62-77, PROF ANIMAL SCI, CORNELL UNIV, 77- *Personal Data:* b Glen Elder, Kans, Jan 12, 29; m 55; c 2. *Educ:* Univ Ill, BS, 51, MS, 53, PhD(meats), 56. *Prof Exp:* Asst prof animal husb, Univ Conn, 55-56. *Mem:* Am Soc Animal Sci; Inst Food Technol; Am Meat Sci Asn. *Res:* Carcass evaluation of meat animals, particularly the relationship of live animal and carcass characteristics. *Mailing Add:* 116 Winston Dr Ithaca NY 14850

STOUFFER, JOHN EMERSON, BIOCHEMISTRY. *Current Pos:* asst prof, 61-66, ASSOC PROF BIOCHEM, BAYLOR COL MED, 67- *Personal Data:* b Sioux City, Iowa, Dec 4, 25; m 55; c 2. *Educ:* Northwestern Univ, BS, 49; Boston Univ, PhD(org chem), 57. *Prof Exp:* Res assoc biochem, Med Col, Cornell Univ, 57-59, instr, 59-61. *Mem:* Am Chem Soc; Am Oil Chemists Soc; Am Soc Biol Chemists; Endocrine Soc; Am Inst Chemists. *Res:* Thyroid hormones; structure function relationships of hormones and mechanism of action; membrane receptor sites. *Mailing Add:* 2703 Albans Houston TX 77005

STOUFFER, RICHARD FRANKLIN, PLANT PATHOLOGY, VIROLOGY. *Current Pos:* RETIRED. *Personal Data:* b Welch, WVa, July 3, 32; m 57; c 2. *Educ:* Vanderbilt Univ, BA, 54; Cornell Univ, PhD(plant path), 59. *Prof Exp:* Asst, Cornell Univ, 54-59; asst prof, Univ RI, 59-60; asst virologist, Univ Fla, 61-65; from asst prof to prof plant path, Fruit Res Lab, Pa State Univ, 76-82; prof & head dept plant path, Univ Ga, 82-87. *Mem:* Am Phytopath Soc; Brit Asn Appl Biol; Asn Appl Biol; Int Comt Fruit Tree Virus Res (secy, 82-85). *Res:* Plant virology; virus diseases of deciduous fruit trees. *Mailing Add:* 1791 Slopewood Bend Marietta GA 30062

STOUFFER, RICHARD LEE, REPRODUCTIVE PHYSIOLOGY. *Current Pos:* SCIENTIST, ORE PRIMATE CTR, 85-, HEAD, DIV REPROD SCI, 96- *Personal Data:* b Hagerstown, Md, July 27, 49; m 73, Gwendolyn M Frush; c Erin E & Brian A. *Educ:* Va Polytech Inst, BS, 71; Duke Univ, PhD(physiol), 75. *Honors & Awards:* Res Career Develop Award, NIH, 82. *Prof Exp:* staff fel endocrinol, Reprod Res Br, Nat Inst Child Health & Human Develop, NIH, 75-77; from asst prof to assoc prof physiol, Col Med, Univ Ariz, 77-85. *Concurrent Pos:* Prin invest, PHS Grants, 78-; mem, NIH Study Sect, 83, 85, & 91; lectr, Reprod Pathophysiol, Ore Health Scis Ctr, 86-; bd dirs, Ovarian Workshop, 88-94 & Soc Study Reprod, 90-93. *Mem:* Soc Study Reprod (pres-elect, 94-95, pres, 96); AAAS; Endocrine Soc; Am Physiol Soc; Am Soc Reprod Med; Am Soc Primatologists. *Res:* Female reproductive endocrinology, with emphasis on the regulation of primate ovarian function; regulation of the corpus luteum; nonhuman primate model for in vitro fertilization and early embryogenesis. *Mailing Add:* Div Reproductive Sci Ore Reg Primate Res Ctr 505 NW 185th Ave Beaverton OR 97006-3448. *Fax:* 503-690-5563

STOUFFER, RONALD JAY, CLIMATE MODELING, CLIMATE DYNAMICS. *Current Pos:* RES METEOROLOGIST, GEOPHYS FLUID DYNAMICS LAB, NAT OCEANIC & ATMOSPHERIC ADMIN, DEPT COM, 77- *Personal Data:* b Hershey, Pa, Feb 3, 54; m 76; c 3. *Educ:* Pa State Univ, BS, 76, MS, 77. *Concurrent Pos:* Mem, Steering Group Global Climate Modeling, Joint Sci Comt, World Meteorol Orgn, 90- *Mem:* Am Meteorol Soc; Am Geophys Union. *Res:* Study of climate variations using mathematical climate models; climate change resulting from increasing greenhouse gases using coupled ocean-atmosphere models. *Mailing Add:* Geophys Fluid Dynamics Lab NOAA Princeton Univ Princeton NJ 08542. *E-Mail:* rjs@gfdl.gov

STOUGHTON, RAYMOND WOODFORD, physical chemistry, nuclear chemistry, for more information see previous edition

STOUT, BARBARA ELIZABETH, NUCLEAR CHEMISTRY, RADIOCHEMISTRY. *Current Pos:* ASST PROF CHEM, UNIV CINCINNATI, 90- *Personal Data:* b Anchorage, Alaska, May 29, 62; m 90. *Educ:* Wesleyan Col, AB, 83; Fla State Univ, MS, 85, PhD(inorg chem), 89. *Prof Exp:* Res assoc, Inst Curie, Paris, France, 85-86 & 87-88; postdoctoral asst, Univ Lausanne, Switz, 89-90. *Mem:* Sigma Xi; Am Chem Soc. *Res:* Actinide and lanthanide solution chemistry; luminescence spectroscopy; environmental chemistry of the f-elements; interactions of polyelectrolytes with the f-elements. *Mailing Add:* Chem Univ Cincinnati 2600 Clifton Ave Cincinnati OH 45220-2872

STOUT, BENJAMIN BOREMAN, FOREST ECOLOGY. *Current Pos:* RETIRED. *Personal Data:* b Parkersburg, WVa, Mar 2, 24; m 45, 89, Elaine Ferguson; c Susan L, David F & Bruce D. *Educ:* WVa Univ, BSF, 47; Harvard Univ, MF, 50; Rutgers Univ, PhD, 67. *Prof Exp:* Forester, Pond & Moyer Co, 47-49; silviculturist, Harvard Black Rock Forest, 50-55, supvr, 55-59; from asst prof to prof forestry, Rutgers Univ, New Brunswick, 59-77, chmn, Dept Biol Sci, 74-77, assoc provost, 77-78; dean, Sch Forestry, Univ Mont, 78-85; mem, Nat Coun Paper Indust Air & Stream Improv, 85-91. *Mem:* Fel Soc Am Foresters; Sigma Xi; Am Inst Biol Sci. *Res:* Ways and means of quantifying vegetations response to environment. *Mailing Add:* 1545 Takena SW Albany OR 97321

STOUT, BILL A(LVIN), agricultural engineering, for more information see previous edition

STOUT, DARRYL GLEN, AGRONOMY, PLANT PHYSIOLOGY. *Current Pos:* res scientist forage prod, 77-93, res scientist & mgr, Agr Can, 93-95, RES SCIENTIST FORAGE PROD, AGR CAN, 95- *Personal Data:* b Carman, Man, Mar 21, 44; m 75; c David & Glenn. *Educ:* Univ Man, BSA, 69, MSc, 72; Cornell Univ, PhD(plant physiol), 76. *Prof Exp:* Res assoc drought tolerance, Univ Sask, 75-77. *Concurrent Pos:* Vis fel, Cornell Univ, 82-83. *Mem:* Am Soc Agron; Can Soc Agron. *Res:* Forage management; seeding rate and cutting management on alfalfa persistence and yield; double cropping and intercropping for hay production and grazing; growth and survival of plants under stress conditions of frost, drought and grazing. *Mailing Add:* Agr Can 3015 Ord Rd Kamloops BC V2B 8A9 Can. *Fax:* 250-554-5229; *E-Mail:* stout@bcrska.agr.ca

STOUT, DAVID MICHAEL, ORGANIC CHEMISTRY, RESEARCH MANAGEMENT. *Current Pos:* sr res scientist neurosci res, 88-90, RES INVESTR, ABBOTT LABS, 90- *Personal Data:* b Flint, Mich, Nov 20, 47; m 69; c 2. *Educ:* Col Wooster, BA, 69; Univ Rochester, MS, 72; Colo State Univ, PhD(org chem), 74. *Prof Exp:* NIH fel, Yale Univ, 74-76; group leader cardiovasc res, Du Pont Critical Care Div, E I du Pont de Nemours & Co, 76-88. *Mem:* Am Chem Soc. *Res:* Neuroscience; organic synthesis. *Mailing Add:* Abbott Labs D 47C AP10 Abbott Park IL 60064

STOUT, EDGAR LEE, MATHEMATICS. *Current Pos:* assoc prof, 69-74, PROF MATH, UNIV WASH, 74- *Personal Data:* b Grants Pass, Ore, Mar 13, 38; m 61; c 1. *Educ:* Ore State Col, BA, 60; Univ Wis, MA, 61, PhD(math), 64. *Prof Exp:* Instr math, Yale Univ, 64-65, asst prof, 65-69, Off Naval Res res assoc, 67-68. *Concurrent Pos:* Vis prof math, Univ Leeds, 72-73. *Mem:* Math Asn Am; Am Math Soc. *Res:* Functions of one or several complex variables; function algebras. *Mailing Add:* Dept Math Univ Wash Box 354350 Seattle WA 98195-4350

STOUT, EDWARD IRVIN, ORGANIC CHEMISTRY. *Current Pos:* chmn, DIR RES DEV & INT SALES, SW TECHNOLOGIES, INC. *Personal Data:* b Washington Co, Iowa, Mar 2, 39; c 3. *Educ:* Iowa Wesleyan Col, BS, 60; Bradley Univ, MS, 68; Univ Ariz, PhD(org chem), 74. *Prof Exp:* Chemist, Lever Bros Co, 61-62; res chemist, Northern Regional Res Ctr, USDA, 62-78; dir res, Spenco Med Corp, 78-80; consult, 81-82; mem staff, 82-86, dir res, Chemstar Prod Co, 81- *Concurrent Pos:* Instr org chem, Bradley Univ, 70-75. *Mem:* Am Chem Soc (secy, 75); Am Burn Asn; Wound Healing Soc. *Res:* Preparation and characterization of starch derivatives including starch graft copolymers; development of absorbent copolymers for wound dressing; development of hydrogel wound dressings; development of hot/cold therapy products; development of wheel chair cushions and bed pads (hospital). *Mailing Add:* Southwest Technol Inc 2018 Baltimore Kansas City MO 64108-1914

STOUT, ERNEST RAY, MOLECULAR BIOLOGY, BIOCHEMISTRY. *Current Pos:* from asst prof to prof molecular biol, 67-97, asst dean, Col Arts & Sci, 78-79, HEAD, DEPT BIOL, VA POLYTECH INST & STATE UNIV, 80-, EMER PROF MOLECULAR BIOL, 97- *Personal Data:* b Boone, NC, Oct 31, 38; m 61; c 3. *Educ:* Appalachian State Univ, BS, 61; Univ Fla, PhD(bot & biochem), 65. *Prof Exp:* Nat Cancer Inst fel biochem genetics, Univ Md, 65-67. *Mem:* AAAS; Am Soc Plant Physiol. *Res:* Mechanism of nucleic acid synthesis in higher plants; control of nucleic acid synthesis; parovirus macromolecular synthesis. *Mailing Add:* 960 Poff School Rd Riner VA 24149

STOUT, GLENN EMANUEL, METEOROLOGY, HYDROLOGY & WATER RESCOURCES. *Current Pos:* asst engr, Ill State Water Surv, 47-52, head atmospheric sci sect, 52-71, asst to chief, 71-74, DIR WATER RESOURCES CENTER, ILL STATE WATER SURV, UNIV ILL, URBANA, 73-, PROF METEOROL, INST ENVIRON STUDIES, 73- *Personal Data:* b Fostoria, Ohio, Mar 23, 20; m 42, Helen L Beery; c Bonnie & Steven. *Educ:* Findlay Col, BS, 42; Univ Chicago, cert, 43. *Hon Degrees:* DSc, Findlay Col, 73. *Prof Exp:* Asst math, Findlay Col, 39-42; instr meteorol, Univ Chicago, 42-43 & US War Dept, Chanute AFB, Ill, 46-47. *Concurrent Pos:* Consult, Crop-Hail Ins Actuarial Assoc, 61-69; prog coordr, Nat Ctr Atmospheric Res, NSF, 69-71; ed-chief, Water Int, 82-86; bd dir, Univ Coun Water Resources, 83-86; exec dir, Int Asn Water Resources, 84-, sec gen, 86-92. *Mem:* Am Meteorol Soc; Am Geophys Union; Am Water Resources Asn; AAAS; Int Asn Water Resources (vpres, 92-94); Int Asn Hydrol Res; Am Water Works Asn; NAm Lake Mgt Asn; Sigma Xi. *Res:* Hail climatology; weather modification; water resources; environmental science; environmental management; hydrology and water resources; Middle East water management. *Mailing Add:* 920 W John St Champaign IL 61821

STOUT, ISAAC JACK, ECOLOGY. *Current Pos:* from asst prof to assoc prof, 72-83, PROF BIOL SCI, UNIV CENT FLA, 83- *Personal Data:* b Clarksburg, WVa, July 20, 39; m 64; c 2. *Educ:* Ore State Univ, BS, 61, Va Polytech Inst & State Univ, MS, 67; Wash State Univ, PhD(zool), 72. *Prof Exp:* Wildlife Mgt Inst fel waterfowl ecol, Va Coop Wildlife Res Univ, 64-65; field ecologist, Old Dominion Univ, 65-67; USPHS fel appl ecol, Wash State Univ, 67-69. *Concurrent Pos:* Mem, Environ Effect & Fate Solid Rocket Emission Prod, NASA, Kennedy Space Ctr, 75. *Mem:* Ecol Soc Am; Brit Ecol Soc; Wildlife Soc; Am Soc Mammalogists; Sigma Xi. *Res:* Population and community ecology; ecology of sand pine scrub; conservation biology. *Mailing Add:* Dept Biol Sci Univ Cent Fla Box 25000 Orlando FL 32816-0001

STOUT, JOHN FREDERICK, ETHOLOGY, ZOOLOGY. *Current Pos:* assoc prof, 69-70, PROF BIOL, ANDREWS UNIV, 70-, CHMN BIOL, 83- *Personal Data:* b Takoma Park, Md, Jan 20, 36; m 56; c 2. *Educ:* Columbia Union Col, BA, 57; Univ Md, PhD(zool), 63. *Honors & Awards:* Alexander von Humboldt Sr US Scientist Award, 75. *Prof Exp:* Instr biol, Walla Walla Col, 62, asst prof, 63-65, dir marine sta, 64-69, assoc prof biol, 66-69. *Concurrent Pos:* USPHS spec fel & vis researcher, Univ Cologne, 69-70; guest res prof, Max Planck Inst Behav Physiol, 75-76. *Mem:* Sigma Xi; Soc Neurosci. *Res:* Neurobiology of acoustic communication; communication during social behavior; behavioral physiology. *Mailing Add:* Dept of Biol Andrews Univ Berrien Springs MI 49104-0001

STOUT, JOHN WILLARD, PHYSICAL CHEMISTRY, CHEMICAL PHYSICS. *Current Pos:* from assoc prof to prof, 46-77, EMER PROF CHEM, UNIV CHICAGO, 77- *Personal Data:* b Seattle, Wash, Mar 13, 12; m 48, Florence L Parsons; c John E. *Educ:* Univ Calif, BS, 33, PhD(phys chem), 37. *Honors & Awards:* Huffman Mem Award, 60. *Prof Exp:* Instr chem, Univ Calif, 37-38, Lalor fel, 38-39; instr chem, Mass Inst Technol, 39-41; investr, Nat Defense Res Comt, Univ Calif, 41-44; group leader, Manhattan Dist, Los Alamos Sci Lab, 44-46. *Concurrent Pos:* Ed, J Chem Physics, 59-82, consult ed, 83-; mem coun, Am Phys Soc, 72-76. *Mem:* AAAS; Am Chem Soc; fel Am Phys Soc. *Res:* Thermodynamics; calorimetry; crystal spectra; cryogenics; paramagnetism and antiferromagnetism. *Mailing Add:* Dept Chem Univ Chicago 5735 S Ellis Ave Chicago IL 60637

STOUT, KOEHLER, MINING & GEOLOGICAL ENGINEERING. *Current Pos:* RETIRED. *Personal Data:* b Deer Lodge, Mont, Sept 1, 22; m 50, Phyllis Storer; c Karen, Carla & Janet. *Educ:* Mont Sch Mines, BS, 48, MS, 49; La Salle Exten Univ, LLB, 57. *Hon Degrees:* DEng, Mont Univ. *Prof Exp:* Asst prof mining eng, Mont Col Mineral Sci & Technol, 52-58, from assoc prof to prof eng sci, 58-84, head dept, 62-84, dean, div eng, 66-84. *Concurrent Pos:* Consult, minerals indust. *Mem:* Am Soc Eng Educ; Nat Soc Prof Engrs; Am Inst Mining, Metall & Petrol Engrs. *Res:* Portland and chemical cements injected into weak, unstable ground to prepare the ground for mining. *Mailing Add:* 1327 W Granite Butte MT 59701. *Fax:* 406-496-4133

STOUT, LANDON CLARKE, JR, PATHOLOGY, INTERNAL MEDICINE. *Current Pos:* assoc prof, 72-74, PROF PATH, UNIV TEX MED BR GALVESTON, 74- *Personal Data:* b Kansas City, Mo, Feb 20, 33; m 54, 81; c 5. *Educ:* Univ Md, MD, 57. *Prof Exp:* Resident internal med, Med Ctr, Univ Okla, 58-61, asst prof, 63-72, dir inst comp path, 65-69, resident path, 66-67, from asst prof to assoc prof, 68-72, chairman chmn dept, 70-72. *Concurrent Pos:* Nat Heart Inst spec fel, Univ Okla, 67-68; consult, Okla Med Res Found, 71-72. *Mem:* Am Asn Path; Am Col Physicians; Am Gastroenterol Asn; Am Heart Asn; Am Diabetes Asn; Int Acad Pathol. *Res:* Atherosclerosis; diabetic renal disease; mitral valve disease. *Mailing Add:* Dept Path Univ Tex Med Br Galveston TX 77555

STOUT, MARGUERITE ANNETTE, PHYSIOLOGY. *Current Pos:* asst prof, 75-82, ASSOC PROF PHYSIOL, NJ MED SCH, UNIV MED & DENT NJ, 82- *Personal Data:* b Marion, Ind, July 17, 43. *Educ:* Univ Wis, BS, 64; Univ Iowa, PhD(physiol & biophys), 74; Pace Univ, MBA, 86. *Honors & Awards:* Nat Heart Lung & Blood Inst Young Investr Award, 78-81. *Prof Exp:* Res scientist I, Galesburg State Res Hosp, 65-70; fel, Univ Iowa, 70-74. *Concurrent Pos:* Guest prof, Cath Univ, Leuven Belg, 90-92; Fogarty Int fel, 90-91. *Res:* Calcium regulation by sarcoplasmic reticulum in chemically skinned vascular smooth muscle. *Mailing Add:* Dept Pharmacol & Physiol NJ Med Sch Univ Med & Dent NJ Newark NJ 07103-2714

STOUT, MARTIN LINDY, geology; deceased, see previous edition for last biography

STOUT, QUENTIN FIELDEN, PARALLEL COMPUTING. *Current Pos:* PROF COMPUT SCI, UNIV MICH, 84-, DIR, SOFTWARE SYSTS RES LAB, 93- *Personal Data:* b Cleveland, Ohio, Sept 23, 49; m 93, Janis Hardwick; c G Nathan & Andrew C. *Educ:* Centre Col, BA, 70; Ind Univ, PhD(math), 77. *Prof Exp:* From asst prof to assoc prof comput sci & math, State Univ NY, Binghamton, 76-84. *Concurrent Pos:* Consult, Parker-Hannifin Corp, 67-72; prin investr, numerous grants, 78- *Mem:* Asn Comput Mach; Am Math Soc; Inst Elec & Electronics Engrs; Soc Indust Appl Math. *Res:* Design and analysis of parallel algorithms; design and analysis of serial algorithms; scientific computing; parallel programming environments; parallel computers. *Mailing Add:* Dept Elec Eng & Comput Sci Univ Mich Ann Arbor MI 48109-2122. *Fax:* 313-763-4617; *E-Mail:* qstout@eecs.umich.edu

STOUT, RAY BERNARD, THERMODYNAMICS OF MATERIAL DEFECTS. *Current Pos:* TECH AREA LEADER, RADIOACTIVE SPENT FUEL & DEFENSE HIGH LEVEL WASTE FORMS, LAWRENCE LIVERMORE NAT LAB, LIVERMORE, 79- *Personal Data:* b Georgetown, Ohio, June 16, 39; m 65, Tanya Kuenzli; c Natasha. *Educ:* Ohio State Univ, BS, 64, MS, 68; Ill Inst Technol, PhD(eng mech), 70; Univ Pittsburgh, MBA, 72. *Prof Exp:* Apprentice, Cincinnati Milling Mach Co, 57-59; fel engr, Bettis Atomic Power Lab, Westinghouse Elec Corp, West Mifflin, 69-79. *Mem:* Am Soc Mech Engrs; Am Phys Soc; Mat Res Soc. *Res:* Applications of numerical analysis and applied mathematics to engineering mechanics and physics of materials. *Mailing Add:* 954 Venus Way Livermore CA 94550

STOUT, ROBERT DANIEL, METALLURGY, WELDABILITY. *Current Pos:* instr, Lehigh Univ, 39-45, from asst prof to assoc prof, 45-50, prof metall, 50-80, head, Dept Metall, 56-60, dean, Grad Sch, 60-80, PROF, LEHIGH UNIV, 81- *Personal Data:* b Reading, Pa, Jan 2, 15; m 39, Elizabeth Allwein; c Elizabeth. *Educ:* Pa State Col, BS, 35; Lehigh Univ, MS, 41, PhD(metall), 44. *Hon Degrees:* ScD, Albright Col, 67. *Honors & Awards:* Lincoln Gold Medal, Am Welding Soc, 43, Spraragen Award, 64, Thomas Award, 75 & Jennings Award, 74, Houdremont lectr, 70; Adams lectr, 60; Hobart Medal, 81; Savage Award, 87. *Prof Exp:* Asst, Carpenter Steel Co, 35-39. *Concurrent Pos:* Deleg, Int Inst Welding, Am Welding Soc, 55-81; mem, Mat Adv Bd, Nat Acad Sci, 64-68; mem, Naval Ship Lab Adv Bd, Dept Navy, 68-74; mem, Pipeline Safety Adv Comt, 69-72. *Mem:* Fel Am Soc Metals; fel Am Welding Soc (pres, 72-73). *Res:* Notch toughness and plastic fatigue properties of steel; weldability of steel. *Mailing Add:* Whitaker Lab No 5 Lehigh Univ Bethlehem PA 18015. *Fax:* 610-758-5553

STOUT, ROBERT DANIEL, IMMUNOPATHOLOGY. *Current Pos:* ASSOC PROF MED IMMUNOL, QUILLEN-DISHNER COL MED, E TENN STATE UNIV, 83-, DIR FLOW, CYTOCHEM RESOURCE, 84-, ASSOC CHMN, DEPT MICROBIOL, 85- *Personal Data:* b Aug 20, 45; m 83. *Educ:* Univ Mich, PhD(immunol), 71. *Prof Exp:* Res fel, Dept Pathology, Harvard Med Sch, 71-73 & Dept Genetics, Stanford Med Sch, 73-76; asst prof, Rosenstiel Res Ctr, Brandeis Univ, 76-83. *Concurrent Pos:* Assoc prof, Grad Fac Prog Molecular Biol, Quillen Dishner Col Med, E Tenn State Univ. *Mem:* AAAS; NY Acad Sci; Am Asn Immunologists. *Res:* T cell-macrophage interaction; cytokines; transmembrane signaling; regulation of immune responses. *Mailing Add:* Dept Microbiol Quillen-Dishner Col Med E Tenn State Univ PO Box 70579 Johnson City TN 37614-0579. *Fax:* 423-929-5847

STOUT, THOMAS MELVILLE, ELECTRICAL ENGINEERING, AUTOMATIC CONTROL SYSTEMS. *Current Pos:* CONSULT, 84- *Personal Data:* b Ann Arbor, Mich, Nov 26, 25; m 47, Marilyn Koebnick; c Martha, Sharon, Carol, James, William & Carol. *Educ:* Iowa State Col, BS, 46; Univ Mich, Ann Arbor, MSE, 47, PhD(elec eng), 54. *Honors & Awards:* Hon mem, Instrument Soc Am, 90. *Prof Exp:* Jr engr, Emerson Elec Mfg Co, 47-48; instr elec eng, Univ Wash, 48-53, asst prof, 53-54; res engr, Schlumberger Instrument Co, 54-56; mgr process anal, TRW Comput Div, 56-64 & Bunker-Ramo Corp, 64-65; pres, Profimatics, Inc, 65-83. *Mem:* Hon mem & fel Instrument Soc Am; sr mem Inst Elec & Electronics Engrs; Am Inst Chem Engrs; Tech Asn Pulp & Paper Indust; Nat Soc Prof Engrs; Soc Computer Simulation. *Res:* Application of computers for simulation and control of industrial processes; application of systems engineering techniques to social problems. *Mailing Add:* 9927 Hallack Ave Northridge CA 91324

STOUT, THOMPSON MYLAN, GEOLOGY, VERTEBRATE PALEONTOLOGY. *Current Pos:* assoc cur, 57-80, EMER, STATE MUS, 80- *Personal Data:* b Big Springs, Nebr, Aug 16, 14; m 40. *Educ:* Univ Nebr, Lincoln, BSc, 36, MSc, 37. *Prof Exp:* Res asst vert paleont, State Mus, 33-38, from instr to prof, 38-57, assoc prof, 57-68, prof, 68-80, emer prof geol, Univ Nebr, Lincoln, 80- *Concurrent Pos:* Res assoc, Frick Lab, Am Mus Natural Hist, New York, NY, 38-; studies of fossil rodents & geol in Europ museums, 48-79; corresp, Nat Mus Natural Hist, Paris, 66. *Mem:* Fel Geol Soc Am; Soc Vert Paleont; Paleont Soc; Am Soc Mammal; NY Acad Sci; Sigma Xi. *Res:* Stratigraphy and vertebrate paleontology, with special reference to the Tertiary and Quaternary and to intercontinental correlations in connection with revisionary studies of fossil rodents; cyclic sedimentation and geomorphology. *Mailing Add:* 214 Bessey Hall Univ Nebr Lincoln NE 68588

STOUT, VIRGIL L, PHYSICS. *Current Pos:* RETIRED. *Personal Data:* b Emporia, Kans, Mar 14, 21; m 46; c 2. *Educ:* Univ Mo, PhD(physics), 51. *Prof Exp:* Res assoc, Stanford Res Inst, 51-52; physicist, Gen Elec Co Res Labs, 52-57, mgr, Phys Electronics Br, Gen Elec Res & Develop Ctr, 57-68, mgr, Solid State & Electronics Lab, 68-75, consult electronics, 75-76, res & develop mgr, electronics sci & eng, Gen Elec Res & Develop Ctr, Gen Elec Co, 76-83. *Concurrent Pos:* Mem adv bd, Cancer Ctr, Univ NMex. *Mem:* Inst Elec & Electronics Engrs. *Res:* Experimental investigations of electronic properties of surfaces. *Mailing Add:* 6100 Caminito Ct NE Albuquerque NM 87111

STOUT, VIRGINIA FALK, ORGANIC CHEMISTRY, ANALYTICAL CHEMISTRY. *Current Pos:* RES CHEMIST, UTILIZATION RES DIV, NORTHWEST & ALASKA FISHERIES CTR, NAT MARINE FISHERIES SERV, NAT OCEANIC & ATMOSPHERIC ADMIN, 61- *Personal Data:* b Buffalo, NY, Jan 5, 32; m 55, 77; c 2. *Educ:* Cornell Univ, AB, 53; Harvard Univ, AM, 55; Univ Wash, PhD(org chem), 61. *Concurrent Pos:* Affil assoc prof, Col Fisheries, Univ Wash, 72-82. *Mem:* AAAS; Asn Women in Sci; Am Chem Soc. *Res:* Synthesis of triglycerides containing only omega-3 fatty acids; fatty acid composition of fish oils from various species of fishes; purification of fish oils by supercritical fluid carbon dioxide extraction. *Mailing Add:* 2822 Tenth E Seattle WA 98102-3926

STOUT, WILLIAM F, MATHEMATICS. *Current Pos:* From asst prof to assoc prof, 67-73, PROF STAT, UNIV ILL, URBANA-CHAMPAIGN, 80- *Personal Data:* b Wilkensburg, Pa, July 3, 40; m 79; c 3. *Educ:* Pa State Univ, BS, 62; Purdue Univ, MS, 64, PhD(probability), 67. *Concurrent Pos:* Prin investr, ONR Psychomet Contracts, 83- *Mem:* Am Statist Asn; Inst Math Statist; fel Inst Math Statist; Psychomet Soc; Am Educ Res Asn. *Res:* Psychometrics, with emphasis on modeling and statistical analysis of psychological test data. *Mailing Add:* 1902 Maynard Dr Champaign IL 61821

STOUTAMIRE, DONALD WESLEY, SYNTHETIC ORGANIC CHEMISTRY, AGRICULTURAL CHEMISTRY. *Current Pos:* RETIRED. *Personal Data:* b Roanoke, Va, Mar 10, 31; m 56; c 3. *Educ:* Roanoke Col, BS, 52; Univ Wis, PhD(org chem), 57. *Prof Exp:* Chemist, Shell Agr Chem Co, 57-86; postdoctoral researcher, Univ Calif, Davis, 91-96. *Mem:* Am Chem Soc; AAAS; Sigma Xi. *Res:* Agricultural chemicals; animal health products; hapten synthesis for development of immunoassays for agricultural chemicals and environmental toxins. *Mailing Add:* 904 Bel Passi Dr Modesto CA 95350

STOUTAMIRE, WARREN PETRIE, PLANT TAXONOMY, EVOLUTION. *Current Pos:* from assoc prof to prof, 66-91, EMER PROF BIOL, UNIV AKRON, 91- *Personal Data:* b Salem, Va, July 5, 28; m 63; c 2. *Educ:* Roanoke Col, BS, 49; Univ Ore, MS, 50; Ind Univ, PhD(taxon), 54. *Prof Exp:* Botanist, Cranbrook Inst Sci, 56-66. *Mem:* Royal Hort Soc; Am Soc Plant Taxon; Bot Soc Am; Sigma Xi; Am Orchid Soc. *Res:* Physiology of orchid seed germination; pollination of terrestrial orchid species. *Mailing Add:* Dept Biol Univ Akron Akron OH 44304

STOUTER, VINCENT PAUL, ZOOLOGY, NEUROENDOCRINOLOGY. *Current Pos:* RETIRED. *Personal Data:* b Jersey City, NJ, Apr 28, 24; m 53; c 5. *Educ:* Spring Hill Col, BS, 49; Fordham Univ, MS, 51; Univ Buffalo, PhD(biol), 59. *Prof Exp:* Instr biol, physiol & genetics, Canisius Col, 51-52; instr biol, anat & genetics, Gannon Col, 52-53; instr gen chem, D'Youville Col, 53-54; from asst prof to prof biol, physiol & anat, Canisius Col, 59-92, chmn, Dept Biol, 59-71, chmn, Health Sci Adv & Recommendation Comt, 62-88. *Mem:* NY Acad Sci; Asn Am Med Cols. *Res:* Hypothalamic neurosecretion; electrolyte and salt balance in mammals. *Mailing Add:* 130 Penwood Dr Apt C Rochester NY 14625-2542

STOVER, DENNIS EUGENE, ELECTROCHEMICAL PROCESSES, HYDROMETALLURGICAL MINING & MINERAL RECOVERY SYSTEMS. *Current Pos:* dir, Isl Technol, 89-96, gen mgr, Wyoming Opers, 93-96, DIR, TECHNOL & PROJ DEVELOP, RIO ALGOM MINING CORP, 96- *Personal Data:* b Benton Harbor, Mich, July 30, 44; m 65, Marianne Calay; c Nicole E & Kathleen E. *Educ:* Kalamazoo Col, BA, 66; Univ Mich, BSE, 67, MSE, 68, PhD(chem eng), 75. *Prof Exp:* Process engr chem process design, Charles E Sech & Assocs, 71-72; sr res engr, Atlantic Richfield Co, 74-78; chief engr in-situ uranium mining, Everest Explor Co, 78-84; chief engr, Everest Minerals Corp, 84-89. *Concurrent Pos:* Mem, Technol Comt, Nat Mining Asn, 96- *Mem:* Am Chem Soc; Am Inst Chem Engrs; Soc Mining Engrs; Sigma Xi. *Res:* Fundamental studies of electrochemical processes; investigation of kinetics and reaction of in situ leaching of uranium ores; development of kinetic/hydrologic models for in situ leaching and solution mining of uranium. *Mailing Add:* 1704 Canary Ct Edmond OK 73034-6117

STOVER, E(DWARD) R(OY), MATERIALS SCIENCE, CARBON-GRAPHITE. *Current Pos:* RES & DEVELOP FEL, AEROSPACE RES & DEVELOP CTR, BF GOODRICH, OHIO, 82- *Personal Data:* b Washington, DC, Apr 9, 29; m 56, Shirley Sheriff; c James E & Terry L. *Educ:* Mass Inst Technol, SB, 50, SM, 52, ScD(metall), 56. *Prof Exp:* Asst metall, Mass Inst Technol, 50-55; ceramist, Res Lab, Gen Elec Co, 55-65; assoc res engr, Dept Mining Technol, Univ Calif, Berkeley, 65-66; consult ceramic engr, Re-entry & Environ Systs Div, Gen Elec Co, Philadelphia, 66-82. *Mem:* AAAS; Am Ceramic Soc; Am Soc Metals; Am Inst Mining, Metall & Petrol Engrs; Soc Advan Mat & Process Eng. *Res:* Mechanical behavior, processing techniques and microstructure of structural materials; carbon-carbon composites; oxidation protection systems; carbon-graphite; pyrolytic graphite; carbides, oxides; reinforced plastics chars; cemented carbides; high temperature application; space and re-entry application; aircraft brake applications; oxidation resistant applications. *Mailing Add:* 1857 Brookwood Dr Akron OH 44313-5062

STOVER, ENOS LOY, BIOLOGICAL SCIENCES. *Current Pos:* PRES, STOVER & ASSOCS, INC, 84- *Personal Data:* b Shawnee, Okla, Nov 19, 48; m 72, Penny Crites; c Suzanna, Aaron & Ross. *Educ:* Okla State Univ, BS, 71, MS, 72, PhD(environ eng), 74. *Prof Exp:* Supvr process develop, Roy F Watson, Inc, 74-78; dir res & develop, Metcalf & Eddy, Inc, 78-80; prof environ eng, Okla State Univ, 80-86. *Concurrent Pos:* Independent consult, 80-84; chmn, Hazardous Waste Comt, Water Pollution Control Fedn, 87-90. *Mem:* Water Environ Fedn; Am Water Works Asn; Int Ozone Asn; Nat Water Well Asn; Int Asn Water Qual. *Res:* Development of improved water and wastewater treatment technologies for environmental pollution control; author of over 200 publications. *Mailing Add:* Rte 4 Box 666 Stillwater OK 74074. *Fax:* 405-624-0019

STOVER, JAMES ANDERSON, JR, ARTIFICIAL INTELLIGENCE, SYSTEMS SCIENCE. *Current Pos:* SR RES ASSOC, APPL RES LAB, PA STATE UNIV, 85- *Personal Data:* b Hayesville, NC, June 9, 37; m 63. *Educ:* Univ Ga, BS, 59; Univ Ala, MA, 66, PhD(math), 69. *Prof Exp:* Physicist, US Army Missile Command, Redstone Arsenal, Ala, 60-62; control systs engr, Marshall Space Flight Ctr, NASA, 62-65; consult systs anal, Anal Serv, Inc, Va, 69; asst prof math, Memphis State Univ, 69-74; prin staff & sr scientist, Ori, Inc, 74-84. *Res:* Artificial intelligence; autonomous systems; systems science and design. *Mailing Add:* 1 RR Long PO Box 33 Spring Mills PA 16875

STOVER, RAYMOND WEBSTER, PHYSICS. *Current Pos:* PRIN SCIENTIST, XEROX CORP, 66- *Personal Data:* b Pittsburgh, Pa, Mar 20, 38; m 60; c 2. *Educ:* Lehigh Univ, BS, 60; Syracuse Univ, MS, 62, PhD(physics), 67. *Concurrent Pos:* Adj fac mem, Rochester Inst Technol, 74- *Mem:* AAAS; Soc Photog Scientists & Engrs. *Res:* Search for an electron-proton charge difference; xerographic development process; electrostatics; triboelectricity; small particle physics. *Mailing Add:* 566 Bending Bough Dr Webster NY 14580

STOVER, SAMUEL LANDIS, MEDICINE. *Current Pos:* assoc prof pediat & prof phys med & rehab, 69-76, PROF REHAB MED & CHMN DEPT, UNIV HOSP & CLINS, UNIV ALA, BIRMINGHAM, 76- *Personal Data:* b Bucks Co, Pa, Nov 19, 30; c 3. *Educ:* Goshen Col, BA, 52; Jefferson Med Col, MD, 59; Am Bd Pediat, dipl, 69; Am Bd Phys Med & Rehab, dipl, 71. *Prof Exp:* Intern, St Luke's Hosp, Bethlehem, Pa, 59-60; gen pract, Ark, 60-61 & Indonesia, 61-64; resident pediat, Children's Hosp, Philadelphia, 64-66; asst med dir, Children's Seashore House, Atlantic City, NJ, 66-67; resident phys med & rehab, Univ Pa, 67-69. *Mem:* Am Acad Pediat; Am Acad Phys Med & Rehab; Am Cong Rehab Med; AMA. *Mailing Add:* Dept PMR Spain Rehab Ctr 1717 Sixth Ave Birmingham AL 35233-7339

STOW, STEPHEN HARRINGTON, GEOCHEMISTRY. *Current Pos:* prog mgr & sr geologist, 80-88, sect head geosci, 88-96, DIR ETHICS OFF, OAK RIDGE NAT LAB, 96- *Personal Data:* b Oklahoma City, Okla, Sept 18, 40; m 65. *Educ:* Vanderbilt Univ, BA, 62; Rice Univ, MA, 65, PhD(geochem), 66. *Prof Exp:* Res scientist, Plant Foods Res Div, Continental Oil Co, 66-69; from asst prof to prof geol, Univ Ala, Tuscaloosa, 69-80. *Concurrent Pos:* Consult, Ala Geol Surv, 69-74 & Indust Co, 73-80. *Mem:* Am Geophys Union; Geochem Soc; Geol Soc Am; AAAS; Int Asn Hydrologists. *Res:* Geochemistry and element distribution in igneous and metamorphic rocks, geology and geochemistry of phosphates; environmental geology; geochemistry of mafic rocks of southern Appalachians; sulfide ore deposits; geology and geochemistry of radioactive and hazardous waste disposal. *Mailing Add:* 9927 McCormick Place Knoxville TN 37923-1960

STOWE, BRUCE BERNOT, PLANT PHYSIOLOGY, BIOCHEMISTRY. *Current Pos:* asst prof bot, 59-63, assoc prof biol, 63-71, dir, Marsh Bot Gardens, 75-78, PROF BIOL, YALE UNIV, 71-, PROF FORESTRY, 74- *Personal Data:* b Neuilly-sur-Seine, France, Dec 9, 27; US citizen; wid, Elizabeth Kwasny; c Mark & Eric. *Educ:* Calif Inst Technol, BS, 50; Harvard Univ, MA, 51, PhD(biol), 54. *Hon Degrees:* MA, Yale Univ, 71. *Prof Exp:* NSF fel, Univ Col NWales, 54-55; instr biol, Harvard Univ, 55-58, lectr bot, 58-59, tutor biochem sci, 56-58. *Concurrent Pos:* Mem, Metab Biol Panel, NSF, 60-61, Subcomt Plant Sci Planning & Comt Sci & Pub Policy, Nat Acad Sci, 64-66; Guggenheim fel, Nat Ctr Sci Res, France, 65-66; vis prof, Univ Osaka Prefecture, Japan, 72 & 73, Waite Agr Res Inst, Univ Adelaide, 72-73 & Japan Asn Advan Sci, 73; vis scientist, Nat Inst Basic Biol, Okazaki, Japan, 85-86; vis investr, Dept Plant Biol, Carnegie Inst Wash, Stanford, Calif, 86 & 89. *Mem:* Am Soc Biol Chemists; Am Soc Plant Physiologists (secy, 63-65); Bot Soc Am; Soc Develop Biol; Phytochem Soc NAm; Sigma Xi; fel AAAS. *Res:* Biochemistry and physiology of plant hormones, especially auxins, gibberellins and their relations to lipids and membrane function. *Mailing Add:* Kline Biol Tower Yale Univ PO Box 208103 New Haven CT 06520-8103. *Fax:* 203-432-6161; *E-Mail:* bruce_stowe@yale.edu

STOWE, CLARENCE M, pharmacology, veterinary medicine; deceased, see previous edition for last biography

STOWE, DAVID F, CARDIOVASCULAR PHYSIOLOGY, ELECTROPHYSIOLOGY. *Current Pos:* asst prof physiol, 76-88, from asst prof to assoc prof anesthesiol, 81-94, PROF ANESTHESIOL, MED COL WIS, 94- *Personal Data:* b Vincennes, Ind, Jan 27, 45. *Educ:* Ind Univ, Bloomington, AB, 68, MA, 69; Mich State Univ, PhD(physiol), 74; Med Col Wis, MD, 83. *Prof Exp:* Fel cardiovasc physiol, Cardiovasc Res Inst, Univ Calif, San Francisco, 74-76. *Concurrent Pos:* Vis prof biol, Marquette Univ, 71; mem circulation comt, Am Heart Asn, circulation fel, Am Physiol Soc. *Mem:* Am Physiol Soc; Sigma Xi; Soc Exp Biol & Med; Am Soc Anesthesiol; Anesthesia Res Soc; Asn Univ Anesthesiologists; Soc Cardiovasc Anesthesiol. *Res:* Preservation of cardiac function for long periods using hypothermia, negative inotropic agents and vasodilators; mechanism of protection of myocardium and coronary vascular endothelium using electromechanical uncoupling, specific inhibitors, agonists and other agents; effects of hypothermia on vascular responsiveness, intracellular calcium transients and contractility. *Mailing Add:* 462 MEB Med Col Wis 8701 W Watertown Plank Rd Milwaukee WI 53226-4801. *Fax:* 414-266-8541

STOWE, DAVID WILLIAM, FIBER OPTIC COMPONENTS & SENSORS, TELECOMMUNICATIONS. *Current Pos:* PRES, ASTER CORP; ASST VPRES, PORTA SYSTS CORP. *Personal Data:* b Three Rivers, Mich, Jan 1, 44; m 93, Estelle Jordan; c 3. *Educ:* Univ Wis, Madison, BS, 66; Univ Ill, Urbana, MS, 67, PhD(physics), 71. *Honors & Awards:* IR 100 Award. *Prof Exp:* Sr physicist, Appl Physics Lab, Johns Hopkins Univ, 71-77; prog mgr fiber optics sensors, surface acoust waves & thin films, Gould Labs Elec & Electronics Res, Gould Inc, 77-83. *Mem:* Optical Soc Am; Soc Photo-Optical Instrumentation Engrs. *Res:* Fiber optic couplers, general fiber optic components, fiber optic sensors and fiber optic communications; inventor of "Stowe" process for single-mode couplers used by major commercial suppliers. *Mailing Add:* 33 Briar Dr Milford MA 01757. *Fax:* 508-435-0220

STOWE, HOWARD DENISON, PATHOLOGY. *Current Pos:* DEPT LARGE ANIMAL CLIN SCI, COL VET MED, MICH STATE UNIV, 80- *Personal Data:* b Greenfield, Mass, Mar 31, 27. *Educ:* Univ Mass, BS, 48; Mich State Univ, MS, 56, DVM, 60, PhD(vet path), 62. *Prof Exp:* Instr animal husb & dairy prod, Bristol County Agr Sch, Mass, 49-53; asst animal husb, anat & vet path, Mich State Univ, 55-60; assoc prof vet sci & chief, Nutrit Sect, Univ Ky, 63-68; from asst prof to assoc prof path, Sch Med, Univ NC, Chapel Hill, 68-73; assoc prof path, Sch Vet Med, Auburn Univ, 73-77, from assoc prof to prof clin nutrit, 77-80. *Concurrent Pos:* Vis researcher, Dunn Nutrit Lab, Cambridge Univ, 62 & Dept Nutrit & Biochem, Denmark Polytech Inst, Copenhagen, 62; pathologist, Div Lab Animal Med, Sch Med, Univ NC, Chapel Hill. *Mem:* Am Vet Med Asn; Conf Res Workers Animal Dis; Am Inst Nutrit. *Res:* Effects of lead upon reproduction in rats; cadmium toxicity in rabbits; canine and avian lead toxicity; genetic influence on selenium metabolism. *Mailing Add:* 8410 Beardslee Rd Owosso MI 48867. *Fax:* 517-353-1699

STOWE, KEITH S, ELEMENTARY PARTICLE PHYSICS. *Current Pos:* PROF DEPT PHYSICS, UNIV WASH. *Personal Data:* b Midland, Mich, Feb 16, 43; m 67; c 2. *Educ:* Ill Inst Technol, BS, 65; Univ Calif, San Diego, MS, 67, PhD(physics), 71. *Prof Exp:* Lectr physics, Calif Polytech State Univ, San Luis Obispo, 71-74, asst prof, 74-76, assoc prof 76-81, prof, 81- *Mem:* Am Phys Soc; Am Asn Physics Teachers. *Res:* Elementary particle theory; oceanography; thermodynamics. *Mailing Add:* Dept Physics Calif Polytech State Univ San Luis Obispo CA 93407

STOWE, ROBERT ALLEN, SURFACE CHEMISTRY, CATALYSIS INDUSTRIAL PROCESS CHEMISTRY. *Current Pos:* CONSULT CATALYTIC & CHEM TECHNOL, 88- *Personal Data:* b Kalamazoo, Mich, July 26, 24; div; c 4. *Educ:* Kalamazoo Col, BA, 48; Brown Univ, PhD(chem), 53. *Honors & Awards:* Victor J Azbe Lime Award, Nat Lime Asn, 64; Joseph Stewart Award, Indust Eng & Chem Div, Am Chem Soc, 84. *Prof Exp:* Res chemist, Ludington Div, Dow Chem USA, 52-58, Res & Develop Lab, 58-64, sr res chemist, 64-69, Hydrocarbon & Monomers Res Lab, 69-71, assoc scientist, 71-74, assoc scientist, 74-79, assoc scientist, Mich Div Res, 79-88. *Concurrent Pos:* Secy, Bd Educ, Luddington, 60-63, pres, 63-69; chmn, Div Indust & Eng Chem, Am Chem Soc, 82, counr, 86- *Mem:* Am Chem Soc; Am Inst Chemists; Sigma Xi; Catalysis Soc. *Res:* Heterogeneous catalysis; hydrocarbon processes; inorganic chemistry; zeolite chemistry; organic fluorine chemistry; statistics; carbon monoxide methanation; Fischer-Tropsch synthesis; coal liquefaction. *Mailing Add:* PO Box 173 5680 Chippewa Dr Cross Village MI 49723-0173

STOWELL, EWELL ADDISON, PLANT PATHOLOGY. *Current Pos:* from instr to prof bot, 53-88, chmn dept biol, 72-77, EMER PROF BOT, ALBION COL, 88- *Personal Data:* b Ashland, Ill, Sept 2, 22; m 53. *Educ:* Ill State Norm Univ, BEd, 43; Univ Wis, MS, 47, PhD(bot), 55. *Prof Exp:* Asst bot, Univ Wis, 46-47; instr, Univ Wis, Milwaukee, 47-49, asst, 49-53. *Concurrent Pos:* Vis lectr, Univ Wis, 63; assoc prof, Univ Mich, 64. *Mem:* Bot Soc Am; Mycol Soc Am; Am Inst Biol Sci; Sigma Xi. *Res:* Taxonomy and morphology of Ascomycetes. *Mailing Add:* Albion Col Albion MI 49224

STOWELL, JAMES KENT, POLYMER CHEMISTRY, ORGANIC CHEMISTRY. *Current Pos:* sr chemist polymer, 78-81, new prod develop supvr, 81-87, RES MGR, MORTON CHEM CO, 87- *Personal Data:* b Elgin, Ill, July 9, 36; m 65, Diane Dunlop; c James & Jeffrey. *Educ:* Knox Col, BA, 58; Univ Iowa, PhD(org chem), 65. *Prof Exp:* Sr res chemist org, PPG Industs Inc, 65-68; sr res chemist polymer, A E Staley Mfg Co, 68-78. *Mem:* Am Chem Soc. *Res:* Development of new polymer products for use in printing inks, coatings, and adhesives; organic chemicals for specialty uses. *Mailing Add:* Morton Chem Co 1275 Lake Ave Woodstock IL 60098-7415

STOWELL, JOHN CHARLES, INSECT CHEMISTRY, NEW REAGENTS. *Current Pos:* from asst prof to assoc prof, 70-80, PROF ORG CHEM, UNIV NEW ORLEANS, 80- *Personal Data:* b Passaic, NJ, Sept 10, 38; div; c Sandra (Baxter) & Alan. *Educ:* Rutgers Univ, New Brunswick, BS, 60; Mass Inst Technol, PhD(org chem), 64. *Prof Exp:* Res specialist, Cent Res Lab, 3M Co, 64-69; NIH fel org chem, Ohio State Univ, 69-70. *Concurrent Pos:* Res Corp & Petrol Res Fund grants, Univ New Orleans, 71-73 & 80-82. *Mem:* Am Chem Soc. *Res:* Organic synthesis; heterocyclic compounds; sterically hindered compounds; three- and four-carbon homologating; carbanions; concurrent strong acid and base catalysis insect pheromones. *Mailing Add:* Chem Univ New Orleans 2000 Lakeshore Dr New Orleans LA 70148-0001. *Fax:* 504-286-6860

STOWELL, ROBERT EUGENE, RESEARCH ADMINISTRATION. *Current Pos:* mem nat adv comt, Nat Ctr Primate Biol, Univ Calif, 67-68, dir, 69-71, chmn dept path, 67-69, asst dean, Sch Med, 67-71, prof, 67-82, EMER PROF PATH, SCH MED, UNIV CALIF, DAVIS, 82- *Personal Data:* b Cashmere, Wash, Dec 25, 14; m 45, Eva Mae Chambers; c Susan & Robert E Jr. *Educ:* Stanford Univ, AB, 36, MD, 41; Wash Univ, PhD(path), 44. *Honors & Awards:* Gold-Headed Cane Award, Am Asn Path, 90; Distinguished Serv Award, 79 & Diamond Jubilee Award, 81 & Stowell-Orbison Award, US-Can Div, Int Acad Path, 82. *Prof Exp:* From asst to assoc prof path, Sch Med, Wash Univ, 42-48; prof path & oncol, Sch Med & dir cancer res, Med Ctr, Univ Kans, 48-59, chmn dept oncol, 48-51, path & oncol, 51-59, pathologist-in-chief, 51-59; sci dir, Armed Forces Inst Path, Washington, DC, 59-67. *Concurrent Pos:* Commonwealth Fund advan med study & res fel, Inst Cell Res, Stockholm, Sweden, 46-47; mem morphol & genetics study sect, NIH, 49-53 & path study sect, 54-55, chmn, 55-57, mem path training comt, div gen med sci, 58-61, chmn animal resources adv comt, Div Res Resources, 70-74; mem, Intersoc Comt Res Potential in Path, 60-80, pres, 57-60; vis prof, Sch Med, Univ Md, 60-67; mem fedn bd, Fedn Am Soc Exp Biol, 63-66; mem subcomt comp path, Comt Path, Nat Acad Sci-Nat Res Coun, 63-69, subcomt manpower needs in path, 64-69 & US Nat comt, Int Coun Socs Path, 66-80, chmn, 72-75; mem, Intersoc Comt Path Info, 65-69, chmn, 66-67; mem adv med bd, Leonard Wood Mem, 65-69; mem div biol & agr, Nat Res Coun, 65-68 & comt doc data anat & clin path, 66-68; mem, Int Coun Socs Path, 66-81; mem bd dirs, Coun Biol Sci Info, Nat Acad Sci, 67-70; ed, Lab Invest, Int Acad Path, 67-72; mem med adv comt & consult, Vet Admin Hosp, Martinez, Calif, 69-72; mem bd dirs, Univ Asn Res & Educ Path, 74-, secy-treas, 78-82; mem sci adv bd, Nat Ctr Toxicol Res, 76-79; vpres, Am Registry Path, 76-78, pres, 78-80; fel, Cytology, Wash Univ Sch Med, 40-42. *Mem:* Col Am Pathologists; Am Soc Clin Path; Am Asn Path & Bact (vpres, 69-70, pres, 70-71); Am Soc Exp Path (vpres, 63-64, pres, 64-65); Int Acad Path (vpres, 57-58, pres elect, 58-59, pres, 59-60); Sigma Xi. *Res:* Cancer; experimental pathology; comparative pathology. *Mailing Add:* Dept Path Univ Calif Sch Med Davis CA 95616

STOWENS, DANIEL, PEDIATRICS. *Current Pos:* RETIRED. *Personal Data:* b New York, NY, Oct 27, 19; m 75; c 2. *Educ:* Columbia Univ, AB, 41, MD, 43; Am Bd Pediat, dipl, 51; Am Bd Path, dipl, 54. *Prof Exp:* Chief, Sect Pediat Path, Armed Forces Inst Path, US Army, Washington, DC, 54-58; assoc prof path, Univ Southern Calif, 58-61 & Univ Louisville, 61-65; pathologist, St Luke's Mem Hosp Ctr, 66-85. *Concurrent Pos:* Registr, Am Registry Pediat Path, 54-58; consult, Walter Reed Army Hosp, 56-58; pathologist, Children's Hosp, Los Angeles, 58-61; dir labs & chief prof servs, Children's Hosp, Louisville, 61-65. *Mem:* Fel Am Soc Clin Path; Soc Pediat Res; Am Asn Path & Bact; Int Acad Path. *Res:* Pediatric pathology, especially pathophysiology of fetus and mechanisms of development; dermatoglyphics. *Mailing Add:* 3214 Fountain St Clinton NY 13323

STOY, WILLIAM S, CHEMISTRY. *Current Pos:* GROUP LEADER, APPLNS RES, ENGELHARD MINERALS & CHEM, MENLO PARK, EDISON, 77- *Personal Data:* b New York, NY, Sept 23, 25; m 49; c 2. *Educ:* Queens Col, NY, BS, 45; Polytech Inst Brooklyn, MS, 50. *Honors & Awards:* Plastics Inst Award. *Prof Exp:* Chemist paint res & develop, Mobil Chem Co, 45-50, supvr, 50-58; sr chemist, Cities Serv Co, Cranbury, NJ, 58-64, mgr plastics applns, 64-71, mgr coatings, plastics & inks, Petrochem Res, 71-77. *Mem:* Am Chem Soc; Soc Plastics Engrs; Am Soc Testing & Mat; Plastics Inst Am. *Res:* Plastics resins and concentrates development; coatings and inks; pigment syntheses and applications; flame retardants; polymer chemistry; extenders-inorganic silicates; catalysis. *Mailing Add:* 221 Herrontown Rd Princeton NJ 08540

ST-PIERRE, CLAUDE, NUCLEAR PHYSICS. *Current Pos:* from asst prof to assoc prof, 62-70, chmn dept, 73-79, dean, Sch Grad Studies, 79-84, PROF PHYSICS, LAVAL UNIV, 70- *Personal Data:* b Montreal, Que, Jan 7, 32; m 54; c 2. *Educ:* Univ Montreal, BSc, 54, MSc, 56, DSc(physics), 59. *Prof Exp:* Sci officer, Defence Res Bd Can, 58-61; Nat Res Coun Can fel, Ctr Nuclear Res, Strasbourg, France, 61-62. *Concurrent Pos:* Vis scientist, AECL, Chalk River, Ont, 86. *Mem:* Can Asn Physicists; Am Phys Soc. *Res:* Nuclear spectroscopy; heavy ion reactions. *Mailing Add:* Dept Physics Laval Univ Ste Foy PQ G1K 7P4 Can

ST-PIERRE, JACQUES, applied statistics, for more information see previous edition

STRAAT, PATRICIA ANN, BIOCHEMISTRY, ENZYMOLOGY. *Current Pos:* chief, Referral Sect & dep chief, Referral & Rev Br, Div Res Grants, 86-96, DEP CHIEF REV, REFERRAL & REV BR, NIH, 96- *Personal Data:* b Rochester, NY, Mar 28, 36. *Educ:* Oberlin Col, BA, 58; Johns Hopkins Univ, PhD(biochem), 64. *Prof Exp:* Lab instr biol, Johns Hopkins Univ, 58-59; USPHS fel, 60-64, res fel radiol sci, 64-67, res assoc, 67-68, asst prof, 68-70; sr res biochemist, Biospherics, Inc, 70-75, res coordr, 75-78, dir res, 78-80; grants assoc, Div Res Grants, NIH, 80-81; chief, Planning & Coord Sect, Prog Opers Br, Nat Toxicol Prog, Nat Inst Environ Health Sci, 81-82; health sci adminr, Molecular & Cellular Biophys Study Sect, NIH, 82-86. *Concurrent Pos:* Lectr, Dept Radiol Sci, Sch Hyg & Pub Health, Johns Hopkins Univ, 70-72; mem, Viking Biol Flight Team & Sci Team & Viking Mission to Mars, NASA, 76. *Mem:* Sigma Xi; Biophys Soc; AAAS. *Res:* Electron transport and inorganic nitrogen metabolism; mechanisms of nucleic acid replication; extraterrestial life detection; biological and chemical aspects of water pollution. *Mailing Add:* Div Res Grants Rm 3048 MSC7766 6701 Rockledge Dr Bethesda MD 20892-7766. *Fax:* 301-480-3962; *E-Mail:* yri@drgpo.drg.nih.gov

STRAATSMA, BRADLEY RALPH, MEDICINE, OPHTHALMOLOGY. *Current Pos:* asst prof surg & ophthal, 59-73, chief, Div Ophthal, 59-68, PROF OPHTHAL, SCH MED, UNIV CALIF, LOS ANGELES, 63-, CHMN DEPT, 68-, PROF SURG, 80-; DIR, JULES STEIN EYE INST, 64- *Personal Data:* b Grand Rapids, Mich, Dec 29, 27; c 3. *Educ:* Yale Univ, MD, 51. *Honors & Awards:* William Warren Hoppin Award, NY Acad Med, 56; co-recipient, Silver Award, Am Soc Clin Path & Col Am Pathologists, 62; co-recipient, Conrad Berens Award, Int Eye Film Festival, 65. *Prof Exp:* Intern, New Haven Hosp, Yale Univ, 51-52; vis scholar, Col Physicians & Surgeons, Columbia Univ, 52, asst resident, 55-58; spec clin trainee, Nat Inst Neurol Dis & Blindness, 58-59. *Concurrent Pos:* Resident, Inst Ophthal, Presby Hosp, New York, 55-58; fel ophthalmic path, Armed Forces Inst Path, Walter Reed Army Med Ctr, DC, 58-59; fel ophthal, Wilmer Inst, Johns Hopkins Univ, 58-59; mem vision res training comt, Nat Inst Neurol Dis & Blindness, 59-63 & neurol & sensory dis prog proj comt, 64-68; consult to Surgeon Gen, USPHS, 59-68; ophthal examr, aid to blind progs, Calif Dept Social Welfare, 59-; mem med adv comt, Nat Coun Combat Blindness, 60-;

consult, Vet Admin Hosp, Long Beach, Calif, 60-75; attend physician, Vet Admin Ctr, Wadsworth Gen Hosp, Los Angeles, 60-; attend physician & consult, Los Angeles County Harbor Gen Hosp, Torrance, 60-; vis consult, St John's Hosp, Santa Monica, 60-; mem courtesy staff, Santa Monica Hosp, 60- & St Vincent's Hosp, Los Angeles, 60-; mem sensory dis serv panel, Bur States Serv, USPHS, 63-65; trustee, John Thomas Dye Sch, Los Angeles, 67-72; prof, New Orleans Acad Ophthal, 68-; ophthalmologist in chief, Univ Calif, Los Angeles Hosp, 68-; mem med adv bd, Int Eye Found, 70-; mem nat adv comt, Pan-Am Cong Ophthal, 71-72 & bd dirs, Conrad Berens Int qye Film Libr, 71- *Mem:* Am Acad Ophthal (pres, 77); AMA; Asn Univ Prof Ophthal (pres, 74); Am Ophthal Soc; Asn Res Vision & Ophthal; Am Bd Ophthal; Pan-Am Ophthal Found. *Res:* Ophthalmology. *Mailing Add:* Jules Stein Eye Inst Los Angeles CA 90024

STRACHAN, DONALD STEWART, INSTITUTIONAL PLANNING, COMPUTER MANAGEMENT. *Current Pos:* From instr to assoc prof oral biol, Sch Dent & Anat, Sch Med, 63-73, asst dean, 69-89, PROF DENT & ORAL BIOL, SCH DENT, UNIV MICH, ANN ARBOR, 73-,. *Personal Data:* b Highland Park, Mich, 32; c 4. *Educ:* Wayne State Univ, BA, 54; Univ Mich, DDS, 60, MS, 62, PhD(anat), 64. *Concurrent Pos:* USPHS res career award, 63-68; consult Vet Admin Hosp, DC, 66-68 & coun dent educ, Am Dent Asn; hon adv bd, Nat Asn Adv Health Professions. *Mem:* Am Dent Asn; Int Asn Dent Res; Am Asn Dent Schs; Sigma Xi. *Res:* Histochemistry of esterase isoenzymes; lactic dehydrogenase in developing teeth and healing bone; data analysis and programming in the analysis of gel electrophoretic patterns; educational research; computer assisted instruction; self instructional media development. *Mailing Add:* 220 Inlets Blvd Nokomis FL 34275-4128

STRACHAN, JAMES DOUGLAS, FUSION EXPERIMENTS, NUCLEAR DIAGNOSTICS. *Current Pos:* PRIN RES PHYSICIST, PRINCETON PLASMA PHYSICS LAB, PRINCETON UNIV, 82- *Personal Data:* b Vancouver, BC, Aug 30, 46; c Douglas R & Gordon D. *Educ:* Univ BC, BSc, 68, MSc, 69, PhD(plasma physics), 72. *Prof Exp:* Res fel, Australian Nat Univ, 72-75. *Mem:* Fel Am Phys Soc. *Res:* Experimental plasma physics; transport and heating of tokamak plasmas; creation of hard x-ray neutron and energetic ion diagnostics; development of high temperature plasmas. *Mailing Add:* Princeton Plasma Physics Lab Box 451 Princeton Univ Princeton NJ 08543

STRACHAN, WILLIAM MICHAEL JOHN, ENVIRONMENTAL ORGANIC CHEMISTRY. *Current Pos:* res environ scientist, Can Ctr for Inland Waters, 70-74, head sect, 74-80, dir, Hazard Assessment Br, 81, res scientist, 82-85, PROJ CHIEF, AIR-WATER INTERACTIONS, CAN CTR FOR INLAND WATERS, 85- *Personal Data:* b Thunder Bay, Ont, Nov 20, 37; div; c 3. *Educ:* Univ Toronto, BA, 59, MA, 60; Queens Univ, PhD(chem), 68. *Prof Exp:* Asst lectr dept chem, Univ Col, London, 60-63; res assoc, Royal Mil Col Can, 63-65; Nat Res Coun Can fel, 68-70. *Concurrent Pos:* Mem, Int Joint Comm, Res Adv Bd, Comt Sci Basis Water Qual Criteria, 74-78; mem, Can Environ Contaminants Act Comt, Dept Environ, Nat Health & Welfare, 75-; mem, Nat Res Coun Special Grants Panel Environ Toxicol, 77-79; Can rep, Orgn Econ Coop & Develop Expert Group, 78-81; chmn, Int Joint Comn, Sci Adv Bd Comt Aquatic Ecosyst Objectives, 78-88, Int Joint Comn, Water Qual Bd Comt Assess Chem, 86-88. *Mem:* Int Asn Great Lakes Res; Soc Environ Toxic Chem. *Res:* Persistent organic chemicals; cycling organic chemicals between air and water; organic contamination of rain and lake-stream waters. *Mailing Add:* Can Ctr Inland Waters PO Box 5050 Burlington ON L7R 4A6 Can. *Fax:* 905-336-6430

STRACHER, ALFRED, BIOCHEMISTRY, MUSCLE & NERVE DEGENERATIVE DISEASES. *Current Pos:* From asst prof to assoc prof, 59-68, PROF BIOCHEM, COL MED, STATE UNIV NY HEALTH SCI CTR AT BROOKLYN, 68-, CHMN DEPT, 72- *Personal Data:* b Albany, NY, Nov 16, 30; m 54, Dorothy Altman; c Cameron, Adam & Erica. *Educ:* Rensselaer Polytech Inst, BS, 52; Columbia Univ, MA, 54, PhD, 56. *Concurrent Pos:* Nat Found Infantile Paralysis fel biochem, Rockefeller Inst, 56-58 & Carlsberg Lab, Copenhagen, 58-59; career scientist, Health Res Coun, 62-69; Commonwealth Fund fel, 66-67, Guggenheim fel, 73-74; mem, NSP-B Rev Comt, Nat Inst Neurol & Commun Disorders & Stroke, 82-85; ed jours, 86-89. *Mem:* Am Soc Biol Chemists; Harvey Soc; Marine Biol Lab; Biophys Soc; fel AAAS. *Res:* Relationship of protein structure to biological activity; contractility in non-muscle systems, muscle and nerve degeneration (molecular basis); membrane-cytoskeleton interaction in platelets; protease inhibitors. *Mailing Add:* Dept Biochem State Univ NY Health Sci Ctr Clarkson Ave Brooklyn NY 11203. *Fax:* 718-270-3316; *E-Mail:* stracher@medlab.hscbklyn.edu

STRADA, SAMUEL JOSEPH, NEUROCHEMISTRY, NEUROBIOLOGY. *Current Pos:* prof & chmn, Dept Pharmacol, 83-94, SR ASSOC DEAN, COL MED, UNIV SALA, 93- *Personal Data:* b Kansas City, Mo, Oct 6, 42; m 71. *Educ:* Univ Mo, Kansas City, BSPharm, 64, MS, 66; Vanderbilt Univ, PhD(pharmacol), 70. *Honors & Awards:* Pharmaceut Mfrs Asn Fac Develop Award, Basic Pharmacol. *Prof Exp:* Asst pharmacol, Univ Mo, Kansas City, 64-66; NIMH staff fel pharmacol, St Elizabeth's Hosp, Washington, DC, 70-72; from asst prof to prof, pharmacol Med Sch, Univ Tex, Houston, 72-83,. *Concurrent Pos:* Assoc fac, Univ Tex Grad Sch Biomed Sci, Houston, 72-83; Fogarty sr int fel, Med Sci Inst, Univ Dundee, Scotland, 80-81; mem grad fac basic med sci, Univ SAla, 83- *Mem:* AAAS; Am Soc Pharmacol & Exp Therapeut; Soc Neurosci; NY Acad Sci; Tissue Cult Asn; Sigma Xi; Asn Med Sch Pharmacol. *Res:* Role of cyclic nucleotides in the nervous system; release of neurotransmitters and synaptic transmission; relation of the nervous system to hormone release mechanisms; role of cyclic nucleotides in cell growth; receptor regulation cyclic nucleotide phosphodiesterases as sites of drug action. *Mailing Add:* Univ SAla Col Med 170 CSAB Mobile AL 36688-0002. *Fax:* 334-460-6073; *E-Mail:* sstrada@jaguar1.usouthal.edu

STRADLEY, JAMES GRANT, CERAMIC ENGINEERING. *Current Pos:* ENG MGR, OAK RIDGE NAT LAB, MARTIN MARIETTA ENERGY SYSTS, 84- *Personal Data:* b Newark, Ohio, Aug 24, 32; m 54; c 3. *Educ:* Ohio State Univ, BCerE, 55, MSc, 58. *Prof Exp:* Res assoc ceramic mat, Res Found, Ohio State Univ, 56-58; res specialist, Cols Div, NAm Rockwell Corp, Ohio, 58-65; develop specialist, Oak Ridge Nat Lab, Tenn, 65-70 & Y-12 plant, Union Carbide Corp, 70-72; vpres, US Nuclear, Inc, 72-77; eng mgr, Oak Ridge Nat Lab, Union Carbide Corp, 77-84. *Mem:* Am Ceramic Soc; Nat Inst Ceramic Engrs; Am Nuclear Soc. *Res:* Management of reprocessing programs, including nuclear fuels, special studies and environmental safeguards; forming, sintering and properties of ceramic materials. *Mailing Add:* 197 Whippoorwill Lane Oak Ridge TN 37830

STRADLEY, NORMAN H(ENRY), CERAMIC ENGINEERING. *Current Pos:* RETIRED. *Personal Data:* b Newark, Ohio, June 28, 24; m 47, Margaret Coy; c Edward R & Pamela J. *Educ:* Ohio State Univ, BCerE & MS, 49. *Prof Exp:* Ceramic engr, Minn Mining & Mfg Co, 50-56, group supvr, 56-59, sr res engr, Am Lava Corp, Tenn, 59-63, proj mgr, 63-68, res supvr, 68-69, proj supvr, 69-74, prod develop specialist, Tech Ceramic Prods Div, 3M Co, Tenn, 74-75, res specialist, Tech Ceramic Prods Div, 75-82, patent liaison, Elec Prod Group, 82-84, sr patent liaison, Electro-Tel Group, 3M Ctr, 3M Co, St Paul, 84-88. *Mem:* Fel Am Ceramic Soc; Nat Inst Ceramic Engrs; fel Am Inst Chemists. *Res:* Coatings for ferrous and non-ferrous alloys and graphite; glass technology; nuclear and electrical ceramics. *Mailing Add:* 5401 Bus 83 No 2117 Harlingen TX 78552-3633

STRADLING, LESTER J(AMES), JR, MECHANICAL & NUCLEAR ENGINEERING. *Current Pos:* RETIRED. *Personal Data:* b Philadelphia, Pa, Aug 21, 16; m 47; c 2. *Educ:* Drexel Inst, BS, 39; Univ Pa, MS, 44. *Prof Exp:* Maintenance engr, Calvert Distillery, 39; design draftsman, Gen Elec Co, 39; jr marine engr, Philadelphia Naval Yard, 39-41; design engr, Bendix Aircraft Corp, 42; instr mech eng, Drexel Inst, 42-45; field engr, Allis Chalmers Mfg Co, 45-49, sales engr, 50-54; vpres eng, Campus Indusrs, Inc, 49-50; from assoc prof to prof mech eng, Drexel Univ, 54-81. *Concurrent Pos:* Mem sci staff, Columbia Univ Div, War Res, Naval Underwater Sound Lab, Conn, 44; consult, Kellett Aircraft Corp, 45 & Mechtronics, Inc, 54-57. *Mem:* Am Soc Eng Educ. *Res:* Application of jet engines to helicopters; fundamental quieting of submarines; diffusion of neutrons in high velocity media and heterogeneous media; study of neutron streaming in holes and vacuua. *Mailing Add:* 3445 Davisville Rd Hatboro PA 19040

STRADLING, SAMUEL STUART, ORGANIC CHEMISTRY. *Current Pos:* From asst prof to assoc prof, 63-74, PROF CHEM, ST LAWRENCE UNIV, 74-, CHMN DEPT, 77- *Personal Data:* b Hamilton, NY, Dec 11, 37; m 63; c 3. *Educ:* Hamilton Col, AB, 59; Univ Rochester, PhD(org chem), 64. *Concurrent Pos:* NSF acad year exten grant, 65-67; vis scholar & vis prof, Univ Va, 76-77; vis prof, Va Tech, 84-85. *Mem:* AAAS; Am Chem Soc; Sigma Xi. *Res:* Reaction mechanisms; natural product chemistry; chemical education. *Mailing Add:* Dept Chem St Lawrence Univ Canton NY 13617-9673

STRAF, MIRON L, NATIONAL STATISTICS FOR PUBLIC POLICY. *Current Pos:* res assoc, 74-77, res dir, 78-87, DIR, COMT ON NAT STATIST, NAT ACAD SCI-NAT RES COUN, 87- *Personal Data:* b New York, NY, Apr 13, 43; m 85, Carolee Bush; c Michael & David. *Educ:* Carnegie-Mellon Univ, BS, 64, MS, 65; Univ Chicago, PhD(statist), 69. *Prof Exp:* Asst prof statist, Univ Calif, Berkeley, 69-74. *Concurrent Pos:* Sr vis res fel, Monitoring Assessment & Res Ctr, Chelsea Col Sci & Technol, London, 77; lectr statist, London Sch Econ & Polit Sci, 77-78; mem, Joseph P Kennedy, Jr Found Comt, 81. *Mem:* Fel Royal Statist Soc; fel Am Statist Asn; Int Statist Inst; Int Asn Off Statist. *Res:* Applied and theoretical statistics; analysis and evaluation of environmental statistics; use of statistics in the courts. *Mailing Add:* Comt Nat Statist Nat Acad Sci 2101 Constitution Ave NW Washington DC 20418. *E-Mail:* mstraf@nas.edu

STRAFFON, RALPH ATWOOD, MEDICINE, UROLOGY. *Current Pos:* staff mem, 59-63, head dept urol, 63-87, chmn div surg, 83-87, VCHMN BD GOV & CHIEF OF STAFF, CLEVELAND CLINIC FOUND, 87- *Personal Data:* b Croswell, Mich, Jan 4, 28; m 81, Shirley Willson; c David, Daniel, Jonathan, Peter & Andrew. *Educ:* Univ Mich, MD, 53; Am Bd Urol, dipl, 62. *Prof Exp:* Intern, Univ Hosp, Ann Arbor, Mich, 53-54, from asst resident to resident gen surg, 54-55, resident surg, 56-57, from jr clin instr to sr clin instr, 57-59. *Concurrent Pos:* Res fel med, Renal Lab, Peter Bent Brigham Hosp, Boston, 56. *Mem:* AMA; fel Am Col Surg; Am Urol Asn; Am Asn Genito-Urinary Surg; fel Am Acad Pediat; Am Surg Asn. *Mailing Add:* Cleveland Clin Found 9500 Euclid Ave Cleveland OH 44195-0001

STRAFUSS, ALBERT CHARLES, COMPARATIVE PATHOLOGY, ONCOLOGY. *Current Pos:* ASSOC PROF PATH, COL VET MED, KANS STATE UNIV, 68- *Personal Data:* b Princeton, Kans, Jan 24, 28; m 54; c 5. *Educ:* Kans State Univ, BS & DVM, 54; Iowa State Univ, MS, 58; Univ Minn, PhD(comp path), 63. *Prof Exp:* Practitioner, Hastings, Nebr, 54-56; instr, Iowa State Univ & pathologist, Iowa Vet Med Diag Lab, 56-59; instr path, Col Vet Med, Univ Minn, 59-63; assoc prof path, Col Vet Med, Iowa State Univ & pathologist, Vet Med Res Inst, 63-64; assoc prof path, Sch Vet Med, Univ Mo-Columbia, 64-68. *Mem:* Am Vet Med Asn; Electron Micros Soc Am; Conf Res Workers Animal Diseases. *Res:* Pathologic and epidemiologic studies of animal neoplasms; ultrastructure studies on the pathogenesis of morphological tissue alterations. *Mailing Add:* 228 Providence Rd Lawrence KS 66049-1630

STRAHL, ERWIN OTTO, MINERALOGY, PETROLOGY. *Current Pos:* RETIRED. *Personal Data:* b New York, NY, July 2, 30; m 52; c 4. *Educ:* City Col, New York, BS, 52; Pa State Univ, PhD(mineral), 58. *Prof Exp:* Res asst mineral, Pa State Univ, 52-58; mineralogist, Mineral Resources Dept, Kaiser Aluminum & Chem Corp, 58-59, Metals Div, Res Lab, 59-69, head, X-ray & Electron Optics Lab, Analytical Res Dept, 69-81, res assoc reduction res, Kaiser Ctr Technol, 81-87. *Mem:* Am Spectrog Soc. *Res:* Mineralogy and petrology of soils and sedimentary rocks; x-ray diffraction analysis of inorganic oxides and hydroxides; quantitative x-ray diffraction and spectographic analysis; phase equilibria studies of aluminum oxide systems. *Mailing Add:* 154 Joaquin Circle Danville CA 94526

STRAHLE, WARREN C(HARLES), combustion, fluid mechanics; deceased, see previous edition for last biography

STRAHM, NORMAN DALE, PHYSICS, ELECTRICAL ENGINEERING. *Current Pos:* PRES, JAMES ORCUTT & CO INC. *Personal Data:* b Toronto, Kans, Feb 22, 40. *Educ:* Mass Inst Technol, SB, 62, SM & EE, 64, PhD(elec sci & eng), 69. *Prof Exp:* Mem tech staff, Lincoln Lab, Mass Inst Technol, 69-70; vis asst prof physics, Univ Ill, Chicago Circle, 70- *Mem:* AAAS; Am Phys Soc; Inst Elec & Electronics Engrs. *Res:* Light scattering; crystal lattice dynamics; quantum optics and quantum electronics. *Mailing Add:* 815 Madison St Evanston IL 60202

STRAHS, GERALD, PHYSICAL CHEMISTRY. *Current Pos:* MED PRES, MERCY CATH MED CTR, 81- *Personal Data:* b New York, NY, May 26, 38; m 60; c 3. *Educ:* Cooper Union Univ, BChE, 60; Univ Ill, MS, 62, PhD(phys chem), 65; Univ Juarez, MD, 80. *Prof Exp:* Assoc chem, Univ Calif, San Diego, 65-68; asst prof biochem, NY Med Col, 68-71; chemist, Crime Lab Sect, NY Police Dept, 72; chemist, US Assay Off, NY, 72-73; chief chemist, Consolidated Refining Co, 73-76; chemist, Brooklyn Hosp, 77-78; intern, USPHS Hosp, 80-81. *Concurrent Pos:* Am Cancer Soc fel, 65-68. *Res:* Precious metals, refining, assaying, recovery. *Mailing Add:* 100 E Marthart Ave Havertown PA 19083

STRAHS, KENNETH ROBERT, CELL BIOLOGY. *Current Pos:* PRES DEVELOP/DIAG, ORTHO PHARM CORP, 89- *Educ:* Univ Pa, PhD(cell biol), 75. *Prof Exp:* Mgr new technol, Beckman Instruments Inc, 84-85, res mgr spec chem & biol methods, Diag Syst Group, 85-89. *Mailing Add:* 39 Bullion Rd Basking Ridge NJ 07920-2420

STRAIGHT, H JOSEPH, MATHEMATICS, STATISTICS. *Current Pos:* asst prof, 77-80, ASSOC PROF MATH, STATE UNIV NY COL FREDONIA, 80- *Personal Data:* b Dunkirk, NY, Jan 26, 51; m 70. *Educ:* State Univ NY, Fredonia, BS, 73; Western Mich Univ, MA, 76, PhD(math-graph theory), 77. *Prof Exp:* Asst math, Western Mich Univ, 73-77. *Concurrent Pos:* Vis prof, Clemson Univ, 80-81. *Mem:* Math Asn Am; NY Acad Sci; Sigma Xi. *Res:* Graph theory, partitions, colorings of graphs; decomposition of graphs into trees. *Mailing Add:* 3231 Cable Rd No 1 Fredonia NY 14063-9758

STRAIGHT, JAMES WILLIAM, MECHANICAL ENGINEERING, EXPLOSIVES ENGINEERING. *Current Pos:* staff mem, Los Alamos Nat Lab, 77-80, assoc group leader, 77-83, dep group leader, 83-85, GROUP LEADER, LOS ALAMOS NAT LAB, 85- *Personal Data:* b Wichita, Kans, Aug 5, 40; m 61, Roberta Cunningham; c William & Suzanne. *Educ:* Univ Kans, BS & MS, 63; Univ Ariz, PhD(mech eng), 67. *Honors & Awards:* Teetor Award, Soc Automotive Engrs, 71. *Prof Exp:* Prog dir underground nuclear testing, Test Command/Defense Atomic Support Agency, 67-69; asst prof mech eng, Vanderbilt Univ, 69-71; from asst prof to assoc prof, Christian Bros Col, 71-77. *Concurrent Pos:* Instr, Los Alamos Br Grad Ctr, Univ NMex; Consult, Ken O'Brien & Assocs, 69-74 & Brown-Straight Consult, 72-77. *Mem:* Am Soc Mech Engrs; Am Soc Eng Educ; Soc Automotive Engrs; Sigma Xi. *Res:* Vibrations; structural dynamics; acoustics; stress analysis; instrumentation; explosives applications; hypervelocity impact. *Mailing Add:* One Comanche Lane Los Alamos NM 87544. *E-Mail:* straight@lanl.gov

STRAIGHT, RICHARD COLEMAN, PHOTOBIOLOGY. *Current Pos:* SUPVRY CHEMIST, MED SERV, VET ADMIN HOSP, 65-, DIR, VET ADMIN VENOM RES LAB, 75-, ADMIN OFFICER RES SERV, VET ADMIN CTR, 80- *Personal Data:* b Rivesville, WVa, Sept 8, 37; m 63; c 3. *Educ:* Univ Utah, BA, 61, PhD(molecular biol), 67. *Prof Exp:* Asst dir radiation biol summer inst, Univ Utah, 61-63. *Mem:* AAAS; Am Chem Soc; Biophys Soc; Am Soc Photobiol; Int Solar Energy Soc. *Res:* Photodynamic action of biomonomers and biopolymers; tumor immunology; effect of antigens on mammary adenocarcinoma of C3H mice; ageing; biochemical changes in ageing; venom toxicology; mechanism of action of psychoactive drugs. *Mailing Add:* 860 S 22nd St Salt Lake City UT 84108

STRAILE, WILLIAM EDWIN, BIOLOGICAL SCIENCE, NEUROSCIENCES. *Current Pos:* MEM STAFF, ORGAN SYSTS PROGS BR, DIV CANCER BIOL, DIAG & CTRS, NAT CANCER INST, 76- *Personal Data:* b Beaver, Pa, Mar 22, 31; m 53; c 4. *Educ:* Westminster Col, AB, 53; Brown Univ, ScM, 55, PhD(biol), 57. *Prof Exp:* Sr cancer res scientist, Springville Labs, Roswell Park Mem Inst, 61-65; assoc prof anat & head cell res sect, Med Sch, Temple Univ, 66-75; grants assoc, Div Res Grants, NIH, 75-76. *Concurrent Pos:* Nat Cancer res fel, Univ London, 57-58; res fel, Brown Univ, 58-61; asst res prof, Grad Sch, State Univ NY Buffalo, 62-65. *Res:* Electron microscopy and electrophysiology of nerve endings; neurotransmitter chemicals in the control of neuronal functions, blood flow and cell division; neural elements in melanotic and epidermal neoplasia. *Mailing Add:* 5700 Granby Rd Derwood MD 20855

STRAIN, BOYD RAY, PHYSIOLOGICAL ECOLOGY. *Current Pos:* from assoc prof to prof, 69-97, dir, Duke Phytotron, 79-89, EMER PROF BOT, DUKE UNIV, 98- *Personal Data:* b Laramie, Wyo, July 19, 35; m 58, Joan Bacon; c Robert Jay & Katherine Evans. *Educ:* Black Hills State Col, BS, 60; Univ Wyo, MS, 61; Univ Calif, Los Angeles, PhD(plant sci), 64. *Prof Exp:* Asst prof bot & plant ecol, Univ Calif, Riverside, 64-69. *Concurrent Pos:* Mem, Panel Ecol Sect, NSF, 72-75 & Comt Mineral Resources & Environ, Nat Res Coun, 73-74; mem, Am Inst Biol Sci Adv Panel, NASA, 76-87, panel biol facil & ctrs, NSF, 87-89; prog mgr co2 res, Dept Energy, 83-89; mem, Int Union Biol Sci, 89-95. *Mem:* Ecol Soc Am; Bot Soc Am; Am Inst Biol Sci(pres, 87-88); AAAS; Sigma Xi. *Res:* Physiological adaptations of plants to extreme environments; ecosystems analysis; effects of global environmental change on plants and ecosystems. *Mailing Add:* Dept Bot Duke Univ Durham NC 27708. *Fax:* 919-660-7425; *E-Mail:* bstrain@acpub.duke.edu

STRAIN, CHARLES A, NUCLEAR PHYSICS. *Current Pos:* RETIRED. *Personal Data:* b Greencastle, Ind, Jan 10, 10. *Educ:* De Pauw Univ, BS, 32; Univ Rochester, PhD(physics), 38. *Prof Exp:* Staff scientist, Naval Res Lab, Washington, 47-71. *Mem:* Am Phys Soc; Sigma Xi. *Mailing Add:* 4904 S Chesterfield Rd Arlington VA 22206

STRAIN, GLADYS WITT, NUTRITION. *Current Pos:* ASSOC PROF MED, MT SINAI MED CTR, 91- *Personal Data:* b Plymouth, Mich, Apr 19, 34; m 56, James J; c Jay, Jeffrey & James. *Educ:* Mich State Univ, BS, 55; Case Western Univ, MS, 60, PhD(nutrit), 64. *Honors & Awards:* Obesity Recognition Award, Obesity Found, 89. *Prof Exp:* Lectr, Columbia Univ, 73-74; res nutritionist, Montifore Med Ctr, 76-81; assoc prof & res nutritionist, Beth Israel Med Ctr, 81-91. *Concurrent Pos:* Nutritionist, Adult Diabetes Prog, Mt Sinai Med Ctr; mem, East Harlem Nutrit Task Force. *Mem:* Am Soc Clin Nutrit; Am Dietetic Asn; NAm Asn Study Obesity; Int Asn Study Obesity; NY Acad Sci; Sigma Xi; Am Soc Nutrit Sa. *Res:* Endocrinology of obesity and the treatment; diabetes in minority groups; improving compliance with behavioral change. *Mailing Add:* Mt Sinai Med Ctr One G Levy Pl PO Box 1055 New York NY 10029. *Fax:* 212-423-0508

STRAIN, JAMES E, PEDIATRICS. *Current Pos:* RETIRED. *Personal Data:* b Apr 23, 23; m; c 4. *Educ:* Phillips Univ, AB, 45; Univ Colo, MD, 47; Am Bd Pediat, cert, 54, 80 & 86. *Honors & Awards:* Clifford Grulee Award, Am Acad Pediat, 85; Excellence in Pub Serv Award, US Surgeon Gen, 88. *Prof Exp:* Intern, Minneapolis Gen Hosp, Minn, 47-48; resident pediat, Denver Children's Hosp, Colo, 48-50, dir, Genetic Serv, 82-86; gen pediat pract, Denver, Colo, 50-86; exec dir, Am Acad Pediat, 86-93. *Concurrent Pos:* Clin prof pediat, Med Ctr, Univ Colo, 69-86, Univ Chicago, 87-; mem, Comn Children & Youth, State Colo, 71-75; mem, Sect Coun Pediat, AMA, 71-, chmn, 74-79; mem, Bd Trustees, Phillips Univ, Enid, Okla, 74-; mem, Task Force Iowa Health Care Stand Proj, 84-85. *Mem:* Sr mem Inst Med-Nat Acad Sci; fel Am Acad Pediat (pres-elect, 81-82, pres, 82-83); AMA; Am Pub Health Asn. *Mailing Add:* Am Acad Pediat PO Box 927 Elk Grove Village IL 60009-0927

STRAIN, JOHN HENRY, POULTRY SCIENCE. *Current Pos:* RETIRED. *Personal Data:* b Worcester, Eng, Oct 28, 22; Can citizen; m 49; c 3. *Educ:* Univ Sask, BSAgr, 49; Iowa State Univ, MS, 60, PhD(poultry breeding), 61. *Prof Exp:* Hatcheryman, Swift Can Co, 49-50; res off, Can Dept Agr, 50-60, scientist poultry genetics, 60-70, head, Animal Sci Sect, Res Br, 70-82. *Mem:* Genetics Soc Can; Poultry Sci Asn; Can Soc Animal Sci. *Res:* Poultry genetics, mainly selection and genotype-environment interaction studies; dwarf broiler breeding management systems. *Mailing Add:* 14 Clark Dr Brandon MB R7B 0T9 Can

STRAIT, BRADLEY JUSTUS, ELECTRICAL ENGINEERING. *Current Pos:* RETIRED. *Personal Data:* b Canandaigua, NY, Mar 17, 32; m 57; c 2. *Educ:* Syracuse Univ, BS, 58, MS, 60, PhD(elec eng), 65. *Prof Exp:* Engr, Eastman Kodak Co, NY, 60-61; from asst prof to prof, Syracuse Univ, 65-96, chmn dept, 74-96. *Mem:* Inst Elec & Electronics Engrs; Sigma Xi. *Res:* Application of computers to antenna problems; array antennas; scattering systems and their effects on antenna performance; electromagnetic theory; microwave measurements. *Mailing Add:* Elec Eng Link Hall Syracuse Univ Syracuse NY 13244

STRAIT, EDWARD J, PHYSICS. *Current Pos:* PRIN SCIENTIST, STABILITY PHYSICS GROUP, GEN ATOMICS. *Honors & Awards:* Excellence in Plasma Physics Res Award, Am Physics Soc, 94. *Mailing Add:* Gen Atomics PO Box 85608 San Diego CA 92186-5608

STRAIT, JOHN, agricultural engineering; deceased, see previous edition for last biography

STRAIT, PEGGY, MATHEMATICS. *Current Pos:* lectr, 64-65, from asst prof to assoc prof, 65-72, PROF MATH, QUEENS COL, NEW YORK, 76- *Personal Data:* b Canton, China, Apr 20, 33; US citizen; m 55; c Paul & David. *Educ:* Univ Calif, Berkeley, BA, 53; Mass Inst Technol, MS, 57; NY Univ, PhD(math), 65. *Prof Exp:* Programmer math, Livermore Radiation Lab, Univ Calif, 54-55 & Lincoln Lab, Mass Inst Technol, 55-57; res assoc, G C Dewey Corp, NY, 57-62. *Concurrent Pos:* Lincoln Lab assoc staff fel, Mass Inst Technol, 56-57; res assoc fel, NY Univ, 62-64; NSF sci fac fel, 71-72. *Mem:* Am Math Soc. *Res:* Stochastic processes; probability theory and applications; mathematical statistics. *Mailing Add:* Dept Math Queens Col Flushing NY 11367

STRAITON, ARCHIE WAUGH, ELECTRICAL ENGINEERING. *Current Pos:* from assoc prof to prof, Univ Tex, Austin, 43-63, dir elec eng res lab, 47-72, chmn dept, 66-71, actg vpres & dean grad sch, 72-73, Asbel Smith prof elec eng, 63-89, EMER ASBEL SMITH PROF, UNIV TEX, AUSTIN, 89- *Personal Data:* b Tarrant Co, Tex, Aug 27, 07; wid; c 2. *Educ:* Univ Tex, BSEE, 29, MA, 31, PhD(physics), 39. *Honors & Awards:* Edison Medal, Inst Elec & Electronics Engrs. *Prof Exp:* Mem inspection dept, Bell Tel Labs, Inc, 29-30; assoc prof eng, Tex Col Arts & Indust, 31-41, prof & dir eng, 41-43. *Mem:* Nat Acad Eng; Am Soc Eng Educ; fel Inst Elec & Electronics. *Res:* Atmospheric refractive index properties; interaction of atmosphere and radio waves; electrical physics; measurement of electrical characteristics of filters; harmonic solution of differential equations. *Mailing Add:* 4212 Far West Blvd Austin TX 78731

STRAKA, THOMAS JAMES, FORESTRY ECONOMICS, FOREST RESOURCE MANAGEMENT. *Current Pos:* assoc prof, 89-95, PROF FOREST RESOURCES, CLEMSON UNIV, 95- *Personal Data:* b Dec 17, 49; m 76, Patricia Ann Casciere. *Educ:* Univ Wis-Madison, BS, 72, MS, 73; Univ SC, MBA, 78; Va Polytech Inst & State Univ, PhD(forest resource mgt & econs), 81. *Prof Exp:* Proj forester, Int Paper Co, 74-78; from asst prof to assoc prof forestry, Miss State Univ, 82-89. *Mem:* Soc Am Foresters; Forest Prod Soc. *Res:* Forest resource management and economics; forest valuation issues; nonindustrial private forest; quantitative forest economics; timberland investment; industrial forestry issues. *Mailing Add:* Dept Forest Resources Clemson Univ PO Box 341003 Clemson SC 29634-1003. *Fax:* 864-656-3304; *E-Mail:* tstraka@clemson.edu

STRAKA, WILLIAM CHARLES, ASTROPHYSICS. *Current Pos:* SR STAFF SCIENTIST, LOCKHEED PALO ALTO RES LAB, 84- *Personal Data:* b Phoenix, Ariz, Oct 21, 40; m 66, Barbara Ellen Thayer; c William Charles III. *Educ:* Calif Inst Technol, BS, 62; Univ Calif, Los Angeles, MA, 65, PhD(astron), 69. *Prof Exp:* Teacher astron & phys sci, Long Beach City Col, 66-70; asst prof astron, Boston Univ, 70-74; from asst prof to prof astron, Jackson State Univ, 74-84, head dept, physics, 77-78. *Concurrent Pos:* Vis staff mem, Los Alamos Nat Lab, 76-81; exec secy astron adv comt, NSF, 78-79. *Mem:* Am Astron Soc; Sigma Xi; AAAS; Am Inst Aeronaut & Astronaut; Am Voice Input-Output Soc; Soc Photo-Optical Instrumentation Engrs. *Res:* Structure and evolution of small mass stars; galactic nebulae; dynamics of supernova shells; computerized voice recognition; planetary exploration. *Mailing Add:* 860 Clara Dr Palo Alto CA 94303. *E-Mail:* bill.strake@lmco.com

STRALEY, JOSEPH PAUL, SOLID STATE PHYSICS. *Current Pos:* from asst prof to assoc prof, 73-81, PROF PHYSICS, UNIV KY, 81- *Personal Data:* b Toledo, Ohio, Jan 22, 42; m 67, Susan Calhoon. *Educ:* Harvard Col, BA, 64; Cornell Univ, PhD(physics), 70. *Prof Exp:* NSF fel chem, Cornell Univ, 70-71; res assoc physics, Rutgers Univ, 71-73; asst prof physics, Univ Ala, 80-81, assoc prof, 81-83. *Concurrent Pos:* NSF res grants, Univ Ky, 76-81 & Univ Ala, 81-; sabbatical leave, Mich State Univ, 79-80. *Mem:* Am Phys Soc. *Res:* Theory of phase transitions; cooperative phenomena; liquid crystals; inhomogeneous conductors; percolation problem. *Mailing Add:* Dept Physics & Astron Univ Ky Lexington KY 40506

STRALEY, JOSEPH WARD, SPECTROSCOPY. *Current Pos:* from asst prof to prof, 44-58, EMER PROF PHYSICS, UNIV NC, CHAPEL HILL, 80- *Personal Data:* b Paulding, Ohio, Oct 6, 14; m 39; c 3. *Educ:* Bowling Green State Univ, BSEd, 36; Ohio State Univ, MSc, 37, PhD(physics), 41. *Prof Exp:* Asst, Ohio State Univ, 37-38, 40-41; actg instr physics, Heidelberg Col, 38-39; instr, Univ Toledo, 41-42, asst prof, 42-44, actg head dept, 43-44. *Concurrent Pos:* Guggenheim fel, 56-57. *Mem:* Am Phys Soc; Am Asn Physics Teachers. *Res:* Spectroscopy; research in science and public policy. *Mailing Add:* S3 Davie Circle Chapel Hill NC 27514

STRALEY, SUSAN CALHOON, MECHANISMS OF PATHOGENESIS OF BACTERIAL INFECTIOUS DISEASES. *Current Pos:* res assoc & lab supvr, 73-79, from asst prof to assoc prof, 83-92, PROF MICROBIOL, DEPT MICROBIOL & IMMUNOL, UNIV KY, 92-, RES PROF, 95- *Personal Data:* b Charlotte, NC, Mar 1, 45; m 67, Joseph P. *Educ:* Univ Rochester, BA, 67; Cornell Univ, PhD(bot), 72. *Prof Exp:* Res assoc fel, Princeton Univ, 72-73, Mich State Univ, 79-80; asst prof microbiol, Univ Ala, Birmingham, 80-83. *Concurrent Pos:* Study sect mem, Bact & Mycol 1, Nat Inst Allergy & Infectious Dis, 88-93; vis scientist, Walter Reed Army Inst Res, 90-91; study comt, Am Heart Asn Immunol & Microbiol, 96- *Mem:* Am Soc Microbiol; AAAS. *Res:* Studying a set of virulence proteins in the plague bacterium Yersinia pestis for their roles in pathogenesis, for the mechanism regulating their expression or secretion and for their potential usefulness in vaccines. *Mailing Add:* 145 Kentucky Ave Lexington KY 40502. *E-Mail:* scstra01@pop.uky.edu

STRALEY, TINA, MATHEMATICS. *Current Pos:* from asst prof to assoc prof math, 73-84, prof math & comput sci, 84-87, PROF MATH & DEPT CHMN, KENNESAW COL, 87- *Personal Data:* b New York, NY, Sept 4, 43; div; c 1. *Educ:* Ga State Univ, BA, 65, MS, 66; Auburn Univ, PhD(math), 71. *Prof Exp:* Teacher math, Miami Beach Sr High Sch, 66-67; instr, Spelman Col, 67-68 & Auburn Univ, 71-73. *Concurrent Pos:* Vis res assoc, Emory Univ, 78-79; prog dir, Div Undergrad Educ, NSF. *Mem:* Am Math Soc; Nat Coun Teachers Math; Math Asn Am; Am Asn Univ Prof; Asn Women Maths. *Res:* Embeddings, extensions and automorphisms of Steiner systems, design theory, scheduling problems. *Mailing Add:* Off Acad Affairs Kennesaw State Col 1000 Chastain Rd Kennesaw GA 30144-5591. *Fax:* 703-306-0445

STRALKA, ALBERT R, MATHEMATICS. *Current Pos:* asst prof, 67-72, assoc prof, 72-76, PROF MATH, UNIV CALIF, RIVERSIDE, 76- *Personal Data:* b Wilkes-Barre, Pa, Jan 18, 40; m 65; c 2. *Educ:* Wilkes Col, AB, 61; Pa State Univ, MA, 64, PhD(math), 67. *Prof Exp:* Instr math, Wilkes Col, 61-62 & Pa State Univ, 66-67. *Mem:* Am Math Soc. *Res:* Ordered structures. *Mailing Add:* Dept Math Univ Calif Riverside CA 92521-0135

STRAMSKI, DARIUSZ, MARINE OPTICS. *Current Pos:* res assoc, 89-92, RES ASST PROF, DEPT BIOL SCI, UNIV SOUTHERN CALIF, 92- *Personal Data:* b Piotrkow, Tryb, Poland, Aug 5, 54; m 78, Malgorzata Zmojdzin; c Wojciech & Jacek. *Educ:* Univ Gdansk, MSc, 78, PhD(natural sci), 85. *Honors & Awards:* Maurycy Rudzki Prize, Polish Acad Sci, 85. *Prof Exp:* Res scientist, Inst Oceanog, Polish Acad Sci, 78-88; vis res scientist, Dept Biol, Univ Laval, 88-89. *Concurrent Pos:* Fr gov & UNESCO fel, Lab Phys & Marine Chem, Univ Pierre & Marie Curie, France, 86-88. *Mem:* Am Soc Limnol & Oceanog; Am Geophys Union. *Res:* Marine optics and bio-optical oceanography; light absorption and scattering by seawater constituents; radiative transfer in the ocean; light-field in the ocean; fluctuations of underwater irradiance; optical processes underlying remote sensing of ocean color; implications of optics in phytoplankton biology. *Mailing Add:* Biol Sci Univ Southern Calif 3616 Trousdale Pkwy Los Angeles CA 90089-0015. *Fax:* 213-740-8123

STRAND, FLEUR LILLIAN, NERVE REGENERATION, NEUROPEPTIDES. *Current Pos:* actg chmn dept, 82, 89, PROF BIOL, NY UNIV, 73- *Personal Data:* b Bloemfontein, SAfrica, Feb 24, 28; US citizen; m 46; c 1. *Educ:* NY Univ, AB, 48, MS, 50, PhD(biol), 52. *Honors & Awards:* Am Med Writers Award, 84. *Prof Exp:* Instr biol, Brooklyn Col, 51-57; NIH fel, Physiol Inst, Free Univ Berlin, 57-59; from asst prof to assoc prof, 61-73. *Concurrent Pos:* Prin investr neuroendocrine res; chmn, NY Acad Sci, 88. *Mem:* AAAS; Am Physiol Soc; Soc Neurosci; Int Soc Psychoneuroendocrinol; Int Soc Develop Neurosci; Sigma Xi; NY Acad Sci (pres, 87). *Res:* Neurohormonal integration; effect of hormones on developing and regenerating nerve and muscle; neuroendocrinology; peptide hormones; editor and author of numerous books and scientific articles. *Mailing Add:* Dept Biol NY Univ Washington Sq 1009 Main Bldg New York NY 10021-7511. *Fax:* 212-998-4015

STRAND, JAMES CAMERON, NEPHROLOGY, HYPERTENSION. *Current Pos:* PRIN INVESTR, DEPT PHARMACOL, PENNWATT CORP, 85- *Personal Data:* b East St Louis, Ill, June 1, 43; m 52; c 2. *Educ:* Monmouth Col, Ill, BA, 66; St Louis Univ, Mo, MS, 73; Univ Nebr, Omaha, PhD(physiol), 77. *Prof Exp:* Nephrol res fel, Mayo Clinic & Found, 77-80; cardiovasc res fel, Georgetown Univ, 80-81; res assoc, A H Robins Co, 81-85. *Mem:* Am Physiol Soc; Am Soc Hypertension; Am Soc Nephrology. *Res:* Mechanisms associated with cardiovascular and renal functions in hypertension and congestive heart failure. *Mailing Add:* Parke Davis Res 2800 Plymouth Rd 755 Jefferson Rd Ann Arbor MI 48105-2495. *Fax:* 313-996-7937

STRAND, JOHN A, III, POLLUTION BIOLOGY. *Current Pos:* WATER QUAL PLANNER, KING CO DEPT NATURAL RESOURCES. *Personal Data:* b Red Bank, NJ, July 22, 38; m 63; c 4. *Educ:* Lafayette Col, AB, 60; Lehigh Univ, MS, 62; Univ Wash, PhD(fisheries biol), 75. *Prof Exp:* Fisheries biologist, NJ Bur Fisheries Lab, 62-63; res scientist, US Naval Radiol Defense Lab, 64-69; sr res scientist aquatic ecol, Pac Northwest Labs, Battelle Mem Inst, 69-90; marine res lab, Sequim, Wash; Off Oil Spill Damage Assessment, Nat Marine Fisheries Serv, 90-93; sr biologist, EA Eng Sci & Tech Inc, 93- *Concurrent Pos:* Auxiliary fac, Sch Fisheries, Univ Wash, 87-92. *Mem:* Sigma Xi; fel Am Inst Fishery Res Biologists; Am Fisheries Soc. *Res:* Aquatic radioecology; biological accumulation of radioisotopes in biological systems and their effects; effects and fate of petroleum residues and other contaminants in biological systems and synthetic fuel; environmental impact assessment; restoration. *Mailing Add:* King Co Dept Natural Resources 700 Fifth Ave Suite 2200 Seattle WA 98104-5022. *Fax:* 425-869-2061

STRAND, KAJ AAGE, ASTRONOMY. *Current Pos:* CONSULT, 77- *Personal Data:* b Hellerup, Denmark, Feb 27, 07; nat US; m 43, 49, Emilie Rashevsky; c Kristina & Vibeke. *Educ:* Univ Copenhagen, BA & MSc, 31, PhD(astron), 38. *Honors & Awards:* Knight Cross First Class, Royal Order Dannebrog, Denmark, 77; Honor Cross, Literis et Artibus, First Class, Austria, 78. *Prof Exp:* Geodesist, Geod Inst, Copenhagen, 31-33; asst to dir observ, Univ Leiden, 33-38; res assoc astron, Swarthmore Col, 38-42, res astronr, 46, Am-Scand Found fel, 38-39, Danish Rask-Orsted Found fel, 39-40; assoc prof astron, Univ Chicago, 46-47; res assoc, 47-67; prof astron, Northwestern Univ & dir, Dearborn Observ, 47-58; dir astrometry & astrophys, US Naval Observ, 58-63, sci dir, 63-77. *Concurrent Pos:* Guggenheim fel, 46; consult, NSF, 53-56 & Lincoln Lab, Mass Inst Technol, 81-86; vis prof, Acad Sinica, China, 87. *Mem:* Int Astron Union; Am Astron Soc; Neth Astron Soc; Royal Danish Acad; Astron Soc Pac; Sigma Xi. *Res:* Photographic observations of double stars; stellar parallaxes; orbital motion in double and multiple systems; instrumentation; astrometric reflector. *Mailing Add:* 3200 Rowland Pl NW Washington DC 20008

STRAND, RICHARD ALVIN, ELECTRICAL ENGINEERING. *Current Pos:* RETIRED. *Personal Data:* b Ridgway, Pa, July 30, 26; m 48; c 3. *Educ:* Pa State Univ, BS, 50, MS, 51, PhD(elec eng), 63. *Prof Exp:* Prod engr, Elliott Co, Pa, 51-56; from instr to assoc prof, Pa State Univ, 56-64; from assoc prof to prof elec eng, Univ Bridgeport, 64-93, chmn dept, 64-81, asst dean eng, 70-79, assoc dean eng, 80-93. *Mem:* Inst Elec & Electronics Engrs; Am Soc Eng Educ. *Res:* Generalized analysis of electromechanical energy converters; curriculum development; educational methods; measurement of effective teaching. *Mailing Add:* 508 Hertiage Village Southbury CT 06488

STRAND, RICHARD CARL, PARTICLE DETECTOR DEVELOPMENT. *Current Pos:* asst physicist, 62-65, assoc physicist, 65-67, PHYSICIST, BROOKHAVEN NAT LAB, 67- *Personal Data:* b Langdon, NDak, Mar 20, 33; m 61, Phyllis Clabaugh; c Andrew & Amanda. *Educ:* NDak State Univ, BS, 55; Johns Hopkins Univ, PhD(physics), 61. *Prof Exp:* Res assoc physics, Johns Hopkins Univ, 61-62. *Concurrent Pos:* Fullbright scholar, Univ Lyons, France, 55-56. *Mem:* Am Phys Soc. *Res:* Experimental sub-nuclear particle physics; software data analysis. *Mailing Add:* Physics Dept Bldg 510A Brookhaven Nat Lab Upton NY 11973. *E-Mail:* strand@bnl.gov

STRAND, TIMOTHY CARL, OPTICAL & MAGNETIC STORAGE TECHNOLOGIES. *Current Pos:* res staff mem, San Jose Res Lab, 83-85, mgr, Mach Vision Sensing, 85-88, mgr explor optics, 88-95, MGR LASER PROCESSING, ALMADEN RES CTR, INT BUS MACH, 96- *Personal Data:* b Marshalltown, Iowa, Apr 17, 48; m 67; c 1. *Educ:* Univ Iowa, BA, 70; Univ Calif, San Diego, MS, 73, PhD(appl physics), 76. *Prof Exp:* Res staff mem, Naval Electronics Lab Ctr, 71-73; res asst physics, Univ Erlangen, WGer, 73-76; res scientist, Univ Southern Calif, 76-79, res asst prof elec eng & optics, 79-83. *Mem:* Fel Optical Soc Am; sr mem Inst Elec & Electronics Engrs; Soc Photo-Optical Instrumentation Engrs. *Res:* Optical storage technologies and integrated optics; machine vision; developing optical inspection and measurement techniques; optical computing; computer generated holography; optical information processing; laser materials processing; magnetic storage. *Mailing Add:* IBM Almaden Res Ctr K63-803E 650 Harry Rd San Jose CA 95120

STRANDBERG, MALCOM WOODROW PERSHING, SOLID STATE PHYSICS, ACOUSTICS. *Current Pos:* Res assoc, Mass Inst Technol, 41-42, mem staff, Off Sci Res & Develop, 42-43, microwave develop, 43-45, res assoc, 45-48, from asst prof to assoc prof, 48-60, prof physics, 60-88, EMER PROF PHYSICS, MASS INST TECHNOL, 88- *Personal Data:* b Box Elder, Mont, Mar 9, 19; m 47, Harriet Elizabeth Bennett; c Josiah R W, Susan A (Berrospe), Elisabeth G (Stith) & Malcom B. *Educ:* Harvard Univ, SB, 41; Mass Inst Technol, PhD(physics), 48. *Concurrent Pos:* Vis scientist, Am Inst Physics, 57-59 & 63-64; Fulbright lectr, Univ Grenoble, 61-62; NATO prof, Univ Palermo, Sicily, 70; invited prof, Univ Geneva, Switz, 70. *Mem:* Fel Am Phys Soc; fel Inst Elec & Electronics Engrs; fel Am Acad Arts & Sci; fel AAAS; NY Acad Sci. *Res:* Design of microwave components, radio transmitters and receivers; biological physics. *Mailing Add:* Mass Inst Technol 26-353 Cambridge MA 02139. *E-Mail:* mwpstr@mit.edu

STRANDHOY, JACK W, RENAL PHARMACOLOGY, VASOPRESSIN. *Current Pos:* asst prof, 75-80, ASSOC PROF PHARMACOL, BOWMAN GRAY SCH MED, WAKE FOREST UNIV, 80- *Personal Data:* b Evanston, Ill, Aug 8, 44; m 67; c 2. *Educ:* Univ Ill, BS, 67; Univ Iowa, MS, 69, PhD(pharmacol), 72. *Prof Exp:* NIH fel physiol, Mayo Clin, 71-73; sr res investr, NC Heart Asn, 73-75. *Concurrent Pos:* Consult, Mead Johnson, 76, Curric Designs, Inc, 77, Wyeth-Ayerst, 80-90 & Ciba-Geigy, 90; prin investr, NIH, 79-; field ed, Pharmacol & Exp Therapeut, 93- *Mem:* Am Soc Pharmacol & Exp Therapeut; Am Soc Nephrology; Int Soc Nephrology; Am Heart Asn. *Res:* Mechanisms by which vasoactive substances, especially catecholamines, prostaglandins, and antihypertensive drugs, affect renal water and electrolyte metabolism; fetal renal development. *Mailing Add:* Dept Physiol & Pharmacol Bowman Gray Sch Med Winston-Salem NC 27157-1083. *Fax:* 919-716-7738

STRANDJORD, PAUL EDPHIL, CLINICAL CHEMISTRY, LABORATORY MEDICINE. *Current Pos:* RETIRED. *Personal Data:* b Minneapolis, Minn, Apr 5, 31; m 53; c 2. *Educ:* Univ Minn, BA, 51, MA, 52; Stanford Univ, MD, 59. *Honors & Awards:* Gerald T Evans Award in Lab Med, 76. *Prof Exp:* Intern med, Sch Med, Univ Minn, 59-60, from instr to assoc prof lab med, 63-69; prof lab med & chmn dept, Sch Med, Univ Wash, 69-94. *Concurrent Pos:* USPHS med fel, Univ Minn, 61-63; pres, Asn Univ Physicians, Univ Wash, 87- *Mem:* AAAS; Acad Clin Lab Physicians & Sci; Am Chem Soc; Am Fedn Clin Res; Am Asn Clin Chem; Am Mgt Asn. *Res:* Diagnostic enzymology. *Mailing Add:* 9410 Lake Washington Blvd NE Bellevue WA 98004

STRANDNESS, DONALD EUGENE, JR, MEDICINE, SURGERY. *Current Pos:* From instr to assoc prof, 62-70, PROF SURG, SCH MED, UNIV WASH, 70- *Personal Data:* b Bowman, NDak, Sept 22, 28; m 57; c 3. *Educ:* Pac Lutheran Univ, BA, 50; Univ Wash, MD, 54. *Concurrent Pos:* Res fel, Nat Heart Inst, 59-60; clin investr, Vet Admin, 62-65; NIH career develop award, 65- *Mem:* Soc Vascular Surg; Am Inst Ultrasonics in Med; Am Col Surg; Am Surg Asn; Int Cardiovasc Soc; Nat Heart, Lung & Blood Inst. *Res:* Peripheral vascular disease and physiology. *Mailing Add:* Dept Surg Univ Wash Sch Med Seattle WA 98195. *Fax:* 425-543-8136

STRANG, GILBERT, APPLIED MATHEMATICS. *Current Pos:* Moore instr math, 59-61, from asst prof to assoc prof, 61-70, PROF MATH, MASS INST TECHNOL, 70- *Personal Data:* b Chicago, Ill, Nov 27, 34; m 58; c 3. *Educ:* Mass Inst Technol, SB, 55; Oxford Univ, BA, 57; Univ Calif, Los Angeles, PhD(math), 59. *Honors & Awards:* Chauvenet Prize, Math Asn Am, 75. *Concurrent Pos:* NATO fel, Oxford Univ, 61-62; Sloan fel, Mass Inst Technol, 66-67; Fairchild scholar, Calif Inst Technol, 81. *Mem:* Am Math Soc; Soc Indust & Appl Math (vpres, 91-96); Math Asn Am. *Res:* Mathematical analysis applied to linear algebra and partial differential equations; author of six textbooks on mathematics. *Mailing Add:* Mass Inst Technol Rm 2-240 Cambridge MA 02139-4307. *Fax:* 617-253-4358; *E-Mail:* gs@math.mit.edu

STRANG, ROBERT M, FOREST & RANGELAND ECOLOGY. *Current Pos:* RETIRED. *Personal Data:* b Gt Brit, 26; m 53; c 5. *Educ:* Univ Edinburgh, BSc, 50; Univ London, PhD(ecol), 65. *Prof Exp:* Res off forestry, Colonial Develop Corp, Swaziland, Nyasaland & Tanganyika, 50-57 & Rhodesian Wattle Co, Ltd, 57-62; forest ecologist, Northern Forest Res Ctr, Forestry Serv, Can Dept Environ, 65-73, biologist, Natural Natural Resources & Environ Br, Arctic Land Use Res, Can Dept Indian & Northern Affairs, 73-74; head, Environ Studies Sect, Northern Natural Resources & Environ Br, 74-75; assoc prof rangeland ecol & mgt, Fac Agr Sci Forestry, Univ BC, 75-81; exec dir, Forest Res Coun BC, 81-87; assoc dean renewable resources, BC Inst Tech, 87-91. *Concurrent Pos:* Hon res assoc, Univ NB, 67-71; secy, Conserv Coun NB, 69-71; adj prof, Simon Fraser Univ, 79-; chmn, Forest Educ Coun BC, 88- *Mem:* Commonwealth Forestry Asn; Soc Range Mgt; Can Inst Forestry. *Res:* Resource and land management. *Mailing Add:* 2456 141st St Surrey BC V4A 4K2 Can

STRANG, RUTH HANCOCK, PEDIATRICS, CARDIOLOGY. *Current Pos:* from asst prof to prof, 62-89, EMER PROF PEDIAT, UNIV MICH, ANN ARBOR, 89- *Personal Data:* b Bridgeport, Conn, Mar 11, 23. *Educ:* Wellesley Col, BA, 44; New York Med Col, MD, 49. *Prof Exp:* Intern, Flower & Fifth Ave Hosps, NY, 49-50, resident pediat, 50-52; from instr to asst prof bact, New York Med Col, 52-57, instr pediat, 52-56, asst clin prof, 56-57. *Concurrent Pos:* Fel cardiol, Babies Hosp, New York, 56-57 & Hopkins Hosp, Baltimore, 57-59; res fel, Children's Hosp, Boston, 59-62. *Mem:* Fel Am Acad Pediat; Am Col Cardiol; Am Heart Asn. *Res:* Congenital heart disease; effect on growth; ventricular performance; echocardiography. *Mailing Add:* 4500 E Huron River Dr Ann Arbor MI 48105-9335

STRANG, W(ILLIAM) GILBERT, MATHEMATICS. *Current Pos:* Moore instr, 59-61, from asst prof to assoc prof, 62-69, PROF MATH, MASS INST TECHNOL, 69- *Personal Data:* b Chicago, Ill, Nov 27, 34; m 58; c 3. *Educ:* Mass Inst Technol, SB, 55; Oxford Univ, BA, 57; Univ Calif, Los Angeles, PhD(math), 59. *Concurrent Pos:* Fels, NATO, 61-62 & Sloan Found, 65-67; Fairchild scholar, 80; pres, Wellesley-Cambridge Press. *Mem:* Am Math Soc; Math Asn Am; Am Acad Arts & Sci. *Res:* Partial difference and differential equations; matrix analysis; optimization. *Mailing Add:* Dept Math Mass Inst Technol Rm 2-240 Cambridge MA 02139-4307

STRANGE, LLOYD K(EITH), ENHANCED OIL RECOVERY. *Current Pos:* ENG CONSULT, 88- *Personal Data:* b Burkburnett, Tex, Dec 17, 22; m 43; c Steven K & George S. *Educ:* Southern Methodist Univ, BS, 50, MS, 56. *Prof Exp:* Petrol eng asst, Magnolia Petrol Co, 50-52; engr, Petrol Prod Eng Co, 52-53; res engr, Mobil Res & Develop Corp, 53-56, sr res engr, 56-63, eng assoc, field res lab, 63-87. *Mem:* Am Soc Mech Engrs; Soc Petrol Engrs. *Res:* Planning, operating and evaluating laboratory and field experiments on improved crude oil recovery processes; application of new research results. *Mailing Add:* 901 Danish Grand Prairie TX 75050

STRANGE, RONALD STEPHEN, INORGANIC CHEMISTRY, EDUCATION. *Current Pos:* from asst prof to assoc prof, 71-84, chmn dept, 75-81, PROF CHEM, FAIRLEIGH DICKINSON UNIV, FLORHAM-MADISON CAMPUS, 84- *Personal Data:* b Covington, Ky, Nov 18, 43; m 70, Virginia Watts; c Stephen, Michael, Malinda & Matthew. *Educ:* Univ Ky, BS, 65; Univ Ill, Urbana, MS, 67, PhD(inorg chem), 71; Stevens Inst of Tech, MS, 87. *Prof Exp:* Instr chem, Ill Inst Technol, 70-71. *Concurrent Pos:* Fac res grant-in-aid, Fairleigh Dickinson Univ, 72-74; NSF teacher training grants, 79-80 & 80-81; vis fel, Princeton Univ, 79. *Mem:* Am Chem Soc; Sigma Xi. *Res:* Molecular modelling; semi empirical self consistent field molecular orbital calculations; graph theory in chemistry; neural networks in chemistry. *Mailing Add:* 121 Park Ave Madison NJ 07940. *Fax:* 973-443-8766; *E-Mail:* strange@aloha.fdu.edu

STRANGES, ANTHONY NICHOLAS, HISTORY OF ENERGY & SYNTHETIC FUELS, HISTORY OF VALENCE THEORY. *Current Pos:* asst prof, 77-83, ASSOC PROF HIST SCI, TEX A&M UNIV, 83- *Personal Data:* b Niagara Falls, NY, Sept 28, 36; m 63, Sonya M Rudy; c Krista & Kara. *Educ:* Niagara Univ, BS, 58, MS, 64; Univ Wis-Madison, PhD(hist sci), 77. *Prof Exp:* Teacher chem & physics, Notre Dame Col Sch, Welland, Ont, 59-62; teacher chem, Lewiston-Porter High Sch, Lewiston, NY, 63-69; archivist & res asst, Univ Wis, Madison, 69-77. *Mem:* Hist Sci Soc; Hist Chem Soc; Soc Hist Technol; Am Hist Asn; Can Sci & Technol Hist Asn. *Res:* History of twentieth-century science, especially electron theories of valence, history of energy, synthetic liquid fuel production from coal and tar using high-pressure liquefaction and Fischer-Tropsch synthesis. *Mailing Add:* 1205 Barak Lane Tex A&M Univ Bryan TX 77802. *Fax:* 409-862-4314

STRANGEWAY, ROBERT JOSEPH, SPACE PLASMA PHYSICS. *Current Pos:* from asst res geophysicist to assoc res geophysicist, 83-92, RES GEOPHYSICIST, INST GEOPHYS & PLANETARY PHYSICS, UNIV CALIF, LOS ANGELES, 92- *Personal Data:* b Preston, Lancashire, Eng, May 27, 53; m 86, Patricia A Timcho; c Matthew R, Rachel K & Kevin P. *Educ:* Univ London, BSc, 74, PhD(space plasma physics), 78. *Prof Exp:* Vis fel, Univ Colo, Nat Oceanic & Atmospheric Admin, 79-80; consult, Lockheed Palo Alto Res Lab, 80-83. *Mem:* Am Geophys Union. *Res:* Plasma wave phenomena in the terrestrial magnetosphere and at the planets; auroral kilometric radiation; the very-low-frequency evidence of lightning on Venus and plasma waves observed in the magnetosheath and upstream of the bow shock of Venus. *Mailing Add:* Inst Geophys & Planetary Physics Univ Calif Los Angeles CA 90024. *Fax:* 310-206-3051; *E-Mail:* strange@igpp.ucla.edu

STRANGWAY, DAVID W, GEOPHYSICS. *Current Pos:* PRES & VCHANCELLOR, UNIV BC, 85- *Personal Data:* b Simcoe, Ont, June 7, 34; m 57; c 3. *Educ:* Univ Toronto, BA, 56, MA, 58, PhD(physics), 60; FRAS, FRSC. *Hon Degrees:* DLittS, Victoria Univ, Univ Toronto, 86; DSc, Mem Univ, NFLD, 86, McGill Univ, Montreal, 89, Ritsumeikan Univ, Kyoto, Japan, 90, Univ Toronto 94; DAgSc, Tokyo Univ Agr, 91. *Honors & Awards:* Medal Except Sci Achievement, NASA, 72; Virgil Kauffman Gold Medal, Soc Explor Geophysicists, 74; Pahlavi lectr, Iran, 78; Logan Gold Medal, Geol Asn Can, 84; J Tuzo Wilson Medal, Can Geophys Union, 87; Officer, Order of Can, 96. *Prof Exp:* Sr geophysicist, Dominion Gulf Co, Toronto, 56; chief geophysicist, Ventures Ltd, Ont, 56-57, sr geophysicist, 58; res geophysicist, Kennecott Copper Corp, Denver, Colo, 60-61; asst prof geol, Univ Colo, Boulder, 61-64; asst prof geophys, Mass Inst Technol, 65-68; from assoc prof to prof physics, Univ Toronto, 68-85, prof, Dept Geol, 72-85, chmn, 72-80, vpres & provost, 80-83, pres, 83-84. *Concurrent Pos:* Consult, Kennecott Copper Corp, Anaconda Co, UN, Alyeska Pipelines & NASA, Environ Res Inst Mich, GTE/Sylvania, Seru Nucleaire & Barringer Res; mem, Subcomt Appl Geophys & Subcomt Geomagnetism, Nat Res Coun, 68-70; mem, Lunar Sample Anal Planning Team, 69-72, chmn, Lunar Sci Coun, 74-76, mem, Lunar Base Working Group, 84; chief, Geophys Br, Johnson Space Ctr, NASA, Houston, Tex, 70-72, Physics Br, 72-73; vis prof, Dept Geol, Univ Houston, 71-73; assoc ed, Geophys, 73-75, Can J Earth Sci, 73-76 & Geophys Res Lett, 77-80; mem, Team Basaltic Volcanism Terrestrial Planets, Lunar & Planetary Inst, 77-80, Nat Acad Planetary Explor, 85-86; pres, Can Geosci Coun, 80; univ space res assoc, Coun Institutions, 84-85; mem, Nat Acad Planetary Explor, 85-86; dir, MacMillan Bloedel, Ltd, Bus Coun BC, Corp Higher Educ Forum; chmn, BC Task Force on Environ & Econ, 89; mem, Premier's Adv Coun on Sci Tech; chair, Nat Mus Sci & Technol, 96; hon fel, Green Col, Oxford Univ, 94; hon adv, Urasenke Fedn, Kyote, Japan, 94; hon prof, Univ Autonoma de Guadalajara, Mex, 96. *Mem:* Hon mem Soc Explor Geophysicists (vpres, 79-80); fel Royal Soc Can; Can Geophys Union; fel Geol Asn Can (vpres, 77-78, pres, 78-79); hon mem Can Explor Geophysicists Soc; Am Geophys Union; Europ Asn Explor Geophysicists; Soc Geomagnetism & Geoelec Japan; fel Royal Astron Soc; AAAS. *Res:* History of the earth's magnetic field; studies of ancient reversals of the field; changes in direction and intensity and secular variation; exploration using electromagnetic techniques; magnetic fields of lunar samples and meteorites; history of magnetic fields in the early solar system. *Mailing Add:* Pres Off Univ BC 6328 Memorial Rd Vancouver BC V6T 1Z2 Can. *Fax:* 604-822-5055

STRANO, ALFONSO J, VIROLOGY, PATHOLOGY. *Current Pos:* CLIN PROF PATH, SCH MED, SOUTHERN ILL UNIV, 73- *Personal Data:* b Ambridge, Pa, Apr 7, 27; m 57; c 1. *Educ:* Hiram Col, BA, 50; Duquesne Univ, MS, 53; Univ Okla, PhD(path), 57; Univ Tex, MD, 60. *Prof Exp:* From instr to asst prof path, Univ Tex Med Br Galveston, 62-67; pathologist, Armed Forces Inst Path & chief, Viro-Path Br, 67-73. *Concurrent Pos:* Am Cancer Soc res fel, 60-62. *Mem:* AMA; Col Am Path; Reticuloendothelial Soc; Int Acad Path; Sigma Xi. *Res:* Immunologic aspects of infectious disease, cellular immunity; histologic reaction to viral infections. *Mailing Add:* 18 Wildwood Rd Springfield IL 62704-4384

STRANO, JOSEPH J, ELECTRICAL & BIOMEDICAL ENGINEERING. *Current Pos:* chmn, Dept Elec Eng, 87, PROF ELEC & COMPUTER ENGR, NJ INST TECHNOL, 87- *Personal Data:* b Newark, NJ, Aug 21, 37; m 62. *Educ:* Newark Col Eng, BS, 59, MS, 61; Rutgers Univ, PhD(elec eng), 69. *Prof Exp:* From instr to assoc prof, Newark Col Eng, 61-76, assoc chmn dept, 75-76, prof elec eng,78-, chmn dept, 76- *Concurrent Pos:* NSF res initiation grant, Newark Col Eng, 71-72. *Mem:* Inst Elec & Electronic Engrs; Am Soc Eng Educ; Sigma Xi. *Res:* Automatic control systems; computer systems; instrumentation. *Mailing Add:* Dept Elec & Comput Eng NJ Inst Technol Newark NJ 07102

STRANSKY, JOHN JANOS, SILVICULTURE. *Current Pos:* RETIRED. *Personal Data:* b Budapest, Hungary, Sept 2, 23; nat US; m 47; c 2. *Educ:* Univ Munich, BF, 47; Harvard Univ, MS, 54; Tex A&M Univ, PhD, 76. *Prof Exp:* Plant propagator, Bussey Inst, Harvard Univ, 54-57; res forester, Southern Forest Exp Sta, US Forest Serv, 57-85. *Concurrent Pos:* Lectr, Sch Forestry, Stephen F Austin State Univ. *Mem:* Soc Am Foresters; Wildlife Soc. *Res:* Silvicultural aspects of combining timber production with wildlife habitat practices in southern forests. *Mailing Add:* 1533 Redbud St Nacogdoches TX 75961

STRASBERG, MURRAY, ACOUSTICS. *Current Pos:* proj coordr, 60-72, SR RES SCIENTIST, DAVID TAYLOR RES CTR, BETHESDA, MD, 72- *Personal Data:* b New York, NY, Aug 11, 17; m 45. *Educ:* City Col New York, BS, 38; Cath Univ, MS, 48, PhD, 56. *Prof Exp:* Patent examr, US Patent Off, 38-42; physicist, David Taylor Model Basin, 42-49 & 52-58; noise consult, US Bur Ships, 49-52; sci liaison officer, Off Naval Res, London, 58-60. *Concurrent Pos:* Fulbright lectr, Tech Univ Denmark, 63; adj prof, Am Univ, 64-70; vis prof, Cath Univ, 74-80; mem gov bd, Am Inst Physics, 77-92. *Mem:* Fel Acoust Soc Am (pres, 74-75, secy, 87-90); Am Inst Physics; Am Phys Soc. *Res:* Underwater acoustics; hydrodynamics; cavitation; hydrodynamic noise; electroacoustic instrumentation; mechanical vibrations. *Mailing Add:* 3531 Yuma St NW Washington DC 20008

STRASSENBURG, ARNOLD ADOLPH, PHYSICS, EDUCATIONAL ADMINISTRATION. *Current Pos:* actg vprovost curric & instr, 80-82, PROF PHYSICS, STATE UNIV NY, STONY BROOK, 77- *Personal Data:* b Victoria, Minn, June 8, 27; m 49, 82; c 5. *Educ:* Ill Inst Technol, BS, 51; Calif Inst Technol, MS, 53, PhD(physics), 55. *Honors & Awards:* Millikan Lectr Award, Am Asn Physics Teachers, 72. *Prof Exp:* From asst prof to assoc prof physics, Univ Kans, 55-66; prof, State Univ NY, Stony Brook, 66-75; head, Mat & Instr Develop Sect, NSF, 75-77. *Concurrent Pos:* Staff physicist, Comn Col Physics, 63-65; dir, Div Educ & Manpower, Am Inst Physics, 66-72; exec officer, Am Asn Physics Teachers, 72-82. *Mem:* AAAS; Am Asn Physics Teachers; Nat Sci Teachers Asn. *Res:* High energy physics; fundamental particles; measurement of educational outcomes resulting from the application of alternative instructional materials and modes. *Mailing Add:* Dept Physics State Univ NY Stony Brook NY 11794-3800

STRASSER, ALFRED ANTHONY, NUCLEAR FUEL & REACTOR TECHNOLOGY. *Current Pos:* MGR FUEL & CORE TECHNOL, VPRES & PRES, S M STOLLER CORP, 72- *Personal Data:* b Budapest, Hungary, Jan 21, 27; US citizen; div; c Christopher. *Educ:* Purdue Univ, BS, 48; Stevens Inst Technol, MS, 52. *Prof Exp:* Metallurgist, M W Kellog & Co, 48-51 & USAF, 51-54; mgr, Mat Dept, Nuclear Develop Assocs & Plutonium Fuels Dept, United Nuclear Corp, 54-72. *Concurrent Pos:* Adj prof, NY Polytech Inst, 79-81. *Mem:* Am Soc Metals; Am Nuclear Soc. *Res:* Technical and economic evaluation of reactor and reactor component performance, specializing in design, fabrication and thermal-mechanical performance; nuclear plant materials technology. *Mailing Add:* 17 Pokahoe Dr North Tarrytown NY 10591

STRASSER, ELVIRA RAPAPORT, MATHEMATICS. *Current Pos:* RETIRED. *Personal Data:* b Hungary; US citizen; wid; c 2. *Educ:* Washburn Univ, BS, 43; Smith Col, MS, 51; NY Univ, PhD(math), 66. *Prof Exp:* Off Naval Res fel, 59-60; lectr math, Hunter Col, 61; from asst prof to assoc prof, Polytech Inst Brooklyn, 61-67; prof math, State Univ NY Stony Brook, 67-83. *Mem:* Am Math Soc. *Res:* Group theory; graph theory; combinatorial problems. *Mailing Add:* 40 Hastings Dr Stony Brook NY 11790-2332

STRASSER, JOHN ALBERT, ENGINEERING, MATERIALS SCIENCE. *Current Pos:* CHIEF MAT ENGR, CANAC, 91- *Personal Data:* b Sydney, NS, Jan 28, 45; m 70, Gayle Moore; c Andrew Albert & Kirby John. *Educ:* NS Tech Col, BME, 67, PhD(metall eng), 72; Pa State Univ, University Park, MS, 68. *Prof Exp:* Spec lectr mat sci, Dalhousie Univ, 69 & 70; res scientist, Phys Metall Div, Can Dept Energy, Mines & Resources, 71-76; dir metall, Sydney Steel Corp, 81-85, vpres mkt, 86-88, pres, 88-91. *Concurrent Pos:* Dir, Atlantic Group Res Indust Metall, 74-78, Brad'or Inst, 75-78 & Atlantic Coal Inst, 80-81. *Mem:* AAAS; Am Soc Metals; Can Inst Mining & Metall; Am Iron & Steel Inst; Can Steel Producers Asn. *Res:* Powder metallurgy; production of powders, their consolidation techniques and their industrial application; rail production. *Mailing Add:* 270 Aumais St Ste-Anne-de-Bellevue PQ H9X 3L2 Can. *Fax:* 514-399-6004

STRASSMANN, JOAN ELIZABETH, EVOLUTION OF SOCIAL BEHAVIOR. *Current Pos:* from asst prof to assoc prof, 80-93, PROF, DEPT ECOL & EVOLUTIONARY BIOL, RICE UNIV, 93- *Personal Data:* b Washington, DC, May 6, 53; m 88, David C Queller; c Anna, Daniel & Philip. *Educ:* Univ Mich, Ann Arbor, BS, 74; Univ Tex, Austin, PhD(zool), 79. *Prof Exp:* NSF fel, Univ Tex, Austin, 79-80. *Mem:* Soc Study Evolution; An Behav Soc; Behav Ecol Soc; Int Union Study Social Insects; AAAS; Int Soc Hymenopterists. *Res:* Evolution of sociality, particularly in wasps (Polistes, Polybia, Parachartergus, Mischocyttarus, Liostenogasta, Parishnogaster) in Texas, Mexico, Italy, Venezuela and Malaysia; origins of social behavior; within-colony conflicts of interest and nepotism; molecular systematics; DNA micro satellite estimators of genetic relatedness. *Mailing Add:* Dept Ecol & Evolutionary Biol Rice Univ 6100 Main St Houston TX 77005. *Fax:* 713-285-5232; *E-Mail:* strassm@pop.rice.edu

STRATFORD, JOSEPH, NEUROSURGERY. *Current Pos:* assoc prof, 62-72, PROF NEUROSURG, McGILL UNIV, 72- *Personal Data:* b Brantford, Ont, Sept 5, 23; m 52; c 2. *Educ:* McGill Univ, BSc, 45, MD, CM, 47, MSc, 51, dipl neurosurg, 54; FRCS(C), 56. *Prof Exp:* Lectr neurosurg, McGill Univ, 55-56; from asst prof to prof surg, Univ Sask, 56-62. *Concurrent Pos:* Dir div neurosurg, Montreal Gen Hosp. *Mem:* Am Asn Neurol Surg; fel Am Col Surgeons; Cong Neurol Surg; fel Royal Soc Med. *Mailing Add:* Montreal Gen Hosp Div Neurosurg 1650 Cedar Ave Montreal PQ H3G 1A4 Can

STRATFORD, RAY P, ELECTRICAL ENGINEERING. *Current Pos:* RETIRED. *Personal Data:* b Pocatello, Idaho, Feb, 25; c 6. *Educ:* Stanford Univ, BSEE, 50. *Prof Exp:* Appln engr indust power systs, Gen Elec, 54, proj engr, Indust Eng Sect, Gen Elec Indust Sales Div, 55-62, Metal Indust Eng Sect, 62-75, consult appln engr, Indust Power Syst Eng Oper, 75-84; mgr, Power Technol Inc, 85-88, sr consult, Indust Power Syst Unit, 88-90. *Concurrent Pos:* Teacher & developer indust power systs eng & indust power syst harmonics & power factor improvement, Power Technol Inc; mem static power converter comt, Inst Elec & Electronics Engrs, Indust Appln soc working group power syst harmonics, Inst Elec & Electronics Engrs, Power Eng Soc; chmn subcomt Harmonics & reactive compensation static power converter comt, Inst Elec & Electronics Engrs Indust Appln Soc, co-chmn task force rev Inst Elec & Electronics Engrs 519 Harmonic Standard. *Mem:* Fel Inst Elec & Electronics Engrs. *Res:* Over 30 technical publications; development of original techniques in analyzing problems caused by harmonic currents from static power converters. *Mailing Add:* PO Box 186 Island Park ID 83429

STRATHDEE, GRAEME GILROY, SURFACE CHEMISTRY. *Current Pos:* mgr res & develop planning, 80-85, DIR RES & DEVELOP, POTASH CORP SASK, 85- *Personal Data:* b Edinburgh, Scotland, June 29, 42; Can citizen; m 67, Barbara; c David. *Educ:* McGill Univ, BSc, 63, PhD(chem), 67. *Prof Exp:* Assoc res officer chem, Whiteshell Nuclear Res Estab, Atomic

Energy Can, Ltd, 67-77, head, Waste Immobilization Sect, 77-80. *Concurrent Pos:* Adj prof civil engr, Univ Sask, 89-; mgr res & develop prog, Sask Potash Producers Asn. *Mem:* Fel Chem Inst Can (vpres); Can Res Mgt Asn; Am Chem Soc; Can Inst Mining & Metall. *Res:* Homogeneous catalysis; catalytic activation of small molecules; hydrogen isotope exchange reactions; enrichment of deuterium; adsorption phenomena; foaming and antifoaming; solidification of high-level liquid waste; glass science and technology; nuclear waste disposal; mineral processing; mine automation. *Mailing Add:* Potash Corp Sask Inc 122 First Ave S Suite 500 Saskatoon SK S7K 7G3 Can. *Fax:* 306-933-8510

STRATHERN, JEFFREY NEAL, GENETICS, MOLECULAR BIOLOGY. *Current Pos:* DIR LAB EUKARYOTIC GENE EXPRESSION, LBI-BRP, NAT CANCER INST-FREDERICK CANCER RES FACIL, 84- *Personal Data:* b Keene, NH, Dec 12, 48. *Educ:* Univ Calif, San Diego, BA, 70; Univ Ore, PhD(biol), 77. *Prof Exp:* Fel, Cold Spring Harbor Lab, 77-78, staff investr genetics, 79-84. *Concurrent Pos:* Damon Runyon/Walter Winchell Cancer Fund fel, 78; adj prof, Dept Biol Sci, Univ Md, Catonsville; ad hoc mem Genetics Study Sect, NIH, 82; mem sci adv comt, Damon Runyon-Walter Winchell Cancer Fund, 84-88; partic, Int Cong Yeast Genetics & Molecular Biol, 84; mem adv comt, Biol Lab Technician Prog, Frederick Community Col, Md, 85. *Res:* Genetics of the control of cell type in yeast, including the demonstration that changes in cell type involve specific DNA rearrangements. *Mailing Add:* 9802 Gas House Pike Frederick MD 21701

STRATHMANN, RICHARD RAY, MARINE BIOLOGY, ZOOLOGY. *Current Pos:* asst prof, 73-80, ASSOC PROF ZOOL, UNIV WASH & RESIDENT ASSOC DIR, FRIDAY HARBOR LABS, 80- *Personal Data:* b Pomona, Calif, Nov 25, 41; m 64; c 2. *Educ:* Pomona Col, BS, 63; Univ Wash, MS, 66, PhD(zool), 70. *Prof Exp:* NIH training grant, Univ Calif, Los Angeles, 70; NSF fel, Univ Hawaii, 70-71; asst prof zool, Univ Md, College Park, 71-73. *Mem:* Am Soc Naturalists; Am Soc Limnol & Oceanog; Am Soc Zoologists; Marine Biol Asn UK. *Res:* Population biology, form and function of marine invertebrates; biology of invertebrate larvae; biology of suspension feeding. *Mailing Add:* 330 Point Caution Dr Friday Harbor WA 98250

STRATMEYER, MELVIN EDWARD, RADIOBIOLOGY, RISK ASSESSMENT. *Current Pos:* res chemist, 69-73, PMS officer, Ionizing Radiation, 73-75, PMS officer, Ultrasound, Exp Studies Br, 75-82, chief, Sonics Br, Div Biol Effects, Bur Radiol Health, 82-84, CHIEF, HEALTH SCI BR, OFF SCI & TECHNOL, CTR DEVICES & RADIOL HEALTH, US FOOD & DRUG ADMIN, 84- *Personal Data:* b Peoria, Ill, Aug 30, 42; m 66; c 1. *Educ:* Purdue Univ, Lafayette, BS, 65, MS, 66, PhD(bionucleonics), 69. *Mem:* AAAS; fel Am Inst Ultrasound Med; Sigma Xi. *Res:* Ionizing radiation effects on nucleic acid and protein metabolism; ionizing radiation effects on mitochrondrial systems; ultrasound effects on growth & development; assessment of risk associated with exposure to medical ultrasound; toxicology of medical device materials. *Mailing Add:* FDA/CDRH Health Sci Br 12709 Twinbrook Pkwy (HFZ-112) Rockville MD 20852. *E-Mail:* mes@fdadr.cdrh.fda.gov

STRATT, RICHARD MARK, STATISTICAL MECHANICS, LIQUIDS. *Current Pos:* from asst prof to assoc prof, 81-88, PROF CHEM, BROWN UNIV, 88-, CHAIR, DEPT CHEM, 96- *Personal Data:* b Philadelphia, Pa, Feb, 21, 54; m 95, Victoria Wilcox. *Educ:* Mass Inst Technol, SB, 75; Univ Calif, Berkeley, PhD(chem), 79. *Honors & Awards:* Apker Award, Am Phys Soc, 90. *Prof Exp:* Res assoc, Univ Ill, Champaign, 79-80, NSF fel, 80. *Concurrent Pos:* Alfred P Sloan fel, 85-89; Fulbright scholar, Oxford Univ, 91-92; chair, Theoret Chem Subdiv, Am Chem Soc, 96- *Mem:* Am Phys Soc; Am Chem soc. *Res:* Statistical mechanics of liquids: the dynamical behavior, the nature of the solvation process, and the character of the electronic structure. *Mailing Add:* Box H Dept Chem Brown Univ Providence RI 02912. *Fax:* 401-863-2594; *E-Mail:* richard_strat@brown.edu

STRATTA, ROBERT JOSEPH, TRANSPLANT SURGERY, PANCREAS TRANSPLANTATION. *Current Pos:* PROF SURG, UNIV NEBR MED CTR, 91-; PROF SURG, UNIV TENN, MEMPHIS, 97- *Personal Data:* b Chicago, Ill, Dec 4, 54; m 77; c 2. *Educ:* Univ Notre Dame, BS, 76; Univ Chicago, Pritzker, MD, 80. *Prof Exp:* Gen surg resident, Univ Utah, 80-86; transplant fel, Univ Wis, 86-88; asst prof to prof surg & dir pancreas transplantation, Univ Nebr Med Ctr, 88-95. *Mem:* Am Col Surgeons; Soc Univ Surgeons; Asn Acad Surg; Am Soc Transplant Surgeons; Surg Infection Soc. *Res:* Pancreas, kidney and liver transplantation including procurement, preservation, organ allocation, technical aspects, immunosuppression, infection prophylaxis, medical and surgical aspects, complications, quality of life and long-term effects; author of over 200 publications. *Mailing Add:* Univ Tenn, Dept Surg 956 Court Ave Suite A202 Memphis TN 38163-2116

STRATTAN, ROBERT DEAN, ELECTRICAL ENGINEERING. *Current Pos:* assoc prof, 68-76, head dept, 68-75, PROF ELEC ENG, UNIV TULSA, 76- *Personal Data:* b Newton, Kans, Dec 7, 36; m 60; c 2. *Educ:* Wichita State Univ, BS, 58; Carnegie-Mellon Univ, MS, 59, PhD(elec eng), 62. *Honors & Awards:* Teetor Award, Soc Automotive Engrs, 82. *Prof Exp:* Res engr, Wichita Div, Boeing Co, Kans, 61-63; mem tech staff elec eng, Tulsa Div, NAm Rockwell Corp, Okla, 63-68. *Mem:* Inst Elec & Electronic Engrs; Am Soc Eng Educ; Nat Soc Prof Engrs; Soc Automotive Engrs; Am Soc Eng Mgt; Int Microwave Power Inst. *Res:* Electromagnetic theory; radar scattering analysis, measurement and camouflage; electrical power system harmonics. *Mailing Add:* Dept Elec Eng 600 S College Tulsa OK 74104. *Fax:* 918-631-3344; *E-Mail:* rds@ohm.ee.utulsa.edu

STRATTON, CEDRIC, INORGANIC CHEMISTRY, ANALYTICAL CHEMISTRY. *Current Pos:* assoc prof, 65-72, PROF INORG & ANALYTICAL CHEM, ARMSTRONG STATE COL, 72- *Personal Data:* b Langley, Eng, Apr 26, 31; US citizen; div; c 1. *Educ:* Univ Nottingham, BSc, 53; Univ London, PhD(inorg chem), 63. *Prof Exp:* Qual control chemist, Richard Klinger, Ltd, Eng, 53-55; develop chemist, Small & Parkes, Ltd, 55-56; sci officer anal res, Brit Insulated Callender's Cables, 57-61; NSF res fel, Univ Fla, 63-65. *Mem:* Am Chem Soc; Royal Soc Chem. *Res:* Chemistry of group V elements, their heterocyclic derivatives; concentration of minerals in local well-water; legal consultancy. *Mailing Add:* Armstrong Res Inst 11935 Abercorn St Savannah GA 31419

STRATTON, CHARLOTTE DIANNE, ORGANIC CHEMISTRY. *Current Pos:* RETIRED. *Personal Data:* b Brooklyn, NY, Mar 7, 29. *Educ:* Bucknell Univ, BS, 51; Pa State Univ, MS, 52. *Prof Exp:* From asst res chemist to res chemist, Parke, Davis & Co, Warner-Lambert Co, Inc, 52-86; consult, Warner-Lambert/Parker Davis, 89-92. *Mem:* Am Chem Soc. *Res:* Medicinal chemistry, especially natural products isolation and organic synthesis of cardiovascular drugs. *Mailing Add:* 1523 Covington Dr Ann Arbor MI 48103

STRATTON, CLIFFORD JAMES, ANATOMY, CELL BIOLOGY. *Current Pos:* prof & chief neuroanatomist, 74-94, ASSOC PROF, CHIEF HISTOLOGIST & ASST CHIEF NEUROANATOMIST, SCH MED, UNIV NEV, 77- *Personal Data:* b Winslow, Ariz, Apr 7, 45; m 68; c 6. *Educ:* Northern Ariz Univ, BS, 68, MS, 70; Brigham Young Univ, PhD(zool, chem), 73. *Prof Exp:* Lab instr, Northern Ariz Univ, 68-70; lect instr & Nat Defense Educ Act fel, Brigham Young Univ, 70-73; res assoc, Sch Med, Univ Calif, Los Angeles, 73-74. *Concurrent Pos:* NIH Young Investr Pulmonary res award, 76-78; researcher, Am Lung Asn, 76-78; res assoc, NIH Lung Cult Conf, W Alton Jones Cell Sci Ctr, NY, 77. *Mem:* Am Asn Anatomists; Electron Micros Soc Am; Tissue Cult Asn; Am Soc Cell Biol; AAAS; Am Fertil Soc. *Res:* Ultrastructural morphology, histochemistry and pharmacology of the human lung surfactant system as studied in vivo and with alveolar cloning, complimented with lipid-carbohydrate embedment procedures; primary interest is infant respiratory distress syndrome. *Mailing Add:* Dept Anat Univ Nev Sch Med Reno NV 89557-0001

STRATTON, DONALD BRENDAN, PHYSIOLOGY, NEUROPHYSIOLOGY. *Current Pos:* From asst prof to assoc prof, 71-80, PROF BIOL, DRAKE UNIV, 81- *Personal Data:* b Escanaba, Mich, Jan 6, 41; m 67. *Educ:* Northern Mich Univ, BS, 63, MA, 64; Southern Ill Univ, PhD(physiol), 71. *Mem:* Am Physiol Soc; Neuroelectrical Soc. *Res:* Cardiovascular physiology with particular interest in vascular smooth muscle; normal physiological responses of vascular smooth muscle; changes in vascular smooth muscle response in pathophysiological states. *Mailing Add:* Dept Biol Drake Univ Des Moines IA 50311

STRATTON, FRANK E(DWARD), ENGINEERING. *Current Pos:* RETIRED. *Personal Data:* b Oceanside, Calif, Dec 20, 37; m 91, Heong L Tan; c Stuart & Marla. *Educ:* San Diego State Col, BS, 62; Stanford Univ, MS, 63, PhD(civil eng), 66. *Prof Exp:* prof eng, San Diego State Univ, 66-97. *Concurrent Pos:* Chmn, Environ Eng Div, Am Soc Civil Engrs, 81; dipl, Am Acad Environ Engrs; regist prof engr, Calif, Nev, Ore & Wash. *Mem:* Fel Am Soc Civil Engrs; Am Water Works Asn; Water Environ Fedn; Am Acad Environ Engrs. *Res:* Water quality management; nutrient removal methods; waste disposal; composting toilets; rain water collection; purification systems; engineering education. *Mailing Add:* Col Eng San Diego State Univ San Diego CA 92182-1324

STRATTON, GLENN WAYNE, ENVIRONMENTAL TOXICOLOGY, NUTRIENT CYCLING. *Current Pos:* From asst prof to assoc prof, 80-89, PROF ENVIRON MICROBIOL, NS AGR COL, 89- *Personal Data:* b Belleville, Ont, Jan 11, 55. *Educ:* Univ Guelph, BSc, 77, MSc, 78, PhD (microbiol), 81. *Concurrent Pos:* Adj prof, Dept Agr Eng, Tech Univ NS & Fac Grad Studies, Dalhousie Univ. *Mem:* Am Soc Microbiol; Can Soc Microbiol. *Res:* Studying the effects of toxicants on the biodegradation of industrial wastes and toxicant interactions towards nutrient cycling and microbiological populations. *Mailing Add:* Dept Biol NS Agr Col PO Box 550 Truro NS B2N 5E3 Can. *Fax:* 902-895-4547; *E-Mail:* gstratton@cox.nsac.ns.ca

STRATTON, JAMES FORREST, PALEONTOLOGY. *Current Pos:* asst prof, 75-77, PROF GEOL, EASTERN ILL UNIV, 77- *Personal Data:* b Chicago Heights, Ill, Nov 29, 43; m 80, Patrice A Fanuko; c James A. *Educ:* Ind State Univ, Terre Haute, BS, 65; Ind Univ, Bloomington, MAT, 67, AM, 72, PhD(paleont), 75. *Prof Exp:* Instr geol, Shippensburg State Col, 67-70. *Concurrent Pos:* Geol consult, Battelle Mem Inst, 88-89, Ill Dept Nuclear Safety, 89- *Mem:* Soc Econ Paleontologists & Mineralogists; Int Bryozool Asn; Am Asn Petrol Geologists; Brit Palaeont Asn; Seismic Soc Am. *Res:* Quantitative analysis of morphological and structural characters of Fenestellidae for the study of taxonomy and functional morphology. *Mailing Add:* RR 4 Box 65 Charleston IL 61920. *E-Mail:* cfjfs@eiu.edu

STRATTON, LEWIS PALMER, BIOCHEMISTRY, BACTERIOLOGY. *Current Pos:* From asst prof to assoc prof, 67-81, PROF BIOL, FURMAN UNIV, 81-, DEPT CHAIR, 91- *Personal Data:* b West Chester, Pa, Aug 22, 37; m 90, Helen M Krizam; c 2. *Educ:* Juniata Col, BS, 59; Univ Maine, MS, 61; Fla State Univ, PhD(chem), 67. *Concurrent Pos:* Vis prof zool chem, Univ Alaska, 75; vis researcher, Ctr Biomolecular Sci & Eng, Naval Res Lab, 88-89; vis fac, Sch Pharm, Health Sci Ctr, Univ Col, 95-96. *Mem:* Asn Southeastern Biologists; Sigma Xi. *Res:* Comparative protein biochemistry; hemoglobin chemistry. *Mailing Add:* Dept Biol Furman Univ Greenville SC 29613. *Fax:* 864-294-2058; *E-Mail:* lew.stratton@furman.edu

STRATTON, MARIANN, NURSING ADMINISTRATION. *Current Pos:* RETIRED. *Personal Data:* b Houston, Tex, Apr 6, 45; wid, Lawrence Mallory Stickney. *Educ:* Sacred Heart Dominican Col, BSN & BA, 66; Webster Col, MA, 77; Univ Va, MSN, 81. *Prof Exp:* Patient care coordr, Naval Regional Med Ctr, USN, 81-83, nurse corps plans officer, Naval Med Command, 83-86, dir nursing serv, US Naval Hosp, Naples, Italy, 86-89, San Diego, Calif, 89-91, chief personnel mgt, Bur Med & Surg, 91-94, dir, US Naval Nurse Corps, 91-94. *Mem:* Am Nurses Asn; Asn Mil Surgeons US. *Mailing Add:* 9364 Blazing Star Trail San Antonio TX 78266-2310

STRATTON, ROBERT, ELECTRONICS ENGINEERING. *Current Pos:* INDEPENDENT CONSULT, 94-; COFOUNDER & RES CONSULT, FINANCIAL MARKET PLACE, INC, 96- *Personal Data:* b Vienna, Austria, Aug 14, 28; US citizen; m 80, Freda Karlberger; c David A & Valerie P. *Educ:* Univ Manchester, BSc, 49, PhD(theoret physics), 52. *Prof Exp:* Res physicist, Metrop Vickers Elec Co, Ltd, Eng, 52-59; mem tech staff, Tex Instruments, Inc, 59-63, dir, Physics Res Lab, 63-71, asst vpres, 70, assoc dir, Ctr Res Lab, 71-72, dir semiconductor res & develop labs, 72-75, dir, Ctr Res Lab, 75-94. *Concurrent Pos:* Vpres, corp staff, Cent Res Labs, Tex Instruments Inc, 82. *Mem:* Nat Acad Eng; fel Inst Elec & Electronics Engrs; fel Brit Inst Physics & Phys Soc; fel Am Phys Soc. *Res:* Solid state theory, including field emission, space charge barriers, thermoelectricity, high electric fields, thermal conductivity, dielectric breakdown and surface energies of solids. *Mailing Add:* Financial Marketplace Inc 12770 Coit Rd Suite 850 Dallas TX 75251. *Fax:* 512-261-9009; *E-Mail:* bobstra@aol.com

STRATTON, ROBERT ALAN, polymer chemistry, for more information see previous edition

STRATTON, ROY FRANKLIN, JR, ELECTRICAL ENGINEERING, PHYSICS. *Current Pos:* electronic engr electromagnetic compatibility, 75-86, ELECTRONIC ENGR SYSTS RELIABILITY, ROME LAB, USAF, 86- *Personal Data:* b Memphis, Tenn, July 23, 29; m 63; c 1. *Educ:* Rhodes Col, BS, 51; Univ Tenn, MS, 53, PhD(physics), 57; Ga Inst Technol, MSEE, 75. *Prof Exp:* Asst dept physics, Univ Tenn, 52-57; res assoc plasma physics, Oak Ridge Nat Lab, 58-70; prof & chmn sci div admin & teaching, Pikeville Col, 70-73; teaching asst elec eng, Ga Inst Technol, 73-75. *Mem:* Inst Elec & Electronics Engrs; AAAS; Sigma Xi. *Res:* Systems reliability techniques; testability and maintainability enhancement techniques for complex electronic systems; monitoring the environment of Air Force Systems. *Mailing Add:* Rome Lab-ERSR 525 Brooks Rd Griffiss AFB NY 13441-4505. *Fax:* 301-330-7083; *E-Mail:* strattonr@rl.af.mil

STRATTON, THOMAS FAIRLAMB, LASERS, NUCLEAR PHYSICS. *Current Pos:* SR PHYSICIST, SUMMER ASSOCS, 93- *Personal Data:* b Kansas City, Mo, Dec 19, 29; m 58, Elaine Doyle; c 2. *Educ:* Union Col, BS, 49; Univ Minn, MS, 52, PhD(physics), 54. *Prof Exp:* Staff mem physics, Los Alamos Sci Lab, 54-66; sr fel, Battelle Columbus Lab, 67; staff mem physics, Los Alamos Nat Lab, 68-75, group leader, Antares Laser Proj, 76-79, dep physics div leader, 80-81, lab fel, 82-93. *Concurrent Pos:* Mem, Atomic Energy Res Estab, UK, 58; mem adv bd pulse power, Nat Acad Sci, 77; atomic energy adv, Dept of Defense, 85. *Mem:* Sigma Xi; fel Am Phys Soc. *Res:* Thermonuclear fusion; soft x-ray spectroscopy; magnetohydrodynamics; plasma acceleration and direct conversion; accelerator applications. *Mailing Add:* 315 Potrillo Los Alamos NM 87544. *Fax:* 505-672-3525; *E-Mail:* stratton@trail.com

STRATTON, WILLIAM R, PHYSICS & NUCLEAR ENGINEERING. *Current Pos:* CONSULT NUCLEAR ENERGY, 82- *Personal Data:* b River Falls, Wis, May 15, 22; m 52; c 3. *Educ:* Univ Minn, PhD(physics), 52. *Honors & Awards:* Spec Award, Am Nuclear Soc, 81, 85. *Prof Exp:* Res assoc, Univ Minn, 52; mem staff, Los Alamos Sci Lab, Univ Calif, 52-92. *Concurrent Pos:* US del, Int Conf Peaceful Uses Atomic Energy, 58 & Fast Reactor Prog, Cadarache, France, 65-66; mem, Adv Comt Reactor Safeguards, Atomic Energy Comn, 66-75; Presidents comn, Accident Three Mile Island; chmn, Spec Comt Source Terms, Am Nuclear Soc. *Mem:* Am Phys Soc; fel Am Nuclear Soc; Sigma Xi. *Res:* Scattering and reaction in nuclear physics; nuclear forces; reactor physics; reactor safety, criticality safety. *Mailing Add:* Two Acoma Lane Los Alamos NM 87544

STRATTON, WILMER JOSEPH, CHEMISTRY. *Current Pos:* assoc prof, 65-70, chmn dept, 65-68, PROF CHEM, EARLHAM COL, 70- *Personal Data:* b Newark, NJ, June 4, 32; m 55; c 3. *Educ:* Earlham Col, AB, 54; Ohio State Univ, PhD(chem), 58. *Prof Exp:* Asst prof chem, Ohio Wesleyan Univ, 58-59 & Earlham Col, 59-64; vis lectr, Univ Ill, 64-65. *Mem:* Am Chem Soc. *Res:* Metal coordination compounds, including synthesis of new polydentate chelates and bonding in chelate systems. *Mailing Add:* 1024 Hidden Valley Dr Richmond IN 47374-5176

STRATY, RICHARD ROBERT, FISHERIES BIOLOGY, OCEANOGRAPHY. *Current Pos:* RETIRED. *Personal Data:* b Milwaukee, Wis, June 21, 29; m 53; c Jill & Joy. *Educ:* Ore State Univ, BS, 54, PhD(fisheries & oceanog), 69; Univ Hawaii, MS, 63. *Honors & Awards:* C Y Conkle Publ Award, Auke Bay Biol Lab, US Dept Interior, 66. *Prof Exp:* Proj leader fish biol, Fish & Wildlife Serv, US Dept Interior, Juneau, 54-55, proj supvr marine fish biol, Bur Com Fisheries, 55-59, proj supvr marine fish biol salmon, Auke Bay Biol Lab, Bur Com Fisheries, 60-61; exped scientist marine biol, Stanford Univ, 64; proj suprv marine biol, Auke Bay Fisheries Lab, Bur Com Fisheries, US Fish & Wildlife Serv, US Dept Interior, 66-74; prog mgr marine invest biol oceanog, Auke Bay Lab, Nat Marine Fisheries Serv, Nat Oceanic & Atmospheric Admin, US Dept Com, 74-86. *Concurrent Pos:* Mem, Alaska Coun Sci & Technol, Off Gov Alaska, 78-; consult, Living Resource Assocs, 86-93. *Mem:* Am Inst Fishery Res Biologists. *Res:* Fishery oceanography; marine ecology; population dynamics; exploratory fishing; fishery assessment; biological oceanography; marine resource survey; fisheries management; fisheries development and dynamics. *Mailing Add:* Living Resource Assocs PO Box 210211 Auke Bay AK 99821

STRAUB, CONRAD P(AUL), SANITARY ENGINEERING, ENVIRONMENTAL HEALTH. *Current Pos:* prof, Univ Minn, Minneapolis, 66-81, dir, Environ Health Res & Training Ctr, 66-81, dir, Div Human Health & Environ, 73-80, dir, Midwest Ctr Occup Health & Safety, 78-81, EMER PROF ENVIRON HEALTH, UNIV MINN, MINNEAPOLIS, 81- *Personal Data:* b Irvington, NJ, June 21, 16; m 45, Anne B Dyak; c Conrad P Jr, Patricia A, Cathleen M & Michael A. *Educ:* Newark Col Eng, BS, 36, CE, 39; Cornell Univ, MCE, 40, PhD(sanit eng), 43. *Hon Degrees:* DEng, Newark Col Eng, 67. *Honors & Awards:* Fuertes Medal, Cornell Univ, 54; Elda Anderson Mem Award, Health Physics Soc. *Prof Exp:* Comput & head comput sect, US Eng Off, NY, 37-39; asst pub health eng, USPHS, NJ, 41, asst sanit engr, NY, 42-44, actg dep chief sanit engr, China, 45-46, chief sanit engr, Poland, 46, sr asst sanit engr, Ohio, 47-48 & Oak Ridge Nat Lab, 48-56, chief radiol health res activ, Robert A Taft Sanit Eng Ctr, 56-64, dep dir, 64-65, dir, 65-66. *Concurrent Pos:* Chmn comt waste disposal, Int Comn Radiol Protection; mem expert comt radiol health & consult, WHO. *Mem:* Am Soc Civil Engrs; Health Physics Soc; Am Pub Health Asn; Am Water Works Asn; Water Pollution Control Asn; NY Acad Scis. *Res:* Industrial wastes; sanitary engineering education; insect control; treatment and disposal of radioactive wastes; radiological health; environmental health; public health implications of water and waste water systems; environmental contaminants. *Mailing Add:* 2330 Chalet Dr NE Columbia Heights MN 55421-2057

STRAUB, DAREL K, INORGANIC CHEMISTRY. *Current Pos:* Instr, 61-62, asst prof, 62-68, ASSOC PROF CHEM, UNIV PITTSBURGH, 68- *Personal Data:* b Titusville, Pa, May 17, 35. *Educ:* Allegheny Col, BS, 57; Univ Ill, PhD(inorg chem), 61. *Mem:* Am Chem Soc; AAAS. *Res:* Iron porphyrins; complexes of sulfur-containing ligands; M-ssbauer spectroscopy. *Mailing Add:* Dept Chem Univ Pittsburgh Pittsburgh PA 15260-0001

STRAUB, KARL DAVID, BIOPHYSICS, BIOCHEMISTRY. *Current Pos:* PROF PHYSICS & ASSOC DIR, FREE ELECTRON LASER LAB, DUKE UNIV, 93-, CLIN PROF MED, 93- *Personal Data:* b Louisville, Ky, Aug 17, 37; m 63, Jeannette Mumford; c 3. *Educ:* Duke Univ, BS, 59, MD, 65, PhD(biochem), 68. *Prof Exp:* Intern, Duke Univ, 68-69; from asst prof to prof med, Univ Ark, 72-93, from asst prof to prof biochem, 72-93. *Concurrent Pos:* Res biophysicist & staff physician, Vet Admin Hosp, Little Rock, 72-74, assoc chief staff res, 74-93; resident internal med, Med Ctr, Univ Ark, 72-76; mem, Exp Prog Stimulate Competitiveness Res, NSF, 80-, actg chmn, 83-; mem, Res Comt, Am Heart Asn, 80-, bd dirs, 83-; consult, Fed Appl Sci Eval Ctr, Washington, 82- *Mem:* Am Soc Biol Chem; Am Chem Soc; Am Fedn Clin Res; Biophys Soc; NY Acad Sci; Int Soc Heart Res; Royal Soc Chem; Sigma Xi. *Res:* Bioenergetics, including active transport oxidative phosphorylation; solid state biophysics; mechanisms of protein hormones; picosecond spectroscopy of porphyrins and hemoproteins. *Mailing Add:* Dept Physics Duke Univ Durham NC 27708-0319

STRAUB, RICHARD WAYNE, HORTICULTURE. *Current Pos:* Res assoc, 71-75, from asst prof to assoc prof, 75-90, PROF ENTOM, NY STATE AGR EXP STA, CORNELL UNIV, 90- *Personal Data:* b Fairfax, Mo, June 5, 40; div; c Christine. *Educ:* Northwest Mo State Univ, BS, 66; Univ Mo, MS, 68, PhD(entom), 72. *Concurrent Pos:* Vis scientist, US Dept Interior, Bur Land Mgt, Washington, DC, 85-86; chmn, Sect F, Entom Soc Am, 92; mem, SC Entom Soc. *Mem:* Entom Soc Am. *Res:* Biology and integrated control of insects of fruit and vegetable crops with emphasis on plant resistance to insect pests and insect transmission of vegetable diseases. *Mailing Add:* PO Box 122 Hellbrook Lane Ulster Park NY 12487. *Fax:* 914-691-2719

STRAUB, THOMAS STUART, BIOORGANIC CHEMISTRY. *Current Pos:* PROF ORG CHEM, LA SALLE UNIV, 72-, CHAIR CHEM, 78- *Personal Data:* b Louisville, Ky, Oct 1, 41; m 65; c 3. *Educ:* Princeton Univ, AB, 63; Univ Minn, MS, 66; Ill Inst Technol, PhD(chem), 70. *Prof Exp:* Chemist, Monsanto Corp, 63-64; NIH postdoctoral biochem, Northwestern Univ, 69-72. *Mem:* Am Chem Soc; AAAS; Sigma Xi. *Res:* Homogenous catalysis; molecular recognition; phase transfer catalysis; chemical models of biologic processes. *Mailing Add:* Dept Chem La Salle Univ Philadelphia PA 19141

STRAUB, WILLIAM ALBERT, ANALYTICAL CHEMISTRY. *Current Pos:* Technologist, 57-67, sr res chemist, 67-75, ASSOC RES CONSULT, USS DIV USX, 75- *Personal Data:* b Philadelphia, Pa, June 21, 31; m 58; c 2. *Educ:* Univ Pa, BA, 53; Cornell Univ, PhD, 58. *Mem:* Am Chem Soc; Soc Anal Chemists. *Res:* Process solution analysis. *Mailing Add:* 1315 Corkwood Dr Monroeville PA 15146-4405

STRAUB, WOLF DETER, SOLID STATE PHYSICS. *Current Pos:* RETIRED. *Personal Data:* b Boston, Mass, Apr 27, 27; m 61, Margrit A Schmuziger; c Sibyl A & Dorothy A. *Educ:* Yale Univ, BS, 50; Univ Mich, MS, 52. *Prof Exp:* Staff mem solid state physics, Res Div, Raytheon Co, 52-65; physicist, Electronics Res Ctr, NASA, 65-70 & M/K Systs, Inc, Mass, 70-72; mgr anal lab, Coulter Systs Corp Inc, Bedford, 72-80, dir advan physics lab, 80-83, 85-90; staff mem, Eaton Corp, 83-85. *Mem:* Am Vacuum Soc; Sigma Xi. *Res:* Galvanometric properties of semiconductors and semimetals; radiation damage and studies of microwave generation in semiconductors; electrical and mechanical properties of dielectric thin films; problems in electrophotography; surface physics. *Mailing Add:* 158 Barton Dr Sudbury MA 01776-2546

STRAUBE, ROBERT LEONARD, RADIOBIOLOGY. *Current Pos:* EXEC SECY RADIATION STUDY SECT, DIV RES GRANTS, NIH, 65- *Personal Data:* b Chicago, Ill, Sept 16, 17; m 44; c 2. *Educ:* Univ Chicago, BS, 39, PhD(physiol), 55. *Prof Exp:* Asst path, Univ Chicago, 43-46; prof radiobiol, Assoc Cols Midwest, 63-64; assoc scientist, Argonne Nat Lab, 47-65. *Mem:* AAAS; Radiation Res Soc; Am Physiol Soc; Soc Exp Biol & Med; Am Asn Cancer Res. *Res:* Nature of radiation effects and their modification by chemical agents; growth processes in neoplastic cells. *Mailing Add:* 96344 Cape Ferrelo Rd Brookings OR 97415-9185

STRAUBINGER, ROBERT M, CELL BIOLOGY. *Current Pos:* Fel, 85-86, ASST RES PHARMACOLOGIST, CANCER RES INST, UNIV CALIF, SAN FRANCISCO, 86- *Personal Data:* b Buffalo, NY, May 29, 53. *Educ:* Univ Calif, San Francisco, PhD(pharmacol), 84. *Mem:* Am Soc Cell Biol. *Mailing Add:* Dept Pharmaceut State Univ NY 539 Cooke Hall Buffalo NY 14260-1200. *Fax:* 716-645-3693; *E-Mail:* rms@acsubuffaledu

STRAUCH, ARTHUR ROGER, III, CONTRACTILE PROTEIN BIOCHEMISTRY, CELL MOTILITY. *Current Pos:* Asst prof, 84-90, ASSOC PROF CELL BIOL, SCH MED, OHIO STATE UNIV, 90- *Educ:* McGill Univ, BSc, 76; State Univ NY, PhD(cell & molecular biol), 81. *Honors & Awards:* Young Investr Award, Am Heart Asn, 86. *Concurrent Pos:* Assoc prof, Prog Molecular, Cellular, Develop Biol, Prog Biochem, Ohio State Univ. *Mem:* Am Soc Cell Biol; AAAS. *Res:* Mechanisms of gene regulation in the cardiovascular system with interests in vascular smooth muscle development and disease. *Mailing Add:* Dept Cell Biol Ohio State Univ 333 W Tenth Ave Columbus OH 43210-1239. *Fax:* 614-292-7659; *E-Mail:* 72010.2261@compuserve.com

STRAUCH, KARL, PARTICLE PHYSICS. *Current Pos:* Soc Fels jr fel, 50-53, from asst prof to prof, 53-75, GEORGE VASMER LEVERETT PROF PHYSICS, HARVARD UNIV, 75- *Personal Data:* b Giessen, Ger, Oct 4, 22; nat US; m 51. *Educ:* Univ Calif, AB, 43, PhD(physics), 50. *Honors & Awards:* Alexander von Humboldt Prize, 83. *Concurrent Pos:* Dir, Cambridge Electron Accelerator, Harvard Univ, 67-74. *Mem:* Am Phys Soc; Am Acad Arts & Sci. *Res:* High energy reactions; elementary particles. *Mailing Add:* Lyman Lab Physics Harvard Univ Cambridge MA 02138-4993. *Fax:* 617-495-0416

STRAUCH, RALPH EUGENE, SOMATICS & MATHEMATICS. *Current Pos:* CONSULT, 76- *Personal Data:* b Springfield, Mass, May 14, 37; m 58, Merna Berkowitz; c Shar & David. *Educ:* Univ Calif, Los Angeles, AB, 59, Univ Calif, Berkeley, MA, 64, PhD(statist), 65. *Prof Exp:* Sr mathematician, Rand Corp, 65-76. *Concurrent Pos:* Feldenkrais Teacher, 76- *Mem:* Feldenkrais Guild; Somatics Soc. *Res:* Dynamic programming; statistical decision theory; national security policy; human perception; paranormal phenomena; policy analysis methodology; mind/body relationship; samatic aspects of human behavior, links between self awareness and human functioning somatic components of post traumatic stress including childhood sexual abuse; post research in perception, mathematics policy analysis methodology. *Mailing Add:* 1383 Avenida de Cortez Pacific Palisades CA 90272. *E-Mail:* rstrauch@somatic.com

STRAUCH, RICHARD G, ENGINEERING ADMINISTRATION. *Current Pos:* PROF ENG, UNIV COLO, 94- *Prof Exp:* Res elec engr, Wave Propagation Lab, Nat Oceanic & Atmospheric Admin, 93. *Mem:* Nat Acad Eng; sr mem Inst Elec & Electronics Engrs. *Mailing Add:* 3390 Fourth St Boulder CO 80304

STRAUGHAN, ISDALE (DALE) MARGARET, ECOLOGY, BIOLOGY. *Current Pos:* PVT CONSULT, 82- *Personal Data:* b Pittsworth, Australia, Nov 4, 39; m 62; c Melanie. *Educ:* Queensland Univ, BSc, 60, Hons, 62, PhD(zool), 66. *Prof Exp:* Demonstr zool, Queensland Univ, 66; sr demonstr, Univ Col, Townsville, 66-67; asst prof & res assoc, Allan Hancock Found, Univ Southern Calif, 69-74, sr res scientist, Inst Marine & Coastal Studies, 74-82. *Concurrent Pos:* Consult biologist, Northern Elec Authority, Queensland, 66-68; Am Asn Univ Women fel, 68-69. *Mem:* AAAS; Sigma Xi; Ecol Soc Am. *Res:* Establishment of natural ecological change in response to natural change in the marine environment and comparison with man-induced ecological change; comparison of man-induced change to natural biological fluctuations. *Mailing Add:* 13688 Park St Whittier CA 90601

STRAUGHN, ARTHUR BELKNAP, PHARMACOKINETICS, BIOPHARMACEUTICS. *Current Pos:* PROF PHARMACEUT & DIR, DRUG RES LAB, UNIV TENN, 74- *Personal Data:* b Durham, NC, Aug 10, 44; m 68, Carol Guthe; c Tate L & C Grant. *Educ:* Univ NC, BS, 72; Univ Tenn, PharmD, 74. *Prof Exp:* Instr therapeut, Univ NC, 72-73. *Mem:* Am Asn Pharmaceut Scientists; Sigma Xi; AAAS; Am Col Clin Pharm; Am Pharmaceut Asn; Am Soc Hosp Pharmacists. *Res:* Pharmacokinetics and biopharmaceutics; develop and conduct studies in humans to define drug absorption and disposition, specifically dosage forms for sustained-release. *Mailing Add:* 2681 Gerald Ford Dr Cordova TN 38018. *Fax:* 901-448-6940; *E-Mail:* astraughn@utmem1.utmem.edu

STRAUGHN, WILLIAM RINGGOLD, JR, BACTERIOLOGY. *Current Pos:* from instr to prof, 44-80, EMER PROF BACT, SCH MED, UNIV NC, CHAPEL HILL, 80- *Personal Data:* b Dubois, Pa, May 21, 13; m 41; c 4. *Educ:* Mansfield State Col, BS, 35; Cornell Univ, MS, 40; Univ Pa, PdD(bact), 58. *Prof Exp:* Teacher high sch, Pa, 35-36 & NY, 36-38; asst bact, Univ NC, 40-42; instr math & chem, Md State Teachers Col, Salisbury, 42-44. *Mem:* Am Soc Microbiol. *Res:* Bacterial physiology and metabolism; antibacterial agents; enzyme synthesis; amino acid decarboxylases-mechanisms of formation and action; bacterial membranes and transport mechanisms. *Mailing Add:* 1016 Highland Woods Chapel Hill NC 27514

STRAUMANIS, JOHN JANIS, JR, PSYCHIATRY. *Current Pos:* PROF & CHMN PSYCHIAT, LA STATE UNIV MED SCH, 85- *Personal Data:* b Riga, Latvia, Apr 22, 35; US citizen; m 59; c 2. *Educ:* Univ Iowa, BA, 57, MD, 60, MS, 64. *Prof Exp:* Intern med, Georgetown Univ Hosp, 60-61; resident psychiat, Univ Iowa, 61-64; asst prof psychiat & Nat Inst Ment Health res career develop grant, Temple Univ, 66-71, assoc prof psychiat, 71-77, prof psychiat, 77-85. *Mem:* Am Psychiat Asn; Soc Biol Psychiat; Am Psychopath Asn; Am Electroencephalographic Soc; Am Col Psychiat. *Res:* Electrophysiology pf psychiatric disorders. *Mailing Add:* Dept Psych, La State Univ Med 1501 Kings Hwy PO Box 33932 Shreveport LA 71130-3932

STRAUMFJORD, JON VIDALIN, JR, MEDICINE, CLINICAL PATHOLOGY. *Current Pos:* RETIRED. *Personal Data:* b Portland, Ore, Feb 23, 25; m 47, Patricia R DeSart; c Jon V III & Jeffrey T. *Educ:* Willamette Univ, BA, 48; Univ Ore, MS & MD, 53; Univ Iowa, PhD(biochem), 58. *Prof Exp:* Res fel biochem, Univ Iowa, 54-58; resident path & consult, Providence Hosp, Portland, Ore, 58-60; asst prof path, Univ Miami, 60-62; assoc prof, Med Col Ala, 62-65; prof clin path & chmn dept, 65-70, dir clin labs, 62-65, clin pathologist-in-chief, Univ Hosp, 65-70; prof path & chmn dept, Med Col Wis, 70-82; prof path, Col Med, Univ SFla, 82-94, dir labs, Clin Lab, 91-93. *Concurrent Pos:* Asst pathologist, Div Clin Path, Jackson Mem Hosp, Miami, Fla, 60-62; consult, Gorgas Mem Inst, Panama, 65, Vet Admin Hosp, Milwaukee, 70-82; dir labs, Milwaukee City Gen Hosp, Wis, 70-82; chief of labs, James A Haley Vet Admin Hosp, 83-91; mem surg adv bd, Shrine Burn Units. *Mem:* AAAS; Am Soc Clin Path; Am Asn Clin Chem; Col Am Pathologists; NY Acad Sci; Asn Am Med Col; Acad Clin Lab Physicians & Scientists; Asn Clin Scientists; Am Asn Clin Scientists; AMA. *Res:* Surface characteristics of cells; clinical chemical screening procedures. *Mailing Add:* 842 Newberger Rd Lutz FL 33549

STRAUS, ALAN EDWARD, ORGANIC CHEMISTRY. *Current Pos:* From asst res chemist to res chemist, 49-67, SR RES CHEMIST, CHEVRON RES CO, 67- *Personal Data:* b Berkeley, Calif, May 14, 24; m 53; c 2. *Educ:* Univ Calif, Berkeley, BS, 49. *Mem:* Am Chem Soc. *Res:* Petrochemicals; hydrocarbon oxidation; surface active agents; hydrocarbon pyrolysis; organic synthesis; polymers; heterogeneous catalysis. *Mailing Add:* 2679 Tamalpais Ave El Cerrito CA 94530

STRAUS, DANIEL STEVEN, BIOCHEMISTRY, CELL BIOLOGY. *Current Pos:* PROF BIOMED SCI & BIOL, UNIV CALIF, RIVERSIDE, 76- *Personal Data:* b May 3, 46; m 83; c 2. *Educ:* Univ Calif, Berkeley, PhD(biochem), 72. *Res:* Endocrinology. *Mailing Add:* Biomed Sci Div Univ Calif Riverside CA 92521-0121. *Fax:* 909-787-5504

STRAUS, DAVID BRADLEY, GENETIC TOXICOLOGY. *Current Pos:* ASSOC PROF CHEM, STATE UNIV NY COL NEW PALTZ, 73- *Personal Data:* b Chicago, Ill, July 26, 30; m 55, Harriett McWethy; c Lisa (Afzal), Lee M & David B. *Educ:* Reed Col, BA, 53; Univ Chicago, PhD(biochem), 60. *Prof Exp:* Asst biochem, Univ Ore, Med Sch, 53-54; asst, Univ Chicago & Argonne Cancer Res Hosp, 55-60; res assoc chem, Princeton Univ, 60-64, res staff mem, 64-65; asst prof biochem, State Univ NY, Buffalo, 65-72. *Concurrent Pos:* Vis asst prof chem, State Univ NY, Albany, 69; adj assoc prof environ med, NY Univ, 84-93. *Mem:* AAAS; Am Chem Soc; Sigma Xi. *Res:* Site specific mutagenesis of viral DNA; nucleic acid enzymology and chemistry. *Mailing Add:* Dept Chem State Univ NY Col New Paltz NY 12561. *Fax:* 914-257-3791; *E-Mail:* strausd@matrix.newpaltz.edu

STRAUS, DAVID CONRAD, BACTERIAL LUNG INFECTIONS BACTERIAL VACCINES, MICROBIOLOGY OF INDOOR AIR. *Current Pos:* assoc prof, 81-95, PROF MICROBIOL, TEX TECH UNIV HEALTH SCI CTR, LUBBOCK, TEX, 95- *Personal Data:* b Evansville, Ind, Apr 27, 47; div. *Educ:* Wright State Univ, BS, 70; Loyola Univ Chicago, PhD(microbiol), 74. *Prof Exp:* Teaching asst microbiol, Sch Med, Loyola Univ Chicago, 70-74; fel, Med Ctr, Univ Cincinnati, 74-75; instr, Univ Tex Health Sci Ctr, San Antonio, 75-76, asst prof microbiol, 76-81. *Concurrent Pos:* Instr microbiol, Ill Col Podiatric Med, 72-73; vis prof microbiol, Univ Calgary, 89-90. *Mem:* Am Soc Microbiol; Sigma Xi. *Res:* Study of mechanisms of bacterial pathogenicity and host response; study of bacterial exotoxins; bacterial lung infections; vaccine for shipping fever in cattle; microbiology of indoor air. *Mailing Add:* 7605 Saratoga Lubbock TX 79424. *Fax:* 806-743-2334

STRAUS, FRANCIS HOWE, II, ENDOCRINE & UROLOGIC PATHOLOGY. *Current Pos:* Intern, Clins, Univ Chicago, 57-58, resident path, 58-62, chief resident, 62-63, from instr to assoc prof, 62-78, PROF PATH, SCH MED, UNIV CHICAGO, 78- *Personal Data:* b Chicago, Ill, Mar 16, 32; m 55, Helen L Puttkammer; c Francis H III, Helen E, Christopher M & Michael W. *Educ:* Harvard Univ, AB, 53; Univ Chicago, MD, 57, MS, 64. *Concurrent Pos:* Am Cancer Soc advan clin fel, 65-68; fel, USPH, 58-60 & Am Cancer Soc Clin, 62-63. *Mem:* Sigma Xi; Am Soc Invest Path; Am Asn Pathologists; Int Acad Path; Int Soc Urol Path; Endocrine Path Soc. *Res:* Morphology in surgical pathology as it relates to diagnosis and prognosis of clinical disease; urologic pathology; endocrine pathology. *Mailing Add:* Dept Path Univ Chicago Billings Hosp 5841 S Maryland Ave Chicago IL 60637. *Fax:* 773-702-9903

STRAUS, HELEN LORNA PUTTKAMMER, ANATOMY, BIOLOGY. *Current Pos:* Fel anat, 62-63, res assoc, 63-64, instr anat & biol, 64-67, asst prof biol & asst dean undergrad students, 67-71, dean undergrad students, 71-82, dean admissions, 75-80, assoc prof, anat, 73-87, PROF, BIOL & ANAT, UNIV CHICAGO, 87- *Personal Data:* b Chicago, Ill, Feb 15, 33; m 55; c 4. *Educ:* Radcliffe Col, AB, 55; Univ Chicago, MS, 60, PhD(anat), 62. *Honors & Awards:* Silver Medalist, Case Prog, 77. *Mem:* Am Soc Zoologists; Am Asn Anatomists; AAAS. *Res:* Teaching biology, science in liberal education. *Mailing Add:* Dept Anat Univ Chicago 5845 Ellis Ave Chicago IL 60637

STRAUS, JOE MELVIN, ATMOSPHERIC PHYSICS, GEOPHYSICAL FLUID DYNAMICS. *Current Pos:* prin dir, Off Res Lab Oper, Aerospace Corp, 86-89, dir, Chem & Physics Lab, 86-91, prin dir, Commun Subdiv, 91-93, gen mgr, Electronics Systs Div, 93-96, GEN MGR, SPACE-BASED SURVEILLANCE DIV, AEROSPACE CORP, 96- *Personal Data:* b Dallas, Tex, May 27, 46; m 71; c 2. *Educ:* Rice Univ, BA, 68; Univ Calif, Los Angeles, MS, 69, PhD(planetary, space physics), 72. *Prof Exp:* Res scientist, 73-80, head, Atmospheric Sci Dept, Space Sci Lab, 80-86. *Mem:* Am Geophys Union; Am Inst Aeronaut & Astronaut; Inst Elec & Electronics Engrs. *Res:* Space systems engineering; atmospheric and ionospheric effects on space systems; communication. *Mailing Add:* Space-Based Surveillance Div The Aerospace Corp PO Box 92957 Los Angeles CA 90009. *E-Mail:* joe.straus@aero.org

STRAUS, JOZEF, EXPERIMENTAL SOLID STATE PHYSICS. *Current Pos:* PRES, JDS FITEL. *Personal Data:* b Velke Kapusany, Czech, July 18, 46; Can citizen. *Educ:* Univ Alta, BS, 69, PhD(physics), 74. *Prof Exp:* Fel, Univ Alta, 69-74; mem sci staff & Nat Res Coun Can Fel, Bell Northern Res Ltd, 74-81. *Res:* Fabrication and study of physical properties of light emitting diodes and of solid state lasers; fiber optics, fiber optics communication; electron tunneling in normal and superconducting metals, Josephson tunneling. *Mailing Add:* 691 Hill Crest Ave Ottawa ON K2A 2N2 Can

STRAUS, MARC J, ONCOLOGY, CHEMOTHERAPY. *Current Pos:* CHIEF ONCOL & PROF MED, NY MED COL, 78- *Personal Data:* b New York, NY, June 2, 43; m 64; c 2. *Educ:* Franklin & Marshall Col, AB, 64; State Univ NY Downstate Med Ctr, MD, 68; Am Bd Internal Med, dipl & cert med oncol, 75. *Prof Exp:* Chief med oncol, Med Ctr, Boston Univ, 74-78, assoc prof med, Sch Med, 75-78. *Concurrent Pos:* Prin investr, Eastern Coop Oncol Group, Med Ctr, Boston Univ, 75-; consult oncol, St Agnes Hosp, Northern West Hosp, St Joseph's Hosp & Peekskill Hosp, 79- *Mem:* Am Soc Clin Oncol; Am Fedn Clin Res; Working Party Ther Lung Cancer; Am Asn Cancer Res. *Res:* Application of cellular kinetics in animal and human tumors to the design of clinical cancer treatment programs; clinical cancer chemotherapy. *Mailing Add:* 707 Westchester Ave No 110 White Plains NY 10604

STRAUS, NEIL ALEXANDER, MOLECULAR BIOLOGY. *Current Pos:* from asst prof to assoc prof, 72-85, PROF MOLECULAR BIOL, UNIV TORONTO, 85- *Personal Data:* b Kitchener, Ont, Apr 29, 43; m 66, Leslie Fujita; c 2. *Educ:* Univ Toronto, BSc Hons, 66, MSc, 67, PhD(molecular biol), 70. *Prof Exp:* Fel biophys, Carnegie Inst, Washington, DC, 70-72. *Concurrent Pos:* Res grant, Natural Sci & Eng Res Coun Can; vis scientist, Du Pont de Demers, Wilmington, Del, 88-89, tech consult, 89-91. *Mem:* Am Soc Microbiol; Int Soc Plant Molecular Biol; Am Soc Plant Physiologists; Can Soc Plant Molecular Biol; Can Soc Plant Physiologists. *Res:* Chloroplast and cyanobacterial molecular genetics; cyanobacterial transformations; gene regulation; recombinant DNA; plant biotechnology. *Mailing Add:* Dept Bot Univ Toronto 25 Willcocks St Toronto ON M5S 3B2 Can. *Fax:* 416-978-5878; *E-Mail:* straus@botany.utoronto.ca

STRAUS, ROBERT, MEDICAL BEHAVIORAL SCIENCE. *Current Pos:* chmn, Dept Behav Sci, 59-87, prof, 59-90, EMER PROF BEHAV SCI, PHARM & SOCIOL, UNIV KY, 90- *Personal Data:* b New Haven, Conn, Jan 9, 23; m 45, Ruth Dawson; c R James, Carol Martin, Margaret & J William. *Educ:* Yale Univ, PhD(sociol), 47. *Honors & Awards:* Lifetime Achievement Award, Am Pub Health Asn, 93. *Prof Exp:* Instr, asst prof & res assoc, Dept Appl Psychol, Yale Univ, 47-53; from asst prof to assoc prof pub health & prev med, Col Med, State Univ NY, Syracuse, 53-56. *Concurrent Pos:* Dir sci develop, Med Res Inst, San Francisco, 90-93. *Mem:* Inst Med-Nat Acad Sci; Sigma Xi; Acad Behav Med Res. *Res:* Alcohol; dependency behaviors; aging; patterns of patient care. *Mailing Add:* 656 Raintree Rd Lexington KY 40502-2874. *Fax:* 606-323-5350; *E-Mail:* rstraus@pop.uky.edu

STRAUS, STEPHEN EZRA, INFECTIOUS DISEASES, VIROLOGY. *Current Pos:* SR INVESTR & HEAD, MED VIROL SECT, LAB CLIN INVEST, NAT INST ALLERGY & INFECTIOUS DIS, NIH, 79-, CHIEF, LAB CLIN INVEST, 91- *Personal Data:* b New York, NY, Nov 23, 46; m 73, Barbara E Portnoy; c Kate, Julie & Benjamin. *Educ:* Mass Inst Techol, BS, 68; Columbia Univ Col Physicians & Surgeons, MD, 72; Am Bd Internal Med, cert, 77. *Honors & Awards:* First Annual Richard H Clemons Mem Lectr, Univ Ala, Birmingham, 94; Morris H Samitz Mem Lectr, Univ Pa, 96. *Prof Exp:* Hemat tech, Presby Hosp, NY, 68-69; counr, NY Methadone Maintenance Treat Prog, 70-71; intern med, Barnes Hosp, St Louis, 72-73, resident, 75-76; res assoc, Lab Biol Viruses, NIH, 73-75; fel infectious dis, Washington Univ, St Louis, 76-78. *Concurrent Pos:* Asst med, Washington Univ Sch Med, St Louis, 72-73 & 75-76, instr med, 78-79; assoc med, Georgetown Univ Sch Med, 74-75; consult staff, Pvt Teaching Serv, Suburban Hosp, 74-75; fel, Nat Res Serv, 76-78; Damon Runyon-Walter Winchell Cancer Fund postdoctoral res fel, 77-78; consult infectious dis, Nat Naval Med Ctr, 79-90; attend staff infectious dis, Clin Ctr, NIH, 79; mem lectr, Nagoya Univ, Japan, 96; vis prof, Beth Israel Hosp, Harvard Univ, 96, Col Univ Col Physicians & Surgeons, 96, Osaka Univ, Japan, 96. *Mem:* Am Soc Microbiol; fel Infectious Dis Soc Am; Am Fedn Clin Res; Am Soc Clin Invest; Asn Am Physicians; Molecular Med Soc. *Res:* Molecular biology; pathophysiology; treatment and prevention of human herpes virus infections. *Mailing Add:* NIH Bldg 10 Rm 11N228 Lab Clin Invest 10 Center Dr MSC 1888 Bethesda MD 20892-1888

STRAUS, THOMAS MICHAEL, applied physics, for more information see previous edition

STRAUS, WERNER, BIOCHEMISTRY, CYTOCHEMISTRY. *Current Pos:* assoc prof, 64-78, prof, 79-81, EMER PROF BIOCHEM, CHICAGO MED SCH, 81- *Personal Data:* b Offenbach, Ger, June 5, 11; nat US. *Educ:* Univ Zurich, PhD(chem), 38. *Prof Exp:* Res assoc path, Long Island Col Med, 47-50; asst prof, State Univ NY Downstate Med Ctr, 50-58; vis scientist, Cath Univ Louvain & Free Univ Brussels, 59-61 & Univ NC, 62-63. *Concurrent Pos:* Estab Investr, Am Heart Asn, 59-61; ed, J Histochem Cytochem, 75-83 & Histochem, 80-90. *Mem:* Fel AAAS; Am Soc Cell Biol; Histochemical Soc. *Res:* Intracellular localization of enzymes; lysosomes and phagosomes; cell biology; immuno-cytochemistry; cell surface receptors. *Mailing Add:* Dept Biochem Chicago Med Sch 3333 Green Bay Road North Chicago IL 60064-3095

STRAUSBAUCH, PAUL HENRY, PATHOLOGY, IMMUNOCHEMISTRY. *Current Pos:* PROF PATH, SCH MED, ECAROLINA UNIV, 78- *Personal Data:* b San Francisco, Calif, Aug 29, 41; m 69; c 1. *Educ:* Univ San Francisco, BS, 63; Univ Wash, PhD(biochem), 69; Univ Miami, MD, 74. *Prof Exp:* Am Cancer Soc fel immunol, Weizmann Inst Sci, 69-71; Med Res Coun Can fel, Univ Man, 71-72; resident path, Dartmouth Med Sch, 74-78. *Res:* Chemical approaches to immunology and cell biology; protein products, especially hormones, produced by tumor cells; macrophage structure and diversity. *Mailing Add:* Dept Path Sch Nursing ECarolina Univ Greenville NC 27858. *Fax:* 919-816-3616

STRAUSBERG, SANFORD I, HAZARDOUS WASTE MANAGEMENT, ENVIRONMENTAL REGULATORY COMPLIANCES. *Current Pos:* SR PROJ MGR, SR HYDROGEOLOGIST, IT CORP, 92- *Personal Data:* b Brooklyn, NY, Nov 13, 31; m 59, Marlene Gurewitz; c Jessica (Carlson) & Marisa. *Educ:* Brooklyn Col, BS, 53; Univ Mich, MS, 55. *Prof Exp:* Geologist ground water, US Geol Survey, 55-57; consult ground water, 57-69, 79-84, 87-89; hydrogeologist, UN, 69-73; dept head ground water, Harza Eng Co, 73-79; mgr geol, Nus Corp, 84-86; mgr earth scis, Ebasco Serv Inc, 86-87; dir hydrogeol, Enviro-Sci Inc, 89-92. *Concurrent Pos:* Expert, UN, Water Grid Mission India, 71-72; consult, Asian Develop Bank, 76-78; site mgr, US Environ Protection Agency superfund, 84-87. *Mem:* Am Inst Prof Geologists; Asn Eng Geologists; Geol Soc Am; Asn Ground Water Scientists Engrs. *Res:* Measurement and evaluation of aquifer parameters for use in estimating subsurface hazardous waste migration, ground water remediation design and cleanup, and ground water supply development. *Mailing Add:* 200 Hana Rd Edison NJ 08817. *Fax:* 732-225-1691

STRAUSE, STERLING FRANKLIN, ORGANIC CHEMISTRY. *Current Pos:* dir, 71-74, VPRES RES & DEVELOP, W H BRADY CO, MILWAUKEE, 74- *Personal Data:* b Summit Station, Pa, Jan 4, 31; m 56; c 4. *Educ:* Lebanon Valley Col, BS, 52; Univ Del, MS, 53, PhD(chem), 55. *Prof Exp:* Develop chemist, Chem Develop Dept, Gen Elec Co, 55-57, spec process develop, 57-58, qual control engr, 58-60, mgr, 60-65, qual control, 65-68, mgr polycarbonate res & develop, 68-71. *Mem:* Am Chem Soc; Sigma Xi; Tech Asn Pulp & Paper Indust. *Res:* Polymeric peroxide and free radical chemistry; polymer processes. *Mailing Add:* N5389 Lily Pad Lane Wild Rose WI 54984

STRAUSER, WILBUR ALEXANDER, PHYSICS, MATHEMATICS. *Current Pos:* RETIRED. *Personal Data:* b Charleroi, Pa, June 15, 24; m 45; c 2. *Educ:* Washington & Jefferson Col, AB, 45. *Prof Exp:* Physicist, Manhattan Eng Dist, Tenn, 46-47; assoc physicist, Oak Ridge Nat Lab, 47-50; sci analyst & chief, Declassification Br, AEC, US Dept Energy, 50-55, asst to mgr, San Francisco Opers Off, 55-56, dep dir, Div Classification, 56-63, asst dir safeguards, Div Int Affairs, 63-70, chief, Weapons Br, Div Classification, 70-79; consult, 79- *Mem:* AAAS. *Res:* Neutron diffraction; security classification; safeguards. *Mailing Add:* 155 Skyline Dr California PA 15419

STRAUSFELD, NICHOLAS JAMES, NEUROBIOLOGY, EVOLUTIONARY BIOLOGY. *Current Pos:* PROF, UNIV ARIZ. *Personal Data:* b Claygate, Eng, Oct 22, 42. *Educ:* Univ Col London, BSc, 65, PhD(neurophysiol), 68; Habilitation, Ger, PhD(neurophysiol), 85. *Honors & Awards:* Excellence in Environ Health Res, Lovelance Inst, 95; MacArthur Fel, John D & Catherine T MacArthur Found, 95. *Concurrent Pos:* John Simon Guggenheim fel, 84. *Mailing Add:* Res Labs Div Neurobiol Univ Ariz Tucson AZ 85721

STRAUSS, ALVIN MANOSH, MECHANICS, APPLIED MATHEMATICS. *Current Pos:* AT DEPT MECH & MATS ENG, VANDERBILT UNIV. *Personal Data:* b Brooklyn, NY, Oct 24, 43; m 67; c 2. *Educ:* Hunter Col, AB, 64; WVa Univ, PhD(theoret & appl mech), 68. *Prof Exp:* Res assoc theoret & appl mech, Univ Ky, 68-70; asst prof eng, Univ Cincinnati, 70-74, head, Eng Sci Dept, 76-80, prof mech, 78- *Concurrent Pos:*

Dir, Div Mech Eng & Appl Mech, NSF, 81- *Mem:* Am Geophys Union; Am Acad Mech; Soc Rheology; Soc Eng Sci; Soc Am Mil Engrs. *Res:* Plasticity; viscoplasticity; biomechanics; phase changes in solids, plasticity, thermomechanics, biomechanics and geomechanics. *Mailing Add:* Dept Mech Eng Vanderbilt Univ Box 1612 Sta B Nashville TN 37240-0001

STRAUSS, ARNOLD WILBUR, PEDIATRIC CARDIOLOGY. *Current Pos:* from asst prof to assoc prof, 77-82, PROF PEDIAT & MOLECULAR BIOL & PHARMACOL, SCH MED, WASH UNIV, 82- *Personal Data:* b Benton Harbor, Mich, Mar 31, 45; m 70; c 2. *Educ:* Stanford Univ, BA, 66; Washington Univ, St Louis, MD, 70. *Honors & Awards:* Mead Johnson Award, 91. *Prof Exp:* Resident pediat, St Louis Children's Hosp, Washington Univ, 70-73, fel, 73-74, fel biochem, 74-75; fel, Res Labs, Merck, Sharp & Dohme, 75-77. *Concurrent Pos:* Estab investr, Am Heart Asn, 79-84. *Mem:* Am Acad Pediat; Soc Pediat Res; Am Col Cardiol; Am Soc Biol Chem; Am Heart Asn; Am Soc Clin Invest; AAAS; Am Pediat Soc; Am Asn Physicians. *Res:* Molecular biology of mitochondrial proteins; compartmentalization of proteins; fatty acid oxidation; human genetic disease. *Mailing Add:* St Louis Children's Hosp One Children's Pl St Louis MO 63110

STRAUSS, ARTHUR JOSEPH LOUIS, PSYCHIATRY. *Current Pos:* MED DIR, NEW ORLEANS REG OFF MENT HEALTH. *Personal Data:* b New York, NY, Jan 25, 33; m 60; c 3. *Educ:* Brooklyn Col, BA, 53; Columbia Univ, MD, 58; Am Bd Psychiat & Neurol, cert psychiat, 85. *Prof Exp:* Postdoctoral fel immunol, Col Physicians & Surgeons, Columbia Univ, NIH, 59-61, investr, Nat Inst Allergy & Infectious Dis, 61-65, sect head autoimmunity, 66-68; resident psychiat, St Elizabeths Hosp, NIMH, 68-71, med dir, 75-85, assoc supt, 85-87; psychiatrist, Bethesda, Md, 71-75; regional med dir psychiat, La Dept Health Hosps, 87- *Concurrent Pos:* Mem, Nat Med Adv Bd, Myasthenia Gravis Found, 64- *Mem:* Am Asn Immunologists; Am Psychiat Asn. *Res:* Organ specific autoantibodies to striated muscle in Myasthenia Gravis. *Mailing Add:* New Orleans Reg Off Ment Health La Dept Health & Hosp 3716 Coliseum St New Orleans LA 70115-3709

STRAUSS, BELLA S, MEDICINE. *Current Pos:* RETIRED. *Personal Data:* b Camden, NJ, May 28, 20. *Educ:* Columbia Univ, BA, 42; Western Res Univ, MD, 53; Am Bd Internal Med, dipl, 61. *Prof Exp:* Intern med, First Div, Bellevue Hosp, NY, 53-54; asst resident path, Univ Hosps, Med Ctr, Univ Mich, Ann Arbor, 54-55; asst resident med, Manhattan Vet Admin Hosp, NY, 55-56; asst resident, First Div, Bellevue Hosp, 56-57, chief resident, Chest Serv Div, 57-58; career scientist, Health Res Coun NY, 62-66; vis specialist, Care/Medico, Avicenna Hosp, Kabul, Afghanistan, 66-67; staff physician, Maine Coast Mem Hosp, Ellsworth, 67-68; assoc prof med, Dartmouth Med Sch, 68-85. *Concurrent Pos:* NY Tuberc & Health Asn Miller fel, Col Physicians & Surgeons, Columbia Univ, 58-60; guest investr, Rockefeller Inst, 62-64; asst prof, Col Physicians & Surgeons, Columbia Univ, 64-66. *Mem:* Fel Am Col Physicians; Sigma Xi. *Res:* Internal and chest medicine; pathophysiology; training of paramedical personnel. *Mailing Add:* 80 Lyme Rd Apt 357 Hanover NH 03755

STRAUSS, BERNARD, MEDICINE. *Current Pos:* assoc prof, 65-72, EMER ASSOC CLIN PROF UROL, DEPT SURG, SCH MED, UNIV SOUTHERN CALIF, 72- *Personal Data:* b Odessa, Russia, Apr 10, 04; nat US; m 64, Lena Wiersbicku. *Educ:* State Univ NY, MD, 27; Am Bd Urol, dipl, 43. *Prof Exp:* Instr urol, Sch Med, Stanford Univ, 39-42; asst prof, Sch Med, Loma Linda Univ, 56-65. *Mem:* Am Urol Asn; fel Am Col Surgeons; corresp mem Belg Soc Urol; Am Med Asn. *Res:* Urology. *Mailing Add:* 9731 Sawyer St Los Angeles CA 90035

STRAUSS, BERNARD S, MOLECULAR BIOLOGY, GENETICS. *Current Pos:* assoc prof, Univ Chicago, 60-64, chmn, Dept Microbiol, 69-84, chmn, Dept Molecular Genetics & Cell Biol, 84-85; prof microbiol, 64-84, dean basic sci, Div Biol Sci, 85-88, PROF MOLECULAR GENETICS & CELL BIOL, UNIV CHICAGO, 84- *Personal Data:* b New York, NY, Apr 18, 27; m 49, Carol Dunham; c Leslie, David & Paul. *Educ:* City Col NY, BS, 47; Calif Inst Technol, PhD(biochem), 50. *Prof Exp:* Hite fel cancer res & biochem genetics, Univ Tex, 50-52; from asst prof to assoc prof, Syracuse Univ, 52-60. *Concurrent Pos:* Fulbright & Guggenheim fels, Osaka Univ, 58; mem, Genetics Training Comt, NIH, 62-68 & 70-74 & Chem Path Study Sect, 85-; vis prof, Univ Sydney, 67 & Hadassah Med Sch, Hebrew Univ, Jerusalem, 81; sr int fel, Fogarty Ctr, NIH, ICRF, London, 91. *Mem:* Am Soc Biol Chemists; Genetics Soc Am; Am Asn Cancer Res. *Res:* Chemical mutagenesis; DNA repair and replication. *Mailing Add:* Dept Molecular Genetics & Cell Biol Univ Chicago 920 E 58th St Chicago IL 60637. *Fax:* 773-702-3172; *E-Mail:* bs19@midway.uchicago.edu

STRAUSS, BRUCE PAUL, CRYOGENICS, LOW TEMPERATURE PHYSICS. *Current Pos:* SR PRIN SCIENTIST & VPRES, COSINE, INC, 90- *Personal Data:* b Elizabeth, NJ, Aug 19, 42; m 83, Suzanne Geller; c Lori (Feldman) & Lisa. *Educ:* Mass Inst Technol, SB, 64, ScD(solid state physics), 67; Univ Chicago, MBA, 72. *Prof Exp:* Prin res engr, Avco-Everett Res Lab, Avco Corp, 67-68; physicist, Argonne Nat Lab, 68-69; sr engr, Nat Accelerator Lab, Batavia, Ill, 69-79; mem staff, Magnetic Corp Am, 79-85; sr prin scientist & vpres, Powers Assocs, Inc, 85-90. *Concurrent Pos:* Vis scientist, Univ Wis-Madison, 71-, Mass Inst Technol, 86- *Mem:* Am Phys Soc; Am Soc Metals; Am Inst Mining, Metall & Petrol Engrs; Cryogenic Soc Am; Mat Res Soc; Sigma Xi. *Res:* Cryogenic magnet systems; optimization of materials and performance. *Mailing Add:* PO Box 1078 Brookline MA 02146-0008

STRAUSS, CARL RICHARD, POLYMER CHEMISTRY. *Current Pos:* advan scientist polyesters, 69-72, sr scientist phenolic binder, 72-74, SR SCIENTIST RESINS & BINDERS, OWENS-CORNING FIBERGLAS CORP, 74- *Personal Data:* b Chicago, Ill, May 18, 36; m 59; c 3. *Educ:* Univ Ill, BS, 58; Univ Akron, MS, 65, PhD(polymer chem), 70. *Prof Exp:* Plant engr chlorinated organics, Pittsburgh Plate Glass Chem Div, 58-63, res chemist reinforcement elastomers, 63-69. *Concurrent Pos:* Instr, Cent Ohio Tech Col, 73-75. *Mem:* Am Chem Soc. *Res:* Cure and mechanical properties of organic binders; glass-binder interaction and mechanical performance of fiberglass composites; binder development. *Mailing Add:* 3380 Milner Rd Granville OH 43023

STRAUSS, CHARLES MICHAEL, computer science, applied mathematics, for more information see previous edition

STRAUSS, ELLEN GLOWACKI, MOLECULAR GENETICS, VIROLOGY. *Current Pos:* from res fel to sr res fel, 69-84, SR RES ASSOC BIOL, CALIF INST TECHNOL, 84- *Personal Data:* b New Haven, Conn, Sept 25, 38; m 69, James H. *Educ:* Swarthmore Col, BA, 60; Calif Inst Technol, PhD(biochem), 66. *Prof Exp:* NIH fel biochem, Univ Wis, 66-68, fel, 68-69. *Mem:* Sigma Xi; Am Soc Microbiologists; Soc Gen Microbiol; Am Soc Virol; Am Trop Med Hyg. *Res:* Molecular biology of the replication of togaviruses, particularly alphavirus Sindbis, primarily through isolation and characterization of conditional lethal mutants; evolution of RNA viruses. *Mailing Add:* Div Biol Calif Inst Technol Pasadena CA 91125. *Fax:* 626-449-0756

STRAUSS, ERIC L, THERMAL PROTECTION SYSTEMS, CRYOGENIC INSULATION. *Current Pos:* CONSULT. *Personal Data:* b Mainz, Ger, Dec 13, 23; m 49, Fay Simon; c Stephen A & Andrea L. *Educ:* Stevens Inst Technol, ME, 49; Univ Va, MME, 53. *Honors & Awards:* Indust Res 100 Award, 63. *Prof Exp:* Mech engr, Nat Adv Comt Aeronaut, Va, 49-53; proj engr, Taylor-Wharton Iron & Steel Co, Pa, 53-54; res & develop scientist, Baltimore Div, Martin Marietta Corp, 54-67, sr res scientist, Astronaut Group, 67-92. *Concurrent Pos:* Lectr, Exten Div, Univ Wis, 65. *Mem:* Soc Plastics Engrs; Am Ceramic Soc. *Res:* Nonmetallics; structural plastics, composites and adhesives, ablators and ceramic heat shield materials for aerospace applications; materials development and investigation of mechanical and thermal properties; heat transfer analysis and polymer degradation. *Mailing Add:* 5052 E Princeton Ave Englewood CO 80110

STRAUSS, FREDERICK BODO, mathematics; deceased, see previous edition for last biography

STRAUSS, GEORGE, BIOPHYSICAL CHEMISTRY. *Current Pos:* Colgate fel, Rutgers Univ, New Brunswick, 55-57, from asst prof to prof, 57-91, res assoc, Inst Microbiol, 57-64, EMER PROF CHEM, RUTGERS UNIV, NEW BRUNSWICK, 91- *Personal Data:* b Vienna, Austria, Nov 27, 21; US citizen; m 54; c 2. *Educ:* Univ London, BSc, 50; Lehigh Univ, PhD(chem), 55. *Prof Exp:* Chemist, A S Harrison & Co, 45-52. *Concurrent Pos:* Rutgers Univ fac fel & USPHS fel, Univ Sheffield, 64-65; vis investr, Fed Inst Technol, Zurich, Switz, 85; vis prof, Univ Rome, Italy, 85. *Mem:* AAAS; Am Chem Soc; Biophys Soc; Sigma Xi. *Res:* Structure and properties of lipid bilayer membranes; macromolecular interactions probed by fluorescence lifetime and polarization and by dynamic light scattering. *Mailing Add:* Dept Chem Rutgers Univ PO Box 939 Piscataway NJ 08855-0939

STRAUSS, H(OWARD) J(EROME), CHEMICAL ENGINEERING. *Current Pos:* PROF, CARLSON SCH MGT, UNIV MINN. *Personal Data:* b New York, NY, July 2, 20; m 50, Nancy Radack; c Michael, Steven & Allen. *Educ:* City Col New York, BChE, 42; Columbia Univ, MS, 47, PhD(chem eng), 49. *Prof Exp:* Chem engr, Tenn Valley Authority, 42-43; metallurgist, Vanadium Corp Am, 43-44; instr chem eng, Cooper Union, 47-50; develop engr, Elec Storage Battery Co, 50-51, res engr, 51-52, supvr res dept, 52-53, asst mgr, 53-55, chief prod engr, 55-58, assoc dir res dept, 58-59, vpres & mgr, ESB-Reeves Corp, 59-62; res dir, Burgess Battery Div, Clevite Corp, Ill, 62-70; assoc dir res & develop, Gould, Inc, St Paul, 70-72, dir mkt & technol develop, 72-76; consult, 76-77; vpres oper improv, ESB Ray-O-Vac Mgt Co, Inc, 77-78; vpres oper & eng, Inco Electroenergy Corp, 78-82. *Mem:* Electrochem Soc; Am Electroplaters Soc; Am Inst Chem Engrs; Franklin Inst; Soc Plastics Engrs; sr mem Inst Elec & Electronics Engrs. *Res:* Industrial electrochemistry; plastics technology. *Mailing Add:* 4967 Devonshire Circle Excelsior MN 55331

STRAUSS, HARLEE S, CHEMISTRY, TOXICOLOGY. *Current Pos:* PRES, H STRAUSS ASSOCS INC, NATICK, MASS, 88- *Personal Data:* b New Brunswick, NJ, June 19, 50; c 1. *Educ:* Smith Col, Mass, BA, 72; Univ Wis, PhD(molecular biol), 79. *Honors & Awards:* Am Inst Chemists Award, 72. *Prof Exp:* Spec asst govt affairs, Am Chem Soc, Washington, DC, 83-84; spec consult, Environ Corp, Washington, DC, 84-85; res, Ctr Technol, Policy & Indust Develop, Mass Inst Technol, 85-86; sr assoc, Gradient Corp, 86-88. *Concurrent Pos:* Consult, 85-; res affil, Ctr Technol Policy & Indust Develop, Mass Inst Technol, 86-92; lectr, Tufts Univ Sch Med, 90-94; exec dir, Silent Spring Inst, Mass, 94-95; mem, Army Sci Bd, 94- *Mem:* AAAS; Am Chem Soc; Asn Women Sci; Am Soc Microbiol; Soc Risk Anal; Int Soc Exposure Assessment. *Res:* Developing methodologies for risk assessment of chemicals in the environment, including examination of sex biases in risk assesssment. *Mailing Add:* 21 Bay State Rd Natick MA 01760-2942. *Fax:* 508-655-5116; *E-Mail:* h strauss@aol.com

STRAUSS, HAROLD C, CARDIOLOGY. *Current Pos:* ASSOC PROF PHARMACOL, SCH MED, DUKE UNIV, 79-, PROF MED, 85- *Personal Data:* b Montreal, Que, Can, Jan 30, 40. *Educ:* McGill Univ, MD, 64. *Mailing Add:* Dept Med & Pharmacol Duke Univ Med Ctr PO Box 3845 Durham NC 27710. *Fax:* 919-681-5392

STRAUSS, HERBERT L, VIBRATIONAL SPECTROSCOPY, MOLECULAR DYNAMICS. *Current Pos:* from asst prof to assoc prof, Univ Calif, Berkeley, 61-73, vchair, 75-81, asst dean, Col Chem, 87-92, vchair, 92-95, PROF CHEM, UNIV CALIF, BERKELEY, 73-, ASSOC DEAN, 95- *Personal Data:* b Aachen, Ger, Mar 26, 36; US citizen; m 60, Carolyn N Cooper; c Michael A, Rebecca A & Ethan E. *Educ:* Columbia Univ, AB, 57, MA, 58, PhD(chem), 60. *Honors & Awards:* Bomen-Michelson Award, Coblentz Soc, 94; Lippincott Award, Am Optical Soc, 94. *Prof Exp:* Ramsey fel, Univ Col, London Univ & NSF fel, Oxford Univ, 60-61. *Concurrent Pos:* Sloan res fel, 66-68; vis prof, Indian Inst Technol, Kanpur, 68, Fudan Univ & Tokyo Univ, 82 & Univ Paris, 86; ed, Ann Rev Phys Chem; mem, Int Union Pure & Appl Biophys Comn I 1, 89-93, Chair, 94- *Mem:* Am Chem Soc; fel Am Phys Soc; fel AAAS. *Res:* Experimental and theoretical spectroscopy; infrared; light scattering; librational motion and phase transitions in solids; coupling of various types of molecular motion. *Mailing Add:* Dept Chem Univ Calif Berkeley CA 94720-1460. *Fax:* 510-643-2156; *E-Mail:* uls@hafnium.cchem.berkeley.edu

STRAUSS, JAMES HENRY, MOLECULAR BIOLOGY, VIROLOGY. *Current Pos:* exec officer, 80-90, from asst prof to prof biol, 69-93, EDITH WILSON & ROBERT BOWLES PROF BIOL, CALIF INST TECHNOL, 93- *Personal Data:* b Galveston, Tex, Sept 16, 38; m 69, Ellen Glowacki. *Educ:* St Mary's Univ, Tex, BS, 60; Calif Inst Technol, PhD, 67. *Prof Exp:* NSF fel, Albert Einstein Col Med, 66-67, res fel, 66-69. *Mem:* AAAS; Am Soc Biol Chemists; Am Soc Microbiol; Sigma Xi; Am Soc Virol. *Res:* Structure and replication of animal viruses; cell surface modification and RNA replication during Togavirus infection; biogenesis of cell plasma membranes; molecular biology of flavivirus replication. *Mailing Add:* Div Biol Calif Inst Technol Pasadena CA 91125. *Fax:* 626-449-0756; *E-Mail:* straussJ@starbase1.caltech.edu

STRAUSS, JEROME FRANK, III, REPRODUCTIVE ENDOCRINOLOGY. *Current Pos:* Intern obstet & gynec, Univ Pa, 75-76, assoc, 76-77, from asst prof obstet, gynec & physiol to assoc prof obstet, gynec, path & physiol 77-85, assoc dean, 90-93, PROF OBSTET, GYNEC, PATH & PHYSIOL, UNIV PA, 85-, ASSOC CHMN DEPT, 87-, LUIGI MASTROIANNI JR PROF & DIR, CTR RES WOMEN'S HEALTH & REPRODUCTION, 93- *Personal Data:* b Chicago, Ill, May 2, 47; m 70, Catherine Blumlein; c Jordan L & Elizabeth J. *Educ:* Brown Univ, BA, 69; Univ Pa, MD, 74, PhD(molecular biol), 74. *Honors & Awards:* President's Achievement Award, Soc Gynec Invest, 90; Res Award, Soc Study Reproduction, 92. *Concurrent Pos:* Dir, Endocrine Lab, Hosp Univ Pa, 81-86, dir, Div Reproductive Biol, Dept Obstet & Gynec, 84-; assoc ed, J Lipid Res, 82-86, J Women's Health, 92-, J Soc Gynec Invest, 93-; mem, Biochem Endocrinol Study Sect, NIH, 83-87, Pop Res Comt, 88-92; assoc chmn, Dept Obstet & Gynec, 87-; corresp ed, J Steroid Biochem & Molecular Biol, 90- *Mem:* Inst Med-Nat Acad Sci; Am Physiol Soc; Am Soc Pathologists; Am Fertility Soc; Soc Study Reproduction; Soc Gynec Invest; Endocrine Soc. *Res:* Regulation of corpus luteum function with special emphasis on the control of cholesterol metabolism; lipoprotein metabolism and intracellular cholesterol transport; luteal cells; placental cell biology. *Mailing Add:* 778 Clin Res Bldg Univ Pa Philadelphia PA 19104. *Fax:* 215-573-5408

STRAUSS, JOHN S, DERMATOLOGY. *Current Pos:* PROF DERMAT & HEAD DEPT, COL MED, UNIV IOWA, 78- *Personal Data:* b New Haven, Conn, July 15, 26; m 50; c 2. *Educ:* Yale Univ, BS, 46, MD, 50. *Honors & Awards:* Stephen Rothman Award, Soc Invest Dermat, 88; Presidential Citation, Am Acad Dermat, 90 & 93. *Prof Exp:* Intern med, Univ Chicago Clins, 50-51; resident dermat, Univ Pa, 51-52, fel, 54-56, instr, 56-57; from asst prof to prof, Sch Med, Boston Univ, 57-78. *Concurrent Pos:* Prin investr, NIH grants, 57-88; assoc dir, Comn Cutaneous Dis, Armed Forces Epidemiol Bd, 65; asst ed, J Am Acad Dermat, 79-88; mem, Nat Inst Arthritis, Musculskeletal & Skin Dis Adv Coun, NIH, 87-90; exec comt, Int Comt Dermat; pres, 18th World Cong Dermat, 92; pres, Int Com Dermat & Int League Dermat Soc, 92-97. *Mem:* Am Acad Dermat (pres 82-83); Soc Invest Dermat (secy-treas, 69-74, pres, 75-76); Am Dermat Asn (secy, 86-91, pres, 91-92); Sigma Xi; hon mem Brit Asn Dermat; hon mem Japan Soc Invest Dermat; hon mem Brazilian Dermat Soc; hon mem Arg Dermat Soc; hon mem Neth Dermat Soc; hon mem Japan Dermat Asn; hon mem Korean Dermat Asn; hon mem Ger Dermat Soc; Asn Am Physicians; hon mem Hong Kong Dermat Soc; hon mem Span Acad Dermat; hon mem Venezuelan Soc Dermat. *Res:* Sebaceous and epidermal cutaneous lipids; sebaceous gland physiology; pathophysiology and methods of treatment of acne. *Mailing Add:* Dept Dermat 2BT Univ Hosps 200 Hawkins Dr Bt 2045-1 Iowa City IA 52242-1090

STRAUSS, LEONARD, electrical engineering, for more information see previous edition

STRAUSS, MARY JO, PHYSICAL CHEMISTRY. *Current Pos:* RETIRED. *Personal Data:* b Columbus, Ohio, June 10, 27; m 57, Simon W; c Jack C & Ruth A. *Educ:* Bowling Green State Univ, BS, 49; Mich State Univ, PhD(phys chem), 54. *Prof Exp:* Phys chemist, US Naval Res Lab, 54-59, pvt consult, 60-71; res assoc, Col Gen Studies, George Washington Univ, 72-76, lectr, Grad Sch Arts & Sci, 77-78; consult, 79-89. *Concurrent Pos:* Res consult, Voc & Tech Div, Md Dept Educ, 85-89. *Mem:* Fel Am Inst Chemists; Women Math Ed; Sigma Xi; AAAS; Asn Women Sci. *Res:* Physical and chemical properties of ammonium amalgam; physical chemistry of the iron-oxygen-water system, particularly corrosion mechanisms; women in higher education; women, science and society; environmental studies; women in mathematics and science education. *Mailing Add:* 4506 Cedell Pl Temple Hills MD 20748

STRAUSS, MICHAEL S, GENETIC RESOURCES CONSERVATION, BIOLOGICAL DIVERSITY. *Current Pos:* DIR, GLOBAL CHANGE PROG, AAAS, 91-, PROG DIR MEETINGS, 94- *Personal Data:* b Los Angeles, Calif, Sept 24, 47; m 72, Kay L Costello. *Educ:* Univ Calif, BS, 69, MS, 74, PhD(biol sci), 76. *Prof Exp:* Researcher, Univ Calif, Irvine, 76-79; asst prof biol & bot, Northeastern Univ, 79-84; proj analyst, US Cong, Off Technol Assessment, 85-86; sr staff officer, Bd Agr, Nat Res Coun, 86-91. *Concurrent Pos:* Proj dir, Comt Managing Global Genetic Resources, Nat Res Coun, 86-91; consult, UN Food & Agr Orgn, 91, 92 & 94; bd dirs, Am Livestock Breeds Conservancy. *Mem:* Am Soc Agron; AAAS; Crop Sci Soc Am; Am Livestock Breeds Conservancy; Seed Savers Exchange. *Res:* In vitro culture and biochemical characterization of tropical tuber crops; germplasm conservation and management, conservation biology, and biological diversity. *Mailing Add:* 4918 King Richard Dr Annandale VA 22003. *Fax:* 202-289-4601; *E-Mail:* mstrauss@aaas.org

STRAUSS, MONTY JOSEPH, PARTIAL DIFFERENTIAL EQUATIONS. *Current Pos:* From asst prof to assoc prof, 71-85, assoc chmn dept, 84-87, PROF MATH, TEX TECH UNIV, 85-, ASSOC DEAN GRAD SCH, 89- *Personal Data:* b Tyler, Tex, Aug 26, 45; m 78, Jane L Winer. *Educ:* Rice Univ, BA, 67; NY Univ, PhD(math), 71. *Mem:* Am Math Soc; Math Asn Am. *Res:* Partial differential equations, particularly the theoretical aspects of existence and uniqueness of solutions and several complex variables; computer literacy. *Mailing Add:* Grad Dean's Off Tex Tech Univ Lubbock TX 79409-1033

STRAUSS, PHYLLIS R, CELL PHYSIOLOGY. *Current Pos:* from asst prof to assoc prof cell physiol, 73-84, prof biol, 84-86, DISTINGUISHED UNIV PROF BIOL, NORTHEASTERN UNIV, 86- *Personal Data:* b Worcester, Mass, Mar 19, 43. *Educ:* Brown Univ, BA, 64; Rockefeller Univ, PhD(life sci), 71. *Prof Exp:* Res fel cell physiol, Harvard Med Sch, 71-73. *Concurrent Pos:* Res career develop award, Nat Cancer Inst, 78-83, & guest worker, 81; vis scholar, Harvard Univ, 88. *Mem:* AAAS; Am Soc Protozoologists; Am Asn Biol Chemists & Molecular Biologists; Soc Am Cell Biologists. *Res:* DNA replication and topoisomerases in eukaryotic cells including Trypanosoma brucei; nucleoside metabolism (adenosine and thymidine) in lymphocytes; thymidine metabolism in lymphocytes; small soluble DNA in eukaryotes. *Mailing Add:* Dept Biol Northeastern Univ 360 Huntington Ave Boston MA 02115-5096

STRAUSS, RICHARD HARRY, INTERNAL MEDICINE. *Current Pos:* ASSOC PROF MED, PREV MED & TEAM PHYSICIAN, OHIO STATE UNIV, 78- *Educ:* Univ Chicago, MD, 64. *Mailing Add:* Dept Prev Med Ohio State Univ Col Med 370 W Ninth Ave Columbus OH 43210-1238

STRAUSS, ROBERT R, BIOCHEMISTRY, MICROBIOLOGY. *Current Pos:* RETIRED. *Personal Data:* b Chelsea, Mass, Nov 4, 29; m 51; c 3. *Educ:* Univ Pa, BA, 54; Hehnemann Med Col, MS, 56, PhD(microbiol), 58. *Prof Exp:* Sr res scientist, Nat Drug Co, Div Richardson-Merrell, Inc, 58-61, dir biochem res, 61, dir, Biochem & Bact Res Labs, 61-67; res microbiologist, St Margaret's Hosp, Boston, 67-73; asst prof, Sch Med, Tufts Univ, 69-73; assoc dir microbiol, Albert Einstein Med Ctr, 73-78; res assoc prof, Sch Med, Temple Univ, 73-86, Clin Path Facil, 86-92. *Concurrent Pos:* Dir, Dept Microbiol, Albert Einstein Med Ctr, 78- *Mem:* AAAS; Am Soc Exp Path; Reticuloendothelial Soc; Am Acad Microbiol; Am Soc Microbiol. *Res:* Biochemistry of inflammation; virus purification; biochemistry of phagocytosis. *Mailing Add:* 12806 Old Bridge Rd Ocean City MD 21842-9242

STRAUSS, ROGER WILLIAM, PAPER TECHNOLOGY. *Current Pos:* RETIRED. *Personal Data:* b Buffalo, NY, Sept 23, 27; m 50; c 4. *Educ:* State Univ NY Col Forestry, Syracuse, BS, 49, MS, 50, PhD(chem), 61. *Prof Exp:* Develop engr, Bauer Bros, Ohio, 50-52; paper sales develop engr, Hammermill Paper Co, Pa, 52-55; instr paper sci, State Univ NY Col Forestry, Syracuse, 55-60; mgr res, Nekoosa-Edwards Paper Co, Wis, 60-66; prof paper sci & eng, State Univ NY Col Environ Sci & Forestry, 66-75; dir res & sci serv, Bowater Inc, Conn, 75-80, dir res & sci serv, Bowater NA Corp, Greenville, SC, 80-88. *Mem:* Tech Asn Pulp & Paper Indust. *Res:* Pulping and bleaching of wood pulp; paper production and coating. *Mailing Add:* 14 Moss Creek Ct Hilton Head Island SC 29926

STRAUSS, RONALD GEORGE, PEDIATRICS, HEMATOLOGY. *Current Pos:* from assoc to PROF PEDIAT, UNIV IOWA COL MED, 76-, PROF PATH, 83- *Personal Data:* b Mansfield, Ohio, Nov 29, 39; m 62, Vivien Douglass; c Dawn, Amy & Heidi. *Educ:* Capital Univ, BS, 61; Univ Cincinnati, MD, 65; Am Bd Pediat, dipl, 70, cert pediat hemat-oncol, 74. *Prof Exp:* Intern pediat, Boston City Hosp, 65-66; from jr resident to chief resident, Children's Hosp, Cincinnati, 66-69; pediatrician, David Grant USAF Med Ctr, 69-71; fel pediat hemat, Children's Hosp Res Found, Cincinnati, 71-73, asst prof pediat, Col Med, Univ Cincinnati, 73-74; asst prof, Col Med, Univ Tenn, Memphis, 74-76; asst mem hemat-oncol, St Jude Children's Res Hosp, 74-76. *Mem:* Soc Pediat Res; Am Acad Pediat; Soc Exp Biol Med; Am Fedn Clin Res; Am Soc Hemat; Am Asn Blood Banks; Am Soc Apheresis. *Res:* Leukocyte physiology and function; neonatal hemaopoiesis and transfusion therapy; automated hemapheresis. *Mailing Add:* Dept Path Univ Iowa Hosp & Clins 144 Med Labs 200 Hawkins Dr Iowa City IA 52242-1087. *Fax:* 319-335-8348

STRAUSS, SIMON WOLF, CHEMISTRY, MATERIALS SCIENCE. *Current Pos:* CONSULT, 80- *Personal Data:* b Poland, Apr 15, 20; nat US; m 57, Mary J Boehm; c Jack C & Ruth A. *Educ:* Polytech Inst Brooklyn, BS, 44, MS, 47, PhD(chem), 50. *Prof Exp:* Inorg chemist, Nat Bur Stand, 51-55; phys chemist, US Naval Res Lab, 55-57, head chem metall sect, 57-63; sr staff scientist, Hq, Air Force Systs Command, 63-80. *Concurrent Pos:* First distinguished scholar-in-residence, Wash Acad Sci, 84-89. *Mem:* Fel AAAS; Am Chem Soc; fel Am Inst Chemists; Math Asn Am. *Res:* Solid state reactions; structure and electrical properties of glass; nature and structure of liquid metals; technical management. *Mailing Add:* 4506 Cedell Pl Temple Hills MD 20748

STRAUSS, STEVEN, PHARMACY, LAW & REGULATORY AFFAIRS. *Current Pos:* From asst prof to assoc prof pharm admin, Long Island Univ, 65-79, alumni dir, 65-70, dir continuing educ, 72-78, PROF PHARM ADMIN, ARNOLD & MARIE SCHWARTZ COL PHARM & HEALTH SCI, LONG ISLAND UNIV, 79-, DIR, DIV PHARM ADMIN & RETAIL DRUG INST, 88- *Personal Data:* b Czech, Dec 4, 30; US citizen; m 59; c 3. *Educ:* Long Island Univ, BS, 55, MS, 65, Univ Pittsburg, PhD(pharm),70. *Honors & Awards:* Rho Chi Pharm Honor Soc. *Concurrent Pos:* Ed, US Pharmacist, 76-89; dir, Grad Pharm Progs, Westchester Campus, Long Island Univ, 77-83; field dir, Mkt Measures, 72-78, IMS Am, Ltd, 73-77; co-dir, Annual Caribbean-US Pharmaceut Conf, 91- *Mem:* Am Pharmaceut Asn; assoc AMA; Am Soc Hosp Pharmacists; Am Soc Pharm Law; Am Asn Cols Pharm. *Res:* Pharmacy administration; marketing; market research; pharmacy law. *Mailing Add:* 39 Prospect Ave Ardsley NY 10502. *Fax:* 718-625-6068; *E-Mail:* stestraphd@aol.com

STRAUSS, ULRICH PAUL, PHYSICAL POLYMER CHEMISTRY. *Current Pos:* from asst prof to prof phys chem, Rutgers Univ, 48-90, dir, Sch Chem, 65-71, chmn dept & dir, Grad Prog Chem, 74-80, EMER PROF PHYS CHEM, RUTGERS UNIV, NEW BRUNSWICK, 90. *Personal Data:* b Frankfort, Ger, Jan 10, 20; nat US; m 43, 50, Elaine Greenbaum; c Dorothy (Politziner), David, Elizabeth & Evelyn. *Educ:* Columbia Univ, AB, 41; Cornell Univ, PhD(chem), 44. *Honors & Awards:* Johnson Wax Sci Achievement Award, 86. *Prof Exp:* Sterling fel, Yale Univ, 46-48. *Concurrent Pos:* NSF sr fel, 61-62; Guggenheim fel, 71-72. *Mem:* Am Chem Soc; fel NY Acad Sci. *Res:* Experimental and theoretical investigations of high polymers and polyelectrolytes. *Mailing Add:* Dept Chem Rutgers Univ New Brunswick NJ 08903. *Fax:* 732-296-1936

STRAUSS, WALTER, MODELING, CIRCUIT SIMULATION. *Current Pos:* RETIRED. *Personal Data:* b Nurnberg, Ger, Nov 6, 23; US citizen; m 59, Phyllis; c Martin & Tobie. *Educ:* City Col New York, BEE, 48; Columbia Univ, PhD(physics), 61. *Prof Exp:* Tutor elec eng, City Col New York, 48-53; asst physics, Columbia Radiation Lab, 53-59; lectr elec eng, City Col New York, 59-60; mem tech staff, Bell Tel Labs, 60-90. *Res:* Magnetic domain devices; magnetoelastic properties of yttrium iron garnet; magnetic materials; piezoelectricity; magnetron oscillators; microwave delay lines; circuit simulation. *Mailing Add:* One Harrison Ct Summit NJ 07901-1713

STRAUSS, WALTER A, MATHEMATICS. *Current Pos:* assoc prof, 66-71, PROF MATH, BROWN UNIV, 71-; PROF MATH & APPL MATH, L H BALLOU UNIV, 95- *Personal Data:* b Aachen, Ger, Oct 28, 37; US citizen; c 2. *Educ:* Columbia Univ, AB, 58; Univ Chicago, MS, 59; Mass Inst Technol, PhD(math), 62. *Prof Exp:* NSF fel, Mass Inst Technol & Univ Paris, 62-63; vis asst prof math, Stanford Univ, 63-66; assoc prof, Brown Univ, 66-71. *Concurrent Pos:* Guggenheim fel, 71; vis scientist, Univ Tokyo, 72; Fulbright Lect, Rio de Janeiro, 67; vis prof, City Univ NY, 68, Mass Inst Technol 78, Univ Md, 81, Yunn U (China), 86, NY Univ, 87 & 88, Univ Houston, 94-95. *Mem:* Soc Indust & Appl Math; Asn Math Physics; Am Math Soc. *Res:* Nonlinear partial differential equations; scattering theory; functional analysis; theory of plasmas. *Mailing Add:* Dept Math Brown Univ Providence RI 02912-0001

STRAUSS, WILLIAM MARK, MOLECULAR BIOLOGY. *Current Pos:* Fel, 89-93, RES SCIENTIST, CTR GENOME RES, WHITEHEAD-MASS INST TECHNOL, 93-; RES SCIENTIST, BETH ISRAEL DEACONESS MED CTR. *Personal Data:* b Dallas, Tex, Oct 21, 53. *Educ:* Columbia Univ, AB, 78; Harvard Univ, PhD(genetics & immunol), 88. *Mem:* Genetics Soc Am; Am Soc Human Genetics. *Res:* The human genome project has facilitated advances in physical and genetic mapping, in order to utilize advances in mapping technology and the explosion in mapping information we are extending the technical boundries of mammalian transgenesis. *Mailing Add:* Beth Israel Deaconess Med Ctr 330 Brookline Ave Boston MA 02215-5400. *Fax:* 617-252-1902; *E-Mail:* wstrauss@genome.wi.mit.edu

STRAUSZ, OTTO PETER, CHEMISTRY. *Current Pos:* Res asst, 62-63, from asst prof to prof, 63-89, dir, Hydrocarbon Res Ctr, 74-77, EMER PROF CHEM, UNIV ALTA, 89- *Personal Data:* b Miskolc, Hungary, 24; Can citizen; c 1. *Educ:* Eotvos Lorand Univ, Hungary, MSc, 52;, Univ Alta, PhD(chem), 62. *Honors & Awards:* E W R Steacie Award, Can Soc Chem, 87. *Mem:* Fel Chem Inst Can; Am Chem Soc; AAAS; NY Acad Sci; Int-Am Photochemical Soc (pres, 75-79). *Res:* Mechanism and kinetics of chemical reactions induced photochemically or thermally and the chemistry of atoms, free radicals and reactive intermediates; chemical composition, analytical chemistry and organic geochemistry of petroleum. *Mailing Add:* Dept Chem Univ Alta Edmonton AB T6G 2G2 Can

STRAW, JAMES ASHLEY, PHARMACOLOGY. *Current Pos:* From asst prof to assoc prof, 65-75, PROF PHARMACOL, SCH MED, GEORGE WASHINGTON UNIV, 75- *Personal Data:* b Farmville, Va, Apr 12, 32; m 54; c 2. *Educ:* Univ Fla, BS, 58, PhD(physiol), 63. *Concurrent Pos:* NIH fel physiol, Univ Fla, 63-64 & res grant, 64-65. *Mem:* Am Asn Cancer Res; Am Soc Pharmacol & Exp Therapeut. *Res:* Pharmacokinetics; cancer chemotherapy; physiological disposition of anticancer drugs; anti-AIDS drugs. *Mailing Add:* Dept Pharmacol George Washington Univ 2300 Eye St NW Washington DC 20037-2803

STRAW, ROBERT NICCOLLS, PROJECT MANAGEMENT. *Current Pos:* Res assoc pharmacol, 67-79, res head med, 79-85, DIR PROJ MGT, UPJOHN CO, 85- *Personal Data:* b Burlington, Iowa, Aug 24, 38; c 3. *Educ:* Univ Iowa, BS, 60, MS, 65, PhD(pharmacol), 67. *Mem:* Am Soc Pharmacol & Exp Therapeut. *Res:* Development of centrally acting drugs. *Mailing Add:* Proj Mgt LOC 7217-258-3 Upjohn Co 301 Henrietta St Kalamazoo MI 49001-0199

STRAW, THOMAS EUGENE, AQUATIC BIOLOGY. *Current Pos:* Asst prof, 68-73, ASSOC PROF BIOL, UNIV MINN, MORRIS, 73- *Personal Data:* b St Paul, Minn, Nov 20, 36; m 57; c 3. *Educ:* Univ Minn, St Paul, BS, 65, PhD(biochem), 69. *Mem:* Am Soc Limnol & Oceanog; Sigma Xi. *Res:* Biochemical limnology; ecology of aquatic bacteria. *Mailing Add:* 855 Lone Oak Rd Morris MN 55121

STRAW, WILLIAM THOMAS, GEOLOGY, GEOMORPHOLOGY. *Current Pos:* RETIRED. *Personal Data:* b Griffin, Ind, Sept 29, 31; m 56; c 3. *Educ:* Ind Univ, BS, 58, MA, 60, PhD(geol), 68. *Prof Exp:* Geologist, Humble Oil & Refining Co, 60-65; lectr geol, Ind Univ, 67-82; from asst prof to prof geol, Western Mich Univ, 68-96, actg chmn dept, 71, chmn, 71-74 & 88-96. *Concurrent Pos:* Actg assoc dir, Geol Field Sta, Ind Univ, 70-81; geologist, Ind Geol Surv, 70 & Mont Bur Mines & Geol, 78-79. *Mem:* Am Asn Petrol Geologists; fel Geol Soc Am; Am Inst Hydrol; Am Inst Prof Geol; Soc Wetland Scientists. *Res:* Glacial geology, hydrogeology, geomorphology and hydrology of wetlands; fluvial sedimentation; geology of valley trains; regional geology of the northern Rocky Mountains; Wetlands hydrology. *Mailing Add:* Dept Geol Western Mich Univ Kalamazoo MI 49008

STRAWDERMAN, WAYNE ALAN, APPLIED MECHANICS. *Current Pos:* RES MECH ENGR, NEW LONDON LAB, NAVAL UNDERWATER SYSTS CTR, 63- *Personal Data:* b Wakefield, RI, Oct 11, 36; m 58, Nancy Lamb; c Suanne & Paul. *Educ:* Univ RI, BS, 58, MS, 61; Univ Conn, PhD(appl mech), 67. *Prof Exp:* Res engr, E I Du Pont de Nemours & Co, Inc, 58-59; teaching asst mech eng, Univ RI, 59-61; mech engr, Elec Boat Div, Gen Dynamics Corp, 61-63. *Concurrent Pos:* Lectr, Univ Conn, 67-69. *Mem:* Acoust Soc Am. *Res:* Response of coupled mechanical-acoustical systems to random excitation, turbulence induced noise, random vibrations and acoustics. *Mailing Add:* 55 Homestead Rd Ledyard CT 06339

STRAWDERMAN, WILLIAM E, STATISTICS. *Current Pos:* instr, 67-69, PROF STATIST, RUTGERS UNIV, 70- *Personal Data:* b Westerly, RI, Apr 25, 41; m 85, Susan L Grube; c Robert L, William E & Heather L. *Educ:* Univ RI, BS, 63; Cornell Univ, MS, 65; Rutgers Univ, MS, 67, PhD, 69. *Prof Exp:* Mem tech staff, Bell Tel Labs, 65-67; prof, Stanford Univ, 69-70. *Mem:* Fel Inst Math Statist; Am Statist Asn. *Res:* Mathematical statistics. *Mailing Add:* Statist Dept Rugters Univ Hill Ctr Busch Campus New Brunswick NJ 08903

STRAWN, OLIVER P(ERRY), JR, MECHANICAL ENGINEERING. *Current Pos:* PARTNER, CONSULT ENG FIRM, 76- *Personal Data:* b Martinsville, Va, Nov 30, 25; wid; c 4. *Educ:* Va Polytech Inst, BS, 50, MS, 65. *Prof Exp:* Sales engr, Richardson-Wayland Elec Corp, 53-57; asst prof mech eng, Va Polytech Inst & State Univ, 57-66, asst prof archit eng, 66-72; pvt consult pract, 72-75. *Concurrent Pos:* Mem, State Bldg Code Tech Rev Bd, 78-82. *Mem:* Am Soc Mech Engrs; Am Soc Heating, Refrig & Air-Conditioning Engrs; Nat Soc Prof Engrs. *Res:* Thermodynamics; heating; ventilating; air conditioning. *Mailing Add:* 601 Turner St NE Blacksburg VA 24060

STRAWN, ROBERT KIRK, ichthyology, for more information see previous edition

STRAYER, DAVID LOWELL, ECOSYSTEMS. *Current Pos:* Postdoctoral assoc, 83-85, asst scientist, 85-91, ASSOC SCIENTIST, INST ECOSYST STUDIES, 91- *Personal Data:* b Toledo, Ohio, Nov 16, 55; m; c 2. *Educ:* Mich State Univ, BS, 76; Cornell Univ, PhD(ecol), 84. *Concurrent Pos:* Assoc mem grad fac ecol, Rutgers Univ, New Brunswick, NJ, 88- *Mem:* Ecol Soc Am; Am Soc Limnol & Oceanog; NAm Benthological Soc; Int Asn Meiobenthologists. *Res:* Limnology; ecology of freshwater invertebrates, especially meiofauna and mollusks; energy flow in freshwater ecosystems. *Mailing Add:* Weatherford Lane Millbrook NY 12545. *Fax:* 914-677-5976

STRAYER, DAVID S, MOLECULAR BIOLOGY. *Current Pos:* PROF PATH, JEFFERSON MED COL, 92- *Personal Data:* b New York, NY, Apr 25, 49; m 91, Skulsky; c Reuben, Rebecca, Rachel & Michelle. *Educ:* Cornell Univ, AB, 70; Univ Chicago, PhD(path), 74, MD, 76. *Prof Exp:* Resident path, Wash Univ Sch Med, 76-80; asst prof, Univ Calif, San Diego, 80-83; assoc prof, Yale Univ Sch Med, 83-85; prof, Univ Tex, 86-92. *Mem:* Am Soc Invest Path; Am Soc Microbiol; Am Soc Urol; Am Asn Immunologists; Int Acad Path. *Res:* Growth factor related tumor development and its inhibition;

virus-cell interactions; surfactant production and regulation of surfactant production in the lung. *Mailing Add:* Dept Path & Cell Biol Jefferson Med Col 1020 Locust St Philadelphia PA 19107. *Fax:* 215-923-2218; *E-Mail:* iepc51w@tjuum.bitnet

STRAZDINS, EDWARD, PHYSICAL CHEMISTRY, POLYMER CHEMISTRY. *Current Pos:* RETIRED. *Personal Data:* b More, Latvia, Sept 19, 18; US citizen; m 43; c 2. *Educ:* Darmstadt Tech Univ, MS, 49. *Prof Exp:* Mill chemist, Baltic Wood Pulp & Paper Mills, 41-42, supvr, 43-44; res chemist, Am Cyanamid Co, 49-62, sr res chemist, 63-66, proj leader chem res, Cent Res Div, 67-68, res assoc, 68-74, prin res scientist, Chem Res Div, 74-85. *Mem:* Am Chem Soc; fel Tech Asn Pulp & Paper Indust; fel Am Inst Chemists. *Res:* Paper chemistry; polyelectrolytes; sizing; retention; flocculation aids; theoretical aspects of paper making process; ecology; electrokinetic phenomena; polymer research and surface chemistry. *Mailing Add:* 5 Spruce Meadow Dr North Hampton NH 03862

STREAMS, FREDERICK ARTHUR, INSECT ECOLOGY. *Current Pos:* asst prof entom, 64-69, assoc prof biol, 69-74, head, ecol sect, 76-79, PROF BIOL, UNIV CONN, 74- *Personal Data:* b Mercer, Pa, Sept 8, 33; m 56; c 3. *Educ:* Indiana State Col, Pa, BS, 55; Cornell Univ, MS, 60, PhD(entom), 62. *Prof Exp:* Teacher pub schs, NY, 57-58; entomologist, Entom Res Div, USDA, 62-64. *Mem:* Fel AAAS; Entom Soc Am; Ecol Soc Am; Am Soc Naturalists. *Res:* Ecology and evolution of populations; biological control of insects; predator-prey interactions in insects. *Mailing Add:* Dept Ecol & Evolutionary Biol Univ Conn U-42 75 N Eagleville Storrs Mansfield CT 06269-0002

STREBE, DAVID DIEDRICH, MATHEMATICS. *Current Pos:* RETIRED. *Personal Data:* b Tonawanda, NY, Oct 6, 18; m 42; c 2. *Educ:* State Univ NY Teachers Col, Buffalo, BS, 40; Univ Buffalo, MA, 49, PhD(math), 52. *Prof Exp:* Instr math, LeTourneau Tech Inst, 46-47 & Univ Buffalo, 47-54; assoc prof, Univ SC, 54-57; prof, State Univ NY Col, Oswego, 57-58, Univ SC, 58-70 & Westmont Col, 70-71; prof math, Columbia Col, SC, 71-74; staff mem, Ariz Col Bible, 84-86; staff mem Southwestern Baptist Bible Col, 84-86. *Mem:* Nat Coun Teachers Math. *Res:* Set theoretic topology. *Mailing Add:* 13244 W Ballad Dr Sun City West AZ 85375

STRECKER, GEORGE EDISON, CATEGORICAL TOPOLOGY. *Current Pos:* assoc prof, 72-77, PROF MATH, KANS STATE UNIV, 77- *Personal Data:* b Ft Collins, Colo, Feb 25, 38; m 60, Julianne Tague; c Cheryl & Marc. *Educ:* Univ Colo, Boulder, BS & BS, 61; Tulane Univ, La, PhD(math), 66. *Prof Exp:* Instr math, Univ Colo, 58-60; teaching asst, Tulane Univ, La, 64-65; res assoc, Univ Amsterdam, 65-66, Fulbright fel, 65-66; fel, Univ Fla, 66-67; asst prof, 67-71; assoc prof, Univ Pittsburgh, 71-72. *Concurrent Pos:* Vis prof math, Vrije Univ, Amsterdam & Inst Univ L'Aquila, Italy, 80, 81; Czech Acad Sci exchange scholar, 80, 87, Hungarian Acad Sci exchange scholar, US Nat Acad Sci, 87. *Mem:* Am Math Soc; Math Asn Am. *Res:* Categorical topology; topological functors; initial and final completions of categories; factorization structures; compactifications of topological spaces; computer sciences; theoretical computer science; Galois connections. *Mailing Add:* Dept Math Kans State Univ Manhattan KS 66506. *E-Mail:* strecker@math.ksu.edu

STRECKER, HAROLD ARTHUR, INORGANIC CHEMISTRY. *Current Pos:* RETIRED. *Personal Data:* b Marietta, Ohio, June 11, 18; m 42; c 5. *Educ:* Cornell Univ, AB, 40, PhD(chem), 48. *Prof Exp:* Chemist, Marietta Dyestuff Co, 40-41 & Nat Defense Comn, 42-45; res assoc, Standard Oil Co, Ohio, 47-58, supvr process res, 58-60, sr res assoc, 60-68, supvr spectros & micros, 69-81. *Mem:* Am Chem Soc; Soc Appl Spectros; Sigma Xi. *Res:* Catalysis; reaction kinetics; atomic spectroscopy; x-ray fluorescence and diffraction; electron microscopy. *Mailing Add:* 7131 Rotary Dr Walton Hills OH 44146-4341

STRECKER, JOSEPH LAWRENCE, THEORETICAL PHYSICS. *Current Pos:* ASSOC PROF PHYSICS, WICHITA STATE UNIV, 68- *Personal Data:* b Kansas City, Mo, Mar 30, 32; m 60; c 2. *Educ:* Rockhurst Col, BS, 55; Johns Hopkins Univ, PhD(physics), 61. *Prof Exp:* Jr instr physics, Johns Hopkins Univ, 55-58, res asst, 58- 61, sr res scientist, Gen Dynamics, Ft Worth, 61-66; assoc prof physics, Univ Dallas, 66-68. *Concurrent Pos:* Adj prof, Tex Christian Univ, 62-67. *Mem:* Am Phys Soc. *Res:* Superconductivity; quantum field theory and application to solid state phenomena; statistical mechanics, especially phase transitions. *Mailing Add:* 161 S Belmont St Wichita KS 67218

STRECKER, WILLIAM D, SOFTWARE SYSTEMS. *Current Pos:* VPRES ENG, DIGITAL EQUIP CORP, 89-, CHIEF TECH OFFICER, 92- *Honors & Awards:* W W McDowell Award, Inst Elec & Electronics Engrs, 85. *Mem:* Nat Acad Eng. *Mailing Add:* 111 Powdermill Rd MSO 2-2/B7 Maynard MA 01754

STRECKFUSS, JOSEPH LARRY, MICROBIOLOGY, IMMUNOLOGY. *Current Pos:* RETIRED. *Personal Data:* b Shirley, Mo, Feb 23, 31; m 52; c 3. *Educ:* Southern Ill Univ, Carbondale, BA, 58, MA, 61, PhD(virol, immunol), 68. *Prof Exp:* Dir diag microbiol, Holden Hosp, Carbondale, Ill 57-66; asst res prof oral microbiol, Univ Tex Dent Br, 68-74, assoc prof microbiol, Dept Path & assoc prof in residence, Dent Sci Inst, 74-90. *Concurrent Pos:* Comt mem curric, Univ Tex Grad Sch Biomed Sci, Houston, 71- *Res:* Mechanism of calcification of Streptococcus mutans, a cariogenic microorganism; effect of fluoride resistance on the organisms adherence potential and carcinogenic properties. *Mailing Add:* 3407 Blue Candle Spring TX 77388

STREEBIN, LEALE E, ENVIRONMENTAL ENGINEERING, MICROBIOLOGY. *Current Pos:* PRES, SEARCH INC, 70- *Personal Data:* b Blockton, Iowa, June 21, 34; m 56; c 4. *Educ:* Iowa State Univ, BS, 61; Ore State Univ, MS, 65, PhD(civil eng), 67. *Prof Exp:* Surveyor, US Army, 51-58; proj engr, Powers, Willis & Assocs, Planners, Engrs & Archit, 61-62, design room supvr, 62-63; from assoc prof to prof civil eng & environ sci, Univ Okla, 66-90, dir, 79-89. *Concurrent Pos:* Lectr, WHO & Pan Am Health Orgn; consult, indust waste treatment & environ probs. *Mem:* Am Soc Civil Engrs; Water Pollution Control Fedn; Am Water Works Asn; Nat Soc Prof Engrs. *Res:* Industrial and hazardous waste treatment; process design; optimization of aerobic biological waste treatment systems; land treatment of industrial wastes; impoundment and stream studies. *Mailing Add:* 2301 Morgan Dr Norman OK 73069

STREET, DANA MORRIS, ORTHOPEDIC SURGERY. *Current Pos:* prof, 75-80, EMER PROF ORTHOP, LOMA LINDA UNIV, 80- *Personal Data:* b New York, NY, May 7, 10; m 40, Elna A Clare; c Rosalyn C, Dana C, Steven M & William M. *Educ:* Haverford Col, BS, 32; Cornell Univ, MD, 36. *Prof Exp:* Chief orthop sect, Kennedy Vet Admin Hosp, Memphis, Tenn, 46-59; prof surg, Sch Med, Univ Ark, 59-62; prof surg in residence, Sch Med, Univ Calif, Los Angeles, 62-75; head orthop div, Harbor Gen Hosp, 62-75 & Riverside Gen Hosp, 75-77; chief orthop sect, Jerry L Pettis Mem Hosp, 77-80. *Concurrent Pos:* Mem staff, Orthop Hosp, Los Angeles, 63-, St Mary's Hosp & Mem Hosp, Long Beach, Calif, 63-75. *Mem:* AMA; Am Orthop Asn; Asn Bone & Joint Surgeons; Am Acad Orthop Surgeons; Western Orthop Asn; Am Fracture Asn. *Res:* Fracture treatment by use of medullary nail, particularly in femur and forearm; treatment and rehabilitation of the paraplegic. *Mailing Add:* 44201 Village 44 Camarillo CA 93012-8935

STREET, KENNETH NORMAN, advanced composite materials, fracture & failure mechanisms, for more information see previous edition

STREET, ROBERT A, PHYSICS. *Current Pos:* RES SCIENTIST, XEROX CORP, CALIF. *Honors & Awards:* David Adler Lectureship Award, Am Physics Soc, 92. *Mailing Add:* Palo Alto Res Ctr Xerox Corp 3333 Coyote Hill Rd Palo Alto CA 94304-1314

STREET, ROBERT ELLIOTT, AERODYNAMICS, NUMERICAL ANALYSIS. *Current Pos:* RETIRED. *Personal Data:* b Belmont, NY, Dec 11, 12; m 41, 69; c 3. *Educ:* Rensselaer Polytech Inst, BS, 33; Harvard Univ, AM, 34, PhD(math, physics), 39. *Prof Exp:* Instr math, Rensselaer Polytech Inst, 37-41; asst physicist, Nat Adv Comt Aeronaut, Langley Field, Va, 41-43; asst prof physics, Dartmouth Col, 43-44; engr, Gen Elec Co, NY, 44-47; assoc prof, Univ NMex, 47-48; from assoc prof to prof, Univ Wash, 48-80, emer prof aeronaut & astronaut, 80-84. *Mem:* Am Inst Aeronaut & Astronaut; Math Asn Am; fel Explorers Club. *Res:* Numerical fluid mechanics. *Mailing Add:* 2818 Old Fairhaven Pkwy Bellingham WA 98225

STREET, ROBERT L(YNNWOOD), fluid mechanics, computational fluid dynamics, for more information see previous edition

STREET, ROBERT LEWIS, industrial engineering, for more information see previous edition

STREET, WILLIAM G(EORGE), AERONAUTICAL ENGINEERING. *Current Pos:* RETIRED. *Personal Data:* b Washington, DC, Dec 1, 17; m 43; c 5. *Educ:* Cath Univ, BAE, 38. *Prof Exp:* Jr aeronaut engr, Nat Adv Comt Aeronaut, 38-39; chief flight test engr, Martin Co, 39-43, preliminary design engr, 45-50; chief flight test engr, Convair Div, Gen Dynamics Corp, 43-45; proj chmn opers res off, Johns Hopkins Univ, 50-53; from proj engr to res & adv tech mkt mgr, Martin-Marietta Corp, 53-67; Wash rep, Bell Aerosysts Co, 67-70; opers res analyst, Tech Anal Div, Nat Bur Standards, 70-74, gen engr, Ctr Bldg Technol, 74-81. *Mem:* Opers Res Soc Am; assoc Am Inst Aeronaut & Astronaut. *Res:* Nuclear propulsion; operations research; aerodynamics; flight testing; weapons systems requirements. *Mailing Add:* 516 Wyngate Rd Timonium MD 21093

STREETEN, DAVID HENRY PALMER, INTERNAL MEDICINE. *Current Pos:* assoc prof, 60-64, PROF MED, STATE UNIV NY HEALTH SCI CTR, 64- *Personal Data:* b Bloemfontein, SAfrica, Oct 3, 21; nat US; m 52, Barbara A Wiard; c Robert D, Elizabeth A & John P. *Educ:* Univ Witwatersrand, MB, BCh, 46; Oxford Univ, DPhil(pharmacol), 51. *Prof Exp:* Intern med & surg, Gen Hosp, Johannesburg, SAfrica, 47; jr lectr med, Univ Witwatersrand, 48; Nuffield demonstr pharmacol, Oxford Univ, 48-51; asst med, Peter Bent Brigham Hosp, Boston, 51-53, jr assoc, 53; from instr to asst prof internal med, Univ Mich Hosp, 53-60. *Concurrent Pos:* Rockefeller traveling fel & res fel med, Harvard Univ, 51-52; investr, Howard Hughes Found, 55-61; consult, Vet Admin Hosp, Syracuse, 61-, Crouse Irving Mem Hosp, 61-, St Joseph's Hosp, 64- & Utica State Hosp, 65- *Mem:* Endocrine Soc; Am Fedn Clin Res; Fel Col Physicians; Fel AAAS. *Res:* Physiology and pathology of adrenal cortex, especially effects of its secretions on water and electrolyte metabolism and their role in causation of disease; normal and abnormal control of blood pressure. *Mailing Add:* Dept Med State Univ NY Hosp Syracuse NY 13210-3000. *Fax:* 315-464-8280

STREETER, JOHN GEMMIL, PLANT PHYSIOLOGY, AGRONOMY. *Current Pos:* From asst prof to assoc prof, 69-78, PROF AGRON, OHIO AGR RES & DEVELOP CTR, OHIO STATE UNIV, 78- *Personal Data:* b Ellwood City, Pa, Feb 25, 36; m 60, Mary A; c Mark E. *Educ:* Pa State Univ,

BS, 58, MS, 64; Cornell Univ, PhD(bot), 69. *Mem:* Fel, Am Soc Agron; Am Soc Plant Physiol; Am Soc Microbiol; fel Crop Sci Soc Am. *Res:* Nitrogen metabolism in plants; amino acid biosynthesis; carbohydrate metabolism in legume nodules. *Mailing Add:* Dept Agron Ohio Agr Res & Develop Ctr Wooster OH 44691. *Fax:* 216-263-3658

STREETER, LYNN ANNE, SOCIAL & BUSINESS IMPACT OF TECHNOLOGY, SOFTWARE ENGINEERING. *Current Pos:* SR DIR, US WEST ADVAN TECHNOL, 93- *Personal Data:* b Midland, Mich; m 85, Thomas Landauer; c Elizabeth Landauer. *Educ:* Univ Mich, BA, 69; Columbia Univ, PhD(psychol), 74. *Prof Exp:* Supvr human factors eng, Bell Labs, 79-81, mem tech staff, Commun Res Dept, 81-83; dir appl res, Bellcore, 84-93. *Concurrent Pos:* Mem, Bd Army Sci & Technol, Comn Eng & Tech Systs, Nat Res Coun, 94-95. *Mem:* Sigma Xi; Asn Comput Mach. *Res:* Business and societal impact of ubiquitous networks; software organization that implements internet applications for end-users. *Mailing Add:* 625 Utica Ave Boulder CO 80304. *E-Mail:* lstreet@advtech.uswest.com

STREETER, ROBERT GLEN, WATERFOWL MANAGEMENT, WILDLIFE RESEARCH. *Current Pos:* ASST DIR REFUGES & WILDLIFE, US DEPT INTERIOR, 95- *Personal Data:* b Madison, SDak, Feb 1, 41; m 64, Karen Johnson; c Shawn & Seth. *Educ:* SDak State Univ, BS, 63; Va Polytech Inst & State Univ, MS, 65; Colo State Univ, PhD(wildlife biol, physiol), 69. *Prof Exp:* Asst biologist avian depredation res, SDak State Dept Game, Fish & Parks, 63; res asst elk range ecol, Va Coop Wildlife Res Unit, US Fish & Wildlife Serv, 63-65; res asst bighorn sheep ecol & mgt, Colo Coop Wildlife Res Unit, 65-69; res physiologist, USAF Sch Aerospace Med, Brooks AFB, Tex, 69-72; wildlife biologist & res asst leader, Colo Coop Wildlife Res Unit, Colo State Univ & US Fish & Wildlife Serv, 72-73; head coop wildlife units, Div Res, US Fish & Wildlife Serv, Washington, DC, 73-75, coal proj res mgr, 75-79, prof design, 79-81, asst team leader tech appln, Western Energy & Land Use Team, 81-83, chief, Off Info Transfer, Res & Develop, 83-88. *Concurrent Pos:* Vis mem grad fac, Tex A&M Univ, 71-72; asst prof, Colo State Univ, 72-73; dep exec dir, NAm Waterfowl Mgt Off, US Secy Interior, exec dir & coordr, NAm Wetlands Conserv Coun, 95. *Mem:* Sigma Xi; Wildlife Soc; Soc Wetlands Scientists. *Res:* Effects of coal extraction, conversion, transportation and related social developments on fish and wildlife populations, development of mitigation options and management decision alternatives; applications of computerized methodologies to wildlife management; national wildlife appraisal methods; scientific information transfer; waterfowl management; population dynamics of bighorn sheep; wetland habitat conservation; altitude physiology in low oxygen and high carbon dioxide environments. *Mailing Add:* Dept Interior 1849 C St NW Rm 3246 Washington DC 20240

STREETMAN, BEN GARLAND, ELECTRICAL ENGINEERING. *Current Pos:* Earnest F Gloyna regents chair Eng, 86-89, PROF ELEC ENG, UNIV TEX, AUSTIN, 82-, DULA D COCKRELL CENTENNIAL CHAIR, 89-, DEANS CHAIR EXCELLENCE, 96- *Personal Data:* b Cooper, Tex, June 24, 39; m 61; c 2. *Educ:* Univ Tex, Austin, BS, 61, MS, 63, PhD(elec eng), 66. *Honors & Awards:* Frederick Emmons Terman Award, Am Soc Eng Educ, 81, AT&T Found Award, 87; Educ Medal, Inst Elec & Electronics Engrs, 89. *Prof Exp:* From asst prof to assoc prof, Univ Ill, Urbana-Champaign, 66-74, res assoc prof, 70-74, prof elec eng, 74-82, res prof, Coord Sci Lab, 74-82. *Concurrent Pos:* Dir, Micro Elec Res Ctr, Univ Tex, Austin, 84- *Mem:* Nat Acad Eng; fel Inst Elec & Electronics Engrs; fel Electrochem Soc; Mat Res Soc. *Res:* Semiconductor materials and devices; molecular beam epitaxy; multilayer heterojunctions in III-V compounds; radiation damage and ion implantation in semiconductors; luminence in semiconductors. *Mailing Add:* Col Eng ECJ10 310 Univ Tex Austin TX 78712. *Fax:* 512-475-7072; *E-Mail:* bstreet@mail.utex.edu

STREETMAN, JOHN ROBERT, physical chemistry, for more information see previous edition

STREETS, DAVID GEORGE, ENVIRONMENTAL SCIENCE, PHYSICAL CHEMISTRY. *Current Pos:* res assoc, 74-75, asst environ scientist, 76-78, environ scientist, Off Environ Policy Anal, 79-85, ENVIRON SCIENTIST, ENERGY & ENVIRON SYSTS DIV, ARGONNE NAT LAB, 85- *Personal Data:* b Lincoln, Eng, Aug 13, 47; m 72; c 2. *Educ:* Univ London, BSc, 68, PhD(physics), 71. *Prof Exp:* NSF fel chem, Univ Rochester, 71-72; Imperial Chem Industs fel physics, Univ London, 72-74. *Mem:* Royal Inst Chem; Brit Inst Physics; Am Chem Soc; Air Pollution Control Asn. *Res:* Environmental policy analysis; acid rain control strategies; renewable energy resources; photoelectron spectroscopy and chemical structure. *Mailing Add:* 1512 Winterberry Lane Darien IL 60561

STREETS, RUBERT BURLEY, JR, electrical engineering; deceased, see previous edition for last biography

STREETT, WILLIAM BERNARD, PHYSICAL CHEMISTRY, HIGH PRESSURE PHYSICS. *Current Pos:* vpres, 94-96, PRES, IMPACT-ECHO CONSULTS, ITHACA NY, 96-; JOS SILBERT EMER DEAN ENG, CORNELL UNIV, 95- *Personal Data:* b Lake Village, Ark, Jan 27, 32; m 55, Jackie Heard; c 4. *Educ:* US Mil Acad, BS, 55; Univ Mich, MS, 61, PhD(mech eng), 63. *Prof Exp:* Instr astron & astronaut, US Mil Acad, 61-62 & 63-64, asst prof, 64-65; NATO res fel low temperature chem, Oxford Univ, 65-67; asst dean acad res & dir, Sci Res Lab, US Mil Acad, W Point, 67-78; sr res assoc, Cornell Univ, 78-81, prof & assoc dean, 81-84, Jos Silbert dean eng, 84-93. *Concurrent Pos:* Guggenheim fel, Oxford Univ, 74-75. *Mem:* Am Concrete Inst; Sigma Xi. *Res:* Experimental measurements of physical and thermodynamic properties of fluids and fluid mixtures at high pressures; computer simulations of liquids; nondestructive testing of concrete and masonry structures. *Mailing Add:* Sch Chem Eng Cornell Univ Olin Hall Ithaca NY 14853. *Fax:* 607-255-9004; *E-Mail:* wbs3@cornell.edu

STREEVER, RALPH L, SOLID STATE PHYSICS. *Personal Data:* b Schenectady, NY, June 7, 34; m 64; c 2. *Educ:* Union Col, NY, BS, 55; Rutgers Univ, PhD(physics), 60. *Prof Exp:* Physicist, Nat Bur Standards, 60-66, US Army Electronics Technol & Devices Lab, 66-82. *Mem:* Am Phys Soc. *Res:* Magnetism and nuclear magnetic resonance in ferromagnetic materials; semiconductor device physics. *Mailing Add:* 11310 Dockside Circle Reston VA 20191

STREHLER, BERNARD LOUIS, BIOLOGY, BIOCHEMISTRY. *Current Pos:* PROF BIOL SCI, UNIV SOUTHERN CALIF, 67- *Personal Data:* b Johnstown, Pa, Feb 21, 25; m 48; c 3. *Educ:* Johns Hopkins Univ, BS, 47, PhD, 50. *Honors & Awards:* Karl August Forster Prize, Ger Acad Sci & Lett, 75. *Prof Exp:* Biochemist, Oak Ridge Nat Lab, 50-53; asst prof biochem, Univ Chicago, 53-56; chief cellular & comp physiol sect, Geront Res Ctr, Nat Inst Child Health & Human Develop, 56-67. *Concurrent Pos:* Dir aging res satellite lab, Vet Admin Hosp, Baltimore, Md, 64-67. *Mem:* Am Soc Biol Chemists; Soc Develop Biol; Geront Soc; Am Soc Naturalists. *Res:* Bioluminescence; photosynthesis; aging; bioenergetics. *Mailing Add:* 2310 Laguna Circle Dr Agoura CA 91301

STREHLER, EMANUEL ERNST, INTRACELLULAR CALCIUM HOMEOSTASIS, MOLECULAR GENETICS OF CALCIUM TRANSPORT-SIGNALLING. *Current Pos:* CONSULT & ASSOC PROF BIOCHEM, MAYO CLIN FOUND, 92- *Personal Data:* b Zurich, Switz, June 17, 54; m 81, Marie-Antoinette Page; c Kevin Y. *Educ:* Swiss Fed Inst Technol, MS, 77, PhD(cell biol), 81. *Honors & Awards:* Latsis Prize, Int Latsis Found, Swiss Fed Inst Technol, 90. *Prof Exp:* Fel, Swiss Fed Inst Technol, 81-82, from asst prof to assoc prof, 86-92; Europ Molecular Biol Orgn fel, Univ Umea, Sweden, 81; fel, Harvard Med Sch, 82-84, instr pediat & res fel cardiol, 84-86. *Concurrent Pos:* High sch chem teacher, Kantonsschule Stadelhofen, Switz, 79; fel young advan researchers, Swiss Nat Sci Found, 82-84; prin investr, Swiss Nat Sci Found, 88-94. *Mem:* Am Soc Cell Biol; AAAS; NY Acad Sci; Swiss Soc Cell Biol, Molecular Biol & Genetics; Swiss Soc Biochem; Am Soc Biochem & Molecular Biol. *Res:* Gene organization, regulation, and alternative splicing options of plasma membrane calcium pumps; distribution and functional significance in normal and diseased cells; molecular genetics of human calmodulin multigene family; structure and function of calmodulin-like protein and its possible role in cell differentiation. *Mailing Add:* Dept Biochem & Molecular Biol Mayo Clin Rochester MN 55905. *Fax:* 507-284-2384; *E-Mail:* strehler@mayo.edu

STREHLOW, CLIFFORD DAVID, environmental sciences, for more information see previous edition

STREHLOW, RICHARD ALAN, CHEMISTRY. *Current Pos:* RES STAFF MEM, UNION CARBIDE NUCLEAR CO, OAK RIDGE NAT LAB, 56- *Personal Data:* b Chicago, Ill, Sept 20, 27; m 77; c 1. *Educ:* Univ Chicago, SB, 48; Univ Ill, PhD(chem), 57. *Mem:* Am Chem Soc; Am Vacuum Soc; Am Soc Testing & Mat; Am Nuclear Soc; Sigma Xi. *Res:* Catalysis and surface chemistry, coal conversion, electro-organic and fused salt chemistry; high vacuum research; mass spectrometry; fusion reactor design; graphite fabrication research. *Mailing Add:* PO Box 52327 Knoxville TN 37950-2327

STREIB, JOHN FREDRICK, PHYSICS. *Current Pos:* from asst prof to prof, 47-80, EMER PROF PHYSICS, UNIV WASH, 80- *Personal Data:* b Avalon, Pa, Mar 21, 15; m 46, 54. *Educ:* Calif Inst Technol, BS, 36, PhD(physics), 41. *Prof Exp:* Asst physicist, Carnegie Inst Technol, 41; asst physicist, Nat Bur Stand, 41-42, assoc physicist, 42-43, physicist, 43; scientist, Los Alamos Sci Lab, 43-46; mem tech staff, Bell Tel Labs, Inc, NY, 46; asst prof physics, Univ Colo, 46-47. *Mem:* Am Phys Soc. *Res:* Nuclear physics; fluorine plus proton reactions; positron absorption. *Mailing Add:* 12507 Greenwood Ave ND Seattle WA 98133

STREIB, W(ILLIAM) C(HARLES), CHEMICAL ENGINEERING. *Current Pos:* RETIRED. *Personal Data:* b Brooklyn, NY, Apr 5, 20; m 47, Doris Watt; c Charles H & John A. *Educ:* Pa State Univ, BS, 42; Newark Col Eng, MS, 53. *Prof Exp:* Jr res engr, Res Ctr, Johns-Manville Corp, 42-44, res engr, 46-50, sr res engr, 50-60, chief, Asbestos Fiber Sect, 60-61, res mgr, Asbestos Fiber Dept, 61-71, dir res & develop, minerals & filtration technol, Manville Corp, 72-82, vpres sales corp, 72-82. *Res:* Diatomaceous earth; perlite and talc, especially new product development for use in filtration and filler applications; asbestos, especially processing, uses and evaluations. *Mailing Add:* 6381 W Fremont Dr Littleton CO 80123

STREIB, WILLIAM E, PHYSICAL CHEMISTRY. *Current Pos:* instr phys chem, 63-64, asst prof chem, 64-68, from assoc prof to prof, 64-79, CRYSTALLOGR, DEPT CHEM, IND UNIV, BLOOMINGTON, 79- *Personal Data:* b New Salem, NDak, Mar 16, 31; m 61; c 2. *Educ:* Jamestown Col, BS, 53; Univ NDak, MS, 55; Univ Minn, PhD(phys chem), 62. *Prof Exp:* Fel, Harvard Univ, 62-63. *Mem:* Sigma Xi; Am Crystallog Asn. *Res:* X-ray crystallography; crystal and molecular structure; low temperature x-ray diffraction techniques. *Mailing Add:* 4501 E Blackstone Ct Bloomington IN 47408

STREICHER, EUGENE, NEUROPHYSIOLOGY. *Current Pos:* neurophysiologist, Sect Aging, NIMH, 54-62, physiologist, Nat Inst Neurol Dis & Stroke, SCIENTIST ADMINR, NAT INST NEUROL DIS & STROKE, 64- *Personal Data:* b New York, NY, Oct 25, 26; m 51. *Educ:* Cornell Univ, BA, 47, MA, 48; Univ Chicago, PhD(physiol), 53. *Prof Exp:* Physiologist, US Army Chem Ctr, Md, 48-50. *Mem:* AAAS; Soc Exp Biol & Med; Am Asn Neuropath; Soc Neuroscience. *Res:* Physiological chemistry of central nervous system. *Mailing Add:* 6521 Greentree Rd Bethesda MD 20817

STREICHER, MICHAEL A(LFRED), METALLURGY, CHEMISTRY. *Current Pos:* CONSULT, CORROSION, 88- *Personal Data:* b Heidelberg, Ger, Sept 6, 21; nat US; m 47, Margaret; c 2. *Educ:* Rensselaer Polytech Inst, BChE, 43; Syracuse Univ, MChE, 45; Lehigh Univ, PhD(phys metall), 48. *Honors & Awards:* Turner Prize & Young Author Prize, Electrochem Soc, 49; Willis Rodney Whitney Award, Nat Asn Corrosion Engrs, 72; Sam Tour Award, Am Soc Testing & Math, 79. *Prof Exp:* Res assoc, Lehigh Univ, 48; res eng, E I du Pont de Nemours & Co, Inc, 49-52, res proj engr, 52-56, res assoc, 56-67, res fel, 67-79; res prof, Dept Mech Eng, Univ Del, 79-88. *Concurrent Pos:* Chmn, Gordon Conf Corrosion, 62 & subcomt corrosion, Welding Res Coun, 66-87; mem review panels, Dept Energy. *Mem:* AAAS; fel Am Soc Metals; fel Nat Asn Corrosion Engrs; Sigma Xi; Am Soc Testing & Mat. *Res:* Corrosion theory; passivity; inhibition; conversion coatings; influence of metallurgical factors on chemical reactivity of metals; corrosion evaluation tests; electrochemistry; stainless steels; nickel-base alloys and development of new alloys. *Mailing Add:* 1409 Jan Dr Wilmington DE 19803

STREIFF, ANTON JOSEPH, PETROLEUM CHEMISTRY. *Current Pos:* sr res chemist, Carnegie-Mellon Univ, 50-71, asst chmn dept chem, 66-74, dir, Am Petrol Inst Res Proj, 58, 60-67, prin res chemist, 72-84, admin officer, dept chem, 74-84, consult dept chem, 84-85, EMER ADMIN OFFICER & PRIN RES CHEMIST, CARNEGIE-MELLON UNIV, 84- *Personal Data:* b Jackson, Mich, Apr 1, 15; m 41, 86; c 4. *Educ:* Univ Mich, BS, 36, MS, 37. *Prof Exp:* Res assoc, Nat Bur Stand, 37-50. *Mem:* Am Chem Soc; Sigma Xi. *Res:* Fractionation, purification, purity and analysis of hydrocarbons; American Petroleum Institute standard reference materials. *Mailing Add:* 1102 Tanbank W Jackson MI 49203

STREIFF, RICHARD REINHART, MEDICINE, HEMATOLOGY. *Current Pos:* from asst prof to assoc prof, 68-74, CHIEF HEMAT UNIT, VET ADMIN HOSP, GAINSVILLE, UNIV FLA, 72-, CHIEF MED SERV, 73-, PROF MED, 74- *Personal Data:* b Highland, Ill, June 1, 29; m 59; c 3. *Educ:* Wash Univ, AB, 51; Univ Basel, MD, 59. *Prof Exp:* Intern med, Harvard Med Serv, Boston City Hosp, 59-60; intern, Mt Auburn Hosp, Cambridge, Mass, 60-61, resident, 61-62; resident, Harvard Med Serv, Boston City Hosp, 62-63; instr med, Harvard Med Sch, 66-68. *Concurrent Pos:* Res fel hemat, Thorndike Med Lab, Harvard Med Sch, 63-68; clin investr, Vet Admin, 69-71. *Mem:* Am Soc Hemat; Am Fedn Clin Res; Am Soc Clin Nutrit; Am Inst Nutrit; Fedn Am Socs Exp Biol. *Res:* Vitamin B-12 and folic acid deficiency anemias; metabolism and biological function of vitamin B-12 and folic acid; synthesis and testing of iron chelators. *Mailing Add:* Dept Med Gainesville Va Hosp 1601 Archer Rd Gainesville FL 32608. *Fax:* 352-374-6116

STREILEIN, JACOB WAYNE, IMMUNOLOGY, GENETICS. *Current Pos:* DIR, SCHEPENS EYE RES INST, HARVARD MED SCH, 93-, PROF & VCHAIR RES, DEPT OPHTHAL. *Personal Data:* b Johnstown, Pa, June 19, 35; m 57, Joan Stein; c Laura A, William W & Robert D. *Educ:* Gettysburg Col, AB, 56; Univ Pa, MD, 60. *Honors & Awards:* Proctor Medal for Outstanding Res in Ophthal & Visual Sci, 66. *Prof Exp:* Intern, Univ Hosp, Univ Pa, 60-61, resident internal med, 61-63, from asst prof to assoc prof med genetics, Sch Med, 66-71; prof cell biol & prof med, Univ Tex Southwestern Med Sch, Dallas, 72-84; prof & chmn, Dept Microbiol & Immunol, Univ Miami Sch Med, 84-93. *Concurrent Pos:* Fel allergy & immunol, Univ Pa, 63-64; fel transplantation immunity, Wistar Inst Anat & Biol, 64-65; Markle scholar acad med, 68-74. *Mem:* Am Asn Immunol; Transplantation Soc; Int Soc Eye Res; Soc Invest Dermat; Asn Res Vision & Ophthal. *Res:* Transplantation immunobiology with special reference to cellular immunity, immunoregulation, graft-versus-host disease, immunogenetic disparity; contact hypersensitivity; immunologic privilege. *Mailing Add:* 44 Neptune St Beverly MA 01915. *Fax:* 617-723-8983; *E-Mail:* waynes@vision.eri.harvard.edu

STREIPS, ULDIS NORMUNDS, MICROBIOLOGY. *Current Pos:* From asst prof to assoc prof, 72-88, PROF MICROBIAL GENETICS, SCH MED, UNIV LOUISVILLE, 88-, VCHAIR, 89- *Personal Data:* b Riga, Latvia, Feb 1, 42; US citizen; m 75; c 2. *Educ:* Valparaiso Univ, BA, 64; Northwestern Univ, PhD(microbiol), 69. *Concurrent Pos:* Damon Runyon Mem Fund Cancer res grant microbial genetics, Scripps Clin & Res Found, 69-70 & Sch Med & Dent, Univ Rochester, 70-72. *Mem:* AAAS; Am Soc Microbiol; foreign mem, Latvian Acad Sci. *Res:* Genetic transformation in Bacillus subtilis; molecular biology of Bacillus thuringiensis; restriction endonucleases; cloning systems; mutagenesis assays; heat shock in prokaryotes. *Mailing Add:* Dept Microbiol & Immunol Univ Louisville Sch Med 2301 S Third St Louisville KY 40292-0001

STREIT, GERALD EDWARD, CHEMISTRY. *Current Pos:* STAFF MEM, LOS ALAMOS NAT LAB, 76-, PROJ LEADER, AIR QUAL STUDIES, 90- *Personal Data:* b Los Angeles, Calif, Dec 22, 48; m 74; c 2. *Educ:* Univ Tex, Austin, BS, 70; Univ Calif, Berkeley, PhD(chem), 74. *Prof Exp:* Nat Res Coun fel, Nat Oceanic & Atmospheric Admin, 74-76. *Mem:* Am Chem Soc. *Res:* Weak plasma interactions; ion-molecule kinetics and mechanisms; electron attachment; small cluster formation; application to chemical ionization mass spectroscometry; kinetics and dynamics of gas-phase neutral systems, particularly in application to atmospheric chemistry and combustion chemistry. *Mailing Add:* Los Alamos Nat Lab PO Box 1663 MS-F604 TSA-4 Los Alamos NM 87545

STREIT, ROY LEON, BAYESIAN INFERENCE NETWORKS, FAULT TOLERANT CONTROL. *Current Pos:* MATHEMATICIAN, SONAR SYSTS RES, US NAVAL UNDERWATER SYSTS CTR, 70- *Personal Data:* b Guthrie, Okla, Oct 14, 47; m 80, Nancy Black; c Adamson, Andrew & Katherine. *Educ:* ETex State Univ, BA, 68; Univ Mo, MA, 70; Univ RI, PhD(math), 78. *Concurrent Pos:* Vis scholar, Stanford Univ, 81-82; vis scientist, Yale Univ, 82-84; exchange scientist, Defense Sci & Technol Orgn, Adelaide, Australia, 87-89. *Mem:* Sr mem Inst Elec & Electronics Engrs; Soc Indust & Appl Math. *Res:* Multitarget tracking and data association; application of Bayesian inference networks and artificial neural networks to sonar detection, classification and localization; emphasis is placed on statistical methods for network characterization and training. *Mailing Add:* US Naval Undersea Warfare Ctr Div 1176 Howell St Code 2002 Bldg 1176 1st Floor Newport RI 02841-1708. *Fax:* 401-841-4749; *E-Mail:* streit@c223.npt.nuwc.navy.mil

STREITFELD, MURRAY MARK, MICROBIOLOGY, CHEMOTHERAPY. *Current Pos:* RETIRED. *Personal Data:* b New York, NY, Sept 16, 22; c 1. *Educ:* City Col New York, BS, 43; McGill Univ, MS, 48; Univ Calif, Los Angeles, PhD(microbiol), 52. *Prof Exp:* Asst chemist toxicol, Off Chief Med Examr, NY, 43; instr, Med Lab, Beaumont Gen Hosp, Tex, 45-46; teaching asst bact, McGill Univ, 47-48 & Univ Calif, Los Angeles, 51-52; from instr to assoc prof microbiol, Sch Med, Univ Miami, 53-97. *Concurrent Pos:* Instr, Med Lab, Brookes Med Ctr, Tex, 45-46; res bacteriologist, Nat Children's Cardiac Hosp, Miami, Fla, 52-57; asst dir, Res Bact Lab, Variety Children's Hosp, 57-59, res assoc, Variety Res Found, 60-; resident attend, Vet Admin Hosp, Coral Gables, 60- *Mem:* Sigma Xi. *Res:* Bacteriology; rheumatic fever; antibiotics; prophylaxis of dental infection; streptococcal and staphylococcal epidemiology; pseudomonas and gonorrhea immunity; gamma globulin; staphylococcal toxins; gonococcal cellular immunity; streptococcal virulence; antibiotics. *Mailing Add:* Dept Microbiol & Immunol PO Box 01690 Univ Miami Sch Med 1600 NW Tenth Ave Miami FL 33101

STREITWIESER, ANDREW, JR, PHYSICAL ORGANIC CHEMISTRY, QUANTUM CHEMISTRY. *Current Pos:* From instr to prof, 52-93, EMER PROF CHEM, UNIV CALIF, BERKELEY, 93- *Personal Data:* b Buffalo, NY, June 23, 27; m 67, Suzanne Cope; c David R & Susan A. *Educ:* Columbia Univ, AB, 48, MA, 50, PhD(chem), 52. *Honors & Awards:* Award, Am Chem Soc, 67 & Phys Org Chem Award, 82; Sr Scientist Award, Humboldt Found, 76; Arthur Cope Scholar Award, Am Chem Soc, 89. *Concurrent Pos:* Sloan Found fel, Univ Calif, Berkeley, 58-62; NSF fac fel, 59-60; Miller Inst fel, 64-65 & 79-80; Guggenheim fel, 69; assoc ed, J Org Chem, 89-97. *Mem:* Nat Acad Sci; AAAS; Am Chem Soc; Am Acad Arts & Sci; corresp mem Bavarian Acad Sci; Ger Chem Soc. *Res:* Theoretical organic chemistry; molecular orbital theory; reaction mechanisms; isotope effects; acidity and basicity; rare earth organometallic chemistry; synthetic inorganic and organometallic chemistry. *Mailing Add:* Dept Chem Univ Calif Berkeley CA 94720-1460. *Fax:* 510-642-0336; *E-Mail:* astreit@socrates.berkeley.edu

STREJAN, GILL HENRIC, IMMUNOLOGY. *Current Pos:* from asst prof to prof, 68-96, EMER PROF IMMUNOL, UNIV WESTERN ONT, 96- *Personal Data:* b Galati, Romania, Sept 24, 30; m 63, Odette Fischer. *Educ:* Univ Bucharest, MS, 53; Hebrew Univ, Jerusalem, PhD(immunol), 65. *Prof Exp:* Instr bact & immunol, Hebrew Univ, Jerusalem, 63-65. *Concurrent Pos:* Res fel, NIH training grant & Fulbright travel grant immunochem, Calif Inst Technol, 65-68. *Mem:* Am Asn Immunol; Can Soc Immunol; Sigma Xi. *Res:* Regulation of immunoglobulin E-mediated hypersensitivity; immunologic aspects of experimental allergic encephalomyelitis and multiple sclerosis. *Mailing Add:* Dept Microbiol & Immunol Univ Western Ont London ON N6A 5C1 Can. *Fax:* 519-661-3499; *E-Mail:* gstrejan@julian.uwo.ca

STREKAS, THOMAS C, INORGANIC & BIOINORGANIC CHEMISTRY. *Current Pos:* asst prof, 78-81, ASSOC PROF CHEM, DEPT CHEM, QUEENS COL, CITY UNIV NEW YORK, 81- *Personal Data:* b Stafford Springs, Conn, May 9, 47; m 78; c 1. *Educ:* Holy Cross Col, BA, 68; Princeton Univ, PhD(chem), 73. *Prof Exp:* Res assoc, IBM Res, Yorktown Heights, NY, 73-75; res assoc, Dept Biochem, Columbia Univ, 75-78. *Mem:* Am Chem Soc; Sigma Xi; AAAS. *Res:* Structure function interrelationship in electron transfer proteins and metalloenzymes; vibrational-electronic spectroscopy of metal complexes; resonance raman spectroscopy. *Mailing Add:* Dept Chem/Biochem Queens Col City Univ NY 65-30 Kissena Blvd Flushing NY 11367-1597

STRELTSOVA, TATIANA D, ENVIRONMENTAL ENGINEERING. *Current Pos:* SR RES SPECIALIST, EXXON PROD RES CO, 77- *Personal Data:* b Leningrad, USSR; Brit & US citizen; c 1. *Educ:* Hydrol Inst, Leningrad, USSR, BS & MS, 59; All-Union Sci Res Inst Hydraul Eng, PhD(hydraul eng), 65. *Hon Degrees:* ScD, Birmingham Univ, 77. *Honors & Awards:* Woman of the Yr, Asn Women Geoscientists, 85-86. *Prof Exp:* Res assoc hydraul, All-Union Sci Res Inst Hydraul Eng, 59-65; sr res assoc underground flows, Moscow State Univ, 65-70; sr res fel flows in porous media, Birmingham Univ, 71-77. *Concurrent Pos:* Fel, Rice Univ, 77; tech ed, Soc Petrol Eng, Am Soc Mech Engrs, 81- *Mem:* Am Geophys Union; Int Asn Water Resources; Soc Petrol Eng. *Res:* Various aspects of fluid flow trough porous media; author or coauthor of 50 publications. *Mailing Add:* 3705 Wakeforest St Houston TX 77098

STRELZOFF, ALAN G, PATTERN RECOGNITION & DIGITAL SIGNAL PROCESSING, IMAGE RECONSTRUCTION & PROCESSING. *Current Pos:* VPRES ARCHIT & TECHNOL COMPUT-AIDED DESIGN & COMPUT-AIDED MFG, COMPUT VISION, 90- *Personal Data:* b Scranton, Pa, Sept 10, 37; m 67; c 4. *Educ:* Mich State Univ, BA, 57; Columbia Univ, PhD(physics), 64. *Prof Exp:* Res assoc physics, Univ Wis, 63-66; asst prof physics & hist sci, Rochester, 66-69; res assoc & asst prof physics & biomed eng, Case Western Res Univ, 69-71 & 73-75; software engr indust control, Allen-Bradley, 75-76 & med image reconstruct, Imaging Syst, Union Carbide, 76-80; dir eng measurement & control mach vision, Systs Div, Analog Devices, 80-88; vpres eng discrete event controllers, Modicon/AEG, 88-90. *Mem:* Inst Elec & Electronics Engrs; Asn Comput Mach. *Res:* Design automation; industrial control; automatic generation of control programs from a computer-aided design database and corresponding inspection programs including machine vision. *Mailing Add:* Modicon/AEG 1 High St North Andover MA 01845

STREM, MICHAEL EDWARD, ORGANIC CHEMISTRY. *Current Pos:* PRES, STREM CHEM INC, 64- *Personal Data:* b Pittsburgh, Pa, Apr 1, 36; m 67. *Educ:* Brown Univ, AB, 58; Univ Pittsburgh, MS, 61, PhD(chem), 64. *Mem:* Am Chem Soc. *Res:* Organometallic chemistry, including its use in organic synthesis. *Mailing Add:* 7 Mulliken Way Newburyport MA 01950-4098

STREMLER, FERREL G, ELECTRICAL ENGINEERING. *Current Pos:* from asst prof to prof, Univ Wis-Madison, 68-96, assoc dean, Col Eng, 78-82, chmn dept, 84-86, EMER PROF ELEC ENG, UNIV WIS-MADISON, 96- *Personal Data:* b Lynden, Wash, Mar 10, 33; m 58; c 2. *Educ:* Calvin Col, AB, 57; Ill Inst Technol, BS, 59; Mass Inst Technol, SM, 60; Univ Mich, PhD, 67. *Honors & Awards:* Western Elec Fund Award, Am Soc Eng Educ, 75. *Prof Exp:* Res asst elec eng, Inst Sci & Technol, Univ Mich, Ann Arbor, 60-61, asst, 61-63, res assoc, 63-65, assoc res engr, 65-68, lectr, 66-67. *Mem:* Inst Elec & Electronics Engrs; Sigma Xi; Am Soc Eng Educ. *Res:* Analytical studies in coherent modulation-detection systems in communications and radar; design of communications and radar equipment; applications of communications and radar principles to remote sensing problems. *Mailing Add:* 249 Maberry Loop Lynden WA 98264-9341

STRENA, ROBERT VICTOR, APPLIED PHYSICS ADMINISTRATION & RESEARCH ADMINISTRATION. *Current Pos:* Asst dir, W W Hansen Lab Physics, 59-91, asst dir, Edward L Ginzton Lab, 81-93, EMER ASST LAB DIR, STANFORD UNIV, 93- *Personal Data:* b Seattle, Wash, June 28, 29; m 57, Rita Brodovsky; c Robert & Adrienne. *Educ:* Stanford Univ, BA, 52. *Mem:* AAAS; Nat Coun Univ Res Adminrs. *Res:* University physical sciences research administration. *Mailing Add:* Edward L Ginzton Lab Stanford Univ Stanford CA 94305

STRENG, WILLIAM HAROLD, PHYSICAL CHEMISTRY. *Current Pos:* RES SCIENTIST, HOECHST MARION ROUSSEL, 92- *Personal Data:* b Milwaukee, Wis, Mar 6, 44; m 67, Barbara York; c 2. *Educ:* Carroll Col, Wis, BS, 66; Mich Technol Univ, MS, 68, PhD(phys chem), 71. *Prof Exp:* Res assoc theoret chem, Clark Univ, 72-73; sr chemist, Merrell Res Ctr, Merrell Dow Pharmaceut, Inc, 73-92. *Concurrent Pos:* Adj asst prof, Sch Pharm, Univ Cincinnati, 84- *Mem:* Am Chem Soc; Am Pharmaceut Asn. *Res:* Elucidation of interactions in electrolyte solution from both theoretical and experimental considerations. *Mailing Add:* 7509 E 229th St Peculiar MO 64078

STRENZWILK, DENIS FRANK, ELECTROMAGNETISM, SOLID STATE PHYSICS. *Current Pos:* RES PHYSICIST, US ARMY BALLISTIC RES LABS, 68- *Personal Data:* b Rochester, NY, Oct 27, 40. *Educ:* Le Moyne Col, NY, BS, 62; Clarkson Col Technol, MS, 65, PhD(physics), 68. *Concurrent Pos:* Teacher, Exten Sch, Univ Del, Aberdeen Proving Ground, Md, 70. *Mem:* Am Asn Physics Teachers; Am Phys Soc. *Res:* Magnetism, effective field theory for yttrium iron garnet, lattice dynamics; clutter simulation of active and passive MMW sensors; statistical studies of IR data. *Mailing Add:* 2823 Meredith Ct Abingdon MD 21009-1850

STRETE, CAROLYN, CLINICAL PSYCHOLOGY, BIOLOGY. *Current Pos:* assignee, NIMH, 80-82, expert, Nat Cancer Inst, 82-84, chief prev epidemiol & cancer, Ctr Rev Sect, 85-91, dep dir, 91-96, ACTG DIR, DIV EXTRAMURAL ACTIV, NIMH, 96- *Personal Data:* b Carthage, Miss, Feb 9, 46; m 66, Dennis B K; c Kiran K & Arun K. *Educ:* Tougaloo Col, BS, 68; State Univ NY, Stony Brook, PhD(psychol), 76. *Prof Exp:* Chair & assoc prof, Dept Psychol Tougaloo Col, 76-80. *Res:* Frontal lobe function in primates; training of monkeys in operant learning situations; surgical lesioning of select cortical reas and post-surgery testing; visual perception and short-term memory in children with learning disabilities. *Mailing Add:* Div Extramural Activities NIMH 5600 Fishers Lane Rm 9-105 Rockville MD 20857. *Fax:* 301-443-0954

STRETTON, ANTONY OLIVER WARD, NEUROBIOLOGY. *Current Pos:* assoc prof, 71-76, PROF ZOOL & MOLECULAR BIOL, UNIV WIS, 76- *Personal Data:* b Rugby, Eng, Apr 24, 36; m 75, Philippa Claude; c Christopher & Richard. *Educ:* Univ Cambridge, BA, 57, MA, 61, PhD(chem), 60. *Prof Exp:* Instr biochem, Mass Inst Technol, 60-61; mem sci staff, Lab Molecular Biol, Med Res Coun, Cambridge, Eng 61-71. *Concurrent Pos:* Stringer fel, King's Col, Cambridge, 64-70; res assoc dept neurobiology, Harvard Med Sch, 66-67; Sloan Found fel, 72-74; John Bascom Prof Zool. *Mem:* Soc Neuroscience; fel AAAS; Brain Res Asn Eng; Genetical Soc Eng. *Res:* Structure and function of the nervous system of simple animals, especially nematodes. *Mailing Add:* Dept Zool 151 Noland Hall Univ Wis 1050 Bascom Mall Madison WI 53706

STREU, HERBERT THOMAS, ENTOMOLOGY, ZOOLOGY. *Current Pos:* assoc res prof, Rutgers Univ, 61-70, res prof entom, 70-88, chmn dept, 76-88, EMER PROF ENTOM, RUTGERS UNIV, 88- *Personal Data:* b Elizabeth, NJ, May 16, 27; c 1. *Educ:* Rutgers Univ, BS, 51, MS, 59, PhD(entom), 60. *Prof Exp:* Nematologist, Agr Res Serv, USDA, 60-61. *Concurrent Pos:* Dir grad prog, Rutgers Univ, 76-81 & 86-88; assoc ed, J NY Entom Soc, 75-83; contrib ed, Am Lawn Appln, 85-88. *Mem:* Fel AAAS; hom mem Entom Soc Am; Acarological Soc Am. *Res:* Ecology and control of arthropods in turfgrass; biology and control of insects, nematodes and other economic arthropod pests attacking ornamental crops. *Mailing Add:* 26 Eastern Pt Salem SC 29676

STREUFERT, SUSAN C, PSYCHOLOGY. *Current Pos:* health scientist adminr, Behav Med Study Sect, Div Res Grants, NIH, 78-80, Human Develop & Aging Study Sect, 84-86, Div Sci Rev, Nat Inst Child Health & Human Develop, 86-93, actg dir, 93-95, DIR, DIV SCI REV, NAT INST CHILD HEALTH & HUMAN DEVELOP, 95- *Personal Data:* b New York, NY, Oct 25, 44. *Educ:* Rutgers-State Univ, New Brunswick, AB, 66; Purdue Univ, MS, 70, PhD(social psychol), 73. *Prof Exp:* Consult, Univ Mannheim, WGer, 73-76; teaching staff, Sch Psychol, Univ Bielefeld, WGer, 74-78; asst prof, Pa State Univ Col Med, 80-84. *Concurrent Pos:* Vis asst prof, Purdue Univ, 73-74; external res mem, Univ Mannheim, WGer, 76- *Mem:* Europ Asn Exp Soc Psychol; Int Asn Appl Psychol; Am Psychol Asn; Acad Behav Med Res; Ger Soc Psychol. *Res:* Author of numerous articles. *Mailing Add:* Nat Inst Child Health & Human Develop Div Sci Rev 6100 Executive Blvd Rm 5E-01 Rockville MD 20852

STREULI, CARL ARTHUR, analytical chemistry; deceased, see previous edition for last biography

STRIBLEY, REXFORD CARL, ORGANIC CHEMISTRY. *Current Pos:* RETIRED. *Personal Data:* b Kent, Ohio, Mar 12, 18; m 45; c 2. *Educ:* Kent State Univ, BS, 39. *Prof Exp:* Chemist, Wyeth Labs Inc, 40-41, res chemist, Mason Lab, 45-50 & 52-55, chief res & develop, 55-70, tech dir, 70-76, nutrit dir & asst vpres mfg, Nutrit Div, Wyeth Labs, Inc Div, Am Home Prod Corp, 76-81, consult, 81- *Concurrent Pos:* US indust adv, Comt Food for Special Dietary Uses, UN Codex Alimentorius Comn, 72-74; mem bd dirs, Infant Formula Coun, 77- *Mem:* Am Chem Soc; Am Oil Chem Soc; Am Dairy Sci Asn; Inst Food Technol. *Res:* Chemistry and development of infant formulas; infant nutrition; milk chemistry; dairy manufacturing technology and engineering; special dietary food products. *Mailing Add:* Box 28334 El Jebel CO 81628

STRICHARTZ, ROBERT STEPHEN, MATHEMATICS. *Current Pos:* from asst prof to assoc prof, 69-77, PROF MATH, CORNELL UNIV, 77- *Personal Data:* b New York, NY, Oct 14, 43; m 68; c 2. *Educ:* Dartmouth Col, BA, 63; Princeton Univ, MA, 65, PhD(math), 66. *Honors & Awards:* First Prize, Math Intel, Fr Mus Competition, 82; Lester R Ford Award, Math Asn Am, 83. *Prof Exp:* NATO fel, Fac Sci, Orsay, France, 66-67; C L E Moore instr math, Mass Inst Technol, 67-69. *Mem:* Am Math Soc. *Res:* Harmonic analysis, partial differential equations, differential geometry. *Mailing Add:* Dept Math Cornell Univ White Hall Ithaca NY 14853-7901

STRICK, ELLIS, GEOPHYSICS, OCEANOGRAPHY. *Current Pos:* RETIRED. *Personal Data:* b Pikeville, Ky, Mar 19, 21. *Educ:* Va Polytech Inst & State Univ, BS, 42; Purdue Univ, West Lafayette, PhD(theoret physics), 50. *Prof Exp:* Physicist radio res, US Naval Res Lab, DC, 42-46; asst prof physics, Univ Wyo, 50-51; res assoc theoret seismol, Shell Explor & Prod Res Lab, Tex, 51-68; assoc prof geophys, Univ Pittsburgh, 68-69. *Concurrent Pos:* Lectr physics, Univ Houston, 51-67; NSF grant, Univ Pittsburgh, 70-71. *Mem:* Soc Explor Geophysicists; Seismol Soc Am. *Res:* Anelastic wave propagation in solids at low frequencies. *Mailing Add:* 2160 Greentree Rd Apt 605 Pittsburgh PA 15220

STRICKBERGER, MONROE WOLF, EVOLUTION, GENETICS. *Current Pos:* assoc prof, 68-71, PROF BIOL, UNIV MO-ST LOUIS, 71- *Personal Data:* b Brooklyn, NY, July 3, 25; m 57; c 2. *Educ:* NY Univ, BA, 49; Columbia Univ, MA, 59, PhD(genetics), 62. *Prof Exp:* Res fel genetics, Univ Calif, Berkeley, 62-63; from asst prof to assoc prof biol, St Louis Univ, 63-66. *Concurrent Pos:* NIH res grant, 63-69. *Mem:* AAAS; Genetics Soc Am; Soc Study Social Biol; Am Genetic Asn; Am Soc Naturalists; Sigma Xi; Soc Study Evolution. *Res:* Evolution of fitness in Drosophila populations; induction of sexual isolation. *Mailing Add:* 1790 Arch St Berkeley CA 94709-1328

STRICKER, EDWARD MICHAEL, BIOPSYCHOLOGY. *Current Pos:* from assoc prof to prof, 71-86, DISTINGUISHED PROF NEUROSCI, UNIV PITTSBURGH, 86- *Personal Data:* b New York, NY, May 23, 41; m 64; c 2. *Educ:* Univ Chicago, BS, 60, MS, 61; Yale Univ, PhD(psychol), 65. *Prof Exp:* Fel, Med Ctr, Univ Colo, 65-66 & Inst Neurol Sci, Med Sch, Univ Pa, 66-67; from asst prof to assoc prof psychol, McMaster Univ, 67-71. *Concurrent Pos:* Consult ed, J Comp & Physiol Psychol, 72-81; NIMH res scientist award, 81-86, Merit award, 87-97; vis prof psychiat, Johns Hopkins Med Sch, 78-79; chmn, Psychobiol Prog, Univ Pittsburgh, 83-86, Dept Neurosci, 86-; consult ed, Am J Physiol, 85-95. *Mem:* Soc Neurosci. *Res:* Physiological and behavioral mechanisms that maintain water and electrolyte balance, body temperature and energy metabolism; the neurochemical basis for recovery of function following brain damage; central controls of motivated behavior. *Mailing Add:* Dept Neurosci Univ Pittsburgh Pittsburgh PA 15260

STRICKER, STEPHEN ALEXANDER, BIOMINERALIZATION, INVERTEBRATE EMBRYOLOGY. *Current Pos:* ASST PROF, UNIV NMEX, 89- *Personal Data:* b Oakland, Calif, Jan 18, 54; m 82; c 1. *Educ:* Univ Calif, Santa Cruz, BA, 76; Univ Wash, MSc, 79, PhD(zool), 83. *Prof Exp:* Teaching fel biol, Univ Calgary, Alta, 83-87; res assoc, Dept Zool, Univ Wis, Madison, 87-88. *Concurrent Pos:* Lectr, Univ Calgary, Alta, 84; instr, Friday Harbor Lab, Wash, 85 & 86; lectr, Univ Calif, Santa Cruz, 89. *Mem:* Am Microscopical Soc; Am Soc Zoologists; AAAS; Am Soc Cell Biologists; Electron Micros Soc Am. *Res:* Biology of nemertean worms; oocyte maturation; nuclear lamins; studies of metamorphosis in marine invertebrates; fertilization histological, ultrastructural and analytical studies of calcifying tissues in marine invertebrates. *Mailing Add:* Dept Biol Univ NMex Main Campus One University Campus Albuquerque NM 87131-0001

STRICKHOLM, ALFRED, BIOPHYSICS, BIOMATHEMATICS. *Current Pos:* assoc prof, 66-72, prof anat & physiol, 72-76, PROF PHYSIOL, MED SCI PROG, CTR NEURAL SCI, IND UNIV, BLOOMINGTON, 76- *Personal Data:* b New York, NY, July 3, 28; m 52; c 3. *Educ:* Univ Mich, BS, 51; Univ Minn, MS, 56; Univ Chicago, PhD(physiol), 60. *Prof Exp:* Fel biophys, Physiol Inst, Univ Uppsala, 60-61; asst prof physiol, Sch Med, Univ Calif, San Francisco, 61-66. *Concurrent Pos:* USPHS grant, 62-; Am Heart Asn grant, 79- *Mem:* AAAS; Am Physiol Soc; Soc Neuroscience; Soc Gen Physiol; Biophys Soc. *Res:* Biophysics of the cell membrane; contraction coupling in muscle; permeability, active transport, and excitation; structure and function of cell membranes; neurobiology; neurotransmitters. *Mailing Add:* Physiol & Biophysics Ind Univ Med Sci Prog Bloomington IN 47405

STRICKLAND, ERASMUS HARDIN, BIOPHYSICS. *Current Pos:* PRES, STRICKLAND COMPUT CONSULT, 82- *Personal Data:* b Spartanburg, SC, May 18, 36; m 66; c 2. *Educ:* Pa State Univ, BS, 58, MS, 59, PhD(biophys), 61. *Prof Exp:* Chief phys chem sect, US Army Med Res Lab, Ft Knox, 61-63; from asst prof to assoc prof biophys, Univ Calif, Los Angeles, 63-70, assoc res biophysicist, Radiation Biol Lab, 69-75. *Mem:* AAAS. *Res:* Nutritional software; circular dichroism and absorption spectroscopy of biological molecules. *Mailing Add:* 30135 Yellow Brick Rd Valley Center CA 92082

STRICKLAND, GEORGE THOMAS, TROPICAL MEDICINE, INFECTIOUS DISEASES. *Current Pos:* PROF MICROBIOL, MED & EPIDEMIOL, & PREV MED, & DIR, INT HEALTH PROG, SCH MED, UNIV MD, BALTIMORE, 82- *Personal Data:* b Goldsboro, NC, Apr 20, 34; m 60, Anne Garst; c George T III, Paul G & James K. *Educ:* Univ NC, Chapel Hill, BA, 56, MD, 60; London Sch Hyg & Trop Med, DCMT, 70, PhD(parasitol), 74. *Prof Exp:* Intern, Nat Naval Med Ctr, Bethesda, Md, 60-61; resident internal med, 63-67, attend physician, 74-82, co-dir & infectious dis fel, 76-80; med officer, US Embassy, Nicosia, Cyprus, 61-63; chief clin invest, Naval Med Res Unit No 2, Taipei, China, 67-70; head immunoparisitol, Naval Med Res Inst, Bethesda, Md, 72-74; prog mgr infectious dis res, Naval Med Res & Develop Command, 74-76; dir res & educ, Dept Med, Uniformed Serv Univ Health Sci, Bethesda, Md, 76-80, prof internal med, 76-82. *Concurrent Pos:* Consult physician & lectr, Tri Serv Gen Hosp, Taipei, 67-70; res assoc, Johns Hopkins Sch Hyg & Pub Health, 74-; sr scientist, Armed Forces Inst Path, 81-82; dir, Int Ctr Med Res Training, Lahore, Pakistan, 83-85; ed, Hunter's Trop Med; sr consult, US Naval Med Res Unit 3, Cairo, 86-90. *Mem:* Am Soc Trop Med & Hyg; Royal Col Trop Med & Hyg; Infectious Dis Soc Am. *Res:* Clinical epidemiology of malaria, schistosomiasis and other endemic infectious diseases; investigating morbidity due to schistosomiasis in Egyptian communities communities; outcomes of antibiotic therapy of Lyme disease in Maryland; costs and cost-effectiveness of treatment of lyme disease; risk factors for hepatitis C in Egypt. *Mailing Add:* Int Health Prog Univ Md Sch Med Baltimore MD 21201. *Fax:* 410-706-8013; *E-Mail:* tstrick@epin.ab.umd.edu

STRICKLAND, GORDON EDWARD, JR, ENGINEERING MECHANICS. *Current Pos:* SR ENG ASSOC, CHEVRON OIL FIELD RES CO, 69- *Personal Data:* b Santa Cruz, Calif, Jan 23, 29; m 56; c 3. *Educ:* Stanford Univ, BS, 54, MS, 55, PhD(eng mech), 60. *Prof Exp:* Mem tech staff, Bell Tel Labs, 59-64; engr, Lawrence Radiation Lab, 64-66; res scientist, Lockheed Missiles & Space Co, 66-69. *Mem:* Sigma Xi. *Res:* Applied mechanics, particularly elasticity and shell theory. *Mailing Add:* 19816 Caprice Dr Yorba Linda CA 92686-4455

STRICKLAND, JAMES SHIVE, EXPERIMENTAL PHYSICS. *Current Pos:* PROF PHYSICS & CHMN DEPT, GRAND VALLEY STATE UNIV, 73- *Personal Data:* b Harrisburg, Pa, Nov 18, 29; m 55; c 3. *Educ:* Franklin & Marshall Col, BS, 51; Mass Inst Technol, PhD(physics), 57. *Prof Exp:* Staff physicist, Phys Sci Study Comt, Mass Inst Technol, 57-58; staff physicist, Educ Develop Ctr, Inc, Mass, 58-72; vis scientist, Mass Inst Technol, 72-73. *Mem:* AAAS; Am Asn Physics Teachers; Am Phys Soc; Am Soc Eng Educ. *Res:* Development of new materials for science education. *Mailing Add:* Dept Physics Grand Valley State Univ Allendale MI 49401. *Fax:* 616-895-3506

STRICKLAND, JOHN WILLIS, PETROLEUM GEOLOGY. *Current Pos:* RETIRED. *Personal Data:* b Wichita, Kans, Mar 23, 25; m 47; c 4. *Educ:* Univ Okla, BS, 46. *Prof Exp:* Geologist, Skelly Oil Co, 47-50; res geologist, Continental Oil Co, 51-55, div geologist, 55-61, explor mgr, Ireland, 61-64, coordr explor res, 64-66, dir adv geol, 66-67, chief geologist, 67-76, mgr, Africa & Latin Am, 76-78, dir geol, 79-81; mgr explor serv, Conoco, Inc, consult geologist, 82-90. *Mem:* Am Asn Petrol Geol. *Res:* Petroleum geology of world; factors controlling generation and distribution of hydrocarbons. *Mailing Add:* 761 W Creekside Dr Houston TX 77024

STRICKLAND, KENNETH PERCY, BIOCHEMISTRY. *Current Pos:* from asst prof to prof biochem, 55-94, prof clin neurol sci, 80-94, EMER PROF CLIN NEUROL SCI, UNIV WESTERN ONT, 94- *Personal Data:* b Loverna, Sask, Aug 19, 27; m 48; c 4. *Educ:* Univ Western Ont, BSc, 49, MSc, 50, PhD(biochem), 53. *Prof Exp:* Nat Res Coun Can fel chem path, Guy's Hosp Med Sch, Univ London, 53-55. *Concurrent Pos:* Lederle med fac award, 55-58; res assoc, Med Res Coun Can, 58-79, career investr, 79- *Mem:* AAAS; Am Soc Biol Chemists; Can Biochem Soc; Can Physiol Soc; Int Neurochemical Soc. *Res:* Biochemistry of central nervous system, especially enzymes (momo- and diacylkinases, CDP-diacylglycerol and phosphatidyl inositol synthetases) of lipid components; biochemistry of muscle, especially triacylglycerol and phosphoglyceride metabolism in differentiating L6 and dystrophic muscle myoblasts. *Mailing Add:* 1478 Adelaide St Unit 56 Univ Western Ont London ON N5X 3Y1 Can. *Fax:* 519-661-3175

STRICKLAND, LARRY DEAN, THERMODYNAMICS, FLUID DYNAMICS. *Current Pos:* proj mgr underground coal gasification, 77-78, prog mgr, press fluid bed combustion, 79-80, chief, gasification proj br, 81-84, chief, Exp Res Br, Dept Energy, 84-90, DIR, GASIFICATION/CLEANUP DIV, MORGANTOWN ENERGY TECHNOL CTR, 90- *Personal Data:* b Elkview, WVa, Nov 6, 38; m 62, Joyce A Carper; c Suzanne & Sharon. *Educ:* WVa Univ, BS, 60, PhD(mech eng), 73; Univ Southern Calif, MS, 62. *Prof Exp:* Prin res engr advan rocket engines, Rocketdyne, NAm Aviation, 62-67; res engr aerodyn, Re-entry Syst, Gen Elec Co, 67-68; instr, WVa Univ, 69-70; res co-op coal gasification, US Bur Mines, 71-73. *Concurrent Pos:* Adj prof, WVa Univ, 78-; mem, Grimthorpe Tech Comt, Int Energy Agency, 79-80, Adv Comt Int Conf Circulatory Fluidized Beds, 85-90; chmn, Joint Classification Prog Operating Comt, Gas Res Inst & Dept Energy, 82-84; co-proj officer, joint US/Ital gasification proj, 86-88. *Mem:* Am Soc Mech Engrs; Sigma Xi. *Res:* Fluid dynamics and heat-transfer as applied to in-situ and above ground coal gasification and other energy related topics; two gasification patents award. *Mailing Add:* 103 Holly Lane Morgantown WV 26505-2515

STRICKLER, STEWART JEFFERY, PHYSICAL CHEMISTRY, CHEMICAL PHYSICS. *Current Pos:* from asst prof to assoc prof, 63-73, chmn dept, 74-77, PROF CHEM, UNIV COLO, BOULDER, 73- *Personal Data:* b Mussoorie, India, July 12, 34; US citizen; m 93, Lynn Y Sorenson; c Janet C & Peter H. *Educ:* Col Wooster, BA, 56; Fla State Univ, PhD(phys chem), 61. *Prof Exp:* Chemist, Radiation Lab, Univ Calif, 61; res assoc, Rice Univ, 61-62, lectr chem, 62-63. *Concurrent Pos:* Hon fel, Australian Nat Univ, 72-73; vis scientist, Nat Renewable Energy Lab, 82-83. *Mem:* Am Chem Soc; Am Phys Soc; fel AAAS; Sigma Xi. *Res:* Molecular spectroscopy; photochemistry; quantum chemistry; lifetimes and properties of excited molecules; laser spectroscopy; photoconversion of solar energy. *Mailing Add:* Dept Chem Univ Colo Box 215 Boulder CO 80309-0215. *E-Mail:* strickler_cubldr.colorado.edu

STRICKLER, THOMAS DAVID, ATOMIC PHYSICS. *Current Pos:* RETIRED. *Personal Data:* b Ferozepur, India, Nov 11, 22; US citizen; m 89; c 4. *Educ:* Col Wooster, BA, 47; Yale Univ, MS, 48, PhD(physics), 53. *Prof Exp:* Instr physics, Yale Univ, 52-53; from asst prof to assoc prof, Berea Col, 53-61, Charles F Kettering prof, 61-86, prof physics & chmn dept, 86-89. *Concurrent Pos:* NSF faculty fel, 60-61; consult, NSF Physics Inst, Chandigarh, India, 66, Gauhati Univ, India, 67 & Calcutta, India, 68; Fulbright lectr, Vidyalankara Univ, Colombo, Sri Lanka, 73-74, De La Salle Univ, Manila, Philippines, 81-82, & Univ Zambia, Lusaka, Zambia, 88-89. *Mem:* AAAS; Am Asn Physics Teachers; Sigma X; Health Physics Soc. *Res:* Neutron and gamma ray scattering; health physics; gaseous electronics. *Mailing Add:* 1468 Rumbaugh Circle Wooster OH 44691

STRICKLIN, BUCK, ORGANIC CHEMISTRY. *Current Pos:* RETIRED. *Personal Data:* b Clovis, NMex, Dec 30, 22; m 42; c 1. *Educ:* Tex Tech Col, BS, 48; Univ Colo, PhD(org chem), 52. *Prof Exp:* Asst, Univ Colo, 48-52; res mgr, Minn Mining & Mfg Co, 52-69, tech dir, Paper Prod Div, 69-76, lab mgr, Disposable Prod Dept, 76-82. *Mem:* Am Chem Soc; Tech Asn Pulp & Paper Indust. *Res:* Fluorocarbons; fluoroethers; chlorination; photochemistry; photoconductivity; polymers. *Mailing Add:* 454 Hilltop Ave St Paul MN 55113

STRICKLIN, WILLIAM RAY, ANIMAL BEHAVIOR, ANIMAL BREEDING. *Current Pos:* ASSOC PROF ANIMAL SCI, UNIV MD, 81- *Personal Data:* b Savannah, Tenn, Apr 17, 46; m 67. *Educ:* Univ Tenn, BSc, 68, MSc, 72; Pa State Univ, PhD(animal sci), 75. *Prof Exp:* asst prof, Animal Sci, Univ Sask, 76-80. *Mem:* AAAS; Animal Behav Soc; Am Genetic Asn; Am Soc Animal Sci; Can Soc Animal Sci. *Res:* Crowding, personal space, and stress. *Mailing Add:* Dept Animal Sci Univ Md College Park MD 20742-0001

STRICKLING, EDWARD, SOILS. *Current Pos:* RETIRED. *Personal Data:* b Woodsfield, Ohio, Oct 20, 16; m 41; c 3. *Educ:* Ohio State Univ, BS, 37, PhD, 49. *Prof Exp:* Instr, High Sch, 37-42; prof soils, Univ Md, College Park, 50- *Mem:* Soil Sci Soc Am; Am Soc Agron. *Res:* Soil physics, especially soil structure and evapotranspiration. *Mailing Add:* 6904 Calverton Dr Hyattsville MD 20782

STRICKMEIER, HENRY BERNARD, JR, MATHEMATICS EDUCATION. *Current Pos:* assoc prof, 70-80, PROF MATH, CALIF POLYTECH STATE UNIV, SAN LUIS OBISPO, 80- *Personal Data:* b Galveston, Tex, Sept 28, 40; m 78. *Educ:* Tex Lutheran Col, BS, 62; Univ Tex, Austin, MA, 67, PhD(math educ), 70. *Prof Exp:* Teacher high sch, Tex, 62-65. *Mem:* Math Asn Am; Am Educ Res Asn; Nat Coun Teachers Math. *Res:* Evaluation of mathematics curricula; analysis of mathematics teaching. *Mailing Add:* 1613 18th St Los Osos CA 93402

STRIDER, DAVID LEWIS, PLANT PATHOLOGY. *Current Pos:* Res asst prof, 59-64, assoc prof, 64-70, PROF PLANT PATH, NC STATE UNIV, 70- *Personal Data:* b Salisbury, NC, Feb 12, 29; m 54; c 4. *Educ:* NC State Col, MS, 57, PhD(plant path), 59. *Concurrent Pos:* Mem, NC State Univ-US AID Mission, Peru, 70-71. *Mem:* Am Phytopath Soc. *Res:* Control of horticultural crops diseases; disease control of greenhouse floral crops. *Mailing Add:* Dept Plant Path NC State Univ Raleigh NC 27695-7616. *Fax:* 919-515-7716; *E-Mail:* david_strider@ncsu.edu

STRIEDER, WILLIAM, CHEMICAL ENGINEERING, PHYSICAL CHEMISTRY. *Current Pos:* asst prof eng sci, 66-70, PROF CHEM ENG, UNIV NOTRE DAME, 70- *Personal Data:* b Erie, Pa, Jan 19, 38; c John, Kathy, Tracy & Joseph. *Educ:* Pa State Univ, BS, 60; Case Inst Technol, PhD, 63. *Prof Exp:* Res fel irreversible thermodyn, Free Univ Brussels, 63-65; res fel statist mech, Univ Minn, 65-66. *Concurrent Pos:* Prin investr, NSF, Air Force Off Sci Res, Petrol Res Fund & Dept Transp grants. *Mem:* Am Inst Chem Engrs; Soc Indust & Appl Math; Am Asn Univ Professors; Am Chem Soc; Am Phys Soc. *Res:* Molecular theory of transport processes; flow through random porous media; transport phenomena; thermodynamics; statistical mechanics. *Mailing Add:* Dept Chem Eng Univ Notre Dame Notre Dame IN 46556. *Fax:* 219-239-8366

STRIEFEL, SEBASTIAN, DEVELOPMENTAL DISABILITIES & FACTORS OF STRESS, NEUROTHERAPY & BEHAVIOR THERAPY. *Current Pos:* coordr, Clin Serv, Exceptional Child Ctr, 74-75, from asst prof to assoc prof, 74-80, DIR SERV, CTR PERSONS DIABILITIES, UTAH STATE UNIV, 75-, PROF, PSYCHOL DEPT, 80- *Personal Data:* b Orrin, NDak, May 18, 41; m 65, Janet Hager; c Marnie R & Seth R. *Educ:* SDak State Univ, BS, 64; Univ SDak, MA, 66; Univ Kans, PhD(psychol), 68. *Honors & Awards:* Shiela Adler Award, Biofeedback Soc Am, 88; Presidential Award, Asn Appl Psychophysiol & Biofeedback, 95. *Prof Exp:* Chief psychol, Ft Riley Ment Hyg, US Army, 68-70; res assoc develop psychol, Bur Child Res, Univ Kans, 70-74. *Concurrent Pos:* Consult ed, Am Jour Ment Deficiency, 75-77, 83-85; assoc ed, J Behav Res Severe Develop Disability, 79-82, guest reviewer, Res Develop Disabilities, 88; chair & vchair, State Bd Mental Health, Utah, 83-91; chair/co-chair, Ethics Comt, Asn Appl Psychophysiol & Biofeedback, 84-90; vis scientist, Fla Ment Health Inst, Univ SFla, 87-88; fel & dipl, Am Bd Med Psycho Therapists, 88-, admin psychol, 89-; treas & mem bd dirs, Asn Appl Psychophysiol & Biofeedback, 89-; mem, Human Rights Comt, Div Servs People with Disabilities, 90-95; mem, Children's Ment Health Task Force, Utah Div Ment Health, 90- *Mem:* Am Psychol Asn; Asn Appl Psychophysiol & Biofeedback (treas, 89-, pres elect, 96-97, pres, 97-98); Asn Behav Analysis; Asn Advan Behav Ther; fel Am Asn Ment Deficiency; Int Asn Right Effective Treat; Am Psychol Soc. *Res:* Stimulus control generalization; mainstreaming of children who have handicaps; effective treatment of abusive parents; restrictiveness of behavioral procedures; stress management; response restriction; impacting poverty; ethics. *Mailing Add:* 1564E 1260N Logan UT 84341. *Fax:* 435-750-2044; *E-Mail:* sebst@cpd2.usu.edu

STRIER, KAREN BARBARA, ANTHROPOLOGY, BIOLOGICAL ANTHROPOLOGY. *Current Pos:* from asst prof to assoc prof, 89-95, chair, 94-96, PROF ANTHROP, UNIV WIS-MADISON, 95- *Personal Data:* b Summit, NJ, May 22, 59. *Educ:* Swarthmore Col, BA, 80; Harvard Univ, MA, 81, PhD(anthrop), 86. *Prof Exp:* Lectr anthrop, Harvard Univ, 86-87; asst prof, Beloit Col, 87-89. *Concurrent Pos:* Presidential young investr award, NSF, 89; adj prof, Beloit Col, 89-; affil prof zool, Univ Wis-Madison. *Mem:* Am Anthrop Asn; Am Asn Phys Anthropologists; AAAS; Animal Behav Soc; Sigma Xi. *Res:* Field research on primates, focusing on the ecological determinants of social organization; relationships between primates and their environments, including seasonal food availability, effects on reproduction, social relationships, and grouping and kinship patterns. *Mailing Add:* Dept Anthrop Univ Wis-Madison 1180 Observ Dr Madison WI 53706. *Fax:* 608-265-4216; *E-Mail:* kbstrier@facstaff.wisc.edu

STRIER, MURRAY PAUL, ENVIRONMENTAL SCIENCE & TECHNOLOGY. *Current Pos:* CONSULT, 86- *Personal Data:* b New York, NY, Oct 19, 23; m 55, Arlene Schimmel; c Sheri, Karen & Robin. *Educ:* City Col New York, BChE, 44; Emory Univ, MS, 47; Univ Ky, PhD(chem), 52; Am Inst Chemists, cert. *Honors & Awards:* Gold Medal, Environ Protection Agency, 79. *Prof Exp:* Asst & instr, Univ Ky, 48-50; res chemist & proj leader, Reaction Motors, Inc, 52-56; sr chemist & head polymers sect, Air Reduction Co, Inc, 56-58; chief chemist, Fulton-Irgon Corp, 58-59; group leader fiber res, Rayonier, Inc, 59-60; supvr develop res, 60-61; res chemist, T A Edison Res Lab, 61-64; sr res scientist, Douglas Aircraft Co, Inc, 64-67, chief fuel cell & battery res sect, 67-69; res assoc, Hooker Res Ctr, 69-71; prin chem engr, Cornell Aeronaut Lab, 71-72; chemist, 72-76, environ & phys scientist, Environ Protection Agency, 76-86. *Concurrent Pos:* Instr, Upsala Col, 63-64; consult, NSF, 73-75. *Mem:* AAAS; Am Chem Soc; Am Inst Chemists; Am Soc Testing & Mat; Electrochem Soc. *Res:* Organic polarography; physical chemistry of rocket propellants; physical properties of organic coatings, plastics and fibers; viscose chemistry; fuel cells and batteries; environmental science; industrial water pollution control-molecular structure-activity correlations. *Mailing Add:* 4114 Meadow Edge Sugar Land TX 77479

STRIETER, FREDERICK JOHN, PHYSICAL CHEMISTRY, SEMICONDUCTOR DEVICES. *Current Pos:* dir, Semiconductor Mat-Gallium Arsenide Venture, 82-87, DIR SENSOR FABRICATION, HONEYWELL, INC, 87- *Personal Data:* b Davenport, Iowa, Sept 14, 34; m 57, Ann Aronson; c Susan & Nancy. *Educ:* Augustana Col, Ill, AB, 56; Univ Calif, Berkeley, PhD, 60. *Prof Exp:* Asst chem, Univ Calif, 56-57, asst crystallog, Lawrence Radiation Lab, 57-59; mem tech staff, Tex Instruments, Inc, 59-75, circuits develop pilot line mgr, 75-82. *Mem:* Electrochem Soc (treas, 73-76, vpres-pres, 79-83); Inst Elec & Electronics Engrs. *Res:* Semiconductor device process technology; impurity diffusion in semiconductors; ion implantation of impurities in semiconductors; electron beam pattern definition; optoelectronic devices, silicon sensors. *Mailing Add:* 7814 Fallmeadow Lane Dallas TX 75248-5328

STRIFE, JAMES RICHARD, COMPOSITE MATERIALS. *Current Pos:* res scientist, United Technol Res Ctr, 78-82, sr res scientist, 82-84, sr mat scientist, 84-86, prin scientist, 86-93, mgr mat processing, 93-96, DIR, CARRIER PROG OFF, UNITED TECHNOL RES CTR, 97- *Personal Data:* b Ilion, NY, Oct 12, 49; m 71; c 2. *Educ:* Rensselaer Polytech Inst, BS, 71, MS, 73, PhD(mat eng), 76. *Prof Exp:* Staff scientist, Union Carbide Corp, 76-78. *Mem:* Am Soc Metals Int; Am Ceramic Soc. *Res:* Advanced composite and ceramic materials for applications in heat engines, optical systems, and space satellite structures; metal, ceramic and carbon matrix composites; development, improvement and application of materials and the processes employed in their manufacture; advanced alloys, coatings and modified surfaces; plastics engineering and manufacturing reliability. *Mailing Add:* United Technologies Res Ctr Silver Lane East Hartford CT 06108. *Fax:* 860-727-7879

STRIFFLER, DAVID FRANK, public health, dentistry; deceased, see previous edition for last biography

STRIFFLER, WILLIAM D, FOREST HYDROLOGY. *Current Pos:* from asst prof to assoc prof Watershed Mgt, 66-75, PROF EARTH RESOURCES, COLO STATE UNIV, 75- *Personal Data:* b Oberlin, Ohio, July 10, 29; m 56; c 4. *Educ:* Mich State Univ, BS & BSF, 52; Univ Mich, MF, 57, PhD(forest hyrdol), 63. *Prof Exp:* Res forester & proj leader groundwater hydrol & steambank erosion, Lake States Forest Exp Sta, Mich, 57-63; hydrologist, Stripmined Areas Restoration Res Proj, Northeastern Forest Exp Sta, Ky, 64-66. *Concurrent Pos:* Consult, Cent soil & Water Conserv Res Inst, India, 75, 77, 80. *Mem:* Am Geophys Union; Am Water Resource Asn; AAAS; Sigma Xi; Indian Soc Soil & Water Conserv. *Res:* Wildland hydrology; land use hydrology; erosion and sedimentation processes; water quality; grassland hydrology; instrumentation. *Mailing Add:* 1201 Lory St Ft Collins CO 80524

STRIGHT, PAUL LEONARD, TEACHING. *Current Pos:* RETIRED. *Personal Data:* b St Paul, Minn, May 12, 30; m 60; c 2. *Educ:* Grinnell Col, BA, 51; Univ Minn, Minneapolis, PhD(org chem), 56. *Prof Exp:* Res chemist, Esso Res & Eng Co, 56-59; res chemist, Allied Chem Corp, 59-65, res supvr, 65-68, res assoc, 68-70; asst prof org chem, Univ Minn, Morris, 70-71; assoc scientist neurochem, Univ Minn, Minneapolis, 71-73; instr chem, Lake Mich Col, 73-93. *Mem:* Sigma Xi; Am Chem Soc. *Mailing Add:* 1758 S Sierra Way Stevensville MI 49127

STRIKE, DONALD PETER, PHARMACEUTICAL CHEMISTRY, ORGANIC CHEMISTRY. *Current Pos:* res chemist, 65-69, res group leader, 69-77, res mgr, 77-84, ASSOC DIR, WYETH-AYERST RES, AM HOME PROD CORP, 84- *Personal Data:* b Mt Carmel, Pa, Oct 24, 36; m 72, Sally Cavanaugh; c Brian & Samantha. *Educ:* Philadelphia Col Pharm & Sci, BS, 58; Iowa State Univ, MS, 61, PhD(org chem), 63. *Prof Exp:* NIH fel, Univ Southampton, 63-64. *Mem:* Am Chem Soc; AAAS. *Res:* Natural products; antibiotics; steroids; prostaglandins; anti-ulcer products; metabolic disorders; anti-viral drugs; antilipemic drugs; antidiabetic drugs; antiosteoporotic drugs. *Mailing Add:* Wyeth-Ayerst Res CN-8000 Princeton NJ 08540

STRIKER, G E, NEPHROLOGY, CELL BIOLOGY. *Current Pos:* DIR DIV KIDNEY, UROL & HEMAT DIS, NIH, NAT INST DIABETES, DIGESTIVE & KIDNEY DIS, 84- *Personal Data:* b Bottineau, NDak, March 7, 34; m, Liliane Z Morel-Maroger. *Educ:* Univ Wash Seattle Sch Med, MD, 59. *Prof Exp:* From asst prof to prof, Dept Path, Wash Univ, Seattle, 66-84. *Concurrent Pos:* Dean curric, Sch Med, Univ Wash, Seattle, 71-77. *Mem:* Am Soc Nephrol; Am Soc Cell Biol; Nat Kidney Found; Am Asn Pathologists; Int Soc Nephrologists; Am Heart Asn. *Res:* Pathology; biochemistry; endocrinology; physiology; nephrology; cell biology. *Mailing Add:* Div Kidney Urol & Hematol Dis Bldg 31 Rm 9A17 NIH 9000 Rockville Pike Bethesda MD 20892-0010

STRIKWERDA, JOHN CHARLES, NUMERICAL ANALYSIS. *Current Pos:* asst prof, 80-84, assoc prof, 84-93, PROF COMPUT SCI, UNIV WIS-MADISON, 93- *Personal Data:* b Grand Rapids, Mich, Mar 15, 47; m 70; c 2. *Educ:* Calvin Col, AB, 69; Univ Mich, MA, 70; Stanford Univ, PhD(math), 76. *Prof Exp:* Res scientist, Inst Comput Applications Sci Eng, 76-80. *Mem:* Soc Indust & Appl Mech; Am Math Soc. *Res:* Numerical methods for partial differential equations, finite difference methods and computational fluid dynamics. *Mailing Add:* Dept Comput Sci Univ Wis 1210 W Dayton St Madison WI 53706-1685

STRIMLING, WALTER EUGENE, PHYSICS, ELECTRONICS ENGINEERING. *Current Pos:* PRES, US DYNAMICS, 55- *Personal Data:* b Minneapolis, Minn, Jan 6, 26; m 57; c 3. *Educ:* Univ Minn, BPhys & MA, 45, PhD(math), 53. *Prof Exp:* Instr math & educ, Col St Catherine, 45-46; asst math, Univ Minn, 49-53; engr, Raytheon Co, 53-55. *Mem:* Am Phys Soc; Math Asn Am; Inst Elec & Electronics Engrs. *Res:* Theoretical physics; chemistry; bioengineering. *Mailing Add:* US Dynamics 160 Bear Hill Rd 02154-1036 MA 02154-4644. *Fax:* 781-895-1900

STRINDEN, SARAH TAYLOR, BIOCHEMISTRY. *Current Pos:* FEL, UNIV WIS-MADISON, 81- *Personal Data:* b Lyons, Kans, Jan 31, 55; m 79. *Educ:* Univ Kans, BS, 76; Univ Southern Calif, PhD(biochem), 81. *Prof Exp:* Technician biochem, Univ Kans, 76-77; res asst, Univ Southern Calif, 78-81. *Mem:* Sigma Xi. *Res:* Various mechanisms controlling gene expression at the post-transcriptional level. *Mailing Add:* 1310 Walnut Bend St Lufkin TX 75904-4228

STRINGAM, ELWOOD WILLIAMS, ANIMAL SCIENCE, AGRICULTURE. *Current Pos:* prof & head, Dept Am Sci, 54-73, prof, 74-83, EMER PROF AM SCI, UNIV MAN, 83- *Personal Data:* b Alberta, Can, Dec 10, 17; m 44, Gabrielle Wellington; c John D, Michael G, Peter E, Richard B, James A & Eve G. *Educ:* Univ Alta, BSc, 40, MSc, 42; Univ Minn, PhD(agr), 48. *Honors & Awards:* Golden Award, Can Feed Indust Asn. *Prof Exp:* Asst, Dom Range Exp Sta, Alta, 40; fieldman, Livestock Prod Serv, 41-42; instr animal husb, Univ Minn, 46-48; assoc prof animal sci, Univ Man, 48-51; prof animal husb, Ont Agr Col, 51-54. *Concurrent Pos:* Mem, Nat Animal Breeding Comt, Can, 58-63 & Nat Genetic Adv Comt Cattle Importations, 69-74; adv comt, Western Vet Col, 66-; dir, Nat Adv Comt Agr, World's Fair, 67. *Mem:* Am Soc Animal Sci; Sigma Xi; Can Soc Animal Sci; fel Agr Inst Can (vpres, 62-63, pres, 66-67). *Res:* Agricultural education; animal genetics and physiology; farm animal production and management; beef cattle production. *Mailing Add:* 209 15300 17th Ave Surrey BC V4A 8Y6 Can

STRINGER, GENE ARTHUR, PHYSICS, ELECTRONICS. *Current Pos:* from asst prof to assoc prof, 71-83, CHMN, DEPT PHYSICS, SOUTHERN ORE STATE COL, 74-, PROF, 83- *Personal Data:* b Yamhill Co, Ore, Nov 16, 39; m 61; c 4. *Educ:* Linfield Col, BA, 61; Univ Ore, MA, 64, PhD(physics), 69. *Prof Exp:* Staff engr & physicist res, Tektronix Inc, Beaverton, Ore, 61-63; res assoc physics, Univ Ore, 69; res assoc & instr, Cornell Univ, 69-71. *Concurrent Pos:* Physics consult, Tektronix Inc, 63-64; NSF grant, Instr Sci Equip, 76-78; proj assoc, Tech Educ Res Ctr, 77-78; NSF LOCI grant, 79-81; Fulbright sr lectr, Univ Philippines, 84-85. *Mem:* Am Asn Physics Teachers; Sigma Xi. *Mailing Add:* 2808 Anderson Creek Rd Talent OR 97540

STRINGER, JOHN, FOSSIL FUEL BURNING SYSTEMS. *Current Pos:* proj mgr, Elec Power Res Inst, 77-82, prog mgr, 82-85, sr prog mgr mat support, 85-87, tech dir explor res, 87-90, dir appl res, 90-96, EXEC TECH FEL, ELEC POWER RES INST, 97- *Personal Data:* b Liverpool, Eng, July 14, 34; m 57, Audrey Lancaster; c Helen C & Rebecca E. *Educ:* Univ Liverpool, Eng, BEng, 55, PhD(metall), 58, DEng, 72; Chartered Eng Inst, UK, CEng, 70. *Honors & Awards:* U R Evans Award, Inst Corrosion, UK, 93. *Prof Exp:* Asst lectr, metall, Univ Liverpool, UK, 57-59, lectr, 59-63, prof, 66-68, prof mat sci, 68-77; sr scientist, Battelle Mem Inst, Columbus, Ohio, 64-65, fel, 65-66. *Concurrent Pos:* Res prof, Dept Mat Sci & Eng, Stanford Univ. *Mem:* Fel Am Inst Metall Engrs; fel Nat Asn Corrosion Engrs; fel Inst Energy UK; fel AAAS; Am Soc Mat Int; fel Royal Soc Arts. *Res:* High temperature oxidation and corrosion of metals and alloys; fossil-fuel burning systems; interaction of oxidation and sulfidation at elevated temperatures; hot corrosion of gas turbines; reactive element effect in high-temperature oxidation; erosion and erosion/corrosion of metals and alloys. *Mailing Add:* 221 Hudson St Redwood City CA 94062-1921. *Fax:* 650-855-2287; *E-Mail:* jstringe@epri.com

STRINGER, L(OREN) F(RANK), electronics engineering, applied mathematics; deceased, see previous edition for last biography

STRINGER, WILLIAM CLAYTON, FORAGE CROP MANAGEMENT. *Current Pos:* ASSOC PROF FORAGE CROPS, DEPT AGRON, CLEMSON UNIV, 84- *Personal Data:* b Athens, Ga, Apr 3, 46; m 69. *Educ:* Univ Ga, BSA, 68, MSc, 72; Va Polytech Inst & State Univ, PhD(agron), 77. *Prof Exp:* Agronomist, NW Ga Br Exp Sta, Univ Ga, 72-74; from asst prof to assoc prof forage corps, Dept Agron, Pa State Univ, 77-84. *Mem:* Crop Sci Soc Am; Am Soc Agron; Am Forage & Grassland Coun. *Res:* Forage crop ecology and physiology; alfalfa management; grazing systems. *Mailing Add:* Dept Agron Clemson Univ Clemson SC 29632-0001

STRINGFELLOW, DALE ALAN, VIROLOGY, IMMUNOBIOLOGY. *Current Pos:* PRES & CHIEF EXEC OFFICER, CELTRIX PHARMACEUT, SANTA CLARA, CALIF. *Personal Data:* b Ogden, Utah, Sept 13, 44; m 66, Jean Racker; c Jennifer, Wendy & Ashley. *Educ:* Univ Utah, BS, 67, MS, 70, PhD(microbiol), 72. *Prof Exp:* NIH fel & instr microbiol, Univ Utah, 72-73; res scientist, UpJohn Co, 73-79, sr scientist virol & head cancer res, 79-82; assoc prof pharmacol, State Univ NY, Upstate Med Ctr, Syracuse, 82-86; vpres cancer res, Bristol Myers, Syracuse, NY, 82-88; prof res molecular & cellular biol, Univ Conn, 86-88; vpres res & develop, Collagen Corp, Palo Alto, Calif, 88-90. *Concurrent Pos:* Mem, Develop Therapeut Contracts Rev Comt, Nat Cancer Inst; mem, Cancer Biol, Immunol Contract Review, Nat Cancer Inst, 85-87; mem, Univ Conn Biotech Adv Bd, 85-88; mem, Ariz Dis Control Res Comm Rev Comt, 87-90; mem, Univ Tex, John Sealy Mem Endowment Fund Rev Comt, 88- *Mem:* Am Soc Microbiol; Am Asn Cancer Res; AAAS; Int Soc Interferon Res; Int Soc Antiviral Res; Soc Biomat Res; Parenteral Drug Asn. *Res:* Antiviral agents; interrelationship between host defense systems and virus infection; pathogenesis of virus infection; mechanisms modulating nonspecific immunity; viral ecology; antineoplastic agents; metastasis; cell cycling; nucleic acid biochemistry; cellular regulation; prostaglandins; cellular communications. *Mailing Add:* 75 Holiday Dr Alamo CA 94507. *Fax:* 408-450-5440

STRINGFELLOW, FRANK, PARASITOLOGY, ZOOLOGY. *Current Pos:* ZOOLOGIST, LIVESTOCK & POULTRY SCI INST, AGR RES CTR, USDA, 67. *Personal Data:* b Cheriton, Va, Oct 27, 40; m 68, Therese Madden; c Mary A & John D. *Educ:* St Louis Univ, BS, 62; Drake Univ, MA, 64; Univ SC, PhD(biol), 67. *Prof Exp:* Asst gen biol, Drake Univ, 63-64; instr anat & physiol, Univ SC, 64-65. *Mem:* Am Soc Parasitol. *Res:* Molecular biology and biochemistry of parasitic nematodes; cultivation of parasitic nematodes. *Mailing Add:* 1 Woodland Ct Greenbelt MD 20770

STRINGFELLOW, GERALD B, MATERIALS SCIENCE, SEMICONDUCTORS. *Current Pos:* PROF ELEC ENG & MAT SCI ENG, UNIV UTAH, SALT LAKE CITY, 80- *Personal Data:* b Salt Lake City, Utah, Apr 26, 42; m 62; c 3. *Educ:* Univ Utah, BS, 64; Stanford Univ, MS, 66, PhD(mat sci), 67. *Honors & Awards:* Alexander von Humboldt US Sr Scientist Award, 79. *Prof Exp:* Mem tech staff, Solid State Physics Lab, Hewlett Packard Labs, 67-71, proj mgr, 71-80. *Concurrent Pos:* Sabbatical, Max Planck Inst, Stuttgart, Ger, 79 & Clarendon Lab, Univ Oxford, Eng, 91; distinguished res award, Univ Utah, 89; guest fel, Royal Soc, London, 90. *Mem:* Am Phys Soc; Electrochem Soc; fel Inst Elec & Electronics Engrs; Mat Res Soc. *Res:* Electrical and optical properties of alloys between III-V compound semiconductors; and III-V compounds; crystal growth and thermodynamics in ternary III-V systems; organometallic vapor phase epitaxy. *Mailing Add:* Dept Mat Sci Univ Utah 304 EMRO Salt Lake City UT 84112. *Fax:* 801-581-4816; *E-Mail:* stringfellow@ee.utah.edu

STRINGHAM, GLEN EVAN, ENGINEERING. *Current Pos:* from asst prof to assoc prof, 57-78, PROF AGR ENG, UTAH STATE UNIV, 78- *Personal Data:* b Lethbridge, Alta, Aug 30, 29; US citizen; m 53; c 4. *Educ:* Utah State Univ, BS, 55; Colo State Univ, PhD(civil eng), 66. *Prof Exp:* Instr agr eng, Calif State Polytech Col, 55-57. *Concurrent Pos:* Chief party, Utah State Univ-Agency Int Develop team, Colombia, 69-71; consult, Honduras, Phillipines, Saudi Arabia, Kenya & Egypt. *Mem:* Am Soc Agr Engrs; Am Soc Civil Engrs; Am Soc Eng Educ; Soil Conserv Soc Am. *Res:* Optimization of surface irrigation. *Mailing Add:* 50 S 100 E Millville UT 84321

STRINGHAM, REED MILLINGTON, JR, PHYSIOLOGY, ORAL BIOLOGY. *Current Pos:* PROF OCCUP HEALTH & ZOOL & DEAN SCH ALLIED HEALTH SCI, WEBER STATE COL, 69- *Personal Data:* b Salt Lake City, Utah. *Educ:* Northwestern Univ, Evanston, DDS, 58; Univ Utah, BS, 64, PhD(molecular & genetic biol), 68. *Prof Exp:* Nat Inst Dent Res fel, 65-68, RES ASSOC PLASTIC SURG, MED SCH, UNIV UTAH, 68- *Concurrent Pos:* Resource person, Intermountain Regional Med Prog, 69, consult, Oral Cancer Screening Proj, 71- *Mem:* Am Dent Asn. *Res:* Salivary gland physiology; health manpower. *Mailing Add:* Weber State Univ Allied Health 3750 Harrison Blvd Ogden UT 84408-0001

STRINTZIS, MICHAEL GERASSIMOS, ELECTRICAL & BIOMEDICAL ENGINEERING, APPLIED MATHEMATICS. *Current Pos:* AT UNIV THESSALONIKI, GREECE, 80- *Personal Data:* b Athens, Greece, Sept 30, 44; US citizen; m; c 1. *Educ:* Nat Tech Univ Athens, BS, 67; Princeton Univ, MA, 69, PhD(elec eng), 70. *Prof Exp:* From asst prof to assoc prof elec eng, Univ Pittsburgh, 70-80. *Concurrent Pos:* Vis prof, Nat Tech Univ, Athens, 78-79; Syracuse Univ, 87-88; grants, NSF, Elec Power Res Inst, NIH & Energy Res & Develop Admin, EC (Esprit). *Mem:* Inst Elec & Electronic Engrs; Soc Indust & Appl Math; NY Acad Sci. *Res:* Signal and image processing; large-scale systems; digital signal processing, image description and processing; detection and estimation theory; biomedical engineering. *Mailing Add:* Dept Elec & Comput Eng Univ Thessaloniki Thessaloniki 540 06 Greece

STRITTMATER, RICHARD CARLTON, PHYSICS. *Current Pos:* RES PHYSICIST MECH, ACOUST & HEAT TRANSFER, BALLISTIC RES LAB, 58- *Personal Data:* b Columbia, Pa, Aug 26, 23; m 50; c 3. *Educ:* Earlham Col, BA, 53; Iowa State Col, MS, 55. *Prof Exp:* Res physicist fluid mech & heat transfer, Remington Arms Co, Ilion, NY, 55-58. *Concurrent Pos:* Mem, Comt Standardization Combustion Instability Measurements, 66-70; Dept Army rep, Steering Comt Interagency Chem Rocket Propulsion Group's Solid Propellant Combustion Group, 67. *Mem:* Sigma Xi. *Res:* Turbulent fluid mechanical interaction at burning surfaces. *Mailing Add:* 2500 Pinehurst Ave Forest Hill MD 21050

STRITTMATTER, CORNELIUS FREDERICK, METABOLIC CONTROL, DIFFERENTIATION. *Current Pos:* chmn dept, 61-78, Odus M Mull prof, 61-89, EMER PROF BIOCHEM, BOWMAN GRAY SCH MED, 89- *Personal Data:* b Philadelphia, Pa, Nov 16, 26; m 55, Carol Entz; c Clare. *Educ:* Juniata Col, BS, 47; Harvard Univ, PhD(biol chem), 52. *Prof Exp:* Instr biol chem, Harvard Med Sch, 52-54, assoc, 55-58, asst prof, 58-61. *Concurrent Pos:* USPHS res fel, Oxford Univ, 54-55; USPHS sr res fel, Harvard Med Sch, 61; consult, New Eng Deaconess Hosp, 58-61; mem fel comt, NIH, 67-70 & 74; consult, NC Alcoholism Res Auth, 74- *Mem:* Am Chem Soc; Am Soc Biol Chemists; Soc Develop Biol; Soc Exp Biol & Med; Am Soc Zool. *Res:* Enzymic differentiation and control mechanisms during embryonic development and aging; characterization of electron transport systems; cellular control mechanisms in metabolism; comparative biochemistry; mechanisms in enzyme systems. *Mailing Add:* 817 Clovelly Rd Winston-Salem NC 27106-5421

STRITTMATTER, PETER ALBERT, TELESCOPES, INSTRUMENTS. *Current Pos:* assoc prof & assoc astronr, 71-73, PROF & ASTRONOMR, STEWARD OBSERV, UNIV ARIZ, 73-, DIR, 75-, REGENTS PROF, 94- *Personal Data:* b Bexleyheath, Eng, Sept 12, 39; US citizen; m 67, Janet

Parkhurst; c Catherine & Robert. *Educ:* Cambridge Univ, BA, 61, MA, 65, PhD(appl math), 67. *Prof Exp:* Mem staff astron, Inst Theoret Astron, Cambridge, 67-68; res assoc, Mt Stromlo & Siding Spring Observ, 69; mem staff, Inst Theoret Astron, Cambridge, 70; res physicist, Univ Calif, San Diego, 70-71. *Concurrent Pos:* Consult, Astron Adv Panel, NSF, 75-79; mem, Bd Asn Univs Res Astron, NSF, 75-85; Alexander Von Humboldt sr scientist award, 79-80; adj sci mem, Max Planck Inst Radioastron, Bonn, 80-; pres, LBT Corp. *Mem:* Am Acad Arts Sci; Am Astron Soc; Royal Astron Soc; Int Astron Union; Ger Astron Soc. *Res:* Quasistellar objects; Seyfert galaxies; radio sources; white dwarfs; novae; speckle interferometry. *Mailing Add:* Steward Observ Univ Ariz Tucson AZ 85721-0065. *Fax:* 520-621-7852; *E-Mail:* pstrittmatter@as.arizona.edu

STRITTMATTER, PHILIPP, BIOCHEMISTRY, ENZYMOLOGY. *Current Pos:* chmn dept, 68-74, PROF BIOCHEM, UNIV CONN, STORRS, 68-, HEAD DEPT, 76- *Personal Data:* b Philadelphia, Pa, July 13, 28; m 56; c 2. *Educ:* Harvard Univ, PhD, 54. *Prof Exp:* From instr to prof biochem, Wash Univ, 54-68. *Mem:* Am Soc Biol Chemists. *Res:* Oxidative enzyme mechanisms. *Mailing Add:* Dept Biochem 23 Old Wood Rd Avon CT 06001

STRITZEL, JOSEPH ANDREW, AGRONOMY. *Current Pos:* RETIRED. *Personal Data:* b Cleveland, Ohio, June 11, 22; m 50; c 9. *Educ:* Iowa State Univ, BS, 49, MS, 53, PhD(soil fertil, prod econ), 58. *Prof Exp:* Exten soil fertil specialist, Iowa State Univ, 50-63, prof soils, 63-76, prof agron, 76- *Mem:* Am Soc Agron. *Res:* Soil fertility; production economics. *Mailing Add:* RR 6 Box 24 Ames IA 50014

STRITZKE, JIMMY FRANKLIN, AGRONOMY. *Current Pos:* asst prof, 70-76, assoc prof, 76-80, PROF AGRON, OKLA STATE UNIV, 80- *Personal Data:* b South Coffeyville, Okla, Sept 9, 37; m 59; c 2. *Educ:* Okla State Univ, BS, 59, MS, 61; Univ Mo, PhD(field crops), 67. *Prof Exp:* Res scientist weed control, Agr Res Serv, USDA, 61-66; asst prof agron, SDak State Univ, 66-70. *Mem:* Am Forest & Grassland Coun; Am Soc Agron; Weed Sci Soc Am; Soc Range Mgt; Coun Agr Sci & Technol. *Res:* Weed control in alfalfa, weed and brush control in pasture and rangelands, herbicide residue and translocation. *Mailing Add:* Agron Okla State Univ Stillwater OK 74078-0001

STRIZ, ALFRED GERHARD, AEROELASTICITY & FINITE ELEMENT ANALYSIS, STRUCTURAL & MULTIDISCIPLINARY DESIGN OPTIMIZATION. *Current Pos:* Asst prof, 81-88, ASSOC PROF AEROSPACE, UNIV OKLA, 88- *Personal Data:* b Rosenheim, WGer, July 25, 52; m 83, Elise Ann Cappentec; c Leonhard, Anneliese & Andrea. *Educ:* Purdue Univ, BS & MS, 76, PhD(aero/astro eng), 81. *Honors & Awards:* Ralph R Teetor Award, 84. *Concurrent Pos:* Res asst aeroelasticity, Purdue Univ, 77-80, instr solid mech, 81; prin investr, Demco, 82, Gulfco, 83, Air Force Off Sci Res, 83-84, Gen Motors Corp, 85-88, USAF, 86, 88 & 91, Fed Aviation Admin, 89-90; co-prin investr, Dept Defense, USAF, 83-85 & 95-96, NASA, 84 & 89-92 & 96, OCAST, 90-91, GRI, 91, Rockwell, 92 & McDonnel Aircraft, 92; jr fac res fel, Univ Okla, 84; sr exp engr, 85, sr proj engr, Gen Motors Corp, 86; vis scholar, Dept Defense, USAF, 82, Air Force Inst Technol, 88, WRDC, 89-90 & 96; Langley Res Ctr, NASA, 94-95. *Mem:* Am Inst Aeronaut & Astronaut; Sigma Xi; assoc fel Am Inst Aeronaut & Astronaut; Int Soc Struct & multidisciplinary Optimization. *Res:* Aeroelasticity; finite element analyses of structures; structural optimization; multidisciplinary design optimization; development of efficient numerical structural analysis and optimization algerithms. *Mailing Add:* FH 206 Sch Aerospace & Mech Eng Univ Okla 865 Asp Ave Norman OK 73019-0601. *Fax:* 405-325-1088; *E-Mail:* striz@ou.edu

STRNISA, FRED V, ENERGY RESEARCH & DEVELOPMENT. *Current Pos:* SELF EMPLOYED. *Personal Data:* b Cleveland, Ohio, Nov 20, 41; c 3. *Educ:* Case Inst Technol, BS, 63; John Carroll Univ, MS, 67; State Univ NY, Albany, PhD(physics), 72; Rensselaer Polytech Inst, MBA, 90. *Honors & Awards:* Pub Serv Leadership Award, Int Dist Heating & Cooling Asn, 92. *Prof Exp:* Engr, Lamp Div, Gen Elec Co, 63-67, physicist, Knolls Atomic Power Lab, 67-69; res assoc, State Univ NY, Albany, 69-73; sr scientist, NY State Atomic Energy Coun, 73-76 & NY State Energy Off, 76-77; prog mgr, NY State Energy Res & Develop Authority, 77- *Mem:* Am Phys Soc; Int Dist Heating & Cooling Asn; Sigma Xi. *Res:* District heating and cooling; cogeneration; electric and gas utility research and development; transportation; radioactive waste management; radiation and impurity defects in solids; circularly polarized electron paramagnetic resonance; mass spectroscopy; lighting technology. *Mailing Add:* 495 Scotch Church Rd Pattersonville NY 12137. *Fax:* 518-432-4630

STRNISTE, GARY F, RADIATION BIOLOGY, MOLECULAR GENETICS. *Current Pos:* group leader, LS-1, 91-95, MEM STAFF, LOS ALAMOS NAT LAB, 75-, CHIEF STAFF, 95- *Personal Data:* b Springfield, Mass, May 31, 44; m 80, Virginia Neal Prater. *Educ:* Univ Mass, BS, 66; Pa State Univ, MS, 69, PhD(biophys), 71. *Honors & Awards:* Jap Gov Res Award,Sci & Technol Agency, 94 & 95. *Prof Exp:* Fel molecular radiobiol, Los Alamos Sci Lab, 71-73; City Univ New York, 73-74. *Concurrent Pos:* Adj prof, Dept Cell Biol, Univ NMex, 92- *Mem:* Radiation Res Soc; Am Soc Biol Chemists. *Res:* Low dose radiation effects; isolation and characterization of human DNA repair genes; somatic cell mutagenesis; in vitro and in vivo repair of DNA. *Mailing Add:* LS-DO MS M888 Life Sci Div Los Alamos Nat Lab Los Alamos NM 87545. *Fax:* 505-665-3024; *E-Mail:* gfs@lanl.gov

STROBACH, DONALD ROY, ORGANIC CHEMISTRY, BIOCHEMISTRY. *Current Pos:* RETIRED. *Personal Data:* b St Louis, Mo, Jan 10, 33; m 60, 83, Barbara Orvis; c Michael & Andrea. *Educ:* Wash Univ, AB, 54, PhD(chem), 59. *Prof Exp:* NIH fels, 60-63; res chemist, Cent Res Dept, E I DuPont de Nemours & Co, Inc, 63-76, int mkt mgr, 76-79, atmospheric sci coordr, 79-82, environ mgr, Freon Prod Div, 82-86, sr res assoc, 86-94. *Mem:* Am Chem Soc. *Res:* Carbohydrates; synthesis and structure determination; synthesis of oligonucleotides; aerosol technology and product development. *Mailing Add:* 2420 W Parris Dr Wilmington DE 19808-4512

STROBECK, CURTIS, POPULATION GENETICS, MOLECULAR EVOLUTION. *Current Pos:* assoc prof, Dept Genetics, 76-84, PROF, DEPT ZOOL, UNIV ALTA, 84- *Personal Data:* b Powers Lake, NDak, Nov 14, 40. *Educ:* Univ Mont, BA, 64, MA, 66; Univ Chicago, PhD(theoret biol), 71. *Prof Exp:* Res fel pop biol, Univ Sussex, Sch Biol Sci, 71-75; vis asst prof, Dept Ecol & Evolution, State Univ NY, Stony Brook, 75-76. *Concurrent Pos:* Vis prof, Ctr Demog & Pop Genetics, Univ Tex, Houston; chmn, Dept Genetics, Univ Alta, 81-82. *Mem:* Genetics Soc Can; Am Genetics Soc; Soc Study Evolution. *Res:* Selection in heterogeneous environments; selection in multi-locus systems; evolution for recombination; effects of linkage in a finite population; evolution of ribosomal DNA in Drosophila and conifers; variation in the mitochondrial DNA of vertebrates. *Mailing Add:* Dept Biol Scis Univ Alta Edmonton AB T6G 2E9 Can

STROBEL, DARRELL FRED, PLANETARY ATMOSPHERES, SPACE PHYSICS. *Current Pos:* PROF PLANETARY SCI, EARTH SCI, PHYSICS & ASTRON, JOHNS HOPKINS UNIV, 84- *Personal Data:* b Fargo, NDak, May 13, 42; m 68; c 2. *Educ:* NDak State Univ, BS, 64; Harvard Univ, AM, 65, PhD(appl physics), 69. *Prof Exp:* Res assoc planetary astron, Kitt Peak Nat Observ, 68-70, asst physicist, 70-72, assoc physicist, 72-73; res physicist, 73-76, supvr res physicist, Naval Res Lab, 76-84. *Concurrent Pos:* Space Sci Bd, Nat Acad Sci-Nat Res Coun. *Mem:* AAAS; Am Astron Soc; Am Geophys Union; Am Meteorol Soc; Int Astron Union. *Res:* Chemistry, dynamics and physics of planetary atmospheres; planetary aeronomy; planetary physics; planetary magnetospheres. *Mailing Add:* Earth Sci Johns Hopkins Univ 3400 N Charles St Baltimore MD 21218-2608

STROBEL, DAVID ALLEN, PSYCHOLOGY. *Current Pos:* chmn dept, 81 & 83-90, PROF PSYCHOL, UNIV MONT, MISSOULA, 73-, ASSOC DEAN, GRAD SCH, 90- *Personal Data:* b Madison, Wis, Jan 17, 42; m 64, 82, Linda Zimmermann; c Laura W. *Educ:* Lake Forest Col, BA, 64; Univ Wis, MA, 71; Univ Mont, PhD, 72. *Prof Exp:* Asst prof, Northwestern Univ, 72-73. *Concurrent Pos:* Grantee, NIH, 73-77, Agr Res Serv, USDA, 77-84; dir, Missoula Primate Lab, 73-92; consult, Missoula Drug Treatment Prog, 78 & Missoula Spec Educ Coop, 83. *Mem:* Am Asn Primatologists; Int Soc Primatologists; Psychologists Ethical Treatment of Animals; Sigma Xi. *Res:* Primatology; human treatment of animals. *Mailing Add:* Dept Psychol Univ Mont Missoula MT 59812

STROBEL, EDWARD, GENETIC ENGINEERING, CYTOGENETICS. *Current Pos:* ASST PROF GENETICS, DEPT BIOL SCI, PURDUE UNIV, 80- *Personal Data:* b Wilkes-Barre, Pa, Mar 18, 47. *Educ:* Towson State Univ, BA, 69; State Univ NY, Stony Brook, PhD(cell & develop biol), 77. *Prof Exp:* Housing inspector, Baltimore City Health Dept, 69-70; instr chem, Boys' Latin Sch, Baltimore, 70-72. *Concurrent Pos:* Consult, Boehringer-Mannheim Biochem, Indianapolis, 80-; fel molecular biol, Sidney Farber Cancer Inst, 77-80; prin investr, Purdue Cancer Ctr, 81-82, NIH, 81-84 & Nat Eye Inst, 81-85. *Res:* Mechanisms involved in maintaining the structural integrity and stability of eukaryotic chromosomes, and how higher order chromosome structure is modulated during development. *Mailing Add:* 25928 Richville Dr Torrance CA 90505

STROBEL, GARY A, PLANT PATHOLOGY. *Current Pos:* From asst prof to prof bot, 63-77, PROF PLANT PATH, MONT STATE UNIV, 77- *Personal Data:* b Massillon, Ohio, Sept 23, 38; m 63; c 2. *Educ:* Colo State Univ, BS, 60; Univ Calif, Davis, PhD(plant path), 63. *Concurrent Pos:* Prin investr, NSF & USDA res grants; NIH career develop award, 69-74. *Mem:* AAAS; Am Soc Biol Chemists. *Res:* Plant disease physiology; biochemistry of fungi and bacteria that cause plant diseases; phytotoxic glycopeptides; metabolic regulation in diseased plants; nature and mechanism of action of host specific toxins. *Mailing Add:* Dept Plant Path Mont State Univ Bozeman MT 59715-5072. *Fax:* 406-994-1848

STROBEL, GEORGE L, THEORETICAL NUCLEAR PHYSICS, OPTICS. *Current Pos:* ASSOC PROF PHYSICS, UNIV GA, 67- *Personal Data:* b Pratt, Kans, May 26, 37; m 57; c 2. *Educ:* Kans State Univ, BS, 58; Univ Pittsburgh, MS, 61; Univ Southern Calif, PhD(physics), 65. *Prof Exp:* Scientist physics, Westinghouse Bettis Atomic Power Lab, 58-61 & Douglas Aircraft Co, 61-64; res assoc, Univ Southern Calif, 65 & Univ Calif, Davis, 65-67. *Concurrent Pos:* Vis prof, Nuclear Res Ctr, Jülich, WGer, 71-72; vis scientist, Lawrence Livermore Lab, 82-93. *Mem:* Am Phys Soc. *Res:* Electromagnetism, x-ray lasers, phase changes, non equilibrium thermodynamics mechanics and explosions. *Mailing Add:* Dept Physics Univ Ga Athens GA 30602. *Fax:* 706-542-2492

STROBEL, HOWARD AUSTIN, ANALYTICAL CHEMISTRY, PHYSICAL CHEMISTRY. *Current Pos:* coordr fedn, 74-81, prof chem, 64-90, EMER PROF, DUKE UNIV, 90- *Personal Data:* b Bremerton, Wash, Sept 5, 20; m 53, Shirley Holcomb; c Paul, Gary & Linda. *Educ:* State Col Wash, BS, 42; Brown Univ, PhD(phys chem), 47. *Prof Exp:* Jr res chemist,

Manhattan Dist, Brown Univ, 43-45, res assoc, 47-48; from instr to assoc prof chem, Trinity Col, 48-64, asst dean, 56-64; dean, Baldwin Residential Fedn, 72-75, fac fel, 75-81. *Concurrent Pos:* Consult, Sci Instrumentation Info Network & Curricula, 81; vis prof, Univ Leicester, 71-72, Univ NC, Chapel Hill, 82; ed, J Chem Educ, 91- *Mem:* Am Chem Soc; Royal Soc Chem. *Res:* Solute-solvent interactions in mixed media; ion exchange phenomena; chemical instrumentation. *Mailing Add:* Dept Chem Duke Univ Durham NC 27708-0346. *Fax:* 919-660-1605; *E-Mail:* strobel@duke.chem.edu

STROBEL, JAMES WALTER, PLANT PATHOLOGY. *Personal Data:* b Steubenville, Ohio, Oct 31, 33; m 55; c 2. *Educ:* Ohio Univ, AB, 55; Wash State Univ, PhD, 59. *Prof Exp:* Asst plant path, Wash State Univ, 55-59; from asst plant pathologist to assoc plant pathologist, Univ Fla, 59-68, prof plant path & plant pathologist, 68-74, chmn ornamental hort-agr exp stas, 70-74, dir agr & res ctr, Brandenton, 68-70; chmn, Dept Hort Sci, NC State Univ, 74-77; pres, Miss Univ Women, 77-88. *Mem:* Am Soc Hort Sci; Am Asn State Cols Univs; Am Phytopath Soc. *Res:* Etiology, epidemiology, and control of vegetable diseases, particularly control of verticillium wilt of tomato and strawberry by breeding for resistance. *Mailing Add:* Erskine Col PO Box 339 Due West SC 29639-1000

STROBEL, RUDOLF G K, PROCESS & PRODUCTS DESIGN. *Current Pos:* res biochemist, 58-75, group leader, 75-81, SECT HEAD, RES DIV, PROCTER & GAMBLE CO, 81- *Personal Data:* b Kiessling, Ger, Feb 7, 27; US citizen; m 58; c 4. *Educ:* Univ Regensburg, BS, 53; Univ Munich, dipl, 55, Dr rer nat, 58. *Prof Exp:* Asst, Max Planck Inst Protein & Leather Res, Ger, 56-58. *Mem:* AAAS; Am Chem Soc; Asn Sci Int Café; Int Apple Inst. *Res:* Histochemistry; histology; protein composition and structure; enzymology; natural products; microbiology; flavor research; flavor analysis; beverage process and products design; emulsion, flour and beverage technologies; machinery/apparatus design. *Mailing Add:* 7305 Thompson Rd Cincinnati OH 45247-2329

STROBER, SAMUEL, IMMUNOLOGY. *Current Pos:* sr asst resident med, 70-71, from instr to assoc prof, 71-82, CHIEF, DIV IMMUNOL, STANFORD UNIV, 78-, PROF MED IMMUNOL, SHC MED, 82- *Personal Data:* b New York, NY, May 8, 40; m 63; c 2. *Educ:* Columbia Univ, AB, 61; Harvard Univ, MD, 66. *Honors & Awards:* Diane Goldstone Mem lectr, Massey Cancer Ctr, Med Col Va, 84. *Prof Exp:* Res fel, Surg Res Lab, Peter Bent Brigham Hosp, Boston, Mass, 62-63 & 65-66 & Oxford Univ, 63-64; intern med, Mass Gen Hosp, Boston, 66-67; res assoc, lab cell biol, Nat Cancer Inst, NIH, Bethesda, Md, 67-70. *Concurrent Pos:* Res Career Develop Award, Nat Inst Allergy & Infectious Dis, NIH, 71-76; investr, Howard Hughes Med Inst, Miami, Fla, 76-81; prin investr, NIH, 76- & State of Calif, 79-; assoc ed, J Immunol, 82-84, Transplantation, 82-85 & Int J Immunotherapy, 84- *Mem:* Am Asn Immunologists; Am Soc Clin Invest; Am Rheumatism Soc; Transplantation Soc; Am Soc Transplantation Physicians. *Res:* Radiotherapy treatments for and causes of rheumatoid arthritis, lupus and organ transplant rejection. *Mailing Add:* Dept Med Div Immunol & Rheumatol Stanford Univ Med Ctr 300 Pasteur Dr Stanford CA 94305-5111. *Fax:* 650-725-4114

STROBER, WARREN, MUCOSAL IMMUNOLOGY. *Current Pos:* HEAD MUCOSAL IMMUNITY SECT, LAB CLIN INVEST, NIH, 82- *Personal Data:* Brooklyn, NY, Oct 17, 37; m; c 3. *Educ:* Univ Rochester, MD, 62. *Mem:* Am Asn Immunologists; Am Soc Clin Invest; Am Bd Allergy & Immunol; Asn Am Physicians; Am Col Allergy. *Mailing Add:* Clin Ctr Bldg 10 Rm 11N250 NI-AID Bldg 10 Rm 11 N238 NIH 9000 Rockville Pike Bethesda MD 20892-1892

STROEBEL, CHARLES FREDERICK, III, PSYCHOPHYSIOLOGY, NEUROPHYSIOLOGY. *Current Pos:* DIR LABS PSYCHOPHYSIOL, INST LIVING HOSP, 62-, DIR CLINS, 74-, DIR RES, 79- *Personal Data:* b Chicago, Ill, May 25, 36; m 59; c 2. *Educ:* Univ Minn, BA, 58, PhD, 61; Yale Univ, MD, 73. *Prof Exp:* Res asst biophys, Mayo Clin, 55-58; res asst, Psychiat Animal Res Labs, Univ Minn, 58-61, actg dir labs & lectr, Univ, 62. *Concurrent Pos:* Adj prof, Univ Hartford, 64-72, res prof, 72-; adj prof, Trinity Col, Conn, 72-; lectr psychiat, Sch Med, Yale Univ, 73-; prof, Dept Psychiat, Univ Conn Health Ctr & Med Sch, 77- *Mem:* Biofeedback Soc Am; Am Psychiat Asn; Sigma Xi; Int Soc Chronobiology; NY Acad Sci. *Res:* Physiologic and behavioral mechanisms of stress and drugs; biologic rhythms; biofeedback; biostatistics; neurophysiology of learning and emotion. *Mailing Add:* PO Box 279 Andover CT 06232

STROEHLEIN, JACK LEE, SOIL SCIENCE. *Current Pos:* Asst prof, Univ Ariz, 62-67, assoc prof agr chem & soils, 67-76, res scientist agr chem, Agr Exp Sta, 74-90, assoc prof, 76-90, EMER PROF SOILS & WATER SCI, UNIV ARIZ, 90- *Personal Data:* b Cobden, Ill, Dec 22, 32; m 65. *Educ:* Southern Ill Univ, BS, 54; Univ Wis, MS, 58, PhD(soils), 62. *Honors & Awards:* Commendation Award, Soil & Water Conserv Soc. *Concurrent Pos:* Adv soils & soil fertil, Brazil Prog, AID, 70-71. *Mem:* Am Soc Agron; fel Soil & Water Conserv Soc. *Res:* Soil-plant-water relationships; soil testing; fertilization and fertilizer use. *Mailing Add:* Dept Soil & Water Environ Sci Univ Ariz 425 Schartz Bldg 38 Tucson AZ 85721. *Fax:* 520-621-1647

STROEVE, PIETER, THIN FILM TECHNOLOGY, COLLOID SCIENCE. *Current Pos:* assoc prof, 82-84, PROF CHEM ENG, UNIV CALIF, DAVIS, 84- *Personal Data:* b Velp, Netherlands, Sept 15, 45; c 3. *Educ:* Univ Calif, Berkeley, BS, 67; Mass Inst Technol, MS, 69, DSc(chem eng), 73. *Prof Exp:* Researcher, Weizmann Inst Sci, Israel, 73-74; sr scientist, 77; res asst prof, Univ Nijmegen, Neth, 74-77; from asst prof to assoc prof chem eng, State Univ NY, Buffalo, 77-82. *Concurrent Pos:* Consult, Los Alamos Nat Lab, 82-87; prin investr grants, NSF, 85-; vis prof, Univ Queensland, Australia, IBM Almaden Res Ctr, 88-89, Max-Planck Inst Polymer Res, 96; consult, Ames Lab, Iowa, 93-95; co-dir, Ctr Polymer Interfaces & Macromolecular Assemblies, NSF. *Mem:* Am Inst Chem Engrs; Am Chem Soc; Am Inst Physics. *Res:* Transport phenomena in multi-phase systems; colloid science; thin film technology. *Mailing Add:* Dept Chem Eng & Mat Sci Univ Calif Davis CA 95616-5294. *E-Mail:* pstroeve@ucdavis.edu

STROH, ROBERT CARL, AFFORDABLE HOUSING POLICY & TECHNOLOGY. *Current Pos:* DIR, CTR AFFORDABLE HOUSING, UNIV FLA, 89- *Personal Data:* b Flint, Mich, July 23, 37; m 79, Kelly A Pascal; c 4. *Educ:* Pa State Univ, BS, 59, MS, 61, PhD(genetics & statist), 64. *Prof Exp:* Grad asst statist, Pa State Univ, 59-64, lectr comput sci, 64-65; sr staff, Auto Biometrics Inc, 64-65; analyst, Vitro Labs, 65-73; vpres, Appl Urbanetics Inc, 73-79; div dir, Nat Asn Home Builders Res Ctr, 79-89. *Mem:* Sigma Xi; Nat Inst Bldg Sci; Soc Res Adminr; Am Inst Constructors. *Res:* Residential and light commercial sector of the construction industry. *Mailing Add:* 8611 SW 23rd Pl Gainesville FL 32607-3464. *Fax:* 352-392-4364; *E-Mail:* struh@nervm.nerdc.ufl.edu

STROH, WILLIAM RICHARD, PHYSICS. *Current Pos:* RETIRED. *Personal Data:* b Sunbury, Pa, May 5, 23. *Educ:* Harvard Univ, SB, 46, AM, 50, PhD(appl physics), 57. *Prof Exp:* Instr physics, Bucknell Univ, 46-49; res fel acoustics, Harvard Univ, 57-58; from asst prof to assoc prof elec eng, Univ Rochester, 58-62; assoc prof physics, Goucher Col, 62-68, prof, 68-81. *Mem:* Am Phys Soc. *Res:* Acoustics; instrumentation. *Mailing Add:* 206 Charmuth Rd Lutherville Timonium MD 21093

STROHBEHN, JOHN WALTER, BIOMEDICAL ENGINEERING. *Current Pos:* From asst prof to assoc prof, Dartmouth Col, 63-74, assoc dean, 76-81, actg provost, 87-89, provost, 89-93, PROF ENG, DARTMOUTH COL, 74- *Personal Data:* b San Diego, Calif, Nov 21, 36; m 58, 80, Barbara Brungard; c 3. *Educ:* Stanford Univ, BS, 58, MS, 59, PhD(elec eng), 64. *Honors & Awards:* Eugene Robinson Award for Outstanding Contrib to Hyperthermia Oncol. *Concurrent Pos:* Partic, Nat Acad Sci-Acad Sci USSR Exchange Prog, 67; mem comn II, Int Sci Radio Union; Inter-Union Comt Radio Meteorol; consult, McGraw-Hill, Inc & Avco Corp; vis res scientist, Stanford Med Sch; distinguished lectr, Ant & Prop Soc, Inst Elec & Electronics Engrs, 79-82; adj prof med, Dartmouth Med Sch, 79; vis fel, Princeton Univ. *Mem:* Fel AAAS; Radiation Res Soc; fel Optical Soc Am; Am Asn Physicists in Med; fel Am Inst Elec & Electronics Engrs. *Res:* Environmental engineering: energy and global warming; image processing and echocardiography; biomedical engineering and cancer. *Mailing Add:* Duke Univ Box 90005 Durham NC 27708. *Fax:* 603-646-3856; *E-Mail:* john.w.strohbehn@dartmouth.edu

STROHBEHN, KIM, ELECTRICAL ENGINEERING. *Current Pos:* ENGR, APPL PHYSICS LAB, JOHNS HOPKINS UNIV, 80- *Personal Data:* b Council Bluffs, Iowa, Oct 17, 53; m 75; c 1. *Educ:* Iowa State Univ, BS, 76, MS, 77, PhD(elec eng), 79. *Prof Exp:* Asst elec eng, Iowa State Univ, 76-80. *Mem:* Inst Elec & Electronics Engrs; Sigma Xi. *Res:* Application of control and estimation theory. *Mailing Add:* 6564 Gayheart Ct Columbia MD 21045-4624

STROHL, GEORGE RALPH, JR, MATHEMATICS. *Current Pos:* From instr to prof, 47-85, chmn dept, 70-76, EMER PROF, US NAVAL ACAD, 85- *Personal Data:* b Ardmore, Pa, Oct 19, 19; m 46; c 2. *Educ:* Haverford Col, BA, 41; Univ Pa, MA, 47; Univ Md, PhD(math), 56. *Mem:* Am Math Soc; Am Soc Eng Educ. *Res:* Topology and analysis. *Mailing Add:* 235 Westwood Rd Annapolis MD 21401-1250

STROHL, JOHN HENRY, ANALYTICAL CHEMISTRY. *Current Pos:* PROF, BIRMINGHAM SOUTHERN COL, 88- *Personal Data:* b Forest City, Ill, Oct 2, 38; m 60; c 2. *Educ:* Univ Ill, BS, 59; Univ Wis, PhD(chem), 64. *Prof Exp:* Asst chem, Univ Wis, 59-64; from asst prof to assoc prof chem, WVa Univ, 70-88. *Mem:* Am Chem Soc. *Res:* Preparative electrochemistry and continuous electrolysis. *Mailing Add:* Birmingham Southern Col PO Box 549022 Birmingham AL 35254

STROHL, KINGMAN P, PULMONARY PHYSIOLOGY, PULMONARY MEDICINE. *Current Pos:* ASSOC PROF MED, CASE WESTERN RESERVE UNIV, 80- *Personal Data:* b Chicago, Ill, Mar 15, 49. *Educ:* Yale Univ, BA, 70; Northwestern Univ, MD, 74. *Mem:* Am Physiol Soc; Am Thoracic Soc; Am Fedn Clin Res. *Mailing Add:* Div Pulm & Critical Care Med VA Med Ctr 111J W 10701 East Blvd Cleveland OH 44106. *Fax:* 216-844-3226

STROHL, WILLIAM ALLEN, VIROLOGY. *Current Pos:* res assoc, 64-66, from asst prof to assoc prof, 66-77, PROF MICROBIOL, RUTGERS MED SCH, COL MED & DENT NJ, 77- *Personal Data:* b Bethlehem, Pa, Nov 1, 33; m 57, Doerga Van Der Kemp; c Durga & Celinde. *Educ:* Lehigh Univ, AB, 55; Calif Inst Technol, PhD(biol), 60. *Prof Exp:* Instr microbiol, Sch Med, St Louis Univ, 59-63. *Concurrent Pos:* Nat Found fel, 59-61. *Mem:* AAAS; Am Soc Microbiol. *Res:* Animal viruses; viral oncogenesis. *Mailing Add:* R W Johnson Med Sch Univ Med & Dent 675 Hoes Lane Piscataway NJ 08854-5635. *Fax:* 732-235-5223

STROHM, JERRY LEE, GENETICS, PLANT BREEDING. *Current Pos:* Head dept, 68-74, PROF BIOL, UNIV WIS-PLATTEVILLE, 64- *Personal Data:* b West Union, Ill, Jan 9, 37; m 57; c 4. *Educ:* Univ Ill, BS, 59; Univ Minn, PhD(genetics), 66. *Res:* Soybean genetics. *Mailing Add:* 425 S Hickory St Platteville WI 53818

STROHM, PAUL F, AGRICULTURAL CHEMISTRY, ORGANIC CHEMISTRY. *Current Pos:* res chemist, 68-72, group leader, 72-77, MGR QUAL CONTROL, AMCHEM PROD, INC, 77- *Personal Data:* b Pennsauken, NJ, Jan 13, 35; m 57; c 5. *Educ:* La Salle Col, BA, 56; Temple Univ, PhD(org chem), 61. *Prof Exp:* Res chemist, Atlantic Refining Co, 60-62 & Houdry Labs, Air Prod & Chem Inc, 62-68. *Mem:* Am Chem Soc; Am Soc Qual Control. *Res:* Organic synthesis: agricultural chemicals, especially herbicides and plant growth regulators; kinetics of urethane reactions; mechanism of epoxy curing reactions; bicyclic amine chemistry. *Mailing Add:* Henkel Corp 300 Brookside Ave Ambler PA 19002-3438

STROHMAN, RICHARD CAMPBELL, ZOOLOGY. *Current Pos:* from asst prof to assoc prof, 58-70, chmn dept, 73-77, PROF ZOOL, UNIV CALIF, BERKELEY, 70- *Personal Data:* b New York, NY, May 5, 27; m; c 2. *Educ:* Columbia Univ, PhD, 58. *Prof Exp:* Instr zool & cell physiol, Columbia Univ, 55-56. *Mem:* Soc Gen Physiol. *Res:* Physiology and biochemistry of muscle growth and development. *Mailing Add:* Dept Molecular Cell Biol Univ Calif Berkeley Berkeley CA 94720-4759

STROHMAN, ROLLIN DEAN, AGRICULTURAL ENGINEERING. *Current Pos:* assoc prof, 69-80, PROF AGR ENG, CALIF POLYTECH STATE UNIV, SAN LUIS OBISPO, 80- *Personal Data:* b Geneseo, Ill, Oct 29, 39; m 69; c 2. *Educ:* Univ Ill, BS(agr eng) & BS(agr sci), 62, MS, 65; Purdue Univ, PhD(agr eng), 69. *Prof Exp:* Agr engr, Western Utilization Res & Develop Div, Agr Res Serv, USDA, 68-69. *Mem:* Am Soc Agr Engrs; Am Soc Photogram. *Res:* Surveying and mapping; microcomputer interfacing. *Mailing Add:* Dept Agr Eng Calif Polytech State Univ San Luis Obispo CA 93407

STROJNY, EDWIN JOSEPH, INDUSTRIAL CHEMISTRY. *Current Pos:* ORG CHEMIST, DOW CHEM CO, 57- *Personal Data:* b Chicago, Ill, Jan 1, 26; m 55; c 2. *Educ:* Ill Inst Technol, BS, 51; Univ Ill, PhD(chem), 55. *Prof Exp:* Asst instr gen chem, Univ Ill, 51-52; org chemist, G D Searle & Co, 54-57. *Mem:* AAAS; Am Chem Soc; Sigma Xi. *Res:* Phenolic compounds and derivatives; aromatic chemistry; heterogeneous and homogeneous catalysis; oxidation of organic compounds by oxygen; reaction mechanisms. *Mailing Add:* 4695 Gully Rd Harbor Springs MI 49740-9610

STROJNY, NORMAN, CHROMATOGRAPHY, ULTRA VIOLET-VISIBLE SPECTROPHOTOMETRY & FLUORESCENCE. *Current Pos:* sr scientist, 85-88, group leader method develop & validation, 88-90, SUPVR, ANAL RES & DEVELOP, DANBURY PHARMACAL, INC, 91- *Personal Data:* b Edwardsville, Pa, June 14, 43. *Educ:* Wilkes Col, BS, 66; Montclair State Col, MA, 74; Rutgers Univ PhD(anal chem), 80, MBA, 85. *Prof Exp:* From jr chemist to sr chemist, Hoffman La Roche, Inc, 65-85. *Mem:* Am Chem Soc; Am Asn Pharmaceut Scientists; Soc Appl Spectros; Am Inst Chem; Anal Lab Mgr Asn. *Res:* Cryogenic photo luminescence of pharmaceuticals; drug metabolism; drugs in biological fluids and pharmaceutical analysis method development; author of over 25 publications and 10 presentations. *Mailing Add:* Danbury Pharmacal Inc 1033 Stoneleigh Ave Carmel NY 10512

STROKE, HINKO HENRY, ATOMIC SPECTROSCOPY, NUCLEAR PHYSICS. *Current Pos:* assoc prof physics, 63-68, chmn, Dept Physics, 88-91, PROF PHYSICS, NY UNIV, 68- *Personal Data:* b Zagreb, Yugoslavia, June 16, 27; US citizen; m 56, Norma Bilchick; c Ilana & Marija. *Educ:* NJ Inst Technol, BS, 49; Mass Inst Technol, MS, 52, PhD, 55. *Honors & Awards:* Sr US Scientist Award, Alexander von Humboldt Found, 77. *Prof Exp:* Res assoc physics, Princeton Univ, 54-57; res staff & lectr physics, Mass Inst Technol, 57-63. *Concurrent Pos:* Assoc prof, Univ Paris, 69-70 & 78; Ed, Comments Atomic & Molecular Physics, 73-; sci assoc, Euro Ctr Nuclear Res, Geneva, 83-; sr fel NATO, 75; mem, Publ Oversight Comt, Am Phys Soc, 91-93. *Mem:* Fel AAAS; fel Am Phys Soc; fel Optical Soc Am; Fr Phys Soc; Europ Phys Soc. *Res:* Hyperfine structure and isotope shifts of stable and radioactive atoms by magnetic resonance and optical spectroscopy; nuclear moments; charge and magnetization distribution; coherence in atomic radiation; solar spectra; spectroscopic instrumentation; laser systems; low temperature bolometric particle spectrometers. *Mailing Add:* Dept Physics NY Univ New York NY 10003. *Fax:* 212-995-4016; *E-Mail:* stroke@acf2.nyu.edu

STROM, BRIAN LESLIE, PHARMACOEPIDEMIOLOGY, CLINICAL EPIDEMIOLOGY. *Current Pos:* asst prof pharmacol, 80-88, assoc prof med, 88-93, PROF MED, UNIV PA SCH MED, 93-, PROF BIOSTATIST & EPIDEMIOL, 95- *Personal Data:* b New York, NY, Dec 8, 49; m 78, Elaine Moskowitz; c Shanra & Jordan. *Educ:* Yale Univ, BS, 71; Johns Hopkins Univ, MS, 75; Univ Calif, Berkeley, MPH, 80. *Hon Degrees:* MA, Univ Pa, 88. *Prof Exp:* Intern med, Univ Calif, San Francisco, 75-76; resident med, 76-78; fel clin pharmacol, 78-80. *Concurrent Pos:* Consult, many law firms, 79-, most major pharmaceut co, 80- & US & foreign govt agencies, 80-; prin investr, NIH, Food Drug Admin grants & others, 80-; lectr, all over the world, 80-; adj prof clin pharm, Philadelphia Col Pharm & Sci, 81-90, adj assoc prof, 90-93, adj prof, 93-; assoc, Leonard Davis Inst Health Econs, 84-89, sr fel, 89-; vis scientist, Dept Clin Pharmacol, Hoddinge Hosp, Sweden, 87; mem, JCAHO, Medication Use Task Force, 89- & US Pharmaceutics Drug Utilization Rev Adv Panel, 90-; Pfizer vis prof clin pharmacol, Georgetown Univ Med Ctr, 92; vis prof, Univ Mich Sch Pub Health, 92-, adj prof, epidemiol, 93. *Mem:* Fel Am Col Physicians; fel Am Col Epidemiol; Am Epidemiol Soc; Am Soc Clin Pharmacol & Therapeut; Am Soc Clin Invest; Int Soc Pharmacol & Epidemiol. *Res:* Clinical epidemiology; pharmacoepidemiology; epidemiologic methods to study the effects of drugs. *Mailing Add:* Hosp Univ Pa 3400 Spruce St Philadelphia PA 19104-4228. *E-Mail:* strom@cceb.med.upenn.edu

STROM, E(DWIN) THOMAS, POLYMER CHEMISTRY, PHYSICAL ORGANIC CHEMISTRY. *Current Pos:* ADJ PROF CHEM, UNIV TEX, ARLINGTON, 96- *Personal Data:* b Des Moines, Iowa, June 11, 36; m 58, Charlotte F Williams; c Laura C & Eric W. *Educ:* Univ Iowa, BS, 58; Univ Calif, Berkeley, MS, 61; Iowa State Univ, PhD(phys org chem), 64. *Honors & Awards:* W T Doherty Award, Am Chem Soc, 89. *Prof Exp:* Res technologist, Dallas Res Lab, Mobil Res & Develop Corp, 64-67, sr res chemist, 67-92, sr staff chemist, 92-95. *Concurrent Pos:* Vis lectr, Dallas Baptist Col, 69-70, El Centro Community Col, 70-72 & Univ Tex, Dallas, 74; adj prof, Univ Tex, Arlington, 78-79, 82-91 & 93-; ed, Southwest Retort, 83- *Mem:* Am Chem Soc; Soc Petrol Engrs; Int Electron Paramagnetic Resonance Soc. *Res:* Polymers for petroleum recovery; free radicals; magnetic resonance. *Mailing Add:* 1134 Medalist Dr Dallas TX 75232. *Fax:* 817-272-3808

STROM, ERIC WILLIAM, COMPUTER MODELING OF GROUND-WATER FLOW. *Current Pos:* intern, 88, phys sci technician, 89, HYDROLOGIST, US GEOL SURV, 93- *Personal Data:* b Ames, Iowa, May 1, 63; m 90, Kathy Kirchhoff. *Educ:* Rice Univ, BS, 88; Tex A&M Univ, MS, 93. *Prof Exp:* Teaching asst, geol, Tex A&M Univ, 90-93. *Mem:* Am Water Resources Asn; Am Geophys Union. *Res:* Investigation of ground-water resources and computer modeling of ground-water flow. *Mailing Add:* US Geol Surv Water Resources Div 308 S Airport Rd Pearl MS 39208. *Fax:* 601-965-5782; *E-Mail:* ewstrom@mod1dmsjkn.usgs.er.gov

STROM, OREN GRANT, TRANSPORTATION SYSTEMS, CONTINUING EDUCATION. *Current Pos:* actg dean, 88-92, ASSOC DEAN, COL ENG & APPL SCI, UNIV COLO, DENVER, 82-88 & 92- *Personal Data:* b Groton, SDak, Aug 1, 31; m 53, Natalie Ellsworth; c Brian, Randie, Kevin & Celia. *Educ:* SDak State Univ, BS, 53; Univ Wyo, MS, 65; Univ Tex, Austin, PhD(civil eng), 72. *Prof Exp:* Hwy engr, State Hwy Dept Wis, 53-54; engr-mgr, USAF, 54-82. *Concurrent Pos:* Dean, Sch Civil Eng, Air Force Inst Technol, USAF, 77-81. *Mem:* Am Soc Civil Engrs; Soc Am Mil Engrs; Am Soc Eng Educ. *Res:* Transportation engineering research; computer-based management of the construction, maintenance and repair of systems so that resources are programmed, allocated and used according to the actual requirements. *Mailing Add:* 16920 E Berry Pl Aurora CO 80015. *Fax:* 303-556-2511; *E-Mail:* ostrom@cvdnvr.denver.colordo.edu

STROM, RICHARD NELSEN, ENVIRONMENTAL GEOCHEMISTRY, CLAY MINERALOGY. *Current Pos:* prin scientist, 90-93, FEL SCIENTIST, SAVANNAH RIVER LAB, 93- *Personal Data:* b Schenectady, NY, June 5, 42. *Educ:* Union Col, BS, 66; Univ Del, MS, 72, PhD(geol), 76. *Prof Exp:* Dep route mgr, Off Interoceanic Canal Studies, Corps Engrs, 67-69; asst prof geol, Univ Wis-Parkside, 75-77; from asst prof to assoc prof geol, Univ SFla, 77-90. *Concurrent Pos:* Prog mgr geosci, Savannah River Site. *Mem:* Sigma Xi; Asn Ground Water Sci & Engrs. *Res:* Environmental geochemistry of metals and radonuclides; hydrogeology and ground water geochemistry. *Mailing Add:* Westinghouse-Savannah River Co Savannah River Site Bldg 773-42A Aiken SC 29808. *E-Mail:* richard.strom@srs.gov

STROM, ROBERT GREGSON, ASTROGEOLOGY. *Current Pos:* from asst prof to assoc prof, Lunar & Planetary Lab, 63-81, PROF PLANETARY SCI, UNI ARIZ, 81- *Personal Data:* b Long Beach, Calif, Oct 1, 33; m 55; c 1. *Educ:* Univ Redlands, BS, 55; Stanford Univ, MS, 57. *Prof Exp:* Geologist, Stand Vacuum Oil Co, 57-60; asst res geologist, Univ Calif, Berkeley, 61-63. *Concurrent Pos:* Mem, Apollo Lunar Oper Working Group, 68-69, Imaging Sci Team, Mariner Venus/Mercury Mission, 69-75, Lunar Sci Inst, Lunar Sci & Cartog Comn, 74-79, NASA Comet Working Group, Jet Propulsion Lab Jupiter Orbiter Sci Working Group & NASA Mercury Geol Mapping Prog, 75-78; rep, Planetary Prog, Jet Propulsion Lab Imaging Syst Instrument Develop Prog, 75-79; mem, NASA Venus Orbital Imaging Radar Sci Working Group, Jet Propulsion Lab, 77-78, assoc mem, Voyager Imaging Sci Team, 78-; mem, Planetary Geol Working Group, 80-82 & NASA Planetary Geol Rev Panel, 80-82; chmn, NASA Planetary Cartog Working Group, 83-85; NASA Planetary Geol & Geophys Working Group, 86-, NASA Mercury Orbiter Sci Working Team, 88- *Mem:* Am Geophys Union; Int Astron Union; Am Astron Soc. *Res:* Lunar and planetary geology; origin and evolution of lunar and planetary surfaces; space craft imaging of planetary surfaces. *Mailing Add:* 5331 S Camino De la Tierra Tucson AZ 85746

STROM, ROBERT MICHAEL, ORGANIC CHEMISTRY, PHOTOCHEMISTRY. *Current Pos:* chemist, Dow Chemical Corp, 80-81, proj leader monomers, 81-82, res leader epoxies, 82-84, group leader thermosets & monomers, 84-85, GROUP LEADER ION EXCHANGE, DOW CHEM CORP, 85- *Personal Data:* b Detroit, Mich, Aug 6, 51; m 74. *Educ:* Grand Valley State Col, BS, 74; Univ Colo, PhD(org chem), 78. *Prof Exp:* Res asst org photochem, Univ Colo, 74-78; res chemist synthetic org chem, Arapahoe Chem Inc, 78-80. *Mem:* Am Chem Soc; Sigma Xi. *Res:* Synthetic organic chemistry; physical organic photochemistry; process development of aromatic and heterocyclic synthesis; determination of structural features of short lived ground and excited state intermediates, monomers, thermosets, flame retardants and epoxies ion exchange. *Mailing Add:* 789 W Chippewa River Rd Midland MI 48640

STROM, STEPHEN, ASTRONOMY, ASTROPHYSICS. *Current Pos:* AT DEPT PHYSICS, UNIV MASS. *Personal Data:* b Bronx, NY, Aug 12, 42; m 60; c 4. *Educ:* Harvard Univ, AB, 62, AM & PhD(astron), 64. *Honors & Awards:* Bart J Bok Prize, 71; Helen B Warner Prize, Am Astron Soc, 76. *Prof Exp:* Astrophysicist, Smithsonian Astrophys Observ, 62-69; lectr astron, Harvard Univ, 64-69; assoc prof physics & earth & space sci, State Univ NY Stony Brook, 69-71, prof astron, 71-72; coordr astron & astrophys, 69-72; astronr, Kitt Peak Nat Observ, 72-, chmn galactic & extragalactic prog, 75- *Concurrent Pos:* Alfred P Sloan Found res fel, 70-72; mem at large, Assoc Univs Res Astron, 71-72; res assoc, Smithsonian Astrophys Observ, 69-71. *Mem:* Am Astron Soc; Int Astron Union. *Res:* Evolution of stars; structure and evolution of galaxies. *Mailing Add:* Grad Res Tower No 518 Amherst MA 01003

STROM, TERRY BARTON, IMMUNOLOGY RESEARCH. *Current Pos:* DIR CLIN IMMUNOL, MED DIR KIDNEY TRANSPLANTATION & PHYSICIAN, BETH ISRAEL HOSP, BOSTON, 83- *Personal Data:* b Chicago, Ill, Nov 30, 41; m 64; c 2. *Educ:* Univ Ill Col Med, MD, 66. *Hon Degrees:* DSc, Hahnemann Univ, 91. *Prof Exp:* Intern med, Univ Ill Hosps, 66-67, jr resident, 67-68; assoc prof med, 78-88, prof med, Harvard Univ, 88-; physician, Brigham & Women's Hosp, Boston, 73- *Concurrent Pos:* Career Develop Award, NIH, 75. *Mem:* Am Soc Transplant Physicians (pres, 83-84); Am Soc Clin Invests; Int Transplant Soc; Am Asn Immunologists; Int Soc Nephrology; Am Soc Nephrology; Clin Immunol Soc (pres, 89-90); Asn Am Prof. *Res:* Mechanisms of transplant rejection and T-lymphocyte activation; clinical transplantation; basic immunology research; development of immunopharmacologic principles and molecules. *Mailing Add:* Dept Med Harvard Med Sch Beth Israel Hosp 330 Brookline Ave Boston MA 02215-5491. *Fax:* 617-735-3547

STROMAN, DAVID WOMACK, FERMENTATION PRODUCTS. *Current Pos:* DIR MICROBIOL RES & DEVELOP, ALCON LABS, INC, 90- *Personal Data:* b Corpus Christi, Tex, June 1, 44; m 65; c 1. *Educ:* Bethany Nazarene Col, BS, 66; Univ Okla, PhD(biochem), 70. *Prof Exp:* NIH fel microbiol, Sch Med, Washington Univ, 70-72; res scientist antibiotic discovery & develop, Upjohn Co, 72-81; sr res scientist biotechnol, Phillips Petrol Co, 81-88. *Mem:* Am Chem Soc; Am Soc Microbiol. *Res:* Molecular biology and biochemical genetics with emphasis on fermentation derived products especially involving recombinant DNA technology. *Mailing Add:* Alcon Labs Inc 6201 S Freeway Ft Worth TX 76134

STROMATT, ROBERT WELDON, ANALYTICAL CHEMISTRY. *Current Pos:* RETIRED. *Personal Data:* b Muskogee, Okla, Mar 27, 29; m 56; c 3. *Educ:* Emporia State Teachers Col, BS, 54; Kans State Univ, PhD(chem), 58. *Prof Exp:* Res chemist, Hanford Labs, Gen Elec Co, 57-66; sr res scientist, Pac Northwest Lab, Battelle Mem Inst, 66-70; fel scientist, Westinghouse-Hanford, 70-87; Pac Northwest Lab, Battelle Mem Inst, 87-95. *Mem:* Am Chem Soc. *Res:* Automation and general methods development. *Mailing Add:* 411 Franklin Richland WA 99352-2003

STROMBERG, BERT EDWIN, JR, PARASITE IMMUNOLOGY. *Current Pos:* assoc prof, 79-86, interim chair, 89-93, PROF PARASITOL & IMMUNOL, UNIV MINN, 86-, DIR GRAD STUDIES, 90- *Personal Data:* b Trenton, NJ, May 19, 44; m 68; JoAnn Earling; c B Erik & Kristin L. *Educ:* Lafayette Col, BA, 66; Univ Mass, MA, 68; Univ Pa, PhD(parasitol), 73. *Prof Exp:* Instr biol, Trenton State Col, 68-70; asst prof parasitol, Univ Pa, 73-79. *Concurrent Pos:* Prin investr, NIH & USDA formula grants, Minn Agr Exp Sta, 79-; dir, Ctr Comp Biomed Res, 84-90; adj prof, Hassan II Agron & Vet Inst, Morocco, 85- *Mem:* Am Soc Parasitol; Am Asn Vet Parasitol (vpres, 87-88, pres-elect, 88-89, pres, 89-90); World Asn Advan Vet Parasitol; Conf Res Animal Dis (vpres, 95-96, pres, 96-97). *Res:* Immune response to helminth parasites; parasite antigens; immune protective response; in vitro cultivation; epidemiology of gastro-intestinal helminths and coccidia and their control. *Mailing Add:* Univ Minn Col Vet Med 1971 Commonwealth Ave St Paul MN 55108. *E-Mail:* b_stro@tc.umn.edu

STROMBERG, KARL ROBERT, mathematics; deceased, see previous edition for last biography

STROMBERG, KURT, PATHOLOGY. *Current Pos:* PROF PATH, UNIFORMED SERVS UNIV HEALTH SCI, BETHESDA, 88-, HEAD, CELL PATH SECT, DIV CYTOKINE BIOL. *Personal Data:* b Albuquerque, NMex, Mar 3, 39; m 93, Jean Wilbur Gleason; c Blake, Peter & Kris. *Educ:* Amherst Col, BA, 61; Univ Colo, MD, 66; Am Bd Path, dipl, 74. *Prof Exp:* Intern path, Yale-New Haven Hosp, 66-67; res assoc, Nat Cancer Inst, 68-72; resident path, Columbia Univ, 72-74; mem res staff, Inst Cancer Res, Delafield Hosp, NY, 72-74; sr staff investr, Nat Cancer Inst, 74-88. *Concurrent Pos:* Sr staff investr, Lab Cytokine Biol, Food & Drug Admin, 88- *Mem:* Am Asn Cancer Res; Am Asn Path; Int Acad Path. *Res:* Epidermal growth factor/erbB family receptors and ligands in carcinogenesis; recombinant biologics in wound healing. *Mailing Add:* FDA CBER Ctr Biologics Eval & Res 8800 Rockville Pike Bldg 29A Rm 3B-20 HFM-511 Bethesda MD 20892

STROMBERG, LAWAYNE ROLAND, MEDICAL DEVICES & DEVELOPMENT. *Current Pos:* PRES, L R STROMBERG MD LTD, 95- *Personal Data:* b Minneapolis, Minn, Nov 18, 29; m 54, Patricia Rivers; c Richard, Kirsten & Eric. *Educ:* Univ Calif, Berkeley, BA, 51; Univ Calif, Los Angeles, MD, 55; Univ Rochester, MS, 63. *Prof Exp:* Intern & resident gen surg, Univ Calif Med Ctr, Los Angeles, 55-58; resident, Vet Admin Hosp, Los Angeles, 58-60; cmndg officer & surgeon, 11th Evacuation Hosp, Korea, US Army, 61-62, nuclear med res officer, Walter Reed Army Inst Res, 65-68, cmndg officer, US Army Nuclear Med Res Detachment, Europe, Landstuhl, Ger, 68-71, dep dir & dir, Armed Forces Radiobiol Res Inst, Nat Naval Med Ctr, 67-77; assoc med dir, Baxter Healthcare Corp, 77-80, vpres med affairs, 80-90; vpres med & sci affairs, Expertech Assoc, 90-95. *Concurrent Pos:* Res fel radiation biol, Walter Reed Army Inst Res, 63-65. *Mem:* Fel Am Col Physician Execs; Asn Military Surg US; fel Royal Soc Med; Int Soc Technol Assessment Health Care. *Res:* Clinical research on new medical devices and drugs for Food & Drug Administration approval. *Mailing Add:* L R Strombera MD Ltd 120 Edgemont St Mundelein IL 60060. *Fax:* 847-949-8686; *E-Mail:* lrstrmbrg@aol.com

STROMBERG, MELVIN WILLARD, GROSS ANATOMY, NEUROANATOMY. *Current Pos:* RETIRED. *Personal Data:* b Quamba, Minn, Nov 2, 25; m 48, Beatrice E Palm; c Peter, Andrew, Elizabeth, Arnold, John & Maija. *Educ:* Univ Minn, BS, 53, DVM, 54, PhD(vet anat), 57. *Prof Exp:* Asst vet anat, Univ Minn, 53-54; from instr to assoc prof, 54-60; assoc prof, Purdue Univ, West Lafayette, 60-62, head dept, 63-81, prof vet anat, 62-93. *Concurrent Pos:* NIH spec fel anat, Karolinska Inst, Sweden, 70-71; adj prof, Ind Univ Sch Med, Indianapolis, 75; vis prof, Univ Munich Sch Med, WGer, 78-79, study & res, 85-86, vis prof, Massey Univ, Fac Vet Sci, Palmerston North, New Zeal, 91. *Mem:* Am Asn Vet Anat (pres, 66-67); Am Asn Anat; World Asn Vet Anat (secy, 91-95); Soc Marine Mammal. *Res:* Histology of cetacean and avian skin; neuroanatomy of domestic and laboratory animals; extra cellular lipids. *Mailing Add:* Dept Anat Sch Vet Med Purdue Univ West Lafayette IN 47906. *Fax:* 765-494-1772

STROMBERG, ROBERT REMSON, POLYMER SCIENCE, BLOOD & TISSUE BANKING. *Current Pos:* head biochem eng sect, Biomed Eng Lab, 80-84, PROD MGR, PROD DEVELOP DEPT, AM RED CROSS, 84- *Personal Data:* b Buffalo, NY, Feb 2, 25; m 47, Joyce White; c Earl, Eileen, Mark & Steven. *Educ:* Univ Buffalo, BA, 48, PhD(phys chem), 51. *Honors & Awards:* Silver Medal, US Dept Com, 73. *Prof Exp:* Asst phys chem, Univ Buffalo, 48-50; phys chemist, Nat Bur Stand, 51-62, chief phys chem br, Off Saline Water, 62, phys chemist, 62-67, chief polmer interface sect, 67-75, dep chief polymers div, 69-76; actg assoc bur dir device res & testing, Bur Med Devices, Food & Drug Admin, 76-80. *Concurrent Pos:* Chmn, Gordon Res Conf Sci Adhesion, 66; US Dept Com fel sci & technol, 75-76. *Mem:* Soc Biomaterials; Am Chem Soc; Am Asn Blood Banks; Int Soc Blood Transfusions. *Res:* Polymer and blood protein; surface interactions; surface chemistry; blood plasma separations; viral inactivation; mechanical properties of bone; platelet shedding by magakeryocytes; plasmapheresis; removal of leukocytes and platelets from red blood cells by filtration; photoactive dyes. *Mailing Add:* 15115 Interlochen Dr #807 Silver Spring MD 20906. *Fax:* 301-738-0704; *E-Mail:* stromberg@usa.red cross.org

STROMBERG, THORSTEN FREDERICK, LOW TEMPERATURE PHYSICS. *Current Pos:* asst prof, 67-74, ASSOC PROF PHYSICS, NMEX STATE UNIV, 74- *Personal Data:* b Aberdeen, Wash, Aug 13, 36. *Educ:* Reed Col, BA, 58; Iowa State Univ, PhD(physics), 65. *Prof Exp:* Res fel, Los Alamos Sci Lab, 65-67. *Mem:* Am Phys Soc. *Res:* Thermal and magnetic properties of superconductors, particularly type-II superconducting materials. *Mailing Add:* 2434 Westwind Rd Las Cruces NM 88005

STROMBOTNE, RICHARD L(AMAR), ENERGY CONVERSION, ATOMIC PHYSICS. *Current Pos:* head div, 65-81, prof chem & chmn, Dept Sci & Math, 76-81, PROF CHEM, CHADRON STATE COL, 81- *Personal Data:* b Watertown, SDak, May 6, 33; m 52; c 4. *Educ:* Pomona Col, BA, 55; Univ Calif, Berkeley, MA, 57, PhD(physics), 62. *Prof Exp:* Res assoc nuclear magnetic resonance, Univ Calif, Berkeley, 59-61; physicist, Radio Stand Lab, US Nat Bur Standards, 61-68; physicist, 68-71, asst for phys sci, 71-73, chief, Energy & Environ Div, 73-78, DIR, OFF AUTO FUEL ECON STANDARDS, US DEPT TRANSP, 78- *Concurrent Pos:* Finder of the Bayard, USA meteorite. *Mem:* AAAS; Soc Automotive Engrs; Am Phys Soc; Meteoritics; Soc Vertebrate Paleontology. *Res:* Automotive fuel economy; energy requirements of transportation systems; geochemical studies related to uranium, radium and radon; air pollution associated with transportation; measurement of fine structure of singly ionized helium; longitudinal spin-spin relaxation in low fields. *Mailing Add:* 24401 Peach Tree Rd Clarksburg MD 20871

STROME, FORREST C, JR, LASERS, INFORMATION RECORDING. *Current Pos:* proj physicist, Apparatus & Optical Div, 53-60, sr res physicist, Res Labs, 60-68, RES ASSOC, EASTMAN KODAK CO, 68- *Personal Data:* b Kalamazoo, Mich, May 19, 24; m 45; c 2. *Educ:* Univ Ill, BS, 45; Univ Mich, MS, 48, PhD(physics), 54. *Prof Exp:* Test engr, Gen Elec Co, 46-47. *Mem:* Am Phys Soc; Optical Soc Am. *Res:* Information recording using lasers. *Mailing Add:* 20 Stuyvesant Rd Pittsford NY 14534-3042

STROMER, MARVIN HENRY, CELL BIOLOGY, ELECTRON MICROSCOPY. *Current Pos:* assoc prof, 68-76, PROF, IOWA STATE UNIV, 76- *Personal Data:* b Readlyn, Iowa, Sept 1, 36; m 60, Shirley L Roepke; c Craig. *Educ:* Iowa State Univ, 59, PhD(cell biol), 66. *Honors & Awards:* Distinguished Res Award, Am Meat Sci Asn, 89; Meats Res Award, Am Soc Animal Sci, 96. *Prof Exp:* Foreman prod develop, George A Hormel & Co, Minn, 59-62; res asst cell biol, Iowa State Univ, 62-66; fel, Carnegie-Mellon Univ, 66-68. *Concurrent Pos:* Lectr, Tex A&M Univ, 71; Humboldt fel, 74; vis scientist, Max Planck Inst Med Res, Heidelberg, WGer, 74-75, Fulbright fel, 88; vis prof, Univ Ariz, 79-80; pres, Iowa Microbeam Co, 84-85, Iowa Affil, Am Heart Asn, 84-86; vis scientist, Univ Montreal, Que, 87, Inst Molecular Biol Austrian Acad Scis, Salzburg, Austria, 96; Fulbright fel, 96. *Mem:* Micros Soc Am; Am Heart Asn; Am Soc Cell Biol; Am Soc

Animal Sci. *Res:* Ultrastructure and biochemistry of filaments and filament attachment sites in striated and smooth muscle and other movement systems. *Mailing Add:* Dept Animal Sci Iowa State Univ 3116 Molecular Biol Bldg Ames IA 50011-3260. *Fax:* 515-294-0453; *E-Mail:* mstromer@iastate.edu

STROMINGER, ANDREW EBEN, PHYSICS. *Current Pos:* Mem, Inst Advan Study, 82-87, PROF PHYSICS, INST THEORET PHYSICS, UNIV CALIF, SANTA BARBARA, 86- *Personal Data:* b Cambridge, Eng, July 30, 55; US citizen. *Educ:* Harvard Col, BA, 77; Univ Calif, Berkeley, MA, 79; Mass Inst Technol, PhD, 82. *Concurrent Pos:* Alfred P Sloan Found fel, 86-90; outstanding jr investr, Dept Energy, 87-89. *Res:* Physics. *Mailing Add:* Dept Physics Univ Calif Santa Barbara CA 93106

STROMINGER, JACK L, IMMUNOLOGY. *Current Pos:* prof biochem, 68-83, chmn, Dept Biochem & Molecular Biol, 70-73, HIGGINS PROF BIOCHEM, HARVARD UNIV, 83-; HEAD, TUMOR VIROL DIV, DANA-FARBER CANCER INST, 77- *Personal Data:* b New York, NY, Aug 7, 25; c 4. *Educ:* Harvard Univ, AB, 44; Yale Univ, MD, 48. *Hon Degrees:* Trinity Col, Dublin, DSc, 75; Wash Univ, DSc, 88. *Honors & Awards:* John J Abel Award Pharmacol, 60; Paul-Lewis Lab Award Enzyme Chem, 62; Nat Acad Sci Award Microbiol, 68; Selman Waxman Award in Microbiol, Nat Acad Sci, 68; Rose Payne Award, Am Soc Histocompat & Immunogen, 86; Hoechst-Roussel Award, 90; Pasteur Medal, 90. *Prof Exp:* From asst prof to prof pharmacol, Sch Med, Washington Univ, St Louis, Mo, 55-61, prof pharmacol & microbiol, 61-64; prof pharmacol & chem microbiol, Med Sch, Univ Wis-Madison, 64-68. *Mem:* Inst Med-Nat Acad Sci; Am Soc Biol Chemists; Am Soc Pharmacol & Exp Therapeut; AAAS; Am Asn Immunologists; Am Soc Microbiologists; Sigma Xi; Am Chem Soc; Am Acad Arts & Sci; Europ Molecular Biol Orgn. *Mailing Add:* 2030 Massachusetts Ave Lexington MA 02173

STROMINGER, NORMAN LEWIS, NEUROANATOMY. *Current Pos:* from asst prof to prof anat, 65-94, PROF OTOLARYNGOL, ALBANY MED COL, 94- *Personal Data:* b New York, NY, June 1, 34; m 57; c 3. *Educ:* Univ Chicago, AB, 55, BS, 56, PhD(biopsychol), 61. *Prof Exp:* Trainee neuroanat, Columbia Univ, 62-65. *Concurrent Pos:* Prof neurosci, Sch Pub Health, State Univ NY, Albany. *Mem:* AAAS; Am Asn Anat; Soc Neuroscience. *Res:* Neuroanatomical studies of auditory and motor systems; mechanisms of emesis. *Mailing Add:* Dept Surg Div Otolaryngol A-135 Albany Med Col Union Univ 47 New Scotland Ave Albany NY 12208. *Fax:* 518-262-5136; *E-Mail:* normanstrominger@ccgateway.amc.edu

STROMMEN, DENNIS PATRICK, INORGANIC CHEMISTRY, RAMAN SPECTROSCOPY. *Current Pos:* PROF CHEM, IDAHO STATE UNIV, 92-, CHMN, 92- *Personal Data:* b Milwaukee, Wis, Sept 2, 38; m 68, Carol Hanson. *Educ:* Wis State Univ, Whitewater, BA, 66; Cornell Univ, PhD(chem), 71. *Prof Exp:* Res assoc spectros, Ctr Mat Res, Univ Md, 70-71; from asst prof to prof chem, Carthage Col, 71-92. *Concurrent Pos:* Vis prof, Univ Ore, 78-80, Nuclear Energy Ctr, Grenoble, France, 86-87; adj prof, Marquette, Univ Milwaukee, Wis. *Mem:* Soc Appl Spectros; Am Chem Soc; Coblentz Soc. *Res:* Characterization of compounds through vibrational analysis, especially with regard to their Raman spectra; drug interactions with polynucleotides; intercalation compounds; ruthenium complexes in zeolites. *Mailing Add:* Dept Chem Carthage Col Idaho State Univ Pocatello ID 83209-0001

STROMMEN, NORTON DUANE, meteorology, climatology, for more information see previous edition

STROM-OLSEN, JOHN OLAF, SOLID STATE PHYSICS. *Current Pos:* PROF PHYSICS, MCGILL UNIV, 67- *Personal Data:* UK & Can citizen. *Educ:* Cambridge Univ, PhD(physics), 66. *Mem:* Am Phys Soc; Can Asn Phys; Mat Res Soc. *Res:* Metallic glasses; nanocrystalline alloys; fine ceramics and metal fibers. *Mailing Add:* Dept Physics Rutherford Bldg McGill Univ 3600 University St Montreal PQ H3A 2T8 Can

STROMSTA, COURTNEY PAUL, speech pathology, audiology; deceased, see previous edition for last biography

STRONACH, CAREY E, MUON SPIN ROTATION SOLIDS & MEDIUM-ENERGY NUCLEAR PHYSICS, MAGNETIC LEVITATION & PHYSICS EDUCATION. *Current Pos:* From instr to assoc prof, 65-80, PROF PHYSICS, VA STATE UNIV, 80- *Personal Data:* b Boston, Mass, Aug 8, 40; m 66, Joan A Venner; c John M & Howard S. *Educ:* Univ Richmond, BS, 61; Univ Va, MS, 63; Col William & Mary, PhD(physics), 75. *Concurrent Pos:* Guest scientist, Los Alamos Naat Lab, 77-87, Brookhaven Nat Lab, 83-; guest scientist, Los Alamos Nat Lab, 77-, Brookhaven Nat Lab, 83-; vis assoc prof, Univ Alta, 78-79; mem bd trustees, Southeastern Univs Res Asn, 83-, Sci Adv Comt, Europ Workshop Spectros Subatomic Species Solids, 85, Continuous Electron Beam Accelerator Facil Users Group & Alt Gradient Synchrotron Users Group, Tri-Univ Meson Facil Users Group, Local Organizing Comt, Int Symp Physics & Chem Finite Syst, Richmond, Va, 91, Maglev Task Force, High-Speed Ground Transp Asn, 94-; dir, Solid State Physics Res Inst, Va State Univ, 84-; prin investr, USA & France Muon Spin Rotation Res Prog, 85-; tv lect high-sch physics, Va State Univ, Network & Black Col Satellite Network, 91-94. *Mem:* Am Phys Soc; Am Asn Physics Teachers; AAAS; Sigma Xi; NY Acad Sci. *Res:* Muon spin rotation studies of solids; concentrating on superconductors and related materials and magnetically ordered materials; medium-energy nuclear physics, primarily pion-nucleus reactions and heavy-ion reactions; author of 98 publications. *Mailing Add:* Box 9325 Va State Univ Petersburg VA 23806. *Fax:* 804-524-5914; *E-Mail:* stronach@cebaf.gov

STRONG, ALAN EARL, REMOTE SENSING, TEACHING & CLIMATOLOGY. *Current Pos:* Res oceanogr-meteorologist, Nat Environ Satellite Serv, 68-86, ADJ PROF & RESEARCHER, NAT OCEANIC & ATMOSPHERIC ADMIN & US NAVAL ACAD, 86- *Personal Data:* b Boston, Mass, May 30, 41; m 66, 84, Nancy Troupe; c Michael, Susan, Kathryn, Julie & Christopher. *Educ:* Kalamazoo Col, BA, 63; Univ Mich, MS, 65, PhD(oceanog), 68. *Prof Exp:* Asst res meteorologist, Great Lakes Res Dist, Mich Univ, 61-68. *Concurrent Pos:* Proj mgr, Coop Prof Oceanic Remote Sensing, Nat Oceanic & Atmospheric Admin & US Naval Acad. *Mem:* AAAS; Am Meteorol Soc; Am Geophys Union; Sigma Xi; Oceanog Soc. *Res:* Lake and sea breezes, air-sea interface; marine meteorology; develop applications of earth satellite data to oceanography; remote sensing-infrared microwave, visible; sea surface temperature measurements by satellite; ocean color measurements by satellite; El Nino studies; submesoscale eddy research; global climate change. *Mailing Add:* US Naval Acad Oceanog Dept Navy/NOAA Annapolis MD 21402. *Fax:* 410-293-2137; *E-Mail:* alan.e.strong@.noaa.gov

STRONG, CAMERON GORDON, INTERNAL MEDICINE, NEPHROLOGY. *Current Pos:* resident internal med, Mayo Grad Sch Med, 61-64, from instr to assoc prof, 67-77, chmn, Div Nephrology, 73-78, PROF MED, MAYO MED SCH, 77-, CONSULT, DIV NEPHROLOGY & INTERNAL MED, MAYO CLIN & FOUND, 66-, CHMN, DIV HYPERTENSION, 77- *Personal Data:* b Vegreville, Alta, Sept 18, 34; m 59; c 2. *Educ:* Univ Alta, MD, 58; McGill Univ, MS, 66. *Prof Exp:* Resident internal med & path, Queens Hosp, Honolulu, 59-61. *Concurrent Pos:* Fel nephrology, Hotel Dieu Montreal, 64-66; res assoc hypertension, dept physiol, Univ Mich, Ann Arbor, 66-67; fel, Coun High Blood Pressure Res,Am Heart Asn, 71- *Mem:* Fel Am Col Physicians; fel Am Col Cardiol. *Res:* Hypertension; renal disease; vascular smooth muscle physiology; prostaglandins; renin-angiotensin system. *Mailing Add:* Div Hypertension Mayo Clin Found Mayo Med Sch 200 First St SW Rochester MN 55901

STRONG, DAVID F, PURE & APPLIED SCIENCES. *Current Pos:* PRES & VICE CHANCELLOR, UNIV VICTORIA, 90- *Personal Data:* b Botwood, Nfld, Feb 26, 44; m; c 2. *Educ:* Mem Univ Nfld, BS, 65; Lehigh Univ, MS, 67; Univ Edinburgh, PhD, 70. *Honors & Awards:* Distinguished Serv Award, Can Inst Mining & Metall, 79; Past Pres Medal, Geol Asn Can, 80; Swiney lectr, Univ Edinburgh, 81. *Prof Exp:* From asst prof to prof, Mem Univ Nfld, 70-90, actg head, Dept Geol, 74-75, univ res prof, 85-90, spec adv to pres, 86-87, vpres acad, 87-90; WF James prof pure & appl sci, St Francis Xavier Univ, NS, 81-82. *Concurrent Pos:* Vis prof, Univ Montpellier, France, 76-77; assoc ed, Can J Earth Sci, 77-83, Transactions of the Royal Soc Edinburgh, 80-; mem, Natural Sci & Eng Res Coun Can, 82-88; past pres medal comt, Geol Asn Can, 85; mem, Res Coun, Can Inst Advan Res & bd dirs, Seabright Corp Ltd, 86-; mem, Nfld & Labrador Adv Coun Sci & Technol, 88-, Res Prog Adv Comt, Centre Cold Ocean Resources Eng, 90- *Mem:* Fel Geol Soc Am; fel Soc Econ Geologists; Can Inst Mining & Metall. *Res:* Natural environment; geological phenomena; processes which form volcanoes and their products, particularly mineral deposits; author of many publications. *Mailing Add:* Univ Victoria PO Box 1700 Victoria BC V8W 2Y2 Can. *Fax:* 250-721-8654

STRONG, DONALD RAYMOND, JR, ECOLOGY, ENTOMOLOGY. *Current Pos:* PROF, DEPT ZOOL, UNIV CALIF, DAVIS, 91- *Personal Data:* b Chelsea, Mass, May 22, 44; m 75, Karin Benson; c Sophia & Erik. *Educ:* Univ Calif, Santa Barbara, BA, 66; Univ Ore, PhD(biol), 71. *Prof Exp:* Res fel pop biol, Univ Chicago, 71-72; from asst prof to prof biol, Fla State Univ, 72-91. *Concurrent Pos:* Assoc ed, Ecol Entom, 80-92. *Mem:* Ecol Soc Am; Am Soc Naturalists; Soc Study Evolution; Royal Entom Soc. *Res:* Ecology of herbivorous insects; biological control; salt marsh ecology; general topics in population and community ecology. *Mailing Add:* Bodega Marine Lab Univ Calif Box 247 Westside Rd Bodega Bay CA 94923. *Fax:* 707-875-2089; *E-Mail:* drstrong@ucdavis.edu

STRONG, E(RWIN) R(AYFORD), CHEMICAL ENGINEERING. *Current Pos:* CONSULT, 84- *Personal Data:* b San Antonio, Tex, Aug 19, 19; m 50, Anabel Scanlon; c Marvin, Catherine & Daniel. *Educ:* Tex Arts & Industs Univ, BS, 40; Ill Inst Technol, MS, 45. *Honors & Awards:* Judson S Swearingen Award Sci Res, 54. *Prof Exp:* Engr, Lone Star Gas Co, 40-42; asst, Inst Gas Tech, Ill Inst Technol, 42-45, assoc res engr, 45-48; res engr in chg waste disposal sect, Southwest Res Inst, 48-56; chem engr, Am Oil Co, 56-62, group leader, 62-63, proj mgr, 63-70, mgr process eng, Amoco Deutschland GmbH, 70-73, sr chem engr, Amoco Europe Inc, London, 73-74, proj mgr, 74-84. *Concurrent Pos:* Gas tech fel, Inst Gas Technol, 42-45; mem task forces sulfur & nitrogen oxides control, mem stationary source emissions comt & mem solid waste mgt comt, Am Petrol Inst, 75-84. *Mem:* Am Chem Soc; Sigma Xi; Am Inst Chem Engrs. *Res:* Fuels technology; production of synthesis and distribution gases from coal and oil; industrial wastes; plant steam surveys; toxicity assays; laboratory and pilot plant treatment; superactivated sludge process; petroleum refining and petrochemical processes; desulfurization and hydrotreatment of heavy oils; air pollution control; hydrocarbon processing economics; alternate fuels and energy conversion systems. *Mailing Add:* 1007 Thunderbird Lane Naperville IL 60563-2244

STRONG, FREDERICK CARL, III, METHODS DEVELOPMENT IN FOOD ANALYSIS. *Current Pos:* FAC ASSOC, DEPT CHEM, BUCKNELL UNIV. *Personal Data:* b Denver, Colo, Nov 17, 17; m 41, Hilda Krader; c Nancy (Weyant) & Frederick C IV. *Educ:* Swarthmore Col, BA, 39; Lehigh Univ, MS, 41; Bryn Mawr Col, PhD, 54. *Honors & Awards:* Medal, Soc Appl Spectros, 60. *Prof Exp:* Chief chemist, Superior Metal Co, 40-42; res chemist, Lea Mfg Co, 42-43, Enthone Co, 45; asst, Wesleyan Univ, 43-45;

instr chem, Cedar Crest Col, 45-47; asst prof, Villanova Col, 47-51; from asst prof to assoc prof chem & chem eng, Stevens Inst Technol, 51-60; prof chem & chmn dept, Inter-Am Univ PR, 60-63 & Univ Bridgeport, 63-68; vis prof chem, Nat Tsing Hua Univ, Taiwan, 69 & Univ El Salvador, 70-72; tech expert, UN Indust Develop Orgn, Asuncion, Paraguay, 72-73; prof titular, Univ Estadual de Campinas, Brasil, 73-87. *Concurrent Pos:* Ed-in-chief, Appl Spectros, 55-60; Leverhulme fel,; Fulbright-Hays lectr, Tribhuvan Univ, Nepal, 68-69; vis prof anal chem, Nat Tsing Hua Univ, Taiwan, 79; tech expert, UN Indust Develop Orgn, Dar-es-Salaam, Tanzania, 81. *Mem:* Fel Am Inst Chemists; Soc Appl Spectros; Am Chem Soc; Sigma Xi; Am Asn Cereal Chemists. *Res:* Spectrochemical analysis; food analysis, copper complexes of proteins and carbohydrates; food intolerance; pharmacology of caffeine. *Mailing Add:* Dept Chem Bucknell Univ Lewisburg PA 17837-1802. *Fax:* 717-524-1739

STRONG, HERBERT MAXWELL, HIGH PRESSURE PHYSICS, PHYSICAL OPTICS. *Current Pos:* RETIRED. *Personal Data:* b Wooster, Ohio, Sept 30, 08; m 35, 83, Virginia Porter; c G Kirk & Steven R. *Educ:* Univ Toledo, BS, 30; Ohio State Univ, MS, 32, PhD(physics), 36. *Honors & Awards:* Award, Soc Mfg Eng, 62; Modern Pioneers Award, Nat Asn Mfrs, 65. *Prof Exp:* Asst, Ohio State Univ, 31-35; res physicist, Bauer & Black Div, Kendall Co, Ill, 35-45 & Kendall Mills Div, Mass, 45-46; res assoc, Res Lab, Gen Elec Co, 46, physicist, Res & Develop Ctr, 46-73; res assoc physics, Union Col, NY, 73-96. *Concurrent Pos:* Consult, Gen Elec Res & Develop Ctr, 73-74; consult technol use of diamond, Lazar Kaplan & Sons, 73-75. *Mem:* AAAS; fel Am Phys Soc; Sigma Xi. *Res:* Technological and industrial applications of diamonds; physical optical studies of rocket motor flames extreme high pressure techniques; measurements and phase equilibria; synthesis of gem diamond; synthesis of industrial diamond; measurement of temperature pressure and gas velocity in rocket motor flames by use of sodium D lines; author of over 40 publications. *Mailing Add:* 1165 Phoenix Ave Schenectady NY 12308

STRONG, IAN B, PHYSICS, ASTRONOMY. *Current Pos:* RETIRED. *Personal Data:* b Cohoes, NY, July 11, 30; m 60; c 1. *Educ:* Glasgow Univ, BSc, 53; Pa State Univ, PhD(physics), 63. *Prof Exp:* Mem tech staff, Bell Tel Labs, Inc, 53-55; staff mem, Ord Res Lab, 55-57; mem staff, Los Alamos Sci Lab, 61- *Mem:* AAAS; Am Phys Soc; Am Geophys Union; Am Astron Soc. *Res:* Acoustics, transmission through solids and liquids, ultrasonics; nuclear physics, particle detection, passage of radiation through matter, multiple scattering; astrophysics, interplanetary medium, high energy astronomy; history; philosophy; sociology of science. *Mailing Add:* 229 Rio Bravo Dr Los Alamos NM 87544

STRONG, JACK PERRY, PATHOLOGY. *Current Pos:* asst, 52-53, from instr to assoc prof, 55-64, PROF PATH, SCH MED, LSUMC, NEW ORLEANS, 64-, HEAD DEPT, 66-, BOYD PROF, 80- *Personal Data:* b Birmingham, Ala, Apr 27, 28; m 51; c 4. *Educ:* Univ Ala, BS, 48; La State Univ, MD, 51; Am Bd Path, dipl, 57 & 58. *Prof Exp:* Intern, Jefferson Hillman Hosp, Birmingham, Ala, 51-52. *Concurrent Pos:* USPHS fel, 57; consult, Southwest Found Res & Educ, 54-55; sabbatical leave, Social Med Res Unit, Med Res Coun, London, Eng, 62-63; mem, path A study sect, USPHS, 65-69, chmn, 67-69; mem, sci adv bd consult, Armed Forces Inst Path, 71-; mem, coun arteriosclerosis, Am Heart Asn; mem epidemiol & biomet adv comt, Nat Heart & Lung Inst, NIH, 71-78 & Panel on Geochemistry of Water in Relation to Cardiovasc Dis, US Nat Comt Geochemistry, Nat Acad Sci, 76-79. *Mem:* Am Asn Path & Bact (asst secy, 59-62); Am Soc Exp Path; Am Soc Clin Path; Col Am Path; US & Can Acad Path (vpres, 77, pres, 78); Int Acad Path (pres, 88-); Sigma Xi. *Res:* Pathology of cardiovascular diseases; atherosclerosis in the human and in primates; epidemiology; geographic pathology and pathogenesis of atherosclerosis; geographic pathology of cancer. *Mailing Add:* Dept Path La State Univ Med Ctr 1901 Perdido St New Orleans LA 70112-1393. *Fax:* 504-568-6037

STRONG, JERRY GLENN, PESTICIDE CHEMISTRY. *Current Pos:* sales mgr, 80-83, TECH MGR, ALBRIGHT & WILSON, UK LTD, 84- *Personal Data:* b Dawson, NMex, Nov 12, 41; m 71. *Educ:* Austin Col, BA, 63; Northwestern Univ, PhD(org chem), 68. *Prof Exp:* Sr res chemist, Mobil Chem Co, 68-76, mgr pesticide synthetics, 77-79, mgr pesticide develop, 79-80. *Mem:* Am Chem Soc. *Res:* Phosphorus chemicals. *Mailing Add:* Albright & Wilson UK Ltd Trinity St PO Box 80 Oldbury Warley West Midlands B69 4LN England

STRONG, JUDITH ANN, PHYSICAL CHEMISTRY, EDUCATIONAL ADMINISTRATION. *Current Pos:* Asst prof, Moorhead State Univ, 69-73, actg chairperson, 77-78, assoc prof, 73-82, chairperson, 84-86, PROF CHEM, MOORHEAD STATE UNIV, 82-, DEAN SOCIAL & NATURAL SCI, 86- *Personal Data:* b Van Hornesville, NY, June 19, 41. *Educ:* State Univ NY Albany, BS, 63; Brandeis Univ, MA, 66, PhD(phys chem), 70. *Concurrent Pos:* Regents fel; NSF fel. *Mem:* Am Chem Soc; Asn Women Sci; Sigma Xi. *Res:* Computer applications in chemical education. *Mailing Add:* Acad Affairs Moorhead State Univ Moorhead MN 56563. *Fax:* 218-236-2168; *E-Mail:* 300jas@mhd5.moorhead.msus.edu

STRONG, LAURENCE EDWARD, PHYSICAL CHEMISTRY. *Personal Data:* b Kalamazoo, Mich, Sept 3, 14; m 38, Ruth Osgerby; c 4. *Educ:* Kalamazoo Col, AB, 36; Brown Univ, PhD(chem), 40. *Hon Degrees:* DSc, Earlham Col, 82. *Honors & Awards:* SAMA Award for Chem Educ, Am Chem Soc, 71. *Prof Exp:* Asst phys chem, Harvard Med Sch, 40-41, res assoc, 41-43, assoc dir pilot plant, 43-46; from assoc prof to prof chem, Kalamazoo Col, 46-52; head dept, Earlham Col, 52-65, prof chem, 52-79, res prof chem, 79-92, chem hygiene off, 91-92. *Concurrent Pos:* Dir, UNESCO Pilot Proj, Asia, 65-66; vis prof chem, Macquarie Univ, Australia, 71-72 & Guilford Col, NC, 81 & 85. *Mem:* Fel AAAS; Am Chem Soc; Sigma Xi. *Res:* Electrical properties of solutions; fractionation of proteins; thermodynamics of acid ionization; precision conductance measurements of substituted benzoic acid in aqueous solution and partial molal volume measurements. *Mailing Add:* 1015 Quaker Knoll Rd Sandy Spring MD 20860. *E-Mail:* larrys2@igc.apc.org

STRONG, LOUISE CONNALLY, MEDICAL GENETICS, CANCER. *Current Pos:* res assoc, Med Genetics Ctr, Grad Sch Biomed Sci, Health Sci Ctr, Univ Tex, Houston, 72-73, from asst prof to assoc prof med genetics, 73-79, from asst prof to assoc prof pediat & biol, MD Anderson Cancer Ctr, 76-90, from asst geneticist to assoc geneticist, 76-90, PROF EXP PEDIAT & GENETICIST, M D ANDERSON CANCER CTR, UNIV TEX, 90- *Personal Data:* b San Antonio, Tex, Apr 23, 44; m 70; c 2. *Educ:* Univ Tex, Austin, BA, 66; Univ Tex, Galveston, MD, 70. *Honors & Awards:* Sam & Bertha Brochstein Award & Margolin Award, Retina Res Found, 83, 87 & 93; Roland J Sadoux Award Outstanding Achievement, Wilms' Tumor Res, 90; Farber Lectr, Soc Pediat Path, 91; Wick R Williams Mem Lectr, Fox Chase Cancer Ctr, Pa, 91; J Walter Junkett Keynote Lectr, Vt Cancer Ctr, 94; Charles A Apffel Mem Lectr, New Eng Deaconess Hosp, Mass, 96. *Prof Exp:* Fel cancer genetics, Univ Tex Grad Sch Biomed Sci & Tex Res Inst Ment Sci, 70-72. *Concurrent Pos:* Consult genetics, Dept Med Pediat, Univ Texas Syst Cancer Ctr, 73-79; mem adv comt, Clearinghouse Environ Carcinogens, Data Eval & Risk Assessment Subcomt, NIH-Nat Cancer Inst, 76-80 & Nat Comt Cancer Prev, Am Cancer Soc, 78-; mem, Grad Fac, Health Sci Ctr, Univ Tex, 77-, dir, Med Genetics Clin, 79-90, Sue & Radcliffe prof, MD Anderson Cancer Ctr, 81-95, vis prof pediat, Med Sch, 88-, Sue & Radcliffe Killan chair, 95-; mem, Bd Sci Coun, Div Cancer Etiology Nat Cancer Inst, 81-84, Nat Cancer Adv Bd, Dept Health & Human Serv, 84-91; assoc ed, Cancer Res, 83-87; Warren E Wheeler vis prof, Children's Hosp, Ohio, 89. *Mem:* Am Soc Human Genetics; fel AAAS; Am Soc Prev Oncol; Am Asn Cancer Res (pres-elect, 95, pres, 96); Am Cancer Soc; Am Med Women's Asn; Asn Women Sci; Leukemia Soc Am. *Res:* Clinical cancer genetics; genetic etiology and epidemiology of cancer; genetic consequences of childhood cancer; author of numerous publications. *Mailing Add:* 338 Hunters Trail Houston TX 77024. *Fax:* 713-794-4421; *E-Mail:* istrong@notes.mdacc.tmc.edu

STRONG, MERVYN STUART, OTOLARYNGOLOGY. *Current Pos:* instr, 52-56, PROF OTOLARYNGOL, SCH MED, BOSTON UNIV, 56- *Personal Data:* b Kells, Ireland, Jan 28, 24; nat US; m 50; c 2. *Educ:* Trinity Col, Dublin, BA, 45; Univ Dublin, MD, 47; FRCS(I), 49; FRCS (Eng), 50. *Honors & Awards:* Newcombe Award, Am Laryngol Asn, 85. *Prof Exp:* Registr otolaryngol, Royal Infirmary, Edinburgh, 49-50. *Concurrent Pos:* Fel otolaryngol, Lahey Clin, Boston, 50-52; asst, Boston Univ Hosp, 52-56, chief serv, 56-85; chief otolaryngol, Boston Vet Admin Hosp, 65-85; chief ambulatory care, Bedford Vet Admin Hosp, 85- *Mem:* Fel Am Soc Head & Neck Surg; AMA; fel Am Col Surgeons; Soc Univ Otolaryngol (pres, 73-74); fel Am Acad Opthal & Otolaryngol. *Res:* Multicentric origins of carcinoma of oral cavity and pharynx. *Mailing Add:* 35 Laurel Rd Weston MA 02193-1610

STRONG, ROBERT LYMAN, PHYSICAL CHEMISTRY. *Current Pos:* from asst prof to assoc prof phys chem, 55-62, PROF PHYS CHEM, RENSSELAER POLYTECH INST, 62- *Personal Data:* b Hemet, Calif, May 30, 28; m 51; c 4. *Educ:* Univ Calif, BS, 50; Univ Wis, PhD(chem), 54. *Prof Exp:* Res fel chem, Nat Res Coun Can, 54-55. *Concurrent Pos:* NSF sci faculty fel, 62-63. *Mem:* AAAS; Am Chem Soc. *Res:* Photochemistry and flash photolysis; atom recombination in gas and solution systems; halogen atom charge-transfer complexes; optical rotary dispersion of excited states and intermediate species in photochemical processes. *Mailing Add:* 8448 135th Ave SE New Castle WA 98059-3314

STRONG, ROBERT MICHAEL, ELECTRICAL ENGINEERING. *Personal Data:* b Pittsburgh, Pa, Mar 12, 43; c 1. *Educ:* Villanova Univ, BEE, 65; Mass Inst Technol, MS, 66, PhD(elec eng), 70. *Prof Exp:* Staff mem, Lincoln Lab, Mass Inst Technol, 69-75; lectr, Health Serv, Sch Pub Health, Harvard Univ, 75-80; mem tech staff, Comput Archit Dept, Sperry Res Ctr, 80-83; consult, 83-90. *Concurrent Pos:* Assoc med, Harvard Med Sch, 71-75. *Mem:* Inst Elec & Electronics Engrs; Asn Comput Mach. *Res:* User-computer interfaces, human factors, computer terminal architecture, data base systems, computer applications in health care research and public health. *Mailing Add:* 9 Hillcrest Rd Medfield MA 02052-2126

STRONG, RONALD DEAN, NONDESTRUCTIVE TESTING. *Current Pos:* MEM STAFF NONDESTRUCTIVE TESTING ENG, LOS ALAMOS SCI LAB, UNIV CALIF, 66- *Personal Data:* b Bremerton, Wash, June 7, 36; m 59; c 2. *Educ:* Wash State Univ, BS, 58. *Prof Exp:* Engr, Boeing Co, 59-61; nondestructive testing engr, Aerojet-Gen Corp, 61-66. *Mem:* Am Soc Nondestructive Testing. *Res:* Investigation of ultrasonic techniques for materials evaluations and implementation of techniques in actual test situations. *Mailing Add:* 199 Venado St Los Alamos NM 87544

STRONG, WILLIAM J, ACOUSTICS OF MUSIC & SPEECH. *Current Pos:* From asst prof to assoc prof, 67-76, PROF PHYSICS, BRIGHAM YOUNG UNIV, 76- *Personal Data:* b Idaho Falls, Idaho, Jan 1, 34; m 59, Charlene Fuhriman; c William, John, Stephen, David, Kathleen & Richard. *Educ:* Brigham Young Univ, BS, 58, MS, 59; Mass Inst Technol, PhD(physics), 64. *Prof Exp:* Scientist, Air Force Cambridge Res Labs, 63-66. *Concurrent Pos:* lectr, Holy Cross Col, 63-64, Northeastern Univ, 64-66; vis scientist, Gallaudet Col, 74, IRCAM, Paris, 89; sr Fulbright fel, Australia, 80. *Mem:* Fel Acoust Soc Am; Inst Elec & Electronics Engrs. *Res:* Physics of musical instruments; analysis and synthesis of instrumental tones and of speech; machine recognition of speech. *Mailing Add:* Dept Physics Brigham Young Univ Provo UT 84602. *Fax:* 801-378-2265; *E-Mail:* strongw@acoust.byu.edu

STRONGIN, MYRON, LOW TEMPERATURE PHYSICS, SURFACE PHYSICS. *Current Pos:* from asst physicist to assoc physicist, 63-67, physicist, 67-74, SR PHYSICIST, BROOKHAVEN NAT LAB, 74- *Personal Data:* b New York, NY, July 27, 36; m 57; c 2. *Educ:* Rensselaer Polytech Inst, BS, 56; Yale Univ, MS, 57, PhD(physics), 62. *Prof Exp:* Mem staff, Lincoln Labs, Mass Inst Technol, 61-63. *Concurrent Pos:* Adj prof, City Univ New York. *Mem:* Fel Am Phys Soc. *Res:* Properties of superconducting materials; analysis of surfaces and influence of surfaces on superconducting properties; epitaxy of films and superconductivity of films; hydrogen on surfaces. *Mailing Add:* Dept Physics Brookhaven Nat Lab Upton NY 11973

STROOCK, DANIEL WYLER, MATHEMATICS. *Current Pos:* PROF MATH, MASS INST TECHNOL, 84- *Personal Data:* b New York, NY, Mar 20, 40; m 62, Lucy Barber; c Benjamin & Abraham. *Educ:* Harvard Col, AB, 62; Rockefeller Univ, PhD, 66. *Honors & Awards:* Steele Prize, Am Math Soc, 96. *Prof Exp:* Vis mem, Courant Inst, NY Univ, 66-69, asst prof, 69-72; assoc prof, Univ Colo, 72-75, prof, 75-84, chmn, Dept Math, 79-81. *Concurrent Pos:* Guggenheim fel, 78-79; ed, Trans of Am Math Soc, 74-80, Ill J Math, 76-82, Annals of Probability, 88-93, Math Zeitschrift, 92-, J Functional Analysis, 94-, Advan in Math, 95-; adj prof, Univ Colo & Beijing Normal Univ. *Mem:* Nat Acad Sci; Am Acad Arts & Sci. *Res:* Author and co-author of various publications; contributed articles on probability theory to professional journals. *Mailing Add:* 55 Frost St Cambridge MA 02140-2247

STROP, HANS R, PROCESS DEVELOPMENT RELATED TO FOOD & FEED PRODUCTION. *Current Pos:* PRES, EPE INC, 82- *Personal Data:* b Bandoeng, Dutch East Indies, Oct 26, 31; US citizen; m 75, Leila M Morey. *Educ:* Delft Univ Technol, Ir, 58. *Prof Exp:* Res engr, Nuclear Reactor Lab, N V Kema, Holland, 59-60, Mats Res Lab, Tyco Inc, 61-62; sr develop engr, Transitron Electronic Corp, 60-61, RCA Corp, 63-64; systs engr, Gen Atomics Div, Gen Dynamics Corp, 62-63, Monsanto Res Corp, 64-70; dir res, Ibec industs Inc, 70-78, vpres res & eng, Anderson Ibec Div, 78-80; sr vpres mkt & sales, Anderson Int Corp, 80-82. *Mem:* Am Oil Chemists Soc; Inst Food Technologists; Am Inst Chem Engrs; Am Chem Soc. *Res:* Research and development related to chemical, polymer, food and feed processing equipment and to chemical processes. *Mailing Add:* 12418 The Bluffs Strongsville OH 44136. *Fax:* 440-238-4687

STROSBERG, ARTHUR MARTIN, PHARMACOLOGY, RESEARCH ADMINISTRATION. *Current Pos:* Pharmacologist, Syntex Res, 70-72, sect head cardiovasc pharmacol, 72-75, prin scientist, 75-83, dept head, 83-90, sr dept head, Cardiovasc Pharmacol & Inst Opers, 90-92, sr dept head, Cardiovascular Pharmacol, Regulatory Pharmacol & Inst Opers, 92-93, HEAD ADMIN POLICIES, SYNTEX RES, 93- *Personal Data:* b Albany, NY, Sept 16, 40; m 73, Sheila Lamoan; c Darryl & Mark. *Educ:* Siena Col, NY, BS, 62; Univ Calif, San Francisco, PhD(pharmacol), 70. *Mem:* AAAS; Am Soc Pharmacol & Exp Therapeut; Sigma Xi; Am Heart Asn; Am Soc Hypertension. *Res:* Cardiovascular pharmacology, cardiotonic agents, antianginal agents, antihypertensive agents; antiarrhythmic agents; contractile properties of cardiac muscle; cardiac muscle contraction mechanisms, cardiac muscle ultrastructure and oscillations; research administration; research policies. *Mailing Add:* Roche Biosci 3401 Hillview Ave Palo Alto CA 94304-1397. *Fax:* 650-852-1700

STROSCIO, MICHAEL ANTHONY, PHYSICS, ELECTRICAL ENGINEERING. *Current Pos:* SR RES SCIENTIST, OFF DIR, US ARMY RES OFF, RES TRIANGLE PARK, NC 85- *Personal Data:* b Winston-Salem, NC, June 1, 49; c Elizabeth (de Clare), Charles M & Gautam D. *Educ:* Univ NC, Chapel Hill, BS, 70; Yale Univ, MPhil, 72, PhD(physics), 74. *Honors & Awards:* Issai Lefkowitz Award. *Prof Exp:* Physicist space sci, Air Force Cambridge Res Labs, 74-75; physicist staff mem, Los Alamos Sci Lab, 75-78; sr staff physicist, Appl Physics Lab, Johns Hopkins Univ, 78-80; prof mgr electromagnetic res, Air Force Off Sci Res, Wash, 80-83; spec asst to res dir, Off of Under Secy Def, Wash, 82-83; policy analyst, White House Off Sci & Tech Policy, Wash, 83-85. *Concurrent Pos:* Instr, Middlesex Community Col, 74-75; res grant, Los Alamos Sci Lab, 77; chmn, Dept Def Res Instrumentation Comt, Wash, 82; vchmn, White House Panel Sci Commun, Wash, 83-84; liaison, Nat Laser Users Facil, Rochester, Ny, 84; assoc mem, Adv Group Electron Devices, 85-; cons, US Dept Energy, Wash, 85-; adj prof, dept elec & comput eng, NC State Univ, Raleigh, 85-, & dept elec eng & physics, Duke Univ, 86-; panel sci commun & nat security, Nat Acad Sci, 82; sr scientist, US Army, 90-; adj prof, Dept Elec Eng, Univ Va, 91-96, Univ Md, 96-97. *Mem:* Am Phys Soc; fel Inst Elec & Electronics Engrs. *Res:* Carrier-phonon interactions in confined nanostructures, quantum transport, and phonon interactions in quantum-well lasers. *Mailing Add:* Off Dir Army Res Off Box 12211 Research Triangle Park NC 27709

STROSS, FRED HELMUT, ANALYTICAL CHEMISTRY, ARCHAEOMETRY. *Current Pos:* PARTIC GUEST, LAWRENCE BERKELEY NAT LAB, UNIV CALIF, 75-, RES ASSOC, DEPT ANTHROP, 70-75, 81-, FAC ASSOC. *Personal Data:* b Alexandria, Egypt, Aug 22, 10; nat US; m 36, Helen Colter; c Brian & Barbara. *Educ:* Case Inst Technol, BS, 34; Univ Calif, PhD(chem), 38. *Prof Exp:* Stand Oil fel, 37-38; chemist, Shell Develop Co, 38-52, supvr res, 52-70. *Concurrent Pos:* Consult, Lowie Mus & Univ Art Mus, Berkeley, 70-93; chmn Nat Res Coun subcomt gas chromatography group, Int Union Pure & Appl Chem; affil prof chem, Univ Wash, Seattle, 75-88; tour speaker, Am Chem Soc, 73-91. *Mem:* Am Chem Soc; Sigma Xi. *Res:* Photochemistry; asphalt technology; catalytic industrial processes; physical chemistry of solids; gas chromatography; analytical physical chemistry, including applications to characterization of polymers; archaeometry, (application of physical sciences to archaeology). *Mailing Add:* 44 Oak Dr Orinda CA 94563. *E-Mail:* fhstross@aol.com

STROSS, RAYMOND GEORGE, PHOTOPERIODISM, HYDROBIOLOGY. *Current Pos:* ASSOC PROF ZOOL, STATE UNIV NY ALBANY, 67- *Personal Data:* b St Charles, Mo, July 2, 30; m 64; c 3. *Educ:* Univ Mo, BS, 52; Univ Idaho, MS, 55; Univ Wis, PhD(zool), 58. *Prof Exp:* Res asst, Univ Wis, 54-58; NIH fel, Oceanog Inst, Woods Hole, 58-59; from asst prof to assoc prof zool, Univ Md, 59-67. *Concurrent Pos:* Prog officer, NSF, 77-78. *Mem:* AAAS; Sigma Xi; Ecol Soc Am; Am Soc Limnol & Oceanog; Am Soc Photobiol; Phycol Soc Am. *Res:* Photoecology; germination control of plant prodagules; biological limnology; experimental ecology; arctic ecology. *Mailing Add:* Dept Biol Sci State Univ NY Albany 1400 Washington Ave Albany NY 12222-1000

STROTHER, ALLEN, PHARMACOLOGY, ANIMAL SCIENCE & NUTRITION. *Current Pos:* from asst prof to assoc prof pharmacol, 65-95, EMER PROF PHYSIOL & PHARMACOL, SCH MED, LOMA LINDA UNIV, 95- *Personal Data:* b Sweetwater, Tex, Feb 20, 28; m 57, Julie A Gutch; c Wesley A & Lori A. *Educ:* Tex Tech Col, BS, 55; Univ Calif, Davis, MS, 57; Tex A&M Univ, PhD(biochem, nutrit), 63. *Prof Exp:* Assoc animal sci, Univ Calif, Davis, 56-57; asst to trustee, Burnett Estate, Ft Worth, Tex, 58; dir nutrit res, Uncle Johnny Feed Mills, Houston, 59; res biochemist, Food & Drug Admin, DC, 63-65. *Concurrent Pos:* vis scientist, Dept Pharm, Kings Col, Univ London, UK, 86. *Mem:* Am Soc Pharmacol & Exp Therapeut; Sigma Xi. *Res:* Large and small animal nutrition; dietary energy levels; mineral requirements; drug and pesticide metabolism; drug interactions and drug-nutrient interactions; effect on drug metabolism. *Mailing Add:* 74448 Nevada Circle E Palm Desert CA 92260

STROTHER, GREENVILLE KASH, BIOPHYSICS. *Current Pos:* Asst prof physics, 57-61, from assoc prof to prof, 61-83, EMER PROF BIOPHYS, PA STATE UNIV, UNIVERSITY PARK, 83- *Personal Data:* b Huntington, WVa, July 27, 20; m 50; c 3. *Educ:* Va Polytech Inst, BS, 43; George Washington Univ, MS, 54; Pa State Univ, PhD(physics), 57. *Mem:* Biophys Soc. *Res:* Microspectrophotometry of cellular systems; biophysical instrumentation. *Mailing Add:* PO Box 243 Aaronsburg PA 16802

STROTHER, J(OHN) A(LAN), AEROSPACE ELECTRO-OPTICS. *Current Pos:* CONSULT, 86- *Personal Data:* b Hartford, Conn, Dec 27, 27; m 51; c 3. *Educ:* Trinity Col, Conn, BS, 50; Princeton Univ, MSE, 54. *Prof Exp:* Electronic scientist, US Navy Underwater Sound Lab, 50-52; mem tech staff, RCA Labs, 54-57; group leader, RCA Defense Electronic Prod Div, RCA, 57-58, unit & prog mgr, RCA Astro-Electronics Div, 58-61, proj engr, Systs Div, EMR, Inc, 61-62, mgr instrumentation eng, Photoelec Div, 62-66; sr mem tech staff, RCA Corp, 66-69, proj mgr, 69-73, mgr electro-optics, 73-75, staff scientist, 75-79, mgr sensor design, Astro-Electronics Div, 79-84; founder/pres, Stron Corp, 84-86. *Res:* Sensing, processing and reproduction of images; speech and hearing; pattern recognition; digital signal processing; satellite systems engineering and program management. *Mailing Add:* 201 Grover Ave Princeton NJ 08540

STROTTMAN, DANIEL, NUCLEAR PHYSICS. *Current Pos:* staff mem, 78-87, group leader, 87-92, DEP DIV DIR, THEORY DIV, LOS ALAMOS NAT LAB, 92- *Personal Data:* b Sumner, Iowa, Apr 15, 43; m 66, Theresa Short; c Nissa. *Educ:* Univ Iowa, BA, 64; State Univ NY, Stony Brook, MA, 66, PhD(physics), 69. *Prof Exp:* Niels Bohr fel nuclear physics, Niels Bohr Inst, Copenhagen, Denmark, 69-70; res officer, Oxford Univ, 70-73; asst prof physics, State Univ NY, Stony Brook, 74-78. *Concurrent Pos:* Vis Nordita prof, Physics Inst, Univ Oslo, 73-74. *Mem:* Fel Am Phys Soc; AAAS. *Res:* Theoretical physics. *Mailing Add:* 613 47th St Los Alamos NM 87544. *Fax:* 505-665-4055; *E-Mail:* dds@lanl.gov

STROUBE, EDWARD W, AGRONOMY. *Current Pos:* res asst, 58-60, from instr to assoc prof, 60-70, PROF AGRON, OHIO STATE UNIV & OHIO AGR RES & DEVELOP CTR, 70- *Personal Data:* b Hopkinsville, Ky, Apr 2, 27; m 54; c 3. *Educ:* Univ Ky, BS, 51, MS, 59; Ohio State Univ, PhD(agron), 61. *Prof Exp:* Agr exten agent, Univ Ky, 54-57, res asst agron, 57-58. *Mem:* Am Soc Agron; Weed Sci Soc Am. *Res:* Weed control of field crops involving the evaluations of herbicides, tillage practices, flaming and crop rotations; soil and crop residue studies involving herbicides. *Mailing Add:* 2688 Mt Holyoke Rd Columbus OH 43221

STROUBE, WILLIAM BRYAN, JR, PHARMACEUTICAL & NUTRITIONAL TECHNICAL MANAGEMENT, MARKETING RESEARCH, MARKETING. *Current Pos:* group leader pharm qual, Bristol-Myers Squibb Co, 86-90, assoc mgr, Pharm Tech Serv, 90-91, sr mkt analyst, mkt res, 91-95, MKT MGR, BRISTOL-MYERS SQUIBB CO, 95- *Personal Data:* b Princeton, Ky, Oct 29, 51; m 73, Katharine Kaiser; c Bryan & Samuel. *Educ:* Murray State Univ, BS, 73; Univ Md, MBA, 86; Univ Ky, PhD(anal & nuclear chem), 77. *Prof Exp:* Anal chemist, Allied Gen Nuclear Serv, 78; res staff fel, US Food & Drug Admin, 78-79, res chemist, 79-86. *Mem:* Am Nuclear Soc; Am Chem Soc; Asn Off Anal Chemists. *Res:* Pharmaceutical analysis; multi-element analysis methodology for neutron activation analysis; trace analysis of biological samples. *Mailing Add:* Bristol-Myers Squibb Co 2400 W Lloyd Expressway Evansville IN 47721-0001

STROUD, CARLOS RAY, QUANTUM OPTICS. *Current Pos:* From asst prof to assoc prof, 70-84, PROF OPTICS, UNIV ROCHESTER, 84-, PROF PHYSICS, 92- *Personal Data:* b Owensboro, Ky, July 9, 42; m 62, Patricia T Stroud; c 3. *Educ:* Centre Col Ky, AB, 63; Wash Univ, PhD(physics), 69. *Concurrent Pos:* Sr vis scientist, Univ Sussex, Gt Brit, 79-80. *Mem:* Fel Am Phys Soc; fel Optical Soc Am. *Res:* Quantum and semiclassical radiation theory; interactions of electromagnetic fields with matter; laser instabilities; Rydberg atomic states. *Mailing Add:* Inst Optics Univ Rochester Rochester NY 14627

STROUD, DAVID GORDON, SUPERCONDUCTIVITY, DISORDERED SYSTEMS. *Current Pos:* from asst prof to assoc prof, 71-81, PROF PHYSICS, OHIO STATE UNIV, 81- *Personal Data:* b Glasgow, Scotland, July, 6, 43; US citizen; m 67; c 2. *Educ:* Stanford Univ, BS, 64; Harvard Univ, MA, 66, PhD(solid state physics), 69. *Prof Exp:* Postdoctoral researcher, Cornell Univ, 69-71. *Concurrent Pos:* Prin investr, NSF, 72-; vis fel, Harvard Univ, 77-78; vis prof, Tel Aviv Univ, 80 & Univ Paris, 85. *Mem:* Am Phys Soc; Mat Res Soc; Am Ceramic Soc. *Res:* Theoretical condensed matter physics; transport and optical properties of granular matter; superconductivity in granular systems; glassy behavior in high-temperature superconductors; liquid-vapor and liquid-solid surfaces. *Mailing Add:* Dept Physics Ohio State Univ 174 W 18th Ave Columbus OH 43210. *Fax:* 614-292-8140

STROUD, JACKSON SWAVELY, EXPERIMENTAL SOLID STATE PHYSICS, ENGINEERING. *Current Pos:* asst mgr, 79-83, SCIENTIST, SCHOTT GLASS TECH, 83- *Personal Data:* b Cabarrus Co, NC, June 1, 31; m 61; c 2. *Educ:* Union Col, BS, 53; Ohio State Univ, MS, 57. *Prof Exp:* Physicist, Corning Glass Works, 57-67 & Bausch & Lomb, Inc, 67-79. *Mem:* Am Phys Soc; Am Ceramic Soc; Optical Soc Am. *Res:* Solid state physics with specialized knowledge of glass; radiation chemistry; glass tank design; optical properties of solids. *Mailing Add:* Schott Glass Technol 400 York Ave Duryea PA 18642

STROUD, JUNIUS BRUTUS, ALGEBRA. *Current Pos:* from instr to prof math, Davidson Col, 60-76, chmn dept, 83-89, Richardson prof math, 85-94, EMER PROF MATH, RICHARDSON DAVIDSON COL, 94- *Personal Data:* b Greensboro, NC, June 9, 29; m 55, Ruby Masincup; c Timothy Brian, Jonathan McIver & Cynthia Lee. *Educ:* Davidson Col, BS, 51; Univ Va, MA, 62, PhD(math), 65. *Prof Exp:* Instr math & sci, Fishburne Mil Sch, 53-57; teacher, High Sch, 57-58. *Concurrent Pos:* Vis lectr, Sec Schs, 62-63, 65-66, 89-90 & 90-91; vis prof, Dartmouth Col, 73, St Andrews Univ, Scotland, 87. *Mem:* Am Math Asn. *Res:* Simple Jordan algebras of characteristic two; finitely generated modules over a Dedekind ring. *Mailing Add:* PO Box 94 Davidson NC 28036-0094

STROUD, RICHARD HAMILTON, ZOOLOGY, FISHERIES. *Current Pos:* asst exec vpres, Sport Fishing I, Aquatic Resources, 53-55, exec vpres, 55-81, consult, 82-88, FISHERIES SCI ED, AQUATIC RESOURCES, 82- *Personal Data:* b Dedham, Mass, Apr 24, 18; m 43, Genevieve DePol; c William & Jennifer. *Educ:* Bowdoin Col, BS, 39; Univ NH, MS, 42. *Honors & Awards:* Pentelow lectr, Univ Liverpool, Eng, 75; Conserv Achievement Award, Nat Wildlife Fedn, 76; Outstanding Achievement Award, Am Inst Fishery Res Biol, 81 & Am Fisheries Soc, 90. *Prof Exp:* Asst bot, Bowdoin Col, 39; asst zool, Univ NH, 40-42; jr aquatic biologist, Tenn Valley Authority, 42, aquatic biologist, 46-47; chief aquatic biologist, Mass Dept Conserv, 48-53. *Concurrent Pos:* Vpres, Sport Fishery Res Found, 62-81, trustee, 82-88; consult, Calif Fish & Game Dept, 65-66, Ark Game & Fish Comn, 69, Iowa Conserv Comn, 70-71 & Tenn Valley Authority, 71-72; mem, World Panel Fishery Experts, Food & Agr Orgn, UN, Ocean Fisheries & Law of Sea Adv Comts, Dept State; chmn, Natural Resources Coun Am, 69-71; mem, NAm Atlantic Salmon Coun & Marine Fisheries Adv Comt, Dept Com; fishery expert adv to Sen Select Comt Govt Opers; bd dir, Nat Coalition Marine Conserv, 75-96; sr science, Aquatic Ecosysts Analysts, 83-88; guest lectr, Japan Sport Fishing Found, 76; ed, Marina Recreational Fisheries Symp, ann series, 82-94. *Mem:* Am Fisheries Soc (pres, 79-80); Fisheries Soc Brit Isles; Freshwater Biol Asn UK; Am Inst Fishery Res Biologists; Int Asn Fish & Wildlife Agencies; hon mem Nat Resources Coun Am. *Res:* Fish population dynamics, behavior, ecology and life history. *Mailing Add:* Consult Aquatic Resources & Fisheries Sci Ed PO Box 1772 Pinehurst NC 28370

STROUD, RICHARD KIM, VETERINARY PATHOLOGY. *Current Pos:* SR FORENSIC SCIENTIST, FISH & WILDLIFE FORENSICS LAB, FISH & WILDLIFE SERV, ASHLAND, ORE, 90- *Personal Data:* b Ann Arbor, Mich, Aug 8, 43; div; c 3. *Educ:* Ore State Univ, BS, 66, MS, 78; Wash State Univ, DVM, 72. *Prof Exp:* Biologist, Marine Mammal Lab, Nat Marine Fisheries Serv-Nat Ocean & Atmospheric Admin, 66-68; vet, Willamette Vet Clin, 72-73; res assoc aquatic animal path, Ore State Univ, 73-79; diag pathologist, Nat Wildlife Health Lab, Madison, Wis, 80-86. *Mem:* Inst Asn Aquatic Animal Med (pres, 77-78); Wildlife Dis Asn; Am Fisheries Soc; Am Vet Med Asn. *Res:* Wildlife and aquatic animal pathology. *Mailing Add:* 1490 E Main Ashland OR 97520

STROUD, ROBERT CHURCH, PHYSIOLOGY. *Current Pos:* RETIRED. *Personal Data:* b Oakland, Calif, Jan 5, 18; m 47. *Educ:* Princeton Univ, AB, 40; Univ Rochester, MS, 50, PhD(physiol), 52. *Prof Exp:* Chemist, Calco Chem Div, Am Cyanamid Co, 40-44 & Lederle Labs Div, 44-48; instr physiol, Grad Sch Med, Univ Pa, 52-53; assoc med physiol, Brookhaven Nat Lab, 53-54; asst prof pharmacol & res assoc aviation physiol, Ohio State Univ, 54-55; asst prof physiol, Heart, 55-56; supvr physiologist, US Naval Med Res Lab, 56-61; pulmonary physiologist, Occup Health Res & Training Facil, USPHS, 61-62; chief res prog mgr life sci, Ames Res Ctr, NASA, 62-64; chief, Sci Rev Sect, Health Res Facil Br, NIH, 64-69, chief, Health Res Facil Br, Div Educ & Res Facil, 69-70, chief, Training Grants & Awards Br, Nat Heart, Lung & Blood Inst, 70-73; exec secy, Rev Br, 73-88. *Concurrent Pos:* Lectr, Stanford Univ, 63-64. *Mem:* Am Physiol Soc. *Res:* Cardiopulmonary and respiratory physiology; physiology of adaptation to high altitudes and submarine environments; physiology of diving; aerospace physiology. *Mailing Add:* 4450 S Park Ave Apt 1811 Chevy Chase MD 20875

STROUD, ROBERT MALONE, IMMUNOLOGY, RHEUMATOLOGY. *Current Pos:* SEMI-RETIRED, 91- *Personal Data:* b St Louis, Mo, Mar 12, 31; m 55, Gloria Flowers; c Robert M Jr & Katherine S (Ware). *Educ:* Harvard Univ, BA, 52, MD, 56. *Prof Exp:* Intern med, Cook County Hosp, Chicago, Ill, 56-57; resident, Barnes Hosp, St Louis, Mo, 59-61; USPHS fel, Johns Hopkins Univ Sch Med, 61-63; Helen Hay Whitney fel, 63-65; dir rheumatology, Ga Warm Springs Found, 65-66; from asst prof to assoc prof med, Univ Ala, Brimingham, 66-71, assoc prof microbiol & prof med, Med Sch, 71-81; pvt practice, 81-91. *Mem:* Am Asn Immunol; Am Col Rheumatology; Am Soc Clin Invest; Am Acad Allergy. *Res:* Food allergy as a cause of arthritis. *Mailing Add:* 32 Iroquois Trail Ormond Beach FL 32174

STROUD, ROBERT MICHAEL, STRUCTURAL BIOLOGY. *Current Pos:* PROF BIOCHEM, UNIV CALIF, SAN FRANCISCO, 77- *Personal Data:* b Stockport, Eng, May 24, 42. *Educ:* Cambridge Univ, BA, 64, MA, 68; London Univ, PhD(crystallog), 68. *Prof Exp:* Fel protein crystallog, Calif Inst Technol, 68-71, assoc prof chem, 75-77. *Concurrent Pos:* Prin investr, NIH & NSF, 71-; consult, NIH, 77-; fel, Sloan Found, 77. *Mem:* Am Crystallog Soc; Brit Biophys Soc; Am Soc Biophys Chem; Biophys Soc. *Res:* Membrane protein structure; structure and function of complex regulatory macromolecular DNA and protein interactions; development of new methodology in macromolecular structural biology. *Mailing Add:* 32 Iroquois Trail Ormond Beach FL 32174-4332

STROUD, ROBERT WAYNE, TEXTILE CHEMISTRY. *Current Pos:* RETIRED. *Personal Data:* b Jonesboro, Ark, May 24, 29; m 57; c 2. *Educ:* Ark Col, BS, 50; Ga Inst Technol, MSCh, 54; Univ Tex, Austin, PhD(org chem), 63. *Prof Exp:* Teacher, Pub Schs, Ark, 49-50; chemist, Carbide & Carbon Chem Co, Tex, 53-54 & 56-58; res chemist, E I DuPont de Nemours & Co, Inc, 62-72, sr res chemist, 72-91. *Mem:* Am Chem Soc. *Res:* Textile fibers chemistry and engineering. *Mailing Add:* 188 S Crest Rd Chattanooga TN 37404-5517

STROUD, THOMAS WILLIAM FELIX, STATISTICS. *Current Pos:* RETIRED. *Personal Data:* b Toronto, Ont, Apr 7, 36; m 83; c 4. *Educ:* Univ Toronto, BA, 56, MA, 60; Stanford Univ, PhD(statist), 68. *Prof Exp:* Asst prof math, Acadia Univ, 60-64; from asst prof to assoc prof, Queens Univ, Ont, 68-92, prof math & statist, 92. *Concurrent Pos:* Res asst, Sch Educ, Stanford Univ, 66-68; Nat Res Coun Can res grant, Queen's Univ, Ont, 69-; vis res fel, Educ Testing Serv, 72-73; invited prof, Fed Polytech Sch Lausanne, 77-78; vis prof, Univ Col Wales, Aberystwyth, 89-90. *Mem:* Am Statist Asn; Statist Soc Can; Inst Math Statist. *Res:* Multivariate analysis; Bayesian inference; statistical analysis of mental test data; generalized linear models; small area estimation; sample survey analysis. *Mailing Add:* Dept Math & Statist Queen's Univ Kingston ON K7L 3N6 Can

STROUGH, ROBERT I(RVING), PHYSICS, ENGINEERING. *Current Pos:* ENG MGR ADVAN PROD, UNITED TECH CORP, 76- *Personal Data:* b Akron, Ohio, June 22, 20; m 45; c 2. *Educ:* Case Western Reserve Univ, BS, 42, MS, 48, PhD(physics), 50. *Prof Exp:* Proj engr, Airborne Instrument Lab, 42-44; develop engr, Arma Corp, 44-46; asst proj engr, Pratt & Whitney Aircraft Div, United Aircraft Corp, 50-51, reactor proj engr, 51-60, develop engr, 60-62, chief develop eng, 62-63, prog mgr SNAP-50 nuclear elec spacer powerplant proj, 63-65, chief adv concepts develop, 65-69, mgr advan mil progs, 69-76. *Concurrent Pos:* Adj prof, Hartford Grad Ctr, Rensselaer Polytechnic Inst, 55-71; assoc dir aircraft nuclear propulsion proj, Oak Ridge Nat Lab, 54-55; mem res adv comt nuclear energy systs, NASA, 61-62. *Mem:* Am Phys Soc; Inst Elec & Electronics Engrs; Am Inst Aeronaut & Astronaut. *Res:* Management and technical direction of nuclear aircraft and spacecraft propulsion and power systems development including reactor, liquid metal and power conversion systems; engineering and design of advanced aircraft powerplants; aerothermodynamics; development of electrical machinery and electromagnetic devices. *Mailing Add:* 55 Ledgewood Dr Glastonbury CT 06033

STROUP, CYNTHIA ROXANE, EXPOSURE ASSESSMENT SURVEYS. *Current Pos:* BIOSTATISTICIAN & CHIEF, STATIST DESIGN & OPERS SECT, ENVIRON PROTECTION AGENCY, 76- *Personal Data:* b Norfolk, Va, Sept 21, 48. *Educ:* Longwood Col, BS, 71; Georgetown Univ, MS, 81. *Honors & Awards:* Silver Medal, Environ Protection Agency. *Prof Exp:* Teacher biol, Arlington County pub schs, 72-74. *Mem:* Am Pub Health Asn; Soc Occup & Environ Health; Am Asn Univ Women. *Res:* Design and analysis of human and environmental exposure studies on selected chemicals, such as formaldehyde, asbestos and dichloromethane; statistical design; quality assurance; sampling; data analysis; environmental monitoring. *Mailing Add:* 29 N Garfield St Arlington VA 22201

STROUS, GER J, BIOCHEMISTRY. *Current Pos:* fac mem, 78-85, lectr, 85-91, PROF & DEPT HEAD CELL BIOL, UNIV UTRECHT, 91- *Personal Data:* b Haelen, Aug 13, 44; Dutch citizen; m 70, Margriet Janssen; c Marc Jonas Job. *Educ:* Univ Nymegen, Neth, MSc, 69, PhD(biochem), 73. *Prof Exp:* Res fel biochem, Univ Nymegen, 70-73; fel cell biol, Dutch Res Coun, 74-78. *Concurrent Pos:* Vis scientist biol, Mass Inst Technol, Cambridge, Mass, 79-80; Harvard Med Sch Childrens Hosp, Boston, Mass, 80-86 & Sch Med, Washington Univ, St Louis, 86-; consult, Physiol Rev Comt, Dutch Res Coun, 86-; Fulbright prof, Wash Univ, Md, 95-96. *Mem:* Dutch Soc Cell Biol; Dutch Soc Biochem; Dutch Soc Glycoconjugates; Am Soc Cell Biol; Brit Biochem Soc; Am Soc Biochem & Molecular Biol. *Res:* Sorting mechanisms of membrane glyco-protein of the Golgi complex and the endosomal system; ubiquitin conjufation system, endocytosis and downregulation of signalling receptors. *Mailing Add:* Dept Cell Biol Univ Utrecht AZU-H02-314 Utrecht 3584CX Netherlands. *Fax:* 31-30-254-1797; *E-Mail:* strous@med.ruu.nl

STROUSE, CHARLES EARL, CHEMISTRY. *Current Pos:* from asst prof to assoc prof, 71-84, PROF CHEM, UNIV CALIF, LOS ANGELES, 84- *Personal Data:* b Ann Arbor, Mich, Jan 29, 44; m 72; c 2. *Educ:* Pa State Univ, University Park, BS, 65; Univ Wis-Madison, PhD(phys chem), 69. *Prof Exp:* AEC fel, Los Alamos Sci Lab, 69-71. *Mem:* AAAS; Am Chem Soc; Am Crystallog Asn. *Res:* Structural chemistry. *Mailing Add:* 10573 W Pico Blvd Suite 106 Los Angeles CA 90064

STROUT, RICHARD GOOLD, ZOOLOGY, PARASITOLOGY. *Current Pos:* Instr poultry sci, 54-60, from asst prof to prof, 60-90, parasitologist, 63-90, EMER PROF PARASITOL, UNIV NH, 90- *Personal Data:* b Auburn, Maine, Nov 11, 27; m 50; c 2. *Educ:* Univ Maine, BS, 50; Univ NH, MS, 54, PhD(parasitol), 61. *Concurrent Pos:* Fel, Sch Med, La State Univ, 67. *Mem:* Sigma Xi; Wildlife Dis Asn; Am Soc Parasitol. *Res:* In vitro culture and pathogenicity of avian coccidiosis; immunity mechanisms; blood parasites of birds and fishes. *Mailing Add:* Dept Animal & Nutrit Sci Rm 203 Kendall Hall Univ NH Durham NH 03824

STROVINK, MARK WILLIAM, EXPERIMENTAL HIGH ENERGY PHYSICS. *Current Pos:* from asst prof to assoc prof, 73-80, PROF PHYSICS, UNIV CALIF, BERKELEY, 80- *Personal Data:* b Santa Monica, Calif, July 22, 44; div; c 2. *Educ:* Mass Inst Technol, BS, 65; Princeton Univ, PhD(physics), 70. *Prof Exp:* From instr to asst prof physics, Princeton Univ, 70-73. *Concurrent Pos:* Vis asst prof physics, Cornell Univ, 71-72; mem, High-Energy Physics Adv Panel, Dept Energy, 88- *Mem:* Fel Am Phys Soc. *Res:* Searches for right-handed charged currents; muon interactions and charm production at high energy; principles of invariance to changes of energy scale and charge-parity inversion; collider detector instrumentation. *Mailing Add:* 6911 Norfolk Rd Berkeley CA 94705

STROYNOWSKI, IWONA T, CELL-CELL INTERACTIONS IMMUNE SYSTEM, MAJOR HISTOCOMPATABILITY COMPLEX ANTIGENS. *Current Pos:* from res fel to sr res fel, 81-88, SR RES ASSOC BIOL, CALIF INST TECHNOL, 88- *Personal Data:* b Bydgoszcz, Poland, Aug 8, 50; US citizen; m 70; c 2. *Educ:* Univ Geneva, Switz, BSc & MSc, 75; Stanford Univ, PhD(genetics), 79. *Prof Exp:* Postdoctoral fel biol, Stanford Univ, 79-81. *Concurrent Pos:* mem, NIH Immunol, Virol & Pathol Study Sect, 90-94. *Mem:* Am Asn Immunol; AAAS. *Res:* Cell mediated self-nonself recognition in the immune system of mice; Isn I transplantation antigens; non-ismcol MHC antigens; alternative splicing; T cell activation; regulation of expression of MMC genes. *Mailing Add:* Ctr Diabetes Res Microbiol Dept Microbiol Int Med & C Dr Univ Tex SW Med Ctr 5323 Harry Hines Blvd Dallas TX 75235-8854. *Fax:* 214-688-8291

STROYNOWSKI, RYSZARD ANDRZEJ, HEAVY LEPTON, EXPERIMENTS IN ELECTRON-POSITRON ANNIHILLATIONS. *Current Pos:* PROF PHYSICS, SOUTHERN METHODIST UNIV, 91- *Personal Data:* b Lodz, Poland, June 11, 46; US citizen; m 70, Iwona Fleszar; c Dorothee & Eva. *Educ:* Univ Warsaw, Poland, MSc, 68; Univ Geneva, Switz, PhD(physics), 73. *Prof Exp:* Staff physicist, European Ctr Nuclear Res, 69-75, Stanford Linear Accelerator Ctr, 75-80; sr res assoc, Calif Inst Technol, 80-91. *Mem:* Fel Am Phys Soc. *Mailing Add:* 7234 Brookshire Dr Dallas TX 75230-4206

STROZIER, JAMES KINARD, AEROSPACE ENGINEERING, MECHANICAL ENGINEERING. *Current Pos:* RES PROF, UNIV UTAH, 84- *Personal Data:* b Rock Hill, SC, May 21, 33; m 56; c 2. *Educ:* US Mil Acad, BS, 56; Univ Mich, Ann Arbor, MSE, 66, PhD(aerospace eng), 66; Long Island Univ, MBA, 84. *Prof Exp:* Instr mech, US Mil Acad, US Army, 64-66, asst prof, 66-67, exec officer, 1st Battalion, 92nd Artil, Vietnam, 68, systs analyst, First Field Force, 68-69, assoc prof mech, US Mil Acad, 70-82, prof aerospace eng, 82-84. *Mem:* Am Inst Aeronaut & Astronaut; Am Soc Eng Educ; Am Soc Mech Engrs; Soc Automotive Engrs. *Res:* Telemetry; wing design; adhesive testing; education methods. *Mailing Add:* 4637 Ledgemont Dr Salt Lake City UT 84124

STROZIER, JOHN ALLEN, JR, SURFACE PHYSICS. *Current Pos:* physicist, Brookhaven Nat Lab, 74-80. *Personal Data:* b Miami, Fla, June 3, 34; m 62; c 3. *Educ:* Cornell Univ, BEP, 58; Univ Utah, PhD(physics), 66. *Prof Exp:* Instr physics, Univ Utah, 66-67; res assoc mat sci, Cornell Univ, 67-69; sr res assoc, State Univ NY, Stony Brook, 69-71, asst prof, 71-74. *Mem:* Am Phys Soc. *Res:* Surface physics; low energy electron diffraction, catalysis. *Mailing Add:* NY State Off Bldg Rm 2B44 State Univ NY Empire State Col Vet Mem Hwy Hauppauge NY 11788

STRUB, MIKE ROBERT, FOREST BIOMETRY, STATISTICS. *Current Pos:* FOREST BIOMETRICIAN, WEYERHAEUSER CO, 77- *Personal Data:* b Alliance, Ohio, Dec 26, 48; m 69. *Educ:* Va Polytech Inst & State Univ, BS, 71, MS, 72, PhD(statist), 77. *Prof Exp:* Instr forestry, Va Polytech Inst & State Univ, 72-74; asst prof forest mgt, Pa State Univ, 75-77. *Mem:* Am Statist Asn; Biomet Soc; Soc Am Foresters. *Res:* Modeling growth and yield of forest stands, especially loblolly pine plantations; general qualitative model and applications to forestry. *Mailing Add:* 1662 Treasure Isle Rd Hot Springs Nat Park Hot Springs AR 71913

STRUBLE, CRAIG BRUCE, AGRICULTURAL CHEMICAL METABOLISM. *Current Pos:* STUDY DIR PHARM CHEM, HAZELTON WIS, 90- *Personal Data:* b Mt Pleasant, Mich, Oct, 30, 50; m 73; c 2. *Educ:* Jamestown Col, BS, 73; NDak State Univ, PhD(zool), 79. *Prof Exp:* Res assoc, Dept Path, Univ Wis-Madison & Wis Regional Primate Ctr, 78-79; res assoc, Dept Animal Sci, NDak State Univ, 79-83; res physiologist, Agr Res Serv, USDA, 83-90. *Mem:* Sigma Xi; Int Soc Study Xenobiotics; Am Chem Soc. *Res:* Metabolism, biliary secretion, and enterohepatic circulation of xenobiotics and agricultural chemicals in laboratory and farm animals; experimental surgery. *Mailing Add:* Hazelton Wisconsin PO Box 7545 MS13 Madison WI 53702-7545

STRUBLE, DEAN L, insect sex pheromones, management of agricultural research, for more information see previous edition

STRUBLE, GEORGE W, COMPUTER SCIENCE. *Current Pos:* PROF COMPUT SCI, WILLAMETTE UNIV, 82- *Personal Data:* b Philadelphia, Pa, July 6, 32; m 55; c 3. *Educ:* Swarthmore Col, AB, 54; Univ Wis, MS, 57, PhD(math), 61. *Prof Exp:* Proj supvr, Numerical Anal Lab, Univ Wis, 60-61; from asst prof to assoc prof math, Univ Ore, 61-69, res assoc, 61-65, assoc dir statist lab & comput ctr, 65-69, dir comput ctr, 69-74, assoc prof comput sci, 69-82. *Concurrent Pos:* Consult, Comput Mgt Serv, Inc, Portland, Ore, 74-78. *Mem:* Asn Comput Mach; Sigma Xi. *Res:* Algorithms. *Mailing Add:* Dept Computer Sci Willamette Univ Salem OR 97301. *E-Mail:* gstruble@willamette.edu

STRUBLE, GORDON LEE, NUCLEAR CHEMISTRY. *Current Pos:* staff chemist, 71-75, sect leader, 75-79, assoc div leader, 80-84, group leader, 84-89, DEP ASST TO DIR, LAWRENCE LIVERMORE NAT LAB, 89- *Personal Data:* b Cleveland, Ohio, Mar 7, 37; m 61; c 4. *Educ:* Rollins Col, BS, 60; Fla State Univ, PhD(chem), 64. *Prof Exp:* Fel, Lawrence Berkeley Lab, Univ Calif, 64-66; asst prof chem, Univ Calif, Berkeley, 66-71. *Concurrent Pos:* Prof physics, Univ Munich, 75. *Mem:* AAAS; Am Chem Soc; Am Phys Soc. *Res:* Experimental and theoretical low energy nuclear structure and reaction physics, determination of characteristics of low energy excitations in nuclei by nuclear reactions and decay processes and their description by theoretical many body techniques; high energy heavy-ion reactions. *Mailing Add:* LDRD L-3 Lawrence Livermore Lab PO Box 808 Livermore CA 94551-0808. *Fax:* 510-424-4820; *E-Mail:* struble@llnl.gov

STRUBLE, RAIMOND ALDRICH, MATHEMATICS. *Current Pos:* RETIRED. *Personal Data:* b Forest Lake, Minn, Dec 10, 24; m 46; c 5. *Educ:* Univ Notre Dame, PhD(math), 51. *Prof Exp:* Aerodynamicist, Douglas Aircraft Co, 51-53; asst prof math, Ill Inst Technol, 53-56; from assoc prof to prof, NC STATE UNIV, 58-88. *Concurrent Pos:* Consult, Armour Res Found, 54-60. *Res:* Fourier analysis; almost periodic functions; nonlinear differential equations; applied mathematics. *Mailing Add:* PO Box 50376 Raleigh NC 27650-6376

STRUCHTEMEYER, ROLAND AUGUST, soils, for more information see previous edition

STRUCK, CURTIS JOHN, EXTRAGALACTIC ASTRONOMY, STAR FORMATION. *Current Pos:* asst prof, 83-89, ASSOC PROF ASTROPHYS, IOWA STATE UNIV, 89- *Personal Data:* b Minneapolis, Minn, May 19, 54; c 2. *Educ:* Univ Minn, BS(physics) & BS(math), 76; Yale Univ, MPhil, 79, PhD(astron), 81. *Prof Exp:* Res fel, McDonald Observ, Univ Tex, 81-83. *Mem:* Am Astron Soc; Int Astron Union; Sigma Xi. *Res:* Theoretical studies of galaxy evolution; computer modeling of large-scale gas dynamics and star formation in galaxies; collisions between galaxies. *Mailing Add:* Dept Physics & Astron Iowa State Univ Ames IA 50011

STRUCK, ROBERT FREDERICK, PHARMACOLOGY, DRUG METABOLISM. *Current Pos:* res scientist, Southern Res Inst, 61-64, sr scientist, 64-80, head, Metabol Sect, 80-87, head, Biol Chem Div, 88-93, DIR, BIOCHEM DEPT, SOUTHERN RES INST, 94- *Personal Data:* b Pensacola, Fla, Jan 9, 32; m 63, Ruby Richardson; c Lesley & Bert. *Educ:* Auburn Univ, BS, 53, MS, 57, PhD(org chem), 61. *Prof Exp:* Assoc scientist, Southern Res Inst, 57-58; org chemist, Fruit & Veg Prod Lab, Agr Res Serv, USDA, 61. *Concurrent Pos:* Mem, Exp Therapeut Study Sect, NIH, 83-86, Study Sec 2, 96- *Mem:* Am Asn Cancer Res; Am Soc Pharmacol Exp Therapeut. *Res:* Metabolism, pharmacology, mechanism of action and medicinal chemistry of anticancer drugs; organophosphorus and organic heterocyclic chemistry. *Mailing Add:* Southern Res Inst PO Box 55305 Birmingham AL 35255-5305. *Fax:* 205-581-2877

STRUCK, ROBERT T(HEODORE), CHEMICAL ENGINEERING. *Current Pos:* RETIRED. *Personal Data:* b Harrisburg, Pa, Apr 26, 21; m 93, Clara Pearson; c Paul C & James N. *Educ:* Pa State Univ, BS, 42, MS, 46, PhD(fuel tech), 49. *Prof Exp:* Res asst petrol refining, Pa State Univ, 42-46, res asst fuel technol, 46-48; chem engr, Consol Coal Co, 48-74; mgr process develop, Conoco Coal Develop Co, 74-81, mgr res admin, 81-83. *Mem:* Am Chem Soc. *Res:* Diffusional processes in hydrocarbon processing; developing processes for converting coal to other fuels; air pollution control processes; development of new routes to metallurgical coke. *Mailing Add:* 2347 Morton Rd Pittsburgh PA 15241-3301

STRUCK, WILLIAM ANTHONY, ANALYTICAL CHEMISTRY. *Current Pos:* RETIRED. *Personal Data:* b Paterson, NJ, Mar 17, 20; m 43, Esther Doverman; c 3. *Educ:* Calvin Col, AB, 40; Univ Mich, MS, 62, PhD, 63. *Prof Exp:* Microanalyst, Upjohn Co, 41-48, head chem res anal, 48-62, mgr phys & analysis chem res, 62-68, from asst dir to dir supportive res, 68-74, vpres, Int Pharmaceut Res & Develop, 74-79, pres, Pharmaceut Res & Develop, 79-83. *Mem:* AAAS; Am Chem Soc. *Res:* Organic electrochemistry; organic analysis; optical rotatory dispersion. *Mailing Add:* 2102 Waite Ave Kalamazoo MI 49008-1718

STRUEMPLER, ARTHUR W, ANALYTICAL CHEMISTRY. *Current Pos:* head div, 65-81, chmn, Dept Sci & Math, 76-81, PROF CHEM, CHADRON STATE COL, 76- *Personal Data:* b Lexington, Nebr, Dec 12, 20; m 50; c 2. *Educ:* Univ Nebr, BS, 50, MS, 55; Iowa State Univ, PhD, 57. *Prof Exp:* Asst prof, Chico State Col, 57-60; fel biochem, Univ Calif, Davis, 60-62; opers analyst, Strategic Air Command Hq, Nebr, 62-65. *Concurrent Pos:* Finder, Bayard Meteorite. *Mem:* Am Chem Soc; Sigma Xi; AAAS; Meteorics Soc; Soc Vert Paleontol. *Res:* Weather modification studies relating to element concentrations in precipitation; geochemical studies related to uranium, radium, and radon. *Mailing Add:* 813 Maxwell Ct Ft Collins CO 80525-4861

STRUHL, KEVIN, MOLECULAR BIOLOGY. *Current Pos:* Asst prof, 82-85, ASSOC PROF BIOCHEM, HARVARD MED SCH, 86- *Personal Data:* b New York, NY, Sept 2, 52. *Educ:* Mass Inst Technol, BS, 74, MS, 74; Stanford Univ, PhD(biochem), 79. *Concurrent Pos:* Searle scholar, Chicago Community Trust, 83. *Res:* Regulation of eukaryotic gene expression; protein-DNA interactions; molecular mechanism of transcriptional activation in yeast. *Mailing Add:* Dept Biol Chem Harvard Univ Med Sch 25 Shattuck St Boston MA 02115-6027

STRUIK, DIRK JAN, HISTORY OF MATHEMATICS. *Current Pos:* from lectr to prof, 26-60, EMER PROF, MASS INST TECHNOL, 60- *Personal Data:* b Rotterdam, Neth, Sept 30, 94; US citizen; wid, Saly Ruth Rambler; c Ruth R, Anne N (Macchi) & Gwendolyn J (Bray). *Educ:* Univ Leiden, Neth, PhD(math), 22. *Honors & Awards:* Kenneth O May Award, Int Comn Hist of Math, 89; Golden Medal, Inst Math, Univ Nac Canton Mex, 75. *Prof Exp:* Asst, Dept Math, Tech Univ Delft, 17-24; Rockefeller fel, Rome, Italy & Goettingen, Ger, 24-26. *Concurrent Pos:* Lectr, Nat Univ Mex & other univs, PR, Costa Rica, Bielefeld, Ger, 34-; prof hist sci, Univ Utrecht, 63-64; from res assoc to assoc, Hist Sci Dept, Harvard Univ. *Mem:* Am Math Soc; Math Asn Am; Hist Sci Soc; Soc Hist Med, Math, Natural Sci & Tech Heth; Am Acad Arts & Sci; Int Acad Hist Sci. *Res:* Differential geometry and tensor analysis; history of science and especially history of mathematics; author of various books. *Mailing Add:* 52 Glendale Rd Belmont MA 02178

STRUIK, RUTH REBEKKA, MATHEMATICS, ALGEBRA. *Current Pos:* actg asst prof, 61-62, from asst prof to assoc prof, 62-80, PROF MATH, UNIV COLO, BOULDER, 80- *Personal Data:* b Mass, Dec 15, 28; div; c Marion, Margo & Louise. *Educ:* Swarthmore Col, BA, 49; Univ Ill, MA, 51; NY Univ, PhD(math), 55. *Prof Exp:* Digital comput programmer, Univ Ill, 50-51; asst, Univ Chicago, 52; lectr math, Sch Gen Studies, Columbia Univ, 55; asst prof, Drexel Inst Technol, 56-57; lectr, Univ BC, 57-61. *Mem:* Math Asn Am; Asn Women Math; Am Math Soc; Sigma Xi. *Res:* Groups; modern algebra. *Mailing Add:* Dept Math Campus Box 395 Univ Colo Boulder CO 80309-0395. *E-Mail:* struik@euclid.colorado.edu

STRULL, GENE, INTEGRATED CIRCUITS, SENSORS. *Current Pos:* RETIRED. *Personal Data:* b Chicago, Ill, May 15, 29; m 52, Joyce Lanosbaum; c David & Brian. *Educ:* Purdue Univ, BSEE, 51; Northwestern Univ, MS, 52, PhD(cadmium sulfide films), 54. *Honors & Awards:* Gov Indust Serv Award, Frederick Philips Awards, 91, Inst Elec & Electronics Engrs, 87. *Prof Exp:* Engr, Mat Eng Dept, Westinghouse Elec Corp, 54-55, sr engr, Semiconductor Div, Pa, 55-58, supvr, Solid State Lab, Md, 58-60, mgr solid state technol, Aerospace Div, 60-68, mgr sci & technol, 68-70, mgr, Advan Technol Labs, Systs Develop Div, 70-79, gen mgr, Advan Technol Div, 81-93, vpres technol, 87-93. *Concurrent Pos:* Lectr, Univ Pittsburgh, 54-58; assoc mem defense sci bd, Nat Res Coun/Nat Acad Sci, 80-82; NASA adv, 67-87; consult, NSF, 92- *Mem:* Fel Inst Elec & Electronics Engrs; Sigma Xi. *Res:* Solid state devices; advanced sensors; integrated systems; patent review; technical presentations; proposal review. *Mailing Add:* 1 Gristmill Ct Suite 606 Baltimore MD 21208

STRUM, JUDY MAY, ULTRASTRUCTURE, IMMUNOCYTOCHEMISTRY. *Current Pos:* from asst prof to assoc prof, 75-82, PROF ANAT, UNIV MD, 82- *Personal Data:* b Seattle, Wash, Mar 27, 38. *Educ:* Univ Wash, Seattle, BS, 63, PhD(anat/biol struct), 68. *Prof Exp:* Teaching res fel, Harvard Med Sch, Boston, Mass, 68-70; asst res anatomist, Cardiovasc Res Inst, San Francisco, Calif, 70-75. *Concurrent Pos:* Prin investr, NIH grants, 76-83, co-investr, 83-95; assoc ed, Am J Anat, 78-80; consult, Johns Hopkins Med Sch, 80. *Mem:* Am Soc Cell Biol; AAAS; Am Asn Anatomists; Electron Micros Soc Am; Int Asn Breast Cancer Res. *Res:* Development and differentiation of cell types in the airways and lung; cardiac muscle structure and function; biology and pathology of the mammary gland. *Mailing Add:* Dep Anat & Neurobiol Univ Md Sch Med 685 W Baltimore St Baltimore MD 21201. *Fax:* 410-706-2512; *E-Mail:* jstrum@umabnet.ab.umd.edu

STRUMWASSER, FELIX, PHYSIOLOGY, NEUROBIOLOGY. *Current Pos:* SR SCIENTIST, MARINE BIOL LAB, WOODS HOLE, 85- *Personal Data:* b Trinidad, WI, Apr 16, 34; nat US. *Educ:* Univ Calif, Los Angeles, BA, 53, PhD(zool), 57. *Honors & Awards:* Penn lectr, Univ Pa, 67; Carter-Wallance lectr, Princeton Univ, 68; 17th Bowditch lectr, Am Physiol Soc, 72; Lang lectr, Marine Biol Lab, 80; Swammerdam lectr, Amsterdam, holland, 86. *Prof Exp:* Asst, Univ Calif, Los Angeles, 56-57; from asst scientist to sr asst scientist, Lab Neurophysiol, NIMH, 57-60; res assoc neurophysiol, Walter Reed Army Inst Res, 60-64; assoc prof, Calif Inst Technol, 64-69, prof, 69-84; prof, Dept Physiol, Sch Med, Boston Univ, 84-87. *Concurrent Pos:* Res assoc, Washington Sch Psychiat, 60-64 & hon res assoc, Dept Biophys, Univ Col, London, 73-74; mem fel comt, NIH, 68-70; mem biochronometry comt, NSF, 69; sr fel, NATO, 73-74; mem, Neurol B Study Sect, NIH, 78-82 & Nat Comn Sleep Dis Res, 90- *Mem:* Fel AAAS; Soc Neuroscience; Soc Gen Physiol; Am Physiol Soc; Biophys Soc; Soc Res Biol Rhythms. *Res:* Neurophysiology; neurocellular basis of behavior, sleep-waking, reproduction; molecular and cellular mechanisms of circadian rhythms in nervous systems; long-term studies on single identifiable neurons in organ and dissociated cell culture; integrative mechanisms of the neuron; second messengers; pacemaker mechanisms in neurons; physiology and biochemistry of peptidergic neurons. *Mailing Add:* 10674 Muirfield Dr Potomac MD 20854. *Fax:* 301-295-3295

STRUNK, DUANE H, ANALYTICAL CHEMISTRY. *Current Pos:* RETIRED. *Personal Data:* b Irene, SDak, Mar 14, 20; m 45, Elizabeth Walker; c Ann (Jost) & Elizabeth (Traxel). *Educ:* Univ SDak, BA, 42; Univ Louisville, MS, 51. *Prof Exp:* Res supvr, Joseph E Seagram & Sons, Inc, 42-43, prod supvr, 43-44, maintenance supvr, 43- 45, res chemist, 46-65, control labs adminstr, 66-83. *Res:* Microanalytical methods, especially colorimetric, flame spectrophotometry and atomic absorption methods for copper and magnesium; water, food and wood chemistry; high accuracy particle counter; proof by density meter. *Mailing Add:* 1751 Lake Place Venice FL 34293

STRUNK, MAILAND RAINEY, CHEMICAL ENGINEERING. *Current Pos:* from assoc prof to prof, 57-79, chmn dept, 64-79, EMER PROF CHEM ENG, UNIV MO, ROLLA, 79- *Personal Data:* b Kansas City, Kans, Aug 17, 19; m 49; c 3. *Educ:* Kans State Univ, BS, 41; Univ Mo, MS, 47; Wash Univ, DSc(chem eng), 57. *Prof Exp:* Technologist, Shell Oil Co, Inc, 47-51, 52-54; instr chem eng, Wash Univ, 54-57. *Mem:* AAAS; Am Soc Eng Educ; Nat Soc Prof Engrs; Am Inst Chem Engrs. *Res:* Applied physical chemistry; heat and mass transfer. *Mailing Add:* 5744 Grand Ave Kansas City MO 64113

STRUNK, RICHARD JOHN, ORGANIC CHEMISTRY, AGROCHEMICAL SYNTHESIS. *Current Pos:* SR RES SCIENTIST, RES CTR, UNIROYAL CHEM CO, 67- *Personal Data:* b Jamaica, NY, July 6, 41; m 68; c 3. *Educ:* Gettysburg Col, AB, 63; State Univ NY Albany, PhD(org chem), 67. *Mem:* Am Chem Soc; Sigma Xi. *Res:* Organic chemistry; agrochemical synthesis in herbicides and insecticides. *Mailing Add:* 16 Briarwood Circle Cheshire CT 06410-2628

STRUNK, ROBERT CHARLES, PEDIATRIC ASTHMA & ALLERGIES. *Current Pos:* PROF PEDIAT, SCH MED, WASHINGTON UNIV, 87- *Personal Data:* b Evanston, Ill, May 29, 42; m 71, Alison L Gans; c Christopher & Alix. *Educ:* Northwestern Univ, BA, 64, MS & MD, 68. *Prof Exp:* Dir clin serv, Nat Jewish Ctr Immunol & Respiratory Med, Denver, Colo, 79-87, actg chmn, Dept Pediat, 85-87. *Concurrent Pos:* Dir, Div Allergy & Pulmonary Med, St Louis C's Hosp. *Mem:* Am Acad Allergy; Am Asn Immunologists; Soc Pediat Res; Am Pediat Soc. *Res:* Asthma mortality; delivery of care in asthma. *Mailing Add:* Dept Pediat Washington Univ Med Sch 400 S Kingshighway Blvd St Louis MO 63110

STRUNZ, G(EORGE) M(ARTIN), NATURAL PRODUCTS CHEMISTRY. *Current Pos:* from res scientist I to res scientist III, 67-91, RES SCIENTIST IV, CAN FOREST SERV, 91- *Personal Data:* b Vienna, Austria, Mar 10, 38; m 72, Annette P Knoppers; c Stella E & Sylvia H. *Educ:* Trinity Col, Dublin, BA, 59; Univ NB, PhD(org chem), 63. *Prof Exp:* Res assoc org chem, Univ Mich, 63-64; res fel, Harvard Univ, 64-65; lectr, Univ NB, 65-67. *Concurrent Pos:* Hon res assoc, Univ NB, 70-; vis scientist, Imp Chem Industs Pharmaceuts, Cheshire, UK, 75-76 & CNR Rome, Italy, 89; adj prof, Univ NB, 88- *Mem:* Fel Chem Inst Can; Am Chem Soc; fel Royal Soc Chem; Phytochem Soc NAm; affil Int Union Pure & Appl Chem. *Res:* Chemistry of microbial metabolites; plant hormones and other natural products; host-insect and host-pathogen interactions in the forest; control of forest insects; pathogens and competing vegetation by natural products. *Mailing Add:* Can Forest Serv PO Box 4000 Fredericton NB E3B 5P7 Can

STRUPP, HANS H, PSYCHOTHERAPY RESEARCH & CLINICAL PSYCHOLOGY, PSYCHOANALYSIS. *Current Pos:* prof, 66-76, distinguished prof psychol, 76-94, DISTINGUISHED EMER PROF PSYCHOL, VANDERBILT UNIV, 94- *Personal Data:* b Frankfurt Am Main, Ger, August 25, 21; m 51, Lottie Metzger; c Karen, Barbara & John. *Educ:* George Washington Univ, AB, 45, AM, 47, PhD(psychol), 54. *Hon Degrees:* MD, Univ Ulm, Ger, 86. *Honors & Awards:* Distinguished Prof Contrib Knowledge Award, Am Psychol Asn, 87; Distinguished Career Contrib Award, Soc Psycother Res, 86. *Prof Exp:* From assoc prof to prof, Univ NC, Chapel Hill, 57-66. *Concurrent Pos:* Co-ed, Psychother Res, Soc Psychother Res, 89-94. *Mem:* Fel Am Psychol Asn; Soc Psycother Res (pres, 72-73); fel AAAS. *Res:* Research on psychotherapy process and outcome. *Mailing Add:* Dept Psychol Vanderbilt Univ Nashville TN 37240. *Fax:* 615-343-8449; *E-Mail:* strupphh@ctrvax.vanderbilt.edu

STRUTHERS, BARBARA JOAN OFT, INTRAUTERINE & ORAL CONTRACEPTION, TOXICOLOGY & GASTROINTESTINAL PHARMACOLOGY. *Current Pos:* dir, Gyn Prods, G D Searle & Co, 87-88, dir GI & Anti-Infective Prods, 88-90, sr sci adv, corp med & sci affairs, 91-95, med dir sleep therapeut team, 95-96, DIR, FEMALE HEALTHCARE COMMUN, G D SEAREL & CO, 96- *Personal Data:* b Bend, Ore, May 4, 40; m 59; c 3. *Educ:* Wash State Univ, BS, 62; Ore State Univ, MS, 68, PhD(food sci), 73; Am Bd Toxicol, cert, 81. *Prof Exp:* Instr sci educ, Ore State Univ, 68-69, chemist food sci, 69-70; proj leader, Ralston Purina Co, 73-75, sr proj leader, 75-78, assoc scientist, 79-81, mgr toxicol, 81-82; assoc dir sci affairs, Monsanto Co, 82-87. *Concurrent Pos:* Radiation safety officer, Ralston Purina Co, 74-82; mem ethics comt, Soc Toxicol; mem bd dir, Soc Advan Contraception, 86-; dir, arthritis & prostaglandin grant prog, 91-93. *Mem:* AAAS; Sigma Xi; Am Inst Nutrit; Soc Toxicol; Soc Advan

Contraception. *Res:* Soy protein-processing toxicology and biochemistry; soybean trypsin inhibitor biological effects; mycotoxin effects in domestic animals; biochemical effects of lysinoalanine; intrauterine contraception; sexually transmitted disease; epidemiology; prostaglandins as ulcer preventives. *Mailing Add:* Healthcare Resource Group GD Searle Co 5200 Old Orchard Rd Skokie IL 60077. Fax: 847-470-6944; E-Mail: bjstru@searle.monsanto.com

STRUTHERS, ROBERT CLAFLIN, COMPARATIVE ANATOMY, DEVELOPMENTAL ANATOMY. *Current Pos:* RETIRED. *Personal Data:* b Syracuse, NY, June 2, 28; m 52; c 6. *Educ:* Syracuse Univ, BA, 50, MA, 52; Univ Rochester, PhD(biol), 56. *Prof Exp:* Asst comp & develop anat, Syracuse Univ, 50-56; from instr to asst prof anat, Ohio State Univ, 56-61; assoc prof, Wheelock Col, 61-62, prof, 62-81, prof natural sci, 81-93. *Res:* Morphology of early embryonic stages of vertebrate animals, particularly on the pharynx and its derivatives. *Mailing Add:* 25 South St Townsend MA 01469

STRUVE, WALTER SCOTT, ULTRAFAST LASER SPECTROSCOPY. *Current Pos:* instr, 74-76, from asst prof to assoc prof, 76-88, PROF CHEM, IOWA STATE UNIV, 88- *Personal Data:* b Wilmington, Del, Feb 22, 45; m 71. *Educ:* Harvard Univ, AB, 67, MA, 69, PhD(phys chem), 72. *Prof Exp:* Postdoctoral fel, AT&T Bell Labs, Murray Hill, NJ, 72-74. *Concurrent Pos:* Vis assoc prof, Univ Chicago, 82. *Mem:* Am Chem Soc; Am Phys Soc; AAAS; Am Soc Photobiol. *Res:* Ultrafast laser spectroscopy of electronic excitation transport in photosynthetic antenna systems; environment-sensitive fluorophores of biological significance. *Mailing Add:* Dept Chem Iowa State Univ Ames IA 50011-0061

STRUVE, WILLIAM GEORGE, CHEMICAL LABORATORY, AUTOMATION. *Current Pos:* RETIRED. *Personal Data:* b Milwaukee, Wis, Mar 19, 38; c 9. *Educ:* Lake Forest Col, BA, 62; Northwestern Univ, PhD, 66; Memphis State Univ, MS, 86. *Prof Exp:* Res chemist, Am Cyanamid Co, 66-68; assoc prof biochem, Univ Tenn, Memphis, 68-87; lab automation specialist, Compuchem, 87-90. *Concurrent Pos:* Vis scholar, Stanford Univ, 69-70. *Res:* Electronics; computer music composition; laboratory automation. *Mailing Add:* 1206 N 23rd St Wilmington NC 28405

STRUVE, WILLIAM SCOTT, ORGANIC CHEMISTRY. *Current Pos:* RETIRED. *Personal Data:* b Utica, NY, May 1, 15; m 39, Elizabeth Miller; c Guy M, Walter S & Edwin B. *Educ:* Univ Mich, BS, 37, MS, 38, PhD(org chem), 40. *Prof Exp:* Du Pont fel, Univ Mich, 40-41; chemist, Jackson Lab, E I du Pont de Nemours & Co, 41-49, res supvr, 49-58, lab dir, Color Res Lab, 58-73, dir, Newark Lab & mgr, Colors Res & Develop, 73-80. *Mem:* Am Chem Soc. *Res:* Carcinogenic hydrocarbons; organic fluorine compounds; dyestuffs; pigments. *Mailing Add:* 29 Dellwood Ave Chatham NJ 07928-1701

STRUZAK, RYSZARD G, ELECTROMAGNETIC COMPATIBILITY, ELECTROMAGNETIC METROLOGY. *Current Pos:* CONSULT, WORLD BANK, 93- *Personal Data:* b Janow, Poland, Apr 2, 33; m 56; c 2. *Educ:* Tech Univ, Wroclaw, BachSci (eq), 54, MSci, 56; Tech Univ, Warsaw, Dr, 62, Dr Habil, 68. *Honors & Awards:* Gold Emblem of Distinction, Asn Elec Engrs, 87. *Prof Exp:* Res asst antennas, Radio & TV Res & Devlop Ctr, Wroclaw, 53-54; lectr telecommun, Tech Univ, Wroclaw, 54-56; head scientist, RFI Lab, Telecommun Res Inst, 63-67, head, Electromagnetic Compatibility Div, 67-73, head, Telecommun Res Inst, Wroclaw Br, 73-85; sr counr & head, Tech Dept, Int Telecommun Union-CCIR, 85-93. *Concurrent Pos:* From asst prof to prof, Tech Univ, Wroclaw, 71-85; mem, Comn Electronics & Telecommun, Polish Acad Sci, 69-78, officer, 78-85; vchmn, SG1, Int Radio Consult Comt, CCIR, 74-85, chmn IWP1/4, 80-85; vchmn, Comn E, Int Union Radio Sci, URSI, 84-87; invited lectr, Int Ctr Theoret Physics, Trieste, 89 & 91. *Mem:* Fel Inst Elec & Electronics Engrs; NY Acad Sci. *Res:* Radio science and engineering; electromagnetic compatibility engineering and standards; RF spectrum monitoring, engineering, planning & management; computer-aided radio engineering and design of radio systems; computer simulation; electromagnetic metrology; electromagnetism. *Mailing Add:* Int Telecomm Union CCIR Place Des Nations BP 820 Geneve 20 CH 1211 Switzerland

STRUZYNSKI, RAYMOND EDWARD, PHYSICS. *Current Pos:* From instr to asst prof, 64-70, ASSOC PROF PHYSICS, BROOKLYN COL, 70- *Personal Data:* b Jersey City, NJ, Dec 10, 37; m 65; c 2. *Educ:* Stevens Inst Technol, BEng, 59, MS, 61, PhD(physics), 65. *Concurrent Pos:* Res scientist, Hudson Labs, Columbia Univ, 65-67. *Mem:* Am Asn Physics Teachers; Sigma Xi. *Res:* Radiative beta decay; liquid helium; quantum mechanics of many boson systems. *Mailing Add:* Dept Physics Brooklyn Col Bedford Ave & Ave H Brooklyn NY 11210

STRYCKER, STANLEY JULIAN, RESEARCH ADMINISTRATION, PHARMACEUTICAL CHEMISTRY. *Current Pos:* RETIRED. *Personal Data:* b Goshen, Ind, Aug 30, 31; m 52; c 4. *Educ:* Goshen Col, AB, 53; Univ Ill, PhD(org chem), 56. *Prof Exp:* Res chemist, Dow Chem Co, 56-63, sr res chemist, 63-68, group leader, 68-69, res mgr pharmaceut sci, 69-74, res mgr chem & indust pharm, 74-80, lab dir chem, 80-82, lab dir res admin, Merrel Dow Pharmaceut, Inc, 82-9090. *Concurrent Pos:* Sabbatical, Col Med, Univ Iowa, 67-68. *Res:* Organic synthesis; heterocyclics; medicinal chemistry. *Mailing Add:* 54928 County Rd 27 Bristol IN 46507

STRYER, LUBERT, MOLECULAR AND CELL BIOLOGY. *Current Pos:* chmn dept, 76-79, WINZER PROF CELL BIOL, SCH MED, STANFORD UNIV, 76-, PROF NEUROBIOL, 93- *Personal Data:* b Tientsin, China, Mar 2, 38; US citizen; m 58, Andrea Stenn; c Michael & Daniel. *Educ:* Univ Chicago, BS, 57; Harvard Univ, MD, 61. *Hon Degrees:* DSc, Univ Chicago, 92. *Honors & Awards:* Eli Lilly Award, Am Chem Soc, 70; Newcomb Cleveland Prize, AAAS, 92; Distinguished Inventors Award, Intellectual Property Owners Asn, 93. *Prof Exp:* From asst prof to assoc prof biochem, Stanford Univ, 63-69; prof molecular biophys & biochem, Yale Univ, 69-76. *Concurrent Pos:* Helen Hay Whitney fel, Harvard Univ & Med Res Coun Lab Molecular Biol, Cambridge, Eng, 61-63; consult, NIH, 67-71; consult, Protein Design Labs, Inc. *Mem:* Nat Acad Sci; Am Soc Biol Chemists; Biophys Soc; fel Am Acad Arts & Sci; fel AAAS. *Res:* Protein structure and function; visual excitation; spectroscopy; x-ray diffraction; signal transduction. *Mailing Add:* Dept Neurobiol Stanford Med Sch Fairchild Bldg D135 Stanford CA 94305

STRYKER, LYNDEN J, COLLOID CHEMISTRY, SURFACE CHEMISTRY. *Current Pos:* PAPER APPL MGR, SPECIALTY MINERALS INC, 93- *Personal Data:* b Stamford, NY, Feb 19, 43; div; c Joel & Jesse. *Educ:* Clarkson Col Technol, BS, 64, PhD(chem), 69. *Prof Exp:* Asst, Clarkson Col Technol, 67-68; lectureship, Brunel Univ, 69-70; sr res chemist, Westvaco Corp, 70-77; assoc prof chem, Inst Paper Chem, 77-79; prog mgr, Hammermill Paper Co, 79-89; prog mgr, Int Paper, 89-93. *Concurrent Pos:* Leverhulme fel, 69-70; chmn papermaking additives, Paper & Bd Div, Tech Asn Pulp & Paper Indust, 91-93, secy, 93-95, vchair, 95- *Mem:* Am Chem Soc; Tech Asn Pulp & Paper Indust. *Res:* Chemistry of papermaking systems; alkaline papermaking; stability of colloidal dispersions; solid-liquid interactions; metal ion hydrolysis and complexation; water pollution abatement; paper sizing and retention; surface characterization of solids; emulsion technology. *Mailing Add:* 635 Barclay Dr Bethlehem PA 18017. Fax: 610-250-3178

STRYKER, MARTIN H, quality control, plasma proteins; deceased, see previous edition for last biography

STRYKER, MICHAEL PAUL, NEUROBIOLOGY, NEUROOPHTHALMOLOGY. *Current Pos:* asst prof, 78-87, PROF PHYSIOL & CO-DIR NEUROSCI, UNIV CALIF, SAN FRANCISCO, 87- *Personal Data:* b Savannah, Ga, June 16, 47; m 78; c 3. *Educ:* Univ Mich, AB, 68; Mass Inst Technol, PhD(psychol, brain sci), 75. *Prof Exp:* Res fel neurobiol, Harvard Med Sch, 75-78. *Concurrent Pos:* Instr neurobiol, Cold Spring Harbor Labs, 76-78; NSF Develop Neuroscience panel mem, 85-88; vis prof, Univ Oxford, 83-88; mem, Mass, Inst Technol Corp, vis comt, Whitlaker Col & dept brain & cognitive sci. *Mem:* Soc Neuroscience; AAAS. *Res:* Neurobiology of the central nervous system; developing visual system. *Mailing Add:* Dept Physiol Univ Calif San Francisco Med Sch 513 Parnassus Ave San Francisco CA 94122-2722

STUART, ALFRED HERBERT, PHOTOGRAPHIC CHEMISTRY. *Current Pos:* RETIRED. *Personal Data:* b Farmville, Va, 13; m 44; c 2. *Educ:* Hampden-Sydney Col, BS, 33; Univ Va, PhD(org chem), 37. *Prof Exp:* Res fel, Univ Va, 37-39; res chemist, Schieffelin & Co, NY, 39-43; dir chem res, 43-47; develop mgr, Charles Bruning Co, Ill, 47-65, chief chemist, Bruning Div, Addressograph-Multigraph Corp, 65-80. *Res:* Diazotype and electrostatic copying processes. *Mailing Add:* 726 Superior St Oak Park IL 60302-2117

STUART, ALFRED WRIGHT, REGIONAL ANALYSIS, REGIONAL GEOGRAPHY. *Current Pos:* chmn, Dept Geog & Earth Sci, 69-77 & 79-88, interim chmn, Dept Criminal Justice, 91-92, PROF GEOG & DEPT GEOG & EARTH SCI, UNIV NC, CHARLOTTE, 69- *Personal Data:* b Pulaski, Va, Nov 16, 32; m 60, Mary L Moyers; c Sarah Park (Sloan), Amy (Madison), Julia (Maynard) & Peter. *Educ:* Univ SC, BS, 55; Emory Univ, MS, 56; Ohio State Univ, PhD(geog), 66. *Honors & Awards:* Polar Medal, US Govt, 65. *Prof Exp:* Glaciologist, US Antarctic Res Prog, NSF, 58-60; res assoc, Inst Polar Studies, Ohio State Univ, 60-61; asst instr geog, 61-63; community planner, City of Roanoke, Va, 63-64; asst prof geog, Univ Tenn, Knoxville, 64-69. *Concurrent Pos:* Urban analyst, US Bur Mines, 68-70; researcher, Oak Ridge Nat Lab, 69; consult, Charlotte-Mechlenburg Planning Comn, 84-85; dir, Ctr Appl Community Res, 88- *Mem:* Asn Am Geographers; Am Chamber Com Res Asn. *Res:* Economic and demographic change in the southern United States; analytical atlas production; polar regions. *Mailing Add:* Dept Geog & Earth Sci Univ NC Charlotte NC 28223. Fax: 704-547-3182; E-Mail: awstuart@email.uncc.edu

STUART, ANN ELIZABETH, NEUROBIOLOGY. *Current Pos:* MEM FAC, DEPT PHYSIOL, UNIV NC, 80-, PROF, 87- *Personal Data:* b Harrisburg, Pa, Oct 5, 43; m 78; c 1. *Educ:* Swarthmore Col, BA, 65; Yale Univ, MS, 67, PhD(physiol), 69. *Prof Exp:* Res fel neurophysiol, Dept Physiol, Univ Calif, Los Angeles Med Ctr, 71-73; res fel neurochemistry, Dept Neurobiol, Harvard Med Sch, 69-71, asst prof, 73-78, assoc prof, 78. *Mem:* Soc Neuroscience; Soc Gen Physiologists; Asn Res Vision & Ophthal. *Res:* Synaptic mechanisms; integration and synaptic transmission between single cells of small populations of neurons; integration in invertebrate central nervous systems; invertebrate vision photoreceptor synapses. *Mailing Add:* Dept Physiol 261 Med Res Bldg 206 Univ NC Chapel Hill NC 27599-7545

STUART, CHARLES EDWARD, OCEAN ACOUSTICS. *Current Pos:* DIR MARITIME SYSTS OFF, ADVAN RES PROJ AGENCY, ARLINGTON, 85- *Personal Data:* b Durham, NC, Feb 9, 42; m 82, Margaret A Robinson; c Marjorie K & Heather A. *Educ:* Duke Univ, BSEE, 63. *Prof Exp:* Engr,

Westinghouse Elec Corp, 63-65; sr engr, Booz Allen Hamilton, 66-68; res dir, B-K Dynamics Inc, 69-78; oceanogr, Off Naval Res, 79-84. *Concurrent Pos:* Trustee, Asn Unmanned Vehicle Systs, 89-93. *Mem:* Sr mem Inst Elec & Electronics Engrs; Asn Unmanned Vehicle Systs; Acoust Soc Am. *Res:* Development of unmanned undersea vehicle technology. *Mailing Add:* Maritime Systs Technol DARPA/UWO 3701 N Fairfax Dr Arlington VA 22203

STUART, DAVID MARSHALL, PHARMACY, CHEMISTRY. *Current Pos:* PROF PHARMACEUT CHEM, COL PHARM, OHIO NORTHERN UNIV, 64- *Personal Data:* b Ogden, Utah, May 20, 28; m 51; c 5. *Educ:* Univ Utah, BS, 51; Univ Wis, PhD(pharmaceut chem), 55. *Prof Exp:* Asst prof pharmaceut chem, Univ Tex, 55-57 & Ore State Col, 57-60; coordr sci info, Neislar Labs, 60-64. *Concurrent Pos:* Pharm consult, Ohio Dept Pub Welfare, 71-77; pres, Pharm Health & Related Mgt, Inc, 74- *Mem:* Am Pharmaceut Asn; NY Acad Sci. *Res:* Scientific literature research and writing; health care research. *Mailing Add:* 92 San Andreas Ct West Jordan UT 84088

STUART, DAVID W, METEOROLOGY. *Current Pos:* from asst prof to prof, Fla State Univ, 62-95, assoc chmn dept, 67-72, chmn, 85-94, UNIV SERV PROF METEOROL, FLA STATE UNIV, 95- *Personal Data:* b Lafayette, Ind, June 15, 32; m 64, Diane Sivertson; c James, Robert & Melissae. *Educ:* Univ Calif, Los Angeles, BA, 55, MA, 57, PhD(meteorol), 62. *Prof Exp:* Res meteorologist, Univ Calif, Los Angeles, 55-61, teaching asst meteorol, 57-61. *Concurrent Pos:* Assoc prof, Naval Postgrad Sch, 66-67. *Mem:* Am Meteorol Soc; Sigma Xi; Am Geophys Union; Oceanog Soc. *Res:* Synoptic meteorology; numerical weather prediction, especially diagnostic studies and air-sea interaction; meteorology of coastal upwelling areas. *Mailing Add:* Dept Meteorol Fla State Univ Tallahassee FL 32306-3034. *Fax:* 850-644-9642; *E-Mail:* stuart@met.fsu.edu

STUART, DERALD ARCHIE, SOLID STATE PHYSICS. *Current Pos:* CONSULT SOLID STATE PHYSICS, 88- *Personal Data:* b Bingham Canyon, Utah, Nov 9, 25; m 48; c 2. *Educ:* Univ Utah, BS, 47, MS, 48, PhD(physics), 50. *Honors & Awards:* Meyer Award, Am Ceramic Soc, 54; Wyld Propulsion Award, Am Inst Aeronaut & Astronaut; Montgomery Award, Nat Soc Aerospace Prof, 64. *Prof Exp:* Asst physics, Univ Utah, 47-50; asst prof eng mat, Cornell Univ, 50-52, assoc prof eng mech & mat, 52-58; propulsion staff mgr & resident rep to Aerojet-Gen Corp, 58-59, asst to Polaris Missile syst mgr & Polaris resident rep to Aerojet-Gen Corp, 59-61, mgr propulsion staff, Missile Systs Div, 61-62, dir propulsion systs, 62-64, asst chief engr, 64-66, asst gen mgr eng & develop, 66-67, vpres & asst gen mgr, 67-70, vpres corp & vpres & gen mgr Missile Systs Div, Lockheed Missiles & Space Co, Lockheed Corp, 70-87. *Concurrent Pos:* Consult, Cornell Aeronaut Lab, 52-54, Allegany Ballistics Lab, 52-58, Lincoln Lab, Mass Inst Technol & Ramo-Wooldridge Corp, 54-56. *Mem:* Nat Acad Eng; fel Am Inst Aeronaut & Astronaut; Soc Logistics Engrs; Soc Women Engrs; Am Contract Managing Asn. *Res:* Glassy state; plastic behavior of materials; solid fuel rockets. *Mailing Add:* 9841 N 107th St Scottsdale AZ 85258

STUART, DOUGLAS GORDON, PHYSIOLOGY. *Current Pos:* PROF PHYSIOL, COL MED, UNIV ARIZ, 70- *Personal Data:* b Casino, NSW, Australia, Oct 5, 31; US citizen; m 57; c 4. *Educ:* Mich State Univ, BS, 55, MA, 56; Univ Calif, Los Angeles, PhD(physiol), 61. *Prof Exp:* Res fel anat, Univ Calif, Los Angeles, 61-63; asst prof physiol in residence, 63-65, assoc prof, Univ Calif, Davis, 65-67. *Mem:* Am Physiol Soc. *Res:* Neural control of posture and locomotion. *Mailing Add:* Dept Physiol Univ Ariz Sch Med Health Sci Ctr 1501 N Campbell Ave Tucson AZ 85724-0001. *Fax:* 520-626-4884; *E-Mail:* dgstuart@arizrvax

STUART, GEORGE WALLACE, THEORETICAL PHYSICS. *Current Pos:* CONSULT, 79- *Personal Data:* b New York, NY, Apr 5, 24; m 48; c 3. *Educ:* Rensselaer Polytech Inst, BEE, 49, MS, 50; Mass Inst Technol, PhD(physics), 53. *Prof Exp:* Head theoret physics unit, Hanford Atomic Prod Oper, Gen Electric Co, 52-57; res adv spec nuclear effects lab, Gen Atomic Div, Gen Dynamics Corp, Calif, 58-67; sr res scientist, Systs, Sci & Software, 67-72; staff scientist, Sci Applns Inc, 72-79. *Mem:* Fel Am Phys Soc. *Res:* Nuclear reactors; plasma theory; atomic physics. *Mailing Add:* PO Box 134 Rancho Santa Fe CA 92067. *Fax:* 619-756-5704

STUART, JAMES DAVIES, ANALYTICAL SEPARATIONS, LIQUID & GAS CHROMATOGRAPHY. *Current Pos:* asst prof, 69-75, ASSOC PROF ANALYTICAL CHEM, UNIV CONN, 75- *Personal Data:* b Elizabeth, NJ, Sept 30, 41; m 64, Carol Morrison; c James E & Jean A (Smith). *Educ:* Lafayette Col, BS, 63; Lehigh Univ, PhD(analytical chem), 69. *Prof Exp:* Instr, Lafayette Col, 67-69. *Concurrent Pos:* Prin investr, Nat Inst Environ Sci grants, 75-77; vis lectr, Chem Dept, Univ Ga, 76; prin investr grant, Dept Interior to Conn Inst Water Resources, 80-88; vis lectr chem eng, Yale Univ, 83; consult, IBM Instruments, Danbury, Conn, 83-85, Olin Corp, Cheshire, Conn, 88, HNV Corp, 91-94, Tekmar-Dohrman, 95-; prin investr grant, Environ Protection Agency, 87-94; lab dir, Marine Environ Lab, Avery Point, 90-92, Univ Conn; bd dirs, New England Chromatography Coun, 90-96, pres, 96- *Mem:* Am Chem Soc. *Res:* Development of modern separation methods using gas and high performance liquid chromatography separately and with mass spectrometry; development of accurate rapid and sensitive methods to determine amino acids and neurotransmitters in human, and animal fluids; assessing the reliability of analyses of air and groundwater around leaking underground gasoline tanks; general analysis method of organic pollutants, flagrants and explosives; involved in the teaching of environmental chemistry. *Mailing Add:* Dept Chem Univ Conn U-60 215 Glenbrook Rd Storrs CT 06269-4060. *Fax:* 860-486-2981; *E-Mail:* stuart@uconnvm.uconn.edu

STUART, JAMES GLEN, BACTERIAL GENETICS, MICROBIOLOGY. *Current Pos:* asst prof biol, 77-85, ASSOC PROF BIOL SCI, MURRAY STATE UNIV, 85- *Personal Data:* b Enid, Okla, Aug 23, 48; m 68; c 2. *Educ:* Cameron State Col, BS, 70; Okla Univ, MS, 72, PhD(med microbiol), 75. *Prof Exp:* Lectr biol, Millikin Univ, 75-77. *Concurrent Pos:* Grant dir, Ky Heart Fund, 78-79 & grant reviewer, 83- *Mem:* Am Soc Microbiol; Sigma Xi. *Res:* Bacterial genetics, specifically the phenomena of genetics and mechanisms of antibiotic resistance in group A streptococci. *Mailing Add:* Dept Biol Murray State Univ Murray KY 42071

STUART, JEFFREY JAMES, HESSIAN FLY GENETICS & STUDY OF AVIRULENCE GENES IN HESSIAN FLY TO WHEAT, GENOMIC ORGANIZATION & DEVELOPMENT GENETICS IN BEETLES. *Current Pos:* ASST PROF INSECT GENETICS, DEPT ENTOM, PURDUE UNIV, 90- *Personal Data:* m 82, Cynthia L Sulsar. *Educ:* Washburn Univ, BA, 78; Kans State Univ, MS, 82, PhD(entom/genetics), 87. *Honors & Awards:* Young Investr Award, Dow Elanco, 92. *Prof Exp:* From grad res asst to res asst, Dept Entom, Kans State Univ, 80-87, res assoc, Div Biol, 88-90. *Mem:* AAAS; Genetics Soc Am; Am Genetics Asn; Entom Soc Am. *Res:* Molecular genetic analysis of important loci in non-Drosophilid insect species; gene conferring virulence in the Hessian fly to resistance genes in wheat; homeotic genes in beetles; insecticide resistance loci. *Mailing Add:* Dept Entom Purdue Univ West Lafayette IN 47907-1968. *E-Mail:* jeff_stuart.entm@mailhost.entm.purdue.edu

STUART, JOE DON, EXPERT SYSTEMS, COMPUTER SCIENCE. *Current Pos:* sr scientist, 72-76, asst vpres, 76-82, PRIN SCIENTIST, RADIAN CORP, 82- *Personal Data:* b Brownsboro, Tex, Feb 28, 32; m 63; c 2. *Educ:* Univ Tex, BA, 57, PhD(physics), 63. *Prof Exp:* Sr physicist appl physics lab, Johns Hopkins Univ, 63-65; sr scientist, Tracor, Inc, 65-72. *Mem:* Am Meteorol Soc; Am Asn Artificial Intel; Inst Elec & Electronic Engrs Computer Soc; Asn Comput Mach. *Res:* Knowledge engineering; computer modeling; the formulation and development of practical expert systems in the fields of equipment fault diagnostics, chemical analysis, weather forecasting, and financial services. *Mailing Add:* 4009 Knollwood Dr Austin TX 78731

STUART, JOHN G, SYNTHETIC, ORGANIC & NATURAL PRODUCTS CHEMISTRY. *Current Pos:* DIV CHAIR & ASSOC PROF ORG CHEM, WILEY COL, 93- *Personal Data:* b Dominica, WI, July 12, 53; US citizen; m 79, Joyce J Webster; c Holly, Dean & Jonathan. *Educ:* Univ Virgin Islands, BA, 79; Univ Houston, MSc, 85; Univ Okla, PhD(org chem), 90. *Mem:* Am Chem Soc; Int Cong Heterocyclic Chem. *Res:* Use of transition medicated process to synthesize intermediates which can be elaborated into interesting natural and synthetic compounds. *Mailing Add:* 711 Wiley Ave Marshall TX 75670. *Fax:* 903-938-8100

STUART, JOHN W(ARREN), ELECTRICAL ENGINEERING. *Current Pos:* CONSULT, 88- *Personal Data:* b Logansport, Ind, Jan 5, 24; m 46; c 5. *Educ:* Purdue Univ, BSEE, 48. *Prof Exp:* Asst elec apparatus, Westinghouse Elec Corp, 48-50, appln engr, 50-55, proj engr, 55-58; chief engr, Accuray Corp, 58-62; mgr, Arthur D Little, Inc, 62-80, vpres mech eng, 62-88. *Mem:* Inst Elec & Electronics Engrs. *Res:* Digital control; solid state device development; digital applications of magnetic devices; research & development management; technical audits; equipment engineering. *Mailing Add:* 137 Sherburn Circle Weston MA 02193

STUART, KENNETH DANIEL, MOLECULAR PARASITOLOGY, GENE EXPRESSION. *Current Pos:* AFFIL PROF MICROBIOL & PATHOBIOL, UNIV WASH, 84- *Personal Data:* b Boston, Mass, 1940; m; c 3. *Educ:* Northeastern Univ, BA, 63; Wesleyan Univ, MA, 65; Univ Iowa, PhD(zool), 69. *Prof Exp:* Res biochem, Nat Inst Med Res, London, 69-71 & State Univ NY, Stony Brook, 71-72; res biol, Univ SFla, 72-76; dir, Seattle Biomed Res Inst, 82- *Concurrent Pos:* Consult, WHO, NIH & Agency Int Develop. *Mem:* Fel AAAS; Am Soc Microbiol; Am Soc Parasitol; Am Soc Cell Biol; Am Adv Sci. *Res:* Molecular parasitology with emphasis on gene organization and expression; antigenic variation and mitochondrial gene expression in African trypanosomes; viruses in Leishmania. *Mailing Add:* Pathobiol Box 357238 Univ Wash Seattle WA 98195

STUART, ROBLEY VANE, SPUTTERING, THIN FILMS. *Current Pos:* pres, 69-89, CONSULT, KORAL LABS INC, 89- *Personal Data:* b Jasper, Minn, Nov 4, 24; m 64, Evelyn M Ekland; c Janet, Jacqueline, William & Judith. *Educ:* Morningside Col, BS, 52. *Prof Exp:* Physicist, Gen Mills Elec Div, 55-59, Appl Sci Div, Litton Indust, 59-66; physicist & vpres, Modern Controls Inc, 66-69. *Mem:* Am Phys Soc; Am Vacuum Soc. *Res:* High altitude gas samplings to study debris from atomic bomb tests; spectroscopic studies of sputtering to measure yields at very low ion energies and ejection energies of sputtered atoms. *Mailing Add:* 7961 230 St Lane N Forest Lake MN 55025-8503

STUART, RONALD S, ORGANIC CHEMISTRY. *Current Pos:* RETIRED. *Personal Data:* b Tingley, NB, Mar 26, 19; m 46, Mary Vanstone; c Brian, David, Robert & Craig. *Educ:* Univ NB, BA, 40; Univ Toronto, MA, 41, PhD(org chem), 44. *Hon Degrees:* DSc, Univ NB, 93. *Prof Exp:* Demonstr chem, Univ Toronto, 40-42; res assoc, Nat Res Coun Can, 43-45; asst dir res, Dom Tar & Chem, 45-48; mgr chem & biol control, Merck & Co, Ltd, 48-53, mgr sci develop, 53-60, mgr tech & prod opers, 60-63, dir res, Merck Sharp & Dohme Can, 63-65, Charles E Frosst & Co, 65-68, dir res, Merc Frosst Labs, 68-78, exec dir, 78-81; dir, Res Serv & Ctr Res Eng & Appl Sci, Univ NB, 82-93. *Mem:* Am Chem Soc; Chem Inst Can; Can Res Mgt Asn. *Res:* Medicinal chemistry; oxidation of aromatic hydrocarbons; organic synthesis of stable isotope labelled compounds; initiating centers of excellence at the university in a wide variety of engineering & scientific disciplines. *Mailing Add:* 340 Springhill Rd Fredericton NB E3C 1R6 Can

STUART, THOMAS ANDREW, ELECTRICAL ENGINEERING. *Current Pos:* PROF ELEC ENG, UNIV TOLEDO, 75- *Personal Data:* b Bloomington, Ind, Feb 6, 41; m 63; c 2. *Educ:* Univ Ill, Urbana, BS, 63; Iowa State Univ, ME, 69, PhD(elec eng), 72. *Prof Exp:* Engr, Martin Co, 63-64 & Honeywell, Inc, 64-65; design engr, Collins Radio Co, 65-69; asst prof elec eng, Clarkson Col Technol, 72-75. *Mem:* Inst Elec & Electronics Engrs. *Res:* Computer applications for electrical power systems; power electronics. *Mailing Add:* Dept Elec Eng Univ Toledo Toledo OH 43606

STUART, WILLIAM DORSEY, GENETIC ENGINEERING, MEMBRANE TRANSPORT. *Current Pos:* asst prof, 78-83, ASSOC PROF GENETICS, SCH MED, UNIV HAWAII, 83-, DEAN RES, 90-; PRES & CHIEF EXEC OFFICER, NEUGENESIS CORP, 92- *Personal Data:* b St Louis, Mo, Mar 28, 39. *Educ:* Fla State Univ, BA, 69, MS, 70, PhD(biol & genetics), 73. *Prof Exp:* Res fel genetics, Dept Biol, Stanford Univ, 73-76; Fel, Melbourne Univ, Australia, 76-78. *Concurrent Pos:* Consult, Cetus Corp, 81-83; co-founder, Hawaii Biotechnol Group, 82-, consult, 83-; vis scholar, Dept Biol Sci, Stanford Univ, 85-86. *Mem:* Genetics Soc Am; Am Soc Microbiol; Sigma Xi; Am Chem Soc; Am Asn Adv Sci. *Res:* Investigation of membrane transport genes and gene products; involvement of ribonucleoproteins complexes in membrane transport; immunohistochemical identification of nucleic acid hybrid molecules; expression of heterologous genes in fungal cells. *Mailing Add:* Neugenesis Corp 2800 Woodlawn Rd Suite 251 Honolulu HI 96822-1865

STUART-ALEXANDER, DESIREE ELIZABETH, GEOLOGY. *Current Pos:* RETIRED. *Personal Data:* b London, Eng, Apr 6, 30; US citizen. *Educ:* Westhampton Col, BA, 52; Stanford Univ, MSc, 59, PhD(geol), 67. *Hon Degrees:* Dr, Univ Richmond, 80. *Prof Exp:* Geologist, Explor Dept, Utah Construct & Mining Co, 58-60; asst prof geol, Haile Selassie Univ, 63-65; geologist, US Geol Surv, 66-86, res geologist, 86- *Concurrent Pos:* Prog scientist, NASA Hq, 74-75; chief, Br Western Regional Geol, 80-85; consult geologist; staff mem, Smith Evenderson Assoc, 89-92. *Mem:* AAAS; fel Geol Soc Am; Am Geophys Union; Earthquake Eng Res Inst. *Res:* Lunar and Martian geology including studies based on remote sensing data and petrology of lunar rocks; terrestrial studies of metamorphic problems and lunar analogs; problems of reservoir-induced seismicity; faulting in the Sierra Nevada Mountains, California. *Mailing Add:* 120 Sea Breeze Pl Aptos CA 95003

STUBBE, JOANNE, CHEMISTRY EDUCATION. *Current Pos:* ELLEN SWALLOW PROF CHEM, MASS INST TECHNOL. *Honors & Awards:* Arthur C Cope Scholar Award, Am Chem Soc, 93. *Mem:* Nat Acad Sci. *Mailing Add:* Dept Chem Mass Inst Technol 77 Massachusetts Ave Cambridge MA 02139-4301

STUBBE, JOHN SUNAPEE, MATHEMATICS. *Current Pos:* asst prof, 49-53, dir comput ctr, 64-70, ASSOC PROF MATH, CLARK UNIV, 53- *Personal Data:* b New York, NY, Feb 21, 19; m 43; c 4. *Educ:* Univ NH, BS, 41; Brown Univ, MS, 42; Univ Cincinnati, PhD(math), 45. *Prof Exp:* Instr math, army specialized training prog, Univ Cincinnati, 43-44; instr, Univ Ill, 45-47; asst prof, Univ NH, 47-49. *Concurrent Pos:* Prof, Worcester Polytech Inst, 69-72. *Mem:* Am Math Soc; Math Asn Am. *Res:* Summability; Fourier series. *Mailing Add:* 101 S Flagg St Worcester MA 01602

STUBBEMAN, ROBERT FRANK, PHYSICAL CHEMISTRY. *Current Pos:* GEN LAW PRACT, 90- *Personal Data:* b Midland, Tex, May 9, 35; m 56; c 3. *Educ:* Austin Col, BA, 57; Univ Tex, MA, 61, PhD(chem), 64, JD, 89. *Prof Exp:* Res chemist, Esso Res & Eng Co, 63-66; sr res chemist, Celanese Chem Co, Tech Ctr, 66-71; sect leader, Spectros Lab, 71-80, mgr, Safety Health & Environ Sect, 80-85. *Mem:* Am Chem Soc; fel Am Inst Chemists; Am Bar Asn. *Res:* Shock tube kinetics; mass spectrometry, including qualitative and quantitative low and high resolution; process research; environmental health and safety. *Mailing Add:* 43 River Ranch Dr Bandera TX 78003

STUBBERUD, ALLEN ROGER, ELECTRICAL ENGINEERING. *Current Pos:* assoc prof, Univ Calif, Irvine, 69-72, assoc dean, Eng Sch, 72-77, dean, 78-83, interim dean, Eng Sch, 94-96, PROF ENG, UNIV CALIF, IRVINE, 72-, CHAIR, ELEC & COMPUT ENG DEPT, 93- *Personal Data:* b Glendive, Mont, Aug 14, 34; m 61, May B Tragus; c Peter A & Stephen C. *Educ:* Univ Idaho, BSEE, 56; Univ Calif, Los Angeles, MS, 58, PhD(eng), 62. *Honors & Awards:* Centennial Medal, Inst Elec & Electronics Engrs. *Prof Exp:* Asst prof eng, Univ Calif, Los Angeles, 62-67, assoc prof, 67-69. *Concurrent Pos:* Consult, 63-; chief scientist, USAF, 83-85; div dir, NSF, 87-88. *Mem:* Fel Inst Elec & Electronics Engrs; fel Am Inst Aeronaut & Astronaut; Int Ref Orgn Forensic Med & Sci; fel AAAS. *Res:* Optimal filtering theory; digital signal processing; system approximation and identification; neural control systems. *Mailing Add:* 19532 Sierra Soto Irvine CA 92612. *Fax:* 714-824-3779; *E-Mail:* arstubbe@uci.edu

STUBBINS, JAMES FISKE, MEDICINAL CHEMISTRY. *Current Pos:* from asst prof to assoc prof, 63-76, PROF MEDICINAL CHEM, MED COL VA, 76- *Personal Data:* b Honolulu, Hawaii, Feb 19, 31; m 59; c 3. *Educ:* Univ Nev, BS, 53; Purdue Univ, MS, 58; Univ Minn, PhD(pharmaceut chem), 65. *Prof Exp:* Asst prof pharmaceut chem, Univ Fla, 62-63. *Mem:* Am Chem Soc; Am Asn Col Pharm Coun Fac. *Res:* Synthesis of medicinal agents; pharmacology of drugs in the autonomic and central nervous systems; antimetabolite theory and chemotherapy; drugs acting on blood cells. *Mailing Add:* 7003 Monument Ave Richmond VA 23226-3546

STUBBINS, JAMES FREDERICK, MATERIALS SCIENCE ENGINEERING. *Current Pos:* FAC MEM NUCLEAR ENG, UNIV ILL, 80- *Personal Data:* b Cincinnati, Ohio, Sept 2, 48; m 86; c 1. *Educ:* Univ Cincinnati, BS, 70, MS, 72, PhD(mat sci), 75. *Prof Exp:* Res assoc mat sci, Univ Oxford, Eng, 77-78; engr, Gen Elec Co, Schenectady, NY, 78-80. *Concurrent Pos:* Fac assoc, Northwest Orgn Cols & Univs Sci, 77- & Argonne Nat Lat, 79-; consult, Los Alamos Nat Lab, 77- *Mem:* Am Nuclear Soc; Am Soc Metals Int. *Res:* Materials development for and application in engineering design; materials application in energy, including nuclear energy, systems; mechanical properties, elevated temperature performance, corrosion and radiation effects. *Mailing Add:* 808 Ayrshire Champaign IL 61820

STUBBLEBINE, WARREN, CHEMICAL ENGINEERING. *Current Pos:* RETIRED. *Personal Data:* b Reading, Pa, Jan 18, 17; m 38, Janee Kemmerling; c Warren Jr, James M, Judith E, Margaret A & Scott D. *Educ:* Pa State Col, BS, 38, MS, 40, PhD, 42. *Prof Exp:* Asst textile chem, Pa State Col, 38-42; head, Flooring Develop Sect, Armstrong Cork Co, 42-47; res dir, Chem & Plastics Div, Off Qm Gen, DC, 47-52; dir develop, Conn Hard Rubber Co, 52-55; dir res & develop, Stowe-Woodward, Inc, 55-61, vpres co, 61-63; vpres, Sandusky Foundry & Mach Co, 63-82. *Concurrent Pos:* Mem, Comt Mat & Equip & Panel Org & Fibrous Mat Res & Develop Bd, Dept Defense, 48-52; mem, Comt Plastics & Elastomers & Comt Chem & Adv Bd Qm Res & Develop, Nat Acad Sci-Nat Res Coun, 52-60, Tech Adv Panel Rubber, 52-57, mem, Comt Elastomers, Adv Bd Mil Personnel Supplies, 61-82; consult, 82-92. *Mem:* AAAS; Sigma Xi; Am Chem Soc; fel Am Inst Chem. *Res:* Centrifugal castings in ferrous and nonferrous alloys and their use and application in the paper and nuclear power industries. *Mailing Add:* 4111 Galloway Rd Sandusky OH 44870

STUBBLEFIELD, BEAUREGARD, topology, for more information see previous edition

STUBBLEFIELD, CHARLES BRYAN, TECHNICAL MANAGEMENT, MARKETING COMMUNICATIONS. *Current Pos:* RETIRED. *Personal Data:* b Viola, Tenn, Sept 14, 31; m 60; c James & Jane. *Educ:* Mid Tenn State Univ, BS, 53; Univ Tenn, MS, 60. *Prof Exp:* Res chemist, PPG Corp, 60-65, group leader anal chem, 65-67; res chemist, Lithium Corp Am, 67-72, dir qual control, 72-81, mgr planning & asst to pres, 81-83, mgr mkt commun, 84, mgr planning & asst to pres, 85, mgr mkt commun, 86-88, mgr tech & mkt serv, 89-93, mgr, Mkt Serv, FMC Corp Lithium Div, 93-97. *Mem:* Am Chem Soc; Sigma Xi; Am Inst Chemists; Soc Competitive Intel Professionals. *Res:* Chemical and instrumental analysis; product and promotional literature; product safety; technical service. *Mailing Add:* 1607 Nottingham Dr Gastonia NC 28054

STUBBLEFIELD, ROBERT DOUGLAS, ANALYTICAL CHEMISTRY. *Current Pos:* RETIRED. *Personal Data:* b Decatur, Ill, Mar 4, 36; m 58; c 3. *Educ:* Eureka Col, BS, 59. *Prof Exp:* Analytical chemist, Agr Res Serv, USDA, 59-62, chemist, 62-64, res chemist, Northern Regional Res Ctr, 64-91. *Concurrent Pos:* Co-dir int collab study aflatoxin M methods milk, Int Union Pure & Appl Chem-Asn Off Anal Chemists, 72-73 & 78-79. *Mem:* Am Oil Chemists Soc; fel Asn Off Anal Chemists; Am Asn Cereal Chemists; Sigma Xi. *Res:* Identification, preparation, and determination of known and unknown toxic compounds produced by the action of molds on agricultural commodities and products. *Mailing Add:* 4134 N Chelsea Pl Peoria IL 61614

STUBBLEFIELD, TRAVIS ELTON, CELL BIOLOGY, CYTOGENETICS. *Current Pos:* RETIRED. *Personal Data:* b Austin, Tex, May 27, 35; m 57, Jacqueline G Ellis; c 2. *Educ:* NTex State Univ, BS, 57; Univ Wis, MS, 59, PhD(exp oncol), 61. *Prof Exp:* NSF fel animal virol, Max Planck Inst Virus Res, Tubingen, WGer, 62-63; asst prof biol, Univ Tex Grad Sch Biomed Sci, Houston, 65-68, assoc prof, 68-73, prof, 74-92. *Concurrent Pos:* Asst biologist, Univ Tex, M D Anderson Hosp & Tumor Inst Houston, 63-68, assoc biologist, 68-73, biologist, 74-90. *Mem:* Am Soc Cell Biol; AAAS. *Res:* Structure and physiology of mammalian chromosomes; synchronized cell culture; cell differentiation; structure and function of centrioles; chromosome transfer; oncogenes. *Mailing Add:* Dept Molecular Genetics M D Anderson Cancer Ctr Box 45 Houston TX 77030

STUBBLEFIELD, WILLIAM L, MARINE GEOLOGY. *Current Pos:* assoc prog dir, Marine Geol Resources, Nat Sea Grant Col Prog, Nat Oceanic Atmospheric Admin, 83-85, chief scientist, Nat Undersea Res Prog, 85-86, exec dir, 86-92, DEP DIR, OFF NAT OCEANIC ATMOSPHERIC ADMIN CORPS OPER, SILVER SPRING, MD, 92- *Personal Data:* b Apr 5, 40; m 75. *Educ:* Memphis State Univ, BA, 62; Univ Iowa, MS, 71; Tex A&M Univ, PhD(geol), 80. *Prof Exp:* Chmn prog, Miami Geol Soc, 79-81, vpres, 82-83. *Mem:* AAAS; Soc Econ Paleontologists & Mineralogists; Am Asn Petroleum Geologists. *Res:* Continental shelf sedimentary processes; dynamics of sediment transport in submarine canyons; stability of continental slope material; sand and gravel resources on continental shelf. *Mailing Add:* Off NOAA Corps Oper 1315 East-West Hwy Rm 12837 Silver Spring MD 20910-3282

STUBBS, DONALD WILLIAM, MEDICAL PHYSIOLOGY. *Current Pos:* from instr to assoc prof, 63-75, PROF PHYSIOL, UNIV TEX MED BR GALVESTON, 75- *Personal Data:* b Seguin, Tex, Sept 26, 32; m 53, Hetty Sutton; c 5. *Educ:* Tex Lutheran Col, BA, 54; Univ Tex, MA, 56, PhD(physiol), 64. *Prof Exp:* Instr zool, Auburn Univ, 56-60. *Concurrent Pos:* NIH res grant, 65-71; multidisciplinary res grant ment health, 74-77; course dir, 74-94; mem, Nat Bd Med Examrs, 83-86. *Mem:* AAAS; Am Physiol Soc; Sigma Xi; NY Acad Sci. *Res:* Biosynthesis of ascorbic acid; hormonal induction of enzyme activities; co-author of textbook of medical physiology. *Mailing Add:* Dept Physiol-Biophys Univ Tex Med Br 301 University Blvd Galveston TX 77555-0641

STUBBS, GERALD JAMES, VIRUS STRUCTURE, FIBER DIFFRACTION. *Current Pos:* from asst prof to assoc prof, 83-90, PROF MOLECULAR BIOL, VANDERBILT UNIV, 90- *Personal Data:* b Hobart, Tasmania, Australia, May 9, 47; m 90, Rebecca Harris; c Andrew, Tamsin, Anneliese & Rachel. *Educ:* Australian Nat Univ, BSc, 68; Oxford Univ, DPhil, 72. *Prof Exp:* Wissenschaftliche asst, Max-Planck Inst Med Res, Ger, 72-76; from res assoc to sr res assoc, Brandeis Univ, 77-83. *Concurrent Pos:* Core expert analyst, J Chemtracts-Biochem & Molecular Biol, 91- *Mem:* Am Crystallog Asn. *Res:* Structure determination of helical plant viruses using x-ray crystallography and fiber diffraction; study of viral assembly and disassembly and host viral interactions. *Mailing Add:* Vanderbilt Univ Dept Molecular Biol PO Box 1820 Sta B Nashville TN 37235. *Fax:* 615-343-6707; *E-Mail:* stubbsgj@ctrvax.vanderbilt.edu

STUBBS, JOHN DORTON, MOLECULAR BIOLOGY, BIOCHEMISTRY. *Current Pos:* from asst prof to assoc prof molecular biol, Calif State Univ, San Francisco, 68-75, chmn, Dept Cellular & Molecular Biol, 72-82, chmn, Univ Grad Comn, 82-85, PROF MOLECULAR BIOL, SAN FRANCISCO STATE UNIV, 75-, COORDR CELL SCI, 92- *Personal Data:* b Cape Girardeau, Mo, Oct 9, 38; m 62; c 2. *Educ:* Wash Univ, BA, 60; Univ Wis-Madison, MA, 62, PhD(biochem), 65. *Prof Exp:* USPHS fel genetics, Univ Wash, 65-67. *Mem:* AAAS. *Res:* Regulation of gene expression; molecular mechanisms of membrane assembly; developmental biochemistry. *Mailing Add:* Biol Dept 1600 Holloway Ave San Francisco State Univ San Francisco CA 94132-1722

STUBBS, NORRIS, COMPOSITE MATERIALS, STRUCTURAL & RISK ANALYSIS. *Current Pos:* AT DEPT CIVIL ENG, TEX A&M UNIV. *Personal Data:* b Nassau, Bahamas, Nov 8, 48. *Educ:* Grinnell Col, BA, 72; Columbia Univ, BS, 72, MS, 74, ScD, 76. *Prof Exp:* Asst prof civil eng, Columbia Univ, 76- *Concurrent Pos:* Consult, Govt Nigeria, 76; instr, Columbia Univ, 78-81 & Barnard Col, 80-81; proj mgr, Leroy Callender Consult Engrs, 80-; Thomas J Watson Jr fel, 72. *Mem:* Soc Exp Stress Analysis; Am Soc Civil Engrs; Am Soc Testing & Mat; Am Inst Aeronaut & Aerospace. *Res:* Nonlinear constitutive models for fabric reinforced composites; continuum modeling of large discrete structural systems; motion control of floating platforms; experimental analysis of structural systems; risk analysis; nondestructive evaluation; quality management. *Mailing Add:* 1608 Armistead St College Station TX 77840

STUBER, CHARLES WILLIAM, GENETICS. *Current Pos:* from asst prof to assoc prof, 65-75, PROF GENETICS, NC STATE UNIV, 75-; SUPVRY RES GENETICIST, AGR RES SERV, USDA, 62- *Personal Data:* b St Michael, Nebr, Sept 19, 31; m 53, Marilyn Cook; c Charles Jr. *Educ:* Univ Nebr, BS, 52, MS, 61; NC State Univ, PhD(genetics, exp statist), 65. *Honors & Awards:* Crop Sci Res Awards; Crop Sci Soc Am, 95; Genetics & Plant Breeding Award, Nat Coun Com Plant Breeders, 97. *Prof Exp:* Instr high sch, Nebr, 56-59. *Concurrent Pos:* Ed, CROP SCI, 86-89; ed-in-chief, Crop Sci Soc Am, 86-91. *Mem:* Genetics Soc Am; fel Am Soc Agron; fel Crop Sci Soc Am (pres, 92-93); Am Genetic Asn; Coun Agr Sci & Technol; AAAS. *Res:* Quantitative genetics; quantitative trait investigations in maize using molecular markers. *Mailing Add:* Dept Genetics NC State Univ Raleigh NC 27695-7614. *Fax:* 919-515-3355

STUBER, FRED A, PHYSICAL ORGANIC CHEMISTRY. *Current Pos:* PROD DEVELOP MGR, OLIN CORP, 89- *Personal Data:* b Paris, France, Dec 7, 33; m 64, Audrey Torrance; c Heidi. *Educ:* Univ Zurich, ChemEng, 57, DSc(nuclear chem), 61. *Prof Exp:* Res assoc mass spectros, Inst Reactor Res, Switz, 61-62; fel, Univ Notre Dame, 62-63 & Mellon Inst, 63-64; res chemist, Ciba, Switz, 64-67; res chemist, D S Gilmore Res Lab, Upjohn Co, North Haven, 67-75, mgr, 75-85; mgr, Dow Chem USA, 85-89. *Mem:* Am Chem Soc. *Res:* Ionization and appearance potentials; analysis of nuclear magnetic resonance spectra; photopolymers; catalysis; polyurethanes (rigid foam, flexible foam, coatings). *Mailing Add:* 350 Knotter Dr Cheshire CT 06410

STUBICAN, VLADIMIR S(TJEPAN), MATERIALS SCIENCE, SOLID STATE CHEMISTRY. *Current Pos:* RETIRED. *Personal Data:* b Bjelovar, Yugoslavia, June 23, 24; US citizen; m 46; c 2. *Educ:* Univ Zagreb, Dipl Ing, 48, PhD(phys chem), 51, DSc(inorg chem), 58. *Prof Exp:* Res asst phys chem, Univ Zagreb, 48-52, asst prof, 52-55; vdir silicate chem, Inst Silicate Chem, Zagreb, Yugoslavia, 55-58; fel, Pa State Univ, 58-60, vis assoc prof geochem, 60-61, from asst prof to prof mat sci, 61-93. *Concurrent Pos:* Consult, Perkin-Elmer Corp, 80-; vis profr, Tech Univ, Tronheim, Norway, 67-68 & Max Planck Inst, Stuttgart, WGer, 77-78. *Mem:* Fel Am Chem Soc; fel Am Ceramic Soc; fel Am Inst Chemists; fel Mineral Soc Am; Croatian Chem Soc. *Res:* Solid state reactions; high temperature materials; inorganic synthesis; solid state technology; chemistry and properties of high melting inorganic materials; material transport in solids; solid state electrolytes. *Mailing Add:* 662 Franklin St State College PA 16803

STUCHLY, MARIA ANNA, ELECTRICAL ENGINEERING, ELECTROMAGNETICS. *Current Pos:* PROF, UNIV VICTORIA, 92- *Personal Data:* b Warsaw, Poland, Apr 8, 39; Can citizen; m 72. *Educ:* Warsaw Tech Univ, BSc & MSc, 62; Polish Acad Sci, PhD(elec eng), 70. *Prof Exp:* Asst prof elec eng, Warsaw Tech Univ, 62-64; sr res & develop engr microwaves, Polish Acad Sci, 64-70, sr researcher, Inst Physics, 70; res assoc elec eng & food sci, Univ Man, 70-76; res scientist, Health & Welfare Can, 76-92. *Concurrent Pos:* Fel, Dept Elec Eng, Univ Man, 70-72, adj prof, 76; non-resident prof, Dept Elec Eng & dir, Inst Med Eng, Univ Ottawa, 78-; expert consult, Telecom, Australia, 83-84; guest scientist, Nat Bur Stand, 87. *Mem:* Fel Inst Elec & Electronics Engrs; Bioelectromagnetics Soc. *Res:* Interaction of electromagnetic waves with living systems, medical applications; numerical modeling, measurement techniques, biological effects and safety standards. *Mailing Add:* Elec & comput Eng Dept Univ Victoria PO Box 3055 Victoria BC V8W 3P6 Can. *E-Mail:* mstuchly@ece.uvic.ca

STUCHLY, STANISLAW S, ELECTRICAL ENGINEERING. *Current Pos:* assoc prof, 76-80, PROF ELEC ENG, UNIV OTTAWA, 80- *Personal Data:* b Nov 20, 31; Can citizen. *Educ:* Tech Univ Gliwice, Poland, BScEng, 53; Warsaw Tech Univ, MScEng, 58; Polish Acad Sci, DScEng, 68. *Prof Exp:* Res engr, Indust Inst Telecommun, Warsaw, Poland, 53-56, sr res engr, 56-59; asst prof, Warsaw Tech Univ, 59-63; head microwave instrument dept, Sci Instruments, Polish Acad Sci, 63-70; assoc prof agr eng & adj prof elec eng, Univ Man, 70-76. *Concurrent Pos:* Adj prof elec eng, Carleton Univ, 76-80. *Mem:* Fel Inst Elec & Electronics Engrs. *Res:* Electromagnetic theory and technique; applications of electromagnetic radiations; industrial and medical applications of radio frequency and microwave radiations; electronic instrumentation, especially transducers for measuring nonelectrical quantities. *Mailing Add:* Dept Elec Eng Univ Victoria PO Box 3055 MS 8610 Victoria BC V8W 3P6 Can

STUCK, BARTON W, ELECTRICAL ENGINEERING. *Current Pos:* PRES, BUS STRATEGIES, 86- *Personal Data:* b Detroit, Mich, Oct 25, 46; m 75, Mary J Cross. *Educ:* Mass Inst Technol, BS & MS, 69, ScD(elec eng), 72. *Prof Exp:* Mem tech staff, Math & Statist Res Ctr, Bell Labs, Am Tel & Tel Co, 72-; pres, Viatel, 84-85. *Concurrent Pos:* Dir-at-large, Inst Elec & Electronics Engrs Commun Soc. *Mem:* Soc Indust & Appl Math; Math Asn Am; sr mem Inst Elec & Electronics Engrs; Asn Comput Mach; Inst Math Statist. *Res:* Digital systems; applied probability theory; co-author one book. *Mailing Add:* 578 Post Rd E Suite 667 Westport CT 06880. *Fax:* 203-454-7142; *E-Mail:* spi!bart@bcr.cc.bellcore.com, barts@aol.com

STUCKER, HARRY T, ENGINEERING, PHYSICS. *Current Pos:* Mem res staff, Gen Dynamics/Ft Worth, 47-54, supvr automatic controls, 54-57, supvr preliminary design, 57-58, supvr electronics lab, 58-59, adv navig guid, 59-61, chief reconnaissance & info syts, 61-63, proj mgr missiles&& space systs, 63-67, mgr spec projs, 67-75, dir electronics progs, 75-82, D-DIR F-111 PROG, GEN DYNAMICS/FT WORTH, 82- *Personal Data:* b Lawrence, Kans, Oct 7, 25; m 47; c 3. *Educ:* Univ Kans, BS, 47, MS, 48; Tex Christian Univ, MBA, 75. *Mem:* Am Inst Aeronaut & Astronaut. *Res:* Control systems; microwave devices; communications; ground based radar systems; avionics systems. *Mailing Add:* 3817 Arroyo Rd Ft Worth TX 76109

STUCKER, JOSEPH BERNARD, CHEMISTRY. *Current Pos:* RETIRED. *Personal Data:* b Chicago, Ill, Feb 28, 14; m 41, Isabelle Breen; c Catherine, John & Andrew. *Educ:* Univ Chicago, BS, 35. *Honors & Awards:* Achievement Award, Nat Lubricating Grease Inst, 85; Fel, Soc Automotive Engrs, 86. *Prof Exp:* Chemist, Pure Oil Co, 35-41, asst supt grease plant, 41-43, group leader prod develop, 43-50, sect supvr, 50-52, div dir, 52-65, sr res assoc, Res Dept, Union Oil Co, Calif, 65-68, mgr prod develop, Pure Oil Div, 68-69 & Union 76 Div, 69-71, mgr prod qual, Refining Div, 71-86, prod mgr mkt, 86-88. *Mem:* Soc Automotive Eng; Am Soc Testing & Mat; Am Petrol Inst; fel Nat Lubricating Grease Inst. *Res:* Product development of lubricants, particularly greases, gear and crankcase oils and industrial lubricants. *Mailing Add:* 421 Marshall Des Plaines IL 60016

STUCKER, ROBERT EVAN, PLANT BREEDING, STATISTICS. *Current Pos:* asst prof agron & plant genetics, corn breeding & quant genetics, 68-72, assoc prof agron & plant genetics, 72-77, PROF AGRON & PLANT GENETICS, UNIV MINN, ST PAUL, 77- *Personal Data:* b Burlington, Iowa, Jan 28, 36; m 56; c 3. *Educ:* Iowa State Univ, BS, 59; Purdue Univ, MS, 61; NC State Univ, PhD(genetics), 66. *Prof Exp:* Res geneticist, Forage & Range Br, Crops Res Div, Agr Res Serv, USDA, 65-68. *Concurrent Pos:* Statist design experiments & consult statistician agr & hort, 72-78; quant genetics consult, Alberta Forest Serv, 82-84. *Mem:* Am Soc Agron; Crop Sci Soc Am; Sigma Xi. *Res:* Wild rice (zizania) breeding; application of quantitative genetics in plant breeding. *Mailing Add:* 3316 N Victoria St St Paul MN 55126

STUCKEY, JOHN EDMUND, PHYSICAL CHEMISTRY, INORGANIC CHEMISTRY. *Current Pos:* PROF CHEM, HENDRIX COL, 58- *Personal Data:* b Stuttgart, Ark, Dec 6, 29; m 55; c 3. *Educ:* Hendrix Col, BA, 51; Univ Okla, MS, 53, PhD(chem), 57. *Prof Exp:* Res chemist, Oak Ridge Nat Lab, Union Carbide Corp, 57; asst prof chem, La Polytech Inst, 57-58. *Mem:* Am Chem Soc. *Res:* Preparations and properties of monofluorophosphate compounds; solution chemistry in the critical temperature region; x-ray crystallography. *Mailing Add:* 46 Meadowbrook Dr Conway AR 72032-2624

STUCKEY, RICHARD E, PROVIDING SOUND SCIENCE TO LEGISLATORS REGULATORS & THE MEDIA, RESEARCH & EXTENSION OF DISEASE ON AGRONOMIC CROPS. *Current Pos:* EXEC VPRES, COUN AGR SCI & TECHNOL, 92- *Personal Data:* b Archbold, Ohio, Feb 29, 44; m 66; Judith A Stealy; c Jeffrey J & Jon D. *Educ:* Biol Educ Goshen Col, BA, 66; Mich State Univ, MS, 70, PhD(plant path), 73. *Prof Exp:* Asst prof bot & plant path, Mich State Univ, 73-75; asst exten prof plant path, Univ Ky, 75-79, assoc exten prof, 79-84, exten, prof, 84-89; dir, Nat Asn Wheat Growers Found, 89-92. *Mem:* AAAS; ASP; Am Soc Agr Engrs; Am Agr Econ Asn. *Res:* Researching and extending predictive systems and pesticiides to manage plant diseases in the US, South America and Europe; research and education programs for the National Association of Wheat Growers; identify and interpret scientific research information on food and fiber, environmental, and other agricultural issues for legislators, regulators, and the media. *Mailing Add:* CAST 40 New Hampshire St Lawrence IA 66044. *Fax:* 515-292-4512; *E-Mail:* b1cast@exnet.iastate.edu

STUCKEY, RONALD LEWIS, BOTANY, VASCULAR PLANT TAXONOMY. *Current Pos:* from asst prof to prof bot, Ohio State Univ, 65-91, cur herbarium, 67-75, assoc dir, Franz Theodore Stone Lab, 77-85, EMER PROF BOT, OHIO STATE UNIV, 91- *Personal Data:* b Bucyrus, Ohio, Jan 9, 38. *Educ:* Heidelberg Col, BS, 60; Univ Mich, MA, 62, PhD(bot), 65. *Prof Exp:* Instr bot, Univ Mich, 65. *Concurrent Pos:* Pres, Ohio Acad Sci, 94-95. *Mem:* Am Soc Plant Taxon; Int Asn Plant Taxon; Bot Soc Am. *Res:* Taxonomy and distribution of angiosperms; history of American botany; monographic studies in the Cruciferae, particularly Rorippa; Ohio vascular plant flora and phytogeography; history of plant taxonomy in North America; taxonomy and distribution of angiosperms, particularly aquatic and marsh flora. *Mailing Add:* Mus Biol Diversity Ohio State Univ 1315 Kinnear Rd Columbus OH 43212-1192. *Fax:* 614-292-7774

STUCKEY, WALTER JACKSON, JR, internal medicine, hematology & oncology; deceased, see previous edition for last biography

STUCKI, JACOB CALVIN, ENDOCRINOLOGY, RESEARCH ADMINSTRATION. *Current Pos:* RETIRED. *Personal Data:* b Neillsville, Wis, Nov 30, 26; m 48; c 3. *Educ:* Univ Wis, BS, 48, MS, 51, PhD(zool, physiol), 54. *Prof Exp:* Res asst, Univ Wis, 50-54; endocrinologist, Wm S Merrell Co, 54-57; res assoc, Upjohn Co, 57-60, dept head endocrinol, 60-61, mgr pharmacol res, 61-68, dir res planning & admin, Pharmaceut Res & Develop, 68-79, dir admin & support opers, 79-81, corp vpres pharmaceut res, 81-89. *Concurrent Pos:* Pharmaceut consult, 89- *Mem:* AAAS; Soc Exp Biol & Med; Endocrine Soc. *Res:* Reproduction; inflammation; pharmacology; research management. *Mailing Add:* 2842 Bronson Blvd Kalamazoo MI 49008-2360

STUCKI, JOSEPH WILLIAM, SOIL CHEMISTRY, PHYSICAL CHEMISTRY. *Current Pos:* Asst prof, 76-80, ASSOC PROF SOIL CHEM, UNIV ILL, 80- *Personal Data:* b Rexburg, Idaho, Feb 4, 46; m 68; c 6. *Educ:* Brigham Young Univ, BS, 70; Utah State Univ, MS, 73; Purdue Univ, PhD(soil chem), 75. *Mem:* Asn Int Etude Argiles; Clay Minerals Soc; Soil Sci Soc Am; Int Soil Sci Soc; Mineral Soc Gt Brit. *Res:* Clay colloid chemistry, clay-water interactions, affects of structural iron oxidation states in clays and soils on their colloidal properties; advanced spectroscopic methods for analysis and characterization of soils and clays; physical-inorganic chemistry of clays. *Mailing Add:* 3704 Meadow Lane Champaign IL 61821

STUCKI, WILLIAM PAUL, BIOCHEMISTRY. *Current Pos:* res biochemist, 67-75, SR RES BIOCHEMIST, PARKE DAVIS & CO, 75- *Personal Data:* b Neillsville, Wis, Sept 28, 31; m 55; c 5. *Educ:* Univ Wis, BS, 57, MS, 59, PhD(biochem), 62. *Prof Exp:* Asst prof Univ Puerto Rico & scientist, PR Nuclear Ctr, Mayaguez, 62-63; asst prof, Antioch Col & assoc biochem, Fels Res Inst, 63-67. *Mem:* Am Chem Soc; NY Acad Sci. *Res:* Protein and amino acid nutrition and metabolism; plant biochemistry; biochemistry of natural products; chemotherapy, immunology and immunochemistry; atherothrombotic disease. *Mailing Add:* 13545 Austin Rd Manchester MI 48158-9573

STUCKWISCH, CLARENCE GEORGE, CHEMISTRY. *Current Pos:* RETIRED. *Personal Data:* b Seymour, Ind, Oct 13, 16; wid; c William, Stephen, David, Deborah & Stephanie. *Educ:* Ind Univ, AB, 39; Iowa State Col, PhD(org chem), 43. *Prof Exp:* Res assoc, Iowa State Col, 43; asst prof chem, Wichita State Univ, 43-44; res chemist, Eastman Kodak Co, 44-45; from asst prof to assoc prof chem, Wichita State Univ, 45-60; assoc prof, NMex Highlands Univ, 60-62, prof & head dept, 62-64, dir, Inst Sci Res, 63-64; prof chem & exec officer dept, State Univ NY, Buffalo, 64-68; chmn, Dept Chem, Univ Miami, 68-74, prof, 68-81, dean grad studies & res, 72-81, assoc vpres advan studies, 80-81, exec vpres & provost, 81-82. *Concurrent Pos:* Adj prof, Dept Chem, ETenn State Univ, 84-92. *Mem:* Am Chem Soc; Sigma Xi. *Res:* Organometallic, psychopharmacological and organophosphorous compounds. *Mailing Add:* 815 Raymon Dr Seymour IN 47274

STUCKY, GALEN DEAN, BIOMATERIALS, ORGANIC-INORGANIC COMPOSITE MATERIALS. *Current Pos:* PROF CHEM, UNIV CALIF, SANTA BARBARA, 85-; PROF, MAT DEPT, COL ENG. *Personal Data:* b McPherson, Kans, Dec 17, 36; m 61; c 2. *Educ:* McPherson Col, BS, 57; Iowa State Univ, PhD(chem), 62. *Prof Exp:* Fel physics, Mass Inst Technol, 62-63; NSF fel, Quantum Chem Inst, Fla, 63-64; from asst prof to assoc prof chem, Univ Ill, Urbana, 64-72, prof, 72-79; group leader, Sandia Nat Lab, 79-81; group leader, Cent Res & Develop Dept, E I du Pont de Nemours & Co, Inc, 81-85. *Concurrent Pos:* Consult div univ & col, Argonne Nat Labs, 66; vis prof physics, Univ Uppsala, Sweden, 71; assoc ed, Inorg Chem, 77-85; chmn, Inorg Div, Am Chem Soc, 86. *Mem:* Am Chem Soc; Mat Res Soc; fel AAAS. *Res:* Materials synthesis; biomimetics; zeolites and molecular sieves; nonlinear optic materials; environmental chemistry; biomaterials synthesis by biogenesis; mesoporous materials; organic-inorganic composite material design and synthesis. *Mailing Add:* Dept Chem Univ Calif Santa Barbara CA 93106-9510. *E-Mail:* stucky@sbxray.ucsb.edu

STUCKY, GARY LEE, BIOINORGANIC CHEMISTRY. *Personal Data:* b Murdock, Kans, May 18, 41. *Educ:* Bethel Col, Kans, AB, 63; Kans State Univ, PhD(inorg chem), 67. *Prof Exp:* Instr chem, Halstead Sch Nursing, Kans, 62-63 & Kans State Univ, 63-65; res scientist bioinorg chem, Miles Labs, Ind, 67-70 & Kivuvu Inst Med Evangel, Kimpese, Zaire, 71; from asst prof to prof bioinorg chem, Eastern Mennonite Col, 72-95. *Concurrent Pos:* Am Leprosy Mission res grant, Eastern Mennonite Col, 72; vis prof chem, Univ Rochester, 81-82 & Bethel Col, Kans, 86-87; res assoc & vis prof, Univ Notre Dame, Ind, 87-88. *Mem:* AAAS; Am Chem Soc; Royal Soc Chem. *Res:* Electrochemistry of leprosy; inorganic synthesis; ion-selective electrodes; hemoglobin variants; chemistry of oxadiazoles. *Mailing Add:* PO Box 1053 Harrisonburg VA 22801. *Fax:* 540-432-4444

STUCKY, RICHARD K(EITH), EVOLUTIONARY PALEOECOLOGY, BIOSTRATIGRAPHY. *Current Pos:* DEPT HEAD & CUR PALEONT, DENVER MUS NATURAL HIST, 89- *Personal Data:* b Newton, Kans, Dec 11, 49; m 69, Barbara J Krehbiel. *Educ:* Univ Colo, Denver, BA, 75, MA, 77; Univ Colo, Boulder, PhD(anthrop), 82. *Prof Exp:* Preparator vert paleont, Denver Mus Natural Hist, 71-76; instr anthrop, Metrop State Col, Denver, 77; Honorarium instr archaeol, Univ Colo, Denver, 77; res fel, Carnegie Mus Natural Hist, 82-84, collection mgr vert paleont, 84-87, asst cur, 87-88. *Concurrent Pos:* Res assoc, Carnegie Mus; adj assoc prof, Univ Colo. *Mem:* Soc Vertebrate Paleont; Am Asn Phys Anthropologists; Ecol Soc Am; Soc Am Nat; Geol Soc Am; AAAS. *Res:* Paleontology (systematics and evolution) of marsupials, primates, artiodactyls and perissodactyls; evolutionary paleoecology of mammals; geological remote sensing. *Mailing Add:* 2226 Birch St Denver CO 80207. *Fax:* 303-331-6492; *E-Mail:* rstucky@csn.org

STUDDEN, WILLIAM JOHN, MATHEMATICAL STATISTICS. *Current Pos:* from asst prof to assoc prof statist, 64-71, PROF STATIST, PURDUE UNIV, LAFAYETTE, 71- *Personal Data:* b Timmins, Ont, Sept 30, 35. *Educ:* McMaster Univ, BSc, 58; Stanford Univ, PhD(statist), 62. *Prof Exp:* Res assoc math, Stanford Univ, 62-64. *Concurrent Pos:* NSF fels, Purdue Univ, Lafayette, 68-71, 72-75. *Mem:* Fel Inst Math Statist; Sigma Xi. *Res:* Optimal designs; Tchebycheff systems. *Mailing Add:* Dept Statist Purdue Univ Lafayette IN 47907

STUDEBAKER, GERALD A, AUDIOLOGY. *Current Pos:* DISTINGUISHED PROF SPEECH & HEARING SCI, UNIV MEMPHIS, 79- *Personal Data:* b Freeport, Ill, July 22, 32; div; c 5. *Educ:* Ill State Univ, BS, 55; Syracuse Univ, MS, 56, PhD(audiol), 60. *Honors & Awards:* Jacob K Javits Award; James F Jerger Career Res Award, 97- *Prof Exp:* Supvr clin audiol, Vet Admin Hosp, DC, 59-61, chief audiol & speech path serv, Syracuse, NY, 61-62; supvr clin audiol, Med Ctr, Univ Okla, 62-66, from asst prof to assoc prof audiol & consult, Dept Otorhinolaryngol, 62-72, res audiologist, 66-72; res prof audiol, Memphis State Univ, 72-76; prof audiol, PhD Prog Speech & Hearing Sci, City Univ New York, 76-79. *Mem:* fel Am Speech & Hearing Asn; fel Acoust Soc Am; fel Am Acad Audiol; Sigma Xi. *Res:* Bone-conduction hearing thresholds, auditory masking; loudness estimation procedures and adaptation; speech discrimination; ear mold acoustics. *Mailing Add:* Memphis Speech & Hearing Ctr 807 Jefferson Ave Memphis TN 38105. *Fax:* 901-525-1282; *E-Mail:* gstudbkr@memphis.edu

STUDER, REBECCA KATHRYN, CELL CALCIUM METABOLISM, SEXUAL DIMORPHISM. *Current Pos:* res assoc med & physiol, 79-81, RES ASST PROF PHYSIOL, MED SCH, UNIV PITTSBURGH, 82- *Personal Data:* b Hannibal, Mo, Feb 22, 43; m 64; c 2. *Educ:* Northeast Mo State Univ, BS, 64; Tex Christian Univ, MS, 66; Univ Pittsburgh, PhD(physiol), 78. *Prof Exp:* Res instr nuclear med, Sch Med, Wash Univ, 66-73. *Mem:* Am Physiol Soc; Endocrine Soc. *Res:* Differences between males and females in their hepatocytes' response to adrenergic stimulation; sexual dimorphism in adrenergic response; effect of diabetes on calcium mediated metabolism in the liver. *Mailing Add:* Dept Physiol Univ Pittsburgh Med Sch 2W-1A Vet Admin Med Ctr Pittsburgh PA 15240

STUDIER, EUGENE H, PHYSIOLOGICAL ECOLOGY. *Current Pos:* assoc prof, 72-74, assoc chmn dept, 78-85, PROF BIOL, UNIV MICH, FLINT, 74- *Personal Data:* b Dubuque, Iowa, Mar 16, 40; div; c 2. *Educ:* Univ Dubuque, BS, 62; Univ Ariz, PhD(zool), 6S. *Prof Exp:* From asst prof to assoc prof biol, NMex Highlands Univ, 65-72. *Concurrent Pos:* USPHS grant, 66-67; Sigma Xi res grant-in-aid, 69; Am Philos Soc grant, 69. *Mem:* Fel AAAS; Am Soc Mammalogists; Am Soc Zoologists. *Res:* Mammalian physiology; physiological adaptation in bats and rodents. *Mailing Add:* Dept Biol Univ Mich Flint 303 E Kearsley St Flint MI 48502-1907

STUDIER, FREDERICK WILLIAM, BIOPHYSICS, MOLECULAR BIOLOGY. *Current Pos:* from asst biophysicist to biophysicist, 64-74, SR BIOPHYSICIST, BIOL DEPT, BROOKHAVEN NAT LAB, 74-, CHMN, 90- *Personal Data:* b Waverly, Iowa, May 26, 36; m 62; c Susan Cook; c Frederick & Carol. *Educ:* Yale Univ, BS, 58; Calif Inst Technol, PhD(biophys), 63. *Honors & Awards:* Ernest O Lawrence Mem Award, US Dept Energy, 77. *Prof Exp:* NSF fel biochem, Med Ctr, Stanford Univ, 62-64. *Concurrent Pos:* Adj assoc prof, State Univ NY, Stony Brook, 71-75, prof, 75- *Mem:* Nat Acad Sci; Biophys Soc; Am Soc Biochem & Molecular Biol; Am Soc Microbiol; Am Soc Virol; Am Acad Arts & Sci. *Res:* Physical and chemical properties of nucleic acids; genetics and physiology of bacteriophage T7; large-scale DNA sequencing. *Mailing Add:* 37 Bonnie Lane Stony Brook NY 11790-2547

STUDIER, MARTIN HERMAN, CHEMISTRY. *Current Pos:* res chemist, 43-36, SR CHEMIST, ARGONNE NAT LAB, 46- *Personal Data:* b Leola, SDak, Nov 10, 17; m 44; c 4. *Educ:* Luther Col, BA, 39; Univ Chicago, PhD(chem), 47. *Prof Exp:* Asst, Iowa State Col, 39-41, instr, 41-42. *Mem:* AAAS; Am Chem Soc; Am Phys Soc; Sigma Xi. *Res:* Nuclear chemistry of the heavy elements; chemical nature of coals; mass spectrometry; organic matter in meteorites. *Mailing Add:* 4429 Downers Dr Downers Grove IL 60515-2729

STUDLAR, SUSAN MOYLE, BRYOLOGY. *Current Pos:* ADJ ASSOC PROF BIOL, WVA UNIV, 93- *Personal Data:* b St Paul, Minn, May 4, 44; m 79, Donley T; c Carl & Ross. *Educ:* Carleton Col, BA, 66; Univ Tenn, Knoxville, PhD(bot), 73. *Prof Exp:* Instr biol, Wellesley Col, 71-72; asst prof, Va Commonwealth Univ, 72-74; asst prof, Centre Col Ky, 74-77, assoc prof, 78-82; adj assoc prof, Okla State Univ, Stillwater, 89-93. *Concurrent Pos:* Vis prof, Mountain Lake Biol Sta, Univ Va, 77, 79 & 80; tech dir, Cent Ky Wildlife Refuge, 79-82 & 84-; adj assoc prof biol, Centre Col Ky, 82- *Mem:* Am Bryol & Lichenological Soc; Brit Bryological Soc; Bot Soc Am; Am Inst Biol Sci. *Res:* Floristics and ecology of bryophytes of West Virginia & Oklahoma. *Mailing Add:* Dept Biol WVa Univ Morgantown WV 26506-6057. *E-Mail:* studla@wvnvm.wvnet.edu

STUDT, WILLIAM LYON, MEDICINAL CHEMISTRY. *Current Pos:* SECT HEAD RES MED CHEM, RORER-AMCHEM INC, 74- *Personal Data:* b Ypsilanti, Mich, Mar 12, 47; m 66; c 3. *Educ:* Eastern Mich Univ, BA, 69; Univ Mich, PhD(org chem), 73. *Prof Exp:* Res fel org chem, Yale Univ, 73-74. *Mem:* Am Chem Soc. *Res:* The organic synthesis of natural products and biologically active compounds. *Mailing Add:* 611 Store Rd Harleysville PA 19438-2717

STUDTMANN, GEORGE H, ELECTRO-MECHANICAL, POWER ELECTRONICS. *Current Pos:* CONSULT, 91- *Personal Data:* b Chicago, Ill, Nov 3, 30; m 61, Judith Gaver; c 4. *Educ:* Purdue Univ, BSEE, 56, MSEE, 57. *Honors & Awards:* Tech Innovation Award, Borg-Warner. *Prof Exp:* Prin elec engr, Battelle Mem Inst, 57-61; sr elec engr, Borg-Warner Res Ctr, 61-62, supvr res eng, 62-73, mgr electronics & elec eng, 73-78, mgr power electronics, 78-83, sr scientist & mgr, 83-88; tech dir, Power Electronics, Square D Co, 88-91. *Mem:* Inst Elec & Electronics Engrs. *Res:* Electromagnetic actuators; variable frequency alternating current motor drives; automotive applications and includes advanced actuators, sensors and systems involving both rotating machinery and power electronics; solid state circuit breakers; granted 31 patents. *Mailing Add:* 413 S Pine Mt Prospect IL 60056

STUDZINSKI, GEORGE P, EXPERIMENTAL PATHOLOGY, CELL BIOLOGY. *Current Pos:* PROF PATH & CHMN DEPT, NJ MED SCH, 76- *Personal Data:* b Poznan, Poland, Oct 30, 32; m 59; c 4. *Educ:* Glasgow Univ, BS, 55, MB, 58, PhD(exp path), 62. *Prof Exp:* Brit Empire Cancer Campaign res fel path, Glasgow Royal Infirmary, 59-60, resident, 60-62; from instr to prof path, Jefferson Med Col, 62-75. *Mem:* Tissue Cult Asn; Am Soc Exp Path; Histochem Soc; Am Asn Cancer Res; Am Soc Cell Biol. *Res:* Study of effect of cancer chemotherapeutic agents on cultured diploid and aneuploid mammalian cells by a combination of cytochemical and biochemical methods; clinical pathology. *Mailing Add:* MSBC 546 Dept Path NJ Med Sch 185 S Orange Ave Newark NJ 07103-2484

STUEBEN, EDMUND BRUNO, PARASITOLOGY. *Current Pos:* assoc prof, 54-63, PROF ZOOL & PHYSIOL, UNIV SOUTHWESTERN LA, 63- *Personal Data:* b Cuxhaven, Ger, Apr 22, 20; nat US; m 4S; c 4. *Educ:* NY Univ, BS, 41; Baylor Univ, MA, 49; Univ Fla, PhD(zool), 53. *Prof Exp:* Instr biol lab & parasitol lab, Univ Fla, 50-53; asst prof biol, Arlington State Col, 53. *Mem:* Sigma Xi. *Res:* Larval development of filariae in arthropods; physiology of filaria larva; transmission of infective state filaria larva; antihistamine effect on coronary circulation. *Mailing Add:* 1405 E Bayou Pkwy Lafayette LA 70508

STUEBER, ALAN MICHAEL, GEOCHEMISTRY. *Current Pos:* RES GEOCHEMIST, OAK RIDGE NAT LAB, 77- *Personal Data:* b St Louis, Mo, Apr 18, 37. *Educ:* Wash Univ, BS, 58, MA, 61; Univ Calif, San Diego, PhD(earth sci), 65. *Prof Exp:* Res assoc earth sci, Wash Univ, 65-66; fel geochem, Carnegie Inst Washington, 66-67; from asst prof to assoc prof geol, Miami Univ, 67-75. *Mem:* Geochem Soc; Sigma Xi. *Res:* Earth sciences; strontium isotope studies. *Mailing Add:* 6804 Prairietown Rd Edwardsville IL 62025-5378

STUEBING, EDWARD WILLIS, AEROSOL OPTICS, AEROSOL CHARACTERIZATION. *Current Pos:* Res physicist, US Army Frankford Arsenal, 70-74, res chemist, Pitman-Dunn Labs, 74-77, RES PHYSICAL SCIENTIST & MGR AEROSOL RES, US ARMY CHEM RES DEVELOP & ENG CTR, 77- *Personal Data:* b Cincinnati, Ohio, Sept 9, 42; m 82; c Barbara J & Jennifer Jane. *Educ:* Univ Cincinnati, BS, 65; Johns Hopkins Univ, MA, 69, PhD(chem physics), 70. *Honors & Awards:* Res & Develop Achievement Award, US Army, 74 & 85. *Concurrent Pos:* Adj asst prof chem, Drexel Univ, 74-77. *Mem:* Am Phys Soc; Asn Comput Mach; Int Soc Quantum Biol; Am Chem Soc; Sigma Xi; Am Asn Aerosol Res. *Res:* Aerosol light scattering; remote sensing of chemical and biological species in the atmosphere and on surfaces; theoretical study of molecular structure, excited states and energy transfer; interaction of matter with laser light at high power density; mathematical modeling and operations research analyses; computer automation of research administration. *Mailing Add:* PO Box 233 Gunpowder MD 21010

STUEDEMANN, JOHN ALFRED, ANIMAL NUTRITION. *Current Pos:* RES ANIMAL SCIENTIST, SOUTHERN PIEDMONT CONSERV RES CTR, AGR RES SERV, USDA, 70- *Personal Data:* b Clinton, Iowa, Oct 3, 42; m 67, Patricia A Wiseman. *Educ:* Iowa State Univ, BS, 64; Okla State Univ, MS, 67, PhD(ruminant nutri), 70. *Mem:* Am Soc Animal Sci; Am Forage & Grassland Coun. *Res:* Ruminant nutrition; forage production and utilization; waste disposal and land fertilization; health problems of beef cattle; forage finishing of cattle; cow-calf management; internal parasitism; environmental impact of the presence of cattle. *Mailing Add:* Southern Piedmont Conserv Res Ctr USDA 1420 Experiment Station Rd Watkinsville GA 30677. *Fax:* 706-769-8962; *E-Mail:* jstuedem@uga.cc.uga.edu

STUEHR, JOHN EDWARD, BIOPHYSICAL CHEMISTRY. *Current Pos:* from asst prof to assoc prof, 64-74, chmn dept, 77-81, PROF CHEM, CASE WESTERN RES UNIV, 74- *Personal Data:* b Aug 30, 35; US citizen; m 62; c 4. *Educ:* Western Res Univ, BA, 57, MS, 59, PhD(chem), 61. *Prof Exp:* NIH res fel chem, Max Planck Inst, Gottingen, WGer, 62-63. *Mem:* Am Chem Soc; Sigma Xi; Fedn Biol Chemists. *Res:* Reaction kinetics of fast processes in solution; relaxation spectroscopy; metal complexing; biochemical kinetics; elementary steps in enzyme kinetics. *Mailing Add:* Dept Chem Case Western Res Univ 10900 Euclid Ave Cleveland OH 44106-1712

STUELAND, DEAN T, EMERGENCY CARE, OCCUPATIONAL MEDICINE & INJURY PREVENTION. *Current Pos:* dir emergency serv, 81-88, STAFF PHYSICIAN, MARSHFIELD CLIN, 81-, DIR EMERGENCY SERV, 81- *Personal Data:* b Viroqua, Wis, June 24, 50; m 72, Marlene McCling; c Jeffrey, Michael, Nancy & Kevin. *Educ:* Univ Wis-Madison, BS, 72, MS, 73, MD, 77; Am Bd Intenal Med, cert, 80; Am Bd Emergency Med, cert, 87 & 96. *Prof Exp:* Internal med resident, Marshfield Clin/St Joseph's Hosp, Univ Wis, 77-80; staff emergency physician, Riverview Hosp, Wisconsin Rapids, Wis, 80-81. *Concurrent Pos:* Dir, Nat Farm Med Ctr, 84-; clin prof, Univ Wis, 84-89, assoc clin prof, 89-; chmn, Trauma Comt, Am Col Emergency Physicians, 86 & 87, Pre-Hosp Subcomt, 88-89; med dir, AODA Unit, Marshfield Clin, 88-, Basic Trauma & Life Support, 89-; mem, Sexual Assault Task Force, Dept Health & Soc Serv, 89-90 & Legis Coun Spec Com to review Emergency Med Serv, 93. *Mem:* Fel Am Col Physicians; fel Am Col Emergency Physicians; Am Pub Health Asn; Soc Critical Care Med; Am Occup Med Asn; fel Am Col Prev Med; Am Soc Addiction Med; Inst Elec & Electronics Engrs; Asn Comput Mach. *Res:* Agricultural health and safety; injury prevention; addiction treatment and prevention. *Mailing Add:* 1000 N Oak Marshfield WI 54449. *Fax:* 719-387-5240; *E-Mail:* stueland@mfldclin.edu

STUELPNAGEL, JOHN CLAY, MATHEMATICS. *Current Pos:* sr engr, 64-66, fel engr, Aerospace Div, 66-76, prog mgr, Syst Develop Div, 76-86, DEPT MGR, DIGITAL SYSTEMS, WESTINGHOUSE ELECTRIC CORP, 86- *Personal Data:* b Houston, Tex, Nov 12, 36; m 59; c 3. *Educ:* Yankton Col, BA, 55; Johns Hopkins Univ, PhD(math), 62. *Prof Exp:* Fel math, Res Inst Advan Studies, Martin-Marietta Corp, 61-64. *Mem:* Am Defense Preparedness Asn. *Res:* Lie groups; linear algebra; differential equations; computation and computer design; radar development. *Mailing Add:* 5306 Tilbury Way Baltimore MD 21212

STUESSE, SHERRY LYNN, NEUROSCIENCES. *Current Pos:* from instr to assoc prof, 77-88, PROF NEUROBIOL, NE OHIO UNIV COL MED, 88- *Personal Data:* b Aruba, Neth, WI, Feb 2, 44; US citizen; m 66; c David, Angela & Patrick. *Educ:* Vanderbilt Univ, Tenn, BA, 66; Washington Univ, St Louis, Mo, MA, 68; State Univ NY, Albany, PhD(biol), 72. *Prof Exp:* Postdoctoral fel, Case Western Reserve Univ, 71-76 & Mt Sinai Med Ctr, 76-77. *Concurrent Pos:* Vis scientist, Salk Inst, La Jolla, Calif, 85-86 & Friday Harbor, Univ Wash, 89-90; prof, Biomed Eng, Univ Akron & Biol Dept, Kent State Univ, 88- *Mem:* Am Physiol Soc; Am Asn Anatomists; Soc Neurosci; Asn Women Sci. *Res:* Neural control of the heart; comparative neuroanatomy; author of over 40 publications. *Mailing Add:* Neurobiol Dept Northwestern Ohio Univ Rootstown OH 44272-0095

STUESSY, TOD FALOR, SYSTEMATIC BOTANY. *Current Pos:* from asst to assoc prof, 68-79, chmn, 88-89, PROF PLANT BIOLOGY, OHIO STATE UNIV, 79-, DIR MUS BIOL DIVERSITY, 91- *Personal Data:* b Pittsburgh, Pa, Nov 18, 43; m 88; c Mary, Alan & Daniel. *Educ:* DePauw Univ, BA, 65; Univ Tex, Austin, PhD(bot), 68. *Honors & Awards:* Wilks Award, Southwestern Asn Naturalists. *Concurrent Pos:* Res assoc, Field Mus Nat Hist, 70-94; Maria Moors Cabot res fel, Gray Herbarium, Harvard Univ, 71-72; assoc dir, Syst Biol Prog, NSF & collabr, Dept Bot, Smithsonian Inst, 77-78. *Mem:* AAAS; Int Asn Plant Taxon; Am Soc Plant Taxon (pres, 87-88); Bot Soc Am; Soc Study Evolution; Sigma Xi. *Res:* Systematics and evolution of Compositae; island biology; flora of southern South America. *Mailing Add:* Nat Hist Mus Los Angeles County 900 Exposition Blvd Los Angeles CA 90007. *Fax:* 614-292-3009; *E-Mail:* estuessy@magnus.aer.ohio-state.edu

STUEWER, ROGER HARRY, HISTORY OF PHYSICS. *Current Pos:* assoc prof, 72-74, PROF HIST SCI & TECH, UNIV MINN, MINNEAPOLIS, 74- *Personal Data:* b Sept 12, 34; US citizen; m 60, Helga Schmeidel; c Marcus L & Suzanne A. *Educ:* Univ Wis, BS, 58, MS, 64, PhD(hist sci & physics), 68. *Honors & Awards:* Distinguished Serv Citation, Am Asn Physics Teachers, 90. *Prof Exp:* Instr physics, Heidelberg Col, 60-62; from asst prof to assoc prof hist physics, Univ Minn, Minneapolis, 67-71; assoc prof hist sci, Boston Univ, 71-72. *Concurrent Pos:* Mem, adv panel hist & philos sci, NSF, 70-72, res support, 70-, hon res assoc, Harvard Univ, 74-75; Am Coun Learned Soc fel, 74-75, 83-84, chmn, Am Inst Physics, adv comn hist physics, 80-93; Volkswagen Found vis prof, Deutsches Mus, Munich, 81-82, chmn, Am Phys Soc, div hist physics, 87-88; vis prof, Univ Vienna & Graz, 89; chmn, Sect L, AAAS, 93-94; distinguished lectr, Sigma Xi, 96- *Mem:* Hist Sci Soc (secy, 72-78); fel AAAS; Sigma Xi; Brit Soc Hist Sci; Am Asn Physics Teachers; fel Am Phys Soc. *Res:* History of twentieth century physics, especially radiation theory, quantum theory, and nuclear physics; Compton effect as a turning point in physics; nuclear physics between WWI and WWII. *Mailing Add:* Sch Physics & Astron Univ Minn Minneapolis MN 55455. *Fax:* 612-624-4578; *E-Mail:* rstuewer@physics.spa.umn.edu

STUFFLE, ROY EUGENE, SEMICONDUCTOR DEVICE MODELING. *Current Pos:* PROF ENG & ASSOC DEAN ENG, IDAHO STATE UNIV, 89- *Personal Data:* b Elwood, Ind, Oct 14, 44; m 85; c 1. *Educ:* Rose Polytech Inst, BSEE, 66 MSEE, 69; Ind Univ, Ft Wayne, MSBA, 75; Purdue Univ,

PhD(elec eng), 79. *Prof Exp:* Adv develop engr, Appl Res & Develop Lab, Gen Elec Co, 68-69 & 72-75; asst prof elec eng, Mich Technol Univ, 79-85; asst prof, Univ Mo-Rolla, 84-89. *Concurrent Pos:* Vis asst prof, Univ Mo-Rolla, 84-85; mem, Steering Comt, Midwest Symp, Circuits & Systs. *Mem:* Inst Elec & Electronics Engrs; Sigma Xi; Am Soc Eng Educ. *Res:* Computer-aided circuit analysis and design; automated modeling procedures for semiconductor devices; adaptation to microcomputers; educational applications of microcomputers. *Mailing Add:* 586 University Dr Pocatello ID 83201-3468

STUFFLEBEAM, CHARLES EDWARD, ANIMAL GENETICS, BIOCHEMISTRY. *Current Pos:* PROF ANIMAL SCI, SOUTHWEST MO STATE UNIV, 69- *Personal Data:* b St Louis, Mo, Feb 22, 33; m 52; c 3. *Educ:* Univ Mo, BS, 58, MS, 61, PhD, 64. *Prof Exp:* Asst county agent, Exten Div, Univ Mo, 59-61, instr animal husb & agr biochem, 62-64; assoc prof range animal sci, Sul Ross State Col, 64-65; assoc prof animal sci, Northwestern State Univ, 65-69. *Mem:* Am Soc Animal Sci; Nat Asn Cols & Teachers Agr (past pres). *Res:* Genetics; biochemistry, physiology and nutrition of domestic animals and their application to agriculture; animal husbandry. *Mailing Add:* Dept Agr SW Mo State Univ 901 S Nat Springfield MO 65804-0027

STUHL, LOUIS SHELDON, TRANSITION METAL CHEMISTRY, COLLOID CHEMISTRY. *Current Pos:* scientist, 88-93, SR SCIENTIST, POLAROID CORP, 93- *Personal Data:* b New York, NY, Feb 5, 51; m 77, Sheila Kojm; c 2. *Educ:* Mass Inst Technol, SB, 73; Cornell Univ, MS, 76, PhD(chem), 78. *Prof Exp:* NSF fel chem, Univ Calif, Berkeley, 78-79; asst prof chem, Brandeis Univ, 79-86; chemist, Am Optical Co, 87-88. *Mem:* Am Chem Soc. *Res:* Metal and colloid chemistry and their application to problems of catalysis, photography, and organic synthesis, including exploratory work, mechanistic studies and model systems. *Mailing Add:* Chem Motif Inc 60 Thoreau St Suite 211 Concord MA 01742. *Fax:* 617-577-5221; *E-Mail:* stuhl%hydra@leia.polaroid.com

STUHLINGER, ERNST, PHYSICS. *Current Pos:* CONSULT, SPACE RES & TECHNOL, INDUST CORP, 82- *Personal Data:* b Niederrimbach, Ger, Dec 19, 13; nat US; m 50; c 3. *Educ:* Univ Tubingen, PhD(physics), 36. *Honors & Awards:* Roentgen Prize; Galabert Prize, Paris, 62; Hermann Oberth Award, 62 & Medal, 64; Propulsion Award, Am Inst Aeronaut & Astronaut, 60; Wernher von Braun Prize, 85. *Prof Exp:* Asst prof, Berlin Inst Technol, 36-41; res asst guid & control, Rocket Develop Ctr, Peenemuende, 43-45; asst res & develop, Ord Corps, US Army, Ft Bliss, Tex & White Sands Proving Ground, NMex, 46-50, astronaut res adminr & supvry phys scientist, Army Ballistic Missile Agency, Redstone Arsenal, Ala, 50-60; dir, Space Sci Lab, Marshall Space Flight Ctr, NASA, 60-68, assoc dir sci, 68-76; sr res scientist, Univ Ala, Huntsville, 76-82. *Mem:* Fel Am Inst Aeronaut & Astronaut; fel Am Astronaut Soc; Ger Phys Soc; Ger Soc Rockets & Space Flight; Brit Interplanetary Soc; Sigma Xi. *Res:* Feasibility and design studies of electrical propulsion systems for space ships; scientific satellites and space probes; electric automobiles; manned missions to Mars. *Mailing Add:* 3106 Rowe Dr SE Huntsville AL 35801-6151

STUHLMAN, ROBERT AUGUST, laboratory animal medicine, medical research, for more information see previous edition

STUHLMILLER, GARY MICHAEL, TUMOR ASSOCIATED ANTIGENS & IMMUNOLOGY. *Current Pos:* ASST PROF MED RES, DUKE UNIV, MED CTR, 76- *Personal Data:* m 80; c 2. *Educ:* Duke Univ, PhD(immunol), 76. *Mem:* Am Asn Immunologists; Am Asn Cancer Res. *Res:* Monoclonal antibodies; tumor associated antigens. *Mailing Add:* Dept Paternity Eoal Roche Biomed Labs 147 York Ct Burlington NC 27215-2230

STUHMILLER, JAMES HAMILTON, PHYSICS. *Current Pos:* SR VPRES, JAYCOR, 75- *Personal Data:* b Cincinnati, Ohio, Apr 1, 43. *Educ:* Mass Inst Technol, BS, 65; Queens Col, City Univ New York, MA, 68; Univ Cincinnati, PhD(physics), 73. *Prof Exp:* Engr, Electronics Div, AVCO, 68-73; scientist, Sci Appln Inc, 73-75. *Mem:* Am Phys Soc; Am Soc Mech Engrs; Am Inst Chem Engrs; Am Metereol Soc; Am Inst Aeronaut & Astronaut. *Res:* Underlying physical phenomena controlling unusual behavior in engineering systems (nuclear power plants, submerged vehicles, space vehicle launches); mathematical representation to predict and correct associated problems. *Mailing Add:* Jaycor 9775 Town Ctr Dr San Diego CA 92121-1190

STUIVER, MINZE, EARTH SCIENCE. *Current Pos:* prof geol & zool, 69-81, PROF GEOL & QUATERNARY SCI, UNIV WASH, 81- *Personal Data:* b Vlagtwedde, Neth, Oct 25, 29; m 56; c 2. *Educ:* State Univ Groningen, MSc, 53, PhD(biophys), 58. *Honors & Awards:* Alexander v Humboldt Award, WGer, 83-84. *Prof Exp:* Res assoc & fel geol, Yale Univ, 59-62, sr res assoc geol & biol & dir radiocarbon lab, 62-69. *Res:* Biophysics of sense organs; low level counting techniques; carbon cycle and radiocarbon time scale calibration; isotopic applications in pleistocene geology, oceanography, limnology and climatology. *Mailing Add:* Geol Sci A J-20 Univ Wash 3900 7th Ave NE Seattle WA 98195-0001

STUIVER, W(ILLEM), ANALYTICAL MECHANICS, SPACE FLIGHT DYNAMICS. *Current Pos:* assoc prof, 61-65, PROF MECH ENG, UNIV HAWAII, 65- *Personal Data:* b Breda, Netherlands, Aug 1, 27; m 57, Chitra Premaratne. *Educ:* Delft Univ Technol, Mech engr, 51; Stanford Univ, PhD(eng mech), 60. *Prof Exp:* Asst mech engr, NZ Ministry Works, 52-54; res engr, NZ Dept Sci & Indust Res, 54-55; anal design engr, Gen Elec Co, 56-58; mem res staff, IBM Corp, 59-61. *Concurrent Pos:* Consult, Stanford Res Inst, 62-67; vis prof, Indian Inst Sci, India, 64-65; Univ New SWales, Australia, 75; Univ Western Australia, 76 & Univ Peradeniya, Sri Lanka, 82-83. *Mem:* Am Inst Aeronaut & Astronaut; Am Astronaut Soc. *Res:* Development of dual state-variable approach to response analysis of discrete dynamical systems; dynamics and control of geostationary satellite systems; interplanetary and interstellar space flight. *Mailing Add:* Dept Mech Eng Univ Hawaii 2540 Dole St Honolulu HI 96822

STUKEL, JAMES JOSEPH, ENGINEERING. *Current Pos:* from asst prof to prof civil eng & mech eng, Univ Ill, Chicago, 68-85, dir off coal res, 75-76, dir, Off Energy Res, 76-80, dir, Off Interdisciplinary Proj, 78-80, dir Pub Policy Prog, Col Eng, 80-85, vchancellor res & dean Grad Col, 85-86, exec vchancellor & vchancellor acad affairs, 86-91, chancellor, 91-95, PRES, UNIV ILL, CHICAGO, 95- *Personal Data:* b Joliet, Ill, Mar 30, 37; m 58; c 4. *Educ:* Purdue Univ, BSME, 59; Univ Ill, Urbana-Champaign, MS, 63, PhD(mech eng), 68. *Honors & Awards:* State of the Art of Civil Eng Award, Am Soc Civil Engrs, 75. *Prof Exp:* Res engr, Westvaco, 59-61. *Concurrent Pos:* Consult, Westvaco, 61-63 & var govt agencies, 68-; prin investr, US Environ Protection Agency training grant, 70-76, res grants, Kimberly Clark Corp, 75-76, Bur Mines & US Environ Protection Agency, 76-82. *Mem:* Am Soc Civil Engrs; Am Soc Mech Engrs; Sigma Xi. *Res:* Aerosol science; air resources management; impact assessment. *Mailing Add:* 2650 N Lakeview Chicago IL 60614

STUKUS, PHILIP EUGENE, MICROBIAL PHYSIOLOGY, ENVIRONMENTAL MICROBIOLOGY. *Current Pos:* asst prof, 68-80, PROF BIOL, DENISON UNIV, 80- *Personal Data:* b Braddock, Penn, Oct 22, 42; m 66; c 3. *Educ:* St Vincent Col, BA, 64; Cath Univ Am, MS, 66, PhD(microbiol), 68. *Mem:* AAAS; Am Soc Microbiol; Sigma Xi; Soc Indust Microbiol. *Res:* Autotrophic and heterotrophic metabolism of hydrogen bacteria; degradation of detergent additives and pesticides by soil microorganisms; distribution of microorganisms in air. *Mailing Add:* Dept Biol Denison Univ PO Box M Granville OH 43023-0613

STULA, EDWIN FRANCIS, VETERINARY PATHOLOGY, SAFETY EVALUATION PATHOLOGY. *Current Pos:* CONSULT SAFETY EVAL PATH, 92- *Personal Data:* b Colchester, Conn, Jan 3, 24; m 55, Elizabeth Konig; c Edwin J. *Educ:* Univ Conn, BS, 50, PhD(animal path), 63; Univ Toronto, DVM, 55. *Prof Exp:* Instr vet med & exten vet, Univ Conn, 55-62; chief res pathologist, Haskell Lab Toxicol & Indust Med, E I du Pont de Nemours & Co, Inc, 63-92. *Mem:* Am Vet Med Asn; Soc Toxicol; NY Acad Sci; Int Acad Path; Soc Toxicol Pathologists. *Res:* Bovine vibriosis, mastitis and infertility; leptospirosis in chinchillas and guinea pigs; spontaneous diseases of laboratory animals; industrial medicine; pathologic effects in animals exposed to various chemicals by various routes; morphologic effects using both light and electron microscopes; carcinogenicity and embryotoxicity. *Mailing Add:* 235 Mercury Rd Newark DE 19711

STULBERG, MELVIN PHILIP, BIOCHEMISTRY. *Current Pos:* RETIRED. *Personal Data:* b Duluth, Minn, May 17, 25; m 55, Dorothy Bonnell; c Laurie, Lisa & Lynn. *Educ:* Univ Minn, BS, 49, MS, 55, PhD(biochem), 58. *Prof Exp:* Res assoc, Biol Div, Oak Ridge Nat Lab, 58-59, biochemist, 59-61, biochemist, Biol Div, 63-89; biochemist, AEC, 61-63; prof, Oak Ridge Grad Sch Biomed Sci, Univ Tenn, 73-89. *Mem:* Am Soc Biol Chemists & Molecular Biologists. *Res:* Protein biosynthesis; isolation and function of transfer RNA; enzyme mechanisms; mechanisms of aging. *Mailing Add:* 122 Breakwater Dr Knoxville TN 37922

STULL, DEAN P, ANALYTICAL CHEMISTRY, NATURAL PRODUCTS PROCESS DEVELOPMENT. *Current Pos:* CHIEF CHEMIST, HAUSER LABS, 76-, DIR SPEC PROJS. *Personal Data:* US citizen. *Educ:* Colo State Univ, BS, 72; Univ Colo, MS, 74, PhD(phys org chem), 76. *Prof Exp:* Res asst, Colo State Univ, 70-71, Univ Calif, San Francisco, 72 & Univ Colo, Boulder, 76. *Mem:* Am Chem Soc; Sigma Xi. *Res:* Methods development of chemical analysis of crude and refined petroleum products; fire retardant technology; natural products. *Mailing Add:* Hauser Inc 5555 Airport Blvd Boulder CO 80301-2339

STULL, ELISABETH ANN, ENVIRONMENTAL IMPACT ANALYSIS, LIMNOLOGY. *Current Pos:* ECOLOGIST, ENVIRON ASSESSMENT DIV, ARGONNE NAT LAB, 78- *Personal Data:* b Fayette, Mo, Jan 7, 43. *Educ:* Lawrence Univ, BA, 65; Univ Ga, MS, 69; Univ Calif, Davis, PhD(zool), 72. *Prof Exp:* Asst prof biol sci, Univ Ariz, 71-75, asst prof ecol & evolutionary biol, 75-78. *Mem:* Am Soc Limnol & Oceanog; Phycol Soc Am; Soc Int Limnol; Int Asn Impact Assessment. *Res:* Energetics and trophic ecology of unicellular taxa; algal floristics; regional and geographical patterns in limnology and water quality; environmental analysis of energy-related technologies; cumulative effects analysis; restoration ecology; ecological risk assessment. *Mailing Add:* Environ Assessment Div Argonne Nat Lab 9700 S Cass Ave Argonne IL 60439

STULL, G(EORGE) A, EXERCISE PHYSIOLOGY. *Current Pos:* PROF & DEAN EXERCISE SCI, SCH HEALTH RELATED PROFS, STATE UNIV NY, BUFFALO, 88- *Personal Data:* b Easton, Pa, Jan 26, 33; m, Jeanine Joosten; c Bobbi A & John D. *Educ:* E Stroudsburg Univ, BS, 55; Pa State Univ, MS, 57, EdD(phys educ), 61. *Honors & Awards:* Asn Res, Admin & Prof Coun & Soc Award, 74; Am Alliance Health, Phys Educ, Recreation & Dance Award, 81. *Prof Exp:* From instr to asst prof phys educ, Pa State Univ, 58-66; from assoc prof to prof phys educ, Univ Md, 66-72; prof educ psychol & phys educ, Univ Ky, 72-77; prof & dir educ psychol & phys educ,

Sch Phys Educ, Recreation & Sch Health Educ, Univ Minn, 77-85; prof & dean allied health, Sch Allied Health Profs, Univ Wis-Madison, 85-88. *Concurrent Pos:* Assoc ed, J Motor Behav, 69-81, Clin Kinesiol, 70- & Res Quart Exercise & Sport, 72-75; chair res sect, Am Asn Health, Phys Educ & Recreation, 72-73, mem bd gov, 76-79, 81-82; pres assoc res admin, Prof Coun & Soc, 76-77; chair, position stands comt, Am Col Sports Med, 79-81, res quarterly exercise & sport adv comt, 79-80; assoc ed, J Motor Behav, 69-81, Clin Kinesiol, 70- & Res Quart Exercise & Sport, 72-75. *Mem:* Am Acad Kinesiol & Phys Educ (pres, 85-86); Am Alliance Health, Phys Educ, Recreation & Dance; Am Col Sports Med; Asn Schs Allied Health Profs; Nat Asn Phys Educ Higher Educ. *Res:* Effects of exercise on muscular and cardiorespiratory systems; locus of and recovery from local fatigue; prognostic value of exercise testing following myocardial infraction and coronary bypass surgery. *Mailing Add:* Health Educ State Univ NY Buffalo S Kimball Tower Buffalo NY 14214-3001. *Fax:* 716-829-2034; *E-Mail:* prohrp@ubvmsd.bitnet

STULL, JAMES TRAVIS, PHARMACOLOGY, BIOCHEMISTRY. *Current Pos:* PROF & CHMN PHYSIOL, UNIV TEX SOUTHWESTERN MED CTR, DALLAS, 86- *Personal Data:* b Ashland, Ky, Feb 7, 44; m 66; c 3. *Educ:* Rhodes Col BS, 66; Emory Univ, PhD(pharmacol), 71. *Prof Exp:* Adj asst prof biol chem, Sch Med, Univ Calif, Davis, 73-74; from asst prof to assoc prof med, Sch Med, Univ Calif, San Diego, 74-78; assoc prof to prof pharmacol, Univ Tex Health Sci Ctr, Dallas, 78-86. *Concurrent Pos:* Damon Runyon Mem Fund Cancer Res fel, Univ Calif, Davis, 71-73; estab investr, Am Heart Asn, 73; assoc dean, Grad Sch Biomed Sci, Univ Tex Health Sci Ctr, Dallas, 80-86; Wellcome vis prof, 90. *Mem:* Am Heart Asn; Am Soc Pharmacol & Exp Therapeut; fel AAAS; Am Soc Biol Chemists; Sigma Xi; Am Physiol Soc; Biophys Soc. *Res:* Protein phosphorylation reactions in regulation of muscle metabolism, contraction and responses to hormones and adrenergic drugs. *Mailing Add:* Physiol Dept Univ Tex Southwestern Med Ctr Dallas 5323 Harry Hines Blvd Dallas TX 75235-9040. *Fax:* 214-648-2974

STULL, JOHN LEETE, PHYSICS, ASTRONOMY. *Current Pos:* Res assoc ceramics, Alfred Univ, 52-58, from asst prof to prof, 58-92, dir observ, 68-90, chmn dept, 72-75, EMER PROF PHYSICS, ALFRED UNIV, 92- *Personal Data:* b Dansville, NY, June 2, 30; m 52; c Marylee (Ashby) & Peter H. *Educ:* Alfred Univ, BS, 52, MS, 54, PhD(ceramics), 58. *Mem:* AAAS; Am Asn Physics Teachers. *Res:* Astronomy; development of physics teaching apparatus; design of small optical observatories and equipment; ccd photometry of various objects. *Mailing Add:* Alfred Univ Dept Physics Saxon Dr Alfred NY 14802. *Fax:* 607-871-2342; *E-Mail:* fstull@biguax.alfred.edu

STULTING, ROBERT DOYLE, JR, MICROBIOLOGY, IMMUNOLOGY. *Current Pos:* ASSOC PROF, WINSHIP CANCER CTR, 88- *Personal Data:* b Knoxville, Tenn, Nov 24, 48; c 2. *Educ:* Duke Univ, BS, 70, MD, 76, PhD(microbiol & immunol), 75; Am Bd Ophthalmol, cert, 82. *Prof Exp:* Intern, Barnes Hosp, St Louis, 76-77, resident, 77-78; resident, Bascom Palmer Eye Inst, Miami, 78-81; fel ophthal, 81-82, asst prof, 82-85, assoc prof ophthal, Emory Univ, 86- *Concurrent Pos:* Consult, Southeastern Regional Organ Procurement Found, 70-76, Med Sch Curriculum Comt, Duke Univ, 73-75; promotions comt & med records comt, Emory Clinic, Emory Univ, 85-; med advisory bd, Eye Bank Asn Am & Ambulatory Surg Ctr Comt, Emory Clin, 86-; consult, Ophthalmic Devices Panel, ctr devices and radiol health, US Food & Drug Admin, 87-88, mem, 88, bd dirs, Eye Bank Asn Am, 88- *Mem:* Am Med Asn; Am Asn Immunol; Am Acad Ophthalmol; Eye Bank Asn Am. *Res:* Collaborative corneal transplantation studies; research to prevent blindness; pathogenesis of herpes simplex keratitis. *Mailing Add:* Emory Eye Ctr Emory Univ Sch Med 1327 Clifton Rd NE Atlanta GA 30322. *Fax:* 404-248-5128

STULTS, FREDERICK HOWARD, TOXICOLOGY. *Current Pos:* AT FIRMENICH INC. *Personal Data:* b Seattle, Wash, Nov 11, 48; m 69; c 3. *Educ:* San Diego State Univ, BS, 71; Univ Calif, Davis, PhD(biochem), 76. *Prof Exp:* Fel toxicol, Med Sch, Duke Univ, 76-77; res toxicologist, 77-80, dir, corp safety, Int Flavors & Fragrances, 80- *Mem:* Am Chem Soc; Inst Food Technologists; Am Col Toxicol. *Res:* Human dermal toxicity, allergenicity, biodegradation & photobiology. *Mailing Add:* Firmenich Inc PO Box 5880 Princeton NJ 08543-5880

STULTS, VALA JEAN, NUTRITION. *Current Pos:* CONSULT NUTRIT. *Personal Data:* b Oklahoma City, Okla, Aug 16, 42. *Educ:* Calif State Univ, Long Beach, BA, 65, MA, 67; Mich State Univ, PhD(human nutrit), 74. *Prof Exp:* Teacher home econ, Lawndale High Sch, 66-68; consult nutritionist, Head Start Prog, Off Econ Opportunity, 69; NIH fel, 73-74; asst instr nutrit, Cen Mich Univ, 74; sales mgr & asst to gen mgr potatoes in retort pouches, Nu Foods Inc, 75-76; nutritionist, Kellogg Co, 77-; chmn, Dept Home Econ, Whittier Col, 83-88. *Mem:* Am Home Econ Asn; Am Dietetic Asn; Soc Nutrit Educ; Soc Nutrit Today; Inst Food Technologists. *Res:* Subjects of interest to the ready-to-eat cereal industry, soft drinks industry and exposing health fraud. *Mailing Add:* 16333 Grenoble Lane Apt 55 Huntington Beach CA 92649

STULTZ, WALTER ALVA, ANATOMY. *Current Pos:* from asst prof to prof, 37-69, EMER PROF ANAT, COL MED, UNIV VT, 69- *Personal Data:* b St John, NB, Mar 14, 04; nat US; m 31, 50, Rhoda Fogg; c Mariel, Arthur, Melanie, Kevin & Natalie. *Educ:* Acadia Univ, BA, 27; Yale Univ, PhD(zool, anat), 32. *Prof Exp:* Prin sch, NB, Can, 22-24; asst biol, Yale Univ, 27-30; instr, Spring Hill Sch, Conn, 30-31; instr & actg head dept, Trinity Col, Conn, 31-32; prof, Mt Union Col, 32-33; asst, Yale Univ, 33-34; fel anat, Sch Med, Univ Ga, 34-35, fel histol & embryol, 35-36; instr anat, Med Col SC, 36-37. *Concurrent Pos:* Sr lectr gross anat & histol, Sch Med, Univ Calif, San Diego, 69-77; vis prof anat, Dartmouth Med Sch, 77-83. *Mem:* Am Asn Anat. *Res:* Experimental embryology of Amblystoma, localization of hind limb; relations of symmetry in fore and hind limbs; interrelationships between limbs and nervous system. *Mailing Add:* B Joy Dr No 5 South Burlington VT 05403

STUMP, BILLY LEE, PHYSICAL CHEMISTRY, POLYMER CHEMISTRY. *Current Pos:* from assoc prof, to prof, 66-92, EMER PROF CHEM & COORDR GEN CHEM, VA COMMONWEALTH UNIV, 92- *Personal Data:* b Morristown, Tenn, Jan 11, 30; m 58, Phyllis Fox; c Vicki L, Elizabeth (Hill) & Marilyn (Burns). *Educ:* Carson-Newman Col, BS, 52; Univ Tenn PhD(chem), 59. *Prof Exp:* Res chemist, Carson-Newman Col, 52-53; res technician, Oak Ridge Inst Nuclear Studies, 53-54; chemist, Redstone Div, Thiokol Chem Corp, 59-60; res chemist, Film Res Lab, E I du Pont de Nemours & Co, 60-62 & Spruance Film Res & Develop Lab, 62-63; assoc prof chem, Carson-Newman Col, 63-66. *Mem:* Am Chem Soc; Sigma Xi. *Res:* Kinetics and reaction mechanisms; catalysis and kinetics of catalytic hydrogenation; polymer chemistry. *Mailing Add:* Va Commonwealth Univ Dept Chem PO Box 2006 Richmond VA 23284-2006. *Fax:* 804-828-8599

STUMP, EDMUND, GEOLOGY. *Current Pos:* ASST PROF GEOL, ARIZ STATE UNIV, 76- *Personal Data:* b Danville, Pa, Dec 28, 46. *Educ:* Harvard Col, AB, 68; Yale Univ, MS, 72; Ohio State Univ, PhD(geol), 76. *Mem:* Geol Soc Am; AAAS. *Res:* Geology of Antarctica and Gondwanaland. *Mailing Add:* Geol Ariz State Univ Tempe AZ 85287-0002

STUMP, EUGENE CURTIS, JR, ORGANIC CHEMISTRY, FLUORINE CHEMISTRY. *Current Pos:* Dir contract res, 60-70, vpres contract res div, 70-76, VPRES RES & DEVELOP, PCR, INC, 76- *Personal Data:* b Charleston, WVa, May 19, 30; m 58; c 3. *Educ:* WVa Univ, BS, 52; Columbia Univ, MA, 53; Univ Fla, PhD(org chem), 60. *Mem:* Am Chem Soc; Royal Soc Chem. *Res:* Synthesis of fluorine containing compounds, particularly ethers, olefins, nitroso and difluoramine compounds; synthesis of fluorine-containing polymers as low temperature elastomers; synthesis of thermally and oxidatively stable fluids. *Mailing Add:* 3131 NW 37 St Gainesville FL 32605-2038

STUMP, JOHN EDWARD, VETERINARY ANATOMY. *Current Pos:* from instr to assoc prof vet anat, 61-76, PROF VET ANAT, PURDUE UNIV, WEST LAFAYETTE, 76- *Personal Data:* b Galion, Ohio, June 3, 34; m 55; c 2. *Educ:* Ohio State Univ, DVM, 58; Purdue Univ, PhD, 66. *Prof Exp:* Private vet pract, Ohio, 58-61. *Concurrent Pos:* Vis prof, Dept Physiol Sci, Sch Vet Med, Univ Calif, Davis, 80, Dept Vet Anat, Col Vet Med, Tex A&M Univ, 81. *Mem:* Am Asn Anatomists; Am Vet Med Asn; World Asn Vet Anat; Am Asn Vet Anat (pres, 77-78); Asn Am Vet Med Cols; Am Soc Vet Ethology; Sigma Xi. *Res:* Gross anatomy of domestic animals. *Mailing Add:* Dept Anat Sch Vet Med Purdue Univ 2955 Newman Rd West Lafayette IN 47906

STUMP, JOHN M, PHARMACOLOGY. *Current Pos:* Res pharmacologist, E I Du Pont de Nemours & Co, 64-72, sr res pharmacologist, 72-78, res assoc, pharmaceut res div, 78-85, MGR, PHARMACEUT RES & DEV ADMIN, E I DU PONT DE NEMOURS & CO, 85- *Personal Data:* b Charleston, WVa, June 26, 38; m 64. *Educ:* WVa Univ, BS, 61, MS, 62, PhD(pharmacol), 64. *Res:* Cardiovascular pharmacology. *Mailing Add:* 38 Aronomink Dr Newark DE 19711

STUMP, ROBERT, PHYSICS. *Current Pos:* From asst prof to assoc prof, 50-60, prof physics, 60-88, EMER PROG PHYSICS, UNIV KANS, 88- *Personal Data:* b Indianapolis, Ind, Oct 16, 21; m 43; c 4. *Educ:* Butler Univ, BA, 42; Univ Ill, MS, 48, PhD(physics), 50. *Concurrent Pos:* Consult, Aeronaut Radio, Inc, DC, 52-53; vis scientist, Midwestern Univs Res Asn, Wis, 59, Europ Orgn Nuclear Res, Geneva, 63-64 & Polytech Sch, Paris, 70-71; vis physicist, Brookhaven Nat Lab, 62-63. *Mem:* Fel Am Phys Soc. *Res:* Experimental nuclear and elementary particle physics; angular correlations; low temperature effects; hydrogen and heavy liquid bubble chamber experiments; atmospheric physics; atmospheric dynamics. *Mailing Add:* PO Box 1241 West Falmouth MA 02574

STUMPE, WARREN ROBERT, INDUSTRIAL RESEARCH & DEVELOPMENT MANAGEMENT. *Current Pos:* VPRES, RADIAN CORP, 87- *Personal Data:* b Bronx, NY, July 15, 25; m 52; c 3. *Educ:* US Mil Acad, BS, 45; Cornell Univ, MS, 49; NY Univ, MIE, 65. *Prof Exp:* Var positions to dep gen mgr, AMF, Stamford, Conn, 54-63; exec vpres, Dortech Inc, Stamford, 63-69; dir systs mgt, Mat Handling Group, Rexnord Darien, Conn, 69-71; vpres res & technol & Bus Develop Sector, Rexnord Inc, 71-87. *Concurrent Pos:* Mem, Indust Adv Bd, Col Eng, Univ Wis, Milwaukee, 79-, Wis Gov's Energy Task Force, 80-81 & Indust Liaison Coun, Col Eng, Univ Wis, Madison, 81-; civilian aide to Secy of Army, Wis, 81-85. *Mem:* Indust Res Inst (pres, 85); Soc Am Mil Engrs; Water Pollution Control Fedn. *Res:* Electronics; design-manufacturing productivity; bio-engineering processes; electro-optics and lasers; microprocessor controls. *Mailing Add:* 1531 Greenbrier Lane Thiensville WI 53092

STUMPERS, FRANS LOUIS H M, ELECTROMAGNETIC NOISE OF TERRESTRIAL ORIGIN APPLIANCES. *Current Pos:* RETIRED. *Personal Data:* b Stratum, Neth, Aug 30, 11; m 54, Maria A Driessen; c Hans, Ingrid, Annette, Marc & Monique. *Educ:* Utrecht Univ, Neth, MSc, 37; Delft Univ, Neth, DSc(tech sci), 46. *Hon Degrees:* DSc, Wroelaw, Poland, 94. *Honors & Awards:* Int Commun Award, Inst Elec & Electronics Engrs, 78; Janusz Groskowski Medal, 88. *Prof Exp:* Res scientist, Philips Res Labs,

Eindhoven, Neth, 27-54, res group leader, 54-68, sci adv, 68-74. *Concurrent Pos:* Res assoc, Mass Inst Technol, 52-53; chmn, Comn VI Circuit Info, Int Union Radio Sci, 63-69 & Comn E Electromagnetic Noise Interference, 81-87; prof, Cath Univ Nymegh, 68-82, Bochum Rohr Univ, Ger, 74-75 & State Univ Utrecht, 76-82. *Mem:* Fel Inst Elec & Electronics Engrs; Int Union Radio Sci (vpres, 75-81, hon pres, 90-); Royal Acad Arts & Sci Neth; Hungarian Acad Sci. *Res:* Multiplex telephony; electromagnetic noise; frequency modulation; radio interference; modulation systems; information theory; control theory; software. *Mailing Add:* Elzentlaan 11 Eindhoven 5611 Lg Netherlands. *Fax:* 31-40-743365

STUMPF, DAVID ALLEN, NEUROLOGY, PEDIATRIC NEUROLOGY. *Current Pos:* BENJAMIN BOSHES PROF, CHMN NEUROL & PROF PEDIAT, NORTHWESTERN UNIV MED SCH, 89- *Personal Data:* b Los Angeles, Calif, May 8, 45; m Elizabeth H Dusenbery; c Jennifer F, Kaitrin E, Todd I Coleman & Shilo E Walker. *Educ:* Lewis & Clark Col, Portland, Ore, BA, 66, BA, 67; Univ Colo, MD, 72, PhD(med), 72; Am Bd Pediat, dipl, 78; Am Bd Psychiat & Neurol, dipl, 79. *Honors & Awards:* Chester H Elliott Mem Award, 68; Nat Merit Award, March of Dimes, 68; Gold Reflex Hammer Award, 71. *Prof Exp:* Fel pediat, Univ Rochester, 72-74 & neurol, Harvard Med Sch, 74-77; dir pediat neurol, Univ Colo Health Sci Ctr, 77-85, asst prof pediat & neurol, 77-80, assoc prof, 80-85; dir pediat neurol, Div Pediat Neurol, Children's Mem Hosp, 85-89. *Concurrent Pos:* Vis prof at numerous univs & cols, 79-; assoc ed, Yearbook of Neurol & Neurosurg, 91- *Mem:* Am Acad Neurol; Child Neurol Soc (pres, 85-87); Am Neurol Asn; Soc Pediat Res; Int Child Neurol Asn; Am Pediat Soc; Am Asn Hist Med; AAAS; Asn Univ Prof Neurol; Am Acad Pediat. *Res:* Enzymology of arylsulfatase A in metachromatic leukolystrophy and studies of related lysosomal disorders; biochemical mechanisms underlying mitochondrial disorders; biochemical parameters in Friedreich's disease; brain death in children and on anencephaly; author of numerous publications. *Mailing Add:* 645 N Michigan Ave Suite 1058 Chicago IL 60611. *Fax:* 312-503-0872; *E-Mail:* stumpf@merle.acns.nwu.edu

STUMPF, FOLDEN BURT, PHYSICS. *Current Pos:* From asst prof to assoc prof, 56-66, PROF PHYSICS, OHIO UNIV, 66- *Personal Data:* b Lansing, Mich, Aug 18, 28; m 54, Margaret H Duncan; c Elizabeth & John. *Educ:* Kent State Univ, BS, 50; Univ Mich, MS, 51; Ill Inst Technol, PhD(physics), 56. *Mem:* Fel Acoust Soc Am; Am Asn Physics Teachers; Sigma Xi. *Res:* Ultrasonic transducers; application of ultrasonics to liquids. *Mailing Add:* 71 Mulligan Rd Athens OH 45701. *E-Mail:* fstumpf1@ohiou.edu

STUMPF, H(ARRY) C(LINCH), METALLURGICAL ENGINEERING. *Current Pos:* RETIRED. *Personal Data:* b Buffalo, NY, June 29, 18; m 43; c 2. *Educ:* Univ Mich, BS, 39, MS, 41, PhD(metall eng), 43. *Prof Exp:* Asst prof chem eng, Univ Del, 42-44; Tech engr, Allegany Ballistics Lab, Md, 44-45; sci assoc, Alcoa Res Labs, Aluminum Co Am, 46-76, sci assoc, Alcoa Lab, Alcoa Tech Ctr, 76-80. *Mem:* Am Inst Mining, Metall & Petrol Engrs; Sigma Xi. *Res:* Physical metallurgy, especially of aluminum alloys; x-ray diffraction. *Mailing Add:* 810 Carl Ave New Kensington PA 15068

STUMPF, PAUL KARL, LIPID BIOCHEMISTRY. *Current Pos:* prof & chmn dept, 58-61, 67-68, 70 & 81, EMER PROF BIOCHEM, UNIV CALIF, DAVIS, 84- *Personal Data:* b New York, NY, Feb 23, 19; m 47, Ruth Rodenbeck; c Ann C, Kathryn L, Margaret, David K & Richard F. *Educ:* Harvard Univ, AB, 41; Columbia Univ, PhD(biochem), 45. *Honors & Awards:* Stephen Hales Award, Am Soc Plant Physiologist, 74; Lipid Chem Prize, Am Oil Chemists Soc, 74, Charles Reid Barnes Life Mem Awrd, 92. *Prof Exp:* Chemist, Div War Res, Columbia Univ, 44-46; instr epidemiol, Sch Pub Health, Univ Mich, 46-48; from asst prof to prof plant biochem, Univ Calif, Berkeley, 48-58. *Concurrent Pos:* NIH sr fel, 54-55; NSF sr fel, 61, 68; Guggenheim fel, 62 & 69; ed, J Phytochem, 60-72 & Archives Biochem & Biophys, 60-65, exec ed, 65-88; ed, J Lipid Res, 63-66, 85-, Anal Biochem, 69-80; mem, Physiol Chem Study Sect, NIH, 60-64; metab biol panel, NSF, 65-68; mem, City of Davis Planning Comn, 67-69; vis scientist, Commonwealth Sci & Indust Res Orgn, Canberra ACT, Australia, 75-76; sr US Sci fel, von Humboldt Fedn, Ger, 76; chief scientist, Coop State Res Serv, Competitive Res Grant Off, USDA, 88-90, NRICGO, 90-91. *Mem:* Nat Acad Sci; Am Soc Plant Physiol (pres, 80); Am Oil Chem Soc; Am Soc Biol Chem; foreign mem Royal Danish Acad Arts & Sci. *Res:* Lipid biochemistry of higher plants; photobiosynthesis; developmental biochemistry. *Mailing Add:* Sect Molecular & Cellular Biol Univ Calif Davis CA 95616. *Fax:* 530-752-3085; *E-Mail:* pkstumf@ucdavis.edu

STUMPF, WALTER ERICH, NEUROENDOCRINOLOGY, PHARMACOLOGY. *Current Pos:* assoc prof anat & pharmacol & mem, Lab for Reproductive biol, 70-73, PROF ANAT & PHARMACOL, UNIV NC, CHAPEL HILL, 73- *Personal Data:* b Oelsnitz, Ger, Jan 10, 27; m 61; c 4. *Educ:* Univ Berlin, MD, 52, cert neurol & psychiat, 57; Univ Chicago, PhD(pharmacol), 67. *Hon Degrees:* Dr rer biol hum hc, Ulm, Ger, 87. *Prof Exp:* Intern, Charite Hosp, Univ Berlin, 52-53; resident neurol & psychiat, 53-57; sci asst, Univ Marburg, 58-60 & Lab Radiobiol & Isotope Res, 61-62; res assoc pharmacol, Univ Chicago, 63-67, asst prof, 67-70. *Concurrent Pos:* Trainee psychother & psychoanal, Inst Psychother, WBerlin, 54-56; lectr clin neurol, Charite Hosp, Univ Berlin, 56-57; vis psychiatrist, Maudsley Hosp, London, 57-59; consult, Microtome-Cyrostats, 69-; mem, Neurolbiol Prog, 70-; assoc, Carolina Pop Ctr, 72-; res scientist, Biol Sci Res Ctr, 72-; consult, Life Sci Inst, Res Triangle Park, NC, 73-; mem coun, Inst Lab Animal Resources, 78-81; mem US subcomt, Int Ctr Cybernetics & Systs, World Orgn Gen Systs & Cybernetics; Humboldt Award, 89. *Mem:* AAAS; Am Soc Zoologists; Histochemical Soc; Int Brain Res Orgn; Am Asn Anatomists; Endocrinol Soc; Soc Xenobiotics. *Res:* Development of histochemical techniques; low temperature sectioning and freeze-drying; dry-mount autoradiography for the localization of hormones and drugs in the brain and other tissues; autoradiography of diffusible substances; anatomic neuroendocrinology; vitamin D; sites and mechanisms of action of hormones and drugs; seasonal regulator concept. *Mailing Add:* Dept Cell Biol Anat Univ NC Chapel Hill 108 Taylor Hall Chapel Hill NC 27599-7090

STUMPH, WILLIAM EDWARD, REGULATION OF GENE EXPRESSION. *Current Pos:* PROF CHEM, SAN DIEGO STATE UNIV, 83- *Personal Data:* b Indianapolis, Ind, Dec 20, 48. *Educ:* Purdue Univ, BS, 72; Calif Inst Technol, PhD(biochem), 79. *Prof Exp:* Asst molecular biol, Baylor Col Med, 79-83. *Mem:* Am Soc Cell Biol; AAAS; Am Soc Biochem & Molecular Biol; Am Soc Microbiol. *Res:* Transcriptional regulation of gene expression; DNA sequences and protein factors that regulate the expression of genes encoding the small nuclear RNAs in prosophila. *Mailing Add:* Dept Chem San Diego State Univ San Diego CA 92182-0328. *Fax:* 619-594-4634; *E-Mail:* wstumph@sciences.sdsu.edu

STUNKARD, ALBERT J, PSYCHOSOMATIC MEDICINE, EATING DISORDERS & OBESITY. *Current Pos:* PROF PSYCHIAT, UNIV PA, 76- *Personal Data:* b New York, NY, Feb 7, 22; m 80. *Educ:* Yale Univ, BS, 43; Columbia Univ, MD, 45. *Hon Degrees:* MD, Univ Edinburgh, Scotland, 92. *Honors & Awards:* Menninger Award, Am Col Physicians; Res Award, Am Psychiat Asn, 60 & 80; Goldberger Award, AMA. *Prof Exp:* Resident physician, Johns Hopkins Hosp, 48-51; fel psychiat, 51-52; res fel med, Col Physicians & Surgeons, Columbia Univ, 52-53; Commonwealth fel med, Med Col, Cornell Univ, 53-56, asst prof, 56-57; assoc prof, 57-62, prof psychiat & chmn dept, Sch Med, Univ Pa, 62-73; prof, Stanford Univ, 73-76. *Concurrent Pos:* Fel, Ctr Advan Study Behav Sci, Calif, 71-72. *Mem:* Inst Med-Nat Acad Sci; Am Psychosom Soc (pres, 74); Am Asn Chmn Departments Psychiat (pres, 86); Asn Res Nerv & Ment Dis (pres, 82); Acad Behav Med Res (pres, 86); Soc Behav Med (pres, 90). *Res:* Genetic, metabolic, psychologic, sociologic studies of obesity; behavioral, psychanalytic, pharmacoligic, dietary and surgical treatment of obesity. *Mailing Add:* Dept Psychiat Univ Pa Philadelphia PA 19104-3246

STUNKARD, JIM A, LABORATORY ANIMAL MEDICINE, VETERINARY MICROBIOLOGY. *Current Pos:* RETIRED. *Personal Data:* b Sterling, Colo, Jan 25, 35; m 67; c 1. *Educ:* Colo State Univ, BS, 57, DVM, 59; Tex A&M Univ, MS, 66. *Prof Exp:* Vet, Glasgow Animal Hosp, Ky, 59-61; vet in charge, Sentry Dog Procurement, Training & Med Referral Ctr, USAF Europe, 61-64 & Lab Animal Colonies & Zoonoses Control Ctr, 61-64, resident, Lab Animal Med, Sch Aerospace Med, Brooks AFB, Tex, 64-66, dir, Vet Med Sci Dept, Naval Med Res Inst, Nat Naval Med Ctr, Md, 66-71. *Concurrent Pos:* Vet consult, Turkish Sentry Dog Prog, USAF Europe, 61-63, Can Air Force Europe, 62-64, Bur Med & Surg, US Navy, Washington, DC, Navy Toxicol Unit, Md, 66-71 & AEC, 68-71; US Navy rep ad hoc comt, Dept Defense, 66-67 & Inst Lab Animal Resources, Nat Acad Sci-Nat Res Coun, Washington, DC, 66-71; consult to dean vet med, Colo State Univ, 69-71. *Mem:* Am Vet Med Asn. *Res:* Veterinary medicine, dentistry and surgery, especially all phases of laboratory animal medicine. *Mailing Add:* 3428 Crain Hwy Bowie MD 20716

STUNTZ, CALVIN FREDERICK, CHEMISTRY. *Current Pos:* from asst prof to prof, 46-79, EMER PROF CHEM, UNIV MD, COLLEGE PARK, 80- *Personal Data:* b Buffalo, NY, Aug 6, 18; m 51, Shirley Mason; c Gordon, Janet & Carol. *Educ:* Univ Buffalo, BA, 39, PhD(chem), 47. *Prof Exp:* Teacher high sch, NY, 39-40; anal chemist, Linde Air Prods Co, Union Carbide & Carbon Corp, 40-41; asst, Univ Buffalo, 41-43, 45-46. *Mem:* Am Chem Soc; Sigma Xi. *Res:* Quantitative analysis; chemical microscopy. *Mailing Add:* 13705 Carlisle Ct Silver Spring MD 20904-1101

STUNTZ, GORDON FREDERICK, INORGANIC CHEMISTRY, PETROLEUM CHEMISTRY. *Current Pos:* SECT HEAD, EXXON RES & DEVELOP LABS, EXXON CORP, 78- *Personal Data:* b Washington, DC, Dec 7, 52; m 73, Sue-Anne Emory; c Lori E & Neal F. *Educ:* Pa State Univ, BS, 74; Univ Ill, PhD(inorg chem), 78. *Mem:* Am Chem Soc. *Mailing Add:* Exxon Res & Develop Labs PO Box 2226 Baton Rouge LA 70821-2226

STUPER, ANDREW JOHN, THEORETICAL CHEMISTRY, ANALYTICAL CHEMISTRY. *Current Pos:* AT ICI AMERICAS. *Personal Data:* b Chicago, Ill, Dec 19, 50; m 77. *Educ:* Univ Wis-Superior, BS, 72; Pa State Univ, PhD(anal chem), 77. *Prof Exp:* Vis scientist, Nat Ctr Toxicol Res, 75-76; consult, Parke Davis Co, 76; sr scientist, Rohm & Haas Co, 77- *Mem:* Am Chem Soc; Sigma Xi; Asn Comput Mach. *Res:* Development of methods which enhance understanding of the relationship between chemical structure and biological activity; use of computers in chemistry. *Mailing Add:* ICI Americas GOIE/N-PINS Dept Wilmington DE 19897-0002

STUPIAN, GARY WENDELL, SOLID STATE PHYSICS, SURFACE PHYSICS. *Current Pos:* MEM TECH STAFF, AEROSPACE CORP, 69- *Personal Data:* b Alhambra, Calif, Oct 17, 39. *Educ:* Calif Inst Technol, BS, 61; Univ Ill, Urbana, MS, 63, PhD(physics), 67. *Prof Exp:* Res asst physics, Univ Ill, Urbana, 61-67; res assoc mat sci, Cornell Univ, 67-69. *Mem:* AAAS; Am Phys Soc; Am Vacuum Soc. *Res:* Auger spectroscopy; solid state devices; analytical instrumentation; tunneling microscopy. *Mailing Add:* 1257 Tenth St Hermosa Beach CA 90254. *Fax:* 310-336-1636

STUPP, EDWARD HENRY, DISPLAY, SOLID-STATE PHYSICS. *Current Pos:* MEM TECH STAFF, SR PROG LEADER COMPONENTS & DEVICES GROUP, GROUP DIR DEVICE RES & DEPT HEAD, THIN FILM MAT RES DEPT & DEPT HEAD DISPLAY RES DEPT, PHILIPS LABS DIV, N AM PHILIPS CO, 62- *Personal Data:* b Brooklyn, NY, Dec 10, 32; m 54, Roberta Hendelman; c Lori A & Steven E. *Educ:* City Col New York, BS, 54; Syracuse Univ, MS, 58, PhD(physics), 60. *Prof Exp:* Asst physics, Columbia Univ, 54-55, Watson Lab, 55-56 & Syracuse Univ, 56-59; staff physicist, Thomas J Watson Res Ctr, 59-62. *Concurrent Pos:* Consult infrared imaging, Philips Broadcast Equip Cor, 72-73. *Mem:* Am Phys Soc; Inst Elec & Electronics Engrs; Soc Info Display (vpres). *Res:* Semiconductor device research management and direction including display systems, thin film transistors and flat panel displays, SOI devices/circuits, EPID, displays, high voltage power integrated circuits; solid-state ballast circuits; photoemission; visible and infrared camera tubes, photodetectors, electron multiplication, image tubes; cold cathodes. *Mailing Add:* Philips Labs 345 Scarborough Rd Briarcliff Manor NY 10510. *Fax:* 914-945-6330; *E-Mail:* ehs@philabs.research.philips.com

STUPP, SAMUEL ISAAC, MATERIAL SCIENCE, POLYMER CHEMISTRY. *Current Pos:* PROF, DEPTS MAT SCI & ENG, CHEM & BIO ENG, UNIV, ILL 89- *Personal Data:* b San Jose, Costa Rica, 51. *Educ:* Univ Calif, Los Angeles, BS, 72; Northwestern Univ, PhD(math sci eng), 77. *Mem:* Fel Am Phys Soc; Am Chem Soc; Am Soc Biomat; AAAS. *Res:* Material science; polymer chemistry. *Mailing Add:* Univ Ill 1304 W Green St Urbana IL 61801

STURBAUM, BARBARA ANN, PHYSIOLOGY. *Current Pos:* RESIDENT PASTORAL MINISTER, SACRED HEART CATH CHURCH, LOUISVILLE, 93- *Personal Data:* b Cleveland, Ohio, June 10, 36. *Educ:* Marquette Univ, BS, 59, MS, 61; Univ NMex, PhD(zool), 72. *Prof Exp:* From asst prof to assoc prof biol & earth sci, St John Col, Ohio, 61-75; from asst prof to assoc prof physiol & biol, Sch Med, Oral Roberts Univ, 75-87; assoc prof physiol, Southeastern Col Osteopath Med, 87-93. *Concurrent Pos:* Consult radionuclide metab & toxicity, Lovelace Found Med Educ & Res, 74-75. *Mem:* Radiation Res Soc; Am Soc Zoologists; Inst Theol Encounter with Sci & Technol; AAAS. *Res:* Environmental physiology, particularly behavioral and physiological responses of animals to environmental factors, especially effects of temperature and pollutants on animals. *Mailing Add:* Lion Spring Ave Louisville MS 39339

STURCH, CONRAD RAY, ASTRONOMY. *Current Pos:* mem tech staff, Comput Sci Corp, 76-80, section mgr, 81-86, asst dept mgr, 86-88, dept mgr, 88-90, SR MGR, COMPUT SCI CORP, 90- *Personal Data:* b Cincinnati, Ohio, Nov 5, 37; m 62; c 1. *Educ:* Miami Univ, BA, 58, MS, 60; Univ Calif, Berkeley, PhD(astron), 65. *Prof Exp:* Res asst astron, Lick Observ, Univ Calif, 65; from instr to asst prof, Univ Rochester, 65-73; vis asst prof, Univ Western Ont, 73-74; vis asst prof, Clemson Univ, 74-76. *Mem:* Am Astron Soc; Int Astron Union. *Res:* Variable stars; stellar populations; interstellar reddening; star catalogs. *Mailing Add:* Comput Sci Corp Space Telescope Sci Inst 3700 San Martin Dr Baltimore MD 21218

STURDEVANT, EUGENE J, LIGHT SCATTERING OPTICS & MATH SURFACE ANALYSIS. *Current Pos:* RETIRED. *Personal Data:* b Newton, Kans, Dec 27, 30; m 58, 84, Mollie A Boyd; c Eugene J II, Mark T, Michael W & Jennifer L (Showers). *Educ:* Univ Calif, Berkeley, BSEE, 63. *Prof Exp:* Engr, Eng Physics Lab, E I du Pont de Nemours & Co, Inc, 63-65, res engr, 65-68; res engr, Holotron Corp, 68-71; dir res & develop, Display Enterprises, Inc, 71-74; advan res engr, Proctor-Silex Div, SCM Corp, 76-80, sr scientist, 80-83; sr res engr opticsa, Spitz, Inc, 84-94. *Concurrent Pos:* Consult electro-optics, 71-80; contract res & develop electro-mech optics & heat/mass transfer, Sturdyco, Inc, 83- *Mem:* Optical Soc Am; Soc Photo-Optical Instrument Engrs. *Res:* Applied research, development and design of electro-optical systems and instruments for display, product inspection and process control; planetarium projection light scattering to develop new projection surfaces; electrohemodynamics enhancement of heat & mass transfer; optics and systems, light scattering; surfaces; transfer. *Mailing Add:* 140 Biddle Rd Paoli PA 19301-1104

STUREK, WALTER BEYNON, AEROSPACE & MECHANICAL ENGINEERING. *Current Pos:* Aerospace engr, Wind Tunnels Br, 65-77, br chief, Comput Aerodyn Br, Launch & Flight Div, US Army Ballistic Res Labs, Aberdeen Proving Ground, 77-93, DIV CHIEF COMPUT SCI & TECHNOL DIV, ACISD, ARL, 93- *Personal Data:* b Bartlesville, Okla, July 14, 37; m 65; c 2. *Educ:* Okla State Univ, BS, 60; Mass Inst Technol, SM, 61; Univ Del, PhD(appl sci), 71. *Mem:* Am Soc Mech Engrs; Am Inst Aeronaut & Astronaut. *Res:* Aerodynamics and flight mechanics of projectiles and missiles; computational fluid dynamics of flow over shell at transonic and supersonic velocity. *Mailing Add:* 3500 Carsinwood Dr Aberdeen MD 21001

STURGE, MICHAEL DUDLEY, EXPERIMENTAL SOLID STATE PHYSICS. *Current Pos:* PROF PHYSICS, DARTMOUTH COL, 86- *Personal Data:* b Bristol, Eng, May 25, 31; nat US; m 56, Mary Balk; c David, Thomas, Benedict & Peter. *Educ:* Cambridge Univ, BA, 52, PhD(physics), 57. *Hon Degrees:* MA, Dartmouth Col, 89. *Prof Exp:* Mem staff, Mullard Res Lab, 56-58; sr res fel, Royal Radar Estab, 58-61; mem tech staff, Bell Labs, 61-83, mem Bellcore, 84-86. *Concurrent Pos:* Res assoc, Stanford Univ, 65; vis scientist, Univ BC, 69; vis prof, Technion, Haifa, 72, 76, 81 & 85, Univ Fourier, Grenoble, France, 89 & 91, Trinity Col, Dublin, 89 & 93; exchange visitor, Philips Res Labs, Eindhoven, Neth, 73-74; vis lectr physics, Drew Univ, 75; ed, J Luminescence, 84-90; vis scholar, Univ Sheffield, Eng, 96. *Mem:* Fel Am Phys Soc; Am Asn Physics Teachers. *Res:* Optical properties of solids; semiconductor luminescence; excitons; superlattices; picosecond spectroscopy; plasmas in solids. *Mailing Add:* Physics Dept Wilder Lab Dartmouth Col Hanover NH 03755. *Fax:* 603-646-1446; *E-Mail:* m.sturge@dartmouth.edu

STURGEON, EDWARD EARL, FOREST RECREATION. *Current Pos:* head dept, 66-73, prof, 66-81, EMER PROF FORESTRY, OKLA STATE UNIV, 81- *Personal Data:* b Irving, Ill, Apr 28, 16; m 43, Geraldine (James); c Thomas E & James C. *Educ:* Univ Mich, BSF, 40, MF, 41, PhD(forestry), 54. *Prof Exp:* Instr forest policy, Univ Mich, 50-51; assoc prof forestry & head dept forestry & biol, Mich Technol Univ, 51-59; assoc prof forestry, Humboldt State Col, 59-66, coordr dept, 60-66. *Concurrent Pos:* Chmn, Okla Bd Regist Foresters, 78-80, Ouachita Soc Am Foresters-Natural Areas Com, 81-86. *Mem:* Nat Wildlife Fedn; fel Soc Am Foresters; Am Forestry Asn. *Res:* Public-private balance in forest land ownership; forest environment; cottonwood reproduction and management. *Mailing Add:* 2616 Quail Ridge Ct Stillwater OK 74074

STURGEON, GEORGE DENNIS, SOLID STATE CHEMISTRY, HIGH TEMPERATURE CHEMISTRY. *Current Pos:* asst prof, 64-73, ASSOC PROF CHEM, UNIV NEBR, LINCOLN, 73- *Personal Data:* b Sioux Falls, SDak, Sept 21, 37; m 67; c 2. *Educ:* Univ NDak, BS, 59; Mich State Univ, PhD(chem), 64. *Prof Exp:* Instr chem, Mich State Univ, 64. *Mem:* AAAS; Am Chem Soc; Sigma Xi. *Res:* Chemistry of refractory materials; high-temperature thermodynamics; chemistry of complex fluorides. *Mailing Add:* Dept Chem Univ Nebr Lincoln NE 68588-0304

STURGEON, MYRON THOMAS, PALEONTOLOGY, STRATIGRAPHY. *Current Pos:* from asst prof to prof 46-78, EMER PROF GEOL, OHIO UNIV, 78- *Personal Data:* b Salem, Ohio, Apr 27, 08; m 46; c 2. *Educ:* Mt Union Col, AB, 31; Ohio State Univ, AM, 33, PhD(paleont), 36. *Honors & Awards:* Mather Award, Ohio Div Geol Surv, 87. *Prof Exp:* Found inspector, US Corps Engrs, Ohio, 34; from asst to assoc prof geol, Mich State Norm Col, 37-46. *Mem:* AAAS; Paleont Soc; assoc Soc Econ Paleont & Mineral; fel Geol Soc Am; Am Ornith Union. *Res:* Stratigraphy and invertebrate paleontology of the Pennsylvanian system of eastern Ohio. *Mailing Add:* 13220 Robinson Ridge Rd Athens OH 45701

STURGEON, RALPH EDWARD, ATOMIC ABSORPTION SPECTROMETRY, TRACE ELEMENT ANALYSIS. *Current Pos:* Res assoc, Nat Res Coun Can, 77-80, asst res officer, 80-83, assoc res officer, 83-89, SR RES OFFICER, DIV CHEM, NAT RES COUN CAN, 89- *Personal Data:* m 73, Dorothy Bischoff; c Christopher & Stephanie. *Educ:* Carleton Univ, Ottawa, BSc, 73, PhD(analytical chem), 77. *Honors & Awards:* Barringer Award, Spectros Soc Can, 86; WAE McBryle Medal, Chem Inst Can, 90. *Concurrent Pos:* Adj prof, Dept Chem, Carleton Univ, 93-; varian univ lectr analytical chem, Univ Western Ont, 93. *Mem:* Fel Chem Inst Can. *Res:* Development of new improved methods for trace metal analysis including sample processing procedures, analytical techniques and instrument development; investigations into the fundamental parameters of operation of the graphite furnace and mechanisms of atom formation. *Mailing Add:* Nat Res Coun Can Ottawa ON K1A 0R6 Can. *Fax:* 613-993-2451; *E-Mail:* ralph.sturgeon@arc.ca

STURGEON, ROY V, JR, PLANT PATHOLOGY. *Current Pos:* FIELD CONSULT, OKLA PEANUT COMN, 86- *Personal Data:* b Wichita, Kans, July 1, 24; m 50; c 2. *Educ:* Okla State Univ, BS, 61, MS, 64; Univ Minn, Minneapolis, PhD(plant path), 67. *Prof Exp:* Instr bot & plant path, Col Agr & Agr Exten, Okla State Univ, 63-65, from instr to assoc prof, 67-74, prof plant path, 74-86, exten plant pathologist, Fed Exten Serv, 67-86. *Concurrent Pos:* Private Plant Health Consult Serv, Okla, 67- *Mem:* Am Phytopath Soc; Soc Nematol; Am Soc Agron. *Res:* Program development and chemical evaluation for disease control, especially fungicides and nematicides. *Mailing Add:* 1729 Linda Ave Stillwater OK 74075

STURGES, LEROY D, FLUID MECHANICS, RHEOLOGY. *Current Pos:* ASSOC PROF ENG MECH, AEEM DEPT, IOWA STATE UNIV, 77- *Personal Data:* b Slayton, Minn, 1945; m 69, Sue A Davis; c Jeffrey L & Jason L. *Educ:* Univ Minn, BAeroE, 67, MS, 75, PhD(eng mech), 77. *Prof Exp:* Space syst analyst, Foreign Technol Div, Systs Command, USAF, 68-72; lectr, AEM Dept, Univ Minn, 77. *Mem:* Sigma Xi; Am Soc Eng Educ; Soc Rheol; Am Acad Mech. *Res:* Investigating flow characteristics of non-linear fluids and their relationship to the rheological properties of the fluids. *Mailing Add:* Iowa State Univ 2019 Black Eng Bldg Ames IA 50011-2162. *E-Mail:* sturges@iastate.edu

STURGES, STUART, NUCLEAR ENGINEERING. *Current Pos:* RETIRED. *Personal Data:* b Altamont, NY, July 1, 13; wid; c 2. *Educ:* Rensselaer Polytech Inst, ChE, 35, MS, 39, PhD(phys chem), 41. *Prof Exp:* Asst instr biochem, Albany Med Col, 35-37, instr, 39-41; asst instr chem eng & chem, Rensselaer Polytech Inst, 37-39; sr chem res engr, Merck & Co, Inc, 41-42, Winthrop Chem Co, 42; prin chem engr, Manhattan Dist, Corps Engrs, US War Dept, 42-46; mgr var opers, Knolls Atomic Power Lab, Gen Elec Co, 48-78. *Concurrent Pos:* Mem staff, Joint Task Force One (Bikini Test), 46; instr chem, Adirondack Community Col, 74-76. *Mem:* Sigma Xi; Am Chem Soc; Am Inst Chemists; AAAS. *Res:* Physical properties of biological compounds; continuous process designs for organic preparations; chemical and metallurgical research; nuclear engineering. *Mailing Add:* 32 Stewart Ave South Glens Falls NY 12803-5127

STURGES, WILTON, III, PHYSICAL OCEANOGRAPHY. *Current Pos:* assoc prof, 72-76, chmn dept, 76-82 & 85-88, PROF OCEANOG, FLA STATE UNIV, 76- *Personal Data:* b Dothan, Ala, July 21, 35; m 57, Mary P Kennedy; c James W, William G & Sarah F. *Educ:* Auburn Univ, BS, 57; Johns Hopkins Univ, MA, 63, PhD(oceanog), 66. *Prof Exp:* Res asst phys oceanog, Johns Hopkins Univ, 63-66; from asst prof to assoc prof, Univ RI, 66-72. *Concurrent Pos:* Instr, US Naval Res Off Sch, 63-66; assoc ed, J Geophys Res, 68-70; mem ocean-wide surv panel, Comt Oceanog, Nat Acad Sci, 68-71, Buoy Technol Assessment Panel Marine Bd, Nat Acad Eng, 72-74, Ocean Sci Comt, Nat Acad Sci, 75-77 & Comn Marine Geodesy, Am Geophys Union, 74-78, Comn Global & Environ Change, 93-; mem adv panel oceanog, NSF, 75-77; mem, Panel on Sea-Level Change, Geophys Study Comm, Nat Res Coun, 84-90; Comm Eng Implications changes in relative mean sea level, Marine Bd, Nat Res Coun, 84-89; mem, Fla Task Force on Oil Spill Risk Assessment, 88-90; mem adv comt climate & global change, Nat Oceanic & Atmospheric Admin, 90-93. *Mem:* Am Geophys Union; Am Meteorol Soc; Oceanog Soc. *Res:* Ocean circulations, especially Gulf of Mexico and North Atlantic; rise of sea level. *Mailing Add:* Dept Oceanog Fla State Univ Tallahassee FL 32306-3048. *E-Mail:* sturges@ocean.fsu.edu

STURGESS, GEOFFREY J, AERONAUTICAL RESEARCH ENGINEERING. *Current Pos:* SR RES ENGR, PRATT & WHITNEY ENG, CONN. *Honors & Awards:* Energy Systs Award, Am Inst Aeronaut & Astronaut, 94. *Mailing Add:* 1747 Lesourd Dr Beaver Creek OH 45432-2478

STURGESS, JENNIFER MARY, MICROBIOLOGY, PATHOLOGY. *Current Pos:* assoc prof path, 71-90, assoc dean res, Fac Med, 90-93, PROF PATH, UNIV TORONTO, 90-; MED DIR, PARKE DAVIS CAN. *Personal Data:* b Nottingham, Gt Brit, Sept 26, 44; m 66, Robert W; c Claire, Paul & Hugh. *Educ:* Bristol Univ, BSc, 65; Univ London, PhD(path), 70. *Honors & Awards:* Sci Award, Can Asn Pathologists, 75. *Prof Exp:* Res asst, Clin Res Unit, Med Res Coun Eng, 65-66; lectr exp path, Inst Dis Chest, Brompton Hosp, Univ London, 66-70. *Concurrent Pos:* Res fel path, Hosp for Sick Children, Toronto, 70-71, Med Res Coun Can term grants & scholar, 71-85; sr scientist, Hosp Sick Children, 71-79; ed, Proceedings Micros Soc Can, 73-90 & Perspectives in Cystic Fibrosis, 80; Cystic Fibrosis Term grant, 74-80; Ont Thoracic Soc grant, 75-80, Med Res Coun term grant, 76-85; dir, Warner Lambert Res Inst, 79-86, vpres sci affairs, Warner Lambert Can Inc, 86-90; consult scientist, Hosp Sick Children, 79-80; dir, Versax Serv Ltd, 82-; WHO adv, Cystic Fibrosis, 83 & Gen; mem, Sci Coun Can, 87-91; mem, Med Res Coun, 90-97; dir, Princess Margaret Hosp, 92-93. *Mem:* Int Acad Path; Am Acad Path; Micros Soc Can. *Res:* Defense mechanisms in the normal lung and in chronic lung diseases; ciliary defects and human respiratory disease; cystic fibrosis. *Mailing Add:* 80 Hazelton Ave Toronto ON M5R 2E2 Can

STURGILL, BENJAMIN CALEB, MEDICINE, PATHOLOGY. *Current Pos:* from instr to assoc prof, 64-76, actg chmn dept, 74-76, PROF PATH, SCH MED, UNIV VA, 76-, ASSOC DEAN & DIR ADMIS, 91- *Personal Data:* b Wise Co, Va, Apr 27, 34; m 55, Eleanore Burchell; c Rebecca K & Benjamin C II. *Educ:* Berea Col, BA, 56; Univ Va, MD, 60. *Prof Exp:* Intern med, NY, Hosp-Cornell Med Ctr, 60-61; resident path, Univ Va, 61-62; clin assoc, NIH, 62-64. *Concurrent Pos:* Traveling fel, Royal Soc Med, 72. *Mem:* Int Acad Path; Am Asn Path; Am Soc Nephrology; Int Soc Nephrology. *Res:* Immunopathology and renal diseases. *Mailing Add:* Pathol Dept Sch Med Univ Va Med Ctr Box 214 Charlottesville VA 22908-0001

STURGIS, BERNARD MILLER, PETROLEUM CHEMISTRY. *Current Pos:* RETIRED. *Personal Data:* b Butler, Ind, Nov 27, 11; m 36; c 2. *Educ:* DePauw Univ, AB, 33; Mass Inst Technol, PhD(org chem), 36. *Honors & Awards:* Horning Mem Award, Soc Automotive Eng, 56; Rector Award, 58. *Prof Exp:* Res chemist, Jackson Lab, E I Du Pont de Nemours & Co, Inc, 36-42, group leader auxiliary chem sect, Elastomer Div, 42-46, head petrol chem div, 46-51 & combustion & scavenging div, Petrol Lab, 51-53, from asst dir to dir, 53-62, mgr mid-continent region, Petrol Chem Div, 62-64, mgr, Patents & Contracts Div, 64-76. *Mem:* Am Chem Soc; Combustion Inst; Licensing Exec Soc. *Res:* Synthetic organic and rubber chemicals; accelerators; antioxidants; sponge blowing agents; peptizing agents; nonsulfur vulcanization of rubber; petroleum additives; tetraethyl lead; combustion; lead scavenging from engines. *Mailing Add:* 407 Hawthorne Dr Wilmington DE 19802-1200

STURKIE, PAUL DAVID, PHYSIOLOGY. *Current Pos:* from assoc prof to prof, Rutgers Univ, 44-77, chmn, Dept Poultry Sci, 60-63 & Dept Environ Physiol, 71-77, EMER PROF PHYSIOL, BARTLETT HALL COOK COL, RUTGERS UNIV, 77- *Personal Data:* b Proctor, Tex, Sept 18, 09; m 40, 64, Betty W Welch; c Robin, Stephanie & Victor Jr. *Educ:* Tex A&M Univ, BS, 33, MS, 36; Cornell Univ, PhD(genetics, physiol), 39. *Honors & Awards:* Poultry Sci Res Award, 47; Borden Award, 56. *Prof Exp:* Res asst, Tex A&M Univ, 34-36 & Cornell Univ, 36-39; assoc prof, Auburn Univ, 39-44. *Concurrent Pos:* Guest reseacher, Agr Res Coun, Gt Brit, 60. *Mem:* Fel AAAS; Am Physiol Soc; fel Poultry Sci Asn; Am Heart Asn; Microcirculatory Soc; fel Royal Soc Edinburgh. *Res:* Physiology of reproduction, heart and circulation of birds; author of more than 170 technical reports and several textbook editions. *Mailing Add:* 103 Fern Rd East Brunswick NJ 08816

STURLEY, ERIC AVERN, MATHEMATICS. *Current Pos:* instr, 57-61, actg head div sci & math, 58-60, asst dean grad sch, 62-64, prof, 61-84, EMER PROF MATH, SOUTHERN ILL UNIV, EDWARDSVILLE, 84- *Personal Data:* b Dibden Hants, Eng, June 9, 15; nat US; m 47, 81; c 3. *Educ:* Yale Univ, BA, 37, MA, 39; Univ Grenoble, cert, 45; Columbia Univ, EdD, 56. *Prof Exp:* Instr, Berkshire Sch, 41-42 & Lawrenceville Sch, 46-47; from instr to assoc prof math, Allegheny Col, 47-57. *Concurrent Pos:* Consult, Talon, Inc, Pa, 55-57; chief party, Southern Ill Univ Contract Team, Mali, WAfrica, 64-67, Nepal, 70-71; chief acad adv, 59-, coordr, Deans Col, Southern Ill Univ, Edwardsville, 67- *Mem:* Am Math Soc; Math Asn Am. *Res:* Statistics; history of mathematics. *Mailing Add:* 553 Buena Vista Edwardsville IL 62025-2070

STURM, EDWARD, GEOLOGY, MINERALOGY. *Current Pos:* RETIRED. *Personal Data:* US citizen; m 50; c 3. *Educ:* NY Univ, BA, 48; Univ Minn, MSc, 50; Rutgers Univ, PhD(geol), 57. *Prof Exp:* Res geologist, Hebrew Univ Jerusalem, 51-52; asst res specialist crystallog, Bur Eng Res, Rutgers Univ, 56-58; asst prof geol, Tex Technol Col, 58-63; from asst prof to prof geol, Brooklyn Col, Pub Higher Educ, 74-85. *Mem:* Geol Soc Am; Mineral Soc Am; Am Crystallog Asn. *Res:* Clay mineralogy; crystallography of silicates; preferred orientation studies; geochemistry of solids. *Mailing Add:* 1079 E 21st St Brooklyn NY 11210

STURM, JAMES EDWARD, PHOTOCHEMISTRY, MASS SPECTROMETRY. *Current Pos:* from asst prof to prof, 56-95, EMER PROF PHYS CHEM, LEHIGH UNIV, 95- *Personal Data:* b New Ulm, Minn, Mar 28, 30; m 55, Margaret R Adams; c 7. *Educ:* St John's Univ, Minn, BA, 51; Univ Notre Dame, PhD(chem), 57. *Prof Exp:* Res assoc, Univ Wis-Madison, 55-56. *Concurrent Pos:* Res assoc, Brookhaven Nat Lab, 57 & Argonne Nat Lab, 58; consult, Edgewood Arsenal, US Army, 68-69; fac res participant, Air Force Geophys Lab, 85, 86 & ARDEC, 87. *Mem:* Am Chem Soc; Sigma Xi. *Res:* Photochemical kinetics; rates of elementary processes, especially reactions of excited or high-velocity (hot) atoms; vacuum ultraviolet photochemistry; photochemistry of metal-ligand complexes; radiation chemistry. *Mailing Add:* Dept Chem No 6 Lehigh Univ Bethlehem PA 18015. *Fax:* 610-758-6536; *E-Mail:* jesd@lehigh.edu

STURM, WALTER ALLAN, computer science, for more information see previous edition

STURM, WILLIAM JAMES, NUCLEAR PHYSICS, SOLID STATE PHYSICS. *Current Pos:* RETIRED. *Personal Data:* b Marshfield, Wis, Sept 10, 17; m 51; c 2. *Educ:* Marquette Univ, BS, 40; Univ Chicago, MS, 42; Univ Wis, PhD(physics), 49. *Honors & Awards:* Commemorative Medal, Atomic Indust Forum, Am Nuclear Soc, 62; Nuclear Pioneer Award, Soc Nuclear Med, 77. *Prof Exp:* Asst nuclear physics, Manhattan Proj, Metall Lab, Univ Chicago, 42-43, jr physicist, 43-46; assoc physicist & group leader, Argonne Nat Lab, 46-47; consult physicist, 49-51; from physicist to sr physicist, Oak Ridge Nat Lab, 51-56; assoc physicist, Int Inst Nuclear Sci & Eng, Argonne Nat Lab, 56- 60, Off Col & Univ Coop, 65-67, asst dir, Appl Physics Div, 67-84. *Mem:* AAAS; Am Phys Soc; Am Nuclear Soc. *Res:* Neutron cross sections and diffraction; nuclear reactions, reactor physics and absolute nuclear particle energies; irradiation effects in solids; subcritical and critical reactor studies; reactor safety. *Mailing Add:* 5400 Woodland Ave Western Springs IL 60558

STURMAN, JOHN ANDREW, BIOCHEMISTRY, NUTRITION. *Current Pos:* Assoc res scientist, 67-79, RES SCIENTIST, DEVELOP NEUROCHEM LAB, DEPT DEVELOP BIOCHEM, INST BASIC RES DEVELOP DISABILITIES, 80-, DEPT CHMN, 84- *Personal Data:* b Hove, Eng, Aug 10, 41. *Educ:* Univ London, BSc, 62, MSc, 63, PhD(biochem), 66. *Concurrent Pos:* Res study grant red cell metab, King's Col Hosp, Med Sch, Univ London, 63-67; lectr, Can Nat Inst Nutrit, 85. *Mem:* AAAS; Am Inst Nutrit; Brit Biochem Soc; Am Soc Neurochem; Int Soc Neurochemistry; Int Soc Develope Neurosci; Am Soc Biol Chem; Am Soc Neurosci; Am Asn Mental Deficiency. *Res:* Sulfur amino acid metabolism in normal and vitamin B-6 deficiency, in fetal, neonatal and adult tissue and in inborn errors of metabolism; axonal transport in developing nerves; nutrition and brain development. *Mailing Add:* Develop Neurochem Lab Inst Basic Res Ment Retardation 1050 Forest Hill Rd Staten Island NY 10314-6330

STURMAN, LAWRENCE STUART, BIOMEDICAL RESEARCH & PUBLIC POLICY. *Current Pos:* res physician virol, 70-92, dir, Div Clin Sci, 89-92, DIR, WADSWORTH CTR, NY STATE DEPT HEALTH, 92-; PROF, DEPT BIOMED, SCH PUB HEALTH, NY STATE UNIV, ALBANY, 95- *Personal Data:* b Detroit, Mich, Mar 13, 38; m 59, Audrie Summers; c Rachel, Serena, Nicole & David. *Educ:* Northwestern Univ, BS, 57, MS & MD, 60; Rockefeller Univ, PhD(virol), 68. *Prof Exp:* Intern, Hosp Univ Pa, 60-61; staff assoc virol, Nat Inst Allergy & Infectious Dis, 68-70; from asst prof microbiol & immunol, Albany Med Col, 79-93; assoc prof microbiol & immunol, Med Col, NY State Univ, Albany, 79-93, chmn, Dept Biomed Sci, Sch Pub Health, 85-95. *Concurrent Pos:* Exec dir, NY State Health Res Coun, 86- *Mem:* Am Soc Microbiol; Am Soc Virol; AAAS; NY Acad Sci; Sigma Xi. *Res:* Viral pathogenesis; public health; scientific basis of public health practice; biomedical research and public policy; laboratory regulation/quality assurance; graduate education in biomedical sciences; viral disease. *Mailing Add:* Wadsworth Ctr PO Box 509 Albany NY 12201-0509. *Fax:* 518-474-3439; *E-Mail:* lawrence.sturman@wadsworth.org

STURMER, DAVID MICHAEL, SOLID STATE CHEMISTRY & PHOTOGRAPHIC CHEMISTRY. *Current Pos:* sr chemist, Eastman Kodak, 67-72, res assoc, 72-77, res lab head, 77-93, PATENT SPECIALIST, EASTMAN KODAK CO RES LABS, 93- *Personal Data:* b Norfolk, Va, July 27, 40; m 64; c 2. *Educ:* Stanford Univ, BS, 62; Ore State Univ, PhD(org chem), 66. *Prof Exp:* NSF fel chem, Yale Univ, 66-67. *Concurrent Pos:* Adj prof, Dept Photog Sci, Rochester Inst Technol, 77-82. *Mem:* Am Chem Soc;

Sigma Xi; Soc Photog Scientists & Engrs. *Res:* Molecular orbital calculations; heterocyclic dye synthesis; spectral sensitization of silver halides; solid state chemistry; radiotracer methods; chemical catalysis. *Mailing Add:* 41 Parkridge Pittsford NY 14534

STURR, JOSEPH FRANCIS, VISUAL SCIENCE. *Current Pos:* from asst prof to assoc prof, 64-72, PROF PHYSIOL PSYCHOL, SYRACUSE UNIV, 72- *Personal Data:* b Syracuse, NY, Apr 29, 33; m 60; c 4. *Educ:* Wesleyan Univ, BA, 55; Fordham Univ, MA, 57; Univ Rochester, PhD(psychol), 62. *Prof Exp:* Asst exp psychol, Fordham Univ, 56-57 & Univ Rochester, 57-58, asst vision res lab, 58-61; USPHS res fel psychophysiol lab, Ill State Psychiat Inst, 61-64. *Concurrent Pos:* Consult, Vet Admin Hosp, Syracuse, 65- *Mem:* AAAS; Optical Soc Am; Asn Res Vision & Ophthal; Sigma Xi. *Res:* Vision; psychophysics; spatio-temporal factors; flicker, increment thresholds; target detection; visual masking and excitability; sensitivity; rapid adaptation. *Mailing Add:* 114 Dorset Rd Syracuse NY 13210-3048

STURROCK, PETER ANDREW, ASTROPHYSICS, PLASMA PHYSICS. *Current Pos:* res assoc, Stanford Univ, 59-60, prof eng sci & appl physics, 61-66, chmn, Inst Plasma Res, 64-74, dep dir, Ctr Space Sci & Astrophys, 83-92, PROF SPACE SCI & ASTROPHYS, DEPT APPL PHYSICS, STANFORD UNIV, 66-, DIR, CTR SPACE SCI & ASTROPHYS, 92- *Personal Data:* b Grays, Eng, Mar 20, 24; US citizen; m 63, Marilyn F Stenson; c 3. *Educ:* Cambridge Univ, BA, 45, MA, 48, PhD(math), 51. *Honors & Awards:* Gravity Found Prize, 67; Hale Prize, Am Astron Soc, 86; Arctowski Medal, Nat Acad Sci, 90; Space Sci Award, Am Inst Aeronaut & Astronaut, 92. *Prof Exp:* Harwell sr fel, Atomic Energy Res Estab, Eng, 51-53; fel, St John's Col, Cambridge Univ, 52-55; res assoc microwaves, Stanford Univ, 55-58; Ford fel plasma physics, Europ Orgn Nuclear Res, Switz, 58-59. *Concurrent Pos:* Consult, Varian Assocs, Calif, 57-64 & NASA Ames Res Ctr, 62-64; dir, Enrico Fermi Summer Sch Plasma-Astrophys, Varenna, Italy, 66; chmn, Plasma Physics Div, Am Phys Soc, 67, Solar Physics Div, Am Astron Soc, 72-74 & advocacy panel, Physics Sun, 80-83; mem, Phys Sci Comt, NASA; dir solar flare, Skylab Workshop, 76-77. *Mem:* Fel AAAS; Am Astron Soc; Int Astron Union; fel Am Phys Soc; fel Royal Astron Soc; Soc Sci Explor (pres, 82-). *Res:* Plasma astrophysics; solar physics; high-energy astrophysics; scientific inference; anomalous phenomena. *Mailing Add:* 802 Cedro Way Palo Alto CA 94305-4055. *Fax:* 650-723-4840

STURROCK, PETER EARLE, ANALYTICAL CHEMISTRY, ELECTROCHEMISTRY. *Current Pos:* From asst prof to assoc prof, 60-78, EMER PROF CHEM, GA INST TECHNOL, 78- *Personal Data:* b Miami, Fla, Dec 6, 29; m 58, Elizabeth Zapf; c Kenneth. *Educ:* Univ Fla, BS, 51, BA, 51; Stanford Univ, MS, 54; Ohio State Univ, PhD(chem), 60. *Mem:* Am Chem Soc. *Res:* Instrumental chemical analysis; equilibria of complex ions; kinetics of electrode reactions; applications of computers to chemical instrumentation. *Mailing Add:* Dept Chem Ga Inst Technol Atlanta GA 30332-0400. *Fax:* 404-894-7452

STURTEVANT, BRADFORD, FLUID MECHANICS. *Current Pos:* Res fel fluid mech, 60-62, from asst prof to assoc prof, 62-72, exec officer aeronaut, 71-76, PROF AERONAUT, CALIF INST TECHNOL, 71- *Personal Data:* b New Haven, Conn, Nov 1, 33; m 58; c 1. *Educ:* Yale Univ, BS, 55; Calif Inst Technol, PhD(fluid mech), 60. *Concurrent Pos:* Res fel & Gordon McKay vis lectr, Harvard Univ, 65-66. *Mem:* AAAS; Am Phys Soc; Am Inst Aeronaut & Astronaut. *Res:* Experimental fluid mechanics; shock waves; vapor explosions; nonlinear acoustics. *Mailing Add:* 1419 E Palm St Altadena CA 91001-2023

STURTEVANT, FRANK MILTON, REPRODUCTIVE MEDICINE, CHRONOBIOLOGY. *Current Pos:* PHARMACEUT CONSULT, 90- *Personal Data:* b Evanston, Ill, Mar 8, 27; m 50, Ruthann Patterson; c Jill (Rovani), Jan (Cassidy) & Barbara (deceased). *Educ:* Lake Forest Col, BA, 48; Northwestern Univ, MS, 50, PhD(biol), 51. *Honors & Awards:* Pres Award, Mead Johnson & Co, 67. *Prof Exp:* Asst, Northwestern Univ, 49-51; sr investr, G D Searle & Co, 51-58; sr pharmacologist, Smith Kline & French Labs, 58-60; dir sci & regulatory affairs, Mead Johnson & Co, 60-72; lectr genetics, Univ Evansville, 72; assoc dir res & develop, G D Searle & Co, 72-80, dir, Off Sci Affairs, 80-86, sr dir, Med Sci Info Dept, 87-90. *Mem:* Drug Info Asn; Soc Exp Biol & Med; Am Soc Pharmacol & Exp Therapeut; Am Fertil Soc; Am Col Toxicol; Fallopius Int Soc; Int Soc Chronobiology; US Int FNDN Studies Reproduction; Soc Adv Contraception. *Res:* Hypertension; pharmacokinetics; biochemorphology; glucoregulation; genetics; reproduction; central nervous system; chronobiology; natural history. *Mailing Add:* 5760 Midnight Pass Rd Suite 610-D Sarasota FL 34242. *Fax:* 941-346-0262; *E-Mail:* fsturtevan@aol.com

STURTEVANT, JULIAN MUNSON, BIOPHYSICAL CHEMISTRY. *Current Pos:* from assoc prof to prof chem, Yale Univ, 46-77, chmn dept, 59-62, assoc dir, Sterling Chem Lab, 50-59, prof, 62-77, EMER PROF CHEM, MOLECULAR BIOPHYS & BIOCHEM, YALE UNIV, 77-, SR RES SCIENTIST, 77- *Personal Data:* b Edgewater, NJ, Aug 9, 08; m 29, Elizabeth Reihl; c Ann S (Ormsby) & Bradford. *Educ:* Columbia Univ, AB, 27; Yale Univ, PhD(chem), 31. *Hon Degrees:* ScD, Ill Col, 62; Regensburg Univ, WGer, 79. *Honors & Awards:* Huffman Award, Calorimetry Conf US, 68; William Clyde DeVane Award, 78; Wilbur Lucius Cross Award, 87; Alexander von Humboldt Sr Scientist Award, Regensburg Univ, WGer, 78-79. *Prof Exp:* From instr to asst prof chem, Yale Univ, 31-43; staff mem, Radiation Lab, Mass Inst Technol, 43-46. *Concurrent Pos:* Consult, Mobil Oil Co, 46-69; Guggenheim fel & Fulbright scholar, Cambridge Univ, 55-56; Fulbright scholar, Univ Adelaide, 62-63; vis prof, Univ Calif, San Diego, 66-67 & 69-70; vis fel, Seattle Res Ctr, Battelle Mem Inst, 72-73; mem, US Nat Comt Data Sci & Technol, 76; vis scholar, Stanford Univ, 75-76. *Mem:* Nat Acad Sci; Am Chem Soc; fel Am Acad Arts & Sci; AAAS. *Res:* The study of biochemical problems by physiochemical methods, with particular application of microcalorimetry. *Mailing Add:* Sterling Chem Lab Yale Univ New Haven CT 06520. *Fax:* 203-432-6144

STURTEVANT, RUTHANN PATTERSON, GROSS ANATOMY, BIOLOGICAL RHYTHMS. *Current Pos:* from asst prof to prof, 75-89, EMER PROF ANAT & SURG, STRITCH SCH MED, LOYOLA UNIV, CHICAGO, 89- *Personal Data:* b Rockford, Ill, Feb 7, 27; m 50, Frank M; c Jill (Rovani), Jan (Cassidy) & Barbara (deceased). *Educ:* Northwestern Univ, Evanston, BS, 49, MS, 50; Univ Ark, Little Rock, PhD(anat), 72. *Prof Exp:* From instr to asst prof life sci, Ind State Univ, Evansville, 65-74; adj asst prof, Sch Med, Ind Univ, 72-74; lectr, Sch Med, Northwestern Univ, 74-75. *Mem:* Am Asn Anatomists; Int Soc Chronobiology; Sigma Xi; AAAS; Soc Exp Biol & Med; Int Soc Biomed Res Alcoholism; Am Soc Pharmacol Exp Ther. *Res:* Chronobiology; chronopharmacokinetics; anatomy; fetal alcohol syndrome. *Mailing Add:* 5760 Midnight Pass Rd No 610D Sarasota FL 34242. *Fax:* 941-346-0262

STURZENEGGER, AUGUST, ORGANIC CHEMISTRY, CHEMICAL ENGINEERING. *Current Pos:* OWNER SEVERAL INVEST COS, 82- *Personal Data:* b Switz, May 3, 21; nat US; m 55; c 3. *Educ:* Swiss Fed Inst Technol, MS, 45, PhD, 48. *Prof Exp:* Chemist, Royal Dutch Shell Co, Holland, 48; chemist, Steinfels, Inc Switz, 49; chemist, 49-59, dir advan technol, Hoffman-La Roche Inc, 59-77, dir, Pharmaceut & Diag Opers, 77-82. *Mem:* Am Chem Soc; Am Astronaut Soc; Am Inst Chem Eng; Swiss Chem Soc; Am Phys Soc; Sigma Xi. *Res:* Process development; detergents; petroleum chemistry; pharmaceuticals; systems analysis and automation; multidisciplinary interactions. *Mailing Add:* E 25 Rensselaer Rd Essex Fells NJ 07021-1403

STUSHNOFF, CECIL, COLD STRESS PHYSIOLOGY, CRYOPRESERVATION. *Current Pos:* sr res scientist, Biochem Dept, 89-90, PROF HORT & BIOCHEM, COLO STATE UNIV, FT COLLINS, 90- *Personal Data:* b Saskatoon, Sask, Aug 12, 40; m 63, Jeannette P Baptist; c Shawna M & Stafan B. *Educ:* Univ Sask, BSA, 63, MSc, 64; Rutgers Univ, PhD(hort, embryol), 67. *Honors & Awards:* Paul Howe Shepard Award; Joseph Harvey Gourley Award; G Darrow Award; C J Bishop Award. *Prof Exp:* Res asst, Dept Hort, Rutgers Univ, 64-67; asst prof fruit breeding, Univ Minn, 67-70, assoc prof, 70-75, prof hort sci & landscape archit, 75-80; prof hort & head dept, Univ Sask, 81-89. *Concurrent Pos:* Consult, Walter Butler Corp & North Gro, Inc, St Paul, Minn; vis prof & guest researcher, Inst Biol & Geol, Univ Tromso, Norway; prin horticulturist res admin, Sci & Educ Admin, USDA, Washington, DC; owner & mgr, White Rock Lake Farm & Berry Patch, St Paul, Minn; int travel grant, Hill Family Found; assoc ed, Can J Plant Sci, 83-; vis scientist, USDA Nat Seed Storage Lab, 87-88, affil tac adminr, CSRS. *Mem:* Fel Am Soc Hort Sci; Am Chem Soc; Am Soc Plant Physiol; Soc Crybiol; Am Pomol Soc; AAAS. *Res:* Cryopreservation and genetic stability of germplasm; preservation of fruit crop genetic resources; transformation of strawberry; biochemistry of endogenous cryoprotectants; plant biotechnology of environmental stresses. *Mailing Add:* Dept Hort Colo State Univ Ft Collins CO 80523-0001. *Fax:* 970-491-7745; *E-Mail:* stushnof@lamar.colostate.edu

STUSNICK, ERIC, ACOUSTICS. *Current Pos:* prog mgr, 77-87, dept mgr, 87-93, DEP DIR RES, WYLE LABS, 93- *Personal Data:* b Edwardsville, Pa, Aug 18, 39; m 67, Madeline Seidelle; c Harold S. *Educ:* Carnegie-Mellon Univ, BS, 60; NY Univ, MS, 62; State Univ NY Buffalo, PhD(physics), 71. *Prof Exp:* Asst prof physics, Niagara Univ, 69-72; assoc physicist, Cornell Aeronaut Lab, Inc, 72-73; res physicist, Calspan Corp, 73-75, sr physicist, 75-77. *Concurrent Pos:* Lectr, Niagara Univ, 72-77. *Mem:* AAAS; Am Phys Soc; Am Asn Physics Teachers; Acoust Soc Am; Sigma Xi; Inst Noise Control Eng. *Res:* Applications of acoustic intensity measurement; acoustic simulation and modeling; digital signal processing and analysis; noise source identification techniques. *Mailing Add:* Wyle Labs 2001 Jefferson Davis Hwy Suite 701 Arlington VA 22202. *Fax:* 703-415-4556; *E-Mail:* estusnic@arl.wylelabs.com

STUTEVILLE, DONALD LEE, PLANT PATHOLOGY. *Current Pos:* asst prof, 64-69, assoc prof, 69-79, PROF PLANT PATH, KANS STATE UNIV, 79-, RES FORAGE PATHOLOGIST, AGR EXP STA, 64- *Personal Data:* b Okeene, Okla, Sept 7, 30; m 52, Lorene J Dringenburg; c Susan A (Carlson), Donald B & Robert V. *Educ:* Kans State Univ, BS, 59, MS, 61; Univ Wis, PhD(plant path), 64. *Prof Exp:* Res asst plant path, Univ Wis, 61-64. *Mem:* Am Phytopathological Soc. *Res:* Diseases of forage crops; improving disease resistance in forage crops, particularly alfalfa. *Mailing Add:* 2006 Stillman Dr Manhattan KS 66502. *Fax:* 785-532-5692; *E-Mail:* dls@plantpath.pp.ksu.edu

STUTH, CHARLES JAMES, ALGEBRA. *Current Pos:* chmn dept, 70-83, PROF, STEPHENS COL, 83- *Personal Data:* b Greenville, Tex, Jan 9, 32; m 53, 75; c 5. *Educ:* East Tex State Univ, 51, MEd, 53; Univ Kans, PhD(math), 63. *Prof Exp:* Instr math, E Tex State Univ, 56-58, from asst prof to prof, 62-66; asst instr, Univ Kans, 58-62; from asst prof to prof, East Tex State Univ, 62-66; asst prof, Univ Mo-Columbia, 66-70. *Concurrent Pos:* Math Avoidance Prog, 78-80; comput info syst, 83-85. *Mem:* Math Asn Am. *Res:* Group theory; theory of semigroups. *Mailing Add:* 506 Arbor Dr Columbia MO 65201-6553

STUTHMAN, DEON DEAN, PLANT GENETICS, PLANT BREEDING. *Current Pos:* From asst prof to assoc prof, 66-79, PROF OAT GENETICS & BREEDING, UNIV MINN, ST PAUL, 79- *Personal Data:* b Pilger, Nebr, May 7, 40; m 62; c 2. *Educ:* Univ Nebr, BSc, 62; Purdue Univ, MSc, 64, PhD(genetics of alfalfa), 67. *Mem:* Fel Am Soc Agron; Crop Sci Soc; Coun Agr Sci & Technol (pres). *Res:* Breeding and genetics of oats. *Mailing Add:* Agron 411 Borlaug Hall Univ Minn St Paul 1991 Upper Buford Circle St Paul MN 55108-6024. *Fax:* 612-625-1268

STUTMAN, LEONARD JAY, hematology, cardiology, for more information see previous edition

STUTMAN, OSIAS, IMMUNOLOGY. *Current Pos:* MEM & SECT HEAD, SLOAN-KETTERING INST CANCER RES, 73-, CHMN, IMMUNOL PROG, 83-; PROF IMMUNOL, GRAD SCH MED SCI, CORNELL UNIV, 75- *Personal Data:* b Buenos Aires, Arg, June 4, 33. *Educ:* Univ Buenos Aires, MD, 57. *Prof Exp:* Lectr, Inst Med Res, Univ Buenos Aires, 57-63; mem res staff physiol, Inst Biol & Exp Med, Buenos Aires, 63-66; from instr to assoc prof path, Med Sch, Univ Minn, Minneapolis, 66-72. *Concurrent Pos:* USPHS res fel, Med Sch, Univ Minn, Minneapolis, 66-69; Am Cancer Soc res assoc, 69-74. *Mem:* Am Asn Immunol; Am Soc Exp Path; Am Asn Cancer Res; Transplantation Soc. *Res:* Development of immune functions in mammals, especially role of thymus and mechanisms of cell-mediated immunity in relation to normal functions and as defense against tumor development. *Mailing Add:* Mem Sloan-Kettering Cancer Ctr 1275 York Ave New York NY 10021-6007. *Fax:* 212-794-4352

STUTT, CHARLES A(DOLPHUS), ELECTRICAL ENGINEERING. *Current Pos:* RETIRED. *Personal Data:* b Avoca, Nebr, Nov 12, 21; m 55; c 2. *Educ:* Univ Nebr, BSc, 44; Mass Inst Technol, ScD(elec eng), 51. *Prof Exp:* Res engr, Stromberg-Carlson Co, NY, 44-46; asst, Res Lab Electronics, Mass Inst Technol, 48-50, instr elec eng, 50-52, mem staff & asst group leader commun, Lincoln Lab, 52-57; res assoc, 57-66, mgr signal processing & commun, Res & Develop ctr, Gen Elec Co, 66-85. *Mem:* sr mem Inst Elec & Electronics Engrs. *Res:* Signal theory; signal processing; data transmission; radar; sonar; radio propagation. *Mailing Add:* 643 Riverview Rd Rexford NY 12148

STUTTE, CHARLES A, PLANT PHYSIOLOGY, AGRONOMY. *Current Pos:* asst prof, 67-71, prof, 71-79, DISTINGUISHED PROF AGRON & BEN J ALTHEIMER CHAIR SOYBEAN RES, UNIV ARK, FAYETTEVILLE, 79- *Personal Data:* b Wapanucka, Okla, July 19, 33; m 55; c 3. *Educ:* Southeastern Okla State Univ, BS, 55; Okla State Univ, MS, 61, PhD(bot, plant physiol), 67. *Prof Exp:* Teacher high schs, Okla, 55-64; instr biol & ecol, E Cent Univ, 64-65; adv plant physiol, forest physiol & gen plant physiol, Okla State Univ, 65-67. *Mem:* Plant Growth Regulator Soc Am; Am Soc Plant Physiologists; Am Soybean Asn; Sigma Xi; Am Soc Agron. *Res:* Physiological stress and growth regulator responses in soybeans, cotton, rice and other crop plants; role of phenolics in natural resistance to insects and disease. *Mailing Add:* 1605 Cedar St Fayetteville AR 72703

STUTTE, LINDA GAIL, EXPERIMENTAL ELEMENTARY PARTICLE PHYSICS. *Current Pos:* SCIENTIST, FERMILAB, 76- *Personal Data:* b Chicago, Ill, Oct 31, 46; m 84. *Educ:* Mass Inst Technol, SB, 68; Univ Calif, Berkeley, PhD(physics), 74. *Prof Exp:* Fel, Calif Inst Technol, 74-76. *Mem:* Am Phys Soc; AAAS. *Res:* High energy neutrino interactions; charged particle beam design; heavy quark physics; rich detectors. *Mailing Add:* Fermilab WH13N Batavia IL 60510. *Fax:* 630-840-2950; *E-Mail:* stutte@fnal.gov

STUTZ, CONLEY I, PHYSICS. *Current Pos:* from asst prof to assoc prof, 69-74, PROF PHYSICS, BRADLEY UNIV, 74- *Personal Data:* b Currie, Minn, Aug 18, 32; m 55; c 2. *Educ:* Wayne State Col, BSE, 57; Univ NMex, MSE, 60; Univ Nebr, PhD(physics), 68. *Prof Exp:* High sch teacher, Iowa, 59; asst prof physics, Pac Univ, 60-64. *Concurrent Pos:* State Coun Am Asn Univ Prof. *Mem:* Sigma Xi; Am Phys Soc; Am Asn Physics Teachers; Am Physics Soc; Am Asn Univ Prof. *Res:* Study of the approach to equilibrium of quantum mechanical systems; nuclear magnetic resonance and nuclear quadrupole resonance of solids. *Mailing Add:* Dept Physics Bradley Univ Peoria IL 61614

STUTZ, HOWARD COOMBS, GENETICS. *Current Pos:* asst prof, 56-67, PROF BOT, BRIGHAM YOUNG UNIV, 67- *Personal Data:* b Cardston, Alta, Aug 24, 18; nat US; m 40; c 7. *Educ:* Brigham Young Univ, BS, 40, MS, 51; Univ Calif, PhD, 56. *Prof Exp:* Prin, High Sch, Utah, 42-44; chmn dept biol, Snow Col, 46-51. *Concurrent Pos:* Guggenheim fel, 60; vis prof, Am Univ Beirut, 67. *Mem:* Bot Soc Am; Soc Study Evolution; Sigma Xi. *Res:* Cytogenetic studies of Secale L and related grasses; phyllogenetic studies of western browse plants; origin of cultivated rye; dominance-penetrance relationships; phylogenetic studies within the family Chenopodiaceae. *Mailing Add:* 531 W 3700 N Provo UT 84604

STUTZ, ROBERT L, SURFACTANT SCIENCE, WHEAT PROCESSING. *Current Pos:* PRES, VANGUARD CORP, 74- *Personal Data:* b Kansas City, Kans, Aug 1, 31; m 60, Janet Mangan; c Susan E (Blackburn) & Kathryn A (Franklin). *Educ:* Univ Kans, BA, 53, MS, 57, PhD(org chem), 61. *Prof Exp:* Asst chemist, Stand Oil Co, Ind, 56-57; sr chemist, Minn Mining & Mfg Co, 61-64; res chemist, 64-65, head chem sect, C J Patterson Co, Kansas City, MO, 65-73. *Concurrent Pos:* Frederick Gardner Cottrell grant, 58-59; consult, 74- *Mem:* Am Chem Soc; Am Oil Chem Soc; fel Am Inst Chem; Sigma Xi; NY Acad Sci. *Res:* Surfactants; food emulsifiers; sucrose esters; specialty chemicals. *Mailing Add:* Vanguard Corp 7301 Mission Rd Suite 315 Shawnee Mission KS 66208

STUTZENBERGER, FRED JOHN, MICROBIOLOGY, ENZYMOLOGY. *Current Pos:* assoc prof, 74-79, PROF MICROBIOL, CLEMSON UNIV, 79- *Personal Data:* b Louisville, Ky, Nov 10, 40; m 70; c 1. *Educ:* Bellarmine Col, BS, 62; Univ Houston, MS, 64; Mich State Univ, PhD(microbiol), 67. *Honors & Awards:* Sigma Xi Res Award, 67. *Prof Exp:* Microbiologist, USPHS, 67-69; asst prof microbiol, Weber State Col, Ogden, Utah, 69-71; Nat Adv Res Coun fel, NZ Dept Agr, Hamilton, 71-73. *Mem:* Sigma Xi; Am Soc Microbiol. *Res:* Extracellular enzymes of thermophilic actinomycetes; cellulose degradation; effect of herbicides on actinomycetes; hypersensitivity pneumonitis antigens and activation of alternate complement pathway; streptococcal immuno-globulin A protease production. *Mailing Add:* Microbiol Dept Clemson Univ Clemson SC 29631

STUTZMAN, LEROY F, CHEMICAL ENGINEERING. *Current Pos:* head chem eng dept, 63-70, PROF CHEM ENG, UNIV CONN, 63- *Personal Data:* b Indianapolis, Ind, Sept 5, 17; m 39; c 3. *Educ:* Purdue Univ, BS, 39; Kans State Col, MS, 40; Univ Pittsburgh, PhD(chem eng), 46. *Prof Exp:* Instr chem, Hillyer Jr Col, 40-41; res fel, Mellon Inst, 41-43; dir rubber res, Pittsburgh Coke & Iron Co, 43; from asst prof to assoc prof chem eng, Tech Inst, Northwestern Univ, 43-50, prof & chmn dept, 50-56; dir res, Remington Rand Univac Div, Sperry-Rand Corp, 56-59; prof chem eng & chief party Univ Pittsburgh res team, Univ Santa Maria, Chile, 59-63. *Concurrent Pos:* Consult, US Off Naval Res, Pure Oil Co, Corn Prod Refining Co & Remington Rand Univac Div, 43-56; consult, 57-; mem bd dirs, Control Data Corp, 74-; Fulbright lectr, Hacettepe Univ, Turkey, 77; vis prof, Univ Vienna, 77-78. *Mem:* AAAS; Am Chem Soc; Am Soc Eng Educ; Am Inst Chem Engrs. *Res:* Mass transfer; oil reservoirs; digital computers; process control; computer graphics; numerical analysis; non-linear optimization; process modelling and simulation. *Mailing Add:* Dept of Chem Eng Univ of Conn Storrs CT 06268

STUTZMAN, WARREN LEE, ELECTRICAL ENGINEERING. *Current Pos:* From asst prof to prof, 69-92, THOMAS PHILLIP PROF ELEC ENG, VA POLYTECH INST & STATE UNIV, 92- *Personal Data:* b Elgin, Ill, Oct 22, 41; m 64, Claudia Morris; c Darren & Dana. *Educ:* Univ Ill, Urbana, AB & BS, 64; Ohio State Univ, MS, 65, PhD(elec eng), 69. *Mem:* Fel Inst Elec & Electronics Engrs; Int Sci Radio Union. *Res:* Wirless communication, propagation; antennas. *Mailing Add:* Dept Elec Eng Va Polytech Inst & State Univ Blacksburg VA 24061-0111. *E-Mail:* stutzman@vt.edu

STUVE, ERIC MICHAEL, SURFACE SCIENCE, ELECTROCHEMISTRY. *Current Pos:* asst prof, 85-90, ASSOC PROF CHEM ENG, UNIV WASH, 90- *Personal Data:* b Billings, Mont, Oct 7, 56. *Educ:* Univ Wis-Madison, BSChE, 78; Stanford Univ, MSChE, 79, PhD(chem eng), 84. *Honors & Awards:* NSF Presidential Young Award, 86. *Prof Exp:* Guest scientist, Fritz-Haber-Max Planck Inst, 84. *Concurrent Pos:* Alexander von Humboldt fel, 84. *Mem:* Am Inst Chem Engrs; Am Chem Soc; Am Vacuum Soc; Electrochem Soc; Am Soc Eng Educ. *Res:* Surface science of electrochemistry; combined ultrahigh vacuum and electrochemical investigations of electrode processes and ultrahigh vacuum studies of double layer modelling; double layer structure, electrodeposition, electrocatalysis, and electric field induced surface chemistry. *Mailing Add:* Dept Chem Eng Univ Wash Box 351750 Seattle WA 98195. *Fax:* 206-543-3778; *E-Mail:* stuve@u.washington.edu

STUY, JOHAN HARRIE, BACTERIOLOGY. *Current Pos:* assoc prof biol, 65-74, PROF BIOL SCI, FLA STATE UNIV, 74- *Personal Data:* b Bogor, Indonesia, Jan 17, 25; m 52; c 2. *Educ:* State Univ Utrecht, Bachelor, 48, Drs, 52, PhD(microbiol), 61. *Prof Exp:* Mem res staff radiobiol, N V Philips Labs, Netherlands, 52-65. *Concurrent Pos:* Fel, biol dept, Brandeis Univ, 57-58, biol div, Oak Ridge Nat Lab, 58-59 & biophys dept, Yale Univ, 59-60; vis prof, Fla State Univ, 62-63; US Atomic Energy Comn grant, 68-74. *Mem:* Am Soc Microbiol. *Res:* Recombination in bacteria and bacteriophages at the DNA level. *Mailing Add:* Dept Biol Sci Fla State Univ 600 W College Ave Tallahassee FL 32306-1096

STWALLEY, WILLIAM CALVIN, ATOMIC MOLECULAR & OPTICAL PHYSICS. *Current Pos:* PROF PHYSICS, UNIV CONN, 93-, HEAD, DEPT PHYSICS, 93-, PROF CHEM, 93-, DIR, CONN USER FACIL, 93- *Personal Data:* b Glendale, Calif, Oct 7, 42; m 63, Mauricette Frisius; c Kenneth W & Steven E. *Educ:* Calif Inst Technol, BS, 64; Harvard Univ, PhD(phys chem), 68. *Prof Exp:* From asst prof to prof chem, Univ Iowa, 68-93, prof physics, 77-93, dir, Iowa Laser Facil, 79-93, dir, Ctr Laser Sci & Eng, 87-89. *Concurrent Pos:* A P Sloan fel, 72-75; assoc prog dir quantum chem, NSF, 75-76. *Mem:* Am Chem Soc; AAAS; fel Am Optical Soc; fel Am Phys Soc; fel Japan Soc Prom Sci. *Res:* Intermolecular forces; gas phase chemical reaction kinetics; molecular beams; laser applications; low temperature physics; atomic and molecular scattering and spectroscopy; laser development. *Mailing Add:* Dept Physics Univ Conn Storrs CT 06269-3046. *Fax:* 860-488-3346; *E-Mail:* stwalley@uconnvm.uconn.edu

STYBLINSKI, MACIEJ A, COMPUTER AIDED DESIGN OF ELECTRONIC CIRCUITS, STATISTICAL DESIGN OF INTEGRATED CIRCUITS. *Current Pos:* ASSOC PROF ELEC ENG, TEX A&M UNIV, 81- *Personal Data:* b Sosnowiec, Poland, Jul 7, 42; c 3. *Educ:* Tech Univ Warsaw, Poland, MSc, 67, PhD(electron), 74, Tech Univ Warsaw, Poland, DSc, 81. *Honors & Awards:* Polish Acad Sci Res Award, 80. *Prof Exp:* Asst, electron, Tech Univ Warsaw, 67-74, asst prof electron, 74-81. *Concurrent Pos:* Vis asst prof electron, Univ Calif, Berkeley, 80; prin investr, Tex Advan Technol Prog, 88-; Fulbright fel, 74-75. *Mem:* Sr mem Inst Elec & Electron Eng. *Res:* Statistical circuit design; intelligent design systems; computer-aided circuit design; very-large-scale integration design for quality and manufacturability; circuit performance variability reduction; manufacturing yield optimization. *Mailing Add:* Dept Elec Eng Texas A&M Univ College Sta TX 77843

STYER, DANIEL F, STATISTICAL MECHANICS, QUANTAL CHAOS. *Current Pos:* asst prof, 85-90, ASSOC PROF PHYSICS, DEPT PHYSICS, OBERLIN COL, 90- *Personal Data:* b Abington, Pa, Jan 31, 55; m 77, Katherine Pozorski; c Gregory M & Colla F. *Educ:* Swarthmore Col, BA, 77; Cornell Univ, PhD(theoret physics), 83. *Prof Exp:* Res fel statist mech, Rutgers Univ, 83-85. *Concurrent Pos:* Vis asst prof physics, Case Western Res Univ, 88 & Univ Colo, Boulder, 91. *Mem:* Am Phys Soc. *Res:* Statistical mechanics and theoretical condensed matter physics; derivation and analysis of series expansions by partial differential approximants; systems with highly degenerate ground states; quantal chaos in phase space. *Mailing Add:* 110 Woodhaven Pl Oberlin OH 44074. *Fax:* 440-775-8960; *E-Mail:* dstyer@physics.oberlin.edu

STYLES, ERNEST DEREK, GENETICS. *Current Pos:* from asst prof to prof, 66-92, EMER PROF GENETICS, UNIV VICTORIA, 92- *Personal Data:* b Canterbury, Eng, Oct 19, 26; m 65; c 2. *Educ:* Univ BC, BSA, 60; Univ Wis, PhD(genetics), 65. *Prof Exp:* Res asst genetics, Univ Wis, 60-64, from proj asst to proj assoc, 64-66. *Mem:* AAAS; Genetics Soc Am; Genetics Soc Can; Am Genetics Asn. *Res:* Maize genetics; genetic control of flavonoid biosynthesis; paramutation. *Mailing Add:* Victoria BC V8N 6B8 Can

STYLES, MARGRETTA M, NURSING. *Current Pos:* PRES, ANCC, 89- *Personal Data:* b Mt Union, Pa, Mar 19, 30. *Educ:* Juniata Col, BS, 50; Yale Univ, MN, 54; Univ Fla, DEd, 68. *Hon Degrees:* LHD, Valparaiso Univ, 86; Dr, Univ Athens, 91. *Honors & Awards:* Anise Sorrel Lectr, Troy State Univ, 82; Harriet Cook Carter Lectr, Duke Univ, 83; Elizabeth Kemble Lectr, Univ NC, Chapel Hill, 85. *Prof Exp:* Assoc prof & dir undergrad studies, Sch Nursing, Duke Univ, NC, 67-69; prof & dean, Sch Nursing, Univ Tex, San Antonio, 69-73; Wayne State Univ, Mich, 73-77; dean, Univ Calif, San Francisco, 77-87, prof, Sch Nursing, 77-92, assoc dir nursing servs, Hosp & Clin, 77-92, coordr, Grad Prog Bus Admin, Dept Ment Health & Community Nursing, 79-85. *Concurrent Pos:* Mem, Nat Comn Nursing, 80-83; proj dir, Study Regulation, Int Coun Nurses, Geneva, 84; mem, Secretary's Comn Nursing, US Dept Health & Human Serv, 88; mem bd dirs, Int Coun Nurses, 89-, chair, Prof Serv Comt, 89-; Fulbright fel, Univ Athens, 90; Int Coun Nurses, 93-97. *Mem:* Inst Med-Nat Acad Sci; fel Am Acad Nursing; Am Nurses Asn (pres, 86-88); Am Orgn Nurse Exec; Am Asn Univ Women. *Mailing Add:* ANCC 600 Maryland Ave SW Suite 100 W Washington DC 20024-2571

STYLES, TWITTY JUNIUS, PARASITOLOGY, BIOLOGY. *Current Pos:* from asst prof to assoc prof, 65-93, PROF BIOL & CHMN DEPT, UNION COL, NY, 93- *Personal Data:* b Prince Edward Co, Va, May 18, 27; m 62; c 2. *Educ:* Va Union Univ, BS, 48; NY Univ, MS, 57, PhD(biol), 63. *Prof Exp:* Jr bacteriologist, New York Health Dept, 53-54, jr scientist, State Univ NY Downstate Med Ctr, 55-64; fel parasitol, Nat Univ Mex, 64-65. *Concurrent Pos:* Lectr, City Col New York, 64; consult off higher educ planning, NY State Educ Dept, 70-71; lectr, Narcotics Addiction Control Comn, NY State, 71-72; NSF course histochem, Vanderbilt Univ, 72; sabbatical, Dept Vet Microbiol & Immunol, Univ Guelph, 72. *Mem:* Am Soc Parasitologists; Soc Protozool; Am Soc Microbiol; Nat Asn Biol Teachers; NY Acad Sci. *Res:* Effect of marine biotoxins on parasitic infections; effect of endotoxin of Trypanosoma lewisi infections in rats and Plasmodium berghei infections in mice. *Mailing Add:* Dept Biol Scis Union Col 807 Union St Schenectady NY 12308-3103

STYLOS, WILLIAM A, IMMUNOCHEMISTRY. *Current Pos:* RETIRED. *Personal Data:* b Lowell, Mass, July 23, 27. *Educ:* State Univ NY, Buffalo, PhD(microbiol & immunol), 67. *Prof Exp:* Exec secy, Immunobiol Study Sect, NIH, 80-92. *Mem:* Sigma Xi; AAAS; Am Asn Immunologists; Am Soc Microbiol. *Mailing Add:* 6 Windward Way Fairhaven MA 02719-1228

STYNES, STANLEY K, CHEMICAL ENGINEERING, COMPUTER GRAPHICS. *Current Pos:* instr chem eng, Wayne State Univ, 56-60, from asst prof to assoc prof, 63-70, asst dean, 69-70, actg dean, 70-72, dean, Col Eng, 72-85, prof, 70-93, EMER PROF CHEM ENG, WAYNE STATE UNIV, 93- *Personal Data:* b Detroit, Mich, Jan 18, 32; m 55, Marcia A Meyers; c Peter, Pamela & Suzanne. *Educ:* Wayne State Univ, BSChE, 58; MSChE, 58; Purdue Univ, PhD(chem eng), 63. *Prof Exp:* Pub health engr, USPHS, 56. *Concurrent Pos:* Fac res fel, Wayne State Univ, 64; dir, Energy Conversion Devices, 77-; pres, Mich Soc Prof Engrs, 88, Eng & Sci Develop Found, 92- *Mem:* AAAS; fel Am Inst Chem Engrs; Am Chem Soc; Am Soc Eng Educ; Nat Soc Prof Engrs; Sigma Xi. *Res:* Transport phenomena in multi-phase systems; control and identification of environmental pollution from industrial sources; tribology (non-metallics and lubrication). *Mailing Add:* 20161 Stamford Dr Livonia MI 48152-1246. *Fax:* 313-577-3810

STYRING, RALPH E, CHEMICAL ENGINEERING. *Current Pos:* RETIRED. *Personal Data:* b Bessemer, Ala, Apr 13, 21; wid. *Educ:* Auburn Univ, BS, 43, Univ Mich, MS, 48. *Prof Exp:* Assoc chem engr, Atlantic Refining Co, 48, asst chem engr, 48-54, supvr engr, 54-61, tech supvr, 61, prin res engr, 61-80, spec proj adv, 80-85. *Mem:* Am Inst Chem Engrs; Soc Petrol Engrs; Am Inst Mech Engrs. *Res:* Natural gas and oil shale processing; liquefied natural gas; in situ recovery of crude oil by thermal methods; tar sand processing. *Mailing Add:* 800 Rollingwood Richardson TX 75081

STYRIS, DAVID LEE, EXPERIMENTAL PHYSICS. *Current Pos:* sr res scientist, 74-89, STAFF SCIENTIST, BATTELLE NORTHWEST LAB, 89- *Personal Data:* b Pomona, Calif, Apr 21, 32; m 58; c 1. *Educ:* Pomona Col, BA, 57; Univ Ariz, MS, 62, PhD(physics), 67. *Prof Exp:* Dynamics engr, Airframe Design, Convair-Pomona, 56-58; res physicist, Weapons Testing, Edgerton, Germeshausen & Grier, 58-60; res assoc, Field Ion Micros, Cornell Univ, 67-69; asst prof physics, shock physics & surface sci, Wash State Univ, 69-74. *Mem:* AAAS; Fedn Am Scientists; NY Acad Sci; Am Soc Mass Spectrometry; Can Spectros Soc; Am Soc Chem Spectrometry. *Res:* Radiation damage of materials related to controlled thermonuclear reactor systems; surface science; mass spectroscopy; atomic absorption spectroscopy; high temperature surface chemistry and physics. *Mailing Add:* 205 Craighill St Richland WA 99352

STYRON, CLARENCE EDWARD, JR, RADIATION ECOLOGY OF NATURAL COMMUNITIES, SAFETY HEALTH & ENVIRONMENTAL COMPLIANCE. *Current Pos:* CHIEF SCIENTIST & RADIATION SAFETY DIR, R M WESTER & ASSOC, INC, 93- *Personal Data:* b Washington, NC, Sept 14, 41; m 69, Patricia Putman; c Hilary C & Joshua P. *Educ:* Davidson Col, BS, 63; Emory Univ, MS, 65, PhD(ecol), 67. *Prof Exp:* Radiation ecologist, Oak Ridge Nat Lab, 67-69; asst prof biol, St Andrews Presby Col, 69-77; environ serv mgr, Monsanto Co, 77-93. *Concurrent Pos:* Consult, Oak Ridge Nat Lab, 69-76; pres, Tech Presentations, 88-; mem, Inst Biosafety Comt, Univ Mo, St Louis, 89- & Wash Univ, 91- *Mem:* Ecol Soc Am; Am Inst Biol Sci; Am Soc Limnol & Oceanog; Sigma Xi; Health Physics Soc. *Res:* Population and community ecology of invertebrates, especially freshwater and marine systems. *Mailing Add:* 43 Wildwood Dr Pacific MO 63069. *Fax:* 314-928-9857; *E-Mail:* styron@compuserve.com

ST-YVES, ANGELE, AGRICULTURAL ENGINEERING. *Current Pos:* DIR RES STA, AGR CAN, QUE, 91- *Personal Data:* b Charette, Que, Can, Apr 30, 40; m 61, Denis Desilets; c Luc, Marie-Christine & Valerie. *Educ:* Laval Univ, BA, 73, BS, 77, MS, 83. *Honors & Awards:* Orger Agr Merit Award, Que Govt, 89; Spec Merit Award, Environ Que, 90. *Prof Exp:* Teacher Comn Scolaire Shawinigan-Sud, Que, 58-61; pvt pract, Que, NS & Mich, 61-70; corr Farmer's Union, Que, 70-72; engr, SNC, Morocco, 77, Roche & Assoc, Que, 79, Comn de Protection des Terres Agricoles, Que, 79-82; engr, Ministere de l'Environ de Que, 82-85, chief div mgmt agr nonpt source pollution, 85-89, chief div agr sector, 89-90, dir agr sector & pesticide mgmt, 90-91. *Concurrent Pos:* Sci coordr res & develop, Sludge Utilization Agr Consortium. *Mem:* Am Soc Agr Engrs; Que Order Agronomists (vpres, 87-89, pres, 89-91); Can Soc Agr Eng; Soil Conserv Soc Am. *Mailing Add:* Agr Can Res Sta 2560 Blvd Hochelaga Sainte-Foy PQ G1V 2J3 Can

SU, CHAU-HSING, FLUID MECHANICS, WATER WAVES. *Current Pos:* assoc prof, 67-75, PROF APPL MATH, BROWN UNIV, 75- *Personal Data:* b Fukien, China, Nov 23, 35; m 60; c 4. *Educ:* Nat Taiwan Univ, BS, 56; Univ Minn, MS, 59; Princeton Univ, PhD(eng), 64. *Prof Exp:* Asst prof eng, Mass Inst Technol, 63-66; res assoc plasma physics, Princeton Univ, 66-67. *Concurrent Pos:* Consult, AT&T Lab. *Mem:* AAAS; Am Phys Soc. *Res:* Nonlinear wave theory. *Mailing Add:* 14 Devonshire Dr Barrington RI 02806

SU, CHEH-JEN, POLYMER CHEMISTRY, PAPER CHEMISTRY. *Current Pos:* RETIRED. *Personal Data:* b Taipei, Taiwan, June 11, 34; US citizen; m 67; c 3. *Educ:* Taipei Inst Technol, Taiwan, BS, 55; NC State Univ, BS, 60; State Univ NY Col Forestry, Syracuse Univ, MS, 63. *Prof Exp:* Chem engr, Taiwan Pulp & Paper Co, 55-59; res chemist, Owens-Ill, Inc, Ohio, 65-67; sr res scientist II paper & polymers, Continental Can Co, Inc, 67-75, sr res scientist I polymer & forest prod, 75-90. *Mem:* Am Chem Soc. *Res:* Characterization of polymers and plastic molded articles; chemicals and materials from renewable sources. *Mailing Add:* 1136 Florence Dr Apt B Westmont IL 60559-2712

SU, GEORGE CHUNG-CHI, ANALYSIS OF ENVIRONMENTAL POLLUTANTS, POLLUTION CONTROL & REGULATION. *Current Pos:* chief tech serv, air pollution control, 74-85, DIR, ENVIRON LAB, MICH DEPT NATURAL RESOURCES, 85- *Personal Data:* b Amoy, China, Aug 8, 39; m 91, Anita Tam; c Janine & Gina. *Educ:* Hope Col, AB, 62; Univ Ill, MS, 64, PhD(org chem), 66. *Prof Exp:* Res chemist plastics dept, E I duPont de Nemours & Co, 66 -69; NIH fel, Dept Biochem, Mich State Univ, 69-70, res assoc, Pesticide Res Ctr, 70-72; biochemist, Pesticide Sect, Bur Labs, Mich Dept Pub Health, 72-74. *Mem:* Am Chem Soc; Chem Soc; NY Acad Sci. *Res:* Organic reaction mechanisms; air monitoring techniques; analytical techniques for isolation, detection, identification and quantitation of environmental pollutants; environmental fate of pollutants and toxicology. *Mailing Add:* Dept Environ Qual PO BOX 30270 Lansing MI 48909-7770. *Fax:* 517-335-9600

SU, HELEN CHIEN-FAN, ORGANIC CHEMISTRY. *Current Pos:* RETIRED. *Personal Data:* b Nanping, China, Dec 26, 22; nat US. *Educ:* Hwa Nan Col, China, BA, 44; Univ Nebr, MS, 51, PhD(chem), 53. *Honors & Awards:* Indust Res Magazine IR-100 Award, 66. *Prof Exp:* Asst chem, Hwa Nan Col, 44-47, instr, 47-49; prof, Lambuth Col, 53-55; res asst, Res Found, Auburn Univ, 55-57; res chemist, Borden Chem Co, 57-63; from assoc scientist to res scientist, Lockheed-Ga Co, 63-68; res chemist, Stored Prod Insects Res & Develop Lab, Agr Res Serv, USDA, 68-90. *Mem:* AAAS; fel Am Inst Chem; Am Chem Soc; NY Acad Sci; Entom Soc Am. *Res:* Heterocyclic nitrogen and sulfur compounds; unsaturated aliphatic compounds; natural products; naturally occurring pesticides; insect pheromones; insect repellents and attractants. *Mailing Add:* 5978 Robin Hood Lane Norcross GA 30093

SU, JIN-CHEN, TOPOLOGY. *Current Pos:* assoc prof, 66-72, PROF MATH, UNIV MASS, AMHERST, 72- *Personal Data:* b Anhwei, China, Dec 30, 32; US citizen; m 60; c 3. *Educ:* Nat Taiwan Univ, BS, 55; Univ Pa, PhD(math), 61. *Prof Exp:* Asst prof math, Univ Va, 61-64; math mem, Inst Advan Study, 64-66. *Mem:* Am Math Soc. *Res:* Transformation groups. *Mailing Add:* Dept Math Univ Mass Box 31545 Amherst MA 01003-0102

SU, JUDY YA-HWA LIN, MUSCLE PHYSIOLOGY, PHARMACOLOGY & BIOCHEMISTRY. *Current Pos:* res assoc cardiovasc pharmacol, 76-77, from actg asst prof to res assoc prof pharmacol, 77-89, RES PROF, DEPT ANESTHESIOL, UNIV WASH, 89- *Personal Data:* b Hsinchu, Taiwan, Nov 20, 38; US citizen; m 62, Michael W; c Marvin D. *Educ:* Nat Taiwan Univ, BS, 61; Univ Kans, MS, 64; Univ Wash, PhD(pharmacol), 68. *Prof Exp:* Asst prof biol, Univ Ala, 72-73. *Concurrent Pos:* Res fel, San Diego Heart Asn, 70-72; prin investr, Wash State Heart Asn, 76-77, Pharmaceut Mfg Asn, 77, NIH, 77- & Am Heart Asn, 80-82; mem Coun Basic Sci, Am Heart Asn, 81-; vis scientist, Max-Planck Inst Med Res, Heidelberg, WGer, 82-83; res career develop award, Nat Heart, Lung & Blood Inst, NIH, 82-87; mem surg, Anesthesiol & Trauma Study Sect, 87-91; vis prof, Mayo Clin, 88. *Mem:* Biophys Soc; Am Soc Pharmacol & Exp Therapeut; Am Soc Anesthesiologists; AAAS; Am Physiol Soc. *Res:* Mechanisms of action of pharmacological agents on the striated and smooth muscles; effects of drugs on the intracellular mechanisms of muscle contraction; modulation of ryanodine-receptor channels and IP3-receptor channels in muscle contraction. *Mailing Add:* Dept Anesthesiol Box 356540 Sch Med Univ Wash Seattle WA 98195. *Fax:* 206-543-2958; *E-Mail:* jsu@u.washington.edu

SU, KENDALL L(ING-CHIAO), ELECTRICAL ENGINEERING. *Current Pos:* From asst prof to prof elec eng, 54-70, regents prof, 70-94, EMER REGENTS PROF ELEC ENG, 94- *Personal Data:* b Nanping, China, July 10, 26; nat US; m 60; c 2. *Educ:* Xiamen Univ, BS, 47; Ga Inst Technol, MS, 49, PhD(elec eng), 54. *Mem:* Fel Inst Elec & Electronics Engrs. *Res:* Network theory; electronics; active filters. *Mailing Add:* Sch Elec Eng Ga Inst Technol 225 N Ave NW Atlanta GA 30332-0250

SU, KENNETH SHYAN-ELL, PHARMACEUTICS. *Current Pos:* RES SCIENTIST, ELI LILLY & CO, 71- *Personal Data:* b Taipei, Taiwan, Nov 26, 41; US citizen; m 70; c 2. *Educ:* Taipei Med Col, BS, 65; Univ Wis, MS, 69, PhD(pharmaceut), 71. *Prof Exp:* Res fel biochem, US Naval Med Res Unit 2, 64-65; pharmaceut chemist, William S Merrell Co, 71. *Mem:* Am Asn Pharmaceut Sci; Am Med Asn. *Res:* Transmucosal drug delivery systems (including nasal, bronchial and sublingual systems), transport microparticles and macromolecules across nasal membranes, aerosol delivery systems, monagneons dosage form, and sustained release drug delivery systems. *Mailing Add:* Lilly Res Labs Eli Lilly & Co Indianapolis IN 46285

SU, KWEI LEE, LIPID BIOCHEMISTRY. *Current Pos:* DIR, MIDAMERICA LABS & FORENSIC CONSULT, 88- *Personal Data:* b Ping Tong, Taiwan, Mar 18, 42; m 68; c 1. *Educ:* Nat Taiwan Univ, BS, 64; Univ Minn, PhD(biochem), 71. *Prof Exp:* Instr pharmacog, Col Pharm, Nat Taiwan Univ, 64-66; Hormel fel, Hormel Inst, Univ Minn, 70-72; from res fel to res assoc lipid chem, 72-74, asst prof, 74-75; res asst prof neurochem, Sinclair Comp Med Res Farm, Univ Mo, Columbia, 75-76; forensic chemist crime lab, Mo State Hwy Patrol, Jefferson City, 76-87. *Mem:* Am Chem Soc; Am Oil Chemists Soc; Am Acad Forensic Sci. *Res:* Isolation, structural determination, biosynthesis and function of ether lipids in mammals; effects of neurotransmitters on lipid metabolism in brain subcellular membranes. *Mailing Add:* 2712 Plaza Dr Jefferson City MO 65109-1147

SU, LAO-SOU, PHYSICAL CHEMISTRY. *Current Pos:* sr res chemist, 69-80, res assoc, 80-84, SR RES ASSOC, S C JOHNSON & SON, INC, 84- *Personal Data:* b Kaohsung, Taiwan, Dec 13, 32; m 45; c 2. *Educ:* Taiwan Norm Univ, BS, 57; Ind Univ, MS, 63, PhD(phys chem), 67. *Prof Exp:* Fel, Univ Mich 67-69 & Ind Univ, 69. *Mem:* Am Chem Soc. *Res:* Corrosion study of aerosol products; elemental analysis by means of x-ray fluorescence spectrometry; electron diffraction study of molecular structure; electrical property determination of substance by dielectric spectroscopy; biological alternating current impedance measurement. *Mailing Add:* S C Johnson & Soc Inc 1525 Howe St Racine WI 53403-2237

SU, ROBERT TZYH-CHUAN, CELLULAR TRANSFORMATION & DIFFERENTIATION, CHROMOSOME STRUCTURE & FUNCTION. *Current Pos:* SCI REV ADMINR, NIH, 90- *Personal Data:* b Szechuan, China, Dec 14, 45; US citizen; m 74. *Educ:* Fujen Univ, Taiwan, BS, 68; Univ Ill, MS, 71; Ind Univ, PhD(microbiol), 75. *Prof Exp:* Assoc instr, Ind Univ, 73-75; res fel biochem, Harvard Med Sch, 75-78; from asst prof to assoc prof, Univ Kans, 78-90. *Concurrent Pos:* Vis scientist, NIH, 81, Johns Hopkins Univ, 83; microbiologist, Food & Drug Admin, 89-90. *Mem:* Am Soc Microbiol; Am Soc Cell Biol. *Res:* Study cell growth and regulation using viral vector, drugs or monoclonal antibodies to probe and identify the changes which occur during cell growth and differentiation. *Mailing Add:* 10434 44th Ave Beltsville MD 20705

SU, STANLEY Y W, COMPUTER SCIENCE & ENGINEERING. *Current Pos:* asst prof, Dept Elec Eng & Commun Sci Lab, 70-74, assoc prof comput & info eng, Dept Elec Eng & Inst Advan Study Commun Processes, 74-78, PROF, DEPT COMPUT & INFO SCI, DEPT ELEC ENG, UNIV FLA, 78- *Personal Data:* b Fukien, China, Feb 18, 40; US citizen; m 65, Phek; c 2. *Educ:* Tamkang Col Arts & Sci, BA, 61; Univ Wis, MS, 65, PhD(comput sci), 68. *Prof Exp:* Proj asst syst prog, Comput Ctr, Univ Wis, 64-67, res asst regional Am English proj, 67, res asst natural lang processing, 67-68; mathematician comput ling, Rand Corp, 68-70. *Concurrent Pos:* Mem, Spec Interest Group Operating Syst & Spec Interest Group Mgt Data, Asn Comput Mach, 73-; consult, Creativity Ctr Consortium, 73-74, Fla Keys Community Col, 74-75 & Cent Fla Community Col, 74-; staff consult, Queueing Systs, Inc, 74-75, Dept Energy, 82-84, Navy Ships Control Ctr, 84-85, Kings Res, 84, General Elec Corp Res & Develop Ctr, 85-; lectr continuing educ, George Washington Univ, 75-80; assoc ed, Transacting Software Eng, Int J Comput Lang, Inst Elec & Electronics Engrs, 81-, Int J Info Sci, 82-; area ed, J of Parallel Distrib & Comput, 84- *Mem:* Asn Comput Mach; Conf Data Systs Lang; Inst Elec & Electronic Engrs. *Res:* Distributed ad parallel database systems; computer architecture for data base management; data base translation and program conversion; data base semantics; application of microprocessor network to non-numeric processing; man-machine communications; object-oriented systems; knowledge base management. *Mailing Add:* Datacase Systs Res Develop Ctr 470 Cse Bldg Gainesville FL 32611

SU, STEPHEN Y H, FAULT-TOLERANT COMPUTING, DESIGN AUTOMATION. *Current Pos:* PROF DESIGN AUTOMATION & FAULT TOLERANT COMPUT, BINGHAMTON UNIV, 78- *Personal Data:* b Anchi, China, July 6, 38; US citizen; m 64; c 2. *Educ:* Nat Taiwan Univ, BS, 60; Univ Wis-Madison, MS, 63, PhD(comput eng), 67. *Honors & Awards:* Alexander von Humboldt Sr Scientist Award, 84-85. *Prof Exp:* Asst prof switching theory, New York Univ, 67-69, comput archit, Univ Calif, Berkeley, 69-71, design automation, Univ Southern Calif, 71-72; assoc prof design automation, Case Western Res Univ, 72-73, syst design, City Col NY, 73-75; prof fault diag, Utah State Univ, 75-78. *Concurrent Pos:* Electronic engr, Air Force Radar Sta, Taiwan, 60-61; logic designer, Fabri-Tek, Inc, 65; proj specialist, Med Sch, Univ Wis, 66; consult, IBM, UNIVAC, & E & H Res, 68-78; mem tech staff, Bell Labs, 69; staff consult, UNIVAC, 73-74; engr, IBM, 74. *Mem:* Sr mem Inst Elec & Electronics Engrs. *Res:* Fault tolerant design; fault diagnosis; computer aided logic/system design of digital systems and computer architecture; developing new algorithms for testing very large scale integration. *Mailing Add:* Dept Comput Sci Eng Bldg T-18 Binghamton NY 13902-6000

SU, TAH-MUN, ORGANIC CHEMISTRY, MICROBIOLOGY. *Current Pos:* STAFF SCIENTIST CHEM & BIOENG, CORP RES & DEVELOP CTR, GEN ELEC CO, 72- *Personal Data:* b Taiwan, July 22, 39; c 3. *Educ:* Chen Kung Univ, Taiwan, BSc, 62; Univ Nev, MS, 65; Princeton Univ, PhD(chem), 70. *Prof Exp:* Res fel geochemistry, Biodyn Lab, Univ Calif, Berkeley, 69-70; res fel chem, Union Carbide Res Inst, 70-71. *Mem:* Am Chem Soc; Am Soc Microbiol. *Res:* Single cell protein from cellulosic fiber; biodegradation of chlorinated hydrocarbons; enzymatic saccharification of cellulose; mechanism of organic chemical reactions; ethanol from biomass. *Mailing Add:* 2259 Berkley Ave Schenectady NY 12309

SU, WEN-PO DANIEL, MEDICINE, DERMATOLOGY & DERMATOPATHOLOGY. *Current Pos:* STAFF CONSULT DERMAT, MAYO CLIN, 76-; PROF DERMAT, MAYO MED SCH, 89- *Personal Data:* b Tainan, China, May 31, 43; US citizen; m 71, Man-Mei Nadine Lee; c Lowell & Anita. *Educ:* Nat Taiwan Univ, MD, 68; Univ Hawaii, MS, 72. *Concurrent Pos:* Vis prof & lectr, numerous US & foreign univs, 76-; spec fel dermatopath, Med Ctr, NY Univ, 77; dir, Diag Qual Control Lab Proficiency Prog, Am Soc Dermatopath, 86-91, Am Bd Dermat, 97-; mem Int Affair Comt, Am Acad Dermat, 94- *Mem:* Sigma Xi; Am Dermat Asn; Asian Dermat Asn; hon mem Chinese Dermat Soc; hon foreign mem Brit Asn Dermatolgoists; Dermat Found; Int Soc Dermatopath (secy, 91-94, pres, 94-97). *Res:* Clinical dermatology; skin pathology, panniculitis, connective tissue disease and infectious diseases. *Mailing Add:* Dept Dermat Mayo Clin 200 First St SW Rochester MN 55905

SU, YAO SIN, ANALYTICAL CHEMISTRY. *Current Pos:* sr res chemist, Corning Glass Works, 63-73, res supvr, 73-79, MGR, CORNING INC, 79- *Personal Data:* b Ping-tung, Taiwan, Oct 17, 29; US citizen; m 54; c 2. *Educ:* Taiwan Univ, BS, 52; Univ Pittsburgh, PhD(chem), 62. *Prof Exp:* Chemist, Union Res Inst, Taiwan, 53-58. *Mem:* Am Chem Soc; Am Ceramic Soc; Am Soc Testing & Mat. *Res:* Inorganic chemical analysis; electroanalysis; classical wet methods. *Mailing Add:* Chem Analysis/Res Develop Corning Inc SP-FR-41 Corning NY 14831-0001

SUAREZ, KENNETH ALFRED, PHARMACOLOGY, TOXICOLOGY. *Current Pos:* from instr to assoc prof pharmacol, 72-82, asst dir, 80-82, PROF PHARMACOL & DIR, RES AFFAIRS, CHICAGO COL OSTEOP MED, 82-, ASST VPRES RES, 92- *Personal Data:* b Queens, NY, June 27, 44; m 68, Eileen Lynch; c Christina. *Educ:* Univ RI, BS, 67, MS, 70, PhD(pharmacol), 72. *Prof Exp:* Nat Defense Educ Act fel, 67-70. *Concurrent Pos:* Major, US Army Res. *Mem:* AAAS; Sigma Xi; Toxicol Soc. *Res:* Drug induced hepatic injury. *Mailing Add:* Pharm Midwestern Univ 555 31st St Downers Grove IL 60615-1235. *Fax:* 630-971-6414

SUAREZ, THOMAS H, RESOURCE MANAGEMENT. *Current Pos:* export & licensing mgr, 88-89, MGR PURCHASING & DISTRIB, EXPLOSIVES & TECHNOL INT, INC, 90- *Personal Data:* b Temperley, Arg, Dec 7, 36; m 61; c 3. *Educ:* Univ Buenos Aires, MS, 59, PhD(phys org chem), 61. *Prof Exp:* Teaching asst org chem, Univ Buenos Aires, 59-61; head lab course, 61; res chemist, Textile Fibers Dept, Dacron Mfg Div, E I du Pont de Nemours & Co, 61-66, anal res supvr, 66-69, supvr process develop, 69-71, tech supt, Polymer Intermediates Dept, 71-74, planning mgr, Polymer Intermediates Dept, 74-77, sales mgr-Latin Am, Petrol Chem Div, 78-81, mgr, Gen Prod Dept, Du Pont de Venezuela, 81-82, sales mgr, Latin Am Explosive Prod Div, 82-85, export & licensing mgr, 85-87. *Mem:* AAAS; Am Chem Soc; Arg Chem Asn. *Res:* Nucleophylic aromatic substitution; reaction kinetics and mechanisms; polymer chemistry; melt spinning synthetic fibers; physical and chemical characterization of polymers. *Mailing Add:* 731 Burnley Rd Wilmington DE 19803

SUBACH, DANIEL JAMES, ANALYTICAL & POLYMER CHEMISTRY, PHYSICAL CHEMISTRY. *Current Pos:* TECH DIR CORP RES & DEVELOP, H B FULLER CO, 89- *Personal Data:* b Shenandoah, Pa, July 7, 47; m 70; c 2. *Educ:* Lebanon Valley Col, BS, 69; Marshall Univ, MS, 71; Tex A&M Univ, PhD(phys chem), 74; Rensselaer Polytech Inst, MBA, 81. *Prof Exp:* Qual control chemist, Campbell's Soup Co, 69-70; sr anal develop chemist, Ciba-Geigy Corp, 75-77; proj mgr anal & phys res & develop, Springborn Labs Inc, 77-78; mgr anal res & develop, Gen Elec Co, 78-80, mgr qual control, Silicon Prod Div, 80-81, mgr, new prod commercialization, res & develop & prod develop, 81-84; mgr new bus develop, NL Industs Inc, 85-86, bus mgr, 86-88. *Concurrent Pos:* NASA fel, Rice Univ, 74-75. *Mem:* Sigma Xi; Am Chem Soc; Am Inst Chem; Fedn Socs Coating Technol. *Res:* Thermodynamics and thermophysical properties; nonelectrolyte mixture and liquid theory; trace analysis of organics and inorganics; chromatography including gas, liquid and thin-layer; adhesives, sealants, coatings polymer performance and formulation. *Mailing Add:* Barrisville Rd RR 2 Box 320 Beaver Falls PA 15010-9423

SUBBAIAH, PAPASANI VENKATA, LIPOPROTEIN RESEARCH, ATHEROSCLEROSIS. *Current Pos:* assoc prof med, 85-89, assoc prof biochem, 86-94, PROF MED, RUSH UNIV, 89-, PROF BIOCHEM, 94- *Personal Data:* b Karumanchi, AP, India, July 1, 43; US citizen; m 65. *Educ:* Andhra Univ, BSc, 63; Nagpur Univ, MSc, 65; Indian Inst Sci, PhD(biochem), 71. *Prof Exp:* Res asst prof, Univ Wash, 78-84. *Mem:* Am Chem Soc; Am Heart Asn; AAAS; Am Soc Biochem & Molecular Biol. *Res:* Lipoprotein metabolism and mechanisms of atherosclerosis; role of phospholipids in atherogenesis; mechanism of action of omega 3 fatty acids; plasma acyltrans ferases; platelet-activating factor. *Mailing Add:* Dept Med Rush-Presby St Luke's Med Ctr 1653 W Congress Pkwy Chicago IL 60612. *Fax:* 312-455-9814; *E-Mail:* psubbaia@rpslmc.edu

SUBBARAO, SALIGRAMA C, CHEMISTRY. *Current Pos:* from asst prof to assoc prof, 69-82, PROF CHEM, LINCOLN UNIV, 82-, CHMN, NATURAL SCI & MATH DIV, 84- *Educ:* Univ Mysore, Ind, BS, 58; Univ Bombay, India, MS, 64; Univ London, Eng, PhD(phys chem), 66. *Prof Exp:* Demonstr/lectr chem, Bhavans Col, India, 62-64; fel, Dept Chem Eng, Toronto Univ, 67-68, Dept Chem, Carleton Univ, 68-69, res fel, Dept Pharmacol, NIH, 76-78. *Concurrent Pos:* Prin investr, AEC, 70-76, Solar Energy Res Inst, 84-86, Dept Energy, 85-86, Off Naval Res, 85-87, Environ Protect Agency, 88-91, US Dept Agr, 92-; dir, Comp Asst Undergrad Sci Educ, NSF, 82-83, Minority Access to Res Careers Prog, NIH, 83-93; assoc dir, Minority Inst Sci Improvement, Dept Educ, 85-88; coordr, minority biomed res prog, NIH, 88-93; actg vpres acad affairs, Lincoln Univ, 89-90; assoc dir, Lincoln advan sci & eng reinforcement prog, Off Naval Res Nat Aeronaut & Space Admin, 83-; actg dir, Lincoln Univ Res Establishment, 85- *Mem:* Fel Am Inst Chemists; Am Chem Soc; AAAS; Am Heart Asn. *Res:* Phsyical chemistry; extraction of veterinary drug residuces from animal tissues; author of 18 publications. *Mailing Add:* 19 Beacon Lane Cotswold Hills Newark DE 19711

SUBBASWAMY, KUMBLE R(AMARAO), THEORETICAL CONDENSED MATTER PHYSICS. *Current Pos:* from asst prof to assoc prof, 78-88, PROF PHYSICS, UNIV KY, LEXINGTON, 88-, Chair, 93- *Personal Data:* b Soraba, India, Mar 18, 51; US citizen; m 86; c 2. *Educ:* Bangalore Univ, India, BSc, 69; Delhi Univ, MSc, 71; Ind Univ, Bloomington, PhD(physics), 76. *Prof Exp:* Res physicist, Univ Calif, Irvine, 76-78. *Concurrent Pos:* Vis scientist, Int Ctr Theoret Physics, Trieste, Italy & 84-85, Oak Ridge Nat Lab, 85. *Mem:* Fel Am Phys Soc. *Res:* Theoretical condensed matter physics; optical properties; ab initio computation of electronic properties; clusters; coal chemistry; first-principles molecular dynamics. *Mailing Add:* Dept Physics Univ Ky Lexington KY 40506-0055

SUBBIAH, RAVI M T, STEROID PHARMACOLOGY, CHOLESTEROL METABOLISM. *Current Pos:* assoc prof internal med, 78-81, PROF MED & PATH, UNIV CINCINNATI MED CTR, 81- *Personal Data:* b Karnataka, India, June 30, 42; m, Deachu; c Jeevan & Rekha. *Educ:* Univ Mysore, India, BSc, 62; Univ Baroda, India, MSc, 64; Univ Toronto, Can, PhD(biochem), 70. *Prof Exp:* Fel atherosclerosis, Mayo Clin, Minn, 70-71, res assoc physiol, 71-73, assoc consult internal med, 73-74, consult, 74-78, asst prof biochem & med, 75-78. *Concurrent Pos:* Grant awards, NIH; dir, Artherosclerosis-Nutrit Training Prog, Univ Cincinnati Med Ctr, 80-; vis prof, Univ Cambridge, 85, Univ Salfurd, 91; consult, UN Develop Prog, 87. *Mem:* Fel Am Heart Asn; Am Chem Soc; Soc Exp Biol & Med; Fedn Am Socs Exp Biol; Am Asn Clin Chem. *Res:* Pathogenesis of atherosclerosis with particular interest on the role of lipid peroxidation in the disease process; potential benefits of estrogens. *Mailing Add:* 146 Ridgeview Dr Cincinnati OH 45215. *Fax:* 513-558-2979

SUBERKROPP, KELLER FRANCIS, MICROBIAL ECOLOGY, PHYSIOLOGY. *Current Pos:* assoc prof, 86-89, PROF BIOL SCI, UNIV ALA, 89- *Personal Data:* b Wamego, Kans, Apr 12, 43; m 71; c 4. *Educ:* Kans State Univ, BS, 65, MS, 67; Mich State Univ, PhD(bot), 71. *Prof Exp:* Res assoc microbial ecol, Kellogg Biol Sta, Mich State Univ, 71-75; asst prof biol sci, Ind Univ-Purdue Univ, Ft Wayne, 75-78; asst prof, 78-84, assoc prof biol sci, NMex State Univ, 84-86. *Mem:* Mycol Soc Am; Ecol Soc Am; Brit Mycol Soc; Sigma Xi; Am Soc Microbiol. *Res:* Role of fungi in decomposition of leaf litter in aquatic habitats; effects of environmental factors on growth and sporulation of these fungi. *Mailing Add:* Dept Biol Univ Ala Box 870344 Tuscaloosa AL 35487-0344

SUBJECK, JOHN ROBERT, RADIATION BIOLOGY, HEAT SHOCK. *Current Pos:* CANCER RES SCIENTIST, DEPT RADIATION MED, ROSWELL MEM INST, 77- *Educ:* Univ Buffalo, PhD(biophysics), 74. *Mem:* Am Soc Cell Biol; Radiation Res Soc. *Res:* Heat shock protein. *Mailing Add:* Radiation Biol PO 84563 Roswell Park Cancer Inst Buffalo NY 14263-0001

SUBLETT, BOBBY JONES, ORGANIC CHEMISTRY, POLYMER CHEMISTRY. *Current Pos:* RETIRED. *Personal Data:* b Paintsville, Ky, Aug 27, 31; m 56, Sonja S Lykius; c John, Melissa, Christopher & Steven. *Educ:* Eastern Ky State Col, BS, 58; Univ Tenn, MS, 60. *Prof Exp:* From res chemist to sr res chemist, Tenn Eastman Co, 60-75, res assoc, 75-90, sr res assoc, 90-97. *Mem:* Am Chem Soc; Sigma Xi. *Res:* Reaction mechanisms; tobacco smoke analysis; condensation polymers; textile chemicals; adhesives. *Mailing Add:* 1205 Jerry Lane Kingsport TN 37664

SUBLETT, ROBERT L, CHEMISTRY. *Current Pos:* assoc prof, 56-70, PROF CHEM, TENN TECHNOL UNIV, 70-, CHMN DEPT, 72- *Personal Data:* b Columbia, Mo, Apr 10, 21; m 46; c 3. *Educ:* Univ Mo, AB, 43, PhD, 50; Ga Inst Technol, MS, 48. *Prof Exp:* Instr chem, Ga Inst Technol, 47; res chemist, Chemstrand Corp, 52-55; assoc prof chem, Ark State Teachers Col, 55-56. *Mem:* Am Chem Soc. *Res:* High polymers; Friedels-crafts; organic and high polymer analytical chemistry; instrumental analysis. *Mailing Add:* 1218 N Maple Ave Cookeville TN 38501

SUBLETTE, IVAN H(UGH), COMPUTER SCIENCE, ELECTRICAL ENGINEERING. *Current Pos:* RETIRED. *Personal Data:* b Urbana, Ill, May 15, 29. *Educ:* Purdue Univ, BS, 49; Univ Pa, MS, 51, PhD(elec eng), 57. *Prof Exp:* Engr, RCA, 49-59, mem tech staff, RCA Labs, 59-74, sr systs programmer, RCA Solid State Div, 74-92. *Mem:* Inst Elec & Electronics Engrs; Asn Comput Mach. *Res:* Computer operating systems; performance measurement and evaluation. *Mailing Add:* Pickwick Apts Maple Shade NJ 08052

SUBLETTE, JAMES EDWARD, zoology, for more information see previous edition

SUBRAMANI, SURESH, CELL BIOLOGY. *Current Pos:* From asst prof to assoc prof, 82-91, PROF BIOL, UNIV CALIF, SAN DIEGO, 91- *Personal Data:* b Jabalpur, India, Feb 21, 52; m 81, Feroza Ardeshir; c Anand & Praveen. *Educ:* Fergusson Col, India, BSc, 72; Indian Inst Tech, MSc, 74; Univ Calif, Berkeley, PhD(biochem), 79. *Concurrent Pos:* Postdoctoral biochem, Stanford Univ, 82; Searle scholar, Searle, 85-90; John Simon Guggenheim fel, 93-94. *Mem:* Am Soc Microbiol; AAAS. *Res:* DNA repair and recombination; gene therapy; biotechnology; protein sorting to subcellular compartments; virology. *Mailing Add:* Biol Dept 0322 Bonner Hall Univ Calif La Jolla CA 92093-0322

SUBRAMANIAN, ALAP RAMAN, ORGANELLE RIBOSOMES & EVOLUTION, CHLOROPLAST PROTEIN SYNTHESIS SYSTEM. *Current Pos:* GROUP LEADER, MAX PLANCK INST MOLECULAR GENETICS, 74-; RES PROF BIOCHEM, UNIV ARIZ, 96- *Personal Data:* b India, Mar 13, 35; US citizen; m 65, Rita Mitra; c Suman & Ranjan. *Educ:* Univ Madras, BSc, 55, MA, 57; Univ Iowa, PhD(biochem), 64. *Prof Exp:* Jr scientist radiol chem, Atomic Energy Estab, India, 58-61; postdoctorate biochem, Northwestern Univ, 65-67; res assoc microbiol, Harvard Med Sch, 67-69, res asst prof molecular genetics, 69-74. *Concurrent Pos:* Vis assoc prof, Univ Rochester, 78; vis scholar, Harvard Univ, 82-83; standing adv comt, Dept Biotechnol, Govt India, 88-; hon prof, Jawaharlal Nehru Univ, New Delhi, India, 94- *Mem:* Am Soc Biochem & Molecular Biol; Ger Biochem Soc; Int Soc Plant Molecular Biol. *Res:* Cloning/characterization/ organization of higher plant chloroplast ribosomal protein genes; basis for nuclear:chloroplast gene allocation; gene transfer and gene accretion; protein structural alterations compared to bacterial homologues; regulating coordinate expression of nuclear and organellar genes. *Mailing Add:* Dept Biochem Univ Ariz Tucson AZ 85721-0088

SUBRAMANIAN, GOPAL, NUCLEAR MEDICINE, CHEMICAL ENGINEERING. *Current Pos:* res assoc radiopharmaceut, 65-68, from instr to assoc prof, 68-76, PROF RADIOL, STATE UNIV NY UPSTATE MED CTR, 72- *Personal Data:* b Madras, India, Apr 4, 37; m 66, Kalyani Margabanduswamy; c Uma, Vinodhini & Manjula. *Educ:* Univ Madras, BSc, 58 & 60; Johns Hopkins Univ, MSE, 64; Syracuse Univ, PhD(chem eng), 70. *Honors & Awards:* Gold Medal, Soc Nuclear Med, 72; Paul C Aubersold Award, Soc Nuclear Med, 82. *Prof Exp:* Chem engr, Prod Dept, E Asiatic Co (India) Pvt, Ltd, 60-62; res assoc radiochem, Med Insts, Johns Hopkins Univ, 64-65. *Concurrent Pos:* NIH grant, State Univ NY Upstate Med Ctr, 69-; consult, Am Nat Stand Inst, 71-; mem, adv panel radiopharmaceut, US Pharmacopeia, 71-; asst prof, Syracuse Univ, 71- *Mem:* AAAS; Soc Nuclear Med; fel Am Inst Chem; Am Inst Chem Eng; Sigma Xi. *Res:* Radiochemistry; radiopharmaceuticals; fluid dynamics as applied to chemical engineering. *Mailing Add:* Dept Nuclear Med-Radiol State Univ NY Health Sci Ctr Syracuse NY 13210. *Fax:* 315-464-7068

SUBRAMANIAN, K N, METALLURGY, MATERIALS SCIENCE. *Current Pos:* From asst prof to assoc prof, 65-85, PROF METALL, MECH & MAT SCI, MICH STATE UNIV, 85- *Personal Data:* b Cuddalore, India, Aug 13, 38; m; c 1. *Educ:* Annamalai Univ, Madras, BSc, 58; Indian Inst Sci, Bangalore, BE, 60; Univ Calif, Berkeley, MS, 62; Mich State Univ, PhD(metall), 66. *Mem:* Am Ceramic Soc; Metall Soc. *Res:* Plastic deformation of crystals; dislocation theory with specific reference to fatigue, work hardening, crystal growth and fracture; two phase materials; phase separation in glasses; erosion; composites. *Mailing Add:* Dept Metall Mech & Mat Sci A304 Eng Bldg Mich State Univ East Lansing MI 48824

SUBRAMANIAN, KRISHNAMOORTHY, MANUFACTURING TECHNOLOGY, ABRASIVE MACHINING PROCESSES. *Current Pos:* res mgr, Norton Co, 83-85, dir, Tech & Bus Develop, 85-88, Ceramics Market Develop, 88-92, DIR, TESTING & APPLN DEVELOP, NORTON CO, 92- *Personal Data:* b Lalgudi, India, July 25, 49; m, Durga V; c Ganesh V. *Educ:* Osmania Univ, BEng, 70; Mass Inst Technol, ME, 76, ScD, 77. *Prof Exp:* Indust engr, Nat Productivity Coun, India, 71-72; res assoc mat processing, Mass Inst Technol, 76-77; sr res engr machining & wear, Sci Res Lab, Ford Motor Co, 77-79, sr res engr adv concepts & energy syst, 79-81; res mgr, Int Harvester Co, 81-83. *Concurrent Pos:* Adj lectr, Univ Mich, Dearborn, 78, adj prof, 79. *Mem:* Am Soc Mech Engrs; fel Soc Mfg Engrs; Am Soc Mat. *Res:* Machining processes; grinding systems; materials and their response to finishing processes; research results in new products, novel processes, technology transfer, productivity improvement & global market development. *Mailing Add:* 643 Longley Rd Groton MA 01450

SUBRAMANIAN, KUNNATH SUNDARA, BIOLOGICAL TRACE ELEMENT RESEARCH, ENVIRONMENTAL TRACE METAL RESEARCH. *Current Pos:* vis fel, 76-78, RES SCIENTIST, HEALTH CAN, 80- *Personal Data:* b Calicut, Kerala State, India, Apr 1, 44; m 74, P H Thylambal; c Sundar & Sheela. *Educ:* Kerala Univ, BSc(Hons) 65; Brock Univ, MSc, 71; McMaster Univ, PhD(anal chem), 75. *Prof Exp:* Trainee, Brabha Atomic Res Ctr, India, 65-66, sci officer, 66-70; fel, Carleton Univ, 74-76; sr scientist, Barringer Res, 78-80. *Concurrent Pos:* Ed, Elsevier, 88-89, Am Chem Soc, 91; Adj prof, Carleton Univ, 89-93; Proj coord, Health Can, 90-93, leader, Surveillance Unit, 90-; prin co-investr, Univ Ottawa, 93- *Mem:* Chem Inst Can; Spectros Soc Can. *Res:* Conduct analytical investigations into the indentification, determination and speciation of trace and ultratrace inorganic contaminants, especially metals, in environmental and biological media such as human blood, urine, tissues, drinking water and house dust. *Mailing Add:* 146 Foxfield Dr Nepean ON K2J 2T1 Can. *Fax:* 613-941-4545

SUBRAMANIAN, MANI M, TELECOMMUNICATIONS, ELECTRICAL ENGINEERING. *Current Pos:* PROF, GEO INST TECHNOL, 91- *Personal Data:* b Madras, India, Jan 11, 34; m 64; c 2. *Educ:* Univ Madras, BSc, 53; Madras Inst Technol, dipl, 56; Purdue Univ, MSEE, 61, PhD(elec eng), 64. *Prof Exp:* Engr, G Janshi & Co, India, 56; trainee, All India Radio, 57; jr sci officer, Electronics Res Inst, 57-59; tech asst & instr elec eng, Purdue Univ, 59-64, asst prof, 64-66; mem tech staff laser res, Bell Tel Labs, Holmdel, 66-83, dist mgr, Bell Commun Res, Inc, 84-87; digital comm assoc, Atlanta, Ga, 87-91. *Concurrent Pos:* Consult, Bell Tel Labs, 64-66. *Mem:* Inst Elec & Electronics Engrs. *Res:* Receivers, parametric amplifiers, ferroelectric materials and propagation through plasma in microwaves; nonlinear optics, cathodoluminescence, lasers, laser systems and propagation through turbulent media in quantum electronics; digital transmission systems; minicomputer systems; software development. *Mailing Add:* 1652 Harts Mill Rd NE 6630 Bay Circle Atlanta GA 30319

SUBRAMANIAN, MARAPPA G, PROLACTIN PHYSIOLOGY, ENDOCRINOLOGY. *Current Pos:* res assoc, Dept Physiol, Sch Med, Wayne State Univ, Detroit, 74-77, res assoc, Dept Obstet-Gynec, 77-78, instr, 78-81, from asst prof to assoc prof obstet-gynec, 81-92, DIR RADIOIMMUNOASSAY LAB, DEPT OBSTET-GYNEC, C S MOTT CTR HUMAN GROWTH & DEVELOP, WAYNE STATE UNIV, DETROIT, 77-, PROF OBSTET-GYNEC, 92- *Personal Data:* b Sungakkarampatti, Madras, India, Dec 12, 38; m 67, Sagunthala Karuppana; c Sendhil & Raj. *Educ:* Madras Vet Col, India, BVSc, 61, MVSc, 67; Rutgers Univ, PhD(reproductive physiol), 74. *Prof Exp:* Asst lectr nutrit, Madras Vet Col, India, 68-70. *Mem:* Endocrine Soc; Am Fertil Soc; Soc Study Reproduction; Soc Exp Biol & Med; Soc Gynec Invest; Res Soc Alcoholism. *Res:* Suckling induced release of prolactin and effects of drugs on prolactin secretion; prolactin measurement, radioimmunoassay versus bioassay; use of zona pellucida as target antigen for immunocontraception; alcohol and lactation. *Mailing Add:* Dept Obstet & Gynec C S Mott Ctr Human Growth & Develop 275 E Hancock Detroit MI 48201. *Fax:* 313-577-8554

SUBRAMANIAN, PALLATHERI MANACKAL, ORGANIC CHEMISTRY, POLYMER CHEMISTRY. *Current Pos:* res chemist, Electrochem Dept, Chestnut Run Labs, E I du Pont de Nemours & Co, Inc, 64-70, sr res chemist, Plastics Dept, 70-72, from res assoc to sr res assoc, 72-85, res fel, 85-90, SR RES FEL & SR TECHNOL FEL, POLYMER PRODS DEPT, EXP STA, WILMINGTON, DEL, E I DU PONT DE NEMOURS & CO, INC, 85- *Personal Data:* b Ottapalam, India, Jan 10, 31; m 66; c 2. *Educ:* Univ Madras, BSc, 50; Univ Bombay, MSc, 58; Wayne State Univ, PhD(org chem), 64. *Prof Exp:* Chemist, Godrej Soaps, India, 50-58. *Mem:* Am Chem Soc; Chem Soc; Sigma Xi; Soc Plastics Engrs. *Res:* Physical organic chemistry; kinetics of elimination reactions in organic bicyclic systems; nuclear magnetic resonance spectroscopy of organic compounds; synthetic organic high polymers; adhesives and coatings; synthesis and process of plastics; diffusion; transport in polymers; permeability; packaging; plastic processing; containers; engineering polymers, polymer blends & processing. *Mailing Add:* 110 Cameron Dr Hockessin DE 19707-9684

SUBRAMANIAN, RAM SHANKAR, TRANSPORT & INTERFACIAL PHENOMENA. *Current Pos:* from asst prof to assoc prof, 73-82, Chair, 86-96, PROF CHEM ENG, CLARKSON UNIV, 82- *Personal Data:* b Madras, India, Aug 10, 47; US citizen; m 73, Jane Gatta; c Laura S & Erin S. *Educ:* Univ Madras, India, BTech, 68; Clarkson Univ, MS, 69, PhD(chem eng), 72. *Honors & Awards:* John Graham Jr Res Award, 78. *Prof Exp:* Instr fac eng & appl sci, State Univ NY, Buffalo, 72-73. *Concurrent Pos:* Prin investr numerous grants & contracts, 75-; vis assoc, Calif Inst Technol, 79-80; mem tech staff, Jet Propulsion Lab, 79-80. *Mem:* Am Inst Chem Engrs; fel AAAS; Sigma Xi; Am Ceramic Soc; Am Soc Eng Educ. *Res:* Interfacial phenomena; transport phenomena associated with bubbles, drops and particles. *Mailing Add:* Dept Chem Eng Clarkson Univ PO Box 5705 Potsdam NY 13699-5705

SUBRAMANIAN, RAVANASAMUDRAM VENKATACHALAM, POLYMER CHEMISTRY, POLYMER SCIENCE. *Current Pos:* res chemist, Mat Chem Sect, Col Eng Res Div, 69-73, assoc prof, 73-78, PROF MAT SCI, WASH STATE UNIV, 78- *Personal Data:* b Kalakad, India, Jan 16, 33; m 53, Chellam Balaji; c Venkatachalam & Balaji. *Educ:* Presidency Col, Madras, India, BSc, 53; Loyola Col, Madras, India, MSc, 54; Univ Madras, PhD(polymer chem), 57. *Prof Exp:* Jr res fel polymer chem, Nat Chem Lab, Poona, India, 57, Coun Sci & Indust Res India sr res fel, 57-59, jr sci officer, 59-63; res assoc chem, Case Inst Technol, 63-66 & Inst Molecular Biophys, Fla State Univ, 66; pool officer, Dept Phys Chem, Madras Univ, 66-67; asst prof, Harcourt Butler Tech Inst, Kanpur, India, 67-69. *Concurrent Pos:* NSF fel, Case Inst Technol, 63-66; AEC fel, Inst Molecular Biophys, Fla State Univ, 66; Coun Sci & Indust Res India grant, 68-69; head, Polymer Mat Sect, Wash State Univ, 74-85, Boeing distinguished prof, 81. *Mem:* Sigma Xi. *Res:* Kinetics and mechanisms of polymerization; polymer structure and proper properties; electropolymerization; interphase modification in carbon fiber reinforced composites; basalt fibers; organotin monomers and polymers; controlled release from polymer matrix; ceramic thin films on fibrous substrates. *Mailing Add:* Dept Mech & Mat Eng Wash State Univ Pullman WA 99164-2920

SUBRAMANIAN, SATCHITHANANDAM, GASTROINTESTINAL MUCIN, LIPID ABSORPTION IN LYMPH. *Current Pos:* RES BIOLOGIST, FOOD & DRUG ADMIN, 87- *Personal Data:* b Sri Lanka; US citizen; m 66, Puvaneswary; c Thushita & Laju. *Educ:* Univ London, PhD(biol), 91. *Prof Exp:* Res assoc, George Washington Univ, 78-87. *Mem:* Am Soc Nutrit Sci. *Res:* Dietary fiber and gastrointestinal mucin levels; feeding rats with diets containing dietary fibers and checking the gastrointestinal mucin levels; effect of plant oils on liver and serum lipids. *Mailing Add:* Off Pre-Market Approval Food & Drug Admin 200 C St SW Washington DC 20204. *Fax:* 202-418-3126

SUBRAMANIAN, SESHA, ELECTRON PARAMAGNETIC RESONANCE OF TRANSITION METAL COMPLEXES, DYNAMICS OF RIGID BODY ROTATION. *Current Pos:* RETIRED. *Personal Data:* b Wadakanchery, Kerala, India, July 19, 35; Can citizen; m 68; c 2. *Educ:* Univ Madras, India, BSc, 56, MA, 58; Indian Inst Sci, Bangalore, PhD(light scattering), 63. *Prof Exp:* Lectr physics, Col Militaire Royal, 63-73, from asst prof to assoc prof, 73-90, prof, 90- *Concurrent Pos:* Sr res fel, Indian Inst Sci, Bangalore, 63-65; fel, Cath Univ Leuven, Belg, 65-68, vis prof, 87-88; adj prof, Concordia Univ, Montreal, Can, 87- *Mem:* Int Soc Magnetic Resonance. *Res:* Electron paramagnetic resonance of transition metal ions; calculation of the intensity of the paramagnetic resonance lines; statistical determination of the errors in the spin Hamiltonian parameters of the paramagnetic ions. *Mailing Add:* 90 Reine des Pres La Prairie PQ J5R 4T5 Can

SUBRAMANIAN, SETHURAMAN, BIOPHYSICAL CHEMISTRY, BIOTECHNOLOGY. *Current Pos:* SR DEVELOP SCIENTIST, CULTOR FOOD SCI INC, 96- *Personal Data:* b Mattur, India, May 16, 40; US citizen; m 69, Anathi; c Sumathi, Sukanya & Mekhala. *Educ:* Univ Madras, BSc, 60, MSc, 65; Indian Inst Technol, Kanpur, India, PhD(phys chem), 69; Ind Univ, South Bend, MBA, 85. *Prof Exp:* Fel phys chem, Med Ctr, Univ Kans, 70-74; Nat Res Coun resident res assoc biophys, Naval Med Res Inst, Bethesda, 74-75; vis scientist phys chem, NIH, 75-82; res scientist, Biotechnol Group, Miles Labs Inc, 82-84, sr res scientist, 84-86, staff scientist, 86, supvr protein chem, 86-90; staff mem, Solvay Enzymes, 90-92 & Pfizer, Inc, 92-96. *Concurrent Pos:* Adj fac, Ind Univ, South Bend; workshop leader, Univ Wis-Madison, 87. *Mem:* Am Chem Soc; Am Soc Biol Chemists; AAAS. *Res:* Protein chemistry; enzymology; microcalorimetry; thermodynamics; spectroscopy; sickle cell hemoglobin; alcohol dehydrogenase; biotechnology; protein engineering; nutraceuticals; food science. *Mailing Add:* Cultor PO Box 8266 Terre Haute IN 47808-8266. *Fax:* 812-299-6864; *E-Mail:* ssubramanian@cultorfs.com

SUBRAMANYA, SHIVA, SPACE SYSTEMS, COMMAND CONTROL SYSTEM. *Current Pos:* ASST PROJ MGR SPACE SYSTS C3, DEFENSE & SPACE SECTOR, TRW, 73-, ADVAN C3I SYSTS MGR & LEAD SYSTS ENGR LARGE SYSTS, 73- *Personal Data:* b Hole Narasipur, India, Apr 8, 33; US citizen; m 67, Lee Silva; c Paul K & Kevin S. *Educ:* Mysore Univ, BS, 56; Karnatak Univ, MS, 62; Clark Univ, PhD(physics), 63; Calif State Univ, Dominguez Hills, MBA, 76; Nova Southeastern Univ, PhD(org theory), 87. *Honors & Awards:* Meritorious Serv Award, Armed Forces Commun Electronics Asn, 85, Medal of Merit, 89; Tech Execellance Award, Asn Engrs, India, 90. *Prof Exp:* Res fel physics, Clark Univ, 63-64; chief engr commun & elec, Alcatel/Transcom Elec, 64-67; prin eng commun, Electronics Div, General Dynamics, 67-73. *Concurrent Pos:* Presidential appointment, AEC, 62. *Mem:* Inst Elec & Electronics Engrs; Am Inst Physics; Am Phys Soc; Armed Forces Commun Electronics Asn. *Res:* Matrix organization structures of aerospace and electronics companies of 1950's to 1980's must be changed to be cost effective; mutation theory suggested by case studies indicate degenerated matrix structure, outsourcing, guru-novice structures are ways for the 1990's; military strategic systems. *Mailing Add:* 12546 Inglenook Lane Cerritos CA 90703

SUBRAMANYAM, VINAYAKAM, ORGANIC CHEMISTRY, PROCES SCALE-UP CHEMISTRY. *Current Pos:* group leader chem, 78-86, sr res chemist, 86-92 RES ASSOC, EI DUPONT DE NEMOURS & CO, 92- *Personal Data:* m 72, Rajeshwari N Rao; c Seema N. *Educ:* Annamalai Univ, India, MS, 67; Northeastern Univ, PhD(org chem), 73. *Prof Exp:* Assoc prof org & inorg chem, Presidency Col, Madras, 57-67; adj prof org chem, Northeastern Univ, 73-78. *Res:* Helped design technitium based cardiac imaging agent and hepatobiliary agent in diagnostic nuclear medicine; projects for process improvements and yield improvements; organic synthesis. *Mailing Add:* 3676 Marian Dr Boothwyn PA 19061. *Fax:* 609-540-4944; *E-Mail:* subramv@jlcloi.dnet.dupont.com

SUBUDHI, MANOMOHAN, CONTINUUM MECHANICS, MECHANICAL VIBRATIONS. *Current Pos:* assoc mech engr struct anal, 76-79, ENG SCIENTIST, BROOKHAVEN NAT LAB, 79- *Personal Data:* b Daspalla, India, Sept 27, 46; m 71, Shanti; c Sumit. *Educ:* Banaras Hindu Univ, India, BSc, 69; Mass Inst Technol, SM, 70; Polytech Inst NY, PhD(vibrations), 74. *Prof Exp:* Sr stress analyst pipe stress, Nuclear Power Serv Inc, 74-75; sr mech engr stress anal, Bechtel Power Corp, 75-76. *Concurrent Pos:* Adj prof, Manhattan Col, Bronx, NY. *Mem:* Am Soc Mech Engrs; Sigma Xi. *Res:* Fracture mechanics; structural analysis using numerical techniques; nuclear plant aging. *Mailing Add:* Brookhaven Nat Lab Bldg 130 PO Box 5000 Upton NY 11973-5000

SUCEC, JAMES, HEAT TRANSFER. *Current Pos:* from asst prof to assoc prof, 64-76, PROF MECH ENG & HEAT TRANSFER, UNIV MAINE, 76- *Personal Data:* b Bridgeport, Conn, June 15, 40; m 64; c 2. *Educ:* Univ Conn, BS, 62, MS, 63. *Prof Exp:* Instr mech eng & thermodynamics, Univ Conn, 63-64. *Concurrent Pos:* Asst proj engr, Pratt & Whitney Aircraft, Div United Technol Corp, 65-68; fac fel, NASA Lewis Res Ctr, 72-73; NSF res proj prin investr, Univ Maine, 79-81. *Mem:* Am Soc Mech Engrs. *Res:* Analytical and finite difference work in transient forced convection heat transfer, particularly conjugate problems; prediction of heat transfer across turbulent boundary layers. *Mailing Add:* 5711 Boardman Hall Rm 202 Univ Maine Orono ME 04469-5711

SUCHANNEK, RUDOLF GERHARD, EXPERIMENTAL ATOMIC PHYSICS. *Current Pos:* ASST RESEARCHER PHYSICS, UNIV CALIF, LOS ANGELES, 80- *Personal Data:* b Hindenburg, Ger, Oct 17, 21. *Educ:* Univ Hamburg, dipl(physics), 58; Univ Alaska, PhD(physics), 74. *Prof Exp:* Engr, Westinghouse Elec Corp, 58-62; eng specialist, Microwave Comp Lab, Sylvania Co, 62-64; physicist, Unified Sci Asn Inc, 64-66; sr res asst atomic collision, Geophys Inst, Univ Alaska, 66-73, fel, 74; res assoc atomic physics, Res Lab Electronics, Mass Inst Technol, 75-77; res assoc, Dept Physics & Astron, Rutgers Univ, 77-80. *Mem:* Am Phys Soc; Inst Elec & Electronic Engrs. *Res:* Excitation transfer collisions of laser excited atoms and molecules; charge exchange collisions of protons with atoms and molecules. *Mailing Add:* 1215 11th St Santa Monica CA 90401

SUCHARD, STEVEN NORMAN, LASERS. *Current Pos:* prog mgr, 86-89, MGR ADVAN PROGS, GM-HUGHES, 89- *Personal Data:* b Chicago, Ill, Feb 8, 44; m 64, Phyllis Shenkin; c David, Jeffrey, Heidi & Marc. *Educ:* Univ Calif, Berkeley, BS, 65; Mass Inst Technol, PhD(chem physics), 69. *Prof Exp:* Res asst, Lawrence Berkeley Lab, 64-65; teaching asst chem, Mass Inst Technol, 65-69; lectr, Univ Calif, Berkeley, 69-70; assoc dept head chem physics, Aerospace Corp, 70-76; prog mgr, Dept Energy, 76-78; tech mgr, Dept Chem, Hughes Aircraft Co, 78-80; prog mgr, TRW, 80-86. *Concurrent Pos:* Fel chem physics, Univ Calif, Berkeley, 69-70. *Mem:* Am Phys Soc. *Res:* Effect of system variables on the output of pulsed and continuous wave chemical lasers; flash photolysis; energy transfer in molecular systems; laser optics in high gain media; determination of the feasibility of producing new chemically and electrically pumped electronic transition lasers; measurement of molecular and kinetic parameters effecting optical gain of potential laser systems; development of advanced surveillance and communications technologies and applications. *Mailing Add:* 9912 Star Dr Huntington Beach CA 92646. *Fax:* 310-616-8262

SUCHER, JOSEPH, THEORETICAL PHYSICS, ELEMENTARY PARTICLE PHYSICS. *Current Pos:* asst prof, 57-61, assoc prof, 61-64, PROF PHYSICS, UNIV MD, 64- *Personal Data:* m, Dorothy Glassman; c Gabriel, Michael, Anatol & Anne. *Educ:* Brooklyn Col, BS, 52; Columbia Univ, PhD, 57. *Prof Exp:* Lectr, Brooklyn Col, 53; res asst & fel, Columbia Univ, 52-57. *Concurrent Pos:* Vis scientist, Brookhaven Nat Lab, 60 & 73, Lawrence Berkeley Lab, 93; NSF fel, 63-64; Guggenheim fel, Cambridge Univ, 68-69; NATO fel, 71; vis scholar, Univ Wash, 70, Chalmer & Uppsala Univ, 92; vis prof, Univ Paris, 71-72, Columbia Univ, 85-86, New York Univ, 86; Sr associateship, Nat Res Coun, 78-79; Ernest Kempton Adams fel, Columbia Univ, 84. *Mem:* Fel Am Phys Soc. *Res:* Scattering theory; elementary particle physics; quantum electrodynamics; quantum theory of composite systems; long-range forces; many-electron atoms. *Mailing Add:* Dept Physics Univ Md College Park MD 20742. *Fax:* 301-314-9525

SUCHESTON, MARTHA ELAINE, DEVELOPMENTAL ANATOMY. *Current Pos:* MEM STAFF, DEPT ANAT, OHIO STATE UNIV, 75-, DIR, MEDPATH, 89- *Personal Data:* b Bowling Green, Ky, June 17, 39; m 68; c 2. *Educ:* Western Ky Univ, BSc, 60; Ohio State Univ, MSc, 61, PhD(anat), 65. *Prof Exp:* Asst prof gross anat & embryol, Ohio State Univ, 67-68; asst prof gross anat, Stanford Univ, 68-69; from asst prof to assoc prof gross anat & embryol, Univ of BC, Vancouver, 70-75. *Concurrent Pos:* Bremer Found Fund fel, Ohio State Univ, 71-73; vis assoc prof gross anat, Univ BC, 74-75; Small Univ grant, 78; Cent Ohio Heart Asn grant, 78-79; NIDR, 85-87 & HCOP, 90-93. *Mem:* AAAS; Am Asn Anat; Teratology Soc; Soc Craniofacial Genetics. *Res:* Birth defects associated with anticonvulsant drugs. *Mailing Add:* Dept Anat 4072 Graves Hall Ohio State Univ Col Med 333 W Tenth Ave Columbus OH 43210-1239

SUCHMAN, DAVID, METEOROLOGY. *Current Pos:* Proj assoc meteorol, 74-76, asst scientist, 76-79, ASSOC SCIENTIST METEOROL, SPACE SCI & ENG CTR, UNIV WIS-MADISON, 79- *Personal Data:* b New York, NY, June 23, 47; m 70; c 2. *Educ:* Rensselaer Polytech Inst, BS, 68; Univ Wis-Madison, MS, 70, PhD(meteorol), 74. *Mem:* Am Meteorol Soc; Sigma Xi. *Res:* Application of geostationary satellite data to the study of the dynamics of mesoscale systems; practical applications of meteorology. *Mailing Add:* 722 Wedgewood Way Madison WI 53711

SUCHOW, LAWRENCE, SOLID STATE INORGANIC CHEMISTRY. *Current Pos:* from asst prof to prof, 64-91, EMER PROF CHEM, NJ INST TECHNOL, 91- *Personal Data:* b New York, NY, June 24, 23; m 68, Rosalyn Hirsch. *Educ:* City Col New York, BS, 43; Polytech Inst Brooklyn, PhD(chem), 51. *Prof Exp:* Anal chemist, Aluminum Co Am, 43-44; res chemist, Baker & Co, Inc, 44, Manhattan Proj, Oak Ridge, Tenn, 45-46, Baker & Co, Inc, 46-47, Signal Corps Eng Labs, US Dept Army, 50-54 & Francis Earle Labs, Inc, 54-58; sr res chemist, Westinghouse Elec Corp, 58-60; mem res staff, Watson Res Ctr, IBM Corp, 60-64. *Concurrent Pos:* NSF grants, 67-74; sabbatical leave, Imp Col, Univ London, 74. *Mem:* Am Chem Soc; Sigma Xi; fel NY Acad Sci. *Res:* High temperature inorganic reactions; physical properties of solids; x-ray crystallography; crystal growth, semiconductors, thin films; phosphors; rare earths; high Tc superconductors. *Mailing Add:* 6 Horizon Rd Ft Lee NJ 07024

SUCHSLAND, OTTO, WOOD TECHNOLOGY. *Current Pos:* from asst prof to assoc prof forest prod, 57-71, PROF FORESTRY, MICH STATE UNIV, 71- *Personal Data:* b Jena, Ger, June 18, 28; US citizen; m 56; c 2. *Educ:* Univ Hamburg, BS, 52, Dr nat sci(wood technol), 56. *Prof Exp:* Res engr, Swed Forest Prod Lab, Stockholm, 52-55; tech dir, Elmendorf Res, Inc, Calif, 55-57. *Mem:* Forest Prod Res Soc. *Res:* Adhesives; gluing of wood; technology of composite wood products. *Mailing Add:* 2699 Cahill Dr East Lansing MI 48823

SUCIU, GEORGE DAN, CHEMICAL ENGINEERING, ORGANIC CHEMISTRY. *Current Pos:* mgr, process res, 75-77, VPRES, RES & DEVELOP, PROCESS DEVELOP, ABBLUMMUS CREST, INC, BLOOMFIELD, NJ, 77- *Personal Data:* b Blaj, Romania, July 30, 34; WGerman citizen; m 59; c 3. *Educ:* Polytech Inst, Bucharest, MS, 57, PhD(chem eng), 59. *Prof Exp:* Shift engr petrol refining, Teleajen Refinery, Ploiesti, Romania, 58-60; pilot plant head, Icechim Res Inst, Bucharest, Romania, 61-68; prin researcher fundamental res chem eng, Res Ctr Romanian Acad, Bucharest, 68-70; assoc prof unit oper petrol refining, Inst Petrol, Ploiesti, Romania, 70-74; sect leader process develop, Akzo Res Lab, Obernburg, WGermany,. *Mem:* Am Chem Soc; Am Inst Chem Engrs. *Res:* Development of new technologies for the petroleum, petrochemical and chemical industries; aromatic alkylation using zeolite catalysts; catalytic reactors; maleic anhydride in fluidized bed reactor; ammoxidation of alkyl aromatics; epoxidation; processing of petroleum residues. *Mailing Add:* 417 Prospect St Ridgewood NJ 07450-5100

SUCIU, S(PIRIDON) N, MECHANICAL ENGINEERING. *Current Pos:* RETIRED. *Personal Data:* b Genesse County, Mich, Dec 11, 21; m 49; c 5. *Educ:* Purdue Univ, BSME, 44, MS, 49, PhD(mech eng). 51. *Honors & Awards:* Akroyd Stuart Award, Royal Aeronaut Soc, 72. *Prof Exp:* Res engr, Flight Propulsion Div, Gen Elec Co, NY, 51-52, Ohio, 52-54, supvr basic combustion res, 54-56, mgr appl rocket res, 56-58, mgr appl res oper, 58-63, mgr aerodynamic & component design oper, 63-67, mgr design technol oper, 67-71, gen mgr gas turbine eng dept, NY, 71-76, mgr energy technol oper, Energy Systs & Technol Div, 76-78, gen mgr neutron devices dept, 78-87. *Concurrent Pos:* Chmn, NASA Airbreathing Propulsion Comt, 67-70; mem Air Force Sci Adv Bd, 70-75; consult, NASA, 70- *Mem:* Am Soc Mech Engrs; Am Inst Aeronaut & Astronaut; Am Mgt Asn. *Res:* Power generation components and systems for utility, industrial, aircraft and marine use in commercial and military applications; electrical, mechanical and neutron devices for nuclear weapons; materials and manufacturing process development; general management of high technology businesses. *Mailing Add:* 4524 Pond Apple Dr N Naples FL 33999-8583

SUCKEWER, SZYMON, PLASMA PHYSICS, ATOMIC PHYSICS. *Current Pos:* mem staff, Princeton Univ, 75-77, res physicist, 77-80, SR RES PHYSICIST, PLASMA PHYSICS LAB, PRINCETON UNIV, 80-, PROF, DEPT MECH & AEROSPACE ENG & HEAD X-RAY LASER DIV PLASMA PHYSICS LAB, 87- *Personal Data:* b Warsaw, Poland, Apr 10, 38; US citizen; c 1. *Educ:* Moscow Univ, MS, 62; Inst Nuclear Res, Warsaw PhD(plasma physics), 66; Warsaw Univ, Dr, 71. *Honors & Awards:* IR-100 Award, 87, 89; Excellence Plasma Physics Award, Am Phys Soc, 90. *Prof Exp:* Head spectros lab plasma physics, Inst Nuclear Res, 66-69; pvt researcher, 69-71; assoc prof, Inst Nuclear Res, Warsaw Univ, 71-75. *Mem:* Fel Am Phys Soc; Optical Soc Am. *Res:* Plasma spectroscopy; ionization, excitation and radiation processes in high and low temperature plasmas; lasers (high power lasers and short wave-length lasers); tokamaks. *Mailing Add:* Dept Mech/Aerospace Eng Princeton Univ Eng Quad Rm D410 Olden St Princeton NJ 08544. *Fax:* 609-258-6109

SUCOFF, EDWARD IRA, PLANT PHYSIOLOGY, FORESTRY. *Current Pos:* asst & assoc prof, 60-71, PROF FORESTRY, UNIV MINN, ST PAUL, 71- *Personal Data:* b NJ, Nov 17, 31. *Educ:* Univ Mich, BS, 55, MS, 56; Univ Md, PhD(bot), 60. *Prof Exp:* Res forester, US Forest Serv, 56-60. *Mem:* AAAS; Am Soc Plant Physiologists. *Res:* Tree growth; stress physiology. *Mailing Add:* 110 Green Hall Forestry Univ Minn St Paul 1530 Cleveland Ave St Paul MN 55108-1027

SUCOV, E(UGENE) W(ILLIAM), LUMINESCENCE & LASERS, FUSION & ELECTROMAGNETIC LAUNCH. *Current Pos:* SR RES ASSOC, UNIV PITTSBURGH, 88- *Personal Data:* b Waterbury, Conn, Oct 27, 22; m 49, 82, Ellen G Benswanger; c Joshua H, Henry M & Andrew N. *Educ:* Brooklyn Col, BA, 43; NY Univ, MS, 54, PhD(physics), 59. *Prof Exp:* Electronics engr, 43-53; asst solid state physics, NY Univ, 53-58; res physicist, Glass Res Ctr, Pittsburgh Plate Glass Co, 58-63; res physicist, Westinghouse Res Labs, 63-66, mgr luminescence res, 66-70, fel physicist, 70-72, mgr behav res, 72-74, adv physicist, 75-78, mgr inertial confinement fusion progs, 78-83, mgr electromagnetic launch progs, 84-88. *Concurrent Pos:* Lectr, Univ Pittsburgh, 78-79; mem prog comt, Inertial Confinement Fusion Topical Meeting, 79-80. *Mem:* Am Phys Soc; Inst Elec & Electronics Engrs; fel Illuminating Engrs Soc; Sigma Xi. *Res:* Fusion physics; gas discharges; lasers; plasmas; electromagnetic launchers; solid state luminescence. *Mailing Add:* 1065 Lyndhurst Dr Pittsburgh PA 15206

SUCZEK, CHRISTOPHER ANNE, SEDIMENTARY GEOLOGY, PHYSICAL STRATIGRAPHY. *Current Pos:* asst prof, 77-82, chair, 90-96, ASSOC PROF GEOL, WESTERN WASH UNIV, 82- *Personal Data:* b Detroit, Mich, Sept 6, 42; c 1. *Educ:* Univ Calif, Berkeley, BA, 72; Stanford Univ, PhD(geol), 77. *Prof Exp:* Actg instr geol, Stanford Univ, 76. *Concurrent Pos:* Adj prof, Univ Nev, Reno, 83-84. *Mem:* Geol Soc Am; Soc Sedimentary Geologists; Geol Asn Can; Int Asn Sedimentologists; Am Geophys Union. *Res:* Tectonics of western North America; sedimentary petrology. *Mailing Add:* Dept Geol Western Wash Univ Bellingham WA 98225-9080. *Fax:* 360-650-7295

SUD, ISH, ENERGY MANAGEMENT, HVAC DESIGN & INDOOR AIR QUALITY. *Current Pos:* PRES, SUD ASSOCS, 79- *Personal Data:* b Calcutta, India, Oct 6, 49; m 85, Anu Agarwal; c Ishani & Shivani. *Educ:* Indian Inst Technol, India, BTech, 70; Duke Univ, MS, 71, PhD(mech eng), 75. *Prof Exp:* Res assoc, Duke Univ, 75, sr engr & systs analyst, 75-77, from res asst prof to res assoc prof, 78-83, adj assoc prof mech eng, 83-87. *Concurrent Pos:* Design engr, T C Cooke, P E, Inc, 74-77, dir, Energy Mgt & Special Proj, 77-78. *Mem:* Am Soc Heating, Refrig & Air Conditioning Engrs; Am Soc Mech Engrs; Sigma Xi; Nat Soc Prof Engrs. *Res:* Development of procedures for estimating building energy usage; research and application of techniques for reducing building energy usage, peak electrical demand and energy costs; research and application of waste heat recovery; humidity control in buildings, indoor air quality. *Mailing Add:* 3004 Montgomery St Durham NC 27705. *Fax:* 919-493-5549; *E-Mail:* sudassoc@concentric.com

SUDAN, RAVINDRA NATH, PLASMA PHYSICS. *Current Pos:* res assoc, Cornell Univ, 58-59, from asst prof to assoc prof elec eng, 59-63, dir, Lab Plasma Studies, 75-85, dep dir, Cornell Theory Ctr, 85-87, PROF ELEC ENG & APPL PHYSICS, CORNELL UNIV, 68-, IBM PROF ENG, 75- *Personal Data:* b Kashmir, India, June 8, 31; m 59, Dipali Ray; c Rajani & Ranjeet. *Educ:* Panjab Univ, India, BA, 48; Indian Inst Sci, dipl, 52; Univ London, DIC & PhD(elec eng), 55. *Honors & Awards:* James Clerk Maxwell Prize, Am Phys Soc, 89; Gold Medal Phys Sci, Acad Sci, Czech Repub, 93. *Prof Exp:* Elec engr, Brit Thomson Houston Co, Eng, 55-57; instruments engr, Imp Chem Industs, Ltd, India, 57-58. *Concurrent Pos:* Vis scientist Int Ctr Theoret Physics, Trieste, 65-66, 70-73; vis res physicist, Plasma Physics Lab, Princeton Univ, 66-67; head theoret plasma physics, Naval Res Lab, DC, 70-71, sci adv, 74-75; consult, Lawrence Radiation Lab, Univ Calif, Maxwell Lab, Los Alamos Sci Lab, Physics Int Co, Sci Appl, Inc; vis physicist, Inst Advan Study, Princeton, 75; sr res fel, Inst Fusion Studies, Univ Tex, 83; co-ed Handbook of Plasma Physics, N Holland. *Mem:* Fel AAAS; fel Am Phys Soc; fel Inst Elec & Electronics Engrs. *Res:* Thermonuclear fusion and space physics; high powered pulsed particle beams; magnetohydrodynamics; plasma turbulence; solar physics. *Mailing Add:* Lab Plasma Studies 369 Upson Hall Cornell Univ Ithaca NY 14853. *Fax:* 607-255-3004

SUDARSHAN, ENNACKEL CHANDY GEORGE, THEORETICAL PHYSICS. *Current Pos:* dir, 70-93, PROF PHYSICS, CTR PARTICLE THEORY, UNIV TEX, AUSTIN, 69- *Personal Data:* b Kottayam, India, Sept 16, 31; m 54; c 3. *Educ:* Univ Madras, BSc, 51, MA, 52; Univ Rochester, PhD(physics), 58. *Hon Degrees:* DSc, Univ Wis-Milwaukee, 69, Univ Delhi, 73, Chalmers Univ Tech, Sweden, 84, Univ Madras, 86, Univ Burwan, 91 & Cochin Univ Sci & Technol, 92. *Honors & Awards:* Padma Bhushan Award, 75; Third World Acad Prize Physics, 85. *Prof Exp:* Demonstr physics, Christian Col, Madras, 51-52; res asst, Tata Inst Fundamental Res, 52-55 & Univ Rochester, 55-57; res fel, Harvard Univ, 57-59; from asst prof to assoc prof, Univ Rochester, 59-64; prof, Syracuse Univ, 64-69. *Concurrent Pos:* Guest prof, Univ Bern, 63-64; vis prof, Brandeis Univ, 64; Sir C V Raman distinguished vis prof, Univ Madras, 70-71; dir, Inst Math Sci, Madras, 84-90. *Mem:* Fel Indian Nat Acad Sci; fel Am Phys Soc; fel Indian Acad Sci; fel Int Acad Philos Sci; fel Third World Acad Sci. *Res:* Quantum field theory; elementary particles; high energy physics; classical mechanics; quantum optics; Lie algebras and their application to particle physics; foundations of physics; philosophy and history of contemporary physics. *Mailing Add:* RLM Bldg 9-328 Univ Tex Austin TX 78712

SUDARSHAN, T S, SURFACE MODIFICATION TECHNOLOGIES, DIAMOND TECHNOLOGY. *Current Pos:* TECH DIR, MAT MODIFICATION INC, 87- *Educ:* IIT Madras, BTech, 76; Va Tech, MS, 78, PhD(mat sci), 84. *Honors & Awards:* Outstanding Young Mfg Engr, Soc Mfg Engrs, 90. *Prof Exp:* Sr metallurgist, Ashok Leyland Ltd, 79-81; dir res & develop, Synergistic Technologies Inc, 84-86. *Concurrent Pos:* Prin investr, Brookhaven Nat Labs Progs, Navy, Army, Air Force, NSF, 85-; vis prof, IIT Madras; chmn, Surface Modification Technologies, 88-; consult, NSF, 89-, Ultramet, 90- & Off Technol Assessment, US Cong, 90-94; chmn, Surface Eng Div, Am Soc Metall; co-ed, J Mat & Mfg Process, J Surface Engr. *Mem:* Am Soc Metall; Metall Soc. *Res:* Surface modification technologies; diamond technology; materials and manufacturing processes; chemical vapor deposition; nanoparticle materials. *Mailing Add:* 2929-P1 Eskridge Rd Fairfax VA 22031

SUDARSHAN, TANGALI S, SOLID, LIQUID & COMPRESSED GAS INSULATION, PHOTOCONDUCTING MATERIAL BREAKDOWN. *Current Pos:* from asst prof to assoc prof, 79-87, PROF, ELEC ENG, UNIV SC, 87- *Personal Data:* Can citizen; m 77; c 2. *Educ:* Univ Bangalore, India, BSc, 68; Univ Mysore, MSc, 70; Univ Waterlooo, Can, MASc, 72, PhD(electrical eng), 74. *Prof Exp:* Res officer, Nat Res Coun Can, 74-79. *Concurrent Pos:* Prin investr, NSF, 80-82, Dept Energy, 80-85, INTELSAT, Wash, DC, 84-87, Sandia Nat Labs, 79-81, Off Naval Res, 87- *Mem:* Sr mem Inst Elec & Electronics Engrs. *Res:* Solid, liquid and gas insulated systems for high voltage power system and pulsed power applications; surface flashover of solid insulator and photoconductor materials; fast high voltage and current diagnostics; insulator degradation and aging; electrical surface properties of insulators. *Mailing Add:* Col Eng Univ SC Columbia SC 29208

SUDBOROUGH, IVAN HAL, INFORMATION SCIENCE. *Current Pos:* FOUNDERS PROF & HEAD COMPUT SCI PROG, UNIV TEX, DALLAS, 85- *Personal Data:* b Royal Oak, Mich, Dec 19, 43; m 69; c 2. *Educ:* Calif State Polytech Col, BS, 66, MS, 67; Pa State Univ, PhD(comput sci), 71. *Prof Exp:* From asst prof to assoc prof comput sci, Northwestern Univ, 71-85. *Concurrent Pos:* NSF res grant, 74. *Mem:* Asn Comput Mach; Soc Indust & Appl Math. *Res:* Computational complexity; formal languages; automata theory; theory of computation. *Mailing Add:* 13309 Rolling Hills Lane Dallas TX 75240

SUDBURY, JOHN DEAN, PHYSICAL CHEMISTRY, SURFACE CHEMISTRY. *Current Pos:* PRES, RELIGIOUS FOUND, 83- *Personal Data:* b Natchitoches, La, July 29, 25; m 47, Jean Jung; c Byron, James (deceased) & Linda. *Educ:* Univ Tex, BS, 44, MS, 47, PhD(phys chem), 49. *Honors & Awards:* Speller Award, Nat Asn Corrosion Engrs, 66. *Prof Exp:* Sr res chemist, Develop & Res Dept, Continental Oil Co, 49-56, supv res chemist, 56-66, dir, Petrochem Res Div, Okla, 66-69, gen mgr, C/A Nuclear Fuels Div, Calif, 69-70, asst to vpres res, NY, 70-72, asst dir res & vpres Res Div, Conoco Coal Develop Co, 72-83. *Mem:* Am Chem Soc; Nat Asn Corrosion Engrs; NY Acad Sci; Electrochem Soc; AAAS. *Res:* Advanced systems for liquified natural gas, arctic transport; development of conversion processes to get coal into more desirable energy sources; conversion of coal to liquids and gases; removal of sulfur from combustion products of coal; corrosion processes associated with petroleum production. *Mailing Add:* 42 Cascade Springs Pl Spring TX 77381

SUDDARTH, STANLEY KENDRICK, STRUCTURAL WOOD PRODUCTS. *Current Pos:* RETIRED. *Personal Data:* b Westerly, RI, Oct 22, 21; m 88, Mary H Comus. *Educ:* Purdue Univ, BSF, 43, MS, 49, PhD(agr econ forestry), 52. *Honors & Awards:* Res Award, Truss Plate Inst, 70; Markwardt Eng Res Award, Forest Prod Res Soc, 71; Markwardt Award, Am Soc Testing & Mat, 72. *Prof Exp:* Assoc dir bomb effectiveness res, US Dept Air Force Proj, Res Found, Purdue Univ, West Lafayette, 51-54, from asst prof to assoc prof forestry, 54-60, prof wood eng, 60-81, Hillenbrand prof wood eng, Agr Exp Sta, 81-86. *Concurrent Pos:* Consult home mfg indust, 55- & US Forest Prod Lab, Madison, Wis, 70-72; tech adv, Am Inst Timber Construct & Truss Plate Inst. *Mem:* Forest Prod Res Soc; Int Acad Wood Sci; Am Soc Agr Engrs; Am Soc Civil Engrs. *Res:* Applied mathematics in engineering and economic problems; engineering properties and uses of wood. *Mailing Add:* 31675 NE Canter Lane Sherwood OR 97140

SUDDERTH, WILLIAM DAVID, MATHEMATICS PROBABILITY, MATHEMATICAL STATISTICS. *Current Pos:* asst prof statist, 69-71, assoc prof, 71-77, PROF STATIST, UNIV MINN, MINNEAPOLIS, 77- *Personal Data:* b Dallas, Tex, Apr 29, 40; m 62; c 2. *Educ:* Yale Univ, BS, 63; Univ Calif, Berkeley, MS, 65, PhD(math), 67. *Prof Exp:* Asst prof statist, Univ Calif, Berkeley, 67-68; asst prof math, Morehouse Col, 68-69. *Mem:* Am Math Soc; fel Inst Math Statist. *Res:* Probability, especially the study of finitely additive probability measures and abstract gambling theory, which is also known as dynamic programming and stochastic control; foundations of statistics; stochastic games. *Mailing Add:* Sch of Statist Univ Minn 270 Vincent 206 Church St SE Minneapolis MN 55455

SUDDICK, RICHARD PHILLIPS, PHYSIOLOGY. *Current Pos:* PROF COMMUNITY DENT, DENT SCH & PROF PHYSIOL, GRAD SCH BIOMED SCI, UNIV TEX HEALTH SCI CTR, SAN ANTONIO, 80- *Personal Data:* b Omaha, Nebr, Feb 3, 34; m 55; c 4. *Educ:* Creighton Univ, BS, 58, MS, 59, DDS, 61; Univ Iowa, PhD(physiol), 67. *Prof Exp:* Instr physiol, Univ Iowa, 63-65; asst prof biol sci, Creighton Univ, 65-68, from assoc prof to prof oral biol & head dept, 68-74, assoc prof physiol, Sch Med, 70-74; assoc prof physiol & asst dean res, Col Dent Med, Med Univ SC, 74-76; prof oral biol & chmn dept & asst dean res, Sch Dent, Univ Louisville, 76-80. *Mem:* AAAS; Int Asn Dent Res; Am Physiol Soc. *Res:* Physiology of exocrine secretion, primarily secretion of saliva; function of the saliva in the oral cavity and the alimentary tract and its relationship to normal and diseased states; etiology of dental caries and periodontal disease; behavioral constructs and neurophysiological correlates in humans. *Mailing Add:* 9226 Bingham St San Antonio TX 78230

SUDERMAN, HAROLD JULIUS, BIOCHEMISTRY. *Current Pos:* RETIRED. *Personal Data:* b Myrtle, Man, July 24, 21; m 47; c 3. *Educ:* Univ Man, BSc, 49, MSc, 52, PhD, 62. *Prof Exp:* Demonstr biochem, Univ Man, 51-52, lectr, 52-56, asst prof, 56-63; asst prof, Ont Agr Col, 63-65; from asst prof to assoc prof biochem, Univ Guelph, 65-86. *Mem:* Can Biochem Soc. *Res:* Molecular properties, structure and function of proteins; comparative biochemistry of hemoglobins. *Mailing Add:* Six Rickson Ave Guelph ON N1G 2W7 Can

SUDHAKARAN, GUBBI RAMARAO, FAR INFRARED LASERS, LASER STARK SPECTROSCOPY. *Current Pos:* PROF & CHMN PHYSICS, UNIV WIS, 93- *Personal Data:* b Bangalore, India, May 29, 49; m 83, Pushpa V Doddaballapur; c Sunil & Shaan. *Educ:* Bangalore Univ, BS, 69, MS, 72; Univ Idaho, PhD(physics), 82. *Prof Exp:* Lectr physics, Jr Col, India, 72-75; chmn, Physics Deptt, S K Col, India, 75-78; fel, Tex Tech Univ, 82-83; asst prof physics, Univ Idaho, 83-88; assoc prof, State Univ NY, Oswego, 88-93. *Mem:* Am Phys Soc; Sigma Xi; NY Acad Sci. *Res:* Development of direct discharge hydrogen cyanide and water vapor lasers in the far infrared region; investigate the molecular structure using the far infrared lasers and laser stark spectroscopy. *Mailing Add:* 610 Tenth Ave N Onalaska WI 54650. *Fax:* 608-785-8403; *E-Mail:* sudhak@physics.uwlax.edu

SUDIA, THEODORE WILLIAM, ENVIRONMENTAL PHYSIOLOGY. *Current Pos:* chief ecol serv, Off Natural Sci, US Nat Park Serv, 69-73, chief scientist, 73-77, actg assoc dir sci & technol, 77-80, dep science adv, Int Sect, 80-81, SR SCIENTIST, US NAT PARK SERV, 81- *Personal Data:* b Ambridge, Pa, Oct 10, 25; m 49; c 3. *Educ:* Kent State Univ, BS, 50; Ohio State Univ, MS, 51, PhD(bot), 54. *Prof Exp:* Asst prof biol sci, Winona State Col, 55-58; res fel plant physiol, Univ Minn, St Paul, 58-59, res assoc physiol ecol, 59-61, asst prof, 61-63, assoc prof plant path & bot, 63-67; assoc dir, Am Inst Biol Sci, Washington, DC, 67-69. *Mem:* AAAS; Ecol Soc Am; Am Soc Plant Physiologists; Bot Soc Am; NY Acad Sci. *Res:* Research administration. *Mailing Add:* 1117 E Capitol St SE Washington DC 20003-1438

SUDIA, WILLIAM DANIEL, ENTOMOLOGY, VIROLOGY. *Current Pos:* RETIRED. *Personal Data:* b Ambridge, Pa, Aug 19, 22; m 49; c 2. *Educ:* Univ Fla, BS, 49; Ohio State Univ, MS, 50, PhD(entom), 58. *Prof Exp:* Entomologist, Med Entom Unit, Ctr Dis Control, USPHS, 51-53, asst chief arbovirus vector lab, 53-65, lab consult & develop sect, 66, chief, Arbovirus Ecol Lab, 67-73, dep dir, Lab Training Div, Ctr Dis Control, 73-84. *Mem:* Sigma Xi; Am Soc Trop Med & Hyg; Am Mosquito Control Asn. *Res:* Ecology of arthropod-borne encephalitis viruses; mosquito vectors and vertebrate hosts. *Mailing Add:* 1445 Diamond Head Dr Decatur GA 30033

SUDMEIER, JAMES LEE, ANALYTICAL CHEMISTRY. *Current Pos:* SR LECTR, TUFTS NEW ENG MED CTR, 86- *Personal Data:* b Minneapolis, Minn, Feb 14, 38; m 62; c 2. *Educ:* Carleton Col, BA, 59; Princeton Univ, MA, 61, PhD(chem), 66. *Prof Exp:* Actg asst prof chem, Univ Calif, Los Angeles, 65-66, asst prof, 66-70; asst prof, Univ Calif, Riverside, 70-71, assoc prof, 71-84. *Mem:* Am Chem Soc. *Res:* Nuclear magnetic resonance studies of coordination compounds and metal binding to biopolymers. *Mailing Add:* Dept Biol Chem Tufts Univ 136 Harrison Ave Boston MA 02111

SUDWEEKS, EARL MAX, ANIMAL NUTRITION, DAIRY NUTRITION. *Current Pos:* PROF & DAIRY EXTEN SPECIALIST, TEX A&M UNIV, 81- *Personal Data:* b Richfield, Utah, Dec 27, 33; m 60, Dorene M Collett; c Jed, Karen, Ruth, Earlene, Susan, William, Marie, Nanette & David. *Educ:* Utah State Univ, BS, 60, MS, 62; NC State Univ, PhD(nutrit biochem), 72. *Prof Exp:* Res assoc animal nutrit, Utah State Univ, 62-65, from asst prof to assoc prof animal exten, 65-68; res asst animal nutrit, NC State Univ, 68-72; asst prof animal nutrit, Univ Ga, 72-80; dir nutrit, Watkins Inc, Winona, Minn & Prof Prods, Inc, Sauk City, Wis, 80-81. *Concurrent Pos:* Consult, US Feed Grains Coun, Taiwan, Gilas Dairy Coop, Mex & Voca, Brazil. *Mem:* Am Dairy Sci Asn; Am Soc Animal Sci; Sigma Xi; Am Inst Nutrit. *Res:* The role of roughages in rumen physiology, energy utilization, feed conversion of beef and dairy cattle. *Mailing Add:* Tex A&M Univ Res & Exten Ctr Box 38 Overton TX 75684. *Fax:* 903-834-7140; *E-Mail:* m_sudweeks@tamu.edu

SUDWEEKS, WALTER BENTLEY, INDUSTRIAL CHEMISTRY, EXPLOSIVES. *Current Pos:* sr res scientist, Ireco Chem, 76-79, dir prod develop, 79-82, asst dir res & develop, 82-84, DIR RES & DEVELOP, IRECO CHEM, 84- *Personal Data:* b Buhl, Idaho, May 22, 40; m 65; c 2. *Educ:* Brigham Young Univ, BS, 65, PhD(org chem), 70. *Prof Exp:* Res chemist, Polymer Intermediates Dept, E I du Pont de Nemours & Co, Inc, 69-76. *Mem:* Am Chem Soc; Nat Defense Preparedness Asn. *Res:* Organic synthesis; hydrometallurgical processes; explosives research; management of commercial explosives research and development. *Mailing Add:* Dyno Nobel Inc 3000 W 8600 S West Jordan UT 84088-9627

SUELTER, CLARENCE HENRY, SCIENCE EDUCATION. *Current Pos:* From asst prof to assoc prof, 61-69, PROF BIOCHEM, MICH STATE UNIV, 69- *Personal Data:* b Lincoln, Kans, Dec 15, 28; m 55; c 3. *Educ:* Kans State Univ, BS, 51, MS, 53; Iowa State Univ, PhD(biochem), 59. *Concurrent Pos:* USPHS fel, Univ Minn, 59-61; res career develop award, Mich State Univ, 65-75. *Mem:* AAAS; Am Chem Soc; Am Soc Biochem & Molecular Biol. *Res:* Science education; structure and function of enzymes. *Mailing Add:* Dept Biochem Mich State Univ Col Human Med 110 E Fee Hall East Lansing MI 48824-1316

SUEMATSU, YASUHARU, OPTICAL COMMUNICATIONS, OPTICAL DEVICES. *Current Pos:* Res assoc, Tokyo Inst Technol, 60-61, from assoc prof to prof, 61-89, dean eng fac, 86-88, pres, 89-93, EMER PROF, TOKYO INST TECHNOL, 93-; PRES, KOCHI UNIV TECHNOL, 97- *Personal Data:* m 62, Hiroko; c Hisayuki & Yoshinori. *Educ:* Tokyo Inst Technol, BS, 55, MS, 57, PhD(elec eng), 60. *Hon Degrees:* DEng, Univ Maryland, 92; Dr, Surry Univ, 94. *Honors & Awards:* Valdmer Paulsen's Gold Medal, Danish Acad Tech Sci, 83; David Sarnoff Award, Inst Elec & Electronics Engrs, 86; Prime Minister Award, Japanese Govt, 83; Tejima Mem Invention Award, 84; Tore Sci & Technol Award, 89; John Tyndall Award, Am Optical Soc, 93; C&C Prize, C&C Found, Japan, 94. *Concurrent Pos:* mem, Coun Univ Found & Sch Coop, Ministry Educ & Cult, 91-, Coun Broadcasting Technol, UK, 94- & Comt Space Develop, 94-, pres, Asn Univ Accreditation, 93; auditor, Japan Soc Prom Sci, 94-95. *Mem:* Foreign assoc mem Nat Acad Eng; fel Optical Soc Am; Inst Electronic, Info & Commun Engrs Japan (pres, 92-93); Inst Elec Engrs Japan; Inst Appl Physics Japan; fel Inst Elec & Electronics Engrs. *Res:* Optical communications, especially for semiconductor lasers, integrated optics and optical waveguides. *Mailing Add:* Kochi-Univ Technol 185 Miyano Kuchi Toseyamada Kochi 782 Japan. *Fax:* 81-8875-7-2001; *E-Mail:* suematsu@ng.kochi-tech.ac.jp

SUEN, CHING YEE, COMPUTER APPLICATIONS, PATTERN RECOGNITION. *Current Pos:* From asst prof to assoc prof, 72-79, chmn dept, 80-84, PROF COMPUT SCI, CONCORDIA UNIV, 79-, DIR CENPARMI, 88-, ASSOC DEAN, RES, 93-; CONSULT, 79- *Personal Data:* b Chung Shan, China, Oct 14, 42; Can citizen. *Educ:* Univ Hong Kong, BSc, 66, MSc 68; Univ BC, PhD(elec eng), 72. *Honors & Awards:* Merit Award, Fed Chinese Can Prof, 88; Meritorious Merit Award, Chinese Lang Comput Soc, 88; Info Technol Award, Natural Scis & Eng Coun Can, 92. *Concurrent Pos:* Chmn comt character recognition, Can Stand Asn, 77-; vis scientist, Res Lab Electronics, Mass Inst Technol, 78-80; dir, Recognition Technol Users Asn, 84-86; gov, Int Asn Pattern Recognition. *Mem:* Fel Inst Elec & Electronics Engrs; Can Image Processing & Pattern Recognition Soc (pres, 84-90); Recognition Technol Users Asn; Chinese Lang Comput Soc (pres, 90-92). *Res:* Character recognition and data processing; computational linguistics and text processing; expert systems. *Mailing Add:* Dept Comput Sci Concordia Univ 1455 Maisonneuve W Suite GM-606 Montreal PQ H3G 1M8 Can. *Fax:* 514-848-4522

SUEN, T(ZENG) J(IUEQ), POLYMER CHEMISTRY. *Current Pos:* CONSULT, 77-; CHMN, ATC ASSOCS, INC, 88- *Personal Data:* b Hangzhou, China, June 7, 12; nat US; m 44, Ming-Tung Chang; c Caroline (Shookhoff) & Theodore M. *Educ:* Tsinghua Univ, China, BS, 33; Mass Inst Technol, MS, 35, ScD, 37. *Prof Exp:* Fel, Mass Inst Technol, 37-38; asst prof chem eng, Chongqing Univ, 38-39; head dept res, Tung Li Oil Works, Chongqing, China, 39-44; mem staff, Radiation Lab, Mass Inst Technol, 44-45; chem engr, Stamford Res Labs, Am Cyanamid Co, 45-56, group leader in charge polymer chem, 56-60, mgr thermoplastics res, 61, dir plastics & polymers res, 61-70, proj mgr div res, 71-77. *Mem:* Am Chem Soc; AAAS. *Res:* Synthetic fuels and lubricants; plastics; condensation and addition polymers; environmental improvement. *Mailing Add:* 349 Mariomi Rd New Canaan CT 06840-3318. *Fax:* 516-674-0272

SUENAGA, MASAKI, METALLURGY, ELECTRICAL ENGINEERING. *Current Pos:* div head metall, 78-86, FROM ASST METALLURGIST TO SR METALLURGIST, BROOK HAVEN NAT LAB, 69- *Personal Data:* b Hohoku, Japan, Sept 15, 37; m 72; c 2. *Educ:* Univ Calif, Berkeley, BSEE, 63, MSEE, 64, PhD(metall), 69. *Prof Exp:* Fel metall, Lawrence Berkeley Lab, 69. *Mem:* Am Phys Soc; AAAS; Am Soc Metals. *Res:* Superconducting materials; mechanical properties of metals and alloys. *Mailing Add:* Bldg 480 Brookhaven Nat Lab Upton NY 11973

SUENRAM, RICHARD DEE, PHYSICAL CHEMISTRY, CHEMICAL PHYSICS. *Current Pos:* RES CHEMIST PHYS CHEM, NAT INST STANDARDS & TECHNOL, 77- *Personal Data:* b Halstead, Kans, Feb 2, 45; m 65; c 1. *Educ:* Kans State Univ, BS, 67; Univ Wis, MS, 69; Univ Kans, PhD(chem), 73. *Prof Exp:* Res chemist phys chem, Rohm & Haas Co, 69-70; res assoc, Harvard Univ, 73-75; res assoc, Nat Bur Standards, 75-77. *Res:* Molecular spectroscopy of transient molecular species found in gas phase chemical reactions; molecular species associated with atmospheric and interstellar chemistry; molecular spectroscopy of van der Waals and hydrogen bonded clusters. *Mailing Add:* Physics B208 Dept Com USG/NIST Gaithersburg MD 20899

SUEOKA, NOBORU, GENETICS. *Current Pos:* PROF BIOL, UNIV COLO, BOULDER, 72- *Personal Data:* b Kyoto, Japan, Apr 12, 29; m 57; c 1. *Educ:* Kyoto Univ, BS, 53, MS, 55; Calif Inst Technol, PhD(biochem genetics), 59. *Prof Exp:* Fulbright grant, 55-56; res fel biochem genetics, Harvard Univ, 58-60; asst prof microbiol, Univ Ill, 60-62; from assoc prof to prof biol, Princeton Univ, 62-72. *Mem:* Am Soc Biol Chemists; Am Soc Microbiol; Genetics Soc Am. *Res:* Biochemical genetics; molecular biology, particularly genetic aspects of biological macromolecules, nucleic acids and protein. *Mailing Add:* Dept Biol MC D Univ Colo Campus Box 347 Boulder CO 80309-0347. *Fax:* 303-492-0388

SUER, H(ERBERT) S, instrumentation, engineering mechanics, for more information see previous edition

SUESS, GENE GUY, MEAT SCIENCE. *Current Pos:* Res technologist, Oscar Mayer & Co, 68-73, new prod develop supvr, 73-78, prod develop mgr, 78-85, ASSOC DIR RES & DEVELOP & VPRES QUAL ASSURANCE, OSCAR MAYER FOODS CORP. *Personal Data:* b Beaver, Okla, Apr 16, 41; m 68; c 2. *Educ:* Tex Tech Univ, BS, 63; Univ Wis-Madison, MS 66, PhD(meat sci, animal sci), 68. *Mem:* Am Meat Sci Asn; Inst Food Technologists. *Res:* Meats processing. *Mailing Add:* 3006 Pelham Rd Madison WI 53713

SUESS, HANS EDUARD, chemistry; deceased, see previous edition for last biography

SUESS, JAMES FRANCIS, PSYCHIATRY. *Current Pos:* prof, 62-82, EMER PROF PSYCHIAT, SCH MED, UNIV MISS, 82- *Personal Data:* b Rock Island, Ill, Nov 27, 19; m 46; c 3. *Educ:* Northwestern Univ, BS, 50, MD, 52. *Prof Exp:* Resident psychiat, Warren State Hosp, Warren, Pa, 53-56, clin dir, 56-62. *Concurrent Pos:* Fel psychiat, Med Sch, Univ Pa, 53; exchange teaching fel, Med Sch, Univ Pittsburgh, 55; Col Physicians & Surgeons fel, Columbia Univ, 58; consult, Vet Admin, 62-82 & Gov Drug Coun, Miss, 72-75; vis prof, Inst Psychiat & Royal Free Hosp Sch Med, London; assoc chief staff educ, Vet Admin Ctr, 78-82. *Res:* Medical education in psychiatry; use of television and videotape in medical education; programmed teaching with television; short term psychotherapy of neurotic and personality disorders; use of videotape in teaching managerial and supervisory skills in business. *Mailing Add:* 1415 Radcliffe St Jackson MS 39211-4824

SUESS, STEVEN TYLER, FLUID DYNAMICS, MAGNETOHYDRODYNAMICS. *Current Pos:* PHYSICIST, MARSHALL SPACE FLIGHT CTR, NASA, HUNTSVILLE, AL, 83- *Personal Data:* b Los Angeles, Calif, Aug 4, 42; m 93, Louis C Alexander; c 2. *Educ:* Univ Calif, Berkeley, AB, 64, PhD(planetary, space sci), 69. *Prof Exp:* Nat Acad Sci-Nat Res Coun res assoc, Environ Sci Serv Admin Res Labs, Boulder, Colo, 69-71; physicist, Space Environ Lab, Nat Oceanic & Atmospheric Admin, 71-83. *Concurrent Pos:* Guest worker, Max Planck Inst Aeronomy, 75; vis scholar, Stanford Univ, 80-81; vis scholar, Inst Astrophys, Arcetri, Italy, 91 & 93. *Mem:* Am Geophys Union; Am Astronom Soc; Sigma Xi; Int Astron Union. *Res:* Dynamics of the sun and stars; oscillations of stars; stellar winds; magnetohydrodynamics of rotating fluids. *Mailing Add:* Space Sci Lab ES82 Marshall Space Flight Ctr NASA Huntsville AL 35812

SUFFET, I H (MEL), ENVIRONMENTAL CHEMISTRY, ANALYTICAL CHEMISTRY. *Current Pos:* PROF ENVIRON SCI & ENG, UNIV CALIF, LOS ANGELES, 91- *Personal Data:* b Brooklyn, NY, May 11, 39; m 62, Eileen Shustermen; c Alison & Jeffrey. *Educ:* Brooklyn Col, BS, 61; Univ Md, Col Park, MS, 64; Rutgers Univ New Brunswick, PhD, 69. *Honors & Awards:* F J Zimmerman Award, Am Chem Soc, 83; Distinguished Serv Award, Environ Chem Div, Am Chem Soc, 90. *Prof Exp:* From asst prof to prof chem & environ sci, Drexel Univ, 69-90. *Concurrent Pos:* Consult & grants, Western Elec Co, 70-72, City Philadelphia, 72-75, Nat Sci Found-Res Appl Nat Needs, 76-77 & 79-80, Environ Protection Agency, 78, 80-97, Health Effects Inst, 82-83, Am Water Works Res Found, 83-88, 96-; mem safe drinking water comt, Nat Acad Sci, 78-79, chmn subcomt efficiency use activated carbon for drinking water treatment; mem, Water Reuse Comt, Am Water Works Asn, 80-88, Organics Contaminants Comt, 82-96, Health Effects Comt, 85-96; comt fate chem environ, Int Asn Water Pollution Res & Control, 82-97. *Mem:* Sigma Xi; Am Chem Soc (treas, 83-86); Am Water Works Asn; Int Asn Water Qual; Asn Environ Eng Profs; Int Humic Substance Soc (secy, 91-95). *Res:* Environmental chemistry and analysis of trace organics; water, water reuse treatment; activated carbon and other water treatment processes; taste and odor problems in drinking water; disinfection byproducts; fate of pollutants in the environment; chemical nature of water and wastes; nonpoint source runoff. *Mailing Add:* Univ Calif Sch Pub Health Environ Sci & Eng Prog 10833 LeConte Ave CHS Rm 46-081 Los Angeles CA 90095-1772. *Fax:* 310-206-3358; *E-Mail:* msuffet@ucla.edu

SUFFIN, STEPHEN CHESTER, PHARMACOLOGY. *Current Pos:* DIR PATH, LAB PROCEDURES INC, 80- *Personal Data:* b Los Angeles, Calif, Aug 13, 47; m 69; c 2. *Educ:* Univ Calif, Los Angeles, BA, 68, MD, 72. *Prof Exp:* Fel immunopath, Univ Calif, Los Angeles, 75-77, asst prof path, 77- *Concurrent Pos:* Sr investr immunopathology, Lab Infectious Dis, Nat Inst Allergy & Infectious Dis, NIH, 78-80; consult, Armed Forces Inst Path, 78-80, Jet Propulsion Lab, Calif Inst Technol, 80- *Mem:* Int Acad Path; Am Soc Clin Pathologists; Col Am Pathologists; Am Asn Immunologists; Am Soc Microbiol. *Mailing Add:* Ventura Inst Psychiat 250 Lombard St Suite 1 Thousand Oaks CA 91360. *Fax:* 818-997-8828

SUFIT, ROBERT LOUIS, NEUROMUSCULAR DISEASES. *Current Pos:* ASST PROF, UNIV WIS-MADISON, 82- *Personal Data:* b Washington, DC, July 16, 50; div; c 3. *Educ:* John Hopkins Univ, BA, 72, MA, 72; Univ VA, MD, 76. *Mem:* Am Acad Neurol; Am Soc Neurol Invest. *Res:* Muscle disease; motor performance of patients with muscle disease. *Mailing Add:* 564 Toepfer Ave Madison WI 53711

SUFRIN, JANICE RICHMAN, BIOORGANIC CHEMISTRY, MOLECULAR & BIOCHEMICAL PHARMACOLOGY. *Current Pos:* cancer res scientist IV, Surg Oncol & Exp Therapeut Dept, 82-88, CANCER RES SCIENTIST IV, EXP THERAPEUT DEPT, ROSWELL PARK CANCER INST, 88-; ASST RES PROF PHARMACOL, ROSWELL PARK GRAD DIV, STATE UNIV NY, BUFFALO, 91- *Personal Data:* b New York, NY, May 5, 41; m 68; c 3. *Educ:* Bryn Mawr Col, AB, 62; Brandeis Univ MA, 67, PhD(chem), 72. *Prof Exp:* Fel, Pharmacol Dept, Sch Med, Johns Hopkins Univ, 72-74; cancer res scientist, Exp Therapeut Dept, Roswell Park Mem Inst, 75-77; res instr physiol & biophys, Sch Med, Wash Univ, 77-80, res asst prof, 80-82; res asst prof chem, Roswell Park Grad Div, State Univ NY, Buffalo, 82-91. *Mem:* Am Chem Soc; Am Soc Biochem & Molecular Biol; Am Asn Cancer Res; Sigma Xi. *Res:* Synthesis and biological evaluation of agents which interfere with the biosynthesis and metabolism of the key biological intermediate, S-adenosylmethionine, thus affecting cellular transmethylation reacionts and polyamine pathways. *Mailing Add:* Grace Cancer Drug Ctr Roswell Park Cancer Inst 666 Elm St Buffalo NY 14263. *Fax:* 716-845-8857; *E-Mail:* rosufrin@ubvms.cc.buffalo.edu

SUGA, HIROYUKI, CARDIAC PHYSIOLOGY, CARDIAC BIOENGINEERING & BIOMEDICAL ENGINEERING. *Current Pos:* PROF & CHMN PHYSIOL, OKAYAMA UNIV MED SCH, 91- *Personal Data:* b Japan, Oct 4, 41; m 69, Atsuko; c Kiyomi & Harumi. *Educ:* Okayama Univ, MD, 66; Univ Tokyo, DMedSc, 70. *Honors & Awards:* Res Encour Award, Japanese Med Eng Soc, 75; Satoh Award, Japanese Circulation Soc, 85; Ueda Award, Japanese Heart J Asn, 85; P D White Int Lectr, Am Heart Asn, 93; Konrad Witzig Lectr, Ctr Control Sci & Dynamical Systs, 94; Mashimo Mem Lectr, Japan Cire Soc, 96. *Prof Exp:* Asst prof physiol, Tokyo Med & Dent Univ, 70-71; fel biomed eng, Johns Hopkins Univ Med Sch, 71-73, asst prof, 75-78; asst prof physiol, Univ Tokyo Med Sch, 73-75; chief, Dept Cardiovasc Dynamics, Nat Cardiovasc Ctr Res Inst, 78-82, dir, 82-91. *Concurrent Pos:* Fel biomed eng, Case Western Res Univ, 71; chmn, Study Group Cardiac Mech, 85-91; ed, Heart & Vessels J, 88-; vis scientist, Nat Cardiovasc Ctr Res Inst, 91-92; mem, Circulation Coun, Am Heart Asn; Upjohn Sci fel award, 93. *Mem:* Fel Am Heart Asn; Am Physiol Soc; Int Cardiovasc Syst Dynamics Soc; Japanese Physiol Soc; Japanese Circulation Soc. *Res:* Physiology and biomedical engineering of heart mechanics and energetics primarily in terms of end-systolic pressure-volume relation and systolic pressure-volume area of the left ventricle; cardiology. *Mailing Add:* Second Dept Physiol Okayama Univ Med Sch Shikatacho Okayama 700 Japan. *Fax:* 81-86-222-5306; *E-Mail:* hirosuga@cc.okayama-u.ac.jp

SUGA, NOBUO, PHYSIOLOGY. *Current Pos:* assoc prof, 69-75, PROF BIOL, WASH UNIV, 76- *Personal Data:* b Japan, Dec 17, 33; m 63; c 2. *Educ:* Tokyo Metrop Univ, PhD(physiol), 63. *Prof Exp:* NSF fel hearing physiol, Harvard Univ, 63-64; res zoologist, Brain Res Inst, Univ Calif, Los Angeles, 65; res neuroscientist, Sch Med, Univ Calif, San Diego, 66-68. *Mem:* AAAS; Int Soc Neuroethology; Acoust Soc Am; Soc Neuroscience; Asn Res Otolaryngol. *Res:* Auditory physiology. *Mailing Add:* Dept Biol Wash Univ Campus Box 1137 One Brookings Dr St Louis MO 63130-4862

SUGAI, IWAO, ELECTRICAL ENGINEERING. *Current Pos:* PRES, SOVIET ELECTRONICS DIGEST DISSEMINATION SERV, 90- *Personal Data:* b Tokyo, Japan, Oct 19, 28; US citizen; m 58, Noriko Obata; c Edward, Emily & Eileen. *Educ:* Univ Calif, Los Angeles, BS, 55; Calif Inst Technol, MSEE, 56; George Washington Univ, DSc, 71. *Prof Exp:* Assoc engr, IBM Res Ctr, 58-60; tech specialist, ITT Lab, 60-63; computer scientist, Comput Sci Corp, 63-73; sr staff engr, Appl Physics Lab, Johns Hopkins Univ, 73-89. *Concurrent Pos:* Asst prof lectr, George Washington Univ, 68-69; lectr, Am Univ, 82-83; asst vpres pac region, Soc Comput Simulation Int, 89-, co-gen chmn, Summer Comput Simulation Conf, Baltimore, 91. *Mem:* Sigma Xi; sr mem Inst Elec & Electronics Engrs; Soc Comput Simulation. *Res:* Analytical solutions of a certain class of a general scalar Riccati's nonlinear differential equation; wave propagation problems; developing vast high technical level computerized data boxes of Soviet and Russian electronic papers for on-line voucher. *Mailing Add:* 14637 Stonewall Dr Silver Spring MD 20905-5857

SUGAM, RICHARD JAY, ENVIRONMENTAL COMPLIANCE, STRATEGIC ENVIRONMENTAL PLANNING. *Current Pos:* Researcher, Pub Serv Elec & Gas Co, 79-89, prin environ engr, 89-92, mgr strategic environ planning & info, 92, MGR, CORP ENVIRON COMPLIANCE & PLANNING, PUB SERV ELEC & GAS CO, 92- *Personal Data:* b New York, NY, Nov 16, 51; m 76, Shelley K Hartz; c Daniel M, Jonathan A & Matthew D. *Educ:* Rutgers Col, AB, 73; Univ Md, PhD(chem), 77. *Prof Exp:* Scientist marine chem, Lockheed Ctr Marine Res, 78-79. *Mem:* Am Chem Soc; AAAS; Int Ozone Asn. *Res:* Environmental chemistry; fate and effects of oxidative biocides in natural waters; performance of power plant auxiliary systems, power plant chemistry and water management, waste disposal and resource recovery; environmental management. *Mailing Add:* Pub Serv Elec & Gas PO Box 570 80 Park Plaza Mail Code T17F Newark NJ 07101. *Fax:* 973-624-9047

SUGAR, GEORGE R, DATA COMMUNICATIONS, ELECTRONIC INSTRUMENTATION. *Current Pos:* RETIRED. *Personal Data:* b Winthrop, Mass, Oct 12, 25; m 61, 85, Margaret Hawkins; c Robert & David. *Educ:* Univ Md, BS, 50. *Honors & Awards:* Silver Medal, US Dept Com. *Prof Exp:* Asst, Inst Fluid Dynamics & Appl Math, Univ Md, 50-51; physicist, Upper Atmosphere & Space Physics Div, Nat Bur Stand, 51-65; electronic engr, Aeronomy Lab, Nat Oceanic & Atmospheric Admin, 65-70; electronic engr automation & instrumentation sect, Electromagnetics Div, Nat Bur Stand, 71-77; electronic engr, Wave Propagation Lab, Nat Oceanic & Atmospheric Admin, 77-79; pres, Pragmatronics Inc, 79-84, consult, 84-85; pres, RDS Enterprises, 79-84. *Concurrent Pos:* Vis lectr, Univ Colo, 73-74. *Mem:* Sigma Xi; Inst Elec & Electronics Engrs. *Res:* Laboratory automation; application of minicomputers to laboratory measurements; management of computers; organization development; electronic instrumentation; meteor-burst propagation and communication. *Mailing Add:* 770 Lincoln Pl Boulder CO 80302-7531

SUGAR, JACK, ATOMIC SPECTROSCOPY. *Current Pos:* PHYSICIST, NAT INST STAND & TECHNOL, 60- *Personal Data:* b Baltimore, Md, Dec 22, 29; m 56, Judith; c Ross, Eve & Erica (Tubbs). *Educ:* Johns Hopkins Univ, BA, 56, PhD(physics), 60. *Honors & Awards:* Silver Medal, US Dept Com, 71. *Concurrent Pos:* Fulbright res traveling grant, 66-67, NATO res grant, 90-91. *Mem:* Fel Optical Soc Am. *Res:* Spectra of solids; atomic spectra and energy levels; nuclear moments; ionization energies. *Mailing Add:* 11014 Kenilworth Ave Kensington MD 20895. *E-Mail:* sugar@enh.nist.gov

SUGAR, OSCAR, physiology, neurosurgery, for more information see previous edition

SUGAR, ROBERT LOUIS, THEORETICAL PHYSICS. *Current Pos:* from asst prof to assoc prof, 66-73, PROF PHYSICS, UNIV CALIF, SANTA BARBARA, 73- *Personal Data:* b Chicago, Ill, Aug 20, 38; m 66, Joan Haley; c Catherine & Elizabeth. *Educ:* Harvard Univ, AB, 60; Princeton Univ, PhD(physics), 64. *Prof Exp:* Res assoc physics, Columbia Univ, 64-66. *Concurrent Pos:* Dep dir, Inst Theoret Physics, 79-81 & 83-85. *Mem:* Fel Am Phys Soc. *Res:* High energy physics. *Mailing Add:* Dept Physics Univ Calif Santa Barbara CA 93106. *Fax:* 805-893-8839; *E-Mail:* sugar@sarek.physics.ucsb.edu

SUGARBAKER, EVAN ROY, NUCLEAR REACTION MECHANISMS. *Current Pos:* asst prof, 81-86, ASSOC PROF PHYSICS, OHIO STATE UNIV, 86- *Personal Data:* b Mineola, NY, Nov, 17, 49; m 85; c 1. *Educ:* Kalamazoo Col, BA, 71; Univ Mich, PhD(physics), 76. *Prof Exp:* Res assoc, Nuclear Struct Res Lab, Univ Rochester, 76-78; vis asst prof physics, Univ Colo, 78-80. *Concurrent Pos:* Co-prin investr NSF grant, 81-88, prin investr, 88- *Mem:* Am Phys Soc; Am Asn Physics Teachers; AAAS. *Res:* Mechanisms in light-ion induced nuclear reactions; nuclear structure. *Mailing Add:* Dept Physics Ohio State Univ 1302 Kinnear Rd Columbus OH 43212. *Fax:* 614-292-7557

SUGATHAN, KANNETH KOCHAPPAN, COATINGS & ADHESIVE CHEMISTRY, SYNTHETIC RESIN CHEMISTRY. *Current Pos:* PRIN, NEW TECH CONSULT, 96- *Personal Data:* b Palliport, India, Mar 23, 26; nat US; m 56, Saraswathy; c Geetha, Prasanna, Gopakumar & Rajagopal. *Educ:* Univ Kerala, BSc, 51, PhD(terpene chem), 67; Univ Saugar, MSc, 53. *Prof Exp:* Demonstr chem, SKV Col, Trichur, India, 53-54, lectr, 54-64; lectr, S N Col, Quilon, India, 64-68; Nat Res Coun-Agr Res Serv fel, USDA Naval Stores Lab, Olustee, Fla, 68-70; Am Cancer Soc res fel, Univ Miss, 71-72; res chemist, Crosby Chem, Inc, 72-76, chief chemist, 76-78; chief chemist, Zielger Chem & Mineral Corp, 78-80; sr scientist & proj mgr, Polymer Res Corp Am, 81-96. *Concurrent Pos:* Sr demonstr, Christian Med Col, Vellore, India, 61-64. *Mem:* Am Chem Soc. *Res:* Product and process development in the fields of polymers, coatings and adhesives; applying graft polymerization techniques to impart special effects to substrates like metals, plastics, rubber and paper; industrial trouble shooting. *Mailing Add:* 39 Ross Hall Blvd S Piscataway NJ 08854. *Fax:* 732-247-2888

SUGAYA, HIROSHI, MAGNETIC RECORDING, VIDEO RECORDING. *Current Pos:* PROF, DIV AUDIO & VISUAL COM, KYUSHU INST DESIGN, UNIV, 88- *Personal Data:* b Hyogo-Ken, Japan, Mar 13, 31; m 59, Hiroko; c Morihiro & Yasuhiro. *Educ:* Osaka Univ, Japan, BSc, 54, Dr Sci(physics), 64; Eindhoven Int Inst, MDipl comput, 61. *Honors & Awards:* Ohkouchi Prize, 69 & 73. *Prof Exp:* Prin researcher acoust, Matsushita Elec Indust, 54-60, Cent Res Lab, 55-69, gen mgr, Video Rec, 70-75, Corp Plan, Eng Div, 75-81 & Audio & Video Div, 81-88. *Concurrent Pos:* Chmn, EIA-J Video Tech Comt, 68-81; mem & chmn, IEC TC60 SC 60B WG-5, 70-94. *Mem:* Fel Inst Elec & Electronics Engrs; Soc Motion Picture & TV Engrs; Inst TV Engrs Japan; Acoust Soc Japan. *Res:* Magnetic recording; developed hot-pressed-ferrite head, high speed video tape contact duplicator and many types of video tape recorders; overwrite recording and re-recording phenomenon. *Mailing Add:* Kansai Univ 3-3-35 Yamate-Cho Osaka Suite 564 Japan. *Fax:* 81-92-553-4569

SUGDEN, EVAN A, ENTOMOLOGY. *Current Pos:* VIS RES SCIENTIST, KY STATE UNIV, 92- *Personal Data:* b Salt Lake City, Utah, Sept 17, 52; c 1. *Educ:* Univ Utah, BA, 76; Univ Calif, Davis, PhD(entom), 84. *Prof Exp:* Apicult consult, Honey Prod Int, 84-85; postdoctoral researcher, Australian Mus, 85-87; biol aide, Calif Dept Food & Agr, Plant Indust, Anal & ID, Exotic Pests, 87-88; postdoctoral, Agr Res Serv, USDA, 88-90, entomologist, Subtrop Agr Res Lab, 90-92. *Concurrent Pos:* Biol sci collabr, USDA. *Mem:* Entom Soc Am; Int Union Study Social Insects; Am Asn Prof Apiculturists; Xerces Soc. *Res:* Feral honey bee and Africanized honey bee monitoring program; bee ecology; pollination of crops and native plants; alternative pollinator species; bee and social hymenoplera systematics and ecology; honey bee parasitology. *Mailing Add:* 98011 NE 10040th St Bothel WA 98011. *Fax:* 502-227-6381

SUGERMAN, ABRAHAM ARTHUR, PSYCHIATRY, PSYCHOPHARMACOLOGY. *Current Pos:* CLIN PROF, ROBERT WOOD JOHNSON MED SCH, 78- *Personal Data:* b Dublin, Ireland, Jan 20, 29; nat US; m 60, Ruth Alexander; c Jeremy, Michael, Adam & Rebecca. *Educ:* Univ Dublin, BA, 50, MB, BCh & BAO, 52; RCPS dipl psychol med, 58; State Univ NY, DSc(psychiat), 62; Univ Newcastle, dipl, 66; Am Bd Psychiat & Neurol, dipl, 69. *Prof Exp:* House officer, Meath Hosp, Dublin, Ireland, 52-53 & St Nicholas Hosp, London, 53; sr house physician, Brook Gen Hosp, 54; registr psychiat, Kingsway Hosp, Derby & Med Sch, King's Col, Newcastle, 55-58; clin psychiatrist, Trenton State Hosp, NJ, 58-59; chief sect invest psychiat & dir clin invest unit, NJ Neuropsychiat Inst, 61-73; res consult & assoc psychiatrist, Carrier Found, 68-72, dir, Outpatient Serv, 72-74 & 77-78, med dir, 74-77, res dir, 72-79, assoc psychiatrist & dir, Med Student Training, 78-90, dir, Affective Disorders Prog, 82-90; med dir, Addiction Recovery Serv, Univ Med & Dent NJ-Community Ment Health Ctr, 90-93. *Concurrent Pos:* Res fel psychiat, State Univ NY Downstate Med Ctr, 59-61; res consult, Trenton Psychiat Hosp, 64-; clin assoc prof, Rutgers Med Sch, 72-78; consult, Med Ctr, Princeton, 72-; contrib fac, Grad Sch Appl & Prof Psychol, Rutgers Univ, 74-78; vis prof, Hahnemann Med Col, 78-93 & Ctr Alcohol Studies, Rutgers Univ, 77-83. *Mem:* Fel Royal Col Psychiatrists; fel Am Psychiat Asn; fel Am Col Clin Pharmacol; fel Am Col Psychiatrists; fel Am Col Neuropsychopharmacology; fel AAAS. *Res:* Evaluation of new psychiatric drugs; nosology; psychology and prognosis in schizophrenia and alcoholism; quantitative analysis of the electroencephalogram. *Mailing Add:* 125 Roxboro Rd Lawrenceville NJ 08648. *E-Mail:* sugerman@pluto.njcc.com

SUGERMAN, HARVEY J, GASTROINTESTINAL SURGERY, CRITICAL CARE MEDICINE. *Current Pos:* From asst prof to prof, 78-87, DAVID M HUME PROF & VCHMN DEPT SURG, MED COL VA, 88- *Personal Data:* b Pittsburgh, Pa, Apr 13, 38; m 68, Elizabeth Levine; c Kathryn, Andrew, David & Elizabeth. *Educ:* Johns Hopkins Univ, BS, 59; Thomas Jefferson Univ, MS, 63, MD, 66. *Mem:* Am Surg Asn; Am Asn Surg Trauma; Soc Univ Surgeons; Surg Infection Soc; Asn Acad Surg; Shock Soc. *Res:* Sepsis induced pulmonary injury; white blood cell activation; adhesion to enothelial cells and membrane injury with permeability; evaluation of surgical techniques for treatment of inflammatory bowel disease; morbid obesity; intra-abdonimal pressure. *Mailing Add:* Med Col Va Sta PO Box 980519 Richmond VA 23298. *Fax:* 804-828-9299

SUGERMAN, LEONARD RICHARD, NAVIGATION. *Current Pos:* ASST DIR RESOURCES MGT, PHYS SCI LAB, NMEX STATE UNIV, 75- *Personal Data:* b New York, NY, June 24, 20; m 40; c 4. *Educ:* Mass Inst Technol, BS, 55; Univ Chicago, MBA, 60. *Honors & Awards:* Norman P Hays Award, Am Inst Navig, 72. *Prof Exp:* USAF, 42-75, supvr bomb-navig br, Dept Armament Training, Lowry AFB, Colo, 50-53, air staff off, Off Dep Chief Staff Develop, Hq USAF, Pentagon, DC, 55-59, res & develop staff off hqs, Syst Command, Andrews AFB, 60-62, hqs, Res & Tech Div, Bolling AFB, 62-64, exec off, Cent Inertial Guid Test Facil, Missile Develop Ctr, Holloman AFB, 64-68, chief, Athena Test Field Off, Ballistic Reentry Systs Prog, 68-70, Air Force Dep to Comdr, White Sands Missile Range & chief, Air Force Range Opers Off, 70-72, dep chief staff, Plans & Requirements, Air Force Spec Weapons Ctr, 72-75. *Concurrent Pos:* US rep guid & control panel, Adv Group Aerospace Res & Develop, NATO, 66-76. *Mem:* Am Defense Preparedness Asn; Am Inst Navig (pres, 70-71); assoc fel Am Inst Aeronaut & Astronaut; Sigma Xi. *Res:* Guidance and control of aerospace vehicles; bombing and navigation systems for aerospace vehicles. *Mailing Add:* 3025 Fairway Dr Las Cruces NM 88011-4912

SUGGITT, ROBERT MURRAY, physical chemistry, for more information see previous edition

SUGGS, CHARLES WILSON, AGRICULTURAL & HUMAN FACTORS ENGINEERING. *Current Pos:* res farm supt, NC Agr Exp Sta, 51-53, from instr to assoc prof, 54-66, PROF AGR ENG, NC STATE UNIV, 66- *Personal Data:* b NC, May 30, 28; m 49; c 3. *Educ:* NC State Col, BS, 49, MS, 55, PhD(agr eng), 59. *Prof Exp:* Instr, Dearborn Motors, 49; asst serv supvr, Int Harvester, 49-51. *Concurrent Pos:* Consult several law firms & foreign countries. *Mem:* Fel Am Soc Agr Engrs; Human Factors Soc. *Res:* Ergonomics; vibration; noise; human performance; tobacco mechanization; vehicle safety; servosystems; environment; machine and workplace safety. *Mailing Add:* 1507 Trailwood Dr Raleigh NC 27606. *Fax:* 919-515-7760

SUGGS, JOHN WILLIAM, ORGANOMETALLIC CHEMISTRY, ORGANIC CHEMISTRY. *Current Pos:* asst prof, 81-86, ASSOC PROF, DEPT CHEM, BROWN UNIV, 86- *Personal Data:* b Highland Park, Mich, Aug 17, 48; m; c 1. *Educ:* Univ Mich, BS, 70; Harvard Univ, PhD(chem), 76. *Honors & Awards:* Res Career Develop Award, Nat Cancer Inst. *Prof Exp:* Woodrow Wilson fel, 70; mem tech staff org chem, Bell Labs, AT&T, 76-81. *Mem:* Am Chem Soc; AAAS. *Res:* Use of organometallic compounds in organic synthesis; mechanisms of and reactive intermediates in organometallic reactions; drug-nucleic acid interactions. *Mailing Add:* Dept Chem Brown Univ Providence RI 02912

SUGGS, MORRIS TALMAGE, JR, MICROBIOLOGY. *Current Pos:* RETIRED. *Personal Data:* b Ft Myers, Fla, June 17, 27; m 52; c 3. *Educ:* Wake Forest Col, BS, 50; Fla State Univ, MS, 57; Univ NC, MPH, 65, DrPH, 67. *Prof Exp:* Teacher, Fla Pub Sch, 52-54; microbiologist, Ctr Dis Control, USPHS, Ala, 57, asst chief tissue cult unit, 58-59, res asst, 60-62, res asst virol training unit, 62-68, spec asst biol reagents sect, Lab Prog, 68, dir biol prod prog, Ctr Infectious Die, 68-85. *Mem:* Am Soc Microbiologists; Conf of State & Prov Pub Health Lab Dirs. *Res:* Standardization and quality assurance of in vitro diagnostic products. *Mailing Add:* 2424 Coralwood Dr Decatur GA 30033

SUGGS, WILLIAM TERRY, QUALITY ASSURANCE & GOOD MANUFACTURING, PRACTICES, REGULATORY AFFAIRS. *Current Pos:* supvr, Anal Develop Qual Control Dept, Parke-Davis, Div Warner-Lambert, 75-77, mgr, Anal Devel Qual Control Dept, 77-82, mgr, Anal Devel Chem Develop Dept, 82-85, sr mgr, 85-91, SECT DIR, ANAL DEVELOP CHEM DEVELOP DEPT, PARKE-DAVIS, DIV WARNER-LAMBERT, 91- *Personal Data:* b Orange, NJ, Dec 7, 45; m 83; c 2. *Educ:*

Seton Hall Univ, BS, 67; Mich State Univ, PhD(org chem), 73; Grand Valley State Univ, MBA, 81. *Prof Exp:* Postdoctoral res assoc hort, Plant Biochem Res, Mich State Univ, 73-75. *Mem:* Am Chem Soc. *Res:* Development of analytical methods for the control of raw materials, chemical intermediates and bulk substances; experimental drug substances produced for use in toxicology, formulations studies and clinical research to support IND and NDA filings. *Mailing Add:* Parke-Davis Warner Lambert 188 Howard Ave Holland MI 49424-6517

SUGIHARA, JAMES MASANOBU, ORGANIC CHEMISTRY, ACADEMIC ADMINISTRATION. *Current Pos:* dean, Col Chem & Physics, NDak State Univ, 64-73, dean, Col Sci & Math, 73, dean, Grad Sch & dir Res Admin, 74-85, dean, Col Sci & Math, 85-86, prof chem, 64-89, interim chair, dept polymers & coatings, 90-91, EMER PROF CHEM, NDak State Univ, 89- *Personal Data:* b Las Animas, Colo, Aug 6, 18; m 44, May Murakami; c John & Michael. *Educ:* Univ Calif, BS, 39; Univ Utah, PhD(chem), 47. *Prof Exp:* From instr to prof chem, Univ Utah, 43-64. *Concurrent Pos:* Fel, Ohio State Univ, 48. *Mem:* Am Chem Soc; Geochem Soc Am. *Res:* Reaction mechanisms; porphyrin chemistry; origin of petroleum. *Mailing Add:* 1001 Southwood Dr Fargo ND 58103

SUGIHARA, KAZUO, ALGORITHMS & COMPLEXITY, DISTRIBUTED COMPUTING. *Current Pos:* Asst prof, 85-92, ASSOC PROF INFO & COMPUT SCI, UNIV HAWAII, MANOA, 92- *Personal Data:* b Hiroshima, Japan, Nov 27, 55; US citizen. *Educ:* Hiroshima Univ, Japan, BS, 80, MS, 82, PhD(systs eng), 85. *Mem:* Inst Elec & Electronics Engrs; Inst Electronics Info & Commun Engrs Japan. *Res:* Design and analysis of algorithms; study of distributed computing in intelligent robots, multimedia systems and internet applications. *Mailing Add:* Dept Info & Comput Sci Univ Hawaii Manoa Honolulu HI 96822. *E-Mail:* sugihara@hawaii.edu

SUGIHARA, THOMAS TAMOTSU, nuclear chemistry, for more information see previous edition

SUGIMURA, TAKASHI, BIOCHEMISTRY, HEALTH SCIENCES. *Current Pos:* pres, 84-91, EMER PRES, NAT CANCER CTR, TOKYO, 92-; PRES, TOHO UNIV, 94- *Personal Data:* b Tokyo, Japan, Apr 20, 26. *Educ:* Med Bd Dipl Health & Welfare, Japan, 50; Univ Tokyo, DMS, 57. *Honors & Awards:* Imperial Prize, Japan Acad, 76; Charles S Matt Prize, Gen Motors Cancer Res Found, 81; Ernst W Bertner Mem Award, 81; Japan Prize, 97. *Prof Exp:* Instr, Dept Radiol, Sch Med, Univ Tokyo, 50-54; vis scientist, Biochem Lab, Nat Cancer Inst, NIH, 57-59; res assoc, Dept Biochem, Sch Med, Case Western Res Univ, 59-60; sr res mem, Chem Div, Cancer Inst, Japanese Found Cancer Res, 60-62; chief, Biochem Div, Nat Cancer Ctr Res Inst, 62-74, dir, 72-74 & 74-84. *Concurrent Pos:* Prof, Dept Molecular Oncol, Dept Cancer Cellular Res, Univ Tokyo, 70-85; adv, Ministry Health & Welfare, Tokyo, 92-94. *Mem:* Foreign assoc Inst Med-Nat Acad Sci; Japan Cancer Soc (pres, 93); Am Asn Cancer Res; Japan Acad. *Mailing Add:* Nat Cancer Ctr 1-1 Tsukiji 5 Chrome-Ku Tokyo 104 Japan

SUGIOKA, KENNETH, ANESTHESIOLOGY. *Current Pos:* PROF PHYSIOL & ANESTHESIOL, DUKE UNIV, 85- *Personal Data:* b Hollister, Calif, Apr 19, 20; m 47, 66, Mary Hinternhoff; c Stephanie, Colin, Kimi, Nathan & Brian. *Educ:* Univ Denver, BS, 45, Wash Univ, MD, 49; Am Bd Anesthesiol, dipl, 55; FFARCS. *Prof Exp:* Intern, Univ Iowa Hosp, 49-50, resident anesthesiol, 50-52, instr, 52; actg chief anesthesiol, Vet Admin Hosp, Des Moines, 52; resident & instr, Vet Admin Hosp, Iowa City, 52; from asst prof to prof anesthesiol, Sch Med, Univ NC, Chapel Hill, 54-83, chmn dept, 69-83. *Concurrent Pos:* NIH spec res fel, 62; consult, Vet Admin Hosp, Fayetteville, NC; vis prof, Inst Physiol, Univ Gottingen, 62, Med Sch, King's Col, Univ London, 63, Max Planck Inst Physiol, Dortmund, Ger, 76-77 & Royal Col Surgeons, 83-84. *Mem:* Soc Acad Anesthesiol Chmn; Am Soc Anesthesiol; Soc Exp Biol & Med; Am Physiol Soc; Asn Univ Anesthetists; Int Soc Oxygen Tissue Transport. *Res:* Application of electronic instrumentation to physiological measurements; electrochemical methods of biological analysis; cation sensitive glass electrodes; oxygen transport. *Mailing Add:* Dept Anesthesiol Box 3094 Duke Univ Med Ctr Durham NC 27710. *Fax:* 919-681-8398

SUGITA, EDWIN T, PHARMACEUTICS. *Current Pos:* From asst prof to assoc prof, 64-72, PROF PHARM, PHILADELPHIA COL PHARM & SCI, 72-, CHMN DEPT PHARMACEUT, 87- *Personal Data:* b Honolulu, Hawaii, Feb 1, 37; m 59; c 2. *Educ:* Purdue Univ, BS, 59, MS, 62, PhD(pharmaceut), 63. *Concurrent Pos:* Res grant, Smith, Kline & French Labs, 65-67; NIH grant, 65-71 & 74-77; Kapnek Charitable Trust fel, 76-81. *Mem:* Acad Pharmaceut Res & Sci; Sigma Xi; Am Asn Pharmaceut Scientists. *Res:* Facilitated absorption of drugs; absorption of drugs: in vitro-in vivo correlations; bioequivalency testing; pharmacokinetics of drugs in humans. *Mailing Add:* 2941 Raspberry Lane Gilbertsville PA 19525

SUGIURA, MASAHISA, SPACE PHYSICS. *Current Pos:* PROF, INST RES & DEVELOP, TOKAI UNIV, TOKYO, JAPAN, 89- *Personal Data:* b Tokyo, Japan, Dec 8, 25; m 62, Keiko Adachi; c Michi. *Educ:* Univ Tokyo, MS, 49; Univ Alaska, PhD, 55. *Honors & Awards:* Tanakadate Prize, 50, Soc Terrestrial Magnetism & Elec Japan, 50; Except Sci Achievement Medal, NASA, 85. *Prof Exp:* Asst prof geophys res, Geophys Inst, Univ Alaska, 55-57, assoc prof geophys, 57-62, prof, 62; Nat Acad Sci sr assoc, NASA, 62-64, mem staff, Goddard Space Flight Ctr, 64-85; prof, Geophys Inst, Fac Sci, Kyoto Univ, Japan, 85-89. *Concurrent Pos:* Guggenheim fel, 59; prof, Univ Wash, 66-67. *Mem:* Fel Am Geophys Union; Soc Geomagnetism & Earth, Planetary & Space Sci; AAAS. *Res:* Magnetospheric physics, geophysics. *Mailing Add:* Inst Res Develop Tokai Univ 2-28 Tomigaya Shibuya-ku Tokyo 151 Japan. *Fax:* 81-3-3467-6177; *E-Mail:* sugiura@jspan. kugi.kyoto-u.ac.jp

SUH, CHUNG-HA, MECHANICAL ENGINEERING, BIOMECHANICS. *Current Pos:* from asst to assoc prof, 66-77, chmn, Dept Eng Design & Econ Eval, 70-78, PROF, UNIV COLO, BOULDER, 77-, DIR, BIOMECH LAB, 70- *Personal Data:* b Chinnampo City, Korea, Sept 11, 32; m 61; c 3. *Educ:* Seoul Nat Univ, BS, 59; Univ Calif, Berkeley, MS, 64, PhD(mech eng), 66. *Prof Exp:* From mech engr to chief engr, Hwan-Bok Indust Co, Ltd, Korea, 59-61; dept head mach design & shop, Atomic Energy Res Inst, 61-62; res engr, Biomech Lab, Univ Calif, Berkeley, 63-66. *Concurrent Pos:* Res consult, Int Chiropractors Asn, 72-88 & Hyundai Motor Co, 84-; dir, Ctr Automotive Res, Univ Colo, Boulder, 89- *Mem:* Am Soc Mech Engrs; Am Gear Mfrs Asn; Soc Automotive Engrs. *Res:* Computer-aided design of mechanisms; optimum design; biomechanics of human joints and system. *Mailing Add:* 900 28th St Boulder CO 80303

SUH, EDWARD MARTIN, ORGANIC & PHARMACEUTICAL CHEMISTRY. *Current Pos:* Sr scientist, 93-96, RES INVESTR, GLAXO WELLCOME, 93- *Educ:* Yale Univ, BA, 86; Harvard Univ, PhD(chem), 93. *Mem:* Am Chem Soc. *Res:* Synthesis of natural products; development of reaction methods followed by application of methods to a specific synthetic problem; design, synthesis and analysis of drug candidates in metabolic disease and diabetes. *Mailing Add:* 2457 Sedgefield Dr Chapel Hill NC 27514

SUH, JOHN TAIYOUNG, MEDICINAL CHEMISTRY, ORGANIC CHEMISTRY. *Current Pos:* RES & DEVELOP CONSULT, 90- *Personal Data:* US citizen; m 58, Ruth Theine; c Mary, Thomas, Edward & Anne. *Educ:* Butler Univ, BS, 53; Univ Wis, MS, 56, PhD(org chem), 58. *Prof Exp:* Teaching asst, Univ Wis, 55; sr res chemist, Res Ctr, Johnson & Johnson, 58-59 & McNeil Labs, Inc, 59-63; group leader res, Colgate-Palmolive Co, 63-65, sect head res, Dept Med Chem, Lakeside Labs Div, 63-75; mgr chem res, Freeman Chem Corp, 76-77; sect head res, Dept Med Chem, USV Pharmaceut Corp, 77-78, assoc dir, Dept Med Chem, Res & Develop, Revlon Health Care Group, 78-84; med chem dir, 84-86; dir, Chem Res Serv Dept, Rorer Pharmaceut Corp, 86-90. *Concurrent Pos:* Vis lectr chem, Marquette Univ, 72-77. *Mem:* Am Chem Soc. *Res:* Medicinal chemistry in areas of cardiovascular, psychopharmacological and hematinic agents; organic chemistry in areas of stereochemistry, natural products, heterocyclic and organometallic chemistry; pulmonary and allergy research. *Mailing Add:* 59 Stanwich Rd Greenwich CT 06830

SUH, NAM PYO, MECHANICAL ENGINEERING. *Current Pos:* assoc prof mech, 70-75, PROF MECH ENG & DIR, MFG & PRODUCTIVITY LAB, MASS INST TECHNOL, 75-, RALPH E & ELOISE F CROSS PROF, 89- *Personal Data:* b Seoul, Korea, Apr 22, 36; US citizen; m 61; c 4. *Educ:* Mass Inst Technol, SB, 59, SM, 61; Carnegie Inst Technol, PhD(mech eng), 64. *Hon Degrees:* Dr Eng, Worcester Polytech Inst, 86; LHD, Univ Lowell, 88. *Honors & Awards:* Larsen Mem Award, Am Soc Mech Engrs, 76, Blackall Award, 82; F W Taylor Award, Soc Mech Engrs, 86; Fed Engr Award, NSF, 87; Soc Petrol Engr Award, 81. *Prof Exp:* Develop engr, Sweetheart Plastics, Inc, 58-59; lectr mech eng, Northeastern Univ, 64-65; sr res engr, United Shoe Mach Corp, Mass, 65-61; from asst prof to assoc prof mech & mat, Univ SC, 65-70. *Concurrent Pos:* Consult, govt agencies & indust firms, 70-; asst dir, NSF, 84-88; co-ed in chief, Robotics & Computer Integrated Mfg; chmn bd, Axiomatics Corp, Woburn, Mass, Sutek Corp, Hudson, Mass; foreign mem, Royal Swed Acad Eng Sci, 89- *Mem:* Am Soc Mech Engrs; Am Soc Eng Educ; Int Inst Prod Eng Res. *Res:* Materials processing; mechanical behavior of materials; solid propellants; manufacturing processes and systems; tribology; design; author four books. *Mailing Add:* Dept Mech Eng Rm 35-237 Mass Inst Technol Cambridge MA 02139

SUH, TAE-IL, ALGEBRA. *Current Pos:* assoc prof, 65-68, PROF MATH, E TENN STATE UNIV, 68- *Personal Data:* b Chungdo, Korea, June 1, 28; m 55; c 3. *Educ:* Kyung-Pook Nat Univ, Korea, BS, 52; Yale Univ, PhD(math), 61. *Prof Exp:* Asst prof math, Kyung-Pook Nat Univ, Korea, 61-63; assoc prof, Sogang Univ, Korea, 63-65. *Mem:* Am Math Soc; Math Asn Am. *Res:* Non-associative algebras. *Mailing Add:* 3407 Berkshire Circle Johnson City TN 37604

SUHADOLNIK, ROBERT J, BIOCHEMISTRY. *Current Pos:* PROF BIOCHEM, SCH MED, TEMPLE UNIV, 70- *Personal Data:* b Forest City, Pa, Aug 15, 25; m 49; c 5. *Educ:* Pa State Univ, BS, 49, PhD, 56; Iowa State Univ, MS, 53. *Prof Exp:* Res assoc biochem, Univ Ill, 56-57; asst prof, Okla State Univ, 57-61; res mem, Albert Einstein Med Ctr, 61-70, head, Dept Bio-Org Chem, 68-70. *Mem:* Am Chem Soc; Am Soc Biol Chemists; Sigma Xi. *Res:* Alkaloid biogenesis; metabolism of allose and allulose; biosynthesis and biochemical properties of nucleoside antibiotics; mechanism of protein synthesis; role of interferon in development of antiviral-anticancer state in normal and DNA repair-deficient mammalian cells. *Mailing Add:* Dept Biochem Temple Univ Health Sci Campus Philadelphia PA 19140. *Fax:* 215-221-3515

SUHAYDA, JOSEPH NICHOLAS, OCEANOGRAPHY. *Current Pos:* Asst prof, 72-75, ASSOC PROF MARINE SCI, COASTAL STUDIES INST, LA STATE UNIV, BATON ROUGE, 75- *Personal Data:* b Flint, Mich, Feb 23, 44; m 66; c 2. *Educ:* Calif State Univ, Northridge, BS, 66; Univ Calif, San Diego, PhD(phys oceanog), 72. *Mem:* Am Geophys Union; Am Shore & Beach Preserv Asn. *Res:* Coastal oceanography, primarily nearshore processes on beaches and reefs, and the influence of storm waves on sediment on the continental shelf. *Mailing Add:* Civil Eng La State Univ Baton Rouge LA 70803-0001

SUHIR, EPHRAIM, MICROELECTRONIC & FIBER OPTIC SYSTEMS, DYNAMIC & PROBABILISTIC PROBLEMS. *Current Pos:* MEM TECH STAFF & PRIN INVESTR BASIC RES, AT&T BELL LABS, NJ, 84- *Personal Data:* b Odessa, USSR, May 17, 37; US citizen; m 68, Raisa Greenberg; c Elena & Eugene. *Educ:* Odessa Polytech Inst, USSR, MS, 66; Moscow Univ, PhD(appl mech), 68. *Honors & Awards:* Outstanding Contribr Award, Am Soc Mech Engrs. *Prof Exp:* Prof appl mech, Nikolaev Inst Naval Archit, Ukraine, 70-75; head lab, reliability & statist, Res Inst Engine Bldg, Lithuania, 75-80; sr proj engr, Exxon Corp, NJ, 80-84. *Concurrent Pos:* Consult, Nikolaev Inst Naval Archit, 70-75; vis prof, Kaunas Polytech Inst, 75-80; prin investr, AT&T Bell Labs, 84-; lectr thermal anal & failure prev, 88-; sr ed, Am Soc Mech Engrs J Electronic Packaging, 93-, ed, Inst Elec & Electronics Engrs CHMT Transactions, 93. *Mem:* Sr mem Inst Elec & Electronics Engrs; Am Soc Mech Engrs; Mat Res Soc; sr mem Soc Plastic Engrs. *Res:* Mechanical behavior, reliability and physical design of microelectronic and fiber optic components, structures, and systems. *Mailing Add:* 21 Leigh Ct Randolph NJ 07869. *Fax:* 908-582-5570

SUHL, HARRY, PHYSICS. *Current Pos:* vis lectr, 60, prof, 61-91, EMER PROF PHYSICS, UNIV CALIF, SAN DIEGO, 91- *Personal Data:* b Leipzig, Ger, Oct 18, 22; nat US; wid. *Educ:* Univ Wales, BSc, 43; Oxford Univ, PhD(theoret physics), 48. *Prof Exp:* Exp officer, Admiralty Signal Estab, Eng, 43-46; mem tech staff, Bell Tel Labs, Inc, 48-60. *Concurrent Pos:* Alexander von Humboldt Award, Humboldt Found, 91. *Mem:* Nat Acad Sci; fel Am Phys Soc. *Res:* Theoretical solid state physics. *Mailing Add:* Dept Physics Univ Calif San Diego La Jolla CA 92093

SUHM, RAYMOND WALTER, STRATIGRAPHY. *Current Pos:* CONSULT GEOLOGIST & GEOPHYSICIST, 81- *Personal Data:* b Springfield, Mass, June 9, 41; m 64, June; c Karen. *Educ:* Southeast Mo State Col, BS, 63; Southern Ill Univ, Carbondale, MS, 65; Univ Nebr-Lincoln, PhD(geol), 70. *Prof Exp:* Instr geol, Southern Ill Univ, Carbondale, 65; geophysicist, Humble Oil Co, Calif, 65-67; asst prof geol, Tex A&I Univ, 70-75, assoc prof, 75-80; explor geologist, Tex Oil & Gas Corp, Oklahoma City, 80-81. *Concurrent Pos:* Consult, Cockrell Corp, 72, Int Oil & Gas, 76-78 & Tenneco Oil, 77, Tex Gas Explor, 82-86. *Mem:* Am Asn Petrol Geologists; Soc Econ Paleontologists & Mineralogists; Int Asn Sedimentologists. *Res:* Ordovician stratigraphy and paleontology; Ozark/Ouachita geology; coastal sedimentation and geomorphology; geologic and geophysical investigations of petroleum basins in the Southern Mid continent. *Mailing Add:* 11716 128th St Oklahoma City OK 73165-9432. *Fax:* 405-794-1701

SUHR, NORMAN HENRY, SPECTROSCOPY, GEOCHEMISTRY. *Current Pos:* spectroscopist, Labs, 58-65, asst dir, 65-70, res assoc, Univ, 63-67, asst prof, 67-69, ASSOC PROF GEOCHEM, PA STATE UNIV, 69-, DIR MINERAL CONST LABS, 70- *Personal Data:* b Chicago, Ill, June 13, 30; m 53; c 4. *Educ:* Univ Chicago, AB, 50, MS, 54. *Prof Exp:* Spectroscopist & mineralogist, Heavy Minerals Co, Vitro Corp Am, 56-58. *Mem:* AAAS; Soc Appl Spectros; Geochem Soc. *Res:* X-ray and emission spectroscopy and atomic absorption, primarily in the fields of earth sciences. *Mailing Add:* 111 Willowbrook Dr Boalsburg PA 16827

SUHRLAND, LEIF GEORGE, HEMATOLOGY, ONCOLOGY. *Current Pos:* prof, 67-89, EMER PROF MED, COL HUMAN MED, MICH STATE UNIV, 89- *Personal Data:* b Schroon Lake, NY, Apr 9, 19; m 50; c 3. *Educ:* Cornell Univ, BS, 42; Univ Rochester, MD, 50. *Hon Degrees:* DM, Univ Rochester, 50. *Prof Exp:* Bacteriologist, USPHS, 42-43; intern & jr asst med, Univ Hosps, Cleveland, 50-52; instr, Western Reserve Univ, 57-59, asst prof med & asst clin pathologist, 59-67. *Concurrent Pos:* Am Cancer Soc fel, Univ Hosps, Cleveland, 52-54; Howard M Hanna & Anna Bishop fels, Sch Med, Western Reserve Univ, 54-57; prof clin oncol, Am Cancer Soc, 78. *Mem:* Am Fedn Clin Res; Am Soc Hemat; Am Soc Clin Oncol; Am Col Physicians. *Res:* Host tumor relationships; clinical trials. *Mailing Add:* 351 Sherwood Rd Williamston MI 48895

SUIB, STEVEN L, INORGANIC PHOTOCHEMISTRY, SOLID STATE CHEMISTRY. *Current Pos:* from asst prof to assoc prof, 80-89, PROF, UNIV CONN, STORRS, 89- *Personal Data:* b Olean, NY, May 1, 53; m 77, Brenda R Shaw; c Walker Jay. *Educ:* State Univ NY, Fredonia, BS, 75; Univ Ill, Urbana, PhD(chem), 79. *Prof Exp:* Res asst, State Univ NY Fredonia, 74-75; teaching asst, Univ Ill, Urbana, 75-77, res asst, 78-79, vis lectr, 79, assoc, 79-80. *Concurrent Pos:* Fel, Univ Conn, 80. *Mem:* Am Chem Soc; Sigma Xi; Mat Res Soc. *Res:* Solid state inorganic chemistry including surface, structural, electrochemical and catalytic properties of semiconductors, ceramics and heterogeneous zeolite compounds; zeolite chemistry and catalysis. *Mailing Add:* Dept Chem U 60 Univ Conn Storrs CT 06269-4060. *Fax:* 860-486-2981; *E-Mail:* suib@uconnvm.uconn.edu

SUICH, JOHN EDWARD, INFORMATION SCIENCE. *Current Pos:* WESTINGHOUSE SAVANNAH RIVER CO, 91- *Personal Data:* b Bridgeport, Conn, Sept 28, 36; m 57; c 2. *Educ:* Harvard Univ, BA, 58; Mass Inst Technol, PhD(nuclear eng), 63. *Prof Exp:* Sr physicist, Savannah River Lab, E I DuPont de Nemours & Co, Inc., 63-65, res supvr, 65-66, res mgr appl math, 66-68, dir comput sci sect, 68-71, mgr telecommun planning, Gen Servs Dept, 71-72, asst mgr comput sci div, Cent Systs & Servs Dept, Del, 72, mgr com systs div mgt sci, 72-75, res assoc, Savannah River Lab, 75-89. *Res:* Relational data base and logic programming. *Mailing Add:* 692 Storm Branch Rd North Augusta SC 29841

SUICH, RONALD CHARLES, STATISTICS. *Current Pos:* MEM FAC MATH, CALIF STATE UNIV, 80- *Personal Data:* b Cleveland, Ohio, Nov 16, 40; m 62; c 3. *Educ:* John Carroll Univ, BSBA, 62; Case Western Reserve Univ, MS, 64, PhD(statist), 68. *Prof Exp:* Mkt researcher, Cleveland Elec Illum Co, 62-64; from instr to asst prof statist, Case Western Reserve Univ, 64-70; asst prof, Univ Akron, 70-77, assoc prof math, 77-80. *Mem:* Am Statist Asn. *Res:* Sequential tests. *Mailing Add:* 522 N Wilson Ave Fullerton CA 92631

SUINN, RICHARD M, BEHAVIOR THERAPY, CLINICAL PSYCHOLOGY. *Current Pos:* PROF, COLO STATE UNIV, 68- *Personal Data:* b Honolulu, Hawaii, May 8, 33; m 58, Grace Toy; c Susan, Randall, Staci & Bradley. *Educ:* Ohio State Univ, BA, 55; Stanford Univ, MA, 57, PhD(psychol), 59. *Prof Exp:* Asst prof, Whitman Col, 59-64; res assoc psychol, Stanford Med Sch, 64-66; assoc prof fac, Univ Hawaii, 66-68. *Concurrent Pos:* Vis prof, Univ Vera Cruz, Mex, 71; mem city coun & mayor, 75-79; bd dirs, Asian Am Psychol Asn, 84-87; vis scholar, Peoples Rep China, 86; chair, Educ & Training Bd, Am Psychol Asn, 86-88, bd dirs, 90-93. *Mem:* Fel Am Psychol Asn; Asn Advan Behav Ther (pres, 93); Asian Am Psychol Asn; Sigma Xi. *Res:* Anxiety management training. *Mailing Add:* Dept Psychol Colo State Univ Ft Collins CO 80523. *Fax:* 970-491-1032; *E-Mail:* suinn@lamar.colostate.edu

SUIT, HERMAN DAY, RADIOTHERAPY. *Current Pos:* HEAD DEPT RADIATION MED, MASS GEN HOSP, 71- *Personal Data:* b Houston, Tex, Feb 8, 29. *Educ:* Univ Houston, AB, 48; Baylor Univ, SM & MD, 52; Oxford Univ, DrPhil(radiobiol), 56. *Prof Exp:* Intern, Jefferson Davis Hosp, Houston, Tex, 52-53, resident radiol, 53-54; house surgeon radiother, Churchill Hosp, Oxford, Eng, 54, res asst radiobiol lab, 54-56, registr radiother, 56-57; sr asst surgeon, Radiation Br, Nat Cancer Inst, 57-59; asst radiotherapist, Univ Tex M D Anderson Hosp & Tumor Inst Houston, 59-63, assoc radiotherapist, 63-68, radiotherapist, 68-71, chief sect exp radiother, 62-70; prof radiation ther, Harvard Med Sch, 70- *Concurrent Pos:* Nat Cancer Inst res career develop award, Univ Tex M D Anderson Hosp & Tumor Inst Houston, 64-68; gen fac assoc, Univ Tex Grad Sch Biomed Sci, 65-70, prof radiation ther, 68-71; staff mem, NASA Manned Spacecraft Ctr, 69-71; subcomt radiation biol, Nat Acad Sci. *Mem:* AAAS; Am Col Radiol; Am Soc Therapeut Radiol (secy, 70-72); AMA; Am Asn Cancer Res. *Mailing Add:* Dept Radiation Ther Mass Gen Hosp Boston MA 02114

SUIT, JOAN C, MICROBIOLOGY. *Current Pos:* res assoc biol, 73-80, RES SCIENTIST, DEPT BIOL, MASS INST TECHNOL, 80- *Personal Data:* b Ontario, Ore, Apr 14, 31; m 60. *Educ:* Ore State Col, BS, 53; Stanford Univ, MA, 55, PhD(med microbiol), 57. *Prof Exp:* Res assoc biochem, Biol Div, Oak Ridge Nat Lab, 57-59; res assoc sect molecular biol, Univ Tex M D Anderson Hosp & Tumor Inst, Houston, 59-66, assoc biologist & assoc prof biol, Univ Tex Grad Sch Biomed Sci, Houston, 66-73. *Mem:* Am Soc Microbiol; Am Soc Cell Biol; Sigma Xi. *Res:* Microbial genetics; DNA replication; microbial growth. *Mailing Add:* 165 Merriam St Weston MA 02193-1356

SUITER, MARILYN J, HUMAN RESOURCE MANAGEMENT GEOSCIENCE. *Current Pos:* PROG ADMINR, AM GEOL INST, 87- *Personal Data:* b Philadelphia, PA. *Educ:* Franklin & Marshall Col, BS, 78; Wesleyan Univ, MS, 81. *Prof Exp:* Geologist, US Geol Surv, 77-81; explor geologist, Cities Serv Oil & Gas, 82-86. *Mem:* Asn Women Geoscientists (pres, 88-); Asn Women in Sci; Asn Earth Sci Ed. *Res:* Trace element geochemistry, surficial geology, neotectonics and petroleum exploration; assessing the status of women and ethnic minorities in the geosciences and developing programs that supports their increased participation in the geosciences. *Mailing Add:* 4210 31st St No 833 Arlington VA 22206

SUITS, BRYAN HALYBURTON, NUCLEAR MAGNETIC RESONANCE APPLIED TO MATERIALS, NUCLEAR MAGNETIC RESONANCE IMAGING OF MATERIALS. *Current Pos:* Asst prof, 85-89, head, Dept Physics, 90-95, ASSOC PROF PHYSICS, MICH TECHNOL UNIV, 89- *Personal Data:* b Ann Arbor, Mich, Dec 29, 54. *Educ:* Carleton Col, BS, 77; Univ Ill, Urbana, MS, 79, PhD(physics), 81. *Prof Exp:* Res assoc, Univ Ill, Urbana, 81-82, Univ Pa, 82-85. *Mem:* Am Phys Soc; Mat Res Soc. *Res:* Nuclear magnetic resonance studies of lattice defects and interfaces in materials with an emphasis on nanoscale materials; nuclear magnetic resonance of non-hydrogen containing materials as a non-destructive evaluation technique. *Mailing Add:* Dept Physics Mich Technol Univ 1400 Townsend Dr Houghton MI 49931-1295

SUITS, JAMES CARR, PHYSICS. *Current Pos:* RETIRED. *Personal Data:* b Schenectady, NY, May 29, 32; m 54, Rosella; c David L, William G & James II. *Educ:* Yale Univ, BS, 54; Harvard Univ, PhD(appl physics), 60. *Prof Exp:* Staff physicist, Res Lab, IBM Corp, San Jose, 60-76, mgr, Garnet Mat Dept, Gen Prods Div, 76-80, res staff mem, Res Lab, 80-92; litigation consultant, 92-94. *Mem:* Fel Am Phys Soc; Inst Elec & Electronics Engrs. *Res:* Magnetism, ultra-high vacuum evaporated thin films, magneto- optics, discovery and development of novel magnetic materials, garnet film growth; magnetic bubble development, electroplating development, process automation and electromigration; magnetic recording materials; computer simulation and modeling. *Mailing Add:* 16130 Kennedy Rd Los Gatos CA 95032. *Fax:* 408-358-3111; *E-Mail:* jimsuits@aol.com

SUK, WILLIAM ALFRED, MUTAGENESIS & CARCINOGENESIS, ENVIRONMENTAL SCIENCES. *Current Pos:* PROG ADMINR, SUPERFUND BASIC RES PROG, NAT INST ENVIRON HEALTH SCI, NIH, 87- *Personal Data:* b New York, NY, July 9, 45; m 84; c 1. *Educ:* Am Univ, BS, 68, MS, 70; George Wash Univ, PhD(microbiol), 77; Univ NC, MPH, 90. *Prof Exp:* Res biologist fisheries & algae, Nat Fisheries Ctr, 68-69; field res hydrologist, remote sensing, Am Univ & US Geol Surv, 69-70; sr technician chem viral cocarcinogenesis, Microbiol Assocs, Inc, 71-72, supvry technician, 72-74, asst proj dir, 74-76; staff scientist cell biol & retrovirol, Frederick Cancer Res Facil, NC, 76-80; prog mgr & sr res scientist occup health assessment, Geomet Technol, Inc, 80-81; sr proj scientist & head lab cell & molecular biol, Environ Sci Div, Northrop Serv, Inc, 81-87. *Concurrent Pos:* NSF fel, Juneau Icefield Res Proj, Glaciol & Arctic Sci Inst, Juneau, Alaska & Atlin, BC, Can, 70; adj prof & mem, Lineberger Cancer Res Ctr, Univ NC Sch Med, Chapel Hill, 83-; consult risk assessment, Indust & Govt Agencies, 81-; prin investr & co-prin investr, Nat Cancer Inst, Nat Inst Environ Health Sci & Environ Protection Agency Contract Awards; mem, Int Prog Chem Safety Collab Study, WHO, 83 & Sci Group Methodologies for Safety Eval of Chemicals, 90; mem, Family Health Int, 87. *Mem:* Am Asn Cancer Res; Am Soc Cell Biol; Sigma Xi; Tissue Cult Asn; Environ Mutagen Soc; Found Glaciol & Environ Res; AAAS; NY Acad Sci; Am Soc Microbiol. *Res:* Carcinogens as modulators of cellular gene expression and how these changes relate to the process of carcinogenesis and differentiation; health hazard assessment of occupational and environmental concerns; retrovirology; molecular toxicology; health policy and administration; biotechnology and technology transfer; public health associated with environmental release of hazardous substances. *Mailing Add:* 3608 Penhurst Pl Raleigh NC 27613

SUKANEK, PETER CHARLES, INTEGRATED CIRCUITS, POLYMER PROCESSING. *Current Pos:* PROF & CHAIR, DEPT CHEM ENG, UNIV MISS, 91- *Personal Data:* b Flushing, NY, Sept 15, 47; m 69, Kathleen L Lambert; c 3. *Educ:* Manhattan Col, BChE, 68; Univ Mass, MS, 70, PhD(chem eng), 72. *Prof Exp:* Proj engr chem eng, Rocket Propulsion Lab, USAF, 72-76; asst prof chem eng, Clarkson Col Technol, 76-82, assoc prof, Clarkson Univ, 82-90. *Concurrent Pos:* Consult, Foreign Technol Div, USAF, 76-79, IBM Corp, 82; engr, Philips Res Labs, 86-87, IBM Corp, 88. *Mem:* Am Inst Chem Engrs; Soc Rheology; Sigma Xi; Electrochem Soc. *Res:* Polymer rheology and processing; holographic interferometry; photolithography; plasma etching; mass transfer. *Mailing Add:* 126 Cedar Hill Dr Oxford MS 38655. *Fax:* 601-232-7023; *E-Mail:* cmpcs@umsvm.edu

SUKAVA, ARMAS JOHN, PHYSICAL CHEMISTRY, CHEMICAL THERMODYNAMICS. *Current Pos:* instr, Univ Western Ont, 54-55, lectr, 55-56, from asst prof to prof, 56-82, EMER PROF CHEM, UNIV WESTERN ONT, 82- *Personal Data:* b Elma, Man, Mar 1, 17; m 50; c 2. *Educ:* Univ Man, BSc, 46, MSc, 49; McGill Univ, PhD, 55. *Prof Exp:* Lectr chem, Univ Man, 47-49; res & develop chemist, Consol Mining & Smelting Co, 49-50; lectr chem, Univ BC, 50-51 & Univ Alta, 51-52. *Mem:* Electrochem Soc; fel Chem Inst Can. *Res:* Thermodynamics of solutions; physicochemical properties of electrolyte systems. *Mailing Add:* Dept Chem Univ Western Ont London ON N6A 5B7 Can

SUKHATME, BALKRISHNA VASUDEO, STATISTICS. *Personal Data:* b Poona, India, Nov 3, 24; m 56; c 1. *Educ:* Univ Delhi, BA, 45, MA, 47; Inst Agr Res Statist, New Delhi, dipl, 49; Univ Calif, Berkeley, PhD(statist), 55. *Prof Exp:* Sr res statistician, Indian Coun Agr Res, 55-58, prof statist, 58-65, dep statist adv, 62-63, sr prof statist, 65-67; from assoc prof to prof statist, Iowa State Univ, 67-80. *Concurrent Pos:* Vis assoc prof statist, Mich State Univ, 59-60; ed jour, Indian Soc Agr Statist, 59-67; consult, FAO, Rome, 65; mem, Int Statist Inst, The Hague, 72- *Mem:* Inst Math Statist; fel Am Statist Asn; Int Asn Surv Statisticians; Indian Soc Agr Statist (joint secy, 56-58). *Res:* Sampling theory and its applications; nonparametric tests for scale and randomness and asymptotic theory of order statistics and generalized U-statistics; planning, organization and conduct of large-scale sample surveys. *Mailing Add:* 1505 Wheeler Ames IA 50010

SUKHATME, SHASHIKALA BALKRISHNA, MATHEMATICAL STATISTICS. *Current Pos:* asst prof, 67-83, ASSOC PROF STATIST, IOWA STATE UNIV, 83- *Personal Data:* b Karad, Maharashtra, India; c 1. *Educ:* Univ Poona, BSc, 53, Hons, 54, MSc, 55; Mich State Univ, PhD(statist), 60. *Prof Exp:* Lectr statist, Univ Delhi, 63-67. *Concurrent Pos:* Univ Grants Comn, India Fel, Univ Delhi, 61-63; Daxina fel, Poona Univ. *Mem:* Inst Math Statist; Am Statist Asn; Indian Statist Asn. *Res:* Nonparametric statistical theory; goodness of fit tests; order statistics. *Mailing Add:* Dept Statist 315 F Snedecor Iowa State Univ Ames IA 50011-1414

SUKHATME, UDAY PANDURANG, ELEMENTARY PARTICLE PHYSICS. *Current Pos:* from asst prof to assoc prof, 80-89, PROF PHYSICS, UNIV ILL, CHICAGO, 89- *Personal Data:* b Pune, India, June 16, 45; m 69; c 2. *Educ:* Univ Delhi, India, BSc, 64; Mass Inst Technol, Cambridge, SB, 66, ScD(physics), 71. *Prof Exp:* Teaching fel physics, Univ Wash, Seattle, 71-73, Univ Mich, Ann Arbor, 73-75, Univ Cambridge, UK, 75-77 & Univ Paris, Orsay, France, 77-79. *Concurrent Pos:* Vis assoc prof, Iowa State Univ, Ames, 79-80. *Res:* Theoretical high energy research with emphasis on the phenomenology of strongly interacting particles and models for multiparticle production. *Mailing Add:* 460 Parkview Pl Hinsdale IL 60521

SUKHODOLSKY, JACOB, SYSTEMS CONTROL THEORY, ENVIRONMENTAL MONITORING SYSTEM CONTROL. *Current Pos:* ASST PROF COMPUT SCI, ST LOUIS UNIV, 95- *Personal Data:* b Odessa, Ukraine, May 20, 52; US citizen. *Educ:* Moscow State Univ, Russia, MS, 74; Yereuan State Univ, Armenia, PhD(bybernetics), 86. *Prof Exp:* Res fel, Food Indust & Automation Inst, 74-80, Ukranian Acad Sci, Econ & Ecol Inst, 80-85; from asst prof to assoc prof comput sci, Kalmyek State Univ, 85-89; programmer & analyst, Hussmann Corp, 90-95. *Res:* Development of a rational agent whose function is to collect data about an object state. *Mailing Add:* 12938 Ferntop Lane Creve Coeur MO 63141

SUKI, BELA, NONLINEAR SYSTEM IDENTIFICATION, RESPIRATOR MECHANICS. *Current Pos:* fel, 90-92, RES ASST PROF BIOMED ENG, BOSTON UNIV, 92- *Personal Data:* b Szeged, Hungary, May 27, 58. *Educ:* Juzsef Attila, Hungary, MS, 82, PhD, 87. *Prof Exp:* Fel biomed eng, Juzsef Atilla, 87-92 & McGill Univ, 90. *Mem:* Biomed Eng Soc. *Mailing Add:* Dept Biomed Eng Boston Univ 44 Cummington St Boston MA 02215

SUKI, WADI NAGIB, INTERNAL MEDICINE, NEPHROLOGY. *Current Pos:* assoc prof, 68-71, CHIEF, RENAL SECT, BAYLOR COL MED, 68-, PROF MED, 71-, PROF PHYSIOL, 82-; SR ATTEND PHYSICIAN, METHODIST HOSP, CHIEF, RENAL SECT, 69- *Personal Data:* b Khartoum, Sudan, Oct 26, 34; US citizen; m 85; c 4. *Educ:* Am Univ Beirut, BS, 55, MD, 59. *Prof Exp:* Resident internal med, Parkland Mem Hosp, Dallas, 61-63; fel exp med, Univ Tex Southwestern Med Sch, Dallas, 59-61, fel nephrology, 63-65, asst prof, 65-88. *Concurrent Pos:* Res fel exp med, Dallas Heart Asn res grant, 67-68; Nat Heart & Lung Inst res grant, Baylor Col Med, 68-72, training grant, 71-76, Nat Inst Arthritis, Diabetes, Digestive & Kidney Dis res grant, 74-88, Nat Inst Allergy & Infectious Dis contract, 74-78, NASA contract, 75-94; attend physician, Ben Taub Gen Hosp, 68-; consult, Vet Admin Hosp, 68- & Wilford Hall, USAF Med Ctr, 72-; chmn, Nat Med Adv Coun, Nat Kidney Found, 71-73, trustee-at-large, 71-76, secy, Sci Adv Bd, 77-78, chmn, 79-80; mem, Exec Comt, Coun Kidney in Cardiovasc Dis, Am Heart Asn, 71-74; mem, Rev Bd Nephrology, Vet Admin Cent Off Med Res Serv, 74-77, chmn, 76-77; secy-treas, Southern Soc Clin Invest, 74-77, pres, 78-79; mem, Gen Med B Study Sect, NIH, 75-79 & 81-85, chmn, 83-85; prog chmn, Am Soc Nephrology, 80; mem, Nephrology Comt, Am Bd Internal Med, 82-88; founder & first pres, Houston & Gulf Coast Area Nephrology Asn, 87-88; chmn, Clin Pract Comn, 91-92, counr, 92-. *Mem:* Am Fedn Clin Res; Am Soc Clin Invest; Int Soc Nephrology; fel Am Col Physicians; Am Soc Nephrology; Renal Physicians Asn; Asn Am Physicians; Am Physiol Soc; Am Soc Transplant Physicians; Am Heart Asn; Nat Kidney Found. *Res:* Renal, fluid and electrolyte physiology and pathophysiology; renal disease, dialysis and transplantation. *Mailing Add:* Dept Med & Physiol Baylor Col Med 6550 Fannin No 1275 Houston TX 77030

SUKOW, WAYNE WILLIAM, MOLECULAR BIOPHYSICS, BIOPHYSICAL CHEMISTRY. *Current Pos:* PROG DIR, DIV TEACHER PREP & ENHANCEMENT, NSF, 88- *Personal Data:* b Merrill, Wis, Dec 9, 36; m 59, Carol J Nelson; c Catherine & David. *Educ:* Univ Wis, River Falls, BA, 59; Case Inst Technol, MS, 63; Wash State Univ, PhD(chem physics), 74. *Prof Exp:* From assoc prof to prof physics, Univ Wis, River Falls, 61-84, chmn dept, 77-84; exec dir, W Cent Wis Consortium, 84-88. *Concurrent Pos:* Vis prof physics, Macalester Col, 67, vis assoc prof chem, Univ Ore, 75 & 76; physicist, 3M Co, 67; NSF sci fac fel, Wash State Univ, 70-72; mem, Instrnl Media Comt, Am Asn Physics Teachers, 82-88; sci educ teacher in-serv presenter, (K-12), 82-91. *Mem:* Biophys Soc; Am Asn Physics Teachers; Nat Sci Teachers Asn; Nat Asn Res In Sci Teaching. *Res:* Protein-ligand binding, particularly the mechanism of detergent binding to membrane proteins; conformational changes of proteins monitored by electron paramagnetic resonance using spin probe molecules; photoelectron microscopy of biological materials; improvement of undergraduate science education using innovative and interdisciplinary approaches; formation of arborescent copper inclusions in Lake Superior agates and Michigan Datolite; science education using interactive science exhibits. *Mailing Add:* 3156 Eakin Park Ct Fairfax VA 22031. *E-Mail:* wsukow@nsf.gov

SUKOWSKI, ERNEST JOHN, PHYSIOLOGY, PHARMACOLOGY. *Current Pos:* ASSOC PROF PHYSIOL, UNIV HEALTH SCI-CHICAGO MED SCH, 63- *Personal Data:* b Chicago, Ill, Nov 17, 32; c 4. *Educ:* Loyola Univ Chicago, BS, 54; Univ Ill, MS, 58, PhD(physiol, pharmacol), 62. *Mem:* NY Acad Sci; Am Physiol Soc; Am Heart Asn; Am Asn Univ Professors; Sigma Xi. *Res:* Cardiac and liver metabolism; cardiovascular physiology; hypertension; sub-cellular physiology; renal physiology. *Mailing Add:* Finch Univ Chicago Med Sch 3333 Green Bay Rd North Chicago IL 60064-3037

SULAK, LAWRENCE RICHARD, EXPERIMENTAL ELEMENTARY PARTICLE PHYSICS. *Current Pos:* PROF PHYSICS & DEPT CHMN, BOSTON UNIV, 85- *Personal Data:* b Columbus, Ohio, Aug 29, 44; m 70; c 2. *Educ:* Carnegie-Mellon Univ, BS, 66; Princeton Univ, AM, 68, PhD(physics), 70. *Prof Exp:* Res physicist, Univ Geneva, 70-71; from asst prof to assoc prof physics, Harvard Univ, 71-79; from assoc prof to prof physics, Univ Mich, 79-85. *Concurrent Pos:* Vis scientist, Europ Orgn Nuclear Res, 70-73; vis physicist, Fermi Nat Accelerator Lab, 71-77; guest assoc physicist, Brookhaven Nat Lab, 74-; vis prof, Harvard Univ, 84-85; prin investr, US Dept Energy contract, 79-, proj dir, 85-; mem, Dept Energy High Energy Physics Adv panel, 87. *Mem:* Am Phys Soc; AAAS. *Res:* Experimental K-meson physics, elementary particle production studies, neutrino physics, studies of deep inelastic scattering, scaling, neutral currents, dimuons and elastic neutrino-proton scattering; proton decay experiments; instrumentation for high energy physics; acoustic signals from particle beams, astrophysical sources of neutrinos, g-2 of moon; precision superconducting storage ring. *Mailing Add:* 111 Carlton St Brookline MA 02146. *Fax:* 617-353-9383

SULAKHE, PRAKASH VINAYAK, PHYSIOLOGY. *Current Pos:* asst prof, Univ Sask, 73-76, assoc prof, 76-80, Med Res Coun Can res prof, 77-78, PROF PHYSIOL, UNIV SASK, 80- *Personal Data:* b Nov 18, 41; Indian citizen; m 73. *Educ:* Bombay Univ, BS, 62, MS, 65; Univ Man, PhD(physiol), 71. *Prof Exp:* Lectr physiol, Topiwala Nat Med Col, India, 66; sci officer med div, Bhaha Atomic Res Ctr, India, 66-67; demonstr & teaching fel physiol, Univ Man, 68-71; Med Res Coun Can fel pharmacol, Univ BC, 71-73. *Mem:* Can Physiol Soc; Int Soc Heart Res; NY Acad Sci; Soc Neurosci; Can Biochem Soc. *Res:* Regulation and metabolism and function of contractile tissues and brain; cyclic nucleotides, calcium ions, autonomic receptors and membranes. *Mailing Add:* Dept Physiol Univ Sask Col Med Saskatoon SK S7N 5E5 Can

SULAVIK, STEPHEN B, MEDICINE. *Current Pos:* PROF & HEAD DIV PULMONARY MED, UNIV CONN, 77- *Personal Data:* b New Britain, Conn, Aug 11, 30; m 55; c 8. *Educ:* Providence Col, BS, 52; Georgetown Univ, MD, 56. *Prof Exp:* Asst chief chest dis, Vet Admin Hosp, Bronx, NY, 61-62; clin instr, 62-63; from instr to asst prof, 63-69, assoc clin prof med, Sch Med, 69-78, clin prof med, Yale Univ Sch Med, 78- *Concurrent Pos:* Mem med adv comt, Dept HEW; assoc prof med & actg head pulmonary div, Univ Conn, 69-77; chmn dept med, St Francis Hosp, Hartford, 69-77. *Mem:* Am Thoracic Soc; AMA. *Res:* Anatomy and physiology of intrathoracic lymphatic system. *Mailing Add:* Div Pulmonary Med Univ Conn Sch Med Farmington CT 06032

SULENTIC, JACK WILLIAM, ASTRONOMY, EXTRAGALACTIC ASTRONOMY. *Current Pos:* from asst prof to assoc prof, 80-88, PROF, DEPT PHYSICS & ASTRON, UNIV ALA, 88- *Personal Data:* b Waterloo, Iowa, Apr 10, 47; m 75. *Educ:* Univ Ariz, BS, 69; State Univ NY Albany, PhD(astron), 75. *Prof Exp:* Fel astron, Hale Observ, 75-78; instr physics & astron, Sierra Nev Col, 78-79; asst prof, Mich State Univ, 79-80. *Concurrent Pos:* Vis prof, Univ Padova, Italy, 87. *Mem:* Am Astron Soc; Sigma Xi; Int Astron Union. *Res:* Application of optical and radio observations to understanding the origin and evolution of galaxies and quasars. *Mailing Add:* Dept Physics & Astron Univ Ala Tuscaloosa AL 35487-0324. *E-Mail:* giacomo@merlot.astr.ua.edu

SULERUD, RALPH L, GENETICS, ZOOLOGY. *Current Pos:* from instr to assoc prof, 64-77, PROF BIOL, AUGSBURG COL, 77-, CHMN DEPT, 74- *Personal Data:* b Fargo, NDak, June 6, 32. *Educ:* Concordia Col, Moorhead, Minn, BA, 54; Univ Nebr, MS, 58, PhD(zool), 68. *Prof Exp:* Instr biol, St Olaf Col, 58-59. *Mem:* AAAS; Genetics Soc Am; Am Genetic Asn; Am Inst Biol Sci; Soc Study Evolution. *Res:* Taxonomy; genetics of Drosophila. *Mailing Add:* 549 Otis Ave St Paul MN 55104

SULEWSKI, PAUL ERIC, OPTICAL PROPERTIES, SYSTEMS ENGINEERING FOR TELECOMMUNICATIONS NETWORKS OPERATIONS SYSTEMS. *Current Pos:* MEM TECH STAFF, SYST ENG, LUCENT TECHNOL, 96- *Personal Data:* b Hempstead, NY, Nov 16, 60; m 85, Jennifer Kamrass. *Educ:* Princeton Univ, AB, 82; Cornell Univ, MS, 85, PhD(physics), 88. *Prof Exp:* Postdoctorate physics, AT&T Bell Labs, 88-90, mem tech staff physics, 90-94, mem tech staff systs eng, 94-96. *Res:* Systems engineering for telecommunications networks operations systems. *Mailing Add:* Lucent Technol Rm 3W-T07 184 Liberty Corner Rd Warren NJ 07059-0908

SULIK, KATHLEEN KAY, TERATOLOGY. *Current Pos:* ASST PROF ANAT, UNIV NC, CHAPEL HILL, 80- *Personal Data:* b Estherville, Iowa, Oct 15, 48; m 77; c 1. *Educ:* Drake Univ, BS, 70; Univ Tenn, PhD(anat), 76. *Prof Exp:* Guest scientist, Gerontol Res Ctr, NIH, 74-75; instr anat, Univ Tenn, 75-76; fel teratol, Dent Res Ctr, Univ NC, 76-78; res assoc, Georgetown Univ, Wash, DC, 78-79, asst prof, 79-80. *Mem:* Teratology Soc; AAAS. *Res:* Embryology and teratology of the craniofacial region emphasizing the teratogenic effect of ethanol, defining critical exposure periods and mechanisms of malformation. *Mailing Add:* Dept Anat Univ NC Chapel Hill Sch Med Chapel Hill NC 27599-7090

SULING, WILLIAM JOHN, ANTIMICROBIAL & ANTICANCER CHEMOTHERAPY. *Current Pos:* res microbiologist, 75-78, sr microbiologist, 78-86, HEAD, BACT-MYCOL SECT, SOUTHERN RES INST, 86- *Personal Data:* b New York, NY, June 12, 40; m 65; c 3. *Educ:* Manhattan Col, BS, 62; Duquesne Univ, MS, 65; Cornell Univ Med Col, PhD(microbiol), 75. *Prof Exp:* Res asst cancer chemother, Sloan-Kettering Inst Cancer Res, 64-70; sr bacteriologist, Biol Lab, Mass Dept Pub Health, 74-75. *Mem:* NY Acad Sci; Am Soc Microbiol; Soc Indust Microbiol. *Res:* Folate metabolism and its inhibition by folate analoguess; the biochemistry of antimicrobial drug resistance and the use of microorganisms for studies involving cancer chemotherapy; drug metabolism and disposition; mechanisms of action of anticancer agents. *Mailing Add:* 537 Canterberry Rd Pelham AL 35124

SULKES, MARK, PHYSICS, CHEMISTRY. *Current Pos:* from asst prof to assoc prof, 81-92, PROF CHEM, TULANE UNIV, 92- *Educ:* Univ Chicago, BA, 71; Cornell Univ, MS, 75, PhD(physics), 78. *Prof Exp:* Fel res assoc, James Franck Inst, Univ Chicago, 77-81. *Concurrent Pos:* Vis scientist, Dept Phys Chem, Ctr Nuclear Studies, France, 82, 84, prof, Sch Physics, Ga Inst Technol. *Mailing Add:* Chem Tulane Univ 6823 St Charles Ave New Orleans LA 70118-5665

SULKIN, STEPHEN DAVID, MARINE BIOLOGY. *Current Pos:* PROF & DIR, SHANNA POINT MARINE CTR, WESTERN WASH UNIV, 85-, ACTG PROVOST, 93- *Personal Data:* b Topeka, Kans, Aug 14, 44; m 70, Shelley S Turpin; c Kimberly, Tracy & Matthew. *Educ:* Miami Univ, Ohio, AB, 66; Duke Univ, MS & PhD, 71. *Prof Exp:* Res asst prof, Chesapeake Biol Lab, Univ Md, Solomons, 71-76, asst prof & head, Horn Point Environ Lab, Cambridge, 76-82, prof, 84-85. *Concurrent Pos:* Ed, Estuarine Coastal Shelf Sci, 90- *Mem:* AAAS; Estuarian Res Fedn; Nat Asn Marine Labs. *Res:* Marine sciences; nutritional requirements of larval crabs. *Mailing Add:* Shannon Point Marine Ctr 1900 Shannon Point Rd Anacortes WA 98221-4042. *E-Mail:* sulkin@henson.cc.wwn.edu

SULKOWSKI, EUGENE, BIOCHEMISTRY. *Current Pos:* prin cancer res scientist, 65-91, RES PROF, ROSWELL PARK CANCER INST, 97- *Personal Data:* b Plonsk, Poland, May 22, 34; US citizen; m 64, Nancy Belter; c Mark & Paul. *Educ:* Univ Warsaw, MS, 56, PhD(biochem), 60. *Prof Exp:* Res asst biochem, Inst Biochem & Biophys, Polish Acad Sci, 56-60; exchange scientist, Univ Sorbonne, 62-63; res asst, Polish Acad Sci, 63-65. *Concurrent Pos:* Res fel, Marquette Univ, 60-62. *Mem:* AAAS; Am Soc Biol Chemists; Polish Biochem Soc. *Res:* Enzymology; human interferon; affinity chromatography. *Mailing Add:* Biophysics Roswell Park Cancer Inst, Elm & Carlfam Buffalo NY 14263. *Fax:* 716-845-8899

SULLENGER, DON BRUCE, SOLID STATE CHEMISTRY. *Current Pos:* ADJ PROF, CHEM DEPT, MIAMI UNIV, OXFORD, OHIO, 92- *Personal Data:* b Richmond, Mo, Feb 8, 29; m 64; c Mark O'Brian, Bruce Alan & Paul Eric. *Educ:* Univ Colo, AB, 50; Cornell Univ, PhD, 69. *Prof Exp:* Trainee, Chemet Prog, Chem Div, Gen Elec Co, 50-51 & 53, res chemist, Res Lab, 53-54; sr res chemist, Monsanto Res Corp, 62-74, res specialist, 74-85, sr res specialist, Mound Lab, 85-88; sr res specialist, EG&G Mound Appl Technologies, 88-92. *Mem:* AAAS; Am Chem Soc; Am Crystallog Asn. *Res:* X-ray crystallographic structural characterization of inorganic and organic substances; materials science; solid state chemistry of inorganic materials. *Mailing Add:* 135 Bethel Rd Centerville OH 45458. *E-Mail:* sullengerdb@worldnet.att.net

SULLIVAN, ALFRED DEWITT, FORESTRY, BIOMETRICS. *Current Pos:* DEAN, COL NATURAL RESOURCES, UNIV MINN, 93- *Personal Data:* b New Orleans, La, Feb 2, 42; m 62; c 2. *Educ:* La State Univ, BS, 64, MS, 66; Univ Ga, PhD(forest biomet), 69. *Prof Exp:* Asst prof statist, Va Polytech Inst & State Univ, 69-73; from assoc prof to prof forestry, Miss State Univ, 78-88; dir, Sch Forest Resources, Pa State Univ, 88-93. *Mem:* Soc Am Foresters. *Res:* Prediction of forest growth and yield; application of statistical methodology to natural resource problems. *Mailing Add:* Col Natural Resources Univ Minn 235 NRAB 2003 Upper Buford Circle St Paul MN 55108

SULLIVAN, ANDREW JACKSON, BIOCHEMISTRY, FOOD CHEMISTRY. *Current Pos:* res chemist, Campbell Soup Co, 53-55 & 57-59, head, Div Flavor Biochem Res, 59-71, div head environ sci & chem technol, Campbell Inst for Food Res, 71-76, dir sci resources, 76-77, dir flavor sci & nutrit, 77-87, DIR, TECHNOL ASSESSMENT & ACQUISITION, CAMPBELL INST RES & TECHNOL, 87- *Personal Data:* b Birmingham, Ala, Mar 3, 26; m 53. *Educ:* Univ Richmond, BS, 47; Univ Mo, PhD(bot), 52. *Prof Exp:* USPHS fel, Univ Pa, 52-53. *Mem:* Inst Food Technologists; NY Acad Sci; fel Am Inst Chemists; Am Chem Soc; Asn Chemoreception Sci. *Res:* Chemistry of microorganisms; food and flavor chemistry. *Mailing Add:* 99 Oak Ridge Dr Haddonfield NJ 08033-3514

SULLIVAN, ANNA MANNEVILLETTE, METALLURGY. *Current Pos:* RETIRED. *Personal Data:* b Washington, DC, Aug 18, 13. *Educ:* George Washington Univ, AB, 35; Univ Md, MS, 55. *Honors & Awards:* Burgess Award, Am Soc Metals, 78. *Prof Exp:* Asst metallurgist, Geophys Lab, Carnegie Inst Wash, 42-45; metallurgist, Nat Bur Stand, 45-46; metallurgist, Naval Res Lab, 47-78; dep tech ed, J Eng Mat Technol, Am Soc Mech Engrs, 78-81. *Concurrent Pos:* Consult; Naval Ord Develop Award. *Mem:* Sigma Xi; Am Soc Metals; Am Soc Testing & Mat; Am Soc Mech Engrs. *Res:* Fracture of metals with special reference to fracture mechanics. *Mailing Add:* 9500 W State Hwy 15 Belleville IL 62223-1023

SULLIVAN, ARTHUR LYON, EDUCATION ADMINISTRATION. *Current Pos:* PROF, TEX A&M UNIV, 92- *Personal Data:* b Atlanta, Ga, May 29, 40; m 62; c 2. *Educ:* Univ NH, BA, 63, MS, 66; Cornell Univ, PhD(natural resources), 69. *Prof Exp:* Asst prof regional planning, Univ Pa, 69-74; asst prof environ mgt, Duke Univ, 74-76; from assoc prof to prof landscape archit, NC State Univ, 76-92, head dept, 78-92. *Concurrent Pos:* Mem, res bd, Regional Sci Res Inst, 72-74; assoc ed, Environ Prof, 79-81; vis prof, Kyoto Univ, Japan, 81; fel, NC Japan Ctr, 81- *Mem:* AAAS; Am Soc Landscape Archit; Coun Educr Landscape Archit; Asian Studies Soc. *Res:* Biogeography of urban development; Japan United States comparative land-use systems; agricultural alternatives. *Mailing Add:* Urban Regional Planning Tex A&M Univ College Station TX 77843-0100

SULLIVAN, BETTY J, PROTEIN CHEMISTRY, PROTEOLYTIC ENZYMES. *Current Pos:* RETIRED. *Personal Data:* b Minneapolis, Minn, May 31, 02. *Educ:* Univ Minn, BS, 22, PhD(biochem), 35. *Honors & Awards:* Thomas Burr Osborne Medal, Am Asn Cereal Chemists, 48; Garvan Medal, Am Chem Soc, 54. *Prof Exp:* Lab asst, Russell Miller Milling Co, 22-24, 26-27, chief chemist, 27-47, dir res, 47-58; vpres & dir res, Peavey Co, 58-67; vpres, Experience Inc, 67-69, pres, 69-73, chmn bd, 73-75, dir, 75-92. *Concurrent Pos:* Scholar biochem, Univ Paris, 24-25. *Mem:* Am Chem Soc; Am Asn Cereal Chemists (pres, 43-44); Sigma Xi; AAAS. *Res:* Chemistry of wheat gluten; sulfhydryl and disulfide groups and interchange as related to function. *Mailing Add:* 8441 Irwin Rd Minneapolis MN 55437

SULLIVAN, BRIAN PATRICK, ELECTROCHEMISTRY, CATALYSIS. *Current Pos:* ASSOC PROF CHEM, UNIV WYO, 90- *Personal Data:* b Brookings, SDak, Oct 10, 49; m 71; c 2. *Educ:* Univ Calif, Irvine, BS, 71, Univ Calif, Los Angeles, MS, 86; Univ NC, Chapel Hill, PhD(chem), 88. *Prof Exp:* Res assoc chem, 75-88, res asst prof chem, Univ NC, Chapel Hill, 88-90. *Concurrent Pos:* Consult, Allied Chem Co, 81-82, Dept Pharm, Univ NC, 85-86, Igen Corp, 87-88; vis assoc chem, Calif Inst Technol, 89. *Mem:* Am Chem Soc; Electrochem Soc. *Res:* Areas of novel inorganic synthesis, reactivity of coordinated ligands and small molecule transition metal complexes; solvent effects on electron and atom transfer reactions, photo chemistry of inorganic molecules and inorganic surface chemistry; the reduction of carbon dioxide to fuels; author of over 70 publications; photochemistry. *Mailing Add:* Dept Chem Univ Wyo Laramie WY 82071-3838. *Fax:* 307-766-2875

SULLIVAN, CHARLES H, DEVELOPMENTAL BIOLOGY. *Current Pos:* asst prof, 86-92, dept chair, 92-94, ASSOC PROF BIOL, GRINNELL COL, 92- *Personal Data:* b Needham, Mass, June 25, 52; m 79, Donna J Norton; c Matthew C & Peter W. *Educ:* Univ Maine, Orono, BA, 74; Univ Md, MS, 79, PhD(zool), 83. *Prof Exp:* Teaching asst zool, Univ Md, 75-82; postdoctoral fel develop biol, Univ Va, 83-86. *Concurrent Pos:* Prin investr grants, Grinnell Col, Res Corp, 87-89, NIH, 88-90, NSF, 91-93 & 95- *Mem:* Soc Develop Biol; Am Soc Cell Biol; Coun Undergrad Res. *Res:* Developmental and cellular biology of vertebrate development with emphasis on cell and tissue interactions in lens development. *Mailing Add:* Dept Biol Grinnell Col Grinnell IA 50112. *E-Mail:* sullivac@ac.grin.edu

SULLIVAN, CHARLES IRVING, ORGANIC POLYMER CHEMISTRY. *Current Pos:* sr scientist, 69-70, res assoc, 70-79, RES FEL, POLAROID CORP, 79- *Personal Data:* b Milwaukee, Wis, Nov 18, 18; m 48; c 2. *Educ:* Boston Univ, AB, 43. *Prof Exp:* Chemist, UBS Chem Co Div, A E Staley Mfg Co, 43-46, supvr indust chem & develop sect, 46-58, mgr res & develop, 58-67, res assoc, 67-69. *Mem:* AAAS; Am Chem Soc; fel Am Inst Chemists. *Res:* Emulsion polymerization; paints; floor finishes; paper coatings and binders; wood coatings; adhesives; textile backings; aqueous polymer research and development related to membrane-like structures, functional coatings, binders and colloids. *Mailing Add:* 148 Bellevue Ave Melrose Boston MA 02176-2818

SULLIVAN, CHARLOTTE MURDOCH, ANIMAL PHYSIOLOGY. *Current Pos:* RETIRED. *Personal Data:* b St Stephen, NB, Dec 18, 19. *Educ:* Dalhousie Univ, BSc, 41, MSc, 43; Univ Toronto, PhD(zool), 49. *Prof Exp:* Nat Res Coun Can overseas fel, Cambridge Univ, 49-50; from lectr to assoc prof zool, Univ Toronto, 50-85. *Res:* Physiology of animal behavior. *Mailing Add:* Ten Avoca Ave Toronto ON M4T 2B7 Can

SULLIVAN, CORNELIUS PATRICK, JR, METALLURGY. *Current Pos:* RETIRED. *Personal Data:* b Schenectady, NY, Sept 28, 29; m 55; c 3. *Educ:* Univ Notre Dame, BS, 51; Mass Inst Technol, SM, 55, ScD(metall), 60. *Honors & Awards:* William A Spraragen Award, Am Welding Soc, 67. *Prof Exp:* Engr metall, Pratt & Whitney, 62-91. *Mem:* Am Soc Metals Int. *Res:* Mechanical behavior of high temperature alloys and their properties. *Mailing Add:* 74 Coach Rd Glastonbury CT 06033

SULLIVAN, DANIEL JOSEPH, ENTOMOLOGY, ANIMAL BEHAVIOR. *Current Pos:* from asst prof to assoc prof, 69-83, PROF ZOOL, FORDHAM UNIV, 83- *Personal Data:* b New York, NY, Apr 22, 28. *Educ:* Fordham Univ, BS, 50, MS, 58; Univ Vienna, cert Ger, 58; Univ Strasbourg, cert French, 62; Univ Innsbruck, cert theol, 62; Univ Calif, Berkeley, PhD(entom), 69. *Prof Exp:* Teacher, NY High Sch, 55-57. *Concurrent Pos:* Fulbright res fel, Nigeria, WAfrica, 84-85; Int Inst Trop Agr fac fel, Cali, Colombia, 88-89. *Mem:* AAAS; Entom Soc Am; Ecol Soc Am; Animal Behav Soc; Am Inst Biol Sci; Sigma Xi. *Res:* Biological control of insect pests, with special reference to the primary parasites and hyperparasites of aphids; ecology and behavior of aphids and parasites; evolution. *Mailing Add:* Dept Biol Sci Fordham Univ Bronx NY 10458. *Fax:* 718-817-3645; *E-Mail:* sullivan@murray.fordham.edu

SULLIVAN, DAVID ANTHONY, ENDOCRINOLOGY, OPHTHALMOLOGY. *Current Pos:* ASST SCIENTIST, EYE RES INST, HARVARD MED SCH, 83- *Educ:* Dartmouth Med Sch, PhD(physiol), 80. *Mailing Add:* Schepens Eye Res Inst Immunization Unit Havard Med Sch 20 Staniford St Boston MA 02114-2500. *Fax:* 617-720-1069

SULLIVAN, DAVID THOMAS, BIOCHEMICAL GENETICS. *Current Pos:* from asst prof to assoc prof, 70-81, PROF BIOL, SYRACUSE UNIV, 81- *Personal Data:* b Salem, Mass, Mar 20, 40; m 66; c 2. *Educ:* Boston Col, BS, 61, MS, 63; Johns Hopkins Univ, PhD(biol), 67. *Prof Exp:* USPHS res fel biochem, Calif Inst Technol, 67-69. *Mem:* Genetics Soc Am; Soc Develop Biol. *Res:* Eukaryotic gene structure, evolution and expression. *Mailing Add:* Syracuse Univ 100 University Pl Syracuse Univ Syracuse NY 13244-0001

SULLIVAN, DENNIS P, MATHEMATICS. *Current Pos:* EINSTEIN PROF SCI, QUEENS COL & CITY UNIV NEW YORK GRAD SCH, 81- *Personal Data:* b Port Huron, Mich, Feb 12, 41. *Educ:* Rice Univ, BA, 63; Princeton Univ, PhD, 65. *Honors & Awards:* Oswald Veblen Prize in Geom, Am Math Soc, 71; Elie Cartan Priz en Geom, French Acad Sci, 81. *Prof Exp:* NATO fel, Warwick Univ, Eng, 66; from lectr to assoc prof, Princeton Univ, 67-69; Sloan fel math, Mass Inst Technol, 69-72, prof, 72-73. *Concurrent Pos:* Miller fel, Berkeley, 67-69; assoc prof, Univ Paris, Orsay, 73-74; Stanislaw Ulam vis prof math, Univ Colo, Boulder, 80-81. *Mem:* Nat Acad Sci; Am Math Soc (vpres, 89-); fel AAAS; corresp mem Nat Acad Sci Brazil. *Mailing Add:* Dept Math Grad Ctr City Univ New York 33 W 42nd St New York NY 10036. *Fax:* 212-642-1823; *E-Mail:* dpsgc@cunyvm.bitnet

SULLIVAN, DONALD, MATHEMATICS. *Current Pos:* asst prof, 61-66, ASSOC PROF MATH, UNIV NB, 66- *Personal Data:* b Merthyr Tydfil, Wales, Mar 23, 36; m 61; c 2. *Educ:* Univ Wales, BSc, 57, PhD(appl math), 60. *Prof Exp:* Asst lectr math, Univ Col, Univ Wales, 60-61. *Mem:* fel Inst Math & Appln. *Res:* Fluid mechanics; phase plane analysis of differential equations; functional equations; integral equations. *Mailing Add:* Dept Math Univ NB Fredericton NB E3B 5A3 Can

SULLIVAN, DONALD BARRETT, LOW TEMPERATURE PHYSICS, ATOMIC PHYSICS. *Current Pos:* Nat Res Coun assoc, 67-69, physicist & chief cryoelectronic metrol sect, 69-84, CHIEF, TIME & FREQUENCY DIV, NAT BUR STANDARDS, 84- *Personal Data:* b Phoenix, Ariz, June 13, 39; m 59; c Deborah, Christine & Michael. *Educ:* Tex Western Col, BS, 61; Vanderbilt Univ, MA, 63, PhD(physics), 65. *Honors & Awards:* Stratton Award, Nat Bur Stand, 85; Gold Medal, Dept Com. *Prof Exp:* Res assoc physics, Vanderbilt Univ, 65; physicist & br chief, Radiation Physics Br, US Army Nuclear Defense Lab, 65-67. *Mem:* Am Phys Soc; Inst Elec & Electronics Engrs. *Res:* Josephson effect and quantum interference in superconductors; development of measurement instruments using these and other low temperature phenomena; development of atomic clocks and methods for clock synchronization. *Mailing Add:* 3594 Kirkwood Pl Boulder CO 80304

SULLIVAN, DONITA B, PEDIATRICS. *Current Pos:* clin instr, 59-62, asst prof pediat & dir birth defects treatment ctr, 62-69, assoc prof, 69-77, PROF PEDIAT & DIR PEDIAT REHAB & RHEUMATOLOGY SECT, MED SCH, UNIV MICH, ANN ARBOR, 77-, PROF PEDIAT & DIR PEDIAT RHEUMATOLOGY, 79-, ASSOC CHMN PEDIAT DEPT & DIR PEDIAT EDUC, 81- *Personal Data:* b Marlette, Mich, Feb 11, 31. *Educ:* Siena Heights Col, BS, 52; St Louis Univ, MD, 56; Am Bd Pediat, dipl, 61. *Hon Degrees:* DHH, Siena Heights Col, 80. *Prof Exp:* Intern, Henry Ford Hosp, Detroit, Mich, 56-57; resident pediat, Children's Hosp of Mich, 57-59, sr resident, 59; res assoc, Sch Med, Wayne State Univ, 59. *Concurrent Pos:* Pediat consult, Wayne Co Gen Hosp, 62-80; Field Clins, Mich Crippled Children's Comn, 64-68 & Cath Social Servs, 66-80; mem med adv comt, Washtenaw Co Chapters, Nat Found & Nat Cystic Fibrosis Res Found, 60-74; prog consult, Nat Found, 66-69; bd trustees, Siena Heights Col, 70-75. *Res:* Handicapped children; children with birth defects; clinical and immunologic aspects of connective tissue disease in children. *Mailing Add:* MPB Univ Hosp D3215 PO Box 0718 Ann Arbor MI 48109

SULLIVAN, EDMUND JOSEPH, UNDERWATER ACOUSTIC SIGNAL PROCESSING, ACOUSTIC ARRAY PROCESSING. *Current Pos:* physicist, 71-85, basic res mgr, 88-94, SR SCIENTIST, NAVAL UNDERSEA WARFARE CTR, 94- *Personal Data:* b Newport, RI, Aug 8, 35; div; c Sean P & Erin A. *Educ:* Univ RI, BSEE, 65, MSEE, 67, PhD(nuclear physics), 70. *Honors & Awards:* Distinguished Tech Achievement Award, Inst Elec & Electronics Engrs Oceanic Eng Soc, 94. *Prof Exp:* Head, Signal Processing Group, Saclant Ctr, LeSpezia, Italy, 85-88. *Concurrent Pos:* Assoc ed, J Acoust Soc Am, 83-85, Circuits, Systs & Signal Processing, 91-, Inst Elec & Electronics Engrs J Oceanic Eng, 93- *Mem:* Fel Acoust Soc Am; sr mem Inst Elec & Electronics Engrs; Am Soc Physics Teachers; Oceanic Eng Soc. *Res:* Underwater acoustic signal processing including statistical signal processing, array processing matched field processing and higher order spectral analysis. *Mailing Add:* 46 Lawton Brook Lane Portsmouth RI 02871. *Fax:* 401-841-2146; *E-Mail:* sullivanej@medelros4.npt.nuwc.navy.mil

SULLIVAN, EDWARD AUGUSTINE, INORGANIC CHEMISTRY. *Current Pos:* RETIRED. *Personal Data:* b Salem, Mass, July 5, 29; m 59; c 6. *Educ:* Col Holy Cross, BS, 50; Mass Inst Technol, MS, 52. *Prof Exp:* Asst, Sugar Res Found, 50-52; res chemist, Metal Hydrides, Inc, 52-63, sr res chemist, Metal Hydrides Div, Ventron Corp, 63-71, tech mgr, res chem, 71-79, sr scientist, Morton Int, 79-92. *Mem:* Am Chem Soc; Tech Asn Pulp & Paper Indust. *Res:* Chemistry of hydrides; inorganic synthesis; industrial applications of hydrides. *Mailing Add:* 43 Brimbal Ave Beverly MA 01915

SULLIVAN, EDWARD T, FOREST ECONOMICS. *Current Pos:* ASSOC PROF FOREST ECON, UNIV FLA, 59-, ASSOC FORESTER, 71- *Personal Data:* b Flushing, NY, June 28, 20; m 54; c 1. *Educ:* NC State Col, BSF, 46; Duke Univ, MS, 47, DF, 53. *Prof Exp:* Acct, Southern Woodlands Dept, WVa Pulp & Paper Co, 47-50; vis instr forest econ, Sch Forestry, Duke Univ, 50-51; asst prof forestry, Univ Minn, 54-59. *Mem:* Am Econ Asn; Soc Am Foresters. *Res:* Marketing of forest products; demand for pulpwood. *Mailing Add:* 755 NW 18th St Gainesville FL 32603

SULLIVAN, F(REDERICK) W(ILLIAM), III, CHEMICAL ENGINEERING. *Current Pos:* RETIRED. *Personal Data:* b Ann Arbor, Mich, June 24, 23; m 48, Ruth Swavely; c Elizabeth, Sarah, Frederick & Edward. *Educ:* Pa State Univ, BS, 47; Univ Del, MS, 49, PhD(chem eng), 52. *Prof Exp:* Chem engr process develop, Houdry Process Corp, 51-56; chem engr process develop & design, Halby Chem Co, 56-63; dir process eng, Maumee Chem Co, 63-70; mgr process eng sect, Chem Div, Sherwin Williams Co, 70-78, mgr process develop, 78-80. *Mem:* Am Chem Soc; Inst Chem Engrs. *Res:* Petroleum refining; heat transfer; manufacture of inorganic and organic chemicals. *Mailing Add:* 208 Sean Way Hendersonville NC 28792

SULLIVAN, FRANCIS E, FAST ALGORITHMS, NONLINEAR DYNAMICS. *Current Pos:* DIR, CTR COMPUT SCI, BOWIE. *Personal Data:* b Brooklyn, NY, May 12, 41; m 69. *Educ:* Pa State Univ, BS, 62; Univ Pittsburgh, PhD(math), 68. *Honors & Awards:* Gold Medal, Dept Com, 88. *Prof Exp:* Chmn, Catholic Univ, 73-82; dir admin, Comput & Appl Math Lab, Nat Inst Stand & Technol, 86- *Concurrent Pos:* Adj prof, Catholic Univ, 82-; sci policy bd, Soc Indust & Appl Math. *Mem:* Soc Indust Appl Math. *Res:* Supercomputer algorithms; parallel computing nonlinear analysis. *Mailing Add:* Ctr Comput Sci 17100 Science Dr Bowie MD 20715

SULLIVAN, GEORGE ALLEN, INFORMATION SCIENCE, STATISTICS. *Current Pos:* criminal justice systs planner & eval coordr, Pa Bd Probation & Parole, 71-74, actg dir, 74-75, sr statist anal, 75-80, sr statist anal, res unit, 80-89, CHIEF RES, PA BD PROBATION & PAROLE, 89- *Personal Data:* b Bronxville, NY, Jan 6, 35; m 60, Virginia Weir; c Bonnie & Timothy. *Educ:* Grinnell Col, AB, 57; Univ Rochester, AM, 59; Univ Nebr, PhD(solid state physics), 64; Univ Pa, MGovt Admin, 76. *Prof Exp:* Res asst solid state physics, Rensselaer Polytech Inst, 64-66; sr physicist, Electronic Res Div, Clevite Corp, Cleveland, 66-69; asst prof elec eng, Air Force Inst Technol, Wright Patterson AFB, 69-70; vis scientist, Physics Inst, Chalmers Univ Technol, Sweden, 70-71. *Mem:* Am Statist Asn; Nat Speleol Soc; Sigma Xi. *Res:* Point defects and diffusion in metals; thermal mass transport and electromigration in solids; semiconductors; properties of semiconducting materials; physics of solar cells; criminal justice information statistics; social rehabilitation programs; criminological research; operations and program planning; multivariate statistical analysis with software packages; design of parole decision making guidelines instruments; risk classification instruments. *Mailing Add:* Mgt Info Div Probation & Parole Box 1661 3101 N Front St Harrisburg PA 17105-1661

SULLIVAN, HARRY MORTON, UPPER ATMOSPHERE PHYSICS. *Current Pos:* RETIRED. *Personal Data:* b Winnipeg, Man, Apr 14, 21; m 49, Dorothy M Austin; c Arthur M, Michael C & Madeleine A. *Educ:* Queen's Univ, Ont, BSc, 45; Carleton Univ, BSc, 50; McGill Univ, MSc, 54; Univ Sask, PhD(upper atmosphere physics), 62. *Prof Exp:* Chemist, Can Civil Serv, 45-47; engr, Canadair Ltd, 54-56; physicist, Can Civil Serv, 56-59 & Nat Ctr Sci Res, France, 62-64; from asst prof to assoc prof physics, Univ Victoria, 64-86. *Mem:* Can Asn Physicists. *Res:* Upper atmosphere; airglow and related phenomena, particularly twilight glow and day glow; rarer constituents of upper atmosphere; photometer calibration techniques; standard radiation sources. *Mailing Add:* 4037 Hollydene Pl Victoria BC V8N 3Z8 Can

SULLIVAN, HUGH D, MATHEMATICS. *Current Pos:* from asst prof to assoc prof, Eastern Wash State Col, 67-82, chmn dept, 70-76, interim dean, Sch Math & Technol, 83-85, dir, Ctr Technol Develop, 85-88, vprovost, Exten Univ Prog & Serv, 88-92, PROF MATH, EASTERN WASH STATE COL, 83- *Personal Data:* b Butte, Mont, June 16, 39; m 61; c 4. *Educ:* Univ Mont, BA, 62, MA, 64; Wash State Univ, PhD(math), 68. *Prof Exp:* Teaching asst math, Univ Mont, 62-64 & Wash State Univ, 64-67. *Concurrent Pos:* Exec dir, Joint Ctr Higher Educ & dir, Spokane Intercol Res & Technol Inst, 92-95. *Mem:* Am Math Soc; Math Asn Am; Sigma Xi. *Res:* Abstract systems theory; topology; probability and statistics. *Mailing Add:* Eastern Wash Univ Mail Stop 32 Cheney WA 99004

SULLIVAN, HUGH R, JR, DRUG METABOLISM. *Current Pos:* RETIRED. *Personal Data:* b Indianapolis, Ind, Apr 8, 26; m 48, Betty Smith; c Hugh III, Kathleen, Mark, Marianne & Kevin. *Educ:* Univ Notre Dame, BS, 48; Temple Univ, MA, 54. *Prof Exp:* Assoc res chemist, Socony-Vacuum Oil Co, 48-51; from assoc res chemist to sr res chemist, Eli Lilly & Co, 51-69, res scientist, 69-72, res assoc, Res Labs, 72-87, sr res scientist, 87-88. *Mem:* Am Chem Soc; Am Soc Pharmacol & Exp Therapeut; Am Soc Mass Spectrometry. *Res:* Mechanism of drug action and detoxication; analgesics; antibiotics; pharmocokinetics; quantitative mass fragmentography. *Mailing Add:* 7135 Kingswood Circle Indianapolis IN 46256

SULLIVAN, J AL, mechanical engineering, for more information see previous edition

SULLIVAN, JAMES BOLLING, BIOCHEMISTRY, ZOOLOGY. *Current Pos:* Asst prof, 70-76, ASSOC PROF BIOCHEM, DUKE UNIV, 77- *Personal Data:* b Rome, Ga, Mar 19, 40; m 63; c 3. *Educ:* Cornell Univ, AB, 62; Univ Tex, Austin, PhD(zool), 66. *Concurrent Pos:* USPHS fel biochem, Duke Univ, 67-70. *Mem:* AAAS; Soc Study Evolution; Am Soc Biol Chemists; Lepidop Soc. *Res:* Comparative protein chemistry. *Mailing Add:* Dept Biochem Duke Univ Sch Med Duke Med Ctr Durham NC 27710-7599

SULLIVAN, JAMES DOUGLAS, physics, space science, for more information see previous edition

SULLIVAN, JAMES HADDON, JR, ENVIRONMENTAL ENGINEERING. *Current Pos:* PRES, SULLIVAN SOFTWARE, 87- *Personal Data:* b Claxton, Ga, Apr 3, 37; m 60; c 1. *Educ:* Ga Inst Technol, BChE, 59; Univ Fla, MS, 68, PhD(eng), 70. *Prof Exp:* Proj engr, Union Bag-Camp Paper Corp, 59-63; develop engr, Cities Serv Corp, 63-66; pres environ eng, Water & Air Res Inc, 70-71, vpres, 72-97. *Mem:* Am Water Works Asn; Am Acad Environ Engrs; Water Pollution Control Fedn; Nat Soc Prof Engrs. *Res:* Water chemistry; waste and water treatment; environmental impact studies. *Mailing Add:* 11126 SW Eighth Ave Gainesville FL 32607

SULLIVAN, JAMES THOMAS, PHYSICAL CHEMISTRY. *Current Pos:* from asst prof to assoc prof, 55-67, exec asst acad affairs, 72-78, vpres, 78-83, PROF CHEM, UNIV ST THOMAS, TEX, 67-, DIR COMPUT SERV, 84- *Personal Data:* b Seekonk, Mass, May 30, 28; m 55; c 4. *Educ:* Providence Col, BS, 50; Cath Univ Am, PhD, 55. *Prof Exp:* Asst, Cath Univ Am, 53-54, res assoc, 54-55. *Mem:* AAAS; Am Chem Soc. *Res:* Teaching. *Mailing Add:* 1811 Portsmouth Houston TX 77098-4301

SULLIVAN, JAY MICHAEL, CARDIOVASCULAR DISEASES. *Current Pos:* PROF MED & CHIEF, DIV CARDIOVASCULAR DIS, COL MED, UNIV TENN, MEMPHIS, 74- *Personal Data:* b Brockton, Mass, Aug 3, 36; m 64, Suzanne Baxter; c Elizabeth, Suzanne & Christopher. *Educ:* Georgetown Univ, BS, 58, MD, 62. *Prof Exp:* House officer med, Peter Bent Brigham Hosp, 62-63, resident, 63-67; res assoc biochem, Harvard Med Sch, 67-69, from instr to asst prof med, 69-74. *Concurrent Pos:* Nat Heart Inst res fel med, Harvard Med Sch, 64-66; res fel, Med Found, 67-69; fel, Coun High Blood Pressure Res, 75; dir hypertension unit, Peter Bent Brigham Hosp, 70-74; dir med serv, Boston Hosp Women, 73-74; consult, Nat Heart & Lung Inst, 74 & Vet Admin Cent Off, 82-85; fel, Coun Circulation, Am Heart Asn, 75; prin investr, Nat Heart, Lung & Blood Inst, 78-90; bd govs, Am Col Cardiol, 94-95; pres, Tenn Affil, Am Heart Asn, 94-95. *Mem:* AAAS; fel Am Col Cardiol; Am Fedn Clin Res; fel Am Col Physicians; Int Soc Hypertension; Sigma Xi; Asn Univ Cardiologists. *Res:* Hypertension, hemodynamics of hypertension, clinical pharmacology of antihypertensive drugs; sodium sensitivity; estrogens and cardiovascular disease. *Mailing Add:* 517 Magnolia Mound Dr Memphis TN 38103

SULLIVAN, JEREMIAH D, ARMS CONTROL. *Current Pos:* from asst prof to assoc prof, 67-73, PROF PHYSICS, LOOMIS LAB PHYSICS, UNIV ILL, 73-, DIR, PROG ARMS CONTROL DISARMAMENT & INT SECURITY. *Personal Data:* b Nov 15, 38. *Educ:* Carnegie Inst Technol, BS, 60; Princeton Univ, PhD(physics), 64. *Prof Exp:* Res assoc, Stanford Linear Accelerator Ctr, 64-67. *Concurrent Pos:* A P Sloan undergrad fel, 56-60, fac res fel, 68-70, NSF grad fel, 60-64; actg asst prof, Stanford Univ, 66-67; vis scientist, Univ Calif, Santa Barbara, Aspen Ctr for Physics, Wiezman Inst, Israel, Univ Rome, CERN Lab, Geneva & Fermilab. *Mem:* Fel Am Phys Soc; Am Asn Physics Teachers; Sigma Xi; AAAS. *Res:* Over 60 articles to publications. *Mailing Add:* 604 Burkwood Ct E Urbana IL 61801. *Fax:* 217-244-5157; *E-Mail:* jdsacdis@ux1.cso.uiuc.edu

SULLIVAN, JERRY STEPHEN, COMPUTER SCIENCES. *Current Pos:* VPRES, MICRO ELECTRONIC & COMPUT TECHNOL CORP, 88- *Personal Data:* b Havre, Mont, July 17, 45; m 67; c 3. *Educ:* Univ Colo, Boulder, BSc, 67, MSc, 69, PhD(physics), 70; Harvard Univ, AMP, 86. *Prof Exp:* Res scientist solid state devices, N V Philips Gloeilampenfabrieken, Eindhoven, 71-75, group dir comp systs res, Philips Labs, 75-80; corp dir, Comput Tech Ctr, Tektronix, 81-83, div gen mgr, 83-88. *Concurrent Pos:* Mem adv bd, Ctr Int Syst, Stanford Univ, 82-; bd dirs, Sherpa Corp, 83-; chmn adv bd, Col Elec Eng & Civil Eng, Univ Tex, 88- *Mem:* Inst Elec & Electronic Engrs; AAAS; Am Phys Soc; Europ Phys Soc; Asn Comput Mach. *Res:* Numerical analysis; network theory; application of computers to semiconductor device modeling and integrated circuit analysis; electron paramagnetic and nuclear magnetic resonance and exchange interactions of ion pairs; microcomputer architecture and microprocessor design; software engineering; system engineering; computer-aided design and manufacturing; computer science. *Mailing Add:* Design Technol Inc 107 Ranch Rd 620 S Austin TX 78734

SULLIVAN, JOHN BRENDAN, MATHEMATICS. *Current Pos:* from asst prof to assoc prof, 73-87, PROF MATH, UNIV WASH, 87- *Personal Data:* b Lynn, Mass, Aug 6, 44; m 70; c 2. *Educ:* Harvard Univ, AB, 66; Cornell Univ, PhD(math), 71. *Prof Exp:* Lectr math, Univ Calif, Berkeley, 71-73. *Concurrent Pos:* NSF grant, 74-79; mem, Inst Advan Study, 79-80; vis prof, Univ Mass, Amherst, 86-87. *Res:* Algebraic groups, lie algebras, and Hopf algebras; cohomology and representations of algebraic groups. *Mailing Add:* Dept Math Univ Wash Box 354350 Seattle WA 98195-4350

SULLIVAN, JOHN HENRY, PHYSICAL CHEMISTRY. *Current Pos:* CHEMIST, LOS ALAMOS SCI LAB, UNIV CALIF, 50- *Personal Data:* b New Haven, Conn, May 18, 19; m 47; c 2. *Educ:* Calif Inst Technol, PhD(chem), 50. *Mem:* Am Chem Soc. *Res:* Kinetics of gaseous reactions. *Mailing Add:* 3536-A Arizona Ave Los Alamos NM 87544-1521

SULLIVAN, JOHN JOSEPH, REPRODUCTIVE PHYSIOLOGY. *Current Pos:* Res assoc, Am Breeders Serv, Inc, W R Grace & Co, 63-65, assoc dir labs & res, 65-79, dir, labs & res, 79-81 & dir prod, 81-84, vpres, 84-89, PRES PROD, AM BREEDERS SERV, INC, W R GRACE & CO, 89- *Personal Data:* b New York, NY, Mar 28, 35; m 63; c 2. *Educ:* Rutgers Univ, BS, 57, PhD(dairy sci, physiol), 63; Univ Tenn, MS, 59. *Mem:* Am Soc Animal Sci; Soc Cryobiology; Soc Study Reproduction. *Res:* Physiology of reproduction and related fields; artificial insemination of domestic animals; low temperature biology. *Mailing Add:* W 8728 Stevenson Dr Poynette WI 53955

SULLIVAN, JOHN LAWRENCE, behavioral neuropharmacology, neurochemistry; deceased, see previous edition for last biography

SULLIVAN, JOHN M, ORGANIC CHEMISTRY. *Current Pos:* PROF CHEM, EASTERN MICH UNIV, 58- *Personal Data:* b Philadelphia, Pa, June 21, 32; m 56; c 9. *Educ:* Dartmouth Col, AB, 54; Univ Mich, MS, 56, PhD(org chem), 60. *Mem:* Am Chem Soc. *Res:* Heterocyclics; conformational analysis. *Mailing Add:* Dept Chem Eastern Mich Univ Ypsilanti MI 48197-2207

SULLIVAN, JOHN W, CEREAL CHEMISTRY. *Current Pos:* DIR RES, ROMAN MEAL CO, 74-, VPRES RES & DEVELOP, 79- *Personal Data:* b Fargo, NDak, Nov 1, 32; m 64; c 3. *Educ:* NDak State Univ, BS, 54, MS, 58; Kans State Univ, PhD(cereal chem), 66. *Prof Exp:* Proj leader food res, John Stuart Res Labs, Quaker Oats Co, 61-68, sect mgr food res, 68-74. *Mem:* Am Chem Soc; Am Asn Cereal Chemists; Inst Food Technologists. *Res:* Physical and chemical changes in starch and associated carbohydrates; enzyme changes in physical structure of starches and proteins. *Mailing Add:* 8010 SE Middle Way Vancouver WA 98664

SULLIVAN, JOHN WILLIAM, central nervous systems, for more information see previous edition

SULLIVAN, JOSEPH ARTHUR, MATHEMATICS. *Current Pos:* prof, 60-93, EMER PROF MATH, BOSTON COL, 93- *Personal Data:* b Boston, Mass, June 5, 23; m 46, Mary Peterson; c Brian, Paul, James & Gregory. *Educ:* Boston Col, AB, 44; Mass Inst Technol, SM, 47; Ind Univ, PhD(math), 50. *Prof Exp:* From instr to assoc prof math, Univ Notre Dame, 50-60. *Mem:* Am Math Soc; Math Asn Am. *Res:* Mathematical analysis. *Mailing Add:* 92 Earle St Norwood MA 02062-1522

SULLIVAN, JOSEPH HEARST, PHOTOBIOLOGY, PHYSIOLOGICAL ECOLOGY. *Current Pos:* res assoc, 85-88, from res scientist to sr res scientist, 88-96, ASST PROF, UNIV MD, 96- *Personal Data:* m 82, Marian Toth. *Educ:* Erskine Col, AB, 78; Western Carolina Univ, MS, 80; Clemson Univ, PhD(plant physiol), 85. *Concurrent Pos:* Adj instr, Univ Md Univ Col, 88-92, asst adj prof, 92-; res grant, US Environ Protection Agency, 88-91 & 92-, NASA, 92-97 & US Dept Agr, 92- *Mem:* Asn Southeastern Biologists; Bot Soc Am; Ecol Soc Am; Am Soc Photobiol; Scand Soc Plant Physiol. *Res:* Physiological and ecological responses of terrestrial plant species to factors associated with global climate change such as carbon dioxide, ultraviolet-beta radiation; study these effects on photosynthesis, leaf chemistry and productivity. *Mailing Add:* Dept Natural Resource Sci Univ Md College Park MD 20742. *Fax:* 301-314-9308; *E-Mail:* js128@umail.umd.edu

SULLIVAN, KAREN A, TRANSPLANTATION. *Current Pos:* res asst prof, 83-87, RES ASSOC PROF, DEPT MED, TULANE UNIV MED CTR, 87- *Personal Data:* b Bronxville, NY. *Educ:* N Adams State Col, BS, 66; Duke Univ, PhD(immunol, microbiol), 74. *Hon Degrees:* DSc, N Adams State Col, 90. *Prof Exp:* Cancer Res Inst Inc NY fel, McIndoe Mem Res Unit, Blond Lab, Queen Victoria Hosp, Sussex, Eng, 73-75; fel, Div Lab & Res, NY State Dept Health, 75-78; asst prof immunol, Med Ctr, W Va Univ, 78-80; asst mem, Mem Sloan Kettering Cancer Ctr, 80-83. *Concurrent Pos:* United Network Organ Sharing Histocompatibility Comt, 89-91. *Mem:* Am Asn Immunologists; Am Soc for Histocompatibility & Immunogenetics; NY Acad Sci; Am Soc Transplant Physicians; Clin Immunol Soc. *Res:* Immunogenetics; cellular immunology; lymphoid cell differentiation; regulation of the immune response. *Mailing Add:* Dept Med & Clin Immunol SL 75 Tulane Univ Med Ctr 1430 Tulane Ave SL 75 New Orleans LA 70112-9826. *Fax:* 504-584-3636

SULLIVAN, KATHRYN D, GEOLOGY, ASTRONAUTICS. *Current Pos:* Mission specialist, Flight STS-41G, 84, Flight STS-31, 90, MEM STAFF, NASA, 78-, ASTRONAUT, 79- *Personal Data:* b Paterson, NJ, Oct 3, 51. *Educ:* Univ Calif, Santa Cruz, BS, 73; Dalhousie Univ, PhD(geol), 78. *Hon Degrees:* Dr, Dalhousie Univ, 85. *Honors & Awards:* Haley Space Flight Award, Am Inst Aeronaut & Astronaut, 91. *Concurrent Pos:* Adj prof, Rice Univ, 85; mem, Nat Comn Space, 85- *Mem:* Am Inst Aeronaut & Astronaut; Geol Soc Am; Am Geophys Union; Soc Women Geogr. *Res:* First American woman to perform extra-vehicular activity. *Mailing Add:* Ctr Sci & Indust 280 E Broad St Columbus OH 43215-2674

SULLIVAN, LAWRENCE PAUL, RENAL PHYSIOLOGY, EPITHELIAL TRANSPORT. *Current Pos:* from asst prof to assoc prof, 61-69, PROF PHYSIOL, MED CTR, UNIV KANS, 69- *Personal Data:* b Hot Springs, SDak, June 16, 31; m 55, Florence Collins; c Paul, Timothy & Ann. *Educ:* Univ Notre Dame, BS, 53; Univ Mich, MS, 56, PhD(physiol), 59. *Prof Exp:* Asst physiol, Univ Mich, 55-59, instr, 59-60; asst prof, George Washington Univ, 60-61. *Concurrent Pos:* USPHS career develop award, 65-70; vis prof, Sch Med, Yale Univ, 69-70; dep ed, J Am Soc Nephrology, 90-96. *Mem:* Am Soc Nephrology; Am Physiol Soc; Sigma Xi. *Res:* Membrane transport; cell volume and pH regulation; potassium transport; acid-base transport mechanisms. *Mailing Add:* Dept Physiol WHE 3021 Univ Kans Med Ctr 3901 Rainbow Blvd Kansas City KS 66160-7401. *Fax:* 913-588-7430; *E-Mail:* lsulliva@kumc.edu

SULLIVAN, LLOYD JOHN, BIOCHEMISTRY, PHYSICAL ORGANIC CHEMISTRY. *Current Pos:* RETIRED. *Personal Data:* b Lowell, Ariz, Sept 6, 23; m 48; c 4. *Educ:* Univ Ariz, BS, 50; Univ Pittsburgh, MS, 54. *Prof Exp:* Res asst phys chem, Mellon Inst Sci, 50-52, res assoc, 52-54, jr fel, 54-56, fel, 56-58; mem tech staff, Cent Res Lab, Tex Instruments, 58-60, sect head & dir energy conversion, Apparatus Div, 60-61; fel phys & anal chem, Mellon Inst Sci, 61-67, sr fel phys & anal chem & head chem & biochem sect, Chem Hyg Fel, 67-80. *Mem:* Fel AAAS; fel Am Inst Chemists; NY Acad Sci; Am Chem Soc. *Res:* Physical properties of organic materials; separation and purification of organic compounds, particularly natural products; gas, liquid and thin layer chromatography; analytical biochemistry; metabolism of organic compounds in vivo and by tissue culture techniques. *Mailing Add:* 2750 Old St Augustine Rd T-210 Tallahassee FL 32301

SULLIVAN, LOUIS WADE, INTERNAL MEDICINE. *Current Pos:* pres, 77-89, dean, 77-85, PRES, SCH MED, MOREHOUSE COL, 93- *Personal Data:* b Atlanta, Ga, Nov 3, 33; m 55; c 3. *Educ:* Morehouse Col, BS, 54; Boston Univ, MD, 58; Am Bd Internal Med, dipl, 66. *Hon Degrees:* 17 from var insts. *Prof Exp:* Intern, NY Hosp-Cornell Med Ctr, 58-59, resident med, 59-60; resident gen path, Mass Gen Hosp, 60-61; instr, Harvard Med Sch, 63-64; asst prof, NJ Col Med, 64-66, asst attend physician, 64-65, assoc attend physician, 65-66; asst prof med, Sch Med, Boston Univ, 66-70, assoc prof med & physiol, 70-77; dean & pres, Sch Med, Morehouse Col, 77-85, pres, 85-89; secy, Dept Health & Human Serv, 89- *Concurrent Pos:* Res fel med, Thorndike Mem Lab, Boston City Hosp & Harvard Med Sch, 61-63; res assoc, Thorndike Mem Lab, Boston City Hosp, 63-64; dir hemat & proj dir, Boston Sickle Cell Ctr, 72-75; USPHS res career develop award, 65-66, 67-71; asst vis physician, Boston Univ Hosp, 66-; assoc ed, Nutrit Reports Int, 69-73; vchmn, Comn Health & Human Serv, Southern Regional Educ Bd, 85-87; Martin Luther King Jr vis prof, Univ Mich, 86. *Mem:* Inst Med-Nat Acad Sci; Soc Exp Biol & Med; Am Fedn Clin Res; AAAS; Fedn Am Socs Exp Biol; Am Soc Clin Invest. *Res:* Metabolism of vitamin B-12 and folic acid in man. *Mailing Add:* Morehouse Sch Med 720 Westview Dr SW Atlanta GA 30310

SULLIVAN, MARGARET P, PEDIATRICS, MEDICINE. *Current Pos:* from asst pediatrician to pediatrician, 56-73, ASHBEL SMITH PROF PEDIAT & PEDIATRICIAN, M D ANDERSON CANCER CTR, UNIV TEX, HOUSTON, 73- *Personal Data:* b Lewistown, Mont, Feb 7, 22. *Educ:* Rice Inst, BA, 44; Duke Univ, MD, 50; Am Bd Pediat, dipl, 56. *Prof Exp:* Pediatrician, Atomic Bomb Casualty Comn, Japan, 53-55. *Mem:* AAAS; Am Asn Cancer Res; Am Acad Pediat; AMA; Am Med Women's Asn (vpres, 72, pres, 74). *Res:* Pediatric oncology. *Mailing Add:* 4606 Waynesboro Dr Houston TX 77035-3646

SULLIVAN, MARY LOUISE, inorganic chemistry, for more information see previous edition

SULLIVAN, MAURICE FRANCIS, PHARMACOLOGY. *Current Pos:* RETIRED. *Personal Data:* b Butte, Mont, Feb 15, 22; m 51; c 6. *Educ:* Mont State Col, BS, 50; Univ Chicago, PhD(pharmacol), 55. *Prof Exp:* Scientist, Hanford Labs, Gen Elec Co, 55-56, sr scientist, 56-65; mgr, Physiol Sect, Pac Northwest Labs, Battelle Mem Inst, 65-71, staff scientist, 71-85, consult, 85-86. *Concurrent Pos:* NIH fel, Med Res Coun, Harwell, Eng, 61-; consult, Battelle Mem Inst, 85-; task groups, Int Comn Radiol Protection, 83-86; expert group on Orgn Econ Coop & Develop, Nuclear Energy Agency, 85- *Mem:* Fel AAAS; Am Physiol Soc; Radiation Res Soc. *Res:* Biological effects of radiation, especially on the gastrointestinal tract; biochemistry; physiology; pathology; pharmacology. *Mailing Add:* 2125 Harris Ave Richland WA 99352-2020

SULLIVAN, MICHAEL FRANCIS, PHOTOGRAPHIC CHEMISTRY. *Current Pos:* Sr chemist, 67-73, res lab head, 73-81, supvr prod & develop, Film Emulsion & Plate Mfg Div, 81-84, DIR MFG STAFF, FILM SENSITIZING DIV, EASTMAN KODAK CO, 84- *Personal Data:* b New Paltz, NY, Aug 20, 42; m 67; c 3. *Educ:* St Lawrence Univ, BS, 63; Univ NC, Chapel Hill, PhD(chem), 68. *Res:* Production and development of black and white and color photographic films. *Mailing Add:* Eastman Kodak Co 1669 Lake Ave Rochester NY 14652-3210

SULLIVAN, MICHAEL JOSEPH, JR, MATHEMATICS. *Current Pos:* from asst prof to assoc prof, 65-77, PROF MATH, CHICAGO STATE UNIV, 77- *Personal Data:* b Chicago, Ill, Jan 8, 42; wid; c Katjleen (Murphy), Michael III, Dan, & Colleen (O'Hara). *Educ:* DePaul Univ, BS, 63; Ill Inst Technol, MS, 64, PhD(math), 67. *Prof Exp:* Teaching asst math, Ill Inst Technol, 62-65. *Concurrent Pos:* Am Coun Educ acad admin internship, 70-71. *Mem:* Am Math Soc; Math Asn Am; Textbook & Acad Authors Asn. *Res:* Differential geometric aspects of dynamics; polygenic functions; applications of mathematics in the management and behavioral sciences; mathematics education; Author numerous mathematics textbooks. *Mailing Add:* 9529 Tripp Oak Lawn IL 60453. *Fax:* 773-995-3767

SULLIVAN, NEIL SAMUEL, LOW TEMPERATURE PHYSICS. *Current Pos:* PROF PHYSICS, UNIV FLA, 82-, CHAIR, DEPT PHYSICS, 89-; CO-PRIN INVESTR, NHMFL, 90- *Personal Data:* b Wanganui, NZ, Jan 18, 42; m 65; c 3. *Educ:* Otago Univ, NZ, BSc, 64, MSc, 65; Harvard Univ, PhD(physics), 72. *Honors & Awards:* Prix Saintour, 78; Prix La Caze, 83. *Prof Exp:* Assoc physics, Ctr Nuclear Studies, Saclay, France, 72-74, res physicist, 74-82. *Concurrent Pos:* Fullbright Exchange Grant, US Educ Found, 65; Frank Knox fel, Harvard Univ, 65-70. *Mem:* Am Phys Soc; French Physics Soc; Inst Physics London; Europ Phys Soc; Groupement Ampere. *Res:* Fundamental properties of solid hydrogen and solid helium at very low temperatures; studies of molecular motions using nuclear magnetic resonance; cosmic axion detectors. *Mailing Add:* Physics Dept Univ Fla Gainesville FL 32611. *Fax:* 352-392-0524; *E-Mail:* Sullivan@phys.ufl.edu

SULLIVAN, PATRICIA ANN NAGENGAST, BIOLOGY. *Current Pos:* PROF BIOL & ACAD DEAN, SALEM COL, 81- *Personal Data:* b New York, NY, Nov 22, 39; m 66. *Educ:* Notre Dame Col Staten Island, BA, 61; NY Univ, MS, 64, PhD(biol), 67. *Prof Exp:* Part-time instr, Notre Dame Col Staten Island, 64-67; asst prof biol, Wagner Col, 67-68; NIH trainee anat & cell biol, State Univ NY Upstate Med Ctr, 68-69 & fel cell biol, 69-70; asst prof biol, Wells Col, 70-74, assoc prof, 74-79, chairwoman, Div Life Sci, 75-76; assoc prof biol, Tex Woman's Univ, 79-81, prof, 87-94, interim pres, 93-94. *Concurrent Pos:* State liaison, Am Asn State Cols & Univ, 95- *Mem:* AAAS; NY Acad Sci; Am Soc Hemat; Sigma Xi; Am Asn Univ Women. *Res:* Bioethics and implications of biological research; hematopoiesis and its regulation; chromatin structure and function. *Mailing Add:* Univ NC 303 Mossman Greensboro NC 27412

SULLIVAN, PAUL JOSEPH, APPLIED MATHEMATICS, ENGINEERING. *Current Pos:* Asst prof, 68-80, PROF APPL MATH & ENG, UNIV WESTERN ONT, 80- *Personal Data:* b Merrickville, Ont, Mar 2, 39; m 62; c 2. *Educ:* Univ Waterloo, BSc, 64, MSc, 65; Cambridge Univ, PhD(appl math), 68. *Concurrent Pos:* Res fel, Calif Inst Technol, 69-70. *Mem:* Am Acad Mech; Can Soc Mech Eng. *Res:* Dispersion within turbulent fluid flow; convection phenomena in fluids; turbulent fluid flow generally. *Mailing Add:* Dept Appl Math Univ Western Ont London ON N6J 1M5 Can

SULLIVAN, PETER KEVIN, LABORATORY SAFETY, POLYMER PHYSICS. *Current Pos:* SAFETY MGR, MT SINAI MED CTR, 86-; SAFETY-DIR, MID-ISLAND HOSP, BETHPAGE, NY. *Personal Data:* b San Francisco, Calif, June 14, 38. *Educ:* Univ San Francisco, BS, 60; Cornell Univ, MS, 63; Rensselaer Polytech Inst, PhD(phys chem), 65. *Prof Exp:* Res fel, Nat Bur Stand, 65-67, chemist, 67-73; phys chemist, Celanese Res Co, 74-79; prin scientist & mgr, Int Nickel Co, 79-82; mgr, Exel Plastics, 82-86. *Mem:* Am Phys Soc; Am Chem Soc. *Res:* Physics, chemistry and mechanical properties of polymers. *Mailing Add:* One Clinton Pl Suffern NY 10901-5603

SULLIVAN, PHILIP ALBERT, AEROSPACE ENGINEERING, PHYSICS. *Current Pos:* asst prof teaching & res, 65-71, assoc prof aerospace sci & eng, 71-82, PROF, INST AEROSPACE STUDIES, UNIV TORONTO, 82- *Personal Data:* b Sydney, Australia, Dec 25, 37; m 62; c 1. *Educ:* Univ New South Wales, BE, 60, ME, 62; Univ London, DIC & PhD(aeronaut eng), 64. *Prof Exp:* Res assoc aeronaut res, Imp Col, Univ London, 62-64; res assoc hypersonics res, Gas Dynamics Lab, Princeton Univ, 64-65. *Concurrent Pos:* Consult, Atomic Energy Can Ltd. *Mem:* Assoc fel Can Aeronaut & Space Inst; Am Inst Aeronaut & Astronaut. *Res:* Air cushion technology with applications to air cushion landing systems, amphibious vehicles and trains. *Mailing Add:* Inst Aerospace Studies 4925 Dufferin St Downsview ON M3H 5T6 Can

SULLIVAN, RAYMOND, GEOLOGY. *Current Pos:* from asst prof to assoc prof, 62-74, assoc dean natural sci, 69-72, PROF GEOL, SAN FRANCISCO STATE UNIV, 74- *Personal Data:* b Ebbw Vale, Wales, Oct 27, 34; m 62; c 2. *Educ:* Univ Sheffield, BSc, 57; Glasgow Univ, PhD(geol), 60. *Prof Exp:* Demonstr geol, Glasgow Univ, 57-60; paleontologist, Shell Oil Co Can, 60-62. *Concurrent Pos:* NSF res grant, 66-67. *Mem:* Am Asn Petrol Geologists; Nat Asn Geol Teachers; fel Geol Soc Am. *Res:* Upper Paleozoic biostratigraphy; sedimentary petrology of carbonate and clastic rocks; environmental geology. *Mailing Add:* San Francisco State Univ Dept Geosci 1600 Holloway Ave San Francisco CA 94132-1722

SULLIVAN, RICHARD FREDERICK, HYDROCARBON CHEMISTRY. *Current Pos:* INDEPENDENT CONSULT, 92- *Personal Data:* b Olathe, Colo, Dec 26, 29; m 68, Judith Jones; c Erin & Amy. *Educ:* Univ Colo, BA, 51, PhD(chem), 56. *Prof Exp:* Res chemist, Calif Res Corp, 55-68, from sr res chemist to sr res assoc, 68-89; res scientist, Chevron Res & Technol Co, 89-92. *Concurrent Pos:* UN Develop Prog; exper consult, Nat Chem Lab, Pune, India, 90. *Mem:* Am Chem Soc; Am Inst Chem Eng. *Res:* Photochemistry; mechanisms of hydrocarbon reactions; catalysis; petroleum process research and development; conversion of shale oil and liquids derived from coal to transportation fuels. *Mailing Add:* 23 Upper Oak Dr San Rafael CA 94903-1731

SULLIVAN, RICHARD HARRISON, NUCLEAR MAGNETIC RESONANCE SPECTROSCOPY, COMPUTATIONAL CHEMISTRY. *Current Pos:* PROF & CHAIR, CHEM DEPT, JACKSON STATE UNIV, 74- *Personal Data:* b Laurens, SC, Apr 27, 41; m 93, Hursie Davis; c Richard A, Jamal O, R Jomar, Eboni J & Emmanuel J. *Educ:* SC State Col, BS, 63; Howard Univ PhD(chem), 72. *Prof Exp:* Asst prof chem, Fayetteville State Univ, 72-74. *Concurrent Pos:* Sabbatical res, Columbia Univ, Bell Labs, 81-82; consult math content & prof develop, Algebra Proj, Inc, 97-; computational chemical techniques. *Mem:* Am Chem Soc; AAAS; Sigma Xi; Asn Comput Mach. *Res:* Molecular dynamics in small molecular systems; structures, energenics and interactions probing. *Mailing Add:* PO Box 17910 Jackson MS 39217-0510. *Fax:* 601-973-3730; *E-Mail:* sullivan@tiger.jsums.edu

SULLIVAN, ROBERT EMMETT, DENTISTRY, PEDIATRIC DENTISTRY. *Current Pos:* From instr to assoc prof pedodont, 63-72, ASSOC PROF PEDIAT, UNIV NEBR-LINCOLN, 69-, PROF PEDODONT, 72-, CHMN, 82- *Personal Data:* b Sioux City, Iowa, May 28, 32; m 61, Mary Ann Haeser. *Educ:* Morningside Col, BA, 54; Univ Nebr, DDS, 61, MSD, 63; Am Bd Pedodont, dipl, 67. *Honors & Awards:* Excellence in Childrens Dentistry Award, Am Soc Dent Children. *Concurrent Pos:* Consult, Omaha-Douglas Co Dent Pub Health, 62-93 & Omaha-Douglas Co Children & Youth Proj, 68-82. *Mem:* Am Acad Pedodont; Am Dent Asn; Am Soc Dent for Children; Am Col Dentists; Int Col Dentists. *Res:* Vital staining of teeth; mechanism of action of dental preventative materials; changes in dental and oral environments due to drug intake. *Mailing Add:* 1201 Piedmont Rd Lincoln NE 68510. *E-Mail:* msulliv@lps.esu18-k12ne.us

SULLIVAN, ROBERT LITTLE, genetics, for more information see previous edition

SULLIVAN, SAMUEL LANE, JR, CHEMICAL ENGINEERING. *Current Pos:* ASSOC PROF CHEM ENG, TULANE UNIV, 61-, ASSOC DEAN ENG, 76- *Personal Data:* b Victoria, Tex, May 25, 35; div; c 4. *Educ:* Tex A&M Univ, BS, 57, MS, 59, PhD(chem eng), 63. *Mem:* Am Inst Chem Engrs; Am Soc Eng Educ; Sigma Xi. *Res:* Multicomponent distillation; chemical process simulation; computer applications in chemical engineering; multicomponent diffusion. *Mailing Add:* Chem Engr Dept Tulane Univ New Orleans LA 70118

SULLIVAN, SEAN MICHAEL, DRUG DELIVERY, GENE THERAPY. *Current Pos:* SECT MGR, SYNTHETIC VECTOR DEVELOP, SOMATIX THER CORP, 94- *Personal Data:* Elizabeth, NJ, Feb 19, 53; m 88, Layla R Fakhuri; c Alexander V & Lawrence M. *Educ:* Maryville Col, BA, 74; Univ Tenn, MS, 81, PhD(biochem), 85. *Prof Exp:* Assoc scientist, Hottan LaRoche, 74-75; asst scientist, Roche Diag, 75-77; fel, Calif Inst Technol, 85-87; scientist, Vestar Inc, 87-91; sr scientist, US Biochem Corp, 91-92, Ribozyme Pharmaceut Inc, 92-94. *Concurrent Pos:* Sci adv bd mem, Dept Cellular & Molecular Biol, Univ Tenn, 95- *Mem:* Biophys Soc; Am Asn Cell Biol; Controlled Release Soc. *Res:* The development of targeted drug delivery systems using liposomes as the delivery vehicle; monoclonal antibodies, sulfated glycolipid and recombinant viral receptors have been used as targeting ligands; cell targets have been tumor cells and virus infected cells; delivered drugs have been chemotherapuetic agents and synthetic aligonucleotides. *Mailing Add:* 850 Marina Village Pkwy Alameda CA 94501. *Fax:* 510-769-8533; *E-Mail:* smsullivan@apple.somatix.com

SULLIVAN, STUART F, ANESTHESIOLOGY. *Current Pos:* prof & vchmn anesthesiol, 73-91, actg chmn, 83-84, 87-88 & 90-91, EMER PROF ANESTHESIOL, UNIV CALIF, LOS ANGELES, 91- *Personal Data:* b Buffalo, NY, July 15, 28; m 59, Dorothy Faytol; c John, Irene, Paul & Ikathryn. *Educ:* Canisius Col, Buffalo, BS, 50; State Univ NY, Syracuse, MD, 55. *Prof Exp:* Instr anesthesiol, Col Physicians & Surgeons, Columbia Univ, 61-62, assoc, 62-64, from asst prof to assoc prof, 64-73. *Concurrent Pos:* Res fel, NIH, 60-61, res career develop award, 66-69. *Mem:* Am Physiol Soc; Am Soc Anesthesiologist; Asn Univ Anesthesiologists. *Res:* Effects of anesthesia and operation on cardiopulmonary function; oxygen and carbon dioxide transport during anesthesia. *Mailing Add:* Dept Anesthesiol Sch Med Univ Calif Los Angeles CA 90095-1778. *E-Mail:* ssull@ucla.edu

SULLIVAN, SUSAN JEAN, endocrinology, biochemistry, for more information see previous edition

SULLIVAN, THOMAS ALLEN, CHEMICAL PROCESSING OF LUNAR SOIL & MARTIAN ATMOSPHERE, LIFE SCIENCE & MATERIALS SCIENCE EXPERIMENTS IN SPACE. *Current Pos:* space scientist, 89-94, MISSION SCIENTIST, NASA, 94- *Personal Data:* b Chicago, Ill, Aug 8, 55; m 90, Carey Naylor; c Shane. *Educ:* Valparaiso Univ, BS, 77; Univ Ill, PhD(org chem), 81. *Prof Exp:* Res chemist, E I DuPont, 81-83, sect chemist, 83-88, sr chemist, 88-89. *Mem:* Am Inst Aeronaut & Astronaut. *Res:* Effect of microgravity in life sciences and materials science. *Mailing Add:* NASA-Johnson Space Ctr Mail Code SD3 Houston TX 77058. *E-Mail:* tom.sullivan@spmail.jsc.nasa.gov

SULLIVAN, THOMAS WESLEY, POULTRY NUTRITION, BIOCHEMISTRY. *Current Pos:* prof, 65-93, mem fac, Animal Sci dept, 76-93, EMER PROF POULTRY SCI, UNIV NEBR-LINCOLN, 93- *Personal Data:* b Rover, Ark, Sept 30, 30; m 55; c 4. *Educ:* Okla State Univ, BS, 51; Univ Ark, MS, 56; Univ Wis, PhD, 58. *Honors & Awards:* Res Award, Nat Turkey Fedn, 68. *Prof Exp:* Instr, Ark Pub Schs, 51-52; res asst poultry nutrit, Univ Ark, 54-55; res asst, Univ Wis, 55-58, from asst prof to assoc prof, 58-65. *Concurrent Pos:* Consult feed mfg & ingredients. *Mem:* Poultry Sci Asn; Am Inst Nutrit; Soc Exp Biol & Med. *Res:* Mineral nutrition and skeletal problems in poultry; nutritional value of cereal grains. *Mailing Add:* Animal Sci Univ Nebr 2317 W Fifth St Russellville AR 72801-5540

SULLIVAN, TIMOTHY PAUL, PLANT PHYSIOLOGY, AGRONOMY. *Current Pos:* SR AGRONOMIST, 3M CO, 76- *Personal Data:* b Duluth, Minn, Dec 3, 45; m 67. *Educ:* Univ Minn, Duluth, BS, 67, MS, 69, PhD(plant physiol), 72. *Prof Exp:* Assoc prof biol, West Chester State Col, 72-76. *Mem:* Plant Growth Regulator Working Group; Int Weed Sci Soc; Am Soc Plant Physiologists; Sigma Xi; Weed Sci Soc Am. *Res:* Host-parasite relationships involving microsurgery of the host cells parasitized by haustoria of an obligate parasite; effects of water stress on photosynthesis, stomatal aperature and water potential during different stages of soybean development. *Mailing Add:* 3824 Willow Way St Paul MN 55122

SULLIVAN, VICTORIA I, biosystematics, for more information see previous edition

SULLIVAN, W(ALTER) JAMES, PHYSIOLOGY, BIOPHYSICS. *Current Pos:* from asst prof to assoc prof, 63-71, actg chmn dept, 71-76, PROF PHYSIOL, SCH MED, NY UNIV, 73- *Personal Data:* b New York, NY, Apr 27, 25; m 51; c 3. *Educ:* Manhattan Col, BS, 46; Cornell Univ, MD, 51. *Prof Exp:* Instr physics, Manhattan Col, 46-47; intern med, Univ Va, 51-52; instr, Cornell Univ, 54-55; vis investr, Rockefeller Inst, 55-56; group leader, Lederle Labs, 56-63. *Concurrent Pos:* Fel physiol, Cornell Univ, 52-54; vis prof physiol, Sch Med, Yale Univ, 77-78. *Mem:* Am Physiol Soc; Biophys Soc; Soc Gen Physiol; Am Soc Nephrology. *Res:* Renal physiology; micropuncture study of renal ion transport. *Mailing Add:* Dept Physiol & Biophys NY Univ Sch Med 550 First Ave New York NY 10016-6402

SULLIVAN, WALTER SEAGER, SCIENCE WRITING. *Current Pos:* RETIRED. *Personal Data:* b New York, NY, Jan 12, 18; m 50; c 3. *Educ:* Yale Univ, BA, 40. *Hon Degrees:* LHD, Yale Univ, 69; Newark Col Eng, 74; Univ Ala, 87; DS, Hofstra Univ, 75; Ohio State Univ, 77; Muhlenberg Col, 87. *Honors & Awards:* George Polk Mem Award in Jour, 59; Westinghouse-AAAS Writing Awards, 63, 68 & 72; Int Nonfiction Book Prize, Frankfurt Fair, Ger, 65; Grady Award, Am Chem Soc, 69; Am Inst Physics-US Steel Found Award in Physics & Astron, 69; Washburn Award,

Boston Mus Sci, 72; Daly Medal, Am Geog Soc, 73; Ralph Coats Roe Medal, Am Soc Mech Engrs, 75; Distinguished Pub Serv Award, US NSF, 78; Pub Welfare Medal, Nat Acad Sci, 80; Bromley Lectr, Yale Univ, 65; McGraw Lectr, Princeton Univ, 88; John Wesley Powell Award, US Dept Interior, US Geol Surv, 90. *Prof Exp:* Mem staff, New York Times, 40-48, foreign corresp, 48-56, sci news ed, 60-63, sci ed, 64-87. *Concurrent Pos:* Mem bd gov, Arctic Inst NAm, 59-65; mem, Univ Coun, Yale Univ, 70-75; mem, Adv Comt Pub Rels, Am Inst Physics, 65-; partic, Sem Technol & Social Change, Columbia Univ & mem adv coun, Dept Geol & Geophys Sci, Princeton Univ, 71-77, mem exped, Arctic, 35 & 46 & Antarctic, 46, 54, 56 & 77. *Mem:* Fel AAAS; fel Arctic Inst NAm; Am Geog Soc; Am Geophys Union. *Mailing Add:* 66 Indian Head Rd Riverside CT 06878-2420

SULLIVAN, WILLIAM DANIEL, biochemistry; deceased, see previous edition for last biography

SULLIVAN, WOODRUFF TURNER, III, ASTRONOMY, HISTORY OF SCIENCE. *Current Pos:* asst prof, 73-78, assoc prof, 78-86, PROF ASTRON, UNIV WASH, 86- *Personal Data:* b Colorado Springs, Colo, June 17, 44; m 68, Barbara Phillips; c Rachel & Sarah. *Educ:* Mass Inst Technol, SB, 66; Univ Md, PhD(astron), 71. *Prof Exp:* Res astronr radio astron, Naval Res Lab, 69-71; fel, Neth Found Radio Astron, 71-73. *Concurrent Pos:* Sr vis fel, Inst Astron, Cambridge, Eng, 80-81 & 87-88; mem, Sci Working Group on Search for Extraterrestrial Intel, NASA, 80-94; chmn hist comt, Astron Soc Pac, 86-92; chmn, Hist Astron Div, Am Astron Soc, 95-97. *Mem:* Int Astron Union; Int Union Radio Sci; Am Astron Soc; Hist Sci Soc. *Res:* Galactic and extragalactic microwave spectroscopy; evolution of galaxies and clusters of galaxies; history of radio astronomy; search for extraterrestrial life, astronomy and culture. *Mailing Add:* Dept Astron Univ Wash Box 351580 Seattle WA 98195

SULLIVAN-KESSLER, ANN CLARE, biochemistry, for more information see previous edition

SULLWOLD, HAROLD H, GEOLOGY, PETROLEUM. *Current Pos:* RETIRED. *Personal Data:* b St Paul, Minn, Dec 22, 16; m 40, Mayla Sandbeck; c Eric & Wende. *Educ:* Univ Calif, Los Angeles, BA, 39, MA, 40, PhD(geol), 59. *Prof Exp:* Geologist, Wilshire Oil Co, 41, US Geol Surv, 42-44 & W R Cabeen & Assocs, 44-52; instr, Univ Calif, Los Angeles, 52-58; consult geologist, 58-60; geologist, George H Roth & Assocs, 60-80; independent geologist, 80-96. *Concurrent Pos:* Adj prof, Univ SC, 70-71; pres, bd dirs, Carpinteria Co Water Dist. *Mem:* Am Inst Prof Geol; fel Geol Soc Am; Am Asn Petrol Geologists; Sigma Xi. *Res:* Petroleum geology; exploration for oil and gas; turbidites; illustrated and published book of geological cartoons. *Mailing Add:* 900 Calle de Los Amigos N-11 Santa Barbara CA 93105

SULSER, FRIDOLIN, PHARMACOLOGY. *Current Pos:* DIR, TENN NEUROPSYCHIAT INST, 74- *Personal Data:* b Grabs, Switz, Dec 2, 26; m 55; c 4. *Educ:* Univ Basel, MD, 55. *Prof Exp:* Asst prof pharmacol, Univ Berne, 56-58; head, Dept Pharmacol, Wellcome Res Labs, NY, 63-65; dir, Psychopharmacol Res Ctr & prof pharmacol, Sch Med, Vanderbilt Univ, 80- *Concurrent Pos:* Int Pub Health Serv fel, NIH, 59-62. *Mem:* AAAS; Am Soc Pharmacol; Am Col Neuropsychopharmacol; Am Fedn Clin Res; NY Acad Sci. *Res:* Pharmacology of psychotropic drugs; neurochemistry; biochemical mechanisms of drug action. *Mailing Add:* Dept Psychiat Vanderbilt Univ Sch Med A2215 Med Ctr Nashville TN 37237-0001. Fax: 615-343-8639

SULTAN, HASSAN AHMED, CIVIL & GEOTECHNICAL ENGINEERING, SOIL MECHANICS. *Current Pos:* assoc prof civil eng, 67-71, PROF CIVIL ENG, UNIV ARIZ, 71- *Personal Data:* b Cairo, Egypt, Dec 12, 36; m 83, Beth Fisher; c Tarik, Timur & Taj. *Educ:* Cairo Univ, BSc, 58; Univ Utah, MS, 61; Univ Calif, Berkeley, PhD(civil eng), 65. *Prof Exp:* Instr civil eng, Ein-Shams Univ, Egypt, 58-59; asst specialist in res, Univ Calif, Berkeley, 63-64; proj engr, Woodward, Clyde, Sherard & Assoc, 65-67. *Concurrent Pos:* Pvt consult, 58-59 & 68-; UN expert, 75; consult, World Bank & Govt of Saudi Arabia, 77-; mem dept soils, geol & found, Trans Res Bd, Nat Acad Sci-Nat Res Coun, mem comt soil & rock properties & chmn comt chem stabilization; res grants, NSF, US Air Force, US Dept Transp, US Nat Park Serv & Govt of Saudi Arabia. *Mem:* Fel AAAS; Am Soc Civil Engrs; Sigma Xi; Nat Soc Prof Engrs. *Res:* Foundation engineering; slope stability; collapsing soils; earth dams; fluid mechanics; soil stabilization; dust and erosion control. *Mailing Add:* 4640 E Avenida Shelly Tucson AZ 85718

SULTZER, BARNET MARTIN, MICROBIOLOGY, IMMUNOLOGY. *Current Pos:* from asst prof to assoc prof, State Univ NY, Downstate Med Ctr, 64-76, prof microbiol & immunol, 76-94, interim chmn, 80-82, EMER PROF, STATE UNIV NY, DOWNSTATE MED CTR, 94- *Personal Data:* b Union City, NJ, Mar 24, 29; m 56, Judith Moreinis; c Steven. *Educ:* Rutgers Univ, BS, 50; Mich State Univ, MS, 51, PhD(bact), 58. *Prof Exp:* Asst bact, Mich State Univ, 56-58; res assoc microbiol, Princeton Labs, Inc, 58-64. *Concurrent Pos:* Prin investr, Nat Inst Allergy & Infectious Dis grants, 67-69, 69-73, 75-78, 78-82, 80-83 & 89-94, Off Naval Res, 84-86; vis scientist, Karolinska Inst, Sweden, 71-72; vis prof, Pasteur Inst, 79-80; assoc ed, J Immunol, 83-86. *Mem:* AAAS; Am Asn Immunologists; Am Soc Microbiol; NY Acad Sci; Harvey Soc; Sigma Xi. *Res:* Lymphocyte activation; immunobiology of bacterial cell wall proteins and lipopolysacchorides. *Mailing Add:* Dept Microbiol & Immunol 395-12J Southbend Ave State Univ NY Health Ctr Brooklyn 450 Clarkson Ave Brooklyn NY 11203-2098. Fax: 718-270-2656

SULYA, LOUIS LEON, BIOCHEMISTRY. *Current Pos:* assoc prof, 45-50, prof 50-78, EMER PROF BIOCHEM & CHMN DEPT, SCH MED, UNIV MISS, 78- *Personal Data:* b North Monmouth, Maine, Aug 17, 11; m 37; c 2. *Educ:* Col Holy Cross, BS, 32, MS, 33; St Louis Univ, PhD(org chem), 39. *Prof Exp:* Instr chem, Spring Hill Col, 34-36; res chemist, Reardon Co, Mo, 40-42. *Mem:* AAAS; Endocrine Soc; Am Chem Soc; Am Soc Biol Chemists; Int Soc Nephrol. *Res:* Endocrinology and comparative biochemistry. *Mailing Add:* 1076 Parkwood Pl Jackson MS 39206-6154

SULZER, ALEXANDER JACKSON, MALARIAOLOGY, MEDICAL PARASITOLOGY. *Current Pos:* RETIRED. *Personal Data:* b Emmett, Ark, Feb 13, 22; m 42; c D L & H E. *Educ:* Hardin-Simmons Univ, BA, 49; Emory Univ, MSc, 60, PhD(parasitol), 62. *Hon Degrees:* DHC, Univ Cayetano Heredia, Peru, 77. *Honors & Awards:* Science Award, Bausch & Lomb, 40; First Prize, Med Res, Inst Hipolito Unanue, Lima, Peru, 81. *Prof Exp:* Med parasitologist, Commun Dis Ctr, Ctr Dis Control, 52-62, res parasitologist, 62-74, res microbiologist, 74-90. *Concurrent Pos:* Res fel, Atomic Energy Comn, Vanderbilt Univ, 50-51; Ctr Dis Control fel, Emory Univ, 59-60 & NIH fel, 60-62; hon prof, Univ Cayetano Heredia, Lima, Peru, 73; adj prof, Sch Pub Health, Univ NC, Chapel Hill, 78- *Mem:* Sigma Xi; Am Soc Trop Med & Hyg; Am Soc Parasitol; Nat Registry Microbiologists; fel Indian Soc Malaria & Commun Dis; fel Royal Soc Trop Med & Hyg; fel Am Acad Microbiol; hon mem Peruvian Soc Microbiol. *Res:* Malaria; diagnostic serology of parasitic diseases of man and animals; tagged systems in serology especially fluorescent tagged materials; fine structure of protozoan parasites; immunoparasitology. *Mailing Add:* 1304 New Mexico Rd Bowdon GA 30108

SULZER-AZAROFF, BETH, APPLIED BEHAVIOR ANALYSIS, PERSONALIZED INSTRUCTION. *Current Pos:* prof psychol & prof educ, 73-92, EMER PROF, UNIV MASS, 92-; PRIN, BROWNS GROUP. *Personal Data:* m 72, Leonid Azaroff; c David, Richard & Lenore. *Educ:* City Col New York, BS, 50, MA, 53; Univ Minn, PhD, 66. *Honors & Awards:* Lifetime Achievement Award, Asn Behav Anal Int; Keller Award, Div 25, Am Psychol Asn. *Prof Exp:* Assoc prof guid & educ psychol, Southern Ill Univ, 66-72; res assoc, Univ Conn Health Ctr, 72-73. *Concurrent Pos:* Consult, psychol training, Mansfield Training Sch, 72-73, Aubrey Daniels & Assoc, 86-, Gen Telephone & Elec, 88-; adv bd, May Inst Autistic Children, 82; adv bd, Groden Ctr, Southern Ill Col Human Serv, 82; chmn, Bd Sci Affairs, Am Psychol Asn, 86-87. *Mem:* Fel Am Psychol Asn; fel Am Acad Behav Med; Asn Behav Anal (pres, 81-82); fel Am Psychol Soc. *Res:* Occupational safety; training strategies for developmentally disabled; promoting staff participation in organizations; incidental teaching of academic subjects; numerous articles published in various journals. *Mailing Add:* PO Box 103 Storrs CT 06268. E-Mail: 75463.1745@compuserve.com

SULZMAN, FRANK MICHAEL, CIRCADIAN RHYTHMS, SPACE BIOLOGY. *Current Pos:* mgr, Biomed Res Prog, NASA Hq, Washington, DC, 85-87, chief, Space Med & Biol Br, 87-89, chief, Life Support Br, 89-93, CHIEF, RES PROGS BR, NASA HQ, WASHINGTON DC, 93- *Personal Data:* b Norfolk, Va, Nov 3, 44; m 69. *Educ:* Iona Col, BS, 67; State Univ NY, Stony Brook, PhD(biol), 72. *Prof Exp:* Res fel biol, Harvard Univ, 72-74, res fel biophysics, Moscow State Univ, 74-75; res fel physiol, Med Sch, Harvard Univ, 75-76, instr, 76-79; from asst prof to assoc prof biol, State Univ NY, Binghanton, 79-86. *Concurrent Pos:* Prin investr, Circadian Rhythm Exp, NASA Spacelab I, 78-84 & Cosmos Circadian Rhythm, USSR-NASA, 80-85; prog scientist, cosmos biosufillite prop NASA, 85-93, scientist, space lab life 2, 91-94, Neurolab prog scientsit, 92- *Mem:* Am Physiol Soc; Am Soc Photobiol; Aerospace Med Asn; Int Soc Chronobiol; AAAS. *Res:* Biological rhythms; space biology; photobiology; thermoregulation psychobiology; primate physiology; space physiology. *Mailing Add:* Life Sci Div NASA Hq Code ULR 300 E St SW Washington DC 20546-0001. Fax: 202-358-4168

SUMAN, DANIEL OSCAR, ENVIRONMENTAL LAW, CHEMICAL OCEANOGRAPHY. *Current Pos:* ASSOC PROF MARINE AFFAIRS, UNIV MIAMI, 91- *Personal Data:* b Panama City, Panama, Sept 16, 50; US citizen. *Educ:* Middlebury Col, BA, 72; Columbia Univ, MA & MEd, 78; Univ Calif, San Diego, PhD(oceanog), 83; Univ Calif, Berkeley, JD(environ law), 91. *Prof Exp:* Fel, Smithsonian Trop Res Inst, 83-84; asst prof oceanog phys sci, Boston Univ, 85-87; dir environ studies, World Col West, 87-88. *Concurrent Pos:* Fulbright sr scholar, 94. *Mem:* AAAS; Am Geophys Union; Oceanog Soc. *Res:* Record of tropical biomass burning in coastal marine sediments and the fluxes of carbonaceous particulates to the troposphere; user group conflicts in marine protected areas; natural resource damage assessment. *Mailing Add:* Div Marine Affairs IRSMAS Univ Miami 4600 Rickerbacker Causeway Miami FL 33149. Fax: 305-361-4675; E-Mail: dsuman@rsmas.miami.edu

SUMARTOJO, JOJOK, SEDIMENTARY PETROLOGY, ECONOMIC GEOLOGY. *Current Pos:* VPRES, UST ENVIRON, 91- *Personal Data:* b Surabaya, Indonesia, July 5, 37; Australian citizen; m 66, Esther M Davenport; c Shanti & Rini. *Educ:* Bandung Inst Technol, BS, 61; Univ Ky, MS, 66; Univ Cincinnati, PhD(geol), 74. *Prof Exp:* From instr to lectr geol, Bandung Inst Technol, 59-62; lectr geol, Univ Pajajaran, 68-69; instr geol, Univ Adelaide, 69-75; asst prof geol, Vanderbilt Univ, 75-80; res specialist, Exxon Prod Res Co, 80-82, res assoc, 82-86; eng, Law Environ, 86-91. *Concurrent Pos:* Vpres, Atlanta Geol Soc, 94-; mem, Houston Geol Soc. *Mem:* Am Asn Petrol Geol; Clay Mineral Soc; Environ Info Asn. *Res:* Petrography, geochemistry and mineralogy of fine-grained detrital sedimentary rocks especially black shales, red-beds and coals; well-log analysis of shales; computer geological mapping; statistical geology. *Mailing Add:* 2236 Carlyle Dr Marietta GA 30062. Fax: 770-955-3308

SUMBERG, DAVID A, EDUCATION, ADMINISTRATION. *Current Pos:* asst prof, 74-80, ASSOC PROF PHYSICS, ST JOHN FISHER COL, 80- *Personal Data:* b Utica, NY, June 28, 42; m 64; c 1. *Educ:* Utica Col, BA, 64; Mich State Univ, MS, 66, PhD(physics), 72. *Prof Exp:* Physicist, Eastman Kodak Co, 72-74. *Mem:* Am Asn Physics Teachers; Am Phys Soc. *Res:* Molecular spectroscopy. *Mailing Add:* Dept Elect Eng Rochester Int Tech 79 Lomb Mem Dr Rochester NY 14623-5603

SUMERLIN, NEAL GORDON, NUCLEAR CHEMISTRY. *Current Pos:* From asst prof to assoc prof, 76-88, CHMN DEPT, 83-, PROF CHEM, LYNCHBURG COL, 88- *Personal Data:* b Freeport, Tex, July 1, 50; m 74; c 2. *Educ:* Ouachita Univ, BS, 72; Univ Ark, PhD(chem), 77. *Mem:* AAAS; Sigma Xi; Am Chem Soc. *Mailing Add:* Dept Chem Lynchburg Col Lynchburg VA 24501

SUMMER, GEORGE KENDRICK, BIOCHEMISTRY, NUTRITION. *Current Pos:* Fel, pediat metab, Univ NC, Chapel Hill, 54-57, from instr to asst prof pediat, 57-65, from asst prof to assoc prof biochem & nutrit, 65-72, prof biochm & nutrit, 72-88, assoc clin prof pediat, 66-88, res sci, Child Develop Inst, 71-88, EMER PROF, UNIV NC, CHAPEL HILL, 88- *Personal Data:* b Cherryville, NC, May 8, 23; m 52, Elizabeth Koch; c David E & Carol A (Velasco). *Educ:* Univ NC, BS, 44; Harvard Med Sch, MD, 51. *Concurrent Pos:* NIH res career develop award, 65-70; vis scientist, Galton Lab, Univ Col, London & Med Res Coun human biochem genetics res unit & dept biochem, King's Col, London, 62-63; vis scientist, Lab Neurochem, NIMH, Bethesda, 76-77, 86. *Mem:* Am Inst Nutrit; Am Soc Hum Genetics; Am Acad Pediat. *Res:* Analytical biochemistry; study of inborn errors of metabolism; pathophysiology of disease; pediatrics. *Mailing Add:* CB 7260 Dept Biochem & Nutrit Univ NC Sch Med Fac Lab Off Bldg Rm 405 Chapel Hill NC 27599-7260. *Fax:* 919-966-2852

SUMMER, WARREN R, PULMONARY MEDICINE, CRITICAL CARE MEDICINE. *Current Pos:* HOWARD A BUCHNER PROF MED, LA STATE UNIV, 83-, ASSOC DIR, GEN-CLIN RES CTR. *Personal Data:* b Bayonne, NJ, Apr 22, 40; m 62, Lillian; c Lori, Renee & Ross. *Educ:* Georgetown Univ, MD. *Prof Exp:* Dir, Med Intensive Care Unit & clin dir pulmonary, Johns Hopkins Hosp, 73-83, assoc prof med, 78. *Concurrent Pos:* Sect chief pulmonary critical care, La State Univ Med Ctr, 83-; dir respiratory serv, Univ Hosp & Charity Hosp, 83-; dir, intensive care unit & pulmonary Ochsner Med Inst. *Mem:* Am Thoracic Soc; fel Am Col Chest Physicians; Am Heart Asn. *Res:* Effects of alcohol on pulmonary host defense role of cytokines in cell trafficking during pulmonary infection sepsis and shock; pulmonary hypertension and pulmonary edema. *Mailing Add:* 1901 Perdido St New Orleans LA 70112

SUMMERFELT, ROBERT C, FISH BIOLOGY. *Current Pos:* chmn dept, 76-85, PROF ANIMAL ECOL, IOWA STATE UNIV, 76- *Personal Data:* b Chicago, Ill, Aug 2, 35; m 60, Deanne Walsh; c Scott, Steven & Sloan. *Educ:* Univ Wis-Stevens Point, BS, 57; Southern Ill Univ, MS, 59, PhD(zool), 64. *Honors & Awards:* Spec Achievement Award, US Fish & Wildlife Serv, 69, 71 & 76; Sport Fish Restoration Award, Fisheries Admin Sect, Am Fisheries Soc, 96. *Prof Exp:* Lectr zool, Southern Ill Univ, 62-64; asst prof zool, Kans State Univ, 64-66; assoc prof zool, Okla State Univ, 66-71, prof zool & leader Okla Coop Fishery Res Unit, 71-76. *Concurrent Pos:* Grants, Bur Com Fisheries, 66-69, Nat Marine Fisheries Serv, Off Water Resources Res, 70-71, 74-76 & 79-81, Environ Protection Agency, 71-72, 77-78 & Bur Reclamation, 72 & 74-75; hon lectr, Mid-Am State Univ Asn, 87-88; assoc dir, NCent Regional Aquaculture Ctr, 88-90. *Mem:* NAm Lake Mgt Soc; Fisheries Soc Brit Isles; Am Fisheries Soc; World Aquacult Soc; fel Am Inst Fishery Res Biologists. *Res:* Biology of fishes; microsporidan parasites of fishes; fish biotelemetry; aquaculture; fish biology. *Mailing Add:* Dept Animal Ecol Iowa State Univ Ames IA 50011. *Fax:* 515-294-7874; *E-Mail:* rsummerf@iastate.edu

SUMMERFIELD, GEORGE CLARK, physics, nuclear engineering; deceased, see previous edition for last biography

SUMMERFIELD, MARTIN, physics; deceased, see previous edition for last biography

SUMMERLIN, LEE R, CHEMISTRY, SCIENCE EDUCATION. *Current Pos:* assoc prof chem & sci educ, 72-77, interim dean, Sch Natural Sci & Math, 80-82, PROF CHEM, UNIV ALA, BIRMINGHAM, 72- *Personal Data:* b Sumiton, Ala, Apr 15, 34; m 58; c 4. *Educ:* Samford Univ, AB, 55; Birmingham Southern Col, MS, 60; Univ Md, College Park, PhD(sci educ), 71. *Honors & Awards:* James Conant Award, Am Chem Soc, 69; Ingalls Award, 85. *Prof Exp:* Chemist, Southern Res Inst, 56-59; teacher, Fla State Univ, 59-61, asst prof chem, 62-71; asst prof sci educ, Univ Ga, 71-72. *Concurrent Pos:* Chemist, US Pipe & Foundry Co, 53-55; consult, Chem Educ Mat Study, 63-70, Cent Treaty Orgn, 64-, US Agency Int Develop, 66-68 & India Proj, NSF, 68-; teaching assoc, Univ Md, 70-71. *Mem:* AAAS; Am Chem Soc; Am Inst Chemists; Nat Asn Res Sci Teaching; Nat Sci Teachers Asn. *Res:* Computer assisted instruction; developing chemistry material for nonscience majors; autotutorial and individualized instruction in chemistry; chemical demonstrations. *Mailing Add:* 1786 Cornwall Rd Birmingham AL 35226-2610

SUMMERS, ANNE O, MECHANISMS OF GENE REGULATION, BIOLOGICAL-METAL INTERACTIONS. *Current Pos:* From asst prof to prof, 77-93, RES PROF MICROBIOL, UNIV GA, 93- *Personal Data:* b Jacksonville, Fla, Mar 15, 42. *Educ:* Washington Univ, St Louis, Mo, PhD(molecular biol), 73. *Concurrent Pos:* Consult, Environ Protection Agency, 85, NSF, 85-87, Envirogen, Inc, 89-, NIH Study Sect MBC-2, 93-; Guggenheim fel, 86-87; vis prof biol, Mass Inst Technol, 86-87. *Mem:* Am Soc Microbiol; Genetics Soc Am; Am Soc Biol Chemists; AAAS. *Res:* Regulation of genes involved in the biotransformation of metals; molecular population biology of the primate normal microbial flora. *Mailing Add:* Dept Microbiol Univ Ga 527 Biol Sci Bldg Athens GA 30602-2605. *Fax:* 706-542-6140; *E-Mail:* summers@bscr.uga.edu

SUMMERS, AUDREY LORRAINE, mathematics, computer science; deceased, see previous edition for last biography

SUMMERS, CHARLES GEDDES, economic entomology, for more information see previous edition

SUMMERS, CLAUDE M, design of transformers; deceased, see previous edition for last biography

SUMMERS, DAVID ARCHIBOLD, MINING, ROCK MECHANICS. *Current Pos:* Asst prof mining eng, Univ Mo, Rolla, 68-74, assoc prof mining, 74-77, sr invstr, Rock Mech & Explosives Res Ctr, 70-76, prof mining, 77-80, dir, Rock Mech & Explosives Res Ctr, 76-84, CUR PROF, UNIV MO-ROLLA, 80-, DIR, HIGH PRESSURE WATER JET LAB, 84-, DIR, ROCK MECH & EXPLOSIVES RES CTR, 96- *Personal Data:* b Newcastle-on-Tyne, Eng, Feb 2, 44; m 72; c 2. *Educ:* Univ Leeds, BSc, 65, PhD(mining), 68. *Mem:* Am Inst Mining, Metall & Petrol Engrs; Am Soc Mech Engrs; fel Brit Inst Mining Engrs; Brit Inst Mining & Metall; Brit Tunneling Soc; Cleaning Equipment Mfr Asn; Water Jet Technol Asn (pres, 86-87); hon mem Brit Hydromech Res Asn. *Res:* Water jet cutting; surface energy of rock and minerals; novel methods of excavation; cavitation at high pressure; coal mining; geothermal development; strata control. *Mailing Add:* 808 Cypress Dr Rolla MO 65401

SUMMERS, DENNIS BRIAN, PLANT BREEDING. *Current Pos:* RES PLANT SCIENTIST, ASGROW SEED CO, 74- *Personal Data:* b Natrona Heights, Pa, Aug 4, 43; m 63; c 3. *Educ:* Ind Univ, Pa, BS, 66, MEd, 68; Pa State Univ, PhD(bot), 73. *Prof Exp:* Teacher pub sch, Pa, 66-67; mem staff & fac chem & biol warfare, US Army Chem Ctr & Sch, 67-69. *Mem:* Nat Sweet Corn Breeders Asn; Am Seed Trade Asn; Am Soc Hort Sci. *Res:* Breeding for disease resistance at the cell culture level. *Mailing Add:* 4068 Union Church Rd Salisbury MD 21801

SUMMERS, DONALD F, VIROLOGY. *Current Pos:* PROF MOLECULAR BIOL & CHMN DEPT CELL, VIRAL & MOLECULAR BIOL, SCH MED, UNIV UTAH, 74- *Personal Data:* b Pekin, Ill, July 10, 34. *Educ:* Univ Ill, MD, 59. *Mem:* Am Soc Virol; Am Soc Microbiol; Am Soc Biol Chemists. *Mailing Add:* Dept Microbiol Molecular Genetics Univ Calif Irvine Irvine CA 92717

SUMMERS, DONALD LEE, APPLIED MATHEMATICS, PHYSICS. *Current Pos:* SR MEM TECH STAFF, SANDIA NAT LABS, 89- *Personal Data:* b North Platte, Nebr, Apr 6, 33; m 66; c 3. *Educ:* Univ Nebr, BS, 55, MA, 57. *Prof Exp:* Analyst math & physics, Air Force Weapons Lab, Kirtland AFB, 57-60; res mathematician, Dikewood Corp, 60-70; sr res mathematician, Falcon Res & Develop Co, Whittaker Corp, 70-77; sr res mathematician, Math & Physics, Dikewood Industs, 77-89. *Mem:* Am Phys Soc; Math Asn Am. *Res:* Applied mathematical modeling using computer simulation techniques; analysis of biological effects of ionizing nuclear radiation; development of casualty prediction using mathematical and statistical methods; psychological test development and evaluation; real time satellite data reduction and simulation modeling of real time physical systems. *Mailing Add:* 3713 Moon NE Albuquerque NM 87111

SUMMERS, GEOFFREY P, SOLID STATE PHYSICS. *Current Pos:* CHAIR, DEPT PHYSICS, UNIV MD, 95- *Personal Data:* b London, Eng. *Educ:* Oxford Univ, BA, 65, PhD(physics), 69. *Prof Exp:* Res asst physics, Univ NC, 70-72; from asst prof to assoc prof physics, Okla State Univ, 73-77. *Mem:* Am Phys Soc. *Res:* Experimental investigation of the electronic structure of defects in solids by means of photoconductivity, luminescence, optical absorption and lifetime studies. *Mailing Add:* Dept Physics Univ Md Baltimore Co Campus 1000 Hilltop Circle Baltimore MD 21250

SUMMERS, GEORGE DONALD, TECHNICAL MANAGEMENT, ENGINEERING. *Current Pos:* DIR, CEREX CORP, 87- *Personal Data:* b Eldorado, Ill, Jan 16, 27; m 50, 79, Sachino; c 2. *Educ:* US Mil Acad, BS, 49. *Honors & Awards:* IR-100 Award, 74. *Prof Exp:* US Army, 49-56; proj engr, Arma Div, Am Bosch, Arma Corp, 56-58; systs analyst & proj engr, Missile Systs Div, Repub Aviation Corp, 58-69; prog mgr, Space Systs Div, Fairchild Industs, 69-72; dir, Advan Prog Div, Atlantic Res Corp, 72-80, div gen mgr & vpres, Electronics & Commun Div, 80-85, consult, 85-92. *Mem:* Inst Elec & Electronics Engrs; Am Inst Aeronaut & Astronaut; Optical Soc Am. *Res:* Systems design and analysis of aerospace, electronics, communications, optics and bio-medical; program and general management. *Mailing Add:* 2150 South Bay Lane Reston VA 20191

SUMMERS, GREGORY LAWSON, RESERVOIR FISHERIES RESEARCH, FISHERIES BIO-TELEMETRY. *Current Pos:* Technician, 74-75, biologist I, 75-77, biologist II, 77-82, DIR, OKLA FISHERY LAB, DEPT WILDLIFE, 82- *Personal Data:* b San Mateo, Calif, Oct 25, 51; div; c 2. *Educ:* Univ Okla, BS, 73 & MS, 78. *Mem:* Am Fisheries Soc. *Res:* Reservoir fisheries research dealing with sportfish management and enhancement. *Mailing Add:* 500 E Constellation Norman OK 73072

SUMMERS, HUGH B(LOOMER), JR, CHEMICAL ENGINEERING. *Current Pos:* RETIRED. *Personal Data:* b Lake City, Fla, Aug 5, 21; m 46, Betty JJ Karstedt; c Hugh B III & Carole A. *Educ:* Univ Fla, BChE, 43. *Prof Exp:* Res chem engr, Naval Stores Res Lab, Southern Utilization Res & Develop Div, Agr Res Serv, USDA, 47-65; process engr, Chem Div, Union Camp Corp, 65-86. *Mem:* Am Chem Soc; Am Inst Chem Engrs. *Res:* Gum naval stores processing; crude tall oil production; tall oil fractionation. *Mailing Add:* 17 Biscayne Blvd Lake City FL 32025

SUMMERS, JAMES THOMAS, TEXTILE FIBER DEVELOPMENT, NONWOVEN FABRIC DEVELOPMENT. *Current Pos:* res chemist, 65-68, sr res chemist, 68-85, RES ASSOC, TEXTILE FIBERS DEPT, E I DU PONT DE NEMOURS & CO, INC, 85- *Personal Data:* b Nashville, Tenn, Nov 4, 38; m 58, Mary Joyce Long; c Amanda, Caroline & Sarah. *Educ:* Vanderbilt Univ, AB, 60; Fla State Univ, PhD(inorg chem), 63. *Prof Exp:* Res assoc, Fla State Univ, 64; res fel, Univ Tex, 64-65. *Mem:* Am Chem Soc; Tech Asn Pulp & Paper Indust. *Res:* Coordination chemistry; polymer chemistry. *Mailing Add:* 1066 Hillview Dr Hendersonville TN 37075

SUMMERS, JAMES WILLIAM, POLYMER SCIENCE. *Current Pos:* Sr res & develop assoc & supvr, 62-80, res & develop fel, 80-94, SR RES & DEVELOP FEL, 94- *Personal Data:* b Logansport, Ind, July 10, 40; m 66, Isabel Caraballo; c David & Marie. *Educ:* Rose Hulman Inst Technol, BS, 62; Case Western Reserve Univ, MS, 66, PhD(polymer eng), 71. *Mem:* Fel Soc Plastics Engrs; Am Chem Soc; Soc Plastics Indust. *Res:* Polymer weatherability; polymer rheology and die design; polymer morphology and physical properties; polymer testing; polymer blends; polymer engineering and weathering; extrusion, effects of sun's heating on plastics; injection molding. *Mailing Add:* 29751 Wolf Rd Bay Village OH 44140-1865. *Fax:* 440-930-1671

SUMMERS, JERRY C, EMISSION CONTROL CATALYSIS. *Personal Data:* b Charleston, WVa, Dec 8, 42; m 62; c 6. *Educ:* WVa Univ, BS, 64; Univ Fla, PhD(inorg chem), 68. *Prof Exp:* Postdoc fel, Univ Fla, 68-69; res chemist, Celanese Chem Co, 69-70; staff res scientst, Gen Motors Corp, 70-79; Res mgr, Engelhard Corp, 79-86; tech dir, Allied Signal Automotive Catalyst Co, 86-94. *Mem:* Soc Automotive Engrs; Am Chem Soc; N Am Catalysis Soc. *Res:* Develop technology to control gaseous emissions from both mobile and stationary sources through heterogeneous catalysis. *Mailing Add:* 212 Sentinel Rd Newton PA 18940

SUMMERS, JOHN CLIFFORD, PESTICIDE CHEMISTRY. *Current Pos:* Res chemist & sr res assoc, 63-89, RES FEL, EXP STA, E I DU PONT DE NEMOURS & CO INC, 90- *Personal Data:* b Chicago, Ill, Dec 4, 36; m 71, Mary A Garrett; c Barbara. *Educ:* Augustana Col, Ill, BA, 58; Univ Ill, PhD(org chem), 63. *Mem:* Am Chem Soc; Soc Environ Toxicol & Chem. *Res:* Coordination for pesticide toxicology studies. *Mailing Add:* Exp Sta Bldg 402 E I Du Pont de Nemours & Co Inc Wilmington DE 19880-0402

SUMMERS, JOHN DAVID, POULTRY NUTRITION. *Current Pos:* PROF NUTRIT, UNIV GUELPH, 56- *Personal Data:* b St Catherines, Ont, Mar 28, 29; m 55; c 5. *Educ:* Univ Toronto, BSA, 53, MSA, 59; Rutgers Univ, PhD(animal nutrit), 62. *Honors & Awards:* Agr Award, Ontario Agr Col. *Mem:* Fel Agr Inst Can; fel Poultry Sci Asn. *Res:* Nutrient requirements of poultry and feeding methods. *Mailing Add:* Dept Animal & Poultry Sci Univ Guelph Guelph ON N1G 2W1 Can

SUMMERS, LUIS HENRY, ARCHITECTURAL ENGINEERING. *Current Pos:* PROF ARCHIT ENG & ENVIRON DESIGN, UNIV COLO, 88- *Personal Data:* b Lima, Peru, Sept 6, 39; div; c 1. *Educ:* Univ Notre Dame, BArch, 61, MSc, 65, PhD(struct eng/appl math), 70. *Honors & Awards:* Cardinal Ledcaro Gold Medal, Cardinal Ledcaro Ecclesiastical Design Found, 60. *Prof Exp:* Architect housing, Dino Mortara Assoc, Rome, Italy, 61-62; architect, Corp Renovacion Urbana, PR, 62-63; instr struct, Univ Notre Dame, 65-66; asst prof, Yale Univ, 66-70; assoc prof, Univ Okla, 70-72; prof struct, Energy Mgt & Solar Passive Design, Pa State Univ, 72-86. *Concurrent Pos:* Teacher art, Notre Dame Int, Rome Italy, 61-62 & Stanley Clark Sch, South Bend, Ind, 62-63; comput consult, Assoc Eng, New Haven, Conn, 67; comput graphics consult, Yale Univ & Conn Hwy Dept, 68; architect engr, Comprehensive Design Assoc Int Inc, 72-78; comput syst consult, Army Construct Eng Lab, Urbana, Ill, 76; pres, CDA Int Archit Engrs, State Col, Pa, 78-90 & Boulder, Colo, 87- *Mem:* Sigma Xi; Environ Designers Res Asn; Am Soc Heating Refrig & Air Conditioning Eng; Am Soc Eng Educ; Am Inst Architects; Nat Soc Prof Engrs; Nat Soc Archit Engrs; Sigma Xi. *Res:* Reduction of buildings energy loss; computer aided modeling of thermal comfort using mean radiant temperature; Colorado Institutions Energy Bonding Project; Dept of Energy-energy efficient lighting systems; HVAC systems energy thermal modeling; development of industrial energy conservation software; integration of building system. *Mailing Add:* Dept Civil & Archit Eng Eng Ctr Ecot 441 Campus Box 428 Univ Colo Boulder CO 80309-0428

SUMMERS, MAX DUANE, INSECT VIRUS MOLECULAR BIOLOGY, GENE EXPRESSION. *Current Pos:* PROF ENTOM, DEPT ENTOM, TEX A&M UNIV, 77-, PROF GENETICS, 83-, DISTINGUISHED PROF ENTOM & PROF BIOCHEM & BIOPHYSICS, 83-, CHAIR AGR BIOTECHNOL, 86-, DIR, CTR ADVAN INVERTEBRATE MOLECULAR SCI, 88-, DISTINGUISHED PROF BIOL, 91- *Personal Data:* b Wilmington, Ohio, June 5, 38; m 56; c 2. *Educ:* Wilmington Col, AB, 62; Purdue Univ, PhD(entom), 68. *Honors & Awards:* J E Bussard Mem Award, Entom Soc Am, 83 & 86; I M Lewis Lectr, Am Soc Microbiol, 86. *Prof Exp:* NSF postdoctoral fac assoc, Cell Res Inst & Dept Bot, Univ Tex, Austin, 68-69, from asst prof to assoc prof bot, 69-77. *Concurrent Pos:* Vis assoc prof & assoc insect pathologist, Dept Entom, Univ Calif, Berkeley, 76; chmn-elect, Bact, Plant, & Insect Virus Div, Am Soc Microbiol, 80; counr, Am Soc Virol, 82-85; ed, Virol, 83-; mem, Biotechnol Tech Adv Comt, US Dept Com, 86-90, Sci Adv Bd Inst Biosci & Technol, Tex A&M Univ, 87-88, Nat Acad Sci Comt Human Rights, 89-90; lectr, Found Microbiol, Am Soc Microbiol, 86; chair, Invert Virus Subcomt, Int Comt Taxonomy Viruses, Tex A&M Univ, 88-; adv, Sericult Biotechnol Inst, Bangladesh, India, 88- *Mem:* Nat Acad Sci; Am Soc Microbiol; Soc Invert Path; Entom Soc Am; Am Soc Virol (pres, 91-92); fel AAAS; fel Am Acad Microbiol. *Res:* Molecular biology of baculoviruses and polydnaviruses; development of the only DNA virus cloning and expression vector system for insect cells and insects. *Mailing Add:* Tex A&M Univ Rm 324 Entom Bldg College Station TX 77843-2475

SUMMERS, MICHAEL EARL, ORIGIN & EVOLUTION OF PLANETARY ATMOSPHERES, GLOBAL ATMOSPHERIC CHANGE. *Current Pos:* PHYSICIST, NAVAL RES LAB, 89- *Personal Data:* b Paducah, Ky, Dec 12, 54; m 87, Diana Wilson. *Educ:* Murray State Univ, BA, 76; Univ Tex, Dallas, MS, 78; Calif Inst Technol, PhD(planetary sci), 85. *Prof Exp:* Res fel, Johns Hopkins Univ, 86-88; physicist, Computational Physics Inc, 88-89. *Concurrent Pos:* Adj prof physics, George Mason Univ, 91- *Mem:* Am Astron Soc; Am Geophys Union; Am Meteorol Soc. *Res:* Atmospheric chemistry and physics: chemistry of atmospheric ozone and active trace constituents; global atmospheric change, global warming and atmospheric dynamics; chemistry of atmospheres of Mars, Io, Uranus, Neptune, Triton, Titan and Pluto; stability of planetary atmospheres. *Mailing Add:* Space Sci Div Naval Res Lab 7641 S Washington DC 20375-5000

SUMMERS, PHILLIP DALE, SYSTEMS DESIGN & SYSTEMS SCIENCE, COMPUTER SCIENCES. *Current Pos:* Res staff, 67-87 & 90-93, exec secy, Sci Adv Comt, Corporate Hq, 87-89, PROG DIR QUAL, IBM RES, 93- *Personal Data:* b Decatur, Ill, Mar 21, 43; m 65, Linda Smith; c Eric & Michael. *Educ:* Mass Inst Technol, BS, 65; Syracuse Univ, MS, 71; Yale Univ, MS, 73, MPhil, 74, PhD(computer sci), 75. *Concurrent Pos:* Adj prof, Dept Computer Sci, NY Univ, Westchester, 78-80. *Mem:* Asn Comput Mach; Inst Elec & Electronics Engrs; Am Asn Artificial Intel; Am Soc Eng Educ. *Res:* Systems aspects of manufacturing; manufacturing strategies; technology management and assessment. *Mailing Add:* 37 Sands St Mt Kisco NY 10549-1324

SUMMERS, RANDY SCOTT, ENVIRONMENTAL SCIENCES. *Current Pos:* ASSOC PROF, DEPT CIVIL & ENVIRON ENG, UNIV CINCINNATI. *Concurrent Pos:* Fulbright scholar, Chem Dept, Univ Crete, Greece, 95. *Res:* Drinking-water disinfection; by-product formation and control. *Mailing Add:* Dept Civil & Environ Eng Univ Cincinnati Cincinnati OH 45221-0071

SUMMERS, RAYMOND, neurological research, for more information see previous edition

SUMMERS, RICHARD JAMES, ALLERGY, PEDIATRICS. *Current Pos:* asst chief, 76-80, CHIEF, ALLERGY-IMMUNOL SERV, WALTER REED ARMY MED CTR, 80- *Personal Data:* b Kendallville, Ind, Nov 13, 43. *Educ:* Ind Univ, AB, 65, MD, 68; Am Bd Pediat, cert, 73; Am Bd Allergy-Immunol, cert, 74. *Prof Exp:* Rotating intern, Fitzsimons Gen Hosp, Denver, 68-69; pediat resident, Fitzsimons Army Med Ctr, 69-71; allergy-immunol fel, Nat Jewish Hosp & Res Ctr, Univ Colo Med Ctr, Fitzsimons Army Med Ctr, 71-73; chief allergy-immunol serv, 97th Gen Hosp, Frankfurt, WGer, 73-76. *Concurrent Pos:* US Army Europe consult allergy-immunol, 7th US Army Surgeon Gen Consult, Heidelberg, WGer, 73-76; asst prof pediat & med, Uniformed Serv Univ Health Sci, 73-76; consult allergy-immunol, Nat Inst Allergy & Infectious Dis, NIH, 79-; assoc prof pediat & assoc prof med, Uniformed Services Univ Health Sci, 83- *Mem:* Fel Am Acad Pediat; Am Acad Allergy; Am Fedn Clin Res; Am Thoracic Soc. *Res:* Penicillin allergy; ampicillin allergy; infectious mononucleosis; catecholamines, especially epinephrine and ephedrine; cyclic nucleotides; histamine; immunotherapy; radioallergosorbent testing; insect sting allergy. *Mailing Add:* 3460 Olney Laytonville Rd Olney MD 20832

SUMMERS, RICHARD LEE, hyperbaric chamber experiment design & control, for more information see previous edition

SUMMERS, ROBERT GENTRY, JR, ZOOLOGY. *Current Pos:* assoc prof, 76-83, PROF ANAT, STATE UNIV NY, BUFFALO, 83- *Personal Data:* b Sonora, Calif, Jan 10, 43; m 70. *Educ:* Univ Notre Dame, BS, 65, MS, 67; Tulane Univ, PhD(anat), 71. *Prof Exp:* Fel, Univ Maine, Orono, 70-71, from asst prof to assoc prof zool, 75-76. *Mem:* Am Soc Zoologists; Am Asn Anatomists; Am Soc Cell Biol; Soc Develop Biol. *Res:* Developmental biology, particularly invertebrate embryology and morphogenesis; electron microscopy of developing invertebrates and their gametes; control systems in growth and regeneration. *Mailing Add:* Dept Anat Sci Farber Hall State Univ NY Sch Med 317 Farber Hall Buffalo NY 14214-0001. *Fax:* 716-831-3395; *E-Mail:* anargs@ubvms.edu

SUMMERS, ROBERT WENDELL, GASTROENTEROLOGY. *Current Pos:* NIH gastroenterol res fel, 68-70, asst prof, 71-74, assoc prof gastroenterol, 74-, PROF GASTROENTEROL, DEPT MED, DIV GASTROENTEROL, UNIV IOWA HOSPS, 74- *Personal Data:* b Lansing, Mich, July 28, 38; m 61, Edith Brenneman; c Kristine, Rebecca & Rachel. *Educ:* Mich State Univ, BS, 61; Univ Iowa, MD, 65. *Concurrent Pos:* Assoc dir, Gastroenterol Prog, Gastroenterol Div, Dept Med, Vet Admin Hosp, Iowa City, 70-71, consult, 71-77; Burroughs Wellcome Res Travel grant, 79; Fogerty Sr Int fel, NIH, 80; dir, Digestive Dis Ctr, Diag & Therapeut Unit, 85. *Mem:* Am Gastroenterol Asn; Am Col Physicians; Am Soc Gastrointestinal Endoscopy; Soc Neurosci; Am Physiol Asn. *Res:* Interrelationships of electrical and motor activity of the small intestine, and intestinal flow as modulated by physiologic, pharmacologic, and pathologic influence; inflammatory bowel disease. *Mailing Add:* Dept Internal Med Univ Iowa Hosp & Clins Iowa City IA 52242. *E-Mail:* robert_summers@uiowa.edu

SUMMERS, WILLIAM ALLEN, INDUSTRIAL ORGANIC CHEMISTRY, GENERAL MANAGEMENT. *Current Pos:* MANAGING DIR, MGT SOLUTIONS LC, 91- *Personal Data:* b Atlanta, Ga, Dec 4, 44. *Educ:* Wabash Col, AB, 66; Northwestern Univ, PhD(chem), 71; Ind State Univ, MBA, 81. *Prof Exp:* Res assoc photochem, Okla Univ, 70-72, vis asst prof, 70-71, sr res assoc photochem, 73-74; prog dir & group leader nucleotide synthesis, Ash Steven Inc, 72-73; develop chemist heterogeneous catalysis, Pitman-Moore, Inc, 74-79, mgr new prod develop, 79-82, dir new prod develop, Animal Prod Group, 82-84, dir com develop-growth hormone, 84-89; group dir, Gustafson Inc, 89-91; group dir new bus develop, Ambico Inc, 94-96. *Concurrent Pos:* Mem bd dirs, Predation Inc, 95- *Mem:* Am Chem Soc; Sigma Xi; Coun Agricultural Sci & Tech. *Res:* Research and development involving heterogeneous catalysis particularly catalytic reduction and photochemistry of nitroparaffins and their derivatives; applications of and design of new catalytic reduction reactions; livestock vaccines in high technology fields of tissue culture and recombinant DNA. *Mailing Add:* PO Box 41231 Des Moines IA 50311-0004

SUMMERS, WILLIAM ALLEN, SR, parasitology, medical microbiology; deceased, see previous edition for last biography

SUMMERS, WILLIAM CLARKE, MARINE ECOLOGY. *Current Pos:* ASSOC PROF ECOL, HUXLEY COL ENVIRON STUDIES, WESTERN WASH UNIV, 72- *Personal Data:* b Corvallis, Ore, Sept 13, 36; m 64; c 2. *Educ:* Univ Minn, BME, 59, PhD(zool), 66. *Prof Exp:* Res assoc & investr squid biol, Marine Biol Lab, 66-72, NIH contract squid ecol, 69-72; dir, Shannon Point Marine Ctr, 72-76. *Concurrent Pos:* Corp mem, Marine Biol Lab. *Mem:* AAAS; Am Soc Mech Engrs; Am Soc Zoologists; Sigma Xi; Am Asn Univ Profs. *Res:* Physiological ecology of aquatic mollusks; life history, autecology and population biology of the squid, Loligo pealei; similar studies on Puget Sound octopus species; marine ecology; coastal ecosystems; aquatic biology; coastal management environmental impact assesstment. *Mailing Add:* Huxley Col Western Wash Univ Bellingham WA 98225

SUMMERS, WILLIAM COFIELD, MOLECULAR BIOLOGY, HISTORY OF SCIENCE & MEDICINE. *Current Pos:* From asst prof radiobiol to assoc prof radiobiol, molecular biophys & biochem, 68-78, PROF THERAPEUT RADIOL, MOLECULAR BIOPHYS, BIOCHEM & HUMAN GENETICS, YALE UNIV, 78-, PROF HIST MED & SCI, 92- *Personal Data:* b Janesville, Wis, Apr 17, 39; m 65, Wilma Poos; c Emily A. *Educ:* Univ Wis-Madison, BS, 61, MS, 63, PhD(molecular biol) & MD, 67. *Hon Degrees:* MA, Yale Univ, New Haven. *Concurrent Pos:* NSF fel, Mass Inst Technol, 67-68. *Mem:* Am Soc Microbiol; Am Soc Biochem & Molecular Biol; Hist Sci Soc. *Res:* Molecular virology; history of science and medicine. *Mailing Add:* 333 Cedar St New Haven CT 06510-8039

SUMMERS, WILLIAM HUNLEY, MATHEMATICS. *Current Pos:* From asst prof to assoc prof, 68-78, PROF MATH, UNIV ARK, FAYETTEVILLE, 78- *Personal Data:* b Dallas, Tex, Feb 5, 36. *Educ:* Univ Tex, Arlington, BS, 61; Purdue Univ, West Lafayette, MS, 63; La State Univ, Baton Rouge, PhD(math), 68. *Concurrent Pos:* Fulbright-Hayes travel grant, Brazil, 73; vis prof, Inst Math, Fed Univ Rio de Janeiro, 73-75; NSF travel grant, India & Ger, 81; vis prof, Univ-GH-Paderborn, 81 & 83 & Univ Essen, 84. *Mem:* Am Math Soc; Math Soc France. *Res:* Asymptotic and weak asymptotic almost periodicity. *Mailing Add:* Dept Math Univ Ark Fayetteville AR 72701

SUMMERS, WILMA POOS, BIOCHEMICAL GENETICS, MOLECULAR VIROLOGY. *Current Pos:* fel pharmacol, Yale Univ, 68-69, res assoc, 69-72, res assoc virol, 72-78, sr res assoc, 78-83, res scientist, Dept Therapeut Radiol, 83-96, RES AFFIL, DEPT THERAPEUT RADIOL, SCH MED, YALE UNIV, 96- *Personal Data:* b Richmond, Ind, Dec 8, 37; m 65, William C; c Emily A. *Educ:* Ohio Univ, BS, 59; Univ Wis-Madison, PhD(oncol), 66. *Prof Exp:* Fel oncol, McArdle Lab Cancer Res, Univ Wis-Madison, 66-67; fel biochem, Harvard Med Sch, 67-68. *Concurrent Pos:* Consult, Nat Cancer Inst, NIH, 73-74. *Mem:* Am Soc Biol Chemists; Am Soc Virol. *Res:* Mechanism of response of mammalian cells to radiation damage; structure and function of herpes simplex virus thymidine kinase. *Mailing Add:* Dept Therapeut Radiol Sch Med Yale Univ 333 Cedar St New Haven CT 06510. *Fax:* 203-785-6309

SUMMERS-GILL, ROBERT GEORGE, EXPERIMENTAL NUCLEAR PHYSICS. *Current Pos:* RETIRED. *Personal Data:* b Sask, Can, Dec 22, 29. *Educ:* Univ Sask, BA, 50, MA, 52; Univ Calif, PhD(physics), 56. *Prof Exp:* From asst prof to prof physics, McMaster Univ, 56-90. *Mem:* Am Phys Soc; Can Asn Physicists. *Res:* Atomic beam resonances; nuclear spectroscopy; direct reactions; nuclear shell model calculations; heavy ion reactions. *Mailing Add:* 94 Whitney Ave Hamilton ON L8S 2G5 Can

SUMMERVILLE, RICHARD MARION, MATHEMATICS. *Current Pos:* prof math & dean, Sch Lib Arts & Sci, 80-82, PROF MATH & VPRES, ACAD AFFAIRS, CHRISTOPHER NEWPORT COL, 82- *Personal Data:* b Shippenville, Pa, May 20, 38; m 62; c 2. *Educ:* Clarion State Col, BS, 59; Wash Univ, AM, 65; Syracuse Univ, PhD(math), 69. *Prof Exp:* Instr math, Clarion State Col, 60-64; asst prof, State Univ NY Col Oswego, 68-69; res assoc, Syracuse Univ, 69-70; assoc prof math & chmn dept, Armstrong State Col, 70-73, prof math & head, Dept Math & Comput Sci, 73-80. *Mem:* Am Asn Univ Profs; Math Asn Am; Am Math Soc; Sigma Xi. *Res:* Complex analysis; conformal and quasiconformal mapping; Schlicht functions. *Mailing Add:* Dept Math Christopher Newport Col Shoe Lane Newport News VA 23606

SUMMITT, ROBERT L, PEDIATRICS, MEDICAL GENETICS. *Current Pos:* from instr to assoc prof, 64-71, assoc dean acad affairs, 79-81, PROF PEDIAT & ANAT, COL MED, UNIV TENN, MEMPHIS, 71-, DEAN COL MED, 81- *Personal Data:* b Knoxville, Tenn, Dec 23, 32; m 55, Joyce Sharp; c Robert L Jr, Susan K (Pridgen) & John B. *Educ:* Univ Tenn, MD, 55, MS, 62; Am Bd Pediat, dipl, 62, recert, 83 & 92; Am Bd Med Genetics, Cert Clin genetics & clin cytogenetics, 82. *Prof Exp:* Intern, Mem Res Ctr & Hosp, Univ Tenn, Knoxville, 56; asst resident pediat, Col Med, Univ Tenn, Memphis, 59-60, chief resident, 60-61, USPHS trainee pediat endocrine & metab dis, Univ, 61-62; fel med genetics, Univ Wis, 63. *Concurrent Pos:* NIH, Children's Bur, State Ment Health Dept & Nat Found res grants; mem pediat staff, City of Memphis, Le Bonheur Children's Hosp; pediat consult, Baptist Mem, St Josph's, Methodist, US Naval, St Jude Children's Res & Arlington Hosps, Baroness Erloyer Hosp & T C Thompson Children's Hosp Med Ctr; mem, Mammalian Genetics Study Sect, NIH, 80-; mem, Coun Grad Med Educ, US Dept Health & Human Servs, 90-94; prin investr, NIH. *Mem:* AAAS; Am Acad Pediat; Am Soc Human Genetics; Soc Pediat Res; Am Pediat Soc; Am Col Med Genetics. *Res:* Clinical genetics and cytogenetics; author of over 140 journal articles. *Mailing Add:* Dept Pediat Univ Tenn Med Group Inc 800 Madison Ave Memphis TN 38163. *Fax:* 901-448-7683

SUMMY-LONG, JOAN YVETTE, PHARMACOLOGY. *Current Pos:* sr res technician, 69-72, res asst, 72-78, asst prof, 78-83, ASSOC PROF PHARMACOL, PA STATE UNIV, 83- *Personal Data:* b Harrisburg, Pa. *Educ:* Bucknell Univ, BS, 65; Pa State Univ, MS, 72, PhD(pharmacol), 78. *Prof Exp:* Jr scientist pharmacol, Smith Kline Pharmaceut Labs, 65-69. *Concurrent Pos:* Res asst, co-investr NASA grant, 77-78, asst prof, 78-79; speaker, Gordon Res Conf, Angiotensin, 80, Subfornical Orgn Workshop Soc Neurosci, 84, 10th Int Symp Neurosec, 87, Brain-Opioid Systs & Reprod, 87; prin investr, grants NIH-HLBI & HD, Am Heart Asn & NSF. *Mem:* Sigma Xi; Soc Neurosci; Soc Pharmacol Exp Therapeut; Endocrine Soc. *Res:* Neuroendocrinology; central nervous system regulation of blood pressure and hydration; endogenous opioid peptide effects on blood pressure, oxytocin and vasopressin neurosecretion; circumventricular organs. *Mailing Add:* Dept Pharmacol Milton S Hershey Med Ctr PO Box 850 Hershey PA 17033-0850. *Fax:* 717-531-5013

SUMNER, BARBARA ELAINE, PHYSICAL CHEMISTRY, MATERIALS SCIENCE. *Current Pos:* RES CHEMIST MAT, NIGHT VISION & ELECTRO-OPTICS LABS, 68- *Personal Data:* b Alexandria, Va, Dec 23, 42. *Educ:* Howard Univ, BS, 66; Am Univ, MS, 74, PhD(chem), 77. *Prof Exp:* Chemist chem warfare, Melpar Inc, 66-68. *Mem:* Am Chem Soc; Electrochem Soc; Sigma Xi; Am Phys Soc. *Res:* Metallurgical analysis, design, fabrication and coordination of intrinsic and extrinsic photosensors and auxiliary components for use in infrared imaging systems. *Mailing Add:* 417 N Alfred St Alexandria VA 22314

SUMNER, DARRELL DEAN, METABOLISM, ENVIRONMENTAL CHEMISTRY & TOXICOLOGY. *Current Pos:* RETIRED. *Personal Data:* b Kansas City, Mo, Jan 1, 41; m 63, Karen; c 3. *Educ:* Univ Kans, AB, 63, PhD(med chem), 68; Am Bd Toxicol, dipl, 80. *Prof Exp:* Sr scientist drug metab, McNeil Labs, Inc, 68-71; sr metab chemist, CIBA-Geigy Corp, 71-75, proj scientist, 75-77, from toxicologist to sr toxicologist, 77-82, mgr environ invest, Agr Div, 82-88, mgr animal metab, 88-91, environ issues mgr, Crop Protection Div, 91-97. *Concurrent Pos:* Vis asst prof, Univ NC, Greensboro, 75-76; adj assoc prof pharmacol & toxicol, Bowan Gray Sch Med, Winston Salem, NC, 82- *Mem:* Am Chem Soc; Inst Food Technologists; Am Indust Hyg. *Res:* Environmental toxicology; food safety. *Mailing Add:* Dept Physiol Pharmacol Bowman Gray Sch Med 115 S Chestnut St Winston Salem NC 27101

SUMNER, DAVID SPURGEON, PERIPHERAL VASCULAR SURGERY, NONINVASIVE DIAGNOSIS OF VASCULAR DISEASE. *Current Pos:* prof, 75-84, DISTINGUISHED PROF SURG, SOUTHERN ILL UNIV, 84- *Personal Data:* b Asheboro, NC, Feb 20, 33; m 59, Martha Sypher; c David V, Mary E & John F. *Educ:* Univ NC, BA, 54; Johns Hopkins Univ, MD, 58. *Prof Exp:* From asst prof to assoc prof surg, Univ Wash, 70-75. *Concurrent Pos:* Clinical investr, Vet Admin, 70-73; Vis prof, numerous med cols, 76-92. *Mem:* Soc Univ Surgeons; Soc Vascular Surg; Int Soc Cardiovasc Surg; Am Surg Asn; Am Col Surgeons. *Res:* Pathophysiology and noninvasive testing of peripheral vascular disease. *Mailing Add:* 800 N Rutledge St Springfield IL 62781. *Fax:* 217-524-1793

SUMNER, DONALD RAY, PLANT PATHOLOGY, SOILBORNE PLANT PATHOGENS. *Current Pos:* from asst prof to assoc prof, 69-83, PROF PLANT PATH, COASTAL PLAIN EXP STA, UNIV GA, 83- *Personal Data:* b Studley, Kans, Sept 20, 37; m 68, Jo Ann Troyer; c Karena. *Educ:* Kans State Univ, BS, 59; Univ Nebr, MS, 64, PhD(plant path), 67. *Prof Exp:* Plant pathologist, Green Giant Co, Minn, 67-69. *Concurrent Pos:* Pres, Southern Div, Am Phytopath Soc, 92-93. *Mem:* Am Phytopath Soc; Sigma Xi. *Res:* Ecology and control of soil-borne pathogenic fungi on vegetables, cotton and corn in irrigated, multiple-cropping systems with integrated pest management and conservation tillage. *Mailing Add:* Dept Plant Path Coastal Plain Exp Sta Tifton GA 31793-0748. *Fax:* 912-386-7285; *E-Mail:* path-tif@tifton.cpes.peachnet.edu

SUMNER, EDWARD D, pharmacy, for more information see previous edition

SUMNER, JOHN RANDOLPH, geophysics, for more information see previous edition

SUMNER, MALCOLM EDWARD, AGRICULTURE, SOIL PHYSICS. *Current Pos:* prof agron, 77-91, REGENTS PROF & COORDR ENVIRON SOIL SCI PROG, DEPT CROP & SOIL SCI, UNIV GA, ATHENS, 91- *Personal Data:* b June 7, 33. *Educ:* Univ Natal, SAfrica, BSc, 54, MSc, 58; Oxford Univ, Eng, PhD(soil chem), 61. *Honors & Awards:* Res Award, Soil Sci Soc Am, 91; Werner L Nelson Award, Am Soc Agron, 91, Soil Sci Award, 91. *Prof Exp:* Sr lectr, Dept Soil Sci, Univ Natal, 55-57, assoc prof, 61-71, prof & head, Dept Soil Sci & Agrometeorol, 71-77. *Concurrent Pos:* Consult, Brit Commonwealth Develop Corp, 67-82, SAfrican Chamber Mines, 69-76, FAO-UNDP Prog, India, 86-87, Food & Fertilizer Tech Ctr, Taiwan, 86, Combustion Chem Corp, 87-90, Agrilab, 87-93, Masstock Inc, 88, Stand Fruit Co, Honduras, 92 & Australian Ctr Int Agr Res, 92; hon prof, Dept Agr & Environ Sci, Univ Newcastle-upon-Tyne, Eng, 89-; Sir Frederick McMaster fel, 92. *Mem:* Fel Soil Sci Soc Am; fel Am Soc Agron. *Res:* Soil acidity and crusting; interactions at the soil colloid-soil solution interface; sustainable land management in the tropics; author and co-author of numerous publications; contributed 208 articles to professional journals. *Mailing Add:* Dept Crop & Soil Sci Univ Ga Athens GA 30602

SUMNER, RICHARD LAWRENCE, HIGH ENERGY PHYSICS. *Current Pos:* Res assoc physics, 72-73, MEM RES STAFF PHYSICS, PRINCETON UNIV, 73- *Personal Data:* b Albany, NY, May 28, 38; m 64; c 2. *Educ:* State Univ NY Albany, BS, 59; Univ Chicago, SM, 65, PhD(physics), 75. *Res:* High energy elementary particle studies; direct muon production and particle production at large transverse momentum. *Mailing Add:* 24 Halley Dr Pomona NY 10970

SUMNERS, DEWITT L, APPLICATION OF TYPOLOGY, MOLECULAR BIOLOGY. *Current Pos:* From asst prof to assoc prof math, 67-75, PROF MATH, FLA STATE UNIV, 75- *Personal Data:* b Ferriday, La, Dec 2, 41. *Educ:* La State Univ, BS, 63; Cambridge Univ, PhD(math), 67. *Concurrent Pos:* Vis prof math, Kwansei Gakuan Univ, Japan, 88. *Mem:* Inst Advan Sci; Sigma Xi; AAAS; Am Math Soc. *Res:* Researching new application using Knot theory in DNA experiments; use of mathematics to describe enzyme action. *Mailing Add:* Dept Math Fla State Univ Tallahassee FL 32306-3027. *Fax:* 850-644-4053

SUMNEY, LARRY W, NATIONAL RESEARCH & TECHNOLOGY NEEDS. *Current Pos:* PRES, CHIEF EXEC OFFICER, SEMICONDUCTOR RES CORP, 82- *Personal Data:* b Wash, Pa, Aug 8, 40; div; c 1. *Educ:* Wash & Jefferson Col, BA, 62; George Washington Univ, MS, 69. *Prof Exp:* Res, microelect advan systs, Naval Res Lab, 62-70; staff, Naval Elec Systs Command, 72-77, res dir, 77-80; dir, Very High Speed Integrated Circuits Prog, Dept Defense, 80-82. *Concurrent Pos:* Managing dir, Sematech, 87. *Mem:* Fel Inst Elec & Electronic Engrs. *Mailing Add:* Semiconductor Res Corp 1101 Slater Dr Box 12053 Durham NC 27703

SUMPIO, BAUER E, VASCULAR SURGERY, SURGERY. *Current Pos:* ASSOC PROF VASCULAR SURG, YALE UNIV, SCH MED, 87- *Personal Data:* b New York, NY, Jan 17, 56. *Res:* Vascular surgery. *Mailing Add:* Dept Surg 137 FMB Yale Univ Sch Med 333 Cedar St PO Box 208062 New Haven CT 06520-8062

SUMRALL, H GLENN, PLANT PHYSIOLOGY, MICROBIOLOGY. *Current Pos:* assoc prof, 73-77, assoc acad dean, 73-84, PROF BIOL, LIBERTY UNIV, 77-, DEAN COL ARTS & SCI, 84- *Personal Data:* b Macon, Miss, Nov 8, 42; m 63; c 2. *Educ:* Southeastern La Univ, BS, 64; La State Univ, MS, 66, PhD(plant path), 69. *Prof Exp:* Asst prof biol, Cornell Col, 69-73. *Mem:* Am Phytopath Soc. *Res:* Fecal coliform pollution in streams and lakes; physiology of plant disease. *Mailing Add:* PO Box 7001 Le Tournea Univ Longview TX 75607-7001

SUMRELL, GENE, ORGANIC CHEMISTRY. *Current Pos:* sr chemist, Southern Utilization Res & Develop Div, 64-67, head invests, 67-73, res leader, 73-84, COLLABR, SOUTHERN REGIONAL RES CTR, AGR RES SERV, USDA, 84- *Personal Data:* b Apache, Ariz, Oct 7, 19. *Educ:* Eastern NMex Col, AB, 42; Univ NMex, BS, 47, MS, 48; Univ Calif, PhD(chem), 51. *Prof Exp:* Asst, Univ NMex, 47-48, asst, Univ Calif, 48-51; asst prof, Eastern NMex Univ, 51-53; res chemist, J T Baker Chem Co, 53-58; sr org chemist, Southwest Res Inst, 58-59; proj leader chem & plastics div, Food Mach & Chem Corp, 59-61; res sect leader, El Paso Natural Gas Prod Co, Tex, 61-64. *Mem:* AAAS; Am Chem Soc; fel Am Inst Chem; Am Oil Chem Soc; Am Asn Textile Chemists & Colorists. *Res:* Fatty acids in tubercle bacilli; organic synthesis; pharmaceuticals; branched-chain compounds; triazoles; petrochemicals; fats and oils; monomers and polymers; cellulose chemistry; cereal chemistry. *Mailing Add:* PO Box 24037 New Orleans LA 70184-4037

SUMSION, H(ENRY) T(HEODORE), MATERIALS SCIENCE ENGINEERING. *Current Pos:* RETIRED. *Personal Data:* b Chester, Utah, Mar 7, 12; m 38; c 4. *Educ:* Univ Utah, BS, 38, PhD(phys metall), 49; Univ Ala, MS, 39. *Honors & Awards:* Apollo Award, NASA, 69. *Prof Exp:* Engr, US Bur Mines, 39-42; asst phys metall, Univ Calif, 46-47 & Univ Utah, 47-49; sr engr, Carborundum Co, 49-51; res assoc, Knolls Atomic Power Lab, Gen Elec Co, 51-56, nuclear fuels metallurgist, Atomic Power Equip Dept, 56-57; res scientist, Lockheed Missiles & Space Co, 57-62; res scientist, Ames Res Ctr, NASA, 62-84. *Mem:* AAAS; Am Soc Metals; fel Am Inst Chem; Am Inst Mining, Metall & Petrol Engrs; fel NY Acad Sci. *Res:* Space environment-materials reactions; space materials applications; solid state structures; x-ray diffraction. *Mailing Add:* 5378 Harwood Rd San Jose CA 95124

SUN, ALBERT YUNG-KWANG, BIOCHEMISTRY, NEUROCHEMISTRY. *Current Pos:* assoc prof, Biochem Dept & res prof, Sinclair Comp Med Res Farm, 74-89, assoc prof, 89-91, PROF, DEPT PHARMACOL, UNIV MO, 91- *Personal Data:* b Amoy, Fukien, China, Oct 13, 32; m 64; Grace Y Cheung; c Aggie Y. *Educ:* Nat Taiwan Univ, BS, 57; Ore State Univ, PhD(biochem), 67. *Prof Exp:* AEC fel & res assoc biochem, Case Western Res Univ, 67-68; res assoc, Lab Neurochem, Cleveland Psychiat Inst, 68-72, proj dir, 72-74. *Concurrent Pos:* NIH gen res support grant, Cleveland Psychiat Inst, 68-73; Cleveland Diabetic Fund res grant, 72; alcohol grant, Nat Inst Alcohol Abuse & Alcoholism, 74-; aging grant, Nat Inst Neurol Commun Dis & Strokes, 75-78. *Mem:* AAAS; Am Chem Soc; Biochem Soc; Am Soc Neurochem; Soc Neurosci; Int Soc Neurochem; Int Soc Biomed Res Alcoholism; Am Soc Biochem Molecular Biol. *Res:* Functional and structural relationship of the central nervous system membranes; active transport mechanism; drug effects on synaptic transmission of the central nervous system. *Mailing Add:* Dept Pharmacol Univ Mo Columbia MO 65212. *Fax:* 573-884-4558; *E-Mail:* pharmags@muccmail.missouri.edu

SUN, ALEXANDER SHIHKAUNG, BIOCHEMISTRY, CELL BIOLOGY. *Current Pos:* PROF, YALE UNIV MED SCH, 92- *Personal Data:* b Feb 21, 39; US citizen; m 68; c 1. *Educ:* Taiwan Normal Univ, BS, 63; Univ Calif, Berkeley, PhD(biochem), 71. *Prof Exp:* Guest investr, Dept Biochem Cytol, Rockefeller Univ, 71-72; asst res physiologist, Dept Physiol & Anat, Univ Calif, Berkeley, 72-75; asst prof path, Mt Sinai Med Ctr, 75-77, asst prof neuroplastic dis, 77-92. *Mem:* Am Soc Cell Biol; Am Soc Photobiol; Geront Soc Am. *Res:* Biochemistry of human aging, especially the effects of oxidative damage generated by subcellular organelles on cell aging, the mechanism controlling the different lifespans of normal and tumor cells in vitro. *Mailing Add:* 123 York Sq New Haven CT 06511. *Fax:* 203-777-3069

SUN, ANTHONY MEIN-FANG, ENDOCRINOLOGY, ARTIFICIAL ORGANS. *Current Pos:* adj prof, 72-88, PROF PHYSIOL, UNIV TORONTO, 88- *Personal Data:* b Nanking, China, April 10, 35; m 64, Irene Ma; c Alexander & Elizabeth. *Educ:* Nat Taiwan Univ, BSc, 58; Univ Toronto, MSc, PhD(physiol), 72. *Prof Exp:* Res assoc, Hosp Sick Children, 72-75. *Concurrent Pos:* Res consult, Res Int Hosp Sick Children, 75-77; sr res scientist, Connaught Res Inst, 74-88; hon prof, Shanghai Med Univ, 88, Nat Defense Univ, 92. *Mem:* Int Soc Artificial Organs; Am Diabetes Asn; Can Physiol Soc; Can Diabetes Asn; Can Biomat Soc. *Res:* Long term culture of pancreatic islets of langerhans; the development of a bioartificial endocrine pancreas and bioartificial liver; differentiation of endocrine cells (somatotrophs and pancreatic beta cells); gene therapy. *Mailing Add:* Dept Physiol Fac Med Med Sci Bldg 1 Kings Col Circle Toronto ON M5S 1A8 Can. *Fax:* 416-978-4940

SUN, BERNARD CHING-HUEY, COMPOSITE FOREST PRODUCTS, ADHESION. *Current Pos:* RETIRED. *Personal Data:* b Nanking, China, Aug 23, 37; m 64; c 2. *Educ:* Nat Taiwan Univ, BSA, 60; Univ BC, MS, 67, PhD(wood-pulp sci), 70. *Prof Exp:* Jr specialist, Nat Taiwan Univ Res Forest, 61-63; demonstr wood pulp sci, Univ BC, 68-70; asst prof wood sci, Mich Technol Univ, 70-75, assoc prof wood sci, Dept Forestry, 75-97. *Mem:* Forest Prod Res Soc; Soc Wood Sci & Technol. *Res:* Performance-driven wood and fiber composites; wood composite materials; wood-pulp relationships; adhesion and adhesives. *Mailing Add:* RR 1 Box 245 Chassell MI 49916-9711

SUN, CHANG-TSAN, ENGINEERING MECHANICS, MATERIALS SCIENCE. *Current Pos:* PROF, UNIV FLA, 79- *Personal Data:* b Shen-Yang, China, Feb 20, 28; US citizen; m 63; Jenny M Ling; c Barry, Karen & Nancy. *Educ:* Nat Taiwan Univ, BS, 53; Stevens Inst Technol, MS, 60; Yale Univ, PhD(solid mech), 64. *Prof Exp:* Sr engr, Atomic Power Develop Assocs Inc, Mich, 64-65; asst prof eng mech, Iowa State Univ, 65-68, assoc prof, 68-77; sr res engr, General Motors Res Labs, Mich, 77-79. *Mem:* Am Soc Mech Engrs; Am Soc Testing & Mat; Am Soc Eng Educ. *Res:* Wave propagation; composite materials; fiber reinforced plastics; stress analysis. *Mailing Add:* Dept Aerospace Eng Mech & Eng Sci Col Eng 231 Aerospace Bldg PO Box 116250 Gainesville FL 32611

SUN, CHAO NIEN, EXPERIMENTAL PATHOLOGY. *Current Pos:* assoc prof to prof, 69-85, chief, Electron Microscope Lab, Vet Admin Hosp, 69-85, EMER PROF PATH, UNIV ARK MED SCI, LITTLE ROCK, 85- *Personal Data:* b Hopeh, China, Dec 4, 14; m 46; c 2. *Educ:* Nat Peking Univ, BSc, 40; Univ Okla, MSc, 50; Ohio State Univ, PhD, 53. *Prof Exp:* Asst biol, Nat Peking Univ, 40-45, lectr, 45-48; asst, Univ Okla, 48-50, Ohio State Univ, 50-51; asst biophys, St Louis Univ, 52-53, res assoc biol & biophys, 54-57; fel anat, Wash Univ, 57-62; from asst prof to assoc prof path, St Louis Univ, 62-67; res assoc prof, Baylor Univ, 67-69. *Concurrent Pos:* Fel, Inst Divi Thomae Found, 53-54. *Mem:* Am Soc Cell Biol; Electron Micros Soc Am. *Res:* Experimental virology; histochemistry; differentiation; tissue culture; biological and pathological ultrastructure; electron microscopy. *Mailing Add:* 2104 Gunpowder Rd Little Rock AR 72207

SUN, CHENG, ELECTRICAL ENGINEERING. *Current Pos:* MEM TECH STAFF, ELECTRON DYNAMICS DIV, HUGHES AIRCRAFT CO, 71- *Personal Data:* b Kiang Su, China, Apr 12, 37; m 62; c 1. *Educ:* Nat Taiwan Univ, BS, 58; Cornell Univ, MS, 62, PhD(microwaves), 65. *Prof Exp:* Mem tech staff microwave appl res, RCA David Sarnoff Res Ctr, 64-71. *Mem:* Inst Elec & Electronics Engrs. *Res:* Microwave solid state circuits and devices. *Mailing Add:* Elec Eng Dept Calif Polytech State Univ San Luis Obispo CA 93407

SUN, CHIH-REE, HIGH ENERGY PHYSICS, NUCLEAR PHYSICS. *Current Pos:* RETIRED. *Personal Data:* b Hsu-Chen, China, May 6, 23; m 56; c 3. *Educ:* Univ Calcutta, BSc, 47; Univ Calif, Los Angeles, MS, 51, PhD(physics), 56. *Prof Exp:* Teacher, Overseas Chinese High Sch, India, 47-49; mem res staff physics, Princeton Univ, 56-62; asst prof, Northwestern Univ, 62-65; assoc prof, Queens Col, NY, 65-68; from assoc prof to prof physics, State Univ NY, Albany, 68-94. *Concurrent Pos:* Consult, Princeton Univ, 66-69. *Mem:* Am Phys Soc. *Res:* High energy experiments with bubble chambers study of elementary particles; channeling in crystals; accelerator; nuclear instrumentation. *Mailing Add:* 4127 Cocoplum Circle Coconut Creek FL 33063

SUN, CHIN-TEH, ENGINEERING MECHANICS. *Current Pos:* from asst prof to assoc prof aeronaut & astronaut, 68-76, PROF AERONAUT & ASTRONAUT, PURDUE UNIV, WEST LAFAYETTE, 76- *Personal Data:* b Taiwan, China, Apr 9, 39; m 68; c 1. *Educ:* Nat Taiwan Univ, BS, 62; Northwestern Univ, MS, 65, PhD(mech), 67. *Prof Exp:* Fel, Northwestern Univ, 67-68. *Mem:* Am Inst Aeronaut & Astronaut; Am Acad Mech; Am Soc Mech Engrs; Seismol Soc Am. *Res:* Mechanics of composite materials; stress waves; structures; fracture mechanics. *Mailing Add:* Dept Aero & Astronaut 1282 Grissom Hall Purdue Univ West Lafayette IN 47907-1282

SUN, DEMING, AUTOIMMUNE DISEASE. *Current Pos:* ASST MEM IMMUNOL, DEPT IMMUNOL, ST JUDE CHILDREN'S RES HOSP, 89-; ASSOC PROF, DEPT NEUROL, UNIV ALA, BIRMINGHAM, 96- *Personal Data:* b Shanghai, China, Jan 30, 47; m 72, Xihe Liu; c Shu Sun. *Educ:* Shanghai First Med Col, MD, 71; Albert-Ludwig Univ, Ger, MD, 82. *Prof Exp:* Postdoctoral immunol, Nat Jewish Hosp, Denver, Colo, 85-86; res staff, Max-Planck Inst, Ger, 86-88. *Concurrent Pos:* Res award, Nat Multiple Sclerosis Soc, 91-94 & 96-, NIH, 91-96. *Mem:* Am Asn Immunologists; Int Soc Neuroimmunol. *Res:* Pathogenesis of demyelinating autoimmune disease. *Mailing Add:* 4611 Melissa Way Birmingham AL 35243. *E-Mail:* sun@email.neuro.uab.edu

SUN, FANG-KUO, DYNAMIC SYSTEMS ANALYSIS. *Current Pos:* STAFF ANALYST, SYSTS ENG, ANALYTIC SCI CORP, 77- *Personal Data:* b Taiwan, Repub China, May 8, 46; US citizen; m 70; c 3. *Educ:* Nat Chiao-Tung Univ, Taiwan, BS, 69; Univ Pittsburgh, MS, 72; Harvard Univ, PhD(decision & control), 76. *Prof Exp:* Res assoc syst eng, Sci Res Lab, Ford Motor Co, 76-77. *Mem:* Inst Elec & Electronics Engrs; Soc Indust & Appl Math; Sigma Xi. *Res:* Systems analysis and design; statistical analysis; operations research. *Mailing Add:* 44 Chesquessett Rd Reading MA 01867-1832

SUN, FRANK F, BIOCHEMISTRY. *Current Pos:* res biochemist, Dept Lipid Res, 68-86, RES BIOCHEMIST, DEPT HYPERSENSITIVITY DIS RES, UPJOHN CO, 87- *Personal Data:* b Kiangshi, China, July 26, 38; c 2. *Educ:* Tunghai Univ, Taiwan, BS, 59; Tex Tech Univ, MS, 63; Univ Tex, Austin, PhD(biochem), 66. *Prof Exp:* NIH fel biochem, Purdue Univ, Lafayette, 66-68. *Concurrent Pos:* Vis scientist, Harvard Med Sch, Boston, 84-85. *Mem:* Am Chem Soc; Am Soc Biol Chemists. *Res:* Lipid biochemistry; biochemistry of protagladins, leukohienes and related compounds; drug metabolism. *Mailing Add:* Cell Biol Inflammation Res Upjohn Co Kalamazoo MI 49001-3298

SUN, HUAI, APPLICATION OF QUANTUM MECHANICS AND ACCURATE FORCE FIELD DEVELOPMENT FOR POLYMERS, METAL OXIDES & INTERPHASES. *Current Pos:* SR SCIENTIST, MOLECULAR SIMULATIONS INC, 90- *Personal Data:* b Nanjing, China, Mar 1, 55; US citizen; c 1. *Educ:* Sichuan Univ, BS, 83, MS, 85; Univ Wash, PhD(phys chem), 90. *Concurrent Pos:* Adj prof, Sichuan Univ, 95- *Mem:* Am Chem Soc; Am Phys Soc; Mat Sci Res Soc. *Res:* Quantum mechanics calculations and molecular dynamics simulation of liquids and crystals are combined to develop highly accurate molecular force field that enables large scale computer simulation of materials. *Mailing Add:* 8826 Calle Perico San Diego CA 92129. *E-Mail:* huai@msi.com

SUN, HUGO SUI-HWAN, ALGEBRA, NUMBER THEORY. *Current Pos:* from asst prof to assoc prof, 70-78, PROF MATH, CALIF STATE UNIV, FRESNO, 78- *Personal Data:* b Hong Kong, Oct 19, 40. *Educ:* Univ Calif, Berkeley, BA, 63; Univ Md, College Park, MA, 66; Univ NB, Fredericton, PhD(math), 69. *Honors & Awards:* First Award Anthology, 5th World Cong Poets. *Prof Exp:* Asst prof math, Univ NB, Fredericton, 69-70. *Concurrent Pos:* Vis res prof, Acad Sinica & Peking Univ; hon prof math & lit, Fuyang Teachers Col, 87. *Mem:* Am Math Soc; Math Asn Am; Soc Indust & Appl Math. *Res:* Group theory, number theory, combinatorial analysis, and finite geometry; combinatorics. *Mailing Add:* Dept Math Calif State Univ Fresno CA 93740-0001

SUN, HUN H, ELECTRICAL ENGINEERING. *Current Pos:* from asst prof to assoc prof, 53-59, prof elec eng, 58-78, dir biomed eng & sci prog, 64-73, chmn dept, 73-78, ERNEST O LANGE PROF ELEC ENG, DREXEL UNIV, 78- *Personal Data:* b Shanghai, China, Mar 27, 25; m 51; c 1. *Educ:* Nat Chiao Tung Univ, BS, 46; Univ Wash, MS, 50; Cornell Univ, PhD, 55. *Prof Exp:* Asst elec eng, Cornell Univ, 51-53. *Concurrent Pos:* Mem, Franklin Inst, 60-80; NIH spec fel & res assoc, Mass Inst Technol, 63-64; ed-in-chief, Trans Biomed Eng, Inst Elec & Electronics Engrs, 72-79; mem study comt, Surg & Bioeng Sect, NIH, 81-85; ed-in-chief, Annals Biomed Eng, 84-90. *Mem:* Am Soc Eng Educ; Inst Elec & Electronics Engrs; Biomed Eng Soc; Sigma Xi. *Res:* Biomedical engineering; network analysis and synthesis; feedback control system. *Mailing Add:* Dept Elec Eng Drexel Univ Philadelphia PA 19104

SUN, JAMES DEAN, INHALATION TOXICOLOGY, BIOCHEMICAL TOXICOLOGY. *Current Pos:* ASSOC DIR, BUSHY RUN RES CTR, UNION CARBIDE CORP, 90- *Personal Data:* b Denver, Colo, Feb 8, 51; m 74. *Educ:* Univ Calif, Davis, BS, 73, Riverside, PhD(biochem), 78. *Prof Exp:* Asst, Chem Indust Inst Toxicol, 78-80; inhalation toxicologist, Lovelace Inhalation Toxicol Res Inst, 80-90. *Concurrent Pos:* Mem, comt on fire toxicol, Nat Acad Sci, 85-87, Toxicol Res Task Group, Chem Mfr Asn, 93-; counr, Mt West Chap Soc Toxicol. *Mem:* Soc Toxicol; NY Acad Sci; Sigma Xi. *Res:* Biological fate of inhaled organic compounds associated with insoluable particles; biomarkers of human exposures to organic compounds; chemical metabolite identification; pharmacokinetic modelling; over 60 publications. *Mailing Add:* 833 Babcock Ct Raleigh NC 27609. *Fax:* 412-733-4804

SUN, JAMES MING-SHAN, mineralogy, geophysics, for more information see previous edition

SUN, JIAN, THORACIC DISEASE. *Current Pos:* RES SCIENTIST, OCHSNER MED INST, 94-; ASSOC PROF, SUZHOU MED COL HOSP, 95- *Personal Data:* b Suzhou, China, May 23, 57; US citizen. *Educ:* Suzhou Med Col, MD, 83; Nanjing Med Col, MSc, 89; Univ London, PhD(life sci), 94. *Prof Exp:* Res asst, Suzhou Canglang Hosp, 76-78; resident, Critical Care Unit, Suzhou Med Col Hosp, 83-86, attend physician/lectr, 89-91; vis res fel, Nat Heart & Lung Inst, London, 92. *Mem:* Fel Am Col Chest Physicians; Chinese med Asn. *Res:* Animal models of thoracic disease; investigate mechanisms of their development. *Mailing Add:* BH 616/618 1516 Jefferson Hwy New Orleans LA 70121. *Fax:* 504-842-4906; *E-Mail:* jsuh@ochsner.org

SUN, LU, INTERNAL MEDICINE, CLINICAL PHARMACOLOGY. *Current Pos:* instr, 90-92, HOUSE STAFF & RESIDENT, CREIGHTON MED SCH, 95- *Personal Data:* m 85, Shume Nang; c David & Angela. *Educ:* Nanjing Med Sch, MD, 82; Creighton Univ, PhD(molecular biol), 90. *Prof Exp:* Asst prof, Zhejiang Med Sch, 86-90; fel, NIH, 92-95. *Mem:* Am Soc Pharmacol; Am Soc Molecular Biol. *Res:* Molecular mechanism of genetic disease; endocrinology; hypertension; medical science. *Mailing Add:* 7700 Howard St No 4 Omaha NE 68114

SUN, MING, IMMUNOCHROMATOGRAPHICAL TEST DEVELOPMENT, IMMUNOSENSORS & DIAGNOSTIC DEVICES. *Current Pos:* PRES & CHIEF EXEC OFFICER, SUN BIOMED LABS, INC, 93- *Personal Data:* b Hunan, China; US citizen; m 72, Alice Lo; c Erica R. *Educ:* Univ Colo, BA, 69; Tex Tech Univ, PhD(biochem), 74. *Prof Exp:* Assoc med, Sch Med & Dent, Univ Rochester, 74-76, asst res prof, 76-78; proj mgr, Abbott Labs Inc, 78-84; prog mgr, Becton Dickenson Inc, 84-87; vpres & bd dirs, Drug Screening Systs Inc, 89-92. *Concurrent Pos:* Robert A Welch res fel chem, Tex Tech Univ, 71-72; Am Heart Asn res fel biochem, Univ Rochester, 74-76, NIH res fel med, 76-77; res grant, Rochester Eye & Human Part Bank Inc, 78-79. *Mem:* NY Acad Sci; Am Asn Clin Chemists; Am Chem Soc. *Res:* Developing immunodiagnostics kits for drugs of abuse screening; device design for immunosensors; rapid nonisotopic immunoassay test development; dry chemistry; membrane based reaction system. *Mailing Add:* PO Box 1821 Cherry Hill NJ 08003

SUN, PU-NING, MECHANICAL ENGINEERING. *Current Pos:* asst prof & acting head dept, 64-65, head dept mech eng, 65-68 & 72-84, actg chmn eng div, 68-72, PROF MECH ENG, CHRISTIAN BROS COL, 65- *Personal Data:* b Tientsin, China, Oct 23, 32; m 67; c 2. *Educ:* Nat Taiwan Univ, BS, 54; Tex A&M Univ, MS, 60, PhD(mech eng), 64. *Prof Exp:* Sr inspector, Taiwan Bur Weights & Measures, China, 54-59. *Concurrent Pos:* Am Soc Eng Educ-Ford Found resident fel, Ford Motor Co, 71-72; NSF fel, Nat Bur Standards, 76. *Mem:* AAAS; Am Soc Mech Engrs; Soc Exp Mech; Inst Elec & Electronics Engrs; NY Acad Sci; Am Soc Engr Educ. *Res:* Theoretical and experimental stress analysis; engineering design. *Mailing Add:* Dept Mech Eng Christian Bros Col 650 E Pkwy S No 50 Memphis TN 38104

SUN, RICHARD C, FOUNDRY MELTING & CASTING, ALUMINUM ALLOY HEAT TREATING. *Current Pos:* TECH DIR FOUNDRY RES & DEVELOP, AM RACING CUSTOM WHEELS, 86- *Personal Data:* b Jan 5, 35; US citizen; m 67, Shirley Chiang; c Juliana L & William C. *Educ:* Univ Mo, Rolla, BS, 59; Northwestern Univ, MS, 62; Univ Wis-Madison, PhD(metal eng), 67. *Prof Exp:* Res scientist/metallurgist, Hayes Int Inc, 66-79; metallurgist, Cert Alloy Prods, 79-81; sr res engr, Smith Tool, 81-82; process engr, Coastcast Corp, 83-84; tech dir, V & W Castings, 84-86. *Mem:* Am Foundrymens Soc; Am Soc Metals; Eng Soc Advan Mobility. *Res:* Study and solve the technical problems in relation to casting of aluminum wheels for automobiles; melting permanent mold preparation; foundry operation and heat treating; alternatives including new alloys, different casting and metal working approaches. *Mailing Add:* 13501 Dalewood Ct La Mirada CA 90638-6539

SUN, SAMUEL SAI-MING, AGRIBIOTECHNOLOGY, PLANT MOLECULAR BIOLOGY. *Current Pos:* assoc prof, 87-91, PROF, UNIV HAWAII, 92- *Personal Data:* b Canton, China, Sept 15, 42; m 75; c 1. *Educ:* Chinese Univ Hong Kong, BSc, 66; Univ Hong Kong, BSc, 68, MSc, 71; Univ Wis-Madison, PhD(bot & hort), 75. *Honors & Awards:* Res Award, Arco, 84. *Prof Exp:* Demonstr plant biochem, Dept Bot, Univ Hong Kong, 69-71; res asst, Dept Hort, Univ Wis, 71-74; fel, Univ Wis-Madison, 75-79, asst scientist, 79-80; sr scientist plant biochem, Arco Plant Cell Res Inst, 80-86, prin scientist & dir molecular biol, 86-87. *Concurrent Pos:* Teacher & leader, molecular biol workshop, China, US, 80, 84, 89 & 91; consult, Food & Agr Orgn, 84, 89; vis prof, Beijing Agr Univ, 88-, acad coun mem biotechnol, 91- *Mem:* Int Soc Plant Molecular Biol; Am Soc Plant Physiologists; AAAS; Am Chinese Bioscientist Soc. *Res:* Plant enzyme and protein chemistry; enzyme and protein biosynthesis and their regulation during plant development; structure, organization, and expression of plant genes; agricultural biotechnology. *Mailing Add:* 7008 Niumalu Loop Honolulu HI 96825

SUN, SHUWEI, MAGNETIC THIN FILMS INTERFACE & SURFACE MAGNETISM, III & V NITRIDE THIN FILMS & HARD COATINGS. *Current Pos:* SR DEVELOP ENG, SEAGATE TECH, 95- *Personal Data:* b Qingdao, China. *Educ:* Chinese Acad Scis, MS, 81; Mass Inst Technol, PhD(mat sci), 91. *Prof Exp:* Lectr physics magnetism, Univ Sci & Technol China, 81-84; vis scientist, Mass Inst Technol, 84-85, res asst, 85-91; lab researcher, Boston Univ, 91-95. *Mem:* Am Phys Soc; Mat Res Soc. *Res:* Magnetic-mechanical interactions and magnetic anisotropy at surface, interface and ultrathin films; giant magneto resistance of thin films; wide bandgap semi-conductor films; antiwear and anticorrosive overcoatings. *Mailing Add:* 10309 Portland Ave S Bloomington MN 55420

SUN, SIAO FANG, PHYSICAL CHEMISTRY. *Current Pos:* from asst prof to prof, 64-92, ADJ PROF CHEM, ST JOHN'S UNIV, NY, 92- *Personal Data:* b Shaoshing, China, Feb 19, 22; m 51; c 3. *Educ:* Nat Chengchi Univ, LLB, 45; Univ Utah, MA, 50; Loyola Univ Chicago, MS, 56; Univ Chicago, PhD, 58; Univ Ill, PhD, 62. *Prof Exp:* Prof math, Northland Col, 60-64. *Concurrent Pos:* Vis scientist, Nat Ctr Sci Res, Strasbourg, 75 & Meudon-Bellevue, France, 78; scientist, Max Planck Inst Biophys Chem, Gottingen, WGer, 76 & Carlsberg Lab, Copenhagen, Denmark, 81. *Mem:* Am Chem Soc. *Res:* Theoretical molecular kinetics; physical chemistry of macromolecules. *Mailing Add:* 185 47 80th Rd Jamaica NY 11432-5806

SUN, TUNG-TIEN, BIOCHEMISTRY, CELL BIOLOGY. *Current Pos:* assoc prof dermat & pharmacol, NY Univ Sch Med, 82-86, prof, 86-90, assoc dir, NIH Skin Dis Res Ctr, 88-93, PROF PHARMACOL, NY UNIV SCH MED, 86-, RUDOLF L BAER PROF & DIR, EPITHELIAL BIOL GROUP, DEPT DERMAT, 90-, PROF UROL, 96- *Personal Data:* b China, Feb 20, 47; m 71, Brenda Shih-Ying Bao; c I-Hsing & I-Fong. *Educ:* Nat Taiwan Univ, BS, 67; Univ Calif, Davis, PhD(biochem), 74. *Honors & Awards:* Angus Lectr, Univ Toronto, 86; Pinkus Lectr, Am Acad Dermatpath, 86; Liu Lectr, Stanford Med Sch, 87; Montagna Lectr, Soc Invest Dermat, 89; Susan Swerling Lectr, Harvard Med Sch, 91; Alcon Award for Ophthal Res, 93. *Prof Exp:* Res assoc biol, Mass Inst Technol, 74-77; asst prof dermat, cell biol & anat, Sch Med, Johns Hopkins Univ, 78-81, assoc prof cell biol & anat, dermat & ophthal, 81-82. *Concurrent Pos:* NIH res career develop award, 78, Nat Eye Inst, 84-88; Monique Weill-Caulier career develop award, 83, scientist award, 84-89; bd dirs, Int Soc Differentiation, 85-86; Hair Res Soc, 92-94; Soc Investigative Dermat, 93; assoc ed, J Investigative Dermat, 90-; adj prof, Dept Dermat, Univ Pa Med Sch, 92-; vchair, Gordon Conf Keratinization & Epithelial Differentiation, 93; bd dir, soc invest Dermatol, 93-97; bd sci coun, Nat Inst Arthritis Musculoskeletal & Skin Dis, NITT, 96- *Mem:* Int Soc Differentiation; Soc Investigative Dermat; Asn Res Vision & Ophthal; fel AAAS; Am Soc Biol Chemists; Am Soc Cell Biol; NY Acad Sci. *Res:* Biochemical studies of mammalian epithelial differentiation. *Mailing Add:* 107 Edgemont Rd Scarsdale NY 10583-2715

SUN, WEN-YIN, METEOROLOGY, FLUID DYNAMICS. *Current Pos:* from asst to assoc prof, 79-88, PROF ATMOSPHERIC SCI, DEPT GEOSCI, PURDUE UNIV, 88- *Personal Data:* b I-Lan, Taiwan; c 2. *Educ:* Nat Taiwan Univ, BS, 68; Univ Chicago, MS, 72, PhD(meteorol), 75. *Prof Exp:* Res asst prof, Meteorol Lab Atmospheric Res, Univ Ill, 75-78; vis scientist, Geofluid Dynamics Prog, Princeton Univ, 78-79. *Mem:* Am Meteorol Soc. *Res:* Theoretical and numerical studies of dynamic mesoscale meteorology, boundary layer meteorology, turbulences and pollution modeling. *Mailing Add:* Geo Sci Purdue Univ 600 Essex West Lafayette IN 47907-1968

SUN, XIAOGUANG GEORGE, OPTICAL FIBER COMMUNICATIONS, ELECTROMAGNETIC WAVE PROPAGATION & SCATTERING. *Current Pos:* CHIEF FIBER OPTICS ENGR, C-COR ELECTRONICS INC, 97- *Personal Data:* b Shanxi, China, June 1, 62; m 88, Shaoyun Hong; c Karen, Aaron & Diana. *Educ:* Beijing Inst Technol, BS, 83; Univ Pa, MSE, 86, PhD(elec eng), 89. *Prof Exp:* Postdoctoral fel, Univ Pa, 90-91; sr engr, AEL Industs Inc, 92-95; staff engr, Tracor Aerospace Inc, 96. *Mem:* Inst Elec & Electronics Engrs; Int Soc Optical Eng; Asn Old Crows. *Res:* Optical modulator linearization; fiber nonlinearity suppression; rare earth doped fiber amplifiers; device applications of high temperature superconductivity; advanced radiation detection and location techniques. *Mailing Add:* 2260 Red Oak Lane State College PA 16803. *E-Mail:* xgs@technologist.com

SUN, YAN, molecular physics, for more information see previous edition

SUN, YUN-CHUNG, CHEMICAL ENGINEERING, MATHEMATICS. *Current Pos:* PRES, WESTECH INC, 91- *Personal Data:* b Shaoton, China, Feb 18, 37; US citizen; m 68; c 1. *Educ:* Tunghai Univ, Taiwan, BS, 61; Univ Mo, MS, 64, PhD(chem eng), 66. *Prof Exp:* Instr chem, Univ Mo, 63-66; sr res engr, Dow Chem Co, 66-91. *Concurrent Pos:* Asst prof chem eng, Saginaw Valley Col, 68. *Mem:* Am Inst Chem Engrs; Am Chem Soc. *Res:* Chemical reaction kinetics; component purification and crystallization; polymer sciences. *Mailing Add:* 108 Wilmington Folsom CA 95630

SUNADA, DANIEL K(ATSUTO), WATER RESOURCES. *Current Pos:* PROF CIVIL ENG, COLO STATE UNIV, 65- *Personal Data:* b Newcastle, Calif, Apr 3, 36; m 60; c 3. *Educ:* Univ Calif, Berkeley, BS, 59, MS, 60, PhD(civil eng), 65. *Concurrent Pos:* Res grants, 66-72. *Mem:* Am Soc Civil Engrs; Sigma Xi; Int Comn Irrigation & Drainage. *Res:* Fundamentals of fluid flow through porous media; institutional building of international organization; water resources. *Mailing Add:* 4709 Chippendale Dr Ft Collins CO 80526-3803

SUNAHARA, FRED AKIRA, PHYSIOLOGY. *Current Pos:* prof, 64-89, EMER PROF PHARMACOL, UNIV TORONTO, 89- *Personal Data:* b Vancouver, BC, Jan 22, 24; m 52, Grace Akiko; c Geoffrey I, Pamela R, Ellen H & Roger K. *Educ:* Univ Western Ont, BSc, 48, PhD(physiol), 52. *Prof Exp:* Fel physiol, Univ Western Ont, 52-53; sci officer aviation med, Defence Res Med Lab, Toronto, 53-61; sr pharmacologist, Ayerst Res Lab, Montreal, 61-64. *Concurrent Pos:* Assoc physiol, Univ Toronto, 59-61; Ont Heart Found res grants, 65- *Mem:* Am Physiol Soc; Pharmacol Soc Can. *Res:* Cardiovascular and respiratory physiology with reference to problems in hypobaric environment and disorientation; autonomic and cardiovascular pharmacology; interrelationship of autonomic drugs and eicosanoid group of substances. *Mailing Add:* Dept Pharmacol Med Sci Bldg Univ Toronto Fac Med Toronto ON M5S 1A8 Can. *Fax:* 416-978-6395

SUNAHARA, YOSHIFUMI, theory of vibration & application to engineering problem, for more information see previous edition

SUND, ELDON H, ORGANIC CHEMISTRY. *Current Pos:* RETIRED. *Personal Data:* b Plentywood, Mont, June 6, 30; m 57, Roberta Faulkner; c Sharon, Elizabeth, Phillip & Nancy. *Educ:* Univ Ill, Urbana, BS, 52; Univ Tex, Austin, PhD(org chem), 60. *Prof Exp:* Res chemist, E I du Pont de Nemours & Co, Del, 59-66; asst prof chem, Ohio Northern Univ, 66-67; from asst prof to prof chem, Midwestern State Univ, 67-95, chmn, 84-89. *Concurrent Pos:* Hardin prof, Hardin Found, 75-76; consult, NTex Chem Consult; Fulbright exchange prof, Hat Field Polytech, Eng, 85-86; vis prof, Univ Hawaii, Manoa, Honolulu, Hawaii, 89-90. *Mem:* AAAS; Sigma Xi; Int Soc Heterocyclic Chem; Am Chem Soc. *Res:* Synthesis of heterocyclic compounds. *Mailing Add:* Dept Chem Midwestern State Univ Wichita Falls TX 76308. *E-Mail:* fsunde@nexus.mwsu.edu

SUND, PAUL N, OCEANOGRAPHY, MARINE ZOOLOGY. *Current Pos:* mariculture syst construct, 89-90, LAB TECHNICIAN & RES ASST, HOPKINS MARINE STA, STANFORD UNIV, 93-; AQUARIST, MONTERAY BAY AQUARIUM, 96- *Personal Data:* b Thief River Falls, Minn, Nov 13, 32; m 56, Lorraine M Pilon; c Paul E, Alan C. *Educ:* Univ Calif, Santa Barbara, BA, 54; Univ Wash, Seattle, MA, 56. *Prof Exp:* Biol oceanogr, Inter-Am Trop Tuna Comn, 56-63; oceanogr, Nat Marine Fisheries Serv, 63-67, asst chief br marine fisheries, 67-71, nat coordr, Platforms of Opportunity Progs, 71-77, oceanogr, Pac Environ Fisheries Group, 78-89. *Concurrent Pos:* Mem plankton adv comt, Smithsonian Inst, 64-; adj prof, Fla Atlantic Univ, 66-68; fel, Nat Inst Pub Affairs, 69; CONSULT, 90-95. *Mem:* AAAS; fel Am Inst Fishery Res Biol; Marine Technol Soc; Am Soc Limnol & Oceanog; Marine Biol Asn UK. *Res:* Fishery and zooplankton ecology; chaetognath taxonomy and ecology; biological oceanography relative to biological indicators of water mass; oceanographic and climatological influences on tunas; billfishes and marine mammals; ecology and life history of tropical tunas; aerial remote sensing of marine mammals; satellite oceanography; environmental influences on fertilization of marine invertebrates; bacteria symbionts of marine invertebrate embryos and eggs; tuna husbandry. *Mailing Add:* 56 Country Club Gate Pacific Grove CA 93950

SUND, RAYMOND EARL, NUCLEAR PHYSICS & ENGINEERING. *Current Pos:* RETIRED. *Personal Data:* b Capac, Mich, Dec 14, 32; m 61, Nancy Thomas; c Mark, Laura, Steven & Susan. *Educ:* Univ Mich, BSE(physics) & BSE(math), 55, MS, 56, PhD(physics), 60. *Prof Exp:* Assoc res physicist, Univ Mich Res Inst, 60-61; staff assoc, Gen Atomic Co, San

Diego, 61-63, staff mem, 63-77; engr, Toledo Edison Co, Ohio, 77-80, res & develop dir, 80-86, sr engr, 86-92. *Concurrent Pos:* Mem Radiation Adv Coun, State Ohio, 83-90; chmn, B & W Owners Group Core Performance Comt, 90 & 91. *Mem:* Am Phys Soc. *Res:* Investigation of decay schemes of radioactive isotopes; studies of photonuclear reactions and of prompt and delayed gamma rays from fission; afterheat and shielding studies for reactors; nuclear fuel for commercial reactors. *Mailing Add:* 6014 Glenbeigh Dr Sylvania OH 43560

SUNDA, WILLIAM GEORGE, TOXICOLOGY, CHEMICAL OCEANOGRAPHY. *Current Pos:* RES CHEMIST, BEAUFORT LAB, NAT MARINE FISHERIES SERV, NAT OCEANIC & ATMOSPHERIC ADMIN, 75- *Personal Data:* b Washington, DC, Oct 18, 45. *Educ:* Lehigh Univ, BS, 68; Mass Inst Technol, PhD(chem oceanog), 75. *Concurrent Pos:* Sci officer, Off Naval Res, 91-93. *Mem:* Am Soc Limnol & Oceanography; Am Geophys Union. *Res:* Trace metal chemistry in natural waters; the interaction between trace metal chemistry and aquatic organisms; trace metal nutrition and toxicology. *Mailing Add:* Nat Marine Fisheries Serv Beaufort Lab Beaufort NC 28516

SUNDAHL, ROBERT CHARLES, JR, FIBER OPTICS, ELECTRONIC MATERIALS. *Current Pos:* MGR, INTEL CORP, 88- *Personal Data:* b Minneapolis, Minn, Dec 6, 36; m 58; c 5. *Educ:* Univ Minn, Minneapolis, BS, 58, MS, 64, PhD(metall), 66. *Prof Exp:* Mem tech staff, Bell Lab, 66-73, supvr piezoelec devices, 73-77, ferrite mat, 77-80 & optical & magnetic mat, 80-84; dir mat sci, Signal Res Ctr, 84-88. *Concurrent Pos:* Mem publ comt, Metall Transactions, 70-76; mem ferroelec comt, Inst Elec & Electronics Engrs, 84-87, tech ed bd, Mat Res Soc, 88-90. *Mem:* Am Ceramic Soc; Mat Res Soc; Optical Soc Am. *Res:* Segregation of impurities at ceramic grain boundaries and surfaces; development of high frequency ferrites for telecommunications; design and fabrication of Lithium Niobium Trioxide integrated optic devices; chemical sensors; electronic polymers; structural ceramics; amorphous alloys; advanced non-destructive testing; electronic packaging. *Mailing Add:* Intel Corp 5000 W Chandler Blvd MS C5-137 Chandler AZ 85226

SUNDAR, P, MATHEMATICS, PROBABILITY. *Current Pos:* ASST PROF MATH, LA STATE UNIV, 85- *Personal Data:* b Tirukkoilur, India, Nov 23, 54. *Educ:* Purdue Univ, PhD(statist), 85. *Mailing Add:* La State Univ Baton Rouge LA 70803-0001

SUNDARAM, K M SOMU, ENVIRONMENTAL DISTRIBUTION PERSISTENCE & FATE OF PEST-CONTROL PRODUCTS, ANALYTICAL METHODS DEVELOPMENT. *Current Pos:* PROJ LEADER ENVIRON CHEM, FOREST PEST MANAGEMENT INST, 72- *Personal Data:* b Kanthayapalayam, Madras, India, Oct 13, 27; Can citizen; m 53, Alam; c RS. *Educ:* Annamalai Univ, BSc, 52, MSc, 55, PhD(phys chem), 59; Univ Sydney, PhD(org chem), 62. *Prof Exp:* Asst prof, Annamalai Univ, 52-58; res fel, Sydney Univ, 59-62; assoc prof, Univ Ghana, 63-66, prof, 67-70; res scientist, Can Forest Serv, Govt Can, 71-72, proj leader pesticides, Chem Contaminant Res Inst, 72-76. *Concurrent Pos:* Adj prof chem, Laurentian-Algoma Univ, 78-; adj prof environ chem, Univ Guelph, 86- *Mem:* Fel Royal Australian Chem Inst; fel Royal Inst Chem; fel Am Chem Soc; charter mem Soc Environ Contaminant Toxicol; fel Asn Off Anal Chemists; Chem Inst Can. *Res:* Analytical methods, distribution, deposition, persistence and fate of pesticides and their additives in all the four compartments of the environment; establish their metabolic fate, toxicity, bioaccumulation, biological consequences and impacts on nontarget organisms, including humans and evaluate the risks and benefits. *Mailing Add:* Forest Pest Mgr Inst 1219 Queen St E Box 490 Sault Ste Marie ON P6A 5M7 Can. *Fax:* 705-759-5700

SUNDARAM, KALYAN, BIOCHEMISTRY. *Current Pos:* SCIENTIST, POPULATION COUN, 67- *Personal Data:* b Hyderabad, India, Nov 22, 32; US citizen; m 67; c 2. *Educ:* Osmania Univ, India, BVSc, 55; Univ Man, Can, MSc, 63; Purdue Univ, PhD(animal physiol), 66. *Prof Exp:* Vet, Govt Andhra Pradesh, India, 55-61; fel cancer res, Sloan Kettering Inst, 66-67. *Mem:* Endocrine Soc; Soc Study Reproduction; Am Soc Andrology. *Res:* Hypothalamus, pituitary and gonadal axis; effects of Luteinizing-hormone releasing hormone, and its analogs on pituitary and testicular function; investigation of new methods of chemical contraception in the male; preclinical testing of contraceptive drugs. *Mailing Add:* 75 Southgate Ave Hastings on Hudson NY 10706

SUNDARAM, PANCHANATHAM N, ROCK MECHANICS, SOIL MECHANICS. *Current Pos:* GEOTECK SUPVR, BECHIEL INC, 82- *Personal Data:* b Madras, India, Aug 23, 39; m 66; c 2. *Educ:* Alagappa Col Eng & Technol, India, BE, 61; Col Eng Guindy, India, MSc, 65; Univ Calif, Berkeley, PhD(civil eng), 77. *Prof Exp:* Jr engr civil eng, Public Works Dept, Govt Madras, 61-63; lectr, Indian Inst Technol, Bombay, 66-72; asst prof, Univ Wis, Milwaukee, 78-80; scientist rock mech, Lawrence Berkeley Lab, 80-82. *Concurrent Pos:* Geotech engr, Hallenbeck-McKay Assoc, 73; vis engr, Univ Calif, Berkeley, 78; res award, US Comt Rock Mech, Nat Res Coun, 78. *Mem:* Am Soc Civil Engrs; Int Soc Rock Mech; Underground Space Asn. *Res:* Hydraulic flow through rock fractures; determination of rock properties; electro-osmosis in soils; properties of spent oil-shale. *Mailing Add:* 130 Violet Rd Hercules CA 94547

SUNDARAM, R MEENAKSHI, MATHEMATICAL STATISTICS, OPERATIONS RESEARCH. *Current Pos:* PROF INDUST ENG, TENN TECHNOL UNIV, 80- *Personal Data:* b Salem, India, June 20, 42; US citizen; m 71; c 2. *Educ:* Tex Tech Univ, PhD(indust eng), 76. *Prof Exp:* Asst prof mfg & eng mgt, Old Dominion Univ, 76-78; assoc prof indust & mfr eng, State Univ NY Col Technol, 79. *Mem:* Sr mem Soc Mfg Engrs; sr mem Inst Indust Engrs; Am Soc Mech Engrs; Am Soc Eng Educ. *Res:* Computer aided process planning; selection of sequence of operations in process planning; design and operation of cellular manufacturing systems; machining of free-form surfaces; computer numerical control machining agile manufacturing. *Mailing Add:* 2809 Old Salem Dr Cookeville TN 38501. *Fax:* 615-372-6172; *E-Mail:* mrs2351@tntech.edu

SUNDARAM, SWAMINATHA, OPTICS-MATERIALS RESEARCH, ACADEMIC ADMINISTRATION. *Current Pos:* RETIRED. *Personal Data:* b Madras, India, Oct 22, 24; US citizen; m 46; c 2. *Educ:* Annamalai Univ, India, BSc Hons, 45, MA, 47, PhD(physics), 57, DSc(physics), 60; Ill Inst Technol, MS, 60. *Honors & Awards:* Spectros Award, Soc Appl Spectros, 72. *Prof Exp:* Assoc prof physics, Ill Inst Technol, Chicago, 62-65; prof, Univ Ill, Chicago, 65-82, head dept, 67-76; prof physics & chmn dept, Univ SFla, Tampa, 82-96. *Concurrent Pos:* Lectr, Annamalai Univ, India, 45-57; instr, Ill Inst Technol, Chicago, 57-59; res assoc, Univ Chicago, 59-60; res physicist, BC Res Coun, Vancouver, Can, 60-61; assoc prof mech eng, Univ Sask, Saskatoon, Can, 61-62. *Mem:* Fel Am Phys Soc; Soc Photo-Optical Instrumentation Engrs. *Res:* Electronic materials and high temperature superconductors; optical studies, thin films, III-V and II-VI related MBE, MOCVD heterostructures, ternaries, superlattices, and multiple quantum wells for device applications. *Mailing Add:* Dept Physics Univ SFla Box 30601 Tampa FL 33620. *Fax:* 813-974-5813

SUNDARARAJAN, PUDUPADI RANGANATHAN, POLYMER PHYSICS, BIOPHYSICS. *Current Pos:* res scientist polymer & paper physcis, 75-79, proj leader mat characterization, 79-81, mgr mat characterization, 81-88, PRIN SCIENTIST, XEROX RES CTR CAN LTD, 88- *Personal Data:* b Madras, India, Sept 16, 43; m 70; c 2. *Educ:* Univ Madras, India, BSc, 63, MSc, 65, PhD(biophys). *Hon Degrees:* DSc Univ Madras, India, 81. *Prof Exp:* Res assoc chem, Univ Montreal, 69-71 & 73-75; res assoc, Stanford Univ, 71-73. *Concurrent Pos:* Consult, Biochem Nomenclature, Int Union Pure & Appl Chem, 71-79; adj prof, Univ Waterloo, 89- *Mem:* Am Chem Soc; Chem Inst Can; Am Phys Soc. *Res:* Studies on solution and solid state conformations; structure and morphology of polymers, blends and composites using microscopy diffraction and theoretical methods and relating them to the properties of polymers. *Mailing Add:* Xerox Res Ctr Canada 2660 Speakman Dr Mississauga ON L5K 2L1 Can

SUNDARESAN, MOSUR KALYANARAMAN, ELEMENTARY PARTICLE PHYSICS. *Current Pos:* from asst prof to prof physics, 61-95, prof physics, DISTINGUISHED RES PROF, CARLETON UNIV, 95- *Personal Data:* b Madras, India, Sept 2, 29; Can citizen; m 57, C S Bharathy; c Sudhir & Sujata. *Educ:* Delhi Univ, India, BSc, 47, MSc, 49; Cornell Univ, NY, PhD(theoret physics), 55. *Prof Exp:* Jr res officer, Dept Atomic Energy, Bombay, India, 55-57; fel, Nat Res Coun Can, 57-59; reader physics, Panjab Univ, Chandigarh, India, 59-61. *Mem:* Can Asn Physicists; Am Phys Soc; Am Asn Physics Teachers. *Res:* Theoretical physics, particularly research in quantum field theory. *Mailing Add:* Physics Dept Carleton Univ Ottawa ON K1S 5B6 Can

SUNDARESAN, PERUVEMBA RAMNATHAN, NUTRITIONAL BIOCHEMISTRY. *Current Pos:* toxicologist-biochemist, Div Toxicol, 77-82, RES CHEMIST, DIV NUTRIT, CTR FOOD & APPL NUTRIT, FOOD & DRUG ADMIN, 82- *Personal Data:* b Madras, India, Aug 11, 30; m 70; c 2. *Educ:* Univ Banaras, BSc, 50, MSc, 53; Indian Inst Sci, Bangalore, PhD(biochem), 59. *Prof Exp:* Res asst biochem, Coun Sci & Indust Res, New Delhi, 56-58; res asst, Indian Inst Sci, Bangalore, 58-59; sr res fel, Coun Sci & Indust Res, 59-61; res assoc, Nutrit Biochem Radio Carbon Lab, Univ Ill, Urbana, 61-62; res assoc, Mass Inst Technol, 62-64; Nat Acad Sci-Nat Res Coun res assoc environ biochem, US Army Res Inst Environ Med, Mass, 64-66, res biochemist, 66-68; chief, Lipids Lab, Res Inst, St Joseph Hosp, 68-77. *Concurrent Pos:* NIH res grants co-investr, Dept Animal Sci, Univ Ill, 60-61 & Dept Nutrit & Food Sci, Mass Inst Technol, 61-64; res consult, Millersville Univ, 72-77; consult biochem, Vet Admin Hosp, 73-77, consult tech dir, Infant Metab Diag Lab, 78-82; vis scientist, Vet Admin Hosp, 83- *Mem:* Am Soc Biochem & Molecular Biol; Am Soc Nutrit Sci; Brit Biochem Soc; Am Col Toxicol; Int Asn Vitamin & Nutrit Oncol; fel Am Inst Chemists. *Res:* Biochemical function and metabolism of vitamin A. *Mailing Add:* Div Sci & Appl Technol Off Spec Nutrit, Ctr Food Safety & Appl Nutrit 465 8301 Muirkirk Rd Laurel MD 20708

SUNDARESAN, SANKARAN, CATALYSIS & REACTION ENGINEERING. *Current Pos:* ASST PROF CHEM ENG, PRINCETON UNIV, 80- *Personal Data:* b Madurai, India, June 9, 55. *Educ:* Indian Inst Technol, BS, 76; Univ Houston, MS, 78, PhD(chem eng), 80. *Prof Exp:* Res engr, E I du Pont de Nemours & Co, 81. *Mem:* Am Inst Chem Eng; Am Chem Soc. *Res:* adsorption processes. *Mailing Add:* 652 Paxson Ave Mercerville NJ 08619

SUNDARRAJ, NIRMALA, ophthalmology, corneal development, for more information see previous edition

SUNDBERG, DAVID K, NEURAL CHEMISTRY, PHARMACOLOGY. *Current Pos:* ASSOC PROF PHARMACOL, BOWMAN GRAY SCH MED, WAKE FOREST UNIV, 82- *Educ:* Univ Tex, Dallas, PhD(physiol), 74. *Res:* Neuro-Endocrinology. *Mailing Add:* Dept Physiol & Pharmacol Bowman Gray Sch Med Wake Forest Univ 300 S Hawthorne Rd Winston-Salem NC 27103-2796

SUNDBERG, DONALD CHARLES, POLYMER SCIENCE. *Current Pos:* asst prof, 78-82, dir indust res, 87-90, ASSOC PROF CHEM ENG, UNIV NH, 82-, EXEC DIR SPONSORED RES, 90- *Personal Data:* b Worcester, Mass, Dec 23, 42; m 66; c 2. *Educ:* Worcester Polytech Inst, BSChE, 65; Univ Del, MChE, 68, PhD(chem eng), 70. *Prof Exp:* Sr chem engr, Monsanto Co, Indian Orchard, 69-74; asst prof chem eng, Univ Idaho, 74-78. *Concurrent Pos:* Consult, Chem Polymer Indust; vis scientist, Swed Inst Surface Chem, 84-85. *Mem:* Am Inst Chem Eng; Am Chem Soc; NAm Thermal Anal Soc. *Res:* Polymer science and engineering; emulsion polymerization; polymer composites; polymer morphology. *Mailing Add:* Univ NH Res & Pub Serv Durham NH 03824-3547

SUNDBERG, JOHN EDWIN, FUEL ADDITIVE FORMULATING, PETROLEUM ANALYSIS. *Current Pos:* res chemist polymer chem, Chevron Res & Tech Co, 77-80, res chemist, Process Develop, 80-83, supvr, Safety & Health, 83-85, sr res chemist, Fuel Chem, 85-87, res assoc, Fuel Additive Chem, 87-90, sr res assoc, 90-93, STAFF SCIENTIST, FUEL ADDITIVE CHEM & TECH TEAM LEADER, FUEL ADDITIVE FORMULATING & APPLN TEAM, CHEVRON CHEM CO, 93- *Personal Data:* b China, Nov 21, 47; US citizen; m 71, Carol A Falkenberg; c Heather & Amy. *Educ:* Col Wooster, BA, 70; Univ Calif, PhD(phys org chem), 75. *Prof Exp:* Asst res chemist org chem, United Technol Corp, 75-77. *Mem:* Am Chem Soc; Soc Automotive Engrs. *Res:* Hydroprocessing; heavy oil processing; analysis of heavy oil; coatings; waterproof membranes; chelating agents; polyurethanes; insulation; adhesion; diesel fuel stability; petroleum low-temperature properties; fuel additive formulating; hydrocarbon fuel analysis; fuel additive applications. *Mailing Add:* Chevron Res Co 576 Standard Ave Richmond CA 94801-2021. *Fax:* 510-242-5544

SUNDBERG, KENNETH RANDALL, PHYSICAL CHEMISTRY, GEOLOGICAL CHEMISTRY. *Current Pos:* res chemist, Phillips Petroleum Co, 80-86, sr chem specialist, 86-88, supvr geo-technol, 88-93, SR RES SCIENTIST, PHILLIPS PETROLEUM CO, 93- *Personal Data:* b Coalville, Utah, Dec 4, 45; m 72; c 2. *Educ:* Univ Utah, BS, 68; Iowa State Univ, PhD(phys chem), 75. *Prof Exp:* Res assoc biophys, Dept Biochem & Biophys, Iowa State Univ, 76-77; NSF fel, Dept Chem, Harvard Univ, 77-78. *Mem:* Am Chem Soc; Sigma Xi; Asn Petrol Geochem Explorationists; Am Asn Petrol Geologists. *Res:* Quantum chemistry and electronic structure theory; molecular optics; geochemistry; remote sensing; reservoir engineering; well transient analysis. *Mailing Add:* 2130 S Dewey Bartlesville OK 74003

SUNDBERG, MICHAEL WILLIAM, PHYSICAL CHEMISTRY. *Current Pos:* RES CHEMIST, EASTMAN KODAK CO RES LABS, 73- *Personal Data:* b Battle Creek, Mich. *Educ:* Albion Col, BA, 69; Stanford Univ, PhD(phys chem), 73. *Honors & Awards:* Von Hevesy Prize Nuclear Med, Soc Nuclear Med, 74. *Mem:* Am Chem Soc; AAAS. *Mailing Add:* 200 Fishers Rd Pittsford NY 14534-9745

SUNDBERG, RICHARD J, ORGANIC CHEMISTRY. *Current Pos:* From asst prof to assoc prof, 64-74, PROF CHEM, UNIV VA, 74- *Personal Data:* b Sioux Rapids, Iowa, Jan 6, 38; m 63; c 2. *Educ:* Univ Iowa, BS, 59; Univ Minn, Minneapolis, PhD(org chem), 62. *Concurrent Pos:* NIH res fel, Stanford Univ, 71-72; Fulbright-Hays fel, Inst Chimie Substances Naturelles, CNRS, Gif/Yvette, France, 78-79. *Mem:* Am Chem Soc. *Res:* Synthetic methods in nitrogen heterocyclic chemistry; synthesis of biologically active compounds; photochemical methods of synthesis; anti-cancer compounds; anti-parasitic compounds. *Mailing Add:* Dept Chem Univ Va McCormick Rd Charlottesville VA 22901-1000. *Fax:* 804-924-3710

SUNDBERG, RUTH DOROTHY, ANATOMY. *Current Pos:* RETIRED. *Personal Data:* b Chicago, Ill, July 29, 15; div. *Educ:* Univ Minn, BS, 37, MA, 39, PhD(anat), 43, MD, 53; Am Bd Path, dipl, 60. *Prof Exp:* Technician anat, Univ Minn, 37-39; instr path, Wayne Univ, 39-41; asst, Univ Minn, Minneapolis, 41-43, from instr to assoc prof anat, 43-60, hematologist, Univ Hosps, 42, dir, Hemat Labs, 45-74, prof lab med, Univ, 63-73, prof, 60-84, prof lab med & path, 73-84, hematologist, Univ Hosps, 45-84, co-dir, Hemat Labs, 74-84, emer prof anat, 84. *Mem:* Am Asn Anatomists; Sigma Xi. *Res:* Morphologic hematology; diagnosis by aspiration or trephine biopsy of marrow; lymphocytogenesis in human lymph nodes; histopathology of lesions in the bone marrow; agnogenic myeloid metaplasia; sideroblastic anemia and hemochromatosis; fatty acid deficiency; laboratory medicine. *Mailing Add:* 1255 Shenandoah Ct Marco Island FL 34145

SUNDBERG, WALTER JAMES, MYCOLOGY. *Current Pos:* from asst prof to assoc prof, 72-90, PROF PLANT BIOL, SOUTHERN ILL UNIV, CARBONDALE, 90- *Personal Data:* b San Francisco, Calif, Sept 16, 39; m 64; c 2. *Educ:* San Francisco State Univ, BA, 62, MA, 67; Univ Calif, Davis, PhD(bot), 71. *Prof Exp:* Lectr bot, Univ Calif, Davis, 71-72. *Concurrent Pos:* Consult, Cent & Southern Ill Regional Poison Resource Ctr; counr, Mycol Soc Am, 81-83. *Mem:* Mycol Soc Am; Brit Mycol Soc; NAm Mycol Asn; Nat Educ Asn; Int Mushroom Soc Trop. *Res:* Mycology; cytology; systematics; ecology; ultrastructure of fungi with emphasis on Basidiomycetes. *Mailing Add:* Dept Plant Biol Southern Ill Univ Mail Code 6509 Carbondale IL 62901-6509

SUNDE, MILTON LESTER, POULTRY NUTRITION. *Current Pos:* From asst prof to prof, 51-87, EMER PROF POULTRY SCI, UNIV WIS-MADISON, 87- *Personal Data:* b Volga, SDak, Jan 7, 21; m 46, Genevieve C Larson; c Roger, Scott & Robert. *Educ:* SDak State Col, BS, 47; Univ Wis, MS, 49, PhD, 50. *Honors & Awards:* Res Award, Am Feed Mfrs Asn, 61; Teaching Award, Poultry Sci Asn, 62, Poultry Hist Award, 96. *Concurrent Pos:* Res scientist, Rockefeller Found, Colombia, SAm, 60; mem animal nutrit comt, Nat Res Coun, 70; Int Feed Ingredient Asn travel grant, 71; Am Feed Ingredient Asn travel fel, 72. *Mem:* Am Chem Soc; Soc Exp Biol & Med; Am Inst Nutrit; fel Poultry Sci Asn (2nd vpres, 65, 1st vpres, 66, pres, 67-68); NY Acad Sci; World's Poultry Sci Asn (US br pres, 84-88, vpres, 88-). *Res:* Unidentified factors; vitamins; amino acids; energy for chickens, turkey and pheasants. *Mailing Add:* Poultry Sci Univ Wis 1056 Animal Sci Bldg Madison WI 53706

SUNDE, ROGER ALLAN, NUTRITIONAL BIOCHEMISTRY, SELENIUM BIOCHEMISTRY. *Current Pos:* PROF NUTRIT & BIOCHEM, UNIV MO, COLUMBIA, 90-, NUTRIT CLUSTER LEADER, 90- *Personal Data:* b Madison, Wis, Jan 31, 50; m 88; c 1. *Educ:* Univ Wis-Madison, BS, 72, PhD(biochem), 80. *Honors & Awards:* Archer-Daniels-Midland Award, Am Oil Chemists' Soc, 85; Bio-Serv Award, Am Inst Nutrit, 90. *Prof Exp:* Res assoc biochem, Univ Wis-Madison, 80-81; NIH fel nutrit biochem, Rowett Res Inst, Aberdeen, Scotland, 81-83; asst prof nutrit, Univ Ariz, Tucson, 83-88, assoc prof nutirt & biochem, 88-89. *Concurrent Pos:* Contrib ed, Nutrit Rev, 84-89; nutrit panel mgr, Comptetitive Grants Prog, USDA-Nutrit Res INst, 90-91; vis prof, Japan Sc Prom Sci, 91; mem, Inorg Discussion Group, Royal Soc Chem. *Mem:* Am Inst Nutrit; Am Soc Biochem & Molecular Biol; Am Chem Soc. *Mailing Add:* Nutrit Cluster Univ Mo 217 Gwynn Hall Columbia MO 65211-0001. *Fax:* 573-882-0185; *E-Mail:* hesrds@mizzou1.edu

SUNDEEN, DANIEL ALVIN, PETROLOGY, GEOCHEMISTRY. *Current Pos:* PROF GEOL, UNIV SOUTHERN MISS, 71- *Personal Data:* b Manchester, NH, Sept 25, 37; m 59; c 2. *Educ:* Univ NH, BA, 65; Ind Univ, MA, 67, PhD(geol), 70. *Concurrent Pos:* Geologist Gulf Mex, Standard Oil Co, Tex, 66; explor geologist, SW USA, Chevron, 69-71; SE Alaska, Pac Cordillera Explor, 76 & Us Geol Surv Kilauea eruption, Hawaii, 83; mem, Joint Comt Powder Diffraction Stand, Int Ctr Diffraction Data. *Mem:* Geol Soc Am; Mineral Soc Am. *Res:* Subsurface volcanic province and tectonism and associated mineralization in the Gulf Coastal Plain of Mississippi; igneous and metamorphic petrology; Mesozoic dikes and other plutons in Southeast New Hampshire; boracite mineralization in salt formations. *Mailing Add:* Dept of Geol Southern Sta MSS Box 5044 Hattiesburg MS 39406-0002. *Fax:* 601-266-5026

SUNDEEN, JOSEPH EDWARD, ORGANIC CHEMISTRY. *Current Pos:* investr cardiovasc res, 69-76, INVESTR ANTI-INFLAMMATORY RES, SQUIBB INST MED RES, 76- *Personal Data:* b Manchester, NH, Nov 5, 43; m 64; c 3. *Educ:* Rensselaer Polytech Inst, BS, 64; Purdue Univ, PhD(chem), 68. *Prof Exp:* Fel org chem, Syntex Res Div, Syntex Corp, 68-69. *Mem:* Am Chem Soc. *Res:* Cardioactive medicinals; anti-arthritics; anti-ulcer compounds. *Mailing Add:* 1108 Pratt Dr Yardley PA 19067-2835

SUNDELIN, KURT GUSTAV RAGNAR, ORGANIC CHEMISTRY, MEDICINAL CHEMISTRY. *Current Pos:* CHEMIST, AGR PROD, E I DUPONT DE NEMOURS INC, 86- *Personal Data:* b Pitea, Sweden, Dec 21, 37; US citizen; m 63; c 5. *Educ:* Idaho State Univ, BS, 62 & 65, MS, 65; Univ Kans, PhD(med chem), 69. *Prof Exp:* Chemist Biol Sci Res Ctr, Shell Develop Co, 69-86. *Mem:* Am Chem Soc. *Res:* Organic chemical synthesis of biologically active agents in area of crop protection chemicals. *Mailing Add:* 25 Longspur Dr Wilmington DE 19808-1972

SUNDELIN, RONALD M, RADIO FREQUENCY SUPERCONDUCTIVITY. *Current Pos:* ASSOC DIR, CONTINUOUS ELECTRON BEAM ACCELERATOR FACIL, 87- *Personal Data:* b New York, NY, Oct 20, 39; m 67, Esther M Frew; c Beth & John. *Educ:* Mass Inst Technol, BS, 61; Carnegie Inst Technol, MS, 63, PhD(physics), 67. *Prof Exp:* Res physicist, Carnegie-Mellon Univ, 67-69; res assoc elem particle physics, Wilson Lab, 69-75, sr res accoc elem particle physics, Newman Lab, Cornell Univ, 75-87. *Concurrent Pos:* Consult, Continuous Electron Beam Accelerator Facil Nat Adv Bd, 86, mem, 85-87, prin investr, 86-87; gov distinguished CEBAF prof, Va Polytech Inst & State Univ, 87- *Mem:* Fel Am Phys Soc; Sigma Xi. *Res:* Medium energy experimental physics, especially muon physics; high energy experimental physics; accelerator physics; normal and superconducting radio frequency. *Mailing Add:* 210 Artillery Rd Yorktown VA 23692-4224

SUNDELIUS, HAROLD WESLEY, GEOLOGY. *Current Pos:* RETIRED. *Personal Data:* b Escanaba, Mich, July 6, 30; m 55, Charlene Swanson; c Karin & Kristine. *Educ:* Augustana Col, AB, 52; Univ Wis, MS, 57, PhD(geol), 59. *Prof Exp:* Geologist mil geol br, US Geol Surv, 59-61, regional geologist eastern br, 61-65; from asst prof to prof geol, Wittenberg Univ, 65-75, assoc dean col, 71-75; vpres acad affairs & dean col, Augustana Col, Ill, 75-88, prof geol, 88-95. *Concurrent Pos:* Consult, Exxon Minerals Dept, 68-75. *Mem:* Fel Geol Soc Am; fel Soc Econ Geol; Nat Asn Geol Teachers; Sigma Xi. *Res:* Appalachian geology, especially Piedmont; economic geology and mineral economics; military geology; geology of the Carolina slate belt; Precambrian geology of the Lake Superior region; massive sulfide deposits in greenstone belts. *Mailing Add:* Augustana Col Rock Island IL 61201

SUNDELL, HAKAN W, PEDIATRICS, NEWBORN MEDICINE. *Current Pos:* instr pediat, 70-71, asst prof pediat neonatology, 71-79, ASSOC PROF PEDIAT NEONATOLOGY, SCH MED, VANDERBILT UNIV, 79- *Personal Data:* b Stockholm, Sweden, July 22, 36; US citizen; m 66; c 3. *Educ:* Karolinska Inst, Stockholm, MD, 63. *Prof Exp:* Resident pediat, Milwaukee Children's Hosp, Marquette Univ, 64-66; fel, neonatal physiol, Sch Med, Vanderbilt Univ, 66-68; pediatrician, Karolinska Inst, Stockholm, 69-70.

Mem: Soc Pediat Res; Microcirculatory Soc; Am Physiol Soc; AMA; Am Acad Pediat. *Res:* Total and newborn pulmonary pathophysiology; hyaline membrane disease and Group B streptococcal pneumonia; apnea reflexes in the newborn period. *Mailing Add:* Dept Pediat Vanderbilt Univ Sch Med U1212 MCN Nashville TN 37232-2585

SUNDER, SHAM, SPECTROSCOPY, SURFACE CHEMISTRY. *Current Pos:* assoc res officer, 79-85, RES OFFICER, ATOMIC ENERGY CAN, LTD, 86- *Personal Data:* b June 5, 42; Can citizen; m 79, Heather Martin; c 2. *Educ:* Univ Delhi, BSc Hons, 62, MSc, 64; Univ Alta, Can, PhD(chem), 72. *Prof Exp:* Fel res, Univ Alta, Can, 72-73 & Nat Res Coun Can, 73-75; res assoc, Nat Res Coun, 75-78; lectr, Heidelberg Univ, Ger, 78-79. *Mem:* Can Inst Chem; Spectros Soc Can; Can Chem Soc; Can Nuclear Soc; Can Inst Synchrotron Radiation. *Res:* Surface chemistry; spectroscopy; electrochemistry; corrosion; nuclear fuel; waste management; nuclear chemistry; radiolysis effects; kinetics; modelling. *Mailing Add:* Atomic Energy Can Ltd Pinawa MB R0E 1L0 Can. *Fax:* 204-753-2455; *E-Mail:* sunders@aecl.ca

SUNDERLAND, JAMES EDWARD, MECHANICAL ENGINEERING. *Current Pos:* PROF MECH ENG, UNIV MASS, AMHERST, 72- *Personal Data:* b Philadelphia, Pa, Oct 26, 32; m 57; c 9. *Educ:* Mass Inst Technol, SB, 54; Purdue Univ, MS, 56, PhD(eng), 58. *Prof Exp:* Instr, Purdue Univ, 57-58, asst prof mech eng, Northwestern Univ, 58-62; assoc prof, Ga Inst Technol, 62-65, prof, 65-67; prof mech & aerospace eng, NC State Univ, 67-72. *Concurrent Pos:* Pub Health Serv grant, 62-69; NSF grant, 66-68; consult engr; US Army grant, 81- *Mem:* Fel Am Soc Mech Engrs; Am Soc Heating, Refrigerating & Air-Conditioning Engrs; Inst Food Technologists; Am Solar Energy Soc. *Res:* Conduction, convection and radiation heat transfer; heat and mass transfer in biological systems; energy conservation; two-component external flow; freeze-drying; computer aided engineering; seasonal storage of solar energy; heat transfer in injection molding. *Mailing Add:* Dept Mech & Indust Eng Univ Mass Amherst MA 01003. *Fax:* 413-545-2178; *E-Mail:* sunderland@ecs.umass.edu

SUNDERLIN, CHARLES EUGENE, ORGANIC CHEMISTRY. *Current Pos:* RETIRED. *Personal Data:* b Reliance, SDak, Sept 28, 11; m 36, Sylvia Sweetman; c Anne E, Mary C, Katherine P & William D. *Educ:* Univ Mont, AB, 33; Oxford Univ, BA, 35; Univ Rochester, PhD(chem), 39. *Prof Exp:* Instr chem, Union Col, NY, 38-41; instr, US Naval Acad, 41-43, from asst prof to assoc prof, 45-46; sci liaison officer, US Off Naval Res, London, 46-47, from dept sci dir to sci dir, 48-51; dep dir, NSF, 51-57; dep dir, Union Carbide Europ Res Assocs, SA, Belg, 57-62; res mgr, Defense & Space Systs Dept, Union Carbide Corp, 62-65; spec asst to pres, Nat Acad Sci, 65-69; vpres & secy, Rockefeller Univ, 69-76; spec asst, Nat Sci Bd, 76-78. *Concurrent Pos:* US deleg gen assembly, Int Coun Sci Unions, Amsterdam, 52 & Oslo, 55; US deleg, Dirs Nat Res Ctrs, Milan, 55; mem, Comt Experts Scientists' Rights, Paris, 53; Workshop Indust Develop Taiwan, Repub China, Nat Acad Sci, 68; chmn, Am Inst Aeronaut & Astronaut & Am Soc Mech Engrs Ninth Struct, Struct Dynamics & Mat Comt, 68. *Mem:* Fel AAAS; Am Chem Soc; Royal Soc Chem; Royal Inst Gt Brit; Brit Soc Chem Indust. *Res:* Research administration and management; international cooperation in science and technology. *Mailing Add:* 3036 P St NW Washington DC 20007

SUNDERMAN, DUANE NEUMAN, RESEARCH ADMINISTRATION. *Current Pos:* sr vpres, 83-90, EXEC VPRES, MIDWEST RES INST, 90-; DIR, SOLAR ENERGY RES INST, 90- *Personal Data:* b Wadsworth, Ohio, July 14, 28; m 53; c 3. *Educ:* Univ Mich, AB, 49, MS, 54, PhD(chem), 56. *Prof Exp:* Res chemist, Argonne Nat Lab & E I du Pont de Nemours & Co, 51-52; res chemist, Savannah River Proj, 52-54; res asst, Univ Mich, 54-55; prin chemist, 56, proj leader, 56-58; asst div chief, 58-59; chief chem physics div, 59-65, assoc mgr physics dept, 65-69; coordr basic res, 67-69; asst dir, 69-70, mgr soc & mgt systs dept, 70-73, assoc dir, 73-74, dir tech develop, 74-75, assoc dir res, 75-79, dir prog develop, Battelle Mem Inst, 83- *Concurrent Pos:* Partic prog mgt develop, Harvard Bus Sch, 69; trustee, Columbus Area Leadership Prog, 75-78; trustee, Mo Corp Sci & Technol & Univ Kans. *Mem:* Am Chem Soc; Am Nuclear Soc; hon mem Am Soc Testing & Mat. *Res:* Nuclear fuel development; environmental research; energy research; technical management. *Mailing Add:* 4187 Stellar Dr Hilliard OH 43026-2556

SUNDERMAN, F WILLIAM, JR, CLINICAL PATHOLOGY, TOXICOLOGY. *Current Pos:* PROF LAB MED & DEPT HEAD, SCH MED, UNIV CONN, 68-, PROF PHARM, 80-, PROF TOXICOL, 86- *Personal Data:* b Philadelphia, Pa, June 23, 31; m 63, Carolyn Reynolds; c Frederick, Elizabeth & Emily. *Educ:* Emory Univ, BS, 52; Jefferson Med Col, MD, 55. *Honors & Awards:* Clin Sci Award, 77; Ames Res Award, 78; Nickel Res Award, Int Union Pure & Appl Biophys, 93. *Prof Exp:* Intern, Jefferson Med Col Hosp, 55-56, instr med, 60-63, assoc, 63-64; from assoc prof to prof path & dir clin lab, Col Med, Univ Fla, 64-68. *Mem:* Am Asn Cancer Res; Am Asn Clin Chem; Am Asn Path; Soc Toxicol; Am Soc Clin Path; Am Col Physicians; Asn Clin Scientists (pres, 64-65); Col Am Pathologists; Endocrine Soc; Am Soc Pharmacol Exp Therapeut. *Res:* Experimental carcinogenesis, trace metal metabolism, and toxicology; clinical biochemistry; environmental teratogens. *Mailing Add:* Depts Lab Med & Pharmacol Univ Conn Health Ctr Farmington CT 06030-2225

SUNDERMAN, FREDERICK WILLIAM, INTERNAL MEDICINE, CLINICAL PATHOLOGY. *Current Pos:* prof, 71-88, EMER PROF PATH & LAB MED, HAHNEMANN MED COL, 88- *Personal Data:* b Altoona, Pa, Oct 23, 98; m 25, 80, Martha-Lee Taggart; c Louise (deceased), Frederick W Jr & Joel B (deceased). *Educ:* Gettysburg Col, BS, 19; Univ Pa, MD, 23, MS, 27, PhD(phys chem), 29; Am Bd Internal Med, dipl, 37; Am Bd Path, dipl, 44. *Hon Degrees:* ScD, Gettysburg Col, 52. *Honors & Awards:* Gold Headed Cane Award, Asn Clin Scientists, 74; Claude P Brown Mem Lectr, 77; Ward Burdick Award, Am Soc Clin Pathologists, 75; Silver-Plate Award, 76; Henry M Scharf Mem Lectr, Gettysburg Col, 77; Outstanding Contrib Clin Chem Educ Award, Am Asn Clin Chem, 81; Pres Hon Award, Col Am Pathologists, 84; Pres Richard von Weizsacker Order Merit, Fed Republic Ger, 89. *Prof Exp:* Instr, Gettysburg Acad, 19; asst dermat, Univ Pa, 23, from instr to assoc prof res med, 25-47, lectr, 34-47, ward physician, Univ Hosp, 34-40, from assoc to chief chem div, Wm Pepper Lab, Univ Pa Sch Med, 33-47; prof clin path & res med, Sch Med, Temple Univ & dir lab clin med, Univ Hosp, 47-48; head, clin path, Cleveland Clin Found, 48-49; dir clin res, Univ Tex MD Anderson Hosp & Tumor Inst, 49-50; prof clin med, Emory Univ, 49-51; prof clin med & dir div metab res, Jefferson Med Col, 51-67, attend physician, 51-76, co-chmn dept, lab med, 71-74, hon clin prof, 75-, dir, Inst Clin Sci, 65- *Concurrent Pos:* Consult metab res, Vet Admin Hosp, Philadelphia, Pa, 53-70; med dir explosives res lab, US Bur Mines, Carnegie Inst Technol, 43-46; actg med dir & med consult, Brookhaven Nat Lab, 47-50; consult, Los Alamos Sci Lab, 47-50, US Army Ord, Redstone Arsenal, 47-69; trustee & vpres, Am Bd Path, 48-51, life trustee, 61-; prof, Post-Grad Sch Med, Univ Tex, 49; dir clin labs, Grady Mem Hosp, Atlanta, 49-51; dir educ, Asn Clin Scientists, 49-; chief clin path, Commun Dis Ctr, USPHS, 50-; med adv, Rohm & Haas Co, 50-71; consult & lectr path, US Naval Med Sch, 54-55, 57-59 & 62-63; dir, Int Seminars Clin Chem & Path, 54-; mem, Pa Governor's Task Force Environ Health, 68-75; ed-in-chief, Annals Clin Lab Sci, 71-; consult path, Pa Hosp, 88-; assoc ed, Am J Clin Path, 40-50, ed-in-chief, Annals Clin & Lab Sci, 71-, cons ed, Am J Occup Med, 79-85. *Mem:* Fel Am Soc Clin Path (pres, 50); fel Am Soc Clin Invest; fel Am Chem Soc; Asn Clin Scientists (pres, 56-58); fel Col Am Path; Int Union Pure & Appl Chem; AAAS; Sigma Xi; Am Inst Biol Sci; AMA; Am Indust Hyg Asn; fel Am Asn Clin Chem; Asn Clin Biochemists; Int Soc Hemat; fel Am Col Physicians; Am Occup Med Asn; Am Soc Biol Chemists; hon mem Soc Pharmacol & Environ Pathologists; Am Soc Clin Pharmacol & Therapeut; hon mem Soc Toxicol Pathologists. *Res:* Serum electrolytes; hazards of nickel and nickel carbonyl exposure; metabolism; clinical chemistry; research medicine; author of numerous publications. *Mailing Add:* Inst Clin Sci Duncan Bldg Suite 3A Pa Hosp 301 S Eighth St Philadelphia PA 19106. *Fax:* 215-829-3094

SUNDERMAN, HERBERT D, SOIL FERTILITY, TILLAGE SYSTEMS. *Current Pos:* asst prof, 75-82, ASSOC PROF AGRON, KANS STATE UNIV, 82- *Personal Data:* b Horton, Kans, Sept 19, 37; m 62, JoAnne Jenison; c Matthew O & Tara J. *Educ:* Kans State Univ, BS, 65, MS, 67; Tex A&M Univ, PhD(soil fertility), 76. *Prof Exp:* Res asst agron, Kans State Univ, 65-67; res assoc, Tex A&M Univ, 67-75. *Concurrent Pos:* Agronomist, Cotton Inc, 82; actg head, Colby Branch Exp Sta, Kans State Univ, 86-87. *Mem:* Am Soc Agron; Soil Sci Soc Am. *Res:* Soil fertility and cultural practices in reduced- and no-tillage systems; transitions from irrigated to dryland cropping; rotations; alternative crops. *Mailing Add:* 105 Experiment Farm Rd Colby KS 67701

SUNDET, SHERMAN ARCHIE, MEMBRANES, TEXTILE FIBERS. *Current Pos:* RETIRED. *Personal Data:* b Litchville, NDak, Sept 25, 18; m 44; c 5. *Educ:* Concordia Col, BS, 39; Univ Idaho, MS, 41; Univ Minn, PhD(org chem), 48. *Prof Exp:* Chemist, B F Goodrich Co, Ohio, 42-45; instr org chem, Univ Calif, Los Angeles, 48-50; res chemist, Textile Fibers Dept, Pioneering Res Div, E I Du Pont De Nemours & Co Inc, 50-54, res supvr, 54-70, res assoc, Polymer Prod Dept, 70-85, sr res assoc, 85-90. *Mem:* AAAS; Am Chem Soc; Sigma Xi. *Res:* Membranes for water desalination. *Mailing Add:* 4485 Yarrow St Wheat Ridge CO 80033-3251

SUNDFORS, RONALD KENT, SOLID STATE PHYSICS. *Current Pos:* Res assoc, 63-65, from asst prof physics to assoc prof, 65-76, PROF PHYSICS, WASH UNIV, ST LOUIS, 76- *Personal Data:* b Santa Monica, Calif, June 3, 32; m 63; c 3. *Educ:* Stanford Univ, BS, 54, MS, 55; Cornell Univ, PhD(exp physics), 63. *Mem:* AAAS; Am Phys Soc; Am Asn Physics Teachers. *Res:* Nuclear magnetic resonance; low temperature physics; semiconductor research; ultrasonics; acoustic coupling to nuclear spins. *Mailing Add:* Dept Physics Wash Univ St Louis MO 63130

SUNDGREN, JAN-ERIC, PHYSICS. *Current Pos:* PROF PHYSICS, LINKOPING UNIV, SWEDEN. *Honors & Awards:* John A Thornton Mem Award & Lectr, Am Vacuum Soc, 95. *Mailing Add:* Dept Tech Linkoping Univ Linkoping 58183 Sweden

SUNDICK, ROY, IMMUNOLOGY. *Current Pos:* asst prof, 74-79, ASSOC PROF IMMUNOL & MICROBIOL, SCH MED, WAYNE STATE UNIV, 79- *Personal Data:* b Brooklyn, NY, May 8, 44; m 81; c 1. *Educ:* Harpur Col, BA, 65; State Univ NY Buffalo, MA, 69, PhD(microbiol), 72. *Prof Exp:* Austrian Res Coun fel, Inst Gen & Exp Path, Univ Vienna, 71-73. *Mem:* Am Asn Immunol; Am Thyroid Asn. *Res:* Pathogenesis of autoimmune thyroid disease. *Mailing Add:* Dept Immunol & Microbiol Wayne State Univ Sch Med 540 E Canfield Ave Detroit MI 48201-1908. *Fax:* 313-577-1155

SUNDIN, DAVID A, OCCUPATIONAL SAFETY & HEALTH. *Current Pos:* Chief, Hazard Surveillance Sect, 71-91, CHIEF, HAZARD EVALUATIONS & TECH ASSISTANCE BR, DIV SURVEILLANCE HAZARD EVALUATIONS & FIELD STUDIES, 91- *Personal Data:* b Cheyenne, Wyo, June 19, 1950. *Educ:* Univ Wyo, BA, 71; Harvard Univ, MBA, 76; NKy Univ, JD, 83. *Mem:* Am Indust Hyg Asn. *Mailing Add:* 4676 Columbia Pkwy Cincinnati OH 45226. *Fax:* 513-841-4488

SUNDSTEN, JOHN WALLIN, NEUROSCIENCES. *Current Pos:* from instr to asst prof, 62-70, ASSOC PROF ANAT, SCH MED, UNIV WASH, 70- *Personal Data:* b Seattle, Wash, Jan 16, 33; m 63; c 6. *Educ:* Univ Calif, Los Angeles, AB, 56, PhD(anat), 61. *Prof Exp:* Asst anat, Sch Med, Univ Calif, Los Angeles, 57-59; NSF fel, 61-62. *Concurrent Pos:* Vis scientist, USPHS, 64-66; USPHS res grant, 64-70; NIH spec fel, Bristol, Eng, 68-69; vis prof, Univ Malaya, 73-74. *Mem:* AAAS; Am Asn Anatomists; Soc Neurosci. *Res:* Structural informatics: preparation of neuroanatomical digital database for multimedia access and 3D reconstruction; quantitation of developing central nervous system. *Mailing Add:* Dept Biol Structure Univ Wash Sch Med Seattle WA 98195. *E-Mail:* jws@u.washington.edu

SUNG, ANDREW HSI-LIN, SOFTWARE ENGINEERING, EXPERT SYSTEMS. *Current Pos:* asst prof, 87-89, chmn comput sci, 88-93, ASSOC PROF COMPUT SCI, NMEX INST MINING & TECHNOL, 89- *Personal Data:* b Taipei, Taiwan, Nov 29, 53; m 83, Cindy Lin; c David L. *Educ:* Nat Taiwan Univ, BS, 76; Univ Tex-Dallas, MS, 80; State Univ NY-Stonybrook, PhD(computer sci), 84. *Prof Exp:* Asst prof comput sci, Univ Tex, Dallas, 84-87. *Mem:* Asn Comput Mach; Inst Elec & Electronics Engrs. *Res:* Testing and validation of computer software; parallel processing and supercomputing; neural networks; software engineering; computational complexity theory; neural networks. *Mailing Add:* Comput Sci Dept NMex Tech Socorro NM 87801-4682. *Fax:* 505-835-5587; *E-Mail:* sung@nmt.edu

SUNG, AN-MIN JASON, INSULATION MATERIALS FOR ELECTRONIC & ELECTRICAL APPARATUS, ELECTRONIC PACKAGING. *Current Pos:* MAT ENGR MGR, ROCKWELL AUTOMATION, 97- *Personal Data:* m, Jie Ren. *Educ:* Fu-Jen Cath Univ, BS, 82; Univ Chin-Hua, MS, 84; Univ Akron, PhD(polymer sci), 91. *Prof Exp:* Prin engr, Chung-Shen Res Inst Sci Technol, 84-87; polymer scientist, Reliance Elec, 92-94, supvr, 94-96. *Res:* Develop insulation materials for electrical and electronic apparatus. *Mailing Add:* 24451 Lakeshore Blvd No 811 Euclid OH 44123. *Fax:* 216-266-7714; *E-Mail:* ajsung@re.re.rockwell.com

SUNG, CHANGMO, ELECTRON MICROSCOPY, ADVANCED CERAMICS. *Current Pos:* MEM TECH STAFF ELECTRON MICROS, GTE LABS, 90- *Personal Data:* b Seoul, Korea, Mar 15, 55; m 81; c 1. *Educ:* Seoul Nat Univ, Korea, BS, 79, MS, 81; Ohio State Univ, MS, 84; Lehigh Univ, PhD(mat sci & eng), 88. *Prof Exp:* Res fac ceramics, Mat Res Ctr, Lehigh Univ, 88-90. *Mem:* Electron Micros Soc Am; Am Soc Metals; Am Ceramic Soc; Mat Res Soc. *Res:* Characterization of ceramics, composites, thin films of GTE Incorporation using analytical transmission electron microscopy. *Mailing Add:* 21 Oak Hill Rd Wayland MA 01778

SUNG, CHENG-PO, BIOCHEMISTRY, BIOCHEMICAL PHARMACALOGY. *Current Pos:* assoc sr investr, Smith Kline & French Labs, 69-77, SR INVESTR, DEPT PHARMACOL & BIOL SCI, SMITH-KLINE LABS, 78- *Personal Data:* b Hsinchu, Taiwan, Oct 21, 35; m 65; c 2. *Educ:* Chung Hsing Univ, Taiwan, BSc, 59; McGill Univ, PhD(biochem), 67. *Prof Exp:* Fel biochem, McGill Univ, 66-67; res scientist, Food & Drug Directorate, Dept Nat Health & Welfare, Can, 67-68; res assoc, dept pharmacol, Univ Wis, 68-69. *Mem:* AAAS; NY Acad Sci; Am Chem Soc. *Res:* Receptor binding and study of vasoactive compounds; endothelial cell biology. *Mailing Add:* Smith Kline Beckman Corp L510 709 Swedeland Rd King of Prussia PA 19406

SUNG, CHEN-YU, DRUG METABOLISM & PHARMACOKINETICS, HEPATOPHARMACOLOGY. *Current Pos:* asst prof, 54-63, PROF PHARMACOL, CHINESE ACAD MED SCI, BEIJING, 63- *Personal Data:* b Anguo Xian, China, May 22, 15; m 45; c 4. *Educ:* Yenching Univ, Beiping, China, BS, 41; George Washington Univ, Washington, DC, MS, 49; Univ Calif, San Francisco, PhD(pharmacol), 52. *Prof Exp:* Asst, chem, Yenching Univ, Beiping, China, 41; res assoc, chem, Oriental Chem Co, Tianjin, China, 42-46; lectr, pharmaceut chem, Dept Pharm, Med Col, Peking Univ, 46-48; postdoctoral, pharmacol, Univ Calif San Francisco, 52-53; instr, pharmacol, Med Sch, Tufts Col, Boston, 53-54. *Concurrent Pos:* Ed-in-chief, Acta Pharmaceut Sinica, 78-; adv, Expert Comt Selection Essential Drugs, WHO, 79-83; mem, Exec Comt Int Union Pharmacol Sect Drug Metab, 86-90; assoc ed-in-chief, J Biomed & Environ Sci, 89- *Mem:* Am Soc Pharmacol & Exp Therapeut; Int Soc Study Xenobiotics; Chinese Pharmacol Soc; Chinese Pharmaceut Asn. *Res:* Pharmacology and phasmacokinetics of some constituents isolated from Chinese folk medicine or Chinese traditional medicine in cooperation with chemists with the purpose of discovering new drugs for the treatment of diseases. *Mailing Add:* Dept Pharmacol Inst Mat Med One Xian Nong Tan St 3R 53 Beijing 100050 China. *Fax:* 86-01-3017757

SUNG, CHI CHING, THEORETICAL PHYSICS. *Current Pos:* assoc prof, 72-78, PROF PHYSICS, UNIV ALA, HUNTSVILLE, 78- *Personal Data:* b Nanking, China, Mar 5, 36; m 68. *Educ:* Taiwan Nat Univ, BS, 57; Univ Calif, Berkeley, PhD(physics), 65. *Prof Exp:* Res assoc physics, Ohio State Univ, 65-67, lectr, 67-68, asst prof, 68-72. *Concurrent Pos:* Consult, Oak Ridge Nat Lab & US Army Missile Command, Hunstville, Ala. *Mem:* Fel Am Optical Soc. *Res:* Optics; quantum electronics. *Mailing Add:* Dept Physics Univ Ala Huntsville AL 35899

SUNG, CHIA-HSIAING, SYSTEMS ENGINEERING, SOFTWARE ENGINEERING. *Current Pos:* sr staff engr, 78-86, SCIENTIST/ENGR, HUGHES AIRCRAFT CO, LOS ANGELES, 86- *Personal Data:* b Ping-Tung, Taiwan, Sept 4, 39; US citizen; m 68; c 3. *Educ:* Univ Tex, Austin, BSEE, 66, MSEE, 68, PhD(elec eng), 71. *Prof Exp:* Sr mem tech staff, Taiwan Telecommun Admin, 61-64; asst res engr, Univ Tex, Austin, 66 & 71; asst prof elec eng & comput sci, Tex A&I Univ, 71-72; vis asst prof elec eng & vis res asst prof, Coord Sci Lab, Univ Ill, Champaign-Urbana, 72-74; asst prof comput sci & elec eng, Univ Louisville, 74-78. *Mem:* Inst Elec & Electronics Engrs; Asn Comput Mach; Am Soc Eng Educ. *Res:* Fault-tolerant spaceborne data processing systems; distributed sytems; microprocessor-based system for improving automobile fuel economy; software satellite-spacecraft simulator. *Mailing Add:* 4721 Steele St Torrance CA 90503

SUNG, CHONG SOOK PAIK, PHYSICS. *Current Pos:* vis prof, Dept Chem, 83-84, PROF PHYSICS, UNIV CONN, 84- *Educ:* Seoul Nat Univ, BS, 68; Polytech Inst NY, MS, 69, PhD(polymer chem), 72. *Prof Exp:* Asst prof, Dept Mat Sci & Eng, Mass Inst Technol, 76-79, assoc prof, 79-83, prin res assoc, 83-84. *Concurrent Pos:* Vis prof, Sch Advan Physics & Chem, Paris, 89, Dept Polymer Sci, Kyoto Univ, Inst Chem Res, 90. *Mem:* Am Chem Soc; fel Am Phys Soc. *Res:* Experimental polymer physical chemistry; development and applications of reactive labeling technique and ultraviolet/VIS fluoroscopy and Fourier transfer infrared internal reflection dichroism for characterization of polymerization Kinetics-mechanisms; water-uptake; oxidation; free volume distribution; surface structure and polymer adsorption. *Mailing Add:* IMS U-136 Univ Conn 97 N Eagleville Rd Storrs CT 06269-3136

SUNG, CYNTHIA, BIOMEDICAL ENGINEERING, PHARMACOLOGY. *Current Pos:* SR STAFF FEL, BIOMED ENG & INSTRUMENTATION PROG, NIH 89- *Personal Data:* b New York, NY. *Res:* Biomedical engineering; pharmacology; drug transport. *Mailing Add:* Biomed Eng & Instrumentation Prog Bldg 13 Rm 3W13 NIH Bethesda MD 20892

SUNG, JOO HO, PATHOLOGY, NEUROPATHOLOGY. *Current Pos:* from asst prof to assoc prof, 62-69, PROF NEUROPATH, MED SCH, UNIV MINN, MINNEAPOLIS, 69- *Personal Data:* b Korea, Feb 18, 27; US citizen; m 59; c 3. *Educ:* Yonsei Univ, Korea, MD, 52. *Prof Exp:* Resident path, Newark Beth Israel Hosp, 54-57; fel neuropath, Col Physicians & Surgeons, Columbia Univ, 57-61, asst prof, 61-62. *Concurrent Pos:* Nat Inst Neurol Dis & Stroke fel, Columbia Univ, 59-61; consult, Minneapolis Vet Admin Hosp, 62-68; mem, NIH Neurol Sci Res Training Comt, 70-73; vis prof, Med Col, Yonsei Univ, Korea, 72. *Mem:* Am Asn Neuropath; Am Acad Neurol; Asn Res Nerv & Ment Dis. *Res:* Aging changes in the nervous system; x-radiation effects on the nervous system. *Mailing Add:* Path Box 198 Mayo Univ Minn Med Sch 420 Delaware St SE Minneapolis MN 55455-0374

SUNG, KUO-LI PAUL, BIOLOGICAL ENGINEERING. *Current Pos:* assoc res bioengr III & lectr, Dept Appl Mech & Eng Sci, 88-92, ASSOC PROF, ORTHOP DEPT & ASSOC PROF, BIOENG DEPT, UNIV CALIF, 92- *Educ:* Col William & Mary, MA, 75; Columbia Univ, MS, 77; Rutgers-Columbia Univ, PhD(physiol), 82. *Hon Degrees:* PhD, Chongqing Univ, China, 93. *Honors & Awards:* Melville Medal, Am Soc Mech Engrs, 90; Lamport Award, Biomed Eng Soc, 92. *Prof Exp:* Res asst, Dept Physiol, Columbia Univ, 74-77, res worker, 77-81, staff assoc sci, Dept Physiol & Cellular Biophys, 82-88, lectr, Div Circulatory Physiol & Biophys, Col Physicians & Surgeons, 86-87; lectr, Inst Biomed Sci, Academia Sinica, 87. *Concurrent Pos:* New investr res award, NIH, 84-87; mem, Cancer Ctr, Univ Calif, San Diego, 91, Inst Biomed Eng, 91-; lectr Bioeng Ctr, Chongqing Univ, China, 93. *Mem:* AAAS; Am Physiol Soc; NAm Soc Biorheology; Int Soc Biorheology; Biomed Eng Soc; Microcirculatory Soc; Sigma Xi. *Res:* Influence of tumor suppressor genes on tumor cell metastasis; biophysical properties and molecular organization of cell membranes; healing mechanism of human ligament cells; adhesion between osteoblast and biomaterials; biophysical properties of blood cells and endothelial cells in inflammatory response; energy balance and molecular mechanisms of cell-cell interactions in immune response; intracellular ions, intracellular transmition and cell activation. *Mailing Add:* Dept Orthop Univ Calif Bioeng Div R-012 9500 Gilman Dr La Jolla CA 92093-0412

SUNG, LANPING AMY, MOLECULAR BIOLOGY. *Current Pos:* ASSOC RES BIOENG & LECTR, UNIV CALIF, SAN DIEGO, 88-, MEM, CTR MOLECULAR GENETICS, 89-, MEM, INST BIOMED ENG, 90- *Personal Data:* b Taiwan. *Educ:* Taiwan Univ, BS, 71; Col William & Mary, MA, 74; Columbia Univ, MPharm, 80, PhD(genetics), 81. *Mem:* Int Soc Biorheology; Sigma Xi; Am Physiol Soc; Am Soc Hemat; Biomed Eng Soc; Am Soc Cell Biol. *Mailing Add:* Dept Anesthesiol-Bioeng Basic Sci Univ Calif San Diego EBUL 6406 MC 0412 La Jolla CA 92093-0412

SUNG, MICHAEL TSE LI, MOLECULAR BIOLOGY, BIOCHEMISTRY. *Current Pos:* asst prof, 71-75, ASSOC PROF BIOCHEM, SOUTHERN ILL UNIV, 75- *Personal Data:* b Chung King, China, Mar 5, 40; US citizen; m 68; c 2. *Educ:* Kans State Col, BA, 62; Univ Wis, PhD(molecular biol), 68. *Prof Exp:* Helen Hay Whitney Found fel, Dept Biochem, Univ BC, 68-71. *Mem:* Am Chem Soc; Sigma Xi. *Res:* Chromatin structure and function; structure and function of nuclear proteins. *Mailing Add:* Bioanaltika Labs Inc 2300 Englert Dr Suite A Durham NC 27713-4450

SUNG, SHEN-SHU, PEPTIDE FOLDING SIMULATION, MOLECULAR MODELING. *Current Pos:* ASST STAFF, CLEVELAND CLIN FOUND RES INST, 90-; ASST PROF, CASE WESTERN RES UNIV, 95- *Personal Data:* b Beijing, China, Sept 19, 47; US citizen; m 78, Lulu Xu; c Annie Xiaoyin Xu. *Educ:* Beijing Univ Chem Technol, BS, 75; Cornell Univ, MS, 81, PhD(theoret chem), 84. *Prof Exp:* Postdoctoral res assoc, Brandeis Univ, 84-88; computational chemist, Stanford Res Inst, 88-90. *Mem:* Am Chem

Soc; Am Phys Soc; Biophys Soc; Protein Soc; AAAS. *Res:* Protein structures and folding, including molecular modeling of proteins and peptide folding simulations; Monte Carlo simulations and molecular dynamics simulations at constant temperature. *Mailing Add:* Cleveland Clin Found FF3 Cleveland OH 44195. *Fax:* 216-444-9263; *E-Mail:* sungs@cesmtp.ccf.org

SUNG, SHUNG H, ACOUSTICS, STRUCTURAL DYNAMICS. *Current Pos:* assoc res engr, 76-85, STAFF RES ENGR, GEN MOTORS RES & DEVELOP CTR, 85- *Personal Data:* b Taipei, Taiwan, Mar 20, 50; US citizen; m 83, Donald J Nefske. *Educ:* Nat Taiwan Univ, BS, 72; Purdue Univ, MS, 74, PhD(aeronaut eng), 76. *Prof Exp:* Res asst, Physics Lab, Acad Sinica, Taiwan, 72; teaching asst, Sch Aeronaut & Astronaut, Purdue Univ, 73-76. *Mem:* Am Soc Mech Engrs; Sigma Xi. *Res:* Acoustics, dynamics and vibration; structural analysis and design; finite element methods; solid-fluid interaction. *Mailing Add:* 4178 Drexel Dr Troy MI 48098-4310

SUNG, YUN-CHEN, COMPUTER SOFTWARE. *Current Pos:* SOFTWARE DEVELOPER, METROLIGHT STUDIOS, LOS ANGELES. *Educ:* Calif Inst Technol, BS; Univ Calif, Los Angeles, MS. *Prof Exp:* staff, Digital Prod, Whitney/Demos Prod. *Res:* Contributed to opening animation sequence in the film Labyrinth. *Mailing Add:* Metrolight Studios 5724 W Third St Suite 400 Los Angeles CA 90036-3078

SUNG, ZINMAY RENEE, PLANT DEVELOPMENTAL BIOLOGY. *Current Pos:* from asst prof to assoc prof, Dept Genetics, 76-89, PROF, DEPT PLANT BIOL, UNIV CALIF, BERKELEY, 89-, ASSOC DEAN, GRAD DIV. *Personal Data:* b Shanghai, China, Feb 16, 47; m 74, Nelson Teng. *Educ:* Nat Taiwan Univ, BS, 67; Univ Calif, Berkeley, PhD(plant physiol), 73. *Prof Exp:* Res asst cell physiol, Max Planck Inst Cell Physiol, WBerlin, Ger, 67-68; res assoc, Univ Calif, Berkeley, 68-73; res assoc somatic genetics, Dept Biol, Mass Inst, Technol, 73-76. *Mem:* Am Soc Plant Physiologists; Am Soc Develop Biologists; Int Soc Plant Molecular Biologists. *Res:* Plant somatic genetics; developmental genetics of plants; genetics of shoot maturation and flowering. *Mailing Add:* Dept Plant Biol Univ Calif Berkeley CA 94720-0001

SUNKARA, SAI PRASAD, tumor biology, enzyme inhibitors, for more information see previous edition

SUNLEY, JUDITH S, NUMBER THEORY. *Current Pos:* assoc prof dir, 80-81, prog dir algebra & number theory, 81-84, DIR, DEP DIV, NSF, 84- *Personal Data:* b Detroit, Mich, July 26, 46. *Educ:* Univ Mich, BS, 67, MS, 68; Univ Md, PhD(math), 71. *Prof Exp:* Asst prof math, Dept Math, Statist & Comput Sci, Am Univ, 71-75, assoc prof, 75-81. *Mem:* Am Math Soc. Res; Math Asn Am; Asn Women Math; AAAS. *Res:* Eisenstein series of Siegel Modular Group; generalized prime discriminants in totally real fields; class numbers of totally imaginary quadratic extensions of totally real fields. *Mailing Add:* 5421 Duvall Dr Bethesda MD 20816

SUNSHINE, GEOFFREY H, TOLERANCE INDUCTION, ACTIVATION IMMUNE RESPONSE. *Current Pos:* ASSOC PROF IMMUNOL, DEPT SURG, VET MED SCH, TUFTS UNIV, 85- *Personal Data:* b May 17, 48; div; c 2. *Educ:* Univ Col London, Eng, BSc(biochem), 69, PhD(biochem), 73. *Mem:* Am Asn Immunologists. *Res:* Antigen Presentation. *Mailing Add:* 16 Laudholm Rd Newton MA 02158. *Fax:* 781-466-6010

SUNSHINE, IRVING, CLINICAL CHEMISTRY, TOXICOLOGY. *Current Pos:* RETIRED. *Personal Data:* b New York, NY, Mar 17, 16; m 39; c 2. *Educ:* NY Univ, BS, 37, MA, 41, PhD, 50, Am Bd Clin Chem, dipl; Am Bd Forensic Toxicol, dipl. *Honors & Awards:* Ames Award, Am Asn Clin Chemists, 73; Toxicol Award, Am Acad Forensic Sci, 80. *Prof Exp:* Instr chem, Newark Col Eng, 41-47; asst prof, NJ State Teachers Col, 47-50; toxicologist & clin chemist, City of Kingston Lab, NY, 50-51; sr instr path & pharmacol, 51-54, from asst prof to assoc prof, 54-73, prof toxicol in path & med, Case Western Res Univ, 73-86; toxicologist, Cuyahoga County Coroners Lab, 51-86. *Concurrent Pos:* Toxicologist, Univ Hosp, Cleveland, Ohio; Fulbright fel, Vrije Univ, Brussels, 79; toxicol consult, WHO, 83. *Mem:* Am Chem Soc; Am Asn Clin Chemists; Am Acad Forensic Sci; Am Asn Poison Control Ctrs; Soc Forensic Toxicologists; Int Asn Forensic Toxicologists. *Res:* Alcohol; barbiturates; toxicology methodology; poison prevention programming; drug abuse. *Mailing Add:* 28150 S Woodland Rd Cleveland OH 44126

SUNSHINE, MELVIN GILBERT, MOLECULAR BIOLOGY. *Current Pos:* res assoc, 73-78, RES SCIENTIST MICROBIOL, UNIV IOWA, 78- *Personal Data:* b Chicago, Ill, Oct 14, 36; m 70; c 2. *Educ:* Univ Ill, BS, 58; Univ Southern Calif, PhD(bact), 68. *Prof Exp:* Res microbiologist, San Diego State Col, 67-68; Jane Coffin Childs Mem Fund Med Res fel, Karolinska Inst, Sweden, 68-70; USPHS trainee, Dept Molecular Biol & Virus Lab, Univ Calif, Berkeley, 70-72; vis asst prof microbiol, Sch Med, Univ Southern Calif, 72-73. *Mem:* Am Soc Microbiol. *Res:* Bacterial genetics; genetics of the temperate bacterial viruses P2 and P4; host factors associated with phages P2 and P4. *Mailing Add:* 340 Raven St Iowa City IA 52245

SUNSHINE, WARREN LEWIS, ORGANIC CHEMISTRY. *Personal Data:* b Passaic, NJ, Sept 10, 47; m 72; c 1. *Educ:* Columbia Univ, AB, 68; Rutgers Univ, MS, 70, PhD(org chem), 74; Fairleigh Dickinson Univ, MBA, 88. *Prof Exp:* NIH res fel natural prods, Univ Va, 74-76; sr chemist cosmetic prods, Am Cyanamid Co, 76-79; sr res scientist, Johnson & Johnson, 79-89; sr res scientist, McNeil Consumer Prod Co, 89-96. *Mem:* Am Chem Soc; Am Asn Pharmaceut Scientists. *Res:* Natural products; medicinal chemistry; consumer product formulations in pharmaceuticals and toiletries. *Mailing Add:* 256 Westwind Way Dresher PA 19025-1417

SUNTHARALINGAM, NAGALINGAM, RADIOLOGICAL PHYSICS. *Current Pos:* from instr radiol physics to assoc prof radiol, 62-72, prof radiol & radiation therapy, 72-97, EMER PROF, THOMAS JEFFERSON UNIV MED COL, 97- *Personal Data:* b Jaffna, Ceylon, June 18, 33; m 61; c 3. *Educ:* Univ Ceylon, BSc, 55; Univ Wis, MS, 66, PhD(radiol sci), 67. *Prof Exp:* Asst lectr physics, Univ Ceylon, 55-58. *Concurrent Pos:* Vis lectr, Grad Sch Med, Univ Pa, 67-72, consult dept physics, 68-72; consult, WHO, 72; chmn bd, Am Col Med Physics, 88. *Mem:* Am Asn Phys Med (pres, 83); Health Physics Soc; fel Am Col Radiol; fel Am Col Med Physics. *Res:* Radiation dosimetry; thermoluminescence dosimetry; clinical dosimetry. *Mailing Add:* 7 Clifton Ct Vorhees NJ 08043

SUNUNU, JOHN HENRY, HEAT TRANSFER, FLUID MECHANICS. *Current Pos:* PRES, JHS ASSOC LTD, 92- *Personal Data:* b Havana, Cuba, July 2, 39; US citizen; m 58; c 8. *Educ:* Mass Inst Technol, BS, 61, MS, 63, PhD(mech eng), 66. *Prof Exp:* Chief engr, Astro Dynamics, Inc, 60-65; from asst prof to assoc prof mech eng, Tufts Univ, 66-82, assoc dean, Col Eng, 68-73; chief of staff, White House, 89-91. *Concurrent Pos:* Consult various indust & govt; pres, JHS Eng Co, 66-83 & Thermal Res, Inc, 68-83; mem, Coun Environ Qual Adv Comt Advan Automotive Power Systs; chmn bd, Student Competitions on Relevant Eng, Inc, 71-; chmn, New Technol Educ Task Force, Nat Gov Asn, 87; mem, Pub Eng Policy Comt, Nat Acad Eng; mem, Pres Coun Environ Qual Adv Comt. *Mem:* Nat Acad Eng; Am Soc Mech Engrs; Acad Appl Sci; Sigma Xi; AAAS. *Res:* Heat transfer and temperature control; slow viscous fluid dynamics; approximate methods of mathematical analysis of fluid phenomena; design and optimization of heat transfer equipment. *Mailing Add:* JHS Assoc Ltd 815 Connecticut Ave NW Suite 1200 Washington DC 20006. *Fax:* 202-835-1674

SUOMI, STEPHEN JOHN, DEVELOPMENTAL PSYCHOBIOLOGY, PRIMATOLOGY. *Current Pos:* CHIEF, LAB COMP ETHOLOGY, NAT INST CHILD HEALTH & HUMAN DEVELOP, 83- *Personal Data:* b Chicago, Ill, Dec 16, 45; m 75. *Educ:* Stanford Univ, BA, 68; Univ Wis, MA, 69, PhD(psychol), 71. *Honors & Awards:* Effron Lectr, Am Col Neuropsychopharmacol, 81; Prokasy Lectr, Univ Utah, 83. *Prof Exp:* Res assoc primatology & lectr psychol, Univ Wis-Madison, 71-75, from asst prof to prof psychol, 75-84. *Concurrent Pos:* Prin investr, NSF & NIMH res grants, 75-83; vis scientist, Ctr Interdisciplinary Studies, Univ Bielefeld, 77-78; affil scientist, Wis Regional Primate Res Ctr, 77-; asst dir, res primate behav NIMH, 84-87; adj prof psychol, Univ Wis-Madison, 84-; gov coun, Soc Res Child Develop, 85-; assoc ed, Psychiatry, 86-91; distinguished sci lectr, Am Psychol Asn, 91. *Mem:* Soc Res Child Develop; Int Primatological Soc (secy Americas, 76-84); fel Am Psychol Asn; Int Soc Study Behav Develop; Int Soc Develop Psychobiol; Am Soc Primatologists. *Res:* Biological and behavioral features of development in human and nonhuman primates; genetic and environmental influences on developmental processes; comparative ethology. *Mailing Add:* 9200 Bardon Rd Bethesda MD 20814

SUOMI, VERNER EDWARD, meteorology; deceased, see previous edition for last biography

SUOZZI, JOSEPH JOHN, ELECTRICAL ENGINEERING. *Current Pos:* mem tech staff, 55-60, supvr magnetic memories, 60-65, dept head magnetic power components, 65-80, DEPT HEAD MAGNETIC BUBBLE MEMORIES, BELL TEL LABS, 80- *Personal Data:* b New York, NY, Mar 2, 26; m 52; c 5. *Educ:* Cath Univ, BEE, 49, MEE, 54; Carnegie Inst Technol, PhD(elec eng), 58. *Prof Exp:* Instr elec eng, Cath Univ, 49-50; test planning engr, Western Elec Co, 50-52; electronic engr, US Naval Ord Lab, 52-55. *Concurrent Pos:* Prog chmn, Int Conf Magnetics, 63, vchmn, 64, gen chmn, 65 & 67; ed-in-chief, Trans on Magnetics, Inst Elec & Electronics Engrs, 65-67; chmn, Int Elec Conf Exec Comt, 80-82. *Mem:* Inst Elec & Electronics Engrs. *Res:* Magnetic amplifiers, especially on feedback in magnetic amplifiers; magnetic power components; energy management systems; computer magnetics. *Mailing Add:* 81 Chimmey Ridge Dr Convent Station NJ 07961

SUPERSAD, JANKIE NANAN, CIVIL & TRANSPORTATION ENGINEERING. *Current Pos:* from asst prof to assoc prof, 70-75, coordr civil eng, 76-81, chmn civil & surv eng, 82-83, PROF CIVIL ENG, SCH ENG, CALIF STATE UNIV, FRESNO, 75- *Personal Data:* b Chaguanas, Trinidad, Feb 8, 29; m 57; c 3. *Educ:* Glasgow Univ, BS, 53; Northwestern Univ, Evanston, MS, 58; Ariz State Univ, PhD(civil eng), 65. *Prof Exp:* Eng asst, Crouch & Hogg, Consult Civil Engrs, Glasgow, Scotland, 53-54; asst engr, Considere Constructions Ltd, Scotland, 55; exec engr, Ministry of Works, Trinidad, WI, 55-60, sr roads engr, 61-64, chief planning engr, 64-68; asst prof faculty eng, Sir George Williams Univ, 68-70. *Concurrent Pos:* Faculty assoc eng, Col Eng, Ariz State Univ, 62-64. *Mem:* Am Soc Civil Engrs; Inst Traffic Engrs; Brit Inst Hwy Engrs; Am Soc Eng Educ; Am Road & Transp Builders Asn. *Res:* Urban transportation planning techniques; highway economics with special reference to under-developed countries. *Mailing Add:* 6237 N Colonial Ave Fresno CA 93704

SUPLINSKAS, RAYMOND JOSEPH, CHEMISTRY. *Current Pos:* PRIN STAFF SCIENTIST, TEXTRON, 77- *Personal Data:* b Hartford, Conn, Aug 29, 39; m 59, Janet Mainello; c Paul, Deborah & Michael. *Educ:* Yale Univ, BS, 61; Brown Univ, PhD(chem), 65. *Prof Exp:* Mem tech staff, Bell Tel Labs,

64-65; assoc prof chem, Yale Univ, 65-72; assoc prof & chmn, Swarthmore Col, 72-77. *Concurrent Pos:* Prin staff scientist, Spec Mat Div, Avco, 77-86. *Mem:* Sigma Xi; AAAS. *Res:* Chemical vapor deposition of ceramic fibers and their use in high-performance structural composites; inorganic polymer precursors for ceramics and fibers; carbon-carbon composites. *Mailing Add:* Textron Specialties Mat Div 2 Indust Ave Lowell MA 01852

SUPPE, FREDERICK (ROY), NATURE OF SCIENTIFIC KNOWLEDGE, AGRARIAN PHILOSOPHY. *Current Pos:* assoc prof philos, 73-83, chairperson comt hist & philos sci, 75-83, PROF PHILOS, UNIV MD, COLLEGE PARK, 83- & PROF, SCH NURSING, BALTIMORE, 84- *Personal Data:* b Los Angeles, Calif, Feb 22, 40. *Educ:* Univ Calif, Riverside, AB, 62; Univ Mich, AM, 64, PhD(philos), 67. *Honors & Awards:* Amicus Poloniae Award, Poland, 75. *Prof Exp:* Instr philos, Univ Mich, 64-67; asst prof, Univ Ill, Urbana, 67-73. *Concurrent Pos:* Educ adv, Indo-Am Prog, USAID, Kanpur, India, 65-67; NSF res grant, 73; Am Coun Learned Soc int travel award, 74; mem adv bd, Nat Workshop Teaching Philos, 74-75; lectr, Sch Nursing, Univ Md, Baltimore, 80-84. *Mem:* Philos Sci Asn (chmn, 76); Sigma Xi; Soc Agr Food & Human Values. *Res:* Nature of scientific knowledge, including structure of theories and models, explanation, facts and scientific observation; growth of scientific knowledge; scientific realism, history of the philosophy of science; automata theory; sexual morality and sex research methodology; nursing theory; agrarian philosophy. *Mailing Add:* RR 2 Mt Jackson VA 22842

SUPPE, JOHN, GEOLOGY, GEOPHYSICS. *Current Pos:* from asst prof to prof, 71-85, BLAIR PROF GEOL, PRINCETON UNIV, 85- *Personal Data:* b Los Angeles, Calif, Nov 30, 42; m 65; c 2. *Educ:* Univ Calif, Riverside, BA, 65; Yale Univ, PhD(geol), 69. *Prof Exp:* Assoc res geologist, Yale Univ, 69; NSF fel geol, Univ Calif, Los Angeles, 69-71. *Concurrent Pos:* Assoc ed, Am J Sci, 75-81; vis prof, Nat Taiwan Univ, 78-79 & 82-83, Calif Inst Technol, 88-89 & Univ Barcelona, 95; Guggenheim fel, 78-79; guest investr, NASA Magellan Mission Venurs. *Mem:* Nat Acad Sci; Geol Soc Am; Am Geophys Union; Am Asn Petrol Geologists. *Res:* Structural geology; tectonics; regional structural geology. *Mailing Add:* Dept Geosci Princeton Univ Guyot Hall Princeton NJ 08544-1003

SUPPES, PATRICK, STATISTICS. *Current Pos:* From instr to assoc prof, Stanford Univ, 50-59, prof, Dept Philos, 59-92, chmn, 63-69, Lucie Stern prof, 75-92, LUCIE STERN EMER PROF, STANFORD UNIV, 92- *Personal Data:* b Tulsa, Okla, Mar 17, 22; m 46, 70, 79; c 4. *Educ:* Univ Chicago, BS, 43; Columbia Univ, PhD, 50. *Hon Degrees:* Dr Soc Sci, Univ Nijmegen, Neth; Dr, Univ Paris, 82. *Honors & Awards:* Palmer O Johnson Mem Award, Am Educ Res Asn, 67; John Smyth Mem lectr, Victorian Inst Educ Res, Australia, 68; Distinguished Sci Contrib Award, Am Psychol Asn, 72, E L Thorndike Award for Distinguished Psychol Contrib Educ, 79; S Richardson Silverman Lectr Hearing & Deafness, Cent Inst Deaf, Washington Univ, St Louis, Mo, 79; Nat Medal Sci, 90. *Concurrent Pos:* Fel, Ctr Advan Study Behav Sci, 55-56; fel, NSF, 56-57; dir, Inst Math Studies Social Sci, Stanford Univ, 59-, prof by courtesy, Dept Statist, 60-, Sch Educ, 67-, Dept Psychol, 73-; res award, Social Sci Res Coun, 59; pres, Comput Curric Corp, Palo Alto, Calif, 67-90; fel, John Simon Guggenheim Mem Found, 71-72; vis prof, Col France, Paris, 79 & 88; William James fel, Am Psychol Soc, 89. *Mem:* Nat Acad Sci; fel Am Psychol Asn; fel AAAS; Am Asn Univ Profs; Am Educ Res Asn (pres, 73-74); Sigma Xi; Nat Acad Educ (pres, 73-77); fel Am Acad Arts & Sci; Soc Exp Psychologists; Int Union Hist & Philos Sci (pres 76, 78). *Res:* Theory of measurement; computer-assisted instruction; mathematical psychology; author of numerous publications. *Mailing Add:* Ventura Hall Stanford Univ Stanford CA 94305-4115

SUPPLE, JEROME HENRY, ORGANIC CHEMISTRY. *Current Pos:* PRES & PROF CHEM, SW TEX STATE UNIV, 89- *Personal Data:* b Boston, Mass, Apr 27, 36; m 64; c 3. *Educ:* Boston Col, BS, 57, MS, 59; Univ NH, PhD(org chem), 63. *Prof Exp:* Res chemist, Univ Calif, Berkeley, 63-64; asst prof org & gen chem, 64-69, assoc dean arts & sci, 72-73, actg assoc provost, State Univ NY Cent Admin, 74-75, assoc vpres acad affairs, 73-78, chmn dept chem, 75-76; assoc prof org & gen chem, State Univ NY, Fredonia, 69-78, vpres acad affairs & prof, Col Plattsburgh, 78-79, acting provost & vpres acad affairs, Potsdam, 88-89. *Concurrent Pos:* NSF sci fac fel, Univ E Anglia, 70-71. *Mem:* AAAS; Am Chem Soc; Sigma Xi. *Res:* Heterocyclic chemistry; natural products; stereochemistry; organic spectroscopy; conformational studies in the heterocyclic systems; narcotic antagonists; homogeneous catalysis. *Mailing Add:* Southwest Tex State Univ 601 University Dr San Marcos TX 78666. *Fax:* 512-245-8088; *E-Mail:* jsol@a1.swt.edu

SUPRENANT, BRUCE A, CONCRETE, CONSTRUCTION. *Current Pos:* ASSOC PROF CIVIL ENG, UNIV S FLA, 86- *Personal Data:* b Dec 29, 52; c 1. *Educ:* Bradley Univ, BS; Univ Ill, Urbana, MS; Mont State Univ, Bozeman, PhD(civil eng). *Prof Exp:* Struct engr, Suerdrup & Parcel, 74-76; instr, Dept Civil Eng & Eng Mech, Mont State Univ, Bozeman, 78-84; assoc prof civil eng, Univ Wyo, Laramie, 85-86; pres, Suprenant Consult Serv, 78- *Concurrent Pos:* Consult, Portland Cement Asn, Concrete Construct Inst; ed-in-chief, J Forensic Eng, 85-; vis assoc prof, Univ Colo. *Mem:* Sigma Xi; Am Soc Civil Engrs; fel Am Concrete Inst; Am Soc Testing & Mat; Nat Asn Corrosion Engrs; Mat Res Soc; Transp Res Bd; Nat Forensic Soc; Prestressed Concrete Inst. *Res:* Failure analysis of concrete and masonry structures, materials and construction. *Mailing Add:* 7720 Ferris Way Boulder CO 80303

SUPRUNOWICZ, KONRAD, MATHEMATICS. *Current Pos:* assoc prof, 61-69, PROF MATH, UTAH STATE UNIV, 69- *Personal Data:* b Pulkovnikov, Siberia, Mar 3, 19; US citizen; m 52; c 1. *Educ:* Univ Nebr, BSc, 52, MA, 53, PhD(math), 60. *Prof Exp:* Instr physics, Minot State Col, 54-55; instr math, Univ Nebr, 57-60; asst prof, Univ Idaho, 60-61. *Concurrent Pos:* Vis assoc prof, Univ Nebr, 62-63. *Mem:* Asn Symbolic Logic; Math Asn Am; Am Math Soc. *Res:* Application of symbolic logic to the study of relational systems; methodology of science. *Mailing Add:* 246 N300E Providence Providence UT 84332

SUPRYNOWICZ, VINCENT A, ENGINEERING HISTORY, ELECTRONICS. *Current Pos:* res prof, 64-90, EMER PROF ELEC ENG, UNIV CONN, 90- *Personal Data:* b Middletown, Conn, Sept 1, 23; m 47; c 3. *Educ:* Ohio State Univ, BSc, 47, MSc, 49; Yale Univ, PhD(physics, biophys), 53. *Prof Exp:* Anal engr, Pratt & Whitney Nuclear Aircraft Proj, 52-54; asst prof physics, Bucknell Univ, 54-56; assoc prof appl sci, Univ Cincinnati, 56-59; head instrumentation, United Aircraft Res Labs, 59-62, prin scientist, 62-64. *Concurrent Pos:* Consult, United Aircraft Res Labs, 64-65. *Res:* Raman and ultraviolet spectroscopy; reactor shielding; bioelectronics; ultrasonics; lasers; experimental quantum mechanics; author of electronics and general engineering books. *Mailing Add:* PO Box 235 Marlborough CT 06447

SURAK, JOHN GODFREY, INTERNATIONAL STANDARDS. *Current Pos:* assoc prof food sci, 86-89, PROF FOOD SCI, CLEMSON UNIV, CLEMSON, SC, 89- *Personal Data:* b Milwaukee, Wis, July 13, 48; m 71; Judith Koepp; c Kristin M & Sarah M. *Educ:* Univ Wis-Madison, BS, 71, MS, 72, PhD(food sci & toxicol), 74. *Prof Exp:* Res asst food sci, Univ Wis-Madison, 70-74; asst prof toxicol, Univ Fla, 74-80; sr scientist, Food Prod Res Dept, Mead Johnson & Co, Evansville, 80-83; supvr prod develop, Wyeth Ayerst Labs, 83-86. *Concurrent Pos:* Prof continuing eng educ, Clemson Univ, 86-89; Malcolm Baldridge Nat Qual Award, Bd Examrs, 90-93; sci lectr, Inst Food Technologists, 91-, chair, Dixie Sect, 92-93, chair, Qual Assurance Div, 94-95. *Mem:* Inst Food Technologists; Sigma Xi; Am Soc Qual Control. *Res:* Quality and productivity improvement as related to its measurement and implementation in manufacturing and service industries. *Mailing Add:* Clemson Univ 223 P & AS Bldg Clemson SC 29634-0371. *Fax:* 864-656-0331; *E-Mail:* jsurak@clemson.edu

SURAMPALLI, RAO YADAGIRI, WATER & WASTEWATER TREATMENT ENGINEERING, HAZARDOUS WASTE MANAGEMENT. *Current Pos:* RES & TECHNOL PROG MGR ENVIRON ENG, US ENVIRON PROTECTION AGENCY, 86- *Personal Data:* b Zaheerabad, India, July 17, 49; US citizen; c 3. *Educ:* Okla State Univ, MS, 78; Iowa State Univ, PhD(environ eng), 85. *Honors & Awards:* Philip Morgan Award, Water Pollution Control Fedn, 86; Commendation Medal, USPHS, 90. *Prof Exp:* Environ engr sanit eng, Environ Eng Consults, Inc, 76-78; res assoc waste water treatment, Okla State Univ, 76-78; environ engr solid & hazardous waste mgt, Ky Dept Environ Protection, 78-80; sr environ engr water & wastewater treatment, Iowa Dept Environ Protection, 80-86. *Concurrent Pos:* Dipl, Am Acad Environ Engrs, 85-; mem, Water Pollution Control Fedn Nat Prog Comt, 87-, Task Force on MOP: 8 & 11-Design & Oper of Wastewater Treatment Plants, 88- & US Environ Protection Agency, Water Res Comt, 89-; consult, World Health Orgn, 87- *Mem:* Am Soc Civil Engrs; Water Pollution Control Fedn; Am Acad Environ Engrs. *Res:* Published 25 papers on design and operation of wastewater treatment plants. *Mailing Add:* PO Box 14241 Shawnee Mission KS 66285

SURAN, JEROME J, ELECTRICAL ENGINEERING. *Current Pos:* SR LECTR, GRAD SCH ADMIN, UNIV CALIF, DAVIS, 82- *Personal Data:* b New York, NY, Jan 11, 26; m 52. *Educ:* Columbia Univ, BS, 49. *Hon Degrees:* Dr Eng, Syracuse Univ, 76. *Prof Exp:* Develop engr, J W Meaker & Co, 49-51; engr res & develop, Motorola, Inc, 51-52; mgr adv circuits, Electronics Lab, Gen Elec Co, 52-62, consult, 54-57, mgr, Electronic Appln & Devices Lab, 62-76, mgr, Electronics Lab, 73-78, staff exec, Tech Systs & Mat Sector, 78-82. *Concurrent Pos:* Instr, Mass Inst Technol, 56-59; mem, Ad Hoc Comt Electronic Mat, Nat Acad Sci, 70-72; adj prof, Syracuse Univ, 76-; US Army Sci Bd, 84-86. *Mem:* Sigma Xi; Inst Elec & Electronics Engrs (pres, 79); fel AAAS. *Res:* Solid state circuit development for applications to the broad field of electronics, including computers, communications, control systems, detection systems. *Mailing Add:* Sch Mgmt Davis CA 95616

SURANYI, PETER, HIGH ENERGY PHYSICS. *Current Pos:* assoc prof, 71-74, PROF PHYSICS, UNIV CINCINNATI, 74- *Personal Data:* b Budapest, Hungary, Jan 31, 35; m 60; c 2. *Educ:* E-tv-s Lorand Univ, Budapest, BS, 58; Acad Sci, USSR, PhD(physics), 64. *Honors & Awards:* Schmidt Award, Hungarian Phys Soc, 68. *Prof Exp:* Jr res fel cosmic ray physics, Cent Res Inst Physics, Budapest, Hungary, 58-61, sr res fel,theoret high energy physics, 65-69; res fel theoret physics, Joint Inst Nuclear Studies, Moscow, 61-65; vis lectr physics, Johns Hopkins Univ, 69-70, res assoc, 70-71. *Concurrent Pos:* Sr fel, Brit Sci Coun, 78-79, 87-88; vis prof, Bonn Univ, 87. *Mem:* Am Phys Soc. *Res:* Quantum field theory; group theoretic methods in elementary particle physics; statistical mechanics. *Mailing Add:* Dept Physics Univ Cincinnati ML11 Cincinnati OH 45221

SURAWICZ, BORYS, INTERNAL MEDICINE, CARDIOLOGY. *Current Pos:* PROF MED, KRANNERT INST CARDIOL, INDIANAPOLIS, 81- *Personal Data:* b Moscow, Russia, Feb 11, 17; nat US; m 46, Frida Van Klaveren; c 2. *Educ:* Stefan Batory Univ, Poland, MD, 39; Am Bd Internal Med, dipl; Am Bd Cardiovasc Dis, dipl. *Honors & Awards:* Sir William Osler Award, 97; Distinguished Scientist Award, NAm Soc Pacing & Electrophysiol, 92. *Prof Exp:* Instr cardiol, Sch Med, Univ Pa, 54-55; instr med, Col Med, Univ Vt, 55-57, asst prof exp & clin med, 56-62; assoc prof med, Col Med, Univ Ky, 62-66, dir, Cardiovasc Div, 62-81, prof, 66-81. *Concurrent Pos:* Fel, Coun Clin Cardiol, Am Heart Asn; master teacher, Am Col Cardiol, 71 & 74. *Mem:* Fel Am Col Physicians; fel Am Col Cardiol; AMA; Am Physiol Soc; Asn Univ Cardiologists; Venezuela Cardiac Soc; Poland Cardiac Soc; Hungary Cardiac Soc; Cardiac Electrophysiol Soc. *Res:* Electrocardiology; role of electrolytes in cardiac arrhythmias; Cardiac Electrophysiology; electropharmacology. *Mailing Add:* Krannert Inst Cardiol Sch Med Ind Univ 1110 W Tenth St Indianapolis IN 46202-2859. *Fax:* 317-338-6019

SURBEY, DONALD LEE, ORGANIC CHEMISTRY. *Current Pos:* RES CHEMIST, LUBRIZOL CORP, 67- *Personal Data:* b North Canton, Ohio, July 19, 40; m 61; c 2. *Educ:* Manchester Col, BS, 61; Univ Notre Dame, PhD(org chem), 68. *Prof Exp:* Control chemist, Miles Labs, Inc, 61-63. *Mem:* Am Chem Soc. *Res:* Organic chemistry as related to process and product development in field of polymer chemistry and lubricant additives. *Mailing Add:* 5648 Ridgebury Blvd Lyndhurst OH 44124-1453

SURBIS, ALBINA Y, ANATOMY. *Current Pos:* asst prof anat, 61-93, ASST PROF, DEPT CELL BIOL & ANAT, SCH MED, UNIV MIAMI, 93- *Personal Data:* b Harvey, Ill, Feb 16, 23; wid. *Educ:* Univ Chicago, BS, 45, MS, 49; Univ Minn, PhD(anat), 55. *Prof Exp:* Instr biol, Univ Akron, 46-47; instr, Univ Minn, 47-49, asst anat, 49-54; res assoc path, Med Sch, Univ Mich, 59-61. *Concurrent Pos:* George fel, Detroit Inst Cancer Res, 56-58; res assoc, Vet Admin Hosp, Miami, 64-69. *Res:* Oncology; electron microscopy; pathology. *Mailing Add:* Dept Cell Biol & Anat R124 Univ Miami Sch Med PO Box 016960 Miami FL 33101

SURESH, MAVANUR RANGARAJAN, CANCER RESEARCH, IMMUNOCHEMISTRY. *Current Pos:* PROF MED RES COUNC, INDUST CHAIR, FAC PHARM, UNIV ALA, 93- *Personal Data:* b Shimoga, India, Apr 22, 53; Can citizen; m 82; c 2. *Educ:* Bangalore Univ, India, BSc Hons, 71, MSc, 73; Indian Inst Sci, Bangalore, PhD(biochem), 78. *Prof Exp:* Postdoctoral res assoc & Am Cancer Soc jr fel, Scripps Clin & Res Fedn, La Jolla, Calif, 78-82; sr postdoctoral fel, Fac Pharm, Univ Alta, 82-84; Usher fel, Med Res Coun Lab Molecular Biol, Cambridge, UK, 84-85; group leader, Summa Biomed Can Ltd, 85; chief scientist, Biomira Inc Edmonton, Can, 85-93. *Concurrent Pos:* Secy, Biochem Soc, Indian Inst Sci, 75-76; vpres, Soc Fels, Scripps Clin & Res Found, La Jolla, Calif, 79-80; vis scientist, Indian Inst Sci, Bangalore, 82; vis fel, Clare Hall, Univ Cambridge, UK, 84; adj assoc prof, Fac Pharm, Univ Alta, 85-; chmn, Biotechnol Adv Comt, Northern Alta Inst Technol, Alta, 87-90, mem, Biol Sci Comt, 90- *Mem:* Am Asn Immunologists; Soc Complex Carbohydrates. *Res:* Cancer associated antigens with special reference to carbohydrate antigens-bispecific monoclonal antibodies; cancer diagnostics and therapeutics in the industrial sector; asthma and allergy diagnostics and therapeutics in the academic university sector. *Mailing Add:* Fac Pharmacy Univ Ala Edmonton AB T6N 2N8 Can. *Fax:* 403-492-8241

SURESH, SUBRA, FRACTURE & FATIGUE, MICROSTRUCTURAL EFFECTS. *Current Pos:* RICHARD P SIMMONS PROF, MASS INST TECHNOL, 93- *Personal Data:* US citizen; m 86, Mary D. *Educ:* Indian Inst Technol, B Technol, 77; Iowa State Univ, MS, 79; Brown Univ, 87. *Hon Degrees:* ScD, Mass Inst Technol, 81. *Honors & Awards:* Robert Lansing Hardy Gold Medal, 83; Champion Mathewson Gold Medal, 85; Pres Young Investr Award, NSF, 85; Ross Coffin Purdy Award, Am Ceramic Soc, 92. *Prof Exp:* Asst res engr, Univ Calif, Berkeley, 81-83; from asst prof to prof eng, Brown Univ, 83-93. *Concurrent Pos:* Co-chmn, Int Symp Interfaces, RI, 88; mem, Int Comt, Fr Metall Soc, 88-; chmn, Ceramics Comt, Am Soc Mech Engrs. *Mem:* Metall Soc Am; Am Ceramic Soc; Am Soc Mech Engrs; Mat Res Soc. *Res:* Theoretical and experimental study of the mechanics and mechanisms of microstructural development, deformation, fracture, and fatigue in advanced engineering materials; composites; ceramics. *Mailing Add:* 8 Ox Bow Rd Wellesley MA 02181. *Fax:* 617-253-0868; *E-Mail:* ssuresh@mit.edu

SURGALLA, MICHAEL JOSEPH, MEDICAL MICROBIOLOGY. *Personal Data:* b Nicholson, Pa, May 12, 20; m 48; c 4. *Educ:* Univ Scranton, BS, 42; Univ Chicago, PhD(bact), 46. *Prof Exp:* Bacteriologist, E R Squibb & Sons, NJ, 46-48; res assoc, Univ Chicago, 48-54; bacteriologist, Biol Sci Lab, Dept of Army, Ft Detrick, Md, 54-71; dir, clin microbiol, Roswell Park Mem Inst, 71-91. *Mem:* AAAS; Am Soc Microbiol; Am Acad Microbiol; NY Acad Sci; Am Soc Clin Pathologists. *Res:* Medical bacteriology; staphylococcus food poisoning; influenza virus; experimental plague; bacterial virulence; pathogenic mechanisms; host resistance; endotoxins; fibrinolysis; opportunist pathogens; hospital infection epidemiology. *Mailing Add:* 163 Hedstrom Dr Buffalo NY 14226

SURGENOR, DOUGLAS MACNEVIN, BIOCHEMISTRY. *Current Pos:* SR INVESTR, CTR BLOOD RES, BOSTON, 72- *Personal Data:* b Hartford, Conn, Apr 7, 18; m 46, Lois Hutchinson; c Peter, Sarah, Johathan, Timothy & Stephen. *Educ:* Williams Col, AB, 39; Mass State Col, MS, 41; Mass Inst Technol, PhD(org chem), 46. *Prof Exp:* Mem staff, Div Indust Coop, Mass Inst Technol, 42-45; res assoc phys chem, Harvard Med Sch, 45-50, asst prof, 50-55, asst prof biol chem, 55-60; sr investr, Protein Found, 56-60; head, Dept Biochem, Sch Med, State Univ NY, Buffalo, 60-64, dean, 62-68, provost, Fac Health Sci, 67-70, prof biochem, 60-77, res prof, Sch Mgt, 71-77; Pres & dir, Am Red Cross Blood Serv, Northeast Red, Boston, 77-83. *Concurrent Pos:* Assoc mem, Lab Phys Chem Related to Med & Pub Health, Harvard Univ, 50-54; consult, Vet Admin Hosp, Buffalo, 60-, chmn, Dean's Comt, 62-68; mem, Med Bd, Buffalo Gen & Buffalo Children's Hosps, 62-68; mem, Med Coun, NY State Educ Dept, 62-68; bd sci counr, Div Biol Stand, NIH, 63-68; mem, Int Comt Thrombosis & Haemostasis, 63-, chmn, 70-72; mem, Nat Heart Inst Prog Proj Comt B, 65-68; consult, Med Bd, Millard Fillmore Hosp, 66-70; mem, Nat Blood Resource Prog Adv Comt, Nat Heart & Lung Inst, 69-73, chmn, 70-73; mem, Med Adv Comt, Am Nat Red Cross, 70-76; pres, 72-87, chmn, Ctr Blood Res, Boston 87-; mem, Bd Trustees, Children's Hosp Med Ctr, Boston, 75-80, overseer, 80-; vis prof pediat, Harvard Med Sch, 77-88; mem, Adv Coun, Nat Heart, Lung & Blood Inst, NIH, 80-84; mem, Expert Adv Panel Human Blood Prods, WHO, 80-87. *Mem:* AAAS; Am Soc Biol Chemists; Am Heart Asn; Am Soc Hemat; Int Soc Thrombosis & Haemostasis. *Res:* Blood biochemistry; blood and public policy; blood coagulation; transfusion medicine. *Mailing Add:* 213 Indian Hill Rd Carlisle MA 01741-1748

SURGI, MARION RENE, GAS CHROMATOGRAPHY-MASS SPECTROMETRY-IDENTIFICATION OF ORGANIC UNKNOWNS, ENVIRONMENTAL REGULATORY CHEMICAL METHODS. *Current Pos:* ANALYTICAL & ENVIRON SERVS INC, 94- *Personal Data:* b New Orleans, La, Dec 19, 56; m 81, Elizabeth Benson; c Renee E & Sara E. *Educ:* Univ New Orleans, BS, 79; La State Univ, PhD(anal chem), 84. *Prof Exp:* Sr res chemist, Signal Res Ctr, 84-86; res specialist, Allied Signal, 86-90, mgr & res scientist, 90-94. *Mem:* Am Chem Soc. *Res:* Environmental impact of ash residues of combustion processes, hazardous waste, regulatory methodology; laboratory auditing and compliance with regulatory methods, data validation, statistical methods in waste identification and characterization. *Mailing Add:* 503 Oakdale Ave Glencoe IL 60022. *Fax:* 847-835-9404; *E-Mail:* renesurgi@aol.com

SURI, ASHOK, software systems, technical management; deceased, see previous edition for last biography

SURI, RAJAN, MANUFACTURING SYSTEMS MODELING & ANALYSIS, FLEXIBLE MANUFACTURING SYSTEMS. *Current Pos:* PROF, INDUST ENG, UNIV WIS, 85- *Personal Data:* b Dec 18, 52; India citizen; c 2. *Educ:* Cambridge Univ, Eng, BA, 74; Harvard Univ, SM, 75, PhD(eng), 78. *Honors & Awards:* Donald P Eckman Award, 81. *Prof Exp:* Fel decision & control, Div Appl Sci, Harvard Univ, 78-80, asst prof, 80; managing dir, SAN Ltd Locomotive Co, Bangalore, India, 81; asst prof systs eng, Div Appl Sci, Harvard Univ, 82-85. *Concurrent Pos:* Consult & database mgr, Multinational Enterprise Proj, Harvard Bus Sch, 75-78; mgt consult, Fiat SPA, Turin, Italy, 76-78; consult, Charles Stark Draper Lab, 76-82; dir, Network Dynamics Inc, Cambridge, Mass, 83-; consult, IBM Corp, 84- *Mem:* Inst Elec & Electronics Engrs; Inst Indust Engrs; Soc Mfg Engrs; Oper Res Soc Am; Inst Mgt Sci. *Res:* Modeling and analysis of manufacturing systems; flexible manufacturing systems; queueing network models and simulation discrete event systems. *Mailing Add:* Indust Eng Dept Univ Wis 1513 University Ave Madison WI 53706

SURIA, AMIN, NEUROPHARMACOLOGY, PSYCHOPHARMACOLOGY. *Current Pos:* PROF, PHARMACOL DEPT, SCH MED, AGA KHAN UNIV, PAKISTAN, 83- *Personal Data:* b Dhoraji, India, Aug 24, 42; US citizen; m 74, Khairunnisa Vimawala; c Nausheen, Sabrina, Raheel & Nida. *Educ:* Univ Karachi, Pakistan, BS, 63, MS, 64; Vanderbilt Univ, Nashville, PhD(pharmacol), 71. *Prof Exp:* Chemist, United Paints Ltd, Karachi, Pakistan, 64; chemist & in-chg lab, Textile Dyes & Auxiliary Dept, Hoechst Pharmaceut Co, Ltd, Karachi, Pakistan, 64-66; vis fel biochem, Pharmacol Lab, Nat Heart & Lung Inst, NIH, Bethesda, Md, 71-72; fel, Lab Preclin Pharmacol, NIMH, St Elizabeth's Hosp, Washington, DC, 72-74, staff fel, 74-75; assoc prof pharmacol, George Washington Univ, Washington, DC, 75-80; prof pharmacol, King Saud Univ, Riyadh, Saudi Arabia, 80-83. *Concurrent Pos:* Guest worker, Lab Preclin Pharmacol, St Elizabeth's Hosp, NIMH; consult, Pakistan Med Res Coun. *Mem:* Am Soc Pharmacol & Exp Therapeut; Soc Neurosci; NY Acad Sci; Pakistan Pharmacol Soc; fel Pakistan Acad Med Sci; Med Res Soc Pakistan (pres, 95-); fel Acad Pharmaceut Sci. *Res:* Molecular mechanisms by which anti-anxiety, anticonvulsant cns active drugs and antidepressant drugs exert their actions on complex neuronal pathways, research entails using electrophysiological and biochemical techniques; arachidonic acid metabolism in health and disease. *Mailing Add:* Pharmacol Dept Sch Med Aga Khan Univ PO Box 3500 Stadium Rd Karachi 5 74800 Pakistan

SURIANO, F(RANCIS) J(OSEPH), MECHANICAL ENGINEERING. *Current Pos:* MEM STAFF AERODYNAMICS-PRELIMINARY DESIGN, AIRESEARCH MFG CO ARIZ, PHOENIX, 68- *Personal Data:* b Kenosha, Wis, July 17, 37; m 59; c 4. *Educ:* Univ Notre Dame, BS, 59, PhD(mech eng), 66; Ga Inst Technol, MS, 61. *Prof Exp:* Asst mech eng, Ga Inst Technol, 59-60; res engr, Wood River Res Lab, Shell Oil Co, 60-61; mem staff aerodyn preliminary design, AiRes Mfg Co, Ariz, 66-67; mem tech staff, Aerospace Corp, 67-68. *Mem:* Am Soc Mech Engrs. *Res:* Heat transfer and fluid mechanics. *Mailing Add:* 8626 E Meadowbrook Ave Scottsdale AZ 85251

SURKAN, ALVIN JOHN, NEURAL NETWORKS, GENETIC ALGORITHMS. *Current Pos:* mem, Inst Water Resources Res, 69-73, PROF COMPUT SCI, UNIV NEBR, LINCOLN, 69- *Personal Data:* b Drumheller, Alta, June 5, 34; m 67, Marna R Cacossa; c Kimberly J & Pamela J. *Educ:* Univ Alta, BSc, 54; Univ Toronto, MA, 56; Univ Western Ont, PhD(physics), 59. *Prof Exp:* Sr demonstr geophys, Univ Western Ont, 58-59; Nat Res Coun Can fel, Univ Alta, 59-61; sci officer marine physics, Can Defence Res Bd, 61-62; fac mem physics, Univ BC, 62-63; staff consult geophys comput, Res & Develop Ctr, IBM Corp, 64-65, mem res staff environ sci group, Phys Sci Dept, Watson Res Ctr, 65-69. *Concurrent Pos:* Fel, Nat Res Coun Can, 61-62;

consult geophys comput & resident visitor physics dept, AT&T, Bell Tel Labs, 72; vis scientist, IBM, Palo Alto Sci Ctr, 77; vis scholar, Stanford Univ, 78; res scientist, HDR Sci, Santa Barbara, Calif; commun statistician, AT&T Bell Labs, 82, circuit routing res, 86; sr scientist, Ames Res Ctr, Res Inst Advan Comput Sci, Moffett Field Col, NASA, 88; neural networks consult, SIR-Gallup, 90. *Mem:* Am Geophys Union; Soc Explor Geophysicists; Int Neural Network Soc; Inst Elec & Electronics Engrs; Am Asn Intel; NY Acad Sci. *Res:* Computer science applications and education; artificial intelligence with non-algorithmic and subsymbolic problem solving; machine learning; simulation of neural networks and genetic programming for both numeric and symbolic data interpretation and analysis; econometric, financial and psychologic forecasting and prediciton. *Mailing Add:* 1940 Devonshire Dr Lincoln NE 65806

SURKO, CLIFFORD MICHAEL, EXPERIMENTAL STUDIES OF NONLINEAR & NONEQUILIBRIUM SYSTEMS, POSITRON PLASMAS & POSITRON MATTER INTERACTIONS. *Current Pos:* PROF PHYSICS, UNIV CALIF, SAN DIEGO, 88- *Personal Data:* b Sacramento, Calif, Oct 11, 41; m 65, Pamela Hansen; c 2. *Educ:* Univ Calif, Berkeley, AB, 64, PhD(physics), 68. *Prof Exp:* Res assoc physics, Univ Calif, Berkeley, 68-69; mem tech staff physics, Bill Labs, 69-82, head, Semiconductor & Chem Physics Res Dept, 82-88. *Concurrent Pos:* Vis sr res physicist, Ecole Polytech, France, 78-79; vis scientist, Plasma Fusion Ctr, Mass Inst Technol, 77-85. *Mem:* AAAS; fel Am Physics Soc; NY Acad Sci; Sigma Xi. *Res:* Experimental research in nonlinear and nonequilibrium systems, including plasmas and fluids; physics of positrons in traps and positron plasmas; physics of patterns and dynamics in fluid convection and catalysis. *Mailing Add:* Physics Dept 0319 Univ Calif San Diego La Jolla CA 92093-0319

SURKO, PAMELA TONI, RULE-BASED EXPERT SYSTEMS, ARTIFICIAL NEURAL & LIFE SYSTEMS. *Current Pos:* sr scientist, 88-94, CHIEF SCIENTIST, SCI APPLNS INT CORP, 95- *Personal Data:* b Britton, SDak, June 15, 42; m 65, Clifford; c 2. *Educ:* Univ Calif, Berkeley, AB, 63, PhD(physics), 70. *Prof Exp:* Asst prof physics, Princeton Univ, 70-80; Distinguished mem tech staff, AT&T Bell Labs, 80-88. *Concurrent Pos:* Chercher Etranger, Ecole Polytechnique, Paris, 79. *Mem:* Am Asn Artificial Intel; Inst Elec & Electronics Engrs; AAAS; Asn Women Sci. *Res:* Knowledge-based systems; bioinformatics; artificial neural systems. *Mailing Add:* Sci Appln Int Corp Mail Stop C5 10260 Campus Point Dr San Diego CA 92121. *E-Mail:* pamela.t.surko@cpmx.saic.com

SURMACZ, CYNTHIA ANN, CELL PHYSIOLOGY, EXERCISE PHYSIOLOGY. *Current Pos:* ASSOC PROF ANAT & PHYSIOL, BLOOMSBURG UNIV, PA, 83- *Personal Data:* b Wilkensburg, Pa, June 26, 57; m 81; c 2. *Educ:* Pa State Univ, BS, 78; Milton S Hershey Med Ctr, PhD(physiol), 82. *Prof Exp:* Instr physiol, Dept Continuing Educ & res fel, Milton S Hershey Med Ctr, 83. *Mem:* AAAS; Nat Asn Biol Teachers; Am Physiol Soc. *Res:* Alterations in plasma electrolytes and the cardiac cycle during exercise. *Mailing Add:* Dept Biol & Allied Health Sci Hartline Sci Ctr Bloomsburg Univ Bloomsburg PA 17815

SURREY, ALEXANDER ROBERT, ORGANIC CHEMISTRY, DRUG RESEARCH. *Personal Data:* b New York, NY, Mar 13, 14; m 39, Rosalie; c Janet L. *Educ:* City Col New York, BS, 34; NY Univ, PhD(chem), 40. *Honors & Awards:* Townsend Harris Medal, 81. *Prof Exp:* Nat Defense Res Comt fel, Cornell Univ, 40-41; res chemist, Sterling-Winthrop Res Inst, 41-57, sect head, 57-60, asst dir chem res, 60-64, sr res fel & dir new prod, 64-67, dir develop res, 67-72, vpres res & develop, 72-76, vpres prod develop, 76-77, vpres tech affairs, 77-81. *Concurrent Pos:* Lectr & adj prof, Rensselaer Polytech Inst, 58-64; law & med consult; consult, 81- *Mem:* Am Chem Soc; fel NY Acad Sci; fel Royal Chem Soc. *Res:* Medicinals. *Mailing Add:* 7090 Fairway Bend Circle Sarasota FL 34243-3622

SURREY, KENNETH, PHYTOCHEMISTRY. *Current Pos:* HEALTH SCIENTIST ADMINR, NIH, 66- *Personal Data:* b India, Dec 6, 22; nat US; m 52; c 4. *Educ:* Univ Punjab, India, BSc, 46, MA, 52; Univ Mo, MA, 55, PhD(phytochem), 57. *Prof Exp:* Lab instr chem, Forman Christian Col, Pakistan, 49-53; asst bot, Univ Mo, 54-57; asst plant physiologist, Argonne Nat Lab, 57-66. *Res:* Histochemistry of protein constituents by azo-coupling reactions in plants; metabolic responses of regenerating meristems and germinating seeds as influenced by visible and ionizing radiation; action and interaction of red and far-red radiation on metabolic processes of developing seedlings; physiological bases for morphological development; neurosciences (neurotoxicology, neuroendocrinology, pain); administration of federally grant-supported research in neurosciences. *Mailing Add:* 5302 Bangor Dr Kensington MD 20895

SURVER, WILLIAM MERLE, JR, DEVELOPMENTAL GENETICS. *Current Pos:* asst prof, 78-81, ASSOC PROF BIOL, CLEMSON UNIV, 81- *Personal Data:* b Altoona, Pa, June 26, 43. *Educ:* St Francis Col, BA, 66; Univ Notre Dame, PhD(genetics), 72. *Prof Exp:* Instr biol, Univ Notre Dame, 71-72; asst prof zool, Univ RI, 72-78. *Mem:* AAAS; Nat Sci Teachers Asn; Nat Asn Biol Teachers; Genetics Soc Am. *Res:* Genetic effects on developing systems; genetics of kelp fly, Coelopa frigida; innovative teaching for general biology. *Mailing Add:* Dept Biol Clemson Univ 201 Sikes Hall Clemson SC 29632-0001

SURWILLO, WALTER WALLACE, PSYCHOPHYSIOLOGY. *Current Pos:* DIR, EEG LAB, BINGHAM CHILD GUID CLIN, 83- *Personal Data:* b Rochester, NY, Nov 25, 26; m 55. *Educ:* Wash Univ, St Louis, BA, 51, MA, 53; McGill Univ, PhD(psychol), 55. *Prof Exp:* Asst psychol, Wash Univ, St Louis, 50-53; asst, McGill Univ, 53-55; res assoc psychophysiol, Allan Mem Inst Psychiat, 55-57; res psychophysiologist gerontol br, NIH, 57-65; assoc prof psychiat, 65-70, prof psychiat Sch Med, Univ Louisville, 70-, assoc prof psychol, grad sch, 71- *Concurrent Pos:* Mem, NIH Exp Psychol Study Sect, 70-74; consult, NSF, 73-, Can Res Coun, 78- *Mem:* Am Psychol Asn; Soc Psychophysiol Res; NY Acad Sci; Soc Neurosci. *Res:* Nervous system function and its relation to behavior; psychophysiological and electrophysiological methods of investigation; instrumentation; central nervous system and behavioral changes with development and senescence; electroencephalography. *Mailing Add:* 3051 Rio Dosa Dr Lexington KY 40509

SURWIT, RICHARD SAMUEL, BEHAVIORAL MEDICINE, CLINICAL PSYCHOLOGY & NEUROENDOCRIMOLOGY. *Current Pos:* from asst prof to assoc prof, 77-83, prof med psychol, Dept Psychiat, 83, ASST PROF EXP MED & PROF PSYCHOL, DUKE UNIV MED CTR, DURHAM, 91-, VCHMN RES, 93- *Personal Data:* b New York, NY, Oct 7, 46; m 82; c 1. *Educ:* Earlham Col, AB, 68; McGill Univ, Can, PhD(clin psychol), 72. *Prof Exp:* Res fel psychol, Dept Psychiat, Harvard Med Sch 72-74, instr, 74-76; dir, Psychophysiol Lab, Mass Ment Health Ctr, Boston, 74-77; asst prof psychol, Dept Psychiat, Harvard Med Sch, 76-77. *Concurrent Pos:* Assoc ed, Health Psychol, 86-90. *Mem:* Fel Am Psychol Asn; fel Acad Behav Med Res; Am Psychosom Soc; fel Soc Behav Med (pres, 94-); Am Diabetes Asn; Am Asn Study Obesity; Am Col Mech. *Res:* Investigation of role of the autonomic and central nervous systems in the pathophysiology of type II diabetes mellitus and study of how behavioral variables relate to chronic glucose control in both type I and type II diabetes; study of the pathophysiology of obesity and type II diabetes including the genetics of both disorders; neuroendocrimology. *Mailing Add:* Duke Univ Med Ctr Box 3322 Durham NC 27710. *Fax:* 919-681-7347; *E-Mail:* surwi001@mc.duke.edu

SURYANARAYANA, NARASIPUR VENKATARAM, MECHANICAL ENGINEERING. *Current Pos:* asst prof, 70-75, assoc prof, 75-79, PROF MECH ENG, MICH TECHNOL UNIV, 79- *Personal Data:* b Bangalore, India, Apr 12, 31; m 59; c 2. *Educ:* Univ Mysore, BE, 54; Columbia Univ, MS, 66; Univ Mich, PhD(mech eng), 70. *Prof Exp:* Tech asst mech eng, Hindustan Shipyard, Visakhapatnam, 55-63; lectr, Indian Inst Technol, Kharagpur, 63-64; training off, Lucas-TVS, Madras, 64-65. *Concurrent Pos:* NSF res grants, 71-72 & 77-79. *Res:* Heat transfer with change of phase; convective heat transfer with turbulence; solar energy. *Mailing Add:* 7 Violin Pl Houghton MI 49931

SURYANARAYANAN, RAJ GOPALAN, SOLID STATE PHARMACEUTICS, DRUG DELIVERY. *Current Pos:* asst prof, 85-92, ASSOC PROF, UNIV MINN, 92- *Personal Data:* b Cuddalore, Tamil Nadu, India, Apr 19, 55; m 85, Shanti Venkates-Waran; c Priya M & Meera S. *Educ:* Banaras Hindi Univ, Varanasi, India, BPharm, 76, MPharm, 78; Univ BC, Vancouver, Can, MSc, 81, PhD(pharmaceut), 85. *Honors & Awards:* Horace T Morse Award. *Prof Exp:* Mgt trainee, Indian Drugs & Pharmaceut Ltd, 78; supvr, Roche Prods, 79; teaching asst, Univ BC, 79, 82-83. *Concurrent Pos:* Consult, several pharmaceut co, 87-; vis res scholar, Sch Pharm, Univ Bradford, UK, 89-90; invited lectr, several pharmaceut co USA & UK, 90- & prof socs, 90- *Mem:* AAAS; Am Asn Pharm Scientists; Am Asn Cols Pharm. *Res:* Solid state properties of drugs and dosage forms; novel methods of drug delivery; quantitative powder x-ray diffractometric studies of pharmaceutical systems. *Mailing Add:* Col Pharm 308 Harvard St SE Minneapolis MN 55455. *Fax:* 612-624-2974; *E-Mail:* surya001@maroon.tc.umn.edu

SURYARAMAN, MARUTHUVAKUDI GOPALASASTRI, ANALYTICAL CHEMISTRY, PHYSICAL CHEMISTRY. *Current Pos:* from asst prof to assoc prof, 66-75, PROF CHEM, HUMBOLDT STATE UNIV, 75- *Personal Data:* b Madras, India, Mar 2, 25; m 52; c 3. *Educ:* Univ Madras, BSc, 46, MS, 52; Univ Colo, PhD(chem), 61. *Prof Exp:* Demonstr chem, Madras Christian Col, 46-49 & Vivekananda Col, Madras, 52; lectr, Sri Venkateswara Univ Cols, Andhra, 52-57; asst, Univ Colo, 57-59, 60-61; sr res chemist, Monsanto Co, Mo, 61-66. *Mem:* Am Chem Soc; fel Royal Inst Chem; fel Indian Chem Soc. *Res:* Analytical chemistry, electrochemistry and ion exchange; general inorganic chemistry. *Mailing Add:* 2118 Daina Ct Arcata CA 95521-5420

SURZYCKI, STEFAN JAN, MOLECULAR BIOLOGY, BIOCHEMISTRY. *Current Pos:* ASSOC PROF, DEPT BIOL, IND UNIV, 75- *Personal Data:* b Krakow, Poland, Jan 13, 36; US citizen; m 70; c 4. *Educ:* Odessa Univ, MS, 60; Warsaw Univ, PhD(genetics), 64. *Prof Exp:* Asst genetics, Warsaw Univ, 61-63; researcher, Genetics Inst Polish Acad Sci, Warsaw, 63-64; fel molecular biol, Harvard Univ, 64-65, res fel, 65-68, Maria Moor Cabot Found fel, 69-70; from asst prof to assoc prof, Univ Iowa, 70-75. *Mem:* Am Soc Cell Biol; Am Soc Microbiol; Plant Molecular Biol Soc. *Res:* Mechanism of transcription initiation by eucaryotic RNA Polymerase II; regulation of gene expression in chloroplast of C. reinhardi. *Mailing Add:* Dept Biol Ind Univ Bloomington IN 47405

SUSAG, RUSSELL H(ARRY), ENVIRONMENTAL ENGINEERING. *Current Pos:* PRES, SUSAG ENVIRON CONSULT, INC, 96- *Personal Data:* b Minneapolis, Minn, Dec 22, 30; m 57; c 6. *Educ:* Univ Minn, BCE, 56, MSCE, 65, PhD, 65. *Honors & Awards:* Radebaugh Award, Cent States Water Pollution Control Asn, 66; Eng of Year, Fla Sect, Am Soc Civil Engrs, 70; Arthur Sidney Bedell Award, Water Pollution Control Fedn, 77; George

J Schroepfer Award, Cent States Water Pollution Control Asn, 87; W R "Bill" Coffin Mem Pub Serv Award, Minn Soc Prof Engrs, 89; Distinguished Serv Award, Prof Engrs Indust, Nat Soc Prof Engrs, 90; Chairman's Award, Am Asn Eng Socs, 96. *Prof Exp:* Teaching asst sanit eng, Univ Minn, 56-57, asst prof, 65-68; assoc prof environ eng, Univ Fla, 68-70; mgr qual control, Metrop Sewer Bd, Minneapolis, 70-74; mgr environ affairs, 3M, 74-78, dir environ regulatory activ, 78-80, dir environ opers, 80-83, dir environ reg affairs, 83-96. *Mem:* Am Soc Civil Engrs; Nat Soc Prof Engrs; Water Environ Fedn; Am Acad Environ Engrs. *Res:* Industrial enviornmental compliance; environmental site remediation; sewer service rates; solid and hazardous waste management; water pollution control, deoxygenation and reaeration characteristics of waste waters and receiving waters. *Mailing Add:* 7305 First Ave S Richfield MN 55423. *Fax:* 612-866-0783

SUSALLA, ANNE A, PLANT ANATOMY, EMBRYOLOGY. *Current Pos:* Asst prof, 72-75, chairperson dept, 77-80, ASSOC PROF BIOL, ST MARYS COL, 75- *Personal Data:* b Parisville, Mich. *Educ:* Madonna Col, BA, 62; Univ Detroit, MS, 67; Ind Univ, Bloomington, PhD(bot), 72. *Mem:* Bot Soc Am; Sigma XI. *Res:* Ultrastructure of plastids in phenotypically green leaf tissue of a genetic albino strain of Nicotiana; tissue culture work is being employed to study the developmental stages of these plastids. *Mailing Add:* Dept Biol St Marys Col Notre Dame IN 46556

SUSCA, LOUIS ANTHONY, GENERAL PEDIATRICS & PEDIATRIC ALLERGY, GENETICS. *Current Pos:* instr pharmacol, 49-53, ASST CLIN PROF PEDIAT, NY MED COL, 60- *Personal Data:* m 55, Mary J Rizzi; c Francis, Mary J, Nancy E & Kathleen A. *Educ:* Fordham Univ, BS, 45, MS, 47, PhD(physiol), 49; NY Med Col, MD, 55. *Honors & Awards:* Encaenia Award, Fordham Univ, 60; Nat Geriat Soc Award, 62. *Prof Exp:* Instr pharm, Fordham Sch Pharm, 47-49. *Mem:* Sigma Xi. *Res:* Cardiology; genetics; cerebral palsy; pharmacology; nutrition in young and old; author of numerous articles. *Mailing Add:* 213-18 Hillside Ave Queens Village NY 11427-1814

SUSI, FRANK ROBERT, ANATOMY, ORAL PATHOLOGY. *Current Pos:* Instr anat, Sch Med, Tufts Univ, 67-68, from asst prof to assoc prof oral path, 67-74, asst prof anat, 68-82, asst dean, 77-82, assoc dean, Acad Affairs, 82-92, PROF ORAL PATH, SCH DENT MED, TUFTS UNIV, 74-, DIR DIV, 73-, DIR BASIC HEALTH SCI, 70-, PROF ANAT, SCH MED, 82-, SR ASSOC DEAN, ACAD AFFAIRS, 92- *Personal Data:* b Boston, Mass, Dec 10, 36. *Educ:* Boston Col, BS, 58; Harvard Univ, DMD, 62, cert, 65; Tufts Univ, PhD(anat), 67. *Concurrent Pos:* Fel anat, McGill Univ, 68-69. *Mem:* Am Asn Anat; Histochem Soc; Am Acad Oral Path; Int Asn Dent Res; Am Asn Dent Schs (vpres, 84-87, pres, 88-89); Am Dent Asn. *Res:* Histochemistry; autoradiography; electron microscopy; keratinization, carcinogenesis; spermiogenesis; dentistry. *Mailing Add:* Dept Oral Path Sch Dent Med Tufts Univ One Kneeland St Boston MA 02111

SUSI, PETER VINCENT, ORGANIC CHEMISTRY, RESEARCH ADMINISTRATION. *Current Pos:* From res chemist tosr res chemist, 56-63, group leader, 63-76, proj leader, 76-81, GROUP LEADER, AM CYANAMID CO, 81- *Personal Data:* b Philadelphia, Pa Apr 26, 28; m 54; c 2. *Educ:* Univ Pa, BA, 50; Univ Del, MS, 51, PhD(chem), 57. *Mem:* AAAS; Am Chem Soc. *Res:* Synthesis and applications research in field of plastics additives, light stabilizers, antioxidants, antistatics; ultraviolet and infrared absorbers; flame retardants, antioxidants and photoinitators. *Mailing Add:* 17 Starlit Dr Middlesex NJ 08846-1443

SUSINA, STANLEY V, PHARMACY, PHARMACOLOGY. *Current Pos:* RETIRED. *Personal Data:* b Berwyn, Ill, Apr 14, 23; m 48, Betty Knauss; c Jan Christopher, David Alan & Margaret Alexander. *Educ:* Univ Ill, BS, 48, MS, 51, PhD(pharmacol), 55; Cumberland Law Sch, Samford Univ, JD, 71. *Prof Exp:* Asst pharm, Univ Ill, 48-50, from instr to assoc prof, 50-62, actg head dept, 61-62; prof pharm law, Sch Pharm, Samford Univ, 62-, assoc dean, 86-90, actg dean, 84-85. *Mem:* Acad Pharmaceut Sci; Am Asn Cols Pharm; Am Pharmaceut Asn; Sigma Xi. *Res:* Antihistamines; neuromuscular blocking agents; local anesthetics; radioactive isotopes. *Mailing Add:* 1912 Greenvale Rd Birmingham AL 35226

SUSKI, HENRY M(IECZYSLAW), ELECTRONIC & COMMUNICATION ENGINEERING. *Current Pos:* RETIRED. *Personal Data:* b Camden, NJ, July 14, 18; m 43. *Educ:* City Col New York, BEE, 41. *Prof Exp:* Switchboard engr, Western Elec Co, 41; electronics scientist, Electronics Div, 46-67, electronics engr, Tactical Electronic Warfare Div, US Naval Res Lab, DC, 67-87; consult, Locus, Inc, 87-89. *Concurrent Pos:* Vpres, NAm Res Corp & Corp Systs Res, 67-77. *Mem:* Sr mem Inst Elec & Electronics Engrs; Sigma Xi. *Res:* Development of long range facility plans, which include construction and installation, for electronic warfare simulation, research, development, and laboratory test; design management and funding organization, considering the assessment of technology and its impact on society. *Mailing Add:* Two Whittington Dr Palm Coast FL 32164

SUSKIND, RAYMOND ROBERT, MEDICAL SCIENCE, HEALTH SCIENCES. *Current Pos:* res fel, Kettering Lab, Univ Cincinnati, 48-50, from asst prof to assoc prof prev med & indust health, 49-62, prof environ health & med, 69-85, chmn, Dept Environ Health, 69-85, dir, Kettering Lab, Col Med, 69-85, EMER J G SCHMIDLAPP PROF MED & DERMAT, UNIV CINCINNATI, 85-; DIR, OCCUP & ENVIRON DERMAT PROG, CTR OCCUP HEALTH, HOLMES HOSP, 85- *Personal Data:* b New York, NY, Nov 29, 13; m 44, Ida Richardson; c Raymond R Jr & Stephen A. *Educ:* Columbia Univ, AB, 34; State Univ NY, MD, 43; Am Bd Dermat & Syphil, dipl, 49. *Honors & Awards:* Mitchell Award, State Univ NY Med Ctr, 43; Health Achievement in Indust Award, 77; Proj Hope Award, 84; Daniel Drake Medalist, Univ Cincinnati, 85; R A Kehoe Award of Merit, Am Acad Occup Med, 87; Presidential Citation, Am Acad Dermat, 90. *Prof Exp:* Resident dermat & syphil, Cincinnati Gen Hosp, 44-46; prof dermat & head, Div Environ Med, Med Sch, Univ Ore, 62-69. *Concurrent Pos:* Res fel dermat, Col Med, Univ Cincinnati, 48-49, asst prof, 50-62, dir dermat res, Kettering Lab, 48-62; attend physician, Univ Hosp, Cincinnati Med Ctr, 69-; attend physician, Univ Ore Hosp, 62-69; mem, Cincinnati Air Pollution Bd, 72-76, chmn, 74-75; rep, USSR-USA Collab Res Prog, Biol & Genetic Effects Pollutants, 73-79; mem, Task Force Res Planning Comt, Nat Inst Environ Health Sci, 75-77; consult, Occup Med to the Surgeon Gen, Dept Navy, 75-80, Bur Drugs & Dermat Adv Comt, Food & Drug Admin, 76-81; chmn, Occup Safety Health Act Standards Adv Comt Cutaneous Hazards, 78; mem, Certifying Bd, Am Bd Toxicology, 78-83, Vet Admin Comt Health Related Effects Herbicides, 79-84, Adv Panel Toxicology, Am Med Asn Coun Sci Affairs, 80-85; assoc ed, Am J Indust Med, 79-86; contrib ed, Bd Chemosphere, 86-, ed, 87-; master/trustee, Ferhold Settlement Fund & Program, 89- *Mem:* Am Col Physicians; NY Acad Sci; fel Am Acad Dermat; Am Col Occup & Environ Med; Am Dermat Asn; Sigma Xi; Soc Investigative Dermat. *Res:* Environmental medicine and dermatology; percutaneous absorption; cutaneous hypersensitivity; effects of physical environment on skin reactions to irritants and allergens; environmental cancer; environmental problems of chemical origin; mechanisms and patterns of cataneous responses to irritants and antigenic stimuli; percutaneous absorption; chemical carcinogenesis; biological effects of heavy metals. *Mailing Add:* Environ Health Univ Cincinnati 3223 Eden Ave Cincinnati OH 45267. *Fax:* 513-558-4397

SUSKIND, SIGMUND RICHARD, MICROBIOLOGY. *Current Pos:* from asst prof to prof, Johns Hopkins Univ, 56-65, dean grad & undergrad studies, 71-77, dean fac arts & sci, 78-83, prof, 83-97, Univ Ombudsman, 88-91, EMER UNIV PROF, JOHNS HOPKINS UNIV, 97- *Personal Data:* b New York, NY, June 19, 26; m 51, Ann P Loewenberg; c Richard, Mark & Steven. *Educ:* NY Univ, AB, 48; Yale Univ, PhD(microbiol), 54. *Prof Exp:* Asst microbiol, Yale Univ, 50-54; USPHS fel, NY Univ, 54-56. *Concurrent Pos:* Consult, Am Inst Biol Sci, 57-59, indust, 57-60, Coun Grad Schs & Med States Asn Cols & Sec Schs, 73-, NSF, 86-; spec consult, USPHS, 66-70; head, Molecular Biol Sect, USPHS, 70-71; vis scientist, Weizmann Inst Sci, Israel, 85; mem adv bd, La Geriat Educ Ctr, 90- *Mem:* Am Soc Microbiol; Genetics Soc Am; Am Asn Immunol; Am Soc Biol Chem; fel AAAS. *Res:* Molecular biology and gene expression. *Mailing Add:* Dept Biol McCollum-Pratt Inst Johns Hopkins Univ Charles St & 34th St Baltimore MD 21218. *Fax:* 410-516-5213; *E-Mail:* suskind@jhuvms.hcf.jhu.edu

SUSLICK, KENNETH SANDERS, SONOCHEMISTRY, BIOINORGANIC CHEMISTRY. *Current Pos:* from asst prof to assoc prof, 78-88, PROF CHEM, UNIV ILL, URBANA-CHAMPAIGN, 88-, PROF, BECKMAN INST, 89-, PROF MAT SCI ENG, 93-, ALUMNI RES SCH PROF CHEM, 95- *Personal Data:* b Chicago, Ill, Sept 16, 52; m 75, Adele Mazuret; c Benjamin A. *Educ:* Calif Inst Technol, BS, 74; Stanford Univ, PhD(chem), 78. *Honors & Awards:* Silver Medal, Royal Soc Arts, Mfgs & Com; Res Career Develop Award, NIH; Nobel Laureate Signature Award, Am Chem Soc; Mat Res Soc Medal, 94. *Prof Exp:* Res asst, Calif Inst Technol, 71-74; chemist, Lawrence Livermore Lab, 74-75. *Concurrent Pos:* Res asst, Univ Calif, Berkeley, 72; Hertz fel, Stanford Univ, 74-78; Sloan Found res fel; vis fel, Balliol Col & Inorg Chem Lab, Oxford Univ, 86. *Mem:* Am Chem Soc; fel AAAS; fel Acoust Soc Am. *Res:* Synthetic analogs of heme proteins, porphyrins and macrocycles; homogeneous catalysis; chemical effects of high intensity ultrasound, sonochemistry and sonocatalysis; sonoluminescence; biochemistry; materials science engineering. *Mailing Add:* Dept Chem Univ Ill 505 S Mathews Ave Urbana IL 61801. *E-Mail:* ksuslick@uiuc.edu

SUSMAN, LEON, ELECTRICAL ENGINEERING. *Current Pos:* CHIEF SCI, ADVAN POWER TECHNOL, INC, 88- *Personal Data:* b Brooklyn, NY, Oct 10, 36; m 58; c 3. *Educ:* City Col NY, BEE, 58, MEE, 62; Polytech Inst Brooklyn, PhD(elec eng), 69. *Prof Exp:* Engr, Ford Instrument Co Div, Sperry Rand Corp, 58 & Airborne Instruments Labs Div, Cutter Hammer Corp, 58-61; sr engr, Sperry Gyroscope Div, Sperry Rand Corp, 61-68, res staff mem microwave & antenna res, 68-80, mgr, Electromagnetics Dept, 80-88. *Mem:* Inst Elec & Electronics Engrs. *Res:* Microwave and antenna theory, in particular the application of transient performance to a wideband theory for radar; traffic control sensor; altimetry applications. *Mailing Add:* Adv Power Technol Inc 1250 24th St NW Washington DC 20037

SUSMAN, MILLARD, GENETICS. *Current Pos:* from asst prof to assoc prof, Univ Wis-Madison, 62-73, chmn dept, 71-75 & 77-86, assoc dean, Med Sch, 86-94, actg dean, Sch Allied Health Professions, 88-90, assoc dean, Med Sch, 86-94, spec adv to dean, Med Sch, 94-95, PROF GENETICS, LAB GENETICS, UNIV WIS-MADISON, 72-, DIR, CTR BIOL EDUC, 95- *Personal Data:* b St Louis, Mo, Sept 1, 34; m 57, Barbara B Fretwell; c 2. *Educ:* Wash Univ, AB, 56; Calif Inst Technol, PhD(genetics), 62. *Prof Exp:* NIH fel, Med Res Coun Microbial Genetics Res Unit, Hammersmith Hosp, London, Eng, 61-62. *Concurrent Pos:* Actg dean, Sch of Allied Health Professions, 88-90. *Mem:* AAAS; Genetics Soc Am; Sigma Xi. *Res:* Bacteriophage genetics and developmental genetics; effects of acridines on bacteriophage growth, recombination and mutation; role of the host cell in phage growth. *Mailing Add:* Lab of Genetics 507 Genetics Bldg Univ Wis-Madison 445 Henry Mall Madison WI 53706. *Fax:* 608-262-2976

SUSMAN, RANDALL LEE, ANATOMY, PHYSICAL ANTHROPOLOGY. *Current Pos:* Lectr & fel, 76-77, ASSOC PROF ANAT SCI, STATE UNIV NY, STONY BROOK, 77- *Personal Data:* b Houston, Tex, Jan 19, 48; m 69; c 2. *Educ:* Univ Calif, Davis, BA, 70; Univ Chicago,

MA, 72, PhD(anthrop), 76; Touro Col, ID, 88. *Mem:* Am Asn Phys Anthropologists; AAAS; Soc Syst Zoologists; Am Anthrop Asn; Soc Vert Paleont. *Res:* Evolution of apes and humans; functional morphology of primates; natural history of the primates; electromyography; gross anatomy; field study of pygmy chimpanzee in Zaire. *Mailing Add:* Dept Anat Sci State Univ NY Health Sci Col Med 100 Nicholls Rd Stony Brook NY 11794-0001

SUSSDORF, DIETER HANS, IMMUNOLOGY. *Current Pos:* from asst prof to assoc prof microbiol, 64-95, ASSOC DEAN, CORNELL UNIV, 84-, ASSOC EMER PROF, MED COL & GRAD SCH MED SCI, 95- *Personal Data:* b Neustadt, Ger, Aug 16, 30; nat US; m 54, Eleanor Stano; c Claudia, Wendy & Ellen. *Educ:* Univ Mo, BA, 52; Univ Chicago, PhD(microbiol), 56. *Honors & Awards:* David Anderson-Berry Prize, 61. *Prof Exp:* Logan fel, Univ Chicago, 57-58; resident res assoc biol, Argonne Nat Lab, 58-59; res fel immunochem, Calif Inst Technol, 59-61; res immunochemist, NIH, 61-63. *Concurrent Pos:* Consult, Travenol Labs, 78-81; course dir & lectr, Ctr Prof Advan, 72-; consult, Diamond Shamrock Chem Corp, 85-88. *Res:* Function of thymus and non-thymic tissues in humoral and cellular immunity; anti-tumor activities of macrophages. *Mailing Add:* Dept Microbiol Cornell Univ Med Col 1300 York Ave New York NY 10021

SUSSENGUTH, EDWARD H, COMPUTER NETWORKING. *Current Pos:* Res & development, 59-70, div dir, 70-81, IBM FEL, IBM, 81- *Personal Data:* b Holyoke, Mass, Oct 10, 32; m 59; c 2. *Educ:* Harvard Univ, AB, 54, PhD(appl math), 64; Mass Inst Technol, MS, 59. *Concurrent Pos:* Adv, Nat Bur Standards, 86-89 & Columbia Univ, Ctr Telecommun Res, 88- *Mem:* Inst Elec & Electronic Engrs; Asn Comput Mach; Sigma Xi. *Res:* Computer networking; high speed data communications. *Mailing Add:* 411 Rutherglen Dr Cary NC 27511

SUSSER, MERVYN W, EPIDEMIOLOGY, SOCIAL MEDICINE. *Current Pos:* ED, AM J PUB HEALTH, 92- *Personal Data:* b Johannesburg, SAfrica, Sept 26, 21; m 49, Zena Stein; c 3. *Educ:* Univ Witwatersrand, MB, BCh, 50, DPH, 60; FRCP(Ed) 57, MRCP(E), 70. *Hon Degrees:* DSc, Witwatersrand Univ, 93. *Honors & Awards:* John Snow Award, Am Pub Health Asn, 94. *Prof Exp:* Med officer, Alexandria Health Ctr & Univ Clin, Johannesburg, 51-55; from lectr to reader social med, Univ Manchester, 57-65; Asn Aid Crippled Children Belding scholar, 65-66; prof, Columbia Univ, 66-77, Gertrude H Sergievsky emer prof epidemiol & dir, Sergievsky Ctr, 77-92. *Concurrent Pos:* Clin tutor med, Univ Witwatersrand, 51-55; John Simon Guggenheim fel, 72-73; mem comt, Sect Epidemiol & Community Psychiat, World Psychiat Asn; vis prof, Univ Sydney, 75, Inst of Social Med, Brazil, 79, Nat Inst Ment Health, Peru, 88, Superior Inst, Italy, 89; ed, Am J Pub Health, 92-, SAfrican J Pub Health, 95- *Mem:* Sr mem Inst Med-Nat Acad Sci; Am Sociol Asn; Soc Epidemiol Res; NY Acad Med; Am Epidemiol Soc; fel Am Col Epidemiol; Fel Am Pub Health Asn; fel Royal Col Physicians; Nat Med & Dent Asn. *Res:* Developmental brain disorders; social and cultural factors in human development and disease. *Mailing Add:* Sergievsky Ctr Columbia Univ 630 W 168th St New York NY 10032

SUSSEX, IAN MITCHELL, BOTANY. *Current Pos:* assoc prof, 60-73, PROF BOT, YALE UNIV, 73- *Personal Data:* b Auckland, NZ, May 4, 27. *Educ:* Univ NZ, BS, 48, MSc, 50; Manchester Univ, PhD, 52. *Prof Exp:* Asst lectr bot, Victoria Univ Col, 54-55; asst prof, Univ Pittsburgh, 55-60. *Mem:* AAAS; Soc Develop Biol; Bot Soc Am; Int Soc Plant Morphol; Am Soc Cell Biol; Am Genetics Soc; Soc Plant Molecular Biol. *Res:* Plant development; tissue culture. *Mailing Add:* Dept Plant Biol Univ Calif Berkeley 345 Mulford Hall Berkeley CA 94720-0001

SUSSEX, JAMES NEIL, PSYCHIATRY. *Current Pos:* RETIRED. *Personal Data:* b Northcote, Minn, Oct 2, 17; m 43; c 4. *Educ:* Univ Kans, AB, 39, MD, 42. *Prof Exp:* Resident psychiat, US Naval Hosp, Mare Island, Calif, 46-49; asst clin prof psychiat, Sch Med, Georgetown Univ, 53-55; assoc prof, Med Col Ala, 55-59, prof & chmn dept, 59-68; chmn, Dept Psychiat, Sch Med, Univ Miami, 70-83, prof psychiat, 68-89, emer chmn, 83-89. *Concurrent Pos:* Fel child psychiat, Philadelphia Child Guid Clin, Univ Pa, 49-51; dir, Ment Health Serv Div, Jackson Mem Hosp, Miami, 70-83; consult, NIMH; consult, Vet Admin, mem, Ment Adv Coun; pres, Am Asn Psychiat Serv Children, 72-74; dir, Am Bd Psychiat & Neurol, 75-82, pres, 82; bd dir, Coun Med Specialty Soc, 85-, pres, 88-89; mem, Coun Med Affairs, 88- *Mem:* AMA; Am Psychiat Asn; Am Col Psychiat; Am Acad Child & Adolescent Psychiat; Am Bd Med Specialties. *Res:* Child psychiatry; child development in cross-cultural perspective; atypical culture-bound syndromes; dissociative states. *Mailing Add:* 6950 SW 134th St Miami FL 33156-6975

SUSSKIND, CHARLES, BIOENGINEERING, HISTORY OF TECHNOLOGY. *Current Pos:* from asst prof to prof, 55-91, asst dean eng, 64-68, EMER PROF ENG SCI, UNIV CALIF, BERKELEY, 91- *Personal Data:* b Prague, Czech; nat US; m 45, T Teresa; c Pamela (Pettler), Peter & Amanda. *Educ:* Calif Inst Technol, BS, 48; Yale Univ, MEng, 49, PhD(elec eng), 51. *Honors & Awards:* Clerk Maxwell Premium, Brit Inst Electronic & Radio Eng, 52. *Prof Exp:* Res assoc, Stanford Univ, 51-55; lectr elec eng, univ & asst dir, Microwave Lab, 53-55. *Concurrent Pos:* Consult ed & dir, San Francisco Press Inc, 59-; govt consult, 68-; coordr acad affairs, Statewide Univ, 69-74. *Mem:* Biomed Eng Soc; Hist Sci Soc; AAAS; fel Inst Elec & Electronics Engrs; Brit Inst Elec Engrs. *Res:* Bioelectronics; bioeffects of nonionizing radiation; history and sociology of technology and science. *Mailing Add:* Col Eng Univ Calif Berkeley CA 94720

SUSSKIND, HERBERT, BIOMEDICAL ENGINEERING. *Current Pos:* mem, Med Radionuclide Develop Group, 70-77, mem, Nuclear Med Div, 77-94, RES COLLABR, BROOKHAVEN NAT LAB, 94- *Personal Data:* b Ratibor, Ger, Mar 23, 29; US citizen; m 61, E Suzanne Lieberman; c Helen J, Alex M & David A. *Educ:* City Col New York, BChE, 50; NY Univ, MChE, 61; NY State, PE, 55. *Prof Exp:* Mem shielding group, Brookhaven Nat Lab, 50-52, fuel processing group, 52-57, assoc sect supvr, 57-58, sect supvr, Slurry Group, 58-59, mem, Reactor Eval & Advan Concepts Group, 59-61, head, Org Cooled Reactor Prog, 61-63, head, Packed Bed Reactor Eng Studies, 63-66, mem, Reactor Eval & Advan Concepts Group, 66-70. *Concurrent Pos:* Biomed engr med staff, Brookhaven Clin Res Ctr, 75 -; assoc prof med, Dept Med, State Univ NY, Stony Brook, 79 - *Mem:* Am Inst Chem Engrs; Am Nuclear Soc; Soc Nuclear Med; Biomed Eng Soc; Am Thoracic Soc. *Res:* Application of chemical engineering to medical problems, principally in pulmonary physiology and nuclear medicine. *Mailing Add:* Med Dept Brookhaven Nat Lab Upton NY 11973-5000

SUSSMAN, ALFRED SHEPPARD, BIOLOGY. *Current Pos:* instr bot, Univ Mich, Ann Arbor, 50-52, from asst prof to assoc prof, 53-61, prof, 61-90, chmn dept bot, 63-68, assoc dean col lit, sci & arts, 68-70, actg dean, 70-71, assoc dean, H H Rackham Sch Grad Studies, 72-74, dean, 74-85, actg vpres acad affairs, 79-80, intern vpres grad studies res, 83-85, EMER PROF BOT, UNIV MICH, ANN ARBOR, 90- *Personal Data:* b Portsmouth, Va, July 4, 19; m 48, Selma Feinman; c Jean, Paul & Harold. *Educ:* Univ Conn, BS, 41; Harvard Univ, AM, 48, PhD(biol), 49. *Prof Exp:* Instr microbiol, Mass Gen Hosp, 48-49. *Concurrent Pos:* Nat Res Coun fel, Univ Pa; Lalor Found fel, 56; NSF sr fel, Calif Inst Technol, 59-60; consult panel develop biol, NSF, 63-65, mem steering comt & comt innovation in lab instr, Biol Sci Curric Study, comnr comn undergrad educ biol sci, 66-69; chmn comt educ, Am Inst Biol Sci; mem biol comt, Argonne Univ Asn, 69-71, chmn, 70-71, examr, NCent Asn Col & Univ, 71-, exec comt, 79-; mem, Grad Rec Examr Bd, Res Comt, 78, chmn, 79-80, mem comt bio & med, 72-78, trustee, 74-78. *Res:* Physiological mycology; microbial physiology and development; dormancy in microorganisms. *Mailing Add:* 1615 Harbal Dr Ann Arbor MI 48105

SUSSMAN, DANIEL JESSE, SIGNAL TRANSDUCTION, DEVELOPMENTAL NEUROBIOLOGY. *Current Pos:* ASST PROF, DIV HUMAN GENETICS, UNIV MD SCH MED, 92- *Personal Data:* b Evanston, Ill, Oct 11, 57. *Educ:* Brandeis Univ, BA, 79; Johns Hopkins Univ, PhD(biochem), 86. *Honors & Awards:* Shannon Award, NIH, 93. *Prof Exp:* Res assoc, Harvard Med Sch, 86-90; sr scientist, W Alton Jones Cell Sci Ctr, 90-93. *Concurrent Pos:* Adj fac, Univ Vt, 92-; sci adv, Disney prod TV ser, 94- *Mem:* AAAS; Am Soc Human Genetics; Soc Develop Biol. *Res:* Investigating the signal transduction pathway mediated by the wnt-1 proto-oncogene. *Mailing Add:* 655 W Baltimore St Baltimore MD 21201. *Fax:* 410-706-6105; *E-Mail:* daniel@genetics.ab.umd.edu

SUSSMAN, HOWARD H, PATHOLOGY, LABORATORY MEDICINE. *Current Pos:* from asst prof to assoc prof, 69-85, PROF PATH, SCH MED, STANFORD UNIV, 85- *Personal Data:* b Portland, Ore, Oct 21, 34; m 70; c 3. *Educ:* Univ Ore, BS, 57, MS, 60, MD, 60. *Prof Exp:* Surgeon, USPHS, 61-69. *Concurrent Pos:* Sci adv, John Muir Cancer & Aging Inst. *Mem:* NY Acad Sci; Am Asn Clin Chem; Int Soc Oncodevelop Biol & Med; Am Found Clin Res; Acad Clin Lab Physicians & Scientists; Am Fed Med Res; Am Soc Clin Path. *Res:* Elucidation of cellular mechanisms of gene regulations which relate to the neoplastic process in humans; phenomenon of ectopic proteins synthesis in human cancer; transferin reception; ions and copper cellular metabolism and activity; fetal cells monitoring in maternal circulation; medical informatics; laboratory information systems. *Mailing Add:* Dept Path L217A Stanford Univ Sch Med Stanford CA 94305-5324. *Fax:* 650-725-6902

SUSSMAN, KARL EDGAR, MEDICINE, ENDOCRINOLOGY. *Current Pos:* RETIRED. *Personal Data:* b Baltimore, Md, May 29, 29; m 55, Joan Flah; c Paula & Ann. *Educ:* Johns Hopkins Univ, BA, 51; Univ Md, MD, 55. *Prof Exp:* Chief med serv, Denver Vet Admin Hosp, 72-75, clin investr, 75-80; from instr to assoc prof med, Univ Colo Med Ctr, Denver, 62-73, head, Div Endocrinol, 69-72, prof med, 73-94; assoc chief staff res & develop, Vet Affairs Med Ctr, Denver, 82-94. *Mem:* Am Col Physicians; Am Diabetes Asn; Am Fedn Clin Res; Am Physiol Soc; Endocrine Soc. *Res:* Factors controlling insulin secretion in isolated rat islets; hormonal control of carbohydrate-lipid metabolism; relationship of intermediary metabolism to insulin secretion; somatostatin-effect on hormone secretion; regulation of somatostation binding. *Mailing Add:* 3769 S Glencoe Denver CO 80237. *Fax:* 303-377-5686

SUSSMAN, M(ARTIN) V(ICTOR), CHEMICAL ENGINEERING, THERMODYNAMICS. *Current Pos:* chmn dept, 61-71, PROF CHEM ENG, TUFTS UNIV, 61- *Personal Data:* b New York, NY; m 53; c 3. *Educ:* City Col NY, BChE; Columbia Univ, MS, 52, PhD(chem eng), 58. *Honors & Awards:* Fulbright-Hays sr lectr, 77; Distinguished Vis Lectr, Va Polytech Inst, 80. *Prof Exp:* Instrument engr, Lummus Co, 47-48 & A G McKee & Co, 48-49; instr chem & res assoc, Fordham Univ, 49-50; asst prof, Columbia Univ, 51; sr engr, Textile Fiber Div, E I du Pont de Nemours & Co, Inc, 53-58; founder, Chem Eng Dept-Turkey, Robert Col, Istanbul, 58-61. *Concurrent Pos:* consult, USAID, 63 & 65, mem, NSF liaison staff, USAID, India, 67-68; NIH spec res fel, Weizmann Inst Sci, 68-69; Ford Found consult curric develop, Birla Inst Technol, India, 71-; vis prof, Mass Inst Technol, 75, Univ Capetown, 90; Erskine prof, Univ Canterbury, NZ, 83; Meyerhoff fel, Weizmann Inst, 83; hon res assoc, Exeter Univ, 90; Sch, Univ Cambridge. *Mem:* Fel Am Inst Chem Engrs; Am Chem Soc; Am Soc Eng Educ; Sigma Xi. *Res:* Thermodynamics; synthetic fibers; biotechnology; cell culture; holder of over 20 patents; holder of patents in fiber processing and biotechnology under active commercial licenses. *Mailing Add:* Dept Chem Eng Tufts Univ 00098264xv Medford MA 02155

SUSSMAN, MAURICE, DEVELOPMENTAL BIOLOGY, MOLECULAR BIOLOGY. *Current Pos:* PROF & CHMN DEPT BIOL SCI, UNIV PITTSBURGH, 76- *Personal Data:* b New York, NY, Mar 2, 22; m 48; c 3. *Educ:* City Col New York, BS, 42; Univ Minn, PhD(bact), 49. *Honors & Awards:* NIH career develop award, 66. *Prof Exp:* USPHS fel & instr bact, Univ Ill, 49-50; instr biol sci, Northwestern Univ, 50-53, from asst prof to assoc prof, 53-58; assoc prof, Brandeis Univ, 58-60, prof, 60-73; prof inst life sci, Hebrew Univ Jerusalem, 73-76. *Concurrent Pos:* Instr, Marine Biol Lab, Woods Hole, 56-60 & 67-70. *Mem:* Am Soc Microbiol; Soc Gen Physiol; Soc Develop Biol; Am Soc Biol Chem; Brit Soc Gen Microbiol. *Res:* Cellular differentiation and morphogenesis; molecular genetics. *Mailing Add:* 72 Carey Lane Falmouth MA 02540-1604. *Fax:* 508-540-6902

SUSSMAN, MICHAEL R, ENERGY TRANSDUCTION, PROTEIN ENGINEERING. *Current Pos:* from asst prof to assoc prof, 83-89, PROF PLANT MOLECULAR BIOL, DEPT HORT, UNIV WIS-MADISON, 91-, INTERIM DIR, BIOTECHNOL CTR, 96- *Personal Data:* b New York, NY, Sept 3, 50; m 83, Nancy J Gaedke; c 2. *Educ:* Bucknell Univ, BS, 71; Mich State Univ, PhD(bot), 76. *Prof Exp:* Fel plant phys, Biol Dept, Yale Univ Med Sch, 76-78, assoc biochem & genetics, Dept Human Genetics, 79-82. *Concurrent Pos:* Res award plant biol, McKnight Found, 83-86; var res grants, Dept Energy, US Dept Agr & NSF, 85-96; consult plant molecular biol, 89-96; vis prof, Cath Univ Louvain, Belg, 90; Fulbright res scholar, 90; Romnes Mid-Career Res Award, 96. *Mem:* Am Soc Plant Physiologists; Int Soc Plant Molecular Biol; AAAS. *Res:* Molecular basis of ion transport across membranes, especially plasma membrane; mechanism of action of plant hormones; molecular regulation of plant growth and development; author of numerous publications. *Mailing Add:* Dept Hort Univ Wis 1575 Linden Dr Madison WI 53706

SUSSMAN, MYRON MAURICE, NUMERICAL ANALYSIS. *Current Pos:* MATHEMATICIAN, BETTIS ATOMIC POWER LAB, WESTINGHOUSE ELEC CO, 75- *Personal Data:* b Trenton, NJ, Oct 7, 45; m 70. *Educ:* Mass Inst Technol, SB, 67; Carnegie-Mellon Univ, MS, 68, PhD(math), 75. *Prof Exp:* Instr math, Carnegie-Mellon Univ, 68-69 & Robert Morris Col, 69-71. *Mem:* Soc Indust & Appl Math; Sigma Xi; Am Math Soc. *Res:* Numerical analysis of partial differential equations and iterative solution of large linear systems of algebraic equations. *Mailing Add:* 5026 Belmont Ave Bethel Park PA 15102-2002

SUSSMAN, RAQUEL ROTMAN, MOLECULAR BIOLOGY. *Current Pos:* ASSOC SCIENTIST, MARINE BIOL LAB, 87- *Personal Data:* b Arg, Oct 22, 21; nat US; m 48, Maurice; c Paul, Michael & Daniel. *Educ:* Univ Chile, BS, 44; Univ Ill, PhD(bact), 52. *Prof Exp:* Asst viruses, Inst Bact Chile, 44-48; asst microbiol, Univ Minn, 48-49 & Univ Ill, 49-50; res assoc, Northwestern Univ, 50-58 & Brandeis Univ, 58-73; sr lectr, Dept Molecular Biol, Hadassah Med Sch, Hebrew Univ, Israel, 73-75; assoc prof, dept biol sci, Univ Pittsburgh, 76-87. *Concurrent Pos:* Hon mem, Chile Soc Microbiol, 71. *Mem:* Sigma Xi; fel AAAS; Am Soc Microbiol. *Res:* Molecular biology, chiefly genetics microbiology. *Mailing Add:* Marine Biol Lab Woods Hole MA 02543. *E-Mail:* rsussman@mbl.edu

SUSSMAN, ROBERT WALD, PRIMATOLOGY, CONSERVATION BIOLOGY. *Current Pos:* PROF ANTHROP, WASH UNIV ST LOUIS, 73- *Personal Data:* b Brooklyn, NY, July 4, 41; m 71, Linda K; c Katya J & Diana W. *Educ:* Univ Calif, Los Angeles, BA, 65, MA, 67; Duke Univ, PhD(anthrop), 72. *Prof Exp:* Asst prof anthrop, Hunter Col, City Univ NY, 71-73. *Concurrent Pos:* Adj res prof anthrop, NY Univ, 73; mem, Sci Rev Comt, Nat Cancer Inst, 75-78; consult, Can Broadcasting Co, 79; assoc ed, Am J Phys Anthrop, 86-90; vis prof anthrop, Sch Agron, Univ Madagascar, 87-88. *Mem:* Am Asn Phys Anthropologists; Orgn Trop Studies; Asn Am Anthropologists; Am Soc Primatologists; Int Soc Primatologists; Defenders of wildlife. *Res:* Naturally occurring primate populations, focusing mainly on ecology and behavior; primate evolution and the relationship between behavior and anatomy. *Mailing Add:* 360 N Mosley Rd St Louis MO 63141

SUTCLIFFE, SAMUEL, civil engineering, mathematics, for more information see previous edition

SUTCLIFFE, WILLIAM GEORGE, PHYSICS. *Current Pos:* PHYSICIST, LAWRENCE LIVERMORE LAB, 68- *Personal Data:* b Detroit, Mich, Nov 25, 37; m 60, Sally H Harris; c Laura A, Catherine L, William H & Michael G. *Educ:* Univ Mich, BS, 60; Univ Del, PhD(physics), 69. *Prof Exp:* Instr physics, US Naval Nuclear Power Sch, 62-64. *Mem:* Am Asn Physics Teachers; Am Nuclear Soc; Inst Nuclear Mat Mgt; AAAS. *Res:* Analysis of nuclear fuel cycles, safeguards and nonproliferation issues. *Mailing Add:* Lawrence Livermore Lab L-19 PO Box 808 Livermore CA 94551

SUTCLIFFE, WILLIAM HUMPHREY, JR, ZOOLOGY. *Current Pos:* RETIRED. *Personal Data:* b Miami, Fla, Nov 8, 23; m 45, 49, 64, Elizabeth P Wilson; c 5. *Educ:* Emory Univ, BA, 45; Duke Univ, MA, 47, PhD(zool), 50. *Prof Exp:* Instr zool, Duke Univ, 49-50; investr marine biol, NC Inst Fisheries Res, 50-51, 50-51; staff biologist lobster invests, Bermuda Biol Sta, 51-53, dir, 53-63; head, Fisheries Oceanog Sect, Bedford Inst Oceanog, 75-76, res scientist, 67-81. *Concurrent Pos:* Assoc, Woods Hole Oceanog Inst, 57; dir marine sci ctr, Lehigh Univ, 64-67. *Mem:* Fel AAAS; NY Acad Sci. *Res:* Dynamics of plankton populations; air-sea interaction; marine food chains. *Mailing Add:* Rte 4 Box 449 Bakersville NC 28705

SUTER, BRUCE WILSEY, SIGNAL PROCESSING, WAVELETS. *Current Pos:* asst prof, 89-91, ASSOC PROF, AIR FORCE INST TECHNOL, 91- *Personal Data:* b Paterson, NJ, Sept 15, 49; m 74, Deborah S Boudinet. *Educ:* Univ SFla, BS, 72, MS, 72, PhD(computer sci), 88. *Prof Exp:* Design engr, Honeywell, Inc, 72-77; sr design engr, Litton Industs, 77-80; res asst, Univ SFla, 80-85; from instr to asst prof, Univ Ala, Birmingham, 85-89. *Mem:* Sr mem Inst Elec & Electronics Engrs. *Res:* Wavelets; time-frequency analysis; multirate signal processing. *Mailing Add:* Dept Elec Eng Air Force Inst Technol 2950 P Street Wright-Patterson AFB OH 45433-7765. *Fax:* 937-656-4055; *E-Mail:* bsuter@afit.af.mil

SUTER, DANIEL B, HUMAN ANATOMY, PHYSIOLOGY. *Current Pos:* Asst prof to prof, Eastern Mennonite Col, 48-85, chmn Div Natural Sci & Math, 64-85, chmn, Dept Life Sci, 72-76, assoc dean, 76-77, EMER PROF BIOL, EASTERN MENNONITE COL, 63-, CHMN DIV NATURAL SCI & MATH, 85- *Personal Data:* b Hinton, Va, Apr 25, 20; m 41, Grace Fisher; c Janice (Showalter), David R, Mary L (Tierney) & Daniel B. *Educ:* Bridgewater Col, BA, 47; Vanderbilt Univ, MA, 48; Med Col Va, PhD(anat), 63. *Concurrent Pos:* NIH fel, Univ Calif, Davis, 70-71. *Mem:* Asn Am Med Cols; Am Asn Anat; Am Sci Affiliation. *Res:* Effects of radiation and pesticides, especially organophosphates, on the central nervous system. *Mailing Add:* 102 Old 33 St W Harrisonburg VA 22801

SUTER, GLENN WALTER, II, TOXICOLOGY. *Current Pos:* RES STAFF MEM, ENVIRON SCI DIV, OAK RIDGE NAT LAB, 75- *Personal Data:* b Harrisonburg, Va, May 1, 48; m 68. *Educ:* Va Polytech Inst, BS, 69; Univ Calif, Davis, PhD(ecol), 76. *Mem:* AAAS; Ecol Soc Am; Soc Environ Toxicol & Chem; Soc Risk Anal. *Res:* Ecological risk assessment. *Mailing Add:* 1521 N Campbell Station Rd Knoxville TN 37932

SUTER, ROBERT WINFORD, CHEMISTRY. *Current Pos:* Assoc prof, 69-80, PROF CHEM, BLUFFTON COL, 80- *Personal Data:* b Warren, Ohio, Aug 3, 41; m 63; c 2. *Educ:* Bluffton Col, BA, 63; Ohio State Univ, MS, 66, PhD(chem), 69. *Mem:* Am Chem Soc. *Res:* Inorganic chemistry, particularly nonmetals; solution phenomena. *Mailing Add:* 10620 Bixel Rd Bluffton OH 45817-0506

SUTER, STUART ROSS, MEDICINAL CHEMISTRY, TECHNOLOGY TRANSFER. *Current Pos:* CONSULT CHEM & PHARMACEUT PATENTS & TECHNOL TRANSFER. *Personal Data:* b Harrisonburg, Va, Apr 1, 41; m 63, Lorraine Helmick; c 2. *Educ:* Bridgewater Col, BA, 63; Univ Mich, Ann Arbor, MS, 65; Univ Va, PhD(org chem), 71; Temple Univ, DJur, 76. *Prof Exp:* Assoc chemist, Smith Kline & French Labs, 65-67; patent chemist, Smithkline Beecham Corp, 71-76, patent atty, 76-88, vpres & patent coun, 88-96. *Mem:* Am Chem Soc; Am Bar Asn; Am Int Property Asn; Licensing Exec Soc. *Res:* Aryl nitrenes; synthetic organic chemistry; medicinal chemistry. *Mailing Add:* 336 Woods Rd Glenside PA 19038

SUTERA, SALVATORE P, MECHANICAL ENGINEERING. *Current Pos:* PROF MECH ENG & CHMN DEPT, WASHINGTON UNIV, 68- *Personal Data:* b Baltimore, Md, Jan 12, 33; m 58, Celia A Fielden; c 3. *Educ:* Johns Hopkins Univ, BSc, 54; Calif Inst Technol, MSc, 55, PhD(eng), 60. *Hon Degrees:* MA, Brown Univ, 65. *Prof Exp:* From asst prof to assoc prof eng, Brown Univ, 60-68, exec off div eng, 66-68. *Concurrent Pos:* Nat Heart Inst res grants, 65-67 & 69-94; consult, Nat Heart, Lung & Blood Inst, 70- *Mem:* Fel Am Soc Mech Engrs; Am Soc Eng Educ; AAAS; Am Soc Artificial Internal Organs; Int Soc Biorheology; Am Soc Heating Refrig & Air Conditioning Engrs. *Res:* Fluid mechanics of blood flow; artificial organs; rheology of suspensions. *Mailing Add:* Dept Mech Eng Wash Univ Box 1185 St Louis MO 63130

SUTHERLAND, BETSY MIDDLETON, BIOCHEMISTRY, CELL BIOLOGY. *Current Pos:* SCIENTIST DNA REPAIR, DEPT BIOL, BROOKHAVEN NAT LAB, 77- *Personal Data:* b New York, NY, Oct 19, 43; m 65. *Educ:* Emory Univ, BS, 64, MS, 65; Univ Tenn, PhD(radiation biol), 67. *Honors & Awards:* Edna M Rowe Mem Lectr Int Photobiol Cong; E O Lawrence Award. *Prof Exp:* NIH fel DNA chem, Lab Molecular Biol, Walter Reed Res Inst, 67-69; fel enzymol, Molecular Biol-Virus Lab, Univ Calif, Berkeley, 69-72; from asst prof to assoc prof molecular biol, Univ Calif, Irvine, 72-77. *Concurrent Pos:* Assoc ed, Photochem & Photobiol, 74-77; mem, Nat Comt Photobiol, Nat Acad Sci, 74-78; Nat Cancer Inst, NIH res career develop award, 75-80. *Mem:* Am Soc Photobiol; Tissue Cult Asn; AAAS; Am Soc Biochem & Molecular Biol. *Res:* DNA damage and repair; biology and biochemistry of photoreactivation; transformation of mammalian cells and its relation to oncogenesis; DNA transfection into human cells. *Mailing Add:* Dept Biol Brookhaven Nat Lab Bldg 463 Upton NY 11973-5000. *Fax:* 516-282-3407

SUTHERLAND, BILL, PHASE TRANSITIONS, QUANTUM MANY-BODY THEORY. *Current Pos:* from asst prof to assoc prof, 70-82, PROF PHYSICS, UNIV UTAH, 82- *Personal Data:* b Sedalia, Mo, Mar 31, 42; m 65; c 2. *Educ:* Wash Univ, AB, 63; State Univ NY, Stony Brook, MA, 65, PhD, 67. *Prof Exp:* Res assoc, State Univ NY, Stony Brook, 67-69; asst res physicist, Univ Calif, Berkeley, 69-70. *Mem:* Fel Am Phys Soc. *Res:* Statistical mechanics; phase transitions; critical phenomena; quasi-periodic systems; quantum many-body systems; strongly correlated systems. *Mailing Add:* Dept Physics Univ Utah Salt Lake City UT 84112. *Fax:* 801-581-4801

SUTHERLAND, C A, METALLURGICAL ENGINEERING. *Honors & Awards:* H T Airey Award, Can Inst Mining & Metall, 91. *Mailing Add:* c/o Xerox Tower Suite 1210 3400 de Maisonneuve Blvd W Montreal PQ H3Z 3B8 Can

SUTHERLAND, CHARLES F, forestry economics, for more information see previous edition

SUTHERLAND, DAVID M, PLANT TAXONOMY. *Current Pos:* From asst prof to assoc prof, 67-80, PROF BIOL, UNIV NEBR, OMAHA, 80- *Personal Data:* b Bellingham, Wash, Oct 5, 40. *Educ:* Western Wash State Col, BA, 63; Univ Wash, PhD(bot), 67. *Mem:* AAAS; Int Asn Plant Taxonomists; Bot Soc Am; Am Soc Plant Taxon; Sigma Xi. *Res:* Systematics of Dalea and related genera; floristics of Great Plains; vegetative characters of grasses. *Mailing Add:* Dept Biol Univ Nebr Omaha NE 68182-0040. *Fax:* 402-554-3532

SUTHERLAND, DONALD JAMES, PHYSIOLOGY, BIOCHEMISTRY. *Current Pos:* From asst prof to assoc prof, 60-67, PROF ENTOM, RUTGERS UNIV, NEW BRUNSWICK, 67-, DEPT CHMN, 87- *Personal Data:* b Chelsea, Mass, Oct 5, 29. *Educ:* Tufts Univ, BS, 51; Univ Mass, MS, 57; Rutgers Univ, PhD(entom), 60. *Mem:* Entom Soc Am; Am Mosquito Control Asn (pres, 86-87). *Res:* Management of mosquitoes, particularly chemical measures; biological rhythms of insects. *Mailing Add:* Dept Entom Rutgers Univ New Brunswick NJ 08903

SUTHERLAND, EARL C, ACCIDENT RECONSTRUCTION WITH COMPUTER SIMULATION, FORENSIC ENGINEERING. *Current Pos:* PRIN, EARL C SUTHERLAND & ASSOCS, 75- *Personal Data:* b Detroit, Mich, July 23, 23; m 71, Marion Schultz; c Earl M. *Educ:* Mich Col, BS, 50, MS, 50; Portland State Univ, MBA, 74. *Prof Exp:* Tech engr, Int Bus Mach Corp, 50-52; metallurgist, Fansteel Metall Corp, 52-56; tech dir & vpres, Eriez (BA) Prod Metal & Magnetics, 56-60; res specialist, NASA, 60-62; mfg mgr, Precision Castparts Corp, 62-64; dir res & advan eng, Omark Industs, 64-67; proj dir & vpres, MEI/Charleton Inc, 67-75. *Concurrent Pos:* Prin engr & consult engr, Earl C Sutherland Assocs & MEI/Charleton Inc, 67-; lectr & prof, Ore State Dept Higher Educ. *Mem:* Nat Asn Corrosion Engrs; Soc Automotive Engrs; Am Soc Metals Int; Nat Soc Prof Engrs; Am Consult Engrs Coun; Metal Inst. *Res:* Accident reconstruction of general aircraft and heavy industrial systems and machinery which fail in service; computer simulation of events to failure. *Mailing Add:* 2565 Dexter Ave N No 401 Seattle WA 98109. *Fax:* 206-285-0692

SUTHERLAND, G RUSSELL, ENGINEERING, MECHANICAL-PRODUCT ENGINEERING. *Current Pos:* RETIRED. *Personal Data:* b Rush Lake, Wis, Dec 20, 23; m 45, Leone Witkowski; c Keith A & Glenn E. *Educ:* Univ Wis, BS(mech eng) & BS(agr), 47, MS, 49. *Prof Exp:* Mgr prod eng, Deere & Co, Des Moines, 66-77, dir prod planning, 78-80, prod eng planning, 80-83 & prod eng, 83-84, vpres eng & technol, Moline, 84-88. *Concurrent Pos:* Mem bd dirs, Am Nat Stand Inst, 84-86. *Mem:* Nat Acad Eng; Am Soc Agr Eng; Soc Automotive Eng. *Mailing Add:* 16 Mason Lane Belle Vista Village Bella Vista AR 72715

SUTHERLAND, GEORGE LESLIE, ORGANIC CHEMISTRY. *Current Pos:* RETIRED. *Personal Data:* b Dallas, Tex, Aug 13, 22; wid, Carol B Kaplan; c 3. *Educ:* Univ Tex, BS, 43, MA, 47, PhD(org chem), 50. *Prof Exp:* Lilly fel, Univ Tex, 49-51; chemist, AM Cyanamid Co, 51-57, group leader, 58-62, mgr metab & anal res, 62-66, dir prod develop & govt registr, 66-69, asst dir res & develop, 69-70, dir res & develop, 70-73, vpres res & develop, Lederle Labs Div, 73-78, dir, Chem Res Div 80-81, dir, Med Res Div, 78-86, vpres, Corp Res & Technol, 86-87. *Mem:* AAAS; Am Chem Soc; NY Acad Sci; Royal Soc Chem. *Res:* Organometallic compounds; anticonvulsants; microbiological growth factors; hypotensive agents; anticoccidials; chemical process development; formulation, metabolism and analysis of agricultural chemicals; discovery and development of pharmaceuticals. *Mailing Add:* 42 Sky Meadow Rd Suffern NY 10901-2519

SUTHERLAND, HERBERT JAMES, ENGINEERING MECHANICS, WIND ENERGY. *Current Pos:* DISTINGUISHED MEM TECH STAFF, SANDIA NAT LABS, 70- *Personal Data:* b San Antonio, Tex, Nov 1, 43; m 77, Vivian Brown; c Suzanne & Kenneth. *Educ:* Univ Tex, Austin, BS, 66, MS, 68, PhD(eng mech), 70. *Prof Exp:* Prod engr, Humble Oil Co, 66; assoc aircraft engr, Lockheed Ga Corp, 67; res teaching asst, Univ Tex, 67-70. *Concurrent Pos:* Vis scientist, Kernforschungszentrum Karslsruhe, Fed Repub Ger, 79. *Mem:* Fel Am Soc Mech Engrs; Am Soc Rheology; Am Acad Mech. *Res:* Constitutive formulations; instrumentation development; geomechanics; fatigue analysis; over 100 technical articles on the instrumentation and analysis of wave propagation in composite and viscoelastic materials, nuclear reactor safety studies, mine subsidence and soil stability, and damage accumulation in wind turbines. *Mailing Add:* Sandia Nat Labs PO Box 5800 MS 0708 Albuquerque NM 87185-0708. *Fax:* 505-845-9500

SUTHERLAND, IVAN EDWARD, COMPUTER SCIENCE, MATHEMATICS. *Current Pos:* VPRES & FEL, SUN MICROSYST LABS, 91- *Personal Data:* b Hastings, Nebr, May 16, 38; m 59; c 2. *Educ:* Carnegie-Mellon Univ, BS, 59; Calif Inst Technol, MS, 60; Mass Inst Technol, PhD(elec eng), 63. *Hon Degrees:* MA, Harvard Univ, 66. *Honors & Awards:* First Zworykin Award, Nat Acad Eng, 72; Outstanding Accomplishment Award, Systs, Man & Cybernet Soc, 75; First Steven Anson Coons Award, Asn Comput Mach Siggraph, 83, Am Touring Award, 88, Software Syst Award, 94; Emmanuel R Piore Award, Inst Elec & Electronics Engrs, 86. *Prof Exp:* Dir info processing tech, Defense Adv Res Projs Agency, 64-66; assoc prof, Div Eng & Appl Physics, Harvard Univ, 66-68; vpres & chief scientist, Evans & Sutherland Comput Corp, Salt Lake City, Utah, 68-74; prof & head, Dept Computer Sci, Calif Inst Technol, 76-80; vpres & tech dir, Sutherland, Sproull & Assocs, Inc, 80-91. *Concurrent Pos:* Tech opers officer, US Army Liaison Group, Proj Mich, Univ Mich, Ypsilanti, 63; elec engr, Nat Security Agency, Ft Meade, Md, 63-64; from assoc prof to prof, Dept Elec Eng, Comput Sci Div, Univ Utah, 68-73; mem, Naval Res Adv Comt, Dept Navy, 68-75, Comput Sci & Technol Bd, Assembly Math & Phys Sci, Nat Res Coun, 77-80, Defense Sci Bd, 77-84, vpres, Picture Design Group, Santa Monica, Calif, 74; mem bd dirs, Evans & Sutherland Comput Corp, 74-, Quotron Systs, Inc, Los Angeles, Calif, 80-, Nat Aviation & Technol Corp, NY, 82-85, Nat Telecommun & Technol Fund, NY, 83-85 & Newmarket Co, Ltd, Bermuda, 84-; sr tech staff mem, Rand Corp, 75-76; vis scientist, Robotics Inst, Carnegie-Mellon Univ, 80-84; gen partner, Advan Technol Ventures, Boston, Mass, 80-; vis acad, Imp Col, London Univ, 85- *Mem:* Nat Acad Sci; Nat Acad Eng; Inst Elec & Electronics Engrs; Sigma Xi; Asn Comput Mach. *Res:* Computer graphics; architecture of high performance computing machinery; algorithms for rapid execution of special functions; large-scale integrated circuit design; robots; author or co-author of over 40 publications. *Mailing Add:* Sun Microsystems MTV 29-01 2550 Garcia Ave Mountain View CA 94043. *E-Mail:* ivan@sutherland@eng.sun.com

SUTHERLAND, JAMES HENRY RICHARDSON, PHARMACOLOGY. *Current Pos:* Trainee cardiovasc res prog, Med Col Ga, 55-56, from asst prof to assoc prof pharmacol, 56-64, chmn dept, 64-68, dir div health commun, 68-74, prof, 64-85, EMER PROF PHARMACOL & TOXICOL, MED COL GA, 85- *Personal Data:* b Can, July 6, 23; nat US; div; c 3. *Educ:* Univ Calif, AB, 48, PhD(physiol), 56. *Mailing Add:* 2515 Center W Pkwy Apt 8A Augusta GA 30909

SUTHERLAND, JAMES MCKENZIE, PEDIATRICS, NEONATAL PERINATAL MEDICINE. *Current Pos:* from asst prof to prof, 56-87, EMER PROF PEDIAT, COL MED, UNIV CINCINNATI, 87- *Personal Data:* b Chicago, Ill, Aug 8, 23; m 53, Betty Steele; c Thomas Steele & Ann McKenzie. *Educ:* Univ Chicago, SB, 47, MD, 50; Am Bd Pediat, dipl, 55. *Prof Exp:* Intern, Cincinnati Gen Hosp, 50-51; resident pediat, Children's Hosp, 51-54; instr, Col Med, Univ Cincinnati, 53-54; fel, Harvard Med Sch, 54-56. *Concurrent Pos:* NIH fel, Children's Med Ctr, Boston, 54-56; attend pediatrician, Children's Hosp, Cincinnati, 56-; dir newborn div, Cincinnati Gen Hosp, 56-85; res assoc & head div newborn physiol, Children's Hosp Res Found, 56-85. *Mem:* AAAS; Soc Pediat Res; Am Pediat Soc; AMA; Am Acad Pediat. *Res:* Physiology of normal and abnormal respiration in infants. *Mailing Add:* 1338 Edwards Rd Cincinnati OH 45208

SUTHERLAND, JOHN B(ENNETT), CHEMICAL ENGINEERING. *Current Pos:* dir indust res & exten, 66-80, EMER PROF CHEM ENG, UNIV MO, COLUMBIA, 80- *Personal Data:* b Burlingame, Kans, Feb 21, 18; m 35, Maxine L Turvey; c John W, Max E & Lynn A. *Educ:* Kans State Col, BS, 39, MS, 40; Univ Pittsburgh, PhD(chem eng), 46. *Prof Exp:* Chem engr, Tex Co, Tex, 40-41; fel asst, Mellon Inst, 41-43; asst prof chem eng, Northwestern Univ, 43-46; pres Sutherland-Becker Labs, 46-64; dir res & planning, Butler Mfg Co, 56-65. *Concurrent Pos:* Exec dir, Kans Indust Develop Comn, 53-56, Master Practr Inst, 81-83; assoc dean eng, Kans State Univ, 65-66; consult corp planning, technol transfer & ventures; consult econ develop & corp planning, 80- *Mem:* Am Chem Soc; Am Inst Chem Engrs; Sigma Xi. *Res:* Lubricating oils; synthetic gems; economic development; gels and films; construction materials; statics and dynamics of bulk solids; research administration. *Mailing Add:* 3021 SW Burlingame Rd Topeka KS 66611-2003

SUTHERLAND, JOHN BRUCE, IV, MICROBIOLOGY. *Current Pos:* MICROBIOLOGIST, FOOD & DRUG ADMIN, 88- *Personal Data:* b Tampa, Fla, Nov 9, 45; m 82, Fatemeh Rafii. *Educ:* Stanford Univ, AB, 67; Univ Wis-Madison, MS, 73; Wash State Univ, PhD(plant path), 78. *Prof Exp:* Fel bacteriol, Univ Idaho, 77-81; asst prof biol sci, Tex Tech Univ, 81-83; res scientist, Mich Tech Univ, 84-86; vis assoc prof bacteriol, Univ Idaho, 86-88. *Concurrent Pos:* Instr, Wash State Univ, 78-79. *Mem:* Am Phytopath Soc; Am Soc Microbiol; Mycol Soc Am; Sigma Xi. *Res:* Biodegradation of xenobiotic compounds by fungi and actinomycetes. *Mailing Add:* 810 Green Oak Lane White Hall AR 71602. *Fax:* 870-543-7307; *E-Mail:* jsutherland@nctr.fda.gov

SUTHERLAND, JOHN CLARK, BIOPHYSICS. *Current Pos:* biophysicist, 77-89, SR BIOPHYSICIST, BROOKHAVEN NAT LAB, 89- *Personal Data:* b New York, NY, Sept 2, 40; m 65, Betsy Middleton. *Educ:* Ga Inst Technol, BS, 62, MS, 64, PhD(physics), 67. *Honors & Awards:* IR-100 Award, 87. *Prof Exp:* Biophysicist, Walter Reed Res Inst, 67-69; res fel, Lab Chem Biodyn, Univ Calif, Berkeley, 69-72, USPHS fel, 69-71; res fel chem, Univ Southern Calif, 72-73; from asst prof to assoc prof physiol, Calif Col Med-Univ Calif, Irvine, 73-77. *Concurrent Pos:* Assoc ed, Photochem & Photobiol, 81-84; res career develop award, Nat Cancer Inst, 66-81; adj prof physiol & biophysics, State Univ NY, Stony Brook, 93- *Mem:* Am Soc Photobiol; Am Phys Soc; Biophys Soc; Am Chem Soc; Electmophimiser Soc; Environ Mutagen Soc; Eurp Soc Photobrol. *Res:* Optical spectroscopy and photochemistry of biological molecules; DNA damage and repair synchrotron radiation; gel electrophoresis; electronic imaging; vacuum ultraviolet spectroscopy of metals. *Mailing Add:* Dept Biol Brookhaven Nat Lab Upton NY 11973-5000. *Fax:* 516-282-3407; *E-Mail:* jcs@bnl.gov

SUTHERLAND, JOHN W, MECHANICAL ENGINEERING, MANUFACTURING. *Current Pos:* from asst prof to assoc prof, 91-97, PROF MECH ENG & ENG MECH, MICH TECHNOL UNIV, 97- *Personal Data:* b Oklahoma City, Okla, Sept 18, 58. *Educ:* Univ Ill, Urbana-Champaign, BS, 80, MS, 82, PhD(mech eng), 87. *Honors & Awards:* Young Mfg Eng Award, Soc Mfg Engrs, 92. *Prof Exp:* Vpres consult, 87-91. *Concurrent Pos:* Pres early career grant scientists & engrs, NSF, 96. *Mailing Add:* Mich Technol Univ 1400 Townsend Dr Houghton MI 49931. *Fax:* 906-487-2822; *E-Mail:* jwsuther@mtu.edu

SUTHERLAND, JUDITH ELLIOTT, POLYMER CHEMISTRY. *Current Pos:* RETIRED. *Personal Data:* b Clovis, NMex, June 6, 24; m 47; c 2. *Educ:* Univ Tex, BSChem, 45; Univ Conn, MA, 68; Univ Mass, PhD(polymer chem), 72. *Prof Exp:* Res biochemist, Tex Agr Exp Sta, College Station, 45-46; res chemist biochem, Clayton Found, Biochem Inst, Austin, Tex, 46-48; chemist, Stamford Chem Co, Conn, 60-61 & Am Cyanamid Co, Conn, 61-71; res chemist polymers, Eastman Kodak Co Res Labs, 72-90. *Mem:* Am Chem Soc; AAAS: Am Phys Soc. *Res:* Polymer synthesis and characterization; solution properties; structure-property relationships; solid state properties of polymers and polymer composites. *Mailing Add:* 101 Burkedale Crescent Rochester NY 14625

SUTHERLAND, LOUIS CARR, ACOUSTICS, STRUCTURAL DYNAMICS. *Current Pos:* CONSULT ACOUST. *Personal Data:* b Walla Walla, Wash, June 2, 26; m 49, Marilyn J McLean; c Paul, Nancy & Alan. *Educ:* Univ Wash, BS, 46, MS, 54. *Prof Exp:* Res asst, Eng Exp Sta, Univ Wash, 47-49; res engr electroacoust, Dept Speech, 49-56; res specialist vibroacoust, Boeing Co, 56-64; dep dir & chief scientist res, Wyle Labs, 64-89. *Concurrent Pos:* Chmn, Subcomt Noise Metrics, SAE-Aircraft Noise Comt, 76-89; US deleg, ISO TC43/SCI/WG24 on Sound Propagation; assoc ed, J Acoust Soc Am. *Mem:* Fel Acoust Soc Am; Inst Elec & Electronics Engrs; Am Inst Aeronaut & Astronaut; Inst Noise Control Eng. *Res:* Physical acoustics as it relates to man's environment; sound propagation, aircraft noise, community noise, noise control, vibroacoustics, shock and vibration environments of aerospace systems. *Mailing Add:* 27803 Longhill Dr Rancho Palos Verdes CA 90275-3908. *Fax:* 310-541-7795; *E-Mail:* lou__sutherland@juno.com

SUTHERLAND, PATRICK KENNEDY, PALEOBIOLOGY, STRATIGRAPHY. *Current Pos:* assoc prof, 57-64, PROF GEOL, SCH GEOL & GEOPHYS, UNIV OKLA, 64- *Personal Data:* b Dallas, Tex, Feb 17, 25; div. *Educ:* Univ Okla, BSc, 46; Cambridge Univ, PhD(geol), 52. *Prof Exp:* Geologist, Phillips Petrol Co, 46-49, 52-53; asst prof geol, Univ Houston, 53-57. *Concurrent Pos:* Nat Acad Sci vis exchange fel, USSR, 71. *Mem:* Fel Geol Soc Am; Paleont Soc; Soc Econ Paleont & Mineral; Am Asn Petrol Geol. *Res:* Paleobiology; biostratigraphy; paleoecology; carboniferous Rugose corals and brachiopods. *Mailing Add:* Univ Okla Sch Geol & Geophysics 100 E Boyd Sec 810 Norman OK 73018-0628

SUTHERLAND, PETER GORDON, THEORETICAL ASTROPHYSICS. *Current Pos:* from asst prof to prof physics, 76-96, chair, Physics Dept, 87-91, DEAN SCI, MCMASTER UNIV, 96- *Personal Data:* b Montreal, Que, Oct 19, 46; m 81, Linda R Mills; c Jesse, Hal & Bryn. *Educ:* McGill Univ, BSc, 67; Univ Ill, MS, 68, PhD(physics), 72. *Prof Exp:* Fel, Physics Dept, Columbia Univ, 71-74; asst prof, Univ Pa, 74-76. *Concurrent Pos:* Lectr, Astron Dept, Columbia Univ, 72-74; Alfred P Sloan Found fel, 78-82; vis scientist, Astron Dept, Univ Tex, Austin, 80-81 & Joint Inst Lab Astrophys, Univ Colo, 86-87. *Mem:* Am Astron Soc; Int Astron Union; Can Asn Physicists. *Res:* Neutron stars; pulsars; compact x-ray sources; supernovae. *Mailing Add:* Gen Sci Bldg Rm 114 McMaster Univ 1280 Main St W Hamilton ON L8S 4K1 Can. *Fax:* 905-546-1252; *E-Mail:* pgs@physun.physics.mcmaster.ca

SUTHERLAND, RICHARD LEE, NONLINEAR OPTICS, QUANTUM ELECTRONICS. *Current Pos:* Scientist, 78-81, sr scientist, 81-93, ASST VPRES, SCI APPLNS INT CORP, 93- *Personal Data:* b Oskaloosa, Iowa, Aug 3, 50; m 72, Marcine Johnson; c Kari & Kendra. *Educ:* Olivet Nazarene Univ, BA, 72; Ohio State Univ, MS, 74, PhD(physics), 79. *Concurrent Pos:* Prin investr, Wright Lab, USAF, 78-80 & 83-, optical charicterization group leader, 91-; adj prof physics, Wright State Univ, 88. *Mem:* Am Phys Soc; Optical Soc Am; Soc Photo-Instrumentation Engrs; Mat Res Soc; Sigma Xi. *Res:* Development of novel organic, liquid crystal and polymeric composite materials and devices for optical limiting, tunable filters and optical switches with applications in laser projection, optical information processing, image/information displays. *Mailing Add:* Sci Applns Int Corp 4031 Colonel Glenn Dayton OH 45431. *Fax:* 937-255-1128; *E-Mail:* sutherri@ml.wpafb.af.mil

SUTHERLAND, ROBERT L(OUIS), ENGINEERING DESIGN & CONSULTING. *Current Pos:* PRES, SKYLINE ENG, INC, 71- *Personal Data:* b Fellsmere, Fla, May 15, 16; m 45, Mary-Alice Reed; c Robert H (deceased), Wayne M, Connie Ann, Nancy Lee & John Gary. *Educ:* Univ Ill, BS, 39, MS, 48. *Honors & Awards:* Templin Award, Am Soc Testing & Mat, 52. *Prof Exp:* Develop engr, Firestone Tire & Rubber Co, Ohio, 39-41; res engr, Borg & Beck Div, Borg-Warner Corp, Ill, 41-42; test engr, Buick Motor Div, Gen Motors Corp, 42-43; sr engr res, Aeronca Aircraft Corp, Ohio, 43-45; res assoc, Col Eng, Univ Ill, 45-48; assoc prof mech eng, Univ Iowa, 48-58; prof, 58-79, head dept, 60-70, EMER PROF ENG, UNIV WYO, 79- *Concurrent Pos:* Legis fel, Nat Conf State Legis, 82-84. *Mem:* Fel Am Soc Mech Engrs (vpres, 64-67); Soc Automotive Engrs; Am Soc Mech Engrs; Sigma Xi. *Res:* Engineering analysis, vibrations and machine design. *Mailing Add:* Box 54 Laramie WY 82070

SUTHERLAND, ROBERT MELVIN, CANCER RESEARCH. *Current Pos:* VPRES & EXEC DIR LIFE SCI, SRI INT, 88- *Personal Data:* b Moncton, NB, Oct 21, 40; US & Can citizen; m 62, Karen Webb; c Kathleen, William & Jeffrey. *Educ:* Acadia Univ, BSc, 61; Univ Rochester, PhD(radiation biol), 66. *Hon Degrees:* DSc, Acadia Univ, 85. *Honors & Awards:* Radiation Res Award, Radiation Res Soc, 77; Sr US Scientist Award, Alexander von Humbolt found, 83. *Prof Exp:* Fel radiation biol, Norsk Hydro's Inst Cancer Res, Oslo, Norway, 66-67; fel, Ont Cancer Found, London Clin, Victoria Hosp, London, Ont, 67-68, radiobiologist, 68-76; assoc prof & head, Radiation Biol Sect, Div Radiation, Oncol & Multimodalities Res, Cancer Ctr, Univ Rochester, 76-79, prof radiation biol & biophys, 79-88, from asst to assoc dir, Exp Therapeut Div, Cancer Ctr, 80-88. *Concurrent Pos:* Radiation res fel, James Picker Found, 66-68; hon lectr biophys, Univ Western Ont, 67-68, lectr therapeut radiol & asst prof biophys, 68-72, assoc prof therapeut radiol & biophys, 72-76; res consult, Nat Cancer Inst Can, 74-, NIH, 76-, Med Res Coun Can, 76-, Nat Cancer Inst, 77-, Am Cancer Soc, 79-93 & Am Col Radiol, 82-; assoc ed, Int J Radiation, Oncol, Biol, Physics, 81- *Mem:* Radiation Res Soc; Can Soc Cell Biol; Am Asn Cancer Res; Am Soc Therapeut Radiol & Oncol; Am Soc Cell Biol; Int Soc Differentiation; AAAS. *Res:* Cancer research focused on role of tumor microenvironments in response to therapy and malignant progression using spheroid tumor model; molecular response to microenvironments of cell-cell contracts and growth factors. *Mailing Add:* Varian Assoc 3050 Hansen Way MS/V-220 Palo Alto CA 94304-1000

SUTHERLAND, RONALD GEORGE, CHEMISTRY. *Current Pos:* from asst prof to assoc prof, Univ Sask, 67-73, assoc dean sci, 81-88, spec adv to pres, 92-93, PROF CHEM, UNIV SASK, 73-, DEPT HEAD, 94- *Personal Data:* b Belfast, Northern Ireland, May 4, 35; m 60; c 2. *Educ:* Univ Strathclyde, BSc, 59; Univ St Andrews, PhD(org chem), 62. *Prof Exp:* Res assoc, Columbia Univ, 62-63; fel, Calif Inst Technol, 63-64; Imp Chem Industs res fel chem, Queen's Col, Dundee, 64-67. *Concurrent Pos:* Sci Res Coun UK sr vis fel, Edinburgh Univ, 75-76; consult, Arms Control & Disarmament Div, External Affairs, Ottawa, Can; tech adv, Can Deleg to Conf on Disarmament, Geneva; adj res fel, Ctr Sci & Int Affairs, Harvard Univ, 93-94; res fel, Peace Res Inst, Australian Nat Univ, 93-94. *Mem:* Royal Soc Chem; Royal Inst Chem; fel Can Inst Chem. *Res:* Organometallic chemistry; organic photochemistry; chemical decomposition of pesticides; investigations of alleged use of chemical weapons; verification research in arms control. *Mailing Add:* Dept Chem Univ Sask Saskatoon SK S7N 5C9 Can

SUTHERLAND, WILLIAM NEIL, SOIL FERTILITY & AGRICULTURAL, EDUCATIONAL ADMINISTRATION. *Current Pos:* RETIRED. *Personal Data:* b Linden, Iowa, Aug 10, 27; m 49; c 4. *Educ:* Iowa State Univ, BS, 50, MS, 53, PhD(soil fertil), 60. *Prof Exp:* Soil conserv agent exten serv, Univ Minn, 54-56; res assoc, Iowa State Univ, 56-60; agriculturist, Tenn Valley Authority, 60-78, agronomist, Test & Demonstration Br, 78-80, chief agr field prog, 80-88, assoc dir, Agr Inst, 86-88. *Mem:* Am Soc Agron; Nat Mgt Asn. *Res:* Evaluation of Tennessee Valley Authority's experimental fertilizers agronomically and in fertilizer use systems in cooperation with land grant universities and fertilizer industry firms; educational programs to encourage efficient fertilizer use; research administration; resource management. *Mailing Add:* 110 Robinhood Florence AL 35630

SUTHERLAND, WILLIAM ROBERT, COMPUTER SCIENCE, ELECTRICAL ENGINEERING. *Current Pos:* VPRES, SUN MICROSYSTS, 90- *Personal Data:* b Hastings, Nebr, May 10, 36; m 84, Sylvia Raley; c Andrew, Peter & Amy. *Educ:* Rensselaer Polytech Inst, BEE, 57; Mass Inst Technol, SM, 63, PhD(elec eng), 66. *Prof Exp:* Assoc group leader comput graphics & comput-aided design & mem tech staff, Lincoln Lab, Mass Inst Technol, 64-69; mgr interactive systs dept, Bolt Beranek & Newman, Inc, 69-72, div vpres & dir comput sci div, 72-75; mgr, Systs Sci Lab, Xerox Palo Alto Res Ctr, 75-81; vpres, Sutherland, Sproull & Assoc Inc, 81-90. *Mem:* Inst Elec & Electronics Engrs; Asn Comput Mach. *Res:* Distributed computing; graphics. *Mailing Add:* 2550 Garcia Ave MS MTV29-01 Mountain View CA 94043. *Fax:* 650-691-0756; *E-Mail:* bert.sutherland@eng.sun.com

SUTHERLAND-BROWN, ATHOLL, ECONOMIC & REGIONAL GEOLOGY. *Current Pos:* RETIRED. *Personal Data:* b Ottawa, Ont, June 20, 23; wid; c Brian. *Educ:* Univ BC, BASc, 50; Princeton Univ, PhD(geol), 54. *Prof Exp:* Geologist econ geol, BC Dept Mines & Petrol Resources, 52-69, dep chief geol, 69-74, chief geologist econ geol, Mineral Resources Br, 74-84, consult, 84-93. *Concurrent Pos:* Mem, Geol Soc Am Del, Am Comn Stratig Nomenclature, 69-72; mem, Nat Orgn Comt, 24th Int Geol Cong, 69-72; exec mem, Nat Adv Comn, Res Geol Sci, 69-73; del, Int Union Geol Sci-UNESCO Meeting Govt Experts, Paris, 71; ed, Can Inst Mining & Metall, 74-76; mem, Can Nat Comn, Int Geol Correlation Prog, 74-; mem, Can Geosci Coun Adv Comt, Geol Surv Can, 76-, exec mem, Can Geosci Coun, 77-, pres, 81. *Mem:* Fel Geol Soc Am; fel Geol Asn Can (vpres, 78-79, pres, 79-80); Can Inst Mining & Metall; Soc Econ Geologists. *Res:* Morphology, classification, distribution and tectonic setting of porpityry deposits; metallogeny and distribution of metals in deposits and background, particularly in Canadian Cordillera; geology and tectonics of Queen Charlotte Islands and insular tectonic belt. *Mailing Add:* 546 Newport Ave Victoria BC V8S 5C7 Can

SUTHERS, RODERICK ATKINS, PHYSIOLOGY. *Current Pos:* from asst prof to assoc prof anat & physiol, 65-74, prof anat & physiol, 74-75, PROF, PROG NEUROSCI, IND UNIV, BLOOMINGTON, 75-, PROF PHYSIOL, SCH MED, 76-, HEAD, PHYSIOL SECT, 89- *Personal Data:* b Columbus, Ohio, Feb 2, 37; m; c 2. *Educ:* Ohio Wesleyan Univ, BA, 60; Harvard Univ, AM, 61, PhD(biol), 65. *Prof Exp:* Res fel biol, Harvard Univ, 64-65. *Concurrent Pos:* Vis prof, Dept Zool, Univ Nairobi, Kenya, 73; adj prof biol, Ind Univ, Bloomington, 83- *Mem:* AAAS; Am Ornith Union; Am Physiol Soc; Soc Neurosci; Acoust Soc Am; Asn Res Otolaryngol; Int Soc Neuroethology. *Res:* Neuroethology and behavior; sensory physiology of animal sonar systems; perceptual abilities and auditory processing of information by echolocating animals; physiology and acoustics of vocalization by echolocating bats; physiology, acoustics and motor control of bird song. *Mailing Add:* Ind Univ Med Sch Prog Bloomington IN 47405-4400. *Fax:* 812-855-4436

SUTIN, JEROME, NEUROANATOMY, NEUROPHYSIOLOGY. *Current Pos:* dir, Neurosci Prog, 85-89 PROF ANAT & CHMN DEPT, EMORY UNIV, 66-, CHARLES HOWARD CANDLER PROF, 80- *Personal Data:* b Albany, NY, Mar 12, 30; m 56; c 2. *Educ:* Siena Col, BS, 51; Univ Minn, MS, 53, PhD(anat), 54. *Prof Exp:* Asst anat, Univ Minn, 52-53; hon res asst, Univ Col, Univ London, 53-54; asst, Univ Minn, 54; jr res anatomist, Univ Calif, Los Angeles, 55-56; from instr to assoc prof, Sch Med, Yale Univ, 56-66. *Concurrent Pos:* Vis investr, Autonomics Div, Nat Phys Lab, Middlesex, Eng; vis prof, Inst Psychiat, Maudsley Hosp, London; Nat Found Infantile Paralysis fel anat, Univ Calif, Los Angeles, 55-56; mem, Neurol A Study Sect, NIH, 71-75, chmn, 74-75. *Mem:* Am Asn Anatomists (pres, 89-90); Asn Anat Chmn (pres, 72-73); Soc Neurosci; Sigma Xi. *Res:* Hypothalamic organization; basal ganglia and motor function; plasticity of noradrenergic neurons. *Mailing Add:* 2072 Castleway Dr Atlanta GA 30345

SUTIN, NORMAN, PHYSICAL INORGANIC CHEMISTRY. *Current Pos:* res assoc, Brookhaven Nat Lab, 56-57, from assoc chemist to chemist, 58-66, dept chmn, 88-95, SR CHEMIST, BROOKHAVEN NAT LAB, 66- *Personal Data:* b SAfrica, Sept 16, 28; nat US; m 58, Bonita Sakowski; c Lewis A & Cara R. *Educ:* Univ Cape Town, BSc, 48, MSc, 50; Cambridge Univ, PhD(chem), 53. *Honors & Awards:* Distinguished Serv Award in the Advan of Inorg Chem, Am Chem Soc, 83; Photochem Award, NY Acad Sci, 85. *Prof Exp:* Imp Chem Industs fel, Durham Univ, 54-55. *Concurrent Pos:* Affil, Rockefeller Univ, 58-62; vis fel, Weizmann Inst, 64; vis prof, State Univ NY, Stony Brook, 68, Columbia Univ, 68, Tel Aviv Univ, Israel, 73, Univ Calif, Irvine, 77 & Univ Tex, Austin, 79; mem, Comt Chem Sci, Nat Res Coun, 81-84; mem, Comt Sci, Am Chem Soc, 87-89. *Mem:* Nat Acad Sci; Am Chem Soc; fel Am Acad Arts & Sci. *Res:* Kinetics and mechanisms of inorganic reactions; bioinorganic chemistry; photochemistry of transition metal complexes; solar energy conversion and storage. *Mailing Add:* Dept Chem Brookhaven Nat Lab Upton NY 11973

SUTMAN, FRANK X, CHEMISTRY. *Current Pos:* SR SCHOLAR SCI EDUC, TEMPLE UNIV, 88- *Personal Data:* b Newark, NJ, Dec 20, 27; m 56, Mabel P; c Frank J, Catherine J & Elizabeth A. *Educ:* Montclair State Col, AB, 49, AM, 52; Columbia Univ, EdD, 56. *Honors & Awards:* NJ Govs Award Sci Educ, 87. *Prof Exp:* Instr, Pub Schs, NJ, 49-55; asst prof sci, Paterson State Col, 55-57; assoc prof natural sci chmn div, Inter-Am Univ, PR, 57-58; dean, Col Educ, Fairleigh Dickinson Univ, 82-88. *Concurrent Pos:* NSF-AID lectr, India, 67; observer, Orgn Am States Coun Sci Educ & Cult, 71; vis prof, Hebrew Univ, Jerusalem, Israel, 73, Rutgers Univ, Upsala Col, Univ Mysore, India, Huazhong Univ Sci & Technol, China; consult, Israel Environ Protection Serv, 75, Peoples Repub China, 80-; Rutgers Univ, Upsala Col, Univ Mysore, India, Huazhang Univ Sci & Technol, China; vis scientist, NSF, 89-93. *Mem:* Fel AAAS; Am Chem Soc; Nat Asn Res Sci Teaching (pres, 72); Nat Sci Teachers Asn; Sigma Xi. *Res:* Chemical education research related to seeking a more effective role for laboratory based instruction in producing student learning of higher order skills. *Mailing Add:* 128 Stratton Lane Mt Laurel NJ 08054-3301. *Fax:* 609-256-4918; *E-Mail:* sutman@rowon.edu

SUTNICK, ALTON IVAN, INTERNAL MEDICINE. *Current Pos:* CO-PRIN, SUTNICK ASSOC, 86- *Personal Data:* b Trenton, NJ, July 6, 28; m 58; c 2. *Educ:* Univ Pa, AB, 50, MD, 54. *Honors & Awards:* Schwartz Award, AMA, 76. *Prof Exp:* From intern to resident anesthesiol & med, Hosp Univ Pa, 54-57, USPHS fel, Univ, 56-57; from resident to chief resident med, Marion Co Gen Hosp, Indianapolis, Ind, 57-61; USPHS fel, Temple Univ, 61-63, instr med, 63-64, assoc, 64-65; res physician, Inst Cancer Res, Fox Chase Cancer Ctr, 65-72, assoc dir, 72-75; assoc prof med, Sch Med, Univ Pa, 71-75; dean & prof med, Med Col Pa, 75-89, sr vpres health affairs, 76-89; vpres, Educ Comn Foreign Med Graduates, 89-95. *Concurrent Pos:* Consult, Coun Drugs, AMA, 62-64; mem, US Nat Comt, Int Union Against Cancer, 69-72; mem ed bd, Res Commun Chem Path Pharmacol, 69-, USA Nat Comt, Int Union Against Cancer, 69-72; vis prof med, Med Col Pa, 71-75; asst ed, Ann Internal Med, 72-75; mem, Nat Cancer Control Planning Conf, Nat Cancer Inst, 73, consult, Diag Res Adv Group, 74-78; sect ed for med, Int J Dermat, 74-75; consult, WHO, 79, 80 & 81; vis prof, Univ Belgrade, Yugoslavia, 88; med educ ed, Int J Dermat, 89- *Mem:* Am Asn Cancer Res; Am Fedn Clin Res; Am Col Physicians; AMA; Asn Am Med Cols; Asn Med Educ Europe. *Res:* Cancer epidemiology; susceptibility to cancer; Australia antigen; hepatitis B surface antigen in hepatitis; pulmonary surfactant/adult disease; medical education; risk-based cancer screening; hepatitis C; relationship iron stores/cancer/life expectancy; first foreign graduates symposium; coined "ergasteric" (laboratory-contracted); clinical competence assessment. *Mailing Add:* Sutnick Assoc 2135 St James Pl Philadelphia PA 19103. *E-Mail:* sutnick@allegheny.edu

SUTTER, DAVID FRANKLIN, APPLIED PHYSICS, INSTRUMENTATION. *Current Pos:* PHYSICIST, DIV PHYS RES, US AEC, 75- *Personal Data:* b Ft Wayne, Ind, Nov 21, 35; m 59; c 3. *Educ:* Purdue Univ, BS, 58; Cornell Univ, MS, 67, PhD(physics), 69. *Prof Exp:* Asst, Cornell Univ, 62-69; physicist, Fermi Nat Accelerator Lab, 69-75. *Mem:* Am Phys Soc; AAAS. *Res:* Computer monitoring and control of accelerators; digital and analog instrumentation; theory of operation of accelerators; electron beam optics; development of superconducting magnet systems. *Mailing Add:* 1510 Blue Meadow Rd Potomac MD 20854

SUTTER, GERALD RODNEY, ENTOMOLOGY. *Current Pos:* Res entomologist, European Corn Borer Lab, Arkeny, Iowa, 65, Northern Grain Insect Res Lab, 65-73, RES LEADER ENTOM, ENTOM RES DIV, NORTHERN GRAIN INSECT RES LAB, AGR RES SERV, USDA, 73- *Personal Data:* b Fountain City, Wis, Sept 20, 37; m 58; c 3. *Educ:* Winona State Col, BA, 60; Iowa State Univ, MS, 63, PhD(entom), 65. *Mem:* Entom Soc Am; Soc Invert Path. *Res:* Utilization of microorganisms in the biological control of insects. *Mailing Add:* 2005 Iowa St Brookings SD 57006

SUTTER, JOHN FREDERICK, GEOLOGY, GEOCHRONOLOGY. *Current Pos:* geologist, 79-87, supvry geologist, 87-93, GEOLOGIST, US GEOL SURV, 93- *Personal Data:* b Oak Harbor, Ohio, June 7, 43; m 65, 75, 88; c 2. *Educ:* Capital Univ, BS, 65; Rice Univ, MA, 68, PhD(geol), 70. *Honors & Awards:* Carey Croneis Distinguished Alumni lectr, Rice Univ, 86. *Prof Exp:* Nat Res Coun resident res assoc, Manned Spacecraft Ctr, NASA, 69-70; asst prof earth & space sci, State Univ NY Stony Brook, 70-71; from asst prof to assoc prof geol & mineral, Ohio State Univ, 71-80. *Concurrent Pos:* Lectr geol, George Washington Univ, 87-; mem, Vis Comt Earth & Environ Sci, Lehigh Univ, 89- & Geol & Geophys, Rice Univ, 91- *Mem:* Fel Geol Soc Am; Am Geophys Union. *Res:* Use of 40Ar/39Ar thermochronology in combination with metamorphic petrology and structural geology to solve tectonic problems; application of high-resolution 40Ar/39Ar geochronology to stratigraphic problems, mainly in large silicic volcanic centers. *Mailing Add:* 11621 Clubhouse Ct Reston VA 20190. *Fax:* 703-648-5310

SUTTER, JOHN RITTER, PHYSICAL CHEMISTRY. *Current Pos:* from asst prof to assoc prof, 62-71, PROF CHEM, HOWARD UNIV, 71- *Personal Data:* b Edwardsville, Ill, May 4, 30; m 58; c 3. *Educ:* Wash Univ, St Louis, AB, 51; Tulane Univ, MS, 56, PhD(chem), 59. *Prof Exp:* Asst chem, Tulane Univ, 54-59; jr chemist & AEC grant, Wash State Univ, 59-60; asst prof, La Polytech Inst, 60-62. *Mem:* AAAS; Am Chem Soc; Am Phys Soc. *Res:* Kinetics; fast reactions; thermodynamics; calorimetry. *Mailing Add:* Dept Chem Howard Univ Washington DC 20059-0001

SUTTER, JOSEPH F, AERONAUTICAL ENGINEERING. *Current Pos:* aerodynamicist, Boeing Com Aircraft Co, 45-61, chief technol, Boeing 727, 61-63, chief engr technol, Com Airplane Div, 63-65, chief engr, 747 Prog, 65-71, head, 71-78, vpres opers & prod develop, Com Airplane Co, 78-81, exec vpres, 81-86, CONSULT, BOEING COM AIRCRAFT CO, 86- *Personal Data:* b Seattle, Wash, Mar 21, 21; c 3. *Educ:* Univ Wash, BS, 43. *Honors & Awards:* Aircraft Design Award, Am Inst Aeronaut & Astronaut, 71, Elmer A Sperry Award, 80; Sir Kinsford Smith Award, Australian Royal Aeronaut Soc, 80; US Nat Medal Technol, 85; Lord Found Award, 89; William Littlewood Mem Lectr, 90. *Concurrent Pos:* Team leader, Develop & Prod Panel, Pres Comn Space Shuttle Accident, 86. *Mem:* Nat Acad Eng; hon fel Eng Royal Aeronaut Soc; hon fel Am Inst Aeronaut & Astronaut Soc; fel Royal Aeronaut Soc Eng. *Mailing Add:* Boeing Com Aircraft Co PO Box 3707 Mail Stop 13-41 Seattle WA 98124. *Fax:* 206-655-5981

SUTTER, MORLEY CARMAN, PHARMACOLOGY. *Current Pos:* from asst prof to assoc prof, 66-71, chmn dept, 71-87, PROF PHARMACOL, UNIV BC, 71- *Personal Data:* b Redvers, Sask, May 18, 33; m 57, Virginia F Laidlaw; c Gregory R, F Michelle & Brent M. *Educ:* Univ Man, BSc & MD, 57, PhD(pharmacol), 63. *Prof Exp:* Pvt pract, Souris, Man, 57-58; asst resident med, Winnipeg Gen Hosp, 58-59; demonstr pharmacol, Univ Man, 59-63; Imp Chem Industs fel, Cambridge Univ, 63-65; asst prof, Univ Toronto, 65-66. *Concurrent Pos:* Wellcome Found travel award, 63; supvr, Downing Col, Cambridge Univ, 63-65; Med Res Coun Can scholar, 66-71. *Mem:* AAAS; Pharmacol Soc Can; Can Soc Clin Invest; Brit Pharmacol Soc; Am Soc Pharmacol & Exp Therapeut. *Res:* Effects of adrenergic blocking agents in shock; mechanism of cardiac arrythmias induced by cyclopropane-epinephrine; pharmacology of veins; vascular smooth muscle in hypertension. *Mailing Add:* Dept Pharmacol & Therapeut 2176 Health Sci Mall Univ BC Vancouver BC V6T 1Z3 Can. *Fax:* 604-822-6012

SUTTER, PHILIP HENRY, SOLID STATE PHYSICS, ROBOTICS. *Current Pos:* from asst prof to assoc prof, 64-83, chmn dept, 76-79 & 82-86, PROF PHYSICS, FRANKLIN & MARSHALL COL, 83- *Personal Data:* b Mineola, NY, Dec 8, 30; m 55, Marcia Willemen; c Alan H, Carl F, Steven H & Neil P. *Educ:* Yale Univ, BS, 52, MS, 54, PhD(physics), 59. *Prof Exp:* Res engr res labs, Westinghouse Elec Corp, 58-63, sr res engr, 63-64. *Concurrent Pos:* NZ sr res fel physics & eng lab, Dept Sci & Indust Res, Wellington, NZ, 69-70; vis scientist, Dept Mat Sci & Eng, Univ Pa, 81-82; chmn Am Asn Physics Teachers Comt Physics Higher Educ, 81-83; vis prof biomed eng, Johns Hopkins Sch Med, 87-88. *Mem:* Am Phys Soc; Am Asn Physics Teachers; Sigma Xi; Inst Elec & Electronics Engrs Robotics & Automation Soc. *Res:* Solid state physics; transport properties; ionic crystals; energy conversion; electronics and computers; robotics; biomedical engineering. *Mailing Add:* 203 Mackin Ave Lancaster PA 17602. *E-Mail:* p_sutter@fandm.edu

SUTTER, RICHARD P, CELL & MOLECULAR BIOLOGY. *Current Pos:* from asst prof to assoc prof biol, 67-74, PROF BIOL, WVA UNIV, 74- *Personal Data:* b Birmingham, Ala, Mar 22, 37; m 64; c 3. *Educ:* St Joseph's Col, Ind, BA, 59; Ohio State Univ, MSc, 61; Tufts Univ, PhD(biochem), 67. *Prof Exp:* Instr biochem, Univ Ill, Chicago, 66-67. *Concurrent Pos:* Adj biochemist, Presby St Luke's Hosp, Chicago, 66-67; vis assoc, Calif Inst Technol, 73-74. *Mem:* AAAS; Am Chem Soc; Am Soc Biol Chemists. *Res:* Molecular basis of sexual development; pheromonal communication; fungal metabolism. *Mailing Add:* Dept Biol WVa Univ Morgantown WV 26505-6057

SUTTIE, JOHN WESTON, NUTRITION. *Current Pos:* from asst prof to assoc prof, 61-69, PROF BIOCHEM, UNIV WIS-MADISON, 69-, PROF NUTRIT SCI, 88- *Personal Data:* b La Crosse, Wis, Aug 25, 34; m 55; c 2. *Educ:* Univ Wis, BSc, 57, MS, 58, PhD, 60. *Honors & Awards:* Mead Johns Award, Am Inst Nutrit, 74; Osborne & Mendel Award, Am Inst Nutrit, 80; Hemostasis Career Award, Int Soc Thrombosis & Hemostasis, 89. *Prof Exp:* Fel biochem, Nat Inst Med Res, Eng, 60-61. *Concurrent Pos:* Assoc ed, J Nutrit, 91-; bd agr, Nat Res Ctr, 96; pres, Fedn Am Soc Exp Biol, 96. *Mem:*

Nat Acad Sci; Am Soc Exp Biol & Med; Am Soc Biol Chem; Am Inst Nutrit; Int Soc Thrombosis & Hemostasis; Am Soc Clin Nutrit. *Res:* Vitamin K action-control of prothrombin synthesis, metabolic action of anticoagulants, chemistry of prothrombin and metabolism of vitamin K; vitamin K nutrition. *Mailing Add:* Dept Biochem Univ Wis Madison WI 53706-1569. *Fax:* 608-262-9338; *E-Mail:* suttie@biochem.wisc.edu

SUTTKUS, ROYAL DALLAS, ICHTHYOLOGY, FISH BIOLOGY. *Current Pos:* from asst prof to prof zool, Tulane Univ, 50-60, prof biol, 60-90, dir, Mus Natural Hist, 76-90, EMER PROF BIOL, TULANE UNIV, 90- *Personal Data:* b Fremont, Ohio, May 11, 20; m 47; c 3. *Educ:* Mich State Col, BS, 43; Cornell Univ, MS, 47, PhD(zool), 51. *Prof Exp:* Asst zool, Cornell Univ, 47-50. *Mem:* AAAS; Am Soc Ichthyologists & Herpetologists; Am Fisheries Soc; Soc Syst Zool; Soc Study Evolution. *Res:* Systematics of fresh and salt water fishes; zoogeography; growth and seasonal distribution; environmental biology; water quality and water pollution; biology of mammals. *Mailing Add:* Mus Nat Hist Tulane Univ Belle Chasse LA 70037

SUTTLE, ANDREW DILLARD, JR, RADIOCHEMISTRY, NUCLEAR PHYSICS. *Current Pos:* PROF NUCLEAR BIOPHYSICS & RADIO BIOCHEM & SPEC ASST TO DIR, MARINE BIOMED INST, UNIV TEX MED BR, 71- *Personal Data:* b West Point, Miss, Aug 12, 26. *Educ:* Miss State Univ, BS, 44; Univ Chicago, PhD(chem), 52. *Prof Exp:* Vpres res & grad studies & dir, Miss Res Comn, Miss State Univ, 60-62; vpres res & prof chem, Tex A&M Univ, 62-71. *Concurrent Pos:* Sr scientist, Humble Oil & Refining Co, 52-62; spec asst to dir res & eng, Dept Defense, Washington, DC, 62-64, mem exec comt sci bd res & eng, 67-; mem, Atomic Indust Forum, 55. *Mem:* Am Chem Soc; Am Phys Soc; Am Nuclear Soc; Inst Elec & Electronics Eng. *Res:* Radiation chemistry; nuclear and thermal energy; petroleum industry. *Mailing Add:* 5025 Forest Lane Circle Dallas TX 75244-7902

SUTTLE, CURTIS, MARINE VIROLOGY, BIOLOGICAL OCEANOGRAPHY. *Current Pos:* ASSOC PROF, EARTH & OCEAN SCI, MICROBIOL & BOT, UNIV BC, 96- *Personal Data:* b Vancouver, Can, 55. *Educ:* Univ BC, BSc, 78, PhD(bot)D, 87. *Prof Exp:* Coastal marine scholar, State Univ NY, Stony Brook, 87-88; from asst prof to assoc prof, Marine Sci, Univ Tex, Austin, 90-96. *Concurrent Pos:* Natural Sci & Eng Res Coun fel, State Univ NY, Stony Brook, 87-88, adj asst prof, 88-94; vis prof, Duke Univ, 88; res sci, Univ Tex, Austin, 88-96; vis prof, Univ Constance, Ger, 95. *Mem:* Am Soc Limnol & Oceanog; Am Soc Microbiol; Phycol Soc Am. *Res:* Role of viruses in controlling and structuring marine ecosystems; viruses as pathogens of marine organisms; viruses in the ocean. *Mailing Add:* Oceanog Univ BC 6270 University Blvd Vancouver BC V6T 2G2 Can. *Fax:* 604-822-8610; *E-Mail:* suttle@eos.ubc.ca

SUTTLE, JEFFREY CHARLES, PHYTOHORMONES, PLANT GROWTH REGULATORS. *Current Pos:* Res physiologist, Metab & Radiation Res Lab, 79-91, RES PHYSIOLOGIST, NORTHERN CROP SCI LAB, USDA, 91- *Personal Data:* b Omaha, Nebr, Jan, 28, 52; m 79; c 1. *Educ:* Univ Tex, BA, 74; Mich State Univ, PhD(bot), 79. *Concurrent Pos:* Adj prof, Hort Dept, NDak State Univ. *Mem:* Am Soc Plant Physiol; Plant Growth Regulator Soc Am; Int Plant Growth Substances Asn. *Res:* Mode of action of synthetic plant growth regulators and their interactions with endogenous phytohormones; plant dormancy regulation. *Mailing Add:* 1344 River St West Fargo ND 58078-2639

SUTTLE, JIMMIE RAY, PHYSICS, ELECTRICAL ENGINEERING. *Current Pos:* ASST VCHANCELLOR RES, NC STATE UNIV, 88- *Personal Data:* b Forest City, NC, Dec 26, 32; m 51; c Helen, Ellen & Ken. *Educ:* Presby Col, SC, BS, 58; Duke Univ, MAT, 60, MA, 65; NC State Univ, PhD(elec eng), 72. *Prof Exp:* Instr math, Presby Col, SC, 60-61; phys scientist, Info Processing Off, US Army Res Off, 61-65 & Res-Technol Div, 65-72, assoc dir, Electronics Div, 72-74, actg dir, 74-75, dir, 75-88. *Concurrent Pos:* Asst dir res, Off Secy Defense, 82; adj prof, Elec Eng, NC State Univ, 74-82. *Mem:* Fel Inst Elec & Electronics Engrs. *Res:* Computer architecture; biomathematics; switching theory; electron paramagnetic resonance spectroscopy of organic solids. *Mailing Add:* 7416 Ridgefield Dr Durham NC 27713

SUTTNER, LEE JOSEPH, GEOLOGY. *Current Pos:* From asst prof to assoc prof, 66-78, PROF GEOL, IND UNIV, BLOOMINGTON, 78-, CHMN, DEPT GEOL SCI, 90- *Personal Data:* b Hilbert, Wis, June 3, 39; m 65; c 4. *Educ:* Univ Notre Dame, BS, 61; Univ Wis, MS, 63, PhD(geol), 66. *Honors & Awards:* Niel Miner Teaching Award, Nat Asn Geol Teachers, 88. *Mem:* Nat Asn Geol Teachers; Int Asn Sedimentologists; Soc Econ Paleontologists & Mineralogists; Geol Soc Am. *Res:* Sedimentology and sedimentary petrology. *Mailing Add:* Geol Sci Ind Univ Bloomington IN 47405

SUTTON, BLAINE MOTE, MEDICINAL CHEMISTRY. *Current Pos:* RETIRED. *Personal Data:* b Ft Recovery, Ohio, Jan 23, 21; m 46. *Educ:* Purdue Univ, BS, 42, MS, 48, PhD(pharmaceut chem), 50. *Prof Exp:* Group leader med chem, Smith Kline & French Labs, Philadelphia, 50-68, sr investr med chem, 68-71, asst dir med chem, 71-75, assoc dir med chem, 75-85. *Mem:* AAAS; Am Chem Soc; Am Pharmaceut Asn; NY Acad Sci; Acad Pharmaceut Sci; Am Rheumatism Asn. *Res:* Synthetic medicinal chemistry; sym pathomimetic amines, sedatives, antibiotics, antirheumatics and hypocholesteremics. *Mailing Add:* 2435 Byberry Rd Hatboro PA 19404-3713

SUTTON, CHARLES SAMUEL, MATHEMATICS. *Current Pos:* from asst prof to prof, 40-78, EMER PROF MATH, THE CITADEL, 78- *Personal Data:* b Lima, Peru, July 15, 13; US citizen; m 46. *Educ:* Mass Inst Technol, BS, 35, MS, 37. *Prof Exp:* Instr math, Tufts Col, 39-40. *Mem:* Am Math Soc; Math Asn Am. *Res:* Analysis; iteration; functional equations. *Mailing Add:* 19 Shrewsbury Rd Charleston SC 29407-3324

SUTTON, CHRISTOPHER SEAN, ASTROPHYSICS. *Current Pos:* ASSOC PROF PHYSICS, MT HOLYOKE COL, 87-, CHAIR, PHYSICS DEPT, 91- *Educ:* Univ Pa, BS, 76, MS, 80, PhD(astrophys), 82. *Prof Exp:* Asst prof physics, Smith Col, 82-87. *Mem:* Am Soc Mech Engrs; Am Astronaut Soc; Am Phys Soc; Asn Am Univ Profs. *Res:* Double beta decay in 100 Molybdenum to study neutrino masses in connection with particle astrophysics. *Mailing Add:* Physics Dept Mt Holyoke Col South Hadley MA 01075. *E-Mail:* ssutton@mhc.mtholyoke.edu

SUTTON, DALLAS ALBERT, BIOLOGY. *Current Pos:* prof, 57-76, EMER PROF BIOL & SCI EDUC, CALIF STATE UNIV, CHICO, 76- *Personal Data:* b Grand Junction, Colo, Sept 12, 11; m 35; c 1. *Educ:* Univ Colo, AB, 39, PhD, 53; Northwestern Univ, MS, 40. *Prof Exp:* Prin pub sch, Colo, 34-45; instr biol, Mesa Col, 45-51; assoc prof biol & sci educ, Eastern Mont Col Educ, 54-57. *Concurrent Pos:* NSF grant. *Mem:* Am Soc Mammal. *Res:* Mammalogy; chipmunks of Colorado; chromosomes of the chipmunks, Genus eutamias; female genital bones of chipmunks. *Mailing Add:* PO Box 86 Chico CA 95927

SUTTON, DAVID C(HASE), PHYSICS. *Current Pos:* Asst prof, 61-68, ASSOC PROF PHYSICS, UNIV ILL, 68- *Personal Data:* b Bryn Mawr, Pa, Dec 18, 33; c 1. *Educ:* Haverford Col, BA, 55; Princeton Univ, PhD(physics), 62. *Concurrent Pos:* Vis assoc prof, Stanford Univ, 68-69. *Mem:* Am Phys Soc; Sigma Xi. *Res:* Photonuclear reactions; nuclear structure; accelerator development; radioactivity; particle-radiation detectors. *Mailing Add:* Dept of Physics Univ of Ill Urbana IL 61801

SUTTON, DAVID GEORGE, LASERS. *Current Pos:* tech staff lasers, Aerospace Corp, 72-85, mgr, Laser Effects Sect, 85-88, head, Propulsion & Environ Sci Corp, 88-91, DIR, MAT EVAL & SURVIVABILITY DEPT, AEROSPACE CORP, 91- *Personal Data:* b San Francisco, Calif, Apr 17, 44; m 63, Sandra Vierra; c 1. *Educ:* Univ Calif, Berkeley, BS, 66; Mass Inst Technol, PhD(phys physics), 70. *Prof Exp:* Fel phys chem, Dept Chem, Mass Inst Technol, 70-71, Univ Toronto, 71-72. *Mem:* Am Phys Soc; Soc Appl Spectros. *Res:* Experimental research in gas phase molecular exitation; gas phase molecular energy transfer; analytical applications of molecular energy transfer; laser effects on materials. *Mailing Add:* Aerospace Corp PO Box 92957 Los Angeles CA 90009. *Fax:* 310-336-5846; *E-Mail:* dave_sutton@qmail2.aero.org

SUTTON, DEREK, INORGANIC CHEMISTRY. *Current Pos:* from asst prof to assoc prof, 67-78, PROF CHEM, SIMON FRASER UNIV, 78- *Personal Data:* b Eng, July 15, 37; m 58; c 2. *Educ:* Univ Nottingham, BSc, 58, PhD(chem), 63. *Prof Exp:* Asst lectr chem, Univ Nottingham, 62-64, lectr, 64-67. *Mem:* Royal Soc Chem; Am Chem Soc; Chem Inst Can. *Res:* Aryldiazo and other complexes of transition metals related to the interaction of nitrogen with transition metals. *Mailing Add:* Dept Chem Simon Fraser Univ Burnaby BC V5A 1S6 Can. *Fax:* 604-291-3765; *E-Mail:* dsutton@sfu.ca

SUTTON, DONALD DUNSMORE, MICROBIOLOGY. *Current Pos:* assoc prof, 60-63, chair, Dept Biol, 65-70, PROF MICROBIOL, CALIF STATE UNIV, FULLERTON, 63- *Personal Data:* b Oakland, Calif, June 8, 27; c 3. *Educ:* Univ Calif, AB, 51, MA, 54, PhD(microbiol), 57. *Prof Exp:* Sr lab technician bact, Univ Calif, 50-53, res asst, 53-55; NSF predoctoral fel, 55-57; asst prof & USPHS fel microbiol, Sch Med, Ind Univ, 57-59; Waksman-Merck fel, Inst Microbiol, Rutgers Univ, 59-60. *Concurrent Pos:* Vis prof, Inst Appl Microbiol, Tokyo Univ, 70-71; consult food microbiol & waste water treatment microbiol, 73-; pres, Environ Assocs, Encinitas, Calif, 82- *Mem:* Am Soc Microbiol; Am Inst Biol Sci; Mycol Soc Am; Ecol Soc Am; Audubon Soc. *Res:* Microbial physiology; metabolism of plant disease bacteria; mechanisms of growth inhibitors and antifungal agents; physiological basis of morphogenesis in fungi; location of enzymes in fungi; microbiology of food fermentations; microbiology of waste water treatment and waste conversions. *Mailing Add:* Dept Biol Calif State Univ PO Box 6850 Fullerton CA 92834-6850

SUTTON, EMMETT ALBERT, CHEMICAL DYNAMICS. *Current Pos:* PRES, CONCORD SCI CORP, 76- *Personal Data:* b Toledo, Ohio, May 7, 35; m 58; c 2. *Educ:* Cornell Univ, BEngPhys, 58, PhD(aeronaut eng), 61. *Prof Exp:* Asst prof physics, Hamilton Col, 61-62; asst prof aeronaut & astronaut, Purdue Univ, 62-65; prin res scientist, Avco Everett Res Lab, 65-70; vpres, Aerodyne Res, Inc, 70-76. *Mem:* Am Inst Aeronaut & Astronaut; Am Optical Soc. *Res:* Experimental chemical kinetics; hypersonic wake chemistry; rocket plume radiation; optical and radar field measurements. *Mailing Add:* Concord Sci Corp 88 Hugh Cargill Rd Concord MA 01742. *Fax:* 978-369-3230

SUTTON, GEORGE E, MECHANICAL ENGINEERING. *Current Pos:* RETIRED. *Personal Data:* b Blandville, WVa, June 3, 23; m 59; c 2. *Educ:* Univ WVa, BSME; Univ Fla, MSE; Mich State Univ, PhD(mech eng), 57. *Prof Exp:* Engr, Indust Eng & Construct Co, 48; instr mech eng, Univ Fla, 48-55; instr, Mich State Univ, 55-57; prof, Univ Ariz, 57-59; prof mech eng & chmn dept, Univ Nev, Reno, 61-74; dir prof serv, Nat Coun Eng Examr, 74-76; dean, Sch Eng, Youngstown State Univ, 76-94. *Concurrent Pos:* Secy western zone, Nat Coun State Bd Eng Exam, 66-68. *Mem:* Am Soc Mech Engrs; Nat Soc Prof Engrs; Am Soc Heating, Refrig & Air-Conditioning Engrs; Sigma Xi. *Res:* Thermal environment; heat transfer. *Mailing Add:* 2602 Algonquin Dr Poland OH 44514

SUTTON, GEORGE HARRY, seismology, geophysics, for more information see previous edition

SUTTON, GEORGE W(ALTER), THERMAL PHYSICS. *Current Pos:* RETIRED. *Personal Data:* b NY, Aug 3, 27; m 52, Evelyn D Kunnes; c 4. *Educ:* Cornell Univ, BME, 52; Caltech, MS, 53, PhD(physics & eng), 55. *Honors & Awards:* Arthur D Fleming Award; Distinguished Serv Award, Am Inst Aeronaut & Astronaut; Thermophysics Medal. *Prof Exp:* Engr rockets, JPL, 53-55; scientist rockets, Lockheed Missile Div, 55-56 & reentry, Gen Elec Missile Div, 56-63; sci adv aerospace, Dept Air Force, 63-65; vpres lasers & electro-optics, Avco-Everett Res Lab, 65-83 & electro-optics, Jaycor, 85-90; dir lasers, Helionetics Laser Div, 83-85; dir electro-optics, Kaman Aerospace Corp, 90-92. *Concurrent Pos:* Lectr, Univ Pa, 61-65, Stanford Univ, 64; vis prof, Mass Inst Technol, 61; dir eclectro optics, ANSER, 92- *Mem:* Nat Acad Eng; Am Inst Aeronaut & Astronaut; Am Soc Mech Engrs; AAAS. *Res:* Ablation heat protection system for re-entry through atmosphere; non-equilibrium ionization for MHD power generation; designed first high energy laser over 100 kilowatts, and successful surveillance equipment; high speed interceptor missiles. *Mailing Add:* 1200 Crystal Dr Arlington VA 22202. *Fax:* 703-416-3279

SUTTON, HARRY ELDON, HUMAN GENETICS. *Current Pos:* assoc prof zool, Univ Tex, 60-64, chmn dept, 70-73, assoc dean, Grad Sch, 67-70 & 73-75, vpres res, 75-79, PROF ZOOL, UNIV TEX, AUSTIN, 64- *Personal Data:* b Cameron, Tex, Mar 5, 27; m 62, Beverly Jewell Sutton; c Susan E & Caroline V. *Educ:* Univ Tex, BS, 48, MA, 49, PhD(biochem), 53. *Prof Exp:* Res scientist, Univ Tex, 48-52; asst biologist, Univ Mich, 52-56; instr human genetics, 56-57, asst prof, 57-60. *Concurrent Pos:* Mem comt personnel res, Am Cancer Soc, 61-64; mem genetics study sect, NIH, 63-67; ed, Am J Human Genetics, 64-69; mem adv coun, Nat Inst Environ Health Sci, 68-72, mem sci adv comt, 72-76; mem comt epidemiol & vet follow-up studies, Nat Acad Sci-Nat Res Coun, 69-; mem adv comt, Atomic Bomb Casualty Comn, 70-75; mem Bd Radiation Effects Res, NAS-Nat Res Coun, 85-87. *Mem:* Genetics Soc Am; Am Chem Soc; Am Soc Human Genetics (pres-elect, 78, pres, 79); Am Soc Biochem & Molecular Biol; Am Genetics Asn; fel AAAS. *Res:* Genetic control of protein structure; inherited variations in human metabolism; human population genetics; protein-DNA interactions. *Mailing Add:* 1103 Gaston Ave Austin TX 78703-2507. *Fax:* 512-471-2149; *E-Mail:* eldon.sutton@mail.utexas.edu

SUTTON, J(AMES) L(OWELL), ENGINEERING. *Current Pos:* RETIRED. *Personal Data:* b Petersburg, Ind, Apr 20, 31; m 59, Diane Tincher; c David, JoAnna, Jeffrey, Mark & Alan. *Educ:* Purdue Univ, BSME, 58. *Prof Exp:* Develop engr, E I du Pont de Nemours & Co Inc, 58-60, res engr, 60-62, process develop supvr, 62-65, eng serv supvr, 65-66, on spec assignment, 66-70, engr, Film Dept, 70-78, tech area supt, Plastics Prod & Resins Dept, 78-81, area supt liaison & capacity planning, Polymer Prod Dept, 81-85, process planning mgr, 85-89. *Mem:* Nat Soc Prof Engrs. *Res:* Development and design of mechanical equipment in the chemical industry. *Mailing Add:* 579 Hickory Pl Circleville OH 43113

SUTTON, JOHN CLIFFORD, PLANT PATHOLOGY. *Current Pos:* From asst prof to assoc prof, 69-82, PROF PLANT PATH, UNIV GUELPH, 82- *Personal Data:* b Halstead, Eng, Oct 10, 41; m 64; c 3. *Educ:* Univ Nottingham, BSc, 65; Univ Wis, PhD(plant path), 69. *Concurrent Pos:* Nat Sci & Eng Coun Can grant, 70-91. *Mem:* Can Phytopath Soc; Am Phytopath Soc. *Res:* Epidemiology of foliar pathogens; biological control of plant diseases; disease management. *Mailing Add:* Dept Environ Biol Univ Guelph Guelph ON N1G 2W1 Can

SUTTON, JOHN CURTIS, ORGANIC CHEMISTRY, ANALYTICAL CHEMISTRY. *Current Pos:* Assoc prof chem, 70-80, PROF, DIV NATURAL SCI, LEWIS-CLARK STATE COL, 80- *Personal Data:* b Weiser, Idaho, May 13, 42; m 65; c 4. *Educ:* Univ Idaho, BS, 64, PhD(chem), 72. *Res:* Utilization of tree bark for the sorption of heavy metal ions from aqueous solutions. *Mailing Add:* Dept Chem Lewis-Clark State Col Lewiston ID 83501-2698

SUTTON, LEWIS MCMECHAN, MICROBIOLOGY, ANALYTICAL CHEMISTRY. *Current Pos:* EXEC VPRES & DIR, PET-AG, INC, 87- *Personal Data:* b Chicago, Ill, Apr 13, 46; m 69, Marjorie Tuttle; c Mac, Beth & Steve. *Educ:* Iowa State Univ, BS, 69; Northern Ill Univ, MS, 72, MBA, 80. *Prof Exp:* Chemist org, Borden Chem, 70-72, chief chemist org & vitamin, 72-76, asst tech dir nutrit res, 76-78, asst gen mgr, Pet-Agr Div, Borden Inc, 78-80, gen mgr, Borden Int, 80-85; vpres, Albion Labs, 85-87. *Mem:* Am Chem Soc; Am Soc Microbiol. *Res:* Analytical methods development both chemical and microbiological; nutritional studies with animal models; international research and technical transfer; international marketing. *Mailing Add:* PET-AG 30 W Rt 20 Elgin IL 60120. *Fax:* 847-741-5135

SUTTON, LOUISE NIXON, MATHEMATICS. *Current Pos:* assoc prof, 62-63, head, Dept Phys Sci & Math, 62-78, PROF MATH, ELIZABETH STATE UNIV, 63- *Personal Data:* b Hertford, NC, Nov 4, 25; div; c 1. *Educ:* Agr & Tech Col NC, BS, 46; NY Univ, MA, 51, PhD(math educ), 62. *Prof Exp:* Instr high sch, NC, 46-47; instr math, Agr & Tech Col NC, 47-50, asst prof, 51-57; asst prof, Del State Col, 57-62. *Concurrent Pos:* Asst dean women, Agr & Tech Col, 47-48; mem adv comt cert math & sci, Del State Bd Educ, 59-61, mem adv comt math, 61-62; mem bd dir, Perquimans County Indust Develop Corp, 67-72; mem gen adv comt, NC State Bd Soc Serv, 69-71; mem bd dir, Div Higher Educ, NC Asn Educr, 69-72; co-dir, NSF Inst, 71-72 & 73-74, dir, 72-73 & 74-75, panelist, 71-72, 74 & 77-78, chmn, 77 & 78. *Mem:* Nat Coun Teachers Math; Nat Educ Asn; Nat Asn Univ Women. *Res:* Mathematics education; concept learning in trigonometry and analytical geometry. *Mailing Add:* Dept Math Elizabeth City State Univ Box 811 Elizabeth City NC 27909

SUTTON, MATTHEW ALBERT, AERODYNAMICS, STRUCTURAL DYNAMICS. *Current Pos:* RETIRED. *Personal Data:* b Austin, Minn, Apr 28, 23; m 46; c 4. *Educ:* Univ Minn, BSc, 45; Ohio State Univ, MSc, 52, PhD(aeronaut eng), 58. *Prof Exp:* Stress analyst, McDonnell Aircraft Co, 46-47; instr eng drawing, Ohio State Univ, 47-48, res assoc wind tunnel design, 48-53, from instr to asst prof aeronaut eng, 53-58; prin eng supvr, Ord Div, Honeywell Inc, 58-62, chief engr, 62-65, chief engr, Systs & Res Div, 65-66, dir res, 66-68, gen mgr, Systs & Res Ctr, 68-76, vpres & gen mgr, Defense Systs Div, 78-81, vpres & gen mgr, Avionics Div, 81-90. *Mem:* Am Inst Aeronaut & Astronaut. *Res:* Aircraft structure and flutter; unsteady aerodynamics. *Mailing Add:* 6109 Habitat Ct S Minneapolis MN 55436

SUTTON, PAUL, soil fertility, for more information see previous edition

SUTTON, PAUL MCCULLOUGH, PHYSICS. *Current Pos:* RETIRED. *Personal Data:* b Ohio, Dec 3, 21; m 46, Doris Nichols; c Pamela & Valerie. *Educ:* Harvard Univ, BS, 43; Columbia Univ, MA, 48, PhD(physics), 53. *Prof Exp:* Asst physics, Columbia Univ, 50-52; res assoc physicist, Corning Glass Works, 52-54, supvr ultrasonics res, 54-56, supvr fundamental physics group, 56-59; sr staff scientist, Aeronutronic Div, Ford Motor Co, 59-62, mgr, Appl Physics Dept, Philco Corp, 62-66, mgr, Physics Lab, Philco-Ford Corp, 66-68, mgr, Physics & Chem Lab, 68-72, mgr, Res Lab, 72-74, mgr electro-optics, 74-80, mgr develop plans, 80-83, mgr Electro-Optics, Aeronutronic Div, 83-87. *Concurrent Pos:* Lectr optics, Univ Calif, Irvine, 66. *Mem:* AAAS; fel Am Phys Soc; Am Ceramic Soc; Optical Soc Am; Sigma Xi. *Res:* Solid state physics; elastic constants; photoelasticity; acoustic propagation; glass physics; dielectric properties of glasses; hypervelocity impact; space charge in glass; atmospheric turbulence; lasers; infrared optics. *Mailing Add:* 6097 Deerford Row La Jolla CA 92037-0904

SUTTON, ROBERT GEORGE, GEOLOGY. *Current Pos:* from asst prof to prof, 54-85, EMER PROF GEOL, UNIV ROCHESTER, 85- *Personal Data:* b Rochester, NY, June 17, 25; m 46; c 2. *Educ:* Univ Rochester, AB, 48, MS, 50; Johns Hopkins Univ, PhD, 56. *Prof Exp:* Instr geol, Alfred Univ, 50-52; jr instr, Johns Hopkins Univ, 52-54. *Mem:* AAAS; Geol Soc Am; Soc Econ Paleont & Mineral. *Res:* Paleozoic stratigraphy; sedimentology; sedimentary petrology. *Mailing Add:* 141 Furlong Rd Rochester NY 14623

SUTTON, ROGER BEATTY, experimental high energy physics, for more information see previous edition

SUTTON, RUSSELL PAUL, CHEMISTRY. *Current Pos:* from asst prof to prof chem, 70-91, chmn dept, 77-82, EMER PROF CHEM, KNOX COL, IL, 91- *Personal Data:* b Mo, July 31, 29; m 53, Mary Jo Ponce; c David, Patricia Ann (Nelson), Daniel, Valerie Sue (Morris) & Teresa (Fielder). *Educ:* Univ Mo, Columbia, BS, 51; State Univ Iowa, MS, 53, PhD(chem), 55. *Prof Exp:* Res chemist, E I du Pont de Nemours & Co, Inc, 55-58. *Concurrent Pos:* Consult examr & comnr, N Cent Asn Cols Sec Schs. *Res:* The chemistry of chalcones and flavylium compounds; gas chromatography. *Mailing Add:* 1392D Oquawka IL 61469

SUTTON, TURNER BOND, PHYTOPATHOLOGY. *Current Pos:* res assoc, 74-76, from asst prof to assoc prof, 76-87, PROF PLANT PATH, NC STATE UNIV, 87- *Personal Data:* b Windsor, NC, Oct 24, 45; m 88. *Educ:* Univ NC, BA, 68; NC State Univ, MS, 71, PhD(plant path), 73. *Prof Exp:* Res assoc plant path, Mich State Univ, 73-74. *Mem:* Am Phytopath Soc. *Res:* Apple diseases; epidemiology and control; pest management. *Mailing Add:* Dept Plant Path NC State Univ PO Box 7616 Raleigh NC 27695-0001

SUTTON, W(ILLARD) H(OLMES), CERAMICS. *Current Pos:* sr mat scientist, 85-90, PRIN SCIENTIST, ADVAN CERAMICS, UNITED TECHNOL RES CTR, 90- *Personal Data:* b Pittsburgh, Pa, Jan 12, 30; m 56, Marikay Onefrey; c Jeffrey. *Educ:* Alfred Univ, BS, 52; Pa State Univ, MS, 54, PhD(ceramics technol), 57. *Honors & Awards:* Achievement Award, Nat Inst Ceramic Engrs, 70; F Lonsberry Award, Allegheny Int Corp, 79; H Bidwell Award, Invest Casting Inst, 84; Spec Award, United Technol Res Ctr. *Prof Exp:* Ceramist, Gen Elec Co, 56-63, mgr metall & ceramics res, 63-69; assoc dir technol, Spec Metals Corp, 69-85. *Concurrent Pos:* Mem, Mat Adv Bd, Nat Acad Sci-Nat Res Coun; chmn, Eng Ceramics Div, Am Ceramic Soc, 68-69, mem bd trustees, 82-85. *Mem:* Am Soc Metals; fel Am Ceramic Soc; Nat Inst Ceramic Engrs; Mat Res Soc; Int Microwave Power Inst. *Res:* Superalloy clean-metal processing; melt-crucible reactions; vacuum melting and refining; high temperature melt purification-application of ceramic filters to superalloys and steel alloys worldwide; fiber composite materials; refractory whiskers; ceramic-metal interfaces and surface chemistry; microwave firing of ceramic materials; develop engineered ceramic materials. *Mailing Add:* United Technol Res Ctr 411 Silver Lane MS 29 East Hartford CT 06108. *Fax:* 860-727-7879

SUTTON, WILLIAM WALLACE, PROTOZOOLOGY, CELL BIOLOGY. *Current Pos:* PRES, MISS VALLEY STATE UNIV, 88- *Personal Data:* b Monticello, Miss, Dec 15, 30; m 54, Leatrice Hubbard; c William W Jr, Averell H, Sheryl (Smith), Alan D, Allison M & Gavin J. *Educ:* Dillard Univ, BA, 53; Howard Univ, MS, 59, PhD(zool), 65. *Hon Degrees:* LLD, Dillard Univ, 91. *Honors & Awards:* Josiah Macy Jr Found Fel, 77. *Prof Exp:* Med technician, DC Gen Hosp, 55-59; from instr to prof biol, Dillard Univ, 59-79, actg chmn, Div Natural Sci, 69-70, chmn, 70-79; vpres acad affairs, Chicago State Univ, 79-80, vpres acad affairs & student develop, 80-81, provost & acad vpres, 81-85; prof biol, Kans State Univ, 85-88, vpres educ & student serv, 85-87. *Concurrent Pos:* Consult, NIH, 72-74 & 16 Inst Health Sci Consortium of NC & Va, 74-; assoc & regional liaison officer, Danforth Found, 75-79; reader/reviewer, Am Biol Teacher, 79-80; coordr, Strengthening Develop Inst Prog, Chicago State Univ, 80-82. *Mem:* Soc Protozoologists; Sigma Xi; Nat Inst Sci; AAAS; NY Acad Sci; Am Asn State Cols & Univs. *Res:* Radiation cell biology; responses of peritrichs to ionizing radiations; chemical analysis of the cyst wall and nutrition of peritrichs; isolation of nucleic acids from peritrichs. *Mailing Add:* Miss Valley State Univ Itta Bena MS 38941

SUTTON, WILLIAM WALLACE, ANIMAL PHYSIOLOGY. *Current Pos:* RES PHYSIOLOGIST, US ENVIRON PROTECTION AGENCY, 73- *Personal Data:* b Athens, Ga, Apr 6, 43; m 75; c 4. *Educ:* Mercer Univ, AB, 64; Marshall Univ, MS, 65; WVa Univ, PhD(zool), 70. *Prof Exp:* Animal physiologist, Chem Corps Proving Ground, Dugway, Utah, 71-73. *Concurrent Pos:* Adj asst prof biol, Univ Nev, Las Vegas, 76-78. *Mem:* AAAS; NY Acad Sci; Am Soc for Testing & Mat; Asn Off Anal Chemists; Asn Chem Soc. *Res:* Validation of biological methods for use in pollutant monitoring networks; establish the data quality that can be achieved within a single laboratory. *Mailing Add:* 649 Oglethorpe Ave Athens GA 30606

SUTULA, CHESTER LOUIS, BOTANY & PHYTOPATHOLOGY, GENERAL COMPUTER SERVICES. *Current Pos:* PRES, AGDIA, INC, 81- *Personal Data:* b Erie, Pa, Feb 15, 33; m 55; c 8. *Educ:* Col Holy Cross, BS, 54; Iowa State Univ, MS, 58, PhD(phys chem), 59. *Prof Exp:* Teaching asst, Iowa State Univ, 55-57; res scientist, Ames Lab, Iowa, 57-59; sr res scientist, Marathon Oil Co, Colo, 59-67; sr res scientist, Ames Res Lab, Ames Co Div, Miles Labs, Inc, 67-69, dir, 69-77; vpres Res & Develop, Ortho Diag, Inc, 77-80; mem staff, CLS Radiation, 80-91. *Mem:* AAAS; Am Chem Soc; Am Phytopath Soc. *Res:* Surface chemistry; calorimetry; wetting properties of complex porous materials; structure of colloidal fluids; microbiology; immunoassay; instrumentation; tests for plant pathogens; plant virology. *Mailing Add:* 30380 CR 6 Elkhart IN 46514-5097

SUUBERG, ERIC MICHAEL, COMBUSTION, CHEMICAL KINETICS. *Current Pos:* assoc prof, 81-90, PROF ENG, BROWN UNIV, 90- *Personal Data:* b NY, Nov 23, 51; m 87, Ina Vatuars; c Alessandra. *Educ:* Mass Inst Technol, BS & MS 74, MS, 76, ScD, 78. *Prof Exp:* Asst prof chem eng, Carnegie-Mellon Univ, 77-81. *Concurrent Pos:* Vis, Centre Nat de La Recherche Sci, France, 88; chmn, Div Fuel Chem, Am Chem Soc, 91; dir-at-large, Div Fuel Chem, Am Chem Soc, 96- *Mem:* Combustion Inst; Am Inst Chem Engrs; Am Chem Soc; Am Carbon Soc. *Res:* Coal chemistry; combustion; carbons; reaction kinetics; fire research oxidation processes; oil shale chemistry; nitric oxide chemistry. *Mailing Add:* Div Eng Box D Brown Univ Providence RI 02912. *Fax:* 401-863-1197

SUURA, HIROSHI, THEORETICAL PHYSICS. *Current Pos:* PROF PHYSICS, UNIV MINN, 65- *Personal Data:* b Hiroshima, Japan, Aug 19, 25; m 51; c 2. *Educ:* Univ Tokyo, BS, 47; Hiroshima Univ, PhD(physics), 55. *Prof Exp:* Prof physics, Nihon Univ, 60-65. *Mem:* Fel Am Phys Soc. *Res:* Theory of elementary particles. *Mailing Add:* Sch Physics Univ Minn Minneapolis MN 55455

SUYAMA, YOSHITAKA, MOLECULAR BIOLOGY, BIOCHEMISTRY. *Current Pos:* from asst prof to assoc prof, 64-75, PROF BIOL, UNIV PA, 75- *Personal Data:* b Osaka, Japan, Sept 5, 31; m 60; c 2. *Educ:* Kyoto Univ, Japan, BAgr, 55; Kans State Univ, PhD(microbiol genetics), 60. *Prof Exp:* Fel genetics & microbiol, Sch Med, Yale Univ, 59-60; asst res biologist genetics & biol, Univ Calif, La Jolla, 60-64. *Concurrent Pos:* Vis assoc prof biochem, Univ Bari, Italy, 69; res fel molecular genetics, Inst Molecular Genetics, Gif, France, 71-72. *Mem:* Genetics Soc Am; Am Soc Biol Chemists; Soc Protozoologists. *Res:* Molecular genetics and biogenesis of organelles in eukaryotic cells; elucidations of nucleic acids and protein synthesizing mechanisms in mitochondria. *Mailing Add:* Dept Biol Univ Pa 207/208 Leidy Labs Philadelphia PA 19104-6018. *Fax:* 215-898-8780

SUYDAM, B R, PLASMA PHYSICS, LASER PHYSICS. *Current Pos:* RETIRED. *Personal Data:* b Manalapan Co, NJ, 1916. *Educ:* Pa State Univ, BS, 37; Mass Inst Technol, PhD(physics), 40. *Prof Exp:* Res physicist, Los Alamos Nat Lab, 54-86. *Mem:* Fel Am Phys Soc. *Mailing Add:* 1967 Peach St PO Box 5800 Mail Stop 0708 Los Alamos NM 87544

SUYDAM, FREDERICK HENRY, CHEMISTRY. *Current Pos:* from asst prof to assoc prof, 52-62, chmn dept, 58-69, PROF CHEM, FRANKLIN & MARSHALL COL, 62- *Personal Data:* b Lancaster, Pa, July 30, 23; m 44; c 3. *Educ:* Franklin & Marshall Col, BS, 46; Northwestern Univ, PhD(chem), 50. *Prof Exp:* Instr chem, Franklin & Marshall Col, 46-47; asst, Northwestern Univ, 47-49; instr anat, Med Sch, Johns Hopkins Univ, 50-52. *Mem:* Am Chem Soc. *Res:* Peptide synthesis; reactions of amino acids; infrared absorption. *Mailing Add:* 442 N President Ave Lancaster PA 17603

SUZUE, GINZABURO, CLINICAL TOXICOLOGY. *Current Pos:* CONSULT, 82- *Personal Data:* b Kumamoto, Japan, Feb 14, 32; c 3. *Educ:* Kyoto Univ, PhD, 61. *Prof Exp:* Chief technologist, Univ Chicago Med Ctr, 82-85; res scientist, Travenol Labs, 79-82. *Concurrent Pos:* Translator, 85- *Mem:* Soc Clin Chem. *Res:* Lipoprotein. *Mailing Add:* 33555 N Ivy Lane Grayslake IL 60030-1991

SUZUKI, DAVID TAKAYOSHI, GENETICS. *Current Pos:* from asst prof to assoc prof, 63-69, PROF ZOOL, UNIV BC, 69- *Personal Data:* b Vancouver, BC, Mar 24, 36; m 58, 72; c 5. *Educ:* Amherst Col, BA, 58; Univ Chicago, PhD(zool), 61. *Hon Degrees:* LLD, Univ PEI, 74; DSc, Acadia Univ, Trent Univ, 81 & Lakehead Univ, 85. *Prof Exp:* Res assoc genetics, Biol Div, Oak Ridge Nat Lab, 61-62; asst prof, Univ Alta, 62-63. *Concurrent Pos:* Res grants, Nat Res Coun Can, 62-86, AEC, 64-69 & Nat Cancer Inst Can, 69-78, NIH, 82-85, Supplies & Serv Can, 84- *Mem:* Genetics Soc Am (secy, 80-83); Genetics Soc Can; Can Soc Cell Biol (pres, 69-70). *Res:* Regulation of development and behavior; genetic organization of chromosomes; developmental and behavioral genetics. *Mailing Add:* Dept Zool Univ BC 2211 W 4th Ave Vancouver BC V6K 4S2 Can

SUZUKI, HOWARD KAZURO, ANATOMY. *Current Pos:* RETIRED. *Personal Data:* b Ketchikan, Alaska, Apr 3, 27; m 52; c 4. *Educ:* Marquette Univ, BS, 49, MS, 51; Tulane Univ, PhD(anat), 55. *Prof Exp:* Asst zool & bot, Marquette Univ, 48-51; asst zool & anat, Tulane Univ, 51-55; instr anat, Sch Med, Yale Univ, 55-58; from asst prof to prof, Sch Med, Univ Ark, 58-70; assoc dean, Col Med, Univ Fla, 70-71, prof anat, 70-73 & 89-90, actg dean, 71-72, dean, Col Health Related Professions, 72-79, prof neurosci, 72-90, prof, Col Health Related Professions, 79-90, emer prof, 90- *Concurrent Pos:* Mem gen res support prog adv comt, NIH; mem adv comt, Off Acad Affairs, US Vet Admin. *Mem:* Fel AAAS; Am Asn Anatomists; Asn Am Med Cols; Soc Exp Biol & Med; Am Soc Allied Health Professions. *Res:* Endocrine relations to bone; phagocytosis and reticuloendothelial system; neonatal human anatomy; comparative bone metabolism. *Mailing Add:* 4331 NW 20th Pl Gainesville FL 32605

SUZUKI, ISAMU, MICROBIOLOGY, BIOCHEMISTRY. *Current Pos:* Nat Res Coun Can fel, Univ Man, 62-64, from asst prof to assoc prof, 64-69, head dept, 72-85, PROF MICROBIOL, UNIV MAN, 69- *Personal Data:* b Tokyo, Japan, Aug 4, 30; m 62, Yumiko Kanehira; c Kenji, Miyo & Kohji. *Educ:* Univ Tokyo, BSc, 53; Iowa State Univ, PhD(bact physiol), 58. *Prof Exp:* Fel microbiol, Western Res Univ, 58-60; instr, Univ Tokyo, 60-62. *Mem:* AAAS; Am Soc Microbiol; Can Soc Microbiol; Can Biochem Soc; Sigma Xi. *Res:* Mechanism of the oxidation of inorganic sulfur compounds by Thiobacilli and ammonia by Nitrosomonas; physiology of autotrophic bacteria; mechanism of enzyme reactions; kinetics. *Mailing Add:* Dept Microbiol Univ Man Winnipeg MB R3T 2N2 Can. *Fax:* 204-275-7615

SUZUKI, JON BYRON, MICROBIOLOGY, DENTISTRY. *Current Pos:* DEAN, UNIV PITTSBURGH, 90- *Personal Data:* b San Antonio, Tex, July 22, 47. *Educ:* Ill Wesleyan Univ, BA, 68; Ill Inst Technol, PhD(microbiol), 72; Am Acad Microbiol, dipl, SM, 72; Loyola Univ, DDS, 78; Am Bd Periodontol, dipl, 87. *Honors & Awards:* Oral Path Nat Award, Am Acad Oral Path, 78. *Prof Exp:* Med technologist & res assoc cytogenetics, Augustana Hosp, Chicago, 68-69; res assoc immunol & pediat, Univ Chicago Hosp, 70-71; clin microbiologist, St Luke's Hosp Ctr Columbia Col Physicians & Surgeons, NY, 71-73; dir clin labs, Registry Hawaii, 73-74; fel, Depts Path & Periodont, dentist & mem fac, Univ Wash, 78-80; clin prof periodont & microbiol, Univ MD, Baltimore, 80-90. *Concurrent Pos:* Instr microbiol, Ill Inst Technol, 68-72; chmn clin labs med technol, Univ Hawaii, 73-74; vis lectr microbiol, Sch Dent, Loyola Univ, Chicago, 74- & Northwestern Univ, 83-; adv, NASA, 76-, res award, 80. *Mem:* Am Acad Microbiol; Int Asn Dent Res; Sigma Xi; Am Dent Asn; AAAS. *Res:* Immunodeficiency states during manned-space flights; research in interaction of immunocompetent cells in disease; periodontal diseases. *Mailing Add:* Univ Pittsburgh 3501 Terrace St Pittsburgh PA 15261

SUZUKI, KINUKO, PATHOLOGY, NEUROPATHOLOGY. *Current Pos:* PROF PATH, SCH MED, UNIV NC, CHAPEL HILL, 86- *Personal Data:* b Hyogo, Japan, Nov 10, 33; m 60, Kunihiko; c 1. *Educ:* Osaka City Univ, MD, 59. *Hon Degrees:* MA, Univ Pa, 71. *Honors & Awards:* Jacob Javits Neurosci Award, NINDS, 89. *Prof Exp:* Asst prof path, Albert Einstein Col Med, 68; from asst prof to assoc prof, Sch Med, Univ Pa, 69-72; from assoc prof to prof path, Albert Einstein Col Med, 72-86. *Mem:* Am Soc Neurochem; Am Asn Neuropath; Soc Neurosci; Int Soc Develop Neurosci. *Res:* Study of pathogenesis of developmental disorder of the central nervous system; neuropathology of Myelin disorder. *Mailing Add:* Dept Path Sch Med Univ NC Chapel Hill CB#7525 Chapel Hill NC 27599-7525

SUZUKI, KUNIHIKO, NEUROCHEMISTRY, NEUROGENETIC DISORDERS. *Current Pos:* PROF NEUROL & PSYCHIAT & DIR NEUROSCI CTR, SCH MED, UNIV NC, 86- *Personal Data:* b Tokyo, Japan, Feb 5, 32; m 60, Kinuko Ikeda; c Jun. *Educ:* Univ Tokyo, BA, 55, MD, 59. *Hon Degrees:* MA, Univ Pa, 71. *Honors & Awards:* A Weil Award, 70; M Moore Award, 75; Jacob K Javits Neurosci Investr Award, 85 & 93; Distinguished Scientist Award, Japan Med Soc Am, 85; Alexander Humboldt Sr Scientist Award, 91; RIKEN Eminent Scientist Award, 95. *Prof Exp:* Resident clin neurol, Albert Einstein Col Med, 60-62, instr neurol, 64, asst prof, 65-68; assoc prof, Sch Med, Univ Pa, 69-71, prof neurol & pediat, 71-72; prof neurol & neurosci, Albert Einstein Col Med, 72-86. *Concurrent Pos:* Mem neurol B study sect, 71-75; mem adv bd, Nat Tay-Sachs & Allied Dis Asn; chief ed, J Neurochem, 77-81; mem bd sci counselors, Nat Inst Neurol, Commun Disorders & Stroke, 80-84; mem, US Nat Comt, Int Brain Res Orgn,

Nat Res Coun, 85-89 & Nat Inst Child Health & Human Develop Ment Retardation Res Comt, 89-92; sr scientist award, Humboldt Found, 91. *Mem:* Int Soc Neurochem; Soc Neurosci; Am Soc Human Genetics; Am Soc Biochem Molecular Biol; Am Soc Neurochem. *Res:* Biochemistry of brain lipids, particularly gangliosides; biochemical and molecular biological studies of inherited metabolic disorders of the nervous system. *Mailing Add:* 4929 Boulder Run Hillsborough NC 27278-8300. *Fax:* 919-966-1322; *E-Mail:* kuni@css.unc.edu

SUZUKI, MAHIKO, THEORETICAL HIGH ENERGY PHYSICS. *Current Pos:* assoc prof, 70-74, PROF PHYSICS, UNIV CALIF, BERKELEY, 74- *Personal Data:* b Tokyo, Japan, Oct 3, 38; m 65, Mie Shigeta; c Yuri. *Educ:* Univ Tokyo, BS, 61, MS, 63, DSc, 66. *Prof Exp:* Res fel physics, Calif Inst Technol, 65-67; mem, Inst Advan Study, 67-68; res assoc, Univ Tokyo, 68-69; vis assoc prof, Columbia Univ, 69-70. *Concurrent Pos:* Fullbright grnt, Fullbright Comn, 65-68; R C Tolman fel, Calif Inst Technol, 66-67; J S Guggenheim Mem Found fel, 76-77. *Mem:* Fel Am Phys Soc. *Res:* Theoretical particle physics of weak, electromagnetic and strong interactions. *Mailing Add:* Dept Physics Univ Calif Berkeley CA 94720. *Fax:* 510-486-6808

SUZUKI, MICHIO, PLANT PHYSIOLOGY, BIOCHEMISTRY. *Current Pos:* RETIRED. *Personal Data:* b Taipei, Formosa, Feb 23, 27; Can citizen; m 59; c 3. *Educ:* Tohuku Univ, Japan, BS, 52, PhD(agr chem), 62. *Prof Exp:* Asst plant physiol & biochem, Tohuku Univ, Japan, 52-66; res scientist, res br, Can Dept Agr, 66-93. *Concurrent Pos:* Nat Res Coun Can res fel, 63-65. *Mem:* Can Soc Plant Physiologists; Am Soc Plant Physiologists; Agr Inst Can; Can Soc Agron; Soc Cryobiol. *Res:* Winter survival of perennial crops and winter cereals; vegetative regrowth of forage crops; metabolism of fructan in grasses; plant nutrition; evaluation of feed quality. *Mailing Add:* 6 Messer Dr Charlottetown PE C1A 6N5 Can

SUZUKI, MICHIO, MATHEMATICS. *Current Pos:* from asst prof to assoc prof, 55-59, PROF MATH, UNIV ILL, 59- *Personal Data:* b Chiba, Japan, Oct 2, 26; m 52; c 1. *Educ:* Univ Tokyo, BA, 48, DrS(math), 52. *Honors & Awards:* Japan Acad Prize, 74. *Prof Exp:* Lectr math, Tokyo Univ Educ, 51-55. *Concurrent Pos:* Fel, Univ Ill, 52-53, res assoc, 53-55; res assoc, Harvard Univ, 56-57; fel, Inst Advan Study, Princeton, NJ, 62-63, vis prof, 68-69, mem inst, 81-; vis prof, Univ Chicago, 60-61 & Univ Tokyo, 71 & 81. *Mem:* Am Math Soc; Math Soc Japan. *Res:* Group theory. *Mailing Add:* Dept Math Univ Ill 1409 W Green St Urbana IL 61801-2917

SUZUKI, SHIGETO, ORGANIC CHEMISTRY. *Current Pos:* SR RES ASSOC, CHEVRON RES CO, 60- *Personal Data:* b San Francisco, Calif, Feb 25, 25; m 53; c 1. *Educ:* Univ Calif, Berkeley, BS, 55; Univ Southern Calif, PhD(chem), 59. *Prof Exp:* Sloan Found res fel org chem, Univ Calif, Berkeley, 59-60. *Mem:* Am Chem Soc; The Chem Soc. *Res:* Organic reaction mechanism, especially carbonium and carbanion rearrangements; organo-sulfur and organo-halogen chemistry. *Mailing Add:* 679 12th Ave San Francisco CA 94118-3618

SUZUKI, TSUNEO, IMMUNOLOGY, BIOCHEMISTRY. *Current Pos:* from asst prof to assoc prof, 70-83, PROF MICROBIOL, MOLECULAR GENETICS & IMMUNOL, UNIV KANS MED CTR, KANSAS CITY, 83-, INTERIM CHAIR, 94- *Personal Data:* b Nagoya, Japan, Nov 23, 31; wid; c 3. *Educ:* Univ Tokyo, BS, 54, MD, 57; Hokkaido Univ, PhD(biochem), 69. *Prof Exp:* Japan Fel Asn fel & Fulbright travel grant, Univ Tokyo, 63; fel, Univ Wis, 63-66 & Univ Lausanne, 66-67; Ont Cancer Inst fel, Univ Toronto, 67-69; res assoc immunochem, Univ Wis, 69-70. *Concurrent Pos:* Mem, Exp Immunol Study Sect, 83-87; sr investr, Univ Kans Med Ctr, 90. *Mem:* Am Asn Immunol; Can Soc Immunol; Am Soc Biochem & Molecular Biol; Am Soc Leukocyte Biol. *Res:* Studies of signal transduction mechanisms triggered by cell surface receptors, which lead to the regulation of macrophage functions. *Mailing Add:* Dept Microbiol Molecular Genetics & Immunol Univ Kans Sch Med Kansas City KS 66160-7420. *Fax:* 913-588-7295; *E-Mail:* tsuzuki@kumc.edu

SVACHA, ANNA JOHNSON, NUTRITION, BIOCHEMISTRY. *Current Pos:* ASST PROF NUTRIT, AUBURN UNIV, 72- *Personal Data:* b Asheville, NC, Nov 27, 28; c 3. *Educ:* Va Polytech Inst & State Univ, BS, 50; Univ Ariz, MS, 69, PhD(biochem, nutrit), 71. *Prof Exp:* Indust chemist, Hercules Powder Co, 51-53; physicist, Taylor Model Basin, US Navy, 53; high sch teacher, Tenn, 53-54; res asst anal chem, Tex Agr Exp Sta, 56-58; res asst org chem, Chas Pfizer & Co, Inc, 58-59; res asst nutrit, Univ Ariz, 67-68; asst poultry scientist, Ariz Agr Exp Sta, 71-72. *Mem:* Am Chem Soc; Am Home Econ Asn; Sigma Xi. *Res:* Appetite regulation with respect to protein and amino acid metabolism; nutritional status and requirements of the elderly. *Mailing Add:* 302 Denson Dr Auburn AL 36830

SVANES, TORGNY, ALGEBRA. *Current Pos:* MEM STAFF, MITRE CORP, 80- *Personal Data:* b Norway. *Educ:* Oslo Univ, MA, 65; Mass Inst Technol, PhD(math), 72. *Prof Exp:* Instr math, Oslo Univ, 66-69; NY State Univ Stony Brook, 72-73; asst prof Aarhus Univ, 73-75; asst prof math, Purdue Univ, 75-77; asst prof math, Bradley Univ, 77-80. *Mem:* Am Math Soc. *Res:* Study of Schubert subvarieties of homogeneous spaces. *Mailing Add:* GTE Govt Syst 77 A St Needham MA 02194

SVE, CHARLES, CIVIL ENGINEERING. *Current Pos:* MEM TECH STAFF STRUCT MECH, AEROSPACE CORP, 68- *Personal Data:* b Pana, Ill, Feb 21, 40; m 62; c 2. *Educ:* Mass Inst Technol, BS, 62, MS, 63; Northwestern Univ, PhD(theoret appl mech), 68. *Prof Exp:* Res engr, NAm Aviation, 63-64; sr engr, Avco Corp, 64-66; res asst civil eng, Northwestern Univ, 66-67. *Concurrent Pos:* Lectr, Univ Southern Calif, 70-71. *Mem:* Am Soc Mech Engrs; Am Inst Aeronaut & Astronaut. *Res:* Applied mechanics; wave propagation in composite materials; experimental mechanics; numerical analysis. *Mailing Add:* 2537 Via Carrillo Palos Verdes Peninsula CA 90274-2720

SVEC, HARRY JOHN, PHYSICAL CHEMISTRY, ANALYTICAL CHEMISTRY. *Current Pos:* Asst chem, Iowa State Univ, 41-43, jr chemist, Manhattan Proj, 43-46, res assoc, Inst Atomic Res, 46-50, asst prof chem, Univ & assoc chemist, Inst, 50-55, assoc prof & chemist, 55-60, prof chem, 60-83, sr chemist, Inst Atomic res, 60-83, DISTINGUISHED PROF SCI & HUMANITIES, IOWA STATE UNIV, 78-, EMER PROF CHEM, 83-; ASSOC, AMES LABS, US DEPT ENERGY, 83- *Personal Data:* b Cleveland, Ohio, June 24, 18; m 43, Edna Mary Bruno; c Mary, Peter, Katherine, Jan, Thomas, Jean, Benjamin, Daniel & Lillian. *Educ:* John Carroll Univ, BS, 41; Iowa State Univ, PhD(phys chem), 49. *Honors & Awards:* Zimmerman Award in Environ Sci. *Concurrent Pos:* Lectr, NATO Advan Study Inst Mass Spectros, 64; ed, Int J Mass Spectrometry Ion Physics, Am Soc Mass Spectrometry, 68-, vpres, 72-74, pres, 74-76; prog dir, Ames Lab, US Dept of Energy, 78-83. *Mem:* Am Chem Soc; Am Soc Testing & Mat; Am Soc Mass Spectrometry (pres, 74-76); Geochem Soc; Chem Soc; Sigma Xi. *Res:* Metallurgy of rare metals; mass spectroscopy; mass spectrometry in physical, inorganic and analytical chemistry; corrosion mechanisms; determination of ultra trace levels of organic pollutants in water and air; highly excited neutral species by neutral fragment mass spectroscopy. *Mailing Add:* 2427 S Hamilton Dr Ames IA 50014-8203

SVEC, LEROY VERNON, AGRONOMY, PLANT PHYSIOLOGY. *Current Pos:* TECH SERV AGRONOMIST, ASGROW SEED CO, 80-; MGR, AGRON TECH SERV, US, 85- *Personal Data:* b Columbus, Nebr, Feb 27, 42; m 64; c 4. *Educ:* Univ Nebr-Lincoln, BSc, 64; Purdue Univ, Lafayette, MSc, 68, PhD(agron), 70. *Honors & Awards:* Upjohn Award, Upjohn Co. *Prof Exp:* Asst prof plant sci, Univ Del, 69-76; assoc prof agron & dist exten agronomist, Univ Nebr, 76-79. *Concurrent Pos:* Mem, Coun Agr Sci & Technol. *Mem:* Am Soc Agron; Sigma Xi; Am Soc Plant Physiologists. *Res:* Performance evaluation of new hybrids and varieties; technical training publications; new cultural practices for crop production. *Mailing Add:* Pioneer Hybrid 4445 Corporate Dr Suite 200 West Des Moines IA 50266

SVEDA, MICHAEL, CHEMISTRY. *Current Pos:* RES & MGT COUN TO ACAD, INDUST & GOVT, 65- *Personal Data:* b West Ashford, Conn, Feb 3, 12; m 36; c 2. *Educ:* Univ Toledo, BS, 34; Univ Ill, PhD(chem, math), 39; PhD (biol, biochem, virol). *Prof Exp:* Asst chem, Univ Toledo, 31-34, teaching fel, 34-35; teaching asst, Univ Ill, 35-37, Eli Lilly res fel, 37-39; res chemist, E I du Pont de Nemours & Co, Inc, 39-44, res mgr, 44-47, new prod sales supvr, 47-51, prod mgr, 51-53, spec asst to mgt, 53-54; mgt consult, 55-60; dir acad proj, NSF, 61-62; corp assoc dir res, FMC Corp, New York, 62-64. *Concurrent Pos:* Mem adv comt creativity in scientists & engrs, Rensselaer Polytech Inst, 65-68; res consult, NSF, 70. *Mem:* Am Chem Soc; AAAS. *Res:* Discovered cyclamate sweeteners; first application of Boolean algebra and theory of sets to people problems, and devised 3-dimensional models showing relationships; devised better way to take off human fat in obesity; interdisciplinary organizations broadly, including mathematical treatment for the first time. *Mailing Add:* Revonah Woods 228 W Lane Stamford CT 06905-8014

SVEJDA, FELICITAS JULIA, ORNAMENTAL HORTICULTURE, PLANT BREEDING & GENETICS. *Current Pos:* RETIRED. *Personal Data:* b Vienna, Austria, Nov 8, 20; nat Can. *Educ:* State Univ Agr & Forestry, Austria, MSc, 46, PhD, 48. *Honors & Awards:* John Cabot Silver Medal, Royal Nat Rose Soc, 86. *Prof Exp:* Res asst rural econ, State Univ Agr & Forestry, Austria, 47-51; asst plant breeder, Swed Seed Asn, 52-53; res officer, Can Dept Agr, 53-86. *Res:* Population biology; plant physiology; hybridization of ornamental plants. *Mailing Add:* 604-1356 Meadowlands Dr E Nepean ON K2E 6K6 Can

SVENDSEN, GERALD EUGENE, ECOLOGY, ETHOLOGY. *Current Pos:* asst prof, 73-77, ASSOC PROF ZOOL, OHIO UNIV, 77- *Personal Data:* b Ashland, Wis, June 18, 40; m 61; c 2. *Educ:* Univ Wis-River Falls, BS, 62; Univ Kans, MA, 64, PhD(behav ecol), 73. *Prof Exp:* Biologist, Fish-Pesticide Res Lab, US Fish & Wildlife Serv, 64-66 & Fish Control Lab, 66-68; from instr to asst prof biol, Viterbo Col, 66-70. *Concurrent Pos:* Actg dir, Rocky Mountain Biol Lab. *Mem:* Am Soc Mammalogists; Ecol Soc Am; Am Soc Evolutionists; Am Soc Naturalists. *Res:* Behavioral ecology; ethology of mammals; social systems analysis and evolution; spatial organization and distribution of terrestrial vertebrates; population biology of terrestrial vertebrates; vertebrate communication systems. *Mailing Add:* Dept Bio Sci Ohio Univ Athens OH 45701-2979

SVENDSEN, IB ARNE, COASTAL ENGINEERING, WAVE MECHANICS & NEARSHORE HYDRODYNAMICS. *Current Pos:* prof civil eng & head dept, 87-96, PROF APPL OCEAN SCI, COL MARINE STUDIES, UNIV DEL, 88-, DISTINGUISHED PROF OCEAN ENG, 96- *Personal Data:* b Copenhagen, Denmark, 1937; US cit; c 2. *Educ:* Tech Univ, Lyngby, Denmark, MSc, 60, PhD(coastal eng), 74. *Prof Exp:* Asst prof civil eng, Coast & Port Eng lab, 60-72; assoc prof, Inst Hydrodyn & Hydraul Eng, Tech Univ, Denmark, 72-87. *Concurrent Pos:* Mem, Int Oil Tanker Comt,

Permanent Int Asn Navig Congresses, Brussels, Belg, 71-74 & Int Comm Improving Fender Syst Design, 79-83; vis prof, Ocean Eng Prog, Univ Del, 82-83. *Mem:* Am Soc Civil Eng; Am Geophys Union; Int Asn Hydraul Res; Danish Ctr Appl Math & Mech; Danish Res Acad. *Res:* Water wave mechanics; wave breaking turbulence and wave generated currents related to sediment transport; coastal erosion and protection. *Mailing Add:* Dept Civil Eng Univ Del Newark DE 19716. *E-Mail:* ias@coastal.udel.edu

SVENDSEN, KENDALL LORRAINE, GEOPHYSICS. *Current Pos:* CONSULT, 91- *Personal Data:* b Greenville, Mich, June 24, 19; m 43, Maxine Paulsen; c Jeffrey, Nancy & Jean. *Educ:* Univ Mich, BS, 43. *Honors & Awards:* Bronze Medal, US Dept Com, 70, Silver Medal, 77; Antarctic Medal, NSF, 70; naming of Svendsen Glacier in Antarctica, US Bd Geog Names, 71. *Prof Exp:* Geophysicist, US Coast & Geod Surv, Nat Oceanic & Atmospheric Admin, 46-70, chief, Geomagnetism Div, 70-71, chief, Geomagnetic Data div, Environ Data Serv, 71-72, chief solid earth & marine geophys data serv div, 72-75, tech asst geomagnetism, Solid Earth Geophys Div, Environ Data Serv, 75-81; res assoc, Coop Inst Res Environ Sci, Univ Colo, Boulder, 81-90. *Concurrent Pos:* Am Geophys Union liaison rep, Comn Geophys, Pan Am Inst Geog & Hist, 72-90, alt US mem, 73-90; mem, Comt Int Participation, Am Geophys Union, 87-88. *Mem:* Am Geophys Union; Asn Geoscientists Int Develop; Sigma Xi; fel AAAS. *Res:* Management of geomagnetic data; international cooperation in geomagnetism; exchange of data, information, and expertise. *Mailing Add:* 15311 Beaverbrook Ct Apt 3E Silver Spring MD 20906-1312

SVENNE, JURIS PETERIS, FEW-BODY THEORY, REACTION THEORY. *Current Pos:* from asst prof to assoc prof, Univ Man, 69-80, assoc dept head, 87-88, assoc dean sci, 89-94, PROF PHYSICS, UNIV MAN, 80- *Personal Data:* b Riga, Latvia, Feb 14, 39; Can citizen; m 63, Aija Pulins; c Mara, Helena & Alexander. *Educ:* Univ Toronto, BASc, 62; Mass Inst Technol, PhD(physics), 65. *Prof Exp:* Res assoc nuclear physics, Mass Inst Technol, 65-66; Nat Res Coun Can fels, Niels Bohr Inst, Copenhagen, Denmark, 66-68; res assoc, Inst Nuclear Physics, D'Orsay, France, 68-69. *Concurrent Pos:* Vis prof nuclear physics, Univ Oxford, 76; instr, Sch Music, Univ Man, 80-; vis res scientist, Physics Dept, Galileo Galilei, Padova, Italy, 84-85. *Mem:* Am Phys Soc; Can Asn Physicists. *Res:* Few-body effects in nuclear reaction theory; absorption and scattering of pions from few-nucleon systems; symmetries in nucleon-nucleon interaction. *Mailing Add:* Dept Physics Univ Man Winnipeg MB R3T 2N2 Can. *Fax:* 204-269-8489; *E-Mail:* svenne@physics.umanitoba.ca

SVENSSON, ERIC CARL, CONDENSED MATTER PHYSICS. *Current Pos:* SR RES OFFICER, NAT RES COUN, OTTOWA, 95- *Personal Data:* b Hampstead, NB, Aug 13, 40; m 65, Patricia Huxley; c Gavin & Carl. *Educ:* Univ NB, Fredericton, BSc, 62; McMaster Univ, PhD(physics), 67. *Prof Exp:* From asst res officer to assoc res officer, Atomic Energy Can Ltd, 65-81, sr res officer physics, 82-97. *Concurrent Pos:* Guest scientist, Aktiebolaget Atomenergi, Studsvik, Sweden, 72-73; vis physicist, Brookhaven Nat Lab, Upton, NY, 81-82; lectr, Can Asn Physicists, 83-84; mem, Assoc Grad Fac, Dept Physics, Univ Guelph & assoc mem, Guelph-Waterloo Prog Grad Work Physics, 92-; adj prof, Dept Physics, Univ Waterloo; mem, Int Comn Struct & Dynamics Condensed Matter, Int Union Pure & Appl Physics, 96- *Mem:* Fel Am Phys Soc; Can Asn Physicists (vpres-elect, 95-96, vpres, 96-97, pres, 97-98); Can Inst Neutron Scattering; Neutron Scattering Soc Am; fel Royal Soc Can. *Res:* Neutron scattering; lattice dynamics; magnetic excitations; effects of impurities on excitation spectra; structure and dynamics of liquid helium; alloys and amorphous and crystalline ice. *Mailing Add:* PO Box 128 Deep River ON K0J 1P0 Can. *Fax:* 613-584-4040; *E-Mail:* eric.svensson@nrc.ca

SVERDLOVE, RONALD, DYNAMICAL SYSTEMS, APPROXIMATION THEORY. *Current Pos:* MEM TECH STAFF, DAVID SARNOFF RES CTR, 81- *Personal Data:* b Brooklyn, NY, Dec 6, 48. *Educ:* Princeton Univ, AB, 69; Stanford Univ, MA, 73, PhD(math), 76. *Prof Exp:* Lectr math, Southern Ill Univ, Carbondale, 76-77; fel, Math Clinic, Claremount Grad Sch, 77-78; asst prof math, Univ Notre Dame, 78-81. *Concurrent Pos:* Vis asst prof math, Claremont Men's Col, Harvey Mudd Col, 78; vis lectr comput sci, Rutgers Univ, 82. *Mem:* Am Math Soc; Math Asn Am; Soc Indust & Appl Math. *Res:* Inverse problems for dynamical systems in two and higher dimensions; approximation of functions by sums of Gaussians; models of the human visual system; computer simulation of electron optics in kinescope guns. *Mailing Add:* 52 Hartley Ave Princeton NJ 08540-7210

SVERDRUP, EDWARD F, ELECTRICAL ENGINEERING. *Current Pos:* sr engr & fel engr, 61-67, ADV ENGR, WESTINGHOUSE RES LABS, 67- *Personal Data:* b Buffalo, NY, Feb 24, 30. *Educ:* State Univ NY Buffalo, BS, 51; Carnegie Inst Technol, MS, 53, PhD(elec eng), 54. *Prof Exp:* Asst prof elec eng, Carnegie Inst Technol, 54-55, 59-61. *Concurrent Pos:* Lectr, Carnegie Inst Technol, 65-67. *Mem:* Am Soc Testing & Mat. *Res:* Electrical properties of high temperature materials; vapor deposition processes; fuel cell development; gas and steam turbines for coal burning combined cycle power plants; induced draft fan erosion. *Mailing Add:* 11029 Old Trail St Irwin PA 15642

SVERDRUP, GEORGE MICHAEL, ATMOSPHERIC SCIENCES, PARTICLE MECHANICS. *Current Pos:* RES SCIENTIST ATMOSPHERIC SCI, BATTELLE MEM INST COLUMBUS LABS, 76-, ASSOC SECT MGR, 79- *Personal Data:* b Minneapolis, Minn, Mar 29, 49; m 70; c 2. *Educ:* Univ Minn, BME, 71, MS, 73, PhD(mech eng), 77. *Mem:* AAAS. *Res:* Chemical and physical characteristics of small particles; physico-chemical interaction of gases and particles. *Mailing Add:* 306 Crandall Dr Worthington OH 43085

SVOBODA, GLENN RICHARD, POLYMER CHEMISTRY. *Current Pos:* RETIRED. *Personal Data:* b Racine, Wis, Nov 18, 30; m 57; c 3. *Educ:* Univ Wis, BS, 52, MS, 53, PhD(pharmaceut chem), 58. *Prof Exp:* Instr anal chem, Univ Wis, 58-59; res chemist, Freeman Chem Corp, Port Washington, 59-61, mgr, Res Lab, 62-64, dir res, 64-67, vpres res & develop, 67-95. *Concurrent Pos:* Asst prof, Ore State Col, 57-58. *Mem:* AAAS; Sigma Xi; Am Soc Mech Engrs. *Res:* Natural products; organo-analytical techniques, especially electrochemistry and optical methods; polymer analysis by physical organic techniques; polymer and monomer synthesis; coatings; unsaturated polyester and urethane specialties; electrochemical and radiochemical syntheses. *Mailing Add:* 1525 Beechwood Lane Grafton WI 53024-1626

SVOBODA, JAMES ARVID, INSECT PHYSIOLOGY. *Current Pos:* RETIRED. *Personal Data:* b Great Falls, Mont, June 28, 34; m 60; c 4. *Educ:* Col Great Falls, BS, 58; Mont State Univ, PhD(entom), 64. *Prof Exp:* Resident res assoc, Insect Physiol Pioneering Res Lab, Agr Res Ctr, USDA, 64-65, res entomologist, 65-79, res leader, 79-95. *Res:* Metabolism of lipids in insects, specifically of steroids and their relationships to growth and development; insect hormones and hormonal control mechanisms. *Mailing Add:* 13301 Overbrook Lane Bowie MD 20715. *E-Mail:* jesuoboda@aol.com

SVOBODA, JOSEF, ARCTIC PLANT ECOLOGY. *Current Pos:* From asst prof to prof, 73-94, assoc chmn, Dept Biol, 90-92, EMER PROF PLANT ECOL, ERINDALE COL, UNIV TORONTO, 94- *Personal Data:* b Praha, Czech, July 16, 29; Can citizen; m 76, Miu-Yin L Leung; c Michael Y & Andrew Y. *Educ:* Univ Western Ont, BSc, 70; Univ Alta, PhD(bot), 74. *Concurrent Pos:* Vis scientist, Univ Freiburg, WGer, 79-80; NATO sr fel, 79-80; mem, steering comt, Can Ctr Toxicol, 81; prin investr, Dept Indian Affairs & Northern Develop, 81-84; assoc ed, J Arctic & Alpine Res, 85- & J Ultimate Reality & Meaning, 88-; mem, Long Term Ecosyst Res & Monitoring Panel, Can Global Change Prog, 92-; vis lectr, Palacky Univ & Univ S Bohemia, 93. *Mem:* Can Bot Asn; Ecol Soc Am; fel Arctic Inst NAm; Asn Can Northern Studies. *Res:* Arctic plant ecology; development and productivity of Polar Oases, impact of Global change on arctic ecosystems; persistent radioactivity in northern environments due to atmospheric nuclear fallout; natural radioactivity in uranium mineralization areas in Northern Canada. *Mailing Add:* Dept Bot Erindale Col Univ Toronto 3359 Mississauga Rd Mississauga ON L5L 1C6 Can

SVOBODA, ROBERT CHARLES, NEUTRINO PHYSICS, NEUTRINO ASTROPHYSICS. *Current Pos:* ASSOC PROF, LA STATE UNIV, 89- *Personal Data:* m, Julien. *Educ:* Fla State Univ, BS, 75; Univ Hawaii, MS, 82, PhD(physics), 85. *Honors & Awards:* Rossi Prize, 88. *Prof Exp:* Nuclear Power Officer, USN, 75-80; postdoctoral fel, Univ Calif, Irvine, 85-89. *Concurrent Pos:* Prin investr particle astrophys, La State Univ, 89-97; vis prof, Univ Calif, Irvine, 96-97. *Mem:* Am Phys Soc. *Res:* Particle physics with an emphasis on neutrinos from the sun, supernovae and from cosmic ray interactions. *Mailing Add:* Physics Dept La State Univ Baton Rouge LA 70803-4001

SVOBODA, RUDY GEORGE, MATHEMATICS. *Current Pos:* Asst prof, 70-77, ASSOC PROF MATH, IND UNIV-PURDUE UNIV, FT WAYNE, 77- *Personal Data:* b Berwyn, Ill, Aug 15, 41; m 64; c 2. *Educ:* Northern Ill Univ, BS, 66; Ohio Univ, MS, 67; Purdue Univ, PhD(math), 71. *Mem:* Am Math Soc; Math Asn Am; Int Congress Individualized Instr; Sigma Xi. *Res:* Development of individualized audio-tutorial instructional materials for algebra and trigonometry courses. *Mailing Add:* 7604 Preakness Cv Ft Wayne IN 46815

SVOKOS, STEVE GEORGE, BIOLOGICAL CHEMISTRY. *Current Pos:* dir regulatory affairs, 72-75, dir regulatory & sci affairs, 75-79, VPRES REGULATORY & SCI AFFAIRS, KNOLL PHARMACEUT CO, WHIPPANY, 79- *Personal Data:* b Wierton, WVa, June 22, 34; m 60; c 3. *Educ:* Brooklyn Col, BS, 56; State Univ NY, MS, 62, PhD(bio-org chem), 64. *Prof Exp:* Chemist, Lederle Labs, Am Cyanamid Co, 56-60, res chemist, 65-69; regulatory liaison, Ayerst Labs Div, Am Home Prod Corp, NY, 69-72. *Mem:* Am Chem Soc; fel Royal Soc Chem; NY Acad Sci; Am Phys Asn; Am Inst Chemists. *Res:* Pharmaceutical administration; medicinal chemistry. *Mailing Add:* 59 First Ave Westwood NJ 07675

SVORONOS, PARIS D N, SYNTHETIC ORGANIC CHEMISTRY, ORGANIC ELECTROCHEMISTRY. *Current Pos:* from asst prof to assoc prof, 81-91, PROF ORG CHEM, QUEENSBOROUGH COMMUNITY COL, CITY UNIV NEW YORK, 91- *Personal Data:* b Oct 9, 50; nat US; m 84, Soraya Ghayourmanesh; c Alexandra & Theodore. *Educ:* Am Univ Cairo, BS, 73; Georgetown Univ, PhD(chem), 80. *Prof Exp:* Asst prof org chem, Trinity Col, 79-81. *Concurrent Pos:* Adj asst prof, Prince George's Community Col, 80; Nassau Community Col, 92; vis prof org chem, Georgetown Univ, 81-, vis assoc prof, 87-88. *Mem:* Am Chem Soc. *Res:* Synthesis, spectroscopy and electrochemistry of tricoordinate organic compounds; undergraduate organic laboratory textbook writer; spectroscopy of chlorofluorocarbons. *Mailing Add:* Chem Queensborough Community Col 22205 56th Ave Flushing NY 11364-1432. *Fax:* 718-631-6453, 428-0802

SWAB, JANICE COFFEY, SYSTEMATIC BOTANY. *Current Pos:* VIS PROF BIOL, MEREDITH COL, NC, 92- *Personal Data:* b Lenoir, NC, July 8, 41; m 86, Edward. *Educ:* Appalachian State Univ, BS, 62; Univ SC, MS, 64, PhD(biol), 66. *Prof Exp:* Asst prof biol, Clemson Univ, 66-67; assoc prof biol, Queens Col, NC, 67-78 & St Mary's Col, NC, 79-90. *Concurrent Pos:* Nat Acad Sci exchange scientist, USSR, 73 & 75; Fulbright scholar, Egypt, 80, Sudan, 90 & Zambia, 91-92. *Mem:* Am Soc Plant Taxonomists (secy, 75-76); Am Inst Biol Sci; Bot Soc Am; Int Asn Plant Taxon; Sigma Xi; AAAS. *Res:* Systematics of the Juncaceae, emphasis on Luzula. *Mailing Add:* 1400 Athlone Pl Raleigh NC 27606. *Fax:* 919-829-2819

SWABB, LAWRENCE E(DWARD), JR, CHEMICAL ENGINEERING. *Current Pos:* RETIRED. *Personal Data:* b Dayton, Ohio, Oct 25, 22; m 44, Gertrude L Frazon; c Edward A, Richard J & Eileen L (Albert). *Educ:* Univ Cincinnati, ChE, 48, MS, 49, PhD(chem eng), 51. *Prof Exp:* Chem engr process develop, Esso Res Labs, Humble Oil & Refining Co, Stand Oil Co, NJ, 51-56, sect head, 56-58, asst dir res labs, 58-63, dir res labs, 64-66, mgr new areas planning & coord, 66-68, vpres petrol res, 68-74, vpres synthetic fuels res, Exxon Res & Eng Co, 74-82. *Mem:* Nat Acad Eng; Am Inst Chem Engrs. *Res:* Research and process development in petroleum industry. *Mailing Add:* 621 Laurel Lake Dr Apt B203 Columbus NC 28722-7420

SWADER, FRED NICHOLAS, SOIL SCIENCE. *Current Pos:* prog leader environ qual, extension serv, 81-84, prog leader water resources, 84-91, EXEC SECY, WORKING GROUP WATER QUAL, USDA, 91- *Personal Data:* b Belle Vernon, Pa, Oct 9, 34; m 56, Nancy Fidler; c Cherith & Frederick (deceased). *Educ:* Cornell Univ, BS, 61, MS, 63, PhD(agron, soil sci), 68. *Prof Exp:* Experimentalist, Cornell Univ, 61-63, res assoc agr eng, 63-67, from asst prof to assoc prof soil sci, 67-81. *Concurrent Pos:* Chmn, Cornell Agr Waste Mgt Conf, 70 & 71; exten laison, Environ Protection Agency, 78-79; co-chair, Exten Comt on Orgn & Policy, Groundwater Task Force, 84-88; vis specialist water qual, Univ Hawaii, 90-91. *Mem:* Soil Conserv Soc Am; Am Soc Agr Engrs; Soil Sci Soc Am. *Res:* Plant-soil-water relationships, as influenced by the physical properties of various soils; soil management for recycling agricultural by-products. *Mailing Add:* 10301 Julep Ave Silver Spring MD 20902. *Fax:* 202-720-1767; *E-Mail:* fswader@esusda.gov

SWADLOW, HARVEY A, NEUROPHYSIOLOGY, PSYCHOLOGY. *Current Pos:* ASSOC PROF PSYCHOL, UNIV CONN, 77- *Personal Data:* US citizen. *Educ:* Univ Miami, BA, 64, MS, 67, PhD(psychol), 70. *Prof Exp:* Fel, Ctr Brain Res, Univ Rochester, 70-72; res assoc, Univ Miami, 72-74; res fel neurophysiol, Retina Found, Boston, 74-75; vis asst prof psychol, Univ Western Ont, 75-76. *Concurrent Pos:* Res affil, Res Lab Electronics, Mass Inst Technol, 76-78; lectr neurol, Harvard Med Sch, 76-80. *Mem:* Sigma Xi; Soc Neurosci; AAAS. *Res:* Structure and function of the visual cortex; interhemispheric communication; impulse conduction along axons. *Mailing Add:* Dept Psychol Univ Conn U-20 406 Cross Campus Storrs Mansfield CT 06269-0002

SWAIM, ROBERT LEE, AEROSPACE ENGINEERING. *Current Pos:* assoc dean, Col Eng, Archit & Technol, 78-87, prof, 87-92, EMER PROF MECH & AEROSPACE ENG, OKLA STATE UNIV, STILLWATER, 92- *Personal Data:* b Rensselaer, Ind, Aug 7, 35; m 60, W Charlene Wasson; c 3. *Educ:* Purdue Univ, BS, 57, MS, 59; Ohio State Univ, PhD(elec eng), 66. *Prof Exp:* Assoc engr, Douglas Aircraft Co, 57-58; engr, NAm Aviation, Inc, 59; sr res engr, Air Force Flight Dynamics Lab, 62-67; prof aeronaut & astronaut & assoc head, Sch Aeronaut & Astronaut, Purdue Univ, West Lafayette, 67-78. *Concurrent Pos:* Vis lectr, USAF Inst Technol, 66-67; pres, RLS Prods & Servs, 92- *Mem:* Assoc fel Am Inst Aeronaut & Astronaut; Sigma Xi; Am Soc Eng Educ. *Res:* Advanced flight control concepts for aircraft, missiles and aerospace vehicles. *Mailing Add:* 3202 W 29th Ct Stillwater OK 74074-2214. *E-Mail:* srobert@master.ceat.okstate.edu

SWAIMAN, KENNETH F, NEUROCHEMISTRY, PEDIATRIC NEUROLOGY. *Current Pos:* Fel pediat, 56-57, Nat Inst Neurol Dis & Stroke spec fel pediat neurol, 60-63, from asst prof to assoc prof, 63-69, PROF PEDIAT & NEUROL, MED SCH, UNIV MINN, MINNEAPOLIS, 69-, DIR DIV PEDIAT NEUROL, 68-, EXEC OFFICER DEPT NEUROL, 77- *Personal Data:* b St Paul, Minn, Nov 19, 31; m 73, 85; c 4. *Educ:* Univ Minn, BA, 52, BS, 53, MD, 55; Am Bd Pediat, dipl; Am Bd Psychiat & Neurol, dipl. *Honors & Awards:* Hower Award, Child Neurol Soc, 81. *Concurrent Pos:* Guest worker, NIH, 78-81. *Mem:* Am Neurol Asn; Am Acad Neurol; Am Acad Pediat; Child Neurol Soc (pres, 72-73); Prof Child Neurol (pres, 78-80). *Res:* Neurochemical changes in developing brain; iron and amino acid metabolism of immature brain. *Mailing Add:* Div Pediat Neurol Univ Minn Med Sch Minneapolis MN 55455

SWAIN, DAVID P, EXERCISE PHYSIOLOGY, PREVENTATIVE MEDICINE. *Current Pos:* Assoc PROF & DIR, WELLNESS INST & RES CTR, OLD DOM UNIV, 93- *Personal Data:* b Concord, Mass, Sept 1, 53; m 90, Xiaohong Zhang. *Educ:* Univ SFla, BA, 78; Univ NC, Chapel Hill, PhD(physiol), 84. *Prof Exp:* Fel, Univ Tex, Southwestern Med Ctr, Dallas, 84-86; asst prof & dir, Human Performance Lab, Marshall Univ, 86-90, assoc prof & dir, 90-93. *Mem:* Fel Am Col Sports Med; Am Phys Soc. *Res:* Evaluating cardiovascular responses to acute exercise; exercise as a means of preventing or treating chronic diseases of lifestyle. *Mailing Add:* Wellness Inst & Res Ctr Old Dom Univ Norfolk VA 23529-0196. *Fax:* 757-683-4270

SWAIN, DAVID WOOD, PLASMA PHYSICS, NUCLEAR FUSION. *Current Pos:* res staff mem, 75-78, proj mgr, 78-79, sr res scientist, 79-81, prog mgr, 81-83, ASST SECT HEAD, OAK RIDGE NAT LAB, 83- *Personal Data:* b Raleigh, NC, Jan 10, 42; m 63; c 2. *Educ:* NC State Univ, BS, 63 & MS, 64; Mass Inst Technol, BS, 69. *Prof Exp:* Res staff mem, Sandia Nat Lab, 69-75. *Mem:* Fel Am Phys Soc. *Res:* Experimental investigation of and technology development for high-power radio-frequency heating systems for use in plasma fusion experiment. *Mailing Add:* Oak Ridge Nat Lab Bldg 9201-2 PO Box Y Oak Ridge TN 37830. *Fax:* 423-576-7926

SWAIN, EDWARD BALCOM, MERCURY CONTAMINATION OF THE ENVIRONMENT, ACID RAIN. *Current Pos:* RES SCIENTIST, MINN POLLUTION CONTROL AGENCY, 88- *Personal Data:* m 81, Mary E Keirstead; c John & Daniel. *Educ:* Carleton Col, BA, 74; Univ Minn, PhD(ecol), 84. *Mem:* Sigma Xi; AAAS; Ecol Soc Am; Int Soc Appl & Theoret Limnol. *Res:* Published evidence that virtually all of the mercury contaminating wilderness lakes and fish is a result of air pollution. *Mailing Add:* Minn Pollution Control Agency 520 Lafayette Rd N St Paul MN 55155-4102

SWAIN, ELISABETH RAMSAY, zoology; deceased, see previous edition for last biography

SWAIN, FREDERICK MORRILL, JR, GEOLOGY, PALEONTOLOGY. *Current Pos:* from asst prof to assoc prof geol, Univ Minn, 46-54, assoc chmn, Dept Geol & Geophys, 59-61, prof, 54-79, EMER PROF GEOL & GEOPHYS, UNIV MINN, MINNEAPOLIS, 79-; EMER PROF GEOL, UNIV DEL, 86- *Personal Data:* b Kansas City, Mo, Mar 17, 16; m 38; c 3. *Educ:* Univ Kans, AB, 38, PhD(stratig, paleont), 43; Pa State Col, MS, 39. *Honors & Awards:* Award, Am Asn Petrol Geol, 49; Haworth Award, Univ Kans, 56. *Prof Exp:* Geologist, Phillips Petrol Co, La, 41-43; asst prof mineral econ, Pa State Col, 43-46; prof geol, Univ Del, 79-86, chmn dept, 83-86. *Concurrent Pos:* Assoc geologist, US Geol Surv, 44-46, geologist, 48-51, 61-; consult, Carter Oil Co, 51-53 & Pa RR, 54-57; part-time prof, Univ Del, 69-79. *Mem:* Fel Geol Soc Am; Soc Econ Paleont & Mineral; Paleont Soc; Am Asn Petrol Geol. *Res:* Stratigraphy; micropaleontology; organic geochemistry. *Mailing Add:* Dept Geol Univ Minn Minneapolis MN 55455

SWAIN, GEOFFREY W, MARINE BIOFOULING CONTROL, CORROSION CONTROL. *Current Pos:* ASSOC PROF OCEAN ENG, FLA INST TECHNOL, 84- *Personal Data:* b Poole, Dorset, Eng; m 85; c 2. *Educ:* London Univ, BSc, 71; Southampton Univ, MSc, 73, PhD(eng), 82. *Prof Exp:* Res asst, Southampton Univ, 74-80, res fel, 80-82. *Concurrent Pos:* Consult, Marine Studies Aberdeen Univ, 82-84. *Mem:* Soc Naval Architects & Marine Engrs; Nat Asn Corrosion Engrs; Inst Corrosion Sci & Technol; Marine Biol Asn UK; Marine Technol Soc; Am Soc Testing & Mats. *Res:* Corrosion control; materials testing and evaluation; marine biofouling control; development of non-toxic antifouling methods. *Mailing Add:* 473 Young St Melbourne FL 32935

SWAIN, HENRY HUNTINGTON, PHARMACOLOGY. *Current Pos:* from instr to prof, 54-91, asst dean fac affairs, 82-90, EMER PROF PHARMACOL, SCH MED, UNIV MICH, ANN ARBOR, 91- *Personal Data:* b Champaign, Ill, July 11, 23; m 48, Victoria Prodan; c Carol D (Boyse) & David N. *Educ:* Univ Ill, AB, 43, BS, 49, MS & MD, 51. *Prof Exp:* Instr pharmacol, Univ Cincinnati, 52-54. *Concurrent Pos:* Pres, Am Heart Asn Mich, 84-85. *Mem:* Am Soc Pharmacol & Exp Therapeut. *Res:* Cardiovascular pharmacology, especially cardiac arrhythmias. *Mailing Add:* Dept Pharmacol Univ Mich Med Sch Ann Arbor MI 48109-0626

SWAIN, HOWARD ALDRED, JR, PHYSICAL CHEMISTRY. *Current Pos:* from asst prof to assoc prof, 60-70, PROF CHEM, WILKES COL, 70- *Personal Data:* b New York, NY, Mar 3, 28; m 51; c 3. *Educ:* Grove City Col, BS, 51; Univ Pa, PhD, 61. *Prof Exp:* High sch instr chem, NJ, 54-56; lab technician, Rohm and Haas Co, 56-57; chemist, Socony-Mobile Res & Develop, 57-58; asst chem, Univ Pa, 58-60. *Concurrent Pos:* Oak Ridge Assoc Univs res partic, Savannah River Lab, SC, 67-68; consult, Vet Admin Hosp, Wilkes-Barre, Pa, 71; lectr, Col Miseracordia, 72; res partic water purification proj, Environ Protection Agency. *Mem:* Am Chem Soc. *Res:* Thermodynamics; radiochemistry. *Mailing Add:* 84 W Mt Airy Rd Shavertown PA 18708-1017

SWAIN, JUDITH LEA, CARDIOVASCULAR MEDICINE. *Current Pos:* ARTHUR L BLOOMFIELD PROF & CHAIR, DEPT MED, STANFORD UNIV SCH MED, 96- *Personal Data:* b Long Beach, Calif, Sept 24, 48; m, Edward W Holmes. *Educ:* Univ Calif, Los Angeles, BS, 70; Univ Calif, San Diego, MD, 74; Am Bd Internal Med, dipl cardiovasc dis. *Honors & Awards:* Bristol-Myers Squibb Cardiovasc Achievement Award, 92. *Prof Exp:* Intern med, Duke Univ Med Ctr, 74-75, resident, 75-76, fel cardiol, 76-80, assoc med, 79-81, from asst prof to assoc prof, 81-91, asst prof physiol, 81-88, assoc prof microbiol & immunol, 88-91, Herbert C Rorer prof med sci & prof genetics, 91, mem, Molecular Biol Grad Group, 91; dir, Div Cardiol, dir, Molecular Biol Lab & prof genetics, Univ Pa Sch Med, 92-96. *Concurrent Pos:* Vis asst prof, Dept Genetics, Harvard Med Sch, 85-86; mem, Cardiol Adv Comt, Nat Heart, Lung & Blood Inst, 89-93, adv coun, 95-; dir, USA-Russia Cardiovasc Res Prog, 92-; mem, Task Force on Heart Failure, NIH, 92-93; consult, Neth Res Initiative Molecular Cardiol, 93; mem, Basic Sci Coun, Am Heart Asn, Coun Clin Cardiol, 94-; chair, Cardiovasc Res Comt, Am Col Cardiol, 96- *Mem:* Inst Med-Nat Acad Sci; fel Am Col Cardiol; Asn Am Physicians; Asn Am Physicians; Am Heart Asn; Am Soc Cell Biol; Am Fedn Clin Res; Am Soc Clin Invest (pres-elect, 94-); Int Soc Heart Res. *Res:* Contributed articles to professional journals. *Mailing Add:* Dept Med Stanford Univ S-102-D MC 5109 Stanford CA 94305

SWAIN, RALPH WARNER, SYSTEMS INDUSTRIAL & MANUFACTURING ENGINEERING, HOSPITAL ADMINISTRATION. *Current Pos:* assoc prof, 76-81, PROF INDUST & SYSTS ENG, UNIV FLA, 81-, ASSOC DIR, HEALTH SYSTS RES DIV, 76-, VPRES FACIL & SUPPORT SERV, SHANDS HOSP, UNIV FLA, 87- *Personal Data:* b Orange, NJ, Dec 16, 44; m 67, 85; c 3. *Educ:* Johns Hopkins Univ, BEngSc, 67; Cornell Univ, MS, 69, PhD(environ systs), 71. *Prof Exp:*

Nat Found Med Educ fel, Ctr Environ Qual Mgt, Cornell Univ, 71; asst prof indust & systs eng, Ohio State Univ, 71-76. *Concurrent Pos:* asst to vpres admin, Shands Hosp, Univ Fla, 81-87. *Mem:* Am Inst Indust Engrs; Hosp Mgt Systs Soc. *Res:* Medical systems planning; optimal location of facilities; design and evaluation of health care delivery systems; facility location and layout; information systems design. *Mailing Add:* 6125 NW 58th Pl Gainesville FL 32653

SWAIN, RICHARD RUSSELL, BIOCHEMISTRY, CLINICAL CHEMISTRY. *Current Pos:* SR BIOCHEMIST CLIN BIOCHEM, ELI LILLY & CO, 73- *Personal Data:* b Columbus, Ohio, Mar 1, 39; m 64, Jenne A Emeric; c Cheryl A (Kuzman). *Educ:* Albion Col, AB, 61; Univ Mich, MS, 63, PhD(biochem), 65. *Prof Exp:* Asst prof biol, MacMurray Col, 67-71; fel, State Univ NY, Buffalo, 71-73. *Mem:* Am Chem Soc; Am Asn Clin Chem; Am Bd Clin Chem. *Res:* Clinical chemistry methodology; clinical enzymology; biochemical assessment of hepatotoxicity and nephrotoxicity; animal clinical chemistry; toxicology. *Mailing Add:* 8642 Lansdowne Ct Indianapolis IN 46234-2105. *Fax:* 317-277-4954

SWAIN, ROBERT JAMES, GEOPHYSICS, ELECTRONICS ENGINEERING. *Current Pos:* DIR, OYO GEOSPACE CORP, 91- *Personal Data:* b Waukesha, Wis, Oct 3, 28; m 50, Marjorie Sperry; c Katherine & Todd. *Educ:* Purdue Univ, BS, 51. *Prof Exp:* Jr engr, A C Electronics Div, Gen Motors Corp, 51-53, prod engr, 53-55; sales & contracts mgr, Conrac Corp, 55-57; staff engr, United Electrodynamics, Inc, 58-59, chief struct seismol, 59-60, gen mgr, Geomeasurements Div, 60-61, vpres & gen mgr, Earth Sci Div, 61-64; vpres & gen mgr, Earth Sci, A Teledyne Co, 64-67, pres, 67-69; chmn & pres, Kinemetrics, Inc, 69-91. *Mem:* AAAS; Am Geophys Union; Seismol Soc Am; Sigma Xi; Am Nuclear Soc; Earthquake Eng Res Inst; Soc Explor Geophysists; Am Soc Civil Engrs; Geol Soc Am. *Res:* Ground motion from earthquakes and blasts; response of structures to ground motion; sensing and recording systems. *Mailing Add:* 16271 Typhoon Lane Huntington Beach CA 92649. *Fax:* 714-846-5668

SWAISGOOD, HAROLD EVERETT, PROTEIN BIOCHEMISTRY, ENZYME TECHNOLOGY. *Current Pos:* from asst prof to prof, 64-72, chmn univ biotechnol fac, 87-92, WILLIAM NEAL REYNOLDS PROF FOOD SCI & BIOCHEM, NC STATE UNIV, 84- *Personal Data:* b Ashland, Ohio, Jan 19, 36; m 56, Janet Cromwell; c Mark H & Ronald R. *Educ:* Ohio State Univ, BS, 58; Mich State Univ, PhD(chem), 63. *Honors & Awards:* Dairy Res Found Award, Am Dairy Sci Asn, 85, Borden Award, 87; Advan Agr Food Chem Award, Am Chem Soc, 94. *Prof Exp:* NIH fel, 63-64. *Concurrent Pos:* Vis prof, Univ Lund, Sweden, 74; guest scientist & intergovt personnel act awardee, Nat Inst Arthritis, Diabetes & Digestive & Kidney Dis, NIH, 83-84; vis scientist, Univ Calif, Davis, 89. *Mem:* AAAS; fel Am Chem Soc; Inst Food Technologists; Am Dairy Sci Asn; Am Soc Biochem & Molecular Biol; Am Inst Nutrit. *Res:* Physical-chemical characterization of proteins; protein interactions and the relationship to biological activity; methods of preparation and characterization of enzymes covalently bound to surfaces; analytical affinity chromatography; bioselective adsorption of fusion proteins. *Mailing Add:* Dept Food Sci NC State Univ Box 7624 Raleigh NC 27695-7624. *Fax:* 919-515-7124; *E-Mail:* harold_swaisgood@ncsu.edu

SWAKON, DOREEN H D, RUMINANT NUTRITION. *Current Pos:* asst prof, 80-85, dir, Forage Testing Lab, 81-85, ASSOC PROF ANIMAL SCI, TEX A&M UNIV, 85- *Personal Data:* b Berwyn, Ill, Oct 9, 53; c 1. *Educ:* Univ Ill, BS, 75; Univ Fla, MS, 77, PhD(animal sci), 80. *Prof Exp:* Res asst, Univ Fla, 75-80. *Concurrent Pos:* Adj prof, Corpus Christi State Univ, 91; consult law firms, 90- *Mem:* Am Soc Animal Sci; Coun Agr Sci & Technol; Soc Range Mgt. *Res:* Feed evaluation and utilization by domestic ruminants, aquacultured species, and wildlife. *Mailing Add:* Dept Animal Sci Tex A&M Univ 700 University Blvd Kingsville TX 78363-8203. *Fax:* 512-595-3713

SWALEN, JEROME DOUGLAS, CHEMICAL PHYSICS, OPTICS. *Current Pos:* mgr physics dept, IBM Res Lab, 62-63, lab mgr, 63-67, mgr, Molecular Physics Dept, 67-73, res staff mem, 73-79, mgr excitations in solids, 79-85, mgr thin film mat & devices, 85-93, EMER, IBM RES LAB, 93-; CONSULT, MOLECULAR OPTICS, 93- *Personal Data:* b Minneapolis, Minn, Mar 4, 28; m 52, Mary King; c Douglas & Diana. *Educ:* Univ Minn, BS, 50; Harvard Univ, AM, 54, PhD(chem physics), 56. *Prof Exp:* Fel, Div Pure Physics, Nat Res Coun Can, 56-57; physicist, Shell Develop Co, 57-62. *Concurrent Pos:* Vis prof, Phys Chem Inst, Univ Zurich, 72-73, Fac Sci, Univ Paris VI & Inst Optics, Orsay, 83; guest prof physics, Univ Calif, Santa Cruz, 80-81, adj prof, 93- *Mem:* Fel AAAS; fel Am Phys Soc; Am Chem Soc; Optical Soc Am; Soc Photogram & Instrumentation Engrs. *Res:* Linear and nonlinear optical properties of thin organic films and monolayers. *Mailing Add:* 16231 Matilija Dr Los Gatos CA 95030. *Fax:* 408-927-3310; *E-Mail:* swalen@almaden.ibm.com

SWALES, JOHN E, AGRICULTURE, HORTICULTURE. *Current Pos:* RETIRED. *Personal Data:* b Kaleden, BC, 24. *Educ:* Ont Agr Col, Univ Toronto, BS, 47. *Honors & Awards:* Distinguished Exten Specialist Award, Int Dwarf Fruit Tree Asn, 89; Spec Recognition Award, Can Soc Hort Sci, 90. *Prof Exp:* Staff, BC Dept Agr, 48-49, dist horticulturalist, Nelson, 48-53, Creston, 58-63, Penticton, 63-75; apple specialist, Agr Can Res Sta, 75-79; head field serv, Okanagan Similkameen Coop Grower's Asn, 79-90. *Concurrent Pos:* Fel Award, Agr Inst Can, 92. *Res:* Contributed articles to professional journals. *Mailing Add:* 184 Hwy 97 S1 C4 RR 1 Kaleden BC V0H 1K0 Can

SWALIN, RICHARD ARTHUR, RESOURCE MANAGEMENT, METALLURGY. *Current Pos:* dean, 84-87, prof, 84-94, EMER PROF MGT, UNIV ARIZ, 94- *Personal Data:* b Minneapolis, Minn, Mar 18, 29; m 52, Helen Van Wagenen; c Karen, Kent & Kristin. *Educ:* Univ Minn, BS, 51, PhD(metall), 54. *Prof Exp:* Res assoc metall, Gen Elec Res Lab, 54-55; prof metall, Univ Minn, 55-77, dean, Inst Technol, 71-77; vpres, Eltra Corp, 77-80, Allied-Signal Corp, 80-84; pres, Ariz Technol Develop Corp, 87. *Concurrent Pos:* Mem, Naval Res Adv Bd-Lab, Bd Res, 72-76; dir, Sheldahl Corp, 72-76, BMC Corp & Medtronic Corp, 73-, Donaldson Corp, 74-77; vchmn, Marine Corps Adv Bd, 73-76; NATO sr fel sci, 76; mem adv bd, AMP Corp, 90-93; NATO sr fel sci, 76. *Mailing Add:* 4705 Via de la Granja Tucson AZ 85718

SWALLOW, EARL CONNOR, HIGH ENERGY PHYSICS, EXPERIMENTAL PHYSICS. *Current Pos:* from asst prof to assoc prof, 76-83, chmn, Div Natural Sci & Math, 87-90, CHMN DEPT, ELMHURST COL, 79-, PROF PHYSICS, 83- *Personal Data:* b Montgomery County, Ohio, Dec 27, 41; div; c 1. *Educ:* Earlham Col, BA, 63; Washington Univ, MA, 65, PhD(physics), 70. *Honors & Awards:* Arthur H Compton Lectr, Univ Chicago, 77. *Prof Exp:* Resident student assoc elem particle physics, Argonne Nat Lab, 64 & 65, res staff assoc, 65-69, res asst for Washington Univ, 69-70; res assoc elem particle physics, 70-74, sr res assoc, Enrico Fermi Inst, Univ Chicago, 74-80. *Concurrent Pos:* Teaching asst, Washington Univ, 65; vis mem staff, Argonne Nat Lab, 78, 79 & 81; vis scientist, Enrico Fermi Inst, Univ Chicago, 83- *Mem:* Am Phys Soc; Sigma Xi; AAAS; Am Asn Physics Teachers; NY Acad Sci. *Res:* Fundamental interactions of elementary particles, especially weak interactions; experimental foundations of physical theory; relationship of experimental foundations to public policy. *Mailing Add:* 2005 S Finley Rd Apt 611 Lombard IL 60148-4846. *Fax:* 630-617-3735; *E-Mail:* earls@elmhurst.edu

SWALLOW, JOHN RIEHARD, GALOIS THEORY. *Current Pos:* MACARTHUR ASST PROF MATH, DAVIDSON COL, 94- *Personal Data:* b Houston, Tex, July 30, 70; m 91, Cameron Wallace; c 1. *Educ:* Univ South, BA, 89; Yale Univ, MS & MPhil, 91, PhD(math), 94. *Concurrent Pos:* Prin investr, NSF, 94-97; asst prof, Univ Sci & Technol, Lile, France, 97. *Mem:* Am Math Soc; Math Asn Am. *Res:* Understand the ways in which finite groups may be realized as Galois groups over the rational numbers. *Mailing Add:* PO Box 1719 Davidson NC 28036-1719

SWALLOW, KATHLEEN CLINEDINST, ENVIRONMENTAL ANALYTICAL CHEMISTRY, SUPER-CRITICAL WATER OXIDATION. *Current Pos:* ASSOC PROF CHEM, MERRIMACK COL, 90- *Personal Data:* b Baltimore, Md, Jan 21, 48; m, Stephen Thaxter; c Lindsey E & Clinton P. *Educ:* Univ Richmond, BS, 70; Mass Inst Technol, PhD(anal chem), 78. *Prof Exp:* Asst scientist, Philip Morris, Inc, 70-73; asst prof chem, Wellesley Col, 77-82 & 89-90; mgr, Anal Labs, Modar Inc, 82-85; sr assoc, Gradient Corp, 86-89. *Concurrent Pos:* Pres, Interstate Labs, Inc, 80-82; consult, Modar Inc, 85-92; vis scientist, Mass Inst Technol, 93 & 96-97, vis prof, 94- *Mem:* Am Chem Soc; Sigma Xi. *Res:* Identification and analysis of potentially mutagenic polycyclic aromatic hydrocarbons in combustion products; analytical techniques for studying the products of supercritical water oxidation; pollutants in natural systems including water, soil and sediment. *Mailing Add:* 131 River Rd West Newbury MA 01985

SWALLOW, RICHARD LOUIS, ZOOLOGY, BIOLOGY. *Current Pos:* assoc prof, 73-80, PROF BIOL, COKER COL, 80- *Personal Data:* b Berwyn, Ill, June 16, 39; m 64; c 1. *Educ:* Univ Ill, Urbana, BS, 63; Univ Mo-Columbia, MA, 66, PhD(zool), 68. *Prof Exp:* USPHS fel, Sch Med, Case Western Reserve Univ, 68-69; asst prof biol, Univ Houston, 69-73. *Mem:* Am Soc Zoologists. *Res:* Comparative physiology including control of metabolism by hormones in fish. *Mailing Add:* Dir Acad Comput Coker Col 300 E College Ave Hartsville SC 29550-3742

SWALLOW, WILLIAM HUTCHINSON, LINEAR MODELS, GROUP TESTING. *Current Pos:* assoc prof, 80-87, PROF STATIST & DIR UNDERGRAD PROGS, NC STATE UNIV, 87- *Personal Data:* b Norwalk, Conn, Oct 21, 41; m 82, Louise Rozak Romanow; c Curtis Romanow. *Educ:* Harvard Univ, AB, 64; Cornell Univ, MS, 68, PhD(biomet), 74. *Prof Exp:* Asst prof statist, Rutgers Univ, 73-79. *Concurrent Pos:* Statist assoc ed, J Am Soc, Hort Sci & Hort Sci. *Mem:* Am Statist Asn; Sigma Xi; Biometric Soc; Am Soc Hort Sci. *Res:* Linear models; estimation of variance components; research directed at improving the teaching of statistics; group testing. *Mailing Add:* Dept Statist NC State Univ Box 8203 Raleigh NC 27695-8203. *Fax:* 919-515-1909; *E-Mail:* swallow@stat.ncsu.edu

SWALM, RALPH OEHRLE, economics of industrial engineering, for more information see previous edition

SWAMER, FREDERIC WURL, ORGANIC CHEMISTRY. *Current Pos:* RETIRED. *Personal Data:* b Shawano, Wis, May 16, 18; m 46; c 3. *Educ:* Lawrence Col, BA, 40; Univ Wis, MS, 42; Duke Univ, PhD(chem), 49. *Prof Exp:* Chemist, Appleton Water Purification Plant, Wis, 40; res chemist, Electrochem Dept, E I du Pont de Nemours & Co, 41-45; res assoc, Duke Univ, 49-50; res chemist, E I DuPont De Nemours & Co, Inc, Wilmington, Del, 50-64; res assoc, Org Chem Dept, Exp Sta, 64-80. *Mem:* AAAS; Am Chem Soc. *Res:* Claisen condensation; physical properties of polymers; acetylene organoalkali compounds; fluorocarbons; heterogeneous catalysis. *Mailing Add:* 750 Folly Hill Rd West Chester PA 19382-6910

SWAMINATHAN, BALASUBRAMANIAN, FOOD MICROBIOLOGY, FOOD TOXICOLOGY. *Current Pos:* SECT CHIEF, CTR DIS CONTROL, 88- *Personal Data:* b Madras, India, Nov 24, 46; m 76. *Educ:* Delhi Univ, BSc hon, 66; Univ Ga, MS, 74, PhD(food sci), 77. *Prof Exp:* Bottler's serv chemist qual control, Coca-Cola Export Corp, 67-72, microbiologist qual control & develop, 74; asst prof food sci, Purdue Univ, 77-88. *Concurrent Pos:* Res grant, Ind Agr Exp Sta, 80-82. *Mem:* Inst Food Technologists; Am Soc Microbiol; AAAS; Int Asn Milk, Food & Environ Sanitarians. *Res:* Rapid detection of pathogenic microorganisms in foods and feeds; pathogenic mechanisms associated with Yersinia enterocolitica; mutagenicity of procyanidins present in beverages. *Mailing Add:* Ctr Dis Control Bldg 1 Rm B-354 1600 Clifton Rd Atlanta GA 30333

SWAMINATHAN, SRINIVASA, MATHEMATICS. *Current Pos:* assoc prof, 68-80, PROF MATH, DALHOUSIE UNIV, 80. *Personal Data:* b Madras, India, Aug 24, 26; m 52; c 1. *Educ:* Presidency Col, Madras, India, BA, 47, MA, 48; Univ Madras, MSc, 50, PhD(math), 57. *Prof Exp:* Govt of France fel, Inst Henri Poincare, Paris, 57-58; lectr math, Univ Madras, 59-64; asst prof, Indian Inst Technol, Kanpur, 64-66; vis assoc prof, Univ Ill, Chicago Circle, 66-68. *Concurrent Pos:* Auth & mem comt reorgn curricula math, Nat Coun Educ Res & Training, Govt of India, 64-67; managing ed, Can Math Bull, 79-85; vis prof, Australian Nat Univ, Canberra, 84; prod ed, Can Math J, 86-; vis prof, Univ Limoges, France, 90-91. *Mem:* Am Math Soc; Can Math Soc; Indian Math Soc; Math Asn Am. *Res:* Functional analysis; topology; geometry of Banach spaces; operator theory; paracompact spaces; fixed point theorems in analysis and topology; biomathematics. *Mailing Add:* Dalhousie Univ Halifax NS B3H 3L1 Can. *Fax:* 902-494-5130; *E-Mail:* swami@cs.dal.ca

SWAMY, MAYASANDRA NANJUNDIAH SRIKANTA, ELECTRICAL ENGINEERING, APPLIED MATHEMATICS. *Current Pos:* prof & chmn, Dept Elec Eng, 70-77, dean, Fac Eng, 77-93, RES PROF ELEC & COMPUT ENG, CONCORDIA UNIV, 93- *Personal Data:* b Bangalore, India, Apr 7, 35; m 64, Leela Sitaramaiah; c Saritha, Nikhilesh & Jagadish. *Educ:* Univ Mysore, BSc(Hons), 54; Indian Inst Sci, Bangalore, dipl, 57; Univ Sask, MSc, 60, PhD, 63. *Prof Exp:* Sr res asst electronics, Indian Inst Sci, Bangalore, 58-59; res asst elec eng, Univ Sask, 59-63, sessional lectr math, 61-63, asst prof, 64-65; Govt India scientist, Indian Inst Technol, Madras, 63-64; from asst prof to prof elec eng, NS Tech Col, 65-68; prof, Concordia Univ, 68-69; prof, Univ Calgary, 69-70. *Concurrent Pos:* Adj prof elec, Pa State Univ, 81-83 & City Col, City Univ NY, 91- *Mem:* Fel Inst Elec & Electronics Engrs; Am Math Soc; Math Asn Am; fel Eng Inst Can; fel Inst Engrs India; fel Inst Elec Engrs UK. *Res:* Network theory; graph theory; signal processing; author or coauthor of over 200 research articles. *Mailing Add:* Dept Elec Comput Eng Concordia Univ 1455 Maissoneuve Blvd W Montreal PQ H3G 1M8 Can. *E-Mail:* swamy@ece.concordia.ca

SWAMY, PADMANABHA NARAYANA, ELEMENTARY PARTICLE PHYSICS, THEORETICAL PHYSICS. *Current Pos:* from asst to assoc prof, 69-77, chmn, Physics Dept, 83-92, PROF PHYSICS, SOUTHERN ILL UNIV, 77- *Personal Data:* b India, July 25, 37; m 63; c 2. *Educ:* Delhi Univ, India, BS, 56, MS, 58, PhD(physics), 63. *Prof Exp:* Res fel physics, Delhi Univ, 63-64, res fel, Tata Inst Fund Res, 64-65; vis scientist, Int Ctr Theoret Physics, Trieste, 65-66; res assoc, Syracuse Univ, 66; vis scientist, Ctr Nuclear Res, Geneva, 66-67; fel, Tata Inst Fund Res, 67-68; asst prof, Am Univ Beirut, 68-69. *Mem:* Am Phys Soc. *Res:* Quantum field theory; particle theory; statistical mechanics. *Mailing Add:* Dept of Physics Southern Ill Univ Edwardsville IL 62026-1654

SWAMY, VIJAY CHINNASWAMY, PHARMACOLOGY. *Current Pos:* res assoc, 67-69, actg chair, 85-88, ASSOC PROF BIOCHEM PHARMACOL, STATE UNIV NY BUFFALO, 70-, CHAIR, 93- *Personal Data:* b Bombay, India, Oct 2, 38; m 72; c 2. *Educ:* Bombay Univ, BSc, 59; Nagpur Univ, BPharm, 62; Ohio State Univ, MS, 64, PhD(pharmacol), 67. *Prof Exp:* Res asst pharmacol, Ohio State Univ, 64-67. *Mem:* AAAS; Am Asn Col Pharmacol. *Res:* Smooth muscle pharmacology; hypertension; adrenergic mechanisms. *Mailing Add:* 35 Lawnwood Dr Amherst NY 14228

SWAN, ALGERNON GORDON, physiology, biophysics, for more information see previous edition

SWAN, CATHY WOOD, ARMS CONTROL TREATY IMPLEMENTATION EXPERT, SPACE POLICY ADVISOR & CONSULTANT. *Current Pos:* VPRES, SCI APPL INT CORP, 92-; PRES & CHIEF EXEC OFFICER, SOUTHWEST ANALYTIC NETWORK, 93- *Personal Data:* m 68, Peter A. *Educ:* Univ Albuquerque, BA, 75; Univ Southern Calif, MS, 77; Univ Calif, Los Angeles, PhD(space policy), 84. *Prof Exp:* Asst prof space policy & acquistion mgt, USAF Acad, 79-81; dir for policy, Secy Air Force Office Spec Proj, 84-89; vpres, EOS Technol, 89-92. *Mem:* Pres Adv Coun Space; Am Astronaut Soc; Space Studies Inst; fel Am Inst Strategic Studies; sr mem Am Inst Aeronaut & Astronaut; Armed Forces Commun & Elec Asn; fel Brit Interplanetary Soc. *Res:* Technical evaluations of facilities and technologies vulnerable to on-site inspections under various arms control; inspection protocols; high performance computing evaluating parallel processing applications; contributed numerous articles to publications. *Mailing Add:* 5865 E Sanna Paradise Valley AZ 85253

SWAN, D(AVID), METALLURGY. *Current Pos:* CONSULT, 82- *Personal Data:* b NJ, May 2, 20; m, Jette Loun; c 4. *Educ:* Rensselaer Polytech Inst, BMetE, 40. *Honors & Awards:* Demers Medal, Rensselaer Polytech Inst, 65. *Prof Exp:* Metall observer, Crucible Steel Co Am, 40-41; res engr, Union Carbide Corp, 46-51, dir res, Union Carbide Metals Co, 52-56, Linde Co, 56-57, vpres res, 58-59, mgr planning, Union Carbide Corp, 59-60, vpres tech, Union Carbide Metals Co, 60-64, gen mgr, Defense & Space Systs Dept, Union Carbide Corp, 64-66; vpres tech, Kennecott Copper Corp, 66-79, vpres environ issues, 79-82. *Concurrent Pos:* Mem, Moscow Steel Inst-NY Univ Exchange Prog, 57; mem, Mat Adv Bd, Nat Acad Sci-Nat Res Coun, 58-62; dir, William F Clapp Labs, Inc, Duxbury, Mass, 64-; chmn, Adv Comt Metall & Mat Sci, Polytech Inst NY, 77-; chmn, Dirs Indust Res, 78-79; mem, Develop Coun, Rensselaer Polytech, mem, Gen Tech Adv Comt, Off Coal Res; fel, Polytech Inst, 80. *Mem:* Am Welding Soc; fel Am Soc Metals; fel Metall Soc (pres, 72-73); Am Inst Mining, Metall & Petrol Engrs (vpres, 72-74). *Res:* Extractive metallurgy; environmental; economic; research management. *Mailing Add:* 226B Heritage Village Southbury CT 06488

SWAN, DEAN GEORGE, WEED SCIENCE. *Current Pos:* RETIRED. *Personal Data:* b Wheatland, Wyo, Sept 16, 23; m 48, Rowena White; c Cynthia, John & Daniel. *Educ:* Univ Wyo, BS, 52, MS, 54; Univ Ill, PhD, 64. *Prof Exp:* Instr, Chadron High Sch, 52-53; asst prof & agron weed res, Pendleton Exp Sta, Ore State Univ, 55-65; exten weed specialist, Univ Ariz, 65-66; exten weed scientist & agronomist, Wash State Univ, 66-89. *Concurrent Pos:* Sabbaticals, Weed Res Orgn, Oxford, Eng, 72-73 & 78-79. *Mem:* Weed Sci Soc Am; Sigma Xi. *Res:* Weed biology; weed control in crops and vegetation management. *Mailing Add:* 822 SW Crestview Dr Pullman WA 99163

SWAN, FREDERICK ROBBINS, JR, ECOLOGY, INDUSTRIAL HYGIENE. *Current Pos:* INDUST HYGIENIST, CLAYTON ENVIRON CONSULT INC, 88- *Personal Data:* b Hartford, Conn, Aug 14, 37; m 62, Patricia L; c Peter & Eric. *Educ:* Middlebury Col, BA, 59; Univ Wis, MS, 61; Cornell Univ, PhD(conserv natural resources), 66; WVa Univ, MS, 88. *Prof Exp:* Assoc prof, 66-74, West Liberty State Col, actg chmn, Sch Natural Sci, 70-72, prof biol, 74-88, chmn dept, 78-84. *Concurrent Pos:* Assoc, Dept Natural Resources, Cornell Univ, 74-75. *Mem:* Am Indust Hyg Asn; Am Soc Safety Engrs; Ecol Soc Am; Sigma Xi; Asn Trop Biol. *Res:* Effects of fire on plant communities; measurement of light in forests. *Mailing Add:* 24 Donald Ave Kendall Park NJ 08824-1619. *Fax:* 732-225-4577

SWAN, HAROLD JAMES CHARLES, PHYSIOLOGY, CARDIOVASCULAR DISEASES. *Current Pos:* PROF MED, UNIV CALIF, LOS ANGELES, 66- *Personal Data:* b Sligo, Ireland, June 1, 22; US citizen; m 46; c 7. *Educ:* Univ London, MB, BS, 45, PhD(physiol), 51. *Honors & Awards:* Walter Dixon Award, Brit Med Asn, 50. *Prof Exp:* Res assoc, Mayo Clin, 51-53, Minn Heart Asn res fel, 53-54, consult cardiovasc dis, 55-65; dir cardiol, Cedars-Sinai Med Ctr, Los Angeles, 65- *Concurrent Pos:* Assoc prof, Mayo Grad Sch, Univ Minn, 57-65; consult, Nat Heart Inst, 60-66; mem, Intersoc Comn Heart Dis Resources, 69- *Mem:* Am Physiol Soc; fel Am Col Physicians; fel Am Col Cardiol (pres, 73); Asn Univ Cardiol. *Res:* Ventricular function; myocardial hypertrophy; coronary arterial disease and myocardial ischemia and infarction. *Mailing Add:* Dept Med Univ Calif Los Angeles 1075 Wallace Ridge Beverly Hills CA 90210-2635

SWAN, JAMES BYRON, SOIL PHYSICS. *Current Pos:* PROF AGRON DEPT & ASSOC DIR, LEOPOLD CTR SUSTAINABLE AGR, IOWA STATE UNIV, AMES, 89- *Personal Data:* b Bloomington, Ill, Dec 9, 33; m 62; c 2. *Educ:* Univ Ill, BS, 55, MS, 59; Univ Wis, PhD(soil physics), 64. *Prof Exp:* Exten specialist & prof soil sci, Univ Minn, St Paul, 64-89. *Mem:* Soil Conserv Soc Am; Am Soc Agron; Soil Sci Soc Am. *Res:* Tillage systems; modeling effect of soil temperature and soil water on plant growth; solute transport in soil. *Mailing Add:* Agron Dept Iowa State Univ 3405 Agronomy Ames IA 50011-0001

SWAN, KENNETH CARL, OPHTHALMOLOGY, PHARMACOLOGY. *Current Pos:* SR CONSULT, CASEY EYE INST. *Personal Data:* b Kansas City, Mo, Jan 1, 12; m 42, Virginia Grone; c Stephen, Kenneth & Susan. *Educ:* Univ Ore, BA, 33, MD, 36; Am Bd Ophthal, dipl, 40. *Honors & Awards:* Proctor lectr, Univ Calif, 46; Proctor Medal, Asn Res Vision & Ophthal, 53; Howe Medal, Am Ophthal Soc, 77; Pioneer Award, Lewis & Clark Col, 79. *Prof Exp:* Assoc ophthal, Univ Iowa, 41-42, asst prof, 42-44; assoc prof ophthal, Med Sch, Univ Ore Health Sci Ctr, 44-45, prof & head dept, 45-78. *Concurrent Pos:* Chmn bd, Am Bd Ophthal, 61; chmn, Sensory Dis Study Sect, NIH, 61-63; mem adv coun, Nat Eye Inst, 69-71; consult, Nat Inst Neurol Dis & Blindness. *Mem:* Am Ophthal Soc; Asn Res Vision & Ophthal; AMA; Am Acad Ophthal. *Res:* Ocular physiology, pharmacology and therapeutics; anomalies of binocular vision; tumors of the eyes; ocular manifestations of vascular diseases; surgical anatomy and pathology. *Mailing Add:* Dept Ophthal Ore Health Sci Univ Portland OR 97201

SWAN, KENNETH G, SURGERY. *Current Pos:* dir & assoc prof, Div Gen & Vascular Surg, 73-76, PROF SURG, NJ MED SCH, 76- *Personal Data:* b White Plains, NY, Oct 2, 34; m 65; c 3. *Educ:* Harvard Univ, AB, 56; Cornell Univ, MD, 60. *Prof Exp:* Resident gen surg, New York Hosp-Cornell Med Ctr, 60-65; fel physiol, Gastrointestinal Res Lab, Vet Admin Ctr, Los Angeles, 65-66; resident thoracic surg, New York Hosp-Cornell Med Ctr, 66-68; dep dir div surg, Walter Reed Army Inst Res, 71-72, dir div surg, 72-73. *Mem:* Am Physiol Soc; Am Gastroenterol Asn; Am Col Surgeons; Soc Univ Surgeons; Soc Thoracic Surgeons. *Res:* Splanchnic circulation; shock; vascular surgery and trauma. *Mailing Add:* Dept Surg Univ Med & Dent NJ Med Sci Bldg G590 185 S Orange Ave Newark NJ 07103-2714. *Fax:* 973-982-6803

SWAN, LAWRENCE WESLEY, BIOLOGY. *Current Pos:* from instr to assoc prof, 54-64, PROF BIOL, SAN FRANCISCO STATE UNIV, 64- *Personal Data:* b Bengal, India, Mar 9, 22; m 46; c 3. *Educ:* Univ Wis, PhB, 42; Stanford Univ, MA, 47, PhD(biol), 52. *Prof Exp:* Res officer, Climatic Res Lab, Lawrence, Mass, 43-46; instr biol, Univ Santa Clara, 51-53. *Concurrent Pos:* Mem, Am Himalayan Expeds, Nepal, 54, 60-61, biol surv, Mt Orizaba, Mex, 64 & 65, biol world tour, 66, field studies, EAfrica, 69 & Galapagos Islands, 70; Academia Sinica Exped, Tibet Plateau, 80; field studies, S Cent Africa, 81. *Mem:* Ecol Soc Am; Am Soc Ichthyol & Herpet; Royal Geog Soc; Sigma Xi; Am Inst Biol Sci. *Res:* High altitude ecology and the Aeolian zone; zoogeography of Asia; vertebrate evolution. *Mailing Add:* 1032 Wilmington Way Redwood City CA 94062-4037

SWAN, PATRICIA B, NUTRITION, BIOCHEMISTRY. *Current Pos:* vprovost res & advan studies & dean, Grad Col, 89-91, interim provost, 91-92, VPROVOST RES & ADVAN STUDIES & DEAN, GRAD COL, IOWA STATE UNIV, 92- *Personal Data:* b Hickory, NC, Oct 21, 37; m 62, James B; c Kathryn A & Deborah L. *Educ:* Univ NC, Greensboro, BS, 59; Univ Wis, MS, 61, PhD(biochem, nutrit), 64. *Prof Exp:* Res fel biochem, Univ Minn, St Paul, 64-65, from asst prof to prof nutrit, 65-89, assoc dean, Grad Sch, 87-89. *Concurrent Pos:* Nutrit prog coordr, USDA, 79-80, prog mgr, competitive grants human nutrit, 85-86; mem bd agr, Nat Res Coun. *Mem:* Am Inst Nutrit (secy, 81-84); Nat Agr Biotechnol Coun; Am Chem Soc. *Res:* Amino acid metabolism development and aging; nutrition effects on muscle metabolism; history of nutrition research. *Mailing Add:* 211 Beardshire Hall Iowa State Univ Ames IA 50011

SWAN, PETER A, SATELLITE DESIGN, DYNAMICS & CONTROL FOR SPACE FLIGHT. *Current Pos:* SYSTS DEVELOP MGR, MOTOROLA SATELLITE COMMUN, 96- *Personal Data:* b Tex, Apr 17, 45; m 68. *Educ:* US Mil Acad, 68; Air Force Inst Technol, MS, 70; Univ Southern Calif, MS, 76; Univ Calif, Los Angeles, PhD(eng), 84. *Prof Exp:* Res engr, test engr, prog mgr & proj leader, USAF, 68-88; dir, Wash Syst, Motorola Space Electronics, 88-93, satellite team leader, Iridium Proj, 93-96. *Concurrent Pos:* Instr astronaut, eng & mgt, USAF Acad, 78-80; consult, Jet Propulsion Lab, 81-84; prof mgmt, Capitol Col, 90-93; mem, Int Activ Comt, Am Inst Aeronaut & Astronaut, 91- *Mem:* Fel Brit Interplanetary Soc; assoc fel Am Inst Aeronaut & Astronaut; AAAS; Int Acad Astronaut. *Res:* The dynamics and control of space tethers or strings in space; the management aspects of mobile satellite communications with 66 satellites and pocket telephones. *Mailing Add:* 5865 E Sanna Paradise Valley AZ 85253

SWAN, RICHARD GORDON, MATHEMATICS. *Current Pos:* RETIRED. *Personal Data:* b New York, NY, Dec 21, 33; m 63, Erdmuthe Plesch-Ritz; c Adrian & Irit. *Educ:* Princeton Univ, AB, 54, PhD(math), 57. *Honors & Awards:* Cole Prize, Am Math Soc, 70. *Prof Exp:* NSF res fel, Oxford Univ, 57-58; from instr to prof, Univ Chicago, 58-96, Louis Block prof math, 82-96. *Concurrent Pos:* Sloan fel, 60-65. *Mem:* Nat Acad Sci; AAAS; Math Asn Am; Am Math Soc. *Res:* Algebraic K-theory; homological algebra. *Mailing Add:* 700 Melrose Ave - M3 Winter Park FL 32789-5610. *E-Mail:* swan@math.uchicago.edu

SWAN, ROY CRAIG, JR, ANATOMY. *Current Pos:* from instr to assoc prof physiol, 52-59, prof anat, 59-70, chmn dept, 59-78, JOSEPH C HINSEY PROF ANAT, MED COL, CORNELL UNIV, 70- *Personal Data:* b New York, NY, June 7, 20; m 49, 77; c 2. *Educ:* Cornell Univ, AB, 41, MD, 47. *Prof Exp:* Intern med, New York Hosp, 47-48; asst resident, 48-49, resident endocrinol & metab, 49-50; asst med, Peter Bent Brigham Hosp, 50-52. *Concurrent Pos:* Life Ins Med Res Fund fel, Harvard Med Sch, 50-52; Markle scholar, 54-59; res assoc, Cambridge Univ, 55-56; mem health res coun, City New York; consult, USPHS, 60-65 & Off Sci & Technol, 63-64; sect ed, Biol Abstr; mem & chmn exec bd, Anat Test Comt, Nat Bd Med Examr; vis prof anat, Boston Univ, 77-78. *Mem:* Am Physiol Soc; Am Soc Clin Invest; Am Asn Anat. *Res:* Ion transport; muscle function and structure; neural fine structure. *Mailing Add:* Dept Anat Cell Biol Cornell Univ Med Col 1300 York Ave New York NY 10021-4805

SWAN, SHANNA HELEN, PUBLIC HEALTH. *Current Pos:* AT SCH DEPT PUBLIC HEALTH, UNIV CALIF. *Personal Data:* b Warren, Ohio, May 24, 36; c 3. *Educ:* City Col New York, BS, 58; Columbia Univ, MS, 60; Univ Calif, Berkeley, PhD(statist), 63. *Prof Exp:* Sr biostatistician, Contraceptive Drug Study, Kaiser Health Res, Walnut Creek, Calif, 69-75; assoc prof math, Calif State Univ, Sonoma, 74-79; dir training prog biostatist & epidemiol, Sch Pub Health, Univ Calif, Berkeley, 79-81; chief, Dept Health Serv, State Calif, 81- *Concurrent Pos:* Consult contraceptive eval, WHO, 74; lectr statist, Univ Copenhagen, Denmark, 60-61 & Univ Tel Aviv, Israel, 67-68 & Sch Pub Health, Univ Calif, Berkeley, 79-; vis assoc prof, Dept Statist, Univ Calif, Berkeley, 78-79; mem, Comt Hormonally Active Agents in Environ, Nat Acad Sci. *Mem:* Soc Epidemiol Res; Am Statist Asn; Biometric Soc; Am Pub Health Asn. *Res:* Evaluating reproductive changes associated with environmental exposures and the methodologic problems involved in studying such associations. *Mailing Add:* 964 The Alaneda Berkeley CA 94707. *Fax:* 510-450-3773; *E-Mail:* sswan@igc.org

SWANBERG, CHANDLER A, GEOPHYSICS, GEOLOGY. *Current Pos:* asst prof, 74-78, ASSOC PROF GEOPHYS, NMEX STATE UNIV, 78- *Personal Data:* b Great Falls, Mont, July 7, 42. *Educ:* Southern Methodist Univ, BS, 65, MS, 69, PhD(geophys), 71. *Prof Exp:* Fel geophys, Mus Geol, Univ Oslo, 71-72; geophysicist, US Bur Reclamation, 72-74. *Concurrent Pos:* Prin investr various govt & state agencies, 74-; sr res consult, Teledyne-Geotech, 81-82. *Mem:* Am Geophys Union; AAAS; Geol Soc Am; Geothermal Resources Coun; Sigma Xi. *Res:* Search for, evaluation and development of geothermal energy resources. *Mailing Add:* PO Box 959 Phoenix AZ 85001-0959

SWANBORG, ROBERT HARRY, IMMUNOLOGY, IMMUNOPATHOLOGY. *Current Pos:* from instr to assoc prof microbiol, 66-73, assoc prof immunol & microbiol, 73-77, PROF IMMUNOL & MICROBIOL, MED SCH, WAYNE STATE UNIV, 77- *Personal Data:* b Brooklyn, NY, Aug 27, 38; m 92, Janice Tantony-Olstyn; c 2. *Educ:* Wagner Col, BS, 60; Long Island Univ, MS, 62; State Univ NY Buffalo, PhD(immunol), 65. *Prof Exp:* NIH trainee immunochem, State Univ NY Buffalo, 65-66. *Concurrent Pos:* Vis investr immunol, Wenner-Gren Inst, Sweden, 75-76; Javits neurosci investr, NIH. *Mem:* AAAS; Am Asn Immunol; Am Asn Investigative Path; Am Soc Neurochem; Int Soc Neuroimmunol. *Res:* Cellular interactions in induction and regulation of the immune response; mechanisms of self-tolerance and autoimmunity; neuroimmunology. *Mailing Add:* Dept Immunol & Microbiol Wayne State Univ Med Sch Detroit MI 48201

SWANEY, JOHN BREWSTER, BIOCHEMISTRY. *Current Pos:* PROF BIOCHEM, HAHNEMANN UNIV, 84-, RES PROF MED, 84- *Personal Data:* b Holyoke, Mass, Feb 25, 44; m 66, Nancy Moore; c 3. *Educ:* Amherst Col, AB, 66; Northwestern Univ, PhD(chem, biochem), 70. *Honors & Awards:* Irma T Hirschl Career Scientist Award, 81. *Prof Exp:* Nat Acad Sci res assoc virol, Plum Island Animal Dis Lab, 70-72; instr, Albert Einstein Col Med, 72-74, from asst prof to assoc prof biochem, 74-84, from asst prof to assoc prof med, 81-82. *Concurrent Pos:* Estab investr, Am Heart Asn; Res Coun NY Heart Asn, 79-85; assoc ed, J Lipid Res, 85- *Mem:* Am Heart Asn; Am Soc Biochem & Molecular Biol. *Res:* Protein chemistry; structure and properties of proteins involved in protein-lipid interactions; plasma lipoproteins; lipid metabolism; reverse cholesterol transport. *Mailing Add:* Dept Biochem Allegheny Univ Health Sci MCP-Hahnemann Univ Sch Med Philadelphia PA 10461. *Fax:* 215-843-8849; *E-Mail:* swaneyj@allegheny.edu

SWANEY, LOIS MAE, BACTERIOLOGY, VIROLOGY. *Current Pos:* RETIRED. *Personal Data:* b Pittsburgh, Pa, Jan 2, 28. *Educ:* Univ Pittsburgh, BS, 49, MS, 52, PhD(molecular biol), 74. *Prof Exp:* Microbiologist bact genetics, Biol Labs, US Dept Army, Frederick, Md, 51-71; res asst, Univ Pittsburgh, 72-73; microbiologist cell-virus interactions & genetic eng, Plum Island Animal Dis Ctr, Agr Res Serv, USDA, 73-88. *Mem:* Am Soc Microbiol; Sigma Xi. *Res:* Genetics of bacterial pili; mutants of foot-and-mouth disease virus; assessment of tissue cultures for production of viral vaccines; development of cell lines; expression of viral genes in procaryotic cells. *Mailing Add:* 355 Summit Dr Southold NY 11971-3711

SWANK, RICHARD TILGHMAN, BIOCHEMISTRY, CELL BIOLOGY. *Current Pos:* res assoc mammalian biochem genetics, 70-72, SR CANCER RES SCIENTIST, ROSWELL PARK MEM INST, 72- *Personal Data:* b Drums, Pa, Feb 1, 42; m 66, Kathryn Dunn; c Douglas, David & Elizabeth. *Educ:* Pa State Univ, BS, 64; Univ Wis-Madison, MS, 67, PhD(biochem), 69. *Prof Exp:* NIH fel, Lab Molecular Biol, Univ Wis-Madison, 69-70. *Mem:* AAAS; Am Soc Cell Biol; Sigma Xi. *Res:* Biogenesis of subcellular organelles; biochemical mechanisms of enzyme subcellular localization in mammals; genetic regulation of hemostasis. *Mailing Add:* Dept Cell & Molecular Biol Roswell Park Cancer Inst Elm & Carlton Sts Buffalo NY 14203-0001. *Fax:* 716-845-8169; *E-Mail:* yswank@mcbio.med.buffalo.edu

SWANK, ROBERT ROY, JR, ENVIRONMENTAL EXPOSURE & RISK ASSESSMENT, HAZARDOUS WASTE MANAGEMENT. *Current Pos:* res chem engr, Southeast Environ Res Lab, US Environ Protection Agency, 71-75, supvry res chem engr & chief, Tech Develop & Applns Br, 75-84, supvry res chem engr & chief, Assessment Br, 84-86, supv env eng & chief, Tech Assessment Br, Off Solid Waste, 86-87, dir res, Athens Environ Res Lab Off Res & Develop, 87-89, staff dir human, freshwater & modeling, environ processes & effects, 89-90, staff dir terrestrial & groundwater effects, 90-91, dir res, Environ Res Lab Athens, Ga, 91-95, DIR RES, ECOSYST RES DIV, NAT EXPOSURE RES LAB, OFF RES & DEVELOP, US EVIRON PROTECTION AGENCY, ATHENS, GA, 95- *Personal Data:* b Brooklyn, NY, June 4, 39; m 60, Sandra Morgan; c Lori, Robert III & Debra. *Educ:* Ga Inst Technol, BChE, 59, MSChE, 63, PhD(chem eng), 68; Mass Inst Technol, MS, 60. *Honors & Awards:* Bronze Medal, US Environ Protection Agency, 73, 92. *Prof Exp:* Maintenance engr, Monsanto Chem Co, 59, sr process engr, 68-71. *Concurrent Pos:* Teaching asst & lectr, Mass Inst Technol, 61; guest lectr, US Army Chem Sch, Ft McClellan, Ala, 65-67; consult, UN Indust Develop Orgn, 74-75 & soft drink beverage water treatment indust, 82-89 & combuster technol indust, 82-91; off delegate to People's Repub China, Environ Protection Agency, 80, 86. *Mem:* Am Inst Chem Engrs; Am Chem Soc; Sigma Xi. *Res:* Models to predict human and environmental exposures due to the release into all environmental media (air-water-soil) of hazardous organic chemicals and metals; soil remediation technology, watershed restoration technology. *Mailing Add:* 19 Starboard Tack Dr Salem SC 29676. *Fax:* 706-355-8009

SWANK, ROLLAND LAVERNE, MATHEMATICS. *Current Pos:* DEPT MGR, W P DELONG & CO, 80- *Personal Data:* b Holland, Mich, Dec 31, 42; m 69. *Educ:* Hope Col, BA, 65; Mich State Univ, MS, 66, PhD(math), 69. *Prof Exp:* Asst prof math, Allegheny Col, 69-74; programmer, Power & Power, 74-80. *Mem:* Am Math Soc; Math Asn Am. *Res:* Topology; geometry. *Mailing Add:* 109 Orlando Ave Holland MI 49423-6630

SWANK, ROY LAVER, NEUROLOGY. *Current Pos:* prof, 54-74, EMER PROF NEUROL, SCH MED, ORE HEALTH SCI UNIV, PORTLAND, 74- *Personal Data:* b Camas, Wash, Mar 5, 09; m 37, 87; c 4. *Educ:* Univ Wash, BS, 30; Northwestern Univ, MD & PhD(anat), 35. *Prof Exp:* Asst anat, Med Sch, Northwestern Univ, 30-34; intern, Passavant Mem Hosp, Chicago, 34-35; house officer, Peter Bent Brigham Hosp, 36-41, jr assoc med, 41-42, assoc, 46-48; asst prof neurol, McGill Univ, 48-54. *Concurrent Pos:* Fel, Harvard Med Sch, 37; Commonwealth Fund fel, Sweden & Montreal Neurol Inst, McGill Univ, 39-41; mem attend staff, Cushing Vet Admin Hosp, 46-48; lectr, Montreal Neurol Inst, McGill Univ, 48; first examiner, Swed Doctoral Exam, Goteburg, Swed, 61; hon chmn, 3rd Int Cong Biorleology, 79. *Mem:* Am Physiol Soc; Am Asn Anatomists; Am Neurol Asn; Can Neurol Asn; Sigma Xi. *Res:* Pyramidal tracts; tissue staining; histochemical staining; vitamin deficiencies; electrophysiology; physiology of breathing. epidemiology of multiple sclerosis; fat metabolism and relationship to multiple sclerosis and to viscosity of blood; platelet adhesivesness and aggregation in surgical shock and microembolic filter to remove them from blood; abnormal plasma protein in multiple sclerosis. *Mailing Add:* Med Sch Univ Ore Portland OR 97201

SWANK, THOMAS FRANCIS, COLLOID CHEMISTRY, PHOTOGRAPHIC CHEMISTRY. *Current Pos:* sr chemist, 83-86, prod develop mgr, 86-88, RES & DEVELOP MGR, NYACOL PROD INC, ASHLAND, MASS, 88- *Personal Data:* b Philadelphia, Pa, Nov 3, 37; m 63; c 3. *Educ:* Villanova Univ, BS, 59; Univ Va, PhD(heterogeneous catalysis), 64. *Prof Exp:* Res chemist, Cabot Corp, 63-69; mgr, Ferro Fluidics Corp, 70-71; scientist, Polaroid Corp, Waltham, 71-76, sr scientist, 76-83. *Mem:* Am Chem Soc; Am Ceramic Soc. *Res:* Heterogeneous catalysis; thin films; x-ray diffraction and spectroscopy; electron microscopy; structure of oxides; inorganic pigments; solid state physics; magnetic fluids; photographic science; colloid and surface chemistry. *Mailing Add:* 25 Musket Lane Sudbury MA 01776. *Fax:* 508-881-1855

SWANK, WAYNE T, ECOLOGY. *Current Pos:* supvry ecologist, 78-83, PROJ LEADER, FOREST SERV, USDA, 84- *Personal Data:* b Washington, DC, Mar 8, 36; m 58; c 4. *Educ:* WVa Univ, BS, 58; Univ Wash, MF, 60, PhD(forestry), 72. *Prof Exp:* Forester admin, Forest Serv, USDA, 59-62, res forester, 66-76; prog mgr, NSF, 77-78. *Concurrent Pos:* Adj prof bot & ecol, Univ Ga, 74-; directorate mem, US Man & Biosphere Prog, MAB 2, 75-89; prin investr, Lon-Term Ecol Res Prog Univ Ga, 80-; comt mem, Nat Acad Sci, 87-90; consult & lectr, Univ & Govt Mex, USSR, Eng, Italy & Switz. *Mem:* Ecol Soc Am; AAAS; Sigma Xi. *Res:* Forest hydrology and ecology research with emphasis on biogeochemical cycles and responses to management practices; studies focus on hyrologic processes, microbial transformations in soils, atmospheric deposition, and forest succession from a watershed ecosystem perspective. *Mailing Add:* PO Box 466 Franklin NC 28734

SWANN, CHARLES PAUL, ARCHAEOMETRY, CONDENSED MATTER. *Current Pos:* Bartol prof physics, 76-85, EMER BARTOL PROF & EMER PROF DEPT PHYSICS & ASTRON, BARTOL RES INST, UNIV DEL, 85- *Personal Data:* b Minneapolis, Minn, Dec 4, 18; m 51, Anne Murphy; c 3. *Educ:* Harvard Univ, BS, 41, MS, 43; Temple Univ, PhD(physics), 56. *Prof Exp:* Mech engr, Steam Div, Westinghouse Elec Corp, 43-46; nuclear physicist, Bartol Res Found, Franklin Inst, 46-76. *Concurrent Pos:* Res assoc, Masca, Univ Pa, 88- *Mem:* Fel Am Phys Soc; AAAS; Sigma Xi; Soc Archaeol Sci. *Res:* Proton induced x-ray studies of bi-valve marine life, historical objects of art and archaeological artifacts; surface studies of materials using Rutherford backscattering spectroscopy. *Mailing Add:* Univ Del Bartol Res Found Newark DE 19716

SWANN, DALE WILLIAM, applied mathematics, operations research, for more information see previous edition

SWANN, DAVID A, CONNECTIVE TISSUE BIOCHEMISTRY. *Current Pos:* CHMN, CHIEF EXEC OFFICER & PRES, ANIKA RES, 87- *Personal Data:* b Barnet, England, Sept 8, 36. *Educ:* Univ Leeds, PhD(physiol chem), 63. *Prof Exp:* Res dir biochem, Shriner Burn Inst, 84-87. *Mailing Add:* Anika Res 236 W Cummings Park Woburn MA 01801-6346

SWANN, GORDON ALFRED, GEOLOGY, ASTROGEOLOGY. *Current Pos:* RETIRED. *Personal Data:* b Palisade, Colo, Sept 21, 31; m 75, Joan Stinebaugh; c Steven, Wendy, Randall & Heidi. *Educ:* Univ Colo, Boulder, BA, 58, PhD(geol), 62. *Honors & Awards:* Exceptional Sci Achievement Award, NASA, 71; Prof Excellence Award, Am Asn Prof Geologists, 72; Spec Achievement Astronaut Training Award, Geol Soc Am, 72. *Prof Exp:* Geologist, US Geol Surv, 63-73 & 85-86, staff geologist for telegeol, 73-76, dep regional geologist, 76-81, dep asst chief geologist, 81-85, 85-86. *Concurrent Pos:* Prin investr, Lunar Geol Exp, Apollo missions 14 & 15; adj prof, Northern Ariz Univ. *Mem:* Geol Soc Am; Sigma Xi. *Res:* Lunar geology. *Mailing Add:* 1171 Sunrise Dr Clarkdale AZ 86324

SWANN, HOWARD STORY GRAY, MATHEMATICS. *Current Pos:* ASSOC PROF MATH, SAN JOSE STATE UNIV, 70- *Personal Data:* b Chicago, Ill, Aug 4, 36. *Educ:* Harvard Univ, AB, 58; Univ Chicago, MS, 59; Univ Calif, Berkeley, PhD(appl math), 68. *Prof Exp:* Asst math, Univ Chicago, 59-61; lectr, Univ Nigeria, 61-63; asst & instr, Univ Calif, Berkeley, 64-68; asst prof, Antioch Col, 68-70. *Mem:* Am Math Soc. *Res:* Functional analysis; differential equations; game theory; automata theory. *Mailing Add:* Dept Math & Comp Sci San Jose State Univ San Jose CA 95192-0103

SWANN, MADELINE BRUCE, SOLDIER SYSTEMS, HUMAN FACTORS ENGINEERING. *Current Pos:* phys scientist, Adv Concepts & Plans Directorate, 90-93, PHYS SCIENTIST, HUMAN RES & ENG DIRECTORATE, US ARMY RES LAB, 93- *Personal Data:* b Washington, DC, July 24, 51. *Educ:* Fisk Univ, Nashville, Tenn, BA, 73; Howard Univ, Washington, DC, PhD(biochem), 80. *Honors & Awards:* Outstanding Young Women of Am, 87. *Prof Exp:* Teaching fel gen chem, org chem, biochem lab & res asst, Dept Chem, Howard Univ, 73-80; asst prof phys sci, gen chem & biochem, Dept Chem & Physics, Miss Valley State Univ, 79; chemist, US Army Belvior Res, Develop & Eng Ctr, 81-90. *Concurrent Pos:* Consult, Technol Appln, Inc, 81; prin investr, in-house lab independent res proj, Off Chief Scientist, US Army Belvoir Res & Develop Ctr, 83-85; mem, Women's Exec Leadership Prog, Off Personnel Mgt, 89. *Mem:* Am Chem Soc; Nat Orgn Black Chemists & Chem Engrs; Sigma Xi; NY Acad Sci. *Res:* Initiating, planning and conducting human factors studies to determine the feasibility of advanced approaches or concept; resolve problems in current programs, to fill data voids or to produce new methodological tools and procedures for examining human performance issues related to soldier systems. *Mailing Add:* 1203 Kingsbury Dr Mitchellville MD 20721-2022

SWANSON, ALAN WAYNE, materials science, inorganic chemistry, for more information see previous edition

SWANSON, ANNE BARRETT, BIOCHEMISTRY, CHEMICAL CARCINOGENESIS. *Current Pos:* DEAN, SCH NATURAL SCI, SONOMA STATE UNIV, 92- *Personal Data:* b Joliet, Ill, Dec 23, 48; m 69. *Educ:* Northern Ill Univ, BS, 70; Univ Wis-Madison, PhD(biochem), 75. *Honors & Awards:* Gallantry Award, Easter Seal Soc. *Prof Exp:* NIH res fel, U W McArdle Lab Cancer Res, 75-78, res assoc chem carcinogenesis, 78-79; from asst prof to assoc prof chem, Edgewood Col, Madison, 79-88, med tech coordr, 80-88, chmn, 81-88, assoc acad dean, Col St Catherine, 88-92. *Concurrent Pos:* Assoc prog dir, NSF, Washington, DC, 85-86; NSF grants, 85 & 87. *Mem:* Am Chem Soc; Sigma Xi; AAAS; Nat Sci Teachers Asn; NY Acad Sci; Found Sci & Handicapped. *Res:* Mechanisms of chemical carcinogenesis; metabolism of precarcinogens to ultimate carcinogenic compounds; nutrition and metabolism of trace minerals; relationships of nutritional biochemistry and carcinogenesis. *Mailing Add:* 2538 Mimosa St Santa Rosa CA 95405-8428

SWANSON, ARNOLD ARTHUR, BIOCHEMISTRY, OPHTHALMOLOGY. *Current Pos:* assoc prof, 68-80, PROF BIOCHEM, MED UNIV SC, 80- *Personal Data:* b Rawlins, Wyo, Mar 11, 23; m 50; c 3. *Educ:* Duke Univ, BA, 46; Trinity Univ, Tex, MA, 59; Tex A&M Univ, PhD(biochem), 61. *Honors & Awards:* Alexander von Humboldt-Stiftung Award, WGer. *Prof Exp:* Res chemist, Med Sch, Temple Univ, 46-48; biochemist ophthal, US Air Force Sch Aviation Med, 50-59; sr chemist, USPHS, 61-63; chief res lab, Vet Admin Hosp, McKinney, Tex, 63-65 & Vet Admin Ctr, 65-68. *Concurrent Pos:* Dir, Swanson Biochem Labs, Inc, 52-58; consult, Southwestern Prods, Inc, 57- & Scott & White Hosp, 65-; adj prof, Baylor Univ, 66- *Mem:* Fel AAAS; Am Chem Soc; Fedn Am Soc Exp Biol; Am Soc Biochem & Molecular Biol; Asn Res Vision & Ophthal; Sigma Xi. *Res:* Proteolysis in normal and senile cataract lens; senile changes and mineral metabolism. *Mailing Add:* Dept Biochem Med Univ SC 171 Ashley Ave Charleston SC 29425-0001

SWANSON, AUGUST GEORGE, NEUROLOGY, MEDICAL EDUCATION. *Current Pos:* RETIRED. *Personal Data:* b Kearney, Nebr, Aug 25, 25; m 47; c 6. *Educ:* Harvard Med Sch, MD, 49; Westminster Col, Mo, AB, 51. *Hon Degrees:* DSci, Univ Nebr, 78. *Prof Exp:* Resident med, Sch Med, Univ Wash, 53-55, resident neurol, 55-57; asst resident, Boston City Hosp, 58; instr, Sch Med, Univ Wash, 58-59, asst prof pediat & med, 59-63; vis res fel physiol, Oxford Univ, 63-64; assoc prof med, Sch Med, Univ Wash, 64-70, prof, 70-74; dir, Dept Acad Affairs, Asn Am Med Cols, 71-91, vpres, 87-91. *Concurrent Pos:* Fel, Univ Wash, 55-57, assoc dean, Sch Med, 67-68, assoc dean acad affairs, 68-71; Markle scholar, 59. *Mem:* Sr mem Inst Med-Nat Acad Sci; Am Neurol Asn. *Res:* Facilitation of the development of medical education and biomedical research. *Mailing Add:* 3146 E Portage Bay Pl Apt H Seattle WA 98102

SWANSON, BARRY GRANT, FOOD PROCESSING, FOOD SAFETY. *Current Pos:* from asst prof to assoc prof food sci, 73-83, PROF FOOD SCI HUMAN NUTRIT, FOOD SCIENTIST & FOOD SCI SPECIALIST, WASH STATE UNIV, 83- *Personal Data:* b Green Lake, Wis, Apr 16, 44; m, Darcel M; c Alyssa M, Krista J & Sara B. *Educ:* Univ Wis-Madison, BS, 66, MS, 70, PhD(food sci), 72. *Prof Exp:* Asst prof food sci, Univ Idaho, 72-73. *Concurrent Pos:* Travel award Spain, Inst Food Technologists, 74, sci lectr regional commun, 79-82 & 85-; vis prof, Dept Food Sci, Univ BC & BC Cancer Res Ctr; int res, Guatemala, Ecuador, Colombia, Philippines, India, China & Chile. *Mem:* Inst Food Technologists; Am Oil Chem Soc; Am Chem Soc; Sigma Xi; Can Inst Food Sci Technol; Am Asn Cereal Chemists. *Res:* Biological utilization and availability of legume proteins; non-thermal processes-high voltage pulsed electric fields, oscillating magnetic fields, high pressure technologies, combined methods; synthesis, analysis and functional properties of carbohydrate fatty acid polyester fat substitutes; microstructure of foods; reduced fat cheese, postharvest quality of fruits land and vegetables. *Mailing Add:* Dept Food Sci & Human Nutrit Wash State Univ Pullman WA 99164-6376. *Fax:* 509-335-4815; *E-Mail:* swansonb@wsu.edu

SWANSON, BASIL IAN, INORGANIC CHEMISTRY. *Current Pos:* ASST PROF CHEM, UNIV TEX, AUSTIN, 73- *Personal Data:* b Minn, Feb 13, 44; m 64; c 2. *Educ:* Colo Sch Mines, BA, 66; Northwestern Univ, Evanston, PhD(chem), 70. *Prof Exp:* Fel, Los Alamos Sci Lab, Univ Calif, 70-71; res corp grant, NY Univ, 71-72, asst prof chem, 71-73. *Concurrent Pos:* Vis staff mem, Los Alamos Sci Lab, 70- *Mem:* Am Chem Soc. *Res:* Study of structure and bonding in inorganic systems using crystallographic and vibrational spectroscopic techniques; study of structural phase changes in crystalline solids; valence delocalization and ion transport in crystalline solids. *Mailing Add:* 3463 Urban Los Alamos NM 87544-2026

SWANSON, CARL PONTIUS, cytogenetics; deceased, see previous edition for last biography

SWANSON, CARROLL ARTHUR, plant physiology; deceased, see previous edition for last biography

SWANSON, CHARLES ANDREW, DIFFERENTIAL EQUATIONS. *Current Pos:* from instr to prof, 57-94, EMER PROF MATH, UNIV BC, 95- *Personal Data:* b Bellingham, Wash, July 11, 29; m 57, Carolyn M Dennis; c Laird R & Denise C. *Educ:* Univ BC, BA, 51, MA, 53; Calif Inst Technol, PhD, 57. *Concurrent Pos:* Assoc ed, Can J Math, 71-80. *Res:* Differential equations. *Mailing Add:* Dept Math Univ BC Vancouver BC V6T 1Z2 Can. *Fax:* 604-822-6074; *E-Mail:* math@ubcmtsg.ca

SWANSON, CURTIS JAMES, COMPARATIVE PHYSIOLOGY, BIOCHEMISTRY. *Current Pos:* asst prof, 70-74, ASSOC PROF BIOL, WAYNE STATE UNIV, 74- *Personal Data:* b Chicago, Ill, Dec 8, 41; m 65; c 2. *Educ:* N Park Col, BA & BS, 64; Northern Ill Univ, MS, 66; Univ Ill, Urbana-Champaign, PhD(zool, physiol), 70. *Prof Exp:* Lectr biol, Univ Ill, 70. *Concurrent Pos:* Grants, NSF, Wayne State Univ, 70-75 & NIH, 71-; Riker res fel, Bermuda Biol Sta, 75, NSF, 77-78. *Mem:* AAAS; Am Inst Biol Sci; Am Soc Zoologists; Am Physiol Soc. *Res:* Electron microscopy of muscle tissue; innervation and developmental neuromuscular physiology; control systems in development; protein biochemistry; theoretical and applied biomechanics; comparative ultrastructure of muscle. *Mailing Add:* Dept Biol Wayne State Univ Detroit MI 48202. *Fax:* 313-577-6891

SWANSON, DAVID BERNARD, CHEMICAL ENGINEERING. *Current Pos:* from engr to res supvr, 59-77, dir, Process Develop & Mfg, Engelhard Minerals & Chem Corp, 77-80, DIR RES SERV, ENGELHARD CORP, 80- *Personal Data:* b Newark, NJ, Dec 14, 35; m 58, Marie DelRusso; c Donna M (Padvano), David S & Paul M. *Educ:* Newark Col Eng, BS, 57, MS, 62. *Prof Exp:* Engr, Esso Res & Eng Co, Standard Oil Co, NJ, 57-59. *Concurrent Pos:* Exec comt, Corp Assocs. *Mem:* Catalysis Soc; Mats Res Soc; Am Chem Soc; AAAS; Soc Hist Technol. *Res:* Heat transfer coefficients of non-Newtonian fluids; dehydration and rehydration of kaolin; zeolitic cracking catalyst. *Mailing Add:* Engelhard Corp 101 Wood Ave S Iselin NJ 08830-2722

SWANSON, DAVID G, JR, NUCLEAR CHEMISTRY, PHYSICAL CHEMISTRY. *Current Pos:* CONSULT, 80- *Personal Data:* b Chicago, Ill, Jan 14, 41. *Educ:* Northwestern Univ, BS, 64; Purdue Univ, PhD(nuclear & phys chem), 69. *Prof Exp:* Nuclear chemist, Sandia Corp, NMex, 69-73; nuclear chemist, Aerospace Corp, 73-80. *Concurrent Pos:* Consult, US Nuclear Regulatory Comn, 75-, Brookhaven Nat Lab, Sandia Nat Labs, Rand & Assocs, Logicon Advan Sci, Inc & Carpenter Res Corp. *Mem:* Am Chem Soc; Am Phys Soc; Am Nuclear Soc. *Res:* Response of materials to radiation; nuclear reactions; radiation transport phenomena; high temperature physical chemistry; heat transfer; materials evaluation and characterization; thermodynamics; nuclear reactor safety studies; post accident heat removal; materials science; composite materials; nuclear weapons effects tests; studies of anti-satellite devices. *Mailing Add:* 6868 Los Verdes Dr 12 Palos Verdes Peninsula CA 90274-5654

SWANSON, DAVID HENRY, CONTINUING EDUCATION, TECHNOLOGY TRANSFER. *Current Pos:* RETIRED. *Personal Data:* b Anoka, Minn, Nov 1, 30; m 51, 91; c 2. *Educ:* St Cloud State Univ, BA, 53; Univ Minn, MA, 55; Iowa State Univ Sci & Technol, PhD(adult educ), 87. *Honors & Awards:* Presidents Award, Technol Transfer Soc, 90. *Prof Exp:* Economist, Northern States Power Co, 55-63; dir econ & mkt res, Iowa Southern Utilities Co, 63-70; dir, New Orleans Econ Develop Coun, 70-72; mgr deal develop, Kaiser Aetna, 72-73; dir corp res, United Serv Automobile Asn, 73-76; adminr, Wis Econ Develop Dept, State Wis, 76-78; dir, Ctr Indust Res & Serv, Iowa State Univ Sci & Technol, 78-89; dir, Econ Develop Lab, Ga Res Inst, Ga Inst Technol, Atlanta, 89-93; exec on loan, Nat Inst Stand, 93-96. *Concurrent Pos:* Instr mkt & mkt mgt, Col Bus Admin, Iowa State Univ, 79-83, mgt technol, Hons Prog, 85-87 & comp mgt, Hons Prog, 85-88; chair, Iowa High Technol Task Force, 83 & Iowa High Technol Coun, 83-86; dir, Nat Asn Mgt & Tech Asst Ctrs, 83-87, pres, 85; dir, Iowa Develop Comn, 84-85; guest researcher, Mfg Exten Partnership, Nat Inst Stand & Technol, 93-; mem bd dirs, Am Indust Exten Alliance, 96. *Mem:* Technol Transfer Soc (vpres, 86-91, pre-elect, 91, pres, 92-93); Nat Asn of Mgt & Tech Assistance Ctrs (pres, 84); Nat Univ Continuing Educ Asn; Am Indust Exten Alliance (pres, 93-95). *Res:* Technology transfer in industry, government and education; technical assistance to management. *Mailing Add:* Econ Develop Inst Ga Inst Technol 224 O'Keefe Bldg Atlanta GA 30332

SWANSON, DAVID WENDELL, PSYCHIATRY. *Current Pos:* assoc prof psychiat, Mayo Grad Sch Med & consult, Sect Psychiat, Mayo Clin, 70-74, prof psychiat & head sect, Mayo Med Sch, Univ Minn, 74-79, vchmn, dept psychiat, Mayo Clin, 79-86, CONSULT, PSYCHIAT SECT & PROF PSYCHIAT, MAYO CLIN, 86- *Personal Data:* b Ft Dodge, Iowa, Aug 28, 30; m 53; c 3. *Educ:* Augustana Col, Ill, BA, 52; Univ Ill, MD, 56. *Prof Exp:* Intern, Ill Cent Hosp, 56-57; resident psychiat, Ill State Psychiat Inst, 59-62, asst serv chief, 62-63; assoc prof & asst chmn dept, Stritch Sch Med, Loyola Univ Chicago, 63-70. *Mem:* AAAS; Am Col Psychiatrists; Am Psychiat Asn; Sigma Xi. *Res:* Paranoid and chronic pain disorders. *Mailing Add:* Dept Psychiat W-9 Mayo Clinic Rochester MN 55901

SWANSON, DON R, INFORMATION SCIENCE, ONLINE SEARCHING. *Current Pos:* dean, Grad Libr Sch, 63-72 & 77-79, PROF INFO SCI, UNIV CHICAGO, 63- *Personal Data:* b Los Angeles, Calif, Oct 10, 24; m 76, Patricia Klick; c Douglas, Richard & Judith. *Educ:* Calif Inst Technol, BS, 45; Rice Univ, MA, 47; Univ Calif, Berkeley, PhD(physics), 52. *Prof Exp:* Res physicist, Radiation Lab, Univ Calif, 50-52; mem tech staff, Hughes Res & Develop Labs, 52-55; dept mgr comput appln, Thompson-Ramo-Wooldridge, Inc, 55-63. *Concurrent Pos:* Mem sci info coun, NSF, 59-63; mem vis comt libr, Mass Inst Technol, 64-72; trustee, Nat Opinion Res Ctr, 64-73; mem adv comt, Libr Cong, 64-72, toxicol info panel, President's Sci Adv Comt, 64-65, comt sci & tech commun, Nat Acad Sci, 66-70 & adv comt, Encycl Britannica, 66-76. *Mem:* Am Soc Info Sci; Am Asn Artificial Intel. *Res:* Studies of fragmentation of scientific literature; analysis of complementary literatures that are mutually isolated, but which, if combined, lead to new inferences that cannot be drawn from the separate literatures. *Mailing Add:* Div Humanities Univ Chicago 1010 E 59th Chicago IL 60637. *E-Mail:* swanson@kiwi.uchicago.edu

SWANSON, DONALD ALAN, VOLCANOLOGY, GEOLOGY. *Current Pos:* GEOLOGIST, US GEOL SURV, 65- *Personal Data:* b Tacoma, Wash, July 25, 38; m 74, Barbara White. *Educ:* Wash State Univ, BS, 60; Johns Hopkins Univ, PhD(geol), 64. *Honors & Awards:* Meritorious Serv Award, Dept Interior, 85. *Prof Exp:* NATO fel, Ger, Italy & Canary Islands, 64-65. *Concurrent Pos:* Affil prof, Univ Wash, 92. *Mem:* AAAS; Geol Soc Am; Am Geophys Union; Sigma Xi. *Res:* Petrology and geology of volcanic rocks, especially from northwest United States; deformation studies of active volcanos, particularly Mount St Helens and other Cascade volcanos; physical volcanology. *Mailing Add:* Hawaiian Volcano Observ Hawaii National Park HI 96718. *Fax:* 206-553-5587; *E-Mail:* donswan@geology.washington.edu

SWANSON, DONALD CHARLES, PETROLEUM GEOLOGY, SEDIMENTOLOGY. *Current Pos:* CONSULT, SWANSON GEOL SERV & CHMN, STRATAMODEL, INC, 79- *Personal Data:* b Canon City, Colo, Sept 22, 26; m 50, Helen K Smith; c Jeffrey S & Charles R. *Educ:* Colo State Univ, BS, 50; Univ Tulsa, BS, 55. *Honors & Awards:* Levorsen Award, Am Asn Petrol Geologists, 68 & 79. *Prof Exp:* Geol & geophys tea engr, Carter Oil Co, Okla, 51-56, jr geologist, Kans, 56, geologist, Ark, 56-57 & Okla, 57-60; geologist, Humble Oil Co, 60-62, sr geologist, Tex, 62-63 & Humble Res Ctr, 63-64, staff geologist, Humble Oil Co, Okla, 64-67; sr res geologist, Esso Prod Res Co, 67, sr res specialist, 67-74; res assoc, Exxon Prod Res Co, 74-79. *Mem:* Fel Geol Soc Am; Am Asn Petrol Geologists; Explorers Club; Soc Petrol Engrs. *Res:* Clastic facies; determination of ancient sedimentary environments; paleogeography; methodology of environmental facies analyses; methodology of exploration; computer application to petroleum geology. *Mailing Add:* 510 Sandy Port Houston TX 77079-2417

SWANSON, DONALD G, PLASMA PHYSICS. *Current Pos:* prof, 80-85, ALUMNI PROF PHYSICS, AUBURN UNIV, 85- *Personal Data:* b Los Angeles, Calif, June 11, 35; m 60; c Christopher, Lynne (Yang) & Robert. *Educ:* Northwest Christian Col, BTh, 58; Univ Ore, BS, 58; Calif Inst Technol, MS, 61, PhD(physics), 63. *Prof Exp:* Fel, Calif Inst Technol, 63-64; from asst prof to assoc prof elec eng, Univ Tex, Austin, 64-74; assoc prof elec eng, Univ Southern Calif, Los Angeles, 74-80. *Concurrent Pos:* Consult, Advan Kinetics, Inc, Calif, 63-64, Princeton Plasma Physics Lab, 82-84, Los Alamos Nat Lab, 83-84 & McDonnell-Douglas Corp, St Louis, Mo, 80- *Mem:* fel Am Phys Soc; Sigma Xi. *Res:* Compressional hydromagnetic waves; plasma-filled waveguide; ion cyclotron waves; mode conversion theory; torsatron. *Mailing Add:* Dept Physics Auburn Univ Auburn AL 36849. *E-Mail:* swanson@physics.auburn.edu

SWANSON, DONALD LEROY, ANALYTICAL CHEMISTRY, PHYSICAL CHEMISTRY. *Current Pos:* RETIRED. *Personal Data:* b Montrose, SDak, Mar 24, 23; m 48, Mary Ellyn Owens; c Dorothy, Ellyn & Julie. *Educ:* SDak State Univ, BS, 47; Univ Wis, PhD(chem), 51. *Prof Exp:* Lab asst chem, Agr Exp Sta, SDak State Univ, 46-47; asst, Univ Wis, 47-51; res chemist, Am Cyanamid Co, 51-58, group leader, 58-61, sect mgr, 62-86. *Mem:* Am Chem Soc. *Res:* Physical and mechanical properties of polymers; polymerization kinetics; copolymerization; radiation chemistry; analysis. *Mailing Add:* 15 Dartmouth Rd Cos Cob CT 06807

SWANSON, ERIC RICE, VOLCANOLOGY, METALLIC ORE DEPOSITS. *Current Pos:* PROF GEOL, UNIV TEX, SAN ANTONIO, 79- *Personal Data:* b Frankfort, Mich, Nov 14, 46; m 75, Nancy F; c Travis & Jenny. *Educ:* Western Mich Univ, BS, 68; Univ Tex, Austin, MA, 74, PhD(geol), 77. *Prof Exp:* Asst prof geol, Wayne State Univ, 76-79. *Mem:* Geol Soc Am; Nat Asn Geol Teachers; Am Geophys Union. *Res:* Volcanic stratigraphy of the Sierra Madre Occidental, Western Mexico; metallic ore deposits; volcanology; geology of Mexico; popular science topics and earth science education. *Mailing Add:* Dept Earth & Phys Sci Univ Tex San Antonio TX 78285

SWANSON, ERIC RICHMOND, APPLIED PHYSICS, NAVIGATION. *Current Pos:* CONSULT, 90- *Personal Data:* b San Diego, Calif, May 4, 34; m 67, Ann Don Carlos; c Wendy A (Sutton) & Lorna K (Seitz). *Educ:* Pomona Col, BA, 56; Univ Calif, Los Angeles, MS, 58. *Honors & Awards:* Burka Award, Inst Navig, 71; John Alvin Pierce Award, Int Omega Asn, 89; Kershner Award, Inst Elec & Electronics Engrs, 92; Gold Medal, Royal Inst Navig, 93. *Prof Exp:* Teaching asst, Univ Calif, Los Angeles, 56-58; electronic engr res & develop, Electro Instruments, Inc, San Diego, 59-60; physicist, br head & consult, Naval Ocean Systs Ctr, 60-90. *Concurrent Pos:* Mem, Comt Consult Int Radio Commun US Study Group, 75- & Int Meritime Consult Orgn Working Group Differential Omeg, 77-79; consult, NATO, 76, India, Int Telecommun, 81. *Mem:* Fel Inst Elec & Electronics Engrs; fel Royal Inst Navig; US Inst Navig; Australian Inst Navig; Am Phys Soc; Int Navig Asn. *Res:* Navigation systems and associated radio propagation problems; timing and time dissemination. *Mailing Add:* 3611 Warner St San Diego CA 92106. *Fax:* 619-222-9642; *E-Mail:* eric.swanson@sdcs.org

SWANSON, ERNEST ALLEN, JR, ANATOMY, HISTOLOGY. *Current Pos:* from asst prof to assoc prof, 67-81, PROF ANAT, SCH DENT, TEMPLE UNIV, 81- *Personal Data:* b Miami, Fla, Apr 9, 36; m 67. *Educ:* Emory Univ, BA, 58, PhD(anat), 64. *Prof Exp:* Instr anat, Emory Univ, 64-65; instr, Univ Va, 65-67. *Mem:* Am Asn Anatomists. *Res:* Changes in the dental pulp associated with cholesterol induced arteriosclerosis. *Mailing Add:* Dept Histol Temple Univ Sch Med 3400 N Broad St Philadelphia PA 19140

SWANSON, GEORGE D, RESPIRATORY PHYSIOLOGY. *Current Pos:* ASSOC PROF BIOMETRICS & ANESTHESIOL, SCH MED, UNIV COLO, 78- *Personal Data:* b Eureka, Calif, Sept 19, 42. *Educ:* Univ Chicago, SB, 37, MD, 38. *Mem:* Am Physiol Soc; Inst Elec & Electronics Engrs; Sigma Xi. *Mailing Add:* Div Sci & Health Col Redwoods 9351 Tompkins Hill Rd Eureka CA 95501-9300. *Fax:* 530-898-4932

SWANSON, GUSTAV ADOLPH, wildlife ecology; deceased, see previous edition for last biography

SWANSON, HAROLD DUEKER, CELL BIOLOGY, SCIENCE & RELIGION. *Current Pos:* from asst prof to prof, 60-95, EMER PROF BIOL, DRAKE UNIV, 95- *Personal Data:* b Wichita, Kans, Mar 5, 30; m 55; c Kristin, Mark & Celia. *Educ:* Friends Univ, BA, 53; Univ Kans, MA, 55; Univ Tenn, PhD(zool physiol), 60. *Prof Exp:* Asst zool, Univ Kans, 53-55 & Univ Tenn, 56-58. *Concurrent Pos:* Fulbright scholar, Norway, 55-56. *Mem:* Sigma Xi. *Res:* Nucleocytoplasmic interaction; subcellular component isolation; science and religion; impulses in Mimosa leaves. *Mailing Add:* 3210 Lincoln Ave Drake Univ Des Moines IA 50310. *E-Mail:* hs549lr@.acad.drake.edu

SWANSON, J ROBERT, BIOCHEMISTRY. *Current Pos:* asst prof, 69-74, ASSOC PROF CLIN PATH, MED SCH, UNIV ORE, PORTLAND, 74- *Personal Data:* b Ft Collins, Colo, June 24, 39; m 62; c 1. *Educ:* Colo State Univ, BS, 61; Wash State Univ, PhD(biochem), 65; Am Bd Clin Chem, dipl. *Prof Exp:* Res fel biochem, Duke Univ, 65-67; clin chem training fel, Pepper Lab, Hosp Univ Pa, 67-69. *Mem:* Am Asn Clin Chem; Am Chem Soc. *Res:* Clinical methods for pulmonary surfactant measurement. *Mailing Add:* Dept Clin Path Ore Health Sci Univ Sch Med 3181 SW Sam Jackson Portland OR 97201-3011

SWANSON, JACK LEE, PHYSICAL CHEMISTRY, BIOCHEMISTRY. *Current Pos:* dean, Sch Sci & Technol, Chadron State Col, 71-76, dean, Sch Prof Studies, 76-79, dean, Admin Serv, 80-87, PROF CHEM, CHADRON STATE COL, 71- *Personal Data:* b Aurora, Nebr, Oct 22, 34; m 56; c 3. *Educ:* Kearney State Col, BS, 56; Univ Nebr, MS, 59, PhD(chem), 67. *Prof Exp:* Prof chem, Kearney State Col, 58-71. *Concurrent Pos:* NSF fel. *Mem:* Am Chem Soc; Sigma Xi. *Res:* Infrared and ultraviolet spectroscopy; magneto-optical rotary dispersion; circular dichroism spectroscopy; medicinal chemistry. *Mailing Add:* Dept Chem Chadron State Col 1000 Main St Chadron NE 69337

SWANSON, JAMES A, PHYSICAL CHEMISTRY. *Current Pos:* PROF CHEM, UNIV NEBR KEARNEY, 62- *Personal Data:* b Aurora, Nebr, Oct 25, 35; m 57; c 3. *Educ:* Univ Nebr Kearney, BA, 57; Univ Nebr-Lincoln, MS, 59, PhD(chem), 62. *Prof Exp:* Part-time lab asst, Univ Nebr, 57-62. *Mem:* Am Chem Soc; Sigma Xi. *Res:* Solution thermochemistry; thermodynamics. *Mailing Add:* Dept Chem Univ Nebr Kearney Kearney NE 68849-5320

SWANSON, JOHN L, MICROBIAL STRUCTURE RESEARCH. *Current Pos:* CHIEF, NAT INST ALLERGY & INFECTIOUS DIS, LAB MICROBIAL STRUCT & FUNCTION, ROCKY MOUNTAIN LABS, NIH, 79- *Personal Data:* b Hastings, Nebr, Aug 16, 36. *Educ:* Univ Nebr, BS, 59, MS, 61, MD, 62. *Prof Exp:* Intern, Univ Hosp, Omaha, Nebr, 62-63; residency anat path, Peter Bent Brigham Hosp, Boston, 63-66; mem staff, Armed Forces Inst Path, 66-67; mem staff, Walter Reed Army Inst Res, Washington, DC, 67-68; asst prof, Dept Microbiol, Col Physicians & Surgeons, Columbia Univ, 68-69; from asst prof to assoc prof, Dept Microbiol, Mt Sinai Sch Med, NY, 69-72; from assoc prof to prof, Dept Path & Dept Microbiol, Univ Utah Col Med, 72-79. *Concurrent Pos:* Ad hoc reviewer res grants & fel, Joshiah Macy Found, Univ Tenn, Vet Admin, Can Med Res Coun, NSF & NIH; extramural adv, Nat Inst Allergy & Infectious Dis sponsored Sexually Transmitted Dis Coop Res Ctr, Univ Tex Health Sci Ctr; mem, Bact & Mycol Study Sect, NIH, 78-79. *Mem:* Sigma Xi. *Res:* Virulence and pathogenic factors of Neisseria gonorrhoeae. *Mailing Add:* 1015 S Fourth St Hamilton MT 59840

SWANSON, JOHN WILLIAM, PHYSICAL CHEMISTRY. *Current Pos:* from tech asst to tech assoc, 41-45, from res asst to res assoc, 46-55, group leader surface & colloid chem, 53-55, group leader phys chem, 56-61, sr res assoc, 56-69, chmn phys chem dept, 62-69, dir surface & colloid sci ctr, 81, EMER PROF, INST PAPER CHEM, 81- *Personal Data:* b Sioux City, Iowa, Oct 12, 17; wid; c John F, James W & Barbara R (Templeton). *Educ:* Morningside Col, BA, 40. *Hon Degrees:* DSc, Morningside Col, 72; MSc, Lawrence Univ, 82. *Honors & Awards:* Res & Develop Div Award, Tech Asn Pulp & Paper Indust, 74, Harris O Ware Prize, 83. *Prof Exp:* Asst chem, Iowa State Col, 40-41. *Concurrent Pos:* Lectr, Lawrence Univ, 45-46; consult to numerous paper co, 50- *Mem:* AAAS; Am Chem Soc; fel Tech Asn Pulp & Paper Indust. *Res:* Surface and colloid chemistry of papermaking; polymer sorption at interfaces; surface area and bonding of cellulose fibers; paper sizing, coating; coagulation and retention of resins in aqueous systems; pollution abatement. *Mailing Add:* 236 Camino Del Vate 'NBU 2412 Green Valley AZ 85614-3106

SWANSON, LAWRENCE RAY, SPACE SURVEILLANCE ALGORITHM DEVELOPMENT. *Current Pos:* PRIN RES SCIENTIST, AUTOMETRIC, INC, 93- *Personal Data:* b Omaha, Nebr, Nov 4, 36; m 62, Judith P Thoreen; c Heidi & Erik. *Educ:* Iowa State Univ, BS, 59; Fuller Theol Sem, BD, 63; Calif State Univ, Los Angeles, MS, 66; Univ Calif, Irvine, PhD(physics), 70. *Prof Exp:* Asst prof physics, Pasadena Col, 70-73, vis prof physics, Greenville Col, 73-74; assoc prof physics & math, Azusa Pac Col, 74-76 & Sterling Col, 76-80; sr electronic engr, TRW, Inc, 80-86; systs engr, Contel Fed Systs, 86-87; prin res scientist, Textron Defense Systs, 87-93. *Res:* Develop algorithms for incorporation into work stations used for space surveillance analysis: algorithms for photometric infrared and radar signature analysis. *Mailing Add:* 1305 N 31st St Colorado Springs CO 80904

SWANSON, LEONARD GEORGE, MATHEMATICS. *Current Pos:* From instr to assoc prof, 64-81, PROF MATH, PORTLAND STATE UNIV, 81- *Personal Data:* b Corvallis, Ore, Sept 10, 40. *Educ:* Portland State Univ, BS, 62; Univ Wash, MA, 65; Ore State Univ, PhD(math), 70. *Concurrent Pos:* Vis assoc prof, Dept Math, Mont State Univ, 77-78; vis prof, Dept Math, Ore State Univ, 84-85. *Mem:* Am Math Soc; Math Asn Am; Inst Math Statist; AAAS. *Res:* Fourier series and their application; number theory. *Mailing Add:* Dept Math Portland State Univ PO Box 751 Portland OR 97207-0751

SWANSON, LLOYD VERNON, REPRODUCTIVE ENDOCRINOLOGY. *Current Pos:* PROF DAIRY PHYSIOL, ORE STATE UNIV, 71- *Personal Data:* b Isanti, Minn, Oct 16, 38; m 66; c 2. *Educ:* Univ Minn, St Paul, BS, 60, MS, 67; Mich State Univ, PhD(physiol), 70. *Mem:* Am Dairy Sci Asn; Am Soc Animal Sci; Soc Study Reproduction; Endocrine Soc; Sigma Xi. *Res:* Reproductive physiology of mammalian species, both male and female, with special interest in the endocrine control of ovulation and of spermatogenesis. *Mailing Add:* Dept Animal Sci Ore State Univ Corvallis OR 97331-6702. *Fax:* 541-737-4174; *E-Mail:* swansonl@ccmail.orst.edu

SWANSON, LYNN ALLEN, ANALYTICAL CHEMISTRY. *Current Pos:* DIR QUALITY CONTROL, BOEHRINGER INGELHEIM ANIMAL HEALTH INC, 93- *Personal Data:* b Minneapolis, Minn, July 28, 42; m 67; c 2. *Educ:* Univ Minn, Minneapolis, BChem, 64; Univ Iowa, MS, 68, PhD(anal chem), 70. *Prof Exp:* Res chemist anal chem, Commercial Solvents Corp, 69-77; asst mgr, Int Minerals & Chem Corp, 77-80; res scientist anal serv, Res & Develop, Pitman-Moore Inc, 80-86, mgr anal res, 86-87, mgr res serv, 87-88, dir anal res, 88-92. *Mem:* Am Chem Soc; Sigma Xi; Am Soc Qual Control. *Res:* Trace analysis of pharmaceuticals, drugs and other additives in animal tissues and body fluids; general chromatography; spectrophotometry. *Mailing Add:* c/o Boehringer Ingelheim Animal Health Inc 15th & Oak Elwood KS 66024

SWANSON, LYNWOOD WALTER, PHYSICAL CHEMISTRY. *Current Pos:* PRES, FEI CO, 86- *Personal Data:* b Turlock, Calif, Oct 7, 34; m 55; c 4. *Educ:* Univ of Pac, BSc, 56; Univ Calif, PhD(chem), 60. *Prof Exp:* Asst chemist, Univ Calif, Davis, 56-59; res assoc, Inst Study Metals, Univ Chicago, 59-61; sr scientist, Linfield Res Inst, 61-63; dir basic res, Field Emission Corp, 63-69; prof chem & dean fac, Linfield Col, 69-73; prof appl physics, Ore Grad Ctr, 73-86. *Mem:* Fel Am Phys Soc. *Res:* Photochemistry; surface adsorption; field electron and ion microscopy; electron physics. *Mailing Add:* 2475 SW Timberline Dr Portland OR 97225-4129

SWANSON, MARK THOMAS, STRUCTURE & EVOLUTION OF BRITTLE FAULT ZONES, REGIONAL TRANSPRESSION & THE NORUMBEGA FAULT ZONE. *Current Pos:* PROF & CHAIR GEOSCI, UNIV SOUTHERN MAINE, 83- *Personal Data:* Lawrence, Kans, Aug 17, 52; m 80, Lisa; c Emily, Joseph, Amanda & Matthew. *Educ:* Northeastern Univ, BS, 75; Lehigh Univ, MS, 79; State Univ NY, Albany, PhD(geol), 82. *Prof Exp:* Asst prof, Univ SFla, 82-83. *Res:* Southern coastal and Casco Bay area of Maine; mesazoic dike infusion and Atlantic drifting; brittle fault structure in coastal exposures; regional deformation in relation transpression associated with the Norumbega fault zone. *Mailing Add:* Dept Geosci Univ Southern Maine Gorham ME 04038. *E-Mail:* m.swanson@usm.maine.edu

SWANSON, MAX LYNN, EXPERIMENTAL SOLID STATE PHYSICS. *Current Pos:* RETIRED. *Personal Data:* b Hancock, Mich, Aug 5, 31; Can & US citizen; m 59, Gudrun Brand; c Eric S, Leila G, Norman R & Tanya Y. *Educ:* Univ BC, BA, 53, MSc, 54, PhD(metal physics), 58. *Prof Exp:* Res metallurgist, Metals Res Lab, Carnegie Inst Technol, 58-60; res officer metal physics, Chalk River Nuclear Labs, Atomic Energy Can Ltd, 60-86; res prof, Univ NC, Chapel Hill, 86-97. *Concurrent Pos:* Guest scientist, Max Planck Inst Metal Res, Stuttgart, 65-66; vis prof, Univ Utah, 71-72, Kyoto Univ, 92-93; guest scientist, Hahn-Meither Inst, Berlin, 77-78. *Mem:* Am Phys Soc; Mat Res Soc. *Res:* Defect solid state physics: irradiation damage in metals and semiconductors, ion channeling; defect trapping configurations; ion beam modification of materials; perturbed angular correlation. *Mailing Add:* Dept Physics & Astron Phillips Hall Univ NC Chapel Hill NC 27599-3255. *Fax:* 919-962-0480; *E-Mail:* swanson@physics.unc.edu

SWANSON, PAUL N, RADIO ASTRONOMY, MILLIMETER WAVE RADIOMETRY. *Current Pos:* mem staff, Calif Inst Technol, 75-85, mgr microwave observational, 85-89, mgr, Astrophys & Space Physics Prog, 89-92, mgr, Satellite Test Equivalence Prin Proj, 92-97, MGR, KERK INTERFEROMETA PROJ, JET PROPULSION LAB, CALIF INST TECHNOL, 97- *Personal Data:* b San Mateo, Calif, June 29, 36; m 59; c Kris, Kyle & Brian. *Educ:* Calif State Polytech Col, BS, 62; Pa State Univ, PhD(physics), 68. *Prof Exp:* Asst prof radio astron, Pa State Univ, Univ Park, 69-75. *Mem:* Am Astron Soc; AAAS; Sigma Xi; Am Inst Aeronaut &

Astronaut. *Res:* Millimeter wavelength radio astronomy; radiometer development; space science; project management. *Mailing Add:* Jet Propulsion Lab 233-200 4800 Oak Grove Dr Pasadena CA 91109-8099. *Fax:* 815-393-4219; *E-Mail:* paul.n.swanson@jpl.nasa.gov

SWANSON, PHILLIP D, NEUROLOGY, BIOCHEMISTRY. *Current Pos:* from asst prof to assoc prof, 64-73, head div, 67-95, PROF NEUROL, SCH MED, UNIV WASH, 73- *Personal Data:* b Seattle, Wash, Oct 1, 32; m 57, Sheila Joardar; c 5. *Educ:* Yale Univ, BS, 54; Johns Hopkins Univ, MD, 58; Univ London, PhD(biochem), 64. *Prof Exp:* Fel neurol med, Sch Med, Johns Hopkins Univ, 59-62; Nat Inst Neurol Dis & Stroke spec fel, Univ London, 62-64. *Mem:* Asn Univ Prof Neurol (pres, 75-76); Am Neurol Asn; emer mem Am Soc Clin Invest; Brit Biochem Soc; fel Am Acad Neuro; Movement Disorders Soc. *Res:* Neurochemistry; cation transport and energy utilization in cerebral tissues; enzymes of importance in cation transport. *Mailing Add:* Dept Neurol Box 356465 Univ Wash Sch Med Seattle WA 98195

SWANSON, ROBERT ALLAN, ELEMENTARY PARTICLE PHYSICS. *Current Pos:* from asst prof to assoc prof, 60-70, PROF PHYSICS, UNIV CALIF, SAN DIEGO, 70- *Personal Data:* b Chicago, Ill, Dec 16, 28; m 57. *Educ:* Ill Inst Technol, BS, 51; Univ Chicago, MS, 53, PhD(physics), 58. *Prof Exp:* Res assoc physics, Univ Chicago, 58-59; asst prof, Princeton Univ, 59-60. *Concurrent Pos:* Vis assoc prof, Univ Chicago, 68-69; NSF fel, Univ Calif, 72- *Mem:* Am Phys Soc; Am Asn Physics Teachers. *Res:* Muonic atoms; experimental kaon physics. *Mailing Add:* Dept Physics Univ Calif San Diego Box 019 La Jolla CA 92093. *Fax:* 619-534-0173

SWANSON, ROBERT E, MEDICAL PHYSIOLOGY. *Current Pos:* assoc prof, 61-73, PROF PHYSIOL, MED SCH, UNIV ORE HEALTH SCI CTR, 73- *Personal Data:* b Duluth, Minn, Dec 19, 24; m 47; c 2. *Educ:* Univ Minn, BA, 49, PhD(physiol), 53. *Prof Exp:* Asst physiol, Univ Minn, 50-52, instr, 52-55; asst physiologist, Brookhaven Nat Lab, 55-58; asst prof, Univ Minn, 58-61. *Res:* Renal, water and electrolyte balance. *Mailing Add:* Dept Physiol Univ Ore Health Sci Univ 3181 SW Sam Jackson Park Rd Portland OR 97201-3011

SWANSON, ROBERT HAROLD, FOREST HYDROLOGY, TREE PHYSIOLOGY. *Current Pos:* PROJ LEADER FOREST HYDROL, NORTHERN FOREST RES CTR, 68-; CONSULT. *Personal Data:* b Los Angeles, Calif, Feb 15, 33; m 55, Joanna; c 2. *Educ:* Colo State Univ, BSc, 59, MSc, 66, Univ Alta, PhD, 83. *Prof Exp:* Res forester hydrol, Rocky Mountain Forest & Range Exp Sta, US Forest Serv, 59-68. *Mem:* Can Inst Foresters; Can Geophys Union. *Res:* Plant-water relations; forest arrangements-streamflow interractions; watershed management simulation and evaluation techniques. *Mailing Add:* No 28216 Three Sisters Dr Canmore AB T1W 2M2 Can. *E-Mail:* www.rswanson@banff.nat

SWANSON, ROBERT JAMES, ENDOCRINOLOGY. *Current Pos:* asst prof anat, physiol & endocrinol, Old Dominion Univ, 75-77, asst prof biol, 77-80. *Personal Data:* b St Petersburg, Fla, Nov 13, 45; m 67; c 2. *Educ:* Wheaton Col, Ill, BS, 67; Fla State Univ, MS, 71, PhD(biol), 76. *Prof Exp:* Teacher gen sci, Madison High Sch, Fla, 67-68; instr anat & kinesiology, Fla State Univ, 69-70. *Mem:* AAAS. *Res:* Female reproductive physiology, especially factors involved in ovulation, such as hormones, smooth muscle activity, nerve involvement and blood flow. *Mailing Add:* 1014 Jamestown Crescent Norfolk VA 23508

SWANSON, ROBERT LAWRENCE, PHYSICAL OCEANOGRAPHY, CIVIL ENGINEERING. *Current Pos:* DIR, WASTE REDUCTION MGT INST, STATE UNIV NY, STONY BROOK, 87- *Personal Data:* b Baltimore, Md, Oct 11, 38; m 63, Dana Lamont; c Lawrence D & Michael N. *Educ:* Lehigh Univ, BS, 60; Ore State Univ, MS, 65, PhD, 71. *Honors & Awards:* Silver Medal, US Dept Com, 73; Prog Admin & Mgt Award, Nat Oceanic & Atmospheric Admin, 75, Unit Citation, 81, Corps Dir Ribbon Award, 87, Spec Achievement Award, 87. *Prof Exp:* Comn officer, US Coast & Geodetic Surv & Nat Oceanic & Atmospheric Admin, 60-87, commanding officer, US Coast & Geodetic Surv Ship Marmer Circulatory Estuarine Surv, 66-67, chief, Oceanog Div, Nat Ocean Surv, 69-72, proj mgr, NY Bight Proj, Marine Ecosyst Anal, Environ Res Labs, 72-78, dir, Off Marine Pollution Assessment, 78-83, commanding officer, Nat Oceanic & Atmospheric Admin & ship researcher, Global Climate Res, 84-86, exec dir, Off Oceanog & Atmospheric Res, 86-87. *Concurrent Pos:* Prof asst, Col Gen Studies, George Washington Univ, 70-73; adj prof, State Univ NY, Stony Brook, 78-; chmn, Ocean Pollution Comt, Marine Technol Soc, 82-93; sr exec fel, John F Kennedy Sch Govt, Harvard, 83; lectr & mem, US Deleg Marine Pollution to the People, Repub China, 83; chief scientist, US-French Bilateral in Marine Sci, 86-87; cert hydrographer for inshore & offshore waters, 87-; mem, Suffolk Co Coun Environ Qual, 88-; mem, Tech Adv Comt, NY State Ctr Hazardous Waste Mgt, 88-; chmn, Coastal Comn,Vollagers of Head of the Harbor and Nissequoque, 94-; trustee, Three Village Hist Soc, 94- *Mem:* Am Soc Civil Engrs; Am Geophys Union; AAAS; NY Acad Sci; Sigma Xi. *Res:* Developing interrelationships and understanding between component parts of the coastal marine ecosystem; studying the impact of ocean dumping on marine ecosystem; specific interests in tides, tidal currents, tidal datums, marine boundaries; solid waste management; environmental engineering; science policy. *Mailing Add:* 46 Harbor Hill Rd St James NY 11780. *Fax:* 516-632-8064

SWANSON, ROBERT NELS, MICROMETEOROLOGY, ATMOSPHERIC SCIENCES. *Current Pos:* CONSULT METEOROLOGIST, 93- *Personal Data:* b Ashland, Wis, Feb 4, 32; m 57; c Robert Jr, Richard, Russell & Rosenne. *Educ:* Wis State Univ, River Falls, BS, 53; Univ Mich, MS, 58. *Prof Exp:* Meteorologist, White Sands Missile Range, 58-61; staff scientist, GCA Corp, Utah, 61-72; sr meteorologist, Pac Gas & Elec Co, San Francisco, 72-84, dir, Meteorol Servs, 84-93. *Concurrent Pos:* Chmn, Comt on Atmospheric Measurements, Am Meteorol Soc, 83-85; mem comt, Pvt Sector Meteorol, Am Meteorol Soc, 90-94, Atmospheric Measurements, Am Soc Testing Mats, 93-; cert consult meteorol, Am Meteorol Soc; pres, Nat Coun Indust Meteorol, 96-97. *Mem:* Am Meteorol Soc; Royal Meteorol Soc; Air Pollution Control Asn; Nat Coun Indust Meteorol; Am Soc Testing Mat; AAAS. *Res:* Boundary layer measurements; alternate energy; turbulence and diffusion; technical management; forensic meteorology. *Mailing Add:* 1216 Babel Lane Concord CA 94518. *Fax:* 510-676-2228; *E-Mail:* rnswanson@worldnet.att.net

SWANSON, SAMUEL EDWARD, GEOCHEMISTRY, PETROLOGY. *Current Pos:* asst prof, 79-84, ASSOC PROF GEOL, UNIV ALASKA, FAIRBANKS, 84- *Personal Data:* b Woodland, Calif, Aug 1, 46; m 79. *Educ:* Univ Calif, Davis, BS, 68, MS, 70; Stanford Univ, PhD(geol), 74. *Prof Exp:* Field asst geol, US Geol Surv, 67; res asst geol, Univ Calif, Davis, 70; asst prof earth sci, Univ NC, Charlotte, 74-76; asst prof, Applachian State Univ, Boone, 76-79. *Mem:* Can Mineral Soc; Am Geophys Union; Mineral Soc Am; Soc Environ Geochem & Health; Sigma Xi; Geol Soc Am. *Res:* Application of geochemical techniques to the study of igneous and metamorphic rocks. *Mailing Add:* Dept Geol Univ Ga Athens GA 30602

SWANSON, STEPHEN KING, CELL BIOLOGY, VIROLOGY. *Current Pos:* develop virologist, 85-89, DEPT HEAD, LEDERLE LABS, 89- *Personal Data:* b Jamestown, NY, Oct 12, 46; m 72, Jocelyn Reed; c Christopher. *Educ:* St Lawrence Univ, BS, 68; Univ Ariz, MS, 74; State Univ NY, Buffalo, PhD(microbiol), 78. *Prof Exp:* Fel, Univ Calif, Los Angeles, 78-85. *Mem:* Am Soc Microbiol; AAAS. *Res:* Biological and structural properties of retroviruses; leukemogenesis by retroviruses. *Mailing Add:* 1113 Lord Ivelson Lane Foster City CA 94404

SWARBRICK, JAMES, PHARMACEUTICS, SURFACE CHEMISTRY. *Current Pos:* VPRES RES & DEVELOP & FORMULATION DEVELOP DIV, APPL ANALYTICAL INDUST, 95- *Personal Data:* b London, Eng, May 8, 34; m 60. *Educ:* Univ London, BPharm, 58, PhD(med), 64, DSc(phys chem), 72; FRIC, 72; FRSC (cchem), 75. *Prof Exp:* From asst prof to assoc prof indust pharm, Purdue Univ, 64-66; prof & asst dean pharm, Univ Conn, 66-72; dir prod develop, Sterling-Winthrop Res Inst, 72-75; prof pharmaceut, Univ Sydney, 75-76; dean, Sch Pharm, Univ London, 76-78; prof pharm, Univ Southern Calif, 78-81; prof pharm & chmn, Dept Pharmaceut, Univ NC, Chapel Hill, 81-92. *Concurrent Pos:* Indust consult, 65-; Vis scientist, Astra Labs, Sweden, 71; chmn, USP-NF Panel Dissolution & Disintegration Testing, 72-75; consult, Australian Dept Health, 75-76, Orgn Am States, 78 & Pan-Am Health Orgn, 79 & 81; examr, Sci Univ Malaysia, 77-78; examr, Univ Singapore, 80-81; consult, Al Fateh Univ, Libya, 81; vis prof, Brighton Polytech, UK, 88. *Mem:* Am Pharmaceut Asn; fel Acad Pharmaceut Sci; Am Asn Col Pharm; fel Pharmaceut Soc Great Brit; fel Royal Soc Chem; fel Am Asn Pharmaceut Scientists. *Res:* Dosage form design and drug delivery; percutaneous absorption; formulation of topical products; preformulation studies; interfacial phenomena of pharmaceutical and biological significance. *Mailing Add:* Appl Anal Indust 1206 N 23rd St Wilmington NC 28405

SWARD, EDWARD LAWRENCE, JR, PHYSICAL CHEMISTRY, SOFTWARE SYSTEMS. *Current Pos:* PRES, INTERLINK MKT CORP, 94- *Personal Data:* b Chicago, Ill, Aug 21, 33; m 57; c 2. *Educ:* Augustana Col, Ill, BA, 55; Univ Buffalo, PhD(chem), 61. *Prof Exp:* Res chemist, Mylar Res & Develop Lab, E I du Pont de Nemours & Co, Inc, 60-64, Du Pont de Nemours, Luxembourg, SA, 64-67 & Del, 67-69; mgr mkt develop, Celanese Res Co, 69-72; mgr long range planning, El Paso Hydrocarbons Co, 72-81, dir planning, 81-83, dir, planning & bus anal, 84-87, pres corp invest, 87; pres, Sward Group, 87-94. *Concurrent Pos:* Adj prof, Univ Tex, Permian Basin, 74-84. *Mem:* Commercial Develop Asn; Am Chem Soc; Am Asn Qual Control; Nat Asn. *Res:* Physical chemistry of polymers; kinetics; process development; financial and business planning and analysis; market research; financial planning. *Mailing Add:* PO Box 260795 Plano TX 75026-0795. *Fax:* 972-985-0883; *E-Mail:* smglnk@lx.netcom.com

SWARDSON, MARY ANNE, GENERAL TOPOLOGY, SET THEORY. *Current Pos:* Asst prof, 81-89, ASSOC PROF MATH, OHIO UNIV, 89- *Personal Data:* b College Park, Ga, Sept 10, 28; m 49, Harold R; c Anne, Catherine & Christine. *Educ:* Tulane Univ, BA, 49; Ohio Univ, MS, 69, PhD(math), 81. *Concurrent Pos:* Chmn math dept, Ohio Univ; Ohio Acad Sci. *Mem:* Am Math Soc; Math Asn Am; Asn Women Math; Am Women Sci. *Res:* Character of closed sets; generalizations of F-spaces; topological characterizations of set-theoretical axioms; generalizations of psuedocompactness; insertion, approximation and extension of real-valued functions; stone-cech compactification; integral summability theory, connectifications. *Mailing Add:* Math Ohio Univ Athens OH 45701. *Fax:* 740-593-0406; *E-Mail:* swardson@oucsace.cs.ohiou.edu

SWARIN, STEPHEN JOHN, CHROMATOGRAPHY, ENVIRONMENTAL ANALYSIS. *Current Pos:* Assoc res scientist, Gen Motors Res Labs, 72-76, sr res scientist, 75-79, staff res scientist, 79-81, sr staff scientist, 81-85, asst dept head, 85-87, prin res scientist, 87-92, DEPT HEAD, GEN MOTORS RES & DEVELOP CTR, 92- *Personal Data:* b Plainfield, NJ, July 24, 45; m 69; c 2. *Educ:* Lafayette Col, AB, 67; Univ Mass,

MS, 69, PhD(anal chem), 72. *Mem:* Am Chem Soc; Sigma Xi; Asn Anal Chemists. *Res:* Polymer analysis; polymer additives analysis; liquid chromatography; derivatization for detectability; environmental analysis; near-infrared spectroscopy; instrumentation. *Mailing Add:* Analytical Chem Dept Gen Motors Res & Develop Ctr Warren MI 48090

SWARINGEN, ROY ARCHIBALD, JR, ORGANIC CHEMISTRY. *Current Pos:* sr develop chemist, 70-74, sect head develop res, 74-81, DEPT HEAD, CHEM DEVELOP LABS, BURROUGHS WELLCOME CO, 81- *Personal Data:* b Winston-Salem, NC, Feb 1, 42; m 69. *Educ:* Univ NC, Chapel Hill, AB, 64; Univ Ill, Urbana, MS, 66, PhD(org chem), 69. *Prof Exp:* Res chemist org chem, R J Reynolds Tobacco Co, 69-70. *Mem:* Am Chem Soc; Royal Soc Chem; Sigma Xi. *Res:* Development research in pharmaceutical chemistry; synthetic organic chemistry; heterocyclic compounds. *Mailing Add:* 824 Sandlewood Dr Durham NC 27712-3528

SWARM, RICHARD L(EE), PATHOLOGY, CARCINOGENESIS. *Current Pos:* PATH CONSULT, 82- *Personal Data:* b St Louis, Mo, June 9, 27; m 50; c 2. *Educ:* Wash Univ, BA, 49, BS & MD, 50; Am Bd Path, dipl. *Prof Exp:* Intern, Barnes Hosp, St Louis, Mo, 50-51; instr & resident path, Washington Univ & Barnes Hosp, 51-54; pathologist, USPHS Med Ctr, 54-55 & Nat Cancer Inst, 55-65; assoc prof path, Col Med, Univ Cincinnati, 65-68; dir, Dept Exp Path & Toxicol, Res Div, Hoffmann-LaRoche, Inc, 68-82. *Concurrent Pos:* Clin assoc prof path, Columbia Univ, 70-90; grantee, Am Cancer Soc & USPHS; consult pathologist, 82- *Mem:* Am Soc Toxicol Pathologists; Am Asn Cancer Res; Am Asn Pathologists; fel Am Soc Clin Path; Col Am Pathologists; AMA; Soc Toxicol; Teratol Soc. *Res:* Histopathology and toxicology in man and laboratory animals; morphology of neoplasms and carcinogenesis; radiation injury; transplantation of tissues; chondrosacomas; ultrastructure of neoplastic cells. *Mailing Add:* Health Sci Assoc PO Box 808 Ridgewood NJ 07451-0808

SWAROOP, ANAND, INHERITED EYE DISEASES, GENE EXPRESSION. *Current Pos:* ASST PROF HUMAN GENETICS, KELLOGG EYE CTR, UNIV MICH, 90- *Personal Data:* b Turrah, India, Jan 14, 57; m 82, Manju Kapoor; c Alok & Kanchan. *Educ:* G B Pant Univ, India, MS, 77; Indian Inst Sci, PhD(biochem), 82. *Prof Exp:* Assoc, dept molecular biophys & biochem, Yale Univ, 82-86, assoc res scientist, Dept Human Genetics, 86-87 & 88-90, Nat Res Serv Awards fel, 87-88. *Concurrent Pos:* Co-dir library core, Mich Humane Genome Ctr, Univ Mich, 90-; fac mem, Grad Prog Cellular & Molecular Biol, 91-, mem, Univ Mich Cancer Ctr, 92- *Mem:* AAAS; Am Soc Microbiol; Am Soc Human Genetics; Asn Res Vision & Opthal. *Res:* Applying the techniques of molecular biology and genetics to understand the development of visual system and associated genetic defects in man. *Mailing Add:* 3481 Yellowstone Dr Ann Arbor MI 48105

SWART, EDWARD REINIER, GRAPH THEORY, COMPLEXITY THEORY. *Current Pos:* chair, Dept Comput & Info Sci, 89-92, actg dean, 93-94, PROF COMPUT & INFO SCI, UNIV GUELPH, 87- *Personal Data:* b Cape Town, SAfrica, Aug 30, 28, Can citizen; m 58, Diana Irene Burnell; c Joy, Felicity, Nicholas & Rosalie. *Educ:* Univ Witwatersrand, BSc, 50, PhD(comput sci), 78; Univ Pretoria, DSc(phys chem), 57; Univ SAfrica, MSc, 75. *Honors & Awards:* Lester R Ford Award, Am Math Asn, 81. *Prof Exp:* Dir, Gulbenian Radiocarbon Dubing Lab, Univ Rhodesia, 58-72, Comput Ctr, 66-76; dean, Fac Sci, Univ Rhodesia, 73-75, chair, Dept Comput Sci, 75-77. *Concurrent Pos:* T Wistar Brown fel, Haverford Col, 63; ed, Proc & Trans Rhodesia Sci Asn, 71-72; Found fel, Inst Combinatorics & Applns, 91; adj prof math & statist, Univ Guelph, 96- *Mem:* Inst Elec & Electronics Engrs; fel Royal Soc Chem. *Res:* Graph theory; complexity theory; contribution to the computer assisted solution of four color theorem. *Mailing Add:* Dept Comput & Info Sci Univ Guelph Guelph ON N1G 2W1 Can. *E-Mail:* tswart@snowhite.cis.uoguelph.ca

SWART, WILLIAM LEE, MATHEMATICS. *Current Pos:* FOUNDER, TRICON PUBL, INC, 86- *Personal Data:* b Brethren, Mich, July 13, 30; m 62; c 2. *Educ:* Cent Mich Univ, BS, 58, MA, 62; Univ Mich, Ann Arbor, EdD(math educ), 69. *Prof Exp:* Teacher, Mesick Consol Schs, Mich, 58-61 & Livonia Pub Schs, 61-63; instr math, Eastern Mich Univ, 63-65; consult math educ, Genesee Intermediate Sch Dist, Mich, 65-67; from asst prof to prof math, Cent Mich Univ, 67-86. *Res:* Learning of elementary mathematics; action research in public schools. *Mailing Add:* Tricon Publ Co 2150 Enterprise Dr Mt Pleasant MI 48858

SWART, WILLIAM W, INDUSTRIAL & MANUFACTURING ENGINEERING. *Current Pos:* CHAIR & PROF INDUST ENG, UNIV CENT FLA, 85- *Personal Data:* b Hareu, Holland, July 21, 44; US citizen; m 90. *Educ:* Clemson Univ, BS, 65; Ga Tech, MS, 68, PhD(indust eng), 70. *Prof Exp:* Assoc prof mgt sci, Univ Miami, 73-78; asst dean bus, Calif State Univ Northridge, 78-79; vpres MIS, Burger King Corp, 79-85. *Mem:* Opers Res Soc Am; Inst Indust Engrs; Am Soc Eng Educ. *Res:* Energy efficient, affordable, industrialized housing; space shuttle processing. *Mailing Add:* Off Dean Eng NJ Inst Technol 5700-GITT University Heights Newark NJ 07102

SWARTS, ELWYN LOWELL, PHYSICAL CHEMISTRY, ANALYTICAL CHEMISTRY. *Current Pos:* RETIRED. *Personal Data:* b Hornell, NY, Feb 26, 29; m 54, Rachel Homet; c Heidi, Andrew & Adam. *Educ:* Hamilton Col, NY, AB, 49; Brown Univ, PhD, 54. *Prof Exp:* Mem fac, Alfred Univ, 53-56, res chemist, Knolls Atomic Lab, Gen Elec Co, NY, 56-57, res chemist, Glass Technol Lab, Ohio, 57-59; staff scientist, PPG Glass Tech Ctr, 59-94. *Concurrent Pos:* Consult, 94- *Mem:* Am Chem Soc; Am Ceramic Soc; Soc Glass Technol; Sigma Xi. *Res:* Properties of glass; melting reactions; surface analysis of glass; nuclear waste glass processing. *Mailing Add:* 625 Ravencrest Rd Pittsburgh PA 15215

SWARTZ, BLAIR KINCH, NUMERICAL ANALYSIS. *Current Pos:* res asst, Los Alamos Nat Lab, 58, Mem staff, 59-91, group leader, 68-74, assoc group leader, 78-80, ASSOC, LOS ALAMOS NAT LAB, 92- *Personal Data:* b Detroit, Mich, Nov 5, 32; m 55, Laura Sparks; c Stacey. *Educ:* Antioch Col, BS, 55; Mass Inst Technol, MS, 58; NY Univ, PhD(math), 70. *Prof Exp:* Asst biol, Sch Med & Dent, Univ Rochester, 51-52; asst chem, Detroit Edison Co, 52-53; asst physics, Antioch Col, 53-54; high sch teacher, 54-55; asst math, Mass Inst Technol, 55-58. *Concurrent Pos:* Asst, Am Optical Co, 55-56; lectr, State Univ NY Teachers Col New Paltz, 58 & Univ NMex, 59; ed, SIAM J Numerical Anal, 74-75; fel, Los Alamos Nat Lab, 83- *Mem:* Soc Indust & Appl Math. *Res:* Approximation theory; differential equations. *Mailing Add:* 172 Paseo Penasco Los Alamos NM 87544. *E-Mail:* bks@lanl.gov

SWARTZ, CHARLES, PHYSICS, RHEOLOGY NON-NEWTONIAN FLUID. *Current Pos:* RETIRED. *Personal Data:* b Emporia, Kans, 1936. *Educ:* Kans State Univ, BS, 58; Okla State Univ, PhD(phys chem), 64. *Prof Exp:* Res assoc, Chem Dept, Univ Colo, 64-65; chemist rheology non-newtonian fluid, Conoco Inc, 65-93. *Mem:* Am Chem Soc; Am Inst Chemists. *Mailing Add:* 1501 El Camino Ponca City OK 74601-2199

SWARTZ, CHARLES DANA, PHYSICS. *Current Pos:* from assoc prof to prof, 56-79, EMER PROF PHYSICS, UNION COL, NY, 79- *Personal Data:* b Baltimore, Md, July 25, 15; m 49, Katherine Hunt; c Timothy H, Douglas K & Christina H. *Educ:* Johns Hopkins Univ, AB, 38, PhD(physics), 43. *Prof Exp:* Physicist, Manhattan Proj, SAM Labs, Columbia Univ, 42-46; assoc, Lab Nuclear Studies, Cornell Univ, 46-48; from instr to asst prof physics, Johns Hopkins Univ, 48-56. *Concurrent Pos:* Fulbright lectr, Univ Ankara, 61-62; vis prof physics, Rensselaer Polytech Inst, 69-70. *Mem:* Am Phys Soc. *Res:* Neutron physics; energy levels of light nuclei; science education; low-temperature physics. *Mailing Add:* 1350 Dean St Schenectady NY 12309

SWARTZ, CHARLES W, MATHEMATICS. *Current Pos:* PROF MATH, NMEX STATE UNIV, 65- *Personal Data:* b Jan 1, 1938; m 71. *Educ:* Univ Ariz, PhD (math), 65. *Concurrent Pos:* Vis scholar, Univ Ariz, 71-72, Stanford Univ, 78, Univ NC, 87. *Mem:* Am Math Soc; Math Asn Am. *Res:* Functional analysis; locally convex spaces; continuous linear operators; vector-valve measures. *Mailing Add:* NMex State Univ Las Cruces NM 88003

SWARTZ, CLIFFORD EDWARD, HIGH ENERGY PHYSICS, PHYSICS EDUCATION. *Current Pos:* assoc prof, 57-67, prof, 67-95, EMER PROF PHYSICS, STATE UNIV NY STONY BROOK, 95- *Personal Data:* b Niagara Falls, NY, Feb 21, 25; m 46, Barbara Myers; c 6. *Educ:* Univ Rochester, AB, 45, MS, 46, PhD(physics), 51. *Honors & Awards:* Oersted Medal, Am Asn Physics Teachers, 87. *Prof Exp:* Assoc physicist, Brookhaven Nat Lab, 51-62. *Concurrent Pos:* Ed, The Physics Teacher, 67-85, 89- *Mem:* Am Phys Soc; Am Asn Physics Teachers; fel AAAS. *Res:* Particle physics; high energy accelerators for nuclear physics research; science curriculum revision and textbooks, kindergarten through college. *Mailing Add:* Dept Physics State Univ NY Stony Brook NY 11794. *E-Mail:* eswartz@sunysb.edu

SWARTZ, DONALD PERCY, GYNECOLOGY. *Current Pos:* obstetrician-gynecologist-in-chief, 72-79, chief, Sect Gen Gynec, 79-88, HEAD DIV GEN GYNEC, ALBANY MED CTR, 88- *Personal Data:* b Preston, Ont, Sept, 12, 21; US citizen; m 44, 84; c 2. *Educ:* Univ Western Ont, BA & MD, 51, MSc, 53. *Prof Exp:* Nat Res Coun Can grant, Univ Western Ont, 52-53; Am Cancer Soc fel, Johns Hopkins Hosp, 56-57, instr obstet & gynec, 57-58; lectr physiol, Univ Western Ont, 58-62; clin prof, Columbia Univ, 62-72, prof obstet & gynec, 72; prof obstet & gynec & chmn dept, Albany Med Col, 72-79. *Concurrent Pos:* Markle scholar, Univ Western Ont, 58-62; consult obstet & gynec, St Peter's Hosp, 72- *Mem:* fel Am Gynec Soc; Am Col Obstet & Gynec; Soc Study Reproduction; Am Fertil Soc; fel Royal Col Surg; fel Am Gynec & Obstet Soc. *Res:* Hormonal contraception; new approaches to pregnancy termination; gynecologic endocrinology; menopausal care. *Mailing Add:* Dept Obstet & Gynec Albany Med Ctr Albany NY 12208

SWARTZ, FRANK JOSEPH, ANATOMY, CYTOLOGY. *Current Pos:* from asst prof to prof, 56-90, EMER PROF ANAT, SCH MED, UNIV LOUISVILLE, 90- *Personal Data:* b Pittsburgh, Pa, Mar 22, 27; wid; c Victor & Andrew. *Educ:* Western Reserve Univ, BS, 49, MS, 51, PhD(zool), 55. *Prof Exp:* Asst biol, Western Reserve Univ, 49-52, Nat Cancer Inst fel, 55-56. *Concurrent Pos:* Lectr & USPHS spec fel, Dept Anat, Harvard Med Sch, 69-70; prof anat, Univ Louisville, 90-; post-doctoral fel, USPHS, Karolinska Inst, Stokckholm, Sweden, 55-56. *Mem:* Am Soc Anat; Sigma Xi. *Res:* Human anatomy; cellular differentiation and genetic significance of somatic polyploidy in mammalian tissues. *Mailing Add:* Dept Anat Sci & Neurobiol Sch Med Univ Louisville Louisville KY 40292

SWARTZ, GEORGE ALLAN, PHYSICS. *Current Pos:* RETIRED. *Personal Data:* b Scranton, Pa, Dec 9, 30; m 80; c 3. *Educ:* Mass Inst Technol, BS, 52; Univ Pa, MS, 54, PhD(physics), 58. *Prof Exp:* Mem tech staff, David Sarnoff Res Ctr, RCA Corp, 58-87; mem tech staff, SRI Int, 87-90. *Concurrent Pos:* Adj assoc prof dept metall & mat sci, Stevens Inst Technol, 80-85. *Mem:* Am Phys Soc; Sigma Xi; Inst Elec & Electronic Engrs. *Res:* Solid state microwave devices, particularly impact avalanche, transit time microwave sources and PIN diode switches; photovoltaic solar energy sources; amorphous silicon photovotaic energy sources; very-large scale integration microchip reliability. *Mailing Add:* 323 Woods Ave Tavernier FL 33070-2258

SWARTZ, GORDON ELMER, ZOOLOGY, EMBRYOLOGY. *Current Pos:* From instr to prof, 46-79, EMER PROF BIOL, STATE UNIV NY, BUFFALO, 79- *Personal Data:* b Buffalo, NY, May 12, 17; m 41, E June Miller; c Gary G & Karen J (Root). *Educ:* Univ Buffalo, BA, 39, MA, 41; NY Univ, PhD(biol), 46. *Mem:* Fel AAAS; Am Micros Soc; Am Soc Zoologists; Am Asn Anat; NY Acad Sci. *Res:* Organogenesis; vertebrate experimental embryology; transplantation. *Mailing Add:* 24 Copper Heights Snyder NY 14226

SWARTZ, GRACE LYNN, INORGANIC CHEMISTRY. *Current Pos:* vis asst prof, 77-80, ASST PROF CHEM, MICH TECHNOL UNIV, 80- *Personal Data:* b Coaldale, Pa, 1943. *Educ:* Muhlenberg Col, BS, 65; Dartmouth Col, MA, 67; Fla State Univ, PhD(chem), 77. *Prof Exp:* Vis instr chem, Fla State Univ, 67-72, res assoc, 72-73; vis instr chem, Purdue Univ, 73-74; res asst chem, Fla State Univ, 74-77. *Mem:* Am Chem Soc; AAAS. *Res:* Mechanistic aspects of transition metal carbonyls and substituted metal carbonyls used in catalytic reactions, with the active catalyst generated thermally or photochemically. *Mailing Add:* Dept Chem & Eng Mich Technol Univ Houghton MI 49931

SWARTZ, HAROLD M, RADIOLOGY, ELECTRON SPIN RESONANCE. *Current Pos:* DIR EDUC PROG & DIR RES RADIOL, CTR EVALUATIVE CLIN SCI, DARTMOUTH-HITCHCOCK MED CTR, 91- *Personal Data:* b Chicago, Ill, June 22, 35; m 81; c 4. *Educ:* Univ Ill, BS & MD, 59; Univ NC, MS, 62; Georgetown Univ, PhD(biochem), 69. *Prof Exp:* Fel nuclear med, Walter Reed Army Inst Res, Med Corps, US Army, 62-64, res med officer, 64-68, chief, Dept Biophys, 68-70, chief, Dept Biol Chem, 70; assoc prof radiol & biochem, Med Col Wis, 70-74, prof, 74-80, dir, Radiation Biol & Biophys Lab, 70-80, dir, Nat Biomed Electron Spin Resonance Ctr, 74-80; prof biophys & assoc dean acad affairs, Col Med, Univ Ill, Urbana-Champaign, 80-91. *Mem:* AAAS; Radiation Res Soc; Soc Nuclear Med; NY Acad Sci. *Res:* Free radicals and paramagnetic metal ions in biological systems; oxygen toxicity; radiation biology applied to radiation therapy; carcinogenesis. *Mailing Add:* Dept Family Med 7250 Strasenburgh Hall Rm 308 Ctr Evaluative Clin Sci Dartmouth-Hitchcock Med Ctr Hanover NH 03755-3863

SWARTZ, HARRY, allergy, science communications; deceased, see previous edition for last biography

SWARTZ, JAMES E, ORGANIC ELECTROCHEMISTRY, PHYSICAL ORGANIC CHEMISTRY. *Current Pos:* from asst prof to assoc prof, 80-93, chair, Sci Div, 89-94, PROF CHEM, GRINNELL COL, 93- *Personal Data:* b Washington, DC, June 12, 51; m 88, Cynthia J Mosier. *Educ:* Stanislaus State Col, BS, 73; Univ Calif, Santa Cruz, PhD(chem), 78. *Prof Exp:* Instr chem, Univ Calif, Santa Cruz, 78; res fel, Calif Inst Technol, 78-80. *Concurrent Pos:* Policy analyst, Energy, US Cong, 89. *Mem:* Am Chem Soc; AAAS; Electrochem Soc; Am Solar Energy Soc; Am Wind Energy Asn. *Res:* Nucleophilic aromatic substitution reactions; free radical radical reactions; radical anions. *Mailing Add:* Chem Dept Box 805 Grinnell Col Grinnell IA 50112-0805. *Fax:* 515-269-4285; *E-Mail:* swartz@grin.edu

SWARTZ, JAMES LAWRENCE, electroanalytical chemistry, control engineering, for more information see previous edition

SWARTZ, JOHN CROUCHER, PHYSICS, MATERIALS SCIENCE. *Current Pos:* RETIRED. *Personal Data:* b Syracuse, NY, Oct 25, 24; m 56; c 3. *Educ:* Yale Univ, BS, 46; Syracuse Univ, MS, 49, PhD, 52. *Prof Exp:* Res physicist, Consol Vacuum Corp, 52-55; sr scientist, E C Bain Lab Fundamental Res, US Steel Corp, 55-71 & Tyco Labs, Inc, Mass, 72-75; sr scientist, Mobil Tyco Solar Energy Corp, 75-76 & Westinghouse Res & Develop Ctr, 77-89; scientist, R J Lee Group, Inc, 89-92. *Mem:* Am Phys Soc. *Res:* VLSI processing; infrared detector material; crystal growth; solid state physics. *Mailing Add:* 3201 Cambridge Dr Murrysville PA 15668

SWARTZ, LESLIE GERARD, PARASITOLOGY. *Current Pos:* From assoc prof to prof, 58-88, EMER PROF ZOOL, UNIV ALASKA, FAIRBANKS, 88-, AFFIL PROF, 88- *Personal Data:* b Chicago, Ill, Aug 16, 30; m 58, Mary Margaret McKean; c Susan E (Mitchell), Judith E, David D & Roger L. *Educ:* Univ Ill, BS, 53, MS, 54, PhD(zool), 58. *Mem:* AAAS; Reptor Res Found. *Res:* Helminth parasitology, especially ecology; avian, freshwater and general ecology. *Mailing Add:* 2149 Yankovich Rd Fairbanks AK 99709. *E-Mail:* fflgs@aurora.alaska.edu

SWARTZ, MARJORIE LOUISE, INORGANIC CHEMISTRY. *Current Pos:* Res assoc, 46-53, from instr to assoc prof, 53-69, PROF DENT MAT, SCH DENT, IND UNIV, INDIANAPOLIS, 69- *Personal Data:* b Indianapolis, Ind, Feb 1, 24. *Educ:* Butler Univ, BS, 46; Ind Univ, MS, 59. *Honors & Awards:* Souder Award, Int Asn Dent Res, 68. *Mem:* AAAS; fel Am Col Dent; hon mem Am Dent Asn; Int Asn Dent Mat; hon mem Am Asn Women Dentists; hon mem Int Col Dent; Sigma Xi. *Res:* Physical and chemical properties of dental cements, resins and amalgams; effect of restorative materials on physical and chemical properties of tooth structure. *Mailing Add:* Ind Univ Sch of Dent Dental Mat DS 112 Indianapolis IN 46202

SWARTZ, MORTON N, INFECTIOUS DISEASES, MICROBIOLOGY. *Current Pos:* Chief, Infectious Dis Unit, 56-90, CHIEF JACKSON FIRM, MED SERV, MASS GEN HOSP, 91- *Personal Data:* b Boston, Mass, Nov 11, 23; m 56, Cesia Rosenberg; c Mark & Caroline. *Educ:* Harvard Univ, MD, 47. *Hon Degrees:* MD, Univ Geneve, 88. *Honors & Awards:* Bristol Award, Infectious Dis Soc Am, 84; Distinguished Teacher Award, Am Col Physicians, 89. *Concurrent Pos:* Assoc ed, New Eng J Med, 81- *Mem:* Am Soc Biol Chemists; Am Soc Microbiol; Asn Am Physicians; Am Soc Clin Invest; Am Col Physicians; Infectious Dis Soc Am (pres, 88); Inst Med. *Res:* Mechanisms antibiotic action; bacterial infections. *Mailing Add:* Mass Gen Hosp Fruit St Boston MA 02114

SWARTZ, STUART ENDSLEY, CIVIL ENGINEERING. *Current Pos:* from asst prof to assoc prof, 68-77, PROF CIVIL ENG, KANS STATE UNIV, 77-, HEAD CIVIL ENG, 92- *Personal Data:* b Chicago, Ill, Oct 17, 38; m 63. *Educ:* Ill Inst Technol, BS, 59, MS, 62, PhD(civil eng), 68. *Prof Exp:* Engr, Caterpillar Tractor Co, Ill, 60; res assoc, Ill Inst Tech, 67-68. *Mem:* Am Soc Civil Engrs; fel Am Concrete Inst; Soc Exp Stress Anal. *Res:* Analysis and design of folded plate structures; theoretical and experimental studies on the buckling of folded plates and other concrete shells; buckling of concrete columns; analysis and design of concrete shells; buckling of concrete panels; fracture toughness of concrete. *Mailing Add:* 3033 Dickens Ave Manhattan KS 66503

SWARTZ, THOMAS W, ELECTRICAL ENGINEERING. *Current Pos:* dir, Spec Proj Off, 91-94, dir, Sensor Technol Off, 94-95, DIR, INFO SYSTS OFF, ADVAN RES PROJS AGENCY, 95- *Personal Data:* b Napa, Calif; m, Gladyne; c 2. *Educ:* Univ Ariz, BS; San Jose State Col, MS. *Prof Exp:* Asst vpres & mgr reconnaissance & surveillance, Target Acquisition Technol Div, Sci Appln Int Corp, 84-90; res staff mem syst anal, target detection & recognition & countermeasures, Sci & Technol Div, Inst Defense Anal, 90-91. *Concurrent Pos:* Air Force res & develop prog mgr, Advan Res Projs Agency. *Res:* Technologies against low flying, air breathing airborne threats and ground targets intentionally employing deception and denial techniques. *Mailing Add:* Info Systs Off Defense Advan Res Projs Agency 3701 N Fairfax Dr Arlington VA 22203-1714

SWARTZ, WILLIAM EDWARD, JR, SURFACE ANALYSIS, INSTRUMENTAL METHODS. *Current Pos:* MGR, ANALYTICAL SERVS, CONSTELLATION TECHNOL CORP, 96- *Personal Data:* b Braddock, Pa, Aug 16, 44; m 93, Donna Eshom; c Jennifer, Denise, Edward, Deborah & Jeremy. *Educ:* Juniata Col, BS, 66; Mass Inst Technol, PhD(chem), 71. *Prof Exp:* Res assoc chem, Univ Ga, 71, Univ Md, 71-72; asst prof chem, Univ SFla, 72-77, assoc prof, 77-82, prof & dept chmn chem, 82-85; mgr mat & processes, Martin Marietta, 85-90, mgr polymer & ceramics technol, 90-94, prog mgr, Technol Develop Ctr, Gen Elec Neutron Devices, 94-96. *Concurrent Pos:* Adj prof, St Petersburg Jr Col, 94. *Mem:* Am Chem Soc; Am Vacuum Soc; Sigma Xi. *Res:* Analytical applications of surface analysis techniques with emphasis on x-ray photoelectron spectroscopy; heterogeneous catalysts and surface chemical phenomena in integrated circuit components. *Mailing Add:* Constellation Technol Corp PO Box 3687 Seminole FL 33775-3687. *Fax:* 813-545-6043

SWARTZ, WILLIAM JOHN, MATHEMATICS. *Current Pos:* from asst prof to assoc prof, 55-62, prof, 62-84, EMER PROF MATH, MONT STATE UNIV, 84- *Personal Data:* b Portage, Wis, Aug 9, 20; m 48; c 2. *Educ:* Mont State Univ, BS, 44; Mass Inst Technol, SM, 49; Iowa State Univ, PhD(math), 55. *Prof Exp:* Instr math, Mass Inst Technol, 47-48, Mont State Univ, 49-51 & Iowa State Univ, 51-55. *Mem:* Am Math Soc. *Res:* Differential equations. *Mailing Add:* Northern Mont State Univ PO Box 7751 Havre MT 59501

SWARTZENDRUBER, DALE, SOIL PHYSICS, SOIL WATER. *Current Pos:* PROF SOIL PHYSICS, UNIV NEBR-LINCOLN, 77- *Personal Data:* b Parnell, Iowa, July 6, 25; m 49, Kathleen J Yoder; c Karl G, Myra M, John K & David M. *Educ:* Iowa State Univ, BS, 50, MS, 52, PhD(soil physics), 54. *Honors & Awards:* Soil Sci Award, Soil Sci Soc Am, 75. *Prof Exp:* Asst soil physics, Iowa State Univ, 50-53; instr agr, Goshen Col, 53-54; asst soil scientist, Univ Calif, Los Angeles, 55-56; assoc prof, Purdue Univ, 56-63, prof soil physics, 63-77. *Concurrent Pos:* Vis prof, Iowa State Univ, 59, Ga Inst Technol, 68, Hebrew Univ, Jerusalem, Volcani Inst, Rehovot, Israel, 71, Griffith Univ, Brisbane, Australia, 89-90 & Ctr Environ Mech, CSIRO, Canberra, Australia, 90; assoc ed, Soil Sci Soc Am Proc, 65-70; vis scholar, Cambridge Univ, Eng, 71; consult ed, Soil Sci, 76- *Mem:* AAAS; fel Soil Sci Soc Am; fel Am Soc Agron; Am Geophys Union; Int Soc Soil Sci; Sigma Xi. *Res:* Physics of soil and water, including water movement through saturated and unsaturated soils and porous media; soil air, temperature, and structure; soil-water-plant relationships; hydrology and water resources. *Mailing Add:* Dept Agron Keim Hall E Campus Univ Nebr Lincoln NE 68583-0915. *Fax:* 402-472-7904

SWARTZENDRUBER, DOUGLAS EDWARD, PATHOLOGY. *Current Pos:* PROF & CHAIR BIOL, UNIV COLO, COLORADO SPRINGS, 82- *Personal Data:* b Goshen, Ind, May 3, 46; m 69; c 3. *Educ:* Goshen Col, Ind, BA, 68; Univ Colo Med Sch, PhD(exp path), 74. *Prof Exp:* Postdoctoral exp path, Los Alamos Nat Lab, 74-76, st; fac develop therapeut, M D Anderson Hosp & Tumor Inst, 80-82. *Concurrent Pos:* Vpres, Onco Metrics Inc, 88-,. *Mem:* Int Soc Anal Cytol; AAAS; Am Asn Cancer Res. *Res:* Research and clinical applications of flow cytometry; differentiation of neoplastic cells; computer modelling of cancer, especially breast; biocompatibility of dental materials. *Mailing Add:* Dept Biol Univ Colo 1420 Austin Bluffs Pkwy Colorado Springs CO 80918-3733. *E-Mail:* dswartze@mail.uccs.edu

SWARTZENDRUBER, LYDON JAMES, CONDENSED MATTER PHYSICS. *Current Pos:* PHYSICIST, NAT BUR STAND, 60- *Personal Data:* b Wellman, Iowa, Aug 8, 33; m 49; c 1. *Educ:* Iowa State Univ, BS, 57; Univ Md, PhD(physics), 68. *Mem:* AAAS; Am Phys Soc; Am Soc Testing & Mat; Am Inst Mining, Metall & Petrol Engrs; Am Soc Nondestructive Testing; Sigma Xi. *Res:* Solid state physics; semiconductors; magnetism; metallurgy. *Mailing Add:* PO Box 249 Lanham MD 20703-0249

SWARTZENTRUBER, PAUL EDWIN, ORGANIC CHEMISTRY, INFORMATION SCIENCE. *Current Pos:* RETIRED. *Personal Data:* b Lagrange, Ind, Apr 23, 31; m 55; c 3. *Educ:* Goshen Col, BA, 53; Univ Minn, Minneapolis, MS, 55; Univ Mo, PhD(org chem), 61. *Prof Exp:* Res chemist, Nat Cancer Inst, 56-59; asst ed, Org Indexing Dept, Chem Abstr Serv, 61-63, assoc ed, 63-64, head, Org Indexing Dept, 64-71, mgr, Phys & Inorg Indexing Dept, 71-72, mgr, Chem Substance Handling Dept, 72-73, mgr chem technol, 73-77, asst to ed, 77-79, managing ed, 79-94. *Concurrent Pos:* Bd dir, doc abstr, 88-94. *Mem:* AAAS; Am Chem Soc; Am Soc Indexers. *Res:* Synthetic organic chemistry; chemical nomenclature; storage and retrieval of chemical information; abstracting and indexing of chemical literature. *Mailing Add:* 820 Crestway Dr Columbus OH 43235

SWARTZLANDER, EARL EUGENE, JR, COMPUTER DESIGN, COMPUTER ARITHMETIC. *Current Pos:* PROF ELEC & COMPUT ENG, UNIV TEX, AUSTIN, 90-, SCHLUMBERGER CENTENNIAL CHAIR ENG, 90- *Personal Data:* b San Antonio, Tex, Feb 1, 45; m 68, Joan Vickery. *Educ:* Purdue Univ, W Lafayette, Ind, BS, 67; Colo Univ, Boulder, MS, 69; Univ Southern Calif, PhD(elec eng) 72. *Prof Exp:* Develop eng, Ball Brothers Res Corp, 67-69; Hughes doctoral fel, Hughes Aircraft Co, 69-73; mem res staff, Technol Serv Corp, 73-74; chief eng, Geophy Syst Corp, 74-75; staff engr, 75-79 & proj mgr, 79-85; mgr, Digital Processing Lab, TRW Elec Syst Group, 85-87; dir res & develop, TRW Defense Syst Group, 87-90. *Concurrent Pos:* Ed, Trans on Comput, Inst Elec & Electronics Engrs, 82-86, J Solid-State Circuits, 84-88, Trans on Parellel & Distrib Systs, 89-90, ed-in-chief, Trans on Comput, 91-94; mem, Solid State Circuits Coun, Inst Elec & Electronics Engrs, 86-91, Bd Govs, Comput Soc, 87-91, secy, 92-93, treas, 94-; ed, Comput Rev, Asn Comput Mach, 87; ed, J Real-Time Systs, 89-; ed-in-chief, J VLSI Signal Processing, 89-95; mem rev bd, Microelectronic Info Processing Systs, NSF, 91-; ADCOM, Inst Elec & Electronics Engrs, Signal Processing Soc, 92-94; mem, Solid State Circuits Coun, Inst Elec & Electronics Engrs, 86-91, secy, 92-93, treas, 94- *Mem:* fel Inst Elec & Electronics Engrs; Inst Elec & Electronics Engrs Comput Soc. *Res:* VLSI circuit development for high performance computers; chip and processor architecture, computer arithmetic and design methodologies; author of one book, editor of seven books and over 150 articles. *Mailing Add:* Dept Elec & Comput Eng Univ Tex Austin TX 78712

SWARTZMAN, GORDON LENI, RESOURCE MANAGEMENT, BIOMETRICS. *Current Pos:* res assoc statist ecol models, 73-76, res asst prof matrices ecol models, 76-79, res assoc prof calculus population dynamics, 79-84, RES PROF, UNIV WASH, 84- *Personal Data:* b New York, NY, Sept 2, 43; m 69; c 2. *Educ:* Cooper Union, NY, BS, 64; Univ Mich, MS, 65, PhD(indust eng), 69. *Prof Exp:* Fel ecol modeling, Colo State Univ, 69-72; vis prof agr & ecol models, Univ Reading, 72-73. *Mem:* AAAS; Int Soc Ecol Modelers; Sigma Xi. *Res:* Interaction between fur seals and fisheries on Bering Sea; simulation modeling as a tool in impact assessment; stochastic models for fisheries management; Lake Washington rainbow trout introduction impact; microcosm toxicant effects modeling. *Mailing Add:* Sch Fisheries WH-10 Univ Wash 3900 Seventh Ave NE Seattle WA 98195-0001

SWARTZWELDER, JOHN CLYDE, MEDICAL PARASITOLOGY, TROPICAL PUBLIC HEALTH. *Current Pos:* from instr to prof med parasitol, La State Univ Sch Med, 37-75, head dept trop med & med parasitol, 60-75, educ dir, Interam Training Prog Trop Med, 59-69, assoc dir, Int Ctr Med Res & Training, 61-69, dir, Interam Training Prog Trop Med & Int Ctr Med Res & Training, 69-75, EMER PROF MED PARASITOL, LA STATE UNIV MED CTR, NEW ORLEANS, 75- *Personal Data:* b Lynn, Mass, Apr 1, 11; m 64, 88. *Educ:* Univ Mass, BS, 33; Tulane Univ, MS, 34, PhD(med protozool), 37; Am Bd Med Microbiol, dipl, 64. *Prof Exp:* Asst med parasitol, Sch Med, Tulane Univ, 33-37. *Concurrent Pos:* Scientist, Charity Hosp, New Orleans, 38-75; consult, Vet Admin Hosp, 49-90. *Mem:* Am Soc Trop Med & Hyg (vpres); Am Soc Parasitol; hon mem Mex Soc Parasitol. *Res:* Amebiasis; Chagas' disease; anthelmintics; research training in tropical medicine; medical education. *Mailing Add:* 4605 Tartan Rd Metairie LA 70003

SWATEK, FRANK EDWARD, MICROBIOLOGY, MEDICAL & INDUSTRIAL MYCOLOGY. *Current Pos:* CLIN PROF MED, SCH MED, UNIV CALIF, IRVINE, 80- *Personal Data:* b Oklahoma City, Okla, June 4, 29; m 51, Mary F Over; c Frank Jr, Lorraine B (Butcher), Martha L (Bradshaw), Susan A (Denny) & Cheryl L. *Educ:* San Diego State Col, BS, 51; Univ Calif, Los Angeles, MA, 55, PhD(microbiol), 56. *Honors & Awards:* Carski Award, Am Soc Microbiol, 74. *Prof Exp:* From instr to assoc prof microbiol, Calif State Univ, Long Beach, 56-63, chmn dept, 60-82, prof, 63-93. *Concurrent Pos:* Consult, Long Beach Vet Admin Hosp, 56-; dept allergy & dermat, 60-; lectr, Sch Med, Univ Southern Calif, 62-94. *Mem:* Fel Am Soc Microbiol; NY Acad Sci; fel Royal Soc Health; Sigma Xi. *Res:* Ecology and experimental pathology of deep mycoses, especially Coccidioides, Cryptococcus and Dermatophytes; industrial work on fungus deterioration of man-made products; fresh and swimming pool water. *Mailing Add:* 812 Stevely Ave Long Beach CA 90805

SWATHIRAJAN, S, ELECTROCHEMISTRY. *Current Pos:* RES SCIENTIST, GEN MOTORS RES LABS, 83-, SECT MGR, 87- *Personal Data:* b Bangalore, India, June 5, 52; m 80, Hema; c Jayanth. *Educ:* Bangalore Univ, BSc, 70, MSc, 72; Indian Inst Sci, Bangalore, PhD(electrochem), 76. *Prof Exp:* Res fel, Indian Inst Sci, 72-77; lectr chem, State Univ NY, Buffalo, 77-79, res asst prof, 80-83. *Concurrent Pos:* Prog mgr, Gen Motors Res Prog Fuel Cells, US Dept Energy, 94-97. *Mem:* Electrochem Soc. *Res:* Electrochemical phenomena; development of novel materials for electrochemical systems; electrochemical energy conversion in batteries and fuel cells; electrodeposition and corrosion protection; electrochemical sensors. *Mailing Add:* Phys Chem Dept RCEL Gen Motors NAO Res & Develop Ctr Bldg 1-2 Warren MI 48090-9055. *Fax:* 810-986-2244

SWAZEY, JUDITH P, SOCIAL & ETHICAL ISSUES IN SCIENCE & MEDICINE. *Current Pos:* PRES, ACADIA INST, 84- *Personal Data:* b Bronxville, NY, Apr 21, 39; m 64; c 2. *Educ:* Wellesley Col, AB, 61; Harvard Univ, PhD, 66. *Prof Exp:* Res assoc, Harvard Univ, 66-71; consult, Comt Brain Sci, Nat Res Coun, 71-73; staff scientist, Neurosci Res Prog, Mass Inst Technol, 73-74; from assoc prof to prof, Dept Socio-Med Sci & Community, Boston Univ Med Sch & Ch Public Health, 74-82; pres, Col Atlantic, 82-84; exec dir, Med Pub Interest Inc, 79-82 & 89-91. *Concurrent Pos:* Adj prof, Dept Socio-Med Sci & Community Med, Boston Univ, 80- *Mem:* Inst Med-Nat Acad Sci; Sigma Xi; AAAS. *Res:* Social, ethical and policy aspects of graduate and professional education, medical research and health care; professional ethics. *Mailing Add:* Acadia Inst PO Box 43 Bar Harbor ME 04609

SWEADNER, KATHLEEN JOAN, BIOCHEMISTRY, NEUROBIOLOGY. *Current Pos:* ASSOC PROF PHYSIOL, DEPT SURG, HARVARD MED SCH & MASS GEN HOSP, 87- *Personal Data:* b 1949. *Educ:* Univ Calif, Santa Barbara, BA, 71; Harvard Univ, MA, 74, PhD(biochem), 77. *Honors & Awards:* Louis N Katz Prize, 84. *Prof Exp:* Consult, Millipore Corp, 73-76; instr neurobiol, Harvard Med Sch, 80-81, asst prof physiol, Dept Surg, 81-87; asst prof, Dept Durg, Mass Gen Hosp, 81-87. *Concurrent Pos:* Estab investr, Am Heart Asn, 82-87. *Mem:* Soc Neurosci; Am Soc Biochem & Molecular Biol; Protein Soc; Biophys Soc; Am Heart Asn; AAAS. *Res:* Isozymes of the sodium, potassium ATPase. *Mailing Add:* Neurosci Ctr Mass Gen Hosp 149-6118 149 13th St Charlestown MA 02129-2060

SWEARENGEN, JACK CLAYTON, SCIENCE & SOCIETY STUDIES. *Current Pos:* ASSOC PROF MFG ENG & PROG COORDR, WASH STATE UNIV, 97- *Personal Data:* b Zanesville, Ohio, Feb 11, 40; m 62; c Peter. *Educ:* Univ Idaho, BS, 61; Univ Ariz, MS, 63; Univ Wash, PhD(mech eng), 70. *Honors & Awards:* Secy Defense Award Excellence, 90. *Prof Exp:* Electromech develop engr, FMC Corp, Santa Clara, Calif, 63-66; mem tech staff, Sandia Nat Labs, 70-78, supvr, Mat Sci Div, 78-84, Solar Components Div, 84-86, Advan Systs Div, 86-88, supvr, systs develop div, 91-92, mgr technol, appln dept, 92-96. *Concurrent Pos:* Reviewer, NSF, 78-88, J Mat Energy Systs, 78-86 & Solar Energy Mat; prin investr, US Dept Energy, 79-83, US Navy, 86-87; teaching assoc, Univ Wash, 66-69; mem, Pres Young Investr Awards Panel, NSF, 88; Sci adv arms control, Off Secy Defense, Pentagon, Wash, DC, 88-90; off technol assessment workshop, disposal chem weapons, 92. *Mem:* Fel Am Sci Affil; Am Soc Mech Engrs; Am Defense Preparedness Asn; Soc Mfg Engrs. *Res:* Structure-property relationships in metals, ceramics and glass-ceramics; energy systems; weapons demilitarization and disposal; life cycle design, materials in manufacturing. *Mailing Add:* Wash State Univ Vancouver WA 98686-9600. *E-Mail:* swearjc@vancouver.wsu.edu

SWEARINGEN, JOHN ELDRED, CHEMICAL ENGINEERING. *Current Pos:* RETIRED. *Personal Data:* b Columbia, SC, Sept 7, 18; m 69; c 3. *Educ:* Univ SC, BS, 38; Carnegie Inst Technol, MS, 39. *Hon Degrees:* EngD, SDak Sch Mines & Technol, 60; LLD, Knox Col, Ill, 62, DePauw Univ, 64, Univ SC, 65, Ill Col & Butler Univ, 68; DLH, Nat Col Educ, 67. *Prof Exp:* Chemist, Stand Oil Co, 39-43, group leader, 43-47; proj engr, Pan Am Petrol Corp, 47, develop supt mfg, 47-48, asst to mgr mfg, 48-49, exec asst to exec vpres, 51; gen mgr prod, Stand Oil Co (Ind), 51-54, vpres prod, 54-56, exec vpres, 56-58, pres, 58-65, chmn bd, 65-83, dir, 52-83, chief exec off, 60-83; chmn bd & exec officer, Continental Ill Corp, 83-87. *Concurrent Pos:* Dir, Am Petrol Inst, 51-, chmn bd, 78-79; consult, Nat Petrol Coun & Nat Indust Conf Bd, 60-; consult, Hwy Users Fedn for Safety & Mobility, 69-; chmn, Nat Petrol Coun, 74-75; dir, Lockheed Corp & Aon Corp. *Mem:* Nat Acad Eng; fel Am Inst Chem Engrs; Am Chem Soc; Am Inst Mining, Metall & Petrol Engrs. *Res:* Petroleum production and processing; management. *Mailing Add:* Amoco Bldg Suite 7906 Stand Oil Co 200 E Randolf Dr Chicago IL 60601. *Fax:* 312-616-0930

SWEARINGEN, JUDSON STERLING, CHEMICAL ENGINEERING. *Current Pos:* RETIRED. *Personal Data:* b San Antonio, Tex, Jan 11, 07; m 60. *Educ:* Univ Tex, BS, 29, MS, 30, PhD(chem eng), 33. *Prof Exp:* Partner, San Antonio Refining Co, 33-38; from asst prof to prof chem eng, Univ Tex, 39-42; turbine designer, Elliott Co, 42-43; div engr, Kellex Corp, 43-45; pres, Statham-Swearingen, Inc, 59-62 & Swearingen Bros, Inc, 64-81; pres, Rotoflow Corp, 46-90, Rotoflow, Ag, Switz, 71-90, adv consult, 90-93. *Mem:* Nat Acad Eng; Am Chem Soc; Am Inst Mech Engrs; Am Soc Testing & Mat. *Res:* Low temperature gas separations; turboexpanders; petroleum and gas; seals, pumps and centrifugal compressors; adsorption refrigeration. *Mailing Add:* 3767 Forest Lane Dallas TX 75244

SWEARINGIN, MARVIN LAVERNE, AGRONOMY, SOYBEAN PRODUCTION. *Current Pos:* from asst prof to assoc prof, 61-75, PROF AGRON, PURDUE UNIV, WEST LAFAYETTE, 75- *Personal Data:* b Hamburg, Ill, Jan 23, 31; m 50; c 3. *Educ:* Univ Mo-Columbia, BS, 56, MS, 57; Ore State Univ, PhD(agron), 62. *Honors & Awards:* Soybean Researchers Recog Award, Am Soybean Asn, 83; Super Serv Award, USDA, 89. *Prof Exp:* Asst crops teaching, Univ Mo, 56-57; instr farm crops, Ore State Univ, 57-61. *Concurrent Pos:* Soybean res consult, Purdue Univ-Brazil Proj, Brazil, 67-69 & AID, Brazil, 71- *Mem:* Fel Am Soc Agron, 89; Crop Sci Soc Am. *Res:* Crop management systems for corn, soybeans and small grains; reduced tillage system for soybean production; weed control in soybeans. *Mailing Add:* 245 Timbercrest Rd West Lafayette IN 47906

SWEAT, FLOYD WALTER, BIOCHEMISTRY. *Current Pos:* asst prof, 70-77, ASSOC PROF BIOCHEM, UNIV UTAH, 77- *Personal Data:* b Salt Lake City, Utah, July 21, 41; m 65; c 2. *Educ:* Univ Utah, BS, 64, PhD(org chem), 68. *Prof Exp:* NIH fel, Harvard Univ, 68-70. *Mem:* Am Chem Soc; Sigma Xi. *Res:* Enzyme purification and characterization; structure elucidation; reaction mechanisms. *Mailing Add:* Dept Biochem Univ Utah Sch Med 50 N Medical Dr Salt Lake City UT 84132-0001

SWEAT, ROBERT LEE, VETERINARY MEDICINE, VIROLOGY. *Current Pos:* CONSULT, 95- *Personal Data:* b Lamar, Colo, June 8, 31; m 53, Barbara J Shaffer; c Michael J & Deborah L. *Educ:* Colo State Univ, BS, 54, DVM, 56; Univ Nebr-Lincoln, MS, 62, PhD(med sci), 66. *Prof Exp:* Instr vet sci, Univ Nebr-Lincoln, 58-66, assoc prof, 66; vet virologist, Norden Labs, Inc, Nebr, 67; assoc res prof vet sci, Univ Idaho, 68-70; vet virologist, Ft Dodge Labs Inc, 70-88; res scientist, Land O'Lakes, Inc, 89-95. *Concurrent Pos:* Vet rep, Nebr State Bd Health, 66-67. *Mem:* Am Vet Med Asn; US Animal Health Asn; Conf Res Workers Animal Dis; Am Asn Bovine Practrs. *Res:* Veterinary science with emphasis on diseases of cattle. *Mailing Add:* 1313 Alford St Ft Collins CO 80524-4217

SWEAT, VINCENT EUGENE, FOOD ENGINEERING. *Current Pos:* ASSOC PROF FOOD ENG, TEX A&M UNIV, 77- *Personal Data:* b Kirwin, Kans, July 28, 41; m 65; c 2. *Educ:* Kans State Univ, BS, 64; Okla State Univ, MS, 65; Purdue Univ, PhD(agr eng), 72. *Prof Exp:* Asst prof food eng, Purdue Univ, 71-75, assoc prof, 75-77. *Concurrent Pos:* Mem thermal properties foods comt, Am Soc Heating, Refrig & Air Conditioning Engrs, 72-; assoc ed food eng div, Am Soc Agr Engrs, 76-; NSF eng res equip grant, 78- *Mem:* Am Soc Agr Engrs; Inst Food Technologists; Am Soc Eng Educ. *Res:* Measurement and modeling of thermal properties of foods; food processing; heat and mass transfer in foods; energy utilization in food processing. *Mailing Add:* Agr Eng Dept Tex A&M Univ College Station TX 77843-0100

SWEDBERG, KENNETH C, PLANT ECOLOGY. *Current Pos:* assoc prof, 62-69, PROF BIOL, EASTERN WASH UNIV, 69- *Personal Data:* b Brainerd, Minn, Apr 14, 30; m 58; c 2. *Educ:* St Cloud State Col, BS, 52; Univ Minn, MS, 56; Ore State Univ, PhD(plant ecol), 61. *Prof Exp:* Instr biol, Moorhead State Col, 56-58; asst prof, Wis State Univ-Stevens Point, 60-62. *Mem:* AAAS; Ecol Soc Am; Weed Sci Soc Am; Am Inst Biol Sci; Sigma Xi. *Res:* Plant synecology and autecology; experimental ecology of annual plants. *Mailing Add:* S-19607 Cheney-Spangle Rd Cheney WA 99004

SWEDLOW, JEROLD LINDSAY, SOLID MECHANICS, STRUCTURAL INTEGRITY. *Current Pos:* from asst prof to assoc prof mech eng, 66-73, assoc dean eng, 77-79, PROF MECH ENG, CARNEGIE-MELLON UNIV, 73- *Personal Data:* b Denver, Colo, Aug 31, 35; m 59; c 3. *Educ:* Calif Inst Technol, BS, 57; Stanford Univ, MS, 60; Calif Inst Technol, PhD(aeronaut), 65. *Honors & Awards:* Philip M McKenna Mem Award, 78; Ralph Coats Roe Award, 81. *Prof Exp:* Res engr rock mech, Ingersoll-Rand Co, 57-59; res fel aeronaut, Calif Inst Technol, 65-66. *Concurrent Pos:* Ed, Reports Current Res, Int J Fracture, 69-; sr vis fel, Imp Col Sci & Technol, 73-74. *Mem:* Am Acad Mech; Am Soc Mech Engrs; Am Soc Testing & Mat; Int Cong Fracture. *Res:* Plasticity of metal via computational procedures; applications to fracture-related problems at both the macro and microscale. *Mailing Add:* 223 Parnassus Ave San Francisco CA 94117

SWEDLUND, ALAN CHARLES, BIOLOGICAL ANTHROPOLOGY. *Current Pos:* vis assoc prof, Univ Mass, Amherst, 74-77, field dir, Europ Studies Prog, 81-82, assoc prof, 77-85, chair, 90-95, PROF ANTHROP, UNIV MASS, AMHERST, 85- *Personal Data:* b Sacramento, Calif, Jan 21, 43; m 66; c 2. *Educ:* Univ Colo, Ba, 66, MA, 68, PhD(anthrop), 70. *Prof Exp:* Asst prof anthrop, Prescott Col, 70-74. *Concurrent Pos:* Vis researcher, Biol Anthrop Prog, Oxford Univ, 82; vis prof anthrop, Univ Rome, 92; Weatherhead scholar, Sch Am Res, Santa Fe, NMex, 95-96. *Mem:* AAAS; Am Asn Phys Anthrop; Am Anthrop Asn; Soc Sci Hist Asn; Population Asn Am; Sigma Xi. *Res:* Demographic and medical anthropology; historical demography and paleodemography; osteology. *Mailing Add:* Dept Anthrop Univ Mass Amherst MA 01003

SWEED, NORMAN HARRIS, CHEMICAL ENGINEERING. *Current Pos:* eng assoc, 81-86, SECT HEAD, EXXON RES & ENG CO, 86- *Personal Data:* b Philadelphia, Pa, Apr 11, 43; m 66; c 2. *Educ:* Drexel Univ, BSChE, 65; Princeton Univ, MA, 67, PhD(chem eng), 68. *Prof Exp:* Asst prof chem eng, Princeton Univ, 68-75; sr res engr, Exxon Res & Eng Co, 74-78; mgr process res, Oxirane Int, 78-81. *Concurrent Pos:* Consult, Engelhard Indust, 69-74 & Cities Serv Res, 74. *Mem:* Am Inst Chem Engrs; AAAS; Am Chem Soc. *Res:* Octane processes (catalytic naphtha reforming, alkylation) and thermal conversion processes (coking, residuum upgrading). *Mailing Add:* 15 Branko Rd Berkeley Heights NJ 07922

SWEEDLER, ALAN R, PHOTOVOLTAICS, ENERGY POLICY. *Current Pos:* assoc prof, 80-83, PROF PHYSICS, SAN DIEGO STATE UNIV, 83-, DIR, CTR ENERGY STUDIES, 81- *Personal Data:* b New York, NY, Jan 31, 42. *Educ:* City Univ New York, BSc, 63; Univ Calif, San Diego, PhD(physics), 69. *Prof Exp:* Prof physics, Univ Chile, Santiago, 70-72; res physicist mat sci, Brookhaven Nat Lab, 72-77; assoc prof, dept physics, Calif State Univ Fullerton, 77-80. *Concurrent Pos:* Vis assoc prof physics, Univ Southern Calif, Los Angeles, 75; cong sci fel, Am Phys Soc, 85; sci fel, Int Security, Stanford Univ, 87; co-dir, Inst Int Security & Conflict Resolution, 88- *Mem:* Am Phys Soc; AAAS; Sigma Xi. *Res:* Superconductivity; high transition temperature compounds; irradiation effects in superconducting compounds; metallurgy of superconducting materials; solar energy; photovoltaics; energy policy; international security and arms control; international security arms control. *Mailing Add:* Dept Physics San Diego State Univ San Diego CA 92182

SWEELEY, CHARLES CRAWFORD, BIOCHEMISTRY, ORGANIC CHEMISTRY. *Current Pos:* RETIRED. *Personal Data:* b Williamsport, Pa, Apr 15, 30; m 50, Marilyn Border; c Suzanne L & C Christopher. *Educ:* Univ Pa, BS, 52; Univ Ill, PhD(chem), 55. *Hon Degrees:* Dr, Ghent Univ, Belg, 82. *Prof Exp:* Chemist, Nat Heart Inst, 55-60; asst res prof biochem, Univ Pittsburgh, 60-63, from assoc prof to prof, 63-68, prof, Mich State Univ, 68-85, chmn, 79-85, univ distinguished prof, 89-92. *Concurrent Pos:* Mem comt probs lipid anal, Nat Heart Inst, 58-59; consult, LKB Instruments, 65-71, Med Chem Study Sect, USPHS, 67-71 & Upjohn Co, 68-72; Guggenheim fel, Royal Vet Col, Stockholm, Sweden, 71; vis prof, Ctr Cancer Res, Cambridge, 79; consult, Upjohn, 68-72 & 86-89, Los Alamos Stable Isotope Resource, 88-91; consult & sr dir, Meridian Instruments, 82- *Mem:* Am Chem Soc; Am Soc Biol Chem; Brit Biochem Soc; Soc Complex Carbohydrates (treas, 75-78, pres, 85); Am Soc Mass Spectrometry. *Res:* Chemistry and metabolism of sphingolipids; sphingolipidoses; biochemistry of lysosomal hydrolases; analytical biochemistry; computer applications in gas chromatography and mass spectrometry; biochemistry of complex lipids and hormones of invertebrates. *Mailing Add:* 1895 Live Oak Trail Williamston MI 48895

SWEENEY, DARYL CHARLES, INVERTEBRATE PHYSIOLOGY, NEUROCHEMISTRY. *Current Pos:* from asst prof to assoc prof zool, 65-75, ASSOC PROF PHYSIOL, UNIV ILL, URBANA-CHAMPAIGN, 75- *Personal Data:* b Oakland, Calif, Jan 21, 36; m 59; c 1. *Educ:* Univ Calif, Berkeley, AB, 58; Harvard Univ, AM, 59, PhD(biol), 63. *Prof Exp:* Instr biol, Yale Univ, 63-65. *Concurrent Pos:* Consult, Nat Inst Neurol Dis & Stoke, 66-69. *Mem:* Am Soc Zool. *Res:* Neurochemistry and the behavior of invertebrate physiology. *Mailing Add:* 1101 S Westlawn Champaign IL 61821

SWEENEY, EDWARD ARTHUR, PEDIATRIC DENTISTRY, DENTAL RESEARCH. *Current Pos:* CLIN PROF PEDIAT DENT, UNIV TEX HEALTH SCI CTR, 87- *Personal Data:* b Boston, Mass, Apr 22, 31; m 66; c 2. *Educ:* Harvard Univ, DMD, 61, cert, 64; Children's Hosp Med Ctr, Boston, cert, 64. *Prof Exp:* Fel dent, Inst Nutrit Cent Am & Panama, 63 & 67; fel protein chem, Protein Found, 64-65; assoc dent, Harvard Sch Dent Med, 64-66, from asst prof to assoc prof pediat dent, 66-81, asst dean curric, 77-80; clin assoc prof pediat dent, Univ Pa, 81-87; dir advan educ dent, 82-87. *Concurrent Pos:* Consult, Robert Wood Johnson Found & Educ Testing Serv, 73-79, Nat Inst Med, Nat Acad Sci, 77-78 & Mass Dept Pub Health, 79-81; counr, Int Asn Dent Res, 77-80. *Mem:* AAAS; Int Asn Dent Res; Am Dent Asn; Am Acad Pediat Dent; Am Asn Dent Schs. *Res:* Protein secretion of salivary gland; nutrition and dental decay and enamel hypoplasia; oral pathology of children. *Mailing Add:* Univ Tex Sch Med 7703 Floyd Curl Dr San Antonio TX 78284-6200

SWEENEY, GEORGE DOUGLAS, PHARMACOLOGY, LIVER TOXICOLOGY. *Current Pos:* assoc prof med, 69-81, PROF MED, MCMASTER UNIV, 81- *Personal Data:* b Durban, SAfrica, Dec 21, 34; m 60; c 3. *Educ:* Univ Cape Town, MB, ChB, 58, PhD(biochem), 63. *Prof Exp:* Sr lectr physiol, Univ Cape Town, 64-68; Ont fel, Col Physicians & Surgeons, Columbia Univ, 68-69. *Concurrent Pos:* Vis prof, Liver Unit, King's Col Hosp, 79-80. *Mem:* Can Soc Toxicol; Pharmacol Soc Can; Can Physiol Soc; Am Soc Pharmacol & Exp Therapeut. *Res:* Hemoprotein synthesis and regulation; porphyrin metabolism; liver toxicity of halo-aromatic hydrocarbons; liver cell life cycle; porphyria. *Mailing Add:* Dept Med McMaster Univ Health Sci Ctr Rm 4W8F Hamilton ON L8S 3Z5 Can. *E-Mail:* sweeney@mcmaster.ca

SWEENEY, JAMES LEE, ECONOMIC ANALYSIS, ENERGY ANALYSIS. *Current Pos:* res asst, Dept Eng Econ Systs, Stanford Univ, 67-70, actg instr, 70-71, from asst prof to assoc prof, 71-80, coop prof, Sch Law, 81-82, chmn, Inst Energy Studies, 81-85, dir, Ctr Econ Policy Res, 84-86, AFFIL PROF, DEPT ECON, STANFORD UNIV, 78-, PROF, DEPT ENG ECON SYSTS, 80-, CHMN, ENG ECON SYSTS, 91- *Personal Data:* b Waterbury, Conn, Mar 22, 44; m 71; c 3. *Educ:* Mass Inst Technol, BS, 66; Stanford Univ, PhD(eng econ systs), 71. *Prof Exp:* Consult, Fed Energy Admin, Washington, DC, 74, dir, Off Energy Systs, 74-75, Off Quant Methods, 75 & Off Energy Systs Modeling & Forecasting, 75-76. *Concurrent Pos:* Co-ed, Resources & Energy; mem, sr adv panel, Energy Modeling Forum; consult, Charles River Assocs, Cornerstone Res. *Mem:* Am Econ Asn; Int Asn Energy Economists. *Res:* Economic and policy issues important for natural resource management and use; energy markets, including oil, natural gas and electricity; use of mathematical models to analyze energy markets. *Mailing Add:* Eng Econ Syst & Oper Res Stanford Univ Terman 306 Stanford CA 94305-4023

SWEENEY, JOHN ROBERT, WILDLIFE BIOLOGY. *Current Pos:* Asst prof, Dept Entom & Econ Zool, 75-80, ASSOC PROF, DEPT FISH & WILDLIFE, CLEMSON UNIV, 80- *Personal Data:* b Wichita, Kans, Dec 31, 45. *Educ:* Univ Ga, BSF, 67, MS, 71; Colo State Univ, PhD(wildlife biol), 75. *Concurrent Pos:* Assoc ed, Southeastern Proceedings. *Mem:* Wildlife Soc. *Res:* Effects of forest management on wildlife populations; natural history and management of feral swine; natural history and population dynamics of bobat and gray fox; annual ethograms of eastern bluebird. *Mailing Add:* Dept Aquacult, Fisheries & Wildlife Clemson Univ G08A Lehotsky Hall Clemson SC 29634

SWEENEY, LAWRENCE EARL, JR, ELECTRICAL ENGINEERING. *Current Pos:* VPRES GOVT PROG, ETAK INC, 92- *Personal Data:* b Charleston, WVa, Mar 27, 42; m 69; c 2. *Educ:* Stanford Univ, BS, 64, MS, 66, PhD(elec eng), 70. *Prof Exp:* Res assoc radio sci, Stanford Univ, 70; asst dir, Ionospheric Dynamics Lab, SRI Int, 70-72, dir, Remote Measurements Lab, 72-85, vpres & dir, Syst Technol Div, 85-89. *Concurrent Pos:* Instr, Stanford Univ, 68-69, lectr, 70-71. *Mem:* Inst Elec & Electronics Engrs; Int Union Radio Sci. *Res:* Ionospheric radio propagation; high frequency signal processing; large antenna arrays; digital signal processing; remote sensing; high frequency radar; radar target scattering characteristics. *Mailing Add:* ETAK Inc 1430 O'Brien Dr Menlo Park CA 94025

SWEENEY, MARY ANN, PLASMA PHYSICS, ASTROPHYSICS. *Current Pos:* fel plasma physics & fusion res, 74-76, staff mem, 76-89, SR STAFF MEM, SANDIA NAT LAB, 89- *Personal Data:* b Hagerstown, Md, Sept 25, 45; m 74, Edward R Ricco; c Alanna C & Susanna M. *Educ:* Mt Holyoke Col, BA, 67; Columbia Univ, MPhil, 73, PhD(astron), 74. *Prof Exp:* Instr astron, Fairleigh Dickinson Univ & William Paterson Col NJ, 72-73. *Concurrent Pos:* Pub speaker; vchmn, Plasma Sci & Applications Comt, Inst Elec & Electronic Engrs, 84, chmn, 89-91, mem, 82-84 & 87-92, Admin Comt, 85-92, mem, Educ & Continued Prof Develop Comt, 85-, secy, Nuclear & Plasma Sci Soc, 87-89, vpres, 88, chmn, Subcomt Fusion Policy, 91-92, chmn, Subcomt Const & Bylaws, 93-94, chmn, nominating Comt, 91-92; chmn, Pub Info Comt, Trinity Sect, Am Nuclear Soc, 86-87; mem, Sci Ctr Comt, NMex Acad Sci, 86-88, vpres, 92, pres-elect, 93, Planning Comt, Explor Sci Ctr, 93; mem, Prog Comt, Int Conf Plasma Sci, Inst Elec & Electronics Engrs, 87,92 & 93, Local Orgn Comt, 94; mem, Prog Comt Plasma Physics, Am Phys Soc, 90, 94, mem, Exec Comt, 91, subcomt chmn, Plasma Conf, 91, secy-treas, 93-, Site Selection Comt, 93-; mem, Prog Comt, Third Int Sch Plasma Physics & Controlled Fusion, 92-93. *Mem:* Am Astron Soc; Am Phys Soc; Am Nuclear Soc; fel Inst Elec & Electronics Engrs; AAAS; Sigma Xi. *Res:* Chief theorist for plasma opening switch research; responsible for monitoring research by contractors and organizing workshops; modeling particle beam fusion target experiments; designing targets and reactor chambers for particle beam fusion; determining radiation environment in accelerators, and evaluating effects of electron and photon bombardment on dielectrics; evaluating effects of ion beams on diagnostics; interested in promoting scientific careers and improving quality of science education; editor of technical reports in inertial confinement fusion progam; theory subtask leader for accelerator beam coupling; enetrimarking of intense soft x-ray applications. *Mailing Add:* Sandia Nat Lab Mail Stop 1186 PO Box 5800 Albuquerque NM 87185. *Fax:* 505-845-7890; *E-Mail:* masween@somnet.sandia.gov

SWEENEY, MICHAEL ANTHONY, PHYSICAL CHEMISTRY. *Current Pos:* asst prof, 66-72, ASSOC PROF CHEM, UNIV SANTA CLARA, 72- *Personal Data:* b Los Angeles, Calif, Dec 5, 31; c 3. *Educ:* Loyola Univ, Calif, BS, 53; Univ Calif, Berkeley, MS, 55, PhD(chem), 62. *Prof Exp:* Res chemist, Chevron Res Co, 61-66. *Concurrent Pos:* Vis asst prof, Indiana Univ, 65; instr, Univ Exten, Univ Calif, Berkeley, 65-66; consult, USPHS, 68-71; vis res chemist, UK Atomic Energy Res Estab, Harwell, 72-73, Inst Bioorg Chem, Barcelona, Spain, 79. *Mem:* Am Chem Soc. *Res:* Radiation chemistry; chemical evolution. *Mailing Add:* Dept Chem Daly Sci Bldg Santa Clara Univ 500 El Camino Real Santa Clara CA 95053-0001

SWEENEY, MICHAEL JOSEPH, IMMUNOLOGY, IMMUNOCHEMISTRY. *Current Pos:* assoc prof biol sci, 77-82, prof clin lab sci, 82-86, PROF MOLECULAR & MICROBIOL, UNIV CENT FLA, 86-, PROF & CHAIR, DEPT HEALTH SCI, 92- *Personal Data:* b Philadelphia, Pa, Jan 31, 39; m 62, Geraldine A Arnaudo; c Michael, Linda & Jennifer. *Educ:* Philadelphia Col Pharm & Sci, BSc, 66, BSc, 67; Temple Univ, PhD(microbiol, immunol), 71. *Prof Exp:* Fel immunol, Sch Med, Temple Univ, 71-72; asst prof immunol, Fla Technol Univ, 71-77. *Concurrent Pos:* Fel immunol, Sch Med, Temple Univ, 71-72. *Mem:* Am Soc Microbiol; Sigma Xi. *Res:* Studies of T and B cell populations in peripheral blood of immunosuppressed patients; characterization of antigens; purification and standardization of allergens. *Mailing Add:* Dept Health Sci Univ Cent Fla Box 25000 Orlando FL 32816-0001. *Fax:* 407-823-6138; *E-Mail:* msweeney@pegasus.cc.ucf.edu

SWEENEY, ROBERT ANDERSON, PHYCOLOGY, LIMNOLOGY. *Current Pos:* DIR SPEC PROJS, ECOL & ENVIRON INC, 81-; PRES, R A SWEENEY & ASSOC. *Personal Data:* b Freeport, NY, Oct 11, 40; m 63, 79, Phyllis Lindsey; c Erica, David, Meghan & Kristin. *Educ:* State Univ Col Albany, BS, 62; Ohio State Univ, MS, 64, PhD(water resources), 66. *Honors & Awards:* Anderson-Everett Award, Int Asn Great Lakes Res, 82. *Prof Exp:* From asst prof to prof biol, State Univ NY Col Buffalo, 66-81, dir, Great Lakes Lab, 67-81. *Concurrent Pos:* Consult, NY State Dept Environ Conserv, 70-; consult, US Army Corps Engrs, 71-, mem, Shoreline Erosion Adv Panel, 74-86; adj prof biol, State Univ NY Col Buffalo, 81-; Niagara Univ, 97- *Mem:* AAAS; Int Asn Great Lakes Res (pres, 80); Phycol Soc Am; Am Inst Biol Sci; Am Soc Limnol & Oceanog. *Res:* Evaluation and solution of water pollution and eutrophication problems in the Great Lakes and their tributaries; dredging; public water supplies. *Mailing Add:* R A Sweeney & Assoc 52 Schwartz Rd Elma NY 14059-9730. *Fax:* 716-686-0664; *E-Mail:* lakeerie@aol.com

SWEENEY, THOMAS FRANCIS, PROBABILITY. *Current Pos:* ASSOC PROF MATH, RUSSELL SAGE COL, 78-, CHAIR MATH & COMPUT SCI, 90- *Personal Data:* m 74, Helen Betzios; c Thomas F. *Educ:* Fairfield, Univ, BS, 71; St Louis Univ, MS, 76, PhD(math), 78; Rensselaer Polytech Inst, MS, 85. *Mem:* Math Asn Am; Nat Coun Teachers Math; Asn Comput Mach. *Res:* Probability, geometry, discrete mathematics, and theory of computation; applying technology to teaching and learning. *Mailing Add:* 19 Eastover Rd Troy NY 12180-7124

SWEENEY, THOMAS L(EONARD), CHEMICAL ENGINEERING, RESEARCH ADMINISTRATION. *Current Pos:* ASST VPRES & DIR, OFF RES, UNIV NOTRE DAME, 94- *Personal Data:* b Cleveland, Ohio, Dec 12, 36; m 61, Beverly Starks; c 4. *Educ:* Case Inst Technol, BS, 58, MS, 60, PhD(chem eng), 62; Capital Univ, JD, 74. *Prof Exp:* Tech specialist, Stand Oil Co, Ohio, 62-63; from asst prof to prof chem eng, Ohio State Univ, 63-94, actg assoc vpres res, 82-94, exec dir, res found, 88-94, actg vpres res, 89-91, assoc vpres & emer prof, 94. *Concurrent Pos:* Consult. *Mem:* Am Inst Chem Engrs. *Res:* Air pollution; heat and mass transfer; chemical technology; occupational safety and health; environmental science and technology; regulation of technology; legal aspects of engineering. *Mailing Add:* 312 Main Bldg Univ Notre Dame Notre Dame IN 46556-5601. *E-Mail:* tsweeney@nd.edu

SWEENEY, THOMAS PATRICK, REMOVABLE PROSTHODONTICS, COMBAT DENTISTRY. *Current Pos:* RETIRED. *Personal Data:* b Milwaukee, Wis, Aug 27, 29; c 2. *Educ:* Univ Wis, BS, 51; Marquette Univ, DDS, 55; Brook Gen Hosp, Ft Sam Houston, Tex, MS, 67; Am Bd Prosthodontics, dipl, 70. *Prof Exp:* Pvt pract, Milwaukee, Wis, 57-60; chief prosthodontics, US Army Dent Activ, Ft Knox, Ky, 67-70; consult removable prosthodontics, US Army, Europe, 70-73; clin instr, Sch Dent, Tufts Univ, Boston, 73-77; comdr & dir dent educ, Walson Army Hosp, Ft Dix, NJ, 77-78; comdr & dir dent serv, US Army Dent Activ, Hawaii, 78-80; comdr & dir dent educ, US Army Med Ctr, Washington, DC, 80-85; dep chief res progs, US Army Med Res & Develop Command, Ft Detrick, Md, 85-88. *Concurrent Pos:* Consult removable prosthodontics, First US Army, Ft Knox, Ky, 67-70; clin instr removable prosthodontics, Sch Dent, Univ Louisville, 68-70; guest lectr removable prosthodontics, Walter Reed Army Med Ctr, 76-78; chmn res comt, Am Col Prosthodontists, 80-84. *Mem:* Fel Am Col Prosthodontists; fel Int Col Dentists; Int Asn Dent Res; Am Dent Asn. *Res:* Removable prosthodontics; combat dentistry (maxillofacial injuries). *Mailing Add:* 1015 Spanish River Rd No 307 Boca Raton FL 37432

SWEENEY, THOMAS RICHARD, MEDICINAL CHEMISTRY. *Current Pos:* RETIRED. *Personal Data:* b Albany, NY, Sept 21, 14; wid; c Thomas R Jr & Laurel G. *Educ:* Univ Md, BS, 37, PhD(org chem), 45. *Prof Exp:* Chemist, Briggs Filtration Co, DC, 40-41; chemist, NIH, Md, 41-47; res chemist, Univ Md, 47-50, US Naval Res Lab, 50-59; chemist, Walter Reed Army Inst Res, 59-64, chief, Dept Org Chem, 64-69, dep dir, Div Med Chem, 69-78, dep dir, Div Exp Therapeut, 78-80; consult, 80-94. *Concurrent Pos:* US Army med res & develop command rep, Med Chem Study Sect A, NIH, 65-75; US deleg NATO Army Armaments Group, Nuclear Biol Chem Defense Panel, Group Experts Chemoprophy Laxis, 75-80; consult, Nat Cancer Inst, 75-83; adv & mem sci & tech rev comt, WHO, 81-84; mem adv comt med chem, US Army med Res & Develop Command, 82-85, chmn, 84 & 85. *Mem:* Am Chem Soc; Sigma Xi. *Res:* Antiradiation and antiparasific agents. *Mailing Add:* 1701 N Kent St Apt 801 Arlington VA 22209

SWEENEY, WILLIAM ALAN, PETROCHEMICALS. *Current Pos:* RETIRED. *Personal Data:* b Can, Sept 12, 26; nat US; m 53, Sally L Grant; c Michael A, Peter G & Alison E. *Educ:* Univ BC, BASc, 49; Univ Wash, Seattle, PhD, 54. *Prof Exp:* Chemist, Can Indusrts, Ltd, 49-50; asst to vpres, Chevron Res Co, 75-76; res scientist, Chevron Res & Technol Co, Chevron Corp, Calif, 54-90. *Concurrent Pos:* Consult, Dept Energy, 90. *Mem:* Am Chem Soc; Sigma Xi; NY Acad Sci. *Res:* Petrochemicals exploratory, process and product development, and plant support emphasizing practicality and economics; effect of chemical structure on surfactant performance, biodegradability and paper sizing; alpha olefin processing and applications; synlubes, gasoline oxygenates. *Mailing Add:* 27 Corte del Bayo Larkspur CA 94939

SWEENEY, WILLIAM JOHN, MATHEMATICS. *Current Pos:* ASSOC PROF MATH, RUTGERS UNIV, NEW BRUNSWICK, 71- *Personal Data:* b Oak Park, Ill, July 15, 40; m 64. *Educ:* Univ Notre Dame, AB, 62; Stanford Univ, MS, 64, PhD(math), 66. *Prof Exp:* Instr math, Stanford Univ, 66-67; asst prof, Princeton Univ, 67-71. *Mem:* Math Asn Am; Am Math Soc. *Res:* Over-determined systems of linear partial differential equations. *Mailing Add:* Dept Math Rutgers Univ New Brunswick NJ 08903-2101

SWEENEY, WILLIAM VICTOR, BIOPHYSICS. *Current Pos:* from asst prof to assoc prof, 75-91, PROF CHEM, HUNTER COL, CITY UNIV NEW YORK, 92- *Personal Data:* b Cleveland, Ohio, Jan 31, 47; m 68; c 1. *Educ:* Knox Col, BA, 68; Univ Iowa, MS, 70, PhD(chem), 73. *Prof Exp:* NIH fel biochem, Univ Calif, Berkeley, 73-75. *Concurrent Pos:* chmn, Dept Chem, Hunter Col, City Univ NY, 88- *Mem:* Am Chem Soc. *Res:* Physical properties of iron-sulfur proteins; nuclear magnetic resonance; epidermal growth factor-like domains; blood clotting proteins. *Mailing Add:* Dept of Chem City Univ NY Hunter Col 695 Park Ave New York NY 10021-5024. *E-Mail:* wvshc@cunyum.bitnet

SWEENY, DANIEL MICHAEL, INORGANIC CHEMISTRY. *Current Pos:* PROF INORG CHEM, BELLARMINE COL, KY, 57- *Personal Data:* b Rockville Center, NY, Sept 25, 30; m 60; c 5. *Educ:* Col Holy Cross, BSc, 52; Univ Notre Dame, PhD(chem), 55. *Prof Exp:* Res chemist, E I du Pont de Nemours & Co, 55-57. *Mem:* Am Chem Soc; Mineral Soc Am; Soc Appl Spectros. *Res:* Physical properties and synthesis of coordination compounds; infrared spectroscopy; structural inorganic chemistry; interpretive spectroscopy. *Mailing Add:* 9604 Gateway Dr Jeffersontown KY 40299-2648

SWEENY, HALE CATERSON, MATHEMATICAL STATISTICS. *Current Pos:* CONSULT STATISTICIAN, 90- *Personal Data:* b Anderson, SC, Mar 31, 25; m 48, Anne K; c William S, Sandra L & Brian T. *Educ:* Clemson Col, BME, 49; Va Polytech Inst, MS, 52, PhD, 56. *Prof Exp:* Design engr, Hunt Mach Works, 49-50; indust engr, Eastman Kodak Co, 51-52; instr indust eng, Va Polytech Inst, 52-53, asst prof statist, 53-56; res statistician, Atlantic Ref Co, 56-59; consult, 59-60; sr res statistician, Res Triangle Inst, 60-64, mgr spec res, 64-72; head, Statist Serv Dept, Burroughs Wellcome Co, 72-90. *Mem:* Am Soc Mech Eng; Am Statist Asn; Inst Math Statist; Biomet Soc. *Res:* Development of statistical methodology application to production; chemical and clinical research; design of experiments; design of medical and veterinary clinical trials. *Mailing Add:* 3500 Cambridge Dr Durham NC 27707

SWEENY, JAMES GILBERT, NATURAL PRODUCTS CHEMISTRY. *Current Pos:* RES SCIENTIST, COCA-COLA CO, 74- *Personal Data:* b Philadelphia, Pa, Jan 18, 44. *Educ:* Eckerd Col, BS, 65; Yale Univ, PhD(org chem), 69. *Prof Exp:* Fel chem, Yale Univ, 69-71; R Russell Agr Res Ctr, 71-72, Univ Glasgow, 72-73 & Univ Va, 73-74. *Concurrent Pos:* Prin Investr, Coca-Cola Co. *Mem:* Am Chem Soc; Royal Soc Chem. *Res:* Isolation, structure determination and synthesis of natural colorants; development of artificial sweeteners. *Mailing Add:* Corp Res & Develop-Technol 439 Cola-Cola Co Atlanta GA 30301. *Fax:* 404-515-5112

SWEENY, ROBERT F(RANCIS), CHEMICAL ENGINEERING, PROCESS CONTROL. *Current Pos:* from asst prof to assoc prof, 64-83, prof chem eng & chmn dept, 83-88, PROF CHEM ENG, VILLANOVA UNIV, 88- *Personal Data:* b Ridley Park, Pa, Sept 9, 31; m 52; c 4. *Educ:* Pa State Univ, BS, 53, MS, 55, PhD, 60. *Prof Exp:* Lab mgr, Appl Sci Labs, 55-64. *Mem:* Sigma Xi; Am Inst Chem Engrs; Instrument Soc Am; Am Soc Eng Educr. *Res:* Applied mathematics; process control; separations and purification; wastewater treatment. *Mailing Add:* Dept Chem Eng Villanova Univ Villanova PA 19085

SWEET, ARNOLD LAWRENCE, TIME SERIES FORECASTING, STATISTICAL QUALITY CONTROL. *Current Pos:* from asst prof to assoc prof eng sci, 64-73, PROF INDUST ENG, PURDUE UNIV, 73- *Personal Data:* b New York, NY, Mar 23, 35; m 59, Janet A Rae; c David & Ian R. *Educ:* Col City New York, BME, 56; Md Univ, MSME, 59; Purdue Univ, PhD(eng sci), 64. *Prof Exp:* Mech engr, Emerson Res Lab, 56-58; mech engr struct dynamics, US Naval Res Lab, 58-60. *Concurrent Pos:* Consult, Midwest Appl Sci Corp, 64-67, Autoliv Inc, 93; vis res fel accident anal, Rd Res Lab, Dept Environ, Gt Brit, 70-71; resident res assoc, US Air Force Systs Command Univ, 79-80. *Mem:* Am Inst Indust Engrs; Am Soc Qual Control; Int Inst Forecasters; Am Asn Univ Professors; Int Ref Orgn Forensic Med & Sci. *Res:* Time series forecasting; applications of probability theory to engineering problems; statistical quality control; reliability. *Mailing Add:* Sch Indust Eng Purdue Univ 1287 Grissom Hall West Lafayette IN 47907-1287

SWEET, ARTHUR THOMAS, JR, SYNTHETIC FIBER CHEMISTRY. *Current Pos:* RETIRED. *Personal Data:* b Salisbury, NC, Jan 19, 20; m 43, Frances Daniel; c Thomas D & Frances S (Currin). *Educ:* Univ NC, BS, 41; Ohio State Univ, PhD(chem), 48. *Prof Exp:* Staff chemist, Uranium Isotope Prod Dept, Tenn Eastman Corp, 44-46; res chemist, Nylon Res Div, E I Du Pont de Nemours & Co, Inc, 48-54, Dacron Res Div, 54-57 & Textile Fibers Patent Div, 57-74, patent assoc, Textile Fibers Patent Liaison Div, 74-85. *Mem:* Am Chem Soc. *Res:* Constitution of Grignard reagent; chemical characteristics of synthetic fibers; patent management. *Mailing Add:* 23 Penarth Dr Wilmington DE 19803-2011

SWEET, BENJAMIN HERSH, VIROLOGY, MICROBIOLOGICAL QUALITY ASSURANCE. *Current Pos:* RETIRED. *Personal Data:* b Boston, Mass, Dec 14, 24; m 47; c 3. *Educ:* Tulane Univ, BS, 46; Boston Univ, MA, 48, PhD(med sci), 51. *Prof Exp:* Res assoc virol, Res Found, Children's Hosp, Cincinnati, 51-54; asst prof microbiol, Univ Md, Sch Med, 54-59; sr investr virol, Merck Sharp & Dohme Res Labs, 59-64; dir & mgr res & develop, Flow Labs, Inc, Md, 64-66; assoc dir life sci div, Gulf South Res Inst, 66-75; mgr, sr scientist & doc adminr, qual assurance, Cutter Labs, Div Miles Labs, 75-85. *Concurrent Pos:* Consult, microbiol, virol & qual assurance, 85- *Mem:* Am Soc Microbiol; Am Soc Trop Med & Hyg; Tissue Cult Asn; Soc Exp Biol & Med. *Res:* Arthropod borne, respiratory, oncogenic, latent viruses, vaccine development; viral immunology and diagnostics; ecology and zoonoses; immunology-adjuvants; water pollution; cell biology; quality assurance; biological and immunological assays; limulus amebocyte research and development; good laboratory and manufacturing practices regulations, regulatory affairs. *Mailing Add:* 787 St John's Way Hendersonville NC 28791

SWEET, CHARLES EDWARD, BACTERIOLOGY, MYCOLOGY. *Current Pos:* RETIRED. *Personal Data:* b Elgin, Tex, Dec 27, 33; m 55; c 4. *Educ:* Univ Tex, BA, 55, MA, 63; Univ NC, MPH, 67, DPH(parasitol), 69. *Prof Exp:* Jr bacteriologist, Br Lab, NMex State Health Dept, 60-61; bacteriologist, Tex State Health Dept, 62, Tyler Tex Br Lab, 63-66, spec proj dir, 69-70, asst dir, Lab Servs, 70-73, dir lab, 70-93. *Res:* Laboratory methodology. *Mailing Add:* Lab Sect Tex State Health Dept 1100 W 49th St Austin TX 78756-3194

SWEET, CHARLES SAMUEL, PHARMACOLOGY. *Current Pos:* DIR CLIN RES, MERCK, SHARP & DOHME RES LABS, 90- *Personal Data:* b Cambridge, Mass, Apr 6, 42; wid; c 2. *Educ:* Northeastern Univ, BS, 66, MS, 68; Univ Iowa, PhD(pharmacol), 71. *Prof Exp:* Res asst pharmacol, Warner-Lambert Res Inst, NJ, 66-68; fel, Col Pharm, Northeastern Univ, 66-68; fel, Col Med, Univ Iowa, 68-71; fel res, Cleveland Clin Educ Found, 71-72; res fel, Merck Inst Therapeut Res, 72-75, sr res fel, 75-76, dir, Cardiol Pharmacol, 76-82, sr scientist, 82-89. *Concurrent Pos:* Mem, Med Adv Bd, Coun High Blood Pressure; mem, Coun Thrombosis, Am Heart Asn. *Mem:* Am Soc Pharmacol & Exp Therapeut; Am Heart Asn. *Res:* Renin-angiotensin system in pathogenesis of experimental hypertension; participation of central nervous system in development and maintenance; action of antihypertensive drugs, particularly as they apply to known causes of hypertension; clinical hypertension. *Mailing Add:* Dir Med Affairs New Prod Planning Merck & Co Inc PO Box 100 W52C 80 Whitehouse Station NJ 08889. *Fax:* 215-661-6913

SWEET, DAVID PAUL, ANALYTICAL CHEMISTRY. *Current Pos:* Anal chemist, 74-78, MGR ANAL SERV, DIV SYNTEX, ARAPAHOE CHEM INC, 78- *Personal Data:* b Dixon, Mar 24, 48; m 68. *Educ:* Bradley Univ, BA, 70; Univ Colo, PhD(anal chem), 74. *Mem:* Am Chem Soc; Am Soc Mass Spectrometry. *Res:* Chromatographic separations and trace analysis, especially using combined vapor phase chromatography-mass spectrometry and liquid chromatography-mass spectrometry. *Mailing Add:* 1231 N Fork Hwy Cody WY 82414

SWEET, FREDERICK, BIOCHEMISTRY, ORGANIC CHEMISTRY. *Current Pos:* asst prof reprod biochem, 71-76, res assoc prof, 76-80, assoc prof obstet & gynec, 80-82, PROF REPROD BIOL OBSTET & GYNEC, WASH UNIV, 82-, DIR DIV REPROD BIOL, 87- *Personal Data:* b New York, NY, May 15, 38; m 62, 88; c 4. *Educ:* Brooklyn Col, BS, 60; Univ Alta, PhD(org chem), 68. *Prof Exp:* Substitute instr chem, Brooklyn Col, 60-62; instr, Bronx Community Col, 62-64; NIH res fel nucleoside chem, Sloan-Kettering Inst Cancer Res, 68-70; res assoc reprod biochem, Univ Kans Med Ctr, Kansas City, 70-71. *Concurrent Pos:* lectr, Bronx Community Col, 68-70; vis asst prof biol sci, Southern Ill Univ, Edwardsville, 73-75, vis prof chem, 76-78; res fel, NATO, 74-76 & 77-78; NIH res career develop award, 75; mem int exchange, Nat Acad Sci, Hungary, 77-78 & 79 & Int Res & Exchange Bd, Princeton, NJ, 91; ed, Endocrin Rev, 86-90, steroids, 90- *Mem:* AAAS; Am Chem Soc; Chem Inst Can; Endocrine Soc. *Res:* Reproductive biochemistry, mechanism of steroid action and metabolism; synthesis of affinity-labeling steroids; synthesis of nucleosides and nucleoside analogs; synthesis of boron-estrogens for neutron capture therapy of cancers; daunorubicin-antibody conjugates for immunotherapy of cancer. *Mailing Add:* Dept Obstet Gynec Wash Univ Sch Med 660 S Euclid Ave St Louis MO 63110-1010

SWEET, GEORGE H, IMMUNOLOGY. *Current Pos:* from asst prof to assoc prof, 66-71, PROF BIOL, WICHITA STATE UNIV, 72- *Personal Data:* b Texhoma, Okla, Feb 4, 34; m 55; c 3. *Educ:* Wichita State Univ, BS, 60; Univ Kans, MA. 62, PhD(immunol), 65. *Prof Exp:* Immunologist, Armed Forces Inst Path, 65-66. *Mem:* AAAS. *Res:* Cell biology; fungal serology; viral immunology. *Mailing Add:* Six Crestview Lakes Wichita KS 67220

SWEET, HAVEN C, PLANT PHYSIOLOGY. *Current Pos:* from asst prof to assoc prof, Fla Technol Univ, 71-85, PROF BIOL, UNIV CENT FLA, 85- *Personal Data:* b Boston, Mass, Mar 1, 42; m 63; c 2. *Educ:* Tufts Univ, BS, 63; Syracuse Univ, PhD(plant physiol), 67. *Prof Exp:* Res fel photobiol, Brookhaven Nat Labs, 67-68; res analyst bot, Brown & Root-Northrop, Tex, 68-69, suprv, 69-71. *Mem:* AAAS; Am Soc Plant Physiol; Bot Soc Am; Am Inst Biol Sci; Linnean Soc. *Res:* Effects of light on plant growth; development of computer-assessment of plant taxonomic, remote sensing and ecological information. *Mailing Add:* Dept Biol Univ Cent Fla Box 25000 Orlando FL 32816-0001

SWEET, JOHN W, METALLURGY. *Current Pos:* RETIRED. *Personal Data:* b Seattle, Wash, May 6, 10. *Educ:* Univ Wash, BS, 34. *Prof Exp:* Chief metallurgist, Boeing Co, 46-48. *Mem:* Fel Am Soc Metals Int; Am Soc Testing & Mat. *Mailing Add:* 1605 Fifth Ave N Seattle WA 98109

SWEET, LARRY ROSS, ARCTIC ENGINEERING. *Current Pos:* RETIRED. *Personal Data:* b Fairbanks, Alaska, June 2, 40; m 79; c 2. *Educ:* Wash State Univ, BS, 63; Univ Alaska, MS, 72. *Prof Exp:* Assoc design engr, Lockheed Missiles & Space Co, 63-65; eng aide, Geophys Inst, Univ Alaska, 65, asst design engr, 66-69, head tech serv, 69-70, assoc supvry engr, 70-75, grad lab instr, Physics Dept, 65-66, exec officer to vpres res, 75-76 & exec officer to vchancellor res & advan study, 76-80; statewide res mgr, Alaska Dept Transp & Pub Facil, 80-85, chief spec res projs, 86-; res assoc, Inst Northern Eng, Univ Alaska, 86, chief spec res projs, Alaska Dept Transp & Pub Facil, 86-95, syst engr, Alaska Sat Facil, Geophys Inst, 87-95. *Concurrent Pos:* Mem, Comt Arctic Oil & Gas Resources, Nat Petrol Coun, 80-81, comt res, Am Soc Civil Engrs, 83-88, Adv Comt Snow & Ice, Am Asn State Transp Off, 85 & Comt Conduct Res, Nat Res Coun, Transp Res Bd, 85-87; US Permafrost Deleg to People's Repub China, 84; mem, Alaska State Climate Adv Bd, 83-87; mem adv bd, Univ Alaska Transp Ctr, 83-86, Northwest Technol Transfer Ctr, 84-87. *Mem:* Arctic Inst NAm; AAAS; Inst Elec & Electronics Engrs; Explorers Club. *Res:* Administration and coordination of basic and applied research in science and engineering in cold regions; state, national and international coordination of arctic research. *Mailing Add:* 1923 Swallow Dr Fairbanks AK 99709

SWEET, LEONARD, STATISTICS. *Current Pos:* from asst prof to assoc prof, 59-74, PROF MATH, UNIV AKRON, 74- *Personal Data:* b Akron, Ohio, Aug 28, 25; m 46; c 2. *Educ:* Univ Akron, BA, 49; Kent State Univ, MEd, 54; Case Western Reserve Univ, PhD(statist), 70. *Prof Exp:* Teacher pub schs, Ohio, 49-57, supvr, 57-59. *Concurrent Pos:* Consult, Akron Pub Schs, Ohio, 62-65 & Addressograph Multigraph Corp, 71-; mem panel evaluating of Instr Sci Equip Prog Proposals, NSF, 78; vpres, Greater Akron Math Educators, 79-81; mem admissions comt, Northeastern Ohio Med Sch, 78-80, biostatist comt, 78-80; grant dir, Local Course Improvement Proj, NSF, 78-80. *Mem:* Am Statist Asn; Math Asn Am; Nat Coun Teachers Math; Sigma Xi. *Res:* Experimental design; symmetrical complementation designs; utilization of the microcomputer by the classroom teacher in mathematics and statistics education. *Mailing Add:* 2430 Thurmont Rd Akron OH 44313-5444

SWEET, MELVIN MILLARD, NUMBER THEORY. *Current Pos:* sr staff mem, Hughes Aircraft Co, 78-80. *Personal Data:* b South Gate, Calif. *Educ:* Calif State Univ, Los Angeles, BA, 64, MA, 65; Univ Md, PhD(math), 72. *Prof Exp:* Mathematician, Nat Security Agency, 66-70; vis asst prof math, Univ Md, Baltimore County, 72-74; res staff mem math, Commun Res Div, Inst Defense Anal, 75-78. *Mem:* Am Math Soc; Math Asn Am. *Res:* Diophantine approximations. *Mailing Add:* 1567 Vista Claridad LaJolla CA 92037-7842

SWEET, MERRILL HENRY, II, BIOLOGY. *Current Pos:* asst prof, 63-66, ASSOC PROF BIOL, TEX A&M UNIV, 66- *Personal Data:* b Chicago Heights, Ill, Sept 5, 35; m 58; c 4. *Educ:* Univ Conn, BS, S8, PhD(entom), 63. *Prof Exp:* Res asst entom, Univ Conn, 62-63. *Mem:* Ecol Soc Am; Assoc Trop Biol; Soc Study Evolution; Soc Syst Zool. *Res:* Systematics; ecology; behavior and life cycles of arthropods, especially hemipterous insects. *Mailing Add:* Dept Biol Tex A&M Univ College Station TX 77843-0100

SWEET, RICHARD CLARK, ANALYTICAL CHEMISTRY, PHYSICAL CHEMISTRY. *Current Pos:* Chemist, 52-60, SUPVR METALL SYSTS APPLNS, PHILIPS LABS, N AM PHILIPS CO, BRIARCLIFF MANOR, 60- *Personal Data:* b Tarrytown, NY, Nov 28, 21; m 48; c 3. *Educ:* Wesleyan Col. BA, 44, MA, 48; Rutgers Univ, PhD(chem), 52. *Mem:* Am Chem Soc; Am Vacuum Soc; Sigma Xi; AAAS. *Res:* Spectroscopy; trace levels; ion exchange; polarography; water analysis; analytical methods; electronic components; vacuum techniques; ceramic-metal seals; cryogenic components design and fabrication; metals processing and joining techniques; welding and brazing. *Mailing Add:* 309 N Washington St North Tarrytown NY 10591-2303

SWEET, ROBERT DEAN, VEGETABLE CROPS. *Current Pos:* RETIRED. *Personal Data:* b Fairview, Ohio, Apr 6, 15; m 36, Virginia Kola; c Christine & Charlotte. *Educ:* Ohio Univ, BS, 36; Cornell Univ, MS, 38, PhD(veg crops), 41. *Prof Exp:* Asst, NY State Col Agr & Life Sci, Cornell Univ, 36-40, exten instr, 40-43, asst exten prof, 43-47, assoc prof, 47-49, prof beg crops, 49-82, chmn dept, 75-82. *Concurrent Pos:* Dir, Coun Agr Sci & Technol. *Mem:* Sigma Xi; Am Soc Hort Sci; fel Weed Sci Soc Am. *Res:* Biological and chemical weed control. *Mailing Add:* 1401 1/2 Slaterville Rd Ithaca NY 14850

SWEET, ROBERT MAHLON, MOLECULAR BIOLOGY. *Current Pos:* BIOLOGIST, BROOKHAVEN NAT LAB, 83- *Personal Data:* b Omaha, Nebr, Sept 21, 43; m 66; c 3. *Educ:* Calif Inst Technol, BS, 65; Univ Wis-Madison, PhD(phys chem), 70. *Prof Exp:* Lectr chem, Univ Wis-Madison, 70; fel molecular biol, Med Res Coun Lab Molecular Biol, Cambridge, Eng, 70-73; asst prof chem, Univ Calif, Los Angeles, 73-81, specialist, Molecular Biol Inst, 81-83. *Concurrent Pos:* Damon Runyon Mem Fund fel, 70-72; Europ Molecular Biol Orgn fel, 72. *Mem:* AAAS; Am Crystallog Asn; Sigma Xi. *Res:* Structure and function of enzymes, determined by x-ray diffraction techniques; studies of phycobitiproteins; photosynthetic accessory pigments from algae. *Mailing Add:* Biol Dept Brookhaven Nat Lab Upton NY 11973-5000. *Fax:* 516-282-3407

SWEET, RONALD LANCELOT, ORGANIC CHEMISTRY. *Current Pos:* RETIRED. *Personal Data:* b Bristol, Eng, Feb 6, 23; nat US; m 76. *Educ:* Rutgers Univ, BSc, 44, MSc, 48, PhD, 55. *Prof Exp:* Fel petrol, Mellon Inst, 51-55; chemist, Pigments Dept, E I du Pont de Nemours & Co, 55-82. *Concurrent Pos:* Co-adj & asst prof, Rutgers Univ, 63-74. *Mem:* Am Chem Soc. *Res:* Pigments. *Mailing Add:* 9179 Pine Springs Dr Boca Raton FL 33428

SWEET, THOMAS RICHARD, CHEMISTRY. *Current Pos:* from asst prof to assoc prof, 49-65, PROF CHEM, OHIO STATE UNIV, 65- *Personal Data:* b Jamaica, NY, Sept 27, 21; m 48; c 2. *Educ:* City Col New York, BS, 43; Ohio State Univ, PhD(chem), 49. *Prof Exp:* Asst, Manhattan Proj, War Res Div, Columbia Univ, 43-45 & Carbide & Carbon Chem Corp, 45-46. *Mem:* Am Chem Soc. *Res:* Organic reagents, solvent extraction and trace metal analysis. *Mailing Add:* Dept of Chem Ohio State Univ Columbus OH 43210

SWEET, WILLIAM HERBERT, NEUROSURGERY. *Current Pos:* from instr to asst prof, Harvard Med Sch, 45-54, assoc clin prof, 54-58, from assoc prof to prof, 58-76, EMER PROF SURG, HARVARD MED SCH, 76- *Personal Data:* b Kerriston, Wash, Feb 13, 10; m 37; c 3. *Educ:* Univ Wash, SB, 30; Oxford Univ, BSc, 34; Harvard Univ, MD, 36; Am Bd Psychiat & Neurol, dipl, 46; Am Bd Neurol Surg, dipl, 46; FRCS(E), 86. *Hon Degrees:* DSC, Oxford Univ, 57, Ohio State Univ, 93; DHC, Univ Sci Med, Grenoble, France, 79. *Honors & Awards:* Harvey Cushing Medal, Am Asn Neurol Surgeons, 78, William H Sweet Young Invest Award, 93; John J Bonica Lectr, Eastern Pain Asn, 80; J Jay Keegan Mem Lectr, Univ Nebr, 81; Order of the Rising Sun, Japan, 83; Frank H Mayfield Lectr, Univ Cincinnati, 86; Herbert Olivecrona Lectr, Karolinska Inst, 89; Samuel Clark Harvey Mem Lectr, Yale Univ, 90; F W L Kerr Mem Award Lectr, Am Pain Soc, 90; Distinguished Serv Award, Soc Neurol Surgeons, 91. *Prof Exp:* Instr neurosurg, Billings Hosp, Chicago, 39-40; Commonwealth Fund fel, Harvard Med Sch, 40-41; actg chief neurosurg serv, Birmingham United Hosp, 41-45. *Concurrent Pos:* Regional consult, Brit Emergency Med Serv, 41-45; asst, Mass Gen Hosp, 45-47, asst neurosurgeon, 47-48, assoc vis neurosurgeon, 48-58, vis neurosurgeon, 58-, chief neurosurg serv, 61-76, mem hosp staff & consult vis neurosurgeon, 76-80, sr neurosurgeon, 80-, hon neurosurg, 97-; lectr, Med Sch, Tufts Col, 47-51; neurosurgeon in chief, New Eng Ctr Hosp, 49-51; mem subcomt neurosurg, Nat Res Coun, 49-52 & mem subcomt neurol & neurosurg, 52-59; trustee, Assoc Univs, Inc, 58-; mem sci & technol adv comt, NASA, 64-70; mem neurol sci res training A comt, Nat Inst Neurol Dis & Stroke; honored guest, Cong Neurol Surgeons, 75; vis prof, Royal Soc Med Found, 79, Buenos Aires Univ Med Sch, 81 & Univ Ziekenhuizen, Belg, 87; permanent hon pres, World Fedn Neurosurg Socs, 84. *Mem:* Sr mem Inst Med-Nat Acad Sci; Am Acad Neurol Surg (pres, 76-77); Am Neurol Asn (vpres, 71-72); Am Pain Soc (pres elect, 80-81, pres, 81-82); Soc Neurol Surgeons (pres, 69-70); fel Am Acad Arts & Sci; Sigma Xi; Am Inst Biol Sci; AMA; Am Surg Asn. *Res:* Central nervous system; research in cerebrospinal and intracerebral fluid; brain tumors; mechanisms of pain and its neurosurgical control; abnormal behavior related to organic brain disease; irreversible coma; ethics of experimentation. *Mailing Add:* 309 Goddard Ave Brookline MA 02146-7425

SWEETING, LINDA MARIE, SPECTROSCOPY, ETHICS. *Current Pos:* from asst prof to assoc prof, 70-84, PROF CHEM, TOWSON STATE UNIV, 84- *Personal Data:* b Toronto, Ont, Dec 11, 41. *Educ:* Univ Toronto, BSc, 64, MA, 65; Univ Calif, Los Angeles, PhD(org chem), 69. *Prof Exp:* Asst prof, Occidental Col, 69-70. *Concurrent Pos:* Guest worker, Nat Inst Arthritis, Metab & Digestive Dis, NIH, 77-78; prog dir, chem instrumentation, NSF, 81-82; vis scholar, Harvard Univ, 84-85; Womens Chemist Comt, Am Chem Soc, 83-89; sci council, Md Acad Sci, 75-83, 89-, comt nominations, Sigma Xi, 90-93, US Army Med Res Inst Chem Defense, 90-93; spec mem, Grad Fac, Univ Md Grad Sch, Baltimore, 92- *Mem:* Am Chem Soc; AAAS; Sigma Xi; Asn Women Sci. *Res:* Application of nuclear magnetic resonance spectroscopy to organic chemistry; mechanisms and materials for triboluminescence; stereochemistry; ethics in science. *Mailing Add:* 506 Alabama Rd Baltimore MD 21204-4309. *E-Mail:* sweeting-l@toe.towson.edu

SWEETMAN, BRIAN JACK, ORGANIC CHEMISTRY, PHARMACOLOGY. *Current Pos:* res assoc chem, 66-68, assoc prof, 69-76, RES ASSOC PROF PHARMACOL, VANDERBILT UNIV, 76-, RES PROF ANESTHESIOL IN RESIDENCE, 89- *Personal Data:* b Palmerston North, NZ, May 4, 36; m 61; c 3. *Educ:* Univ NZ, BSc, 58, MSc, 59; Univ Otago, NZ, PhD(org chem), 62. *Prof Exp:* Res officer div protein chem, Commonwealth Sci & Indust Res Orgn, Melbourne, Australia, 63-66. *Concurrent Pos:* Assoc chem, Mass Spectrometry Resource, Vanderbilt Univ, 83- *Mem:* Am Soc Mass Spectroscopy. *Res:* Biomedical mass spectrometry; organic mass spectrometry and analytical pharmacology; prostaglandins; vapor-phase analysis; medicinal and organosulfur chemistry; anti-radiation and anti-arthritic drugs; protein chemistry of keratin; natural products. *Mailing Add:* 2928 Donna Hill Dr Nashville TN 37214

SWEETMAN, LAWRENCE, BIOCHEMISTRY, PEDIATRICS. *Current Pos:* DIR, MASS SPECTROMETRY LAB, MED CTR, BAYLOR UNIV, 97- *Personal Data:* b La Junta, Colo, Feb 17, 42; m 70. *Educ:* Univ Colo, BA, 64; Univ Miami, PhD(biochem), 69. *Prof Exp:* Res assoc biochem, Sloan-Kettering Inst Cancer Res, 68-72, instr, Sloan-Kettering Div, Grad Sch Med Sci, Cornell Univ, 69-72; from asst prof to prof pediat, Univ Calif, San Diego, 72-90; prof pediat & path, Children's Hosp, Los Angeles, 90-96. *Mem:* Am Chem Soc; Sigma Xi. *Res:* Metabolism of inherited diseases in children; organic acidurias. *Mailing Add:* 205 Carriage Hill Lane Heath TX 75087-8921

SWEIGARD, RICHARD JOSEPH, SURFACE MINE RECLAMATION, SLOPE STABILITY. *Current Pos:* CHMN & ASSOC PROF MINING ENG, UNIV KY, 88- *Personal Data:* b Harrisburg, Pa, Aug 18, 52; m 73, Nena Dentler; c Rebecca L & Rachel L. *Educ:* Drexel Univ, BS, 75; Pa State Univ, MS, 79, PhD(mining eng), 84. *Prof Exp:* Eng geologist, Betz-Converse-Murdoch Inc, 78-80; res asst, Pa State Univ, 80-83, instr mining eng, 83-84; asst prof mining eng, Southern Ill Univ, Carbondale, 84-88. *Concurrent Pos:* Reg prof engr, Commonwealth Pa, 82-; mining engr, Consol Inc, 83, 85, 87; consult & instr, Various Mining Co, 84-; prin investr, US Dept Interior, 88-91, EKy Power Coop, 89-90; exec dir, Univ Ky Mining Engr Found, 93- *Mem:* Soc Mining, Metall & Explor; Am Soc Civil Engrs; Am Soc Surface Mining & reclamation. *Res:* Research falls under the category of environmental impacts of mining; specific research topics have included alleviating excessive compaction of reconstructed soil, postmining land use planning, slope stabilization on abandoned mine lands and disposal of coal combustion by products. *Mailing Add:* 4600 Hickory Creek Dr Lexington KY 40515. *Fax:* 606-323-1962; *E-Mail:* rsweigar@uklans.uky.edu

SWEITZER, JAMES STUART, ASTRONOMY, SCIENCE EDUCATION. *Current Pos:* ASTRONR, ADLER PLANETARIUM, 78-, ASST DIR, 84- *Personal Data:* b South Bend, Ind, Mar 27, 51; m 73; c 2. *Educ:* Univ Notre Dame, BS, 73; Univ Chicago, MS, 75, PhD(astron, astrophys), 78. *Mem:* Am Astron Soc; Am Asn Mus; Int Planetarium Soc. *Res:* Interstellar molecules; astronomy education. *Mailing Add:* 311 Park Ave River Forest IL 60305

SWELL, LEON, BIOCHEMISTRY. *Current Pos:* RES PROF BIOCHEM & MED, VA COMMONWEALTH UNIV, 70- *Personal Data:* b New York, NY, July 26, 27; c 3. *Educ:* City Col New York, BS, 48; George Washington Univ, MS, 49, PhD(biochem), 52. *Prof Exp:* Lab asst, George Washington Univ, 49-51; chief biochemist, Vet Admin Ctr, Martinsburg, WVA, 51-64, chief, Lipid Res Lab, Vet Admin Hosp, Richmond, VA, 64- *Concurrent Pos:* Assoc prof lectr, George Washington Univ, 59-; assoc res prof, Med Col Va, 64- *Mem:* AAAS; Am Soc Biol Chemists; Soc Exp Biol & Med; Am Inst Nutrit. *Res:* Cholesterol, lipid and electrolyte metabolism; enzymes. *Mailing Add:* 505 Baldwind Rd Richmond VA 23229-6841

SWENBERG, CHARLES EDWARD, BIOPHYSICS. *Current Pos:* chief, 81-88, PROJ MGR, ARMED FORCES RADIOBIOL RES INST, 88- *Personal Data:* b Meriden, Conn, Mar 11, 40; div; c Charles & Johannes. *Educ:* Univ Conn, BA, 62, MS, 63; Univ Rochester, PhD(physics), 68. *Prof Exp:* Res assoc, Univ Ill, 67-69; res assoc, NY Univ, 69-70, asst prof physics, 70-73, res assoc prof chem, 73-81. *Mem:* Fel Am Phys Soc; Inst Elec & Electronics Engrs; Biophys Soc; Radiation Res Soc; fel AAAS. *Res:* Effects of ionizing radiation on DNA, DNA-drug interactions and mathematical simulations. *Mailing Add:* Armed Forces Radiobiol Res Inst 8901 Wisconsin Ave Bethesda MD 20889-5603

SWENBERG, JAMES ARTHUR, VETERINARY PATHOLOGY, CHEMICAL CARCINOGENESIS. *Current Pos:* PROF PATH, UNIV NC, 89-, PROF ENVIRON SCI & ENG, 90-, PROF NUTRIT, 97- *Personal Data:* b Northfield, Minn, Jan 15, 42; m 63, Sandra Lelanal; c James Daniel & Heather Christine. *Educ:* Univ Minn, DVM, 66; Ohio State Univ, MS, 68, PhD(vet path), 70. *Honors & Awards:* John Barnes lectr, Brit Toxicol Soc, 93. *Prof Exp:* NIH trainee path, Ohio State Univ, 66-70, res assoc, 70, asst prof, 70-72, assoc prof, 72; res scientist path, Upjohn Co, 72-76, res sect head, Path & Genetic Toxicol, 76-78; chief path, Chem Indust Inst Toxicol, 78-84, head, Dept Biochem Toxicol & Pathobiol, 84-89; head, Drug Safety Eval, Glaxo, 89. *Concurrent Pos:* Consult, Battelle Mem Inst, 71-72, Health Effects Inst, 82 & 85 & Environ Protection Agency, 83 & 85; mem, Sci Adv Panel, Chem Indust Inst Toxicol, 77-78; mem, NCI Carcinogenesis Prog Sci Rev Comt, 78-81; adj prof, Dept Path, Univ NC, 78-; adj assoc prof, Duke Univ, 78-; NTP Bd Sci Coun, 82-86, chmn, 85-86; dir curric toxicol, Univ NC, 91- *Mem:* Am Asn Cancer Res; AAAS; Am Asn Neuropathologists; Am Col Vet Pathologists; Soc Toxicol; Am Asn Pathologists. *Res:* Cancer research, including chemical carcinogenesis, neurooncogenesis and chemotherapy, and short-term tests for carcinogens; DNA damage/mutagensis; improved toxicology and data handling methods; inhalation toxicology; mechanisms of toxicity and carcinogenisity; risk assessment; toxicology. *Mailing Add:* Environ Sci Univ NC 357 Rosenau Hall CB 7400 Chapel Hill NC 27599-7400. *Fax:* 919-966-6123

SWENDSEID, MARIAN EDNA, BIOCHEMISTRY. *Current Pos:* assoc prof, 53-72, PROF NUTRIT, UNIV CALIF, LOS ANGELES, 72- *Personal Data:* b Petersburg, NDak, Aug 2, 18. *Educ:* Univ NDak, BA, 38, MA, 39; Univ Minn, PhD(physiol chem), 41. *Prof Exp:* Asst nutrit, Univ Ill, 42; res biochemist, Simpson Mem Inst, Univ Mich, 42-43; sr res chemist, Parke Davis & Co, Mich, 45-48; res biochemist, Simpson Mem Inst, Univ Mich, 48-52. *Mem:* Am Chem Soc; Am Soc Biol Chem. *Res:* Vitamin research; biochemical aspects of hematology; the use of carbon 13 in the study of intermediary metabolism; amino acids in nutrition. *Mailing Add:* Sch Pub Health 2 Faith Univ Calif Irvine CA 92715

SWENDSEN, ROBERT HAAKON, PHYSICS. *Current Pos:* PROF, DEPT PHYSICS, CARNEGIE MELLON UNIV, 84-, ASSOC DEAN, 93- *Personal Data:* b New York, NY, Apr 4, 43; m 71, Carol; c Eric & David. *Educ:* Yale Univ, BS, 64; Univ Pa, PhD(physics), 71. *Prof Exp:* Res asst physics, Univ Cologne, 71-73; physicist, Kernforschungsanlage Julich, Ger, 74-76; assoc physicist, Brookhaven Nat Lab, 76-79; res staff, IBM Zurich Res Lab, Switz, 79-84. *Mem:* Fel Am Phys Soc. *Res:* Solid state physics; phase transitions; magnetism; computer simulations. *Mailing Add:* Dept Physics Carnegie Mellon Univ Pittsburgh PA 15213. *Fax:* 412-681-0648; *E-Mail:* rs3v@andrew.cmu.edu

SWENERTON, HELENE, NUTRITION. *Current Pos:* Res nutritionist, 70-72, nutrit specialist, 72-91, EMER NUTRIT SPECIALIST, UNIV CALIF, DAVIS, 91- *Personal Data:* b Norfolk, Va, Jan 13, 25; m 43; c 3. *Educ:* Univ Calif, Davis, BS, 63, MS. 65, PhD(nutrit), 70. *Mem:* AAAS; Am Inst Nutrit; Soc Nutrit Educ; Am Dietetics Assoc. *Res:* Role of dietary zinc in mammalian growth and development; effects of maternal dietary deficiencies on fetal development; influence of nutrition education on consumer decisions. *Mailing Add:* Dept Nutrit Univ Calif Davis CA 95616-8669. *Fax:* 530-752-8966

SWENSON, CHARLES ALLYN, BIOPHYSICS. *Current Pos:* res assoc, 60-62, from asst prof to assoc prof, 62-72, assoc head dept, 84-87, PROF BIOCHEM, UNIV IOWA, 72- *Personal Data:* b Clinton, Minn, Aug 31, 33; m 60; c 3. *Educ:* Gustavus Adolphus Col, BS, 55; Univ Iowa, PhD(chem), 59. *Prof Exp:* Asst, Univ Iowa, 55-56; asst prof chem, Wartburg Col, 58-60. *Concurrent Pos:* NIH res career devlop award. *Mem:* Am Chem Soc; Biophys Soc; Am Soc Biol Chemists; Protein Soc. *Res:* Physical biochemistry; spectroscopic and thermodynamic approaches for protein structure; energy transduction and regulation in muscle contraction. *Mailing Add:* Dept Biochemistry Univ Iowa Iowa City IA 52242-1109. *Fax:* 319-335-9570

SWENSON, CHRISTINE ERICA, PRE-CLINICAL DRUG DEVELOPMENT. *Current Pos:* scientist, Liposome Co, 84-85, sr scientist, 86-87, group leader, 87-88, dir biol scis, 88-96, EXEC DIR, PRECLIN DRUG DEVELOP, LIPOSOME CO, 96- *Personal Data:* b Wantagh, NY, Apr 27, 53; m, James Yasinski; c Jeff & Emma. *Educ:* Middlebury Col, BA, 75; Cornell Univ, PhD(microbiol), 80. *Prof Exp:* Fel, Pop Coun, Rockefeller Univ, 79-81, Univ Calif, San Francisco, 81-84. *Mem:* Am Soc Microbiol; NY Acad Sci. *Res:* Pharmacology and toxicology of novel, lipid-based formulations of anti-microbial, anti-neoplastic and anti-inflammatory drugs. *Mailing Add:* Liposome Co One Research Way Princeton NJ 08540. *Fax:* 609-520-8250

SWENSON, CLAYTON ALBERT, EXPERIMENTAL SOLID STATE PHYSICS. *Current Pos:* from asst prof to prof, 55-87, chmn dept, 75-82, EMER PROF PHYSICS, IOWA STATE UNIV, 87- *Personal Data:* b Hopkins, Minn, Nov 11, 23; m 50, 80; c 3. *Educ:* Harvard Univ, BS, 44; Oxford Univ, DPhil(physics), 49. *Prof Exp:* Instr physics, Harvard Univ, 49-52; res physicist, Div Indust Coop, Mass Inst Technol, 52-55. *Concurrent Pos:* Consult, Commonwealth Sci & Indust Res Orgn, Sidney, Australia, 64-65; Nat Phys Lab, UK, 74-75 & Los Alamos Nat Lab, 85. *Mem:* Fel Am Phys Soc; AAAS; Sigma Xi. *Res:* Low temperatures; high pressures; low temperature thermodynamics; thermometry; equations of state of solids. *Mailing Add:* 2102 Kildee St Ames IA 50014-7027

SWENSON, DAVID HAROLD, CARCINOGENESIS, CANCER CHEMOTHERAPY. *Current Pos:* ASSOC PROF, SCH VET MED, LA STATE UNIV, 90- *Personal Data:* b Moorhead, Minn, June 16, 48; m 85, Nancy Baughman; c Sonia. *Educ:* Univ Minn, BS, 70; Univ Wis, PhD(oncol), 75. *Prof Exp:* NIH fel carcinogenesis, Inst Cancer Res, Chester Beatty Res Inst, 75-77; res chemist, Nat Ctr Toxicol Res, 77-79; res scientist genetic toxicol, Upjohn Co, 79-84, sr res scientist, Cancer Res, 84-87; vpres, Karkinos Biochem Inc, 87-90. *Concurrent Pos:* Vis & prin scientist, dept biol, Western Mich Univ, 87; pres, Flora Pharm Int Ltd, 92- *Mem:* Am Asn Cancer Res; AAAS; Res Soc NAm; Am Chem Soc. *Res:* Elucidation of the mechanism of interaction of genotoxins, carcinogens and cancer chemotherapeutic agents with nucleic acid. *Mailing Add:* 3880 Johns Lane Midland MI 48642. *Fax:* 504-346-3295; *E-Mail:* utswen@lsuvax.snce.lsu.edu

SWENSON, DONALD OTIS, ENGINEERING. *Current Pos:* CONSULT ENGR, BLACK & VEATCH, 71- *Personal Data:* b Manhattan, Kans, Feb 19, 37; m 62; c 4. *Educ:* Univ Kans, BSME, 63, MSc, 65, PhD(eng mech), 67. *Prof Exp:* Sr res assoc, Advan Mat Res & Develop Lab, Pratt & Whitney Aircraft Div, United Aircraft Corp, Conn, 67-71. *Mem:* Fel Am Soc Mech Engrs; Am Soc Testing & Mat. *Res:* Air pollution control technology and systems for fossil fueled power plants; material behavior; fatigue of materials; control systems; co-author of four books on air pollution control technology, testifies as expert witness on air pollution control technology; energy technology. *Mailing Add:* 9925 Perry Dr Overland Park KS 66212-5417

SWENSON, FRANK ALBERT, HYDROLOGY. *Current Pos:* RETIRED. *Personal Data:* b Davenport, Iowa, Feb 3, 12; m 43, 87; c 2. *Educ:* Augustana Col, AB, 36; Univ Iowa, MS, 40, PhD(geol), 42. *Prof Exp:* Surv man & geologist, US Army Corps Engrs, 37-38; asst geol, Univ Iowa, 38-42; from asst geologist to geologist, Mil Geol Br, US Geol Surv, 42-46, ground water investr, 46-63, res geologist, 63-74. *Concurrent Pos:* Consult, US Dept Justice; geologist, Ground Water Br, US Geol Surv, 42; consult geologist-hydrologist, 75- *Mem:* Fel Geol Soc Am; Int Geol Cong; Int Asn Hydrogeol. *Res:* Geology and ground water investigations in Montana and Wyoming; limestone hydrology; geochemistry. *Mailing Add:* 9906 Hawthorn Dr Sun City AZ 85351-3827

SWENSON, G(EORGE) W(ARNER), JR, ELECTRICAL ENGINEERING, RADIO ASTRONOMY. *Current Pos:* assoc prof, Univ Ill, Urbana, 56-58, prof elec eng & res prof astron, 58-70, actg head astron dept, 70-72, head elect eng dept, 79-85, prof, 56-88, EMER PROF ELEC ENG & ASTRON, UNIV ILL, URBANA, 88- *Personal Data:* b Minneapolis, Minn, Sept 22, 22; m 43; c 4. *Educ:* Mich Col Mining & Technol, BS, 44, EE, 50; Mass Inst Technol, SM, 48; Univ Wis, PhD, 51. *Prof Exp:* Asst elec eng, Mass Inst Technol, 46-48; instr, Univ Wis, 48-51; assoc prof, Washington Univ, St Louis, 51-53; prof, Univ Alaska, 53-54; assoc prof, Mich State Univ, 54-56. *Concurrent Pos:* Res prof, Geophys Inst, Univ Alaska, 54-56; consult, NSF, 59-75, US Army Ballistic Missile Agency, 59-60, NASA & Nat Acad Sci; mem, Adv Comt, Nat Radio Astron Observ, 59-80, vis scientist & chmn, Very Large Array Design Group, 64-68,; vis assoc, Calif Inst Technol, 72-73; Guggenheim fel, 85; sr res assoc acoust, Construct Eng Res Lab, US Army, 88-95; adj prof, Elec Eng, Mich Tech Univ, 96- *Mem:* Nat Acad Eng; fel AAAS; fel Inst Elec & Electronics Engrs; Inst Noise Control Eng; emer mem Am Astron Soc. *Res:* Antenna design; radio astronomy; radio propagation; acoustics. *Mailing Add:* Dept Elec & Comput Eng Univ Ill 1308 W Main St Rm 328 Urbana IL 61801. *E-Mail:* gswenson@uiuc.edu

SWENSON, GARY RUSSELL, ATMOSPHERIC PHYSICS. *Current Pos:* PROF ELEC ENG & ATMOSPHERIC PHYSICS, UNIV ILL, 96- *Personal Data:* b Grantsburg, Wis, June 17, 41; m 67; c 2. *Educ:* Wis State Univ-Superior, BS, 63; Univ Mich, Ann Arbor, MS, 68, PhD(atmospheric sci), 75. *Prof Exp:* Space scientist atmospheric sci, Marshall Space Flight Ctr, NASA, 68-84; space scientist, Lockheed, Calif, 84-96. *Mem:* Am Geophys Union; Sigma Xi. *Res:* Experimental research using remote sensing techniques, upper atmospheric phenomena, including aurora. *Mailing Add:* 107 E Sherwin Dr Urbana IL 61802-7138

SWENSON, HENRY MAURICE, DENTISTRY. *Current Pos:* From instr to assoc prof, 45-62, PROF PERIODONT, SCH DENT, IND UNIV, INDIANAPOLIS, 62-, DIR CLIN, 56- *Personal Data:* b Brooklyn, NY, Aug 13, 16; m 41; c 4. *Educ:* Univ Ill, BS, 41, DDS, 42; Am Bd Periodont, dipl, 51. *Concurrent Pos:* Consult, Vet Admin, 58- & US Dept Army, 59- *Mem:* Am Dent Asn; fel Am Col Dentists; Am Acad Periodont; Int Asn Dent Res. *Res:* Treatment and management of periodontal involvement. *Mailing Add:* 615 W 77th St & North Dr Indianapolis IN 46260

SWENSON, HUGO NATHANAEL, PHYSICS. *Current Pos:* RETIRED. *Personal Data:* b New Richland, Minn, Mar 11, 04; m 56, Astrid Kinnman. *Educ:* Carleton Col, AB, 25; Univ Ill, MS, 27, PhD(spectros), 30. *Prof Exp:* Asst physics, Univ Ill, 25-29; head dept, Earlham Col, 29-30; Am-Scand Found fel, Bohr's Inst, Denmark, 30-31; instr physics, Barnard Col, Columbia Univ, 31-37; instr physics, Queen's Col, 37-41, from asst prof to emer prof, 41-73. *Mem:* AAAS; Am Phys Soc; Am Asn Physics Teachers; Sigma Xi. *Res:* Electronics. *Mailing Add:* 1805 S Balsam St No 227 Lakewood CO 80232

SWENSON, LEONARD WAYNE, PHYSICS. *Current Pos:* assoc prof, 68-81, PROF PHYSICS, ORE STATE UNIV, 81- *Personal Data:* b Twin Falls, Idaho, June 11, 31; m 50; c 3. *Educ:* Mass Inst Technol, BS, 54, PhD(physics), 60. *Prof Exp:* Instr physics, Northeastern Univ, 57-58 & Tufts Univ, 58-59; res assoc, Mass Inst Technol, 60-62; Bartol fel nuclear struct res group, Bartol Res Found, 62-64, res staff mem, 64-66; dir space radiation effects lab, Va Assoc Res Ctr, 67-68. *Concurrent Pos:* Consult, Joseph Kaye & Co, 57-59. *Mem:* Am Phys Soc; Am Sci Affil. *Res:* Nuclear structure and reaction; intermediate energy nuclear physics. *Mailing Add:* 308 NW Eighth St Corvallis OR 97330

SWENSON, MELVIN JOHN, VETERINARY PHYSIOLOGY. *Current Pos:* prof & head dept, 57-73, prof, 73-87, EMER PROF PHYSIOL, IOWA STATE UNIV, 87- *Personal Data:* b Concordia, Kans, Jan 14, 17; m 47, Mildred; c Myron, Pamela & Brita. *Educ:* Kans State Col, DVM, 43; Iowa State Col, MS, 47, PhD(path), 50. *Prof Exp:* Instr vet sci, La State Univ, 43; asst prof path, Iowa State Col, 49-50; from asst to assoc prof physiol, Kans State Col, 50-56; prof, Colo State Univ, 56-57. *Mem:* AAAS; Am Physiol Soc; Am Soc Vet Physiol & Pharmacol; Soc Exp Biol & Med; Am Vet Med Asn; Sigma Xi. *Res:* Need for trace minerals in animals; effect of antibiotics on growth and hematology; nutrient requirements of animals; histophysiology of nutritional deficiencies; anemias of farm animals. *Mailing Add:* 122 SW Countrywood Lane Ankeny IA 50021

SWENSON, ORVAR, PEDIATRIC, SURGERY. *Current Pos:* RETIRED. *Personal Data:* b Halsingborg, Sweden, Feb 7, 09; nat US; m 41, Melva Criley; c Wend, Mimi & Elsa. *Educ:* William Jewell Col, AB, 33; Harvard Med Sch, MD, 37. *Hon Degrees:* Dr, Univ Marseilles France, 75; DSc, William Jewel Col, 93. *Honors & Awards:* Billings Award, AMA, 52; Mead Johnson Award, 52; Ladd Medal Surg Sect, Am Pediat, 68; Dennis Brown Brit Asn Pediat Surg, 79. *Prof Exp:* Intern surg, Ohio State Univ Hosp, 37-38; house officer path, Children's Hosp, Boston, 38-39, house officer surg, 39-41, Peter Bent Brigham chief surg resident, 44-45; Cabot fel, Harvard Med Sch, 41-44, asst surg, 42-44, instr, 44-47, assoc, 47-50; assoc prof, Sch Med, Tufts Univ, 50-54, clin prof pediat surg, 54-57, prof, 57-60; prof surg, Med Sch, Northwestern Univ, Chicago, 60-73 & Sch Med, Univ Miami, 73-77. *Concurrent Pos:* Surg house officer, Peter Bent Brigham Hosp, 39-41, asst res surgeon, 41-42, jr assoc, 44, res surgeon, 44-45, surgeon, 45-50; jr attend surgeon, Children's Hosp, Boston, 45, assoc vis surgeon, 45-47, surgeon, 47-50; vis surgeon, New Eng Peabody Home Crippled Children, 46-50, mem assoc staff, 50; lectr, Simmons Col, 48-50; sr surgeon, New Eng Ctr Hosp, 50-60; surgeon in chief, Boston Floating Hosp Infants & Children, 50-60 & Children's Mem Hosp, Chicago, 60-72. *Mem:* Assoc Asn Thoracic Surg; Am Surg Asn; fel Am Col Surg; fel Am Acad Pediat; fel Am Pediat Surg Asn (pres, 75). *Res:* Gastro-intestinal system; discovered cause and cure of Hirschsprung's Disease (1948). *Mailing Add:* Main St Rockport ME 04856

SWENSON, PAUL ARTHUR, CELL PHYSIOLOGY. *Current Pos:* RETIRED. *Personal Data:* b St Paul, Minn, Feb 5, 20; m 42; c 2. *Educ:* Hamline Univ, BS, 47; Stanford Univ, PhD(biol), 52. *Prof Exp:* Instr physiol, Univ Mass, 50-S4, from asst prof to assoc prof, 54-66; radiation biophysicist, Biol Div, Oak Ridge Nat Lab, 66-85. *Concurrent Pos:* Vis assoc physiologist, Brookhaven Nat Lab, 56-57; USPHS spec fel, Oak Ridge Nat Lab, 62-64. *Mem:* Biophys Soc; Am Soc Photobiol; Radiation Res Soc. *Res:* Effects of ultraviolet and ionizing radiations on metabolic control in bacteria. *Mailing Add:* 100 Ontario Lane Oak Ridge TN 37830

SWENSON, RICHARD PAUL, PROTEIN CHEMISTRY & ENGINEERING, ENZYMOLOGY. *Current Pos:* asst prof, 84-89, dir biochem, Instrument Ctr, 87-94, ASSOC PROF BIOCHEM, OHIO STATE UNIV, 89- *Personal Data:* b Red Wing, Minn, Mar 5, 49. *Educ:* Gustavus Adolphus Col, BA, 71; Univ Minn, PhD(biochem), 79. *Honors & Awards:* Bacaner Basic Sci Res Award, Minn Med Found, 80. *Prof Exp:* Teaching asst, Gustavus Adolphus Col, 68-71; res asst biochem, Dept Endocrinol, Mayo Clinic, 71-74; teaching asst, Univ Minn, 74-77; fel, Univ Mich, Ann Arbor, 79-82, asst prof, Biol Chem Dept, 83-84. *Concurrent Pos:* Mem, Ohio State Biotech Ctr; prin investr, NIH. *Mem:* Am Chem Soc; AAAS; Sigma Xi; Am Soc Biochem & Molecular Biol; Protein Soc. *Res:* Mechanism of enzyme and protein action; protein engineering; structural genes for bacterial flavodoxins; flavoprotein quinone reductases; flavoprotein electron transferases; oxidation-reduction properties; electron transfer mechanisms. *Mailing Add:* Biochem Dept Ohio State Univ 776 Biol Sci Bldg 484 W 12th Ave Columbus OH 43210

SWENSON, RICHARD WALTNER, photographic chemistry, for more information see previous edition

SWENSON, ROBERT J, THEORETICAL PHYSICS. *Current Pos:* prof physics & chmn dept, 70-90, VPRES RES, MONT STATE UNIV, 90- *Personal Data:* b Butte, Mont, Mar 3, 34; m 58; c 3. *Educ:* Mont State Univ, BS, 56; Lehigh Univ, MS, 58, PhD(physics), 61. *Prof Exp:* Res assoc physics, Lehigh Univ, 61-62; Nat Acad Sci fel, 62-63 & res fel, Free Univ Brussels, 62-64; Joint Inst Lab Astrophysics fel, Univ Colo, 64-65; from asst prof to assoc prof physics, Temple Univ, 65-70, chmn dept, 67-70. *Mem:* Fel Am Phys Soc; fel AAAS; Sigma Xi; Am Asn Physics Teachers. *Res:* Thermodynamics; statistical mechanics; relativistic fluid mechanics; general theory. *Mailing Add:* Vpres Res Mont State Univ Bozeman MT 59717-0001. *Fax:* 406-994-2893

SWENSON, THERESA LYNN, ATHEROSCLEROSIS, DIABETES. *Current Pos:* SR RES BIOCHEM, ATHEROSCLEROSIS RES, MERCK SHARP & DOHME RES LABS, 89- *Personal Data:* b Racine, Wis, Sept 17, 57; m 90. *Educ:* Univ Wis-Parkside, BS, 70; Univ Wis-Madison, PhD(physiol chem), 85. *Prof Exp:* Postdoctoral fel med, Columbia Univ, 85-89. *Concurrent Pos:* Mem, Arteriosclerosis Coun, Am Heart Asn. *Mem:* Fel Am Heart Asn; Am Asn Biochem & Molecular Biol; Am Chem Soc; AAAS. *Res:* Biochemical mechanisms of atherosclerosis; biochemical mechanisms and physiological functions of the enzymes and proteins involved in lipoprotein remodeling. *Mailing Add:* Diagnescent Technol Inc 1 Executive Blvd Yonkers NY 10701. *Fax:* 732-594-1169

SWENTON, JOHN STEPHEN, ORGANIC CHEMISTRY. *Current Pos:* from asst prof to assoc prof, 67-77, PROF CHEM, OHIO STATE UNIV, 77- *Personal Data:* b Kansas City, Kans, Dec 8, 40; m; c 2. *Educ:* Univ Kans, BA, 62; Univ Wis, PhD(chem), 65. *Prof Exp:* Nat Acad Sci-Nat Res Coun fel, Harvard Univ, 65-66. *Concurrent Pos:* Grants, Soc Petrol Res Fund, NSF & Eli Lilly, 84-86. *Mem:* Am Chem Soc; Royal Soc Chem. *Res:* Synthetic and mechanistic organic photochemistry, synthetic and mechanistic organic electrochemistry, and natural products synthesis. *Mailing Add:* Dept Chem Ohio State Univ 120 W 18th Ave Columbus OH 43210

SWERCZEK, THOMAS WALTER, VETERINARY PATHOLOGY. *Current Pos:* From asst prof to assoc prof, 69-78, PROF VET SCI COL AGR, UNIV KY, 78- *Personal Data:* b Cedar Rapids, Nebr, May 10, 39; m 64; c 3. *Educ:* Kans State Univ, BS, 62; DVM, 64; Univ Conn, MS, 66, PhD(path), 69. *Mem:* Am Vet Med Asn; Conf Res Workers Animal Dis. *Res:* Comparative pathology; pathogenesis of infectious diseases of horses; nutritional pathology; pathogenesis of gastrointestinal diseases of livestock. *Mailing Add:* 664 Providence Rd Lexington KY 40502

SWERDLOFF, RONALD S, ENDOCRINOLOGY, INTERNAL MEDICINE. *Current Pos:* spec fel endocrinol, Univ Calif, Los Angeles, 67-69, from asst prof to assoc prof med, 69-78, assoc chief, 73-78, CHIEF, DIV ENDOCRINOL & METAB, HARBOR-GEN HOSP CAMPUS, UNIV CALIF, LOS ANGELES, 73-, PROF MED, HARBOR-UCLA MED CTR, 78- *Personal Data:* b Pomona, Calif, Feb 18, 38; m 59; c Jonathan & Peter. *Educ:* Univ Calif, Los Angeles, BS, 59; Univ Calif, San Francisco, MD, 62. *Honors & Awards:* Wyeth Award, Soc Study Reproduction, 74; Serono Distinguished Andrologist Award, Am Androl Soc, 86; Serono Distinguished lectr, Australian Reproductive Biol, 90; Harrison Mem lectureship, Australian Endocrine Soc, 81. *Prof Exp:* Intern internal med, Kings Co Hosp, Univ Wash, 62-63, asst resident med, 63-64; Clin res assoc, Res Metab Sect, NIH, 64-66. *Concurrent Pos:* Dir med residency prog, St Mary's Long Beach Hosp & Harbor Gen Hosp, 69-71; NIH career develop award, 72-77; actg dir, Clin Study Ctr, Harbor Gen Hosp, 78-80; vis prof, Dept Anat, Monash Univ, 80-81; dir, Pop Res Ctr, Univ Calif, Los Angeles, 86-91; ed, J Clin Endocrinol & Metab, 78-83; Consult, UN Family Planning Asn, 83-86, Human Reproductive Prog, WHO, 83-89; dir, WHO Collaborating Ctr, 93- *Mem:* Am Fedn Med Res; Endocrine Soc; Soc Study Reproduction; Am Androl Soc; Am Asn Prof; Am Fertil Soc. *Res:* Reproductive endocrinology; neuroendocrinology; contraceptive development. *Mailing Add:* Div Endocrinol Harbor-Univ Calif Los Angeles Ctr 1000 W Carson St Torrance CA 90509. *Fax:* 310-533-0627

SWERDLOW, MARTIN A, MEDICINE, PATHOLOGY. *Current Pos:* prof & head, Dept Path, 89-93, EMER FRANCES B GEEVER PROF & HEAD, UNIV ILL COL MED, 93- *Personal Data:* b Chicago, Ill, July 7, 23; m 45, Marion Levin; c Steven & Gray. *Educ:* Univ Ill, BS, 45, MD, 47; Am Bd Path, dipl, 52. *Honors & Awards:* Raymond Allen Award for Teaching, Col Med, Univ Ill, 60-72. *Prof Exp:* Resident path, Michael Reese Hosp, Chicago, 48-50 & 51-52; pathologist, Menorah Med Ctr, 54-57; from asst prof to assoc prof path, Univ Ill Col Med, 57-60, clin assoc prof, 60-66, prof, 66-72, assoc dean, Abraham Lincoln Sch Med, 70-72; prof path, Sch Med, Univ Mo-Kansas City, 73-74; chmn, Dept Path, Michael Reese Hosp & Med Ctr, 74-89, vpres, Acad Affairs, 75-88; prof path, Univ Chicago, 74-89, assoc dean, 82-89. *Concurrent Pos:* Pathologist, Englewood Hosp, Chicago; consult, Vet Admin Hosp, Hines & Cook Co Hosp, Chicago; chmn, Dept Path, Kansas City Gen Hosp, 73-74. *Mem:* Am Soc Clin Path; Col Am Pathologists; Am Asn Study Liver Dis; US Can Acad Path; Am Soc Dermat Path. *Res:* Histopathology of skin disorders; experimental skin tumors; diseases of liver; diseases of breast; parasitic diseases. *Mailing Add:* Dept Path M/C 847 Univ Ill Col Med 1819 W Polk St Chicago IL 60612. *Fax:* 312-996-7586

SWERGOLD, GARY DAVID, TRANSPOSCABLE ELEMENT BIOLOGY. *Current Pos:* SR STAFF FEL, DIV CELLULAR & GENE THER, FOOD & DRUG ADMIN, 93- *Personal Data:* b New York, NY, May 20, 55; m 82; c 2. *Educ:* Cornell Univ, BA, 76; Albert Einstein Col Med, MD, PhD, 83. *Prof Exp:* Fel, Nat Cancer Inst, NIH, 86-92, med genetics, 90-92. *Mem:* AAAS; Am Soc Human Genetics; Am Soc Microbiol. *Res:* Biology and regulation of the human LINE-1 transposable element, this element is developmentally regulated and is capable of causing human disease by insertional mutogenesis. *Mailing Add:* FDA/CBER/DCGT/HFM 515 1401 Rockville Pike Rockville MD 20852. *E-Mail:* swergold@helix.nih.gov

SWERLICK, ISADORE, ORGANIC CHEMISTRY. *Current Pos:* RETIRED. *Personal Data:* b Philadelphia, Pa, Jan 23, 21; m 51, Rhoda Weinman; c Anne L & Robert A. *Educ:* Temple Univ, BA, 43; Duke Univ, PhD(chem). 50. *Prof Exp:* Asst, Duke Univ, 46-49; res chemist, E I du Pont de Nemours & Co, Inc, 50-56, res supvr, 56-70, staff scientist, Film Dept, 70-76, res assoc, Polymer Prod Dept, 77-82. *Mem:* AAAS; Am Chem Soc; Sigma Xi. *Res:* Organics and polymers. *Mailing Add:* 614 Loveville Rd C2H Hockessin DE 19707

SWERLING, PETER, ENGINEERING ADMINISTRATION. *Current Pos:* DIR, SWERLING MANASSESMITH, 82-, PRES, 86- *Personal Data:* b New York, NY, Mar 4, 29. *Educ:* Calif Inst Technol, 47; Cornell Univ, BA, 49; Univ Calif, Los Angeles, MA, 51, PhD, 55. *Prof Exp:* Mem tech staff, Rand Corp, 48-61; dept mgr, Conductron Corp, 61-64; adj prof, Univ Southern Calif, 64-66; prof & chmn, Tech Serv Corp, 66-82. *Concurrent Pos:* Asst prof eng, Univ Ill, 56-57. *Mem:* Nat Acad Eng; fel Inst Elec & Electronics Engrs; Sigma Xi. *Mailing Add:* 1136 Corsica Dr Pacific Palisades CA 90272. *Fax:* 818-224-4269

SWERN, FREDERIC LEE, AIRCRAFT CONTROL SYSTEMS. *Current Pos:* ASSOC PROF ENG, STEVENS INST TECHNOL, 84- *Personal Data:* b New York, NY, Sept 9, 47; m 69, Gayle R Unger; c Lauren & Michael. *Educ:* City Col New York, BEE, 69; Newark Col Eng, MSEE, 74; NJ Inst Technol, D Engr Sci, 81. *Prof Exp:* Engr, Navig & Control Div, Bendix, 69-72; Univac Div, Sperry Rand, 72-73, sr engr, Flight Systs Div, 78-84; sr systs analyst, Chubb & Son Inc, 73-78. *Concurrent Pos:* Consult, Swerlin Assocs 81-, Govt Comn Sci & Technol, 85-86; researcher & consult, NASA Langley Res Ctr, 79-82 & 85-90, Gen Motors Corp, 83-84, Hyatt Clark Industs, 84-85, US Army Armament Res & Develop Ctr, 85-92 & Westinghouse Elevator, 87. *Mem:* Inst Elec & Electronics Engrs; Am Soc Mech Engrs; Asn Comput Mach; Am Inst Aeronaut & Astronaut; Sigma Xi. *Res:* Automatic flight control system; aircraft control system; improved flare control for transport aircraft. *Mailing Add:* Mech Eng Lab Castle Point Stevens Inst Technol Hoboken NJ 07030. *Fax:* 201-216-8315; *E-Mail:* fswern@stevens.tech.edu

SWETHARANYAM, LALITHA, TOPOLOGY. *Current Pos:* assoc prof, 69-73, PROF, McNEESE STATE UNIV, 73- *Personal Data:* b Trivandrum, India; nat US; m 71. *Educ:* Annamalai Univ, Madras, PhD(math), 66. *Prof Exp:* Lectr math & head dept, LVD Col, Raichur, India, 56-61; res fel, Annamalai Univ, Madras, 61-65, lectr, 65-69. *Concurrent Pos:* Regional coordr speaker's bur, Asn Women Math, Nat Off, 83-87. *Mem:* Am Math Soc; Indian Math Soc; Math Asn Am; Assoc Women in Math. *Res:* Functional analysis; point set topology. *Mailing Add:* 525 E Jefferson Dr Lake Charles LA 70605-6663

SWETITS, JOHN JOSEPH, MATHEMATICAL ANALYSIS. *Current Pos:* assoc prof, 70-81, PROF MATH, OLD DOMINION UNIV, 81- *Personal Data:* b Passaic, NJ, Oct 1, 42; m 66; c 3. *Educ:* Fordham Univ, BS, 64; Lehigh Univ, MS, 67, PhD(math), 68. *Prof Exp:* Instr math, Lafayette Col, 67-68, asst prof, 68-70. *Mem:* Am Math Soc; Math Asn Am; Soc Indust & Appl Math. *Res:* Summability theory; approximation theory. *Mailing Add:* Dept Math & Statist Old Dominion Univ Norfolk VA 23529-0001

SWETS, DON EUGENE, SOLID STATE PHYSICS, CHEMICAL PHYSICS. *Current Pos:* RETIRED. *Personal Data:* b Grand Rapids, Mich, Oct 7, 30; m 56; c 4. *Educ:* Univ Mich, BSE(physics) & BSE(math), 53, MS, 55. *Prof Exp:* sr res physicist, Res Labs, Gen Motors Corp, 55-80, staff res scientist, 80-87. *Res:* Measurement of diffusion coefficients; hydrogen in steel; helium, neon, and hydrogen fused in quartz; growth of single crystals, especially tetragonal germanium dioxide; ribbon shaped germanium; hexamethylenetetramine IV-VI and III-V compounds; rare earth iron compounds; super conductor compounds. *Mailing Add:* 6900 Timbercrest Washington MI 48094

SWETS, JOHN ARTHUR, PSYCHOLOGY. *Current Pos:* vpres, Bolt Beranek & Newman, Inc, Cambridge, 64-69, sr vpres, 69-74, gen mgr res & develop, consult & dir, 71-74, CHIEF SCIENTIST, BOLT BERANEK & NEWMAN LABS, CAMBRIDGE, 75- *Personal Data:* b Grand Rapids, Mich, June 19, 28; m 49, Maxine R Crawford; c Stephen A & Joel B. *Educ:* Univ Mich, Ann Arbor, BA, 50, MA, 53, PhD, 54. *Honors & Awards:* Howard Crosby Warren Medal, Soc Exp Psychologists, 85; Distinguished Sci Contrib Award, Am Psychol Asn, 90. *Prof Exp:* Instr psychol, Univ Mich, Ann Arbor, 54-56; asst prof psychol, Mass Inst Technol, Cambridge, 56-60, assoc prof, 60-63. *Concurrent Pos:* Vis res fel, Philips Labs, Neth, 58; adv, Vision Comt & Comt Hearing & Bioacoustics, Nat Acad Sci, Nat Res Coun, 60-; lectr, Dept Clin Epidemiol, Harvard Med Sch, 85-88, Dept Health Care Policy, 88-; chmn, Soc Psych Psychologists, 86; mem, Comn Behav Soc Sci & Educ, Nat Res Coun, 88-92, vchair, 92-93, chmn, 93-; adv, consult & lectr numerous govt & prof orgns sci. *Mem:* Nat Acad Sci; fel AAAS; Am Acad Arts & Scis; fel Acoust Soc Am; fel Am Psychol Soc; Psychonomic Soc; Psychometric Soc; Sigma Xi; fel Am Psychol Asn. *Res:* Psychology; acoustics; vision; application of signal detection theory to human perception and decision making and to diagnostic tasks in several fields, predominantly clinical medicine; developed computer-based techniques for instruction. *Mailing Add:* BBN Corp 10 Moulton St Cambridge MA 02138-1191. *E-Mail:* swets@bbn.com

SWETT, CHESTER PARKER, PSYCHOPHARMACOLOGY, BEHAVIOR THERAPY. *Current Pos:* DOCTOR CLIN PSYCHIAT, NH HOSP. *Personal Data:* b Lancaster, Ohio, Aug 16, 39; m 64; c 2. *Educ:* Denison Univ, BS, 61; Harvard Med Sch, MD, 66. *Prof Exp:* Intern, Harvard Surg Serv, Boston City Hosp, 66-67; staff assoc, NIH, 67-69; psychiat resident, Mass Ment Health Ctr, 69-72; scientist, Drug Epidemiol Unit, Boston Univ Med Ctr, 72-74; staff psychiatrist, McLean Hosp, 74-89, serv chief, 83-89; assoc prof, Harvard Med Sch, 83-89; med dir, Brattleboro Retreat, 90-; prof clin psychiat, Dartmouth Med Sch, 90- *Mem:* Am Psychiat Asn; Am Acad Psychiat & Law; Asn Advan Behav Ther; AAAS. *Res:* The causes of impulsive violence and the effects of violence upon victims. *Mailing Add:* c/o APS Bldg 36 Clinton St Concord NH 03301

SWETT, JOHN EMERY, ANATOMY, NEUROPHYSIOLOGY. *Current Pos:* PROF ANAT & CHMN DEPT, COL MED, UNIV CALIF, IRVINE, 76- *Personal Data:* b San Francisco, Calif, Mar 19, 32; m 56; c 4. *Educ:* Univ Wash, AB, 56; Univ Calif, Los Angeles, PhD(anat), 60. *Prof Exp:* NSF fel, Univ Pisa, 60-61, NIH fel, 61-62; neurophysiologist, Good Samaritan Hosp, Portland, Ore, 62-66; assoc prof anat, State Univ NY Upstate Med Ctr, 66-67; assoc prof anat, Med Sch, Univ Colo, Denver, 67-76. *Concurrent Pos:* NIH res grants, 64- *Mem:* Am Asn Anatomists; Am Physiol Soc; Soc Neurosci. *Res:* Organization of the spinal cord; mechanisms of sensory detection; organization of the peripheral nervous system. *Mailing Add:* Dept of Anat Univ of Calif Col of Med Irvine CA 92717

SWETT, KEENE, GEOLOGY. *Current Pos:* asst prof, 66-70, assoc prof, 70-74, PROF GEOL, UNIV IOWA, 74- *Personal Data:* b Wilton, Maine, Nov 6, 32; m 54, Joan D Huston; c Alan & JoAnn (Sheehan). *Educ:* Tufts Univ, BS, 55; Univ Colo, MS, 61; Univ Edinburgh, PhD(geol), 65. *Prof Exp:* Asst lectr geol, Univ Edinburgh, 63-66. *Concurrent Pos:* NSF fel, 67-82. *Mem:* Geol Soc Am; Am Asn Petrol Geol; Soc Econ Paleont & Mineral; Int Asn Sedimentol; AAAS. *Res:* Petrological studies of sediments and sedimentary rocks with especial regard to the post-depositional alterations and patterns of diagenesis; Cambro-Ordovician shelf sediments of western Newfoundland, northwest Scotland, central eastern Greenland and Spitsbergen; late proterozic biostratigraphy and paleo environments of Spitsbergen and Central East Greenland. *Mailing Add:* Geol Univ Iowa Iowa City IA 52242-1000. *Fax:* 319-335-1821

SWEZ, JOHN ADAM, BIOPHYSICS. *Current Pos:* From asst prof to assoc prof physics, 67-77, PROF PHYSICS & DIR RADIATION LAB, IND STATE UNIV, TERRE HAUTE, 77- *Personal Data:* b Cleveland, Ohio, Nov 18, 41; m 65; c 1. *Educ:* Pa State Univ, BS, 63, MS, 65, PhD(biophys), 67. *Mem:* AAAS; Radiation Res Soc; Biophys Soc. *Res:* Degradation studies of DNA in Escherichia coli after ionizing radiation, physical characterization and effect of bacteriophage infection; injection of nucleic acid of bacteriophage T1 into its host Escherichia coli. *Mailing Add:* Dept Physics Ind State Univ Physics Sci Bldg Main Campus 217 N Sixth St Terre Haute IN 47809-0001

SWEZEY, ROBERT LEONARD, INTERNAL MEDICINE, RHEUMATOLOGY. *Current Pos:* prof med & dir div rehab med, 74-78, CLIN PROF MED, SCH MED, UNIV CALIF, LOS ANGELES, 78-, MED DIR, OSTEOPOROSIS PREV & TREAT CTR, 87-; MED DIR, ARTHRITIS & BACK PAIN CTR, 78- *Personal Data:* b Pasadena, Calif, Apr 30, 25; m 49, Annette Maler; c 3. *Educ:* Ohio State Univ, MD, 48; Am Bd Internal Med, dipl, 60; Am Bd Phys Med & Rehab, dipl, 69; Am Bd Rheumatol, dipl, 74. *Honors & Awards:* Harry Bruckel Award, Spondylitis Asn Am, 93. *Prof Exp:* Intern, Los Angeles Co Gen Hosp, Calif, 48-49 & Am Hosp, Paris, 49-50; resident internal med, Wadsworth Gen Med & Surg Vet Admin Hosp, 51-54, fel rheumatol, Wadsworth Gen Med & Surg Vet Admin Hosp & Univ Calif, Los Angeles, 54-55, clin asst med, Univ Calif, Los Angeles, 55-57, clin instr, 57-64, asst prof, 64-65, career fel phys med & rehab, 65 & 66-67; acad career fel, Univ Minn, 65-66; assoc prof internal med, phys med & rehab, Sch Med, Univ Southern Calif, 67-73, prof med, phys med & rehab, 73-74. *Concurrent Pos:* Consult, Nat Arthritis Comn, 75; mem, Am Deleg, US/USSR Comn Arthritis, 77, US/USSR Coop Prog Arthritis, NIH, 77-84; mem, Coun Rehab Rheumatol, Am Rheumatism Asn, 81- *Mem:* AMA; Am Acad Phys Med & Rehab; Am Rheumatism Asn; fel Am Col Physicians; Asn Acad Physiatrists; fel Am Col Rheumatol; Soc Clin Densitometry; Spondylitis Asn Am; Am Acad Algol; Am Acad Pain Med; Am Back Soc; Nat Osteoporosis Found; Am Soc Bone & Joint Mineral Res; Back Pain Soc; Soc Clin Densitometry. *Res:* Rheumatology; clinical aspects of rheumatic diseases; mechanisms of arthritic deformities and their treatments; physical medicine and rehabilitation; conservative treatment of lumbar spinal stenosis; site specific exercise treatments for osteoporosis; evaluation of radiographic absorptiometry in osteoporsis; mechanics of posture and posture correction. *Mailing Add:* 1328 16th St Santa Monica CA 90404

SWIATEK, KENNETH ROBERT, NEUROSCIENCES. *Current Pos:* res scientist, Ill Inst Develop Disabilities, 68-70, admin res sci, 70-75, dir res, 75-76, dir, 76-80. *Personal Data:* b Chicago, Ill, Dec 30, 35; m 60; c 4. *Educ:* NCent Col, BS, 58; Univ Ill Med Ctr, PhD(biol sci), 65. *Prof Exp:* Res assoc biol chem, Dept Pediat, Univ Ill Col Med, 65-68. *Concurrent Pos:* Grant carbohydrate metab newborn animal, NIH, 71-74. *Mem:* Am Chem Soc; Sigma Xi; AAAS; Soc Develop Biol; Am Asn Ment Deficiency. *Res:* Study of growth of nervous system with special emphasis on development of carbohydrate, ketones and amino acid metabolism in fetal and newborn brain tissue as affected by pain-relieving drugs of labor and delivery. *Mailing Add:* 1640 W Roosevelt Rd Chicago IL 60608-1336

SWICK, KENNETH EUGENE, MATHEMATICS. *Current Pos:* asst prof, 70-78, assoc prof, 78-85, PROF MATH, QUEENS COL, NY, 85- *Personal Data:* b Silver Lake, Ind, Jan 20, 36; m 57. *Educ:* Anderson Col, BS, 57; Univ Southern Calif, MA, 64; Univ Iowa, PhD(math), 67. *Prof Exp:* Mathematician, Hughes Aircraft Corp, Calif, 62-64; asst prof, Cornell Col, 66-67 & Occidental Col, 67-70. *Mem:* Math Asn Am; Am Math Soc; Soc Indust & Appl Math. *Res:* Nonlinear differential and integral equations; nonlinear population dynamics. *Mailing Add:* 230 Vineyard Rd Huntington NY 11743

SWICK, ROBERT WINFIELD, BIOCHEMISTRY. *Current Pos:* PROF NUTRIT SCI, UNIV WIS-MADISON, 69-, CHMN DEPT, 85- *Personal Data:* b Jackson, Mich, July 6, 25; m 47; c 4. *Educ:* Beloit Col, BS, 47; Univ Wis, MS, 49, PhD(biochem), 51. *Prof Exp:* Assoc biochemist, Div Biol & Med, Argonne Nat Lab, 51-69. *Mem:* Am Inst Nutrit; Am Soc Biol Chem. *Res:* Control and kinetics of protein metabolism; regulation of enzyme levels and metabolism. *Mailing Add:* N4290 Alpine Village Lane Cambridge WI 53523-9537

SWICKLIK, LEONARD JOSEPH, ORGANIC CHEMISTRY. *Current Pos:* RETIRED. *Personal Data:* b Nanticoke, Pa, Jan 26, 28; m 52; c 3. *Educ:* Wilkes Col, BS, 49; Univ Pittsburgh, PhD(chem), 54. *Prof Exp:* Res chemist, E I du Pont de Nemours & Co, Va, 54; res chemist, Eastman Kodak Co, 56-64, sr res chemist & group leader, 64-68, tech assoc, 68-70, head, Process Improv Lab, 71-73, supvr chem process, 73-78, supvr, Oils Processing Dept, Distillation Prod Div, 78-84, supvr, Develop & Control Lab, 84-86. *Mem:* Am Oil Chemists Soc; AAAS; Am Chem Soc; NY Acad Sci; Sigma Xi. *Res:* Food applications of emulsifiers; fat and oil chemistry as applicable to edible products; food and animal feed applications of vitamins. *Mailing Add:* 92 Northwick Dr Rochester NY 14617

SWICORD, MAYS L, BIOELECTROMAGNETICS RESEARCH. *Current Pos:* DIR, BIOL RES, FLA CORP ELECTROMAGNETICS RES LAB, MOTOROLA, 95- *Personal Data:* b Chunju, Korea, May 5, 38; m 58, Kay Pratt; c Jeffrey & Hwayoung. *Educ:* King Col, BA, 60; Univ NC, MS, 63; Univ Md, PhD(electrophysics), 80. *Prof Exp:* Physicist, Radiation Measurements & Calibration Br, Div Electronic Prods, Ctr Devices & Radiol Health, Dept Health & Human Servs, 69-70, chief, Electromagnetic Sect, 70-72, chief, Microwave Sect, Prod Testing & Eval Br, 72-73, chief, Electromagnetic Br, 73-81, chief, Electromagnetic Radiation Br, Div Risk Assessment, 82-85, chief, Molecular Biol Br, Div Life Sci, 85-89, chief, Radiation Biol Br, 89-95. *Concurrent Pos:* Staff mem, WHO, Geneva, 85-86; chmn, Gordon Res Conf Bioelectrochem, 90; mem, Comt Radiofrequency Radiation Hazards, Inst Elec & Electronics Engrs; mem, Int Comn Nomionizing Radiation Protection, 92-96. *Mem:* Sr mem Inst Elec & Electronics Engrs; Bioelectromagnetics Soc (pres, 91-92); Europ Bioelectromagnetics Asn; Bioelectrochem Soc. *Res:* Measurement of absorption characteristics and electrical properties of biomolecules; interaction of microwaves and extremely low frequency fields with biological systems; biological effects of non-ionizing radiation. *Mailing Add:* Fla Corp Electromagnetic Res Lab Motorola 8000 W Sunrise Blvd Room 2105 Ft Lauderdale FL 33322. *Fax:* 954-723-5611; *E-Mail:* emx029@email.moi.com

SWIDEN, LADELL RAY, INDUSTRIAL CONTROLS, MANAGEMENT INFORMATION SYSTEMS. *Current Pos:* DIR, ENG & ENVIRON RES CTR, SDAK STATE UNIV, 86-; DIR, UNIV/INDUST TECHNOL SERV, 88- *Personal Data:* b Sioux Falls, SD, June 17, 38; m 61, Phyllis Enga; c David, Daniel & Shari. *Educ:* SDak State Univ, BSSE, 61; Univ SDak, MBA, 82. *Prof Exp:* Engr, Honeywell, 62-67; vpres sales, Swiden Appliances & Furn, 67-68; engr, Raven Indust, 68-72, mgr engr, 77-84; vpres engr, Beta Raven Inc, 84-85; pres, Delta Syst Inc, 85-86. *Concurrent Pos:* mem bd dir, Am Indust Ext Alliance, Nat Asn Mgt & Tech Asst Ctrs & SDak Micro Mkt Alliance; pres, SDak Eng Soc, NE Chap. *Mem:* Nat Soc Prof Engrs; Inst Sci Am; Am Indust Ext Alliance; Nat Asn Mgt & Tech Assistance Ctrs. *Res:* Automation of process controls and integration with management information systems; additional emphasis on engineering and research management; granted 2 patents. *Mailing Add:* 105 Heather Lane Brookings SD 57006

SWIDER, WILLIAM, JR, ATMOSPHERIC CHEMISTRY, PHYSICS. *Current Pos:* chmn civilian policy bd, 78-81, actg br chief, 84-85, PHYSICIST, AIR FORCE GEOPHYSICS LAB, 64-, DEP DIV DIR, 89- *Personal Data:* b Brooklyn, NY, Jan 5, 34; m 59, Eileen O'Neill; c Sarah, Michael, Karen, Stacy & Gregory. *Educ:* Lehigh Univ, BS, 55, MS, 57; Pa State Univ, PhD(physics), 63. *Honors & Awards:* Loeser Award, Air Force Geophysics Lab, 77. *Prof Exp:* Assoc physicist, Int Bus Mach Corp, 57-60. *Concurrent Pos:* Res fel, Nat Ctr Space Res, Brussels, Belgium, 63-64; Air Force Rep to Geophysics Res Forum Nat Res Coun; vis prof physics, Utah State Univ, 75. *Mem:* Am Geophys Union; Sigma Xi. *Res:* Ionospheric physics; airglow. *Mailing Add:* 15 Old Stagecoach Rd Bedford MA 01730-1246. *Fax:* 781-377-3160; *E-Mail:* swider@plh.af.mil

SWIDLER, RONALD, electrophotography, chemistry of fats & oils, for more information see previous edition

SWIERSTRA, ERNEST EMKE, ANIMAL PHYSIOLOGY. *Current Pos:* RETIRED. *Personal Data:* b Netherlands, Aug, 14, 30; Can citizen; m 62, Norma Brown; c 2. *Educ:* Univ Groningen, dipl, 51; Univ BC, BSA, 56, MSA, 58; Cornell Univ, PhD(physiol), 62. *Prof Exp:* Asst animal breeding, Cornell Univ, 58-62; sr res scientist, Can Dept Agr, 62-75, head, Animal Sci Sect, 75-84, asst dir, 84-86, dir, Res Sta, 86-91. *Mem:* Am Soc Animal Sci; Can Soc Animal Sci. *Res:* Reproductive physiology. *Mailing Add:* 12 Cedar Bay Brandon MB R7B 0Z4 Can. *E-Mail:* swierstrae@docker.com

SWIFT, ARTHUR REYNDERS, PHYSICS. *Current Pos:* asst prof, 67-70, assoc prof, 70-76, PROF PHYSICS, UNIV MASS, AMHERST, 76- *Personal Data:* b Worcester, Mass, July 25, 38; m 61; c 3. *Educ:* Swarthmore Col, BA, 60; Univ Pa, PhD(physics), 64. *Prof Exp:* NATO fel physics, Cambridge Univ, 64-65; res assoc, Univ Wis, 65-67. *Mem:* Am Phys Soc. *Res:* Elementary particle theory. *Mailing Add:* Dept Physics & Astron Lederle Tower Univ Mass Amherst MA 01003. *Fax:* 413-545-0468

SWIFT, BRINTON L, veterinary medicine, for more information see previous edition

SWIFT, CALVIN THOMAS, ENGINEERING, REMOTE SENSING. *Current Pos:* PROF ELEC & COMPUT ENG, UNIV MASS, 81-; CONSULT ENG, 82- *Personal Data:* b Quantico, Va, Feb 6, 37; m 59; c Pamela & Janet. *Educ:* Mass Inst Technol, BS, 59; Va Polytech Inst & State Univ, MS, 65; Col William & Mary, PhD(physics), 69. *Honors & Awards:* Centennial Award, Inst Elec & Electronics Engrs, 84, Distinguished Sci Award, 92. *Prof Exp:* Res engr, NAm Aviation, Calif, 59-62; aeorspace engr, Langley Res Ctr, NASA, 62-81, leader microwave radiometer group, 75-81. *Concurrent Pos:* Asst lectorial prof, George Washington Univ, 70-; lectr, Col William & Mary, 71-; adj assoc prof, Old Dominion Univ, 75-; ed, Geosci & Remote Sensing Soc, 80-84; chmn, Comn F, Int Union Radio Sci, 87-90. *Mem:* Fel Inst Elec & Electronics Engrs; Antennas & Propagation Soc (secy-treas, 74-77); Geosci & Remote Sensing Soc (pres, 85); Int Union Radio Sci. *Res:* Antennas and propagation, with emphasis on remote sensing of the ocean. *Mailing Add:* Dept Elec & Comp Eng Univ Mass Knowles Eng Bldg Amherst MA 01003

SWIFT, CAMM CHURCHILL, ICHTHYOLOGY. *Current Pos:* ASSOC CUR FISHES, NATURAL HIST MUS LOS ANGELES COUNTY, 70- *Personal Data:* b Oakland, Calif, Sept 29, 40; m 74; c 5. *Educ:* Univ Calif, Berkeley, AB, 63; Univ Mich, Ann Arbor, MS, 65; Fla State Univ, PhD(biol), 70. *Concurrent Pos:* Adj asst prof, Dept Biol Sci, Univ Southern Calif, 72-; bd gov, Am Soc Ichthyologists & Herpetologists, 73-78; secy, S Calif Acad Sci, 81-86, vpres, 87- *Mem:* Am Soc Ichthyologists & Herpetologists; Soc Vert Paleont; Soc Study Evolution; Soc Syst Zool; AAAS; Sigma Xi. *Res:* Systematics and evolution of Recent and fossil, freshwater and marine shore fishes of North America. *Mailing Add:* 346 W Leroy Ave Arcadia CA 91007-6909

SWIFT, CHARLES MOORE, JR, geophysics, for more information see previous edition

SWIFT, DANIEL W, PLASMA PHYSICS, SPACE PHYSICS. *Current Pos:* from asst prof to assoc prof, 63-72, PROF PHYSICS, GEOPHYS INST, UNIV ALASKA, 72- *Personal Data:* b Worcester, Mass, Mar 6, 35; m 61; c 3. *Educ:* Haverford Col, BA, 57; Mass Inst Technol, MS, 59. *Prof Exp:* Mem staff, Lincoln Lab, Mass Inst Technol, 58-59; sr scientist, Res & Adv Develop Div, Avco Corp, 59-63. *Mem:* AAAS; Am Geophys Union; Am Phys Soc. *Res:* Theoretical studies of the earth's magnetosphere and auroral phenomena. *Mailing Add:* 3181 Anella Ave Fairbanks AK 99709

SWIFT, DAVID LESLIE, HEALTH EFFECTS OF AIRBORNE POLLUTANTS, AEROSOL SCIENCE. *Current Pos:* asst prof, 66-70, assoc prof environ med, 70-78, PROF ENVIRON HEALTH SCI, JOHNS HOPKINS UNIV, 78- *Personal Data:* b Chicago, Ill, Aug 7, 35; m 59, Suzanne N Haller; c Charles, Kevin & Austin. *Educ:* Purdue Univ, BS, 57; Mass Inst Technol, SM, 59; Johns Hopkins Univ, PhD(chem eng), 63. *Honors & Awards:* Thomsom Lectr, London Univ, UK, 88. *Prof Exp:* Chem engr, Argonne Nat Lab, Ill, 63-65; USPHS air pollution spec fel, London Sch Hyg, 65-66. *Mem:* Am Soc Affil; Brit Occup Hyg Soc; Am Conf Govt Indust Hyg; Am Indust Hyg Asn; Am Asn Aerosol Res; Sigma Xi. *Res:* Exposure and health effects of airborne pollutants; characterization of airborne particles; basis for environmental standards and the production and delivery of pharmaceutical aerosols; air pollution transport. *Mailing Add:* 1020 Lithfield Rd Baltimore MD 21239. *Fax:* 410-955-9334; *E-Mail:* swift@bigsis.sph.jhu.edu

SWIFT, DONALD J P, SEDIMENTOLOGY, OCEANOGRAPHY. *Current Pos:* SLOVER PROF, DEPT OCEANOG, OLD DOMINION UNIV, 86- *Personal Data:* b Dobbs Ferry, NY, July 26, 35; m 61, Sondra Ford; c Etain, Cecilia & Colin. *Educ:* Dartmouth Col, AB, 57; Johns Hopkins Univ, MA, 61; Univ NC, PhD(geol), 64. *Honors & Awards:* Shepard Medal, 89. *Prof Exp:* Asst prof sedimentology, geol dept, Dalhousie Univ, 63-66; assoc scientist marine geol, P R Nuclear Ctr, 66-67; assoc prof geol, Duke Univ, 67-68; Slover assoc prof, Inst Oceanog, Old Dominion Univ, 68-71; res oceanogr, Atlantic Oceanog & Meteorol Labs, Nat Oceanic & Atmospheric Admin, 71-81; res adv, Arco Explor Technol, 81-86. *Concurrent Pos:* Res grant, Geol Surv Can, 64-65; res assoc, NS Mus, 65-66; assoc ed, Maritime Sediments, 65-66; res grant, Nat Res Coun Can & Defense Res Bd Can, 65-67; Coastal Eng Res Ctr, 69-71; US Geol Surv, 69-71 & NSF, 69-72; mem, Univ Senate, Old Dom Univ, 69-71, chmn, Univ Res Comt, 69-71; res grant, NASA, 70-71; proj leader, Continental Margin Sedimentation Proj, 72-81; consult, Oceanog Panel, NSF, 74-; res assoc, Smithsonian Inst, 74-81; adj prof, Univ Miami, 74-81; asst chmn, dept oceanog, 87-90, Univ Senate, Old Dom Univ, 86-89; res grant, NSF, 89-94, Nat Oceanic & Atmospheric Admin, 89- 93, Off Naval Res, 93- *Mem:* AAAS; Soc Econ Paleont & Mineral; Fel Geol Soc Am; Am Asn Petrol Geol; Int Asn Sedimentologists. *Res:* Formation of the shallow marine sea bed by storm current resuspension and bigenic mixing; high resolution sequence stratigraphy of modern and ancient continental margins: analysis by observation and simulation. *Mailing Add:* Dept Oceanog Old Dominion Univ Norfolk VA 23529-0276. *Fax:* 757-683-5303; *E-Mail:* djsloof@ludwick.naeco.odu.edu

SWIFT, DOROTHY GARRISON, BIOLOGICAL OCEANOGRAPHY, TRACE METALS. *Current Pos:* guest investr, Gran Sch Oceanog, Univ RI, 70-73, res assoc, Dept Chem, 74-76, res assoc, 76-88, ASST MARINE SCIENTIST, GRAD SCH OCEANOG, UNIV RI, 89- *Personal Data:* b Flint, Mich, Aug 1, 39; div. *Educ:* Swarthmore Col, BA, 61; Johns Hopkins Univ, MA, 67, PhD(oceanog), 73. *Honors & Awards:* Bronze Medal, Am Rhododendron Soc, 80. *Prof Exp:* Guest student investr, Biol Dept, Woods Hole Oceanog Inst, 68-69. *Concurrent Pos:* Consult, Bigelow Lab Ocean Sci, 82-84. *Mem:* Am Soc Limnol & Oceanog; Am Geophys Union; Phycol Soc Am; Int Phycol Soc; Sigma Xi. *Res:* Trace metal requirements in phytoplankton; atmospheric input of trace metals biochemistry, nutrition and ecology of marine phytoplankton; bioassay for vitamins in seawater; vitamin bioassay; biogeochemistry; algal culture and plant tissue culture; atmospheric chemistry. *Mailing Add:* URI Grad Sch Oceanog Narragansett Bay Campus RI 02882. *E-Mail:* dorothy@gsosun1.gso.uri.edu

SWIFT, ELIJAH, V, BIOLOGICAL OCEANOGRAPHY. *Current Pos:* asst prof, 69-74, ASSOC PROF OCEANOG, UNIV RI, 74- *Personal Data:* b Boston, Apr 12, 38; m 61. *Educ:* Swarthmore Col, BA, 60; Johns Hopkins Univ, MA, 64, PhD(oceanog), 67. *Prof Exp:* NSF trainee, Woods Hole Oceanog Inst, 68-69. *Concurrent Pos:* NSF grants, 71-76. *Mem:* Phycol Soc Am; Int Phycol Soc; Marine Biol Asn UK; Brit Phycol Soc; Am Soc Limnol & Oceanog; Sigma Xi. *Res:* Morphology, taxonomy, ecology and physiology of phytoplankton, particularly marine species. *Mailing Add:* Dept Oceanog Univ RI S Ferry Rd Narragansett RI 02882-1096

SWIFT, FRED CALVIN, entomology, ecology, for more information see previous edition

SWIFT, GEORGE W(ILLIAM), CHEMICAL ENGINEERING. *Current Pos:* from asst prof to assoc prof, Univ Kans, 61-70, actg assoc dean grad sch, 66-70, prof chem & petrol eng, 70-81, DEANE E ACKERS DISTINGUISHED PROF ENG, UNIV KANS, 81- *Personal Data:* b Topeka, Kans, Nov 28, 30; m 56; c 3. *Educ:* Univ Kans, BS, 53, MS, 57, PhD(chem eng), 59. *Prof Exp:* Res engr, Continental Oil Co, 59-61. *Concurrent Pos:* Consult, Continental Oil Co, 63- & C W Nofsinger Co, 65- *Mem:* Am Inst Chem Engrs; Soc Petrol Engrs; Am Soc Eng Educ; Sigma Xi. *Res:* Transient flow of gas in porous media; transport and thermodynamic properties at low temperature and high pressure; rheology. *Mailing Add:* 1102 Hilltop Dr Lawrence KS 66044

SWIFT, GLENN W(ILLIAM), ELECTRICAL ENGINEERING. *Current Pos:* from lectr to prof, 60-97, EMER PROF ELEC ENG, UNIV MAN, 97- *Personal Data:* b Athabasca, Alta, May 17, 32; m 61; c 2. *Educ:* Univ Alta, BSc, 53, MSc, 60; Ill Inst Technol, PhD(elec eng), 68. *Prof Exp:* Elec engr, Can Westinghouse Co, Ltd, 56-58. *Concurrent Pos:* Consult various firms including Westinghouse Can, Fed Pioneer, 60-; Nat Res Coun Can grants, 60- *Mem:* Sr mem Inst Elec & Electronics Engrs. *Res:* Power system protection and control; microprocessors. *Mailing Add:* Dept Elec Eng Univ Man Winnipeg MB R3T 2N2 Can

SWIFT, GRAHAM, ORGANIC POLYMER CHEMISTRY. *Current Pos:* sr chemist, 68-77, MGR RES SECT, ROHM AND HAAS CO, 77-, RES FEL, 86- *Personal Data:* b Chesterfield, Eng, Apr 16, 39; m 61; c 2. *Educ:* Univ London, BSc, 61, PhD(org chem', 64. *Prof Exp:* NIH fel, Fels Res Inst, Philadelphia, 64-66; sci off, Imperial Chem Industs, Eng, 66-68. *Mem:* Royal Soc Chem; Royal Inst Chem; Am Chem Soc. *Res:* Heterocyclic chemistry; synthesis and reactions of special aziridines, oxiranes and thiiranes; fatty acid chemistry; organic polymer coatings, especially synthesis and evaluation of novel coating compositions; water soluble polymer synthesis; application of polymer in detergents, mining, and water treatment; emulsion polymer synthesis. *Mailing Add:* Rohm and Haas Co Spring House PA 19477-1100

SWIFT, GREGORY WILLIAM, REFRIGERATION. *Current Pos:* Fel, 81-85, TECH STAFF MEM, LOS ALAMOS NAT LAB, 86- *Personal Data:* b Omaha, Nebr, July 7, 52. *Educ:* Univ Nebr, BS, 74; Univ Calif, Berkeley, PhD(physics), 80. *Mem:* Fel Acoust Soc Am; Am Phys Soc. *Res:* Fundamentals and applications of thermoacoustics and other novel heat-engine and refrigeration methods. *Mailing Add:* RR 5 PO Box 287 H Santa Fe NM 87501. *E-Mail:* swift@lanl.gov

SWIFT, HAROLD EUGENE, PHYSICAL INORGANIC CHEMISTRY. *Current Pos:* Chemist, 62-63, res chemist, 62-63, sr res chemist, 63-65, sect supvr, Catalysis Sect, Gulf Res & Develop Co, Pittsburgh, 66-73, res dir & sr scientst, Chem & Minerals Div, 74-77, MGR, CATALYST & CHEM DEPT, GULF SCI & TECHNOL CO, 77- *Personal Data:* b Butler, Pa, Mar 27, 36; m 60; c 3. *Educ:* Allegheny Col, BS, 58; Pittsburgh Univ, PhD(chem), 62. *Concurrent Pos:* Indust bd dir for sch eng & sci, Univ Mass, Amherst, 81-83. *Mem:* Am Chem Soc (chmn, Petrol Chem Div, 77-78). *Res:* Process research for chemical, refining, synthetic fuels and pollution control; heterogeneous and homogeneous catalysis. *Mailing Add:* 1100 Woodhill Dr Gibsonia PA 15044-9238

SWIFT, HEWSON HOYT, CYTOLOGY. *Current Pos:* Instr zool, Univ Chicago, 49-51, from asst prof to prof, 51-71, distinguished serv prof, 71-77, chmn dept, 72-77, Beadle distinguished serv prof biol, 77-84, Beadle distinguished serv prof, Dept Molecular Genetics, Cell Biol & Path, 84-90, EMER PROF, UNIV CHICAGO, 91- *Personal Data:* b Auburn, NY, Nov 8, 20; m 42; c 2. *Educ:* Swarthmore Col, BA, 42; Univ Iowa, MS, 45; Columbia Univ, PhD(zool), 50. *Honors & Awards:* E B Wilson Award, 85. *Concurrent Pos:* Mem, Cell Biol Study Sect, NIH, 58-62, Develop Biol Adv Panel, NSF, 62-65 & Etiology Cancer Adv Panel, Am Cancer Soc, 66-70; vis prof, Harvard Univ, 70-71; chmn, Sect Cellular & Develop Biol, Nat Acad Sci, 75-79; vis sr scientist, Commonwealth Sci & Indust Res Orgn, Canberra, Australia, 77-78. *Mem:* Nat Acad Sci; Am Soc Cell Biol (pres, 64); Histochem Soc (pres, 73); Genetics Soc Am; Am Acad Arts & Sci; hon fel Nat Acad Sci India. *Res:* Cell biology; cytochemistry; molecular structure of chromosomes and chloroplasts. *Mailing Add:* Molecular Genetics & Cell Biol Univ Chicago 1103 East 57th St Chicago IL 60637. *Fax:* 773-702-9270; *E-Mail:* swift@cells.uchicago.edu

SWIFT, HOWARD R(AYMOND), CERAMICS. *Current Pos:* CONSULT, 82- *Personal Data:* b Streator, Ill, Mar 3, 20; m 46; c 5. *Educ:* Univ Ill, BS, 40, MS, 42, PhD(ceramics), 45. *Prof Exp:* Asst eng, Exp Sta, Univ Ill, 40-42, res assoc eng, 43-44; res phys chemist, Libbey-Owens-Ford Glass Co, 45-56, chief glass tech res, Libby-Owens-Ford Co, 55-61, asst dir res, 61-68, dir res & develop, 68-76, chmn, Tech Prod Comt, 76-82, asst to pres, Glass Div, 78-82. *Mem:* Fel Am Ceramic Soc; fel Brit Soc Glass Technol; fel Am Soc Testing & Mat. *Res:* Crystallization of glass; effect of glass composition on properties; stones in glass; manufacturing of flat glass. *Mailing Add:* 3525 Wesleyan Dr Toledo OH 43614

SWIFT, JACK BERNARD, THEORETICAL SOLID STATE PHYSICS. *Current Pos:* assoc prof, 75-81, PROF PHYSICS, UNIV TEX, AUSTIN, 81- *Personal Data:* b Ft Smith, Ark, Jan 3, 42; m 71; c 2. *Educ:* Univ Ark, Fayetteville, BS, 63; Univ Ill, Urbana, MS, 65, PhD(physics), 68. *Prof Exp:* NSF fel, Max Planck Inst Physics & Astrophys, Munich, 68-69; res fel, Harvard Univ, 69-71; vis, Bell Tel Lab, 74; asst prof physics, 71-75. *Concurrent Pos:* Res Fel, A P Sloan Found, 73-75. *Res:* Critical phenomena; light scattering properties of liquids; hydrodynamics. *Mailing Add:* Dept Physics Univ Tex Austin TX 78712

SWIFT, LLOYD HARRISON, PLANT MORPHOLOGY. *Current Pos:* RETIRED. *Personal Data:* b Crete, Nebr, Sept 12, 20. *Educ:* Univ Nebr, AB, 41, MS, 60, PhD(bot), 62; Western Reserve Univ, MA, 42. *Prof Exp:* Lexicographer, World Pub Co, Ohio, 42; instr Eng, Ill Inst Technol, 44 & Univ Mo, 44-45; asst prof bot, Univ Alaska, 62-63; prof & chmn dept Univ Nebr, Ataturk Univ, Turkey, 63-65; res assoc bot, Univ Nebr, 65-78. *Res:* Botanical bibliography and the classification and indexing of information important in botany; etymology and history of botanical terminology and nomenclature; phytography in plant morphology, taxonomy and physiology. *Mailing Add:* 2210 Sewell St Lincoln NE 68502-3850

SWIFT, LLOYD WESLEY, JR, MICROMETEOROLOGY, FOREST HYDROLOGY. *Current Pos:* Jr forester, 54-55, res forester, 57-71, RES METEOROLOGIST, FOREST SERV, USDA, 72- *Personal Data:* b San Francisco, Calif, July 11, 32; m 55; c 4. *Educ:* State Univ NY Col Forestry, Syracuse, BS, 54; NC State Univ, MS, 60; Duke Univ, DF, 72. *Mem:* Am Meteorol Soc. *Res:* Water quality of forested and logged mountain slopes; streamflow and precipitation measurement on steep slopes; air circulation patterns in mountains; effect of slope aspect and inclination on forest microenvironment. *Mailing Add:* Coweeta Hydrol Lab 3160 Coweeta Lab Rd Otto NC 28763

SWIFT, MICHAEL C, HUMAN GENETICS. *Current Pos:* assoc prof med, 72-79, RES SCIENTIST, BIOL SCI RES CTR, UNIV NC, 72-, PROF MED, 79- *Personal Data:* b New York, NY, Feb 5, 35; m 71; c 3. *Educ:* Swarthmore, BA, 55; Univ Calif, Berkeley, MA, 58; NY Univ, MD, 62. *Prof Exp:* Instr med, NY Univ Sch Med, 66-67, asst prof, 70-71. *Concurrent Pos:* Mem, Genetics Curric, 72-; assoc attend physician, Univ NC Hosps, 72-79, attend phys, 79-; dir, Second Yr Course Human Genetics, Univ NC, 80-89. *Mem:* AAAS; Am Soc Human Genetics. *Res:* Identify specific genes that predispose to particular common diseases and characterize them at the molecular level; develop tests to identify susceptible gene carriers; devise new strategies to prevent gene-associated common diseases. *Mailing Add:* 826 Goodrich Ave St Paul MN 55105-3345

SWIFT, MICHAEL CRANE, PREDATOR-PREY INTERACTIONS, ENERGETICS. *Current Pos:* STA MGR, MONTICELLO ECOL RES STA, 87- *Personal Data:* b Berkeley, Calif, Aug 21, 44; m 77. *Educ:* Univ Calif, Davis, BSc, 66, MA, 68; Univ BC, PhD(zool), 74. *Prof Exp:* Fel, Univ Sask, 74-75; res assoc, Inst Animal Res Ecol, Univ BC, 75-76; instr intro biol, Duke Univ, 77-79; asst prof limnol & aquatic ecol, Appalachian Environ Lab, Ctr Environ & Estuarine Studies, Univ Md, 80-87. *Concurrent Pos:* Lectr forestry-fisheries interactions, Fac Forestry, Univ BC, 75-76; vis lectr physiol, Univ NC, Chapel Hill 76; vis scientist, Marine Lab, Duke Univ, 79-81; adj fac, Frostburg State Col, 80-; assoc mem, Grad Fac, Univ Md, 81- *Mem:* AAAS; Am Soc Limnol & Oceanog; Soc Int Limnol; Ecol Soc Am; Sigma Xi; NAm Benthological Soc. *Res:* Limnology; predator-prey interactions among zooplankton; Chaoborus ecology. *Mailing Add:* 826 Goodrich Ave St Paul MN 55105

SWIFT, ROBINSON MARDEN, PHYSICAL CHEMISTRY. *Current Pos:* from asst prof to assoc prof, 56-72, PROF CHEM, ST ANSELM'S COL, 72-; CHIEF CHEMIST, EDISON ELECTRONICS DIV, MCGRAW-EDISON, 57- *Personal Data:* b Wolfeboro, NH, May 6, 18; m 44; c 4. *Educ:* Univ NH, BS, 40; Northwestern Univ, MS, 48; Syracuse Univ, PhD(chem), 56. *Prof Exp:* Chemist, Bird & Son, Inc, Mass, 40-44; instr chem, Thiel Col, 47-53. *Mem:* Am Chem Soc; Sigma Xi. *Res:* Thermodynamics; epoxy resins. *Mailing Add:* 18 Birchhill Dr Hooksett NH 03106-1523

SWIFT, TERRENCE JAMES, PHYSICAL CHEMISTRY, BIOCHEMISTRY. *Current Pos:* from asst prof to assoc prof chem, 63-76, PROF CHEM, CASE WESTERN RESERVE UNIV, 76- *Personal Data:* b Dubuque, Iowa, June 29, 37; m 65; c 2. *Educ:* Loras Col, BS, 59; Univ Calif, Berkeley, PhD(chem), 62. *Prof Exp:* NSF fel, Max Planck Inst Phys Chem, 62-63. *Mem:* Am Soc Biol Chem; Am Chem Soc. *Res:* Magnetic resonance spectroscopy as applied to biological systems and processes. *Mailing Add:* Dept Chem Case Western Res Univ University Circle Cleveland OH 44106-1749

SWIFT, WILLIAM CLEMENT, MATHEMATICS, ANALYSIS & FUNCTIONAL ANALYSIS. *Current Pos:* from assoc prof to prof, 63-90, EMER PROF MATH, WABASH COL, 90- *Personal Data:* b Lexington, Ky, Mar 17, 28; m 50, Ellen Dumbacher; c Thomas, William Jr, Michael, Matthew, Lawrence, Margaret, Joseph & James. *Educ:* Univ Ky, BS, 50, PhD(math), 55. *Prof Exp:* Instr math, Cornell Univ, 55-56; mem tech staff, Bell Tel Labs, Inc, 56-58; asst prof math, Rutgers Univ, 58-63. *Mem:* Math Asn Am. *Res:* Complex variables; linear programming; summability. *Mailing Add:* 116 N Grace Ave Crawfordsville IN 47933-2023

SWIGAR, MARY EVA, PSYCHIATRY. *Current Pos:* ASSOC PROF PSYCHIAT, UMDNJ/ROBERT WOOD JOHNSON MED SCH, NEW BRUNSWICK, NJ, 88-; CHIEF PSYCHIAT, ROBERT WOOD JOHNSON UNIV HOSP, 88- *Personal Data:* b Nesquehoning, Pa, Oct 17, 40. *Educ:* Muhlenberg Col, BS, 62; Health Sci Ctr, Temple Univ, MD, 66. *Prof Exp:* Teaching fel, Yale Univ, Sch Med, 67-70, instr, 70-71, from asst prof to assoc prof psychiat, 71-88. *Concurrent Pos:* Consult, Dept Obstet-Gynec, Sch Med, Yale Univ, 70-73, Gaylord Rehab Hosp, 70-79 & 85-88. *Mem:* Am Med Women's Asn; Am Psychopath Asn; NY Acad Sci; AAAS; fel Int Col Psychosom Med. *Res:* Psychiatric aspects of obstetrics-gynecology; psychoendocrinology; diagnostic imaging and psychiatric syndromes; early response to treatment in psychoses. *Mailing Add:* Clin Acad Bldg CAB2206 125 Paterson St New Brunswick NJ 08901. *Fax:* 732-235-7677

SWIGART, RICHARD HANAWALT, NEUROANATOMY. *Current Pos:* from asst prof to assoc prof, Univ Louisville, 53-57, asst dean student affairs, 69-72, actg dean, Sch Med, 72-73, vpres, Allied Health Affairs, 76-78, actg dean Grad Sch, 76-77, dir, Div Allied Health, 78-92, actg spec asst to pres, Health Affairs, 81-86, PROF ANAT, SCH MED, UNIV LOUISVILLE, 67-, ACTG DEAN, COL HEALTH & SOCIAL SERVS, 86-, ASSOC DEAN, SCH MED, 86- *Personal Data:* b Lewistown, Pa, July 7, 25; m 51; c 3. *Educ:* Univ NC, BA, 47; Univ Minn, PhD(anat), 53. *Prof Exp:* Asst anat, Univ Minn, 48-50, instr, 50-52, res assoc histochem, 52-53. *Mem:* Am Asn Anat; Biol Stain Comn; Histochem Soc; Soc Exp Biol & Med; Sigma Xi. *Res:* Chronic hypoxia, effect on cardiovascular and erythropoietic systems; carbohydrate metabolism in cardiac and skeletal muscle; effect of age on adaptive responses; neurological mutant mice. *Mailing Add:* Dept Anat Sci & Neurobiol Univ Louisville Carmichael Bldg Louisville KY 40292

SWIGER, ELIZABETH DAVIS, PHYSICAL CHEMISTRY, INORGANIC CHEMISTRY. *Current Pos:* Instr math, 54-56, instr chem, 56-60, from asst prof to assoc prof, 60-66, PROF CHEM, FAIRMONT STATE COL, 66- *Personal Data:* b Morgantown, WVa, June 27, 26; m 48; c 2. *Educ:* WVa Univ, BS, 48, MS, 52, PhD, 65. *Mem:* Am Chem Soc; AAAS; Sigma Xi. *Res:* Nuclear quadrupole resonance spectroscopy; computer applications; coordination compounds. *Mailing Add:* 1599 Hillcrest Rd Fairmont WV 26554-4807

SWIGER, LOUIS ANDRE, ANIMAL GENETICS, POPULATION GENETICS. *Current Pos:* PROF & DEPT HEAD ANIMAL SCI, VA POLYTECH INST & STATE UNIV, 80- *Personal Data:* b Waverly, Ohio, Sept 16, 32; m 53; c 3. *Educ:* Ohio State Univ, BSc, 54; Iowa State Univ, MSc, 57, PhD(animal breeding), 60. *Honors & Awards:* Rockefeller Prentice Mem Award. *Prof Exp:* Animal geneticist, USDA, 59-62; assoc prof animal sci & exp sta statist, Univ Nebr, 62-65; assoc prof animal sci, Ohio State Univ, 65-70, prof, 70-80. *Concurrent Pos:* Grad chmn, Dept Animal Sci, Ohio State Univ, 68-80. *Mem:* Am Soc Animal Sci; Biomet Soc; Sigma Xi. *Res:* Population genetics and application to domestic animals. *Mailing Add:* 2600 N Main St Blacksburg VA 24060

SWIGER, WILLIAM F, geotechnical engineering; deceased, see previous edition for last biography

SWIHART, G(ERALD) R(OBERT), STRUCTURAL ENGINEERING. *Current Pos:* RETIRED. *Personal Data:* b Carroll, Nebr, Feb 16, 20; m 44; c 3. *Educ:* Rose Polytech Inst, BS, 47; Yale Univ, MEng, 49. *Prof Exp:* Instr, Rose Polytech Inst, 48; asst instr, Yale Univ, 48-49; from instr to prof civil eng, Univ Nebr, Lincoln, 49-90, teacher exten div, 58 & 59, vchmn dept, 71-73 & 81-82. *Concurrent Pos:* Struct designer, Harold Hoskins & Assocs, Nebr, 55, 57, 59 & 61; struct res engr, US Naval Civil Eng Lab. *Mem:* Am Soc Civil Engrs; Am Concrete Inst; Nat Soc Prof Engrs. *Res:* Ultimate load theories of reinforced concrete structures subjected to static and dynamics loading. *Mailing Add:* 2338 Calumet Ct Lincoln NE 68502

SWIHART, JAMES CALVIN, THEORETICAL SOLID STATE PHYSICS, BIOPHYSICS. *Current Pos:* assoc prof, 66-67, assoc dean grad sch, 71-74, chmn biophys prog, 71-78, PROF PHYSICS, IND UNIV, BLOOMINGTON, 67-, CHMN, PHYSICS DEPT, 80- *Personal Data:* b Elkhart, Ind, Feb 8, 27; m 47; c 2. *Educ:* Purdue Univ, BSChE, 49, MS, 51, PhD(physics), 55. *Prof Exp:* Danish govt fel, Inst Theoret Physics, Copenhagen Univ, 54-55; physicist, Argonne Nat Lab, 55-56; physicist, Res Ctr, Int Bus Mach Corp, 56-66. *Concurrent Pos:* Vis physicist, Lawrence Radiation Lab, Berkeley, 65; visitor, Cavendish Lab & assoc, Clare Hall, Univ Cambridge, 74. *Mem:* AAAS; fel Am Phys Soc; Sigma Xi. *Res:* Theory of solid state physics; superconductivity; many-body problem; biophysics. *Mailing Add:* Dept Physics Ind Univ Swain W Bloomington IN 47405. *Fax:* 812-855-5533

SWIHART, THOMAS LEE, ASTROPHYSICS. *Current Pos:* assoc prof, 63-69, PROF ASTRON, UNIV ARIZ, 69-, ASTRONR, STEWARD OBSERV, 74- *Personal Data:* b Elkhart, Ind, July 29, 29; m 51; c 3. *Educ:* Ind Univ, AB, 51, AM, 52; Univ Chicago, PhD(astrophys), 55. *Prof Exp:* Assoc prof physics & astron, Univ Miss, 55-57; mem staff, Los Alamos Sci Lab, 57-62; prof astrophys, Univ Ill, 62-63. *Concurrent Pos:* Fulbright-Hays lectr, Aegean Univ, Turkey, 69-70. *Mem:* Int Astron Union. *Res:* Theoretical astrophysics; radiation transfer; polarization of radio sources; atmospheric structure of stars. *Mailing Add:* 448 W Hardy Rd Tucson AZ 85737

SWIM, WILLIAM B(AXTER), FLUID DYNAMICS, ACOUSTICS. *Current Pos:* PROF MECH ENG & DIR, NOISE CONTROL FACIL & FAN RES LAB, TENN TECHNOL UNIV, 73- *Personal Data:* b Stillwater, Okla, Nov 18, 31; m 79; c 5. *Educ:* Okla State Univ, BS, 55; Ga Inst Technol, PhD(mech eng), 66. *Prof Exp:* Instr mech eng, Pa State Univ, 55-59; eng res, Okla State Univ, 59-61; sr res engr, Trane Co, 64-73. *Concurrent Pos:* Consult fluid dynamics acousts & turbomach, Holley Automotive, Toro, US Navy, MOOG Automotive, 81-; Fulbright fel, 81. *Mem:* Am Soc Mech Engrs; Acoust Soc Am; Am Soc Heating, Refrig & Air-Conditioning Engrs. *Res:* Fluid dynamics of turbomachinery; analysis of internal flows; generation and suppression of flow-noise; noise reduction of fans and blowers, flow losses in piping and duct systems; axial fan design; centrifugal blower evaluation; noise reduction of fan and blower systems. *Mailing Add:* Dept Mech Eng Tenn Technol Univ Cookeville TN 38505-0001

SWINDALE, LESLIE D, SOIL SCIENCE, RESEARCH ADMINISTRATION. *Current Pos:* ADJ PROF SOIL SCI, UNIV HAWAII, MANOA, 91- *Personal Data:* b Wellington, NZ, Mar 16, 28; m 55; c 3. *Educ:* Univ Victoria, NZ, 48, MSc, 50; Univ Wis, PhD(soil sci), 55. *Prof Exp:* Phys chemist, NZ Soil Bur, 49-57, sr phys chemist, 57-60; dir, NZ Pottery & Ceramics Res Asn, 60-63; prof soil sci, Univ Hawaii, Manoa, 63-76, chmn, dept agron & soil sci, 65-68, soil scientist, agr exp sta, 65-76, assoc dir, 70-75; dir gen, Int Crops Res Inst Semi-arid Tropics, 77-91. *Concurrent Pos:* Fel, Univ Wis, 55-56; chief soil resources, Conserv & Develop Serv, Land & Water Develop Div, Food & Agr Orgn, UN, Rome, 68-70. *Mem:* Fel Soil Sci Soc Am; fel NZ Inst Chem; Royal Soc NZ; Int Soc Soil Sci; fel Am Soc Agron. *Res:* Genesis of soils, their characterization and uses. *Mailing Add:* 2910 Nanihale Pl Honolulu HI 96822. *E-Mail:* l.swindale@cgnet.com

SWINDELL, ROBERT THOMAS, ORGANIC CHEMISTRY. *Current Pos:* CHMN, DEPT CHEM, UNIV ARK, LITTLE ROCK, 92- *Personal Data:* b Greenfield, Tenn, Feb 22, 38; m 61; c 1. *Educ:* Memphis State Univ, BS, 61; Univ SC, PhD(org chem), 65. *Prof Exp:* NIH fel org photochem, Iowa State Univ, 65-66; asst prof chem, Tenn Technol Univ, 66-77, prof, 77-86, chmn, Dept Chem, 86-92. *Mem:* Am Chem Soc; Royal Soc Chem. *Res:* Organic reaction mechanisms; organic photochemistry. *Mailing Add:* Dept Chem Univ Ark 2801 S University Ave Little Rock AR 72204-1099. *Fax:* 501-569-8838; *E-Mail:* rtswindell@ualr.edu

SWINDEMAN, ROBERT W, MATERIALS FOR PRESSURE VESSELS & PIPING, HIGH TEMPERATURE MECHANICAL METALLURGY. *Current Pos:* MEM RES STAFF, MARTIN MARIETTA ENERGY SYSTS, 85- *Personal Data:* b Toledo, Ohio, Jan 18, 33; m 63; c 3. *Educ:* Univ Notre Dame, BS, 55, MS, 57. *Honors & Awards:* Award of Merit, Am Soc Testing & Mat, 85; Bd of Gov Award, Am Soc Mech Engrs, 89; Res & Develop 100 Award, 90. *Prof Exp:* Engr, Large Steam Turbine Div, Gen Elec Co, 55; mem res staff, Nuclear Div, Union Carbide, 57-85. *Concurrent Pos:* Res officer, Australian Atomic Energy Res Estab, 61-63; mem, Mat Properties Coun. *Mem:* Fel Am Soc Metals Int; fel Am Soc Testing & Mat; fel Am Soc Mech Engrs. *Res:* Deformation and fracture of high-temperature alloys; constitutive equations and inelastic analysis methods; pressure vessels and piping for fossil energy applications; fatigue and fracture in high-temperature nuclear applications; development of advanced alloys for heat recovery systems. *Mailing Add:* 125 Amanda Dr Oak Ridge TN 37830

SWINDEN, H SCOTT, EARTH SCIENCES. *Honors & Awards:* Barlow Medal, Can Inst Mining & Metall, 92. *Mailing Add:* c/o Can Inst Mining & Metall 3400 de Maisonneuve Blvd W Montreal PQ H3Z 3B8 Can

SWINDLE, DAVID WESLEY, JR, CHEMICAL MANAGEMENT SERVICES, ENVIRONMENTAL SAMPLING & ANALYSIS. *Current Pos:* prin prog mgr, 92-95, SECTOR MGR, AEROSPACE & DEFENSE INDUST, RADIAN INT, 96- *Personal Data:* b Nashville, Tenn, June 20, 54; m 76, Carolyn Knight; c Mary-Louise & Caroline A. *Educ:* Tenn Tech Univ, BS, 76, Va Inst Technol, MS, 77; Univ Tenn, MBA, 81. *Prof Exp:* Proj engr, Martin Marietta, 77-81, mgr, US Enrichment Safeguards Prog, 81-85, dir, Int Tech Prog Div, 85-89, tech dir environ restoration, 89-92. *Mem:* Nat Mgt Asn; Inst Nuclear Mat Mgt; Sigma Xi; Int Soc Decontamination & Decommissioning. *Res:* Investigation and application of using environmental sampling and collections to defect and measure nuclear, chemical and biological activities. *Mailing Add:* 707 17th St No 3400 Denver CO 80202-3404. *Fax:* 303-292-5860; *E-Mail:* david_swindle@radian.com

SWINDLE, TIMOTHY D, PLANETARY SCIENCE, METEORITICS. *Current Pos:* ASST PROF PLANETARY SCI, UNIV ARIZ, 86- *Personal Data:* b Great Bend, Kans, June 5, 55; m 77; c 2. *Educ:* Univ Evansville, BS, 77, BA, 78; Washington Univ, MA, 81, PhD(physics), 86. *Concurrent Pos:* Mem, Lunar & Planetary Sample Team, NASA, 87-; Meteorite Working Group, NASA/NSF, 89-92; counr, Meteoritical Soc, 91- *Mem:* Meteoritical Soc; Geochem Soc; Am Astron Soc Div Planetary Sci. *Res:* Noble gas geochemistry and geochronology of meteorites and lunar samples. *Mailing Add:* Planetary Sci Univ Ariz 1600 E University Blvd Tucson AZ 85721-0001

SWINEBROAD, JEFF, ZOOLOGY. *Current Pos:* dep assoc dir res & develop progs, US Energy Res & Develop Admin, 74-77, mgr environ prog, Off Asst Secy Environ, 77-79, DEP DIR, OFF PROG COORDINATION, DEPT ENERGY, 80- *Personal Data:* b Nashville, Tenn, Mar 22, 26; m 53; c 2. *Educ:* Ohio State Univ, BA, 49, MA, 50, PhD, 56. *Prof Exp:* Asst ornith, Univ Colo, 46-47; tech asst zool, Ohio Coop Wildlife Res Unit, 48; asst, Ohio State Univ, 49-50, asst instr, 51, instr conserv, Conserv Lab, 51-53 & Nat Audubon Soc, 54-56; zoologist, Rutgers Univ, 55-57, from asst prof to assoc prof, 57-66, prof biol, 66-68, chmn dept biol sci. 60-68. asst res specialist, Col Agr, 59-68; pop ecologist, USAEC, 68-72, chief, Ecol Sci Br, 72-74. *Mem:* AAAS; Animal Behav Soc; Ecol Soc Am; Wilson Ornith Soc(secy, 67-); Cooper Ornith Union. *Res:* Avian anatomy; ecology and migration of birds; animal population behavior. *Mailing Add:* 10423 Kardwright Ct Gaithersburg MD 20879

SWINEHART, BRUCE ARDEN, analytical chemistry, for more information see previous edition

SWINEHART, CARL FRANCIS, INORGANIC CHEMISTRY. *Current Pos:* RETIRED. *Personal Data:* b Bainbridge, Ohio, Aug 26, 07; m 34; c 2. *Educ:* Ohio Wesleyan Col, AB, 29; Western Reserve Univ, PhD(inorg chem), 33. *Prof Exp:* Asst, Western Reserve Univ, 29-32; res chemist, Harshaw Chem Co, 32-52, assoc dir res, 52-60, dir tech develop, Inorg Prod, 60-62 & Crystal-Solid State, 62-67, proj dir crystal growth develop, Harshaw Div, Kewanee Oil Co, Ohio, 67-72; consult, Harshaw-Filtrol Parnership, Ohio, 72-88 & Engelhard, NJ, 89-90. *Res:* Fluoride gases; manufacture of fluorides; synthetic crystal production. *Mailing Add:* 4102 Silsby Rd Univ Heights Cleveland OH 44118

SWINEHART, JAMES HERBERT, INORGANIC CHEMISTRY, BIOINORGANIC CHEMISTRY. *Current Pos:* from asst prof to assoc prof, 68-72, PROF CHEM, UNIV CALIF, DAVIS, 72- *Personal Data:* b Los Angeles, Calif, Nov 22, 36; m 63; c 3. *Educ:* Pomona Col, BA, 58; Univ Chicago, PhD(chem), 62. *Prof Exp:* NSF fel phys inorg chem, Max Planck Inst Phys Chem, Univ Gottingen, Ger, 62-63. *Concurrent Pos:* Fel, John Simon Guggenheim Found, 69-70. *Mem:* Am Chem Soc. *Res:* Mechanisms of inorganic reactions; transition metals in the marine environment. *Mailing Add:* 830 Douglas Ave Davis CA 95616

SWINEHART, JAMES STEPHEN, NUCLEAR MAGNETIC RESONANCE, COMPUTATIONAL CHEMISTRY. *Current Pos:* chmn dept, 70-76, PROF CHEM, STATE UNIV NY COL CORTLAND, 70- *Personal Data:* b Cleveland, Ohio, July 27, 29; m 63, Ann Fundis; c Susan. *Educ:* Western Res Univ, BS, 50; Univ Cincinnati, MS, 51; NY Univ, PhD(chem), 59. *Prof Exp:* Res chemist, Merck & Co, 51-53; from asst prof org chem to assoc prof, Wagner Col, 57-61; assoc prof, Am Univ, 61-65; anal chemist, Atlantic Res Corp, 65-67; sr spectroscopist, Perkin Elmer Corp, 67-69 & Digilab, 69-70. *Mem:* Am Chem Soc. *Res:* Organic synthesis; natural products; instrumentation; infrared and nuclear magnetic resonance spectroscopy; information retrieval; cigarette smoke; gas chromatography; technical writing; computational chemistry. *Mailing Add:* RD 3 820 Gwen Lane Cortland NY 13045. *Fax:* 607-753-2927; *E-Mail:* swinehartj@snycorva.cortland.edu

SWINEHART, PHILIP ROSS, SOLID STATE ELECTRONICS. *Current Pos:* res scientist low temp sensors & radiation detection, 75-84, VPRES, SENSOR DIV, LAKE SHORE CRYOTRONICS INC, 84- *Personal Data:* b Los Alamos, NMex, May 20, 45. *Educ:* Ore State Univ, BS, 67; Ohio State Univ, MS, 68, PhD(elec eng), 74. *Prof Exp:* Res assoc, Electro Sci Lab, Ohio State Univ, 68-69; res engr, Ohio Semitronics Inc, 72-73. *Mem:* Inst Elec & Electronics Engrs. *Res:* Low temperature sensors and radiation detectors; magnetic field, temperature, pressure & radiation sensors. *Mailing Add:* Lake Shore Cryotronics Inc 575 McCorkle Blvd Westerville OH 43082

SWINFORD, KENNETH ROBERTS, FORESTRY. *Current Pos:* from asst prof to prof, 46-75, asst to dir forestry, 71-75, EMER PROF FORESTRY, UNIV FLA, 76- *Personal Data:* b Trader's Point, Ind, July 8, 16; m 38, Marie Wesley; c George W & Sandra S. *Educ:* Purdue Univ, BS, 37; Univ Fla, MSF, 48; Univ Mich, PhD, 60. *Prof Exp:* Exten ranger, State Forest Serv, Fla, 40-41; timber cruiser, Brooks-Scanlon Corp, 46. *Concurrent Pos:* Consult forester, F & W Forestry Serv Inc, Gainesville, Fla & Moses, Hicks, Jowell & Wood, 76-; teacher, Sch Forestry, Univ Fla, 75-76, Woodland Mgrs, Inc, 76-92, Moses, Hicks, Jowell & Wood, 92- *Mem:* Soc Am Foresters; Am Forestry Asn. *Res:* Management of forest lands, especially pine plantations; landscape forestry; outdoor recreational use of forests and wild lands; management and harvesting of forests for energy fuel. *Mailing Add:* 10311 NW 34th Lane Gainesville FL 32606

SWINGLE, DONALD MORGAN, APPLIED PHYSICS, SYSTEMS ENGINEERING. *Current Pos:* RETIRED. *Personal Data:* b Washington, DC, Sept 1, 22; m 43; c 3. *Educ:* Wilson Teachers Col, BS, 43; NY Univ, MS, 47; Harvard Univ, AM, 48, MEngSci, 49, PhD(eng sci, appl physics), 50; George Washington Univ, MBA, 62; Indust Col Armed Forces, dipl, 62. *Prof Exp:* Engr, Signal Corps Eng Labs, US Dept Army, 46-47; res asst, Eng Res Lab, Harvard Univ, 49-50; physicist, Signal Corps Eng Labs, US Dept Army, 50-60, chief, Weather Electronic Res Group, 50-53, chief, Meteorol Techn Sect, 54-57, chief br, 58-60, physicist, sr res scientist & dep dir, Meteorol Div, US Army, Electronics Res & Develop Labs, 61-63, res physicist, sr res physicist & chief, Meteorol Res Team A, US Army Electronics Command, 64-65, res physicist & sr scientist, Atmospheric Sci Lab, 65-66, res physicist & chief tech & explor develop tech area, 66-71, sr scientist, Eng & Explor Develop Tech Area, 71-74, sr scientist, Spec Sensors Tech Area, Combat Surveillance & Target Acquisition Lab, 74-78, sr res physicist, Atmospheric Sci Lab, Army Electronics Res & Develop Command, 78-80. *Concurrent Pos:* US mem, Comn Instruments & Methods Observ, World Meteorol Orgn, 53-65; US deleg, 53 & 57; adv, US Mil Acad, 59; reviewer res proposals, NSF, 60-74; mem, Comt Atmospheric Environ, Comn Unidentified Flying Objects, Am Inst Aeronaut & Astronaut, 62-70; chmn, Nat Task Group Mesometeorol, Interdept Comt Atmospheric Sci, 63-74; Army rep, DOD Forum Environ Sci, 64-65; mem, Chem Comt Meteorol, Nat Ctr Atmospheric Res, 63-65, Nat meso-micrometeorol Res Facil Surv Group, 64; lab mem, Army Res Coun, 64-65; consult, Mark Resources Inc, 81-82, NMex State Univ, 87-88 & NMex Res Inst, 88-; chief, Measurements Lab, NMex Res Inst, 88- *Mem:* Am Meteorol Soc; sr mem Inst Elec & Electronics Engrs; Nat Soc Prof Eng; assoc fel Am Inst Aeronaut & Astronaut; fel NY Acad Sci. *Res:* Radar meteorology; atmospheric propagation, electromagnetic, acoustic waves; radioactive fallout prediction; meteorological techniques, applied meteorology, meteorological system engineering; atmospheric modification, management, mesometeorology; indirect sensory techniques; nuclear surveillance; research and development management. *Mailing Add:* 1765 Pomona Dr Las Cruces NM 88001-4919

SWINGLE, HOMER DALE, OLERICULTURE. *Current Pos:* exten specialist hort, Agr Exten Serv, 46-47, from asst prof to prof, 48-79, EMER PROF, UNIV TENN, KNOXVILLE, 79- *Personal Data:* b Hixson, Tenn, Nov 5, 16; m 42, 62, Ella Porterfield; c Janet (Sciscioli). *Educ:* Univ Tenn, BS, 39; Ohio State Univ, MS, 48; La State Univ, PhD(hort), 66. *Prof Exp:* Teacher high sch, 39-46. *Concurrent Pos:* Consult plant & soil water rels, Oak Ridge Nat Labs, 71-75. *Mem:* Fel Am Soc Hort Sci. *Res:* Evaluation of vegetable varieties; chemical weed control in horticulture crops; mechanization of harvest. *Mailing Add:* 3831 Maloney Rd Knoxville TN 37920

SWINGLE, KARL F, PHARMACOLOGY. *Current Pos:* pharmacologist, 68-73, supvr pharmacol, 73-77, SR RES SPECIALIST, RIKER LABS, MINN MINING & MFG CO, 77- *Personal Data:* b Richland Center, Wis, Feb 16, 35; div; c 4. *Educ:* Univ Wis, BA, 58; Univ Minn, PhD(pharmacol), 68. *Prof Exp:* Asst bacteriologist, Sioux City Dept Health, Iowa, 58-59; med technologist, Vet Admin Hosp, Minneapolis, 61-64. *Mem:* Am Soc Pharmacol & Exp Therapeut; NY Acad Sci; Soc Exp Biol & Med; Am Chem Soc. *Res:* Anti-inflammatory drugs; pulmonary pharmacology. *Mailing Add:* 1510 N Helmo Ave St Paul MN 55128-5527

SWINGLE, KARL FREDERICK, RADIOBIOLOGY. *Current Pos:* res chemist, 69-70, PHYSICIST, VET ADMIN HOSP, 70- *Personal Data:* b Bozeman, Mont, Jan 7, 15; m 40; c 5. *Educ:* Mont State Col, BS, 37; Univ Wis, PhD(biochem), 42. *Prof Exp:* Res chemist, Inst Path, Western Pa Hosp, 42-43; asst res chemist, Univ Wyo, 43-45; assoc chemist, Mont State Col, 45-47, prof vet biochem, 57-61; supvry chemist, US Naval Radiol Defense Lab, 61-69. *Concurrent Pos:* Asst researcher, Univ Calif, Irvine, 70- *Mem:* Sigma Xi; Radiation Res Soc. *Res:* Radiation biochemistry; nucleic acid metabolism. *Mailing Add:* Sr Res Specialist 1510 N Helmo Ave St Paul MN 55128-5527

SWINGLE, ROY SPENCER, ANIMAL SCIENCE, NUTRITION. *Current Pos:* TECH SERVS MGR, SYNTEX ANIMAL HEALTH. *Personal Data:* b Harvey, Ill, Oct 15, 44; m 66, Carmen Roberts; c Brian & Gary. *Educ:* Univ Ariz, BS, 66; Wash State Univ, MS, 69, PhD(nutrit), 72. *Prof Exp:* From asst prof to assoc prof animal sci, Univ Ariz, 72-94. *Mem:* Am Soc Animal Sci; Am Inst Nutrit; Am Dairy Sci Asn. *Res:* Ruminant nutrition; utilization of structural and nonstructural carbohydrates. *Mailing Add:* 7712 Whippoorwill Lane Amarillo TX 85704

SWINGLEY, CHARLES STEPHEN, PHYSICAL CHEMISTRY. *Current Pos:* RES ASSOC RES LABS, EASTMAN KODAK CO, 70- *Personal Data:* b Dallas, Tex, Nov 11, 43; m 64; c 2. *Educ:* Rochester Inst Technol, BS, 65; Wayne State Univ, PhD(chem), 70. *Mem:* Soc Photog Sci & Eng. *Res:* Surface, colloid, polymer and photographic chemistry. *Mailing Add:* 623 Oakridge Dr Rochester NY 14617

SWINK, LAURENCE N, CRYSTALLOGRAPHY. *Current Pos:* PRES, AZ/TEC CONSULT, TEMPE, ARIZ, 89- *Personal Data:* b Enid, Okla, Oct 24, 34; div; c Steven M. *Educ:* Univ Wichita, BA, 57; Iowa State Col, MSc, 59; Brown Univ, PhD(chem), 69. *Prof Exp:* Flight test technician, Cessna Aircraft Co, Kans, 56-57; mat engr, Chance-Vought Aircraft Co, Tex, 57; mat engr, Douglas Aircraft Co, Calif, 59-60; nuclear res officer, McClellan AFB, Calif, 60-63; mem tech staff crystallog, Tex Instruments, Inc, Dallas, 66-75, mgr, Infrared Glass Lab, Electro-Optics Div, 75-78; vpres, Amorphous Mat Inc, Garland, Tex, 79-80; mgr, Advan Systs Develop, Xerox Corp, Dallas, 81-82; tech dir, Multi- Plate Co, Dallas, 82-86; sr proj mgr, GTE/Siemens

Transmission Syst, Tempe/Phoenix, 86-87; sr tech consult, Quadri Corp, Tempe, Ariz, 87-89. *Mem:* Am Crystallog Asn. *Res:* X-ray and electron diffraction techniques; electron microprobe analysis; electron microscopy; auger spectroscopy, x-ray fluorescence; printed circuit technology; semiconductor materials/process technology. *Mailing Add:* 1617 E Julie Dr Tempe AZ 85283-3161

SWINNEN, LODE J, CLINICAL HEMATOLOGY-ONCOLOGY, ANTINEOPLASTIC DRUG DEVELOPMENT. *Current Pos:* fel hemat-oncol, Hines Vet Admin Hosp, 83-86, ASST PROF MED, DIV HEMAT-ONCOL, LOYOLA UNIV CHICAGO, 86- *Personal Data:* b May 9, 55. *Educ:* Univ Cape Town, MB ChB, 78; Am Bd Internal Med, cert 83, cert med oncol, 85, cert hemat, 86. *Prof Exp:* Internal med residency, St Joseph Hosp-Northwestern Univ, 80-83. *Concurrent Pos:* Mem, Lymphoma Comt & Develop Therapeut Comt, SW Oncol Group; mem, Task Force AIDS Malignancies, Nat Cancer Inst-Nat Inst Allergy & Infectious Dis, NIH. *Mem:* Am Soc Clin Oncol; Am Asn Cancer Res; Am Fedn Clin Res; Am Col Physicians. *Res:* Laboratory development of models to overcome anti-neoplastic drug resistance with subsequent implementation of those models in human cancer treatment trials; biology and treatment of lymphoma occuring in immunodeficient individuals, specifically following organ transplantation. *Mailing Add:* Loyola Univ Med Ctr 2160 S First Ave Maywood IL 60153. *Fax:* 708-216-9335

SWINNEY, CHAUNCEY MELVIN, ECONOMIC GEOLOGY, PETROLOGY. *Current Pos:* RETIRED. *Personal Data:* b Riverside, Calif, Sept 3, 18; m 42, Gwen McCluskey; c Steve, Richard & Brian. *Educ:* Pomona Col, BA, 40; Stanford Univ, PhD(geol), 49. *Prof Exp:* Tester, Union Oil Co, Calif, 42; geologist, US Geol Surv, 42-45; instr, Stanford Univ, 47-49, asst prof mineral sci, 49-56; supvr, Prod Res Div, Richfeid Oil Corp, 59-66; mgr energy resources exp & develop, Southern Calif Edison Co, 66-82. *Concurrent Pos:* Geologist, US Geol Surv, 46-53; vpres, Mono Power Co, Subsid Southern Calif Edison Co, 73-82. *Mem:* Geol Soc Am; Am Asn Petrol Geol; Am Inst Mining Metall & Petrol Eng; Sigma Xi. *Res:* Energy resources exploration, development and production. *Mailing Add:* 1354 Seafarer St Ventura CA 93001

SWINNEY, HARRY LEONARD, NONLINEAR DYNAMICS, FLUID PHYSICS. *Current Pos:* prof, 78-84, Trull Centennial Prof, 84-90, SID RICHARDSON FOUND REGENTS CHAIR, UNIV TEX, AUSTIN, 90- *Personal Data:* b Opelousas, La, Apr 10, 39; m 67, Gloria Luyas; c Brent (deceased). *Educ:* Rhodes Col, Memphis, BS, 61; Johns Hopkins Univ, PhD(physics), 68. *Honors & Awards:* Morris Loeb Lectr, Harvard Univ, 82; Fluid Dynamics Prize, Am Phys Soc, 95. *Prof Exp:* Res assoc physics, Johns Hopkins Univ, 68-70, vis asst prof, 70-71; asst prof physics, NY Univ, 71-73; from assoc prof to prof physics, City Col, City Univ New York, 73-78. *Concurrent Pos:* Guggenheim fel, 83-84; dir, Ctr Nonlinear Dynamics, 85- *Mem:* Nat Acad Sci; Am Asn Physics Teachers; Am Acad Arts & Sci; fel Am Phys Soc. *Res:* Instabilities and turbulence are studied in experiments on nonequilibrium systems, particularly fluids and chemical reactions and granular media. *Mailing Add:* Dept Physics Univ Tex Austin TX 78712. *Fax:* 512-471-1558; *E-Mail:* swinney@chaos.ph.utexas.edu

SWINSON, DEREK BERTRAM, PHYSICS, ACCIDENT RECONSTRUCTION. *Current Pos:* From asst prof to prof, 65-95, EMER PROF PHYSICS, UNIV NMEX, 96- *Personal Data:* b Belfast. N Ireland, Nov 5, 38; m 65; c 2. *Educ:* Queen's Univ, Belfast, BSc, 60; Univ Alta, Calgary, MS, 61, PhD(physics), 65. *Concurrent Pos:* Consult, accident reconstruct, 68- *Mem:* Brit Inst Physics; Sigma Xi; Am Geophys Union; Southwestern Asn Tech Accident Investr. *Res:* Cosmic radiation, extensive air showers; mu-mesons underground and variations of their intensity with solar activity; sidereal cosmic ray anisotropies; consultant in accident reconstruction. *Mailing Add:* Dept Physics Univ NMex 800 Yale NE Albuquerque NM 87131. *Fax:* 505-277-1520

SWINTON, DAVID CHARLES, CELL BIOLOGY. *Personal Data:* b St Charles, Ill, May 4, 43; m 70. *Educ:* Brandeis Univ, AB, 65; Stanford Univ, PhD(biol), 72. *Prof Exp:* Res fel biophys, Univ Chicago, 72-74, res assoc, 74-80; mem fac, Dept Biol, Univ Rochester, 80-85. *Mem:* Am Soc Cell Biol. *Res:* Information content of organelle DNA; expression of organelle DNA during mitotic cell cycle and during meiosis. *Mailing Add:* 11 Millwood Ct Pittsford NY 14534

SWINYARD, EWART AINSLIE, PHARMACOLOGY. *Current Pos:* prof pharmacol & dir, Pharmaceut Res, Col Phar, Univ Utah, 47-77, prof pharmacol, Col Med, 67-77, dean, Col Pharm, 70-76, dir, Ctr Early Pharmaceut Drug Eval Antiepileptic Drugs, 75-94, EMER PROF PHARMACOL, COL PHARM & COL MED, UNIV UTAH, 76- *Personal Data:* b Logan, Utah, Jan 3, 09; m 34, Grace Parkinson; c Emma L & Richard E. *Educ:* Utah State Univ, BS, 32; Idaho State Col, BS, 36; Univ Minn, MS, 41; Univ Utah, PhD(pharmacol), 47. *Hon Degrees:* DSc, Utah State Univ, 83 & Univ Utah, 86. *Honors & Awards:* Rennebohm Lectr, Univ Wis, 60; Award & Medal distinguished res & ed alcoholism, Am Med Soc Alcoholism, 77; DuMez lectr, Univ Md, 79; Epilepsy Award, Am Soc Exp Therapeut, 82; Kaufman lectr, Ohio State Univ, 63; Distinguished Basic Neuroscientist Award, Am Epilepsy Soc, 90- *Prof Exp:* From instr to asst prof pharm, Idaho State Col, 36-45, prof pharmacol, 45-47. *Concurrent Pos:* Am Col Apothecaries fac fel; lectr, Col Med, Univ Utah, 45-67, chmn, Dept Biopharmaceut Sci, 65-71, distinguished res prof, 68-69; ed, Am Med Soc Alcoholism, 77. *Mem:* Am Soc Pharmacol & Exp Therapeut; Am Pharmaceut Asn; NY Acad Sci; Am Asn Cols Pharm (hon pres, 81-82); Sigma Xi. *Res:* Arsenical chemotherapy; body water and electrolyte distribution; experimental therapy of convulsive disorders; assay of anticonvulsant drugs; relationship between chemical structure and pharmacological activity of anticonvulsant drugs; antiepileptic drug development program funded by Epilepsy Branch, NIH. *Mailing Add:* Dept Pharmacol & Toxicol Univ Utah 421 Wakara Way Suite 125 Salt Lake City UT 84108-1210

SWIRYN, STEVEN, cardiology, cardiac electrophysiology, for more information see previous edition

SWISCHUK, LEONARD EDWARD, RADIOLOGY. *Current Pos:* assoc prof, 70-73, PROF RADIOL & PEDIAT, UNIV TEX MED BR GALVESTON, 73- *Personal Data:* b Bellevue, Alta, June 14, 37; m 60; c 4. *Educ:* Univ Alta, BS & MD, 60. *Prof Exp:* Asst prof pediat, Med Ctr, Univ Okla, 66-68, assoc prof radiol & pediat, 68-70. *Mem:* Am Med Asn; Am Col Radiol; Am Acad Pediat; Radiol Soc NAm. *Mailing Add:* RAD C264 Child Health Ctr C65 Univ Tex Med Sch 301 Univ Blvd Galveston TX 77550

SWISHER, ELY MARTIN, ENTOMOLOGY. *Current Pos:* RETIRED. *Personal Data:* b Bozeman, Mont, Sept 29, 15; m 40, Marguerite Sorenson; c Kathryn R, Robert M & George D. *Educ:* Willamette Univ, AB, 37; Ore State Col, MS, 41; Ohio State Univ, PhD(entom), 43. *Prof Exp:* Asst zool, Ohio State Univ, 40-43; midwest mgr, Rohm and Haas Co, 43-53, mgr develop sect agr & sanit chem, 53-73, mgr govt regulatory rels, 73-76, mgr agr chem standards, 76-81; mem staff, Regulatory Compliance Serv, 81-89. *Mem:* Entom Soc Am; Weed Sci Soc Am. *Res:* Insecticides; fungicides; field evaluations; development of agricultural pesticide chemicals. *Mailing Add:* 1950 Branch Rd Perkasie PA 18944

SWISHER, GEORGE MONROE, MECHANICAL & CONTROL ENGINEERING. *Current Pos:* assoc prof, 73-79, PROF MECH ENG & ASSOC DEAN ENG, TENN TECHNOL UNIV, 79- *Personal Data:* b Columbus, Ohio, July 17, 43; m 64; c 1. *Educ:* Univ Cincinnati, BSME, 66; Ohio State Univ, MSME, 67, PhD(mech eng), 69. *Prof Exp:* Asst prof systs eng, Wright State Univ, 69-73. *Concurrent Pos:* Consult, United Aircraft Prod, 70- & Missile Systs Div, Rockwell Int Corp, 77. *Mem:* Am Soc Mech Engrs; Am Soc Eng Educ; Sigma Xi. *Res:* Manual control; control theory; stress analysis; dynamic system measurement and control. *Mailing Add:* 1035 E Sixth St Cookeville TN 38501-2830

SWISHER, HORTON EDWARD, food chemistry; deceased, see previous edition for last biography

SWISHER, JOSEPH VINCENT, ORGANIC CHEMISTRY. *Current Pos:* asst prof, 61-69, assoc prof chem, 69-84, PROF, UNIV DETROIT, 84- *Personal Data:* b Kansas City, Mo, Jan 12, 32; m 83; c 3. *Educ:* Cent Methodist Col, AB, 56; Univ Mo, PhD(org chem), 60. *Prof Exp:* Fel chem, Purdue Univ, 60-61. *Mem:* Am Chem Soc. *Res:* Oranosilicon chemistry; stereochemistry of addition reactions; polymer chemistry. *Mailing Add:* 10466 Silver Lake Rd Brighton MI 48116

SWISHER, ROBERT DONALD, organic chemistry, environmental chemistry; deceased, see previous edition for last biography

SWISHER, SCOTT NEIL, INTERNAL MEDICINE, HEMATOLOGY. *Current Pos:* chmn dept, 67-77, assoc dean res, 77-83, PROF MED, COL HUMAN MED, MICH STATE UNIV, 67- *Personal Data:* b Le Center, Minn, July 30, 18; m 45; c 2. *Educ:* Univ Minn, BS, 43, MD, 44; Am Bd Internal Med, dipl, 52. *Prof Exp:* Asst resident & fel med, Sch Med & Dent, Univ Rochester, 47-48, fel med & hemat, 49-51, from instr to prof med, 51-67; fel, med sch, Univ Minn, 48-49. *Concurrent Pos:* From asst resident physician to chief resident physician, Ancker Hosp, St Paul, Minn, 48-49; from asst physician to sr assoc physician & head hemat unit, Strong Mem Hosp, Rochester, NY, 53-67; mem comt blood & related probs, Nat Res Coun, 54-, chmn, 60. *Mem:* AAAS; Am Soc Clin Invest; Asn Am Physicians; Am Col Physicians; Am Fedn Clin Res. *Res:* Mechanisms of destruction of erythrocytes by antibodies; human hemolytic disorders. *Mailing Add:* Mich State Univ Med Sch East Lansing MI 48824

SWISLOCKI, NORBERT IRA, BIOCHEMISTRY, CELL BIOLOGY. *Current Pos:* PROF & CHMN BIOCHEM & MOLECULAR BIOL, MED SCH, UNIV MED & DENT NJ, 78- *Personal Data:* b Warsaw, Poland, Jan 11, 36; US citizen; div; c 2. *Educ:* Univ Calif, Los Angeles, BS, 56, MA, 60, PhD(zool, endocrinol), 64. *Prof Exp:* USPHS fel biochem, Brandeis Univ, 64-66; from instr to assoc prof biochem, Grad Sch Med Sci, Cornell Univ, 67-78, chmn, Biochem Unit, 75-78, assoc, Sloan-Kettering Inst Cancer Res, 66-78, assoc mem, 72-78. *Concurrent Pos:* Pres, Dept Biochem, Assoc Med Sch, 87-88. *Mem:* Am Soc Biochem & Molecular Biol; Endocrine Soc; Biophys Soc. *Res:* Mechanisms of hormone action; membrane function; endocrinology; aging of erythrocytes. *Mailing Add:* Dept Biochem & Molecular Biol NJ Med Sch Univ Med & Dent NJ 185 S Orange Ave Newark NJ 07103-2714. *Fax:* 973-982-5594

SWITENDICK, ALFRED CARL, METAL HYDRIDES, TRANSITION METAL COMPOUNDS. *Current Pos:* RETIRED. *Personal Data:* b Batavia, NY, Oct 8, 31; m 80, Mildred Cook; c Lesley & Suzanne. *Educ:* Mass Inst Technol, SB, 53, PhD(solid state physics), 63; Univ Ill, MS, 54. *Honors & Awards:* Sci Citation Classic, Inst Sci Info, 88. *Prof Exp:* Asst physics, Univ

Ill, 53-54; asst, Mass Inst Technol, 56-62, res staff mem, 62-64; staff mem physics org solids, Sandia Lab, 64-68, staff mem solid state theory, 68-70, supvr, Solid State Theory, 70-80; staff mem, Div Mat Sci, US Dept Energy, Washington, DC, 80-82; sr tech staff mem, Adv Mat Physics, Sandia Lab, 82-94; consult, Quantum Chem Proj, Idaho Nat Eng Labs, 94-95. *Concurrent Pos:* Invited prof, Univ Paris-Sud, Orsay, 92; computational/theoret tech panel, Naval Studies Bd, Nat Acad Sci, 93-94. *Mem:* AAAS; fel Am Phys Soc. *Res:* Electronic energy bands of transition metals and transition metal compounds; intermetallic compounds; hydrogen in metals; boron and boron compounds. *Mailing Add:* 4309 Hannett Ave NE Albuquerque NM 87110-4942. *Fax:* 208-526-8541

SWITKES, EUGENE, QUANTUM CHEMISTRY, VISUAL PSYCHOPHYSICS. *Current Pos:* from asst prof to assoc prof, 71-84, PROF CHEM, PHYSIOL OPTICS GROUP, UNIV CALIF, 89- *Personal Data:* b Newport News, Va, Dec 22, 43; m 69; c 2. *Educ:* Oberlin Col, BA, 65; Harvard Univ, MS & PhD(theoret chem), 70. *Prof Exp:* NSF fels, Univ Edinburgh, 70-71 & Cambridge Univ, 71. *Concurrent Pos:* Fel & responder, Neurosci Res Prog, Boulder Intensive Study Session, 72. *Mem:* Assoc Res in Vision & Ophthal; Sigma Xi. *Res:* Theory of the electronic structure of molecules, quantum mechanics; information processing in the visual system; visual accommodation and perception; environmental visual information content. *Mailing Add:* Dept Chem Univ Calif 1156 High St Santa Cruz CA 95064-1077

SWITZER, BOYD RAY, NUTRITION, BIOCHEMISTRY. *Current Pos:* asst prof, 72-78, ASSOC PROF NUTRIT, SCH PUB HEALTH, UNIV NC, CHAPEL HILL, 78-, ASST PROF BIOCHEM & NUTRIT, SCH MED, 74- *Personal Data:* b Harrisonburg, VA, Oct 3, 43; m 67; c 2. *Educ:* Bridgewater Col, BA, 65; Univ NC, Chapel Hill, PhD(biochem), 71. *Prof Exp:* NIH fel, Univ Southern Calif, 71-72. *Mem:* AAAS; Am Chem Soc. *Res:* Ethanol effects on nutrition, metabolism and biological function; fetal alcohol effects. *Mailing Add:* Dept Nutrit Univ NC 2207 McGauran Greenberg Chapel Hill NC 27599-7400. *Fax:* 919-966-7216; *E-Mail:* switzer@uncsphuy.bitnet

SWITZER, CLAYTON MACFIE, AGRICULTURE, WEED SCIENCE. *Current Pos:* RETIRED. *Personal Data:* b London, Ont, July 17, 29; m 51; c 3. *Educ:* Ont Agr Col, BSA, 51, MSA, 53; Iowa State Univ, PhD, 55. *Hon Degrees:* LLD, Dalhousie Univ. *Prof Exp:* Head dept, Ont Agr Col, 55-70, from assoc prof to prof bot, 65-70, from assoc dean to dean, 70-83; dep minister, Ont Ministry Agr & Food, 84-89; pres, Clay Switzer Consults Ltd, 89-91. *Concurrent Pos:* Chmn, Ont Weed Comt, 62-83; mem, Sci Coun Can, 77-82. *Mem:* Can Soc Pest Mgt; fel Weed Sci Soc Am; Can Soc Hort Sci; fel Agr Inst Can (pres, 83-84); Int Turfgrass Soc (pres, 77-81). *Res:* Physiology of herbicide action; weed control; growth regulation of turfgrass. *Mailing Add:* 16 Tamarack Pl Guelph ON N1E 3Y6 Can

SWITZER, JAY ALAN, ELECTROCHEMISTRY, ELECTRONIC MATERIALS. *Current Pos:* prof chem, 90-96, CUR PROF CHEM, UNIV MO, ROLLA, 96- *Personal Data:* b Cincinnati, Ohio, May 14, 50; m 73; c 1. *Educ:* Univ Cincinnati, BS, 73; Wayne State Univ, MA, 75, PhD(inorg chem), 79. *Prof Exp:* Sr res chemist, Unocal Corp, 79-87; assoc prof mat sci, Univ Pittsburgh, 87-90. *Concurrent Pos:* Sr res investr, Mat Res Ctr, Univ Mo, Rolla, 90- *Mem:* AAAS; Am Ceramic Soc; Am Chem Soc; Electrochem Soc; Mat Res Soc. *Res:* Inorganic materials chemistry; electrodeposition and physical electrochemistry; nanoscale optical and electrical materials; quantum effects in nanoscale materials; electrodeposited ceramic superlattices; superconductors; scanning tunneling microscopy. *Mailing Add:* Dept Chem Univ Mo Rolla MO 65401. *Fax:* 573-341-2071; *E-Mail:* jswitzer@umr.edu

SWITZER, LAURA MAE, PHYSICAL EDUCATION, MATHEMATICS. *Current Pos:* PROF PHYS EDUC, SOUTHWESTERN OKLA STATE UNIV, 71- *Personal Data:* b McLean, Tex, Apr 21, 41. *Educ:* Wayland Baptist Col, Tex, BS, 63; Southwestern Okla State Univ, MEd, 66; Univ Okla, EdD(curric), 71. *Prof Exp:* Teacher & coach phys educ & math, Sanford-Fritch Independent Sch Dist, Tex, 63-65; instr phys educ, Southwestern Okla State Univ, 65-69; asst, Univ Okla, 69-71. *Mem:* Am Alliance Health Phys Educ & Recreation; Nat Educ Asn. *Res:* Comparison of massed versus distributed practice sessions in the learning of recreational activities skills. *Mailing Add:* Dept Health & Phys Educ Southwestern Okla State Univ 100 Campus Dr Weatherford OK 73096-3001

SWITZER, PAUL, APPLIED STATISTICS, SPATIAL MODELS. *Current Pos:* Assoc prof, 65-76, chmn, 79-82, PROF STATIST & EARTH SCI, STANFORD UNIV, 76- *Personal Data:* b St Boniface, Can, Mar 4, 39; m 63; c 1. *Educ:* Univ Man, BA, 61; Harvard Univ, PhD(statist), 65. *Concurrent Pos:* Vis scientist, Environ Protection Agency, Wash, 90; chmn, Panel Statist US Nat Bur Mines, Nat Acad Sci, 81-82; vpres, Int Asn for Math Geol, 84-86; ed, J Am Statist Asn, 86-88 & Statist Sci, 95- *Mem:* Fel Inst Math Statist; fel Am Statist Asn; fel Int Statist Inst; fel Royal Statist Soc; Am Geophys Union. *Res:* Earth sciences; resources; environment. *Mailing Add:* Sequoia Hall Statist Dept Stanford Univ Stanford CA 94305-4065. *E-Mail:* ps@stat.stanford.edu

SWITZER, ROBERT L, CHEMICAL ENGINEERING, MANAGEMENT. *Current Pos:* RETIRED. *Personal Data:* b Long Beach, Calif, June 18, 18; m 41, Margaret E Smith; c William R & Marjorie (Cowan). *Educ:* Univ Calif, BS, 41; Univ Southern Calif, MS, 52. *Prof Exp:* Sr sect leader, Design Div, Res Dept, Union Oil Co, 41-60, sr sect leader eng serv, 60-67, supvr eng serv, Res Dept, 67-83, mgr eng serv, 81-83. *Concurrent Pos:* Eng consult, 83-84. *Mem:* Instrument Soc Am; Am Inst Chem Engrs. *Res:* Petroleum refining development and shale retorting; granted 17 US patents. *Mailing Add:* 241 Euclid Ave Long Beach CA 90803-6019

SWITZER, ROBERT LEE, BIOCHEMISTRY, MICROBIAL PHYSIOLOGY. *Current Pos:* from asst prof to assoc prof, 68-78, head dept, 88-93, PROF BIOCHEM, UNIV ILL, URBANA, 78- *Personal Data:* b Clinton, Iowa, Aug 26, 40; m 65, Bonnie George; c Brian R & Stephanie A. *Educ:* Univ Ill, Urbana, BS, 61; Univ Calif, Berkeley, PhD(biochem), 66. *Prof Exp:* Fel biochem, Nat Heart Inst, 66-68. *Concurrent Pos:* Fel, John Simon Guggenheim Mem Found, 75-76; vis prof, Freiburg Univ, WGer, 75-76, Univ Calif, Davis, 88; mem, Biochem Study Sect, NIH, 85-89, chmn, 87-89. *Mem:* Am Soc Biol Chem; Am Chem Soc; Am Soc Microbiol; AAAS. *Res:* Microbial physiology and enzymology, particularly regulation of branched biosynthetic pathways, mechanisms of regulatory enzymes and regulation of inactivation and turnover of enzymes during bacterial endospore formation; control of gene expression. *Mailing Add:* Dept Biochem 318 Roger Adams Univ Ill 600 S Mathews Urbana IL 61801. *E-Mail:* rswitzer@uiuc.edu

SWITZER, WILLIAM PAUL, ANIMAL PATHOLOGY, MICROBIOLOGY. *Current Pos:* RETIRED. *Personal Data:* b Dodge City, Kans, Apr 9, 27; m 51; c 2. *Educ:* Agr & Mech Col, Tex, DVM, 48; Iowa State Col, MS, 51, PhD, 54 Univ Vienna, DSc, 78. *Prof Exp:* Asst diagnostician, Iowa Vet Diag Lab, Iowa State Univ, 48-52, from asst prof to prof vet hyg, Univ & Vet Med Res Inst, 52-74, prof vet microbiol & pres med, Vet Med Res Inst & assoc dean Col Vet Med, 74-91, distinguished prof, 78-91. *Mem:* Am Soc Microbiol; Am Vet Med Asn. *Res:* Swine enteric and respiratory diseases; tissue culture; myoplasma. *Mailing Add:* 2224 Hilton Dr Ames IA 50014

SWOFFORD, HAROLD S, JR, CHEMISTRY. *Current Pos:* from asst prof to assoc prof, 62-77, PROF CHEM, UNIV MINN, MINNEAPOLIS, 77- *Personal Data:* b Spokane, Wash, July 24, 36; m 58; c 3. *Educ:* Western Wash State Col, BA, 58; Univ Ill, Urbana, MS, 60, PhD(anal chem), 62. *Prof Exp:* Teaching asst chem, Univ Ill, Urbana, 58-60. *Mem:* Am Chem Soc; Sigma Xi. *Res:* High temperature electrochemistry; fused salts. *Mailing Add:* Chem Dept Univ Minn Minneapolis MN 55455-0100

SWOFFORD, ROBERT LEWIS, LASER SPECTROSCOPY. *Current Pos:* proj leader, 77-80, group leader laser res, 80-81, group leader quantum chem, 81-83, group leader chem physics, 83-85, RES ASSOC, STANDARD OIL CO, 85- *Personal Data:* b Charlotte, NC, Jan 29, 48; m 73; c 2. *Educ:* Furman Univ, BS, 69; Univ Calif, Berkeley, PhD(chem), 73. *Prof Exp:* Sr res assoc chem, Cornell Univ, 73-77. *Mem:* Am Chem Soc; Optical Soc Am; AAAS; Laser Inst Am; Soc Appl Spectros. *Res:* Laser techniques to study the forces which control chemical reactions at the molecular level. *Mailing Add:* Dept Chem Wake Forest Univ PO Box 7486 Reynolda Sta Winston Salem NC 27109-7486

SWOOPE, CHARLES C, PROSTHODONTICS. *Current Pos:* dir grad & res prosthodontics, 67-71, assoc prof, 71-73, prof prosthodontics, 73-80, CLIN ASSOC, SCH DENT, UNIV WASH, 80- *Personal Data:* b Jersey City, NJ, July 7, 34; m 55; c 2. *Educ:* Univ Md, DDS, 59; Univ Wash, MSD, 64. *Prof Exp:* Asst chief dent serv, USPHS Hosp, New Orleans, 64-67. *Concurrent Pos:* Asst prof, Loyola Univ, 64-67; consult, USPHS Hosp, Va Hosp & Univ Hosp, Seattle, Wash, 67-68. *Mem:* Am Prosthodont Soc; Am Acad Denture Prosthetics (secy-treas, 86-91); Am Equilibration Soc; Am Acad Maxillofacial Prosthetics. *Res:* Resilient lining materials; emotional evaluation of denture patients; bone changes; speech problems; force transmission to teeth. *Mailing Add:* 1515 116th Ave Bellevue WA 98004

SWOPE, FRED C, FOOD SCIENCE, BIOCHEMISTRY. *Current Pos:* Asst prof, 68-74, ASSOC PROF BIOL, VA MIL INST, 74- *Personal Data:* b Lexington, Va, Mar 25, 35; m 64. *Educ:* Univ Md, BS, 61; Mich State Univ, PhD(food sci), 68. *Mem:* Am Chem Soc. *Res:* Lipoproteins; structural studies on membranes. *Mailing Add:* Dept Biol Va Mil Inst Lexington VA 24450

SWOPE, RICHARD DALE, FLUID MECHANICS, HEAT TRANSFER. *Current Pos:* PROF ENG SCI, TRINITY UNIV, 80-, CHMN, 81- *Personal Data:* b Palmyra, Pa, Sept 27, 38; m 57; c 2. *Educ:* Univ Del, BME, 60, MME, 62, PhD(appl sci), 66. *Prof Exp:* Appl scientist res & develop, Armstrong Cork Co, 66-68; asst prof eng, PMC Cols, 68-71; assoc prof, Ctr Eng, Widener Col, 71-77, prof eng & asst dean, 77-80. *Mem:* Int Solar Energy Soc; Am Soc Mech Engrs; Am Soc Eng Educ; Sigma Xi. *Res:* Energy; turbulence; shear stresses; solar energy; energy storage; bubble mechanics and formation. *Mailing Add:* 14825 Umicron Apt 909 San Antonio TX 78245

SWORD, CHRISTOPHER PATRICK, GRADUATE EDUCATION & RESEARCH ADMINISTRATION, MICROBIOLOGY. *Current Pos:* GRAD DEAN & DIR RES & PROF MICROBIOL, SDAK STATE UNIV, BROOKINGS, 76- *Personal Data:* b San Fernando, Calif, Sept 9, 28; m 59, Mary Gerhardt; c Mary A, Carolyn, Christopher & Jacqueline. *Educ:* Loyola Univ, Calif, BS, 51; Univ Calif, Los Angeles, PhD(microbiol), 59. *Prof Exp:* Fel & res assoc microbiol, Univ Kans, 58-59, from asst prof to prof, 59-70; prof life sci & chmn dept, Ind State Univ, Terre Haute, 70-76. *Concurrent Pos:* President's fel, Soc Am Bact, 60; consult-evaluator, NCent Asn Cols & Schs. *Mem:* AAAS; Am Soc Microbiol; Coun Grad Schs US; Nat Coun Univ Res Adminr. *Res:* Biochemical and immunological mechanisms of pathogenesis; bacterial virulence; host-parasite interactions in Listeria monocytogenes infection; ultrastructure of bacteria and infected cells; science policy. *Mailing Add:* Grad Dean/Dir Res/Prof Microbiol SDak State Univ Box 2201 Univ Sta Brookings SD 57007

SWORD, JAMES HOWARD, ENGINEERING MECHANICS, CIVIL ENGINEERING. *Current Pos:* Instr civil eng, 51, from instr to assoc prof eng mech, 51-66, PROF ENG MECH, VA POLYTECH INST & STATE UNIV, 66- *Personal Data:* b Derby, Va, Jan 1, 24; m 46; c 2. *Educ:* Va Polytech Inst, BS, 50, MS, 64. *Mem:* Am Soc Eng Educ. *Res:* Computer programming; mechanics; interferometry. *Mailing Add:* 1503 Greenwood Dr Blacksburg VA 24060

SWORDER, DAVID D, ENGINEERING. *Current Pos:* PROF APPL MECH & ENG SCI, UNIV CALIF, SAN DIEGO, 77- *Personal Data:* b Dinuba, Calif, Aug 1, 37. *Educ:* Univ Calif, Berkeley, BS, 58, MS, 59; Univ Calif, Los Angeles, PhD(eng), 65. *Prof Exp:* Sr engr, Litton Systs, Inc, 59-64; from asst prof to assoc prof elec eng, Univ Southern Calif, 64-77. *Mem:* Inst Elec & Electronics Engrs. *Res:* Adaptive and stochastic control problems. *Mailing Add:* 9500 Gilman Dr La Jolla CA 92093

SWORSKI, THOMAS JOHN, SCIENTIFIC PROGRAMMING. *Current Pos:* RETIRED. *Personal Data:* b Pittsburgh, Pa, Sept 8, 20; m 44; c 2. *Educ:* Duquesne Univ, BS, 42; Notre Dame Univ, PhD(phys chem), 51. *Prof Exp:* Chemist, Oak Ridge Nat Lab, 51-57 & Nuclear Res Ctr, Union Carbide Corp, 57-63; chemist, Oak Ridge Nat Lab, 64-81, prog analyst comput sci, 81-88. *Concurrent Pos:* Vis lectr, Stevens Inst Technol, Hoboken, NJ, 62. *Res:* Photochemistry; chemical kinetics; entire chemical research career devoted to the radiation chemistry of aqueous solutions, organic liquids and gases. *Mailing Add:* 101 Adelphi Rd Oak Ridge TN 37830

SWOVICK, MELVIN JOSEPH, DRUG & ALCOHOL ANALYSIS, DETECTION OF GUNSHOT RESIDUE. *Current Pos:* RETIRED. *Personal Data:* b Altoona, Pa, Jan, 20, 26; m 68, Maria E Galatz; c Michael W. *Educ:* Detroit Inst Technol, BSc, 74. *Prof Exp:* Med technician, Vet Hosp, Altoona, Pa, 54; lab technician, Allied Chem Inc, 55-60; develop chemist, Napco Chem Co, 60-63; anal chemist, Schwarz BioRes, Inc, 64; anal chemist coatings chem, Reichhold Chem, Inc, 65-80; forensic chemist, Oakland Co Sheriff's Dept, 80-91. *Concurrent Pos:* Instr, Austin Cath Prep Schs, 75-79; fac mem, Notre Dame High Sch. *Mem:* Am Chem Soc. *Res:* Developed methods for the analysis of gunshot residue in forensic chemistry. *Mailing Add:* 345 Folkstone Ct Troy MI 48098

SWOYER, VINCENT HARRY, technical administration, computer science, for more information see previous edition

SWYER, PAUL ROBERT, PEDIATRICS, NEONATOLOGY. *Current Pos:* from asst prof to prof, 65-86, EMER PROF, UNIV TORONTO, 86- *Personal Data:* b London, Eng, May 21, 21; Can citizen; m 47, Rumbaut Fernande; c Sandra & Michele. *Educ:* Cambridge Univ, BA, 40, MB, BChir & MA, 43, MD, 84; FRCP(L); FRCP(C), DCH (Eng), LMC(C), 54, FAAP, 55. *Hon Degrees:* MD, Univ Lausanne, Switz, 84. *Honors & Awards:* Distinguished Serv Award, Can Pediat Soc, 95. *Prof Exp:* Registr, Middlesex Hosp, 47-48; asst resident chest dis & med officer, Brompton Hosp for Dis of Chest, 48-49; registr, SWarwickshire Hosp, 49-50; asst med registr, Hosp Sick Children London, 50-52; registr, Royal Hosp, Wolverhampton, 52-53; fel cardiol, Hosp Sick Children, Toronto, 53-54, res assoc pediat, 54-60, asst scientist, 61-66, sr scientist, Res Inst, & chief, Div Perinatology, 67-86. *Concurrent Pos:* Can Dept Nat Health & Welfare grants, 54-67; sr staff physician, Hosp Sick Children, 64-; Med Res Coun Can grants, 66-86, Phys Serv Inc grants, 79-85 & NIH grants, 85-86; WHO Fel, 84; consult physician, Hosp Sick Children, Toronto, 86-; chair, Integration Comt Maternal, Neonatal & Child Health, Metro Toronto Dist Health Coun Hosp, 93-; founder, soc critical care med. *Mem:* Am Pediat Soc; Am Acad Pediat; Soc Pediat Res; Can Pediat Soc; Can Med Asn; Soc Critical Care Med. *Res:* Investigation of mechanics of breathing; energy metabolism, thermoregulation, blood flow and pressures and methods of treatment of pulmonary disorders in newly born infants; delivery, perinatal care; nutrition and respiration of newborns. *Mailing Add:* Hosp Sick Children 555 University Ave Toronto ON M5G 1X8 Can. *Fax:* 416-813-5245

SWYNGEDOUW, CHRIS, ANALYTICAL CHEMISTRY, CHEMICAL ENGINEERING. *Current Pos:* RES & DEVELOP SUPVR, CITY OF CALGARY, 94- *Personal Data:* b Gent, Belg, Mar 1, 55; m 84, Karen Freimark; c Nicholas. *Educ:* State Univ Ghent, Belg, BSc, 77; Univ Calgary, PhD(org chem), 85. *Prof Exp:* Postdoctoral, Dept Food Sci, Univ Alta, 84-88; lab scientist II, Univ Environ Ctr, 88-89; chief chemist, Chemex Labs Inc, Alta, 89-94. *Concurrent Pos:* Instr environ chem, Mt Royal Col, 90-92. *Mem:* Can Inst Chem. *Res:* Optimization or laboratory processes through automation; internal consulting. *Mailing Add:* PO Box 2100 Sta M Calgary AB T2P 2M5 Can. *Fax:* 403-268-3838; *E-Mail:* cswynged@gov.calgary.ab.ca.

SWYT, DENNIS, PHYSICS. *Current Pos:* CHIEF, PRECISION ENG DIV, NAT INST STAND & TECHNOL, 89- *Personal Data:* b May 25, 43. *Educ:* Case Western Res Univ, PhD(physics), 71. *Mailing Add:* Nat Inst Stand & Technol Precision Eng Div Rte 270 Bldg 220 Gaithersburg MD 20899

SY, JOSE, BIOCHEMISTRY. *Current Pos:* PROF, CALIF STATE UNIV, FRESNO, 85- *Personal Data:* b Sorsogon, Philippines, Dec 10, 44. *Educ:* Adamson Univ, Manila, BS, 64; Duke Univ, PhD(biochem), 70. *Prof Exp:* Res assoc, Rockefeller Univ, 70-74, from asst prof to assoc, 74-85. *Concurrent Pos:* Vis prof, Univ Calif, Irvine, 91-92. *Mem:* Protein Soc; Am Soc Biochemists & Molecular Biologists. *Res:* Nucleic acids and protein synthesis. *Mailing Add:* Dept Chem Calif State Univ Fresno CA 93740

SY, MAN-SUN, CELLULAR IMMUNOLOGY, IMMUNO-REGULATION. *Current Pos:* ASST PROF, SCH MED, CASE WESTERN RES, 92- *Educ:* Univ Colo, PhD(immunol), 79. *Prof Exp:* Asst prof, Med Sch, Harvard Univ, 79-92. *Res:* Auto-immunity. *Mailing Add:* Sch Med Case Western Res 1090 Euclio Ave BRB Rm 933 Cleveland OH 44106-4943

SYAGE, JACK A, LASER SPECTROSCOPY, MOLECULAR BEAM SPECTROSCOPY. *Current Pos:* SCIENTIST, THE AEROSPACE CORP, 84- *Personal Data:* b Rockville Center, NY, Apr 5, 24; m 83, Elizabeth Tallman; c George A & Amber R. *Educ:* Hamilton Col, BA, 76, Brown Univ, PhD(phys chem), 81. *Prof Exp:* Fel, Calif Inst Technol, 82-84. *Mem:* Am Phys Soc; Am Chem Soc; Optical Soc Am; Am Soc Mass Spectrometry. *Res:* Pico second reaction dynamics and molecular beam; atmospheric chemistry; propulsion and combustion chemistry. *Mailing Add:* Aerospace Corp PO Box 92975 Los Angeles CA 90009. *E-Mail:* jack__syage@qmail2.aero.org

SYBERS, HARLEY D, PATHOLOGY, PHYSIOLOGY. *Current Pos:* PROF PATH & LAB MED, UNIV TEX MED SCH, HOUSTON, 83-, PROF PATH & RADIOL, UNIV TEX DENT SCH, 86- *Personal Data:* b Tony, Wis, June 18, 33; m 58; c 2. *Educ:* Univ Wis-Madison, BS, 56, MS & MD, 63, PhD(physiol), 69; Am Bd Path, dipl & cert anat path & clin path, 68. *Prof Exp:* Resident path, Univ Wis-Madison, 64-68; asst prof, Univ Calif, San Diego, 69-75; assoc prof path, Baylor Col Mcd, 75-83. *Concurrent Pos:* USPHS contract, Univ Calif, San Diego, 69-74; Nat Heart & Lung Inst grant, 74-77; NIH res grant, 79-81, mem, Cardiovascular Study Sect, NIH, 80-84. *Mem:* Am Heart Asn; Am Soc Clin Path; Am Physiol Soc; Am Asn Pathologists; Int Acad Path. *Res:* Cardiac pathophysiology. *Mailing Add:* 5223 Valkeith Dr Houston TX 77096. *Fax:* 713-794-4149

SYBERT, JAMES RAY, SOLID STATE PHYSICS. *Current Pos:* Instr, Univ NTex, 56-58, from asst prof to assoc prof, 61-67, chmn dept, 69-80, PROF PHYSICS, UNIV NTEX, 67- *Personal Data:* b Greenville, Tex, Dec 25, 34; div; c 4. *Educ:* Univ NTex, BA, 55, MA, 56; La State Univ, PhD(physics), 61. *Concurrent Pos:* Adj prof, Southwest Ctr Advan Studies, Dallas, 67-70; vis prof, San Diego State Univ, 80, Ind Univ, Malaysia, 89. *Mem:* Am Phys Soc; Am Asn Physics Teachers. *Res:* Media in science education; electron transport in metals and semiconductors. *Mailing Add:* Dept Physics Univ NTex Denton TX 76203

SYBERT, PAUL DEAN, AROMATIC POLYMERS, RIGID-ROD POLYMERS. *Current Pos:* POLYMER RES CHEMIST, GEN ELEC LABS, 84- *Personal Data:* b Joliet, Ill, July 16, 54; m 81. *Educ:* Augustana Col, BA, 76; Univ Iowa, MS, 77; Colo State Univ, PhD(org chem), 80. *Prof Exp:* Sr res chemist, Monsanto, 80-81; polymer chemist, SRI Int, 81-84. *Mem:* Am Chem Soc. *Res:* New polymerization methods for new and existing rod-like aromatic polymers which afford anisotropic solutions; preparation of polymers for use as desalination membranes. *Mailing Add:* 11620 Hwy 66 Evansville IN 47712-8836

SYDEMAN, WILLIAM J, ECOLOGY OF MARINE VERTEBRATES. *Current Pos:* Farallon biologist, 86-90, DIR FARALLON RES, POINT REYES BIRD OBSERV, 90- *Personal Data:* b Hartford, Conn, Aug, 24, 57. *Educ:* Lewis & Clark Col, BS, 79; Northern Ariz Univ, MS, 85. *Res:* Marine bird and mammal population and behavioral ecology; marine birds as indicators of oceanic conditions; marine ecosystem management; coastal marine food-web structure and dynamics; conservation biology and restoration ecology. *Mailing Add:* 540 King Rd Petaluma CA 94952. *Fax:* 415-868-1946; *E-Mail:* wjsydemar@ucdavis.edu

SYDISKIS, ROBERT JOSEPH, VIROLOGY. *Current Pos:* ASSOC PROF MICROBIOL, SCH DENT, UNIV MD, BALTIMORE CITY, 71- *Personal Data:* b Bridgeport, Conn, Sept 19, 36; m 61; c 2. *Educ:* Univ Bridgeport, BA, 61; Northwestern Univ, PhD(microbiol), 65. *Prof Exp:* Fel, Univ Chicago, 65-67; asst prof virol, Sch Med, Univ Pittsburgh, 67-71. *Mem:* Am Soc Microbiol. *Res:* Isolation and identification of natural plant components which inhibit the replication of herpes virus; effect of various glucocorticoid hormones on herpes virus replication. *Mailing Add:* 405 Bent Twig Ct Abingdon MD 21009

SYDNOR, THOMAS DAVIS, ORNAMENTAL & URBAN HORTICULTURE, URBAN FORESTRY & ARBORICULTURE. *Current Pos:* from asst prof to prof ornamental hort, 72-94, PROF NATURAL RES, OHIO STATE UNIV, 95- *Personal Data:* b Richmond, Va, Jan 27, 40; m 62, Ann; c 3. *Educ:* Va Polytech Inst & State Univ, BS, 62; NC State Univ, PhD(plant physiol), 72. *Honors & Awards:* Alfred J Wright Award, 78. *Prof Exp:* Landscape foreman, Southside Nurseries Inc, 62-63, vpres, 65-69. *Concurrent Pos:* Consult landscape & urban hort, 78-; prin investr, Ohio Shade Tree Eval Proj, 78- *Mem:* Sigma Xi; Am Soc Hort Sci; Int Soc Arboricult; Am Soc Consult Arborists; Soc Am Foresters. *Res:* Shade tree evaluation and the effects of environmental conditions on growth and development of woody ornamentals and trees for urban, highway and landscape situations. *Mailing Add:* 6800 Harriott Rd Powell OH 43065

SYDOR, MICHAEL, OPTICAL PROPERTIES OF ELECTRONIC MATERIALS & SMALL PARTICULATE. *Current Pos:* From asst prof to assoc prof, 68-74, PROF PHYSICS, UNIV MINN, DULUTH, 74- *Personal Data:* b Prusseniv, Ukraine, Dec 25, 36; US citizen; m 62, 87, Jacqueline Burnett; c 5. *Educ:* Univ BC, BASc, 59; Univ NMex, PhD(physics), 64. *Mem:* Am Phys Soc; Sigma Xi; Am Geophys Union. *Res:* Modulated photoreflectance; materials growth by molecular beam epitaxy and closed space vapor transport; quantum-well structures; numerical modeling of materials growth processes; light scattering from submicron particles and amorphous materials. *Mailing Add:* Dept Physics Univ Minn Duluth MN 55812. *E-Mail:* msydor@ub.d.umn.edu

SYDORIAK, STEPHEN GEORGE, PHYSICS. *Current Pos:* RETIRED. *Personal Data:* b Passaic, NJ, Jan 6, 18; m 45; c 6. *Educ:* Univ Buffalo, BA, 40; Yale Univ, PhD(physics), 48. *Prof Exp:* Mem staff, Radiation Lab, Mass Inst Technol, 41-45; mem staff, Los Alamos Nat Lab, Univ Calif, 48-80. *Mem:* Am Phys Soc. *Res:* Radar signal threshold studies; liquid helium-three properties; 1962 helium-three vapor pressure scale of temperatures; critical nucleate boiling equation for helium; superconducting magnet design for passive quench arrest. *Mailing Add:* 1192 41st St Los Alamos NM 87544

SYED, ASHFAQUZZAMAN, X-RAY CRYSTALLOGRAPHY, STRUCTURE ANALYSIS. *Current Pos:* PROD SPECIALIST, X-RAY INSTRUMENTATION & CRYSTALLOG, ENRAF-NONIUS, BOHEMIA, NY, 84- *Personal Data:* b Barabanki, India, July 5, 52; m 84; c 2. *Educ:* Gorakhpur Univ, India, BSc, 70, MSc, 72, PhD(physics crystallog), 79. *Prof Exp:* Res asst x-ray crystallog, Dept Physics, Gorakhpur Univ, India, 72-78, sr res asst, 78-79; res chemist instrument anal, Tata Iron & Steel Co, Jamshedpur, India, 79-81, lectr physics, Tech Inst, 79; res asst x-ray crystallog, State Univ NY, Buffalo, 81-83; res assoc x-ray crystallog, Univ New Orleans, 83-84. *Mem:* Am Crystallog Asn. *Res:* Chemical crystallography; accurate x-ray diffraction data and charge-density analysis; computing methods in x-ray crystallography; hardware and software developments and instrumentation in x-ray crystallography. *Mailing Add:* 252 Brunswick St Rochester NY 14607

SYED, IBRAHIM BIJLI, MEDICAL PHYSICS, RADIOLOGICAL HEALTH. *Current Pos:* prof nuclear med, 79-92, PROF MED, MED PHYSICS & NUCLEAR CARDIOL, SCH MED, UNIV LOUISVILLE, 79-, DIR BASIC NUCLEAR MED SCIS, 79-; PHYSICIST & RADIATION SAFETY OFFICER, MED CTR, VET ADMIN, 79- *Personal Data:* b Bellary, India, Mar 16, 39; US citizen; m 64, Sajida Shariff; c Mubin & Zafrin. *Educ:* Univ Mysore, BSc, 60, MSc, 62; Bombay Univ, dipl, 64; Johns Hopkins Univ, DSc(radiol sci), 72; Am Bd Radiol, dipl, 75; Am Bd Health Physics, dipl, 77; Am Bd Hazard Control Officers, dipl, 80. *Hon Degrees:* PhD, Marquis Giuseppe Scicluna Int Univ, 85. *Honors & Awards:* Hind Rattan Jewel of India Award. *Prof Exp:* Lectr physics, Veerasaiva Col, Univ Mysore, 62-63; physicist, Victoria Hosp, Bangalore, India, 64-67; chief physicist, Halifax Infirmary, Can, 67-69; res asst, Johns Hopkins Univ, 69, postdoctoral fel, 72-73; chief physicist, Med Physics Div, Baystate Med Ctr, Wesson Mem Unit, 73-79, admin dir med physics, 77-79; asst clin prof, Sch Med, Univ Conn, 75-79. *Concurrent Pos:* Consult physicist, Bowring & Lady Curzon Hosp & Ministry of Health, India, 64-67, Bangalore Nursing Home, 64-67, Wing Mem Hosp, 73-79 & Mercy Hosp, 73-79; assoc prof, Springfield Tech Community Col, 73-79; adj prof radiol, Holyoke Community Col, 73-79; consult med physicist & radiol safety officer to area hosps in Ky & Ind, 79-; clin prof med, Endocrinol, Metab & Radionuclide Studies, Univ Louisville Sch Med, 80-; dir, Nuclear Med Sci, 80-; vis prof, Banglalore Univ & Gulbarga Univ, India, 87-88 & 96-97; vis scientist, Bhabba Atomic Res Ctr, Bombay, India; consult, Coun Sci & Indust Res, Govt India, 80-, Am Coun Sci & Health, 80-, Gastroenterol & Urol, Div Food & Drug Admin, Human & Health Serv, 88-, radiopharmaceutical div, 89-; tech expert nuclear med, Int Atomic Energy Agency, Rep Bangladesh; govt India scholar, Bhabha Atomic Res Ctr, Bombay, 63-64; consult to govt of India, diag radiol physics, nuclear med physics & radiation oncol physics, UN Develop Prog, 92; tech expert nuclear med, Int Atomic Energy Agy, Guatemala, Cent Am, 94; PhD thesis examr, Am Bd Radiol & Am Bd Health Physics. *Mem:* Fel Brit Inst Physics; fel Royal Soc Health, Eng; Am Asn Physicists in Med; fel Am Inst Chemists; fel Am Col Radiol; Health Physics Soc; Soc Nuclear Med; Am Col Nuclear Med; fel Am Asn Physicists Med. *Res:* Radiopharmaceutical dosimetry; medical health physics; therapeutic radiological physics; effects of caffeine in man; estimation of absorbed dose to embryo and fetus from radiological and nuclear medicine procedures; magnetic resonance imaging and bioeffects; theory of limitations; physicist's concept of God; half value layer of polyenergetic photon emitting radio nuclide; bremsstrahlijng and radioactivity determination; author of one manual and contributor of over 100 articles to science journals; contributed over 50 articles on religion and science; molecular coincidence imaging; healing in spiritual medicine. *Mailing Add:* 7102 Shefford Louisville KY 40242. *Fax:* 502-894-6937 Ext 6908; *E-Mail:* syed.ibrahim@forum.va.gov

SYEKLOCHA, DELFA, MEDICAL BACTERIOLOGY, IMMUNOLOGY. *Current Pos:* RETIRED. *Personal Data:* b Vancouver, BC, Sept 12, 33. *Educ:* Univ BC, BA, 54; McGill Univ, MSc, 62, PhD(microbiol), 64. *Prof Exp:* NIH fel, Ont Cancer Inst, 64-65; asst prof microbiol, Univ BC, 65- *Mem:* Am Soc Microbiol; Can Soc Microbiol; Can Soc Immunol. *Res:* Immunizing potential of attenuated mutants of Pseudomonas aeruginosa strains and characterization of soluble antigens derived from the wild type; biological activities and characterization of a lethal exotoxin produced by Paeruginosa. *Mailing Add:* 940 Keith Rd West Vancouver BC V7T 1M3 Can

SYGUSCH, JURGEN, BIOCHEMISTRY, CRYSTALLOGRAPHY. *Current Pos:* assoc prof, 91-92, PROF BIOCHEM, UNIV MONTREAL, 92- *Personal Data:* b Jablonec, Czech, Aug 8, 45; Can citizen; div; c 1. *Educ:* McGill Univ, BSc, 67, MSc, 69; Univ Montreal, PhD(chem), 74. *Prof Exp:* Med Res Coun Can fel, Dept Biochem, Sch Med, Univ Alta, 74-77; assoc prof biochem, Sch Med, Univ Sherbrooke, 77-91. *Mem:* AAAS; Can Biochem Soc; Am Crystallog Asn; Biophys Soc. *Res:* Structural studies by enzyme kinetics and by x-ray crystallography of conformational changes resulting from substrate or ligand binding. *Mailing Add:* Dept Biochem Univ Montreal CP 6128 Sta Ctr Ville Montreal PQ H3C 3J7 Can. *Fax:* 514-343-2210; *E-Mail:* syguschj@bch.umontreal.ca

SYKES, ALAN O'NEIL, ACOUSTICS, APPLICATION OF MULTITERMINAL NETWORK THEORY TO VIBRATION PROBLEMS. *Current Pos:* RETIRED. *Personal Data:* b St Regis Falls, NY, May 19, 25; m 51, Emily A Adams; c Alan O Jr & Edward A. *Educ:* Cornell Univ, AB, 48; Cath Univ Am, PhD, 68. *Prof Exp:* Physicist, David Taylor Model Basin, USN Dept, US Space Off Naval Res, 48-52, electronic scientist, 52-54, physicist, 54-58, physicist & consult to head acoust div, 58-60, physicist & head, Noise Transmission & Radiation Sect, 60-61, physicist & head, Noise Res & Develop Br, 61-64, physicist & head, Struct Acoust Br, 64-65, physicist & sci officer, 65-81. *Concurrent Pos:* Mem hydroballistic adv comt, Navy Bur Ord, 56-60; mem struct impedence panel, Noise Adv Comt, Navy Bur Ships, 56-64, consult, Soc Automotive Engrs, 57-; consult, vibration anal & control, 81-; pres & founder, Acoust Res & Appln, 83-; head, shock & vibration comt, Acoust Soc Am. *Mem:* Fel Acoust Soc Am; NY Acad Sci; Sigma Xi. *Res:* Underwater acoustics with emphasis on signal processing and propagation; noise reduction, vibration theory and electroacoustic transducer development; instrumentation for measurement of the dynamic and piezoelectric properties of polymeric materials. *Mailing Add:* 304 Mashie Dr SE Vienna VA 22180

SYKES, BRIAN DOUGLAS, BIOPHYSICAL CHEMISTRY. *Current Pos:* assoc prof, 75-80, PROF BIOCHEM, UNIV ALTA, 80- *Personal Data:* b Montreal, Que, Aug 30, 43; m 68; c 2. *Educ:* Univ Alta, BSc, 65; Stanford Univ, PhD(chem), 69. *Honors & Awards:* Ayerst Award, 82; Steacie Prize, 82; Kaplan Award, 92. *Prof Exp:* From asst prof to assoc prof chem, Harvard Univ, 69-75. *Concurrent Pos:* NIH grant, Harvard Univ, 69-75, Alfred P Sloan fel, 71-73; Med Res Coun Can grant, 75- *Mem:* Can Biochem Soc; Am Soc Biol Chemists; Am Chem Soc; Biophys Soc; fel Royal Soc Can. *Res:* Application of nuclear magnetic resonance to problems in biochemistry. *Mailing Add:* Dept Biochem Univ Alta Edmonton AB T6C 2H7 Can

SYKES, DONALD JOSEPH, STATISTICAL QUALITY ANALYSIS, IMAGING SCIENCE & TECHNOLOGY. *Current Pos:* dir & chief oper officer, 83-88, CHMN BD, MARPAC CO, 88- *Personal Data:* b Buffalo, NY, Mar 16, 36; m 60; c 2. *Educ:* Rochester Inst Technol, BS, 58. *Prof Exp:* Dir appl res, Cormac Chem Corp, 59-63; res mgr, P A Hunt Chem Corp, 63-69, asst dir res, 69-75, dir res, 75-77, asst vpres res, 77-78, vpres res & develop, 78-80, sr vpres, 80-83. *Mem:* Am Chem Soc; Am Soc Quality Control; Soc Plastic Eng; Soc Imaging Sci & Technol. *Res:* Super concentrates/polymers; imaging science. *Mailing Add:* 8 Sunset Ct Mahwah NJ 07430

SYKES, JAMES AUBREY, JR, TECHNOLOGY STRATEGY & MANAGEMENT, APPLIED SCIENCE & ENGINEERING OF MATERIALS. *Current Pos:* DIR TECH PLANNING, GLOBAL TECH GROUP, AMP, INC, 94- *Personal Data:* b Washington, DC, Sept 24, 41; m 60, Sharon O'Brien; c David A & Brian F. *Educ:* Univ Md, BS, 64, MS, 65, PhD(chem eng), 68. *Prof Exp:* Engr, W R Grace & Co, 65-68; process eng, Div Shell Oil, Shell Develop Co, 68-71, tech mgr & supvr, 71-74; dir indust chem & technol, Air Prod & Chem, Inc, 74-84, gen mgr, Tech Planning Serv, 84-94. *Concurrent Pos:* Abstractor, Chem Abstracts, Am Chem Soc, 69-71. *Mem:* Am Inst Chem Engrs; Sigma Xi; Inst Elec & Electronics Engrs; Am Chem Soc; World Future Sod; Stratig Mgt Soc. *Res:* Polymers; commodity chemicals; performance chemicals; petroleum processing; materials and metallurgy; heat transfer; process systems; technology management; corporate-level research and development; manufacturing technology; innovation management; research and development efficiency; energy systems. *Mailing Add:* PO Box 314 Old Zionsville PA 18068

SYKES, JAMES ENOCH, FISHERIES. *Current Pos:* RETIRED. *Personal Data:* b Richmond, Va, Apr 12, 23; m 47, Kathryn Porter; c Daniel P. *Educ:* Randolph-Macon Col, 48; Univ Va, MS, 49. *Honors & Awards:* Outstanding Achievement Award, Am Inst Fishery Res Biologists. *Prof Exp:* Lab instr biol, Univ Va, 48-49; fishery res biologist, US Fish & Wildlife Serv, 49-58, chief striped bass invests, 58-62, biol lab dir, Bur Com Fisheries, 62-71; dir, Div Fisheries, Nat Marine Fisheries Serv, Nat Oceanic & Atmospheric Admin, 71-79; mem, NC Coastal Resources Comn, 79-86. *Mem:* Am Fisheries Soc; Am Inst Fishery Res Biologists (pres, 75 & 76). *Res:* Coastal pelagic and offshore sport fisheries; assessment of marine resources; biology of Gulf and Atlantic menhaden. *Mailing Add:* 3105 Country Club Rd Morehead City NC 28557

SYKES, LYNN RAY, GEOPHYSICS, NUCLEAR ARMS CONTROL. *Current Pos:* Res scientist, Lamont Geol Observ, Columbia Univ, 62-65, res geophysicist, Inst Earth Sci, Environ Sci Serv Admin, Lamont Geol Observ, 65-68, from assoc prof to prof, 68-78, head, Seismol Group, 71-85, HIGGINS PROF GEOL, LAMONT-DOHERTY EARTH OBSERV, COLUMBIA UNIV, 78- *Personal Data:* b Pittsburgh, Pa, Apr 16, 37; m 86, Katherine W Flanz. *Educ:* Mass Inst Technol, BS & MS, 60; Columbia Univ, PhD(geol), 65. *Hon Degrees:* State Col NY Potsdam, 88. *Honors & Awards:* Macelwane Award, Am Geophys Union, 70, Bucher Medal, 75; Fed Am Scientists Award for Sci in Pub Serv, 88; John Wesley Powell Award, US Geol Surv, 92. *Concurrent Pos:* Mem comts seismol & earthquake prediction, Nat Res Coun-Nat Acad Sci, 73-75; mem, Earthquake Prediction Eval Coun, US Geol Surv, 79-82, chmn, 84-88; mem comn acad priorities arts & sci, Columbia Univ, 78-79; mem, Earthquake Prediction Eval Coun, US Geol Surv, 79-82, chmn, 84-88; Guggenheim fel, 88- *Mem:* Nat Acad Sci; fel Geol Soc Am; AAAS; fel Am Geophys Union; fel Royal Astron Soc; Am Acad Arts & Sci. *Res:* Investigations of long-period and mantle seismic waves; surface wave propagation across ocean areas; precise location of earthquake hypocenters and relationship of spatial distribution of earthquakes to large-scale tectonic phenomena; field study of aftershocks of 1964 Alaskan earthquake; field study of deep and shallow earthquakes in Fiji-Tonga region; earthquake prediction; plate tectonics; identification of underground nuclear explosions; yield estimation and sizes of Soviet nuclear weapons. *Mailing Add:* Lamont-Doherty Earth Observ Columbia Univ Palisades NY 10964. *E-Mail:* sykes@edeo.columbia.edu

SYKES, PAUL JAY, JR, PHYSICS, NUCLEAR ENGINEERING. *Current Pos:* asst prof, 64-84, EMER PROF PHYSICS, UNIV BC, 84- *Personal Data:* b Hummelstown, Pa, Aug 31, 18; m 48, Dorothy W Kendrick; c 1. *Educ:* Univ BC, BA, 48; Univ Calif, MA, 51. *Prof Exp:* Chief proj off nuclear eng test facil, Wright-Patterson AFB, Ohio, 52-56, chief reactor hazards br, Spec Weapons Ctr, Kirtland AFB, 57-58, proj officer, Anal Div, 58-60, proj officer, Physics Div, Air Force Weapons Lab, 60-64. *Mem:* Am Asn Physics Teachers; Royal Astron Soc Can. *Res:* Design and engineering of nuclear research reactor facilities; reactor hazards and safeguards; nuclear weapon systems analysis. *Mailing Add:* 5616 Westport Pl West Vancouver BC V7W 1T9 Can

SYKES, RICHARD BROOK, MICROBIOLOGY. *Current Pos:* group res & develop dir, 87-94, dep chmn, Glaxo Holdings, 94-95, CHIEF EXEC OFFICER, GLAXO WELCOME PLC, 95- *Personal Data:* b Eng, Aug 7, 42; m 69; c 2. *Educ:* Paddington Col, BS, 65; Queen Elizabeth Col, London Univ, MS, 68; Bristol Univ, PhD, 72. *Prof Exp:* Head, Antibiotic Res unit, Glaxo Res Labs, 72-77; dir, Dept Microbiol, Squibb Inst Med Res, 79-83, vpres infectious & metab dis, 83-86; chief exec, Glaxo Group Res, UK, 86-87. *Concurrent Pos:* Chmn & chief exec, Glaxo Group Res Ltd; pres, Glaxo Inc Res Inst. *Mem:* Brit Soc Antimicrobial Chemother. *Mailing Add:* Welcome Plc Landsdowne House Barkley Sq London WIX 6BP England

SYKES, ROBERT MARTIN, ENVIRONMENTAL ENGINEERING. *Current Pos:* from asst prof to assoc prof, 72-, PROF CIVIL ENG, OHIO STATE UNIV. *Personal Data:* b Lawrence, Mass, July 25, 43; m 65; c 1. *Educ:* Northeastern Univ, BSCE, 66; Purdue Univ, West Lafayette, MSCE, 68, PhD(sanit eng), 70. *Prof Exp:* Asst prof civil eng, Union Col, NY, 70-72. *Concurrent Pos:* Consult, NY State Dept Environ Conserv, 70-71. *Mem:* Water Pollution Control Fedn; Am Water Works Asn. *Res:* Water pollution abatement; biological processes for waste water treatment; ecosystem theory; modeling of aquatic systems. *Mailing Add:* Dept Civil & Environ Geodetic Sci Hitchcock Hall Rm 417-A Ohio State Univ 2070 Neil Ave Columbus OH 43210

SYKORA, OSKAR P, DENTISTRY. *Current Pos:* assoc prof, 71-90, PROF PROSTHODONTICS, DALHOUSIE UNIV, 90- *Personal Data:* b Nachod, Czech, June 22, 29; Can citizen; m 65. *Educ:* Sir George William Univ, BA, 54; Univ Montreal, MA, 55, PhD(slavic hist), 59; McGill Univ, DDS, 59. *Prof Exp:* From asst prof to assoc prof prosthodontics, McGill Univ, 61-71. *Mem:* Am Prosthodontic Soc; Can Dent Asn; Can Inst Int Affairs; Can Acad Prosthodontics; Europ Prosthodontic Asn; Am Acad Hist Dent. *Res:* Fixed and removable prosthetic dentistry. *Mailing Add:* 1584 Rowbie St Halifax NS B3H 3E6 Can

SYLVESTER, ARTHUR GIBBS, NEOTECTONICS, PETROFABRICS. *Current Pos:* PROF, UNIV CALIF, SANTA BARBARA, 66- *Personal Data:* b Altadena, Calif, Feb 16, 38; m 61; c 2. *Educ:* Pomona Col, BA, 59; Univ Calif, Los Angeles, MA, 63 & PhD(geol), 66. *Prof Exp:* Fulbright scholar, US Educ Found, Norway, 61-62; res geologist, Shell Develop Co, 66-68. *Concurrent Pos:* Regional lectr, Sigma Xi, 71-72; assoc dir educ abroad prog, Univ Calif & Study Ctr Bergen Univ, 72-74; lectr, Struct Geol Sch, Am Asn Petrol Geologist, 77-86, dir, 83-86; chmn dept geol sci, Univ Calif, Santa Barbara, 80-86; distinguished lectr, Am Asn Petrol Geol, 82-83; assoc ed, Am Asn Petrol Geologist, 85-88; ed, Geol Soc Am, 89- *Mem:* Norweg Geol Soc; Seismol Soc Am; fel Geol Soc Am; Am Geophys Union; Am Asn Petrol Geologists; Nat Asn Geol Teachers. *Res:* Geodetic investigations of near field crustal movements associated with active and potentially active faults; structure and tectonics of strike-slip faults; deformation of rock-forming minerals. *Mailing Add:* Dept Geol Sci Univ Calif Santa Barbara CA 93106

SYLVESTER, DIANE MARIE, GENERAL & CARDIOVASCULAR PHARMACOLOGY, BIOMARKERS IN TOXICOLOGY. *Current Pos:* ASSOC PROF PHARMACOL & DIV HEAD BASIC & PHARMACEUT SCI DEPT, ALBANY COL PHARM, 97- *Personal Data:* b Boston, Mass, Apr 17, 51; c Erin, Ethan & Evan. *Educ:* Fairleigh Dickinson Univ, BS, 73; Univ Dayton, MS, 75; Wash State Univ, PhD(pharmaceut sci), 81. *Prof Exp:* Clin chem, Harborview Med Ctr, 75-76; med technologist, Pullman Mem Hosp, 77-97; res fel & instr pharmacol, Wash State Univ, 81-84, from asst prof to assoc prof, 84-97. *Mem:* Am Soc Pharmacol & Exp Therapeut. *Res:* Developing biomarkers to monitor exposure to toxins; antiplatelet agents. *Mailing Add:* Dept Pharmacol Albany Col Pharm Albany NY 12208. *Fax:* 518-445-7260; *E-Mail:* sylvestd@panther.acp.edu

SYLVESTER, EDWARD SANFORD, ENTOMOLOGY. *Current Pos:* prin lab asst entom, Univ Calif, Berkeley, 45-47, instr entom univ & jr entomologist exp sta, 47-49, asst prof & asst entomologist, 49-55, lectr & assoc entomologist, 55-61, chmn entom sci, 81-85, PROF ENTOM & ENTOMOLOGIST EXP STA, UNIV CALIF, BERKELEY, 61-, ASSOC DEAN, 87- *Personal Data:* b New York, NY, Feb 29, 20; m 42; c 2. *Educ:* Colo State Univ, BS, 43; Univ Calif, PhD(entom), 47. *Prof Exp:* Lab asst bot, Colo State Univ, 40, asst entom, 41-43. *Mem:* Entom Soc Am; Am Phytopath Soc; Sigma Xi. *Res:* Insect vector-virus relationships; biostatistics; Aphidiae. *Mailing Add:* 366 Ocean View Ave Kensington CA 94707-1224

SYLVESTER, JAMES EDWARD, MOLECULAR BIOLOGY, GENETICS. *Current Pos:* ASSOC PROF, DEPT PATH, HAHNEMANN UNIV, PA, 88- *Personal Data:* b Syracuse, NY, Apr 30, 47; m 84, Linda Struhar; c Scott & Karissa. *Educ:* Le Moyne Col, BS, 68; Univ Del, PhD(chem), 77. *Prof Exp:* Lab dir, Brandt Assocs, Inc, 70-73; staff fel, Lab Molecular Genetics, Nat Inst Child Health & Human Develop, NIH, 77-80; res assoc, dept pediat, Univ Mich, 80-81; res assoc, Dept Human Genetics, Univ Pa, 81-88. *Concurrent Pos:* Mem, biohazard safety comt, Smith, Kline & French, 84- *Mem:* Am Soc Human Genetics; AAAS. *Res:* Molecular and genetic organization of the human genes that code for ribosomal RNA; structure of the nucleolus; genetics of Friedreichs Ataxia. *Mailing Add:* Dept Microbiol & Immunol Hahnemann Univ Sch Med, Broad & Vine Sts Philadelphia PA 19102-1178. *E-Mail:* sylvesterj@hal.hahnemann.edu

SYLVESTER, JOSEPH ROBERT, FISHERIES MANAGEMENT, MARINE BIOLOGY. *Current Pos:* WITH US ENVIRON PROTECTION AGENCY, OFF PESTICIDE PROGS, ARLINGTON, VA, 93- *Personal Data:* b Fayetteville, NC, Nov 3, 42. *Educ:* Univ Hawaii, BA, 65, MS, 69; Univ Wash, PhD(fish biol), 71. *Prof Exp:* Fishery res biologist, Nat Marine Fisheries Serv, Bur Com Fisheries, 65-71; dir, Bur Fish & Wildlife, Govt VI, 71-73 & 76-78; fishery res biologist, Oceanic Inst, 73-76; mgr, Marine Mammal Endangered Species Prog, Nat Marine Fisheries Serv, St Petersburg, Fla, 78-80; leader ecol sect, Nat Fishery Res Lab, LaCrosse, Wis, 80-83; adj fac & asst prof biol, Univ Wis, LaCrosse, 80-83; proj leader & vis prof, Univ Ark, Pine Bluff, 83-89; mgr, Fisheries Habitat Protection Prog, Fisheries Div, Mich Dept Natural Resources, 89-93. *Concurrent Pos:* Res assoc, Hawaii Inst Marine Biol, Univ Hawaii, 65-69; mem, Space Explor Res Rev Panel, Biol, NASA, 75. *Mem:* Am Fisheries Soc; Am Inst Fisheries Res Biologists; Sigma Xi; Ecol Soc Am; Wildlife Soc. *Res:* Fish and wildlife sciences; co-author of numerous publications. *Mailing Add:* PO Box 26192 Arlington VA 22215

SYLVESTER, NICHOLAS DOMINIC, CHEMICAL ENGINEERING. *Current Pos:* assoc prof, 72-75, chmn chem & petrol eng, 77-78, PROF CHEM ENG, UNIV TULSA, 75-, DEAN ENG, 78- *Personal Data:* b Cleveland, Ohio, Apr 16, 42; m 65; c 2. *Educ:* Ohio Univ, BS, 64; Carnegie-Mellon Univ, PhD(chem eng), 69. *Prof Exp:* Asst prof chem eng, Univ Notre Dame, 68-72. *Concurrent Pos:* Res consult, Amoco Prod Res Co, 75- *Mem:* Am Soc Eng Educ; Soc Petrol Engrs; Am Inst Chem Engrs; Soc Rheology; Am Chem Soc. *Res:* Enhanced oil recovery; multi-phase flow; non-Newtonian fluid mechanics; water pollution control; chemical reaction engineering. *Mailing Add:* Col Eng Univ Akron Akron OH 44325-3901

SYLVESTER, ROBERT O(HRUM), CIVIL & ENVIRONMENTAL ENGINEERING. *Current Pos:* from asst prof to assoc prof civil eng, 47-73, head div water & air resources, Dept Civil Eng, 68-73, dir, Inst for Environ Studies, 73-76, prof, 73-78, chmn, Dept Civil Eng, 76-78, EMER PROF CIVIL ENG, UNIV WASH, SEATTLE, 78- *Personal Data:* b Seattle, Wash, Aug 20, 14; m 40, Irene V Olson; c Robert J & James W. *Educ:* Univ Wash, BS, 36; Harvard Univ, SM, 41; Environ Eng Intersoc, dipl, 58. *Honors & Awards:* Arthur Sidney Bedell Award, Water Pollution Control Fedn, 57. *Prof Exp:* Engr, Allis Chalmers Mfg Co, 36-38; instr eng, Univ Wash, 38-39; dist engr, Wash State Dept Health, 39-41, 46-47. *Concurrent Pos:* Consult various industs, US & Can govt; mem study sect res grant review, NIH, 63-67; mem adv panel, BC Dept Lands, Forests, Water Resources, 70-72, mem adv panel water quality criteria, Nat Acad Sci, 71-72, US Nat Comt, Int Asn Water Pollution Res, 71-74 & review panel, US Gen Acct Off Water Res, 73. *Mem:* Fel Am Soc Civil Engrs; Am Water Works Asn; Water Pollution Control Fedn; Int Asn Water Pollution. *Res:* Am Geophys Union. *Res:* Water resources; water supply; water resource and quality management; water pollution control technology; solid waste collection, disposal and resource recovery; environmental aspects of water quality. *Mailing Add:* 10218 Richwood Ave NW Seattle WA 98177

SYLVIA, AVIS LATHAM, CELL PHYSIOLOGY. *Current Pos:* fel, Ctr Aging & Human Develop, 74-76, res assoc, 76-77, asst prof, 77-83, ASSOC PROF, DEPT PHYSIOL, DUKE UNIV MED CTR, 83- *Personal Data:* b Westerly, RI, Nov 16, 38. *Educ:* Univ NC, Greensboro, AB, 60; Univ Conn, MS, 66; Univ NC, Chapel Hill, PhD(physiol), 73. *Prof Exp:* Res assoc cell physiol, Sch Med, Univ NC, 73-74. *Mem:* AAAS; Soc for Neurosci; Geront Soc; Sigma Xi. *Res:* Cellular oxidative metabolism, bioenergetics and redox phenomena; physiological and biochemical aspects of development and aging in the mammalian central nervous system. *Mailing Add:* 3719 Shrewsbury St Durham NC 27707

SYMBAS, PANAGIOTIS N, THORACIC SURGERY, CARDIOVASCULAR SURGERY. *Current Pos:* assoc thoracic surg, 64-65, from asst prof to assoc prof, 66-73, PROF SURG, THORACIC CARDIOVASC SURG DIV, SCH MED, EMORY UNIV, 73-, DIR SURG RES LAB, 70-; DIR THORACIC & CARDIOVASC SURG, GRADY MEM HOSP, ATLANTA, 70- *Personal Data:* b Greece, Aug 15, 25; US citizen; m 65, Hytho Bagatis; c Nikolas, Peter & John. *Educ:* Univ Salonika, MD, 54. *Prof Exp:* Intern surg, Vanderbilt Univ, 56-57, resident surgeon, 60-61, instr surg, 61-62; fel cardiovasc surg, St Louis Univ, 62-63. *Mem:* Am Surg Asn; Am Asn Thoracic Surg; Soc Thoracic Surg; Soc Univ Surgeons; fel Am Col Surgeons. *Mailing Add:* Dept Surg Emory Univ Sch Med 69 Butler St SE Atlanta GA 30303-3056

SYMCHOWICZ, SAMSON, DRUG METABOLISM, BIOCHEMICAL PHARMACOLOGY. *Current Pos:* RETIRED. *Personal Data:* b Krakow, Poland, Mar 20, 23; nat US; m 53, Sarah Nussbaum; c Esther, Beatrice & Caren. *Educ:* Chem Tech Col Eng, Czech, Chem Eng, 50; Polytech Inst Brooklyn, MS, 56; Rutgers Univ, PhD(physiol, biochem), 60. *Prof Exp:* Asst biochem, Allan Mem Inst, McGill Univ, 51-53; asst hormone res, Col Med, State Univ NY Downstate Med Ctr, 53-56; res biochemist, Schering Corp, 56-66, sect leader, 66-70, head dept biochem, 70-73, assoc dir biol res, 73-77, dir drug metab & pharmacokinetics, 77-92. *Mem:* Am Chem Soc; Am Soc Pharmacol & Exp Therapeut; Int Soc Study Xenobiotics; NY Acad Sci; AAAS. *Res:* Biogenic amines; drug metabolism. *Mailing Add:* 44 Laurel Ave Livingston NJ 07039

SYME, S LEONARD, EPIDEMIOLOGY. *Current Pos:* prof, 68-94, EMER PROF EPIDEMIOL, SCH PUB HEALTH, UNIV CALIF, BERKELEY, 94- *Personal Data:* b Dauphin, Man, Can, July 4, 32; m 54; c 3. *Educ:* Univ Calif, Los Angeles, BA, 53, MA, 55; Yale Univ, PhD(med sociol), 57. *Honors & Awards:* James D Bruce Mem Award, Am Col Physicians, 89. *Prof Exp:* Sociologist, Heart Dis Control Prog, USPHS, 57-60; exec secy, Human Ecol Study Sect, NIH, Bethesda, 60-62; sociologist & asst chief, Heart Dis Control Prog, USPHS, San Francisco, 62-65, chief, 66-68. *Concurrent Pos:* Chmn, Dept Biomed & Environ Health Sci, Sch Pub Health, Univ Calif, Berkeley, 75-80. *Mem:* Inst Med-Nat Acad Sci; fel Am Heart Asn; fel Am Sociol Asn; fel Am Pub Health Asn; AAAS; Int Soc Cardiol; Am Epidemiol Soc. *Res:* Published over 90 articles in various journals. *Mailing Add:* Sch Pub Health Univ Calif 140 Warren Hall Berkeley CA 94720

SYMES, LAWRENCE RICHARD, SOFTWARE SYSTEMS, COMPUTER SCIENCE & SOFTWARE ENGINEERING. *Current Pos:* assoc prof, 70-74, dir, Comput Ctr, 70-75, head dept, 72-81, dir acad comput, 80-81, dean sci, 82-92, PROF COMPUT SCI, UNIV REGINA, CAN, 74-, DEAN GRAD STUDIES & RES & ASSOC VPRES RES, 97- *Personal Data:* b Ottawa, Can, Aug 3, 42; m 64; c 3. *Educ:* Univ Sask, BA, 63; Purdue Univ, MS, 66, PhD(comput sci), 69. *Prof Exp:* Asst prof comput sci, Purdue Univ, 69-70. *Concurrent Pos:* Mem bd comput serv, Sask Sch Trustees Asn, Regina, 72-89, Sask Agr Res Fund, 87-88, Sask ADA Asn, 90-93; lectr, Xian Jiaotong Univ, China, 83, Shandong Acad of Sci, China, 87; bd dir, Hosp Syst Serv Group, 78-94, chmn, 80-83; mem adv coun, Can/Sask Advan Technol Agreement, 85-87; mem steering comt, IBM/Sask Agreement, 90-91; mem bd dir, Software Technol Ctr, 93-; exec dir, Post sec Educ, Govt Sask, 94-95; mem bd dir, Sask Commun Network, 96- *Mem:* Asn Comput Mach; Can Info Processing Soc (pres, 79-80); Inst Elec & Electronics Engrs Comput Soc. *Res:* Programming languages; distributed computing; computer networks; software engineering; technology in support of learning. *Mailing Add:* Univ Regina Regina SK S4S 0A2 Can. *Fax:* 306-585-4893; *E-Mail:* symesdcs@uregina.ca

SYMINGTON, JANEY STUDT, VIROLOGY, CELL BIOLOGY. *Current Pos:* res assoc, 78-79, asst res prof, 80-85, ASSOC RES PROF, ST LOUIS UNIV INST MOLECULAR VIROL, 85- *Personal Data:* b St Louis, Mo, June 29, 28; m 49, Stuart; c Anne (Rhodes), Stuart 5th, Sidney S & John S. *Educ:* Vassar Col, AB, 50; Radcliffe Col, PhD(biol), 59. *Prof Exp:* Res assoc & asst prof bot, Washington Univ, 58-71, res asst prof biol, 71-73, Dept Health, Educ & Welfare Pub Health Serv spec trainee cell biol & tissue cult animal cell virol, 73-74, res assoc microbiol, 74-77. *Concurrent Pos:* Guest cur biotechnol, St Louis Sci Ctr, 89-92; prin investr, NSF grant, Informal Sci Educ, 90-92, partic, Nat Meeting, 92; adv, Genetics Gallery, St Louis Sci Ctr, 95-97; sci & tech coun, Regional Com & Growth Asn. *Mem:* Am Soc Microbiol; Sigma Xi; Am Soc Plant Physiol; Am Inst Biol Sci; Am Soc Cell Biol; AAAS. *Res:* Virus structure and replication; interaction of viruses with antibodies and cell surfaces. *Mailing Add:* 745 Cella Rd St Louis MO 63124

SYMKO, OREST GEORGE, LOW-TEMPERATURE PHYSICS. *Current Pos:* from asst prof to assoc prof, 70-79, PROF PHYSICS, UNIV UTAH, 79- *Personal Data:* b Ukraine, Jan 24, 39; US citizen; m 62, Ivanna Mycyk; c Sophia & Martha. *Educ:* Univ Ottawa, BSc, 61, MSc, 62; Oxford Univ, DPhil(physics), 67. *Prof Exp:* Res officer physics, Clarendon Lab, Oxford Univ, 67-68; asst res physicist, Univ Calif, San Diego, 68-70. *Concurrent Pos:* Res Corp grant, Univ Utah, 71; grantee, NSF, 72-84, Dept Army, 80, Rockwell intern, 84-90, NSF intern, 84-92, Air Force, 85-92 & Off Naval Res, 93- *Mem:* Fel Am Phys Soc. *Res:* Low temperature physics; magnetism; superconductivity; dilute alloys; nuclear magnetic resonance; Josephson junctions; thermoacoustics quasicrystals. *Mailing Add:* Dept Physics Univ Utah Salt Lake City UT 84112. *Fax:* 801-581-4801; *E-Mail:* orest@mail.physics.utah.edu

SYMON, KEITH RANDOLPH, ORBIT THEORY, PARTICLE ACCELERATORS. *Current Pos:* from asst prof to prof, 55-89, EMER PROF PHYSICS, UNIV WIS, MADISON, 89- *Personal Data:* b Ft Wayne, Ind, Mar 25, 20; m 43, Mary Louise Reinhardt; c Judith E, Keith J, James R & Rowena L. *Educ:* Harvard Univ, SB, 42, AM, 43, PhD(theoret physics), 48. *Prof Exp:* From instr to assoc prof physics, Wayne Univ, 47-55. *Concurrent Pos:* Head, Advan Res Group, Midwestern Univs Res Asn, 50-57, head, Theoret Sect, 55-57, tech dir, 57-60; actg dir, Madison Acad Comput Ctr, 82-83 & Synchrotron Radiation Ctr, 83-85. *Mem:* Fel Am Phys Soc; Am Asn Physics Teachers; fel AAAS. *Res:* Orbit theory; design of high energy accelerators; plasma stability; numerical simulation of plasmas; theory of energy loss fluctuations of fast particles. *Mailing Add:* Dept Physics Univ Wis Madison WI 53706. *Fax:* 608-262-7205; *E-Mail:* krsymon@facstaff.wisc.edu

SYMONDS, PAUL S(OUTHWORTH), ENGINEERING, MECHANICS. *Current Pos:* from asst prof to prof eng, 47-83, chmn div, 59-62, EMER PROF & PROF ENG RES, BROWN UNIV, 83- *Personal Data:* b Manila, Philippines, Aug 20, 16; US citizen; m 43, Ilese Powell; c Alan Powell & Robin Peter. *Educ:* Rensselaer Polytech Inst, BS, 38; Cornell Univ, MS, 41, PhD(appl mech), 43. *Hon Degrees:* Docteur en Sci Appliquees, Faculte Polytech de Mons, Belgium. *Prof Exp:* Instr mech eng, Cornell Univ, 41-43; physicist, US Naval Res Lab, Washington, DC, 43-47. *Concurrent Pos:* Lectr, Univ Md, 46-47; vis prof, Cambridge Univ, 49-51, Imp Chem Industs fel, 50-51; Fulbright awards, 49, 57; Guggenheim fel, 57-58; NSF sr fel, Oxford Univ, 64-65; vis prof, Univ Ill, 72, Univ Cape Town, 75 & Cambridge Univ, 73 & 80; assoc prof, ENSM, Nantes, 84; vis scholar, Kyoto Univ, 90, Inst Problem Prochnost, Kiev, 90. *Mem:* Fel Am Soc Civil Engrs; fel Am Soc Mech Engrs; Int Asn Bridge & Struct Engrs; fel Am Acad Mech; Sigma Xi. *Res:* Theory of elasticity and plasticity; structural analysis involving plastic deformations; static and dynamic loading; dynamic instability and chaos in elastic-plastic dynamic response; theory of vibrations and wave propagation. *Mailing Add:* Div Eng Brown Univ Providence RI 02912

SYMONDS, ROBERT B, GAS GEOCHEMISTRY, VOLCANOLOGY. *Current Pos:* RES GEOLOGIST, 92- *Personal Data:* b St Louis, Mo, Feb 13, 59; m, Beatrice Ritchie. *Educ:* Beloit Col, BS, 83; Mich Technol Univ, MS, 85, PhD, 90. *Prof Exp:* Field asst gas geochem, Cascades Volcano Observ, US Geol Surv, 82-83; field asst mapping, San Juan Mountains, US Geol Surv, 84; res asst, Mich Technol Univ, 83-90, res assoc, 90-91; guest researcher, Geol Surv, Japan, 91. *Mem:* Am Geophys Union. *Res:* Gas sampling at active volcanoes in the US, NZ, Antarctica and Indonesia; thermochemical modeling of volcanic gases; gas transport and ore deposits. *Mailing Add:* US Geol Surv 5400 MacArthur Blvd Vancouver WA 98661

SYMONS, DAVID THORBURN ARTHUR, GEOPHYSICS, GEOLOGY. *Current Pos:* head, Dept Geol, 73-77 & 79-82, PROF GEOPHYS & GEOTECHNICS, UNIV WINDSOR, 77- *Personal Data:* b Toronto, Ont, July 24, 37; m 64, V Elizabeth Davies; c Elisabeth, Douglas & Brock. *Educ:* Univ Toronto, BASc, 60, PhD(econ geol), 65; Harvard Univ, MA, 61. *Prof Exp:* Nat Res Coun Can overseas fel paleomagnetism, Univ Newcastle, Eng, 65-66; res scientist rock magnetism, Geol Surv Can, 66-70. *Concurrent Pos:* Adj, prof, Univ Western Ont, 86-; pres, 88-91, prin, Canterbury Col, 91- *Mem:* Can Geophys Union; Am Geophys Union; Geol Asn Can. *Res:* Application of paleomagnetic methods to geotectonic, ore genesis and geochronologic problems in the Canadian Cordillera and Shield and to the history of the earth's geomagnetic field; geotechnical geophysics. *Mailing Add:* Dept Earth Sci Univ Windsor Windsor ON N9B 3P4 Can. *Fax:* 519-973-7081; *E-Mail:* dsymons@uwindsor.ca

SYMONS, EDWARD ALLAN, PHYSICAL ORGANIC CHEMISTRY, HETEROGENEOUS CATALYSIS. *Current Pos:* RES OFFICER, CHALK RIVER LABS, AECL RES, 72- *Personal Data:* b Kingston, Ont, Apr 24, 43. *Educ:* Queen's Univ, Kingston, BSc, 65, PhD(chem), 69. *Mem:* Fel Chem Inst Can. *Res:* Hydrogen isotope exchange mechanisms and associated physical/ organic chemistry in systems of potential interest for heavy water production processes; noble metal heterogeneous catalysis of oxidation reactions, especially carbon monoxide; catalytic gas sensors; deuterium isotope exchange. *Mailing Add:* Chalk River Labs AECL Res Chalk River ON K0J 1J0 Can. *E-Mail:* symonsa@aecl.ca

SYMONS, GEORGE E(DGAR), ENVIRONMENTAL ENGINEERING. *Current Pos:* ENG ED & CONSULT, 78- *Personal Data:* b Danville, Ill, Apr 20, 03; m 26, Virginia Thompson; c 1. *Educ:* Univ Ill, BS, 28, MS, 30, PhD(chem), 32; Am Acad Environ Engrs, dipl. *Honors & Awards:* Diven Medal, Fuller Award, Am Water Works Asn, Hall of Fame; Emerson Medalist Water Pollution Control Fedn, Bedell Award. *Prof Exp:* Res chemist, Ill State Water Survey, 28-33; instr, Univ Ill, 32-33; chemist, Freeport Sulfur Co, 33-34; consult, 34-35; engr, Greeley & Hansen, 35-36; chief chemist, Buffalo Sewer Authority, NY, 36-43; consult engr, 43-64; assoc ed, Water & Sewage Works, 43-48, managing ed, 49-51, ed, 57-59; ed, Water & Wastes Eng, 64-70; mgr spec proj, Malcolm Pirnie, Inc, 70-78. *Concurrent Pos:* Adj prof, Canisius Col, 41-42; lectr, Med Sch, Buffalo Univ, 42-43; res assoc, NY Univ, 54-55; contrib ed, Water Eng & Mgt, 78-90. *Mem:* Am Chem Soc; fel Am Pub Health Asn; fel Am Soc Civil Engrs; hon mem Am Water Works Asn (pres, 73-74); Am Inst Chem Engrs; Am Pub Works Asn; Nat Soc Prof Engrs; hon mem Water Pollution Control Fedn. *Res:* Engineering editing and writing. *Mailing Add:* 300 S Ocean Blvd Apt H-3 Palm Beach FL 33480

SYMONS, JAMES M(ARTIN), ENVIRONMENTAL ENGINEERING. *Current Pos:* prof, 82-96, CULLEN DISTINGUISHED PROF CIVIL ENG, UNIV HOUSTON, 96- *Personal Data:* b Champaign, Ill, Nov 24, 31; m 58, Joan Kinsman; c Andrew J, Linda J & Julie A. *Educ:* Cornell Univ, BCE, 54; Mass Inst Technol, SM, 55, ScD(sanit eng), 57. *Honors & Awards:* Harrison P Eddy Award, Water Pollution Control Fedn, 63; Huber Res Prize, Am Soc Civil Engrs, 67; Res Award, Am Water Works Asn, 81; Silver Medal, US Environ Protection Agency, 71. *Prof Exp:* Asst, NIH Proj, Mass Inst Technol, 55-57, instr sanit eng, 65-68, asst prof, 58-62; res pub health engr, USPHS, 62-70; chief, Phys & Chem Contaminants Removal Br, Drinking Water Res Div, Nat Environ Res Ctr, US Environ Protection Agency, 70-82. *Concurrent Pos:* Assoc, Rolf Eliassen Assocs, Mass, 57-61. *Mem:* Nat Acad Eng; Am Soc Civil Engrs; Water Environ Fedn; Asn Environ Eng Prof; Am Acad Environ Engrs; Int Water Supply Asn; Am Water Works Asn. *Res:* Drinking water treatment research. *Mailing Add:* Dept Civil & Environ Eng Univ Houston Houston TX 77204-4791. *Fax:* 713-743-4258; *E-Mail:* jsymons@uh.edu

SYMONS, PHILIP CHARLES, ELECTROCHEMISTRY. *Current Pos:* PRES, PRIN CONSULT, ELECTRO CHEM ENGR CONSULTS INC, 80- *Personal Data:* b Taunton, Eng, June 4, 39; m 89; c 2. *Educ:* Univ Bristol, BSc, 60, PhD(electrochem), 63. *Prof Exp:* Sr chemist, Proctor & Gamble Ltd, Eng, 63-67 & Hooker Chem Corp, 68-69; res dir batteries, Udylite Co, Occidental Petrol Corp, 69-73; chief scientist, Energy Develop Assocs, 73-80. *Concurrent Pos:* Sr proj mgr, Elec Power Res Inst, 92-94. *Mem:* Am Chem Soc; Electrochem Soc; Inst Elec & Electronics Engrs Comput Soc. *Res:* High energy density batteries; electrochemical thermodynamics and kinetics; thermodynamics of phase transitions; electrochemical engineering. *Mailing Add:* Electrochem Eng Consults 1295 Kelly Park Circle Morgan Hill CA 95037-3370

SYMONS, TIMOTHY J, NUCLEAR PHYSICS. *Current Pos:* fel, 77-79, div fel, 79-83, ASSOC DIR, LAWRENCE BERKELEY LAB, 83-, DIV HEAD, NUCLEAR SCI, 85- *Personal Data:* b Southborough, Eng, Aug 4, 51; m 87, Syndi Master; c Henry B & Daniel R. *Educ:* Oxford Univ, BA, 72, MA, 76, PhD (physics), 76. *Prof Exp:* Fel, Oxford Univ, 76-77. *Concurrent Pos:* Vis fel, Inst Nuclear Physics, Heidelberg, 80-81. *Mem:* Fel Am Phys Soc. *Res:* Study of nuclear physics using high energy heavy-ion beams. *Mailing Add:* Lawrence Berkeley Labs B70a-3307 Nuclear Sci Div Berkeley CA 94720. *Fax:* 510-486-4808; *E-Mail:* symons@lbl.gov

SYMPSON, ROBERT F, ANALYTICAL CHEMISTRY, ELECTROCHEMISTRY. *Current Pos:* From asst prof to assoc prof, 54-65, PROF CHEM, OHIO UNIV, 65-, CHMN DEPT, 77- *Personal Data:* b Ft Madison, Iowa, June 21, 27; m '53; c 4. *Educ:* Monmouth Col, BS, 50; Univ Ill, MS, 52, PhD, 54. *Mem:* Am Chem Soc; Electrochem Soc. *Res:* Polarography and amperometric titrations applied to analytical chemistry. *Mailing Add:* Dept Chem Ohio Univ Athens OH 45701-2978

SYNEK, MIROSLAV (MIKE), ATOMIC PHYSICS, PHYSICAL CHEMISTRY. *Current Pos:* INDEPENDENT CONSULT, 95- *Personal Data:* b Prague, Czech, Sept 18, 30; US citizen; c Mary R & Thomas. *Educ:* Charles Univ, Prague, MS, 56; Univ Chicago, PhD(physics), 63. *Prof Exp:* Technician chem, Inst Indust Med, Prague, Czech, 50-51; asst physics, Czech Acad Sci, 56-58; res asst, Univ Chicago, 58-62; asst prof physics, DePaul Univ, 62-65, assoc prof physics, 65-67, assoc prof chem, 66-67; prof physics, Tex Christian Univ, 67-71; regional sci adv & res scientist, Dept Physics, Univ Tex, Austin, 71-73; lectr, exten lectr & res scientist, Depts Physics, Chem, Astron & Math, 73-75; fac mem, Div Earth & Phys Sci, Col Sci & Eng, Univ Tex, San Antonio, 75-95. *Concurrent Pos:* Consult, US Army, 58, Physics Div, Argonne Nat Lab, 66-73 & Brooks AFB, Tex, 83; prin investr, Mat Lab, Wright-Patterson AFB, Ohio, 64-71; prin investr, Robert A Welch Found res grant, 69-71 & 76-83; referee manuscripts, Phys Rev; occasional lectr; adv, Soc Phys Student, Am Inst Phys, 83-; elected adv, Soc Physics Students; nominated judge, Alamo Regional Sci Fair. *Mem:* Fel AAAS; fel Am Phys Soc; Am Asn Physics Teachers; Am Chem Soc; fel Am Inst Chemists; Soc Sci Res; Sigma Xi; NY Acad Sci. *Res:* Educational and computational physics; popularization of science; astronomy and energy; laser-crystal efficiency; energy applications; laser-active ions of rare earths; materials science; atomic wave functions; statistical mechanics; molecular dynamics; global systems of free elections is a historical urgency in the nuclear age; laser fusion. *Mailing Add:* PO Box 4911 San Antonio TX 78280

SYNGE, RICHARD LAURENCE MILLINGTON, BIOCHEMISTRY. *Current Pos:* RETIRED. *Personal Data:* b Liverpool, Eng, Oct 28, 14; m 43, Ann Stephen; c 7. *Hon Degrees:* DSc, Univ E Anglia, 77, Univ Aberdeen, 87; PhD, Univ Uppsala. *Honors & Awards:* Novel Prize in Chem, 52. *Prof Exp:* Biochemist, Wool Industries Res Asn, 41-43, Lister Inst Prev Med, 43-48; head, Dept Protein Che, Rowett Res Inst, 48-67; biochemist, Food Res Inst, 67-76; hon prof, Sch Biol Sci, Univ E Anglia, 68-84. *Concurrent Pos:* Vis biochemist, Ruakura Animal Res Sta, NZ, 58-59. *Mem:* Am Soc Biol Chemists; fel Royal Soc Chem; hon mem Royal Irish Acad; Royal Soc N Z. *Mailing Add:* 19 Meadow Rise Rd Norwich NR2 3QE England

SYNOLAKIS, COSTAS EMMANUEL, TSUNAMI HAZARD MITIGATION, COMPUTER TOMOGRAPHY. *Current Pos:* PROF CIVIL & AEROSPACE ENG, UNIV SOUTHERN CALIF, 85- *Personal Data:* b Athens, Greece, Sept 21, 56; US citizen. *Educ:* Calif Inst Technol, BSc, 78, MS, 79, PhD(civil eng), 86. *Honors & Awards:* Presidential Young Investr Award, NSF, 89. *Concurrent Pos:* Prin investr, NSF, 86-; NSF presidential young investr award, 89. *Mem:* AAAS; Am Phys Soc; Int Tsunami Comn; Am Soc Civil Engrs; NY Acad Sci; Geophys Union. *Res:* Analytical solutions on long wave runup and evolution problems; mixing of elliptic jets in stratified flow; optical flow; non-destructive application of tomography; asphalt core tomography; concrete core tomography; tsunami and tidal wave hazard mitigation; analytical solutions on long wave runup; mixing of elliptic jets in stratified flow; optical flow; ride applications of CT in asphalt and concrete; vibration isolation. *Mailing Add:* Dept Civil Eng 2531 Univ Southern Calif Los Angeles CA 90089-2531. *Fax:* 213-744-1426; *E-Mail:* costas@mizar.usc.edu

SYNOVITZ, ROBERT J, HEALTH SCIENCE. *Current Pos:* prof, 68-89, EMER PROF HEALTH SCI & CHMN DEPT, WESTERN ILL UNIV, 89- *Personal Data:* b Milwaukee, Wis, Feb 3, 31; wid; c 4. *Educ:* Wis State Univ, La Crosse, BS, 53; Ind Univ, Bloomington, MS, 56, HSD, 59. *Prof Exp:* Instr pub schs, Mo, 56-58; asst prof health sci, Eastern Ky Univ, 59-62; assoc prof physiol & health sci, Ball State Univ, 62-68. *Concurrent Pos:* Teaching & res grant, Ball State Univ, 66-67; consult, 89- *Mem:* Am Sch Health Asn (nat pres, 81-82); Soc Pub Health Educ. *Mailing Add:* 1936 Fargo Blvd Geneva IL 60134

SYNOWIEC, JOHN A, MATHEMATICAL ANALYSIS. *Current Pos:* asst prof, 67-74, ASSOC PROF MATH, IND UNIV NORTHWEST, 74- *Personal Data:* b Chicago, Ill, Sept 18, 37; m 67; c 3. *Educ:* DePaul Univ, BS, 59, MS, 61, DMS, 62; Ill Inst Technol, PhD(math), 64. *Prof Exp:* Instr math, DePaul Univ, 61-62; from instr to asst prof, Ill Inst Technol, 63-67. *Mem:* Am Math Soc; Math Asn Am; Soc Indust & Appl Math. *Res:* Generalized functions; partial differential equations; harmonic analysis; history of mathematics. *Mailing Add:* Ind Univ Northwest 3400 Broadway Gary IN 46408

SYPERT, GEORGE WALTER, NEUROLOGICAL SURGERY. *Current Pos:* PRES, SW FLA NEUROSURG ASSOCS, 89-; CHMN, SW FLA NEUROSURG INST, 89- *Personal Data:* b Marlin, Tex, Sept 25, 41; m 73, E Joy Arpin; c Kirsten & Shannon. *Educ:* Univ Wash, BA, 63, MD, 67. *Prof Exp:* Resident neurosurg, Sch Med, Univ Wash, 68-73, instr, 73-74; from asst prof to prof, Col Med, Univ Fla, 74-84, Overstreet Family prof neurosurg & neurosci & eminent scholar, 84-89. *Concurrent Pos:* Asst chief neurosurg, Fitsimons Gen Hosp, US Army, 68-70; staff neurosurgeon, Shands Teaching Hosp, Gainesville & chief neurosurg, Gainesville Vet Admin Med Ctr, 74-89; chmn, continuing med, Am Asn Neurol Surgeons, 82-87, sect spinal dis, 85-87; hon guest, Japanese Cong Neurol Surg, 86 & 89, Royal Australian Col Surg, 89 & SAfrican Neurol Surg Asn, 90. *Mem:* Soc Neurosci; Cong Neurol Surgeons; Am Asn Neurol Surgeons; AAAS; Am Physiol Soc; Soc Neurol Surgeons; Am Soc Stereotactic & Functional Neurosurg (vpres, 81-83, pres, 83-85). *Res:* Neurophysiological and ionic mechanisms involved in synaptic transmission; segmental motor control; synaptic plasticity; neuronal repetitive firing mechanisms; pathophysiology of epilepsy; mammalian cellular neurophysiology. *Mailing Add:* 3677 Central Ave Suite A Ft Myers FL 33901

SYPHERD, PAUL STARR, MICROBIOLOGY, MOLECULAR BIOLOGY. *Current Pos:* assoc prof, 70-72, chmn microbiol, 74-87, PROF MICROBIOL, COL MED, UNIV CALIF, IRVINE, 72-, VICE CHANCELLOR RES, DEAN GRAD STUDIES, 89- *Personal Data:* b Akron, Ohio, Nov 16, 36; m 54; c 4. *Educ:* Ariz State Univ, BS, 59; Univ Ariz, MS, 60; Yale Univ, PhD(microbiol), 63. *Prof Exp:* NIH res fel biol, Univ Calif, San Diego, 62-64; from asst prof to assoc prof microbiol, Univ Ill, Urbana, 64-70. *Concurrent Pos:* USPHS fel, Univ Calif, San Diego, 62-64; mem, Microbiol Chem Study Sect, NIH, 75-81; mem, Nat Bd Med Examr, 82-85; Comt Health Manpower, Nat Res Coun, 82-86; mem, Microbiol Genetics Study Sect, NIH, 87- *Mem:* Am Soc Microbiologists; Am Soc Biol Chemists; Am Acad Microbiol. *Res:* Structure and synthesis of ribosomes; regulation of nucleic acid synthesis; molecular basis of morphogenesis; molecular mechanisms of the regulation of gene expression, with and emphasis on post-transcriptional regulation; post-translational modification of proteins in microorganisms. *Mailing Add:* Univ Ariz Rm 512 Admin Tucson AZ 85721. *Fax:* 520-621-9118; *E-Mail:* sypherd@ccitarizona.edu

SYRETT, BARRY CHRISTOPHER, CORROSION, ELECTROCHEMISTRY. *Current Pos:* tech adv, 79-92, MGR, CORROSION SCI & TECHNOL, ELEC POWER RES INST, 92- *Personal Data:* b Stockton on Tees, Eng, Dec 16, 43; US citizen; m 66,91, Christina J Palm; c Nichola J. *Educ:* Univ Newcastle, BSc, 64, PhD(metall), 67. *Honors & Awards:* Sci Am Award, Am Soc Testing & Mat, 79; Frank Newman Speller Award, Nat Asn Corrosion Engrs, 92, TJ Hull Award, 97. *Prof Exp:* Res scientist corrosion, Dept Energy, Mines & Resources, Govt Can, 67-70 & Int Nickel Co, Inc, 70-72; metall prog mgr, SRI Int, 72-79. *Concurrent Pos:* Chmn publ comt, Nat Asn Corrosion Engrs Int, 89-91, mem bd dirs, 89-97; ed, Corrosion Testing Made Easy Ser; chmn, Int Region Mgt Comt, 95-97. *Mem:* Fel Nat Asn Corrosion Engrs Int; fel Inst Corrosion (UK); prof mem Inst Mat (UK); Eng Coun (UK). *Res:* Corrosion research, including pitting, crevice corrosion, stress corrosion, erosion-corrosion, fretting corrosion, corrosion fatigue, hydrogen embrittlement, corrosion resistant coatings, failure analysis, alloy development and liquid metal embrittlement. *Mailing Add:* 1881 Fulton St Palo Alto CA 94303

SYSKI, RYSZARD, MATHEMATICS, PROBABILITY. *Current Pos:* res assoc mgt sci & lectr math, 61-62, Univ Md, College Park assoc prof, 62-66, chmn, Probability & Statist Div, 66-70, PROF MATH, UNIV MD, COLLEGE PARK, 66- *Personal Data:* b Plock, Poland, Apr 8, 24; m 50, Barbara; c 6. *Educ:* Polish Univ Col, London, Dipl Eng, 50; Imp Col, dipl, 51, BSc, 54, PhD(math), 60. *Prof Exp:* Sci officer, ATE Co, Eng, 51-52, sr sci officer, Hivac Ltd, 52-60. *Concurrent Pos:* Chmn bibliog comt, Int Teletraffic Cong, 55-61, mem organizing comt, 67. *Mem:* Bernoulli Soc Math Statist & Probability; fel Inst Math Statist; Polish Math Soc. *Res:* Queueing and probability theories; stochastic processes; marhow processes; potential theory. *Mailing Add:* 11405 Fairoak Dr Silver Spring MD 20902

SYTSMA, KENNETH JAY, PLANT SYSTEMATICS, MOLECULAR PHYLOGENETICS. *Current Pos:* ASST PROF BOT, UNIV WIS-MADISON, 85- *Personal Data:* b Tokyo, Japan, Jan 23, 54; US citizen; m 75; c 4. *Educ:* Calvin Col, BS, 76; Western Mich Univ, Kalamazoo, MA, 79; Wash Univ, St Louis, PhD(bot), 83. *Honors & Awards:* Cooley Award, Am Soc Plant Taxonomists, 86. *Prof Exp:* Teaching asst bot, Western Mich Univ, Kalamazoo, 76-79; fel bot, Wash Univ, 79-83; cur, Summit Herbarium, Panama City, 80-81; res fel, Univ Calif, Davis, 83-85. *Mem:* Am Soc Plant Taxonomists; Am Soc Bot; Soc Study Evolution. *Res:* Study of evolutionary and systematic relationships of flowering plants by use of DNA analysis, isozymes and pollination biology. *Mailing Add:* Dept Botany 132 Birge Hall Univ Wis Madison 430 Lincoln Dr Madison WI 53706-1381

SYTSMA, LOUIS FREDERICK, ENVIRONMENTAL CHEMISTRY. *Current Pos:* PROF CHEM, TRINITY CHRISTIAN COL, 77- *Personal Data:* b Chicago, Ill, July 20, 46; m 67, Charlene Myroup; c Erick & Anne. *Educ:* Calvin Col, BA, 67; Ohio Univ, PhD(org chem), 71. *Prof Exp:* Chemist, Anderson Develop Co, 71-77; asst prof chem, Siena Heights Col, 73-77; prof environ chem, Au Sable Trails Inst Environ Studies, 82-91. *Concurrent Pos:* Consult, Anderson Develop Co, 77-94; chemist, Argonne Nat Lab, 88- *Mem:* Am Chem Soc; Sigma Xi. *Res:* Cause, movement and analysis of environmental pollutants. *Mailing Add:* Trinity Christian Col 6601 W College Dr Palos Heights IL 60463

SYTY, AUGUSTA, CHEMISTRY. *Current Pos:* PROF ANAL CHEM, INDIANA UNIV PA, 68- *Personal Data:* b Harbin, China. *Educ:* Univ Tenn, Knoxville, BS, 64, PhD(anal chem), 68. *Concurrent Pos:* Guest res chemist, Nat Bur Standards. *Mem:* Am Chem Soc; Soc Appl Spectros. *Res:* Flame emission; atomic absorption; methods of analysis; molecular absorption spectrometry in the gas phase; metal speciation; selective determination of chromium (VI). *Mailing Add:* Dept Chem Indiana Univ Pa Indiana PA 15705-0001

SYVANEN, MICHAEL, MOLECULAR EVOLUTIONARY THEORY. *Current Pos:* PROF, DEPT MED MICROBIOL & IMMUNOL, UNIV CALIF, DAVIS, 87- *Personal Data:* b Vancouver, Wash, Dec 27, 43; m 78, Sue E Greenwald. *Educ:* Univ Wash, BS, 66; Univ Calif, Berkeley, PhD(biochem), 72. *Prof Exp:* Fel, Stanford Univ Med Sch, 72-76; from asst prof to assoc prof, Harvard Med Sch, 76-87. *Concurrent Pos:* Consult, Calif Fish & Game, 93-; pres, Wildlife Forensic DNA Found. *Mem:* Am Soc Microbiol; Am Genetics Soc; AAAS. *Res:* Molecular genetic studies of bacteria and insects; examination of bacteria and flies, isolated from natural sources, that have gained resistance to toxic chemicals; genetic changes that permit resistance; developing theory of the role of horizontal gene transfer in biological evolution. *Mailing Add:* Dept Med Microbiol & Immunol Univ Calif Davis CA 95616. *Fax:* 530-752-8692; *E-Mail:* msyvanen@ucdavis.edu

SYVERTSON, CLARENCE A, RESEARCH ADMINISTRATION, TECHNICAL MANAGEMENT. *Current Pos:* ENG & MGT CONSULT, 88- *Personal Data:* b Minneapolis, Minn, Jan 12, 26; m 53, 82, JoAnn M Caruso; c Marguerite (Schier) & Lynn S (Sechrest). *Educ:* Univ Minn, BS, 46, MS, 48. *Honors & Awards:* Lawrence Sperry Award, Inst Aeronaut Sci, 57; NASA Inventions & Contrib Award, 64, Exceptional Serv Medal, NASA, 71, Distinguished Serv Medal, 84. *Prof Exp:* Res scientist, Ames Aeronaut Lab, Nat Adv Comt Aeronaut, NASA, 48-58, chief, Hypersonic Wind Tunnel Br, Ames Res Ctr, 59-63, chief, Mission Anal Div, 63-65, dir, Mission Anal Div, Off Adv Res & Technol, 65-66, dir astronaut, 66-69, dep dir, Ames Res Ctr, 69-78, dir, 78-84; consult prof, Stanford Univ, 84-88. *Concurrent Pos:* Exec dir civil aviation res & develop policy study, Dept Transp, NASA, 70-71; mem bd gov, Nat Space Club, 78-84, adv bd, Col Eng, Univ Calif, Berkeley, 81-86, Comt Aircraft & Engine Develop Testing, Air Force Studies Bd, Nat Res Coun, 84-85 & Comt Space Sta Eng & Technol, Aeronaut & Space Eng Bd, Nat Res Coun, 84-86; mem, bd dirs, West Valley Mission Cols Found, 84- *Mem:* Nat Acad Eng; fel Am Inst Aeronaut & Astronaut; fel Am Astronaut Soc. *Res:* Civil aviation; mission analysis; entry vehicle research; developed aerodynamic theories and vehicle concepts for high-speed flight; theories used to predict missile and launch vehicle stability; vehicle concepts includes basis for B-70 valkyrie and research precursor to space shuttle. *Mailing Add:* 14666 Spring Ave Saratoga CA 95070

SYWE, BEI-SHEN, metal-organic chemical vapor deposition system design, materials characterization, for more information see previous edition

SYZE, RICHARD LAURENCE MILLINGTON, biochemstry, for more information see previous edition

SZABLYA, JOHN F(RANCIS), ELECTRICAL ENGINEERING. *Current Pos:* VPRES & CONSULT ENGR, SZABLYA CONSULTS, INC, 90- *Personal Data:* b Budapest, Hungary, June 25, 24; US, Canadian & Hungarian citizen; m 51, Helen M Bartha-Kovacs; c Helen A, Janos I, Louis J, Stephen J, Alexandra H, Rita H & Dominique M. *Educ:* Tech Univ Budapest, Dipls, 47-48, DEcon, 48. *Honors & Awards:* Zipernowszky Medal, Hungary, 54. *Prof Exp:* Mem fac, Tech Univ Budapest, 49-56; mem fac, Univ BC, 57-63; prof elec eng, Wash State Univ, 63-82; elec consult engr, Ebasco Servs, Inc, 82-90. *Concurrent Pos:* Engr, Ganz Elec Works, 47-56; consult, Hungarian Elec Res Labs, 52-56, Tech Univ Braunschweig, Ger, 73-74, Univ of the West Indies, Trinidad, 80-81, Univ Wash, 83- & Seattle Univ, 87. *Mem:* Fel Inst Elec & Electronics Engrs; fel Inst Elec Engrs; Tensor Soc; Austrian Inst Elec Engrs. *Res:* Electromechanical energy conversion; electric power transmission; high power, high voltage research; fundamental electromagnetism; energy research. *Mailing Add:* 4416 134th Pl SE Bellevue WA 98006

SZABO, A(UGUST) J(OHN), CIVIL ENGINEERING. *Current Pos:* RETIRED. *Personal Data:* b Baton Rouge, La, Sept 27, 21; m 45; c 3. *Educ:* La State Univ, BS, 43; Harvard Univ, MS, 50. *Honors & Awards:* Arthur Sidney Bedell Award, Water Pollution Control Fedn, 58. *Prof Exp:* Pub health engr, State Bd Health, La, 46-55; assoc prof civil eng, Univ Southwestern La, 55-63; prin engr, Domingue, Szabo & Assocs Inc, 63-64, secy & treas, 64-91, in house consult, 91-96. *Concurrent Pos:* USPHS, 42; aviation engr, US Air Force, 43-46; Corps Engrs, Vicksburg Dist, 56. *Mem:* Water Pollution Control Fedn; Am Soc Civil Engrs; Am Water Works Asn; Nat Soc Prof Engrs; Am Acad Environ Engrs; Am Consult Eng Coun. *Res:* Sanitary and environmental engineering. *Mailing Add:* 1117 Kim Dr Lafayette LA 70503

SZABO, ALEXANDER, LASER SPECTROSCOPY OF SOLIDS AT LOW TEMPERATURE, INFORMATION STORAGE IN CRYSTALS USING HOLE-BURNING. *Current Pos:* RETIRED. *Personal Data:* b Copper Cliff, Ont, Mar 13, 31; m 57, Ethel Semmens; c Susan, John, Eleanor & Jennifer. *Educ:* Queen's Univ, BS, 53; McGill Univ, MS, 55; Tohoku Univ, Japan, DEng(physics), 70. *Prof Exp:* Res officer electron beams, Nat Res Coun Can, 55-59, res officer microwave masers, 59-61, res officer lasers & solid state physics, 61-96. *Concurrent Pos:* Assoc ed, Optical Mat, 91- *Mem:* Fel Japan Soc Prom Sci; Optical Soc Am. *Res:* Coherence lifetimes and optical line widths of impurity ions in solids using fluorescence line narrowing and photon echo techniques. *Mailing Add:* 662 Glenhurst Circle Gloucester ON K1J 7B7 Can. *E-Mail:* alex.szabo@nrc.ca

SZABO, ARTHUR GUSTAV, FLUORESCENCE, SPECTROSCOPY. *Current Pos:* HEAD, DEPT CHEM & BIOCHEM, UNIV WINDSOR, 94- *Personal Data:* b Toronto, Ont, Nov 19, 39; c 3. *Educ:* Queen's Univ, Ont, BSc, 61; Univ Toronto, MA, 63, PhD(chem), 65. *Honors & Awards:* John A Labatt Award, Chem Soc Can. *Prof Exp:* Nat Res Coun Can fel chem, Southampton, 65-67; res officer, Biol Div, Nat Res Coun Can, 67-94. *Concurrent Pos:* Vis scientist, Nat Ctr Sci Res, Orleans, France 77-78; vis prof, Univ Parma, Italy, 82; adj prof, Biochem Dept, Univ Ottawa, 83- *Mem:* Chem Inst Can; Biophys Soc US. *Res:* Protein-membrane studies; molecular dynamics of proteins using fluorescence anisotropy decay technique; biomolecule interactions using spectroscopic techniques; laser excitation and time correlated fluorescence spectroscopy of biomolecules. *Mailing Add:* Dept Chem & Biochem Univ Windsor Windsor ON N9B 3P4 Can

SZABO, ATTILA, THEORETICAL BIOPHYSICAL CHEMISTRY. *Current Pos:* RES SCIENTIST, LAB CHEM PHYS, NIH, 80- *Personal Data:* b Budapest, Hungary, Sept 6, 47; US citizen; div. *Educ:* McGill Univ, BSc, 68; Harvard Univ, PhD(chem physics), 73. *Prof Exp:* Fel, Inst Physicochem Biol, Paris, 72-73; fel, Med Res Coun Lab Molecular Biol, Cambridge, Eng, 73-74; asst prof chem, Ind Univ, Bloomington, 74-78, assoc prof, 78-80. *Mem:* Biophys Soc. *Res:* Nuclear magnetic relaxation and fluorescence depolarization and internal motions in biopolymers; structure-function relations in allosteric systems. *Mailing Add:* 1949 Richards Rd Apt 5 Toledo OH 43607-1040

SZABO, BARNA ALADAR, MECHANICAL ENGINEERING. *Current Pos:* from assoc prof to prof, 68-75, GREENSFELDER PROF MECHS, UNIV WASH, 75-, DIR, CTR COMPUT MECH, 77- *Personal Data:* b Martonvasar, Hungary, Sept 21, 35; US citizen; m 60; c 2. *Educ:* Univ Toronto, BASc, 60; State Univ NY, Buffalo, MS, 66, PhD(civil eng), 69. *Prof Exp:* Mining engr, Int Nickel Co Can Ltd, 60-62; civil engr, H G Acres Ltd Consult Engrs, 62-66; instr eng & appl sci, State Univ NY, Buffalo, 66-68. *Concurrent Pos:* Consult, Asn Am Railroads, 74-77; dir, Washington Univ Technol Assocs, 78-82; chmn tech adv bd, Noetic Tech Corp, St Louis. *Mem:* Am Acad Mech; Am Soc Mech Engrs; Soc Eng Sci. *Res:* Numerical approximation techniques in continuum mechanics; development of adaptive methods in finite element analysis; numerical structure of stress analysis. *Mailing Add:* 48 Crestwood Dr St Louis MO 63105

SZABO, BARNEY JULIUS, geochemistry, for more information see previous edition

SZABO, EMERY D, MEDICAL & HEALTH SCIENCES, TECHNICAL MANAGEMENT. *Current Pos:* TECH DIR, ELLAY INC, LOS ANGELES, 92- *Personal Data:* b Komarom, Hungary, Apr 5, 33; US citizen; m 70; c 1. *Educ:* Univ Budapest, Hungary, ME, 56; Univ NY, MS, 63. *Prof Exp:* Asst mgr, Kentile Floors Inc, 59-69; group leader, Tenneco Chem Inc, tech serv mgr, 77-80; Tech dir, Alpha Chem & Plastics Corp, 81-83, dir technol, 90-92. *Concurrent Pos:* vpres & tech dir, Dexter Plastics, 83-90. *Mem:* Am Chem Soc; fel AAAS; Soc Plastics Engrs. *Res:* Vinyl and olefinic polymers for biomedical and beverage packaging applications; material science of chemicals and additives for polyvinyl chloride and application technology of vinyl plastics; agency regulations relating to vinyl plastics; awarded three US patents. *Mailing Add:* 12400 S Montecito Rd Apt 424 Seal Beach CA 90740

SZABO, GABOR, PHYSIOLOGY, BIOPHYSICS. *Current Pos:* assoc prof, 75-79, PROF PHYSIOL, UNIV TEX MED BR GALVESTON, 79- *Personal Data:* b Mar 20, 41; Can citizen. *Educ:* Univ Montreal, BS, 64; Univ Chicago, PhD(physiol), 69. *Prof Exp:* Asst prof physiol, Med Ctr, Univ Calif, Los Angeles, 71-75. *Mem:* AAAS; Biophys Soc. *Res:* Regulation of cell membrane function. *Mailing Add:* Dept Physiol & Biophys Univ Va Box 449 1300 Jefferson Park Ave Charlottesville VA 22908. *Fax:* 804-982-1616; *E-Mail:* gs32@virginia.edu

SZABO, KALMAN TIBOR, TERATOLOGY. *Current Pos:* CONSULT, 86- *Personal Data:* b Abda, Hungary, July 29, 21; US citizen; m 44, Edith Patka; c Claire & Helen. *Educ:* Univ Budapest, BSc, 47; Rutgers Univ, MS, 62; Univ Vienna, MSc, 71, DSc(teratology), 73. *Hon Degrees:* DSc, Pannonia Univ, Hungary, 91. *Honors & Awards:* Gold Medal, Soc Toxicol, 81. *Prof Exp:* Res scientist genetics, Res Inst, Acad Sci, Fertod, Hungary, 53-56; res assoc reproductive physiol, Rutgers Univ, 60-62; toxicologist, 62-66; sr scientist & unit head teratology, 67-69, sr investr & group leader reproductive toxicol & teratology, 69-70, asst dir toxicol, 71-72, assoc dir, 72-81, dir, 81-83, dir reproductive & develop toxicol, Smith Kline & Fr Labs, 83-86. *Concurrent Pos:* Adv & partic, Adv Comt Protocols on Reproductive Studies, Safety Eval Food Additives & Pesticide Residues, Food & Drug Admin, 67; res assoc prof pediat, Med Col, Thomas Jefferson Univ, 75- *Mem:* Teratology Soc; Behav Teratology Soc; Soc Toxicol; Soc Study Reproduction; Int Acad Environ Safety; Am Col Toxicol. *Res:* Spontaneous and induced anomalies of the central nervous system; role of maternal nutritional deprivation in embryogenesis; evaluation of various factors affecting teratogenic response; drug toxicology; reproductive and developmental toxicology of drugs. *Mailing Add:* 215 Morris Rd Ambler PA 19002

SZABO, PIROSKA LUDWIG, HISTOLOGY, GROSS ANATOMY. *Current Pos:* SCH HEALTH SCI, TOURO COL, 86- *Personal Data:* b Bratislava, Czechoslovakia, Dec 14, 40; US citizen; m 63; c 3. *Educ:* Oberlin Col, BA, 62; Univ Fla, MS, 64, PhD(med sci), 67. *Prof Exp:* Fel gross anat, Col Physicians & Surgeons, Columbia Univ, 67-68; asst prof gross anat & histol, Med Col Va, 68-70, Albert Einstein Col Med, 70-73; instr biol & embryol, Lehman Col, 73-77; prof & chmn anat, NY Col Osteop Med, 77-86. *Concurrent Pos:* Consult, Osteop Nat Bd, 79- *Mem:* AAAS. *Mailing Add:* Sch Health Sci Touro Col 135 Carman Rd Dix Hills NY 11746

SZABO, SANDOR, PATHOLOGY, PHARMACOLOGY. *Current Pos:* asst prof, 77-81, ASSOC PROF PATH, BRIGHAM & WOMEN'S HOSP, HARVARD MED SCH, 81- *Personal Data:* b Ada, Yugoslavia, Feb 9, 44; m 72; c 2. *Educ:* Univ Belgrade, MD, 68; Univ Montreal, MSc, 71, PhD(exp med, pharmacol), 73; Harvard Sch Pub Health, MPH(occupational med), 83. *Honors & Awards:* Milton Fund Award, Harvard Univ, 78. *Prof Exp:* Vis scientist exp med & pharmacol, Inst Exp Med Surg, Univ Montreal, 69-70, res asst, 70-73; resident path, Peter Bent Brigham Hosp, 73-77, res fel, Med Sch, 75-77, res assoc path, Peter Bent Brigham Hosp. *Concurrent Pos:* Chief ed, Sci J Medicinski Podmladak, 67-68; consult to health dir, CZ, Panama, 71; Nat Inst Environ Health Sci grant, 78-; NIH res career develop award, 80-85; FDA gastroint drug adv comt, 84- *Mem:* Soc Exp Biol & Med; Am Soc Pharmacol & Exp Therapeut; Am Asn Pathologists; Endocrine Soc; Pharmacol Soc Can; Royal Col Pathologists. *Res:* Experimental pathology and pharmacology of the gastro-intestinal tract and endocrine glands; development of disease models; duodenal ulcer produced by propionitrile, cysteamine; adrenal and thyroid necrosis caused by acrylonitrile pyrazole; gastric cytoprotection by sulphydryls. *Mailing Add:* Pathol & Lab Med VA Med Ctr 5901 E 7th St Long Beach CA 90822. *Fax:* 617-732-5343

SZABO, STEVE STANLEY, agronomy, for more information see previous edition

SZABO, STEVEN, CURRICULUM DEVELOPMENT OF MATHEMATICS FOR SECONDARY SCHOOLS, CURRICULUM DEVELOPMENT OF COURSES FOR SECONDARY SCHOOL MATH TEACHERS. *Current Pos:* RETIRED. *Personal Data:* b Detroit, Mich, July 28, 29; m 51, Madelyn; c Catherine, Christine, Carol, Colette, Constance, Clarissa & Carla. *Educ:* Univ Toledo, BEd, 51; Wayne State Univ, Mich, MEd, 59; Univ Ill, PhD(math educ), 69. *Prof Exp:* Math teacher, Cass Tech High Sch, Detroit, Mich, 56-62, Dist 204, Joliet, Ill, 74-88; res assoc, Univ Ill, 62-73. *Mem:* Math Asn Am. *Res:* Developed student texts and teacher commentaries for high school geometry and trigonometry courses based on vector methods. *Mailing Add:* 2306 Black Rd Joliet IL 60435

SZABO, TIBOR IMRE, BEHAVIORAL BIOLOGY. *Current Pos:* RES SCIENTIST APICULT, AGR CAN, 74- *Personal Data:* b Tiborszallas, Hungary, July 11, 34; Can citizen; m 66, Eva Faust; c Marton, Emilia, Tibor, Andrew, Daniel, Kristina & Maria. *Educ:* Univ Hort, Budapest, BAE, 58; Univ Guelph, MSc, 69, PhD(apicult), 73. *Prof Exp:* Fel apicult, Univ Guelph, 73-74. *Concurrent Pos:* Res scientist & adj prof, Univ Guelph, 92- *Mem:* Int Bee Res Asn; Sigma Xi. *Res:* Honey bee behavior, biology, physiology & breeding. *Mailing Add:* Environ Biol Univ Guelph Guelph ON N1G 2W1 Can. *Fax:* 519-837-0442

SZABUNIEWICZ, MICHAEL, VETERINARY MEDICINE. *Current Pos:* from asst prof to prof , 62-76, EMER PROF VET PHYSIOL, TEX A&M UNIV, 76- *Personal Data:* b Poland, Oct 11, 09; m 48, Rzeszowska; c Jean M & Charles H. *Educ:* Acad Vet Med, DVM, 34, DVSc(physiol), 37. *Prof Exp:* Dir, Exp Farm Kasese, Belgian Congo, 46-50; dir, Regional Diag Vet Lab & Exten Serv, 50-60; area vet, Agr Res Serv, USDA, 61-62. *Concurrent Pos:* Vis prof, Pahlavi Univ Shiraz, Iran, 76, Univ Cent Venezuela, 77-78. *Mem:* AAAS; Am Vet Med Asn; Am Soc Vet Physiol & Pharmacol; Am Asn Lab Animal Sci. *Res:* Physiology; pharmacology; radiation research. *Mailing Add:* 404 College View St Bryan TX 77801

SZAFRAN, ZVI, BORON HYDRIDE CHEMISTRY. *Current Pos:* PROF CHEM, MERRIMACK COL, 81-, DEAN SCI & ENG, 92- *Personal Data:* b Tel Aviv, Israel, July 15, 55; US citizen; m 76, Jill A Goldstein; c Mark C. *Educ:* Worcester Politech, Inst, BS, 76; Univ SC, PhD(inorg chem), 81. *Concurrent Pos:* Assoc dir, Nat Microscale Chem Ctr, 93- *Mem:* Am Chem soc. *Res:* Microscale chemistry. *Mailing Add:* Dean Sci Merrimack Col 315 Turnpike St North Andover MA 01845-5806. *E-Mail:* zszafran@merrimack.edu

SZAKAL, ANDRAS KALMAN, IMMUNOBIOLOGY, CANCER. *Current Pos:* assoc prof anat, 79-82, FULL PROF ANAT & IMMUNOBIOL, VA COMMONWEALTH UNIV, 82- *Personal Data:* b Szekesfehervar, Hungary, Sept 26, 36; US citizen; m 61, Norma E Skinner; c Andras & Jamas. *Educ:* Univ Colo, Boulder, BA, 61; MS, 63; Univ Tenn, PhD(immunobiol), 72. *Prof Exp:* Res asst histochem, Univ Colo, Boulder, 60-61; res assoc electron micros, Univ Mich, Ann Arbor, 65-66; staff biologist, Oak Ridge Nat Lab, 66-69, consult electron microscopist, 69-70, Oak Ridge Assoc Univs fel, 70-72, res biologist, Div Biol, 72-74; prin scientist lung immunobiol, Life Sci Div, Meloy Labs, Inc, 74-79. *Concurrent Pos:* Adj prof, Dent Sch Med, Col Va, Richmond. *Mem:* AAAS; Am Asn Immunobiologists. *Res:* Aging of the immune system, follicular dendritic cell immunobiology, follicular dendritic cells and HIV infections. *Mailing Add:* Dept Anat Med Col Va MCV Sta PO Box 709 Richmond VA 23298-0709. *Fax:* 804-786-9477; *E-Mail:* aszakal@gems.vcu.edu

SZALAY, JEANNE, TUMOR BIOLOGY. *Current Pos:* asst prof 72-77, ASSOC PROF BIOL, QUEENS COL, NY, 77- *Personal Data:* b Jan 17, 38; US citizen; c 2. *Educ:* Wash Sq Col Arts & Sci, BA, 59; Columbia Univ, PhD(biol), 66. *Prof Exp:* Fel cell biol & cytol, Col Physicians & Surgeons, Columbia Univ, 66-67; fel, Albert Einstein Col Med, 67-69, res asst cell biol & cytol, 69-70, instr, Dept Anat, 70-72. *Mem:* Asn Res Vision & Ophthalmol; Am Assoc Cancer Res; Clin Immunol Soc. *Res:* Tumor biology; tumor dormancy cellular interactions during metastasis; immunology. *Mailing Add:* Dept Biol City Univ NY Queens Col 65-30 Kissena Blvd Flushing NY 11367-1575

SZALDA, DAVID JOSEPH, BIOINORGANIC CHEMISTRY. *Current Pos:* PROF CHEM, BARUCH COL, 78- *Personal Data:* b Buffalo, NY, May 25, 50; m 74, Victoria A Galgano; c Dava & David Jr. *Educ:* Manhattan Col, BS, 72; Johns Hopkins Univ, MA, 74, PhD(inorg chem), 76. *Prof Exp:* Fel bioinorg chem, Columbia Univ, 76-78. *Concurrent Pos:* Res collabr, Brookhaven Nat Lab, 81- *Mem:* Sigma Xi; Am Chem Soc. *Res:* Electron transfer reactions; metal nucleic acid interactions; structural chemistry: x-ray crystallography. *Mailing Add:* Dept Natural Sci Baruch Col PO Box 502 17 Lexington Ave New York NY 10010

SZALECKI, WOJCIECH JOZEF, REACTIVE FLUORESCENT DYES. *Current Pos:* res chemist, 83-88, SR CHEMIST, ORG SYNTHESIS, MOLECULAR PROBES, INC, 88- *Personal Data:* b Kutno, Poland, Mar 18, 35; US citizen; m 77, Danuta Grad; c Dorota & Adam. *Educ:* Univ Lodz, Poland, MS, 59, PhD(org chem), 68. *Prof Exp:* Prof asst org chem, Univ Lodz, Poland, 59-69, adj, 70-79; res assoc, Univ Colo, Boulder, 79-82, prof res assoc biochem, 82-83. *Concurrent Pos:* Res fel, Wayne State Univ, Detroit, 69-70; abstractor, Chem Abstracts Serv, 70-82. *Mem:* Am Chem Soc; fel Am Inst Chemists; AAAS. *Res:* Synthesis of physiological active compounds and reagents for biochemical research; structure determination. *Mailing Add:* 2485 Park Forest Dr Eugene OR 97405. *Fax:* 541-344-6504

SZALEWICZ, KRZYSZTOF, THEORY OF INTERMOLECULAR INTERACTION & MUON CATALYZED FUSION. *Current Pos:* asst prof, 88-90, assoc prof, 90-94, PROF PHYSICS, DEPT PHYSICS, UNIV DEL, 94- *Personal Data:* b Gdansk, Poland, Jan 19, 50; m, Lidia M Jankowska; c Magdalena, Agnieszka & Monika. *Educ:* Univ Warsaw, MS, 73, PhD(quantum chem), 77, DSc, 84. *Prof Exp:* Asst quantum chem, Dept Chem, Univ Warsaw, Poland, 73-77, adj, 77-85; assoc res scientist, Dept Physics, Univ Fla, 85-88. *Concurrent Pos:* Adj res asst prof, Dept Physics, Univ Fla, 80-82; vis scientist, Univ Cologne, 82-84, Univ Uppsala, 90; Joint Inst Lab Astrophysics vis fel, Univ Colo, Boulder, 95-96; vis fel, Inst Theoret Atomic & Molecular Physics, Harvard Univ, 96. *Mem:* Am Phys Soc. *Res:* Theoretical, atomic and molecular physics; quantum chemistry; muon catalyzed fusion; intermolecular interactions; electron correlation; spectroscopy of diatomic molecules; theory of beta decay; many-body methods. *Mailing Add:* Dept Physics & Astron Univ Del Newark DE 19716. *Fax:* 302-831-1637; *E-Mail:* szalewic@udel.edu

SZAMOSI, GEZA, THEORETICAL PHYSICS. *Current Pos:* prof, 64-88, EMER PROF THEORET PHYSICS, UNIV WINSOR, 88-; PRIN SCI COL; CONCORDIA UNIV, MONTREAL, QUE, 88- *Personal Data:* b Budapest, Hungary, Mar 23, 22; Can citizen; m 44, Asnat Sternberg; c Michael & Annie. *Educ:* Univ Budapest, PhD(physics), 47; Hungary Acad Sci, DSc, 56. *Honors & Awards:* Schmid Prize the Hungarian Phys Soc, 59. *Prof Exp:* Assoc prof, Eotvos Univ, Budapest, 47-55, prof, 55-56; prof, Israel Inst Technol, Israel, 57-61; consult, Nat Lab Frascati, Italy, 61-64. *Concurrent Pos:* Nuffield fel, 69-70; A Alberman vis prof, Israel Inst Technol, 70-71; Can-France fel, Inst Henri Poincare, Paris, 74 & 80-81; Can-Japan fel, Dept Physics, Nagoya Univ, Japan, 81. *Mem:* Can Asn Physicists. *Res:* Special theory of relativity and its application to classical and quantum mechanics, statistical mechanics, plasma physics, astrophysics and to classical theories of elementary particles; history and philosophy of science; author or coauthor of over 60 publications. *Mailing Add:* Sci Col Concordia Univ Montreal PQ H3G 1M8 Can. *Fax:* 514-848-2598; *E-Mail:* szam@vax2.concordia.ca.

SZAMOSI, JANOS, PHYSICAL CHEMISTRY, POLYMER CHEMISTRY. *Current Pos:* ASST PROF CHEM, WESTERN ILL UNIV, 85- *Personal Data:* b Gyor, Hungary, Oct 28, 55; m 81; c 2. *Educ:* Tech Univ Budapest, BS, 78; State Univ NY Stony Brook, MS, 81; Univ Tex, Arlington, PhD(math sci & chem), 83. *Prof Exp:* Fel, Stanford Univ, 84-85. *Mem:* Am Chem Soc. *Res:* Polymer chemistry; stochastic processes; mathematical modeling; materials science; chemical kinetics. *Mailing Add:* 441 Jefferson Ave Morrisville PA 19067

SZANISZLO, PAUL JOSEPH, MICROBIOLOGY, MYCOLOGY. *Current Pos:* from asst prof to assoc prof, 68-80, chmn, Div Biol Sci, 76-82, PROF MICROBIOL, UNIV TEX, AUSTIN, 80- *Personal Data:* b Medina, Ohio, June 9, 39; m 60, Susan J Twigg; c P Christopher & Juli A (Powell). *Educ:* Ohio Wesleyan Univ, BA, 61; Univ NC, MA, 64, PhD(bot), 67. *Honors & Awards:* Coker Award, 67. *Prof Exp:* Res fel, Harvard Univ, 67-68. *Concurrent Pos:* Guest res microbiol, Sect Enzymes & Cellular Biochem, Nat Inst Arthritis, Diabetes & Digestive & Kidney Dis, NIH, Bethesda, Md, 83; ed, Biol Metals, 87-91, Mycologia, 91-95 & FEMS Microbiol Lett, 92-93; chair-elect & chair, Div F, Am Soc Microbiol, 95-97. *Mem:* AAAS; Am Soc Microbiol; Int Soc Human & Animal Mycol; Mycol Soc Am; Sigma Xi. *Res:* Growth, development and differentiation in fungi; iron transport in bacteria, fungi and plants; importance of siderophores in plant nutrition; dimorphism in and molecular biology of fungal pathogens of humans. *Mailing Add:* Dept Microbiol Exp Sci Bldg Univ Tex Austin TX 78712-1095

SZAP, PETER CHARLES, ANALYTICAL CHEMISTRY. *Current Pos:* LECTR, GEORGIAN CT COL, NJ, 89- *Personal Data:* b New York, NY, Aug 20, 29; m 57; c 3. *Educ:* Queens Col, NY, BS, 51; Fordham Univ, MS, 53. *Prof Exp:* Res chemist, Lever Bros Res & Develop Co, NJ, 53-59; anal res chemist, Toms River Chem Corp, 59-67, sect leader anal qual control, Ciba-Geigy Corp, 67-77; mgr anal servs, Ciba-Geigy Corp, 77-86, sec sch chem teacher, 86-87; consult, 87-89. *Concurrent Pos:* Chem Abstractor, 51-81. *Mem:* Am Chem Soc; Sigma Xi; Soc Appl Spectros. *Res:* Analytical methods development in detergents, dyestuffs, resins and raw materials; analysis and applications of optical brighteners, especially infrared, ultraviolet and visible absorption spectroscopy; chromatography; liquid chromatography techniques. *Mailing Add:* 333 Killarney Dr Toms River NJ 08753

SZARA, STEPHEN ISTVAN, PSYCHOPHARMACOLOGY. *Current Pos:* CHIEF BIOMED RES BR, DIV RES, NAT INST DRUG ABUSE, 75- *Personal Data:* b Pestujhely, Hungary, Mar 21, 23; nat US; div; c 1. *Educ:* Pazmany Peter Univ, Hungary, DSc(chem), 50; Med Univ Budapest, MD, 51. *Prof Exp:* Sci asst, Microbiol Inst, Univ Budapest, 49-50, asst prof, Biochem Inst, 50-53, chief, Biochem Lab, State Ment Inst, 53-56; vis scientist, Psychiat Clin Berlin, 57; vis scientist, Nat Inst Ment Health, 57-60, chief sect psychopharmacol, Lab Clin Psychopharmacol, Spec Ment Health Res, 60-71, chief clin studies sect, Ctr Studies Narcotic & Drug Abuse, Nat Inst Mental Health, 71-74. *Concurrent Pos:* Assoc clin prof, George Washington Univ. *Mem:* AAAS; Int Col Neuropsychopharmacol; fel Am Col Neuropsychopharmacol; Am Soc Pharmacol & Exp Therapeut; IEEE Computer Soc. *Res:* Metabolism of psychotropic drugs, especially tryptamine derivatives; correlation between metabolism and psychotropic activity of drugs. *Mailing Add:* 10901 Jolly Way Kensington MD 20895-1127

SZAREK, STANLEY RICHARD, PHYSIOLOGICAL ECOLOGY. *Current Pos:* Asst prof, 74-80, ASSOC PROF BOT, ARIZ STATE UNIV, 80- *Personal Data:* b Visalia, Calif, Nov 14, 47; m 77. *Educ:* Calif State Univ, Pomona, BS, 69; Univ Calif, Riverside, PhD(biol), 74. *Concurrent Pos:* Consult, US Biol Prog Desert Biomed, 75-77. *Mem:* Am Soc Plant Physiologists; Ecol Soc Am. *Res:* Physiological ecology of desert plants, emphasizing photosynthetic carbon metabolism and high temperature stress physiology. *Mailing Add:* Dept Botany Ariz State Univ Tempe AZ 85287-0002

SZAREK, WALTER ANTHONY, ORGANIC CHEMISTRY, CARBOHYDRATE CHEMISTRY. *Current Pos:* asst prof org chem, Queen's Univ, 67-71, assoc prof, 71-76, dir, Carbohydrate Res Inst, 76-85, PROF ORG CHEM, QUEEN'S UNIV, ONT, 76-; FOUNDING MEM & PRIN INVESTR, NEUROCHEM INC, 93- *Personal Data:* b St Catharines, Ont, Apr 19, 38; Can citizen. *Educ:* McMaster Univ, BSc, 60, MSc, 62; Queen's Univ, Ont, PhD(org chem), 64. *Honors & Awards:* Claude S Hudson Award, Am Chem Soc, 89, Melville L Wolfrom Award, 92. *Prof Exp:* Res fel chem, Ohio State Univ, 64-65; asst prof biochem, Rutgers Univ, 65-67. *Concurrent Pos:* Premier, Ont Coun Technol Fund; chmn, Div Carbohydrate Chem, Am Chem Soc, 82-83. *Mem:* Am Chem Soc; fel Chem Inst Can; Royal Soc Chem; Soc Glycobiol; AAAS. *Res:* Structure and synthesis of carbohydrates and carbohydrate-containing antibiotics; biochemical aspects; synthesis and chemical modification of nucleosides; conformational and mechanistic studies of carbohydrate reactions; sweeteners; targeted delivery of drugs; natural products synthesis; Alzheimer's disease. *Mailing Add:* Dept Chem Queen's Univ Kingston ON K7L 3N6 Can. Fax: 613-545-6532; E-Mail: szarekw@chem.queensu.ca

SZARKA, LASZLO JOSEPH, BIOENGINEERING. *Current Pos:* SECT HEAD, E R SQUIBB & SONS, 74- *Personal Data:* b Szekesfehervar, Hungary, Sept 6, 35; US citizen; m 63; c 2. *Educ:* Univ Sci, Budapest, Hungary, MS, 61, PhD(phys chem), 67. *Prof Exp:* Asst res investr phys chem, Chinoin Pharmaceut Plant, Hungary, 61-63; sect head bioeng, Res Inst Pharmaceut Chem, Hungary, 64-72; head chemist, Pharmaceut Ctr, Hungary, 72-73; res & develop biochem, Blackman Labs Inc, 74. *Mem:* Am Chem Soc; Am Inst Chem Eng. *Res:* Antibioticum and enzyme fermentation technology; batch, fed batch and continuous cultivation; transport phenomena, process control and reactor designing; optimization and scale-up problems; molecule biotransformations, steroids and hydrocarbons. *Mailing Add:* 5 Wellington Rd East Brunswick NJ 08816-1720

SZASZ, THOMAS STEPHEN, PSYCHIATRY. *Current Pos:* prof, 56-90, EMER PROF PSYCHIAT, STATE UNIV NY HEALTH SCI CTR, 90- *Personal Data:* b Budapest, Hungary, Apr 15, 20; US citizen; div; c 2. *Educ:* Univ Cincinnati, AB, 41, MD, 44; Am Bd Psychiat & Neurol, dipl psychiat, 51. *Hon Degrees:* DSc, Allegheny Col, 75, Univ Francisco Marroquin, Guatemala, 79. *Honors & Awards:* Holmes-Munsterberg Award Forensic Psychol, Int Acad Forensic Psychol, 69; Humanist of Year, Am Humanist Asn, 73; Distinguished Serv Award, Am Inst Pub Serv, 74. *Prof Exp:* Intern med, Boston City Hosp, 44-45; resident psychiat, Clinics, Univ Chicago, 46-48; mem staff, Chicago Inst Psychoanal, 51-56. *Concurrent Pos:* Vis prof psychiat, Sch Med, Marquette Univ, 68; consult, Comt Ment Hyg, NY State Bar Asn, Judicial Conf Comt, Judicial Conf DC Circuit, Comt Laws Pertaining Ment Disorders & Res Adv Panel, Inst Study Drug Addiction; adv ed, J Forensic Psychol; mem bd consult, Psychoanal Rev, mem adv comt, Living Libraries, Inc. *Mem:* Fel Royal Soc Health; fel Am Psychiat Asn; Am Psychoanal Asn. *Res:* Epistemology of the behavioral sciences; history of psychiatry; psychiatry and law. *Mailing Add:* Dept Psychiat State Univ NY Health Sci Ctr Syracuse NY 13210. Fax: 315-464-3163

SZCZARBA, ROBERT HENRY, TOPOLOGY. *Current Pos:* Off Naval Res res assoc math, 60-61, from asst prof to assoc prof, 61-74, PROF MATH, YALE UNIV, 74- *Personal Data:* b Dearborn, Mich, Nov 27, 32; m 55; c 2. *Educ:* Univ Mich, BS, 55; Univ Chicago, MS, 56, PhD(math), 60. *Concurrent Pos:* NSF fel, Inst Advan Study, 64-65. *Mem:* Am Math Soc; Math Asn Am. *Res:* Algebraic and differential topology and geometry of differentiable manifolds. *Mailing Add:* Dept Math Yale Univ PO Box 208283 New Haven CT 06520-8283

SZCZECH, GEORGE MARION, VETERINARY PATHOLOGY, REPRODUCTIVE TOXICOLOGY. *Current Pos:* SR TOXICOL PATHOLOGIST, BURROUGHS WELLCOME CO, 78- *Personal Data:* US citizen; m; c 3. *Educ:* Univ Minn, BS, 64, DVM, 66; Purdue Univ, PhD(vet path), 74; Am Bd Toxicol, dipl; Am Col Vet Pathologists, dipl. *Prof Exp:* Resident vet med, Colo State Univ, 66-67; vet pract, small animals, 67-68; sr scientist toxicol, Res Ctr, Mead Johnson Co, 68-70; res fel vet path, Purdue Univ, 70-74; res scientist path, Upjohn Co, 74-78. *Concurrent Pos:* Assoc ed, Fund Appl Toxicol, 80-85; consult, Nat Toxicol Prog, 80- *Mem:* Am Vet Med Asn; Soc Toxicology; Teratology Soc. *Res:* Toxicologic pathology; clinical pathology and reproductive toxicology. *Mailing Add:* 643 Rock Creek Road Chapel Hill NC 27514

SZCZEPANIAK, KRYSTYNA, MOLECULAR SPECTROSCOPY, LOW TEMPERATURE MATRIX-ISOLATION. *Current Pos:* postdoc fel phys chem, 86-88, RES SCIENTIST, DEPT CHEM, UNIV FLA, GAINESVILLE, 88- *Personal Data:* b Lwow, Poland, Jun 19, 34; m 85. *Educ:* Warsaw Univ, Poland, BS, 58, PhD(physics), 65. *Prof Exp:* Asst, physics, Tech Univ, Warsaw, 58-63; adjunct prof phys, Warsaw Univ, 63-78; docent, Inst Physics, Polish Acad Sci, 78-85. *Concurrent Pos:* Res asst, dept physics, Moscow Univ, USSR, 62-63; Ford Found fel, 68-69; postdoc fel, Nat Res Coun, Halifax, 68-69; dept chem, Univ Fla, Gainsville, 69; vis lectr, dept chem, Salford Univ, Eng, 72-73; vis scientist, dept chem, Marburg Univ, W Ger, 82. *Mem:* Polish Phys Soc (treas, 78-80). *Res:* Structure and molecular interactions of nucleic acid bases and their analogues and related model compounds by means of vibrational and electronic spectroscopy; low temperature matrix isolation spectroscopy and by theoretical, quantum mechanical methods. *Mailing Add:* Dept Chem Univ Fla PO Box 117200 Gainesville FL 32611-7200

SZCZEPANSKI, MAREK MICHAL, EXPERIMENTAL SURGERY & GASTROENTEROLOGY, LABORATORY ANIMAL SCIENCE. *Current Pos:* ASST PROF PHYSIOL & DIR, COMP MED UNIT NORTHEASTERN OHIO UNIV COL MED, ROOTSTOWN, 80- *Personal Data:* b Warsaw, Poland, June 8, 41; Can & US & Poland citizen; m 80; c 2. *Educ:* Agr Univ Warsaw, DVM, 67; Univ Toronto, DVPH(pub health), 72. *Prof Exp:* Asst surg, Agr Univ Warsaw, 67-68; res asst, McGill Univ, 68-70; res fel, Univ Toronto, 70-72; assoc vet small animal pract, Lakeshore Vet Hosp, Toronto, 72-73; staff vet, Toronto Humane Soc, 73-75; asst prof physiol & dir animal care, Fac Med, Mem Univ Nfld, 75-80. *Mem:* Am Asn Lab Animal Sci; Can Vet Med Asn; Can Asn Lab Animal Sci. *Res:* Pathophysiology of the esophagus; achalasia; experimental esophagitis; esophageal replacement by a gastric tube; control mechanisms governing esophageal motor activity; anti-reflux mechanism in hiatus hernia. *Mailing Add:* Physiol Northeastern Ohio Univ Col Med 4209 State Rte 44 Box 95 Rootstown OH 44272-9698

SZCZESNIAK, ALINA SURMACKA, FOOD RHEOLOGY, FOOD TEXTURE. *Current Pos:* RETIRED. *Personal Data:* b Warsaw, Poland, July 8, 25; US citizen; wid; c Andrew. *Educ:* Bryn Mawr Col, AB, 48; Mass Inst Technol, ScD(food sci), 52. *Honors & Awards:* Scientist of the year, NY Sect of Inst Food Technologists, 82; Nicholas Appert Medal, Inst Food Techologist, 85, Fred W Tanner Mem Lectr, 90; Scott Blair Award, Am Asn Cereal Chemists, 89; Mone Sklodowska Curie Award, Pilsurtski Inst Am, 96. *Prof Exp:* Prin scientist, Gen Foods Corp, 52-86. *Concurrent Pos:* Ed-in-chief, J Texture Studies, 68-79; lectr & author. *Mem:* NY Acad Sci; fel Inst Food Technologists; Soc Rheology; Polish Inst Arts & Sci Am; Sigma Xi. *Res:* Instrumental and sensory methods of food texture measurement; meaning of texture to the consumer; texturization and relationship to structure, microscopic and molecular. *Mailing Add:* 22 Wilson Block Mt Vernon NY 10552-1113

SZCZESNIAK, RAYMOND ALBIN, MEDICINAL CHEMISTRY, NUCLEAR MEDICINE. *Current Pos:* PRES, PROF CONSULTS, INC, 77- *Personal Data:* b Buffalo, NY, Nov 28, 40; wid; c 4. *Educ:* Fordham Univ, BS, 63; Univ Mich, Ann Arbor, MS, 65, PhD(med chem), 68. *Prof Exp:* Sr res scientist, E R Squibb & Sons, Inc, New Brunswick, 68-69, res chemist, 69-72, sr res chemist radiopharmaceut, 72-73; radioimmunoassay specialist, Nuclear-Med Labs, Inc, 73-77. *Mem:* Soc Nuclear Med; Am Chem Soc. *Res:* Radioimmunoassay; radiomedicinal synthesis. *Mailing Add:* 4042 Mendenhall Dr Dallas TX 75244

SZE, HEVEN, PLANT PHYSIOLOGY, BIOCHEMISTRY. *Current Pos:* from asst prof to assoc prof, 82-92, PROF, DEPT BOT, UNIV MD, 92- *Personal Data:* b The Hague, Neth, Oct 22, 47; US citizen; m 74. *Educ:* Nat Taiwan Univ, BS, 68; Univ Calif, Davis, MS, 70; Purdue Univ, PhD(plant physiol), 75. *Prof Exp:* Res fel biophys, Harvard Med Sch, 75-78; res assoc, Univ Kans, 78-79, asst prof, 79-82. *Mem:* Am Soc Plant Physiologists; AAAS; Am Soc Cell Biol; Am Soc Biochem & Molecular Biol. *Res:* Membrane structure and function; mechanism of solute transport; biophysics; Ht-translocating ATPases, Ca2t transport. *Mailing Add:* Dept Plant Biol Univ Md College Park MD 20742. Fax: 301-314-9082; E-Mail: hs29@umail.umd.edu

SZE, MORGAN CHUAN-YUAN, CHEMICAL ENGINEERING. *Current Pos:* RETIRED. *Personal Data:* b Tientsin, China, May 27, 17; nat US; m 45, Agnes C Lin; c Karl, Arthur & Morgan. *Educ:* Mass Inst Technol, SB, 39, ScD(chem eng), 41. *Honors & Awards:* Award for Achievement, Chinese Inst Engrs, 69. *Prof Exp:* Chem engr, Universal Trading Corp, 41-42; process engr, Belle Works, E I du Pont de Nemours & Co, Inc, 42-44, Hydrocarbon Res, Inc, NY, 44-45 & Foster Wheeler Corp, 45-47; sr process engr, Hydrocarbon Res, Inc, 47-53, dir process eng dept, 53-59, tech dir, 59-61; exec staff engr, Lummus Co, 61-64, mgr eng develop ctr, 64-71, vpres res & develop, 71-80; vpres adv tech group, Wheelabrator-Frye Inc, 80-83; vpres process, Energy & Environ Technol, Signal Co, 83-85. *Mem:* Nat Acad Eng; AAAS; Am Inst Chem Engrs; NY Acad Sci; Sigma Xi; Am Chem Soc. *Res:* Nitrogen fixation; petroleum refining and processing; petrochemicals; cryogenics. *Mailing Add:* 4 Regina Rd Portsmouth NH 03801

SZE, PAUL YI LING, NEUROSCIENCE, PHARMACOLOGY. *Current Pos:* AT DEPT PHARMACOL, CHICAGO MED SCH. *Personal Data:* b Shanghai, China, June 7, 38. *Educ:* Nat Taiwan Univ, BS, 60; Duquesne Univ, MS, 62; Univ Wis, MS, 64; Univ Chicago, PhD(biochem), 69. *Prof Exp:* From asst prof to prof biobehav sci, Univ Conn, 69- *Concurrent Pos:* Mem, Neurol A Study Sect, NIH, 80-84, Gen Res Support Rev Comt, 85-89, Res Scientist Develop Rev Comt, NIMH, 90-94. *Mem:* AAAS; Am Soc Neurochem; Soc Neurosci; Int Soc Neurochem. *Res:* Biochemistry of neurotransmitters; neurochemical aspects of alcoholism; neurobiological actions of steroid hormones. *Mailing Add:* Dept Pharmacol Chicago Med Sch 3333 Green Bay Rd North Chicago IL 60064. *Fax:* 847-578-3268; *E-Mail:* szep@mis.finchcms.edu

SZE, PHILIP, PHYCOLOGY, AQUATIC BIOLOGY. *Current Pos:* asst prof, 77-83, ASSOC PROF BIOL GEORGETOWN UNIV, 83- *Personal Data:* b Washington, DC, Dec 3, 45. *Educ:* Dickinson Col, BS, 68; Cornell Univ, PhD(phycol), 72. *Prof Exp:* Vis asst prof biol, State Univ NY, Buffalo, 72-73; asst prof phycol, Stockton State Col, 73-74; asst prof biol, State Univ NY, Buffalo, 74-77. *Mem:* Phycol Soc Am; Int Phycol Soc; Brit Phycol Soc. *Res:* Ecology of algae, including studies of phytoplankton in eutrophic lakes and rivers, intertidal macroalgal communities and filamentous algae in streams. *Mailing Add:* Dept Biol Georgetown Univ 1421 37th St NW Washington DC 20057-0001

SZE, ROBERT CHIA-TING, LASERS, NON-LINEAR OPTICS. *Current Pos:* MEM STAFF, LOS ALAMOS NAT LAB, 74-; FOUNDER & PRES, STABLELASE INC, 88- *Personal Data:* b Kowloon, China, Aug 27, 41; US citizen; m 70; c 1. *Educ:* Cornell Univ, BEE, 64; Yale Univ, MS, 66, PhD(appl physics), 70. *Prof Exp:* Fel, Yale Univ, 70-71, State Univ NY, Stony Brook, 71-73; res assoc, Yale Univ, 73-74. *Concurrent Pos:* Consult, Tachisto, Inc, 80-81, Tachisto, 83-85, Summit Technol, 85-88 & XMR, 85; consult & co-founder, Laser Tech, Inc, 81-83. *Mem:* Fel Inst Elec & Electronics Engrs; Am Phys Soc; Optical Soc Am; Sigma Xi. *Res:* Physics of lasers and the generation of coherent light sources; physics of noble gas ion lasers; high energy rare-gas halide excimer lasers; generation of coherent wavelengths via Raman stokes and anti-stokes scattering; development of compact high repetition rate excimer and carbon dioxide lasers. *Mailing Add:* 1042 Stagecoach Rd Santa Fe NM 87501

SZE, SIMON M, ELECTRICAL ENGINEERING. *Current Pos:* PROF ENG, NAT CHIAO TUNG UNIV. *Personal Data:* b Nanking, China, Mar 21, 30. *Educ:* Nat Taiwan Univ, BS, 57; Univ Wash, MS, 60; Stanford Univ, PhD, 63. *Honors & Awards:* J J Ebers Award, Inst Elec & Electronics Engrs Electron Devices Soc, 91. *Mem:* Nat Acad Eng; fel Inst Elec & Electronics Engrs. *Mailing Add:* Inst Electronics Nat Chiao Tung Univ 1000 Ta Hsueh Rd Hsinchu Taiwan

SZE, TSUNG WEI, ELECTRICAL ENGINEERING. *Current Pos:* from asst prof to assoc prof, 54-60, Fessenden prof, 57-62, Westinghouse prof, 62-65, assoc dean eng, 70-77, PROF ENG, UNIV PITTSBURGH, 60- *Personal Data:* b Shanghai, China, Sept 13, 22; nat US; m 52; c 3. *Educ:* Univ Mo, BS, 48; Purdue Univ, MS, 50; Northwestern Univ, PhD(elect eng), 54. *Prof Exp:* Asst elec eng, Northwestern Univ, 50-52, instr, 52-54. *Concurrent Pos:* Consult, Univac Div, Sperry Rand Corp, 56-58, Westinghouse Elec Corp, 59-, MPC Corp, 69-74 & Mellon Inst, 78-; adj prof, Jiaotong Univ, People's Repub China, 79- *Mem:* Am Soc Eng Educ; Asn Comput Mach; Inst Elec & Electronics Engrs. *Res:* Logical design and switching theory; digital computer designs; digital image processing. *Mailing Add:* Univ Pittsburgh Commun Systs High Educ Fifth Ave & Bigelow Blvd Pittsburgh PA 15261

SZEBEHELY, VICTOR, ASTRONOMY, SPACE SCIENCES. *Current Pos:* prof aerospace eng & eng mech, 68-76, chmn dept, 76-81, R B CURRAN CHAIR ENG, UNIV TEX, AUSTIN, 82- *Personal Data:* b Budapest, Hungary, Aug 10, 21; nat US; m 70; c 1. *Educ:* Budapest Tech Univ, DSc, 45. *Honors & Awards:* Sci Res Soc Award, Sigma Xi, 51; D Brouwer Award, Am Astron Soc, 78 & Am Astronaut Soc, 82; Fulbright Lectr, 86 & 90. *Prof Exp:* Asst prof appl math, Budapest Tech Univ, 43-47; res asst, Pa State Univ, 47-48; assoc prof appl mech, Va Polytech Inst, 48-51; head, Ship Dynamics Br, David Taylor Model Basin, US Dept Navy, 51-57; mgr space mech, Missiles & Space Div, Gen Elec Co, 57-62; assoc prof astron, Yale Univ, 62-68. *Concurrent Pos:* Lectr, McGill Univ, 48 & Univ Toronto, 49; prof lectr, Univ Md & George Washington Univ, 51-57; consult, NASA, Gen Elec Co, IT&T Co, Bell Tel Labs & Inst Defense Anal, Tracor, USAF Space Command & Lawrence Berkeley Lab. *Mem:* Nat Acad Eng; Int Astron Union; Am Astron Soc; Am Inst Aeronaut & Astronaut. *Res:* Celestial mechanics; problem of three and n bodies; applied mechanics; analytical dynamics; continuum mechanics; applied mathematics; matrix and tensor analysis. *Mailing Add:* Dept Aerospace Eng Univ Tex Austin TX 78712. *Fax:* 512-471-6788

SZEBENYI, DOLETHA M E, PROTEIN CRYSTALLOGRAPHY. *Current Pos:* RES ASSOC BIOCHEM, CORNELL UNIV, 75- *Personal Data:* b Arlington, Mass, Nov 27, 47; m 72, Thomas; c Gordon. *Educ:* Bryn Mawr Col, AB, 68; Univ Conn, PhD(phys chem), 72. *Mem:* AAAS; Am Crystallog Asn. *Res:* Protein crystallography; structure of calcium binding proteins; other macromolecules; use of synchrotron radiation and Laue diffraction for macromolecular crystallography. *Mailing Add:* Chess Wilson Lab Cornell Univ Ithaca NY 14853. *Fax:* 607-255-9001; *E-Mail:* szebenyi@poopdec.chess.cornell.edu

SZEBENYI, EMIL, COMPARATIVE ANATOMY, EMBRYOLOGY. *Current Pos:* from asst prof to prof, 62-83, chmn, Dept Biol Sci, 71-80, EMER PROF COMP ANAT, EMBRYOL & EVOLUTION, FAIRLEIGH DICKINSON UNIV, 83-, MANAGING DIR, CARIB-BIO-MED INST LTD, 97- *Personal Data:* b Budapest, Hungary, June 9, 20; US citizen; wid; c Tomas, Andrew & Steven. *Educ:* Budapest Tech Univ, dipl, 42, Doctoratus (animal genetics & husb), 43. *Prof Exp:* Asst prof animal genetics, Univ Agr Sci Hungary, 52-53, Hungarian Acad Sci fel & adj, 53-56. *Concurrent Pos:* Pres, Alfacell Corp, 81-86; independent res, 86-; managing dir, Carib Biomed Inst Ltd. *Mem:* AAAS; Sigma Xi; Am Soc Zoologists; Soc Develop Biol; Int Abstracts Biol Sci. *Res:* Anatomy; human embryology; experimental morphogenesis; developed an effective drug against cartinomal and ademo carainouars. *Mailing Add:* Reading PO Box 111 St James Jamaica. *Fax:* 876-952-2828

SZEDON, JOHN R(OBERT), ELECTRICAL ENGINEERING, SOLID STATE PHYSICS. *Current Pos:* Sr engr, 62-67, sr res scientist, 67-68, MGR SURFACE DEVICE STUDIES, WESTINGHOUSE ELEC CORP RES LABS, 68- *Personal Data:* b Elrama, Pa, May 26, 37; m 72. *Educ:* Carnegie-Mellon Univ, BS, 59, MS, 60, PhD(elec eng), 62. *Honors & Awards:* Thomas D Callinan Award, Electrochem Soc, 73. *Concurrent Pos:* Lectr, Carnegie-Mellon Univ, 67-68. *Mem:* Inst Elec & Electronics Engrs; Electrochem Soc. *Res:* Semiconductor device physics; surface controlled semiconductor devices; ion migration in insulators; injection-trapping in metal-insular semiconductor structures; ionizing radiation effects in dielectrics; p-N junction; heterojunction and MIS solar cells. *Mailing Add:* 20 Greenwood Rd Pittsburgh PA 15221

SZEGO, CLARA MARIAN, CELL BIOLOGY, ENDOCRINOLOGY. *Current Pos:* asst clin prof biophys, 48-49, from asst prof to prof, 49-60, PROF BIOL, UNIV CALIF, LOS ANGELES, 60- *Personal Data:* b Budapest, Hungary, Mar 23, 16; US citizen; m 43, Sidney Roberts. *Educ:* Hunter Col, BA, 37; Univ Minn, MS, 39, PhD(physiol chem), 42. *Honors & Awards:* Ciba Award, Endocrine Soc, 53; Gregory Pincus Mem Medallion, Worcester Found Exp Biol, 74. *Prof Exp:* Asst physiol chem, Sch Med, Univ Minn, 40-42, asst physiol, 42, instr, 42-44; fel cancer, Minn Med Found, 44; assoc chemist, Off Sci Res & Develop, Nat Bur Stand, 44-45; res assoc, Worcester Found Exp Biol, 45-47; res instr physiol chem, Yale Univ, 47-48. *Concurrent Pos:* Guggenheim fel, 56; mem, Univ Calif Molecular Biol Inst, 69-, Jonsson Comprehensive Cancer Ctr, 76- *Mem:* Fel AAAS; Am Physiol Soc; Am Soc Zoologists; Endocrine Soc; Am Soc Cell Biol; Biochem Soc; Soc Endocrinol; Int Soc Res Reproduction; Europ Soc Comp Endocrinol. *Res:* Molecular mechanisms of endocrine regulation. *Mailing Add:* Dept Molecular Cellular & Develop Biol Univ Calif Los Angeles CA 90095-1606. *Fax:* 310-459-7587; *E-Mail:* cmszego@ucla.edu

SZEGO, GEORGE C(HARLES), CLEAN RENEWABLE ENERGY, FORENSIC INVESTIGATIONS. *Current Pos:* PRES, GEORGE C SZEGO & ASSOC, INC, 80- & BAY TECHNOLOGIES, INC, 85- *Personal Data:* b Budapest, Hungary, Aug 10, 19; US citizen; c 5. *Educ:* Univ Denver, BS, 47; Univ Wash, MS, 50, PhD(chem eng), 56. *Honors & Awards:* Nat Award Energy Innovative Bldg Complex, Owens-Corning, 80. *Prof Exp:* Prof & chmn, Dept Chem Eng, Seattle Univ, 47-56; mgr space propulsion & power, Gen Elec Co, 56-59; sr staff mem, TRW Space Technol Labs, 57-61 & Inst Defense Anal, 61-70; pres & chmn, Intertechnol Solar Corp, 70-81. *Concurrent Pos:* Consult, var orgn, 51- & White House Off Sci & Technol, 65-68; founding chmn, Int Soc Energy Conversion Eng Conf, 65-; mem, White House Comt Energy, 78-79; distinguished adj prof, Howard Univ, 90. *Mem:* Fel Am Inst Chem Engrs; Solar Energy Industs Asn; Solar Energy Res Found. *Res:* Clean, renewable carbon dioxide-neutral economic energy of its conversion; energy for economic, clean major energy source; granted one patent. *Mailing Add:* 3146 Catrina Lane Annapolis MD 21403

SZEGO, PETER A, SOCIAL IMPLICATIONS OF TECHNOLOGY. *Current Pos:* RETIRED. *Personal Data:* b Berlin, Ger, July 18, 25; nat US. *Educ:* Stanford Univ, BS, 47. *Prof Exp:* Asst prof mech eng, Rice Univ, 51-54 & Univ Santa Clara, 56-63; mgr mech sect, advan technol div, Ampex Corp, Redwood City, 63-76; exec asst, bd supvr, Santa Clara Co, Calif, 76-82; chief consult, State Senate Comt Elections, 82-85, State Senate Comt Pub Employ & Retirement, 85-87, chief consult, State Senate Comt Natural resources & Wildlife, 87-93, chief consult, State Senate Comt Agr & Water Resources, 93-95. *Concurrent Pos:* Lectr mech eng, Univ Santa Clara, 70-82. *Mem:* Am Soc Mech Engrs; Soc Indust & Appl Math; Asn Comput Mach; Inst Elec & Electronics Engrs; Am Math Soc; Prof Eng Soc. *Res:* Scientific programming; applied mathematics; engineering mechanics; science policy. *Mailing Add:* 75 Glen Eyrie Ave Apt 19 San Jose CA 95125

SZEKELY, ANDREW GEZA, PHYSICAL CHEMISTRY. *Current Pos:* RETIRED. *Personal Data:* b Temesvar, Rumania, Apr 15, 25; US citizen; m 51; c 6. *Educ:* Eotvos Lorand Univ, Budapest, dipl chem, 50. *Prof Exp:* Asst electrochem, Physico-Chem Inst, Eotvos Lorand Univ, 49-51; res chemist, High Pressure Res Inst, Budapest, 51-56; dept head petrol refining, 56-57; res chemist, Tonawanda Res Lab, Linde Div, Tarrytown Tech Ctr, Union Carbide Corp, 58-62, sr res chemist, 62-66, develop assoc process metall, Newark Develop Labs, NJ, 67-70, sr develop assoc, Gas Prod Develop, 70-77, corp develop fel, Linde Labs, 78-91. *Mem:* Metall Soc. *Res:* Process metallurgy; thermodynamics and kinetics. *Mailing Add:* 2379 Claire Ct Yorktown Heights NY 10598

SZEKELY, IVAN J, RESOURCE MANAGEMENT. *Current Pos:* PRES, PHARMACEUT RES INT, 71- *Personal Data:* b Budapest, Hungary, Aug 13, 19; nat US;. *Educ:* Pazmany Peter Univ, Hungary, PhD, 43, MS, 44. *Prof Exp:* Asst prof chem, Bowling Green State Univ, 47-48; prof pharm, Univ Calif, 48-51; dir res & prod develop, Barnes-Hind Pharmaceut, Inc, 51-57, from exec vpres to pres, 57-69. *Concurrent Pos:* Pharmaceut mgt consult. *Mem:* Am Chem Soc; Am Pharmaceut Asn; NY Acad Sci. *Res:* Formulation of pharmaceutical dosage forms; ophthalmic solutions; physical-chemical properties of contact lens materials, especially contact lens solutions. *Mailing Add:* 13643 Wildcrest Dr Los Altos CA 94022

SZEKELY, JOSEPH GEORGE, BIOPHYSICS. *Current Pos:* ASSOC RES OFFICER, ATOMIC ENERGY CAN LTD, 68- *Personal Data:* b Cleveland, Ohio, May 7, 40; m 67; c 2. *Educ:* Case Western Reserve Univ, BS, 62; State Univ NY Buffalo, PhD(physics), 67. *Prof Exp:* USPHS fel, Univ Tex M D Anderson Hosp & Tumor Inst, 67-68. *Mem:* Can Soc Cell Biol; Can Micros Soc; Inst Food Technologists; Environ Mutagens Soc. *Res:* Genetic toxicology; cytology; food irradiation. *Mailing Add:* Whiteshell Lab Atomic Energy Can Ltd Pinawa MB R0E 1L0 Can. *Fax:* 204-753-8802

SZEKELY, JULIAN, process metallurgy, chemical engineering; deceased, see previous edition for last biography

SZELESS, ADORJAN GYULA, MECHANICAL ENGINEERING, NAVAL ARCHITECTURE. *Current Pos:* RETIRED. *Personal Data:* b Budapest, Hungary, Dec 7, 27; US citizen; m 53. *Educ:* Budapest Tech Univ, MS, 52; Va Polytech Univ, PhD(mech eng), 67. *Prof Exp:* Marine engr, Obudai Hajogyar, Hungary, 52-54; naval architect, Dunai Hajogyar, 54-56; plant engr, Munchen-Dachauer Papierfabriken GmbH, Ger, 57-58; naval architect, Wasser-u Schiffahrtsdirektion, Ger, 58-59; marine appln engr, Cummins Engine Co, Ind, 59-62; asst prof, Va Polytech Inst & State Univ, 62-72, assoc prof mech eng, 72-92. *Concurrent Pos:* NSF res initiation grant, 68-69; researcher, Naval Res Lab, 69-70; sci analyst, Ctr Naval Anal, Univ Rochester, Va, 69-71. *Mem:* Soc Naval Architects & Marine Engrs. *Res:* Ship hydrodynamics; propulsion; resistance; stability; fishtype propulsion by undulating plates. *Mailing Add:* 512 Southgate Dr Blacksburg VA 24061

SZENT-GYORGYI, ANDREW GABRIEL, BIOCHEMISTRY. *Current Pos:* PROF BIOL, BRANDEIS UNIV, 66- *Personal Data:* b Budapest, Hungary, May 16, 24; nat US; m 47; c 3. *Educ:* Univ Budapest, MD, 47. *Prof Exp:* Instr, Univ Budapest, 46-47; fel, Neurophysiol Inst, Copenhagen, 48; mem, Inst Muscle Res, Marine Biol Lab, Woods Hole, 48-62, instr physiol, 53-58; prof biophys, Dartmouth Med Sch, 62-66. *Concurrent Pos:* Am Heart Asn estab investr, 55-62; USPHS res career award, 62-66; head physiol course, Marine Biol Lab, Woods Hole, 67-71, trustee, 70-76 & 81- *Mem:* Soc Gen Physiol (pres, 70-71); fel AAAS; Am Soc Biol Chem; Biophys Soc (pres, 74-75). *Res:* Regulation of muscle contraction; structure of muscle proteins. *Mailing Add:* Dept Biol Brandeis Univ 415 South St Waltham MA 02254-9110. *Fax:* 781-736-3107; *E-Mail:* zentgyorgyi@binahoc.brandeis.edu

SZENTIRMAI, GEORGE, ELECTRICAL ENGINEERING, COMPUTER AIDED DESIGN. *Current Pos:* RETIRED. *Personal Data:* b Budapest, Hungary, Oct 8, 28; US citizen; m 52, 74, Irene Sharp; c Andrea & Susan. *Educ:* Budapest Tech Univ, dipl elec eng, 51 & Can Tech Sci, 55; Polytech Inst Brooklyn, PhD(elec eng), 63. *Honors & Awards:* Meritorious Serv Award, Inst Elec & Electronics Engrs. *Prof Exp:* From asst prof to assoc prof elec eng, Budapest Tech Univ, 54-56; design engr, Stand Tel & Cables, Ltd, Eng, 57-58; sect leader elec eng, Tel Mfg Co, Ltd, Eng, 58-59; mem tech staff, Bell Tel Labs, Inc, 59-64; supvr elec eng, 64-68; prof elec eng, Cornell Univ, 68-75; staff scientist, Electronics Res Ctr, Rockwell Int Corp, 75-80; vpres adv develop, Compact Div, Comsat Gen Integrated Systs, 80-82; pres, DGS Assocs Inc, 83-96. *Concurrent Pos:* Consult, Cent Phys Res Inst, Budapest, 55-56 & Bell Tel Labs, Inc, 68-75; adj prof elec sci & eng, Univ Calif, Los Angeles, 75-80. *Mem:* Fel Inst Elec & Electronics Engrs; Brit Inst Elec Engrs. *Res:* Synthesis and design of electrical filters and networks; computer-aided circuit and system analysis and design; microwave networks. *Mailing Add:* 772 Ames Ave Palo Alto CA 94303-4131

SZENTIVANYI, ANDOR, PHARMACOLOGY, ALLERGY. *Current Pos:* PROF PHARMACOL & CHMN DEPT, COL MED, UNIV SOUTH FLA, TAMPA, 70-, PROF INTERNAL MED, 73-, ASSOC DEAN GRAD STUDIES, 78-, DEAN, COL MED & DIR MED CTR, 80- *Personal Data:* b Miskolc, Hungary, May 4, 26; US citizen; m 48; c 2. *Educ:* Debrecen Univ Med, MD, 50. *Prof Exp:* Asst prof med, Univ Med Sch Budapest, 53-56; Rockefeller fel med, Univ Chicago, 57-59; USPHS fel allergy & immunol, Univ Colo, Denver, 59-60, asst prof med, 61-65, from asst prof to assoc prof Pharmacol & microbiol, 63-67; prof med & chmn, Dept Microbiol, Sch Med, Creighton Univ, 67-70. *Mem:* Am Asn Immunol; Am Acad Allergy; Am Soc Pharmacol & Exp Therapeut; Am Soc Clin Pharmacol; Am Col Clin Pharmacol. *Res:* Pharmacological aspects of immune and hypersensitivity mechanisms. *Mailing Add:* Dean Med PO Box 19 Univ SFla 12901 Bruce B Downs Blvd Tampa FL 33612-4742

SZEPE, STEPHEN, CHEMICAL ENGINEERING. *Current Pos:* ASSOC PROF ENERGY ENG, UNIV ILL, CHICAGO CIRCLE, 68- *Personal Data:* b Nagykoros, Hungary, June 21, 32; US citizen; m 58; c 1. *Educ:* Veszprem Tech Univ, Dipl Ing, 54; Ill Inst Technol, PhD(chem eng), 66. *Prof Exp:* Res chem eng, Hungarian Petrol & Gas Res Inst, Veszprem, 54-56 & Sinclair Res, Inc, Ill, 57-61; instr chem eng, Ill Inst Technol, 61-64; asst prof, Wash Univ, 65-68. *Mem:* AAAS; Am Chem Soc; Am Inst Chem Engrs; Catalysis Soc. *Res:* Chemical reaction engineering; kinetics and catalysis; optimization; process dynamics. *Mailing Add:* Dept Chem Eng Univ Ill Chicago 810 S Clinton St Chicago IL 60607

SZEPESI, BELA, NUTRITION, MOLECULAR BIOLOGY. *Current Pos:* RES CHEMIST, NUTRIT INST, SCI & EDUC ADMIN, USDA, 69- *Personal Data:* b Ozd, Hungary, Nov 19, 38; US citizen; m 61; c 3. *Educ:* Albion Col, BA, 61; Colo State Univ, MS, 64; Univ Calif, Davis, PhD(comp biochem), 68. *Mem:* Am Inst Nutrit; Brit Biochem Soc; Brit Nutrit Soc; Soc Exp Biol & Med. *Res:* Mechanism of overweight; control of gene expression in rat liver; disaccharide effect on enzyme induction; starvation-refeeding; hormone effect on rat liver enzymes; utilization of carp as food. *Mailing Add:* 2920 Tapered Lane Bowie MD 20715. *Fax:* 301-344-1062

SZEPESI, ZOLTAN PAUL JOHN, ELECTRONICS, SOLID STATE PHYSICS. *Current Pos:* RETIRED. *Personal Data:* b Sarosfa, Hungary, May 13, 12; nat US; m 42, Elisabeth V Dauda; c Juliette & Erna. *Educ:* Univ Szeged, BSc, 32, MSc, 34; Univ Budapest, PhD(physics), 37. *Hon Degrees:* Golden Diplom, Univ Eotvos Lorand, Budapest, 88. *Honors & Awards:* Notworthy Contribution Award, NASA, 70. *Prof Exp:* Mem staff, Inst Theoret Physics, Hungary, 34-36; physicist, Tungsram Res Lab, 36-45; engr, Hungarian Tel & Tel Inst, 45-46; physicist, Pulvari Lab, 46-47; res assoc, Grenoble, 47-51; sr physicist, Can Marconi Co, Que, 51-58; fel engr, Electronic Tube Div, Westinghouse Elec Corp, NY, 58-72, fel scientist, Westinghouse Res Lab, Pa, 72-77. *Concurrent Pos:* Res fel, CNRS France, 47-51; consult, Presby Univ Hosp, 78, Westinghouse Res Lab, 81-83, Panel Vision, 83-85 & Magnascreen, 89. *Mem:* Hon mem, Int Technol Inst, 91. *Res:* Compton effect of gamma rays; noise effects in electron tubes; wave guides; slot antennas; high frequency oscillators; photoconductors; solid state display panels; noise measurements of transistors. *Mailing Add:* 2611 Saybrook Dr Pittsburgh PA 15235-5131

SZEPTYCKI, PAWEL, MATHEMATICS. *Current Pos:* from asst prof to assoc prof, 61-67, PROF MATH, UNIV KANS, 67- *Personal Data:* b Lwow, Poland, Feb 10, 35; m 61; c 3. *Educ:* Univ Warsaw, MSc, 56; Univ SAfrica, PhD(math), 61. *Prof Exp:* Res officer math, SAfrican Coun Sci & Indust Res, 59-61. *Concurrent Pos:* Vis prof math, Univ Nice, 79-80, Polish Acad Sci, 80, Univ Kuwait, 87-88 & Univ Grenoble, 88-89. *Mem:* Am Math Soc. *Res:* Mathematical analysis. *Mailing Add:* Dept Math Univ Kans Lawrence KS 66045

SZER, WLODZIMIERZ, BIOCHEMISTRY. *Current Pos:* PROF BIOCHEM, SCH MED, NY UNIV, 68- *Personal Data:* b Warsaw, Poland, June 3, 24; m 48; c 2. *Educ:* Univ Lodz, MS, 50; Polish Acad Sci, PhD(biochem), 59. *Honors & Awards:* J K Parnas Award, Polish Biochem Soc. *Prof Exp:* Instr org chem, Univ Lodz, 51-53; res assoc, Inst Antibiotics, Poland, 54-56; asst prof biochem, Inst Biochem & Biophys, Polish Acad Sci, 59-62, dozent biochem, 63-67. *Concurrent Pos:* Jane Coffin Childs Mem Fund fel, Sch Med, NY Univ, 63-64; prin investr, US Pub Health Serv grantee, 71- *Mem:* Am Soc Biol Chemists; Harvey Soc. *Res:* Structure of polynucleotides; molecular mechanisms in gene expression; contributed numerous articles to professional scientific journals. *Mailing Add:* Dept Biochem NY Univ Med Ctr 550 First Ave New York NY 10016-6402. *Fax:* 212-263-8166

SZERB, JOHN CONRAD, PHYSIOLOGY. *Current Pos:* Lectr, Dalhousie Univ, 51-52; from asst prof to assoc prof, 52-63, prof pharmacol, 63-93, chmn, Dept Physiol & Biophys, 63-93, prof, Dept Physiol & Biophys, 77-93, EMER PROF, DALHOUSIE UNIV, 93- *Personal Data:* b Budapest, Hungary, Feb 24, 26; nat Can; m 57, Constance Dillam; c 2. *Educ:* Univ Munich, MD, 50. *Concurrent Pos:* Res fel, Pasteur Inst, Paris, 50-51; Nuffield fel, Cambridge Univ, 60-61, vis scientist, 70-71; mem, Med Res Coun Can, 65-70; vis prof, Duke Univ, 84. *Mem:* Soc Neurosci; Pharmacol Soc Can; Can Physiol Soc; fel Royal Col Physicians Can. *Res:* Release of transmitters and electrical activity in the central nervous system. *Mailing Add:* Dept Physiol & Biophys Dalhousie Univ Halifax NS B3H 4H6 Can. *E-Mail:* jszerb@dal.ca

SZERI, ANDRAS ZOLTAN, FLUID MECHANICS, TRIBOLOGY. *Current Pos:* PROF & CHMN, DEPT MECH ENG, UNIV DEL, 94-, ROBERT L SPENCER PROF, 95- *Personal Data:* b Nagyvarad, Hungary, June 6, 34; m 62, Mary J Parkinson; c Andrew, Elizabeth & Maria. *Educ:* Univ Leeds, BSc, 59, PhD(eng), 62. *Prof Exp:* Engr, Dept Appl Mech, Eng Elec Co, Eng, 62-64; prof fluid mech, Valparaiso Tech Univ, Chile, 64-67; from asst prof to assoc prof mech eng, Univ Pittsburgh, 67-77, prof mech eng, 77-94, prof math, 77-93, chmn, Dept Mech Eng, 84-87, William Kepler Whiteford prof eng, 90-94. *Concurrent Pos:* Consult, Westinghouse Res Labs, Pa, 67-82; assoc ed, J Tribol, 78-87, tech ed, 87-93; ext examr, Univ WIndies, 89-; mem, Res Comt Tribol, Am Soc Mech Engrs, 92. *Mem:* Fel Am Soc Mech Engrs; Am Acad Mech; Soc Eng Sci; Soc Natural Philos; Soc Rheol. *Res:* Laminar and turbulent internal flows; solution multiplicity; flow stability; non-Newtonian-fluids; convection; hydrodynamic lubrication; fluid inertia; heat transfer, non-Newtonian behavior, emulsion lubricants, metal working, bearing design. *Mailing Add:* Dept Mech Eng Univ Del Newark DE 19176

SZERI, ANDREW JOHN, FLUID DYNAMICS, NONLINEAR DYNAMICS. *Current Pos:* ACTG ASSOC PROF MECH ENG, UNIV CALIF, BERKELEY, 97- *Personal Data:* b Stafford, Eng, Jan 9, 64; US citizen. *Educ:* Univ Pittsburgh, BS, 84; Cornell Univ, MS, 87, PhD(theory & appl mech), 88. *Prof Exp:* Wiezmann res fel, Calif Inst Technol, 88-89; postdoctoral, Univ Calif, Santa Barbara, 89-91; from asst prof to assoc prof mech eng, Univ Calif, Irvine, 91-96. *Concurrent Pos:* Ed, J Nonlinear Sci, 93-; Young investr award, US Off Naval Res, 93-97. *Mem:* Am Phys Soc; Soc Rheology; Soc Indust & Appl Math; Acoust Soc Am. *Res:* Convective diffusive transport; nonlinear dynamics; perturbation and computational methods; optimal control; mechanics of bubbles; sonoluminescence; suspensions mixing. *Mailing Add:* Dept Mech Eng Univ Calif Berkeley CA 94720-1740. *E-Mail:* aszeri@me.berkeley.edu

SZETO, ANDREW Y J, BIOMEDICAL ENGINEERING, REHABILITATION ENGINEERING. *Personal Data:* b Jan 8, 49; m 79, Vivian Lim Ong; c Jonathan & David. *Educ:* Univ Calif, Los Angeles, BS, 71; Univ Calif, Berkeley, MS, 73, MEngr, 74; Univ Calif, Los Angeles, PhD(man-mach systs), 77. *Honors & Awards:* Outstanding Res Award, Sigma Xi, 81; Centennial Cert Except Contrib, Asn Supvr & Exec Engrs. *Prof Exp:* Postdoctoral scholar & res asst, Biotechnol Lab, Univ Calif, Los Angeles, 75-77; from asst prof to assoc prof, Dept Biomed Eng, La Tech Univ, Ruston, La, 77-82; dir neurol prod res & develop, La Jolla Technol, Inc, San Diego, Calif, 82-83; assoc prof, San Diego State Univ, San Diego, Calif, 83-87, prof & grad adv, dept elec & comput eng, 82-83. *Concurrent Pos:* Prin investr, NSF grant, 78-80; co-prin investr, Rehab Res & Develop, La State Div Voc Rehab, 79-82; comt chmn, Inst Elec & Electronics Engrs-Eng Med & Biol Soc, 83; chmn, Inst Elec & Electronics Engrs-Eng Med & Biol Soc, San Diego, 83 & 84, award comt, 84, 85, 86 & 87; vchmn, Biomed Eng Div, Am Soc Eng Educ, 84-85 & 85-86; consult elec stimulation, La Jolla Technol, Inc, 84-86; conf chair, Inst Elec & Electronics Engrs, Eng Med & Biol Soc, 93, rep-at-large, Advan Coop Counter Measure, 96 & vpres financial planning, 97-98. *Mem:* Sigma Xi; Inst Elec & Electronics Engrs Med & Biol Soc; Biomed Eng Soc; Human Factors Soc; Int Soc Prosthetics & Orthotics; Am Asn Eng Educ; sr mem Inst Elec & Electronics Engrs. *Res:* Biomedical engineering; electrical and computer engineering; human factors; assistive technology. *Mailing Add:* Dept Elec & Comput Eng San Diego State Univ 5500 Campanile Dr San Diego CA 92182-1309. *Fax:* 619-594-6005; *E-Mail:* aszeto@sciences.sdsu.edu

SZETO, GEORGE, MATHEMATICS. *Current Pos:* From asst prof to assoc prof, 68-75, PROF MATH, BRADLEY UNIV, 75- *Personal Data:* b Hong Kong, Aug 10, 38; m 68; c 1. *Educ:* United Col Hong Kong, BSc, 64; Purdue Univ, Lafayette, MA, 66, PhD(math), 68. *Honors & Awards:* Rutherburg Award Math. *Concurrent Pos:* NSF res grant, 72-73. *Mem:* Am Math Soc. *Res:* Separable algebras; Galois theory for rings. *Mailing Add:* Dept Math Bradley Univ Peoria IL 61625-0001

SZETO, HAZEL HON, FETAL PHARMACOLOGY. *Current Pos:* ASSOC PROF PHARMACOL, CORNELL UNIV MED SCH, 79- *Educ:* Cornell Univ, MD & PhD(pharmacol), 74. *Mailing Add:* Dept Pharmacol Cornell Univ Med Campus 1300 York Ave New York NY 10021-4805. *Fax:* 212-746-8835; *E-Mail:* hhszeto@cumc.cornell.edu

SZEWCZAK, MARK RUSSELL, NEUROPHARMACOLOGY, PSYCHOPHARMACOLOGY. *Current Pos:* Pharmacologist, Hoechst-Roussel Pharmaceut Inc, 75-82, res pharmacologist, 82-84, sr res pharmacologist, 84-86, res assoc, 86-88, sr res assoc, 88-90, group leader neurosci, 90-92, SR RES ASSOC, HOECHST-ROUSSEL PHARMACEUT INC, 93- *Personal Data:* b Philadelphia, Pa, July 28, 53; m 75; c 3. *Educ:* Villanova Univ, BS, 75; Rutgers Univ, MS, 82, PhD, 84. *Mem:* AAAS; Soc Neurosci; NY Acad Sci. *Res:* Neuropharmacology; psychopharmacology; neuroscience; pharmacology; drug development; treatments for chronic central nervous system disease. *Mailing Add:* 155 Greenwich St Stewartsville NJ 08886. *Fax:* 908-231-2413; *E-Mail:* szewczak@hrpl6.enet.hcc.com

SZEWCZUK, MYRON ROSS, AGING, INFLAMMATORY BOWEL DISEASE. *Current Pos:* from asst prof to assoc prof, 81-87, PROF IMMUNOL, QUEENS UNIV, 87-, ASSOC PROF MED, 88- *Personal Data:* b Allendorf, Ger, Sept 16, 46; Can citizen; m 73; c 2. *Educ:* Univ Guelph, Ont, BSc, 71, MSc, 72; Univ Windsor, Ont, PhD(biol), 75. *Prof Exp:* Res assoc immunol, Med Col, Cornell Univ, 75-78; asst prof, McMaster Univ, 78-81. *Concurrent Pos:* Killiam res fel immunol, 75-77; NIH res fel, 77-78; Med Res Coun Can scholar, 79-81; Geront Res Coun Ont scholar, 79-81; career scientist, Ont Ministry Health, 84-; invited speaker & NAm co-chair, Int Cong Geront, 85. *Mem:* Can Soc Immunol; Am Soc Microbiol; Am Asn Immunologists; exec mem Can Asn Geront; NY Acad Sci; Can Asn Gastroenterol; Can Asn AIDS Res. *Res:* Mechanisms of age-related decline in B- and T-cell immune responses; idiotype regulation of immunity; mucosal immunity; immune aspects of murine muscular dystrophy; humoral and cell-mediated cytotoxic mechanisms in human inflammatory bowel disease; immunology of HIV infection. *Mailing Add:* Dept Microbiol & Immunol Queen's Univ Kingston ON K7L 3N6 Can. *Fax:* 613-545-6796

SZEWCZYK, ALBIN A, MECHANICAL ENGINEERING, FLUID MECHANICS. *Current Pos:* from asst prof to assoc prof, 62-67, chmn, Dept Aerospace & Mech Eng, 78-88, PROF MECH ENG, UNIV NOTRE DAME, 67- *Personal Data:* b Chicago, Ill, Feb 26, 35; m 56; c Karen M, Lisa A, Andrea J & Terese H. *Educ:* Univ Notre Dame, BS, 56, MS, 58; Univ Md, PhD(fluid mech), 61. *Prof Exp:* Assoc engr, Lab Div, Northrop Aircraft Inc, 56-57; res fel, Inst Fluid Dynamics & Appl Math, Univ Md, 61-62. *Concurrent Pos:* Consult, Argonne Nat Lab, 68-80; fel, Univ Queensland, 71-72. *Mem:* Am Phys Soc; fel Am Soc Mech Engr; Am Soc Eng Educ; Am Inst Aeronaut & Astronaut. *Res:* Fluid mechanics; numerical fluid dynamics; experimental investigations of bluff body flows. *Mailing Add:* Dept Aerospace & Mech Eng Univ Notre Dame Notre Dame IN 46556. *E-Mail:* albin.a.szewczyk.1@nd.edu

SZIDAROVSZKY, FERENC, GAME THEORY, DYNAMIC ECONOMIC MODELS. *Current Pos:* PROF MATH, ECON UNIV, BUDAPEST, 86-, PROF SYSTS ENG, UNIV ARIZ, TUCSON, 85- *Personal Data:* b Budapest, Hungary, July 24, 45; m 69, Gabriella; c Ferenc, Anna, Miklos & Tamas. *Educ:* Eotvos Univ Sci, Budapest, BS, 65, MS, 68, PhD(math), 70; Budapest Econ Univ, PhD(econ), 77. *Hon Degrees:* DEngSci, Hungarian Acad Sci, 86, Can Math Sci, Hungarian Acad Sci, 75. *Prof Exp:* From asst prof to assoc prof numerical methods, Eotvos Univ Sci, Budapest, 68-77; prof & actg head comput sci, Agr Univ, Budapest, 77-86. *Concurrent Pos:* Vis assoc prof, Univ Ariz, 75-76, vis prof, 81-83 & 88-90; prof, Econ Univ, Budapest, 81-86; vis prof, Univ Tex, El Paso, 87-88, technion, Haifa, 84. *Res:* Dynamic systems, numerical methods, optimization and game theory with applications to natural resources management and economics. *Mailing Add:* Dept Systs & Indust Eng Univ Ariz PO Box 210020 Tucson AZ 85721-0020. *E-Mail:* szidar@tucson.sie.arizona.edu

SZIKLAI, GEORGE C(LIFFORD), ELECTRONICS, OPTICS. *Current Pos:* RETIRED. *Personal Data:* b Budapest, Hungary, July 9, 09; nat US; m 34; c 1. *Educ:* Munich Tech Univ, CE, 28; Univ Budapest, absolutorium, 30. *Prof Exp:* Asst chief engr, Aerovox Corp, NY, 30-32; chief engr, Polymet Mfg Corp, NY, 33-35; res & develop engr, Micamold Radio Corp, 35-38; mgr & chief engr, Am Radio H W Corp, 38-39; res & develop engr, Radio Corp Am, 39-56; asst to vpres eng, Westinghouse Elec Corp, 56-65, dir res commun & displays, Pa, 65-67; sr mem res lab, Lockheed Missiles & Space Co, 67-75. *Concurrent Pos:* Consult, US Dept Defense, 58-; independent consult, 76- *Mem:* Am Phys Soc; Optical Soc Am; fel Inst Elec & Electronics Engrs; NY Acad Sci; Sigma Xi. *Res:* Television; colorimetry; solid state circuitry. *Mailing Add:* 26900 St Francis Rd Los Altos Hills CA 94022

SZIKLAI, OSCAR, BIOLOGY, FOREST GENETICS. *Current Pos:* asst prof, Sopron Forestry Sch, Univ BC, 57-59, lectr forestry, 59-61, instr, 61-64, from asst prof to prof, 64-90, EMER PROF FOREST GENETICS, UNIV BC, 90- *Personal Data:* b Repashuta, Hungary, Oct 30, 24; Can citizen; m 49; c Steven, Peter, Leslie & Susan. *Educ:* Sopron Univ, Hungary, BSF, 46; Univ BC, MF, 61, PhD(forest genetics), 64. *Hon Degrees:* Dr, Univ Sopron, Hungary. *Honors & Awards:* Distinguished Serv Award, Int Union Forestry Res Orgn, 90. *Prof Exp:* Instr silvicult, Sopron Univ, Hungary, 46-47; asst forester, Hungarian Forest Serv, 47-49; res officer, Forest Res Inst, Budapest, 49-51; asst prof silvicult, Sopron Univ, Hungary, 51-56. *Concurrent Pos:* Nat Res Coun Can, Res grants forest genetics, 62-; exchange scientist, Forest Res Inst, Japan, 78; vis prof, Forest Genetics, Nanjing, China, 80. *Mem:* Can Inst Forestry. *Res:* Forest biology; selection and hybridization of Salix, Populus and Pseudotsuga genera; variation and inheritance studies in western Canadian conifers. *Mailing Add:* Dept Forest Sci Univ Brit Col 2075 Wes Brook Mall Vancouver BC V6T 1Z2 Can. *Fax:* 604-822-9102

SZILAGYI, JULIANNA ELAINE, HYPERTENSION, NEUROPEPTIDES. *Current Pos:* ASST PROF PHYSIOL, COL PHARMACOL, UNIV HOUSTON, 85- *Educ:* Ohio State Univ, PhD(physiol), 76. *Mailing Add:* Dept Pharmacol Univ Houston 4800 Calhoun Houston TX 77204-5515. *Fax:* 713-743-1229

SZILAGYI, MIKLOS NICHOLAS, ELECTRON & ION OPTICS, NEURAL NETWORKS. *Current Pos:* PROF, DEPT ELEC & COMPUT ENG, UNIV ARIZ, 82- *Personal Data:* b Budapest, Hungary, Feb 4, 36; m 57, 75, Julia S Levai; c Gabor & Zoltan. *Educ:* Tech Univ Leningrad, MS, 60; Electrotech Univ Leningrad, PhD(elec eng), 65; Tech Univ Budapest, DTech, 65. *Hon Degrees:* DSc, Hungarian Acad Sci, 79. *Honors & Awards:* Brody Prize, L Eotvos Phys Soc, 64. *Prof Exp:* Res asst, dept phys electronics, Tech Univ Leningrad, 58-60; res assoc, Res Inst Tech Physics, Hungarian Acad Sci, Budapest, 60-66; head, Lab Electron Optics, Tech Univ Budapest, 66-71; prof & head, dept phys sci, K Kando Col Elec Eng, Budapest, 71-79, col rector, 71-74; vis prof, Inst Physics, Univ Aarhus, Denmark, 79-81; vis sr res assoc, Sch Appl & Eng Physics, Cornell Univ, 81-82. *Concurrent Pos:* Sci adv, Nat Inst Neurosurg, Budapest, 66-70; vis scholar, Enrico Fermi Inst, Univ Chicago, dept elec eng & Lawrence Berkeley Lab, Univ Calif, comput sci dept & Stanford Linear Accelerator Ctr, Stanford Univ, 76-77; fel, UN Indust Develop Orgn, 76; consult, Ger Electron Synchrotron, Hamburg, WGer, 80-81; vis prof, dept appl physics, Univ Heidelberg & Max Planck Inst Nuclear Physics, Heidelberg, WGer, 84; vis prof, Comput Sci Dept, Univ Aahrus, Denmark, 88, 89 & 90 & Dept Appl Physics, Tech Univ, Neth, 88-89. *Mem:* Sr mem Inst Elec & Electronics Engrs; Am Phys Soc; Int Soc Hybrid Microelectronics; Europ Soc Stereotactic & Functional Neurosurg; L Eotvos Phys Soc; J Neumann Soc Comput Sci; Danish Phys Soc; Danish Eng Soc. *Res:* Electron and ion optics; microelectronics; physical electronics; computer-aided design; microfabrication of integrated circuits; biomedical engineering; artificial intelligence; expert systems; neural networks; computer simulation of social phenomena. *Mailing Add:* Dept Elec & Comput Eng Univ Ariz Tucson AZ 85721. *Fax:* 520-621-8076; *E-Mail:* szilagyi@ece.arizona.edu

SZIRMAY, LESLIE V, CHEMICAL & NUCLEAR ENGINEERING. *Current Pos:* from asst prof to assoc prof, 69-84, PROF & CHMN CHEM & NUCLEAR ENG DEPT, YOUNGSTOWN STATE UNIV, 84- *Personal Data:* b Eger, Hungary, Nov 13, 23; US citizen; m 62. *Educ:* Eotvos Lorand Univ, Budapest, Dipl chem, 49; Univ Detroit, MS, 62; Iowa State Univ, ME, 67; Univ Denver, PhD(chem eng), 69. *Prof Exp:* Process engr, Hungarian Sulphuric Acid Factory, 48-49; res engr, Hungarian Mineral Oil Res Inst, Budapest & Veszprem, 49-54, Nitrogen Works of Austria, 55-56, Esso Res Labs, Ont, 56, Palm Oil Recovery, Inc, 56-58 & Falconbridge Nickel Mines Ltd, 58-60; develop engr, Can Gen Elec, 62-64; asst, Iowa State Univ, 64-67; instr chem & nuclear eng, Univ Denver, 67-69. *Concurrent Pos:* Consult, Atomic Energy Comn Can, 62-64, De Havilland Aircraft Can Ltd, 64 & Dravo Eng, 79-; US Atomic Energy Comn fel, Univ Mo-Rolla, 71; vis prof, Polytech Toulouse, France, 88-89. *Mem:* Am Inst Chem Engrs; Am Chem Soc; Am Nuclear Soc. *Res:* Gas separation; exchange adsorption; coal liquefaction. *Mailing Add:* 948 Winona Dr Youngstown OH 44511-1405

SZKODY, PAULA, CATACLYSMIC VARIABLES, ACCRETION DISKS. *Current Pos:* res assoc, Univ Wash, 75-82, sr res assoc, 82-83, res assoc prof, 83-91, res prof, 91-93, PROF ASTRON, UNIV WASH, 93- *Personal Data:* b Detroit, Mich, July 17, 48; m 76, Donald E Brownlee II; c Allison & Carson. *Educ:* Mich State Univ, BS, 70; Univ Wash, MS, 72, PhD(astron), 75. *Honors & Awards:* Annie J Cannon Award, 78. *Concurrent Pos:* Vis scientist, Kitt Peak Nat Observ, 76; vis instr astron, Univ Calif, Los Angeles, 77, adj asst prof, 80 & 81; vis asst prof, Univ Hawaii, 78; vis assoc, Calif Inst Technol, 78, 79 & 80. *Mem:* Fel AAAS; Am Astron Soc; Am Asn Variable Star Observers; Int Astron Union; Astron Soc of Pac. *Res:* Ground and satellite data on close binary stars with mass transfer; physical understanding of the accretion process and the effects on the stars involved. *Mailing Add:* Dept Astron Box 351580 Univ Wash Seattle WA 98195. *Fax:* 206-685-0403; *E-Mail:* szkody@astro.washington.edu

SZLYK-MODROW, PATRICIA CAROL, RESPIRATORY CONTROL & CIRCULATION, THERMOREGULATION. *Current Pos:* co-comdr, 89-91, CAPT, PHYSIOLOGIST & BIOCHEMIST, USAR, 85-, NUCLEAR SCI OFF, 91-; RES PHYSIOLOGIST, US ARMY RES INST ENVIRONMED, NATICK, MASS, 83- *Personal Data:* b Worcester, Mass, Dec 24, 52; m, Harold E III; c Eric. *Educ:* Elmira Col, NY, BA, 74; State Univ NY, Buffalo, PhD(physiol), 80. *Prof Exp:* Res asst pharmacol, Worcester Found Exp Biol, 74-75; lectr physiol, State Univ NY, Buffalo, 77-78 & Queen's Univ, Ont, 80-83. *Concurrent Pos:* Fel, Can Heart Found, Kingston, Ont, 81-83; animal use comnr, US Army Res Inst Environ Med, 83-85, lectr heat res, 84-; reviewer, US Army Res Contracts, 83- & Aviation Space & Environ Med, 85-; contract officer, Inst Chem Defense, 84-88; consult, Dept Defense, 84-; sci fair judge, Int Fair & State, Dept Defense, 88-; Sci Rev Comn, US Army Res Inst Environ Med, 90-; nat deleg, Natick Chap, Sigma Xi, 90. *Mem:* Am Physiol Soc; Can Physiol Soc; NY Acad Sci; Sigma Xi (pres, 90-91); Reserve Officers Asn. *Res:* Examine mechanisms underlying fluid shifts and cardiorespiratory responses to hypoxia, hypocapnia, heat stress and dehydration; provide doctrine for prevention, diagnosis and treatment of dehydration and heat injury. *Mailing Add:* Szlyk-Modrow PO Box 1907 Frederick MD 21702

SZMANT, HERMAN HARRY, polymer chemistry, for more information see previous edition

SZONNTAGH, EUGENE L(ESLIE), ARCHAEOMETRY, INDUSTRIAL HYGIENE. *Current Pos:* COURTESY PROF & MGR ENVIRON FIELD SAMPLING & ANALYSIS LAB, COL PUB HEALTH, UNIV OF SOUTH FLA, 86- *Personal Data:* b Budapest, Hungary, July 31, 24; US citizen; m 50, Nora Jenser; c Dezso & Thomas. *Educ:* Budapest Tech Univ, MEng Sci, 48, PhD(anal chem), 75. *Honors & Awards:* IR-100 Award, Indust Res, 62; Eng Achievement Award, Honeywell, Inc, 74, Star Inventor, 83. *Prof Exp:* Jr chem engr, Hungarian State RR, 48-50; asst prof anal chem, Veszprem Tech Univ, 50-52, assoc prof, 52-56, head electro-chem div, Dept Chem Technol, 56; Rockefeller res fel instrumental anal, Vienna Tech Univ, 57; develop engr, Leeds & Northrup Co, 57-61, develop specialist, 61-62, scientist, 62-63, sr scientist, 63-72; dir, Continuing Educ Inc, 72; prin eng, 73-75, in charge Chem & Mat Labs, Process Control Div, Honeywell, Inc, 75-82, prin eng, avionics, 82-86. *Concurrent Pos:* Consult, Res Inst Chem Indust & Hungarian Petrol & Natural Gas Res Inst, Veszprem, 51-56 & Process Control Div, Honeywell, Inc, 72. *Mem:* Am Chem Soc; sr mem Instrument Soc Am; Am Indust Hygiene Asn. *Res:* Materials testing and analysis; classical and instrumental analytical chemistry; electrical and electronic measurements; polarography; liquid and gas chromatography; instrumental process analysis; electrochemical sensors; archaeometry; industrial hygiene; mercury vapor toxicity; corrosion. *Mailing Add:* 14538 Maplewood Dr N Largo FL 34644-5023. *Fax:* 813-595-6948

SZONYI, GEZA, APPLIED STATISTICS. *Current Pos:* APPL STATISTICIAN & HEAD CO, SZONYI ASSOCS, 85- *Personal Data:* b Budapest, Hungary, Feb 7, 19; US citizen; m 45, Lilly Wolffers; c Petra & David M. *Educ:* Univ Zurich, PhD, 44. *Prof Exp:* Res chemist, W Stark AG, Switz, 45-47; info scientist & head co, Chemolit, 47-51; res chemist, Can Industs, Ltd, 51-53 & Barrett Div, Allied Chem & Dye Corp, 53-57; lit scientist, Socony Mobile Oil Co, Inc, 57-58; info res chemist, Atlas Chem Industs, Inc, 58-64; chief lit chemist, Ciba Corp, NJ, 64-69; sr scientist res comput group, Polaroid Corp, 69-85. *Concurrent Pos:* Adv, Mass Manpower Comn; invited speaker, Simmons Col, Mass Inst Technol, Philip Morris Co & Inst Technol & Higer Studies, Monterrey, Mex; appl statistician, Mass Inst Technol Ctr Adv Eng Study. *Mem:* Am Chem Soc; Sigma Xi; Am Statist Asn. *Res:* Chemical computer operations, molecular mechanics, computer aided synthesis, reaction libraries; usage of applied statistics, particularly experimental design, to solve scientific and engineering problems; scientific computer programming; computerized information retrieval systems; paper chemistry and technology; catalysis; physical and pharmaceutical chemistry; improved information handling; development of computer software for applied statistics; computer simulation and chemical computer graphics; organic chemistry. *Mailing Add:* 177 Cedar St Lexington MA 02173

SZOSTAK, JACK WILLIAM, RIBOZYMES, ORIGIN OF LIFE. *Current Pos:* PROF GENETICS, MASS GEN HOSP & HARVARD MED SCH, 79- *Personal Data:* b London, Eng, Nov 9, 52; Can citizen; m 93, Terri L McCormick. *Educ:* McGill Univ, BSc, 72; Cornell Univ, PhD(biochem), 77. *Honors & Awards:* Nat Acad Scis Award, Molecular Biol, 94. *Prof Exp:* Fel biochem, Cornell Univ, 77-79. *Mem:* AAAS; Am Chem Soc. *Res:* Genetic analysis of ribozyme structure and activity and in vitro evolution of new ribozymes. *Mailing Add:* Dept Molecular Biol Mass Gen Hosp Boston MA 02114. *E-Mail:* szostak@frodo.mgh.harvard.edu

SZOSTAK, ROSEMARIE, ZEOLITE SYNTHESIS, MOLECULAR SIEVES. *Current Pos:* CHIEF SCIENTIST, GA INST TECHNOL, 83- *Personal Data:* b Waukegan, Ill, Oct 7, 52. *Educ:* Georgetown Univ, BSc, 74; Univ Calif, Los Angeles, PhD(inorg chem), 82. *Prof Exp:* Res chemist, Mobil Oil Corp, 79-82; fel, Worcester Polytech Inst, 82-83. *Mem:* Am Chem Soc; Electron Micros Soc; NAm Catalysis Soc; Brit Zeolite Asn; Mat Res Soc. *Res:* Synthesis and characterization of new molecular sieve and zeolite materials for catalytic and absorbent applications. *Mailing Add:* Clark Atlanta Univ 223 James P Brawley Dr Atlanta GA 30314

SZOT, ROBERT JOSEPH, REPRODUCTION TOXICOLOGY, GENETIC TOXICOLOGY. *Current Pos:* INDEPENDENT CONSULT TOXICOL, 96- *Personal Data:* b Passaic, NJ, Sept 23, 38; m 63, Daria M Huk; c Stephen, Andrea, Ellen & Carrie. *Educ:* Rutgers Univ, BA, 60; Long Island Univ, MS, 63; Harvard Univ, ScD, 70. *Prof Exp:* Res scientist, E R Squibb & Sons, 62-67; group leader, Burroughs Wellcome Co, 70-77; dir toxicol, Schering Plough Corp, 77-89; sr assoc toxicol, Psizer, 89-91; sr dir toxicol, R W Johnson Parmaceut Res Inst, 91-96. *Mem:* Am Col Toxicol; Soc Toxicol; Environ Mutagen Soc; Europ Soc Toxicol; NY Acad Sci; Am Bd Toxicol. *Res:* General, reproductive and genetic toxicology pertaining to the development of new drugs. *Mailing Add:* 2 Rolling Lane Flemington NJ 08822. *Fax:* 908-218-0668

SZPANKOWSKI, WOJCIECH, ANALYSIS ALGORITHMS, PERFORMANCE EVALUATION. *Current Pos:* from asst prof to assoc prof, 85-92, PROF COMPUT SCI, PURDUE UNIV, WEST LAFAYETTE, 92. *Personal Data:* b Wapno, Poland, Feb 18, 52; m 78; c 2. *Educ:* Tech Univ, Gdansk, BA & MA, 76, PhD(telecommun & comput sci), 80. *Prof Exp:* Asst prof telecommun, Tech Univ, Gdansk, 80-83; asst prof comput sci, McGill Univ, Montreal, 83-89. *Concurrent Pos:* Vis scientist, Inria, Rocquencourt, France, 89; invited prof, Inria, France, 92-93. *Mem:* Inst Elec & Electronics Engrs; Soc Indust & Appl Math. *Res:* Performance evaluation; analysis and design of algorithms; stability problems in distributed systems; multiaccess protocols queueing theory; operations research; applied probability. *Mailing Add:* Dept Comput Sci Purdue Univ West Lafayette IN 47907. *Fax:* 765-494-0739; *E-Mail:* spa@cs.purdue.edu

SZPILKA, ANTHONY M, CONDENSED MATTER THEORY. *Current Pos:* PROF MATH, CARROLL COL. *Personal Data:* b Detroit, Mich, Nov 3, 57. *Educ:* Princeton Univ, BS, 79; Cornell Univ, PhD(appl physics), 85. *Prof Exp:* Staff physicist, Gen Elec Co, 85-87; instr physics, Univ Utah, 87- *Mem:* Am Phys Soc. *Res:* Ordering in high temperature superconductors and quantized hall effects. *Mailing Add:* 1616 Hudson St Helena MT 59601

SZPOT, BRUCE F, BATTERY EQUIPMENT DESIGN, SYSTEMS COST ANALYSIS. *Current Pos:* BRAKE ENGR, HAYES INDUST BRAKE, 87- *Personal Data:* b Milwaukee, Wis, Feb 15, 45; m 72; c 4. *Educ:* Marquette Univ, BE & ME, 68, MBA, 72. *Prof Exp:* Motor control engr, Square D Co, 65-68; thick film engr, Allen Bradley Co, 68-72, thin film engr, 73-74, prod engr, 74-80; battery engr, Johnson Controls, 80-87. *Res:* Battery manufacturing process analysis and caliper braking systems analysis. *Mailing Add:* 4752 N Cumberland Blvd Milwaukee WI 53211

SZPUNAR, CAROLE BRYDA, ORGANIC CHEMISTRY, ANALYTICAL CHEMISTRY. *Current Pos:* MEM STAFF, ESSO INT AM, INC, 80- *Personal Data:* b Chicago, Ill, July 8, 49; m 72. *Educ:* Univ Ill, Chicago, BS, 71; Northwestern Univ, MS, 75, PhD(chem), 77. *Prof Exp:* Chemist soil, water & bldg mat, Novak, Dempsey & Assocs, Inc, 71-73; fel, Northwestern Univ, 74-76; res chemist coal, Exxon Res & Eng Co, 77- *Mem:* Am Chem Soc; Sigma Xi. *Res:* Coal analysis, research, and characterization. *Mailing Add:* Argonne Natl Lab 9700 Cass Ave Bldg 900 Argonne IL 60439-4803

SZTANKAY, ZOLTAN GEZA, ELECTRO-OPTICS. *Current Pos:* SUPVRY PHYSICIST, ARMY RES LAB, 71- *Personal Data:* b Cleveland, Ohio, Apr 17, 37; m 70, Anda Stager. *Educ:* Valparaiso Univ, BS, 59; Univ Wis, MS, 61, PhD(physics), 65. *Prof Exp:* Physicist, Harry Diamond Labs, 65-71. *Mem:* Inst Elec & Electronics Engrs; Am Phys Soc; Optical Soc Am. *Res:* Development of electrooptical, laser and infrared sensing systems, especially three-dimensional imaging laser radar; the propagation and back-scatter of laser beams in the atmosphere; the phenomology of target and clutter returns and the detection of targets in clutter. *Mailing Add:* EO/IR Technol Br Army Res Lab 2800 Powder Mill Rd Adelphi MD 20783-1197. *Fax:* 301-394-5270; *E-Mail:* sztankay@arl.mil

SZTEIN, MARCELO BENJAMIN, LYMPHOKINES, TRYPANOSOMA. *Current Pos:* res fel, George Washington Univ, 82-83, asst res prof, 83-84, dir, Flow Cytometry Fac, 86-88, assoc prof, IDEM, 88-89, ASSOC PROF HEMAT/GMC, DEPT MED, GEORGE WASHINGTON UNIV, 84-, ASSOC PROF, PEDIAT CHIEF, CELLULAR IMMUNOL & FLOW CYTOMETRY SECT, CTR VACCINE DEVELOP, 89- *Personal Data:* b Buenos Aires, Arg, Mar 11, 55; m 79; c 2. *Educ:* Nicolas Avellaneda Sch, Arg, BS, 70; Univ Buenos Aires, MD, 76. *Prof Exp:* Asst investr endocrinol, Reproduction Res Ctr, Univ Buenos Aires, 71-72; teaching asst histol & cytol, II Cathedral, Sch Med & asst investr immunol, Reproduction Res Ctr, 73-79, jr fel, Nat Coun Sci Res, 77-79, sr fel, 79; vis fel immunol, Lab Microbiol-Immunol, Nat Inst Dent Res, NIH, 79-82. *Concurrent Pos:* Prin investr, Arg Asn against Cancer grant, 80-81 & NIH grant, George Washington Univ, 84-85, 86-89. *Mem:* Am Asn Immunol; Fedn Am Soc Exp Biol; NY Acad Sci; AAAS. *Res:* Basic mechanisms involved in the regulation of immune response in health and disease with particular emphasis on lymphokines and flow cytometry; biochemistry; malaria; flow cytometry. *Mailing Add:* Pediat CMI Ctr Vaccine Develop Univ Md Baltimore 685 W Baltimore St Rm 480 Baltimore MD 21201-1116. *Fax:* 410-706-6205

SZTUL, ELIZABETH SABINA, MEMBRANE BIOGENESIS, INTRACELLULAR TRAFFIC. *Current Pos:* ASST PROF, PRINCETON UNIV, 89- *Personal Data:* b Sept 16, 55; m 80; c 1. *Educ:* Yale Univ, PhD(cell biol), 84. *Concurrent Pos:* Res scientist, Dept Cell Biol, Yale Univ. *Mailing Add:* Dept Cellular Biol Univ Ala Med Sci 1918 Univ Blvd Rm 840 Birmingham AL 35294-0005

SZU, SHOUSUN CHEN, MOLECULAR BIOPHYSICS. *Current Pos:* vis fel biophys, NIH, 75-78, vis assoc biophys, Nat Cancer Inst, 78, sr staff fel, 80-87, RES CHEMIST, NIH, 88- *Personal Data:* b Chunking, China, Sept 25, 45; m 72; c 3. *Educ:* Taiwan Prov Cheng-Kung Univ, BS, 66; Mich Tech Univ, MS, 67; Univ Calif, Davis, PhD(physics), 74. *Prof Exp:* Res assoc polymer hydrodynamics, Dept of Chem, Univ NC, 73-75. *Mem:* AAAS; Biophys Soc; NY Acad Sci. *Res:* Macromolecular conformations, including poly-peptide and polynucleotide kinetics and protein foldings; macromolecular hydrodynamics; polysaccharide vaccine. *Mailing Add:* Lab Develop & Molecular Immunity Nat Inst Child Health & Human Develop Bldg 6 Rm 1A06 Bethesda MD 20892

SZUBINSKA, BARBARA, CELL BIOLOGY. *Current Pos:* res assoc, 68-73, RES ASST PROF ELECTRON MICROS, SCH MED, UNIV WASH, 73- *Personal Data:* b Stanislawow, Poland, Oct 4, 32; m 70. *Educ:* Jagiellonian Univ, Krakow, MS, 57, PhD(zool), 61. *Prof Exp:* From instr to asst prof histol, Jagiellonian Univ, Krakow, 59-66; res asst electron micros, Sch Med, Umea Univ, Sweden, 66-68. *Concurrent Pos:* Rockefeller Found fel, Sch Med, Univ Wash, 63-64. *Mem:* Am Soc Cell Biol. *Res:* Ultrastructure of cells and plasma membrane; wound healing in single cells. *Mailing Add:* PO Box 95829 Seattle WA 98145-2829

SZUCHET, SARA, PHYSICAL BIOCHEMISTRY. *Current Pos:* PROF NEUROL & NEUROBIOL, UNIV CHICAGO, 76- *Personal Data:* b Poland. *Educ:* Univ Buenos Aires, MSc, 56; Cambridge Univ, PhD(phys chem), 63. *Prof Exp:* Res asst, Lister Inst Prev Med, Univ London, 57-58; postdoctoral fel chem, Princeton Univ, 63-66; res assoc biol, State Univ NY, Buffalo, 66-68, asst prof biophys sci, 69-76. *Mem:* NY Acad Sci; Brit Biophys Soc; Biophys Soc; AAAS; Am Soc Cell Biol; Am Soc Neurochem. *Res:* Biology of oligodendrocytes; cell-cell interaction and molecular events that signal myelination in the central nervous system; characterization of receptors involved in myelination; role of oligodendrocytes in multiple sclerosis. *Mailing Add:* Dept Neurol MC 2030 Univ Chicago 5841 S Maryland Ave Chicago IL 60637-1463

SZUHAJ, BERNARD F, BIOCHEMISTRY, LIPID CHEMISTRY. *Current Pos:* scientist, Res Dept, 68-73, DIR FATS & OILS RES, FOOD RES, CENT SOYA CO, INC, 73- *Personal Data:* b Lilly, Pa, Nov 27, 42; m 64; c 3. *Educ:* Pa State Univ, BS, 64, MS, 66, PhD(biochem), 69. *Prof Exp:* Asst biochem, Pa State Univ, 64-68. *Mem:* AAAS; Am Oil Chem Soc; Am Chem Soc; Inst Food Technol; Sci Res Soc NAm. *Res:* Basic lipid research; research and development of fats and oil products; analytical biochemistry. *Mailing Add:* 1946 W Cook Rd Fort Wayne IN 46818-1166

SZUMSKI, STEPHEN ALOYSIUS, MEDICAL ADMINISTRATION. *Current Pos:* RETIRED. *Personal Data:* b DuPont, Pa, Dec 26, 19; m 46; c 10. *Educ:* Univ Ariz, BS, 47, MS, 49; Pa State Univ, PhD(bact), 51. *Prof Exp:* Microbiologist & group leader, Am Cyanamid Co, 51-65, assoc dir med adv dept, Lederle Labs, 65-85. *Mem:* Am Soc Microbiologists. *Res:* Process development; microbial production of antibiotics; vitamins; enzymes; vaccines; reagins. *Mailing Add:* 106 Hunt Ave Pearl River NY 10965

SZURSZEWSKI, JOSEPH HENRY, GASTROINTESTINAL PHYSIOLOGY, NEUROSCIENCES. *Current Pos:* NIH fel, dept physiol & biophys, Grad Sch, 66-68, assoc consult, Med Sch, 71-73, from asst prof to assoc prof pharmacol, 71-77, asst prof pharmacol, 73-77, CONSULT PHYSIOL, DEPT PHYSIOL & BIOPHYS, MED SCH, MAYO CLINIC, 73-, ASSOC PROF PHARMACOL, 77-, PROF PHYSIOL, 77-, CHMN DEPT, 83- *Personal Data:* b Pittsburgh, Pa, May 25, 40; c 2. *Educ:* Duquesne Univ, BS, 62; Univ Ill, Urbana, PhD(physiol), 66; Univ Oxford, BSc, 71. *Honors & Awards:* Bowditch Award, Am Physiol Soc, 79; Distinguished Invest, Mayo Found, 86; Distinguished Achievement Award, Am Gastroenterol Asn, 87. *Prof Exp:* Teaching asst, dept physiol & biophysics, Univ Ill, Urbana, 63-65, fel, 64-65, NIH fel, 65-66. *Concurrent Pos:* Fulbright-Hays scholar, Monash Univ, Australia, 69-70; Burn fel pharmacol, Oxford Univ, 70-71; estab investr, Am Heart Asn, 74-79. *Mem:* Am Physiol Soc; Am Gastroenterological Asn; Brit Physiol Soc; Soc Neurosci; Sigma Xi. *Res:* Cellular control of gastrointestinal motor function. *Mailing Add:* Dept Physiol & Biophys Mayo Clin 200 First St SW Rochester MN 55905-0001. *Fax:* 507-284-0266; *E-Mail:* gijoe@mayo.edu

SZUSZ, PETER, MATHEMATICS. *Current Pos:* prof, 66-94, EMER PROF MATH, STATE UNIV NY, STONY BROOK, 94- *Personal Data:* b Novisad, Yugoslavia, Nov 11, 24; m 73, Margaret Wenner. *Educ:* Eotvos Lorand Univ, Budapest, PhD(math), 51; Hungarian Acad Sci, DMS, 62. *Prof Exp:* Res fel math, Math Inst, Hungarian Acad Sci, 50-65; vis prof, Mem Univ, 65; vis assoc prof, Pa State Univ, 65-66. *Mem:* Am Math Soc. *Mailing Add:* PO Box 877 Glen NH 03838. *E-Mail:* peters2@juno.com

SZUSZCZEWICZ, EDWARD PAUL, IONOSPHERIC PHYSICS, PLASMA PHYSICS. *Current Pos:* res physicist ionospheric physics, 72-75, SUPVRY RES PHYSICIST IONOSPHERIC PHYSICS & ACTIVE PLASMA EXP SPACE, E D HULBURT CTR SPACE RES, NAVAL RES LAB, 75- *Personal Data:* b Philadelphia, Pa, June 19, 41; m 64; c 4. *Educ:* St Joseph's Col, Pa, BS, 63; St Louis Univ, PhD(physics), 69. *Prof Exp:* Alexander von Humboldt Found guest scientist plasma discharges, Physics Inst, Univ Wurzburg, WGer, 69-70; Nat Acad Sci resident res assoc plasma diag, Goddard Spaceflight Ctr, NASA, 70-72. *Concurrent Pos:* Navy sci rep coord activ int magnespheric study, Int Comt Atmospheric Sci, 75-76. *Mem:* Am Phys Soc; Am Geophys Union; Sigma Xi. *Res:* Experimental investigation of turbulent ionospheric plasma phenomena, their fundamental causal mechanisms, and their coupling to solar, geophysical and man-made controls. *Mailing Add:* 10507 Cowberry Ct Vienna VA 22182

SZUTKA, ANTON, analytical chemistry, for more information see previous edition

SZWARC, MICHAEL, PHYSICAL CHEMISTRY. *Current Pos:* RETIRED. *Personal Data:* b Bedzin, Poland, June 9, 09; m 33; c 3. *Educ:* Warsaw Polytech Inst, ChE, 32; Hebrew Univ, Israel, PhD(org chem), 42; Univ Manchester, PhD(phys chem), 47, DSc, 49. *Hon Degrees:* DSc, Univ Leuven, Belg, 74, Uppsala Univ, Swed, 75, Louis Pasteur Univ, France. *Honors & Awards:* Baker Lectr, Cornell Univ, 72; Int Plastic Eng Gold Medal, 76; Benjamin Franklin Gold Medal, Franklin Inst, 78'; Am Chem Soc Award, 70; Herman Mark Award, 90. *Prof Exp:* Asst, Hebrew Univ, Israel, 34-42; lectr, Univ Manchester, 47-52; prof phys & polymer chem, State Univ NY Col Environ Sci & Forestry, 52-56, res prof, 56-64, distinguished prof phys & polymer chem, 64-, dir, Polymer Res Ctr, 67-84; dept chem, Col Environ Sci, State Univ NY, 84. *Concurrent Pos:* Vis prof, Uppsala Univ, Sweden, 69-70; lectr, Univ Ottawa, Can. *Mem:* Am Chem Soc; fel Royal Soc. *Res:* Chemical kinetics; bond dissociation energies; reactivities of radicals; polymerization reactions; living polymers; reactivities of ions and ion-pairs; electron-transfer processes in aprotic solvents. *Mailing Add:* 1176 Santa Luisa Sr Solana Beach CA 92075-1614

SZYBALSKI, WACLAW, BIOCHEMISTRY, MOLECULAR GENETICS. *Current Pos:* PROF ONCOL, MCARDLE LAB CANCER RES, MED SCH, UNIV WIS-MADISON, 60- *Personal Data:* b Lwow, Poland, Sept 9, 21; nat US; m 55, Elisabeth Hunter. *Educ:* LWOW Polytech Inst, ChEng, 44; Gliwice Polytech Inst, MChEng, 45; Gdansk Technol Inst, DSc, 49. *Hon Degrees:* Dr, Univ Marie Curie, Lublin, Poland, 80, Univ Gdansk, Poland, 89. *Honors & Awards:* K-A-Forster Award, German Acad Sci, 71; A Jurzykowski Found Award Biol, 77. *Prof Exp:* Dir chem, Agr Res Sta, Konskie, Poland, 44-45; asst prof indust microbiol & biotechnol, Gdansk Inst Technol, 45-49; pilot plant mgr antibiotics, Wyeth Inc, West Chester, Pa, 50-51; staff mem microbiol genetics, Cold Spring Harbor Lab, NY, 51-54; assoc prof, Inst Microbiol, Rutgers Univ, 54-60. *Concurrent Pos:* Vis prof, Inst Technol, Copenhagen, Denmark, 47-48 & 49-50; dir regional lab, Bur Stand, Gdask, Poland, 48-49; chmn, Gordon Conf Nucleic Acids, 72; mem adv NIH panel recombinant DNA, 75-77. *Mem:* AAAS; Am Soc Microbiol; Am Asn Biol Chemists; hon mem Polish Asn Microbiol; hon mem Polish Med Alliance; Genetic Soc; hon mem Ital Soc Exp Biol. *Res:* Molecular biology; molecular genetics; control of transcription and DNA replication; genetic and physical mapping; universal and rare-cutting restriction enzymes; construction of regulatory circuits; ordered cloning and sequencing of the entire D range genomes. *Mailing Add:* Univ Wis Med Sch 450 N Randall Ave Madison WI 53706-1506. *Fax:* 608-262-2824; *E-Mail:* szybalsk@macc.wisc.edu

SZYDLIK, PAUL PETER, PHYSICS. *Current Pos:* from asst prof to assoc prof, 67-72, PROF PHYSICS, STATE UNIV NY COL PLATTSBURGH, 72- *Personal Data:* b Duryea, Pa, Aug 1, 33; m 62; c 6. *Educ:* Univ Scranton, BS, 54; Univ Pittsburgh, MS, 57; Cath Univ Am, PhD(physics), 64. *Prof Exp:* Res asst nuclear physics, Radiation Lab, Univ Pittsburgh, 54-56; nuclear engr, Knolls Atomic Power Lab, Gen Elec Co, 56-60; res asst cosmic ray physics, Cath Univ Am, 60-63, theoretical nuclear physics, 63-64; res assoc theoret nuclear physics, Univ Calif, Davis, 64-66; appl physicist, Knolls Atomic Power Lab, Gen Elec Co, 66-67. *Concurrent Pos:* Vis res prof physics, Univ Fla, 73-74; vis prof mech eng, State Univ NY, Stony Brook, 78; guest physicist, Brookhaven Nat Lab, 78; fac fel, NASA-Lewis, 85-88; vis res physicist, Univ Durham (UK), 86. *Mem:* Am Phys Soc; Am Solar Energy Soc; Am Asn Phys Teachers. *Res:* Solar energy; transport in semiconductors. *Mailing Add:* Dept Physics State Univ NY Col Plattsburgh NY 12901-2697. *Fax:* 518-564-3152

SZYGENDA, STEPHEN ANTHONY, COMPUTER SCIENCE, ELECTRICAL ENGINEERING. *Current Pos:* DEAN, SCH ENG, UNIV ALA, BIRMINGHAM, 96- *Personal Data:* b McKeesport, Pa, Oct 5, 38; m 60; c 3. *Educ:* Fairleigh Dickinson Univ, BS, 64; Northwestern Univ, MS, 67, PhD(appl math), 68. *Honors & Awards:* CAD Award for Contrib to Computer Aided Design. *Prof Exp:* Mem tech staff, Bell Tel Labs, Inc, 62-68; assoc prof comput sci & elec eng, Univ Mo-Rolla, 68-70; prof, Southern Methodist Univ, 70-73; prof comput sci & elec eng, Univ Tex, Austin, 73-80, Clint Murchison Sr Chair Elec & Computer Eng, 86-96. *Concurrent Pos:* Pres, Commodity Command Standard Systs, Combat Gen Integrated Systs, Rubicon, SBII; consult, more than 40 Int Co. *Mem:* Fel Inst Elec & Electronics Engrs; Asn Comput Mach. *Res:* Digital computer reliability and maintainability; self-repairing digital computers; digital simulation; fault diagnosis; design automation; programming languages; biomedical computing; automatic test pattern generation; software engineering; domain specific automatic programming; automatic model generation; engineering entrepreneurship. *Mailing Add:* Sch Eng Univ Ala Birmingham AL 35242. *E-Mail:* sszygenda@eng.uab.edu

SZYLD, DANIEL BENJAMIN, NUMERICAL ANALYSIS, MODELLING. *Current Pos:* assoc prof, 90-95, PROF MATH, TEMPLE UNIV, 95- *Personal Data:* b Buenos Aires, Arg, Mar 5, 55; m 90, Kathleen A Ross; c Demian & Ana. *Educ:* NY Univ, MS, 79, PhD(math), 83. *Prof Exp:* Assoc res scientist, Inst Econ Anal, NY Univ, 80-85; vis asst prof numerical anal, Duke Univ, 85-86, asst prof dept comput sci, 86-90, dir grad studies, 86-87. *Concurrent Pos:* Vis assoc prof, Dept Math, Sch Exact Sci, Univ Buenos Aires, 84 & 88; adj prof comput sci, Courant Inst Math Sci, New York Univ, 84 & 85; vis researcher, Dept Math, Cath Pontific Univ, Rio de Janeiro, 85-86; consult, Interam Develop Bank, 85-87; NSF grants, 86, 88-90, 89, 90-93 & 92-; vis res scientist, Dept Math Sci, Inst Comput Math, Kent State Univ, 89; assoc ed, Electronic J Linear Algebra, 96-98. *Mem:* Am Math Soc; Soc Indust & Appl Math; Asn Comput Mach; Int Linear Algebra Soc. *Res:* Sparse matrix techniques; linear algebra; Eigen value problems; software for supercomputers; economics models; oil reservoir models; non-negative matrices; graph theory. *Mailing Add:* Dept Math Temple Univ Philadelphia PA 19122-6094. *Fax:* 215-204-6433; *E-Mail:* szyld@math.temple.edu

SZYMANSKI, BOLESLAW K, PARALLEL PROCESSING, COMPILER DESIGN. *Current Pos:* assoc prof, 85-90, actg chairperson, 93-94, PROF COMPUT SCI, RENSSELAER POLYTECH INST, 90- *Personal Data:* b Paslek, Poland, Apr 22, 50; US citizen; m 73, Emilia Haraf; c Piotr R & Witold A. *Educ:* Warsaw Tech Univ, MEng, 73; Nat Acad Sci, Warsaw, PhD(comput sci), 76. *Honors & Awards:* Outstanding Tech Achievements, Polish Engr Soc, 78. *Prof Exp:* Asst prof comput sci, Warsaw Tech Univ, 73-75; researcher, Inst Sci Tech & Econ Info, Warsaw, 76-78, researcher & head, Info Syst Div, 79-81; vis asst prof comput sci, Univ Pa, 82-85. *Concurrent Pos:* Adj lectr, Warsaw Univ, 77-79; vis researcher comput sci, Univ Aberdeen, UK, 78; consult, UNESCO, GE, IBM, 93; sr researcher, Comput Control & Command, Philadelphia, 83-90; prin investr, Army Res Off, NASA & Off Naval Res, 86-, NSF & High Performance Comput, 87-; vis scientist, Inst Comput Appln Sci & Eng, NASA, 89-92; nat lectr, Asn Comput Mach, 89-91; vis prof, Weizmann Inst, Israel, 93. *Mem:* AAAS; Asn Comput Mach; Inst Elec & Electronics Engrs. *Res:* Computer languages and compilers for parallel scientific computation, algorithm design for parallel and distributed systems; computer simulation of systems ranging from computers to ecology. *Mailing Add:* Rensselaer Polytech Inst Troy NY 12180. *Fax:* 518-276-4033; *E-Mail:* szymansk@cs.rpi.edu

SZYMANSKI, CHESTER DOMINIC, BIOCHEMISTRY. *Current Pos:* VPRES, PROCTOR CHEM, 80- *Personal Data:* b Bayonne, NJ, June 2, 30; m 56; c 3. *Educ:* The Citadel, BS, 51; Univ Miami, MS, 58; State Univ NY Col Forestry, Syracuse Univ, PhD(biochem), 62; Fairleigh Dickinson Univ, MBA, 74. *Prof Exp:* From chemist to sr chemist, 61-65, res assoc, 65-67, tech mgr, 67-74, assoc dir appl res, 74-78, mkt mgr Chem Prods Div, 78-80, vpres, Nat Starch & Chem Corp, 80- *Mem:* Am Chem Soc; Royal Soc Chem; Am Asn Cereal Chem. *Res:* Enzymic and chemical modification of starches; application of starches and synthetic polymers in industrial areas; polymer development for water enduses oil field application and photographic systems; dispersants, coagulants, thickeners and specialty chemicals; monomers used in polymer modification as well as in Epstein-Barr and ultraviolet cure systems. *Mailing Add:* 459 Washington Ave Martinsville NJ 08836

SZYMANSKI, EDWARD STANLEY, DIAGNOSTICS. *Current Pos:* MGR QUAL ASSURANCE, BEHRING DIAGNOSTICS. *Personal Data:* b Philadelphia, Pa, Mar 24, 47; m 93, Denise Scala; c Annalisa. *Educ:* St Joseph's Col, Pa, BS, 69; Georgetown Univ, PhD(chem), 74. *Prof Exp:* Sr scientist, Dade Reagents, 79-84; mgr, Instrumentation Labs, 84-89; mgr, Environ Diagnostics, 90-91; mgr, Miles, 91-93. *Mem:* Am Chem Soc; Am Asn Clin Chem. *Res:* Ligand binding to proteins; steroid reductases; enzyme kinetics; protein purification by biospecific affinity chromatography; function of milk proteins and specificity of milk enzymes; diagnostics. *Mailing Add:* 20400 Mariani Ave M/S 9-15 Cupertino CA 95016. *Fax:* 408-366-3725; *E-Mail:* edward.szymanski@bdi.hcc.com

SZYRYNSKI, VICTOR, PSYCHIATRY, NEUROLOGY. *Current Pos:* prof & psychother, 64-79, EMER PROF PSYCHIAT, UNIV OTTAWA, 79- *Personal Data:* b Oct 10, 13; nat Can; m 47; c 2. *Educ:* Univ Warsaw, MD, 38; Univ Ottawa, PhD(psychol), 49; FRCP(C), cert neurol, 52 & psychiat, 53; FRCP, FACP, FRCPsych. *Honors & Awards:* Gold Medal, Am Acad Psychosom Med, 59; Officer, Order of Polonia Restituta, Cross of Merit; Knight, Order Holy Sepulcher. *Prof Exp:* Demonstr neurol & psychiat, Univ Wilno, Poland, 39, sr resident & lectr, 39-40; res neurol & psychiat, Base Mil Hosps, Mid East, 41-46; lectr psychol, Polish Inst, Beirut, 46; consult, Guid Ctr, Univ Ottawa, 48-60, lectr psychiat, 48-49, assoc prof, 49-56, prof psychophilo, 56-60, prof psychother, 58-60; consult, State Dept Health & dir, State Dept Clin, NDak, 60-61; assoc prof neurol, prof psychiat & chmn dept, Univ NDak, 60-61. *Concurrent Pos:* Attend neurologist, Ottawa Civic Hosp, 51-60, asst electroencephalographer, 54-60, consult psychiatrist, 57-60; neurologist & psychiatrist, Royal Can Air Force Hosp, Rockcliffe, 51-56, sr consult, 56-60; neurologist, Dept Vet Affairs, 51-60; consult neurologist & psychiatrist, State Hosp Jamestown, 60-64; chief dept psychiat, Ottawa Gen Hosp, 64-70; dir, Ctr Pastoral Psychiat, St Paul Univ, Ont, 67-70; sr consult in chg supv psychother, Nat Defense Med Ctr, Ottawa, 77-, consult psychiat, Cauachan Forces Med Coun, 84- *Mem:* Fel Am Acad Psychosom Med (pres, 65-66); fel Am Col Physicians; fel Am Psychiat Asn; fel Am Acad Neurol; Sigma Xi; fel Royal Col Physicians Can; fel Brit Psychol Soc. *Res:* Psychotherapy; community psychiatry; child psychiatry; clinical neurology; marital therapy. *Mailing Add:* 33 Cedar Rd Gloucester ON K1J 6L6 Can

WITHDRAWN